Cambridge-Eichborn German Dictionary

Cambridge-Eichborn German Dictionary

Economics
Law
Administration
Business
General

Volume 2

German-English

Cambridge University Press

Cambridge
London New York New Rochelle
Melbourne Sydney

Published by the Press Syndicate of the University of Cambridge
The Pitt Building, Trumpington Street, Cambridge CB2 1RP
32 East 57th Street, New York, NY 10022, USA
296 Beaconsfield Parade, Middle Park, Melbourne 3206, Australia

First published in the Federal Republic of Germany 1982
First published by Cambridge University Press 1983

Printed in Great Britain at the University Press, Cambridge
and in the Federal Republic of Germany at Mohndruck Gütersloh

Library of Congress catalogue card number: 83–10144

British Library cataloguing in publication data

Cambridge-Eichborn German dictionary.
Vol. 2: German-English
1. German language–Dictionaries–English
2. English language–Dictionaries–German
433'.21 PF3640

ISBN 0 521 25846 4

VORBEMERKUNG

I. Alphabetische Anordnung

1. Stichwörter sind grundsätzlich alphabetisch geordnet.

2. Pluralformen sind, soweit sie angeführt werden müssen, hinsichtlich ihrer alphabetischen Anordnung wie Singularformen behandelt.
   Selbständig behandelt sind lediglich die Pluralformen der Wörter auf -y.

3. Verben, bei denen auf die Partikel »to« verzichtet wird, sind durch (v.), Adjektive durch (a.) kenntlich gemacht.

4. Über die Einordnung eines Wortes als Stichwort oder seine Unterordnung unter ein Stichwort entschied der Grad seiner Selbständigkeit.

5. Die Untergruppen sind in nachstehender Reihenfolge angeordnet:

   a) reines Substantiv, ohne Beifügung;

   b) Substantiv, erweitert durch Synonyme und Hinweise auf seinen besonderen Anwendungsbereich (eingeklammerter Kursivtext, in alphabetischer Reihenfolge), z. B. **abatement** *(decrease)* [Ver]minderung, Abnahme, *(deduction)* Abzug, *(discount)* Abschlag, [Preis]nachlaß, Rabatt, *(law of real property)* widerrechtliche Besitzerergreifung;

   c) Substantiv, erweitert durch Präposition, z. B. **for account and risk** auf Rechnung und Gefahr; **for third** ~ für fremde Rechnung; **not taken into** ~ unberücksichtigt;

   d) Substantiv, erweitert durch unverbundene adjektivische oder substantivische Appositionen, durch welche die Bedeutung des Substantivs modifiziert wird, z. B. **account** Konto; **advance** ~ Vorschußkonto; **appropriation** ~ Bereitstellungskonto; **»~ attached«** »Konto beschlagnahmt«; **bank** ~ Bankkonto;

   e) Substantiv, erweitert durch verbundene, nachgestellte Appositionen (alphabetisch, ohne Berücksichtigung der Bindewörter, nach den Anfangsbuchstaben der Appositionen geordnet), z. B. **account | in arrears** Rechnungsrückstand; ~ **in bank** Bankkonto; ~ **of charges** Unkostenkonto; ~ **with customers** Kundenkonto;

   f) Adjektiv (a.), das mit dem Stichwort-Substantiv gleichlautend ist;

   g) einfaches Verb (v.), das mit dem Stichwort-Substantiv gleichlautend ist;

   h) Verb, erweitert durch Synonyme und Hinweise auf seinen besonderen Anwendungsbereich (eingeklammerter Kursivtext, in alphabetischer Reihenfolge), z. B. **abate** *(v.) (decrease)* abnehmen, geringer werden, *(deduct)* herabsetzen, abziehen, nach-, ablassen, *(reduce legacies)* (Legate) verkürzen;

   i) Verb, erweitert zur Phrase durch beliebige grammatische Konstruktionen, alphabetisch geordnet nach dem Anfangsbuchstaben des jeweils wichtigsten Wortes dieser Konstruktion, z. B. **accept** | *(v.)* **a bill** Wechsel akzeptieren, mit Akzept versehen; ~ **bills for collection (discount)** Wechsel zum Einzug (Diskont) hereinnehmen; ~ **in blank** blanko akzeptieren;

   k) Substantiv, erweitert zur Phrase durch verbale Konstruktionen, in alphabetischer Reihenfolge dieser Verben, z. B. **to add to an account** einem Konto zuschlagen; **to age ~s** Konten nach ihrer Fälligkeit aufgliedern; to appear in an ~ auf einer Rechnung stehen; **to audit ~s** Rechnungen überprüfen;

   l) Einfaches Kompositum des Stichworts, alphabetisch geordnet nach den Anfangsbuchstaben des jeweils nachgestellten (unbetonten) Kompositumgliedes, z. B. **account | analysis** Kontenanalyse; ~ **book** Kontobuch; ~ **day** *(stock exchange)* Abrechnungstag.

6. Die Untergruppen eines Stichworts sind im Text jeweils durch einen Absatz hervorgehoben.

II. Erläuterungen der angewandten Abkürzungen und Zeichen

1. Abkürzungen

a.	=	Adjektiv	o.s.	=	oneself
abbr.	=	(abbreviation) = Abkürzung	pl.	=	plural
Br.	=	hauptsächlich in Großbritannien	pol.	=	politisch
	=	gebräuchlich	print.	=	Buchdruck
coll.	=	umgangssprachlich	sociol.	=	Soziologie
dial.	=	dialektisch	s. o.	=	someone
el.	=	elektrisch	s. th.	=	something
[etwa]	=	annähernd entsprechender	Scot.	=	schottisch
	=	Begriff	sl.	=	Slang
fam.	=	familiär	techn.	=	Technik
fig.	=	bildlich	tel.	=	Telefon
j., jds.,			th.	=	thing
jem.	=	jemand, jemandes,	US	=	hauptsächlich in den USA
	=	jemandem		=	gebräuchlich
lat.	=	aus dem Lateinischen	v.	=	Verb
mar.	=	Schiffahrt	v. i.	=	verbum intransitivum
math.	=	Mathematik	v. t.	=	verbum transitivum
med.	=	Medizin	→	=	siehe
mil.	=	Militär			

2. Tildenzeichen

Fettgedruckte Stichwörter werden bei Wiederholungen innerhalb ihres Abschnittes durch eine Tilde (~) ersetzt, wobei sich die Tilde auf die Gesamtheit eines mehrteiligen Stichwortes bezieht. Beginnt das durch die Tilde ersetzte Wort im Gegensatz zum Stichwort mit einem großen Buchstaben oder umgekehrt, so wird dies durch einen Kreis über der Tilde (~̊) angedeutet.

3. Senkrechter Strich

Wird vom Ordnungswort eines mehrteiligen Stichwortes (z. B. **extension agreement)** eine Untergruppe abgeleitet (~ **course** = Fortbildungskursus), so wird das Ordnungswort dieses Stichwortes von seinem restlichen Teil durch einen dünnen senkrechten Strich **(extension | agreement)** abgetrennt.

4. Runde Klammern

a) Steht ein Buchstabe innerhalb eines Wortes in runden Klammern, z. B. bei **hono(u)r,** so deutet die Klammer eine zweite Schreibmöglichkeit an;

b) steht ein Wort innerhalb eines Ausdrucks in runden Klammern, so verweist die Klammer auf ein Synonym, z. B. **current account** laufendes (tägliches) Konto, **to audit (balance) accounts** Konten saldieren (ausgleichen).

5. Eckige Klammern

Sie bedeuten, daß die eingeklammerten Stellen (Buchstaben oder Wörter) mitgelesen oder ausgelassen werden können, z. B. **abandonment** [Verzicht]leistung; **abatement** *(remittance of tax)* [Steuer]erlaß, Nachlaß.

6. Während im Englischen die Wiederholung eines Wortes durch eine Tilde (~) bezeichnet wird, sind kurz nacheinander wiederholt auftretende deutsche Wörter oder Wortteile durch einen kurzen Strich (-) markiert, z. B. **able to earn** dienst-, unterhaltsfähig; **ability to pay** Zahlungs-, Leistungsfähigkeit; **bear account** Baissekonto, -position.

III. Rechtschreibung

Die amerikanische Rechtschreibung weicht häufig von der englischen ab. Den wesentlichen Abweichungen wurde durch nachfolgende Regelung Rechnung getragen;

1. Wörter, die im Amerikanischen verkürzt wiedergegeben werden, bekamen folgendes Druckbild; **hono(u)r, program(me).**
2. Die Wortendung **ise** oder **ize** wurde in Anlehnung an die vom Oxford Dictionary Dictionary durchgeführte Schreibweise meist mit **ise** wiedergegeben.
3. Die amtlichen Regeln für die englische Silbentrennung wurden strengstens beachtet und an Hand von Webster's New International Dictionary kontrolliert.
4. Die Verwendung der Bindestriche zwischen einzelnen selbständigen Substantiven ist heute zwiespaltiger denn je. In der englischen und amerikanischen Literatur finden sich alle Varianten (Bindestrich, kein Bindestrich, Zusammenschreibung).
   Da die Entwicklung mehr in die Richtung geht, den Bindestrich wegzulassen oder Wörter zusammenzuschreiben, wurde dieser Tendenz im allgemeinen entsprochen.

NOTES

I. Alphabetical Order

1. Catchwords are placed in alphabetical order.

2. The plural form has been treated, as far as it has to be mentioned, in the same alphabetical order as the singular. The plural form of words ending with a »y« has been treated separately.

3. Verbs have been marked with a (v.) where the participle »to« has been omitted. Adjectives with an (a.).

4. The classification of a word as catchword has been decided according to the grade of its independency, or its sub-division under a catchword.

5. The sub-grouping is arranged in the following manner:

   a) pure substantives without attributes;

   b) nouns extended by synonyms and indication of their special use (in brackets, text in italics) are in alphabetical order, i.e. **abatement** *(decrease)* [Ver]minderung, Abnahme, *(deduction)* Abzug, *(discount)* Abschlag [Preis]nachlaß, Rabatt, *(law of real property)* widerrechtliche Besitzergreifung;

   c) nouns extended by prepositions, i. e. **for account and risk** auf Rechnung und Gefahr; **for third** ~ für fremde Rechnung; **not taken into** ~ unberücksichtigt;

   d) nouns extended by detached adjectival or substantival appositions in which the meaning of the nouns is modified, i.e.
   account Konto; **advance** ~ Vorschußkonto; **appropriation** ~ Bereitstellungskonto; »~ **attached**« »Konto beschlagnahmt«; **bank** ~ Bankkonto;

   e) nouns extended by joined following appositions (alphabetical order without any regard to the conjunction) are arranged according to the first letter of the apposition, i.e. **account | in arrears** Rechnungsrückstand; ~ **of charges** Unkostenkonto; ~ **with customers** Kundenkonto;

   f) adjectives (a.) which are of homonymous value with the catchword noun;

   g) simple verb (v.) which is of homonymous value with the catchword noun;

   h) verbs extended by synonyms and with explanations as to their special use (in brackets, text in italics) are in alphabetical order, i.e.
   abate *(v.) (decrease)* abnehmen, geringer werden, *(deduct)* herabsetzen, abziehen, nach-, ablassen, *(reduce legacies)* (Legate) verkürzen;

   i) verbs extended into phrases through any grammatical construction have been placed alphabetically according to the first letter of the most important word in this construction, i.e. **accept** | *(v.)* **a bill** Wechsel akzeptieren, mit Akzept versehen; ~ **bills for collection (discount)** Wechsel zum Einzug (Diskont) hereinnehmen; ~ **in blank** blanko akzeptieren;

   k) nouns extended into phrases by means of verbal construction have been placed in alphabetical order of the verbs, i. e. **to add | to an account** einem Konto zuschlagen; **to age ~s** Konten nach ihrer Fälligkeit aufgliedern; **to appear in an** ~ auf einer Rechnung stehen; **to audit ~s** Rechnungen überprüfen;

   l) simple compounds of the catchwords have been placed in alphabetical order according to the first letter of the following unaccentuated part of the compositum, i.e. **account | analysis** Kostenanalyse; ~ **book** Kontobuch; ~ **day** *(stock exchange)* Abrechnungstag.

6. The sub-grouping of a catchword is always shown in the text by a paragraph.

II. Explanation of the use of abbreviations and signs

I. Abbreviations

a.	=	adjective	o.s.	=	oneself
abbr.	=	abbreviation	pl.	=	plural
Br.	=	chiefly used in Great Britain	pol.	=	political
coll.	=	colloquial	print.	=	printing term
dial.	=	dialect	sociol.	=	sociological
el.	=	electrical	s. o.	=	someone
[etwa]	=	approximate translation	s. th.	=	something
fam.	=	familiar	Scot.	=	Scotch
fig.	=	figurative	sl.	=	slang
j., jds.,	=		techn.	=	technical
jem.	=	jemand, jemandes	tel.	=	telephone
	=	jemandem (someone,	th.	=	thing
	=	someone's, to someone)	US	=	chiefly used in the USA
lat	=	Latin	v.	=	verb
mar.	=	marine	v. i.	=	verbum intransitivum
math.	=	mathematical	v. t.	=	verbum transitivum
med.	=	medical	→	=	see

2. **Repetition sign**
   Heavy typed catchwords when repeated in the paragraph are substituted by a repetition mark (~). When the catchword consists of one or more sections, this sign replaces the whole.
   When in contrast with the catchword the repeated word begins with a capital letter or vice versa, this is indicated by a circle put over the repetition mark (~̊).

3. **Perpendicular stroke**
   If however a subdivision is formed of a catchword consisting of one or more words (i. e. **extension agreement**) whose first part determines the alphabetically placed word of the whole the catchword is separated from the remaining part by a thin perpendicular stroke **(extension | agreement).**

4. **Round brackets**
   a) If a letter is placed in round brackets, i. e. **hono(u)r,** then the bracket shows a second form of spelling;
   b) if a word is placed in round brackets, then the bracket refers to the synonym, i. e. **current account** laufendes (tägliches) Konto, **to audit (balance) accounts** Konten saldieren (ausgleichen).

5. **Square brackets**
   These mean that the bracketed letters (or words) can be read or omitted, i.e. **abandonment** Verzicht[leistung]; **abatement** *(remittance of tax)* [Steuer]erlaß, Nachlaß.

6. In order to save space the separation sign (-) is used frequently in the German text and it indicates that the same word is used before and after, i.e. **able to earn** dienst-, unterhaltsfähig; **ability to pay** Zahlungs-, Leistungsfähigkeit; **bear account** Baissekonto, -position.

III. Correct Spelling

The American spelling often differs from the English. The most important differances have been accounted for by the following scheme:

1. Words which are used by Americans in an abbreviated manner have been printed as follows: **hono(u)r, program(me).**
2. The Oxford Dictionary way of spelling has been adopted for words ending in **ise** and **ize.**
3. The recognized rules for dividing syllables in English have been most carefully followed and checked with the Webstar's New International Dictionary.
4. The use of the hyphen between single simple nouns is nowadays even more disputable than ever. One finds all sorts of variations in both English and American literature (hyphen, no hyphen, written together). Since the development tends more to leave the hyphen out or to write words together this tendency has generally been followed.

A

A, von ~ bis Z from beginning to end;
das ~ und O einer Geschichte the crux of a matter; **das ~ und O einer Wissenschaft** the essence of a science;
etw. von ~ - Z kennen to know the ins and outs of s. th.; **von ~ - Z erfunden sein** to be a concoction from beginning to end;
wer ~ sagt, muß auch B sagen in for a penny, in for a pound.
a | conto on account; **~ jour** up to date; **~ eine Mark** at one Mark [each piece]; **~ meta** on joint account;
eins ~ top grade, first quality.
Aal beim Schwanz anfassen to begin at the wrong end.
aalglatt slippery as an eel.
Aas carcass, carrion;
kleines ~ *(fig.)* little rascal.
aasen to graze, to browse;
mit dem Geld ~ to play ducks and drakes with one's money.
Aasgeier *(fig.)* shark, vulture;
wie ~ um die Nachfolge kämpfen to fight like vultures over the succession.
ab *(abzüglich)* minus, less, deducting, *(Versandort)* ex, *(wirksam)* effective, as of *(US)*, as from *(Br.)*, *(Zug)* departure;
vom 1. April ~ beginning April 1; **~ Bahnhof** ex rail; **~ Diskont** less discount; **~ dort** loco your town; **~ heute** from today; **~ hier** to be delivered here; **~ jetzt** from this time; **~ Kai** ex quay; **~ Kai unverzollt** ex quay duties unpaid; **~ Lager** ex store (warehouse); **~ München** from Munich onward; **~ die Post!** off you go!; **~ Schiff** ex ship; **~ Skonto** less discount; **~ diesem Termin** as from this date; **~ Werk** ex works (mill);
sich ~ hier verstehen to be quoted from here.
abänderlich alterable.
abändern to alter, to change, to diversify, *(parl.)* to amend, to emend, *(umarbeiten)* to revise, to recast, to vary, *(verbessern)* to correct, to improve;
Buchung (Eintragung) ~ to alter (adjust, rectify, reverse) an entry; **Entscheidung ~** to revise a decision; **Gesetzentwurf ~** to amend a bill; **teilweise ~** to modify; **erstinstanzliches Urteil ~** to disaffirm the judgment of an inferior court.
Abänderung alteration, change, diversification, *(Richtigstellung)* correction, improvement, revision;
teilweise ~ modification;
~ einer Buchung adjustment of an entry; **~ einer Einheitspolice** endorsement of a policy; **~ eines Gesetzesentwurfs (einer Gesetzesvorlage)** amendment of a bill; **~ eines Haushaltsvoranschlags** amendment of an appropriation bill; **~ der Satzung** modification of articles of association; **~ eines gekreuzten Schecks in einen Barscheck** opening of a crossing *(Br.)*;
~ beantragen to move an amendment; **~ vornehmen** to make a change; **nur eine ~ vornehmen** to make only one qualification.
Abänderungsantrag motion to amend a motion, amendment;
~ annehmen to pass an amendment; **~ einbringen (stellen)** to move an amendment [to a bill], to table an amendment; **von einem ~ Abstand nehmen** to recede from an amendment.
Abänderungs | befugnis power to amend; **~bescheid** *(Patentrecht)* certificate of correction.
abänderungsfähig adaptable, amendable, modifiable, changeable, alterable, capable of alterations.
Abänderungs | klage amendment to pleading; **~klausel** reopening clause, *(Testament)* derogatory clause; **~patent** reissue patent; **~plan** scheme of improvement, improvement scheme, *(Gebäude)* plan of alterations; **~recht** right to amend; **~urkunde** deed of variation; **~vorschlag** opposed amendment; **unwesentlicher ~vorschlag** minor amendment; **~wünsche** demands of amendment.
Abandon *(Seeversicherung)* abandonment [of cargo], dereliction; **~akzept** acceptance of abandonment; **~erklärung** notice of abandonment; **~klausel** abandonment clause.
abandonnieren to abandon, to relinquish, to surrender;
Prämiengeschäft ~ to abandon an option.
Abarbeiten *(Schulden)* working off;
stapelweises ~ von Programmen *(Datenverarbeitung)* batch processing.
abarbeiten, sich to labo(u)r, to slave, to drudge; **sich die Finger ~** to work one's fingers to the bone; **Schuld ~** to work off a debt; **seine Überfahrt ~** to work one's passage.
Abart variety, species, version.
abartig abnormal.
Abbau *(einzelner Beamter)* dismissal, discharge, rundown, axe, *(Beamtenschaft)* reduction, cut, retrenchment, *(Bergwerk)* exploitation, working, mining, getting *(Br.)*, *(Demontage)* disassembly, dismantling, *(Erleichterung)* relaxation, *(Gebäude)* demolition, slash, cut[back] *(US)*, *(Herabsetzung)* reduction, cut, retrenchment;
~ der Auftragspolster working off the backlog of orders; **vorübergehender ~ der Belegschaft** laying off of personnel *(US)*; **~ der Bestände** stock reduction; **~ von Betriebsanlagen** factory removal; **~ von Einschränkungen** removal (lifting) of restrictions; **~ größerer Gebiete im Tagebau** area stripping *(US)*; **~ der Gehälter** reduction of salaries; **~ von Handelsschranken** reduction (dismantling) of trade barriers; **~ einer Hochdruckzone** disintegration of a high pressure area; **~ der Investitionstätigkeit** cutback in investment; **~ der Kontrollfunktion** easing of controls; **~ eines Kreditkontos** reduction of a loan account; **~ des Personals** retrenchment of employees; **~ der Planwirtschaft** decontrol; **~ des militärischen Potentials** military disengagement; **~ der Preisüberwachungsvorschriften** price decontrol; **~ von Steuervergünstigungen** retrenchment of tax privileges; **~ unter Tage** underground working; **~ der Überstunden** cuts in overtime; **~ der Zölle** tariff reduction; **~ der Zollschranken** elimination of customs barriers; **~ der Zwangswirtschaft** gradual decontrol;
~betrieb workings.
abbauen *(Angestellte)* to lay off, *(einzelne Beamte)* to discharge, to dismiss, to axe, *(Beamtenschaft)* to retrench, to cut, *(Bergwerk)* to work, to exploit, to abandon, *(Betriebseinrichtungen)* to dismantle, to discard, to mine, *(demontieren)* to dismantle, to disassemble, to scrap, *(Einschränkungen)* to lift, to remove, *(Gebäude)* to pull down, to demolish, *(Gehälter, Preise, Zölle)* to reduce, to cut [down], *(Lager)* to reduce stocks, *(Preispolster)* to thin down, *(Schulden)* to repay, to reduce, to work off, *(Zwangswirtschaft)* to decontrol;
Auftragsüberhang ~ to work off the backlog of orders; **Ausgabenwirtschaft ~** to put down one's expenditures; **Beamtenschaft ~** to diminish (reduce, retrench) the number of employees; **Belegschaft vorübergehend ~** to lay off personnel *(US)*; **Bewirtschaftungsvorschriften ~** to abolish state planning, to decontrol; **Gehälter ~** to reduce salaries; **Lager ~** to reduce stocks; **Preisüberwachungsvorschriften ~** to decontrol prices; **Steuervorteile ~** to retrench tax privileges; **Zölle ~** to reduce tariffs.
abbaufähiges Vorkommen exploitable deposits.
Abbau | fähigkeit workableness; **~feld** working field, **~förderungsstrecke** hauling gallery; **~front** *(Kohle)* coal face; **~gebiet** mining district; **~gerechtigkeit, ~gerechtsame, ~konzession** mining franchise; **~gesellschaft** mining partnership *(US)*; **~methode** working (mining) method; **~programm** *(Industrie)* dismantling program(me); **~recht** mining concession, surface right, common of digging; **~schacht** working pit; **~sohle** working level; **~stelle** working face; **~strecke** panel entry, heading, gangway *(US)*, heading room; **~verfahren** mining operations; **~verluste** mining losses; **~wirtschaft** exploitation.
abbauwürdig workable, exploitable.
abbekommen, etw. to be damaged; **seinen Teil ~** to come in for one's share;
etw. ~ haben to got a trashing *(coll.)*.
abberufen to recall, to call back, *(vorübergehend)* to suspend;
von einem Amt ~ to remove from office; **Gesandten ~** to recall an envoy; **Vorstandsmitglied ~** to remove a director.
Abberufung recall;
vorläufige ~ suspension from office; **vorzeitige ~** recall *(US)*;
~ des Abwicklers (Liquidators) removal of a liquidator; **~ eines Betroffenen** recall of an ambassador; **~ eines Geschworenen** withdrawing a juror; **~ eines Vorstandsmitglieds** removal of a director.
Abberufungs | abstimmung recall vote; **~feldzug** recall campaign; **~recht** power of removal; **~schreiben** letters of recall.
abbestellbar countermandable.
abbestellen to countermand, to counterorder, to cancel [an order, a reservation], *(Zeitung)* to discontinue, to cancel (stop, *fam.*) a subscription.
Abbestellung cancellation, counterorder, countermand[ing], *(Zeitung)* discontinuance;
~ eines Abonnements discontinuance of a subscription.
abbezahlen to pay (clear) off, *(durch Teilzahlung)* to pay off on the instalment (hire-purchase, *Br.*, deferred-payment, *US*) system, *(tilgen)* to repay.

abbezahlt, noch ~ werden müssen to be subject to a hire-purchase agreement *(Br.)*.
Abbezahlung paying (clearing) off, *(Ratenzahlung)* payment on account, hire-purchase *(Br.)* (deferred-payment, *US*) system, *(Tilgung)* repayment, redemption.
Abbiegen turning.
abbiegen to turn off, *(Straße)* to branch off;
in eine Seitenstraße ~ to turn down a side street; **verkehrt (falsch) ~** to take a wrong turning.
Abbiege|spur turning lane; **~verbot** no turns, turn ban; **~verkehr** turning traffic.
Abbiegung turning;
zweite ~ rechts second turning to the right.
Abbild likeness, portrait;
getreues ~ living image;
~ seines Vaters likeness of his father.
abbilden to copy, to picture, to illustrate, to reproduce.
Abbildung picture, illustration, image, figure, reproduction, *(Kartographie)* mapping;
seitenverkehrte ~ mirror-inverted image; **winkelgetreue ~** conformal projection;
~ im Text text illustration;
mit ~en versehen to illustrate.
Abbitte apology.
abblasen, Unternehmen to beat a retreat.
abblättern to patch (flake, peel) off.
abblenden *(Foto)* to fade out;
Scheinwerfer ~ to dim [out] (dip) the headlights.
Abblend|licht dipped (dimmed) light, antidazzle headlight; **~schalter** dip (dimmer) switch; **~spiegel** nondazzle rear-view mirror; **~vorrichtung** dipper, dimmer; **~vorschriften** antidazzle requirements.
abblitzen, mit seinem Gesuch to meet with a rebuff;
j. ~ lassen to send s. o. packing, to give s. o. the wind.
abbrechen to break away, *(Arbeit)* to stop, to interrupt, to cease, to knock off *(US)*, *(Betriebseinrichtungen)* to disassemble, to dismantle, *(Gebäude)* to pull (take, break) down, to demolish, *(Verbindungen)* to discontinue, to sever, to break off, to drop; **Belagerung ~** to raise a siege; **Beziehungen ~** to break off connections (relations); **alle Brücken hinter sich ~** to burn one's boats; **Diskussion ~** to prevent (gag, *Br.*) a debate; **Gefecht ~** to withdraw from action; **kurz ~** to stop short; **Reise ~** to cut short a journey; **Streik ~** to call off a strike; **Verhandlungen ~** to break off negotiations; **Zeile ~** to break (divide) a line; **Zelte ~** to strike tents.
abbremsen to slow down, to decelerate;
Auto rechtzeitig ~ to brake a car in time; **Düsenflugzeug ~** to parabrake a jet airliner.
abbrennen to burn down (off, away);
Feuerwerk ~ to set off fireworks.
abbringen to dissuade;
j. von einer Gewohnheit ~ to break s. o. off a habit; **Hund von einer Fährte ~** to take a dog off the scent; **j. von einem Plan ~** to persuade s. o. out of his plan.
Abbröckeln der Kurse easing (dropping) off (crumbling) of prices.
abbröckeln *(Kurse)* to crumble [away], to ease off, to drop, to drift down, to give away;
etw. ~ to ease a fraction, to loosen (recede) fractionally.
Abbröckelung *(Kurse)* crumbling, easing off, drop.
Abbruch *(Gebäude)* demolition, pulling down, housebreaking, scrap, *(Maschine)* dismantlement, *(Ruf)* derogation, *(Schaden)* prejudice, damage, *(Statistik)* cut-off, *(Verhandlungen)* breaking off, discontinuance, interruption, rupture;
~ diplomatischer Beziehungen severance (rupture) of diplomatic relations, diplomatic rupture, formal diplomatic breach;
~ eines Gesprächs discontinuance of a conversation; **~ einer öffentlichen Vorstellung** discontinuance of a public performance;
jds. Ansehen ~ tun to cast a slur on s. one's reputation; **jds. Interessen ~ tun** to damage (prejudice, injure, be detrimental, prejudicial to) s. one's interests; **auf ~ verkaufen** to sell as scrap (at demolition value); **Maschinen auf ~ verkaufen** to sell machinery as junk;
~anordnung demolition order; **~arbeiten** demolition [work]; **~arbeiter** demolition worker; **~befehl** demolition order; **~betrieb, ~firma** demolition company (firm), housebreaker; **~bewilligung** demolition permit; **~gebiet** clearance area *(Br.)*; **~kolonne** demolition gang; **~kosten** demolition (dismantling) costs; **~kostenversicherung** demolition cost insurance; **~preis** breakup price.
abbruchreif derelict, dilapidated, *(Gebäude)* due for demolition, condemned, *(Schiff)* condemned.
Abbruch|spezialist demolition engineer; **~unternehmer, ~unternehmen** housebreaker, knacker, demolition company, wrecking company (contractor) *(US)*; **~wert** breakup (scrap) value.
abbrummen, Strafe to do one's time.
abbuchen *(abschreiben)* to get off the books, to write off (down), to charge off, to cut, *(ausbuchen)* to abandon, to retire, to eliminate, *(belasten)* to charge, to debit;
Flugzeug ~ to write off an aircraft as lost; **Forderung ~** to write off a debt, to wipe off a debit balance; **von einem Konto ~** to deduct from an account; **seine Verluste ~** to cut one's losses.
Abbuchung *(Abschreibung)* write-off, *(Ausbuchung)* abandonment, retirement, *(Belastung)* charge, charge-off, debit [entry];
automatische ~ direct debit;
automatische ~ vom Lohnkonto automatic deduction from pay;
~ vornehmen to pass an amount to the debit of an account.
Abbuchungs|beleg debit slip, bank giro credit slip; **~genehmigung** direct debiting; **~verfahren** direct debiting service, direct debit system.
abbummeln to idle away.
abbüßen, Gefängnisstrafe to serve years in prison.
ABC alphabet, *(fig.)* rudiments, elements;
~-Abwehr CBR defence; **~-Abwehroffizier** chemical warfare officer; **~-Buch** primer; **~-Code** telegraphic (CBR) code; **~-Kriegsführung** CBR warfare; **~-Schütze** alphabetarian; **~-Staaten** CBR powers; **~-Waffen** CBR weapons.
abdampfen *(coll.)* to shave off.
abdanken *(Beamter)* to quit service, to resign, to retire, *(Herrscher)* to abdicate, *(Offizier)* to dismiss, to cashier, *(Schiff)* to lay off, to put out of commission;
Mannschaft ~ to pay off the crew.
Abdankung *(Beamter)* retirement, demission, *(Herrscher)* abdication.
Abdankungsurkunde deed (instrument) of abdication.
abdecken *(Kredit)* to repay, *(mil.)* to camouflage, *(Reproduktion)* to mask [out], *(Schulden)* to pay back, to cover, to settle, to repay, to meet, to settle, *(Termingeschäft)* to cover;
Ansprüche aufgrund einer vorhandenen Versicherung ~ to pay on s. th. under the policy; **Dach ~** *(Sturm)* to blow the tiles off the roof; **Debetsaldo ~** to cover a short account; **fälligen Kredit ~** to meet a loan when due; **Tisch ~** to clear the table.
abdeckend, sich automatisch self-liquidating *(US coll.)*.
Abdecker flayer, knacker *(Br.)*.
Abdeckerei knackery.
Abdeck|papier masking (golden-rod) paper; **~platte** cover plate; **~rahmen** mask.
Abdeckung *(Schulden)* covering, settlement;
zur teilweisen ~ des Kontos in partial fulfil(l)ment of the account;
~ eines Kredits repayment of a loan; **~ eines Saldos** payment of a balance; **~ von Schulden** settlement of debts.
abdichten to seal, to make airtight;
Faß ~ to make a cask leakproof; **Leck in einem Rohr ~** to stop a leak in a pipe.
Abdichtungs|ring packing washer; **~streifen** weather strip.
abdienen, seine Zeit to serve one's time.
Abdisponieren drawing on an account, withdrawal of funds.
abdisponieren to redeposit, to dispose;
Gelder ~ to withdraw funds; **von einem Konto ~** to draw on an account.
Abdisposition drawing on an account, withdrawal of funds.
abdrängen to push (force) aside;
Auto beim Überholen ~ to force a car off the road; **Demonstranten in eine Nebenstraße ~** to force demonstrators into a side street.
abdrehen *(Licht, Radio)* to turn off, *(Schiff)* to haul off.
Abdruck *(Exemplar)* print, copy, imprint, *(Nachdruck)* reproduction, reprint, *(Stempel)* impression;
erster ~ galley (first) proof; **fehlerhafter ~** inaccurate copy; **schlechter ~** foul impression, poor copy; **unberechtigter ~** unauthorized reprint, piracy;
~ mit offener Schrift open-letter proof; **~ eines Siegels** impression of a seal; **~ von 5000 Stück** run off of five thousand pieces;
~ machen to print.
abdrucken to print, to imprint, to reproduce, *(veröffentlichen)* to publish;
auszugsweise ~ to reproduce an extract; **Brief ~** to reproduce a letter; **100 Stück ~** to strike off a hundred copies; **unerlaubt ~** to pirate; **wieder ~** to reprint;
~ lassen to run off.

abdrücken to pull the trigger.
Abdruck | recht copyright; **zweites ~recht** serial rights; **~tantieme** reprint royalty, reproduction fee.
Abend, bunter variety show; **geselliger ~** conversable evening; **lustiger ~** spree; **total verlorener ~** thoroughly dull evening; **freier ~ der Hausangestellten** the servant's night out;
am ~ schon vergeben sein to have an engagement for the evening; **~ auswärts verbringen** to have an evening (a night) out; **tödlich langweiligen ~ verbringen** to have a absolutely punk evening *(sl.)*;
man soll den Tag nicht vor dem ~ loben don't count your chickens before they're hatched;
~anzug dinner clothes, evening (formal) dress, dressing suit; **~anzug ist vorgeschrieben** evening dress is de rigueur; **kein Zwang für einen ~anzug** evening dress is optional; **~aufführung** evening performance; **~ausgabe** late edition, evening paper; **~blätter** evening papers; **~börse** evening market; **~dämmerung** dusk of the evening, daylight; **~einladung annehmen** to engage o. s. for dinner; **~essen** supper, dinner, evening meal; **~essen geben** to give a dinner; **Freunde zum ~essen eingeladen haben** to entertain friends to dinner.
abendfüllendes Programm full-length program(me).
Abend | gesellschaft evening (dinner) party, soirée; **zahlreich besuchte ~gesellschaft** crowded party; **formlose ~gesellschaft** quiet dinner; **~gesellschaft mit Tanz** dancing party; **~gesellschaft geben** to give a party; **~imbiß** cold supper; **~kasse** *(Theater)* box office; **kleines ~kleid** semi-evening (cocktail) dress, dinner dress, evening gown *(US)*; **~kurse** evening classes; **~kurssystem** university extension; **~land** Occident, the Western World, the West.
abendländisch occidental, western.
Abend | mantel opera cloak; **~nachrichten** evening bulletin (news); **~post** evening mail; **~presse** evening newspapers; **~programm** evening entertainment; **~schicht** evening shift; **~schoppen [am Sonntag]** sundowner; **zum ~schoppen gehen** to pop into the local for a pint; **~schule** evening (adult, night) school; **~schule besuchen** to join evening classes; **~spaziergang** evening walk; **sich in den ~stunden fortbilden** to burn the midnight oil; **~unterhaltung** evening; **~unterricht** evening school; **musikalische ~veranstaltungen** musical evenings; **~vorstellung** evening (nightly) performance; **~zeitungen** evening papers; **~zug** night train.
Abenteuer adventure, exploit;
tägliches ~ im Berufsverkehr commuting ordeal;
auf ~ ausgehen, ~ suchen to go in search of adventure; **sich auf ein ~ einlassen** to get involved in a risky undertaking; **kopfüber ein romantisches ~ suchen** to leap right into a romance;
~buch adventure book; **seinem ~drang nachgehen** to satisfy one's thirst for adventure; **~film** adventure film; **~geschichte** adventure story, yarn, tale (story) of adventure; **aufregende ~geschichten** stirring tales of adventure; **erfundene ~geschichte** fabricated account of adventures; **~leben** adventurous life.
abenteuerlich adventurous;
~e Geschichte phantastic story; **~er Plan** wildcat scheme; **~e Reise** adventurous voyage; **~es Unternehmen** risky undertaking.
Abenteuer | regierung carpet government; **~roman** adventure novel.
Aber | depot bonds account; **~glaube** superstition; **~glauben beseitigen** to explode a superstition.
aberkennen to deny, to deprive, *(Besitz)* to dispossess, *(Recht)* to deprive, to forejudge;
jem. die bürgerlichen Ehrenrechte ~ to deprive (dispossess) s. o. of civil rights; **Schadensersatz ~** to disallow compensation; **jem. die Staatsangehörigkeit ~** to deprive s. o. of his nationality, to expatriate s. o.; **jem. einen Titel ~** to deprive s. o. of his title.
Aberkennung | der bürgerlichen Ehrenrechte deprivation of civil rights; **~ der Rechtsfähigkeit** incapacitation; **~ des Ruhegehalts** deprivation of a pension; **~ von Schadenersatz** disallowance of compensation; **~ der Staatsangehörigkeit** forfeiture (deprivation) of citizenship, expatriation, denaturalization.
abernten to harvest, to crop.
Abernterecht, vergütetes grain rent.
abfahrbereit ready to start (depart), preparatory to leaving.
abfahren *(Auto)* to drive off, *(Dampfer)* to sail, to clear [port], *(Kolonne)* to move off, *(Zug)* to start, to move (steam) off, to pull out, to leave, to depart;
fahrplanmäßig ~ to start on time (after schedule, *US*); **pünktlich ~** *(Zug)* to draw out of the station promptly; **sich ~** *(Reifen)* to wear [out];
Zug ~ lassen to start a train.
abfahrender Zug outgoing train.
Abfahrt departure, start, setting-out, going, *(Dampfer)* sailing, *(Ski)* downhill running;
bei ~ des Zuges at train time;
fahrplanmäßige ~ scheduled departure *(US)*; **voraussichtliche ~** *(Schiff)* expected to sail;
~en zweimal wöchentlich *(Schiff)* sailings twice weekly;
seine ~ hinauszögern to delay one's departure; **seine ~ vorverlegen** to accelerate one's departure.
Abfahrts | bahnsteig starting (departure) platform; **~befehl** sailing orders; **~flagge** blue Peter; **~gleis** line of departure, departure line; **~hafen** port of departure (sailing); **~hinweis** advance sign; **~ort** starting place (point), place of departure; **~plan** schedule of steamers; **~punkt** starting point; **~rampe** drive-off; **~signal** *(Schiff)* blue Peter, *(Bahn)* green flag; **auf das ~signal warten** to wait for an opening; **~stelle** *(Autobahn)* exit; **~verbot** prohibition from sailing; **~zeit** time of departure, *(Dampfer)* sailing date, *(Zug)* train (starting) time; **fahrplanmäßige ~zeit** scheduled time *(US)*.
Abfall waste, scrap, garbage *(US)*, refuse *(Br.)*, junk, truck, dross, *(von einer Partei)* defection, desertion, secession, backsliding, falling away, *(Plunder)* stuff;
ohne ~ wasteless;
gewerblicher ~ trade refuse *(Br.)*; **herumliegender ~** litter; **radioaktiver ~** radioactive waste, fallout;
~ vom wahren Glauben lapse from true belief; **~ der Niederlande** revolt of the Netherlands; **~ von seiner Partei** desertion from one's party;
~behälter litter bin (basket); **~beseitigung** refuse disposal *(Br.)*, garbage disposal (removal) *(US)*; **~beseitigungsanlage** disposal unit; **~beseitigungsgebühr** disposal tax; **~beutel** refuse bag; **~bewegung** breakaway movement; **~drohung** secessionist threat.
Abfälle odds and ends, odd-come shorts, oddments, waste, rubbish, refusel;
verwertbare ~ salvageable items;
~ verwerten to recycle refuse.
Abfall | eimer, ~kübel dustbin, refuse bin, ash (trash, *US*) can, garbage can *(US)*; **~eisen** scrap iron.
abfallen to decrease, *(el.)* to drop off, *(Gewinn)* to yield, *(Industrieprodukt)* to come off as waste product, *(pol.)* to secede, to desert, to defect, to fall away, *(Straße)* to decline, to descend, to slope, *(sich verschlechtern)* to deteriorate;
gegenüber dem Muster ~ to prove inferior to sample; **von einer Partei ~** to break away (bolt) from (desert) a party; **gegenüber dem ersten Roman ~** to be a comedown against the first novel.
abfallend, steil precipitous;
~e Qualität inferior quality.
Abfall | energie waste energy; **~erzeugnis** waste product; **~gefäß** silent butler; **~grube** dust hole; **~halde** junk yard; **~händler** junk dealer; **~haufen** scrap heap, trash pile *(US)*; **~holz** waste wood.
abfällig derogatory, disparaging, *(Beurteilung)* unfavo(u)rable;
sich über j. ~ äußern to speak disparagingly about s. o.; **j. ~ bescheiden** to rebuff s. o.; **jds. Gesuch ~ bescheiden** to reject (refuse) s. one's request; **etw. ~ beurteilen** to pass an adverse (unfavo(u)rable) judgment on s. th.;
~e Bemerkung derogatory remark; **~e Kritik** adverse criticism.
Abfall | kohle waste coal; **~koks** waste coke, coke breeze; **~korb** wastepaper (scrap, *US*) basket; **~material** waste material, *(radioaktives)* radioactive waste, fallout; **~papier** wastepaper.
Abfallprodukt waste (by-, residual, spinoff) product;
zur Weiterverarbeitung geeignete ~e recycable refuse, shorts; **~e verwerten** to utilize waste products; **~e erneut industriell verwerten** to feed back waste material into the system.
Abfall | stoffe waste substances (materials); **wiederverwertbare ~stoffe** recycable refuse, shorts; **~tonne** garbage barrel *(US)*; **~verkauf** odds-and-ends sale *(US)*; **~vernichter** refuse destructor, trash smasher *(US)*, disposal unit; **~verwertung** recovery (recuperation) of waste, waste utilization, recycling, salvage; **kommunale ~verwertung** municipal waste treatment; **~verwertungsanlage** waste treatment facilities; **~verwertungsunternehmen** waste treatment plant; **~ware** rejects, throwouts; **~wirtschaft** utilization of waste products; **~zerkleinerer** trash masher *(US)*.
Abfangen *(Flugzeug)* flattening out;
~ von Briefen interception of letters; **~ von Kunden** enticement of customers; **~ von Kursschwankungen** price cushioning.
abfangen to catch, *(Balken)* to prop up, *(Briefe)* to intercept, *(Flugzeug)* to flatten out, to right, *(feindliches Flugzeug)* to intercept, *(Schwankungen)* to cushion, *(Rezession)* to level off;

Kunden ~ to entice (steal) customers; **Kurssturz** ~ to cushion the decline; **inflationäre Tendenzen** ~ to check (cushion) inflationary tendencies; **schleudernden Wagen** ~ to pull a car out of a skid.

Abfang|jäger interceptor fighter (plane); **~kanal** branch sewer.

abfärben to come off;
auf j. ~ to rub off on s. o.

Abfassen|von Geschäftsbriefen business-letter writing; ~ **in Kodesprache** coding.

abfassen *(formulieren)* to formulate, to word, to couch, to pen, *(in Kodesprache)* to code, *(Schriftstück)* to draw (get) up, to draft, to compose, to prepare, to write;
artikelweise ~ to article; **freundlich** ~ to couch in polite words; **gemeinverständlich** ~ to couch in a popular style; **Gesuch schriftlich** ~ to couch a request in writing; **Protokoll** ~ to draw up the minutes; **Schriftstück** ~ to put into writing; **Testament** ~ to make (draw up) a will; **Vertrag** ~ to make out (prepare) a contract.

Abfasser draftsman.

Abfassung *(Formulierung)* formulation, wording, embodiment, *(von Schriftstücken)* composition, drafting, drawing up, draftsmanship, preparation;
~ **eines Berichts** report writing; ~ **einer Beschwerde** filing of a complaint; ~ **eines Protokolls** drawing up the minutes; ~ **eines Reklametextes** copy writing; ~ **von Schriftsätzen** pleading; ~ **eines Textes** wording of a text; ~ **von Wirtschaftsbeiträgen** economic writing; ~ **eines Wörterbuches** dictionary making.

abfeiern *(Überstunden)* to idle away.

abfertigen *(absenden)* to forward, to dispatch, to send off, to expedite, *(abweisen)* to snub, to rebuke, *(Flugzeug, Schiff)* to clear, *(zur Post geben)* to post *(Br.)*, to mail *(US)*, to dispatch, *(Zoll)* to clear, *(Zug)* to dispatch, to start;
j. ~ to process s. o. *(US)*; **j. beschleunigt** ~ to dispatch s. o. speedily; **j. bevorzugt** ~ to give s. o. priority (preference); **Bettler kurz** ~ to snap a beggar short; **Boten** ~ to deal with (attend to) a messenger; **Gepäck** ~ to dispatch luggage *(Br.)* (baggage, *US*); **Kunden** ~ to deal with (attend to, serve) a customer; **j. kurz** ~ to be short with s. o., to send s. o. about his business (packing), to be brief with s. o.; **schnell** ~ to expedite; **Waren im Durchgangsverkehr** ~ to convey goods in transit; **zollamtlich** ~ to effect customs clearance, to clear through the customs.

Abfertiger dispatching clerk, dispatcher.

Abfertigung dispatch[ing], expedition, expediting, forwarding, turnround, handling, *(Abweisung)* refusal, rebuff, *(Flugplatz)* clearance, check-in, *(Kunde)* attendance, service, *(zur Post geben)* posting *(Br.)*, mailing *(US)*, dispatch, *(Post)* clearance;
normale ~ ordinary dispatch (handling); **rasche** ~ *(Schiffahrt)* quick turn-round; **schroffe** ~ snub; **zollamtliche** ~ clearance of goods, customs clearance; **zuverlässige** ~ dispatch reliability; ~ **am Flugzeugschalter** check-in; ~ **des Gepäcks** baggage dispatch *(US)*, dispatch of luggage *(Br.)*;
~ **zum freien Verkehr beantragen** to enter for consumption;
hier keine ~ *(Schalter)* position closed.

Abfertigungs|angestellter dispatch clerk; **~antrag zum freien Verkehr** entry for consumption; **~beamter** dispatching (routing, *US*) clerk, *(Bahn)* luggage-office *(Br.)* (baggage, *US*) clerk; **~buch** dispatch book; **~dienst** dispatch service; **~gebäude** *(Flugplatz)* terminal building; **~gebühr** forwarding charges; **zollamtliche ~gebühr** clearance charges; **~hafen** port of clearance; **~schalter** *(Flugzeug)* check-in counter, *(Gepäck)* luggage (baggage, *US*) counter; **~schein** forwarding (dispatch) note, waybill, *(Zoll)* permit, clearance certificate; **~spediteur** forwarding agent; **~stelle** office of dispatch, forwarding (dispatch[ing]) office, *(Güterbahnhof)* platform, *(Post)* dispatching (forwarding) office, handling place; **~tag** day of dispatch; **~tisch** dispatch table; **~vorschriften** forwarding instructions, dispatch regulations (instructions); **~zeit** handling time, *(Flugplatz)* check-in (ground-handling) time, *(Zoll)* hours of clearance.

Abfeuern eines Raumschiffes space launch.

abfeuern to discharge, to let off, *(Raumschiff)* to launch, to fire [off].

abfindbar compoundable.

abfinden to pay off, to satisfy, *(entschädigen)* to compensate, to indemnify;
j. ~ to pay s. o. out; **j. in bar** ~ to pay s. o. a compensation in cash; **sich** ~ to put up with, to swallow *(US)* one's medicine; **sich mit einer Entscheidung** ~ to submit to a decision, to acquiesce in a decision; **Fürsten** ~ to endow a prince with an apanage; **sich mit den Gegebenheiten** ~ to take the world as one finds it; **j. mit Geld** ~ to buy s. o. off; **Gesellschafter** ~ to buy out a partner; **seine Gläubiger** ~ to compound (make an arrangement) with (pay off) one's creditors; **Kind zu Lebzeiten** ~ to portion off (forisfamiliate) a child; **möglichen Konkurrenten** ~ to buy off a potential outside competitor; **sich mit einer Niederlage** ~ to come under the yoke; **sich mit den Tatsachen** ~ to face the facts; **Teilhaber** ~ to buy out a partner; **sich mit dem Unabänderlichen** ~ to make the best of it; **j. für einen Verlust** ~ to recoup s. o. for a loss; **mit leeren Versprechungen** ~ to feed off with empty promises;
sich ~ **lassen** to accept compensation.

Abfindung *(Angestellter)* lay-off benefit, dismissal compensation, severance pay (benefit), *(Entschädigung)* compensation, satisfaction, indemnification, indemnity, commutation payment, *(Gläubiger)* settlement, arrangement, composition, paying off, *(Teilhaber)* buying off, *(Zahlung)* satisfaction;
als endgültige ~ in full and final payment;
globale (pauschale) ~ lump-sum (global) settlement (payment); **hinausgeschobene** ~ deferred compensation; **im Schiedswege zuerkannte** ~ award of compensation;
~ **für frühzeitiges Ausscheiden** golden (silver) handshake; ~ **in bar** settlement (compensation) in cash, cash indemnity; ~ **in Form eines Jahresgehalts** annual compensation; ~ **eines Kindes zu Lebzeiten** forisfamiliation of (separate portion on) a child; **soziale** ~ **im Kündigungsfall** redundancy pay (payment) *(Br.)*; ~ **im Vergleichswege** arrangement, composition;
~ **gewähren** to pay compensation; ~ **vereinbaren** to settle the amount of compensation.

Abfindungs|ansprüche haben to be entitled to compensation; **soziale ~ansprüche haben** to be entitled to a redundancy payment *(Br.)*; **~betrag** [amount of] compensation, indemnity; **~entschädigung** compensation for loss of office; **~fonds** staff severance fund; **~guthaben** withdrawal benefit; **~konto** indemnity account; **soziale ~leistungen** redundancy insurance *(Br.)*; **politische ~leistungen an eine Interessengruppe** political payoff to an interest group; **betriebliche ~regelung** private redundancy scheme *(Br.)*; **~scheck** redundancy cheque *(Br.)*; **~summe** compensation, indemnity, indemnification, [amount of pecuniary] compensation, gratuity, satisfaction, *(Angestellte)* severance pay *(US)*, redundancy payment *(Br.)*; **bei der Pensionierung gezahlte ~summe** post-retirement gratuity; **betriebliche ~vereinbarung** private redundancy agreement *(Br.)*; **~vergleich** nuisance settlement; **~vertrag** [deed of] settlement, settlement agreement, composition deed, compromise, *(Ehepartner)* family settlement *(Br.)*; **~wesen** system of compensation; **~wesen bei Entlassungen** redundancy payments system *(Br.)*; **~zahlung** lump-sum payment, payout, payoff, composition, compensatory (composition, compromise) payment; **~zahlungen bei Stillegungen** redundancy payments *(Br.)*; **~zahlungen an Kinder leisten** to raise portions for children.

abfischen to fish out.

abflachen *(Konjunkturzyklus, Preisgefälle)* to flatten, *(Straße)* to grow smoother.

Abflachung level ground, *(Untiefe)* shoal;
~ **des Preisanstiegs** flattening out of the rising price tendency;
~ **der Wachstumskurve** flattening of economic growth.

Abflauen subsidence, lull, abatement, *(Preise)* sag, recession, decline;
~ **der Börse** stock-exchange reaction; ~ **der Kurse** dropping (sagging, giving way, crumbling) of prices.

abflauen *(Börse)* to sag, to flag, to flatten out, to ease off, to give away, to slacken, to drop, to wane, to crumble, to become easier, *(Interesse)* to be flagging, *(Konjunktur)* to recede, to slump, *(Sturm)* to tail away, *(Wind)* to lull, to abate, to subside, to die down;
~ **lassen** to depress.

abflauende Kurse dropping (crumbling, sagging) prices.

abfliegen to fly (take) off, to start;
Gebiet ~ to patrol an area.

abfließen to flow out, to run off, to drain away, *(Kapital)* to flow out, to be withdrawn.

Abflug flight, start, taking off, take-off, takeoff, get-off;
im ~ outbound;
fahrplanmäßiger ~ scheduled departure *(US)*;
~ **mit Starthilfe** assisted take-off;
~ **verschieben** to delay the departure;
~deck flying-off platform (deck); **~geschwindigkeit** take-off speed; **~gewicht** take-off weight; **~hafen** airport of departure; **~halle** departure lounge; **~karte** embarkation card; **~platz** flight station, take-off area; **~stelle** take-off position, flight station; **~termin** flight date; **~zeit** aircraft departure time; **voraussichtliche ~zeit** estimated time of departure.

Abfluß outflow, runoff, flowoff, *(Abflußrohr)* waste (outlet) pipe, *(Gold, Kapital)* drain, efflux, outflow, *(Kreditzurückziehung)* withdrawal;
langsamer ~ ooze; **verstopfter** ~ clogged waste pipe;
~ **ins Ausland** foreign drain; ~ **heißen Geldes** hot-money outflow; ~ **unserer Goldreserven** drain on our gold reserves;
~**becken** basin, sink; ~**gebiet** catchment area; ~**graben** drain, gutter; ~**hahn** drain cock; ~**kanal** escape drain, waste channel, wasteway; ~**leitung** drainpipe, outlet pipe; ~**möglichkeit** outlet; ~**recht über das Nachbargrundstück** right of drip; ~**rinne** waste drain, gutter; ~**rohr** drainpipe, escape (outlet, discharge, waste) pipe, *(vom Dach)* downpipe; ~**schleuse** water gate; ~**ventil** drain valve.
abforsten to disafforest.
Abfrage|platz *(tel.)* outgoing position; ~**stöpsel** *(tel.)* answering plug; ~**taste** speaking key.
abfressen to feed down, to browse.
Abfühlstation *(Lochstreifenverfahren)* reading station.
Abfuhr disposal, removal, *(Abweisung)* rebuff, turndown, *(Spediteur)* carriage, cartage;
~ **von Müll** refuse *(Br.)* (garbage, *US*) disposal;
schwere ~ **erleiden** to be sent packing; **jem. eine** ~ **erteilen** to send s. o. to the right-about (packing, away with a flea in his ear), to rebuff s. o.; **sich eine** ~ **holen** to meet with a rebuff (repulse).
abführbar payable.
Abführen in die Haft remitment.
abführen to lead away, to march off, *(Geldbetrag)* to pay over (off), *(Schuld)* to clear, to discharge, *(überweisen)* to remit;
Betrag an j. ~ to pay an amount over to s. o.; **Devisen** ~ to surrender foreign currency; **Dieb** ~ to walk a thief off; **j. gefangen** ~ to lead s. o. captive; **Gewinne** ~ to surrender profits; **in die Haft** ~ to remit; **Steuern** ~ to pay taxes; **Steuer gleich vom Ertrag** ~ to pay a tax at the source.
Abfuhr|gesellschaft cesspool-clearing company; ~**kosten** transport charges, removal expenses *(Br.)*; ~**lohn** cartage, carriage; ~**spediteur** cartage contractor; ~**system** *(Fäkalien)* cesspool clearing system.
Abführung *(Geldbetrag)* payment, paying over, *(Überweisung)* remittance;
nach ~ **des Vermögenssteuerertrages** after payment of the proceeds of the property tax;
~ **von Gewinnen** surrender of profits; ~ **von Steuern** payment of taxes; ~ **des Überschusses** surrender of surplus.
abfüllen to fill up;
Bier in Fässer ~ to tun (cask) beer; **auf Flaschen** ~ to bottle.
Abgabe *(Ausgabe)* issue, *(Aushändigung)* delivery, turning over, *(Einreichung)* filing, *(Elektrizität)* output, *(Fahrkarte)* surrender, return, *(Gebühr)* fee, *(Kommunalsteuer)* rate *(Br.)*, lot *(Br.)*, scot *(Scot.)*, *(Steuer)* duty, impost, imposition, tax, direct tax *(US)*, assessment *(Br.)*, *(Tribut)* tribute, *(Umlage)* levy, contribution, surcharge, *(Verbrauchssteuer)* excise, duty, *(Verkauf)* sale, sell-off, *(Zoll)* duty, lot *(Br.)*, toll;
gegen ~ **von** upon delivery of;
~ **von Anteilen** *(Rückversicherung)* ceding of quotas; ~ **einer Einkommensteuererklärung** filing of an income-tax return; ~ **einer Erbschaftssteuererklärung** filing of an Inland Revenue affidavit; ~ **einer Erklärung** issue of (making) a statement; ~ **einer Erklärung des Nichtbestreitens** plea of nole contendere; ~ **von Geboten** bidding; ~ **des Gepäcks** depositing of luggage *(Br.)*, checking of baggage in the baggage room *(US)*; ~ **auf das Grundvermögen** levy on real estate; ~ **einer Meinung** delivery of an opinion; ~ **einer Offerte** making an offer; ~ **auf die Prämieneinkünfte** levy on premium income; ~ **einer Sache an ein anderes Gericht** referring of a case to another court; ~ **von Scheinangeboten** puffing; ~ **unter Selbstkostenpreis** sale below cost; ~ **eines Urteils** pronouncing of a judgment; ~ **einer Wahlstimme** voting, casting of one's vote, polling.
Abgaben [public] dues, *(an der Börse)* sales;
~ **abgerechnet** *(Pächter)* beyond reprises;
frei von ~ duty-free, tax-free, scot-free;
direkte ~ direct taxes; **drückende** ~ heavy burden; **gesetzliche** ~ statutory levies; **gewerbliche** ~ industrial charges; **größere** ~ *(Börse)* heavy sales (selling); **hohe** ~ heavy taxes; **indirekte** ~ indirect taxes; **innere (inländische)** ~ internal taxes (charges); **kommunale** ~ municipal rates; **öffentliche (staatliche)** ~ public charges (taxes), rates and taxes; **soziale** ~ social [security] contributions, compulsory welfare; **städtische** ~ municipal taxes, town rates (taxes, dues), urban rates; **ständige** ~ perpetual taxes; **steuerliche** ~ fiscal burden; **zusätzliche** ~ supplementary charges;
mit ~ **belegen** to impose taxes, to levy [contributions], to tax *(US)*; ~ **erheben** to impose (levy, collect) a duty (tax); **hohe** ~ **bezahlen müssen** to be heavily taxed.
Abgabe|beschränkungen sales restrictions; ~**druck** *(Börse)* sales pressure; ~**frist** filing term; ~**kurs** *(Emission)* issue price; ~**leistung** *(el.)* power output; ~**liste** declaration of goods shipped; ~**marke** revenue stamp; ~**material** *(Börse)* stock offered, offerings.
Abgaben|befreiung immunity (exemption) from taxes; ~**bescheid** tax notice.
Abgabeneigung willingness (inclination) to sell.
Abgabenerhebung collection (gathering) of taxes.
abgabenfrei exempt from taxation (taxes), tax-exempt (-free, *US*), nondutiable, free of duty, duty-free, toll-less (-free), *(Kommunalsteuer)* nonassessable, zero-rated.
Abgaben|freiheit immunity [from taxes], exemption from duties (taxes), franchise *(US)*; ~**freiheit verlangen** to claim immunity from certain taxes; ~**ordnung** tax code, Internal Revenue Code *(US)*; ~**pflicht** taxability, tax liability, rat(e)ability.
abgabenpflichtig dutiable, liable to duty (to pay taxes), assessable, taxable, customable, *(Kommunalsteuer)* rat(e)able.
Abgaben|pflichtiger taxpayer; ~**reform** rating reform; ~**satz** tax rate, rate of duty; ~**umgehung** avoidance of duty (tax); ~**verteilung** assessment of taxes, classification of duties, allocation of revenue; ~**verzeichnis** rolls of the Exchequer; ~**wesen** tax (fiscal) system; ~**wirtschaft** fiscal management, financial economy.
Abgabe|pflicht tax liability; ~**preis** selling (sales) price, *(Gas, Elektrizität)* rate *(US)*, *(Obligation)* issue price; ~**sätze** *(Diskontpolitik)* selling rates; ~**stelle** delivery office *(Br.)*; ~**termin** filing date, *(Einkommensteuererklärung)* return period, *(Steuer)* date of payment; ~**verpflichtung** *(Börse)* firm offer.
Abgang going away, departure, *(Abfahrt)* departure, leaving, start, *(Abnahme)* decrease, reduction, *(Absatz)* market, sale, *(Absatzgebiet)* outlet, market, *(Bilanz)* deletion, *(Flüssigkeit)* leakage, *(Flugzeug)* start, *(Lagerbestand)* quantity issued, *(große Nachfrage)* run, *(Schauspieler)* exit, *(Schiff)* setting out, sailing, *(Schwund)* reduction, *(Tara)* tare, *(Tod)* decease, *(Verlust)* waste, wastage, loss, decrease, *(Warenversand)* dispatch, *(beim Wiegen)* deficiency, short weight, loss;
nach ~ **von der Schule** on leaving school;
üblicher ~ **von Arbeitskräften** natural waste; ~ **vom Goldstandard** abandonment of the gold standard; ~ **von einem Grundsatz** departure from a principle; **gleichmäßiger** ~ **von versicherten Leben** *(Lebensversicherung)* equal decrement of life; ~ **mit bestandener Prüfung** graduation from school (college); ~ **von der Schule** leaving school;
guten ~ **finden** to find a ready market, to go off well; **schlechten** ~ **finden** to have a poor sale, to be a drug in the market; **sich einen guten** ~ **verschaffen** to retire gracefully.
Abgänge deductions, *(Bilanz)* losses, retirements, *(Verkäufe)* sales;
~ **in der Belegschaft** separations;
pro Jahr bis zu 20% ~ **haben** to replace as much as 20% of its faculty each year.
abgängig missing, deficient, lost.
Abgangs|alter *(Schule)* school-leaving age; ~**amt** *(Post)* dispatching office, *(Telegramm)* office of origin; ~**bahnhof** departure (starting) station, station of departure, dispatching station, initial terminus, dispatch (forwarding) point *(US)*; ~**bahnsteig** departure platform; ~- **und Zugangsbericht** change report; ~**datum** date of dispatch; ~**entschädigung** severance pay, layoff benefit; ~**flugsteig** boarding gate; ~**geld** layoff benefit (pay); ~**gewicht** original tare; ~**hafen** port of departure (sailing, clearance); ~**liste** shipping list; ~**ort** place of departure, departure point, *(Fracht)* originating (initial) point; ~**postamt** dispatching office; ~**prüfung** final *(US)* (leaving) examination, finals *(US)*; ~**rate** *(Belegschaft)* separation rate; ~**rechnung** tare account (note, rate); **Zu- und** ~**satz** *(Belegschaft)* replacement rate; ~**schüler** graduate; ~**station** departure station, departure yard, station of departure, *(Flugplatz)* initial terminus, *(Fracht)* dispatching station, dispatch (forwarding) point *(US)*; ~**vergütung** *(Versicherungsrückkauf)* withdrawal benefit; ~**verkehr** outgoing traffic; ~**zeit** time of departure, *(Fracht, Telegramm)* time of dispatch, *(Schiff)* time of sailing; ~**zettel** *(Post)* bag list; ~**zeugnis** *(Angestellter)* clearance card, credit *(US)*, *(Schüler)* leaving (high school) certificate *(Br.)*, diploma *(US)*.
Abgas|e vapo(u)r, exhaust gas;
~**anlage** *(Flugzeug)* exhaust system; ~**schalldämpfer** muffler *(US)*, silencer *(Br.)*.

abgearbeitet worn out, tailworn.
abgebaut *(Baustelle)* dismantled, *(Bergwerk)* exploited, *(entlassen)* discharged, dismissed, fired, laid off *(US)*, *(Zölle)* cut, reduced, *(Zwangswirtschaft)* decontrolled.
abgeben to deliver [up], to give up, to hand over, *(Angebot)* to submit, to tender, *(Fahrkarte)* to surrender, to return, to give up, to hand over, *(Gepäck)* to leave with, to deposit, *(Schriftstück)* to file, to submit, to hand in, *(trassieren)* to value, *(verkaufen)* to sell, to dispose, to supply, to let have;
sich mit etw. ~ to have to do (occupy, deal, busy, concern o. s.) with s. th., to indulge with s. th.; **Akten an eine andere Behörde** ~ to pass records to another department; **Aktien** ~ to sell shares; **guten Anwalt** ~ to be cut out for a lawyer; **Augenzeugen für etw.** ~ to be an eyewitness for s. th.; **billig** ~ to sell cheap, to sell at a low figure; **blanko** ~ *(Börse)* to sell bear *(Br.)* (short, *US*); **eigenhändig** ~ to deliver personally; **Einfuhrerklärung** ~ to submit an import declaration; **Einkommensteuererklärung** ~ to file an income-tax return; **entgeltlich** ~ to sell for value (a consideration); **Erklärung** ~ to make a statement (declaration), to state, to declare; **eidesstattliche Erklärung** ~ to sign an affidavit; **gute Ernte** ~ to yield a good crop; **sein Gepäck** ~ to leave one's luggage at the luggage office *(Br.)*, to check one's baggage in the baggage room *(US)*; **sein Geschäft an seinen Sohn** ~ to make over one's business to one's son; **Gutachten** ~ to give an expert opinion; **Hintergrund** ~ to form the background; **guten Lehrer** ~ to make a good teacher; **Mittelsperson** ~ to play the intermediary; **Nachricht bei jem.** ~ to leave a note with s. o.; **Offerte** ~ to make an offer; **Paket** ~ to drop (leave) a parcel; **Partie zu zurückgesetzten Preisen** ~ to dispose of a lot at reduced prices; **persönlich** ~ to deliver by hand; **sich mit Politik** ~ to be interested (dabble in, bother about) politics; **Prügelknaben für j.** ~ to be s. one's scapegoat; **Sache an ein anderes Gericht** ~ to refer a case to another court; **seine Stimme** ~ to cast one's vote; **Sündenbock** ~ to carry the can (baby, *sl.*); **Telegramm** ~ to hand in a telegram; **Urteil** ~ to pass judgment; **guten Verkäufer** ~ to be a good salesman; **Versicherung** ~ to assure; **Versprechen** ~ to promise; **seine Visitenkarte bei jem.** ~ to leave one's card on s. o.; **seine Waren billig** ~ to sell one's goods cheaply; **Wechsel** ~ to draw value on s. o.; **Willenserklärung** ~ to express one's intention.
Abgeber *(Börse)* seller, giver, marketeer, *(einer Erklärung)* declarant, *(einer eidesstattlichen Erklärung)* deponent, *(eines Ladungsverzeichnisses)* manifestant, *(Wechsel)* drawer.
abgeblendet dimmed, dim-lighted, dipped;
nicht ~ undimmed;
~ **fahren** to drive with dimmed lights.
abgebrannt burned, *(pleite)* on the rocks (nut, *US sl.*), cleaned out, melted out *(sl.)*;
total ~ stone-broke, stony broke *(sl.)*;
völlig ~ **sein** to be without any means (stonybroke, *sl.*, hard up for money).
abgebrüht salted, case-hardened, conscience-proof, hard-boiled *(coll.)*.
abgedroschen stock, oldhat, commonplace, copybook, well-worn, stale, trite;
~**e Gedanken** outworn ideas; ~**e Redensart** stock phrase; ~**er Witz** stale joke.
abgedunkelt fahren, völlig to steam with all lights out.
abgefahrene Reifen badly worn tyres.
abgefaßt worded;
wie folgt ~ conceived as follows;
energisch ~ strongly worded; **höflich** ~ couched in polite terms.
abgefeimt sly, wily, cunning;
~**er Schurke** utter scoundrel.
abgefertigt werden *(Zoll)* to pass the customs;
kurz ~ to meet with a snub (rebuff).
abgefunden indemnified, *(Kind)* forisfamiliated;
~**er Gläubiger** compounded creditor.
abgegangener Beamter ex- (former) official.
abgegeben disposed of;
persönlich ~ delivered by hand.
abgeglichen *(Konto)* balanced, square.
abgegolten satisfied, met.
abgegrast *(Gebiet)* well-covered, thoroughly worked.
abgegrenzter|Begriff clear-cut notion; ~ **Bezirk** specified territory.
abgegriffen *(Buch)* well-thumbed, thumbmarked, *(Münze)* worn, detrited.
abgehackt *(Redeweise)* chopped, jerky.
abgehalftert sacked, fired *(US)*.
abgehalten werden *(Messe)* to be held.
abgehängt *(Speisewagen)* taken off;
~ **sein** *(fig.)* to be out of it.
abgehärtet endured, weather-beaten.
abgehauen off the hook *(sl.)*.
Abgehen von den Regeln deviation from the rules.
abgehen *(Absatz finden)* to sell, *(vom Betrag)* to be deducted, *(fehlen)* to be missing (wanted), *(Flugzeug)* to start, *(Post)* to go, to leave, to be dispatched, *(Schauspieler)* to make one's exit, to go off, *(Schiff)* to sail, to set out, to leave port, *(Straße)* to branch off, *(versandt werden)* to be forwarded (dispatched), *(Zug)* to depart, to go (steam) off, to leave;
von einem Amt ~ to retire from an office; **von einer früheren Ansicht** ~ to come round; **von der Bühne** ~ to leave the stage; **von einer Entscheidung** ~ to change one's opinion; **Gelände** ~ *(mil.)* to patrol the terrain; **glatt** ~ to turn out well, to go swimmingly; **Gleise** ~ to inspect the tracks; **mit einem akademischen Grad** ~ to graduate with a degree; **von einem Grundsatz** ~ to deviate from a principle; **kein Jota von etw.** ~ not to swerve a jota from s. th.; **nur langsam** ~ to go off heavily; **von einer Meinung** ~ to change one's view; **reißend** ~ to sell rapidly (like hot dogs, cakes); **schnell** ~ to yield an easy (quick, short) return; **von der Schule** ~ to leave school; **schwer** ~ to sell badly (heavily); **von einer Summe** ~ to be deducted from a sum; **um 12 Uhr** ~ to go at twelve o'clock.
abgehend|e Ladung outward cargo (freight); ~**e Post** outgoing mail; ~**es Schiff** leaving ship; ~**er Zug** departing train.
abgehetzt dead (dog) -tired, dead-beat.
abgehoben withdrawn, *(Dividende)* cashed, collected;
nicht ~**e Dividenden** unclaimed dividends, dividends not yet collected.
abgeholt fetched, collected, picked up;
~ **werden** to wait to be collected.
ab|geholzt cut-out; ~**gekämpft** worn out, exhausted, dead.
abgekanzelt werden to get a lecture.
abgekartet fixed, put-up, preconcerted, collusive, plotted;
~**es Spiel** underplot, put-up job *(sl.)*, rig; ~**es Spiel treiben** to stack cards *(sl.)*; ~**e Zeugenaussage** collusive evidence.
abgeklappert *(Gebiet)* canvassed.
abgeknipst *(Wochenkarte)* expired.
abgekommen, vom Kurs driven out off one's course.
abgekürzt abbreviated, abridged, concise, condensed, shortened;
~**e Lebensversicherung** limited payment life policy; ~**e Leibrente** temporary life annuity; ~**es Verfahren** summary proceedings, shortened process.
abgelagert *(Wein)* matured, seasoned;
nicht ~ unseasoned;
nicht ~**es Holz** green wood.
abgelaufen expired, exhausted, up, *(fällig)* due, mature, *(Steuerjahr)* ended, *(Verfahren)* summary;
noch nicht ~ unexpired, still valid;
~ **sein** *(Frist)* to have run;
~**er Wechsel** overdue bill.
abgelegen distant, remote, unfrequented, back, out-of-the-way, from the way, lonely, off the beaten track;
weit ~ off the map *(coll.)*;
~**es Dorf** sequestered village; ~**e Stadt** far-off city.
abgelegt filed for record, *(Kleid)* cast-off, discarded;
~**e Akten** dead files (material); ~**e Sache** discard.
abgeleiert hackneyed.
abgeleitetes Einkommen derived income.
ab|gelenkt diverted; **im Dock** ~**geliefert** delivered at dock.
abgelten *(entschädigen)* to reimburse, to compensate, to indemnify, to settle, to pay off, *(Schuld)* to discharge, to satisfy;
Kapitalertragssteuer durch eine 30%ige Pauschalzahlung ~ to meet capital yield tax by a 30 per cent lump-sum payment;
Überstunden ~ to pay for overtime;
sich seinen Urlaubsanspruch ~ **lassen** to accept payment in lieu of a holiday.
Abgeltung discharge, payment, *(Abfindung)* settlement, *(Entschädigung)* compensation, reimbursement, indemnification;
zur ~ **von Barleistungen** in lieu of cash;
pauschale ~ compounded (global) settlement;
~ **von Ansprüchen** settling of claims; ~ **von Leistungen** payment of services rendered; ~ **von Urlaubsansprüchen** vacation allowance *(US)*.
Abgeltungs|betrag indemnity, redemption money; ~**darlehn** redemption loan.
abgemacht understood, agreed, *(geregelt)* arranged, settled;
~! it's a deal, O.K., okay! *(US)*;
~**er Preis** price agreed upon.

abgemagert zum Skelett reduced to a skeleton.
abgemessen measured, *(Redeweise)* stiff, formal.
abgeneigt ill disposed, indisposed, disinclined;
~ **sein** to be averse (disinclined), to jib *(Br.)*; **einem Glas Wein nicht** ~ **sein** to be equal to a glass of wine.
abgenommen detached, *(Strom)* picked up;
fest ~ *(Emissionsgeschäft)* underwritten firm.
abgenutzt obsolete, worn out, used, beat-up, *(Kleider)* threadbare, shabby, *(Papier)* old;
ziemlich ~ **aussehen** to look the worse for wear; ~ **werden** to waste, to wear away;
~**e Schrift** worn-out type; ~**e Stelle** fray, fret.
abgeordnet delegate, delegatory.
Abgeordneten|bank bench; ~**bezüge** parliamentary pay; ~**haus** Chamber of Deputies, House of Commons *(Br.)* (Representatives, *US*); ~**immunität** parliamentary privilege (immunity); ~**kammer** Parliament; ~**liste** return book *(Br.)*; ~**mandat** seat [in Parliament], electoral mandate, parliamentary seat; ~**nötigung** obstruction of members.
Abgeordnetensitz seat [in Parliament], parliamentary seat;
sich um einen ~ **bemühen** to stand for Parliament; **frei gewordenen** ~ **neu besetzen** to fill a vacancy in congress *(US)*; **des** ~**es für verlustig erklären** to unseat a member of Parliament.
Abgeordneten|stimme delegate vote; ~**wahl** parliamentary election; ~**zahl** number of deputies.
Abgeordnete|r deputy, delegate *(US)*, *(parl.)* member of parliament, parlamentarian, frock, representative *(US)*, congressman *(US)*;
bisheriger (ehemaliger) ~**r** retiring deputy; **einflußreiche** ~ members above the gangway; **erfahrener** ~**r** old parliamentarian hand; **nicht zum Kabinett gehöriger** ~**r** backbencher; **gewählter** ~**r** elected representative, member returned; **gewöhnlicher** ~**r** backbencher; **parteiloser** ~**r** unattached deputy;
~**r für A** sitting (hono(u)rable) member for A; ~**r der Arbeiterpartei** labour member *(Br.)*;
~ **beeinflussen** to lobby; ~ **wegen der Erhöhung von Zuschüssen beeinflussen** to lobby for higher subsidies; **einem** ~**n frühere Ausführungen entgegenhalten** to hansardize *(Br.)*; **einem** ~**n das Wort erteilen** to recognize a member *(US)*; **zu wenig** ~ **haben** to be underrepresented; ~**r sein** to have a seat (sit) in Parliament; ~**n stellen** to send a member to Parliament; ~**n wählen** to return a member to Parliament; **sich in einer Sache an seinen** ~**n wenden** to take up a matter with one's MP; ~**r werden** to go into Parliament.
abgepackte Ware packaged goods.
abgerechnet settled;
nicht ~ unsettled;
~**er Betrag** amount deducted; **nicht** ~**e Konten** open accounts.
abgerissen tattered, ragged, shabby, *(Haus)* pulled down, demolished;
völlig ~ **sein** to be down at heel.
abgerufen werden, geschäftlich to be called away on business.
abgerundet rounded off, round, in round figures, *(Stil)* well-rounded;
~**er Betrag** round sum; ~**e Leistung** finished performance.
abgesagt cancelled, *(Konzert)* off.
abgesandt forwarded, shipped *(US)*.
Abgesandter delegate, *(Politik)* envoy, *(geheim)* emissary.
abgeschafft extinct.
abgeschätzt rated, valued, assessed, extended;
nicht ~ unrated, unvalued.
abgeschieden remote, secluded, out of the way, solitary, lonely.
Abgeschiedenheit solitude, seclusion.
abgeschirmt screened;
nicht ~ unscreened.
abgeschlafft knocked out.
abgeschlagen sein to be nowhere.
abgeschlossen private, secluded, quiet, *(beendet)* finished, *(beschlossen)* settled, agreed, *(Bildung)* well-rounded, *(zugeschlossen)* closed;
formgerecht ~ duly completed; **hermetisch** ~ airtight, hermetically sealed; **in sich** ~ self-contained, *(Erzählung)* complete; **nicht** ~ unsettled, uncleared, *(nicht zugeschlossen)* unclosed; **sauber** ~ buttoned up *(sl.)*;
~ **am ...** *(Rechnung)* up to ...;
~ **leben** to live a secluded life;
~**es Börsengeschäft** round transaction; ~**e Geschäfte** business transacted; **mit** ~**em Hochschulstudium** with a degree; ~**es Konto** closed account; **nicht** ~**e Rechnung** unsettled account; ~**e Wohnung** separate dwelling, self-contained flat.
abgeschmackt in bad taste, tasteless;
~**e Bemerkung** fatuous remark.
abgeschnitten cut-off, withdrawn;
vom Verkehr mit anderen ~ incommunicado;
~**e Verbindungen** cut-off communications.
abgeschossen discharged, shot-off, *(Rakete)* launched;
~ **werden** to get a four-penny one *(Br., sl.)*.
abgeschrieben depreciated, written off;
zu 100% ~ **werden können** to qualify for an allowance of 100 per cent; **teilweise** ~ **sein** to be partly depreciated.
abgeschwächt *(Kurse)* easier, weaker, sagged, depressed, worked off;
etw. ~ eased off a fraction;
leicht ~ **eröffnen** to open at a slight discount; ~ **liegen** to rule easier; ~ **sein** to be depressed;
~**e Börse** weaker tendency on the stock exchange, weaker prices; ~**er Markt** sagging market.
abgeschwemmtes Erdreich rainwash.
abgesehen|von apart (aside, *US*) from, except for, save; **von einigen Fehlern** ~ with the exception of a few mistakes; **von den finanziellen Verlusten einmal** ~ not to mention the financial losses.
abgesetzt *(abgesagt)* cancelled, off, *(abgezogen)* deducted, written off, *(Beamter)* removed, dismissed, *(König)* dethroned, *(Manuskript)* in type, paragraphical, *(verkauft)* sold;
~ **sein** *(drucktechn.)* to be in type; ~ **werden** *(Fallschirmtruppen)* to be dropped (landed), *(Theaterstück)* to come off, *(Ware)* to go off, to sell; **flott** ~ **werden** to sell rapidly; **sofort** ~ **werden** *(Aktien)* to be absorbed by the public.
abgesichert, vertraglich covered by contract;
mit Einschränkungen ~ **sein** to be hedged about with qualifications.
abgesondert distinct, separate, solitary, detached, isolated;
~ **verwahren** to keep separately;
~**e Befriedigung** *(Konkurs)* preferential treatment (payment);
~**es Vermögen** *(Ehefrau)* separate property.
abgespaltene Gruppe splinter group.
abgespannt tired, worn out, fagged, washed out *(coll.)*.
abgesperrt, polizeilich cordoned off by the police.
abgespielt *(Schallplatte)* worn.
abgesprochen agreed upon, *(heimlich)* collusive.
abgestanden *(Bier)* stale, flat, *(fig.)* as dry as chip, musty, insipid, stale.
abgestellt *(Fahrzeug)* parked, *(mil.)* detached, *(tel.)* disconnected;
auf das Alter des Erwerbers ~ **sein** to be geared to the purchaser's age; **außerhalb der Straße** ~ **sein** to be standing off the road;
~**er Angestellter,** ~**e Arbeitskraft** borrowed (loaned) employee.
abgestempelt stamped, *(Effekten)* assented *(US)*, *(entwertet)* cancelled, obliterated;
nicht ~ undefaced; **richtig** ~ duly stamped.
abgestimmt *(Konto)* reconciled;
aufeinander ~ correlative; **schlecht** ~ ill-timed; **zeitlich** ~ timed;
~**er Empfänger** tuned receiver.
abgestuft *(Steuer)* gradual, gradational, graduated.
abgestumpft dull, indifferent, apathetic.
abgetakelt *(Schiff)* unrigged.
abgetane Sache off-cast.
abgeteilt partitioned;
~**er Raum** compartment.
abgetragen *(bezahlt)* paid up, *(Kleider)* shabby, out at elbows, threadbare, rusty;
völlig ~ **sein** to be worn to the last thread;
~**e Schuld** liquidated (paid off, paid up) debt.
abgetrennt detached.
abgetreten assigned;
~**es Gebiet** ceded territory.
abgetrieben driven out of one's course.
abgeurteilt tried, convicted;
im Schnellverfahren ~ summarily sentenced;
rasch ~ **werden** to be brought to a speedy justice.
abgewertet devalued, devalorized.
abgewickelt settled, paid off, liquidated;
nicht ~ unsettled.
abgewiesen *(Klage)* dismissed, *(Kläger)* nonsuited;
als rechtlich irrelevant ~ denied on the law;
~ **werden** to come down, to get the mitten *(coll.)*.
abgewimmelt werden to be turned down flat.
abgewinnen, Geschmack to find pleasure in; **dem Meer Land** ~ to recover (reclaim) land from the sea; **einer Sache die beste Seite**

~ to make the best of it; **jem. einen Vorsprung** ~ to steal a march on s. o.; **jem. einen Vorteil** ~ to get the better of s. o.; **der Wüste Ackerland** ~ to wrest arable land from the desert.
abgewirtschaftet run down, broken down, ruined;
~ **haben** to be down and out.
abgewogen balanced, measured, calculated, judicious, poised.
abgewöhnen to disaccustom;
jem. etw. ~ to disaccustom (break, cure) s. o. of s. th.; **sich das Rauchen** ~ to give up smoking.
abgewrackt werden to go to scrap.
abgewürgt *(Motor)* stalled.
abgezahlt paid up;
noch ~ **werden müssen** to be subject to a hire-purchase *(Br.)* (deferred-payment, *US*) agreement.
abgezählt, bitte Fahrgeld ~ **bereit halten** please have the exact fare ready.
abgezeichnet *(Schriftstück)* initialled.
abgezirkelt pinpoint;
wie ~ with clockwise precision.
abgezogen *(Truppen)* withdrawn.
Abglanz reflection.
abgleichen to balance, to adjust, *(drucktechn.)* to justify;
Konten ~ to square accounts.
Abgleichung adjustment;
~ **von Konten** squaring of accounts.
Abgleiten der Kurse weakness in the market, declining (sliding) market.
abgleiten to slip, *(Kurse)* to slide down, to weaken, to slip, to decline, to fall, *(Währung)* to slump, to go down;
ins Banale ~ to lapse into trivialities; **seitlich** ~ *(Flugzeug)* to sideslip, to skid; **sozial** ~ to sink in the social scale.
Abgott | der Familie idol of the family;
Geld zu seinem ~ **machen** to worship money, to make a god of money.
abgöttisch verehren to idolize.
abgraben, jem. das Wasser to cut the ground from under s. one's feet.
abgrasen to browse;
Bezirk ~ to work a district; **Markt** ~ to exploit a selling area; **ganze Stadt** ~ to scour the whole town.
abgreifen, eine Entfernung auf der Karte to measure a distance on the map.
abgrenzen to mark out, to limit, *(Begriff)* to define, to demarcate, *(Hoheitsgewässer)* to delimit, *(Mutung)* to peg out, to stake, *(Vollmacht)* to define, to circumscribe;
Thema ~ to keep one subject distinct from another.
Abgrenzung demarcation, termination, delimitation, *(Begriffe)* definition;
periodische ~ *(von Aufwand und Energie)* matching;
strenge ~ **der Berufsgruppen** demarcation of occupational classes; ~ **der Hoheitsgewässer** delimitation of territorial waters; ~ **der Verkaufsgebiete** division of markets; ~ **von Vollmachten** definition of powers.
Abgrenzungs | kosten deferrals and accruals; ~**linie** boundary line, line of demarcation; ~**merkmale** classification criteria; ~**posten** *(Bilanz)* deferred item; **gewerkschaftliche** ~**probleme** demarcation problems in industry.
Abgrund yawn, abyss, precipice, *(Schlucht)* chasm, gulf;
~ **der Hölle** pit of hell; ~ **der Verworfenheit** abyss of depravity; **in einen** ~ **stürzen** to precipitate into an abyss; ~ **überschreiten** to go over the brink.
abgründige Vorstellung unfathomable idea.
Abguß cast, *(drucktechn.)* plate, stereo[type];
~ **herstellen** to cast a copy.
Abhaken ticking off, tallying.
abhaken to tick off, to mark with a tick, to check off *(US)*, to tally, *(Waggon)* to uncouple;
jds. Namen auf einer Liste ~ to put a tick against s. one's name (to check against a name, *US*) in a list; **Rechnungsposten** ~ to tick off items in an account; **Waren auf einer Liste** ~ to keep tally of goods.
abhalftern, j. to get rid of s. o., to give s. o. the sack *(coll.)*.
abhalten to keep off, to hold off, *(Fest)* to celebrate, to observe, *(hindern)* to detain, to hinder, to prevent, to deter, *(Schiff)* to edge away;
j. von der Arbeit ~ to keep s. o. from (hinder s. o. in) his work; **Hauptversammlung** ~ to hold the statutory meeting; **vom Lande** ~ *(Schiff)* to bear off from the land; **Prüfung** ~ to hold an examination; **Versammlung** ~ to hold a meeting, *(Parlament)* to sit; **öffentliche Versammlung** ~ to meet in public; **Vorlesung** ~ to deliver a lecture.
Abhaltung *(Fest)* celebration, *(Verhinderung)* detention;
~**en** detentions;
anderweitige ~ other business to attend to;
~ **der Hauptversammlung** holding the statutory meeting; ~ **einer Versammlung** holding of a meeting; ~ **einer Vorlesung** delivery of a lecture, lecturing.
Abhaltungsgrund previous engagement, prevention.
abhandeln *(behandeln)* to treat, *(Preisnachlaß erwirken)* to bargain, to obtain a reduction, to beat down, to knock off the price, *(verhandeln)* to negotiate;
jem. etw. ~ to bargain s. th. out of s. o., to knock s. th. off s. one's price, to beat s. o. down by; **Thema** ~ to treat a subject.
abhanden·gekommen lost, missing, mislaid;
~**e Sache** mislaid property; ~**e Wertpapiere** lost securities.
abhanden kommen to get lost, to be mislaid, to go astray.
Abhandlung treatise, treat, tract, essay, dissertation, *(Vortrag)* paper, disquisition;
gedankenreiche ~ thoughtful essay; **gelehrte** ~ learned treatise; **gesammelte** ~**en** *(Gesellschaft)* transactions, proceedings; **kritische** ~ critical treatise; **kurze** ~ prolusion; **wissenschaftliche** ~ scientific treatise, dissertation;
~ **einer Gesellschaft** transactions of a learned society;
~ **schreiben** to dissert.
Abhang slope, incline, gradient, hillside, hang, decline, descent;
sanfter ~ gentle slope.
abhängen *(abhängig sein)* to depend upon, *(Anhänger)* to unlock, to unhitch, *(Konkurrenz)* to out-distance, to give the skip, *(Waggon)* to take off, to uncouple;
j. ~ *(tel.)* to hang up on s. o.; **von einer Erlaubnis** ~ to depend on a permission (permit); **finanziell von jem.** ~ to be financially dependent on s. o.; **immer mehr von jem.** ~ to rest more and more in s. one's hands; **von niemanden** ~ to be on one's own, to be financially independent; **Speisewagen** ~ to unhook the dining car; **von den Umständen** ~ to depend on circumstances; **voneinander** ~ to interdepend; **vom Wetter** ~ to depend on the weather; **vom Zufall** ~ to be at the mercy of chance; **von einer Zustimmung** ~ to be subject to approval.
abhängig conditioned, conditional, contingent upon, *(finanziell)* dependant, *(gegenseitig)* interdependent, *(jur.)* attendant, *(von einer Zustimmung)* subject to;
rechtlich ~ incident at law;
~ **machen von** condition [up]on, to subject; ~ **sein** to depend, to be held subject; **von jem.** ~ **sein** to be in subjection to s. o., to eat s. one's salt; **von jds. Genehmigung** ~ **sein** to be subject to s. one's approval; **von jds. Gutdünken** ~ **sein** to be at s. one's discretion; **von seinem Vater** ~ **sein** to depend on one's father; **in einem** ~**en Arbeitsverhältnis stehen** to belong to the wage-earning group; **voneinander** ~**e Funktionen** interdependent functions; ~**es Gebiet** *(Staat)* dependency; **in** ~**er Stellung sein** to be in a subordinate position; ~**e [Tochter]gesellschaft** controlled (underlying, *US*) company; ~**es Unternehmen** controlled concern.
Abhängiger dependant.
Abhängigkeit dependence, dependency, *(Unterordnung)* subordination, subjection;
in ~ **von** subject to, as a function of;
gegenseitige ~ interdependence; **vollständige** ~ total dependency;
finanzielle ~ **von seinen Eltern** dependence upon one's parents;
~ **zweier Herstellungsverfahren** interdependence of two manufacturing processes;
von der ~ **von der Dollarparität befreien** to unhook from the dollar; **in** ~ **geraten** to lose one's independence; **j. in völliger** ~ **halten** to have absolute control over s. o.; **in** ~ **leben** to live in dependence; **in sklavischer** ~ **von Konventionen leben** to be a slave to convention.
Abhängigkeits | bedürfnis dependency need; ~**gebiet** dependency; ~**grad [vom Arbeitslohn]** partial dependence; ~**verhältnis** dependent relation[ship], dependent condition, dependence, *(Angestellter)* subordinate position; **in einem** ~**verhältnis zu jem. stehen** to be dependent upon s. o.; **in einem völligen** ~**verhältnis existieren** to live in a state of subjection.
Abhängung unterwegs *(Waggon)* dropoff en route.
abhärten to harden, to inure;
sich ~ to harden the body; **sich gegen Kälte** ~ to harden o. s. to the cold *(fam.)*.
Abhauen lam *(US sl.)*.
abhauen to skedaddle, to scat, to fly the scoop, to pop (pike) off, to lam, to scram *(sl.)*, to blow *(sl.)*, to hop it *(sl.)*, to hop the twig *(sl.)*, to cut one's stick *(sl.)*, to hook it *(sl.)*, to beat it *(US sl.)*.

abhebbar, jederzeit subject to check *(US)*; **mit einjähriger Kündigungsfrist** ~ withdrawable at one year's notice; **täglich** ~ at call.

Abheben *(Flugzeug)* take-off, getaway, *(Geld)* withdrawal.

abheben to draw, to withdraw, *(Dividende)* to cash, to collect, *(Flugzeug)* to take off;
mehrere Dächer ~ *(Sturm)* to lift several roofs; **Flugzeug** ~ to pull the aircraft up; **Geld von der Bank** ~ to withdraw funds from the bank; **sich vom Hintergrund** ~ to stand out against the background; **Hörer** ~ to pick up (lift) the receiver; **von seinem Konto** ~ to draw on (withdraw from) one's account; **leicht** ~ *(Flugzeug)* to take off easily; **Telefonhörer** ~ to take off (lift) the receiver; **seine Zinsen** ~ to cash (collect) one's interest.

abhebend, sich outlined.

Abhebung|en withdrawal of funds, drawings;
tägliche ~**en** day-to-day withdrawals;
~ **der Dividende** cashing (collection) of dividends; ~ **eines Geldbetrags** withdrawal of a sum of money; ~ **von einem Konto** drawing on an account; ~ **der Prima** collecting of the first of exchange; ~ **vom Sparkonto** withdrawal from a deposit account, savings withdrawal.

Abhebungs|befugnis authority for withdrawal, drawing authorization, drawing right; ~**beschränkungen** withdrawal restrictions; ~**erfordernisse** withdrawal requirements; ~**formular** withdrawal form; ~**voraussetzung** negotiated order of withdrawal *(US)*.

abheften to file [away], to file in;
Briefe ~ to run letters into a file.

abhelfen to redress, to remedy, to relieve;
einem Bedürfnis ~ to satisfy a need; **einer Beschwerde** ~ to adjust a complaint; **einem Fehler** ~ to correct an error.

abhelfend remedial.

abhetzen, sich to wear o. s. out, exhaust o. s.

Abhilfe relief, redress, remedy;
gesetzliche ~ legal redress;
~ **im Verwaltungswege** administrative remedy; ~ **im Wege einer einstweiligen Verfügung** relief by injunction;
gerichtliche ~ **bekommen** to obtain judicial redress; ~ **schaffen** to remedy, to redress, to take remedial measures;
~**gesetz** remedial statute; ~**maßnahmen** remedial (corrective) measures; **keine gesetzlichen** ~**möglichkeiten haben** to have no remedy at law.

Abhitze waste heat.

abhobeln to plane away.

abholbereit ready for collection;
~ **sein** to be awaiting collection.

Abhol|bezirk collection district; ~- **und Zustelldienst** pickup and delivery service.

Abholen, j. zum ~ **schicken** to send s. o. to meet s. o.

abholen to collect, to fetch, to call for;
j. ~ to call on s. o., to pick up s. o.; **jem. vom Bahnhof** ~ to meet s. o. at the station (off the train); **seine Briefe vom Schließfach** ~ to fetch (collect) one's letters from one's post-office box; **sein Gepäck bei der Gepäckaufbewahrung** ~ to claim one's luggage from the left-luggage office *(Br.)* (baggage from the baggage room, *US*); **j. zu Hause** ~ to pick up s. o. at his house;
~ **lassen** to send for, to pick up *(US)*.

Abhol|fach post-office (letter, private) box; ~**fahrzeug** pickup truck; ~**frist** period for collection; ~**gebühr** collection fee; ~**kommando** *(Flugzeug)* aircraft ferrying department, *(mil.)* fetching party; ~**stelle** collecting service.

Abholung collection, fetching, pickup *(US)*;
~ **am Schalter** general delivery *(US)*; ~ **von Verlegerbeischüssen** collection of publishers' enclosures;
auf seine ~ **warten** to wait to be collected.

Abholungs|dienst *(Spediteur)* pickup and delivery service; ~**fach** post-office (letter) box.

Abholzeit time of collection.

abholzen to deforest, to disafforest.

Abholzung disafforestation, clearance, deforestation, clearing.

Abholzungsplan felling plan.

Abhör|anlage, ~**apparat** monitory (bugging, *US*) device, monitor, recording system; ~**box** *(Fernsehen, Film)* monitoring booth; ~**dienst** monitory service; ~**einrichtung** wire tapping, monitory (bugging, *US*) device.

Abhören *(Telefongespräche)* listening in, interception, telephone (wire) tapping, monitoring, bugging *(US)*, milking.

abhören to listen in, to intercept, to wire, to tap, to monitor, to milk;
Rechnungen ~ to audit accounts; **Schulaufgabe** ~ to hear a lesson; **Telefonleitung [mit Wanzen]** ~ to bug a telephone *(US)*.

Abhörer wire tapper, monitor, milker.

Abhör|gerät monitor, *(tel.)* dictograph, detectaphone, bugging device *(US)*; ~**kabine** listening cubicle; ~**krieg** audio surveillance war; ~**mikrophon** miniphone; ~**raum** monitor room; ~**skandal** bugging scandal *(US)*; ~**stelle** interception (monitor) station, interceptor, *(mil.)* listening post; ~**stromkreis** tapping circuit; ~**system** monitory system; ~**vorfall** bugging case *(US)*; ~**vorrichtung** listening (monitoring) device, bugging device *(US)*, bug *(US)*; ~**vorrichtung einbauen** to bug *(US)*; **mit** ~**vorrichtungen versehen** wired, bugged *(US)*; ~**zelle** control room.

Abirrung aberration.

Abitur examination for the General Certificate of Education *(Br.)*, final examination *(US)*;
sein ~ **machen** to pass one's school-leaving examination, to take one's finals *(US)*.

Abiturient graduate *(US)*, candidate for the General Certificate of Education *(Br.)*.

Abiturienten|examen examination for the General Certificate of Education *(Br.)*, final (leaving) examination *(US)*, finals *(US)*; ~**zeugnis** [etwa] Advanced General Certificate of Education *(Br.)*, diploma *(US)*.

abjagen, jem. etw. to skunk s. o. out of s. th. *(sl.)*; **jem. sein Geld** ~ to swindle money out of s. o.; **jem. die Kundschaft** ~ to alienate s. one's clients.

abkämmen, ganze Stadt nach einem Mörder to comb the whole city to find a murderer.

abkanzeln to rag, to row, to haul over the coals, to tick off, to trim *(sl.)*, to call down *(US)*;
j. ganz gehörig ~ to give s. o. a good ticking-off.

abkapseln, sich to exile o. s., to retire into one's shell; **hermetisch** ~ to seal off.

abkassieren, in wesentlich erhöhten Gewinnen to reap in terms of substantially increased profits.

abkaufen to buy, to purchase from;
seinem Partner den Anteil ~ to buy out a partner; **jem. den ganzen Vorrat** ~ to clear s. one's stock.

Abkehr estrangement, withdrawal;
~ **vom Sozialismus andeuten** to trend away from socialism.

abkehren, sich to dissociate o. s., to take no further interest.

Abkippen dumping.

abkippen to dump, to tip, *(Flugzeug)* to stall, to wing over.

Abkippgeschwindigkeit *(Flugzeug)* stalling speed.

abklappern, Gebiet to canvass an area; **ganze Gegend nach etw.** ~ to scour the whole district for s. th.; **alle Häuser in der Gegend** ~ *(Vertreter)* to do the round of all the houses in an area; **Läden nach etw.** ~ to round (traipse round) the shops looking for s. th.; **alle Straßen nach einer Beschäftigung** ~ to pound the pavement *(sl.)*.

Abklatsch *(drucktechn.)* plate, print, stereotype, *(fig.)* imitation.

abklatschen to copy, to reproduce, to print [off], to strike off, to dab.

Abklingen lull;
~ **der Konjunktur** recession, slackening of economy;
im ~ **sein** to be on the wane, to have run out its string.

abklingen to fade [out], to fade away, *(Epidemie)* to recede, *(Konjunktur)* to recede, to slacken, to wane, to vanish, *(Sturm, Wind)* to die down, to subside, to abate.

abknapsen, sich etw. to stint o. s. of s. th.; **sich Zeit** ~ to take time off.

abknipsen, Film to finish off a film.

abknöpfen, jem. Geld to touch (sting) s. o. for money; **jem. ein Pfund** ~ to sponge on (spring) s. o. for a quid *(Br.)*.

abkommandieren *(mil.)* to detail, to detach, to assign, to draft, to overslaugh *(Br.)*, to second *(Br.)*;
ins Ausland ~ to order abroad; **zu einem Lehrgang** ~ to detach for a course.

abkommandiert detached;
~ **sein** to be on a course.

Abkommandierung detachment, detail, assignment, posting, secondment *(Br.)*;
~ **zu einem höheren Kommando** overslaugh *(Br.)*.

Abkomme descendant, offspring, scion.

Abkommen accord, arrangement, agreement, understanding, treaty, league, convention, compromise, *(Tarif)* bargain;
durch gütliches ~ by mutual agreement; **im Sinne dieses** ~**s** for the purpose of this agreement;
befristetes ~ transient agreement; **betriebsgewerkschaftliches** ~ shopcraft settlement; **dieses** ~ present agreement; **dreiseitiges** ~ triangular agreement; **finanzielles** ~ financial agreement; **formloses** ~ *(Völkerrecht)* accord; **an Bedingungen geknüpftes** ~ conditional agreement; **gütliches** ~ amicable settlement; **inter-**

nationales ~ international convention; **langfristiges** ~ long-term agreement; **laufendes** ~ continuing (standing) agreement; **multilaterales** ~ multilateral agreement; **mündliches** ~ verbal agreement; **schriftliches** ~ written agreement; **stillschweigendes** ~ tacit agreement; **ungebundenes** ~ no-strings agreement; **unwiderrufliches** ~ binding agreement; **vorläufiges** ~ preliminary agreement; **vorübergehendes** ~ temporary agreement; **zweiseitiges** ~ bilateral treaty;
~ **über deutsche Auslandsschulden** London Agreement; ~ **über den Austausch von Kriegsgefangenen** cartel; ~ **mit der Betriebsgewerkschaft** shopcraft settlement; ~ **mit den Gewerkschaften** union agreement; ~ **einer Luftfahrtgesellschaft** civil aviation agreement; ~ **zur gegenseitigen Unterrichtung** information-sharing agreement; ~ **über gegenseitige Verteidigungsaufgaben** mutual defense (defence, *Br.*) agreement; ~ **über gemeinsames Vorgehen** *(dipl.)* concert; ~ **über den Zahlungsverkehr** exchange agreement; ~ **über wirtschaftliche Zusammenarbeit** Agreement on Economic Cooperation (OEC);
~ **zur Unterzeichnung auflegen** to open a convention for signature; ~ **beenden** to determine an agreement; **sich durch ein** ~ **von etw. befreien** to contract o. s. out of s. th.; **einem internationalen** ~ **beitreten** to accede to an international agreement; ~ **bestätigen** to confirm a treaty; ~ **zustande bringen** to mediate a settlement; **einem** ~ **entsprechen** to confirm with an arrangement; **in den Bereich eines ~s fallen** to fall within the ambit of an agreement; **zu einem** ~ **gelangen** to reach an agreement; ~ **kündigen** to terminate a convention; **mit jem. ein** ~ **schließen** to enter into an agreement with s. o.; ~ **treffen** to make an agreement, to come to an arrangement, to reach an understanding, to make a deal; **mit seinen Gläubigern ein** ~ **treffen** to compound (make an arrangement, a composition) with one's creditors; ~ **mit Vorbehalt unterzeichnen** to sign an agreement provisionally; **einem** ~ **nicht zustimmen** to dissent from an arrangement.

abkommen to get away, *(Flugzeug)* to take off, *(Schiff)* to come off;
vom Gegenstand der Verhandlung ~ to digress from the subject; **vom Kurs** ~ to deviate from the course; **von einem Plan** ~ to abandon a plan; **vom Thema** ~ to wander from the subject; **von einer Vorstellung** ~ to get rid of an idea; **vom Wege** ~ to lose one's way, to go astray;
vom Geschäft nicht ~ **können** not to be able to get away from business.

Abkommenschaft descendants, offspring, issue, posterity, progeny.

Abkommens|entwurf draft agreement, draft convention; ~**konto** agreement account; ~**land** *(ECU)* clearing country; ~**verlängerung** extension of an accord; ~**währung** *(ECU)* clearing currency.

abkömmlich dispensable, available;
eine ganze Woche nicht ~ **sein** to be needed for a whole week.

Abkömmling descendant, offspring, scion;
direkter ~ lineal descendant; **eheliche** ~**e** legitimate offspring; **ohne** ~ **sterben** to die intestate.

abkoppeln to uncouple, to unclutch, to detach.

abkratzen to go west *(sl.)*, to kick the bucket *(sl.)*.

abkühlen, sich to cool down *(coll.)*, *(Konjunktur)* to cool off; **jds. Begeisterung** ~ to throw cold water on s. one's enthusiasm.

abkühlend|wirken to have a moderating effect; **auf jds. Begeisterung** ~ **wirken** to cool off s. one's enthusiasm.

Abkühlung cooling;
konjunkturelle ~ cyclical slackening; **merkliche** ~ noticeable decline in temperature;
~ **der Beziehungen** cooling of relations.

Abkühlungs|vertrag *(Völkerrecht)* cooling-off treaty; ~**zeit** *(Tarifauseinandersetzungen)* cooling time, cooling-off period.

Abkunft descent, origin, birth, stock, family, lineage, parentage, extraction;
von adliger ~ of noble descent; **von deutscher** ~ of German extraction; **von niedriger** ~ of mean birth;
von bürgerlicher ~ **sein** to be a commoner; **vornehmer** ~ **sein** to be of noble birth.

abkuppeln to detach, to uncouple.

abkürzen to abbreviate, *(kürzen)* to curtail, to reduce, *(verkürzen)* to abridge, to short-cut, to shorten, to condense;
Frist ~ to shorten a period; **Urlaub** ~ to curtail one's holiday; **Verfahren** ~ to shorten a procedure; **Weg** ~ to take a short cut, to shorten a road.

Abkürzung shortcut, cutoff, *(Kurzform)* abbreviation, short for, *(Verkürzung)* abridg(e)ment;
handelsübliche ~**en** commercial signs;
~ **der Debatte auf bestimmte Punkte** kangaroo closure *(Br.)*; ~ **einer Frist** shortening of a period; ~ **seines Urlaubs** curtailment of one's holiday; ~ **der Versicherungsdauer** shortening of policy;
~ **nehmen** to cut off a corner.

Abkürzungs|system system of abbreviation; ~**verfahren** short-cut method; ~**verzeichnis** list of abbreviations; ~**weg** short cut, crosscut; ~**weg einschlagen** to take a short cut; ~**zeichen** *(Kurzschrift)* grammalog(ue).

Ablade|frist free (unloading) time ; ~**gebühr** unloading charges; ~**gewicht** shipping (delivered) weight; ~**kommando** unloading detail (party); ~**kosten,** ~**lohn** unloading charges, charges for unloading, discharging fees.

Abladen unloading, unlading, discharging, *(Müll)* dumping;
~ **übernehmen** to attend to the unloading;
~ **verboten** no dumping, no rubbish to be shot here *(Br.)*.

abladen to unload, to unlade, to discharge, *(Lastwagen)* to detruck, *(Passagiere)* to offload, *(Schiff)* to unship, to pack out, *(Zug)* to detrain;
Müll ~ to shoot (dump) rubbish; **Schuld auf j. anderen** ~ to shift the blame on s. o. else; **seine Sorgen bei jem.** ~ to unburden one's sorrows to s. o., to pour one's sorrow into s. one's heart *(fam.)*.

Abladeplatz unloading place (platform, rack), *(mil.)* unloading point, *(Schiffsplatz)* port of discharge, unloading port (berth), *(Schutt)* dump, dumping ground, tip.

Ablader unloader, freighter, *(Schiff)* shipper, dock labo(u)rer, docker *(Br.)*, stevedore, lumper, longshoreman *(US)*.

Ablade|recht dumpage *(US)*; ~**risiko** unloading risk; ~**schein** weight certificate, certificate of discharge; ~**termin** date of delivery; ~**vorrichtung** dumping service; ~**zeit** turnaround time.

Ablage store, *(Ablagekorb)* [filing] tray, *(Ablegen)* filing, *(abgelegte Akten)* filed material, files, *(abgelegte Post)* filed mail, *(Theater)* cloakroom;
zur ~ ready for filing;
alphabetische ~ alphabetical filing; **bibliothekarische** ~ lateral filing; **chronologische** ~ chronological filing;
~ **nicht mehr verwendeter Funksendungen** dead book; ~ **nach Orten** geographical filing; ~ **nach Sachgebieten** subject filing; ~**fach** pigeonhole; ~**kartei** filing card; ~**korb** [filing] tray; ~**mappe** folder.

ablagern to store, *(durch Lagern bessern)* to season, to mature.

Ablagerung storage.

Ablage|system filing system; ~**tisch** filing stand, tray; ~**vorrichtung** filing equipment; **zentrales** ~**wesen** central filing system.

ablandig offshore.

Ablaß outlet, *(Abzug)* deduction, allowance.

ablassen to let up, *(abgeben)* to let have, *(abtreten)* to cede, *(aufgeben)* to desist, to give up, *(Ballon)* to send up, to release, *(Preis reduzieren)* to abate, to reduce, to grant a reduction, to give a discount, to make an allowance, to knock off, *(verkaufen)* to sell, *(Wanne)* to empty, to drain;
jem. einen Artikel für ... ~ to do s. o. an article at ...; **billig** ~ to sell cheap; **Luft aus einem Reifen** ~ to deflate a tyre; **von einem Plan** ~ to throw a scheme overboard; **etw. vom Preis** ~ to make an allowance, to give a rebate (discount), to abate the price; **unter dem Selbstkostenpreis** ~ to sell below cost price; **Waren billig** ~ to let goods go cheaply; **Zug** ~ to dispatch (start) a train.

Ablaß|hahn discharge cock; ~**öffnung** drain, outlet; ~**rohr** venting (drain) pipe; ~**ventil** outlet (escape) valve.

Ablauf *(Abfluß)* outflow, efflux, discharge, *(Frist, Vertrag)* expiry, expiration, determination, lapse, running, *(Stapellauf)* launching, *(Verlauf)* devolution, course;
bei ~ **des Mietvertrages** on expiry (expiration) of the lease; **bei** ~ **des Wechsels** when the bill matures; **durch** ~ by maturity; **mit** ~ **der Frist** upon expiration of the term; **nach** ~ **von drei Jahren** after lapse of three years; **nach** ~ **von vier Monaten** at the end of four months, after four months have passed; **noch vor** ~ **einer Stunde** before an hour has passed; **vor** ~ **des Jahres** before the close of the year; **vor** ~ **der Woche** before the end of the week;
reibungsloser ~ efficient working, smooth functioning;
~ **einer Einlösungsfrist** expiration of a period for redemption; **gewöhnlicher** ~ **der Ereignisse** usual course of events; ~ **des Gesellschaftsvertrages** expiration of the term of partnership; ~ **der Kündigungsfrist** fulfil(l)ment of the notice period, *(Bankeinlagen)* withdrawal notice; ~ **eines Patents** expiration (expiry) of a patent; ~ **der Schutzrechte** extinguishment of copyright; ~ **des Verkaufsvorgangs** sales process; ~ **des Waffen-**

stillstands expiration of truce; ~ **eines Wechsels** maturity of a bill; ~ **der festgesetzten Zeit** expiration of the term fixed; ~ **eines Zeitraumes** lapse of time;
~ **der Dinge beschleunigen** to hasten the process; ~ **einer Frist hemmen** to suspend the running of a time; **für einen reibungslosen** ~ **des Programms sorgen** to see that a programme runs smoothly;
~**bahn** *(Flugzeug)* runway, *(beim Stapellauf)* launching ramp (ways), slipway, ground ways; ~**berg** *(Bahn)* incline; ~**diagramm** flow chart.

ablaufen to drain away, *(fällig werden)* to fall (become) due, to mature, to become payable, *(Frist)* to lapse, to expire, to run down, *(Hochwasser)* to recede, to subside, to flow out, to run off (out), *(Pachtvertrag)* to fall in, to expire, to determine, *(Versicherungspolice)* to run out, to cease to exist, *(vonstatten gehen)* to take its course, *(Zeit)* to elapse, to go;
anders ~ to turn out differently; **nicht gut** ~ to end in trouble; **jem. den Rang** ~ to steal a march upon s. o., to leave s. o. behind, to get the better of s. o.; **reibungslos** ~ to go off without a hitch (swimmingly); **sich die Schuhsohlen nach etw.** ~ to run one's legs off; **ganze Stadt nach etw.** ~ to scour the whole town.

Ablauf|frist time limit, *(Wechsel)* due date, maturity; ~**kanal** culvert; ~**klausel** *(Bürgschaft)* determination clause; ~**modell** process model; ~**plan** schedule; ~**planer** progress chaser (clerk); ~**programm** operating cycle; ~**rohr** *(Dachrinne)* drainpipe; ~**termin** expiration (expired) date, term, deadline *(US)*, *(Wechsel)* date of maturity.

Ableben death, decease, demise;
bei Nachweis des ~**s** after proof of death.

Ablege|fach pigeon hole; ~**fehler** *(drucktechn.)* misprint; ~**kasten,** ~**korb** [letter] tray; ~**mappe** filing jacket.

Ablegen *(Schriftsatz)* distribution.

ablegen *(Akten, Briefe)* to [put on] file, to pigeonhole, *(Hut, Mantel)* to take off, *(niederlegen)* to put down, *(Schiff)* to put out to sea;
Briefe in alphabetischer Reihenfolge ~ to file papers in alphabetical order; **chronologisch** ~ to file in date order; **Eid** ~ to take an oath; **veraltete Fachausdrücke** ~ to discard obsolete terminology; **Geständnis** ~ to make a confession; **Gewohnheit** ~ to break o. s. of a habit; **Kinderschuhe** ~ to emerge from childhood; **seinen Namen** ~ to give up using one's name; **Prüfung** ~ to pass (take, sit in) an examination; **Rechnung** ~ to render account; **nach Sachgebieten** ~ to file by subject matter; **Satz** ~ *(Druckerei)* to distribute the type; **Schiff** ~ to put a ship to sea; **Titel** ~ to renounce a title; **Trauer** ~ to come out of mourning; **als unbrauchbar** ~ to discard; **Zeugnis** ~ to give evidence, to testify, to bear witness; **Zeugnis für j.** ~ to bear witness for s. o., to give evidence in s. one's favo(u)r.

Ableger *(Filiale)* offshoot, subsidiary, *(Pflanze)* offshoot, cutting.

Ablege|satz dead matter, matter for distribution; ~**vorrichtung** *(Setzmaschine)* distributor.

Ablegung|des Abschlußexamens graduation; ~ **eines Eides** taking an oath; ~ **einer Prüfung** taking (sitting in) an examination; ~ **einer Rechnung** rendering of account; ~ **des Schlußexamens** graduation; ~ **einer Verklarung** making a ship's protest.

ablehnbar rejectable, *(Zeuge)* challengeable.

ablehnen to decline, to refuse, to turn down, to turn one's thumbs down, to deny, to disown, to disclaim, to deprecate, to veto, to pass up *(US)*, *(mißbilligen)* to disapprove, to condemn, *(verurteilen)* to damn, *(im Wege der Abstimmung)* to reject, to outvote, to vote out, to rule out *(US)*;
Amt ~ to refuse an office; **Angebot** ~ to decline (refuse) an offer; **Antrag** ~ to refuse an application, *(parl.)* to vote down a motion; **Autorschaft** ~ to disclaim authorship; **Buch einhellig** ~ to damn a book; **dankend** ~ to decline with thanks; **Deckung** ~ *(Versicherung)* to disclaim liability; **einstimmig** ~ to refuse with one voice; **Geschworenen wegen Befangenheit** ~ to challenge a juror; **Gesetzesantrag** ~ *(parl.)* to defeat (throw, rule out, *US*) a bill; **Gesuch** ~ to run down a request, to dismiss a petition; **glatt** ~ to refuse outright (downright, point-blank); **höflich** ~ to decline, to shun consent; **Richter wegen Befangenheit** ~ to refuse a judge; **rundweg** ~ to refuse outright; **Verantwortung** ~ to assume no responsibility; **Verpflichtung** ~ to decline a liability; **Vorschlag** ~ to reject a proposal, to nonplacet; **Zeugen** ~ to challenge a witness; **Zuständigkeit** ~ to refuse to acknowledge jurisdiction.

ablehnend negatory;
einer Sache ~ **gegenüberstehen** to look upon a matter with disapproval; **sich** ~ **verhalten** to take up a negative attitude; ~**e Antwort** refusal, negative answer.

Ablehnung nonapproval, refusal, denial, rejection, disapproval, decline, exclusion, *(Mißbilligung)* damnation, *(Zeugen)* challenge, *(Zurückweisung)* repudiation;
ausdrückliche ~ express rejection; **sich aus den Umständen ergebende** ~ implied rejection; **glatte** ~ flat denial, point-blank (distinct) refusal; **höfliche** ~ declination; **mündliche** ~ oral negation; **vermutete** ~ implied rejection;
~ **unter Angabe eines bestimmten Grundes** challenge for cause; ~ **eines Angebots** rejection (refusal) of offer; ~ **der Anklageerhebung** disallowance of a charge; ~ **eines Antrags** defeat of a motion; ~ **wegen Befangenheit** challenge of favo(u)r, principal challenge, recusation, declination *(Scot.)*; **heftige** ~ **im öffentlichen Bereich** public-sector onslaught; ~ **durch den Betrieb** shopfloor dissent; ~ **eines Geschworenen** challenge to the poll *(Br.)*, challenge of a juror; ~ **eines Gesuchs** refusal of a petition; ~ **eines Hilfsersuchens** denial of a request for help; ~ **von Kosten** disallowance of costs; ~ **einer Resolution** rescission of a resolution; ~ **eines Schiedsrichters** objection to an arbitrator; ~ **von Tarifvertragsverhandlungen** failure to bargain collectively; ~ **einer Testamentsvollstreckung** renunciation of an administratorship; ~ **eines Zeugen** challenge of (exception to) a witness; ~ **der Zusammenarbeit mit der Versicherungsgesellschaft [im Prozeßfall]** failure to cooperate with an insurance company; ~ **der Zuständigkeit** refusal to acknowledge a jurisdiction;
~ **eines Gesetzentwurfes beantragen** to move the rejection of a bill; ~ **erfahren** to meet with a rebuff; **glatte** ~ **erfahren** to meet with a square refusal; **Antrag auf** ~ **einer Gesetzesvorlage stellen** to move rejection of a bill.

Ablehnungs|antrag discharge petition; ~**bereich** *(Statistik)* rejection region; ~**bescheid** notice of denial (rejection), negative reply; ~**brief** letter of regret; ~**erklärung** declinatory plea; **im** ~**fall** in case of refusal; ~**grund** reason for refusal; ~**linie** *(Statistik)* rejection line; ~**recht** right to challenge; ~**zahl** *(Statistik)* rejection number.

Ableichtern lightening.

ableichtern to lighten.

ableisten to fulfil(l), to perform;
Eid ~ to take an oath; **seine Lehrzeit** ~ to serve one's time; **Militärdienst** ~ to complete one's military service, to do one's time.

Ableistung fulfil(l)ment, performance;
~ **eines Eides** taking an oath; ~ **des Militärdienstes** serving one's time.

ableiten to derive, *(Blitz)* to arrest, *(el.)* to shunt, *(ling.)* to derive;
Folgerungen ~ to draw conclusions; **Hochwasser** ~ to discharge floods; **logisch** ~ to deduce; **Strom** ~ to deflect a stream, to divert the course of a river; **Wasser** ~ to drain the water away.

Ableitung derivation, *(el.)* earth lead.

Ableitungsrohr outlet pipe.

ablenken to divert, to avert, to detract, to distract, *(Magnetnadel)* to deviate, to turn, *(Radar)* to deflect;
sich ~ to divert o. s.; **j.** ~ to take s. one's mind away; **jem. von seiner Arbeit** ~ to distract s. o. from his work; **jds. Aufmerksamkeit** ~ to divert s. one's attention; **vom Kurs** ~ *(Ballon)* to divert from its course; **rasch vom Thema** ~ to change the subject hastily;
sich leicht ~ **lassen** to be easily distracted.

Ablenkung diversion, distraction, change, *(Magnetnadel)* deviation, *(Radar)* deflection;
~ **des Handels** trade diversion; ~ **von geschäftlichen Interessen** diversion of the mind from business;
~ **brauchen** to need a change.

Ablenkungs|angriff *(mil.)* diversion; ~**manöver** manoeuvre of diversion, red herring, feint, *(mil.)* demonstration; ~**manöver unternehmen** to draw a red herring across the trail, to feint.

Ablese|einrichtung reading device; ~**fehler** reading error; ~**marke** pointer.

Ablesen|der Worte von den Lippen lip reading; ~ **des Zählers** meter reading.

ablesen to read off (out);
Konten ~ to call over accounts; **vom Manuskript** ~ to read off one's speech; **jem. jeden Wunsch von den Augen** ~ to anticipate s. one's wishes; **Zähler** ~ to read the meter.

Ablese|skala direct-reading dial; ~**strich** graduation mark.

Ablesung *(Thermometer)* reading.

ableugnen to deny, to disown, to disavow, to traverse, to contest;
etw. rundweg ~ to give a flat denial; **seine Schuld** ~ to plead not guilty; **Tatsachen** ~ to deny facts; **seine Unterschrift** ~ to disown one's signature.

Ableugnung denial, traverse.
ablichten to blueprint, to photostat, to xerox.
Ablichtung blueprint, photostatic copy, photostat, xerox.
Ablieferer deliverer, deliveryman.
abliefern to deliver, to hand (turn) in, to hand over, to surrender, *(Flugzeug)* to ferry;
Einbrecher bei der Polizei ~ to surrender a burglar to the police; **Fundsachen** ~ to turn in things found; **Kupons** ~ to surrender coupons; **rechtzeitig** ~ to deliver on schedule.
Ablieferung delivery, handing over, surrender;
bei ~ **von** on delivery; **bis zur** ~ pending delivery; **zahlbar bei** ~ cash on delivery (C.O.D.);
bestimmungsgemäße ~ *(Börse)* good delivery; **falsche** ~ misdelivery; **verspätete** ~ delay in (late) delivery;
~ **von Kupons** surrendering of coupons;
bei ~ **bezahlen** to pay on delivery.
Ablieferungs | buch delivery book; ~**frist** time of delivery, delivery date; ~**gewicht** delivery weight; ~**klausel** delivery clause; ~**kontingent** delivery quota; ~**pflicht** delivery obligation; ~**platz** delivery point; ~**prämie** [delivery] bonus, bounty; ~**schein** bill of delivery, dock receipt; ~**soll** delivery quota; ~**termin** day (date) of delivery, deadline *(US)*, *(Börse)* payday, settling day *(Br.)*; ~**verpflichtung** *(ausländischer Aktien)* surrender rule *(Br.)*.
ablisten, jem. etw. to do s. o. out of s. th.
Ablistung des Erbanteils catching bargain.
ablösbar removable, *(abfindbar)* compoundable, *(abtrennbar)* detachable, *(Anleihe)* callable, *(Rente)* redeemable, *(Strafe)* commutable, *(Tapete)* removable;
nicht ~ *(Rente)* irredeemable.
ablösen to detach, to remove, *(Amtsvorgänger)* to replace, to relieve, to supersede, *(Fideikommiß)* to disentail, *(Kapital)* to withdraw, *(Lasten)* to commute, *(Rente)* to redeem, *(Schuld)* to compound, to discharge, to settle, *(Wache)* to relieve;
jem. ~ to take s. one's place; **sich** ~ *(Briefmarke)* to come off (unstick), *(Farbe)* to come off; **Anleihe** ~ to redeem a loan; **sich bei der Arbeit** ~ to work in shifts; **Briefmarke vom Umschlag** ~ to unstick (remove, demount) a stamp from an envelope; **j. im Dienst** ~ to relieve s. o. of his duties; **Dienstbarkeit** ~ to commute an easement; **Hypothek** ~ to satisfy (pay off) a mortgage; **Kredit** ~ to repay a credit; **sich bei einer Nachtwache** ~ to take turns on a night watch; **Postgebühren pauschal** ~ to settle postal charges by block payment; **Schuld** ~ to solve a debt; **fällige Zinsscheine** ~ to detach coupons; **zu einem Zinstermin** ~ to redeem at an interest date.
ablöslich redeemable, recoverable.
Ablösung *(Amortisation)* discharge, settlement, liquidation, *(Anleihe)* redemption, refunding, *(Dienst)* fresh shift, *(Fideikommiß)* disentailment, *(Kapital)* withdrawal, *(mil.)* relief, *(mil., sl.)* washout, *(Pauschalregelung)* composition, block payment, *(Renten)* redemption, *(Schuld)* repayment, *(Strafe)* commutation;
frei durch ~ on Her (His) Majesty's service *(Br.)*;
vorzeitige ~ *(Lastenausgleich)* lump sum payment in advance;
~ **im Amt** supersession; **vorzeitige** ~ **einer Anleihe** anticipatory redemption of a loan; ~ **einer Dienstbarkeit** commutation of a right of user; ~ **einer Hypothek** satisfaction of a mortgage; ~ **von Krediten** repayment of credits;
mit ~ **arbeiten** to work in shifts.
Ablösungs | anleihe redemption loan, consol bonds, sinking fund debentures; ~**berechtigung** redemption right; ~**bestimmungen** redemption provisions; ~**betrag** amount to be redeemed, price of redemption, redemption capital (price); ~**fonds** sinking (redemption) fund; ~**hypothek** refunding mortgage; ~**kapital** redemption capital; ~**mannschaft** relay, *(Marine)* relief, *(Militär)* relieving guard (party), *(Werk)* oncoming shift; ~**pfandbrief** redemption bond; ~**prämie** redemption premium; ~**rate** sinking fund instalment; ~**recht** entitlement to commutation, redeemable (redemption) right, right to redeem (of redemption); ~**recht ausschließen** to clog the equity of redemption; ~**rente** redeemable annuity; ~**schicht** oncoming shift; ~**schuld** commutation debt; ~**schuldverschreibungen** refunding (unified, consolidated, redemption, renewal) bonds; ~**summe** redemption price (capital), commutation; ~**system** *(Schichtarbeit)* relay system; ~**wert** nuisance (redemption) value, *(Lebensversicherung)* surrender value; ~**zahlung** redemption payment; ~**zeitplan** redemption table; ~**zeitpunkt** redemption date.
abluchsen, jem. etw. to bamboozle s. o. out of s. th., to diddle (twist) s. o. out of his money, to take s. o. for s. th. *(US)*, to spring s. o. for a quid *(Br.)*.
abmachen *(Geschäft)* to transact, to bargain, *(vereinbaren)* to arrange, to agree, to settle, to stipulate, to fix up;
mit jem. etw. ~ to arrive at an understanding (come to an arrangement) with s. o.; **gütlich** ~ to settle amicably, to come to an amicable arrangement; **mündlich** ~ to make a verbal agreement; **Paketschnur** ~ to undo the strings of a parcel; **Preis** ~ to settle a price; **seine Probezeit** ~ to be on probation; **schriftlich** ~ to agree in writing; **seine Strafe** ~ to serve a sentence, to do one's time; **jds. Verband** ~ to remove s. one's bandage; **vertraglich** ~ to settle by agreement, to stipulate by contract.
Abmachung *(Geschäft)* transaction, bargain, *(Vereinbarung)* engagement, arrangement, agreement, convention, settlement, covenant, composition, stipulation, deal;
durch vorherige ~ by prearrangement; **mangels besonderer** ~ except as may be otherwise agreed upon;
ausdrückliche ~ express agreement; **bedingungslose** ~ bare contract; **alle Teile befriedigende** ~ mutually satisfactory agreement; **besondere** ~**en** particular covenant; **bindende** ~ binding arrangement, writing obligatory, obligatory pact; **ehrliche (faire)** ~ square deal; **finanzielle** ~ financial arrangement; **frühere** ~ previous arrangements; **geheime** ~ secret understanding; **mündlich getroffene** ~ verbal (unwritten) agreement; **gütliche** ~ amicable arrangement; **interne** ~**en** internal arrangements; **schriftliche** ~ agreement in writing, written agreement; **übliche** ~ regular arrangement; **vertragliche** ~ stipulation, covenant; **vorherige** ~ prearrangement; **wirtschaftliche** ~**en** trade agreement; **zwischenstaatliche** ~ international agreement (convention);
~ **eines Händlerrings** ring settlement;
~ **bestätigen** to confirm an agreement, to caramelize *(sl.)*; ~ **brechen** to break an agreement; ~ **zustande bringen** to transact a deal; **zu einer** ~ **gelangen** to come to an arrangement; **sich an eine** ~ **halten** to abide by an agreement, to keep one's contract; ~ **mit jem. treffen** to come to an agreement with s. o.; ~ **verletzen** to break an agreement; **zu einer** ~ **hinzugezogen werden** to adstipulate.
abmagern to lose weight;
zum Skelett ~ to be worn to a shadow.
Abmagerung loss of weight.
Abmagerungsdiät slimming diet, hunger cure.
Abmagerungskur reducing (starvation) diet, slimming course;
~ **durchführen** to be a weight catcher.
Abmarsch marching off, departure, moving off, *(Fahrzeuge)* start;
~**befehl** marching order.
abmarschbereit ready to move off.
abmarschieren to march (rank) off, *(Fahrzeuge)* to move off, to start;
heimlich ~ to decamp.
Abmarschzeit starting time.
abmeiern, Pächter to turn out a farmer.
Abmeldebescheinigung, polizeiliche leaving permit.
abmelden, sich to notify one's departure.
Abmeldung notice of departure.
abmessen to measure, to dimension, *(eichen)* to gauge, to take the gauge, to gage.
Abmessung dimension, size, location *(US)*, admeasurement;
~**s-, Konstruktions- oder Qualitätsnormen** standards of dimensions, designs or quality.
abmieten to hire, *(Haus)* to rent.
abmontierbar demountable.
Abmontieren dismount, dismantling.
abmontieren to take down (to pieces), to demount, to dismount, *(Werksanlagen)* to scrap, to dismantle, to disassemble, to strip.
abmühen to labo(u)r, to toil and moil.
abmurksen *(fam.)* to kill off, to do away.
abmustern *(Matrose)* to sign off, *(Schiffsbesatzung)* to discharge, to pay off.
Abnahme removal, taking off, *(Absatz)* sale, *(Annahme)* acceptance, receiving, *(Gebäude)* final architect's certificate, *(Gewicht)* loss, *(Kauf)* purchase, acquisition, *(Leckage)* leakage, *(Minderung)* decrease, decline, diminution, reduction, dwindling, decrement, abatement, letdown, *(Übernahme)* taking over, takeover, [physical] acceptance, *(technische Überprüfung)* acceptance test;
bei ~ **von uns** on purchase (orders) of; **bei** ~ **der Maschine** on taking delivery of the machine; **bei** ~ **größerer Mengen** if larger quantities are taken; **vor** ~ before delivered;
~ **der Bestände** decrease in stocks; ~ **einer Bilanz** approval of a balance sheet; ~ **eines Eides** administration of an oath; ~ **einer**

eidesstattlichen Erklärung administration of an affirmation; ~ **der Kräfte** decline of strength; ~ **einer Lieferung** taking delivery; ~ **einer Parade** review; ~ **einer Rechnung** auditing of an account; ~ **der Siegel** removal of the seals; ~ **von Stichproben** acceptance sampling; ~ **durch den Verbrauchermarkt** consumer acceptance; ~ **der Vorräte** shrinkage of stocks; ~ **durch Wiederverkäufer** dealer acceptance;
gute ~ finden to sell well, to find a ready sale (market); **keine ~ finden** not to sell; ~ **verweigern** to refuse to take delivery;
~**beamte** inspection personnel; ~**beamter** quality inspector *(Br.)*, receiving clerk, accepting official *(US)*, *(mil.)* acceptance inspector; ~**bedingungen** terms of acceptance, acceptance specifications; ~**bereitschaft des Verbrauchermarktes** consumer acceptance; ~**bericht** inspector's report; ~**bescheinigung** [acknowledgment of] receipt, certificate of analysis (inspection); ~**bestimmungen** acceptance specifications; ~**bewertungsmaßstäbe** acceptance criteria; ~**fahrt** *(Schiff)* acceptance on trial; ~**flug** acceptance flight; ~**frist** delivery-acceptance period; ~**garantie** *(Anleihekonsortium)* underwriting guarantee; ~**kommission** acceptance committee, inspection commission; ~**kontrolle** check on delivery, quality control; ~**kosten** inspection cost; ~**land** purchasing country; ~**lauf** *(Maschine)* trial run; ~**möglichkeit** capability to take delivery; ~**muster** *(Statistik)* lot-acceptance sampling; ~**pflicht** obligation to accept the goods; ~**prüfung** acceptance (quality) test, quality inspection *(Br.)*, purchase trial *(US)*; ~**prüfung eines Schiffes verlangen** to demand trial of a ship before her acceptance; ~**raum** inspection department; ~**recht** *(im Prämiengeschäft)* right of calling; ~**schein** receipt; ~**spediteur** clearing agent; ~**toleranz** acceptance tolerance; ~**verfahren** inspection procedure; ~**verpflichtung** *(Effektenhändler)* firm bid; **festgelegte** ~**verpflichtung** *(Restaurant)* tie *(Br.)*, obligation of a tied house; ~**verweigerung** power to reject, rejection, refusal of delivery, nonacceptance; ~**verweigerungsrecht** right to reject; ~**verzug** delay in taking over; **im** ~**verzug sein** to be in default; ~**vorschriften** quality specification; ~**zahl** acceptance number; ~**zwang für alle Produkte** full line forcing *(US)*.

abnehmbar removable, detachable, pick-off *(US)*.

Abnehmen decrease, wane;
im ~ begriffen on the decrease;
~ **der wirtschaftlichen Kapazität** economic shrinkage.

abnehmen *(annehmen)* to accept, to take delivery, *(berechnen)* to charge, *(Flut)* to recede, to ebb, *(geringer werden)* to decline, to decrease, to diminish, to abate, to ebb, *(Gerüst)* to take down, *(Geschwindigkeit)* to fall off, *(Gewicht)* to lose weight, *(kaufen)* to buy, to purchase, to order, *(Konjunktur)* to be subsiding, to slow down, to taper off, *(kürzer werden)* to shorten, *(Nachfrage)* to fall off, *(im Preis fallen)* to dwindle, to drop, to decline, to recede, to fall, *(prüfen)* to inspect, *(Wechsel)* to discount, *(Wind)* to lull, to abate;
allmählich ~ to taper off; **Bau** ~ to survey a building; **Eid** ~ to administer an oath, to swear in; **jem. einen Gang in die Stadt** ~ to save s. o. a trip to the town; **jem. sein ganzes Geld** ~ to fleece s. o. of his last halfpenny; **Gerüst** ~ to take down the scaffolding; **Hörer** ~ to lift the receiver, to answer the telephone; **Lieferung** ~ to take delivery; **Parade** ~ to pass a review; **j. den Paß** ~ to confiscate s. one's passport; **den ganzen Posten** ~ to take the whole lot; **Rechnung** ~ to audit an account; **ganze Reihe** ~ to purchase the whole series; **Siegel** ~ to remove (break) the seal; **Strom** ~ to use electricity; **jem. die Verantwortung** ~ to relieve s. o. of his responsibilities; **Waren** ~ to take delivery of goods, to collect (accept) the goods; **Waren in großen Mengen** ~ to take up goods to a large amount; **Warenlieferung** ~ to accept delivery of goods; **jem. zuviel** ~ to overcharge s. o.

Abnehmer taker, *(Benutzer)* user, *(Käufer)* buyer, purchaser, vendee *(US)*, bargainee, *(Kunde)* client, customer, *(pl.)* market, *(Verbraucher)* consumer;
alleiniger ~ sole buyer, **gewerblicher** ~ industrial customer; **keine** ~ *(Börse)* no buyers;
~ **finden** to find (meet with) purchasers; **keine ~ finden** to find no sale (market); ~ **sein** to be in the market;
~**gruppe** consumer group; ~**kartell** buying (purchasing) combine; ~**konto** customer account; ~**kreis** customers, consuming public; ~**land** customer country; ~**liste** list of customers (subscribers); ~**nation** consumer nation, consuming country.

Abneigung disinclination, dislike, aversion, objection;
besondere ~ pet aversion;
~ **gegen j. haben** to take an aversion to s. o.

abnormal abnormal, irregular.

Abnormalitätsindex *(Statistik)* index of abnormality.

abnötigen, jem. eine Entscheidung to worry s. o. into a decision; **jem. sein Geld** ~ to screw money out of s. o.; **Respekt** ~ to command respect; **jem. ein Versprechen** ~ to wring a promise from s. o.

abnutzbar subject to wear, wearable.

Abnutzbarkeit wearability;
geringe ~ good wearing qualities.

abnutzen to outwear, to use up;
sich ~ to wear out, to abrade, to waste, to consume; **sich leicht** ~ to be apt to wear out.

Abnutzung wear and tear, waste, wastage, exhaustion, depreciation, attrition, erosion, *(Münzen)* abrasion;
eingetretene ~ accrued depreciation; **maschinelle** ~ machine wear; **natürliche** ~ fair wear and tear; **übliche** ~ permissive waste;
~ **durch Gebrauch** fair wear and tear;
der ~ unterliegen to be of a wasting character.

Abnutzungs|aufwand depreciation cost (expense); ~**betrag** depreciation amount, amount of depreciation; ~**erscheinungen aufweisen** to show signs of wear; ~**fehler** defect by deterioration; ~**fonds** depreciation reserve; ~**gebühr** depreciation charge, detriment *(Br.)*; ~**grenze** *(Münzen)* limit of abrasion; ~**kampf** battle of attrition; ~**krieg** war of attrition; ~**restwert** scrap value *(US)*; ~**satz** rate of depreciation (wear and tear), depreciation rate.

Abonnement *(Bahn)* season *(Br.)* (commutation, *US*) ticket, *(Zeitschrift)* subscription, standing order;
bei aufgehobenem ~ subscription tickets not available; **im** ~ by subscription;
abgelaufenes ~ lapsed subscription; **im voraus zu bezahlende** ~**s** subscriptions to be paid in advance; **kostenloses** ~ complimentary subscription;
sein ~ abbestellen to give up subscribing, to discontinue one's subscription; ~ **aufgeben (kündigen)** to withdraw (drop) one's subscription; ~ **erneuern** to renew one's subscription; **im ~ essen** to buy luncheon vouchers (meal tickets, *US*);
~**abteilung** subscription department ~**auftrag** subscription order; ~**bedingungen** terms (conditions) of subscription; ~**dauer** period of subscription; ~**erneuerung** renewal of subscription, subscription renewal; ~**exemplar** subscription copy; ~**fahrkarte** season *(Br.)* (commutation, *US*) ticket; ~**fahrpreis** commutation fare *(US)*; ~**formular** subscription form; ~**gebühr** rate of subscription, subscription price; ~**karte** subscription (subscriber's, season, *Br.*, commutation, *US*) ticket, *(Theater)* coupon, *(Mittagessen)* luncheon voucher, meal ticket *(US)*; **mit einer ~karte zur Arbeit fahren** to commute to work *(US)*; ~**konzert** subscription concert; ~**liste** list of subscribers; ~**police** floating policy; ~**preis** subscription [fee, price, rate], package price; ~**reflektant** intending subscriber; ~**stamm** regular subscribers; ~**vereinbarung** arrangement for subscription; ~**verkauf** subscription sale.

Abonnent subscriber, *(Zeitkarteninhaber)* season-ticket holder, commuter *(US)*;
~**, der mindestens 50% bezahlt hat** paid subscriber;
~ **einer Zeitung sein** to take in *(Br.)* (subscribe for, *US*) a newspaper; ~**en für eine Zeitung werben** to canvass for a newspaper, to solicit subscriptions.

Abonnenten|abteilung subscription department; ~**analyse** subscriber research (analysis); ~**brief** subscription letter; ~**kreis** subscriber goodwill; ~**liste** list of subscribers; ~**sammler** subscription agent, solicitor *(US)*, canvasser *(US)*; ~**schwund** downward trend in subscriptions; ~**versicherung** subscriber's (newspaper) insurance; ~**werber** subscription agent *(US)*, subscriptionist *(US)*, canvasser *(US)*; ~**werbung** canvassing *(US)*.

abonnieren to subscribe, to enter a subscription, *(Zeitung)* to take in *(Br.)*, to keep *(US)*.

abonniert sein, auf eine Zeitung to be a subscriber to a newspaper.

abordnen to delegate, to depute, to deputize *(US)*, *(mil.)* to detail, to detach, to assign.

Abordnung delegation, deputation, draft, body of delegates;
mit allen Vollmachten ausgestattete ~ high-powered delegation;
~ **anhören** to hear a deputation; ~ **zu Verhandlungen mit jem. entsenden** to send a deputation to confer with s. o.; ~ **leiten** to head a delegation.

abpachten to lease, to rent.

Abpackanlage packing plant.

abpacken to pack up.

Abpackmaschine packaging machine.

abpassen, j. to lie on s. one's doorstep; **günstige Gelegenheit** ~ to watch one's opportunity; **Zeit** ~ to bide one's time.

abpatrouillieren to [go on] patrol, *(mil.)* to patrol an area.
abpausen to copy, to trace.
abpflücken to pick off, to pluck.
abplacken, sich to toil and moil, to fag, to plug, to drudge.
abplagen, sich to struggle, to sweat *(coll.)*; **sich mit der Lexikonherstellung** ~ to drudge at dictionary making; **sich mit einem schwierigen Problem** ~ to struggle with difficulties.
abprallen, von jem. völlig unberührt to glance off s. o. like water off a ducks back.
abpressen, jem. Geld to extort money from s. o.; **jem. ein Geständnis** ~ to force a confession from s. o.
abrackern, sich für seinen Lebensunterhalt to scrape for one's living, to scrabble for one's livelihood.
abraten, jem. von etw. to advise s. o. against s. th.; **Freund von der Eheschließung bei geringen Bezügen** ~ to dissuade a friend from marrying on a small salary.
Abraum waste.
abräumen to clear away, to remove.
abreagieren, sich to blow off steam; **seine Gefühle** ~ to work off one's feelings.
abrechnen to [give an] account, *(abwickeln)* to settle, to liquidate, to square up, *(abziehen)* to deduct, *(einbehalten)* to recoup, *(Skonto gewähren)* to discount, to make an allowance;
mit jem. ~ to make (square up) one's account (get even) with s. o., *(fig.)* to get upsides with s. o.; **mit jem. eines Tages** ~ to come home on s. o. some day; **4%** ~ to allow (deduct, take off) 4%; **Effekten zum Kurs von ...** ~ to credit (debit) with the proceeds of the securities at the price of ...; **auf Heller und Pfennig** ~ to pay to the last penny; **Kasse** ~ to balance the cash; **Konten** ~ to clear (settle, balance, square) accounts; **netto** ~ to render a net statement; **seine Spesen** ~ to account for one's expenses; **Tara** ~ to allow for the tare; **seine Unkosten** ~ to deduct one's expenses; **Wechsel** ~ to discount a bill of exchange.
Abrechner clearing agent, *(Börse)* settling clerk.
Abrechnung *(Abzug)* deduction, discount, allowance, *(über verkaufte Effekten)* contract *(Br.)* (sold, *US*) note, *(Kommissionär)* ringing up, *(Liquidierung)* liquidation, *(Rechnung)* note, account, bill, *(Rechnungswesen)* accounting, *(Scheckverkehr)* bank clearing, clearance, *(Schlußrechnung)* settlement *(Br.)*, settling (balancing) of accounts;
auf ~ **von** on account; **laut** ~ per account rendered; **nach** ~ **von** after deduction of; **nach** ~ **der inflationsbedingten Erhöhung** after inflation retention; **nach** ~ **der Spesen** after deducting expenses (charges); **nach** ~ **der Steuern** after taxes;
endgültige ~ final settlement; **frisierte** ~ cooked account; **gegenseitige** ~ compensation, offset; **innerbetriebliche** ~ intercompany squaring; **jährliche** ~ annual balance; **monatliche** ~ monthly tally; **nächste** ~ next account; **periodische** ~ periodical settlement; **buchhalterisch richtige** ~ proper accounts; **tägliche** ~ *(Giroausgleich)* daily settlement; **wertmäßige** ~ deliveries accounting; **wöchentliche** ~ weekly settlement;
~ **in regelmäßigen Abständen** periodic accounting; **interne** ~ **der Banken** settlement of interbank debits and credits, clearing; ~ **über den Kauf (Verkauf) von Effekten** contract note *(Br.)*, bought note *(US)*; ~ **des Liquidators** liquidator's account; ~ **der Regionalbanken** country clearing *(Br.)*; ~ **über getätigte Verkäufe** account sales; ~ **zu landesdurchschnittlichen Verleihsätzen** *(Filmverleih)* formula deal; ~ **über Verluste** allowance for losses;
in ~ **bringen** to deduct; **im voraus bezahlte Beträge in** ~ **bringen** to allow for sums paid in advance; **Rabatt von 5% in** ~ **bringen** to take off five per cent; ~ **erteilen** to render account; **seine** ~ **machen** to settle one's accounts; **seine** ~ **zur Revision vorlegen** to send one's accounts for credit; **bei der** ~ **zurückgeben** *(unverkaufte Karten)* to account.
Abrechnungs|bank clearing bank (agent), clearinghouse agent; ~**beamter** settlement clerk; **monatliche** ~**bedingungen** lumped order terms of sales; ~**beleg** clearing voucher; **gesamter** ~**betrag** *(Schecks)* inclearing; ~**blatt** *(Börsenmakler)* contract sheet, *(Konto)* summary sheet; **Kontrollabschnitt und** ~**blatt** counterfoil and leaf; ~**bogen** settlement sheet; ~**börse** clearinghouse; ~**büro** clearinghouse; ~**erleichterungen** clearinghouse facilities; ~**formular** clearing form; ~**konto für Geschäftsreisende** travel(l)ing account for settlement with travel(l)ers; ~**kontor** clearinghouse; ~**kurs** making-up (settling) price, settling rate; ~**methode** accounting method; ~**periode** accounting (settlement) period; ~**posten** clearance item; ~**preis** settling price; ~**rücklage** clearing reserve; ~**saldo** clearing balance; ~**schlüssel** settlement formula; ~**stelle** clearinghouse [agent]; ~**system** clearing (cost) system; ~**system einführen** to install a cost (clearing) system.
Abrechnungstag settling (settlement, bargain, audit, cash) day, day of account, *(fig.)* day of reckoning, *(Börse)* account (prompt, name, settling, ticket) day *(Br.)*, payday *(Br.)*, *(Devisenverkehr)* value date;
~ **für Montanwerte** mining ticket day *(Br.)*.
Abrechnungs|termin settlement day, *(Buchhändler)* settlement date; ~**unterlagen** clearing vouchers; ~**urkunde im Bankverkehr** clearinghouse certificate *(Br.)*; ~**verfahren** clearinghouse system; ~**verkehr** clearing system, clearinghouse business; ~**zeitraum** *(Bank)* charging period, settlement (accounting) period, *(Börse)* account; ~**zettel zustellen** *(Börsenmakler)* to pass a name.
Abrede denial, *(Vereinbarung)* agreement, stipulation, understanding, *(Kartell)* arrangement;
formlose ~ *(Wettbewerbsbeschränkung)* hono(u)rable understanding; **frühere** ~ previous agreement;
der ~ **gemäß handeln** to keep to the terms of an agreement; **in** ~ **stellen** to deny, to disavow; **mit jem. eine** ~ **treffen** to come to an agreement with s. o.
abreden, jem. ~, **etw. zu tun** to persuade s. o. not to do s. th.
abredewidrig contrary to directions.
abregen, sich to cool down *(coll.)*, to simmer down *(sl.)*.
Abreibung rubdown;
jem. eine ~ **verpassen** to give s. o. a sound thrashing.
Abreise departure, parting, getting away, going, start, setting out (off), remove, going off;
plötzliche ~ scuttle;
~ **beschleunigen** to precipitate a journey; **seine** ~ **festsetzen** to fix one's departure; **gerade vor der** ~ **sein** to be on the point of starting; **seine** ~ **vorbereiten** to prepare for departure; **seine** ~ **vorverlegen** to accelerate one's departure.
abreisen to depart, to take one's departure, to get off, to leave, to start [on a journey];
nach New York ~ to sail for New York; **mit dem Schiff** ~ to sail, to embark;
binnen einer halben Stunde ~ **müssen** to have to leave at half an hour's notice.
Abreise|tag day of departure; **mit den** ~**vorbereitungen beschäftigt sein** to be engaged in the preparations for departure.
Abreißblock counterfoil book.
Abreißen eines Hauses demolition of (pulling down) a house, house breaking.
abreißen to pick off, *(Gebäude)* to pull (knock, take) down, to demolish, *(Seil)* to break, *(Werksanlagen)* to dismantle, to strip;
Blatt vom Block ~ to tear a sheet off the pad; **jem. die Maske** ~ to unmask s. o.
Abreiß|kalender tearoff block (calendar), date block; ~**leine** *(Fallschirm)* breaking cord.
abrichten to train.
Abrichter trainer.
abriegeln to bolt, *(Feuer)* to check, to localize, *(Grenze)* to close, *(Polizei)* to cordon off, *(mil.)* to seal off, to isolate;
Angriff ~ to contain an attack; **hermetisch** ~ to shut down like a clam; **Straße** ~ to block a road, to barricade a street.
Abriegelung cordon, *(Feuer)* localization, *(mil.)* interdiction;
~ **einer Straße** blocking of a road.
abringen, jem. to wring (wrest) from s. o.; **dem kargen Boden seinen Lebensunterhalt** ~ to wrest a living from the soil; **jem. ein Zugeständnis** ~ to wring a concession from s. o.
Abriß draft, [rough] sketch, summary, outline, conspectus, *(Buch)* abridgement, compendium, *(Schriftstück)* abstract;
kurzer ~ summary;
~ **geben** to outline, to sketch; **Haus auf** ~ **verkaufen** to sell a house for the breakup value.
Abrollen *(Ablauf)* devolution.
abrollen to unreel, *(Spediteur)* to transport, to deliver, to cart away;
Film ~ to run off a film; **in rascher Folge** ~ to follow quickly upon each other; **reibungslos** ~ to go off without a hitch.
Abroll|kosten carriage, haulage, cartage; ~**spediteur** delivery carrier.
Abrücken *(mil.)* departure, moving off.
abrücken *(mil.)* to move off, to depart;
~ **von** to move away from;
von einer Parteilinie ~ to dissociate o. s. from a party line.
Abruf *(Datenverarbeitung)* call, *(dipl.)* recall;
auf ~ at (on) call, at short notice, at a minute's warning;
~ **von Banknoten** calling in of bank notes; ~ **von Geldern** calling of funds; ~ **von Versorgungsgütern** call for supplies; ~ **von bestellter Ware** request for delivery;

~e aus vorhandenen Lagerbeständen bedienen to meet orders out of stock; **auf ~ liefern** to deliver on request; **jem. auf ~ zur Verfügung stehen** to be at s. one's call; **auf ~ verkaufen** to sell on delivery;
~auftrag off-the-shelf order, make-and-take order *(US)*.
abrufbar, jederzeit callable.
abrufbereit ready for collection.
Abrufbereitschaft call, readiness for collection.
abrufen to call back, *(Computer)* to recall, to fetch, *(Diplomaten)* to recall, *(Zug)* to call out;
nach Belieben ~ to call up at will; **Gelder ~** to call in funds.
abrunden to round off;
Betrag nach oben ~ to bring an amount up to round figures; **Satz ~** to turn (round off) a sentence.
Abrundung *(Statistik)* rounding;
~ einer Summe rounding off an amount.
abrüsten to disarm, *(Flugzeug, Maschine)* to dismantle, *(Schiff)* to unrig, to put out of commission.
Abrüstung disarmament;
allgemeine ~ universal disarmament; **kontrollierte (überwachte) ~** controlled disarmament; **nukleare ~** nuclear disarmament.
Abrüstungs|abkommen disarmament agreement; **~befürworter** disarmer; **~gespräche** arms negotiations; **~kommission** disarmament commission; **~konferenz** disarmament conference; **~plan** plan for disarmament; **~verhandlungen** disarmament talks; **~vertrag** disarmament pact; **~vorschläge** proposals for disarmament.
Abrutschen *(Flugzeug)* stalling;
seitliches ~ side slip;
~ der Währung currency slide.
abrutschen to slide down, to slip, *(Flugzeug)* to stall, to fall off, *(vergammeln)* to be on (hit) the skids *(US sl.)*.
Absacken *(Flugzeug)* stall[ing], pancake.
absacken *(Flugzeug)* to pancake, to stall, *(Schiff)* to subside, *(Straßendecke)* to sag.
Absage *(Auftrag)* countermand, counterorder, cancellation, denial, *(Weigerung)* refusal, turndown, negative reply, rejection;
eindeutige ~ decided refusal; **glatte ~** definite rebuff, flat no;
~ nicht entgegennehmen not to take no for an answer; **glatte ~ erhalten** to receive a definitive no; **~ erteilen** to decline, to refuse; **jem. eine ~ erteilen** to give s. o. a rebuff, to give s. o. a plump „NO" for an answer; **sich eine ~ holen** to meet with a refusal; **zu einer glatten ~ neigen** to be in the mood to refuse point blank;
~brief letter of apology (regret), rejection letter.
absagen to declare off, *(Bestellung)* to counterorder, to countermand, to cancel, to call off, *(ablehnen)* to refuse, to decline;
mit größtem Bedauern ~ to decline with many regrets; **Einladung ~** to decline an invitation; **seinen Gästen ~** to put off one's guests; **Sendung ~** to sign off.
Absägen *(Entlassung)* axe, *(aus politischen Gründen)* decapitation *(US)*.
absägen to cut off, *(entlassen)* to sack, to axe, *(aus politischen Gründen)* to scalp *(US)*, to decapitate *(US)*;
Ast ~, auf dem man sitzt to cut one's throat.
Absatz *(Absatzmarkt)* market, outlet, *(Abschnitt)* paragraph, new line, first line of a paragraph, article, clause, subjection, subclause, *(beim Diktat)* new line, paragraph, *(im Druck)* break, period, *(Einrücken)* indenture, *(Ferse)* heel, *(Korrekturlesen)* run-out, *(statistische Kurve)* trend, *(starke Nachfrage)* run, *(Verbrauch)* consumption, *(Verkauf)* sale, disposal, selling, *(Vertrieb)* marketing, distribution, *(Zeitungssatz)* circulation;
direkter ~ direct selling (marketing); **erhöhter ~** foot-pace; **flauer ~** dead sale; **genossenschaftlicher ~** associative marketing; **großer ~** large (potential) market (sales); **guter ~** heavy sale; **kein ~** *(Korrekturlesen)* run-in; **langsamer ~** slow sales; **an der Rentabilitätsschwelle liegender ~** marginal sales; **neuer ~** fresh paragraph, new line; **reißender ~** rapid sales; **schlanker ~** ready (short) sales; **schlechter ~** poor market; **schneller ~** quick (short) sales, quick return, ready market; **übermäßiger ~** overdraw; **vorhergehender ~** preceding article;
~ landwirtschaftlicher Erzeugnisse agricultural market; **~ an die Industrie** sales to industry; **~ von Industrieerzeugnissen** industrial marketing; **~ je beschäftigte Person** sales per employee; **~ an Private** private offering, *(Banken)* private placement of securities; **~ je qm Verkaufsraum** sales per sq. m. of salesroom; **~ und Vertrieb** distribution, marketing;
~ der Masse der Erzeugnisse beeinflussen to account for the bulk of goods sold; **neuen ~ beginnen** to begin a new paragraph; **~ einfügen** to insert (put in) a clause; **bei jedem ~ die erste Zeile einrücken** to indent the first line of each paragraph; **~ erläutern** to explain a passage; **~ finden** to sell, to be salable, to find a market, to go off; **glänzenden ~ finden** to rub off in great style; **guten ~ finden** to find (meet with) a quick (ready) sale, to find a ready market, to run off (sell) readily; **keinen ~ finden** to find no sale, *(Börse)* to find no buyers; **leichten ~ finden** to find a ready market; **reißenden ~ finden** to be of quick sale, to go off briskly (quickly), to sell like hot cakes (dogs); **schlechten ~ finden** to sell hard (heavily), to go off slowly, to find a poor market; **schnellen ~ finden** to meet with ready sale (a ready market); **schwer ~ finden** to run into heavy selling; **langsamen ~ haben** to go off slowly, to be of slow sale; **weltweiten ~ haben** to achieve world-wide sale; **~ machen** *(Brief, Manuskript)* to begin a new (indent a) line; **auf dem ~ kehrt machen** to turn on one's heels; **~ steigern** to increase the sale; **~ streichen** to cancel a paragraph; **~ vorantreiben** to push sales.
Absätze, mit schiefen ~n worn at the heels;
in ~ einteilen to paragraph.
Absatz|abkommen marketing (distribution) agreement; **~analyse** market (sales) analysis; **~ansporn geben** to give a fresh fillip to sales; **frühjahrsbedingter ~anstieg** spring sales sprint; **sprungartiger ~anstieg** sales jump; **~anstrengungen** sales drive (effort); **~anteil** market coverage; **~apparat** marketing organization; **~aufgliederung** product sales breakdown, *(Zeitung)* circulation breakdown; **~aufteilung** division of markets; **~aufwand** marketing cost; **~ausschuß** marketing board, sales committee; **~aussichten** sales prospects, marketing outlook; **~ausweitung** extension of the market; **übermäßige ~ausweitung** overtrading; **~bedingungen** market[ing] conditions, sales terms *(US)*; **~begriffe** marketing terms; **~belebung** revival of (increase in) sales; **verstärkte ~bemühungen** marketing efforts; **~berater** marketing adviser; **~bereich** market, trading (marketing) area; **~bereitschaft** marketing resource; **~bericht** market (sales) report; **~beschleunigung herbeiführen** to speed up the sales process; **~beschränkungen** sales restrictions; **~beschränkung auf einzelnes Geschäft** exclusive outlet (selling); **~bestimmungen** marketing conditions; **~bewegungen** sales trend.
absatzbewußt sales-minded (-oriented);
~e Mentalität marketing mentality.
Absatz|bewußtsein marketing (sales) mindedness, market orientedness; **~bezirk** marketing territory; **~bild** marketing picture; **~branche** marketing field; **~chance** opening, sales prospect; **~chancen** potential sales, sales prospects (possibilities, opportunities), potential market; **~denken** marketing concept; **sich immer mehr dem ~denken zuwenden** to grow in marketing mindedness; **~diagramm** sales curve (diagram); **~einrichtungen** distribution (distributive, marketing) facilities, sales devices; **~elastizität** sales elasticity; **~entwicklung** market development; **~erfahrung** marketing experience (knowhow); **~erfassung** market coverage; **~ergebnis** sales result(s); **~erhöhung** rise in sales; **~erkundung** marketing research; **~erwägungen** sales considerations, market (sales) prospects; **~fachleute** marketing people; **~fachmann** marketing (market-research) specialist, marketing analyst, marketing man, marketeer; **aufgeschlossener ~fachmann** development markete(e)r.
absatzfähig marketable, salable;
~e Waren marketable commodities.
Absatz|fähigkeit selling capacity, marketability, salability; **~feld** trading area, outlet, market; **~feld haben** to find a market; **~feldzug** marketing (sales, selling) campaign, marketing drive; **~finanzierung** marketing (sales) financing; **~finanzierungsgesellschaft** sales finance company *(US)*; **~finanzierungsinstitut** factor *(US)*; **~finanzierungssystem** factoring system *(US)*; **~finanzierungsvertrag** factoring agreement; **~flaute** dull market, dullness, period of dull sale, letdown in sales, slackness of the market, stagnation of trade.
absatzfördernde Gesamtmaßnahmen für einen Artikel marketing of an article.
Absatzförderung sales promotion, merchandising;
planmäßige ~ sales drive.
Absatz|förderungsverfahren sales promotion technique; **~forscher** market research specialist, marketing researcher; **~forschung** marketing (market) research; **~forschungsabteilung** marketing division; **~frage** marketing problem; **~gag** marketing gimmick; **~garantie** sales guarantee.
Absatzgebiet market, trading (marketing, selling) area, area of destination, sales territory, field, outlet, débouché;
ausländische ~e foreign markets; **beschränktes ~** narrow sales

area; **garantiertes** ~ guaranteed market; **natürliches** ~ natural marketing area; **neues** ~ new channels of trade; **überseeisches** ~ overseas market;
~ **für billige Artikel** economy market; ~**e in der Industrie** industry outlets;
neue ~**e erschließen** to open up new markets, to open up a new territory for trade; ~ **entstehen lassen** to make up a market; ~ **vergrößern** to carve out wider markets; ~ **zurückerobern** to recover a market, to win back markets.

Absatz|gefüge marketing structure; ~**gelegenheit** sales opportunity; ~**gemeinschaft** sales combine (syndicate); ~**genossenschaft** marketing cooperative, cooperative marketing association, *(landwirtschaftliche)* producer (agricultural) cooperative, farm[er's] cooperative *(US)*, producer society *(Br.)*; ~**genossenschaft auf Provisionsbasis** terminal cooperative commission agency *(US)*; ~**gesellschaft** trading company; ~**gliederung** sales classification; ~**gremium** selling group, sales (marketing) conference; ~**grenze** sales limit; ~**höhe** volume of trade; ~**honorar** *(Autor)* royalty; ~**index** sales index; ~**kalender** selling calendar; ~**kalkulation** sales estimate; **sich in eine gewaltige** ~**kampagne stürzen** to launch into a massive sales drive; ~**kanäle** marketing channels; ~**kartell** distribution (sales, marketing) cartel; ~**kenntnis** marketing knowledge; **umfassende** ~**kenntnisse** competence in marketing; ~**kennzahlen** distribution indices, *(Statistik)* standard figures of distribution; ~**klima** state of the market; ~**konjunktur** seller's market; ~**kontingent** market (marketing, sales) quota; ~**kontingentierung** allocation of sale; ~**kontrolle** marketing (sales, progress) control, orderly marketing *(US)*; ~**kontrollstelle** marketing board; ~**konzentration** market concentration; ~**konzeption** marketing conception; ~**kosten** distribution expenses (costs), marketing costs, cost of marketing, cost of sales, expenses of marketing; ~**krise** sales crisis, slump in sales; ~**kunde** marketing knowledge; ~**kurve** distribution curve; ~**lage** sales (market) situation, sales position; **schlechte** ~**lage** poor market situation; ~**leistung** market performance; ~**lenkung** sales control, control of the market, controlled distribution; ~**mangel** selling pressure.

Absatzmarkt market, market (trading) area, outlet;
eng abgegrenzter ~ restricted market; **ausländischer** ~ foreign market; **begrenzter** ~ limited market; **gerade flügge gewordener** ~ fledg(e)ling market; **günstiger (erfolgversprechender)** ~ promising (seller's) market; **industrieller** ~ industrial sales; **inländischer** ~ domestic market; **sicherer (zugesicherter)** ~ assured market;
~ **für industrielle Erzeugnisse** industrial market; ~ **jugendlicher Käufer** youth market; ~ **auf öffentlichen Nahverkehrsmitteln** public transport commuter market;
sich auf einem ~ **durchsetzen** to penetrate a market; ~ **eröffnen** to be the key to sales, to break the ground; ~ **haben** to find a market; ~ **halten** to hold on the market; ~ **öffnen** to be the key to sell; ~ **schaffen** to create a market.

Absatzmärkte outlets, markets;
neue ~ **erschließen** to open up new channels of trade.

absatzmäßig|übernehmen, sich to overtrade; **sich in einem Land** ~ **verankern** to build up one's business in a country.

Absatz|mathematik mathematics of marketing; ~**menge** sales volume, quantity of sales, quantity sold; ~**mentalität** marketing mentality; ~**methoden** distribution (marketing, sales, selling) methods; ~**mittler** functional middleman; ~**möglichkeit** sales (market) opportunity, market [potential], selling possibility, opening; **mit sicheren** ~**möglichkeiten** certain to sell; ~**monopol** sales monopoly; ~**netz** network of dealers; ~**normung** standardization in marketing; ~**ordnung** marketing regulations; ~**organisation** sales (selling) organization; ~**organisation für zukünftige Aufgaben anreichern** to flesh out a marketing organization; ~**plan** plan of distribution, distribution plan, sales projection; ~**planung** marketing planning (mix, *US*); **Kopfzerbrechen bei der** ~**planung bekommen** to run into marketing headaches; ~**planung betreiben** to merchandise; ~**politik** marketing, selling (marketing, sales) policy; **individuelle** ~**politik** direct marketing; **schöpferische** ~**politik** innovative marketing; **selektive** ~**politik** selective selling; ~**potential** sales potential; ~**preis** selling (sales) price; ~**problem** marketing problem; ~**produkt** marketing product; ~**prognose** sales forecast; ~**programm** marketing program(me); ~- **und Vertriebsprogramm** marketing plan; ~**provision** seller's commission; ~**prozeß** marketing process; **neue** ~**quellen eröffnen** to open up new markets; ~**quote** sales (marketing) quota, sales proportion; ~**regulierung** market control; ~**richtung** destination of goods sold; ~**risiko** merchandising risk; ~**rückgang** letdown (decline) in sales, sales decline (reduction); ~**rückgang aufweisen** to be on a downswing; ~**schrumpfung** decrease (decline) in sales, sales decline, dwindling sales; ~**schwierigkeiten** marketing (sales) difficulties; ~**spezialist** marketing specialist; **mengenmäßiger** ~**spielraum** potential market; ~**stab** sales force (people, personnel); ~**statistik** marketing statistics, sales chart, sales statistics; ~**steigerung** increase in sales, increased sales, sales increase; **planmäßige** ~**steigerung** sales drive; ~**steuerung** marketing control; ~**stockung** stagnation in trade, stagnant market, slowing down of sales; ~**struktur** marketing structure; ~**studie** marketing investigation, market (marketing [research]) study; ~**syndikat** seller's cartel; ~**system** selling plan, marketing (distribution) system; ~**tagung** sales convention; ~**tätigkeit** marketing activity (functions); ~**technik** marketing technique.

absatztechnische Fähigkeiten, hervorragende marketing leadership.

Absatz|tendenz sales trend, trend of the market; ~**terminologie** marketing terminology; ~**übereinkommen** marketing agreement; ~**überschuß** marketing surplus; ~**umfang** sales volume, volume of trade; ~**unkosten** cost of sales; ~**unternehmen** sales agency, marketing institution; ~**unterstützung** marketing backing; ~**vereinbarung** marketing agreement, selling arrangement; ~**vereinigung** marketing cooperative (association); ~**verfahren** marketing procedure; ~**verhältnisse** market (marketing) conditions, market situation; **erschwerte** ~**verhältnisse** onerous selling conditions (process); ~**verordnung** *(Agrarprodukte)* marketing order; ~**vertrag** marketing contract; ~**vertretung** marketing (sales [promotion]) agency, distribution; ~**volumen** sales volume, total sales; ~**vorausschätzung** sales forecast[ing]; ~**vorbereitung** sales planning; ~**vorbereitung durch Vertriebsplanung** merchandising *(US)*; ~**vorschau** sales forecasting; ~**vorschlag** marketing proposal; ~**weg** trade (marketing, sales) channels, channels of distribution (trade); **ausschließlicher** ~**weg** exclusive distribution.

absatzweise by paragraphs, paragraph by paragraph.

Absatzwesen marketing [field (system)];
genossenschaftliches ~ associative (cooperative) marketing.

Absatz|wirtschaft [industrial] marketing, distributing (distributive) trade; ~**wirtschaftler** marketing man, markete(e)r.

absatzwirtschaftliche|Funktionen marketing functions; ~ **Maßnahmen** marketing operations (transactions).

Absatz|zahlen sales figures, market (marketing) data; ~**zeichen** *(Druck)* paragraph, mark; ~**zeit** marketing period; ~**zentrum** distribution center *(US)* (centre, *Br.*); ~**ziel** marketing goal; ~**ziffern** sales figures; ~**zone** marketing (distribution) area.

absaufen *(Flugzeug)* to lose weight, *(Grube)* to fill with water, *(Motor)* to be flooded, *(Schiff)* to go to the bottom, to sink.

absaugen to siphon off, *(Gas)* to exhaust.

abschaffbar abatable, abolishable, *(Gesetz)* abrogable.

abschaffen *(Amt)* to abolish, to discontinue, *(Gesetz)* to repeal, to abrogate, to rescind, to annul;
sein Auto ~ to give up one's car; **sein Dienstmädchen** ~ to do without a maid; **Gesetz** ~ to abrogate (repeal, rescind) a law.

Abschaffung cancellation, abolition, abrogation, extinguishment, *(Gesetz)* repeal, annulment, rescission, *(Störung)* abatement;
~ **eines Gesetzes** repeal (annulment) of a law; ~ **der Klassenunterschiede** levelling of classes; ~ **eines Mißstandes** redress of a grievance; ~ **der Sklaverei** abolition of slavery; ~ **des Tarifzwanges** *(Autoversicherung)* tariff abolition; ~ **von Zöllen** abolition of customs;
sich öffentlich für die ~ **eines Gesetzes einsetzen** to agitate for the repeal of a law; ~ **einer einschränkenden Bestimmung ins Auge fassen** to eye deregulation route.

abschaltbar disconnectible.

abschalten to disconnect, *(Maschine)* to put out of action (operation), *(Rundfunk)* to cut out, to turn off, *(Strom)* to cut off, to disconnect, to kill, *(Telefon)* to disconnect.

Abschaltstellung off position.

Abschaltung *(Radio)* switching off, *(Strom)* disconnection, *(Telefon)* cutoff, disconnection;
~ **ganzer Stromnetze** loadshedding *(el.)*.

abschätzbar appraisable, appreciable, estimable, valuable, assessable, rat(e)able.

Abschätzbarkeit rat(e)ability, assessability.

abschätzen *(bewerten)* to value, to valuate, to make a valuation, to form an estimate, to evaluate, to price, *(taxieren)* to appraise, to estimate, to tax, to gauge *(Br.)*, to gage *(US)*, *(steuerlich veranschlagen)* to assess, to rate, *(vergleichen)* to measure;
nach dem Augenmaß ~ to measure by the eye; **Fremden mit einem Blick** ~ to give a stranger the once-over; **Gebäude für die**

Versicherung ~ to rate a building for insurance purposes; **jeden Gegenstand einzeln** ~ to value each object; **gerichtlich** ~ *(verschuldeten Besitz)* to extend; **Grundstück** ~ to estimate an estate; **Kosten** ~ to tax costs; **öffentliche Meinung** ~ to gauge public opinion; **nochmals** ~ to reassess; **Schaden auf fünf Pfund** ~ to value the damage done at five pounds; **nach dem Steuerwert** ~ to assess for taxable value; **Verlust** ~ to assess the extent of a loss; **jds. Vermögen** ~ to estimate s. one's fortune; **etw. unter dem Wert** ~ to undervaluate, to underrate; **Wirkung einer Rede** ~ to gauge the effect of a speech.

Abschätzer appreciator, taxer, appraiser, valuer, prizer, *(Havarie)* average adjuster, *(Steuer)* assessor.

abschätzig disparaging, derogatory;
~**e Bemerkung machen** to make a disparaging remark.

Abschätzung *(Bewertung)* valuation, evaluation, valuing, *(Schätzung)* estimate, appraisal, estimation, appraisement, taxation, *(Schätzung von Grundstücken)* rating, assessment, extend *(Br.)*, *(Situation)* judgment;
nach ungefährer ~ at a rough estimate;
gerichtliche ~ judicial valuation;
~ **zwecks hypothekarischer Beleihung** rating of the entire mortgage pattern; ~ **zur Festlegung der Erbschaftssteuer** appraisal for inheritance taxation purposes; ~ **zur Festlegung öffentlicher Gebührnisse** appraisal for fixing of utility rates; ~ **von Geschäftsgrundstücken** business property appraisal; ~ **eines Grundstücks** land (real-estate) appraisal; ~ **der Kosten** taxing of costs; ~ **eines Kreditrisikos** appraising a credit risk; ~ **des Risikos** calculation of risk; ~ **durch Sachverständige** expert appraisal; ~ **des Schadens** appraisal of damage; ~ **zu Steuerzwecken** appraisal for taxation purposes, assessed valuation *(US)*; ~ **zu Versicherungszwecken** appraisal for insurance purposes, insurance appraisal; ~ **eines Wohngrundstücks** dwelling appraisal;
~ **vornehmen** to make an estimate, to appraise.

Abschätzungs|ausschuß assessment committee, committee of appraisement; ~**beamter** valuation officer, official appraiser; ~**gebühr** valuation fee; ~**klausel** *(Versicherung)* agreed-value (appraisal) clause; ~**kommission** assessment (appraisement) committee.

Abschaum mud (vilest part);
~ **der Gesellschaft (Menschheit)** scum of the earth, dredge (offscourings) of humanity, lees of a society.

Abscheu aversion, disgust;
~ **vor der Öffentlichkeit haben** to have a horror of publicity; **mit** ~ **erfüllt sein** to be filled with nausea.

abscheuerregend disgusting, repugnant, repulsive.

abscheulich vile, disgusting, foul, loathsome, odious;
sich ~ **benehmen** to behave abominably.

Abscheulichkeit flagrancy, loathsomeness, odiousness.

abschicken to send off, to dispatch, to forward, to ship *(US)*;
Brief ~ to post *(Br.)* (mail, *US*) a letter; **Geld** ~ to remit money.

abschieben to sidetrack, *(Ausländer)* to deport;
j. ~ to turn s. o. away, to send s. o. to grass, *(kaltstellen)* to put s. o. on the shelf; **Häftling** ~ to transport a criminal; **Schuld auf j.** ~ to blame s. o.; **Unterstützungsempfänger** ~ to remove a pauper; **Verantwortung** ~ to shift the (get rid of) responsibility, to pass the buck *(US)*.

Abschiebung *(Ausländer)* deportation, removal;
~ **feindlicher Ausländer** expulsion of enemy nationals; ~ **eines unerwünschten Ausländers** deportation of an undesired alien; ~ **eines Unterstützungsempfängers** removal of a pauper.

Abschied farewell, leave-taking, parting, leaving, *(Abreise)* departure, *(Entlassung)* dismissal, retirement, *(mil.)* discharge, leave, *(Rücktritt)* resignation;
schlichter ~ *(mil.)* cashiering, blue ticket *(sl.)*; **unehrenhafter** ~ dishono(u)rable discharge;
seinen ~ **bekommen** to be superannuated, to be dismissed; **um seinen** ~ **einkommen** to apply for one's discharge; **ehrenvollen** ~ **erhalten** to be hono(u)rably retired; **seinen** ~ **erhalten** to be placed on the retired list; **jem. den** ~ **geben** to dismiss s. o., *(mil.)* to cashier; ~ **nehmen** to take one's farewell, to take leave; **seinen** ~ **nehmen** *(Beamter)* to retire, to tender one's resignation, to send in one's papers, *(Offizier)* to quit the service, to resign one's commission; **ohne** ~ **weggehen** to take French leave; **mit schlichtem** ~ **entlassen werden** *(mil.)* to be cashiered.

Abschieds|abend farewell party; ~**ansprache** farewell address, valedictory *(US)*; ~**audienz** farewell (leave-taking) audience; ~**bahnsteig** waving bay; ~**besuch** farewell call (visit), parting (leave-taking) visit; ~**brief** farewell letter; ~**empfang** farewell reception; ~**ermahnung** parting injunction; ~**essen** farewell (leaving, valedictory) dinner; ~**feier** farewell celebration, send-off *(fam.)*; **jem. das** ~**geleit geben** to see s. o. on his way; ~**geschenk** going-away present; **sein** ~**gesuch einreichen** to tender one's resignation, to send in one's papers; ~**kuß** parting kiss; ~**rede** farewell speech, valedictory *(US)*; ~**trunk** stirrup (farewell, grace) cup, one for the road *(coll.)*; ~**vorstellung** farewell performance; ~**worte** parting words, farewell speech; ~**zeugnis** leaving certificate, diploma *(US)*.

Abschießen *(Flugzeug, Rakete)* launching.

abschießen to shoot, to fire [off], to discharge, to kill, *(Flugzeug)* to shoot down, to wing *(coll.)*, *(Rakete, Torpedo)* to launch;
j. ~ to kick s. o. out of his job, *(aus politischen Gründen)* to scalp (decapitate, knife, *US*) s. o.; **einzeln** ~ *(mil.)* to pick off; **feindlichen Panzer** ~ to knock out an enemy tank; **Vogel** ~ *(fig.)* to ring (bear away) the bell, to take the rag off the bush *(US fam.)*.

abschinden, sich to tag, to toil and moil, to work one's fingers to the bone (o. s. to death), to keep one's nose to the grindstone.

Abschirmdienst counterintelligence.

abschirmen to protect, to shade, to shield, to act as curtain, *(tel.)* to screen;
Augen gegen die Sonne ~ to shield one's eyes against the sun; **Haus gegen Einsicht** ~ to screen a house against public view; **gegen Störungen** ~ *(Rundfunkgerät)* to suppress interferences; **heimische Wirtschaft** ~ to protect the economy by tariff barriers.

Abschirmung screening [device], shield protection, *(Gegenspionage)* counterintelligence, *(Sicherheit)* cover;
~ **gegen Störungen** suppression of interferences.

Abschirmvorrichtung *(tel.)* screening device, shield.

abschlachten to kill off, to butcher.

Abschlag *(Abzug)* deduction, reduction, *(im Kurs)* decline, discount, disagio, *(Preisminderung)* abatement, rebate, allowance, discount;
auf ~ on account, in part, *(in Teilzahlungen)* in part payments, by instalments, on hire purchase *(Br.)*, on the deferred payment system *(US)*, *(im voraus)* by anticipation; **mit 12%** ~ less 12%; **ohne** ~ without reduction; **ohne Zuzahlung und** ~ without discount or surcharge; **zu einem festgelegten** ~ *(Schatzwechsel)* through the tap *(Br.)*;
~ **im Listenpreis** chain discount;
Waren mit einem zehnprozentigen ~ **vom Normalpreis anbieten** to offer goods at 10 per cent off the regular price; **auf** ~ **bezahlen** to pay by instal(l)ments; ~ **auf den Preis gewähren** to allow a discount, to make an allowance; **auf** ~ **nehmen** to take on [future] account; **mit einem** ~ **verkaufen** to sell at a decline (reduced price, discount).

abschlagen to knock off, *(Gesuch)* to refuse, to decline, to turn down;
Bürstenabzug ~ to take off a proof; **Format** ~ *(drucktechn.)* to unlock the form; **Gerüst** ~ to take down the scaffolding; **glatt (rundweg)** ~ to turn down (refuse) flatly; **vom Preis** ~ to allow a discount, to grant a reduction; **Zelt** ~ to strike a tent.

abschlägig negative, refusing;
~ **bescheiden** to turn down a request, to rebuff; ~ **beschieden werden** to get an unfavo(u)rable answer;
~**e Antwort** refusal, negative reply; ~**e Antwort erhalten** to meet with a refusal; ~**er Bescheid** rebuff.

abschläglich on account, as part payment *(Br.)*;
~**e Zahlung** payment on account, instalment.

Abschlags|bewilligung, vorläufige *(parl.)* vote on account *(Br.)*; ~**dividende** interim (initial, *Br.*) dividend, dividend at interim (on account); ~**quote** *(Konkurs)* first dividend; ~**quote verteilen** *(Treuhänder)* to declare a dividend; ~**summe** instalment, payment on account; ~**tag** settling day; ~**verteilung** *(Konkurs)* distribution of a dividend; ~**zahlung** partial payment, preliminary distribution, *(Teilzahlung)* part (initial) payment, payment in part, instalment [payment], *(Vorschuß)* anticipation, payment on account, advance; **auf** ~**zahlung kaufen** to buy on hire purchase *(Br.)* (on the deferred payment system, *US*); ~**zahlung leisten** to make a payment on instalment (part payment).

Abschlagung *(Bitte)* refusal.

abschleifen *(fig.)* to polish, to refine;
sich ~ to smooth (refine) one's manners.

Abschleppdienst recovery (breakdown, wrecking, towing, wrecker, *US*) service.

Abschleppen hauling, towing away.

abschleppen *(Auto)* to haul, to tow off (away), to take in tow;
Schiff ~ to tow a ship.

Abschlepp|fahrzeug recovery vehicle, tow truck *(US)*; ~**gerät** towing equipment; ~**kommando** recovery (breakdown, wrecking, *US*) party; ~**kran** breakdown (salvage, wrecking, *US*) crane; ~**mannschaft** breakdown gang, wrecking crew *(US)*; ~**seil** towing line, tow line (rope), drag rope; ~**wagen** recovery vehicle, wrecker *(US)*, salvage truck *(US)*, breakdown van (lorry), tow car (truck, *US*); ~**zone [für falsch geparkte Fahrzeuge]** tow-away zone *(US)*.

Abschließen | einer Debatte closure of a debate; ~ **eines Friedensvertrages** conclusion of peace.

abschließen to lock [up], *(v./i.)* to end, to close, *(Angelegenheit)* to conclude, to terminate, *(Brief)* to close, to end, *(Engagement eingehen)* to sign a contract, *(Geschäft)* to transact, *(Konto, Rechnung)* to settle, to adjust, to wind up, to balance, *(Tür)* to turn the key, to lock;

Abkommen ~ to conclude a treaty; **aktiv** ~ to show a balance in favo(u)r, to close in the black *(US coll.)*; **Anleihe** ~ to contract a loan; **Arbeit** ~ to complete a work; **sich von der Außenwelt** ~ to retire within o. s., to live a secluded life; **Bilanz** ~ to strike (bring down) a balance; **Brief** ~ to bring a letter to a close; **Bücher** ~ to balance (close, make up) the books; **erfolgreich (mit Erfolg)** ~ to crown, to bring to a successful conclusion; **mit einem besseren Ergebnis** ~ to close with a better result; **Essen mit Kaffee** ~ to top the dinner with coffee; **Friedensvertrag** ~ to conclude a treaty of peace; **Geschäft mit jem.** ~ to strike (close, conclude) a bargain (enter into a transaction) with s. o.; **Geschäftsjahr** ~ to close the business year; **mit Gewinn** ~ to show a profit; **Gläubigervergleich** ~ to compound (compose) with one's creditors; **Jahr mit Verlust** ~ to close a year in the red *(US coll.)*; **Krankenversicherung** ~ to insure against illness; **Lebensversicherung** ~ to take out a life insurance policy; **Lieferungsvertrag** ~ to contract for a supply; **Nahrungsmittel luftdicht** ~ to airtight food; **passiv** ~ to show a debit balance, to close in the red *(US coll.)*; **für eigene Rechnung** ~ to trade for own account; **Rechnungsjahr** ~ to close the financial *(Br.)* (fiscal, *US*) year; **Rede mit ...** ~ to wind up by saying ...; **Sache** ~ to set a matter at rest; **sein Studium** ~ to finish one's studies, to take a degree; **Tal von der Außenwelt** ~ *(Erdrutsch)* to isolate a valley from the outer world; **sich von der Umwelt** ~ to shut o. s. off from one's environment; **Vergleich** ~ to arrive at a composition, to execute an accord, to come to an arrangement; **Verhandlungen** ~ to terminate negotiations; **Verkauf** ~ to effect a sale; **mit einem Verlust** ~ to close with a loss, to show a deficit; **Versicherung** ~ to take out an insurance policy, to obtain an insurance; **Vertrag** ~ to come to (sign, conclude, effect, enter into) an agreement, to enter a contract; **Waffenstillstand** ~ to conclude an armistice; **Wette** ~ to lay a wager, to bet; **mit voller Zeile** ~ to make lines even.

abschließend concluding, conclusive, in conclusion, definitive, final, *(Urteil)* definitive;

mit Verlust ~ showing a deficit;

~**e Bemerkung** concluding remarks.

Abschluß *(Abschlußprüfung)* final examination, finals, *(Angelegenheit)* conclusion, *(Bank)* bank return, *(Bilanz)* balance [sheet], *(an der Börse)* bargain, transaction, commitment, *(Brief)* ending, close, *(Debatte)* closure, *(Effektenemission)* underwriting, *(Fertigstellung)* completion, end[ing], termination, *(Geschäft)* deal[ing], business, transaction, bargain, commitment, *(Liquidaton)* settlement *(Br.)*, winding up, *(Rechnungslegung)* adjustment, settlement, *(Rechnungssumme)* balance, *(Verkauf)* sale, *(Verschluß)* shutting up, *(Werbebranche)* contract;

bei ~ **unserer Bücher** on (when) balancing (closing) our books; **beim** ~ **des Berichts** at the time the report went to press; **beim** ~ **der Rechnungsperiode** at the close of the financial period; **nach** ~ **seines Studiums** after having finished one's studies;

betriebswirtschaftlicher ~ diploma in business administration; **endgültiger** ~ final arrangement; **fester** ~ firm bargain (deal); **gemeinschaftlicher** ~ joint bargain; **jährlicher** ~ annual balance; **nichtkonsolidierter** ~ deconsolidated accounts; **provisorischer** ~ provisional booking; **zufriedenstellender** ~ perfect rounding off;

~ **einer Angelegenheit** winding up of an affair; ~ **seiner Ausbildung** completion of one's education; ~ **der Bücher** closing (making up) of the books, balancing of accounts; ~ **von Deckungsgeschäften** hedging; ~ **der Effektentransferbücher einer Gesellschaft** books close; ~ **für weniger als ein Jahr** *(Werbung)* short term; ~ **eines Kontos** closing an account, rest *(Br.)*; ~ **einer Lebensarbeit** consummation of a life's work; ~ **einer Lebensversicherung** taking out a life insurance policy; ~ **auf künftige Lieferung** time bargain, forward deal; ~ **der Rechnungsperiode** fiscal closing; ~ **auf kurze Sicht** short deal; ~ **auf lange Sicht** long-term transaction; ~ **zu einem festen Verkaufspreis** outright sale; ~ **eines Versicherungsvertrages** effecting an insurance, taking out (conclusion of) an insurance contract; ~ **eines Vertrages** signing (conclusion) of an agreement (a contract); ~ **über 10 Millionen Tonnen Weizen** contract for 10 million tons of wheat;

akademischen ~ **anstreben** to study for a degree; ~ **aufstellen** to strike a balance; **zum** ~ **bringen** to bring to a close (conclusion), to terminate, to carry out; **Geschäft zum** ~ **bringen** to make a bargain (deal); **Geschäft zu einem erfolgreichen** ~ **bringen** to bring a business to a successful conclusion; **Vertrag zu einem** ~ **bringen** to complete a contract; **zum** ~ **gelangen** to reach an understanding, to come to an agreement; **zum** ~ **kommen** to end, to draw a close, to be effected; **zu einem raschen** ~ **kommen** to talk a fast trade; **besten** ~ **machen** to pass out highest; **mit jem. einen** ~ **machen** to strike a bargain (make a deal) with s. o.; **seinen** ~ **machen** to go down *(Br.)*; ~ **perfekt machen** to seal a fast trade; **seinen** ~ **in höherer Mathematik machen** to take hono(u)rs in mathematics; **mit einem guten** ~ **rechnen** to calculate on a good trade; **ohne** ~ **sein** *(Börse)* to be a blank; **vor dem** ~ **stehen** to be drawing to a close; ~ **tätigen** *(Börse)* to close (do, negotiate) a deal, to make a commitment; ~ **vermitteln** to secure a business; ~ **veröffentlichen** to publish (disclose) a balance sheet.

Abschlüsse business [done], *(Aufträge)* orders secured, *(Börse)* transactions, commitments;

kleine ~ odd lots; **vereinzelte** ~ spasmodic dealings; **vierteljährliche** ~ quarterly trade accounts; **wenig** ~ few sales;

~ **machen** to make commitments, to do business; ~ **durch Umstellung von Dollar- auf Goldbasis inflationssicher machen** to hedge against inflation by gearing the dollar value of contracts to gold; **größere** ~ **tätigen** to make more sales; ~ **in Devisen tätigen** to effect exchange transactions; ~ **auf London tätigen** to effect exchange deals on London.

Abschluß | abrechnung *(Bank)* closing statement, *(Börse)* contract note *(Br.)*; ~**abteilung** *(Immobilienbüro)* closing department; ~**agent** factor, commission (closing, underwriting, *Br.*) agent, *(Versicherungsgeschäft)* credit agent; ~**anmeldung** *(Umsatzsteuer)* final declaration; **mit** ~**arbeiten beschäftigt sein** to be balancing the books for the year.

abschlußbereiter werden to become more prone to a settlement.

Abschluß | bericht closing statement, final report; ~**bescheinigung** final discharge; ~**bilanz** [annual] balance sheet; ~**bogen** *(Bankwesen)* settlement sheet; ~**buchung** closing entry *(US)*; ~**einheit** *(Börse)* even (full, *US*) lot; ~**ergebnis** result for the year, operating result, closed accounts, *(Versicherungsgesellschaft)* underwriting result; ~**examen** leaving (final) examination, *(Abitur)* examination for the General Certificate of Education *(Br.)*, finals *(US)*, graduation from high school *(US)*; ~**examen an der Handelsschule** commercial examination; **an einer Schule das** ~**examen machen** to graduate at *(Br.)* (from, *US*) a school; ~**feier** *(Schule)* commencement [day] *(US)*, Speech Day *(Br.)*; ~**formalitäten beim Grundstückskauf** real-estate closing, completion; ~**formel** *(Brief)* completory close; ~**gebühr** closing fee, sales charge, *(Bank)* bank charges; ~**geschäft beim Aktienkauf** stock transfer deal; ~**hahn** stopcock; ~**jahr** *(Inserat)* contract (contractual) year; ~**konto** profit and loss summary account; ~**kosten** *(Versicherung)* initial expenses; ~**kurs** sales (closing) rate, closing price; ~**kursus** terminal course; ~**meldung** *(Umsatzsteuer)* final declaration; ~**nota** contract note *(Br.)*; ~**posten** closing item; ~**prämie** sales premium; ~**probebilanz** post-closing trial balance; ~**protokoll** minutes; ~**provision** [sales, new business, final] commission, *(Effektenkommission)* underwriting commission, *(Generalvertreter)* overriding commission; ~**prüfer** auditor; ~**prüfung** graduation, commencement, final examination, finals, *(Revision)* [general] audit; ~**prüfung zum Assistenten im Buchhandel** assistant's leaving examination; ~**prüfung machen** to be in for one's schools *(Br.)*, to take one's finals *(US)*, to graduate at *(Br.)* (from, *US*) a school; ~**rabatt** *(Anzeigenplazierung)* time discount; ~**rechnung** final account, *(Bank)* closing statement, account of settlement; ~**saldo eines Kontos** ultimate balance of an account; ~**sätze** dealing rates; ~**sitzung** closing session; ~**spesen** bank-return charges, bank-balance charges; ~**stichtag** delivery date; ~**tabelle** settlement sheet; ~**tag** *(Bankkonto)* closing date, *(Börse)* settling day *(Br.)*; **erfolgreicher** ~**tag** *(Börse)* break-even date; ~**termin** target day, *(Anleihe)* closing date; ~**veranstaltung** final performance; ~**vereinbarung** final accord; **schriftliche** ~**vereinbarung mit dem Finanzamt** closing agreement *(US)*; ~**vergütung** terminal bonus; ~**verhandlung** closing; ~**verlust** terminal loss; ~**vertreter** factor, commission merchant; **einzelne** ~**verweigerung** *(Kartellrecht)* individual refusal to deal *(US)*; ~**vollmacht**

power to contract, contractual power, authority to negotiate (contract), *(Gewerkschaft)* bargaining power; **~vorschriften** balancing requirements; **~wechsel** [remittance per] appoint; **~zahlung** complete payment, *(letzte Rate)* final instal(l)ment, *(bei der Pensionierung)* severance benefit, *(an ausgediente Soldaten)* terminal leave pay *(US)*; **jährliche ~zahlung an den Gewinn koppeln** to link the minimum bonus to profitability; **~zahlung leisten** to complete payment; **~zeitpunkt** balance-sheet date; **~zeugnis** leaving certificate, *(an der Oberschule)* high-school diploma *(US)*, Advanced General Certificate of Education *(Br.)*; **~ziffern** profit and loss figures.

abschmeicheln, jem. etw. to cozen s. th. out of s. o.

abschmelzen, Sicherung to blow a fuse.

abschmieren to grease, to lubricate, *(Flugzeug)* to crash, to nose-dive, *(Schüler)* to crib, to copy.

Abschmierfett lubricating grease.

abschnallen, sich vom Sitz to unbuckle one's seat.

Abschneiden, schlechtes bad performance, poor showing.

abschneiden to cut off, *(Kupons)* to detach, to detail;
am besten ~ to come off best; **jem. die Ehre ~** to speak ill of s. o.; **jem. den Fluchtweg ~** to cut s. one's way of escape; **gut ~** to do well, to make out *(US)*; **plus minus null ~** to break even; **bei einer Prüfung am besten ~** to come out on top; **schlecht ~** to fare poorly; **einer Stadt die Zufuhr ~** to cut off a town's supplies; **im Vergleich mit anderen günstig ~** to measure up favo(u)rably with others; **Weg ~** to take a shortcut; **jem. das Wort ~** to interrupt s. o., to cut s. o. short.

Abschnitt section, segment, *(Buch)* chapter, section, passage, patch, title, head, [new] paragraph, break, *(Dividendenschein)* dividend warrant, *(Dokument)* clause, particle, *(Epoche)* period, term, epoch, phase, *(Kapitel)* chapter, heading, *(Kontrollblatt)* counterfoil, stub, *(US)*, *(Lebensmittelkarte)* coupon, *(Reise)* stage, leg, *(Scheck)* stub, counterfoil, *(Stoffmuster)* coupon, *(Stück)* item, article, appoint, number, *(Stückelung)* denomination, *(Talon)* counterfoil, *(Vertrag)* paragraph, article, *(Wechsel)* bill of exchange, item, *(Zeit)* period, term, phase, stage, *(Zinsschein)* coupon;
in kleinen ~en by easy stages;
noch nicht eingegangene ~e uncollected items *(US)*; **nicht offiziell an der Börse gehandelter ~** odd (fractional, *US*) lot; **große ~e** large denominations; **noch nicht verrechnete ~e** effects not cleared;
~ einer Anleihe portion (slice) of a loan; **oberer ~ eines Dividendenscheins** dividend top *(Br.)*; **~ mit telegrafischer Eingangsanzeige** wire fate item; **neuer ~ in jds. Leben** new chapter in s. one's life; **~e auf auswärtige Plätze** out-of-town items *(US)* (bills, *Br.*), out items *(US)*; **~ der Tagesordnung** items on the agenda, compartment *(Br.)*; **~e auf uns** bills on us *(Br.)*;
in ~e einteilen to sector; **in vier ~e zerfallen** to fall into four sections; **in fünf ~en ziehen** to draw in five bills.

Abschnitts|leitung *(Flugüberwachung)* radar area control; **~reserve** *(mil.)* local reserve.

abschnittsweise in sections, by paragraphs, *(Anleihe)* in portions (slices).

Abschnittszeichen section mark.

abschnüren, durch eine Blockade to cut off by a blockade; **Handel ~** to put a stranglehold on the trade; **Handel des Feindes ~** to throttle the enemy's trade.

abschöpfen to skim off, *(EG)* to levy, *(Gewinne)* to tax away, to siphon off, *(Kaufkraft)* to absorb, to skim off;
überschüssige Kaufkraft ~ to skim off surplus purchasing power; **Liquidität ~** to absorb liquidity; **Rahm ~** *(fig.)* to skim the cream off.

Abschöpfung absorption, skimming off, *(EG)* [adjustment] levy; **fiskalische (steuerliche) ~** tax take, taxing away;
~ der Kaufkraft absorption of buying power; **~ überflüssiger Kaufkraft** skimming surplus purchasing power; **~ von Liquidität** absorption of liquidity; **~ von Planungsgewinnen** *(Regionalpolitik)* betterment levy; **~ von Übergewinnen** skimming off excess profits;
~ erheben *(EG)* to impose a levy.

Abschöpfungs|anleihe absorption loan; **~beitrag auf Agrareinfuhren** products of agricultural levies; **~betrag** *(EG)* price adjustment levy, rate (amount) of levy; **innergemeinschaftlicher ~betrag** *(EG)* intracommunity levy.

abschotten to bulkhead.

abschrecken to discourage, to intimidate, *(mil.)* to deter.

abschreckend deterrent, exemplary;
als ~es Beispiel dienen to be a warning to others; **~e Strafe** exemplary punishment, deterrent sentence; **~e Wirkung** deterrent effect.

Abschreckung discouragement, *(mil.)* deterrent;
abgestufte ~ graduate deterrent; **nukleare ~** nuclear deterrent.

Abschreckungs|mittel *(Steuerpolitik)* disincentive, *(Strafe)* determent, deterrent; **als ~mittel dienen** to act as a deterrent of crime; **~politik** policy of determent; **~potential** deterrent power; **~strafe** deterrent; **~strategie** strategy of deterrence; **~streitmacht** deterrent, counterforce; **~waffe** deterrent, horror weapon; **~wirkung** deterring effect.

abschreibbar depreciable.

Abschreibegebühren reproduction costs, copying fees.

Abschreiben copying, *(Urkunde)* engrossment.

abschreiben *(abbestellen)* to counterorder, to countermand, to cancel, *(absagen)* to send a refusal, *(Autor)* to plagiarize, to crib, *(Bilanz)* to write (charge) off, to depreciate, to allow for depreciation, to amortize, to cut, *(kopieren)* to copy, *(aus Kurzschrift übertragen)* to transcribe, *(Schüler)* to crib, *(Urkunden)* to engross;
jem. ~ to put s. o. off; **10% ~** to mark down 10 per cent for depreciation; **hohe Anlaufkosten ~** to write off heavy start-up costs; **für Büroeinrichtungen ~** to allow for depreciation of office furniture; **noch einmal ~** to write over again; **kapitalisierte Entwicklungskosten ~** to write off capitalized development cost; **sich die Finger ~** to work one's fingers to the bone; **Flugzeug ~** to write off an aircraft as lost; **zweifelhafte Forderung ~** to write off a doubtful *(Br.)* (bad, *US*) debt, to wipe off a debit balance; **Forschungs- und Entwicklungskosten sofort ~** to write off exploration and development expenses immediately; **gänzlich ~** to write down; **Grundstück ~** to write down property; **Kapital teilweise ~** to write down capital; **Kunden ~** to regard a customer as lost; **neugekaufte Maschine beschleunigt ~** to depreciate a new machine over a shorter period; **für Maschinenbenutzung ~** to write off for depreciation of machinery; **15% des Maschinenwertes ~** to depreciate a machine by 15 per cent; **steuerlich ~** to write off against taxes; **teilweise ~** to write down; **Totalverlust ~** to write off as a total loss; **Verluste ~** to charge off (deduct, cut) losses; **Verluste mit 15% ~** to cut (mark down) 15 per cent for depreciation; **voll (vollständig) ~** to wipe off the books, to write off; **steuerbegünstigt vorzeitig ~** to accelerate depreciation.

Abschreiber copyist, copying clerk, transcriber.

Abschreibfehler clerical error.

Abschreibpolice open policy.

Abschreibung writeoff *(US)*, charge-off, markdown, write-down, *(einzelner Posten)* item written off, *(für Substanzverringerung)* depletion, *(für Wertminderung)* [allowance for] depreciation, capital allowance, amortization, lost usefulness;
nach ~ aller Verluste after charging (writing) off all losses;
7b ~ allowance on premises, [statutory] repairs allowance (deduction); **altersbedingte ~** depreciation for age; **bilanzmäßig anerkannte ~** balance-sheet depreciation; **steuerlich anerkannte ~** tax depreciation (writeoffs); **beschleunigte ~** accelerated depreciation, emergency amortization, rapid writeoff *(US)*; **buchmäßige ~** theoretical depreciation; **degressive ~** declining-balance depreciation; **geometrisch degressive ~** double-declining balance depreciation; **digitale ~** sum-of-the-years digits method *(US)*; **entstandene ~en** depreciation accruals; **auf Grund natürlicher Abnutzung erforderliche ~** physical depreciation; **erhöhte ~en** accelerated allowance *(Br.)*; **genehmigte ~** allowance for depreciation *(Br.)*; **höchstmögliche ~** maximum depreciation; **laufende ~en** writing-down allowances *(Br.)*; **lineare ~** straight-line [method of] depreciation; **normale ~** ordinary depreciation; **ordentliche ~** depreciation according to plan; **übermäßige ~** excessive depreciation; **verdiente ~** amount of depreciation earned; **verkürzte ~** accelerated writeoff *(Br.)*; **vollständige ~** wholesale writing down; **steuerbegünstigte vorzeitige ~** accelerated allowance *(Br.)*, emergency amortization, rapid writeoff *(US)*; **steuerlich zulässige ~en** tax writeoffs *(US)*, capital allowance *(Br.)*;
~ für Abnutzung depreciation for wear and tear *(Br.)*, wear-and-tear allowance *(Br.)*; **~ für Anlagegüter** *(AFA)* annual allowance *(Br.)*; **130%ige ~ für Anlagegüter** investment allowance *(Br.)*; **~ auf das Anlagevermögen** annual depreciation, depreciation on investments; **jährliche ~ auf das Anlagevermögen** capital allowance *(Br.)*, depreciation on fixed assets, annual depreciation (allowance, *Br.*); **~ im Anschaffungsjahr** first-year allowance *(Br.)*; **~ nach Anschaffungswerten** historic-cost depreciation; **~ auf Basis der erbrachten Leistung** service output depreciation method; **~en auf Betriebsanlagen** depreciation of industrial equipment, allowance on plant *(Br.)*; **~ auf die Betriebs- und Geschäftsausstattung** depreciation on office furniture and equipment; **~ vom jeweiligen Buchwert** written-

down value; ~en für Devisenverluste write-offs for losses on foreign exchange *(US)*; ~en auf Einrichtungsgegenstände capital allowances on furniture *(Br.)*; ~ auf Fabrikgebäude mills and factories allowance *(Br.)*; ~ auf Finanzanlagen writedowns and other valuation adjustments of investments; ~en für Gebäude depreciation of buildings; ~ auf gewerblich genutzte Gebäude industrial building allowance *(Br.)*; ~ auf Gebäudekonto (für Gebäudeabnutzung) reduction of premises account; ~en und Gewinne retentions; ~en und nicht ausgeschüttete Gewinne business savings, net cashflow; ~en auf Grundstücke real-estate depreciation, depreciation of premises (property owned); ~en auf das Grundstücksvermögen depreciation on land; ~en auf Industriebauten industrial building allowance *(Br.)*; ~ für Investitionen investment allowance *(Br.)*; ~ von Lagerbeständen inventory writedown; hundertprozentige steuerliche ~en für Maschinen und Betriebsausrüstung im Anlaufsjahr 100% first-year tax relief on new machinery and plant; ~ auf den Maschinenpark depreciation on machinery; ~ im Rahmen der volkswirtschaftlichen Gesamtrechnung maintaining capital intact; ~ auf Rationalisierungsinvestitionen functional depreciation; ~en auf Sachanlagen depreciation on tangible assets; ~ für Substanzverringerung depletion allowance (expense) *(US)*; ~en auf Verwaltungsgebäude reductions of premises account; ~en auf Warenbestände inventory writedowns; ~ auf Werksanlagen depreciation on plant; ~ für Wertminderung allowance for wear and tear *(Br.)*; ~ nach Wiederbeschaffungskosten replacement cost depreciation; ~ vom Wiederbeschaffungswert depreciation on replacement value; ~ auf Wirtschaftsgebäude agricultural building allowance *(Br.)*;

~en auf die Preise abwälzen to charge depreciation of equipment onto costs; ~ aussetzen to interrupt depreciation; mit ~en belasten to charge depreciations; zulässige ~ berechnen to compute allowance *(Br.)* (depreciation); steuerliche ~en vornehmen können to gain relief; steuerlich zulässige ~en in Anspruch nehmen to claim capital allowance *(Br.)*; ~en nicht in Anspruch nehmen to disclaim allowance on depreciation; als steuerlich zulässige ~ anerkannt sein to qualify for capital allowances *(Br.)*; mit ~en belastet sein to be burdened with charges of depreciations; seine ~en verdienen to earn one's depreciation; ~ [zeitlich] verteilen to allocate depreciation; seine ~en steuerlich über mehrere Jahre verteilen to spread one's depreciation over several years; ~en vornehmen to write off (down), to charge depreciations, to depreciate; steuerlich anerkannte ~en vornehmen to depreciate for tax purposes; ~en auf Kapitalanlagegüter steuerlich vortragen to carry forward capital allowance *(Br.)*; 2% des Hauswertes pro Jahr für ~en zulassen to compute the writing-down on the basis of 2% per year of the cost of the building *(Br.)*; für ~en zurückstellen to allow for depreciation.

Abschreibungs|art method of depreciation; ~aufwand depreciation expense (charges); ~ausgleich depreciation adjustment; ~basis capital allowance basis *(Br.)*; ~berechnung depreciation expense computation, capital allowance computation *(Br.)*; ~berechnungsgrundlage service-yield basis [of depreciation].

abschreibungsberechtigt sein to qualify for an allowance *(Br.)*.

Abschreibungsbestimmungen depreciation provisions;
den ~ entsprechen to qualify for an allowance *(Br.)*.

Abschreibungsbetrag amount of depreciation, depreciable amount, amount written off, [allowance for] depreciation, depreciation allowance *(Br.)*, depreciation charge;
zusätzlich gewährter ~ balancing allowance *(Br.)*; jährlicher ~ annual allowance *(Br.)*, annual rate of depreciation; laufender ~ systematic allowance for depreciation; laufender ~ (vom 2. Jahr) writing-down allowance *(Br.)*; voller ~ full allowance *(Br.)*.

Abschreibungsbeträge, aktivierte (bei der Liquidation) balancing charge; angefallene ~ historic depreciation; steuerlich noch nicht ausgenutzte ~ excess allowance *(Br.)*; zukünftige ~ future writing-down allowance *(Br.)*;
~ absetzen to charge depreciation; ~ auf das Anlagevermögen berechnen to compute the capital allowance *(Br.)*; ~ für ein Kraftfahrzeug in Anspruch nehmen to claim allowance for wear and tear of a car; ~ auf siebzehn Jahre verteilen to spread allowance over 17 years *(Br.)*.

Abschreibungs|buchung depreciation accounting; ~einheit depreciation unit; ~erleichterungen depreciation facilities (breaks, *US*).

abschreibungsfähig depreciable, liable to depreciation, entitled to capital allowance *(Br.)*;
voll ~ sein to qualify for an allowance of 100% *(Br.)*; ~e Kosten service costs; ~e Vermögenswerte depreciable property *(US)*.

Abschreibungs|faktoren depreciation factors; ~formel depreciation formula; ~freiheit allowance on depreciation, depreciation allowance; ~grundwert depreciable value; ~konto depreciation account; ~korrekturen adjustment of depreciations; ~kosten depreciation charges (expense), depreciable costs, charge to (cost of) depreciation; ~kosten und Erhaltungsaufwand user costs; ~lasten amortization (depreciation) charges.

Abschreibungsmethode depreciation (retirement) method;
auf dem Umfang der Anlagebenutzung beruhende ~ output method of calculating depreciation *(US)*; degressive ~ declining-balance method of depreciation; arithmetisch degressive (digitale) ~ sum of the years digit method *(US)*; direkte ~ direct method of depreciation; indirekte ~ indirect method of depreciation; kombinierte ~ und Erhaltungsmethode combined depreciation and upkeep method; lineare ~ straight-line (flat-rate) method of depreciation;
gleichmäßige ~ vom Anschaffungswert straight-line method of calculating depreciation *(US)*; ~ vom Anschaffungswert mit fallenden Quoten reducing-fraction method of calculating depreciation; ~ auf der Basis der erbrachten Leistungen service output depreciation method; gleichmäßige ~ vom Buchwert fixed percentage (diminishing-value) method of depreciation; ~ nach Gewinn und Rentabilität output method of calculating depreciation; ~ nach Quoten time method of calculating depreciation *(US)*; ~ mit fallenden Quoten reducing-fraction method of calculating depreciation; ~ mit gleichmäßigen Quoten straight-line method of calculating depreciation; ~ mit steigenden Quoten sinking-fund method of calculating depreciation; ~ nach Terminquoten time-method of calculating depreciation *(US)*.

Abschreibungsmodalitäten, günstigere liberalized rules on depreciation;
~ verbessern (lockern) to loosen rules on depreciation.

Abschreibungsmöglichkeit depreciation allowance;
indirekte ~ indirect method of depreciation; schnellere ~ für Anlagegüter faster capital-goods depreciation;
von ~en keinen Gebrauch machen to disclaim allowance for depreciation; auf ~en stark reagieren to be vulnerable to depreciation.

Abschreibungsobjekt depreciation base, item written of.

abschreibungspflichtig liable to depreciation, depreciable.

Abschreibungs|plan system of depreciation, depreciation (write-off) schedule; ~politik depreciation policies; liberalisierte ~politik liberalisation of depreciation allowances; steuerliche ~politik depreciation tax policy; ~praxis depreciation practice; ~prozentsatz, ~quote rate of depreciation, depreciation rate; ~reform depreciation reform; steuerliche ~regeln depreciation provisions; steuerliche ~regelungen depreciation provisions; ~reserve accrued depreciation reserve (fund); ~restwert scrap (depreciated) value; ~richtlinien depreciation guidelines (rules); abgeänderte ~richtlinien depreciation changes; ~richtlinien lockern to loosen rules on depreciation; ~rücklage reserve for wear, tear, obsolescence or inadequacy, reserve (allowance) for depreciation, depreciation fund; ~rücklagenkonto accrued depreciation (depreciation reserve) account; ~rückstellung [allowance for] depreciation.

Abschreibungssatz depreciation rate (charge), rate of depreciation;
feststehender ~ fixed depreciation; höchstmöglicher ~ maximum depreciation; linearer ~ straight-line rate of depreciation *(US)*; verteidigungsbedingter ~ fast writeoff for defence facilities; zugelassener ~ *(Steuer)* percentage depletion;
maximal zugelassener ~ für Substanzverminderung maximum depreciation;
jährlichen ~ berechnen to compute the annual depreciation charge.

Abschreibungs|sätze, allgemeine composite rates of depreciation; ~sätze steuerlich in Anspruch nehmen to claim capital allowance *(Br.)*; höchste steuerlich zugelassene ~sätze in Anspruch nehmen to take the maximum depreciation allowable for tax purposes; ~sätze variieren to vary writeoffs *(US)*; ~schema depreciation (writeoff, *US*) schedule; ~stichtag depreciation date; ~system depreciation (writeoff, *US*) system; ~tabelle table of depreciation rates; ~ursache obsolescence; ~verfahren depreciation procedure; systematisch durchgeführtes ~verfahren depreciation accounting; ~vergünstigung allowance for (concessions on) depreciation, depreciation break *(US)*; im Rahmen der Einkommensteuer gewährte ~ver-

günstigungen income-tax depreciation allowance; **alle ~vergünstigungen zur Erneuerung des Anlageparks einsetzen** to allocate total depreciation to replace plant and other assets; **durchschnittliches ~verhältnis** average ratio of depreciation; **~verlust** retirement loss; **erleichterte ~vorschriften** depreciation facilities; **~vorteile** depreciation benefits; **~vortrag** capital allowance carried forward *(Br.)*; **~wert** written down (liquidating) value; **~zeitraum** writing-down period, depreciation period; **~zeitraum eines Investitionsbetrages** payout period; **für ~zwecke** for allowance purposes *(Br.)*.

Abschreiten der Gemeindegrenze beating of the grounds.

abschreiten to step off, to measure out;
Ehrenkompanie ~ to inspect the guard of hono(u)r; **Front** ~ to pass down the ranks; **Grenzen eines Grundstücks** ~ to walk along the boundaries of a piece of property.

Abschrift copy, double, duplication, *(Durchschlag)* carbon (typewritten) copy, *(Stenogramm)* transcript, transcription; **für gleichlautende** ~ for copy conform; **für die Richtigkeit der** ~ certified true copy; **laut beigefügter** ~ as per enclosed copy; **amtliche** ~ office copy; **beglaubigte** ~ certified (exemplified, verified, examined) copy, exemplification, conformed document *(US)*; **notariell beglaubigte** ~ notarized (certified) copy; **ordnungsgemäß beglaubigte** ~ **[einer Urkunde]** office copy; **eigenhändige** ~ autograph copy; **amtlich erteilte** ~ office copy; **gleichlautende** ~ true (counterfact, exact, conform) copy, conformed copy *(US)*; **saubere** ~ fair copy; **mit dem Original genau übereinstimmende** ~ diplomatic copy; **mit dem Original verglichene** ~ examined copy; **vollständige** ~ complete copy; **wortgetreue** ~ close (true) copy; **zuverlässige** ~ faithful copy;
~ **eines Testamentsvollstreckungszeugnisses** office-copy probate *(Br.)*;
mehrere ~en anfertigen to make several copies; **saubere ~ eines Briefes anfertigen** to copy a letter out fair; ~ **beglaubigen** to attest a copy of record, to certify a copy; **in ~ beifügen** to attach a copy; ~ **erteilen** to deliver (furnish) a copy; **~en herstellen** to run off copies, to copy, to transcribe; ~ **nehmen** to take a copy; ~ **vergleichen** to check (read over) a copy.

abschriftlich copied [out], in duplicate, by way of copy.

Abschriftnahme copying, duplicating.

Abschub evacuation, *(Ausländer)* expulsion.

abschuften, sich to plod along, to tail, to drudge, to work like a nigger.

Abschuß shot, firing, discharge, *(Flugzeug)* bringing down, *(Jagdstrecke)* bag, kill, *(mil., Panzer)* knocking out, *(Rakete)* launching;
wahrscheinlicher ~ probable;
~anlagen launching facilities; **~basis** launching site, *(für Atomraketen)* atomic base; **~bühne** launching platform; **~flugzeug** parent plane; **~gelände** launching site; **~geschwindigkeit** launching velocity; **~kandidat** prospective flunk; **j. auf die ~liste setzen** to put s. o. on the spot; **~ort** launching point; **~panne** launching failure; **~platz** launching range; **~punkt** *(Flugzeug)* present position; **~rampe** launching pad; **~rohr** *(Torpedoboot)* torpedo tube; **~stelle** launching site; **~vorrichtung** launching device, launcher; **~zeit** *(Jagd)* open season.

abschüssig steep, precipitous;
~ **sein** to decline, to bend aside;
auf die ~e Bahn kommen to go downhill (to the dogs, *coll.*).

Abschütteln eines Gegners shakeout of an assailant.

abschütteln, j. to get rid of s. o., to shake s. o. off; **Last** ~ to throw off a burden.

abschwächen to attenuate, to weaken, to mitigate, to tone (water) down;
sich ~ *(Hoch)* to weaken, *(Konjunktur)* to soften, to depress, to decline, to level off, *(Kurse)* to weaken, to sag, to ease [off], to show a declining tendency, *(Meinungsäußerung)* to qualify; **sich etw.** ~ to ease off a fraction; **Ausdruck** ~ to qualify an expression; **seine Äußerungen** ~ to give a palliative explanation; **Behauptung** ~ to modify a statement; **Dementi** ~ to soften a denial; **Erklärung** ~ to qualify a statement; **Explosionswirkung** ~ to weaken an explosion; **jds. Fehler** ~ to gloss over s. one's faults; **seine Forderungen** ~ to soft-pedal one's claims; **seine Formulierungen in einem Zeitungsartikel** ~ to tone down some of the offensive statements in an article; **die Preise** ~ to weaken the prices.

abschwächende Erklärung palliative declaration.

Abschwächung extenuation, mitigation, *(Äußerungen)* softening, palliation, *(Konjunktur)* softness, decline, levelling off, *(Kurse)* ease, easing, sagging, lowering, weakening, depression, concession;
geringe ~ slight decline; **saisonbedingte** ~ seasonal allowance; ~ **einer Behauptung** modification of a statement; ~ **um einen Bruchteil** fractional ease; ~ **eines Dementis** softening of a denial; ~ **einer Erklärung** qualification of a statement; ~ **der Geldmarktsätze** ease in the money rates; ~ **der Konjunktur** economic slowdown, downward business trend; ~ **der Kurse** weaker tendency in prices; ~ **der Preise** price weakness; ~ **der Sätze für Festgeld** lowering of the time loan rates; ~ **des Umsatzes** drop (falling off, letdown) in sales; ~ **der Wachstumsrate** dampening of rates of growth; ~ **des Zinssatzes für festes Geld** lowering of the time-loan rate;
~en zeigen *(Börse)* to turn soft.

Abschwächungs|hinweise, konjunkturelle signs of slowdown; **~tendenz** weaker (downward, contractive, slackening, flagging, declining) tendency, tendency to decline, downward potential.

abschwatzen, jem. etw. to wheedle s. th. out of s. o.; **jem. sein Geld** ~ to talk s. o. out of his money.

abschweifen to deviate, to digress;
nicht ~ to keep to the point; **von einem Thema** ~ to run away (wander) from a subject; **vom geraden Weg** ~ to leave the beaten path.

abschweifend discursive.

Abschweifung vom Thema digression from the subject.

abschwellen *(Sturm)* to abate, to subside.

Abschwemmen *(von Land)* avulsion.

abschwemmen to wash (sweep) away, to wash out.

abschwenken, nach links *(Truppen)* to wheel to the left.

abschwindeln, jem. etw. to diddle (humbug) s. o. out of s. th.

abschwören to renounce, to forswear, to abjure;
dem Alkohol ~ to take the pledge.

Abschwörung abjuration.

Abschwung, konjunktureller downward business trend, recession, levelling off, cyclical downturn (downswing), downtrend;
~phase downward phase (swing), period of recession.

absegnen to give one's blessing.

absehbar foreseeable, within sight;
kaum ~e Auswirkungen immeasurable consequences; **in ~er Zeit** within reasonable time, in the foreseeable future.

absehen to foresee;
von einer Bestrafung ~ to refrain from punishment; **von Blumenspenden bitte** ~ no flowers, please; **jem. eine Fertigkeit** ~ to learn a trick (knack) from s. o.; **es auf jds. Geld** ~ to be after s. one's money; **es auf eine Professur** ~ to have one's eye on a professorship; **von den Unkosten** ~ to take no account of the expenses; **jem. jeden Wunsch von den Augen** ~ to wait on s. o. hand and foot.

abseilen to rope down.

Abseite *(Münze)* reverse.

abseits [gelegen] out of the way, aside, apart, remote;
~ **der Straße** off the road;
sich ~ **halten** to keep aloof; **in einem sehr** ~ **gelegenen Hause wohnen** to live in a house remote from any town or village.

absenden to send off, to forward, to dispatch, to expedite, to consign, to ship *(US)*, *(Beauftragten)* to delegate, to depute, *(Boten)* to send out, *(Brief)* to post *(Br.)*, to mail *(US)*, *(Geld)* to remit.

Absendeort dispatch (forwarding, shipping, *US*) point.

Absender *(Brief)* sender, return address, *(Güter)* dispatcher, forwarder, consignor, forwarding carrier;
an den ~ **zurück** return to sender; **im Fall der Nichtzustellung an** ~ **zurück** in case of nondelivery return to sender;
fehlender ~ missing return address;
vom ~ **getragen werden** to be shipped prepaid;
~angabe return address, forwarded by, *(Geschäftskuvert)* envelope corner card; **~freistempler** franking machine, postage meter; **~land** country of shipment.

Absende|spediteur forwarding carrier; **~stelle** station of dispatch, forwarding point, *(Post)* office of dispatch, *(Telegramm)* office of origin; **~tag, ~termin** date of mailing (shipment, dispatch).

Absendung sending off, *(Brief)* posting *(Br.)*, mailing *(US)*, *(Güter)* forwarding, dispatch, consignment, shipping *(US)*, shipment *(US)*.

abservieren to kick out *(sl.)*, to axe, *(aus politischen Gründen)* to scalp *(US)*.

abserviert werden to wander in the wilderness.

Abserviertwerden *(pol.)* wandering in the wilderness.

absetzbar *(abschreibungsfähig)* depreciable, liable to depreciation, *(Beamter)* dismissible, removable, dative, deposable, *(börsengängig)* marketable, *(steuerlich)* deductible, allowable for deduction, *(verkäuflich)* vendible, salable, marketable;

leicht ~ easily sold; **nicht** ~ *(Beamter)* nonremovable, irremovable; **steuerlich** ~ allowable for tax purposes;
leicht ~ **sein** to find a ready market; **nicht** ~ **sein** to be unsalable;
~e Ausgaben deductible expenses; **~er Posten** deductible item; **~e Wertpapiere** marketable securities.

Absetzbarkeit sal(e)ability, sal(e)ableness, *(Abzugsfähigkeit)* deductibility, *(Beamter)* removability, *(Börsengängigkeit)* marketability.

Absetzbewegung, planmäßige disengagement, retirement.

Absetzen von Fallschirmspringern air drop of parachuters.

absetzen *(abziehen)* to deduct, to charge off, *(Beamten)* to remove, to relieve from a post, to displace, to discharge, to dismiss, *(vom Budget)* to take (strike) off, *(drucktechn.)* to set type, to compose, *(verkaufen)* to market, to sell, to dispose of, to distribute, *(Wertpapiere)* to place, to sell;
sich ~ to retreat, *(Truppen)* to disengage, to break away; **Aktien von der Notierung** ~ to remove shares from the stock exchange list; **j. mit dem Auto** ~ to drop s. o.; **j. am Bahnhof** ~ to put s. o. down at the station; **Beamten** ~ to remove an official; **Betrag von einer Rechnung** ~ to deduct an item from an account; **billig** ~ to sell cheaply; **vom Budget** ~ to strike off the budget; **sich erfolgreich** ~ *(mil.)* to make good one's retreat; **Falschgeld** ~ to put off a counterfeit note; **mit Gewinn** ~ to sell at a premium; **jem. zu Hause** ~ to drop s. o. at his door; **Herrscher** ~ to depose, to dethrone; **sich gegen den Hintergrund** ~ to stand out against the background; **Koffer** ~ to put down a suitcase; **Kosten steuerlich** ~ to deduct the costs; **vom Lande** ~ to bear off the land; **Lotsen** ~ to drop a pilot; **Luftlandetruppen** ~ to drop parachutists; **Manuskript** ~ to set in type, to compose a manuscript; **Manuskript äußerst schnell** ~ to set type at high speed; **am offenen Markt** ~ to sell in the open market; **von der Notierung an der Börse** ~ to remove from the stock-exchange list; **j. von seinem Posten** ~ to dismiss s. o. from his post; **Punkt von der Tagesordnung** ~ to remove (cut out) an item from the agenda; **sich rechtzeitig** ~ to make off in time; **Spesen** ~ to deduct expenses; **Stück** ~ *(Theater)* to withdraw a play; **Termin** ~ to adjourn a hearing; **Transportkosten vom Gewinn** ~ to deduct the cost of transportation from the profit; **mit Verlust** ~ to sell at a loss (discount); **j. von der Verpflegung** ~ to take s. o. off food; **Vorstandsmitglied** ~ to remove a director; **seine Waren** ~ to place (get off, dispose of) goods, to clear one's stock; **Waren flott (leicht)** ~ to sell goods easily; **sich nach dem Westen** ~ *(Flüchtling)* to cut out West; **Zeile** ~ to begin a new paragraph; **etw.** ~ **lassen** to get s. th. set up in type; **sich leicht** ~ **lassen** to sell readily; **sich nicht leicht** ~ **lassen** to find no sale (buyers); **sich schwer** ~ **lassen** to run into heavy selling, to go off heavily.

Absetzer *(vom Flugzeug)* jump master.

Absetz|gebiet *(mil.)* landing area; **~gleis** unloading siding; **~linie** *(Buchbinder)* fillet.

Absetzung *(Beamter)* remove, removal, dismissal, discharge, supersession, deposition, privation, *(Kosten)* deduction, charge-off, *(mil.)* cashiering, *(Monarch)* deposal, dethronement;
einstweilige (vorläufige) ~ suspension; **steuerlich zulässige ~en** allowable deductions;
~ **für Abnutzung** deduction for depreciation; **jährliche** ~ **für Abnutzung** annual allowance *(Br.)*; **steuerfreie** ~ **für Abnutzung** allowance for wear and tear; ~ **von der Börsennotierung** removal from the stock-exchange list; ~ **eines Prozesses** discontinuance of a lawsuit; ~ **für Substanzverringerung** deduction for depletion, depletion charges (expenses); ~ **von der Tagesordnung** withdrawal from the agenda; ~ **eines Termins** adjournment of a hearing; ~ **des Vorstands** removal of directors.

Absetzungsbeträge von der Einkommensteuer income-tax deductions.

absichern to protect, to safeguard, *(baufälliges Dach)* to support, *(Kursrisiko)* to hedge, *(Risiko)* to guard, to exclude;
durch vertragliche Bestimmungen ~ to guard by clauses; **Forderung hypothekarisch** ~ to secure a debt by mortgage; **heimische Industrie gegen Importe** ~ to safeguard an industry; **Kredit** ~ to cover a loan; **sich nach allen Seiten** ~ to hedge all bets.

Absicherung protection, *(Kursrisiko)* hedge, *(Risiko)* guard, exclusion;
zur ~ **für unvorhergesehene Fälle** to cover unforeseen events; ~ **eines Kredits** providing security for (covering) a loan.

Absicherungsbestimmungen *(Maschinenanlage)* fencing provisions.

Absicht intent, intention, aim, end, notion, purpose, turn, thought;
in benachteiligender ~ with the purpose of injury; **in der besten** ~ with the best of intentions; **in betrügerischer** ~ with fraudulent intent, with intent to defraud; **in böser** ~ in a spirit of mischief, malicious; **in keiner bösen** ~ without evil intent; **in böswilliger** ~ with malice aforethought, with malice prepense, wrongfully intending; **in ehrlicher** ~ with honesty of purpose; **in gewinnsüchtiger** ~ with an eye to profit, with the object of gain, for pecuniary gain (intent), with a view to profit; **in guter** ~ with good intentions; **in redlicher** ~ with honesty of purpose; **in verbrecherischer** ~ feloniously; **mit** ~ on purpose; **mit einer bestimmten** ~ with an express purpose;
betrügerische ~ intent to defraud; **böse** ~ nigger in the wood pile; **auf eine bestimmte Person gerichtete böse** ~ special malice; **vermutete böse** ~ implied malice, constructive malice; **vorbedachte böse** ~ malice aforethought; **böswillige** ~ malicious intent; **erklärte** ~ purport; **gemeinsame** ~ common purpose; **gesetzgeberische** ~ policy of the law *(US)*, purview; **hundsgemeine** ~ misbegotten plan; **rechtsgeschäftliche** ~ contemplation; **unredliche** ~ dishonest intent; **verbrecherische** ~ criminal intent; **wettbewerbsbeschränkende ~en** *(Kartellrecht)* restrictive trading agreement *(Br.)*, pooling agreement in restraint of trade *(US)*;
~ **eines Gesetzes** intention of a law; ~ **der rechtswidrigen Zueignung** intent to steal, constructive taking;
jds. ~en ergründen to fathom s. one's meaning; **jds. böse ~en erkennen** to get next to s. o. *(US coll.)*; **seine ~en zu erkennen geben** to disclose one's designs; ~ **haben** to contemplate; **beste ~en haben** to mean well; **böse ~en haben** to have designs; **ernsthafte ~en haben** to intend marriage, to court a woman with hono(u)rable intentions, to be serious *(sl.)*; ~ **hegen** to harbo(u)r the intent; **freundliche ~en gegenüber jem. hegen** to mean well by s. o.; **mit besten ~en an etw. herangehen** to do s. th. with the best intentions; **j. über seine ~en in keiner Weise im Unklaren lassen** to give s. o. definite information as to one's intentions; **seine ~en mitteilen** to open one's designs; **mit besten ~en gepflastert sein** to be paved with good intentions; **jegliche ~en für ein Vorhaben in Abrede stellen** to disclaim all intention of doing s. th.; **j. über seine ~en täuschen** to mislead s. o. as to one's intentions; **sich mit der** ~ **tragen** to contemplate; **mit voller** ~ **tun** to do on purpose (deliberately); **jem. böse ~en unterstellen** to impute ignoble intentions to s. o.; **jds. ~en vereiteln** to frustrate s. one's plans; **jds. ~en verkennen** to mistake s. one's intention; **seine wahren ~en verraten** to show one's true colo(u)rs.

absichtlich with intent, intentional, wilful, wittingly, on (of) set purpose, voluntary, advisedly, deliberately, designed, *(mutwillig)* malicious, *(vorsätzlich)* by design, wilful, *(vorbedacht)* premeditated;
etw. ~ **überhören** to turn a deaf ear to s. th.; **etw.** ~ **übersehen** to turn a blind eye on s. th.;
~e Beleidigung (Kränkung) deliberate (studied) insult; **~e Vernachlässigung** positive (active) waste; **~es Verschweigen** *(Versicherungsabschluß)* material misrepresentation; **~e Zerstörung** wilful destruction.

Absichtserklärung representation of intention, declaration of policy, posture statement, letter of intent *(US)*.

absichtslos unintentional, casual.

Absichtsnachweis evidence of intention.

Absinken decline, slackening off, *(der Kurse)* decline, fall, drop, slide in values;
~ **der Aktienkurse** stock-market slide; ~ **der Belegschaftsziffern** decline in manpower; **plötzliches** ~ **der Kurse** slump in prices; ~ **der Leistungsfähigkeit** decline in production; ~ **der Löhne** wage deflation;
im ~ **begriffen sein** to be on the decline (downgrade).

absinken *(Kurse)* to decline, to recede, to fall, to drop, to go down;
auf den Grund ~ to sink to the bottom; **völlig** ~ *(fig.)* to touch the bottom.

absitzen, zehn Jahre to do ten years; **seine Strafe** ~ to serve (do) one's time, to do a stretch; **langweiliges Stück** ~ to sit out a stupid play.

absolut absolute, must, dictatorial, plenipotentiary;
~ **keine Bedenken haben** to have no scruples whatever; ~ **zurückgegangen sein** to show an actual fall, *(Spareinlagen)* to have gone down definitely;
~e Konterbande absolute contraband; **~e Mehrheit** absolute majority; **~e Monarchie** absolute monarchy; **~er Narr** positive fool; **~e Schönheit** perfect beauty; **~e Unmöglichkeit** physical impossibility; **~er Versager** flop, washout, slouch *(US sl.)*, lemon *(sl.)*; **~e Wahrheit** gospel truth.

Absolutismus absolutism.

Absolutwert einer Abweichung absolute deviation.
Absolvent school leaver, graduate *(US)*.
absolvieren to complete one's studies, to graduate *(US)*;
Lehrgang ~ to complete (graduate from, *US*) a course; **sein tägliches Pensum** ~ to do one's daily stint; **eine Prüfung** ~ to pass an examination.
Absolvierung completion, graduation *(US)*;
~ **eines Lehrgangs** completion of (graduation from, *US*) a course.
absonderlich peculiar, strange, unusual;
~**er Mensch** eccentric person, screwball *(US sl.)*.
absondern to sever, to separate, to detach, to seclude, to prescind, *(Konkurs)* to set apart (aside), to abstract, *(Kranke)* to isolate;
sich ~ to seclude o. s., *(Parteiflügel)* to cave *(Br.)*; **den Dreißigsten für die Witwe** ~ to set out the widow's thirds; **Gläubigerforderung** ~ to treat a creditor's claim as preferential.
Absonderung segregation, separation, abstraction, detailment, *(im Konkurs)* preferential treatment, setting aside (apart), *(Kranke)* isolation, *(Quarantäne)* quarantine;
~ **eines Parteiflügels** cave *(Br.)*.
Absonderungsanspruch preferential claim, claim of a secured creditor (of exemption, *US*).
absonderungsberechtigt preferential, secured;
~**er Gläubiger** preferential (secured) creditor.
Absonderungs|berechtigter preferential (secured) creditor; ~**recht** preferential right.
absorbieren to absorb, to eat up, to engross, *(Staatsgebiet)* to integrate;
j. völlig ~ to absorb s. o.
absorbierende Wirkung absorbing effect.
absorbiert absorbed;
von seinen Geschäften völlig ~ **werden** to be bound up in business.
Absorption absorption, *(Staatsgebiet)* integration.
Absorptions|theorie *(Zahlungsbilanz)* absorption approach; ~**vermögen** *(Markt)* absorbing capacity (power).
Abspalten separation, secession.
abspalten to wedge off, to separate, *(Gebiet)* to split off;
sich ~ to separate, to split off, to segregate, to hive off; **sich von einer Partei** ~ to split off from a party.
absparen, sich etw. to stint o. s.; **sich sein Studium vom Munde** ~ to pinch and spare for one's study.
abspeisen, mit kleinen Summen to fob off with paltry amounts;
mit leeren Versprechungen ~ to feed with empty promises.
abspenstig machen to estrange, *(Arbeiter)* to pirate *(US)*, *(Kunden)* to entice (draw) away, to alienate, to knock down a customer *(sl.)*, *(Versicherungsnehmer)* to twist.
Abspenstigmachen *(Arbeiter)* piracy *(US)*, *(Kunden)* alienation, enticement, *(Versicherungsnehmer durch scheidenden Agenten)* twisting.
absperren to barrier [off], to block off, *(Bezirk)* to cordon (rope) off, *(el.)* to cut off, *(Gas, Wasser)* to turn (shut) off, *(Straße)* to block, to bar, to barricade, *(Talsperre)* to dam, *(zusperren)* to lock away;
Benzinzufuhr ~ to cut off the petrol (gas, *US*); **sich gegen westliche Einflüsse** ~ to seal off one's land against Western influences.
Absperr|gerät barrier; ~**hahn** stopcock; ~**kette** cordon; ~**kommando** cordon; ~**linie** barrier; ~**posten** cordon of sentries; ~**seil** rope.
Absperrung cordon, blockage, barricade;
sanitäre ~ sanitary cordon;
gegen die ~**en drängen** to be pressing against the barriers.
Absperrungs|gitter crush barrier; ~**ventil** check (stop, wast) valve; ~**vorrichtung** shutter, locking device.
Abspieldauer, einstündige one-hour recording time.
Abspielen, erneutes playback.
abspielen to play [over];
sich ~ to take place, to happen; **sich in jds. Abwesenheit** ~ to go on during s. one's absence; **sich direkt vor jds. Augen** ~ to go on under one's nose; **sich hinter den Kulissen** ~ to take place behind the scenes; **Tonbandaufnahme** ~ to play back a tape recording.
Abspiel|gerät playing machine; ~**tisch** transcription turntable.
absplittern to splinter off, *(von Partei)* to split off.
Absprache understanding, arrangement, working agreement;
laut ~ according to agreement; **mangels** ~ failing agreement;
nach vorheriger ~ according to prior agreement;
anmeldepflichtige ~ *(Kartellrecht)* agreement subject to registration *(Br.)*; **geheime** ~ collusive agreement, collusion; **ministerielle** ~**en** ministerial deals; **mündliche** ~ verbal agreement (contract); **registrierte** ~ *(Kartellrecht)* registered agreement *(Br.)*; **vorherige** ~ preconcert; **wettbewerbsbeschränkende** ~ pooling of profits [in restraint of trade] *(US)*;
~ **mit der Bank** banking agreement; ~**n der Fluggesellschaften** airline cartel; **unzulässige** ~ **zwischen Konzernchefs** intra-enterprise conspiracy *(US)*; ~ **über eine gemeinsame Politik** conference;
sich an eine ~ **halten** to abide by an agreement; ~ **treffen** to make an agreement.
absprachegemäß as per arrangement.
absprechen, sich to come to an arrangement, to agree; **jem. jegliche Begabung** ~ to deny that s. o. has any talent; **sich mit seinen Mitarbeitern** ~ to consult with one's fellow workers; **Recht** ~ to deny (divest of) a right; **Schadensersatz** ~ to disallow damages; **Vorgehen genau** ~ to arrange the steps to be taken; **vorher** ~ to prearrange; **jds. guten Willen** ~ to question s. one's good will.
absprechend, in ~**em Ton über j. sprechen** to speak disparagingly of s. o.
absprengen *(Truppenteil)* to disperse, to cut off, to separate.
abspringen to jump down (off), *(Fahrradkette)* to come off;
mit dem Fallschirm ~ to jump, to bale (bail, *US*) out, to hit the silk *(sl.)*; **von einem Handel** ~ to back out of a bargain; **von einer Partei** ~ to desert a party, to rat *(sl.)*; **vom Thema** ~ to travel out of the record; **von einem fahrenden Zug** ~ to jump out of a moving train.
abspritzen to wash out;
Auto ~ to run the hose over a car.
Absprung jump, leap;
~ **mit einem Fallschirm** parachute descent, jump, baling (bailing, *US*) out; ~ **mit verzögerter Öffnung** delayed jump;
~ **von einer Partei** desertion of a party;
~**gebiet** jump area; ~**gelände** drop[ping] zone (field); ~**hafen** advanced landing ground; ~**höhe** jumping height; ~**platz** advanced landing ground; ~**punkt** jumping-off point.
abspulen to unwind, to unreel.
abspülen, Geschirr to wash the dishes.
abstammen to descend, to be descendent, to issue, to stem;
von den gleichen Eltern ~ to be of the whole blood; **von einer guten Familie** ~ to come of (from) a good family; **in gerader Linie** ~ to be in direct descent.
Abstammung descent, descendance, origin, birth, lineage, parentage, ancestry, genealogy, extraction, root of descent, blood, filiation *(US)*;
in unmittelbarer ~ in the direct line; **von deutscher** ~ of German extraction; **von hoher (vornehmer)** ~ of noble descent; **von niedriger** ~ of humble birth; **von vornehmer** ~ high-born;
eheliche ~ legitimate descent; **gradlinige** ~ lineal descent; ~ **mütterlicherseits** maternal line; **unbekannter** ~ paternity unknown; **unmittelbare** ~ immediate descent; **väterliche** ~ paternal line; **vornehme** ~ high birth;
~ **in gerader Linie** lineal descent; ~ **von einer Nebenlinie (Seitenlinie)** collateral descent; ~ **auf der Vaterseite** paternal side;
seine ~ **herleiten** to deduce one's descent from; **englischer** ~ **sein** to be of English extraction; **vornehmer** ~ **sein** to be of noble origin; **seine** ~ **auf j. zurückführen** to claim descent from s. o.
Abstammungs|linie side, genealogical line; ~**tafel** family tree, pedigree.
Abstand distance, space, *(Bodenabstand)* clearance, *(drucktechn.)* margin, *(Verzicht)* renunciation, abandonment, *(Zeilen)* spacing, *(zeitlich)* interval;
in einigem ~ at some distance; **mit** ~ by far; **mit** ~ **besser** far better; **mit großem** ~ out and away;
bezahlter ~ *(Mieter)* key money, premium *(Br.)*; **einzeiliger** ~ single-line spacing; **qualitätsmäßiger** ~ difference in quality; **regelmäßiger** ~ even spacing; **reichlicher** ~ *(Schiff)* good berth; **zeitlicher** ~ time lag;
~ **der Jahre** disparity of years;
mit ~ **gewinnen** to win by a wide margin; ~ **halten** to stand off (aloof), *(fig.)* to keep one's distance; **guten** ~ **halten** *(Schiff)* to keep good berth; **j. auf respektvollem** ~ **halten** to hold s. o. at bay; ~ **von etw. nehmen** to desist (refrain, abstain, recede) from s. th.; ~ **von einer Forderung nehmen** to abate (relinquish, waive) a claim; **Dinge im richtigen** ~ **sehen** to see things in the right perspective; ~ **zu wahren wissen** to know one's place; ~ **zahlen** to pay by way of compensation.
Abständen, in kurzen at short intervals; **in regelmäßigen** ~ periodical; **in unregelmäßigen** ~ at irregular intervals;
mit ~ **setzen** to print out.

Abstandnahme renunciation.

Abstands|geld recession money, indemnification, compensation, *(Angestellter)* dismissal wage, smart money, severence pay, golden (silver) handshake, *(Börse)* option money, *(Reukauf)* forfeit money, *(Wohnungsmiete)* premium, key money *(Br.)*; **~summe** forfeit money, *(Hausmiete)* premium, key money *(Br.)*; **angemessene ~summe** adequate compensation; **imaginäre ~summe** notional premium; **~zahlung** *(Mieter)* premium, key money *(Br.)*; **gegen eine ~zahlung von 5000 DM** on payment of DM 5000 as an indemnity.

abstatten, Bericht to render account; **jem. einen Besuch** ~ to pay s. o. a visit, to call on s. o.; **Dank** ~ to render thanks.

abstauben *(profitieren)* to snaffle, to sneak, to pinch.

abstechen *(sich abheben)* to contrast, to stand out.

Abstecher excursion, trip, side trip *(US)*, run, sally, detour; ~ **nach München machen** to take a trip to Munich.

Abstecken demarcation, location *(US)*.

abstecken to demarcate, to mark out, to plot out a line, to lay off, to locate *(US)*;
Bauplatz ~ to trace out a building site; **Grundstück** ~ to mark out a claim; **Kurs** ~ *(Schiff)* to plot (prick) the course; **mit Pfählen** ~ to mark off, to peg out; **seine Ziele** ~ to define one's aims.

Absteck|fähnchen surveyor's flag; **~pfahl** alignment picket; **~pflock** peg, pin; **~schnur** tracing line.

abstehen to refrain, to desist, to recede;
sich die Beine ~ to kick one's heels; **von seinen Forderungen** ~ to forgo (waive) one's claims.

Absteige house of call, dump *(sl.)*, shabby house.

absteigen to stop, to put up;
von seinem Fahrrad ~ to get off one's bicycle; **in einem Hotel** ~ to put up at a hotel; **bei Verwandten** ~ to stay with relations.

absteigend descending, descendant, degressive, *(Kurse)* falling, receding, declining;
auf dem ~en Ast sein to be on the downgrade.

Absteigequartier [chance] accommodation, lodgment, stop, pied-à-terre, *(anrüchig)* house of call, *(billiges Hotel)* low-class hotel;
bei jem. sein ~ **nehmen** to stay with s. o.

Abstellbahnhof sidings, railway (railroad, *US*) yard.

Abstellen *(el., tel.)* disconnection.

abstellen to base, to aim at, *(abordnen)* to assign, *(Auto, Flugzeug)* to park, *(Gas, Licht, Wasser)* to turn off, *(Personal)* to detach, to second *(Br.)*, *(Radio)* to switch off, to cut out, *(Reaktor)* to shut down, *(Soldaten)* to detail, to second *(Br.)*, *(Strom)* to cut off, *(tel.)* to disconnect, to cut off, *(Waggon)* to shunt, to sidetrack;
Angestellten ~ to loan an employee; ~ **auf** to gear, to tailor; **Auto** ~ to park a car; **Beeinträchtigung** ~ to abate a nuisance; **Beschwerden** ~ to redress grievances; **sein Fahrrad bei jem.** ~ to leave one's bike with s. o.; **auf monatliche Fälligkeiten** ~ to calculate maturity on a monthly basis; **Fernseher** ~ to switch off the television set; **Flugzeuge getrennt (luftangriffsicher)** ~ to disperse aircraft; **Korruption** ~ to abolish corruption; **auf Kundenwünsche** ~ to aim at the needs of customers; **Mißstand** ~ to abate a nuisance; **Motor** ~ to stall the engine; **auf ausländisches Recht** ~ to apply foreign law; **Versicherungssumme auf die ursprüngliche Kredithöhe** ~ to gear the sum assured to the amount of the original loan; **Wagen in die Garage** ~ to garage a car.

Abstell|gebühr *(Autoverleih)* drop-off charge; **~gleis** storage track, sidetrack, siding, dock *(Br.)*, *(fig.)* sidetrack; **aufs ~gleis geschoben** cast aside; **Zug auf ein ~gleis bringen** to dock a train; **j. aufs ~gleis schieben** to shunt s. o. sideways, to sideline s. o.; **~hahn** stopcock; **~kammer** storeroom, closet *(US)*; **~möglichkeiten** storage facilities; **~platz** *(Auto)* parking area (place, lot, *US*), *(Flugzeug)* aircraft parking, hardstand, location *(US)*; **getrennter ~platz** *(Flugzeuge)* dispersal point bay; **~platz für transportable Häuser** mobile house site; **~raum** storage room, storeroom, closet *(US)*; **~tisch** stand, dumb-waiter.

Abstellung *(Beeinträchtigung)* abatement, *(Beschwerden)* redress, redressing, removal, *(el.)* disconnection, *(Personal)* detachment, assignment, seconding *(Br.)*;
getrennte ~ *(Flugzeuge)* dispersal; **vorübergehende** ~ location; ~ **von Beschwerden** redress of complaints (grievances); ~ **eines Fehlers** elimination of an error; ~ **eines Mißbrauchs** abolition of an abuse.

Abstellvorrichtung shut-off, *(Schreibmaschine)* releasing device.

abstempeln to stamp, to postmark, to hallmark, *(entwerten)* to obliterate, to deface, to cancel, *(Kontrolle)* to check;
j. als Demagogen ~ to label s. o. as demagogue.

Abstempelung stamping, *(Entwertung)* obliteration, defacement, cancellation, *(Kontrolle)* checking;
~ **bei der Post** postmark.

Absterben death.

absterben to die, *(Gliedmaßen)* to numb, *(Motor)* to stall, to peter out, to fail, to die, to conk out *(sl.)*, *(Pflanzen)* to wither.

Absterbeordnung *(Lebensversicherung)* life table.

Abstich *(Hochofen)* tap.

Abstieg descent, *(Familie, Nation)* decline, *(Person)* going down;
im ~ on the downgrade;
gesellschaftlicher ~ drop, social decline.

Abstiegs|bahn *(Raumfahrzeug)* trajectory of descent; **~stollen** adit, entry.

Abstimmanzeiger magic eye, tuning indicator.

Abstimmen voting, vote, ballot[ing], poll;
~ **mit Mehrfachstimmkarten** card voting.

abstimmen to [give one's] vote, to poll, to go to the polls, to ballot *(US)*, *(angleichen)* to adjust, *(Bücher)* to reconcile, to balance, to adjust, to [make] agree, *(kontrollieren)* to check off, *(koordinieren)* to harmonize, to coordinate, *(parl.)* to divide, to come to a division, *(Rundfunkgerät)* to tune in;
sich ~ to come to an agreement; **Berichte aufeinander** ~ to collate reports; **über eine Entschließung** ~ to vote on a resolution; **durch Erheben von den Sitzen** ~ to vote by rising; **Farben aufeinander** ~ to match colo(u)rs; **über eine Frage** ~ to vote on a question; **geheim** ~ to [take a] ballot; **durch Handaufheben** ~ to vote by show of hands; **Konten** ~ to compare (reconcile, balance, square) the accounts; **namentlich** ~ to vote by call-over; **nicht** ~ to abstain from voting; **durch Stimmzettel** ~ to [vote by] ballot; **Termine aufeinander** ~ to correlate dates; **in geheimer Wahl** ~ to take a secret vote, to vote by ballot; **zeitlich aufeinander** ~ to synchronize; **zugunsten von** ~ to vote in favo(u)r of; **durch Zuruf** ~ to vote by acclamation, to exercise voting rights viva voce;
~ **lassen** to take a vote; **über eine Frage** ~ **lassen** to put a question to the vote; **namentlich** ~ **lassen** to divide the house.

abstimmende Politik want-touch policy.

Abstimm|knopf *(Radio)* turning knob; **~schärfe** selectivity.

Abstimmung vote, voting, poll, *(Bücher)* adjustment, balancing, squaring, *(Koordinierung)* coordination, *(Plebiszit)* referendum, plebiscite, *(Rundfunkgerät)* tuning, modulation, *(Sprechfunk)* syntonization, *(Tarife)* harmonization;
bei der ~ during the voting, *(parl.)* on division; **durch** ~ by vote, by ballot;
automatische ~ automatic tuning; **entscheidende** ~ key vote; **ergebnislose** ~ inconclusive vote; **freie** ~ free vote; **geheime** ~ secret (secrecy of) ballot, balloting; **gemeinsame** ~ joint ballot; **monatliche** ~ *(Konten)* monthly reconciliation; **namentliche** ~ roll-call vote, *(parl.)* division *(Br.)*; **schriftliche** ~ voting by mail, *(Hauptversammlung)* [voting on a] poll, *(Versammlung)* poll rate; **überraschende** ~ snap division; **unentschiedene** ~ tie division; **öffentlich vorgenommene** ~ open vote, voting by open ballot; **zeitliche** ~ timing, synchronization;
~ **über Abänderungsanträge** voting on amendments; ~ **durch Abgabe von Stimmzetteln** balloting; **schriftliche** ~ **nach Aktienanteilen** *(Hauptversammlung)* [voting on a] poll; ~ **der Bücher** checking (reconcilement, adjustment) of books; ~ **durch Delegiertenstimmen** *(Gewerkschaft)* card vote; ~ **über eine Entschließung** vote on a resolution; ~ **durch Erheben von den Sitzen** vote by rising; ~ **von Farben aufeinander** matching of colo(u)rs; ~ **unter Fraktionszwang** party-line vote; **freie** ~ **ohne Fraktionszwang** free vote; ~ **mit der Gegenpartei** *(Parlament)* cross voting; ~ **im Hammelsprung** division lobby; ~ **durch Handaufheben** vote by show of hands, show-of-hands vote; ~ **auf der Hauptversammlung** voting at stockholders' meeting; ~ **der Interessen** agreement of interests; ~ **über mehrere Kandidaten auf einer Liste** general ticket *(US)*; ~ **der Konten** reconciliation (squaring, adjustment) of accounts; ~ **nach dem Mehrstimmenwahlrecht** plural voting; ~ **durch Namensaufruf** call of the House; ~ **im Plenum** floor vote; ~ **über den Schluß der Debatte** guillotine vote *(Br.)*; ~ **durch Stellvertreter** voting by proxy; ~ **durch Stimmzettel** voting by ballot, balloting; ~ **über einen Streik** strike vote; ~ **über die Tarifempfehlungen** *(Gewerkschaftsmitglieder)* ballot on the recommendation; ~ **durch Treuhänder** voting trust; ~ **über eine Vertrauensfrage** confidence vote; ~ **in mehreren Wahlgängen** vote in several ballots; ~ **durch Zuruf** vote by acclamation; ~ **zum Zweck der Abberufung** recall election;
durch spätere ~ **aufheben** to unvote; **durch** ~ **aufnehmen** to vote in; ~ **beanstanden** to query a vote; ~ **beantragen** to request a ballot; **durch** ~ **beschließen** to vote; **Haushaltsvoranschlag**

durch ~ beschließen to vote the supplies; **~ bestätigen** to confirm a vote; **Antrag zur ~ bringen** to put a motion to the vote; **auf eine ~ drängen** to press a division; **namentliche ~ durchführen** to take the members; **~ entscheiden** to give the casting vote; **~ für ungültig erklären** to cancel a vote; **~ eröffnen** to open the vote (ballot); **~ nach Mehrheitsgrundsätzen forcieren** to step up majority voting; **zur ~ gelangen** to be put to the vote; **die für eine ~ erforderliche Mehrheit haben** to make a house; **aus der ~ mit großer Mehrheit hervorgehen** to emerge from the voting with a large majority; **zu einer abschließenden ~ kommen** to come to a full vote; **~en des Plenums nicht registrieren lassen** to take unrecorded votes; **sich bei der ~ vertreten lassen** to vote by proxy; **~ provozieren** to challenge a division; **~ schließen** to declare the vote closed; **zur ~ schreiten** to take the (proceed to a) vote, to put a question to the vote; **an der ~ teilnehmen** to cast one's vote; **an der ~ indirekt teilnehmen** to vote by nominees; **~ verhindern** to halt the ballot, to invoke the no-vote procedure; **schriftliche ~ nach Kapitalanteilen verlangen** *(Hauptversammlung)* to demand a poll; **Vorschlag der Betriebsführung der Belegschaft zur ~ vorlegen** to put the company's plan to a ballot of the workforce; **~ vornehmen** to take a poll (the vote); **durch ~ wählen** to vote in, to elect.

Abstimmungs | anweisung ballot order; **~anzeiger** vote indicator; **~apparat** vote recorder; **~art** method of voting; **~befugnis** voting power (privilege).

abstimmungsberechtigt entitled to vote.

Abstimmungs | beschluß, durch ~beschluß beseitigen to vote away; **~blatt** statement *(Br.)*, proof sheet *(US)*; **~block** block vote.

Abstimmungsergebnis result of ballot (vote), voting figure, referendum vote, poll, outcome of a division;
einseitiges ~ lopside vote; **knappes ~** close vote;
~ ausrechnen to take the tally; **~ bekanntgeben** to announce the result of the poll; **bestes ~ erzielen** to head the poll; **~ veröffentlichen** to declare the result of a poll.

Abstimmungs | ersuchen demand for a poll; **~gebiet** voting area, plebiscitary district (area), territory (zone) subject to a plebiscite; **~glocke** division bell; **~leiter** polling clerk; **~liste** polling list; **~lokal** polling station; **~mechanismus** voting machine; **~methode** method of voting; **~modus** method of voting; **~niederlage** voting defeat; **~recht** franchise; **~regeln** voting rules; **~spielraum** voting margin; **~tafel** vote indicator; **~termin** *(Konto)* reconciliation date; **~vereinbarung** voting agreement; **~verfahren** voting procedure, procedure on taking a poll; **~vorschriften** voting rules; **~zettel** voting slip (paper), ballot *(US)*; **~zwang bei allen Gesetzen** compulsory referendum.

Abstimmvorrichtung *(Radio)* tuning device, tuner.

abstinent abstinent, teetotal;
nicht mehr ~ off the [water] waggon *(coll.)*;
völlig ~ sein to be strictly teetotal.

Abstinenz *(von Alkohol)* temperance, teetotalism.

Abstinenzler teetotaler, abstainer, water drinker, pussyfoot *(Br., sl.)*;
~ sein to be on the water waggon *(coll.)*;
~abzeichen blue ribbon; **~bewegung** temperance movement.

abstinenzlerisch teetotal, pussyfoot *(Br., sl.)*.

Abstinenzlertum teetotalism.

abstoppen to pull up, to stop, *(fig.)* to put an end to, *(mit Zeituhr)* to [take the] time;
Produktion ~ to put the brake on production; **Verkehr ~** to stop the traffic.

Abstoßen *(vom Ufer)* push-off;
~ von Aktien unloading (selling off) of stock; **~ unrentabler Betriebseinheiten** disvestment; **~ von Geschäftszweigen** spinoff of product lines.

abstoßen to push (shove) off, *(anwidern)* to disgust, to repel, *(Effekten)* to unload, to sell off, *(Lagerbestände)* to clear, to get rid of, to work off *(sl.)*, *(Schulden)* to liquidate, to discharge, to get rid of;
Aktienpaket ~ to sell a block of shares; **sich die Hörner ~** to sow one's wild oats; **sein Lager ~** to liquidate one's stock of goods; **Mitmenschen ~** to hold off people; **vom Pier ~** to bear off the quay; **Remittenden ~** to remainder; **Waren ~** to sell off (dispose of) goods.

abstoßend ugly, repellant, repellent.

Abstoßung, soziale rejection;
~ unrentabler Betriebseinheiten disinvestment.

Abstottern *(fam.)* hire purchase *(Br.)*, never-never *(Br., sl.)*.

abstottern *(fam.)* to pay by (on, *US*) instalments, to buy on the never-never *(Br., sl.)*.

abstrahieren to abstract, to prescind.

abstrahlen to radiate, to emit, to beam.

abstraktes Schuldanerkenntnis naked promise.

abstrapazieren, sich to wear o. s. out.

abstreichen to tick (charge) off, to check [off];
Posten ~ to check an entry; **etw. von der Rechnung ~** to knock s. th. off the bill; **Stellen ~** to point off places.

abstreiten to deny;
seine Autorschaft ~ to disclaim one's authorship; **jem. das Recht ~** to dispute s. one's right; **Schuld ~** to deny a charge; **Schulden ~** to refuse to acknowledge a debt.

Abstrich *(Abzug)* deduction, discount, allowance, abatement, rebate, slash, *(Ersparnis)* cut, cutback;
~e economies;
~e beim Haushaltsvoranschlag budget economies; **~ von Unkosten** curtailment (cutting down) of expenses;
~e machen (vornehmen) to make cuts in, to retrench, to reduce (curtail) expenses, to economize, to cut; **~e im Haushaltsplan machen** to make cuts in (slash) the budget; **~ vom Preis machen** to knock s. th. off the price.

abströmen to flow off.

abstufen to shade, to tone, to modulate, *(Steuern)* to grade, to graduate;
Farben ~ to shade off colo(u)rs; **Löhne nach den Leistungen ~** to scale pay to output.

Abstufung shading, tone, *(Steuern)* graduation, scale.

abstumpfen to dull, to deaden;
geistig ~ to drowse;
j. ~ lassen to wear s. o. into stubbornness.

Absturz crash, *(Lawine)* downrush, *(Steilhang)* precipice, steep;
~ mit Todesfällen fatal crash;
~ eines Flugzeugs verursachen to crash an aircraft.

abstürzen to plunge, to fall, to drop, *(Flugzeug)* to crash, to pile up;
brennend ~ to come down in flames; **tödlich ~** to write o. s. off *(sl.)*.

Absturzgefahr danger of falling.

abstützen to support, to prop, to underpin, *(versteifen)* to reinforce.

Abstützung support;
großindustrielle ~ suchen to seek shelter with conglomerates.

Abstützungsmaterial underpinning.

Abstützvorrichtung supporting device.

absuchen to search, to scour, to comb;
alle Ecken und Enden ~ to search every nook and cranny; **Gelände ~** to search the ground; **Himmel ~** *(Scheinwerfer)* to sweep the sky; **Horizont ~** to scan the horizon; **ganze Stadt nach einem Mörder ~** to comb a whole city in search of a murderer; **seine Taschen ~** to rummage through one's pockets.

abtakeln *(Schiff)* to dismantle, to unrig.

Abtakelung dismantlement.

Abtast | band *(Fernsehen)* scanning belt; **~blende** scanning diaphragm; **~dose** *(Grammophon)* pickup; **~einrichtung** scanning device.

abtasten to feel, to probe, to test, to try out, *(Fernsehen)* to scan;
Markt ~ to sound the market; **Markt mit kleinen Börsenumsätzen ~** to make a little deal in stocks as a feeler; **Taschen nach dem Schlüssel ~** to feel one's pockets for the key.

Abtaster scanner.

Abtast | feld scanning field; **~fläche** scan area; **~gerät** scanning device, scanner, pickup; **~linie** active line; **~nadel** stylus, recording needle; **~scheibe** scanning disk; **~strahl** scanning beam.

Abtastung *(Radar)* scanning;
punktförmige ~ *(Fernsehen)* direct scanning.

Abtast | vorrichtung scanner, *(Radar)* hunting; **~zeile** [scanning] line.

Abtauautomatik automatic defroster.

abtauen to thaw [off], *(Eisschrank)* to defrost.

abtaxieren to guess, to estimate.

Abteil *(Bahn)* compartment, section *(US)*;
bestelltes ~ reserved compartment;
~ erster Klasse first [-class compartment]; **~ für Raucher** smoker, smoking compartment.

abteilbar divisible.

abteilen to divide, *(absondern)* to separate, *(in Grade)* to graduate, *(in Parzellen)* to parcel, to plot out, *(durch Trennwand)* to partition off, *(Waren)* to parcel [out];
in kleine Einzelmengen ~ to portion off; **in Fächer ~** grade into sections; **Stadt in Bezirke ~** to divide a town in wards; **Teil eines Zimmers ~** to curtain off part of a room; **Zahlenkolonne durch eine Linie ~** to rule off a column of figures.

Abteilfenster compartment window.

Abteilung separation, *(Abschnitt)* section, compartment, *(Betrieb, Verwaltung)* department, division *(US)*, *(drucktechn.)* column, rubric, *(Gefängnis, Krankenhaus)* ward, *(mil.)* party, detachment, detail, section, *(Ministerialbehörde)* government department *(Br.)*, board, division *(US)*, bureau *(US)*, *(Ressort)* desk, *(Schicht)* gang, shift, *(Schiff)* ship's hold;
in ~en aufgeteilt compartmentalized; **in derselben ~** under the same head; **innerhalb einer ~** intradepartmental; **deutschsprachige ~** *(Universität)* department of German; **federführende ~** initiating department; **humanistische ~** *(Schule)* classical side; **internistische ~** medical ward; **juristische ~** legal department; **neusprachliche ~** department of modern languages; **statistische ~** statistical department, *(Bank, Maklerfirma)* analysis department; **technische ~** engineering (technical) department; **verpachtete ~** leased department; **wasserdichte ~** *(Schiff)* watertight department; **wirtschaftspolitische ~** economic-policy department;
~ für sanitäre Einrichtungen sanitation department; **~ Eins des Grundbuchs** [etwa] property register *(Br.)*; **~ Zwei** *(Grundbuch)* [etwa] class A *(Br.)*; **~ Drei des Grundbuchs** [etwa] charges register *(Br.)*, class C *(Br.)*; **~ für Herrenbekleidung** men's clothing department; **~ für Inkassi auswärtiger Plätze** transit department *(US)*; **~ für Konjunkturprognosen** forecasting division; **~ zur Regulierung unbezahlter Rechnungen** *(Warenhaus)* adjustment bureau; **~ Soldaten** body of troops; **~ für jederzeit kündbar angelegte Spargelder** ordinary department; **~ für Vermögensverwaltungen** trust department; **~ für Versicherungsstatistik** actuarial department; **~ für Vertriebsplanung und Verkaufsförderung** commercial development department; **~ für festverzinsliche Wertpapiere** bond department *(US)*;
~ auflösen to do away with a department; **~ zwecks Einsparungen gründlich durchforsten** to comb out a department.

Abteilungs|angehörige departmental personnel; **~aufgaben** departmental duties; **~bericht** departmental record; **~besprechung** divisional meeting *(US)*; **~bibliothek** departmental library; **~chef** department head, chief (head) of a department, departmental chief (manager); **stellvertretender ~chef** assistant department head; **~etat** department budget; **~geschenk** departmental gift; **~kommandeur** *(mil.)* unit commander; **~kosten** department expenses, departmental costs (expenses); **~leiter** department[al] head (chief), division manager *(US)*, vice president *(US)*, departmental manager, head of a department, *(Ministerium)* assistant secretary *(US)*, *(Warenhaus)* floor walker (manager, *US*), shopwalker; **stellvertretender ~leiter** assistant department head (administrator); **~leiter in der Stadtverwaltung** city commissioner *(US)*; **~leiter vertreten** to deputize for the department head; **~leiterbesprechung, ~leitertreffen** divisional meeting, interdepartmental conference; **~personal** department personnel; **~präsident** division president *(US)*; **~vorstand** department head, head of a department, departmental chief.

abteilungsweise departmental.

Abteilungszeichen division mark, hyphen.

abtelefonieren, jem. to cancel an engagement by telephone.

abtelegrafieren to countermand by wire, to wire refusal.

abteufen to deepen;
Schacht ~ to sink a shaft.

abtönen to tint, to shade, *(Farben)* to gradate.

Abtötung von Bakterien germ killing.

abtragen to clear (carry, take) away, to remove, *(Haus, Mauer)* to demolish, to pull (take) down, *(Kleid)* to overwear, *(Kurve)* to plot, *(Passivsaldo)* to work off, to acquit, to liquidate, to discharge;
sich ~ to wear off, to wear away; **Hypothek ~** to sink (amortize, redeem) a mortgage; **Schuld ~** to acquit (compound, sink) a debt; **Schuld in Raten ~** to pay off a debt by instal(l)ments, to stall a debt; **Verpflichtung ~** to redeem an obligation.

abträglich adverse, derogative, detrimental;
dem Ansehen ~ harmful to the reputation; **unseren Interessen ~** detrimental to our interests;
~ sein to be derogatory, to derogate, to prejudice.

Abtragung *(Hypothek)* amortization, redemption, *(Schulden)* paying off, acquittal, discharge, payment, clearing off;
~ einer Mauer demolition of a wall.

Abtransport transport, removal, *(Bevölkerung)* evacuation;
~fahrzeug haulage vehicle.

abtransportieren to transport, to cart away, to remove, *(Bevölkerung)* to evacuate.

abtreiben to bear (drive) away, *(Ballon)* to go adrift, *(Flugzeug)* to given off its course, *(med.)* to procure abortion, *(Schiff)* to make leeway.

Abtreibung abortion;
in besonderen Fällen erlaubte ~ elective abortion; **selbst herbeigeführte ~** self-induced abortion;
~ in Notzuchtsfällen abortion in cases of rape;
~ vornehmen to perform an abortion.

Abtreibungs|beihilfe aid for abortions; **~bestimmungen** abortion stipulations; **~eingriff** criminal operation; **~gesetz** abortion law; **~klinik** abortion clinic; **~mittel** abortive; **~versuch** attempted abortion.

abtrennbar detachable, separable;
nicht ~ undetachable.

abtrennen to separate, to sever, to partition, to mark off, to wedge off, *(Kupon)* to clip, to detach, to cut off, *(Verfahren)* to sever;
Scheck vom Scheckbuch ~ to tear a check *(US)* (cheque, *Br.*) out of the book; **Zimmerteil ~** to wall off part of a room; **hier ~** detach here.

Abtrennung cutting off, severance, *(Kupon)* clipping, detaching;
~ der besetzten Gebiete separation of occupied territories; **~ eines Verfahrens** severance of an action.

Abtrennungsrecht right of severance.

abtretbar transferable, conveyable, assignable, *(Pensionsanspruch)* negotiable;
nicht ~ unassignable, not transferable.

abtreten to assign, to make over (an assignment), to sign over, to cede, to relinquish, to remit, to surrender, to transfer, *(beiseite treten)* to step aside, *(Grundstück)* to convey [away], *(Minister)* to step down, *(Schauspieler)* to make one's exit, *(Treppenstufen)* to tread off, *(Zeuge)* to stand down, *(zurücktreten)* to resign, to retire, to lie down, to give up;
Ansprüche ~ to assign claims; **von der Bildfläche ~** to make one's exit; **blanko ~** to assign in blank; **von der Bühne ~** to make one's exit; **von einem Posten ~** to resign from a post, to relinquish an appointment; **vom Schauplatz ~** to quit the scene; **Schiff dem Versicherer ~** to abandon a ship covered by a policy; **Schuldforderung ~** to transfer a debt; **Versicherungspolice ~** to surrender an insurance policy; **wieder ~** to reassign; **mit Würde ~** to retire gracefully;
~ lassen *(Soldaten)* to dismiss.

abtretend *(Schauspiel)* outgoing.

Abtretender transferor, transferrer, assignor, surrenderer, *(Staat)* cedent state.

Abtreter conveyor, *(Fußmatte)* door mat.

Abtretung assignment, cession, transfer, making over, relinquishment, surrender, *(Grund und Boden)* conveyance, *(Seeversicherung)* abandonment;
vom Eintritt eines Ereignisses abhängige ~ conditional assignment; **beglaubigte ~** certified transfer; **dazwischenliegende ~** mesne assignment; **formlose ~** equitable assignment; **gültige ~** binding assignment; **mehrfache ~** successive assignment; **nichtige ~** invalid assignment; **rechtswirksame ~** legal assignment; **stille ~** [etwa] equitable assignment; **ungültige ~** invalid assignment; **im Ausland vorgenommene ~** foreign assignment; **zu Besicherungszwecken vorgenommene ~** equitable assignment;
~ von Buchforderungen assignment of book debts; **~ des Ersatzanspruches** subrogation assignment; **~ einer Forderung** assignment of a claim; **~ einer bestimmten Forderung** specific assignment of an existing debt; **offene ~ von Forderungen** absolute assignment; **~ zukünftiger Forderungen** assignment of future debts (debts accruing due); **~ von Forderungen gegen einen Sonderfonds** assignment by way of charge; **~ eines Gesellschaftsanteils** assignment of a share in a partnership; **~ immaterieller Güter** assignation of choses in action; **~ einer Hypothek** mortgage assignment; **~ im Konkursverfahren** assignment on bankruptcy; **~ der Mieteinkünfte** assignment of lease; **~ der Pensionsbezüge** assignment of pension; **~ der Rechte aus einer Versicherung** assignment of a policy; **~ des Ruhegehalts** assignment of retired pay; **~ eines Staatsgebietes** cession of a territory; **~ des Versicherungsanspruchs** assignment of the proceeds of a policy; **~ des Versicherungsanspruches an den Hypothekengläubiger** mortgage endorsement; **~ der Versicherungspolice** surrender of policy.

Abtretungs|benachrichtigung notice of assignment; **~empfänger** assignee; **~erklärung** declaration of assignment, subrogation assignment.

abtretungsfähig assignable, transferable, conveyable.

Abtretungs|formular form of assignment; **~recht** right to assign, subrogation right; **~urkunde** assignation, [deed, instrument of] assignment, quitclaim deed *(US)*, *(Grundstücksrecht)* deed of conveyance, *(Verpfändung)* bill of sale; **~vertrag** *(Territorium)* treaty of cession; **~vordruck** form of assignment.

Abtrieb, Abtrift leeway, drift.
Abtriftgeschwindigkeit drift velocity.
Abtritt *(Theater)* exit.
Abtrockentuch tea (dish) towel.
abtrudeln to go into a spin.
abtrünnig unfaithful, renegade, disloyal;
seinem Glauben ~ werden to abandon one's faith; **einer Partei ~ werden** to desert (rat, *sl.*) a party; **einer Sache ~ werden** to desert a cause, to turn one's coat.
Abtrünniger deserter, turncoat, *(Politik)* deviationist, seceder, rat.
Abtrünnigwerden desertion *(fig.)*, breakaway, *(Politik)* ratting.
abtun to dismiss, to discard, to put aside;
j. geringfügig ~ to snub (slight, rebuff) s. o.; **mit einer Handbewegung ~** to wave aside; **Sache als erfolglos ~** to give s. th. up as a bad job; **etw. als unwichtig ~** to pooh-pooh s. th.
aburteilen to sentence, to pronounce;
j. in Abwesenheit ~ to sentence s. o. in absentia; **strafbare Handlung ~** to try an offence; **Verbrecher ~** to bring a criminal to justice.
Aburteilung sentence, *(Verbrecher)* conviction, condemnation;
nach strafgerichtlicher ~ on conviction; **zwecks ~ dem Gericht übergeben** fully committed;
seiner ~ entgegensehen to be shortly sentenced; **für die ~ von Konkursfällen zuständig sein** to have jurisdiction in bankruptcy; **einem Gericht die ~ von Schwurgerichtssachen übertragen** to vest a court with power to try cases of life and death.
abverdienen to work off.
abverlangen to demand;
sich das Äußerste ~ to exert o. s. to the utmost, to set o. s. high standards; **seinen Mietern eine geringe Miete ~** to rent one's tenants low; **jem. einen überhöhten Preis ~** to charge s. o. an excessive price.
abvermieten to sublet.
Abwägen consideration;
kritisches ~ critical attitude; **in Kaufmannskreisen übliches ~** reasonable business judgment;
~ der Wahrscheinlichkeit balance of probabilities.
abwägen to weigh, to balance;
das Für und Wider ~ to weigh the pros and cons; **eine Sache gegen die andere ~** to balance one thing against the other; **sein Urteil sorgfältig ~** to judge carefully; **seine Worte ~** to weigh one's words.
abwägend critical;
sorgsam ~ deliberative.
Abwägung consideration, trade-off, balancing;
bei sorgfältiger ~ after careful consideration;
in Kaufmannskreisen übliche ~ reasonable business judgment;
~ der Kostenvorteile cost-benefit trade-off; **~ des beiderseitigen Verschuldens** *(Ehescheidung)* rectitude comparative *(US)*.
Abwahl *(Aufsichtsrat)* retirement.
abwählen to vote out, *(Aufsichtsrat)* to retire, *(Politiker)* not to re-elect;
j. ~ to vote s. o. out of power.
Abwälzen der Verantwortung buck passing *(US)*.
abwälzen *(Preiserhöhung)* to pass along (on), *(Steuer)* to shift, to pass on;
Arbeit auf einen anderen ~ to push a job off on s. o. else; **Kosten auf die Preise ~** to burden the prices; **erhöhte Lohnkosten auf die Verbraucher ~** to pass on increased labo(u)r cost onto the consumer; **Schuld auf andere ~** to shift the blame on others; **Treibstofferhöhung automatisch auf die Verbraucher ~** to automatically pass on fuel cost increases to consumers; **Unkosten ~** to pass costs on; **Verantwortung ~** to shift the responsibility, to pass the buck *(US)*; **Verbrechen auf einen anderen ~** to lay a crime at s. o. else's door.
Abwälzung passing on (along), shifting;
~ von Steuern shifting (passing on) of taxes; **~ der Verantwortung** buck-passing *(US)*.
abwandeln, leicht to give a slight twist.
abwandelungsfähig modifiable, changeable, alterable.
abwandern to migrate, *(Kunde)* to drift, to drift away;
in Ausland ~ *(Kapital)* to find its way into foreign countries; **zur Opposition ~** *(Wähler)* to switch to the opposition.
Abwanderung migration, *(Kapital)* exodus, *(Kunde)* drift;
~ ländlicher Arbeitskräfte in die Stadt drift of labo(u)r into the towns; **~ aus einem Gebiet** migration from an area; **~ von Kapital** exodus of capital; **~ von Kunden** drift of trade; **~ in die Stadt** exodus from the country; **~ von Stammgästen** switch of loyalties; **~ von Wissenschaftlern** brain drain.
Abwanderungsrate rate of emigration.
Abwärme waste heat.
abwarten to wait for, to lie low;
günstigen Augenblick ~ to bide one's time; **das Ende ~** to stay to the end; **Gang der Ereignisse ~** to await the issue of events; **in Geduld ~** to possess one's soul in patience; **günstige Gelegenheit ~** to wait one's opportunity; **etw. ruhig ~** to wait and see;
~ bis man drankommt to wait one's turn.
abwartend temporizing, cautious, waiting;
sich ~ verhalten to wait and see;
~e Haltung policy of wait and see, wait-and-see attitude; **~e Haltung einnehmen** to sit on the fence, to wait and see.
abwärts downward, downhill;
Fluß ~ fahren to descend a river;
mit seinen Geschäften geht es ~ his business is going down, he is in a bad way.
Abwärtsbewegung *(Konjunktur)* down, downtrend, downturn, *(Kurse)* bearish (downward) tendency, downward trend, *(Preise)* downward movement;
konjunkturelle ~ business (economic) downturn;
in einer ~ ausklingen to end on a downward note; **sich in einer ~ befinden, in einer ~ sein** to be on a downslope (on the downgrade), to trend down.
abwärtsgehen to be going downhill, to be on the downgrade.
Abwärts|hub *(Kolben)* downstroke; **~spirale** downward spiral; **~tendenz** downward trend (tendency).
Abwasch dishwashing, washing up *(Br.)*.
abwaschbar washable.
abwaschen to wash.
Abwasch|küche scullery; **~wasser** dishwater.
Abwässer effluent, sewage, waste water;
~ aus Gewerbebetrieben trade effluent;
~anlagen sewage works, sewer; **~beseitigung** sewage sanitation (disposal); **~führung** sewage engineering; **~kanal** effluent drain; **~reinigung** sewage cleaning; **~system** sewage system.
Abwässerungs|gebiet drainage area; **~graben** drainage ditch; **~leiste** weatherboard.
Abwässer|verwertung utilization of waste water; **~verwertungsanlage** sewage treatment plant.
abwechseln, sich to take turns, to alternate; **sich auf einer langen Autoreise am Steuer ~** to take spells at the wheel; **im Dienst ~** to go on duty alternately; **jährlich ~** *(Vorsatz)* to rotate every year; **turnusmäßig ~** to rotate in office.
abwechselnd alternate, alternately, *(turnusmäßig)* in turns, in rotation, rotary, by turns.
Abwechslung alternation, *(Turnus)* rotation, *(Unterbrechung)* change, variety, diversity;
um der ~ willen for variety's shake; **zur ~** for a change;
willkommene ~ welcome change;
keine ~ bieten to be a monotonous occupation; **~ in das tägliche Leben bringen** to relieve the monotony of everyday life;
~ nötig haben to need a change.
abwechslungslos monotonous, uneventful.
abwechslungsreich varied, diversified;
~ gestalten to diversify.
Abweg wrong way;
j. auf ~e führen to lead s. o. astray; **auf ~e geraten** to err, to be on the wrong track, to go astray, to stray from the right path.
abwegig erroneous, devious, wrong, mistaken, irrelevant, out of the way, *(Bemerkung)* off (beside) the point;
völlig ~ entirely mistaken;
~es Gerücht ill-founded rumo(u)r.
Abwehr defence, defense *(US)*, defensive, *(Gegenspionage)* counterintelligence, counterespionage, military intelligence, *(eines Schlages)* ward;
elastische ~ flexible response;
auf ~ stoßen to meet with resistance;
~agent counterspy; **~angelegenheiten** security matters; **~bereitschaft** stand-by; **~bewegung** parry; **~chef** intelligence director; **~dienst** counterespionage service; **~dienst der Marine** Naval Intelligence Division.
abwehren to fence out, to fend off, *(mil.)* to repel;
Besucher ~ to deny visitors; **Katastrophe ~** to avert disaster; **Vorwurf kühl ~** to reject a reproach coolly.
abwehrende Haltung einnehmen to take up a defensive attitude.
Abwehr|front defensive front; **~jäger** interceptor; **~kämpfe** defensive action; **~kartell** countervailing powers *(US)*; **~krieg** defensive war; **~manöver** evasive action; **~manöver durchführen** to take avoiding action; **~maßnahme** preventive (protective, defensive) measures; **~offizier** intelligence (security) officer, counterspy; **~patent** defensive patent; **~rakete** antiballistic missile; **~schlacht** defensive battle; **~stelle** counterespio-

nage office, intelligence office; ~**stellung** *(mil.)* defensive position; ~**streik** defensive strike; ~**tätigkeit** intelligence operation; ~**werbung** counterpublicity; ~**zoll** protective tariff.

abweichen to differ, to digress, to deviate, to depart, to vary, *(Briefmarke)* to soak off;
von den Bestimmungen ~ to deviate from the rules; **keinen Finger breit** ~ not to budge an inch; **vom Gegenstand der Klage** ~ to depart from the matter in dispute; **kein Jota von etw.** ~ not to swerve an iota (a jot); **vom Kurs** ~ to deviate from the course, to sheer; **von der Norm** ~ to diverge from the beaten track; **von einer Regel** ~ to be an exception to the rule; **im Text (Wortlaut)** ~ to read differently, to differ in wording; **vom Thema** ~ to wander from the subject; **von einer Überzeugung** ~ to yaw; **voneinander** ~ to diverge; **von seiner gewohnten Weise** ~ to go out of one's way.

abweichend different, divergent, discrepant, variant, contra;
vom Üblichen ~ out-of-line; **von der früheren Regelung** ~ unlike the former regulation;
~**e Ansichten** divergent opinions; **völlig** ~**e Darstellung einer Angelegenheit geben** to give quite a different version of an affair; ~**e Entscheidung** dissentient opinion; ~**e Regelung** regulation to the contrary; ~**er Text** different wording.

Abweichler *(vom Kommunismus)* deviationist, *(Parteipolitik)* dissident, diversionist, fractionist, factionalist, insurgent *(US)*.

Abweichlertum deviationism, factionalism, insurgence *(US)*.

Abweichung deviation, divergence, digression, yaw, aberration, *(pol.)* diversionism, *(Statistik)* spread, *(Verschiedenheit)* divergence, difference, *(Widerspruch)* discrepancy;
in ~ **von** notwithstanding this, in derogation of;
durchschnittliche ~ *(Statistik)* mean deviation; **geringfügige** ~ immaterial variance; **gleichsinnige** ~ *(Statistik)* concurrent deviation; **mittlere** ~ standard deviation; **primäre** ~ primary deviation; **unzulässige** ~ error; **zulässige** ~ permissible deviation, allowed variation, *(Münzen)* [remedy] allowance, allowable tolerance *(US)*;
~ **in den Auffassungen** difference of opinion; ~ **vom allgemeinen Bebauungsplan** zoning variance *(US)*; ~**en vom Haushalt** budget variance; ~ **des Kompasses** compass variation; ~ **von der Norm** abnormality, anomaly; ~ **nach oben oder unten** plus or minus variation; ~ **von der Parteilinie** deviation from the party line; ~ **von einer Regel** exception from the rule; ~ **von der Reiseroute** deviation from the voyage; ~ **vom Thema** digression from the subject; ~ **des mündlichen Vorbringens vom Schriftsatz** variance; ~ **durch den Wind** drift, windage.

Abweichungsklausel derogatory clause, *(Warenverkehr)* deviation clause.

abweisen to refuse, to reject, to turn down, to snub;
Anerbieten ~ to dismiss an offer; **Anspruch** ~ to turn down a claim; **Antrag** ~ to reject a motion; **Behandlung eines Gesuchs** ~ to dismiss a petition; **Besucher** ~ to refuse to see a visitor; **Bettler** ~ to send away a beggar; **Bitte** ~ to turn down a request; **Forderung** ~ to set a claim aside; **glatt** ~ to turn down flat; **j. grob** ~ to rebuff s. o.; **Klage** ~ to dismiss (throw out) a case; **Kläger mit der Klage** ~ to enter judgment for the defendant, to nonsuit the plaintiff; **kostenmäßig (kostenpflichtig)** ~ to dismiss (nonsuit) with costs; **Prüfling** ~ to reject a candidate; **j. scharf** ~ to send s. o. packing; **jede Verantwortung von sich** ~ to refuse to take any (assume no) responsibility; **wegen Versäumnis des Klägers** ~ to nonsuit the plaintiff; **Vorschlag** ~ to reject a proposal; **Wechsel** ~ to dishono(u)r a bill;
sich nicht ~ **lassen** to take no denial.

abweisend rejecting, *(Haltung, Miene)* cold, unfriendly.

Abweisung refusal, rejection;
~ **eines Anspruchs** disallowance of a claim; ~ **eines Antrags** rejection of a motion; ~ **einer Berufung** dismissal of an appeal; ~ **einer Klage** dismissal of an action, nonsuit; **kostenpflichtige** ~ **einer Klage** nonsuit with costs.

Abweisungsbescheid nonsuit.

abwendbar preventable, avertible.

abwenden to avert, to prevent, to ward off;
Gefahr ~ to ward off a danger; **Katastrophe** ~ to avert disaster; **sich von einer Sache** ~ to turn one's back on s. th.; **sich von jem. in Verachtung** ~ to turn away from s. o. in contempt.

abwendig machen, Kunden to attract (entice) away customers.

Abwendung prevention, swing away;
~ **eines Schadens** avoidance of a damage.

abwerben, mit dem Angebot höherer Bezahlung to lure away with an offer of better pay; **Angestellte** ~ to entice servants, to poach employees; **Arbeitskräfte** ~ to lure (pirate, *US*) labo(u)rers into other jobs; **Kunden** ~ to drum up (entice away) customers; **Vereinsmitglieder** ~ to raid members of a club *(US)*.

Abwerbung *(Angestellte)* enticement, *(Mitglieder)* raid[ing] *(US)*;
~ **von Arbeitskräften** seducing to leave service, enticement of employees *(Br.)*, labor piracy *(US)*, pirating *(US)*; ~ **von Belegschaftsangehörigen** poaching of staff.

abwerfbar *(Treibstofftank)* jettisonable.

abwerfen *(Benzinkanister)* to jettison, to drop, *(Ertrag)* to yield, to return, to bring in, to recoup;
Ertrag ~ to yield a return; **Gewinn** ~ to leave (yield) a profit, to be profitable, to pay; **seine Maske** ~ to throw off one's mask; **netto** ~ to [yield] net; **nichts** ~ not to pay; **Postsack** ~ to drop a mailbag; **Rakete** ~ to discard a rocket; **gute Rendite** ~ to give a good return on an investment; **5% Zinsen** ~ to bear interest at 5 per cent.

abwerfend, Gewinn remunerative.

abwerten to devalue, to devaluate, to depreciate, to devalorize.

abwertende|Bemerkung derogatory remark; ~ **Stellungnahme** depreciative comment.

Abwertung devalorization, devaluation;
zur Exportsteigerung vorgenommene ~ competitive devaluation;
~ **durch Paritätsveränderung (der Währung)** devaluation (depreciation) of currency.

Abwertungs|anwärter candidate for devaluation; ~**befürworter** advocate of devaluation; ~**gewinn** devalorization profit; ~**kandidat** candidate for devaluation; ~**klausel** devaluation clause; ~**maßnahmen** devaluation measures; ~**politik** devaluation policy; ~**satz** devalorization rate.

abwesend absent, away [from home], missing, *(fig.)* absentminded, lost in thought, absorbed, *(bei Gericht)* nonappearing;
vorsätzlich ~ contumacious;
als ~ **gemeldet sein** to be reported absent;
~**er Besitzer** absent owner.

Abwesender absentee.

Abwesenheit absence, nonattendance, *(vom Arbeitsplatz)* absenteeism, *(vom Gericht)* default of appearance, nonappearance, *(Nichtbestehen)* nonexistence;
im Falle seiner ~ failing him; **in** ~ in absentia; **in jds.** ~ behind s. one's back;
dauernde ~ chronic absence; **gelegentliche** ~ occasional absence; **vereinbarte** ~ arranged absence; **vereinbarte gegenseitige** ~ *(Parlament)* pairing off;
~ **von der Schule** nonattendance at school;
durch ~ **glänzen** to be conspicuous by one's absence; **seine** ~ **vom Tatort nachweisen** to establish one's alibi; **in** ~ **verurteilen** to deliver a judgment in default.

Abwesenheits|liste absentees' list; ~**pfleger** public administrator, curator for an absentee; ~**pflegschaft** public administration, curatorship; ~**protest** [etwa] householder's protest; ~**quote** rate of absenteeism, absentee (absenteeism, absence) rate; ~**satz** rate of absenteeism, absentee (absenteeism, absence) rate; ~**urteil** judgment in default.

abwickeln to adjust, to settle, to transact, to effect, to execute, to complete, to phase out, to handle, *(liquidieren)* to liquidate, to wind up;
Angelegenheit ~ to handle (manage) an affair; **Außenhandel zu Vorkriegspreisen** ~ to conduct foreign trade at a prewar price level; **Film** ~ to feed the film; **Geschäft** ~ to settle a business, to transact (deal with a piece of) business; **sich glatt** ~ to go off smoothly; **Konkurssache** ~ to liquidate a bankrupt's affairs; **Kredit** ~ to repay a credit (loan); **über ein Refinanzierungsinstitut** ~ to effect through a refinancing institution; **Sache gut** ~ to see a business through; **Straßenverkehr** ~ to direct (control, regulate) the traffic; **Unternehmen** ~ to liquidate a company, to wind up a business company; **Verkauf** ~ to effect a sale; **alte Verträge** ~ to work off old contracts; **Zahlungen am Monatsende** ~ to make payments at the end of the month; **zwangsweise** ~ to execute under the rules.

abwickelnder Gesellschafter liquidating partner.

Abwickler liquidator;
~**amt** liquidatorship.

Abwicklung arrangement, management, settlement, adjustment, handling, *(Liquidation)* liquidation, winding up, windup;
bis zur ~ **des Geschäftes** pending transaction of the business; **außergerichtliche** ~ settlement out of court; **bankmäßige** ~ banking transaction; **finanzielle** ~ financial transaction; **zwangsweise** ~ execution under the rules;
~ **einer Angelegenheit** winding up (settlement) of an affair; ~ **unter Aufsicht des Gerichts** winding up subject to the supervision of the court; ~ **eines Geschäfts** windup of a business; ~ **einer Gesellschaft** winding up of a company; **außerkonkurs-**

rechtliche ~ zugunsten der Gläubiger general assignment for the benefit of creditors; **~ eines Kredites** repayment of a loan; **~ von Lagerbestellungen** planned arrangement of stock orders; **~ der Quartalsverbindlichkeiten** quarterly settlements; **~ des Straßenverkehrs** handling (control) of the traffic; **~ von Telefongesprächen** handling of calls;
~ durchführen to carry out a liquidation.
Abwicklungs|amt liquidating office; **~antrag** winding-up petition; **~bank** liquidating bank; **~bedingungen** settlement terms; **~bestimmungen** winding-up rules; **~gebühren** liquidation fee; **~geschäft** winding-up transaction; **~gesellschaft** liquidating company; **~konto** liquidation (settlement, *Br.*) account; **~kosten** handling costs; **~mitteilung** notification of liquidation; **~stelle** liquidating (clearing) office, *(mil.)* demobilization station; **~technik** project engineering; **~termin** *(Börse)* settlement (settling) date; **~verfahren** liquidation (winding-up) proceedings; **~verfahren einer Gesellschaft leiten** to conduct the proceedings in the winding-up of a company; **für das ~verfahren verantwortlich sein** to be responsible for the process of winding-up; **~wert** liquidation value; **~zeitraum** settling period.
abwiegen to weigh out, *(Gepäck)* to weigh in;
verschiedene Pläne gegeneinander ~ to weigh one plan against the other.
Abwimmeln shake *(sl.)*.
abwimmeln to shake (choke, stall, *US sl.*, brush, *US*) off, to give shake *(sl.)*;
j. mit einer Ausrede ~ to fob s. o. off with an excuse; **unangenehme Frage ~** to head off an awkward question.
Abwind downwash.
abwinken to motion away.
abwirtschaften *(Regierung)* to collapse.
abwischen to wipe [off].
Abwracken dismantlement, shipbreaking.
abwracken, Schiff to break up (rip, dismantle) a ship, to strike a ship off the list.
Abwracker shipbreaker.
Abwrackgeschäft shipbreaking.
Abwurf *(Bombe)* release, *(Last)* discharge, *(Notwurf)* jettison;
~ mit dem Fallschirm airdrop, paradrop; **~ von Versorgungsgütern** supply dropping;
~behälter drop tank, *(mit Fallschirm)* paracrate, *(unter Flugzeugrumpf)* belly tank; **~höhe** dropping height; **~meldung** drop message; **~stelle** dropping (drop) point; **~tank** drop tank; **~vorrichtung** *(Bombe)* bomb release, *(Tank)* jettison device; **~zielgerät** bombsight.
Abwürgen einer Debatte gagging of a debate *(Br.)*.
abwürgen, Debatte to prevent (gag, *Br.*) a debate; **Diskussion ~** to throttle a discussion; **Motor ~** to stall (kill) an engine.
abzahlbar redeemable;
monatlich ~ payable in monthly instalments.
Abzahlbarkeit redeemability.
Abzahlen payment by instalments, *(Abstottern)* never-never *(Br., sl.)*.
abzahlen to pay off, to acquit, to discharge debts;
Hypothek ~ to clear off a mortgage; **monatlich ~** to pay in monthly instal(l)ments; **nach und nach ~** to pay by (on, *US*) instal(l)ments; **seine Schulden ~** to discharge (pay off, clear off) one's debts; **seine Schuld in Raten ~** to clear off by instal(l)ments.
abzählen *(Stimmen)* to tell off, to count;
sein Geld ~ to count one's money; **Stimmen ~** to tell the votes.
Abzahlung paying off, paying up, *(in Raten)* part (instalment) payment, payment (paying off, repayment) by instalments (on the instalment, hire-purchase, *Br.*, deferred-payment, *US*) system, *(Tilgung)* payment in full, clearing off, liquidation;
auf ~ on account, *(in Teilzahlungen)* by instalments, on hire-purchase, on deferred terms *(US)*;
~ in bequemen Raten easy payment;
auf ~ kaufen to purchase on account, to buy on the instalment (hire-purchase, *Br.*) (deferred-payment, *US*) system (on trust), to buy by instalments (on the instalment plan); **etw. auf ~ verkaufen** to sell s. th. on the hire-purchase *(Br.)* (deferred-payment, *US*) system; **einem Kunden etw. auf ~ verkaufen** to hirepurchase s. th. to a customer.
Abzahlungs|anzeige hire-purchase advertisement; **~bank** consumer credit agency, personal (small) loan company, hire-purchase finance house *(Br.)*, finance company *(US)*; **auf ~basis** on the instalment plan (hire-purchase, *Br.*); **~bedingungen** hire-purchase terms *(Br.)*; **~bestimmungen** hire-purchase regulations *(Br.)*; **~finanzierung** instalment-plan financing; **~finanzierungsgesellschaft** hire-purchase finance house *(Br.)*, consumer credit agency, personal loan company; **~formular** hire-purchase form; **~frist** repayment period; **Beschränkungen auf dem ~gebiet aufheben** to lift restrictions on instalment buying; **~gebühren** hire-purchase charges *(Br.)*; **~geschäft** hire purchase [sale] *(Br.)*, time selling, tally trade *(Br.)*, instalment business (sale), business on the instalment system, sale on the deferred-payment system *(US)*, investment payment sales, *(einzelnes)* instalment (hire-purchase, *Br.*) transaction, deferred payment sale *(US)*, tally business, *(Firma)* instalment (hire-purchase finance, *Br.*) house, tally shop *(Br.)*; **~geschäfte** hire-purchase activities; **~gesellschaft** hire-purchase company *(Br.)*, consumer credit agency; **abhängige ~gesellschaften** instalment finance subsidiaries; **~gesetz** Hire-Purchase Act *(Br.)*; **~gläubiger** hire-purchase creditor *(Br.)*; **~grundlage** instalment basis; **~hypothek** repayment mortgage; **~karteikarte** hire-purchase card *(Br.)*; **~kauf** instalment buying (sale, selling), hire purchase *(Br.)*, purchase on the deferred-payment system *(US)*; **als ~käufer besitzen** to hold on hire purchase *(Br.)*; **~konto** instalment (hire-purchase, *Br.*, deferred-payment, *US*) account; **~kosten** instalment (hire-purchase, *Br.*) charges.
Abzahlungskredit instalment (hire-purchase, *Br.*, deferred-payment, *US*) credit, instalment loan;
~e *(Bilanz)* (hire-purchase, *Br.*, deferred-payment, *US*) borrowings;
~ für Einzelhändler retail instalment business; **~ für Produktivgüter** productive instalment credit;
~ aufnehmen to borrow through hire purchase *(Br.)* (on the deferred-payment system, *US*);
~geschäft instalment sale (business), hire purchase *(Br.)*, tally trade *(Br.)*, deferred-payment sale *(US)*; **~sätze** consumer loan rates.
Abzahlungs|periode repayment (hire-purchase, *Br.*) period; **~plan** instalment (hire-purchase, *Br.*, deferred-payment, *US*) system, partial payment plan; **~preis** instalment (time, hire-purchase, *Br.*, deferred-payment, *US*) price; **~rate** hire-purchase instalment *(Br.)*, period payment; **Aufschub für die ~raten für sein Auto erhalten** to defer car payments *(US)*; **~raten auf mehere Monate verteilen** to spread instalments over several months; **~risiko** hire-purchase *(Br.)* (deferred-payment, *US*) hazard; **~system** instalment plan (system), deferred-payment *(US)* (hire-purchase, *Br.*) system, tally trade (system) *(Br.)*; **~umsätze** hire-purchase sales *(Br.)*; **~verkauf** instalment (deferred-payment, *US*, hire-purchase, *Br.*) sale, time selling; **hochwertige ~verkäufe** high-ticket instalment sales; **~verpflichteter** hirer *(Br.)*; **~verpflichtungen** hire-purchase *(Br.)* (deferred-payment, *US*) debts (commitments), *(Bilanz)* instalment receivables *(US)*; **~vertrag** instalment contract, contract of hire purchase *(Br.)*, hire-purchase *(Br.)* (deferred-payment, *US*) agreement (contract), *(für 5 und mehr Raten)* credit sale agreement *(Br.)*; **~vertrag mit Eigentumsvorbehalt** hire-purchase and conditional sales agreement *(Br.)*; **~vertrag abschließen** to sign a hire-purchase agreement *(Br.)*; **~verträge** *(Bilanz)* instalment receivables *(US)*; **miteinander verbundene ~verträge** add-ons; **~volumen** instalment-credit outstanding; **Auto im ~wege bezahlen** to buy a motor-car and pay for it by monthly instalments; **im ~wege erwerben** to buy on the instalment plan; **~wesen** instalment buying (deferred-payment, *US*) system, hire-purchase financing *(Br.)*, tally trade *(Br.)*; **~zeitraum** hire-purchase period *(Br.)*.
abzapfen to tap, to broach, to draw;
jem. Geld ~ to bleed (milk) s. o.
Abzapfhahn faucet.
abzäunen to fence off, to hedge (rail) in.
Abzeichen badge, mark, decoration, *(Flugzeug)* nationality marking, *(mil.)* tab, ensign;
~ anstecken to pin on a badge;
~träger badgeman.
abzeichnen to initial, to initialize, to append one's initials, to sign, *(nach Durchsicht)* to check off;
sich ~ *(abheben)* to stand out, to contrast; **sich klar ~** to come into focus; **am Rande ~** to initial in the margin; **Rechnungen ~** to initial accounts.
Abzeichnung initialling.
Abziehapparat proof (galley, *US*) press.
abziehbar allowable, deductible.
Abziehbild transfer picture, decalcomania.
Abziehen *(Kopieren)* printing, *(Kunden)* alienation, enticement.
abziehen to move off, *(abrechnen)* to deduct, to recoup, *(Abziehbild)* to transfer, *(drucktechn.)* to pull off, to strike (print) off,

(Foto) to print, *(Geld)* to withdraw, *(Kunden)* to alienate, to entice, *(vom Lohn)* to withhold, to dock, *(nachlassen)* to abate, to discount, *(Rauch)* to escape, *(subtrahieren)* to deduct, to subtract, *(Wolken)* to disperse;

3% ~ to allow 3 per cent, to strike off 3%; **Betrag ~** to deduct an amount; **Bier auf Flaschen ~** to bottle beer; **unverrichteter Dinge ~** to come away disappointed; **zehn Dollar von einer Rechnung ~** to knock off ten dollars from a bill; **Drittel für Neuwertleistungen ~** to allow the deduction of one third for old upon the balance; **mit leeren Händen ~** to come away empty-handed; **Korrekturbogen ~** to pull a proof; **vom Lohn ~** to retain an amount of the pay; **jem. 100 DM vom Lohn ~** to dock DM 100 off s. one's wages; **Matrize ~** to run off a stencil; **vom Preis ~** to knock off the price, to make an allowance; **Rechnungsposten ~** to deduct an item from an account; **Satz in Fahnen ~** to take proofs in galley; **große Schau ~** to draw the long bow; **mit Schimpf und Schande ~** to leave under a cloud; **Skonto ~** cash discount, to deduct discount; **von einer belagerten Stadt ~** to raise a siege; **Text ~** to duplicate a text; **Truppen ~** to withdraw troops; **seine Unkosten ~** to deduct expenditure; **unsauber ~** to blot, to smut; **zuvor 5% ~** to make a previous deduction of 5%.

Abzieh|papier transfer (proof) paper; **~plakat** transparency, decalcomania; **~presse** proof (galley) press.

abzielen to aim at;
darauf ~ to tend in the direction; **auf eine Unkostenverminderung ~** to be intended to cut expenses.

Abzinsung discounting, deduction of interest accrued.

abzirkeln to measure carefully;
seine Worte genau ~ to weigh one's words.

Abzug deduction reduction, off-reckoning, off-take, *(Abdruck)* copy, *(Druckerei)* print, reproduction, *(Einbehaltung)* recoupment, *(Foto)* [contact] print, *(Gewichtsabzug)* weight deducted, *(Kamin)* vent, outlet, port, *(Lithographie)* transfer, offset, *(Lohn)* withholding, stoppage, docking *(Br.)*, *(Luft, Rauch)* vent, *(Nachlaß)* allowance, discount, abatement, rebate[ment], *(Subtraktion)* subtraction, *(Wetterstörung)* recession;
bar ohne ~ net (spot) cash, cash without discount; **Kassa ohne ~** terms net cash; **nach ~ von** after allowance for; **nach ~ der Einkommensteuer** clear of income tax; **nach ~ der Schulden** clear after debts paid; **nach ~ des Skontos** less discount; **nach ~ aller Spesen** all deductions made; **nach ~ der Steuern** tax deducted; **nach (unter) ~ der Zinsen** less interest accrued; **ohne ~** clear, without deduction, *(Kanal)* ventless; **ohne ~ anteiliger Erbschaftssteuern** free from legacy duty respectively; **ohne ~ von Steuern** tax-free; **unter ~ von** deducting, subject to deduction of, withholding; **unter ~ Ihrer Provision** deducting your commission;
Preise verstehen sich ohne ~ terms strictly cash;
ehrenvoller ~ orderly retreat; **endgültiger ~** final (clean) proof; **erster ~** *(Druckerei)* galley [proof]; **fotografischer ~** photoprint; **gleichmäßiger ~** uniform deduction; **harter ~** *(Foto, drucktechn.)* hard print; **heimlicher ~** *(mil.)* decampment; **hektografischer ~** mimeographed copy, manifold; **letzter ~** foundry proof; **reproduktionsfähiger ~** reproduction proof (pull); **signierter ~** signed proof; **stufenweiser ~** gradual withdrawal; **unkorrigierter ~** foul proof;
3% ~ bei Barzahlung 3% discount for cash; **~ von Betriebsausgaben** deduction from gross income; **~ für Bruchwaren** breakage; **~ vom steuerpflichtigen Einkommen** deduction from taxable income; **~ in Fahnen** slip (galley) proof; **~ von Geldbeträgen** withdrawal of funds; **~ für Geschäftsauslagen (Kosten)** allowance (deduction) for expenses; **zwangsweise durchzuführender ~ von Gewerkschaftsbeiträgen vom Gehalt** automatic checkoff of union dues *(US)*; **~ auf Kunstdruckpapier** art pull, glossary print; **~ für Lebensversicherungsbeiträge** *(Einkommensteuer)* life insurance relief *(Br.)*; **~ an der Quelle** *(Steuer)* deduction (withholding) at the source; **~ für Spesen** allowance for expenses, expense-account deduction; **~ von Truppen** withdrawal of troops;
zum ~ blasen to sound the retreat; **in ~ bringen** to deduct, to make deductions, to allow a discount; **10% vom Lohn in ~ bringen** to stop 10% from wages; **für Unkosten in ~ bringen** to allow for costs; **~ gewähren** to make a reduction, to grant a rebate[ment], to [allow a] discount; **einer Besatzung freien ~ gewähren** to allow the garrison to leave with the hono(u)rs of war; **Finger am ~ halten** to have one's finger on the trigger; **in ~ kommen** to be deducted; **~ machen** *(Druckerei)* to pull off a proof, *(Foto)* to take a print from a negative, to copy; **~ vornehmen** to discount; **~ von 4% vornehmen** to strike off 4 per cent; **j. zum ~ zwingen** to make a place too hot for s. o.

Abzüge *(Geld)* drain;
frei von ~n net; **mit Berücksichtigung aller ~** all deductions made; **ohne ~ jeder Art** free from all deduction;
steuerlich anerkannte ~ allowable deductions; **einkommensteuerfreie ~** exemptions; **gesetzlich feststehende ~** *(Einkommensteuer)* fixed (statutory) deductions *(US)*;
~ vom steuerpflichtigen Einkommen income-tax deductions; **~ von Gold** gold withdrawals; **~ für Kantinenverbrauch** checkoff for canteen expenses; **~ vor Verteilung des Reingewinns** surplus charges; **~ für Werbungskosten** *(Steuererklärung)* allowance for professional expenditure;
schlechte ~ liefern to print badly; **~ machen** to recoup.

abzüglich deducted, less, minus, ex;
~ Diskont less discount; **~ Dividende** ex dividend; **~ aller Kosten** less charges, charges deducted, clear of all expenses; **~ Steuer** tax deducted, less tax; **~ der Zinsen** less interest accrued.

Abzugs|beträge, aufgegliederte *(Einkommensteuer)* itemized deductions; **~bogen** proof [sheet], pull.

abzugsfähig deductible, allowable;
nicht ~ nondeductible;
bei der Einkommensteuererklärung ~ sein to be deductible for federal income-tax purposes *(US)*; **steuerlich ~ sein** to be allowable deductions for tax purposes;
voll ~e Ausgaben darstellen to be fully deductible current expenses; **~er Betrag** deduction; **~e Unkosten** *(Einkommensteuer)* permissible expenses; **~er Verlust** deductible loss.

Abzugs|graben well drain; **~kanal** [box] drain, channel, outlet, culvert, follow (drain); **~loch** vent hole; **~öffnung** outlet, vent; **~öffnung anbringen** to vent; **~papier** photographic (developing, proof) paper; **~post** mimeograph (duplicating, manifold) paper; **~posten** valuation item; **~rohr** waste pipe.

abzwacken, jem. etw. to tweak s. th. from s. o.; **sich etw. ~** to stint o. s. of s. th.

abzweigen to branch off, *(el.)* to derive, to shunt, *(Geldbeträge)* to earmark, to set aside, to divert, *(Rohrleitung)* to tap;
für sich selbst ~ to put aside for o. s.; **Geld für wohltätige Zwecke ~** to divert a sum for charity; **Mittel ~** to earmark funds.

Abzweigung branching off, *(Abzug)* deduction, *(Kapital)* diversion, *(Rohrleitung)* branch line, *(Straße)* fork, junction;
~ von Geldbeträgen earmarking of funds.

abzwingen, jem. ein Geständnis to extort a confession from s. o.; **jem. ein Zugeständnis ~** to force s. o. to make a concession.

Achillesferse vulnerable heel of Achilles, tender spot;
jds. ~ darstellen to be at s. one's most vulnerable; **jds. ~ ausfindig machen** to find s. one's vulnerable spot, to hit a blot.

Achs|abstand wheelbase; **~antrieb** final drive; **~druck** axle load.

Achse axle, *(pol.)* axis;
auf der ~ on track (truck), on the lam *(sl.)*; **per ~** by car (carriage, land), *(Bahn)* per rail, by wag(g)on;
sich um eine ~ drehen to wheel on an axis; **sich um die eigene ~ drehen** *(Flugzeug)* to roll; **Güter per ~ schicken** to send goods by rail (wagon, *US*); **auf ~ sein** to be out (on the road); **auf der ~ sein** *(Ware)* to be on their way; **Drittel des Jahres auf der ~ sein** to be on the road about a third of the year.

Achsel, j. über die ~ ansehen to look down on s. o.; **etw. auf die leichte ~ nehmen** to make light (easy work) of s. th.; **auf beiden ~n tragen** to be a double dealer, to sit on the fence;
~klappe *(mil.)* shoulder strap; **~träger** double dealer, trimmer *(Br.)*; **mit einem ~zucken** with a shrug of one's shoulders; **mit einem ~zucken abtun** to shrug off; **j. mit einem ~zucken abtun** to snap one's fingers at s. o.

Achsen|bruch broken axle; **zugelassenes ~gewicht** axle load.

Achs|kilometer car mile, milage covered; **~schenkel** journal.

Acht ban, outlawry, proscription;
in ~ und Bann tun to ostracize.

acht, außer ~ lassen to cast to the winds, to disregard; **sich vor etw. in ~ nehmen** to guard o. s. against (beware of) s. th.

achtbares Haus respectable firm.

Achtelseite *(Anzeige)* eighth of a page.

achten to respect, to value, to esteem;
sehr auf gutes Benehmen ~ to attach great importance to good manners; **Gesetz ~** to respect (observe) the law; **auf seine Kleidung ~** to be careful of one's clothes; **auf jds. Warnung ~** to heed s. one's warning.

ächten to outlaw, to boycott;
gesellschaftlich ~ to ostracize.

Achter|bahn switchback *(Br.)*, big dipper, roller coaster *(US)*; **~deck** quarter deck, afterdeck; **erhöhtes ~deck** poop deck.

achterlastig stern-heavy.

achtern astern.

Achterschiff stern.
achtgeben to take care, to be careful, to watch, to pay attention.
Achtgroschenjunge nark.
achtlos heedless, inattentive;
~ **behandeln** to trifle;
~**es Benehmen** disrespectful behavio(u)r.
achtsam watchful, observant, circumspect.
Achtstunden|arbeitstag working day of eight hours, eight-hour working day; ~**tag** eight-hours day, 8hr day.
achtstündig eight-hour.
Achtung respect, reputation, esteem;
aus ~ vor in deference of;
~ **vor dem Gesetz** deference of (respect for) the law; ~ **vor sich selbst** self-respect;
~, **Bauarbeiten!** danger, men at work!; ~, **Hochspannung!** danger, high voltage!;
jem. ~ einflößen to fill s. o. with respect; **sich allgemeiner ~ erfreuen** to be held in general esteem; **jds. ~ erringen** to gain s. one's esteem; ~ **seiner Freunde verloren haben** to have fallen into disgraces with his companions; **plötzlich in jds. ~ sinken** to plummet in s. one's esteem; **in jds. ~ steigen** to go up in s. one's estimation; **keine ~ verdienen** to be unworthy of respect; **allgemeine ~ verlieren** to fall in respect; **jds. ~ verlieren** to forfeit s. one's esteem.
Ächtung ban[ishment], proscription, outlawry, act of attainder, boycott;
gesellschaftliche ~ ostracism.
Achtungssignal attention signal.
Acker ploughed (plowed, *US*) field, *(Ackerland)* arable land, farmland, *(Ackerboden)* soil;
fetter ~ rich soil;
~ **bestellen** to till (cultivate) the soil.
Äcker grounds.
Acker|arbeit work in the fields; ~**bau** agriculture, farming, culture; ~**bau und Viehzucht** farming and stockbreeding; ~**bestellung** tillage, cultivation; ~**boden** arable (tillable) soil (land), farm land; ~**gaul** farm horse; ~**gerät** agricultural (farming) implements; ~**krume** topsoil, mold; ~**land** arable (tillable, farm) land, tillage; **bebautes ~land** hookland.
Ackern ploughing, plowing *(US)*.
ackern to plough, to plow *(US)*.
Acker|schlepper agricultural vehicle, farm tractor; ~**wagen** farm wag(g)on; ~**wirtschaft** agriculture, husbandry, farming.
ad acta *(lat.)* into the discard, to be filed;
~ **legen** to lay aside, to shelve.
ad|hoc *(lat.)* for these circumstances; **etw. ~ notam nehmen** to take due notice of s. th.
Adamskostüm, im ~ sein to be in one's birth suit (buff).
adaptieren to adapt.
Adaptionsniveau adaption level.
adäquate Ursache adequate cause.
Addieren einzelner Posten footing, adding up, cast, casting.
addieren to add, to cast (reckon) up, to sum up, *(Konto)* to foot up, *(alles zusammenrechnen)* to total, to tot;
falsch ~ to make a mistake in adding; **richtig ~** to add correctly.
Addiermaschine adding machine, adder, totalizer;
~ **mit Schreibwerk** adding-listing machine.
Addition addition, *(von Kolonnen)* footing;
~ **vornehmen** to perform an addition.
Additions|aufgabe tot *(Br.)*; ~**fehler** error in addition; ~**maschine** adding [-listing] machine; ~**zeichen** plus [sign].
Adel aristocracy, nobility;
niederer ~ gentry *(Br.)*; **verarmter ~** impoverished nobility;
~ **der Arbeit** dignity of labo(u)r.
adeln to raise to the peerage.
Adels|familie county family *(Br.)*; ~**kalender** Red Book *(Br.)*; ~**prädikat** title of nobility; **in den ~stand erhoben werden** to be raised to the peerage.
Ader vein, lead, *(Bergbau)* vein, load, seam, course, *(Blutgefäß)* blood vessel, *(el.)* core, conductor, lead, *(Holz)* vein, grain, streak, *(Stein)* vein, lode, *(Verkehr)* artery;
grausame ~ haben to have a streak of cruelty; **kaufmännische ~ haben** to have a turn for business; **leichte ~ haben** to be a happy-go-lucky fellow;
~**laß** bloodletting.
Adjutant adjutant.
Adjutantur adjutancy.
adlig noble, titled, aristocratic.
adoptieren to adopt;
Sohn ~ to adopt a son.
Adoptierter adoptee.
Adoption adoption;
~ **eines Mündigen** arrogation;
Kind zur ~ weggeben to have a child adopted.
Adoptions|beschluß adoption order; ~**gesetz** Adoption Act *(Br.)*; ~**recht** adoption law; ~**vertrag** legal adoption.
Adoptiv|bruder adoptive brother; ~**eltern** adoptive parents; ~**erbe** heir by adoption; ~**kind** adopted child, adoptee; ~**mutter** foster (nursing) mother; ~**sohn** adopted (foster) son; ~**tochter** foster daughter; ~**vater** adoptive (foster) father, adopter.
Adressant addresser, *(Warensendung)* consignor;
~ **eines Wechsels** drawer of a bill.
Adressat addressee, *(Geldsendung)* payee, *(Warenempfänger)* consignee, *(Wechselbezogener)* drawee.
Adresse address, direction, destination, *(Geldmarkt)* borrower, *(Souverän)* message, *(Wechselrecht)* house;
ohne ~ unaddressed, undirected; **per ~** under cover, care of (c/o);
abgekürzte ~ abbreviated address; **erste ~** *(Geldmarkt)* first-rate borrower, *(Wechsel)* first-class (prime, *US*) name; **falsche ~** wrong address, misdirection; **feststehende ~** registered address; **kurze ~** brief address; **ständige ~** permanent address; ~ **feststellen** to find out an address; **jem. seine ~ geben** to give s. one's address; **an die falsche ~ geraten** to have come to the wrong shop, to put the saddle on the wrong horse; ~ **hinterlassen** to leave one's address; **sich eine ~ notieren** to take note of an address, to write an address down; **bei ersten ~n plazieren** to place at first-class bankers; **an die falsche ~ richten** to misaddress, to misdirect; **sich an die richtige ~ wenden** to apply to the proper quarters.
Adressen|änderung change of address, address changes; **falsche ~angabe** misdirection; **ungenaue ~angabe** directions insufficient; **ohne ~angabe verreisen** to depart without leaving one's address; ~**buch** address book; ~**büro** list broker (house); ~**kartei** mailing list; ~**kontrolle** address (mailing-list) control; ~**lieferant** name supplier; ~**nachweis** list broker; ~**plan** mailing schedule; ~**quelle** address (mailing-list) source; ~**überprüfung** mailing-list revision; ~**verlag** list broker; ~**verlagsinhaber** list owner.
Adressenverzeichnis list [of addresses], mailing list *(US)*;
~ **auf dem neuesten Stand halten** to maintain a list; ~ **leihweise zur Verfügung stellen** to rent lists *(US)*; ~**se verkaufen** to sell lists *(US)*.
Adressenzettel label, docket.
Adressieren von Briefumschlägen envelope addressing.
adressieren to address, to direct, to superscribe, *(Güter)* to consign;
falsch ~ to misaddress, to misdirect.
Adressiermaschine addressing (mailing) machine, mailer *(US)*, addressograph, envelope addresser.
adressiert addressed, directed;
falsch ~ incorrectly addressed, misdirected; **unrichtig ~** incorrectly addressed.
Adreß|karte *(auf Gepäckstück)* paper of direction; ~**umschlag** addressed envelope.
Advocatus diaboli the devil's advocate.
Advokat advocate, barrister-at-law.
Advokaten|kniff pettifoggery; ~**stand** barristership.
Advokatur barristership.
Affäre affair, business, carryings-on;
erniedrigende ~ degrading affair;
~ **beilegen** to settle a dispute; ~ **in allen Verästelungen kennen** to know the ins and outs of a matter; **in eine ~ verwickelt sein** to be mixed up in an affair; **sich aus der ~ ziehen** to save one's bacon; **sich mit Eleganz aus der ~ ziehen** to come out of an affair with hono(u)r; **sich mit Humor aus der ~ ziehen** to make the best of a bad bargain.
Affe monkey, ape, *(Geck)* dandy, fop, *(Schwips)* kick *(US sl.)*;
blöder ~ silly fool; **eingebildeter (lackierter) ~** conceited ass; **wie ein vergifteter ~ abzischen** to dash off like a stuck pig; **seinem ~n Zucker geben** to make a pet of one's whim; **einen ~n haben** to be tipsy.
Affekt affect, affectation, *(strafrechtlich)* uncontrollable impulse;
im ~ in the heat of passion;
~**handlung** sudden heat of passion.
affektiert affected, coy, prim, priggish, unnatural, niminy-piminy, namby-pamby, la-di-da *(fam.)*;
nicht ~ unsophisticated;
~ **reden** to talk prunes and prisms;
~**er Mensch** high-stepper; ~**er Stil** precious style.

Affektiertheit niminy-pimininess, lug *(US coll.)*.
Affektionswert fancy price.
Affektivität *(Marketing)* emotional traits.
Affektpsychose emotional insanity.
affenartige Geschwindigkeit like greased lightning *(coll.)*.
Affen | komödie monkey tricks; ~**liebe zu seinen Kindern haben** to dote on one's children; ~**schande** beastly shame *(coll.)*; ~**spektakel** devil of a noise; ~**tempo** breakneck speed; ~**theater** monkey business, tomfoolery; ~**zahn** breakneck speed.
Affiche poster, bill.
Affront affront, insult.
Agent agent, representative, operative *(US)*, *(Makler)* broker, *(Provokateur)* feigned accomplice;
bezahlter ~ subsidized (paid) agent; **politischer** ~ political agent;
~ **für Grundstückspachten** lease broker *(US)*; ~ **für Wertpapiere** bond salesman *(US)*;
als ~ **auftreten** to agent; ~**en führen** *(Abwehroffizier)* to run an agent.
Agenten | dienste espionage; ~**dienste leisten** to spy, to commit espionage; ~**etat** agency budget; ~**nest** nest of spies; ~**netz** network of agents, spy network; ~**netz auffliegen lassen** to smash a spy ring; **Land mit einem** ~**netz überziehen** to spy out a land; ~**provision** agent's commission, commission fee, brokerage; ~**ring** network of agents, spy ring; ~**tätigkeit** subversive activity, espionage work; ~**zentrum** spy center (capital), espionage basis.
Agentur [commission] agency, agency business (office), factorship, representation, representative office, *(Zweigniederlassung)* branch [office];
vorgeschobene ~ *(Werbung)* house agency;
~ **für Industriewerbung** industrial agency; ~ **für Öffentlichkeitsarbeit** public-relations firm; ~ **einer Versicherungsgesellschaft** insurance agency;
~**bewerbung** agency application; ~**erfahrung** agency experience (background); ~**etat** agency budget; ~**geschäft** agency business; ~**konto** account; ~**kosten** agency fees; ~**leiter** agency manager; ~**leitung** handling an agency; **führende** ~**leute** agency executives; ~**mannschaft** agency team; ~**meldung** news agency report; ~**netto** agency net; ~**provision** agency commission; ~**tätigkeit** agency service; ~**unkosten** agency expenses; ~**vergütung** agency [service] fee; ~**vertrag** agency agreement, agency contract; ~**vertreter** agency representative; ~**wesen** agency world (field).
Agglomerationskosten agglomeration costs.
Aggregat aggregate, set of machines, mass, aggregation;
~**tafel** *(Lebensversicherung)* aggregate table.
Aggression aggression;
~ **abreagieren** to vent aggression; **zu** ~**en herausfordern** to invite aggressive action.
Aggressions | akt, ~**handlung** act of aggression, aggressive action; ~**trieb** aggressiveness.
aggressiv aggressive, militant;
~ **sein** to have a chip on one's shoulder;
~**e Verkaufspolitik** hard (high-pressure) selling; ~**e Werbung** knocking *(Br.)* (competitive, *US*) copy.
agieren to act, to play a role;
hinter den Kulissen ~ to pull the strings.
Agio agio, [exchange] premium, redemption premium, rate of (premium on) exchange, *(bei der Emission)* stock discount;
anstehendes ~ constant premium; **veränderliches** ~ fluctuating premium;
~ **bei der Auslösung einer Kaution** premium on lease; ~ **aus Kapitalerhöhung** premium on capital increase;
~ **genießen** to command (be at) a premium;
~**erlös** paid-in surplus; ~**geschäft** agiotage, premium hunting, stockjobbing; ~**gewinn** exchange profit; ~**konto** agio account; ~**papiere** premium bonds.
Agiotage agiotage, premium hunting, stockjobbing.
Agioteur stock-exchange operator, premium hunter, stockjobber *(US)*.
Agitation agitation, rabble-rousing, flagwaving *(coll.)*.
Agitations | material agitprop material; ~**redner** rabble-rouser.
Agitator agitator, rabble-rouser, flagwaver *(coll.)*;
politischer ~ malcontent, stumper.
agitatorisch agitatorial;
~**e Rede** rabble-rousing speech; ~**e Tätigkeit** stirring up of the masses.
agitieren to agitate, to stir up, to solicit;
gegen etw. ~ to come out against s. th.
Agonie agony, death struggle.
Agrar | abschöpfung *(EG)* agricultural levy; ~**ausschuß** agricultural committee; ~**einfuhren** agricultural (farm) imports; ~**einkommen** agricultural income; ~**erzeugnis** agricultural (farm) product; ~**erzeugnisse** agricultural commodities; **leicht verkäufliches** ~**erzeugnis** cash crop; ~**exporte** agricultural exports; **gemeinsamer** ~**fonds** *(EG)* Common Agricultural Fund; ~**frage** land question.
agrarfreundlich pro-agriculture.
Agrar | gebiet rural (agricultural) area; ~**genossenschaft** Agricultural Cooperative Society; ~**genossenschaftsgesetz** Agricultural Credits Act *(Br.)*; ~**gesetz** Land Act; ~**gesetzgebung** land laws; ~**hilfe** farm subsidies, agricultural support (subsidies, *Br.*); ~**importland** country importing agricultural products; ~**konjunkturen** agricultural fluctuations; ~**kredit** agricultural credit, farm loan (credit), agricultural loan *(US)*; **kurzfristiger** ~**kredit** agricultural short-term credit *(Br.)*; ~**krise** agricultural crisis; ~**land,** ~**staat** agricultural country; ~**markt** agricultural market; ~**marktbereich** agribusiness sector; ~**marktpolitik** agricultural marketing; ~**maßnahmen** agrarian measures; ~**politik** agrarian (agricultural) farm policy; ~**politik der Europäischen Gemeinschaft** Common Agriculture Policy; ~**preise** agricultural (farm) prices; ~**preisniveau** farm-price level; ~**preissubventionen** deficiency payments; ~**problem** land question; ~**produkt** agricultural product; **kriegsunwichtige** ~**produkte** nonbasic commodities; ~**produktion** farm (agricultural) production; ~**reform** agrarian (land) reform; ~**sektor** agricultural sphere; ~**sozialismus** agrarian socialism; ~**soziologie** rural society; ~**stadium** agricultural stage; ~**stadt** agrarian city; ~**statistik** agricultural statistics; ~**struktur** agricultural structure, structure of agriculture; ~**strukturpolitik** agricultural structure policy; ~**subvention,** ~**zuschuß** agricultural *(Br.)* (farm) subsidy; ~**system** agricultural system; ~**technik** agricultural engineering; ~**überschuß** agricultural surplus; ~**verfassung** agrarian structure; ~**wirtschaft** agricultural (agrarian) economy; ~**wirtschaftler,** ~**wissenschaftler** agricultural economist; ~**wissenschaft** agronomy, agricultural science; ~**zoll** agricultural duty; ~**zuschüsse für die von der Natur benachteiligten Gebiete** hill-farming subsidies *(Br.)*.
Agrément erteilen to grant the agreement.
Agronom agricultural (rural) economist.
Ahn parent, ancestor, forefather, *(pl.)* ancestry, forefathers.
ahnden to average, to punish.
ähneln, seinem Vater to favo(u)r one's father *(coll.)*; **sich ziemlich** ~ to be pretty much alike.
ahnen to have a presentiment;
nur ~ to be dimly aware.
Ahnen | bild family portrait; ~**forschung** ancestry (genealogical) research; ~**forschung treiben** to genealogize; ~**reihe** pedigree; ~**tafel** family tree, pedigree; ~**verehrung** ancestor worship.
Ahnfrau ancestress, mother.
ähnlich similar, alike;
wie ein Ei dem anderen ~ **sein** to be as like as two peas; **seinem Vater sprechend** ~ **sein** to be the picture of one's father;
~**e Anschauungen** similar views; **täuschend** ~**es Bild** lifelike portrait.
Ähnlichkeit likeness, similarity, parallel;
entfernte ~ distant likeness; **schwache** ~ distant resemblance; **sprechende** ~ true likeness; **vage** ~ general resemblance; **verblüffende** ~ striking likeness (feature);
~ **der Methoden** similitude of methods; ~**en des Stils** conformities of style;
überhaupt keine ~ **haben** to have no feature in common.
Ahnung presentiment, forewarning;
nicht die blasseste ~ not the ghost of a notion (slightest idea); **dunkle** ~ **von etw. haben** to have an inkling of s. th.; **keine** ~ **von etw. haben** to have no idea of s. th.; **keine** ~ **haben wer gemeint ist** not to know s. o. from Adam; **keine** ~ **von jds. Plänen haben** to be in complete ignorance of s. one's plans; **nicht die leiseste** ~ **von etw. haben** not to have the vaguest notion of s. th.; **von Tuten und Blasen keine** ~ **haben** not to know the first thing about it (beans, *US*).
ahnungslos unknowingly, unsuspicious;
völlig ~ **sein** to have no idea; **sich** ~ **stellen** to play the innocent.
Aide-memoire memory aid, *(dipl.)* aide-mémoire.
Airbus air coach, skytrain *(US)*;
billiger ~ **mit Fahrkartenverkauf unmittelbar vor dem Abflug** walk-on low-price skytrain *(US)*.
Akademie academy, institute, *(Fachschule)* academy, college;
Pädagogische ~ teacher training college *(Br.)*;
~**direktor** director of studies; ~**mitglied** member of an academy, academician; ~**preis** academy award.

Akademiker university man, [college] graduate, academician, professional, post-doctoral fellow *(US)*;
nur für ~ degree-demanding;
~ **sein** to have had a university education;
~**ausbildung** graduate (university) education; ~**kragen** Yale-blue collar *(US)*; ~**nachweis** grading papers; ~**verband** association of professional men.

akademisch academic[al], university, professional, *(theoretisch)* formal;
~ **ausgebildet** university-trained (educated);
~**es Amt** academic position; ~**e Ausbildung** college training, university education; ~**er Bereich** academic field; ~**e Berufe** professions; **rein** ~**e Frage** academic question; ~**e Freiheit** academic freedom; ~**er Grad** [university] degree; ~**en Grad besitzen** to hold a degree; ~**en Grad erlangen** to take one's degree, to graduate *(US)*, to proceed *(Br.)*; ~**en Grad verleihen** to graduate, to cap; ~**e Laufbahn** academic career; ~**e Tracht** academic dress, gown *(Br.)*; ~**e Verbindung** fraternity; ~**es Viertel** 15 minutes grace; ~**e Vorbildung** academical qualification; ~**e Welt** campus; ~**er Werdegang** academic background; ~**e Würde** academic rank; ~**e Würden** academic credentials.

Akklamation acclamation.

akklimatisieren, sich to get acclimatized, to naturalize; **sich rasch** ~ to feel at home soon; **sich völlig** ~ to go native *(US sl.)*.

Akklimatisierung acclimatization.

Akkord *(Lohnform)* contract *(US)* (job) work, piecework, tut *(Br.)*, *(Vergleich)* agreement with one's creditors, *(Vertrag)* settlement, arrangement, composition;
im ~ [by the] job, by contract *(US)*, by the (upon) tut *(Br.)*; **im** ~ **anstellen** to take in contract *(US)*; **im** ~ **arbeiten** to job, to do job work (piecework), to work by agreement (the job, the piece), to work on piece rates; **j. im** ~ **beschäftigen** to put s. o. on piecework; **mit seinen Gläubigern einen** ~ **zustande bringen** to compound with one's creditors; **j. im** ~ **entlohnen** to pay s. o. by the job; **in** ~ **geben** to let out by contract *(US)*; **in** ~ **nehmen** to take in contract *(US)*; **Arbeit auf** ~ **übernehmen** to undertake by contract *(US)*, to contract for work *(US)*; **Arbeit im** ~ **vergeben** to let out work by contract *(US)*, to job; **im** ~ **bezahlt werden** to be paid by the job.

Akkordarbeit job (piece-rate) work, jobbing, piecework, contract work *(US)*, work on contract *(US)*, taskwork, tut (time) work *(Br.)*, incentive operation;
schlecht bezahlte ~ tight job; **überproportionale** ~ high piecework.

Akkord | arbeiter jobber, jobbing hand, job worker, taskworker, piecework employee, pieceworker; ~**berechnung** rate fixing *(US)*; ~**betrieb** contract shop *(US)*; ~**bezahlung** piecework pay, group payment.

akkordieren, mit seinen Gläubigern to compound with one's creditors.

Akkordklasse task group.

Akkordlohn piecework pay, piece-rate wages, piece wage (rate bonus), contractual wages *(US)*;
~ **mit garantiertem Mindestbetrag** piecework with base guarantee;
~**arbeit** piece (task, job, result, statement, unit) wage; **niedrig bezahlte** ~**arbeit** tight job; ~**arbeiter** pieceworker, job worker; ~**bezahlung** contract wage payment *(US)*, piecework pay; ~**formel** piece-rate formula; ~**satz** job rate, piece rate, piece-[work] rate formula; ~**schein** piece-rate ticket; ~**system** piece-rate plan, piece method, wage incentive payment plan, payment by results, piece-work (incentive pay) system, contract system [of wage payment] *(US)*; **überproportionales** ~**system** high piece-rate system; ~**verdienst** piecework earnings; ~**vermittler** piece master *(Br.)*; ~**zuschlag** piece-rate bonus.

Akkord | meister *(Bergbau)* butty; ~**meistersystem** sweating system; ~**prämie** piece-rate bonus; ~**preis** piece (statement) price; ~**[richt]satz** job (piece, piecework) rate; **überhöhter** ~**satz** runaway rate; ~**system** piece-price (incentive pay) system, wage-incentive payment (piece-rate) plan, contract system [of wage payment] *(US)*; ~**tarif** piece rates; ~**tariflohn** piecework payrate; ~**verdienst** piece-rate earnings; ~**vertrag** piecework contract; ~**wesen** wage incentive payment plan, contracting *(US)*; ~**zettel** job ticket; ~**zuschlag** piecework bonus, make-up pay *(US)*.

akkreditieren *(Diplomat)* to accredit;
j. ~ to open a credit in favo(u)r of s. o.; **Gesandten** ~ to accredit an ambassador.

akkreditiert accredited;
nicht ~ unaccredited;
bei einem Staat ~ **sein** to be based to a country.

Akkreditierter accreditee *(Br.)*, accredited [person] *(Br.)*, beneficiary of a letter of credit.

Akkreditierung *(dipl.)* accreditation.

Akkreditiv [letter of] credit;
begebbares ~ negotiable credit; **nur bei bestimmten Banken benutzbares** ~ straight credit *(US)*; **bestätigtes** ~ confirmed letter of credit; **einfaches** ~ clean letter of credit; **sich automatisch erneuerndes** ~ revolving letter of credit; **normales** ~ straight credit; **teilbares** ~ transferable (divisible) credit *(US)*; **unbestätigtes** ~ unconfirmed letter of credit; **unkündbares (unwiderrufliches)** ~ irrevocable letter of credit; **bestätigtes unwiderrufliches** ~ confirmed irrevocable credit; **widerrufliches** ~ revocable letter of credit;
~ **mit Dokumentenaufnahme** documentary letter of credit;
~ **annullieren** to cancel a credit; ~ **bestätigen** to confirm a credit; **jem. ein** ~ **einräumen (stellen)** to open a credit in favo(u)r of (accredit) s. o.; ~ **eröffnen (erstellen)** to open (issue) a letter of credit, to establish a credit; ~ **zurückziehen** to revoke a letter of credit;
~**auftrag** letter of authority, credit instruction; ~**bank** issuing bank, issuing banker; ~**bedingungen** terms of a credit; ~**deckungsguthaben** balance with house and foreign bankers; ~**ermächtigung** letter of authority; ~**eröffnung** opening of a letter of credit; ~**gestellung** opening of a credit in favo(u)r; ~**inhaber** accreditee, accredited [person]; ~**verpflichtungen** customer's liabilities; ~**vorschuß** packing (anticipatory) credit *(Br.)*; ~**widerruf** revocation of a letter of credit.

Akkumulation accumulation, *(el.)* storage.

Akkumulator storage battery, accumulator;
~ **aufladen** to charge an accumulator;
~**raum** *(Schiff)* battery compartment; ~**spannung** battery voltage; ~**zelle** accumulator cell.

akkumulieren to accumulate.

akkumulierend accumulative.

Akkumulierung accumulation;
~ **zur Schuldentilgung** accumulation for payment of debts.

akkurat accurate, exact, tidy;
~ **arbeiten** to work accurately;
~**e Handschrift** neat handwriting.

Akontozahlung payment on account, downpayment, instalment;
als ~ **erhalten** received on account;
~ **an Gläubiger** payment of creditors on account; ~ **eines Teilbetrages** part payment on account;
~ **leisten** to make payments on account.

Akquirieren solicitation, [house-to-house] canvassing.

akquirieren to canvass, to solicit, to tout, to drum up *(US)*.

akquirierend business-getting.

Akquisiteur canvasser, commercial travel(l)er, drummer *(US)*, *(Anzeigen)* space salesman *(US)*, *(Versicherung)* insurance agent, solicitor, tout, producer *(US)*.

Akquisition canvassing, business getting.

Akquisitions | abteilung *(Versicherungsgesellschaft)* new-business (business-getting) department; ~**chancen** acquisition prospects; ~**kosten** *(Versicherung)* acquisition cost (expenses); ~**programm** acquisition program(me).

Akrobat acrobat, tumbler.

Akrobatenkunststück acrobatics, acrobatic feat (trick).

Akt act *(Künstler)* nude, *(Rechtsvorgang)* deed, *(Theater)* act;
feindseliger ~ act of hostility; **notarieller** ~ notarial deed; **richterlicher** ~ judicial act; **unfreundlicher** ~ *(dipl.)* unfriendly act;
~ **der Verzweiflung** act of despair.

Akte file, record, dossier, *(Urkunde)* document, instrument;
fortlaufend geführte ~ continuous record;
~ **anlegen** to open a file; ~ **verlegen** to misplace a file.

Akten files, records, rolls, documents, papers;
bei den ~ on file; **für die dortigen** ~ for your files; **zu den** ~ for our files, to be filed;
abgelegte ~ dead (closed) files, filed material; **alphabetisch geführte** ~ alphabetic (box) files; **doppelte** ~ counter-rolls; **griffbereite** ~ ready-reference files; **übliche** ~ ordinary files;
~ **abteilungsweise ablegen** to file material departmentally; ~ **anfordern** to call in records; ~ **anlegen** to compile (open) files; ~ **aufbewahren** to preserve records (documents); ~ **beiziehen** to consult records; **benötigte** ~ **schnell und leicht beiziehen** to locate wanted files with ease and speed; **bei den** ~ **bleiben** to be retained in the files; **seine** ~ **durchgehen (durchsehen)** to examine one's files; **alte** ~ **durchsehen** to examine old records; ~ **einsehen** to consult official documents; **etw. in den** ~ **eintragen** to put s. th. on record; **nach Lage der** ~ **entscheiden** to judge a case on its merits; ~ **führen** to keep records; ~ **heranziehen** to consult records; **aus den** ~ **hervorgehen** to appear on the

records; **zu den ~ legen** to lay on the shelves, to shelve, to pigeonhole, to subjoin to the files, to file [away]; **in den ~ nachschlagen** to consult one's records; **zu den ~ nehmen** to put on (subjoin to) the files; **Bericht zu seinen ~ nehmen** to place a record on one's files; **Urkunde zu den ~ nehmen** to enter a document into the records; **~ schließen** to close files; **bei den ~ sein** to be on file; **~ verlegen** to misplace files; **in jds. ~ vermerkt werden** to go into s. one's records; **~ zusammenheften** to link up records;

~ablage filing [of records]; **~ablage einer Abteilung** departmental filing; **~ablage in alphabetischer Reihenfolge** filing in alphabetical order; **~ablage in chronologischer Reihenfolge** filing in order of date; **~ablage nach Sachgebieten** classified filing; **~abschrift** transcript of record; **~anforderung** *(Gericht)* writ of certiorari *(US)*, mittimus, invocation of papers; **~auszug** note, abstract of (extract from) records, précis of a set of documents; **~blatt** record sheet *(US)*; **~bock** stand; **~bündel** bundle of files, dossier; **~deckel** binder, filing folder, jacket, file cover; **~doppel, ~durchschlag** file copy; **~duplikat** counterrolls; **~einsicht** inspection (perusal) of documents, inspection of the records; **~einsicht haben** to have access to the files; **~heft** file, dossier; **~hefter** document file, file folder, filing jacket; **kurzgefaßter ~inhalt** abstract of records; **~klammer** paper clip; **~koffer** attaché case, portfolio.

aktenkundig | machen to place on record; **~ sein** to be on (a matter of) record; **~ werden** to appear on record.

Akten | lage, nach according to record; **nach ~lage entscheiden** to decide a case on its merits; **~mappe** brief (dispatch) case, document file, portfolio.

aktenmäßig documentary, on record;
etw. ~ festhalten to [place on] record, to spread s. th. on the record *(US)*; **~ feststehen** to be on (a matter of, appear on the) record; **~ festgehalten sein** to be on (incorporated in) the records.

Akten | mensch bureaucratist, red tapist; **~notiz** memo[randum], note, commentary, constat; **interne ~notiz** interoffice memo, buck slip *(US)*; **~notiz versenden** to route a memo; **~nummer** file number; **~ordner** file folder, binder; **in einen ~ordner einheften** to file away; **~rubrik** file heading; **~rückversand** remittitur of record; **~sammlung** records and files; **~schrank** filing (file) cabinet; **~schrank für abgelegte Korrespondenz** transfer case; **~schwanz** tab; **mit ~schwänzen versehen** to docket; **~spiegel** retention schedule; **~stempel** file mark; **~stoß** pile of documents; **~stück** file, record, document, paper; **politisches ~stück** state paper; **~studium** examination of the files; **~tasche** brief case (bag), portfolio, attaché case; **~umschlag** holder; **~vermerk** memo[randum], note, commentary, constat; **innerbetrieblicher ~vermerk** interoffice memo, buck slip *(US)*; **~vermerk anfertigen** to [make a] memorandum, to make a minute, to minute s. th. down; **~vernichtung** record destruction; **~versandanordnung** *(Gericht)* writ of certiorari, mittimus; **~versendung** forwarding of documents; **~verzeichnis** file index; **~vorgang** subject of records; **~wolf** file destroyer, shredding machine; **~zeichen** file (reference) number, *(im Brief)* ref; **in jedem Schriftwechsel anzugebenes ~zeichen** reference to be quoted in all communications; **unser ~zeichen** our reference; **~zeichen angeben** to quote a reference; **~zimmer** filing room; **~zurückbehaltungsrecht** attorney's lien; **~zusammenstellung** paper book.

Akteur *(Soziologie)* actor.

Aktie share *(Br., Canada)*, stock *(US)*, *(Urkunde)* share *(Br.)* (stock, *US*) certificate;
zu einem Agio abgegebene ~ premium stock *(US)*; **im Clearingverkehr abgerechnete ~** clearinghouse stock *(US)*; **abgestempelte ~n** stamped (marked, *Br.*) shares; **alte ~** original stock *(US)*; **amortisierte ~** redeemed stock *(US)*; **zusätzlich angebotene ~n** excess shares; **ausgegebene ~n** shares outstanding, issued shares (stocks, *US*); **neu ausgegebene ~** baby *(US sl.)*; **über das genehmigte Aktienkapital hinaus ausgegebene ~n** overstocks *(US)*; **an Betriebsangehörige (die Belegschaft) ausgegebene ~n** staff shares *(Br.)*, shares for the staff *(Br.)*, employee shares *(Br.)* (stocks, *US*); **an den Gründer ausgegebene ~** promoter's stock *(US)*; **über dem Nennwert ausgegebene ~** shares issued at premium; **zum Nennwert ausgegebene ~n** shares issued at par; **noch nicht ausgegebene ~n** unissued shares; **in verschiedenen Serien ausgegebene ~n** classified stocks *(US)*; **an Strohmänner ausgegebene ~n** dummy shares *(Br.)* (stocks, *US*); **ausgeliehene ~n** shares (stocks, *US*) loaned; **mit Bezugsrecht ausgestattete ~** stock carrying rights *(US)*; **ausländische ~** foreign share (stock, *US*); **effektiv im Besitz befindliche ~** real (long) stock *(US)*; **begebene ~** issued share (stock, *US*); **im Sanierungsverfahren nicht beteiligte ~n** nonassented stocks *(US)*; **nicht bevorrechtigte ~n** deferred stocks *(US)*; **voll bezahlte ~** paid-up (full-paid) stock *(US)*; **börsengängige ~n** stocks negotiable on the stock exchange *(US)*; **börsennotierte ~n** quoted shares, shares quoted *(Br.)* (stocks listed, *US*) on the stock exchange; **dividendenberechtigte ~** participating share; **nicht sofort dividendenberechtigte ~** deferred stock *(US)*; **eigene ~** own share *(Br.)* treasury stock *(US)*; **eingebrachte ~** vendor's share; **amtlich eingeführte ~n** quoted shares, listed stocks *(US)*, shares officially quoted *(Br.)* (stocks listed, *US*) on the stock exchange; **zur Einziehung eingelieferte ~** surrendered share; **eingetragene ~** registered stock *(US)*; **eingezahlte ~** paid-up stock *(US)*; **zu einem Drittel eingezahlte ~** share on which one third has been paid; **noch nicht eingezahlte ~** partly paid [up] share; **voll eingezahlte ~** fully paid share *(Br.)*, full-paid stock *(US)*; **eingezogene ~** recalled share; **endgültige ~** definite share; **erstklassige ~n** high-grade (gilt-edged) shares *(Br.)*, glamor stocks *(US)*, blue chips *(US)*; **fallende ~n** declining shares (stocks, *US*), sliding stocks *(US)*; **gängige ~n** active shares *(Br.)* (stocks, *US*); **garantierte ~** guaranteed share (stock, *US*); **gebundene ~** restricted share *(Br.)*; **gehandelte ~n** issues traded; **unter einem Dollar gehandelte ~n** penny stocks *(US)*; **im Freiverkehr gehandelte (an der Freiverkehrsbörse notierte) ~n** shares traded over the counter, curb stocks *(US)*; **mit nur 1/4 des Pariwertes gehandelte ~** quarter stock *(US)*; **recht rege gehandelte ~n** active stocks *(US)*; **im Wert geminderte ~** share that shows a depreciation; **gesplittete ~n** split-up stocks *(US)*; **unentgeltlich zur Verfügung gestellte ~** donated stock *(US)*; **gewinnberechtigte ~** participating share *(Br.)*, profit-sharing stock *(US)*; **gewöhnliche ~** common share *(Br.)*, ordinary stock *(US)*; **gezeichnete ~n** shares applied for, subscribed shares *(Br.)* (stocks, *US*); **nicht gezeichnete ~n** unsubscribed stocks *(US)*; **aus dem Verkehr gezogene ~** withdrawn share; **gleichrangige ~n** shares ranking pari passu; **nur buchmäßig gutgeschriebene ~n** phantom stocks *(US)*; **herrenlose ~** unclaimed share *(Br.)* (stock, *US*); **hinterlegte ~** deposited share *(Br.)* (stock, *US*); **im Sammeldepot hinterlegte ~** assented stock *(US)*; **als Sicherheit hinterlegte ~n** shares lodged as collateral; **inländische ~n** home shares *(Br.)*, domestic shares; **junge ~n** new shares (stocks, *US*), junior issues (stocks, *US*); **kaduzierte ~n** forfeited shares (stocks, *US*); **kleingestückelte ~** fractional share; **kumulative ~** cumulative share; **kündbare ~n** callable stocks *(US)*; **auf den Inhaber lautende ~** share warrant (stock certificate, *US*) to bearer; **auf den Namen lautende ~** registered share; **lieferbare ~n** spots; **lombardierte ~** loaned share (stock, *US*); **mehrstimmige ~** stock entitling to a plural vote *(US)*; **mehrstimmige ~ im Besitz der Direktion** management stock *(US)*; **mündelsichere ~** trustee stock *(US)*; **nachschuß- und umlagefreie ~** nonassessable stock *(US)*; **nachschußpflichtige ~** assessable stock *(US)*; **nicht nachschußpflichtige ~** nonassessable stock *(US)*; **in voller Höhe nachschußpflichtige ~** double-liability stock *(US)*; **nennwertlose ~** no-par [value] share (stock, *US*), unvalued share (stock, *US*), nonpar [value] stock *(US)*; **neue ~** fresh (new, junior) share, fresh stock *(US)*; **notierte ~n** shares quoted on the stock exchange, quoted (listed) stocks *(US)*; **an der Börse nicht notierte ~n** displaced shares, unlisted stocks *(US)*; **an der Freiverkehrsbörse notierte ~n** curb stocks *(US)*; **notleidende ~** nondividend-paying stock *(US)*; **rückkaufbare ~n** redeemable shares; **spekulative ~n** speculative stocks *(US)*; **gut stehende ~n** shares at a premium; **steigende ~n** advancing stocks *(US)*; **stimmberechtigte ~** voted stock *(US)*; **nicht stimmberechtigte (stimmrechtlose) ~** nonvoting share (stock, *US*), a-share; **stimmrechtslose festverzinsliche ~n** nonvoting fixed-interest shares; **südafrikanische ~n** South Africans *(Br.)*; **teilbezahlte ~n** partly paid shares *(Br.)* (stocks, *US*); **überemittierte (ungültige) ~** overissue stock *(US)*; **übertragbare ~n** negotiable stocks; **formfrei übertragene ~** street certificate *(US)*; **umtauschfähige ~** convertible stock *(US)*; **unverwertete ~** unissued share (stock, *US*); **jederzeit verkäufliche ~** unrestricted stock *(US)*; **nur an Private verkäufliche ~** restricted stock *(US)*; **auf Baisse verkaufte ~** short stock *(US)*; **im Einzeldepot verwahrte ~n** nonassented stocks *(US)*; **verwässerte ~n** watered stocks *(US)*; **nicht weitergegebene ~** nonnegotiated share; **in Raten zahlbare ~n** instal(l)ment shares; **zinssatzempfindliche ~** interest-rate sensitive stock *(US)*; **zinstragende ~n** interest-bearing shares (stocks, *US*); **zur Börsennotierung zugelassene ~n** shares quoted *(Br.)* (stocks listed, *US*) on the stock exchange, quoted shares *(Br.)*, listed stocks *(US)*; **zum Börsenhandel nicht zugelassene ~n** shares not admitted (listed, *US*) on the stock exchange, unquoted shares; **zum Verrechnungsverkehr zugelassene ~** clearinghouse stock

(US); **nicht zugelassene ~n** unallowed shares; **zugeteilte ~n** shares allotted; **von den Gründern zurückgegebene ~n** donated stocks *(US)*; **zweitklassige ~n** second-line stocks *(US)*; **~n einer Abzahlungsfinanzierungsgesellschaft** hire-purchase finance shares *(Br.)*; **~n auswärtiger Banken zum Anschaffungspreis** shareholding (stockholding, *US*) interest in foreign banks at cost; **~ im Besitz des Publikums** outstanding shares; **~ ohne Besitzerschein** inscribed stock *(US)*; **~n mit geringen Börsenumsätzen** inactive stock *(US)*; **~ mit von anderen AG's garantierter Dividende** guaranteed share *(Br.)* (stock, *US*); **~ mit normaler Dividendenabrechnung** equity share; **~ mit rückwirkender Dividendenberechtigung** cumulative stock *(US)*; **verpachtete ~ mit Dividendengarantie** leased-line share; **~ mit Dividendenschein** share cum rights; **~ mit Dividendenvorzugsberechtigung** stock preferred as to dividends *(US)*; **~n im Eigenbesitz** stocks held in treasury *(US)*; **~n einer Finanzierungsgesellschaft** finance-house shares; **~n von Goldbergwerken** gold shares *(Br.)*; **~n eines nur aus Aktien bestehenden Investmentfonds** common stock funds *(US)*; **~n einer Kapitalanlagegesellschaft** banker's (trustee) shares; **~ mit bevorzugter Liquidationsberechtigung** stock preferred as to assets *(US)*; **~ mit [von anderen Gesellschaften] garantierter Mindestdividende** guaranteed share (stock, *US*); **~ mit Nennwert** par value share *(US)*; **~ ohne Nennwert** unvalued (no-par) share *(Br.)*, no-par value stock *(US)*, unvalued stock *(US)*; **~n unter dem Nennwert** shares at a discount; **~n und Obligationen** stocks and bonds; **~n mit einem Pariwert von 50** half stocks *(US)*; **~ ohne Prämienrechte** share ex rights; **~n mit hoher Rendite** shares that yield high interest; **~n in der Schwerindustrie** heavy-industry shares; **~n von Terraingesellschaften** land shares *(Br.)*; **~n einer Treuhandgesellschaft** trust-company stocks *(US)*; **~n mit beschränkter Verwendungsfähigkeit** letter stocks *(US)*; **~n von Wohnungsbaugesellschaften** housing stocks *(US)*;

~ abnehmen to take delivery of stocks *(US)*; **~n von der Notierung absetzen** to remove shares from the stock-exchange list; **~n abstoßen** to unload stocks *(US)*; **~n vor der Börsenzulassung zum Verkauf anbieten** to beat the gun *(US)*; **den Inhabern von alten ~ junge ~ zum Kurs von ... anbieten** to offer new shares *(Br.)* (stock, *US*) to the holders of old ones at...; **~n zur Generalversammlung anmelden** to deposit shares for the general meeting; **~ niedrig ansetzen** to set a low value on a stock *(US)*; **~n seines Auftraggebers aufkaufen** to run stocks against one's client *(US)*; **~n auflegen** to announce shares; **~n ausgeben** to issue shares; **~n zum Nennwert ausgeben** to issue shares at par; **~n unter dem Nennwert ausgeben** to issue shares at a discount; **~n über Pari ausgeben** to issue shares at a premium; **~n unter Pari ausgeben** to issue shares at a discount; **~n ausleihen** to lend stocks *(US)*; **Bezugsrecht auf junge ~n ausüben** to exercise the right to subscribe (acquire) new shares (stock, *US*); **~ zum Nennwert berechnen** to raise the face value; **~n besitzen** to hold shares (stocks, *US*); **~n beziehen** to take up shares (stocks, *US*); **junge ~n beziehen** to subscribe to (for) new shares (stocks, *US*), to exercise the right to subscribe for shares *(Br.)* (new stock, *US*); **~n unmittelbar bei der Gesellschaft beziehen** to subscribe the memorandum; **~n bei der Börse einführen** to have shares admitted (stocks listed, *US*) at the stock exchange; **alte ~n in neue eintauschen** to exchange old shares (stocks, *US*) for new ones; **~n voll einzahlen** to pay up shares; **~n einziehen** to call in (pay off) shares; **verlorengegangene ~n für kraftlos erklären** to cancel shares; **sich auf eine Vielzahl von ~n erstrecken** to spread over a wide variety of shares; **~n in ungewöhnlich geringen Mengen erwerben** to buy shares in odd lots; **eigene ~n erwerben** to buy its own shares; **~n in Depotverwaltung geben** to place shares in safe custody *(Br.)*; **10.000 Pfund in ~n angelegt haben** to have 10.000 in stocks *(US)*; **noch ~n einzudecken (gefixt) haben** to be short of stocks *(US)*; **~n als Sicherheit haben (halten)** to hold stocks as security *(US)*; **mit ~n handeln** to job shares; **~n hereinnehmen** to take in shares for a borrower, to borrow stock *(US)*; **~n als Deckung hinterlegen** to lodge stocks as cover *(US)*; **~n kaduzieren** to cancel shares; **~n kaufen** to buy in; **~n auf den Namen der Bank überschreiben lassen** to transfer shares into the bank's name; **Einzahlung auf ~n leisten** to make a payment on shares, to pay a call on stocks *(US)*; **~n zu einem zugesicherten Preis liefern** to put stocks at a certain price *(US)*; **~n lombardieren** to lend money on stock *(US)*; **~n als zusätzliche Sicherheit lombardieren** to lodge stock as an additional security *(US)*, to lend money on stock *(US)*; **~n manipulieren** to manipulate stocks *(US)*; **~n mitnehmen** to pick up shares; **auf ~n nachzahlen (nachschießen)** to make additional payment on shares (stocks, *US*); **~n in Prolongation nehmen** to borrow (carry) stocks *(US)*; **~n in Zahlung nehmen** to take delivery of stocks *(US)*; **~n an der Börse notieren** to quote shares *(Br.)* (list stocks, *US*) on the stock exchange; **~ beim Publikum plazieren** to place shares with the public; **mit ~n eingedeckt sein** to be long of stocks *(US)*; **in ~n spekulieren** to play the stock market, to stag the market *(Br.)*; **~ splitten** to split shares (stock, *US*); **~n stückeln** to subdivide shares; **~ um 2 1/4 Punkte auf 178 in die Höhe treiben** to build up a stock 2 1/4 points to 178 *(US)*; **~n übertragen** to assign shares (stocks, *US*); **~n umschreiben** to transfer shares; **aus ~n in hochverzinsliche Obligationen umsteigen** to switch out of stocks into high-yielding bonds *(US)*; **alte ~n in neue umtauschen** to exchange old shares *(Br.)* (stock, *US*) into new ones; **~n umwandeln** to [re]convert shares; **~n unterbringen** to place shares; **~ unterteilen** to split a share (stock, *US*); **~n veräußern** to realize shares; **~n seines Auftraggebers verkaufen** to run stock against one's client *(US)*; **eine ~ dont 1% auf einen Monat verkaufen** to give 1 per cent call on a share for a month; **~n im Kundenauftrag verkaufen** to sell shares on its customer's advice; **~n durch Fehlspekulationen verlieren** to sink stock in speculation *(US)*; **~n vernachlässigen** *(Börse)* to ignore shares; **~ verwahren** to hold shares in safe custody *(Br.)*; **~n als Kreditunterlage verwenden** to apply shares as collateral security; **~n vinkulieren** to restrict shares; **~n auf den Markt werfen** to spin stocks *(US)*; **~n zeichnen** to apply (make application) for shares *(Br.)*, to subscribe to (for) (take up) shares *(Br.)*, to take stock in *(US)*; **neue ~n zeichnen** to subscribe to (for) new shares (stocks, *US*); **~n zur Börsennotierung zulassen** to quote shares *(Br.)* (list stocks, *US*) at the stock exchange; **~n an die Gesellschaft zurückgeben** to surrender shares; **~n für eine Haussebewegung zurückhalten** to hold stocks for a rise *(US)*; **~n zurückkaufen** to pay off (redeem) shares; **~n zusammenlegen** to amalgamate (convert, consolidate) shares; **~n zuteilen** to allocate shares; **~n nach erfolgter Zeichnung zuteilen** to allot shares (stocks, *US*); **~n voll zuteilen** to allot shares to all applicants.

Aktien | abschlüsse stock deals *(US)*, dealing in stocks and shares; **~abschnitt** dividend warrant, coupon; **~agio** share premium *(Br.)*, stock premium *(US)*; **örtliches ~angebot** local equities; **~angebot an die Angestellten** restricted stock option *(US)*; **~anreiz** stock appeal *(US)*; **~anteil** [proprietary] share; **gezeichnete ~anteile** share application money; **~anteil an einem Unternehmen** stock on a company; **~anteile kaduzieren** to forfeit shares; **~anteilschein** share (stock, *US*) certificate; **~aufteilung** [reserve] split-up, splitting, stock split *(US)*; **~ausgabe** share issue *(Br.)*, issuance of stocks *(US)*, stock issue *(US)*; **~auslieferung** delivery of stocks *(US)*; **~aussichten** outlook for stocks *(US)*; **~auswahl** selection of shares (stocks, *US*); **~bank** joint stock bank *(Br.)*, equity bank, banking company (corporation, *US*), incorporated bank *(US)*; **landwirtschaftliche ~bank** joint stock land bank *(US)*; **~bankwesen** corporate banking.

Aktienbesitz holding of shares (stocks, *US*), shareholdings *(Br.)*, stockholdings *(US)*, stock investment (ownership) *(US)*; **für eine Vorstandsstellung erforderlicher ~** qualification shares *(Br.)*; **steuerbegünstigter ~** deferred share ownership; **wechselseitiger ~** cross holdings of shares;
~ der Kundschaft von Versorgungsbetrieben customer ownership; **~ des Staates** state shareholdings; **~ eines Unternehmens** stock ownership *(US)*.

Aktienbesitzer shareholder *(Br.)*, holder (owner) of shares *(Br.)*, stockowner *(US)*, stockholder *(US)*;
registrierter ~ stockholder of record *(US)*.

Aktien | bestand portfolio of shares (stocks, *US*); **eigener ~bestand** treasury stock *(US)*; **~beteiligung** share stake, interest in shares, equity holdings (participation), shareholding interest, stockholdings *(US)*; **auf den Namen von Strohmännern lautende ~beteiligung** nominee shareholdings; **wechselseitige ~beteiligungen** intercorporate stockholdings *(US)*; **gezeichnete ~beträge** share application money; **~betrug** share pushing *(Br.)*, stock bubbling (robbery) *(US)*; **~bewertung** valuation of shares (stocks, *US*), share valuation; **~bezugsrecht** subscription right, stock [purchase] right *(US)*, *(für Betriebsangehörige)* stock option (right) *(US)*; **~bezugsrechtsobligationen** option bonds; **~bezugsrechtsschein** stock-subscription warrant *(Br.)*, stock-allotment warrant *(US)*; **~bezugsrechtswesen** *(Betriebsangehörige)* stock-option plan *(US)*; **~bonus** share bonus; **~börse** stock exchange; **~brauerei** jointstock brewery; **~buch** register of shares *(Br.)*, share register *(Br.)*, stockholder's *(US)* (shareholders', *Br.*) ledger, stock registry (ledger) *(US)*, stock book *(US)*; **~depot** stock deposit *(US)*; **~einführung einer privaten Kapitalgesellschaft vorbereiten** to put a private company on the road to public stock offering

(US); ~**einlage** share stake; ~**einzahlung** payment on shares; **aufgeschobene** ~**einzahlung** deferred call on shares; ~**einziehung** redemption (paying off) of shares; ~**emission** issue of shares *(Br.)*, shares (stock, *US*, equity) issue, *(im Submissionswege)* issue by tenders; ~**erträgnisse** earnings per share, share earnings, profit issuing from stock *(US)*; ~**erwerb** acquisition (purchase) of shares; ~**erwerber** transferee of shares; ~**fachmann** share (security, *US*) analyst; ~**fonds** share[holding] fund; ~**gattung** class of shares, class of stocks *(US)*; ~**geschäft** dealing in stocks and shares, stock business, stockbroking *(US)*; **nur buchmäßig erfaßtes** ~**geschäft** phantom stock deal *(US)*.

Aktiengesellschaft *(AG)* joint stock company *(Br.)*, [business] corporation *(US)*, incorporated company *(US)*, public [limited] company *(Br.)*, stock company *(US)*;
an der Börse eingeführte ~ stock-exchange-listed company; **fehlerhaft errichtete** ~ corporation de facto *(US)*; **fusionierte** ~ consolidated corporation *(US)*; **inländische** ~ domestic corporation *(US)*; **staatliche** ~ government corporation *(US)*;
~, **deren Aktien sich im festen Besitz einiger weniger Personen befinden** closed corporation *(US)*; ~ **ohne Beschränkung des Aktienerwerbs** public company *(Br.)*; ~ **mit Dividendenbeschränkung** limited-dividend corporation *(US)*; ~ **ohne Nachschußpflicht** joint-stock company with limited liabilities *(Br.)*;
als ~ **eintragen** to incorporate *(US)*; ~ **gründen** to promote a joint stock company *(Br.)*, to organize a corporation *(US)*; **in eine** ~ **umwandeln** to convert into a public company.

Aktien|gesetz [etwa] Companies Act *(Br.)*, Corporation Law *(US)*; **nur zu Verrechnungszwecken vorgenommene** ~**gutschriften** phantom stock plan *(US)*; ~**handel** dealing in shares and stocks, share trading (dealings) *(Br.)*, stockjobbing, stockbrokerage, trading in stocks *(US)*, stock trading *(US)*; ~**händler** jobber in shares *(Br.)*, dealer in stocks *(US)*, sharebroker *(Br.)*, stockbroker *(US)*; ~**hausse** share (stock, *US*) -market boom, rise of stocks *(US)*, boom in equities (stocks, *US*); ~**hinterlegung** deposit of shares (stocks, *US*); ~**index** index of stocks *(US)*, average *(US)*, share price index *(Br.)*, *(Industrieaktien)* industrial ordinary share index *(Br.)*, Dow-Jones (Moody's) index *(US)*; **allgemeiner** ~**index** all-share index; ~**inhaber** shareholder *(Br.)*, stockholder *(US)*, holder of a stock *(US)*; ~**kaduzierung** cancellation of shares.

Aktienkapital share (shareholder's) capital *(Br.)*, equity stock (capital), joint *(Br.)* (stock, *US*) capital, *(Effektenkapital ohne Vorrechte)* common stock *(US)*, ordinary share capital *(Br.)*;
effektiv ausgegebenes ~ issued capital *(Br.)*, issued [capital] stock *(US)*, outstanding shares *(Br.)*, outstanding [capital] stock *(US)*; **genehmigtes, noch nicht ausgegebenes** ~ unissued capital *(Br.)*, unissued capital stock *(US)*; **mit zusätzlicher Dividendenberechtigung ausgestattetes** ~ participating capital stock *(US)*; **autorisiertes** ~ authorized [share] capital *(Br.)* (capital stock, *US*), registered capital *(Br.)*, registered [capital] stock *(US)*; **eingezahltes** ~ fully-paid (paid up) shares *(Br.)* (stock, *US*); **nicht eingezahltes** ~ capital not paid up, capital stock not paid up *(US)*; **teilweise eingezahltes** ~ part-paid stock *(US)*; **genehmigtes** ~ authorized capital *(Br.)*, authorized capital stock *(US)*; **gezeichnetes** ~ capital stock subscribed *(US)*; **stimmberechtigtes** ~ voting share capital *(Br.)*, voting capital stock *(US)*, voting stock of a company *(US)*; **nicht stimmberechtigtes** ~ nonvoting stock *(US)*; **verwässertes** ~ watered stock *(US)*;
ausgegebenes ~ **einer Bank** outstanding bank capital; ~ **ohne Vorrechte** ordinary share capital *(Br.)*, common stock *(US)*;
~ **besitzen** to hold shares (stock, *US*); ~ **erhöhen** to increase the share *(Br.)* (stock, *US*) capital; ~ **erwerben** to absorb the capital stock *(US)*; **10% des** ~**s kontrollieren** to control ten per cent of the voting power; ~ **verwässern** to water the stock *(US)*; ~ **zerlegen** to divide the capital; ~ **zusammenlegen** to reduce share capital *(Br.)* (capital stock, *US*), to write down (off) capital.

Aktien|kapitalzeichnung stock subscription *(US)*; ~**kategorie** class of stocks *(US)* (shares, *Br.*); ~**käufe** share purchases, buying of shares (stocks, *US*); **breitgestreute** ~**käufe** broadly diversified share purchases; **selektive** ~**käufe** selective stock purchases *(US)*; ~**kaufpreis** cost of the stock; ~**kaution** qualification in shares; ~**konjunktur** equity boom; ~**konto** share (stock, *US*) account; ~**konzern** corporate trust *(US)*; ~**kupon** coupon.

Aktienkurs share (stock, *US*) price;
abbröckelnde ~**e** easing share prices; **zu hohe** ~**e** top-heavy market;
~**e herunterbringen (herunterdrücken)** to pull (hammer) down the prices of stock *(US)*; ~**e raketenartig hochtreiben** to send the stocks skyward *(US)*;
~**index** share price index *(Br.)*, stock price index *(US)*, Dow Jones index *(US)*; ~**liste** share (stock, *US*) list, stock record *(US)*; ~**niveau** stock-market level; **sich gerade keiner Erfolge bei der** ~**pflege rühmen können** to boast a poor share-price performance; ~**rückgang** decline in stocks *(US)*; ~**schwankungen** fluctuations in the share *(Br.)* (stock, *US*) market; ~**steigerung** stock-market rise *(US)*; ~**treiberei** kiting stocks *(US)*; ~**umtausch** exchange of shares (stocks, *US*); ~**zettel** share *(Br.)* (stock, *US*) list, stock record *(US)*.

Aktien|legat legacy of shares; ~**liste** stock record *(US)*.

Aktienmajorität controlling interest, majority of shares *(Br.)* (stocks, *US*), stock (stockholders') majority *(US)*;
~ **besitzen** to own control of shares, to hold the controlling interest.

Aktien|majoritätsbesitzer controlling shareholder *(Br.)* (stockholder, *US*); ~**makler** sharebroker *(Br.)*, stockbroker *(US)*, stockjobber *(US)*; ~**manipulierung** stock manipulation *(US)*; ~**mantel** certificate of stock *(US)*, share (stock, *US*) certificate; ~**markt** share *(Br.)* (stock, *US*, equity) market; **auf dem** ~**markt spekulieren** to play on the stock exchange, to play the stock market, to stag the market *(Br.)*; ~**marktentwicklung** stock-market trend *(US)*; ~**mehrheit** majority stock *(US)*, majority of shares *(Br.)* (stocks, *US*, stockholders, *US*); ~**mehrheit besitzen** to hold a controlling interest; ~**mittelwert** par line; ~**notierung** quotation of shares, share (stock, *US*) quotation.

Aktienpaket block (portion, parcel) of shares *(Br.)* (stocks, *US*);
auf die Kurse drückendes ~ downside block; **großes** ~ large block of units (stock, *US*); **kontrollierendes** ~ controlling block; **durch Indossament übertragbare** ~**e** amounts of stock negotiable *(US)*; **mehrere hundert Aktien umfassende** ~**e** round lot *(US)*;
~ **mit durch hundert teilbarem Nennwert** even lot *(US)*;
~ **abstoßen** to unload a block of shares; **sein** ~ **auf den Markt bringen** to market one's block of shares; ~ **an einen marktaufkaufenden Konzern veräußern** to sell a stock block to an acquisitive conglomerate *(US)*; **über größere** ~**e verfügen** to deal in larger lines of shares; ~ **verkaufen** to sell a block of stocks *(US)*; **beträchtliches** ~ **zusammenkaufen** to build up a sizable position in stocks *(US)*.

Aktien|plazierung placing (sale) of shares (stocks, *US*), selling of stock *(US)*; ~**polster** cushion of stocks *(US)*; ~**poolvereinbarung** stock-pooling agreement; ~**portefeuille** portfolio [of shares], share (equity) portfolio, stock portfolio *(US)*; ~**preis** share (stock, *US*) price; ~**promesse** share warrant to bearer *(US)*; ~**recht** [etwa] company law *(Br.)*, stock (corporation) law *(US)*.

aktienrechtliche Grundsätze principles of company (corporation, *US*) law.

Aktien|rechtsdirektiven company law directives; ~**rechtsreform** amendment of stock laws *(US)*; ~**register** share register (list) *(Br.)*, stock record (ledger) *(US)*, register of joint-stock companies; ~**rendite** earnings per share, yield on shares (stocks, *US*), redemption yield; ~**rendite beim augenblicklichen Kursstand von 5 zu 1 zum Kapital ergeben** to put the shares at the present price on a price-earnings ratio of just over five; ~**repartierung** allotment of shares (stocks, *US*); ~**rückgabe [an die Gesellschaft]**, ~**verzicht** surrender of shares *(Br.)*; ~**rückkauf [durch die Gesellschaft]** redemption of shares (stocks, *US*), stock repurchase *(US)*, stock redemption *(US)*; ~**schein** share warrant *(Br.)*, stock certificate *(US)*; **auf den Inhaber lautender** ~**schein** share warrant to bearer *(Br.)*; ~**schenkung** donation of capital stock *(US)*; ~**schwindel** share pushing *(Br.)*, stock bubbling (robbery) *(US)*; ~**schwindler** share pusher *(Br.)*, share adventurer *(Br.)*; ~**spekulant** share (stock, *US*) adventurer; ~**spekulation** agiotage, speculation in stocks *(US)* (shares, *Br.*), stock-market speculation, stock adventure *(US)*, stock-jobbery *(Br.)*; ~**spekulationen durchführen** to gamble, to stag the market *(Br.)*, to manipulate stocks *(US)*; ~**spitze** share fraction; ~**split** [reverse] split-up, splitting, stock split *(US)*; ~**stempel** *(Emission)* stamp tax *(US)* (duty, *Br.*); ~**stimmrecht ausüben** to vote [on] the stock; ~**streuung** dispersal of stock ownership *(US)*; ~**stückelung** denomination of shares (stocks, *US*), subdivision of shares, share denomination; ~**sturz** slump in stocks *(US)*; ~**tausch** exchange of shares *(Br.)* (stocks, *US*), share exchange *(Br.)*, stock switch *(US)*, *(zwischen Mutter- und Tochtergesellschaft)* split off *(US)*, spinoff *(US)*; ~**teilung** [reserve] split-up *(US)*, splitting; ~**tip** stock tip *(US)*; ~**übernahmeverpflichtung** association clause; ~**übertragung** assignation (transfer) of shares *(Br.)*, assignment (transfer) of stock *(US)*, stock *(US)* (share, *Br.*) transfer; ~**übertragung mit Gesellschaftssiegel** transfer under seal; ~**übertragung unter Parteien** transfer under hand; ~**übertragungsbuch** stock transfer book

(US); ~**umsätze** turnover in shares (stocks, *US*); ~**umsatzsteuer** tax on stock sales *(US)* (sales of shares, *Br.*); ~**umschreibung** transfer of shares (stock, *US*); ~**umtausch** exchange of shares *(Br.)* (stocks, *US*); ~**umtauschangebot** share exchange offer, capital stock exchange offer *(US)*; ~**umtauschgeschäft** share exchange transaction; ~**umwandlung** reconversion of stock *(US)*; ~**urkunde** share *(Br.)* (stock, *US*) certificate, share warrant to bearer *(Br.)*, certificate of stock *(US)*; ~**verkauf** sale of shares *(Br.)*, selling of stock *(US)*; ~**verkäufer** transferor of shares *(Br.)*, giver of shares (stock, *US*); **betrügerischer ~verkäufer** sharepusher *(Br.)*; **jem. einen telegrafischen ~verkaufsauftrag zukommen lassen** to wire s. o. to sell shares; ~**vermögen** fortune in stocks *(US)*; ~**verpfändung** mortgage of shares, legal mortgage, pledge of stocks *(US)*; ~**versicherungsgesellschaft** joint-stock insurance company; ~**verwahrung** safe custody of shares *(Br.)*; ~**verwässerung** dilution (watering) of stocks *(US)*; ~**verzeichnis** share register *(Br.)*, stock ledger (register) *(US)*; ~**vorkaufsrecht** stock option *(US)*; ~**vorrat** cushion of stocks *(US)*; ~**vorzugspreis eines neugegründeten Unternehmens** ground floor *(US)*; ~**wert** stock value *(US)*, cost of a share *(Br.)*; ~**werte** shares, stocks *(US)*; **variabel verzinsliche ~werte** determinable interest securities; ~**zeichner** applicant (subscriber) for shares *(Br.)*, share applicant *(Br.)*, stock subscriber *(US)*; ~**zeichnung** application (subscription) to shares *(Br.)* (stocks, *US*), share application *(Br.)*, subscription to capital stock *(US)*; ~**zeichnung [ab]schließen** to close a subscription list; **zur ~zeichnung auffordern** to invite application for shares *(Br.)*; ~**zeichnungsbuch** subscription ledger *(US)*; ~**zeichnungsliste** allotment sheet, list of subscribers.

Aktienzertifikat share warrant (certificate) *(Br.)*, stock warrant *(Br.)* (certificate, *US*), certificate of stock *(US)*;
gelochtes ~ punch-card stock *(US)*;
~ auf den Inhaber share warrant [to bearer]; **~ für zum Zweck der Stimmrechtsausübung erfolgte treuhänderische Übertragung des Aktienkapitals** voting trust certificate *(US)*.

Aktien | zertifikatsquittung stock receipt; ~**zusammenlegung** split-back (-down), stock splitdown, reverse split *(US)*; ~**zuteilung** allotment (allocation) of shares *(Br.)*, stock allotment *(US)*; **volle ~zuteilung** allotment of shares (stocks, *US*) to all applicants; ~**zuteilungsbericht** return of allotments; ~**zwischenhändler** jobber.

Aktion action, activity, move, step, drive *(US)*, *(Hilfsaktion)* scheme, project, drive, *(mil.)* action, operation, *(Werbung)* drive, campaign;
erstmalige ~ first-of-a-kind action; **gemeinsame ~** joint action; **konzertierte ~** concerted action; **massierte ~** mass action; **kombinierte militärische ~en** combined operations; **projektorientierte ~** marketing campaign;
~ zur Aufbringung von Geldern campaign for (drive to rise) funds; **großangelegte ~ zugunsten der Flüchtlinge** fund-raising drive for refugees; **~ des Geheimdienstes** intelligence operation;
~ gegen j. durchführen to enforce a course of action upon s. o.; **~ starten** to start (launch) a drive *(US)*; **in ~ treten** *(Ausschuß)* to take action, *(Maschine)* to start working; **voll in ~ treten** to get the lead out of one's pants *(sl.)*; **~ unternehmen** to take action; **politische ~ unterstützen** to support a political campaign.

Aktionär shareholder *(Br.)*, stockholder *(US)*, stockowner *(US)*, holder of stocks *(US)*, member *(Br.)*, proprietor in a joint-stock company *(Br.)*, actionary, *(Gründer)* incorporator;
alle ~e the whole crowd of shareholders; **auswärtiger ~** nonresident shareholder (stockholder, *US*); **einfacher ~** common stockholder *(US)*; **im Hauptbuch eingetragener ~** registered shareholder *(Br.)*, stockholder of record *(US)*; **nicht zur Familie gehöriger (familienfremder) ~** shareholder outside the family; **solidarisch haftender ~** contributory *(Br.)*; **minderjähriger ~** infant shareholder; **opponierender ~** dissenting shareholder (member) *(Br.)*, dissenting stockholder *(US)*, dissentient; **stimmgebundener ~** voting-trust certificate holder *(US)*; **als Strohmann vorgeschobener ~** nominee shareholder;
dem ~ in Form einer Steuergutschrift anrechnen to impute to the shareholder in the form of a tax credit; **~e zur Zeichnung auffordern** to invite shareholders (stockholders, *US*) to subscribe the capital; **als ~ ausscheiden** to cease to be a member *(Br.)*; **~e zu einer Generalversammlung einberufen** to summon shareholders for a general meeting *(Br.)*, to give notice to stockholders of a general meeting *(US)*; **~en mit Bezugsrechten Geld entlocken** to tap shareholders with rights offering; **Ansprache an die ~e halten** to address the shareholders *(Br.)* (stockholders, *US*); **~ einer Gesellschaft sein** to hold (possess) shares in a company *(Br.)*, to hold stocks *(US)*.

Aktionärs | ausschuß shareholders' committee; ~**brief** shareholder (stockholder, *US*) newsletter; ~**dividende** shareholders' dividend; ~**gremium** shareholder body; ~**gruppe** shareholder (stockholder, *US*) group; ~**information** proxy statement; ~**interesse** shareholder (stockholder, *US*) interests; ~**kategorien** classes of shareholders; ~**klage** shareholder suit (action), *(für die Gesellschaft)* representative action, stockholder action *(US)*, stockholder's derivative action *(US)*, *(gegen seine Gesellschaft)* shareholder's bill; ~**korrespondenz** stockholder correspondence *(US)*; ~**liste** list of members; **kapitalmäßige ~mehrheit** majority of stockholders *(US)*; ~**pflege** stockholder relations (communications) *(US)*, service to shareholders *(Br.)* (stockholders, *US*); ~**rechte** shareholder's (stockholder's, *US*) rights; ~**rechte der gleichen Aktiengattung** class rights; ~**register** subscribers' *(Br.)* (stockholders', *US*) ledger, stock book *(US)*; ~**verpflichtungen** liability of stockholders, shareholders' (stockholders', *US*) liabilities; ~**versammlung** meeting of shareholders *(Br.)* (stockholders, *US*); **gruppenweise stattfindende ~versammlung** class meeting; ~**vertreter [im Aufsichtsrat]** management representative; ~**verzeichnis** share list (register) *(Br.)*, nominal list of shareholders *(Br.)*, index of members *(Br.)*, stock ledger (record) *(US)*, list of stockholders *(US)*, *(zur Dividendenauszahlung)* dividend book; ~**vorschlag** shareholder's proposal; ~**zeitschrift** external house organ; ~**zustimmung** shareholder (stockholder, *US*) ratification.

Aktions | ausschuß excutive committee; ~**bereich** range of action, *(Fahrzeug, Flugzeug)* cruising range, *(mil.)* covered area; ~**bereich eine Blockade durchführender Streitkräfte** *(Völkerrecht)* area of operation of blockading naval forces; ~**bereich ausdehnen** to enlarge the area of operations; **im ~bereich eines Flugzeugs liegen** to be within the aircraft's range; ~**entwurf** blueprint for action.

aktionsfähig sein, nicht to be flat on one's back.

Aktions | forschung action research; ~**freiheit** freedom of action; ~**gebiet** zone of action; **jem. ein ~gebiet erschließen** to open up a field of action for s. o.; ~**gruppe** action group; ~**plan ausarbeiten (entwerfen)** to chart (map out) a course of action; ~**programm** program(me) for action; ~**radius** radius of action, *(Flugzeug)* range of action, flying range, *(Schiff)* cruising range.

aktionsunfähig, infolge von Verlusten crippled by its losses;
~ machen to cripple; **j. völlig ~ machen** to bind s. o. to hand and foot.

aktiv active, *(Bilanz)* on the asset side, favo(u)rable, *(zielstrebend)* vigorous, dynamic, energetic, active;
nicht ~ inactive, *(mil.)* retired;
~ legitimiert able to sue, capable of suing;
~ abschließen *(Konto)* to show a credit balance; **sich in einem Verein ~ beteiligen** to take an active part in a club; **~ dienen** *(mil.)* to serve with the colo(u)rs; **sich ~ für eine Sache einsetzen** to go all out for s. th.; **~ sein** *(Vereinsmitglied)* to be an active member; **im Geldmarkt ~ sein** to appear as creditor in the money market; **~ werden** to take active steps;
~e Betriebsangehörige members of the staff; **im ~en Dienst** on active duty; **~e Dienstzeit** service with the colo(u)rs; **~e Handelsbilanz** favo(u)rable balance of trade; **~e Konjunkturpolitk** anticyclical measures; **~er Offizier** regular officer; **~er Soldat** regular soldier; **~e Teilnahme** active part; **~es Wahlrecht** franchise.

Aktiva assets, effects, property, *(Bilanz)* resources *(coll.)*;
in der Substanz abnehmende ~ wasting assets; **antizipative ~** accrued receivables *(US)*; **nur zur Deckung der Sicherungsübereignungsansprüche ausreichende ~** fully pledged assets; **nicht bewertbare ~** *(Versicherungswesen)* unadmitted assets; **ertragbringende ~** earning assets; **festliegende ~** capital (fixed, permanent) assets; **flüssige ~** circulating (current, quick, floating, fluid, *US*) assets; **nicht flüssige ~** frozen assets; **geschäftliche ~** business resources *(coll.)*; **jederzeit greifbare ~** available (tangible) assets, active capital; **leicht greifbare ~** easily realizable assets; **immaterielle ~** *(Patente usw.)* intangible assets; **kurzfristige ~** limited-life assets; **mögliche ~** contingent assets; **leicht realisierbare ~** quick (fluid, *US*) assets; **nicht realisierbare ~** sticky (unmarketable) assets; **reine ~** net assets *(US)*; **scheinbare ~** fictitious assets; **sonstige ~** *(Bilanz)* other assets; **transitorische ~** deferred (suspense) assets, accrued income, unexpired expense; **unzureichende ~** insufficient assets; **veranschlagte ~** estimated assets; **frei verfügbare ~** available assets; **zur Verteilung für die Masse verfügbare ~** *(Konkurs)* unpledged assets, assets on hand; **teilweise zur Masseverteilung verfügbare ~** partly pledged assets; **verpfändete ~** assets pledged as collateral; **werbende ~** productive assets;

~ **einer Bank** bank's recources; ~ **mit überhöhtem Buchwert** watered assets; ~ **hoher Liquiditätsstufe** liquid assets, quick assets *(US)*, near money; ~ **und Passiva** assets and liabilities; **die ~ belaufen sich auf** the assets add up to; **Verhältnis der flüssigen ~ zu den laufenden Verbindlichkeiten** working capital ratio *(US)*;
~ **nach Liquidationsgesichtspunkten aufführen** to arrange assets in the order of liquidity; **als ~ behandeln** to carry as assets; ~ **im Konkurs (Verteilungsplan) feststellen** to marshal assets; ~ **und Passiva übernehmen** to take over accounts receivable and accounts payable *(US)*.

Aktiv|bestand available assets; **~bilanz** favo(u)rable balance of trade; **~forderungen** active debts, accounts receivable *(US)*; **~geschäft** *(Banken)* lending business; **~handel** export trade.

aktivieren to activate, to improve, *(Geschäft)* to get going;
in der Bilanz ~ to carry as assets; **Gewinne** ~ to capitalize profits.

Aktivierung activation, improvement, *(Bilanz)* carrying as assets; ~ **des Außenhandels** achievement of an export surplus; ~ **der Außenpolitik** reinforcement of foreign policy; ~ **von Gewinnen** capitalization of profits; ~ **aller Kräfte** mobilization of all forces; ~ **der Zahlungsbilanz** improvement in the balance of payments.

aktivierungspflichtig|sein to constitute capital expenditure;
~er Aufwand capital expenditure.

Aktivist activist, shock worker.

aktivistisch *(Bilanz)* on the asset side.

Aktivität vigo(u)r, activity;
finanzielle ~ finance activity; **geschäftliche** ~ activity in trade; **übermäßige** ~ overactivation;
große ~ **entwickeln** to be very active; ~ **zeigen** to take an active part.

Aktiv|kapital working assets (capital); **~konto** assets account; **~legitimation** ability (capacity) to sue *(US)*, status; **mangelnde ~legitimation** inability (incapacity) to sue *(US)*; **ohne ~legitimation** out of court; **~legitimation besitzen** to be entitled to sue; **~masse** assets of a bankrupt's estate, mass of assets; **~mittel** working capital; **~pension** pension received.

Aktivposten asset, asset item, *(Bank)* credit item, *(Bilanzierung)* resources, *(Rechnungsabgrenzung)* deferred item;
zeitweilig nicht einlösbarer ~ deferred asset; **potentieller** ~ contingent asset; **sonstige** ~ *(Bilanz)* sundry assets;
zu den laufenden ~ eines Unternehmens zählen to be long-term business assets.

Aktivpotential asset potential.

Aktivsaldo active balance, *(Bank)* credit balance;
~ **im Außenhandel** active foreign trade balance; ~ **im Waren- und Dienstleistungsverkehr** surplus on trade and services; ~ **der Zahlungsbilanz** external surplus.

Aktivschulden accounts payable *(US)*.

Aktivseite *(Bilanz)* active (asset) side;
auf der ~ on the plus side of the account (asset side);
auf der ~ [einer Bilanz] aufführen to carry as assets; **sich auf der ~ der Bilanz niederschlagen** to show up in black on the balance sheet *(US coll.)*.

Aktivum asset;
geschäftliches ~ business resources *(coll.)*;
~ **des Berichtjahrs** favo(u)rable feature of the year under report.

Aktiv|vermögen *(Bilanz)* assets, resources *(coll.)*; **eingesetztes ~vermögen** assets employed, active capital; **~wechsel** bills in hand, billholdings; **~wert** creditors' figure; **~zinsen** *(Bilanz)* interest receivable *(US)* (due); **unbezahlte ~zinsen** outstanding interest.

Aktualität topicality, topical event, *(Buch, Film)* up-to-dateness; **von brennender** ~ of utmost topical importance.

Aktualitäten passing events;
~kino news theatre (cinema); **~schau** topical gazette, topical news film, newsreel, pictures of current events.

aktuell topical, of current event, front-page, *(auf neuestem Stand)* up to date, modern;
~ **sein** to carry the front pages; **wieder ~ werden** to regain topicality;
~e Anspielungen topical allusions; **~en Artikel schreiben** to write an article on current affairs; **~er Bedarf** immediate requirements; **~er Bericht** current-events lecture; **~er Film** topical film; **~e Frage** front-page question; **~er Kapitalbedarf** capital needed immediately; **~e Nachrichten** front-page news; **~es Problem** present-day question; **~e Sendungen** live broadcasts; **~es Thema** topical subject; **~er Zeitungsartikel** article right up to the minute.

Akustik, schlechte poor acoustics;
~ **der Funkübertragung** radioacoustics.

akustisch|es Echolot echo sounder; **~e Werbung** acoustic advertising.

akut acute, intense, crucial, critical;
~er Lehrermangel acute (serious) shortage of teachers.

Akzelerationsprinzip acceleration principle.

Akzent tone, stress, accent, *(Phonetik)* emphasis;
gewöhnlicher ~ common accent; **schwankender** ~ floating accent *(Br.)*; **deutlich spürbarer** ~ very marked accent; **starker** ~ broad accent;
~e setzen to emphasize certain features; **in einer Politik neue ~e setzen** to focus on new ideas; **mit einem gewöhnlichen ~ sprechen** to speak with a plebeian accent.

akzentfrei sprechen to speak without any accent.

akzentuieren to stress, to accentuate.

Akzept [letter (bill) of] acceptance, *(akzeptierter Wechsel)* accepted bill (draft), acceptance bill;
mangels ~ for want (in default) of acceptance; **mangels ~ zurück** returned for nonacceptance; **mit ~ versehen** accepted; **allgemeines** ~ clean (general) acceptance; **bedingtes** ~ qualified acceptance; **bedingungsloses** ~ general acceptance; **vor Fälligkeit bezahltes** ~ acceptance under rebate *(Br.)*, anticipated (rebated) acceptance *(US)*; **eingeschränktes** ~ special acceptance; **einwandfreies** ~ approved acceptance; **erstklassiges** ~ first-class acceptance; **formell gültiges** ~ approved acceptance; **laufendes** ~ outstanding acceptance; **auf Dollar laufendes** ~ dollar acceptance; **teilweises** ~ partial acceptance; **unbedingtes** ~ general (unconditional) acceptance; **unbeschränktes** ~ clean (general) acceptance; **ungedecktes** ~ blank acceptance; **verfallenes** ~ acceptance due; **vorbehaltsloses** ~ clean acceptance;
~ **per Intervention (ehrenhalber)** acceptance for (upon) hono(u)r (supra protest);
~ **decken** to provide for acceptance; ~ **einholen** to obtain (secure) an acceptance, to present a bill for acceptance; **sein ~ einlösen** to meet one's draft, to hono(u)r (meet) an acceptance; ~ **zurückgehen lassen** to return a bill unpaid, to dishono(u)r a bill; **Wechsel mit ~ versehen** to provide a bill with acceptance; **zum ~ vorlegen** to present a bill for acceptance.

akzeptabel acceptable, eligible, desirable;
gesellschaftlich nicht ~ beyond the pale.

Akzeptant acceptor;
~ **eines Ehrenakzepts** acceptor for hono(u)r; ~ **im Konkurs** acceptor bankrupt; ~ **verstorben** acceptor dead; **an den ~en zurück** refer to acceptor.

Akzeptanten-Kontokorrent acceptor's ledger.

Akzeptation acceptance.

Akzeptations|buch bills payable book; **~kredit** acceptance credit.

Akzept|austausch exchange of drafts; **~bank** acceptance house (corporation, *US*), accepting banker (house) *(Br.)*, merchant banker *(Br.)*; **~besorgung** procuring acceptance; **~bestand** holdings of acceptances, bill holdings; **~buch** acceptance ledger; **~datum** date of acceptance; **~einholung** presentment for acceptance; **~einlösung** bill discounting.

akzeptfähig bankable, negotiable.

Akzept|frist term of acceptance; **~gebühr** acceptance charge; **~geschäft** acceptance business, business of accepting bills, bill brokerage *(Br.)*; **~geschäfte machen** to discount bills; **~gläubiger** acceptance creditor; **kaufmännisches ~haus** acceptance house (corporation) *(US)*, accepting house *(Br.)*, merchant banker *(Br.)*; **~höchstkredit** acceptance line.

akzeptieren to accept, to provide with acceptance, *(Wechsel)* to hono(u)r;
blanko ~ to accept in blank; **nicht** ~ to refuse to accept, *(Wechsel)* to dishono(u)r by nonacceptance; **ungedeckt** ~ to accept uncovered; **Vorschlag** ~ to accept a proposal.

akzeptiert [duly] accepted;
gesellschaftlich ~ free of the company of gentlemen; **nicht** ~ unaccepted, *(Wechsel)* unhono(u)red, dishono(u)red;
~ **werden** to go, *(Wechsel)* to find (meet) with due protection; **~er Wechsel** accepted draft; **nicht ~er Wechsel** dishono(u)red bill.

Akzeptierung acceptance, accepting;
~ **eines Angebots auf Kauf eines Effektenpaketes** award of a block of shares.

Akzept|konto acceptance (bills payable, *US*) account; **~kredit** acceptance credit; **~obligo** acceptance liability, *(Bilanz)* bills (trade, acceptances) receivable *(US)*; **~obligobuch** acceptor's ledger, bills payable book *(US)*; **~provision** accepting (acceptance) commission, commission for acceptance; **~schulden**

acceptance commitments, *(Bilanz)* trade account receivables *(US)*; ~**schuldner** acceptance debtor, drawee; ~**umlauf** bills in circulation; ~**verbindlichkeiten** acceptance commitments, bills (trade acceptances) receivable *(US)*; ~**verbindlichkeiten der Kundschaft** *(Bilanz)* customers' liability on acceptances; **mit ~vermerk versehen** to provide with acceptance; ~**verpflichtung** acceptance liability; ~**verweigerung** nonacceptance, dishono(u)r; ~**vorlage** presentment for acceptance.

akzessorisch collateral;
~**er Vertrag** accessory contract.

Akzidenz|arbeit job, jobbing work, display work; ~**arbeiter** jobbing man; ~**druck** job work (printing); ~**drucker** job printer; ~**druckerei** job office; ~**drucksachen** commercial work; ~**satz** jobbing work; ~**schrift** display type, jobbing face; ~**setzer** job (display) compositor, display hand.

Akzise excise, indirect tax, inland duty.

Akzisen|amt excise office *(Br.)*; ~**einnehmer** excise commissioner (officer) *(Br.)*, exciseman *(Br.)*; **unter ~verschluß** under bond.

Aladins Wunderlampe Aladdins's lamp.

Alarm alarm, *(mil.)* alert, warning, *(Fliegeralarm)* airraid warning;
blinder ~ false alarm;
~ **aufheben** *(Luftwarnung)* to give the all-clear; ~ **auslösen** to set off an alarm; ~ **geben** to sound an alert; **bei einer bestimmten Situation ~ geben** to alert to a situation; **blinden ~ schlagen** to cry wolf;
~**anlage** alarm system, police (burglary) alarm; **automatische ~anlage** automatic alarm system; **optische ~anlage** visual alarm system; ~**anlagen angeschaltet haben** to have s. th. wired to alarms; ~**anlagenruf** burglar alarm call.

alarmbereit on the alert, standing by.

Alarm|bereitschaft stand-by, alert, *(Fliegeralarm)* air alert; **in ~bereitschaft** on the alert; **sich in ~bereitschaft halten** to stand by, to be on the alert; **in ~bereitschaft versetzen** to put on the alert; ~**einrichtung** alarm system, burglar (police) alarm; ~**gebiet** *(mil.)* danger area; ~**gepäck** scram-bag *(sl.)*; ~**gerät** alarm; **selbsttätiges ~gerät** *(Radar)* autoalarm device; ~**glocke** alarm bell.

alarmieren to alarm, to [put on the] alert, to sound the alarm (alert);
Feuerwehr ~ to call out the fire brigade; **bei einer bestimmten Situation ~** to alert to a situation.

alarmierende Nachrichten startling news.

Alarm|posten alarm post; ~**ruf** alarm; ~**sammelplatz** *(mil.)* alarm post; ~**signal** alarm, alarm signal; ~**sirene** airraid siren; ~**stufe** alert phase (stage); ~**system** alarm system; ~**tauchen** *(U-Boot)* crash dive; ~**zeichen** alarm signal; ~**zeichen geben** to raise the alarm; ~**zustand** stand-to; **Truppen in ~zustand versetzen** to alert troops.

albern|e Gans silly thing; ~**es Zeug reden** to talk nonsense.

Album album;
Fotos in ein ~ einkleben to mount photographs into an album.

aleatorischer Vertrag aleatory contract.

Alibi alibi;
~ **für mangelnde Investitionsbereitschaft beseitigen** to remove the noninvestment alibi; ~ **nachweisen** to prove (establish, produce) an alibi; **falsches ~ vorbringen** to set up a false alibi.

Alimentation alimony, maintenance.

alimentationsberechtigt entitled to alimony (maintenance).

Alimentations|klage alimentary (alimony, bastardy, *US*) process, action for support *(US)*; ~**klage anstrengen** to file an affiliation petition; ~**kosten** alimony payments; ~**pflicht** liability to pay alimony; ~**verfahren** affiliation (bastardy, *US*) proceedings; ~**zahlungen** alimony payment.

Alimente alimony, maintenance.

Alimenten|abfindung alimony in gross; ~**forderung** claim of (to) alimony, claim for maintenance, maintenance claim.

alimentenpflichtig liable to pay alimony.

Alimenten|prozeß affiliation (bastardy, *US*) case; ~**urteil** affiliation (bastardy, *US*) order.

alimentieren, Kind to maintain a child; **Konto ~** to place an account in funds.

Alkohol alcohol, liquor, spirits, hard stuff *(sl.)*, rum *(US)*;
völlig dem ~ verfallen wholly given to drinking;
unverfälschter (reiner) ~ pure alcohol;
eine Menge ~ vertragen können to be able to take a lot of alcohol; ~ **schmuggeln** to bootleg *(US)*; **j. unter ~ setzen** to make s. o. drunk; **sich unter ~ setzen** to get drunk; **auf ~ verzichten** to forbear to drink alcohol;
~**anteil**, ~**prozentsatz** percentage of alcohol; **illegaler ~ausschank** blind tiger *(US sl.)*; **konzessionierter ~ausschank** public house *(Br.)*, off licence *(Br.)*; ~**ausschank konzessionieren** to license liquor selling; **unter ~einfluß** intoxicated, under the influence of intoxicating liquor; **unter ~einfluß stehen** to be under the influence of drink, to have a brick in one's hat *(sl.)*.

alkoholfeindlich dry *(US)*.

alkoholfrei nonalcoholic, soft *(coll.)*;
~**e Getränke** nonalcoholic beverages, soft drinks *(coll.)*; ~**e Getränkeindustrie** soft-drink industry *(coll.)*; ~**es Restaurant** temperance restaurant.

Alkohol|gegner prohibitionist, dry, teetotal(l)er, pussyfoot *(Br., sl.)*; ~**gegnerverband** anti-saloon league *(US)*; ~**gehalt** alcoholic strength; **von geringem ~gehalt** light; ~**genuß** consumption of alcohol; **übermäßiger ~genuß** excessive or intemperate use of intoxicants; **unter übermäßigem ~genuß stehend** excessively intoxicated; **konzessionierter ~handel** licensed trade.

Alkoholiker habitual drinker, drunkard.

alkoholisch alcoholic, spirituous;
~**e Getränke** alcoholic beverages; ~**e Getränke zu sich nehmen** to drink.

alkoholisieren, j. to make s. o. drunk, to alcoholize.

alkoholisiert under the influence of liquor;
~**es Getränk** stimulant, intoxicating liquor.

Alkoholismus alcoholism, habitual drunkenness.

Alkohol|monopol liquor monopoly; ~**probe** breath test; ~**schmuggel** rumrunning, smuggling of intoxicating liquor, bootlegging *(US)*; ~**schmuggler** bootlegger *(US)*, rumrunner *(US)*; ~**spiegel** level of alcohol; ~**steuer** alcoholic beverage tax, liquor excise *(US)*; ~**süchtiger** alcoholic; ~**test** breath test; ~**verbot** control of drink, prohibition; **unter ~verbot** dry *(US)*; **nicht unter ~verbot** wet *(US)*; ~**verbot für das ganze Land aussprechen** to turn the whole country dry *(US)*; ~**verbot einführen** to introduce prohibition, to go dry *(US)*; ~**verbrauch einschränken** to restrict the consumption of alcohol; ~**vergiftung** alcoholism, alcoholic gastritis; ~**verkauf nur außerhalb des Ladens** package store *(US)*.

All world, universe;
ins ~ vorstoßen to advance into space.

all|abendlicher Besuch regular evening visit; ~**bekannt** widely known, notorious.

Allbeteiligungsklausel *(Völkerrecht)* participation clause.

alle *(aufgebraucht)* sold, out, finished, all gone, used up;
~ **vier Monate** quarterly;
~ **werden** to run out.

Allee avenue, walk, parkway *(US)*.

allein alone, solitary, single, exclusive, *(einsam)* lone, *(entlegen)* apart, alone, *(ohne Unterstützung)* single-handed, by oneself, *(ohne Zeugen)* privately, in private;
für sich ~ per se *(lat.)*; **für sich ~ betrachtet** on its merits;
alles ~ erledigen to do everything by o. s.; ~ **das Wort führen** to do all the talking; ~ **die Geschäftsaufsicht innehaben** to be left in the sole charge of the business; ~ **befugt sein** to have sole power; ~ **berechtigt sein** to have exclusive (sole) rights; ~ **stehen** to be single (unmarried, without dependants); **für sich ~ stehen** to be fighting a lone battle.

Allein|auslieferer sole distributor; ~**auslieferung** sole agency; ~**berechtigung** exclusive (sole) right; ~**besitz** exclusive possession; ~**eigentum** exclusive (full, sole) ownership; **im ~eigentum stehend** independently (wholly) owned; ~**eigentümer** sole owner (proprietor, *US*), single proprietor *(US)*; ~**erbe** sole (universal) heir; ~**erfinder** sole inventor; ~**flug** solo flight; ~**gang** single-handed attempt; **im ~gang handeln** to go it alone, to play a lone hand; ~**handel** exclusive dealing, monopoly; ~**herrschaft** autocracy, monocracy; ~**herrscher** absolute ruler, monocrat; ~**hersteller** sole manufacturer; ~**herstellungsrecht** monopoly.

alleinig sole, exclusive;
~**er Abnehmer** sole buyer; ~**es Benutzungsrecht** sole use; ~**e Geschäftsführung** sole management; ~**es Herstellungsrecht besitzen** to have the exclusive rights of a production; ~**e Publikationsrechte** sole rights of publication; ~**e Rechnung** sole account; ~**er Tarifvertreter** exclusive bargaining agent; ~**er Testamentsvollstrecker** sole executor; ~**er Verfasser** sole author; ~**es Verkaufsrecht** sole right to sell; ~**er Vermächtnisnehmer** sole legatee; ~**e Veröffentlichungsrechte** sole rights of publication; ~**er Vertreter** sole agent, exclusive dealer *(US)*; ~**es Vorführungsrecht** exclusive film.

Allein|inhaber exclusive owner, sole owner (proprietor, *US*), single proprietor *(US)*; ~**lizenz** exclusive licence; ~**mädchen** general maid; ~**meldung** scoop, beat; ~**nutzungsrecht** exclusive right, *(Urheberrecht)* copyright; ~**pächter** sole tenant; ~**reeder** sole owner; ~**schuld** sole responsibility.

alleinstehend standing apart, isolated, *(Anzeige)* island *(US)* (solid) position, solus position *(Br.)*, *(Haus)* detached, insular, isolated, *(unverheiratet)* unmarried, single, relationless, discovert, living alone, without dependants;
für sich ~ discrete; **halb** ~ *(Anzeige)* semi-solus *(Br.)*;
~**e Anzeige** sole advertisement; ~**e Frau** single woman, feme sole.

Allein|stehender single man, bachelor; ~**steuer** single tax *(Br.)*; ~**tarifvertreter** sole bargaining agent *(Br.)*; ~**unterhalter** sole provider; ~**unternehmer** owner-manager.

alleinverantwortlich solely responsible.

Allein|verhandlungspartner für Tarifverhandlungen sole bargaining agent *(Br.)*; ~**verhandlungsrecht** exclusive negotiating right; ~**verkauf** exclusive sale, sales monopoly, franchising *(US)*; ~**verkaufsrecht** exclusive privilege (licence, sale), dealer franchise, *(Makler)* exclusive listing *(US)*; ~**verkaufsvereinbarung** exclusive sales agreement; ~**vermächtnisnehmer** universal legatee; ~**versand** exclusive distribution; ~**vertreter** sole (exclusive) agent, exclusive dealer *(US)*, *(Firma)* sole representative; ~**vertretung** sole (exclusive) agency (franchise, *US*), *(Artikel)* exclusive representation; ~**vertretung haben** to be sole agent; ~**vertretungsrecht** sole distribution rights; ~**vertretungsrecht besitzen** to have the rights of sole distribution; ~**vertretungsvertrag** exclusive agency contract, exclusive sales agreement; ~**vertrieb** exclusive sale, exclusive (sole) distribution, exclusive (sole) agency, sole right to sell, monopoly.

alleinvertriebsberechtigt sein to be sole distributor.

Allein|vertriebsberechtigter exclusive distributor; ~**vertriebsrecht** exclusive distribution franchise *(US)*; ~**vertriebsvertrag** exclusive sales agreement; ~**vorstand** sole director; ~**zeichnungsberechtigung** single signature; ~**zuständigkeit** unity of command.

Alleräußerst|es utmost, extreme limit;
im ~**en** if it comes to the pinch.

alleräußerster Preis rock-bottom price.

Allergie allergy;
~ **gegen j. haben** to be allergic to s. o.

allerhand|Geld a lot of money;
~ **loshaben** to be up to the mark.

allerhöchste Autorität supreme authority.

allerletzt ultimate;
~**e Gelegenheit** the very last chance; ~**e Neuigkeiten** stop-press news.

Allerletzter tail ender *(US)*.

allernächst, in ~**er Nähe** in close proximity; ~**e Verwandte** next of kin.

Allerneueste, das *(Mode)* the last thing;
das ~ **auf dem Gebiet des Komforts bringen** to be the last word in comfort and convenience.

aller|neueste Mode latest fashion; ~**unterst** rock-bottom.

Allerwelts|kerl jack of all trades, man of all works; ~**wort** household word.

allerwenigsten, am least of all.

alles|aussteigen everybody get out, please; ~ **inbegriffen** everything included, terms inclusive, all-in *(Br.)*; ~, **was Rang und Namen hat** all the world and his wife;
jem. ~ **bedeuten** to be all the world for s. o.; **auf** ~ **gefaßt sein** to be prepared for anything; ~ **für j. tun** to go [to] any length for s. o.

Alles|brenner multi-fuel burner; ~**könner** all-round man, smart guy, jack of all trades; ~**sparer** champion hoarder; ~**wisser** know[-it]-all.

allgemein general, overhead, omnibus, overall, common, nation-wide, universal, popular, public;
im ~**en** as a general rule, on the whole, nine times out of ten;
~ **anerkannt** generally accepted; ~ **genommen** generally speaking; ~ **üblich** universal; ~ **verbreitet** current, widespread; ~ **zugänglich sein** *(Patent)* to be in the public domain *(US)*;
~**e Abgabe** levy; ~**e Anwendung** universal application; ~**e Feststellungen treffen** to generalize; ~**e Gütergemeinschaft** community of goods, universal partnership; ~**e Havarie** general average; **von** ~**em Interesse** of general interest; ~**es Konto** general account; ~**e Meinung** general (widespread) opinion; ~**e Redensarten** generalities; ~**er Sprachgebrauch** general usage; ~**e Unkosten** overhead, oncost *(Br.)*; ~**e Unzufriedenheit** nation-wide discontent; ~**es Wahlrecht** universal suffrage; ~**e Wehrpflicht** universal conscription; ~ **gebrauchtes Wort** word in general use, household word; **auf** ~**en Wunsch** by popular request.

Allgemein|befinden general health; ~**begriff** general conception.

allgemeinbildend academic.

Allgemeinbildung general knowledge, wide culture;
gute ~ good general education.

Allgemeines general data.

allgemeingültig generally accepted, generally admitted, general, universal.

Allgemein|gültigkeit generality (general principle), universality; ~**gut** common knowledge; ~**gut sein** to be an open secret; ~**gut werden** to become the norm.

Allgemeinheit community, general public, common (ordinary) run, omnibus, commonalty, [general] public, the massess;
im Interesse der ~ for the common good;
für die ~ **arbeiten** to labo(u)r for the common good; **der** ~ **gehören** to be common property; **im Interesse der** ~ **liegen** to be in the public interest; **für die** ~ **abträglich sein** to be harmful to the community.

Allgemein|platz commonplace; ~**tarif** *(Gemeindeverband)* general rates *(Br.)*; ~**unkosten** overhead [charges], oncost *(Br.)*.

allgemeinverbindlich generally binding.

Allgemeinverbindlichkeit universal validity.

allgemeinverständlich universal, popular.

Allgemein|verständlichkeit intelligibility; ~**wissen** common knowledge; ~**wohl** general (common, public) weal, common good; ~**zustand** general condition.

Allheilmittel cure-all, heal-all, universal remedy, panacea;
~ **für alle Sorgen** plaster for all sores *(fam.)*.

Allianz alliance.

alliierte Streitkräfte allied forces.

Alliierter ally, confederate.

allmählich gradual, progessive;
~ **eine Gewohnheit annehmen** to get into a habit;
~**e Fortschritte machen** to make slow progress.

Allmende common [land, pasture], common fields;
nicht eingefriedete ~ inbound common;
unberechtigte ~**nutzung** disturbance of common; ~**zuweisung** view and delivery.

allodial udal, allodial.

Allodial|eigentum estate in fee simple; ~**gut** fee simple, udal tenure; ~**güter** court (allodial) lands *(Br.)*.

Allonge allonge, rider, *(drucktechn.)* flyleaf.

Allotria treiben to play pranks, to lark about.

Allparteien|gespräche all-party talks; ~**liste** blanket ballot; ~**regierung** all-party government.

Allphasensteuer multistage tax.

Allrad|antrieb all-wheel drive; ~**bremse** all-wheel brake.

allseitig|e Ausbildung allround training; **zur** ~**en Zufriedenheit** to the satisfaction of everybody.

All|strom AC/DC current; ~**tag** everyday life, blue Monday *(US)*; **grauer** ~**tag** monotonous routine.

alltäglich daily, everyday, household, common, commonplace, routine, copybook, trivial;
~**e Erfahrung** daily experience; **nicht** ~**e Geschichte** somewhat unusual story; ~**es Gesicht** ordinary face; ~**es Problem** bread-and-butter issue.

Alltäg|liches matter of course; ~**lichkeit** commonplace, prose.

alltags on workdays;
~ **wie feiertags** on workdays and holidays.

Alltags|beschäftigung daily routine; ~**gesicht** ordinary face; ~**gespräche** casual conversation; ~**kleid** everyday dress, undress; ~**kleidung** everyday (workday) clothes; ~**kost** ordinary fare; ~**leben** everyday life, working-day life, *(Diplomat)* diplomatic round; **monotones** ~**leben** monotonous jog-trot of life; ~**routine** everyday routine; **kleine** ~**sorgen** small worries of life; ~**welt** workaday world; ~**wort** household word.

Allüren, feierliche pontifical airs;
~ **eines Filmstars** manerism of a film star.

All|wellenempfänger all-wave receiving set, multirange receiver; ~**wettereigenschaft** all-weather capability; ~**wetterkarosserie** all-weather body; ~**zuständigkeit** general competence.

Allzweck|behörde all-purpose authority; ~**fahrzeug** all-purpose vehicle; ~**schrank** all-purpose cabinet; ~**traktor** all-duty tractor; ~**verwaltungseinheit** all-purpose unit.

Alm alpine pasture.

Almosen alms, almsgiving, charity, dole, handout *(US sl.)*;
von ~ **lebend** alms-fed;
~ **geben** to give (distribute, bestow) alms; **von** ~ **leben** to live on charity (alms); **auf** ~ **angewiesen sein** to be dependent on alms;
~ **verteilen** to deal out alms, to dispense charity (alms);
~**beitrag** contribution of alms; ~**empfänger** beneficiary, almsman, pauper *(US)*, *(pl.)* almsfolk; **zum** ~**empfänger werden** to join the club of the handouts *(US sl.)*; ~**geber** almsgiver; ~**sammlung** alms collection; ~**spende** almsgiving; ~**verteilung** dispensation of charity.

Alpdruck nightmare.

Alphabet alphabet;
~**schloß** combination (puzzle) lock.
alphabetisch alphabetical;
~ **[an]ordnen** to arrange alphabetically, to alphabetize; ~ **angeordnet sein** to be arranged in alphabetical order; ~ **geordnet sein** to go in alphabetical order;
~**er Katalog** dictionary catalog(ue); ~**e Liste** check list; **in ~er Ordnung** alphabetically; ~**e Reihenfolge** alphabetical order (sequence).
Alptraum nightmare.
Alt und Jung old and young.
alt old, aged, *(gebraucht)* secondhand;
~ **gekauft** bought secondhand;
so ~ wie Methusalem as old as the hills (Methuselah); **so ~ wie die Sintflut** as old as Adam; **so ~ wie die Welt** world-old;
~**er Bürgermeister** ex-mayor, late burgomaster; ~**e Dame** dame; **zum ~en Eisen werfen** to discard as worthless, to junk *(sl.)*; ~**e Firma** long-established firm; ~**er Fuchs** sly dog; ~**er Hase** old stager; ~**es Haus** old boy *(fig.)*, old chap *(coll.)*, old top *(sl.)*; ~**er Junge** old boy *(fam.)*; ~**e Jungfer** old maid, spinster; ~**er Käse** *(fig.)* stale news, old hat *(coll.)*; ~**e Kleider** used clothes; ~**er Knabe** old top (boy, egg) *(coll.)*; **die ~e Leier** the same old cant; **der ~e Mann** *(Bergbau)* goof, gob, waste; ~**e Möbel** secondhand furniture; **zum ~en Preis ablassen** to charge the old price; ~**er Schwede** old egg *(sl.)*; ~**e Sprachen** ancient languages; ~**er Sünder** old sinner (rascal); ~**er Trick** old dodge; ~**en Trott aufgeben** to leave the beaten track; ~**en Trott beibehalten** to travel in the same groove; **die gute ~e Zeit** the piping times of Yore; ~**er Zopf** old school tie.
Altar, mit jem. vor den ~ treten to lead a woman to the altar; **sein Leben auf dem ~ des Vaterlandes opfern** to give one's life as a sacrifice for one's country.
Altbaumiete pre-currency reform rent.
altbekannt ever-familiar.
Altbestände existing stock.
altbewährt time-tested;
~**e Freundschaft** long-standing friendship.
Altbürgermeister late burgomaster.
Alte *(Chefin)* madam;
der ~ the old-man; **häßliche ~** witch; **meine ~** my old lady; **wieder ganz der ~ sein** to be quite o. s. again.
alt|ehrwürdig time-hono(u)red; ~**eingeführt**, ~**eingesessen** long established; ~**eingesessene Familie** old family.
Alt|eisen scrap iron; ~**eisenhändler** junk dealer.
Alten|tagesstätten facilities for old people; ~**teil** farm annuity; ~**teilsvertrag** annuity contract; ~**wohnheim** home (asylum) for the aged (elderly), residential home.
Alter age, *(Dienstalter)* seniority;
bei Ihrem ~ at your time of life; **im ~ von** at the age of; **im arbeitsfähigen ~** of working age; **im besten ~** in the prime of life; **in fortgeschrittenem ~** well advanced in years; **gereiften ~s** of mellow age; **in gesetztem ~** of mature age; **im heiratsfähigen ~** of marriageable age; **in kindlichem ~** while still a child; **im schulpflichtigen ~** schoolable; **in einem schwierigen ~** *(Heranwachsender)* at an awkward age; **unbestimmten ~s** of uncertain age; **im unterscheidungsfähigen ~** at the age of discretion; **im vorgerückten ~** advanced in years, late in life; **im zarten ~** of tender age; **vom ~ gebeugt** stricken in years, time-stricken; **ehemündiges ~** age of consent; **erreichtes ~** age attained; **erwerbsfähiges ~** workable age; **erwünschtes ~** *(Anzeige)* probable age; **geschäftsfähiges ~** responsible age; **heiratsfähiges ~** marriageable age, puberty; **pensionsfähiges ~** retiring age, age of retirement; **rüstiges ~** green old age; **schulpflichtiges ~** legal (compulsory) school age; **unterscheidungsfähiges (zurechnungsfähiges) ~** age (years) of discretion; **vorgerücktes ~** advanced age, declining years; **vorgeschriebenes ~** statutory age; **vorschulpflichtiges ~** preschool age;
hohes ~ erreichen to live to a great age; **unterscheidungsfähiges ~ erreicht haben** to have reached the age of understanding; **im besten ~ sein** to be in the flower of one's age; **im militärpflichtigen ~ sein** to be of military age; **reiferen ~s sein** to be of mature age; **für sein ~ sparen (zurücklegen)** to lay aside money (to be saving) for one's old age; **im pensionsfähigen ~ stehen** to be eligible of age to retire; **im hohen ~ sterben** to die at a good old age.
älter older, elder, *(Anspruch)* prior;
~ **als Durchschnitt** overage;
~**e Fassung** earlier version.
alterfahrener Parlamentarier old parliamentarian hand.
Altern aging.
altern to age, *(Wein)* to mature.
alternativ alternative;
~**e Kosten** opportunity costs.
Alternativ|angebot alternative tender; ~**antwort** alternative reply; ~**bedingung** disjunctive term.
Alternative alternative, option, choice;
~ **im Werbeplan** advertising alternative;
keine ~ haben to have no alternative; **mit einer ~ herausrücken** to come up with an alternative.
Alternativ|entscheidung alternative decision; ~**frage** dichotomous question; ~**hypothese** *(Statistik)* alternative hypothesis; ~**kosten** opportunity costs; ~**lösung** alternative solution; ~**prognose** alternative forecast; ~**vermächtnis** alternative legacy; ~**verpflichtung** alternative obligation; ~**vorschlag** alternative proposal; ~**währung** alternative (alternate, *US*) currency.
alters, von ~ her from time out of mind.
Alters|abschreibung depreciation for age; ~**abstand** age difference; ~**angaben** age data; **falsche ~angaben machen** to state one's age falsely; ~**anzeichen** evidence of age, marks of old age; ~**aufbau der Bevölkerung** age grouping of the population.
altersbedingt senile;
~**e Abschreibung** depreciation for age.
Alters|bedingungen age contingencies; ~**beschränkungen** age restrictions; ~**beschwerden** infirmities of age; ~**bestimmung** age determination; ~**bezüge für Vorstandsmitglieder** directors' pension; ~**blödsinn**, ~**schwachsinn** senile dementia; ~**dispens** waiving of the age limit; ~**durchschnitt** average age; ~**entlastungsbetrag** [etwa] higher age allowance *(Br.)*; ~**erfordernisse** age requirements; ~**erscheinungen** concomitants of old age; ~**folge** seniority; ~**freibetrag** *(Einkommensteuer)* old-age exemption *(US)*, age allowance *(Br.)*, age tax allowance *(Br.)*; ~**freibetrag für über 65jährige** age relief *(Br.)*; ~**freibetrag für Ledige** single age allowance *(Br.)*; ~**freibetragsgrenze** old-age exemption limit *(US)*; ~**fürsorge** relief for old people, *(Betrieb)* retirement provisions; ~**genosse** contemporary, equal in age; ~**genossen sein** to be of the same age.
altersgeschwächt sein weakened by age.
Altersgliederung age distribution.
altersgrau hoary.
Altersgrenze age limit (barrier), *(Beamter)* retirement age;
über der ~ over age;
über die ~ hinaus tätig bleiben to work beyond the age limit; ~ **erreichen** to reach the retirement age, to attain (reach) the age limit; ~ **erreicht haben** to be due to retire.
Alters|gründen, aus for age reasons; ~**gruppe** age grade (group, bracket); ~**heim** old folk's home, old people's home *(Br.)*, almshouse *(Br.)*, asylum (home) for the aged, pogey, pogy *(sl.)*; **sich in ein ~heim einkaufen** to buy a place for one's old age; ~**hilfe** old-age assistance; ~**klasse** age group (bracket, class); ~**klasseneinstufung** age grouping; **anerkannter ~nachweis** *(Versicherung)* age admitted; ~**norm** age norm; ~**pension** superannuation, pension; ~**pensionierung** involuntary retirement, retirement on account of age; ~**pensionsfonds** pension fund; ~**pfennig zurücklegen** to save up for one's old age; ~**präsident** chairman by seniority; ~**präsidium** fatherhood *(Br.)*; ~**pyramide** popularity pyramid; ~**rente** retirement allowance (pension, *Br.*), old-age pension (annuity), old persons' pension, *(Grundrente)* primary benefit, retirement annuity, *(Sozialversicherung)* old-age insurance benefit *(US)*; **monatliche ~rente** monthly retirement benefit; **staatliche ~rente** state retirement pension; ~**rentner** old-age pensioner; ~**schicht** age group.
altersschwach old, infirm, decayed with age, time-stricken.
Alters|schwäche decrepit old age, senile decay, decrepitude of age; **an ~schwäche sterben** to die of decay; **wegen ~schwäche untauglich** disqualified by age; ~**sicherung** provision for old age; ~**sicherung treffen** to provide for the future; ~**sitz** old-age domicile; ~**staffelung** age scale; ~**sterblichkeit** age mortality; ~**stufe** age bracket (group); ~**tabelle** age schedule; ~**unterschied** disparity of (difference, disproportion in) age; ~**unterstützung** relief for old people (the aged), old-age assistance (benefit); ~**verfall** decrepitude; ~**vergünstigung gewähren** to make allowance for age; ~**versicherung** old-age insurance, *(Kasse)* old-age pension fund; **betriebliche ~versicherung** old-age pension fund; **~-, Hinterbliebenen- und Invalidenversicherung** old-age survivors' and disability insurance *(US)*; ~**versicherungsgesetz** Old-Age Pension Act *(Br.)*; ~**versicherungskosten** pension plan benefit costs; **staatlicher ~versicherungsplan** government pension insurance program(me).
Altersversorgung old-age (retirement, *Br.*) pension scheme, old-age (superannuation, retirement) benefit *(US)*, old-age pension *(US)*;

berufliche ~ occupational pension scheme; **betriebliche** ~ self-administrated (company) pension scheme; **staatliche** ~ state pension scheme; **zusätzliche** ~ additional pension scheme;
~ **und Hinterbliebenenversorgung für Selbständige** retirement annuity system for self-employed;
aus der staatlichen ~ ausscheiden to contract out of the state pension scheme; **staatliche ~ im Betrieb einführen** to integrate with the state pension system; **Ansprüche an die betriebliche ~ haben** to belong to a pension scheme.
Altersversorgungs|anteil, bruttobezogener earnings-related part of the state pension; ~**gesetz** Old-Age Pension *(Br.)* (Superannuation, *US*) Act; ~**kasse** provident fund, old-age pension scheme *(US)*; ~**plan** pension plan; **betrieblicher ~plan** industrial pension plan; **maßgeschneidertes ~system** tailoring of pension policy; ~**versicherung** old-age pension fund; ~**werk** pensions system (scheme), superannuation scheme, *(Künstler)* late work; ~**werk eines Verbands** society scheme.
Alters|vorrang seniority; ~**vorrecht** privilege of age; ~**vorsorge** provision for one's old age (retirement), old-age provisions; ~**vorsorge treffen** to provide for one's retirement; ~**weisheit von der Jugend verlangen** to put an old head on young shoulders; ~**zulage** age addition, superannuation (seniority) allowance (pay); ~**zusammensetzung** age distribution (classification); ~**zwangsversicherung** old-age compulsory insurance.
Altertümer relics of the past, antiquities.
Alterung *(Metallurgie)* aging.
Ältestenrat Council of Elders, rules committee *(US)*.
altgedient veteran;
~ **sein** to have seen much service.
altgewohnter Anblick familiar sight.
Alt|gold old gold; **regenerierter ~gummi** reclaimed rubber; ~**guthaben** old-age assets.
althergebracht long-standing, old.
altjüngferlich old-maidish;
~**e Person** old maid.
altklug|sein to have an old head on young shoulders;
~**es Kind** precocious child.
Altmaterial salvage, scrap, junk;
~**erfassung** salvage collection; ~**händler** junk dealer; ~**sammlung** scrap drive, salvage campaign; ~**verwertung** recovery of waste, salvage; ~**wert** breakup value.
Alt|metall scrap; ~**metallhändler** scrap merchant.
altmodisch old-fashioned, old-school, obsolete, out-of-date, outmoded, mouldy, oldhat, fusty, time-worn, passé, square;
sehr ~ sein to be a back number;
~**es Benehmen** the grand manner; ~**e Person** old timer.
Altpapier waste paper;
~**sammlung** waste-paper drive; ~**sammlung durchführen** to collect old newspapers for salvage; ~**verwertung** waste-paper salvage.
altrenommiert old-standing.
Alt|silber old silverware; ~**stadt** old parts of a town, city; ~**stadtsanierung** slum clearance, comprehensive development *(Br.)*; ~**stadtsanierungsgebiet** [etwa] comprehensive development area *(Br.)*; ~**wagen** secondhand (used) car; ~**warengeschäft** old-clothes shop; ~**warenhändler** secondhand (junk) dealer; **alles an den ~warenhändler verkaufen** to peddle out *(sl.)*; ~**warenhandlung** secondhand shop (store, *US*); ~**weibergeschwätz** tittle-tattle; ~**weibersommer** Indian summer; ~**werden** aging, growing old; **absichtliches ~werden** planned obsolescence.
Aluminium aluminium, aluminum;
~**bauweise mit Wandverkleidungselementen** curtain walling.
Alumnat boarding school.
amalgamieren to amalgamate.
Amateur amateur, dilettante;
~**aufführung** amateur theatrical; ~**eigenschaft** amateur status; ~**film** amateur film; ~**fotograf** amateur photographer; ~**fotograf sein** to make a hobby of photography; ~**funk** amateur telecommunication; ~**funker** radio amateur, ham *(coll.)*; ~**funkfrequenz** amateur band; ~**funklizenz** amateur transmitting licence; ~**meisterschaften** open championship; ~**schauspieler** ham actor; ~**sender** amateur transmitter.
ambulant ambulant, itinerant, perambulating, mobile, travel(l)ing;
j. ~ behandeln to treat s. o. as an outpatient;
~**e Behandlung** outpatient treatment; **private ~e Behandlung** private outpatient consultation; ~**es Gewerbe** itinerant trade; ~**er Gewerbebetrieb** street (door-to-door) trading, peddling, peddlery *(Br.)*; ~ **behandelter Patient** outpatient, ambulatory patient *(US)*; ~**e Verkaufseinrichtung** mobile selling unit (shop, *Br.*).
Ambulanz motor ambulance, *(Krankenhausabteilung)* outpatients *(Br.)* (ambulatory, *US*) department.
Ambulatorium health center *(US)* (centre, *Br.*).
Amelioration improvement, betterment;
~**en vornehmen** to effect improvements.
Meliorationsfähigkeit capability of being improved.
Amerika, in ~ hergestellt American-made.
Amerikaner, gebürtiger natural (native) born American citizen, American national by birth; **naturalisierter ~** naturalized (hyphenated) American.
amerikanisch American, Yankee;
~**e Buchführung** columnar (tabular) method of bookkeeping.
amerikanisieren to americanize, to yankeefy.
Amerikanisierung americanization.
Amerikanismus americanism.
Amme wet nurse.
Ammenmärchen old wives' (nursery, fairy) tale, cock-and-bull story, pure invention.
Amnestie amnesty, act of grace, general pardon, *(für Minister)* bill of amnesty;
~ **beschließen** to vote an amnesty; ~ **erlassen** to issue a general pardon (amnesty); **unter eine ~ fallen** to be covered by an amnesty;
~**beschluß** *(für Minister)* bill of indemnity; ~**gesetz** act of indemnity; ~**vorlage** bill of oblivion.
amnestieren to amnesty, to grant amnesty, to pardon.
Amok amok, amuck;
~ **laufen** to run amuck, to go berserk (juramentado, *US*).
Amok|laufen running amok (amuck); ~**läufer** berserker.
Amortisation amortization, redemption, *(durch Auslosung)* redemption by drawing.
Amortisations|anleihe amortization (amortized, redemption, instalment, *US*) loan, instalment bonds *(US)*; ~**aufwand** redemption expenditure; ~**bedingungen** terms of redemption; ~**darlehen** amortized loan; ~**dauer** period of redemption; ~**fonds** sinking (amortization, redemption) fund; ~**fonds zweckentfremden** to raid the sinking fund; ~**fondsreserve** sinking-fund reserve; ~**hypothek** instalment (amortization) mortgage; ~**kasse** sinking fund, redemption office; ~**konto** redemption account; ~**methode** amortization method; ~**plan** redemption table (plan), scheme of redemption (repayment), amortization schedule; ~**prämie** redemption premium; ~**quote**, ~**rate** redemption rate, amortization quota, amortization instalment; ~**rücklagen** sinking-fund reserves; ~**satz** redemption rate, instalment; ~**schein** bill of amortization, redemption voucher; ~**schuld** redeemable bonds; ~**tabelle** redemption table; ~**wert** redemption value; ~**zahlung** instalment, redemption (sinking-fund) payment.
amortisierbar amortizable, redeemable.
amortisieren to amortize, to pay amortization, to redeem, *(bezahlen)* to liquidate, to pay back (off).
amortisiert redeemed.
Amortisierung amortization, redemption.
Ampel traffic signal (light), *(Blumenvase)* hanging flowerpot.
Amperestunde ampere hour.
Amphibien|fahrzeug amphibious vehicle, duck; ~**flugzeug** amphibian; ~**panzer** amphibious tank; **kleiner ~wagen** jeep *(US)*.
amphibisch amphibious;
~**e Operationen** amphibian (combined) operations; ~**e Truppen** landing force (party).
Ampulle ampul, ampoule *(Br.)*.
Amputation amputation.
amputieren to amputate.
Amputierter amputeé, limbless *(US)*.
Amt *(Amtspflicht)* duty, public function, *(Anstellung)* appointment, *(Aufgabe)* business, charge, function, part, task, *(Aufgabenbereich)* province, *(Auftrag)* commission, *(Behörde)* magistracy, board, agency *(US)*, bureau, department, office, *(Beschäftigung)* employment, *(Posten)* place, position, post, station, situation, *(Telefon)* exchange, operator, central *(US)*;
im ~ [befindlich] in office (power), in the saddle; **in Ausübung seines ~es** while an officer; **kraft seines ~es** by virtue of his office; **nicht mehr im ~** out; **ohne ~** on the shelf; **von ~s wegen** officially, ex officio, in ordinary, per curiam;
akademisches ~ academic position; **Auswärtiges ~** Foreign Office *(Br.)*, State Department *(US)*; **bekleidetes ~** office held; **besoldetes ~** salaried (paid, lucrative) office; **einträgliches ~** office of profit, sinecure; **hohes ~** high position; **lebenslängliches ~** office for life; **öffentliches ~** government office; **staatliches ~** public appointment; **Statistisches ~** Statistical Bureau, Bureau of the Census *(US)*; **auf zwei Jahre verliehenes ~** office tenable for two years;

~ **für Denkmalschutz** Ancient Monuments Directorate *(Br.)*; ~ **des Doyen** deanship; ~ **für Internationale Entwicklung** Agency for International Development (AID); ~ **eines Gesandten** ministry; ~ **eines Konsuls** consulship; ~ **auf Lebenszeit** life tenure; ~ **eines Liquidators** liquidatorship; ~ **eines Rechnungsführers** accountantship; ~ **eines Revisors** auditorship; ~ **des Sprechers** speakership; ~ **eines Staatsbeamten** civil service; ~ **des Steuereinnehmers** receivership; ~ **für Technische Hilfe** *(UNO)* Technical Assistance Board; ~ **eines Treuhänders** trusteeship; ~ **des Vorsitzenden** office of a chairman; ~ **für Wetterdienst** meteorological office; ~ **für internationale Zusammenarbeit** International Cooperation Administration (ICA) *(US)*; **sein ~ abgeben** to relinquish an office, to give up one's appointment; **Übernahme eines ~es ablehnen** to decline an appointment; **j. im ~ ablösen** to supersede s. o.; ~ **nicht annehmen** to refuse an office; ~ **anrufen** *(tel.)* to call the exchange; ~ **antreten** to enter upon (accede, succeed to) an office; ~ **aufgeben** to relinquish (resign, vacate) office; ~ **ausfüllen** to serve in an office; ~ **zur Zufriedenheit ausfüllen** to fill an office satisfactorily; **aus dem ~ ausscheiden** to vacate (leave, cease to hold an) office; ~ **ausschlagen** to disclaim an office; ~ **ausüben** to exercise an office, to execute an office, to perform one's functions; **sein ~ behalten** to continue in (retain one's) office; **j. mit einem ~ bekleiden** to invest s. o. with an office; **öffentliches ~ bekleiden** to hold (occupy) a public office (position); ~ **des Schatzmeisters bekleiden** to fill the office of a treasurer; **unfähig sein, ein öffentliches ~ zu bekleiden** to be incapable of holding an office; **j. in seinem ~ belassen** to retain (maintain) s. o. in his office; **sich um ein ~ bemühen** to figure for office *(coll.)*; **j. in ein ~ berufen** to appoint s. o. to an office; **j. wieder in ein ~ berufen** to recall s. o. to an office; **sich um ein ~ bewerben** to run for an office, to apply for a post; **um Entlassung aus dem ~ bitten** to hand in one's resignation; **im ~ bleiben** to continue (remain) in office; **lange im ~ bleiben** to have a long run; **über die festgelegte Zeit im ~ bleiben** to hold over; **j. in ein ~ einführen** to establish (inaugurate) s. o. in an office; **j. in ein ~ einschwören** to swear s. o. in; **j. in ein ~ einsetzen** to institute (establish) s. o. in an office; **ins Auswärtige ~ eintreten** to enter the diplomatic service; **aus dem ~ entfernen** to remove from office, to relieve of his post, to supersede; **des ~es entheben** to depose from office; **j. seines ~es vorläufig entheben** to suspend s. o. from his office; **j. seines ~es entkleiden** to strip s. o. of his office; **j. aus einem ~ entlassen** to relieve s. o. of his office; **eines ~es entsetzen** to depose from (strip of) office, to oust (eject) from office; **zu einem ~ ernennen** to commission, to appoint; **von ~s wegen handeln** to act ex officio; ~ **innehaben** to fill a post, to hold (keep, bear) an office; ~ **auf Bewährung innehaben** to be in office on good behavio(u)r; ~ **zeitweilig innehaben** to be in charge of an office pro tempore; **sich an sein ~ klammern** to cling on to office; **sich in einem ~ halten können** to survive in an office; ~ **leiten** to run an office; **öffentliches ~ in gewinnsüchtiger Weise mißbrauchen** to job; **jem. im ~ nachfolgen** to succeed to s. one's office; **sein ~ niederlegen** to demit (quit, resign) one's office, to vacate office, to give up one's appointment, to resign the seals, *(Minister)* to step down, to leave one's office, *(in Pension gehen)* to retire; **aus dem ~ scheiden** to resign (leave) office; **im ~e sein** to be in office; **nicht jds. ~es sein** not to pertain to s. one's office; **nicht [mehr] im ~ sein** to be out; **mit einem ~ verbunden sein** *(Gehalt)* to go with an office; **in ~ und Würden sein** to be in an established position; **an einer Sitzung von ~s wegen teilnehmen** to be present at a meeting ex officio; **sein ~ einem neuen Vormund übergeben** to resign a ward to a new guardian; ~ **übernehmen** to assume (undertake) an office; **jem. ein ~ übertragen** to receive s. o. into a charge, to commission s. o.; **in seinem ~ verbleiben** to continue in one's (remain in) office; **aus dem ~ verdrängen** to ease out (oust from) of office; **jem. aufgrund seiner Beziehungen zu einem ~ verhelfen** to jockey s. o. into office; **ein ~ versehen** to officiate, to administer an office, to perform the duties of one's office; **aus dem ~ vertreiben** to boot out of office; ~ **verwalten** to execute an office, to perform one's functions; **j. für ein ~ vorschlagen** to name s. o. to an office; **einem ~ vorstehen** to be in charge of an office; **für ein ~ wählen** to elect to an office; **seines ~es walten** to officiate, to perform one's functions, to discharge the duties of one's office; **seines ~es entkleidet werden** to be shorn of one's post; **aus dem ~ entlassen werden** to be dismissed from one's post; **von ~s wegen tätig werden** to act ex officio; **für ein ~ vorgeschlagen werden** to be preferred to an office; **bei einem ~ vorstellig werden** to call at an office; **von einem ~ zurücktreten** to divest o. s. of (resign, lay down, vacate) office.

Ämter, nicht gleichzeitig zu bekleidende incompatible offices; **städtische ~** municipal offices; ~ **für siegreiche Parteiangehörige** jobs for the boys; **mehrere ~ auf sich vereinigen** to hold a plurality of offices; **~handel** office hunting, placemongering; **~häufung** plurality; **~jagd** place hunting; **~kauf** purchase of office, trade *(US)*, maladministration of justice; **~korruption** official corruption; **~patronage** patronage *(US)*; **~tausch** exchange of posts; **~übermut** insolence of offices, plurality; **~vereinigung** combination of offices, plurality; **~verkauf** selling public offices; **~verteiler** spoilsmonger *(US)*; **~verteilung** spoils system *(US)*.

amtieren to be in charge, to officiate, to act, to hold (be in) an office, to function, to serve; **als Richter ~** to discharge judicial functions, to sit as judge; **als Sekretär ~** to act as secretary; **stellvertretend ~** to act as deputy.

amtierend officiating; **~er Präsident** acting president; **~er Richter** sitting judge (magistrate).

amtlich official, magisterial, officiary, ministerial, functional, authorized, authoritative; **nicht ~** nonofficial, unofficial, in an unofficial capacity, inofficial, private; ~ **bescheinigt** signed on authority, certified; ~ **notiert** *(Börse)* officially quoted (listed, *US*); ~ **zugelassen** chartered, certified, licensed; ~ **ankündigen** to announce publicly; ~ **beglaubigen** to legalize; ~ **berichten** to return; ~ **genehmigen** to license; ~ **registrieren** to make an official entry, to enter into an official list; ~ **nicht notiert sein** *(Börse)* not to be quoted (listed, *US*) on the exchange; ~ **notiert werden** to be officially quoted, to be listed on the stock exchange *(US)*; ~ **tätig werden** to act in one's official capacity; ~ **zulassen** to license, to authorize; **sich widerrechtlich ~e Befugnisse anmaßen** to usurp authority; **~e Beglaubigung** legalization, certification, exemplification; **~e Bekanntmachung** official announcement (notice, publication); **~er Bericht** official report; **~e Bescheinigung** governmental authorization, certificate; **~e Darstellung** official version; **~es Dementi** official denial; **in ~er Eigenschaft** in one's official capacity, ex officio; **in ~er Eigenschaft tätig werden** to act in virtue of one's office; **~e Erklärung** official statement; **~er Erlaß** decree; **~e Ermittlungen** official inquiry; **~e Funktion** official capacity; **~e Gebühren** official fees; **~e Genehmigung** official authorization; **~e Hinterlegungsstelle** legal custodian; **~er Konkursverwalter** official receiver; **~e Kreise** government (official) circles; **~er Kurs** official quotation; **~e Mitteilung** bulletin, communiqué; **~e Notierung** *(Börse)* official quotation; **~es Organ** official organ; **mit ~en Papieren ausstatten** to document; **~e Quelle** official source; **aus ~en Quellen** from official quarters; **~er Reiseführer** official guide; **~es Schreiben** official letter; **von ~en Stellen** from official quarters; **~e Untersuchung** official inquiry; **~e Verlautbarung** official announcement; **~e Veröffentlichung** public document; **~es Wahlergebnis** election results (returns); **~er Wechselkurs** official exchange rate; **~e Ziffern** official figures.

amtlicherseits officially; ~ **Beachtung finden** to receive official attention.

Amtmann chief clerk, magistrate *(US)*.

Amts|alter length of service, seniority; **~anklage erheben** to impeach a public officer; **~anmaßung** usurpation of office, assumption of authority, colo(u)r of office; **~anmaßung begehen** to falsely represent o. s. as a person holding office under Her Majesty *(Br.)*; **~antritt** entry upon office, entering office, assumption of (accession to) office, ingoing, *(US, Präsident)* inauguration; **beim ~antritt** upon entering into office; **vor dem ~antritt** before taking office; **~antrittsurkunde** deed of assumption; **~anwalt** district attorney *(US)*, official solicitor *(Br.)*; **~anwärter** candidate for an office; **~arzt** medical officer, health officer *(US)*.

amtsärztliche Bescheinigung medical certificate.

Amts|ausübung conduct of business; **~befugnis** authority; **seine ~befugnisse überschreiten** to exceed one's competence; **~bereich** officialty, field, range, province, incumbency; **~bescheid** official note; **~betrieb** official routine; **~bewerber** candidate; **~bezeichnung** official title; **~bezirk** administrative district, bailiewick *(US)*, magistracy; **~blatt** journal, register *(US)*, Gazette *(Br.)*; **~blatt der Europäischen Gemeinschaften** Official Gazette of the European Communities; **im ~blatt bekanntmachen** to gazette; **~bote** official messenger, beadle, usher, marshal *(US)*; **~bürgermeister** city *(US)* (town) manager; **~bürgermeistersystem** city *(US)* (commission) manager plan; **~bürgschaft** fidelity guarantee; **~charakter** professional (official) character; ~**dauer** duration of appointment, tenure (term, period, run) in office, terms *(US)*, *(Minister)* ministry, administration *(US)*, *(Präsident)* presidency; ~**delikt** misdemeano(u)r (misconduct, malfeasance) in office (by a public officer, *US*); **nach ~deutsch riechen** *(Brief)* to smack of officiousness; ~**diener** beadle, usher, marshal *(US)*; ~**eid** oath of office *(US)*, official oath *(Br.)*, affirmation; ~**eid ablegen** to be sworn in; **jem. den ~eid abnehmen** to swear s. o. in; ~**einführung** inauguration, initiation into office; ~**einkünfte** emoluments; ~**einsetzung** promotion to an office, inauguration, installation, instalment, investiture; ~**enthebung** dismissal from a post, deprivation of (removal from) office, deposition, ejection, deprivation of benefice *(Br.)*; **vorläufige ~enthebung** suspension; **willkürliche ~enthebung** removal without proper cause; ~**entlassung** mittimus; ~**entsetzung** dismissal from a post, ejection from an office; ~**freizeichen** dial tone; ~**führung** tenure (term, period, run) in office, conduct in office, conduct of business; **schlechte ~führung** official misconduct; ~**gebäude** office; ~**gebühren** official fees; ~**geheimnis** official secrecy; ~**genosse** adjunct, colleague; ~**gericht** county *(Br.)* (district, petty sessional, municipal, magistrate) court, sheriff's court *(Scot.)*, *(London)* [etwa] metropolitan court; ~**gerichtsbezirk** magisterial precinct *(US)*; ~**gerichtsrat** [etwa] Solicitor *(US)*; ~**geschäfte** official functions (business); **seine ~geschäfte aufnehmen** to take up one's duties; ~**gewalt** authority, official power, rod; ~**gewand** gown; ~**haftung** official responsibility; ~**handlung** official act (function); **konsularische ~handlungen** consular transactions; ~**handlung vornehmen** to officiate; ~**hilfe** administrative aid; ~**inhaber** office bearer, occupant of an office, officeholder *(US)*; **faktischer ~inhaber** officer de facto; **nomineller ~inhaber** titular; ~**kasse** cashier's office; ~**kette** chain of office; ~**kleid** garb; ~**kleidung** habit, professional dress; **richterliche ~kleidung** court dress; ~**laufbahn** official career; ~**leiter** chief officer, functionary; ~**leitung** *(tel.)* exchange line; ~**lokal** office; ~**miene aufsetzen** to look as solemn as a judge; ~**mißbrauch** malpractice, malversation, abuse of authority, jobbery; **wegen ~mißbrauchs anklagen** to impeach; ~**mißbrauch treiben** to job.

amtsmüde weary of office.

Amts|nachfolge succession to an office; ~**nachfolger** successor to an office; ~**namenwähler** *(tel.)* code switch; ~**niederlegung** vacating an (vacation of) office, retirement, resignation, abdication; ~**ort** official residence; ~**paß** official passport; ~**periode** tenure of office, magistrateship, *(Richter)* judicature; **nach Beendigung seiner ~periode** on completion of his tour of duty; ~**periode des Präsidenten** presidential term; **neue ~periode anfangen** to enter upon another term of office; **für eine dritte ~periode wiederwählen** to elect to a third term; ~**person** office bearer, officeholder *(US)*; **für eine Übergangsperiode eingesetzte ~person** interim officer.

Amtspflicht function, official duty;
strenge ~ strictly ministerial duty;
seinen ~en nachkommen to perform the duties of one's office; **seine ~en verletzen** to prevaricate; **seine ~en vernachlässigen** to be remiss in the performance of one's duties;
~**verletzung** breach of duty, prevarication, official misconduct.

Amts|raum office; ~**räume des Gerichts** offices of a court; ~**richter** district judge, justice of the peace *(US)*; ~**robe** official robe; ~**sache** official business; ~**schimmel** red tape (tapism); **wiehernder ~schimmel** red-tape curtain; ~**schimmel reiten** to be fond of red tape; ~**schreiben** official letter; **als ~schreiben abgefaßt sein** to be written in an official style; ~**schreiber** clerk; ~**siegel** official seal; ~**sitz** seat, location, *(Diplomat)* official residence; ~**sprache** official language, *(ironisch)* officialese, gobbledygook *(US sl.)*, civil service jargon *(Br.)*; ~**stab** *(parl.)* mace; ~**stab des Gerichtsvollziehers** wand of peace *(Scot.)*; ~**stelle** public office, agency; ~**stelleninhaber** office bearer, officeholder *(US)*; **ausscheidender ~stelleninhaber** outgoing officeholder *(US)*; ~**stil** official manner (style); **schwülstiger ~stil** gobbledygook *(US sl.)*; ~**stube** office; ~**stunden** office (official, business) hours; ~**stunden angleichen** to correlate office hours; ~**tag** *(Richter)* court day; ~**tätigkeit** office, function, service; ~**tracht** official uniform (attire), livery, *(Richter)* robe, toga, vestment, *(Universität)* gown; ~**träger** office bearer, officeholder *(US)*, functionary; ~**übernahme** assumption of office; **bei ~übernahme** on accepting office; ~**überschreitung** misuse of authority.

amts|üblich official; ~**unfähig** incapable of holding office.

Amts|unterschlagung malversation, depeculation, positive misprision, extortion in office; ~**vergehen** misfeasance, misdemeano(u)r (malfeasance) in office; ~**verletzung** misconduct in office; ~**verlust** loss (forfeiture) of office; ~**vermittlung** *(Telefon)* telephone exchange; ~**verrichtung** function, office, service; ~**verschwiegenheit** official secrecy; **zur ~verschwiegenheit verpflichtet sein** to be sworn to secrecy; ~**verwaltung** officiation; ~**vorgänger** predecessor; ~**vormund** guardian by appointment of the High Court of Justice, official guardian, committee *(US)*, conservator *(US)*; ~**walter** functionary; **turnusmäßiger ~wechsel** rotation in office; **auf dem ~weg** through [official] channels; ~**weg einhalten** to act through the proper channels; ~**weisheit** official wisdom; ~**wohnung** residency; ~**zeichen** *(tel.)* dial tone; ~**zeit** run, tenure in (term of) office; **gesetzlich vorgesehene ~zeit** statutory term; **in seiner ~zeit** during his term of office; ~**zeit des Präsidenten** presidential term *(US)*; ~**zeit verlängern** to extend the term of office; ~**zimmer** office, bureau, *(US Präsident)* oval room *(US)*.

amüsant witty, amusing, entertaining;
ganz ~ not bad fun *(coll.)*.

Amüsement recreation, diversion, pleasure.

amüsieren, sich glänzend (köstlich, königlich) to have the time of one's life, to enjoy o. s. to the full; **sich längst nicht so gut wie alle anderen ~** not to have a quarter the pleasure as s. o. else; **sich herzlich ~** to have grand time; **sich richtig ~** to amuse o. s., to take one's pleasure, to have a good (high old) time, to be in high spirits, to kick up one's heels *(US sl.)*.

Amüsierlokal dive *(sl.)*.

amüsiert haben, sich köstlich to have had one's whack of pleasure.

Anachronismus anachronism;
sich eines ~ schuldig machen to perpetrate an anachronism.

analog analogous, similar;
~**en Fall zitieren** to quote a case in point.

Analogie analogy;
in ~ behandeln to treat analogously; **aus der ~ schließen** to argue from analogy;
~**schluß** reasoning by analogy, argument from example.

Analogrechner analogue computer.

Analphabet analphabetic, illiterate person, marksman.

analphabetisch illiterate, unlettered.

Analphabetismus illiteracy.

Analyse analysis, breakdown *(US)*, *(chem.)* test;
genaue ~ dissection; **nachträgliche ~** post-check; **qualitative ~** qualitative analysis;
~ der Bilanzverhältniszahlen ratio analysis; **~ abweichender Fälle** deviant case analysis; **~ der Glaubwürdigkeit** credibility test; **~ der Kostenvorteile** cost-benefit analysis; **~ des Vorstands** directorate analysis;
~ einer Angelegenheit fertigen to make a precis of an affair; **~ vornehmen** to analyse, to break down *(US)*.

analysieren to analyse, to break down *(US)*;
genau ~ to dissect.

Analytiker analyst.

Anarchie anarchy.

Anarchismus anarchism.

Anarchist anarchist, Red.

anarchistisch *(gesetzlos)* anarchistic, red.

anbahnen to open, to pave the way, to initiate, to prepare the ground;
sich ~ to be under way; **neue Geschäftsverbindungen ~** to open new business connections; **neue Handelsbeziehungen ~** to open up new trade channels.

anbahnende Preiserhöhungen, sich rise in prices under way.

Anbahnung initiation;
~ eines Geschäfts introduction of business.

anbandeln, mit jem. to get off with s. o.

Anbau side building, lean-to, annex, enlargement, extension, addition *(US)*, *(eines Flügels)* wing, *(Landwirtschaft)* growing, cultivation, culture, tillage, *(Nebengebäude)* outbuilding;
erkerartiger ~ turret;
~**beschränkungen** reduction in acreage, acreage restrictions; ~**beschränkungen erlassen** to restrict cultivation.

anbauen to enlarge (extend) one's premises, *(Landwirtschaft)* to cultivate, to till, to grow;
Flügel ~ to throw out a wing to a house; **Garage ~** to add a garage to the house; **an ein Gebäude ~** to add to a building; **Getreide ~** to grow (cultivate) cereals; **Hotelflügel ~** to build a new wing to a hotel.

anbaufähig arable, tillable, cultivable;
nicht ~ irreclaimable.

Anbau|fläche acreage, cultivable area, arable land; **zugewiesene ~fläche** acreage allotment; ~**fläche verringern** to reduce acreage; ~**flächenbeschränkungen** reduction in acreage; ~**ge-**

biet cultivated area, area under cultivation; **gesamtes ~gebiet** total area of land farmed; **~methoden** cultivation methods; **~möbel** unit (sectional) furniture; **~schrank** cupboard unit.
Anbauten annex, outbuildings, new wing.
anbei herewith, hereby, enclosed, attached.
anbequemen, sich den Verhältnissen to accommodate o. s. to circumstances.
anberaumen to appoint, to assign, to fix, to set, to call to schedule *(US)*;
Sitzung ~ to fix a meeting; **Verhandlungstermin** ~ to assign a day for a hearing in court.
Anberaumung setting, appointment;
ohne ~ eines neuen Termins sine die;
~ eines Verhandlungstermines assigning a day for a hearing in court.
Anbetracht, in considering, in consideration, whereas, aware of.
anbetrifft, was as regards.
anbetteln, j. to pester s. o. with requests.
Anbetung des Reichtums worship of wealth.
anbezahlen to pay on account, to make a first instalment (down-payment), to deposit *(US)*.
Anbiederer backslapper *(US sl.)*.
anbiedern, sich to backslap; **sich bei jem.** ~ to scrape an acquaintance with s. o., to pal up (hobnob) with s. o.
Anbiederung intrusion, ingratiation.
Anbiederungsversuch attempted ingratiation.
Anbieten der Lieferung tender of delivery.
anbieten to proffer, to offer;
sich ~ to offer one's services; **Beweis** ~ to tender an avernment in law, to advance proof; **jem. seine Dienste** ~ to offer (tender) one's services to s. o.; **fest** ~ to offer firm; **Gehalt** ~ to offer a salary; **zum Kauf** ~ to offer for sale, to pitch; **Lieferung** ~ to tender delivery; **Mietschuld zu begleichen** ~ to tender the amount of rent; **seinen Rücktritt** ~ to tender one's resignation; **sich aus freien Stücken** ~ to volunteer; **Waren 15% unter Preis** ~ to offer goods at 15 per cent off the regular price; **als Zahlungsmittel** ~ to tender.
Anbiet[end]er offerer, offeror.
anbinden, j. kurz to keep a tight hold on s. o.
Anblick sight;
beim ersten ~ at first sight, on the first impulse;
gewohnter ~ familiar sight; **großartiger** ~ grand show, majestic spectacle;
jämmerlichen ~ bieten to present a lamentable appearance.
Anbord | nahme der Boote hoisting in of the boats; **~verbringung** placing on board.
anbrechen, Vorräte to break into provisions.
anbrennen to catch fire, to ignite, *(Küche)* to burn.
anbringen to put up, to fasten, to affix, *(verkaufen)* to sell, to dispose, to knock off;
Änderungen ~ to make alterations; **Bemerkung** ~ to have one's say; **Beschwerde** ~ to lodge a complaint; **Kritik** ~ to criticize; **Plakat** ~ to stick a bill, to post a placard; **Siegel** ~ to affix seals to.
Anbringungskosten charge for fixing.
Anbruch *(Grube)* opening;
bei ~ des Tages at daybreak;
~ einer neuen Zeit dawn of a new era.
andauern to last, to go on, to continue.
andauernd continuous, constant, persistent;
~e Bemühungen sustained efforts; **~e Konjunktur** continuing boom; **~e Nachfrage** persistent demand.
Andenken memory, remembrance, reminder, *(Geschenk)* token, souvenir, keepsake;
j. in gutem ~ bewahren to have a pleasant memory of s. o.; **jds. ~ in Ehren halten** to treasure s. one's memory; **bei jem. noch in frischem ~ sein** to be still fresh in s. one's mind; **bei jem. in gutem ~ stehen** to stand high in s. one's esteem;
~laden gift (souvenir) shop.
Anderdepot trust deposit.
anderes, etw. ganz ~ sein to be a different kettle of fish.
Anderkonto client's account *(Br.)*, *(Anwalt)* solicitor's [trust] account *(Br.)*, *(Treuhänder)* trust account;
~ eines Testamentsvollstreckers executorship account;
~ verwalten to hold a client's money *(Br.)*.
ändern to change, to alter, *(anpassen)* to adapt, *(verbessern)* to correct, to rectify;
sich ~ to vary, *(Wetter)* to change, to break; **Eintragung** ~ to rectify an entry; **Entscheid** ~ to revise a decision; **sich von Grund auf** ~ to undergo a radical change; **Haushaltsvoranschlag** ~ to amend an appropriation bill; **Kurs** ~ to alter the course; **seine Meinung** ~ to change one's opinion, to veer; **seine Meinung grundsätzlich** ~ to reverse o. s.; **nachträglich** ~ *(Wechsel)* to alter materially; **Plan** ~ to alter (amend) a plan; **sich plötzlich** ~ to break; **seine Politik von Grund auf** ~ to reverse one's policy; **Satzung** ~ to alter the conditions contained in the memorandum; **seinen Standpunkt** ~ to shift one's ground; **Tagesordnung** ~ to vary the order of the day; **sein Testament** ~ to alter one's will; **seinen Ton** ~ to change one's tune; **sich zu seinem Vorteil** ~ to change for the better.
anders different, otherwise, in another way;
~artig diverse; **~denkend** dissenting, dissentient.
Andersdenkender dissenter, dissentient.
Änderung alteration, change, modification;
gegen jede ~ eingestellt standpat;
~en vorbehalten subject to alteration (revision, modification); **geringfügige** ~ slight modification; **grundlegende** ~ basic change; **rechtserhebliche** ~ material alteration; **wesentliche** ~ material alteration;
~ der Abschreibungsrichtlinien changes in depreciation, depreciation changes; **~ der Adresse** change of address; **~ der Aktienstückelung** conversion of stocks *(US)*; **~ der Anzeigensätze** change in rates; **~en in der Bestandsbewertung** inventory valuation changes; **~ des Besteuerungssystems** tax switch; **~ der Bezugsbedingungen** alteration of terms of supply; **vorgenommene ~en in der Buchführung** accounting changes; **~ des Flächennutzungsplans** rezoning *(US)*, zoning variations *(US)*, zone change *(US)*; **~ des Gerichtsstandes** change of venue; **~ des Gesellschaftszwecks** alteration of objects clause; **~ des Größenverhältnisses** scale-up; **~ des Grundkapitals** alteration of capital; **~ einer Klage** departure of an action at law; **~ der Konzessionsbedingungen** amendment of charter; **~ der Lagerhaltung** inventory changes; **~ seiner Lebensgewohnheiten** break in one's way of living; **~ des Lohntarifs** change in salary scales; **unberechtigte ~ eines Passes** alteration of a passport; **~ durch das Plenum** floor amendment *(US)*; **~ der Politik** political switch; **angebrachte ~en der Politik** expedient change of policy; **~ des Produktionsverfahrens** change in process; **~ des Sachvortrages** trial amendment; **~ der Satzung** modification (alteration) of the articles of association; **~ des Satzungszweckes** alteration of objects clause; **~ der Steuersätze** changes in rates of taxes; **~ der Tagesordnung** variation of the order [of business], amendment of the agenda; **~ der Verfassung** change in the constitution, constitutional amendment; **~ in der Verteilung des Aktienkapitals** reorganization of share capital *(Br.)* (capital stock, *US*); **~ eines Vertrages** alteration of a contract; **~ der Vertragsbedingungen** modification of the terms of a contract; **~ im Vorstand** changes in the direction of a firm; **~ eines Wechselbetrages** alteration of amount; **~en des Wortlauts** verbal changes; **~ der Zinskonditionen** market change in interest rates;
~ erfahren to undergo a change; **einige ~en vornehmen** to make some modifications.
Änderungs | anmeldung memorandum of alteration; **~antrag** amendment; **über einen ~antrag abstimmen** to vote on an amendment; **~anzeige** notification of change; **~buchung** offsetting entry.
änderungsfähig changeable, modifiable, alterable, *(Gesetz)* amendable.
Änderungs | gesetz amendment; **~gesetzgebung** legislation by reference; **~protokoll** protocol of amendment; **~schein** *(Patentgesetz)* certificate of correction; **~tätigkeit** subversive activity; **~vorschlag** proposed amendment.
anderweitig beschäftigt otherwise occupied.
andeuten to indicate, to hint, to intimate, to allude;
unheilvolle Entwicklungen ~ to allude to certain sinister developments; **etw. flüchtig** ~ to make a passing allusion; **jem. etw.** ~ to give s. o. to understand; **seine Pläne kurz** ~ to indicate one's plans; **vorsichtig** ~ to imply cautiously; **Wechsel in der Regierungspolitik** ~ to indicate a change in government policy; **seine Zustimmung zu einem Plan** ~ to intimate one's approval of a plan.
andeutend indicative, suggestive.
Andeutung hint, nudge, indication, intimation, inkling, allusion, wrinkle *(coll.)*;
leise ~ breath; **versteckte** ~ insinuation;
~ eines Lächelns ghost (shadow) of a smile; **~ eines Skandals** breath of a scandal;
~ über seine Absichten fallen lassen to let fall a hint of one's intentions; **~ machen** to indicate, to [drop a] hint; **diskrete ~ über j. machen** to have a quiet dig at s. o., to drop a slight hint; **voller ~en stecken** *(speech)* to be full of allusions.

andeutungsweise zu verstehen geben to hint that.
andienen to tender, to proffer, to deliver, *(Geld)* to provide; **einer Bank Devisenüberschüsse** ~ to pay foreign exchange surpluses into a bank; **Miete** ~ to tender the amount of rent due.
Andienung tender, *(Lieferung)* delivery;
~ **der fälligen Miete** tender of rent due.
andienungspflichtig *(Devisen)* subject to market regulations.
Andrang throng, run, congestion, rush, *(Verkehr)* rush hours, heavy traffic;
~ **auf eine Bank** run on a bank; ~ **auf das Erfrischungszelt** rush to the refreshment tent; ~ **an der Kasse** crush at the box office.
andrehen *(Licht, Radio)* to turn on;
jem. etw. ~ to fob off (foist, unload, palm) s. th. on s. o., to put s. th. off upon s. o.; **als Markenartikel** ~ to palm off as a genuine article.
androhen to threaten;
jem. gerichtliche Schritte ~ to threaten s. o. with legal proceedings.
Androhung | der Beugestrafe commission of rebellion; ~ **der Entlassung** threat of dismissal; **unter** ~ **der Todesstrafe** under pain of death.
Andruck *(Abzug)* pull, proof, preprint, *(Druckbeginn)* going to press;
endgültiger ~ final pull.
andrucken to pull a proof, to point, to print.
anecken, überall to put one's foot into it; **bei jem.** ~ to rub s. o. the wrong way.
aneignen, sich to acquire, to appropriate, to adopt, to pouch, to corral, to collar *(coll.)*; **etw.** ~ to possess o. s. of a thing; **sich eine Fremdsprache** ~ to acquire a foreign language; **sich Geld** ~ to embezzle funds, to misappropriate (convert) money; **sich einen Namen** ~ to adopt a name; **sich rechtswidrig** ~ to appropriate unlawfully, to misappropriate, to arrogate property, to pocket; **sich rücksichtslos** ~ to grab; **sich eine Sprache vollständig** ~ to master a language; **sich den Thron** ~ to usurp the throne.
Aneignung appropriation, acquisition, annexation, occupation; **gewaltsame** ~ seizure, usurpation; **rechtswidrige** ~ conversion, misappropriation, embezzlement, trover;
~ **für eigene Zwecke** constructive taking.
aneinander | anschließen to link together; **~fügen** to tack together; **sich** ~ **gewöhnen** to get used to one (each) another.
aneinandergeraten to clash, to conflict, to come to blows.
aneinandergrenzen to touch each other, to adjoin, to be adjacent.
aneinandergrenzend adjacent, adjoining.
Anekdote anecdote.
Anekdotenerzähler anecdotist.
Anekdotenschatz hoard (mine) of anecdotes;
über einen unerschöpflichen ~ **verfügen** to have a perfect fund of anecdotes.
anempfehlen to recommend.
Anempfehlung recommendation.
Anerbieten offer, offering, tender, advance;
~ **von Diensten** tender of services.
anerkannt admitted, accepted, recognized, acknowledged; **allgemein** ~ generally accepted; **amtlich** ~ officially recognized, stated *(US)*; **nicht** ~ *(Kartellrecht)* overruled *(US)*; **rechtlich** ~ recognized by law; **überall** ~ *(Buchhaltungsprinzip)* generally accepted;
als Erbe ~ **sein** to be owned as heir; ~ **werden** *(dipl.)* to receive recognition; **offiziell** ~ **werden** to get official standing; **staatlich ~e Börse** recognized stock exchange; **~er Fachmann auf seinem Gebiet** recognized authority in one's field; **gesetzlich ~er Feiertag** legal holiday; **~e Forderung** allowed claim, debt on record; **gerichtlich ~er Gläubiger** judgment creditor; **nicht vom Vater ~es Kind** unowned child; **~e Konkursforderung** proved debt; **~er Rekord** official record; **~er Schadensersatzanspruch** admitted claim; **~e Schuld** admitted debt; **gerichtlich ~e Schuld** judgment debt; **~e Tatsache** established (admitted) fact; **~er Text** authentic text; **~er Vertreter** recognized agent; **~er Werbungsmittler** recognized advertising agent; **~es Werk** standard work.
anerkanntermaßen admittedly.
anerkennen to acknowledge, to recognize, to warrant, to approbate, *(Bilanzposten)* to allocate, *(genehmigen)* to ratify, *(zugeben)* to admit, to allow, to avow;
Anspruch ~ to allow a claim, to recognize a claim; **j. als gesetzlichen Erben** ~ to recognize s. o. as the lawful heir; **Forderung** ~ to allow a claim; **förmlich** ~ to confess; **uneheliches Kind** ~ to own a child; **Kind nicht** ~ to disown (repudiate) a child; **jds. Meinung** ~ to approve of s. one's opinion; **nicht** ~ to disclaim, to disallow, to repudiate; **Parteibehauptung** ~ to admit a statement to be true; **Rechnungsposten** ~ to allow an item in an account; **Richtigkeit einer Urkunde** ~ to acknowledge a deed; **Schiedsspruch** ~ to abide by an award; **Schuld** ~ to recognize (admit, own) a debt; **Schuld nicht** ~ to renounce a debt; **Schulden nicht** ~ *(Staat)* to repudiate debts; **als kriegführenden Staat** ~ to recognize a state as a belligerent; **j. als überlegen** ~ to give s. o. best *(Br.)*; **seine Unterschrift** ~ to acknowledge (own) one's signature; **seine Unterschrift nicht** ~ to disown one's signature; **Urteil** ~ to confess judgment; **Vaterschaft** ~ to recognize a natural child; **Verantwortung nicht** ~ to disclaim (assume no) responsibility; **jds. Verdienste** ~ to recognize s. one's services; **jds. Verdienste um etw.** ~ to give s. o. credit for s. th.; **Vertrag nicht** ~ to repudiate an agreement; **Wechsel** ~ to hono(u)r (accept) a bill; **Wechsel nicht** ~ to dishono(u)r (refuse to accept) a bill.
Anerkenntnis acknowledgment, admission, admittance, confession, *(Bilanzposten)* allocation, *(Billigung)* approval, approbation, *(gegenüber einer Behörde)* recognizance;
notarielles ~ certificate of acknowledgement; **schriftliches** ~ acknowledgement by record;
~ **des Bankauszuges** verification form *(Br.)*, reconcilement blank *(US)* (statement, *Br.*); ~ **des Beklagten** confession of judgment; ~ **einer Forderung** allowance of a claim; ~ **einer Gewerkschaft** certification of a union; ~ **eines Kindes** legitimation of a child; ~ **eines Kontostandes** approval of an account; ~ **einer Schuld** acknowledgement of a debt; ~ **mit Stundungsvereinbarung** cognovit; ~ **der Tätigkeitsausübung im öffentlichen Interesse** certificate of public convenience and necessity; ~ **der Unterschrift** confession of signature; ~ **der Vaterschaft** acknowledgement of paternity;
~ **vor Gericht abgeben** to enter into a recognizance;
~formular *(Schuld)* form of acknowledgment; **~urteil** consent decree, decree of registration, judgment by consent (confession, *US*); **~zahlung** acknowledgment, token payment.
Anerkennung admission, acknowledgment, *(öffentliche Erwähnung)* hono(u)rable mention, *(Forderung)* recognition, allowance, *(Genehmigung)* ratification, *(Kind)* legitimation, affiliation, *(Kontoauszug)* verification form, reconcilement blank *(US)* (statement, *Br.*), *(Wechsel)* acceptance, *(Würdigung)* accolade;
in ~ **seiner Dienste** in acknowledgment of his services; **ohne** ~ **einer Rechtspflicht** ex gratia;
de-facto ~ de-facto recognition; **de-jure** ~ dejure recognition; **hohe** ~ golden opinion; **notarielle** ~ acknowledgment; **professionelle** ~ professional recognition; **stillschweigende** ~ implicit recognition; **volle** ~ full faith and credit *(US)*; **vorläufige** ~ de-facto recognition; **weltweite** ~ universal acclaim;
~ **einer Forderung** allowance of a claim; ~ **ausländischer Gerichtsentscheidungen** judicial comity; ~ **einer Gewerkschaft** union recognition; ~ **der Grenze** recognition of the frontier; ~ **der Haftung** assumption of liability; ~ **als kriegführende Macht** recognition of belligerence; ~ **als Markenartikel durch die Verbraucher** brand acceptance (recognition); ~ **besonderer Prozeßkosten** special allowance; ~ **einer Regierung** recognition of a government; ~ **eines Staates** recognition of a new state; **nachträgliche** ~ **einer unberechtigten Unterschriftsleistung** ratification of an unauthorized signature; ~ **einer Urkunde** legalization of a document; ~ **eines Vertreters** certification of an agent;
viel ~ **erhalten** to be greatly acclaimed; ~ **finden** to gain acceptance, *(dipl.)* to win recognition; **öffentliche** ~ **finden** to achieve distinction in public life; **auf der Buchmesse viel** ~ **finden** to be hono(u)rably mentioned at the book fair; ~ **verdienen** to deserve credit; **jem.** ~ **zollen** to pay tribute to s. o.; **jem. höchste** ~ **zollen** to give s. o. full marks.
Anerkennungs | bescheid recognition order; **~betrag für ein Mietverhältnis** nominal rent; **~leistung** part performance; **~schreiben** letter of commendation, testimonial, applause mail *(US)*; **~spalte** *(Zeitung)* credit column; **~urkunde** acknowledgment; **~urkunde im Bankenverkehr** clearinghouse certificate; **~verfahren** recognition procedure (process); **~vermerk** acknowledgment.
anfachen to fan, *(fig.)* to incite, to stir up.
anfahren to drive up, *(Zug)* to start;
j. ~ to go for (let fly at) s. o.; **anderes Auto** ~ to run into another car; **an die Bordsteinkante** ~ to drive against the curb; **Erde** ~ to carry earth; **Fußgänger** ~ to knock down a pedestrian; **j. grob** ~ to snap at s. o.; **mit einem Ruck** ~ to start with a jerk.
Anfahrt drive, approach.
Anfahrtsstraße approach road, driveway.

Anfall *(Erbschaft)* reversion, accession, devolution, *(Ertrag)* yield, *(Fälligwerden)* accrual, *(med.)* fit, attack, touch, *(Steuern)* incidence, *(Warenproduktion)* amount produced;
in einem ~ von Geisteskrankheit in a fit of mental derangement; **in einem ~ von Großzügigkeit** in a burst of generosity;
~ eines Fonds items accruing to a fund; **~ von Grippe** bout of influenza; **~ einer Krankheit** spell (onset, go, *Br.*) of an illness; **~ von Nervosität** willies *(US)*; **~ von Zinsen** accrual of interest.
Anfallberechtigter allottee, *(Erbschaft)* reversioner, remainderman.
Anfälle, gelegentliche occasional fits.
Anfallen vesting.
anfallen to attack, to assault, to assail, *(Arbeit)* to arise, to come to pass, to transpire *(US)*, *(Erbschaft)* to revert, to devolve, to vest, *(sich ergeben)* to occur, to result, *(Gewinn)* to yield, *(Hund)* to go for, *(Steuern)* to arise, *(Waren)* to come on the market, *(Zinsen)* to accrue;
j. aus dem Hinterhalt ~ to ambush s. o.
anfallend incoming;
~e Erbschaft reversion of an estate; **~es Material** material as it becomes available; **~e Nebenprodukte** spinoff products; **~e Zinsen** accruing interest.
anfällig susceptible, sensitive, vulnerable, weak, *(gegen Krankheit)* prone;
gegen Konjunkturschwankungen ~ sensitive to business movements (economic fluctuations); **nicht ~** healthy; **gegen Versuchungen ~** open to temptations;
gegen Infektionen sehr ~ sein to be susceptible to infections; **dem Verrat gegenüber ~ sein** to be vulnerable to betrayal.
Anfälligkeit susceptibility, *(Krankheiten)* liability, proneness.
Anfang start, beginning, commencement, inception, push-off *(coll.)*, *(Brief)* opening, *(Einleitung)* opening, introduction, *(Entstehung)* origin[ation], *(Funkwerbung)* lead-in, *(Krankheit)* access;
am ~ einer neuen Epoche at the dawn of a new era; **am ~ des Festzugs** at the bead of the procession; **am ~ der Seite** at the top of the page; **gleich von ~ an** from the outset, right at the start; **vom ~ bis zum Ende** from first to last, from one end to the other;
erster ~ scratch; **kleiner ~** small beginning; **neuer ~** fresh start, new departure; **vielversprechender ~** promising start;
~ einer Anzeige lead-in of an advertisement; **der ~ vom Ende** the beginning of the end; **~ der fünfziger Jahre** in the early fifties; **~ Juli** early July, at the beginning of July; **~ einer großen Karriere** commencement of a great career; **~ einer Rede** opening of a speech; **~ der Verhandlungen** opening of negotiations; **~ der Vorstellung 8 Uhr** performance begins at 8 o'clock;
keinen ~ finden not to know where to begin; **~ machen** to get in at the thin end of the wedge; **mit der Bauindustrie den ~ machen** to zero in on the construction industry; **erfolgreichen ~ machen** to get off the ground; **neuen ~ machen** to start afresh, to turn over a new leaf *(fam.)*; **verheißungsvollen ~ nehmen** to go off to a good start; **von ~ an dabei sein** to be in on the ground floor; **von ~ an gefragt sein** *(Börse)* to open active; **von ~ an nichtig sein** to be void on its face.
Anfänge, in den ersten ~n in the cradle;
erste ~ einer Industrie infancy of an industry; **~ einer Wissenschaft** rudiments (elements) of a science;
noch in den ~n stecken to be still in one's swaddling clothes.
anfangen to begin, to start, to commence, to initiate, *(entstehen)* to originate, *(eröffnen)* to open;
mit der Arbeit ~ to set to work; **mit 100 Dollar Lohn in der Woche ~** to start at 100 $ a week; **am falschen Ende ~** to start at the wrong end, to put the cart before the horse; **Feindseligkeiten ~** to begin hostilities; **bei einer Firma ~** to start work with a firm; **früh ~** to make an early start; **Geschäft ~** to start a business; **ganz harmlos ~** to start on a low key; **in einem fremden Land von vorn ~** to open up in a new country; **neues Leben ~** to turn over a new leaf; **mit Null ~** to start from scratch; **Prozeß ~** to bring an action, to institute legal proceedings; **zu rauchen ~** to take up smoking; **Streit mit jem. ~** to pick a quarrel with s. o.; **ganz von unten (von vorn) ~** to start from scratch (a shoestring, *US*); **noch einmal von vorn ~** to make a fresh start, to start all over again; **immer wieder davon ~** to be always harping on the same string.
Anfänger alphabetarian, beginner, *(Neuling)* freshman, novice, recruit, initiate, tyro, tenderfoot *(coll.)*, punk *(US sl.)*, rookie *(sl.)*;
~kursus introductory (pipe, *sl.*) course.
anfänglich initial, original, early, first.
anfangs at the beginning, at the start, at first sight.

Anfangs|abschreibung initial capital allowance; **hohe ~belastung** front-end load; **~beruf** entry occupation, beginning job; **~bestand** *(Bilanz)* opening capital (balance), *(Lager)* beginning (opening) inventory, initial (opening) stock; **~bestand einer Bibliothek** nucleus of a library; **~bestellung** initial order; **~betrag** *(Einkommensteuer)* threshold.
Anfangsbuchstabe initial (index) letter;
großer ~ majuscule, two-line (capital) letter;
mit ~n schreiben to capitalize; **mit seinen ~n versehen** to initial.
Anfangs|buchung opening entry; **~datum** starting date; **~dividende** initial dividend; **~einkommen** original income; **~einlage** *(Bank)* initial deposit, invested capital; **~einstufung** initial placing; **~förderung** initial output; **~gehalt** initial (starting, commencing) salary, starting (entrance, probationary) rate; **~gehalt ist Verhandlungssache** starting salary negotiable; **~gehalt in der Größenordnung von 25.000 Dollar und zusätzliche erhebliche Tantiemenvereinbarungen** starting salary in the area of 25.000 Dollars plus significant bonus arrangements; **~gehalt festsetzen** to assess the starting (initial) salary; **~gehaltsunterschied** starting salary differential; **~gründe** ABC, rudiments, elements; **j. in die ~gründe einer Wissenschaft einführen** to initiate s. o. in a science; **in den ~gründen einer Sache stecken** to be only at the ABC of a subject; **erstklassiges ~grundgehalt und zusätzlich eine ungewöhnlich großzügige Aufwandsentschädigung** excellent starting base salary plus unusually generous benefits; **~guthaben** *(ECU)* initial credit balance; **~inventar** beginning (basic, initial, opening, original) inventory, opening stock; **~investitionen** initial investments; **~jahre** initial years; **~kapital** initial (original) capital, original investment, original assets, capital to start with, seed money, *(AG)* capital stock, *(Anlage)* original investment; **~kaution** *(Versicherung)* initial guarantee deposit; **~kosten** initial expenses; **große ~kosten** high first cost; **~kredit** starting credit; **~kurs** *(Ausgabekurs)* issuing price, opening price (quotation, rate), starting price; **gewinnbringende ~kurse** bargain-basement prices; **~lehrbuch** primer; **~lohn** entrance (starting, probationary) rate; **statistisches ~material** basic data; **~plan** planned opener; **ausbaufähige ~position** beachhead; **~prämie** initial (opening) premium, initial rate; **~problem** startup problem; **~produkt** initial product; **~produktion** initial production; **~punkt** starting point; **~rendite** initial yield; **~reserve** *(Lebensversicherung)* initial reserve; **~satz** initial rate; **~satz des Einkommensteuertarifs** basic rate of personal tax; **~schuld** *(ECU)* initial debit balance; **~schwierigkeiten** breaking-in (initial) difficulties, teething troubles; **~stadium** infancy, early period, primary (initial, early, inchoate) stage, cradle, early mist, youth; **im ~stadium** in the embryonic stage, in the egg, infantile; **~stadium einer Nation** infancy of a nation; **~stadium eines Unternehmens** initial stages of an undertaking; **Verschwörung im ~stadium zunichte machen** to kill a plot in the egg; **noch ganz im ~stadium sein** to be in the earliest stages of preparation; **über das ~stadium hinaus sein** to be beyond the horse-and-buggy stage; **im ~stadium stehenbleiben** to get stuck in the early stages; **~- und Endstelle** *(Omnibusroute)* stage points of a bus route; **~stellung** initial assignment, entry (beginning) job; **~stellung suchen** to be looking for one's first job; **~steuersatz** *(Einkommensteuer)* basic rate of personal tax, basic rate band of taxes; **verkürzten ~steuersatz von 20% für Einkünfte bis zu 225 Pfund einführen** to introduce a reduced band of income tax at 20% for the first £ 225 of taxable income; **~studium** inchoateness; **~stufe** first base; **~stufen der Industrialisierung** initial stages of industrialization; **~symptome** initial symptoms; **~tarif** starting rate; **~tarif nach der Einkommensteuertabelle** basic rate income tax; **~termin** commencing (starting) date; **~unterricht** grounding; **~vermögen** original assets (property); **~warenbestand** original inventory; **~wartezeit** *(Versicherung)* initial waiting period; **~wert** initial value; **~zeile** first line; **~zeit** starting (initial) period.
anfassen to touch;
bei der Arbeit mit ~ to take a hand in the work; **j. mit Glacéhandschuhen ~** to handle s. o. with kid gloves; **Problem richtig ~** to tackle a problem; **j. rücksichtsvoll ~** to treat s. o. with consideration; **unangenehme Sache ~** to grasp a nettle; **etw. verkehrt ~** to get hold of the wrong end of the stick.
anfechtbar void, voidable, avoidable, subject to avoidance, rescindable, infirm, defeasible, contestable, contradictable, impugnable, *(zu kritisieren)* open to question, critizable, challengeable;
nicht ~ avoidless, incontestable, *(Urteil)* not subject to review; **mit Rechtsmitteln nicht ~** not appealable, unappealable, not subject to appeal;

~ **sein** to be open to dispute; **wahlweise** ~ **sein** to be voidable at s. one's option;
~**es Rechtsgeschäft** voidable contract, *(Konkursschuldner)* voidable preference; ~**es Urteil** voidable judgment; ~**er Vertrag** impeachable (voidable) contract.

Anfechtbarkeit voidability, voidableness, defeasibility, contestability.

anfechten to avoid, to make void, to contest, to annul, to challenge, to impugn, to dispute;
Echtheit einer Unterschrift ~ to dispute the authenticity of a signature; **Ehe** ~ to contest a marriage; **Entscheidung** ~ to dispute a decision; **Geschworenen** ~ to challenge a juror; **Gültigkeit einer Abstimmung** ~ to challenge a vote; **Patent** ~ to oppose a patent; **Testament** ~ to break (dispute, contest) a will; **Urteil** ~ to appeal against a judgment; **Vertrag** ~ to rescind (impugn, avoid) a contract; **Wahl[ergebnis]** ~ to contest (dispute) an election; **Zeugen** ~ to challenge a witness.

Anfechtender contestant.

Anfechtung trial, *(jur.)* avoidance, voiding, rescission, contestation, *(Patentrecht)* disclaimer, *(Urteil)* appeal;
~ **wegen Betrugs** rescission for fraud; ~ **der Gültigkeit einer Stimme** challenge of a vote; ~ **wegen Irrtums** rescission for mistake, *(Vertrag)* avoidance of contract owing to mistake; ~ **eines Patents** opposition of a patent; ~ **wegen arglistiger Täuschung** rescission for fraudulent misrepresentation; ~ **eines Testaments** breaking a will; ~ **eines Vertrages** repudiation (rescission, avoidance) of a contract;
auf ~ **eines Vertrages klagen** to claim for rescission of a contract; **der** ~ **unterliegen** to be subject to rescission.

Anfechtungsbedingungen conditions of avoidance.

anfechtungsberechtigt sein to be entitled to rescission.

Anfechtungs|berechtigter rescinder, contesting party; ~**erklärung** avoidance; ~**frist** time for repudiation; ~**grund** invalidating causes, cause for rescission; ~**grund abgeben** to be conditioned for avoidance; ~**gründe** grounds of rescission, conditions for avoidance, ground for annulments; ~**klage** action for avoidance of contract, rescissory action, action for rescission, *(Ehe)* action for annulment, nullity suit, *(Patent)* interference proceedings, disclaimer; ~**klage anstrengen** to bring an action in rescission, *(Patentrecht)* to enter a disclaimer; ~**möglichkeit** power of avoidance; ~**recht** right of rescission (avoidance); ~**verfahren** *(Ehe)* nullity suit, *(Patentrecht)* interference proceedings.

Anfeindung hostility, animosity;
vielen ~**en ausgesetzt sein** to be faced with hostilities on all sides.

anfertigen to make, to manufacture, to fabricate, to produce;
auf Bestellung ~ to make to order; **in einer bestimmten Größe** ~ to size; **500 Kopien** ~ to take 500 copies; **Liste** ~ to draw up (prepare) a list; **nach Maß** ~ to make to order; **Niederschrift über eine Unterredung** ~ to take minutes of a conversation; **Notizen** ~ to take notes; **Protokoll** ~ to draw up a protocol; **Übersetzung** ~ to make a translation;
Ersatzteil ~ **lassen** to have a spare part made.

Anfertigung making, fabrication, manufacture, production;
~ **von Notizen** note-taking.

Anfertigungskosten manufacturing costs.

an|feuchten to moisten, to dampen; ~**feuern** to fire, *(fig.)* to animate, to excite, to kindle, to inspire, to pep; **zu höchsten Leistungen** ~**feuern** to speed up.

Anfeuerungsrede rousing speech.

anfinanzieren to provide with initial credit facilities.

anflehen to implore, to beseech, to entreat, to conjure;
j. auf den Knien ~ to fall upon one's knees before one; **Richter um Gnade** ~ to implore a judge for mercy.

anfliegen *(Flugplatz)* to approach, to head for, *(landen)* to land;
auf dem Leitstrahl ~ to come in on the beam; **linienmäßig** ~ to provide regular service to.

Anflug approach, run-up, *(Andeutung)* smack, shade, spasm, touch, trace, tinge, suggestion, *(fig.)* smell, snack, touch, taint, tinge, whiff;
hindernisfreier ~ unobstructed approach; **mißglückter** ~ missed approach;
~ **von Anarchie** smack of anarchy; ~ **von Eifersucht** fit of jealousy; ~ **von Frost** touch of frost; ~ **von Großzügigkeit** fit of generosity; ~ **mit Leitstrahl** beamed approach; ~ **von Mißtrauen** taint of suspicion; ~ **von Mitleid** wave of compassion; ~ **von Prüderie** whiff of prudery; ~ **von Traurigkeit** suspicion of sadness;
~**anzeigegerät** approach path indicator; ~**bake** radio marker; ~**feuer** approach lights; ~**geschwindigkeit** approach speed; ~**hafen** port of call; ~**raum** approach area; ~**richtung** direction of approach; ~**schneise** approach lane; ~**überwachungsradar** approach surveillance radar; ~**weg** approach route (path).

anfordern to call (ask) for, to demand, to claim, *(Bereitstellung verlangen)* to requisition, *(Material)* to require, to request;
weitere Geldmittel ~ to ask for more funds; **polizeiliche Hilfe** ~ to call in the police.

Anforderung demand, claim, request, pretence, *(Erfordernis)* requirement, *(Requisition)* requisition;
betriebstechnische ~**en** manufacturing requirements;
~ **von Akten** invocation of papers *(US)*, *(Prozeßakten)* writ of certiorari; ~**en für Ferien- und Reisegelder** holiday currency demands; ~**en zum Halbjahresultimo** midyear demands; ~**en zum Jahresultimo** yearly demands; ~**en für das Lager** stores requisition; ~**en im Schalterverkehr** over-the-counter *(US)* (current counter) requirements; **strenge** ~**en an die Sorgfaltspflicht** high standard of care; ~**en zum Ultimo** monthly requirements; ~**en der Volkswirtschaft** economic wants;
den ~**en entsprechen** to meet (answer) the requirements; **allen** ~**en entsprechen** to come up to the mark, to fill the bill; **beruflichen** ~**en entsprechen** to match job specifications; **den** ~**en der Praxis entsprechen** to meet practical requirements; **allen** ~**en genügen** to fill every requirement; **den** ~**en genügen** to be up to standard; **den** ~**en nicht genügen** to be below standard; **den gesetzlichen** ~**en einer Wahl genügen** to be qualified for the vote; ~**en herabsetzen** to relax requirements; **den gestellten** ~**en Genüge leisten** to have the necessary qualification(s); **den** ~**en nicht Genüge leisten** to be below standard; ~**en nicht gewachsen sein** not to be up to standards; ~**en stellen** to lay claim to; **harte** ~**en an sich selbst stellen** not to spare o. s.; **hohe** ~**en an j. stellen** to require a great deal of s. o.; **zu hohe** ~**en an j. stellen** to be too exacting with s. o.; **hohe** ~**en an jds. Geduld stellen** to tax s. one's patience; **hohe** ~**en an die Geschäftsmoral stellen** to set a high standard of business morality; **den** ~**en gerecht werden** to meet the challenge; **um den** ~**en dieser schwierigen Zeit gerecht zu werden** to meet the exigencies of this difficult period.

Anforderungs|beamter *(mil.)* procurement officer *(US)*; ~**formular** requisition blank; ~**schein** requisition.

Anfrage inquiry, enquiry, question, *(parl.)* question, interpellation;
auf ~ upon inquiry; **bezüglich Ihrer** ~ regarding your enquiry; ~**n erbeten** enquiries solicited;
briefliche ~ inquiry by letter; **parlamentarische** ~ interpellation;
~ **über die Kreditfähigkeit** credit inquiry (enquiry, *Br.*);
schriftliche ~ **beantworten** to handle a written request; **parlamentarische** ~ **einbringen** to interpellate; **parlamentarisch** ~ **schriftlich einbringen** to table a question; **einer** ~ **für bessere Bedingungen entsprechen** to grant a request for better terms; ~ **richten** to make an inquiry, to inquire, *(parl.)* to address a question;
Preise auf ~ prices upon request.

anfragen to inquire, to enquire, to ask;
schriftlich ~ to enquire by letter (in writing); **telefonisch** ~ to enquire by telephone.

anfreunden, sich mit jem. to chum up with s. o., to strike up a friendship (pal up) with s. o., to become friends; **sich mit einflußreichen Leuten** ~ to get in with influential people.

anfügen to annex, to join, to affix, to attach, to enclose, to suffix;
seinem Testament einen Nachtrag ~ to annex a codicil to one's will.

Anfügung *(Schriftstück)* attachment, appendage;
unter ~ **einer Liste** enclosing a list.

Anfuhr carriage, transport[ation], delivery, *(Versorgung)* supply;
~ **zum Bauplatz** transport to building site.

anführbar citable, adducible.

anführen *(angeben)* to state, to allege, *(Beweis, Zeugen)* to adduce, *(führen)* to head, to be at the head, to lead, *(zitieren)* to cite, to quote;
j. ~ to take s. o. for a ride, to dupe s. o.; **zum Beweis** ~ to put in as evidence; **zu seiner Entschuldigung** ~ to plead in one's defence; **als Erklärung** ~ to put forward as an explanation; **falsch** ~ to misquote; **Gesetzesbestimmung** ~ to quote a law; **Gründe** ~ to state reasons, to argue; **Liste** ~ to [stand first on a] list; **Meuterei** ~ to lead a mutiny; **Stelle falsch** ~ to misquote a passage; **Tatsachen** ~ to state facts; **Truppe** ~ to command troops; **zu jds. Verteidigung** ~ to state in s. one's defence; **Zeugen namentlich** ~ to name a witness.

Anführer leader, head, cock, standard bearer, principal, chief, boss *(US)*, *(Rädelsführer)* ringleader, principal actor;
~ **eines Aufruhrs** instigator of a riot.

Anfuhr | kosten cartage; ~**rechnung** cartage note.

Anführung allegation, quotation, citation, *(von Quellen)* reference;
unter ~ eines Generals under the command of a general; **~ höchstrichterlicher Entscheidungen** citation of authorities; **~ einer Gesetzesstelle** quoting a law; **~ seiner Quellen** quotation of one's authorities.

Anführungs | striche inverted commas; ~**zeichen** quotation mark.

anfüllen to fill up, to cram, *(Speicher)* to stock;
seinen Kopf mit Fachwissen ~ to cram up a subject.

anfunken to wireless, to radio.

Angabe indication, *(Anweisung)* instruction, order, *(Aufschneiden)* blow *(US sl.)*, *(Auskunft)* information, brag, *(Behauptung)* allegation, assertion, *(Darstellung)* account, representation, specification, *(Einzelheit)* datum, detail, *(Erklärung)* statement, declaration, *(beim Zoll)* declaration;
laut ~ according to statement; **nach ~ der Sachverständigen** according to the experts; **nach ~ des Zeugen** according to the witness's statements; **ohne ~** *(Zoll)* undeclared; **ohne ~ des Erscheinungsjahres** *(Buch)* with no indication of the year, no date; **ohne ~ von Gründen** without giving (stating) reasons; **unter ~ des Namens und der Adresse** giving name and address;
beschreibende ~ descriptive term *(US)*; **genaue ~** definitive statement; **zu niedrige ~** understatement; **summarische ~** summary;
~ von Einzelheiten specification; **~ von Gründen** assignment of reasons; **~ des Inhalts** statement of contents; **irrtümliche ~ eines Miterfinders** misjoinder of inventor; **~ von Referenzen** indication of references; **~ der Seitenzahl des Hauptbuches** posting folio; **~ des Standorts** *(Flugzeug, Schiff)* position report; **~ des Versicherungswertes** declaration of the value insured; **~ des Wertes** declaration of value.

Angaben data, particulars;
nach seinen ~ according to his statement, by his own account; **nach den ~ des Antragstellers** according to the applicant; **nicht den ~ entsprechend** *(Versicherung)* not according to representations; **ohne nähere ~ zu machen** without going into details; **allgemeine ~** general data; **betrügerische ~** false (fraudulent) statement; **detaillierte ~** full particulars, disclosure; **einschränkende ~** qualifications; **falsche ~** false declaration (accounts, statement), misstatement, *(Versicherungsrecht)* false representations, *(bei Vertragsabschluß)* misdescription; **erheblich falsche ~** *(Schuldrecht)* actionable misrepresentation; **wissentliche falsche ~** untrue statement; **finanzielle ~** financial data; **genaue ~** full details; **irreführende ~** fraudulent representation, misleading statements; **kurze ~** brief data; **nähere ~** details; **qualitative ~** qualitative data; **quantitative ~** quantitative data; **sachdienliche ~** pertinent data; **statistische ~** statistical data, return; **unter Geheimschutz stehende ~** restricted data *(US)*; **ungenaue ~** inaccurate information; **vertrauliche ~** confidential information; **wahrheitsgetreue ~** true statement; **weitere ~** further particulars; **wesentliche ~** material data; **sich widersprechende ~** conflicting (two irreconcilable) statements; **wirtschaftliche ~** economic (trade) data; **zugesicherte ~** *(Versicherungsabschluß)* affirmative warranty; **zusätzliche ~** further information (details); **zuverlässige ~** reliable information; **zweckdienliche ~** pertinent information;
falsche ~ im Börsenprospekt misstatement in prospectus; **statistische ~ über die Geldversorgung** money supply figures; **~ über die Leserschaft** audience data; **~ zur Person** name and description, personalia, personal data (history), particulars; **~ von Referenzen** indication of references; **~ des Versicherten** statement of the insured;
nähere ~ erbitten to ask for further information (particulars); **nähere ~ folgen** particulars follow; **detaillierte (nähere) ~ machen** to give details; **wissentlich falsche ~ machen** to knowingly make false statements; **seine ~ spezifizieren** to be more explicit in one's statement; **sich für die Richtigkeit seiner ~ verbürgen** to vouch for the truth of one's statement; **sich auf ~ verlassen** to rely upon a statement; **sich durch betrügerische ~ verschaffen** to obtain under false pretences; **jem ~ vorlegen** to register data with s. o.;
ich versichere die Richtigkeit obiger ~ I warrant that the above answers are true.

angängig practicable, feasible.

angebaut in tillage, under cultivation (crop), *(Haus)* built-on, semi-detached;
nicht mehr ~ werden to go out of cultivation;
~**er Hausflügel** wing to a house; ~**er Schuppen** lean-to shed.

Angeben show, showing off, big talk, splurge.

angeben to state, to declare, to indicate, to name, to appoint, to allege, *(aufschneiden)* to boast, to put on side, to talk large (tall) *(sl.)*, to brag, to shoot a line *(sl.)*, to blow *(coll.)*, to act up *(US)*, *(festlegen)* to assign, *(Preise)* to quote, *(Wert)* to declare, *(als Zeuge)* to state, to allege, to declare;
Buchinhalt kurz ~ to sum up a book; **sein Einkommen ~** to make an income-tax statement; **seine Einkünfte zu niedrig ~** to understate one's income; **einzeln ~** to particularize, to specify, to give particulars; **falsch ~** to misstate; **gewaltig ~** to draw the long bow *(coll.)*; **Gründe ~** to give (state, assign) reasons, to show cause; **zu hoch ~** to overstate; **näher ~** to specify, to itemize *(US)*; **seinen Namen und Adresse ~** to give one's name and address; **Paketwert ~** to declare the value of a parcel; **äußersten Preis ~** to quote the outside price; **einzelne Rechnungsposten ~** to itemize accounts; **Referenzen ~** to quote references; **Richtung ~** to indicate the direction; **Tempo ~** to set the pace; **Todesursache ~** to state the cause of death; **Ton ~** to set the pace; **unrichtig ~** to misrepresent; **sein Vermögen ~** to declare one's property; **voll ~** to state fully; **Warenwert beim Zoll ~** to enter goods at the customhouse; **zu wenig ~** *(Zoll)* to enter short, to understate; **Wert ~** to declare the value; **als Zahlstelle ~** to name as paying agents; **genaue Zeit ~** to state a precise time; **Zeugen ~** to name a witness.

Angeber boaster, swaggerer, braggert, swank, spread eagle, line-shooter *(sl.)*, dazzler *(sl.)*.

Angeberei showing off, bragging, boasting, splurge.

angeberisch pretentious, swanky, spread-eagle, boastful, bragging, windy;
~**e Aufmachung** pretentious layout.

angeblich supposed, purported, alleged, pretended, would-be, *(Recht)* putative, reputed;
~ krank sein to be reputed to be ill; **~ reich sein** supposed to be wealthy; **~ in eine Affäre verwickelt sein** to be rumo(u)red to be involved in an affair;
~ neue Erfindung allegedly new invention; ~**e Forderung** pretended claim; ~**er Graf** self-styled count; ~**e Neutralität** professed neutrality; ~**e Rechte** assumed rights; ~**er Sachkenner** would-be connoisseur; ~**er Täter** alleged culprit; ~**e Verbesserungen** so-called improvements; ~**er Wert** nominal value, *(Wechsel)* face value; ~**er Zweck** ostensible purpose.

angeboren inborn, innate, inherent, native, inhered, connate;
~**es Recht** inherent right.

Angebot offer, offering, overture, *(Auktion)* first (opening) bid, *(Lieferungsvertrag)* tender, bid *(US)*, *(Vorschlag)* proposal, proposition, *(Warenangebot)* supply;
im ~ on offer; **jedem vernünftigen ~ zugänglich** open to any reasonable offer;
vorher abgesprochenes ~ collusive price, *(Banken)* syndicate bid *(Br.)*; **bemustertes ~** sample[d] offer; **bindendes ~** firm offer; **einige ~e** *(Börse)* a few buyers; **elastisches ~** fluctuating (variable) tender; **ernstgemeintes ~** serious offer; **erstes ~** first bid; **festes ~** firm offer (bid), binding (positive, definitive) offer; **fingiertes ~** sham bid; **freibleibendes ~** free (conditional, not binding) offer, offer subject to prior sale (without obligation, without engagement, subject unsold), quotation without obligation; **gekoppeltes ~** combination offer; **mündlich gemachtes ~** verbal offer; **gemeinsames ~** joint supply; **an die Allgemeinheit gerichtetes ~** offer made to the world at large; **gesamtwirtschaftliches ~** aggregate supply; **gleichbleibendes ~** standing offer; **großzügiges ~** liberal offer; **höheres ~** higher bid; **kaufmännisches ~** industrial offer; **lächerliches ~** derisive offer; **laufendes ~** current supply, *(Börse)* floating supply; **öffentliches ~** general offer, offer to the public; **reichhaltiges ~** abundant offers, sample offerings, variety; **reizvolles ~** attractive offer; **solides ~** bona-fide offer; **spärliches ~** *(Börse)* few offers; **spontanes ~** voluntary offer; **stärkeres ~** *(Börse)* more sellers than buyers; **stillschweigendes ~** implied offer; **tägliches ~** *(Börse)* floating supply; **telegrafisches ~** telegraphic offer; **umfassendes ~** comprehensive offer; **unelastisches ~** inelastic supply; **unverbindliches ~** not binding offer, offer without engagement; **unverlangtes ~** voluntary offer; **ursprüngliches ~** original offer; **vergleichbares ~** comparable offer; **vernünftiges ~** reasonable offer; **verschlossenes ~** sealed proposal; **verstecktes ~** buried offer; **vorbehaltloses ~** unconditional offer; **nicht wettbewerbkonformes ~** noncompetitive offer; **zusammengesetztes ~** composite supply;
~ und Annahme offer and acceptance; **~ an Arbeitskräften** supply of labo(u)r; **rückläufiges ~ an Arbeitskräften** decline in jobs; **~ am Arbeitsmarkt** positions offered, unfilled jobs offering; **~ am Frachtenmarkt** freight offer; **~ am Geldmarkt** supply of money; **~ zur Genugtuung** offer of amends *(Br.)*; **~ und**

Nachfrage supply and demand; **großzügiges ~ von Sondervergütungen** generous range of benefits; **~ offener Stellen** unfilled jobs offering, positions offered; **~ aus der Vorjahresernte** carryover;
~ abgeben to make an offer, to tender, to put in a bid, to put a bid on the table; **~ für einen Brückenbau abgeben** to bid on a new bridge, to tender for the construction of a bridge; **von ~ und Nachfrage abhängen** to depend on supply and demand; **~ ablehnen** to reject (decline, set aside, refuse) an offer; **augenblickliches ~ ablehnen** to decline an offer as it stands; **besseres ~ abwarten** to hold out for a higher price; **~ annehmen** to accept (close with, embrace) an offer; **~ schnellstens annehmen** to snatch at an offer; **~ telefonisch annehmen** to telephone one's acceptance; **zu ~en auffordern** to invite offers (tenders); **~ aufrechterhalten** to hold an offer open; **~ ausschlagen** to reject (repel, refuse) an offer; **sein ~ beifügen** to enclose one's tender; **billigstes ~ berücksichtigen** to allocate to the lowest tenderer; **~ einholen** to obtain an offer; **~ einreichen** to lodge (submit) a tender; **~ entgegennehmen** to be open to an offer; **sein ~ erhöhen** to raise one's bid, to up one's offer; **für sein ~ eine Annahmefrist festlegen** to lay down a time limit on one's acceptance; **sich über ein ~ freuen** to jump at an offer; **~e hinauftreiben** to run up the bidding; **~ unbeachtet lassen** to treat an offer with neglect; **~ machen** to propose, to offer, to make (submit, put in, send in) a tender; **mündliches ~ machen** to make an offer orally; **schriftliches ~ machen** to make an offer in writing; **von einem ~ Gebrauch machen** to avail o. s. of an offer, to make use of s. one's services; **vernünftiges ~ zur Schuldenbegleichung machen** to tender money in discharge of a debt; **sich jds. ~ zunutze machen** to improve on s. one's offer; **an sein ~ gebunden sein** to be bound by one's offer; **auf einem ~ sitzenbleiben** to stick to an offer; **sich auf ein ~ stürzen** to leap (jump) at an offer; **einem ~ näher treten** to entertain (avail o. s. of) an offer; **~ übermitteln** to communicate an offer; **~ übersteigen** to outstrip the supply; **~e unterbreiten** to submit offers; **~ verlangen** to ask for a quotation; **~ in Betracht ziehen** to be open (entertain, consider) an offer; **jds. ~ zurückweisen** to rebut s. one's offer; **~ zurückziehen** to revoke (withdraw) an offer, to retract a bid;
dieses ~ gilt sieben Tage for acceptance within seven days.

angeboten for sale, *(Börse)* offered;
fest ~ offered firm; **stark ~** freely offered;
billig ~ sein *(Effekten)* to be on the bargain counter; **~ werden** to be up for sale, *(Börse)* to be on (come into, come out of) the market;
~e Menge quantity offered; **~e Ware** goods for sale.

Angebots|abänderung variation of offer; **manipulierte ~abgabe** collusive bidding; **~adressat** offeree; **~annahme** offer acceptance; **~ausschließungsvertrag** bidding agreement; **~ausschreibung** public invitation to tender; **~bedingungen abändern** to vary the terms of an offer; **~begrenzung** termination of offer; **~beschränkung** restriction of supply; **~blankett** form; **~buch** *(Effektenmaterial)* offer book; **~elastizität** elasticity of supply; **~empfänger** tenderee *(US)*; **~formular** form; **~gegenüberstellung** summary of forms; **~knappheit** shortage of supplies; **~kurve** supply curve; **regressive ~kurve** backward-bending supply curve; **~lage** supply position (situation); **~liste** *(Effektenemission)* sheet offer *(US)*; **~lücke** gap in supplies; **~mappe eines Handelsreisenden** salesman's advertising portfolio; **~muster** sample offer; **~potential** potential supply; **~preis** supply (offer, offering, tender) price; **~reserve** reserve of supply; **~sortiment** set of demands; **~tabelle** supply schedule; **~überhang** backlog of orders, excessive supply; **~unterlagen** specifications; **~verschiebung** shift in supply, supply shift; **~verzeichnis** list of offers; **~verzögerung** demand lag.

angebracht advisable, appropriate, suitable, befitting, apt;
nicht ~ out of place;
~e Reaktion suitable reaction.

angebrannt burnt.

angebrochen *(Konservendose)* opened.

angebunden, kurz short.

angedeihen lassen, seinen Kindern eine gute Erziehung to give one's children a good education.

angefallen accrued, *(Erträge)* earned;
noch nicht ~ unaccrued;
~e Kosten costs incurred.

angefangen haben, schon to be under way.

angefault partly rotten.

angefertigt made to order;
einzeln ~ custom-built *(US)*; **vom Schneider ~** tailor-made.

angefochtene Wahl contested election.

angefügtes Muster sample attached.

angeführt headed;
wie oben ~ as stated (quoted) above.

Angeführter victim, dupe.

angegangen, leicht *(Fleisch)* slightly off.

angegeben, nicht undesignated; **wie ~** as indicated; **zu hoch ~** overstated;
~er Preis quoted price.

angegliedert affiliated.

angegossen sitzen, wie to fit like a glove.

angegraute Schläfen greying *(Br.)* (graying, *US*) temples.

an|gegriffen, heftig under fire; **~gehängt** *(drucktechn.)* run-on.

angehaucht tinged, tinted;
kommunistisch ~ prick *(US sl.)*; **patriotisch ~** imbued with patriotism.

an|geheftet *(Zinsschein)* attached; **~geheiratet** [related] by marriage; **~geheiratete Tante** aunt by marriage; **~geheitert** tipsy, down by the head, fresh, merry, high, happy, mellow *(sl.)*;
~geheitert sein to be slightly elevated *(coll.)*.

angehen to concern, to regard, *(anfangen)* to begin, *(beginnen)* to start, to commence, *(Feuer)* to catch fire;
j. ~ to concern s. o.; **j. um etw. ~** apply to s. o. for s. th.; **Chef um Gehaltserhöhung ~** to tackle the boss for a raise *(US coll.)* (rise, *Br.*); **seine Freunde um finanzielle Unterstützung ~** to lay one's friends under a contribution; **gegen etw. ~** to fight against (resist, oppose) s. th.; **j. um Geld ~** to tap s. o. for money; **seine Nachbarn um Beträge für wohltätige Zwecke ~** to solicit one's neighbo(u)rs for a charitable contribution; **nicht ~** *(Pockenimpfung)* not to take; **j. nichts ~** not to be s. one's cup of tea *(Br., coll.)*; **uns nichts ~** to be none of our funeral; **Problem ~** to approach (tackle) a problem; **j. um einen Rat ~** to seek s. one's advice; **Thema methodisch ~** to study a subject on sound lines; **j. um Zahlung ~** to press s. o. for payment.

angehend beginning;
~er Anwalt intending lawyer; **~er Käufer** prospective buyer; **~er Star** star in the making.

angehören to belong to, to pertain;
einem Ausschuß ~ to sit (be) on a committee; **als Mitglied ~** to be a member; **der Vergangenheit ~** to belong to the past.

angehörig belonging;
keiner Gewerkschaft ~ nonunion.

Angehörige|r family member, relative, dependant, kin, kinsman, dependant;
meine ~n my family; **nächster ~r** next of kin; **unterhaltspflichtiger ~r** dependant relative; **vollbezahlter ~r** paid-up member; **~ der freien Berufe** professional classes (men), professional people; **~r des rechten Flügels** right winger; **~r der Handelsmarine** merchant seaman; **~r der Kampftruppen** combatant; **~r des Küstenwachdienstes** coastguardman; **~r einer Minderheit** minority member; **~r des Mittelstandes** member of the middle classes; **~r der weißen Rasse** white [man]; **~r eines ausländischen Staates** foreign subject; **~r eines befreundeten Staates** alien-ami; **~r eines Vereins** member of a society, club member; **~ der oberen Zehntausend** socialite *(US)*.

angehört werden to gain (get) a hearing.

angeht, wen es to whom it may concern.

angeklagt accused;
nicht zum zweiten Mal ~ werden können not to be in jeopardy of life on the same offence; **~ sein** to stand accused.

Angeklagte|r defendant *(US)*, accused, culprit, panel *(Scot.)*;
inhaftierter ~r prisoner on trial;
~r in der Hauptverhandlung prisoner at the bar; **~r in der Revisionsverhandlung** defendant in error;
~n aburteilen to pass judgment on a prisoner, to deal with a culprit; **gegen einen ~n aussagen** to witness against an accused; **~n freisprechen** to find for the defendant, to dismiss the accused; **~n verurteilen** to pass sentence upon the accused.

angeknackst cracked, slightly damaged, *(leicht verrückt)* slightly cracked;
moralisch ~ lax in morals.

angekommen, gerade fresh in; **soeben ~** new-come;
gerade ~ sein *(Zug)* to be in.

angekränkelt, moralisch defective in moral sense.

Angel fishing rod (tackle);
aus den ~n off the hinges; **zwischen Tür und ~** in a hurry;
Welt aus den ~n heben to shake the world to its foundations.

angelaufene|Schulden run-up debts; **~ Zinsen** interest accrued.

Angeld earnest [money], bargain money, handsel, *(Anzahlung)* deposit, forfeit money.

angelegen sein lassen, sich to take an interest, to make it one's object (a feature of doing).

Angelegenheit matter, affair, business, concern, line, pidgin *(Br., coll.)*, *(Rechtsfall)* case;
endgültig abgeschlossene ~ closed account; **aufreibende** ~ wearying business; **außergewöhnliche** ~ nobody's business; **auswärtige** ~**en** external (foreign) affairs; **dienstliche** ~ official business; **dringende** ~ pressing matter; **dunkle** ~ fishy business; **ehrenrührige** ~ degrading affair; **ernsthafte** ~ serious matter, no laughing matter; **faule** ~ bad egg; **finanzielle** ~ financial affair; **fragliche** ~ matter of dispute; **reichlich gemischte** ~ mixed bag *(fam.)*; **geschäftliche** ~ matter of business, business matter; **häusliche** ~**en** domestic affairs; **heikle** ~ matter of delicacy; **hochoffizielle** ~ command performance; **innere** ~**en** home *(Br.)* (internal) affairs; **kitzlige** ~ nice affair, ticklish business, tickler; **kostspielige** ~ costly affair; **öffentliche** ~**en** public affairs; **offizielle** ~ formal; **parlamentarische** ~ parliamentary business; **peinliche** ~ embarrassment; **persönliche** ~**en** personal matters, private affairs; **private** ~ private affair; **schmutzige** ~ unfair (dirty) business; **schwebende** ~ pending (unsettled) question; **schwierige** ~ tough proposition, long row to hoe *(US)*; **städtische** ~**en** urban affairs; **strittige** ~ matter in issue; **übliche** ~ routine matter; **unbedeutende** ~ smalltime affair; **unerledigte** ~ outstanding matter; **verwickelte** ~ involvement; **vordringliche** ~ matter calling for attention; **weltliche** ~**en** mundane affairs; **wesentliche** ~ primary business; **wichtige** ~ matter of consequence, high affairs; **wirtschaftliche** ~ business (trade) matter; **zähflüssige** ~ cumbersome process; ~ **der freiwilligen Gerichtsbarkeit** nonlitigious (noncontentious) business; ~ **des Gesetzgebers** legislative business;
das ist meine ~ that's my funeral;
~ **sorgfältig im Auge behalten** to give a matter every care; ~ **vollkommen beherrschen** to master a subject; ~ **freundschaftlich beilegen** to settle a matter amicably; **jds.** ~**en besorgen** to manage s. one's affairs; **seine** ~**en in Ordnung bringen** to set one's affairs (one's house) in order; ~ **ins reine bringen** to settle a business; ~ **zur Sprache bringen** to raise a matter; **j. mit einer** ~ **in Verbindung bringen** to link s. o. with an affair; **sich in jds.** ~**en einmischen** to meddle in s. one's concern, to intermeddle in s. one's business, to interfere with s. o. (in s. one's affairs); ~ **erledigen** to deal with a piece of business; **seine eigenen** ~**en erledigen** to manage one's own affairs; ~ **außergerichtlich erledigen** to settle a matter without going to law; **seine finanziellen** ~**en selbst erledigen** to handle one's own financing; **jds.** ~**en fördern** to promote s. one's interests; ~ **erledigt haben** to have disposed of an affair; **seine** ~**en geordnet hinterlassen** to leave one's affairs in perfect order; **j. für eine** ~ **interessieren** to gain s. o. over for a cause; ~ **klären (klarstellen)** to clear up a matter; **in geschäftlichen** ~**en kommen** to come on business; **seine eigenen** ~**en nicht mehr besorgen können** to be incapable of managing one's own affairs; **sich um seine eigenen** ~**en kümmern** to mind one's own (go about one's) business, to hoe one's own row *(US)*, to peddle one's own papers *(US sl.)*; **wichtige** ~ **aus etw. machen** to make an affair of s. th.; ~ **manipulieren** to gerrymander a piece of business; **seinen eigenen** ~**en nachgehen** to attend to one's own affairs; **seine** ~**en ordnen** to settle one's affairs; ~ **prüfen** to look into a matter; ~ **regeln** to settle a matter; ~ **richtigstellen** to adjust a matter; **jds. eigene** ~ **sein** to be s. one's own business; **reichlich verworrene** ~ **sein** to be a mixed bag *(fam.)*; **über eine** ~ **nicht unterrichtet sein** to be uninformed about a matter; **seine Nase in anderer Leute** ~**en stecken** to poke one's nose into other people's business; **jem. alle finanziellen** ~**en überlassen** to leave all money matters to s. o.; ~ **sorgfältig überlegen** to give a matter careful consideration; ~ **überprüfen** to look into (check up on, *US*) a matter; **jem. die Erledigung seiner** ~**en übertragen** to place a matter in s. one's hands; ~ **genauestens untersuchen** to look closely into an affair; ~ **weiter (genauer) untersuchen** to go further into a matter; ~ **zurückstellen** to let a matter lie over.
angelegentlich intently, earnestly, *(dringend)* pressing, urgent;
sich ~ **in ein Buch vertiefen** to immerse o. s. in a book;
~**e Empfehlungen** cordial recommendation.
angelegt invested;
fest ~ locked (tied) up; **groß** ~ on a grand scale; **nicht** ~ uninvested, idle; **verteilt** ~ *(Kapital)* diversified.
angelernter Arbeiter semi-skilled worker.
Angelgerät fishing gear.
Angeln nicht erlaubt fishing is prohibited.
angeln to fish, to angle;
sich einen Ehemann ~ to land s. o. for a husband; **sich einen Millionär** ~ to catch a millionnaire; **Schlüssel aus der Tasche** ~ to fish the key out of one's pocket.
Angelplatz fishing ground.
Angelpunkt pivot, central, pivotal point, hinge, hub, issue;
~ **der Finanzwelt** hub of the financial world;
~ **einer Politik sein** to be the cardinal point of a policy.
Angel|schein rod (fishing) licence, fishing permit *(US)*; ~**sport** gentle craft.
angemaßt self-constituted.
angemeldet registered, incorporated *(US)*, *(Konkursforderung)* proved, *(Warenzeichen)* registered;
nicht ~ unregistered; **Patent** ~ patent pending.
angemessen suitable, fair and reasonable, adequate, competent, appropriate, just, proportionate, worthily, worthy, suitable, due, moderate, *(Strafe)* condign;
es für ~ **halten** to think it right; **den Bedürfnissen der Bewohner** ~ **sein** to be suited to the requirements of the inhabitants; **nicht ganz** ~ **sein** not to be quite in place; **jds. Geldbeutel** ~ **sein** to suit s. one's purse;
~**e Abstandssumme** adequate compensation; ~**e Belohnung** adequate reward (remuneration); ~**e Besuchsregelung** reasonable access; ~**es Einkommen** fair income; **in** ~**er Form** in appropriate form; **innerhalb** ~**er Frist** within reasonable time; ~**e Kündigung** reasonable notice; ~**er Preis** reasonable price; ~**es Verfahren** proper procedure; ~**e Vergütung** fair and reasonable compensation; **in** ~**er Weise** in a suitable way; ~**er Zeitraum** reasonable length of time.
Angemessenheit moderation, moderateness, adequacy, suitability, *(Preis)* fairness, reasonability;
~ **der Reserven** reserve adequacy; ~ **des Werbeaufwands** advertising accountability.
angemietet rented;
kurzfristig ~ time-shared.
angenagelt, wie ~ **dastehen** to stay like a post.
angenagt, vom Wasser worn by water.
angenähert approximate.
Angenehme|im Leben, das the pleasant things in life;
das ~ **mit dem Nützlichen verbinden** to combine business with pleasure.
angenehm pleasant, pleasing, agreeable;
~ **warm** nice and warm;
~**en Eindruck hinterlassen** to leave a favo(u)rable impression; **sich ein** ~**es Leben machen** to take life easy; ~**es Wesen** engaging manners; ~**e Zeit verbringen** to spend a pleasant time.
angenommen assumed, fictitious, *(Gesetz)* adopted, accepted, carried, *(Recht)* constructive;
einstimmig ~ carried unanimously, passed without a dissentient voice; **nicht** ~ unadopted;
~ **sein** to be approved of; ~ **werden** to go, to be accepted, *(Gesetz)* to be carried, to pass; **als gültig** ~ **werden** *(Münze)* to pass as current; **fast überall [als Zahlungsmittel]** ~ **werden** to go almost anywhere;
~**er Antrag** motion carried; ~**es Kind** adopted child; ~**er Name** pseudonym, assumed (suppositious) name; **unter einem** ~**en Namen reisen** to travel incognito; ~**er Wechsel** accepted (hono(u)red) bill; ~**er Wert** fictitious value.
angepackt werden müssen, fest to need a tight hand.
angepaßt adapted.
Anger meadow, pasture.
angeregt animated, lively;
in ~**er Stimmung sein** to be in high spirits.
angesammelt accumulated, *(Erträge)* earned, *(Zinsen)* accrued.
angesäuselt, leicht half-seas over *(coll.)*.
angeschlagen *(fig.)* out on one's feet, groggy;
~**en Eindruck machen** to seem to be groggy; ~**er Produktionsapparat** impaired productive system.
angeschlossen affiliated, *(el.)* in circuit, *(Telefon)* connected;
~**e Bank** member bank; ~**e Firmen** member firms; ~**e Sender** linked-up broadcasting stations.
Angeschlossensein *(Rundfunkstationen)* hookup, linkup.
angeschmutzt shop-soiled, shopworn.
angeschnittene|Anzeige bleed advertisement; ~ **Seite** bleed-off page.
angeschrieben, bei jem. gut ~ **sein** to be in s. one's good books, to stand high in s. one's favo(u)r, to have a good standing with s. o., to be in good odo(u)r with s. o.; **bei jem. schlecht** ~ **sein** to be in s. one's black books; **bei seinem Chef schlecht** ~ **sein** to be in a tough spot with one's boss.
Angeschuldigter accused [person], suspect.
an|geschwemmt alluvial; ~**geschwollen** *(Fluß)* proud, up.
angesehen of good reputation, reputable, well-reputed, respectable, esteemed, renowned, weighty, having influence, worthy;
hoch ~ highly reputed; **nicht** ~ looked down upon, disrespectable;

bei jem. gut ~ sein to have a good standing with s. o.; **bei jem. schlecht ~ sein** to be in s. one's black books; **sehr ~ sein** to be of recognized standing;
~er Bürger hono(u)rable citizen; **~e Firma** renowned (respectable) firm; **~e Leute** people of position; **~e Stellung** well-established position.
Angesehenheit high reputation, repute.
angesessen settled, resident, domiciled.
angesetzt *(Preis)* quoted, *(Termin)* fixed, appointed, scheduled; **zu hoch ~** excessive in amount; **zu niedrig ~** short-posted, understated; **zum Verkauf ~** put up for sale;
für Montag ~ sein *(Termin)* to be down for Monday;
~er Arbeiter employed worker; **~er Verhandlungstermin** day fixed for a hearing.
angesichts in view of;
~ von in the light of; **~ der Gefahr** in the face of danger.
angespannt strained, tense, intense;
einer Rede ~ folgen to follow a speech closely; **aufs Äußerste ~ sein** to be under great strain; **stark ~ sein** to be under pressure; **mit ~er Aufmerksamkeit** with close attention; **~er Geldmarkt** tightness of money (in the money market); **~e Lage** tight situation; **~e Lage des Kapitalmarktes** stringency of the capital market.
angestammt ancestral, rooted, hereditary;
~es Recht birthright.
angestaubt shopworn.
angesteckt infected.
angestellt employed, in the employ (pay) of, on the payroll; **im Büro ~** black-coated *(Br.)*, white-collar *(US)*; **fest ~** salaried, in a permanent position, established, on the regular staff, permanently appointed, ordinary;
~ sein to be employed (in employment); **bei jem. ~ sein** to be in s. one's pay; **fest ~ sein** to be permanently appointed (a permanent employee, on the establishment), to be on a regular salary; **auf Lebenszeit (lebenslänglich) ~ sein** to hold an office (a post) for life; **für zwei Jahre fest ~ werden** to be engaged for a term of two years.
Angestellte employee, lady clerk, *(pl.)* staff, salaried (black-coated, *Br.*, white-collar, *US*) men (people), salaried staff; **kaufmännische ~** lady clerk; **leitende ~** *(pl.)* senior (supervisory) staff *(Br.)*, executive (supervisory) personnel *(US)*, office management people *(US)*; **zahlreiche ~** *(Haushalt)* establishment of servants;
~ im gehobenen und mittleren Bereich senior and semi-senior level officers; **~ der öffentlichen Hand** public-sector employees; **~ des Hotel- und Gaststättengewerbes** hotel and catering employees; **leitende ~ und sonstiges Personal** officers and staff; **~ auf Zeit** temporary staff (employees);
kurz vor der Entlassung stehende leitende ~ beraten to counsel about-to-be-booted executives; **seine leitenden ~n an sich binden** to hold one's management team; **~ loswerden** to rid o. s. of employees.
Angestellten | zu jem. abbestellen to lend an employee to s. o.; **~ ausbezahlen** to pay off an employee; **~ aussteuern** to drop out an employee; **seine ~ bei der Wahl beeinflussen** to vote one's employees; **~ mit vollen Bezügen beurlauben** to suspend an employee on full pay; **~ entlassen** to discharge (dispose of) an employee; **zu den ~ gehören** to be on the establishment; **einem ~ kündigen** to give an employee warning, to give notice to an employee; **~ zur disziplinarischen Bestrafung melden** to report an employee for misconduct; **~ versetzen** to move an employee;
~ausbildung employee training; **~beratung** counselling employees; **~bestechung** commercial bribery; **~beurteilung** employee appraisal; **abgeschriebenes ~darlehen** loan to employee written off; **~einstufung** employee rating *(US)*; **~erfindung** invention made by an employee; **~fluktuation** employee turnover; **~gehalt** salary rate; **~gehälter** salaries to staff, office (staff) salaries; **~gewerkschaft** [etwa] National and Local Government Officers' Association, Clerical and Administrative Workers' Union *(Br.)*, white-collar union *(US)*, public employee union; **~klasse** salary group; **einem ~konto Aktien gutschreiben** to credit an employee on the company books with shares of stock; **~liste** establishment list; **~moral** employee morale; **~pension** employee pension *(Br.)*; **~pensionierung** employee retirement; **~pensionskasse** staff pension fund *(Br.)*; **~position** salaried post (position); **~rabatt** employee discount; **~rente** employee pension; **~schaft** employees, staff, salaried personnel; **~tantieme** employee's bonus; **~verband** staff association *(Br.)*; **~verhältnis** ordinary; **im ~verhältnis** on the payroll *(US)*; **im ~verhältnis stehen** to be employed (on the establishment); **~verpflegung** catering for employees; **~versicherung** employee's insurance, social security (insurance); **~versicherungsgesetz** Social Security Act *(US)*; **~versicherungskarte** social security card; **~vertretung** employee representation; **~verzeichnis** list of employees; **~zeitschrift** personnel periodical.
Angestellter employee, employe *(US)*, white collar worker, officer, official, functionary, placeholder, salaried employee *(Br.)*, *(AG)* corporate (corporation) official *(US)*, *(Diener)* man servant, *(Korrespondent)* correspondent, [correspondence] clerk; **abgestellter ~** loaned employee; **ganztägig beschäftigter ~** full-time employee; **nicht ganztägig (halbtägig) beschäftigter ~** part-time employee; **hoch bezahlter ~** high-salaried employee; **bezugsberechtigter ~** *(Belegschaftsaktien)* eligible employee; **streng kaufmännisch eingestellter ~** articulate commercially aware senior executive; **gewerkschaftsfreundlich eingestellter ~** pro-union employee; **festbesoldeter ~** salaried employee; **führender ~** executive; **im Rang gleichstehender ~** level executive; **hochbezahlter ~** high-salaried employee; **hochgestellter ~** high-ranking executive; **hochqualifizierter ~** top-calibre employee; **höherer ~** executive, white collar *(US)* (black-coated, *Br.*) employee; **initiativer ~** take-charge executive; **kaufmännischer ~** clerk; **langjähriger ~** long-service employee; **leitender ~** senior (business) executive, executive [employee], top executive *(US)*, managerial employee, business manager, line (operating, senior, executive) official (officer) *(US)*, *(AG)* corporation (corporate) officer (executive) *(US)*, old head *(sl.)*, *(Luftverkehrsgesellschaft)* air executive; **täglich pendelnder leitender ~** commuting executive; **nicht gewerkschaftlich organisierter ~** nonunion employee; **pensionsfähiger ~** superannuated employee; **auf Probe ~** probationer; **rangältester ~** senior officer *(US)*; **städtischer ~** town clerk *(Br.)*, city employee *(US)*; **statistischer ~** census employee; **untergeordneter ~** inferior clerk, nonpolicy-making functionary, nonofficer, understrapper, subordinate officer *(US)*; **in die Zentrale versetzter ~** relocated employee; **versicherter ~** covered employee; **vorübergehend ~** temporary; **zeichnungsberechtigter ~** confidential (signing) clerk;
~ mit Aufsichtsfunktionen supervisory employee; **~ für Außenarbeiten** outdoor servant; **~ einer Bank** bank clerk *(Br.)*; **leitender ~ in der Bauindustrie** construction executive; **~ im öffentlichen Dienst** government employee, public (state) employee *(US)*; **~ als Erfinder** employee inventor; **~ der Handelsmarine** merchant navy officer; **~ einer Luftfahrtgesellschaft** airline official (executive); **~ einer Speditionsgesellschaft** mail clerk *(US)*; **~ in leitender Stellung** executive [officer] *(US)*; **~ des Telegrafenamtes** telegraph operator; **~ mit Überwachungsfunktion** supervisory executive;
als ~ arbeiten to have a white-collar *(US)* (black-coated, *Br.*) job.
ange | stochen, heute frisch *(Bierfaß)* tapped today; **~stoßen** *(Ladung)* dented; **von Scheinwerfern ~strahlt** floodlit; **~strahlte Werbefläche** floodlight advertisement; **~strengt arbeiten** to work hard; **frisch ~strichen** wet paint; **rot ~strichen** rubric; **~tan** apt, likely; **~tan sein** to be fond of s. th.; **von einer Idee sofort ~tan sein** to take an idea at once; **von einer Batterie ~trieben** run by battery; **~troffen** found; **~trunken** slightly intoxicated, tipsy; **~wachsen** *(Zinsen)* accrued; **~wandt** applied, mixed; **~wandte Wissenschaft** applied science.
angewiesen dependent;
auf j. ~ sein to depend on s. o.; **ganz auf sich selbst ~ sein** to be entirely thrown upon one's own resources; **auf wohltätige Spenden ~ sein** to be reduced to charity; **auf Unterstützung ~ sein** to be dependent on alms; **auf seinen Vater ~ sein** to depend on one's father.
Angewiesensein dependence.
angewöhnen, sich etw. to pick up a habit, to accustom o. s. to s. th.; **sich langsam ~** to drop into the habit; **sich das Trinken ~** to take to drinking.
Angewohnheit habit;
aus ~ habitually;
schlechte ~en ablegen (aufgeben) to leave off (forswear) bad habits.
angewurzelt, wie rooted to the spot.
angezeigt werden, wegen ... to be booked on charges of *(fam.)*.
angezogen haben, sich unmöglich to be dressed up to kill.
angleichen to adapt, to adjust, to assimilate, to approximate, *(Handels- an Steuerbilanz)* to match, *(Rechtsvorschriften, Steuern)* to harmonize;
Amtsstunden aneinander ~ to correlate office hours; **Einheitswerte ~** to equalize assessments; **Einkommen ~** to equalize

incomes; **Frachtsätze** ~ to standardize (adjust) freight rates; **widerstreitende Interessen** ~ to accommodate conflicting interests; **Löhne** ~ to equalize wages, to adjust existing wage rates; **Mittel den Zwecken** ~ to adjust the means to an end; **Preise schrittweise** ~ *(EG)* to approximate prices progressively; **die Produktion der Nachfrage** ~ to gear production to demand; **innerstaatliche Rechtsvorschriften** ~ *(EG)* to approximate municipal laws; **Währungen** ~ to align currencies; **Zinsen** ~ to adjust interest.

Angleichung assimilation, adjustment, adaptation, approximation, *(Einkommen)* equalization, *(Handels- an Steuerbilanz)* matching, *(Europäische Rechtsvorschriften)* harmonization;
~ **der Einheitswerte** equalization of assessments; ~ **der Frachtsätze** standardization of freight charges, adjustment [and relationship] of rates; ~ **der Gehälter** salary adjustment; ~ **der Getreidepreise** *(EG)* grain price adjustment; ~ **widerstreitender Interessen** accommodation of conflicting interests; ~ **der bestehenden Lohnsätze** adjustment of existing wage rates; ~ **der Preise** adjustment of prices, price adjustment; **schrittweise** ~ **der Preise** *(EG)* progressive approximation of prices; ~ **innerstaatlicher Rechtsvorschriften** *(EG)* approximation of municipal laws; ~ **von Steuern** harmonization of taxes; ~ **der Währungen** monetary alignment.

Angleichungsperiode period of adjustment.

Angler angler, fisherman.

angliedern to affiliate, *(annektieren)* to annex, *(eingliedern)* to integrate, to incorporate, *(wirtschaftlich)* to assimilate, to attach; **Truppen einem Verband** ~ to attach troops to a formation.

Angliederung affiliation, incorporation, *(Annektion)* annexation; **wirtschaftliche** ~ economic assimilation (attachment).

Angreifen | des Kapitals incursions into the capital; ~ **der Reserven** raid on the reserves.

angreifen to attack, to assail, to take the offensive, *(Kapital)* to draw on, *(mil.)* to attack, to engage, *(Rost)* to attack, to corrode;
die Augen ~ to affect (strain) the eyes; **unbefestigtes Dorf** ~ to descend upon a defenceless village; **jds. Ehre** ~ to impeach s. one's hono(u)r; **seine Ersparnisse** ~ to make inroads on one's savings; **sein Kapital** ~ to make holes (incursions) in one's capital; **Kasse** ~ to break into the till; **mit überlegenen Kräften** ~ to attack with superior forces; **Land** ~ to invade a country; **von neuem** ~ to recharge; **j. in der Öffentlichkeit** ~ to go for (attack) s. o. in the papers (in public); **j. plötzlich** ~ to fly at s. one's throat; **Rede scharf** ~ to criticize a speech severely; **Reserven** ~ to raid the reserves; **selbst mit** ~ to lend a hand; **tätlich** ~ to commit an assault; **überraschend** ~ to attack without warning; **j. verbissen** ~ to make a dead set upon s. o.; **sein Vermögen** ~ to touch one's capital; **j. wie ein Verrückter** ~ to be down on s. o. like a hammer; **Vorräte** ~ to draw on a stock, to touch supplies; **Vorschläge des Premierministers scharf** ~ to attack the Prime Minister's proposals; **in einander folgenden Wellen** ~ to attack in waves; **an der Westfront** ~ to make a push on the Western front; **j. in der Zeitung** ~ to attack (go for) s. o. in a newspaper.

angreifend offensive, aggressive;
~**es Flugzeug** attacking aircraft; ~**er Staat** aggressor nation.

Angreifer aggressor, assailant;
~**staat** aggressor nation.

Angrenzen abutment, adjacency, contiguity.

angrenzen to border, to abut, to adjoin, to bound, to be contiguous;
an ein Land ~ to border a state; **an einen öffentlichen Weg** ~ to touch a public road, to adjoin a highway.

angrenzend adjoining, adjacent, abutting, neighbo(u)ring, bordering, bounding, *(anstoßend)* contiguous;
unmittelbar ~ fronting and abutting; ~ **und zusammenhängend** *(Schulbezirk)* contiguous and compact;
~**es Gebiet** neighbo(u)ring country; ~**es Grundstück** adjoining estate; ~**e Zone** contiguous zone.

Angriff attack, onslaught, onrush, onset, assault, thrust, *(mil.)* attack, offensive, charge;
~**en ausgesetzt** vulnerable (exposed) to attack;
bewaffneter ~ armed attack; **erneuerter** ~ renewed attack; **gewalttätiger** ~ assault and battery; **großangelegter** ~ large-scale attack; **heimtückischer** ~ vicious attack; **hinterhältiger** ~ stab in the back; **katalytischer** ~ catalytic attack; **körperlicher** ~ offence against a person; **leidenschaftlicher** ~ vehement attack; **massierter** ~ *(mil.)* mass attack; **niederträchtiger** ~ pot-shot; **nicht provozierter** ~ unprovoked aggression; **rollender** ~ *(mil.)* relay attack; **tätlicher** ~ assault, battery;
~ **der Baissepartei** bear campaign (raid, *Br.*); ~ **nach Bereitstellung** deliberate attack; ~ **der Haussepartei** bull campaign (raid, *Br.*); **plötzlicher** ~ **auf ein Lager** sudden raid on a camp; ~ **auf jds. Leumund** imputation of s. one's character; ~ **aus Zufall** accidental attack;
~ **ist die beste Verteidigung** attack is the best form of defence; ~ **abbrechen** to break off an attack; ~ **abschlagen** to repulse an attack; **sich** ~**en aussetzen** to leave o. s. open to attacks; **jedem** ~ **Trotz bieten** *(Festung)* to defy every attack; ~ **eröffnen** *(mil.)* to develop; **den feindlichen** ~**en Stand halten** to withstand the onset of the enemy; **in** ~ **nehmen** to break ground, to go about, to set one's hand to, to plunge ahead with, to proceed with s. th., to take s. th. in hand, to tackle s. th.; **das Dringendste zuerst in** ~ **nehmen** to attend to the most urgent things first; **Sache in** ~ **nehmen** to put one's hand to a task; **heftigen** ~ **gegen den Premierminister richten** to make a savage onslaught on the Prime Minister; ~**en ungeschützt ausgesetzt sein** to lie open to attacks; **einem** ~ **standhalten** to hold out against an attack; **zum** ~ **übergehen** to proceed to attack, to take the offensive; ~ **unternehmen** to make an attack; ~ **vortragen** to mount an offensive.

Angriffs | abschnitt attack sector; ~**bündnis** offensive alliance; ~**fläche bieten** to lay o. s. open to attack; ~**flug** raid, sortie; ~**front** battle front; ~**geist** fighting spirit; ~**handlung** offensive, act of aggression; ~**hubschrauber** attack helicopter; ~**krieg** offensive (invasive) war, war of aggression.

angriffslustig with one's hackle up, out for scalps.

Angriffs | plan plan of attack; ~**punkt** weak point, *(Vorwand)* handle, pretext; **keinen** ~**punkt bieten** to give no offence; ~**raum** zone of attack; ~**signal** signal to attack; ~**spitze** spearhead; ~**streik** attack strike; ~**termin** zero day; ~**vorbereitungen** *(Amphibienkräfte)* prelanding operations; ~**waffen** aggressive (offensive) weapons, weapons of offense (offence, *Br.*); ~- **und Verteidigungswaffen** offensive and defensive arms; ~**zeit** zero hour; ~**ziel** objective.

Angst fear, alarm, dread, terror;
höllische ~ dreadful fear, blue funk; **lähmende** ~ paralysing fear; **panikartige** ~ panic fear;
irgendwie ~ **bekommen** to get sort of frightened; **mit der** ~ **zu tun bekommen** *(coll.)* to get the wind up; **j.** ~ **einjagen** to put the wind up s. o.; **in** ~ **geraten** to become filled with distress; **überhaupt keine** ~ **haben** to be wholly void of fear; **wahnsinnige** ~ **haben** to be in a blue funk *(sl.)*; **in ständiger** ~ **leben** to live in constant fear; **vor** ~ **wie von Sinnen sein** to be scared out of one's senses (wits); **j. in** ~ **und Schrecken versetzen** to terrify s. o.; **voller** ~ **auf etw. warten** to sweat it out *(sl.)*; **vor** ~ **zittern** to quake in one's shoes;
~**geschrei** screams of fear; ~**hase** funk.

ängstigen to alarm, to frighten;
sich zu Tode ~ to worry o. s. to death; **j. zu Tode** ~ to frighten s. o. out of his wits.

Angst | käufe panic buying, funk buying *(sl.)*; ~**käufe tätigen** to panic-buy; ~**klausel** *(Wechsel)* safety (without recourse) clause.

ängstlich fearful, timid, *(besorgt)* anxious, afraid, apprehensive;
~ **um seinen guten Ruf bedacht** anxious about one's reputation; **sich** ~ **an die Vorschriften halten** to stick scrupulously to the rules.

Ängstlichkeit timidity, timidness, anxiety;
übergroße ~ oversolicitude.

Angst | macher panicmonger; ~**preise** panic prices; ~**psychose** panic; ~**röhre** *(Zylinder, fam.)* top (silk) hat, topper *(coll.)*, tile, plug hat *(US sl.)*; ~**traum** nightmare; ~**verkäufe** panic sale (selling); ~**zustände bekommen** to feel sick with fear.

anhaben to be dressed, to wear;
jem. nichts ~ **können** to have nothing on s. o. *(coll.)*.

anhaften, einer Sache to cling to s. th.

anhaftend adhesive, adherent, sticky;
~**er Fehler** inherent vice; **einem Kompromiß** ~**e Mängel** imperfections inherent in a compromise.

anhaken to tick (check) off.

Anhalt foothold, *(fig.)* clue;
als ~ **dienen** to serve as a hint; ~ **finden** to gain a footing.

Anhaltelager detention (concentration) camp.

Anhalten *(Auto)* pull-up, *(Maschine)* stop, stoppage;
plötzliches ~ crash halt (stop);
~ **und Ausrauben von Zügen** trainjacking; ~ **eines Kraftfahrers durch einen Verkehrspolizisten** detention of a motorist by a traffic officer; ~ **der Krise** continuing crisis; ~ **von Post durch die Zensur** interception of mail by the censor.

anhalten to arrest, to halt, to put to a stand, *(Auto)* to stop, to pull up, *(dauern)* to continue, to last, *(Verkehr)* to hold up, to block;

jem. zur Arbeit ~ to urge s. o. to work; Auto zum Mitfahren ~ to hitchhike *(coll.)*, to thumb a lift; bei Bedarf ~ to stop by request; Luft ~ to hold one's breath; plötzlich ~ to pull up short, to stop dead; ruckartig ~ to stop with a jerk; Verfahren ~ to stay proceedings.

anhaltend continuous, increasing, continual, continued, persistent;
~er Beifall sustained applause; ~er Fleiß assiduity; ~es Interesse continued interest; ~e Konjunktur continuous boom; ~e Nachfrage steady demand.

Anhalter hitchhiker;
per ~ on the thumb;
per ~ fahren to hitchhike *(coll.)*, to thumb a lift (ride, *US*), to get a ride *(US)*, to beat one's way *(US)*, to long-arm *(sl.)*.

Anhalte|recht right of (to) stoppage in transit; ~stelle stopping place, stop, *(Autobus)* bus stop.

Anhaltspunkt indication, criterion, clue, lead *(US)*, pointer *(fam.)*;
nachstehende ~e clues given below; statistische ~e statistical evidence;
~ für eine Erklärung abgeben to offer a clue for an explanation; j. einen ~ geben to put s. o. on the track; keine ~e haben to have nothing to go by (on).

Anhaltswert approximate (reference) value.

anhand haben, etw. to be commissioned to sell s. th.

Anhandgeben firm offer;
~ von Grundstücken bei mehreren Maklern multiple listing *(US)*.

Anhang appendix, appendage, appendant, subjoinder, supplement, adjunct, *(Beilage)* annex, enclosure, schedule, addendum, pendant, *(Gefolgschaft)* supporters, adherents, followers, following, *(Gesetz)* schedule, *(Testament)* codicil, *(zur Urkunde)* rider, *(Wechsel)* slip, allonge;
ohne ~ without [family] encumbrance.

Anhänge|adresse, ~etikett tag, tally, tie-on label.

anhängen to affix, to join, to annex, *(Wagen)* to attach, to couple;
jem. etw. ~ to land s. o. with s. th., to attach to s. o., to give a dog a bad name [and hang him]; Klausel ~ to add a clause; jem. wie eine Klette ~ to stick like wax to s. o.; einem Kunden alte Ladenhüter ~ to fob off old stock on a client; Null ~ to add a zero; jem. einen Prozeß ~ to involve s. o. in a lawsuit; ein paar Sätze an seine Rede ~ to add a few more sentences to one's speech; Sonderwagen ~ to put on an extra coach; einem Unschuldigen einen Mord ~ to saddle a murder on an innocent person; Zettel an ein Paket ~ to tie a label on a parcel.

anhängend *(Zinsschein)* attached;
~es Muster attached sample.

Anhänger adherent, supporter, follower, partisan, sympathizer, satellite, henchman, *(pl.)* following, *(Anhängeadresse)* tie-on label, tag, tally, tab, *(Gepäck)* luggage-label holder, *(des Kommunismus)* fellow traveller, *(Lastwagen)* trailer, *(Lokomotive)* tender;
begeisterter ~ devotee, fan *(coll.)*, buff *(US fam.)*; blind ergebener ~ heeler *(US coll.)*; glühender ~ strong partisan; leidenschaftlicher ~ warm supporter; loyaler ~ loyal supporter; sturer ~ diehard; treuer ~ firm partisan, true blue; kaum vorhandene ~ marked absence of supporters; zuverlässige ~ thick supporters;
~ der Doppelwährung bimetallist; überzeugter ~ der Etikette strict observer of etiquette; ~ des Freihandelssystems free trader; ~ der Geburtenkontrolle birth controller; ~ des Kollektivismus collectivist; ~ der Linken leftist; überzeugter ~ der freien Marktwirtschaft free-market fundamentalist; ~ des Merkantilismus mercantilist; ~ der Planwirtschaft statist; ~ der Politik der kleinen Schritte gradualist; ~ der konstitutionellen Regierungsform constitutionalist; ~ des Syndikalismus syndicalist; ~ einer Untergrundbewegung undergrounder; ~ der Verhältniswahl proportionalist; ~ der britischen Zugehörigkeit zur Europäischen Gemeinschaft pro-marketeer *(Br.)*; ~ der Zwangswirtschaft coercionist;
~ befestigen to tie on a label; ~ gewinnen *(Idee)* to catch on; ~ im Mittelstand haben *(pol.)* to be recruited from the middle classes; zahlreiche ~ haben to have a numerous following; jds. glühender ~ sein to sit at s. one's feet; von seinen ~n umringt sein to be surrounded by his devotees; ~ moderner Musik sein to have a prejudice in favo(u)r of modern music; mit einem ~ versehen to tag;
~bremse trailer brake; ~schaft following, partisanship, followers, adherents; sich eine ~schaft in der großen Masse sichern to build up a popular following; ~schar in allen Altersgruppen broad-based following; ~wagen trailer.

Anhänge|schildchen tag; ~schloß padlock; ~zettel tie-on label, tag, tally.

anhängig pending, pendent, ancillary;
vor Gericht ~ pending before the court; während der Prozeß ~ ist pendente lite;
Klage (Prozeß) ~ machen to bring an action, to institute legal proceedings; gegen j. ~ sein *(Verfahren)* to lie against s. o.; ~er Prozeß pending lawsuit; ~e Sache cause pending.

Anhängigkeit, Anhängigsein *(Prozeß)* pendency.

anhänglich primitive, devoted, faithful;
~ sein to cling.

Anhänglichkeit devotion, faithfulness.

Anhängsel appendage, appendicle, tag.

Anhängung zusätzlicher Waggons putting on of more coaches.

anhäufen to mass, to agglomerate, to store (pile) up, *(Reichtum)* to accumulate, to amass, to aggregate, *(Waren)* to hoard, to amass, to aggregate, to stockpile, *(Zinsen)* to accrue.

anhäufend cumulative.

Anhäufung cumulation, mass, conglomerate, agglomeration, *(Geschäft)* block, cluster, *(Kapital)* accumulation, aggregation, *(Waren)* hoarding, *(Zinsen)* accrual;
~ von Kapital accumulation of capital; ~ von Rechtsansprüchen increase in claims; ~ von Rückständen accumulation of arrears; ~ von Vermögenswerten conglomeration of assets.

anheben to lift, to raise;
Preise ~ to increase (raise, jack up, *coll.*) prices.

Anhebung *(Preise)* increase, raise;
~ der Lebenshaltungskosten cost-of-living rise; globale ~ des Lohnniveaus round-of-wage increase; generelle ~ des Preisniveaus mounting prices; ~ der Steueranfangsbeträge threshold increase.

anheften to tack, to fasten, to affix, *(mit Büroklammer)* to clip on, *(Zinsschein)* to attach, to affix;
Bekanntmachung ~ to put up a notice; Preiszettel ~ to label, to ticket *(US)*.

anheimfallen to revert (fall) to, to devolve upon;
der Fürsorge ~ to fall upon the parish, to be reduced to charity; der Vergessenheit ~ to fall into oblivion.

anheimstellen to submit, to leave;
jem. ~ to defer to s. one's opinion, to leave it to s. o.; jds. Ermessen ~ to leave to s. one's discretion.

Anheirat affinity.

anheischig machen, sich to pledge o. s.;
~ zu kaufen to profess to purchase.

anheizen to heat, to fire;
Konjunktur ~ to boost business, to heat up the economy.

anheuern to engage, to enrol, to hire, to recruit *(US)*, *(Seeleute)* to sign on;
sich ~ lassen *(Matrose)* to sign the ship's articles.

Anheuerung hiring, enrolment, recruitment *(US)*.

Anhieb, auf den ersten at the first push.

anhimmeln to idolize.

Anhöhe elevation, height, rising ground, eminence, up, hill, high ground.

anhören to hear;
j. ~ to give (grant) s. o. a hearing; j. bis zu Ende ~ to hear s. o. out; sich gut ~ to sound all right; j. nicht ~ to refuse s. o. a hearing; Sendung ~ to listen to a programme; j. unparteiisch ~ to give s. o. a fair hearing.

Anhörung hearing, audience;
nach ~ der Zeugen after hearing the witnesses;
öffentliche ~ hearing in public, public hearing; verweigerte ~ denial of hearing;
~ durch das Gericht court hearing; ~ im Schiedsgerichtsverfahren arbitration hearing; ~ hinter verschlossenen Türen closed-door hearing;
bei öffentlichen ~en äußerst scharf behandeln to grill at public hearings; keine ~ finden to be refused a hearing; j. ohne ~ verurteilen to condem s. o. without a hearing.

Anhörungs|termin *(Insolvenzverfahren)* date of hearing, hearing date; ~verfahren hearing.

Animierdame taxi dancer, B girl.

animieren to encourage, to incite, *(Alkohol)* to stimulate, to panic *(US sl.)*.

Animositäten, unbedeutende petty animosities.

ankämpfen, gegen Schwierigkeiten to row against the tide; gegen den hohen Seegang ~ to struggle against the waves.

Ankauf buying, purchasing, acquisition, *(Land)* land purchase;
günstiger ~ good buy;
~ von Firmenwagen fleet buying; ~ von Industrieunternehmungen asset backing; ~ einer Prise preemption; ~ zu Spekula-

tionszwecken purchase on speculation; ~ **durch den Staat** state buying; ~ **und Verkauf** purchase and sale; ~ **und Verkauf gebrauchter Industrieausrüstungen** purchase and sale of second-hand industrial equipment; ~ **offener Warenforderungen** factoring; ~ **von Wertpapieren** purchase of investment securities; **über den ~ entscheiden** to make the buying decision; ~ **genehmigen** to okay a purchase *(US)*; **über den ~ eines Hauses verhandeln** to negotiate for the purchase of a house; ~ **eines Wagens in Erwägung ziehen** to consider buying a car.

ankaufen to purchase [land], to buy, to acquire;
sich ~ to settle; **Wechsel** ~ to discount a bill.

Ankäufer purchaser, buyer, acquirer, *(im Vertragstext)* vendee.

Ankaufs|entscheidung buying (purchasing) decision; ~**ermächtigung** *(Wechsel)* authority to negotiate, *(Außenhandel)* authority to purchase; ~**etat** purchase fund.

ankaufsfähig purchasable, *(Wechsel)* discountable, rediscountable *(US)*;
~**e Wechsel** *(Landeszentralbank)* bills eligible for discount (rediscount, *US*).

Ankaufs|fonds purchase fund; ~**genehmigung** purchase approval; ~**kommission** purchasing commission; ~**kosten** *(Kapitalanlagegesellschaft)* acquisition cost, sales charge; ~**kredit** vendor credit; ~**kurs** buying rate; **zu ~kursen** at cost; ~- **und Verkaufskurs** *(Börse)* double price; ~**möglichkeiten** acquisition possibilities; ~**option** option to purchase; ~**preis** purchase (cost) price, purchasing rate, *(EG)* buying-in price; **zum ~preis** at first cost; ~**preise von Versicherungspolicen** insurance policy acquisition costs; ~**projekt** acquisiton project; ~**sätze** *(Landeszentralbank)* buying (discount, rediscount, *US*) rates; ~**spesen** *(Kapitalanlagegesellschaft)* acquisition cost, sales charge; ~**stelle für ungemünztes Gold** bullion office; ~**summe** purchase money; ~**syndikat** original syndicate; ~**wert** original cost, outlay for assets; **zum ~wert** at cost price.

Anker|aufnehmen (hochziehen) to pick up an anchor; ~ **auswerfen** to cast (drop) anchor; **vor ~ gehen** to cast (drop) anchor, to berth; **Schiff vor ~ legen** to moor (anchor) a ship; ~ **lichten** to loose (weight, get up the) anchor, to heave the anchor; **vor ~ liegen** to ride at anchor (the road), to lie at anchor, to be in the road; ~ **an Bord nehmen** to take the anchor inboard; **vor ~ treiben** to drag its anchor, to ride at ease; ~**boje** anchor buoy; ~**gebühr**, ~**geld** anchorage *(Br.)*, duty of anchorage; ~**grund** anchorage, berth, holding ground; **vom ~grund abbringen** to unmoor; ~**kette** anchor chain; ~**licht** riding light; ~**mast** mooring mast.

ankern to cast (drop) anchor.

Anker|platz anchorage, berth; ~**recht** right of anchorage; ~**ruf** lever watch; ~**trosse** mooring rope, [anchor] cable.

anklagbar indictable, prosecutable, impeachable.

Anklage charge, accusation, criminal charge, incrimination, information, plaint, *(vor dem Parlament)* impeachment, arraignment, *(vor dem Schwurgericht)* indictment;
begründete ~ true bill; **fehlerhafte** ~ mischarge; **formelle** ~ information; **öffentliche** ~ penal (criminal) action, prosecution; **schwebende** ~ pending charge;
~ **wegen Bestechung** charge of extortion; ~ **wegen Fahrerflucht** hit-and-run charge; ~ **wegen Mißachtung des Gerichtes** contempt charge; ~ **wegen Schmuggels** smuggling charge; ~ **vor dem Schwurgericht** presentment;
~ **glatt ableugnen** to meet a charge with a stiff denial; ~ **als unbegründet abweisen** to ignore a bill; ~ **begründen** to substantiate a charge; **sich gegen eine ~ behaupten** to purge o. s. of a charge; **gegen einen Einzelpunkt einer ~ keinen Widerspruch einlegen** to plead no contest to a single charge; ~ **erheben** to prefer (bring) a charge, to bring in (lay down) an indictment, to file an information *(Br.)*, to prefer a bill of indictment, to bring an accusation, to present *(US)*; **öffentliche ~ erheben** to indict; ~ **für begründet erklären** to bring in (find, *US*) a true bill; ~ **fallenlassen** to ignore a bill, to quash an indictment, to exclude from indictment, to drop (throw out) a charge; **j. von einer ~ freisprechen** to acquit s. o. of a charge; **sich wegen einer ~ zu verantworten haben** to answer a charge; **einer ~ stattgeben** to sustain a charge; **unter ~ stehen** to stand trial, to be under a charge; **unter ~ des Diebstahls stehen** to be accused of theft; **sich der ~ stellen** to meet a charge; **j. wegen Mordes unter ~ stellen** to charge s. o. with murder; **sich gegen eine ~ verteidigen** to answer a charge; ~ **vertreten** to be counsel for the prosecution; ~ **verwerfen** to ignore a bill of indictment; ~ **widerlegen** to rebut an accusation; ~ **zurückziehen** to quash the indictment, to ignore a bill;
~**bank** dock; **auf der ~bank sitzen** to be in the dock; ~**behörde** the prosecution, Director of Public Prosecution *(Br.)*; ~**beschluß** indictment; ~**beschluß verkünden** to return an indictment; ~**erhebung** indictment, presentment *(US)*, impeachment, commencement of prosecution; ~**erhebung ablehnen** to disallow a charge.

anklagefähig indictable, chargeable.

Anklagejury grand jury *(US)*.

anklagen to charge, to accuse, to indict, to prosecute, to criminate, to incriminate, to inculpate, to emplead, to libel *(Scot.)*;
j. wegen Amtsmißbrauchs ~ to impeach s. o.; **des Aufruhrs** ~ to indict as a rioter (on a charge of rioting); **des Diebstahls** ~ to accuse of theft; **erneut** ~ to reaccuse, to recharge; **des Mordes** ~ to charge with murder; **j. eines Verbrechens** ~ to charge s. o. with a crime.

anklagend accusatory.

Anklagepunkt count, *(pl.)* particulars of criminal charge;
~**e gegen j. beweisen** to bring a charge home to s. o.; **j. in allen ~en schuldig erklären** to find guilty on all charges; ~ **fallenlassen** to desert the diet *(Scot., law)*; **in allen ~en für schuldig befunden werden** to be found guilty on all counts.

Ankläger indictor, arraigner, accuser, public prosecutor, district attorney *(US)*, pursuer *(Scot.)*;
öffentlicher ~ Director of public prosecutions, Counsel for the Crown *(Br.)*, public prosecutor;
~ **im Kriegsgerichtsverfahren** judge advocate *(Br.)*.

Anklagerede statement declaration.

anklägerischerseits on the part of the prosecutor.

Anklägerrolle role of a prosecutor;
~ **übernehmen** to assume the role of indicter.

Anklage|schrift bill of indictment *(Br.)*, special presentment, charge, *(mil.)* charge sheet; **begründete ~schrift** true bill *(US)*; **förmliche ~schrift** indictment; ~**schrift vorlegen** to prefer an indictment; ~**verfügung** indictment; ~**vertreter** prosecuting attorney, council for the prosecution, publich prosecutor; ~**vertretung** prosecution; **j. in den ~zustand versetzen** to commit s. o. for trial.

anklammern to pin, to peg, to fasten;
sich an eine Hoffnung ~ to cling to a hope.

Anklang vogue, echo, appeal;
allgemeiner ~ general appeal;
allgemeiner ~ bei den Wählern general voter appeal;
~ **finden** to catch on, to go down, to find favo(u)r, *(Ware)* to meet with approval, to find a ready market, to be approved of, *(Theaterstück)* to take; **keinen ~ finden** to have no appeal, to prove unpopular; **nicht überall ~ finden** to have no broad appeal; **beim Publikum ~ finden** to get across (go down) with the audience, to hit down *(US)*; ~ **bei jem. finden** to go down well with s. o., to appeal to s. o.

ankleben to stick, to affix, to paste, to glue;
Tapeten ~ to hang wallpaper; **Zettel** ~ to stick (post, *US*) bills.

Ankleber billposter, sticker.

Ankleide|frau dresser; ~**kabine** fitting room, *(Badeanstalt)* cubicle; ~**puppe** doll; ~**raum** dressing room, changeroom *(US)*, toilet *(US)*; ~**räume** cloakroom facilities.

anklingeln, j. to phone (ring up) s. o.

anklingen to remind of, to sound like an echo.

anklopfen to knock, to rap;
bei jem. ~ to look in on s. o., to pay a short visit to s. o., *(fig.)* to sound (tap) s. o.

anknipsen to switch (turn, put) on.

anknüpfen *(Beziehungen)* to enter into, to form, to establish, to open;
Bekanntschaft mit jem. ~ to make s. one's acquaintance; **neue Geschäftsbeziehungen** ~ to enter into new business relations; **Gespräch mit jem.** ~ to enter into a conversation with s. o.; **an alte Traditionen** ~ to continue traditions; **Verhandlungen** ~ to initiate (enter into) negotiations; **an den Vorredner** ~ to take up the remarks of the speaker.

Anknüpfung, in referring to, with reference to.

Anknüpfungs|punkt link, common interest; ~**werbung** tie-in advertising.

Ankommen arrival, incoming.

ankommen to arrive at, *(Anklang finden)* to catch, to go over (down), *(Waren)* to get in, to meet with approval, *(Zug)* to come (pull) in, to be due;
bei jem. ~ to be acceptable to s. o.; **bei einer Firma** ~ to find employment with a firm; **gut** ~ *(fig.)* to go down, to catch on, to find favo(u)r, *(Verkaufsartikel)* to find a ready market; **nicht** ~ *(Verkaufsartikel)* to fall flat, not to register; **beim Provinzpublikum besonders gut** ~ to go down very well with a provincial audience; **beim Publikum** ~ to get across with the audience, to hit down *(US)*, *(Theaterstück)* to be a winner; **pünktlich** ~ to

arrive on time (as scheduled, *US*); **bei den Schülern schlecht** ~ not to go down well with the pupils; **mit einem Theaterstück** ~ to put a play across; **auf die Umstände** ~ to depend on the circumstances; **unbeschädigt** ~ *(Waren)* to arrive in fair condition; **auf das Wetter** ~ to depend on the weather;
es drauf ~ **lassen** to take (stand) one's chance, to chance (risk) it; **es auf jds. Entscheidung** ~ **lassen** to rely on s. o.; **es auf ein paar Mark nicht** ~ **lassen** not to be particular to a few pounds; **es auf einen Prozeß** ~ **lassen** to venture a lawsuit.
ankommend arriving, *(Telefongespräch)* incoming.
Ankömmling newcomer, comer, incomer, arrival.
ankoppeln to couple, *(Raumschiff)* to dock.
Ankratz beim Publikum finden to put o. s. over.
ankreiden to chalk up;
jem. etw. ~ to give s. o. bad marks for s. th.
ankreuzen to [mark with a] tick (a cross), to mark, *(rot)* to red-letter, to rubricate.
ankündigen to announce, to intimate, to bill, to give out, *(Ware)* to advise, *(in der Zeitung)* to advertise, to publish;
Buch ~ to announce the publication of a book; **jem. etw. formell** ~ to notify s. o. of s. th.; **öffentlich** ~ to announce publicly, to proclaim; **ordnungsgemäß** ~ to give due notice of; **durch Plakate** ~ to placard, to poster; **rechtzeitig** ~ to give due notice; **gerichtliche Schritte** ~ to threaten proceedings.
Ankündigung announcement, notice, proclamation, intimation, card, *(Aktienausgabe)* prospectus, *(Buch, Reklame)* advertisement, advertising, *(Ware)* advice;
ohne vorherige ~ without previous notice;
öffentliche ~ official (public) announcement; **schriftliche** ~ written notice; **vorherige** ~ advance notice;
~ **des Ausnahmezustands** emergency action notification; ~ **der zu ergreifenden Maßnahmen** notice of measures to be taken; ~ **im Rundfunk** broadcast announcement.
Ankündigungs | effekt announcement effect; ~**schreiben** letter of advice.
Ankunft arrival, coming;
bei ~ on arrival; **bei** ~ **des Zuges** on arrival of the train, when the train comes in;
nicht bekannte ~ uncertain arrival; **glückliche** ~ safe arrival; **planmäßige** ~ scheduled arrival *(US)*; **rechtzeitige** ~ seasonable arrival;
~ **und Abfahrt** *(Schiffe)* arrival and sailing, *(Züge)* arrival and departure;
bei ~ **weiterbefördern** reforward on arrival.
Ankunfts | anzeige *(Güter)* notice of arrival; ~**bahnhof** station of arrival; ~**bahnsteig** arrival platform; ~**gleis** arrival track; ~**hafen** port of arrival; ~**halle** arrival side (station); ~**ort** place of arrival; ~**tafel** arrival board; ~~ **und Abfahrtstafel** train indicator; **mutmaßlicher** ~**tag** probable date of arrival; ~**zeit** time of arrival, arrival time; ~~ **und Abfahrtszeiten** arrivals and departures.
ankuppeln to couple, to connect.
ankurbeln to stimulate, *(Motor)* to crank (wind) up;
Arbeitstempo ~ to step up the pace of work; **Konjunktur** ~ to enliven business; **Produktion** ~ to step (crank, pep, *US*) up (stimulate) production; **Wirtschaft** ~ to invigorate (stimulate) business, to pep up the economy, to prime the pump *(US)*, to give the economy a shot in the arm *(US)*, to boost business.
Ankurbelung | der Ausfuhr boosting of exports; ~ **der Konjunktur** stimulation of business activity; ~ **der Wirtschaft** stimulation (reorganization, invigoration) of business, priming the pump *(US)*, pump priming *(US)*.
Ankurbelungs | kredit reconstruction (pump-priming, *US*) credit; ~**programm** pump-priming program *(US)*.
Anlage *(angelegtes Geld)* invested capital, *(Anordnung)* disposition, arrangement, plan, *(grafische Anordnung)* layout, *(Begabung)* endowment, gift, talent, faculty, vein, disposition, *(Beilage)* enclosure, inclosure, exhibit, attached letter, supporting document, *(zu einem Bericht)* annex, appendix, exhibit, *(Betrieb)* plant, factory, works, *(Einbau)* installation, equipment, facility, *(Einheit)* unit, *(Entwurf)* design, outline, plan, draft, *(Gebäude)* construction, *(Gründung)* establishment, foundation, *(Investition)* placement, placing, investment, *(Können)* faculty, *(Montage)* assembling, package, *(Roman)* composition, *(Urkunde)* annex, rider, *(Verwendung)* employment [of funds];
in der ~ **vorhanden** rudimentary;
~**n** *(Bauten)* works, *(Bilanz)* assets, facilities, *(Stadt)* public gardens (park), green belt, pleasure ground;
abgeschriebene ~ retirement unit; **ausgesuchte** ~ choice investment; **außerbetriebliche** ~**n** nonoperating assets; **im Bau befindliche** ~**n** construction (sites) in progress; **betriebsfertige** ~ factory at work; **dem Geschäftsbetrieb dienende** ~**n** assets for use in the business; **elektrische** ~ electric plant, wiring; **ererbte** ~**n** heredity; **erneuerte** ~ replacement unit; **nicht ersetzbare** ~**n** nonreplaceable assets; **aus der Bilanz ersichtliche** ~**n** balance-sheet assets; **erste** ~**n** A-rating; **erstklassige** ~ high-grade investment; **ertragreiche** ~**n** profitable investment; **später erworbene** ~**n** after-acquired assets; **feste** ~**n** fixtures, fixed (permanent, capital, slow) assets; **festverzinsliche** ~ fixed [-interest bearing] investment; **vom Verteidigungsministerium finanzierte** ~**n** defense (defence, *Br.*) -financed facilities; **gebäudeähnliche** ~ structure in the nature of a building; **geistige** ~**n** abilities; **genehmigungsbedürftige** ~**n** installations subject to approval; **außer Betrieb genommene** ~ retirement unit; **neu in Betrieb genommene** ~ newly established plant; **im Leasingverfahren gepachtete** ~**n** leased facilities; **getrennte** ~**n** *(Pensionsfonds)* separate accounts; **gewinnbringende** ~**n** earning assets, profitable (paying) investment; **industrielle** ~**n** industrial installations; **installierte** ~ installation; **kurzfristige** ~ short-term investment; **kurzfristige spekulative** ~ speculation *(Br.)*, turn *(US)*, round transaction *(US)*; **landwirtschaftliche** ~**n** agricultural assets; **langfristige** ~**n** long-term (long-time) investments (holdings); **liquide** ~**n** quick (floating, fluid, liquid, *US*) assets; **lukrative** ~ profitable (remunerative) investment; **maschinelle** ~**n** machinery, plant equipment; **militärische** ~**n** military installations; **mittelfristige** ~**n** medium-term investments; **moderne** ~**n** modern equipment; **mündelsichere** ~**n** gilt-edged *(Br.)* (legal, *US*) security, legal (eligible, *US*, trustee, *Br.*) investment, trustee loan *(Br.)*; **öffentliche** ~**n** public gardens *(US)* (parks), recreation ground; **risikoärmere** ~**n** *(Investmentfonds)* defensive portion *(US)*; **risikoreiche** ~**n** *(Investmentfonds)* aggressive portion *(US)*, aggressive investments; **sanitäre** ~**n** hygienic facilities; **sichere** ~**n** safe (nonspeculative) investments; **spekulative** ~**n** aggressive (speculative, special-situation) investments; **städtische** ~**n** public garden *(US)*, pleasure ground, grounds, park; **stillgelegte** ~**n** discarded assets; **technische** ~**n** plant; **unabhängige** ~**n** self-contained units; **unbelastete** ~**n** available assets; **unproduktive** ~**n** dead assets; **verborgene** ~ *(med.)* taint; **verbrecherische** ~ criminal disposition; **verteidigungsbedingte** ~**n** defense (defence, *Br.*) -financed facilities; **verteilte** ~**n** diversification; **verzinsliche** ~**n** interest-bearing investments; **vorteilhafte** ~**n** good (paying, remunerative) investments; **vorübergehende** ~ current investment; **wertschaffende** ~**n** productive investments;
~ **in Aktien** share investment *(Br.)*, investment in stock *(US)*; ~**n im Ausland** foreign investments; ~**n im Bau** *(Bilanz)* installation (plant) under construction, construction in progress; ~**n auf Depositenkonto** fixed-deposit investments; ~**n in Ersthypotheken** first-mortgage investments; ~ **mit festem Ertrag** fixed [-yield] investment; ~ **von Geldbeträgen** investment of funds; ~ **in Grundstücken** real-estate investments; ~ **einer Investmentgesellschaft** investment trust buying; ~ **von Kapitalien** investment of funds, capital investment; ~ **einer Kartei** card indexing; ~ **überschüssiger Mittel** employment of surplus funds; ~ **mit verteiltem Risiko** diversification of one's investments; ~ **in Staatspapieren** funding; ~ **einer Steinkohlenzeche** colliery plant; ~ **einer Untersuchung** research design; ~ **zu einem Vertrag** enclosure (schedule) to a contract; ~ **in Wertpapieren** investment in securities;
~ **abschreiben** to write down an asset; **in der** ~ **beifügen** to enclose, to attach; ~**n im Licht des Liquidationstermins bewerten** to value assets on a gone-concern basis; **zur** ~ **empfehlen** to single out for investment; **als langfristige** ~ **empfehlen** to advise retention of longer commitments; ~**n erneuern** to replace fixed assets; **abgenutzte** ~ **ersetzen** to replace worn-out equipment; ~**n erweitern** to expand its plant; **lediglich die** ~**n eines anderen Betriebes erwerben** to acquire only the assets of another business; **als** ~ **für lange Sicht gelten** to have long-term appeal, to be a purchase for the long pull *(US)*; **hervorragende** ~**n haben** to be gifted with rare talents; ~ **zum Geschäftsmann haben** to have a turn for business; ~**n zum Schauspieler haben** to have the makings of an actor; **Wert einer** ~ **heraufsetzen** to write up the value of an asset; ~ **außer Betrieb nehmen** to retire (discard) a unit; **städtische** ~**n schützen** to patrol the parks; **für eine langfristige** ~ **attraktiv sein** to have long-term appeal, to be a purchase for the long pull *(US)*; ~ **außer Betrieb setzen** to discard (retire) an asset; **in eine steuerfreie** ~ **umwandeln** to convert an investment into a nontaxable form.
anlageähnlicher Charakter investment-like feature.
Anlage | aktien investment stocks; ~**art** type of investment; ~**aufwand** investment expense; ~**ausgliederung** investment elimina-

tion; ~**ausschuß** capital issue committee, *(Kapitalanlagegesellschaft)* investment committee; ~**bank** investment bank[er], investment trust.

anlagebedingt *(Krankheit)* constitutional.

Anlage | bedingungen terms of investment; **attraktive ~bedingungen für industriell weniger erschlossene Gebiete schaffen** to attract investment to poorer regions; ~**bedürfnis** investment demand; ~**befugnis** power of investment; ~**begeisterung** investment enthusiasm; ~**berater** investment adviser (consultant, counsellor, *US*), financial investment manager, security analyst *(US)*, *(Kapitalanlagegesellschaft)* investment manager; ~**beratung** investment advisory service, investment counselling *(US)*, investment advice *(Br.)*, security (investment) analysis *(US)*, *(Investmentfonds)* investment management; ~**beratungsfirma** investment house (counselling firm, *US*); ~**beratungsvertrag** investment advisory contract (agreement); ~**bereich** investment area; ~**bereitschaft** propensity (inclination, readiness) to invest; ~**bereitschaft der Kapitalanlagegesellschaften animieren** to put back into the investment trust sector; ~**bereitschaft zeigen** to be ready to invest; ~**beschränkungen** restrictions on investment, investment restrictions; ~**beschränkung in Richtung auf bestimmte Sparten** *(Versicherungsgesellschaft)* restriction on investment of special classes; ~**bestimmungen** investment clauses, *(Kapitalanlagegesellschaft)* investment policy; **weitgestreute ~beteiligungen** diversified holdings; ~**betrag** amount invested; ~**bewertung** *(Effekten)* investment rating, appraisal of investments; ~**blatt** *(Korrekturbogen)* rider; ~**buchführung** investment accounting; ~**chancen im Immobiliengeschäft** property investment opportunities; ~**dauer** period of investment; ~**deckung** investment recovery; ~**entschluß** investment decision, *(Anlagegesellschaft)* fund decision; ~**erfahrung** investment experience; ~**erlöse** investment earnings; **ausländische ~erlöse devisenmäßig vereinnahmen** to repatriate earnings from foreign investments; ~**erneuerungsplan** replacement program(me); ~**erneuerungssatz** replacement rate; ~**erträgnisse** investment earnings; ~**fachmann** security analyst *(US)*; ~**fonds** investment trust, *(Kapitalanlagegesellschaft)* fund money, investment fund; ~**form** type of investment; **vorgeschriebene liquide ~formen** specific reserve assets; ~**fragen** investment matters; ~**gegenstand** fixed asset.

Anlagegeschäft investment banking (business);
riesiges ~ gigantic scale of buying of securities.

Anlagegeschäftsaufgaben investment-banking functions.

Anlagegesellschaft investment trust, trust company, unit trust *(Br.)*;
~ **mit Austauschrecht der Investitionseffekten** flexible managed-list (management) trust *(US)*; ~ **mit festgelegtem Effektenbestand** rigid (fixed) trust *(US)*.

Anlage | gesichtspunkte investment angles; ~**gewinn** investment gain, return, yield; ~**gewohnheiten** investment habits; ~**grundsätze** investment standards.

Anlagegüter *(Bilanz)* assets, capital goods (equipment);
in der Bilanz nicht aufgeführte ~ nonledger assets; **im Liquidationsfall geringwertige ~** inadmitted assets; **kurzfristige ~** limited-life (short-life, short-lived) assets; **langfristige ~** permanent investments; **langlebige ~** long-lived assets; **mittelfristige ~** medium-term assets; **veraltete ~** out-of-date capital; **verschiedene ~** *(Bilanz)* miscellaneous assets;
~ **mit schnell erzielbarem Barerlöswert** assets with rapid rates of cash return; ~ **mit einer zehnjährigen Nutzungsdauer** investment with a useful life of ten years;
~ **höher bewerten** to appreciate fixed assets; ~ **beim Ankauf wirtschaftlich nutzbar machen** to make an asset viable on acquisition.

Anlage | informationsbrief investment newsletter; ~**interesse** investment interest; ~**interessent** would-be investor; ~**investitionen** capital investment, investment placing, investment in plant and equipment, investment in fixed assets; ~**kapital** invested (investment, permanent) capital, capital (fixed) assets, fixed (stock) capital, *(Kapitalanlagegesellschaft)* investment fund; **flüssiges ~kapital** moneyed (money) capital; ~**kapitalaufwand** fixed capital expenditure; ~**kauf** asset purchase, purchasing of assets; ~**käufe** investment (portfolio) buying, *(Investmentgesellschaft)* investment trust buying; **gutes ~klima** attractive climate for investment; **nicht für den Markt bestimmte ~konten melken** to churn captive accounts; ~**konto** investment account, *(Kontobuch)* investment ledger; ~**konzentration** concentration of investments; ~**kosten** initial capital expenditure, first (prime) cost, *(Baukosten)* cost of construction, *(Einbauten)* cost of installation, *(Effektenkauf)* fixed capital expenditure, *(Gründungskosten)* promotion money (cost), initial outlay; ~**kostenschätzung** capital expenditure appraisal; **[langfristiger] ~kredit** investment credit; ~**kundschaft** buying (investing) public, investing community, stockholding elements; ~**land für Investitionskapital** target country for investment capital; ~**leistung** *(Kapitalanlagegesellschaft)* management performance; ~**liste** panel of shares *(Br.)*; ~**markt** investment market; ~**medium** investment vehicle; ~**möglichkeiten** investment opportunities (media, *US*); ~**möglichkeiten im Aktienmarkt** equity market investment.

Anlagen | abbau running down of assets; ~**abgang** loss in assets; ~**abschreibung** capital allowance, depreciation of equipment, depreciation of fixed assets, writeoff of assets; ~**abschreibungsgesetz** Capital Allowance Act *(Br.)*; ~**analyse** investment analysis; ~**ausschlachtung** assets stripping; ~**auswahl** *(Kapitalanlagegesellschaft)* portfolio selection; **sanitärer ~bau** sanitary engineering; ~**bedarf** investment requirements; ~**besitz** investment holdings; ~**bewerter** investment analyst; ~**bewertung** asset valuation, investment appraisal, investment analysis, valuation of assets; ~**buch** property ledger; ~**buchhaltung** property accounting, *(Abteilung)* property-accounting department; ~**einheit** fixed-asset unit; ~**erneuerung** asset replacement, revival of investment; ~**erneuerungskonto** replacement account; ~**erwerb** acquisition of capital assets; ~**erwerb durch eine Leasinggesellschaft bei gleichzeitiger Vermittlung an den Verkäufer** salesback leasing *(US)*; ~**finanzierung** fixed-assets (investment) financing; ~**institut** investment institution; ~**kartei** fixed-assets register, property cost record cards; ~**käufe** acquisition of capital assets, assets purchase; ~**komplex** mass of assets; ~**konstruktion** design engineering; ~**konto** fixed-asset (property, investment) account; ~**neubewertung** revaluation of assets; ~**nutzung** use of assets; ~**pachtung** lease of assets, leasing; ~**planung** plant layout; ~**publikum** investing public; ~**schutzgesetz** Prevention of Fraud Investment Act *(Br.)*; ~**schwund** dwindling assets; ~**seite** *(Bilanz)* asset side; ~**sicherheit** capital safety; ~**status** assets status; ~**streuung** spread of assets, diversification (diversity) of investment, diversifying; **größere ~streuung der Kapitalanlagegesellschaft** wider range investment; **große Investitionen zur ~streuung sowohl geographisch wie auf dem Produktionsgebiet vornehmen** to spend heavily on both geographical and product diversification; ~**streuungspolitik** policy of diversification; **eingeschränkter (weniger weisungsgebundener) ~teil** *(Treuhandvermögen)* narrower-range part *(Br.)*; ~**überschreibung**, ~**übertragung** transfer of assets, asset transfer; ~**umfang** size of assets; ~**veränderungen** changes in fixed assets; ~**veräußerung** disposal of an asset; ~**verkauf**, ~**verwertung** liquidation (sale) of assets; ~**vermietung** plant leasing; ~**vermittler** investment middleman; ~**verringerung** running down of assets; ~**verwaltung** asset (investment) management; ~**verwaltungsabteilung** asset management department; ~**verzinsung** yield, return; ~**volumen** size of assets; ~**wert** value of capital stock; **wirklichen ~wert darstellen** to represent the true value of the assets; ~**zugang** accretion to fixed assets.

Anlageobjekt investment object (project).

Anlagepapier investment paper (security, bill);
~**e** securities, investment bonds (stock);
erstklassige ~e gilt-edged (trustee) securities *(Br.)*, savings investment *(US)*, blue chips *(US)*; **festverzinsliche ~e** interest-bearing investments (securities); **mündelsichere ~e** gilt-edged securities *(Br.)*, gilts *(Br.)*, trustee stocks *(US)*, legal investments *(US)*;
~**e auf lange Sicht** strongbox securities *(US)*.

Anlage | pessimismus investor's pessimism; ~**plan** layout; ~**politik** investment policy; **bewegliche ~politik** flexible investment approach; **zielbewußte ~politik** selective investing; ~**posten** asset items; **feststehende ~posten** fixed asset units; ~**programm** investment program(me); ~**projekt** construction (investment) project; **heiß begehrtes ~projekt** hot property; ~**publikum** buying (investing) public, stockholding elements, investment community, capital-seeking investors; **in den Blickpunkt eines breiteren ~publikums rücken** to come to the attention of a broader section of the investing public; ~**rendite** return of assets, investment return, yield; ~**richtlinien** investment rules; ~**risiko** investment risk, risk of investment; ~**schätzung** *(Effekten)* investment rating.

Anlagestreuung diversification, dispersal of assets;
~ **vornehmen** to diversify; **einzelne Betriebe zur ~ zwingen** to force some outfits into diversification.

anlagesuchendes Publikum investing (buying) public, investment community, stockholding elements, capital-seeking investors.

Anlage | tätigkeit investment performance; **~termin** vesting day; **~titel** securities, investment papers, *(kurzfristige)* short-term investments; **~überwachung** investment supervision; **~veränderungen im Effektenportefeuille** portfolio changes; **~veränderungen vornehmen** to switch investments; **~verfügung** investment disposition (disposal); **~verlust** investment loss, loss on investments; **~vermögen** capital (permanent, fixed) assets, tangible fixed (equity) assets, invested capital, investment estate, fixed capital (property) investment; **wertberichtigtes ~vermögen** net book amount; **~vermögen abschreiben** to depreciate fixed assets; **5% des ~vermögens in Beleihungen beweglichen Vermögens investieren** to invest 5% of their assets in chattel paper; **~verpflichtungen** investment commitments; **~verwaltung** investment (property) management; **~verzinsung** investment return, yield; **laufende ~verzinsung** flat yield of an investment; **~voraussetzungen für ein Treuhandvermögen** trust requirements; **langfristiges ~vorhaben** long-term capital project; **~vorteil** investment merit; **~wert** asset value, *(Effekten)* investment value.

Anlagewerte invested capital, investment securities, capital goods;
ausgesuchte ~ selected investments *(Br.)*, blue chips *(US)*, glamor stocks *(US)*; **diverse ~** *(Bilanz)* other investments; **erstklassige ~** gilt-edged *(Br.)* (trustee, *US*) stocks, blue chips *(US)*; **ertragreiche ~** live assets; **festverzinsliche ~** interest-bearing investment (securities); **hochwertige ~** high-grade securities; **immaterielle ~** intangible assets; **kapitalähnliche ~** investmenttype assets; **kurzfristige ~** short-maturing securities; **mündelsichere ~** gilt-edged stock (securities) *(Br.)*, trustee *(Br.)* (legal, *US*) securities, trustee investments *(Br.)*, *(Börsenbericht)* the gilt-edged list *(Br.)*; **schlechte ~** poor investments; **unsichere ~** dubious securities; **höher verzinsliche ~** higher-yielding investments; **wohlfundierte ~** live assets;
~ mit begrenzter Lebensdauer limited-life assets;
~ heraufsetzen to write up the value of assets; **in ~n investieren** to place in investments.

Anlage | wertminderung capital depreciation; **~wertsteigerung** capital appreciation *(Br.)*; **~williger** would-be investor; **~zeitraum** period of investment; **~ziel** investment objective (goal); **~zinsen** interest on capital outlay; **~zuwachs** addition to plant; **zu ~zwecken** for investment purposes; **für langfristige ~zwecke billig liegen** to offer good value for long-range investment purposes.

Anlandebrücke landing stage.

Anlandgewicht landed weight.

anlangen, gut to arrive safely; **an einem toten Punkt ~** *(Verhandlungen)* to reach a deadlock.

Anlaß occasion, rise, provocation, turn, *(Veranlassung)* notice, inducement, room;
aufgrund dieses besonderen ~es on this particular occasion; **aus nichtigem ~** for a trivial reason; **bei gewichtigem ~** on great occasions; **beim geringsten ~** at the drop of a hat;
besonderer ~ special occasion; **feierlicher ~** solemn occasion; **förmlicher ~** ceremonial occasion;
kein ~ zur Beschwerde no grounds of complaint; **~ zur Besorgnis** cause for concern; **~ zu einem Familientreffen** occasion for a family gathering; **~ zum Kaufen** buying motive; **kein ~ zur Klage** no grounds for complaint; **~ für scharfe Kontroversen** matter of controversy;
j. ohne ~ beleidigen to insult s. o. gratuitously; **~ geben** to cause; **~ zur Beunruhigung geben** to be a matter of concern; **~ zur öffentlichen Entrüstung geben** to give occasion to an outburst of popular indignation; **~ zur Klage geben** to give cause (room) for complaint; **~ zur Kritik geben** to lay o. s. open to criticism; **allen ~ haben** to have every reason; **aus besonderem ~ kommen** to call on particular business; **beim geringsten ~ beleidigt sein** to take offence at the slightest thing;
~einspritzanlage engine primer; **~einspritzung** priming.

anlassen *(Gerät)* to leave on, *(laufen lassen)* to leave running (on), *(starten)* to start, to set going, *(Wasser)* to turn on;
sich gut ~ to bid fair, to look promising; **sich ganz gut ~** to promise well, to work out quite well; **Motor ~** to start the engine.

Anlasser *(Auto)* motor starter, starter knob (lever, *Br.*);
automatischer ~ self-starter;
~ betätigen to press the starter;
~druckknopf starter button; **~kraftstoff einspritzen** to prime.

anläßlich on the occasion of.

Anlaßmotor starter.

anlasten to charge, to debit;
jem. die Spesen ~ to charge the expenses to s. o.; **einem Dritten ein Verbrechen ~** to lay a crime at s. one else's door.

Anlauf startup, start, *(Flugzeug)* takeoff run;
gleich beim ersten ~ at the first onset; **im ersten ~** at one go (the first onset);
stürmischer ~ dash, sudden rush;
~ der Produktion starting of production.

Anlaufbetrag initial cost, launching (startup) costs.

Anläufe unternehmen, mehrere to have several goes at.

Anlaufen *(Hafen)* call;
~ eines Nothafens forced call.

anlaufen *(Betrieb)* to start, *(Film)* to run, *(Glas)* to mist, *(Produktion)* to warm up, *(Silber)* tarnish;
auf 2000 DM ~ to amount (add up) to DM 2000; **Hafen ~** to make for (call at) a port; **vor Kälte blau ~** to turn blue with cold;
~ lassen *(Betrieb)* to put into operation, to start (set) working; **Maschine ~ lassen** to set a machine going; **Rechnung ~ lassen** to run up a score (bill).

Anlauf | hafen port of call, call port; **~kapital** initial circulating capital; **~klausel** calling clause; **~kosten** launching (startup) costs, *(Produktion)* initial development expenses; **~kredit** opening (starting) credit; **~leistung** first output; **~schwierigkeiten** initial difficulties, teething troubles; **~verzögerung** internal (intermediate) lag; **~zeit** starting (initial) period, setup (setting up, start) time, *(Produktion)* warming-up time.

anläuten, j. to ring s. o. up, to give s. o. a ring (call, tinkle).

Anlege | brücke wharf, pier, quay, jetty, landing stage; **~gebühren** pier dues, anchorage, berthage, quayage; **~hafen** port of call.

anlegen *(bezahlen)* to spend, to pay, *(drucktechn.)* to feed, *(Fabrik)* to set up, to erect, to establish, *(Kapital)* to place, to invest, to embark, *(planen)* to plan, to design, *(Schiff)* to land, to harbo(u)r, to berth, to call, *(Schiff)* to touch;
zu 8% ~ to put out at 8 per cent; **sich mit jem. ~** to have a rumpus with s. o.; **befristet ~** to invest at short notice; **es darauf ~, jem. zu schaden** to be out to harm s. o.; **Erträge erneut ~** to redeploy proceeds; **fest ~** to sink; **auf drei Monate fest ~** to fix a deposit for ninety days notice; **Garten ~** to [lay out a] garden; **Geld ~** to invest money; **Geld in einem Geschäft ~** to embark capital in a trade; **sein Geld gut ~** to invest one's money to good account; **sein Geld in Grundstücken ~** to invest one's money in real estate; **sein Geld in Hausgrundstücken ~** to invest one's money in house property; **sein Geld mit verteiltem Risiko ~** to diversify one's investments; **sein Geld vorteilhaft ~** to invest one's money to advantage; **sein Geld in Wertpapieren ~** to invest one's money in stocks and shares; **gewinnbringend ~** to invest advantageously, to invest one's money to good account; **in einem Hafen ~** to call at a harbour; **selbst mit Hand ~** to take a hand in the work oneself; **jem. Handschellen ~** to handcuff s. o.; **am Kai ~** to dock, to berth, to wharf; **Kapital ~** to invest capital, to embark money; **sein Kapital fest ~** to tie (lock) up one's capital; **sein Kapital langfristig ~** to make a long-term investment; **Kartei ~** to card-index; **Konto ~** to open an account; **beim Kunden wieder ~** to recycle; **kurzfristig ~** to invest [money] at short notice; **langfristig ~** to make long-term investments; **längseits ~** to come alongside; **Liste ~** to make up (compile) a list; **anderen Maßstab ~** to apply another standard; **strengen Maßstab an die Geschäftsmoral ~** to set a high standard of business morality; **mündelsicher ~** to acquire gilt-edged (trustee) securities *(Br.)*; **planmäßig ~** to lay out, to plan; **Reserven ~** to stockpile, *(Bilanz)* to make provisions; **an ein Schiff ~** to come alongside a ship; **sicher ~** to invest safely; **seinen Sonntagsstaat ~** to put on one's best bib and tucker; **in Staatspapieren ~** to invest in public funds, to fund one's money *(Br.)*; **Straße ~** to construct a road; **Trauer ~** to go into mourning; **verteilt ~** to diversify; **verzinslich ~** to put out at interest; **sich einen Vorrat ~** to lay in a stock (store), to take in supplies, to stockpile; **zinstragend ~** to invest advantageously, to place money at interest.

Anlegeplatz, öffentlicher public wharf, landing stage, dock.

Anleger investor, *(drucktechn.)* feeder;
institutionelle ~ institutional investors (lenders, *US*); **private ~** private investors;
~bedürfnisse investor demand; **~pflege** investor relations; **~schutz** protection of investors.

Anlege | schiene *(drucktechn.)* guide rail; **~schloß** padlock; **~stelle** anchorage, landing place (platform), wharf, quay, jetty, stop; **~tisch** *(drucktechn.)* horse.

Anlegung | von Kapital placing of funds, placement of capital, investment; ~ **von Mündelgeldern** trusteeship investment.

anlehnen, sich to rest, to base, *(mil.)* to lean upon; **sich an die Hügel** ~ to nestle among the hills; **Leiter an die Wand** ~ to lean a ladder against the wall; **sich im Stil** ~ to follow the style.

Anlehnung *(pol.)* dependence, support;
in ~ **an** with reference to;
~ **an einen Autor** borrowing from an author.

Anleihe loan, *(Autor)* borrowing, *(Darlehn)* advance, lend *(fam.)*, *(Staat)* stock *(Br.)*, bond *(US)*;
abgelöste ~ retired (redeemed) loan; **ablösbare** ~ redeemable loan, loan redeemable by allotment (lot); **achtprozentige** ~ loan bearing interest at 8%; **aufgewertete** ~ revalorized loan; **auslosbare** ~ redeemable loan, loan redeemable by allotment; **äußere** ~ foreign (external) loan; **in Umlauf befindliche** ~**n** loans in circulation; **auf dem Eurobondmarkt begebene internationale** ~**n** Eurobonds; **besicherte** ~ secured loan; **hypothekarisch besicherte** ~ mortgage loan; **nicht besicherte** ~ unsecured loan; **dreiprozentige** ~ three per cent loan; **jederzeit einlösbare** ~ optional bond; **festverzinsliche** ~ fixed interest-bearing loan; **freigegebene** ~ unfrozen loan; **fundierte** ~ consolidated (funded) loan; **garantierte** ~ secured loan; **nicht garantierte** ~ unsecured loan; **im Freiverkehr gehandelte** ~ outside loan; **gekündigte** ~ redemption loan; **voll gezeichnete** ~ fully subscribed loan; **nicht in voller Höhe gezeichnete** ~ undersubscribed loan; **indexgebundene** ~ indexed loan; **innere** ~ internal (inland) loan, internal bonds; **internationale** ~ international loan; **kommunale** ~ local authority loan (bonds) *(Br.)*, municipal bonds (stock, securities), municipal loan; **konsolidierte** ~ funded (consolidated) loan, consolidated funds, unified stock *(Br.)*; **kündbare** ~ demand loan; **kurzfristige** ~**n** short-term loan, deficiency bills *(Br.)*; **landwirtschaftliche** ~**n** agricultural loans; **langfristige** ~ long-term loan; **mündelsichere** ~ gilt-edged *(Br.)* (trustee, *US*) loan; **notierte** ~ quoted (listed) loan; **amtlich nicht notierte** ~ outside loan; **öffentliche** ~ public (government, civic, *US*) loan; **staatliche** ~**n** state bonds; **städtische** ~ municipal bond *(US)*, corporation loan *(Br.)*, city bonds; **steuerbegünstigte** ~ privileged loan; **steuerfreie** ~ tax-exempt (free) loan; **überzeichnete** ~ oversubscribed loan; **unbesicherte** ~ unsecured loan; **unkündbare (untilgbare, unbefristete)** ~ irredeemable (perpetual) loan; **unveränderliche** ~ closed issue; **unverzinsliche** ~ noninterest-bearing loan; **verzinsliche** ~ interest-bearing loan, loan at interest; **wertbeständige** ~ fixed-value loan; **über zwanzigjährige** ~ long bond; **zweckgebundene** ~ tied loan; ~**n der Länder** state bonds; ~**n und verzinsliche Schatzanweisungen** loan issues and interest-bearing treasury bonds; ~ **mit freigegebenem Wechselkurs** floating-rate loan;
~ **abschließen** to contract a loan; ~ **auflegen** to float (launch) a loan, to float a bond issue; ~ **in Tranchen auflegen** to issue a loan in instalments, to split a loan in tranches; ~ **zur Zeichnung auflegen** to offer a loan for subscription, to invite subscriptions for a loan; ~ **aufnehmen** to raise (contract) a loan; ~ **aufwerten** to revalidate a loan; ~ **ausgeben** to issue loan stock *(Br.)*; ~ **in Tranchen ausgeben** to issue a loan in instalments; ~ **begeben** to issue (negotiate) a loan, to dispose of an issue; ~ **bewilligen (gewähren)** to grant (award) a loan; ~ **auf den Markt bringen** to place a loan; ~ **konsolidieren** to fund (consolidate) a loan; ~ **kontrahieren** to contract a loan; ~ **konvertieren** to convert a loan; ~ **kündigen** to call in a loan, to give notice of redemption; ~ **lancieren** to float a loan; **bei jem. eine** ~ **machen** to borrow money from s. o.; ~ **in Abschnitten in Anspruch nehmen** to draw a loan in tranches; ~ **tilgen** to redeem (retire) a loan; ~ **fest übernehmen** to underwrite a loan; ~ **teilweise übernehmen** to take a portion of a loan; ~ **an ein Konsortium übertragen** to put a loan into the hands of a syndicate; ~ **überzeichnen** to cover over (oversubscribe) a loan; ~ **umwandeln** to convert a loan; **alte** ~**n in neue umwandeln** to reschedule old loans into new ones; ~ **unterbringen** to negotiate (place) a loan; ~ **zum Kurse von 98% unterbringen** to place a loan at 98 per cent; ~ **vermitteln** to negotiate a loan; ~ **zeichnen** to subscribe to *(Br.)* (for) a loan; ~ **zurückzahlen** to redeem (repay) a loan; ~ **vorzeitig zurückzahlen** to return a loan ahead of schedule;
~**abkommen** loan agreement; ~**ablösung** loan redemption, redemption of a loan, liquidation of a loan; ~**absatz** sale of a loan; ~**abschnitt** slice of a loan; ~**abteilung** loan (bond, *US*) department; ~**agio** premium on a loan, loan premium; ~**angebot** loan offer; ~**aufnahme** raising of a loan; ~**ausgabe** issue of a loan; **mit Vorrechten ausgestattete** ~**ausgabe** senior issue; ~**ausschuß** loan committee; ~**ausstattung** terms of a loan, loan terms; ~**bank** public loan bank, loan society; ~**bedarf** loan demand; ~**bedingungen** loan terms, terms of a loan; ~**begeber** issuer of a loan, lender; ~**begebung** floating of a loan; **konsortiale** ~**begebungen** syndication of loans; ~**begebungskosten** flotation costs of a loan; ~**bericht** loan report; ~**beschaffung** procuration of a loan; ~**besitzer** loan subscriber (holder), bondholder *(US)*; ~**bestimmungen** loan regulations; ~**beteiligung** loan participation; ~**betrag** amount of a loan, bond amount *(US)*; ~**betreuung** loan administration; ~**bündel** loan package; ~**dienst** servicing of a loan, loan (bond, *US*) service, service of a loan (bond, *US*), redemption (loan) service; ~**emission** issue of a loan, bond issue *(US)*; ~**emission garantieren** to underwrite a loan; ~**erlös** proceeds of a loan, proceeds of an issue; ~**finanzierung** loan [account] financing; ~**fonds** loan fund; ~**fonds für währungsschwache Länder** soft loan fund; ~**garant** bond underwriter *(US)*; ~**garantie** guarantee of a loan, loan guarantee, underwriting; ~**genehmigung** loan sanction; ~**geschäft** loan business (function); ~**gespräche** loan talks; ~**gewährung** award of a loan; ~**gläubiger** loan stockholder; ~**gremium** loan council; ~**kapital** loan fund (capital, *Br.*), bond (debenture) capital, debenture stock *(Br.)*, bonded debt *(US)*, stock *(Br.)*; **genehmigtes** ~**kapital** loan (debenture) capital, authorized bonds; ~**klausel** loan clause; ~**konsortium** underwriting syndicate; **sich aus einem** ~**konsortium zurückziehen** to pull out of a loan; ~**konto** *(Kontobuch)* loans (loan, *US*) ledger; ~**konversion** loan (debt) conversion; ~**kündigung** call for redemption of a loan, notice of redemption; ~**kurs** quotation of a loan; ~**kurszettel** stock list *(Br.)*, bond record *(US)*; ~**laufzeit** period (term) of a loan; ~**los** lottery bond; ~**markt** bond market; **kommunaler** ~**markt** local authority negotiable bond market; ~**markt für kurzfristige Papiere** yearly bond market *(Br.)*; ~**mittel** loans, bonds *(US)*; ~**nehmer** loan subscriber; ~**notierung** quotation of a loan; ~**papier** stock, bond *(US)*, *(Staat)* government security (stock); **öffentliche** ~**papiere** public bonds; ~**plazierung** placing of a loan; ~**projekt** loan project; ~**rechnung** loan account; ~**rückkauf** retirement of a loan; ~**rückzahlung** loan redemption; ~**schuld** bond obligation, funded (bonded, *US*) debt, debenture stock *(Br.)*, funded (bonded) indebtedness; ~**schulden[last]** funded (bonded, *US*) indebtedness; ~**schuldner** loan (bond) debtor; ~**skandal** loan scandal; ~**steuer** sinking-fund tax, loan capital duty *(Br.)*; ~**stock** capital stock; **konvertierbarer** ~**stock** convertible loan stock; ~**stockgesetz** capital stock law *(Br.)*.

Anleihestücke loans, debenture stock *(Br.)*, bonds *(US)*;
zur Plazierung anstehende ~ gilts on tap *(Br.)*; **noch nicht abgehobene ausgeloste** ~ allotted loans not yet collected;
~ **zurückzahlen** to retire a loan.

Anleihe | stückelung denomination of a loan; ~**tausch vor Fälligkeit** refunding at maturity; ~**tilgung** redemption (amortization) of a loan, loan redemption, bond amortization (redemption) *(US)*; ~**tilgungsfonds** sinking (redemption) fund; ~**tilgungsplan** redemption table; ~**titel** loans, bonds *(US)*; ~**tranche** portion (slice) of a loan; ~**übernahme** negotiation of a loan; ~**übernahmegarantie** underwriting guarantee; ~**übernahmekonsortium** underwriting syndicate; ~**umwandlung** conversion of a loan, loan conversion; ~**unterbringung** placing of a loan; ~**verhandlungen** loan negotiations; ~**verkäufe** sales of loans; ~**vermittler** loanmonger; ~**verpflichtungen** loan commitments; ~**verschuldung** bonded indebtedness *(US)*; ~**vertrag** loan agreement (contract); ~**verzinsung** yield of a loan, *(Zinsendienst)* loan service; ~**währung** bond issue currency; **Kapital auf dem** ~**wege aufbringen** to raise capital by the issue of a loan; ~**zeichner** subscriber to a loan, loan subscriber, loan stockholder; ~**zeichnung** loan subscription, subscription for (to, *Br.*) a loan; ~**zeichnungskurs** loan subscription price; ~**zinsen** loan (stock) interest; ~**zinsen und Vorzugsdividenden** *(Bilanz)* prior charges; ~**zuteilung** allotment of a loan; ~**zuteilung mit Teilzahlungssystem** instalment allotment *(Br.)*.

anleiten to direct, to guide, to instruct, to initiate, to conduct.

Anleitung instruction, direction, guidance, *(technisch)* manual, *(Textbuch)* primer, guide, textbook;
~ **zum Fotografieren** guide to photography.

Anleitungs | heft instruction booklet; ~**verfahren für die Berufsausbildung** job instruction training.

Anlernberuf semi-skilled occupation.

anlernen to train, to school;
j. ~ to put a certain polish on s. o.

Anlern | ling learner, beginner, trainee, improver; ~**lohn** learner's wage rate; **planmäßige** ~**methode** planned approach to training; ~**verhältnis** trainee status; ~**werkstätte** training shop; ~**zeit** training period.

anlesen, Buch to begin a book.
Anlieferer deliver.
anliefern to supply, to deliver;
frei Haus ~ to deliver at s. one's door.
Anlieferung supply, delivery;
~ **frei Haus** delivery free at residence, home delivery; ~ **im Luftfrachtwege** use of airfreight in delivery; ~ **auf der Schiene** delivery by rail; ~ **an Schiffsseite** delivery shipside; ~ **auf dem See- und Binnenwasserweg** delivery by sea or inland waterway; ~ **auf der Straße** delivery by road.
Anlieferungs | kosten delivery charge; ~**preis** *(Zoll)* landed costs; ~**schein** delivery (shipping, *Br.*) note; ~**zustand** delivered condition.
Anliegen request, concern, business, cause, entreaty, desire, solicitation;
dringendes ~ urgent request; **grundlegendes nationales** ~ fundamental national purpose;
mit einem ~ **herausrücken** to come forward with a request; **sein** ~ **unterstreichen** to make one's point; ~ **vorbringen** to express a wish.
anliegen to abut, to border, to be adjacent;
eng ~ to fit closely.
anliegend adjacent, adjoining, abutting, bordering, joined, *(anbei)* attached, enclosed, inclosed *(US)*, herewith, annexed, *(im Brief)* annexed;
~**e Felder** abutting fields; ~**es Grundstück** adjacent land, neighbo(u)ring lot.
Anlieger abutter, abutting (adjacent, adjoining) owner, borderer, contiguous occupier, *(Fluß)* riverain, *(Nachbar)* neighbo(u)r, *(Straße)* wayside owner, *(Verkehrsregelung)* local resident;
~**beiträge** neighbo(u)rhood improvements, assessment bonds; ~**gebühr** road charge; ~**grundstück** adjacent (abutting) land, neighbo(u)rhood lot, *(Straßenanlieger)* wayside property; ~- **und Kanalisationskosten** *(Bilanz)* roads and sewers; ~**staat** border (bordering, neighbo(u)ring) state (country); ~**straße** access road, byroad, private highway; ~**verkehr** *(Straßenschild)* residents only.
anlocken, Alt und Jung to draw the town; **Kunden** ~ to attract (entice, tout, draw, lure, bait) customers into the store.
Anlockung enticement, attraction.
anmachen *(Licht)* to turn (switch) on;
Bild an die Wand ~ to fasten a picture to the wall; **Feuer** ~ to make fire.
Anmachholz kindling.
anmahnen to admonish, to urge;
rückständige Steuern ~ to issue a warning to pay taxes; **Zahlung** ~ to send s. o. a reminder.
Anmarsch approach, advance;
bereits im ~ to be already on the way;
auf dem ~ **auf die Hauptstadt sein** to converge on the capital; ~**weg** *(mil.)* route of advance, approach.
anmaßen, sich to arrogate, to assume, to usurp; **sich ein Recht** ~ to arrogate (assume) a right to o. s.; **sich jds. Rechte** ~ to usurp s. one's rights; **sich einen Titel** ~ to usurp a title.
anmaßend presumptious, assuming, assumptive, dogmatic[al], top-lofty, pretentious, arrogant, highhanded, fishly *(fig.)*;
~**es Benehmen** arrogance, presumption.
Anmaßung arrogance, presumption, highhandedness, usurpation, overbearance;
~ **eines Rechts** usurpation of a franchise.
anmeckern, j. to carp at s. o.
Anmelde | bestimmungen *(Patentamt)* instructions to applicants; ~**buch** visitors' book; ~**datum** date of application (registration), *(Konkursantrag)* filing date; ~**erklärung** registration statement.
anmeldefähige Forderung *(Konkurs)* provable debt.
Anmeldeformular registration (application) form (blank), *(Wettbewerb)* entry form;
polizeiliches ~ police form;
~ **ausfüllen** to enter one's name in the visitors' book, *(Hotel)* to sign a registration form, to register with a hotel.
Anmelde | frist time (closing date) of application, period set for declaration, *(Patent)* filing period; ~**frist bis zum 15. März** closing date for applications March 15th; ~**gebühr** application (registration) fee, *(Konkurs)* filing fee; ~**gegenstand** *(Patentrecht)* object of invention; ~**gesuch** application; ~**karte** application card; ~**liste** registration list.
anmelden to announce, to declare, to report, to give notice, *(ansteckende Krankheit)* to notify, *(Warensendung)* to advise of, *(beim Zoll)* to enter;
sich ~ to check in, to register, *(zur Teilnahme)* to enter one's name; **Aktien zur Generalversammlung** ~ to deposit shares for the general meeting; **Anspruch (Forderung)** ~ to file (lodge) a claim; **seinen Bankrott** ~ to declare o. s. bankrupt; **Erfindung zum Patent** ~ to apply for a patent; **Ferngespräch** ~ to book a trunk call *(Br.)*, to put in (place) a long-distance call *(US)*; **Forderung beim Konkursverwalter** ~ to lodge a proof of debt with the official receiver; **Gesellschaft zur Eintragung** ~ to register a company (corporation, *US*); **Gewerbe** ~ to register a trade; **sich im Hotel** ~ to register with a hotel, to sign a registration form; **Kind beim Standesamt** ~ to notify a birth, to register a new-born child (the birth of a child, *US*); **Konkurs** ~ to file a petition for a receiving order in bankruptcy, to strike a docket, to declare o. s. bankrupt, to go through the hoops *(sl.)*; **Konkursforderung** ~ to lodge a proof of debt; **Kraftfahrzeug** ~ to register a motor vehicle; **sich zu einem Kursus** ~ to enrol(l), to enlist; **Ladung** ~ to manifest a cargo; **Patent** ~ to apply for (take out) a patent, to file an application for a patent; **sich polizeilich** ~ to register o. s. with the police; **j. zu einer Prüfung** ~ to put in s. o. for an examination; **Schaden** ~ to give notice of a claim; **Schüler** ~ to enter a child as a pupil; **Telefongespräch** ~ to make (place) a call; **Todesfall** ~ to report a death to the registrar's office *(Br.)* (the authorities, *US*); **Tratte** ~ to advise a draft; **sich bei einem Verein** ~ to apply for membership of a club; **Vermögen** ~ to declare one's property; **Waren zur Verzollung** ~ to enter goods at the customhouse; **Warenzeichen** ~ to register a trademark; **sich zu einem Wettbewerb** ~ to go in for a competition; **seine Zahlungsunfähigkeit** ~ to declare o. s. insolvent;
sich ~ **lassen** to send in one's name (up one's card), *(beim Arzt)* to have an appointment made; **sich beim Vorstand** ~ **lassen** to report o. s. to the manager.
Anmelde | nummer application number; ~**pflicht** compulsory registration.
anmeldepflichtig notifiable, reportable, subject to registration, *(Krankheit)* certifiable;
~ **sein** to require one's registration;
~**e Absprache** *(Kartellrecht)* agreement subject to registration; ~**e Betriebsunfälle** reportable accidents in industry.
Anmeldepflichtiger notifyee.
Anmelder applicant, notifier, *(Patentgesetz)* claimant, applicant, *(Zoll)* declarer;
früherer ~ *(Patent)* prior applicant; **gemeinsame** ~ *(Patentgesetz)* joint applicants.
Anmelde | raum reception; ~**schein** application blank, entry form, *(Polizei)* registration card, *(Wettbewerb)* entry form; ~**schluß** application close, deadline for application *(US)*; ~**stelle** booking (filing, register, registration) office, *(für Ferngespräche)* booking operator; ~**tag** *(Patent)* application date; **letzter** ~**tag** closing day for applications; ~**termin** application date, *(Student)* graduation time, *(Patentrecht)* filing date; ~**unterlagen** enrol(l)ment records, *(Patentrecht)* documents for application, application documents; ~**voraussetzungen** form requirements; ~**vordruck** application blank, *(Wettbewerb)* entry form; ~**zeit** period set for declaration; ~**zettel im Hotel ausfüllen** to register with a hotel; ~**zwang** compulsory registration.
Anmeldung notification, notice, report, announcement, filing, registration, application, enrol(l)ment, *(beim Arzt)* appointment, *(Empfangsbüro)* reception, *(im Hotel)* enquiries, reception, *(zwecks Teilnahme)* entry, *(Vermögen, Verzollung)* declaration;
bei der ~ *(Patentrecht)* upon filing; **nach vorheriger** ~ by appointment;
ausgeschiedene ~**en** *(Patentrecht)* divisional applications; **frühere** ~ prior application; **kollidierende** ~ interfering application; **polizeiliche** ~ report to (registration with) the police; **rechtzeitige** ~ due application; **schwebende** ~ *(Patent)* pending application; **bisher vorliegende** ~**en** applications received so far;
~ **von Aktien zur Hauptversammlung** depositing of shares for the general meeting; ~ **im Ausland** foreign application; ~ **eines Ferngesprächs** booking of a telephone call; **handelsgerichtliche** ~ **einer Firma** registration of a company (corporation, *US*); **doppelte** ~ **einer Forderung** *(Konkurs)* double proof; ~ **eines Kindes beim Standesamt** registration of a new-born child; ~ **des Konkurses** petition in bankruptcy; ~ **einer Konkursforderung** proof of a debt; ~ **eines Kraftfahrzeugs** registration of a motor vehicle; ~ **zu einem Kursus** enrol(l)ment, enlistment, enlisting; ~ **von Neufahrzeugen** registration of new cars; ~ **eines Patents** application for a patent; ~ **zu einem Studienlehrgang** registra-

tion for a course of studies; ~ **zum Tagesheim für Kleinstkinder** day-care enrol(l)ment; ~ **für den ausgeschiedenen Teil** *(Patentrecht)* divisional application; ~ **eines Verfahrens** *(Patentrecht)* process application; ~ **eines Warenzeichens** registration of a trademark; ~ **von Wertpapieren** registration of securities;
j. ohne vorherige ~ aufsuchen to call on s. o. without an appointment; ~ **durchführen** to prosecute an application; ~ **einreichen** to file an application; **jds. polizeiliche ~ entgegennehmen** to lodge in the registry; ~ **zurückweisen** *(Patent)* to reject an application; ~ **zurückziehen** *(Patentantrag)* to withdraw an application.

anmerken to mark;
jem. etw. ~ to notice s. th. on s. o.; **als Fußnote** ~ to make a footnote;
sich nichts ~ lassen to dissemble one's emotions.

Anmerkung annotation, [marginal] note, gloss, *(Fußnote)* foot note;
kritische ~ comment;
erklärende ~ zu einem Buchungsposten postil *(US)*; **~en zu Gerichtsentscheidungen** notes *(US)*; **~en des Verfassers** author's notes;
~en machen to comment; **mit ~en versehen** to annotate, to make one's comments upon s. th.

Anmerkungszeichen reference mark, asterisk.

Anmieten und Vermieten leasing, renting and hiring.

anmieten, Konzerthalle to hire a concert hall; **Unterkunftsräume vorübergehend** ~ to rent temporary accommodation.

Anmietstelle renting station.

anmustern to enrol(l), to enlist, to sign on;
Mannschaft ~ to hire a crew.

Anmusterung enrol(l)ment, enlistment;
~ **von Seeleuten** engagement of seamen.

an|muten, heimatlich to remind of home; **~nageln** to nail.

annähern to approximate;
verschiedene Standpunkte aneinander ~ to reconcile different points of view; **Zolltarife** ~ *(EG)* to harmonize customs tariffs.

annähernd approximate, general, rough, near, approximative;
~ **veranschlagt** on a rough calculation;
~e Berechnung approximation.

Annäherung approach, approximation, accession, *(pol.)* rapprochement;
schrittweise ~ *(EG)* progressive approximation;
~ **eines Flugzeugs** approach of an airplane; ~ **zweier Staaten** rapprochement between two states; ~ **der Zolltarife** *(EG)* harmonization of customs tariffs.

Annäherungs|abschnitt approach section; **~bahn** *(Raumschiff)* rendezvous flight path; **~manöver** *(Raumschiff)* rendezvous manoeuvre; **~methode** show-business approach; **~politik** policy of rapprochement; **~rechnung** approximate calculation, approximation; **~versuch** approaches, advances, overture; **~versuch machen** *(pol.)* to seek a rapprochement; **~versuche bei jem. unternehmen** to make approaches to s. o., to make a pass to a woman *(sl.)*; **~wert** approximate value, approximation.

Annahme acceptance, accepting, taking, approval, *(Depositen)* reception, *(Gesetz)* passing, passage *(US)*, *(Quittung)* receipt, *(Reisegepäck)* counter, *(Vermutung)* assumption, presumption, conjecture, *(Voraussetzung)* supposition, *(Waren)* acceptance, receiving, receipt;
auf einer bloßen ~ beruhend hypothetical; **gegen** ~ against acceptance; **in der** ~ on the presumption, believing that; **mangels** ~ *(Wechsel)* returned for want of [non]acceptance; **mangels ~ protestiert** protested for nonacceptance; **mangels ~ zurück** returned for want of acceptance; **nach** ~ upon acceptance; **unter der** ~ on the assumption; ~ **verweigert** *(Brief)* refused, *(Wechsel)* acceptance declined; **wegen nicht erfolgter** ~ for nonacceptance;
bedingte ~ conditional acceptance, *(Wechsel)* qualified (enlarged) acceptance; **bedingungslose** ~ general acceptance; **bereitwillige** ~ due hono(u)r (protection); **auf Erfahrung beruhende** ~ educated guess; **einstimmige** ~ unanimous adoption; **nicht erfolgte** ~ nonacceptance; **fragwürdige** ~ precarious assumption; **spätere** ~ after-acception; **stillschweigende** ~ tacit acceptance; **tatsächliche** ~ physical acceptance; **teilweise** ~ partial acceptance; **unbedingte** ~ absolute (unreserved) acceptance, *(Wechsel)* general (unqualified, clean) acceptance; **willkürliche** ~ gratuitous assumption;
Angebot und ~ offer and acceptance; ~ **eines Antrags** carriage of a motion; ~ **unter einer Bedingung** qualified acceptance; ~ **eines Berichtes** adoption of a report; ~ **einer Bestechung** acceptance of a bribe; ~ **nur durch eingeschriebenen Brief** acceptance by registered letter only; ~ **ehrenhalber** *(Wechsel)* acceptance supra protest (for hono(u)r); ~ **von Einlagen** reception of deposits; ~ **einer Erbschaft** entering upon an inheritance; ~ **eines Geschenks** approbation of a gift; ~ **einer Gesetzesvorlage** carriage (passing, passage, *US*) of a bill; ~ **schlechter Gewohnheiten** getting into bad habits; ~ **der Haushaltsvorlage** budget grant; ~ **an Kindes Statt** adoption of a child, legal adoption; ~ **eines Namens** assumption of a name; ~ **eines anderen Namens** changing one's name; ~ **durch die Post** acceptance by post; ~ **eines Urteils** acceptance of a judgment; ~ **unter Vorbehalt** acceptance under reserve, *(Wechsel)* conditional (qualified) acceptance; ~ **eines Vorschlages** acceptance of a proposal;
j. zur ~ eines Angebots drängen to urge s. o. to accept an offer; **einstimmige ~ erfahren** to be adopted by a unanimous vote; ~ **finden** to go through, to pass; **sich zur ~ eines Angebots nicht verpflichtet fühlen** not to feel bound to accept an offer; **Wechsel mangels ~ protestieren** to protest (note) a bill for nonacceptance; **einem Gesetz zur ~ verhelfen** to get a bill through; ~ **verweigern** to decline (refuse) acceptance, to refuse [to take] delivery, *(Wechsel)* to dishono(u)r a bill for nonacceptance; ~ **eines Briefes verweigern** to refuse to accept a letter; ~ **von Waren verweigern** to refuse goods; ~ **vorbereiten** *(Wechsel)* to prepare due hono(u)r; **zur ~ vorlegen** *(Wechsel)* to present for acceptance;
~beamter receiving clerk; **~bedingungen** conditions (terms) of acceptance; **~bereich** *(Statistik)* acceptance region; **~bescheinigung** receipt; **~bestätigung** acknowledgement of receipt, acceptance note; **~erklärung** [letter of] acceptance; **ausdrückliche ~erklärung** express acceptance; **~frist** *(Wechsel)* period of (time for) acceptance; **für sein Angebot eine ~frist festlegen** to lay down a time limit on one's acceptance; **~grenze** *(Statistik)* acceptance boundary line; **~protest** protest for nonacceptance; **~stelle** *(Bank)* subscription agency, *(Briefschaften)* posting office, *(Pakete)* receiving office; **~stempel** receipt stamp; **~tarif** *(Spediteur)* differential tariff; **~übermittlung** communication of acceptance; **~urkunde** [instrument of] acceptance; **mit ~vermerk versehen** to provide with acceptance; **~vermutung** implied acceptance; **~vertrag** *(Adoption)* legal adoption; **~verweigerung** *(Waren)* rejection, refusal [of goods], *(Wechsel)* dishono(u)red by nonacceptance, refused acceptance; **~verzug** delayed acceptance; **sich im ~verzug befinden** to have been put on notice to take delivery, not to take delivery in due time; **im ~verzug sein** to be in default of acceptance; **~zahl** *(Statistik)* acceptance number.

Annalen annals, records.

annehmbar acceptable, reasonable, receivable, adoptable, presentable, *(anzeichend)* sufficient, adequate;
~e Bedingungen reasonable terms; **~er Preis** fair (reasonable) price.

annehmen to accept, *(genehmigen)* to approve, to okay *(US)*, *(Lieferung)* to accept, to receive, to take delivery, *(Namen)* to assume, *(vermuten)* to suppose, to think, to assume, to presume, to calculate *(US)*, to guess *(US)*, *(Wechsel)* to accept, to hono(u)r, to provide with acceptance;
sich jds. ~ to take an interest in s. o.; **Amt nicht** ~ to refuse an office; **Angebot** ~ to accept an offer; **Antrag** ~ to carry (adopt) a motion; **sich der Armen** ~ to take up the cause of the poor; **Auftrag** ~ to undertake (accept) an order; **bereitwillig** ~ to embrace; **Bestellung** ~ to take an order; **Einladung zum Abendessen** ~ to accept an invitation to dinner; **Einladung nicht** ~ to decline an invitation; **einstimmig** ~ to adopt unanimously; **Entschließung** ~ to pass a resolution; **Erbschaft** ~ to enter upon an inheritance; **sich der Flüchtlinge** ~ to take up the cause of the refugees; **gern** ~ to welcome; **Geschenk** ~ to approbate a gift; **Gesetzentwurf** ~ to carry a law, to pass a bill; **Gesetzesvorlage nicht** ~ to reject (throw out) a bill; **schlechte Gewohnheiten** ~ to slide into bad habits; **drohende Haltung** ~ to assume a threatening attitude; **Herausforderung** ~ to take up a challenge; **Kind (an Kindes Statt)** ~ to adopt a child; **einen anderen Namen** ~ to change one's name; **Resolution** ~ to adopt a resolution; **sich einer Sache** ~ to take care of s. th., to see about s. th., to attend to a matter; **Schüler** ~ to take pupils; **als selbstverständlich** ~ to take for granted; **mit Sicherheit** ~ to take for granted; **unverändert** ~ to adopt as it stands; **Urteil** ~ to submit to a judgment; **Vernunft** ~ to listen to reason; **unter Vorbehalt** ~ to accept under reserve; **Vorschlag einstimmig** ~ to carry a vote unanimously; **als wahr** ~ to presume; **Waren** ~ to take delivery of goods; **Warensendung nicht** ~ to refuse to accept a consignment, to refuse delivery; **Wechsel** ~ to hono(u)r (accept) a bill; **Wechsel nicht** ~ to refuse to accept a bill, to dishono(u)r a bill by nonacceptance *(US)*; **Wette** ~ to take up a wager, to take on a bet.

Annehmender receiver, adopter, offeree.
Annehmer *(Wechsel)* acceptor, drawee.
Annehmlichkeit commodity, convenience, ease;
~**en des Lebens** amenities of life;
jede ~ **bieten** to afford every comfort.
Annehmlichkeitswert *(Grundstück)* amenity value.
annektieren to annex.
Annexion annexation.
Annexionsgelüste annexionist tendency.
Annonce advertisement, insertion, ad *(US coll.)*;
fingierte ~ dummy advertisement; **zweispaltige** ~ double column;
~ **in die Zeitung einrücken lassen** to advertise, to put an advertisement (a notice) in the papers.
Annoncen|agent, ~**akquisiteur** advertising agent, canvasser; ~**annahme** newspaper office; ~**blatt** advertising paper; ~**büro,** ~**expedition** advertising office (agency), publicity agent, space broker *(US)*; ~**gebühren,** ~**preisstaffel** advertising rates, rate card *(US)*; ~**seite** advertising sheet; ~**tarif** advertising rates (charges), rate card *(US)*; ~**vertreter,** ~**werber** advertising (publicity) agent, canvasser; ~**wesen** advertising.
Annoncieren advertising, insertion.
annoncieren to advertise, to insert.
Annuität annuity;
~**en** consolidated funds;
ewige ~ perpetual annuity, annuity in perpetuity; **hinausgeschobene** ~ deferred annuity; **lebenslängliche** ~ life annuity; **nachschüssige** ~ ordinary annuity; **unendliche** ~ annuity in perpetuity; **vorschüssige** ~ annuity due;
~ **mit sofort beginnender Laufzeit** immediate annuity; ~ **mit begrenzter Laufzeit** terminable annuity; ~ **mit bestimmter Laufzeit** annuity certain; ~ **mit unbestimmter Laufzeit** contingent annuity.
Annuitäten|hypothek instal(l)ment mortgage; **fundierte** ~**schuld** temporary (terminable) annuity.
annullierbar annullable, voidable, avoidable, cancellable, defeasible, *(Urteil)* recallable.
annullieren *(Aufträge)* to cancel, to countermand, *(Gesetz)* to defeat, to render null, *(umstoßen)* to rescind, *(Urteil)* to quash, to vacate, *(Vertrag)* to make void, to avoid, to annul, to rescind, to set aside, to nullify, to invalidate, to vitiate, to evacuate;
Heiratsvertrag ~ to evacuate a contract of (annul a) marriage.
annullierend diriment.
annulliert cancelled;
irrtümlich ~ cancelled in error.
Annullierung annulment, voidance, vitiation, rescission, invalidation, undoing, *(Aufträge)* cancellation, countermanding, *(Gesetz)* defeasance *(Br.)*, defeat, *(Urteil)* quashing, *(Wechsel)* nullification;
~ **einer Bürgschaft** revocation of a guarantee; ~ **eines Geschäfts** calling off a deal; ~ **einer Registereintragung** cancellation of a registration; ~ **eines Testaments** cancellation of a will; ~ **einer Urkunde** setting aside of a deed; ~ **und Festlegung neuer Vertragsbestimmungen** rescission of terms; ~ **einer Vertragsvereinbarung** avoidance of an agreement.
Annullierungs|anspruch right of rescission; ~**gebühr** cancellation charge.
Anode anode, plate *(US)*, positive electrode.
Anodenbatterie high-tension battery, B battery.
Anomalität *(Statistik)* abnormality.
anonym anonymous;
~ **bleiben** to remain anonymous; ~ **reisen** to travel under an alias (incognito);
~**er Brief** anonymous letter.
Anonymität anonymity.
anordnen to order, to dispose, to appoint, *(anweisen)* to conduct, to direct, to institute, *(gruppieren)* to arrange, to group, *(regeln)* to direct, to rule, *(unterbringen)* to place, *(Vermögenssteuer)* to marshal;
alphabetisch ~ to arrange in alphabetical order; **Aufhebung der Zwangsvollstreckung** ~ to vacate an attachment; **ausdrücklich** ~ to order expressly; **Beschlagnahme** ~ to levy an attachment order; **Freigabe** ~ to release an attachment; **Freigabe des Vermögens** ~ to release property; **Kontosperre** ~ to block an account; **neu** ~ to rearrange; **paarweise** ~ to pair off; **Rückzug** ~ to order the retreat; **Ruhen des Verfahrens** ~ to stay proceedings; **nach Sachgebieten** ~ to arrange by subject matter; **Sitzungspause** ~ to declare a recess; **testamentarisch** ~ to dispose of by will; **vorher** ~ to predispose (preordain); **wertmäßig** ~ to arrange in order of value.
Anordnung order, direction, instruction, regulation, *(Grafik)* design, layout *(US)*, *(Gruppierung)* arrangement, form, formation, system, economy, getup, grouping, *(Muster)* design, *(Statistik)* order, array, *(System)* form, frame, system, plan, *(Truppen)* disposition, *(Vermögenswerte)* marshal(l)ing, *(Verwaltung)* decree;
auf ~ **von** at the instance (order) of; **auf** ~ **des Gerichts** by order of the court; **entgegen früheren** ~**en** against previous arrangements; **entsprechend Ihren** ~ in obedience to your orders; **gemäß Ihren** ~**en** in compliance with your orders (instructions); **laut** ~ as ordered;
allgemeine ~ standing order; **alphabetische** ~ arrangement in alphabetical order; **asymetrische** ~ *(Anzeige)* informal balance; **behördliche** ~ administrative order (regulation), government regulation; **einstweilige** ~ decretal order, provisional remedy, restraining interim order; **falsche** ~ misarrangement; **gerichtliche** ~ commandment, fiat *(Br.)*, court order, judicial writ; **gewerbepolizeiliche** ~**en** factory regulations; **polizeiliche** ~ police ordinance; **pyramidenförmige** ~ *(Anzeige)* pyramid; **befristete richterliche** ~ temporary injunction *(US)*; **systematische** ~ orderly arrangement; **übersichtliche** ~ well-ordered arrangement; **vorläufige** ~ provisional arrangement, interim order; **zeitliche** ~ time series; **zwingende** ~ peremptory notice;
~ **der Betriebsanlage** departmental layout; ~ **einer Bibliothek** arrangement of a library; ~ **der Entlassenenbetreuung** aftercare arrangement; ~ **mit Gesetzeskraft** statutory order *(Br.)*; ~ **des Getrenntlebens** matrimonial (separation) order *(Br.)*; ~ **der Haftentlassung** writ of privileges *(Br.)*; ~ **der Haftentlassung gegen Kautionsgestellung** writ of mainprize *(Br.)*; ~ **eines Haftprüfungstermins** writ of Habeas Corpus; ~ **eines Leitwegs** routing order; ~ **der Liquidation** dissolution order; ~ **der Nachlaßverwaltung (Nachlaßpflegschaft)** grant (letters) of administration; ~ **der Polizeiaufsicht** supervision order *(Br.)*; ~ **von Ratenzahlungen** instalment order; ~ **der Rechnungslegung** order for an account; **einstweilige** ~ **zum Schutz des Vorbehaltsguts der Ehefrau** protection order; ~ **der Untersuchungshaft** interim committitus, commitment for trial, remand in custody; ~ **der Vermögensverwaltung** administration order *(Br.)*; ~ **der zwangsweisen Vorführung** *(Zeuge)* warrant; ~ **der Vormundschaft** letters of guardianship; ~ **der Zwangsliquidation** compulsory winding-up order; ~ **eines Zwangsvergleichs** composition order; ~ **der Zwangsvollstreckung** attachment order;
~ **nicht beachten** to ignore an order; ~ **befolgen** to give heed to an order; ~**en billigen** to acquiesce in an arrangement; ~**en erlassen** to make (emit) orders, to give instructions; **den ärztlichen** ~**en folgen** to follow the doctor's advice; **sich an** ~**en halten** to conform with orders, to act upon instructions; **gegen jds.** ~**en handeln** to act (go, run) counter to s. one's orders; **sich mit seinen** ~**en über j. hinwegsetzen** to give orders over s. one's head; ~**en Folge leisten** to obey orders; ~**en des Gerichts mißachten** to fail to comply with the court's order; ~**en nachkommen** to comply with instructions; ~ **außer Kraft setzen** to suspend a rule; ~**en treffen** to give instructions, to arrange, to make arrangements; **notwendige** ~**en treffen** to make all necessary arrangements; **auf** ~**en warten** to await instructions; ~**en zuwiderhandeln** to act contrary to (in defiance of) instructions; ~**en des Gerichts zuwiderhandeln** to fail to comply with the orders of the court.
Anordnungs|befugnis authority; ~**meßzahl** *(Statistik)* order statistic; ~**plan** layout.
anormal anomalous, abnormal;
unter ~**en Verhältnissen leben** to live in abnormal circumstances.
anpacken to treat, to handle;
energisch ~ to put one's shoulders to the wheel; **Sache falsch** ~ to tackle a matter the wrong way; **tüchtig** ~ to sail into *(sl.)*; **Übel an der Wurzel** ~ to strike at the root of an evil.
anpassen to adapt, to adjust, to fit, to accommodate, to assimilate, *(Handels- und Steuerbilanz)* to match, *(Politik)* to realign;
sich ~ to conform, to trim; **seine Bedürfnisse dem internationalen Gegenwert der eigenen Waren und Dienstleistungen** ~ to tailor one's requirements to the international value of goods and services one provides; **Kosten den Erträgen** ~ to match costs and revenues; **Löhne** ~ to equalize wages; **sich jds. Meinung** ~ to fall in with s. one's opinion; **Mittel dem Zweck** ~ to adapt the means to the end; **Produktion der Nachfrage** ~ to gear production to demand; **Rente automatisch den Bruttolöhnen** ~ to uprate a pension regularly in line with earnings; **Rente nach Ausscheiden aus dem Berufsleben laufend dem Preisniveau** ~ to

revalue a pension post-retirement in line with prices, to index-link a pension; **Rente während der Beschäftigungszeit laufend dem Bruttolohn** ~ to revalue a pension pre-retirement in line with earnings; **seinen Stil den Zuhörern** ~ to suit one's style to the audience; **sich seiner Umgebung** ~ to fit o. s. into one's surroundings; **sich den Verbraucherbedürfnissen** ~ to gear to consumer needs; **sich den Verhältnissen** ~ to accommodate (adapt) o. s. to circumstances; **sich den veränderten Verhältnissen** ~ to dance to another tune; **Zinsen** ~ to adjust the interest.

Anpassung adaptation, accommodation, assimilation, *(Handels- und Steuerbilanz)* matching, *(automatische Lohnangleichung)* escalation *(US)*, *(Politik)* realignment, *(Preise, US)* escalation, adaptation, adjustment;
automatische ~ *(Löhne)* escalator clause, escalator adjustment, *(Steuersystem)* built-in flexibility; **beste** ~ *(Statistik)* best fit; **schlechte** ~ maladjustment; **soziale** ~ social adaption (adjustment); **strukturelle** ~ structural adaption; **stufenweise** ~ gradualism; **vorübergehende** ~ temporization; **wirtschaftliche** ~ economic adjustment;
~ **der Agrarpolitik an die Europäische Gemeinschaft** farm policy alignment; ~ **der Anzeigensätze** adjustment in advertising rates; ~ **der Löhne** equalization of wages, adjustment of existing wage rates; ~ **der Preise** adaptation of prices, price adjustment; ~ **der Rente an das Preisniveau** index-linking of a pension; ~ **der Sozialversicherungsleistungen** social security adjustment; **automatische** ~ **der Steuertabelle an die Inflationsrate** automatic adjustment of tax schedule to the rate of inflation; ~ **an den ermäßigten Tarif** short-rate adjustment; ~ **an die Verbraucherbedürfnisse** gearing to consumer needs; ~ **an die Verhältnisse** accommodation to circumstances; ~ **der Währungen** alignment (adjustment) of currencies; ~ **der Wechselkurse** exchange adjustment;
~**en durchführen** to make adjustments.

Anpassungsbeihilfe adaptation allowance.

anpassungsfähig flexible, elastic, adaptable, adaptive;
nicht ~ inadaptable.

Anpassungsfähigkeit flexibility, elasticity, adaptability;
automatische ~ *(Steuersystem)* built-in flexibility; **geistige** ~ versatility; **wirtschaftliche** ~ economic adaptiveness;
~ **der Preise** flexibility of prices.

Anpassungs|gesetz amendment law; ~**klausel** rise and fall clause, *(Löhne)* escalator clause, *(Steuersystem)* matching clause; **automatische** ~**klausel** *(Versicherungswert)* self-reducing clause; ~**maßnahmen** *(EG)* measures of adjustment; ~**mechanismus** adjustment mechanism; ~**phase** settling-down phase; ~**politik** time-serving policy, opportunism; ~**prozeß** process of accommodation, adjustment (assimilative) process; ~**reaktion** phase of adjustment; ~**schwierigkeiten** assimilative difficulties; ~**verfahren** adjustment process; ~**vermögen** adaptability; ~**zeitraum** period of adjustment.

Anpfiff *(fig.)* dressing room, *(coll.)* tingler.

anpflanzen to plant, to cultivate, to grow.

Anpflanzung plantation, cultivation.

anpflaumen, j. to kid s. o.

an|pöbeln to barrack *(fam.)*; ~**prangern** to pillory.

anpreisen to recommend, to promote, to write up, to sell *(US)*;
wie saures Bier ~ to offer at a knockdown price; **marktschreierisch** ~ to puff *(Br.)*, to boost, to quack, to crack up, to push *(US)*.

Anpreisung recommendation, claptrap;
marktschreierische (übertriebene) ~ puff[ing], boost[ing], puff *(Br.)*, patter, ballyhoo *(coll.)*, push *(US)*.

Anprobe try-on;
zum Schneider zur ~ **gehen** to go to the tailor's for a fitting.

anprobieren, Anzug to try on a suit.

anprobiert, nicht not tried on.

anpuffen to jostle.

Anpumpen touch *(sl.)*.

anpumpen to touch for money, to pump for money *(fam.)*;
j. ~ to touch (tap, stick, *US*, strike, *sl.*) s. o., to put the bee (bite) on s. o. *(US)*; **j. auf der Straße** ~ to put the sleeve on s. o. *(sl.)*.

anquatschen, j. to accost s. o.

Anrainer abutter, abutting owner, neighbo(u)ring peasant;
~**recht** right of contiguity; ~**staat** bordering state.

anranzen, j. to snap s. one's nose off.

Anraten advice, recommendation.

anraten to advise, to recommend;
jem. etw. dringend ~ to urge s. o. to do s. th.

anrechenbar chargeable, attributable, *(Gerichtskosten)* taxable.

anrechnen to reckon, *(abziehen)* to allow, to deduct, *(belasten)* to charge, *(debetieren)* to debit, *(gutschreiben)* to credit;
auf das Erbteil ~ to throw (bring) into hotchpot; **jem. etw. hoch** ~ to give s. o. credit for s. th.; **jem. zehn Jahre Dienstzeit** ~ to allow s. o. ten years seniority; **auf eine Schuld** ~ to appropriate money to a debt; **Steuer** ~ to impute (credit) a tax; **Untersuchungshaft** ~ to make allowance for custody; **sich als Verdienst** ~ to count it one's glory, to take credit to o. s.; **zuviel** ~ to overcharge, *(Steuer)* to overrate.

Anrechnung *(Abzug)* allowance, deduction, *(Belastung)* charge, charging, debit[ing], *(Gutschrift)* credit[ing], placing to account, *(Rechnungsstellung)* invoicing;
~ **des Altwertes** *(Versicherung)* deduction new for old; **steuerliche** ~ **außergewöhnlicher Belastungen** excess relief *(Br.)*, relief for excess charges *(Br.)*; ~ **bei der Einkommensteuer** tax credit *(US)*; ~ **aufs Erbteil** bringing into hotchpot; ~ **der Ersitzungszeit des Vorbesitzers** tacking; ~ **auf die Pensionszeit** retirement credit; ~ **auf eine Schuldsumme** appropriation of money to a debt; ~ **im Ausland gezahlter Steuern** allowance as a credit of a tax, double taxation relief *(Br.)*, foreign tax credit *(US)*, *(insgesamt gezahlte Steuern)* overall limitation *(US)*; ~ **des Vorausempfängers** advance brought into hotchpot;
in ~ **bringen** to allow, to deduct; **jem. in** ~ **bringen** to put down (charge, debit) to s. one's account; **auf das Erbteil in** ~ **bringen** to throw (bring) into hotchpot; **Satz von 4% in** ~ **bringen** to apply a rate of 4 per cent.

anrechnungsfähig countable;
~**e Dienstjahre** pensionable years of service; ~**es Jahr** *(Sozialversicherung)* year of coverage.

Anrechnungs|punkt *(Schule)* credit *(US)*; ~**system** *(Körperschaftssteuer)* imputation system *(Br.)*; ~**verfahren** *(Doppelbesteuerung)* indirect relief.

Anrecht right, title, claim;
bedingtes ~ conditional interest; **erstes** ~ first refusal;
~ **auf einen Streik** right to strike;
~ **auf etw. haben** to be eligible (qualified) for (entitled to) s. th.; **kein** ~ **haben** to have no business doing; **sein** ~ **geltend machen** to assert one's claim; **auf ein** ~ **verzichten** to renounce a claim.

Anrede [form of] address, style, *(im Brief)* salutation, greeting, *(des Gerichts in der Klageschrift)* direction, address;
~**form** style (form) of address.

anreden to address, to style.

anregen to suggest, to initiate, to foster, to bring up, to prompt, *(Alkohol)* to stimulate;
Arbeitslust ~ to animate to greater efforts; **Dissertationsthema** ~ to suggest the subject of a dissertation; **Konjunktur** ~ to stimulate business activity; **j. zum Nachdenken** ~ to make s. o. think.

anregend|es Buch stimulating book; ~**es Mittel** stimulant, exhilaration.

Anregung initiation, initiative, instigation, suggestion, stimulation, fosterage;
auf ~ **von** on the initiative of; **einer ersten** ~ **folgend** under the impulse of the moment;
~ **der Konjunktur** stimulation of business activity;
auf jds. ~ **handeln** to act on the impulsion of s. o.; **für eine** ~ **dankbar sein** to appreciate a suggestion.

Anregungsmittel stimulant, exhilarant.

anreichern to enrich;
unzureichende Rücklagen ~ to rebuild inadequate reserves.

Anreicherung enrichment;
~ **unzureichender Rücklagen** rebuilding inadequate reserves.

Anreise journey;
~**tag** day of arrival.

anreißen, Fünfpfundnote to break into a five-pound note.

Anreißer tout, cheap-jack, clicker *(Br., sl.)*, puller-in *(US)*.

anreißerisch gaudy, loud;
~**e Werbung** puffing publicity *(Br.)*, ballyhoo *(coll.)*.

Anreiz incentive, inducement, impulsion, stimulus, fillip, premium, *(Waren)* appeal, whet;
finanzielle ~**e** financial incentives; **materieller** ~ pecuniary incentive; **preislicher** ~ price appeal;
steuerliche ~**e für Investitionen** investment tax incentives; ~ **zum Kauf** inducement to buy, buying incentive; **keinerlei** ~ **für die Unternehmerschaft** disincentive to members of the managerial classes;
jem. etw. als ~ **bieten** to hold out an inducement to s. o.; **im nächsten Jahr stärkere steuerliche** ~**e schaffen** to take more positive fiscal action next year;
~**artikel** eye-catcher, loss leader; ~**blockierung** disincentive; ~**effekt** *(steuerlich)* incentive; ~**prämie** incentive premium; ~**reaktion** stimulus response; ~**system zur Produktivitätssteigerung** productivity incentive system.

anrempeln to jostle, to bump against.
Anrichte cupboard, sideboard, buffet, dresser *(Br.)*.
anrichten to bring about, to course, *(Speisen)* to dress, to prepare;
etw. schönes ~ to make a nice mess of it; **Verwüstungen** ~ to ravage.
Anrichte|raum pantry; ~**tisch** waiting table; ~**zimmer** pantry.
anrollen to cart, *(Flugzeug)* to taxi up.
anrüchig obnoxious, of ill repute, ill-reputed, shady *(coll.)*;
~**es Hotel** ill-reputed hotel; ~**er Lebenswandel** disreputable conduct; ~**e Methoden** wildcat methods.
anrücken *(mil.)* to advance.
Anruf call, ring, buzz *(coll.)*;
fernmündlicher ~ telephone call; **gebührenfreier** ~ call toll-free; **nächtlicher** ~ night call;
~ **durch den Wachposten** challenge;
~ **entgegennehmen** to take a call; **ohne** ~ **schießen** to shoot without warning; **auf einen** ~ **warten** to wait for a call;
automatischer ~**beantworter** *(tel.)* automatic telephone answering machine, responder *(US)*.
anrufen *(Posten)* to challenge;
j. ~ to call s. o., to give s. o. a ring (call, blast, *sl.*), to ring s. o. up on the telephone, to phone (buzz) s. o.; **funktelefonisch** ~ to radiotelephone; **Gericht** ~ to appeal (have recourse) to the law;
j. um Hilfe ~ to appeal to s. o. for help; **höhere Instanz** ~ to appeal to a higher court; **Schiedsgericht** ~ to go to arbitration.
Anrufer caller.
Anrufklappe call indicator.
Anrufung |der Gerichte appeal at law, reference to a court; ~ **einer höheren Instanz** appeal to a higher court; ~ **eines Schiedsgerichtes** submission of an affair to arbitration.
Anrufungsverfahren *(Personalverwaltung)* appeal procedure.
Ansage *(Rundfunk)* announcement, lead-in.
ansagen to announce, to compère *(Br.)*;
sich ~ to make an appointment; **Zeit** ~ to give the time.
Ansager *(Rundfunk)* announcer, *(Veranstaltung)* emcee, compère *(Br.)*.
ansammeln *(Kapital)* to accumulate, *(Vorräte)* to assemble, *(Vorräte)* to hoard, to amass, to pile (hoard) up, to stockpile, to lay (store) up;
sich ~ to pile up, *(Menschenmassen)* to gather round, to assemble, *(Zinsen)* to accrue; **Reichtümer** ~ to amass riches; **Reserven** ~ to build up reserves; **Truppen** ~ to concentrate troops.
Ansammlung mass, amassment, head *(Br.)*, aggregation, concentration, *(Kapital)* accumulation, *(Verkehr)* congestion, *(Vorräte)* hoard[ing], stockpiling, *(Zinsen)* accrual;
~ **von Fahrzeugen** mass of traffic; ~ **von Gerümpel** collection of rubbish; ~ **von Menschen** throng (aggregation) of people; ~ **von Reserven (Rücklagen)** building up of reserves; ~ **von Truppen** concentration of troops.
ansässig resident, residing, domiciled, settled, based;
im Ausland ~ resident (living) abroad; **in Großbritannien** ~ resident *(Br.)*; **nicht** ~ nonresident, nonresidential;
sich ~ **machen** to establish o. s., to settle down, to take up one's abode; ~ **sein** to be resident, to reside, to domicile; **im Ausland** ~ **sein** to reside abroad; **an einem Platz seit Generationen** ~ **sein** *(Familie)* to have lived at a place for generations; ~ **werden** to become a resident, to take up one's residence.
Ansässiger inhabitant, resident.
Ansässigkeit residence.
Ansässigwerden domestication.
Ansatz amount set up, *(Abschätzung)* valuation, appraisement, *(Anzeichen)* inception, beginning, symptom, sign, *(Haushaltungsvoranschlag)* appropriation, amount budgeted, *(Kurve)* trend, *(in einer Rechnung)* rate, entry, *(Versuch)* attempt, *(Voranschlag)* estimate, assessment, *(Wertschätzung)* valuation;
im ersten ~ right away, straight off, at the first onset;
erster ~ first go; **gelegentlich glücklicher** ~ occasional lucky stab; **der im Etat vorgesehene** ~ the appropriation provided for in the budget;
~ **des Haushaltsplans** budgetary appropriation; ~ **eines Lächelns** trace of a smile; ~ **eines Preises** fixing of a price; ~ **zum Reden** attempt to speak;
außer ~ **bleiben** to be left out of account; **in** ~ **bringen** to place to account; **leichten** ~ **zur Besserung zeigen** to show signs of improvement.
Ansätze rudiments, first beginnings;
~ **des Tarifs** tariff rates; ~ **konjunktureller Verschlechterung** signs of a slowdown;
in den ~**n steckenbleiben** to get bogged down at the very outset; **gute** ~ **zeigen** to promise well.
Ansatz|berichtigung rectification of an account; ~**fehler** *(Statistik)* error in equations; **systematischer** ~**fehler** specification bias; ~**punkt** starting point; ~**rohr** extension pipe; ~**stück** extension, *(Ausziehtisch)* draw leaf, *(Wechsel)* allonge; ~**teil** nozzle.
ansaufen, sich einen to get plastered *(coll.)*.
Ansaug|pumpe suction pump; ~**rohr** suction pipe; ~**schlauch** suction hose; ~**ventil** inlet (suction) valve.
anschaffen to provide, to procure, to make provision for, to furnish, *(Geldbetrag)* to remit, to make remittance, *(kaufen)* to purchase, to acquire;
sich [selbst] etw. ~ to furnish (equip) o. s. with s. th., to invest in s. th. of one's own; **sich ein Auto** ~ to purchase a car; **Betrag bei einer Bank** ~ to remit a sum to a bank; **Deckung** ~ to furnish with cover; **Deckung für einen Wechsel** ~ to make provision for cover of a bill; **Gegenwert** ~ to make remittance, to remit the proceeds; **Gelder für den Zinsendienst** ~ to provide funds for payment of interest; **Vorräte** ~ to lay in stocks, to stockpile, to purvey.
Anschaffung provision, procurement, *(bei einer Bank)* remittance, *(Erwerb)* purchase, acquisition, *(Währungsguthaben)* delivery;
gemeinsame ~**en** jointly-acquired property;
~ **in bar** remittance in cash; ~ **zwecks Deckung** providing cover;
~ **des Gegenwertes** remittance of proceeds; ~ **in Schecks** return remittance *(US)*; ~ **von Vorräten** stockpiling, purveyance; ~ **zum Zweck der Weiterveräußerung** purchase for resale;
notwendige ~**en beschließen** to decide upon a necessary purchase; **größere** ~**en gemacht haben** to have bought a lot of things; **für** ~ **sorgen** to provide for payment; **keine** ~ **vornehmen** to leave without cover.
Anschaffungs|basis, auf *(Kapitalanlagegesellschaft)* at cost; ~**betrag** purchase price; ~**kosten** costs of acquisition, cost of purchase, acquisition (prime, original, first) cost, first (initial) outlay, purchase money, outlay for assets; **nicht abgeschriebene** ~**kosten** unallowed expenditure; ~**kosten eines Kraftfahrzeuges** cost of a car; ~**kosten eines Wirtschaftsgutes auf die Nutzungsdauer verteilen** to spread the cost of an asset over its useful life; **steuerbegünstigter** ~**kredit** qualifying loan *(Br.)*;
~**preis** cost of acquisition, acquisition price, purchase (original, cost, first) price, initial cost, *(Bilanz)* cost; ~**tag** purchase (vesting) date, date of acquisition (purchase); ~**wert** value at cost, cost (acquisition, original, initial,) value, purchasing value of money, prime cost; ~- **und Unterhaltungszuschuß für ein Kraftfahrzeug** motor vehicle advance and basic allowance.
anschaulich graphic, descriptive, vivid, visual;
~ **darstellen** to depict; **durch Beispiele** ~ **machen** to illustrate by examples.
Anschauung view, opinion;
rückständige ~**en** stuffy views;
etw. aus eigener ~ **kennen** to know s. th. from one's own experience; **jds. politische** ~**en teilen** to share s. one's political opinions; **fortschrittliche** ~**en vertreten** to hold progressive views.
Anschauungs|material illustrative data, *(Schule)* demonstration material; ~**material für den Schulunterricht** visual aids in teaching; ~**modell** mockup; ~**unterricht** object lessons (teaching), visual instruction.
Anschein look, appearance, air, semblance;
allem ~ **nach, beim ersten** ~ to all appearances, on the face of it; **dem** ~ **nach** apparently; **den** ~ **wahrend** face-saving; **nach dem ersten** ~ [at the] first blush; **unter dem** ~ **des Rechtes** under the colo(u)r of law;
äußerer ~ feigned appearance, front *(coll.)*; **falscher** ~ make-believe;
~ **der Glaubwürdigkeit** semblance of credibility;
falschen ~ **erwecken** to give the wrong impression; **sich den** ~ **geben** to assume an appearance; **sich den** ~ **geben krank zu sein** to pretend to be ill; **den** ~ **wahren** to keep up appearances.
anscheinend apparent, seeming, ostensible, colo(u)rable;
~**e Besserung** seeming improvement; ~**e Gefahr** apparent danger.
Anscheins|beweis half proof, prima facie evidence; ~**vollmacht** ostensible (constructive) authority.
anschicken, sich to get ready to do.
anschieben, Auto to push a car.
Anschiß dressing down, giving hell;
~ **verpassen** to tell of *(mil., sl.)*.
Anschlag notice, announcement, *(Berechnung)* calculation, estimate, valuation, computation, *(Plakat)* poster, posting, bill, placard, placarding, affiche, *(Reklame)* advertisement, *(Steuer)* rate, assessment, *(Verschwörung)* plot, conspiracy;

nach dem niedrigsten ~ at the lowest calculation; **tückischer** ~ machination; **verdeckter** ~ obstructed site; **wilder** ~ fly posting;
~ **auf das Botschaftsgebäude** attack on the embassy; ~ **auf die Freiheit des Volkes** attempt against the liberty of the people; ~ **einer Tür** door step; ~ **in Verkehrsmitteln** car-card advertising; **durch** ~ **bekanntgeben** to placard; **Versteigerung durch** ~ **bekanntmachen** to advertise a sale; **in** ~ **bringen** to allow for, to make an allowance; ~ **der Reparaturkosten einreichen** to hand in an estimate of the costs of repair; **leichten** ~ **haben** *(Schreibmaschine)* to have a light touch; ~ **auf j. machen** to make an attempt on s. one's life; ~ **am schwarzen Brett machen** to put up a notice on the bulletin board; ~ **an eine Mauer machen** to stick up a bill on a wall; ~ **auf j. vorhaben** to have designs on s. o.; ~ **der Kosten vornehmen** to make an estimate of the costs;
~**bogen** bill, poster; ~**brett** notice *(Br.)* (bulletin, *US*) call, board, billboard *(US)*, hoarding *(Br.)*, *(Bahn, Theater)* call board; ~**dauer** period of display.

Anschlagen *(Plakat)* billing, posting, placing a poster.

anschlagen to fasten, to fix, *(bewerten)* to calculate, to value, *(Plakat)* to post (put) up, to placard, to stick [up], to bill, *(für Steuer)* to assess, to rate;
Bekanntmachung ~ to put (pin) up a notice; **Flügel leicht** ~ to touch the keys of a piano; **gut** ~ to answer well; **gut bei jem.** ~ *(Kur)* to have a great effect on s. o.; **zu hoch** ~ to overestimate; **an gut sichtbarer Stelle** ~ to post in a conspicuous place; **schnelleres Tempo** ~ to quicken one's pace; **einen anderen Ton** ~ to change one's (sing another) tune; **warnenden Ton** ~ to strike a note of warning; **Versteigerung** ~ to advertise a sale.

Anschlag|kontrolle site inspection; ~**kontrolleur** site inspector; ~**kosten** space charges; ~**leiste** fence; ~**papier** poster paper; ~**säule** advertising (poster) pillar.

Anschlags|einheit *(Außenwerbung)* showing; ~**preis** *(Auktion)* upset price.

Anschlag|stelle [poster] site, billboard *(US)*; **allgemeine** ~**stelle** usual used site; ~**stellenblock** *(Anzeige)* poster showing.

Anschlagswert estimated (appraised) value.

Anschlag|tafel notice board *(Br.)*, [poster] hoarding *(Br.)*, poster site (panel), show (bulletin, *US*) board, billboard *(US)*; ~**werbung** posting, poster advertising; ~**zaun** poster (billboard, *US*) hoarding; ~**zettel** posting bill, poster placard.

anschleichen, sich an die feindliche Stellung to sneak up to the enemy position.

anschließen to link, *(el.)* to put in circuit, to wire [up], *(mit Kette)* to chain, *(Satz)* to close up;
sich an j. ~ to align o. s. with s. o.; **sich den Ausführungen des Redners** ~ to concur with the speaker; **sich der Berufung** ~ to cross-appeal; **sich einer politischen Bewegung** ~ to associate o. s. with a political movement; **sich enger** ~ to join more closely; **einer Fabrik ein Forschungsinstitut** ~ to affiliate a research institute to a factory; **Fahrrad** ~ to padlock a bicycle; **sich einer Gesellschaft** ~ to make one of the party; **Haus an die Gasversorgung** ~ to connect a house to the gas mains; **sich der Mehrheit** ~ to join the majority, to swim with the tide (stream); **sich einer Meinung** ~ to adopt a view; **sich einer Partei** ~ to join (throw in one's lot with) a party; **sich einer Sache** ~ to climb on the bandwaggon; **sich schnell** ~ to make easily social contacts; **Sender** ~ to link up transmitters; **ans Stromnetz** ~ to connect to the mains.

Anschluß *(Bahn, Flugzeug)* connexion, connection *(US)*, *(Einverleibung)* incorporation, *(el.)* connexion, contact, *(Glas, Wasser)* supply, *(Telefon)* [telephone] line, *(Verein)* affiliation;
im ~ **an mein Schreiben** referring (with further reference) to my letter;
besetzter ~ line engaged;
~ **an Europa** joining Europe; ~ **an das Fernsprechnetz** connection of a new telephone; ~ **an das Gasleitungsnetz** connection with the gas pipe; ~ **eines Staates** accession of a state; ~ **an das Stromnetz** connection to the mains;
seinen ~ **bekommen** *(tel.)* to get through (a connection, *US*, connexion); ~ **an den Leistungsstandard einer Klasse bekommen** to catch up with the rest of a class; **seinen** ~ **erreichen** *(Zug)* to make one's connection *(US)*, to catch (meet) a train; **leicht** ~ **finden** to be a good mixer, to make contacts easily; **schwer** ~ **finden** not to be a sociable person; ~ **haben** to cross a train, to run in connection with; **überall** ~ **haben** to meet all trains; ~ **verpaßt haben** *(fig.)* to have missed the boat (bus); ~ **herstellen** *(tel.)* to switch; ~ **suchen** to seek company; **auf einen anderen** ~ **umstellen** *(Anruf)* to forward a call; ~ **unterbrechen** *(tel.)* to switch off; ~ **verlieren** to get left behind; ~ **versäumen** to miss one's connection; ~ **wiederherstellen** to reconnect;
~**auftrag** follow-up order, follow-on contract; ~**bahn** branch (feeder) line; ~**bahnhof** junction; ~**bereich** *(tel.)* telephone area; ~**berufung** cross appeal, counterappeal; ~**buchstaben** abutting letters; ~**buchung** *(Flug)* onto booking, booking onward, continuing plane reservation; ~**dose** *(el.)* wall socket, outlet (junction) box; ~**fahrkarte** transfer ticket, *(Bus und Bahn)* combined rail and road ticket.

anschlußfertig *(sl.)* fully wired.

Anschluß|finanzierung follow-up financing; ~**firma** *(Faktorei)* client; ~**flug** plane connection, interconnecting flight; ~**flüge im Inland** domestic transfer flights; ~**flugzeug** connecting flight; ~**flugzeug erreichen** to catch a plane; ~**gleis** siding, side line, junction [line], sidetrack *(US)*; ~**kabel** subscriber's cable; ~**kasten** *(el.)* pull box; ~**klemme** *(el.)* terminal; ~**klinke** *(tel.)* jack; ~**kompanie** flank company; ~**leitung** *(tel.)* subscriber's line; ~**linie** branch line, *(Flugverkehr)* feeder line; ~**nummer** call number; ~**pacht** reversionary lease; ~**pfändung** second distress, junior execution; ~**programm** successor plan; ~**punkt** junction; ~**reederei** connecting carrier; ~**revision** cross-errors; ~**rohr** connecting pipe; ~**schnur** *(el.)* flex *(Br.)*, connecting cord *(US)*; ~**station** junction; ~**stecker** plug; ~**stelle** terminal, *(el.)* wiring point; ~**stöpsel** plug; ~**strecke** connecting (feeder) line; ~**stück** *(el.)* coupling; ~**vertrag** follow-on contract; ~**zug** connecting (corresponding) train, *(an Dampferlinie)* boat train.

anschmiegen, sich an die Berge to cling to the mountains.

anschmiegsam pliant, supple.

anschmieren, j. to sell s. o. a gold brick, to take s. o. in.

anschnallbar strap-on.

anschnallen to buckle (strap) on;
sich ~ to fasten one's seat belt.

Anschnallgurt safety (seat) belt;
~**vorrichtung** safety-belt mechanism.

anschnauzen, j. to snap at s. o., to dress s. o. down, to haul s. o. over the coals.

anschneiden *(Anzeige)* to bleed;
Frage ~ to raise a question; **Thema** ~ to broach a subject; **Thema am Rande** ~ to touch upon a subject.

Anschnitt *(Anzeige)* bleed;
im ~ **verkaufen** to sell by the piece;
~**zuschlag** bleed premium (charge).

Anschreibe|block scorebook; ~**buch** passbook.

Anschreiben accompanying (covering) letter, letter of transmittal.

anschreiben *(belasten)* to charge, to debit, to book, to score, to chalk, to note down, to put down to a customer's account, to mark up;
~ **lassen** to take on credit (tick, *Br.*, the cuff, *US*), to run up a book (a score, bills in a store, *US*); **Kunden** ~ **lassen** to carry a customer.

Anschreibenlassen beim Kaufmann scoring of debts, score credit *(US)*.

Anschreibkonto *(beim Kaufmann)* credit (charge, *US*, monthly, *Br.*) account.

Anschrift address, direction;
ohne ~ unaddressed;
falsche ~ wrong address, *(auf Brief)* misdirection; **namentliche** ~ form of address;
~**en potentieller Kunden liefern** to supply names of prospects; **sich jds. Namen und** ~ **notieren** to take down s. one's name and address.

Anschriften|ermittlung säumiger Schuldner skip tracing; ~**sammelpunkt** address point; ~**verzeichnis** list of addresses.

Anschriftsänderung change of address.

anschuldigen to charge, to accuse;
j. des Mordes ~ to accuse s. o. of murder, to impute a murder to s. o.

Anschuldigung accusation, indictment, incrimination, charge, imputation;
falsche ~ aspersion, trumped-up charge, calumny; **leichtfertige (falsche)** ~ malicious prosecution; **versteckte** ~ oblique accusation;
~ **gegen j. erheben** to frame an accusation against s. o.; ~ **hundertprozentig zurückweisen können** to have a complete answer to an accusation; ~ **präzisieren** to specialize an accusation; **seine** ~ **zurücknehmen** to withdraw one's charge, to retract an accusation.

anschwärzen, j. to put the finger on s. o., to blacken s. one's character, to denigrate s. o.; **j. laufend** ~ to be always running s. o. down; **Konkurrenz** ~ to disparage a competitor, to defame a competitor's reputation.

Anschwärzung disparagement, backbiting, blackwash, denigration, aspersion, malicious falsehood *(Br.)*;

~ **der Konkurrenz** defamation of a competitor's reputation, disparagement of a competitor, trade libel *(US)*; ~ **von Konkurrenzerzeugnissen** running down the goods of a competitor.
anschwellen to swell, *(Fluß, Kosten)* to rise.
anschwemmen to wash ashore.
Anschwemmung alluvion, reliction, aggradation.
anschwindeln to bamboozle, to diddle, to cheat.
Ansehen [established] reputation, repute, respect, standing, authority, account, face, credit, weight, clout, prestige, cachet, social importance;
bei flüchtigem ~ at first glance; **ohne** ~ **der Person** without exception of persons; **von großem** ~ of great authority, of high standing;
geschäftliches (kaufmännisches) ~ sound commercial credit, business reputation (standing), goodwill; **öffentliches** ~ public credit;
~ **einer Firma** reputation of a firm; **hohes** ~ **einer Firma** high standing of a firm; **internationales** ~ **eines Landes** international prestige of a country;
wieder zu ~ **gelangen** to recover one's credit; **geringes** ~ **genießen** to be of little account; **höchstes** ~ **genießen** to enjoy the highest reputation; **hohes** ~ **genießen** to be held in high repute (esteem); **großes** ~ **in der Öffentlichkeit genießen** to rank high in public favo(u)r; ~ **gewinnen** to win a reputation; **jds.** ~ **bei allen gerecht und billig Denkenden herabsetzen** to lower s. o. in the estimate of right-thinking members of society generally; **j. vom** ~ **kennen** to know s. o. by sight; **in hohem** ~ **stehen** to enjoy a good reputation; **im** ~ **steigen** to gain; **schnell im** ~ **steigen** to boom *(US)*; **jds.** ~ **steigern** to add to s. one's credit; **an** ~ **verlieren** to come down; **an** ~ **bei jem. verlieren** to fall in s. one's good opinion; **sein** ~ **in der Öffentlichkeit verlieren** to lose one's credit with the public; **sein** ~ **wahren** to save one's face.
ansehen, sich eine Ausstellung to go to an exhibition; **etw. flüchtig** ~ to give s. th. a cursory glance, to glance at s. th.; **j. kritisch von der Seite** ~ to look at s. o. from the corner of one's eye; **es jem. an der Nasenspitze** ~ to tell it by s. one's face; **j. prüfend** ~ to let one's glance dwell on s. o.; **j. scheel** ~ to look with an evil eye on s. o.; **j. über die Schulter** ~ to look down on s. o.; **j. als Schwindler** ~ to regard s. o. as an imposter; **sich die Sehenswürdigkeiten** ~ to go sightseeing; **sich ein Theaterstück bis zum Ende** ~ to see out a play; **sich ganz verdutzt** ~ to look at one another like stuck pigs; **Vertrag genau** ~ to examine a contract closely; **sich eine Wohnung** ~ to look at an apartment (flat); **j. wütend** ~ to look black at s. o.; **Zeitung flüchtig** ~ to scan through a newspaper;
Schaufenster ~ **gehen** to go window-shopping.
ansehnlich respectable, handsome, considerable, plump;
~**es Gehalt** handsome salary; ~**e Summe** important sum; ~**es Vermögen** sizable fortune.
Ansehung der Person, ohne without respect of persons.
Ansetzblatt flyleaf.
ansetzen *(abschätzen)* to rate, to assess, to value, *(berechnen)* to charge, to debit, *(Preis)* to quote, to fix, *(Termin)* to appoint, to fix, to schedule *(US)*;
Aktie niedrig ~ to set a low value on a stock; **noch einmal** ~ to start anew, to begin again; **zum Endspurt** ~ to smell one's oats; **geschichtliches Ereignis** ~ to date a historical event; **zu hoch** ~ to overestimate, to overvalue; **Kosten** ~ to tax the costs; **zur Landung** ~ to come in to land; **zu niedrig** ~ to understate, to undervalue; **500.000 Pfund für die Einrichtung von Schulneubauten** ~ to appropriate 500.000 pounds for the new school buildings; **Sache X gegen Y** ~ to docket the case of X vs. Y; **Sitzung** ~ to fix a meeting; **Termin für eine Sache** ~ to set a case down for hearing; **Termin zur mündlichen Verhandlung** ~ to assign a day for a hearing in court; **Vorstellung für Sonnabend** ~ to set a performance for Saturday.
Ansetzung *(Preis)* quotation, fixing, *(Termin)* appointment, fixing;
~ **eines Verhandlungstermins** assigning a day for a hearing in court.
Ansicht [point of] view, opinion, mind, outlook, ground, sight, *(Schaubild)* diagram, *(Skizze)* sketch, *(Zeichnung)* drawing;
nach allgemeiner ~ by common repute; **nach** ~ **der Geschäftsführung** in the judgment of the management; **nach** ~ **der Sachverständigen** in the opinion of (according to) the experts; **zur** ~ *(Kauf)* on approval (approbation), for inspection; **zur gefälligen** ~ for your kind inspection;
abweichende ~ divergent opinion, *(Richter)* dissentient opinion; **allgemeine** ~ general reputation, common repute; **aufgeschlossene** ~**en** forward opinions; **bestrittene** ~ controversial opinion; **feste** ~ decided opinions; **schriftlich festgehaltene** ~ position paper; **gegenteilige** ~ opposite opinion, counterview; **geteilte** ~**en** divided opinions; **liberale** ~**en** broad views; **moderne** ~**en** advanced views, modernism; **politische** ~**en** political views (opinions); **radikale** ~**en** extreme opinions; **rückständige** ~**en** stuffy views; **schwankende** ~**en** fluid opinions; **übereinstimmende** ~ consensus of opinion; **überholte** ~**en** outmoded views (outlook); **vernünftige** ~ just opinion; **redaktionell vertretene** ~ editorial opinion; **weitherzige** ~**en** large [-scale] views; **weitverbreitete** ~ widely held opinion;
allgemein vertretene ~ **zu einer Frage** prevalent idea on a question; ~ **in natürlichem Maßstab** full-scale view; ~ **der Minderheit** dissent[ing] (minority) opinion; ~ **von oben** top view;
seine ~ **ändern** to change one's mind; **sich einer** ~ **anschließen** to endorse an opinion, to adopt a view; **sich weitgehend jds.** ~**en anschließen** to fall in with s. one's views; **anderen Leuten seine** ~**en aufdrängen** to force one's ideas on other people; **zur** ~ **auslegen** to expose for inspection; ~ **äußern** to advance (voice, forward) an opinion, to air one's views; **jds.** ~ **beipflichten** to agree with s. one's views; **seine** ~ **unmißverständlich zum Ausdruck bringen** to make one's meaning clear; **seine** ~ **an den Mann bringen** to get one's own views across; **seine** ~ **darlegen** to state one's views, to discourse; **mit seiner** ~ **allein dastehen** to stand alone; **seine** ~ **durchsetzen** to press (carry) one's point; **jds.** ~ **erforschen** to sound s. one's views; **seine** ~ **zu erkennen geben** to signal one's views; **sehr bestimmte** ~**en haben** to have very pronounced views; **entschiedene** ~**en haben** to feel strongly about; **vernünftige** ~**en haben** to have sound views; **mit seiner** ~ **hinter dem Berge halten** to hide one's view; **seine** ~ **kundtun** to disclose one's point of view; **sich den augenblicklichen** ~**en zu eigen machen** to take up current opinions; **seine** ~**en schriftlich niederlegen** to express one's thoughts on paper; **zur** ~ **schicken** to send on approval; **anderer (verschiedener)** ~ **sein** to take a different view, to dissent; **jds.** ~ **teilen** to be of s. one's mind, to share s. one's view; ~ **vertreten** to hold a view (opinion), to take the line *(coll.)*; **andere** ~ **vertreten** to take a different view; **extreme** ~**en vertreten** to hold extreme opinions; **ganz entschieden seine gegenteilige** ~ **vertreten** to express strong dissent; **jem. etw. zur** ~ **vorlegen** to lay s. th. before s. o.; ~ **des Autors wiedergeben** to express the author's meaning.
Ansichts|album *(Briefmarken)* approval book; ~**besorgung** *(Buchhändler)* approval acquisition; ~**bogen** *(Philatelie)* approval sheet; ~**exemplar** specimen copy; ~**gebühr** *(Buchhändler)* on-approval fee; ~**kartenladen** pooch *(sl.)*; ~**muster** sample for inspection; ~**nummer** specimen copy; ~**postkarte** picture postcard; ~**sache** matter of opinion; **vorwiegend** ~**sache sein** to rest largely on personal opinions; ~**sendung** consignment (articles sent) on approval, consignment for inspection, *(Philatelie)* approval sheet; ~**versand** dispatch on approval.
ansiedeln to settle, to establish, to colonize, to plant;
sich ~ to take one's abode, to establish o. s.; **Geschichte** ~ to lay a story; **Industriebetriebe** ~ to locate industries; **sich ohne Rechtstitel** ~ to squat.
Ansiedler settler, colonist.
Ansiedlung settlement, establishment, colony;
überseeische ~**en** overseas settlements;
aufgelockerte ~ **industrieller Fertigungsbetriebe** dispersal of industrial facilities; ~ **von Industriebetrieben** location (localization) of industry.
Ansiedlungs|kommission land-settlement board; ~**politik** industrial location policy.
Ansinnen request, demand;
~ **von sich weisen** to repel a suggestion.
anspannen to harness, to hitch, to yoke, *(Kredit)* to strain, *(Reserven)* to tax, to draw;
alle seine Fähigkeiten ~ to strain every nerve, to go at it hammer and tongs.
Anspannung tightening, pressure, exertion, strain, stretch;
unter aller ~ with every faculty on the stretch;
konjunkturelle ~**en** cyclical strains;
~ **des Arbeitsmarktes** pressure on the labo(u)r market; ~**en am Geldmarkt** strain in the money market, monetary strain; ~ **der Liquidität** tightening of the money market, pressure on liquidity, money squeeze; ~ **des Notenumlaufs** over-issue of currency notes; ~ **der Reserven** draw on the reserves; ~ **der gesamten Wirtschaft** strain on the economy.
an|sparen to save, to put by; ~**spielen** to hint, to allude; **auf etw.** ~**spielen** to get at s. th. *(fam.)*.
Anspielung reference, hint, allusion, insinuation, innuendo;
aktuelle ~**en** topical allusions; **bedeutungsvolle** ~ rich allusion; **beiläufige** ~ side glance;
~**en machen** to make allusions, to insinuate.

Ansporn spur, stimulus, incentive, incitement, whet, prod.
anspornen to inspire, to urge, to stimulate, to incite, to egg on; **jds. Ehrgeiz** ~ to spur s. one's ambition.
anspornend incentive.
Anspornrabatt incentive rebate.
Ansprache address, speech, harangue, talk, message; **am Schluß seiner** ~ at the conclusion of his speech; **aufrührerische** ~ inflammatory speech; **bewegende** ~ moving speech; **feierliche** ~ allocution; **grundlegende** ~ keynote speech; **informelle** ~ causerie; **persönliche** ~ *(Anzeige)* personal approach; **unvorbereitete** ~ extemporaneous speech; **für die Vertretertagung vorbereitete** ~ talk prepared for salesmen; ~ **des Präsidenten** presidential address; ~ **der Zielgruppen** *(Werbung)* cream plan;
~ **des Premierministers [im Rundfunk] anhören** to listen to the Prime Minister; ~ **halten** to make an address (a speech), to deliver an oration (a speech), to harangue, to address a gathering; **kurze** ~ **halten** to deliver a short address; **offizielle** ~ **halten** to make a formal speech; ~ **an eine Versammlung halten** to address a meeting; **seine** ~ **auswendig lernen** to memorize one's lines.
ansprechbar responsive, easily approachable.
Ansprechen | menschlicher Gefühle *(Werbung)* human appeal; ~ **snobistischer Gefühle** *(Werbung)* snob appeal.
ansprechen to talk to, *(Bremse, Schaltgerät)* to respond, *(Prostituierte)* to solicit, to pick up, *(Ware)* to appeal;
j. ~ to reach s. o.; **auf freundliche Behandlung** ~ to react to kind treatment; **als Fälschung** ~ to pronounce to be a forgery; **generell** ~ to have a universal appeal; **j. um Hilfe** ~ to appeal to s. o. for help; **Jugend** ~ to appeal to young people; **auf Schmeicheleien** ~ to be susceptible to flattery; **sofort** ~ to give instant response; **gut auf den Steuerknüppel** ~ to respond well to the controls; **j. auf der Straße** ~ to accost s. o. in the street.
ansprechend appealing, attractive, pleasing, *(Beispiel)* contagious;
eine ~e Art winning ways; **~es Äußeres** attractive appearance; **~e Manieren** winning manners; **~e Werbung** advertising appeal.
Ansprech | funkfeuer responder beacon; **~vermögen** *(Mikrophon)* responsivity; **~wiederholung** callback.
Anspruch claim, *(Anrecht)* interest, right, *(Behauptung)* pretension, pretence, *(Forderung)* demand, call, *(Recht)* title, right; **in** ~ **genommen** bound up, engrossed;
abgetretener ~ assigned claim; **älterer** ~ prior (anterior) claim; **anerkannter** ~ *(Konkurs)* proved claim (debt); **vertraglich anerkannter** ~ liquidated damages; **befristeter** ~ deferred claim; **begründeter** ~ sound (valid, substantiated) claim; **schlecht begründeter** ~ bad claim; **berechtigter** ~ lawful (valid, legitimate, rightful) claim, rightful action; **billigkeitsrechtlicher** ~ equitable interest; **dinglicher** ~ claim ad rem; **einklagbarer** ~ enforceable claim, right to bring action; **nicht einklagbarer** ~ unenforceable claim; **entgegenstehender** ~ adverse claim, *(Patentrecht)* conflicting claim; **erster** ~ first claim; **fälliger** ~ mature debt; **sofort fälliger** ~ immediate right; **festgestellter** ~ liquidated claim, *(gerichtlich)* judgment debt; **fingierter** ~ fictitious claim; **geheimgehaltener** ~ secret (latent) equity; **zu spät geltend gemachter** ~ nonclaim; **gemeinschaftlicher** ~ joint right; **gesetzlicher** ~ lawful claim; **durch den Stand der Technik neuheitsschädlich getroffener** ~ *(Patentrecht)* claim met by the art; **kollidierender** ~ *(Patentrecht)* conflicting claim; **obligatorischer** ~ chose in action; **persönlicher** ~ personal right; **plausibler** ~ specious claim; **rechtmäßiger** ~ equitable claim; **rechtsgültiger** ~ good (just) title, legal claim; **schuldrechtlicher** ~ debt claim; **seerechtlicher** ~ maritime claim; **territorialer** ~ territorial claim; **unbegründeter** ~ bad claim; **unberechtigter** ~ false claim; **noch unentschiedener** ~ dormant claim; **unverjährbarer** ~ indefeasible title; **verdeckter** ~ latent (secret) equity; **verfallener** ~ forfeited claim; **verjährter** ~ stale demand, nonclaim, outlawed claim *(US)*, claim barred by the Statute of Limitations; **vermögensrechtlicher** ~ pecuniary claim, interest in property; **vollgültiger** ~ good claim; **vollstreckbarer** ~ enforceable claim; **vorgehender** ~ prior claim; **vorrangiger** ~ *(Grundbuch)* prior charge; **wahlweiser** ~ alternative claim; **zusammenfassender** ~ omnibus claim *(Br.)*; **zusätzlicher** ~ supplemental claim; **rechtlich zweifelhafter** ~ doubtful claim; ~ **auf Anordnung eines Haftprüfungstermins** privilege of the writ of habeas corpus; ~ **auf Beförderung zu verbilligten Frachtsätzen** transit privilege; ~ **auf bevorrechtigte Befriedigung** *(Konkursrecht)* privileged debt, preferential claim; ~ **auf Erstattung der Kosten für die Anreise der Familienmitglieder und den Gepäcktransport** family passage and baggage entitlement; ~ **in Höhe des Anteils** pro rata benefit; ~ **auf Invalidenrente** disablement claim; ~ **auf eine Pension** pension claim; ~ **auf Schadensersatz** claim for damages; ~ **auf Schadensfreiheitsrabatt** no-claim discount entitlement *(Br.)*; ~ **aus einer Sterbeversicherung** death claim; ~ **auf Unterstützung** right of support; ~ **auf Vertragsbeendigung** right to end the agreement; **gesetzlicher** ~ **auf Wiederanstellung** legal right to reinstatement; ~ **auf betriebliche Zuschüsse zur Arbeitslosenunterstützung** supplementary unemployment insurance credit;
~ **in bar abfinden** to buy up a claim for cash; ~ **abtreten** to assign a claim; ~ **abweisen** to disallow a claim; ~ **anerkennen** to admit (allow, validate, recognize) a claim; **jds.** ~ **anerkennen** to sustain s. o. in a claim; ~ **dem Grunde nach anerkennen** to admit a claim on its merits; ~ **anmelden** to notify a claim, *(Konkurs)* to file a claim, to prove a debt; ~ **aufrechterhalten** to sustain a claim; ~ **befriedigen** to satisfy (answer, settle) a claim; ~ **voll befriedigen** to make satisfaction of a debt; ~ **im Wege des Vergleichs befriedigen** to compromise a claim; **sich eines ~s begeben** to remise a claim; ~ **begründen** to support (constitute) a claim; ~ **näher begründen** to substantiate a claim; **seinen** ~ **behaupten** to hold (keep) one's ground; ~ **bestreiten** to reject (dispute, resist) a claim; ~ **beweisen** to deraign; ~ **bewerten** to assess a claim; ~ **zu Fall bringen** to defeat a claim, to rebut an equity; ~ **durchsetzen** to enforce a claim; ~ **einklagen** to file a claim in court; ~ **auf Schadensersatz erhalten** to be awarded entitlement in damages; ~ **erheben** to lay (vindicate, advance, raise, put forward, prefer, set up) a claim to, to pretend; ~ **als Gläubiger erheben** to rank as creditor; **keinen** ~ **erheben auf** to make no pretences to; ~ **fallenlassen** to abandon a claim; ~ **feststellen** to establish a claim; ~ **geben** to entitle; **eines ~s verlustig gehen** to forfeit a right; ~ **auf etw. haben** to be eligible for s. th.; **ersten** ~ **auf etw. haben** to have the first refusal on s. th.; **obligatorischen** ~ **gegen j. haben** to own a claim against s. o. *(US)*; ~ **auf ein Patent haben** to be entitled to a patent; ~ **auf Unterhalt haben** to be entitled to an allowance, to have a right of support; **Kapitalmarkt in** ~ **nehmen können** to have access (recourse) to the capital market; ~ **geltend machen** to advance (put in, raise, assert, set up) a claim; ~ **in ordentlichen Gerichtsverfahren geltend machen** to raise a claim in ordinary proceedings; ~ **auf Schadensersatz geltend machen** to lodge a claim for compensation, to make a claim for damages; **seinen** ~ **glaubhaft machen** to establish (authenticate) one's claim; ~ **als berechtigt nachweisen** to establish one's claim, *(Konkurs)* to prove a debt; **in** ~ **nehmen** to make use of, *(mil.)* to put in requisition; **etw. für sich in** ~ **nehmen** to claim s. th.; **j. beruflich in** ~ **nehmen** to consult s. o. professionally; **j. für etw. in** ~ **nehmen** to indent on s. o. for s. th.; **jds. Dienste in** ~ **nehmen** to enlist s. one's services; **Dienste eines Anwalts in** ~ **nehmen** to engage the service of a lawyer; **j. finanziell in** ~ **nehmen** to be a strain on s. one's resources; **jds. Freizeit in** ~ **nehmen** to trespass upon s. one's spare time; **jds. Freundschaft in** ~ **nehmen** to make a draft on s. one's friendship; **jds. Geduld in** ~ **nehmen** to tax s. one's patience; **meinen Geldbeutel in** ~ **nehmen** to be a drain on my purse; **j. gerichtlich in** ~ **nehmen** to go to law with s. o.; **Hilfe eines Anwalts in** ~ **nehmen** to retain a lawyer; **Kredit in** ~ **nehmen** to take up (make use of) a credit; **Kredite bei der Bank in erhöhtem Maße in** ~ **nehmen** to increase the borrowings at the bank; **viel Platz in** ~ **nehmen** to occupy much space; **ärztlichen Rat in** ~ **nehmen** to take medical advice; **seine Reserven in** ~ **nehmen** to fall back on one's reserves; **Schutz des Gesetzes in** ~ **nehmen** to take the benefit of an act; **zu sehr in** ~ **nehmen** to overtax; **vollständig in** ~ **nehmen** to preoccupy; **mindestens fünf Jahre Zeit in** ~ **nehmen** to require at least five years; **jds. Zeit in** ~ **nehmen** to trespass upon s. one's time; **viel Zeit in** ~ **nehmen** to take up much time; ~ **regulieren** *(Versicherung)* to adjust a claim; **in** ~ **genommen sein** to be wrapped up; **geschäftlich ununterbrochen in** ~ **genommen sein** to have no vacation from business; ~ **mit unseriösen Mitteln sichern** to maverick a claim *(US)*; **einem** ~ **stattgeben** to allow a claim; **seinem** ~ **Abbruch tun** to prejudice one's claim; ~ **verfolgen** to prosecute a claim; **auf einen** ~ **verzichten** to abandon (quit) a claim, to renounce one's title; **außerordentlich in** ~ **genommen werden** to be taxed to the utmost; ~ **zedieren** to assign a claim.
Ansprüche, althergebrachte vested interests; **berechtigte** ~ legitimate claims; **beteiligungsähnliche** ~ *(Bilanz)* interest in the nature of investments; **gerichtlich einklagbare** ~ legal debts; **kollidierende** ~ *(Patentrecht)* interfering claims; **mäßige** ~ moderate claims; **nachträgliche (spätere)** ~ subsequent claims; **territoriale** ~ territorial pretentions; **widerstreitende** ~ *(Patentrecht)* interfering (contending) claims; **wohlbegründete** ~ wellfounded claims; **zukünftige** ~ future interests;

~ Dritter third-party claims; ~ **aus der Kraftfahrzeugversicherung** motor claims; ~ **während der Lebenszeit eines Dritten** interest pour autre vie; ~ **für festgestellte Schäden** claims for damage observed;
seine ~ **aufgeben** to waive one's right, to remise, release and forever quitclaim; ~ **befriedigen** to satisfy claims; **seine** ~ **durchsetzen** to push one's demands; ~ **aus einer Unfallversicherung erheben** to put in a claim after an accident; ~ **für ungültig erklären** to divest of rights; **allen ~n genügen** *(Hotel)* to satisfy all possible requirements; **höchsten ~n genügen** to have reached a high degree of excellence; **überhaupt keine ~ gegen j. haben** to have no claim whatsoever against s. o.; **sich über jds. ~ hinwegsetzen** to override s. one's claims; **seine ~ gerichtlich geltend machen** to enforce one's claims; **seine ~ mäßigen** to moderate one's claims; ~ **regulieren** to adjust claims; **bescheidene ~ stellen** to be modest in one's requirements; **keine besonderen ~ stellen** not to ask for favo(u)rs, to be easy to please; **nur geringe ~ stellen** to be a man of low wants; **große ~ stellen** to be difficult to please; **weniger hohe ~ stellen** to take in sail; **literarische ~ stellen** to have pretensions to literary taste; **hohe ~ an j. stellen** to make great demands on s. o.; ~ **an jds. Geduld stellen** to tax s. one's patience; **hohe ~ an die Geschäftsmoral stellen** to set a high standard of business morality; **auf alle ~ verzichten** to remise, release and forever quitclaim; **seine ~ vorbringen** to put up (advance) one's claims; **den ~n gerecht werden** to meet the demands; **unbegründete ~ nicht zulassen** to exclude unfounded claims; **seine ~ zurückstecken** to cut one's comb *(coll.)*.

Anspruchs | abtretung assignment of an interest; **~befriedigung** satisfaction of a claim; **~begründung** proof of debt (claim); **mehrfache ~begründung** double pleading.

anspruchsberechtigt sein to become eligible to, to have [the legal right to file] a claim.

Anspruchs | berechtigter person entitled, party entitled to a claim, rightful claimant, *(auf den Rest)* residual claimant; **~berechtigung nachweisen** to file a proof for a claim, to prove a debt; **~bewertung** claims assessment; **~entstehung** arisal of a claim; **bei der ~entstehung** at the time the claim arose; **~erhebung** presentation (arisal) of claim; **~formular** form of a claim, claim form, claim blank *(US)*; **~gläubiger** *(Erbschaft)* person of inheritance; **~gruppe** class of claims; **~häufung** double pleading; **~kürzung** reduction of claims.

anspruchslos unpretending, humble, modest;
~e Kost plain fare; **~er Mensch** lowbrow.

Anspruchs | nachweis proof of claim; **~nehmer** claimant; **~niveau** level of aspiration; **~regulierung** *(Versicherung)* claim payment, claim settlement; **~schuldner** person of incidence, claim debtor; **~steller** claimant; **~unterlagen** claim papers; **~verjährung** extinction (barring, limitation) of a claim; **der ~verwirkung nicht unterworfen** *(Lebensversicherung)* nonforfeiting; **~verwirkung herbeiführen** to work for a forfeiture; **~verzicht** abandonment (waiver) of a claim, quitclaim.

anspruchsvoll pretentious, fastidious, difficult to please;
~e Leser critical readers; **~e Unterhaltung** high-brow conversation; **~es Wesen** pretentious ways.

Anspruchs | voraussetzung prerequisite for a claim; **~vorrang** *(Eigentumsrecht)* overreaching of interests; **~zurückweisung** disallowance of claim.

anstacheln to stimulate, to spur, to prod;
zu weiteren Anstrengungen ~ to stimulate to further efforts; **zum Aufruhr** ~ to prompt to riot.

Anstalt institute, [public] institution, home, establishment, corporation, *(Irrenanstalt)* mental hospital (institution) *(US)*, asylum, *(Stiftung)* foundation, endowment, endowed institution, *(Vorbereitung)* provision;
gemeinnützige ~ public utility establishment (undertaking); **geschlossene** ~ detention hospital; **lithographische** ~ lithographic printing office; **öffentliche (öffentlich-rechtliche)** ~ public institution, body corporate; **schulgeldfreie** ~ charitable educational institution (school); **typographische** ~ printing house (establishment, shop, *US*);
~en treffen to make provisions (preparations); **die notwendigen ~en treffen** to make all necessary arrangements; **in eine ~ verbringen** to confine to an asylum, to commit to a mental institution *(US)*.

Anstalts | abteilung ward; **~arzt** resident physician; **~ärzte** house staff; **~behandlung** institutional treatment; **~chirurg** house surgeon; **~fürsorge, ~pflege** institutional care; **~gebäude** institute, institution; **~leiter** *(Schule)* headmaster *(Br.)*, principal *(US)*; **~patient** inpatient; **~unterbringung, ~verbringung** confinement in an asylum, commitment to a mental institution *(US)*.

Anstand form, decency, propriety;
natürlicher ~ common decency;
an jds. ~ appellieren to appeal to s. one's finer feelings; **allen ~ fahrenlassen** to throw propriety to the wind; **keinen ~ haben** to have no manners; **j. ~ lehren** to teach s. o. manners; **mit ~ verlieren** to be a good loser; ~ **wahren** to keep within the bounds of propriety, to observe the decencies, to preserve decency; **den ~ wahren** to keep one's foot.

anständig fair, decent, proper, tidy, seemly, correct, white *(US coll.)*;
sich ~ aufführen to play fair; **j. ~ behandeln** to treat s. o. decently; **sich ~ benehmen** to behave decently; **sich als sehr ~ erweisen** to come down handsomely; **als ~ gelten** to have a name for honesty; **j. für ~ halten** to take s. o. for an honest man;
~es Benehmen mannerliness, decent (proper) behavio(u)r; **~es Gehalt** respectable salary; **~er Kerl** decent type *(Br.)*, nice chap *(Br.)*, square shooter *(US coll.)*; **~e Kleidung** decent clothes; **~e Leute** decent people; **~e Preise** reasonable prices; **jem. eine ~e Tracht Prügel verabreichen** to give s. o. a good thrashing; **~es Vermögen** sizable property.

Anständigkeit propriety, decency, seemliness;
sich für jds. ~ verbürgen to certify s. one's character.

Anstands | besuch formal call; **jem. einen ~besuch machen** to pay one's respects to s. o.; **~brief** grace note; **~dame** chaperon, duenna; **~dame spielen** to play the chaperon (gooseberry); **~formen** convenance, proprieties; **~gefühl** tact; **~gefühle verletzen** to outrage all decency; **j. dazu bringen, aus ~gründen zurückzutreten** to persuade s. o. of the propriety of resigning.

anstandshalber for decency's sake;
~ **tun müssen** to be bound in hono(u)r (in courtesy bound) to do s. th.

anstandslos unhesitatingly, without hesitation;
Grenze ~ überschreiten to cross the frontier freely; ~ **zahlen** to pay up readily; **Ware ~ zurücknehmen** to take back articles without objection.

Anstands | pflicht moral obligation; **~regeln** respectabilities of life, ethical standards, convention, custom, decorum; **allgemeine ~regeln** rules of courteous conduct; **gegen die ~regeln verstoßen** to offend against the proprieties; **~regeln wahren** to observe the proprieties; **~vermächtnis** legacy of shame; **~verstoß** offence against decency; **~wauwau** *(fam.)* chaperon, dragon, gooseberry; **~wauwau spielen** to play propriety (the chaperon, gooseberry).

anstandswidrig improper, indecent, improper.

anstechen, Faß to tap a barrel.

anstecken to infect, to taint;
sich eine Zigarette ~ to light a cigarette.

ansteckend contagious, infectious, catching;
~e Krankheit contagion, infectious disease.

Anstecknadel pin, badge.

Ansteckungs | gefahr risk of infection; **~verdächtiger** contact.

anstehen to queue *(Br.)* (line, *US*) up, to stand in line *(US)*, *(angesetzt sein)* to be pending (up), *(sich verzögern)* to stand over, to be delayed, *(sich ziemen)* to befit;
schon lange zur Beschlußfassung ~ to have been delayed for a long time; **zur Debatte** ~ to be down for debate; **zur Entscheidung** ~ to be up for a decision; **morgen** ~ *(Termin)* to be fixed for tomorrow; **zur Pensionierung** ~ to qualify for a pension; **zur mündlichen Verhandlung** ~ to be up for trial;
~ **lassen** to postpone, to put off; **Schuld ~ lassen** to defer (hold over) payment.

anstehend issuable, pending, under consideration;
~es Erz outcrop; **~e Fragen** matters to be dealt with; **~e Sache** business at issue; **~er Termin** day assigned for a hearing.

Anstehende, für Brot bread queue *(Br.)* (line, *US*).

Ansteigen rise, increase, advance, improvement, jump;
~ **der Kurse** recovery of prices; **raketenartiges ~ der Kurse** skyrocketing of prices *(US)*; **stetiges ~ der Kurse** steady increase of prices; **explosionsartiges ~ der Mietpreise** rental explosion; ~ **der Preise** rising of prices, price increase (climb, recovery, hike, *US*);
im ~ begriffen sein to be on the rise.

ansteigen *(Kurse, Preise)* to rise, to increase, to advance, to climb, to improve, to head (swing) up, to swell, to recover, *(Straße)* to ascend, to tower, *(Temperatur)* to go up, to rise;
~ **bis** to mount to; **hausseartig** ~ to rise sharply; **raketenhaft** ~ to zoom upward; **sprunghaft** ~ to jump, to hop upwards, to rise by leaps and bounds; **steil** ~ to rocket, to skyrocket *(US)*; **übermäßig** ~ *(Kurse)* to go through the roof; **wieder** ~ to be back on the rise;
schnell ~ lassen to zoom.

ansteigend on the upward plane;
sanft ~es Gelände gently rising ground; **~e Preise** increasing prices.

anstellen to engage, to enlist, to enrol(l), to employ, to recruit *(US)*, to hire *(US)*, *(ernennen)* to appoint, to place, *(Rundfunk)* to turn (switch) on;
~ **und entlassen** to hire and fire *(sl.)*;
etw. ~ to get into mischief; **sich** ~ to queue *(Br.)* (line, *US*) up, to stand in line *(US)*, *(fig.)* to put it on, to make bones about; **hundert Arbeiter** ~ to sign on a hundred workmen; **Berechnungen** ~ to make a calculation; **Betrachtungen** ~ to take into consideration; **Butler** ~ to put in a butler; **sich für Fahrkarten** ~ to queue *(Br.)* (line, *US*) up to buy tickets; **j. fest** ~ to put s. o. on the establishment; **sich geschickt** ~ to get about cleverly; **j. monatlich** ~ to employ s. o. on a month-to-month basis; **j. neu** ~ to take a new employee; **nach einer Probezeit fest** ~ to appoint s. o. during good behavio(u)r; **j. als Sekretärin** ~ to engage s. o. as secretary; **Untersuchungen** ~ to make inquiries; **Untersuchung an Ort und Stelle** ~ to make investigations on the spot; **Vergleich** ~ to draw a comparison; **Versuche** ~ to carry out experiments, to experiment; **weitere Versuche mit einer Maschine** ~ to put a machine to further trials; **Vertreter** ~ to appoint an agent; **vorübergehend** ~ to employ temporarily; **wieder** ~ to reappoint, to reengage, to rehire *(US)*;
sich ~ **lassen** to sign on.

anstellig handy, clever;
sehr ~ **sein** to turn one's hand to anything.

Anstellung employment, situation, job, post, position, place, *(Einstellung)* engagement, enlistment, enrol(l)ment, recruitment *(US)*, hiring *(US)*, *(Ernennung)* appointment, placement; **feste** ~ permanent (definite) appointment (assignment), regular employment (post); **lebenslängliche** ~ life tenure; **sichere** ~ fixed appointment; **staatliche** ~ public appointment, government employment;
~ **von Arbeitskräften** recruitment of labo(u)r *(US)*; ~ **und Entlassung** hiring and firing *(sl.)*; ~ **und Gewinnbeteiligung** *(Walfischfang)* lay; ~ **auf Lebenszeit** appointment for life;
sich um eine staatliche ~ **bewerben** to solicit a government post; **dreijährige feste** ~ **erhalten** to be engaged for a term of three years; ~ **ins Auge fassen** to consider an appointment; **feste** ~ **haben** to be on the establishment (regular staff); **keine feste** ~ **haben** to have no regular work.

Anstellungs|bedingungen conditions of employment; **~befähigung** eligibility for appointment; **~behörde** appointing authority.

anstellungsberechtigt qualified (eligible) for a post (appointment).

Anstellungs|bestimmungen hiring regulations *(US)*; **~büro** employment agency, recruiting office *(US)*; **~eignung** eligibility for appointment; **~methoden** recruitment practices *(US)*; **~prüfung** [qualifying] test, competitive examination; **~schreiben** letter of appointment (engagement); **~verhältnis kündigen** to cancel an employment contract; **~vertrag** articles of employment, employment contract; **~vertrag abschicken** to make the appointment in writing; **~voraussetzungen** eligibility for appointment; **~zeitraum** employment period, period of engagement; **~zuschuß** appointment grant.

ansteuern to head (make) for, to access.

Ansteuerungsfeuer homing beacon, *(Hafen)* entrance light.

Anstich *(Brauerei)* tap.

Anstieg uprise, *(Kurve)* ascent, *(Preise, Kurse)* rise, rising, increase, advance, improvement, buildup, growth, recovery, hike *(US)*;
inflationsbedingter ~ *(Steuern)* buoyancy; **plötzlicher** ~ jump; **prozentualer** ~ increment per cent; **raketenartiger** ~ skyrocketing *(US)*; **saisonbedingter** ~ seasonal upswing (upturn); **schneller** ~ spurt; **steiler** ~ *(Börse)* upsurge; **überraschender** ~ surprise jump;
~ **der Aktienkurse** stock-market rise, upward movement of stocks, run-up of prices; ~ **der Bauarbeiterlöhne** construction-wage increase; ~ **der Kriminalität** jump in crime; ~ **der Lebenshaltungskosten** cost-of-living rise; **explosionsartiger** ~ **der Mieten** rental explosion; ~ **der Reallöhne** real wage growth; ~ **der Zinssätze** hike in interest rates *(US)*;
sich in einem ~ **des Umlaufvermögens niederschlagen** to find its way into an increase of current assets.

anstiften to instigate, to incite, to induce, *(Verbrecher)* to abet, to encourage;
Aufruhr ~ to work up a rebellion, to urge a revolt; **j. zum Meineid** ~ to suborn s. o.; **zur Patentverletzung** ~ to induce infringement of a patent; **zu einem Streik** ~ to instigate a strike.

Anstifter instigator, inciter, plotter, *(Strafrecht)* accessory before the fact;
~ **zum Meineid** suborner of perjury; ~ **eines Verbrechens** instigator of a crime.

Anstiftung instigation, incitement, solicitation *(US)*, *(Verbrecher)* abetment, encouragement;
~ **zum Meineid** subornation; ~ **zur Patentverletzung** inducement of infringement of a patent; ~ **zur Unzucht** solicitation of chastity; ~ **zum Vertragsbruch** inducing breach of contract.

Anstoß impulse, impulsion, impact, impetus, shove, initiative, *(Ärgernis)* offence, offense *(US)*, arrogance, *(neuer)* push;
auf ~ **von** on the initiative of;
~ **erregen** to give offence, to raise a scandal, to knock *(US sl.)*; ~ **geben** to initiate, to originate, to give an impulse (occasion) to; **ersten** ~ **geben** to make the first move; ~ **nehmen** to take amiss, to take umbrage, to be scandalized, to take exception to (offence at); **an allem** ~ **nehmen** to stumble at a straw;
~effekt impact effect.

anstoßen to push, *(ermuntern)* to encourage, *(angrenzen)* to border, to abut, to neighbo(u)r;
auf die Braut ~ to drink to the bride; **auf jds. Gesundheit** ~ to propose s. one's health.

anstoßend contiguous, adjacent, adjoining, abutting.

anstoßerregendes Gewerbe offensive trade.

anstößig offensive, scandalous, indecent, improper, vile;
nicht ~ unoffending;
~es Benehmen shocking (offensive) behavio(u)r; **~e Praktiken** vile practices; **~e Reden führen** to use indecent language; **~e Stellen ausmerzen** to bowdlerize; **~e Werbung** indecent advertising.

anstrahlen to floodlight, to spotlight;
Springbrunnen bunt ~ to play colo(u)red lights on a fountain.

Anstrahler floodlight projector.

Anstrahlung floodlighting, spotlighting.

anstreben to aspire, to follow, to strive for, to be after;
Einfluß ~ to be eager to get influence.

anstreichen to paint, to coat, *(kenntlich machen)* to mark, to check up;
dünn ~ to wash; **rot** ~ to rubricate; **Tag rot im Kalender** ~ to make it a red-letter day.

Anstreicher painter, whitewasher.

anstrengen, sich to endeavo(u)r, to exert o. s., to labo(u)r, to be at pains, to make an effort; **die Augen** ~ to be trying on the eyes; **sich energisch** ~ to make a push; **sich gehörig** ~ to make good play; **sich geistig** ~ to yoke one's mind; **sich gewaltig** ~ to make a long arm; **Klage (Prozeß) gegen j.** ~ to institute legal proceedings (bring an action) against s. o.; **alle Kräfte** ~ to leave no stone unturned, to strain every nerve.

anstrengend exacting, strenuous, laborious, killing, weariful;
~e Arbeit trying (collar) work; **~es Korrekturenlesen** trying proofreading; **~e Reise** wearing journey; **~er Tag** wearing day.

Anstrengung endeavo(u)r, exertion, effort, strain, stretch, push, trouble;
durch ~ **eines Prozesses** by going to law; **mit äußerster** ~ by supreme effort; **ohne** ~ easily;
enorme **~en** all-out efforts; **geringe** **~en** simple efforts; **geschäftliche** **~en** business tensions; **große** **~en** tug, arduous efforts; **größte** ~ heat *(US sl.)*; **körperliche** ~ labo(u)r exertion; **massierte** **~en** mass efforts; **übermäßige** **~en** superhuman efforts; **mit einer Reise verbundene** ~ fatigues incidental to a journey; **vereinigte** ~ joint effort; **vergebliche** ~ dead lift; **wilde** **~en** frantic efforts;
~ **zur Absatzsteigerung** sales promotional efforts (practices) *(US)*; **~en zur Ausweitung des Produktionsprogramms** diversification move; **kurzfristig unternommene** **~en zur Sicherung von Arbeitsplätzen** short-term job-saving exercise; **~en des Stadtlebens** pressure of city life; **erhöhte** **~en zur Verbesserung der Führungsmethoden** upgrading of management efforts;
erneute **~en machen** to renew one's efforts; **gemeinsame** **~en machen** to combine one's efforts; **alle nur möglichen** **~en machen (unternehmen)** to go all out for s. th., to strain every nerve, to leave no stone unturned; **in seinen** **~en nachlassen** to relax (slacken) in one's efforts; **den geschäftlichen** **~en nicht mehr gewachsen sein** to be no longer equal to the strain of business; ~ **unternehmen** to make an effort; **letzte** ~ **unternehmen** to make a final effort; **seine** **~en verdoppeln** to redouble one's exertions (efforts), to mend one's efforts.

Anstrich paintwork, tincture, wash, *(fig.)* smack, colo(u)r, tinge, savo(u)r;
~ **von Bildung** veneer of culture; ~ **von Ehrbarkeit** gloss of respectability;

~ **haben** to relish, to smack of; **einer Sache einen neuen ~ verleihen** to put a fresh complexion on s. th.
anstückeln to patch on.
Ansturm run, rush, onslaught, stampede, charge, onset, attack;
~ **auf eine Bank** run on a bank; ~ **am Eingang** crush at the gate; ~ **auf Erdölaktien** run on oil stocks; ~ **auf das Erfrischungszelt** rush to the refreshment tent; ~ **der Gläubiger** run of creditors;
~ **auf einen Laden** wild rush on a shop;
~ **auf eine Bank machen** to make a run on a bank.
Ansuchen request, application, petition, instance;
auf ~ on request; **auf ~ von sieben Mitgliedern** on application of seven members.
ansuchen, um Geldmittel to solicit for funds.
Antagonismus antagonism.
antasten *(Sparkonto)* to touch;
jds. Rechte ~ to encroach upon s. one's rights; **Vorräte** ~ to break into provisions.
Anteil stake, [proportional] share, part, portion, percentage, proportion, slice, participation, *(Aktie)* share certificate, share of stock *(US)*, *(Beteiligung)* interest, share, concern, stock, holding, quotum, *(Beute)* cut *(US sl.)*, *(Erbschaft)* portion, *(Genußschein)* participating share, *(Quote)* quota, contingent, contribution pro rata, *(Zuteilung)* allotment, lot;
nach ~en proportionally, according to quotas;
bestimmter ~ stated proportion; **beträchtlicher** ~ good share; **börsengängige ~e** shares marketable on a stock exchange; **gemeinschaftliche ~e** joint shares; **gerechter** ~ fair share; **gewinnberechtigter** ~ participating share; **gleiche ~e** even shares, aliquot parts; **halber** ~ half share; **rechtmäßiger** ~ lawful share; **stimmberechtigte ~e** voting shares; **treuhänderischer** ~ fiduciary interest; **verfügbarer** ~ available portion; **verhältnismäßiger** ~ pro rata share, quota; **durch Verlosung zugeteilter** ~ allotment, lot;
~ **am Aktienkapital** share of stock *(US)*; ~ **weiblicher Arbeitskräfte** female participation rate; ~ **am Ertrag** portion of proceeds; **~e und Geldbeträge von Tochtergesellschaften** *(Bilanz)* shares and amounts owing from subsidiary companies *(Br.)*; **festverzinslicher ~ am Gesamtkapital** gearing, leverage; ~ **am Geschäftsgewinn** percentage on profits; ~ **am Gesellschaftsvermögen** share (capital interest) in a partnership; ~ **am Gewinn** share of the profit, profit share; ~ **am Konsortium** underwriting share; **hoher ~ von Obligationen und Vorzugsaktien am Gesellschaftskapital** high leverage factor *(US)*; **im nächsten Jahr rückzahlbarer ~ langfristiger Schulden** current portion of long-term debts;
~ **größerer Abteilungen am Umsatz und Ertrag aufschlüsseln** to break down the contribution of major divisions to sales and pretax earnings; **jem. seinen ~ auszahlen** to pay s. o. out, to disburse s. one's full and entire part; **seinen [vollen] ~ beanspruchen** to claim one's proportionate share; **seinen ~ beitragen** to contribute one's share; **seinen verhältnismäßigen ~ beitragen** to contribute pro rata; **seinen vollen ~ an etw. bekommen** to come in for a full share of s. th.; **seinen ~ bezahlen** to pay one's due, to contribute one's quota; **seinen ~ an der Rechnung bezahlen** to pay one's shot; **um seinen ~ bringen** to kiss out *(US sl.)*; **auf jds. ~ entfallen** to fall to s. one's lot; **gleichen ~ haben** to go equal shares; **~e an einem Geschäft haben** to have an interest in a business; ~ **am Gewinn haben** to participate (share) in the profit; **keinerlei ~ an einer Sache haben** to have no part or lot in s. th.; **großen ~ an einem Unternehmen haben** to take an active part in an undertaking; ~ **nehmen** to sympathize sincerely; **~e nehmen** to take stock in; **an einem Gebrechlichen ~ nehmen** to show concern for an invalid; **regen ~ an der politischen Entwicklung nehmen** to take an active interest in the political events; **zu gleichen ~en berechtigt sein** to be entitled to equal shares; **~e übernehmen** to take over shares; **auf seinen ~ verzichten** to waive (renounce, abandon) a claim; **aufrichtigen ~ an jds. Problemen zeigen** to show sincere concern for s. one's problems.
anteilig proportionate, proportional, in proportion to, pro rata.
Anteilnahme care, interest, *(aufrichtige)* sincere sympathy;
mit ~ solicitously;
jem. seine ~ aussprechen to express one's sympathy with s. o.; **allgemeine ~ zum Siedepunkt bringen** to excite interests to the highest pitch; **aufrichtige ~ an jds. Geschick nehmen** to feel a kindly interest towards s. o.
Anteil|nehmer beneficiary; **~satz** *(Steueraufkommen)* proportion.
Anteilsaufstellung rate schedule.
anteilsberechtigt participating;
~ **sein** *(Erbe)* to be coparcener.
Anteils|berechtigter portioner, beneficiary; **~bewertung** *(Investmentfonds)* unit evaluation; **~bezeugung** token of concern.
Anteilschein share [certificate], participation, certificate *(US)*, participating receipt, *(Aktie)* share (scrip, *US*) certificate, scrip, share of stock *(US)*, *(Zinsschein)* coupon;
~ **mit Ausschüttung von Erträgen** income unit *(Br.)*; ~ **einer Kapitalanlagegesellschaft** investment [trust] certificate, unit *(Br.)*, unit certificate *(Br.)*, unit trust unit *(Br.)*, collateral trustee share *(US)*; ~ **ohne Nennwert** nonpar value share (stock, *US*); ~ **mit Wiederanlage der Erträge** accumulation unit *(Br.)*; **~besitzer** shareholder *(Br.)*, stockholder *(US)*, *(Kapitalanlagegesellschaft)* unitholder *(Br.)*, certificate holder *(US)*.
Anteilseigner shareholder *(Br.)*, shareholding member, stockholder *(US)*, *(Kapitalanlagegesellschaft)* shareholder *(US)*, certificate holder *(US)*, unitholder *(Br.)*;
~seite representation of ownership.
Anteils|empfänger portionist; **~gebühr** percentage, proportionate charge; **~kapital** equity stock.
anteilsmäßig rat(e)able, pro rata, on a prorata basis, proportionate, proportional, proratable *(US)*;
Gewinn ~ aufteilen to distribute the profits proportionally, to prorate profits *(US)*; ~ **verteilen** to proportion, to prorate;
~e Veranlagung proportional assessment.
Anteils|pacht percentage lease; **~papiere** equity; **~prämie** percentage premium; **~recht** interest, share; **~rechte an einer Gesellschaft** corporate shares (stocks, *US*); **~register** *(Investmentfonds)* stock register *(US)*; **~übereignung**, **~übertragung** assignment of interests; **~zeichner** subscriber, applicant; **~zeichnung** subscription.
antelefonieren *(fam.)* to call (ring) up.
Antenne aerial, antenna, sky wire *(sl.)*;
automatisch ausfahrbare ~ electrically operated aerial; **geerdete** ~ grounded antenna; **gerichtete** ~ directional antenna; **herausfahrbare** ~ telescopic aerial; **schwundmindernde** ~ fading-reducing antenna;
keine ~ für etw. haben to have no feelings for it.
Antennen|ableitung antenna down-lead, lead-in; **~abstimmung** aerial tuning; **~buchse** antenna jack, aerial socket; **~draht** aerial wire; **~einführung** lead-in; **~mast** [radio] mast; **~zuführung** down lead.
Anthologie omnibus.
Anthrazit hard (anthracite, glance, blind) coal.
Anti|alkoholiker total abstainer, water drinker; **~biotikum** antibiotic.
anti|bürokratisch anti-red tape; **~chambrieren** to dance attendance.
Anti|dumpingzoll antidumping duty; **~faschismus** antifascism; **konstante ~haltung** bloodymindedness.
anti|inflationär counterinflationary; **~inflationistische Vollmachten** antiinflationary powers.
Anti|inflationspolitik counterinflation policy; **~inflationsprogramm** antiinflation plan; **~kapitalismus** anticapitalism.
antikapitalistisch anticapitalistic.
Anti|kolonialismus anticolonialism; **~kommunismus** anticommunism; **~kommunist** anticommunist.
antikommunistisch anticommunistic.
Anti|militarismus antimilitarism; **~pathie** antipathy, repugnance.
Antippen, kurzes touch and go.
antippen, Thema kurz to touch a subject.
Antiqua *(Druckschrift)* Roman type (letter);
fette (schmale) ~ bold (narrow) roman; **moderne** ~ modern;
~buchstaben Roman letters.
Antiquar antiquarian (secondhand) bookseller, dealer in secondhand books.
Antiquariat antiquarian (secondhand) bookshop;
bibliophiles ~ bibliophile antiquarian bookselling; **wissenschaftliches** ~ scientific antiquarian bookselling.
antiquarisch antiquarian, secondhand.
Antiquaschrift Roman type (letters), *(breit)* expanded type.
antiquiert antiquated, obsolete, out-of-date, mouldy.
Antiquitäten antiques, [old] curiosities, curios;
~ **sammeln** to collect curios;
~bummel machen to go curio hunting; **~geschäft** antique (curio) shop; **~handel** antique trade; **~händler** antique (curio) dealer, dealer in antiques; **~laden** antiquarian's shop, antique (curiosity) shop; **etw. in einem ~laden auftreiben** to come across s. th. in a curio shop; **~läden abgrasen** to hunt curios; **~markt** antique market; **~sammler** antiquarian, curio hunter, antique collector, collector of antiques; **~sammlung** antiquarian collection.

Anti|raketen-Rakete anti-ballistic missile; **~selektion** *(Statistik)* adverse selection; **~streikbewegung** back-to-work movement; **~streikgesetzgebung** antistrike legislation; **~these** antithesis.

antizipando in anticipation (advance).

Antizipandozinsen anticipated (anticipatory) interest.

antizipativ *(Rente)* anticipative;
~e Aktiva accrued assets (receivables, *US*); **~e Passiva** accrued payables *(US)*; **~er Posten** accrued item.

antizipieren to anticipate.

antizyklisch countercyclical, contracyclical, anticyclical;
sich wie üblich ~ verhalten to play its usual countercyclical role; **~e Finanzpolitik** compensatory finance; **~e Konjunkturpolitik** countercyclical compensatory government (fiscal) policy; **~e Methode** anticyclical approach; **~e Werbung** anticyclical advertising.

Antrag offer, *(Börse)* marrying *(Br.)*, *(Gesuch)* application, petition, request, *(Offerte)* tender, *(parl.)* motion, move, *(Vorschlag)* proposal, proposition;
auf ~ ex parte, on application, at the instance of; **auf ~ des Schuldners** upon the application of the debtor; **durch ~ beim Gericht** by application to the court; **zur Begründung des ~s** in support of a motion;
als rechtlich unbegründet abgewiesener ~ motion denied on law *(US)*; **vorrangig zu behandelnder ~** motion having priority; **heute eingebrachter ~** motion down for today; **im Parlament eingebrachter ~** parliamentary motion; **einseitiger ~** undefended petition; **ohne mündliche Verhandlung entschiedener ~** motion of course; **erneuerter ~** reapplication; **formeller ~** formal application; **ordnungsgemäßer ~** legal demand; **schriftlicher ~** mailed *(US)* (written) application, application in writing; **ursprünglicher ~** original motion; **zurückgezogener ~** abandoned (dropped) motion;
~ zur Abänderung eines ~s motion to amend a motion; **~ auf schriftliche Abstimmung nach Kapitalanteilen** demand for a poll; **~ auf Aufhebung des Konkursverfahrens** petition for discharge *(US)*; **~ auf Behandlung des nächsten Tagesordnungspunktes** next business motion; **~ in der Berufungsinstanz** motion on appeal; **~ auf Bestellung eines Konkursverwalters** application for receiver; **~ auf Beugehaft** judgment summons *(Br.)*; **~ auf Ehescheidung** petition of divorce; **~ auf offizielle Einführung von Aktien an der Börse** application for official quotation *(Br.)* (listing, *US*) on the stock exchange; **~ auf Einsichtnahme** requisition for a search; **~ auf Einstellung des Untersuchungsverfahrens** arrest of inquest; **~ auf Einstellung des Verfahrens** motion for adjournment, motion to arrest a judgment; **~ auf Entmündigung** petition in lunacy; **~ auf Entscheidung** motion for decree; **~ auf Erteilung einer Gewerbelizenz (auf Geschäftseröffnung)** business application; **~ bei Gericht** application to the court; **~ zur Geschäftsordnung** procedural motion; **~ auf ein Hypothekendarlehen** mortgage loan application; **~ auf Klageabweisung** motion to dismiss; **~ auf Konkurseröffnung** petition in bankruptcy, bankruptcy petition; **~ auf Liquidation der Gesellschaft** winding-up petition; **~ auf Offenlegung und Urkundenvorlage** bill of discovery; **~ auf Prozeßverbindung** bill of peace; **~ zur Sache** substantive motion; **~ auf Sachentscheidung** tender of issue; **~ auf Schadenersatz** claim for damages; **~ auf Übergang zur Tagesordnung** previous-question motion; **~ auf Verfahrenseinstellung** application to stay proceedings; **~ auf erneute Verhandlung** motion for reargument *(US)*; **~ auf mündliche Verhandlung** moving for an argument; **~ über den nur in mündlicher Verhandlung entschieden werden kann** special motion; **~ auf Vertagung** motion to adjourn; **~ auf Vorlage eines Vergleichs durch das Gericht** amicable action; **~ auf Wiederaufnahme des Verfahrens** motion to set aside judgment, bill for a new trial; **~ auf Zuteilung von Wertpapieren** application for allotment, letter of application *(Br.)*;
~ ablehnen to defeat, (reject, dismiss, deny, vote down, throw out, overrule) a motion, *(Gericht)* to refuse a petition; **über einen ~ abstimmen** to put a motion to the vote; **~ abweisen** to deny a motion; **~ annehmen** to accept an offer, *(parl.)* to carry (adopt) a motion; **~ ohne Debatte annehmen** to accept a motion undebated; **~ mit großer Mehrheit annehmen** to adopt a motion by a large majority; **~ aufsetzen** to draft an application; **sich gegen einen ~ aussprechen** to oppose a motion; **~ bearbeiten** to proceed with an application; **~ bewilligen** to grant an application; **~ zur Abstimmung bringen** to put a motion to the vote; **~ zur Annahme bringen (durchbringen)** to carry a motion; **~ einbringen** to propose (forward, bring forward, table, *Br.*) a motion, to move a vote (resolution); **~ schriftlich einbringen** to submit a motion in writing; **~ einreichen** to file a petition; **~ entgegennehmen** to secure an application; **über einen ~ entscheiden** to act on an application; **einem ~ entsprechen** to act favo(u)rably on a petition; **nach ~ erkennen** to find for the plaintiff; **~ für zulässig erklären** to declare a demand admissible; **~ erledigen** to dispose of a motion; **~ fallenlassen** to table a motion *(US)*; **~ auf die Tagesordnung setzen** to put a resolution on the record; **einem ~ stattgeben** to grant a petition, to grant a motion; **~ stellen** to file a motion, to make (put, present) an application, to move, to propose **~ auf Ablehnung einer Vorlage stellen** to move the rejection of a bill; **~ auf Behandlung der Tagesordnung stellen** to move the previous question; **~ auf gerichtliche Bestätigung eines Testaments stellen** to propound a will; **~ zur Debatte stellen** to take a motion from the table; **~ auf Eintragung eines Grundpfandrechts stellen** to make application for the registration of a charge; **~ auf Eröffnung des Vergleichs- und Sanierungsverfahrens stellen** to file a petition (apply for permission) for reorganization under Chapter 10 *(US)* (to reorganize under the Bankruptcy Act); **~ bei Gericht stellen** to petition the court; **~ auf Geschäftsaufsicht stellen** to make application for receivership, to petition for the appointment of a receiver *(US)*; **~ auf Gewährung des Armenrechts stellen** to petition for leave to sue in forma pauperis; **~ auf Konkurseröffnung (Erlaß eines Konkurseröffnungsbeschlusses) stellen** to file a petition [for a receiving order] in bankruptcy, to petition the court to make a receiving order, to strike a docket, *(gegen j.)* to initiate bankruptcy proceedings against s. o.; **~ auf Schluß der Debatte und Abstimmung stellen** to move that the question be now put (closure of the debate, *US*); **~ auf Vertagung stellen** to put a motion for adjournment; **~ auf Zurückstellung der Sacherörterung stellen** to move that the meeting postpone consideration of subject; **~ überstimmen** to defeat (deny) a motion; **~ unterstützen** to support (speak for, second, back) a motion; **auf ~ einer Partei verhandeln** to proceed ex parte; **über einen ~ verhandeln** to hear a motion; **~ erneut vorlegen** to resubmit an application; **~ auf unbestimmte Zeit zurückstellen** to shelve a motion; **~ zurückweisen** *(Gericht)* to dismiss a petition; **~ zurückziehen** to drop (withdraw, abandon) a motion;
der ~ ist angenommen the ayes have it.

Anträge, nicht bearbeitete application backlogs; **eingegangene ~** proposals received.

antragen, auf etw. to apply for s. th.; **jem. eine Stellung ~** to offer s. o. a job.

Antrags|ablehnung defeat (rejection) of a motion; **~annahme** carriage (acceptance) of a motion; **~bearbeiter** referee; **~befürwortung** seconding a motion; **~begründung** grounds for an application; **schriftliche ~begründung** case for motion; **~datum** date of filing, filing date; **~erledigung** disposal of a motion; **~form** form of motion.

Antragsformular application (entry, claim, inquiry, proposal) form, *(für Aktien)* letter (form) of application, application blank;
~ zur Eröffnung eines Kundenkreditkontos charge account application form;
~ ausfüllen to fill in an application form.

Antrags|frist time of application, *(Patentrecht)* filing term; **~gebühr** application fee, *(Patentrecht)* filing fee; **~gegner** respondent, opposing party, opponent, noncontent; **~gegner sein** to resist a motion.

antragsgemäß erkennen (entscheiden) to find for the plaintiff.

Antrags|genehmigung consent to a request; **~kopie** copy of petition (application); **~recht** initiative *(US)*; **~rücknahme** withdrawal of a motion; **~stadium** application stage.

Antragsteller applicant, proponent, moving party, submitter, *(Anspruchsberechtigter)* claimant, *(Beschwerdeführer)* appellant, *(bei Gericht)* petitioner, *(Hauptversammlung)* requisitionist, *(für Kursus)* enrollee, *(parl.)* proposer of a motion, proponent, mover, *(Prozeßpartei)* party moving, *(im Rubrum)* ex parte;
geschädigter ~ *(Versicherung)* injured claimant;
~ bei einer Versicherung applicant for insurance.

Antragstellerin female petitioner, *(Firma)* applicant company.

Antragstellung introduction (representation) of a motion, filing of an application;
binnen einem Monat nach ~ within a period of one month from the date of requirement;
~ auf Bestätigung eines Testaments propounding a will; **~ auf Einberufung einer Hauptversammlung** requisition of shareholders.

Antrags|unterstützung seconding a motion; **~vordruck** application form (blank); **~zettel** application slip; **~zunahme** pickup in filings.

antreffen to find, to meet;
niemanden ~ to find everybody out.
antreiben to urge, to hurry on, to extort, to impel, to egg on; **Arbeiter** ~ to urge the workmen; **elektrisch** ~ to operate electrically.
Antreiber inciter, driver *(coll.)*;
~**methode** sweatshop system.
Antreten zum Appell muster.
antreten, sein Amt to accede to (enter upon) one's office; **zur Arbeit** ~ to turn out for duty; **Besitz** ~ to enter into possession; **Beweis** ~ to tender (adduce) evidence, to furnish proof; **Dienst** ~ to report for work, to clock in, to punch the clock *(US)*; **zum Dienst** ~ *(Soldat)* to report for duty; **Erbschaft** ~ to enter upon (come into possession of) an inheritance; **der Größe nach** ~ to line up according to size; **Macht** ~ to come into power; **Regierung** ~ *(Monarch)* to come (ascend) to the throne, *(Partei)* to come into power, to take office; **Reise** ~ to start (set out) on a journey; **Stellung** ~ to take up a job (position), to start on a job, to take up one's duty; **Strafe** ~ to begin serving one's time.
Antrieb impulse, urge, drive, impetus, incentive, *(Soziologie)* drive, *(techn.)* motion, drive, propulsion;
aus eigenem ~ of one's own volition, spontaneous, voluntary; **aus natürlichem** ~ by instinct; **mit elektrischem** ~ electrically operated;
~ **drosseln** to reduce the power; **jem. inneren** ~ **geben** to make s. o. tick; **zusätzlichen** ~ **geben** to furnish additional impetus; **aus eigenem** ~ **handeln** to act from an inner push; **etw. aus eigenem** ~ **tun** to do one's own thing.
Antriebs|aggregat prime mover; ~**kraft** motive power, drive, driving force, propulsion; ~**kraft eines Unternehmens sein** to be the live wire in a concern.
antrinken, sich Mut to give o. s. Dutch courage *(coll.)*.
Antritt entering, beginning, start;
~ **eines Amtes** assumption of (entrance upon) an office; ~ **eines Beweises** furnishing of proof; ~ **einer Erbschaft** entering into (entrance upon) an inheritance; ~ **eines Kabinettpostens** entrance upon a ministerial office; ~ **der Macht** assumption of power; ~ **der Regierung** *(Monarch)* accession to the throne, *(Partei)* coming into power; ~ **einer Reise** setting out on a journey; ~ **einer Stellung** taking up a job; ~ **eines Urkundenbeweises** putting in of a document.
Antritts|audienz first audience; ~**besuch** first visit, formal call; ~**datum** date of appointment; ~**rede** inaugural (inauguration) address, *(Parlament)* maiden speech; **frühester** ~**termin** earliest date available; ~**vorlesung** inaugural lecture.
Antwort answer, reply, return, response;
Ihrer gefälligen ~ **entgegensehend** awaiting the favo(u)r of your reply; ~ **nur bei Absage erforderlich** regrets only; **sofern nicht eine ausreichende** ~ **eingeht** failing a satisfactory reply; **heute abgehende** ~ reply leaving today; **abgelehnte** ~ *(Interview)* nonrespondent; **abschlägige** ~ rebuff, negative answer, repulse, denial; **ausstehende** ~ missing reply; **ausweichende** ~ evasive (noncommittal, shuffling) answer, evasive reply; **baldige** ~ early reply; **barsche** ~ short answer; **befriedigende** ~ satisfactory reply; **bejahende** ~ answer in the affirmative; **beleidigende** ~ offensive answer; ~ **bezahlt** reply paid, *(Telegramm)* answer prepaid (A. P.); **briefliche** ~ reply by mail; **definitive** ~ final answer; **eingegangene** ~ reply received; **endgültige** ~ definitive answer; **entscheidende** ~ final answer; **ergänzende** ~ supplemental answer; **auf Prestigegründen beruhende falsche** ~ *(Meinungsumfrage)* prestige bias; **freche** ~ smart answer (backlet) *(sl.)*; **frostige** ~ frosty answer; **aus dem Ärmel geschüttelte** ~ off-the-cuff response; **klare** ~ direct (plain) answer; **positive** ~ favo(u)rable answer; **postwendende** ~ reply by return of post *(Br.)* (mail, *US*); **präzise** ~ precise answer; **nicht präzise** ~ vague answer; **prompte** ~ ready (prompt, expeditious) reply (answer); **richtige** ~ correct answer; **schlagfertige** ~ crisp answer, repartee; **schnelle** ~ speedy reply; **sofortige** ~ immediate reply; **stereotype** ~ stock answer; **umgehende** ~ prompt answer, answer by return of post *(Br.)* (mail, *US*), reply on receipt; **ungenügende** ~ frivolous answer; **unverbindliche** ~ noncommittal (evasive) answer; **unverblümte** ~ round answer; **vage** ~ uncertain answer; **verneinende** ~ answer in the negative; **vorsichtige** ~ guarded answer; **zustimmende** ~ positive answer, answer in the affirmative; **zweideutige** ~ dubious answer;
auf ~ **drängen** to press for an answer; ~ **einleiten mit** to precede an answer with; **abschlägige** ~ **erhalten (bekommen)** to meet with a refusal, to take a denial; ~ **erteilen** to reply; **abschlägige** ~ **erteilen** to rebuff; **richtige** ~ **finden** to hit the right answer; ~ **geben** to return; **jem. eine scharfe** ~ **geben** to snap s. one's nose off; **unklare** ~ **geben** to hedge; **keine** ~ **gestatten** to permit with no reply; **keine** ~ **von jem. herausbekommen** to draw no reply from s. o.; **um eine** ~ **verlegen sein** to be at fault for an answer; **um keine** ~ **verlegen sein** not to be backward in coming forward; **jem. eine** ~ **suggerieren** to prompt s. o. with an answer; **auf jds.** ~ **warten** to look forward to s. one's reply; **zu einer** ~ **gedrängt werden** to be pushed for an answer; **j. keiner** ~ **würdigen** to vouchsafe s. o. no reply;
um ~ **wird gebeten (uAwg)** an answer is requested (R.S.V.P.);
~**brief** letter of reply.
antworten to [give an] answer, to respond, to reply;
ablehnend ~ to give a negative reply; **bejahend** ~ to answer in the affirmative; **ziemlich erregt** ~ to reply with some heat; **frech** ~ to answer back; **grob** ~ to give an offensive answer; **postwendend** to answer by return of post *(Br.)* (mail, *US*); **schriftlich** ~ to write back, to return in writing; **in gereiztem Ton** ~ to snap; **ungezwungen** ~ to answer in an easy manner; **zustimmend** ~ to reply in the affirmative.
Antwortenkontrolle *(Meinungsbefragung)* scrutiny.
Antwort|karte double postcard, reply (return) card; ~**kupon** reply coupon; ~**note** *(dipl.)* counter note, note in reply; **internationaler** ~**schein** international reply coupon; ~**schreiben** reply, letter sent in response, answer in writing; ~**telegramm** reply-paid telegram; ~**telegrammformular** form of authority.
anvertrauen to [deliver in] trust, to deposit, to entrust, to commit to the charge of, to consign, *(Geheimnis)* to confide;
jem. ~ to give in charge of s. o., to recommend to s. one's care; **jem. etw.** ~ to put one's trust in s. o.; **sich jem.** ~ to put o. s. in the hands of s. o.; **jem. eine Aufgabe** ~ to assign a task to s. o., to put a matter in s. one's hands; **Brief einem zuverlässigen Boten** ~ to send a letter by a sure messenger; **sich einem Freund** ~ to fling o. s. on a friend; **jem. ein Geheimnis** ~ to confide a secret to s. o., to let s. o. into a secret; **jem. einen Geldbetrag** ~ to entrust s. o. with a sum; **jem. etw. zu treuen Händen** ~ to commit s. th. to the trust of s. o.; **Kind einer Tante** ~ to give a child in custody of an aunt; **jem. seine Sorgen** ~ to unbosom one's troubles to s. o.
anvertraut fiduciary;
~**es Geld** trust fund, money held on trust.
Anvertrauter charge.
Anverwandte relations;
nächste ~ next of kin.
Anverwandtschaft kinship, relationship.
anvisieren *(mar.)* to take a bearing on.
Anwachsen accretion, growth, increase, *(Staatsgebiet)* accession;
~ **des Anlagevermögens** increase in fixed assets; ~ **der Bevölkerung** swell in the population; ~ **von Schulden** accumulation of debts; ~ **der Studentenschaft seit Kriegsende** postwar bulge in student numbers; ~ **von Zinsen** accrual of interest.
anwachsen to grow, to augment, to increase, to bulge, *(sich ansammeln)* to accumulate, *(Betrag)* to run up, *(Flut)* to swell, to rise, *(Zinsen)* to accrue;
lawinenartig ~ to snowball;
Schuldkonto ~ **lassen** to run up debts.
Anwachsungs|klausel clause of accrual; ~**recht** accruing right.
anwählen, direkt *(tel.)* to dial direct.
Anwalt lawyer, solicitor *(Br.)*, attorney at law *(US)*, law agent *(Scot.)*, *(im Prozeß)* pleader, barrister-at-law *(Br.)*, counsel *(Br.)*, counsellor [at-law] *(US)*;
von einem ~ **präpariert** primed by a lawyer;
aufstrebender ~ rising lawyer; **auf Schadensersatzklagen ausgehender** ~ ambulance chaser *(US)*; **mit der ständigen Vertretung beauftragter** ~ standing counsel *(Br.)*; **bedeutender** ~ leading counsel *(US)*; **beratender** ~ special pleader, counsel in chambers *(Br.)*, chamber counsel *(Br.)*, consulting barrister *(Br.)*, office lawyer *(US)*; **engagierter** ~ paid attorney *(US)*; **erfahrener** ~ case lawyer, lawyer of wide experience; **als Treuhänder fungierender** ~ solicitor-trustee *(Br.)*; **gegnerischer** ~ opposing counsel *(Br.)*; **gerissener** ~ Philadelphia *(US)* (quirky) lawyer; **junger** ~ stuff gown, colt *(Br.)*; **klägerischer** ~ counsel for the plaintiff *(Br.)*, plaintiff's counsel *(Br.)*; **plädierender** ~ barrister *(Br.)*, pleader, counsel *(Br.)*, counsellor *(US)*; **nicht plädierender** ~ chamber barrister; **praktizierender** ~ practising lawyer; **prozeßbevollmächtigter** ~ attorney of record *(US)*, senior counsel *(Br.)*; **raffinierter** ~ slick lawyer; **auf Gesellschaftsrecht spezialisierter** ~ corporation lawyer; **auf Immobilienrecht spezialisierter** ~ property (real-estate) lawyer; **auf internationales Recht spezialisierter** ~ international lawyer; **auf Zivilrecht spezialisierter** ~ common lawyer; **versierter** ~ full-blown (-fledged) lawyer (barrister, *Br.*); **weiblicher** ~ barristress; **zugelassener** ~ authorized counsellor *(US)*; **an allen Gerichten zugelassener** ~ attorney at large *(US)*;

~ **des Beklagten** counsel for the defence *(Br.)*, attorney for the defendant *(US)*; ~ **des Klägers** plaintiff's counsel *(Br.)*; ~ **für Steuersachen** tax lawyer (attorney, *US*); **begeisterter** ~ **der Verstaatlichung** enthusiastic advocate for nationalization;
~ **anweisen** to direct (instruct, brief) a counsel *(Br.)*; **für j. als** ~ **auftreten** to act as counsel for s. o. *(Br.)*; **sich als** ~ **ausgeben** to pass o. s. off as a lawyer; ~ **aus der Anwaltschaft ausschließen** to disbar a barrister *(Br.)*, to strike s. o. off the roll *(Br.)*; ~ **beauftragen** to brief a counsel (barrister) *(Br.)*, to instruct an attorney *(US)*; ~ **befragen** to take counsel's opinion *(Br.)*, to consult a lawyer; **sich mit seinem** ~ **beraten** to confer with one's counsel *(Br.)*; ~ **beschäftigen** to employ a solicitor *(Br.)*, to retain a lawyer; **sich mit einem** ~ **besprechen** to confer with one's counsel *(Br.)*; **[zum]** ~ **bestellen** to constitute s. o. one's attorney *(US)*, to brief (retain) a counsel (barrister, solicitor, *Br.*); ~ **für laufende Beratung engagieren** to retain a counsel *(Br.)* (lawyer); **seinem** ~ **Weisungen erteilen** to brief (instruct) one's lawyer; **seine Sache durch einen** ~ **vortragen lassen** to be heard by counsel *(Br.)*; **sich als** ~ **einen Namen machen** to establish one's reputation as a lawyer; **sich einen** ~ **nehmen** to retain (brief) a barrister (counsel) *(Br.)*, to engage the services of a lawyer, to hire an attorney *(US)*, to brief instructions to a barrister *(Br.)*; **als** ~ **nicht reüssieren** to be a failure as a lawyer; **vollbeschäftigter** ~ **sein** to have plenty of briefs; **als** ~ **tätig sein** to practise at the bar; **durch einen** ~ **vertreten sein** to be represented by counsel *(Br.)*; **als** ~ **beim Patentamt zugelassen sein** to be recognized to practise before the Patent Office *(US)*; **jem. einen** ~ **stellen** to provide s. o. with an attorney *(US)*; **Angelegenheit einem** ~ **übergeben (übertragen)** to put a matter (place a case) in the hands of a lawyer; ~ **mit Weisungen versehen** to give instructions to a solicitor *(Br.)*; **j. als** ~ **vertreten** to hold a brief for s. o. *(Br.)*; **sich an einen** ~ **wenden** to apply to a solicitor *(Br.)*; ~ **werden** to go to the bar; **zum** ~ **einer Sache werden** to become the advocate of a cause; **als** ~ **zugelassen werden** to be called *(Br.)* (admitted, to go) to the bar, to be admitted to the roll *(Br.)*; ~ **zu Rate ziehen** to call in the aid of an attorney *(US)*, to consult a lawyer; **als** ~ **zulassen** to admit a solicitor *(Br.)*, to call to the bar, to license a lawyer, to admit an attorney to practise law *(US)* (to the roll, *Br.*); ~ **zuziehen** to consult a solicitor *(Br.)* (an attorney, *US*), to employ a counsel *(Br.)*.

Anwältin barristress *(Br.)*.

anwaltlich, sich ~ **beraten lassen** to seek legal advice; ~ **tätig sein** to practise at the bar *(Br.)* (as attorney, *US*); ~ **vertreten sein, sich** ~ **vertreten lassen** to be represented by counsel *(Br.)*, to appear by counsel *(Br.)*; ~ **vertreten** to act as counsel for s. o. *(Br.)*, to hold a brief *(Br.)*;
~**e Tätigkeit** advocacy, attorneyship *(US)*.

Anwalts|anderkonto solicitor's client account *(Br.)*; ~**assessor** [etwa] junior lawyer (counsel, *Br.*); ~**auftrag** dock brief *(Br.)*; ~**beruf** legal profession, bar; ~**beruf ausüben** to practise law (at the bar, *Br.*); ~**beruf vorübergehend nicht ausüben dürfen** to be suspended from practice; **sich für den** ~**beruf vorbereiten** to study (read) for the bar; ~**bescheinigung** practising certificate; ~**besprechung** conference with one's lawyer; ~**bestallung** practising certificate; ~**bestellung** retainer, briefing of a lawyer; ~**brief** letter from a lawyer, *(vor Prozeßbeginn)* letter before action; ~**büro** lawyer's (law, *US*) office, barrister's [writing] chamber *(Br.)*, chambers *(Br.)*, *(Anwaltsfirma)* law firm, firm of solicitors *(Br.)*; **im** ~**büro arbeiten** to serve a term under articles *(Br.)*; ~**büro eröffnen** to hang out one's shingle *(coll.)*; **sich in einem** ~**büro die Sporen verdienen** to serve a hitch with a law firm.

Anwaltschaft legal profession, attorneyship *(US)*, *(Gesamtheit der Anwälte)* the bar, advocacy, Faculty of Advocates;
Anwalt aus der ~ **ausschließen** to disbar a barrister *(Br.)*.

anwaltschaftlich|vertreten sein to be represented by counsel *(Br.)*; **j.** ~ **vertreten** to hold a brief (act as counsel) for s. o. *(Br.)*.

Anwalts|firma law firm, firm of solicitors *(Br.)* (lawyers); ~**gebühr fällig werden lassen** to authorize an attorney's fee; ~**gebühren** lawyer's (counsel's, *Br.*) fee, legal fees, legal charges *(Br.)*, solicitor's charges *(Br.)*, *(Vorschuß)* retainer, retaining fee; ~**gebührenrechnung** bill of costs *(Br.)*; ~**gebührentabelle** scale of solicitor's charges *(Br.)*; ~**gehilfe** articled (solicitor's, *Br.*) clerk, writer; ~**gutachten** counsel's opinion *(Br.)*, lawyer's opinion; ~**honorar** attorney's *(US)* (lawyer's, solicitor's, counsel's, *Br.*) fee; **vorläufiges** ~**honorar** retainer, retaining fee; **zusätzliches** ~**honorar** refresher *(Br.)*; ~**honorar teilen** to split a fee; ~**kammer** incorporated law society *(Br.)*, bar council *(Br.)*, Faculty of Advocates *(Scot.)*; **Anwalt aus der** ~**kammer ausschließen** to disbar a barrister; **j. aus der** ~**kammer ausschließen** to strike s. o. off the roll *(Br.)*; ~**kanzlei** chambers *(Br.)*, lawyer's (law, *US*) office, barrister's chamber *(Br.)*; ~**kollegen vertreten** to devil a colleague; ~**konto** solicitors' account *(Br.)*.

Anwaltskosten legal expense, attorney's fee *(US)*, solicitor's costs (fee) *(Br.)*, retainer, retaining fee, costs due to a solicitor *(Br.)*;
erstattungsfähige ~ party-and-party costs; **nicht erstattungsfähige** ~ overriding charges; **notwendig gewordene** ~ party-and-party cost;
~ **festsetzen** to tax costs;
~**vorschuß** retaining fee, retainer.

Anwalts|laufbahn, seinen Sohn für die ~**laufbahn bestimmen** to intend to make one's son a barrister; ~**laufbahn einschlagen** to go to the bar; **sich zur** ~**laufbahn entschließen** to elect to become a lawyer; ~**liste** roll [of solicitors, *(Br.)*], law list *(Br.)*; **von der** ~**liste streichen** to strike s. o. off the roll *(Br.)*, to disbar a barrister *(Br.)*; ~**plädoyer** counsel's *(Br.)* (attorney's, *US*) speech; ~**praxis** law (solicitor's, *Br.*) practice; ~**praxis ausüben (betreiben)** to go to law (the bar), to practise law; ~**privileg** attorney-client privilege *(US)*; ~**prüfung** law-society examination *(Br.)*; ~**rechnung** solicitor's bill *(Br.)*; ~**robe** long robe.

Anwaltstand legal profession, *(Gesamtheit der Anwälte)* the bar, Faculty of Advocates;
in den ~ **aufnehmen** to admit an attorney to practise law *(US)*.

Anwalts|tätigkeit advocacy, attorneyship *(US)*, practice of law, solicitorship *(Br.)*; **beratende** ~**tätigkeit** office practice *(US)*; ~**tätigkeit ausüben** to practise law; ~**verein** society of lawyers, Law Society *(Br.)*, Inns of Chancery *(London)*, bar association; ~**vereinbarung auf Erfolgshonorarbasis** champertous contract; ~**vertreter** devil; ~**verzeichnis** law list *(Br.)*, roll [of solicitors]; **im** ~**verzeichnis aufgeführt sein** to appear on the roll; ~**vorschuß** retaining fee; **aus dem** ~**vorstand ausstoßen** to disbench *(Br.)*; ~**wechsel** change of solicitor; ~**zulassung** calling to the bar, admission as solicitor *(Br.)* (attorney, *US*).

Anwandlung fit, impulse, streak;
in einer ~ **von Schwäche** in a weak moment; **in einer** ~ **von Schwermut** in a mood of melancholy;
~ **von Großzügigkeit** generous streak; ~ **von Sparsamkeit** qualms of economy;
alle humanitären ~**en abwürgen** to kill all feelings of humanity;
~ **von Faulheit haben** to have a lazy fit.

Anwärter candidate, expectant, aspirant, probationer, *(eines Rechtes)* reversioner, remainderman, *(Verein)* candidate [for membership];
~ **auf den ersten Arbeitsplatz** first job seeker; ~ **für den gehobeneren Dienst** probationer for higher grade; ~ **auf eine Erbschaft** expectant heir, reversioner; ~ **auf die Staatsbürgerschaft** declarant *(US)*;
~**liste** list of candidates, *(Versicherung)* waiting list.

Anwartschaft expectancy, expectation, remainder, reversion, possibility coupled with an interest, abeyance, future right, future estate, future interest, *(Befähigung)* qualification, *(Sozialversicherung)* qualifying period, *(Staatsdienst)* candidateship;
entfernte ~ possibility on a possibility; **gesetzliche** ~ legal expectancy; **in Wirksamkeit getretene** ~ present fixed right of future enjoyment, vested remainder; **nähere** ~ near (ordinary) possibilities;
~ **auf eine Erbschaft** reversion (expectancy) of an inheritance *(US)*; ~ **des Hinterbliebenen** survivorship; ~ **auf eine Leibrente** deferred [life] annuity;
~ **auf eine Stelle erwerben** to qualify as a probationer for a post.

anwartschaftlich reversionary.

anwartschaftsberechtigt entitled in remainder.

Anwartschafts|berechtigter prospective beneficiary, reversioner, remainderman; ~**dividende** reversionary dividend; ~**eigentum** remaindership; ~**gut** estate in expectancy (remainder), remainder estate; ~**patent** reversionary patent.

Anwartschaftsrecht beneficial (expectant) estate, inchoate (expectant, equitable, contingent, reversionary) right, remainder (reversionary, contingent) interest, right in reversion, interest in expectancy;
bedingtes ~ contingent remainder; **auflösend bedingtes** ~ remainder vested subject to being divested; **feststehendes** ~ executed remainder; **gesetzliches** ~ legal remainder; **unentziehbares** ~ vested remainder; **wechselseitiges** ~ cross remainder;
~ **auf die eigenen Aktien** equitable interest in its own shares;
~ **besitzen** to have a reversionary interest [in an estate].

Anwartschafts|regeln remainder rules; ~**rente** reversion, deferred (reversionary) annuity; ~**übertragung** transfer of expectancy; ~**vermächtnis** executory bequest; ~**vermögen** property in expectancy, fortune in reversion; ~**zeit** waiting time.

anweisen *(anordnen)* to direct, to order, to enjoin, *(beauftragen)* to instruct, *(übertragen)* to transfer, *(überweisen)* to remit, to transfer, *(zuweisen)* to assign, to allot, *(Mittel zuweisen)* to appropriate, to provide;
jem. einen Betrag ~ to remit (send) an amount to s. o.; **Betrag auf eine Bank** ~ to make a sum payable at a bank; **Etatstitel zur Zahlung** ~ to pass an account for payment; **Geld telegrafisch** ~ to transfer money by cable; **jem. einen Platz** ~ to show s. o. a seat; **postwendend** ~ to remit by return of post; **jem. ein Zimmer** ~ to assign a room to s. o.;
Betrag auf ein Konto ~ lassen to have an amount credited to s. one's account.

Anweisung *(Anordnung)* order, direction, *(schriftliche Aufforderung)* order in writing, *(Auftrag)* charge, commission, *(Beauftragung)* instruction, *(Geldanweisung)* money order, *(Orderpapiere)* bill (check) to order, *(Übertragung)* transfer, *(Überweisung)* remittance, assignment, draft, *(Vorschrift)* regulation, specification, *(Zuweisung)* assignment, allocation, appropriation;
auf ~ von under instructions of; **auf gemeinsame** ~ by joint order; **auf ~ des Stadtrats** by order (under instructions) of the town council; **bis auf weitere ~en** until further orders; **gegen ausdrückliche ~en** contrary to instructions; **laut** ~ conformably to instructions, as per advice;
amtliche ~ precept; **ausdrückliche** ~ strict order; **detallierte ~en** poop sheet *(sl.)*; **genaue ~en** exact directions; **kaufmännische** ~ trade acceptance; **laufende** ~ standing order; **ministerielle** ~ departmental order; **mündliche** ~ verbal order; **schriftliche ~en** instructions in writing, letter of instruction; **strenge** ~ strict order; **telegrafische** ~ cable order (transfer); **umfassende ~en** blanket instructions; **verbindliche ~en** mandatory instructions *(US)*; **weitere** ~ follow-up instructions;
~ **zur Abonnementsverlängerung** renewal instructions; **~en beim Abschied** parting injunctions; **~en an den Anwalt** instructions to counsel *(Br.)*, briefing of a lawyer; ~ **zur Auflösung nicht verbrauchter Etatstitel** surplus fund warrant; ~ **zur Auslieferung von Lagergut** delivery order; ~ **zur Befriedigung einzelner Gläubiger** special assignment; **~en an ein unteres Gericht** writ of mandate *(US)*; ~ **auf den Inhaber** bearer warrant (scrip); **~en für Notfälle** emergency instructions; ~ **an Order** bill made out to order; **~en auf auswärtige Plätze** orders payable at foreign banks; **~en an die Polizei** directions to the constables; ~ **auf Waren** delivery order;
~en abwarten to await instructions; **auf ~en achten** to attend to directions; **nach jds. ~en arbeiten** to work under s. one's directions; ~ **ausstellen** to draw a check *(US)* (cheque, *Br.*); **~en befolgen** to comply with instructions; **~en übergenau befolgen** to carry out orders too literally; **durch ~ bezahlen** to remit; **~en von jem. entgegennehmen** to place o. s. under s. one's orders; ~ **erhalten** to receive a note; **detaillierte ~en erhalten** to receive full and particular instructions; **~en erteilen** to give instructions; **~en geben** to give instructions (directions); **jem. genaue ~en geben** to lay strict instructions on s. o.; **sich an ~en halten** to go by instructions (directions); **sich nicht an gegebene ~en halten** to go flat against s. one's orders; **~en Folge leisten** to act upon instructions, to go by the directions; **sich nach den erteilten ~en richten** to go by directions (instructions); **sich völlig nach den ~en seines Anwalts richten** to go entirely by what one's solicitor says *(Br.)*; **seine ~en überschreiten** to go beyond one's instructions.

Anweisungs|bank deposit bank; **~betrag** amount transferred, remittance; **~empfänger** payee, assignee; **~gebühr** transfer charge; **~schein** assignment.

anwendbar applicable, employable, exercisable, adoptable, usable, *(einschlägig)* relevant;
nicht ~ unadoptable; **praktisch** ~ practical, practicable;
auf alle Fälle ~ sein to apply to all cases; **nicht ~ sein** *(Gesetz)* not to apply.

Anwendbarkeit applicability;
praktische ~ practicability.

anwenden to apply, to employ, to exert, to exercise, to dispose (make use) of, *(aufwenden)* to spend;
falsch (verkehrt) ~ to misapply, to misemploy; **sein Geld schlecht** ~ to make bad use of one's money; **Gesetz** ~ to administer the law, to put the law into force (operation); **Gewalt** ~ to use (resort to) force; **alle Kräfte** ~ to strain every nerve; **falsche Methode** ~ to go the wrong way about s. th.; **praktisch** ~ to reduce to practice; **Recht** ~ to apply the law; **schlecht** ~ to make bad use of; **große Sorgfalt** ~ to bestow great diligence; **Steuertabelle** ~ to operate a tax table; **Verfahrensvorschriften** ~ to follow the rules of procedure; **verkehrt** ~ to misapply, to misemploy; **vorteilhaft** ~ to employ to advantage.

Anwendung application, appliance, appropriation, employment, use, utilization, exercise;
in ~ dieser Verordnung in pursuance of this decree; **unter ~ eines Abkommens** in operation of a convention; **unter ~ von Gewalt** by force; **unter ~ unerlaubter Mittel** employing unfair means; **unter ~ von Zwang** by [using] force; **zur äußerlichen** ~ for outward (external) application;
begrenzte ~ registered application; **falsche** ~ misuse; **praktische** ~ reduction to practice, economic (practical) application; **sinngemäße** ~ analogical application; **unrichtige** ~ wrong application; **willkürliche** ~ arbitrary use;
~ **eines Abkommens** operation of a convention; ~ **der Akkordschere** rate cutting; ~ **der konsolidierten Bilanzierungsmethode** consolidation policy; ~ **eines Durchgangstarifs für die auf der Strecke formveränderten Frachtgüter** fabrication-in-transit; **[strenge] ~ eines neuen Gesetzes** [strict] application of a new law; ~ **von Gewalt** resort to force; ~ **einer Methode** adoption of a method; ~ **in der Praxis** practical application of a process; **vernünftige ~ der Steuergesetze** fiscal prudence; ~ **einer Steuertabelle** operation of a tax table; ~ **eines Systems** application of a system; ~ **eines Verfahrens** practical application of a process; ~ **besonders intensiver Verkaufsmethoden** high-pressure salesmanship; ~ **von Waffengewalt** use of armed force; **unterschiedliche ~ des Zolltarifs** flag discrimination;
in ~ bringen to put in [to] force; **Gesetz in ~ bringen** to put a law into operation; **Regel zur ~ bringen** to apply a rule; ~ **eines Gesetzes durchsetzen** to enforce a law; ~ **finden** to apply, to be applicable; **zeitlich unbegrenzt ~ finden** to apply without any time limit; **zur ~ kommen** to be applied; ~ **eines Gesetzes verhindern** to interfere with the operation of a law.

Anwendungs|beispiel illustrative phrase; **~bereich** range (scope, field, area) of application, ambit; **innerhalb des gesetzlichen ~bereichs** within the meaning of the act; **~bereich eines Gesetzes** scope of a law; **~form** embodiment; **~gebiet** range (field) of application, *(Zolltarif)* application; **betriebliches ~gebiet** company-wide coverage; **~modalitäten** implementation clauses; **~möglichkeit** applicability; **~technik** application technics; **~verfahren** method of application; **~vorschriften** directions for use.

Anwerbe|büro recruiting firm; **~feldzug** recruiting drive; **~formular** application blank.

Anwerben von Führungskräften executive recruiting.

anwerben, Arbeitskräfte to enlist (recruit) labo(u)r; **Matrosen gewaltsam** ~ to impress sailors;
sich ~ lassen to sign on.

Anwerber recruiting officer;
~ **von Arbeitskräften** labo(u)r scout, industry recruiter.

Anwerbe|technik, ~verfahren recruiting technique; **~versuch** recruiting attempt; **~zeit** recruiting season; **~zettel** enlistment.

Anwerbung enlistment, engagement, enrolment, recruitment, recruiting;
gewaltsame ~ impressment;
~ **von Arbeitskräften** labo(u)r recruitment; ~ **auf der Hochschule** university recruiting.

Anwerbungs|kommission recruitment committee; **~plan** hiring scheme *(US)*; **~programm** recruitment program(me).

anwerfen *(Motor)* to crank up, to throw into gear;
Flugzeugmotor ~ to swing the propeller.

Anwerfer *(Auto)* starting handle.

Anwerfkurbel starting crank.

Anwesen premises, property, real estate;
kirchlichen Zwecken dienendes ~ religious house; **das gesamte** ~ all and hail *(Scot., law)*; **landwirtschaftliches** ~ estate, farm; **verlassenes** ~ deserted premises; **nicht mehr vorhandenes** ~ toft; **schönes ~ haben** to own a fine place; ~ **nur für Wohnzwecke nutzen** to use a property for residential purposes only.

anwesend attendant, present;
~ **sein** to be present (in attendance), to attend; **persönlich ~ sein** to appear in person; **ständig ~ sein** to be on hand at all times; **bei einer Versammlung ~ sein** to attend (assist by) a meeting; **zufällig ~ sein** to chance to be there.

Anwesende those present, audience, onlookers;
~r attendant;
~ **ausgenommen** present people excepted;
verehrte ~ ladies and gentlemen;
Zahl der ~n feststellen *(parl.)* to count the house.

Anwesenheit presence, attendance.

Anwesenheits|appell roll call; **~buch** attendance book; **~geld** attendance (call, reporting) fee, *(Dockarbeiter)* fall-back pay *(Br.)*; **steuerfreies ~geld** tax-free daily allowance for attendance; ~**kontrolle** floor check; ~**liste** roll, names of those present, attendance sheet, record of attendances, *(Arbeiter)* time sheet *(US)*; ~**liste verlesen** to call the roll; ~**nachweis** attendance record; ~**prämie** attendance bonus; ~**vergütung** attendance money; ~**verzeichnis** attendance sheet.

Anwohner borderer, neighbo(u)r, adjacent owner, *(Fluß)* riverain, *(Straße)* resident;
~ **des Flughafens** people living next to the airport.

Anzahl number, quantity, head *(Br.)*, *(Statistik)* absolute frequency;
in großer ~ in great numbers;
geringe ~ small quantity;
~ **der Beschäftigten** number of persons employed; **große** ~ **der Bevölkerung** large part of the population; ~ **von Kunden** traffic, flow of customers;
nur in beschränkter ~ **vorhanden sein** to be in short supply.

anzahlen to pay *(Br.)* (make, *US*) a deposit (on account), to make a first instalment (downpayment), to deposit, to pay down *(US)*;
100 DM ~ to leave DM 100 as deposit; **für eine Lieferung** ~ to pay a deposit on goods.

Anzahlung payment on account, downpayment *(US)*, earnest money, deposit *(US)*, part (advance) payment, pay down *(US)*, *(Mietvorauszahlung)* key money *(Br.)*, *(Ratenzahlung)* first instalment, *(Vorauszahlung)* advance, prepayment *(US)*;
bis zur Höhe der geleisteten ~ to extent of such payment;
1/3 ~ one-third down; **erhaltene** ~**en** *(Bilanz)* payments on account (advances) received; **geleistete** ~**n** *(Bilanz)* deposits with suppliers, advances paid, accounts paid up; **keine** ~ nothing down; **bei Nichtabschluß zurückzahlbare** ~ deposit subject to contract;
~**en auf Anlagen** *(Bilanz)* advances for plants; ~**en bei Lieferanten** *(Bilanz)* prepayments *(US)*, prepays *(US)*; ~**en für Neuanlagen** *(Bilanz)* prepayments for capital additions *(US)*;
~**en in Abzug bringen** to allow for sums paid in advance; ~ **leisten** to pay a (an amount as) deposit (in a sum as a security), to make a downpayment *(US)*; **100 DM** ~ **leisten** to leave DM 100 as deposit.

Anzahlungs|bedingungen instalment (downpayment, *US*) requirements; ~**garantie** advance guarantee; ~**kauf** will-call purchase *(US)*; ~**summe** payment on account, deposit *(US)*; ~**tabelle** prepayment table *(US)*.

anzapfen *(Telefon)* to tap, to wiretap, to bug *(US)*, to milk;
Faß heimlich ~ to tap the admiral *(marine, sl.)*.

Anzapfung von Telefonleitungen wire tapping, milking, bugging *(US)*.

Anzeichen sign, symptom, indication, mark, evidence, trace, token, foreboding, foretoken;
nach allen ~ according to all indications; **wenn nicht alle** ~ **trügen** unless we are greatly mistaken;
bedrohliches ~ ugly symptom; **ermutigendes** ~ healthy sign; **günstiges** ~ favo(u)rable auspices; **positives** ~ plus sign; **unfehlbares (zuverlässiges)** ~ true sign;
~ **böser Absichten** evidence of ill will; ~ **von Unzufriedenheit** symptoms of discontent; ~ **konjunktureller Verschlechterungen** signs of slowdown.

Anzeige [press] advertisement, ad *(US)*, insert, insertion, *(Ankündigung)* announcement, *(Avis)* advice [note], letter of advice, *(bei der Behörde)* declaration, charge, denouncement, denunciation, report, *(Bekanntmachung)* notification, *(bei Gericht)* information, denouncement, denunciation, delation, criminal charge, *(Mitteilung)* notice, *(Wertangabe)* declaration of value;
laut ~ as per advice; **ohne weitere** ~ without further notice;
amtliche ~ official announcement; **angeschnittene** ~ *(Werbung)* bleed page; **redaktionell aufgemachte** ~ editorial style of (editorialized) advertisement, advertorial *(US sl.)*; **sensationell aufgemachte** ~ flaring advertisement; **briefliche** ~ advice; **doppelseitige** ~ double-page spread; **Neugier erregende** ~ teaser advertisement *(US)*; **feuilletonistische** ~ advertisement in feuilleton style (in a short story); **terminlich fixierte** ~ fixed-date advertisement; **ganzseitige** ~ spread, full-page ad *(US)*; **nicht gebrachte** ~ holdover; **gedruckte** ~ printed advertisement; **besonders gestaltete** ~ display-type advertisement; **redaktionell gestaltete** ~ editorial style of (editorialized) advertisement; **großformatige** ~ big-splurge advertisement, spectacular; **halbseitige** ~ half-page advertisement; **kleine** ~**n** classified advertisements, small (want) ads *(US)*; **laufende kleine** ~**n** rate holders *(US)*; **mehrfarbige** ~ colored ad *(US)*; **unmittelbar über und neben dem Rand plazierte** ~ over and next matter; **gegenüber dem Text plazierte** ~ matter facing text; **redaktionelle** ~ reader advertisement, reading notice; **rubrizierte** ~**n** smalls; **seitenbeherrschende** ~ page dominance; **seitenteilige** ~ space advertisement; **einzeln stehende** ~ sole advertisement; **telegrafische** ~ wire (cable) message; **textanschließende** ~ following (next to reading, facing) matter; **überladene** ~ buckeye; **umrandete** ~ boxed advertisement; **unverzügliche** ~ *(Versicherungsfall)* immediate notice; **zum Plakat vergrößerte** ~ blowup; **zusätzliche** ~ additional advertisement, additional insertion; **zweiseitige** ~ two-page advertisement;
~ **der Akzeptverweigerung (Annahmeverweigerung)** notice of dishono(u)r; ~ **mit eingefalteten Blättern** fold-in; ~ **von Gefahrenumständen** *(Versicherung)* material representation; ~ **in der Gesamtausgabe** full-run advertisement; ~ **über die erfolgte Geschäftsverlegung** notice of removal; ~ **mit fortgesetzter Handlung** continuity panel; **doppelseitige** ~ **in Heftmitte** center *(US)* (centre, *Br.*) spread position advertisement; ~ **der Nichterfüllung** notice of default; ~ **bei der Polizei** report to the police; ~ **im Rahmen einer Serie** following-on advertisement; ~ **auf einer Skala** scale reading; **fingierte** ~ **zu Testzwecken** dummy advertising; ~ **eines Unfalls** notification of an accident; ~ **des Vertragrücktritts** notice of recission; ~ **eines Todesfalls** notification of death;
~ **aufgeben** to advertise, to insert an advertisement in a newspaper; **zur** ~ **bringen** to bring before the authority, to give notice, to denounce, to report, to inform; **j. zur** ~ **bringen** to lay an information (bring a charge) against s. o.; **nicht plazierte** ~ **in der nächsten Woche bringen** to roll over an advertisement to the next week; ~ **erstatten** to give (lay, lodge an) information *(Br.)*; ~ **gegen j. erstatten** to file criminal charges (lodge, lay information) against s. o.; ~ **gegen j. bei der Polizei erstatten** to report s. o. to (lay an information against s. o. with) the police; ~ **laufen haben** to run an advertisement; ~ **kennzeichnen** to key an advertisement; ~ **bei verschiedenen Werbeträgern unterbringen** to place advertisements in various media; ~ **zurückziehen** to dismiss a charge;
~**erstatter** reporting person; ~**erstattung** reporting.

anzeigen to indicate, *(ankündigen)* to announce, *(avisieren)* to advise, *(Gerät)* to record, to register, *(bei Gericht)* to denounce, to inform, to lay (lodge) an information against *(Br.)*, *(inserieren)* to advertise, to insert, to publish, *(mitteilen)* to inform, to notify, to give notice, *(Thermometer)* to read, to register, *(Versicherungsfall)* to disclose;
j. bei der Behörde ~ to denounce s. o. to the authorities; **beabsichtigten Besuch** ~ to notify of an intended visit; **Buch** ~ to notice a book; **Eheschließung** ~ to announce a marriage; **Empfang** ~ to acknowledge receipt; **Neuauflage eines Buches** ~ to advertise the new edition of a book; **j. bei der Polizei** ~ to report s. o. to the police; **Preise** ~ to quote prices; **Protest** ~ to give notice of dishono(u)r; **rechtzeitig** ~ *(Wareneingang)* to advise in due course; **sich selbst** ~ to give o. s. up; **Todesfall** ~ to notify (report) a death; **Verlust bei der Polizei** ~ to notify the police of a loss; **Wareneingang** ~ to acknowledge the receipt of goods.

Anzeigen|abruf release; ~**abschluß** [advertising] contract; ~**abteilung** advertisement *(Br.)* (advertising, *US*) department; ~**agentur** advertising agency; ~**akquisiteur** [advertisement] canvasser, advertising agent (solicitor, *US*), adman *(US)*; ~**annahme[stelle]** advertising agency, publicity bureau; **im redaktionellen Teil enthaltener** ~**appell** copy appeal; **geringes** ~**aufkommen** low advertising; ~**auftrag** advertisement (space, *US coll.*) order, order for advertising, advertising contract; **zu einem bestimmten Zeitpunkt abberufener** ~**auftrag** wait order; **schriftlicher** ~**auftrag mit genauer Plazierung** insertion (advertising) order; ~**beilage** advertisement supplement; ~**beleg** voucher copy; ~**belegung** space buying *(US coll.)*; ~**blatt** advertiser, advertising paper, newspaper having many advertisements, admag *(US coll.)*, *(Amtsblatt)* gazette; ~**blatt der Wirtschaft** industrial advertiser; ~**büro** advertising (advertisement, *Br.*) office.

Anzeigender denouncer, relator, reporting person;
~ **einer Straftat** private prosecutor.

Anzeigen|direktor advertising (advertisement, *Br.*) director; ~**disposition** placing space orders *(US coll.)*; ~**einnahmen** ad revenues *(US)*; ~**einstufung nach dem Werbetext** order of merit-rating; **wiederkehrendes** ~**element** standing detail; ~**erinnerungstest** blind product text; ~**erscheinungsplan** schedule of insertions; ~**erstatter** informant; ~**expedition** advertising agency, publicity agent, space buyer *(US coll.)*; ~**fachblatt** advertising paper; ~**fachmann** advertising expert, adman *(US)*; ~**festpreis** flat rate; ~**flaute** flatness in the advertising business; ~**fließsatz** undisplay *(US)*; ~**format** size of an advertisement, linage *(US)*, space size *(US coll.)*; ~**friedhof** newspaper graveyard, cocktail of ads *(US)*; ~**gebühren** advertising charges (fees), adrates *(US)*; ~**gestaltung** creative copy and art work; ~**gestaltung an verschiedene freiberuflich tätige Grafiker vergeben** to order art work from free lancers; ~**größe** space size *(US coll.)*, size of an advertisement, linage *(US)*; **verschiedene** ~**größen** mixed space units *(US coll.)*; ~**grundmaß** inch, agate line *(US)*; ~**grundpreis** open (basic) rate, open time rate *(US)*; ~**häufigkeit** frequency of insertion; ~**jahr** contract year; ~**käufer** space buyer *(US coll.)*; ~**kennzeichnung** keying an advertisement; ~**klischee** advertising block; ~**kosten** space charges (fees) *(US coll.)*; **bedeutsamer** ~**kunde** large newspaper space user *(US coll.)*; ~**kunde der Hauptausgabe** national advertiser; ~**leerraum belegen** to buy remnant (standby) space *(US coll.)*; ~**leiter** advertisement director *(Br.)*, advertisement (publicity, advertising, *US*) manager; **auf der Auflage beruhende** ~**liste** circulation rate base; ~**maß** inch, agate line *(US)*; ~**mittler** space broker *(US coll.)*; ~**plantage** newspaper graveyard, cocktail of ads *(US)*; ~**planung nach Verlegerwahl** run-of-paper; **reservierter** ~**platz** reserved position; ~**plazierung** placing of advertising, ad position *(US)*.

Anzeigenpreis [advertising] rate;
kombinierter ~ combination rate; **verbilligter** ~ remnant (reduced) rate;
~ **für Schwarzweißseite** one-time black-and-white page rate; **billigere** ~**e für Lokalausgabe berechnen** to run advertisements at a lower local rate.

Anzeigenpreisliste advertisement rates *(Br.)*, rate announcement (card, *US*);
auflagenbedingte ~ circulation rate base; **z. Zt. gültige** ~ temporary rate sheet.

Anzeigen|preiswechsel change in rates; ~**rabatt beim Belegen mehrerer Zeitschriften** clubbing offer *(US)*.

Anzeigenraum [advertising (newspaper)] space;
~ **auf dem Umschlag** cover;
~ **verbilligt abgeben** to sell at a discount outside the normal advertising channels; ~ **belegen (in Auftrag geben)** to reserve (book) space *(US coll.)*; **ganzen** ~ **vergeben haben** to be booked to capacity; ~ **sicherstellen** to contract for space *(US coll.)*; ~**abnahme in Teileinheiten zum Tarif des Gesamtauftrags** space charged against a block booking *(US coll.)*; ~**belegung** space buying *(US coll.)*; ~**vermittler** advertising (space, *US coll.*) salesman.

Anzeigen|reservierung advertising reservation; ~**richtsatz** advertising rate base; **kombinierter** ~**richtsatz** combination rate; ~**satz** advertising composition; ~**schluß** [copy] deadline *(US)*, closing date, publisher's deadline *(US)*, [editorial] closing, forms close, copy (closing) date; ~**seite** advertising page (sheet), page of advertising; **angeschnittene** ~**seite** bleed-page advertisement; ~**sektor** advertising sector; ~**serie** serial advertisement; ~**serie auf Abzahlungsbasis** hire-purchase advertisement *(Br.)*; ~**spalte** advertising (advertisement) column; ~**spiegel** advertising page plan (type area); ~**split** split run.

Anzeigentarif advertisement *(Br.)* (space, *US coll.*) rates, advertising charges, advertising rate base (schedule), rate card *(US)*, *(Zeitungskopf)* business notice;
z. Zt. gültiger ~ temporary rate sheet; **kombinierter** ~ combination rate;
~ **für Einzelinsertionen ohne Rabatt** one-time (transient) rate; ~ **für ortsansässige Firmen** local rates.

Anzeigen|teil *(Zeitung)* advertisement columns, advertising section, classified advertising, space *(US coll.)*, small ads *(US)*; ~**teil kaufen** to buy press space *(US coll.)*; ~**teil pachten** to lease the advertising business; ~**termin** date of insertion, copy date (deadline, *US*); ~**test** impact test; ~**text** copy; **druckfertigen** ~**text bereithalten** to have a print-ready copy; ~**texter** copywriter, ad writer *(US)*; ~**untersuchung** copy testing; ~**vermittler** advertising agent (operator); ~**vermittlung** advertising agency; ~**vertreter** newspaper (advertising, advertisement, *Br.*) representative, advertising (space, *US coll.*) salesman, advertising sales executive, ad representative *(US)*; ~**vertretung** newspaper (advertising) agency; **reine** ~**verwaltung** sole advertising representation; ~**volumen** advertising volume; **mit seinen Einkünften vom** ~**volumen abhängen** to rise and fall with the advertising cycle; ~**vorabdruck** preprint; ~**vordruck** advertising form; ~**vortest** pretest; ~**werbeleiter** advertisement (sales promotion) manager; ~**werber** canvasser, solicitor *(US)*.

Anzeigenwerbung [press] advertising;
klassische ~ above-the-line advertising;
~ **ortsansässiger Geschäfte** local advertising; ~ **in Teilauflagen** split run.

Anzeigen|wesen advertising; ~**wiedererkennungstext** recognition; ~**zeilenkosten pro Umsatz von 1 Milliarde Dollar** marline rate *(US)*; ~**zeitschrift** advertising paper, admag *(US coll.)*; ~**zunahme** advertising growth.

Anzeigepflicht duty (obligation) to disclose;
anzeigepflichtige Krankheit notifiable disease.

Anzeigepflichtverletzung *(Versicherung)* nondisclosure, concealment.

Anzeiger gazette, advertiser, *(Gerät)* recording instrument, gauge.

Anzeige|spielraum für Verluste discovery period; ~**tafel** indicator board, scoreboard; ~**vorrichtung** indicator.

anzetteln to instigate, to contrive, to machinate;
Verschwörung ~ to hatch a conspiracy.

Anzettelung instigation, machination, contrivance.

Anziehen *(Kurse, Preise)* advance, rise, rising, recovery, hardening, improvement, upward movement;
~ **der Aktienkurse** upward movement of stock; ~ **der Bremse** application of the brake; **plötzliches leichtes** ~ **der Effektenkurse** bulge of the stock market; **gleichzeitiges** ~ **der Preise** simultaneous increase in prices.

anziehen to put on, *(Kunden)* to attract, to appeal, to draw, to allure, *(Feuchtigkeit)* to absorb, to draw in, *(Kurse, Preise)* to rise, to go (move) up, to [be on the] advance, to harden, to recover, to rally, to firm up, to stiffen, *(zitieren)* to quote, to refer to, to cite;
j. ~ to dress s. o.; **Bremse** ~ to [apply the] brake; **sich zu elegant** ~ to overdress; **sich extravagant** ~ to be peculiar in one's dress; **sich geschmacklos (miserabel)** ~ to dress badly; **gut** ~ *(Auto)* to pull away well; **Kapital** ~ to attract capital; **anderes Kleid** ~ to change one's dress; **kräftig** ~ to recover smartly (sharply); **langsam** ~ to edge up; **drei Punkte** ~ to advance three points; **raketenartig** ~ to skyrocket *(US)*; **rasch** ~ to advance (go up) sharply, to rise strongly, to move briskly ahead, to go ahead sturdily; **trotz kleiner Umsätze scharf** ~ to move sharply on little business; **Spendierhosen** ~ to be in a spending mood; **stark** ~ to rally briskly; **Steuerschraube** ~ to put the tax screw (bite) on; **jeden Tag etw. anderes** ~ to wear a different suit every day; **sich den Umständen entsprechend** ~ to dress as befits the occasion; **sich warm** ~ to wrap o. s. up; **weiter** ~ to increase further; **ein wenig** ~ *(Kurse)* to advance a fraction; **wieder** ~ to stiffen again; **den Zügel** ~ to tighten the reins, to rein up.

anziehend attractive, appealing, engaging, prepossessing, winning;
nicht ~ unattractive;
bei ~**en Preisen** in a rising market, with attractive prices; ~**es Wesen** winning ways.

Anziehung attraction, appeal;
starke ~ **auf j. ausüben** to attract s. o. strongly.

Anziehungskraft appeal, attraction, attractive power, pulling power, allurement;
doppelte ~ twin appeal; **große** ~ big draw;
~ **eines Gebietes** amenity of an area; ~ **auf Kunden** appeal to customers, customer appeal;
~ **ausüben** to appeal; **starke** ~ **auf j. ausüben** to attract s. o. strongly; **große** ~ **auf das Publikum ausüben** to take the fancy of the public; **seine** ~ **verloren haben** to have lost one's appeal.

Anziehungs|moment *(Werbung)* appeal; ~**punkt** pole of attraction, *(Ausstellung)* point, chief attraction, real draw.

Anziennität seniority.

Anziennitäts|liste seniority list; ~**rechte abschaffen** to crack the seniority system.

anzu|bändeln suchen, mit jem. to set one's cap at s. o.; **leicht** ~**bringen sein** to sell readily.

Anzug *(Annäherung)* approach, advance, *(Kleidung)* suit, dress;
im ~ in the wind;
fertiger ~ ready-made suit, reach-me-down *(sl.)*; **korrekter** ~ correct dress; **modischer** ~ modish dress; **zweireihiger** ~ double-breasted suit; **zweitbester** ~ second-best suit;
~ **anprobieren** to try [on] a suit; **sich einen** ~ **von der Stange kaufen** to buy a ready-made (off-the-peg, *Br.*) suit; **sich einen** ~ **machen lassen** to have a suit made [to measure]; **sich zu einem** ~ **Maß nehmen lassen** to get measured for a suit of clothes; **im** ~ **sein** to be brewing (afoot), to be waiting in the wings, to be in the wind, *(Erkältung)* to come on, *(Gewitter)* to be approaching (gathering), *(Krieg)* to draw on; **j. aus dem** ~ **stoßen** to knock the daylights out of s. o. *(sl.)*.

anzüglich personal, pointed;
~ **werden** to become personal;
~**e Bemerkungen** offensive (personal) remarks, personalities;
~**e Witze erzählen** to tell off-colo(u)red (smutty) jokes.

Anzugs|ordnung dress regulation; **rasches (rasantes) ~vermögen** smart pickup.
anzünden fire, to kindle, to light;
Licht ~ to light the lamp; **Streichholz** ~ to strike a match.
Anzupumpender, leicht easy touch.
anzuschaffen, noch short.
anzuziehen, nichts geeignetes ~ **haben** to have nothing fit (suitable) to wear; **sich hervorragend** ~ **wissen** to have excellent taste in dress.
anzweifeln to doubt;
Beschlußfähigkeit ~ to challenge the quorum; **Beweismaterial** ~ to suspect the truth of evidence.
apart striking, distinctive, *(Mode)* stylish, smart.
Aperitif appetizer, aperitif, short drink.
Apfel, haltbarer long-keeping apple;
~ **der Zwietracht** apple of discord;
in den sauren ~ **beißen** to bite on the bullet, to swallow the pill; **der** ~ **fällt nicht weit vom Stamm** like father, like son, chip of the old block.
Apotheke dispensary, dispenser, chemist's shop *(Br.)*, drugstore *(US)*, pharmacy *(US)*;
eine ~ **sein** to charge fancy prices.
Apothekenbesitzer drugstore owner *(US)*.
Apotheker chemist *(Br.)*, druggist *(US)*;
geprüfter ~ dispensing chemist *(Br.)*;
~**buch** dispensatory; ~**gewicht** apothecaries' (troy) weight; ~**preise** fancy (stiff) prices; ~**preise bezahlen** to pay through the nose; ~**rechnung** stiff (swingeing) bill; ~**ware** pharmaceuticals, drugs.
Apparat apparatus, machine, machinery, set, contrivance, mechanical device, *(Ausrüstung)* equipment, outfit, *(Meßgerät)* instrument, *(Organisation)* setup, organization, body, *(Politik)* machine, *(Telefon)* telephone, *(Vorrichtung)* appliance, device;
am ~ *(tel.)* speaking;
bürokratischer ~ red-tapism; **übermäßig aufgeblähter bürokratischer** ~ overblown bureaucracy; **gut eingespielter** ~ well-functioning machinery; **fotografischer** ~ camera;
gesamter ~ **einer Fabrik** manufacturing stock; ~ **der Verwaltung** machine of government, administration machinery;
am ~ **bleiben** *(Telefon)* to hold on (the line); **j. an den** ~ **rufen** to call s. o. to the telephone; **am** ~ **sein** to be on the telephone (line); **über den notwendigen** ~ **verfügen** to be duly equipped.
Apparatebau apparatus industry.
Apparatur equipment, outfit.
Appartement flat *(Br.)*, apartment *(US)*, *(Hotel)* suite (set) of rooms;
~**bewohner** apartment *(US)* (flat, *Br.*) dweller; ~**haus** block of flats *(Br.)*, apartment (condominium) building *(US)*, flatted house *(Br.)*; ~**hotel** apartment hotel *(US)*; ~**wohnung** flat dwelling *(Br.)*, apartment *(US)*.
Appell appeal, *(mil.)* roll-call, inspection, muster;
feierlicher ~ conjuration, solemn appeal;
~ **in letzter Minute** last-minute appeal;
~ **abhalten** to call the roll; **zum** ~ **antreten** to fall in for roll-call;
~ **an j. richten** to direct an appeal to s. o.
Appellant defendant in error.
Appellationsgericht court of appeal, Court for the Correction of Errors.
appellieren to [make an] appeal;
an den Kapitalmarkt ~ to turn to private sources of capital; **an das Volk** ~ to appeal (go) to the country.
Appetit appetite, stomach;
herzhafter ~ hearty appetite; **ungezügelter** ~ insatiable appetite;
~ **anregen** to sharpen (whet, stimulate) the appetite; **guten** ~ **haben** to eat well; **keinen** ~ **haben** to be off one's feed; **jem. den** ~ **verderben** to spoil s. one's appetite;
~**anreger** appetizer, whet; ~**brötchen** savo(u)ry, roll, canapé, titbit.
appetitlich appetizing, savoury looking delicious, attractive, *(fig.)* pleasant.
applanieren to level, to flatten.
applaudieren to clap, to applaud;
nicht ~ to sit on one's hands.
Applaus applause, clapping;
stürmischer ~ enthusiastic applause;
~ **bekommen** to meet with applause; **einem Darsteller großen** ~ **zollen** to give a performance a big hand *(coll.)*.
Appoint item, number;
per netto ~ **ziehen** to draw the exact amount.

Approbation *(Arzt)* licence to practise as a doctor;
ärztliche ~ **besitzen** to qualify as a doctor; **jem. die** ~ **entziehen** to revoke s. one's licence, to strike off the Medical Register; ~ **erteilen** to license a doctor to practise medicine.
approbiert licensed, qualified;
~**er Apotheker** registered pharmacist; ~**er Arzt** qualified physician.
April, erster All Fools Day;
j. in den ~ **schicken** to send s. o. on a fool's errand, to make an April fool of s. o.;
~**wetter** April weather.
Aquarellmalerei water colo(u)r.
Äquator equator, the line.
Äquivalent equivalent, consideration, quid pro quo;
~ **in Geld** pecuniary (valuable) consideration.
äquivalent equivalent.
Äquivalenz|lehre *(Patentrecht)* doctrine of equivalence; ~**prinzip** cost-of-service principle; ~**wert** equivalent value.
Ära era, epoch;
neue ~ **einleiten** to inaugurate a new era.
Arbeit work, labo(u)r, *(Aufgabe)* task, assignment, *(Ausführung)* workmanship, craftsmanship, handiwork, *(Beschäftigung)* employment, achievement, job, occupation, *(Dienst)* service, *(Erzeugnis)* product, make, *(Geschäft)* concern, business, *(Leistung)* performance, output, *(Mechanik)* work, *(Mühe)* effort, trouble, pains, toil, exertion, *(Schule)* exercise, essay, theme *(US)*, composition, *(Stück)* piece of work, job, *(Tätigkeit)* activity, operation, *(Universität)* paper, dissertion, thesis;
auf dem Weg zur ~ *(Versicherungsrecht)* on the way to business; **bei der** ~ on the job, at work; **in der täglichen** ~ in harness; **mit** ~ **überlastet** overwhelmed with work; **ohne** ~ unemployed, jobless, out of work; **während der** ~ in course of one's employment;
~**en** pursuits;
anhaltende ~**en** close work; **anstrengende** ~ exacting task; **auferlegte** ~ task; **wieder aufgenommene** ~ return to plant; **sich auftürmende** ~ work piling up; **auserwählte** ~ delicate workmanship; **schlampig ausgeführte** ~ slipshod work; **in der Ausführung begriffene** ~ work in progress; **bequeme und lukrative** ~ sweet job; **bezahlte** ~ paid work; **im Akkord bezahlte** ~ work at piece rates; **schlecht bezahlte** ~ badly paid (journeyman) work; **nach Stunden bezahlte** ~ time work; **untertariflich bezahlte** ~ scab work; **eigene** ~ personal labo(u)r; **in den Tarif einbezogene** ~ bargain work; **einträgliche** ~ fat job; **entfremdete** ~ alienation of labo(u)r; **in nächtlicher Tätigkeit entstandene** ~ work that smells of lamp oil; **noch zu erledigende** ~ jobs awaiting attention; **rasch erledigte** ~ fast work; **ermüdende** ~ tedious work; **erstklassige** ~ finest workmanship; **fertiggestellte** ~ [accomplished] work; **freiwillige** ~ labo(u)r of love; **ganztägige** ~ full-time job; **gebundene** ~ restricted job; **geistige** ~ mental work, headwork, brainwork; **geleistete** ~ work done, hours worked; **im Stücklohn geleistete** ~ contract work; **tatsächlich geleistete** ~ hours worked; **in Angriff genommene** ~ job in hand; **gewöhnliche** ~ ordinary labo(u)r; **hervorragende** ~ first-rate workmanship, excellent piece of work; **hochwertige** ~ high-class workmanship; **kinderleichte** ~ child's play; **körperliche** ~ manual labo(u)r; **langweilige** ~ dry work, boring job, a chore *(US)*; **langwierige** ~ long job; **laufende** ~ work in progress; **leichte** ~ light work; **seine ersten literarischen** ~**en** his early productions as a writer; **mäßige** ~ feeble work; **mechanische** ~ unskilled labo(u)r, routine job; **mißratene** ~ misfit; **monotone** ~ humdrum work; **öffentliche** ~**en** public works; **penible** ~ exacting work; **primitive** ~ rough work; **produktive** ~ productive work; **saure** ~ uphill work; **schlampige** ~ a lick and a promise; **schlechte** ~ poor workmanship; **schludrige** ~ badly finished (rush) work; **schriftstellerische** ~ literary work, *(Erzeugnis)* writing paper; **schweres Stück (schwierige)** ~ hard (warm) work, grind *(fam.)*, tough job; **selbständige** ~ occupation of a professional nature; **sorgfältige** ~ sound workmanship; **systematische** ~ systematic (methodical) work; **termingebundene** ~ *(Werbung)* traffic; **übermäßige** ~ excessive labo(u)r; **global übernommene** ~ lump work; **vertraglich übernommene** ~ contract labo(u)r; **unbezahlte** ~ unremunerative work; **undankbare** ~ thankless task; **unerledigte** ~ unfinished work; **ungelernte** ~ common labo(u)r, manual (unskilled) work; **unselbständige** ~ employment, *(Doppelbesteuerungsabkommen)* dependent personal service; **unzureichende** ~ underwork; **vergütete** ~ work against payment; **vorausbezahlte** ~ dead horse; **vorbereitete** ~ dead work; **vordringliche** ~ work of immediate urgency, priority (key) job; **vorgetane** ~ preserved work; **vorzügliche** ~ first-class work;

wissenschaftliche ~ treatise, paper; **nicht enden wollende** ~ endless task; **nicht zusagende** ~ uncongenial job; **zusätzliche** ~ supplementary (excess of) work;
~ **im Akkord** task wage (work), job work, piecework; ~ **am laufenden Band** work on the assembly line, serial production; ~ **für den Fachmann** skilled job; ~ **von Führungskräften** managerial work; ~ **als landwirtschaftlicher Gehilfe** farm labo(u)ring; ~ **und Kapital** Capital and Labo(u)r; ~ **auf Prämienbasis** work on the bonus system; **wissenschaftliche ~en nach der Promovierung** post-graduate work; ~ **außerhalb der Saison** off-season work; ~ **in wechselnden Schichten** split shift; ~ **unter Tage** underground work; ~ **im Tagelohn** daywork; ~ **unter Tariflohn** scab work; ~ **mit geringer Verdienstspanne** low-profit work; ~ **nach Vorschrift** go-slow *(Br.)*, work-to-rule *(Br.)*;
~ **an einen Untergebenen abgeben** to devolve work on a subordinate; **j. von der** ~ **abhalten** to keep s. o. from work; **jem. von der** ~ **ablenken** to entice s. o. from his duty; **j. bei einer** ~ **ablösen** to give s. o. a spell; **sich mit seiner** ~ **abplagen** to sliver away with one's work; **mit der** ~ **ernsthaft anfangen** to buckle down to work; **zur** ~ **anhalten** to keep in harness; ~ **annehmen** to take an employment; ~ **auf dem Lande annehmen** to swallow the anchor *(sl.)*; **j. zur** ~ **antreiben** to incite s. o. to work; **ganz in seiner** ~ **aufgehen** to burn with love for one's work, to be utterly devoted to one's work; **mit der** ~ **aufhören** to knock off work; ~ **aufnehmen** to set to (take up) work; ~ **wieder aufnehmen** to go back to work; ~ **aufteilen** to divide up the work; ~ **auf mehrere Leute aufteilen** to break up a piece of work among several people; ~ **ausführen** to execute work; **von der** ~ **ausruhen** to lie up; **~en und Lieferungen ausschreiben** to invite tenders; ~ **aussetzen** to stop working, to walk out *(US)*; **sich äußerst lobend über jds.** ~ **aussprechen** to refer to s. one's work in terms of high praise; ~ **beenden** to cease work; **von der** ~ **befreien** to release from working; **sich wieder an die** ~ **begeben** to return to work; **seine** ~ **beginnen** to start working; **bei der Ernte** ~ **bekommen** to get a turn of work at the harvest; **j. mit zusätzlicher** ~ **belasten** to put additional work on s. o.; ~ **beschaffen** to procure (provide) employment; **seine** ~ **beschleunigen** to speed up one's work; **j. in seiner** ~ **bestärken** to encourage s. o. in his studies; **um** ~ **bitten** to ask for work; **in** ~ **bringen** to fit into a job; **j. an die** ~ **bringen** to put s. o. to work; **großen Teil der** ~ **hinter sich bringen** to get through a lot of work; **sich für eine** ~ **nicht eignen** not to be up to a job; **bei der** ~ **einschlafen** to sleep over one's work; ~ **einstellen** to stop working, to knock off, *(kündigen)* to quit work, *(streiken)* to turn out, to lay down tools, to come out on strike, to walk out *(US)*; **sich mit** ~ **entschuldigen** to make work one's excuse; ~ **erhalten** to obtain employment, to get work; ~ **erledigen** to manage a piece of work; **seine** ~ **flüchtig erledigen** to hurry over a task, to scurry through one's work; ~ **innerhalb einer Woche erledigen** to finish a job within (inside of, *US*) a week; **in** ~ **ersticken** to be smothered with work; **in der** ~ **ertrinken** to be immersed in one's work; **scharenweise der** ~ **fernbleiben** to stay away from the assembly line in droves; ~ **fertigstellen** to finish off a job; **in seinem Beruf keine** ~ **finden** to find no work in one's line; **seine** ~ **fortsetzen** to carry on with one's work, to keep working; ~ **zu Ende führen** to carry out a job; **während der** ~ **schnell etw. futtern** to put on the nose bag *(fam.)*; ~ **geben** to put in work, to give employment; **Auftrag in** ~ **geben** to put an order in hand; **an die** ~ **gehen** to proceed (take) to business; **auf** ~ **gehen** to go out (take) to work; **mit Eifer an die** ~ **gehen** to get to work dingdong, to wire away *(coll.)*; **ernsthaft an die** ~ **gehen** to go roundly to work; **zur** ~ **gehen** to go to one's work; **ernsthafter** ~ **aus dem Wege gehen** to shy away from hard work; ~ **haben** to have a job, to be employed; **neues Buch in** ~ **haben** to have a new book on the stocks; **keine** ~ **haben** to be out of work (unemployed); ~ **wieder aufgenommen haben** to be back on the job; **viel Ärger mit einer** ~ **gehabt haben** to have spent a good deal of trouble over a job; **wieder seine geregelte** ~ **haben** to be in regular work again; ~ **hinter sich haben** to be through with a job; **unerledigte** ~ **liegen haben** to fall behind with one's work; **sein Äußerstes bei der** ~ **hergeben** to work to the full at one's task; **an der** ~ **hindern** to ratten *(Br., sl.)*; **eine** ~ **hinschmeißen** to fling up a task; **durch seine** ~ **hinzulernen** to learn on the job; ~ **schreiben lassen** to set a paper; **von seiner Hände** ~ **leben** to live by one's hands (by the sweat of one's brow), to be left to one's purchase; **Hand an die** ~ **legen** to put one's right hand to the work; **ausgezeichnete** ~ **leisten** to do a first-class job; **bahnbrechende** ~ **leisten** to do pioneer work; **ganze** ~ **leisten** to make a thorough job of it, to go the whole hog; **gute** ~ **leisten** to give good service, to make a good job of it; **Hervorragendes bei seiner** ~ **leisten** to do one's work with distinction; **nützliche** ~ **leisten** to perform useful work; **schlechte** ~ **leisten** to tinker; **schludrige** ~ **leisten** to scamp; **untergeordnete** ~ **leisten** to devil; ~ **leiten** to direct a job; **seine** ~ **liebgewinnen** to reconcile o. s. to one's work; **im Rahmen einer** ~ **liegen** to fall within the scope of a job; **sich an die** ~ **machen** to get (buck, settle) down to work, to go about one's work, to hitch up to a job *(US)*, to get down to it, to roll up one's sleeves; **sich mit Eifer an die** ~ **machen** to wire in *(coll.)*; **sich ernsthaft an die** ~ **machen** to set to work in earnest; **jem.** ~ **machen** to put s. o. to inconvenience (trouble); **sich selbst an die** ~ **machen** to put one's hand to the plough (plow, *US*), to take a hand in the work o. s.; **sich tüchtig an die** ~ **machen** to pitch into work; **seiner täglichen** ~ **nachgehen** to go about one's usual work (business), to do one's daily stint; **seiner** ~ **im Ausland nachgehen** to work on assignment abroad; **in** ~ **nehmen** to take in hand, to put on the stocks; **sofort in** ~ **nehmen** to have work started at once; **seine** ~ **niederlegen** to drop one's work, to stay off one's job, to down tools *(Br.)*, to walk out *(US)*; **sehr nach** ~ **riechen** to smell of the lamp (midnight oil); ~ **sabotieren** to make a bad job; **sich vor keiner** ~ **scheuen** to be willing to do anything; **an der** ~ **sein** to be at work; **auf** ~ **sein** to be out at work; **in** ~ **sein** to be in hand (process) of manufacture; **mit Freude bei der** ~ **sein** to have one's heart in one's work; **mit ganzer Seele (ganzem Herzen) bei der** ~ **sein** to have one's heart in (lend one's soul to) one's work; **tüchtig an der** ~ **sein** to be hard at it; **an seine** ~ **gefesselt sein** to be pegged down to one's work; **an selbständige** ~ **gewöhnt sein** to be accustomed to working independently; **mit seiner** ~ **im Rückstand sein** to be behind (in arrears) with one's work; **mit** ~ **überladen (von** ~ **überhäuft) sein** to be up to the ears in work, to be snowed under; **in seine** ~ **ganz vertieft sein** to be wrapped (bound) up in one's work; **j. an die** ~ **setzen** to set s. o. about a task (to work); **über der** ~ **sitzen** to sit at work; **bis zum Hals in der** ~ **stecken** to be up to one's neck in work; **bei jem. in Lohn und** ~ **stehen** to be in s. one's employ; **mitten in der** ~ **stehen** to be in harness; **sich in die** ~ **stürzen** to throw o. s. into work, to plunge into business; ~ **suchen** to look for (seek) a job, to seek work (employment); **bei der** ~ **trödeln** to slack at one's job; ~ **übernehmen** to undertake a job, to undertake a piece of work; **zusätzliche ~en übernehmen** to take on extra work; ~ **zum Verpusten unterbrechen** to stop work to have a few whiffs; **in der** ~ **untergehen** to be immersed in one's work; **an j.** ~ **vergeben** to place a contract with s. o.; ~ **im Akkord vergeben** to let out a job of work on contract; **~en und Lieferungen vergeben** to let out a work in contract, to give on contract; **seine** ~ **vernachlässigen** to be negligent in one's work; ~ **verpfuschen** to butcher a job; ~ **verrichten** to do a job, to perform work; **allerlei** ~ **verrichten** to do odd jobs; ~ **seiner Angestellten verrichten** to keep a dog and bark o. s.; ~ **verschaffen** to procure labo(u)r; **jem.** ~ **verschaffen** to find s. o. work; **sich ganz in die** ~ **vertiefen** to bury o. s. in work; ~ **vollenden** to execute a job of work; **mit seiner** ~ **gut vorankommen** to make progress in one's studies; ~ **vorantreiben** to press on the work; **sich eine** ~ **vornehmen** to plan a piece of work; ~ **vorwärtstreiben** to press on with the work; **mit niedrigen ~en beschäftigt werden** to be employed at a lower status; **mit seiner** ~ **fertig werden** to get through one's work; **mit der** ~ **vertraut werden** to get one's hand in; **mitten in der** ~ **weggerafft werden** to die with one's boots on; **sich seiner** ~ **widmen** to apply o. s. (attend) to one's work; ~ **wiederaufnehmen** to fall to work again; ~ **bei Fortsetzung der Lohnverhandlungen wiederaufnehmen** to negotiate a return to work pending further talks; ~ **nicht machen wollen** to jib at a job; **Material für eine wissenschaftliche** ~ **zusammenstellen** to collect material for a scientific work; ~ **zuweisen** to place in work; **sich zu harter** ~ **zwingen** to force o. s. to work hard.

Arbeiten working, *(Maschine)* running, functioning; **einwandfreies** ~ *(Maschine)* smooth running.

arbeiten to [be at] work, to labo(u)r, *(dienen)* to serve, *(herstellen)* to produce, to make, to manufacture, *(Holz)* to warp, *(Kapital)* to yield, *(Maschine, Mechanismus)* to go, to run, to operate, to function, to work;
im Akkord ~ to work by the job (piece), to do job (piece) work; **angestrengt** ~ to work one's fingers to the bone; **für einen Apfel und ein Ei** ~ to work for peanuts *(sl.)*; **wieder im gleichen Arbeitstempo** ~ to resume normal working schedules; **im Bankfach** ~ to be in the banking line; **unter ungünstigen Bedingungen** ~ to labo(u)r under a disadvantage, to work under difficult conditions; **wie besessen (wie ein Besessener)** ~ to work like a nigger, to work like a madman, to be working like the devil; **im Betrieb seines Vaters** ~ to work in one's

father's firm; **billiger** ~ to work for less; **für ein Butterbrot** ~ to work all day for a mere pittance; **einwandfrei** ~ *(Maschine)* to run smoothly, to function without friction; **gegen Entgelt** ~ to work for hire; **aufgrund eigener Erfahrungen** ~ to work on experience; **nach jds. Erfahrungen** ~ to work on the lines of s. o.; **mit Erfolg** ~ to work to good purpose; **ernsthaft** ~ to knuckle down *(US sl.)*; **nur in Etappen** ~ to work by fits and starts; **in einer Fabrik** ~ to be a factory hand, to work in the shops; **für seine Familie** ~ to maintain one's family; **fieberhaft** ~ to work at a white-hot speed; **fleißig** ~ to be hard at work (on the job); **am Fließband** ~ to work on the assembly line; **freiberuflich** ~ to work free-lance; **ganztägig** ~ to work full-time; **nicht ganztägig** ~ to work short (half) -time; **rein gefühlsmäßig** ~ to work almost by feel; **mit jem. geschäftlich** ~ to do business (deal) with s. o.; **mit Gewinn** ~ to operate at a profit; **halbtags** ~ to work part (half) -time; **Hand in Hand** ~ to work in close cooperation (hand in glove); **jem. in die Hände** ~ to play into s. one's hands; **sich die Hände wund** ~ to work one's fingers to the bone; **hart** ~ to show application in one's studies; **hart** ~ **müssen** to work for one's living; **hauptamtlich** ~ to work on a full-time basis; **sechs Stunden hintereinander** ~ to work six hours without let-up (interruption); **mit Hochdruck** ~ to work at high pressure; **mit großem Kapital** ~ to dispose of a large capital; **sich kaputt** ~ to work one's tail off *(US)*; **mit dem Kopf** ~ to be a brainworker; **mit ganzer Kraft und Energie** ~ to put one's back into s. th.; **wie ein Kümmeltürke** ~ to work like a nigger (beaver, *US*); **lange** ~ to work long hours; **planmäßig langsam** ~ to work to rule *(Br.)*; **nur nach Laune** ~ to be on and off with s. th.; **methodisch** ~ to work on a system; **bis spät in die Nacht** ~ to burn the midnight oil; **nicht** ~ to rest, *(Kapital)* to lie idle; **nicht mehr** ~ to have retired; **wie ein Pferd** ~ to work like a horse (dog, slave); **ohne Plan und Überlegung** ~ to work on a piecemeal plan; **für eigene Rechnung** ~ to work for (open up) one's own account; **an einem Roman** ~ to be working on a novel, to have a novel on the stocks; **nach der Schablone** ~ to work mechanically; **in Schichten** ~ to work in shifts; **schludrig** ~ to skimp; **schwer** ~ to plod, to pound, to keep one's nose to the grindstone; **an sich selbst** ~ to improve o. s.; **gegen freie Station** ~ to work au pair *(Br.)*; **stoßweise** ~ to work in sudden bursts; **zwölf Stunden hindurch ununterbrochen** ~ to work twelve hours without a let-up; **ganzen Tag schwer** ~ to go hard all day; **Tag und Nacht** ~ to work day and night, to work round the clock, to work double tides *(Br.)*; **im Tagelohn** ~ to hack; **in fieberhaftem Tempo** ~ to work at white-hot speed; **wie der Teufel** ~ to work like hell (the devil), to work with all one's might; **sich zu Tode** ~ to kill o. s. with work, to work o. s. to death; **tüchtig** ~ to do a good job; **übermäßig** ~ to work too hard; **bis zum Umfallen** ~ to work till one drops; **umschichtig** ~ to take turns; **umsonst** ~ to waste one's labo(u)r, to be engaged in a profitless task, to work on even terms, to work for love; **praktisch umsonst** ~ to have nothing for one's pains; **unentgeltlich** ~ to operate on a nonprofit basis; **ungleichmäßig** ~ to work by fits and starts; **unregelmäßig** ~ to work in snatches; **mit Unterbrechungen** ~ to work at it off and on; **in einem Unternehmen** ~ to work for a firm; **ununterbrochen** ~ to work without intermission; **als Verkäufer** ~ to clerk *(US)*; **mit Verlust** ~ to operate at a loss; **ohne Verlust** ~ to break even; **weniger** ~ to slack off; **wirtschaftlich** ~ to work economically; **halben Tag zusätzlich** ~ to work an extra half day; **zuverlässig** ~ to be thorough in one's work; **für zwei** ~ to do two men's work; **zu** ~ **aufhören** to pack up; **jem. zu** ~ **geben** to give s. o. a job; ~ **lassen** to employ; **Kapital** ~ **lassen** to put out money at interest; **Maschine** ~ **lassen** to operate a machine; **j. schwer** ~ **lassen** to keep s. one's nose to the grindstone.

arbeitend labo(u)ring, working, *(Betrieb)* going;
im Akkord ~ jobbing; **nicht** ~ *(Kapital)* idle;
~**e Bevölkerung** working classes; ~**es Kapital** employed (invested) capital.

Arbeiter worker, workman, working man, labo(u)rer, hand, employee, *(Arbeitspotential)* manpower, *(Handwerker)* artisan, *(an der Maschine)* operative, operator, attendant, *(pl.)* workpeople, workmen, workfolk, blue-collar people *(US)*;
angelernter ~ semi-skilled worker; **ausgebeuteter** ~ sweatee; **besonders ausgebildeter** ~ specialized worker; **unterdurchschnittlich ausgebildeter** ~ substandard worker; **ausgesperrter** ~ locked-out worker (workman); **bedächtiger** ~ slow worker; **im Stundenlohn beschäftigter (bezahlter)** ~ hourly worker; **bester** ~ first hand; **niedrig bezahlter** ~ low-salaried worker; **eingeborene** ~ native labo(u)r; **eingewanderter** ~ immigrant labo(u)rer; **erwachsener** ~ adult worker; **fähiger** ~ able worker; **farbige** ~ colo(u)red labo(u)r; **fleißiger** ~ steady (hard) worker; **flinker** ~ swift worker; **flotter** ~ quick (ready) worker; **fluktuierender (unsteter)** ~ turnover-prone employee; **geistiger** ~ brainworker, white-collar man (worker) *(US)*, black-coated worker *(Br.)*; **gelernter** ~ skilled worker; **geschickter** ~ facile worker, good workman; **gewerblicher** ~ industrial labo(u)rer; **gewerkschaftsfreier** ~ free rider; **gewinnbeteiligter** ~ profit-sharing employee; **gewissenhafter** ~ careful workman; **gründlicher** ~ thorough worker; **guter** ~ fine workman; **harter** ~ earnest worker; **durch eine Stechuhr kontrollierter** ~ clock puncher; **körperbehinderter** ~ handicapped worker; **landwirtschaftlicher** ~ farmhand, agricultural (farm) labo(u)rer; **männlicher** ~ male worker; **minderjähriger** ~ underage worker *(US)*; **gewerkschaftlich organisierte** ~ unionized labo(u)r, unionist workers, workmen organized into trade unions; **nicht [gewerkschaftlich] organisierter** ~ nonunion labo(u)rer, nonunionist; **qualifizierter** ~ qualified worker (operator); **schludriger** ~ slapdash worker; **streikender** ~ striking employee; **träger** ~ klupper *(US sl.)*; **überbezahlter** ~ overpaid workman; **überzähliger** ~ redundant worker; **unausgebildeter** ~ unskilled (substandard) worker; **unbeschäftigter** ~ idle (unemployed) workman; **unerfahrener** ~ threshold worker *(US)*; **ungelernter** ~ manual (unskilled, inexperienced) worker, common labo(u)rer, dilutee, plug *(sl.)*; **ungeschickter** ~ clumsy workman; **vollbeschäftigter** ~ full-timer; **zäher** ~ arduous worker; **zuverlässiger** ~ reliable worker;
~ **mit zwei Berufen** two-job worker; ~ **in einer Maschinenfabrik** engine worker; ~ **der Nachtschicht** night man; ~ **der Stirn** brainworker;
~ **anwerben** to engage (recruit, *US*) workers; ~ **ausbeuten** to sweat labo(u)r; **ungelernte** ~ **auskämmen** to decasualize; ~ **im Stücklohn bezahlen** to pay workman by the piece; ~ **einstellen** to take (sign) on hands, to recruit (hire) labor *(US)*; **ungelernte** ~ **einstellen** to dilute labo(u)r; **in der Woche hundert** ~ **einstellen** to sign on a hundred workmen a week; **zusätzlich zweihundert** ~ **einstellen** to take on 200 extra hands; ~ **entlassen** to discharge a workman, to lay off a worker; **seine** ~ **kurzfristig entlassen** to fire (sack) one's workmen; **in Zeiten wirtschaftlicher Depression** ~ **vorübergehend entlassen** to lay off workmen during a business depression; **sich ertragsmäßig beim** ~ **niederschlagen** to hit the worker's pocket; **unermüdlicher** ~ **sein** to be a demon for work; ~ **auf die Straße setzen** to put workers on the street; ~ **umsetzen** to reallocate workers; ~ **unterbringen** to place workers; ~ **zum Streik verleiten** to induce men to strike; ~ **wiedereinstellen** to reinstate a worker.

Arbeiter|abordnung workers' delegation; ~**anwerbung** recruitment of labor *(US)*; ~**aufstand** labo(u)r uprise; ~**ausbildung** worker training; ~**ausschuß** shop council, workers' committee; ~**aussperrung** lockout; ~**ausstand** [labo(u)r] strike, walkout *(US)*; ~**bank** labor bank *(US)*; ~**baracke** bunkhouse; ~**bedarf** manpower requirements; ~**bevölkerung** working (labo(u)ring) classes, working (manufacturing, working-class) population; ~**bewegung** labo(u)r movement; ~**bus** workers' bus; ~**dauerkarte** workmen's season ticket; ~**einsatz** labo(u)r employment, manpower management, *(Arbeitslenkung)* direction of labo(u)r; ~**fahrschein** workmen's ticket; ~**familie** working-class family; ~**feiertag** Labor Day *(US)*.

arbeiterfeindlich antilabo(u)r.

Arbeiter|fortbildungsprogramm workers' education program(me); ~**frage** labo(u)r question (problem); ~**freizeitklub** working-men's club *(Br.)*.

arbeiterfreundlich prolabo(u)r.

Arbeiter|führer labo(u)r leader, boss *(US)*; ~**fürsorge** industrial welfare [work]; ~**gegend** working-class district (area); ~**gewinnbeteiligung** profit-sharing by the workmen, industrial partnership; ~**gruppe** group of workmen; ~**haus** working-class house; ~**haushalt** workman's budget; ~**herrschaft** ergatocracy; ~**hilfsverein** friendly society *(Br.)*; ~**hochschule** labo(u)r college.

Arbeiterin female (woman) worker, female operative, workwoman, working woman, factory (work) girl.

Arbeiter|interessen vertreten to look after the interests of the workers; ~**karte** workmen's return ticket; ~**klasse** working (operative, labo(u)ring) class, Labo(u)r; **wohlhabende** ~**klasse** worker affluence; ~**klasse ausbeuten** to exploit the working class; ~**kolonie gründen** to colonize labo(u)rers; ~**kolonne** gang; ~**lebensversicherung** industrial insurance; ~**mangel** labo(u)r (manpower) shortage, labo(u)r scarcity; **unter** ~**mangel leiden** to be shorthanded; ~**mannschaft** crew of labo(u)rers; ~**mitbestimmung** employee participation.

Arbeiterorganisation labo(u)r organization;
internationale ~ International Labo(u)r Organization; **vom Arbeitgeber kontrollierte** ~ company union.

Arbeiter|partei Labour Party *(Br.)*; ~**rat** company (shop) council; ~- **und Soldatenrat** soviet; ~**regierung** Labour Government *(Br.)*; ~**rente** workers' surplus; ~**rentenversicherung für begrenzte Erwerbsunfähigkeit** permanent partial disability insurance *(US)*; ~**rückfahrkarte** workmen's return ticket.

Arbeiterschaft working people (classes), workers, labo(u)r force, Labo(u)r;
nicht organisierte ~ nonunion (free) labo(u)r.

Arbeiterschutz prevention of labo(u)r accidents;
~**gesetz** Factories Act *(Br.)*; ~**gesetzgebung** protective labo(u)r legislation *(US)*, factory legislation *(Br.)*, Factories (Factory) Acts *(Br.)*.

Arbeiter|siedlung, ~kolonie labo(u)r colony (settlement), workers' housing estate, *(einzelnes Haus)* homecraft *(Br.)*; ~**stand** working classes, Labo(u)r; ~**stimmen** working-class (labo(u)r) vote; ~**stimmen verlieren** to lose the labo(u)r vote; ~**stimmenunterstützung im ganzen Land** labo(u)r's national support; ~**streik** labo(u)r strike, stick *(Br.)*, walkout *(US)*; ~**stunde** working hour, manhour; ~**trupp** working force; ~**tum** working classes; ~**überschuß** surplus labo(u)r.

Arbeiterunfall industrial accident;
~**gesetz** Workmen's Compensation Act *(US)*; ~**verhütung** prevention of labo(u)r accidents; ~**versicherung** workmen's compensation *(US)* (employer's liability) insurance; **staatlicher** ~**versicherungsfonds** state workmen's compensation insurance fund *(US)*; ~**versicherungsgesetz** Workmen's Compensation Act *(US)*; ~**versicherungsprämie** compensation insurance premium *(US)*.

Arbeiteruniversität workers' campus.

Arbeiterunruhen labo(u)r unrest (trouble, disturbances);
unter ~ zu leiden haben to suffer from labo(u)r troubles.

Arbeiter|verein workmen's club; **Internationale** ~**vereinigung** International Working Men's Association; ~**versicherung** industrial insurance; ~**vertreter** labo(u)r representative (official); ~**vertretung** labo(u)r representation; ~**viertel** working-class district (quarter); ~**wochenkarte** workmen's return ticket; ~**wohlfahrt** workers' welfare organization; ~**wohnung** worker housing, workman's dwelling, working-class flat, cottage, tenement, *(mit landwirtschaftlichem Nebenerwerbsbetrieb)* homecroft *(Br.)*; ~**zeitung** labo(u)r paper; ~**zug** workmen's (workpeople's) train.

Arbeitgeber employer [of labo(u)r], master, job provider, hirer *(US)*, boss *(coll.)*, *(pl.)* management;
anspruchsvoller ~ exacting employer; **augenblicklicher** ~ current employer; **früherer** ~ ex- (previous) employer; **gemeinschaftlicher** ~ joint employer; **letzter** ~ most recent employer; **zeitweiliger** ~ temporary employer;
~ **und Arbeitnehmer** employers and employed, employer and his people, masters and men (servants);
seinen ~ auf Gehaltserhöhung ansprechen to ask one's employer for a rise *(Br.)* (raise, *US*); **es mit seinem ~ verscherzt haben** to be out of favo(u)r with one's employer; **seinem ~ kündigen** to give notice to one's employer (one's master warning); **seinen ~ auf jeden Fall zufriedenstellen wollen** to be zealous to please one's employer; **dem ~ zufallen** to accrue to the employer;
~**anteil** *(Arbeitslosenunterstützung)* Federal Unemployment Tax *(US)*, *(Sozialversicherung)* employer's national insurance contribution *(Br.)*, social security payroll tax *(US)*; ~-**Arbeitnehmerausschuß** labo(u)r-management committee; ~-**beisitzerliste** employers' panel; ~**beiträge zur Arbeiterrentenversicherung** social security payroll tax *(US)*, employer's national insurance contribution *(Br.)*; ~**bescheinigung** employer's certificate; **in ~betrieben** on the employers' premises; ~-**Arbeitnehmerbeziehungen** personnel relations; ~**erfinder** employee inventor; ~-**Arbeitnehmergremium der öffentlichen Hand** national joint council *(Br.)*; ~**gruppe** employer group; ~**hut** hard hat, homburg; **schwarze ~liste** unfair list *(US)*; ~**lizenz** shop right *(US)*; ~**organisation** organization of employers *(Br.)*; ~**schaft** employers, management; ~**verband** employers' association (organization), Federation of British Industries *(Br.)*, Federation of Employer's Organization, [etwa] National Union of Manufacturers; ~**vereinigung** mastership; ~-**Arbeitnehmerverhältnis** employee-employer relations; ~**vertreter** employers' representative.

Arbeitnehmer wage earner, working man, worker, employee, employed person, jobholder, employe *(US)*;
an der Pensionskasse nicht beteiligter ~ employee outside a pension scheme; **gewinnbeteiligter** ~ profit-sharing employee; **überflüssig gewordener** ~ redundant employee; **gewerkschaftlich organisierte** ~ organized labor *(US)*; **versicherungspflichtiger** ~ employee contributor;
Arbeitgeber und ~ capital (management) and labo(u)r, employers and employed, masters and men;
~ **zum Eintritt in die Gewerkschaft veranlassen** to unionize employees;
~**aktien** employee shares (stocks, *US*); ~**anteil** *(Sozialversicherung)* personal contribution to social insurance *(US)*; **vom Arbeitgeber bezahlter ~anteil** *(Sozialversicherung)* employee benefit paid by company; ~**anteil zur Krankenkasse** National Health Service employees' contribution *(Br.)*; ~**beisitzerliste** employees' panel; ~**beitrag** *(Arbeitslosenversicherung)* federal unemployment tax *(US)*; ~**beratung** job counselling; ~**eigentum** employee ownership; ~**einkünfte für zusätzliche Steuerzahlungen ausgleichen** to leave employees no worse off after tax; ~**einstellung** employee attitude; ~**erfinder** employee inventor; ~**erfindung** employee invention; **in ~hand sein** to be employee-owned.

Arbeitnehmerin working woman.

Arbeitnehmer|moral employee morale; ~**organisation** organization of workers *(Br.)*, employee organization, organized labo(u)r; ~**politik** industrial relations policy; ~**rechte** employee's rights; ~**schaft** employees; **tariflich festgelegte** ~**schutzbestimmungen** minimum terms order; **in Ausübung einer ~tätigkeit** engaged in employment; ~**verband** employees' association, federation of workers' organization, trade union *(Br.)*, National Federation of Employees *(Br.)*; ~**verhalten** employee attitude; ~-**Arbeitgeberverhältnis** labo(u)r [management] relations, industrial *(US)* (employee-employer) relations; ~**versicherung durch den Arbeitgeber** split dollar insurance *(US)*; ~**vertreter** shop steward, employees' representative, *(im Aufsichtsrat)* personnel (staff) representative.

Arbeits|abgänge labo(u)r separations; ~**abkommen** wage agreement, employment contract, *(Tarif)* collective bargaining agreement; ~**ablauf** flow of work, workflow, flow process; **normaler ~ablauf** usual course of employment; ~**ablaufbogen,** ~**ablaufdiagramm** flow-process chart; ~**ablaufkarte** route card; ~**ablaufstudie** flow-process study; ~**abneigung** disinclination to work; ~**abrechnungskarte** operation job card; ~**abteilung** *(mil.)* working party; **ungenehmigte ~abwesenheit** quit; **schleppende ~abwicklung** shuffle.

arbeitsam diligent, industrious, steady.

Arbeitsamt labo(u)r exchange *(Br.)*, unemployment office;
Internationales ~ International Labo(u)r Office; **Statistisches** ~ Bureau of Labor Statistics *(US)*;
sich beim ~ melden to report to the labour exchange *(Br.)* (unemployment office); **beim ~ geführt werden** to be registered at a labo(u)r office.

Arbeits|amtsnachweis labo(u)r office report; ~**analyse** work (operation) analysis; ~**andrang** pressure of work; ~**anfall** volume of work, work to be done, work requirements, demand of one's job; **immer noch zunehmenden ~anfall bewältigen** to cope with the growing amount of work; ~**anfang** commencement of work; ~**anforderung** labo(u)r (manpower) supply; ~**angebot** labo(u)r supply; ~**anhäufung** pressure of work; ~**anreiz** incentive to work; **fehlender ~anreiz** disincentive to work; ~**anstrengung** work effort; **gewaltige ~anstrengung unternehmen** to pull the labo(u)ring oar *(fam.)*; ~**antritt** taking up work, commencement of work; ~**anweisung** instruction card, briefing, *(Schema)* layout; **jem. ~anweisungen erteilen** to instruct s. o. how to do his work; ~**anzug** working clothes, overalls, jeans, *(Soldat)* fatigue dress (clothes), fatigue uniform; ~**atmosphäre** working climate; ~**auffassung** attitude to work; ~**aufgabe** job assignment; ~**aufnahme** commencement of work; ~**aufruf** work call; ~**aufteilung** labo(u)r division, distribution of labo(u)r, breaking up of work; ~**aufteilungsverfahren** labo(u)r-division process; ~**auftrag** work (job) order; ~**auftragskostenrechnung** job-order cost accounting; ~**auftragsnummer** job number.

Arbeitsaufwand effort, energy, *(Lohnkosten)* labo(u)r costs;
unmittelbarer ~ direct labo(u)r costs; **unnützer** ~ waste of labo(u)r;
~ **pro Produktionseinheit** unit labo(u)r costs.

Arbeitsausfall man-hours lost, loss of working hours;
~**entschädigung** fall-back pay.

Arbeitsausführung workmanship, operation;
für gute ~ bekannt sein to have a name for good workmanship.

Arbeits|ausrüstung working equipment; ~**ausschuß** study group (committee), working (executive, *US*) committee, working party; ~**ausstand** strike, walkout *(US)*; ~**ausweispapiere** working papers; ~**band** *(Terminal)* job tape; ~**bank** workbench; ~**basis** working basis; ~**beanspruchung** *(Maschine)* load; ~**bedarf** labo(u)r demand, manpower requirements; ~**bedingungen** working (job, employment) conditions, labo(u)r conditions

(standards, *US*), conditions of labo(u)r, working facilities, *(technisch)* operating conditions; **normale ~bedingungen standard conditions; sichere ~bedingungen gewährleisten** to provide a safe system of work; **seine ~bedürfnisse registrieren lassen** to list one's employment demands; **~beendigung** completion of work (service); **~befähigung für eine bestimmte Arbeit** labo(u)r grade.
arbeitsbefreit exempt from work.
Arbeits|befreiung release (exemption) from working; **~befriedigung** job joy (satisfaction) *(US)*.
Arbeitsbeginn commencement of work, *(Arbeiter)* starting time, time when work begins;
möglicher ~ date available;
~ und Arbeitsschluß starting and finishing time;
verschiedene Zeiten für den ~ festlegen to stagger one's employees' starting times; **~ registrieren (stempeln)** to clock in, to punch the clock *(US)*.
Arbeits|behinderung encroachment of jobs, rattening *(Br., sl.)*; **~belastung** workload; **~bereich** field of action (operation), sphere of activities; **~bereich einer Stabskraft** staff responsibility; **Angestellten in seinen neuen ~bereich einführen** to schedule an employee for organization; **~bericht** job (labo(u)r) report; **täglicher ~bericht** daily performance report; **~beschaffung** job (work) creation, creation of work, relief work.
Arbeitsbeschaffungs|aufwand, ~kosten public works expenditure; **~ausschuß** public works committee; **~behörde** Public Works Administration *(US)*; **~etat** procurement budget; **~maßnahme** job-creating measure; **~möglichkeit** job-creating power; **~politik** make-job policy; **~praktiken** *(Gewerkschaft)* make work; **~programm** relief (public works, employment, manpower, job-creation) program(me); **~projekt** relief (public works, manpower) project; **~stelle** job-creating agency.
Arbeits|bescheinigung certificate of employment *(US)*, employment certificate *(US)*, clearance card, *(nach Entlassung)* discharge paper, leaving certificate *(Br.)*, certificate from last employer; **~beschleunigung** pushing on of the work.
arbeitsbesessen sein to be a demon for work.
Arbeits|besprechung work session, committee meeting; **~besuch** working visit; **~beutel** workbag; **~bewertung** employment rating *(US)*, job evaluation (rating) *(US)*, evaluation of a job *(US)*, efficiency rating; **~bewertungsmethode, ~bewertungsverfahren nach dem Punktsystem** job evaluation (rating) system (plan) *(US)*; **~bewilligung** labo(u)r permit; **~bezeichnung** job identification; **völlig ruhiger ~bezirk** district free from labo(u)r troubles; **~blatt** work sheet, *(Lohnabrechnung)* time sheet *(US)*; **~boykott** labor boykott *(US)*; **~buch** workbook, time book (sheet, *US*); **~bühne** platform; **~charakteristiken** job characteristics; **~dauer** working time; **~definition** working definition; **~diagramm** diagram.
Arbeitsdienst *(mil.)* fatigue [duty], employment youth service *(Br.)*;
~pflicht labo(u)r (industrial) conscription; **~verpflichtung** recruiting labor *(US)*.
Arbeits|direktor labo(u)r-relations director, director of labo(u)r relations (affairs), worker director *(Br.)*; **~disziplin** shop discipline; **~durchlauf** flow; **~durchlaufdiagramm** flow diagram; **~effekt** labo(u)r effectivity; **~eifer** work urge, zeal.
arbeitseifrig full of zeal.
Arbeits|einheit unit of labo(u)r (work), erg; **~einkommen** earned (occupational) income *(Br.)*, emoluments of employment.
Arbeitseinsatz employment of labo(u)r, labo(u)r employment, placement, manpower management, *(Arbeitszuweisung)* labo(u)r allocation;
gleichmäßigen ~ im ganzen Jahr gewährleisten to spread work more evenly throughout the year; **zum ~ befohlen werden** to be liable to labo(u)r conscription;
~büro placement bureau; **~lenkung** direction of labo(u)r.
Arbeitseinstellung *(Arbeitsauffassung)* attitude to work, *(Anstellung)* employment, appointment, recruiting *(US)*, *(Betriebsschließung)* shutdown, *(Streik)* strike, cessation of work, turnout *(Br.)*, stoppage from work, labo(u)r stoppage, tie-up *(US)*, walkout *(US)*, layoff, play *(sl.)*;
vorübergehende ~ suspension of work;
~en in einer Streikphase hiring during a strike *(US)*; **~ auf unbestimmte Zeit** hiring at will *(US)*.
Arbeitseinstellungspraktiken, gewerkschaftliche featherbedding practices.
Arbeitseinteilung organization of labo(u)r;
~ nach Befähigungen job dilution *(US)*.
Arbeits|einweisung job instruction, escort; **~einzugsgebiet** labo(u)r market area; **~elemente** work (operation) elements.
Arbeitsentgelt wage[s], pay, remuneration;
~e *(Bilanz)* labo(u)r costs;
niedrigeres ~ lower rate of remuneration.
Arbeits|erfahrung work experience; **~erfahrung bekommen** to get the feel of work; **erste ~erfolge** first fruits; **~ergebnis** outcome of one's labo(u)r; **~erlaubnis** work permit, working papers, *(für Ausländer)* alien's labo(u)r permit *(Br.)*; **~erlaubnisschein** labo(u)r pass; **~ermüdung** fatigue.
arbeitsersparende Maßnahmen labo(u)r-saving devices, motion economy *(US)*.
Arbeits|ersparnis economy (saving) of labo(u)r, labo(u)r saving, motion economy *(US)*; **~ertrag** yield, output; **~essen** working dinner (lunch), business luncheon, luncheon meeting session; **~etat** working budget; **~exemplar** *(Buch)* working copy.
arbeitsextensiv having a low labo(u)r content.
arbeitsfähig employable, able-bodied, able to work (earn);
nur bedingt ~ nondescript; **vorübergehend nicht ~** temporarily incapacitated;
~es Alter working age; **~e Mehrheit** *(parl.)* majority required, working majority.
Arbeits|fähigkeit employability, ability to perform labo(u)r, ability to work, working capacity, capacity to work; **~faktoren** job factors; **~feld** sphere (field) of action, vineyard; **~fertigkeit** skill; **~folge** sequence of operations; **~folgenplan** routing sheet.
arbeitsfördernder Faktor employee motivation *(US)*.
Arbeitsfortschritt, entsprechend dem ~ bezahlen to pay as the work proceeds.
Arbeitsfortschritts|abrechnung, wöchentliche ~ weekly account of work done; **~bericht** progress report; **~bescheinigung** progress certificate; **~bild** *(Statistik)* Gantt progress chart.
Arbeitsfragen labo(u)r problems.
arbeits|freier Tag playday *(Br.)*; **~freien Tag nehmen** to take a day off.
Arbeitsfreude enjoyment of work, job joy (satisfaction) *(US)*.
arbeitsfreudig sein to have one's heart in one's work.
Arbeitsfrieden industrial (labo(u)r, job) peace;
~ stören to cause labo(u)r troubles.
Arbeitsfrühstück working breakfast.
Arbeitsgang process, turn, bout, period of work, cycle, operation;
üblicher ~ office (business) routine;
~ abschließen to finish off a piece of work; **in einem ~ erledigen** to finish a job in one standing.
Arbeits|gebiet province, sphere (area) of work, field of study (activity), line district, demesne, domain, department, *(Bank)* sphere of operations; **nicht in jds. ~gebiet fallen** to be outside s. one's field; **~gelände** work area; **~gelegenheit** opportunity for work, job opportunity; **~gemeinschaft** team, working pool, *(mehrerer Industriebetriebe)* joint venture [agreement], *(Rundfunkanstalten)* corporation, *(Schule, Universität)* study (working) group, seminar; **kommunale ~gemeinschaft** joint committee *(Br.)*; **~genehmigung** authorization to start work, *(Einzelner)* labo(u)r (work) permit; **~gerät** medium, tools, equipment; **~geräte** implements of trade; **~gericht** industrial tribunal *(Br.)*, labor court *(US)*; **~gerichtsbeschluß** labo(u)r court order; **~gerichtsverfahren** labor jurisdiction *(US)*; **~gerüst** scaffold; **~gesetzgebung** labo(u)r legislation; **~gesuch** application blank; **~grundlage** working basis; **~gruppe** working group (party, *Br.*), study group (commission), team, detail *(US)*, *(Druckerei)* companionship; **sorgfältig ausgewählte ~gruppe** hand-picked team; **~häufung** peak load; **~haus** penitentiary, workhouse *(US)*, industrial prison.
arbeitshemmend disincentive to work;
~er Faktor disincentive.
Arbeits|hingabe devotion to one's work; **~höchstzeit** maximum working hours; **~hub** power stroke; **~hygiene** industrial health; **~hypothese** working hypothesis; **~impuls** incentive to work; **~inhalt** job content; **~intensität** manpower requirements.
arbeitsintensiv labo(u)r-intensive;
~ sein to have a high labo(u)r content.
Arbeits|intensivierung ohne Lohnerhöhung stretch-out *(US)*; **~jahr** business year; **~jahre** working life; **~kamerad** fellow worker, workfellow, mate; **~kämpfe** industrial strife (action, disputes), labo(u)r (trade) disputes; **~kämpfe im Wege gemeinsamer Besprechungen beilegen** to settle trade disputes by joint consultation; **unlautere ~kampfmethoden** unfair industrial practices *(Br.)*, unfair labor practices *(US)*; **~kapazität** working capacity; **~kapital** working capital; **mit ~kapital ausstatten** *(Bergbau)* to habilitate *(US)*; **~karte** operation card, work ticket (map); **~karteikarte** job card; **~kasten** workbox; **~kittel, ~kleid** overall *(Br.)*, smock; **~kleidung** working (work) clothes,

overalls, *(grob)* dungaree; ~**klima** working climate; ~**knappheit** shortage of manpower, manpower shortage; ~**kollege** mate, workfellow, workmate, fellow worker (labo(u)rer, employee, servant, *US*); ~**kolonne** working party *(Br.)*, detail *(US)*, *(Druckerei)* companionship; **fliegende** ~**kolonne** flying squadron; ~**kommando** labo(u)r battalion, fatigue party, detail *(US)*; ~**konflikt** industrial conflict, labo(u)r dispute; ~**kontrolle** check on the operation *(US)*; ~**konzept** pattern of working; ~**kosten** cost of labour, labo(u)r (employment) costs; ~**kostenbelastung** labo(u)r charge; ~**kostenentwicklung** labo(u)r cost trend; ~**kostensteigerung** rise in labo(u)r costs.

Arbeitskraft working capacity (potential), *(Arbeiter)* worker, workman;
ausgeliehene ~ borrowed employee; **fallweise eingestellte** ~ extra; **freiberufliche** ~ professional worker; **männliche** ~ male worker; **menschliche** ~ manpower; **überschüssige** ~ redundant employee; **unentbehrliche** ~ key man; **weibliche** ~ female (woman) worker;
neu angeworbene ~ **anlernen** to process a recruit *(US)*; **seine** ~ **einbringen** *(in Firma)* to contribute one's services; **seine volle** ~ **einsetzen** to work to the full extent of one's power; **menschliche** ~ **durch Maschinen ersetzen** to displace (replace) human labo(u)r by machinery.

Arbeitskräfte workmen, labo(u)r [force], manpower, body of workers;
knapp an ~**n** short of hands (labo(u)r), shorthanded; **mangels** ~**n** owing to shortage of staff; **mit ungenügenden** ~**n versehen** underhanded;
angelernte ~ semi-skilled labo(u)r; **ausgebildete** ~ skilled manpower; **ausländische** ~ foreign labo(u)r; **nicht benötigte** ~ redundance of workers; **für den Rohbau benötigte** ~ infraconstruction workers; **am Streik nicht beteiligte** ~ strike-free labo(u)r; **bezahlte** ~ paid labo(u)r; **dienstverpflichtete** ~ drafted labo(u)r; **einheimische** ~ native labo(u)r; **im Ausland einsatzfähige** ~ exportable manpower; **familieneigene** ~ family-employed workers; **farbige** ~ colo(u)red labo(u)r; **fehlende** ~ manpower shortage; **freigesetzte** ~ workers released; **gelernte** ~ skilled labo(u)r; **geschulte** ~ qualified labo(u)r; **inländische** ~ domestic workers; **knappe** ~ shortage of labo(u)r, manpower shortage; **kostbare** ~ fringe executives; **landwirtschaftliche** ~ peasant labo(u)r, rural manpower; **gewerkschaftlich organisierte** ~ union (organized) labo(u)r; **gewerkschaftlich nicht organisierte** ~ unorganized labo(u)r; **hoch qualifizierte** ~ highly qualified workers; **höher qualifizierte** ~ better quality labo(u)r supply; **ständige** ~ permanent labo(u)r; **im öffentlichen Bereich tätige** ~ public-sector manpower; **nicht in der Landwirtschaft tätige** ~ nonagricultural working force; **überschüssige** ~ surplus manpower (labo(u)r); **am Streik unbeteiligte** ~ strike-free labo(u)r; **ungelernte** ~ untrained *(Br.)* (unskilled) labo(u)r; **unrentable** ~ marginal labo(u)r; **verfügbare** ~ supply of labo(u)r, labo(u)r supply, manpower available; **weibliche** ~ female labo(u)r; **weiße** ~ white labo(u)r; **zusätzliche** ~ additional employees; **zwangsverpflichtete** ~ conscript (indentured) labo(u)r;
~ **abbauen** to reduce the labo(u)r force; ~ **von einem Konkurrenzbetrieb abwerben** to raid rival organizations; ~ **abziehen** to call off workers; ~ **ausbeuten** to sweat labo(u)r; **seine** ~ **übermäßig ausnutzen** to drive one's workmen too hard; ~ **beaufsichtigen** to direct the workmen; ~ **einsetzen** to direct (deploy) labo(u)r; **ausländische** ~ **einsetzen** to immigrate foreign labo(u)r; ~ **einsparen** to save labo(u)r; ~ **einstellen** to enrol(l) workers, to hire labo(u)r *(US)*, to recruit manpower *(US)*; **unnötige** ~ **einstellen** to featherbed; **zusätzliche** ~ **einstellen** to take on extra workers; **effektiv nicht mehr benötigte** ~ **entlassen** to clean out the deadwood; **menschliche** ~ **ersetzen** to displace human labo(u)r by machinery; ~ **freisetzen** to release surplus labo(u)r; **überschüssige** ~ **freisetzen** to shed surplus labo(u)r; **ausländische** ~ **heranziehen** to import labo(u)r; ~ **aus einem anderen Bezirk heranziehen** to import labo(u)r from another district; ~ **in Anspruch nehmen** to make a call on manpower; ~ **sparen** to save labo(u)r; ~ **umdisponieren (umgruppieren)** to redeploy the labo(u)r force; ~ **umsetzen** to transfer employees, to dislocate workers; ~ **zum Berufswechsel verführen** to lure labo(u)r into other jobs; ~ **direkt von der Universität wegengagieren** to recruit labor on campus *(US)*; ~ **zuweisen** to allocate labo(u)r (manpower);
~**abbau** cutback on manpower, laying off of workers, job cutback; ~**abwerbung** labo(u)r piracy *(US)*; ~**analyse** worker analysis; ~**angebot** labo(u)r supply; ~**anwerber** industry recruiter *(US)*; ~**anwerbung** recruitment of labo(u)r; ~**bedarf** demand for labo(u)r, manpower need, direct labo(u)r budget, manpower (labo(u)r) requirements, labo(u)r demand; ~**bedarfsansatz** manpower [forecasting] approach; ~**beschaffungsstelle** recruiting firm *(US)*; ~**einsatz** employment of labo(u)r, manpower planning; ~**einsatz lediglich im Zuliefererverhältnis** labo(u)r-only subcontracting; ~**ersatz** labo(u)r displacement; ~**ersparnis** labo(u)r saver (saving); ~**front** manpower front; ~**mangel** shortage (scarcity) of labo(u)r, manpower (labo(u)r) shortage; ~**material** human resources; ~**mobilität** spatial mobility of labo(u)r; **berufsbedingte** ~**mobilität** occupational mobility of workers; ~**potential** human resources, working potential, potential labo(u)r force; ~**reserve**, ~**reservoir** reserve of labo(u)r, manpower reserve, potential labo(u)r force, recruitment sources *(US)*, total possible labo(u)r force; ~**rückgang** worker decline; ~**überbesatz** overstaffing, overmanning; ~**überschuß** excess labo(u)r supply, redundant labo(u)r; ~**verteilung** diversion of manpower, allocation of labo(u)r (manpower); ~**vorschau** labo(u)r outlook.

Arbeits|kreis study group (committee); ~**lage** employment picture; **angespannte** ~**lage** labo(u)r-tight economy; ~**lager** labo(u)r (work) camp; ~**laufzettel** job ticket.

Arbeitsleistung labo(u)r efficiency, labo(u)r (work) performance, service rendered, *(Fabrik)* output, *(Fähigkeit)* working capacity, *(Maschine)* load, payload, power, *(Produktivität)* productivity, productiveness, *(aufgewandte Zeit)* man hours; **hervorragende** ~ excellent piece of work; **zusätzliche** ~**en** additional work;
~ **pro Arbeitsstunde** output per work hour.

Arbeitslenkung manpower control, planned (direction of) labo(u)r.

Arbeitslohn pay, wage[s], earnings, hire, labo(u)rage, *(Rechnungsposten)* labo(u)r costs;
~ **kürzen** to dock a workman's wages.

Arbeitslöhne wages, labo(u)r costs, labo(u)rage;
Material und ~ materials and labo(u)r.

arbeitslos unemployed, nonemployed, workless, out of employ (work, job), [thrown] out of employment, jobless;
geld- und ~ down and out;
~ **machen** to toss (throw) out of a job; ~ **sein** to be out of work (a job), to be in dry dock *(fam.)*, to be unemployed (off the payroll, thrown out of employment); **ganzes Jahr** ~ **gewesen sein** to have been out of work for a whole year; ~ **werden** to fall (be thrown) out of work, to be thrown out of employment;
~**e Jugendliche** young unemployed persons.

Arbeitslosen|anstieg increase in unemployment; ~**armee** jobless army, army of the jobless; ~**entwicklung positiv (negativ) beurteilen** to be bullish (bearish) about unemployment; ~**forderung** jobless claims; ~**fürsorge** unemployment relief, unemployment assistance *(Br.)*, work relief; **in die** ~**fürsorge einbeziehen** to cover in the unemployment relief; ~**geld** unemployment relief, dole *(Br.)*; **gehaltsabhängiges (lohnabhängiges)** ~**geld** earnings-related unemployment benefit *(Br)*; **nicht von nachgewiesener Mittellosigkeit abhängiges** ~**geld** non-means-tested unemployment assistance *(Br.)*; ~**gesamtzahl** jobless total; ~**gesetz** Unemployment Workmen's Act *(Br.)*, Unemployment Compensation Law *(US)*; **über ein strukturell bedingtes** ~**heer von etwa 1/2 Million verfügen** to have a structural basis of about half a million unemployed; ~**hilfe** unemployment assistance *(Br.)*, redundancy fund contribution *(Br.)*; **ins Ermessen gestellte** ~**hilfe** uncovenanted benefit *(Br.)*; **lohnabhängige** ~**hilfe** earnings-related unemployment benefit *(Br.)*; ~**hilfe für ausgesteuerte Arbeitslose** extended unemployment benefit *(Br.)*; **keinen Anspruch auf** ~**hilfe haben** to be disqualified from receiving unemployment benefit *(Br.)*; ~**höchstziffer** unemployment peak; ~**kartei** jobless (unemployment) roll; ~**problem** unemployment problem; ~**prozentsatz** unemployment (jobless) rate, unemployment ratio, rate of unemployment, jobless percentage (rate); **saisonbereinigter** ~**prozentsatz** seasonally adjusted unemployment rate; **saisonal nicht bereinigter** ~**prozentsatz** crude unemployment rate; ~**quote** rate of unemployment, unemployment rate, unemployment ratio; ~**restsatz** hard core; ~**rückgang** drop in unemployment; ~**schätzungen** unemployment estimates; ~**schlange** unemployment line, job (dole, *Br.*) queue; ~**schub** unemployment projection; ~**spitze** peak of unemployment; ~**statistik** unemployment statistics; ~**unruhen** unemployment disturbances.

Arbeitslosenunterstützung unemployment benefit *(Br.)* (pay, compensation, *US*), work relief, dole *(Br.)*, out benefit (pay), out-of-work relief;
auf Beitragszahlungen beruhende ~ covenanted benefit; **ins Ermessen gestellte weitere** ~ extended benefit *(Br.)*; **vom Betrieb gezahlte** ~ plant unemployment benefit;

höchste ~ full rate of unemployment benefit; **staatliche** ~ state unemployment benefit; **zusätzliche** ~ supplementary unemployment insurance;
~ **beanspruchen** to register for unemployment benefits; ~ **beziehen** to be on unemployment rolls, to draw unemployment benefit *(Br.)*, to receive unemployment compensation *(US)*, to be on (draw) the dole *(Br.)*; **Voraussetzungen für die** ~ **erfüllen** to qualify for unemployment insurance; **seine** ~ **kassieren** to collect one's dole *(Br.)*; **zur** ~ **berechtigt sein** to qualify for unemployment insurance, to be entitled to the dole *(Br.)*.
Arbeitslosenunterstützungs | anspruch unemployment claim; ~**beiträge** unemployment contributions; ~**empfänger** recipient of unemployment relief, dole drawer *(Br.)*; ~**fonds** unemployment [reserve] fund; ~**gesetz** Unemployment Compensation Law *(US)*, Unemployed Workmen Act *(Br.)*; ~**programm** unemployment compensation program(me); ~**wesen** unemployment benefit scheme.
Arbeitslosenversicherung unemployment insurance.
Arbeitslosenversicherungs | beitrag unemployment insurance contribution, *(des Arbeitgebers)* federal unemployment tax *(US)*; ~**fonds** unemployment [reserve] fund; ~**gesetz** Unemployment Insurance Act *(Br.)*.
Arbeitslosen | zahl unemployment figures; **abnehmende** ~**zahlen** decline in unemployment; ~**zahl anschwellen lassen** to swell the unemployment register; ~**zählung** census of unemployment; ~**ziffer** number of unemployed, unemployment (jobless) rate; ~**zunahme** unemployment growth; ~**zuschußfonds** unemployment subsidy fund.
Arbeitsloser unemployed person, vag *(sl.)*;
akademischer ~ university-trained unemployed person; **ausgesteuerter** ~ unemployed person on relief; **gemeldeter** ~ registered unemployed person.
Arbeitslosigkeit unemployment, joblessness;
von ~ **betroffen (heimgesucht)** unemployment-ridden (-bedevilled); **unter der** ~ **leidend** unemployment-burdened;
anhaltende ~ prolonged (sustained) unemployment; **entwicklungsmäßig (technisch) bedingte** ~ technological unemployment; **örtlich bedingte** ~ local unemployment; **dauernde** ~ chronic unemployment; **erhöhte** ~ rise in unemployment; **fluktuierende** ~ frictional unemployment; **konjunkturbedingte (konjukturell bedingte)** ~ cyclical unemployment; **langfristige** ~ long-run (-term) unemployment; **partielle** ~ partial unemployment; **rezessionsbedingte** ~ recession unemployment; **rückläufige** ~ decline in unemployment; **saisonbedingte** ~ seasonal unemployment; **sektionale** ~ local unemployment; **nicht sichtbare** ~ hidden unemployment; **strukturbedingte (strukturelle)** ~ structural unemployment; **temporäre** ~ frictional unemployment; **unfreiwillige** ~ forced unemployment; **versteckte** ~ concealed unemployment; **vorsätzliche** ~ voluntary unemployment; **vorübergehende** ~ intermittent unemployment; **zeitbedingte** ~ secular unemployment; **zunehmende** ~ unemployment advance (trend);
~ **unter den Erwachsenen** adult unemployment;
~ **beseitigen (beheben)** to alleviate unemployment; ~ **durch weitere Staatsverschuldung beseitigen** to spend one's way out of unemployment; **alle Mittel zur Verringerung der** ~ **einsetzen** to focus on reducing unemployment; **der** ~ **mit Exportsteigerungen zu Leibe rücken** to mop up unemployment by means of export growth; ~ **vergrößern** to add to unemployment.
Arbeitslosigkeits | bescheinigung unemployment certificate; ~**kurve** unemployment curve; **hohe** ~**ziffer als gegeben hinnehmen** to live with high unemployment rates.
Arbeitslust enthusiasm for work, work urge, job joy *(US)*.
arbeitslustig sein to be in the mood to work.
Arbeitsmarkt labo(u)r (wage, employment, manpower) market, job market;
gut besetzter ~ free labo(u)r market; **leerer** ~ tight labo(u)r market;
~ **leer pumpen** to raid the labo(u)r market;
~**anspannung** pressure on the labo(u)r market; ~**ausgleich** labo(u)r market clearing; ~**belebung** reemployment; ~**lage** situation of the labo(u)r market, labo(u)r [market] situation, job situation; **angespannte** ~**lage** strained situation on the labo(u)r market, labo(u)r-tight economy; **stabile** ~**lage** employment stability; ~**politik** employment policy, labo(u)r-market policy.
arbeitsmarktpolitische Maßnahmen labo(u)r-market policy measures.
arbeitsmäßig | einsetzen to employ manpower; ~ **nicht verplant sein** to be leisured; **über das ganze Unternehmen** ~ **verteilen** to redistribute workers throughout the company.
Arbeits | material labo(u)r material, stock in trade; ~**menge** amount of work.
Arbeitsmethode method of work (operation), working system, operational method, work habit;
untaugliche ~**n** restrictive practices *(Br.)*;
sich für eine ~ **entscheiden** to decide upon a method of working.
Arbeits | minister Minister of Labo(u)r, Minister of Employment *(Br.)*, Secretary of State for Employment, Secretary of Labor *(US)*; ~**ministerium** Ministry of Labo(u)r *(Br.)*, Department of Employment *(Br.)*, Employment Department *(Br.)*, Labo(u)r Department *(US)*, Department of Labor *(US)*; ~**mittel** instruments of labo(u)r; ~**modell** working model; ~**möglichkeit** job opportunity, employment possibility; **angebotene** ~**möglichkeiten ablehnen** to turn down jobs on offer; ~**moral** morale at work, employee morale; ~**moral heben** to boost the morale.
Arbeitsnachweis *(Bescheinigung)* certificate of employment, *(Behörde)* employment agency (bureau, exchange, *Br.*);
staatlicher ~ employment (labo(u)r) exchange *(Br.)*; **täglicher** ~ daily performance record;
~**stelle** labo(u)r (employment) exchange *(Br.)*.
Arbeits | niederlegung cessation of work, work stoppage, *(Streik)* downing tools *(Br.)*, down-tools strike *(Br.)*, walkout *(US)*; **fristlose** ~**niederlegung** summary departure; ~**normen** work norms; **gerechte** ~**normen** fair labo(u)r standards; ~**ökonomie** labo(u)r economics; ~**ordnung** labo(u)r scheme, shop rules, work's rule-book; ~**ort** place of work; ~**papiere** employment (working) papers, employment records *(US)*; **von unbedeutenden Mitarbeitern erstelltes** ~**papier** low-level working paper; **sich die** ~**papiere geben lassen** to ask for one's cards; ~**partie** job lot *(US)*; ~**paß** labo(u)r permit.
Arbeitspause rest pause (period), break, recess *(US)*;
ohne ~ **arbeiten** to work without intermission; **sich eine halbstündige** ~ **genehmigen** to enjoy a break from work for half an hour; **sich eine** ~ **gönnen** to take a rest [from work], to take off.
Arbeitspensum task, load;
bestimmtes ~ stint *(Br.)*;
sein ~ **schaffen** to peg one's production.
Arbeits | periode shift, action cycle, swing *(coll.)*, *(Maschine)* run; ~**pferd** *(fig.)* work horse, work beast, slogger, fag *(Br.)*; **reinstes** ~**pferd sein** to work like a horse; ~**pflicht** industrial conscription; ~**pflichten** duties of a job.
arbeitspflichtig liable to work.
Arbeitsphasen, verwandte associated operations.
Arbeitsplan [working] program(me), [working] scheme, work schedule, *(Fabrikation)* production plan, *(Konstruktion)* functional diagram, *(Werkzeugmaschine)* tooling layout;
maschineller ~ operations plan, operating chart;
~ **für die Errichtung eines Gebäudes** schedule for the construction of a building;
~ **aufstellen** to draw up a program(me).
Arbeitsplanung im Rahmen der Fertigungsplanung manufacturing analysis.
Arbeitsplatz workplace, yard *(US)*, *(Stellung)* job [opening], situation, place of employment (to work), *(Bergbau)* stall;
am ~ on the floor;
angesehener ~ prestige job; **außerlandwirtschaftlicher** ~ job outside agriculture; **gefährlicher** ~ hazardous situation; **sicherer** ~ safe place to work; **unbesetzter** ~ job vacancy;
~ **in der Fabrik** plant job; ~ **zu Hause** home office;
seinen ~ **aufgeben** to resign voluntarily; **j. um seinen** ~ **bringen** to jockey s. o. out of his job; ~ **ergattern** to land a job; **am** ~ **erscheinen** to get on the job; **pünktlich am** ~ **erscheinen** to turn up early for work; **seinen** ~ **aufgrund ökonomischer Entwicklungen verloren haben** to have been made redundant by economic factors; ~ **ausfindig machen** to scent a job; ~ **für j. schaffen** to create a job for s. o.; **nicht am** ~ **sein** to be off work; **am** ~ **umschulen** to re-educate on the job; **seinen** ~ **verlassen** to throw up one's job; **seinen** ~ **wechseln** to change one's employment, *(häufiger)* to job-hop; **in unmittelbarer Nähe seines** ~**es wohnen** to live within distance of one's work;
~**ablösung** job rotation *(US)*; ~**analyse** ergonomics; ~**ausschreibung** contract for public works, bidding; **mit nur geringen** ~**aussichten** with little prospect of finding a job; ~**ausweitung** job enlargement; ~**beschaffung** creation of new jobs; ~**beschaffungsplan für Schulabgänger** school-leaver job-creation scheme; ~**beschreibung** job specification *(US)*; ~**bewertung** job evaluation *(US)*, job rating *(US)*.
Arbeitsplätze | bewirkend employment-creating;
gefährdete ~ jobs threatened; **offene** ~ jobs available; **höher qualifizierte** ~ higher-grade jobs;

~ **in der Flugzeugindustrie** aircraft-industry jobs; ~ **in der Privatwirtschaft** private-sector jobs;
sich empfindlich auf ~ auswirken to be job-sensitive; ~ **örtlich bereitstellen** to provide local employment; ~ **freimachen** to free jobs; **neue ~ schaffen** to create additional employment (new jobs); **nützliche ~ schaffen** to give work helpful to the community; ~ **tauschen** to trade jobs.

Arbeitsplatz|einweisung job orientation; ~**geber** job provider; ~**gesetz** Shops and Offices Act *(Br.)*; ~**gestaltung** job (workplace) layout, human engineering *(US)*; **regionale ~prämie** regional employment premium *(Br.)*; ~**sicherung** job security, occupational safety; ~**untersuchung** job analysis; ~**verknappung** job shortage; ~**verlust** loss of job, job loss; ~**vernichtung** displacement of human labo(u)r by machinery; ~**wechsel** change of employer (job), labo(u)r flux (turnover), job changes, *(innerhalb eines Betriebs)* job rotation *(US)*; **häufiger ~wechsel** job-hopping; ~**wechselformel** labo(u)r-flux formula; ~**zuweisung** placement.

Arbeits|podest working platform; ~**politik** employment policies; ~**potential** potential labo(u)r force; ~**prämie** work incentive; ~**prämienprogramm** work incentive program(me); ~**produktivität** productivity of labo(u)r, labo(u)r (worker) productivity; ~**programm** program(me) of work, work[ing] program(me).

Arbeitsprozeß operation, procedure, [working] process, *(Rechtsstreit)* labo(u)r case;
entscheidender ~ policy-making procedure;
in den ~ wieder eingliedern to rehabilitate; **neue Kräfte in den ~ eingliedern** to absorb new workers in the labo(u)r force.

Arbeits|psychologie industrial psychology; ~**qualität** workmanship, quality of work; ~**raum** workroom, workplace, *(Büro)* office, bureau, *(Schule)* study; ~**räume** work [working] premises; ~**recht** labor law *(US)*, industrial law *(Br.)*, law of master and servant *(Br.)*.

arbeits|rechtliche Auseinandersetzung labo(u)r (trade) dispute; ~**reiche Woche** busy week.

Arbeits|reserve labo(u)r pool (reserve), working potential, potential labo(u)r force; ~**richtlinien** rules of work, work rules; ~**richtlinienvereinbarung** work-rules settlement.

Arbeitsrückstände work in arrear, arrears of work;
~ **haben** to fall behind with one's work; **erhebliche ~ haben** to have a good deal of work outstanding.

Arbeits|ruhe recreation, rest pause (period); **sonntägliche ~ruhe** Sunday closing; ~**saal** workroom; ~**schema** layout, working regulations; ~**scheu** aversion to labo(u)r, idleness, dodging.

arbeitsscheu workshy, averse to (afraid of [hard]) labo(u)r, idle, dodging *(Br.)*;
~ **sein** to shirk one's share of work.

Arbeitsscheue|r work dodger *(Br.)*, shirker;
sich für ~ nachteilig auswirken to be penal for the workshy.

Arbeitsschicht [work] shift, turn;
nicht durchgehende ~ split shift; **gleichbleibende ~** fixed shift; **unterbrochene ~** split shift; **zusätzliche ~** relief shift *(US)*.

Arbeits|schiedsgericht industrial arbitration; **ständig tagendes ~schiedsgericht** joint industrial council *(Br.)*; ~**schiene** *(el., Bahn)* third rail; ~**schluß** stopping (finishing) time, leaving-off time, time when work ends, quitting time *(US)*; ~**schluß registrieren (stempeln)** to clock out, to sign off; ~**schlußklausel** quitting clause *(US)*; ~**schutz** safe system of work; ~**schutzgesetz** Employment Protection Act *(Br.)*, Factory Act *(Br.)*; **nicht den ~schutzgesetzen unterliegen** to fall outside the protection of the statutory and common-law rules relating to safety; ~**sicherheit** industrial safety; ~**sitzung** committee meeting, work session; ~**soziologie** sociology of work.

arbeitssparend labo(u)r-saving;
~**e Einrichtungen** labo(u)r-saving devices (appliances).

Arbeits|speicher *(Datenverarbeitung)* working storage; ~**spitze** *(el.)* peak load; **offizielle ~sprache** working language.

Arbeitsstab setup, study group, task force *(US)*, planning staff, team;
hochdotierter ~ blue-ribbon task force *(US)*; **bei der Universität tätiger ~** university workforce;
~ **für Öffentlichkeitsarbeit** public-relations setup.

Arbeits|statistik labo(u)r statistics; ~**stätte** workplace, workshop, business; ~**stelle** place of work, workplace; **nicht unbedingt notwendige ~stelle** nonessential business; ~**stimmung** working climate; ~**stock** unemployment fund; ~**streckung** work spreading, spreading of work, employment spread; ~**streckungsverfahren** spreadwork system; ~**streitigkeit** labo(u)r (trade, industrial) dispute, labor conflict *(US)*, ~**streitigkeiten** grievances of the workers *(US)*; ~**strom** operating current; ~**stromkreis** *(el.)* operating circuit.

Arbeitsstück workpiece, piece [of work], job;
~ **ausfeilen** to go over a piece of work;
~**liste** work program(me).

Arbeits|studie motion study, job analysis *(US)*; ~**stufe** stage, process, operation.

Arbeitsstunde man-hour, workhour;
effektive ~n actual hours of work; **festgelegte ~n** scheduled hours of work; **geleistete ~n** man-hours worked; **tatsächlich geleistete ~n** total actual hours worked; **verlorene ~n** man-hours lost; **gewerkschaftlich vorgeschriebene ~n** union hours; **die Herstellungskosten in ~n berechnen** to calculate the cost of production in man-hours.

Arbeits|stundenanpassung spreadover; ~**stundenbuch** time book, workbook; ~**stundenverkürzung** shortening of one's working hours; **auf ~suche gehen, auf ~suche sein** to apply for a job, to look for work (job), to hump; ~**suchender** employment applicant, job seeker *(US)*; ~**system** working system.

Arbeitstag office (lawful, working) day, day's work, workday *(US)*;
halber ~ half holiday; **verlorene ~e** man-days lost.

arbeitstäglich per working day.

Arbeits|tagung business meeting; ~**takt** *(Maschine)* operation cycle.

Arbeitstätigkeit job, labo(u)r;
gelegentlich am Wochenende erforderliche ~ occasional weekend shift; **frühere ~en** employment history;
~ **im Rahmen öffentlich erteilter Aufträge** public works job; **psychologische Schwierigkeiten auf seine ~ zurückführen** to blame one's job for one's psychological ills.

Arbeits|technik industrial engineering; **seinen ~teil bewältigen** to do one's proportion of work; ~**teilung** division (differentiation) of labo(u)r (employment); **sein ~tempo verlangsamen** to slacken up one's work-pace; ~**therapie** occupational therapy; ~**tier** plodder, wheel horse, plugger, toiler, grub, bustler *(coll.)*, hustler *(coll.)*, fag *(Br.)*; ~**tisch** worktable, desk, writing table, bench; ~**titel** *(Buch)* tentative title; ~**trupp** working party, detail *(US)*; ~**turnus** turn, rotation; ~**überlastung** excess of work; ~**umwelt** working environment.

arbeitsunfähig unemployable, disabled, incapable of work, incapacitated, ineffective, unable (unfit) to work;
dauernd ~ invalid, permanently unemployable; **teilweise ~** nondescript; **vorübergehend ~** incapable of working, temporarily incapacitated;
~ **machen** to crock up; **j. mehrere Monate ~ machen** to invalid s. o. for several months; ~ **werden** to become disabled; **dauernd ~ werden** to become permanently incapacitated; ~ **geschrieben werden** to be returned unfit for work.

Arbeitsunfähigkeit unemployability, incapacity (incapability) to (unfitness for) work, physical disability, incapacitation for work, disablement, disability for service, inefficiency of labo(u)r;
dauernde ~ permanent disability (invalidity); **teilweise ~** partial disability; **vorübergehende (zeitweilige) ~** temporary disablement;
Unternehmen praktisch zur ~ verurteilen to produce a state of deadlock in a firm.

Arbeitsunfähigkeits|bescheinigung certificate of disability; ~**grad** degree of disability; ~**rente** invalidity (industrial injury) benefit.

Arbeitsunfall industrial injury, on-the-job (industrial) accident, accident at work, injury contracted in the course of employment;
~ **erleiden** to sustain an industrial injury;
~**entschädigung** worker's compensation; ~**verletzung** occupational (industrial) injury; ~**versicherung** disability insurance, workmen's compensation insurance *(US)*.

Arbeitsunlust disinclination to work, job boredom, worker dissatisfaction, marginal disutility of labor *(US)*.

arbeitsunlustig not in the humo(u)r for work.

Arbeitsunlustiger shirker, quitter *(US)*.

arbeitsuntauglich unemployable, incapable of work, disabled.

Arbeitsunterbrechung suspension of employment, interruption in working hours, stoppage of work, work stoppage, *(Betriebsstillegung)* shutdown;
unvermeidbare ~ *(Verfahren)* inherent delay; **vorübergehende ~** temporary cessation of work;
~ **infolge vorübergehender Entlassung** layoff.

Arbeits|unterlagen working papers (sheet); ~- **und Diskussionsunterlagen** green paper *(Br.)*; ~**unterweisung** job instruction; ~**verdienst** wage [earnings], pay; ~**vereinbarungen** labo(u)r arrangements; ~**vereinfachung** work (job) simplification;

~**verfahren** manner of working, working (operating) process, working method, *(Produktionsverfahren)* production method; ~**vergleichsskala** job-comparison scale; ~**vergütung** remuneration, pay.
Arbeitsverhältnis employment, job, situation, place, working relationship;
~**se** working (labo(u)r) conditions;
gemeinsames ~ common service; **gutes** ~ good working relationship; **privates** ~ private employment;
aus dem ~ **erwachsen** to arise out of the employment conditions; **Fortsetzung des** ~**ses nicht zumutbar erscheinen lassen** to prevent further satisfactory continuance of the relationship; **im Zusammenhang mit dem** ~ **stehen** *(Einkommen)* to go with the job.
Arbeitsverlangsamung work restriction, slowing down on the job, slowdown, soldiering, *(Dienst nach Vorschrift)* go-slow [strike] *(Br.)*, slowdown strike *(US)*;
durch ~ **streiken** to strike on the job, to go slow *(Br.)*.
Arbeits|verlust man-hours lost; ~**vermittler** employment agent.
Arbeitsvermittlung procurement of work, *(Behörde)* employment agency (bureau);
staatliche ~ employment exchange *(Br.)*.
Arbeitsvermittlungs|büro employment agency (bureau, exchange, *Br.*); ~**dienst** United States Employment Service; ~**nachweis**, ~**stelle** employment exchange (agency), recruiting agent *(US)*; ~**zentrale** job center *(US)* (centre, *Br.*).
arbeitsverpflichtet werden to be liable to labo(u)r (industrial) conscription.
Arbeits|verpflichtung industrial conscription; ~**versäumnis** absenteeism; ~**verschleppung** go-slow tactics; ~**verteilung** division of labo(u)r (employment), assignment of activities.
Arbeitsvertrag employment contract, contract of employment;
einheitlicher ~ master contract; **Gewerkschaftszugehörigkeit voraussetzender** ~ close-shop contract *(US)*;
~ **ein Jahr zuvor abschließen** to sign up a year in advance.
Arbeits|verweigerung refusal to work, standout, *(Sitzstreik)* sitdown (stay-in) strike; **absichtliche** ~**verzögerung** ca'canny, goslow *(Br.)*; ~**vitalität** working vitality; ~**volumen** volume of work; ~**vorbereiter** planning engineer; ~**vorbereitung** scheduling; ~**vorgang** operation, working process; **zeitlich nicht beeinflußbare** ~**vorgänge** restricted elements; ~**vorrat** stock of labo(u)r; ~**vorrechte** work privileges; **auf dem** ~**wege** *(Versicherungsrecht)* on the way to business.
Arbeitsweise method of operation, manner of working, operative characteristics, *(Maschine)* function[ing];
selbständige ~ autonomous course of study; **nicht standesgemäße** ~ unprofessional work;
~ **des Verstandes** wheels of thought.
arbeitswillig willing (ready) to work.
Arbeits|wissenschaft labo(u)r economics; ~**woche** work week; ~**wut** passion for work.
arbeitswütig sein to be a demon for work;
~**er Mensch** glutton for work.
Arbeitszeit working hours (period, time), job time, hours of employment, spell, *(Betrieb)* operating time, *(Maschine)* machining time, run, *(Produktion)* period of production, *(für einzelnes Stück)* time spent on a job;
in der ~ in the course of one's employment; **während der** ~ during working hours;
benötigte ~ length of time needed for a job; **durchgehende** ~ continuous operations; **effektive** ~ actual hours of work; **festgesetzte** ~ scheduled hours of work; **garantierte** ~ guaranteed employment; **unmittelbar geleistete** ~ direct labo(u)r; **gleitende** ~ staggering of hours, flexible working hours, flextime *(Br.)*; **lange** ~ long hours; **nachgeholte** ~ make-up work; **normale (regelmäßige)** ~ straight time; **reine** ~ hours actually worked; **tägliche** ~ working day; **tarifliche** ~ collectively agreed working hours; **verkürzte** ~ part-time employment, short (part) time; **vertragliche (vertraglich vereinbarte)** ~ contractual (contract) hours of work; **volle** ~ full time; **nach dem Tarif vorgesehene** ~ nominal hours;
~ **mit Überstunden** overtime;
~ **registrieren** to keep time, to clock; ~ **verkürzen** to shorten one's working time, to reduce hours;
~**abkommen** hours convention *(US)*; ~**beschränkung** limitation of hours; ~**ermittlung** work measurement; ~**ersparnis** useful saving of time; ~**gesetz** wage-hour law *(US)*; ~**kontrolle** timekeeping; ~**kontrolleur** timekeeper, timetaker, check clerk *(US)*; ~**ordnung** working-time regulations; **bewegliches** ~**programm** flexible schedule; ~**vereinbarung über gleitende** ~ flexible working agreement; ~**verkürzung** shortening of one's working hours (time), short time, reduction of working hours *(US)*; ~**verlängerung** lengthening of working hours; ~ **verlust** broken time.
Arbeits|zettel time *(US)* (work) sheet; ~**zeug** tools, gear, equipment; ~**zeugnis** leaving certificate, certificate of employment, employment certificate (character, testimonial); ~**zimmer** study [hall], sanctum, workroom, closet *(Br.)*, den *(fam.)*, *(Künstler)* studio, atelier; **sich in seinem** ~**zimmer vergraben** to immure o. s. in one's study; ~**zuordnung** assignment of activities; ~**zuteilung**, ~**zuweisung**, labo(u)r allocation, allocation of labo(u)r; ~**zwang** compulsory labo(u)r; ~**zwangsverpflichtung** industrial conscription, recruitment of labor *(US)*; ~**zyklus** operation cycle.
Arbitrage arbitrage, arbitration;
direkte ~ direct arbitration (arbitrage); **indirekte** ~ indirect (triangular, *US*) arbitrage;
~ **in drei verschiedenen Währungen** indirect (triangular, *US*) arbitrage; ~ **über mehrere Zwischenplätze** compound arbitrage;
~ **treiben** to arbitrate, to straddle.
arbitragefähig admitted to arbitrage dealings.
Arbitrage|geschäft arbitrage dealings (transactions), back spread; ~**händler** arbitrage dealer, arbitrager, arbitragist; ~**klausel** arbitration clause; ~**rechnung** arbitration of exchange; ~**syndikat** arbitrage syndicate; **ermittelter** ~**umrechnungskurs** arbitrated rate.
Arbitrageur arbitrage(u)r, arbitragist, arbitrage broker, shunter.
Arbitragewerte arbitrage stocks.
Architekt architect.
Architekten|büro architect's office, architectural practice; ~**diplom** diploma in architecture; ~**gebühr**, ~**honorar** surveyor's fee; **tonangebende** ~**gruppe** architectural establishment.
Architektur architecture.
Archiv archives, [old] records, depository for records, *(Film, Platte)* library, *(Gebäude)* archives, *(Raum)* filing (muniment) room, *(Zeitung)* morgue *(US)*;
für unser ~ for our files;
~ **leiten (verwalten)** to keep the records (archives);
~**aufnahme** *(Film)* stock shot; ~**beamter** archivist, recorder, keeper of the records; ~**exemplar** file (record) copy, copy on file; ~**leiter** archivist, registrar; ~**material** records, archives; ~**unterlagen** permanent files.
Archivar keeper of the archives, filing clerk, *(Behörde)* archivist, registrar, recorder;
~**beamter** archivist, recorder, keeper of the records; ~**exemplar** file (record) copy, copy (on file); ~**unterlagen** permanent files.
Archivierung record keeping.
Arena arena, circle, cockpit, *(Zirkus)* circle, ring;
politische ~ arena of politics;
~ **mit den besten Ausgangschancen betreten** to enter the ring with most of the advantages.
arg, im ~**en liegen** *(Vermögensverhältnisses)* to be in a bad state; **in** ~**er Verlegenheit sein** to be in a tight corner; **jem. einen** ~**en Streich spielen** to play a nasty trick on s. o.
Ärger annoyance, vexation, anger, provocation, irritation;
zum ~ **seiner Nachbarn** to the annoyance of one's neighbo(u)rs; **häuslicher** ~ domestic troubles (worries);
seinen ~ **am Büroboten auslassen** to vent one's anger on the office boy; **vor** ~ **platzen** to blow one's top *(coll.)*.
ärgerlich annoyed, vexed, irritated, cross *(coll.)*;
~ **werden** to lose one's temper (wool, *coll.*);
~**e Bestimmungen** vexatious rules and regulations; ~**es Gesicht machen** to look irritated; **was für eine** ~**e Sache** what a nuisance.
ärgern to annoy, to vex, to irritate, to give offence, to nettle;
sich ~ to feel annoyed, to fly into a temper; **sich grün und gelb** ~ to fly into a blue rage; **sich maßlos** ~ to be boiling; **sich über eine Verzögerung** ~ to be irritated by a delay.
Ärgernis annoyance, nuisance, offence;
~ **erregend** disorderly;
öffentliches ~ public nuisance;
~ **erregen** to give offence; **öffentliches** ~ **erregen** to offend public decency; ~ **hervorrufen** to give rise to a scandal, to scandalize; ~ **an etw. nehmen** to take offence at s. th.; **wahres** ~ **sein** to be a positive nuisance.
Arglist malice, mala fide, malevolence, dolose, fraudulent, malicious, deceitful;
wegen ~ **anfechten** to vitiate for fraud.
arglistig|e Täuschung actionable (moral, positive) fraud, wilful deception, wilful deceit, *(bei Vertragsabschluß)* fraud in treaty, fraudulent (false) statement; ~**es Verschweigen** fraudulent concealment.

Argument argument, point, contention;
brauchbares ~ answerable argument; **entscheidendes** ~ clincher; **rein gefühlsbetontes** ~ emotional argument; **gegenteiliges** ~ contrary point; **handfeste** ~**e** solid arguments; **hieb- und stichfestes** ~ tight argument; **hinkendes** ~ halting argument; **schwaches** ~ feeble (flimsy) argument; **stichhaltiges** ~ valid argument; **nicht stichhaltiges** ~ frivolous (unsound) argument; **wenig stichhaltige** ~**e** arguments of little substance; **überzeugende** ~**e** powerful arguments; **nicht überzeugendes** ~ invalid argument; **übliches** ~ stock argument; **unfundiertes** ~ infirm argument; **unwiderlegbare** ~**e** impregnable arguments; **verbrauchtes** ~ worn-out argument;
~**e dafür und dagegen** pros and cons; ~**e aus der Gosse** kitchen-sink arguments;
~ **entkräften** to invalidate an argument; ~ **erhärten** to strengthen a case; ~ **ad absurdum führen** to make hay of an argument; **gutes** ~ **für etw. haben** to have a fair case for saying; **alle** ~**e widerlegt haben** to have disposed of all arguments; **einem** ~ **seine Schärfe nehmen** to take the edge off an argument; **über starke** ~**e verfügen** to have a strong case; ~ **verstehen** to grasp an argument; ~ **vorbringen** to advance (put out) an argument; **die üblichen** ~**e vorbringen** to dish up the usual arguments; ~ **für etw. vorbringen** to make out a case for s. th., to put out an argument; **jds.** ~**e vorwegnehmen** to cut the ground from under s. one's feet; ~ **gründlich widerlegen (zerpflücken)** to tear an argument to shreds.
Argumentation reasoning;
dürftige ~ threadbare arguments;
jds. ~ **begreifen** to catch s. one's point; ~ **vertiefen** to expand an argument.
argumentieren to argue, to reason, *(bei Gericht)* to plead;
zwingend ~ to clinch an argument.
Argusaugen, mit Argus-eyed.
Argwohn distrust, suspicion;
jds. ~ **erwecken** to arouse s. one's suspicion.
argwöhnisch suspicious, distrustful.
Aristokrat aristocrat, blue blood.
Aristokratie aristocracy.
aristokratisch aristocratic, patrician, upper-crust, silk-stocking *(US)*.
Arithmetik arithmetic.
arithmetisch | e Mitte arithmetical average; ~**er Mittelwert** arithmetic mean; ~**e Reihe** arithmetic progression.
Arkaden | gang arcade, portico; ~**läden** shopping arcade; ~**viertel** amusement arcade.
Arktik arctic.
Arm | des Gesetzes arm (limb, tentacles) of the law; ~ **voller Pakete** armful of parcels;
j. mit offenen ~**en aufnehmen** to receive s. o. open-armed, to welcome s. o. with open arms; **jem. in den** ~ **fallen** to put a spoke in s. one's wheel; **jem. unter die** ~**e greifen** to give s. o. a long leg, to lend a helping hand, to stake s. o. *(US)*; **langen** ~ **haben** to have far-reaching influence; **einem alten Freund in die** ~**e laufen** to tumble into an old friend; **j. auf den** ~ **nehmen** to play s. o. up, to pull s. one's leg, to trifle with s. o., to take s. o. for a camel ride *(US)*.
arm poor, indigent, needy, penniless, *(bemitleidenswert)* poor, pitiable, miserable, *(gehaltlos)* thin, weak, meager, meagre *(Br.)*, *(Qualität)* poor, low-grade;
ganz ~ dead poor;
~ **wie eine Kirchenmaus** as poor as a church mouse;
sich als ~ **ausgeben** to wear the mantle of the poor; **j.** ~ **essen** to eat s. o. out of house and home *(coll.)*;
~**er Boden** unproductive (poor, infertile) soil; ~**es Erz** low-grade ore; ~**e Kohle** lean coal.
Armamputierter basket case.
Armaturen fittings, mountings;
~ **eines Dampfkessels** boiler fittings;
~**anzeige** dashboard display; ~**beleuchtung** dashboard light; ~**brett** instrument board (panel), dashboard; **stoßgedämpftes** ~**brett** anti-impact dashboard.
Arm | band bracelet, *(Uhr)* watch band (strap); ~**banduhr** wristwatch; ~**binde** sling.
Arme poor persons, paupers *(US)*;
mittellose ~ destitute people; **öffentlich unterstützter** ~**r** pauper; **verschämte** ~ the new poor;
~ **aussaugen** to grind the faces of the poor; **für die** ~**n sammeln** to collect for the poor; ~ **unterstützen** to render aid to (relieve) the poor.
Armee army, military forces;
marschbereite ~ route army;
bei der ~ **dienen** to serve in the army (with the colo(u)rs); ~ **einsetzen** to bring in the troops; **in die** ~ **eintreten** to join the army (colo(u)rs); ~ **unterhalten** to subsidize an army; ~ **verproviantieren** to furnish an army with supplies, to victual an army;
~**bereich,** ~**gebiet** army area (zone); **rückwärtiges** ~**gebiet** communications zone, army service area; ~**korps** army corps; ~**kreise** armed force sources; ~**lieferant** army contractor; ~**lieferant sein** to purvey for the (victual an) army; ~**oberkommando** army headquarters.
Ärmel, seine ~ **hochkrempeln** to roll up one's sleeves; **aus dem** ~ **schütteln** to play it off the cuff *(coll.)*.
Armeleute | geruch whiffs of the slums; ~**viertel** low-income neighbo(u)rhood, slums, poor quarter.
Ärmelstreifen *(mil.)* stripe.
Armen | abgabe poor rate; **Bestallung eines** ~**anwalts** dock brief *(Br.)*; ~**asyl** pauper asylum *(US)*, union (county, *US*) house, workhouse *(Br.)*; ~**begräbnis** pauper burial *(US)*; ~**fürsorge** maintenance of the poor, poor relief *(Br.)*, public *(US)* (national, *Br.*) assistance; ~**gesetzgebung** pauper legislation *(US)*, poor laws *(Br.)*; ~**grab** the paupers' grave *(US)*; ~**hilfe** alms, poor relief *(Br.)*; ~**kasse** alms purse, relief fund; ~**küche** soup kitchen; ~**pflege** social welfare, poor relief *(Br.)*; ~**pfleger** overseer of the poor *(Br.)*, reliever, relieving officer.
Armenrecht pauper's right *(US)*, [free] legal aid *(Br.)*, poor (poverty) law;
im ~ in forma pauperis;
~ **beantragen** to petition for leave to sue in forma pauperis *(US)*; ~ **entziehen** to dispauper *(US)*; ~ **erlangen** to obtain legal aid *(Br.)*; **im** ~ **klagen** to sue in forma pauperis *(US)*; **Antrag auf Erteilung des** ~**s stellen** to petition for leave to sue in forma pauperis *(US)*.
Armenrechts | antrag pauper petition *(US)*; ~**beratungsstelle** Poverty Law Centre *(US)*; ~**berechtigter** poor prisoner *(Br.)*, pauper *(US)*; ~**bewilligung** legal aid (poor persons) certificate *(Br.)*; ~**gesetz** Legal Aid Act *(Br.)*; ~**gesuch stellen** to petition for leave to sue in forma pauperis *(US)*; ~**kläger** poor (assisted, *Br.*) person, poor litigant *(US)*; ~**kosten** pauper costs *(US)*; ~**partei** assisted person *(Br.)*, pauper; ~**prüfungsausschuß** certifying committee.
Armen | sachen poor-law matters; ~**siedlung** poor farm *(US)*; ~**unterstützung** pauper *(US)* (poor, *Br.*) relief, alms *(Br.)*; **gemeindliche** ~**unterstützung** parish relief; ~**unterstützungsfonds** community chest *(US)*; ~**ursachen beseitigen** to remove the causes of poverty; ~**viertel** poor quarter, low-income neighbo(u)rhood; **aus dem** ~**viertel stammend** on the wrong side of the [rail]road track; ~**wesen** legal aid system *(Br.)*.
armieren to reinforce, *(Kabel)* to armo(u)r.
ärmlich poor, miserable, shabby, necessitous;
~**e Behausung** wretched house; ~**es Dasein** miserable existence; ~**e Kleidung** shabby clothes; **in** ~**en Verhältnissen leben** to live in narrow circumstances.
Armprothese mechanical arm.
armselig poorly, twopenny, wretched, little, miserable;
~**e Entschuldigung** paltry excuse; ~**es Gehalt** miserable salary; ~**es Haus** wretched house; ~**e Kreatur** poor creature; ~**es Mäntelchen** threadbare coat.
Armseligkeit paltriness, wretchedness, miserableness.
Armut poverty, poorness, need, destitution, indigence, penury, a light purse;
in drückender ~ under the pressure of poverty;
äußerste ~ abject poverty; **drückende** ~ pinch of poverty, grinding poverty; **geistige** ~ lack of intellect; **größte** ~ dire need (distress), deep poverty;
~ **des Bodens** poorness of the soil;
~ **beseitigen** to abolish pauperism; **j. vor der** ~ **bewahren** to rescue s. o. from poverty; **seine geistige** ~ **dokumentieren** to show no sign of intelligence; **in** ~ **geraten** to fall into (be reduced to) poverty; ~ **kennengelernt haben** to know the pressure of poverty; **in** ~ **leben** to be living in poverty (want); ~ **lindern** to relieve distress among the poor; **von der** ~ **bedrängt sein** to be under pressure of poverty; **Geld zur Steuerung der** ~ **zur Verfügung stellen** to apply money for the benefit of poor people; **der** ~ **steuern** to cure poverty; ~ **vorschützen** to make a poor mouth.
Armuts | gebiet poverty area, slums, poor quarter; ~**grenze** poverty trap; ~**ursachen beseitigen** to remove the causes of poverty.
Armutszeugnis poor person's certificate *(Br.)*, certificate of poverty *(US)*, means test *(Br.)*;
sich ein ~ **ausstellen** to betray one's ignorance, to reveal one's incapacity.

Aroma aroma, fragrance, *(Tee)* nose *(Br.)*.
Arrangement arrangement, setout;
künstlerisches ~ artistic arrangement;
~ **mit seinen Gläubigern treffen** to compound with one's creditors.
Arrangeur arranger, *(Festlichkeit)* marshal.
arrangieren to make arrangements, to arrange, to organize, *(Festlichkeit)* to marshal, *(Regisseur)* to state-manage;
etw. für j. ~ to make the necessary arrangements for s. o.; **sich mit jem.** ~ to fix things up with s. o.; **sich mit seinen Gläubigern** ~ to compound (come to an arrangement) with one's creditors; **Schaufenster neu** ~ to dress a shop window.
Arrest *(Haft)* detention, confinement, *(mil.)* arrest, *(Schüler)* keeping in detention, *(Zwangsvollstreckung)* attachment order *(US)*, seizure, distraint, distress, attachment;
dinglicher ~ distraint (charging, *Br.*) order, attachment; **einfacher** ~ open arrest; **leichter** ~ *(mil.)* open arrest; **offener** ~ *(Konkurs)* receiving order *(Br.)*; **persönlicher** ~ attachment, committal order; **strenger** ~ *(mil.)* solitary confinement, detention on bread-and-water-diet *(mil.)*;
~ **eines Schiffes** arrest (embargo) of a vessel; ~ **zur Vollziehung einer Beugestrafe** arrest in civil practice;
~ **anordnen** to [levy a] distress, to distrain, to attach, to seize; ~ **aufheben** to discharge (release) an attachment; ~ **eines Schiffes aufheben** to raise the embargo of a ship; **mit** ~ **belegen** to [levy a] distress; **Schiff mit** ~ **belegen** to embargo a ship; **Schüler mit** ~ **bestrafen** to keep a pupil in, to detain a pupil; **mit** ~ **belegt sein** to be under distraint; **im** ~ **sitzen** to be under arrest; **j. in den** ~ **stecken** to place (put) s. o. under arrest;
~**anordnung** distress warrant; ~**anstalt** *(mil.)* detention barracks, guardhouse, remand home *(Br.)*; ~**antrag** motion in arrest of judgment.
Arrestbefehl writ of attachment, attachment order *(US)*;
~ **erwirken** to obtain a distraint.
Arrestbeschluß attachment order;
~ **verkünden** to give notice of distraint.
Arrest|bruch pound breach; ~**gläubiger** attaching creditor, distraining party; ~**gründe** grounds of attachment; ~**hypothek** execution (judgment) lien.
arrestieren to arrest, *(Schiff)* to seize, to arrest, *(technisch)* to stop, to lock, to arrest.
Arrest|lokal *(mil.)* guardhouse, remand home *(Br.)*, cooler *(sl.)*; ~**strafe** *(mil.)* arrest; ~**verfahren** attachment proceedings *(US)*; ~**vollziehung** attachment of execution.
arriviert sein to have arrived.
arrogant arrogant, with a high hand, haughty, highty-tighty, hoity-toity, upstart;
j. ~ **behandeln** to be highhanded with s. o.; ~ **proklamieren** to lay down the law about *(fig.)*;
~**es Benehmen** overbearing behavio(u)r; ~**er Ton** arrogant tone.
Arroganz arrogance, overbearingness, haughtiness, toploftiness.
arrondieren, sein Gelände to round off one's property.
Arsenal arsenal, ordnance depot;
~ **der Schwerindustrie** center (centre) of heavy industry.
Art *(Ausführung)* manner, *(Beschaffenheit)* kind, nature, shape, cast, type, *(Form)* form, fashion, style, *(Marke)* brand, make, *(Qualität)* quality, description, stripe *(US)*, *(Sorte)* class, sort, order, species, category, variety, *(Verfahren)* method, procedure;
auf die eine oder andere ~ some way or other; **auf ruhige** ~ quietly; **auf eine verletzende** ~ in an offensive manner; **in seiner unbeholfenen** ~ in his awkward manner; **nach** ~ after the fashion; **nach** ~**en** classified; **nach** ~ **des Hauses** *(Restaurant)* homemade; **nach** ~ **eines Verhörs** in the nature of a trial; **von gleichmäßiger** ~ **und Güte** of uniform kind; **von mittlerer** ~ **und Güte** of average kind or quality, middling;
ausgestorbene ~ extinct species; **bewährte** ~ approved method; **persönliche** ~ way; **weitschweifige** ~ circuitous way;
~ **der Aufführung** brand of showmanship; ~ **der Beförderung** mode (manner) of conveyance; ~ **der Berechnung** manner of calculation; ~ **der Bewirtschaftung** method of exploitation; **eine** ~ **Börsenmakler** a sort of stockbroker; ~ **der Erwerbseinkünfte** earned-income category; ~ **einer Krankheit** nature of a disease; ~ **und Weise** manner, method, mode, modus, line; **vorschriftsmäßige** ~ **und Weise** proper way;
jem. eine Nachricht auf schonende ~ **beibringen** to break the news gently to s. o.; **gewinnende** ~ **haben** to have a winning way; **aus der** ~ **schlagen** to go one's own ways; **in jds.** ~ **schlagen** to take after s. o.; **auf alle möglichen** ~**en versuchen** to try every possible way.
artfremde Einflüsse alien influences.
Artigkeiten polite words, compliments;
~ **sagen** to make pretty speeches, to pay compliments.
Artikel article, commodity, merchandise, product, line, item, match, lot, *(Bestimmung)* clause, paragraph, *(gram.)* article, *(Kommentar)* comment[ary], *(in der Zeitung)* article, [news] item, stuff;
laut ~ under article;
~ *(pl.)* wares, goods, commodities;
schwer abzusetzender ~ product difficult to sell, dead stock; **einzeln angefertigter** ~ one off; **groß aufgemachter** ~ feature article; **ausführlicher** ~ write-up; **ausgegangener** ~ out-of-stock item; **ausländischer** ~ product of foreign make; **begehrter** ~ called-for article; **bestellter** ~ article demanded; **hoch besteuerte** ~ high-duty goods; **bewirtschafteter** ~ rationed item; **billige** ~ low-priced lines (goods); **gut eingeführte** ~ established products, well-known commodities; **neu eingeführte** ~ novelties; **in mehreren Zeitungen gleichzeitig erscheinender** ~ syndicated article; **fertiger** ~ finished product; **gängiger** ~ runner, seller, salable type; **gebrauchte** ~ secondhand articles; **glänzend gehender** ~ runner; **geschützter** ~ branded commodity; **hergestellter** ~ manufacture[d article]; **im Gefängnis hergestellte** ~ prison-made goods; **hochbesteuerte** ~ high-duty goods; **hochwertiger** ~ article of high quality; **salopp geschriebener informeller** ~ chatty piece; **inländischer** ~ domestic product; **kontingentierte** ~ quota (rationed) goods; **kurzer** ~ paragraph, *(Zeitung)* pamphlet; **lancierter** ~ inspired article; **lebenswichtige** ~ articles of first necessity; **neueste** ~ up-to-date merchandise; **provozierender** ~ think-piece *(sl.)*; **rationierter** ~ rationed item; **seriengefertigte** ~ mass-produced articles; **nicht sortierte** ~ nongraded products; **unmoderner** ~ plug *(US)*; **einem Alleinvertriebsrecht unterliegender** ~ proprietary article; **unwirtschaftliche** ~ onerous goods; **schnell verkäuflicher** ~ fast-selling item; **schwer verkäufliche** ~ articles (items) hard to get rid of; **verwandte** ~ complimentary line; **vollwertige** ~ articles of high quality; **stets vorrätige** ~ stock articles; **wirtschaftlicher** ~ money saver; **zugkräftiger** ~ popular line; **wegen Platzmangels zurückgesetzter** ~ crowded-out article; **zuverlässiger** ~ reliable article; **zwanzigzeiliger** ~ twenty-line article;
~ **in Fortsetzungen** serial story; ~ **mit größter Gewinnspanne** most profitable purchase; ~ **des Parteiprogramms** plank in the party platform; ~ **mit stabilen Preisen** price-maintained products; ~ **mit hoher Umschlagsgeschwindigkeit** article of quick sale; ~ **mit hohen Verkaufspreisen** high-prices commodities; ~ **für eine Zeitung** contribution to a newspaper;
~ **vollständig abdrucken** to reproduce an article entirely; ~ **zum Verkauf aufmachen** to get up an article for sale; ~ **bei einer Firma bestellen (in Auftrag geben)** to place an order for an article with a firm; ~ **vor Veröffentlichung durchsehen** to subedit an article; ~ **einführen** to put an article on the market; ~ **zur Veröffentlichung freigeben** to release an article for publication; ~ **führen** to deal in an article (a line), to keep an article in stock (store), to stock an article, to carry goods *(US)*; ~ **nicht führen** not to keep an article; ~ **nicht mehr führen (auf Lager haben)** to be out of an article; **neuen** ~ **lancieren** to put a new article on the market; ~ **für eine Zeitung schreiben** to contribute to a newspaper; **sich auf einen** ~ **spezialisieren** to specialize in a line; ~ **überfliegen** to skim an article; **billige** ~ **verkaufen** to run a cheap line; ~ **veröffentlichen** to write an article; ~ **zusammenstreichen** to shorten an article;
~**einzelspanne** markup; **pro Zeile bezahlter** ~**schreiber** space writer, penny-a-liner *(Br.)*; ~**serie** set of articles.
artikelweise in sections.
artikulieren to articulate, to enunciate;
lautstark ~ to be in full throat.
artikuliert articulate, articulated;
~ **sprechen** to articulate.
Artikulierung articulation.
Artillerie, leichte light artillery; **motorisierte** ~ motorized artillery; **schwere** ~ heavy artillery (armament);
~**feuer** cannonade, shelling.
Artist [variety] artist, performer *(US)*.
Artisten|beruf life of a performer; ~**kunststück** artistic performance.
Artistik artistry.
Arznei medicine, medicament, drug, preparation, physic;
ohne ~ drugless;
seine ~ **einnehmen** to take one's prescription; ~ **geben** to administer a medicine; ~ **schlucken** to dose; **jem. seine** ~ **verabreichen** to give s. o. his medicine; ~ **verschreiben** to prescribe a drug (medicine);

~**abgabe** dispensing; ~**buch** dispensatory; ~**hersteller** dispenser; ~**kapsel** capsule.

Arzneimittel medicament, medicine, pharmaceutical preparation, physic, drug;
warenzeichenrechtlich geschützte ~ patent medicine;
~ **eines Kurpfuschers** quack remedy;
~**bereitung** preparation of drugs; ~**industrie** pharmaceutical industry; ~**kosten senken** to cut down the drug bill; ~**kunde** pharmacy; **amtliche** ~**liste** pharmacopoeia.

arzneimittelpflichtig ethical.

Arzneimittelschrank medicine cabinet (chest).

Arzt doctor, medical practitioner, medical attendant, physician;
approbierter ~ regular (licensed) physician *(US)*, qualified medical practitioner; **behandelnder** ~ attending physician; **diensttuender** ~ doctor in charge; **operierender** ~ operating surgeon; **praktischer** ~ general (medical) practitioner;
~ **aufsuchen** to attend a doctor, to take medical advice, to consult a doctor; **sich als** ~ **ausgeben** to pass o. s. off as a doctor, to pretend to be a doctor; **einem** ~ **die Approbation erteilen** to license a doctor to practise medicine; **den** ~ **holen** to go for a doctor; ~ **konsultieren** to consult a doctor, to meet a doctor in consultation, to take medical advice; ~ **holen lassen** to send for a doctor; **sich an einen** ~ **wenden** to run to a doctor; ~ **zuziehen** to consult a doctor, to call in a physician;
~**beruf** medical profession, profession of medicine; ~**besuch** doctor's call (visit), *(beim Arzt)* visit to (attendance of) the doctor.

Ärzte|besucher detailman *(US)*; ~**gremium** panel of physicians; ~**kammer** general medical council *(Br.)*; ~**kollegium** council of physicians; ~**kongreß** medical congress; ~**schaft** the medical profession, medical establishment.

Arzt|helferin doctor's attendance; ~**honorar** medical fees; **vom staatlichen Gesundheitsamt gezahlte** ~**honorare** health service fees *(Br.)*; **im Krankenhaus anfallende** ~**kosten** in-hospital medical expenses.

ärztlich medical;
~ **empfohlen** medically recommended; ~ **verordnet** prescribed;
~ **behandeln** to attend, to give medical treatment, to prescribe for; **sich** ~ **behandeln lassen** to take medical treatment;
~**e Approbation entziehen** to strike off the Medical Register; ~**es Attest** medical certificate; ~**e Behandlung** medical treatment; **in** ~**er Behandlung sein** to be under medical care; ~**e Bemühungen** medical attendance (attention); ~**er Berater** medical adviser; ~**e Beratung** medical advice; ~**en Beruf ausüben** to practise medicine; ~**es Beschwerdegericht** medical appeal tribunal; ~**e Betreuung** medical attendance (attention); ~**e Fakultät** medical faculty; ~**e Fürsorge** medical assistance; ~**es Honorar** medical fee; ~**e Kenntnisse** medical knowledge; ~**e Leistungen** medical benefits; ~**en Rat einholen** to have (take) medical advice; ~**e Standespflichten** medical etiquette; **eingehende** ~**e Untersuchung** thorough medical examination, checkup; ~**e Verrichtung** medical services; ~**e Versorgung** medical attention; ~**es Versorgungswerk** medical aid scheme; ~**es Zeugnis** medical certificate; ~**e Zulassung** licence (license, *US*) to practise as doctor.

Arzt|praxis haben to practise medicine; ~**rechnung** doctor's fee (bill); **durch** ~**rechnungen fast am Bettelstab** impoverished by doctor's bills; ~**tasche** doctor's case; **als** ~**vertreter fungieren** to act as locum tenens for a doctor; ~**visite** doctor's visit (call); **freie** ~**wahl** free choice of a physician.

Asche ash, *(Kohlenrest)* cinders;
glühende ~ [smouldering] embers;
in Sack und ~ **gehen** to wear sackcloth and ashes; **in Schutt und** ~ **legen** to coventrize.

Aschen|bahn dirt track; ~**puttel** Cinderella; ~**puttel sein** to be the drudge.

asozial antisocial, unsocial;
~**e Familie** slum family; **aus einem** ~**en Stadtteil kommen** to be born on the wrong side of the track.

Asoziale|r social outcast;
zu den ~**n gehören** to live on the fringe of society.

Aspekt facet, aspect, bearings, view;
unter sozialen ~**en** under its social aspect;
der humanitäre ~ the personal element;
fachliche ~**e eines Berufs** technical aspects of a job; **politischer** ~ **einer Frage** political phase of a problem; **wesentliche** ~**e eines Unternehmens** major facets of a business;
etw. unter einem anderen ~ **betrachten** to look at s. th. from a different point of view.

Asphalt asphalt, mineral pitch;
~**arbeiter** asphalter, asphalt layer (paver); ~**beton** asphalt cement; ~**decke** asphalt macadam; ~**pappe** asphaltic felt; ~**presse** gutter (yellow) press.

asphaltieren, Straße to asphalt a road.

Aspirant aspirant, seeker.

Assekurant assurer *(Br.)*, underwriter.

Assekuranz assurance *(Br.)*, insurance, underwriting;
~**büro** insurance office; ~**geschäft**, ~**versicherung** insurance business, underwriting; ~**makler** insurance broker.

assekurieren to assure *(Br.)*, to insure, to underwrite.

Asservaten|konto suspense account; ~**raum** property room.

Assessor *(beim Anwalt)* junior barrister (counsel), *(bei Gericht)* assistant judge;
sich für das ~**examen vorbereiten** to prepare for the barrister examination.

Assimilation, gesellschaftliche social adoption (adaptation).

assimilieren to assimilate.

Assimilierung assimilation.

Assimilierungsprozeß process of assimilation.

Assistent assistant, aid, research fellow, sidekicker *(Br.)*;
nicht fest angestellter ~ unestablished assistant; **unermüdlicher** ~ rowing assistant.

Assistenten|stab *(Krankenhaus)* house staff; ~**stelle** assistanceship.

Assistenz|arzt junior hospital doctor, medical assistant, intern *(US)*; **als** ~**arzt tätig sein** to intern *(US)*; ~**professor** senior lecturer.

assortieren to assort, to lay in stock.

assortiert, wohl ~**er Laden** well-stocked shop.

Assortiment assortment of goods.

Assoziation association, *(Teilhaberschaft)* partnership.

Assoziations|abkommen *(EG)* association agreement; ~**ausschuß** Association Committee; ~**index** index of association; ~**test** association test; ~**zentrum** association center *(US)* (centre, *Br.*).

assoziieren, sich to associate, to partner; **sich mit jem.** ~ to go into partnership with s. o.

assoziiert associate[d];
~ **sein** to be in partnership;
~**e Länder** associated countries; ~**er Staat** associated state.

Assoziiertenstatus associate status.

Assoziierung *(EG)* association, adhesion.

Assoziierungsverhandlungen association negotiations.

Ast branch, limb, *(Flugbahn)* branch;
auf dem absteigenden ~ *(fig.)* on the downgrade, over the hills; ~ **absägen, auf dem man sitzt** to cut off one's nose to spite one's face; **sich einen** ~ **lachen** to split one's sides with laughter; **etw. auf den** ~ **nehmen** to put one's back into s. th.

Astrologe astrologer, stargazer.

Astrologie astrology.

Astronaut astronaut, spaceman.

Astronautik astronautics.

Astronom astronomer.

astronomisch|er Schiffsort astronomical position; ~**e Summe** astronomical sum, enormous figure.

Asyl asylum, shelter, refuge, sanctuary, retreat, haven, home, franchise;
politisches ~ political asylum;
~ **für Obdachlose** casual ward, pauper asylum, night (reception, *Br.*) shelter, stretch house *(sl.)*;
um politisches ~ **bitten** to ask for political asylum; ~ **erhalten** to be granted asylum; ~ **gewähren** to grant asylum.

asylberechtigt entitled to asylum.

Asyl|gesuch application for asylum; **jederzeit widerrufliche** ~**gewährung** extradition warrant; ~**gewährung durch ein neutrales Land** neutral asylum; ~**land** asylum; ~**ort** privileged place; ~**recht** right of asylum; ~**recht verletzen** to violate sanctuary; ~**sucher** asylum-seeker.

Atelier studio [apartment], atelier, workshop, designing department;
fotografisches ~ photographer's parlo(u)r;
ins ~ **gehen** *(Film)* to go into production;
~**arbeiter** stagehand, sceneshifter; ~**aufnahme** studio shot; ~**kamera** stand camera *(Br.)*; ~**leiter** *(Architekt)* patron, *(einer Werbeagentur)* art director; ~**wohnung** studio flat.

Atem, außer puffed, breathless;
längerer ~ more staying power;
~ **anhalten** to catch (hold) one's breath; **jem. den** ~ **benehmen (verschlagen)** to take s. one's breath away; **langen** ~ **haben** to have a long wind; **j. in** ~ **halten** to keep s. o. on the go; **wieder zu** ~ **kommen** to get one's second wind (breath again); **j.** ~ **schöpfen lassen** to give s. o. a breather.

atemberaubend breathtaking.
atemlos breathless, out of breath, puffed;
in ~er Folge in rapid succession; **~e Stille** dead silence.
Atempause breathing time, breathing space;
jem. einen kleine ~ gewähren to give s. o. a breather.
Atemzug, im gleichen in the same breath;
mit seinem Bruder nicht im gleichen ~ genannt werden können not to be named in the same breath with his brother; **seinen letzten ~ tun** to breath one's last.
Ätherkrieg war of the airwaves.
Atlantik Atlantic, pond *(sl.)*;
über den ~ fliegen to fly the Atlantic;
~charta Atlantic Charta; **~flugpreise senken** to cut Atlantic fares; **~frachtverkehr** ocean shipping; **~frachtvertrag** ocean shipping; **~hafen** Atlantic port; **~küste** Eastern Seaboard; **~pakt** North Atlantic Treaty, Atlantic Pact.
Atlantisch|e Gemeinschaft Atlantic Community; **~er Ozean** the Atlantic.
Atlas *(Landkarte)* atlas, *(Textilien)* satin;
~format large square folio, atlas folio; **~papier** satin paper.
Atmosphäre *(fig.)* atmosphere, climate, air, flavo(u)r, feel;
geschäftige ~ air of bustle; **gespannte ~** tense atmosphere; **gespenstige ~** ghostly atmosphere; **vertraute ~** homely atmosphere; **zwanglose ~** relaxed atmosphere;
~ von Frieden und Ruhe atmosphere of peace and calm; **~ eines Platzes** genius loci;
~ von Reichtum atmen to smell rich; **~ ausstrahlen** to generate an atmosphere; **~ entspannen** to relax the tension.
Atmosphärendruck atmospheric pressure.
atmosphärisch *(Radio)* static, atmospheric;
~e Bedingungen atmospheric conditions; **~e Störungen** atmospheric disturbances, atmospherics, strays.
Atom|abfall nuclear waste; **~aktien** atomic shares (stocks, *US*); **~angriff** nuclear attack; **~anlagen** nuclear facilities; **mit ~antrieb** nuclear-powered.
atomar atomic, nuclear;
~e Abrüstung nuclear disarmament; **~e Abschreckung** nuclear deterrent; **~e Kriegsführung** atomic warfare; **~e Waffen** nuclear weapons.
Atom|ausrüstung nuclear equipment; **~bombe** [nuclear] fission (atomic) bomb, nuclear device; **~bomben einsetzen** to atom-bomb; **~bombenangriff** nuclear attack; **~bombenexplosion** atomic explosion, nuclear burst; **~bomber** nuclear bomber; **~brüter** breeder pile; **~deponie** nuclear burial ground; **~energie** atomic (nuclear) energy; **~energiebehörde** Atomic Energy Authority *(Br.)*; **~energiekommission** Atomic Energy Commission; **~forschung** nuclear research; **~forschungszentrum** center *(US)* (centre, *Br.*) for nuclear research; **~garantieversprechen** nuclear guarantee; **~gefechtskopf** atomic (nuclear) warhead; **~gemeinschaft** atomic pool; **Europäische ~gemeinschaft** European Atomic Energy Community (EURATOM).
atomgetrieben nuclear-powered;
~es Flugzeug nuclear aircraft.
Atom|gewicht atomic weight; **~kern** atomic nucleus; **~klub** Atomic Club; **~kraft** atomic (nuclear) power; **mit ~kraft angetrieben** atomic (nuclear) powered; **~kraftwerk** nuclear power station (plant), atomic power plant (station); **~kraftwerksgelände** atomic power plant sites; **~krieg** atomic (nuclear) warfare; **begrenzter ~krieg** limited-strategy war; **zur Ausweitung des ~kriegs zwingen** to put on the nuclear escalator; **~kriegsführung** nuclear warfare; **~macht** nuclear power; **~meiler** atomic pile, nuclear energy plant; **~motor** nuclear-powered engine; **~müll** nuclear waste, radioactive waste material; **~müllbeseitigung** nuclear waste disposal; **~-patt** nuclear stalemate; **~physik** nuclear physics; **~pilz** fireball; **~politik** nuclear policy; **~rakete** atomic rocket; **~reaktor** nuclear [power] reactor; **~schiff** nuclear ship; **~schlag** nuclear strike; **~spaltung** nuclear fission; **~sperrvertrag** Nonproliferation Treaty, Test Ban Treaty; **~sprengkopf** nuclear (atomic) warhead; **mehrfacher ~sprengkopf** multiple warhead; **~streitmacht** nuclear strike force; **~-U-Boot** nuclear-(atomic-) powered submarine; **~versuch** nuclear test; **~waffe** ultimate deterrent; **~waffen** nuclear (atomic) weapons (force); **~-, biologische und chemische Waffen** ABC weapons; **~waffenabkommen** nuclear weapon deal.
atomwaffenfreie Zone atom-free (denuclearized) zone.
Atom|waffenlager nuclear weapons stock; **~waffenversuchsstopp** suspension of nuclear tests; **~werk** nuclear station; **~zeitalter** nuclear (atomic) age; **~zerfall** atomic decay (disintegration); **~zertrümmerung** nuclear fission.
Attaché attache, studied interpreter *(Br.)*.
Attacke attack, onset, charge;
heftige ~ violent attack; **rigorose ~n** unrelenting attacks;
~ auf die Geldbörse *(fam.)* call on the purse; **scharfe ~ gegen die Regierungspolitik** strong attack against the government's policy;
~ reiten *(fig.)* to launch an attack.
attackieren to attack, to charge;
j. in gemeiner Weise ~ to take a pot-shot at s. o.
Attentat attentate, attack, outrage, attempt on s. one's life;
~ auf j. begehen to make an attempt on s. one's life; **einem ~ zum Opfer fallen** to be assassinated.
Attentäter assassin.
Attentats|klausel assassination clause; **~plan** assassination plot.
Attest certificate, attestation;
ärztliches ~ doctor's (medical, health) certificate;
~ ausstellen to grant a certificate.
attestieren to attest, to certify.
Attraktion attraction, pull, draw;
effektvolle ~ showmanship; **große ~** big draw; **kurzfristige ~** a passing fancy.
Attraktivität|einer Anzeigenaussage copy appeal; **~ eines Gebietes** amenity of an area.
Attrappe dummy [pack], (display, sham) package.
ätzen to etch, to engrave, to bite.
Ätz|ung etching, block *(Br.)*, engraving *(US)*; **~verfahren** etching (engraving, *US*) process; **~zeichnung** etched copperplate.
Audienz hearing, audience, presence *(Br.)*;
öffentliche ~ public audience;
~ erhalten to come to the presence; **~ gewähren** to grant an audience; **um eine ~ nachsuchen** to request a hearing; **sich eine ~ verschaffen** to gain a hearing; **in ~ empfangen (zur ~ vorgelassen) werden** to be received in audience (admitted to the presence); **sich rückwärts aus einer ~ zurückziehen** to retire backward out of the presence *(Br.)*;
~saal presence chamber (room) *(Br.)*.
audiovisuell audiovisual;
~e Geräte audiovisual equipment; **~e Güter** audiovisual goods; **~er Sprachunterricht** audiolingual methods; **~e Verkaufshilfen** audiovisual aids.
Auditorium audience, *(Saal)* auditory, lecture room.
Auf und Ab|des Krieges contingencies of war; **~ des Lebens** vicissitudes (ups and downs, rough and smooth) of life.
aufarbeiten to finish, *(Material)* to use up;
unerledigte Korrespondenz ~ to work off one's arrears of correspondence; **alte Möbelstücke ~** to refurbish old furniture; **Rückstände ~** to work (clear) off arrears.
aufbahren to lay out [in state].
Aufbahrung laying out, lying-in-state.
Aufbahrungshalle mortuary, funeral home (parlo(u)r).
Aufbau erection, building-up, construction, getup, *(Montage)* assembly, mounting, *(Struktur)* structure, setup, organization, system, *(Waren)* getup, *(Wirtschaft)* rehabilitation, reorganization;
im ~ begriffen in the initial stages;
vorläufiger ~ preliminary structure;
~ eines Briefes composition of a letter; **~ eines Dramas** texture of a play; **~ eines Gerüstes** scaffolding; **~ zerstörter Häuser** reconstruction of damaged houses; **~ der Industrie** industrial organization (rehabilitation); **~ eines Lagers** buildup of stocks; **~ einer Organisation** structure of an organization; **~ einer Rüstungsindustrie** military buildup; **~ eines Theaterstücks** mechanics of play-writing; **~ der Wirtschaft** economic structure;
gleichen ~ aufweisen *(Roman)* to be essentially of the same pattern; **~ einer Gesellschaft finanzieren** to rehabilitate a company financially;
~anleihe rehabilitation loan; **soziale ~arbeit** social improvement; **~arbeiten** reconstruction work.
aufbauen to build up, to upbuild, to arrange, to construct, to erect, *(Bühne)* to set, *(Maschine)* to assemble, *(Organisation)* to set up, to organize;
Anklage auf einem Gutachten ~ to base a charge on an opinion; **Gebäude schnell ~** to run up a building; **sein Geschäft auf einer soliden Grundlage ~** to build up one's business on a sound basis; **j. [politisch] ~** to build s. o. up; **leistungsfähigen Verband ~** to develop a strong organization; **wieder ~** to rebuild, to reconstruct, to reedify, *(Gesellschaft)* to organize, to rehabilitate; **Zelt ~** to pitch a tent.
aufbauende Kritik constructive criticism.
Aufbau|finanzierung financial rehabilitation; **~gesetz** zoning act (law) *(US)*; **~hilfsfonds** rehabilitation fund; **~klasse** continua-

tion class; ~**kredit** reconstruction credit, rehabilitation loan; ~**kursus** advanced training course; ~**lehrgang** continuation course; ~**möbel** sectional (unit) furniture; ~**programm** reconstruction program(me), rehabilitation plan; ~**schule** continuation school; ~**schulunterricht** continuation teaching; ~**skizze** layout; **noch im** ~**stadium sein** to be still in its infancy.
aufbauschen to play up;
weit über Gebühr ~ to blow up way out of proportion; **Sache** ~ **richtig** to make a mountain out of a molehill.
Aufbauten *(Flugzeug)* framework, *(Schiff)* superstructure;
windschlüpfrige ~ streamlined superstructure.
aufbereiten to prepare, to process, *(Altöl)* to recondition, *(Erz)* to dress, *(Kohle)* to clean, to prepare, *(Trinkwasser)* to refine, to cleanse;
statistisches Material ~ to develop statistical information, to process data; **Tabellen** ~ to prepare tables.
Aufbereitung, redaktionelle editorial preparation; **statistische** ~ data processing.
Aufbereitungs|anlage processing plant, *(Bergbau)* dressing plant; ~**fehler** processing error.
aufbessern *(Gehalt)* to raise, to increase, *(Kurse)* to improve, *(Möbel)* to refurbish;
seine Einkünfte durch das Verfassen von Kurzgeschichten ~ to augment one's income by writing short stories; **seine Englischkenntnisse** ~ to brush up one's English.
Aufbesserung|des Gehaltes salary increase, rise *(Br.)*, raise *(US)*; ~ **der Kurse** improvement of prices.
Aufbewahren, zum for store;
jem. zum ~ **geben** to give in s. one's charge, to deposit with s. o.; **einer Bank Geld zum** ~ **geben** to deposit money in a bank.
aufbewahren to keep, to save [up], to pressure, to hive, *(Bank)* to deposit, to keep in safe custody *(Br.)*, *(Lager)* to store;
als Andenken ~ to keep as a souvenir; **geordnet** ~ to keep on [the] file; **getrennt** ~ to keep apart; **seine Korrespondenz verschlossen** ~ to keep one's letters unter lock and key; **kühl** ~ to refrigerate; **etw. sicher** ~ to keep s. th. safe (in safe custody); **auf dem Speicher** ~ to loft; **amtliche Unterlagen** ~ to keep records; **Urkunden** ~ to preserve documents;
sein Gepäck ~ **lassen** to leave one's luggage at the cloakroom *(Br.)*, to check one's baggage in the baggage room *(US)*; **Urkunden bei der Bank** ~ **lassen** to place documents on deposit with a bank.
Aufbewahrer keeper, custodian.
Aufbewahrung keeping, preservation, trust, *(Bank)* depositing, deposition, safe custody *(Br.)*, safekeeping, *(Lagerung)* storage;
zur sicheren ~ for safekeeping;
ordnungsgemäße ~ proper custody;
~ **in Stahlkammern** safe deposit, safe facilities *(US)*; ~ **von Wertpapieren** safe custody of securities *(Br.)*;
jem. Geld zur ~ **geben** to leave a sum of money in s. one's custody; **zur** ~ **übergeben** to warehouse, to deposit, to leave in s. one's custody; **sein Gepäck zur** ~ **übergeben** to leave one's luggage at the cloakroom *(Br.)*, to check one's baggage *(US)*; **Sachen dem Gastwirt zur** ~ **übergeben** to deliver goods into the personal custody of an innkeeper; **einer Bank Urkunden zur** ~ **übergeben** to deposit documents with a bank.
Aufbewahrungs|frist safekeeping period; ~**gebühr** fee for safekeeping, *(Bank)* safe-deposit fee, safe custody fee, *(Gepäck)* cloakroom fee *(Br.)*, checkroom fee *(US)*, *(Lager)* storage charge; ~**gepäck** left luggage *(Br.)*, checked baggage *(US)*.
Aufbewahrungsort depository, repository, store, depot, place of deposit;
derzeitiger ~ *(Katalog)* present location; ~ **unbekannt** whereabouts unknown;
~ **für Diebesgut** fence *(sl.)*; ~ **für alte Rechnungen** depository for old bills.
aufbewahrungspflichtig sein to be liable to keep old records.
Aufbewahrungs|raum storage room, storeroom, *(Gepäck)* checkroom *(US)*, left-luggage room *(Br.)*; ~**schein** *(Depot)* safe-custody receipt, *(Gepäck)* luggage receipt *(Br.)*, baggage check *(US)*; ~**vertrag** safe-custody (safekeeping) contract; ~**zeit** retention period.
Aufbieten levy, ordering, mobilization.
aufbieten to bring into play, *(Zinsscheine)* to summon;
alles ~ to turn on the heat *(US)*; **seine ganze Beredsamkeit** ~ to exert all one's eloquence; **Brautpaar** ~ to put up the banns; **seinen ganzen Einfluß** ~ to bring every influence to bear; **bedeutende Kapitalien** ~ to invest considerable capital; **seine ganze Kraft** ~ to summon up one's energy; **Truppen** ~ to call up (levy) troops.
Aufbietung, unter ~ **aller Kräfte** with the utmost effort;
~ **eines Brautpaars** publication of the banns; ~ **des gesamten Volkes** levee en masse; ~ **von Zinsscheinen** summoning of coupons.
aufbinden, jem. einen Bären to take s. o. in nicely.
aufblähen to inflate, to swell, *(Währung)* to inflate;
sich wie ein Truthahn ~ to swell like a turkey cock.
aufblasen, sich to puff o. s. up, to put on airs (side), to give o. s. airs.
aufblättern, Zeitung to unfold a newspaper.
aufbleiben to stay up, *(Tür)* to remain open;
lange ~ to sit (stop) up late, to keep late hours; **bis 11 Uhr** ~ to wait up until 11 o'clock.
aufblitzen to flash.
aufblühen *(Handel)* to revive, to prosper, to thrive, to flourish, to expand.
aufblühend flourishing, thriving, prospering;
~**er Handel** flourishing trade; ~**e Stadt** rising town.
aufbrauchen to consume, to use up, to exhaust, to drain;
gesamtes Kapital ~ to draw out all the principal.
Aufbrausen flare, huff.
aufbrausen to fly into a temper;
bei der kleinsten Kleinigkeit ~ to flare up at the least thing; **leicht** ~ to easily fly off the handle.
aufbrausend explosive, volcanic, hotheaded, quick-tempered.
Aufbrechen breakup, forcing;
~ **eines Geldschranks** safeblowing, safecracking; ~ **von Landstraßen** breaking up highways.
aufbrechen to break [open], to pry, *(fortgehen)* to make a move, to set off, to sally forth (out), *(Safe)* to blow, to break up, to force, *(Straße)* to burst, to crack;
Brief ~ to open (unseal) a letter; **eilig** ~ to way *(coll.)*; **früh am Morgen** ~ to start early in the morning; **Kiste** ~ to prize a box open; **zu einer Reise** ~ to set out on a journey; **Schloß** ~ to pick a lock; **sofort** ~ to leave without delay; **Tür durch einen Keil** ~ to wedge a door open; **um 10 Uhr** ~ to disperse at ten o'clock; **früh** ~ **wollen** to be determined to start early.
aufbringen to get open, *(beschaffen)* to get up, to procure, to provide;
j. ~ to get s. one's back up; **Abfindungszahlungen** ~ to raise portions (composition payments); **hundert Dollar** ~ to raise a hundred dollars; **Geld** ~ to raise the money; **Gerücht** ~ to set a rumo(u)r afloat; **Interesse** ~ to show interest; **Kapital** ~ to procure capital; **Kosten** ~ to afford (defray, meet) costs, to find the money; **Mittel** ~ to raise (mobilize) funds; **Mode** ~ to introduce (set, start, create) a fashion; **seinen ganzen Mut** ~ to pluck up one's courage; **als Prise** ~ to make a prize of (bring in) a ship; **Steuern** ~ to raise (gather) taxes; **Truppen** ~ to levy troops; **3000 DM jährlich für die Unterhaltung eines Autos** ~ **müssen** to cost 3000 DM a year to run a car.
Aufbringung *(Kapital)* raising, *(Mode)* introduction, *(Schiff)* capture at sea, seizure, *(bei Verlustanteil)* contribution;
~ **von Abfindungszahlungen** raising portions (composition payments); ~ **von Kapitalien** capital flo(a)tation; ~ **von Mitteln** mobilization (procurement) of funds; ~ **von Steuern** collection of taxes, tax levy, tax gathering.
Aufbringungsklausel *(Feuerversicherung)* contributory clause;
~ **und Beschlagnahmeklausel** free of capture and seizure clause.
aufbringungspflichtig contributory.
Aufbringungs|pflichtiger contributory; ~**schuld** contribution; ~**schuldner** contributory; ~**soll** production target; ~**umlage** levy, contribution.
Aufbruch start[ing], departure, kickoff, setting-out *(coll.)*;
allgemeiner ~ general exodus;
jem. den sofortigen ~ **befehlen** to tell s. o. to start at once; **sich im** ~ **befinden** *(Land)* to be on the point of emerging; **zum** ~ **rüsten** to get ready to leave.
aufbruchsbereit ready to leave.
Aufbruchsstimmung, allgemeine general disposition to leave early.
aufbrummen to inflict upon;
jem. die Kosten ~ to land s. o. with the expenses; **jem. eine Strafe** ~ to inflict a punishment on s. o.
aufbürden to [impose] a burden, to load;
jem. etw. ~ to inflict s. th. upon s. o.; **sich jem.** ~ to inflict one's company on s. o. *(fam.)*; **sich etw.** ~ to burden o. s. with s. th.; **seinen Mitarbeitern viel Arbeit** ~ to load a lot of work onto one's staff; **jem. die Schuld** ~ to lay (put) the blame on s. o.; **sich eine Verantwortung** to saddle o. s. with a responsibility; **sich zu viel** ~ to take too much on one's shoulders, to bite off more than one can chew.

Aufbürdung imposition.
aufdecken to reveal, to divulge, to disclose, to nail to the counter, to detect, to expose, to dig up, to bring to light;
Betrug ~ to show up a fraud; **seine Karten** ~ to show one's hand; **Mängel** ~ to notify a defect; **Unangemessenheit der Rücklagen** ~ to disclose the inadequacy of reserve; **Verbrechen** ~ to detect a crime; **eine Verschwörung** ~ to expose a plot.
Aufdeckung discovery, disclosure, exposure, bringing to light, revelation, detection;
unter ~ aller Scheußlichkeiten with the lid off;
~ **eines Abhörfalles** bugging disclosure; ~ **eines Betruges** disclosure of a fraud; ~ **eines Verbrechens** detection of crime; ~ **einer Verschwörung** exposure of a plot.
aufdonnern, sich to dress up, to doll o. s. up *(coll.)*, to trim.
Aufdrängen intrusion;
~ **seiner Meinung** obtrusion of one's opinions on others.
aufdrängen to force (thrust) upon;
jem. etw. ~ to force (thrust) s. th. on s. o.; **sich jem.** ~ to make intrusions upon s. o., to obtrude o. s. upon s. o., to hoist upon s. o.; **sich Freunden unangenehm** ~ to be pushing with strangers; **minderwertige Waren** ~ to impose inferior goods.
aufdrehen to turn on, *(Radio)* to turn up;
Gashahn ~ to turn on the gas tap, *(sich umbringen)* to gas o. s.; **Motor** ~ to open up, to rev up; **voll** ~ to turn on the heat.
aufdringlich too familiar, importunate, obtrusive, urgent, solicitous, *(Parfüm)* pungent;
~**er Bettler** importunate beggar; ~**er Mensch** pushing person.
Aufdringlichkeit intrusion, importunity, *(Parfüm)* pungency.
Aufdruck impression, imprint, lettering, enfacement, *(auf Postkarten)* surcharge, *(Stempel)* stamp.
aufdrucken to enface, *(stempeln)* to imprint, to stamp.
aufdrücken, sein Siegel to impose one's seal.
aufeinander on top of one another;
~ **angewiesen sein** to be dependent upon one another; **gegenseitig ~ ziehen** to counterdraw;
~ **abgestimmte Farben** matched colo(u)rs.
aufeinanderfolgend consecutive, successive;
turnusmäßig ~ by rotations, rotational;
während dreier ~er Tage on three successive (consecutive) days.
aufeinander|stapeln to pile up; ~**stoßen** *(Autos)* to crash together, to collide.
Aufenthalt quarters, living, rest, commorancy, *(Schiff)* stay, *(Wohnsitz)* abode, residence, domicile, *(Zug)* stop, wait;
dauernder ~ dwelling place, habitancy; **fünf Minuten** ~ five minutes stop; **ordnungsgemäßer** ~ lawful residence; **ständiger** ~ legal residence; **unbefristeter** ~ residence unlimited in time; **unbekannten ~s** of unknown abode; **vorübergehender** ~ brief sojourn, stay, temporary residence;
~ **im Ausland** foreign sojourn; ~ **an einem Ort** continuance in a place; **unfreiwilliger ~ während einer Reise** detention on a journey;
Strecke ohne ~ durchfahren to make a journey without stop; ~ **angenehm gestalten** to make a stay a success; **kurzen ~ haben** *(Schiff)* to touch; **längeren ~ auf dem Bahnhof haben** to have a long wait at the station; **vorübergehend ~ nehmen** to stay, to stop, to stop over *(US)*, to quarter; **weder seinen gewöhnlichen noch ständigen ~ in England nehmen** to be not resident or ordinarily resident in the United Kingdom; **seinen ~ verlängern** to prolong one's stay.
Aufenthalts|anzeige notification of residence; ~**beschränkung** restriction on residence; ~**beschränkung auf ein bestimmtes Gebiet** restriction to a certain area; ~**bestätigung** *(Ausländer)* residence certificate (permit); ~**dauer** duration (length) of stay; **beabsichtigte ~dauer** period of proposed stay; ~**erlaubnis** residence (stay) permit, *(für Ausländer)* registration certificate, alien's residence permit; **kurzfristige ~erlaubnis** visitor's permit; ~**genehmigung** *(Universität)* green card *(US)*; **schriftliche ~genehmigung** written permission to reside; **jederzeit widerrufliche ~genehmigung** *(Asylrecht)* executive warranty; ~**kontrolle von Ausländern** supervision of aliens; ~**kosten** subsistence expenses.
Aufenthaltsort whereabouts, domicile, local habitation, place [of abode], residence, abidal, home, repair;
ohne festen ~ of no fixed abode; **jetziger ~ unbekannt** present location unknown;
zur Sozialhilfe berechtigender ~ settlement; **dauernder** ~ dwelling place; **gesetzlicher** ~ legal residence; **gewöhnlicher** ~ usual place of abode, habitual residence; **gesetzlich zugelassener** ~ legal stopping place;
seinen gewöhnlichen ~ haben to be ordinarily resident.
Aufenthaltsraum *(Betrieb)* rest (recreation) room, swing room *(sl.)*, *(Hotel)* dayroom, lounge, *(Jugendherberge)* common room;
~ **für durchreisende Touristen** economy room;
lediglich ein ~ für Lehrer sein to be a room for the use of teachers only.
Aufenthalts|verbot banishment; ~**verlängerung** lengthening of stay; ~**wechsel** change of residence; ~**zulage** lodging allowance.
auferlegen to impose, to inflict, to entail, to lay upon;
jem. Bedingungen ~ to impose conditions upon s. o.; **jem. einen Eid** ~ to put s. o. on his oath; **einem Flugzeug Startverbot** ~ to ground an airplane; **Geldstrafe** ~ to fine, to mulct; **Kontribution** ~ to levy a contribution; **einem Land Kontributionen** ~ to lay a country under contribution; **Kosten** ~ to order to bear the costs; **jem. die Kosten des Verfahrens** ~ to award the costs against s. o.; **Steuern** ~ to impose taxes; **jem. strengstens Stillschweigen** ~ to enjoin strict silence upon s. o.; **Strafe** ~ to inflict a punishment; **jem. eine Verpflichtung** ~ to lay s. o. under an obligation; **sich Zwang** ~ to restrain o. s.; **sich keinen Zwang** ~ to be free and easy.
Auferlegung imposition, infliction;
unter ~ der Kosten with costs, on payment of (awarding the) cost;
~ **einer Geldstrafe** infliction of a fine; ~ **hoher Steuern** heavy (harsh) taxation; ~ **von Steuern** laying on of taxes.
aufessen to eat up, to finish one's meal;
alles bis auf den letzten Krümel ~ to eat every bit of one's dinner.
auffächern to diversify;
sein Produktionsprogramm ~ to diversify one's manufacturing (production) program(me); **einseitig auf Bedürfnisse der Raumfahrtindustrie abgestelltes Produktionsprogramm** ~ to diversify out of aerospace industry into manufacturing; **sein Warensortiment** ~ to diversify one's product lines.
Auffächerung|des Produktionsprogramms diversification of products; ~ **des Warensortiments** diversification of product lines.
Auffächerungsmöglichkeit way to diversify.
Auffahren *(Zusammenstoß)* rear-end collision;
zu dichtes ~ driving bumper to bumper.
auffahren to draw (drive) up, *(aufprallen)* to run into, *(Geschütz)* to bring into action, *(Schiff)* to run aground;
beim geringsten Anlaß ~ to flare up at the slightest provocation; **schweres Geschütz** ~ *(fig.)* to bring heavy artillery into play; **auf einen Güterzug** ~ to crash into a freight train; **Menge Kuchen** ~ to dish up a lot of cake; **nahe** ~ to ride close behind; **aus dem Schlaf** ~ to wake up with a start; **voll auf etw.** ~ to plough into s. th.;
Fahrzeuge ~ lassen to bring vehicles in position.
Auffahrt rising ground, access, ascent, *(Auffahren)* approach [ramp], drive, driving up, driveway *(US)*.
Auffahrts|rampe approach (access) ramp; ~**weg** access route.
Auffahrunfall rear-end collision.
auffallen to be conspicuous, to attract interest (attention);
jem. ~ to strike s. o.; **immer** ~ to step off; **lästig** ~ to stick out like a sore thumb; **unangenehm** ~ to attract unfavo(u)rable notice, to make a bad impression (spectacle) of o. s.
auffallend striking, remarkable, particularly;
~ **gut besucht** notably well attended;
sich ~ benehmen to cut a caper.
auffällig conspicuous, ostentatious, noticeable, *(Farbe, Kleidung)* showy, loud, gaudy, flashy;
~**es Benehmen** peculiar behavio(u)r;
sich ~ benehmen to behave oddly; **sich ~ kleiden** to dress extravagantly.
Auffälligkeit conspicuousness, *(Kleidung)* loudness.
Auffang|becken, ~behälter catch basin.
Auffangen von Kosten absorption of cost, cost absorption.
auffangen to cushion, *(Erschütterung)* to cushion, *(Funksignal)* to pick up, *(Kosten)* to absorb, *(Regenwasser)* to collect;
inflatorische Ausstrahlungen ~ to cushion inflationary factors; **den Ball** ~ *(fig.)* to keep the conversation going (ball rolling); **Flüchtlinge** ~ to receive refugees; **einige Gesprächsfetzen** ~ to catch a few words of the conversation; **Kosten teilweise** ~ to pick up (absorb) part of the costs; **steigende Kosten** ~ to absorb rising costs; **Kostenerhöhungen** ~ to absorb increases in costs; **feindliche Kräfte** ~ to contain enemy forces; **Kurssturz** ~ to cushion the decline; **Schwankungen** ~ to cushion fluctuations; **konjunkturelle Talfahrt** ~ to cushion the downswing; **Verluste** ~ to absorb losses.

Auffang|gebiet *(Flüchtlinge)* reception area, *(Raumkapsel)* recovery area; ~**gesellschaft für notleidende Industriebetriebe** Securities Management Trust *(Br.)*; ~**graben** catchwater (interception) ditch; ~**lager** reserve position, *(Flüchtlinge)* reception camp; ~**netz** *(Schiff)* save-all; ~**position** *(mil.)* reserve position.
auffassen to understand, to comprehend, to grasp, to conceive; **etw. anders** ~ to see s. th. differently; **als Beleidigung** ~ to take as an insult; **etw. falsch** ~ to take s. th. in the wrong spirit, to misunderstand s. th.; **langsam** ~ to be slow in the uptake; **Stelle richtig** ~ to put a right construction on a passage; **schnell** ~ to be quick on the uptake (of comprehension), to be quick-witted; **Schweigen als Zustimmung** ~ to read silence as consent; **schwer** ~ to be slow of apprehension.
auffassend, leicht apprehensive; **schnell** ~ quick of apprehension, nimble.
Auffassung opinion, outlook, view, *(Begreifen)* uptake, comprehension, understanding, concept;
nach meiner ~ in my view (opinion), to my mind;
abweichende ~ dissenting (dissentient) opinion *(US)*; **falsche** ~ misunderstanding; **geteilte** ~ divided opinion; **vernünftige** ~ just opinion; **weitverbreitete** ~ widely held opinion;
~ **des Gerichts** judicial opinion; ~ **der Minderheit** minority opinion; **falsche** ~ **einer Textstelle** misinterpretation of a passage;
falsche ~ **von seinen Pflichten haben** to misconceive one's duty; ~ **teilen** to share a view; **strenge** ~ **in Disziplinarangelegenheiten vertreten** to be strict in the matter of discipline; **klägerische** ~ **vortragen** to argue the case for the plaintiff.
Auffassungsgabe perceptive faculty, apprehension;
rasche ~ **haben** ready wit, quickness (readiness) of mind, to be a quick learner.
Auffassungsvermögen apprehension, understanding;
gutes ~ **haben** to be quick on the uptake.
auffindbar discoverable, findable, traceable.
auffinden to discover, to locate.
Auffindung von Bodenschätzen discovery of natural resources.
aufflackern *(Aufruhr)* to flare up;
wieder ~ to recrudesce.
auffliegen to go up in smoke;
~ **lassen** to shop *(sl.)*.
auffordern to request, to invite, to summon, to call up;
zur Einzahlung von Kapital ~ to call up capital; **Stadt zur Kapitulation** ~ to demand the surrender of a town; **jem. zur Zahlung** ~ to request payment from s. o., *(dringend)* to dun s. o.
Aufforderung request, appeal, call, calling, invitation, requisition, summoning;
auf ~ on demand (request);
ausdrückliche ~ express request; **dringende** ~ urgent request; **gerichtliche** ~ summons; **öffentliche** ~ public notice, ban; **schriftliche** ~ demand in writing, request in writing; **wiederholte** ~**en** repeated requests;
~ **zur Abgabe von Geboten** invitation to contract (treat); ~ **zur Beteiligung an einer Ausschreibung** bid invitation *(US)*; ~ **zur Einzahlung auf Aktien** call on shares *(Br.)* (stocks, *US*), *(schriftlich)* call letter; ~ **zu erscheinen** *(Fraktionsführer)* one-line whip *(Br.)*; ~ **zur Klageeinlassung** optional writ; ~ **zur Leistung einer Einschußzahlung im Effektendifferenzgeschäft** margin call *(US)*; ~ **zur Nachschußzahlung** stock assessment; ~ **zur Rechnungsvorlage** requisition for the production of accounts; ~ **zur Rückzahlung** call (recall) for redemption; ~ **zur Vorlage des Bankausweises** bank call *(US)*; ~ **zur Vorlage von Urkunden** notice to produce documents; ~ **zur Zahlung** call for funds, summons to pay; **öffentliche** ~ **zur Zeichnung von Effekten** public offering (issue).
Aufforderungsschreiben written request, *(Bank)* call letter.
aufforsten to afforest, to reforest, to wood.
Aufforstung reforestation, afforestation;
~ **vom Staatsland** timber culture entry.
auffressen, das ganze Vermögen to swallow up all the money.
auffrischen to furbish [up], to refurbish, to renovate;
sich ~ to refresh o. s.; **sein Englisch** ~ to brush up (dish up, refresh, *US*) one's English; **alte Erinnerungen** ~ to go back to one's old haunts; **sein Gedächtnis** ~ to refresh one's memory; **seine Kohlenvorräte** ~ to renew one's supplies of coal; **Vorräte** ~ to replenish one's stocks.
Auffrischung refreshment, *(Sprache)* brush-up;
zur ~ **Ihres Gedächtnisses** to refresh your memory; **zur** ~ **der Kenntnisse** to brush up one's knowledge;
~ **der Lagerbestände** replenishment of stocks;
ein bißchen der ~ **bedürfen** to be a bit rusty.
Auffrischungskurs refresher course *(US)*.
aufführbar *(Theaterstück)* playable, performable.
aufführen *(Bau)* to build, to erect, *(Film)* to show, to produce, *(Posten)* to enter, to book, to record, to list, *(Theater)* to perform, to show, to enact, to represent, to put on the stage; **detailliert (einzeln)** ~ to specify, to specialize, to detail, to itemize *(US)*; **sich kümmerlich** ~ to cheapen o. s.; **listenmäßig** ~ to itemize *(US)*; **sich schäbig** ~ to make o. s. cheap; **sich schlecht** ~ to behave badly, to misbehave; **sich seltsam** ~ to behave in a strange fashion; **Stück** ~ to put a play on the stage; **sich tyrannisch (despotisch)** ~ to act with a high hand; **sich in einer Bar ungehörig** ~ to be disorderly in a bar; **wieder** ~ to react; **Stück wieder** ~ to put a play on again.
Aufführung *(Buchung)* entry, *(Errichtung)* construction, erection, *(Film, Theater)* performance, presentment, production, [re]-presentation;
ausführliche (detaillierte) ~ specialization, itemization *(US)*; **bevorstehende** ~**en** upcoming plays; **öffentliche** ~ performance in public;
~ **eines einzelnen Buchungspostens** itemization of an account *(US)*; ~ **eines Dramas** dramatic performance; ~ **beruflich erforderlicher Eigenschaften** job specification; ~ **von Gründen** assignment of reasons; ~ **der Gründe gegen die Entlastung des Konkursschuldners** specialization of grounds of opposition to a bankrupt's discharge; ~ **der strittigen Punkte** specification of the points at issue; ~ **eines Stückes** putting on of a play;
Theaterstück zur ~ **bringen** to put a play on the stage; **Theaterstück zur** ~ **freigeben** to license a play; **hundert** ~**en erlebt haben** to have a run of one hundred performances.
Aufführungs|rechte performing (stage, dramatic) rights, rights of representation and performance; ~**zeitraum** run.
Auffülladung berth cargo.
auffüllen to refill, to replenish, to restock, to fill up, to cram; **Fonds** ~ to reestablish a fund; **Lager** ~ to restock, to replenish one's inventory; **Mannschaftsbestand** ~ to complete a crew; **Reserven** ~ to replenish (fill up) reserves; **Schiffsvorräte** ~ to replenish a ship's stores; **Warenlager wieder** ~ to renew a stock of goods; **wieder** ~ *(Belegschaft)* to recruit *(US)*.
Auffüllung *(Reserven)* replenishment;
~ **eines Fonds** reestablishment of a fund; ~ **des Lagers (Lagerbestands)** replenishment of stocks, replacement of inventories, restocking; ~ **der Vorräte** replenishment of supplies.
Aufgabe task, business, office, concern, job, assignment *(US)*, part, *(Absendung)* dispatch, *(Aufgeben)* abolition, departure, abandonment, *(Auftrag)* advice, *(Mitteilung)* advice, *(Pflicht)* duty, business, function, responsibility, *(Preisgabe)* relinquishment, release, waiver, renunciation, abandonment, *(Rechenaufgabe)* mathematical problem, sum, *(Schule)* homework, assignment *(US)*, *(Telegramm)* handing in;
~ **folgt** advice in due course; **einer** ~ **nicht gewachsen** unequal to a task; **laut** ~ as per advice, advised, as advised by;
nach dem Dienstplan anfallende ~**n** rostered duties; **berufliche** ~ job assignment; **doppelte** ~ double function; **praktisch durchführbare** ~ practical proposition; **ehrenamtliche** ~**n** honorary duties; **erste** ~ *(Kapitalmarkt)* first-rate borrower; **geschichtliche** ~ historical mission; **im Augenblick gestellte** ~ task at hand; **grundsätzliche** ~**n** basic functions; **geistig interessierende** ~ work that interests; **kapitalmarktpolitische** ~**n** objectives of capital market policy; **konsularische** ~**n** consular functions; **ministerielle** ~**n** ministerial duties; **schriftliche** ~**n** *(Schule)* written homework; **schwierige** ~ onerous task; **staatliche** ~**n** governmental duties; **unangenehme** ~ chore; **untergeordnete** ~**n** ancillary duties; **unternehmerische** ~ company task; **verschiedenartige** ~ multifarious duties; **vielseitige** ~**n** manifold duties; **vordringlichste** ~ priority task, top priority job; **vorgeschriebene** ~ prescribed task; **vorrangige** ~ primary duty; **wichtigste** ~ primary business; **zugewiesene** ~ assigned task;
~ **eines Amtes** vacation of an office; ~ **von Ansprüchen** relinquishment (abandonment) of claims, *(fam.)* backdown; ~ **einer Anzeige** insertion (placing) of an advertisement; ~**n des Bankgeschäfts** banker's functions; ~**n und Befugnisse** functions and powers; ~ **einer Bestellung** placing of an order; ~**n der Betriebsleitung** managerial functions; ~ **eines alten Brauches** departure from an old custom; ~ **eines Briefes** posting *(Br.)* (mailing, *US*) a letter, *(Sinn)* purport of a letter; ~ **des Gepäcks** booking of luggage *(Br.)*, checking of baggage *(US)*; ~ **eines Geschäfts** giving up business, breaking up of an establishment, closing down, *(Ruhestand)* retiring from business, retirement from business; ~ **der Geschäftstätigkeit** de facto dissolution; ~ **der Geschworenen** province of the jury; ~ **der Gesellschaft**

functions of a society; ~ **eines belasteten Grundstücks** abondonment of a mortgaged estate; ~ **einer Gutschriftsstornierung** credit returns account; ~ **von Kauf- und Verkaufsorders zu verschiedenen Zeiten** *(Börse)* selling on a scale *(US)*; ~ **einer [Konkurs]vorzugsstellung** surrender of preference; **~n eines Liquidators** liquidator's duties; **klassische ~n der Nationalökonomie** classical types of economics; ~ **einer Omnibuslinie** discontinuance of a bus line; ~ **bei der Post** posting *(Br.)*, mailing *(US)*; ~ **des Preises** price quotation; ~ **eines Prinzips** departure from a principle; ~ **unrentabler Produktionsgebiete** elimination of unprofitable operations; ~ **eines Rechtes** relinquishment of a right, waiver, remise; ~ **der Staatsangehörigkeit** renouncement of one's citizenship, renunciation of one's nationality *(Br.)*; ~ **einer guten Stellung** vacation of a good position; ~ **der Tarifbindungen** tariff abandonment; ~ **eines Unternehmens** abandonment of an enterprise; ~ **einer Versicherungspolice** surrender of policy;
einem Kind seine ~n abfragen to hear a child his lesson; **einem Schüler die ~n abhören** to hear a pupil's lesson; **j. mit einer ~ betrauen** to assign s. o. with a task; **schwierige ~ bewältigen** to tackle a difficult task; ~ **durchführen** to conduct an assignment; **jem. von einer ~ entbinden** to release s. o. from a task, *(j. entfernen)* to strip s. o. of a job; ~ **erfüllen** to perform (complete) a task; **informatorische ~n erfüllen** to handle informations; **richterliche ~n erfüllen** to exercise judicial functions; ~ **erledigen** to tackle a job; **seine ~n erledigen** to pursue one's duties, *(sorgfältig)* to be exact in one's duties; **jds. ~ erleichtern** to lighten s. one's task; **jem. eine bestimmte ~ geben** to set s. o. a job; **zu jds. ~n gehören** to be part of s. one's functions; **nicht zu den ~n eines Ausschusses gehören** to be outside the reference of a commission; **sich zur ~ des Rauchens verpflichtet haben** to be under a vow not to smoke; **an eine ~ herangehen** to approach a task; ~ **machen** to send advice; **es sich zur ~ machen** to make it one's business; **seine ~n machen** *(Schüler)* to do one's homework, to prep *(fam.)*; **jds. ~ sein** to be s. one's place; **für eine ~ nicht geeignet sein** not to be up to a job; **für eine ~ wie geschaffen sein** to be cut out (tailor-made) for a job; **einer ~ gewachsen sein** to cope with a task, to be up to one's job (equal to a task), to measure up to one's task *(US)*; **einer ~ nicht gewachsen sein** to be unequal to a task; **zur ~ seines Amtes gezwungen sein** to walk the plank; ~ **stellen** to assign a task; **leichte ~ stellen** to give an easy task; ~ **übernehmen** to take over an assignment; **jem. eine ~ übertragen** to vest s. o. with a function; **bestimmte ~n wahrnehmen** to carry out agency duties; **dienstliche ~n wahrnehmen** to carry out official functions; **mit der gestellten ~ fertig werden** to have one's work cut out for one; **sich einer ~ widmen** to settle down to a task; **sich einer ~ nicht gewachsen zeigen** to prove unequal to one's task; **jem. eine ~ zuweisen** to allot duties to s. o., to assign a task to s. o.;
~amt *(Post)* office of dispatch, *(Telegramm)* office of origin; **~bahnhof** dispatch point (station); **~formular** telegram form.

aufgabegemäß as per advice.

aufgabeln, altes Bild to pick up an old painting.

Aufgabenausweitung des Bankgeschäfts bank diversification.

Aufgabenbereich sphere of action (activities), field of work, duties, functions, competence, province, domain, scope, purview, line, vires, *(Ausschuß)* order (terms) of reference;
innerhalb des ~s within the province of;
nichtkommunaler ~ proprietary duties; **redaktioneller ~** editorial duties;
~ **eines Gesetzgebungskörpers** purview of a legislative body; ~ **der Wirtschaft** economic functions;
~ **beschränken** to limit functions; **zu jds. ~ gehören, in jds. ~ liegen** to come within s. one's functions (duties, activities), to fall within s. one's province, to come (lie) within the purview of s. o.; **neuen ~ übernehmen** to enter upon new duties; **seinen ~ übernehmen** to take up one's duties; **sich auf seinen neuen ~ vorbereiten** to fit o. s. out for one's new duties; ~ **wahrnehmen** to discharge duties; **jem. einen ~ zuweisen** to assign a duty to s. o.

Aufgabenbuch *(Schüler)* prep book.

Aufgabengebiet domain, purview, field of action (activities), scope, duties of a job, assignment of duties, province, competence, line, *(Ausschuß)* order (terms) of reference;
unterschiedliche ~e discriminative duties; **wirtschaftliches ~** economic business;
~ **im Vorstandsbereich** general management field in industry;
in jds. ~ fallen to come into s. one's domain; **in das ~ der Gewerkschaft fallen** to be within the scope of trade-union activities; **viele ~e außerbetrieblich erledigen lassen** to job out many functions.

Aufgabenkreis scope, functions, activities, duties, domain, province, purview, line;
normaler ~ normal activity (operations);
jem. in seinen ~ einführen to acquaint s. o. with his duties; **außerhalb von jds. ~es liegen** to lie outside the scope of s. one's address; **innerhalb des normalen ~es liegen** to come within the scope of normal functions; **jem. einen bestimmten ~ zuweisen** to detail s. o. for a duty.

Aufgaben|spezialisierung functional specialization; **~stellung** assignment of duties.

Aufgabenummer registration number.

Aufgaben|verteilung task distribution; **~wahrnehmung** discharge of duties; **~zuweisung** assignment of functions, assignment of a task.

Aufgabe|ort place of origin; **~postamt** office of dispatch, *(Telegramm)* office of origin; **~schein** *(Gepäck)* receipt, check *(US)*, *(Post)* postal receipt; **~spediteur, ~spedition** initial carrier; **~station, ~stelle** place of dispatch, dispatching (sending) station; **~stempel** postmark, cancellation stamp; **~tag** day of dispatch; **~zeit** time of dispatch, *(Datengerät)* code time.

Aufgang way up, flight of steps, staircase, stairway.

aufgebahrt liegen, öffentlich to lie in state.

aufgebauscht *(Bericht)* played up, magnified;
leicht ~ slightly exaggerated.

aufgebaut sein, sorgfältig *(Buch)* to have a pattern.

aufgeben to give up, to toss in the towel, *(absenden)* to dispatch, *(ad acta legen)* to lay aside, *(anzeigen)* to advise, to give notice, *(Patient)* to condemn, *(belasten)* to debit, *(Besitz)* to abandon, to peg out, *(kreditieren)* to credit, *(Rechtsanspruch)* to release, to abandon, to relinquish, to waive, to abnegate, to resign, *(Schiff)* to desert, to abandon, to cast away, *(verzichten)* to give up, to abandon, to renounce, to part with, to relinquish;
j. ~ to give s. o. up; **Amt ~** to resign office; **Anlage ~** to retire a unit; **Annonce ~** to put an advertisement in the paper; **Annonce [in einer Zeitung] ~** to insert (run) an advertisement [in a newspaper]; **Anspruch ~** to resign (waive, give up) a claim; **Bedingungen ~** to quote terms; **Bestellung ~** to [place an] order; **Brief ~** to post *(Br.)* (mail, *US*) a letter; **Einzelheiten ~** to furnish with particulars; **seinen Geist ~** to breath one's last, to give up the ghost; **Gepäck ~** to register (book) luggage *(Br.)*, to check baggage *(US)*; **Geschäft ~** to give up one's (retire from) business; **Gewohnheit ~** to break with a habit; **belastetes Gründstück ~** to abandon a mortgaged estate; **Hausarbeiten ~** to give (assign, *US*) homework; **zum Kauf ~** to give a buying order; **Konkursvorzugsstellung ~** to surrender a preference; **Kurse ~** to quote prices; **nicht ~** to hang on, to show perseverance; **Optionsrecht ~** to abandon an option; **Paket ~** to take a parcel to the post; **Plan endgültig ~** to hang up a plan definitively, to throw a scheme overboard; **jem. ein Rätsel ~** to ask s. o. a riddle; **Rauchen ~** to give up (cut out) smoking; **sein Rechtsstudium ~** to leave off studying law; **das Rennen ~** *(fig.)* to throw up the sponge; **Saldo ~** to state the balance of an account; **am Schalter ~** to hand in at the counter; **Schiff ~** to surrender (abandon) a ship; **Staatsangehörigkeit ~** to renounce one's citizenship *(US)* (nationality, *Br.*); **seine Stellung ~** to resign from one's post, to throw (give, pack) up (quit, *US*) one's job, to relinquish one's appointment; **Telegramm ~** to wire, to send (hand in) a telegram; **Unternehmen ~** to abandon an enterprise; **zum Verkauf ~** to give a selling order; **seinen Widerstand ~** to give up one's resistance; **Wohnsitz ~** to abandon a domicile, to relinquish a residence.

Aufgeber sender, consignor, *(Anzeige)* advertiser, *(Fernspruch)* drafter, *(Postanweisung)* remitter.

aufgeblasen swollen-headed, gassy, boastful, puffed up [with wind], intoxicated with pride, inflated, with a high hand;
~ **wie ein Zinshahn** as proud as a peacock (punch);
~ **sein** to be on one's high horse, to suffer from a swollen head, to get the swelled head *(US)*.

Aufgeblasenheit conceit, arrogance, self-sufficiency, inflation, putting on, toploftiness *(coll.)*;
jem. seine ~ abgewöhnen to knock the stuffing out of s. o.; **jds. ~ dämpfen** to settle s. one's hash *(sl.)*.

Aufgebot *(Eheschließung)* public notice, asking, banns of matrimony, *(mil.)* mobilization, levy, calling up, draft, *(Polizei)* posse, *(Vorladung)* summons, *(Wertpapiere)* cancellation;
mit einem großen ~ in strength; **unter ~ aller Kräfte** with might and main, by straining every nerve;
starkes ~ von Polizei strong body (force) of police; **starkes ~ von Wagen** imposing array of cars;
~ **bestellen (verkünden lassen)** to publish (put up, ask) the banns.

aufgeboten *(Wertpapiere)* called in, withdrawn;
~ **sein** *(Truppen)* to be out.
Aufgebots|buch marrying notice book; ~**verfahren** publication, summons, *(Wertpapiere)* cancellation proceedings.
aufgebracht excited, upset, wild, hot under the collar;
über j. ~ sein to be out of patience with s. o.
aufgebraucht used up, spent, consumed;
~**es Geld** spent money.
auf|gedonnert dressed (got) up to the nines (to hill), flossy *(US sl.)*, jazzed up *(sl.)*; ~**gefischt werden** to be picked up by; ~**geflogen** *(Ballon)* up; **wieder** ~**geforstet** reafforested; **nachstehend** ~**geführt** specified below; **zuerst** ~**geführt** first-named; **wieder** ~**geführt werden** to come on again; ~**gegangen** *(Kuvert)* unstuck.
aufgegeben *(Schiff)* abandoned, derelict;
~**es Gepäck** registered luggage *(Br.)*, checked baggage *(US)*.
aufgegliedert analysed, broken down *(US)*;
~**e Geburtenziffer** crude birth rate.
aufgehalten detained, windbound;
hier geschäftlich ~ werden to be kept here by business; **durch unangemeldete Besucher im Büro ~ werden** to be detained in the office by unexpected callers.
Aufgehen *(Fusion)* merger;
völliges ~ in seiner Arbeit complete devotion to one's work;
~ **der Klageansprüche** merger of rights of action.
aufgehen *(Fusion)* to merge, to be absorbed, *(Mond, Sonne)* to rise, to ascend, *(math.)* to be even, to come out, *(Saat)* to spring up, to shoot, to germinate, *(Tür)* to open, *(Vorhang)* to rise; **ganz in seiner Arbeit** ~ to be utterly devoted to (engrossed in) one's work; **ganz in seiner Familie** ~ to have no life apart from one's family; **in einer anderen Firma** ~ to be incorporated in another firm; **ganz in ihren Kindern** ~ to be wrapped up in their children; **in Rauch** ~ to end up in smoke; **in einem Reich** ~ to be merged in an Empire.
aufgehender Stern *(fig.)* rising star.
aufgehoben *(Gesetz)* abrogated, extinct, *(Urteil)* reversed, *(Vertrag)* cancelled;
gut ~ well looked after; **nicht** ~ unrevoked, unabrogated, unrepealed, not cancelled;
~ **werden** *(Versammlung)* to break up.
aufgeklärt enlightened.
aufgekratzt in high spirits, in full feather, chirpy *(Br., coll.)*.
aufgelassen *(Grundstück)* conveyed, assured;
~**e Grube** shut-down mine.
aufgelaufen accrued, accumulated;
~**e Dividende** accumulated (accumulation) dividend; ~**e Etatsbewilligungen** amounts voted; ~**e Kosten** accrued costs (charges), accumulated charges; ~**e Zinsen** interest accrued.
Aufgeld *(Börse)* premium, agio, price of exchange, over-agio *(Br.)*, *(Handgeld)* earnest (odd) money, *(Reportgeschäft)* report, backwardation, contango *(Br.)*, *(Zuschlag)* extra charge;
~**konto** agio account.
aufgelegt *(Anleihe)* issued, *(Schiff)* laid up, disposed, inclined, in the mood (mind);
gut ~ well-disposed; **nicht** ~ indisposed;
zum Schreiben ~ in the mood to write; **zur Zeichnung** ~ open for subscription;
zum Arbeiten ~ sein to be in the mood to work; **nicht zum Arbeiten ~ sein** not to feel like working; **nicht ~ sein** to be not in tune for; **schlecht ~ sein** to be out of sorts;
~**er Schwindel** barefaced swindle.
aufgelockerte Bebauung low-density housing.
aufgelöst, in Tränen dissolved in tears.
aufgemacht dressed, made up;
groß ~ *(Nachricht)* featured, full blown;
hübsch ~**e Geschenkartikel** gift packages.
aufgenommen accepted, received;
glänzend ~ large, well accepted;
~ **sein** to be one of the crowd; **allenthalben wohlwollend ~ worden sein** to have been well received throughout the country; **freundlich ~ werden** to meet with a kind reception; **von den Zeitungen gut ~ werden** to have a good press; **kühl ~ werden** to win a cold reception; **höheren Orts ungünstig ~ werden** to find no favo(u)r in high quarters;
~**e Gelder** debts, accounts payable *(US)*; **tatsächlich** ~**es Inventar** physical inventory; ~**e Stimme** recorded voice.
aufgeräumt in good humo(u)r, cheerful.
aufgeregt excited, agitated, nervous, in a flurry, hot and bothered;
~ **sein** to be put about; **völlig ~ sein** to be in a flutter;
die ~**en Gemüter beruhigen** to allay popular excitement.
aufgerichtet, hoch upright.
aufgerufen called, *(Obligationen)* recalled;
nicht ~ uncalled;
~ **werden** *(Prozeß)* to be put up;
~**e Banknoten** notes withdrawn from circulation; **zur Einzahlung** ~**es Kapital** called-up capital.
aufgeschlagenes Buch open book.
geschlossen open-minded, hospitable, *(Markt)* receptive;
j. gegenüber einer Sache sehr ~ finden to find s. o. amenable to s. th.; **für alles ~ sein** to keep an open mind; **sich ganz ~ zeigen** *(Börse)* to be in sunny mood.
Aufgeschlossenheit open-mindedness, *(Markt)* receptivity.
auf|geschlüsselt nach broken down by; ~**geschmissen** *(fam.)* up the pole *(sl.)*; ~**geschmissen sein** to be stuck in a fix.
aufgeschoben postponed, delayed, put off;
~ **werden** to lie over;
~**er Bedarf** deferred (pent-up, *US*) demand; ~**e Lebensversicherung** deferred [life] assurance *(Br.)*; ~**e Leibrente** deferred annuity; ~**e Lieferung** *(Börse)* deferred delivery; ~**e Reparaturen** deferred maintenance; ~**e Zahlung** deferred payment.
aufgeschreckt, von schlechten Nachrichten troubled by bad news.
aufgestauter Bedarf pent-up demand *(US)*.
aufgestellter|Kandidat nominee; ~ **Saldo** balance struck.
aufgetakelt rigged up, *(fig.)* dressed fit to kill (up to the nines, to death), with bells *(sl.)*;
sich mächtig ~ haben to be in full feather.
aufgetankt filled up.
aufgetragen, ein bißchen zu stark laid on a bit too thick.
aufgewärmt warmed-over *(US)*, warmed up *(Br.)*.
Aufgewärmtes *(fig.)* rehash.
aufgeweckt bright, quick-witted, sharp, clever, wide *(Br., sl.)*.
aufgewendet spent, expended;
nicht ~ unexpended;
~**er Betrag** amount spent.
aufgewertet revalued, revalorized.
aufgeworfen werden *(Frage)* to come up.
auf|gezählt, einzeln specified, itemized; ~**gezeichnet sein** to stand on record; ~**gezogen** *(Foto)* mounted; **von oben** ~**gezwungen** imposed from on high.
Aufgleitfläche anafront, warm front.
aufgliedern to subdivide, to split up into, *(analysieren)* to analyse, to break down *(US)*, to classify;
nach Abteilungen ~ to departmentalize; **anteilsmäßig** ~ to average; **Bilanz** ~ to analyse a balance sheet; **Konten** ~ to dissect (classify) accounts; **Konten nach ihrer Fälligkeit** ~ to age accounts; **Kosten** ~ to itemize costs.
Aufgliederung splitting up, analysis, itemization, breakdown *(US)*;
berufliche ~ occupational distribution, breakdown by occupations; **fachliche** ~ departmentalization;
~ **in Abteilungen** departmentalization; ~ **der Bankpassiva** analysis of a bank's liabilities; ~ **einer Bilanz** analysis sheet; ~ **der Buchungen** classification of entries; ~ **eines Etats** breakdown of a budget *(US)*; ~ **von Konten** classification (dissection) of accounts; ~ **von Kosten** itemization (breakdown, *US*) of costs; ~ **der Produktionskosten** manufacturing statement; ~ **nach Sachgebieten** functional classification; ~ **der Spesen** breakdown of expenses.
aufgreifen to pick up, to seize;
Faden der Erzählung wieder ~ to pick up the thread of the discussion; **Fall** ~ to move into a case; **Idee sofort** ~ to jump at an idea; **Sache** ~ to take up a matter; **Verbrecher** ~ to pick up a criminal.
aufhaben *(Geschäft)* to be open;
viel ~ *(Schüler)* to have plenty of homework.
aufhacken, Boden to peck up the ground.
aufhalsen, jem. etw. to thrust (saddle) s. th. on (land s. th. with) s. o., to pass s. th. on to s. o., to let s. o. in for s. th.
aufhaltbar barrable.
Aufhalte|aktion holding action; ~**linie** *(mil.)* stop line.
aufhalten to stop, to hinder, to balk, to check, *(Fahrzeug)* to hold up, to halt, *(Schiff)* to detain;
sich ~ to dwell, to reside, to linger, *(vorübergehend)* to sojourn; **sich über etw.** ~ to find fault with s. th.; **sich über j.** ~ to take exception to s. o.; **sich im Ausland** ~ to stay abroad; **Feind** ~ to check the enemy; **Flut** ~ to stem the tide; **Fortschritt** ~ to retard progress; **sich im Freien** ~ to spend one's time in the open; **an der Grenze** ~ to detain at the frontier; **sich mit Kleinigkeiten** ~ to waste one's time with trifles; **sich lange mit etw.** ~ to linger over s. th.; **sich in der Nähe** ~ to stay around; **sich in der Nähe des Hauses** ~ to linger round the house; **sich länger bei einem**

Punkt ~ to dwell at greater length on a subject; **sich ständig** ~ to haunt; **sich kurz an der Tür** ~ to pause at the door; **Verkehr** ~ to hold up (block, obstruct, delay) the traffic; **sich vorübergehend** ~ to sojourn; **sich im Winter im Ausland** ~ to spend the winter abroad; **Zug** ~ to stop a train.

Aufhängekreuz *(drucktechn.)* peel.

aufhängen to hang up, *(Zeitungsartikel)* to peg;
Bild an der Wand ~ to hang a picture on the wall; **an der Decke** ~ to suspend from the ceiling; **Frage an einer Tatsache** ~ to pivot a question on a fact; **Mantel** ~ to hang up one's coat; **an gut sichtbarer Stelle** ~ to put up in a conspicuous place; **j. symbolisch** ~ to hang s. o. in effigy; **jem. schlechte Ware** ~ to hoist one's wares upon s. o.

Aufhänger hanger, *(fig.)* pretext, approach, cover, *(Journalismus)* peg, curtain raiser, feature;
~ **für eine Beschwerde** peg to hang a grievance on; ~ **für eine Forderung** peg to hang a claim on;
als ~ **benutzen** to peg.

Aufhängevorrichtung hanger, suspender.

Aufhängung suspension;
kardanische ~ cardanic suspension.

aufhebbar cancellable, voidable, annullable, abatable, rescindable, divestible, forfeitable, defeasible, defeasanced, *(Gesetz)* abolishable, repealable.

aufheben to pick up, to lift, *(aufbewahren)* to keep, to preserve, *(auflösen)* to dissolve, *(ausgleichen)* to compensate, to counterbalance, *(Bestellung)* to countermand, to cancel, *(Gültigkeit)* to void, to avoid, to annul, to invalidate, to abate, to make void, to rescind, *(Verordnung)* to abrogate, to revoke, *(Waren)* to store, to lay up, to warehouse;
sich ~ to balance, to compensate each other, to set off, to offset *(US)*; **gerichtliche Anordnung** ~ to discharge a court order; **Baubeschränkungen** ~ to rezone *(US)*; **Belagerung** ~ to raise the siege; **Beschlagnahme** ~ to release (remove) an attachment, *(Staat)* to lift an embargo; **Beschluß** ~ to rescind a decree; **Beschränkungen** ~ to lift restrictions; **testamentarische Bestimmungen** ~ to defeat the provisions of a will; **Blockade** ~ to raise a blockade; **Boykott** ~ to call off (lift) a boycott; **Briefe** ~ to keep letters; **Ehe** ~ to annul a marriage; **Embargo** ~ to take off (lift) an embargo; **Entscheidung** ~ to reverse (disaffirm) a decision; **Fehdehandschuh** ~ to pick up the gauntlet; **sich gegenseitig** ~ *(Buchungen)* to cancel each other; **Geheimhaltungsbestimmungen** ~ to declassify; **Gesetz** ~ to abrogate (abolish) a law; **Haushaltstitel** ~ to deobligate; **Immunität** ~ to revoke the liberty of freedom from arrest; **Konkursverfahren** ~ to grant the bankrupt's discharge; **Kontensperre** ~ to release blocked accounts; **Quarantäne** ~ to remove the quarantine; **Rassentrennung** ~ to desegregate; **Sitzung** ~ to close (break up) a meeting, to leave the chair, *(Gericht)* to break up the court, *(vertagen)* to adjourn a meeting; **Steuer** ~ to abolish a tax; **Streik** ~ to call off a strike; **Testament** ~ to revoke a will; **Testament gerichtlich** ~ **lassen** to break a will; **Urteil** ~ to quash (reverse, rescind, vacate) a judgment; **erstinstanzliches Urteil** ~ to disaffirm the judgment of an inferior court; **Verfassung** ~ to subvert the constitution; **einstweilige Verfügung** ~ to discharge (dissolve) an injunction; **letztwillige Verfügung** ~ to set aside a will; **Vergleich** ~ to set aside a composition; **Verlöbnis** ~ to break off an engagement; **Verordnung vorübergehend** ~ to suspend a regulation; **Vertrag** ~ to cancel (rescind, dissolve, annul, avoid, set aside) a contract; **Vorbehalt** ~ to abolish a reserve; **Wahlversammlung** ~ to dismiss a congregation; **negative Wirkung** ~ to neutralize a negative effect; **etw. für einen späteren Zeitpunkt** ~ to keep s. th. for a later date; **Zwangswirtschaft** ~ to decontrol.

aufhebende Bestimmung rescinding clause.

Aufhebens, großes great fuss;
viel ~ **um nichts** much ado about nothing;
viel ~ **machen** to noise abroad; **nicht viel** ~ **um etw. machen** to be offhand about s. th.; **keines** ~ **wert sein** nothing to make a song and dance (write home) about.

Aufhebung lifting, picking up, *(Annullierung)* annulment, cancellation, nullification, abolishment, invalidation, rescission, *(Beschränkungen)* removal, lifting, *(Bestellung)* countermanding, cancellation, *(Gesetz)* abolition, abrogation, repeal, *(Sitzung)* adjournment, closing, *(Steuer)* abolishment, *(Unterbrechung)* discontinuance, *(erstinstanzliches Urteil)* defeasance, disaffirmance, reversal, cessation, *(Vertrag)* avoidance, rescission, disaffirmance, invalidation, cancellation, *(Vollmacht, Testament)* revocation, revoke;
einstweilige ~ suspense, suspension; **gegenseitige** ~ compensation, setoff, offset *(US)*; ~ **des Bankgeheimnisses** lifting of banking secrecy; ~ **von Baubeschränkungen** rezoning *(US)*; ~ **einer Beschlagnahme** release of an attachment, derequisition *(Br.)*, *(fremder Staat)* raising (lifting) of an embargo; ~ **von Beschränkungen** removal (abolition) of restrictions; ~ **einschränkender Bestimmungen** deregulation; ~ **einer Blockade** raising of a blockade; ~ **einer Ehe** annulment of marriage; ~ **eines Fideikommisses** discontinuance of an estate; ~ **von Geheimhaltungsbestimmungen** declassification; ~ **der ehelichen Gemeinschaft** judicial separation; ~ **der Geschäftsordnung** suspension of standing orders; ~ **einer Gesellschaft** dissolution of a partnership, winding up of a company; ~ **eines Gesetzes** repeal (invalidation, abolition, abrogation) of a law; **vorübergehende** ~ **eines Gesetztes** suspension of a statute; ~ **der Goldeinlösungspflicht** suspension of specie payment; ~ **des Goldstandards** suspension of the gold standard; ~ **eines Haftbefehls** replevin; ~ **von Handelsbeschränkungen** dropping of trade barriers; ~ **von Haushaltstiteln** deobligation; ~ **der Immunität** withdrawal of s. one's immunity, revocation of the liberty of freedom from arrest; ~ **einer Kartellabsprache** determination of an agreement; ~ **einer Klage** withdrawal of an action; ~ **einer Konkursanordnung** [order of] discharge, discharge of a receiving order; ~ **von Kontingentskontrollen** lifting of quota controls; ~ **einer Kontosperre** release of a blocked account; ~ **der Ladenverkaufspreise** lifting of fixed retail prices; ~ **des Mieterschutzes** decontrol of rents; ~ **eines Mietverhältnisses** forfeiture of a tenancy; ~ **eines Pachtvertrages** cancellation of a lease; ~ **eines Pfändungsbeschlusses** cancellation of a garnishee order; ~ **der Preisbindung** abolition of resale price maintenance; ~ **der Preisüberwachungsvorschriften** price decontrol; ~ **der Rassentrennung** desegregation, integration; ~ **eines Schiedsspruchs** setting an award aside, annulment of an award; ~ **einer vergleichsweisen Schuldenregelung** annulment of a scheme of arrangement; ~ **des Sichtvermerkzwanges** abolition of visas; ~ **eines Sparkontos** withdrawal of a deposit account *(Br.)*; ~ **einer Steuer** abolition of a tax; ~ **eines Strafverfahrens** discontinuance of prosecution; ~ **eines Testamentes** revocation of a will; ~ **der Todesstrafe** abolition of capital punishment; ~ **eines Treuhandverhältnisses** setting aside of a trust; ~ **eines Urteils** quashing (reversal) of a judgment; ~ **der Verfassung** subversion (cassation) of the constitution; ~ **einer einstweiligen Verfügung** dissolution of an injunction; ~ **einer richterlichen Verfügung** reversal of an order of the court; ~ **eines Verlöbnisses** breaking off an engagement; ~ **einer Versammlung** dissolution of an assembly; ~ **eines Vertrages** rescission (invalidation, nullification, avoidance, annulment) of a contract; ~ **der Wohnungszwangswirtschaft** derequisition *(Br.)*; ~ **der Zwangsverwaltung** desequestration; ~ **der Zwangswirtschaft** decontrol, derationing;
~ **des Konkursverfahrens beantragen** to apply to the court for an order of discharge; **Vertrag im Wege der Anfechtung zur** ~ **bringen** to avoid a contract; ~ **erbrechtlicher Bindungen durchführen** to execute a disentailing assurance; **zur** ~ **kommen** to be cancelled.

Aufhebungs|antrag motion in arrest of judgment; ~**beschluß** decree of annulment; ~**bestimmung** rescinding (cancellation) clause; ~**grund** *(Wandlung)* redhibitory defect (vice); ~**gründe** *(Urteil)* grounds for annulment; ~**klage** *(Ehe)* nullity suit, *(Vertrag)* redhibitory action; ~**klausel** overriding (repeating, determinative) clause.

aufheitern, j. to humo(u)r s. o., to liven s. o. up; **sich** ~ *(Wetter)* to clear up, to brighten; **sich gebietsweise** ~ to clear in some areas.

Aufheiterung cheer, brightening, *(Wetter)* clearing up, bright interval;
mit zeitweiligen ~**en** with sunny spells (bright periods).

Aufheiterungsgebiet area with bright periods.

aufhellen *(Problem)* to eludicate, to clear up.

Aufhellung eludication.

aufhetzen to incite, to instigate, to stir up;
Arbeiter gegen ihre Arbeitgeber ~ to incite workmen against their masters *(Br.)*; **Menschen gegeneinander** ~ to set people at loggerheads; **Pöbel** ~ to stir up the mob; **zu einem Streik** ~ to instigate a strike.

aufhetzende Ansprache rabble-rousing (inflammatory) speech.

Aufhetzung incitement, instigation, rabble-rousing *(coll.)*, abetment.

Aufholarbeit make-up work.

aufholen to make up for, to recover, *(mar.)* to haul up;
jem. gegenüber ~ to catch up with s. o.; **Verluste** ~ to make up for (recover) losses; **das Versäumte** ~ to make up leeway; **Verspätung** ~ *(Zug)* to make up for lost time.

Aufholkonjunktur backlog boom.
Aufhören cessation, cesser, discontinuance.
aufhören to end, to cease, to stop, to sit up and take notice *(fam.)*, to discontinue, to leave off, to let up, to come to an end, to desist, *(Aufträge)* to dry up;
allmählich ~ to peter out, *(Sturm)* to subside; **mit der Arbeit** ~ to cease working, to knock off, to tie it up *(sl.)*; **plötzlich** ~ to stop short; **zu rauchen** ~ to forsake smoking; **mitten im Satz** ~ to break off in the middle of a sentence; **rechtzeitig mit dem Spekulieren** ~ to stop one's losses; **mit den Zahlungen** ~ to discontinue (cease, put off) payment.
Aufkauf buying up, cornering;
spekulativer ~ forestalling the market;
~ **von Industrieunternehmungen** asset backing.
Aufkäufe, durch ~ **den Markt berherrschen** to forestall (corner) the market.
aufkaufen to buy up, *(zur Verteuerung)* to corner, to forestall;
Wechsel ~ to buy up bills; **ganzes Weizenangebot** ~ to make a corner in wheat.
Aufkäufer buyer-up, forestaller, coemptor, corner man, cornerer *(Br.)*, *(Häuser)* house knacker;
~**gruppe** corner, ring, pool, *(bei Auktionen)* sales ring; **Richtwerte setzender** ~**markt** primary market *(US)*; ~**ring bilden** to forestall (corner) the market.
Aufkauftour acquisition binge.
aufklappbar tie-up.
aufklappen to unfold, *(Verdeck)* to open up;
Buch ~ to open a book.
aufklaren *(Wetter)* to clear up.
aufklären to illuminate, to enlighten, *(mil.)* to reconnoitre, to scout, *(vom Flugzeug)* to spot;
j. ~ to show s. o. the light; **Geheimnis** ~ to solve a mystery; **Gelände** ~ to reconnoitre the ground, to make a reconnaissance; **Mißverständnis** ~ to clear up a misunderstanding; **sich** ~ *(Wetter)* to clear up; **Verbrechen** ~ to throw light on (detect) a crime.
Aufklärer scout, *(Flugzeug)* reconnaissance aircraft, scouting plane, *(elektronisch gesteuert)* surveillance aircraft, reconnaissance drone.
Aufklärung clarification, illumination, information, *(mil.)* reconnaissance, scouting, *(explanation)* information;
erhaltene ~ information obtained; **gewaltsame** ~ reconnaissance in force; **taktische** ~ tactical reconnaissance; **überraschende** ~ eye opener;
~ **eines Geheimnisses** solution of a mystery; ~ **der Öffentlichkeit** public enlightenment; ~ **über ein Produkt** product publicity; ~ **eines Verbrechens** detection of a crime; **keiner** ~ **bedürfen** to need no explanation; ~ **durchführen** to be (go) on the scout; **sich für die** ~ **der Menschen einsetzen** to work for the enlightenment of mankind; ~ **über etw. geben** to give an explanation of s. th.; **sich** ~ **über etw. verschaffen** to gather information about s. th.
Aufklärungs|abteilung reconnaissance unit; ~**arbeit** educational work; ~**bomber** reconnaissance bomber; ~**fahrt** reconnaissance cruise; ~**fahrzeug** scout car; ~**feldzug** public-relations campaign, *(für die Kundschaft)* customer information campaign; ~**flug zu Bildaufnahmezwecken** photoreconnaissance; ~**flugzeug** reconnaissance plane, scout, scouting plane; **ferngesteuertes** ~**flugzeug** reconnaisance drone; ~**material** information material; **prozessuale** ~**pflicht** discovery of documents; ~**prospekt** poop sheet; ~**prozentsatz** detection rate; ~**raum** reconnaissance area; ~**satellit** reconnaissance satellite; ~**schiff** scout [ship]; ~**spähtrupp** reconnoitring party; ~**tätigkeit** information activity, *(mil.)* reconnaissance.
Aufklärungswerbung educational advertisement *(Br.)*, reason-why advertising *(US)*;
~ **über ein Produkt** product publicity.
Aufklärungszeitalter age of enlightenment.
Aufklebe|adresse gummed (paste-on) label; ~**marke** label, adhesive stamp.
aufkleben to gum down, *(Etikett)* to stick [on], to label;
Wechselmarke ~ to furnish a bill with a stamp.
Auf|kleber, ~**klebezettel** [stick-on] label, facing slip *(US)*, sticker *(US)*.
Aufkommen emergence, *(Kranker)* recovery, *(Steuer)* yield, accrual;
vorzeitiges ~ **[bei der Landung]** undershoot;
~ **an Einkommensteuer** income-tax receipts; ~ **für die Kosten** defrayal of expenses; ~ **einer Mode** coming into fashion; ~ **an direkten Steuern** indirect revenue *(Br.)*; ~ **der Verkehrswirtschaft** transportation money.
aufkommen to come into being, to arise, *(bezahlen)* to answer (pay) for, to compensate, *(Brise)* to spring up, *(Kranker)* to regain one's health, to recover, *(Mode)* to come into fashion (up), *(Wind)* to spring up;
für etw. ~ to answer (be responsible) for s. th.; **für die Beiträge eines Mitglieds** ~ to carry a member; **gegen eine Konkurrenz** ~ to contend with competition; **für die Kosten** ~ to assume (defray) the costs (expenses), to meet (bear, pay) the expenses; **vor der Landebahn** ~ to undershoot the runway; **für keine Schäden** ~ to disclaim responsibility for any damage; **für jds. Unkosten** ~ to defray s. one's expenses; **für einen Verlust** ~ to be liable (responsible) for a loss;
keinen Rivalen gegen sich ~ **lassen** to keep all rivals down; **keinen Zweifel** ~ **lassen** to admit of no doubt; **für entstehende Schäden** ~ **müssen** to be held liable for damage.
aufkommende Mode rising fashion.
Aufkommensspitze *(Steuern)* peak in tax yield.
aufkrempeln, sich die Ärmel *(fig.)* to pitch into work.
aufkreuzen, in voller Kriegsbemalung auf der Mole to parade on the pier in full dress *(fam.)*; **plötzlich** ~ to show (pop) up.
aufkündigen *(Anleihe, Kapital, Kredit)* to call in, to recall, *(Hypothek)* to foreclose;
jem. den Dienst ~ to give notice to s. o.; **Handel** ~ to break a bargain; **Hypothek** ~ to foreclose a mortgage; **Staatsvertrag** ~ to denounce (withdraw) from a treaty.
Aufkündigung *(Dienste)* notice to quit, *(Hypothek)* foreclosure, *(Kapital)* recall, calling, *(Vertrag)* termination, revocation;
~ **eines Staatsvertrags** denouncement of a treaty.
Aufladegebühren loading (packing) charges.
Aufladen loading, *(Batterie)* charging, boosting.
aufladen to load, to lade, *(Flugzeugmotor)* to supercharge, to boost, *(verladen)* to pack up;
jem. etw. ~ to burden (load) s. o. with s. th.; **Batterie** ~ to charge (boost, power up) a battery; **sich selbst eine Last** ~ to make a rod for one's own back; **jem. die ganze Schuld** ~ to put (lay) the blame on s. o.; **sich eine große Verantwortung** ~ to saddle o. s. with a big responsibility.
Aufladeplatz loading point.
Auflader loader, packer.
Auflage *(Anweisung)* direction, injunction, instruction, *(Bedingung)* condition, *(Belastung)* charge, *(Buch)* edition, impression, *(auf die Sitze)* pad, *(Steuer)* imposition, levy, duty, tax, custom, *(Testament)* charge, *(Zeitung)* circulation;
mit einer hohen ~ with a wide circulation; **unter einer** ~ with a charge;
in der Geschäftswelt (bei der Wirtschaft) abgesetzte ~ circulation among businessmen; **tatsächlich abgesetzte** ~ net paid circulation, certified net sales; **ausgelieferte** ~ delivered circulation; **beschränkte** ~ *(Buch)* limited edition; **durchgesehene und verbesserte** ~ revised and improved edition; **dritte** ~ [book in the] third edition; **erweiterte** ~ enlarged edition; **gerichtliche** ~ court ban, injunction; **hohe** ~ *(Zeitung)* wide circulation; **kleine** ~ short number; **neubearbeitete (überarbeitete)** ~ revised edition, revision; **neue, unveränderte** ~ new impression; **verbesserte** ~ corrected edition; **tatsächlich verkaufte** ~ certified net sale; **vermehrte und verbesserte** ~ enlarged and revised edition;
hohe ~ **haben** to have a wide circulation; **jem. etw. zur** ~ **machen** to make it a condition for s. o.
Auflagen|zu Lasten des Kunden disbursements to client's debit; **sechs** ~ **erleben** to get through (run into, reach) six editions; **drei** ~ **haben** to go through three editions; **zwanzig** ~ **erlebt (erzielt) haben** to have run up (reached) 20 editions; ~ **machen** to impose conditions;
~**analyse** circulation analysis; ~**anstieg** circulation growth; ~**beschränkung** restriction on circulation; ~**bestätigung** publisher's statement, certified report; ~**bonus** circulation bonus; ~**höhe** circulation basis, print run; **wirkliche** ~**höhe** reader circulation; ~**kontrolle** circulation control; **geprüfte** ~**meldung des Verlages** publisher's statement; ~**methode** circulation method; ~**prüfung** audit of circulation; ~**rekorde aufstellen** to set publishing records; **über Zeitungskioske abgesetzter** ~**teil** newsstand sales; ~**teilung** *(Anzeige)* splitting; ~**überwachung** audit of circulation; ~**überwachungsstelle** Audit Bureau of Circulations *(US)*; ~**veränderung** change in circulation; ~**vergleich** circulation comparison.
Auflage|schwankungen fluctuations in circulation; ~**tafel für Zolltarife** toll board; ~**ziffer** *(Buch)* reprint, printing, *(Zeitung)* circulation rate.
auflassen to leave open, *(Ballon)* to release, *(Grundstück)* to assure, to convey, to transfer, to surrender, to sasine *(Scot.)*;

Grube ~ to shut down (abandon) a mine; **Grundstück an einen Käufer** ~ to convey land to a purchaser.

Auflassung assurance of property, common assurance, primary conveyance, transfer, surrender, closing of title *(US)*;
außergerichtliche ~ ordinary conveyance; **notariell beurkundete** ~ act of sale *(Louisiana)*; **lastenfreie** ~ overreaching conveyance *(Br.)*; **unentgeltliche** ~ voluntary conveyance;
~ **von Amts wegen** office grant; ~ **einer Grube** abandonment of a mine;
der ~ **bedürfen** to lie in livery.

Auflassungs|erklärung conveyance; ~**genehmigung erteilen** to grant, bargain and sell; ~**urkunde** transfer deed, quitclaim deed, deed of conveyance, record by way of conveyance, instrument of sasine *(Scot.)*; ~**verfahren** [etwa] common recovery; ~**verpflichtungsschein** bond for a deed.

Auflauf concourse, confluence, run, gathering, crowd, *(Landfriedensbruch)* unlawful assembly, riot;
~ **verursachen** to cause a riot, to create a disturbance.

Auflaufen accumulation, accrual, increase, *(Flut)* rise, inflow;
~ **von Kosten** accruing costs, accumulation of charges; ~ **von Zinsen** accrual of interest.

auflaufen to amount to, to pile up, *(Kosten)* to accumulate, *(Schiff)* to strike ground, to run upon rocks, to run aground (ashore), *(Schulden)* to run up, *(Zinsen)* to accrue;
auf Land ~ to run ashore; **auf eine Mine** ~ to hit a mine; **auf eine Sandbank** ~ to strike a sandbank;
Betrag ~ **lassen** to run up an amount; **Schiff** ~ **lassen** to strand (beach) a ship, to run a ship aground.

Aufleben *(Handel)* revival, recovery, *(Versicherungsvertrag)* reinstatement.

aufleben to liven up, *(Handel)* to revive, to recover, to look up, *(alte Rechte)* to revive;
alte Traditionen wieder ~ **lassen** to revive old traditions; **abgelaufene Versicherung wieder** ~ **lassen** to reinstate a lapsed policy.

auflegen *(Buch)* to bring out, to publish, to print, *(Produktionsserie)* to start, to launch, *(Schallplatte)* to put on, *(Schiff)* to lay up, *(Steuern)* to impose, to levy, to tax, *(Strafe)* to inflict;
Anleihe ~ to float (raise, issue) a loan; **Anleihe neu** ~ to refloat a loan; **Anleihe zur Zeichnung** ~ to offer a loan for subscription, to invite subscriptions for (float) a loan; **Buch wieder (neu)** ~ to republish a book; **Bücher zum Verkauf** ~ to display books for sale; **Gedeck** ~ to lay a plate; **Hörer** ~ to replace (restore) the receiver, to hang up, to ring off *(Br.)*; **neu** ~ to reissue, to reprint, to republish; **Obligationsanleihe** ~ to float a bond issue; **einem Pferd den Sattel** ~ to saddle a horse; **Schiff** ~ to put a ship out of commission; **Schiff zum Bau** ~ to lay a ship on the stocks; **Subskribentenliste** ~ to open a subscription list; **Tischtuch** ~ to spread a tablecloth; **zum Verkauf** ~ to display for sale; **Wahllisten zur Einsicht** ~ to open the list of voters for inspection; **Werk wieder** ~ to issue a new edition of a book; **zur Zeichnung** ~ to offer for subscription; **zur öffentlichen Zeichnung** ~ to issue for public subscription.

Auflegung *(Anleihe)* issue, flotation;
~ **zur Zeichnung** opening for subscription, *(durch Prospekte)* issue by prospectus *(Br.)*.

auflehnen, sich to revolt, to rebel, to rise in rebellion.

Auflehnung insurgence, insubordination, revolt, rebellion.

auflesen to pick up;
verstreute Ähren ~ to glean scattered ears; **j. aus der Gosse** ~ to take s. o. out of the gutter.

aufleuchten to light up.

Auflieferer consignor, sender.

aufliefern *(bei der Bahn)* to consign, to send, to dispatch, to ship *(US)*, *(Briefe)* to post *(Br.)*, to mail *(US)*.

Auflieferung *(Bahn)* consignment, dispatch, sending, shipping *(US)*, *(Briefe)* posting *(Br.)*, mailing *(US)*.

aufliegen to be open for inspection (available), *(Kondolenzbuch)* to be open, *(Schiff)* to lie up, *(Zeitungen)* to be kept (taken in);
zur Einsicht ~ *(Wahllisten)* to be available for inspection; **öffentlich** ~ to be open for inspection; **zur Zeichnung** ~ to be open (offered) for subscription.

auflockern to disperse, to ease, to relax, *(Boden)* to loosen, to break up, to mellow, *(Verwaltung)* to decentralize;
Kapitalmarkt ~ to ease the capital market; **Situation** ~ to ease off the situation, to relax the tension; **gesellschaftliche Veranstaltung** ~ to liven up a party.

Auflockerung ease, relaxation, dispersion, *(Verwaltung)* decentralization;
industrielle ~ dispersion of industry; **konjunkturelle** ~ easing of cyclical conditions;
~ **von Bestimmungen** relaxation of restrictions; ~ **des Kapitalmarktes** easing of the capital market; ~ **eines Programms** dissemination of a program(me).

auflodern to flare (blaze, flame) up.

auflösbar dissolvable, *(chemisch)* soluble, *(Ehe)* dissoluble, *(Rätsel)* solvable, *(Vertrag)* determinable, terminable.

auflösen to dissolve, *(Firma)* to liquidate, to wind up, *(Konzern)* to split (break) up, *(Körperschaft)* to disincorporate *(US)*, *(Menschenmenge)* to break up, to disperse, *(Vertrag)* to cancel, to annul, to rescind, to invalidate, *(zersetzen)* to disintegrate;
sich ~ *(Firma)* to go into liquidation, *(Parlament)* to dissolve; **sich in seine Bestandteile** ~ to break up into its components; **sich in blauen Dunst** ~ to dissolve in thin air; **Fonds** ~ to wind up a fund; **Geschäft** ~ to liquidate a business; **Gesellschaft** ~ to wind up (liquidate) a company, to dissolve a partnership; **sich in kleine Gesprächsgruppen** ~ to split up into small groups; **Handelsgesellschaft** ~ to wind up a business company (partnership); **seinen Haushalt** ~ to break up one's household; **Heer** ~ to demobilize (disband) an army; **Konto** ~ to close (eliminate, *US*) an account; **Menschenmenge** ~ to disperse a crowd; **Monopole** ~ to break up monopolies; **sich in nichts** ~ to end in smoke *(fam.)*, to take to itself wings, to come to nothing; **Parlament** ~ to dissolve parliament; **Rücklage** ~ to release (dispose of) a reserve; **sich selbst** ~ *(Firma)* to wind up voluntarily; **sich in Tränen** ~ to melt into tears; **Verein** ~ to disincorporate a club; **Verlobung** ~ to break off an engagement; **Versammlung** ~ to dissolve (break up, dismiss) a meeting; **Wertberichtigungen und Rückstellungen** ~ to reduce prior provisions *(US)*; **sich in Wohlgefallen** ~ to be settled to everybody's satisfaction; **Wohnung** ~ to vacate (relinquish, abandon) one's residence; **Zug** ~ *(Bahn)* to split up a train.

auflösende Bedingung resolutory (resolutive) condition.

Auflösung dissolution, liquidation, winding up, cancellation, *(Nebel, Wolke)* dissipation, *(Zerfall)* dissolution, decomposition, breakup;
selbst beantragte ~ voluntary winding-up;
~ **einer Armee** disbandment (demobilization) of an army; ~ **einer Ehe** dissolution of a marriage, absolute divorce; ~ **von Einkommensteuerrückstellungen** disposition of deferred income tax; ~ **eines Fonds** winding up of a fund; ~ **eines Geschäfts** liquidation (winding-up, wind-up, *US*) of a business; ~ **einer Handelsgesellschaft** dissolution of a partnership, liquidation (winding up) of a company; ~ **eines Haushalts** breaking up of a household; ~ **eines Kontos** closing (elimination, *US*) of an account; ~ **des Parlaments** dissolution of Parliament *(Br.)*; ~ **eines Rätsels** key to a riddle; ~ **von Rücklagen** reduction in (release of, disposition of) reserves; ~ **von Rückstellungen** writing back of provisions, reversal of accruals; ~ **eines Vereins** disincorporation of a club; ~ **einer Versammlung** breakup (dissolution) of a meeting; ~ **eines Vertrages** cancellation (termination, invalidation) of a contract; ~ **von Wertberichtigungen und Rückstellungen** reduction of prior provision *(US)*;
~ **einer Versammlung anordnen** to order the dispersal of an assembly.

Auflösungs|antrag *(Gemeinschuldner)* petition for bankruptcy, winding-up petition; ~**bescheinigung** certificate of dissolution; ~**beschluß** dissolution order, *(Gericht)* winding-up order, *(Körperschaft)* resolution of surrender; ~**bestimmungen** provisions for dissolution, winding-up regulations; ~**erscheinungen** signs of decay; ~**gründe** grounds for dissolution; ~**stab** *(mil.)* demobilization staff; ~**termin** date of dissolution; ~**verfügung** dissolution (winding-up) order; ~**voraussetzungen** *(Pensionskasse)* termination requirements.

aufmachen to open, *(Anzeige)* to lay out, to make up, *(Buch)* to get up;
sich ~ to start on a journey; **sich nach ...** ~ to take one's way to...; **Artikel zum Verkauf** ~ to get up an article for sale; **Bericht tendenziös** ~ to give a report a tendentious flavo(u)r; **Bilanz** ~ to make up (strike) a balance sheet; **Brief** ~ to open a letter; **Bücher** ~ to make up the books; **Flasche** ~ to open (uncork) a bottle; **Geschäft** ~ to start a business, *(Laden)* to open a shop; **geschenkmäßig** ~ to giftwrap; **Geschichte groß** ~ to run a big story; **Hahn** ~ to turn on a tap; **Havarie** ~ to adjust the average; **Konto** ~ to open an account; **Laden** ~ to open one's shop, to set up shop; **Nachricht groß** ~ to play up (feature, splash, *Br.*) a piece of news; **Paket** ~ to untie (undo) a parcel; **Post** ~ to open the post *(Br.)* (mail, *US*); **Rechnung** ~ to make out an invoice; **Schirm** ~ to put up an umbrella; **um 10 Uhr** ~ *(Ladengeschäft)* to open at ten o'clock; **Zeitungsartikel groß** ~ to feature an article.

Aufmachung make-up, set-out, window dressing, laying out, *(Anzeige)* presentation, layout, *(Buch)* getup, layout, turnout, presentation, *(Kleidung)* outfit, rig-out, getup, *(Schaupackung)* dummy, mannequin *(US)*, *(Seeschadensberechnung)* average adjustment, *(Waren)* packaging;
nicht in ~en für den Einzelverkauf not put up for retail sale;
appetitanregende ~ appetizing appeal; **äußere ~** *(Ware)* outward appearance; **betrügerische ~** false colo(u)r; **bloße ~** mere show, eyewash; **geschmackvolle ~** attractive packaging; **redaktionelle ~** editorial preparation;
~ einer Bilanz striking of a balance sheet; **~ von Produkten** make-up of goods; **~ einer Rechnung** making up of an invoice; **große ~ eines Zeitungsartikels** featuring of an article; **~ einer [Zeitungs]seite** [page] layout;
Nachricht in großer ~ bringen to play up (feature, highlight, splash, *Br.*) a piece of news.

Aufmachungs|bestimmungen *(Post)* make-up regulations; **~muster [für Drucksachen]** dummy.

Aufmarsch line-up, parade;
~ von Truppen concentration (assembly) of troops, *(zum Gefecht)* deployment;
~flugplatz base airfield; **~gebiet** assembly (deployment, concentration) area.

aufmarschieren to march up, to deploy.

aufmarschieren lassen *(mil.)* to assemble, to concentrate;
seine Gründe ~ to deploy one's arguments; **Zeugen ~** to call in witnesses.

Aufmarsch|plan assembly plan; **~raum** deployment (concentration) area.

aufmerksam attentive, with open ears, *(höflich)* obliging, thoughtful, *(wachsam)* alert, watchful, vigilant;
einer Beweisführung ~ folgen to follow an argument closely; **dem Lauf der Ereignisse ~ folgen** to have one's ears to the ground; **j. auf sich ~ machen** to catch s. one's eye; **j. auf die Gefahr ~ machen** to warn s. o. of a danger; **etw. ~ verfolgen** to follow s. th. closely; **~ zuhören** to listen attentively;
~e Bedienung prompt service; **~e Zuhörer** attentive audience.

Aufmerksamkeit attention, notice;
~en tokens of concern, attentions;
äußerste ~ last attention; **gespannte ~** close (marked) attention; **kleine ~** small token, courtesy; **mangelnde ~** lack of attention; **nachlassende ~** slackening of attention; **volle (ungeteilte) ~** undivided attention;
~ ablenken to detract attention, to call off the attention; **seine ~ von etw. abwenden** to take one's mind off s. th.; **jds. volle ~ beanspruchen** to engross s. one's whole attention; **jds. ~ entgehen** to slip s. one's attention; **~ erregen** to attract (capture, catch) attention; **jds. ~ erregen** to win s. one's ear; **nur geringe ~ finden** to command scant attention; **jds. ~ auf etw. lenken** to draw (direct) s. one's attention to s. th., to catch s. one's eye; **~ richten auf** to call attention to; **nicht der ~ wert sein** to be beneath notice; **~ des Gerichts zu erregen suchen** to seek court attention; **j. mit ~en überhäufen** to wait on s. o. hand and foot; **jds. ~ auf sich ziehen** to draw s. one's attention to o. s., to make o. s. conspicuous; **jem. mit größter ~ zuhören** to listen to s. o. with profound interest; **seine ~ anderen Dingen zuwenden** to shift one's attention to other matters.

Aufmerksamkeits|erreger advertising approach, eye catcher, eye stopper, attention getter; **~faktor** attention (interest) factor; **~prüfung** impact test; **~wert** attention-getting value.

auf|möbeln, j. to buck (perk) s. o. up *(coll.)*; **~montieren** to set up, to assemble; **~mucken** to kick over the traces, to kick against the pricks; **~muntern** to animate, to cheer (pep) up.

Aufmunterung animation, encouragement.

Aufnahme acceptance, reception, *(auf Band)* [tape] recording, *(Beherbergung)* accommodation, *(Einbau)* installation, *(Eingliederung)* incorporation, integration, *(Einschreibung)* enrol(l)ment, enlistment, *(Eintritt)* admission, admittance, acceptance, *(Film)* shooting, *(Foto)* photograph, picture, shot, exposure, snapshot, view, *(in der Gesellschaft)* initiation, affiliation, *(Kapital)* taking up, raising, *(Krankenhausabteilung)* reception [office], *(Kredit)* borrowing, *(in Liste)* entry, listing, *(eingetretenen Schadens)* assessment, *(auf Schallplatte)* pickup, transcription *(US)*, *(einer Tätigkeit)* start, taking up, assumption, *(Vermessung)* surveying, *(Warenangebot)* absorption, *(von Wertpapieren)* assimilation;
freundliche ~ friendly reception; **gastfreundliche ~** entertainment; **tatsächliche ~** *(Lagerbestand)* physical inventory; **topografische ~** mapping; **unfreundliche ~** sour-spirited reception; **vergrößerte ~** *(Foto)* enlargement;
Achtung ~! *(Film)* action!;
~ einer Anleihe taking up (raising) a loan; **~ von Ausländern** admission of aliens into a country; **~ von Bedingungen** inclusion of conditions; **~ der Bestände** stocktaking, inventory taking; **~ des Betriebs** going into operation; **~ von Betriebsmitteln** borrowing of corporate cash; **~ von Beweisen** hearing of (taking) evidence; **~ diplomatischer Beziehungen** entering into (establishment of) diplomatic relations; **~ einer Diskussion** taking up of a discussion; **~ in eine Firma** initiation into a business, admission as partner; **~ einer ausländischen Gesellschaft** adoption of a foreign corporation *(US)*; **~ einer Hypothek** raising a mortgage; **~ des Inventars** inventory taking, stocktaking; **effektive ~ des Inventars** physical inventory; **~ von Kapital** taking up (raising) of capital; **~ einer Klausel** insertion of a clause; **~ ins Krankenhaus** admission into hospital; **~ aus dem täglichen Leben** life shot; **~ neuer Mitglieder** admission of new members; **~ in der Öffentlichkeit** public acceptance; **negative ~ in der Presse** hostile press reception; **~ eines Protests** protestation; **~ in das Protokoll** entry into the minutes, *(Gericht)* recording of evidence; **~ von Schulden** contraction of debts; **~ in die deutsche Sprache** adoption into the German language; **~ in die Tagesordung** inclusion in the agenda; **~ eines Teilhabers** admission into a partnership; **~ des Transatlantikverkehrs** opening of transatlantic traffic; **~ einer Tratte** hono(u)ring a bill of exchange; **~ der Verbindung mit jem.** establishing contact with s. o.; **~ in einen Verein** initiation into a society; **~ von Verhandlungen** entering into (initiation of) negotiations; **~ der Verwundeten** picking up of the wounded; **~ eines Wortes in ein Lexikon** inclusion of a word into a dictionary; **~ eines Wortes in eine Sprache** absorption of a word into a language;
für seine ~ bezahlen to pay one's entrance; **günstige ~ finden** to have a favo(u)rable reception, *(Mode)* to come into fashion, to catch on, *(Waren)* to meet with a ready market (sale); **kühle ~ finden** to meet with a cool reception; **günstige ~ in der Öffentlichkeit finden** to create a favo(u)rable public opinion; **gute ~ in der Presse finden** to be favo(u)rably noticed in the press; **jem. ~ gewähren** to take s. o. in; **~n machen** to take views; **~ von jem. machen** to snapshot s. o.; **um ~ nachsuchen** to make an application for membership; **~ vergrößern** to enlarge a photograph; **jem. die ~ versagen** to deny s. o. admission; **zur ~ vorschlagen** to propound (propose) for admission;
~antrag application for admission (membership), membership application; **einem ~antrag stattgeben** to approve an application; **~antrag stellen** to make an application for membership; **~apparat** camera, film motion picture *(US)*, *(Schallplatten)* recorder; **~atelier** studio, *(Schallplatten)* recording studio; **~ausschuß** *(Verein)* membership committee; **~bedingungen** terms of admission, entrance requirements; **~bedingungen erfüllen** to be eligible for admission; **~beitrag** initial contribution.

aufnahmebereit receptive, *(Filmkamera)* ready to shoot, *(gastfreundlich)* hospitable.

Aufnahme|bereitschaft *(Zuhörer)* receptiveness, receptivity; **~bereitschaft der Verbraucher** consumer acceptance; **~bescheinigung** entrance certificate; **~bezirk** *(für Flüchtlinge)* receiving district; **~dauer** *(Bandgerät)* recording session; **~- und Übertragungseinrichtung** pickup.

aufnahmefähig *(Börse)* buoyant, *(kauflustig)* inclined to buy, *(Markt)* ready, active, receptive, broad, *(in Verein)* admissible;
nicht ~ *(Markt)* unreceptive; **nicht mehr ~** *(Markt)* saturated; **sich als ~ erweisen** to prove itself absorbent;
beschränkt ~er Markt limited market; **nicht mehr ~er Markt** long market *(US)*; **nicht sehr ~er Markt** soft market.

Aufnahmefähigkeit acceptance, receptivity, learning, capacity, *(Antenne)* pickup performance, *(Börse)* buoyancy of the market, *(Markt)* absorption (absorptive) capacity, absorption power, *(Radar)* pickup performance, *(im Verein)* admissibility;
~ von Lagerräumen capacity of storage.

Aufnahme|feierlichkeiten initiation ceremonies; **~freudigkeit** *(Markt)* consumer acceptance, receptivity; **~gebiet** receiving district.

Aufnahmegebühr entrance (admission, registration, initiation, *US*) fee;
seine ~ zahlen to pay one's entrance.

Aufnahme|gelände *(Film)* lot, location; **~gerät** *(Band)* recorder, *(Foto)* camera; **~gesuch** application for membership (admission); **~grenze** *(des Marktes)* marginal increment; **~kamera** film (pickup, *US*) camera; **~land** *(für Flüchtlinge)* host country; **~leiter** *(Film)* production manager; **~mikrophon** pickup transmitter; **~neigung** *(Börse)* willingness to absorb, *(Verbraucher)* consumer acceptance; **~objektiv** photographic lens.

Aufnahmeprüfung entrance (previous) examination, admission test, competitive (qualifying) examination, *(Universität)* university examination, responsions *(Br.)*, smalls *(Br.)*;
~ **in die höhere Schule** eleven-plus examination *(Br.)*; ~ **in den höheren Verwaltungsdienst** competitive civil-service examination *(Br.)*;
~ **bestehen** to pass the entrance examination.

Aufnahme|raum *(Fotograf)* studio, *(Schallplattenfirma)* recording room, studio; ~**richtlinien** acceptance rules; ~**staat** host country; ~**stellung** *(mil.)* rallying (covering) position; ~**studio** recording studio; **zweites ~team** *(Film, Fernsehen)* second unit; ~**technik** recording technique; ~**termin** time of admission; ~**verfahren** *(Band)* recording technique, *(Universität)* university examination; ~**voraussetzungen** entrance requirements; ~**voraussetzungen erfüllen** to be eligible for admission; ~**wagen** sound truck, recording van (car, *US*); ~**willigkeit des Verbrauchers** consumer acceptance; ~**zeremonie** initiation ceremony; ~**zettel** *(Buchhändler)* order-acceptance slip.

aufnehmen to receive, to take up, to take in, *(auf Band)* to record, to take on tape, *(beherbergen)* to accommodate, to shelter, *(in die Bilanz)* to include into, to extend, *(Eindrücke)* to grasp, to receive, to take in, to apprehend, *(einfügen)* to insert, *(eingliedern)* to incorporate, to integrate, *(Fahrgäste)* to pick up, *(fotografieren)* to photograph, to shoot, *(als Gast)* to lodge, *(Markt)* to absorb, to take up, *(Mitglied)* to affiliate, to initiate, *(Soziologe)* to assimilate, *(Telegramm)* to copy, *(vermessen)* to survey, *(Wertpapiere)* to assimilate, *(in Zeitung)* to insert, *(zulassen)* to take into, to enrol(l), to admit, to enlist, to initiate *(US)*;
j. ~ to put s. o. up; **j. bei sich** ~ to give s. o. a home; **es ~ mit** to cope with; **es mit allen** ~ to take on all comers; **es geistig mit jem.** ~ to match one's wits with s. o.; **Anleihe** ~ to raise (contract, float) a loan; **Arbeit** ~ to set to (take up) work; **Arbeit wieder** ~ to resume work; **Artikel in eine Zeitschrift** ~ to accept an article for publication in a periodical; **begeistert** ~ to receive with enthusiasm; **Besatzung eines gestrandeten Schiffes** ~ to pick up a shipwrecked crew; **Bestellung** ~ to take (book) an order; **Bestimmungen in eine Vereinbarung** ~ to embody terms in an agreement; **Betrag in eine Rechnung** ~ to include an amount in an account; **Betrieb** ~ to go into operation, to start working; **Beweis** ~ to hear (take down) evidence; **diplomatische Beziehungen** ~ to enter into (establish) diplomatic relations; **Diktat** ~ to take down in shorthand; **Dinge mit Gelassenheit** ~ to take things calmly; **Diskussion wieder** ~ to pick up the thread of (resume) a discussion; **Dokumente** ~ to list documents; **Ermittlungen** ~ to start investigations; **Fahrt** ~ to get under way; **j. in seine Familie** ~ to receive s. o. into one's family; **Fehdehandschuh** ~ to take up the gauntlet; **Feindseligkeiten [wieder]** ~ to [re]open hostilities; **fürs Fernsehen** ~ to telerecord; **Flüchtling in sein Haus** ~ to take in a refugee; **Friedensverhandlungen** ~ to enter into a treaty of peace; **Funkspruch** ~ to receive (pick up) a wireless message; **gastfreundlich** ~ to entertain; **Gebiet** ~ to survey a district; **Geld** ~ to borrow (raise) money; **Geld gegen hypothekarische Sicherheit** ~ to borrow on mortgage; **als Gesellschafter** ~ to introduce as partner; **gierig in sich** ~ to devour; **in Gnaden wieder** ~ *(Partei)* to depurge; **Grundsätze in ein Gesetz** ~ to embody principles in a law; **Grundstück** ~ to survey a property; **etw. gut** ~ to take s. th. in good part; **Handelsbeziehungen** ~ to enter into trade relations; **Hypothek auf ein Haus** ~ to raise a mortgage on (mortgage) a house; **Inventar** ~ to [take an] inventory, to draw up an inventory, to take stock; **Kampf gegen etw.** ~ to go into battle against s. th.; **Kapital** ~ to raise funds; **Katalog** ~ to [draw up a] catalog(ue); **Klausel** ~ to insert a clause; **es mit der Konkurrenz** ~ to cope with one's competitors, to sustain competition; **mit jem. Kontakt** ~ to contact (get in touch) with s. o.; **Kredit** ~ to raise a credit; **Kurs** ~ to trace the course; **in eine Liste** ~ to [enter into a] list; **als Mitglied in einen Verein** ~ to affiliate a member to a society, to admit s. o. to a club; **jds. Personalien** ~ to take down s. one's particulars; **Programm zwecks späterer Sendung** ~ to transcribe a program(me); **Protest** ~ to draw up a protest; **Protokoll** ~ to draw up the minutes, to protocolize; **in ein Protokoll** ~ to enter into the minutes; **Rede ungünstig** ~ to give a speech a hostile reception; **etw. richtig** ~ to get the message; **Schaden** ~ to assess the damage; **Schulden** ~ to contract debts; **Seekabel** ~ to pick up a cable; **Seeschadensberechnung** ~ to average; **Spur** ~ to pick up the scent; **in einen Staatsverband** ~ to naturalize; **stenografisch** ~ to take down in shorthand; **Studium wieder** ~ to resume one's studies; **in die Tagesordnung** ~ to include in the agenda; **jem. als Teilhaber** ~ to admit (take in) s. o. as a partner, to take s. o. into partnership; **Urkunde** ~ to draw up a document; **Verbindung mit jem.** ~ to establish contact with s. o.; **Verfolgung** ~ to take up the pursuit; **Verhandlungen** ~ to enter into negotiations; **nur wenig Verkehr** ~ *(Straße)* to be unfit for heavy traffic; **Verkehrsunfall** ~ to take down the details of an accident; **jds. Vorbringen äußerst freundlich** ~ to turn a sympathetic ear to s. one's request; **Vorschlag sehr kühl** ~ to welcome a suggestion coldly; **herauskommende Ware glatt** ~ *(Börse)* to absorb all offerings; **Wort ins Lexikon** ~ to include a word into a dictionary; **Wort in eine Sprache** ~ to absorb a word into a language; **Zahlungen wieder** ~ to resume payments;
es mit jem. ~ **können** to be able to cope with s. o., to be a match for s. o., to work with the best; **es leicht mit jem.** ~ **können** to be more than a match for s. o.; **sich in eine Gesellschaft** ~ **lassen** to join a society; **Protest** ~ **lassen** *(Wechselrecht)* to note (notify) a protest, to have a bill protested, to enter protest of a bill.

aufopfern to sacrifice;
sich völlig für eine Sache ~ to be wholly devoted to a cause.

aufopfernd devoted, loyal, self-sacrificing;
~**e Fürsorge** devoted care; ~**e Hingabe** selfless devotion.

Aufopferung|en der großen Havarie general average sacrifices; ~ **einer Mutter für ihre Kinder** devotion of a mother for her children.

aufpacken to load;
jem. etw. ~ to saddle s. o. with s. th.

aufpäppeln, j. to feed s. o. up.

aufpassen to keep [a] watch on (over), to watch, to watch out *(US coll.)*, to pay attention, to look out for;
auf j. ~ to take care of (look after) s. o.; **auf Kinder** ~ to take care of children; **auf die Rechtschreibung** ~ to mind the spelling; **wie ein Schießhund** ~ to keep one's eyes peeled *(sl.)*; **in der Schule nicht** ~ to be inattentive at school.

Aufpasser watchdog.

aufpeitschen to work up, to excite.

Aufpeitschungsmittel stimulant.

aufpflanzen, sich vor jem. to plant o. s. in front of s. o. *(coll.)*, to square up to s. o.

aufplustern, sich to give o. s. airs.

aufpolieren to polish up, to refurbish, to revamp;
seine Englischkenntnisse ~ to brush up (furbish) one's English.

Aufpolierung revampment.

aufpolstern to upholster.

aufprägen to imprint.

Aufprall impact, shock, collision.

aufprallen to hit (strike) on, to collide;
auf eine Lokomotive ~ to crash into a railway engine.

Aufpreis additional (extra) price, surcharge, premium, markup;
gegen geringen ~ for a little extra, against an extra charge;
~ **fürs Schiebedach** sliding roof extra.

aufpulvern to enliven, to buck up.

Aufpulverungsmittel energizer, pep pill *(coll.)*.

aufpumpen to pump up, to inflate.

aufputschen to stir up, to incite, to ferment;
Massen ~ to rouse the masses; **Volk** ~ to raise the mob.

Aufputschmittel energizer, pep pill *(coll.)*.

aufraffen, sich to shake one's ears, to buck up, to scramble to one's feet, to rouse o. s. to do, to nerve o. s.; **sich zur Beendigung einer Arbeit** ~ to make a push to finish a job; **sich zu einem Entschluß** ~ to bring o. s. to make a decision.

Aufräumen *(Arbeitsplatz)* cleanup.

aufräumen to clear, to tidy up, to clean up, to do out;
mit überholten Ansichten ~ to do away with oldfashioned ideas; **unter der Bevölkerung** ~ *(Seuche)* to thin out (decimate) the population; **gründlich** ~ to clean house *(US)*; **mit veralteten Ideen** ~ to get rid of obsolete ideas; **sein Lager** ~ to sell off, to clear one's stock; **mit einem Mißbrauch** ~ to abolish an abuse; **Zimmer** ~ to put a room straight (in order); **Zimmer gründlich** ~ to give the rooms a good turnout, to prim up a room.

Aufräumezeit cleanup period (time).

Aufräumungs|arbeiten clearance, clearing away; ~**kommando** clearing squad; ~**kosten** demolition costs.

aufrechenbar compensable, subject to compensation.

aufrechnen to balance, to settle, to square, to cast up amounts, *(belasten)* to charge, *(in Gegenrechnung bringen)* to compensate, to set off *(Br.)*, to offset *(US)*, *(zusammenrechnen)* to cast, to reckon (add) up;
mit einem Anspruch ~ to set off with *(Br.)* (offset against, *US*) a claim; **Posten gegeneinander** ~ to set off (balance) one item against the other.

Aufrechnung *(Addition)* cast, *(Gegenrechnung)* compensation, setoff *(Br.)*, offset *(US)*, stoppage, *(Kontoabschluß)* settlement per contra, balancing (squaring) of accounts, *(Zuschlag)* additional charge, charging, markup;
im Prozeß ~ geltend machen to set off a claim in an action.
Aufrechnungs|anspruch, nicht bestrittener admitted setoff; **~einwand** defence of setoff; **~vereinbarung** *(Bank)* letter of setoff.
aufrecht upright, erect, *(Charakter)* hono(u)rable, honest;
~er Freund staunch friend; **~er Patriot** loyal patriot.
aufrechterhalten to maintain, to sustain;
Angebot ~ to hold open an offer; **seine Behauptung ~** to stick to one's view; **gute Beziehungen ~** to maintain good relations; **seine Entscheidung ~** to abide by a decision; **Forderung ~** to insist on a claim (demand); **Frieden ~** to keep the peace; **künstlich ~** to bolster; **Preisgefüge ~** to maintain prices; **seinen Standpunkt ~** to stick to one's view; **Urteil ~** to uphold (confirm) a decision; **Versicherung ~** to carry an insurance.
Aufrechterhaltung maintenance, upkeep;
~ eines Preisgefüges maintenance of prices; **~ der öffentlichen Ruhe und Ordnung** keeping the peace, maintenance of order and security, policing; **~ eines Urteils** confirmation of a judgment; **~ einer Versicherung** carrying of an insurance;
~ der öffentlichen Sicherheit gefährden to endanger the maintenance of public order; **~ der Regierungstätigkeit und der öffentlichen Ordnung sicherstellen** to preserve the organizational fabric of human society.
aufregen to excite, to agitate, to stir up, to work up, to send;
sich ~ to get excited, to trouble; **sich leicht ~** to be easily upset emotionally, to steam easily *(sl.)*; **die Nachbarschaft ~** to scandalize the neighbo(u)rs; **sich nicht darüber ~** to take it easy; **j. schrecklich ~** to give s. o. a fit *(coll.)*.
aufregend exciting, thrilling;
~e Nachricht hot (exciting piece of) news.
Aufregendes rouser;
nichts ~ nothing to write home about;
nichts ~ sein to be hardly worth troubling about.
Aufregung flutter, excitement, fret, agitation, dust, flurry;
in heller ~ in a fever;
fieberhafte ~ febrile excitement; **unnötige ~** tizzy;
in ~ geraten to get excited; **große ~ hervorrufen** to cause great excitement; **in ~ versetzen** to torment, to excite, to alarm; **~ zügeln** to sit on the lid *(coll.)*.
Aufregungszustand state of excitement.
aufreiben *(Gesundheit)* to undermine;
j. völlig ~ to wear s. o. out; **sich völlig ~** to knock o. s. up *(fam.)*; **den Feind ~** to annihilate (destroy) the enemy; **Nerven ~** to fray the nerves.
aufreibend exhausting, wearisome;
~e Arbeit exhausting work; **~er Tag** trying day.
aufreihen, sich to line up.
aufreißen to tear open, *(Straße)* to tear up a road;
Briefumschlag ~ to rip open an envelope; **seine Klappe ~** to talk big; **ein Loch ~ um damit ein anderes zu stopfen** to rob Peter to pay Paul; **Mund und Nase ~** to stand aghast; **alte Wunden wieder ~** to rip up old grievances.
Aufreißpackung tear-open wrapper.
aufreizen to stir up, to instigate, to incite;
j. zum Widerstand ~ to rouse s. o. to resistance.
aufreizend provocative, provoking, irritating;
sich ~ anziehen to wear sexy clothes.
Aufreizung instigation, incitement, incendiarism, fomentation.
aufrichten to put (set) up, to erect, *(Flugzeug)* to straighten (pull) out;
j. ~ to encourage s. o.; **sich zur vollen Größe ~** to draw o. s. up to full height; **sich an jds. Worten ~** to take heart from s. one's words.
aufrichtig sincere, upright, honest, open-hearted, veracious, true;
es ~ mit jem. meinen to be sincere with s. o.;
jem. sein ~es Beileid aussprechen to offer s. o. one's condolence; **~e Bewunderung** genuine admiration.
Aufrichtigkeit uprightness, honesty, sincerity, cando(u)r, plain speaking, truth.
aufriegeln to unbar, to unbolt.
Aufriß vertical section, *(Anzeige)* layout, *(Gebäude)* front view, elevation;
~ der Geschichte outline of history.
aufrollen to coil [up], to roll up;
alte Affäre wieder ~ to dig out an affair again; **Fahne ~** to furl a flag; **Flanke ~** to roll up the flank; **Frage erneut ~** to bring up a question again; **feindliche Front ~** to roll up the enemy front; **ganze Problematik ~** to point out all problems involved; **Prozeß wieder ~** to reopen a trial; **Stückware ~** to wind up piece goods; **Thema erneut ~** to bring up a subject again.
Aufrücken promotion, advance[ment].
aufrücken to advance, to promote;
in höhere Einkommensschichten ~ to move up into higher income brackets; **in eine höhere Klasse ~** to be moved up to a higher form (class, *US*); **in eine höhere Stelle ~** to rise (be promoted) to a better position; **zum Vorgesetzten ~** to move up to a superior position.
Aufruf public notice, *(zur Einziehung)* call, recall, *(Geschworene)* array, proclamation, *(Gläubiger)* summons, *(zur Hilfeleistung)* appeal, *(Jahrgang)* call-up, calling-up;
namentlicher ~ roll call; **öffentlicher ~** proclamation, appeal to the public;
~ zur namentlichen Abstimmung *(parl.)* calling of the House *(Br.)*; **~ von Banknoten** calling in (withdrawal) of bank notes; **~ der anstehenden Fälle** calling the docket; **~ des Klägers** calling of the plaintiff; **~ einer Sache** calendar call; **~ an das Volk** appeal to the country *(Br.)*; **~ von Wertpapieren** retirement of securities; **~ der Zeugen** calling of witnesses;
~ erlassen to issue a proclamation, to proclaim, *(zur Hilfeleistung)* to launch an appeal; **~ richten an** to address an appeal to.
aufrufen to call up, *(Banknoten)* to call in, to withdraw from circulation, *(Gläubiger, Obligationen)* to recall, to summon;
zur Einlösung ~ to call for redemption; **zur Einzahlung auf Aktien ~** to make a call on shares *(Br.)* (stocks, *US*); **Jahrgang ~** to call up an age group; **namentlich ~** to roll-call, to call the roll; **Obligationen ~** to call in bonds; **zum Streik ~** to call a strike; **zur Tilgung ~** to call for redemption; **Verhandlung ~** to call the plaintiff, to call a case *(Br.)*; **Wertpapiere ~** to retire securities; **Zeugen ~** to call a witness.
ausruf|fähig callable; **~pflichtig** subject to call.
Aufruftafel *(Bahn)* call board.
Aufruhr riot, uproar, agitation, commotion, turmoil, unlawful assembly, insurrection, insurgence, disorder, distemper, tumult, unrest, revolt, rebellion, run, hurlyburly, kick-up *(US sl.)*;
in offenem ~ up in arms;
~ der Elemente war of the elements; **~ und bürgerliche Unruhen** riot and civil commotion;
zum ~ anstacheln to urge a revolt; **~ anstiften (anzetteln)** to make an uproar, to create (raise) a disturbance, to incite a riot, to disturb the peace; **~ auslösen** to touch off (excite) a riot; **sich in ~ befinden** to be up, to be in a state of commotion; **~ ersticken** to smother a rebellion, to stifle a revolt; **~ hervorrufen** to occasion a rising; **~ niederschlagen** to squash a riot, to crush a revolt, to break a rebellion; **~ in der Hauptstadt niederwerfen** to deal with the disorders in the capital; **in ~ sein** to be in a ferment state; **in hellem ~ gegen etw. sein** to be up in arms against s. th.; **~ unterdrücken** to squash a riot; **in ~ versetzen** to throw into disorder; **Stadt in ~ versetzen** to raise the town;
~akte Riot Act *(Br.)*; **~klausel** civil-commotion clause; **~schäden** riot damage; **~versicherung** civil-commotion insurance.
aufrühren, alte Geschichte wieder to rake up old quarrels (grievances); **vergessene Geschichte lieber nicht ~** to let sleeping dogs lie; **viel Staub ~** to raise a lot of dust.
Aufrührer rioter, rebel, insurgent, insurrectionist, stirrer, revolter, seditionary;
~bande riotry.
aufrührerisch rioting, riotous, revolted, insurgent, rebellious, seditious, subversive, incendiary, insurrectional, disorderly;
~e Gesinnung insurrectionalism; **~e Massen** disorderly crowds; **~e Menge** turbulent mob; **~e Rede** subversive (rabble-rousing) speech; **~es Verhalten** mutinous behavio(u)r.
Aufruhr|gebiet riot area; **~versicherung** civil-commotion insurance; **~zeichen sein** to be the signal for a revolt.
aufrunden to round up.
Aufrundung rounding up.
aufrüsten to rearm, to arm.
Aufrüstung, moralische moral rearmament.
Aufrüstungs|plan rearmament plan; **~programm** armament program(me).
aufrütteln to stir (shake) up;
öffentliche Meinung ~ to mobilize public sentiment, to stir up public opinion; **j. aus seiner Untätigkeit ~** to rouse s. o. from indolence.

aufsagen to recite, to say, to repeat;
jem. den Dienst ~ to warn s. o. away.
aufsammeln to gather, to collect.
aufsässig rebellious, contumacious, recalcitrant;
~**e Untertanen** rebellious subjects.
Aufsässigkeit contumacy, rebelliousness, recalcitrancy.
Aufsatz article, *(Abhandlung)* essay, treatise, *(Kühler)* cowl, *(Möbel)* top, *(Schule)* free composition, paper, thesis, theme *(US)*, *(techn.)* top, crown, superstructure;
historischer ~ history paper; **juristischer** ~ legal writing; **preisgekrönter** ~ prize essay; **von Fehlern strotzender** ~ composition studded with errors;
~ **von unnötigem Ballast befreien** to prune an essay; ~ **veröffentlichen** to publish a treatise.
Aufsätze, vermischte miscellanies.
Aufsatzschrank court cupboard.
aufsaugen *(Markt)* to absorb;
Kleinbetriebe ~ to swallow small firms.
aufschalten, sich *(Radar)* to lock on.
aufschiebbar, nicht ~ **sein** not to be delayed.
aufschieben to push (shove) open, *(verschieben)* to postpone, to defer, to [use] delay, to put off, to prolong, to shunt, to waive, *(Urteil)* to stay, to suspend, *(vertagen)* to adjourn;
Frage für später ~ to leave a question till later; **Reise** ~ to postpone a journey; **etw. auf später** ~ to defer s. th. to a later date; **Termin** ~ to extend a time limit; **bis zur nächsten Woche** ~ to put off until next week; **Zahlung** ~ to defer (postpone) payment; **Zwangsvollstreckung** ~ to stay execution;
etw. beliebig lange ~ **können** to postpone s. th. to one's pleasure; **sich nicht** ~ **lassen** to brook no delay.
aufschiebend dilatory, suspensive;
~**e Bedingung** suspensive (suspensory) condition, condition precedent; ~**e Einrede** dilatory plea; ~**es Veto** suspensible (suspensory) veto; ~**e Wirkung** suspensory (delaying) effect.
Aufschiebung postponement, delay, suspension, *(Vertagung)* adjournment.
aufschießen, wie Pilze aus der Erde to spring up like mushrooms.
Aufschlag impact, hit, thump, *(Abzahlungssystem)* loading, *(Flugzeug)* crash, *(Kurs)* rise, advance, improvement, *(mil.)* table, *(Prämie)* premium, *(Prämienzuschlag)* loading, *(Preis)* additional charge, markup, *(Steuer)* surtax, additional tax, *(Zuschlag)* extra charge;
~ **für kleinere Aktienposten** *(Börse)* trading difference; ~ **auf den Einfuhrpreis** import markup; ~ **in Zielnähe** *(mil.)* near miss;
mit einem kleinen ~ **liefern** to supply at a small extra cost.
Aufschlagen auf die Preise markup.
aufschlagen to raise, to surcharge, *(Flugzeug)* to crash, *(im Kurs)* to look up, to advance, to improve, to rise, *(Prozente)* to add, to put on;
Buch ~ to open (turn up) a book; **Kosten** ~ to charge extra cost; **auf den Preis** ~ to increase the price, to mark up; **8% auf den Preis** ~ to add 8% to the price; **sein Quartier** ~ to take up one's quarters; **seinen Wohnsitz** ~ to take up one's abode, to settle down; **Zelt** ~ to pitch (put up) a tent.
Aufschlags|gewinn markup, *(Versicherung)* loading profit; ~**seite** eye-catching right-hand page, spread, *(vordere)* front cover.
aufschließen to open, to unlock, *(Bergwerk)* to develop, to win, *(Grundstücke)* to develop, to improve, *(Märkte)* to open up, to develop, *(Marschkolonne)* to close up;
jem. sein Herz ~ to unbosom o. s. to s. o.; **zur Spitzengruppe** ~ to catch up with the leading group.
Aufschließung *(Bergwerk, Grundstücke)* development, improvement, *(Märkte)* opening, opening up, development;
~ **eines Marktes** development of a trade area.
Aufschließungs|arbeiten development work; ~**gebiet** development area; ~**gewinn** development gain; ~**kosten** property development costs; **örtlich begrenzte** ~**maßnahmen** local improvements.
Aufschluß information, enlightenment, explanation;
um näheren ~ **bitten** to ask for full information (further particulars); **jem.** ~ **über etw. geben** to give s. o. an explanation about s. th.
Aufschlüsse, interessante sidelights;
~ **über einen Charakter gewähren** to throw light on a character.
aufschlüsseln to subdivide, to apportion, to classify, to analyse, to break down *(US)*;
Anteil größerer Abteilungen am Umsatz und Ertrag ~ to break down the contribution of major divisions to sales and pretax earnings *(US)*; **Aufstellungen** ~ to break down listings *(US)*; **Gemeinkosten der Muttergesellschaft auf die Auslandstöchter entsprechend ihrem Umsatzanteil** ~ to allocate corporate overhead expenses to overseas subsidies in proportion to their share of sales; **Kosten** ~ to allocate costs, to apportion (pool) expenses; **Unkosten** ~ to break down expenditure *(US)*; **Verkaufsgebiete** ~ to divide sales areas.
Aufschlüsselung apportionment, subdivision, breakdown *(US)*; **berufliche** ~ job analysis (breakdown, *US*); **prozentuale** ~ breakdown by percent *(US)*;
~ **nach Berufen** breakdown by occupations *(US)*; ~ **der Geschäftsunkosten** overhead allocation; ~ **von Kosten** allocation (breakdown, *US*) of expense; ~ **der gesamten Produktionszahlen** breakdown of the global output figures *(US)*; ~ **von Verkaufsgebieten** division of sales areas.
aufschlußreich informative, revealing, illuminating;
~ **für einen Charakter sein** to reveal a character.
aufschnappen, Bruchstücke von Wissen to pick up scraps of knowledge.
aufschneiden *(fig.)* to throw the hatchet, to talk large *(sl.)*, to boast, to act up, to shoot a line *(sl.)*;
tüchtig ~ to draw the longbow *(coll.)*, to lay it on thick.
Aufschneider braggart, show-off, line-shooter *(sl.)*.
Aufschneiderei bragging, big talk, ballyhoo, gas *(coll.)*.
Aufschnitt cold cuts *(US)*.
aufschrecken, aus dem Schlaf to wake up with a start.
Aufschrei der Empörung outcry of indignation.
aufschreiben to write (jot, stick) down, to put down in writing, to [make a] note;
jem. ~ *(Polizei)* to take s. one's name.
Aufschrift inscription, enfacement, legend *(US)*, *(Brief)* direction, address, *(Münze)* legend, *(Überschrift)* superscription, heading, title, *(Waren)* ticket, label;
mit ~ **versehen** to label, to ticket.
Aufschub prolongation, postponement, continuance, suspension, deferment, deferral, *(Stundung)* respite, grace, *(Vertagung)* adjournment, *(Verzögerung)* delay, retardation;
mit ~ **zahlbar** reversionary; **ohne** ~ without delay;
kurzer ~ short shrift; **unvermeidbarer** ~ unavoidable delay;
~ **des Konkursantrages** adjournment of a petition in bankruptcy; ~ **der Zahlungsfrist** extension of time; ~ **der Zwangsvollstreckung** stay of execution;
~ **bewilligen** to grant a delay; **um** ~ **bitten** to ask for time (a delay); **keinen** ~ **dulden** to bear (admit of) no delay; ~ **erlangen** to obtain an adjournment; ~ **erwirken** *(Strafurteil)* to procure a reprieve; ~ **gewähren** to allow time, to grant a respite;
~**gewährung** allowance of respite; ~**vereinbarung** suspension agreement.
aufschütten, Weg to gravel a path.
aufschwänzen *(Börse)* to corner, to squeeze.
aufschwätzen, jem. etw. to hoist s. th. upon s. o., to talk s. o. into buying s. th., to sell s. o. a pup.
aufschwindeln, jem. Waren to palm off goods on s. o.
aufschwingen, sich zu einem Brief to bring o. s. to write a letter;
sich vom Statisten zum Filmstar ~ to rise from an extra to a film star.
Aufschwung impetus, impulse, *(Konjunktur)* upswing, uptrend, upturn *(US)*, prosperity, *(Kurse)* rise, advance, improvement, *(Preise)* rally, lift, recovery, revival;
~ **nehmend** improving, booming *(US)*;
konjunktureller ~ cyclical upswing (uptrend), upward business trend, upturn in the business cycle; **lagerzyklischer** ~ step-up in inventory growth *(US)*; **saisonaler** ~ seasonal upswing; **selbstbewirkter** ~ home-made upswing; **wirtschaftlicher** ~ economic progress, boom, recovery, upswing;
~ **des Handels** increase in (impulse to) trade; ~ **der Preise** upward tendency of prices; **plötzlicher** ~ **der Preise** sudden advance in prices;
~ **erleben (nehmen)** *(Kurse)* to go up, to advance, to rise, to improve, to be on the upswing *(US)*; **großen** ~ **geben** to give great impetus; ~ **erkennen lassen** to show signs of improvement; ~ **nehmen** *(Konjunktur)* to take an upward trend; **bedeutenden** ~ **nehmen** to improve considerably, to be booming, to take a considerable turn for the better; **neuen** ~ **nehmen** to revive, to show renewed activity; **rapiden** ~ **nehmen** to boom; **im** ~ **begriffen sein** to be booming (on the upswing, *US*); ~ **verlangsamen** to slow down the upward price trend; **zusätzlichen** ~ **verleihen** to give fresh impetus.
Aufschwungs|aussichten recovery prospects; ~**jahr** high (booming, upswing) year; ~**phase** stage in upswing, upswing phase; ~**phase fortsetzen** to continue its upward advance; ~**tendenz** rising (upward) tendency.

Aufsehen stir, sensation, noise, splash;
~ **erregen** to attract publicity, to make a splash; **großes** ~ **erregen** to set tongues wagging *(coll.)*; **kaum** ~ **erregen** to raise barely a flutter of interest.

aufsehenerregend|er Mord shocking murder; ~**e Nachrichten** sensational news; ~**er Trick** stunt.

Aufseher overseer, overman, controller, surveyor, foreman, supervisor, superintendent, surveillant, super, guardsman, overlooker *(Br.)*, gaffer *(Br.)*, *(Bahn)* inspector, *(Gefängnis)* warden *(US)*, warder, jailor, goaler *(Br.)*, guard *(US)*, *(Laden)* shopwalker, floorwalker *(US)*;
~**amt** inspectorate, overseership, controllership, surveyorship, *(Gefängnis)* wardship, foremanship.

Aufseherin matron.

Aufsetzen *(Flugzeug)* touchdown.

aufsetzen to draw up, to draft, to minute, to compose, *(Flugzeug)* to touch down, to land, *(Schiff)* to run aground;
Bewerbung ~ to write an application; **Erklärung** ~ to draw up a statement; **Protokoll** ~ to draw up the minutes, to protocolize; **Rechnung** ~ to make out an invoice; **Rede** ~ to draft a speech; **schriftlich** ~ to consign to writing; **neues Stockwerk** ~ to add another storey; **Testament** ~ to make a will; **Übertragungsurkunde** ~ to draft a conveyance; **Vertrag** ~ to draw (prepare, write) up a contract (an agreement).

Aufsicht oversight, inspection, supervision, control, charge, running, custody, *(auf Gebäude)* top view, *(Kinder)* care, custody, *(Schulklasse)* invigilator, proctor *(US)*, *(Vormund)* guardianship, tutorage;
ohne ~ uncontrolled; **unter** ~ under control; **unter gesundheitspolizeilicher** ~ under sanitary inspection; **unter staatlicher** ~ state (government) controlled;
ärztliche ~ medical supervision; **in Form der Beratung ausgeübte** ~ consultative supervision; **elterliche** ~ parental control; **innerbetriebliche** ~ internal control; **staatliche** ~ state control;
~ **im Laden** shopwalker *(Br.)*, floorwalker *(US)*;
seine ~ **mangelhaft ausüben** to be negligent in one's supervision; **jem. mit der** ~ **von etw. betreuen** to give s. o. the charge of s. th.; ~ **führen** to watch, to control, to superintend, *(Schulklasse)* to be in charge, to invigilate, to proctor *(US)*; ~ **über etw. haben** to supervise, to preside over a system, to have the charge of (keep an eye on) s. th.; ~ **über jem. haben** to have charge of s. o.; **unter strenger** ~ **halten** to keep under close guard; **unter** ~ **stehen** *(Geisteskranker)* to be under restraint; **unter ärztlicher** ~ **stehen** to be under medical care; **unter polizeilicher** ~ **stehen** to be under police surveillance; **unter** ~ **eines Vormunds stehen** to be under s. one's guardianship; ~ **über etw. übernehmen** to take charge of s. th.; **einer** ~ **unterstehen** to be subject to control (supervision).

Aufsichtsamt intendency, supervisorship, supervisory board *(Br.)*, control commission (board), superintendentship;
kommunales ~ board of supervisors *(US)*;
~ **für Einhaltung von Abwässerungsbestimmungen** court of commissioners of sewers; ~ **für das Kreditwesen** Credit Control Board; ~ **für Landwirtschaftskredite** Farm Credit Administration *(US)*; ~ **für betriebliche Pensionskassen** occupational pension board, Pension Benefit Guaranty Corporation *(US)*; ~ **für das Sparkassenwesen** Registrar of Friendly Societies *(Br.)*; ~ **für das Versicherungswesen** [etwa] insurance section *(Br.)*, State Insurance Commission (Commissioner, *US*), Industrial Assurance Commissioner *(Br.)*.

Aufsichts|beamter inspector, superintendent, supervisor, supervising official, control (regulatory) officer, checker, surveyor, conservator, *(Eisenbahn)* railway superintendent, train dispatcher, *(Fürsorge)* welfare supervisor; ~**befugnis** supervisory jurisdiction, *(Lehrer)* visatorial power.

Aufsichtsbehörde controlling (supervising, supervisory) authority, control office, controlling (regulatory, *US*) body, general overseer;
staatliche ~ state regulatory commission *(US)*;
~ **für Kleinlebensversicherer** Industrial Assurance Commissioner *(Br.)*; ~ **für Nervenheilanstalten** master in lunacy *(Br.)*; ~ **öffentlicher Versorgungsbetriebe** public service commission;
der ~ **den Nachweis einer Schadensversicherung erbringen** to file an indemnity policy from an insurance company with the department.

Aufsichts|beschwerde administrative complaint; ~**bezirk** inspector's district, inspectorate.

aufsichtsführend in control, controlling, superintendent, supervisory, regulatory *(US)*;
~**e Richter** supervising judge *(Br.)*.

Aufsichts|führender control officer; ~**führung** supervision; ~**funktionen** oversight powers; **alleinige** ~**funktion** exclusive control; ~- **und Überwachungsfunktionen** oversight powers; ~**instanz** administrative chief, supervisory jurisdiction; **als** ~**instanz tätig werden** to exercise supervisory jurisdiction; **mit dem** ~**knüppel drohen** to wield the regulatory club; ~**kompetenz** supervisory power; ~**maßnahmen** control measures; ~**organ** supervisory organ, controlling body; ~**person** supervisor, controller; **als** ~**person** in a supervisory capacity; ~**personal** supervising (inspectoral, superintendency, *US*) staff; ~**pflicht** supervising (supervisory) duty; **gesetzliche** ~**pflicht** statutory control.

aufsichtspflichtig subject to supervision.

Aufsichtsrat board of directors (governors, the company), industrial (supervisory) board *(Br.)*, *(Einzelperson)* board member, member of the board of directors;
~ **einer Gesellschaft mit beschränkter Haftung** supervisory board of a close corporation under German law;
im ~ **sein** to be represented on the board.

Aufsichtsrats|bericht director's report; ~**beschluß** director's resolution; **mehreren** ~**gremien angehören** to sit on various supervising boards.

Aufsichtsratsmitglied board member, member of the board [of directors];
nominelles ~ guinea pig *(Br.)*; **staatliches** ~ government director on the board.

Aufsichtsrats|posten directorship, directorate, chair on the supervisory committee; ~**protokoll** board minutes, corporate minutes *(US)*; ~**sitz** seat on the board, board seat; ~**sitzung** meeting of the board of directors, board meeting; ~**steuer** tax on directorship; ~**tantieme**, ~**vergütung** director's fee (remuneration); ~**vorsitz** chairmanship of the supervisory committee; ~**vorsitzender** chairman of the board of directors (supervisory board); ~**wahl** board elections, election of directors.

Aufsichts|recht visitatorial right; ~**stellung** supervisory position.

Aufsichtstätigkeit supervisory control, regulatory job *(US)*;
~ **der Gesundheitsbehörde** sanitary control;
~ **ausüben** to exercise supervisory controls.

Aufsichtswirkung regulatory impact.

Aufsitzen, in einem in a stretch.

aufsitzen lassen, j. to let s. o. down.

Aufspaltbarkeit eines Patentrechts divisibility of a patent.

aufspalten to split, to break down *(US)*;
konfessionell ~ to denominationalize.

Aufspaltöl cracked oil.

Aufspaltung split, split-up, breakdown *(US)*;
~ **der Eigentumsrechte** dispersion of ownership.

aufspannen *(Landkarte)* to mount, *(Schirm)* to put up.

aufspeichern to stock, to warehouse, to magazine, to store [up], to pile up, *(el.)* to accumulate, *(Getreide)* to garner.

Aufspeicherung storage, stocking, warehousing *(US)*, *(Elektrizität)* accumulation.

aufspielen, sich to give o. s. airs, to put it on, to put on an independent air, to feel one's oats, to splurge, to act up *(US)*, to put on the high-and-mighty; **sich gegenüber jem.** ~ to lord it over s. o.; **sich als Held** ~ to pose as a hero.

aufsplittern *(Partei)* to split [up];
sich in mehrere Lager ~ to split up into several parties.

Aufsplitterung split-up, splitting;
~ **der Partei nicht zulassen** not to hold with splitting the party.

aufspringen to jump (leap, spring) up, *(Autotür)* to jar open;
auf einen Zug ~ to jump a train.

aufspulen to wind (reel) up.

Aufspüren von Verbrechern tracking-down of criminals.

aufspüren to ferret out, to hunt up;
j. ~ to track s. o. down; **Verbrecher** ~ to hunt down a criminal.

aufstacheln to incite, to instigate;
j. zum Widerstand ~ to goad s. o. to resistance.

Aufstand insurrection, insurgence, rising, uprising, rebellion, upheaval, commotion, revolt;
politischer ~ political upheaval; **sozialpolitischer** ~ social rebellion; **volkstümlicher** ~ grassroot rebellion;
Volk zum ~ **anstacheln** to incite people to sedition; ~ **anzetteln** to work up a rebellion; ~ **auslösen** to lead to a rebellion; ~ **beenden** to quiet a tumult; **zu einem nationalen** ~ **führen** to touch off a national uprising; **bewaffneten** ~ **machen** to rise up in arms; ~ **niederschlagen (niederwerfen)** to quell (throttle) a sedition (revolution), to crush a rising; **im** ~ **sein** to be in a state of revolt, to rise in rebellion; ~ **verursachen** to work up a rebellion.

aufständisch rebellious, seditious, insurgent, insurrectional, revolted, rioting;
~**e Kräfte** rebel forces; ~**e Truppen** insurgent troops.
Aufständische | r rebel, insurgent, insurrectionist, revolter;
in den Händen der ~**n sein** to be in secessionist hands.
Aufstands | bekämpfung counterinsurgence; ~**bewegung** insurgent movement; ~**versicherung** riot and civil commotion insurance.
aufstapeln to arrange in stock, to store (pile, lay) up, to hoard, to stack, to stockpile;
auf dem Deck ~ to deck up; **unordentlich** ~ to lumber.
Aufstapelung stockpiling, hoarding.
aufstauen *(Fluß)* to dam (bank) up;
sich ~ to pile up, to accumulate.
aufstecken, jem. ein Licht to open s. one's eyes; **Sache** ~ to throw up the sponge, to turn up *(sl.)*.
Aufstehen getting up, rising;
sehr gegen frühes ~ **eingestellt sein** to have a strong aversion to getting up early.
aufstehen to get up, to rise;
gewöhnlich (aus Gewohnheit) früh ~ to practise early rising; **mit den Hühnern** ~ to rise with the lark; **vom Krankenbett** ~ to leave one's sick bed; **spät** ~ **und spät schlafen gehen** to keep late hours; **mit dem linken Fuß zuerst** ~ to get out of bed on the wrong side.
Aufsteigen upgrade;
im ~ **begriffen sein** to be in the ascendant.
aufsteigen *(befördert werden)* to be promoted, *(Ballon)* to go up, *(Flugzeug)* to be airborne, to take the air, *(Nebel)* to rise, *(im Rang)* to ascend;
in einem Ballon ~ to ascend in a balloon; **zum Direktor** ~ to rise as high as the position of a director; **zur nächsten Klasse** ~ to move to the next class; **sozial** ~ to advance in the social scale; **zu den höchsten Würden** ~ to attain the highest hono(u)rs.
Aufstellen fixing, fitting.
aufstellen to set (put) up, to establish, to station, *(Bauten)* to erect, to construct, to situate, *(Bilanz)* to prepare, to make, to strike, *(entwickeln)* to elaborate, *(Kandidaten)* to nominate, to set up, to put forward, *(Kosten)* to specify, to itemize, *(Maschine)* to instal(l), to mount, to erect, to assemble, *(mil.)* to post, to assemble, to troop, *(Rechnung)* to make out (up), *(Waren)* to display, to expose;
Bedingungen ~ to make (stipulate) conditions; **Behauptung** ~ to make a statement; **Bett** ~ to set up a bed; **sich vor dem Eingang** ~ to take one's stand in front of the entrance; **erneut** ~ to reconstitute; **Etat** ~ to make a budget, to prepare the estimates; **Fahrplan** ~ to make out a timetable (schedule of trains, *US*); **Falle** ~ to set a trap; **Gerüst** ~ to [furnish] a scaffold; **sich hintereinander** ~ *(mil.)* to fall into line; **Höchstkurse** ~ to establish high records; **neue Höchstkurse an der Börse** ~ to reach a new high; **Inventar** ~ to [take an] inventory, to take stock; **Kandidaten** ~ to nominate (set up, put up) a candidate, to state for nomination *(US)*; **Kostenanschlag** ~ to make an estimate; **Liste** ~ to make out a list; **als Norm** ~ to set up as a norm; **Programm** ~ to draw up (formulate, make) a program(me); **Regel** ~ to state a rule; **sich in einer Reihe** ~ to line (queue, *Br.*) up; **Rekord** ~ to set up a record; **in Schlachtordnung** ~ to marshal troops; **sich längs der Straße** ~ to line the roads; **Streikposten** ~ to throw a picket line, to picket; **Tabellen** ~ to compile (dress) tables; **Tagesordnung** ~ to fix the agenda; **Theorie** ~ to elaborate a theory; **Truppen** ~ to arrange troops, to raise forces; **seine Waren zum Verkauf** ~ to display one's goods for sale; **Zelt** ~ to put up a tent;
sich als Kandidat ~ **lassen** to stand as candidate, to run for an office *(US)*, *(für das Parlament)* to run in an election, to stand for Parliament (a constituency) *(Br.)*, to run for Congress *(US)*.
Aufsteller eines Etats budget maker.
Aufstell | gleis *(Bahn)* siding; ~**plakat** show (window) card.
Aufstellung statement, schedule, eludication, *(Anordnung)* arrangement, disposition, drawing up, *(Bericht)* report, *(Kandidat)* nomination, *(Liste)* list, bill, account, *(Maschine)* assembly, installation, instal(l)ment, erection, mounting, *(mil.)* formation, line-up, *(zum Verkauf)* display, exposure;
laut ~ as per account [rendered]; **laut umstehender** ~ as stated overleaf; **laut untenstehender** ~ as per statement below;
amtliche ~ register; **beiliegende** ~ annexed statement; **detaillierte (genaue)** ~ detailed statement, specification, itemized schedule *(US)*, itemization *(US)*; **kurze** ~ summary schedule; **staffelförmige** ~ *(mil.)* echelon; **statistische** ~ statistical table, statement, *(Listen)* returns; **steuerliche** ~ tax statement; **tabellarische** ~ tabular statement, table, tabulation; **taktische** ~ *(mil.)* disposition; **vergleichende** ~ comparative statement;
~ **der Abgangsdaten** list of sailings; ~ **der Aktiva und Passiva** statement of assets and liabilities, schedule *(US)*; ~ **von Bedingungen** making conditions; ~ **einer Behauptung** making a statement; ~ **einer Bilanz** striking a balance, preparation of a balance sheet; ~ **einer versicherungstechnischen Bilanz** actuarial valuation; ~ **über die Einkommensverteilung** statement of distribution of income; ~ **von Flächenabnutzungsplänen** zoning *(US)*; ~ **eines Gerüsts** erection of a scaffolding; ~ **des Inventars** inventory taking, stocktaking; ~ **von Investitionsplänen** capital budgeting; ~ **eines Kandidaten** putting in of a candidate; ~ **einer Konkurstabelle** marshal(l)ing of securities; ~ **der Kosten** statement of accounts, statement of charges; **erläuternde** ~ **für die Steuererklärung** supporting schedule for an income-tax return; ~ **in Tabellenform** tabular statement, tabulation, table; ~ **einer Tagesordnung** fixing the agenda; ~ **einer Theorie** elaboration (putting forward) a theory; ~ **über früher gezahlte Vergütungen** compensation history; ~ **der Verlustquellen** *(Konkursverfahren)* deficiency account; ~ **eines Verteilungsplans** *(Konkurs)* marshalling of assets; ~ **eines gemeinsamen Zolltarifs** establishment of a common customs tariff;
~ **anfertigen** to draw up a list; **Richtigkeit einer** ~ **bestätigen** to verify a list; ~ **auf den neuesten Stand bringen** to bring a statement up to date; **feindliche** ~**en durchbrechen** to break through the enemy's rank and file.
Aufstellungs | kosten cost of installation, assembly (setting up) cost, installation cost; **bauseitig anfallende** ~**kosten** on-site installation cost; ~**ort** *(Maschine)* erection site.
aufstemmen to pry (force, break) open, to prize, to force with a lever.
aufstempeln, Aktien to raise the face value of shares (stocks, *US*).
Aufstieg ascent, climb, upgrade, rise, uprise, advancement;
im ~ on the upgrade (rise);
kometenhafter ~ meteoric progress; **rasanter** ~ speedy climb; **sozialer** ~ **der Arbeiterklasse** social advancement of labo(u)r; ~ **und Untergang** rise and fall; **kontinuierlicher** ~ **der Wirtschaft** steady upward trend of the economy;
sich nach dem ~ **undankbar erweisen** to kick down the ladder; **jds.** ~ **mit allen Mitteln fördern** to groom s. o. for advancement; **im** ~ **sein** to be on the way up (upgrade).
Aufstiegs | bahn *(Rakete)* launching trajectory; ~**bild** progress chart.
Aufstiegschance promotional opportunity;
~**n in der Betriebshierarchie** attractive openings on managerial levels;
keine ~**n haben** to be at a dead end in one's job, to have a blind-alley job.
Aufstiegsmöglichkeit prospects, promotional opportunity, opportunity to advance (for growth), upside potential;
keine ~ blind-alley job;
~**en haben** to have prospects of moving to a position of greater responsibility.
Aufstiegs | möglichkeitstabelle fortune sheet; **in einer** ~**phase sein** to be in a fair way to succeed; ~**prüfung** promotional examination.
aufstiegswillig wishing to grow.
aufstöbern to run to earth, to unearth, to track;
entsprungenen Flüchtling in einem Versteck ~ to drag an escaped prisoner out of a hiding place; **alte Manuskripte** ~ to discover old manuscripts.
aufstocken to build up, *(Gebäude)* to add another stor(e)y;
Kapital ~ to increase the capital stock *(US)*; **Kredit** ~ to increase a credit line (limit); **Produktion** ~ to raise production; **Rohstoffvorräte** ~ to stockpile.
Aufstockung *(Gebäude)* addition, *(Kapital)* increase of capital, *(Vorräte)* stockpiling.
Aufstockungsaktie bonus share (stock, *US*).
aufstoßen to push (fling) open.
Aufstrandsetzen eines Schiffes beaching a ship.
aufstrebend rising, budding;
~**e Stadt** booming town.
aufsuchen to look up, to call on, to visit, to see;
j. ~ to go and see s. o.; **Arzt** ~ to consult a doctor; **alte Freunde** ~ to hunt up old friends; **sein Stammlokal häufig** ~ to frequent a public house.
auftakeln to rig up;
sich ~ to trim o. s. up.
Auftakt send-off, prelude;
~ **einer Konferenz** prelude to a conference;
~ **sein** to [be a] prelude.
Auftanken in der Luft flight refuelling.
auftanken to tank, to refuel, to fill up, to petrol *(Br.)*.

Auftank|station refuel(l)ing base (stop); **~vorrichtung in der Luft** flying boom; **~zeit** refueling time.
Auftauchen emergence.
auftauchen to emerge, *(Frage)* to come up, *(U-Boot)* to surface; **aus dem Nebel** ~ to loom through the fog; **plötzlich** ~ to pop up; **im Verlauf des Gesprächs** ~ to crop up in the course of conversation; **wieder** ~ to come to the front (topic) again; **immer wieder** ~ to turn up like a bad halfpenny, to keep turning up; **so als ob nichts gewesen wäre wieder** ~ to turn up again as large as life.
Auftauen eingefrorener Guthaben (Forderungen) unblocking of frozen assets, unfreezing of accounts.
auftauen to thaw, *(Autoscheibe)* to defrost;
Konto ~ to unfreeze an account; **eingefrorenen Kredit** ~ to unblock a frozen credit; **Kühler** ~ to thaw out the radiator.
aufteilbar allocable, apportionable.
aufteilen to divide, to distribute, to [re]partition, to apportion, to portion (share) out, to split up, to whack, *(parzellieren)* to parcel, *(zuteilen)* to allot, to allocate, to share out;
anteilig ~ to distribute pro rata; **Arbeit auf mehrere Leute** ~ to break up a piece of work among several people; **Betrag** ~ to prorate an amount; **Betrag gleichmäßig** ~ to split a sum into equal shares; **Betrag unter verschiedene Leute** ~ to allocate a sum of money among several people; **Erbschaft** ~ to parcel out an inheritance; **Gerichtskosten anteilmäßig auf die Parteien** ~ to apportion the costs to the sides; **Gewinne steuerlich** ~ to apportion part of profits to a particular tax year; **Gewinne untereinander** ~ to split the profits; **gleichmäßig** ~ to distribute equally; **Kontingent** ~ to allocate the shares in a quota, to quota; **Kosten** ~ to apportion (assign) the costs; **in Landgüter** ~ to parcel into farms; **unter mehrere Leute** ~ to distribute among several people; **nach einem bestimmten Schlüssel** ~ to prorate *(US)*; **Sicherheiten** ~ to marshal securities (assets); **Staatsgebiet aufteilen** to dismember a territory; **Unkosten** ~ to lump the expenses; **Urlaub** ~ to stagger the holiday; **Verluste** ~ to share losses; **Verluste gleichmäßig über das ganze Jahr** ~ to apportion losses evenly over the year; **sein Vermögen unter seinen Erben** ~ to divide one's property (share one's estate) amongst one's heirs; **Vorräte** ~ to share out provisions.
Aufteilung distribution, partition, portionment, breakdown, *(Gebiet)* dismemberment, repartition, *(Grundstücke)* parcel(l)ing, *(Unkosten)* allocation, apportionment;
anteilsmäßige ~ prorata apportionment, proration *(US)*; **prozentuale** ~ distribution on a percentage basis; **regionale** ~ regional division;
~ **des Absatzmarktes** market segmentation; ~ **der Arbeit** breaking up of work; ~ **eines Betrages unter verschiedene Leute** allocation of a sum among several people; ~ **des Frachtgeschäfts** cargo sharing; ~ **der Generalunkosten** overhead allocation; ~ **des Gesellschaftsgewinns** distribution of partnership profit; ~ **unter den Gläubigern** distribution among the creditors; ~ **der Grundstückspacht** apportionment of rent; ~ **im Innenverhältnis** equitable apportionment; ~ **von Kontingenten** allocation (division) of quotas; ~ **der Kosten** allocation (distribution) of costs; ~ **der Provisionsgebühr** diversion of commission; ~ **der Schulden** distribution of debts; ~ **der Sicherheiten** marshalling of securities (assets); ~ **eines Staates** dismemberment of a territory; ~ **eines Steuerbetrages** apportionment of a tax; ~ **des Urlaubs** staggering of the holiday; ~ **in Verwaltungsbezirke** regionalization; ~ **des Werbeetats** assignment of advertising expenditure; ~ **auf verschiedene Werbeträger** media allocation;
~ **des Marktes vornehmen** to allocate the market.
Aufteilungs|bogen apportionment sheet; **~plan** allocation scheme; **~vertrag** repartition treaty.
auftischen to serve, to dish up;
die üblichen Argumente neuverpackt ~ to dish up the usual arguments in new form; **alte Geschichte immer wieder** ~ to rehash an old story, to dine out on a story.
Auftrag *(Anwalt)* brief, *(Anweisung)* direction, order, orders, line, instruction, mandate, indent, assignment, *(Aufgabe)* mission, task, *(Bestellung)* sales order, *(Botengang)* errand, *(Botschaft)* message, *(Geschäftsbesorgung)* commission, commitment, appointment, *(Mandat)* mandate, *(Pflicht)* charge, duty, *(Verdingung)* contract;
entsprechend (gemäß) ihrem ~ subject to your order, in conformity with your instructions; **im** ~ **[von]** by order (attorney, procuration), in charge, on (by way of) commission, on the authority of; **für und im** ~ **von** for and on behalf of; **im** ~ **eines Dritten** by order of a third party; **im** ~ **und für Rechnung** by order and for account of; **im** ~ **der Regierung** by order of the government; **in amtlichem** ~ in an official capacity, in discharge of official duty; **in besonderem** ~ on special mission; **in höherem** ~ on orders from above; **in** ~ **gegeben** on order, ordered; **laut** ~ by (according) to order; **ohne** ~ uncommissioned; **ohne offiziellen** ~ without any official status;
abgegrenzter ~ limited authority; **bindender** ~ firm order; **eingehender** ~ incoming order; **darin enthaltener** ~ order contained therein; **noch nicht erledigter** ~ back order; **fester** ~ definite (binding, firm) order; **freibleibender** ~ conditional order; **gekoppelter** ~ contingent order; **genauer** ~ distinct order; **geschäftlicher** ~ commercial order; **großer** ~ large (tall) order; **bis zum Widerruf gültiger** ~ open (good-until-cancelled) order; **Ihr** ~ **vom** your favo(u)r of; **innerbetrieblicher** ~ shop order; **laufender** ~ standing order; **limitierter** ~ *(Börse)* limited order, stop-loss order *(US)*; **offener** ~ back order; **öffentlicher** ~ government (public) contract; **periodischer** ~ periodical order; **rückständiger** ~ back order; **schriftlicher** ~ written order; **schwerer** ~ hard assignment; **umfangreicher** ~ huge order; **unbeschränkter (unlimitierter)** ~ unlimited (discretionary) order; **unerledigter** ~ outstanding order; **unlimitierter** ~ unlimited (discretionary) order; **vordringlicher** ~ rush order; **zusätzlicher** ~ additional order;
~ **auf Abruf** option order; ~ **zum Bau eines Krankenhauses** hospital contract; ~ **per Fernschreiben** telex order; ~ **zum regulären Festpreis** straight-fixed price contract *(US)*; ~ **durch die Post** mail order *(US)*; ~ **mit Preisbegrenzung** closed order; ~ **zur Überweisung der Dividende an die Bank** dividend mandate *(Br.)*; ~ **zur Zahlungseinstellung** stop-payment order;
~ **ablehnen** to decline an order; **nach** ~ **anfertigen** to make to order; ~ **annehmen** to book an order; ~ **annullieren** to cancel (countermand) an order; ~ **aufgeben** to order; ~ **ausführen** to deal with (execute, effect, act upon, attend to, fill, *US*) an order, to do (carry out, discharge) a commission; ~ **bestens ausführen** to execute an order to the best advantage; ~ **buchstabengetreu ausführen** to carry out an order to the letter; ~ **Punkt für Punkt ausführen** to execute an order in every detail; **seinen** ~ **ausrichten** to tell one's errand; ~ **ausschreiben** to invite bids *(US)*; ~ **bearbeiten** to put a matter in hand; ~ **als vordringlich behandeln** to deal with an order as one of special urgency; ~ **bekommen** to get an order, *(mil.)* to receive an assignment; **sich um einen** ~ **bemühen** to be in the running for a contract, to make (put in, send in, submit) a tender; ~ **für jem. besorgen** to do a commission for s. o.; ~ **bestätigen** to confirm an order; **sich um einen im Submissionsweg vergebenen** ~ **bewerben** to tender for a contract; **jds.** ~ **buchen** to book (enter, secure) s. one's order; ~ **durchführen** to perform a mission, to go on assignment; ~ **einholen** to call for an order; **jds.** ~ **eintragen** to enter up (book) s. one's order; **sich eines ~s entledigen** to carry out an order, to execute a commission; ~ **erhalten** to obtain (secure) an order; ~ **erledigen** to fill *(US)* (attend to) an order, to execute (carry out) a commission; ~ **erteilen** to give (place, release) an order, *(Ausfuhr)* to indent, *(Behörde)* to confer (award) a commission; **jem. einen** ~ **erteilen** to instruct s. o., to give s. o. instructions; **einem Anwalt einem** ~ **erteilen** to brief a barrister; **einer Firma einen** ~ **erteilen** to contract with a firm; **postalisch** ~ **erteilen** to mail in one's order *(US)*; ~ **brieflich erteilen** to send an order by letter; ~ **unmittelbar erteilen** to place an order direct; **in** ~ **geben** to commission, to commit, to [place an] order; **Artikel bei einer Firma in** ~ **geben** to place an order for an article with a firm; **Studie in** ~ **geben** to contract out a study; **den** ~ **haben** to be commissioned to do; **keinen** ~ **für etw. haben** to have no business to do s. th.; **sich an seinen** ~ **halten** to stick to one's instructions; **im** ~ **von jem. handeln** to act on behalf of s. o.; **in jds.** ~ **kommen** to come on s. one's behalf; ~ **rückgängig machen** to cancel (revoke) an order; **von einem** ~ **Vormerkung nehmen** to note an order; **an einem** ~ **hälftig beteiligt sein** to share an order on a 50 - 50 basis; **in** ~ **gegeben sein** to be on order; **sich einen** ~ **sichern** to snag a contract; ~ **stornieren** to cancel (revoke, withdraw) an order; ~ **übermitteln** to transmit an order; ~ **verbuchen** to book an order; ~ **vergeben** to [place an] order, *(Behörde)* to let out s. th. on contract; ~ **an seine Lieferanten weitergeben** to job a contract; ~ **widerrufen** to withdraw a contract; ~ **zurücknehmen** to cancel (remand) an order, to countermand; ~ **zusammenstellen** to make up an order.
Aufträge orders;
bei Vergabe von ~n when ordering; **Ihrer** ~ **gewärtig** awaiting your orders; **mit ~n überhäuft** overwhelmed with orders;
abgewickelte und noch laufende ~ orders completed and still in work; **ausgeführte** ~ filled orders; **eingehende** ~ incoming orders; **erledigte** ~ filled orders; **telefonisch erteilte** ~ orders placed by telephone; **erwartete** ~ orders to come; **gebuchte** ~

orders on the book; **keine** ~ no orders; **öffentliche** ~ public (government) contracts; **schriftliche** ~ orders placed by letter; **umfangreiche** ~ heavy orders; **unerledigte** ~ unfilled (outstanding) orders, backlog of orders; **vorliegende** ~ orders on hand; **weitere** ~ further orders; **zukünftige** ~ future orders; **zurückgehaltene** ~ reserve orders;
~ **vom Festland** Continental orders *(Br.)*;
~ **annehmen** to undertake orders; **jds.** ~ **prompt ausführen** to give one's best attention to s. one's orders; **große** ~ **bearbeiten** to handle large orders; **sich um** ~ **bemühen** to solicit orders; ~ **buchen** to write orders; ~ **durchführen** to perform a mission; ~ **einholen** to canvass orders; ~**n entgegensehen** to await orders; **jem. seine** ~ **entziehen** to withdraw one's orders from s. o.; ~ **erbitten** to call for orders; **alle** ~ **in der Reihenfolge des Eingangs erledigen** to execute (meet) all orders in strict rotation; **große** ~ **erteilen** to order large quantities; ~ **nur zögernd erteilen** to go slow on orders; ~ **hereinholen** to canvass (solicit) orders; ~ **kassieren** to scoop up orders; ~ **sammeln** to call for (canvass, collect) orders; ~ **im größeren Ausmaß produktionsmäßig vergeben** to farm out orders for many products; ~ **verlagern** to shift orders; ~ **zurückziehen** to shorten commitments.

auftragen *(Kleider)* to wear out, *(Kurve)* to trace, *(Meßwerte)* to plot, *(Speisen)* to serve;
jem. etw. ~ to charge s. o. with s. th., to instruct s. o. to do s. th.; **jem. eine Arbeit** ~ to give s. o. a job; **zu dick** ~ to lay it on with a trowel (thick, *sl.*); **jem. eine delikate Sache** ~ to entrust s. o. with a delicate task; **ganz schön** ~ to pitch it strong; **zu stark** ~ to overstate one's case.

Auftraggeber contractor, party ordering, constituent, *(Arbeitgeber)* employer [of labo(u)r], principal, *(Geschäftsabschluß)* committer, *(jur.)* mandator, *(Kunde)* client, customer, *(eines Künstlers)* patron, *(Warenversand)* consignor, *(Werbung)* sponsor;
ausländischer ~ foreign principal; **industrieller** ~ industrial client; **öffentlicher** ~ contract-placing authority; **ungenannter (verdeckter)** ~ undisclosed principal;
~ **und Auftragnehmer** employer and his agent;
~ **benennen** to disclose the name of the principal, *(Börse)* to give up; **sich mit seinem** ~ **besprechen** to consult one's principal; ~ **unzureichend vertreten** to misrepresent s. o.;
~**gruppe** supporting group.

auftragloser Geschäftsführer agent of necessity.

Auftragnehmer consignee, successful bidder, contractor, mandatary;
~ **und Auftraggeber** principal and agent, employer and his agent.

Auftrags|ablehnung denial (rejection, declining) of an order; ~**abrechnungskarte** operation (job) card; ~**abteilung** order department; ~**abwicklung** filling a contract; ~**angebot telegrafisch bestätigen** to cable one's acceptance; ~**annahme** taking (acceptance of) an order; ~**annullierungen** cancellation of orders; ~**anstieg** jump in orders; **saisonbedingter** ~**anstieg** seasonal upturn in demand; ~**bau** building on contract; ~**bearbeitung** handling of an order, order handling (processing); ~**bearbeitungssystem** order processing system; ~**bedingungen** terms of a contract; ~**beendigung** *(Werbung)* end of series; ~**bereinigung** elimination of unfilled orders; ~**beschaffung** bidding for orders; ~**besorgung** solicitation of orders; ~**besprechung** briefing conference; ~**bestand** orders on hand, orders booked, order backlog, unfilled orders *(US)*; **unerledigter** ~**bestand** backlog, reserve of unfilled orders; **wachsender** ~**bestand** lengthening order book; ~**bestandbuch** order book; ~**bestätigung** confirmation (acknowledgement) of an order, *(Makler)* contract note *(Br.)*, *(schriftliche)* confirmation note, *(Spediteur)* confirmatory note *(US)*; ~**betrieb** commission manufacture; ~**bild** order picture; **neuen** ~**boom auslösen** to rush in with new orders; ~**brief** order letter; ~**buch** order (commission) book, book of commissions; ~**buchhalter** order clerk; ~**buchung** writing orders; ~**datum** order date; ~**dienst** *(Telefon)* telephone-answering service; ~**eingang** receipt of an order, order entry (intake); **nachlassender** ~**eingang** slowdown in orders; **hinter dem** ~**eingang herhinken** to lag behind incoming orders; ~**eingänge** incoming orders, new orders received, orders booked; **mangels** ~**eingänge** owing to lack of orders; ~**eingänge zügig erledigen** to keep pace with the rush of orders; ~**einholung** getting an order; ~**empfang** receipt of order; ~**entwicklung** trend of orders; ~**erhalt** receipt of an order; ~**erholung** pick-up in orders; ~**erledigung** order filling, order service, filling of orders; **sofortige** ~**erledigung** prompt attention to an order; **sich persönlich um eine** ~**erledigung kümmern** to personally handle an order; ~**erneuerung** renewal of orders.

Auftragserteilung placing an order, *(Behörde)* allocation of contract, contract award;
bei ~ when ordering (placing an order); **zahlbar bei** ~ cash with order;
~ **nur im Bedarfsfall vornehmen** to switch to a hand-to-mouth ordering pace.

Auftrags|erweiterung extension of an order; ~**fertigung** custom order, job (jobbing) production; ~**flaute** stagnation of orders; ~**flut** surge in orders; ~**formular** order form (sheet, slip, blank, *US*); **übliches** ~**formular** standard form of order; **kombiniertes** ~ **und Versandrechnungsformular** combination sales-order-shipper invoice form.

auftragsgemäß to (in pursuance of an) order, according to (in accordance with) orders (instructions), as instructed (ordered);
~ **handeln** to act in compliance with s. one's orders.

Auftrags|geschäft, ~**handel** commissional business; **wirtschaftliche** ~**größe** economic order quantity; ~**höhe** order level; ~**index** index of orders booked, order index; ~**karte** order card; ~**kartei** order register; ~**kassierer** order taker; ~**käufer** personal shopper; **unberechnete** ~**kosten** cost of unbilled contracts; ~**kostenbuch** job cost ledger; ~**kostenrechnung** job costing; ~**kostensammelblatt** job cost sheet; ~**kürzung** cutback in orders; ~**lage** order position, order picture; ~**lenkung** allocation of contracts, distribution of orders; ~**liste** list of orders, order book; ~**lücke** lag in orders; ~**makler** drop shipper, two-dollar-broker *(US)*; ~**mangel** shortage of work.

auftragsmäßig wieder interessant werden to go back on the books.

Auftrags|nummer register (order) number; ~**planung und** ~**steuerung** production planning; ~**polster** backlog of orders, back (cushion of) orders; **vorgedruckte** ~**postkarte** postcard order form; ~**produktion** one-off production; **öffentliches** ~**programm** relief works program(m)e; ~**prüfung** order checking; ~**rest** remainder of order; ~**rückgang** falling off of orders, fall in demand; ~**rückstand** back (unfilled) orders, orders on hand, backlog, decline (fall-off, downtrend) in new orders; ~**schein** order form (sheet); ~**sendung** drop shipment; ~**sperre** embargo on orders; ~**stopp** *(Makler)* stop[-loss] order; ~**stornierung,** ~**streichung** withdrawal (cancellation) of an order; ~**strom** rush (flush) of (surge in) orders, order flow; ~**tätigkeit** ordering activity; **unerledigter** ~**überhang** backlog of orders, reserve of unfilled orders; ~**umfang** size of an order, *(Anzeige)* insertion and size; ~**vergabe** placing an order, order placing, *(Behörde)* award of a contract, contract award, granting of contracts, letting of works and supplies, allocation (placing, letting, *US*) of a contract; **freihändige** ~**vergabe** free adjudication; ~**verhältnis** contract of agency, agency contract; ~**verlagerung** shifting of orders; ~**verweigerung** refusal to supply; ~**verzögerung** delays in execution; ~**volumen** size of orders.

auftragsweise by way of commission;
~ **Einziehung** collection on a commission basis.

Auftrags|welle wave of incoming orders; ~**werbung** solicitation of orders, canvass; ~**wert** value of the goods ordered.

auftragswidrig contrary to instructions.

Auftrags|wiederholung repetition of an order; ~**zahlen** order-book figures; ~**zettel** order slip (form, sheet, blank, *US*), requisition form *(Br.)*; ~**zugang** order flow, flow of incoming orders; ~**zuteilung,** ~**zuweisung** *(Behörde)* awarding of a contract, contract award; **bei einer** ~**zuteilung leer ausgehen** to lose out on a bidding.

auftreiben to obtain, to get hold of, to pick up, to find;
Beweise ~ to hunt up evidence; **etw. zum Essen für unerwarteten Besuch** ~ to rustle up some food for unexpected visitors; **Geld** ~ to raise money.

Auftreten behavio(u)r, conduct, manner, air, presence, demeano(u)r, *(vor Gericht)* appearance, *(Schauspieler)* appearance;
autoritäres ~ heavy-father tone; **effektvolles** ~ showmanship; **erfolgreiches** ~ lifemanship; **erstes** ~ début; **forsches** ~ swagger; **gesetztes** ~ gravity of an appearance; **großkotziges** ~ high-handed proceeding; **halbwöchentliches** ~ *(Ensemble)* split week; **herrisches** ~ overbearance; **höfliches** ~ soft manners; **unbefangenes** ~ liberal manner;
erstes ~ **in der Gesellschaft** debut in society; **erstes** ~ **einer Krankheit** first occurrence of a disease; ~ **in der Öffentlichkeit** public appearance;
forsches ~ **haben** to have a brisk manner.

auftreten to act, to appear, *(sich benehmen)* to behave, to conduct o. s., *(auf der Bühne, Schauspieler)* to go on, *(Film)* to come on, *(Theater)* to enter, to make one's entry, to tread the stage, to pose, to appear, *(vorkommen)* to occur;

für j. ~ to stand up for s. o.; **bescheiden** ~ to bear low sail; **Kindern gegenüber bestimmt** ~ to be firm with children; **energisch** ~ to assert o. s., to go it; **sehr entschieden** ~ to take a firm stand; **als Erbe** ~ to claim to be the heir; **mit einer Forderung** ~ to present a claim; **gebieterisch** ~ to lay down the law; **in einer Gegend nicht** ~ not to be found in a region; **gemeinsam** ~ to co-star; **für jem. vor Gericht** ~ to appear for s. o.; **als Anwalt vor Gericht** ~ to practise in court; **als Kandidat** ~ to stand as candidate, to run for an office *(US)*; **als Kläger** ~ to appear for the plaintiff; **als Kreditgeber** ~ to function as creditor; **zum ersten Mal** ~ to make one's debut; **zum ersten Mal öffentlich** ~ to make one's first appearance; **zum letzten Mal** ~ to take one's last curtain; **im Namen von ...** ~ to go under the name of ...; **öffentlich** ~ to appear in public; **persönlich** ~ to act in person; **als Prozeßbevollmächtigter für den Beklagten** ~ to appear for the defence; **selbstherrisch** ~ to lay down the law about; **[selbst]sicher** ~ to act with (have plenty of) assurance; **selten** ~ to occur rarely; **wieder** ~ to recur; **würdig** ~ to deport o. s. with dignity; **als Zeuge** ~ to take the witness box.

auftretend, lokal stationary.

Auftrieb impulse, impetus, spur, *(Börse)* buoyancy, *(Flugzeug)* lift, *(Preise)* rising tendency (trend), upswing, upsurge, boost; **hydrostatischer** ~ buoyancy, buoying lift; **konjunktureller** ~ business improvement, upturn in the business cycle, cyclical uptrend, cyclical boom (upswing), upsurge; **neuer** ~ fresh impetus, second wind;
~ **in der Wohnungswirtschaft** upsurge in housing;
raketenartigen ~ **erfahren** *(Kurse)* to turn in stellar performance; **erneuten** ~ **erhalten** *(Kurse)* to turn in another strong performance; **starken** ~ **erhalten** to be given strong impetus; ~ **geben** to quicken, to make more lively; **konjunkturellen** ~ **geben** to buoy up the economic index; **einer Sache starken** ~ **geben** to give s. th. a major boost; **den Truppen neuen** ~ **geben** to put fresh heart into the troops; **zusätzlichen** ~ **geben** to furnish additional impetus; ~ **haben** *(Konjunktur)* to boom.

Auftriebs|faktoren stimulating factors; ~**reserve** reserve buoyancy.

Auftriebstendenz upward trend (tendency), upward phase, upswing, upsurge, pickup *(US sl.)*;
konjunkturelle ~ upward trend;
~ **des Pfundes abschwächen** to relieve the upward pressure on sterling; ~ **erkennen lassen** to show a tendency to improve.

Auftritt scene, appearance, spot *(Br., coll.)*, *(Theater)* entry, scene, appearance;
erster ~ debut; **peinlicher** ~ embarrassing scene;
jem. einen ~ **machen** to make s. o. a scene; **seinen** ~ **verpassen** to miss (miscue) one's entrance; **auf seinen** ~ **warten** to wait in the wings.

Auftrittsmöglichkeiten in einem Amt voll ausspielen to have a natural grasp for the theatrical side of an office.

auftrumpfen, mit etw. to play one's trump card.

aufwachsen to grow up, to spend one's childhood.

Aufwallung flush.

Aufwand expenditure, expense, outlay, cost, *(Luxus)* extravagance, luxury, show, pomp;
mit großem ~ **verbunden** entailing great expenses; **mit einem unnötigen** ~ **von Energie** with an unnecessary expenditure of energy; **ohne** ~ without circumstance (any great outlay);
aktivierungspflichtiger ~ capital expenditure; **außerordentlicher** ~ sundry expenditure; **betriebsfremder** ~ nonoperating expenses, income deductions; **bürokratischer** ~ bureaucratic expenditure; **erfolgswirksamer** ~ revenue expenditure; **großer** ~ large expenditure; **großer technischer** ~ major engineering; **an der Grenze der Wirtschaftlichkeit liegender** ~ marginal costs; **neutraler** ~ *(Bilanz)* other deductions, income deductions; **ruinöser** ~ ruinous expenditure; **sonstiger** ~ *(Bilanz)* other charges; **übermäßiger** ~ extravagant expenses; **unnützer** ~ waste; **zukünftiger** ~ future expense; **zusammengefaßter** ~ pool of expenditure;
~ **für das Erziehungswesen** education expenditure; ~ **der Gemeinden** local expenditure *(US)*; ~ **der öffentlichen Hand** government spending; ~ **für eine Hausangestellte** cost of domestic services; ~ **von Nettoeinkünften** net revenue expenditure; ~ **vor Produktionsaufnahme** preparation expense; **bei der Parlamentseröffnung entfalteter** ~ **und Prunk** pomp and ceremony of the state opening of parliament; ~ **für die Raumfahrt** space outlays; ~ **für Steuern von Einkommen, Ertrag und Vermögen** expenditure for taxes on income, earnings and property; ~ **für Wertpapierbesitz** security expense; ~ **der gewerblichen Wirtschaft für Bauleistungen** nonresidential building outlay; **unnützer** ~ **an Zeit** waste of time;
über ~ **abrechnen** to expense; **aufdringlichen** ~ **treiben** to be fond of vulgar display; **großen** ~ **treiben** to live in state (at rack and manger), to spend a great deal; **keinen** ~ **treiben** to live in a small way; **unnützen** ~ **treiben** to throw (fling) one's money away.

Aufwands|angaben cost data; ~**entschädigung** expense (office, service) allowance, allowance for special expenditure, entertainment expenses, *(Abgeordneter)* salary of a member of parliament *(Br.)*, *(leitender Angestellter)* fringe benefit, *(Behörde)* office (entertainment, representation) allowance; ~**entschädigung gewähren** to allow for special expenditure; ~**entwicklung** spending trend; ~**faktoren** expense factors; ~**konto** expense (expenditure) account; **bleibende** ~**kosten** basic expenditure accounts.

Aufwandsposten expense item;
bleibende ~ basic expenditure accounts.

Aufwands|prinzip *(Steuer)* sumptuary principle; ~**programm** spending plan; **periodenechte** ~- **und Ertragsrechnung** accrual accounting; **verzögerte** ~**regelung** postponement of expense; ~**steuer** tax on consumption (expenditure), sumptuary (expenditure) tax, use tax *(US)*; ~**zahlen** expense figures.

Aufwärmen warm[ing].

aufwärmen to warm up (over, *US*);
alte Geschichten ~ to rake up (rehash) old stories, to furbish up old tales.

Aufwartefrau charwoman, daily cleaner, cleaning woman *(US)*.

aufwarten to serve, to wait, to tend;
jem. ~ to attend (wait on) s. o.; **mit einer interessanten Neuigkeit** ~ to come up with an interesting piece of news; **bei Tisch** ~ to serve at table; **mit einigen Überraschungen** ~ to have some surprises in store.

Aufwärterin waitress.

aufwärts upwards, uphill;
fünf Dollar und ~ from five Dollars up;
sich ~ **bewegen** *(Kurse, Preise)* to rise, to move, to go up, *(Geschäft)* to be improving (looking up, booming); **Fluß** ~ **fahren** to go upstream.

Aufwärtsbewegung *(Börse)* advance, up, upward push, buoyant tone of the market, *(Kurse)* upward trend (tendency), rise, improvement, *(Preise)* upward movement;
allgemeine ~ forward movement; **konjunkturelle** ~ upward business trend, cyclical upward movement;
~ **am Aktienmarkt** advances on the stock market; ~ **des Pfundes** sterling's upward float;
~ **anführen** to be in the van of advance; **der** ~ **nur langsam folgen** to lag behind the advance; ~ **fortsetzen** to continue its upward trend; **gleichmäßige** ~ **der Wirtschaft herbeiführen** to keep the economy on a stable upward path; **leichte** ~ **erkennen lassen** to tend to rise.

Aufwärtsentwicklung improvement, upward surge, upsurge, uptrend, upswing.

aufwärtsgehen *(fig.)* to improve.

Aufwärts|kurve curve upward; ~**strich** upstroke; ~**tendenz** upward tendency, improvement; ~**tendenz erkennen lassen** to show a tendency to improve.

Aufwartung attendance, service;
jem. seine ~ **machen** to call on (pay one's respects, devoirs to) s. o.

aufweichen, Währung to soften the currency.

Aufweichung der Währung softening of the currency.

aufweisen to show, to produce;
Beschädigungen ~ to show signs of damage; **Gewinn** ~ to show a profit; **große Mängel** ~ to have many defects; **genügend Mittel** ~ to produce sufficient funds; **Saldo** ~ to show a balance; **Verlust** ~ to show a loss.

aufwenden to spend, to expend, to employ, *(anwenden)* to use, to employ;
viel Geld ~ to go to great expense; **Kosten** ~ to defray expenses; **große Mühe** ~ to take great pains.

aufwendig expensive, costly, sumptuous, extravagant, *(Buch)* lavish, luxurious;
~ **leben** to live in grand style (at heck and manger), to live high on the hog *(sl.)*;
~**es Geschenk** lavish gift; ~**e Lebensführung** extravagant (high-style, sumptuous) living; ~**e Verwaltung** wasteful administration.

Aufwendungen expenditure, expense, disbursements, improvements, outgoings;
andere ~ *(Bilanz)* other expenses; **steuerlich anerkannte (steuerabzugsfähige)** ~ allowable expenditure (deduction); **außerordentliche** ~ extraordinary expenses (income); **außerordentliche und betriebsfremde** ~ extraordinary and outside

expenditure; **betriebliche** ~ operating expenses; **betriebsfremde** ~ nonoperating expenses; **aus dem Erfolg zu deckende** ~ expenditure to be charged to income; **entstandene** ~ expenditure occasioned; **entstandene, aber noch nicht fällige** ~ accrued expense (account payables, *US*); **erstmalige** ~ initial expenditure; **freiwillige** ~ voluntary contributions; **im voraus gezahlte** ~ prepaid expenses; **periodenfremde** ~ periodic charges (cost, expense), time cost; **private** ~ private expenditure; **soziale** ~ social expenditure (disbursements); **andere soziale** ~ *(Bilanz)* other social expenditure; **unnütze** ~ waste; **werterhöhende** ~ valuable improvements; **wertsteigernde** ~ improvements;
~ **für die Altersversorgung** expenditure on retirement pensions; ~ **für die Altersversorgung und Unterstützung** pensions and assistance; **zusätzliche** ~ **für leitende Angestellte** executive fringes; ~ **für ärztliche Behandlungen** medical costs; ~ **für Bürobedarf** expense on office requirements; ~ **für die Errichtung von Wohnhäusern** residential outlay; ~ **für Forschungsarbeiten** investment in research; ~ **für Rohstoffe** cost of raw materials; ~ **für Unterstützungen** expenditure for relief; ~ **aus Verlustübernahme von Konzerngesellschaften** transfer of losses from affiliates; ~ **nach Verrechnung mit Bestandsveränderungen** *(Bilanz)* cost of materials including changes in inventories; ~ **für bezogene Waren** outlay for goods supplied; ~ **für Wertpapierbesitz** security expenses; ~ **für den Wohnungsbau** housing expenditure;
~ **bestreiten** to defray the expenses; **beträchtliche** ~ **machen** to incur heavy expenses.

Aufwendungs|anspruch right of indemnity; ~- **und Instandhaltungskosten** upkeep and improvements.

aufwerfen *(Damm)* to throw up, to build;
sich als jds. Beschützer ~ to pose as s. one's protector; **Frage** ~ to come up with a question, to state an issue, to raise a question; **sich zum Richter** ~ to act the part of a judge.

aufwerten to revalue, to [re]valorize, to upvalue, *(Anlagegüter)* to write up, to appreciate *(Br.)*, *(Grundstück)* to appreciate, to reassess.

Aufwertung [upward] revaluation, upvaluation, valorization, revalorization, *(Grundstück)* appreciation, reassessment;
~ **von Anlagen** appreciation *(Br.)* (writing up) of assets; ~ **des Pfundes** revaluation of the pound; ~ **einer Währung** currency revaluation.

aufwertungsähnliche Maßnahmen quasi-revaluation measures.

Aufwertungs|anhänger upvaluer; ~**anleihe** stabilization loan; ~**erlös** revaluation profit; ~**gewinn** revaluation surplus; ~**kandidat** candidate for revaluation; ~**satz** rate of revaluation; ~**verlust** revaluation loss.

aufwickeln to wind (coil) up;
Film ~ to take up a film.

aufwiegeln to stir, to agitate, to incite, to instigate, to work up;
Seeleute zur Meuterei ~ to incite (stir) sailors to mutiny; **Volk** ~ to stir up the people, to foment rebellion.

Aufwiegelung incitement, instigation, agitation, sedition, incendarism.

aufwiegen to offset, to counterbalance, to match against;
alle Nachteile ~ to make up for all shortcomings; **Verlust** ~ to compensate a loss;
man kann ihn nicht mit Gold ~ he is worth his weight in gold.

Aufwiegler stirrer, instigator, agitator, *(fig.)* firebrand.

aufwieglerisch incendiary, seditious, agitating.

Aufwind upwind, upcurrent, updraft, anabetic wind.

aufwirbeln, Staub *(fig.)* to kick up a dust, to set tongues going wagging.

aufwischen to wipe off, *(Fußboden)* to clean.

aufwühlen to churn up *(fig.)* to stir the blood;
alte Geschichten ~ to rake up old scandals.

aufzählen to enumerate, to numerate;
Beispiele ~ to give examples; **Geld** ~ to count down money; **sein Geld auf den Tisch** ~ to count (plank) down money; **in einer Liste** ~ to list, to specify, to itemize *(US)*.

Aufzählung enumeration, listing, itemization *(US)*;
~ **der Klagepunkte** allegation of counts; **einfache** ~ **der Tatumstände** bare statement of the facts.

aufzehren to use up, to consume, *(Kräfte)* to exhaust;
sich ~ to become exhausted; **gesamte Einkünfte** ~ to absorb the whole of the available income; **sein Kapital** ~ to eat up one's capital.

aufzeichnen to write (mark, take, set) down, to note, *(anreißen)* to trace, *(eintragen)* to book, to record, to register, to list, to chronicle, *(Meßwerte)* to plot, *(Rundfunk)* to transcribe, *(zeichnen)* to design, to draw, to sketch;
Flugzeugbewegungen auf dem Radarschirm ~ to plot aircraft movement by radar; **genau** ~ to map out; **Grundriß eines Hauses** ~ to make a sketch of a house; **auf Tonband** ~ to record on tape, to can *(coll.)*.

Aufzeichnung memorandum, record, note, notation, *(Band)* recording, record, *(in Geschäftsbüchern)* registration, register, recording, *(Meßgerät)* trace, record, *(Rundfunk)* transcrip[tion], platter;
~ **von Kurs und Entfernung** air plot.

Aufzeichnungen notes, papers;
laufend geführte ~ progressive records; **kurze** ~ memorandum; **schriftliche** ~ memorandum in writing; **stenografische** ~ shorthand notes, stenographs; **unsere** ~ our records;
~ **über den Kassenausgang** cash disbursement records; ~ **der Kundenbuchhaltung** accounts receivable records *(US)*; ~ **über den Wareneinkauf** purchase records;
mit seinen ~ **herumhantieren** to shuffle one's notes; **seine** ~ **konsultieren** to refer to one's notes; **sich** ~ **machen** to take notes (a record); **anhand von** ~ **sprechen** to speak from (with) notes; **seine** ~ **verbrennen** to commit one's manuscripts to the flames.

Aufzeichnungs|einrichtungen transcription service; ~**kontrolle** monitoring; ~**methode** recording method; ~**nadel** recording needle; ~**system** notetaking system.

aufzeigen to disclose, to point up, to indicate, to show;
Problematik ~ to point out the problems involved.

Aufziehen|eines Reifens fitting on of a tyre; ~ **einer Uhr** winding up a clock; ~ **der Wache** changing of the guard.

aufziehen *(Gefahr)* to be brewing, *(Gewitter)* to come up, *(Kinder)* to raise, to bring up, *(Last)* to hoist, *(necken)* to kid, to tease, to needle, *(organisieren)* to arrange, to organize, to get up, *(Wache)* to mount;
j. ~ to pull s. one's leg, to roast s. o., to play on s. o.; **Fahne** ~ to hoist a flag; **falsch** ~ to go about the wrong way; **neues Geschäft** ~ to start a new business enterprise; **groß** ~ to get up in grand style; **Nachricht groß** ~ to splash a piece of news *(Br.)*; **Messe** ~ to organize a fair; **neu** ~ *(Karte)* to remount; **Reifen** ~ to fit a tyre; **strengere Saiten** ~ to adopt another tone; **Uhr** ~ to wind up a watch; **Vorhang** ~ *(Theater)* to raise the curtain; **Wohltätigkeitsveranstaltung** ~ to get up a performance for charity.

Aufzieh|karton mount; ~**leine** *(Fallschirm)* release cord, static line; ~**leinwand** mount; ~**vorrichtung** hoisting apparatus.

Aufzucht breeding, rearing;
~ **von Vieh** raising of livestock.

Aufzug lift *(Br.)*, elevator *(US)*, hoistaway *(US coll.)*, *(Aufmachung)* rigout, turnout, getup, *(Prozession)* procession, *(Theater)* act;
ohne ~ walk-up *(US)*;
elektrischer ~ electric elevator *(US)*;
~ **bedienen** to operate the lift *(Br.)* (elevator, *US*).

Aufzugs|arbeiter hoisting engineer; ~**führer** lift attendant *(Br.)*, elevator operator *(US)*; ~**gesellschaft** elevator company *(US)*; ~**schacht** lift *(Br.)* (elevator, *US*) shaft, hoistway; ~**versicherung** elevator public liability insurance *(US)*.

aufzuregen, ohne sich weiter without troubling any further.

aufzuweisen haben, etw. to have s. th. to one's name.

aufzwingen to impose (force) upon;
jem. etw. ~ to huff s. o. into s. th.

Augapfel ihres Vaters the apple of her father's eye.

Auge eye;
direkt vor jds. ~ right under s. one's very nose; **in die ~n fallend** conspicuous; **mit anderen ~n** with a fresh eye; **mit bloßem** ~ with the naked eye; **soweit das** ~ **reicht** as far as the eye can see; **um jds. schöner ~n willen** for s. one's fair face; **unter vier ~n** face to face, between ourselves;
blaues ~ black eye, bruise; **kauflüsterne ~n** came-to-bid eyes; **magisches** ~ *(Rundfunkgerät)* magic eye, tuning eye; **scharfes** ~ quick eye;
~ **um** ~ an eye for an eye; ~ **des Gesetzes** eye of the law; ~ **eines Wirbelsturms** eye of a storm, storm center *(US)* (centre, *Br.*); **jem. jeden Wunsch von den ~n ablesen** to wait on s. o. hand and foot; **mit scheelen ~n ansehen** to look askance at; **sich die ~n ausweinen** to cry one's heart out; **im** ~ **behalten** to keep an eye on; **jem. dauernd im** ~ **behalten** to keep s. o. under one's eye; **Sache im** ~ **behalten** to keep track of a matter; **jds. Schritte im** ~ **behalten** to watch s. one's movements; **das** ~ **beleidigen** to be an eyesore; **mit argwöhnischen ~n betrachten** to eagle-eye; **Problem mit anderen ~n betrachten** to look on a problem with a different eye; **gerade noch mit einem blauen** ~ **davonkommen** to escape by the skin of one's teeth, to get away with murder *(sl.)*, to get off lightly; **den ~n entschwinden** to vanish from sight; **ins** ~ **fallen** to

catch the eye; **am meisten ins ~ fallen** to be most obvious; **sofort ins ~ fallen** to spring to the eye; **etw. ins ~ fassen** to envisage s. th.; **vor jds. ~n Gnade finden** to find favo(u)r in s. one's eyes; **jem. etw. vor ~n führen** to make it clear for s. o.; **ins ~ gehen** to turn out crabs, to go haywire; **im ~ haben** to consult, to consider; **nur die Gegenwart im ~ haben** to take a short view; **hinten und vorn ~n haben** to have eyes in the back of one's head; **Spesenwirtschaft im ~ haben** to keep tabs on the expenses; **seine ~n überall haben** to be all eyes; **wachsames ~ auf j. haben** to keep a watchful eye on s. o.; **wachsames ~ auf etw. haben** to keep a wary eye on s. th.; **seine ~n offen halten** to keep one's eyes peeled; **große ~n machen** to open one's eyes; **jem. schöne ~n machen** to make eyes at s. o., to give s. o. the glad eye; **jem. die ~n öffnen** to open (unseal) s. one's eyes, to bring s. th. home to s. o.; **ein ~ riskieren** to risk a glance; **jem. offen ins ~ schauen** to look s. o. straight in the eye; **etw. mit eigenen ~n sehen** to witness s. th. in person; **einer Gefahr ins ~ sehen** to face a danger; **jem. ein Dorn im ~ sein** to be a thorn in s. one's side (flesh); **j. unter vier ~n sprechen** to speak to s. o. privately, to talk to s. o. in privacy; **ins ~ springen** to leap to the eye; **besonders ins ~ springen** to jump off the page; **jem. vor ~n stehen** to be present to s. one's mind; **jem. Sand in die ~n streuen** to throw (cast) dust in s. one's eyes, to pull the wool over s. one's eyes *(US)*; **kaum seinen ~n trauen** hardly to believe one's eyes; **mit offenen ~n träumen** to day-dream; **sich die ~n verderben** to pore one's eyes out; **aus den ~n verlieren** to lose view (sight, track) of; **Kinder aus den ~n verlieren** to trust children out of doors; **seine ~n vor den Fehlern eines anderen verschließen** to close one's eyes to the faults of s. o.; **seine ~n vor der Wirklichkeit verschließen** to turn a blind eye; **j. mit den ~n verschlingen** to devour s. o.; **ein ~ werfen auf** to lay eyes on; **aller ~n auf sich ziehen** to attract general attention; **ein ~ zudrücken** to stretch a point, to turn one's blind eye on; **kein ~ zutun** not to get a wink of sleep; **mit den ~n zwinkern** to blink one's eyes; **aus den ~n aus dem Sinn** out of sight, out of mind.

Augenarzt eye specialist.

Augenblick moment, instant, bit, snatch, twinkle;
einer der seltenen ~e one of the rare occasions; **im ~ aufgeführt** going at present; **im ersten ~** at first; **im kritischen ~** at a push; **in diesem ~** at this juncture; **zum rechten ~** in the nick of time; **alle ~e** any moment; **entscheidender ~** zero hour; **kritischer ~** critical (crucial) moment; **kurzer ~** instant; **lichter ~** *(Geisteskranker)* lucid interval; **schwacher ~** misguided moment;
günstigen ~ abpassen to bide one's time; **im letzten ~ absagen** to cry off at the last moment; **Zug im letzten ~ erreichen** to catch a train in the nick of time; **lichte ~e haben** to have one's brighter moments; **im ~ beschäftigt sein** to be busy just now; **im ~ geschehen sein** to be the work of a moment.

augenblicklich immediate, actual, *(sofort)* right (straight) off;
~e Lage current situation; **einer ~en Regung folgen** to act on the spur of the moment.

Augen|brauenstift eyebrow pencil; **~diener** eyeservant; **~dienerei** eyeservice; **~fehler** defect of eyesight; **~fenster** *(Gasmaske)* eyepiece; **in ~höhe** at eye level; **j. seines ~lichts berauben** to deprive s. o. of his eyesight.

Augenmaß ocular estimate;
nach ~ bauen to build by eye; **überhaupt kein ~ haben** *(fig.)* to have no eye for proportion.

Augenmerk attention;
sein ~ auf etw. richten to have s. th. in view.

Augenschein ocular (local) inspection, inspection of property *(Br.)*, real evidence, surface value;
dem ~ nach to all appearances;
richterlicher ~ judicial inspection (survey);
j. in ~ nehmen to take stock of s. o., to view; **~ vornehmen** to make a visit to the scene.

augenscheinlich manifest, evident, apparent, obvious;
~ sein to go without saying.

Augenscheinnahme local inspection, view, *(Gericht)* judicial survey;
erste ~ on-the-spot check.

Augenscheins|beauftragter *(Gericht)* viewer; **~beweis** ocular proof, *(Gericht)* evidence by inspection, demonstrative evidence, prima facie evidence.

Augen|schirm eyeshade, visor *(US)*; **~verbindung** eye contact; **~weide** feast, banquet; **wahre ~weide sein** to be a sheer delight, to present a fine spectacle to the eyes; **~zeuge** ocular (eye-) witness; **~zeugenbericht** eye-witness account.

Auguren|der öffentlichen Meinung pundits of public opinion; **~lächeln** knowing smile.

Auktion auction [sales], outcry, vendue *(US)*;
in der ~ verkauft sold by auction;
gerichtlich ausgesetzte ~ adjourned sale;
zur ~ bringen, in die ~ geben to auction, to sell by (at, *US*) auction, to put up for sale, to set up, to bring to the hammer; **auf einer ~ erwerben (kaufen)** to buy by (at, *US*) auction; **Waren auf einer ~ kaufen** to buy goods at the sales; **im Wege der ~ verkaufen** to [sell by, at, *US*] auction, to sell at the spear.

Auktionator auctioneer, appraiser *(US)*.

auktionieren to sell by (at, *US*) auction, to [put up for] auction.

Auktions|ankündigung auction notice (sign); **~bedingungen** terms of auction, auction terms; **~firma** auction house; **~gebühren** auction (auctioneer's) fees, lot money; **~geschäft beleben** to spur auction activity; **~gesetz** Auctions Act *(Br.)*; **~hammer** gavel *(US)*; **~katalog, ~liste** auction bill, catalog(ue) of sale, sale catalog(ue); **~kosten** auction (auctioneer's) fee, auctioneer's commission; **~lokal** auction room (mart), saleroom; **~markt** auction market; **~posten** auction (odd) lot; **~preis** auction (hammer) price; **~raum, ~saal** auction room (mart); **~stand** commercial pitch; **~termin** auction day; **seinen Anteil an ausgeweiteten ~umsätzen steigern** to increase one's share of the bigger auction pie; **~verkauf** auction sale, sale by (at, *US*) auction.

Aula aula, assembly room, lecture theatre, common hall, auditorium *(US)*, *(Schule)* school (assembly) hall.

ausarbeiten to work out in detail, to work up, to plan, to elaborate, to compose;
Plan ~ to work out (conceive, develop) a plan; **Roman in seinen Grundlinien ~** to work up the plot of a novel; **schriftlich ~** to compose; **sorgsam ~** to elaborate; **Vertrag ~** to draw up a contract;
sich richtig ~ wollen to be in trim for rough work.

Ausarbeitung|eines Planes work-out (formulation) of a plan; **~ eines Vertrages** drafting of a contract;
~ mit Zitaten spicken to cram an essay with quotations.

ausarten, in Geiz to degenerate in avarice; **in einen Krieg ~** to develop into a war.

ausbaden müssen, es to be on the mat *(sl.)*, to be landed with (hold, carry) the baby, to hold the bag for s. th. *(US)*.

ausbaggern to excavate, to trench, to unsilt, *(Hafen)* to dredge.

ausbalancieren to poise;
verschiedene Meinungen ~ to balance different opinions.

ausbaldowern *(fam.)* to find (pry, ferret) out.

Ausbau development, enlargement, expansion, *(Demontage)* dismantlement, *(Entwicklung)* development, improvement, *(Haus)* extension, outbuilding, *(Maschine)* dismantling, dismantlement, *(Maschinenteile)* disassembly, removal, *(mil.)* consolidation, development;
~ des Betriebes factory extension; **~ des Dachgeschosses** building of an attic; **~ einer Eisenbahnlinie** extension of a railway *(Br.)*, continuation of a railroad *(US)*; **~ des Flughafens** development of an airport; **~ der Gemeindeanlagen** local improvements; **~ eines Geschäfts** expansion of business; **~ eines Krankenhauses** enlargement of a hospital; **~ der Laufbahnmöglichkeiten** career progression; **~ seiner Stellung** consolidation (strengthening) of one's position; **~ des Straßennetzes** completion of the road system;
~arbeiten interior work; **~aufwand** *(Mineralien)* development expenditure *(US)*; **~bedarf des Straßennetzes** highway needs.

ausbauen *(entwickeln)* to develop, to improve, *(Gelände)* to develop, to enlarge one's premises, *(Geschäft)* to extend, to enlarge, to expand, *(Haus)* to enlarge, to extend, *(maschinelle Anlagen abbauen)* to disassemble, to dismantle, to dismount, to remove;
Dachgeschoß ~ to build a room in the attic; **Eisenbahn ~** to complete (extend) a railway (railroad, *US*) line; **Flughafen ~** to develop an airport; **Handelsbeziehungen ~** to strengthen trade relations; **Schuppen ~** to convert a shed; **seine Stellung ~** to consolidate (strengthen) one's position; **Straße ~** to improve a road; **Strecke zweigleisig ~** to double an existing track; **Theorie ~** to elaborate a theory; **seinen Vorsprung ~** to extend one's lead; **Wirtschaftsbeziehungen ~** to improve economic relations.

ausbaufähig developable, extensible, *(Stellung)* promising, progressive, expandable, capable of improvement;
~e Stellung position with good prospects.

Ausbau|firma finishing contractor; **~gewerbe** finishing trade; **~kosten** *(Mineralien)* development expenditure *(US)*; **~plan** development scheme; **~plan für das Bundesfernstraßennetz** [etwa] national interurban road programme *(Br.)*; **~programm** *(betriebliches)* plant expansion program(me).

Ausbauten vornehmen to build extensions.
Ausbauvorhaben expansion plan.
ausbedingen to stipulate, to condition for, to make s. th. a condition, *(vorbehalten)* to reserve.
Ausbedingung stipulation.
ausbedungen conditional, stipulated;
~**e Qualität** stipulated quality.
ausbeißen, sich die Zähne daran to find it a hard nut to crack.
ausbessern to [put into] repair, to mend, to piece, to fix *(US)*, *(Tippfehler)* to correct.
Ausbesserung repair, reparation;
behelfsmäßige ~ *(Straße)* roadside repairs;
sich in ~ **befinden** to be under repair.
Ausbesserungsarbeiten repairs, repair work, *(Straße)* road repairs;
während der ~ **geschlossen sein** to be closed during repairs.
ausbesserungsbedürftig in need of (not in good) repair;
~ **sein** to be out of repair.
ausbesserungsfähig repa(i)rable, mendable.
Ausbesserungs|kosten cost of repair; ~**werft** repair yard; ~**werkstatt** repair shop.
ausbeulen *(Auto)* to flatten, to bump out.
Ausbeute yield, output, gain, result, *(Kux)* dividend;
wissenschaftliche ~ scientific results.
ausbeuten to turn to account, to make capital out of, *(Arbeiter)* to sweat, to exploit, *(Bergwerk)* to work, to exploit, *(mißbrauchen)* to exploit, *(Notlage)* to take undue advantage, *(Unternehmen)* to deplete, to milk *(US)*;
Arbeiterklasse ~ to exploit the working classes; **Archive** ~ to exploit archives; **die Armen** ~ to grind the faces of the poor; **Bodenschätze eines Landes** ~ to exploit the national resources of a country; **jds. Unwissenheit** ~ to trade on s. one's ignorance; **versuchsweise** ~ *(Bergwerk)* to prospect.
Ausbeuter exploiter, vampire, *(Arme)* grinder, *(Arbeiter)* sweater.
Ausbeutezeche productive mine.
Ausbeutung exploitation, depletion, *(Bergwerk)* working, mining, *(Bodenschätze)* exhaustion, depletion;
kommerzielle ~ industrial exploitation; **monopolistische** ~ monopolistic exploitation; **rücksichtslose** ~ ruthless exploitation;
~ **von Arbeitern** exploitation (sweating) of workers; ~ **eines Unternehmens** milking of an enterprise *(US)*.
Ausbeutungs|abkommen exploitation contract; ~**betrieb** sweatshop *(sl.)*.
ausbeutungsfähig exploitable.
Ausbeutungs|kosten cost of exploitation, exploitation costs; ~**recht** exploitation right; ~**system** *(Arbeiter)* sweating system; ~**theorie** *(Marx)* theory of surplus value.
ausbezahlen to pay out (off);
bar ~ to pay cash down; **jds. Gehalt voll** ~ to pay s. one's salary in full; **jem. seinen Lohn** ~ to pay s. o. his wages; **am Schalter** ~ to pay over the window; **Teilhaber** ~ to buy out a partner.
ausbezahlt paid out.
ausbieten, zum Verkauf to put up (offer) for sale.
ausbilden to school, to instruct, to train, to educate;
j. besonders ~ to process s. o.; **Angestellten als Buchhalter** ~ to instruct a clerk in bookkeeping; **seinen Geschmack** ~ to cultivate one's taste; **in erster Hilfe** ~ to train in first aid; **als Krankenschwester** ~ to train to be a nurse; **methodisch** ~ to drill; **sich** ~ to study; **System weiter** ~ to elaborate a system; **Truppen** ~ to exercise troops; **umsonst** ~ to train for free; **Sohn zum Juristen** ~ **lassen** to educate a son for the bar.
Ausbilder, Ausbildender [training] instructor, trainer, *(mil.)* driller.
Ausbildung education, instruction, training;
akademische ~ academic (university) training; **nur auf den Broterwerb ausgerichtete** ~ bread-and-butter education; **außerbetriebliche** ~ outside training; **berufliche** ~ professional (pre-employment, occupational) training, *(Einkommensteuer)* training for a trade, profession or vocation; **berufsbezogene** ~ job-oriented education; **betriebswirtschaftliche** ~ business administration background; **einsatzmäßige** ~ operational training; **erstklassige** ~ slap-up education; **fachliche** ~ vocational (industrial, occupational) training; **ganztägige** ~ full-time instruction; **gründliche** ~ thorough education (training); **handwerkliche** ~ manual training, training in craftsmanship; **innerbetriebliche** ~ employee (in-service, in-plant, *US*) training; **juristische** ~ legal education (training), education for the bar; **kaufmännische** ~ commercial education, business (mercantile) training; **kostenlose** ~ free education; **methodische** ~ drill; **militärische** ~ military training; **praktische** ~ on-the-job training *(US)*; **praxisbezogene** ~ end-on course; **technische** ~ technical training; **vielseitige** ~ manysided education; **weitere** ~ further education (training); **zusätzliche** ~ additional training;
~ **leitender Angestellter** executive (cold storage, *US*) training; ~ **von Arbeitskräften** manpower training; ~ **am Arbeitsplatz** instruction (training, *US*) on the job, on-the-job (in-plant) training *(US)*; ~ **der Besatzungsmitglieder** air-crew training; ~ **im eigenen Betrieb** in-house training; ~ **des Betriebspersonals** staff training; ~ **während der Dienstzeit** in-service training; ~ **von Führungskräften** training of management, management training; ~ **an der technischen Hochschule** technical education; ~ **in Kurzlehrgängen** short-course training; ~ **von Lehrlingen** apprenticeship training; ~ **in der Lehrlingswerkstatt** vestibule school training *(US)*; ~ **von Nachwuchskräften** management (cold storage, *US*) training; **vorsorgliche** ~ **für gehobenere Positionen** cold-storage training *(US)*; ~ **in Schnellkursen** intensive courses, blitz training *(US)*; ~ **in neuen technologischen Verfahren** training in new technology; ~ **von Vorarbeitern** training of foremen; ~ **und Praxis in periodischem Wechsel** recurrent education;
seine ~ **abschließen** to complete one's education; **mit der** ~ **anfangen** to be launched into training; **mitten in der** ~ **aufhören** to quit in mid-term; **für jds.** ~ **aufkommen** to pay for s. one's schooling; **sich noch in der** ~ **befinden** to be still learning; ~ **bekommen** to receive training; ~ **am Arbeitsplatz bekommen** to learn on the job; **gründliche** ~ **erhalten** to have a thorough education; **jds.** ~ **finanzieren** to finance s. one's education; **akademische** ~ **haben** to have been through the university; **noch in der** ~ **stecken** to be in the learning process; ~ **eines Schülers vorantreiben** to force a pupil.
Ausbildungs|abschnitt phase of training; ~**abteilung** staff training department; ~**ausschuß** educational panel; ~**bedürfnisse** training needs; ~**beihilfe** educational (training) grant, educational endorsement (aid), training subsidy *(US)* (allowance), training benefit; ~**beihilfeplan** aid-to-education program(me); ~**bereich** field of training; ~**bestimmungen für Lehrlinge** apprenticeship regulations; ~**dauer** training time; ~**ergebnisse** training results; ~**fachmann** training specialist.
ausbildungsfähig accomplishable;
nicht ~ unaccomplishable.
Ausbildungs|film training film; ~**förderung** training (educational) grant; ~**förderungsstelle** grant-paying authority.
Ausbildungsgang training course, *(Lebenslauf)* educational background;
praxisbezogener ~ end-on course; **zusammengefaßter** ~ summary of one's education; **zweigleisiger** ~ two-tier form of education.
Ausbildungs|grad nachweisen, hohen to have high educational qualifications; ~**gruppe** training group; ~**investitionen** investment in training; ~**kosten** training costs, investment in men, *(Lehrlinge)* premium of apprenticeship; ~**kursus** training course, course of training; **innerbetrieblicher** ~**kursus** in-company course; ~**kursus für Nachwuchskräfte** management trainee (training) course; ~**lager** training camp; ~**lehrgang** training course; ~**leiter** chief instructor, training director (coordinator, supervisor); ~**mängel** training needs; **aus mehreren Fakultäten zusammengesetzte** ~**mannschaft** multidisciplinary team; ~**material** training material; ~**methode** instructional (training) method; ~**möglichkeiten** training facilities (activities); ~**nachweis** training records; ~**offizier** instructor; ~**ordnung** training arrangements; ~**personal** training personnel; ~**plan** training schedule (scheme), curriculum.
Ausbildungsprogramm apprentice (training) program(me), educational training scheme;
~ **für Führungskräfte** executive training program(me); ~ **zur Verbesserung des Betriebsklimas** job-relations training; ~ **für Verkaufsleiter** sales training program(me).
Ausbildungs|reise training tour; ~**rücklage** savings for education; ~**schiff** training (receiving) ship; ~**stätte** training center *(US)* (centre, *Br.*, facilities), training location; ~**stufe** training level; ~**stufen** basic training pattern; ~**tätigkeit** training activity; ~**unterstützung** training benefit; **berufliches** ~**verfahren** job-training process; **in ein** ~**verhältnis eintreten** to take up one's indenture; ~**versicherung** educational endowment assurance *(Br.)* (insurance).
Ausbildungsvertrag indenture of apprentice, apprenticeship contract, contract of training (apprenticeship);
staatlicher ~ government training contract;
~ **für jem. abschließen** to bind s. o. out as apprentice; ~ **besitzen** to be trained full-time for a trade or profession.

Ausbildungs|vorschrift training manual; ~**vorteile** training benefits; ~**weg** educational background; ~**zeit** term of articles; **berufliche** ~**zeit** training time on a job; ~**zentrale** training center *(US)* (centre, *Br.*); ~**zentrum** training center *(US)* (centre, *Br.*); ~**zentrum für Führungskräfte** management center *(US)* (centre, *Br.*); ~**ziel** training objective; ~**zuschuß** training benefit (grant, subsidy, *US*), education allowance.

ausbitten, sich Bedenkzeit to request time for consideration; **sich eine Gunst von jem.** ~ to ask a favo(u)r of s. o.; **sich absolute Ruhe** ~ to insist on absolute silence.

Ausbleiben absence, nonattendance, failing, *(im Termin)* nonappearance, default;
~ **beim Gerichtstermin** failure of a party to appear; ~ **der Zahlung** default of payment, nonpayment; ~ **eines Zuges** nonarrival of a train;
jds. langes ~ **entschuldigen** to account for s. one's absence.

ausbleiben *(Aufträge)* to dry up, *(bei Gericht)* to fail to appear, to default, *(Post)* to fail to come in, *(Zug)* to be overdue;
die ganze Nacht ~ to stay out all night; **mit der Zahlung** ~ to make default, to be in arrears with one's payment.

ausblenden to fade out;
Vorhang ~ to fade a curtain.

Ausblendung *(Filmszene)* fade-out.

Ausblick view, outlook, prospect, vista, perspective;
herrlicher ~ wonderful view; **panoramaartiger** ~ big-picture (panoramic) view;
~ **auf die weitere Entwicklung** future prospects.

Ausblutung, finanzielle financial bleeding;
~ **einer Armee** depletion of an army.

ausbojen to buoy off.

ausbomben to bomb out.

ausbooten, j. to unship s. o., *(fig.)* to chuck s. o. out; **Minister aus der Regierung** ~ to chuck a minister out of government; **Passagiere** ~ to disembark passengers.

ausbrechen to break out (gaol), to cut loose, *(Auto)* to swerve, to veer, *(Feuer)* to break out, *(Krieg, Vulkan)* to erupt;
aus einer Koalition ~ to break away from a coalition; **nicht** ~ *(Sturm)* to hold off.

ausbreiten to spread [out];
sich ~ to overspread, to open out, to spread o. s., to outspread; **sich kilometerweit** ~ to stretch for miles; **sich über das ganze Land** ~ *(Wetterzone)* to cover the whole country; **sich über ein Thema** ~ to enlarge upon a subject; **seine Ware zum Verkauf** ~ to spread (sort) out (display) one's goods for sale; **sein Werkzeug** ~ to lay out one's tools; **Zeitung** ~ to unfold a newspaper.

Ausbreitung spread, *(fig.)* expansion, dissemination, propagation;
~ **in andere Energiebereiche** diversification into other energy sources;
~ **sozialistischer Ideen genauestens verfolgen** to watch the spread of socialism; ~ **einer Krankheit verhindern** to prevent the spread of a disease.

ausbrennen to burn out.

ausbringen, Boot to launch a boat; **Trinkspruch** ~ to propose a toast.

Ausbruch *(Begeisterung, Zorn)* outburst, flare, *(Fluchtversuch)* outbreak, break, escape;
bei ~ **des Krieges** when war broke out;
~ **der Feindseligkeiten** outbreak of hostilities; ~ **aus dem Gefängnis** prison breaking (breach), breach of prison, jailbreaking *(US)*; ~ **des Krieges** outbreak of war; ~ **von Rassenunruhen** racial outbreak; ~ **eines Vulkans** eruption (outbreak) of a volcano;
zum ~ **kommen** *(Krankheit)* to become apparent, to manifest itself.

Ausbruchsversuch attempted escape.

Ausbrüten incubation, *(fig.)* concoction.

ausbrüten *(fig.)* to hatch;
Plan ~ to concoct a scheme.

ausbuchen to abandon, to retire;
fast völlig ~ to book nearly solid.

Ausbuchung abandonment, retirement;
feste ~ solid booking.

Ausbuchungsverlust retirement loss.

ausbügeln, Anfangsschwierigkeiten to iron out initial difficulties; **Fehler** ~ to smooth over a fault.

Ausbund personification, paragon, incarnation;
~ **der Höflichkeit** pink of politeness; ~ **von Tugend** model (paragon) of virtue;
~ **der Tugend sein** to be a pattern of virtue.

ausbürgern to expatriate, to deprive of citizenship (nationality); **wieder** ~ to denaturalize, to disnaturalize.

Ausbürgerung expatriation, deprivation of citizenship (nationality), *(naturalisierte Staatsbürger)* denaturalization, denaturalysation.

Ausdauer endurance, persistence, hardiness, patience;
große ~ **besitzen** to have great patience; **sein Studium mit** ~ **verfolgen** to persevere in one's studies; **sein Ziel mit** ~ **verfolgen** to pursue one's object to the end; **für seine** ~ **belohnt werden** to get a fair reward for one's labo(u)r; ~ **bei seiner Arbeit zeigen** to persevere in one's work.

ausdauernd persevering, persistent, unremitting, tenacious;
~ **sein** to show perseverence, to hang on.

Ausdecken *(Reproduktion)* masking out.

ausdecken *(Reproduktion)* to mask out.

ausdehnbar expandable, expansible.

ausdehnen to extend, to expand, to enlarge, to step up, to widen;
sich ~ to dilate, to open out, *(Stadt)* to spread out, to outspread, to grow; **seinen Aufenthalt über die vorgesehene Zeit hinaus** ~ to stay longer than originally intended; **seinen technischen Beratungsdienst weltweit** ~ to expand its engineering consultation service on an international basis; **seinen Einflußbereich auf andere Gebiete** ~ to extend one's influence to other territories; **seine Ferien** ~ to prolong (extend) one's holiday; **sein Geschäft** ~ to extend (expand, enlarge) one's business; **industrielle Kapazität** ~ to increase (enlarge) the industrial capacity; **sich bis ans Meer** ~ to stretch to the sea; **sich meilenweit** ~ to stretch for miles; **sich ständig** ~ *(Absatz)* to be constantly growing; **sich über viele Stunden** ~ to be dragged on for several hours; **seine Tätigkeit auf bankfremde Geschäfte** ~ to diversify outside banking (into nonbanking financial areas); **sich bis 4 Uhr** ~ *(Sitzung)* to last till four o'clock; **sich sehr weit** ~ *(Stadt)* to cover a wide area; **seinen Wirkungsbereich** ~ to extend one's sphere of activities.

ausdehnend extensive;
~**e Auslegung** extensive interpretation.

Ausdehnung extension, extent, growth, expansion, prolongation, incidence, reach, enlargement, spread, dimension;
horizontale ~ horizontal expansion; **territoriale** ~ territorial expansion; **wirtschaftliche** ~ economic expansion;
~ **des Einflußbereiches** extension of influence; ~ **seines Geschäfts** enlargement of one's business; ~ **der Geschäftstätigkeit** spread of business; ~ **des Handels** expansion of trade; ~ **der Streckensätze** extension of carrier's lines; ~ **der Tätigkeit auf bankfremde Finanzgebiete** diversification into outside banking (to other financial areas); ~ **eines Unternehmens** company growth;
gewaltige ~ **annehmen** to assume colossal proportions; **an** ~ **zunehmen** to increase in size.

Ausdehnungs|bedürfnis expansionism; ~**politik** policy of expansion.

ausdenken to concert, to devise, to conceive, to design;
sich zahlreiche Entschuldigungen ~ to offer numerous excuses; **Plan** ~ to conceive a plan; **sich einige Überraschungen** ~ to have some surprises in store.

ausdiskutieren to discuss thoroughly;
Punkt für Punkt ~ to dispute the ground inch by inch.

Ausdruck expression, term, *(fig.)* voice, vent, *(Stil)* style, mode of expression;
beschönigender ~ euphemism; **bildhafter** ~ figurative expression; **familiärer** ~ informal expression; **fehlerhafter** ~ faulty expression; **gewählter** ~ literary expression; **unglücklich gewählter** ~ unguarded expression; **idiomatischer** ~ idiom; **juristischer** ~ legal term; **kaufmännischer** ~ business (trade) term; **literarischer** ~ bookish expression; **ordinärer** ~ low expression; **ortsgebundener (ortsüblicher)** ~ local expression (term); **schiefer** ~ unhappy expression; **allgemein üblicher** ~ common expression; **veralteter** ~ obsolete expression; **vulgärer** ~ vulgarism;
~ **des Mißfallens** frown; ~ **der Umgangssprache** colloquial expression; ~ **tiefster Verachtung** unmistakable expression of contempt; ~ **der modernen Zeit** characteristic of our time; **sich eines gelinden** ~**s bedienen** to put it mildly; **seine Meinung zum** ~ **bringen** to express one's opinion; **seiner Dankbarkeit** ~ **geben** to voice one's gratitude; **seiner Empörung** ~ **geben** to give voice to one's indignation; **in seinen Worten zum** ~ **kommen** to find voice in one's words; **viel** ~ **in etw. legen** to put much feeling into s. th.; ~ **einer starken Überzeugung sein** to bear the mark of a strong conviction; **um einen** ~ **verlegen sein** to be at a loss for a word; **seiner Dankbarkeit voller Beschämung** ~ **verleihen** to pour out one's thanks; **seinen Gefühlen in einer**

leidenschaftlichen Ansprache ~ verleihen to give vent to one's feelings in an impassioned speech; **seinem Zorn ~ verleihen** to give vent to one's anger.
ausdrückbar expressible.
Ausdrücke, beleidigende defamatory language, words actionable in themselves; **unflätige ~** four-letter Saxon words; **volkstümliche ~** folksay;
anstößige ~ benutzen to use objectionable language.
ausdrücken to express, to voice, to frame, to phrase, to couch, *(auspressen)* to squeeze, to press;
es anders ~ to put it otherwise; **Bereitschaft der Regierung ~** to demonstrate the readiness of the government; **in Dollars ~** to state in terms of dollars; **sich geistreich ~** to speak brilliantly; **sich gemäßigt ~** to observe moderation in what one says, to put it mildly; **sich sehr gewählt ~** to call things by fine names; **sich nicht gerade gewählt ~** not to put too fine a point on it; **sich kurz ~** to be brief; **sich maßvoll ~** to speak in measured terms; **es so ~** to put it that way; **sich schwer verständlich ~** to have swallowed a dictionary; **vorsichtig ~** to express in guarded terms; **sich vulgär ~** to adopt the common parlance.
ausdrücklich express, explicit, specific, definite, positive, formal;
~ einen Unterschied machen to make a clear distinction; **~e Abmachung** express agreement; **~e Anweisung** strict order, positive instruction; **~ festgelegte Bedingungen** express conditions; **~es Dementi** formal denial; **~e Erklärung** specific statement; **auf Grund ~er Ermächtigung** by express authority; **~e Genehmigung** express permission; **~es Verlangen** express request; **~e Vertragserfüllung** specific performance.
Ausdruckskraft phraseology, style.
ausdruckslos inexpressive, vacant, blank.
Ausdrucksweise expression, language, speech, term;
ordinäre ~ bad language; **schwülstige ~** inflated language; **unhöfliche ~** unparliamentary language; **vornehme ~** usage in language *(Br.)*; **vulgäre ~** vile language;
~ der Gosse language of the gutter;
sich einer korrekten ~ befleißigen to use correct language.
Ausdruckzeit print-out time.
auseinander apart, asunder, *(Ehe)* on the rocks *(coll.)*;
weit ~ wide apart.
auseinanderbrechen to break apart, *(Geleitzug)* to fall in disorder, *(Schiff)* to break her back.
Auseinanderfallen | einer Partei split of a party; **~ einer Regierung** disruption of a government.
auseinanderfallen to fall to pieces, *(Partei)* to disintegrate, to break up, to split, *(Regierung)* to disrupt.
Auseinandergehen divergence, *(Versammlung)* breaking up;
beim ~ on parting;
zum friedlichen ~ auffordern to read the Riot Act.
auseinandergehen to rise, to adjourn, to disperse, *(Meinungen)* to differ, *(Parlament)* to dissolve, *(Versammlung)* to break up;
als Freunde ~ to part friends.
auseinander | genommen, zu Transportzwecken knocked down; **~gerissene Familie** separated family.
auseinanderhalten to distinguish, to tell apart;
anscheinend ähnliche Fälle ~ to distinguish between cases apparently similar; **zwei Menschen ~** to know one from the other.
auseinanderhaltend discriminating.
auseinander | kommen, im Gedränge to get lost (separated) in the crowd; **sich ~leben** to become estranged; **~nehmbar** dismountable.
auseinandernehmen to take to pieces, to disassemble;
j. völlig ~ to give s. o. a piece of one's mind, to criticize s. o. severely.
Auseinanderreißen einer Familie disruption of a family.
auseinanderreißen, Familie to disrupt a family.
Auseinanderrücken *(Machtblöcke)* disengagement.
auseinanderrücken *(Zeilen)* to space.
auseinandersetzen to explain, to set forth, to state, to declare, to expound, to explicate;
sich ~ to arrange, to settle, *(Erben)* to partition, *(Partner)* to distribute the assets; **sich mit jem. ~** to be at grips with s. o.; **sich detailliert ~** to dispute the ground inch by inch; **sich mit seinen Gläubigern ~** to come to terms (compound) with one's creditors; **jem. etw. lang und breit ~** to explain s. th. to s. o. at great length; **sich mit dem Leben ~** to face life; **sich mit einem Problem ~** to grapple with a problem; **sich mit jem. wegen einer Sache ~** to have it out (come to an understanding) with s. o.; **sich erneut mit einem größeren Komplex von Sachgebieten ~** to struggle again over a lot of ground; **sich mit einem Thema ~** to deal with a subject.
Auseinandersetzung arrangement, settlement, final settlement of accounts, *(Abwicklung)* liquidation, winding up, *(Erbteilung)* distribution and partition *(US)*, *(Partner)* distribution of assets, *(Meinungsverschiedenheit)* dispute, argument, contestation, conflict, cross, quarrel;
arbeitsrechtliche ~ labo(u)r dispute; **außergerichtliche ~** extrajudicial settlement, settlement out of court; **bewaffnete ~** armed conflict; **gerichtliche ~** court litigation, jurisdictional dispute; **handelspolitische ~** trade clash; **heftige ~** violent controversy; **innerpolitische ~en** domestic struggles; **kriegerische ~** armed conflict; **lohnpolitische ~** wage dispute; **parlamentarische ~en** parliamentary debate; **religiöse ~** religious disputes; **vermögensrechtliche ~** property settlement; **wortreiche ~** wordy conflict;
~ mit den Gewerkschaften trade dispute; **~ mit seinen Gläubigern** composition with one's creditors; **~ eines Nachlasses** partition of a succession *(US)*, distribution [and partition] of an estate; **innere ~en einer Partei** party quarrels; **~ über eine Rechtsfolge** dispute over a point of law; **~en in der Wahlzeit** eve-of-the-poll issues;
heftige ~ beginnen to plunge into an argument; **~ bereinigen** to pluck a crow; **sich in eine ~ einschalten** to interfere in a dispute; **~en haben** to run into battles; **~ mit jem. haben** to have a dust-up with s. o. *(coll.)*; **heftige ~ mit jem. haben** to have a fierce argument with s. o.; **~ provozieren** to provoke a controversy; **vor ernsthaften ~en stehen** to be going to have a hot time; **kurz vor einer militärischen ~ stehen** to be back on the verge of a shooting match; **~ vornehmen** *(Erben)* to partition an estate among the heirs.
Auseinandersetzungs | anspruch distribution share *(US)*, settlement right; **~anteil** purparty; **~bilanz** liquidating balance sheet; **~guthaben** settlement assets; **~plan** liquidation plan; **~verfahren** liquidation proceedings; **~vertrag** final settlement, deed of partition (separation, settlement); **~zeugnis** clearing certificate.
auseinandertreiben, Menschenmenge to disperse a crowd.
auseinanderziehen *(Fahrzeuge)* to disperse, to string out;
sich ~ *(Kolonne)* to tail away.
auserlesen choice, first class (-rate), select, *(Geschmack)* exquisite;
~e Gesellschaft select company; **~e Qualität** prime quality; **~e Ware** choice (picked) goods.
ausersehen to choose, to select, to mark, to earmark;
~ sein für to be marked out for;
~ *(a.)* designate, predestinated.
auserwählt select;
viele sind berufen, aber nur wenige sind ~ many are called but few are chosen.
Auserwählte, ein paar a privileged few.
ausfahrbar *(Fahrgestell)* extendable, *(Periskop)* raisable;
~e Antenne telescopic antenna.
Ausfahren | der Landeklappe extension of the landing gear; **~ der Post** delivery of the mail (post).
ausfahren to go for a drive (ride, *US*), *(Fahrgestell, Landeklappe)* to extend, to drive out, *(Periskop)* to raise, to lift, *(Schiff)* to put to sea, to leave port, *(Zug)* to pull out, to leave the station;
Kapazität fast voll ~ to operate at close to capacity, to gear productions to the capacity of a plant; **Kranken im Rollstuhl ~** to take an invalid out in a wheelchair (bath chair, *Br.*); **Kurven ~** to take curves on the outside; **Motor ~** to run up to top speed; **Pakete ~** to deliver parcels.
ausfahrendes Schiff outgoing ship.
Ausfahr | gleis departure track; **~signal** starting signal.
Ausfahrt drive, ride, excursion, *(Autobahn)* exit point, *(Bergwerk)* ascent, *(aus einem Grundstück)* [point off] exit, way-out, *(Hafen)* mouth, outlet, *(Schiff)* departure, *(Tor)* gateway, *(Zug)* departure;
auf der ~ ins Ausland begriffen *(Schiff)* outward-bound;
Achtung ~! caution, concealed drive!;
zur ~ bereitstehen *(Zug)* to be ready to leave; **~ freihalten!** keep exit clear!; **~ unternehmen** to go for a ride.
Ausfall *(Abfall)* refuse parts, waste, scrap, rejects, *(Atomphysik)* fall-out, *(Ergebnis)* result, issue, outcome, *(Fehlbetrag)* deficit, deficiency, shortage, *(Maschine)* breakdown, failure, *(mil.)* sally, *(Verlust)* loss, nonpayment;
durch einen ~ des Motors due to a breakdown of the engine; **~ von Einnahmen** revenue shortfall; **~ eines Erben** lapse of an heir; **~ an Gewicht** loss of weight; **~ der Produktion** loss (falling off) of production; **~ einer Prüfung** result of an examination; **~ an Steuern** revenue deficit; **~ des Stromes (der Funkverbindungen)** blackout; **~ eines Unternehmens** loss of an adventure; **~ eines Zuges** annulment of a train;

~ **decken** to cover a deficit (loss); ~ **ergeben** to show a decrease; ~ **erleiden** to suffer a loss; ~ **aus der Festung machen** to make a sortie from a fortress, to sally;
~**betrag** *(im Zwangsvollstreckungsverfahren)* deficiency; ~**bürge** surety, bail absolute, absolute guarantor.
Ausfallbürgschaft indemnity letter (bond, *US*), bond of indemnity *(US)*, deficiency guarantee, conditional (deficit) guaranty, guaranty of collection *(US)*;
öffentlich-rechtliche ~ official bond *(US)*;
~ **übernehmen** to give a letter of indemnity, to execute a bond *(US)*.
Ausfälle *(mil.)* casualties, losses;
sich ~ **erlauben** to lapse into invectives; **große** ~ **haben** to suffer heavy losses; **wütende** ~ **gegen j. machen** to launch fierce attacks against s. o.
ausfallen *(Auto)* to break down, to fail, *(Einnahme)* not to be forthcoming, *(Ernte)* to turn out, *(aus Festung)* to make a sortie, to sally, *(Maschine)* to fail, to be out of action, to pack up *(sl.)*, to go dead, *(mil.)* to become a casualty, *(Muster)* to sample out, *(Signal)* not to function, *(Sitzung)* not to take place, *(Stromversorgung)* to break down, *(versagen)* to fail, to break down, *(Vorlesung)* to be cancelled [off], *(aus einem Wettbewerb)* to drop out, *(Zug)* to be cancelled;
zu jds. Gunsten ~ to be in s. one's favo(u)r; **gut** ~ to turn out well, to be a success, to prove satisfactory; **heute** ~ *(Zug)* not to be running today; **zu klein** ~ *(Anteil)* to be too small; **wegen Krankheit** ~ to drop out because of illness; **schlecht** ~ to turn out badly, to be a failure; **nach Wunsch** ~ to answer well; **alles zur Zufriedenheit** ~ to turn out to satisfaction.
ausfallen lassen *(streichen)* to kill;
Dividende ~ to omit a dividend; **Sitzung** ~ to drop a meeting; **Unterricht** ~ to cancel a lesson.
Ausfallhaftung deficit guarantee, secondary liability *(US)*.
ausfällig offensive, insulting, abusive;
~ **werden** to become abusive;
~**e Bemerkungen** rude remarks, insulting language, invectives.
Ausfall|klausel indemnity clause; ~**muster** reference (outturn) sample (pattern), outsample, pattern reference; ~**quote** *(mil.)* attrition rate; ~**rate** failure rate; ~**risiko** abnormal (business) risk; ~**straße** arterial road (highway), main street; ~**stunden** man-hours lost, nonproductive hours; ~**urteil** deficiency jugdment; ~**zeit** *(Computer)* downtime.
ausfeilen, Aufsatz stilistisch to improve the style of an article.
ausfertigen to draft, to draw up, *(Abschrift)* to copy, to exemplify, to engross, *(Rechnung)* to make out, to invoice, *(Sendung)* to dispatch;
doppelt ~ to make out (deliver) in duplicate; **in richtiger Form** ~ to draw up; **Kreditbrief** ~ to issue a letter of credit; **Paß** ~ to make out a passport; **Rechnung** ~ to [make out an] invoice; **Urkunde** ~ to execute an instrument; **Vertrag** ~ to draw up (make out) a contract; **vierfach** ~ to quadruplicate; **Wechsel doppelt** ~ to draw a bill of exchange in duplicate.
ausfertigende Stelle drafting office.
Ausfertigung make, form, *(Abschrift)* copy, engrossment, exemplified copy *(US)*, exemplification, *(Sendung)* dispatch, *(Urkunde)* execution, copy, *(Vertrag)* drawing up, making out, draft, *(Wechsel)* issue;
für die Richtigkeit der ~ certified true copy; **in doppelter** ~ [signed] in duplicate, bipartite; **in dreifacher** ~ in triplicate; **in fünffacher** ~ in five copies (quintuplicate); **in vierfacher** ~ in quadruplicate; **in zweifacher** ~ done in duplicate;
alle ~**en** full set; **dritte** ~ third copy; **erste** ~ original; **erste vollstreckbare** ~ first authentic copy; **amtlich erteilte** ~ office copy *(Br.)*; **vollstreckbare** ~ special execution, authority to execute a deed; **zweite** ~ duplicate, *(Wechsel)* second of exchange;
~ **beglaubigter Abschriften** delivery of certified copies; ~ **von Abtretungsurkunden** conveyancing; ~ **einer öffentlichen Urkunde** transcript of a legal document;
zweite ~ **einer Urkunde anfertigen** to make a copy of a deed; **Urkunde in doppelter** ~ **ausstellen** to make out a document in duplicate; ~ **erteilen** to deliver a copy; **in drei** ~**en liefern** to make in three styles.
Ausfertigungs|datum, ~**tag** date of issue; ~**datum einer Urkunde** date of execution of a document; ~**gebühr** official fee.
ausfindig machen to trace out, to discover, to detect, to locate, to descry, to dope (pry) out;
j. ~ to trace down s. o.; **Brief** ~ to trace a letter; **Eigentümer** ~ to trace the owner; **Mittel und Wege** ~ to contrive ways and means; **Platz** ~ to find a place; **säumigen Schuldner** ~ to skiptrace a debtor; **neue Tatsachen** ~ to unearth new facts.

Ausfindigmachung location, discovery;
~ **der Adressen säumiger Schuldner** skip-tracing.
ausfischen, zu stark to overfish.
ausflaggen, Schiff to dress a ship.
ausfliegen to evacuate by air, *(Ausflug machen)* to make an excursion.
Ausflucht evasion, pretext, excuse, shuffle, subterfuge, put-off, get-off, come off *(coll.)*;
leere ~ shallow argument.
Ausflüchte *(fig.)* fencing;
~ **gebrauchen** to evade the issue, to resort to subterfuge, to prevaricate, to use shift, to fence.
ausfluchten to align.
Ausfluchtung alignment.
Ausflug outing, jaunt, [pleasure] trip, drive, tour, [holiday] excursion, ride, sally;
erster ~ first setting out;
~ **zu verbilligten Preisen** cheap trip; **kurzer** ~ **ins Verlagsgeschäft** fling in the publishing business;
~ **machen** to go for (make) a trip (an excursion, a jaunt).
Ausflügler excursionist, holidayer, tripper *(Br.)*, tourist *(US)*;
~**zug** excursion train.
Ausflugs|autobus charabanc; ~**dampfer** excursion steamer; ~**fahrkarte** excursion ticket; ~**gesellschaft** pleasure party; ~**lokal** tourist inn, roadhouse; ~**lokal am Fluß** riverside inn; ~**ort** place of popular resort, pleasure resort (spot); ~**preise** excursion fares; ~**schneise** departure corridor; ~**tarif** round-trip excursion fare *(US)*, excursion rates; ~**verkehr** excursion traffic; **beliebtes** ~**ziel** place of popular resort; ~**zug** excursion (pleasure) train.
Ausfluß outflow, discharge, *(Abfluß)* outlet.
ausfolgen to deliver, to hand over (out);
Waren ~ to deliver goods.
Ausfolgeschein bill of delivery.
Ausfolgung delivery [up];
~ **gestellter Sicherheiten** delivery of securities.
ausforschen, j. to sound s. o.
Ausforsten thinning.
ausforsten to thin, to cut over.
Ausfracht outward freight.
Ausfragen examination, pump[ing].
ausfragen to interrogate, to examine, to question, to pump.
ausfräsen *(drucktechn.)* to rout.
ausfressen to eat out (up);
ganze Sache ~ **müssen** to be on the mat *(sl.)*, to hold the bag for s. th.
Ausfuhr export [trade], exportation;
für die ~ **bestimmt** earmarked for exportation; **zur** ~ **geeignet** exportable;
gesteigerte ~ increased exports; **sichtbare** ~ visible trade (exports); **staatlich subventionierte** ~ bounty-fed exports; **unsichtbare** ~ invisible exports, indirect exporting; **vorübergehende** ~ temporary export; **zusätzliche** ~ additional export; **Ein- und** ~ imports and exports;
~ **auf dem Luftwege** air-borne exports; ~ **in Rezessionszeiten** export of recession; ~ **auf dem Seewege** sea-borne exports;
~ **erhöhen** to increase (step up) exports; ~ **fördern** to subsidize export trade; ~ **kontingentieren** to fix export quotas; **für die** ~ **bestimmt sein** to go for export; ~ **steigern** to raise exports;
~**abfertigung** export clearance; ~**abgabe** export duty (levy, tax), duty (levy) on exports; ~**absprache** *(Kartellgesetz)* export agreement; ~**abteilung** export department; ~**agent** export broker; ~**angebot** export tender; ~**ankurbelung** boosting of exports; ~**anreiz** export incentive; **plötzlicher** ~**anstieg** jump in exports; ~**anstrengungen** export efforts; ~**anteil** export ratio; ~**antrag** application for export.
Ausfuhrartikel article of exportation, export article, *(pl.)* exports, export goods;
industrielle ~ manufactured exports.
Ausfuhr|auftrag export order; ~**ausgangskontingent** initial export quota; ~**ausweitung** export expansion; **Einfuhr- und** ~**bank** Export-Import Bank of Washington.
ausführbar workable, practicable, executable, performable, feasible, *(zur Ausfuhr geeignet)* exportable.
Ausführbarkeit practicability, workability, feasibility.
Ausfuhr|bedingungen export regulations; ~**bedürfnisse** export demands (requirements); ~**beihilfe** export bonus; ~**belebung** upturn in exports; ~**bescheinigung** certificate of clearance outwards; ~**beschränkungen** restrictions (curb) on export, export restrictions; ~**bestimmungen** export regulations; ~**bewilligung** export licence (license, *US*, permit), transire *(Br.)*.

ausfuhrbewußt export-minded.

Ausfuhr|bürgschaft export guarantee; ~**defizit** export deficit; ~**deklaration** declaration (entry) outwards *(Br.)*, shipper's manifest *(US)*, export specification *(Br.)*, export declaration *(US)*; ~**embargo** embargo on exports, export prohibition (bar, ban).

Ausführen von Geschäftsfreunden business entertaining of clients.

ausführen to accomplish, to achieve, to do, to [bring into] effect, to carry out (in execution), to implement, to outcarry, to execute, to fulfil, to fulfill *(US)*, to perform, to get over, to put through, *(Bau)* to construct, to erect, *(Redner)* to say, to state, to remark, *(Verbrechen)* to perpetrate, to commit, *(Waren)* to export, to sell abroad;
Anweisungen ~ to act upon orders; **Auftrag** ~ to execute (carry out, fill, *US*) an order, to discharge a duty, *(Botengang)* to discharge an errand; **sämtliche Bankgeschäfte** ~ to transact banking business of every description; **detailliert** ~ to particularize; **j. zum Essen** ~ to take s. o. out; **etw. fachgemäß** ~ to make a professional job of s. th.; **folgendes** ~ to point out the following, to make the following remarks; **fristgemäß** ~ to carry out within a given time; **seine Gedanken nochmals** ~ to explain one's ideas once again; **Hund** ~ to take a dog out for a walk; **ins Kino** ~ to take to the cinema; **näher** ~ to go into detail, to elaborate; **Plan** ~ to carry out (realize) a plan (project); **Skizze weiter** ~ to elaborate a sketch; **Thema weiter** ~ to dwell at greater length on a subject; **Vorhaben** ~ to effect one's purpose; **wieder** ~ to reexport; **zufriedenstellend** ~ to fulfil, to fulfill *(US)*;
sich ~ **lassen** to be practicable (feasible).

ausführend executive;
~**e Behörde** enforcement agency, executive body; ~**e Gewalt** executive power; ~**er Ingenieur** field engineer; ~**es Organ** executive body, executory.

Ausführender doer, performer.

Ausfuhr|entwicklung export trend; ~**erfahrung** export-business experience; **unerwartet hoher** ~**erfolg** export bonanza; ~**erfolge** export achievements; ~**erhöhung** rise in exports; ~**erklärung** declaration (entry) outwards, shipper's manifest, export specification *(Br.)*; ~**erlaubnis** export licence (permit), transire *(Br.)*; ~**erlöse** export earnings; ~**erweiterung** expansion of exports; ~**faktoring** export factoring; ~**finanzierung** export financing; ~**finanzierungsanleihe** export financing loan; ~**firma** exporter; ~**förderung** export drive (promotion), promotion of (boost to) exports, export subsidy, *(in Dollarraum)* dollar drive.

Ausfuhrförderungs|ausschuß export-promotion committee; ~**gremium** export council; ~**maßnahmen** export promotion measures; ~**verfahren** export-subsidy system.

Ausfuhrgarantie export guarantee.

Ausfuhrgenehmigung export permit (licence, authorization), transire *(Br.)*;
~ **erteilen** to pass (grant) an export licence.

Ausfuhr|geschäft export business; ~**gewinnspanne** export profit margin; ~**güter** exports, export (exported) goods (commodities); ~**hafen** shipping port, port of exportation; ~**handel** export (active, outward) trade; ~**händler** export merchant, exporter; ~**hindernis** export bar; ~**industrie** export industry; ~**institut** Institute of Export; ~**kartell** export cartel; ~**kaution** *(Zoll)* export bond; ~**kolli** export packages *(US)*; ~**kommissär** export commission house; ~**konnossement** export bill of lading; ~**kontingent** export quota; ~**kontrolle**, ~**kontrollmaßnahmen** export control.

Ausfuhrkredit export credit;
~**garantie** export credit guarantee; ~**versicherung** export credit insurance.

Ausfuhr|land country of exportation, exporting country; ~**lenkung** export control.

ausführlich in full, detailed, circumstantial, exhaustive, comprehensive;
sehr ~ at great length, in great detail, full-length;
~ **begründen** to give full reasons; ~ **beschreiben** to give a detailed description; ~ **darstellen** to give full particulars; **auf einen strittigen Punkt** ~ **eingehen** to labo(u)r a point; ~ **explizieren** to explain; ~ **schreiben** to write at greater length; ~ **über etw. sprechen** to speak at some length about a subject; **sich** ~ **über ein Thema verbreiten** to enlarge on a subject; ~**e Begründung** full reasons; ~**er Bericht** circumstantial account; ~**en Bericht erstatten** to give a detailed report; ~**e Beschreibung** detailed description; ~**e Erklärung** full statement; ~**es Protokoll** verbatim record.

Ausführlichkeit fullness, circumstantiality, detailedness;
mit großer ~ **beschreiben** to describe in great detail.

Ausfuhr|liste export list; ~**lizenz** licence outward, export permit (licence), transire *(Br.)*, Federal export licence *(US)*; ~**markt** export market; ~**meldung** export declaration; ~**möglichkeiten** export possibilities; ~**monopol** foreign staple, export monopoly; ~**musterlager** export sample store; ~**nachrichten** export intelligence *(Br.)*; ~**nummer des statistischen Warenverzeichnisses** statistical number; ~**offerte** export tender; ~**papiere** export (shipping) documents; ~**politik** export policy; ~**prämie** export premium, export subsidy, subsidy to exports, bounty on exportation, [king's] bounty *(Br.)*; ~**prämienschein** export bounty certificate; ~**preisindex** price index of exports; ~**programm** export program(me); ~**quote** export quota; ~**rekord** export record; ~**rückgang** export fall, decline (fall, cut) in exports; **scharfer** ~**rückgang** sharp drop in export orders; ~**schein** certificate of clearance outward; ~**schlacht** export drive (battle); ~**sperre** embargo on exports, export prohibition, export ban; ~**statistik** export statistics; ~**steigerung** export increase, increased exports; **wertmäßige** ~**steigerung** rise in value of exports; ~**steuer** export tax; ~**steuerrückvergütung** export rebate, tax rebate for exporters, reimbursement for exports; ~**subvention** export subsidy; ~**tarif** export rates (tariff); ~**tonnage** export tonnage; ~**überschuß** export surplus, excess of exports; ~**überschußfaktor** export earner.

Ausführung execution, carrying out, handling, performance, fulfil(l)ment, discharge, deed, hand, *(Bauvorhaben)* design, construction, *(Fertigstellung)* achievement, completion, fulfilment, *(Gesetz)* implementation, *(Kleid)* version, *(Modell)* type, model, make, design, style, *(Qualität)* workmanship, quality, finish, *(Thema)* exposition;
in doppelter ~ in duplicate;
erstklassige ~ finest workmanship; **fehlerhafte** ~ defective execution; **luxuriöse** ~ more luxurious finish; **schlechte** ~ faulty workmanship; **technische** ~ technique;
~ **eines Auftrages** execution of an order; ~ **eines Planes** realization (elaboration) of a plan; ~ **eines Verbrechens** perpetration of a crime;
zur ~ **bringen** to [carry into] effect; **zur** ~ **gelangen** to be accomplished (carried out); **längere** ~ **machen** to dwell at length; ~ **der Baupläne einer Firma übertragen** to place the contract for a building with a firm.

Ausführungen statements, speech, comments, remarks;
in seinen ~ in the course of his remarks; **in verschiedenen** ~ *(Ware)* of every variety, of different designs;
ergänzende ~ complimentary statement; **tatsächliche und rechtliche** ~ statement of claim;
an die ~ **des Vorredners anknüpfen** to take up the remarks of the speaker; **sich in keiner Weise den** ~ **des Vorredners anschließen können** to strongly dissent from what the last speaker said; **seine** ~ **mit einer Anekdote beginnen** to preface one's remarks with an anecdote; **längere** ~ **machen** to deal (dwell) at length.

Ausführungs|angelegenheiten regulatory matters; ~**anzeige** advice note, confirmation slip, *(Makler)* broker's memorandum, contract note, advice of deal *(Br.)*; ~**art** modality; ~**behörde** enforcement agency, executive body.

Ausführungsbestimmungen implementing (implemental) provisions (regulations), administrative regulations, directives, executive orders *(US)*, *(fam.)* marching orders, *(Satzung)* regulatory statute;
~ **enthaltend** self-executing;
ministerielle ~ regulations of an executive department, departmental regulations; ~ **zur Satzung** corporation bylaws;
~ **befolgen** to comply with regulations.

Ausführungs|buch *(Makler)* sales blotter; ~**datum** date of execution; ~**entwurf** working design; ~**fragen** regulatory matters; ~**frist** period of performance; ~**garantie** performance bond; ~**gesetz** declaratory statute, carrying law, executive order *(US)*; ~**kollektiv** collective executive; ~**kommando** *(mil.)* executive command.

ausführungsreif ripe for execution.

Ausführungs|verordnung bylaw, executive order *(US)*, rule, statutory instrument *(Br.)*; ~**zeichnung** working drawing.

Ausfuhr|verbot prohibition of exports, export prohibition (bar, ban), embargo on exports; ~**vergütung** bounty on exportation, drawback, refund of duty; ~**verkaufsrechnung** export sales note; ~**verpflichtungen** export obligations; ~**versandliste** pricking note; **staatliche** ~**versicherung** government export credit insurance; ~**vertrag** export contract; ~**volumen** export volume; ~**waren** export commodities, exports; ~**werbung** export publicity; ~**wert** export value; ~**wirtschaft** export trade; ~**ziel** exporting goal; ~**ziffern** export figures; ~**zoll** export duty (tariff), customs outwards, exitus.

ausfuhrzoll|frei free of export duty; ~**pflichtig** liable to export duty.

Ausfuhr|zolltarif export rates (tariff); ~**zunahme** growth of export, export increase; ~**zuschuß** subsidy on exports; ~**zuteilung** export allocation; **für** ~**zwecke beladen** shipped for exportation.

ausfüllen *(Formular)* to fill in (up, out, *US*), to complete; **Antragsformular** ~ to fill in an application blank; **Einkommensteuererklärung** ~ to prepare an income-tax return; **falsch** ~ *(Formular)* to phony up; **Formular** ~ to complete a form; **Formular flüchtig** ~ to fill in a form carelessly; **Fragebogen** ~ to fill in (out, *US*) a questionnaire; **j. ganz** ~ to absorb s. o. completely; **Lücke** ~ to fill (stop) a gap; **Mauerfugen** ~ to smooth (flush) the joints; **nicht** ~ to leave void; **Öffnung mit Sandsäcken** ~ to sandbag an opening; **Posten** ~ to fill a position; **leere Stellen** ~ to fill in blank spaces; **Vordruck** ~ to fill in (up) a form.

Ausfülltarif *(Fluggesellschaft)* superapex tariff.

Ausfüllung filling in (up, *Br.*, out, *US*);
vor ~ before preparing;
~ **eines Formulars** preparation (completion) of a form; ~ **eines Fragebogens** filling in a questionnaire; ~ **eines Steuerformulars** tax preparation.

Ausfüllungsbefugnis authorization to fill in a blank.

Ausgabe expense, expenditure, outlay, *(Ausgabestelle)* booking office, *(Aushändigung)* giving (handing) out, *(Auslage)* disbursement, outlay, *(Briefe)* delivery, *(Briefmarken)* issue, *(Buch)* edition, set, *(Datenverarbeitung)* output, *(Emission)* issue, issuing, issuance *(US)*, emission, *(Gepäck)* counter, *(Verteilung)* distribution, *(Zeitung)* number, edition;
alte ~ *(Heft)* back issue, *(Zeitung)* back number; **mit Vorrechten ausgestattete** ~ *(Anleihe)* senior issue; **bearbeitete** ~ revised edition; **berechtigte** ~ copyrighted edition; **bibliophile** ~ cabinet edition; **billige** ~ cheap edition; **broschierte** ~ pamphlet copy; **durchgesehene** ~ revised edition, revision; **einbändige** ~ single (one) -volume edition; **endgültige** definitive edition; **erweiterte** ~ enlarged edition; **zweispaltig gedruckte** ~ double-column edition; **gekürzte** ~ abridged edition; **amtlich genehmigte** ~ sealed form; **urheberrechtlich (verlagsrechtlich) geschützte** ~ copyright edition, copyrighted publication; **heutige** ~ *(Zeitung)* current number; **unzulässig hohe** ~ *(Anleihe)* overissue; **kleine** ~ petty cash; **letzte** ~ *(Zeitschrift)* current number, latest edition, final; **unberechtigt nachgedruckte** ~ pirated edition; **neue** ~ reprint; **revidierte** ~ revised edition, revision; **textkritische** ~ text; **ungekürzte** ~ unabridged edition; **unveränderte** ~ reprint; **vollständige** ~ complete edition; **vordatierte** ~ predate; **zweisprachige** ~ bilingual edition, diglot; **zweite** ~ still contingent second edition;
~ **im Folioformat** folio edition; ~ **von Gratisaktien** bonus (scrip, *Br.*) issue; ~ **von Gratisaktien bei Kapitalerhöhung** capitalization issue; ~ **im Großformat** library edition; ~ **letzter Hand** definitive edition; ~ **von mit variablen Zinssätzen ausgestatteten Kommunalanleihen** floating rate issue in the local authority negotiable bond market; ~ **nur für Lehrer** teacher edition; ~ **in Miniform** pony edition; ~ **neuer Münzen** issue of new coinage; ~ **von Obligationen** floating (issue) of bonds; ~ **eines Passes** issue of a passport; ~ **von Sonderziehungsrechten** *(Weltwährungsfonds)* special drawing rights issue; ~ **einer Zeitung** run of a paper;
~ **als aktivierungspflichtigen Aufwand behandeln** to treat an expenditure as properly attributable to capital; **in** ~ **bringen** to enter as expenditure; **sich eine** ~ **leisten können** to afford an expense; ~ **von Gratisaktien vornehmen** to declare a stock dividend; **auf eine** ~ **zeichnen** to subscribe to an issue;
~**abstrich** expenditure cut; ~**ansatz** budget item; ~**automat** *(Fahrscheine)* vending machine; ~**bank** bank of issue; ~**bedingungen** terms of issue, *(Obligation)* debenture conditions; ~**bereich** *(Datenerfassung)* output area; ~**bewilligung** budgetary appropriation; ~**daten** *(Datenverarbeitung)* output data; ~**datum** publication (issue) date, date of issue; ~**dispositionen im laufenden Rechnungsjahr** budgetary allocations for the current year; ~**drang** propensity to spend; ~**ermäßigung** *(Konsortium)* concession; ~**erstattung** reimbursement for expenses; ~**etat** budget.

ausgabefreudig ready to spend;
~ **sein** to burn in one's pocket.

Ausgabe|jahr year of issue; ~**konstanten** expense constants; ~**kostenzuschlag zuzüglich Erwerbskosten der Wertpapiere** *(Kapitalanlagegesellschaft)* loading; ~**kurs** issue price, rate of issue, *(Investmentzertifikat)* offer price; ~**land** issuing country; **übertragbare** ~**mittel** transferable funds.

Ausgaben expenditure, expense, outgoings *(Br.)*, outlay, spending;
mit all den damit verbundenen ~ with all its attendant expenses; **abnehmende** ~ declining expenditure; **abzugsfähige** ~ deductible expenses; **aktivierte** ~ capitalized expenses; **steuerlich nicht anerkannte** ~ expenditure not allowable for tax purpose, disallowable expenditure; **vor der Gründung angefallene** ~ preliminary expenses; **außerordentliche** ~ extra-budgetary (extraordinary) expenditure, extras; **außerplanmäßige** ~ unbudgeted expenditure, expenditure not provided for in the budget; **bare** ~ cash expenditure (expenses), out-of-pocket expenses; **bedeutende** ~ high expenses; **betriebliche** ~ operating expenditure; **effektive** ~ out-of-pocket expenses; **in nichtgewerblicher Eigenschaft eingegangene** ~ expenses incurred by a trader in another capacity; **einmalige** ~ nonrecurring charges (expenses); **entstandene** ~ expenses incurred; **entstandene oder mit der Geschäftsführung notwendigerweise entstehende** ~ costs necessarily incurred in the conduct of business; **erstattungsfähige** ~ refundable expenditure; **noch nicht fällige** ~ accrued expenses; **feste (fortlaufende)** ~ constant expenses, nonvariable expenditure, fixed charges; **in den Römischen Verträgen nicht festgelegte** ~ *(EG)* nonobligatory spending; **gehabte** ~ incurred expenses; **zu Lasten der Gemeinde gehende** ~ expenses defrayable out of local contributions; **gelegentliche** ~ casual expenses; **gemeine** ~ ordinary expenses; **geplante** ~ spending plan; **geringe** ~ light expense; **geringfügige** ~ petty expenses; **gleichbleibende** ~ expense constants; **große** ~ heavy expenditure; **indirekte** ~ indirect expenses; **kapitalisierte** ~ capitalized expenses; **kleine** ~ minor expenses, petty charges, petty cash; **kleinere** ~ minor expenses; **laufende** ~ fixed (current, running) expenses, current (returning) expenditure; **notwendige** ~ connected expenses, expenses necessarily incurred; **öffentliche** ~ government expenditure; **ordentliche** ~ ordinary expenses; **persönliche** ~ private expenses; **private** ~ private expenditure; **sachliche** ~ material cost; **sonstige** ~ other payments, *(Bilanz)* nonoperating expenses; **tägliche** ~ daily expenses, routine expenditure; **tatsächliche** ~ out-of-pocket expenses, actual expenditure; **übermäßige** ~ profuse expenditure; **auf das Kapitalkonto übernommene** ~ capitalized expenses; **unerwartete** ~ contingent expenses; **ungedeckte** ~ uncovered expenses; **unvorhergesehene** ~ unforeseen expense (expenditure), contingent expenses, contingencies, incidentals; **veranschlagte** ~ expenditure budgeted for; **verschiedene** ~ *(Bilanz)* sundries, sundry expenses; **verschwenderische** ~ profuse expenditure; **tatsächlich vorgenommene** ~ actual expenditure outturns; **wachsende** ~ growing expenditure; **werbende** ~ productive expenses; **wiederkehrende** ~ fixed charges, recurring expenditure; **nicht wiederkehrende** ~ nonrecurring expenditure, nonrecurring expenses; **regelmäßig wiederkehrende** ~ recurrent expenses; **zusätzliche** ~ additonal expenses;
~ **pro Kopf der Bevölkerung** per capita costs; **Einnahmen und** ~ income and expenditure; ~ **durch Ferienreisende** tourist expenditure; ~ **der öffentlichen Hände** government spending, governmental (public) expenditure; **jährlich neu zu finanzierende** ~ **der öffentlichen Hand** supply services *(Br.)*; **konjunkturbelebende** ~ **der öffentlichen Hand** deficit budgeting; ~ **für Investitionszwecke** investment spending; ~ **für den Lebensunterhalt** consumption expenditure; ~ **außer der Reihe** extras; ~ **im Reiseverkehr** tourist spending; ~ **auf dem Sozialversicherungssektor** social security spending; ~ **der Verbraucherschaft** consumer spending; ~ **zur freien Verfügung** discretionary spending; ~ **für die innere Verwaltung** internal administrative expenditure; ~ **im Vorgriff** anticipatory expenditure;
~ **abdecken** to clear expenses; ~ **auf j. abwälzen** to board the gravy train *(US)*; **seine** ~ **den Einnahmen anpassen** to proportion one's expenses to one's income, to equate the expenses with the income; **sich in den** ~ **Beschränkungen auferlegen** to show spending forbearance; ~ **aufgliedern** to classify expenses, to break down expenses *(US)*; **seine** ~ **aufschlüsseln** to allocate one's expenditure; ~ **beschneiden** to cut (axe) expenditure; **seine** ~ **beschränken** to restrict one's expenses, to limit expenditure; ~ **bestreiten** to defray the costs; **als** ~ **buchen** to enter as expenditure (expense); ~ **in konstanten Preisen darstellen** to express expenditure in constant prices; ~ **decken** to cover expenses; ~ **einschränken** to cut down (reduce the, limit) expenses, to curtail, to retrench expenses, to make retrenchments, to curtail one's expenses, to take in a reef; **sich in seinen** ~ **einschränken** to draw in one's expenditure; ~ **auf ein vernünftiges Maß einschränken** to keep one's expenditure within reasonable limits; **unsinnige** ~ **einschränken** to do away with wasteful expenditure; ~ **erhöhen** to increase the expenditure; ~ **erstatten**

to refund the expenses; **120 Dollar wöchentliche ~ haben** to sit at $ 120 a week; **~ zu verantworten haben** to be responsible for the expenditure; **~ radikal herabsetzen** to axe expenditure; **~ machen** to spend; **große ~ machen** to incur heavy expenses; **größere ~ scheuen** to avoid heavy spending; **~ senken** to cut expenditure; **geringere ~ tätigen** to underspend; **~ übernehmen** to bear the costs; **als ~ verbuchen** to enter as expenditure; **überflüssige ~ vermeiden** to economize; **große ~ verursachen** to entail large expenditure; **große ~ vornehmen** to spend a great deal; **~ wiedereinbringen** to recover the expenses; **für unvorhergesehene ~ zurückstellen** to allow (provide) for contingencies; **~abbau** limitation of spending; **~abrechnung** expense sheet; **~abstriche** expenditure cut; **~ansätze** budget appropriations (items); **~anstieg** rise in spending; **rapider ~anstieg** spending splurge; **~aufgliederung** classification of expenses, breakdown of costs *(US)*; **~aufstellung** statement (return) of expenses; **~aufwand** outlay; **~ausschuß** expenditure committee; **~begrenzung** cash (spending) ceilings; **~begrenzung im öffentlichen Bereich** cash limits in the public sector; **~beleg** voucher jacket, voucher for payment, expense voucher, disbursement voucher, receipt; **abgezeichneter ~beleg** [club] chit; **~bereitschaft** propensity to spend; **~beschleunigung** acceleration of spending; **~beschneidung** cost cutting, retrenchment (curtailment) of expenses, axe of expenditure, spending axe, expenditure cut; **~beschränkung** restriction (retrenchment, restraint) of expenditure; **~beschränkungen anordnen** to clamp limits on spending; **~beschränkungen bei der Etatsfeststellung festsetzen** to produce cash limits around budget time; **~bewilligung** budgetary appropriation; **~buch** housekeeping book; **Einnahmen- und ~buch** receipts and expenses book; **Einnahmen-~buchführungssystem** cost-book principle; **~budget** budget, estimates, appropriation bill *(Br.)*; **~deckung** cost recovery; **~dispositionen im laufenden Rechnungsjahr** budgetary allocations for the current year; **~drang** propensity to spend; **~einschränkung** expenditure cut, retrenchment of expenses; **~entscheidung** spending decision; **~entwicklung** trend of spending; **~erstattung** reimbursement for expenses; **~etat** budget, estimates, appropriation bill *(Br.)*; **~etat nicht völlig ausschöpfen** to keep the spending program(me) short of its target; **~formular** voucher jacket; **~freibetrag** expenditure exemption.

ausgabenfreudig free-spending, ready to spend.

Ausgaben|freudigkeit free spending; **~freudigkeit der Verbraucherschaft** consumer spending; **~gesetz** spending bill; **~gewohnheit** spending habit; **amtlich festgelegte ~grenzen** cash ceilings; **~größe** level of spending; **~gruppe** category of expenditure; **~höchstgrenze festsetzen** to set a limit to expenses, to put a ceiling on spending; **~höhe** expenditure ceiling; **~konto** expense account; **~kontrollbogen** check register; **steuerlich anerkannte ~kosten** allowable expenditure; **~kurve** expenditure curve; **~kürzung** cut in expenditure, expenditure (spending) cut, curtailment (retrenchment) of expenses; **~neigung** propensity (willingness) to spend, marginal propensity to spend; **wiederbelebte ~neigung** spending revival; **~nummer** *(Banknote)* issue number; **~plafond** expenditure ceiling; **~posten** expense item, item of expense; **vordringliche ~posten** spending priorities; **~prioritäten** spending priorities; **staatliches ~programm** government spending program(me); **~programm der öffentlichen Hand** public spending plan; **~programm der Regierung** government's spending program(me); **~quote** spending rate; **~rechnung** calculation of expenses (expenditure), bill of costs; **~rückgang** spending shortfall; **~schalter** *(Post)* delivery counter; **~schätzung** budget (spending) estimate; **~schema** scheme of expenditure; **~schwerpunkt** budget emphasis; **~seite** payment (spending) side; **~sektor der öffentlichen Hand** sector of public expenditure; **~spielraum** scope for spending; **~stelle** *(Emission)* issue department, *(Fahrkarten)* ticket (booking, *Br.*) office, *(Gepäck)* luggage *(Br.)* (baggage, *US*) office; **~steuern** outlay taxes; **~stimmung** spending mood; **staatlicher ~stopp** ceiling to government spending; **~streichung** disallowance of disbursement, spending axe; **~struktur** expenditure (cost) pattern; **gesteigertes ~tempo** acceleration of spending; **~trend** trend of spending; **~überhang** excess of expenditure over revenue; **~übernahme auf Kapitalkonto** capitalization of expenditure; **~überschüsse** excessive spending; **~verhalten der Verbraucher** spending behavio(u)r of consumers; **~verteilung** distribution of expenses; **~verzeichnis** list (schedule) of expenses; **~verzögerung** expenditure lag; **~vollmacht** spending power; **~volumen** total expenditure, volume of spending; **~voranschlag** estimates of expenditure; **~vorgabe** expenditure target.

Ausgabenwirtschaft economy in spending, spending, expenditure;
hemmungslose ~ *(Regierung)* spending spree; **schlechte ~** poor management of expenditure; **zügellose ~** lavish expenditure; **gesamte ~ der öffentlichen Hand** total public expenditure; **~ der Regionalfonds** *(EG)* regional fund spending;
~ ankurbeln to increase one's spending; **jds. hemmungsloser ~ ein Ende bereiten** to check s. one's extravagant spending; **seine ~ beschränken** to put down one's expenditure; **seine ~ in Ordnung bringen** to regulate one's expenditure; **seine ~ einschränken** to put down one's expenditure, to hold spending down; **~ zu verantworten haben** to be responsible for the expenditure; **seine ~ in engen Grenzen halten** to impose tight cash limits on its own spending; **~ im festgelegten Rahmen halten** to spend up to plan; **öffentliche ~ während einer längeren Wachstumsperiode auf gleichem Niveau halten** to hold public spending level during a period of prolonged growth; **~ des gesamten Regierungsapparates überblicken** to oversee the spending of all government departments.

Ausgaben|wünsche, seine ~wünsche nach seinen Einnahmemöglichkeiten ausrichten to measure one's spending by one's means; **~zunahme** outlay growth; **jährliche ~zunahme auf 1% beschränken** to limit the growth in its spending to 1% a year.

Ausgabeort issuing place.

Ausgabeposten expense (spending) item, item of expense (expenditure);
bei der Steuer abzugsfähiger ~ expenditure qualifying for relief *(Br.)*; **vordringliche ~** spending priorities;
~ verschwinden lassen to draw the curtain on outlays.

Ausgabe|preis issue price, *(Investmentzertifikat)* offering (offer) price; **~programm** program(me) of expenditure; **~spesen** *(Investmentfonds)* initial charge; **~stelle** issuing office, *(Fahrscheine)* ticket office, *(Gepäck)* counter; **~stelle für postlagernde Sendungen** general delivery *(US)*; **~tag** day (date) of issue, publication (issue) date; **~wert** issue value; **~zentrum** *(mil.)* distribution center.

Ausgang result, issue, outcome, upshot, end, conclusion, going out, *(Ausgehen)* outing, *(drucktechn.)* break, *(geographisch)* outlet, mouth, *(Prozeß)* exitus, *(Tür)* exit, way-out, *(Urlaub)* day (time) off, leave, *(Waren)* outturn, outgo;
am ~ des Dorfes at the end of the village; **am ~ des Jahrhunderts** towards the close of the century;
mit tödlichem ~ fatal;
~! exit, way out!; **kein ~!** no exit!;
tödlicher ~ fatality; **ungünstiger ~** unfavou(r)able issue;
guter ~ eines Unternehmens good issue of an undertaking; **~ einer Zeile** end of a line;
~ haben to have one's day off, *(mil.)* to be on pass; **auf einen glücklichen ~ der Verhandlungen hindeuten** to point to a happy issue of the negotiations; **guten ~ erwarten lassen** to be in a promising state; **guten ~ nehmen** to turn out well; **seinen ~ nehmen** to take root from; **~ der Wahlen voraussagen** to predict the result of the elections.

Ausgangs|ader discovery vein; **~bahnhof** terminal station, terminus; **~basis** initial position, starting base; **~basis für Friedensverhandlungen** launching platform for peace; **~basis für die Wahlen** good voting base; **~baumuster** prototype; **~beschränkung** *(mil.)* curfew, confinement to barracks; **~datum** date basis; **~deklaration** clearance outwards; **~erzeugnis** primary product; **~fakturenbuch** sales book; **~fracht** outward freight, outbound transportation, outgoing freight; **~frachtsatz** basing rate; **~gebot** *(Auktion)* upset price; **~gesamtheit** *(Statistik)* parent population; **~hafen** shipping port, port of embarkation; **~industrie** basic industry; **~kapital** initial capital, original investment; **~kasse** check-out counter *(US)*; **~körbchen** out-tray (basket); **~lage** initial position; **sich in einer guten ~lage befinden, sich in eine günstige ~lage bringen** to manoeuvre for position; **~lager** base camp; **~leistung** *(el.)* power output; **~linie** *(mil.)* jumping-off line; **~maß** *(Statistik)* basic dimensions; **~material** raw material; **~parität** initial par value; **~position** initial position; **günstige ~position haben** *(bei Verhandlungen)* to get (be let) in on the ground floor; **günstigere ~position für neue Wählerstimmen haben** to have the edge in vote-getting terms; **~produkt** primary product; **~punkt** starting point, place to begin, takeoff, zero, center, *(Bahn)* point of departure, *(Luftflotte)* base, *(Preisbestimmung)* basing point; **günstiger ~punkt** vantage point; **~punkte** *(Angestelltenbewertung)* basic points; **~rechnung** sales invoice; **~sperre** *(mil.)* confinement to barracks, *(Bevölkerung)* curfew; **totale ~sperre** all leave is stopped; **unter ~sperre** confined to barracks; **~stellung** *(mil.)* initial position, *(Fallschirmtruppen)* jumping-off position; **günstigere ~stellung** comparative advantage; **~stellung zurücknehmen** *(mil.)* to recover; **~stichprobe** *(Statistik)* master sample; **~stoff** basic material, *(Atom)* source material; **~tarif** *(Versicherung)* manual rate; **~urlaub** leave to go out; **~werkstoff** parent material; **~wert** starting value; **~werte** *(Arbeitsplatzbewertung)* basic points, *(Programmierung)* output, *(Zeitstudie)* basic data; **~zeile** *(Terminal)* loose line; **~zeitpunkt** base period; **~zeitraum** reference period; **~zoll** export duty; **~zollsatz** basic duty.

ausgearbeitet worked out;
sorgfältig ~ elaborate.

ausgebaute Mansardenwohnung attic flat.

ausgebbar issuable;
wieder ~ reissuable.

ausgeben *(Geld)* to spend, to expend, to disburse, to lay out, to outlay, *(Banknoten)* to issue, to circulate, *(Briefe)* to deliver, *(in Umlauf setzen)* to issue, to emit, to utter, *(verteilen)* to give (hand) out, to distribute;
sich ~ to spend one's energy; **Aktien ~** to issue shares; **alles ~** to live up to one's income; **sich als ~** to pretend to be ..., to pass o. s. off as ...; **sich für j. anders ~** to figure (personate) o. s. as; **Anleihe ~** to float (issue, negotiate) a loan; **sich als Bankier ~** to pass o. s. off as a banker; **Banknoten ~** to issue bank notes; **40.000 Dollar im Jahr ~** to live at the rate of $ 40.000 (spend $ 40.000) a year; **einen ~** *(fam.)* to stand a drink; **Falschgeld ~** to utter counterfeit money; **sich fälschlich für j. ~** to falsely personate o. s. for s. o.; **Geld ~** to lay out money; **sein ganzes Geld ~** to spend all one's money; **Geld leicht ~** to spend money with a free hand; **Geld mit vollen Händen ~** to throw money away right and left, to spend money like water; **sich als Gesellschafter ~** to hold o. s. out as a partner *(Br.)*; **Gratisaktien ~** to declare a stock dividend; **Kreditbrief ~** to issue a letter of credit; **Losung ~** *(mil.)* to give the password; **Obligationen ~** to issue bonds; **Paß ~** to issue a passport; **Rationen an die Truppen ~** to serve out rations to the troops; **Runde ~** to stand treat (a drink to all); **sich als Sachverständigen ~** to pretend to be an expert; **in Stücken von 10.000 Dollar ~** to issue in denominations of $ 10.000; **sich zu Unrecht als Professor ~** to have no right to term o. s. a professor; **sich als unzurechnungsfähig ~** to stultify o. s.; **seinen ganzen Verdienst ~** to live up to one's income; **Vermögen für Bücher ~** to spend a fortune on books; **viel für etw. ~** to spend a lot of money on s. th.; **Vorräte ~** to issue provisions; **für Werbungszwecke ~** to spend on advertising; **zuviel ~** to overspend;
~ müssen to be at the expense of.

ausgebendes Konsortium distributing syndicate *(US)*.

Ausgeber issuer, disburser.

ausgebessert mended, repaired;
~e Stelle mend, mended place.

ausgebeutet sweated, *(Bergwerk)* worked out;
~ sein *(Bergwerk)* to be no longer workable.

ausgebildet accomplished, trained, skilled, schooled, educated;
beruflich ~ professional; **fachlich ~** skilled in the art, specialized; **juristisch ~** learned in the law; **nur mittelmäßig ~** low-skilled; **nicht [fachlich] ~** unspecialized, unaccomplished; **nicht genügend ~** *(mil.)* nonefficient; **voll ~** fully qualified; **nicht voll ~** rudimentary;
fachlich ~ sein to be skilled in a business; **im falschen Beruf ~ sein** to be trained in the wrong skills.

Ausgebildeter, in erster Hilfe first aider.

ausgeblichen discolo(u)red.

ausgeblieben *(Post)* overdue.

ausgebombt bombed out.

ausgebrannt burnt-out;
~e Persönlichkeit a spent firework.

ausgebucht booked;
bis Ende 1979 ~ sein to be booked through 1979;
~er Tag full day.

ausgebürgert expatriate;
~ werden to be expatriated.

Ausgebürgerter expatriate.

Ausgeburt | der Hölle fiend (spawn) of hell; **~ der Phantasie** figments of phantasy.

ausgedacht, raffiniert trickily devised.

ausgedehnt extensive, broad, large, wide, spacious, wide-stretched, vast;
~e Forschungen large-scale research; **~er Grundbesitz** large estates; **~er Handel** extensive trade; **~er Spaziergang** long walk; **~es Waldgebiet** far-flung tract of wood.

ausgedient retired, pensioned off, *(Sachen)* worn-out.

Ausgedinge farm annuity.

ausgedorrt dry, torrid.

ausgedruckt printed off;
~er Druckbogen folded printed sheet.

ausgedrückt in terms of;
gelinde ~ to say the least of it; **in Pfunden ~** in terms of pounds; **prozentual ~** expressed as percentage.

ausgefahren rutty;
~e Gleise verlassen *(fig.)* to leave the beaten track; **~e Straße** road full of ruts.

ausgefallen out of the way (ordinary), unusual, eccentric, queer, *(Dividende)* passed, *(Konzert)* off;
~er Buchstabe dropped letter; **~e Idee** odd idea; **~er Motor** dead engine; **~e Vorstellung** cancelled performance; **~e Wörter** rare words.

ausgefeilt *(Stil)* polished, refined;
nicht ~ *(Stil)* unfinished; **technisch ~** sophisticated;
sorgfältig ~ sein to smell of the lamp.

ausgefertigt *(Urkunde)* given, done;
einfach ~ in a single copy.

ausgeflippt psyched up.

ausgefräster Druckstock routed plate.

ausgefressen haben, etw. to have got up to some monkey business.

ausgefuchst cunning, sly, artful, wily.

ausgeführt executed, *(ins Ausland verkauft)* exported;
nicht ~ unexported;
~e Aufträge filled orders.

ausgegangen out, *(drucktechn.)* out of sorts, *(Restaurantgericht)* off, *(Ware)* out, off, sold out.

ausgegeben spent, disbursed, *(emittiert)* issued;
nicht ~ unexpended, *(nicht emittiert)* unissued; **in Stücken ~** issued in denominations.
~ sein to be off;
effektiv ~es Aktienkapital outstanding shares *(Br.)*, issued (outstanding) [capital] stock *(US)*; **nicht ~es Aktienkapital** unissued [capital] stock *(US)*.

ausgeglichen even, square, liquidated, in balance, well-balanced, selfbalancing, *(fig.)* levelheaded, at ease, on an even keel, quiet, well-disposed;
nicht ~ unsettled, unliquidated;
~ sein to balance, *(fig.)* to have a level head;
~es Konto balanced (settled) account; **~er Mensch** man of poise; **~er Staatshaushalt** balanced budget.

Ausgeglichenheit levelness, quiet, ease, tranquility, poise.

Ausgeh | abend evening out; **~anzug** go-to-meeting clothes.

ausgehen to go out, to leave the house, to step out *(sl.)*, to go among people, *(Geld)* to run short [of money], *(Resultat haben)* to turn out, *(Stoff)* to lose colo(u)r, *(Vorräte)* to run low, *(Waren)* to run short, to sell out;
abends ~ to have an evening on the town; **auf Abenteuer ~** to go in search of adventure; **nur auf Betrug ~** to be bent on fraud; **auf Beute ~** to go plundering; **vom Chef ~** *(Anordnung)* to come from the boss; **darauf ~, die Aufmerksamkeit der Hausfrauen zu erregen** to be calculated to attract the attention of housewives; **frei ~** to get off scot-free; **gesellschaftlich ~** to go into society; **groß ~** to make a night of it; **für den Kläger günstig ~** to turn out favo(u)rably for the claimant; **in einem Hause ein- und ~** to have the run of the house; **leer ~** to go empty-handed, to be left out, *(Gläubiger)* to obtain (get) nothing by it; **nicht ~** to keep the house; **von einem Platz ~** *(Straßen)* to radiate from a place; **von der Regierung ~** to originate with the government; **schlecht ~** to end bad; **von dem Standpunkt ~** to work from the principle; **straffrei ~** to go unpunished; **unentschieden ~** to end in a draw; **viel ~** to go out a great deal; **ziemlich viel ~** to go about a good deal; **vom Volk ~** *(Staatsgewalt)* to originate with the people; **von falschen Voraussetzungen ~** to start from false presupposition; **wenig ~** to go very little in society; **von X ~** to start from X;
bei jem. ein- und ~ können to be free of s. one's house, to have the run of the house.

ausgehend | e Fracht outward freight; **im ~en 20. Jahrhundert** towards the close of the 20th century; **~e Ladung** outward cargo; **~e Post** departing (outgoing) mail; **~es Schiff** outward-bound vessel; **~e Vorräte** provisions running low (out).

Ausgehendes *(Bergbau)* crop.

Ausgeh | erlaubnis *(mil.)* pass; **~kleid** party (going-out, *US coll.*) dress.

ausgehoben *(mil.)* drafted;
von der Polizei ~ pulled up by the police;
~er Rekrut conscript; **~e Truppen** levy.

ausgehöhlt, vom Meer washed out by the sea.

Ausgehtag day off.

ausgehungert hunger-stricken.
Ausgeh|uniform class A uniform *(US)*, dress uniform; **~verbot** *(Bevölkerung)* curfew, *(mil.)* confinement to barracks; **~verbot verhängen** to impose a curfew.
ausgeklagte Forderung judgment debt.
ausgeklügelt well-thought out, well-contrived, wiredrawn; **raffiniert ~er Plan** cleverly devised plan; **~es Überwachungssystem** ingenious system of surveillance.
ausgekocht *(fig.)* salted, shrewd, tricky, artful;
~er Bursche deep card *(sl.)*; **~er Politiker** thoroughpaced politician; **~er Verbrecher** utter rogue.
ausgekommen sein, nie miteinander to have never hit it off.
ausgelassen boisterous, wild, rollicking, exuberant;
sehr ~ sein to be in high spirits, to hold high jinks;
~e Gesellschaft gay society.
Ausgelassenheit wildness, jinks, hilarity, exuberance, frolic;
~ der Gäste loud mirth of the guests.
ausgelastet fully occupied, booked, *(Betrieb)* working to capacity;
total ~ sein to be full up with business; **voll ~ sein** *(Betrieb)* to be working to capacity; **zu 85% ~ sein** *(Betrieb)* to operate at a rate of 85% of capacity.
ausgelegt, eng strictly construed;
~er Betrag money disbursed; **~e Kredite** loans granted.
ausgeleiert|es Gewinde worn thread; **~es Gummiband** worn-out elastic.
ausgelernt haben to have served one's time (finished one's apprenticeship).
ausgeliefert delivered, *(Person)* extradited;
den Blicken der Menge ~ sein to be exposed to the full view of the crowd; **den Elementen hilflos ~ sein** to be at the mercy of the elements.
ausgeliehen sein *(Bibliotheksbuch)* to be out.
ausgelost drawn;
~er Betrag prize money; **~e Pfandbriefe (Schuldverschreibungen)** bonds called for redemption.
ausgelotet sounded.
ausgemacht settled, agreed, positive, *(coll.)* certain, it's a deal;
~er Idiot perfect idiot; **~er Preis** price agreed upon; **~e Sache** dead certainty, sure thing, foregone conclusion; **~er Schuft** utter rogue; **~er Schwindel** regular swindle.
ausgenommen excluding, free, exempt, except, excepting;
keiner ~ without exception, bar none *(coll.)*;
~ es regnet unless it rains;
~ sein to be exempted from.
ausgenutzt used;
nicht ~ unused, unavailed, *(Gesetz)* dormant;
sich ~ fühlen to think o. s. ill-used.
Ausgenutzter exploitee.
ausgepfändet sold up.
ausgepichter Kerl slyboots.
ausgeplündert impoverished, stripped, desolated.
ausgeprägt coined, marked, distinct;
~er Wesenszug distinctive characteristic, marked feature.
ausgepumpt pumped out, *(fig.)* worn-out, all-in, pooped *(US coll.)*;
vollkommen ~ fagged out.
ausgerechnet just, of all things.
ausgereift mature;
nicht ~ unseasoned;
noch nicht ~ sein *(Wein)* to have not matured properly.
ausgerichtet oriented;
~ sein auf to be geared to; **stark links ~ sein** to have a strong tendency to the left.
ausgerüstet, schlecht badly equipped; **ungenügend ~** inadequately provided.
ausgeschaltet [switched] off, *(Gang)* thrown out of gear.
ausgeschieden dismissed, retired, *(Sache)* discarded, put away, *(Teilnehmer)* eliminated;
~ sein to be out of the running.
Ausgeschiedener out.
ausgeschlossen excluded, *(nicht zugelassen)* inadmissible, ineligible, *(unmöglich)* impossible, out of the question;
~, nichts zu machen nothing doing; **aus dem Parlament ~** unseated;
~ sein to kiss the post; **aus der Anwaltskammer ~ sein** to be disbarred; **von einem Wettbewerb ~ sein** to be disqualified from a competition; **~ werden** to be precluded.
ausgeschmückt decorated.
ausgeschrieben written in full, in full letters, *(Preis)* awarded;
sich ~ haben *(Schriftsteller)* to have drained o. s. dry;
~er Betrag *(Anzeige)* amount stated; **~e Handschrift** developed handwriting; **voll ~er Name** name in full; **~e Stelle** advertised post.
ausgeschüttet *(Dividende)* divided;
~er Gewinn distributed profit.
ausgesetzt exposed, *(vertagt)* deferred;
dem Gelächter ~ subject to ridicule;
hilflos ~ stranded;
der Kritik ~ sein to be open to criticism; **einer Sache ~ sein** to lie open to s. th.; **Veränderungen ~ sein** to undergo changes;
~er Betrag allowance; **~er Preis** offered price.
Ausgesetztsein exposure.
ausgesiedelt evacuated.
Ausgesiedelter evacuee.
ausgesparter Raum *(drucktechn.)* whites.
ausgesperrt *(Arbeiter)* locked out;
~ sein to have got the key of the street.
ausgespielt haben to have had one's day.
ausgesprochen distinct, pronounced, marked;
~e Ansichten decided views, pronounced opinions; **~e Begabung** marked ability; **~ englische Einrichtung** typical English institution; **~er Gegner** declared opponent; **~es Pech** definitely bad luck; **~er Plagegeist** positive torment *(coll.)*; **~e Vorliebe** distinct partiality.
ausgestalten to arrange, to lay out, to shape, to turn into.
Ausgestaltung *(Verkaufsraum)* layout.
ausgestattet provided, furnished, endowed, equipped;
gut ~ *(Revue)* highly spectacular; **nicht ~** unfurnished; **schlecht ~** badly appointed;
mit zahlreichen Illustrationen ~ sein *(Buch)* to contain numerous illustrations; **reichlich ~ sein** to be endowed with ample means; **schlecht ~ sein** to be poorly provided for;
mit schönen Möbeln ~es Zimmer beautifully appointed room.
ausgestellt *(Kreditbrief)* issued, *(auf einer Messe)* on show, exhibited, on exhibition, *(Wechsel)* made out;
dauernd ~ on permanent display; **dreifach ~** made out in triplicate; **an Order ~ und blanko giriert** made out to order and indorsed in blank; **ordnungsgemäß ~** duly drawn;
~ sein to be on show, *(Wechsel)* to be drawn; **öffentlich ~ sein** to be on public display; **~ werden** to go on exhibit;
~er Wechsel drawn (issued) bill.
ausgesteuert *(el.)* modulated;
nicht ~ unmodulated;
~ sein *(Arbeitsloser)* to be out of benefit (unemployment relief), to have exhausted one's benefit rights *(Br.)*.
ausgestochen, von der Konkurrenz supplanted by a rival firm.
Ausgestoßener outcast, pariah.
ausgesucht first choice, first-class (-rate), selected, exquisite, picked;
~e Höflichkeit extreme politeness; **~e Ware** choice quality (goods, articles).
ausgetauscht interchanged.
ausgetreten, sich in ~en Bahnen bewegen to keep to the beaten track; **~er Weg** beaten track.
ausgewachsen full grown, adult;
voll ~ sein to reach full growth.
ausgewählt picked, choice, select, first-rate;
~e Anlagewerte selected investments; **~es Kapital** select chapter; **~e Stellen** *(Buch, usw.)* selected passages.
ausgewandert emigrated.
ausgewechselt, wie completely changed.
ausgewiesen expelled, *(dokumentiert)* evidenced by, accounted for, *(Flüchtling)* expelled;
nicht ~ unaccounted for; **nicht gesondert ~** *(Bilanz)* not shown separately below;
~er Betrag declared amount; **~e Dividende** declared dividend.
Ausgewiesener displaced person, expellee.
ausgewogen [well] balanced, *(Luftschiff)* [well-] trimmed;
~e Diät balanced diet.
Ausgewogenheit balance, *(Index)* weighting.
ausgezahlt, in bar with cash alternative;
~er Betrag disbursement.
ausgezeichnet excellent, distinguished, eminent, superb, outstanding, A I, first-class (-rate), classic, fine, boss *(US sl.)*, *(mit Preis versehen)* priced at;
nicht ~ *(im Schaufenster)* unpriced;
jem. ~ passen to suit s. o. to a T; **nicht ~ sein** *(im Schaufenster)* to be unpriced; **sorgfältig ~ sein** to be clearly priced; **unmißverständlich ~ sein** to be marked in plain figures;
~e Arbeit excellent piece of work; **von ~er Qualität** of superior quality.

Ausgleich *(Abrechnung)* balance, balancing, squaring, *(Berichtigung)* adjustment, *(Bezahlung)* payment, *(Deckung)* cover, *(Entschädigung)* compensation, *(Gegenkonto)* setoff *(Br.)*, offset *(US)*, *(Glattstellung)* evening up, *(Gläubigervergleich)* composition, *(Gleichstellung)* equalization, *(Preise)* equation, *(Vergleich)* conciliation, accommodation, arrangement, settlement;
als ~ (zum ~ für) compensational, by way of compensation, as payment for; **zum ~ aller Forderungen** in settlement of all claims; **zum harmonischen ~** for better rapport; **zum ~ unserer Rechnung** in order to balance (in settlement of) our account; **zum ~ unserer Tratte** as cover for our draft; **zum vollen ~** in full discharge; **zum völligen ~ dieser Sache** for the closing of this transaction;
als ~ für erlittene Verluste as compensation for losses suffered;
automatischer ~ built-in balancing effect, *(Lohnklausel)* escalator clause; **finanzieller ~** financial adjustment; **güterrechtlicher ~** settlement *(Br.)*; **gütlicher ~** amicable arrangement; **sozialer ~** social adjustment; **vollständiger ~** full settlement; **wirtschaftlicher ~** economic adjustment;
~ von Angebot und Nachfrage equilibrium of supply and demand; **~ in bar** cash adjustment; **~ der steuerlichen Belastungen** equalization of the tax burden; **~ der Handelsbilanz** redressing the balance of trade; **~ unter Miterben** hotchpot, collation; **~ für Nervenbelastung** nuisance costs; **~ der nach erfolgter Clearingabrechnung verbleibenden Salden** clearinghouse settlement *(US)*; **anderweitiger ~ von Sonderausgaben** absorption of extras; **~ der Steuern** equalizing assessment of taxes; **~ der Versicherungsrisiken** spread of risk; **~ der Zahlungsbilanz** balance-of-payments adjustment; **~ des Zahlungsverkehrs** settlement of transactions;
~ zwischen zwei Gegnern zustande bringen to effect a compromise between two contestants; **~ finden** to strike a balance; **~ der Interessen herbeiführen** to bring about a conciliation of interests; **für einen ~ sorgen** to provide for a counterbalance; **zum ~ zur Verfügung stellen** to grant in return; **~ vornehmen** *(Erbschaft)* to put into hotchpot.
ausgleichbar compensable, adjustable.
Ausgleichen balancing, levelling, equalization, adjustment.
ausgleichen to equate, to make equal, to equalize, to adjust, to level, *(decken)* to cover, to reimburse, to countervail, *(entschädigen)* to compensate, to redeem, *(Gegenposten)* to balance, to square, to make up, to settle by contra account, to set off *(Br.)*, to offset *(US)*, *(glattstellen)* to even up, to settle, *(Gläubiger befriedigen)* to compound, *(Kräfte)* to counterweigh, to counterpoise, *(Satz)* to underlay, *(Streit)* to compose, to compound, to settle, to heal, *(Verpflichtungen)* to discharge;
sich ~ to balance, to be balanced; **in bar ~** to settle in cash; **gegenseitige Forderungen ~** to set off claims; **etw. gegeneinander ~** to counterbalance s. th.; **Haushalt ~** to balance the budget; **Haushaltsdefizit ~** to balance an adverse budget; **durch Kompromiß ~** to compound; **Konto ~** to settle an account; **nach oben ~** to level up; **nach unten ~** to level down; **Nachteile ~** to offset disadvantages; **Rechnung ~** to settle a bill; **Risiken ~** to spread risks; **Verlust ~** to make up for a loss; **Verlust durch einen Gewinn ~** to set off a gain against a loss.
ausgleichend countervailing, compensatory, compensative;
~e Gerechtigkeit retributive justice; **~e Regelung** compensatory adjustment.
Ausgleichs|abgabe equalization levy, countervailing (compensatory) charge; **~abkommen** clearing agreement; **~abzug** offset allowance *(US)*; **~amt** board of equalization; **~anspruch** equalization claim, equitable damages, *(Mitbürge)* right to contribution; **~anspruch der Ehefrau gegen das Vermögen des Ehemannes** equity to a settlement; **~anspruch eines Gesellschafters** equity of partner; **~ansprüche** contribution rights; **~ansprüche erhalten** *(Mitbürgen)* to obtain contributions; **~ansprüche haben** to be entitled to a composition; **~antenne** aerial screen; **~arbitrage** arbitration of exchange; **~ausschlußklausel** *(Seeschadensversicherung)* American clause; **~berechnung** *(Nachlaß)* hotchpot calculation (computation); **~bestimmung** *(Grundstücksteilung)* rule of apportionment; **~bestimmungen** *(Nachlaßregelung)* hotchpot provisions; **~betrag** balance, compensation, equalization sum; **geldwerter ~betrag** money compensatory amount; **~betrag für Abschreibungsverluste** balancing allowance; **~buchung** balancing entry; **~dividende** equalizing dividend; **~einrede** *(Bürge)* benefit of division; **~entschädigung** compensatory damages, equalization benefit; **~finanzierung von Ausfuhrschwankungen** *(Weltwährungsfonds)* compensatory financing of export fluctuations; **~finanzierungsmöglichkeiten** compensatory financing facility; **~folgesteuer** equalization tax; **~fonds** equalization (compensation) fund; **~forderung** equalization claim, equitable damages; **~frist** equalization period; **~gebühr** equalization fee; **~getriebe** *(Auto)* equalizing (differential) gear; **~kasse** equalization office, compensation fund, *(Bankwesen)* clearinghouse; **~klausel** *(Lohnfestsetzung)* escalator clause *(US)*; **~klauseln** *(Nachlaßregelung)* hotchpot clauses; **~koeffizient** *(EG)* coefficient of equivalence; **~konto** compensatory balance, over-and-short (variance, adjustment) account; **~kredit** stopgap loan; **~kurs** equalization price, clearing rate; **~leistung** compensatory payment, equalization benefit, *(Erbe)* putting in hotchpot; **~leistungen an finanzschwache Gemeinden** Exchequer Equalization grant *(Br., till 1959)*, rate deficiency grant *(Br.)*; **~lohn** *(Akkordlohn)* make-up wages; **~maßnahmen** adjustment (compensatory) measures, adjustment action; **~moment** redeeming feature; **gesetzliche ~pflicht** *(Nachlaßregelung)* statutory hotch-pot requirement.
ausgleichspflichtig *(Erbe)* liable to put into hotchpot.
Ausgleichs|pflichtiger *(Erbe)* collator; **~plan** compensation scheme; **~pool** buffer pool; **~posten** compensating item, setoff *(Br.)*, offset *(US)*, special assets, *(Bilanz)* deferred (adjustment) item, balancing item; **~posten für Anteile in Fremdbesitz** minority interests; **~preis** temporary equilibrium price, *(EG)* compensatory price, levelling price; **~punkt** equalization point; **~quittung** receipt in full discharge; **~quote** equalization rate; **~rechnung** method of compensation; **~regelung** compensatory adjustment, compensation scheme; **~rücklage** equalization reserve; **~schuld** equalization debt; **~stelle** equalization board; **~steuer** equalization (compensatory) tax; **~stock** equalization fund; **~strom** *(el.)* transient current; **~summe** equalization sum, compensation balance; **~tarif** equalizing rate; **~transformator** balancer transformer.
Ausgleichsumlage equalization fee, *(Montanunion)* levy;
kommunale ~ rate-in-aid *(Br.)*.
Ausgleichs|urlaub für Überstunden compensatory time off; **~verfahren** equalizing process, *(Konkurs)* composition in bankruptcy, *(Nachlaßregelung)* hotchpot; **~verfahren für Weidenutzungen** admeasurement of pasture; **~vorrat** *(EG)* buffer stock; **~vorratsfinanzierung** *(EG)* buffer stock financing; **~wechsel** remittance per appoint; **~zahlung** equalization (compensation) payment, *(bei Entlassungen)* coordination allowance *(US)*, severance pay *(US)*, redundancy pay *(Br.)*, *(Feuerversicherung)* contribution, *(an Landwirte)* deficiency payment; **~zahlung an finanzschwache Gemeinden** rate deficiency grant *(Br.)*; **~zeitraum** equalization period; **~ziffer** balancing figure; **~zoll** countervailing duty; **~zoll für Schleuderausfuhr** dumping duty; **~zugeständnis** compensatory concession; **~zulage** cost-of-living allowance; **staatliche ~zuweisung** rate deficiency grant *(Br.)*.
Ausgleichung balancing, equalization, equation, *(Banken)* clearance, clearing, *(Entschädigung)* compensation, *(Erben untereinander)* [putting in] hotchpot, *(mit Gläubigern)* settlement, arrangement, composition, *(Richtigstellung)* adjustment;
zur ~ unserer Rechnung in full discharge of our account;
~ der Buchung accounting equation; **~ des Marktes** evening out of the market;
~ vornehmen *(Nachlaßregelung)* to put into hotchpot.
Ausgleichungspflicht *(Erben)* hotchpot.
ausgliedern to separate, *(Konzerngesellschaft)* to disembody, to disincorporate, to eliminate;
Konto ~ to eliminate an account; **unrentable Produktionsgebiete ~** to eliminate unprofitable operations.
Ausgliederung separation, *(Konzerngesellschaft)* disembodiment, disincorporation;
~ von Konten elimination of accounts; **~ von Konzernkonten** intercompany elimination *(US)*.
ausgraben to dig up, to excavate, *(exhumieren)* to disinter, to unbury, to exhume;
alte Dokumente ~ to dig out old manuscripts; **Familiengeheimnis ~** to unearth a family secret; **eingeschneites Haus ~** to tunnel out a snowbound house; **Kriegsbeil ~** to take up the hatchet; **Ruinen ~** to excavate a buried city; **alte Streitereien wieder ~** to rake up old quarrels; **neue Tatsachen ~** to unearth new facts.
Ausgrabung excavation, *(Exhumiering)* disinterment, exhumation;
~en vornehmen to excavate a buried city.
ausgreifend, mit ~en Schritten with long strides.
ausgründen to disincorporate, to disembody.
Ausgründung disincorporation, disembodiment.

Ausguck lookout, crow's nest.
Ausguß sink, kitchen drain;
verstopfter ~ plugged sink;
~**eimer** slop pail; ~**rohr** waste (discharge, outlet) pipe; ~**ventil** discharge valve; ~**wasser** waste water.
aushaben, Buch to have finished a book.
aushalten to bear, to endure, to stand, to stick it out, to tolerate, to hold out;
höchstens einen Monat an einem Arbeitsplatz ~ to stick to a job only for a month; **Belagerung** ~ to withstand a siege; **Belastung** ~ to sustain a burden; **bis zum letzten Blutstropfen** ~ to endure to the end; **lange** ~ *(Kleidungsstück)* to last a long time; **bis zum Umfallen** ~ to hang on like grim death; **Vergleich** ~ to hold a candle to, to stand a comparison; ~, **bis Verstärkungen kommen** to hang on until reinforcements come; **Zahnschmerzen** ~ to endure toothache;
sich ~ **lassen** to live at the expense of others; **viel** ~ **müssen** to have a lot to put up with.
aushandelbar negotiable.
Aushandelbarkeit negotiability.
Aushandeln negotiating, bargaining;
~ **von Luftfahrt-Angestelltentarifen** airline bargaining.
aushandeln to bargain, to barter, to negotiate (confer) with;
besondere Kurse für Aktienpakete ~ to negotiate prices on block trades; **Preis** ~ to negotiate a price; **Tarif** ~ to bargain collectively; **Vertrag bis in die kleinsten Einzelheiten** ~ to negotiate a contract in exhausting detail;
noch ~ **müssen** to be left to negotiation.
aushändigen to deliver [up], to hand over (out), *(Urkunde)* to surrender.
Aushändigung delivery up, handing over, disposition, *(Dokumente)* surrender;
bei ~ on delivery (surrender); **zahlbar gegen** ~ **der Begleitpapiere** payable against surrender of shipping documents; **bedingungslose** ~ absolute delivery;
~ **von Wertpapieren** delivery of stocks;
~ **verweigern** to refuse delivery.
Aushändigungs|schein receipt of delivery; ~**verbot** *(Post)* fraud order.
Aushandlung bargaining, negotiating;
~ **von Luftfahrt-Angestelltentarifen** airline bargaining.
Aushang notice, bulletin, *(Plakat)* poster, placard, placarding, *(Tafel)* notice board *(Br.)*.
Aushänge|bogen advance sheet; ~**fahrplan** time poster (table), schedule *(US)*.
aushängen to placard, to post [up], to put up, *(Fahnen)* to have been hung out, *(Namen)* to be on the bulletin board;
Tür ~ to unhinge a door.
Aushänge|schild sign, signboard, ticket, shingle, shop bill *(Br.)*, *(fig.)* front, *(Wirtshaus)* bush; ~**zettel** label, ticket, bill, poster, placard.
Aushangs|brett bulletin board, newsboard *(Br.)*; ~**plakat** display poster.
ausharren to persist, to persevere, to hold out, to stand one's ground;
unter demütigenden Bedingungen ~ to eat humble pie; **bis zum Ende** ~ to fight to the bitter end; **auf seinem Posten** ~ to stay at one's post.
aushauchen, sein Leben to breath one's last.
aushauen to chisel out;
Stufen im Eis ~ to hew steps out of the ice.
aushäusig sein, viel to be rarely at home.
ausheben to dig, *(mil.)* to recruit, to levy, to conscript, to draft *(US)*, to enlist, to enrol(l), *(Polizei)* to knock off *(US sl.)*;
Gräben ~ to dig trenches; **Tür** ~ to unhinge a door; **Verbrechernest** ~ to round up a band of criminals.
Aushebung|von Truppen call (recruitment, conscription, enlistment, draft, *US*) of soldiers; ~ **von Verbrechern** roundup of criminals *(US)*.
Aushecken concoction, hatching *(fig.)*.
aushecken to plan, to hatch, to concoct, to cook up, to frame up *(coll.)*;
Komplott ~ to form a conspiracy; **Streich** ~ to run a rig, to think out a prank.
ausheilen to heal.
aushelfen to help out, to make shift, to assist, to accommodate;
jem. mit 100 Dollar ~ to lend s. o. $ 100 to tide over; **jem. mit Geld** ~ to accommodate s. o. with money; **seinem Vater im Geschäft** ~ to help one's father in the shop.
Aushilfe aid, *(Geld)* accommodation, *(Laden)* counter hand, sales assistant, [sales] assistance, *(Notbehelf)* makeshift, stopgap, *(Person)* temporary, handyman, help, substitute, stopgap, extra, hired man *(US)*;
zur ~ as a makeshift;
als ~ **arbeiten** to help out; **j. als** ~ **haben** to employ s. o. as a stopgap; **als** ~ **kommen** to come to take s. one's place; **als** ~ **tätig sein** to come as a stopgap *(coll.)*; **zur** ~ **geholt werden** to be called in for relief.
Aushilfs|arbeit temporary work, odd job; ~**arbeiter** handyman, part-timer, hired help (man, *US*), casual [labo(u)rer], temporary, stopgap; ~**bestimmungen** subsidiary provisions; ~**charakter** *(Beschäftigung)* subsidiary nature; ~**gerüst** temporary scaffolding; ~**kellner** temporary waiter; ~**kraft** temporary [employee], handyman, help, casual [worker], hired man *(US)*, dogsbody *(sl.)*, *(Hausangestellte)* betweenmaid *(Br.)*; ~**lehrer** assistant teacher; ~**personal** auxiliary personnel, help, helpers, temporary staff; ~**sekretärin** relief secretary; ~**stellung** temporary position, emergency job, grass *(sl.)*; ~**telefonist** relief telephonist.
aushilfsweise temporarily, as a stopgap, as makeshift;
~ **bei jem. arbeiten** to help s. o. out; ~ **kommen** to come as a stopgap *(coll.)*.
aushöhlen *(Wasser)* to erode, to undermine, to wear away, to sap;
Staat ~ to undermine the power of a state.
Ausholen *(fig.)* pumping.
ausholen, j. to sound (pump) s. o.; **weit** ~ *(fig.)* to go far back.
aushorchen, j. to suck s. one's brains, to pump s. o.;
j. ~ **wollen** to tap s. o. for information.
Aushub excavation, excavated material.
aushungern to starve;
Stadt ~ to famish a town; **Volk wirtschaftlich** ~ to starve a country's economic system.
ausixen to cancel.
auskalkulieren to cost.
auskämmen *(ungelernte Arbeiter)* to decasualize, *(Betrieb)* to comb out;
Gelände ~ to comb out an area.
Auskämmung combing out *(Br., sl.)*;
~ **ungelernter Arbeiter** decasualization.
Auskämmungsprozeß *(zur Freimachung von Arbeitskräften)* comb[ing] out *(Br., sl.)*.
auskaufen *(aufkaufen)* to forestall, *(Teilhaber)* to buy out;
Laden ~ to buy the whole stock.
auskehren to clear out, to pay out;
in bar ~ to pay out in cash.
auskennen, sich to know one's way about, to know one's stuff;
sich bestens ~ to know a trick or two (the ropes, *sl.*); **sich in einem Gebiet bestens** ~ to be intelligent on a subject; **sich in einer Gegend nicht** ~ to be unfamiliar with a district (a stranger in these parts); **sich in seinem Geschäft** ~ to know one's business; **sich in Entwicklungsfragen gründlich** ~ to have experience of the nuts and bolts in development; **sich gründlich in einem Fach** ~ to be thoroughly familiar with s. th., to know the ropes *(sl.)*, to be well versed in a subject; **sich in geschäftlichen Dingen gut** ~ to be well versed in business; **sich in einem Lande gut** ~ to be quite at home in a country; **sich hier nicht** ~ to be a stranger to these parts; **sich in einem Ort** ~ to know one's way about a place; **sich in den Struktur-, Steuer- und Preisproblemen ihrer spezialisierten Märkte für Investitionspapiere** ~ to be knowledgeable of the structure, taxation and pricing in their particular financial markets; **sich überhaupt nicht mehr** ~ to be completely at a loss; **sich in der Welt** ~ to know one's onions *(sl.)*; **sich in der großen Welt nicht** ~ to have no knowledge of the ways of the world.
auskippen to dump, to tip over.
ausklagen to sue, to take legal action;
Hauptschuldner ~ to discuss a principal debtor.
Ausklagung eines Hauptschuldners discussion of a principal.
ausklammern to remove the brackets;
Frage ~ to leave a question in the cold.
ausklamüsern *(fam.)* to pry (dope) out.
Ausklang epilogue, end.
ausklappbare Seite *(Buch)* pull-out.
Ausklarieren outclearance, clearance (declaration, *Br.*) outward.
ausklarieren *(Schiff)* to clear for sailing, *(Zollrecht)* to take out of bond.
Ausklarierungsschein *(Schiff)* clearance certificate.
auskleiden, Raum mit Holz to wainscot (panel) a room.
ausklingen to die (fade) away;
mit einem Appell ~ to end with an appeal; **mit einem herrlichen Feuerwerk** ~ to culminate in a magnificent firework display; **traurig** ~ to end on a sad note;

seine Rede in einer Mahnung ~ lassen to conclude one's speech with an admonition.
ausklinken to release, *(Buchstaben)* to mortise, *(Tür)* to unlatch.
Ausklinkvorrichtung breakaway link, release device.
ausklügeln, etw. raffiniert to think out a shrewd scheme.
ausknobeln to puzzle one's brains, to figure out *(US)*.
Auskommen livelihood, living, support, subsistence, sustenance; **genügendes ~** competence, competency; **hinlängliches (hinreichendes) ~** sufficiency, independence;
sein ~ haben to get (earn, make) a living, to have (enjoy) a competence (sufficiency), to pay one's way, to gain one's subsistence; **anständiges ~ haben** to live in decent conditions; **bequemes ~ haben** to be well off; **gerade sein (sein knappes) ~ haben** to make both ends meet, to have just enough to live on, to have a bare competence, to pick up a scanty livelihood *(Br.)*; **sein gutes ~ haben** to enjoy a competence, to be in easy circumstances; **sein ~ suchen** to seek a livelihood.
auskommen, mit etw. to manage (do) with s. th.; **mit jem. ~** to get along (on) with s. o.; **gut mit jem. ~** to hit it off (cotton on) with s. o.; **mit seinem Einkommen ~** to live up to one's income; **mit seinem Einkommen knapp ~** to make both ends meet; **mit seinem Gehalt ~** to manage on one's pay; **mit seinem Geld ~** to make both ends meet, to live within one's means; **mit seinem Geld lange ~** to make one's money go far; **mit seinem Geld nicht ~** to earn a bare living; **mit wenig Geld ~** to live (manage) with little money; **gerade so ~** to make both ends meet, to have enough to live on, to rub along (on); **glänzend mit jem. ~** to hit it off with s. o.; **mit 5000 Pfund im Jahr ~** to live on £ 5000 a year; **schlecht mit den Leuten ~** not to mix well; **mit einem niedrigen Lohn ~** to get by on a low wage; **schlecht miteinander ~** to make together badly; **ohne etw. ~** to go without; **mit ganz wenig ~** to exist on very little; **mit weniger ~** to manage on less.
auskömmlich sufficient, adequate;
~es Gehalt haben to earn enough to live on; **~e Pension** satisfactory pension; **~er Preis** paying price.
Auskopierpapier printing-out paper.
auskorrigieren *(drucktechn.)* to cancel.
auskosten müssen, bis zur Neige to have one's fill of s. th., to drain the cup of sorrow to the dregs.
auskramen *(Schublade)* to empty, *(Spielzeug)* to pull out;
alte Erinnerungen ~ to call up old memories; **alte Geschichten wieder ~** to rake up old grievances.
auskundschaften to trace, to scout, to locate, *(Geheimnis)* to ferret out, *(Land)* to explore, *(mil.)* to spy out, to reconnoitre.
Auskunft information, intelligence, *(Schalter)* inquiry office, information desk *(US)*, *(über Kreditfähigkeit)* credit information, report, *(Telefon)* directory enquiries;
nach eingeholter ~ upon inquiry;
befriedigende ~ favo(u)rable report, satisfactory information; **detaillierte ~** detailed information; **erschöpfende ~** exhaustive information; **telefonisch erteilte ~** telephoned inquiry; **falsche ~** misinformation, false information; **genaue ~** full (precise) information; **nähere ~** details, particulars, further inquiry (information); **persönliche ~** personal character; **telefonische ~** telephone inquiry; **zuverlässige ~** reliable information; **zweckdienliche ~** relevant information; **zweifelhafte ~** vague information;
~ über die Finanzlage status report; **~ in Postangelegenheiten** postal information; **~ in Zollangelegenheiten** tariff information;
~ besorgen (einholen) to collect (seek, procure, take) information, to make inquiries; **um ~ bitten** to request information, *(Arbeitgeber)* to make reference to; **um genaue ~ bitten** to ask for detailed information; **jem. um ~ über einen Dritten bitten** to ask s. o. for particulars about s. o.; **um ~ einkommen** to apply for information; **~ über eine Firma erhalten** to receive a report on a firm; **~ von dritter Seite erhalten** to obtain information from outside sources; **~ erteilen** to give (render, furnish) information; **~ geben** to give information; **jem. eine falsche ~ geben** to direct s. o. wrongly; **~ einziehen lassen** to have inquiries made; **~ verweigern** to decline information; **sich an jem. um ~ wenden** to apply to s. o. for information;
sofortige ~ über Deckung erbeten *(für einen Scheck)* advise fate; **genaue ~ erteilt** full details obtainable from; **nähere ~ erwünscht** full particulars will be appreciated.
Auskünfte|einholen to collect information, to make inquiries; **zusätzliche ~ erhalten** to receive news from another quarter; **einfache ~ geben** to give basic advice; **jem. mit stets griffbereiten ~n versorgen** to put information at s. one's fingertips.
Auskunftei inquiry office (agency), information bureau *(US)*, *(Kreditauskunft)* credit agency.
Auskunftgeber informant, reference, referee;
~ anschreiben to take up references.
Auskunfts|abteilung information department, *(Bank)* commercial intelligence department; **~beamter** information officer, inquiry clerk; **~buch** *(zur Eintragung von Auskünften über Kunden)* opinion book *(Br.)*; **~büro** inquiry office, information centre *(Br.)* (bureau, *US*); **~büro des Fremdenverkehrsvereins** tourist office *(Br.)* (bureau, *US*); **~ersuchen** inquiry; **schriftliches ~ersuchen** letter of inquiry; **~erteilung** supply of information, giving information, discovery; **~kartei auf den neuesten Stand bringen** to revise the credit files *(US)*; **~person** informant; **~pflicht** obligation to disclose, *(Versicherung)* liability to discover.
auskunftspflichtig liable to render information, liable to discover (discovery);
~ sein to be required to give information.
Auskunfts|quelle fund (source) of information; **~schalter** inquiry office, information desk (window, *US*); **~stand** *(Messe)* information stand; **~stelle** intelligence (inquiry) office, information desk *(Br.)* (booth, bureau, *US*); **zentrale ~stelle** central information office.
Auskuppeln declutching.
auskuppeln to disengage the clutch, to declutch.
auskurieren, Krankheit to cure a disease.
Auslade|bahnsteig unloading platform; **~brücke** handling platform; **~hafen** port of discharge; **~kosten** unloading expenses (charges).
Ausladen unloading, discharge, *(Schiff)* unshipping, unshipment, landing;
Ein- und ~ loading and unloading;
~ besorgen to do the unloading.
ausladen to unload, to unlade, to discharge a cargo, to clear, *(Balkon)* to project, *(Flugzeug)* to deplane, *(Lastwagen)* to detruck, *(Omnibus)* to debus *(US)*, *(Schiff)* to unship, to land, to lighten;
seine Gäste ~ to put off one's guests.
Auslade|ort unloading point, place of discharge; **~platz** unloading place, *(Schiff)* unloading berth, wharf.
Auslader unloader, discharger, *(Schiff)* ship deliverer.
Auslade|rampe unloading platform; **~risiko** unloading risk; **~stelle** unloading place, *(Schiff)* wharf.
Ausladung unloading, *(Balkon)* nosing;
~ über Schiffsseite discharge overside.
Auslage expense, outlay, laying out, disbursement, *(Schaufenster)* shop front (window), *(Schaustellung)* sales display, window dressing, *(ausgestellte Waren)* goods exhibited, window display;
in der ~ in the [shop]window;
~ industrieller Erzeugnisse industrial display; **~ innerhalb des Ladens** interior display; **~ in Pyramidenform** pyramid display;
~ herrichten to dress a shop window, to set up the display;
~fenster display (show, *US*) window; **~geld** spending money; **~geld geben** to place in funds *(Br.)*; **~gestaltung** display work; **~kasten** showcase, display case; **~material für Schaufenster** window material.
Auslagen expenses, expenditure, outlay, cost[s], mise, paid-on charges *(Br.)*;
allgemeine ~ ordinary expenses; **angemessene ~** reasonable expenses; **bare ~** out-of-pocket expenses *(Br.)*, cash advances (disbursements); **erstattungsfähige ~** reimbursable expenses; **kleine ~** sundries, petty expenses; **sonstige ~** *(Bilanz)* sundry expenses; **tatsächliche ~** out-of-pocket expenses;
~ zu Lasten des Kunden expenses charged to client's account, disbursement to client's debit;
die ~ ansehen to go window shopping; **seine ~ aufschreiben** to keep a record of one's expenses; **seine ~ vergütet bekommen** to recover one's disbursements; **~ bestreiten** to bear (defray, cover) the expenses; **~ ersetzen (erstatten)** to reimburse (refund) the expenses; **seine ~ wieder hereinbekommen** to recoup one's disbursements; **~ tragen** to bear the expenses; **seine ~ zurückerhalten** to recover one's outlay; **~ zurückerstatten** to refund the expenses (disbursements);
~abrechnung expense account, statement of expenses; **~aufstellung** specification of disbursements, disbursement account; **~ersatz, ~erstattung** reimbursement of expenses (outlays); **~kurve** outlay curve; **~material** display equipment; **~material für Händler** dealer display.
Auslagenota disbursement account.
Auslagen|rechnung note of disbursements (expenses, *Br.*); **~stand** display stand; **~vorauszahlungen** advance, prepayment; **~werbung** *(auf Ladentisch)* counter display.

auslagern to take out of store, to withdraw from a warehouse, *(sicherstellen)* to dislocate, to evacuate.

Auslagerung withdrawal from a warehouse, *(Sicherstellung)* dislocation, evacuation.

Auslagerungsplan withdrawal plan.

Ausland foreign countries (parts), foreign country;
für das ~ bestimmt outward-bound, outbound; **im ~** in foreign parts, abroad; **im ~ geboren** foreign-born; **im ~ getätigt** offshore *(US)*; **im ~ hergestellt** foreign-built (made); **im ~ lebend** absentee; **im ~ zahlbar** payable abroad; **In- und ~** at home and abroad;
feindliches ~ enemy countries; **neutrales ~** neutral countries; **im ~ anlegen** to plough (plow, *US*) in foreign investments; **sich ständig im ~ aufhalten** to abide abroad; **Waren im ~ billig auf den Markt bringen** to dump goods on a foreign market; **sich im ~ eindecken** to draw one's supplies from abroad; **ins ~ gehen** to go abroad; **Beziehungen mit dem ~ haben** to have relations with foreign countries; **im ~ reisen** to travel abroad; **ins ~ schicken** to send abroad; **im ~ sein** to be in foreign parts *(Br.)*; **im ~ ansässig sein** to be domiciled abroad; **nach dem ~ bestimmt sein** to be bound for foreign parts; **vom ~ kontrolliert werden** to be controlled by foreign interests; **im ~ wohnen** to reside abroad; **aus dem ~ zurückkehren** to return from abroad.

Ausländer foreigner, foreign subject (national), alien, nonnational, outlander;
ansässiger ~ alien resident *(US)*; **befreundeter ~** friendly alien; **eingebürgerter ~** naturalized citizen, denizen *(US)*; **teilweise eingebürgerter ~** denizen; **feindlicher ~** enemy alien, alien enemy; **lästiger (unerwünschter) ~** undesirable person; **unerfahrener ~** greener *(sl.)*;
~ von Geburt alien née;
~ abschieben (ausweisen) to expel (deport) an alien; **~ abweisen** to turn back an alien; **~n gehören** to be under foreign ownership;
~amt aliens' registration office; **~ausweis** registration certificate *(Br.)*; **~behandlung** treatment of foreigners; **~eigenschaft** alienage, status of an alien, foreign nationality; **~erfassung** registration of foreign nationals *(Br.)*.

ausländerfeindlich hostile to foreigners.

Ausländer|gesetz Aliens Order *(Br.)*; **~gesetzgebung** alien laws; **~guthaben** external account; **~jury** half-tongue; **~konto** external account; **beschlagnahmtes ~konto** enemy property account; **~-DM-Konto** nonresident DM-account; **~kontrolle** aliens' control; **~konvertierbarkeit** convertibility for nonresidents, nonresident convertibility; **~polizei** aliens' registration office; **~registrierung** registration of aliens, alien registration; **~status** alienage; **~steuer** alien duty; **~vermögen** alien (foreign-owned) property.

ausländisch foreign, of foreign growth, alien, external, extraneous;
~e Absatzmärkte foreign markets; **~e Aktien** foreign shares (stocks) *(US)*; **~e Bankkredite** bank lendings abroad; **in ~em Besitz** foreign-owned; **in ~em Besitz stehen** to be under foreign ownership; **~e Besucher** visitors from abroad, foreign visitors; **~e Devisen** foreign currency; **~es Erzeugnis** foreign product; **~es Fabrikat** foreign [-made] product; **~es Gericht** foreign court; **~e Gerichtsbarkeit** foreign jurisdiction; **~e Gesellschaft** foreign (alien, *US*) corporation; **~e Guthaben** foreign-owned balances; **von ~em Kapital kontrolliert werden** to be controlled by foreign interests; **~es Konto** external account; **~e Presse** foreign press; **~e Pressestimmen** extract of foreign newspapers; **~es Schiff** foreigner; **~e Schuldverschreibungen** foreign currency bonds; **~e Vereinigung** external association; **~es Vermögen** alien (foreign-owned) property; **~e Vermögensverwaltung** alien property custodian *(US)*; **~e Verteilerstelle** offshore marshalling yard; **~e Währungen** foreign (offshore, *US*) currencies; **~e Wertpapiere** foreign securities (stocks); **~e Zahlungsmittel** foreign money (currency).

Auslands|absatz export (foreign) sales, sales abroad, foreign market; **~abteilung** foreign department; **~akkreditive** credits in foreign countries; **~aktie** foreign share (stock); **~akzept** foreign bill, bill accepted abroad; **~anfrage** foreign inquiry; **~anlagen** foreign investments, foreign assets, external assets; **~anleihe** external (foreign) loan; **DM-~anleihen** foreign DM bonds; **~aufenthalt** residence (stay, time spent) abroad, foreign sojourn; **vorübergehender geschäftsbedingter ~aufenthalt** temporary residence abroad for business.

Auslandsauftrag indent, export order, *(Rüstungsauftrag)* offshore order;
~ mit freier Einkaufsmöglichkeit open indent;
~ erteilen to indent.

Auslands|bank foreign (overseas, *US*) bank, foreign banking corporation *(US)*; **~beamter** foreign service officer; **~bedarf** foreign demand; **~belegenheit** offshore location; **~berichte** foreign coverage; **~berichterstatter** foreign correspondent; **~besitz** foreign holdings (ownership), assets held abroad, foreign-held assets; **~bestellung** indent, export order; **~bestellung einer Gattungsware** open indent; **~bestellung eines bestimmten Markenerzeugnisses** closed (specific) indent; **~besucher** foreign visitor; **~beteiligungen** foreign interests; **~beteiligung an einer Messe** foreign exhibitors; **~bevollmächtigter** foreign agent; **~beziehungen** foreign relations; **~beziehungen haben** to have connections abroad; **~bonds** external (foreign-currency) bonds; **~börse** foreign stock exchange; **~brief** foreign letter; **~briefverkehr** foreign mail service *(Br.)*; **~debatte** foreign-affairs debate; **~deutscher** German living abroad, German expatriate; **~dienst** service abroad, foreign service *(US)*; **~dienststelle** diplomatic agency; **~dollar** foreign dollar; **~einkommen** overseas income; **~einlagen** foreign deposits; **~emission** foreign [bonds] issue; **~emissionsgeschäft** international issuing business; **~engagements** foreign engagements (commitments); **~erfahrungen** experience acquired abroad; **~erträge** foreign earnings; **~erzeugnisse** foreign products; **~fabrikat** foreign make; **~fahrten** driving abroad; **~ferienreise** foreign holiday; **~filiale** foreign (overseas) branch; **~firma** foreign firm; **~forderungen** claims against foreign debtors, *(Bundesbank)* foreign assets; **~gebühr** *(Post)* foreign postage; **~gelder** foreign (floating) capital; **~geschäft** offshore (export) trade, *(einzelnes)* export business, external transaction; **~gesellschaft** foreign (overseas) company; **~gespräch** *(Telefon)* external (foreign, *US*) call, overseas (continental) call *(Br.)*, long-distance call; **~gläubiger** foreign creditor; **~gruppe** external group; **~guthaben** foreign assets (deposits, credit, balances), foreign-owned balances, assets held abroad; **saldierte ~guthaben** foreign assets position; **~guthaben auflösen** to repatriate foreign assets; **~hafen** foreign port; **~handel** export (foreign, external) trade.

Auslandshilfe foreign aid (assistance), foreign relief, external aid;
amerikanische ~ US-financed foreign aid;
~ einstellen to drop foreign aid; **~ gewähren** to pump in foreign aid.

Auslandshilfs|abkommen foreign-aid program(me); **~amt der USA** Foreign Operations Administration; **~etat** foreign-aid budget; **~fonds** foreign-aid fund *(US)*; **~gelder** foreign-aid spending *(US)*; **~gesetz** Foreign Aid Appropriations Act *(US)*; **~programm** foreign-aid program *(US)*; **~projekt** foreign-aid project; **~zusagen** foreign-aid grants.

Auslandsinvestitionen capital invested abroad, foreign investments, investments abroad;
~ vornehmen to plough (plow, *US*) in foreign investments.

Auslandsinvestitionsgesetz Foreign Investment Law.

Auslandskapital foreign (outside) capital;
~ anziehen to bring foreign capital to a country;
~anlagen investments abroad.

Auslands|kartell foreign cartel; **~käufe** *(Kriegsmaterial)* offshore purchases *(US)*; **~konkurrenz** foreign competition, competition from abroad; **~konkurrenz eindämmen** to curb foreign competition; **~kontenbereich** external accounts area; **~konto** foreign deposit, *(Ausländer)* nonresident account; **nicht angegebenes ~konto** undeclared foreign bank account; **~kontrolle** foreign control; **~korrespondent** *(Bank)* foreign correspondent clerk; **~korrespondenz** foreign correspondence; **~kredit** external (foreign) credit, foreign loan; **~kredite** lending to nonresidents (foreigners); **~kunde** foreign customer; **~kundschaft** foreign clients; **~lieferungen** export shipments, deliveries overseas; **~luftverkehr** extraterritorial air traffic; **~markt** export (foreign) market, outlet for export trade; **vom ~markt ausschließen** to shut out of the foreign market; **~märkte mit allen Mitteln erschließen** to grab markets abroad; **~mitteilungen** external communications; **~nachfrage** external (foreign) demand; **~nachrichten** foreign news, news from abroad, external communications; **~niederlassung** overseas branch; **~notierung** quotation on a foreign market; **~obligation** foreign bonds, foreigners *(Br.)*, securities of a foreign government; **~paket** foreign parcel; **~paketgebühr** overseas parcel rate; **~paß** passport; **~patent** foreign patent; **~patent anmelden** to file an application for a patent abroad; **~pension** foreign pension; **~porto, ~posttarif** foreign rate (postage), foreign postage rates, overseas postage rates *(Br.)*; **~post** overseas postage (post) *(Br.)*, overseas mail *(Br.)*, outward (foreign) mail *(US)*; **~postanweisung** international (foreign) money order, overseas ordinary money order.

Auslandsposten *(Diplomat)* overseas post (assignment), posting.

Auslandspost | karte foreign postcard; ~**tarif** foreign (overseas, *Br.*) postage, overseas postage rates *(Br.)*; ~**verkehr** external mail service *(US)*.

Auslands | präsenz presence abroad; ~**preis** foreign price; ~**presse** foreign press; ~**produkt** foreign product; ~**projekt** foreign-aid project *(US)*; ~**redakteur** foreign-news editor.

Auslandsreise foreign voyage (journey, excursion, travel), foreign trip, journey abroad;
sich eine ~ leisten to afford o. s. a trip abroad; **auf ~ sein** *(Schiff)* to be in the foreign trade; **auf eine ~ geschickt werden** to be ordered abroad.

Auslands | reiseverkehr foreign travel; ~**reserven** off-shore reserves; ~**scheck** foreign check *(US)* (cheque, *Br.*); ~**schrifttum** foreign literature; ~**schulden** debts abroad, foreign debts, external debts; ~**schuldendienst** foreign-debts service; ~**schuldverschreibungen** external bonds; ~**schule** foreign school; ~**sender** foreign station; ~**sendung** foreign shipment, *(Rundfunk)* foreign broadcast; ~**spediteur** foreign shipper; **bezahlte ~steuer** foreign tax suffered; ~**stimmen** *(Zeitung)* extract of foreign newspapers; ~**stipendiat** British Council scholar *(Br.)*; ~**stipendium** travelling fellowship; ~**telefongespräch** external (foreign, long-distance) call, overseas (continental, *Br.*) call; ~**telegramm** international telegram; ~**testamentsvollstrecker** foreign administrator; ~**tochter** foreign subsidiary (affiliate), nonresident subsidiary; ~**tournee machen** to tour foreign countries; ~**überweisung** remittance abroad; **besteuerte ~überweisung** remittance assessed; **steuerlich den Tatbestand einer ~überweisung erfüllen** to constitute a remittance; ~**umsatz** export (foreign) sales; **umfangreiche ~umsätze** extensive sales overseas; ~**urlaub** foreign vacation; ~**urteil** foreign judgment; ~**verbindlichkeiten** external (foreign) liabilities; **mindestreservepflichtige ~verbindlichkeiten** reserve-carrying foreign liabilities; ~**verbindungen** foreign relations; ~**verhandlungen** overseas negotiations; ~**verkäufe** export (foreign) sales, *(Börse)* foreign liquidations; ~**verkehr** export (external, foreign) traffic; ~**vermögen** external assets (property), assets held abroad, foreign property (possessions); ~**verpflichtungen** foreign liabilities; ~**verschuldung** foreign debts (indebtedness); ~**vertreter** foreign representative (agent); ~**vertretung** diplomatic representation, *(Firma)* representation abroad, representative office abroad; ~**verwendung** *(dipl.)* overseas assignment, posting; ~**vorhaben** foreign-aid project *(US)*; ~**währung** foreign currency; ~**ware** foreign goods; ~**wechsel** foreign bill of exchange, bill in foreign currency; ~**werbung** foreign advertising; ~**wert** foreign value, *(beim Zoll)* foreign valuation; ~**werte** *(Börse)* external assets, foreign stock (securities), foreigners; ~**wohnsitz** foreign domicile; ~**wohnsitz haben** to be resident abroad; ~**wohnung** foreign domicile; ~**zahlung** foreign payment; ~**zahlungsverkehr** foreign payments (transfer); ~**zufuhr** imports; ~**zulage** [foreign service] expatriation allowance *(US)*.

auslassen to omit, to leave out, *(überspringen)* to skip, to pass over;
sich über etw. ~ to express o. s. about s. th.; **Gelegenheit ~** to miss a chance; **seine schlechte Laune an jem. ~** to vent one's ill temper upon s. o.; **Mittagessen ~** to cut out lunch; **sich negativ über j. ~** to speak disparagingly about s. o.; **keinen Tanz ~** not to miss a dance; **sich weitläufig über etw. ~** to branch out into dissertation, to dwell at length on s. th.

Auslassung omission, skip, *(Bericht)* diminution, *(Text)* gap; ~**en** *(Äußerungen)* remarks, utterances;
Irrtümer und ~en vorbehalten errors and omissions excepted; **langatmige ~en** expatiations;
stillschweigende ~ von Einzelheiten jumping over of details; **sich in längeren ~en ergehen** to deal at length about.

Auslassungs | punkte pause dots; ~**zeichen** *(drucktechn.)* caret.

Auslaßventil outlet (escape, exhaust).

auslasten to balance, to equalize, *(Werk)* to employ (run, use) to capacity;
Maschinenanlage restlos ~ to utilize the whole power of a machine.

Auslastung *(Betrieb)* working to capacity, *(Flugzeug)* load factor; **~ der Fertigungsanlagen** production load.

Auslastungsgrad der industriellen Kapazitäten, geringer low level of industrial capacity utilization.

Auslauf outlet, drain, discharge, *(Flugzeug)* landing run, *(Tiere)* run, space, room;
~**ausgaben** deferred budget expenditure; ~**befehl** sailing orders.

auslaufbereit ready to sail.

Auslaufen spillage, *(Flugzeug)* landing run, *(Investition)* fade-out, *(Produktion)* phasing out, *(Schiff)* sailing, leaving a port, departure, start, *(Vertrag)* expiration, expiry;
am ~ verhindert *(Schiff)* weather-bound;
~ eines Patents expiry (lapse) of a patent;
zum ~ bereit sein to be ready to sail.

auslaufen *(Artikel)* to be discontinued, *(Fahrzeug)* to stop running, *(Farben)* to bleed, *(Flüssigkeit)* to spill, to run (flow) out, *(Investition)* to fade out, *(Lager)* to wear out, *(Patent)* to expire, to phase out, *(Produktion)* to be on its way out, *(Schiff)* to sail, to go under sail, to put to sea, to clear the harbo(u)r, to leave port, to put forth (off) to sea, *(Tank)* to run dry, *(Vertrag)* to run out, to expire, *(Wärmflasche)* to be leaking, *(Zug)* to leave the station;
fahrplanmäßig ~ to sail to schedule *(US)*; **mit dem Gezeitenstrom ein- und ~** to tide; **aus einem Sack ~** to spill out of a sack; **sich tüchtig ~ können** to have plenty of exercise; **Auto ~ lassen** to let the car coast; **Erzeugnisse mit niedriger Gewinnspanne produktionsmäßig ~ lassen** to phase out low- margin products; **Produktion ~ lassen** to stop (taper off) production.

auslaufend *(Schiff)* outward bound, outbound, *(Vertrag)* expiring;
~e Termingelder maturing time deposits.

Ausläufer errand boy, messenger, *(Erdbeben)* coda, *(Gebirge)* foothills, *(Hoch)* spur, ride, *(Tief)* trough;
~ einer Stadt outskirts (fringes) of a city.

Auslauf | formel fade-out formula; ~**genehmigung** clearance; ~**hafen** port of departure; ~**hahn** drain cock; **auf ~kurs liegen** to stand out [to sea]; ~**modell** discontinued line; ~**rohr** outlet (discharge) pipe; ~**strecke** *(Flugzeug)* landing run.

ausleben, sich richtig to sow one's wild oats.

ausleeren to empty, to drain;
Briefkasten ~ to clear a letter (pillar, *Br.*) box.

auslegbar interpretable, construable, explicable;
verschieden ~ capable of varying interpretations.

Auslegen *(Bogen)* taking off, delivery, *(Waren)* display, layout, exposition;
~ der bedruckten Bogen delivery of the printed sheets.

auslegen *(deuten)* to interpret, to construe, *(drucktechn.)* to deliver, *(Geld)* to lay out, to disburse, to expend, to outlay, *(Patent)* to lay open, *(vorstrecken)* to advance, *(Ware)* to exhibit, to dispose, to display for sale;
für j. etw. ~ to pay for s. o.; **Bücher zum Verkauf ~** to display books for sale; **buchstäblich ~** to literalize; **einschränkend (eng) ~** to put a restrictive interpretation on, to interpret strictly; **zur Einsicht ~** to make available for inspection; **falsch ~** to construe wrongly, to misinterpret, to misread, to misconstrue; **Boden mit Fliesen ~** to tile a floor; **Geld ~** to make outlays of money *(US)*; **Gesetz ~** to expound a law; **Gesetz einschränkend ~** to interpret a law restrictively; **Kabel ~** to lay out a cable; **Netze ~** to put out nets; **Punkt zu jds. Gunsten ~** to stretch a point in s. one's favo(u)r; **Schublade mit Papier ~** to line a drawer with paper; **jds. Schweigen falsch ~** to misunderstand s. one's silence; **Stelle anders ~** to interpret a passage differently; **Testament ~** to construe a will; **Text ~** to open a text; **Tonnen ~** to stream buoys; **jds. Verhalten als Schwäche ~** to interpret s. one's behavio(u)r as weakness; **Vertrag ~** to interpret a contract; **Waren im Schaufenster ~** to exhibit goods in a shop window; **weit ~** to put a wide interpretation on, to interpret extensively; **Bestimmung weit ~** to construe a clause extensively (liberally); **jds. Worte ganz anders ~** to put quite another construction on s. one's words; **jds. Worte zu weit ~** to press s. one's words too far; **Zimmer mit Linoleum ~** to lay down a floor with linoleum; **Zimmer mit Teppichen ~** to cover a room with carpets;
sich so und so ~ lassen to read both ways.

Ausleger *(mar.)* boom, *(drucktechn.)* flyer, fly;
~**brücke** cantilever bridge.

Auslege | schrift *(Patent)* patent specification; ~**tisch** *(drucktechn.)* delivery table; ~**ware** articles shown in the window.

Auslegung interpretation, reading, construction, exposition;
amtliche ~ statutory exposition; **anerkannte ~** established interpretation; **ausdehnbare ~** extensive interpretation; **buchstäbliche ~** literalism; **einschränkende ~** restrictive interpretation; **enge ~** limited (close, rigid, narrow) interpretation, narrow construction; **extensive ~** extensive (liberal) construction; **falsche ~** wrong construction, misinterpretation, misconstruction; **freie ~** free interpretation; **freundliche ~** charitable construction; **gekünstelte ~** artificial construction; **gerichtliche ~** court interpretation; **gewaltsame ~** violent interpretation; **gezwungene (forcierte) ~** strained interpreta-

tion, strain, distortion; **großzügige** ~ wide definition; **individuelle** ~ private interpretation; **maßgebliche** ~ authentic interpretation, authoritative construction; **moralische** ~ moralization; **richterliche** ~ judicial interpretation; **richtige** ~ proper interpretation; **strenge** ~ strict construction; **übliche** ~ customary interpretation; **unberechtigte (unzulässig weite)** ~ extravagant interpretation; **ungezwungene** ~ liberal interpretation; **vergleichende** ~ comparative interpretation; **weite** ~ extensive (liberal) construction; **weitgehende** ~ broad interpretation; **wörtliche** ~ literal construction, literalization; **zwingende** ~ necessary implication;
möglichst wohlwollende ~ **des Erblasserwillens** *(Erbrecht)* Cyprès doctrine; ~ **von Gesetzen** statutory interpretation; ~ **eines Textes** exposition of a text;
falsche (unrichtige) ~ **von etw. vornehmen** to put a false interpretation on s. th.; **zwei** ~**en zulassen** to admit (to be patient) of two interpretations.

Auslegungs|bestimmungen interpretation clause; ~**frage** matter of construction; ~**grundsätze** principles of interpretation; ~**grundsätze bei Testamentsnachträgen** dependent relative revocation; **mehrere** ~**möglichkeiten** several interpretations; **zwei** ~**möglichkeiten zulassen** to admit of two interpretations; ~**protokoll** protocol of interpretation; ~**regeln** rules (canons) of construction; ~**spielraum** permissiveness; ~**weise** method of interpretation.

ausleihbar borrowable.

Ausleihbücherei lending library.

Ausleihe|von Büchern issuing of books; ~ **von 10 - 12** *(Bibliothek)* books are issued between ten and twelve.

Ausleihemöglichkeiten borrowing facilities.

Ausleihen lending, borrowing, loan.

ausleihen to lend [out], to hire out *(US)*, to loan [out] *(US)*;
Bücher ~ to lend out books; **Bücher aus der Bibliothek** ~ to borrow books from a library; **Geld auf Zinsen** ~ to lend money on (at) interest; **sich Geld** ~ to borrow money; **an kreditbedürftige Kaufleute** ~ to lend to cash-hungry businessmen; **langfristig** ~ to borrow long; **auf Zinsen** ~ to loan (lend) on interest.

Ausleiher lender, borrower, *(Pfandleiher)* pawnbroker.

Ausleiheverpflichtungen lending obligations.

Ausleih|karte *(Bibliothek)* book card; ~**schalter** *(Bibliothek)* loan desk.

Ausleihung lending, borrowing.

Ausleihungen lendings, borrowings, loans;
langfristige ~ long-term borrowing;
~ **am Geldmarkt** short-term borrowings; **langfristige** ~ **im Hypothekenbankgeschäft** long-term mortgage bank business; ~ **mit einer Laufzeit von mindestens vier Jahren** loans for a term of at least four years; ~ **im Kontokorrentverkehr** lending on current account; ~ **im kurzfristigen Kreditgeschäft** short-term borrowings; ~ **an Kunden** advances to customers; ~ **an Nichtbanken** lending to nonbank customers; ~ **zu gleichbleibenden Zinssätzen** fixed-interest borrowing.

Ausleihungs|bedingungen lending terms; ~**befugnis** public lending right, lending power; ~**höchstgrenze für Personalkredite anheben** to raise the limit on personal loans; **gebührenpflichtiges** ~**recht** public lending right; ~**sätze** borrowing (lending, *US*) rates; ~**verpflichtungen** lending obligations; ~**volumen zurückschrauben** to reduce the volume of lending.

auslernen to finish (serve) one's apprenticeship.

Auslese selection, choice, pick, flower, elite, sorting, cream, *(literarisch)* digest, anthology, *(Sortiment)* assortment;
natürliche ~ natural selection;
~ **treffen** to make a selection;
~**bedingungen** screening standards *(US)*.

auslesen *(aussortieren)* to sort [out], to single out, *(auswählen)* to choose, to select, to pick, to cull, *(Buch)* to finish reading.

Auslese|prozeß sifting process; ~**prüfung** competitive examination, screening test *(US)*; ~**verfahren** selection process (procedure), screening process; ~**vorrichtung** sorter.

ausleuchten to illuminate, to floodlight.

Ausleuchtung illumination.

auslieferbar extraditable.

Auslieferer deliverer, supplier.

ausliefern to hand over, to surrender, *(Dokumente)* to surrender, *(Staatsangehörige)* to extradite, to surrender, *(Ware)* to deliver, to supply;
Bücher ~ to deliver books; **Festung** ~ to surrender a fortress; **j. dem Gericht** ~ to turn s. o. over to the law; **sich jem. auf Gnade und Ungnade** ~ to throw o. s. upon s. one's mercy, to place o. s. in s. one's power; **Verbrecher an seinen Heimatstaat** ~ to extradite a criminal to his own country.

Auslieferung completed delivery, supply, *(Effekten)* surrender, delivery, *(fremde Staatsangehörige)* extradition;
gegen ~ **von** against delivery of; **zahlbar bei** ~ cash on delivery; **zur** ~ **zum ...** to be delivered at ...;
bevorzugte ~ priority delivery;
~ **per LKW** delivery by road; ~ **auf dem Luftwege** use of airfreight in delivery; ~ **flüchtiger Straftäter** surrender of fugitives; ~ **der Verladepapiere (Schiffspapiere) gegen Bezahlung** documents against payment;
~ **ablehnen** *(dipl.)* to refuse extradition.

Auslieferungs|abteilung delivery (traffic) department; ~**antrag,** ~**begehren** *(dipl.)* requisition, extradition order; ~**anweisung** delivery (pickup) order; ~**aufgaben auf das Speditionsgewerbe übertragen** to subcontract the delivery functions to professional carriers; ~**auftrag** delivery order; ~**bedingungen** terms of delivery; ~**bescheinigung** certificate of delivery, delivery ticket; ~**bestimmungen** *(dipl.)* extradition rules; ~**buch** delivery book; ~**depot** *(mil.)* general depot; ~**ersuchen** *(dipl.)* requisition, extradition order; ~**fahrer** deliveryman; ~**gebiet** area of supply; ~**gebühr** delivery charge; ~**gewicht** delivered weight; ~**gründe** *(dipl.)* grounds for extradition; ~**hafen** delivery port; ~**klausel** delivery clause; ~**lager** deposit, repository, supply store, field inventory, local supply station, distribution warehouse, distributing stock, receiving house *(Br.)*, *(Buchhandel)* trade department; ~**leiter** warehouse manager; ~**ort** delivery place.

auslieferungspflichtiges Verbrechen extraditable offence.

Auslieferungs|prämie delivery bonus; ~**recht** *(dipl.)* extradition law; ~**schein** delivery note (slip, ticket), mate's receipt; ~**stelle** distribution centre *(Br.)* (center, *US*), delivery station *(US)*; ~**stelle eines Versandhausunternehmens** mail-order store *(US)*; **gemeinsames** ~**system mehrerer Firmen** consolidated delivery system; ~**tag** day of delivery, delivery date; ~**verfahren** *(dipl.)* extradition proceedings; ~**vertrag** delivery contract, *(dipl.)* extradition treaty, cartel; ~**verweigerung** refusal to deliver; ~**zettel** delivery note (slip).

ausliegen to lie on the desk, *(Waren)* to be exposed for sale, to be displayed, *(Zeitungen)* to be available, to be kept (taken in, *Br.*);
zur öffentlichen Einsicht ~ to be open to public inspection; **in der Hotelhalle** ~ to be found in the lobby; **zur Prüfung** ~ to be available for examination.

ausliquidieren to liquidate a bankrupt's affairs.

ausloben to offer a reward.

Auslobung offer made to the world at large, general offer, award;
~ **vornehmen** to offer an award.

auslöffeln, was man sich eingebrockt hat to lie in the bed one has made, to have to face the music.

auslosbar callable by lot.

auslösbar redeemable.

auslöschbar effaceable.

auslöschen to extinguish, to quench, to efface, *(Schrift)* to efface, to obliterate, to blur out, *(vernichten)* to annihilate, to extinguish, to wipe out, *(Worte)* to erase;
Feuer ~ to put out (quench) a fire; **Kerze** ~ to snuff out a candle; **elektrisches Licht** ~ to switch off the electric light; **seine Zigarette** ~ to stub (put) out one's cigarette.

Auslöschung defacement, effacement, obliteration;
~ **eines ganzen Volkes** annihilation of a people.

Auslöse|hebel release lever; ~**knopf** releaser.

auslosen to draw by lot, to allot, *(mit einer Münze)* to toss;
Obligationen ~ to draw bonds.

auslösen to touch off, to ungear, to remove, to release, *(hervorrufen)* to arouse, to spark off, to call forth;
Alarm ~ to release an alarm; **Aufstand** ~ to work up a rebellion; **allgemeine Bewunderung** ~ to elicit universal admiration; **Bomben** ~ to release bombs; **Gefangenen** ~ to ransom a prisoner; **Kettenreaktion** ~ to start a chain reaction; **Kupplung** ~ to declutch, to disengage the clutch; **Mechanismus** ~ to release a mechanism; **Pfand** ~ to redeem a pawn; **Revolution** ~ to spark off a revolution; **kostspieligen Streik** ~ to trigger off a costly strike; **soziale Unruhen** ~ to create social unrest; **Verschluß** ~ to release a shutter, to trigger.

Auslöser *(phot.)* release.

Auslöse|schalter trip switch; ~**vorrichtung** trip, tripper, release gear.

Auslosung *(Effekten)* drawing [by lot], drawing for redemption, *(Lotterie)* [prize] draw, *(Preise)* prize drawing;
im Wege der ~ by drawing;
nächste ~ current drawing;

~**en dieses Monats** this month's draw; ~ **zur Rückzahlung** drawing for redemption; ~ **der Schöffen** calling of the jury; ~ **von Wertpapieren** raffle;
an der ~ teilnehmen to be eligible for inclusion in the draw.

Auslösung release, redemption, *(Lösegeld)* ransom, *(Trennungsgeld)* severance pay, separation allowance;
~ **von Bomben** release of bombs; ~ **einer Kettenreaktion** start of a chain reaction; ~ **der Ladung** ransom of cargo; ~ **eines Pfandes** redemption of a pledge; ~ **eines Verschlusses** release of a shutter.

Auslosungs|anleihe prize (lottery) bonds; ~**fonds** prize fund; ~**liste** list of drawings; ~**nummer** number drawn; ~**preis** redemption price.

Auslösungsrecht redemption right, right of redemption;
vertragliches ~ contractual right to redeem;
~ **des Hypothekenschuldners** right of equity of redemption *(US)*.

Auslosungs|schein letter of allotment, drawing certificate; ~**termin** drawing date; ~**verfahren** *(Statistik)* lottery sampling.

ausloten to sound, to plumb.

Auslotsen pilotage.

auslotsen *(Schiff)* to pilot a ship.

Auslotsung pilotage.

ausmachen to amount (come, run up) to, to reach, to total, *(ausbedingen)* to stipulate, to condition, to fix *(US)*, *(ausschalten)* to turn (switch) off, *(bilden)* to constitute, to form, to make up, *(entdecken)* to trace, to find, *(Flugzeug, Schiff)* to locate, to spot, *(vereinbaren)* to settle, to arrange, to agree;
jds. ganzen Besitz ~ to constitute s. one's entire estate; **wesentlichen Bestandteil von etw.** ~ to be part and parcel of s. th.; **Erhebliches** ~ to matter a good deal; **etw.** ~ to make a difference; **etw. fest** ~ to make a definite arrangement; **etw. mit jem.** ~ to arrange with s. o.; **kaum etw.** ~ to hardly matter at all; **Licht** ~ to turn out (switch off) the light; **j. in einer Menschenmenge** ~ to distinguish (spot) s. o. in a crowd; **Preis** ~ to settle (agree on) a price; **Schiff am Horizont** ~ to discern a ship on the horizon; **beträchtliche Summe** ~ to amount to quite a lot of money; **größeren Teil der Einkünfte** ~ to form the greater part (bulk) of s. one's income; **wesentlichen Teil der Produktion** ~ to form the bulk of production; **Termin** ~ to agree about a date; **Treffpunkt** ~ to arrange for a meeting place; **untereinander** ~ to settle between themselves; **viel** ~ to matter a lot.

ausmachender Betrag final amount.

ausmalen to paint, *(Erzählung)* to embroider, to amplify;
Plan in allen Einzelheiten ~ to work out every detail of a plan; **sich die Zukunft in den rosigsten Farben** ~ to picture the future to o. s. in the rosiest colo(u)rs.

ausmanövrieren to outmanoeuvre;
j. ~ to outflank s. o.; **seine Gegner** ~ to dish one's opponents *(coll.)*.

Ausmarsch departure.

Ausmaß degree, extent, scope, scale;
in einem erschreckenden ~ at a fearful rate; **in geringem** ~ to a slight degree; **in einem großen** ~ on a large scale, to a large extent; **in größerem** ~ to a higher degree; **größten** ~**es** full-scale; **von gewaltigem** ~ of huge proportions;
~**e** proportions;
~ **einer Katastrophe** scale of a disaster; ~ **des Schadens** extent of damage; ~**e eines Zimmers** dimensions of a room;
ungeahnte ~**e annehmen** to take on vast dimensions; **Reformen größten** ~**es durchführen** to carry out sweeping reforms; ~ **des Erträglichen übersteigen** to be beyond endurance.

ausmerzen to eliminate, to weed out;
anstößige Buchstellen ~ to expurgate (bowdlerize) a book.

Ausmerzung elimination, *(anstößiger Stellen)* expurgation, bowdlerization.

ausmessen to [ad]measure, to take the measurements, to gauge, to lay off, *(Faß)* to gauge, to take the gauge;
Entfernung ~ to measure a distance; **Grundstück** ~ to survey property for its extent; **Zimmer der Länge nach** ~ to measure the length of a room.

Ausmessung [ad]measurement.

ausmisten *(fig.)* to weed, to muck out;
Augiasstall ~ to cleanse the Augean stables; **Augiasstall einer Stadt** ~ to clean up a city.

ausmünzen to coin, to mint.

Ausmünzung mintage, coinage.

ausmustern to reject, to discard, to single out, to cast off, *(mil.)* to exempt from military service, *(Ware)* to reject, to discard, to single out, to cast off.

Ausmusterung *(mil.)* exemption from military service, *(Soldat)* discharge, *(Ware)* rejection, discarding.

Ausnahme exception, *(Vorbehalt)* reserve, proviso;
mit ~ gegenteiliger Bestimmungen save as otherwise provided for; **mit einigen** ~**n** with a few exceptions; **mit wenigen** ~**n unverändert** *(Börse)* spotted; **ohne** ~ without reserve;
einzige ~ solitary exception; **geringe** ~**n** marginal exceptions; **gesetzliche** ~ statutory exception;
~ **von der Regel** exception to a rule;
~ **bilden** to be exceptional; **bei jem. eine** ~ **machen** to make an exception in s. one's case; **keine** ~ **zulassen** to admit of no exception;
~**n bestätigen die Regel** the exceptions prove the rule;
~**angebot** special (exceptional) offer; ~**bescheinigung** exempting certificate; ~**bestimmung** exception, saving (exceptive) clause, exemption (exceptional) provision; ~**bewilligung** exceptional grant, dispensation; ~**bewilligung erteilen** to dispense; ~**erlaubnis** special licence, permit; ~**fall** case for exemption, exception to the rule, special (exceptional) case; ~**frachtsätze** differential rates; ~**genehmigung** special licence (permit), *(Bauvorhaben)* nonconfirming use; ~**genehmigung von den Bebauungsvorschriften** zoning variance *(US)*; ~**genehmigung erteilen** to dispense, to grant an exemption; ~**gericht** court of special jurisdiction; ~**gerichtsbarkeit** special jurisdiction; ~**gesetz** special (exceptive) law; ~**gesetzgebung** emergency measures; ~**gründe** special reasons; ~**klausel** exemption clause *(Br.)*; ~**preis** special (extra, exceptional) price; ~**prinzip** principle of exemption; ~**recht** exemption privilege; ~**regelung** exemption; **mit** ~**sätzen besteuert werden** to be subject to special income-tax rules; ~**stellung** special privilege, exemption, exceptional position; ~**tarif** differential (special) rates, exceptional rates, exceptional tariff, preferential tariff; ~**verfügung**, ~**verordnung** exemption (provisional) order; ~**vorrecht** exemption privilege.

Ausnahmezustand state of national emergency;
im ~ under martial law;
~ **über ein Gebiet verhängen** to proclaim a district.

ausnahms|los all and singular, hard and fast; ~**weise** by want of exception.

Ausnehmen der Ladenkasse knockdown *(US sl.)*.

ausnehmen to except, to exempt, to do up brown *(sl.)*;
j. ~ to make an exception of s. o., *(Geld abnehmen)* to clean s. o. out, to fleece s. o.; **sich in einem Aufzug sonderbar** ~ to cut a queer figure in a getup; **jds. Geldbeutel** ~ to drain s. one's purse; **sich gut** ~ to look well; **Nest** ~ to rob (take) a nest; **feindliche Stellung** ~ to destroy an enemy position; **j. nach Strich und Faden** ~ to turn and rend s. o.; **j. total** ~ to take s. o. to the cleaners *(sl.)*; **j. von einer Verordnung** ~ to exempt s. o. from a regulation.

ausnehmend exceptional, outstanding, extreme, exceeding.

Ausnüchterungszelle detoxification cell, fish tank *(sl.)*.

ausnutzen to make use of, to use, to utilize, *(Arbeiter)* to sweat, *(Bergwerk)* to exploit, to work, *(profitieren)* to turn to account, to make profit of;
j. ~ *(fam.)* to sponge on s. o., to make a convenience of s. o., to take undue advantage of s. o., to weather upon s. o.; **neue Bekanntschaft dreist** ~ to presume on a short acquaintance; **Betriebsanlagen** ~ to operate facilities, to utilize plant capacities; **seine Freunde** ~ to exploit one's friends; **jds. Geduld** ~ to tax s. one's patience; **Gelegenheit** ~ to make the most of an opportunity; **jds. Gutgläubigkeit** ~ to play upon s. one's good nature; **Idee** ~ to cash in on an idea; **jds. ungünstige Lage** ~ to get the drop on s. o. *(US coll.)*; **jds. Leichtgläubigkeit** ~ to practise upon s. one's credulity; **j. bis zum letzten** ~ to work s. o. for all he is worth *(sl.)*; **Monopolstellung** ~ to discriminate a monopoly; **rationell** ~ to utilize effectively; **jds. Schwäche** ~ to take unfair advantage of s. one's weakness; **Skonto** ~ to take cash discount; **seine gesellschaftliche Stellung** ~ to pull rank *(sl.)*; **jds. Unwissenheit** ~ to trade upon s. one's ignorance; **voll** ~ to make full use of; **j. in gemeiner Weise** ~ to play it low on s. o.; **in sittenwidriger Weise** ~ to take undue advantage; **j. in der widerlichsten Weise** ~ to take a mean advantage of s. o.; **seine Zeit gut** ~ to make the most of (improve) one's time; **seine Zeit restlos** ~ to run things fine.

Ausnutzung use, utilization, employment, *(Arbeiter)* sweating, *(Bergwerk)* exploitation, *(Wirtschaftlichkeit)* economy;
mißbräuchliche ~ improper advantage; **rationelle** ~ rational (efficient) employment, effective utilization; **schamlose** ~ naked exploitation; **sittenwidrige** ~ taking undue advantage;
~ **von Betriebsanlagen** operation of facilities, utilization of plant capacities; ~ **von Betriebserfindungen durch den Firmen-**

inhaber shop right; **volle ~ der Betriebskapazität** full utilization of plant capacity; **diskriminierende ~ einer Monopolstellung** discriminating monopoly.
Ausnutzungsfaktor efficiency factor.
auspacken to unpack, to unwrap, to pack out;
gründlich ~ to let fly, to speak one's mind, to squeal *(coll.)*; **Waren aus dem Ballen ~** to unbale (uncase) goods; **Waren aus einer Kiste ~** to uncase (unbox) goods.
auspendeln, sich *(Zinssätze)* to stabilize at a certain level.
auspfänden, j. to sell s. o. up; **Schuldner ~** to inquire into the assets of a debtor.
auspfeifen to boo;
j. ~ *(Theater)* to hiss off the stage, to give s. o. the bird.
Auspizien auspices;
unter den ~ des Bürgermeisters under the patronage of the mayor.
ausplappern, Geheimnis to blurt out a secret.
Ausplaudern giveaway.
ausplaudern to let out, to give away, to open one's mouth, to tell *(coll.)*;
Geheimnis ~ to reveal a secret; **öffentlich ~** to put it on the street.
ausplazieren, j. to make a nonhero of s. o.
ausplündern to plunder, to loot, to ransack, *(Kasse)* to rob, to pillage;
Haus ~ to gut a house; **j. bis aufs Hemd ~** to strip s. o. to the skin; **j. völlig ~** to suck s. o. dry, to bleed s. o. white, to clean s. o. out; **Land völlig ~** to drain a country, to strip a country of its wealth; **Markt durch Spekulationsmanöver ~** to milk the market.
Ausplünderung pillage, plunder, loot, sack.
auspolstern to pad;
Auto ~ to upholster a car.
ausposaunen to trumpet, to blazon;
Sache überall ~ to broadcast a business, to cry from the housetops.
Ausposauner trumpet.
ausprägen to coin, to monetize, to mint;
geringwertig ~ to coin below standard; **sich in einem Gesicht ~** to be stamped on s. one's face.
Ausprägung mintage, coinage.
auspressen *(Früchte)* to wring;
Apfelsine ~ to press juice out of an orange; **j. bis auf den letzten Tropfen ~** to drain s. o. dry.
Ausprobieren trial, testing;
Maschine kostenlos zum ~ zusenden to send a machine for free trial.
ausprobieren to try [out], to test, *(Wein)* to taste;
etw. ~ to have a go (try) at s. th., to try s. th. out, to give s. th. a whirl *(US)*; **Maschine weiter ~** to put a machine to trial;
~, wie weit man bei jem. gehen kann to try it on with s. o. *(sl.)*.
ausprobiert tested;
nicht ~ unexperienced.
Auspuff exhaust;
~klappe cutout; **~kontrolle** exhaust control; **~rohr** exhaust pipe; **~topf** silencer *(Br.)*, muffle *(US)*; **~ventil** exhaust (escape) valve.
auspumpen to pump out;
Schiff ~ to free a ship.
ausquartieren to dislocate, to dislodge, to lodge elsewhere, to turn out of a lodging.
Ausquartierung dislodgement, dislocation.
ausquatschen, alles to spill the beans *(US sl.)*.
ausquetschen to wring;
j. ~ to pump s. o., to suck s. one's brains; **Verdächtigen ~** to pump (grill, *US*) a suspected person.
ausradieren to delete, to erase, to scratch out;
ganze Stadt ~ to coventrize (coventrate) a town, to wipe a whole city off the map.
ausradiert off the map *(sl.)*;
~e Stelle erasion, rasure.
Ausradierung erasement.
Ausrangieren scrapping, *(Betriebseinheit)* discarding, discardment, *(Schiff)* disrating.
ausrangieren to sort out, to scrap, to cast [out], to throw away, to junk *(sl.)*, *(Betriebseinheit)* to discard, *(Schiff)* to disrate, *(Waggon)* to shunt off;
alten Anzug ~ to discard an old suit; **Überflüssiges ~** to weed out dead wood.
ausrangiert cast off, discarded, on the shelf.
ausrauben to rob, to plunder, to pillage, to mug *(US sl.)*, to kick over *(US sl.)*;
Bank ~ to stick up a bank *(sl.)*; **Wohnung vollständig ~** to ransack a flat completely.
ausräuchern, Feind to smoke out an enemy; **Verbrechernest ~** to round up a band of criminals.
ausräumen to clear, to empty, *(Dieb)* to strip an apartment;
Bedenken ~ to remove scruples; **Haus ~** to remove the furniture from a house; **Meinungsverschiedenheiten ~** to overcome differences of opinion; **Mißverständnisse ~** to clear up misunderstandings; **Schwierigkeiten ~** to clear (smooth) away difficulties; **Wohnung ~** to unfurnish an apartment; **Zweifel ~** to dispel doubts.
ausrechnen to compute, to calculate, to count out, to work (figure) out, *(zusammenzählen)* to cast (add) up, to reckon;
falsch ~ to miscalculate; **Betrag im Kopf ~** to do (work out) a sum in one's head; **Kosten ~** to calculate (figure up) the cost; **jds. Unkostenanteil ~** to work out s. one's share of expenses; **Zinsen ~** to work out (cast) interest.
Ausrechnung calculation, computation, *(Zusammenzählung)* reckoning;
~ der zu zahlenden Einkommensteuern income-tax computation; **~ des Wechselkurses** computation of exchange.
Ausrede evasion, [professed] excuse, pretext, subterfuge, put off, alibi;
billige ~ poor (thin) excuse; **faule ~** shuffling answer, cop-out, lame excuse; **jämmerliche ~** fine excuse; **wenig überzeugende ~** slim excuse;
sich eine ~ ausdenken to concoct an excuse; **~ für eine Absage erfinden** to find a pretext for refusing; **zu einer ~ greifen** to lower o. s. to a subterfuge; **jederzeit ~n bei der Hand haben** to be fertile in excuses.
ausreden to finish speaking;
sich ~ to make excuses; **jem. etw. ~** to explain s. th. away; **jem. das Heiraten mit einem kleinen Gehalt ~** to dissuade s. o. from marrying on a small salary; **jem. einen Plan ~** to talk s. o. out of a plan;
j. ~ lassen to hear s. o. out; **j. nicht ~ lassen** to snap s. o. out, to cut s. o. short.
ausreichen to last, to be sufficient (enough);
für alle ~ to go round (supply all); **mit seinem Geld ~** to live within one's means; **sparen und mit dem Geld ~** to economize in order to make one's money spin out; **kaum ~** to be hardly enough; **zur Schilderung eines Sachverhalts kaum ~** to be not the word for it; **trotz nicht vorhandener Mittel ~** to manage in spite of lack of funds; **drei Tage ~** *(Vorräte)* to last three days.
ausreichend sufficient, competent, adequate, ample, enough, *(Begründung)* conclusive, *(Zensur)* fair[ly good];
nicht ~ insufficient, inadequate, *(Begründung)* inconclusive;
~es Baukapital haben to have ample money for building; **~e Beweise liefern** to furnish sufficient proof; **~e Entschuldigung** reasonable excuse; **über ~e Geldmittel verfügen** to have sufficient means; **~es Guthaben** sufficient funds; **~e Kenntnisse** adequate knowledge; **~e Mittel** sufficiency of money; **~e Sicherheit** ample bail; **~e englische Sprachkenntnisse** competent knowledge of English; **~e Versorgung** sufficient supply of provisions; **~e Vorräte** adequate supplies, competent supply of provisions.
ausreifen to mature, to ripen.
Ausreise departure, leaving, *(Schiff)* exit, outward voyage (passage, journey) *(Br.)*;
auf der ~ ins Ausland begriffen *(Schiff)* outbound, outward-bound; **bei der ~** on leaving the country;
auf der ~ über N. fahren to travel outward via N; **bei der ~ die Pässe kontrollieren** to examine the passports on leaving the country; **~ verweigern** to refuse an exit permit;
~beschränkung exit restriction; **~bewilligung** exit permit; **~fracht** outbound freight; **~gebühren** *(Schiff)* outward charges; **~genehmigung** exit permit, *(Visum)* exit visa.
ausreisen to leave the country.
Ausreise|sperre exit embargo; **~visum** exit visa.
Ausreißen running away, guy *(Br.)*.
ausreißen to tear (pull) out, *(weglaufen)* to bolt, to run off (away), to run for it;
Bäume ~ können to feel full of vim; **sich kein Bein ~** not to break one's neck; **sich ein Bein für j. ~** to fall over o. s. for the service of s. o., to bend over backwards to help s. o.
Ausreißer escapee, runaway, fugitive, eloper, crawfish *(US sl.)*.
ausrichten to adjust, to straighten, to pattern on, *(drucktechn.)* to align, *(erreichen)* to accomplish, to get, *(Feier)* to arrange, to organize, *(mil.)* to line up, to dress the lines, *(Mitteilung)* to pass on, to deliver, *(nivellieren)* to level out, *(techn.)* to adjust;

jem. etw. ~ to take a message to (leave a message with) s. o.; **jem. einen Auftrag** ~ to pass on an order to s. o.; **Botschaft** ~ to deliver a message; **jem. schöne Grüße** ~ to remember s. o. kindly; **seine Politik nach der Parteilinie** ~ to follow the party line; **Produktion auf den Absatz** ~ to coordinate production with sales; **seiner Tochter die Hochzeit** ~ to arrange for one's daughter's wedding; **wenig** ~ to have little success;
viel bei jem. ~ **können** to have great influence with s. o.

Ausrichtung der landwirtschaftlichen Erzeugnisse *(EG)* guidance of agricultural production.

ausrollen to roll up, *(Auto)* to coast, *(Flugzeug)* to taxi;
Kabel ~ to run (pay) out a cable.

Ausroll|strecke *(Flugzeug)* landing run (strip); ~**winkel** landing angle.

ausrotten to exterminate, to extirpate, to wipe out, to kill off, to pluck out;
ganze Bevölkerung ~ to wipe out the entire population; **Seuche** ~ to stamp an epidemic disease out; **etw. mit Stumpf und Stiel** ~ to destroy s. th. root and branch; **Typhus** ~ to eradicate typhoid; **Verbrechen** ~ to weed out (eradicate) crime; **Volk** ~ to delete a nation; **Vorurteil** ~ to eradicate a prejudice; **mit der Wurzel** ~ to uproot.

Ausrottung extermination, extirpation, destruction;
~ **eines Volkes** deletion of a nation; **systematische** ~ **eines Volkes** genocide.

ausrücken to march out;
von zu Hause ~ to bolt from home.

Ausrückhebel disengaging lever.

Ausruf exclamation, shout, cry, *(über Lautsprecheranlage)* shout, paging, shot;
durch öffentlichen ~ by public proclamation;
durch ~ **bekanntmachen** to proclaim, to issue a proclamation.

Ausrufanlage auf dem Flugplatz airport page.

ausrufen, j. to call out s. one's name, to page s. o.; **Haltestellen** ~ to call the stops; **zum Kaiser** ~ to proclaim emperor; **Krieg** ~ to proclaim war; **Lose** ~ *(Auktion)* to call out the lots; **Streik** ~ to call a strike; **seine Waren** ~ to cry out one's wares.

Ausrufenlassen paging.

Ausrufer [town] crier, herald, proclaimer;
öffentlicher ~ common crier, bellman; **städtischer** ~ town crier.

Ausrufung proclamation;
~ **der Republik** proclamation of the republic.

Ausrufungszeichen exclamation mark (point, *US*).

ausruhen, sich to [take a] rest, to relax, to rest up *(US)*; **sich auf seinen Lorbeeren** ~ to rest upon one's laurels; **fünf Minuten** ~ to take five *(sl.)*.

ausrüsten to outfit, to equip, to accommodate, to furnish, to stock, to fit (rig) out;
Expedition ~ to furnish an expedition; **mit modernsten Maschinen** ~ to equip with modern machinery; **Schiff** ~ to man (furnish, fit) a vessel.

Ausrüster fitter, outfitter, *(Schiff)* owner pro tempore.

Ausrüstung equipment, outfit, fitout, furnishing, turnout, set, apparatus, harness, rig, tackle, fixings *(US)*, *(Ausrüsten)* outfitting, *(Buch)* turnout, *(Handwerker)* kit, *(mil.)* ordnance, *(Papierindustrie)* finish;
in feldmarschmäßiger ~ in full marching order;
feldmarschmäßige ~ *(mil.)* field equipment; **gemietete** ~ rented equipment;
~ **eines Bergsteigers** mountaineering outfit; ~ **eines Schiffes** fitting out (equipment) of a ship;
zur ~ **gerechnet werden** to be classified as equipment.

Ausrüstungs|dock fitting-out dock; ~**gegenstände,** ~**güter** equipment [goods], fittings, fixings *(coll.)*, *(mil.)* stores; ~**investitionen** producers' durable equipment; ~**konto** equipment account; ~**nachweis** *(mar.)* establishment *(Br.)*; ~**vermietung** equipment leasing; ~**werkzeuge für Reparaturzwecke** repairing outfit.

ausrutschen to slip, *(fig.)* to drop a brick, to make a bloomer.

Ausrutscher gaffe, bloomer, blunder.

Aussaat dissemination.

Aussage *(Erklärung)* statement, declaration, *(Zeuge)* testimony;
nach seinen bisherigen ~**n** according to his own statements; **nach seinen eigenen** ~**n** according to his own showing; **nach den** ~**n des Zeugen** according to testimony (evidence);
beeidigte ~ sworn statement; **beeidigte schriftliche** ~ affidavit; **beglaubigte schriftliche** ~ deposition; **falsche** ~ untrue statement; **nichteidliche** ~ unsworn statement; **unklare** ~ oracle; **dem Zeugnisverweigerungsrecht unterliegende** ~ legal privileged evidence *(US)*; **widersprechende** ~**n** divergent testimonies; **einander widersprechende** ~**n** inconsistent statements;
~ **unter Eid** sworn declaration, affidavit, deposition under oath; ~ **vor Gericht** statement made in court; ~ **auf dem Sterbebett** dying declaration; ~ **vor dem Untersuchungsrichter** declaration; ~ **eines unmittelbaren Zeugen** positive testimony;
~ **zur Beweissicherung aufnehmen** to perpetuate evidence; **seine** ~ **beeiden** to swear to one's statement; **bei seiner** ~ **bleiben** to adhere to one's statement, to abide by what one has said, to stand one's ground; **jds.** ~ **bestätigen** to corroborate s. one's statement; ~ **eidlich erhärten** to make a deposition on oath; ~**n der Zeugen erschüttern** to shake the witnesses' evidence; ~ **machen** to testify, to give evidence, to make a statement (deposition), *(schriftlich)* to depose *(Scot.)*; **beeidete** ~ **machen** to make a statement under oath, to give sworn evidence; **falsche** ~ **machen** to give false evidence; **jds.** ~ **protokollieren** to take down s. one's deposition; **jds.** ~ **umstoßen** to put s. o. out of court; **sich auf jds.** ~ **verlassen** to rely on s. one's evidence; **zur falschen** ~ **verleiten** to suborn; ~ **verweigern** to refuse to give evidence, to stand mute *(Br.)*; **wegen evtl. Selbstbezichtigung die** ~ **verweigern** to plead the Fifth Amendment; ~ **widerrufen** to back down (withdraw) from a statement, to withdraw the testimony.

aussagen to make a statement, to state, to declare, *(Zeuge)* to testify, to depose, to give evidence;
unter Eid ~ to depose; **eidlich** ~ to declare s. th. [up] on oath; **falsch** ~ to give false evidence; **für j.** ~ to give evidence for s. o., to testify on s. one's behalf; **gegen j.** ~ to give evidence (witness, testify) against s. o.; **falsch gegen j.** ~ to misinform against s. o.; **vor Gericht** ~ to testify before court; **zu jds. Gunsten** ~ to testify in s. one's favo(u)r, to give evidence in favo(u)r of s. o.; **nichts** ~ *(Vertragsbestimmungen, Zeitungsartikel)* to be silent; **als Zeuge** ~ to be called on to give evidence.

Aussagender deponent.

aussagepflichtiger Zeuge compellable witness.

Aussage|verweigerung refusal to give evidence; **anwaltliches** ~**verweigerungsrecht** legal professional privilege; ~**zwang für einen Zeugen** compellability of witness.

Aussatz leprosy.

Aussätzigen|politik leper policy; ~**spital** pest house.

Aussätziger leper.

aussaugen to suck out, *(Boden)* to exhaust, to impoverish;
Land ~ to drain the wealth of a country; **j. bis aufs Mark** ~ to bleed s. o. white.

Aussaugung impoverishment.

ausschachten to excavate, to dig up, to tunnel.

Ausschachtung tunnelling.

Ausschachtungsarbeiten excavation;
mit den ~ **beginnen** to break ground.

ausschalten to eliminate, to exclude, to cut out, *(el.)* to switch off, *(Getriebe)* to throw out, *(Maschine)* to disengage, to stop;
kleine Geschäftsleute ~ to cut out the small traders; **Konkurrenz** ~ to eliminate competition; **Risiko** ~ to eliminate risks; **alle Zweifel für immer** ~ dismiss all doubt once and for all; **Zwischenhandel** to eliminate the middlemen.

Ausschalter *(el.)* circuit breaker.

Ausschaltung elimination, exclusion, *(el.)* cutoff, disconnection, *(Maschine)* disengagement, stop;
~ **der Konkurrenz** elimination of competition; ~ **von Risiken** elimination of risk; ~ **des Zwischenhandels** elimination of the middlemen.

Ausschaltvorrichtung bei Übergeschwindigkeit overspeed gear.

Ausschank public house, tavern *(US)*, dispense, pub *(fam.)*, *(Bar)* bar, counter *(Br.)*, alehouse *(Br.)*;
billiger ~ one-arm joint *(sl.)*; **heute** ~ beer on tap today; **konzessionierter** ~ licensed premises; **verbotener** ~ illegal sale of alcoholic drinks;
~ **über die Straße** off-licence *(Br.)*;
~**zeiten** licensing hours.

Ausschau halten to watch, to be on the outlook, to keep an eye out (look out) for.

Ausscheiden retirement, resignation;
turnusmäßiges ~ retirement by rotation;
~ **ungeeigneter Bewerber** screening of candidates (competitors); ~ **aus dem Dienst** retiring from office; ~ **eines Direktors** retirement of a director; ~ **aus einer Firma** withdrawal from a company; ~ **eines Gesellschafters** withdrawal (retirement) of a partner; ~ **aus der Regierung** wandering in the wilderness; ~ **der besseren Risiken** *(Versicherungsgesellschaft)* adverse selection.

ausscheiden to retire, to go out, *(absondern)* to separate, *(ausschalten)* to eliminate, *(ausschließen)* to exclude, to remove, to rule out, *(aussortieren)* to sort out, *(Gase)* to liberate;

aus dem Amt ~ to relinquish (withdraw from, leave) office, to retire; **ungeeignete Bewerber** ~ to screen competitors; **aus dem Dienst** ~ to retire from active service; **aus einer Firma** ~ to retire from (leave) a company (firm); **Frage** ~ to rule out a question; **aus einer Koalition** ~ to withdraw from a coalition; **aus der Regierung** ~ to resign from government *(Br.)*, to wander (walk) in the wilderness; **als Teilhaber** ~ to leave a partnership; **turnusmäßig** ~ to retire by rotation; **aus einem Unternehmen** ~ to withdraw from an undertaking; **aus einem Verband** ~ to retire from an association; **aus einem Verein** ~ to withdraw from a society; **völlig** ~ to be entirely out of the question; **aus einer Vorrunde** ~ to fail to qualify in the preliminary round; **aus dem Vorstand** ~ to leave the board; **als wertlos** ~ to reject; **aus einem Wettbewerb** ~ to drop out of (be eliminated from) a contest; **aus dem Wettlauf für neue Abonnenten** ~ to drop out of the race for subscribers;
bei der Preisverteilung ~ **müssen** not to qualify for a prize.

ausscheidend outgoing;
~**es Vorstandsmitglied** retiring director.

Ausscheidetafel *(Lebensversicherung)* decrement table;
~ **mit zwei Ausscheideursachen** double decrement table.

Ausscheidungs|frage *(Interview)* screening question; ~**grund** cause for leaving; ~**kampf** elimination contest; ~**prüfung** competitive examination; ~**runde** qualifying round; ~**system** knockout system; ~**termin** date of leaving; ~**wettkampf** knockout competition.

ausscheren to deviate, to diverge, *(Auto)* to jackknife, to jump the queue, to swerve, *(Schiff)* to fall out, to leave formation; **aus der Kolonne** ~ to pull out of the line of traffic; **aus einem Verband** ~ to leave a formation.

Ausschießen *(drucktechn.)* imposition.

ausschießen *(drucktechn.)* to impose.

ausschiffen to debark, to disembark, to land, to put ashore, to set sail, to leave the harbo(u)r, to interleave, *(Ladung)* to unload; **Truppen** ~ to disembark troops.

Ausschiffung debarkation, disembarkation, landing.

Ausschiffungs|befehl discharge note; ~**hafen** port of disembarkation; ~**kosten** landing charges.

ausschimpfen, j. gehörig to pepper s. o. with abuse.

ausschlachten *(Betrieb, Kraftfahrzeug)* to cut up for sale, to break up, to scrap, to cannibalize *(US)*, *(fig.)* to capitalize;
Betriebsanlagen ~ to strip assets; **Fall politisch** ~ to make capital out of a case; **Schiff** ~ to break up (scrap) a ship; **Werk** ~ to pluck up a plant.

Ausschlachter *(Schiff)* shipbreaker.

Ausschlachtung exploitation, breaking up, cutting up for sale, cannibalization *(US)*, *(Schiff)* ship breaking;
~ **von Anlagen** asset stripping.

Ausschlachtungswert recovery (breakup) value.

ausschlafen, sich richtig to have one's sleep out.

Ausschlag *(Entscheidung)* decision, decisive factor, *(Magnetnadel)* deflection, *(Meßinstrument)* response, reaction, *(Pendel)* swing;
~ **des Preisbarometers** movement of prices;
~ **geben** to turn the scale, to decide the issue, to clinch a matter, *(Stimmen)* to have the casting vote; **entscheidenden** ~ **geben** to tip the scale.

ausschlagbare Seite gatefold.

Ausschlagen|eines Angebots refusal (rejection) of an offer; ~ **der Waage** turn of the scales.

ausschlagen to decline, to disclaim, to reject, to renounce, to refuse, *(Magnetnadel)* to deflect, to deviate, *(Pendel)* to swing, *(Waage)* to turn;
Amt ~ to disclaim an office; **Angebot** ~ to decline (reject) an offer; **Erbschaft** ~ to disclaim an estate, to renounce (resign) an inheritance *(US)*, to renounce a succession; **zum Nachteil** ~ to be detrimental, to turn out to be a disadvantage; **Schublade mit Papier** ~ to line a drawer with paper; **Stellung** ~ to refuse a job; **jem. zum Vorteil** ~ to turn out to s. one's advantage, to turn up trumps for s. o.

ausschlaggebend decisive, material, essential, determinant, prime, payoff;
~ **sein** to turn the scale, to prevail, *(Kapitalanteil)* to be controlling; **bei jem.** ~ **sein** to weigh with s. o.; ~ **für j. sein** to have a decisive influence upon s. o.; **nicht** ~ **sein** to cut no ice *(coll.)*; **von** ~**er Bedeutung sein** to turn the balance, to tip the scales; **von** ~**er Bedeutung für jds. Laufbahn sein** to determine (be decisive for) s. one's career; ~**er Beweis** decisive proof; ~**er Einfluß** controlling vote; ~**er Kapitalanteil** controlling interest; **im** ~**en Moment** at the critical moment; ~**e Stimme** casting (decisive) vote.

Ausschlagung refusal, rejection, *(Erbschaft)* disclaimer;
~ **eines Angebots** rejection (decline) of an offer; ~ **einer Erbschaft** disclaimer of estate, renunciation of an inheritance *(US)*; ~ **der Mitgift** renunciation of dower; ~ **des Testamentsvollstreckeramtes** renunciation of an executorship.

Ausschlagungsfrist *(Erbschaft)* term for deliberating.

ausschleusen to lock out.

ausschließen to exclude, to seclude, to preclude, *(ablehnen)* to rule (vote) out, *(Arbeiter)* to lock out, to eliminate, *(ausscheiden)* to eliminate, *(ausstoßen)* to expel, to debar, *(disqualifizieren)* to disqualify, *(Einrede)* to estop, *(Teilhaber)* to freeze out, *(Zeilen)* to justify;
j. ~ to lock s. o. out, to close one's door against s. o.; **Anwalt aus der Anwaltschaft** ~ to disbar a barrister *(Br.)*; **alle Bedingungen des Käufers** ~ to override any forms or conditions referred to by the buyer; **von einer Bewerbung** ~ to debar from applying for a position; **Firma von der Beteiligung an Ausschreibungen der Regierung** ~ to blacklist a company from receiving government contracts; **sich gegenseitig** ~ to be incompatible; **Haftung** ~ to exonerate o. s. from liability; **j. vom gesellschaftlichen Leben** ~ to ostracize s. o.; **Mißverständnisse** ~ to preclude a misunderstanding; **Mitglied von der Inanspruchnahme der Fondsmittel** ~ to declare a member ineligible to use the resources of the fund; **von der Mitgliedschaft** ~ to deny s. o. admission; **Möglichkeit** ~ to rule out the possibility; **j. wegen Nichtzahlens seiner Mitgliederbeiträge** ~ to drop s. o. for nonpayment of dues; **Öffentlichkeit** ~ to exclude the general public, *(Gericht)*to order the case to be heard in closed session (camera); **Presse und Öffentlichkeit** ~ to exclude both press and public; **Rechtsweg** ~ to bar legal proceedings; **Richter von der Ausübung des Richteramtes** ~ to disqualify a judge; **gerichtliche Schadensersatzforderung** ~ to preclude recovery by suit; **Kind vom Schulbesuch** ~ to expel a child from school; **vom Universitätsbesuch** ~ to send down *(Br.)*, to rusticate *(US)*; **j. aus einem Verein** ~ to expel (exclude) s. o. from a society; **Vereinsmitglied vorübergehend** ~ to suspend a member of a club; **j. von einer Verhandlung** ~ to put s. o. out of court; **Verjährung** ~ to bar prescription; **sich vertraglich** ~ to contract out; **von einem Wettbewerb** ~ to disqualify from a contest; **j. zeitweilig** ~ to suspend s. o.; **von der Zuteilung [bei der Aktienemission]** ~ to preclude from allotment.

ausschließlich exclusive, sole, only, without;
nicht ~ nonexclusive;
~ **Dividende** dividend off; ~ **der Heizungskosten** *(Miete)* exclusive of heating; ~ **der Kosten** exclusive of costs; ~ **Verpackung** exclusive packing;
~ **zuständig** to have exclusive (original) jurisdiction in all cases; ~**e Beschäftigung** sole occupation; **im** ~**en Besitz von etw. sein** to be sole possessor of s. th.; ~**e Gerichtsbarkeit** exclusive jurisdiction; ~**e Lizenz** exclusive licence; ~**es Recht** exclusive (sole) right.

Ausschließlichkeit exclusiveness, exclusivity.

Ausschließlichkeits|abkommen tying *(US)* (solus, exclusive) agreement; ~**aufhänger** *(Werbung)* exclusive angle; ~**bindung,** ~**geschäft** exclusive dealing *(US)*; ~**klausel** exclusive clause; ~**nutzung eines Patents** monopolistic use of a patent; ~**police für Berufstätige** commercial policy; ~**recht** exclusive right, sole right of negotiation; ~**rechte verletzen** to infringe monopoly rights; ~**vereinbarungen** exclusive dealings; ~**verhältnis** exclusive feature; ~**verpflichtung** exclusive franchise *(US)*; ~**vertrag** tying agreement, *(Vertreter)* exclusive agency contract (dealer arrangement, *US*); ~**vertrag mit einem Autor abschließen** to take an option on all the future works of an author.

Ausschließung exclusion, preclusion, exception, *(Mitglied)* exclusion, expulsion, debarment, shutout, *(Anwaltschaft)* disbarment;
~ **von der Erbschaft** exclusion from an inheritance *(US)*; **zeitweilige** ~ **eines Mitglieds** suspension of a member; ~ **von der Teilnahme an Ausschreibungen** debarment of tender.

Ausschließungs|einrede *(Nachlaß)* plene administrative; ~**frist** time limit; ~**grund** disqualification; ~**klausel** preclusion clause; ~**system** prohibitive system; ~**verfahren** foreclosure proceedings.

Ausschluß exclusion, elimination, debarment, ruling out, *(Ausnahme)* exception, *(Aussperrung)* lockout, *(Disqualifikation)* disqualification, ruling out, *(drucktechn.)* spacing material, *(Einrede)* estoppage, estoppel, *(Präklusion)* preclusion, foreclosure;
mit ~ **von** with the exception; **mit** ~ **dieser Waren** exclusive of these goods; **unter** ~ **von** to the exclusion of, excluding; **unter** ~

aller persönlichen Einwendungen free from the equities; **unter ~ der Konkurrenz** noncompetitive; **unter ~ der Öffentlichkeit** in chambers, in camera *(Br.)* (closed session); **unter ~ des Rechtsweges** disbarring legal actions; **unter ~ der Verantwortung** without responsibility;
~ aus der Anwaltschaft disbarment of a barrister *(Br.)*; **~ der Ausgleichspflicht des Versicherers** policy exclusion of contribution; **~ der Gewährleistung** caveat emptor, nonwarranty clause; **~ der Gütergemeinschaft** separation of property; **~ der Haftung** exemption from liability, nonliability; **~ eines Kindes vom Schulbesuch** expulsion of a child from school; **~ der Konsumentenkonkurrenz** nonrivalness in consumption; **~ vom gesellschaftlichem Leben** ostracism; **~ von Leistungsansprüchen** *(Sozialversicherung)* exclusion of benefits; **~ der Öffentlichkeit** nonadmission of the general public, exclusion of the general public; **~ von Presse und Öffentlichkeit** exclusion of press and public from a meeting; **~ des Rechtsweges** ouster of jurisdiction, precluding recovery by suit; **~ vom Richteramt** disqualification of a judge *(US)*; **~ der Sachmängelhaftung** nonwarranty clause; **durch geschickte Manöver erreichter ~ eines Teilhabers** freeze-out of a partner; **~ von der Universität** suspension from university, sending down *(Br.)*, rustification *(US)*; **~ eines Vereinsmitgliedes** expulsion (exclusion) of a member of a club; **~ vom passiven Wahlrecht** ineligibility; **~ des Wettbewerbs** restraint of trade, exclusivity stipulation;
~ der Öffentlichkeit anordnen to clear the court; **~ der Öffentlichkeit beantragen** *(Parlament)* to spy strangers *(Br.)*; **Beweisaufnahme unter ~ der Öffentlichkeit durchführen** to hear evidence in camera *(Br.)* (closed session); **Verhandlung unter ~ der Öffentlichkeit führen** to hear a case in chambers *(Br.)*; **unter ~ der Öffentlichkeit stattfinden** to be heard in camera *(Br.)* (closed session); **Antrag auf ~ der Öffentlichkeit stellen** to ask that a case may be heard in camera *(Br.)* (closed session); **unter ~ der Öffentlichkeit tagen** to sit in closed court (camera, *Br.*), to be heard in camera *(Br.)*; **Sache unter ~ der Öffentlichkeit verhandeln** to try a case in camera *(Br.)* (closed session);
~bestimmung exclusive clause; **~frist** time limit, bar date, *(Erbe)* term for deliberating, *(Strafverfahren)* limitation of time, *(Verjährung)* period of limitation, *(vor Streikverkündung)* cooling time; **~frist für schriftliche Klagevorbringen** circumduction *(Scot.)*; **~klage** foreclosure action; **~klausel** *(Seetransport)* preclusion clause, exclusivity stipulation *(Br.)*, *(Versicherung)* memorandum clause; **~prinzip** *(Preis)* exclusion principle; **~recht** exclusive right, monopoly; **~taste** *(drucktechn.)* spacing key; **~termin** time limit; **~urteil** foreclosure decree, order for foreclosure *(Br.)*, forejudger *(Br.)*; **~verfahren** foreclosure proceedings; **~zwang** *(Wasserversorgung)* compulsory connection.

ausschmücken to decorate, to adorn, to ornament, to drape, to enrich;
Geschichte ~ to embellish a story.

Ausschmückung adornment, decoration, ornamentation, *(Gebäude)* enrichment;
~ einer Geschichte embellishment of a story.

Ausschneiden cutting.

ausschneiden to cut out;
Bild aus der Zeitung ~ to cut a picture out of a newspaper; **Zeitungsartikel ~** to clip *(US)* (cut out) newspaper articles.

Ausschnitt extract, excerpt, *(Film)* cutout, *(Kleid)* neck, *(Stanze)* trimming, cut-out, *(Zeitung)* cutting, cutout, clipping *(US)*;
~ vergrößern to enlarge a cropped negative area.

Ausschnitts|büro, **~dienst** [press] clipping bureau *(US)*, clipping agency *(US)*, press-cutting agency, newspaper clipper *(US)*; **innerbetrieblicher ~dienst** reader *(US)* (research, abstract) service; **~redakteur** exchange editor; **~stelle** cutout, clipping.

ausschnittsweise wiedergeben, Sendung to reproduce extracts from a program(me).

ausschnüffeln to nose out, to smoke out *(sl.)*.

ausschöpfen to scoop out;
seine Mittel ~ to exhaust one's resources.

Ausschöpfung von Reserven exhaustion of reserves.

Ausschreiben von Neuwahlen going to the country *(Br.)*.

ausschreiben to write in full (at full length), *(ankündigen)* to announce, *(einberufen)* to call, to convoke, to convene, *(Aufträge)* to put out to tender, to advertise for (solicit) bids *(US)*, *(Kurzschrift)* to extend, *(Steuern)* to impose, to levy, *(im Subskriptionswege)* to invite bids *(Br.)* (tenders);
sich ~ to overwrite; **Abkürzungen ~** to expand abbreviations; **Auftrag ~** to invite tenders (bids, *US*); **Belohnung ~** to offer a reward; **Gebäude im Submissionswege ~** to invite tenders for a building; **Lieferauftrag ~** to invite tender for suppliers; **Neuwahlen ~** to call a new election, to go (appeal) to the country *(Br.)*; **öffentlich ~** to put out on open tender; **Preis ~** to offer a prize; **Quittung ~** to sign a receipt; **Rechnung ~** to make out an invoice; **Scheck ~** to fill (make, write) out a check *(US)* (cheque, *Br.*); **offene Stelle ~** to advertise a vacant position (a vacancy); **neue Steuer ~** to impose a tax on the people; **Stipendium ~** to exhibit a foundation (prize); **Submission ~** to invite tenders for a subscription; **Wettbewerb ~** to put up for competition, to invite public competition; **Zahlen ~** to write out the numbers.

Ausschreibung *(Bekanntmachung)* announcement, *(Einberufung)* convocation, calling, *(Rechnung)* making out, *(Scheck)* filling out, *(Stelle)* advertisement, *(Steuern)* imposition, *(im Submissionswege)* invitation to tender, invitation to bid *(US)*, bid invitation *(US)*, solicitation for bids *(US)*, bidding *(US)*, call for tenders, public tender, contract by tender, competitive tendering;
durch ~ by tender;
beschränkte ~ closed (restricted) invitation for tenders; **freie (freihändige) ~** competitive bidding *(US)*, invitation for tenders with discretionary award of contracts; **öffentliche ~** public invitation to tender;
~ öffentlicher Arbeiten contract for public works; **~ von Neuwahlen** appeal to the country *(Br.)*;
sich an staatlichen ~en beteiligen to tender for a contract, to bid on a government contract *(US)*; **sich an einer ~ für eine neue Autobahn beteiligen** to tender for the construction of a new motorway *(Br.)*; **an einer ~ teilnehmen** to participate in a tender; **~ veranstalten (vornehmen)** to put out to tender, to invite tenders (bids, *US*) for a piece of work.

Ausschreibungs|absprache collusive tendering; **~angebot** tender offer; **~ausschuß** tender board; **~bedingungen** terms of tender, specifications of work to be done; **~bestimmungen** tender instructions; **~beteiligter** contract bidder *(US)*; **~frist** deadline for tenders, closing date *(US)*; **~garantie** participating (tender) guarantee, bid bond *(US)*; **~protest** bid protest *(US)*; **~schluß** closing date of tender; **~teilnehmer** contract bidder *(US)*; **~termin** deadline for tenders, closing date *(US)*; **~unterlagen** documents of a tender; **~verfahren** competitive bidding process *(US)*; **staatliches ~verfahren** government bidding process *(US)*; **~wettbewerb** bid competition *(US)*.

Ausschreitungen outrages, excesses;
von den Truppen verübte ~ excesses committed by the troops; **~ begehen** to commit excesses (outrages).

Ausschuß commission, committee, board, panel, *(beim Druckvorgang)* spoilage, spoiled work, *(Produktion)* waste, wastage, scrap, refuse, reject(s), junk, rummage, *(Waren)* substandard goods;
an einen ~ verwiesen committed;
auswärtiger ~ foreign-relations committee; **beratender ~** advisory council (panel); **beschließender ~** decision-making committee; **vom Präsidenten eingesetzter ~** presidentially-appointed panel; **vorübergehend eingesetzter ~** provisional committee; **engerer ~** select *(Br.)* (small) committee; **erweiterter ~** enlarged committee *(US)*; **gemeinsamer ~** joint committee; **gemischter ~** joint commission (committee, *Br.*), hybrid committee; **geschäftsführender ~** executive (managing, management) committee; **informeller ~** informal commission; **interministerieller ~** interagency group (committee), interdepartmental committee; **interparlamentarischer ~** interparliamentary committee; **koordinierender ~** coordinating committee; **ministerieller ~** department committee; **nachgeordneter ~** subordinate committee; **paritätischer ~** joint committee; **parlamentarischer ~** parliamentary commission; **schiedsrichterlicher ~** arbitration committee; **städtischer ~** city commission; **ständiger ~** standing (permanent) committee, *(Parlament)* sessional committee; **statistischer ~** statistical committee; **vollziehender ~** steering committee; **gesetzlich vorgeschriebener ~** statutory committee; **vorläufiger ~** temporary committee; **besonders zusammengestellter ~** blue-ribbon panel *(US)*; **zwischenstaatlicher ~** interstate committee;
~ für Abwässerbeseitigung sewerage committee; **~ für auswärtige Angelegenheiten** foreign affairs committee; **~ zur Bekämpfung des unlauteren Wettbewerbs** Federal Trade Commission *(US)*; **~ zur Einvernahme ausländischer Zeugen** commission to examine witnesses *(US)*; **~ für wirtschaftliche Entwicklungsfragen** economic development committee *(Br.)*; **~ zur Festlegung der Geschäftspolitik** policy committee; **~ für Fragen des Industrieschutzes** safety committee; **~ für Fragen des Umweltschutzes** council on environmental quality; **~ für Minderheitsfragen** minorities committee; **~ der Präsidenten** *(EG)* Presi-

dential Committee; **ausdrücklicher ~ des ordentlichen Rechtsweges** contracting-out; **örtlicher ~ für Schankkonzessionen** excise commission *(US)*; **~ zur Wahrung von Arbeitnehmerrechten** employee rights committee; **~ für Wirtschaft und Finanzen** *(UNO)* Economic and Financial Committee; **~ der gewerblichen Wirtschaft** trades council; **internationaler ~ für Wirtschaftsprüferrichtlinien** International Accounting Standards Committee;
einem ~ angehören to be (serve, sit) on a committee, to form part of a commission; **~ auflösen** to put a committee out of business, to disband a committee; **aus einem ~ ausscheiden** to cease to form part of a commission, to throw off a committee; **aus einem ~ ausschließen** to throw off a committee; **in einen ~ berufen** to appoint to a committee; **~ bilden** to constitute (resolve itself into) a committee; **~ einsetzen** to constitute (establish, name) a committee, to appoint a commission; **~ gründen** to form a committee; **~ konstituieren** to constitute a committee; **sich zu einem ~ konstituieren** *(parl.)* to form themselves into a committee, to resolve itself into committee (a commission); **~ konstruieren** to constitute (strike) a committee; **~ leiten** to head a commission; **in einem ~ sitzen** to serve (serve, sit) on a committee, to be on a panel (board); **einem ~ zur Verfügung stehen** to attend on a committee; **unter ~ der Öffentlichkeit tagen** to sit in closed court (camera, *Br.*); **an einen ~ überweisen** to refer to a committee, *(Gesetzesvorlage)* to commit a bill; **einem ~ die Möglichkeit einer Arbeitsaufnahme verschaffen** to put a committee into working shape; **Frage an einen ~ verweisen** to refer a question to a committee; **seinen Fall einem ~ vorlegen** to lay one's case before a commission; **dem ~ vorliegen** to be in the committee stage; **in einen ~ gewählt werden** to be elected to a committee; **~ nach folgenden Grundsätzen zusammensetzen** to set up a committee on the following lines;
mit geheimen ~abstimmungen aufräumen to sweep away secrecy from committee votes; **~akten** committee files; **~arbeit leisten** to serve on a commission; **~berater** committee council; **~beratungen** committee discussions (consultations); **~beratungen beschleunigen** to expedite the business of a committee; **~bericht** committee (panel) report, report of a committee; **~bericht entgegennehmen** to receive a report of a committee; **~beschluß** committee determination, commission ruling; **~besetzung** committee assignment; **~bogen** *(drucktechn.)* waste sheet; **~diskussion** committee discussion (debate).

Ausschüsse aufteilen, sich in to go into committees.

Ausschuß | einsetzung setting up a committee; **~empfehlungen** committee's recommendations (proposal); **~entscheidung** committee ruling; **~ernennung** committee (commissional) appointment; **~errichtung** setting up of a committee; **~funktion** function of a committee; **~funktionen wahrnehmen** to serve on a panel; **~holz** rejected timber, culls *(US)*; **~interesse** committee attention; **~kollege** committee colleague; **~lager** junk pile; **~mehrheit** majority of a committee; **~meldung** scrap report; **~mitglied** member of the board, committee (commission, board) member, commissioner, committeeman *(US)*, panel member; **verschiedene ~mitglieder** several members of a committee; **letzte ~mitglieder auswählen** to pick the rest of the commission; **~mitglied sein** to be (sit, serve) on a committee; **~papier** waste paper, broke; **~personal** committee staff; **~prognose** commission projection; **~protokoll** committee record; **~protokoll veröffentlichen** to publish the commission's proceedings; **~quote** percentage of rejects; **~resolution herbeiführen** to pass a measure through a committee; **~sitz** seat on a committee; **Anspruch auf einen ~sitz haben** to be entitled to a seat on a committee; **~sitzung** conference (session) of a committee, committee meeting; **öffentliche ~sitzung** congressional hearing *(US, senate)*; **an einer ~sitzung teilnehmen** to attend a committee meeting; **~stadium** committee stage; **noch nicht im ~stadium** *(Gesetz)* uncommitted; **unbesetzte ~stelle** commission vacancy; **~stück** waste; **~tätigkeit beginnen** to open a commission; **~untersuchungen, ~vernehmungen** committee hearings (investigations), *(parl.)* legislative investigation *(US)*; **~vereinbarung** committee arrangement; **übliches ~verfahren** usual procedure at committee meetings; **~ verhandlungen** commission's proceedings; **~verwaltung** commission's proceedings, commission government, committee system *(Br.)*; **~verweisung** committal, devolution; **~vollmachten** powers of a committee; **~vorschlag** committee's (commission) proposal (recommendations); **~vorschläge für Kürzungen** committee cuttings; **~vorsitz** committee chairmanship; **~vorsitzender** chairman of a committee, committee (commission, panel) chairman, convener *(Scot.)*; **~vorsitzender sein** to head a commission; **~ware** job (damaged, rummage) goods, trumpery wares, substandard goods, junk, manufacturing rejects, as-is merchandise; **~zimmer** committee room; **~zugehörigkeit** committeeship.

ausschütten to pour (empty) out, *(zahlen)* to distribute, to pay; **Börsengewinne ~** to distribute trading profits; **Dividende ~** to declare (strike, pay) a dividend; **außerordentliche Dividende ~** to cut a melon *(US)*; **zusätzliche Dividende ~** to distribute an additional (supplementary) dividend; **60% der Erträgnisse an die Aktionäre ~** to pay out 60 per cent of profit to shareholders (stockholders, *US*); **Gewinn ~** to distribute the proceeds; **sein Herz ~** to unbosom one's heart; **Konkursmasse ~** to liquidate the assets of a bankrupt; **Konkursquote ~** to divide a bankrupt's property (estate); **Konkursquote von 40% ~** to pay 40% out of the estate; **Sack Korn ~** to empty (spill) a sack of corn.

Ausschüttung distribution, payment;
anteilige ~ prorata distribution; **radioaktive ~** fallout;
~ von Börsengewinnen distribution of trading profits; **~ einer Dividende** declaration (payment) of a dividend; **~ einer außerordentlichen Dividende** cutting a melon *(US)*; **~ von Gewinnen** distribution of profits; **~ von Kapitalgewinnen** *(Investmentgesellschaft)* capital distribution; **~ der Konkursmasse** distribution of a bankrupt's estate; **~ realisierter Kursgewinne** capital-gains distribution; **~ des Nettogewinns** apportionment of the net profit; **~en aus einem Treuhandvermögen** distribution of a trust fund; **~ von Zwischendividenden** declaration of interim dividends.

Ausschüttungs | benachrichtigung notice of distribution; **~erwartung** expected distribution of profits.

ausschüttungsfähig distributable.

Ausschüttungs | formular distribution form; **~termin** distribution date.

ausschwärmen *(mil.)* to fan out, to deploy.

ausschweben *(Flugzeug)* to flatten out.

Ausschwebestrecke float.

ausschweifend wanton, extravagant, dissolute;
~es Leben führen to lead a dissolute life.

Ausschweifungen debauch, dissipations;
sich ~ hingeben to fall into dissipate ways.

Aussehen exterior, appearance, look, aspect, presence, complexion, cachet;
nach seinem ~ by the look of him;
gefälliges ~ *(Waren)* good appearance; **großstädtisches ~** city look; **schlampiges ~** slovenly appearance;
anderes ~ bekommen to assume a different look; **nach dem ~ beurteilen** to judge by appearances; **gefälliges ~ geben** to gild; **nach dem ~ gehen** to go by looks; **wieder sein normales ~ haben** to look o. s. again; **im ~ zu wünschen übrig lassen** to be lacking in personal presence; **über ein gutes ~ verfügen** to have a good presence, to be good-looking.

aussehen, ziemlich abgenutzt to look the worse for wear; **sich die Augen nach jem. ~** to stare o. s. blind looking for s. o.; **bedeutend ~** to have an air of importance; **nach etw. Besonderem ~** to have a distinguished air about one; **düster ~** to look blank; **entrüstet ~** to raise one's eyebrows; **glänzend ~** to look like a million; **wie ein gerupftes Huhn ~** to look like a dying duck in a thunderstorm; **wie Milch und Blut ~** to look in the pink of health; **miserabel ~** to look like a drowned rat; **schlecht ~** to look like nothing on earth; **sehr schlecht ~** to be looking very poorly; **wie drei Tage Regenwetter ~** to look down in the mouth; **wie der Tod ~** to look as pale as death; **ungünstig ~** to have taken an unfavo(u)rable turn; **unheimlich ~** to have the gallows in one's face; **verboten ~** to look a sight; **vernachlässigt ~** to wear a neglected look, to look a sight; **in Wirklichkeit nicht so alt ~** not to look one's age;
Sache ganz anders ~ lassen to make all the difference.

aussehend, verboten disreputable-looking;
verdächtig ~es Individuum suspicious character.

außen exterior, outside, outward, external.

Außen | abmessungen outside dimensions; **~abteilung** field office; **~anschluß** *(tel.)* outside number; **~anschnitt** *(Anzeige)* outside bleed; **~ansicht** exterior [view]; **~antenne** outdoor aerial *(Br.)* (antenna, *US*); **~arbeit** field (outside, outdoor) work, outdoor job; **~aufnahme** *(Film)* exterior, outdoor scene, location filming, *(Fernsehen)* exterior shot; **im Studio gedrehte ~aufnahme** rear screen projection; **~aufnahmen machen** to film on location; **~bahn** outer lane; **~bahnhof** outer station; **~beamter** field officer; **~beitrag** net exports; **~beleuchtung** outdoor lighting, *(Auto)* head and tail lamps; **~bereich** *(Regionalplanung)* [etwa] white land *(Br.)*; **~beziehungen** external affairs *(Australia)*; **~bezirk** purlieu, outlying district, suburb, outskirts, suburban area; ~**bezirk eines Gefängnisses** rules of a prison; ~**bilanz** balance of payments; ~**bordmotor** outboard motor, putt-putt *(coll.)*.

aussenden, Funkspruch to send a message by radio.

Außendienst outdoor (field) service, fieldwork, *(Bahn)* line service;
im ~ in the field;
~ **und Filialen** fields and branches;
im ~ **beschäftigt sein** to work in the field; **auf verschiedenen Plätzen im** ~ **gewesen sein** to have a background in various places of the world;
~**kräfte** field force; ~**mitarbeiter** fieldworker, field representative; ~**mitarbeiter im Angestelltenverhältnis** travelling salesman on straight salary; ~**tätigkeit** field service.

Außen|durchmesser external (outer) diameter; ~**einsatz** fieldwork; ~**geltung** external validity, *(Akzept)* foreign acceptance; ~**gewässer** extraterritorial waters; ~**hafen** outer harbo(u)r, outport.

Außenhandel foreign (external) trade, export trade, commerce;
sichtbarer ~ visible trade;
~ **mit eigenen Schiffen** active commerce; ~ **mit fremden Schiffen** passive commerce;
im ~ **tätig sein** to be engaged in export; ~ **treiben** to traffic with other countries.

Außenhandels|abkommen foreign-trade agreement; ~**abschlüsse** foreign-trade dealings; ~**abteilung** export (foreign-trade) department; ~**analyse** study of foreign trade; ~**anteil** share of export trade; ~**bank** export bank; ~**beamter** foreign-trade official; ~**bedürfnisse** export demands; ~**beschränkung** restraint(s) of foreign trade; ~**beziehungen** external commercial relations; ~**beziehungen eigener mit fremden Staatsangehörigen** commerce with foreign nations *(US)*; ~**bilanz** foreign-trade balance; **ausgeglichene** ~**bilanz** foreign trade equilibrium; ~**defizit** foreign-trade (export) deficit; ~**entwicklung** development of foreign trade; ~**finanzierung** financing of foreign trade, foreign-trade financing; ~**firma** international trader, export company; ~**förderung** export promotion; ~**geschäfte durchführen** to carry out foreign trading; ~**gesetz** Export Trade Act *(US)*; ~**kartelle** export cartel; ~**kaufmann** import and export merchant; ~**kontrolle** export (foreign-trade) control; ~**lücke** trade gap; ~**monopol** export monopoly, monopoly for foreign trade, foreign-trade monopoly; ~**organisation** overseas trade service; ~**papiere** foreign-trade documents; ~**passivsaldo** adverse foreign-trade balance; ~**platz** foreign-trade (export) center *(US)* (centre, *Br.*); ~**politik** foreign-trade policy; ~**politik auf der Basis gegenseitiger Vorteile** fair trade policy; ~**schulden** overseas debt; ~**statistik** export statistics; ~**stelle** foreign-trade department (agency), overseas trade agency; ~**tätigkeit** foreign-trade activities; ~**überschuß** foreign-trade (export trade) surplus, trade gain; ~**unternehmen** export company, international trader; ~**vertrag** foreign-trade (export) contract; ~**volumen** export volume, volume of foreign trade; ~**ziffern** export (foreign sales) figures; **nicht bereinigte** ~**ziffern** crude trade.

Außen|haut *(Schiff)* skip, shell; ~**haut aus Aluminium** aluminium airframe; ~**institut** research institute; ~**klosett** outhouse *(US)*; ~**kräfte** field staff, fieldworkers; ~**lager** field inventory (warehouse, *US*), *(techn.)* outbearing; ~**landung** off-field landing; ~**leitung** open (overhead) line; ~**leuchte** outdoor lamp; ~**linien eines Gebäudes** exterior features of a building; ~**maße** outside measurements; ~**mauer** outwall.

Außenminister Secretary of State for Foreign Affairs *(Br.)*, Foreign Secretary *(Br.)*, Secretary of State *(US)*, Foreign Affairs Minister;
~**ebene** Foreign Minister level; ~**konferenz** council of foreign ministers; ~**rat** Council of Foreign Ministers; ~**stellvertreter** Deputy Foreign Minister.

Außenministerium Ministry of Foreign Affairs, Foreign Office *(Br.)*, State Department *(US)*;
im ~ **vorsprechen** to call on the Foreign Minister.

Außen|organisation field staff (organisation); ~**passagier** outside [passenger]; ~**pier** jetty; **gemaltes** ~**plakat** painted bulletin; ~**politik** foreign politics (policy, affairs).

außenpolitisch|er Ausschuß foreign-affairs committee, Foreign Relations Committee *(US)*; ~**er Druck** foreign pressure; **in** ~**en Entschlüssen frei bleiben** to remain free to determine its own foreign policy; ~**e Kursänderung** reorientation of foreign policy; ~**e Lage** foreign situation; ~**e Probleme** international problems; ~**e Verpflichtungen** foreign commitments.

Außen|posten *(Diplomat)* outpost; **rückständiger** ~**posten** backward outpost; ~**rand** top margin; ~**reede** outer harbo(u)r; ~**reparatur** outside repairs; ~**revisor** travelling (field) auditor, sales supervisor; **leitender** ~**revisor** accountant in charge; ~**schalter** *(Bank)* night safe deposit, *(Zoll)* outside service; ~**schild** outdoor sign; ~**seite** outside, exterior, front, surface; **an der** ~**seite des Bürgersteiges gehen** to walk on the outside of the pavement.

Außenseiter dark horse, outsider, *(Marketing)* newcomer, *(Soziologie)* marginal man;
als ~ **geltend** marginal;
geldgebender ~ angel *(sl.)*; **krasser** ~ rank outsider; **völliger** ~ dark horse;
als ~ **gelten** *(Soziologe)* to be marginal;
~**rolle** outside role.

Außen|sitz outside seat, outside *(Br.)*; ~**spalte** outside position; ~**spiegel** *(Auto)* external mirror; **innen verstellbarer** ~**spiegel** internally adjustable mirror.

Außenstände outstanding (active) debts, outstanding accounts, book debts, outstandings, outs, debts, receivables *(US)*, *(Bilanz)* sums of money due and owing;
abgeschriebene ~ debts written off; **abgetretene** ~ accounts receivable discounted *(US)*, pledged accounts receivable *(US)*; **beitreibbare** ~ recoverable debts; **zeitweilig nicht einbringliche (eingefrorene)** ~ frozen (deferred) assets (debts); **seine** ~ his outstanding bills; **sichere** ~ good debts; **nach der Fälligkeit sortierte (überfällige)** ~ aging accounts receivable *(US)*; **uneinbringliche (verlorene)** ~ bad (irrecoverable) debts; **unsichere (zweifelhafte)** ~ bad *(Br.)* (doubtful, *US*), debts; **verbürgte** ~ guaranteed accounts; **verlorene** ~ irrecoverable debts; **verschiedene** ~ *(Bilanz)* sundry debtors;
~ **und sonstige Forderungen** book or other debts;
~ **abtreten** to assign outstanding debts; ~ **eintreiben (einziehen)** to collect money due (outstanding amounts, outstanding debts), to pull in the cash; ~ **haben** to have money owing.

Außen|standsliste schedule of accounts receivable *(US)*; ~**station** outside (outer) station, *(Krankenhaus)* outward, *(mil.)* outstation; ~**steg** *(Buch)* fore edge.

außenstehend outside.

Außen|stehender outsider, outside person, looker-on; ~**stelle** branch [office], agency, field office, service depot, substation, *(Behörde)* outstation, suboffice; ~**stellenleiter** field sales manager; ~**tarif** external tariff; ~**temperatur** open-air temperature; ~**tür** outer door; ~**übertragung** remote pickup; ~**umsatz** external turnover (sales); ~**verhältnis** external relationship *(US)*; ~**vertreter** outside agent; ~**wand** outer wall, *(Stahlskelettbau)* clothing; **nichttragende** ~**wand** curtain wall; ~**welt** outside (outer) world; ~**werbung** outdoor advertising (display), *(an öffentlichen Verkehrsmitteln)* parade poster *(US)*; ~**werbungsunternehmen** outdoor advertising plant; ~**werk** *(mil.)* outwork; ~**wert des Geldes** external value of money; ~**werterhöhung des Pfundes** increased external value of sterling; ~**wirtschaft** external (foreign) trade, external economy.

außenwirtschaftlich external;
~**es Gleichgewicht** external equilibrium, foreign-trade equilibrium; ~**e Lage** external economic situation; ~**e Position** external position.

Außenwirtschafts|bereich foreign sector; ~**lehre** international economics.

Außen|zimmer outward room; ~**zoll** external tariff (duty); **gemeinsamer** ~**zoll** *(EG)* common external tariff.

außer outside, out of;
völlig ~ **sich** out of one's wits;
~ **Landes gehen** to leave the country; **völlig** ~ **sich sein** to be in a great way *(Br., coll.)*; ~ **Betrieb setzen** to put out of action.

Außerachtlassen der gesetzlich vorgeschriebenen Sorgfalt legal negligence.

Außerachtlassung ignoring;
~ **seiner Pflichten** evasion of one's duties; ~ **von persönlichen Überlegungen** elimination of personal considerations;
wegen ~ **der im Berufsleben erforderlichen Sorgfalt verklagen** to sue for professional negligence.

außer|akademisch outside; ~**amtlich** unofficial, private, nonofficial *(Br.)*; ~**beruflich** outside, extraprofessional, extracurricular, extraofficial.

außerbetrieblich external, nonoperating;
~**e Anlagen** nonoperating assets; ~**e Ausbildung** outside training; ~**er Benutzer** *(Werksbibliothek)* outside user; ~**e Unterlagen** external data.

Außerbetrieb|nahme von Anlagegütern retirement (removal) of fixed assets; ~**setzung** putting out of operation, *(Anlagegut)* discardment.

außerbörslich unofficial, on the curb (kerb, *Br.*) rate, in the outside market, over-the-counter *(US)*;
~**er Kurs** curb (kerb, *Br.*) rate.
außerdienstlich off-duty, unofficial, private, outside one's official functions, extraofficial, off the record.
Außerdienststellung eines Schiffes laying up (decommissioning) of a ship, mothballing.
äußere | Angelegenheiten foreign affairs; ~ **Anleihe** external loan; ~ **Einflüsse** outside influences; ~ **Erscheinung** outward appearance; ~**r Hafen** outer port; **nach dem** ~**n Schein beurteilen** to judge by appearances; ~ **Staatsschuld** external debt; ~ **Umstände** external conditions; ~ **Verletzung** external injury.
außerehelich illegitimate, extramarital, extramatrimonial;
~**es Kind** illegitimate child, bastard; ~**er Sohn** son born out of wedlock; ~**er Verkehr** criminal conversation.
Äußer | es exterior, outside, surface, *(Erscheinung)* outward appearance;
unansehnliches ~**es** plainness;
nicht auf sein ~**es achten** to take no thought of one's appearance; **Menschen nur nach dem** ~**en beurteilen** to look only on the surface of men; **durch Verpackung ein besseres** ~**es geben** to face; **auf sein** ~**es viel Wert legen** to pay much attention to one's outward appearance.
außer | etatsmäßig not included in the budget, extrabudgetary, *(überzählig)* supernumerary, noncommissioned; ~**europäisch** extra-European; ~**fahrplanmäßig** special, off schedule *(US)*, not as scheduled *(US)*, unscheduled *(US)*.
außergerichtlich extrajudicial, nonlitigious, in pais, deplano, out of court;
Sache ~ **beilegen (vergleichen), sich** ~ **vergleichen** to settle (arrange) a case out of court, to settle a matter without going to law, to arrange privately;
j. gerichtlich und ~ **vertreten** to represent s. o. in and out of court;
~**e Beilegung** amicable arrangement; ~**e Kosten** extrajudicial costs; ~**er Vergleich** settlement out of court, out-of-court composition.
außer | geschäftlich private, unofficial; ~**gesetzlich** outside the law, extralegal.
außergewöhnlich extra, out of the way, unusual, exceptional, out of the ordinary;
~ **billig** exceptionally cheap;
~**er Fall** *(Strafrecht)* extraordinary case; ~**e Funktion** offbeat role; ~**e Gefahr** *(durch Arbeitgeber verursacht)* extraordinary risk; ~**e Sorgfalt** extraordinary care.
außerhalb outside, out of, exterior;
~ **meines Bereiches** beyond my province; ~ **der Dienststunden** out of office hours; ~ **der Stadt** out of the town (center);
sich ~ **eindecken** to draw one's supplies from abroad; **von** ~ **kommen** to come from outside the town; ~ **wohnen** to live out of town.
außer | irdisch extraterrestrial; ~**kirchliche Trauung** common-law marriage.
außerkonkursliche Abwicklung zugunsten der Gläubiger general assignment for the benefit of creditors.
Außerkraftsetzung abrogation, suspension, repeal, invalidation;
ausdrückliche ~ express abrogation;
~ **eines Abkommens** termination of a convention; ~ **eines Gesetzes** repeal (suspension) of a law.
Außerkrafttreten eines Gesetzes suspension of a statute.
Außerkurssetzung withdrawal from circulation, retirement, *(Zahlungsmittel)* demonetization.
außerlehrplanmäßig extracurricular.
äußerlich exterior, external, outward;
rein ~ **betrachtet** on the face of it; ~ **unversehrt** undamaged on the outside;
~ **in Ordnung sein** *(Scheck)* to be regular on its face;
~**e Erscheinung** outward appearance; **nur zum** ~**en Gebrauch** for external use only.
Äußerlichkeit outward appearance, superficiality.
Äußerlichkeiten matter of form, formality;
bloße ~ mere formalities;
nur auf ~ **bedacht sein** to have everything in the shopwindow;
nach ~ **urteilen** to judge s. th. from the outside.
äußern to express, to utter, to voice, to speak one's mind, to give one's opinion, to give forth, to talk;
sich zu etw. ~ to put forward one's opinion about s. th.; **sich abfällig** ~ to speak unfavo(u)rably; **sich amtlich** ~ to go on record; **seine Ansicht** ~ to express one's opinion; **sich ausführlich über etw.** ~ to be specific about s. th.; **Bedenken** ~ to express doubts; **sich begeistert** ~ to rave *(sl.)*; **seine Bewunderung laut** ~ to be loud in one's admiration; **sich dahingehend** ~ to express o. s. to the effect; **sich gegen jem.** ~ to pronounce against s. o.; **sich gutachtlich** ~ to give one's opinion; **sich herabsetzend** ~ to speak disparagingly; **sich klar und offen** ~ to speak one's mind clearly and to the point; **Kritik** ~ to criticize; **seine Meinung** ~ to express one's view, to speak for o. s.; **sich zu einem Problem** ~ to square up to a problem; **sich zu einem Thema** ~ to express one's views on a subject; **im gereizten Ton** ~ to snap out; **sich überheblich** ~ to lay down the law; **Verdacht** ~ to voice a suspicion; **Vermutung** ~ to venture a guess; **sich vertraulich** ~ to speak off the record.
außerordentlich extraordinary, extra, out of the common, exceptional, exceeding, special, out of all measure;
~**e Aktionärsversammlung einberufen** to call an extraordinary meeting of shareholders (stockholders, *US*); ~**e und betriebsfremde Aufwendungen** extraordinary and outside expense; ~**e Ausgaben** extraordinary expenses, extras, *(Haushalt)* extrabudgetary expenses; ~**e Dividende** superdividend, surplus dividend *(US)*, melon *(US)*; ~**e Erträge** extraordinary income; ~**e Fähigkeiten** unusual abilities; ~**er Gesandter** extraordinary ambassador; ~**e Hauptversammlung** extraordinary general meeting *(Br.)*; ~**e Kündigung** dismissal for exceptional reasons; ~**e Leistung** exceptional achievement; ~ **anziehendes Mädchen** extremely attractive girl; ~**er Professor** associate professor, professor extraordinarius, senior lecturer *(Br.)*; ~**e Reserve** *(Versicherungswesen)* reserve; ~**e Rücklage** surplus (extraordinary) reserve, contingency fund; ~**e Vollmachten** special powers; ~**e Zahlung** extra payment.
außerparlamentarisch extraparliamentary, outdoor, out-of-door *(Br.)*.
außerplanmäßig supernumerary, extracurricular, noncommissioned, *(Haushalt)* extrabudgetary, nonbudgetary *(Br.)*;
~**e Ausgaben** expenditure not budgeted for; ~**er Beamter** unestablished civil servant, supernumerary; ~**er Halt** unscheduled stop *(US)*; ~**e Stelle** supernumerary post.
außerschulisch out-of-school, extracurricular.
Äußerst | en, bis zum to the full;
das ~**e befürchten** to fear the worst; **bis zum** ~**en gehen** to go the whole length, to run to an extreme, to go to extremes (the limit, *US*); **zum** ~**en kommen** to come to a pitch; **jeden sein** ~**es tun lassen** pull devil, pull baker; **zum** ~**en entschlossen sein** to be ready to go to the bitter end; **zum** ~**en gebracht sein** to be reduced to extremities; **auf das** ~**e gefaßt sein** to be prepared for the worst; **zum** ~**en getrieben sein** to stand at bay; **zum** ~**en treiben** to bring to the last push, to take extreme measures; **zum** ~**en getrieben werden** to be driven to extremities;
wenn es zum ~**en kommt** when it comes to the push, if the worst comes to the worst.
äußerst utmost, utter, extreme, exceeding, farthest, ultimate, last, knockdown, outside;
~ **gewissenhaft** conscientious to a degree; ~ **überrascht** immensely surprised;
in ~**er Armut leben** to live in dire need; ~**e Belastung** maximum load; **im** ~**en Falle** in the extreme case (utmost); ~**e Gefahr** extraordinary danger; ~**e Grenze** deadline *(US)*; **bis zu den** ~**en Grenzen der Erde** to the farthermost ends of the earth; **im** ~**en Norden** in the extreme North; ~**er Preis** bottom (lowest) price; ~**er Termin** final date, deadline *(US)*; **von** ~**er Wichtigkeit** of utmost importance; **im** ~**en Winkel der Erde leben** to live in the uttermost corner of the earth.
außer | staatlich extrastate; ~**stande sein etw. zu tun** to be unable to do s. th.
äußerstenfalls if the worst comes to the worst.
außertariflich outside the agreed scale;
~**e Zahlungen** payments over and above.
Äußerung expression, utterance, voice, vent, *(Bemerkung)* observation, comment, remark;
durch behördliche ~**en** through the government organ; **amtliche** ~ official comment; **beleidigende** ~ actionable words, defamatory statement; **der Rechtsverfolgung entzogene** ~ privileged communication (libel action); **gutachtliche** ~ expert opinion; **leichtfertige** ~**en** flippant remarks; **mündliche** ~ verbal act; **richterliche** ~**en** deliverances of a judge; **unwahre** ~**en** injurious falsehoods;
~**en, zu denen [keine] Erklärungen oder Berichtigungen veröffentlicht werden müssen** statement privileged [subject] [without] explanation or contradiction; ~**en in Wahrnehmung berechtigter Interessen (der Immunität)** privileged communication;
sich jeder ~ **enthalten** to refrain from comments; **unvorsichtige** ~ **fallen lassen** to drop a careless remark; **sich zu keiner** ~ **ver-**

leiten lassen to refuse to be drawn; ~ **in Wahrnehmung berechtigter Interessen machen** to make a statement on a privileged occasion; **beleidigende ~en zurücknehmen** to withdraw an offending expression.

außervertraglich noncontractual;
~**e Haftung** tortuous liability.

Aussetzen *(Motor)* failure, misfiring.

aussetzen *(Flugzeugmotor)* to stall, to pack up *(sl.)*, *(Kind)* to expose, to abandon, *(Maschine)* to stop, *(Motor)* to fail, to misfire, to stall, to conk out *(sl.)*, *(Passagiere)* to disembark, to land, to put ashore, *(Summe)* to settle, *(Tätigkeit)* to discontinue, *(unterwerfen)* to subject, to expose, *(verschieben)* to postpone, to defer, to put off, *(vertagen)* to adjourn, to suspend;
an jem. etw. ~ to find fault with s. o.; **an jem. nichts** ~ to have no objection against s. o.; **mit der Arbeit** ~ to stop working; **Motor höchster Beanspruchung** ~ to impose great stress on an engine; **mit der Behandlung** ~ to discontinue a treatment; **Belohnung** ~ to offer (hold out) a reward; **Beschluß** ~ to stay a decree, to stop execution; **Boot** ~ to launch (hoist out) a boat; **Entscheidung über die Konkursanordnung** ~ to stay a petition; **sich einer Gefahr** ~ to expose o. s. to a danger; **sich dem allgemeinen Gelächter** ~ to expose o. s. to universal ridicule; **sich einer Haftung** ~ to incur a liability; **neugeborenes Kind** ~ to expose a new-born child; **sich der Kritik** ~ to subject o. s. (lay o. s. open) to criticism; **Kursnotierung** ~ to suspend a quotation; **jem. eine Leibrente** ~ to settle a life annuity on s. o.; **Matrosen auf einer unbewohnten Insel** ~ to maroon a sailor; **seiner Tochter ein Nadelgeld** ~ to allow a stipend to one's daughter; **Preis** ~ to offer a prize; **Preis auf jds. Kopf** ~ to put a prize on s. one's head; **Rente** ~ to settle an annuity; **sich einem Risiko** ~ to run a risk; **Ruhegehalt** ~ to settle a pension; **Strafvollziehung** ~ to suspend execution of a sentence; **mit dem Studium** ~ to interrupt one's studies; **Summe** ~ to appoint (settle) a sum; **Tag** ~ to take a day off; **Termin** ~ to adjourn a hearing; **Urteilsverkündung** ~ to reserve judgment, *(Strafurteil)* to suspend a sentence; **Verfahren** ~ to abate (suspend) proceedings, to stay execution; **Vermächtnis** ~ to bequeath, to bequest; **Vollstreckung eines Urteils** ~ to suspend a judgment (the execution); **an einem Vorschlag etw.** ~ to have objections to a proposal; **dem Wetter** ~ to weather; **Wirtschaft großen Belastungen** ~ to place great strains on the economy; **seiner Frau ein Wittum** ~ to settle a jointure on one's wife; **Zahlung** ~ to suspend payment; **zeitweilig** ~ to intermit; **Zwangsvollstreckung** ~ to stay execution.

Aussetzung *(Aufschub)* postponement, deferment, *(Kind)* exposure, exposition, abandonment, *(Preis)* offer, promise, *(Unterbrechung)* discontinuance, interruption, *(Verfahren)* stay of proceedings, *(Vertagung)* adjournment, *(Zahlung)* suspension, moratorium;
einstweilige ~ writ of probable cause; **vorübergehende** ~ temporary suspension, stay;
~ **einer Belohnung** offer of (offering) a reward; ~ **der Entscheidung über die Konkursanordnung** stay of a petition; ~ **eines neugeborenen Kindes** exposure (exposition) of a newborn child; ~ **der Kursnotierung** suspension of the quotation; ~ **einer Leibrente** settlement of an annuity; ~ **eines Nadelgeldes für seine Tochter** allowance of a stipend to one's daughter; ~ **der Notierung** suspension of a quotation; ~ **einer Pension** settling a pension; ~ **des Rechts auf richterliche Haftprüfung** suspension of the writ of habeas corpus; ~ **einer Rente** settlement of an annuity; ~ **eines Ruhegehalts** settling of a pension; ~ **der Strafvollstreckung** suspension of execution; ~ **eines Termins** adjournment of a hearing; ~ **der Todesstrafe** respite *(Br.)*; ~ **des Urteils** reserving a (arrest, suspension) of judgment; ~ **eines Verfahrens** abatement and revival, abatement (suspension, stay) of proceedings, supersedeas; ~ **eines Vermächtnisses** bequeathal, bequest; ~ **der Vollstreckung** respite of a sentence; ~ **von Zahlungen** suspension of payments; ~ **der Zwangsvollstreckung** stay of execution;
~ **des Verfahrens beantragen** to apply for a stay of court proceedings.

Aussetzungs|antrag motion to set aside judgment; ~**beschluß** discontinuing order.

Aussicht view, prospect, outlook, aspect, vista, *(Chance)* opening, expectation, chance;
mit der ~ späterer Beteiligung with a view to partnership; **mit ~ auf einen zukünftigen Vertragsabschluß** looking forward to a future contract;
allgemeine ~en general outlook; **nicht die geringste** ~ not a dog's (not a ghost of a) chance; **glänzende ~en** bright prospects; **günstige** ~ opening; **herrliche** ~ superb view; **politische ~en** political outlook; **schlechte ~en** bad (poor) outlook, poor prospects; **schöne** ~ fine view; **trostlose ~en** dull prospects; **trübe** ~ blue lookout, gray (sombre) view; **unverbaubare** ~ unrestricted view; **vielversprechende ~en** healthy (promising) future; **weitere ~en** *(Wetter)* further outlook; **wirtschaftiche ~en** prospects of the economy;
~ **von einem Berg** view of a mountain; **gute ~en im Beruf** a job with good prospects; ~ **auf schwere Bestrafung** possibility of severe penalties; ~ **nach hinten** *(Zimmer)* retrospective view; ~**en auf kurze Sicht** short-term prospects;
herrliche ~ gewähren to command a fine view; **in ~ haben** to have in prospect; **glänzende ~en haben** to make out for a brilliant future; **gute ~en haben** to stand (run) a good chance, to have fair prospects in life; **gute ~en haben, gewählt zu werden** to stand a good chance of being elected; **Stellung in ~ haben** to have a job in prospect; **in ~ nehmen** to envisage; **j. für einen wichtigen Posten in ~ nehmen** to consider s. o. for an important position; **jem. eine Belohnung in ~ stellen** to promise s. o. a reward; **etw. direkt in ~ stellen** to hold out an immeditate prospect; **neue Wohnung in ~ stellen** to hold out the prospect of a new flat; ~ **verbauen** to obstruct the view, to stop a neighbo(u)r's light; ~ **versperren** to intercept (interrupt) a view.

Aussichts|aufnahme *(Film)* distance shot; ~**bus** sightseeing bus, rubberneck waggon *(sl.)*; **großes ~fenster** view (picture) window; ~**hügel** watch *(Scot.)*; ~**kuppel** *(Bahn)* vista dome.

aussichtslos hopeless, without prospects, desperate, futile;
~ **sein** *(Beruf)* to offer no prospects; **völlig ~ sein** to be a dead end;
~**er Beruf** terminal (blind-alley) job; ~**er Beruf sein** to offer no prospects, to be a dead end *(fam.)*; ~**er Fall** hopeless case; ~**er Kampf** losing fight; **in einer ~en Lage sein** to be in a desperate state; ~**e Sache** lost case; **sich um eine ~e Sache bemühen,** ~**e Sache betreiben** to flog a dead horse, to play a losing game; **von vornherein ~er Versuch** experiment doomed to be a failure; ~**e Versuche unternehmen** to make futile attempts.

Aussichtslosigkeit desperateness, futility.

Aussichtspunkt viewpoint, lookout *(US)*, overlook.

aussichtsreich fair, favo(u)rable, promising, odds-on, likely-looking;
~ **sein** to offer good prospects;
~**er junger Mann** a young hopeful; ~**e Stellung** job (position) with good prospects; ~**es Unternehmen** promising undertaking.

Aussichts|turm observation tower, belvedere; ~**wagen** observation car; ~**zug** observation train *(US)*.

Aussieben screening, washout *(US sl.)*.

aussieben to reject, to eliminate, to wash out *(US sl.)*, *(Radio)* to filter out;
Kandidaten ~ to screen candidates.

aussiedeln to transplant, to depopulate, to evacuate.

Aussiedler evacuee, emigrant, refugee.

Aussiedlung evacuation, depopulation, transplantation.

aussöhnen, sich to reconcile; **sich mit seinem Schicksal** ~ to become reconciled with one's fate.

Aussöhner healer.

Aussöhnung zustande bringen to bring about a reconciliation.

aussondern *(abtrennen)* to separate, to set apart, *(ausmustern)* to cast off (out), to reject, to eliminate, *(aussortieren)* to single out, to sort [out], *(Geldbeträge)* to appropriate, to earmark, *(im Konkurs)* to parcel (sort) out;
ungeeignete Bewerber ~ to screen candidates; **sein Eigentum aus dem Konkurs** ~ to take as true owner goods out of the bankrupt's possession; **Waren aus dem Vermögen des Konkursschuldners** ~ to take the goods out of the order and disposition of the bankrupt.

Aussonderung separation, selection, *(Geldbeträge)* appropriation, earmarking, *(im Konkurs)* parcelling (sorting) out;
~ **von Anlagegütern** segregation of assets; ~ **von Betriebsmitteln für Versorgungszwecke** *(Pensionsplan)* funding; ~ **ungeeigneter Bewerber** screening of candidates.

Aussonderungs|anspruch, ~**recht** *(Konkurs)* colo(u)rable claim, preferential claim.

aussonderungsberechtigt|e Forderung colo(u)rable claim; ~**er Gläubiger** creditor with a colo(u)rable claim.

aussonderungsfähig *(Konkurs)* recoverable, colo(u)rable;
~**e Vermögenswerte** equitable (colo(u)rable) assets.

Aussonderungs|fähigkeit *(Konkurs)* recoverableness, colo(u)rableness; ~**recht** *(Konkurs)* colo(u)rable claim; ~**verfahren** reclamation proceedings *(US)*.

aussortieren to sort out, to assort, to grade, *(Unbrauchbares)* to reject, to cast out.
Aussortierung sorting, assortment, *(Unbrauchbares)* rejection;
~ **mit der Hand** handsorting.
ausspähen, feindliche Stellung to develop an enemy's position.
Ausspannen recreation, relaxation, *(Versicherungskunden)* twisting.
ausspannen to recreate, to relax, to go (take it) easy, to unbend the mind, *(Kunden)* to entice, *(Versicherungskunden)* to twist;
Bogen aus der Maschine ~ to take a sheet out of the typewriter; **richtig** ~ to have a good slack; **ganzen Tag** ~ to dedicate a day for pleasure.
aussparen *(im Text)* to leave blank;
Gelände bei der Bombardierung ~ to leave an area unbombed; **Streitfrage** ~ to avoid a controversial question.
aussperren to shut (lock) out, *(Arbeiter)* to lock out, *(Zeilen)* to space out.
Aussperrung lockout.
Aussperrungsmaßnahmen lockout actions.
ausspielen *(Gegner)* to outmanoeuvre, *(Lotteriegewinn)* to raffle;
einen gegen den anderen ~ to play one off against the other, to play games with *(sl.)*; **Karte** ~ to play a card; **sein ganzes Können gegen j.** ~ to throw one's skill into the scales against s. o.; **seine Rolle zu stark** ~ to overdo one's part in a play; **letzten Trumpf** ~ to play one's trump card.
Ausspielung lottery, raffle;
~ **vornehmen** to draw a lottery.
ausspinnen, Geschichte lang und breit to spin out a story.
ausspionieren to spy out;
Geheimnis ~ to peep out a secret.
Aussprache *(ling.)* pronunciation, accent, articulation, *(parl.)* [floor] debate, *(Unterredung)* talk, conversation, discussion, debate;
allgemeine ~ *(parl.)* full-dress debate; **buchstabengetreue** ~ spelling pronunciation; **deutliche** ~ distinct pronunciation, articulation; **falsche** ~ faulty articulation, mispronunciation; **gezierte** ~ precious pronunciation; **heftige** ~ heated debate; **korrekte** ~ diction *(US)*; **vertrauliche** ~ intimate talk; **zwanglose** ~ informal talk;
~ **im Plenum** floor debate;
in eine ~ **eintreten** to commence a debate; **j. an seiner** ~ **als Ausländer erkennen** to recognize s. o. by his foreign accent; **offene** ~ **mit jem. haben** to be quite frank with s. o.; **schlechte** ~ **haben** to pronounce badly; ~ **leiten** to lead a debate; ~ **schließen** to close a debate; **an einer** ~ **teilnehmen** to take part (a hand) in a debate; ~ **zusammenfassen** to summarize a discussion;
~**abend** evening forum *(US)*; ~**bezeichnung** phonetic transcription; ~**wörterbuch** pronouncing dictionary.
aussprechen to express, to voice, *(ling.)* to utter, to deliver, to pronounce;
sich ~ to talk o. s. out; **seine Ansicht** ~ to speak one's mind, to state one's view, to have one's say; **sein Bedauern** ~ to express one's regrets; **jem. sein Beileid** ~ to offer s. o. one's condolences; **sich dagegen** ~ to make objections, to argue in the negative; **sich klar und deutlich dagegen** ~ to swing round into clear disapproval; **seinen Dank** ~ to tender (express) one's thanks; **seine Dankbarkeit** ~ to voice one's gratitude; **deutlich** ~ to articulate; **sich einmal über alles** ~ to make a clean breast of it; **falsch** ~ to mispronounce, to pronounce wrongly; **sich für etw.** ~ to speak for (in support of) s. th.; **sich lobend über j.** ~ to speak highly of s. o.; **sich mit jem.** ~ to unburden o. s. to s. o.; **sich gründlich miteinander** ~ to have a heart-to-heart talk with s. o.; **seine Meinung deutlich (offen)** ~ to express one's view clearly, to speak one's mind; **sich für einen Plan** ~ to advocate a plan; **der Regierung das Vertrauen** ~ to pass a motion (a vote) of confidence; **sich für Sozialreformen** ~ to profess o. s. to be a social reformer; **sich gegen einen Tarifvertrag** ~ to come out against a tariff; **sich gegen die Todesstrafe** ~ to declare o. s. against capital punishment; **Todesurteil über ein Unternehmen** ~ to sign the death warrant for an enterprise; **Urteil** ~ to pass judgment; **Verdacht** ~ to raise a suspicion; **sich vorbehaltlos für etw.** ~ to favo(u)r s. th. without reservation; **sich für ein Vorhaben** ~ to advocate a plan.
Ausspruch statement, utterance, saying, dictum.
ausstaffieren to kit up, to fit out, to equip, to heel *(US sl.)*, *(Film)* to make up, to dress *(coll.)*;
sich ~ to rig o. s. out, to be dressed up to kill.
Ausstaffierung equipment, outfit, *(Film)* makeup, *(Kleidung)* getup, *(verächtlich)* rig;
seltsame ~ queer rig.
Ausstand [labo(u)r] strike, standout, tie-up, turnout *(Br.)*, walkout *(US)*;
sich im ~ **befinden** to be on strike; **in** ~ **treten** to [go on] strike, to come (walk, *US*) out.
ausständig on strike.
Ausstanzstück cut-out.
ausstatten to equip, to outfit, to fit (rig) out, to fit up, to endow, to provide with, to accommodate, to find, *(Film, Stück)* to stage, to mount, *(mil.)* to activate, *(Wohnung)* to furnish;
mit großen Begabungen ~ to endow with great talents; **Fabrik** ~ to equip a factory; **gut** ~ *(Buch)* to get up richly; **Haus** ~ to furnish a house; **Hotel mit allem Komfort** ~ to fit up a hotel with modern conveniences; **mit Kapital** ~ to endow with capital, to capitalize; **j. mit Rechten** ~ to vest s. o. with rights; **reichlich** ~ *(Buch)* to get up richly; **Schiff mit amtlichen Papieren** ~ to document a ship; **Tochter** ~ to portion off a daughter, to give a dowry to a girl, to dower a daughter; **mit Vollmachten** ~ to vest (clothe) with authority.
Ausstatter outfitter, equipment builder.
Ausstattung fitting out, outfitting, rig, kit, equipment, furnishing, turnout, *(Aussteuer)* dowry, marriage portion, trousseau, *(Auto)* trimmings, *(Film)* make-up, setting, *(Geschäftseinrichtung)* outfit, fittings, *(Haus)* apparel, *(Möbel)* furniture, *(Schiff)* appointments, *(Theater)* decor, *(Versorgung)* provision, supply, *(Zubehör)* appurtenance;
in feiner ~ fancy-packed; **in kostbarer** ~ lavishly got up; **mit moderner** ~ with all modern conveniences;
äußere ~ *(Waren)* getup; **erste** ~ *(Bankwesen)* initial allocation; **feine** ~ fancy packing; **günstige** ~ *(Anleihe)* attractive terms; **künstlerische** ~ artistic getup; **personelle** ~ personnel strength; **technische** ~ machinery; **zusätzliche** ~ *(Auto)* optional equipment;
~ **mit verschiedenen Aktien** *(Kapitalanlagegesellschaft)* multiple capital structure; ~ **einer Anleihe** terms of a loan; ~ **eines Betriebes** factory equipment; ~ **eines Buches** getup (turnout) of a book; ~ **eines Hotels** appointments for a hotel; ~ **mit Kapital** capital equipment, capitalization; **großzügige** ~ **eines Krankenhauses** liberal endowment of a hospital; ~ **einer Pensionskasse** funding of a pension fund; ~ **für die Tropen** tropical outfit; ~ **eines Zimmers** appointments of a room;
Laden mit gesamter ~ **erwerben** to buy a shop with all fixtures; **zur** ~ **gerechnet werden** to be classified as equipment.
Ausstattungs|abteilung outfitting department; ~**arbeiten** shop-fitting work; ~**film** feature (costume) film, spectacular; ~**gegenstände** fitting (equipment) goods; **Möbel- und** ~**geschäft** house-furnishing firm; **Betriebs- und** ~**hauptbuch** plant and equipment ledger; ~**investitionen** equipment investments; ~**karton** fancy box; ~**kosten** cost of equipment (installation), outfit; ~**leiter** *(Theater)* designer; ~**papier** boxed stationery; ~**politik** packaging policy; ~**stück** *(Theater)* costume piece, spectacular, extravagancy; **besondere** ~**wünsche** *(Auto)* optional extras.
ausstechen *(verdrängen)* to oust, to supplant, to outrival;
Konkurrenten ~ to outdistance (oust) a rival; **alle Konkurrenten** ~ to be preeminent above all one's rivals; **Nebenbuhler** ~ to supplant (oust) a rival; **Torf** ~ to cut (dig) peat.
ausstehen *(aushalten)* to endure, to bear, to stand, *(Entscheidung)* to be pending, *(Forderung)* to be outstanding (overdue);
Angst ~ to suffer anxiety;
j. nicht ~ **können** to have no patience with s. o., to have s. o. in one's hairs *(US)*; **j. für den Tod nicht** ~ **können** not to be able to stand s. o. at any price; **etw.** ~ **müssen** to have to go through with (put up with a lot); **furchtbare Schmerzen** ~ **müssen** to undergo terrible pain.
ausstehend outstanding, delinquent, receivable, *(Sendung)* overdue;
~ **sein** to stand out, to be in arrears;
~**er Bericht** report yet to come; ~**e Entscheidung** pending decision; ~**e Forderungen** outstanding debts, outs; ~**e Zahlung** arrears, account receivables *(US)*.
aussteigen to get out (off, *US*), to alight, to climb out, *(Flugzeug)* to deplane, *(aus einem Geschäft)* to bale (bail, *US*) out, *(Schiff)* to disembark;
aus ausländischen Anlagewerten ~ to switch out of foreign assets; **aus einem Bus** ~ to get down from a bus, to debus; **j. an der Ecke** ~ **lassen** to put s. o. down at the corner; **aus einem Geschäft** ~ to declare a bargain off, to back out of a deal; **aus dem Geschäft der Errichtung von Bürogebäuden** ~ to jump off one's office blocks; **aus einer Sache** ~ to get (back, *US*) out of s. th.; **bei der nächsten Station** ~ to get off the train next station; **aus einem Zug** ~ to alight from (get off) a train.

Aussteigeöffnung *(Dach)* trap door.
Ausstellen *(Ware)* exhibiting, exposing, display, *(Scheck)* drawing.
ausstellen to make out, to issue, *(auf einer Ausstellung)* to exhibit, to expose, *(Gas, Radio)* to turn off, *(im Schaufenster)* to [set on] show, to display, *(Urkunde)* to draw up;
sich ein Armutszeugnis ~ to betray one's ignorance; **Attest (Bescheinigung)** ~ to furnish (hand) a certificate; **etw. blanko** ~ to make out in blank; **auf den Inhaber** ~ to make out to bearer; **Konnossement** ~ to make out a bill of lading; **Kreditbrief** ~ to issue a letter of credit; **auf jds. Namen** ~ to make out in s. one's name; **öffentlich** ~ to exhibit s. th. to the public; **Paß** ~ to issue a passport; **Quittung** ~ to [give a] receipt; **Rechnung** ~ to [make out an] invoice; **Reitwechsel** ~ to fly a kite *(Br.)*; **Scheck** ~ to draw (write out, make out) a check *(US)* (cheque, *Br.*); **Schuldschein** ~ to sign a bond; **Schuldverschreibungen** ~ to issue bonds; **Totenschein** ~ to issue a death certificate; **Urkunde in dreifacher Ausfertigung** ~ to make out a document in triplicate; **Versicherungspolice** ~ to issue a policy; **Waren auf einer Messe** ~ to exhibit goods at a fair; **Waren im Schaufenster** ~ to put goods on show, to display goods in the shop window; **Wechsel** ~ to draw (make out) a bill of exchange; **Wechsel an Order** ~ to make a bill payable to order; **Zeugnis** ~ to furnish (hand) a certificate.
ausstellende | Behörde issuing authority; ~ **Firma** exhibiting company.
Aussteller *(Emittent)* issuer, emitter, *(Kreditbrief)* issuing bank, *(Messe)* exhibitor, shower, *(Wechsel, Scheck)* drawer, maker, writer, *(Vollmachtgeber)* constituent;
~ **im Konkurs** drawer bankrupt; ~ **verstorben** drawer dead; **an den** ~ **zurück** refer to drawer;
~ **einer Bescheinigung** certifier; ~ **eines Gefälligkeitswechsels** accommodation maker, kiteflyer *(Br., sl.)*; ~ **einer Konzession** licenser; ~ **eines Passes** issuer of a passport; ~ **eines Solawechsels** maker of a promissory note; ~ **einer Urkunde** drawer of a document; ~ **ungedeckter Wechsel** kiteflyer *(Br., sl.)*;
~**haftung** liability for endorsement; ~**provision** drawing commission; ~**verzeichnis** *(Messe)* list of exhibitors, fair directory.
Ausstellfenster *(Auto)* quarter windows.
Ausstellung making out, drawing, *(Akkreditiv)* issue, issuing, *(Messe)* fair, exhibition, exposure, exposition *(US)*, *(Schau)* show, shopping parade, pitching, *(im Schaufenster)* display, exhibiting;
internationale ~ international exhibition; **landwirtschaftliche** ~ agricultural fair, regional show;
~ **eines Akkreditivs** issue of a letter of credit; ~ **überhöhter Einfuhrrechnungen** overinvoicing of imports; ~ **eines Ersatzfrachtbriefes** memorandum billing *(US)*; ~ **eines Frachtbriefes** making out a consignment; ~ **von Gefälligkeitswechseln** kiteflying *(Br.)*; ~ **einer Geldanweisung** issue of an order of money; ~ **eines Kreditbriefes** issue of a letter of credit; ~ **eines Lagerscheines** issuing of a warehouse warrant; ~ **von Leihgaben** loan collection; ~ **eines falschen Lieferscheines** misbilling; ~ **eines Passes** making out a passport; ~ **einer Rechnung** invoicing, making out a bill, billing; ~ **eines Schecks** making out (drawing) a check *(US)* (cheque, *Br.*); ~ **eines Solawechsels** making a note; ~ **eines Überziehungschecks** overcertification; ~ **einer Urkunde** execution (issuance, *US*) of a deed; **betrügerische** ~ **einer Urkunde** fraud in the execution; ~ **eines Versicherungsscheins** execution of a policy; ~ **eines Wechsels** making out a bill of exchange;
~ **beschicken** to take space at an exhibition; ~ **besuchen** to attend a fair; ~ **eröffnen** to open an exhibition; **in eine** ~ **gehen** to go to an exhibition; ~ **gestalten** to arrange an exhibition; ~ **veranstalten** to stage (make) an exhibition.
Ausstellungs | artikel goods exhibited for sale, exhibits; ~**behörde** exhibition board; ~**datum** date of issue, issuing date; ~**einwand** *(Wechsel)* real defence *(Br.)*; ~**fläche** [stand]space, exhibition (floor) space; ~**gebäude** fair (exhibition) buildings; ~**gebühr** space rate; ~**gegenstand** exhibition subject, show piece, exhibit; ~**gelände** exhibition grounds (site), fair site (ground) *(US)*; ~**gesellschaft** exhibition (exposition) corporation; ~**gut**, ~**güter** exhibited articles, exhibits; ~**halle** exhibit hall; ~**insel** exhibition island; ~**jahr** year of issue; ~**kasten** display case, showcase; ~**katalog** fair catalog(ue); ~**kosten** exhibition expenses; ~**leitung** exhibition board (officials), fair authorities; ~**material zum Selbstkostenpreis** self-liquidating display; **geliehenes** ~**material** loaned display; ~**objekt** exhibition, exhibit, showpiece; ~**ort** *(Wechsel)* drawer's domicile, place of exchange (issue), issuing place; ~**pavillon** pavilion; ~**plakat** show card; ~**platz** exhibition grounds, show place; ~**postamt** issuing post office.
Ausstellungsraum showroom, exhibition (display) room, salon, *(in einer Ausstellung)* space in an exhibition, *(Hotel)* stock (sample) room;
~ **eines Händlers** dealer showroom;
~ **belegen** to take space; ~ **vergeben** to farm out a right to space in an exhibition.
Ausstellungs | räume exhibition premises; ~**schachtel** display box; ~**stand** stand in a trade exhibition, exhibition stand; ~**stück** exhibit, showpiece, showroom model; ~**tag** *(Wechsel)* date of issue; ~**unternehmen** display contractor; ~**vertrag** trading contract; ~**vitrine** display case, showcase; ~**wagen** show waggon, van, *(bei Umzügen)* floater; ~**ware** goods displayed; ~**wesen** exhibitionism; ~**zelt** pavilion.
Aussterbeetat, auf dem ~ **stehen** to be about to be abolished.
Aussterben, im on the wane; **kurz vor dem** ~ close to extinction.
aussterben to die out.
Aussteuer advancement by portion, trousseau, bottom drawer, bridal outfit, dowry, dotation, marriage portion;
~**befugnis** *(Treuhänder)* power of advancement.
aussteuern *(el.)* to modulate, to control, *(Tochter)* to portion off, to endow.
Aussteuer | police endowment (portion) policy; ~**truhe** hope chest *(US sl.)*.
Aussteuerung *(el.)* level control, modulation, *(mar.)* approach, *(Tochter)* endowment, *(Trägerwelle)* modulation.
Aussteuer | versicherung endowment (marriage portion) insurance; ~**versicherungsplan** endowment assurance scheme *(Br.)*.
Ausstieg exit, *(Dach)* trap door, *(Flugzeug, Schiff)* disembarkation;
~**luke** *(Raumschiff)* escape hatch.
Ausstoß output, outturn, production, run, manufacture, make, *(mar.)* torpedo tube;
jährlicher ~ annual output; **mengenmäßiger** ~ physical output; **täglicher** ~ daily output;
~ **pro Arbeitsstunde** manhour output; **potentieller** ~ **einer Volkswirtschaft** potential gross national output;
~ **den Aufnahmemöglichkeiten des Marktes anpassen** to tailor output to the market; ~ **steigern** to step up its output; ~ **verringern** to cut back (reduce the) output;
~**beschränkung** restriction of output.
ausstoßen *(Abfallprodukt)* to eject, to expel, *(ausschließen)* to expel, *(Fabrikat)* to turn out, to produce, to manufacture, *(Vulkan)* to emit, to eject, to throw out;
Fluch ~ to utter a curse; **Offizier aus dem Heer** ~ to cashier an officer; **täglich eine Tonne Stahl** ~ to produce a ton of steel daily.
Ausstoß | rohr *(Torpedo)* torpedo tube; ~**steigerung** step-up in output *(US)*; ~**vorrichtung** *(Schiff)* torpedo launching gear; ~**zahlen** output (production) figures; ~**ziffer** rate of output.
ausstrahlen to radiate, to emit, *(Rundfunk)* to transmit, to flash; **Heiterkeit** ~ to radiate gaiety; **Sendung** ~ to beam out a program(me); **Sendung über Kurzwelle** ~ to transmit a program(me) on short wave; **Wärme** ~ to radiate warmth.
Ausstrahlung radiation, emission, *(mehrere Kanäle)* syndication, *(Persönlichkeit)* personality, *(Rundfunk)* transmission;
inflatorische ~ **auffangen** to cushion inflationary factors; **negative** ~**en spüren** to feel bad vibrations.
Ausstrahlungstermin play date.
ausstrecken to stretch [out], to reach out;
Fühler ~ *(fig.)* to throw out a feeler; **sich** ~ *(Ebene)* to extend, to stretch.
Ausstreichen cancellation, deletion.
ausstreichen to strike (blot, mark, rule, scratch) out, to efface, to cancel, to delete, to obliterate, to expunge, to kill, *(auf Wechsel)* to cross out;
jds. Namen auf einer Liste ~ to cancel a name on a list; **Rechnungsposten** ~ to scratch an item from an account; **Zahlen** ~ to cancel figures.
Ausstreichung deletion, defacement, cancellation, obliteration, *(auf Wechsel)* crossing out.
ausstreuen to spread, to diffuse, to disseminate;
Gerücht ~ to spread (disseminate) a rumo(u)r; **Nachrichten** ~ to circulate news.
Ausstreuung dissemination.
ausströmen *(Gas)* to escape, to issue, to leak out, to exhaust, *(Wasser)* to stream (pour, flow) out;
aus einem beschädigten Tank ~ to pour out of a damaged tank; **Wärme** ~ to radiate warmth.

ausstudieren to take one's degree, to graduate *(US)*.
ausstudiert haben to have finished one's studies.
aussuchen to choose, to select, to pick [out];
sich je nach Bedarf ~ to have it both ways; **sich ganz in Ruhe** ~ to pretty much take one's choice.
Austastpegel *(Fernsehen)* black level.
Austausch *(Auswechslung)* [inter]change, commutation, *(Ersatz)* replacement, substitution, *(Tauschgeschäft)* exchange, barter;
im ~ **für** in exchange (return) for;
kultureller ~ cultural exchanges;
~ **von Bemerkungen** *(über den ganzen Sitzungssaal)* cross talk *(Br.)*; ~ **von Erinnerungen** reminiscent talk; ~ **von Ferienplätzen** holiday interchange; ~ **von Fertigprodukten gegen Rohstoffe** exchange of finished goods against raw materials; ~ **von Gefangenen** exchange of prisoners; ~ **von Höflichkeiten** interchange of civilities, reciprocation of courtesies; ~ **von Informationen** exchange of information; **wechselseitiger** ~ **von Krediterfahrungen** credit interchange; ~ **von Landbesitz** exchange (reciprocal transfer) of estates; ~ **vertraulicher Nachrichten** passage of confidence; ~ **von Noten** exchange of notes; ~ **der Ratifizierungsurkunden** exchange of ratifications; ~ **von Vollmachten** exchange of powers; ~ **von Vorstandsmitgliedern** management switch;
Rohstoffe im ~ **gegen Maschinen erhalten** to receive raw materials in exchange for machinery; **im** ~ **kommen** to come on an exchange basis; ~ **technischer Erfahrungen vereinbaren** to agree upon the exchange of technical know-how;
~**abkommen** two-way agreement; ~**anzeige** barter (exchange) advertisement.
austauschbar exchangeable, interchangeable, commutable, replaceable, mutual;
gegenseitig ~ *(Effekten)* interconvertible, interchangeable.
Austauschbarkeit interchangeability, *(Effekten)* interconvertibility.
Austausch|bedingungen terms of trade; ~**dozent** exchange lecturer.
austauschen to change for, to exchange, to barter, to commute, to interchange;
zwei Bücher ~ to replace one book by another; **alte Erinnerungen** ~ to exchange old memories.
Austausch|gruppe exchange group; ~**güter** merchandise; ~**inserat** exchange advertising; ~**lehrer** exchange teacher; ~**offizier** relief officer; ~**prinzip** interchangeability principle; ~**professor** exchange (guest) professor; ~**programm** exchange program(m)e; ~**recht** option of exchange; ~**relationen** *(Handel)* terms of trade; ~**scheck** exchange check *(US)* (cheque, *Br.*); ~**stelle** *(Lehrer)* exchange teaching job; ~**stück** exchange copy, *(Ersatzstück)* spare [part]; ~**student** exchange student; ~**verhältnis** *(Handel)* terms of trade; ~**werkstoff** alternative (alternate, *US*) material, substitute.
austeilen to deal (measure, share, portion) out, to outportion, to distribute, to allot;
Almosen (Liebesgaben) ~ to dispense (distribute) alms; **Lebensmittelrationen** ~ to share out food rations; **Schläge** ~ to deal out blows; **sparsam** ~ to dole out.
Austeilung dispensation, distribution, share-out, issuance *(US)*.
Austeritätsprogramm austerity program(m)e.
Austern|fang oyster fishing; ~**zucht** oyster farm; ~**züchter** oyster farmer.
austoben, sich to sow one's wild oats, to have one's fling, *(Sturm)* to spend itself.
Austrag, Sache zum ~ **bringen** to settle a matter.
austragen *(Briefe)* to deliver, *(Posten)* to retire, to abandon;
Meinungsverschiedenheiten mit jem. ~ to settle a difference (to have it out) with s. o.; **Meisterschaft** ~ to hold a championship; **Pakete in der ganzen Stadt** ~ to distribute parcels all over the town; **Sache außergerichtlich** ~ to settle a matter out of court; **Wettbewerb** ~ to contest for a prize; **Zeitung** ~ to do a newspaper round (route, *US*).
Austräger deliverer, deliverman, deliveryman, errand boy, roundsman, *(Zeitung)* newspaper boy.
Austragung *(Briefe)* delivery, *(Posten)* retirement, abandonment;
bis zur ~ **der Sache** pending arrangement.
austreiben, jem. den Hochmut to cure s. o. of his conceit.
austreten to withdraw, to retire, *(WC)* to pay a penny, to go and wash one's hands;
aus einer Gesellschaft ~ to withdraw from a partnership; **aus dem Glied** ~ to leave the ranks; **aus der Kirche** ~ to leave the church; **aus einer Partei** ~ to leave (bolt from, *US*) a party; **aus einem Verein** ~ to discontinue (cancel) one's membership, to resign from a club.
austrinken to empty a glass;
sein Glas bis auf den letzten Tropfen ~ to drain one's glass to the dregs.
Austritt withdrawal, retirement, resignation, *(Gas)* escape, *(Öffnung)* exit, outlet;
~ **aus einem Staatenverband** secession from a union; ~ **aus einem Verein** withdrawal from membership;
seinen ~ **erklären** to resign from membership, to declare (give notice of) one's withdrawal.
Austritts|alter age at exit (withdrawal); ~**anzeige** notice of withdrawal; ~**bescheinigung** leaving certificate, *(Versicherung)* confirmation of withdrawal; ~**erklärung** resignation, retirement, *(Gewerkschaft)* letter of resignation, resignation letter; ~**klausel** *(Gewerkschaft)* escape clause; ~**recht** right of withdrawal; ~**ventil** outlet valve.
austrixen to trip out.
austrocknen *(Flußbett)* to dry up, to drain.
Austrocknung drainage.
austüfteln to puzzle out, to figure out *(US)*;
Sache ~ to fiddle over a job.
ausüben *(berufsmäßig)* to practise, *(Kontrolle)* to exercise, *(Tätigkeit)* to follow, to pursue, to conduct, to perform, to carry on, to exert;
Amt ~ to exercise an office; **Anwaltsberuf** ~ to practise law; **geringe Anziehungskraft** ~ to have little attraction; **starke Anziehungskraft** ~ to be a big draw; **Aufsichtstätigkeit** ~ to exercise supervisory control; **Beruf** ~ to pursue an occupation, to follow (ply) a trade; **Bezugsrecht** ~ to exercise subscription rights; **Druck auf j.** ~ to bring pressure to bear on s. o.; **seinen Einfluß** ~ to exert one's influence; **richterliches Ermessen** ~ to exercise judicial discretion; **Funktion** ~ to fulfil(l) a function; **Gerichtsbarkeit** ~ to exercise jurisdiction; **Gewerbe** ~ to carry on (follow, ply) a trade; **Kontrolle** ~ to exercise control; **Nebenbeschäftigung** ~ to moonlight; **Option** ~ to exercise an option; **Option nicht** ~ to abandon an option; **Praxis** ~ to [carry on a] practice; **Recht** ~ to exercise (enjoy) a right; **sein Stimmrecht** ~ to exercise one's voting rights; **gewerbliche Tätigkeit** ~ to pursue (ply) a trade; **Verbrechen** ~ to perpetrate a crime; **Vetorecht** ~ to veto; **Vorkaufsrecht** ~ to make use of a right of preemption; **Zwang auf j.** ~ to bring pressure to bear on s. o.
ausübend executive, practising;
nicht ~ nonpractising;
~**er Arzt** practitioner; ~**e Gewalt** executive power.
Ausübung exercise, execution, pursuit, carrying on;
aufgrund der ~ **eines Bezugsrechts** on the exercise of an option; **in** ~ **meines Berufes** in pursuance (line, *US*) of my vocation; **in** ~ **seines Dienstes** in performance of his duties, in line of his duty *(US)*;
~ **einer Amtspflicht** discharge of duty; ~ **des Anwaltsberufes** practice of law; **öffentliche** ~ **eines Berufes** public calling; ~ **des richterlichen Ermessens** exercise of judicial discretion; ~ **treuhänderischer Funktionen** exercise of trusteeship functions; ~ **der Gerichtsbarkeit** administration (exercise) of justice; ~ **eines Geschäftsbetriebes** doing business *(Br.)*; ~ **eines Gewerbes** commercial pursuit, carrying on (pursuit of) a trade; ~ **eines im Kriege verbotenen Gewerbes** licence; ~ **einer Kaufoption** exercise of an option to purchase; ~ **von Machtbefugnissen** exercise of power; ~ **einer Nebenbeschäftigung** moonlighting; ~ **eines Nutzungsrechts** enjoyment of a right; ~ **des Prämienrechts** exercise of option; ~ **eines Rechts** use of a right; ~ **der Staatsgewalt durch ein Ministerium** consolidated government; ~ **des Vetos** veto; ~ **des Vorkaufsrechtes** preemption entry;
jem. die Lizenz zur ~ **eines Gewerbes erteilen** to accord permission to transact business, to grant a licence; **in** ~ **seines Amtes handeln** to act in one's official capacity; **j. an der** ~ **seiner Pflichten hindern** to obstruct s. o. in the execution of his duty; **in** ~ **seines Berufes sterben** to die in harness; **auf die** ~ **des Pfandrechts verzichten** to waive the lien.
ausufern to overflow its banks.
Ausverkauf selling off (out), clearance sale, clearing of goods, winding-up sale, sellout *(sl.)*, closeout *(US)*, *(Geschäftsaufgabe)* closing-down (winding-up) sale, *(Ramschverkauf)* rummage (jumble, *Br.*) sale, *(Saisonausverkauf)* seasonal sale, *(Sonderverkauf)* cheap (bargain) sale, White Sale;
~ **einer Auflage** remainder sale; ~ **von Beteiligungen** selloff of holdings; ~ **wegen Geschäftsaufgabe** closing-down sale *(US)*; ~ **durchführen** to sell out, to clear a shop, to close out *(US)*;
Waren im ~ **erwerben** to buy goods at the sales.
ausverkaufen to sell out (off), to clear off (a shop), to close out *(US)*.

Ausverkaufs|abteilung im Erdgeschoß bargain sale basement; ~**anzeigen** White Sale ads; ~**preis** sale (bargain, groundfloor) price, special sales (clearance) price; ~**reklame** bargain sale advertising; ~**ware** reduced (sale) goods; ~**werbung** bargain sale advertising.

ausverkauft cleared, sold (closed, *US*) out, out of stock, outsold, *(Theater)* filled to capacity, full house *(US)*;
zur Zeit ~ temporarily sold out;
~ **sein** to be run out, *(Theater)* to be fully booked; ~ **werden** to be selling out;
vor einem ~en Haus spielen to play to a full house; ~**es Parkett** capacity crowd.

auswachsen to grow into, to grow up, to reach one's full growth; **sich zu einem größeren Krieg** ~ to develop into a major war; **sich zu einem Skandal** ~ to develop into a scandal.

Auswahl choice, assortment, selection, pick, *(Delegation)* draft, *(Marktforschung)* sample, *(Musterkollektion)* variety, assortment, *(Theater)* repertory;
bewußte ~ *(Statistik)* judgment sampling (sample); **geschichtete** ~ *(Statistik)* stratified sample; **große** ~ wide choice (range); **gute** ~ comprehensive range; **kleine** ~ narrow range of choice; **mehrphasige** ~ multistage sampling; **reiche (reichhaltige)** ~ rich (large, varied) assortment, rich selection; **repräsentative** ~ representative selection, *(Statistik)* controlled sampling; **systematische** ~ systematic sample; **für den Versicherer ungünstige** ~ selection against the insurer;
repräsentative ~ **von Exportgütern** representative selection of exports; ~ **der Frachtstrecke** buyer's right of routing; ~ **von Führungskräften** executive selection; ~ **eines repräsentativen Querschnitts** sampling; ~ **der besseren Risiken** *(Versicherung)* selection by the company; ~ **von Werbeträgern** media selection;
reiche ~ **bieten** to offer a wide range; **vollkommene** ~ **haben** to have the best choice; **Werke in** ~ **herausgeben** to publish a selection; **sich für die** ~ **genügend Zeit lassen** to take pretty much one's choice; **jem. Muster zur** ~ **schicken** to send s. o. patterns to choose from; ~ **treffen** to take one's choice, to select, to make a selection; **sorgfältige** ~ **treffen** to choose carefully, to make a careful choice;
~**abstand** sampling interval; ~**band** selection; ~**befragung** *(Händler)* selection poll; ~**einheit** *(Statistik)* sampling unit.

auswählen to select, to choose, to pick [out], to cull, *(Statistik)* to sample;
Buch als Weihnachtsgeschenk ~ to select a book as a Christmas present; **Buchpassagen** ~ to select passages; **seine Freunde sorgfältig** ~ to choose one's friends carefully; **ungeeigneten Kandidaten** ~ to pick the least deserving candidate; **in Ruhe** ~ to take pretty much one's choice; **sorgfältig** ~ to make a careful choice; **stichprobenweise** ~ to select at random; **richtigen Zeitpunkt** ~ to time it rightly.

Auswahl|experiment, binäres binary choice experiment; ~**fehler** sampling error; ~**frage** multiple choice question *(US)*; ~**funktion** selective function; ~**gremium** selection board; ~**grundlage** *(Statistik)* frame; ~**käufe** selective buying; ~**kommission** selection board; ~**lager** shunting depot; ~**lehrgang** selective course; ~**liste** short list; ~**maßstäbe** standards of selectivity; ~**methoden** methods of selection; ~**möglichkeit** selective device, alternative; ~**muster** reference sample; ~**plan** sample design; ~**prozeß** selection process; ~**prüfung** competitive examination; ~**recht der Frachtstrecke durch den Käufer** buyer's right of routing; ~**satz** *(Statistik)* sampling fraction (ratio); ~**sendung** consignment on approval, samples, sampled offer; **Einheit der ersten** ~**stufe** *(Statistik)* first-stage (primary) unit; **Einheit der zweiten** ~**stufe** second-stage (secondary) unit; ~**system** selective system; **wissenschaftlich einwandfreies** ~**system** scientifically selective sampling; ~**test** selection test; ~**umfang** latitude in selection.

Auswahlverfahren selection procedure;
systematisches ~ systematic sampling;
~ **für die Einberufung zum Militärdienst** selective service system *(US)*; **statistisches** ~ **für Marktforschungszwecke** controlled sampling.

auswalzen to roll thin, to flatten, *(Papier)* to mill;
Geschichte unendlich ~ to make a song about.

Auswanderer emigrant, emigree, migrant;
~**beratungsstelle** emigration information center *(US)* (centre, *Br.*); ~**logis** emigrant's quarters.

auswandern to emigrate, to migrate, to expatriate, to leave the country;
~ **müssen** to have to leave the country.

Auswanderung emigration, expatriation.

Auswanderungs|behörde emigration office; ~**büro** emigration office (agency); ~**erlaubnis** emigration permit; ~**problem** emigration issue; ~**schiff** emigrant ship; ~**steuer** emigration tax; ~**strom** stream of emigrants; ~**überweisungen** immigrant remittances; ~**verbot** ban on emigration; ~**verkehr** emigrant traffic; ~**vermittler** emigrant agent; ~**zahlen** emigration figures.

Auswärtig|es Amt Foreign Office *(Br.)*, State Department *(US)*; **in das ~e Amt eintreten** to enter the diplomatic service.

auswärtig from outside (another place), nonlocal, foreign, external, extraneous, *(nicht ansässig)* nonresident, *(aus der Provinz)* out-of-town;
~**e Angelegenheiten** foreign (external) affairs; ~**er Ausschuß** *(parl.)* foreign relations committee; ~**er Besuch** out-of-town visitors; ~**e Beziehungen** foreign relations; ~**e Clearings** out-of-town clearings *(US)*; ~**er Dienst** foreign service *(US)*; ~**e Gäste** nonresident guests; ~**er Handel** foreign trade; ~**er Korrespondent** foreign correspondent; ~**e Kunden** out-of-town customers; ~**er Leihverkehr** *(Bibliothek)* interlibrary loan; ~**es Mitglied** associate (corresponding, nonresident) member; ~**e Schüler** out-of-town (nonresident) pupils; ~**es Verrechnungssystem** out-of-town clearing system *(US)*; ~**er Vertreter** agent in the field; ~**e Währungen** offshore currencies.

auswärts outward;
~ **essen** to eat out; **von** ~ **kommen** to come from abroad; ~ **wohnen** to live out of town; **nach** ~ **ziehen** to move to another place.

Auswärtsessen boarding out.

auswechselbar exchangeable, interchangeable, interconvertible, commutative, *(erneuerungsfähig)* renewable;
~**e Sicherheit** floating security.

auswechseln to interchange, to exchange, to commute, to replace;
Batterie ~ to replace a battery; **Reifen** ~ to change a tyre (tire, *US*); **Sicherheiten** ~ to shift liens; **durchgebrannte Sicherung** ~ to replace a blown fuse.

Auswechslung exchange, interchange, commutation, *(Ersatz)* replacement;
~ **von Sicherheiten** shifting of liens; ~ **eines Treuhänders** replacement of a trustee.

Auswechslungskosten cost of replacement.

Ausweg way-out, out *(coll.)*, shift, loophole;
als letzter ~ in the last resort;
~ **finden** to hit upon an expedient; **keinen** ~ **finden** to find no way; **sich einen** ~ **lassen** to leave o. s. a loophole (an out); **keinen** ~ **mehr wissen** to be at the end of one's resources (tether).

Ausweich|bahnhof by-station; ~**beruf** alternate job; ~**betrieb** emergency operating center *(US)* (centre, *Br.*); ~**bewegung** evading movement, *(Auto)* swerving.

Ausweichen evasion, shunt;
~ **vor der Verantwortung** evasion of responsibility.

ausweichen to evade, to elude, to hedge, to get out of the way, to avoid;
einer Entscheidung ~ to side-step a decision; **vor einem Fahrzeug** ~ to make way for a vehicle; **dem Feind** ~ to avoid contact with the enemy; **einer Frage** ~ to evade (shirk, dodge, blink) a question; **immer** ~ to play least in sight; **nach rechts** ~ to swerve to the right; **dem wahren Sachverhalt** ~ to beg the question; **einem anderen Schiff** ~ to give way to another ship; **einer Verantwortung** ~ to shuffle out of a responsibility.

ausweichend evasive, cagey *(fam.)*;
~**e Antwort** evasive reply, noncommittal answer.

Ausweich|flughafen alternate (alternative, satellite) airport, alternative aerodrome; ~**frachtrouten** alternative routing; ~**frachtsatz** alternative tariff (rate); ~**frequenz** alternative frequency; ~**gleis** siding, shunting line, turnout; ~**hafen** alternative base; ~**klausel** *(internationale Abmachungen)* escape clause; ~**krankenhaus** reserve hospital; ~**kurs** *(mar.)* avoiding course; ~**lager** outstore, reserve store; ~**lazarett** evacuation hospital *(US)*; ~**manöver** evasive action; ~**manöver durchführen** to take evasive action; ~**mittel** substitute; ~**möglichkeit** loophole; **letzte** ~**möglichkeit** *(Auto)* last clear chance; ~**plan** alternative plan; ~**platz** *(Bahn)* passing place, *(Straße)* road widening, turnout *(US)*; ~**programm** replacement program(m)e; ~**stelle** bypass, lay-by, road widening, *(Bahn)* passing place, loop, turnout, *(Kanal)* basin; ~**stellung** *(mil.)* alternative (alternate, *US*) position; ~**stoff** substitute, ersatz; ~**straße** bypass, detour *(US)*; ~**treibstoff** alternative fuel; ~**ziel** *(Bomber)* alternative (alternate, *US*) target.

Ausweis permit, identity card, identification [card (papers)] *(US)*, pass, credentials, *(Aufstellung)* statement, *(Bank)* bank

return, statement, *(Beleg)* voucher, *(Berechtigungsschein)* warranty, *(Bescheinigung)* certificate, *(Beweis)* proof, *(Bibliothek)* ticket, *(mil.)* pass, *(Mitglied)* membership card, *(Paß)* passport, *(Student)* card, *(Verein)* membership card;
nach ~ der Bücher according to the books;
monatlicher ~ *(Bank)* monthly statement (return); **polizeilicher ~** pass, identity card, identification [card] *(US)*; **statistischer ~** return;
~ der Bank von England Bank of England return *(Br.)*; **~ des Statistischen Bundesamtes** Board of Trade Returns *(US)*; **~ der Bundesnotenbank** [etwa] Bank of England return *(Br.)*; **~ über die Entwicklung des Eigenkapitals** statement of net worth *(US)*; **~ der Girozentralen** clearinghouse statement; **~ der Landeszentralbanken** [etwa] Federal Statement *(US)*; **~ des Steuereinziehers** tax warrant; **~ über die Verwendung von Barmitteln** capital reconciliation statement *(Br.)*; **~ über die Verwendung des Grundkapitals** flow of funds statement *(US)*, funds-flow statement *(US)*, statement of [sources and] application of funds *(US)*, summary of balance sheet changes, statement of stockholder's equity (investment net worth) *(US)*;
~ besitzen to hold an identification (identity) card; **Reisenden mit den erforderlichen ~en versehen** to document a traveller; **seinen ~ vorzeigen** to show one's identity card.

ausweisen to exile, *(aufführen)* to show, to present, *(Ausländer)* to deport, to expel, *(im Bebauungsplan)* to allocate, *(in Büchern)* to give account of, *(verbannen)* to exile, to banish;
j. ~ to prove s. one's identity; **sich ~** to identify o. s., to prove one's identity, to produce one's papers; **als unerwünschten Ausländer ~** to deport as an undesirable alien; **sich mit seinem Führerschein ~** to prove one's identity with one's driving licence; **sich als guter Geschäftsmann ~** to prove o. s. a good businessman; **Gewinn ~** to show a profit; **Saldo ~** to turn out (show) a balance; **Saldo von 100 Dollar zu Ihren Gunsten ~** to leave (present) a balance of $ 100 to your credit; **Verlust ~** to show a loss.

Ausweis|hülle identification card case; **~karte** identity (identification, *US*) card, pass; **~karte für gewerkschaftspflichtige Betriebe** union shop card; **~kontrolle vornehmen** to check the identification papers; **~papiere** document [identification] papers, credentials; **~papiere besitzen** to hold an identification (identity) card.

ausweispflichtiger Rohertrag obligatorily published gross profit.

Ausweis|stichtag bank-return date; **~tasche** identification card case.

Ausweisung banishment, *(Ausländer)* expulsion, exile, expelling, deportation, renvoi, *(im Bebauungsplan)* allocation, *(aus Wohnung)* eviction, ejection;
jds. ~ veranlassen to order s. o. out of the country.

Ausweisungs|befehl order of removal, *(Ausländer)* deportation (expulsion) order; **~gründe** reasons for deportation.

ausweiten to expand, to extend, to enlarge, to enhance, to broaden, to step up, to widen;
sich zu einer allgemeinen Debatte ~ to widen out into a general discussion; **sein Geschäft ~** to expand one's business; **seinen Horizont ~** to broaden (enlarge) one's mind; **Notenumlauf ~** to expand the currency; **Produktion ~** to step up (expand) production; **sein Produktionsprogramm ~** to broaden (diversify) its line of production; **Staatsausgaben ~** to expand government spending; **Umsatz ~** to expand sales; **sein Warensortiment ~** to diversify one's product lines; **Zahlungsmittelumlauf ~** to expand the currency.

Ausweitung enlargement, extension, expansion, enhancement;
industrielle ~ industrial expansion; **übermäßige ~** overexpansion;
~ des Abzahlungsgeschäftes instalment credit extension; **berechtigte ~ des Aufgabenbereiches** legitimate diversification; **~ von Bankkrediten** overextension of banking credits; **~en auf dem Gebiet der Dienstleistungsbetriebe** utilities expansion; **~ des Dienstleistungsfächers** extension of operation; **~ des Fremdumsatzes** external turnover expansion; **~ der Geldversorgung** expansion of the money supply; **~ des Geschäfts** extension of business; **~ der Kapazität** expansion (extension) of capacity; **~ eines Konflikts** extension of a conflict; **übermäßige ~ des Kreditgeschäfts** undue expansion of credit transactions; **~ der Produktion** expansion of production; **~ des Produktionsprogramms** diversification into manufacturing; **~ des Sortiments** expansion of assortment; **~ der Währung** expansion (inflation) of the currency; **~ des beruflichen Wirkungskreises** career enlargement; **~ des Zahlungsmittelumlaufs** expansion of currency;
in bestimmten Wirtschaftsgebieten zu einer beschleunigten ~ der Produktionsprogramme beitragen to spur broad diversification moves in certain industries; **~ der Streckensätze genehmigen** to extend carriers' lines.

Ausweitungs|anstrengungen diversification efforts; **~prozeß** diversification process, process of expansion.

auswendig by heart, from memory;
~ hersagen to repeat without books; **Sache in- und ~ kennen** to know s. th. inside out (the rights of a case); **etw. ~ können** to have s. th. by heart; **~ lernen** to learn by heart; **seine Ansprache ~ lernen** to memorize one's lines.

Auswendiglernen memorization.

auswerfen *(Anker)* to cast, to drop, *(Gehalt)* to fix, to appoint, to throw out, *(Rente)* to settle, *(Vulkan)* to vomit, to belch forth, to eject;
Angel ~ to cast the line; **Betrag ~** to allocate a sum, to set aside an amount; **Köder ~** to put out bait; **Prämie für besondere Leistungen ~** to grant a bonus for special work; **500.000 $ für die Einrichtung von Schulneubauten ~** to appropriate $ 500.000 for new school building.

auswertbar *(Patent)* workable, utilizable, *(Statistik)* evaluable, analysable.

auswerten to exploit, *(analysieren)* to analyze, to evaluate, *(verwerten)* to utilize;
kommerziell ~ to commercialize; **Erfindung kommerziell ~** to reduce an invention to practice; **Luftaufnahmen ~** to interpret air photographs; **Statistik ~** to interpret statistics; **Untersuchungsergebnisse ~** to turn findings to account; **voll ~** to make full use of.

Auswerter evaluer, *(Kurven)* plotter.

Auswerte|stelle *(mil.)* interpretation center *(US)* (centre, *Br.*), plotting station; **~verfahren** plotting method.

Auswertung exploitation, utilization, *(Antworten)* evaluation, analysis, *(Auslegung)* interpretation;
sekundäre ~ desk research; **wirtschaftliche ~** economic evaluation;
~ einer Meinungsbefragung opinion rating; **~ eines Patents** exploitation (working) of a patent; **~ von Statistiken** interpretation of statistics.

Auswertungs|tätigkeit evaluation work; **~verfahren** *(mil.)* plotting method.

auswetzen, Scharte to wipe out a disgrace.

auswickeln to unwrap, to undo.

auswiegen to scale, to weigh, to tare.

auswintern *(Holz)* to season.

auswirken, sich to bear upon, to take effect, to work out, to tell upon, to operate; **sich auf j. ~** to affect s. o.; **sich auf das Betriebsergebnis ~** to come through into the results; **sich gegen j. ~** to operate to s. one's disadvantage; **sich günstig auf j. ~** to have a great effect on s. o.; **sich hemmend auf den Fortgang einer Geschichte ~** to get in the way of a story line; **sich kostenmäßig ~** to make a showing on costs; **sich auf die öffentliche Meinung ~** to sway public opinion; **sich in einer Preiserhöhung ~** to result in a price increase; **sich ungünstig ~** to have an unfavo(u)rable effect; **sich verheerend ~** to play havoc with; **sich voll ~** to be in full swing; **sich als Vorteil ~** to turn out to be an advantage.

Auswirkung bearing, effect, consequence, result, *(Rückwirkung)* repercussion;
globale ~en world-wide consequences; **handelspolitische ~en** trade-policy effects; **politische ~en** reactions of a policy; **positive geschäftliche ~en** business efficacy; **steuerliche ~en** tax effects, effects on taxation;
kostenmäßige ~en auf den Haushalt budgetary costs; **~en der Nachfrageentwicklung** scale effect; **~en eines Vertrages** effect of a contract; **~en der Wahlen** election effects;
~en dämpfen to cushion the effects; **große ~en auf die Zukunft haben** to affect the future greatly; **~en zeitigen** to come on stream; **~en auf den Markt zeitigen** to have effect on the market; **kostenmäßige ~en zeitigen** to make a showing on costs.

Auswirkungssymptome coming on stream.

auswischen to wipe out;
jem. eins ~ to play a dirty trick on (score off) s. o. *(Br.)*, to give s. o. a dig.

auswringen, nasse Kleider to wring out wet clothes.

Auswüchse der Phantasie, krankhafte figments of imagination.

Auswurf *(Vulkan)* ejectamenta;
~ der Menschheit dregs (scum) of society.

auszahlbar disbursable;
bei Nachweis der Legitimation ~ payable upon submission of proof of identity.

auszahlen to pay off (out, away), to disburse;
sich ~ to pay, to be worth-while, to produce dividends, to pan out *(US sl.)*; **sich für alle** ~ to be profitable for all; **Angestellten** ~ to pay off (out) an employee; **in bar** ~ to pay cash down; **Betrag voll** ~ to pay the full amount; **jds. Gehalt voll** ~ to pay s. one's salary in full; **jem. seinen Gewinnanteil** ~ to pay out s. one's share; **Gläubiger** ~ to pay off creditors; **sich längerfristig gesehen** ~ to pay in the long run; **1000 DM gegen Legitimation** ~ to pay the sum of DM 1000 upon submission of proof of identity; **jem. seinen Lohn** ~ to pay s. o. his wages; **Postanweisung** ~ to cash a postal (money) order; **Restbetrag** ~ to pay out the balance; **Teilhaber** ~ to buy out a partner; **j. voll** ~ to pay s. o. outright;
sich einen Scheck ~ **lassen** to cash a check *(US)* (cheque, *Br.*).
auszählen to count the votes cast, *(Raketenstart)* to count down.
auszahlende Bank cash-paying bank.
Auszahler disburser, payer.
Auszahlung paying out (off), payout, payment, outpayment, disbursement, *(Gläubiger)* reimbursement, *(Überbringer)* remittance, transfer;
~**en** moneys paid out;
briefliche ~ remittance by mail *(US)*, payment by letter, mail transfer *(US)*; ~ **gesperrt** payment stopped; **telegrafische** ~ telegraphic (cable) transfer; **umfangreiche** ~**en** heavy disbursements; **vollständige** ~ outright payment, payment in full; ~**en nur im Erlebensfall** payment conditional to survival; ~ **der Gehälter** salary disbursements; ~ **durch die Gerichtskasse** payment out of court; ~ **der Gläubiger** satisfaction of creditors; ~ **absonderungsberechtigter Gläubiger** payment of secured creditors *(US)*; ~ **in voller Höhe** full payment; ~ **der Invalidenrente** disablement pay; ~ **der Löhne** wage payment, pay-off *(sl.)*; ~ **von Massegläubigern** payment of unsecured creditors *(Br.)*; ~ **New York** New York exchange; ~**en zum Parikurs** parity payments; ~ **der Schadenssumme** loss payment; ~ **eines Teilhabers** buying out a partner; ~ **der Versehrtenrente** disablement pay;
Betrag zur ~ **anweisen** to order a sum to be paid; **zur** ~ **gelangen** to be paid out; ~ **sperren** to stop payments.
Auszählung *(Raketenstart)* countdown;
~ **der Stimmen** counting the votes.
Auszahlungs | abschnitt pay voucher; ~**abteilung** payment department, *(Finanzministerium)* division of disbursement; ~**anweisung** disbursement voucher, disbursing order, payment order; ~**beauftragter** disbursing agent; ~**belege** vouchers payable, disbursement vouchers; ~**belege prüfen** to preaudit vouchers.
auszahlungsberechtigt authorized to make payments.
Auszahlungs | bescheinigung pay voucher; ~**bestätigung** acknowledgement of receipt; ~**betrag** amount paid, disbursement, amount payable; ~**datum** pay date; ~**ermächtigung** authorization to pay, withdrawal warrant; ~**ermächtigungen für Pensionen** pension warrants; ~**kasse** paying teller's department *(US)*; ~**kassierer** paying teller *(US)*; ~**klausel** *(Versicherung)* facility-of-payment clause; ~**konto** disbursing account; ~**kurs** *(Anleihe)* percentage rate; **bei einem** ~**kurs von 97%** at a rate of 97 per cent; ~**liste** pay sheet; **verschiedene** ~**möglichkeiten** payout variations; ~**postamt** money-order office, office of payment *(Br.)*; ~**richtlinie** payment terms; ~**schalter** paying counter, pay desk, cashier's counter *(US)*; ~**schein** pay slip; ~**sperre** stop payment order, stopping payment; ~**stelle** disbursing (paying) office, paying agent, *(Post)* office of payment *(Br.)*; ~**termin** date of payment, pay date; ~**überschuß** excess of withdrawal; ~**verbot** stop payment; ~**verfügung** disbursing order, accountable warrant; ~**wert einer Anleihe** net proceeds of a loan.
Auszeichnen eines Textes display of text matter.
auszeichnen to tag, to label, to ticket, to mark [out], *(ehren)* to distinguish, to honour *(Br.)*, to dignify, to price, *(mit Orden)* to decorate, *(Schrift)* to display, to accentuate;
sich ~ to exceed, to excel, to distinguish o. s., to come to the front; **j.** ~ to confer an hono(u)r on s. o.; **sich durch Abwesenheit** ~ to be conspicuous by one's absence; **Artikel** ~ to label an article for sale; **Film mit einem Oskar** ~ to award the Oscar to a film; **sich durch geschickte Handelspolitik** ~ to be characterized by a clever economic policy; **sich durch Ideenarmut** ~ to be outstanding by the absence of ideas; **sich im Leben** ~ to make one's mark in life; **sich im öffentlichen Leben** ~ to win distinction in public life; **maschinell** ~ to mark by machine; **neu** ~ to reprice; **niedrig** ~ to price low; **niedriger** ~ to mark down; **j. mit dem Nobelpreis** ~ to award the Nobel prize to s. o.; **mit einem Preis** ~ to award a prize; **preislich** ~ to mark with a selling price; **sich durch Tapferkeit** ~ to be conspicuous for one's bravery; **Text** ~ to display text matter; **mit einem Verkaufspreis** ~ to mark with a selling price; **j. mit seinem Vertrauen** ~ to hono(u)r s. o. with one's confidence; **Vorstellung durch seine Anwesenheit** ~ to hono(u)r a performance by one's presence; **Ware billiger** ~ to mark down goods.
Auszeichnung *(drucktechn.)* display, *(Ehrung)* hono(u)rable distinction, hono(u)r, *(Medaille)* decoration, medal, *(Preis)* award, prize, *(Textstellen)* display, *(von Waren)* labelling, marking, ticketing, pricing, tag;
mit ~ *(Schule)* with distinction; **mit** ~**en bepflastert** plastered with decorations;
akademische ~**en** academic hono(u)rs (distinctions); **besondere** ~ *(Schule)* hono(u)r; **ehrenvolle** ~ feather in one's cap; **höchste** ~ blue ribbon; **höchstmögliche** ~ highest possible award; **höhere** ~ *(Preise)* markup; **niedrigere** ~ *(Preise)* markdown; **verdeckte** ~ *(im Geschäft)* pricing in code;
~ **für gute Führung** *(mil.)* Good Conduct Medal;
mit ~ **bestehen** to pass with (obtain first-class) hono(u)rs; **in einem Fach mit** ~ **bestehen** to major in a subject *(US)*; **Prüfung mit** ~ **bestehen** to distinguish o. s. in an examination; **sich um eine** ~ **bewerben** to enter for an award; ~ **erhalten** to receive a distinction; **erste** ~**en erhalten** to make first honors *(US)*; **persönliche** ~ **erhalten** to receive a distinction, to receive an individual award; ~ **verleihen** to award a decoration, to confer a distinction; **j. für eine** ~ **vorschlagen** to put s. o. forward for a decoration.
Auszeichnungs | bestimmungen labelling provisions; ~**fehler** mistake in labelling; ~**schrift** display (bold) type; ~**system** hono(u)rs system; ~**zeile** display line; ~**zettel** price tag.
ausziehbar extractable;
~**es Bett** truckle bed, divan bed; ~**e Leiter** extension ladder; ~**es Stativ** tripod; ~**er Tisch** draw-leaf table.
Auszieh | bett, ~**liege** truckle (divan) bed.
Ausziehen moving out, move, removal;
~ **bei Nacht und Nebel** moonlight flitting;
jem. beim ~ **des Mantels helfen** to help s. o. out of his coat; **im** ~ **begriffen sein** to be on the move.
ausziehen to pull out, to extract, *(Auszüge machen)* to extract, to docket, to excerpt, to abstract from, *(kürzen)* to abridge, to condense, to extract, *(umziehen)* to quit the premises, to move [out], to evacuate, *(Zeichnung)* to trace, to plot;
sich ~ to undress; **alten Adam** ~ to turn over a new leaf; **Buchstellen** ~ to make extracts from a book; **Fernrohr** ~ to extend a telescope; **j. bis aufs Hemd** ~ to fleece s. o. of every halfpenny; **Kinderschuhe** ~ to cut one's eye teeth, to emerge from childhood; **Konto** ~ to make a statement (abstract, *Br.*) of account; **nicht** ~ *(Mieter)* to retain possession; **Posten** ~ to take out an item; **Stellen aus einem Buch** ~ to make extracts from a book; **Tisch** ~ to pull out the drawleaf of a table; **Uniform** ~ to leave military service; **aus einer Wohnung** ~ to move out of a flat (apartment, *US*);
~ **müssen** to have notice to quit.
ausziehender Mieter outgoing tenant.
Auszieh | fallschirm auxiliary parachute; ~**leiter** extension ladder; ~**platte** table leaf; ~**sitz** pull-out seat; ~**tisch** sliding (telescope, extending, draw-leaf, *Br.*) table; ~**tusche** Indian (Chinese, drawing) ink.
auszischen to hiss down;
Schauspieler ~ to give an actor the bird.
Auszubildend | er, kaufmännisch business (commercial) trainee;
~**en an einen anderen Lehrherrn abtreten** to turn an apprentice to another master.
auszudrücken, um es vornehm to express (put) it delicately.
Auszug extract, extraction, excerpt, *(Aufstellung)* status, statement, *(Konto)* statement, extract, abstract *(Br.)*, *(Patent)* abridgment, *(Volk)* exodus, *(aus der Wohnung)* removal *(Br.)*, move, moving out, *(Zusammenfassung)* summary, compendium, epitomization;
beim ~ **aus der Wohnung** on moving out of the flat *(Br.)*; **beglaubigter** ~ duly certified extract; **regelmäßiger** ~ *(Bank)* periodical statement;
~ **aus der Bilanz** condensed (summary) balance sheet, condensed statement *(US)*; ~ **aus dem Geburtenregister** birth certificate; ~ **aus dem Grundbuch** abstract of title, land certificate, office copy of the Land Registry *(Br.)*, certificate of title *(US)*; ~ **aus dem Handelsregister** extract from a registered statement; ~ **für das Klavier** piano arrangement; ~ **aus dem Parlament** walkout from parliament; ~ **aus der Sitzungsniederschrift** extract of the minutes; ~ **aus dem Sterberegister** abstract of the register of deaths; ~ **aus den Vertragsbestimmungen** memorandum;

~ anfertigen (machen) to make (take) an extract from, *(Konto)* to make a statement (an abstract, *Br.*) of account, to abstract, to contract, to docket, to extract, to excerpt, *(Patent)* to abridge; **j. einen Brief im ~ mitteilen** to tell s. o. the gist of a letter; **~ prüfen** to verify a statement (an abstract, *Br.*); **~ verweigern** *(Mieter)* to hold over.

Auszüge | aus Leserbriefen points from letters;
~ machen to abstract from, to extract, to make (take) an extract from; **ausgewählte ~ der besten Autoren veröffentlichen** to cull extracts from the best authors.

Auszugsverweigerung *(Mieter)* holding over.

auszugsweise in abstracts (an abridged from), by way of excerpt;
~ wiedergeben to reproduce an extract.

auszusetzen, nichts an jem. no flies on s. o.;
an jem. etw. ~ haben to pick a hole in s. one's coat (jacket), to find fault with s. o.; **etw. an einer Sache ~ haben** to be critical of s. th.

auszuziehen, sich ~ weigern to hold over.

autark autarchic, autarkic, self-sufficient.

Autarkie autarchy, economic (national) self-sufficiency;
wirtschaftliche ~ economic self-sufficiency;
~anhänger autarkist; **~streben** economic nationalism.

authentisch authentic, genuine, good;
nicht ~ *(Buch)* unfathered;
~e Quelle reliable source; **von ~er Seite** from good (reliable) authority; **~er Text** genuine (authentic) text; **~e Unterschrift** genuine signature.

authentisieren to authenticate, to certify, to legalize.

Auto [motor]car *(Br.)*, motor vehicle, auto *(US)*, automobile *(US)*;
aus dem ~ geworfen *(Unfallpolice)* thrown from automobile;
ohne ~ without transport;
abgasfreies ~ pollution-free automobile, nonpolluting car; **auf dem Autofriedhof abgestelltes ~** knockdown kit; **ausrangiertes ~** junk auto (car); **billigeres ~** lesser-priced car; **billiges ~** low- (popular-) priced car, flivver *(sl.)*; **frisiertes ~** hot rod *(sl.)*, souped car *(US sl.)*; **in Zahlung gegebenes ~** trade-in car; **gepanzertes ~** armo(u)red car; **gestohlenes (kurzgeschlossenes) ~** hot short *(sl.)*; **in Massen hergestelltes ~** volume car; **herrenloses ~** dumped car; **dringend reparaturbedürftiges ~** dilapidated car; **schrottreifes ~** junk heap *(sl.)*; **im Verbrauch sparsames ~** economical car; **überholtes ~** overhauled car; **vorbeifahrendes ~** passing car; **den Sicherheitsbestimmungen gerecht werdendes ~** safety car; **wirtschaftliches ~** economic car; **zugelassenes ~** licensed car, legally operating automobile *(US)*;
~ für gehobenere Ansprüche executive-class car; **~ mit neuer Bereifung** car with new tires (tyres, *Br.*); **~ für Körperbehinderte** invalid car; **~ der Mittelklasse** intermediate-sized car;
~ abmelden to suspend a licence; **~ abschleppen** to pick up a (tow a broken) car; **~ abschmieren** to grease the axle of a car; **~ abspritzen** to wash a car, to hose down a car; **~ polizeilich anmelden** to register a car, to take a car's number; **~ aufbocken** to jack up a car; **sein ~ beherrschen** to understand how to drive a car; **jds. ~ benutzen** to operate s. one's automobile; **~ für Privatfahrten benutzen** to use a car for personal travel; **sein ~ mit Verstand benutzen** to use one's car more sensibly; **j. mit dem ~ nach Hause bringen** to motor (drive) s. o. home; **wieder in sein ~ einsteigen** to get back into one's car; **~ ohne Garantie erwerben** to buy a car with all faults; **~ fahren (lenken)** to drive (operate) a car; **im ~ fahren** to go (travel) by car; **im ~ nach A fahren** to drive to A; **mit dem ~ gegen einen Baum fahren** to race one's car against a tree; **nicht mit dem ~ fahren** to keep one's car off the road; **sein eigenes ~ fahren** to have a car of one's own; **~ in den Straßengraben fahren** to ditch a car; **~ frisieren** to tune (doll) up a car; **gebrauchtes ~ in Zahlung geben** to trade in a used car; **~ im Griff haben** to keep the car straight; **jem. aus dem ~ helfen** to help s. o. out of a car; **neues ~ herausbringen** to style a new car; **sein ~ herausfahren** to get out one's car; **~ aus dem Schlamm herausholen** to extricate a car from the mud; **aus dem ~ herausschleudern** to shell out *(sl.)*; **~ fahren können** to know how to drive a car; **sich per Anhalter im ~ mitnehmen lassen** to hitch a ride, to hitch-hike, to thumb a lift (ride); **~ registrieren lassen** to register a car; **~ mieten** to rent a car *(US)*; **~ auf Kilometerabrechnung mieten** to hire a car by distance; **j. im ~ mitnehmen** to give s. o. a lift, to take s. o. for a ride; **~ nehmen** to take a taxi; **~ rammen** to bump a car; **~ stehlen** to shoplift a car; **sein ~ zur Verfügung stellen** to permit one's car to be used; **~ überladen** to stuff a car with people; **~ von der Fabrik übernehmen** to take over a car from the factory; **~ unterhalten** to run a car; **~ unterstellen** to lay up a car; **~s verschrotten** to de-junk cars; **~ zu steuern verstehen** to understand how to drive a car; **~ vorführen** to demonstrate a car; **~ waschen** to give the car a wash; **von einem ~ angefahren werden** to be knocked down by a motorcar; **neue ~s aus Schrottwagen zusammenbauen** to assemble cars from knockdown bits; **mit einem ~ zusammenstoßen** to run foul with a car;
~abgase auto exhaust; **~abmeldung** suspension of licence; **~abzahlungsgeschäft** floor-plan service; **~aktien** motor (automobile, *US*) shares, motors *(Br.)*; **~angebot** auto (car) supply; **~anhänger** automobile truck, auto carrier *(Br.)*, trailer, *(Wohnwagen)* motor caravan; **~anlasser** car starter; **~anruf** taxicab call; **~anschaffung** purchase of a car; **zinsloser ~anschaffungskredit** interest-free car loan; **~antenne** car aerial; **~arbeiter** car (auto) worker; **~atlas** road map; **kurzer ~ausflug** joyride; **~ausstellung** motor exhibition (show), auto (automobile) show *(US)*; **~ausstoß** auto output.

Autobahn freeway *(US)*, motorway *(Br.)*, special road *(Br.)*, [automobile] expressway *(US)*, superhighway *(US)*, express highway *(US)*;
gebührenpflichtige ~ turnpike road, tollway *(US)*; **vierspurige ~** four-lane expressway *(US)* (motorway, *Br.*); **nur für PKW zugelassene ~** parkway;
~ mit sechs Fahrbahnen six-lane freeway *(US)*; **~ mit Parallelbahnen** multistrip highway *(US)*;
überlastete ~ verkehrsmäßig entlasten to siphon off traffic from an overcrowded motorway *(Br.)*;
~abfahrt gate.

autobahnähnliche Qualität near motorway standard *(Br.)*.

Autobahn | auffahrt access point, freeway ramp *(US)*; **~ausbau** motorway extension *(Br.)*; **~ausfahrt** exit point; **~bau** motorway construction *(Br.)*; **~bauamt** motorwayification board *(Br.)*; **~gang** overdrive; **~gebäude** expressway building *(US)*; **~gebühr** turnpike money *(US)*, intermediate (road) toll; **~geschwindigkeit** highway speed *(US)*; **~kleeblatt** cloverleaf; **~markierungen** carriageway lane markings; **20 ~minuten Fahrt** 20 motorway minutes *(Br.)*; **~netz** network of motorways, freeway *(US)* (motorway, *Br.*) system; **~programm** motorway programme *(Br.)*, freeway program *(US)*; **~raststätte** transport café, truck shop; **~ring** motorway ring road *(Br.)*; **~überführung** overpass; **~unterführung** underpass; **~verkehr** motorway *(Br.)* (freeway, *US*) traffic; **~zubringer** motorway feeder road *(Br.)*.

Auto | batterie car (automobile) battery *(US)*; **~batterie aufladen** to top up a car battery *(Br.)*; **~benutzung für Geschäftszwecke** use of a car for business; **~beschädigung** damage to a car; **~besitz** car ownership; **~besitzer** car owner.

Autobiograph autobiographer.

Autobiographie autobiography.

autobiographisch autobiographical.

Auto | blech motor-body sheet; **~box** lockup *(Br.)*, rented garage; **in der ~branche sein** to be in the motor business; **~brille** motoring goggles; **~bücherei** mobile library.

Autobus omnibus, autobus *(US)*, bus *(fam.)*, *(Überlandfahrt)* [motor] coach;
mit Liegemöglichkeiten ausgestatteter ~ restroom-equipped bus; **billiger ~** jitney; **zweistöckiger ~** double-decked bus;
mit dem ~ fahren to go by bus; **~ in Betrieb nehmen** to put a bus on the road; **~ aus dem Verkehr ziehen** to take a bus off the road;
~bahnhof, ~endstation bus terminal; **~benutzer** bus passenger (rider); **~fahrer** bus driver, busman; **~fahrplan** bus guide (schedule, *US*, timetable); **~fahrschein** bus ticket; **~fahrt** bus ride, omnibus journey; **~gesellschaft** line; **~haltestelle** bus stop; **~linie** bus line; **~reklame** bus advertising; **~schaffner** bus conductor; **~werbung** bus advertising.

Autodach roof of a car.

Autodafé auto-da-fé, act of faith.

Autodidakt self-educated person, autodidact;
~ sein to be entirely self-educated.

autodidaktisch self-educated (-taught).

Auto | dieb clouter *(sl.)*; **~diebstahl** theft of a car, car theft; **~dienst** car service; **~droschke** taxicab, motorcab; **~einfuhren, ~importe** car imports; **~empfänger** car radio; **~ersatzteile** automotive replacement parts *(US)*, car parts, motorcar spares *(Br.)*; **~export** auto export; **~fabrik** car factory (plant), auto plant (factory); **~fabrikant** carmaker, motorcar manufacturer *(Br.)*; **~fachleute** auto experts; **~fahrbahn** lane; **~fährdienst** car-ferry (autocarrier) service; **~fähre** automobile *(US)* (car) ferry.

Autofahren motoring, driving;
sicheres ~ safe motoring;
~ unter Alkoholeinfluß driving under the influence of drink.

Autofahrer [car] driver, motorist, *(pl.)* motoring public; **geringeres Risiko darstellender** ~ lower risk motorist; **hohes Risiko darstellender** ~ high-risk driver; **hervorragender** ~ demon driver; ~ **der Anhalter mitnimmt** picker-upper *(sl.)*; **sich als hervorragender** ~ **entpuppen** to turn out to be an excellent driver; **harte Maßnahmen gegen rücksichtslose** ~ **ergreifen** to take strong measures against reckless drivers; ~**gruß** V-sign *(Br.)*.

Auto|fahrt drive, car ride; ~**fahrt machen** to go for a drive (ride); ~**falle** road trap, plant for motorists, *(Polizei)* speed trap; ~**fenster** car window; ~**firma** car (motor, auto) company; ~**friedhof** junk yard, car dump, breaker's yard; ~**gangster** motor bandit; ~**garage** [automobile] garage; ~**garantie** car guarantee; ~**gepäckträger** roof rack; ~**geschäft** car (automobile, *US*) business; ~**giro** autogyro, gyroplane.

Autogramm autograph;
mit einem ~ **versehen** to autograph;
~**jäger** autograph hunter; ~**markt** autograph market; ~**preis** autograph price; ~**sammler** autograph collector; ~**sammlung** autography.

autographieren to autograph.

autographisch autographic;
~ **vervielfältigen** to autograph.

Autohaftpflichtversicherung motorcar *(Br.)* (automobile, *US*, collision, public liability motor, *Br.*) insurance;
~ **für Unfälle von Erfüllungsgehilfen** nonownership liability insurance;
~ **unterhalten** to carry a public liability motor insurance *(Br.)*.

Auto|halle [motor] garage; ~**haltestelle** cab (taxi) rank, cabstand ~**händler** motorcar *(Br.)* (automobile, auto dealer, motor) trader; ~**hersteller** carmaker, auto manufacturer; ~**herstellung** fabrication of automobiles, carmaking, auto manufacturing; ~**hupe** hooter; ~**import** auto import; ~**importeur** car importer; ~**industrie** motor (automotive, auto, car) industry, automobile industry *(US)*; ~**inspektion durchführen** to inspect a car; ~**karosserie** automobile *(US)* (car) body, bodywork; ~**karte** road map; ~**kauf** purchase of a car, car purchase, car buying; ~**kauf zu Sonderpreisen** cut-price car buying; ~**kino** drive-in cinema, ozoner, passion pit *(sl.)*; ~**koffer** trunk of a car; ~**kolonne** autocade, motor cavalcade, fleet of motor cars; ~**konzern** auto concern; ~**korso** car parade, motorcade *(US)*.

autokrank carsick.

Autokrankheit car sickness.

Autokrat autocrat, despot.

Autokratie autocracy, despotism.

Auto|kredit motorcar credit *(Br.)*, auto loan *(US)*; ~**kundendienst** auto servicing *(US)*; ~**luftfährdienst** car air ferry; ~**marke** make of a car; ~**markt** auto *(US)* (car) market.

Automat automatic [selling] machine, penny-in-the-slot (vending) machine;
reinster ~ **sein** to be a mere machine.

Automaten|büffet self-service restaurant, automat *(US)*; ~**mißbrauch** misuse of slot machines; ~**restaurant** self-service restaurant, cafeteria *(US)*, automat *(US)*; ~**verkauf** automatic selling.

Automatik automatic working, automation, self-action, *(Autoradio)* automatic tuning.

Atomation automation;
~ **der Büroarbeit** office automation.

Automations|aufwand automation spending; ~**prozeß** process of automation.

automatisch automatic, penny-in-the-slot, push-button, self-acting, self-driven, mechanical;
~**er Anrufbeantworter** automatic telephone answering machine; ~**er Ausgleich,** ~**e Anpassung** *(Lohnklausel)* escalator [adjustment], *(Rundfunkgerät)* fading control; ~**es Getriebe** automatic gearbox; **sich** ~ **abdeckender Kredit** self-liquidating credit.

automatisieren to automate, to automatize.

automatisiert automated.

Automatisierung automation, automatization;
~ **der Büroarbeit** office automation.

Auto|mechaniker motor (auto) mechanic, motor fitter, grease monkey *(US sl.)*; ~**miete** car rental; ~**mietgebühr** car rental costs; ~**mietverleih** rent-a-car, car-hire service *(US)*; ~**minute** driving minute; **15** ~**minuten vom Flugplatz** 15 minutes drive from the airport.

Automobil [passenger] car, motorcar *(Br.)*, motor vehicle, auto[mobile] *(US)*;
~**aktien** automobile shares, auto (motor) stocks *(US)*; ~**arbeiterstreik** auto strike; ~**ausstellung** motor show (exhibition) *(Br.)*; ~**bau** car (automobile, *US*) manufacturing; ~**club** motoring organization; ~**fabrikant** manufacturer of cars; ~**firma** auto establishment; ~**hersteller** carmaker, motor (automobile, *US*) manufacturer; ~**herstellung** fabrication of automobiles, carmaking; ~**industrie** motorcar (automotive, automobile, *US*) industry.

Automobilist motorist, autorist *(US)*.

Automobil|konzern motor concern; ~**pendler** commuting motorist; ~**produktion** motorcar (automobile, *US*) production; ~**produktionsprogramm** auto schedule; ~**produzent** auto manufacturer, carmaker; ~**verband** Automobile Association; ~**versicherung** motorcar insurance; ~**werte** motor shares (stocks, *US*), motors *(Br.)*.

Auto|modelle car lines; **neue** ~**modelle auf dem Markt einführen** to place new cars on the market; **neues** ~**modell zum Verkauf freigeben** to release a car for delivery; ~**montage** auto assembly *(US)*; ~**montagefabrik,** ~**montagewerk** car assembly plant, auto-assembly plant *(US)*, auto assembler *(US)*.

autonom autonomic, autonomous, self-governing;
~ **werden** to achieve autonomy.

Autonomie autonomy, self-government, home rule *(Br.)*;
~ **gewähren** to grant autonomy;
~**gesetz** statute of autonomy; ~**vorkämpfer** home ruler *(Br.)*.

Auto|nummer car (licence) number; ~**nummernschild** licence (license, *US*) plate, number plate; ~**panne** breakdown, *(Reifen)* flat tire (tyre, *Br.*), puncture; ~**papiere** car (driving) papers; ~**park** car (vehicle, *Br.*) park, fleet of cars, truck fleet; ~**parkplatz** parking place (lot, *US*); ~**pilot** *(Flugzeug)* automatic pilot, auto pilot; ~**politur** car (auto, *US*) polish; ~**produktion** auto (motorcar, *Br.*, automobile, *US*) manufacturing, automobile production *(US)*; ~**produzent** motorcar manufacturer; ~**prüfung** driving test, auto trial.

Autopsie autopsy, post-mortem examination.

Autor author, writer, bookwright, composer;
mit den besten Empfehlungen des ~**s** with kind regards from the author; **mit Genehmigung des** ~**s** with the sanction of the author;
fest bezahlter ~ *(Film)* staff writer;
sich als ~ **bekennen** to avow o. s. the author, to father a book, to admit the paternity of a book; ~ **in Grund und Boden kritisieren (verreißen)** to pull an author to pieces; **einem** ~ **zuschreiben** to impute to an author.

Auto|rad car wheel; ~**radio** car radio; ~**rasthaus** roadside inn, drive-in (curb-service, *US*) restaurant; ~**rechnung** automobile bill; ~**reifen** motorcar tyre *(Br.)* (tire, *US*), rubber *(sl.)*; **schlauchloser** ~**reifen** tubeless tyre; **platten** ~**reifen wechseln** to change a flat tire *(US)* (tyre, *Br.*); ~**reiseführer** roadbook, motoring guide; ~**reisezug** car sleeper train, autotrain.

Autoren|anteil royalty, seigniorage, author's fee, copy money; ~**aufführung,** ~**eintrag** author's entry; ~**exemplar** author's copy; ~**honorar** royalty, seigniorage, author's fee, copy money; ~**katalog** author's catalog(ue); ~**korrekturen** author's proof (corrections, alterations).

Auto|rennbahn racing track, motordrome; ~**rennen** motor race.

Autoren|rechte copyright, literary property; ~**verzeichnis** author catalog(ue).

Auto|reparatur car (motor, auto) repairs; ~**reparaturkosten** auto repair costs; ~**reparaturwerkstatt** car (automobile, *US*) repair shop, service station; ~**restaurant** roadside inn, drive-in (curb service, *US*) restaurant.

autorisierbar authorizable.

autorisieren to authorize, to empower, to qualify.

autorisiert authorized, accredited;
nicht ~ unauthorized;
~**e Übersetzung** official translation.

autoritär authoritarian, dogmatic[al];
~**es Auftreten** air of authority; ~**e Lösung** authoritarian solution; ~**es System** authoritarian system.

Autorität authority, *(Fachmann)* expert;
überlegene moralische ~ lofty moral authority; **unfehlbare** ~ oracle; **versicherungsstatistische** ~ actuarial consultant; **verlorene** ~ spent force;
anerkannte ~ **auf seinem Gebiet** recognized authority in one's field;
j. mit ~ **ausstatten** to gird s. o. with authority; ~ **ausstrahlen** to project authority; **seine** ~ **entschlossen bewahren** to be very firm in upholding one's authority; **jds.** ~ **erschüttern** to bring discredit to s. one's authority; ~ **genießen** to carry authority; **keine** ~ **bei jem. genießen** to have no control over s. o.; **seine** ~ **geltend machen** to exert one's authority; ~ **auf einem Gebiet sein** to be an authority (expert) on a subject; **jds.** ~ **in Frage**

stellen to buck s. one's authority; **jds. ~ untergraben** to undermine s. one's authority; **seine ~ wiedergewinnen** to recover one's authority.

autoritativ authoritative.

Autoritäts|entfremdung alienation from authority; **~person sein** to be in authority; **~verlust** relinquishment of authority.

Autorodeo rodeo.

Autorschaft authorship.

Auto|sachschadenversicherung auto property damage insurance; **~sattler** car upholsterer; **~schaden** damage to a car; **~schalter** *(Bank)* drive-in window, drive-in; **~schau** motor show; **~scheinwerfer** headlight, head lamp; **~schlange** line (string) of cars; **~schlepp** *(Segelflugzeug)* catapult; **~schloß** car lock; **~schlosser** motor (automobile, *US*) mechanic, motor fitter, grease monkey *(US sl.)*; **~schlüssel** car key; **~schnellstraße** expressway *(US)*, speedway *(US)*; **~schnellwäscherei** car wash; **~schuppen** car shed; **~silo** autosilo; **~sitz** car seat; **~spedition** trucking *(US)*; **~sport** motoring; **~spur** car track; **~steckbrief** particulars of a car; **~steuer** car (motor, *Br.*) tax, motor-vehicle duty *(Br.)*; **~stopp** hitchhiking; **per ~stopp fahren** to hitchhike, to thumb; **~straße** motor road, motorway *(Br.)*, highway *(US)*; **zwei ~stunden entfernt** two hours drive; **~tankstelle** [automobile] service station; **~tarifabkommen** auto wage settlement; **~tarifvertragsverhandlungen** auto contract bargaining; **~telefon** car telephone; **~transporter** motorcar hauler, automobile transport vehicle; **~tunnel** vehicular tunnel; **neuer ~typ** new sort of a car; **neue ~typen auf dem Markt einführen** to place new cars on the market.

Autotypie *(drucktechn.)* autotype, half-tone engraving;
flachgeätzte ~ shallow half-tone; **freistehende ~** silhouette half-tone;
~klischee halftone block.

Auto|umsatz auto sales; **~unfall** motor[car] (automobile) accident, stack-up *(sl.)*, car crash; **~unfall haben** to stack up *(sl.)*; **~unfallversicherung** motorcar (automobile, *US*) insurance; **~unglück** motorcar *(Br.)* (automobile, *US*) accident; **~unterhaltungskosten** cost of motoring, car expenses, automobile operating costs *(US)*; **~verkäufe** auto sales; **~verkäufer** car salesman; **~verkaufszahlen** car sales; **~verkehr** motor traffic; **~verleih, ~vermietung** renting of cars, car rental service *(US)*, *(Firma)* rent-a-car corporation *(US)*, car hire firm *(Br.)*, hire car service *(Br.)*; **~vermietung mit gestelltem Chauffeur** auto livery service; **~vermietung für Selbstfahrer** self-drive cars for hire; **~vermietungsunternehmen** rent-a-car corporation *(US)*, car-hiring organization *(Br.)*; **~verschrottungsgebühr** junk-car tax; **~versicherung** motorcar (motor) insurance *(Br.)*, car (auto, automobile, *US*) insurance; **internationale ~versicherung** international motor insurance; **~versicherungspolice** motor policy; **kurzfristige ~- und Krankenhausversicherungspolice** short-term automobile and hospitalization policy *(US)*; **~versicherungssätze** auto-insurance rates; **~versicherungsschutz** auto coverage; **~versicherungsvertrag** automobile insurance contract *(US)*; **~vertreter** car salesman, auto dealer; **~vertretung** auto dealership; **~waschanlage** car wash; **~waschanstalt** carwash service; **~weltmacht** world auto power; **~wrack** wreck, dilapidated vehicle, auto scrap; **~zeitalter** auto age; **~zentrum mit Sonderpreisen** cut-price car center; **~zubehör** auto components, automotive components *(US)*, motor-vehicle accessories; **~zubehörindustrie** auto components industry; **~zulassung** car licence; **~zulieferer, ~zulieferungsbetrieb** car accessories firm, car components manufacturer (firm), auto (automotive) industry supplier *(US)*; **~zulieferungsindustrie** auto industry supplier (auto components, parts) industry; **~zusammenstoß** smash with a car, car crash, smash-up; **~zusammenstoßversicherung** automobile collision insurance *(US)*.

Aval surety, guarantee *(Br.)*, aval *(Canada)*, guaranty *(US)*, *(Wechselbürge)* guarantor;
per ~ guaranteed by;
~ geben to stand surety;
~akzept collateral acceptance.

avalieren to guarantee [due payment of a bill].

avalierter Wechsel guaranteed bill of exchange.

Avalist guarantor.

Aval|konto guarantee account; **~kredit** surety credit; **~linie** line of guarantee; **~provision** guarantee commission; **~rechnung** guarantee account; **~wechsel** guaranteed bill of exchange.

Avancement promotion, preferment.

Avancen machen, jem. to make approaches to s. o.

avancieren to advance, to be promoted;
zum Bestseller ~ to become a bestseller.

Avantgarde vanguard.

Avantgardist pioneer, vanguard;
~ sein to be in the vanguard.

Avers face of a coin.

Avis advice, letter of advice;
bis auf weiteres ~ until further notice; **laut ~** as per advice; **mangels ~es** for nonadvice; **mangels ~es zurück** returned for want of advice, no advice;
~brief letter of advice.

avisieren to give advice, to advise, to notify;
rechtzeitig ~ to advise in due course; **Tratte ~** to advise a draft.

Avisierung advice, notification.

Aviso dispatch boat (vessel).

Avistawechsel sight bill.

Aviszettel advice slip.

Axt an etw. legen to set an axe to s. th.

B

babbeln to babble, to prattle.
Babel, das reinste a hotbed of vice.
Baby|ausstattung layette; ~**bonds** savings (premium treasury, baby, *US*) bonds.
babylonisches Sprachengewirr babel.
Babysitter baby sitter (minder);
~ **abgeben** to babysit.
Bach brook, streamlet;
reißender ~ torrent;
den ~ **heruntergehen** to go down the drain *(fam.)*;
~**bett** water course.
Back forecastle.
Backbord port;
~**motor** port engine; ~**seite** port side, larboard *(US)*.
Backenbremse block (shoe) brake.
Bäcker baker.
Bäckerei bakery, baker's shop.
Bäckerhandwerk baker's trade.
Back|fisch teenager, teenage girl, flapper *(Br.)*, bobby soxer *(US)*; ~**stein** brickwork; ~**steine regnen** to rain cats and dogs; ~**steinmauer** brick wall; ~**stube** bakehouse; ~**werk** pastry, confectionery.
Bad bath, *(Kurort)* health resort, spa, *(Foto)* tank;
eigenes ~ *(Hotel)* private bathroom; **öffentliches** ~ public baths; **tägliches** ~ daily dip;
Kind mit dem ~ **ausschütten** to empty (pour) the baby away with the bath-water; **in ein** ~ **gehen** to take the waters (a cure), to go to a spa.
Bade|anstalt bathing establishment, bathhouse, [public] swimming pool; ~**gast** bather, *(Kurgast)* cure guest; ~**kabine** bathing cabin, bathhouse; ~**kur** cure, balneotherapy; ~**kur machen** to [visit a] bath, to undergo a cure; ~**meister** swimming-pool attendant; ~**möglichkeiten** bathing facilities.
baden gehen to go bathing (swimming), *(fig.)* to go by the wayside, to end up in smoke.
Bade|ofen water heater, geyser; ~**ort** health (bathing) resort, watering place, spa.
Bäder|amt baths department; ~**heilkunde** balneotherapy.
Bade|stelle bathing place; ~**strand** bathing beach; ~**unfälle** bathing casualties; ~**wanne** bathtub; ~**zimmer** bathroom, toilet *(US)*; ~**zimmereinrichtung** bathroom fittings.
baff sein to be dumbfounded.
Bafög-Student [etwa] student in receipt of a grant from public funds.
Bagage *(Gesindel)* riffraff, rabble, *(mil.)* baggage;
die ganze ~ the whole lot, ragtag and bobtail, kit and caboodle *(US)*.
Bagatell|betrag petty amount, drab; ~**beträge** petty cash; ~**delikt** minor (petty, trivial, trifling) offence; ~**diebstahl** petty larceny *(US)*.
Bagatelle flea-bite, picayune, pin, trifle, mere bagatelle, one gallus *(US sl.)*;
~**n** airy nothings;
sich nicht mit ~**n abgeben** not to stick at trifles; **keine** ~ **sein** to be no trifling matter.
Bagatell|gericht small debts court; ~**gerichtsbarkeit** summary jurisdiction.
bagatellisieren to make light of, to minimize.
Bagatellisierung minimization.
Bagatell|klage summary action; ~**klausel** *(Versicherung)* franchise clause *(Br.)*; ~**konkurs** summary case, small estate *(Br.)*; ~**sache** summary offence *(US)*; ~**schaden** petty (minimal) damage, minor (trivial) loss; ~**schulden** small (petty) debts; ~**strafsachen** petty offences; ~**stücke** *(Wertpapiere)* small securities, baby bonds *(US)*; ~**vergehen** trivial (petty, minor) offence.
Bagger dredger, dredge, excavator, digger, *(Löffelbagger)* power shovel, navvy *(US)*;
mit dem ~ **wegräumen** to dredge away;
~**arbeiten** dredging operations; ~**eimer** dredge bucket, basket-dipper; ~**firma** dredging contractor.
Baggern dredging.
baggern to dredge, to excavate.
Bagger|schiff, ~**schute** dredge boat.
Bahn way, path, road, *(Eisenbahn)* rail, railway *(Br.)*, railroad *(US)*, *(fig.)* channel, *(Rennbahn)* course, *(Stoff, Tapete)* width, breadth, *(Strecke)* line, track *(US)*;
an der ~ at the station; **aus der** ~ **geworfen sein** to be thrown out of gear; **ausschließlich mit der** ~ by an all-rail route; **frei** ~ free on rail, free on board *(US)*; **mit der** ~ by rail (train); **nicht im Gewahrsam der** ~ off the line;
eingleisige ~ single-line (track, *US*), one-track railway;
~ **eines Raumschiffes** track of a spacecraft; ~ **eines Sturms** path of a storm;
~ **frei!** out of the way!;
mit der ~ **befördern** to [forward by] rail, to railroad *(US)*; ~ **beschreiben** *(Raumschiff)* to describe an orbit; **sich in ähnlichen** ~**en bewegen** to take a similar course; ~ **für j. brechen** to pave the way for s. o.; **sich eine** ~ **brechen** to forge ahead; **j. zur** ~ **bringen** to see s. o. off; **freie** ~ **für ein Projekt erhalten** to receive green light for a project, to receive the go-ahead on a project; **mit der** ~ **fahren** to go by train (rail); **frühzeitig auf die falsche** ~ **geraten** to go wrong in early life; **auf die schiefe** ~ **geraten** to go off the rails, to go to the bad, to backslide; **Angelegenheit in andere** ~**en lenken** to direct a matter into other channels; **j. aus seiner** ~ **reißen** to throw s. o. off his balance; **sich in mehrere** ~**en verbreitern** to be extended to several lanes; **wieder in geregelten** ~**en verlaufen** to be back to normal; **in ruhigen** ~**en verlaufen** to take a calm course; **mit der** ~ **verschicken** to send by rail; **sich in ähnlichen** ~**en vollziehen** to take a similar course; **in jds.** ~**en wandeln** to follow in s. one's footsteps; **neue** ~**en weisen** to open new prospects; **aus der** ~ **werfen** to knock sideways; **j. aus seiner** ~ **werfen** to throw s. o. off his balance; **in gewohnte** ~**en zurückfallen** to fall back into the same rut;
~**abfertigung** railway dispatch office; ~**abzweigung** branch line; ~**aktien** railway shares, railroad stocks *(US)*, rails, railroads *(US)*.
bahnamtlich|geprüft examined by the railway authorities;
~**e Bestimmungen** railway regulations; ~**e Mitteilungen** official communications; ~**es Rollfuhrunternehmen** contract carrier, regular cartage company, railway express agency; ~**e Vorschriften** railway regulations.
Bahn|angestellter railway (railroad, *US*) employee; ~**anlagen** railway installations *(Br.)*, rail facilities; ~**anlagen für Gleisanlieger** accommodation works; ~**anleihe** railway loan; ~**anschluß** connection, connexion, *(Gleis)* siding, industrial track; ~**arbeiter** railway (railroad, *US*) man, railroader *(US)*; ~**ausstattungsgegenstände** work equipment, company service equipment; ~**beamter** railway (railroad, *US*) official; ~**beförderung** railway transport *(Br.)*, transport by rail, railway (rail, railroad, *US*) transportation; ~**begleitpapiere** goods invoice; ~**benutzer** rail passenger; ~**benutzungsrecht** running powers; ~**betrieb** operation of a railway line, railroading *(US)*.
bahnbrechend epoch-making, pioneering, trail-blazing;
~ **sein (wirken)** to do pioneer work, to pioneer, to blaze a trail;
~**e Erfindung** epochmaking discovery.
Bahn|brecher pioneer, pathfinder, waymaker; ~**brücke** railway bridge, viaduct; ~**bus** railway company's bus, railroad bus *(US)*; ~**damm** embankment; ~**depot** railway depot; **im** ~**dienst tätig sein** to work on the railway; ~**eigentum** railway (railroad, *US*) property; ~**einrichtungen** railway equipment.
bahnen, sich einen Weg to tread a path, to blaze a trail; **jem. einen Weg** ~ to clear the way for s. o.; **sich einen Weg durch die Menge** ~ to force one's way through the crowd; **sich einen Weg durch den Urwald** ~ to hew one's way through dense jungle.
Bahnfahrt trip, train ride (journey).
Bahnfracht railway carriage *(Br.)*, railage, railway (railroad, *US*) freight;
~**brief** bill of carriage, railroad bill of lading *(US)*, waybill *(US)*; ~**dienst** railway parcel service; ~**gut** railway parcels; ~**sätze**, ~**tarif** railway (railroad, *US*) rates; ~**sendung** rail carloading; ~**verkehr** transportation by rail *(Br.)*, railway (railroad, *US*) freight transportation.
bahnfrei carriage paid, [delivered] free station.
Bahn|gebäude, ~**grundstück** railway premises; ~**gelände** railway property; ~**gleis** rail track.
Bahnhof [train] station, railway (railroad, *US*) station, depot *(US)*;
frei ~ free station; **vom** ~ **leicht zu erreichen** within easy reach of the station;
für Personen- und Güterverkehr geeigneter ~ good and substantial depot *(US)*; **großer** ~ *(fig.)* red carpet;
~ **zur Ergänzung des Eisvorrats** icing station; ~ **für den Personenverkehr** passenger station;

j. vom ~ **abholen** to meet s. o. at the station; **j. am ~ absetzen** to land s. o. at the station; ~ **durchfahren** to pass a station; **sich einem großen ~ gegenübersehen** to find o. s. courteously carpeted; **seine Koffer zum ~ bringen lassen** to have one's luggage (baggage, *US*) taken to the station; **großen ~ für j. veranstalten** to roll out the red carpet for s. o., to give s. o. a red-carpet reception, to escort s. o. with great pomp; **immer nur ~ verstehen** to be Greek to s. o.

Bahnhofs|anlagen station premises; ~**buchhandel** station booksellers; ~**buchhändler** keeper of a railway bookshop; ~**buchhandlung** railway bookshop (bookstall); ~**droschke** privilege cab *(Br.)*; ~**gaststätte** station restaurant; ~**gebäude** station (railway) building, depot grounds *(US)*; ~**halle** station (waiting) hall, concourse *(US)*; ~**hotel** station hotel; ~**kommandant** *(mil.)* Railway Transport Officer (R.T.O.); ~**mission** travel(l)er's aid.

bahnhofsnahe within easy reach of the station.

Bahnhofs|nähe proximity to the station; ~**niederlage** depot; ~**polizei** railway police *(Br.)*; ~**restaurant** station restaurant; ~**spediteur** transfer company, contract carrier; ~**vorsteher** stationmaster, station agent *(US)*, ornament *(sl.)*; ~**wirtschaft** station restaurant, refreshment room.

Bahn|kilometer, gefahrene miles travel(l)ed; ~**knotenpunkt** [railway] junction; ~**körper** roadbed, permanent way *(Br.)*; ~**körpererhaltung** roadbed maintenance; ~**korrektur** *(Raumschiff)* orbit correction; ~**kreuzung** railway crossing, crossover.

bahnlagernd left at station to be called for, to be called for at station office.

Bahnlieferung railway carriage, transport by rail.

Bahnlinie railway (railroad, *US*)line;
eingleisige ~ single line (track); **in die Stadt führende** ~ up line; ~ **zwischen zwei Städten** intercity railway;
~ **stillegen** to close a line; ~ **dem Verkehr übergeben** to open a line for traffic.

bahnmäßig verpackt packed for railway transport.

Bahn|meister roadmaster, trackmaster *(US)*, permanent-way inspector *(Br.)*; ~**oberbau** permanent way; ~**papiere** goods invoice; ~**polizei** railway police *(Br.)*.

Bahnpost|amt railway (travel(l)ing) post office; ~**beamter** postal clerk *(US)*; ~**dienst** rail mail service *(US)*; ~**klassen** surface mail categories *(Br.)*.

bahnpostlagernd to be called for at station office.

Bahn|postwagen post-office (post, mail, *US*) car, mail van *(US)*; ~**preis** railway fare; ~**rampe** [railway] platform; ~**räumer** rail guard, cowcatcher *(US)*; ~**schranke** level-crossing barrier, grade-crossing gate *(US)*; ~**schranke öffnen (schließen)** to open (close) the gate; ~**schwelle** sleeper *(Br.)*, tie *(US)*; **amtlicher** ~**spediteur** contract (rail) carrier, railway contractor, regular cartage (transfer) company, railway express agency, goods agent *(Br.)*; **mit Hilfe (unter Inanspruchnahme) eines** ~**spediteurs** through the medium of a goods agent *(Br.)*; ~**station** railway (railroad, *US*) station; **frei** ~**station des Empfängers** free railroad station of consignee *(US)*.

Bahnsteig [railway] platform, landing.
auf dem ~ auf und ab laufen to march up and down (pace) the railway platform; **frei ~ zugeliefert werden** to be delivered free railway station;
~**brücke** footbridge; **von der** ~**kante zurücktreten!** please step back!; ~**karte** platform ticket; ~**schaffner** ticket porter (collector), gateman *(US)*; ~**sperre** platform barrier, ticket gate; ~**unterführung** subway.

Bahn|strecke railway line (track, *US*); **eingleisige** ~**strecke** single line (track); ~**tarif** railway tariff, railroad rates *(US)*; ~**telegramm** railway (railroad, *US*) station telegram; ~**transport** rail carriage, railway (railroad, *US*) transport, conveyance by rail; **lediglich im** ~**transport** allrail; ~**transportversicherung** rail transportation insurance *(US)*; ~**überführung** overhead way, dry bridge.

Bahnübergang grade (level, *Br.*) crossing;
beschrankter ~ crossing with gates; **niveaugleicher** ~ farm crossing; **schienengleicher** ~ grade *(US)* (level, *Br.*) crossing; **unbeschrankter** ~ ungated level crossing *(Br.)*.

Bahn|unterführung subway, underpass; ~**verbindung** train connection (service), rail link; **~- oder Busverbindungen** rail or bus travel; ~**verkehr** railway (railroad, *US*) traffic; ~**versand** dispatch by rail, railway (rail) transportation, forwarding (shipping, *US*) by rail; ~**versandvorschriften** dispatch regulations; ~**vorschriften** regulations of the railway, railway regulations; ~**wärter** linesman, signalman, gatekeeper *(US)*, guard *(US)*, flagman *(US)*; ~**wärterhäuschen** linesman's lodge, gatehouse *(US)*; **heimische** ~**werte** *(Börse)* home rails, railways *(Br.)*, railroads *(US)*; ~**zeit** station time; ~**zustellung** rail delivery.

Bai bay, bight, fleet.

Baisse decline [in prices], depression, fall, drop, slump, bear market;
konjunkturelle ~ cyclical depression; **plötzliche** ~ sudden decline;
erwartete ~ im voraus berücksichtigen to undersell *(Br.)* (underdiscount, *US*) the market; **sich in einer ~ eindecken** to raid the bears *(Br.)*; **während der ~ kaufen** to buy (purchase) for a fall; **auf ~ spekulieren** to operate (gamble) for a fall, to speculate on (for) a fall, to [go a] bear *(Br.)*, to sell a bear *(Br.)*, to bear the stocks *(Br.)*, to sell short *(US)*; **im Zeichen der ~ stehen** to be marked by a decline in prices; ~ **herbeizuführen trachten** to bear the market *(Br.)*; **in der ~ verkaufen** to go bear *(Br.)* (short, *US*);
~**angebot** short offer *(US)*; ~**angriff** bearish operation (demonstration, *Br.*), drive *(US)*; ~**angriff machen** to hammer the market; ~**bewegung** bearish demonstration *(Br.)*; ~**clique** operators for a fall; ~**engagement** bear account *(Br.)*, short sale *(US)*; ~**engagements** bear accounts *(Br.)*, short engagements (interests of the market) *(US)*, short stock (position) *(US)*; ~**gerücht** bear rumo(u)r *(Br.)*; ~**geschäft** bear transaction *(Br.)*; ~**haltung** bearish attitude *(Br.)* ~**klausel** slump clause; ~**konto** bear account *(Br.)*; ~**manöver** bear raid, bearish operation; ~**markt** bear[ish] (falling, depressed, short, *US*) market; ~**moment** bear point; ~**partei** bear, bearish clique, operators for a fall, short side *(US)*, shorts *(US)*, short interest of the market *(US)*; ~**position** bear position (account) *(Br.)*, short account *(US)*; ~**position hereinnehmen (vortragen)** to take in bear accounts *(Br.)*; ~**spekulant** speculator for a fall, bear [seller] *(Br.)*, short *(US)*; ~**spekulation** bear[ish] speculation *(Br.)*, bearish operation *(Br.)*, bear transaction *(Br.)*, operation (speculation, dealing) for a fall, selling a bear *(Br.)* (stocks short, *US*), going short *(US)*, short sale *(US)*; ~**stimmung** bearish mood (market) *(Br.)*, bearishness *(Br.)*, depression of the market; ~**strömung,** ~**tendenz** bearish tendency (tone) *(Br.)*, bearishness *(Br.)*, downward tendency.

baissetendenziös bearish *(Br.)*, short *(US)*.

Baisse|termingeschäfte trading on the short side *(US)*; ~**verkauf** bear sale *(Br.)*, short sale *(US)*; **offene** ~**verkäufe durchführen** to bang the market; ~**verkäufer** bear seller *(Br.)*; ~**vorhersage** forecast of a slump; **konjunkturelle** ~**zeit** business slump.

Baissier bear *(Br.)*, stale, short [seller] *(US)*;
~**s** short interest of the market *(US)*;
~ **werden** to turn bear *(Br.)*.

Bajonett bayonet;
~ **aufpflanzen** to fix bayonet;
~**sockel** *(el.)* bayonet-joint base.

Bake buoy, mark, navigation guide, beacon, *(Verkehrszeichen)* signal light, beacon;
mit ~n versehen to beacon [off].

Baken|antenne beacon antenna (aerial, *Br.*); ~**blindlandung** instrument landing system; ~**boje** beacon (leading) buoy; ~**feuer** beacon light; ~**geld** beaconage; ~**tonne** beacon buoy.

Bakterie germ, bug *(coll.)*.

Bakterien|forschung bacteriology; ~**krieg** germ warfare.

baldmöglichst prompt.

Balg skin, hide;
jem. den ~ abziehen to fleece (skin) s. o.

balkanisieren to balcanize.

Balkanstaaten Balkan States, Near East *(US)*.

Balken girder, beam, timber, *(Dach)* rafter, *(drucktechn.)* thick rule;
lügen, daß sich die ~ biegen to lie like a trooper (gasmeter);
~**decke** timbered ceiling; ~**diagramm** bar chart; ~**schlagzeile** streamer; ~**überschrift** banner [headline].

Balkon balcony, alcove, *(Theater)* balcony, dress circle;
~**fenster** balcony window; ~**tür** french window; ~**zimmer** alcove room.

Ball ball, dance;
~ **nur für geladene Gäste** private dance;
am ~ bleiben to keep the ball rolling; ~ **ins Rollen bringen** to start the ball rolling; ~ **eröffnen** to open the ball; **am ~ sein** to be in command.

Ballast ballast, lastage;
ohne ~ unballasted;
fliegender ~ shifting ballast; **überflüssiger** ~ lumber;
~ **abwerfen** to discharge ballast; **unnötigen ~ abwerfen** to jettison; **mit ~ beladen** ballast; **vom ~ befreien** to unballast; ~

einnehmen to take in ballast; **mit ~ fahren** to sail in ballast; **~ löschen** to discharge (throw out) ballast;
~einnahme ballasting; **~eisen** kentlage, kentledge; **~fracht** dead freight; **~gebühren** ballastage.
ballastgeladen ballast-laden, going in ballast.
Ballastladung ballast, dead freight;
nur mit ~ in ballast.
Ballast|reise ballast passage; **~schiff** ballast lighter; **~tank** ballast tank.
Ballempfang *(Radio)* relay reception.
Ballen bale, pack, package, parcel, bundle;
nach tatsächlichem Gewicht berechnete ~ running bales; **~ Baumwollstoff** piece of cotton cloth; **~ Papier** ten reams; **~ Tuch** twelve pieces of cloth;
Waren in ~ verkaufen to sell in bale; **in ~ verpacken** to make up in bales, to bale;
~binder packer; **~gut** bale (pack) goods; **~presse** baling press, baler; **~schnur** bale tie, packing cord; **~ware** bale goods.
ballenweise in bales, by the bale.
Ballenzeichen bale mark.
Ballet ballet;
~meister choreographer, ballet master; **~truppe** corps de ballet.
Ballon balloon, *(weiche Birne, fam.)* nut;
im ~ aufsteigen to [go up in a] balloon; **eins auf den ~ bekommen** to get a crack on the head; **~ aufsteigen lassen** to launch a balloon;
~aufstieg ascent in a balloon, balloon ascent; **~fahrer** balloonist; **~flug** flight in a balloon; **~hülle** envelope; **~korb** nacelle; **~reifen** balloon tyre *(Br.)* (tire, *US*), *(großer)* doughnut tyre *(US sl.)*; **~sperre** balloon (aerial) barrage; **~stoff** balloon fabric.
Ballotage voting by ballot, secret ballot.
ballotieren to [vote by] ballot.
Ball|robe ball dress; **~saal** ballroom, assembly room; **~sendung** *(Rundfunk)* rebroadcast.
Ballung *(Statistik)* concentration.
Ballungs|gebiet, ~raum agglomeration, congested (overcrowded, conurbation) area; **städtisches ~gebiet** urban center *(US)* (centre, *Br.*).
Balsam für meine Seele honey to my soul.
Bambus|papier chinese paper; **~vorhang** Bamboo Curtain.
Bammel|bekommen to get the wind up *(sl.)*; **~ haben** *(fam.)* to be in a blue funk, to shake in one's shoes.
banal stock, commonplace, trite, trivial, banal.
banalisieren to vulgarize.
Banause slob *(US sl.)*, low-brow.
Band band, cord, *(Bandgerät)* tape, *(Buch)* volume, *(Buchbinder)* band, *(Faß)* hoop, *(Fließband)* assembly line, *(Förderband)* conveyor belt, *(Metall)* strip, iron strap, *(Rundfunk)* wave band, *(Schreibmaschine)* ribbon, *(Sender)* waveband, frequency band, *(Textilien)* sliver;
am laufenden ~ on the assembly line, *(fig.)* one after the other, thick and fast *(sl.)*;
das Blaue ~ *(Atlantik)* the Blue Ribbon; **eheliches ~** marriage tie; **einzelner ~** odd volume; **endloses ~** endless (continuous) belt; **familiäre ~e** family ties; **gemustertes ~** fancy ribbon; **leeres ~** blank tape; **vorliegender ~** present; **[vorweg]aufgenommenes ~** [pre]recorded tape;
~ der Ehe marriage knot;
auf ~ aufnehmen to [punch (record) on] tape, to can *(coll.)*; **außer Rand und ~ geraten** to get out of hand; **~e der Freundschaft knüpfen** to form links of friendship; **~ löschen** to erase the tape; **Bücher am laufenden ~ schreiben** to turn (churn) out books one after the other; **außer Rand und ~ sein** to kick up a row; **aufs ~ sprechen** to record one's voice; **~ zerschneiden** *(Zeremonie)* to cut the tape.
Bandage bandage;
die ~n beim Kampf ums Leben nie ablegen to fight one's way through life with kid gloves; **mit harten ~n arbeiten** to play hard.
bandagieren to bandage.
Band|arbeit assembly-line technique; **~aufnahme** tape recording, *(Aufgenommenes)* canned speech, *(Rundfunksendung)* prerecorded broadcast; **~aufnahme machen** to record on tape; **~aufnahmeproduktion, ~aufzeichnung** tape recording, taping session, *(Rundfunk)* delayed broadcast.
Bandbreite *(Kursschwankungen)* band, margin, spread *(US)*, *(Radio)* band[path] width, *(Vorhersage)* prediction interval;
feste ~n *(Wechselkurs)* fixed margins (limits); **große ~** wide range; **zugelassene ~** *(Wechselkurse)* adjustable peg;
~ der Wechselkurse margin (spread, *US*) of exchange rates; **größere ~n der Wechselkurse** wider-band exchange rates; **höchstzugelassene ~ der Wechselkurse** maximum range of permitted fluctuations.
Bandbreitensatz *(Währungen)* floating rate.
Bande band, crew;
fröhliche ~ merry crowd; **jugendliche ~** rat pack;
~ von Brandstiftern fire gang; **~ Jugendlicher** band of youth;
~ ausheben to break up a gang; **mit einer ~ kooperieren** to mix up with a gang; **sich zu einer ~ vereinigen** to band together.
Bände sprechen to speak volumes.
bändefüllend voluminous.
Band|einsteller *(Schreibmaschine)* ribbon switch; **~einteilung** distribution of volumes; **~eisen** band (strap, hoop) iron, metal strapping; **~eisensicherung** metal strapping.
Bändel haben, j. am to have s. o. on a string.
Banden|bildung guerilla network; **~diebstahl** robbery; **~führer** ringleader, leader of a gang, guerilla (gang) leader; **~krieg** guerilla (gang) war; **~mitglied** gangster *(US)*, thug, guerilla; **~organisation** guerilla network; **~wesen** gangsterism, thuggery.
Banderole revenue stamp *(US)*, fiscal stamp *(Br.)*.
Banderolensteuer stamp duty (tax).
Band|fabrikation assembly-line technique; **~filter** directional (wave band, band-pass) filter; **~förderanlage** belt *(Br.)* (band) conveyor; **~geschwindigkeit** recording (tape) speed.
bändigen to tame, *(fig.)* to keep in cherk;
nicht zu ~ sein to be quite out of hand.
Bandit bandit, gangster, outlaw, bad man *(US sl.)*;
~ werden to take to the heather *(Scot.)*.
Banditen|führer bandit leader; **~tum** banditry, brigandage.
Band|maß tape line (measure), measuring tape; **~mikrophon** ribbon microphone; **~montage** flow system; **~musik** canned music; **~produktion** assembly-line production; **~sperre** band-stop filter; **~spreizung** *(Radio)* band spreading; **~stahl** band strip; **~übertragung** recorded broadcast; **~waren** narrow goods; **~wurmrede** endless speech; **~wurmsatz** run-on sentence; **~zuführung** tape feed.
bange|Ahnungen uneasy forebodings; **~ Stunde** anxious hour.
Bank bank[ing house], banker, banking firm (establishment), moneyed corporation *(US)*, *(Bankreihe)* row, *(Flöz)* seam, vein, *(Schulbank)* desk, *(Sitz)* seat, bench, *(Untiefe)* shoal, *(Verkaufstisch)* stand;
auf der ~ at the bank; **bei einer ~ zahlbar** payable at a bank; **durch die ~** *(fig.)* allround; **knapp an ~en** underbanked; **nur an eine ~ zahlbar** *(Scheck)* crossed specially; **ohne Angabe einer bestimmten ~** *(Scheck)* crossed generally;
dem Abrechnungsverkehr (Giroverkehr) angeschlossene ~ clearing bank *(Br.)*, associated bank *(US)*; **ausstellende ~** issuing bank; **auswärtige ~** out-of-town bank; **auszahlende ~** paying bank[er]; **avisierende ~** notifying bank; **barzahlende ~** cash (specie)-paying bank; **beauftragte ~** paying (payor, *US*) bank; **bekannte ~** renowned bank; **am Landeszentralbanksystem beteiligte ~** member bank *(US)*; **Effektenemissionsgeschäfte betreibende ~** investment bank; **bezogene ~** drawee bank; **durchleitende (eingeschaltete) ~** intermediary bank *(US)*; **einlösende ~** cashing banker; **einziehende ~** collecting bank (banker) *(US)*; **federführende ~** leading underwriter, syndicate manager, originating banker; **als Hinterlegungsstelle fungierende ~** depositary bank *(US)*; **fusionierte ~** merged bank; **geschlossene ~** closed bank; **halbstaatliche ~** semi-private bank; **konsortialführende ~** originating banker, syndicate manager; **staatlich konzessionierte ~** state-chartered (state, *US*) bank; **korrespondierende ~** reporting bank; **landwirtschaftliche ~** rural (land, farmer's, farm loan) bank; **negoziierende ~** negotiating bank; **öffentlich-rechtliche ~** bank incorporated under public law; **privilegierte ~** chartered bank; **ruinierte ~** wrecked bank; **seriöse ~** sound bank; **Akkreditiv stellende ~** opening bank; **überweisende ~** remitting bank; **verwahrende ~** depositary bank, custodian *(US)*; **zahlende ~** paying (payor, *US*) bank; **zahlungsunfähige ~** insolvent bank, bank in failing condition; **zwischengeschaltete ~** intermediary bank *(US)*;
~ für Außenhandel British Trade Corporation *(Br.)*; **~ mit Beratungsdienst auf allen Gebieten** full-service bank; **~ von England** Bank of England, the Bank *(Br.)*, Old Lady of Threadneedle Street *(fam.)*; **~ für Überseehandel** overseas bank; **~en und Versicherungen** financial corporations *(US)*; **~ für Wohnungsbaufinanzierungen** housing bank; **~ für internationalen Zahlungsausgleich** Bank for International Settlements; **~ der oberen Zehntausend** top-drawer exclusive bank;

von der ~ abheben to withdraw from a bank; **~ auf Überziehungsmöglichkeiten ansprechen** to approach a bank for an overdraft; **seine ~ anweisen** to instruct one's bank; **bei einer ~ arbeiten** to be employed in a bank; **mit einer ~ arbeiten** to bank with; **~ ausrauben** to stick up (to turn off) a bank *(sl.)*, to nick a bank *(sl.)*; **bei seiner ~ eine Kreditlinie beantragen** to ask a bank for a line of credit *(US)* (credit limit, *Br.*); **seine ~ mit der Bezahlung anfallender Steuern beauftragen** to commission one's bank to pay one's taxes; **~ zur Hausbank einer Firma bestimmen** to appoint a bank as bankers to the company; **~ einschalten** to interpolate a bank; **Geld bei der ~ einzahlen** to put money in (pay money into) a bank, to bank an amount; **Konto bei einer ~ eröffnen** to open an account with a bank; **~en fusionieren** to incorporate one bank with another, to absorb a bank, to consolidate banks; **Geld bei einer ~ stehen haben** to keep money at a bank; **~ halten** *(Spielsaal)* to hold (keep) the bank; **bei einer ~ hinterlegen** to deposit at a bank; **auf der ~ liegen** to lie at the bank; **ungenutzt in der ~ liegen** to lie idle in the bank; **Kredite bei der ~ in erhöhtem Maße in Anspruch nehmen** to increase the borrowings at the bank; **auf die lange ~ schieben** to put into cold storage (on the shelf), to shelve; **in der ~ sein** to lie at the bank; **bei der ~ im Debet sein** to be overdrawn at the bank; **stark bei den ~en verschuldet sein** to be deeply in hock to the banks; **auf der ~ der Spötter sitzen** to scoff at anything; **~ sprengen** *(Spielbank)* to break the bank; **durch eine ~ überweisen** to remit through a bank; **Konto bei einer ~ unterhalten** to have (keep) an account with a bank; **einer ~ vorlegen** to exhibit to a bank;

~abhebungen bank withdrawals; **~abrechnungsbuch** bankbook; **~abschluß** balance of a bank, bank return *(Br.)* (statement); **~abteilung** *(Notenbank)* banking department; **~agent** bank broker; **~agentur** bank agent (broker), *(Depositenkasse)* branch; **ausländische ~agentur** foreign agency *(US)*; **~aktien** bank shares (stocks, *US*); **in ~aktien spekulieren** to speculate in bank stocks *(US)*; **~aktiengesellschaft** joint stock bank, banking corporation *(US)*; **~aktionär** bank shareholder, holder of bank stock *(US)*; **~akzept** bank (banker's) acceptance; **erstklassiges ~akzept** fine bank acceptance *(Br.)*, prime banker's acceptance *(US)*.

Bankangestellter bank assistant (clerk, *Br.*, employee, official), banking employee, city man;
leitender ~ officer of a bank, bank's officer;
~ sein to be employed in a bank.

Bank|anleihe bank loan, post-notes; **konsortialiter gewährte zinsvariable ~anleihe** syndicated floating-rate bank loan; **~anstalt** banking house (establishment); **~anteil** banking interest; **~anteilseigner** shareholder (stockholder, *US*) in a bank; **~antwort** bank reply; **~anweisung** bank check *(US)* (cheque, *Br.*, bill, draft); **durch ~anweisung bezahlt** paid by check *(US)* (cheque, *Br.*); **~aufsichtsbehörde** banking regulator, state superintendence of banks *(US)*; **~auftrag** bank money order, banker's order; **~ausbildung** bank education; **~auskunft** bank's enquiry *(Br.)*, banker's reference (inquiry); **~auskünfte über ein Kundenkonto** bank disclosure; **~ausleihungen** bank lending *(US)*; **~ausweis** balance of a bank, bank report (return, *Br.*, statement); **wöchentlicher ~ausweis** weekly bank statement; **wöchentlicher ~ausweis der Notenbank** bank return *(Br.)*, Return for the Week *(Br.)*; **regelmäßiger ~auszug** periodical statement; **~aval** bank guarantee (guaranty, *US*); **~beamter** bank clerk *(Br.)*; **leitender ~beamter** bank officer (official); **allgemeine ~bedingungen** charge account terms; **~beleg** bank receipt (slip), record of a bank, bank record; **~bericht** bank return *(Br.)*, bank report (statement); **~betriebslehre** science of banking; **~betriebswirt** bank economist; **~betriebs[wirtschafts]lehre** bank economy; **~bevollmächtigter im Verrechnungsverkehr** inclearer *(Br.)*; **~bilanz** balance sheet of a bank, bank's balance sheet, bank report (statement, return, *Br.*); **~bonifikation** underwriting fee; **~bote** bank messenger (porter, runner); **~briefkasten** bank's letter box; **~buch** bankbook, *(Gegenkonto)* passbook; **~buchhalter** bank accountant; **~buchhaltung** bank accounting; **~bürge** bank guarantor; **~bürgschaft** bank guarantee; **~darlehn** banker's (bank[ing]) advance, bank loan (credit), bank borrowing, *(kurzfristig an Wechselmakler)* night money *(Br.)*; **~depositen** banker's balance, bank deposits; **~depot** bank deposit, deposit in a bank, lodgment; **~direktor** bank manager (president), manager of a bank; **~diskont[satz]** bank *(Br.)* (banker's) discount, bank *(Br.)* (discount, rediscount, *US*) rate, official rate of discount; **gültiger ~diskontsatz** current bank rate *(Br.)*; **~diskontsatz herabsetzen** to reduce the bank (discount, rediscount, *US*) rate.

Bänke, vor leeren ~n spielen to play to empty benches.

bankeigenes Gebäude bank premises.

Bank|einbruch bank burglary, raid on a bank; **~einbruchsversicherung** bank burglary insurance; **~einkünfte** bank earnings; **~einlage** deposit [in bank], bank deposit; **~einlagen in größeren Mengen verschwinden lassen** to spirit away large quantities of the bank's deposits; **~einleger** depositor.

Bänkelsänger street singer.

Banken|abrechnung bank clearing; **~abrechnungsstelle** clearinghouse; **~abteilung** *(Notenbank)* banking department; **~apparat** banking system (machinery); **~aufgabe** banking function; **~aufsicht** banking control (supervision); **~ausschuß** banking committee; **~dezentralisation** decentralization in banking; **~freiheit** free banking system *(US)*; **~funktion** banking function; **~fusion** merger (incorporation) of banks, amalgamation of banks, banking amalgamation, bank merger.

Bankengagements bank's commitments.

Bank|gesetzgebung banking legislation; **~gruppe** group of banks, bank group; **~intervention** *(Börse)* banking support; **~kommissar** bank commissioner *(US)*, commissioner of banking *(US)*, conservator *(US)*, *(Staatsbanken)* controller of the currency *(US)*; **~kommission** banking committee; **~konsortium** bank consortium, banking syndicate, group (consortium) of banks; **~konsortium für Krisenzeiten** money pool *(US)*; **~konzentration** money trust *(US)*; **~kooperation** cooperation between banks; **~liquidität** bank liquidity, easy money market *(US)*; **~markt** market for bank shares (stocks, *US*); **~pfandrecht** banker's lien; **~privileg** free banking system *(US)*.

Bankenquete Royal commission on the banking system *(Br.)*, legislative probe of banking practice *(US)*.

Banken|schließung bank closure; **~sektor** banking sector; **~system** banking system; **~vereinigung** association of banks, banking association (organization); **~viertel** financial district; **~zentrum** financial center *(US)* (centre, *Br.*), financial district.

Bankerfahrung banking experience.

Bankett banquet, feast, *(für j.)* complimentary dinner, *(Straße)* shoulder;
~ für j. veranstalten to give s. o. a testimonial dinner.

Bankfach *(Gewerbe)* banking [business], banking field, business of banking, *(Stahlfach)* safe [deposit box];
im ~ tätig sein to be in the banking line;
~leute bank experts; **~mann** financial expert; **~sprache** bankerese.

bankfähig bankable, eligible, negotiable;
nicht ~ unbankable, nonnegotiable;
~es Papier bank paper; **~e Sicherheiten** bankable securities.

Bank|fähigkeit eligibility, negotiability; **~fazilitäten** banking accommodations (facilities); **ausreichende ~fazilitäten sicherstellen** to ensure adequate banking accommodations; **~feiertag** bank holiday *(Br.)*; **~filiale** branch [bank]; **kontoführende ~filiale** account-holding branch; **~finanzierung** financing through banks; **~firma** banking house (establishment, partnership, company, corporation, *US*); **~forderung** bank's claim; **gegenseitige ~forderungen** interbank balances; **~formular** bank['s] form.

bankfremd|es Geschäft nonbanking business (activity); **~e Interessen** nonbanking interests; **~es Risiko** nonbanking venture; **~e Tätigkeit** nonbanking activity.

Bank|funktionen banker's (banking) functions; **~garantie** guarantee (guaranty, *US*), banker's guaranty *(US)*; **~gebäude** bank building (premises); **~gebäudekonto** bank premises account; **~gebühr für Guthabenkonto** cash-holding charge; **~gebühren** bank charges; **~geheimnis** bank[ing] secrecy, banker's duty of secrecy; **zum Schutz des ~geheimnisses erlassene Bestimmungen umgehen** to get around the bank secrecy laws; **~geld** *(Giralgeld)* bank money *(US)*; **~gelder unterschlagen** to abstract bank funds.

Bankgeschäft banking [business], business of banking, bank job, *(Bankfirma)* banking house (establishment), *(einzelnes Geschäft)* banking transaction, banking operation;
alle ~e complete banking facilities; **irreguläre ~e** supplementary banking functions; **kaufmännisches ~** commercial banking;
~ in Anlagewerten investment banking;
sämtliche ~e ausführen to transact all types of banking; **~ betreiben** to bank, to carry on a banking business, to carry on the business of banking, to do business as a banker; **staatlich genehmigtes ~ betreiben** to carry on a bona fide banking business *(Br.)*; **~e mit jem. machen** to bank with s. o.; **für ~e des**

Staates zur Verfügung stehen to act as the banker of the government; über solide Kenntnisse des gesamten ~s verfügen to have a sound general banking knowledge.

bankgeschäftlich | genutzt werden to be used for banking purposes;
~e **Betreuung** allround banking service; **unter ~n Gesichtspunkten** under banking aspects.

Bank | gesellschaft banking company (partnership, corporation, *US*), moneyed corporation *(US)*; **[nicht] in der Form der AG betriebene ~gesellschaft** [non]stock banking corporation *(US)*; **~- und Versicherungsgesellschaft** moneyed corporation *(US)*; **~gesetz** Bank Charter Act *(Br.)*, Banking Act *(Australia)*, *(Landeszentralbanken)* Federal Reserve Act *(US)*, Banking and Financial Dealings Act *(Br.)*; **~gewerbe** banking business, business of banking, banking trade; **~gewinn** banking profit.

bankgiriert endorsed by a bank.

Bank | giro bank transfer, endorsement of a bank; **~grundstück** bank (bank's) premises; **~gruppe** bank group, syndicate banking; **~gruppensystem** chain (group, *US*) banking.

Bankguthaben balance (sum) at the bank, bank balance (funds, holdings), credit bank balance, cash account, cash at bankers (in bank), money in the bank, *(Bilanz)* cash assets (in bank), bank balances, sums due from banks, *(Kreditkonto)* credit at the bank;
nicht abgehobenes ~ unclaimed balance; **terminlich abgesprochene ~** balances with banks for agreed periods; **unbeanspruchtes ~** dormant bank balance; **wechselseitige ~** interbank deposits; **zweckgebundene ~** earmarked balances at banks;
~ des Staates government deposits *(US)*;
~ pfänden to garnish a bank account.

Bankhalter *(Spielbank)* croupier.

Bankhaus bank, banking house, *(Privatbankhaus)* private banker;
bekanntes ~ renowned banking company.

Bankier [private] banker, money agent;
~ sein to bank, to do business as a banker.

Bankiers | beruf banking profession; **~bonifikation** underwriting fee; **~provision** banker's commission; **~vereinigung** bankers' association *(Br.)*, Institute of Bankers *(Br.)*.

Bank | indossament bank stamp *(US)*; **~inhaber** proprietor of a bank, private banker.

Bankinstitut banking institution, bank establishment, national banking association *(US)*;
ausländisches ~ foreign bank; **örtliches ~** local bank.

bankinterner Abrechnungsverkehr bank clearing system.

Bank | justiziar legal adviser of a bank; **~kapital** bank's capital, bank assets (stock); **~kassierer** cashier of a bank, bank cashier, [bank] teller *(US)*; **~kenntnisse** banking experience; **~konditionen** conditions of a bank, banking conditions; **~konkurs** bank failure.

Bankkonto bank[ing] account, checking account *(US)*;
vom Ehemann alimentiertes ~ bank account fed by the husband; **persönliches ~** private banking account; **überzogenes ~** [bank] overdraft;
~ eines Gemeinschuldners account of a bankrupt; **~ in laufender Rechnung** current account;
von seinem ~ abheben to withdraw from a bank; **sein ~ abschließen** to close one's account with a bank; **~ besitzen** to bank with, to have a bank account, to be a creditor on the bank books; **Betrag auf ein ~ einzahlen** to pay an amount into a banking account; **~ eröffnen** to open a bank account; **~ bei ... haben** to have a bank account with ...; **~ pfänden** to garnish a bank account; **~ sperren** to block an account; **vom ~ überweisen** to remit through a bank; **~ überziehen** to make an overdraft, to overdraw one's account; **~ unterhalten** to keep one's account open at a bank, to keep an account with a bank;
~abstimmung bank reconciliation; **~auszug** bank statement; **~inhaber** owner (holder) of a bank[ing] account, bank depositor.

Bank | kontor banking office; **~kontrollbehörde** banking regulator; **~konzern** banking concern, bank group (trust).

Bankkonzession bank charter, state charter *(US)*;
~ entziehen to revoke a bank charter; **~ gewähren** to charter a bank.

Bankkredit bank (commercial) credit, banker's (bank, banking) advance;
~e bank lendings;
revolvierend eingesetzte ~e roll-over bank loans; **über den gesetzlichen Höchstbetrag hinausgehender ~** excess loan *(US)*; **~e in Form direkt beglichener Kundenrechnungen** traders' credits; **~ mit 30 - 90 Tagen Laufzeit** commercial bank loan; **~ für bargeldlose Überweisungen** deposit loan; **~ an die Wirtschaft** business lendings;
~ aufnehmen to take up money at a bank; **~ einräumen (gewähren)** to open a credit with a bank; **~e revolvierend einsetzen** to roll over bank loans on a continuing basis; **~ eingeräumt erhalten** to obtain credit at a bank; **~ haben** to be in credit at (have credit with) the bank; **~ in erhöhtem Maße in Anspruch nehmen** to increase the borrowing at a bank; **über einen ~ verfügen** to have credit with a bank.

Bank | kreise banking circles (interest), bank experts; **in ~kreisen allgemein bekannt sein** to be common knowledge among bankers; **~krise** banking crisis; **~kunde** bank's client, bank borrower, customer (depositor) of a bank, banking customer; **~kundschaft** customers of a bank; **~lehrling** banking student; **~leitung** bank management; **~leitzahl** transit number, bank code number; **~liquidität** liquidity of a bank, bank liquidity.

bankmäßig banking, *(Wertpapiere)* bankable, negotiable;
~e Sicherheit collateral security *(US)*; **~er Überweisungsverkehr** clearing system.

Bank | methoden, mit der Praktizierung unlauterer ~methoden Schluß machen to tidy up loose banking practices; **~nähe** proximity to a bank; **~nebenplatz** nonbank place.

Banknote bank note *(Br.)* (bill, *US*), paper, greenback *(US)*;
echte ~ good bank note; **falsche ~** dud note, stumer *(Br., sl.)*; **gefälschte ~** forged (dud, falsified) note; **ungedeckte ~** fiduciary note *(Br.)*;
~ fälschen to forge a bank note.

Banknoten paper currency (money);
im Inland ausgegebene ~ home currency issues; **ausländische ~** foreign [currency] notes; **nicht einlösbare ~** insolvable bank notes; **falsche ~** bogus money, green goods *(US sl.)*; **als gesetzliches Zahlungsmittel geltende ~** legal tender notes, lawful money *(US)*; **nur im Inland gültige ~** home currency issues; **umlaufende ~** notes in circulation; **in Gold zahlbare ~** gold notes *(US)*;
~ und Kleingeld notes and small change; **~ mit kleinem Nennwert** money of small denominations;
~ ausgeben to issue [bank] notes; **~ einlösen** to redeem notes; **~ einziehen (aus dem Verkehr ziehen)** to withdraw bank notes; **~ in Umlauf setzen** to issue bank notes.

Banknoten | ausgabe note issue *(Br.)*, emission of bank notes; **ungedeckte ~ausgabe** fiduciary note issue *(Br.)*; **~ausgabe kontingentieren** to limit the fiduciary issue *(Br.)*; **~ausweis** note return *(Br.)*; **~bündel** bundle of notes, bank roll; **einem ~bündel entnehmen** to weed off *(sl.)*; **~druck** bank-note printing; **~druck autorisieren** to authorize the issue of money; **~druckerei** note press; **~einziehung** withdrawal of bank notes; **~fälscher** note forger, forger (counterfeiter) of bank notes, greenback goods dealer *(US sl.)*; **~fälschung** counterfeiting, forgery of bank notes, bill forgery *(US)*; **~monopol** note-issuing monopoly; **~papier** currency (note) paper; **~presse** note press; **~privileg** right to issue bank notes *(Br.)*, note-issuing privilege *(US)*; **~umlauf** circulation (currency) of bank notes, paper currency, bank notes in circulation, credit circulation.

Bank | panik run on a bank; **~papier** bank paper, banker's note; **~pfandrecht** banker's lien; **~platz** banking centre (place); **~pleite** bank smash (failure), collapse of a bank; **~politik** banking policy; **~portefeuille** bank portefeuille, portfolio of a bank; **~praxis** practice of banking, banking practice; **~privileg** bank charter; **~provision** banker's (banking, bank's) commission, bank charges; **~quittung** bank receipt; **~rate** discount (bank, *Br.*) rate; **~raub** bank robbery (raid); **~räuber** bank robber; **~referenz** banker's reference; **~reform** banking reform; **goldene ~regeln** golden rules of banking, banker's rule; **~rembours** commercial credit; **~revision** bank examination (audit); **~revisor** bank's inspector (auditor, examiner, *US*).

Bankrott bankruptcy, burst-up, bust, wall *(Br.)*, blowup *(US)*, failure, *(Zahlungsunfähigkeit)* insolvency;
am Rande des ~s verging on bankruptcy;
vom Schuldner beantragter ~ voluntary bankruptcy; **betrügerischer ~** fraudulent bankruptcy; **einfacher ~** failure, casual (simple) bankruptcy; **fahrlässiger ~** reckless bankruptcy; **offenkundiger ~** notur bankrupt *(Scot.)*; **unverschuldeter ~** casual (simple) bankruptcy; **völliger ~** smash, smashup, crash; **seinen ~ anmelden** to file a petition in bankruptcy; **seinen ~ erklären** to declare o. s. bankrupt; **~ machen** to break, to fail, to go bust (to the wall, *Br.*); **vom völligen ~ bedroht sein** to be up against utter bankruptcy.

bankrott bankrupt, bust, in chancery, broke, sold up *(fam.)*, all to pieces, in the tub *(sl.)*, *(zahlungsunfähig)* insolvent;
fast ~ near bankrupt; **gänzlich** ~ dead (stone) broke *(US)*; **sich ~ erklären** to file a petition in bankruptcy; **j. ~ erklären** to adjudge s. o. (declare s. o. a) bankrupt; **j. öffentlich ~ erklären** to declare (adjudicate) s. o. judicially to be bankrupt, to declare s. o. at the exchange; ~ **machen** to [become (go)] bankrupt, to smash [up], to fail in business, to break, to go to the wall *(Br.)* (scat), to bust, to fold up *(Br.)*, to wind up *(US)*; ~ **sein** to be in Queer Street *(Br.)*, to be (become) bankrupt, to have one's name (appear) in the gazette; **geistig ~ sein** to be bankrupt of ideas, to have exhausted one's intellectual resources; ~ **werden** to go into receivership, to fail; **für ~ erklärt werden** to be adjudged (gazetted, bankrupt, insolvent), to have one's name in the gazette, to be adjudicated bankrupt (hammered on the exchange);
~er Aktionär bankrupt member of a company.

Bankrotterklärung petition in (declaration of) bankruptcy.

Bankrotteur [adjudicated] bankrupt, defaulter;
betrügerischer ~ fraudulent bankrupt.

Bankrott|masse assets of a bankrupt's estate; **~prozentsatz** bankruptcy rate.

Bank|ruhezahlungen in-bank pensions; **~saldo** bank balance; **~satz** bank *(Br.)* (discount) rate; **~schalter** counter, window *(US)*; **~schalterstunden** banking hours; **~schaltertag** clear business day; **~scheck** bank check *(US)* (cheque, *Br.*), check drawn on a bank, bank[er's] draft, cashier's check *(US)* (cheque, *Br.*), treasurer's cheque *(Br.)*; **~schein** banker's note; **~schließfach** safe [deposit box]; **~schließung** bank shutdown (closure); **nach ~schluß** after banking hours; **~schulden** bank (banking) indebtedness, bank debt, *(Bilanz)* due to banks; **mit den ~schulden hinter den Lieferantenschulden zurücktreten** to subordinate bank debt to trade debt; **~schuldner** bank borrower, debtor of a bank; **~schuldverschreibungen** bank bonds; **~sicherheit** bank's security, collateral *(US)*.

Bankspesen bank charges (commission), banking charge (commission), service and activity charge;
besondere [nachgewiesene] ~ actual rates; **monatliche** ~ maintenance charge; **übliche** ~ posted rate, normal service charges.

Banksprache bank parlance.

bankstatistische Erhebungen banking statistics.

Bank|statut bank charter; **~system** banking system.

Banktätigkeit banking activity (activities);
~ **ausüben** to bank; **private ~ einschränken** to curb private banking operations.

banktechnisch banking;
~e Einrichtungen banking facilities; **~er Gesichtspunkt** banking point of view.

Bank|theorie banking theory *(Br.)*; **~transaktion** banking transaction (operation); **~tratte** bank (banker's, *Br.*) draft; **~tresor** safe deposit, strong room, bank vault; **seinen Schmuck im ~tresor verwahren** to keep one's jewels in a vault of the bank; **~überfall** bank raid, bank robbery; **~überfallversicherung** bank robbery insurance; **~überweisung** bank (banker's) transfer, banker's order; **~überziehung** overdraft.

banküblich according to established banking practice.

Bank|umsatz bank turnover; **~umsätze auf der Debetseite** bank debits *(US)*; **~unkosten** bank charges, banking charges (commission); **~unterlagen** banker's books; **~unternehmen** banking establishment (concern); **~unterschlagung** bank embezzlement; **~usance** practice of banking; **~valuta** bank money *(US)*; **~verbindlichkeiten** *(Bilanz)* due to banks, bank loans and overdrafts *(Br.)*; **~verbindung** banker, bank, *(einer Bank)* banker's correspondent, *(Bankkonto)* bank[ing] account; **~verbindungen außerhalb des Landes unterhalten** to bank outside the state; **~verkehr** banking [business], business of banking; **im ~verkehr** in interbank *(US)* dealings; **~vermögen** bank assets; **~verpflichtungen** *(Bilanz)* due to banks; **gegenseitige ~verpflichtungen** interbank balances; **~verschuldung** banking indebtedness, bank indebtedness, bank borrowing; **~vertreter** representative of a bank; **~vollmacht** authority to sign an account, mandate; **schriftliche ~vollmacht** written mandate; **~volumen** banking capacity; **~vorschuß** bank loan; **kurzfristige ~vorschüsse** day-to-day advances from banks; **~vorstand** bank management; **~währung** bank money *(US)*.

Bankwechsel bank acceptance (bill, draft), banker's draft *(Br.)*, bank paper;
erstklassiger ~ fine bank bill, prime banker's bill *(US)*;
~ **der Bank von England** bank post bill *(Br.)*.

Bank|welt banking world (community); **~werte** bank stock *(US)*; **in ~werten spekulieren** to speculate in bank stocks.

Bankwesen banking [technique], banking system (business);
genossenschaftliches ~wesen cooperative banking; **internationales** ~ international banking; **unabhängiges** ~ independent banking system;
~ **und Finanzwesen** banking and public finance.

Bank|zahlung banker's payment; **~zentrum** banking center *(US)* (centre, *Br.*); **internationales ~- und Finanzzentrum** centre of banking and international finance; **~zinsen** bank interest, interest on deposits, *(Sollzinsen)* interest on loan capital (bank loans); **bezahlte ~zinsen** bank interest paid; **erhaltene ~zinsen** bank interest received; **~zinssatz** bank rate; **~zinssatz für erstklassige Firmen** prime [lending] rate *(US)*, key rate *(Br.)*; **~zusammenbruch** bank failure, smash; **von einem ~zusammenbruch betroffen sein** to be embarrassed by a bank failure; **~zusammenschlüsse** banking concentration.

Bann spell, sway, charm;
in den ~ von etw. geraten to be under the spell of s th.; **jem. in seinen ~ schlagen** to cast a glamo(u)r over s. o.; **seine Zuhörer in seinen ~ schlagen** to hold the attention of an audience (have a grip on one's audience); **unter dem ~ des Alkohols stehen** to be in the grip of alcohol; **gesellschaftlich in den ~ tun** to hunt out of society, to ostracize; **j. in seinen ~ ziehen** to captivate (fascinate, enthral(l)) s. o.

bannen to ward (keep) off;
Not ~ to banish want.

Banner banner, standard, *(Werbung)* streamer;
~ **des Freihandels hochhalten** to raise the standard of free trade;
~träger standard bearer.

Bann|kreis verge *(Br.)*; **in jds. ~kreis geraten** to be under s. one's spell; **~meile** precinct of parliament; **innerhalb der ~meile des Parlaments** within the verge of parliament; **~strahl** thunder; **kirchlicher ~strahl** thunder of the church; **~ware** contraband articles (goods).

Bar [saloon] bar, taproom, nightclub, *(Hotel)* cocktail lounge.

bar bare, nacked, *(Geld)* cash [down], cash in hand, prompt, ready, *(rein)* pure, sheer;
gegen ~ terms cash, money (cash) down, for ready money (money out of hand); **gegen ~ gekauft** bought for cash; **gegen ~ verkauft** sold for cash; **in ~** in cash (specie); **nicht in ~** otherwise than for cash; **nur gegen ~** on the cash system; **Verkauf nur gegen ~** cash sales only;
~ **ohne Abzug** cash without discount, net cash; ~ **gegen 2% Diskont** cash less 2 per cent discount; ~ **gegen Dokumente** cash against documents; ~ **aller Mittel** without any means; ~ **gegen Nachnahme** cash on delivery; **in ~ oder in Sachleistungen** in cash or in kind; ~ **auf den Tisch** cash down; ~ **jeglicher Vernunft** devoid of any sense; ~ **zu zahlen** payable in cash;
~ **auf den Tisch bezahlen** to pay [cash] down (in cash), to pay in ready money; **gegen ~ kaufen** to buy for cash (ready money), to purchase for cash (ready money); **in ~ übersenden** to make remittance in cash; **gegen ~ verkaufen** to sell for cash (for current payment); ~ **zahlen** to pay cash (money) down;
~e Ausgaben cash expenditure; **~e Auslagen** cash disbursement; **~es Geld** ready (present) money, [spot] cash; **~es Gold** pure gold; ~ **zahlender Kunde** cash customer; **alles für ~e Münze nehmen** to take s. th. for gospel truth, to swallow a story; **~er Rückkaufwert** *(Lebensversicherung)* cash surrender value; **~er Unsinn** bare (sheer) nonsense; **~es Vermögen** pecuniary property.

Bär bear;
hungrig wie ein ~ as hungry as a hunter; **stark wie ein** ~ as strong as an ox;
jem. einen ~en aufbinden to play a practical joke on s. o., to taradiddle s. o., to tell s. o. a whopping lie; **wie ein ~ schlafen** to sleep like a log.

Bar|abdeckung settlement in cash; **~abfindung** settlement in cash, cash settlement, cash (money) compensation, monetary indemnity, pecuniary compensation, compensation in cash; **~abhebung** cash withdrawal (cash withdrawn, drawing); **~ablösung** settlement in cash; **~ablösungswert** cash surrender value; **~abrechnung** cash settlement; **~abschluß** cash transaction, cash bargain, bargain for cash; **~abzug** cash reduction.

Baracke hut, shack *(US)*, *(mil.)* blockhouse;
~n barracks;
elende ~ hovel, shanty;
in ~n leben to live in huts; **in ~n unterbringen** to hut.

Baracken|aufsteller hut builder; **~lager** hutted camp, hutment; **~räumung** hut clearance; **~reihe** *(mil.)* line *(Br.)*; **~viertel** slum quarter; **~wohnung** barrack flat.

Bar|anforderung cash requirements; ~**angebot** cash offer; **alternatives** ~**angebot** cash alternative; ~**ansammlung** cash buildup; ~**anschaffung** remittance (payment) in cash, cash payment (remittance); ~**anzahlung** *(Leihwagen)* prepayment; ~**artikel** ready-money article; ~**aufwand** cash outlay, cash expenditure; ~**aufwendungen** out-of-pocket costs; ~**ausgleich** cash adjustment, cash settlement; ~**auslagen** actual (out-of-pocket, *Br.*) expenses, actual expenditure, cash expenditure (outlay); ~**ausschüttung** cash distribution, cash share-out; ~**ausschüttung an die Aktionäre** cash to shareholders; ~**ausstattung** cash allocation; ~**auszahlung** payment in cash, cash payout; ~**auszahlung aus einer Gewinnvereinbarung** profit-sharing payment in cash.

barbarisch wild, barbarous, brutal;
~**en Hunger haben** to have a wolf in one's stomach; ~ **kalt** frightfully cold; ~**e Sitten** barbarous habits; ~**es Verbrechen** brutal crime.

Bar|besitzer nightclub owner; ~**bestand** amount of cash, cash on (in) hand, balance in cash; ~**bestand einer Bank** cash in vaults, vault cash, hard cash, cash reserve, effects, cash holdings *(US)*; ~**bestände** cash assets, cash funds; **Erhöhung der** ~**bestände vornehmen** to increase one's holdings of cash; ~**betrag** amount in cash, cash value; **weitere** ~**beträge der Regierung in Anspruch nehmen** to draw another dollop of government cash; ~**bezüge** remuneration in cash.

Barbier barber.

barbieren, j. über den Löffel to fleece s. o. of his money.

barbiert, völlig über den Löffel done brown *(coll.)*.

Bar|darlehn cash loan, advance in cash; ~**deckung** cash cover (security); ~**deckung anschaffen** to deposit a margin in cash *(US)*; ~**depot** cash deposit; ~**depotpflicht** compulsory cash deposit; ~**devisen** foreign cash, spot exchange; ~**diskont** cash (time) discount; ~**dividende** *(Lebensversicherung)* cash benefit (bonus); ~**eingang** cash item, specie payment *(US)*; ~**eingänge** cash receipts; ~**einkauf** cash purchase; ~**einkommen** cash income (earnings); ~**einlage** cash deposit, *(Kapitalanteil)* contribution in cash, cash investment; ~**einlage leisten** to contribute cash; ~**einnahmen** cash earnings (income, receipts), cash takings; **gesamte** ~**einnahmen** total cash received; ~**einschuß leisten** to contribute cash, to deposit a margin in cash *(US)*; ~**einzahlung** cash item; ~**einzahlungspflicht zum Nennwert** *(Aktienausgabe)* true value rule.

Bären|dienst erweisen to do a disservice, to be ill-serving; ~**führer** bear leader, cicerone; ~**hunger** wolfish appetite; ~**hunger haben** to have a wolf in one's stomach; **über** ~**kräfte verfügen** to be as strong as an ox; ~**natur haben** to have a strong constitution.

Bar|entlohnung remuneration in cash; ~**entnahme** cash drawings, withdrawal of cash; ~**erlös**, ~**erträgnisse** proceeds in cash, cash proceeds; ~**faktura** cash invoice; ~**finanzierung** direct financing; ~**fonds** cash on hand; ~**forderung** money claim; ~**freimachung** *(Post)* bulk franking; ~**gebot** cash purchase offer.

Bargeld cash [in (on) hand], ready cash, the ready, dry (ready, current, cash) money, down money, specie, stuff;
so gut wie ~ as good as ready money;
im Haus vorhandenes ~ cash in house;
~ **auf der Reise** travel cash;
~ **abheben** to draw cash; ~ **auf den Tisch legen** to plank down the ready; **auf** ~ **aus (versessen) sein** to be in cashbind; **knapp an** ~ **sein** to be short of cash; ~ **eines Landes aus dem Verkehr ziehen** to drain away the specie of a country (a country of money);
~**abzug** drain of specie; **investierte** ~**anlagen** cash investment; ~**anleger** cash investor; ~**automat** cash dispensing machine, cash dispenser; **hohe** ~**bedürfnisse haben** to be squeezed for cash; ~**bestand** cash balance; ~**deckungsrate** *(Bankwesen)* cash ratio; ~**geschäft** cash management; ~**guthaben** cash balance; ~**hortung** hoarded money; ~**karte** cash card; ~**kartensystem** cash-card service.

bargeldlos without ready money, paid by check (cheque, *Br.*), noncash, cashless *(US)*;
~ **zahlen** to transfer;
~**e Überweisung** transfer by check *(US)* (cheque, *Br.*); ~**es Verkaufssystem** credit-coupon plan; ~**er Verkehr** *(Kaufhaus)* drawback system; ~**e Zahlung** money transfer, cashless payment *(US)*; ~**er Zahlungsverkehr** cash transactions, *(Kaufhaus)* drawback system.

Bargeld|mangel shortage of cash; ~**position** cash position; ~**reserve** cash reserve; ~**reserven freisetzen** to free up bogged-down cash; ~**rückfluß** reflux of notes and coins; ~**schwemme** cash mountain; ~**sendung** cash remittance; ~**spende** cash donation; **unterhaltene** ~**summen** amount of cash held; ~**umlauf** cash in circulation, circulation of notes and coins, note and coin circulation; ~**verkehr** cash transactions, trade on cash terms; ~**volumen** total notes and coins in circulation.

Bar|geschäft cash transaction (business, purchase, sale), ready money purchase, transaction for cash; **gesamter** ~**gewinn** gross cash earnings; ~**guthaben** balance in cash, cash balance (assets), *(Bilanz)* cash in bank (at bankers); ~**gutwerte** cash assets; ~**hinterlegung** cash deposit; ~**hocker** bar stool; ~**kapital** cash capital (equity); ~**kasse** petty cash, *(Boot)* launch, longboat; ~**kauf** purchase for cash, cash purchase; ~**käufer** cash purchaser; ~**kellner** bartender, barkeeper, barman; ~**kredit** cash credit; ~**kreditkarte** cashcard; ~**legat** cash legacy; ~**leistungen** cash assets brought in, *(Sozialamt)* benefits in cash; ~**liquidität** cash liquidity ratio, financial liquidity; ~**lohn** wage paid in cash.

Barmittel cash [funds], cash resources, *(Investmentfonds)* cash reserve;
mangels ~ for lack of funds;
brachliegende ~ idle cash; **eigene** ~ internal cash;
~ **zum günstigen Augenblick aufnehmen** to spot the optimum moment for raising cash; ~ **beim Börsentiefstpunkt einsetzen** to commit cash near the bottom end;
kurzfristige ~**anlage** short-term harbo(u)r for one's cash; ~**bedarf** cash demand; ~**ergebnisabrechnung** cash operating statement; ~**zufluß** influx of cash, flow of cash, cash fund flow.

Barmixer bartender.

barocker Geschmack eccentric taste.

Barometer barometer, rain glass, weatherglass;
~ **ablesen** to read the barometer;
~**ablesung** barometer reading; ~**druck** barometric pressure; ~**höhe** barometer height; ~**stand** barometer reading; ~**sturz** rapid fall of the barometer.

barometrisches Gefälle barometric gradient.

Bar|posten, kleine petty cash; ~**prämie** cash bonus, cash incentive; ~**preis** cash price, price for cash; ~**preisbedingungen** cash terms; ~**rabatt** cash discount, anticipation; ~**rabattsatz** discount rate; ~**regulierung** cash adjustment (settlement).

Barren bar, ingot, *(Gold, Silber)* bullion;
zu ~ **verarbeiten** to ingot;
~**gold** [gold] bullion; ~**silber** bar silver, silver bullion.

Barreserve money reserve, *(Bank)* minimum cash reserve;
übermäßige ~**n haben** to have cash galore.

Barriere bar, barrier, wall, hedge, gate, *(Bahn)* grade *(Br.)* (level, *US*) crossing.

Barrikaden, auf die ~ **steigen** to get on the barricades.

barrikadieren to barricade.

Bar|rückkaufswert *(Lebensversicherung)* cash surrender value; ~**saldo** cash balance; ~**schaft** cash stock, ready money; ~**schatz** metallic money; ~**scheck** open check (cheque, *Br.*), cash cheque *(Br.)*, uncrossed check *(US)* (cheque, *Br.*), customer's check *(US)*; ~**schuldner** *(Bilanz)* advances; ~**sendung** cash remittance, remittance in cash, specie consignment; ~**sicherheit** cash collateral (security), cash overs *(US)*; ~**sortiment** book distribution; ~**sortimenter** book distributor.

Bart beard;
jem. um den ~ **gehen** to scratch s. one's back, to butter s. o. up, to soft-soap s. o.; **einen** ~ **haben** *(Witz)* to be a chestnut (as old as hills); **in seinen** ~ **murmeln** to mumble (mutter) away to o. s.; **sich den** ~ **raufen** to tear one's hair; **sich um des Kaisers** ~ **streiten** to quarrel over a mere trifle.

Bar|überschuß balance in hand, cash balance; ~**überweisung** cash remittance; ~**umsätze** *(Börse)* cash trades; ~**vergütung** allowance in money, money (cash) allowance, cash refund (compensation), *(Lebensversicherung)* cash bonus; ~**verkauf** cash deal, cash (money) sale, *(Börse)* spot sale; ~**verkauf ohne Zustellung** cash-and-carry system *(US)*; ~**verkaufswert** cash value; ~**verkehr** business on cash terms, *(Börse)* spot market; ~**verlust** net (clear) loss; ~**vermächtnis** cash legacy; ~**vermögen** cash, cash assets (capital); ~**verpflichtung** cash obligation; ~**verteilung** cash distribution, cash share-out; ~**vorrat** amount in cash, cash on hand, stock, cash reserve, effects; ~**vorräte der Bank** bullion at the bank; ~**vorschuß** cash advance, imprest fund *(Br.)*; ~**vorschuß für die Portokasse** petty cash fund; ~**wert** cash (present) value; ~**werte** cash assets; ~**wertrechnung** discounted cashflow method.

Barytpapier baryta paper.

Barzahlung cash [payment], payment in cash, cash settlement, cash down-payment, *(Kassamarkt)* spot payment, spot cash *(US)*;

gegen ~ for prompt cash, for money, cash down; **nur gegen ~** for cash only, terms [strictly for] cash, cash terms only, on the cash system;
bei ~ 5% Rabatt five per cent discount for cash;
sofortige ~ prompt cash payment, spot cash; **unverbuchte ~** unrecorded cash payment; **~ vorgesehen** terms cash;
~ bei sofortiger Abrechnung spot payment; **~ ohne Abzug** net cash; **~ bei Auftragserteilung (Bestellung)** cash with (less) order; **~ unter Diskontabzug** cash with discount; **~ gegen Dokumente** cash against documents; **~ bei Lieferung** cash on delivery; **~ New York** New York funds; **~ gegen Papiere** cash against documents; **~ und Selbstabholung** cash and carry;
auf ~ berechnen to base on cash; **~ einstellen** to suspend cash payment; **4% Diskont bei ~ gewähren** to allow 4 per cent off for ready money; **gegen ~ verkaufen** to sell for cash (value, *US*); **sofortige ~ verlangen** to demand cash on the barrelhead.
Barzahlungs|basis cash-settlement basis; **~bedingungen** cash terms, *(Börse)* spot conditions; **~beleg** petty cash voucher; **~diskont** cash discount; **~geschäft** spot firm, cash-and-carry store *(US)*; **~grundlage** cash-settlement basis; **~kunde** cash customer; **~preis** cash price; **~rabatt, ~skonto** cash discount, discount for cash; **vom ~system zum Kontokorrentverkehr übergehen** to transfer a business from payment of invoices to open-account terms; **~[verkaufs]system** cash (cash-and-carry, *US*) system; **~vertrag** cash contract.
Bar|zeichnung subscription in cash; **~zuschuß** cash allowance (grant).
Basar baza(a)r, variety show;
~ für wohltätige Zwecke church bazar.
basieren to base, to be based upon, *(Ansicht)* to ground, to found, to take root from.
Basis base, basis, pedestal foundation, substratum;
auf abgestufter ~ on a graduated basis; **auf anteiliger ~** on an equitable basis; **auf gleicher ~** on equal terms; **auf paritätischer ~** on a 50/50 basis; **auf privater ~** privately;
auf der ~ der Gegenseitigkeit on a basis of reciprocity; **gemeinsame ~** common ground (platform); **geschäftliche ~** business base; **tragfähige ~** sound basis;
~ für den Erfolg cornerstone for success; **~ für Preissenkungen** basis of prices;
Geschäft auf gesunder ~ aufbauen to build up a business on a sound basis; **~ bilden** to form the foundation; **gemeinsame ~ finden** to find a common approach; **~ eines Unternehmens verbreitern** to spread its business basis; **auf der ~ der Kostenteilung zusammenarbeiten** to work on a cost-sharing basis;
~einkommen basic income; **~einstandspreis** standard cost price; **~jahr** base year; **~kurs** initial rate; **~linie** *(Vermessung)* base line; **~periode** base period; **~preis** basic [material] price, base price; **~punktsystem** *(Verkehrstarif)* basing point system; **~region** *(EG)* basis region; **~vokabularschatz** basic vocabulary; **~wert** base (intrinsic) value; **~zeitraum** base period.
Bassin receptable, reservoir, tank, *(Bad)* swimming pool.
Bastard bastard *(US)*, illegitimate (bastard) child, hybrid, mongrel;
~schrift *(drucktechn.)* bastard type.
Bastel|artikel, ~ware do-it-yourself items.
basteln to rig up.
Basteltätigkeit do-it-yourself.
Bataillon battalion.
Bataillons|abschnitt batallion sector; **~stab** batallion headquarters; **~stärke** strength of a batallion.
Batterie storage battery, accumulator, *(mil.)* battery;
entladene ~ discharged battery; **erschöpfte ~** run-down battery; **geladene ~** charged battery;
ganze ~ von Flaschen whole regiment of bottles;
~ aufladen to refresh (recharge) a battery; **~ nicht voll aufladen** to undercharge a battery; **~ erschöpfen** to run down a battery; **~ kurzschließen** to short-circuit a battery; **~ kurzzeitig stark laden** to boost a battery; **mit normaler ~ laufen** to run off standard batteries; **~ überladen** to milk a battery;
~aufladung battery charging.
batteriebetrieben battery-operated.
Batterie|element battery cell; **~empfänger** battery-operated set; **~gehäuse** *(Auto)* battery case; **~klemme** *(Auto)* battery clip; **~ladegerät** battery charger; **~ladestelle** battery charging station; **~spannung** voltage; **~zündung** *(Auto)* battery-coil ignition.
Batzen chunk;
~ Gold lump of gold;
~ Geld kosten to cost a pretty penny.

Bau *(Bauart)* fabric, fabrication, structure, *(Bauen)* construction, building, erection, *(Baustelle)* building site, *(Bauwerk)* building, structure, edifice, works, *(Gefängnis, fam.)* glasshouse *(Br., sl.)*, *(Maschinen)* manufacture, construction;
am ~ on the building site; **im ~ begriffen (befindlich)** in course (process) of construction, under construction, on the stocks; **solange das Haus im ~ ist** while the house is being built;
imposanter ~ noble pile; **verlassener ~** *(Bergwerk)* abandoned mine;
~ sanitärer Anlagen sanitary engineering; **~ einer Bahnlinie** construction of a railway line, railway engineering; **~ einer neuen Brücke** construction of a new bridge; **~ von Eigentumswohnungen** condominium building; **~ von Fabriken** factory construction; **~ einer Straße** road construction;
mit dem ~ anfangen to commence a building; **auf dem ~ arbeiten** to be in the building line; **~ rasch errichten** to run up a building; **drei Tage ~ haben** *(mil.)* to be three days confined to barracks; **niemals aus seinem ~ kommen** to bury o. s. alive; **im ~ sein** to be in course of construction; **vom ~ sein** *(fam.)* to be in the racket; **~ vergeben** to let a building contract; **mit dem ~ einer schwierigen Straße fertig werden** to negotiate a difficult road;
~abgabe building tax.
Bauabnahme [quantity, *Br.*] surveying;
~ durchführen to survey a building;
~beamter building (quantity, *Br.*) surveyor; **~gebühren** surveyor's fees; **~schein** final architect's certificate.
Bau|abrechnung builder's account; **~abschnitt** section, stage; **~absicht** determination to build; **~abstand** space between two buildings; **~abteilung** construction department; **~akademie** school of architecture; **~aktien** buildings issues (shares, stocks, *US*); **~amt** surveyor's office, Board of Works *(Br.)*, superintendent of public works; **~amtsleiter** surveyor of buildings, building surveyor (inspector); **~amtsleitung** surveyorship; **~anschlag** building estimate, quantity surveying *(Br.)*; **~arbeiten** structural (construction) work, works of construction, *(Straßenarbeiten)* road repairs.
Bauarbeiter building trade operative, building (construction) worker;
~gewerkschaft building trade (construction) union; **~lager** construction camp; **~löhne** construction wages, building pay *(US)*; **~streik** construction strike.
Bauart constructive form, type of construction, *(Auto)* type, model, *(Maschine)* making;
modernste ~ latest type; **übliche ~** orthodox construction.
Bau|auflage building preservation order; **regionale ~auflagen** local building regulations; **~aufseher, ~aufsicht** [district] surveyor, building inspector, clerk of the Board of Works; **~aufsichtsamt, ~aufsichtsbehörde** inspector of works, superintendent of public works, surveyor's office, Dean of Guild Court *(Scot.)*.
Bauauftrag agreement (contract) to build, building (housing) order;
öffentlicher ~ construction contract;
~ im Submissionswege vergeben to job out a building contract; **rote Dachziegel im ~ vorschreiben** to specify red tiles for a roof.
Bau|auftragserteilung construction contract award; **~aufwand** cost of construction, building costs; **~ausführung** execution of a building, building operations, development *(Br.)*; **~ausnahmegenehmigung** exception, *(für Geschäftshäuser)* spot zoning *(US)*; **~ausnahmegenehmigung für Geschäftshäuser erteilen** to spot-zone; **~ausschreibung** calling for tenders; **~ausschuß** building board, zoning board *(US)*; **~baracke** building shed; **~bedarf** building material (supplies); **~beginn** commencement of a building, *(Schiff)* laying down; **~behörde** surveyor's office, board of works *(Br.)*; **~beschädigung** dilapidations.
baubeschränktes Gebiet restricted district.
Baubeschränkungen building (zoning, *US*) restrictions;
~ aufheben to rezone *(US)*; **~ erlassen** to restrict [real estate], to zone *(US)*; **keinen ~ unterliegen** to be free from building restrictions (zoning, *US*).
Bau|beschränkungsvereinbarung restrictive covenant; **~beschreibung** specification; **~bestimmungen** *(Generalbebauungsplan)* zoning law *(US)*, building byelaw *(Br.)*, local building regulations; **~bewilligung** building permit *(US)*; **~bewilligung erteilen** to authorize development *(Br.)*; **in verschiedene ~bezirke einteilen** to zone *(US)*; **~block** building block; **~bude** building shed; **~büro** site office.
Bauch|binde *(Buch)* blurb; **~landung** belly lending; **~landung machen** to belly-land; **~redner** ventriloquist.

Bau|darlehn building (construction) loan; ~**denkmal** monument; **kulturhistorisches** ~**denkmal** ancient building; ~**dezernat** engineer's department; ~**diebstahlsversicherung** builder's risk insurance; ~**dispens** spot zoning *(US)*; ~**dispens erteilen** to spot-zone *(US)*; ~**dock** *(Schiff)* stocks, building slip; **fertige** ~**einheit** package; ~**eisen** structural iron; ~**element** [building] component, element, unit.

Bauen building.

bauen *(anbauen)* to grow, to cultivate, *(errichten)* to build, to erect, to construct, to ground, to raise, to found, *(Maschinen)* to make, to fabricate, to manufacture;
auf j. ~ to rely (build, depend) on s. o.; **jem. goldene Brücken** ~ to build golden bridges for s. o.; **seinen Doktor** ~ to take one's degree; **Eisenbahnlinie** ~ to build a railroad *(US)*; **sein Examen** ~ to take one's examination; **auf sein Glück** ~ to trust to luck; **auf festem Grund** ~ to build on firm ground; **auf fremde Hilfe** ~ to lean on others for support; **Luftschlösser** ~ to build castles in the air; **mit schlechtem Material** ~ to jerry-build *(Br.)*; **sich ein Nest** ~ to feather one's nest; **zu niedrigsten Preisen** ~ to build down to prices; **auf Sand** ~ to rely upon a broken reed; **Unfall** ~ to have an accident;
sich einen Anzug ~ **lassen** to have a suit made, to go to the tailor's to be measured for a suit.

Bauer peasant, farmer, husbandman, countryman, hind *(Br.)*; **freier** ~ yeoman *(Br.)*; **kleiner** ~ smallholder *(Br.)*;
~ **sein** to follow the plough (plow, *US*).

bäuerlich rural, countrified.

Bauern|bewegung farmer's movement; ~**dorf** farm village; ~**familie** farm family; ~**fänger** skinner, duper, confidence man *(US)*, conman *(US)*; ~**fängerei** confidence trick (game), dupery, skin game *(US sl.)*; ~**gut** farmstead, farmhold, farmyard; ~**haus** farmhouse, cottage.

Bauernhof farmyard, farmstead, farmplace, agricultural holding, peasant property holding;
armer ~ county farm (house) (local, *US*); **durch die Familie bewirtschafteter** ~ family-sized farm;
~ **bewirtschaften** to manage (operate) a farm.

Bauern|junge country lad; ~**partei** peasants' party; ~**stand** peasantry; ~**stolz** upstart pride; ~**tölpel** country bumpkin, hobnail; ~**tum** peasantry; ~**verband** Peasants (National Farmer's, *Br.*) Union.

Bauersfrau country woman, farmwife.

Bauerwartungsland land ripe for development, development land;
~ **erwerben** to obtain land for development;
~**abgabe** development land tax *(Br.)*.

Baufach building trade (line);
~**mann** construction authority, building consultant.

baufähig *(Bergbau)* workable, exploitable;
~**es Land** ploughland, plowland *(US)*, arable land, *(bebauungsfähig)* building estate (site).

baufällig dilapidated, derelict, ramshackle, tumbledown, crazy, ruinous, in bad (out of) repair;
~ **sein** to be in decay; ~ **werden** to get out of repair, to fall into disrepair.

Bau|fälligkeit decay, disrepair, unrepair, dilapidation, ruinous state; ~**fehler** structural defect; ~**feld** pitch; ~**finanzierung** constructional financing; ~**finanzierung aus einer Hand** single-source building financing; ~**finanzierungsgenossenschaft** savings and loan association *(US)*; ~**firma** building constructor, building construction company; ~**flucht** alignment; ~**fluchtlinie** straight (building) line, row; ~**fluchtlinie abstecken** to plot a line; ~**fluchtlinie überschreiten** to project beyond the building line; ~**form** constructive form; ~**fortgangsbescheinigung** architect's certificate; ~**führer** assistant architect, site supervisor *(US)*; ~**führung** site supervision *(US)*; **freies** ~**gebiet** unrestricted (architectural-free) zone; **saniertes** ~**gebiet** upgraded area, development area; ~**gebiet mit Sondergenehmigungen** spot zone *(US)*; ~**gebühren** surveyor's fee; ~**gelände** building site (plot), site [land], construction site (yard), development area; **nicht erschlossenes** ~**gelände** undeveloped *(Br.)* (unimproved, *US*) land; ~**geld** building capital, *(Kredit)* building loan, building advance; ~**gelder** building capital (funds); ~**geldhypothek** development (construction) mortgage; ~**geldkredit** building loan; ~**geldkreditvertrag** building loan agreement; ~**genehmigung** housing permit, building permit (licence); **um** ~**genehmigung nachsuchen** to submit a plan to the city council; ~**genossenschaft** cooperative building society *(Br.)*, terminating building society *(Br.)*, building and loan association *(US)*; ~**gerät** construction equipment; ~**gerippe** skeleton, shell; ~**gerüst** scaffold[ing], stagging; ~**geschäft** building contractors; ~**gesellschaft** building society; ~**gesellschaft zur Erstellung von Häusern mit Kostenmiete** cost-rent society *(Br.)*; ~**gesuch** application for a building permit; ~**gesuch einreichen** to ask for a building permit, to submit a plan to the city council; ~**gewerbe** building line (trade), construction (building) industry; ~**grube** excavation; ~**grund** building lot (site, ground), site land; **abgesteckter** ~**grund** consolidated plot; ~**grundstück** plot of land, building plot (lot, estate, site), piece of ground, groundplot; **durchgehendes** ~**grundstück** through lot; ~**haftpflichtversicherung** builder's risk insurance; ~**handwerk** building trade; ~**handwerker** building operative (tradesman); ~**herr** builder-owner; ~**hilfsarbeiter** bricklayer's helper; ~**hof** timberyard; ~**holz** wood timber *(Br.)*; ~**hütte** building shed; ~**hypothek** building (development, construction) mortgage; ~**index** construction cost index; ~**industrie** building trade, building (construction) industry; **mit der** ~**industrie den Anfang machen** to zero in on the construction industry; ~**ingenieur** architectural (structural) engineer, *(Tiefbau)* civil engineer; ~**inspektor** building inspector, district surveyor; ~**investitionen** expenditure on building, construction spending; ~**investitionen der öffentlichen Hand** public investment in building; ~**jahr** year of construction (manufacture); ~**jahr 1981** 1981 model; ~**kapital** building capital; **ausreichendes** ~**kapital haben** to have ample money for building; ~**kasten** construction set; ~**kastensystem** unit construction system; ~**komplex** complex of buildings, building complex; ~**konjunktur** building boom; **rückläufige** ~**konjunktur** building slump; ~**kontingent** building quota; ~**konto** construction account; ~**kontrakt** building contract; ~**konzession** building permit *(US)*; ~**körper** body of a building.

Baukosten building expenses, builder's price, construction costs (prices), cost of construction (building), expenses of building;
~ **einer Garage berechnen** to give a quotation for building a garage;
~**index** index of building (construction) costs, construction cost index; ~**kalkulation** quantity surveying *(Br.)*; ~**kalkulation durchführen** to survey a building for quantities *(Br.)*; ~**voranschlag** building (contractor's) estimate, bill of quantities *(Br.)*, specifications, schedule, quantity surveying *(Br.)*; ~**voranschlag machen** to predetermine the costs of a building, to survey a building for quantities *(Br.)*; ~**voranschlag für einen Garagenbau vorlegen** to give a quotation for building a garage; ~**zuschuß** subsidy to building cost; **verlorener** ~**zuschuß** *(Mieter)* key money *(Br.)*.

Baukredit building loan;
~**vertrag** building loan contract; ~**vorhaben** housing loan scheme.

Bauland building ground (plot, site, land), developed land, groundplot;
billigeres ~ back land; **zentral gelegenes** ~ central urban land; **für Zwangsenteignung in Frage kommendes** ~ land subject to compulsory acquisition;
~ **erschließen** to develop (improve, *US*) land;
~**abgabe** development charge; ~**beschaffung** release of land, assembling of plots; ~**beschaffungsgesetz** Community Land Act *(Br.)*; **kommunaler** ~**beschaffungsplan** community land scheme *(Br.)*; ~**besteuerung** site value rating; ~**erschließung** development of building lots, development (improvement, *US*) of land, land (site) development; ~**erschließungsabgabe** development land tax *(Br.)*; ~**erschließungsgesellschaft** real-estate developer; ~**erschließungsprojekt** development plan, site land; ~**förderungsgesellschaft** development corporation *(Br.)*; ~**konjunktur** land boom; ~**preise** building land prices; ~**wert** development (site) value.

Bau|leiter builder's manager, builder, surveyor *(Br.)*, *(öffentliche Bauten)* superintendent of public works, clerk of works *(Br.)*; ~**leitplan** development plan *(Br.)*; ~**leitplanung** development planning *(Br.)*, zoning *(US)*; ~**leitung** site supervision *(US)*.

baulich architectural, structural, constructive;
in ~ **gutem Zustand erhalten** to keep in good repair;
~**e Änderungen** structural alterations; ~**e Anordnung** architecture, architectural arrangement; **in** ~**er Hinsicht** from an architectural point of view, architecturally; ~**e Verbesserungen** structural improvements.

Bau|lichkeiten constructions, buildings; ~**linie** straight (building) line; ~**lücke** gap; ~**markt** building (construction) market, market for construction; ~**maschinen** construction machines; ~**maschinenindustrie** construction machines industry; **unterstützende** ~**maßnahmen** underpinning operations; ~**material**

construction (building) material, builder's hardware; ~**materialienhändler** builder's hardware merchant; ~**materialienzug** construction (work) train.

Baumbestand tree population (stock).

Baumeister building constructor, [master] builder;
~ **sein** to build.

Baumethode method of construction.

Baum | grenze timber line *(US)*; ~**hecke** hedgerow.

Baumittel, über ausreichende ~ verfügen to have ample money for building.

Baum | schule nursery garden, horticulture; ~**stamm** trunk; **gefällter** ~**stamm** log.

Baumuster model.

Baumwoll | artikel cotton goods; ~**börse** cotton (wool, *Br.*) exchange; ~**druck** calico (cotton) printing.

Baumwolle cotton;
~ **zu Tuch verarbeiten** to work cotton into cloth.

Baumwoll | ernte cotton harvest; ~**fabrik** cotton factory; ~**flanell** cotton flannel; ~**garn** cotton yarn; ~**gebiet** cotton belt; ~**industrie** cotton industry; ~**kämmerei** cotton combing; ~**markt** cotton market; ~**pflanzung** cotton plantation; ~**pflücker** cotton picker; ~**samen** cotton seed; ~**samenöl** cottonseed oil; ~**samt** cotton velvet; ~**spinnerei** cotton mill; **bedruckter** ~**stoff** printed cotton; ~**textilien** Manchester goods; ~**waren** cottons, cotton goods; ~**wechsel** cotton bill.

Bau | nummer serial number; ~**objekt** building project; ~**obligationen** constructions bonds; ~**ordnung** building law (code), zoning act *(US)*; **örtliche** ~**ordnung** building byelaw; ~**ordnungsamt** surveyor's office; ~**orgie** building spree; ~**parzelle** building plot (lot, *US*), building site, site land; ~**periode** building time, period of erection; ~**plan** plan of a building, ground (architect's) plan, working drawing, groundplot, *(Projekt)* building project; **genehmigter** ~**plan** certificate of occupancy; ~**platz** building ground (site, yard, lot, *US*), site, ground, groundplot, lot *(US)*, plot [of land, ground]; ~**platzsteuer** undeveloped land duty *(Br.)*; ~**polizei** building and repair police.

baupolizeiliche | Genehmigung building permit (licence); ~ **Übertretung** building-code violation; ~ **Vorschriften** local building regulations.

Bau | polizeiordnung building (housing) code; ~**preise** building (construction) prices, building costs; ~**programm** building (housing) program(me), construction schedule; **sorgfältig kalkuliertes** ~**programm** correctly costed construction program(me); ~**projekt** scheme of development, building development scheme, construction project; ~**rechnung** construction account; ~**recht** building laws.

baureif ripe for development, developed, improved *(US)*;
noch nicht ~ undeveloped *(Br.)*, unimproved *(US)*;
~**es Gelände** building estate (lot, site).

Bau | reihe series; ~**richtlinien** building standards; ~**risikopolice** builder's risk policy; ~**risikoversicherung** builder's risk insurance; ~**riß** working drawing, architect's plan, blueprint; ~**sache** *(Gericht)* building case; ~**sachverständiger** building (quantity, *Br.*) surveyor, building consultant; ~**saison** building season.

Bausch und Bogen, in in bulk (blocks), in the gross (lump), by the gross, wholesale;
in ~ kaufen to buy by [the] bulk (one lot, by the gross, lump), to purchase wholesale; **Bücher in ~ kaufen** to buy a job lot of books; **in ~ verkaufen** to sell by bulk, to sell outright, to make a clean sweep.

Bauschäden structural damage;
~**versicherung** builder's risk insurance.

Bausch | betrag lump sum; ~**gebühr** lump fee; ~**preis** lump-sum purchase, bulk price.

Bau | schlosser locksmith; ~**schreiner** joiner; ~**schuppen** building shed; ~**schutt** refuse material of a building, rubble, debris; ~**sektor** building sector; **öffentlicher** ~**sektor** public building sector; ~**sohle** *(Bergwerk)* working level.

Bauschverkauf sale by bulk, bulk sale.

Bauspar | darlehen building agreement loan *(US)*; ~**darlehnssätze** borrowing rates of building societies *(Br.)*, building society rates *(Br.)*; ~**einlagen** building society deposits.

Bausparen, prämienbegünstigtes cash savings plan with bonus.

Bausparer investor, building society depositor *(Br.)*, investing member *(Br.)*;
zugeteilter ~ advanced (borrowing) member *(Br.)*; **noch nicht zugeteilter** ~ unadvanced (investing) member *(Br.)*;
~ **ohne Inanspruchnahme einer Bausparhypothek** free shareholder.

Bauspar | gelder building society deposits; ~**guthaben** deposits with building societies, investors' balance; ~**hypothek** building society mortgage *(Br.)*, member's mortage *(Br.)*; ~**hypothek aufnehmen** to effect a mortgage with a building society; ~**kasse** building society *(Br.)*, building and loan association *(US)*, house owners' loan corporation *(US)*, home building and loan (homestead-aid benefit) association *(US)*, permanent building society *(Australia)*; ~**kassengesetz** building societies act *(Br.)*; ~**kassenmittel** building society deposits; ~**kassenzinssätze** building society rates; ~**konto** investment account *(Br.)*; ~**mittel** building society funds *(Br.)*; ~**summe** building society money, investment; ~**vertrag** building loan agreement; ~**vertrag abschließen** to open an ordinary share account; ~**vertrag voll ansparen** to save the full deposit; ~**vertragsnummer** roll number; **fällige** ~**zinsen** building society interest payable; **vereinbarte** ~**zinsen** interest from building society, building society (investor's) interest *(Br.)*; **vereinnahmte** ~**zinsen** interest from building societies; ~**zinsen und Tilgung** interest paid to a building society.

Bau | spekulant jerrybuilder; ~**sperre verfügen** to put a freeze on building; ~**sperrgebiet** restricted district; **sich im** ~**stadium befinden** to be under construction; ~**stahl** constructional (structural) steel; ~**stahlgewebe** mesh; ~**stein** building stone (block), brick; ~**stelle** [building] ground (site), excavation site, works; **Vorsicht** ~**stelle!** *(Straßenarbeiten)* danger, road up!; ~**stellenleiter** site foreman; ~**stil** constructive form; **klassischer** ~**stil** classical architecture; ~**stoffabgabe** building material tax; ~**stoffe** building material; ~**stoffhändler** material man; ~**stoffindustrie** building material producers; ~**stofflager** building yard; ~**stopp verfügen** to put a freeze on building; ~**streitigkeit** building case; ~**summe** overall costs of a building; **gewerbliche** ~**tätigkeit** building (construction) activities; **öffentliche** ~**tätigkeit** public construction; **private** ~**tätigkeit** private building; ~**technik** constructural (construction, structural) engineering; ~**techniker** civil (architectural) engineer.

bautechnisch architectural, constructional;
~**e Probleme** building technicalities.

Bauteil structural member;
abgrenzendes ~ party structure; **tragende** ~**e** supporting members.

Bautempo rate of building.

Bauten constructions, works, buildings;
öffentliche ~ public (capital) works;
~ **auf fremden Grundstücken** *(Bilanz)* buildings on real estate not owned by the company.

Bau | terrain building lot *(US)* (site); ~**tischler** joiner; ~**tischlerei** joinery; ~**träger** builder, builder-owner; ~**trägervorhaben** builder's project; ~**trupp** gang; ~**überhang** unfinished building projects; ~**unternehmen** building (construction) company (contractors), building enterprise, [firm of] building contractors; ~**unternehmer** [master] builder, house builder, building contractor, developer *(Br.)*; **unseriöser** ~**unternehmer** speculative builder, jerrybuilder; ~**unternehmerkaution** construction bond; ~**unternehmerversicherung** builder's risk insurance; ~**unternehmervertrag** building contract; ~**verbot** building prohibition; ~**verbot erlassen** to put a freeze on building; **modernes** ~**verfahren** modern construction technique; ~**vergabe** construction contract award; ~**verordnung** building (construction) code, building law; ~**versicherung** builder's risk insurance; ~**vertrag** contract to build, building contract; **schlüsselfertiger** ~**vertrag** turnkey contract *(US)*; ~**volumen** construction volume; ~**vorbereitungszeit** preconstruction time; ~**vorhaben** building operations (purpose, project), development *(Br.)*; **in Ausführung befindliche** ~**vorhaben** building contracts in progress; **öffentliches** ~**vorhaben** public construction project.

Bauvorschriften *(Flächenplan)* building byelaws (regulations) *(Br.)*, zoning ordinances *(US)*;
örtliche ~ local building regulations; **städtische** ~ building codes.

Bau | weise method of construction; **geschlossene** ~**weise** terracing; **konventionelle** ~**weise** conventional construction; **offene** ~**weise** detached building; ~**werk** building or structure, edifice, construction, architecture; **historisches (unter Denkmalsschutz stehendes)** ~**werk** ancient building; **aufgrund der Belegenheit störendes** ~**werk** nuisance in fact; ~**werk als Ganzes** entire structure; ~**werkstatt** workshop; ~**werkzeuge** tools; ~**werte** *(Börse)* building issues (shares, stocks); ~**wesen** building industry, constructional (structural, civil) engineering; **öffentliches** ~**wesen** public building; ~**wirtschaft** building trade (business), construction industry; ~**wirtschaft gerade noch aufrecht erhalten** to keep the construction sector afloat; ~**zaun** hoarding; ~**zeichner** draftsman, draughtsman; ~**zeichnung** working drawing; ~**zeit** construction time, period of erection (construction); **mitten in der** ~**zeit** in mid-construction; **in einer** ~**zeit von fünf Monaten entstanden sein** to be built in five months; ~**zuschuß** aid for building; ~**zustand** structural condition; **für** ~**zwecke** for building purposes; ~**zwischenkredit** building advance.

Bazille bacillus, bug *(US coll.)*.

Bazillenkrieg biological warfare.

beabsichtigen to intend, to have in view, to plan, to mean; **nichts Böses** ~ to intend no harm.

beabsichtigt intentional, calculated;
~ **sein** to be done on purpose;
~**e Beleidigung** studied insult; ~**e Wirkung** desired effect; ~**er Zweck** object in view.

beachten to attend, to pay attention (regard), to regard, to heed; **Einwand nicht** ~ to ignore an objection; **Folgen wenig** ~ to take little notice of the consequences; **nicht** ~ to take no notice, to take no account of; **jds. Ratschläge** ~ to attend to s. o. one's recommendations, to follow s. one's advice; **sorgfältig** ~ to pay particular attention (heed to s. th.); **Vorschriften** ~ to observe regulations; **Warnung** ~ to heed a warning; **wenig** ~ to pay little heed.

beachtenswert remarkable, noteworthy, on the map;
kaum ~ trifling.

beachtlich considerable, remarkable;
ganz ~ pretty good;
~**es Geburtstagsgeschenk** handsome birthday present.

Beachtung regard, notice, attention, heed;
unter ~ **von** in consideration of; **unter gebührender** ~ with due observance; **zur** ~ please note; **zur besonderen** ~ for special consideration;
~ **pro Anzeigenseite** adpage audience *(US)*; ~ **des Gesetzes** compliance with the law;
keine besondere ~ **erfahren** to receive no particular notice; **sich größter** ~ **erfreuen** *(Zeitung)* to respond to more support; **oberflächliche** ~ **finden** to receive perfunctory attention; **wenig** ~ **finden** to be hardly noticed; **der öffentlichen Meinung keine** ~ **schenken** to be heedless of public opinion; **einer Sache große** ~ **schenken** to devote great care to s. th.; **einer Sache keine** ~ **schenken** to pay no attention to, to let s. th. go by; ~ **verdienen** to be worth considering.

beackern to plough, to till;
Brachfeld ~ to fallow.

Beamter official, officer, officeholder, executive *(US)*, *(höherer)* executive, functionary, magistrate *(US)*, *(Staatsbeamter)* civil servant *(Br.)*, government official *(US)*, government employee, public servant *(US)*;
amtierender ~ acting officer; **provisorisch angestellter** ~ probationer; **aufgeblasener** ~ pompous official; **mit Unterschriftsbefugnis ausgestatteter** ~ officer authorized to sign; **außerplanmäßiger** ~ supernumerary, unestablished civil servant *(Br.)*; **Amtmißbrauch ausübender** ~ oppressor *(US)*; **beauftragter** ~ officer in charge; **in Ausbildung befindlicher** ~ administration trainee *(Br.)*; **über die Amtszeit hinaus bleibender** ~ holdover; **diensttuender** ~ official in charge; **neu eintretender** ~ incoming officer; **im Dienst ergrauter** ~ veteran officer; **festangestellter** ~ permanent (salaried) officer, established civil servant *(Br.)*; **hochbezahlter** ~ highly-paid executive *(US)*; **hochgestellter** ~ highly placed official; **hochqualifizierter** ~ high-grade executive *(US)*; **höherer** ~ high-grade official (officer) *(Br.)*, senior official (officer, *Br.*), senior (higher) executive officer *(Br.)*, high-ranking official, major executive, functionary *(US)*, top-grade civil servant *(Br.)*, mandarin *(coll.)*; **kleiner** ~ petty official; **korrupter** ~ grafter; **leitender** ~ chief officer, commissioner, top-ranking officer; **Ausbildung leitender** ~ training executive *(US)*; **mittlerer** ~ subordinate (minor) officer; **pensionierter** ~ old civil servant, pensionary [on the government]; **pflichtvergessener** ~ delinquent magistrate *(US)*; **planmäßiger** ~ career *(US)* (established, *Br.*) civil servant; **richterlicher** ~ magistrate; **staatlicher** ~ government official, civil servant *(Br.)*, officeholder; **städtischer** ~ municipal (local government, *Br.*) officer, city (official) clerk *(US)*, town officer; **subalterner** ~ junior (inferior) officer; **unabsetzbarer** ~ perpetual officer; **untätiger** ~ inactive official; **untergeordneter** ~ minor (lower-grade, -level, *Br.*) official, clerical officer *(Br.)*, inferior officer; **vorgesetzter** ~ superior officer; **zuständiger** ~ official in charge; **zweithöchster** ~ second-ranking officer;
~ **des Auswärtigen Dienstes** foreign-service officer *(US)*; ~ **des gehobenen Dienstes** higher-echelon official; ~ **des mittleren Dienstes** minor (lower-grade, lower-level, *Br.*) official, clerical officer *(Br.)*; ~ **im öffentlichen Dienst** public (civil) servant, public officer; ~ **auf Dienstreise** itinera[n]cy; ~ **am Eingangsschalter** receiving teller; ~ **bei der Eisenbahn** railway official; ~ **für Erteilung von Konzessionen** licensing magistrate; ~ **am Fahrkartenschalter** ticket (booking) agent; ~ **des Geheimdienstes** intelligence officer; ~ **des Gesundheitsdienstes** health officer; ~ **der Handelsmarine** navy (naval) officer; ~ **des Innenministeriums** interior ministry official; ~ **des Kartellamtes** antitrust official *(US)*; ~ **auf Lebenszeit** established civil servant, career civil servant *(US)*; ~ **der Personalabteilung** *(AA)* assignments officer; ~ **des Rechnungshofes** government auditor; ~ **mit Residenzpflicht** official of whom residence is required; ~ **im Ruhestand** retired civil servant; ~ **in einer Schlüsselposition** key official; ~ **im höheren Staatsdienst** civil servant *(Br.)*, officeholder *(US)*; ~ **in leitender Stellung** top-grade civil servant *(Br.)*, executive officer *(US)*, policy-making official *(US)*; ~ **einer Treuhandgesellschaft** trust officer; ~ **des Umweltschutzes** environmental officer; ~ **des Versicherungsamtes** state regulator *(US)*; ~ **in der öffentlichen Verwaltung** executive officer *(Br.)*; ~ **des Zollfahndungsdienstes** preventive officer *(Br.)*;
~ **des Auswärtigen Amtes sein** to be in the diplomatic service; **als** ~ **angestellt sein** to be in the civil service; ~ **werden** to become a civil servant *(Br.)*; **als** ~ **eingestellt werden** to get a position in the government (civil service, *Br.*).

Beamten|ablösen to supersede an official; ~ **absetzen** to remove an official; ~ **vorübergehend abstellen** to second an official; ~ **seiner Stellung entheben** to divest an official of power and authority; ~ **entlassen** to shelve (dismiss) an officer; ~ **rehabilitieren** to whitewash an official; ~ **versetzen** to move an official; ~ **einstweilig versetzen** to second an official;
~**abbau** civil service cut; **radikalen** ~**abbau durchführen** to axe a number of officials; ~**anwärter** applicants for civil service jobs; ~**apparat** civil service (servants); ~**besoldung** civil service pay *(Br.)*; ~**bestechung** bribery (favo(u)r) of officials; ~**bürokratie** civil service bureaucracy; ~**deutsch** officialese; ~**dünkel** bumbledom; ~**eid** oath of allegiance, oath of office *(US)*; ~**eid ablegen** to be sworn in; ~**eigenschaft** civil service status; ~**eigenschaften** qualifications of an official; ~**einstellung kurz vor dem Regierungswechsel** midnight appointment; ~**entlassung** removal of an official; ~**gehalt** government salary; ~**gehälteranhebung** government pay increase; ~**gesetz** Civil Service Law *(Br.)*, National Civil Service Act *(US)*; ~**haftung** liability of an official; ~**herrschaft** bureaucracy; ~**hierarchie** hierarchy; ~**jargon** bureaucratic jargon; ~**kategorie** division *(Br.)*; ~**körper** service staff corps; ~**laufbahn** official career; **mittlere** ~**laufbahn** second division *(Br.)*; ~**laufbahn einschlagen** to enter the civil service; ~**pension** civil-service pension; ~**pension beziehen** to be pensioned on the government; ~**pensionsfonds** employees' pension fund; ~**position** civil-service job; **guten** ~**posten bekommen** to get a good position in the civil service; ~**rangstufen** civil service grades; ~**reform** civil service reform *(Br.)*; ~**schaft** civil establishment; **höhere** ~**schaft** higher-grade officials; ~**stand** officialdom, the civil servants *(Br.)*; ~**status**, ~**stellung** government situation, official position; **gute** ~**stellung** good post in the civil service; ~**tum** civil servants, officialism, officialdom; ~**verhältnis** civil service relationship; **im** ~**verhältnis stehen** to be in the civil service *(Br.)* (public service, *US*); ~**versicherung** civil service insurance; ~**wechsel** rotation of officers; ~**wirtschaft** officialdom, red tapism; ~**witwe** service widow.

beamtet appointed;
~ **(in** ~**er Stellung) sein** to hold an office (a permanent post).

beanspruchbar claimable.

beanspruchen to lodge a claim, to demand, to reclaim, to vindicate, to arrogate, *(Maschine)* to stress, to strain;
jds. Dienste ~ to avail o. s. of s. one's services; **Eigentum** ~ to claim a title; **jds. Geduld übermäßig** ~ to tax s. one's patience; **jds. Geldbörse** ~ to be a strain on s. one's resources; **öffentliche Mittel** ~ to have recourse to public money; **Nachlaß** ~ to lay claim to an estate; **Reifen sehr** ~ to put great strain on tyres; **Schadenersatz** ~ to put in a claim for damages; **j. finanziell sehr** ~ to be a great strain on s. one's resources; **Steuervergünstigungen** ~ to claim tax relief; **vier Stunden** ~ to take four hours; **ganzen Tag** ~ to take a whole day; **unrechtmäßig** ~ to usurp; **Vorrang** ~ to claim priority; **Vorrecht** ~ to claim a privilege; **Wirtschaft stark** ~ to place great strains on the economy; **jds. Zeit über Gebühr** ~ to encroach (trespass) upon s. one's time.

beansprucht claimed;
sehr ~ sein to have many demands on one's time; **~ werden** *(Material)* to be stressed.

Beanspruchung claim, demand, vindication, *(Maschine)* stress, strain;
höchste ~ heavy-duty service, highest stress; **statische ~** static stress; **steuerliche ~** tax demands; **zulässige ~** safe load, *(Material)* allowable stress;
starke ~ von jem. a strain on s. one's resources; **~ des Aktienmarktes** resort to the share (stock) market; **~ der Bremsen** brakeload; **~ des Geldbeutels** strain on the purse; **starke ~ des Geldmarktes** strong demand on the money market; **~ öffentlicher Mittel** recourse to public money; **bedenkliche ~ des Staatsvermögens** serious draft on national resources; **~ von jds. Zeit** demand upon s. one's time;
den ~en des modernen Lebens kaum gewachsen sein to suffer from the great strains of modern life; **starker ~ standhalten** to withstand handwear.

Beanspruchungsgrenze limit of stress.

beanstanden to take exception to, to find fault with, to query, to protest, to object, to complain;
nichts zu ~ bei jem. no flies on s. o.; **Rechnung ~** to question an invoice; **Rechnungsposten ~** to query the items of an account; **Revisionsbericht ~** to take exception to the auditor's report; **Warenlieferung ~** to reject goods delivered.

beanstandete | Postsendung rejected mail; **~ Waren** rejects.

Beanstandung objection, complaint, query, protest, claim, finding fault;
bei ~en in case of complaint;
berechtigte ~ legitimate complaint;
~ der Fragestellung *(bei Zeugen)* demurrer to interrogatories; **~ von Waren** rejection of goods delivered;
ohne ~ annehmen to accept without dissent; **~en bei einer geleisteten Arbeit beseitigen** to put one's own job right; **~en erheben** to raise objections; **zu ~en Anlaß geben** to give cause for complaint; **zu ~en keinen Anlaß geben** to offer no reason for objections; **~en bei jem. geltend machen** to bring a complaint to s. one's notice; **~en vorbringen** to lodge complaints; **~en gegen Sonntagsarbeit vorbringen** to demur at working on Sundays; **~en zurückweisen** to overrule objections.

beantragen to apply for, to make an application, to request, to demand, to petition, *(in Sitzung)* to bring forward, to put (present) a motion, to move (motion) for, to propose;
Abänderung ~ to move an amendment; **Bezugsschein ~** to apply for a purchasing permit; **Einleitung eines Konkursverfahrens ~** to file a petition in bankruptcy; **Erstattung ~** to claim repayment; **als Erster ~** to initiate; **kurze Fristverlängerung ~** to request a brief delay; **Gebührenerlaß ~** to apply for a remission of fees; **Geldmittel bei der Regierung ~** to put in a claim for a grant; **Gerichtsbeschluß ~** to sue out a writ; **Klageabweisung ~** to direct a nonsuit; **Kredit ~** to request a loan; **Kreditlinie ~** to apply for a credit line *(US)* (limit, *Br.*); **Schadenersatz ~** to make a claim for (demand) damages; **Schließung der Debatte ~** to move closure; **schriftlich ~** to apply by letter; **Stipendium ~** to apply for a scholarship; **Unterstützung ~** to claim benefits; **einstweilige Verfügung ~** to ask for (claim) an injunction; **Vertagung für eine Woche ~** to move that the case be adjourned for a week.

Beantragung application, request, petition, *(Parlament)* motion;
~ einer gerichtlichen Entscheidung motion of decree; **~ eines Haftprüfungstermins** petition for a writ of habeas corpus; **~ des Konkursverfahrens** filing of a bankruptcy petition, striking a docket *(Br.)*; **~ eines Stipendiums** application for a scholarship; **~ einer einstweiligen Verfügung** seeking an injunction; **~ eines Verhandlungstermins** entry of a cause for trial; **~ eines Versäumnisurteils** statement of particulars.

beantworten to answer, to respond, to reply;
Klage ~ to file an answer; **schriftlich ~** to give a written reply, to write an answer, to answer in writing.

beantwortet werden müssen, sofort to demand an immediate answer.

Beantwortung answer, reply, response;
in ~ Ihres Briefes in reply (replying) to your letter; **in ~ Ihres geehrten Schreibens** in answer of your favo(u)r;
wenig beachtete ~ einer parlamentarischen Anfrage little-notice parliamentary reply; **~ der Klageschrift** statement of defense (defence, *Br.*);
j. von der ~ eines Briefes abhalten to hinder s. o. answering a letter; **bei ~ eines Briefes eine Nummer angeben** to quote a number in reply to a letter; **höflichst um ~ bitten** to request the favo(u)r of an answer.

Beantwortungsfrist *(Klageerhebung)* notice to plead.

bearbeitbar workable, machinable.

Bearbeitbarkeit workability, machinability.

bearbeiten to handle, to work, *(Akten)* to treat, to deal with, *(Boden)* to cultivate, *(Kunden)* to canvass, *(maschinell)* to tool, to machine, *(Rohstoff)* to process, *(Stück für Theater)* to adapt, *(mit Werkzeugen)* to tool;
j. ~ to work on s. one's mind; **Abgeordnete ~** to lobby members of parliament; **Anfrage ~** to handle an inquiry; **Angelegenheit ~** to handle a case, to have a matter in hand, to deal with a matter; **Antrag ~** to take charge of an application; **Auftrag ~** to deal with an order; **Bezirk ~** *(Vertreter)* to work a district, to cover a territory; **Buch neu ~** to revise a book; **Dinge beschleunigt ~** to expedite matters; **Fall ~** to handle (process) a case; **fehlerhaft ~** to mishandle; **fertig ~** to finish; **grob ~** to rough-machine; **Kredit ~** to process a loan; **Kunden ~** to canvass (high-pressure) customers; **Manuskript ~** to prepare a manuscript; **nochmals ~** to do over again, to remake; **für den Rundfunk ~** to adapt to broadcasting; **Sachgebiet ~** to deal with a subject; **Wahlbezirk ~** to canvass (work, *fam.*) a constituency; **Wähler ~** to electioneer, to campaign *(US)*, to canvass for votes; **Wörterbuch ~** to compile a dictionary;
sich nach dem Regen leicht ~ lassen *(Boden)* to work easily after the rain.

Bearbeiter official in charge, referee, *(Theaterstücke)* adapter, *(Wörterbuch)* compiler;
~ von Kundenwerbungen account executive.

bearbeitet worked, machined, processed, *(Stück)* adapted;
nicht ~ unworked;
~ werden to be in hand.

Bearbeitung work, handling, preparation, *(Akten)* treatment, handling, *(Boden)* cultivation, tillage, *(Film)* production, *(Buch)* adaptation, *(Kunden)* canvassing, *(mechanisch)* tooling, *(Rohstoffe)* processing, manufacture, *(Theaterstück)* adaptation, adaption;
in ~ in hand, on the docket *(fam.)*;
chemische ~ chemical treatment; **fertige ~** finishing; **freie ~** free adaptation; **maschinelle ~** machining, mechanical treatment; **zweite ~** revision;
~ einer Angelegenheit handling of an affair; **~ eines Auftrages** processing an order, order handling (processing); **~ eines Bezirks** working a district; **~ von Kundenbestellungen** handling of customers' orders; **~ eines Manuskripts** preparation of a manuscript; **~ an Ort und Stelle** in-place treatment; **~ von Steuerunterlagen** tax work; **englische ~ des Urtextes** English adaption of the original; **~ von Versicherungsansprüchen** handling of claims; **~ eines Wahlbezirkes** canvassing (working) of a constituency; **~ eines Wörterbuches** compilation of a dictionary;
mit der ~ eines Falles beauftragt sein to be put in charge of a case; **jem. etw. zur ~ übergeben** to place s. th. into the hands of s. o.

Bearbeitungsbeschränkungen processing restrictions.

bearbeitungsfähig workable.

Bearbeitungs | gebühr handling (processing) fee (charge), *(Bank)* service charge; **~genehmigung** processing permit; **~kosten** handling costs, *(Maschine)* tooling costs, *(Versicherung)* claim expenses; **~methode, ~möglichkeit** manufacturing method, machining method; **~plan** *(Kostenberechnung)* operation plan; **~stelle** workshop; **~verbot** processing prohibition; **~verfahren** treatment, manufacturing method, *(Maschine)* tooling method; **~vorgang** machining (mechanical) operation; **~zeit** staff (handling) time, *(Maschine)* machining time; **~zugabe** machining allowance; **~zuschlag** industrial accession, machining allowance.

Beatmung, künstliche artificial respiration.

beaufsichtigen to supervise, to superintend, to control, to direct, to manage;
Arbeit ~ to oversee work; **Arbeiten persönlich ~** to superintend work personally; **Examensarbeiten ~** to invigilate *(US)* (proctor, *US*) at an examination; **Gefangenen schärfer ~** to keep a better watch over a prisoner; **Kinder ~** to look after (take charge of) children.

Beaufsichtigung superintendence, supervision, control management, inspection, tab, *(von Prüfungen)* invigilation, proctoring *(US)*;
staatliche ~ government (state) control;
~ von Gefangenen surveillance of prisoners; **~ einer Schulklasse** supervision of a class; **~ der für Minderjährige bestehenden Vormundschaften** supervision of guardianship of infants.

beauftragen to charge, *(anweisen)* to instruct, to direct, *(Auftrag geben)* to order, *(bestellen)* to appoint, to institute, to constitute, *(bevollmächtigen)* to authorize, to commission, *(ermächtigen)* to commission, to empower;
j. mit etw. ~ to entrust s. o. with s. th., to charge s. o. with a commission; **Anwalt** ~ to retain (brief) a barrister, to instruct an attorney *(US)* (solicitor, *Br.*); **Angestellten mit Führungsaufgaben** ~ to entrust an employee with executive functions; **seine Bank mit der Bezahlung seiner Steuern** ~ to commission one's bank to pay one's taxes; **j. mit dem Einkauf von etw.** ~ to commission s. o. to buy s. th.; **j. mit einem Fall** ~ to put a case into s. one's hands; **Grundstücksmakler** ~ to place in the hands of (list with, *US*) a broker; **j. mit der Kabinettsbildung** ~ to charge s. o. to form a government; **Kommission** ~ to appoint a commission; **Korrespondenten mit etw.** ~ to entrust a matter to one's correspondent; **jem. mit dem Verkauf** ~ to entrust s. o. with the sale; **mit dem Verkauf seiner Effekten** ~ to authorize with the sale of one's effects; **j. mit seiner Vertretung** ~ to make s. o. one's deputy; **j. mit Vorlesungen** ~ to invite s. o. to deliver lectures.

beauftragt commissioned, appointed, in charge, authorized, delegate;
~ **durch** by order;
~ **sein** to be in charge; **mit Vorlesungen** ~ **sein** to be invited to hold lectures;
~**er Richter** commissioned judge.

Beauftragter mandatary, commissioner, authorized person, assign, *(Bevollmächtigter)* attorney in fact, mandatary, representative, trustee, designee *(US)*, agent, *(Vertreter)* deputy, proxy;
persönlich ~ personal representative, private attorney; **mit einer Untersuchung** ~ investigator;
~ **für Frauenfragen** commissioner for women's affairs; ~ **der öffentlichen Hand** public agent; ~ **auf Kabinettsebene** Cabinet-level appointee; ~ **für den Umweltschutz** environmental officer;
als ~ **handeln** to act as agent.

Beauftragung instruction, direction, commission, authorization, mandate;
~ **eines Anwaltes** retaining (briefing, instructing) a solicitor (lawyer).

beaugenscheinigen to inspect, to view, to examine closely.

bebauen to build on, to develop *(US)*, *(anbauen)* to cultivate, to till, to farm;
zu dicht ~ to overbuild; **Gelände** ~ to build up an area; **landwirtschaftlich** ~ to cultivate, to till, to farm.

bebaut cultivated, tilled, tame *(US coll.)*;
~**e Fläche,** ~**es Gelände** built-up area; ~**es Grundstück** developed land (real estate, *US*); ~**e und unbebaute Grundstücke** *(Bilanz)* real estate.

Bebauung building, construction, development, *(Landwirtschaft)* cultivation, tillage, culture, farming, cropping, *(Städteplanung)* town planning;
mehrfache ~ multiple cropping; **regellose** ~ haphazard development.

Bebauungs|beschränkungen zoning *(US)* (planning, *Br.*) restrictions; ~**bestimmungen** zoning classification *(US)*; ~**bezirk** zoning district *(US)*; ~**dichte** density of development.

bebauungsfähig *(Grundstück)* developable, *(Land)* cultivable, fertilizable, tillable, arable.

Bebauungs|grenze margin of cultivation; ~**plan** plan for zoning *(US)*, zoning ordinance *(US)*, street (development, *Br.*) plan, *(Einzelvorhaben)* building project (scheme); ~**plan aufstellen** to zone *(US)*, to plan a city; **gesamtes** ~**projekt** general building scheme; ~**status** zoning status *(US)*; ~**vorschriften** zoning legislation *(US)*, zoning *(US)*, building byelaw (ordinances); **wieder dem normalen** ~**zweck zugeführt werden** to be zoned back into its proper economic classification *(US)*.

beben *(Erde)* to quake.

bebildern to illustrate.

bebildert, reich richly illustrated.

Becher cup, mug;
~ **bis zur bitteren Neige leeren** to drain the cup to the lees;
~**werk** bucket conveyor.

bedacht careful, throughtful, *(im Testament)* put down;
auf etw. ~ **sein** to be tender of s. th.; **von der Natur mit hervorragenden Anlagen** ~ **sein** to be endowed by nature with great talents; **auf seinen Ruf** ~ **sein** to be mindful of one's good name; **auf seinen Vorteil** ~ **sein** to always have an eye to one's interests;
~ **sein, zu gefallen** to be anxious to please.

Bedachter beneficiary, recipient, *(Legatsnehmer)* legatee;
alternativ ~ alternative legatee; **gemeinschaftlich** ~ joint beneficiaries; **testamentarisch** ~ beneficiary under a will.

bedanken, sich überströmend to be effusive (profuse) in one's thanks.

Bedarf need, want, supply, demand, occasion, *(Erfordernis)* requirement, *(Verbrauch)* consumption;
bei ~ if required, on request; **für sofortigen** ~ for immediate requirements; **nach** ~ when required, as occasion may require; **zur Deckung unseres** ~**s** to cover our requirements;
aktueller ~ current requirements; **aufgeschobener** ~ deferred demand; **aufgestauter** ~ pent-up *(US)* (replacement) demand; **außerordentlicher** ~ nonrecurrent requirements; **dringender** ~ urgent need; **eigener** ~ personal requirements; **einheimischer** ~ home demand, home requirements; **elastischer** ~ elastic demand, discretionary wants; **mittelbar entstandener** ~ derived demand; **gegenwärtiger** ~ present needs; **geringer** ~ not much required; **gesteigerter** ~ increased demand; **heimischer** ~ home requirements; **inländischer** ~ domestic (home) demand; **lebensnotwendiger** ~ bare necessaries of life; **lebenswichtiger** ~ essential supply, requirements of primary importance; **lokaler** ~ local requirements; **menschlicher** ~ human necessities; **möglicher** ~ potential demand; **nachträglicher** ~ additional requirement; **notwendiger** ~ necessary requirements; **öffentlicher** ~ public requirements (expenditure); **ordentlicher** ~ recurrent requirements; **örtlicher** ~ local consumption (wants); **persönlicher** ~ personal use (requirements, wants); **potentieller** ~ potential demand; **pro-Kopf** ~ per capita demand; **spezifischer** ~ selective demand; **staatlicher** ~ government consumption; **ständiger** ~ constant demand; **täglicher** ~ everyday consumption; **tatsächlicher** ~ actual demand; **unelastischer** ~ inelastic demand; **gesamter volkswirtschaftlicher** ~ schedule demand; **voraussichtlicher** ~ anticipated need (requirement); **vordringlicher** ~ primary demand; **ständig wachsender** ~ constantly increasing demand; **zukünftiger** ~ future needs; **zurückgestellter** ~ deferred demand; **zusätzlicher** ~ additional demand;
~ **an Arbeitskräften** labo(u)r requirements; **täglicher** ~ **an Lebensmitteln** daily supply of food; ~ **an Menschen und Material** need for men and material; ~ **am Platze** local requirements; **großer** ~ **an Stenotypistinnen** great demand for typists; ~ **der Verbraucher** consumer needs; ~ **an Wohnhäusern** deficiency of houses;
Produktion auf den ~ **abstellen** to gear (tailor) production to demand; ~ **schriftlich angeben** to record the requirements; **dem täglichen** ~ **anpassen** to bring in line with actual needs; **nur für den eigenen** ~ **arbeiten** to produce only for its own requirements; ~ **befriedigen** to meet the demand; **seinen** ~ **bei ... beziehen** to draw one's supplies from ...; ~ **decken** to cover (comply with) the requirements, to supply (satisfy) the needs, to satisfy (meet) the demand; **jds.** ~ **decken** to meet s. one's requirements; **steigenden** ~ **decken** to meet the increasing demand; ~ **des Handels decken** to meet the needs of trade; **seinen** ~ **an Kleidungsstücken decken** to make provisions for one's clothing; **seinen** ~ **für die kommende Saison decken** to order one's supplies for the season; **über** ~ **einkaufen** to overstock, to buy in excess of demand; **seinen** ~ **an Lebensmitteln wöchentlich einkaufen** to buy one's supply of food weekly; ~ **haben** to need, to require, to be in the market for; **nach** ~ **halten** *(Zug)* to stop when required; ~ **hervorrufen (schaffen)** to create a demand; **gesamten** ~ **liefern** to furnish the total supply; ~ **übersteigen** to outstrip (outpace) the demand; **bei** ~ **ausgegeben werden** to be issued upon request; **hinter den** ~ **zurückfallen** to fall short of the requirements.

Bedarfs|abnahme reduced demand; ~**analyse** demand analysis; ~**anflugshafen** flag station (stop, *US*).

Bedarfsartikel necessaries, requisites, consumer goods, articles of consumption;
gehobene ~ high-quality products; **kaufmännische** ~ trade supplies; **lebensnotwendige** ~ vital necessities; **notwendige** ~ necessaries, essentials; **tägliche** ~ daily needs;
~ **für Buchdruckereien** printing necessaries; **persönliche** ~ **für die Schiffsmannschaft** small stores;
~**geschäft** convenience store.

Bedarfs|ausgleich equalization of supplies; ~**ballung** accumulated demand; ~**berechnung** calculation of requirements; ~**deckung** commodity coverage; **unmittelbare** ~**deckung** hand-to-mouth buying; ~**deckungsgüter** convenience goods *(US)*; ~**deckungsmöglichkeit** supply capacity; ~**deckungsvertrag** requirement contract; ~**deckungswirtschaft** subsistence economy, consumer economics; ~**elastizität** elasticity of demand;

~**entwicklung** demand trend; ~**erhöhung** improved (increased) demand; **im** ~**fall** in case of need, when required; ~**fehlentwicklung** misdirected demand; ~**frage einer Lizenz prüfen** to examine the need for granting a licence; ~**gegenstand** requisite, commodity, implement; ~**gegenstände** necessaries, requisites; ~**gruppe** consumer group; ~**güter** consumer (consumption) goods; **gehobene** ~**güter** luxuries and semi-luxuries; ~**güterindustrie** consumption (consumer) goods industry; ~**haltestelle** flag station (stop, *US*), halt *(Br.)*, request (whistle, *US*) stop; **reiner** ~**kauf** hand-to-mouth buying; ~**lage** state of demand; ~**land** consumer country; ~**lenkung** consumption control, consumer guidance; ~**liste** list of requirements, demand schedule; ~**lücke** gap in supplies; ~**massierung** accumulated demand; ~**meldung** purchase notice (requisition); ~**nachfrage** consumer demand; ~**nachweis** certificate of convenience and necessity; **abstrakte** ~**police** valued policy; ~**quelle** source of requirements; ~**quote** vacancy rate; ~**rechnung** cash budgeting; ~**reserve** backlog of orders, backlog demand; ~**schätzung** consumption forecast; ~**schöpfung** demand creation; ~**schule** selective school; ~**spitze im Saisonverkauf** peak of demand; ~**träger** user, consumer; ~**verschiebung** shift in consumption; ~**vorwegnahme** anticipation of demand; ~**wandel** change of requirements; ~**weckung** want creation, consumptionism; ~**wirtschaft** consumer economics; ~**zug** auxiliary train; ~**zunahme** increased demand.

bedauerlich regrettable, unfortunate;
~**er Vorfall** deplorable incident.

Bedauern, mit größtem ~ **absagen** to decline with many regrets; **sein** ~ **äußern** to express one's regrets; **sinnloses** ~ **äußern** to cry over spilled milk *(coll.)*; **sein** ~ **zum Ausdruck bringen** to testify one's regrets.

bedeckt *(Himmel)* cloudy, overcast.

Bedeckung convoy, escort;
unter ~ **von zwei Polizisten** escorted by two policemen.

Bedenken doubt, concern, qualms;
nicht ohne ~ not without misgivings;
~ **äußern** to demur, to express doubt; **j. ohne** ~ **empfehlen** to recommend s. o. unhesitatingly; ~ **erregen** to raise doubts; ~ **bei etw. haben** to be wary of doing, to hesitate; **starke** ~ **gegen j. haben** to have a strong objection to s. o.; **noch** ~ **hegen** to hesitate, to have some doubts left; **erhebliche** ~ **hegen** to be in serious doubt; **keine** ~ **tragen** to have no scruples.

bedenken to consider, to weigh, to think over, to ponder;
sein Alter ~ to bear in mind s. one's age; **sich eines anderen** ~ to change one's mind; **Folgen einer Handlung** ~ to weigh up the consequences of an action; **j. reichlich mit Geschenken** ~ to shower gifts upon s. o.; **j. testamentarisch (in seinem Testament)** ~ to remember (include) s. o. in one's will; **sich eine Weile** ~ to deliberate for a while;
jem. etw. zu ~ **geben** to draw s. one's attention to s. th.

bedenklich questionable, doubtful, delicate, *(gefährlich)* serious, critical;
~**e Handlungsweise** conduct open to question; ~**e Lage** delicate position; **j. in eine** ~**e Lage bringen** to put s. o. in a precarious position; ~**es Licht auf j. werfen** to reflect badly on s. one's character; ~**e Schulden** staggering debts; ~**er Verlauf** dangerous course; ~**e Wendung nehmen** to take a serious turn; ~**er Zustand** critical situation.

bedenkt, wenn man alles so recht taking one thing with another.

Bedenkzeit time for consideration (to consider), *(Aufschub)* respite, grace, delay.

bedeppert *(fam.)* abashed, in a maze, abashed;
leicht ~ thin in the upper crust *(sl.)*;
ganz ~ **aussehen** to have a face as long as a fiddle.

bedeuten to mean, to signify;
jem. etw. ~ to give s. o. to understand; **in der Fachwelt etw.** ~ to be a recognized authority in one's field; **nichts Gutes** ~ to bode no good; **jds. Ruin** ~ to bring about (mean) s. one's ruin; **jem. viel** ~ to mean a great deal to s. o.; **zweierlei** ~ to have a double meaning;
nichts zu ~ **haben** to be irrelevant.

bedeutend significant, meaning, relevant, *(prominent)* powerful, eminent, outstanding, great;
sich ~ **bessern** to improve considerably; **sich für sehr** ~ **halten** to think no end (no small beer) of o. s.; **nicht gerade** ~ **sein** to amount to very little;
~**e Aufträge** heavy orders; ~**en Einfluß ausüben** to exercise considerable influence; ~**es Ereignis** important event; ~**e Persönlichkeit** outstanding personality; ~**e Rolle spielen** to cut a dash; ~**e Stelle einnehmen** to take a prominent place; ~**es Vermögen** respectable competence.

bedeutsam significant, important;
als ~ **hinstellen** to make much of;
welthistorisch ~**es Ereignis** event of world-wide importance.

Bedeutung significance, signification, importance, bearing, consequence, concernment, value, weight, mark, moment, worth, interest, *(Sinn)* meaning, purport,*(Wirkung)* effect;
ohne ~ of no account; **ohne rechtliche** ~ irrelevant; **von allergrößter** ~ of capital (paramount) importance; **von seiner eigenen** ~ **erfüllt** imbued with one's own importance; **von entscheidender** ~ of vital importance; **von großer** ~ of great weight; **von sekundärer** ~ of secondary importance; **von untergeordneter** ~ of secondary importance; **von ziemlicher** ~ of considerable interest;
allgemeine ~ common intent; **anerkannte** ~ acceptation; **eigentliche** ~ proper (inward) meaning, proper (narrow) sense; **fachliche** ~ technical meaning; **gegenwärtige** ~ present-day significance; **große** ~ great value; **allein in Betracht kommende** ~ necessary implication; **laienhafte** ~ popular sense; **lokale** ~ topicality; **rechtliche** ~ relevancce, legal effect; **relative** ~ *(Statistik)* weight; **übermäßige** ~ overriding importance; **überragende** ~ overriding importance; **übertragene** ~ figurative meaning; **ursprüngliche** ~ primary meaning; **versteckte** ~ hidden meaning; **wahre** ~ common intendment, intent; **wirtschaftliche** ~ economic prominence; **wörtliche** ~ literal sense (meaning of a word); **zwingende** ~ necessary implication;
~ **für die Allgemeinheit** public importance; ~ **einer Partei** party's weight;
keine ~ **beimessen** to attach no importance to; **einer Sache** ~ **beimessen** to attach importance to s. th.; **einer Sache große** ~ **beimessen** to give weight to s. th.; ~ **einer Sache erhöhen** to add to the weight; **relative** ~ **geben** *(Statistik)* to weight; **neue** ~ **gewinnen** to take a new meaning; ~ **haben** to matter; **große** ~ **haben** to have a strong bearing on; **internationale** ~ **haben** to be an international force; **jem. seine geringfügige** ~ **klarmachen** to tell s. o. where to get off; **Dinge nicht in ihrer relativen** ~ **sehen** to have no perspective; **von** ~ **sein** to weigh, to carry weight, to count, to have a bearing on, to bear a sense, to be relevant; **von grundlegender** ~ **sein**to be of basic importance; **von geringer** ~ **sein** to be of little interest; **für j. von** ~ **sein** to matter to s. o.; **von ziemlicher** ~ **sein** to make a great deal of difference; **von seiner** ~ **völlig überzeugt sein** to be full of o. s. (one's importance); **j. von seiner** ~ **zu überreden suchen** to come the heavy swell over s. o. *(sl.)*.

bedeutungslos insignificant, empty of meaning, irrelevant;
völlig ~ **sein** not to matter in the least, not to make two straws' difference *(coll.)*; **völlig** ~ **werden** to shrivel into nothing.

Bedeutungsnuancen shades of meaning.

bedeutungs|schwere Entscheidung momentous decision; ~**voll** ominous, pregnant with meaning; **j. einen** ~**vollen Blick zuwerfen** to look at s. o. with meaning.

bedienen to wait upon, to serve, to tend, to attend, to manage, *(Maschine)* to operate, to work, to run;
j. ~ to attend to s. o.; **sich** ~ to help o. s.; **sich jds.** ~ to make use of s. o.; **Anleihe** ~ to serve a loan; **Aufzug** ~ to operate an elevator *(US)* (lift, *Br.*); **Ehemann von hinten bis vorne** ~ to wait upon one's husband hand and foot; **Käufer (Kunden)** ~ to serve (attend to) a customer; **im Laden** ~ to serve in a shop; **sich einer List** ~ to use a stratagem; **sich einer bestimmten Methode** ~ to work on a system; **sich jds. Namen** ~ to use s. one's name; **reell** ~ to give good value; **sich einer fremden Sprache** ~ to speak in a foreign language; **Telefonzentrale** ~ to take telephone calls, to answer the telephone; **bei Tisch** ~ to wait on at table.

Bedienstete|r employee, servant, footman, *(Botschaft)* staff member;
fest angestellter ~**r** regular employee; **leitender** ~**r** chief officer; **ranghöchster** ~**r** senior officer; **überflüssige** ~ unprofitable servants; **fachlich vorgebildeter** ~**r** professional employee;
über zahlreiche ~ **verfügen** to have a large household.

bedient served;
restlos ~ **sein** to be cheesed off; **mit etw. schlecht** ~ **sein** to get poor value for s. th.

Bedienung attendance, service, serving, *(Laden)* shop assistant[s] *(Br.)*, *(Maschinen)* attendance, operation, running, control;
einschließlich ~ attendance (service) included;
ausgezeichnete ~ excellent service; **prompte (schnelle)** ~ prompt service (attention); **schlechte** ~ *(Hotel)* poor do;
~ **im Auto (Autorestaurant)** carshop, curb service *(US)*; ~ **ist im Preis einbegriffen** service included; **technische** ~ **eines Schiffes** management of a ship;
15% für die ~ 15 per cent for service.

Bedienungs|anleitung, ~anweisung operating (working, service) instructions, instruction sheet; **~aufschlag** service charge; **~bühne** operating platform; **~eigenschaft** handling characteristic; **~feld** control panel; **~geld** service charge, drink money (penny); **10% ~geld zahlen** to add 10 per cent to the bill for service; **~hebel** operating lever; **~knopf** control button; **~kraft** *(einer Maschine)* operator; **~mannschaft** operators, operating personnel; **~personal** operating personnel, operators, *(im Laden)* shop assistants *(Br.)*; **~pult** control panel (desk); **~schalter** control switch; **~schild** instruction plate; **~tafel** operating panel; **~vorschriften** operating instructions; **~zeit** handling time; **~zeiten** service times, *(Laden)* holding times; **~zentrale** operations center; **~zuschlag** service charge.

bedingen to condition, to determine;
Fracht ~ to engage the freight; **technische Vorbildung ~** to require technical training.

bedingt conditioned, qualified, limited, conditional;
~ arbeitsfähig partially disabled, nondescript; **auflösend ~** defeasible;
durch Überfluß ~ sein to be caused by abundance; **durch die Umstände ~ sein** to depend on the circumstances; **einem Plan nur ~ zustimmen** to give a scheme one's qualified approval;
~e Annahme conditional acceptance, *(Wechsel)* qualified acceptance; **~es Eigentum** conditional estate, qualified property; **~e Freilassung** probation; **~er Kauf** conditional purchase; **~e Konterbande** conditional contraband; **~es Lob** restricted praise; **~e Richtigkeit einer Behauptung** relative truth of a statement; **~es Sortiment** restrictive indorsement; **~e Strafaussetzung zur Bewährung** probation, parole; **sehr ~es Übereinkommen** agreement subject to numerous qualifications; **~es Urteil** conditional judgment; **~e Wahrscheinlichkeit** conditional probability; **~e Zustimmung** qualified approval.

Bedingt|bezug und ~abrechnung conditional purchase and settlement; **~buchhaltung** *(Buchhalter)* conditional purchase bookkeeping; **~geschäft** conditional transaction; **~gut** *(Buchhändler)* books on sale or return; **~lieferung** sale on approval.

Bedingung condition, clause, provision, proviso, *(Voraussetzung)* qualification, stipulation;
unter der ~ with [a] proviso, on condition (the stipulation) that; **unter einer ~** subject to one condition; **unter keiner ~** not on any account, on no account, under no circumstances, in no case; **unter ~ einer Gegenleistung** on reciprocal terms;
auflösende ~ resolutive (resolutory, subsequent) condition; **aufschiebende ~** condition precedent, suspensory condition; **ausdrückliche ~** express (explicit) condition; **ausreichende ~** sufficient condition; **einschränkende ~** restrictive covenant; **nachher zu erfüllende ~** subsequent condition; **wahlweise zu erfüllende ~** disjunctive condition; **an den Eintritt eines Ereignisses geknüpfte ~** positive condition; **gemischte ~** mixed condition; **gesetzliche ~** legal condition, statutory provision; **am Grundstück haftende ~** inherent condition; **konforme ~** consistent condition; **lästige ~** onerous clause; **mögliche ~** possible condition; **notwendige ~** essential condition; **positive ~** positive condition; **schwierige ~** rough going; **selbständige ~** independent condition; **selbstverständliche (stillschweigende) ~** implied condition; **strenge ~** stringent condition; **unerfüllte ~** unfulfilled condition; **unerläßliche ~** necessary condition; **ungesetzliche (unzulässige) ~** unlawful condition; **ungewisse ~** contingent condition; **unmögliche ~** impossible condition; **mit einem Vertrag unvereinbare ~** repugnant condition; **rechtlich unzulässige ~** illegal condition; **zwingend vorgeschriebene ~** compulsory condition; **wesentliche ~** essential condition; **ausdrücklich zugesicherte ~** affirmative condition; **rechtlich zulässige ~** lawful condition; **zwingende gesetzliche ~** mandatory statutory provision;
unter einer ~ annehmen to accept under reserve; **unter jeder ~ annehmen** to accept without any qualification; **~ erfüllen** to meet (satisfy, observe) a condition; **zur ~ machen** to condition, to specify, to make it a proviso; **~ stellen** to set up a condition; **Kurzschrift erwünscht, aber nicht ~** *(Anzeige)* shorthand an advantage but not essential.

Bedingungen terms;
gemäß nachstehenden ~ subject as hereafter provided; **nach den ~ dieser Bestimmung** under the terms of this clause; **unter ähnlichen ~** on similar terms; **unter günstigen ~** on easy terms; **unter den jetzigen ~** as its stands; **unter normalen ~** under existing (normal) conditions; **zu seinen eigenen ~** on its own terms; **zu gleichen ~** on equal terms; **zu leichten ~** on easy conditions; **zu schweren ~** on onerous conditions; **zu den üblichen ~** on usual terms; **zu unveränderten ~** on equal (same unchanged) conditions; **zu vernünftigen ~** on reasonable terms; **zu vorteilhaften (günstigen) ~** on advantageous terms;
allgemeine ~ general (standard) terms; **angenommene ~** conditions agreed upon; **annehmbare ~** fair (reasonable) terms; **äußerste ~** best terms; **besondere ~** special terms; **drückende (erschwerte) ~** onerous terms; **Zug um Zug zu erfüllende ~** concurrent (mutual) conditions; **ausdrücklich festgelegte ~** express conditions; **vertraglich festgelegte ~** conditions set forth in a contract; **festgesetzte ~** fixed conditions; **gegen das öffentliche Interesse gerichtete ~** conditions which are contrary to public policy; **gleichartige ~** concurrent conditions; **gleiche ~ für alle** fair field and no favo(u)r; **günstige ~** optimum conditions, easy terms; **kulante ~** liberal settlement; **mörderische ~** ruinous terms; **präzise ~** unambiguous terms; **sittenwidrige ~** conditions contra bonos mores; **unvorteilhafte ~** unfavo(u)rable terms; **vorgedruckte ~** printed conditions; **wettbewerbsneutrale ~** conditions remaining neutral regarding competitions; **zufriedenstellende ~** satisfactory terms;
~ bei sofortiger Bezahlung (Barzahlung) spot conditions; **~ für Kundenkonten** charge account terms; **~ eines Waffenstillstandsvertrages** terms of an armistice; **~ für monatliche Zahlungsweise** end-of-month terms;
~ annehmen to accept the terms; **bestimmte ~ annehmen** to agree upon certain conditions; **jds. ~ ohne Vorbehalt annehmen** to accept s. one's conditions without reserve (qualification); **unter ungünstigen (schwierigen) ~ arbeiten** to labo(u)r under a disadvantage, to work under difficult conditions; **jem. ~ auferlegen** to impose (lay down) conditions on (dictate terms to) s. o.; **auf ~ eingehen** to yield to conditions; **~ einhalten** to adhere to terms; **~ nicht einhalten** to fail to comply with conditions; **sich auf bestimmte ~ einigen** to settle certain conditions; **gesetzlichen ~ entsprechen** to comply with legal requirements; **~ erfüllen** to comply with conditions, *(beim Vertrag)* to execute; **bestimmte ~ erfüllen** to perform certain conditions; **vorteilhafte ~ erhalten** to obtain favo(u)rable conditions; **~ für j. festlegen** to lay down conditions for s. o.; **jem. vorteilhafte ~ gewähren** to make good terms with s. o.; **~ an etw. knüpfen** to make reservations with repect to s. th., to attach conditions to s. th.; **~ eines Heereslieferungsvertrages modifizieren** to renegotiate an army supply contract *(US)*; **seine ~ nennen (stellen)** to make (name) one's terms, to make one's conditions; **sich ~ unterwerfen** to submit to conditions; **~ stillschweigend zustimmen** to acquiesce in the terms;
~ bleiben auszuhandeln *(Inserat)* terms are for discussion.

bedingungsfeindliches Geschäft unconditional bargain.

Bedingungskauf conditional sale.

bedingungslos unconditional, absolute, unqualified, bare, without reserve;
~ annehmen to accept without reservation; **~ kapitulieren** to surrender unconditionally; **jem. ~ vertrauen** to trust s. o. unreservedly;
~e Kapitulation unconditional surrender.

bedrängen to press, to urge, to plague, to badger;
j. mit Fragen ~ to pester s. o. with questions; **j. hart ~** to press s. o. hard; **Schuldner mit der Rückzahlung ~** to push s. o. for payment, to dun (crowd) a debtor; **j. von allen Seiten ~** to close in on s. o.

Bedrängnis distress, hardship, need;
finanzielle ~ embarrassment, narrow straits, difficulties;
in ~ bringen to distress; **in ~ sein** to be pinched (in boiling water); **in großer ~ sein** to be reduced to great straits, to be at bay, to feel the draught *(Br., sl.)*.

bedrängt pressed, distressed, oppressed;
auf äußerste ~ pressed to the utmost; **von Feinden ~** embarassed by enemies; **von seinen Gläubigern ~** hounded (pressed) by one's creditors;
~ sein to be embarassed; **hart ~ werden** to be hard pressed;
in ~er Lage in straitened circumstances (narrow straits); **in ~er Lage sein** to be hard up (in a state of distress), to be in a predicament; **in ~en Verhältnissen leben** to live in cramped conditions.

bedrohen, jds. Existenz to endanger s. one's existence; **mit dem Tode ~** to threaten with death.

bedrohlich threatening, menacing;
~ aussehen to look precarious;
~e Anzeichen ominous signs; **in ~e Nähe kommen** to come dangerously near; **~es Schweigen** ominous silence.

Bedrohung threat, menace, intimidation;
~ des Weltfriedens menace to world peace;
~ der Sicherheit darstellen to constitute a threat to security; **in ständiger ~ leben** to live in constant danger of one's life.

Bedrucken der Rückseite backing up.
bedrucken to impress, to print, to imprint, to pull;
Stoff mit Muster ~ to print patterns on material.
bedrücken to depress, to vex, to wring, *(Steuern)* to squeeze; **j.** ~ to weigh on s. one's mind.
bedrückt low, blue, depressed, down in the mouth;
von der Hitze ~ oppressed by the heat; **von Sorgen** ~ weighed down with cares; ~ **von Steuern** crushed by taxation;
in ~er Stimmung sein to be depressed, to look blue, to have the blues.
Bedrücktheit depression.
bedungene Prämie stipulated premium.
bedürfen to require, to need, to want;
ärztlicher Behandlung ~ to require medical care; **keiner Erklärung** ~ to need no explanation; **dringend der Hilfe** ~ to badly want help; **der Ruhe** ~ to need a rest; **sorgfältiger Überprüfung** ~ to want careful consideration; **keiner weiteren Worte** ~ to go without saying.
Bedürfnis need, want, necessity, requirement, turn, *(Nachfrage)* demand;
dringendes ~ exigency; **individuelles** ~ private want; **kollektives** ~ social want; **öffentliches** ~ public necessity, public want, reasonable public demand; **tiefgefühltes** ~ heart-felt wish; **öffentliches** ~ **auf Erteilung einer Bankkonzession** reasonable public demand for a bank;
einem ~ **abhelfen** to meet a want; **um einem langempfundenen** ~ **abzuhelfen** to supply a want that has long been felt; **langjähriges** ~ **befriedigen** to meet a long-felt want; **einem** ~ **entsprechen** to fill a need; **neues** ~ **erwecken** to create a new want; **dringendes** ~ **nach etw. fühlen** to have a strong desire for s. th.; **einem öffentlichen** ~ **genügen** to supply a public demand; ~ **nach etw. haben** to stand in need of s. th.; **dringendes** ~ **haben** to feel an urge;
~ **haben, die Wahrheit zu sagen** to feel bound to tell the truth.
Bedürfnisse, augenblickliche present needs; **elastische** ~ variable requirements; **finanzielle** ~ financial needs, pecuniary wants; **leibliche** ~ bodily wants; **meritorische** ~ merit wants; **örtliche** ~ spot (local) needs; **persönliche** ~ one's personal needs; **tägliche** ~ daily wants;
~ **des Einzelhandels** retail [trade] demands; **dringendste** ~ **des Lebens** the bare necessities; ~ **des zivilen Sektors** civilian needs; ~ **des Verkehrs** traffic requirements;
auf jds. ~ **abstellen** to tailor to s. one's specific needs; **auf die** ~ **der Kunden abstellen** to aim at the needs of customers; ~ **befriedigen** to provide for the needs; **seine** ~ **befriedigen** to satisfy one's needs; **jds. ~n entsprechen** to correspond to s. one's needs, to serve s. one's turn; **nur geringe** ~ **haben** to be a man of few wants; **für jds.** ~ **sorgen** to minister to s. one's needs, to supply the needs of s. o., to purvey for s. o.; **den ~n Rechnung tragen** to take account of the needs.
Bedürfnis|anstalt, öffentliche public convenience (lavatory, toilet room), communal toilet, sanitary convenience *(US)*, public comfort station *(US)*; **Wände einer ~anstalt mit Unanständigkeiten beschmieren** to scribble dirty words on W.C. walls; **~erregung** want creation; **~koinzidenz** coincidence of wants; **~losigkeit** absence of wants; **~pyramide** hierarchy of needs.
bedürftig poor and needy, necessitous, one-horse *(US coll.)*, indigent;
~ **sein** to be in want, to stand in need; **der Ruhe** ~ **sein** to need a rest;
~e Angehörige poor relations; **~e Familie** needy family.
Bedürftiger poor (needy) person, destitute, pauper.
Bedürftigkeit neediness, indigence, distress, *(Armenrecht)* poverty;
~ **einwenden** to plead poverty; **in großer** ~ **leben** to live in straitened circumstances (dire need); **seine** ~ **nachweisen** to prove one's lack of means.
Bedürftigkeits|grad poverty level; **~grenze** means test limit *(Br.)*; **~nachweis, ~prüfung** means (needs) test *(Br.)*; **~rente** assistance pension *(Br.)*.
beduselt tipsy, drowsy.
beehren to hono(u)r, to favo(u)r;
sich ~ to have the hono(u)r; **mit Aufträgen** ~ to favo(u)r with orders.
beeiden, seine Aussage to declare on oath, to take on (swear an) oath.
beeidigt|e Aussage sworn testimony (statement), affidavit; **~er Bücherrevisor** chartered (certified, *US*) accountant; **~er Makler** sworn broker; **~er Schätzer** sworn appraiser, licensed valuer *(Br.)*.
beeilen, sich to hurry up, to hasten, to make haste, to get a hump (hustle) *(sl.)*; **sich mit seiner Arbeit** ~ to be quick about a job; **sich mit einem Auftrag** ~ to rush with an order; **sich ~, nach Hause zu kommen** to make a push to get home, to hasten home.
beeindrucken to impress, to make an impression;
gewaltig ~ to hit like a ton of bricks, to make a strong impression; **j. kaum (nur schwach)** ~ to move s. o. very little; **j. ungemein** ~ to knock s. o. for a row *(sl.)*.
beeindruckt affected;
günstig ~ prepossessed in favo(u)r; **tief** ~ deeply impressed.
beeinflußbar suggestible;
so ~, daß Pflegschaft angeordnet werden muß facile *(Scot., law)*.
beeinflussen to affect, to inspire, to have influence on, to reach, *(Parlament)* to influence, to lobby, *(störend)* to interfere with, *(ungünstig)* to warp, *(Urteil)* to bias, *(Wähler)* to canvass;
j. ~ to get at (sway) s. o.; **Abgeordnete wegen der Erhöhung von Zuschüssen** ~ to lobby M. P.'s for higher subsidies; **j. gegen einen anderen** ~ to prejudice s. o. against s. o.; **Börse (Markt)** ~ to have an effect on the market; **sich gegenseitig** ~ to interact; **gerichtliche Entscheidung** ~ to affect the findings; **Geschworene** ~ to tamper with the jury; **j. zu jds. Gunsten** ~ to exercise one's influence on behalf of s. o.; **j. günstig** ~ to have a great effect on s. o.; **künstlich** ~ to manipulate; **öffentliche Meinung** ~ to sway public opinion; **nachteilig** ~ to have a bad influence on, to affect prejudicially; **j. gegen einen Dritten negativ** ~ to poison s. one's mind against s. o.; **Konjunktur in zunehmendem Maße negativ** ~ to take a bigger bite out of the economy; **in stärkerem Maße politisch** ~ to use more political muscle; **j. positiv** ~ to influence s. o. for the good; **Richter** ~ to weigh with the judge; **schädlich** ~ to taint; **j. ungehörig** ~ to exert an undue influence on s. o.; **ungünstig** ~ to affect unfavo(u)rably; **j. unzulässig** ~ to exercise undue influence upon s. o.; **auf unehrliche Weise** ~ to fix *(US)*; **jem. bei der Abfassung eines Testamentes in unzulässiger Weise** ~ to use undue influence with the maker of a will; **Zeugen** ~ to suborn (tamper with, get at, *fam.*) a witness; **leicht zu** ~ waxy, *(Börse)* soft.
beeinflußt influenced, affected;
von einer Hochdruckzone ~ influenced by an anticyclone; **von der Meinung Dritter** ~ governed by what other people say; **von jem.** ~ **werden** to be under the influence of s. o.; **von außen** ~ **werden** to be controlled by influence from outside;
~er Zeuge tampered witness.
Beeinflussung influence, *(Wähler)* canvassing;
erlaubte ~ due influence; **hypnotische** ~ hypnotic suggestion; **künstliche** ~ manipulation; **moralische** ~ morale persuasion; **sittenwidrige** ~ improper influence; **unzulässige** ~ undue influence;
~ **von Abgeordneten** lobbying of members of parliament; ~ **der Börsenkurse durch Konzertzeichnungen** stagging the market; ~ **der Geschworenen** tampering with the jury; ~ **des Lohnniveaus** wage leadership; ~ **der öffentlichen Meinung** sway of public opinion; ~ **eines Zeugen** subornation (tampering with) a witness;
Gesetz durch ~ **durchbringen** to lobby a bill through the house; **sich von** ~ **freimachen** to break free from an influence.
beeinträchtigen to injure, to interfere with, to infringe, to encroach, to vitiate, *(schmälern)* to impair, *(Wert)* to discount, to prejudice, to be derogatory, to derogate;
Aufrechterhaltung der öffentlichen Sicherheit ~ to endanger the maintenance of public safety; **Erwerbsfähigkeit** ~ to impair one's earning capacity; **jds. Gesundheit** ~ to impair s. one's health; **jds. Interessen** ~ to affect (prejudice, injure, interfere with, impair) s. one's interests; **jds. Rechte** ~ to encroach upon (be of prejudice to) s. one's rights; **jds. Ruf** ~ to be injurious to (detract from) s. one's reputation; **jds. Vertrauen** ~ to disturb s. one's faith; **Wert** ~ to impair the value.
beeinträchtigt prejudiced, interfered, touched;
durch Saisonschwankungen ~ seasonally unstable;
~e Gesundheit impaired health; **~er Wert** nuisance value.
Beeinträchtigung impairment, encroachment, infringement, affection, interference, abridgement, curtailment, prejudice, vitiation, detriment, *(Ruf)* detraction, *(Schädigung)* damnification, damage, injury, *(Störung)* disturbance, trespass, nuisance;
ohne ~ **irgendwelcher Ansprüche** without prejudice to any claim; **ohne** ~ **der Belange** without detriment to the interests;
~ **der Disziplin** breach of discipline; ~ **des Empfangs durch ausländische Rundfunkstationen** interference from foreign broadcasting stations; ~ **der Ertragsfähigkeit** impeachment of annuity *(Br.)*; ~ **der geistigen Fähigkeiten** impairment of s.

one's mental faculties; ~ **der Gesundheit** impairment (deprivation) of health; ~ **einer Konzession** disturbance of franchise; ~ **der Lebensgemeinschaft** loss of consortium *(Br.)*; ~ **des Pächters** *(Verpächter)* constructive eviction; ~ **vertraglicher Pflichten** impairing the obligations of a contract; ~ **eines Rechtes** encroachment of a right; ~ **der ungehinderten Religionsausübung** disturbance of public or religious worship; ~ **von jds. gutem Ruf** detraction from (hurt of) s. one's reputation; ~ **der Verkehrssicherheit** endangering the safety of road traffic; ~ **der Verstandeskräfte** impairment of a mental nature; ~ **eines Vorrechtes** derogation from a privilege; ~ **des Wertes** impairment of value; ~ **des körperlichen Wohlbefindens** impairment of a physical nature;
~ **beseitigen** to quiet, to abate a nuisance.

beenden, beendigen to close, to end, to conclude, to complete, to accomplish, to finish, to determine, to stop;
Arbeit ~ to finish with a piece of work; **schwierige Aufgabe erfolgreich** ~ to bring off a difficult task; **seine Ausbildung** ~ to complete one's education; **Beweisaufnahme** ~ to close a case; **Debatte** ~ to close a debate; **Dienstverhältnis** ~ to terminate an employment; **Dienstverhältnis fristlos** ~ to terminate an employment contract without notice *(US)*; **Gesellschaftsverhältnis** ~ to dissolve a business partnership; **jds. Karriere** ~ to be the end of s. one's career; **Krieg** ~ to bring war to an end; **seine Laufbahn** ~ to end one's career; **seine Lehrzeit** ~ to conclude (finish) one's apprenticeship; **Rede** ~ to conclude a speech; **Rede mit einem Zitat** ~ to end up a speech with a quotation; **Sitzung** ~ to break up a meeting; **Streit** ~ to bring a quarrel to an end; **Versammlung mit einer kurzen Ansprache** ~ to wind up a meeting with a short speech; **Vertrag (Vertragsverhältnis)** ~ to discharge (conclude, determine, terminate) a contract; **Vertretungsverhältnis** ~ to terminate an agency; **Vortrag** ~ to conclude a speech.

beendet finished;
fast ~ **sein** to be near its fag end.

Beendigung completion, conclusion, end, ending, determination, termination, discontinuance, *(Aufhören)* cessation;
kurz vor ~ near completion; **nach** ~ **des Krieges** after the war; **nach** ~ **des Vertrages** on completion of contract, cessation of an agreement; **vor** ~ **der Revision** before the close of the audit;
gesetzliche ~ constructive revocation;
~ **einer Amtszeit** expiration of a term of office; ~ **der Arbeit** completion of work; ~ **des Beschäftigungsverhältnisses** termination of employment, employment termination; ~ **der Debatte** termination of a debate; **automatische** ~ **des Deckungsschutzes** *(Kriegsausbruch)* automatic termination of cover; ~ **des Dienstverhältnisses** cessation (completion) of service, termination of employment, employment termination; ~ **der Einreichung von Schriftsätzen** close of pleadings; ~ **der Gewalttaten** end to violence; ~ **des Klagevorbringens** close of the case; ~ **eines Mietverhältnisses** termination of a lease; **selbsttätige** ~ **eines Nutzungsrechtes** special limitation; ~ **eines Pachtvertrages** ending a lease, expiration (determination) of a lease; ~ **einer Rede** termination (conclusion) of a speech; ~ **einer Sitzung** breaking up of a meeting; ~ **eines Streiks** cessation from strike; **einverständliche** ~ **eines Vertragsverhältnisses** termination of agreement, discharge of a contract; ~ **eines Vertretungsverhältnisses** termination of agency; ~ **des Waffenstillstands** expiration of truce; ~ **des Wahlvorgangs** closing of polls.

beengen to restrict, to confine, to pinch, to hamper.

beengt cramped for space, confined;
räumlich ~ cramped for space;
~**er Raum** confined space; **in** ~**en Verhältnissen leben** to live in cramped conditions.

beerben, j. to succeed to s. one's property, to become (be) s. one's heir, to inherit from s. o. *(US)*.

beerdigen to bury, to inter.

Beerdigung funeral, burial, interment;
kirchliche ~ Christian burial;
einer ~ **beiwohnen** to attend a funeral.

Beerdigungs|feier funeral ceremony; ~**geld** funeral benefit; ~**gottesdienst** funeral service, dead office; ~**institut** undertaker's business, funeral home (parlor, *US*); ~**kosten** funeral cost (expenses); ~**ort** burial place; ~**unternehmer** funeral director.

Beerenobst soft fruit.

befähigen to enable, to qualify, to fit.

befähigt fit, qualified, able, *(begabt)* gifted, talented, *(geeignet)* eligible;
~ **sein** to have the necessary qualifications.

Befähigung qualification, capacity, fitness, *(Befugnis)* competence, *(Eignung)* ability, aptitude, *(Geschick)* ability, *(Leistungsfähigkeit)* efficiency;
berufliche ~ occupational competence; **erforderliche** ~ necessary qualification; **juristische** ~ legal qualification;
~ **für einen akademischem Beruf** professional qualification; ~ **für den Staatsdienst erwerben** to qualify for a civil-service position; ~ **zur Bekleidung eines öffentlichen Amtes haben** to be qualified to hold a public office; ~ **zum Richteramt haben** to qualify as a judge;
die nötigen ~**en haben** to have the necessary qualifications; **seine** ~ **nachweisen** to qualify.

Befähigungs|auswahl selection on the basis of aptitude; ~**erfordernisse** ability requirements.

Befähigungsnachweis qualifying certificate, ability requirements, certificate of competency (proficiency), *(Spediteur)* certificate of convenience and necessity *(US)*, *(Universität)* licence;
kein ~ **erforderlich** no qualifications required;
~ **erbringen** to qualify; **beruflichen oder fachlichen** ~ **erbringen können** to possess professional or technical qualifications; **jem. hohe Punkte beim** ~ **zuerkennen** to give s. o. a high credit rating for competence *(US)*;
~**klausel** *(Spediteur)* grandfather clause *(US)*.

Befähigungs|prüfung qualification (aptitude) test; ~**schein** certificate of competency; ~**zeugnis** licence.

befahrbar passable [by vehicles], carriageable, trafficable *(US)*, *(Gewässer)* navigable;
nicht ~ *(Gewässer)* unnavigable, *(Straße)* impassable, impracticable; **nur mit Schneeketten** ~ negotiable only with chains;
~**er Fluß** navigable river; ~**e Straße** vehicular road; **nicht** ~**e Straße** impassable road.

Befahrbarkeit passableness, trafficability *(US)*, *(Fluß)* navigability.

befahren to drive on, to travel, *(Bus)* to cover [a route];
Feld mit Mist ~ to manure a field; **Fluß regelmäßig** ~ to ply a river; **Grube** ~ to descend into a mine, *(besichtigen)* to inspect a mine; **Küste** ~ to sail along the coast; **Land mit dem Auto** ~ to cover a country by car; **Meere** ~ to plough the seas; **Straße häufig** ~ to use a road frequently; **Strecke regelmäßig** ~ *(Bus)* to cover a route regularly;
~ *(a.)* used, travelled;
stark ~**e Straße** frequented road.

befallen, von einer Krankheit attacked by a disease.

befangen partial, biassed, prejudiced, ill at ease, *(verlegen)* bashful, embarrassed, shy;
im Streit ~ contentious;
sich für ~ **erklären** to plead partiality, to disqualify o. s. *(US)*; **j.** ~ **machen** to embarrass (abash) s. o.; **in einem Irrtum** ~ **sein** to labo(u)r under a delusion; **in Vorurteilen** ~ **sein** to be blinded by prejudices, to be prejudiced;
~**er Richter** partial judge; ~**er Zeuge** challengeable witness.

Befangenheit constraint, embarrassment, bashfulness, *(jur.)* prejudice, bias, partiality, prejudgment, disqualification *(US)*;
Richter wegen ~ **ablehnen** to challenge a judge; **Zeugen wegen** ~ **ablehnen** to take exception to (challenge) a witness; **jem. die** ~ **nehmen** to put s. o. at ease.

befassen, sich mit etw. to engage in (deal, concern, take up s. th., occupy o. s.) with s. th.; **sich mit einer Angelegenheit eingehend** ~ to give a matter one's special attention; **sich mit einer Angelegenheit nicht** ~ not to touch an affair; **sich mit einem Gegenstand** ~ to deal with a subject; **sich intensiv mit etw.** ~ to go into s. th. in detail, to deal with a matter at some length; **sich mit Politik** ~ to deal in politics; **sich mit der eingegangenen Post** ~ to attend to the correspondence; **sich mit einem Problem** ~ to look into a problem; **sich mit der Übersetzung eines Romans** ~ to be occupied in translating a novel; **sich ständig mit etw.** ~ to have s. th. on one's brain; **sich mit einem Thema** ~ to approach a subject;
sich mit etw. nicht ~ **müssen** to be spared s. th.

befaßt occupied, busy with;
mit einer Angelegenheit nicht ~ **sein** to have no concern in a matter; **mit einer Sache** ~ **sein** to have a matter in hand;
das Gericht ist mit der Sache ~ the matter is before the court.

Befehl order, decree, call, mandate, charge, *(mil.)* command;
ausdrücklicher ~ positive order; **dienstlicher** ~ official order; **keine** ~**e** no orders; **richterlicher** ~ judicial order, writ, bench warrant, court order; **schriftlicher** ~ written order;
~ **zum Auslaufen** sailing orders; ~ **von höchster Stelle** top-level order;

jds. ~ ausführen to execute s. one's commands; **~e von jem. entgegennehmen** to take orders from s. o.; **~ erlassen** *(mil.)* to issue an order; **jem. dauernd ~e erteilen** to order s. o. about; **jem. ohne richterlichen ~ festnehmen** to arrest s. o. without a warrant; **auf ~ handeln** to act according to instructions; **~ übermitteln** to signal an order; **~ übernehmen** to assume the (take) command; **jds. ~ unterstehen** to be put under s. one's command, to be subordinated to s. o.; **~ verweigern** to refuse to obey an order.

befehlen to command, to order, to direct;
jem. strengstes Stillschweigen ~ to enjoin s. o. to strictest secrecy.

befehlend commanding.

Befehls | ausgabe issuance of orders, briefing; **~bereich** command; **~buch** orderly book; **~ebene** echelon; **reiner ~empfänger** mere puppet.

befehlsgemäß to order;
~ handeln to act according to instructions.

Befehlsgewalt power of command, authority;
~ über jem. haben to have authority over s. o.; **jem. ~ übertragen** to place s. o. in command.

befehlshabend *(mil.)* commanding.

Befehls | haber commander, commanding officer; **jds. dauernde ~haberei satt haben** to be tired of s. one's constant dictations; **~mißbrauch** abuse of authority; **~sprache** computer language; **~stand** command post; **~stelle** head-quarters; **vorgeschobene ~stelle** advance command post; **~ton** peremptory tone; **~verweigerung** refusal to obey an order.

befehlswidrig contrary to instructions.

Befehls | wirtschaft command planning system; **~zentrale** nerve center *(US)* (centre, *Br.*).

befeinden, sich to be at loggerheads.

befestigen to fix, to fasten, to attach, to affix, *(mil.)* to fortify;
sich ~ *(Kurse)* to strengthen, to firm up, to show a rising tendency, to stiffen, to harden; **aneinander ~** to connect with s. th.; **Anhänger an einem Koffer ~** to label a suitcase; **Boot an einem Pfahl ~** to fasten a boat to a post; **mit Nägeln ~** to nail; **Straßendecke ~** to consolidate the road surface.

befestigt fast;
~es Lager fortified camp; **~e Stadt** fortified city; **~e Start- und Landebahn** hard-surface runway; **~e Straße** paved road.

Befestigung attachment, *(Kurse)* consolidation, hardening, stiffening, strengthening, *(mil.)* fortification;
vorgeschobene ~ outwork.

Befestigungs | anlagen, ~werk fortification, walls; **~gürtel** ring of forts.

befeuern to beacon.

Befeuerung *(Schiffahrt)* lights.

Befinden *(Gesundheit)* health, *(Gutachten)* judgment, opinion;
nach meinem ~ in my judgment (view);
sich nach jds. ~ erkundigen to inquire (ask) after s. one's health.

befinden to find, *(Gericht)* to judge, to rule, to determine, to decree, to hear;
sich ~ to be, *(enthalten)* to contain; **sich im Ausland ~** to be abroad; **sich unmittelbar an der Bushaltestelle ~** to be next to the bus stop; **für gut ~** to deem good; **sich in einer heiklen Lage ~** to be in a tricky situation; **über eine Rechtsfrage ~** to decide a point of law; **sich auf Reisen ~** to be away; **für richtig ~** to find correct; **in einer Sache ~** to make a decision on s. th., to rule in a case; **für schuldig ~** to find guilty; **sich in einer finanziellen Verlegenheit ~** to be in pecuniary embarrassment, to be financially embarrassed;
über etw. nicht zu ~ haben to have nothing to do with s. th.

befindlich contained, to be found;
außerhalb ~ outside; **im Bau ~** under construction; **im Umlauf ~** in circulation.

beflaggen to flag, to deck with flags, to put out bunting;
Schiff ~ to dress a ship.

beflaggt flagged;
~es Schiff ship dressed overall; **~e Straße** street gay with bunting.

beflecken to defile, to stain, to spot, to foul;
seine Hände mit Blut ~ to stain one's hands with blood, to commit murder.

befleißigen, sich to strive for, to be solicitous, to put o. s. out, to endeavo(u)r; **sich ~, seinen Brötchengeber zufriedenzustellen** to take great pains to please one's employer; **sich größter Höflichkeit ~** to be the pick of politeness; **sich einer Sache ~** to give one's mind to s. th.; **sich des Studiums der Rechte ~** to study for the bar *(Br.)*, to study law *(US)*.

beflissen solicitous of, eager, assiduous.

beflügeln, seine Phantasie to give wings to one's phantasy; **seine Schritte ~** to quicken one's pace.

befolgen to follow, to observe, to adhere, to be observant, to comply with;
ärztliche Anordnungen streng ~ to strictly follow the doctor's order; **Anweisungen ~** to comply with orders, to act upon instructions; **Gesetz ~** to abide by the law; **nicht ~** to disobey; **Regeln ~** to comply with rules.

Befolgung compliance, observation.
genaue ~ strict observance;
peinliche ~ aller Gepflogenheiten des politischen Lebens niceties in politics; **~ der Regeln** abidance by the rules.

Beförderer carrier, conveyer.

befördern to carry, to transfer, to convey, to haul, *(absenden)* to dispatch, to forward, to consign, to expedite, to route, to handle, to ship *(US)*, *(Angestellte, Beamte)* to promote, to advance, to prefer to a higher post, to upgrade, *(bringen)* to take, to bring, *(transportieren)* to transport, to transmit;
j. ~ to appoint s. o. to a higher post, to advance s. o.; **mit der Bahn ~** to transport (send) by rail, to rail goods; **mit einem Omnibus zum Bahnhof ~** to convey to the station in a bus; **bevorzugt ~** to promote with priority; **j. zum Direktor ~** to make s. o. a director; **als Eilgut ~** to forward by express train; **im Flugzeug ~** to fly, to airlift; **Güter zur Bahn ~** to transport (carry) goods to the station; **Güter an ihren Bestimmungsort ~** to dispatch goods to their destination; **j. ins Jenseits ~** to send s. o. [in]to eternity; **durch einen Kanal ~** to channel; **auf dem Landwege ~** to convey by land; **mit Lastwagen ~** to lorry *(Br.)*, to [ship by] truck *(US)*; **an die frische Luft ~** to chuck s. o. out; **auf dem Luftwege ~** to airlift; **Pakete zur Post ~** to take parcels to the post *(Br.)*, to mail parcels *(US)*; **in den Papierkorb ~** to throw into the wastepaper basket; **Personen ~** to carry passengers for a consideration; **Personen und Fracht ~** to convey both passengers and goods; **mit der Post ~** to forward goods by post *(Br.)* (mail, *US*), to post, to mail; **Post mit dem Flugzeug ~** to transport post (mail, *US*) by airplane; **durch ein Privatunternehmen ~** to express *(US)*; **auf eigenes Risiko ~** to carry at one's own risk; **40% des Handels in eigenen Schiffen ~** to carry (trade on) 40 per cent of its own ships; **schnell ~** to hurry to; **Telegramm ~** to transmit (handle) a telegram; **Waren per Achse ~** to cart goods; **Güter auf dem Wasserwege ~** to ship goods.

befördert transported, carbonized *(sl.)*, *(im Rang)* promoted;
im Flugzeug ~ airborne; **mit Luftpost ~** airspeeded;
~ werden to advance, to be promoted, to be advanced, to get one's promotion, to come to preferment, *(mil.)* to rise to a higher rank, to get one's stripes (step); **vor jem. ~ werden** to be promoted over s. one's head; **bevorzugt ~ werden** to be preferentially promoted; **nach dem Dienstalter (nach Dienstjahren) ~ werden** to be promoted by seniority (in order of age); **in einen höheren Rang ~ werden** to be promoted to a higher rank.

Beförderung carriage, carrying, conveyance, conveying, transfer, *(Absendung)* dispatch, forwarding, *(Güter)* haul, haulage, freightage, shipment *(US)*, *(mil.)* step, promotion, *(Rang)* step, promotion, *(in einer Stellung)* promotion, preferment, advance, advancement, lift, elevation, *(Telegramm)* handling, transmission, *(Transport)* transport, transportation;
zur ~ übernommen received for shipment *(US)*;
durchgehende ~ through transportation; **öffentliche ~** public transport; **private ~** express *(US)*; **spätere ~** future advancement;
~ per Achse road transport; **~ per Bahn** rail (railway) transport, transportation by rail; **~ im Binnenschifffahrtsverkehr** river transport *(Br.)*, inland waterway transportation *(US)*; **~ von Briefen** carriage of letters; **~ nach dem Dienstalter** advance (promotion) by seniority, seniority basis; **~ als Drucksache** book post *(Br.)*; **~ als Eilgut** carrying express; **~ gegen Entgelt** carriage on hire; **kostenlose ~ der Familienangehörigen** free family passage; **~ von Freikarteninhabern** deadhead transportation; **~ von Führungskräften** executive promotion; **~ von Gepäck** transportation of baggage; **~ von Haus zu Haus** door-to-door transport; **~ auf dem Landwege** land carriage (transport); **~ mit Lastkraftwagen** motor-truck transport, road transport (haulage, *Br.*); **~ auf dem Luftwege** transport[ation] by air, air transport, air transportation; **~ von Massengütern** transport in bulk, conveyance in bulk (mass); **~ im Nahverkehr** short-distance transport; **~en zum Neujahrstag** New Year's hono(u)rs *(Br.)*; **~ von Personen** conveyance of passengers, passenger transport; **~ durch die Post** postal transport, carriage by mail; **~ außer der Reihe** prepromotion; ~

der Reihe nach lineal promotion; ~ per Schiff waterborne transport; direkte ~ von Seefracht freighting voyage; ~ auf dem Seewege carriage by sea, waterborne transport, marine transport; ~ von und zum Speicher *(Spediteur)* elevating service; tariffreie ~ für Stauung dunnage allowance; ~ im Straßenfernverkehr haulage, highway transportation; ~ von Stückgut transportation of general cargo; ~ eines Telegramms transmission of a telegram; ~ im Transitverkehr through transport; ~ mit Umladung transshipment; ~ durch öffentliche Verkehrsmittel public transport, common carrier transportation; gewerbsmäßige ~ von Waren haulage-contracting (carrier's) business; ~ auf dem Wasserwege sea (waterborne) transport, water carriage, waterage;
~ sperriger Güter ablehnen to refuse to carry bulky goods; zur ~ anstehen to be about to be promoted, to be on one's promotion, to be in line for promotion, to be eligible for promotion; ~ erfahren to get one's promotion; auf seine ~ hinarbeiten to urge one's promotion; mit einer ~ rechnen to calculate on preferment; in der ~ an der Reihe sein to be in line for promotion; jds. ~ im Wege stehen to prove an obstacle to s. one's promotion; j. bei der ~ übergehen to supersede s. o., to pass over s. one's head; andere bei der ~ übergehen to be put over s. one's head; ~ verdienen to merit promotion; ~ veröffentlichen to gazette an appointment *(Br.)*; zur ~ vorsehen to mark out for promotion.

Beförderungs|alter seniority; ~**anspruch** *(Stellung)* seniority right; ~**anweisungen** forwarding (dispatching) instructions; ~**art** mode (manner) of conveyance, *(in Stellung)* type of promotion; ~**arten** express classes; ~**aussichten** *(Stellung)* promotional status; ~**bedingungen** conditions of carriage, terms of conveyance, *(Stellung)* terms of promotion; ~**bestimmungen** forwarding conditions, *(Post)* service instructions, *(Stellung)* terms of promotion, promotional arrangements; ~**chance** opportunity for promotion; ~**dauer** period of transport; ~**eignung** capacity for advancement, qualification; ~**entgelt** transport charge; staatliches ~**ersuchen** government transportation request; ~**frist** period allowed for carriage; ~**gebühr** carriage, transport[ation] charge, *(Post)* postage; ~**gebührensätze** carriage (transportation) rates; ~**gefahr** risk of carriage, transport risk; ~**gesellschaft** highway carrier *(US)*; ~**klassifizierung** express classification; ~**kosten** carrying (forwarding) costs, cost of carriage (transportation), charges of carriage, transport charges, transportation charges (costs), porterage, *(Straße)* haulage; ~**leistungen** transportation service; ~**liste** *(Stellung)* promotion list, advancement (promotion) roster; ~**mittel** vehicle, [means of] conveyance (transportation, *US*), transportation *(US)*; öffentliches ~**mittel** hackney carriage, public conveyance (transportation, *US*); ~**möglichkeiten** transport facilities, *(Angestellter)* opportunity to advance; ~**plan** *(Stellung)* advancement roster, promotion plan (roster), promotional program(me); ~**politik** *(Stellung)* promotional policy; ~**preis** freight and passenger rates; ~**problem** *(Stellung)* seniority problem; ~**programm** promotional program(me); ~**richtlinien** *(Stellung)* lines of promotion; ~**risiko** transport risk; ~**roheinnahmen** *(Bahn)* gross traffics *(US)*; ~**rohr** dispatch tube; ~**schein** waybill; ~**steuer** transport tax, transportation tax *(US)*, railway passenger duty *(Br.)*; ~**strecke** route of travel; ~**system** *(Stellung)* promotional system; ~**tabelle** opportunity (promotional) chart; ~**tag** day of nomination; ~**tarif** passenger tariff, *(Güter)* freight *(US)* (goods, *Br.*) tariff; ~**unterlagen** *(Stellung)* promotional material *(US)*; ~**unternehmen** haulage contractor, transport company *(Br.)*, carrier, forwarding (shipping, *US*) agent, common carrier, haulage contractor; ~**verbot** prohibited transport, *(Post)* fraud order; ~**verfahren** *(Stellung)* promotion practice; ~- **und Transportverhältnis** transportation ratio *(US)*; ~**vertrag** contract of carriage, passage contract, shipping contract *(US)*; ~**vorschriften** dispatch (forwarding) instructions; ~**weg** way of transportation, route of travel, forwarding route, *(Telegramm)* route; ~**wesen** public transport service, transportation, *(Stellung)* promotional system; allein auf Fähigkeiten und Leistungen beruhendes ~**wesen** merit system *(US)*.

beförderungswürdig eligible for promotion.

Beförderungs|zeit period of transport; ~**zulage** *(Stellung)* seniority pay; ~**zwang** compulsory conveyance.

befrachtbar charterable.

befrachten to charter, to [engage the] freight, to let, to load;
in Bausch und Bogen ~ to charter in a lump sum; Schiff ~ to take a ship to freight; mit Stückgütern ~ to freight by parcels; nach dem Wert ~ to freight ad valorem.

Befrachter sender, shipper, charterer, freighter;
Reeder und ~ owner and charterer.

Befrachtung charter[ing], charterage, freighting, freightage, affreightment;
~ in Bausch und Bogen lump-sum freighting; ~ nach dem Gewicht freighting on weight; ~ für eine ganze Reise voyage (trip) charter; ~ mit Stückgütern berth freighting, freighting by the case; ~ nach dem Wert freighting ad valorem; ~ für einen bestimmten Zeitraum time charter.

Befrachtungs|bedingungen freighting conditions; ~**büro**, ~**kontor** shipping agency; ~**makler** chartering broker; ~**provision** freighting commission; ~**tarif** charter rates; ~**vertrag** contract of affreightment, freight contract, charterparty.

befragen *(Meinungsumfrage)* to question, to interview, to [take a] poll, *(Zeugen)* to hear, to interrogate, to examine, to question;
sein Gewissen ~ to consult one's conscience; Sachverständigen ~ to consult an expert.

Befrager [field] interviewer, fieldworker, interrogator.

Befragte *(Meinungsbefragung)* sample.

Befragtengruppe panel, persons reviewed.

Befragter informant, respondent *(Br.)*, interviewee, interrogatee, pollee *(US)*;
~ innerhalb einer ausgewählten Stichprobe sample respondent *(Br.)*.

Befragung *(Meinungsumfrage)* poll, survey, field interview, *(Zeuge)* questioning, hearing, examination, interrogation;
direkte ~ direct examination; im einzelnen festgelegte ~ quantitative interview; gegabelte ~ split ballot; individuelle ~ fieldwork; mündliche ~ oral interview; nachfassende ~ follow-up; telefonische ~ telephone interview;
~ in Form eines mündlichen Gesprächs face-to-face interview; ~ eines beschränkten Personenkreises sample testing; ~ auf dem Postwege mail survey.

Befragungs|einheit interviewing unit; indirekte ~**methode** indirect opinion method; ~**protokoll** account of interrogation; ~**schema** pattern of interrogation; ~**vorschrift** instruction sheet.

befreien to exonerate, to release, to free, to clear, *(von Verbindlichkeiten)* to disengage, *(Volk)* to liberate;
sich von einer Belastung ~ to ease o. s. of a burden; von einem Eid ~ to release from an oath; sich von jds. Einfluß ~ to break free from s. one's influence; sich von unerwünschten Elementen ~ to weed of less desirable people; Gefangenen (gewaltsam) ~ to rescue a prisoner, to deliver out of captivity; aus dem Gefängnis ~ to release from prison; von Gemeindesteuern ~ to derate of local taxes *(Br.)*; von der Haftpflicht ~ to discharge (relieve) from liability; j. aus einer schwierigen Lage ~ to help a lame dog over a stile, to intangle s. o.; sich aus einer schwierigen Lage ~ to extricate o. s. from a difficulty; unterdrücktes Land ~ to free a country from oppression; Land von Banditen ~ to rid a country from bandits; j. von einer Last ~ to free s. o. of a burden; vom Militärdienst ~ to exempt from military service; von einem lästigen Rivalen ~ to rid of a troublesome rival; j. von seinen Schulden ~ to extricate s. o. from debts; Sklaven ~ to emancipate slaves; j. von einer Sorge ~ to free s. o. of a burden; von einer Steuer ~ to exempt from a tax; j. von der Teilnahme ~ to excuse s. o. from attendance; sich von seinen Verbindlichkeiten ~ to rid o. s. from obligations; j. aus den Händen von Verbrechern ~ to rescue a man from bandits; j. von einem Verdacht ~ to purge s. o. from a suspicion; j. von einer Verpflichtung ~ to exonerate s. o. from an obligation; von der Verpflichtung zur Leistung ~ to discharge from performance.

Befreier liberator, emancipator.

befreit free, exempt, quit, *(entschuldigt)* excused;
vom Militärdienst (Wehrdienst) ~ draft-exempt *(US)*; von Steuern ~ tax-exempt, duty-free;
sich ~ fühlen to feel relieved;
~er Vormund general guardian.

Befreiter exempt.

Befreiung liberation, disengagement, discharge, *(Entlastung)* exoneration, *(Gefängnis)* release, *(Steuern)* exemption, *(Strafverfolgung)* immunity, *(Verbindlichkeiten)* discharge, release;
gewaltsame ~ rescue;
~ von der Allmendepflicht inclosure; ~ von der Dividendenbegrenzungsvorschrift exemption from dividend restraints *(Br.)*, dividend freedom *(Br.)*; ~ von der Doppelbesteuerung double-taxation relief *(Br.)*; ~ von einem Ehehindernis marriage dispensation; ~ von der Eintragungspflicht exemption from filing accounts; ~ von einer festgelegten Erbfolge disentail; gewaltsame ~ von Gefangenen jail delivery; ~ von Gemeinde-

steuern derating of local taxes *(Br.)*; ~ **von der Mehrwertsteuer** vat exemption; ~ **vom Militärdienst** exemption from military service; ~ **von Steuern** freedom from tax, exemption of taxation; ~ **eines Volkes** liberation of a nation; ~ **von der Zollrevision des Gepäcks** courtesy of the port *(US)*; ~ **von Steuern bewilligen** to grant exemption.

Befreiungs|anspruch right of indemnity; ~**armee** army of liberation, liberation organization; ~**bestimmungen** *(Steuer)* exemption provisions; ~**bewegung** liberation movement; ~**front** liberation organization; ~**klausel** exemption clause *(Br.)*; ~**krieg** war of independence; ~**methode** *(Doppelbesteuerungsabkommen)* exemption method.

Befremden surprise, astonishment, amazement, displeasure; ~ **ausdrücken** to show marked surprise; **allgemeines** ~ **auslösen** to cause general astonishment.

befremden to take aback, to displease, to seem strange, to strike as odd.

befremdet sein to be astonished (surprised, amazed).

befremdlich odd, queer, strange; ~**es Benehmen** strange behavio(u)r.

befreunden, sich mit etw. to cotton on to s. th., to get accustomed; **sich mit jem.** ~ to make a friend of. s. o., to make friends with s. o.; **sich mit einem Gedanken** ~ to get used to an idea.

befreundet intimate, friendly; ~ **sein** to be friends with; **eng** ~ **sein** to hobnob; **mit jem. gut** ~ **sein** to be on good terms (intimately acquainted) with s. o.; **mit jem. intim** ~ **sein** to rub noses with s. o.; ~**e Familie** friends of ours; ~**e Firma** business correspondent; ~**es Land** friendly nation.

befrieden to pacify, to appease, to quiet.

befriedigen to satisfy, *(bezahlen)* to pay off, to give satisfaction, *(Nachfrage)* to meet; **schwer zu** ~ hard to please; **Anspruch** ~ to satisfy a claim, to comply with a request; **Bedürfnisse** ~ to supply the needs; **bevorzugt** ~ to prefer; **jeden Geschmack** ~ to suit every taste; **seine Gläubiger** ~ to satisfy (meet the claims of) one's creditors; **seine Gläubiger im Vergleichswege** ~ to compound with one's creditors; **Gläubigeranspruch voll** ~ to make satisfaction of a debt; **seinen Hunger** ~ to satisfy one's hunger; **jds. Launen** ~ to gratify s. one's whims; **Nachfrage** ~ to meet (satisfy) the demand; **seine Neugier** ~ to yield to (appease s. one's) curiosity; **sich aus einem Vermögensstück** ~ to satisfy a debt out of a property; **j. voll** ~ to pay s. o. in full; **Wissensdurst eines Kindes** ~ to gratify a child's thirst for knowledge; **Zahlungsansprüche** ~ to meet demands for payment.

befriedigend satisfactory, *(Prüfung)* passing; **Examen** ~ **bestehen** to get a pass in an examination; **alle Teile** ~**e Abmachung** mutually satisfactory arrangement; **Verhandlungen zu einem** ~**en Abschluß bringen** to bring negotiations to a satisfactory conclusion; ~**es Gefühl** gratifying feeling; ~**en Nachweis erbringen** to establish to the satisfaction; ~**e Note** a passing grade *(US)*.

befriedigt satisfied, pleased; ~ **aussehen** to look pleased with o. s.; **sich** ~ **über etw. äußern** to express one's satisfaction about s. th.; **von seiner Arbeit** ~ **sein** to find satisfaction in one's work; **sehr** ~ **sein** to be very much gratified; ~ **sein zu wissen** to have the gratification of knowing.

Befriedigung satisfaction, gratification, content, *(Bezahlung)* payment; **zur** ~ **der Gläubiger** for the purpose of paying creditors; **abgesonderte** ~ *(im Konkurs)* preferential treatment (payment); **anteilmäßige** ~ prorata settlement, proportionate share; **aufrichtige** ~ unfeigned satisfaction; **bevorzugte** ~ preferential payment, prior satisfaction; **quotenmäßige** ~ payment pro rata; **teilweise** ~ payment in part; **vollständige** ~ settlement in full; **vorzugsweise** ~ preferential assignment; ~ **eines Anspruchs** satisfaction of a claim; ~ **der Gläubiger** satisfaction of (paying off) creditors; ~ **eines Gläubigers auf Grund eines Urteils** satisfaction of a judgment; ~ **seiner Wünsche** satisfaction of one's desires; **güterwirtschaftliche** ~ **finden** to be satisfied by more goods; **volle** ~ **in seinem Beruf finden** to find complete satisfaction in one's work; ~ **gewähren** to render satisfaction, to respond; **vorzugsweise** ~ **gewähren** to give a preference; **Anspruch auf bevorzugte** ~ **haben** to be entitled to preference; ~ **der Gläubiger vereiteln** to defeat the creditors.

Befriedigungsvorrecht preferential right.

Befriedung pacification, regional neutralization.

Befriedungs|aktion *(mil.)* containing action; ~**politik** appeasement policy.

befristen to set a time limit (deadline, *US*); **Lieferzeit** ~ to stipulate a time for delivery; **Zahlungsaufforderung** ~ to grant (accord) a respite.

befristet limited, timed, for a fixed time, terminable; **zeitlich** ~ limited in time; ~ **anlegen** to invest at short notice; ~**e Einlage** *(bei Bank)* time deposit; ~**es Eintrittsrecht** option; ~**e Forderung** deferred claim; ~**er Kredit** time loan; ~**er Scheck** memorandum check *(US)*; ~**e Spareinlagen** time deposits; ~**e Verbindlichkeiten** time liabilities; ~**er Wechsel** sight draft.

Befristung postponement, deferment, terminability.

befruchten to fertilize, to fecundate, *(künstlich)* to inseminate; **Diskussion** ~ to enhance (enrich) the discussion.

Befruchtung, künstliche insemination.

befugen to authorize, to warrant.

Befugnis *(Berechtigung)* faculty, warrant, authorization, *(Vollmacht)* authority, power, *(Zulassung)* licence, *(Zuständigkeit)* competence, jurisdiction; **außerhalb der** ~**se** ultra vires; **gesetzliche** ~ statutory authority; **hoheitsrechtliche** ~**se** sovereign powers; **originäre (aus der Rechtsnatur sich ergebende)** ~ inherent power *(US)*; **rechtsgeschäftliche** ~ disposing capacity; **satzungsmäßige** ~**se** corporate powers *(US)*; **stillschweigend zuerkannte** ~ implied power; **zugewiesene** ~**se** delegated powers; **einem Gericht zugewiesene** ~**se** definite powers of a court; **unbeschränkte** ~ **zur Einsetzung eines Begünstigten** *(Treuhänder)* general power of appointment; ~ **zu Ermessensentscheidungen** discretionary jurisdiction; ~ **der Etatstitelübertragung** virement; ~ **zur Gestellung von Sicherheiten** capacity to charge security; ~ **zur Kreditaufnahme** *(Vorstand)* borrowing power; ~**se des Kurators einer Stiftung** power of visitation; **sich amtliche** ~**se anmaßen** to usurp authority; ~ **besitzen** to be authorized; **innerhalb seiner** ~**se bleiben** to keep within one's proper sphere; **in jds.** ~ **eingreifen** to encroach upon s. one's functions; ~**se einschränken** to restrain powers; **jem. die** ~ **erteilen** to authorize s. o.; ~ **festlegen** to prescribe powers; **außerhalb (in Überschreitung) seiner** ~ **handeln** to act beyond the scope of one's authority, *(Vorstand)* to act ultra vires; **außerhalb von jds.** ~ **liegen** to lie beyond s. one's competence, to be outside the terms of s. one's reference; **im Rahmen der satzungsmäßigen** ~ **liegen** to be intra (within) vires; **seine** ~**se überschreiten** to act beyond the scope of one's authority, to exceed one's powers (authority); **satzungsgemäße** ~ **überschreiten** to be ultra (outside) vires; ~**se auf j. übertragen** to delegate powers (confer authority) upon s. o.; ~**überschreitung** excess of power.

befugt empowered, authorized, entitled, *(zugelassen)* licensed, *(zuständig)* competent, *(Vorstand)* intra vires; **nicht** ~ incompetent; ~ **sein** to have authority; **allein** ~ **sein** to have sole power; **nicht zu einer Auskunft** ~ **sein** not to be authorized to give information; **rechtlich** ~ **sein** to be in capacity; ~**er Beamter** competent public officer.

Befugter duly authorized person.

Befund findings, *(Test)* result; **ohne** ~ no evidence; **ärztlicher** ~ medical report; **einer Arbeit einen wissenschaftlichen** ~ **zugrundelegen** to base one's thesis on scientific data.

befürchten to be afraid of, to have fears; **das Schlimmste** ~ to fear (be prepared for) the worst.

Befürchtung fear, apprehension; ~**en hegen** to have fears; ~**en um jds. Sicherheit hegen** to feel apprehension for s. one's safety; **jds.** ~**en zerstreuen** to dispel s. one's fears.

befürworten to recommend, to advocate, to support, to promote, to sponsor, to endorse, to back; **Antrag** ~ to second (support) a motion, to speak in support of a motion; **jds. Bewerbung** ~ to back s. one's application; **Entschließung** ~ to support a resolution; **Ernennung** ~ to advocate an appointment; **Gesetzentwurf** ~ to sponsor a bill; **Kandidaten** ~ to support (back up) a candidate; **Volksbefragung** ~ to advocate a referendum.

befürwortend with a favo(u)rable recommendation.

Befürworter advocate, supporter, furtherer, seconder, subscriber; **aufrichtiger** ~ devout supporter; **unbedingter** ~ thick-and-thin advocate; ~ **der Abwertung** advocate of devaluation; ~ **einer konzilianten**

Auslandspolitik im Außenministerium State Department Beavers *(US)*; ~ **des Gemeinsamen Marktes** Common Marketeer; ~ **der freien Marktwirtschaft** free enterpriser; ~ **einer harten Politik** hard-liner;
zum ~ **werden** to enter the list as an advocate.
Befürwortung recommendation, promotion, advocacy, endorsement, backing, support;
in ~ **von** in support of;
~ **eines Antrags** support of a motion; ~ **eines Bewerbers** backing up of a candidate;
jem. eine ~ **schreiben** to write on s. one's behalf.
Befürwortungsschreiben letter of recommendation, letters recommendatory.
begabt able, talented, gifted, endowed;
schwach ~ poorly gifted; **überdurchschnittlich** ~ accelerated; **mathematisch** ~ **sein** to have a gift for mathematics; **für Sprachen** ~ **sein** to have a gift for languages;
~**er Schüler** apt (bright) pupil.
Begabten|förderung upgrading of talented students; ~**prüfung** intelligence test; ~**reserve** unexploited talents, untapped educational potential.
Begabung endowment, gift, capacity, aptitude, talent, instinct, flair;
durchschnittliche ~ moderate capacities; **erfinderische** ~ inventive faculty; **geistige** ~ intellectual character; **manuelle** ~ manual aptitude; **mittelmäßige** ~ medium capacity; **natürliche** ~ natural selection (gift); **persönliche** ~ talent, personal capital, qualification; **schauspielerische** ~ histrionic ability;
~ **für Verwaltungsaufgaben** good administrative ability;
seine natürliche ~ **durch Lernen fördern** to improve one's natural gifts by study; ~ **für Sprachen haben** to have a gift for languages; **seine** ~ **frühzeitig erkennen lassen** to give early indications of one's talent.
begangen, nicht *(Tat)* uncommitted.
begaunern to do in, to cheat, to swindle.
begebbar negotiable, endorsable, transferable, *(börsenfähig)* marketable;
nicht ~ not transferable, unnegotiable, nonnegotiable;
~**es Akkreditiv** negotiable credit; ~**es Wertpapier** negotiable (marketable) instrument.
Begebbarkeit negotiability, transferability, *(Börsenfähigkeit)* marketability.
Begebbarkeitsklausel negotiable words.
begeben to negotiate, to value, *(girieren)* to indorse, to endorse, *(übertragen)* to transfer;
Aktien ~ to market securities; **Anleihe** ~ to issue (float) a loan; **Anleihe an ein Konsortium** ~ to put a loan into the hands of a syndicate; **sich eines Anspruchs** ~ to relinquish a claim; **sich an die Arbeit** ~ to set to work; **sich wieder an die Arbeit** ~ to return to work; **sich in ärztliche Behandlung** ~ to place o. s. under medical treatment; **sich zeitig zu Bett** ~ to go to bed early; **sich zu einer Einheit** ~ to join one's unit; **Emmission** ~ to dispose of an issue; **sich in Gefahr** ~ to expose o. s. to danger; **sich aufs Glatteis** ~ to skate on thin ice; **sich nach Hause** ~ to make for home; **sich nach Paris** ~ to proceed to Paris; **sich eines Rechtes** ~ to waive (abandon, forgo, renounce) a right; **sich auf eine Reise** ~ to start on one's journey; **sich unter jds. Schutz** ~ to place o. s. under s. one's protection; **Wechsel** ~ to negotiate a bill; **wieder** ~ to reissue;
tatsächlich ~ *(Wertpapiere)* actually outstanding;
~**es Kapital** issued capital.
Begebender indorser, endorser.
Begebenheit event, occurrence, incidence, happening.
Begebung issue, negotiation;
bedingte ~ conditional delivery; **gültige** ~ valid delivery;
~ **von Aktien** issue of shares (stocks, *US*); ~ **einer Anleihe** issue (floating, flotation, negotiation) of a loan; ~ **von Obligationen** issue of loan capital; ~ **von Rechten** waiver of rights; ~ **eines Wechsels** negotiation of a bill of exchange; ~ **von Wertpapieren** sale of securities.
Begebungsaviso advice of negotiation.
begebungsfähig negotiable.
Begebungs|fähigkeit negotiability, negotiable character; ~**konsortium** issuing syndicate; ~**kosten** issuing expenses; ~**kurs** issue price; ~**recht** power to negotiate; ~**tag** day of issue; ~**vertrag** transfer deed; **für** ~**zwecke** for the purpose of negotiation.
begegnen to meet, to come across;
allgemeiner Ablehnung ~ to meet with general disapproval; **einem Angriff** ~ to counter an attack; **jem. feindlich** ~ to treat s. o. badly, to give s. o. a hostile reception; **jem. freundlich** ~ to be nice to s. o.; **einer Gefahr mit Umsicht** ~ to meet a danger with circumspection; **jem. höflich** ~ to treat s. o. with politeness; **der gesteigerten Nachfrage** ~ to meet the increased demand; **Schwierigkeiten** ~ to obviate difficulties; **unhöflich** ~ to disoblige; **jem. zufällig** ~ to stumble upon s. o., to meet s. o. by chance; **jem. mit Zurückhaltung** ~ to receive s. o. with reserve.
Begegnung meeting, encounter;
flüchtige ~ brief encounter.
begehbar walkable, passable;
~**er Schrank** walk-in closet.
Begehen|eines Festes celebration of a feast; ~ **eines Verbrechens** commission (perpetration) of a crime.
begehen *(Fest)* to celebrate, *(Flur)* to inspect, to visit, *(Verbrechen)* to perpetrate, to commit;
Diebstahl an öffentlichem Eigentum ~ to steal public property; **Dummheit** ~ to do s. th. foolish; **unerlaubte Handlung** ~ to commit a tort; **Irrtum** ~ to make an error; **Konkursdelikt** ~ to commit an act of bankruptcy; **Selbstmord** ~ to commit suicide; **Taktlosigkeit** ~ to drop a brick; **Verbrechen** ~ to commit (perpetrate) a crime; **Weihnachtsfest traditionell** ~ to celebrate Christmas in the old style.
Begeher einer Amtsanmaßung usurper of a public office.
Begehren wish, desire, demand, request.
begehren to seek, to desire, to covet;
j. zur Frau ~ to seek s. one's hand in marriage; **heftig** ~ to long (crave) for.
begehrlich covetous, desirous, longing, *(lüstern)* lewd, lustful, lascivious;
~**e Blicke auf etw. werfen** to look with greedy eyes at s. th.
begehrt requested, inquired for, sought, in demand (request), in favo(u)r, *(Geld)* scarce;
wenig ~ dull, in little demand;
~ **sein** to be in great favo(u)r; **lebhaft** ~ **sein** to be in brisk demand; **sehr** ~ **sein** to be in great demand (request), to have the call; **wenig** ~ **sein** to be hard to sell, to be in little demand (request); **gesellschaftlich überall** ~ **werden** to be a pet of society;
~**er Artikel** popular line; ~**es Fotomodell** model much sought after.
Begehung commitment, perpetration;
~ **eines Diebstahls** commission of a theft; ~ **einer Flur** inspection of a field, perambulation; ~ **einer unerlaubten Handlung** commission of a tort; ~ **einer Übertretung** commission of an offence; ~ **eines Verbrechens** perpetration of a crime.
Begehungsort place of commission, place of crime, venue.
begeistern to rouse enthusiasm, to fire;
j. ~ to turn s. o. on *(fam.)*; **sich** ~ *(fig.)* to take fire; **sich für j.** ~ to go into raptures over s. o.; **Publikum** ~ to carry the audience away; **sich für eine Sache** ~ to be on a new kick; **j. zu einer Tat** ~ to inspire s. o. to action; **sich übermäßig** ~ to go overboard.
begeisternde Rede rousing speech.
begeistert enthusiastic;
leicht ~ easily moved;
~ **sein to be delighted** (enchanted); **nicht gerade** ~ **sein** to be less than eager to do;
~**er Anhänger** enthusiast, fan, fervent supporter; **jem. einen** ~**en Empfang bereiten** to give s. o. an enthusiastic welcome.
Begeisterung fire, enthusiasm;
in der ersten ~, **im ersten Ansturm der** ~ in the first glow of enthusiasm (flush of victory);
mäßige ~ temperate enthusiasm;
mit ~ **annehmen** to accept enthusiastically; ~ **auslösen** to set the senses afire; **jds.** ~ **bremsen (dämpfen)** to contain s. one's enthusiasm, to throw cold water on s. th.; **in** ~ **geraten** to go into raptures; ~ **hervorrufen** to radiate enthusiasm; **abkühlend auf jds.** ~ **reagieren** to quench s. one's enthusiasm; **von** ~ **erfüllt sein** to be fired with enthusiasm; **voller** ~ **über j. sprechen** to sing s. one's praise, to speak in glowing terms of s. o.; **etw. ohne** ~ **tun** to do s. th. in a half-hearted way; **sich vor** ~ **überschlagen** to go overboard *(fig.)*; **j. in** ~ **versetzen** to throw s. o. into raptures.
Begeisterungs|ausbruch outburst of enthusiasm; ~**fähigkeit der Jugend** fire of youth; ~**sturm** flame of enthusiasm; **j. zu** ~**stürmen hinreißen** to carry s. o. off his feet.
Begierde ardent desire, appetite;
fleischliche ~**n** lusts of the flesh;
~ **nach Lob** craving for praise;
sündhafte ~**n erwecken** to arouse covetous desires.
begierig desirous, eager, keen, itching;
~, **j. zu sehen** anxious to see s. o.

begießen, sich die Nase to wet one's whistle.

Beginn beginning, inception, startup, start, outset, commencement, initiation, threshold, *(Steuertarif)* threshold, *(Verhandlung)* opening;
von ~ an from the beginning; **zu ~** at the start; **zu ~ seiner Laufbahn** at the outset of his career; **zu ~ der Vorstellung** when the curtain rises;
suggestiver ~ *(Interview)* lead-in;
~ des Entladens breaking bulk; **~ der Hauptverhandlung** opening of the trial; **~ einer Krankheit** onset of a disease; **~ einer Laufbahn** commencement of a career; **~ der Laufzeit einer Police** commencement of a policy; **~ einer neuen Politik** adoption of a new policy; **~ des Rechtsstreits** litis contestation; **~ des Risikos** *(Versicherung)* attachment of risk; **~ des Semesters** beginning of the term; **~ der Versicherungslaufzeit** inception date of policy; **~ der Vorstellung 8 Uhr** performance begins at 8 o'clock;
am ~ seiner Laufzeit stehen to be at the threshold of one's career.

beginnen to begin, to start, to commence, to initiate, to undertake, *(Versicherungsrisiko)* to attach;
seine Arbeit ~ to set to work; **Gespräch ~** to enter into a conversation; **bei Börseneröffnung mit höheren Kursen ~** to advance from the start in brisk dealings; **neues Leben ~** to turn over a new leaf; **von neuem ~** *(Gemeinschuldner)* to start again after a failure; **Rechtsstreit ~** to commence an action, to initiate legal proceedings; **Rede mit einem Zitat ~** to open a speech with a quotation; **um 8 Uhr ~** to commence at 8 o'clock; **Verhandlungen ~** to start (initiate) negotiations; **Vorstellung ~** to ring up.

beglaubigen to attest, to certify, to certificate, to docket, to prove, to docket, to homologate, *(Gesandten)* to accredit, *(Kontoauszug)* to verify, *(Unterschrift)* to certify;
Abschrift ~ to attest a copy; **amtlich ~** to legalize, to exemplify; **gerichtlich ~** to exemplify, to make an attested copy; **Gesandten bei einer Regierung ~** to accredit an ambassador; **notariell ~** to notarize, to attest; **öffentlich ~** to authenticate; **mittels Schlüsselzahl ~** to authenticate by keyword; **Testament ~** to prove a will;
seine Unterschrift ~ lassen to have one's signature legalized; **Urkunde ~ lassen** to have a document authenticated.

beglaubigend certificatory.

Beglaubigender attestor.

beglaubigt authenticated, attested, certified, proved, verified, accredited, *(Unterschrift)* witnessed;
amtlich (öffentlich) ~ witnessed by official means, legally attested, legalized, exemplified; **nicht ~** unaccredited; **notariell ~** certified (attested) by a notary, notarized;
notariell ~ sein to be authenticated by seal;
~e Abschrift attested (certified, exemplified) copy; **amtlich ~e Abschrift** office copy; **notariell ~e Abschrift** notarized copy; **~e Abtretung** certified transfer; **~er Nettoverkauf** *(Zeitung)* certified net sales; **~er Scheck** certified (guaranteed) check *(US)* (cheque, *Br.*); **~e Unterschrift** attested signature; **~e Vollmacht** authenticated power of attorney.

Beglaubigung authentication, verification, certification, acknowledgement, attestation, caption, attestation;
zur ~ dessen in witness whereof (thereof); **zur ~ der Echtheit** in pledge of good faith;
amtliche ~ legalization, exemplification, certifying, certification; **eidliche ~** verification; **notarielle ~** authentic (notarial) act;
~ einer Abschrift certificate of a copy; **~ eines Botschafters** accreditation of an ambassador; **~ der Unterschrift** verification (attestation) of signature; **~ von Urkunden** attestation of deeds;
der öffentlichen ~ bedürfen to have to be legalized (certified); **einem Botschafter die ~ erteilen** to accredit an ambassador.

Beglaubigungs|brief letter certificatory; **~formel** attestation (testing) clause; **~formular** *(Aktien)* verification form; **~gebühr** legalization fee; **~klausel** attestation (testing, witnessing) clause; **mit der ~klausel versehen** to attach authentication; **~papiere** identification papers; **~schreiben** certificate of authentication, *(dipl.)* letter of credence, credentials; **~schreiben eines Gesandten entgegennehmen** to receive a foreign minister; **sein ~schreiben überreichen** to present one's credentials; **~stempel** seal; **~vermerk** certificate of acknowledgement, attestation clause, countersign.

begleichen to quit, to pay back, to settle, to discharge, to pay, to meet, to clear, to liquidate;
Konto ~ to square (clear) an account; **Rechnung ~** to meet a bill, to settle an account; **Rechnung vollständig ~** to settle a bill in full; **Rückstände ~** to pay up arrears; **Schulden ~** to liquidate (discharge, settle) debts; **vollständig ~** to settle in full.

Begleichung payment, settlement, clearance, satisfaction, liquidation;
zur ~ von in discharge of; **zur teilweisen ~ des noch ausstehenden Betrages** in part payment of the outstanding balance;
restlose ~ settlement in full;
~ der Miete payment of rent; **~ einer Rechnung** settlement of an account, payment of a bill; **~ von Schulden** liquidation of debts; **~ von Verbindlichkeiten** discharge of liabilities.

Begleit|adresse accompanying address, declaration form, dispatch note *(Br.)*; **~band** companion volume; **~blatt** summary sheet; **~brief** accompanying (cover[ing]) letter, *(bei Schriftstück)* letter of transmittal, transmittal letter.

begleiten to accompany, to go with, to follow, *(Anstandsdame)* to chaperone, *(Polizei)* to escort;
j. zum Bahnhof ~ to see s. o. off; **j. nach Hause ~** to escort (see) s. o. home; **Dame nach Hause ~** to squire a lady; **öffentlich ~** to take about *(coll.)*; **mit einem großen Polizeiaufgebot ~** to escort by a large body of policemen (police complement, *US*); **Reisegesellschaft ~** to escort a party; **j. ein Stück Weges ~** to set s. o. on his way.

begleitend attendant.

Begleiter companion, attendant, attender, *(Anstandsdame)* chaperone, *(Begleitperson)* escort;
ständiger ~ appendage, running mate.

Begleiterscheinung concomitant phenomenon, implication, attendant;
unangenehme ~en discomforts;
~en eines Krieges implications of a war;
~en der Wohlstandsgesellschaft sein to accompany the affluent society.

begleitet escorted, attended;
von Erfolg ~ successful.

Begleit|fahrzeug escort; **~flugzeug** escort plane, air escort; **~jäger** escort fighter; **~karte** accompanying form; **~kommando** covering party; **~mannschaft** escort; **~musik** background music; **höfliche ~notiz** compliment slip; **~papiere** accompanying documents; **~person** *(Post)* mailguard *(Br.)*; **~personal** *(Zug)* train staff (crew, *US*); **~personen** companions; **~schein** covering (consignment) note, delivery note (slip), bill of delivery, *(bei Fahrzeug)* waybill; **zollamtlicher ~schein** customs permit, bond note; **~schiff** escort vessel, convoy ship; **~schreiben** accompanying (covering) letter; **~schutz** escort; **~umstände** concomitant (attending, surrounding) circumstances; **aufgrund von ~umständen beweisen** to circumstantiate.

Begleitung attendance, attendants, retinue, escort, company, *(König, Präsidenten)* entourage, *(mil.)* convoy, escort, *(Musik)* accompaniment;
in ~ seiner Sekretärin accompanied by his secretary;
jem. seine ~ anbieten to offer to accompany s. o.; **in jds. ~ sein** to be in s. one's company.

Begleit|wagen escort waggon *(US)*; **~zettel** bill of delivery, waybill, *(Post)* post bill, dispatch note *(Br.)*, *(Zoll)* transire.

beglichen settled.

beglücken, j. to make s. o. happy, to bless s. o.;
j. mit einem Besuch ~ to favo(u)r s. o. with a visit.

beglückt happy, delighted.

beglückwünschen to congratulate, to felicitate;
sich ~ to hug o. s., to cross o. s.

Beglückwünschung gratulation.

begnadet, mit etw. ~ sein to be blessed with s. th.;
~er Künstler highly gifted artist.

begnadigen to show clemency, to [grant] pardon, to reprieve, to respite, *(Amnestie)* to amnesty;
j. zu lebenslänglichem Zuchthaus ~ to commute a death sentence into one of penal servitude for life.

begnadigt werden to be granted a pardon, to receive pardon (quarter).

Begnadigter pardoned.

Begnadigung pardon, reprieve, respite, mercy, *(Amnestie)* amnesty;
bedingte ~ conditional pardon; **unbeschränkte ~** absolute pardon; **volle ~** full pardon;
~ ablehnen to deny a pardon.

Begnadigungs|akt act of clemency; **~ausschuß** clemency board, Board of Pardons *(US)*; **~befugnis** prerogative of mercy *(Br.)*.

begnadigungsfähig remissible.

Begnadigungs|fähigkeit remissibility; ~**gesuch** petition for a reprieve; ~**gesuch einreichen** to petition for mercy; ~**kommission** clemency board, Board of Pardons *(US)*; ~**recht** power of pardon, prerogative of pardon *(Br.)*; ~**recht ausüben** to be vested with power to pardon.

begnügen, sich mit etw. to content o. s. with s. th., to settle for s. th.; **sich mit der Hälfte** ~ to make do with half the amount; **sich mit wenigem** ~ to be content with little;
sich damit ~ **müssen** to have to make shift with it.

begraben to bury, to inter, to entomb;
etw. ~ *(fig.)* to draw the curtain over s. th., to wipe s. th. off the slate; **j. mit militärischen Ehren** ~ to give s. o. a military funeral; **jds. Hoffnungen** ~ to shatter s. one's hopes; **das Kriegsbeil** ~ *(fig.)* to bury the hatchet; **seine Meinungsverschiedenheiten** ~ to sink one's differences; **etw. in seinen Papieren** ~ to find s. th. buried in one's papers; **Plan in Vergessenheit** ~ to sink a plan in oblivion; **auf hoher See** ~ to bury at sea; **seinen Streit** ~ to end one's quarrel;
auf dem Friedhof ~ **liegen** to be buried in the cemetery; **lebendig** ~ **sein** to be buried alive;
Du kannst dich ~ **lassen** go and hang yourself.

Begräbnis funeral, burial, interment, entombment, committal;
christliches ~ Christian burial; **feierliches** ~ solemn burial; **militärisches** ~ military funeral;
das ~ **hat in aller Stille stattgefunden** the funeral has been private; **an jds.** ~ **teilnehmen** to attend s. one's funeral; ~ **verschieben** to postpone a burial;
~**feier,** ~**feierlichkeiten** obsequies, funeral ceremonies; ~**kasse** burial society; ~**kosten** funeral cost (expenses); ~**ort** cemetery; ~**platz** burial ground (place, spot); ~**riten** funeral rites; ~**schein** burial permit *(US)*; ~**schulden** death debts; ~**stätte** burial (resting) place, grave, burial vault; ~**vorkehrungen** funeral arrangements; ~**zuschuß** funeral benefit.

Begreifen uptake, comprehension, understanding.

begreifen to comprehend, to understand, to grasp, to conceive, to take in;
Idee ~ to conceive an idea; **in sich** ~ to imply; **plötzlich** ~ to realize suddenly; **Pointe nicht** ~ to miss a point; **Sache** ~ to get the picture; **schnell** ~ to be quick in (on) the uptake; **schwer** ~ to be slow on the uptake; **schwer zu** ~ hard (difficult) to understand.

begreiflich comprehensible, understandable, apprehensible, intelligible;
jem. ~ **machen** to make s. o. understand; **jem. die Vorteile eines Unternehmens** ~ **machen** to point out clearly the advantage of a project to s. o.;
leicht ~**e Tatsache** easily understood fact; ~**es Verlangen** natural desire.

begrenzen to confine, to define, *(Geschwindigkeit)* to limit, to restrict;
seine Interessensgebiete ~ to circumscribe one's interests; **[räumlich]** ~ to terminate; **Redezeit** ~ to limit the time allotted to each speaker; **Spesenaufwand** ~ to put a stop to expenditure; **zeitlich** ~ to set a time limit.

begrenzt limited, restricted, confined, close, narrow;
zeitlich ~ terminable;
~ **haltbar** perishable;
~ **sein** to be restricted (limited); **in seiner Zeit** ~ **sein** to be limited in time; ~ **werden** to be bounded;
~**er Absatzmarkt** limited (narrow) market; ~**e Anwendung** restricted application; ~**e Auflagenhöhe** limited edition; ~**es Fassungsvermögen** limited capacity; ~**e Geschwindigkeit** restricted speed; ~**e Haftung** limited liability; ~**er Horizont** narrow (restricted) horizon; ~**en Kredit genießen** to enjoy restricted credit; ~**e Mittel** limited means; ~**e Redezeit** allotted time; ~**e Vollmacht** limited authority; ~ **haltbare Waren** nondurable goods, nondurables; **über ein** ~**es Wissen verfügen** to have scanty knowledge.

Begrenzung limit[ation], restriction, boundary, terminability, circumscription;
zeitliche ~ limit of time, time limit;
~ **eines Besitzrechtes** limitation; ~ **des Bevölkerungszuwachses** population limitation; **jährliche** ~ **des Dividendenanstiegs auf 10%** 10% a year limitation on dividend increases; ~ **der Fernsehwahlkosten** limit on television spending in campaigns; ~ **auf eine Fluglinie** single destination; ~ **der Geschwindigkeit** speed limit; ~ **der Haftung** limitation of liability; ~ **der Kinderzahl** family limitation; ~ **der Ladung** loading gauge; ~ **der Mitgliederzahl (Mitgliedschaft)** limitation of membership, membership limitation; ~ **der atomaren Rüstung** nuclear arms control.

Begrenzungs|abkommen auf dem Gebiet strategischer Waffen strategic arms limitation agreement; ~**bake** boundary beacon; ~**feuer** boundary lighting; ~**leuchte** side light, side marker *(US)*; ~**licht** *(Auto)* position light; **seitliches** ~**licht** *(Flugzeug)* clearance light; ~**linie** boundary line.

Begriff idea, term, notion, concept, *(Werbung)* conception;
im ~ **zu** on the edge, on the point of; **nach allgemein gültigen** ~**en** according to common standards; **nach herkömmlichen** ~**en** according to received notions; **nach menschlichen** ~**en** humanly speaking; **schwer von** ~ inapt, slow in the uptake;
abstrakter ~ abstraction; **allgemeiner** ~ universal concept; **bedeutungsgleicher** ~ synonym; **juristischer** ~ legal term; **relativer** ~ comparative term;
~**e des Absatzwesens** marketing terms;
hohen ~ **von seinen Pflichten haben** to have a high conception of one's duties; **keinen** ~ **von etw. haben** to have no idea of s. th.; **klaren** ~ **von etw. haben**to have a clear conception of s. th.; **merkwürdige** ~**e von der Arbeit haben** to have a curious idea of work; **ungefähren** ~ **von etw. haben** to have a vague notion of s. th.; **sich einen** ~ **von etw. machen** to imagine (visualize) s. th.; **sich einen falschen** ~ **über jds. Vermögenslage machen** to have a wrong estimate about s. one's financial position; **sich einen richtigen** ~ **machen** to form a true notion of s. th.; **schwer von** ~ **sein** to be slow in the uptake (of wit), to be dull of comprehension, to be dull-witted; **im** ~ **sein, ein Vermögen zu machen** to be on the high road to fortune; **im** ~ **stehen, abzureisen** to be on the point of departure; **falschen** ~ **verwenden** to misuse a term;
das geht über meine ~**e** that's beyond me; **das übersteigt alle** ~**e** that beats everything.

begriffen, mitten in der Arbeit in the midst of one's work; **im Aufbruch** ~ on the point of leaving; **in der Ausführung** ~ under way, in the making; **im Bau** ~ being built; **in der Entwicklung** ~ in process of formation; **auf einer Reise** ~ on a journey; **in Reparatur** ~ under repair; **in Verhandlungen** ~ engaged in negotiations; **auf dem Weg zum Erfolg** ~ on the road to success.

begrifflich notional, conceptual, abstract.

Begriffsbestimmung definition;
elastische ~ elastic definition; **zwingende** ~ absolute definition.

Begriffs|bildung formation of a concept, concept formation; ~**definitionen** glossary of terms; ~**erläuterung** explanation of terms.

begriffsstutzig dull, slow-witted, hard-thinking.

Begriffsumfang terminal quantity.

Begriffsvermögen understanding, comprehension, comprehensiveness;
über mein ~ over my head, beyond me;
über jds. ~ **gehen** to be beyond s. one's depth; ~ **der Zuhörer übersteigen** to be above the heads of an audience.

Begriffsverwirrung, an ~ **leiden** to be a little confused.

begründen *(Geschäft)* to found, to establish, to set up, *(Gesellschaft)* to float, *(motivieren)* to warrant, to motivate, *(substantiieren)* to give the reasons, to set forth, to substantiate;
Anklage ~ to substantiate a charge; **Anspruch näher** ~ to substantiate a claim; **Antrag** ~ to speak in support of a motion; **ausführlich** ~ to give detailed reasons; **Dynastie** ~ to be the founder of a dynasty; **Entscheidung** ~ to state the reasons for a decision; **späteren Erfolg** ~ to lay the foundation for future success; **Gerichtsstand** ~ to establish jurisdiction; **Haftung** ~ to create liability; **neuen Lehrstuhl** ~ to establish a new chair; **Mietverhältnis** ~ to enter into a lease; **Motiv** ~ to predicate a motive; **näher** ~ to substantiate; **Recht** ~ to constitute a right; **seinen Ruf** ~ to lay the foundations for one's reputation; **seine Sache** ~ to make out one's case; **Schadensersatzanspruch** ~ to sound in damages; **Teilhaberschaft** ~ to organize a partnership; **Treuhandverhältnis** ~ to create a trust; **Urteil** ~ to give (state) the reasons for a judgment; **Vermutung** ~ to establish (raise) a presumption; **Verpflichtung** ~ to create an obligation; **seinen Wohnsitz** ~ to elect domicile at a place, to establish a domicile.

begründend constituting.

Begründer founder, promoter, originator, starter;
~ **des Reichtums** founding father.

begründet founded, substantiated, *(berechtigt)* legitimate, justified;
nicht ~ unfounded; **schlecht** ~ ill-founded; **vertraglich** ~ founded on contract;
gesetzlich ~ **sein** to derive its sanction; **nicht** ~ **sein** *(Anspruch)* to have no merits; **rechtlich und sachlich** ~ **sein** to be good in law and in fact;

~er Anspruch legitimate claim; **~e Rechte** vested rights; **~er Verdacht** well-founded suspicion; **~e Zweifel** reasonable doubts.

Begründung foundation, establishment, *(Beweisführung)* argumentation, *(Motivierung)* motivation, reasons, arguments, ground;
mit der ~ on the ground; **ohne jede ~** without giving any reasons; **zur ~ von** in support of;
bestechende ~ specious reasoning; **eingehende ~** detailed reasons; **nähere ~** substantiation; **rechtliche ~** legal arguments; **schlüssige ~** conclusive argument, cause shown; **schriftliche ~** reasons in writing; **schwache ~** shaky arguments; **wenig stichhaltige ~** arguments of little substance;
~ eines Anspruchs substantiation of a claim; **~ einer Behauptung** substantiation of a statement; **~ einer Berufung** reasons for an appeal; **~ einer Dynastie** foundation of a dynasty; **~ für angeforderte Etatsmittel** justification for budgetary means; **~ von Gebräuchen** institution of customs; **~ eines Gerichtsstandes** establishment of jurisdiction; **~ eines Gesellschaftsverhältnisses** establishment of a partnership; **~ eines Gesetzes** preamble of a law; **erstmalige ~ eines Grundstücksrechts** original conveyance; **~ der Haftpflicht** creation of liabilities; **~ einer Lebensstellung** settlement; **~ eines Nutzungsrechtes** raising a use, creation of a licence; **~ eines Rechts** constitution of a right; **~ eines Schuldverhältnisses** creation of an obligation; **schriftliche ~ eines Treuhandverhältnisses** declaration of trust (use); **~ eines Urteils** reasons adduced, opinion of the court, grounds for a judgment; **~ einer Verordnung** preamble of a decree; **~ eines Versprechens** raising a promise; **~ eines Vertreterverhältnisses** creation of agency; **~ seines Wohnsitzes** establishment of residence;
gute ~ bereithalten to have good reasons ready; **~ für seine Entscheidung geben** to state one's reasons for a decision; **~ für etw. vorbringen** to advance arguments for s. th.; **~ vortragen** to state a case.

begrüßen to greet, *(auf einer Tagung)* to welcome;
j. ~ to howdy s. o.; **j. erfurchtsvoll ~** to touch s. o. forelock; **j. freundlich ~** to make s. o. welcome; **j. mit Handschlag ~** to shake hands with s. o.; **Vorschlag wärmstens ~** to welcome a suggestion warmly.

Begrüßung salutation, salute, greeting, welcome;
übliche ~ conventional greeting;
zu jds. ~ erscheinen to turn out to welcome s. o.

Begrüßungs|ansprache, ~rede salutatory, address of welcome, welcome (salutational) address; **~brief** welcome letter; **~feier** welcoming reception; **~formel** salutation; **~geschenk** handsel; **~worte** words of welcome.

begünstigen to favo(u)r, to encourage, to aid, to benefit, to patronize, to countenance, *(Feind)* to give aid and comfort, *(fördern)* to promote, to foster, to bring forward, *(Gläubiger)* to give a preference, to prefer, *(Verbrechen)* to abet;
Flucht eines Verbrechers ~ to connive at an escape from prison; **Gläubiger ~** to favo(u)r a creditor, to prefer one creditor over another; **einheimische Industrie ~** to benefit local industry; **j. in seinen Plänen ~** to favo(u)r s. one's plans; **Entstehung der Schwerindustrie ~** to foster the growth of heavy industries; **j. nach der Tat ~** to be an accessory after the fact.

begünstigende Stelle benefiting body.

Begünstiger abettor.

begünstigt, vom Glück favo(u)red by fortune; **von der Nacht ~** under cover of the night.

Begünstigtenrecht beneficial interest, equitable interest.

Begünstigte|r beneficiary, accommodated party, recipient of a favo(u)r, *(Akkreditiv)* payee, *(Gläubiger)* preferred creditor, *(Lebensversicherung)* nominee, *(Sicherstellung)* guarantee, *(Verbrechen)* accessory after the fact, *(Vermächtnis)* legatee;
im Ermessungswege ~r discretionary beneficiary; **eventuell ~r** *(Versicherung)* contingent beneficiary; **lebenslänglich ~r** life beneficiary; **wirklicher ~r** ultimate beneficiary;
per Saldo ~r net beneficiary;
~r bei einer Grundstücksüberlassung cestui que use; **~r eines treuhänderisch gebundenen Sondervermögens** settlement beneficiary; **~r einer Stiftung (Vermögensverwaltung)** beneficiary under a settlement; **~r eines Versicherungsvertrages** beneficiary of an insurance; **~r eines Vertrages** covenantee; **~r eines Vertrages zugunsten Dritter** third party beneficiary (creditor, donee); **~r einer Versorgungsstiftung** benefciary in a profident fund;
selbst ~r bleiben *(Versicherung)* to retain ownership in one's policy; **~n einsetzen** *(Lebensversicherer)* to nominate a beneficiary.

Begünstigung favo(u)r, favo(u)ritism, encouragement, *(Förderung)* promotion, furtherance, support, *(Gläubiger)* preference, preferential treatment, *(Lebensversicherung)* nomination of beneficiary, *(Verbrechen)* connivance, aiding, abetting;
gleichmäßige ~ equal benefit; **steuerliche ~** tax privilege;
~ im Amt favo(u)ritism; **~ Dritter** third-party benefit; **~ der Einheimischen** nativism *(US)*; **~ einer Person** discrimination in favo(u)r of s. o.;
j. wegen ~ anklagen to arraign s. o. as accessory after the fact; **j. ~ gewähren** to be an accessory after the fact to s. one's crime.

Begünstigungs|klausel *(Versicherung)* benefit clause; **~motiv** motive to prefer; **~recht der Ehefrau am Vermögen des Ehemannes** equity to a settlement; **~tarif** preferential tariff; **~zeitraum** *(Steuer)* tax concession period; **~zertifikat** beneficial interest.

begutachten to give an expert opinion, *(abschätzen)* to appraise, to evaluate, *(Versicherungsgeschäft)* to survey;
Schaden ~ to assess the damage.

Begutachter expert, appraiser, valuer, surveyor.

Begutachtung expert opinion, appraisement, *(Versicherung)* survey;
schriftliche ~ written opinion;
~ eines Schadens assessment of damage.

begütert opulent, wealthy, acred, rich, propertied, [well-]landed, well-to-do *(Br.)*;
~e Klassen leisured classes; **~er Mann** man of property, moneyed man.

Begüterten, die the well-to-do.

behaftet, mit Mängeln full of faults; **mit Schulden ~** encumbered (loaded) with debts.

Behagen ease, pleasure, relish, comfort, enjoyment.

behaglich cosy, snug, homely *(Br.)*, easy;
sich ~ fühlen to feel at ease; **es sich in einem Lehnstuhl ~ machen** to nestle down in an armchair;
~e Atmosphäre homelike atmosphere; **~e Kabine** snug cabin; **~es Leben führen** to live in comfort, to lead an easy life; **~es Stübchen** snug little room.

behalten to retain;
seinen französischen Akzent ~ not to lose one's French accent; **j. im Amt ~** to retain s. o. in office; **j. in ehrendem Angedenken (Andenken) ~** to hono(u)r s. one's memory, to keep s. one's memory green; **etw. im Auge ~** not to lose sight of s. th.; **j. im Auge ~** to keep an eye on s. o.; **Briefdurchschlag ~** to keep a copy of a letter; **j. im Dienst ~** to retain s. one's services; **seine Fassung ~** to keep one's head cool; **Fülle von Einzelheiten ~** to hold a mass of details in one's head; **etw. zum eigenen Gebrauch ~** to keep s. th. for one's own spending; **im Gedächtnis ~** to retain in one's mind; **restliches Geld ~** to keep the odd money; **seine Meinung für sich ~** to keep one's counsel; **seinen guten Namen ~** to maintain one's reputation; **Oberhand über j. ~** to prevail over s. o.; **seinen guten Ruf ~** to maintain one's reputation; **etw. für sich ~** to keep s. th. to oneself (under one's hat); **seine Stellung ~** to retain one's position; **etw. übrig ~** to have s. th. left; **seinen Wagen in der Gewalt ~** to retain control of one's car; **seinen Wert ~** to maintain its value, to have a fixed value.

Behälter case, casket, tank, vessel, repository, container;
verschlossener ~ sealed case; **versiegelter ~** sealed bag; **mehrfach verwendbarer ~** container premium;
in ~n transportieren to containerize;
~anlagen container facilities; **~anlegestelle** container berth; **~bahnhof** container terminal; **~bau** tank and container construction; **~betrieb** container operation; **~frachtversand** container shipment; **~inhalt** tank capacity.

Behälterisierung containerization.

Behälter|partie container lot; **~schiff** container ship; **~umfang** volume of a container; **~verkehr** container shipment (traffic, car service), fishyback service; **~verschraubung** *(Auto)* filler cap; **~wagen, ~waggon** container car, tank waggon (car, *US*); **~zug** container train.

Behältnis repository, vessel, storeroom.

behandeln to handle, to manage, to manipulate, to treat, to cover, *(pflegen)* to nurse, to attend, *(Rohstoffe)* to process, to work;
j. ambulant ~ to treat s. o. as an outpatient; **j. anständig ~** to give s. o. fair play (a fair deal), to level with s. o. *(sl.)*; **ausführlich ~** to elaborate; **j. bevorzugt ~** to treat s. o. differently; **brutal ~** to rough-handle; **Thema delikat ~** to handle a subject delicately; **j. despotisch ~** to rule s. o. with a high hand; **j. wie Dreck ~** to treat s. o. like dirt; **Frage ~** to deal with a question; **Gegenstand erschöpfend ~** to treat a subject

exhaustively; **j. gemein** ~ to do s. o. a dirty trick *(Br.)*; **j. gerecht** ~ to deal with s. o. according to his deserts; **j. mit Glacéhandschuhen** ~ to handle s. o. with kid gloves; **zwei Menschen gleichberechtigt** ~ to place two people on the same footing; **gönnerhaft** ~ to patronize; **j. gut** ~ to do well by s. o., to treat s. o. well; **j. lässig** ~ to treat s. o. in an offhand manner; **leichtfertig** ~ to make light of; **j. menschlich** ~ to treat s. o. with humanity; **j. mit Milde** ~ to deal leniently with s. o.; **j. miserabel** ~ to put the boot into s. o.; **Vertrag als nichtig** ~ to consider a contract void; **pfleglich** ~ to nurse; **Kapitalmarkt pfleglich** ~ to nurse the capital market; **Maschine pfleglich** ~ to handle a machine with care; **schlecht** ~ to neglect; **j. schlecht** ~ to use s. o. ill, to deal badly by s. o.; **j. schonungslos** ~ to handle s. o. without gloves; **als nicht schwierig** ~ to make light of; **j. stiefmütterlich** ~ to give s. o. a raw deal, to treat s. o. shabbily; **unfair** ~ to hit below the belt; **unfreundlich** ~ to lift up the heel against; **ungerecht** ~ to wrong; **j. äußerst unmanierlich** ~ to give s. o. a rough ride; **j. unsanft** ~ to pull (bang) s. o. about; **unterschiedlich** ~ *(Zollgüter)* to discriminate; **vertraulich** ~ to treat in strictest confidence; **vordringlich** ~ to give urgent attention; **beim Transport vorsichtig** ~ to handle with care in carriage; **Thema auf verschiedene Weise** ~ to view a subject in various ways; **Werkstoff** ~ to process material;
sich ärztlich ~ **lassen** to have medical treatment; **schwer zu** ~ **sein** to be hard to handle.

behandelnder Arzt doctor in attendance.

behandelt, sich schlecht ~ **fühlen** to think o. s. ill-used; **grob** ~ **werden** to meet with harsh usage; **unfair** ~ **werden** to get a raw deal; **in einem Zusatzabkommen** ~ **werden** to be subject to supplementary agreement.

behändigen to deliver, to hand over, to consign.

Behandlung treatment, manipulation, handling, management, work, *(Arzt)* treatment, attendance, attention;
in ~ under cure; **in stationärer** ~ confined as a patient; **ambulante** ~ outpatient treatment; **anständige** ~ fair do; **ärztliche** ~ doctor's attendance, medical attention (care); **ausführliche** ~ detail, detailed treatment; **bevorzugte** ~ *(Konkursgläubiger)* preferential treatment; **diskriminierende** ~ discriminating treatment, discrimination, discriminatory treatment; **elende** ~ shabby treatment; **erfolglose** ~ ineffectual treatment; **fachgerechte** ~ good and workmanlike manner; **fiktive** ~ *(Statistik)* dummy treatment; **grobe** ~ punishment *(coll.)*; **großzügige** ~ handsome treatment; **medizinische** ~ medication, medical treatment; **miserable** ~ low-key treatment; **rücksichtsvolle** ~ deferential treatment; **sachgemäße** ~ proper usage, proper handling; **schlechte** ~ ill-treatment (usage), maltreatment; **stationäre** ~ *(Kranker)* stationary treatment; **steuerliche** ~ fiscal treatment; **thermische** ~ heat-treatment; **unerfreuliche** ~ short end of the stick *(sl.)*; **unfaire** ~ rough dealing, raw deal, unfair treatment; **unmenschliche** ~ *(Scheidungsrecht)* inhuman treatment; **unsachgemäße** ~ rough handling; **unterschiedliche** ~ difference in treatment, *(Preis)* price discrimination *(US)*, *(Zolltarif)* discrimination, discriminating treatment; **zollrechtliche** ~ customs treatment; **einheitliche** ~ **für Erbschaftsteuerrechte** aggregation for estate duty; ~ **im Krankenhaus** hospitalization; ~ **als Kuriersache** courier handling; ~ **eines Postens** handling of an item; ~ **als Privatkassenpatient** private medical treatment; ~ **durch die Regierung** government's handling;
~ **eines Gesuchs ablehnen** to dismiss a petition; **auf eine** ~ **ansprechen** to recover under a treatment; **j. zur stationären** ~ **aufnehmen** to admit s. o. for treatment as inpatient, to hospitalize s. o. *(US)*; **strapaziöse** ~ **aushalten** to take a beating; **sich zur** ~ **ins Krankenhaus begeben** to go to have treatment in a hospital; **eingehende** ~ **erfahren** to be treated exhaustively; **mit einer neuen** ~ **Erfolge erzielen** to get results from a new treatment; **sich schlechte** ~ **nicht gefallen lassen** to kick against the treatment one is receiving; **in ärztlicher** ~ **sein** to have medical treatment, to stand in cure; **sich gegen parteiische** ~ **wehren** to kick against partiality.

Behandlungs|kosten handling charges, *(Arzt)* medical costs, cost of treatment; ~**methode** treatment; ~**weise** way of treating, usage; **unvorschriftsmäßige** ~**weise** rough (improper) usage; ~**zimmer** consulting room.

beharren, auf einer Forderung to persist in a demand; **auf seiner Meinung** ~ to stick to one's guns; **auf seinem Recht** ~ to stand on one's rights.

beharrlich insistent, persevering, persistent, unremitting, steadfast;
~ **behaupten** to insist on saying; **etw.** ~ **leugnen** to deny s. th. steadfastely; **sich** ~ **weigern** to refuse persistently.

Beharrlichkeit perseverance, assiduity.

behaupten to maintain, to allege, to assert, to make an assertion, *(Zeuge)* to claim;
sich ~ to stand one's ground, *(Kurse)* to hold their ground, to keep its head, to keep (remain) steady, to remain firm; **sich eisern** ~ to sit tight *(fam.)*; **das Feld** ~ to hold the field; **das Gegenteil** ~ to maintain the contrary; **sich gut** ~ *(Wechselkurs)* to hold fairly steady; **j. zu kennen** ~ to claim s. one's acquaintance; **weiterhin hohe Kurse** ~ to continue to rule high; **seine Rechte** ~ to safeguard (defend, assert) one's rights; **seine Schuldlosigkeit in einer Strafsache** ~ to maintain that one is innocent of a charge; **hohen Stand** ~ to continue high; **sich in seiner Stellung** ~ to hold one's position; **seinen Thron** ~ to remain upon one's throne; **zu Unrecht** ~ to state falsely.

behauptend, sich steady.

behauptet *(Börse)* maintained.

Behauptung assertion, averment, *(Anspruch)* claim, pretension, *(Erklärung)* statement, declaration, *(Vorbringen)* allegation, contention;
nach seinen eigenen ~**en** according to his own statement; **abträgliche** ~ harmful assertion; **abwegige** ~ frivolous claim; **anfechtbare** ~ refutable statement; **diffamierende** ~ defamatory statement; **ehrenrührige** ~ scandalous matter; **einseitige** ~ partial statement; **falsche** ~ jactitation; **fragwürdige** ~ questionable assertion; **geschäftsschädigende** ~**en** injurious falsehood *(Br.)*; **herabsetzende** ~ disparaging statement; **kühne** ~ bold statement; **negative** ~ negative assertion; **positive** ~ positive assertion; **rechtserhebliche** ~**en** allegations good in law; **tatsächliche** ~ material allegation, allegation (statement) of facts; **unbewiesene** ~ unproved allegation; **uneingeschränkte** ~ positive asservation; **unerhebliche** ~ immaterial averment; **unwiderlegliche** ~ peremptory assertion; **verleumderische** ~ libelous statement;
~**en tatsächlicher Art** statement of facts; ~ **gegen** ~ one's man's word against another; ~ **ohne Beweisantritt** nude matter;
seine ~ **aufrechterhalten** to adhere to one's statement; ~ **aufstellen** to make a statement (an assertion); **dogmatische** ~**en aufstellen** to dogmatize; **jds.** ~ **bestätigen** to bear out an assertion; ~ **bestreiten** to deny an assertion, to dispute (contest) a statement; ~ **der Gegenseite bestreiten** to tender an issue; **Unrichtigkeit einer** ~ **beweisen** to disapprove a statement; ~ **beweisen können** to have evidence for a statement; **bei seiner** ~ **bleiben** to persist in saying; ~ **als gegeben hinnehmen** to accept a statement as fact; **jds.** ~**en sorgfältig prüfen** to go into s. one's statements; ~ **rechtfertigen** to sustain an allegation; **seine** ~**en substantiieren** to be more explicit in one's statement; ~ **widerlegen** to refute a statement; **einer** ~ **widersprechen** to gainsay a statement, to contradict (take exception to) a statement.

Behausung dwelling, tabernacle, lodgings, accommodation, diggings *(Br., coll.)*, digs *(Br., sl.)*;
armselige ~ humble cottage, kennel *(US sl.)*; **menschliche** ~**en** human habitations.

beheben to repair, to mend, to remedy, *(Geld)* to withdraw;
Arbeitslosigkeit ~ to alleviate unemployment; **Gefahr** ~ to remove a danger; **Mangel** ~ to remedy a fault; **Notlage** ~ to relieve an emergency; **Schaden** ~ to repair a damage; **Schwierigkeiten** ~ to remove (smooth away) difficulties; **Verkehrsstockung** ~ to relieve a traffic jam; **Zweifel** ~ remove doubts.

Behebung|der Arbeitslosigkeit alleviation of unemployment; ~ **der Hungersnot** famine relief; ~ **eines Mißstands** abatement of a nuisance; ~ **eines Schadens** repair of a damage; ~ **von Schwierigkeiten** removal of difficulties; ~ **einer Verkehrsstockung** relief of a traffic jam; ~ **der Versorgungsschwierigkeiten** famine relief; ~ **eines Zweifels** resolution of a doubt.

beheimatet domiciled, resident, *(Schiff)* registered;
in H. ~ **sein** *(Schiff)* to hail from H.

beheizen to heat, to warm;
zentral ~ to have central heating.

beheizt sein, zentral to have central heating.

Beheizung heating, warming.

Beheizungsanlage heating system.

Behelf expedient, makeshift, shift;
als ~ makeshift, jerrybuilt;
als ~ **dienen** to serve as a makeshift.

behelfen, sich to do without, to makeshift, to manage, to resort, to expedients; **sich irgendwie** ~ to manage somehow; **sich kümmerlich** ~ to scrape along; **sich ohne jem.** ~ to get on without s. o.; **sich ohne Sekretärin** ~ to do without the services of a secretary; **sich mit wenig** ~ to live with little money.

Behelfs|antenne temporary antenna; **~ausgabe** emergency edition; **~bauten** makeshift construction; **~bett** improvised bed; **~brücke** temporary (emergency, hasty) bridge; **~dienst** emergency service; **~flugplatz** emergency landing field, airstrip; **~garage** carport; **~heim** makeshift home; **~konstruktion** makeshift construction; **~landeplatz** emergency landing field (ground); **zu einer ~lösung greifen** to resort to an expedient.

behelfsmäßig makeshift, picknicky, in a rough-and-ready manner, by way of expedient, temporary;
~ reparieren to patch up; **j. ~ unterbringen** to put s. o. up; **~es Bett** improvised bed.

Behelfs|maßnahmen emergency actions; **~mittel** expedient; **~unterbringung** temporary housing; **~unterkunft** makeshift home, temporary accommodation.

behelligen to bother, to molest, to trouble, to badger, to importune, to vex;
j. mit Fragen ~ to pester s. o. with questions; **mit Geldforderungen ~** to importune with requests for money.

Behelligung importunity.

beherbergen to host, to lodge, to house, to accommodate, to harbo(u)r, to take in;
Bibliothek ~ to house a library, **Obdachlose ~** to harbo(u)r homeless people.

Beherberger harbo(u)rer.

Beherbergung housing, lodging, accommodation;
~ und Beköstigung boarding.

Beherbergungs|gewerbe hotel industry; **~wesen** hotel industry.

beherrschen to rule, to govern, to dominate, to master, to control, to direct;
sich ~ to master one's feelings, to control o. s.; **allein ~** to monopolize; **etw. asshaft ~** to be a nailer at it; **Englisch genauso gut ~ wie Französisch** to speak English and French with equal ease; **sein Fach ~** to know one's trade; **das Feld ~** to be in full command of a situation; **Gebiet ~** *(mil.)* to control an area; **kompliziertes Gebiet der Kommunalfinanzen ~** to master the intricacies of municipal finances; **sowohl den Hafen wie die Stadt ~** *(mar.)* to command both harbo(u)r and city; **Land ~** to rule over a country; **Luftraum ~** to have air supremacy; **Markt ~** to hold (command, control, dominate) the market; **alles meisterhaft ~** to be perfect in everything; **Sache gründlich ~** to know a subject inside out; **Sache wie am Schnürchen ~** to have s. th. at one's finger tips; **See ~** to have naval supremacy; **Situation ~** to be master of a situation, to master a situation; **Situation meisterhaft ~** to handle a situation in a masterly manner; **mehrere Sprachen ~** to have a command of several languages; **Stadt ~** *(Festung)* to dominate the town; **Volk ~** to rule over a country; **vollständig ~** to have at one's finger tips; **j. vollständig ~** to have the whip hand over s. o., to have s. o. under one's thumbs; **zahlenmäßig ~** to dominate numerically; **seine Zunge ~** to be careful of what one says;
sich nicht ~ können to have no self-control, to be unable to control one's feelings.

beherrschend commanding, dominating.

Beherrscher dominator, ruler.

beherrscht cool, restrained, self-possessed;
von Furcht ~ ridden by fear; **von seinen Leidenschaften ~** ruled by one's passions;
~es Auftreten disciplined manner; **~es Unternehmen** controlled company (concern).

Beherrschtheit self-control.

Beherrschung domination, command, control, *(Luftraum)* supremacy;
monopolistische ~ monopolistic control; **vollständige ~** *(Kfz)* immediate control;
~ des Luftraums air supremacy; **~ der Programmzeiten** domination of program(me) ownership; **sichere ~ einer Situation** the Nelson touch; **~ einer Sprache** command of a language; **~ des Weltmarktes** command of the world market; **seine ~ verlieren** to lose one's self-control (nerves, cool, *sl.*), to hit the ceiling.

Beherrschungsvertrag controlling agreement.

beherzigen to lay to heart;
Warnung nicht ~ to take no heed of a warning.

behilflich helpful, willing, assistant;
jem. ~ sein to lend s. o. a helping hand, to aid s. o., to throw a rope to s. o.; **bei etw. ~ sein** to be instrumental in doing s. th.

behindern to handicap, to obstruct, to impede, to disturb, to hinder, to hamper;
j. in der Ausübung seiner Pflichten ~ to obstruct s. o. in the execution of his duties; **Fortschritt ~** to stand in the way of progress; **Handel ~** to handicap trade; **Pfandauslösung ~** to clog the equity of redemption *(Br.)*; **jds. Pläne ~** to impede s. one's plans; **Schiffahrt ~** to obstruct navigation; **Sicht ~** to obstruct the view; **Verkehr ~** to hold up (impede, disturb) traffic, to cause an obstruction; **Wettbewerb ~** to restrain trade.

behindert handicapped;
körperlich ~ disabled; **durch einen schweren Mantel ~** hampered by a heavy overcoat.

Behindertenfürsorge welfare of the handicapped.

Behinderung hindrance, obstacle, obstruction, impediment, disturbance, crimp *(US sl.)*, *(Arbeitsfähigkeit)* disablement;
ohne jede ~ without let or hindrance;
körperliche ~ physical disability;
~ in der Ausübung einer Grunddienstbarkeit obstruction of an easement; **~ in der Ausübung des Wahlrechts** obstruction of polling; **~ der Betätigungsfreiheit** impeding of the liberty to work; **~ der Erfassung zum Wehrdienst** obstructing the recruiting or enlistment *(US)*; **~ im Genuß eines Rechtes** disturbance of s. o. in the lawful enjoyment of a right; **~ des Handels** impediment to trade; **~ des Konkursverfahrens** obstruction of bankruptcy; **~ des Pfandauslöserechts** clog on the equity of redemption *(Br.)*; **~ der Pressefreiheit** restriction of the liberty of the press; **~ der Rechtspflege** obstructing justice; **~ von Regierungsmaßnahmen** obstructing governmental operations; **~ der Schiffahrt** obstructing navigation; **~ des Straßenverkehrs** obstruction of the highway; **~ eines Wegerechts** disturbance of right of way; **~ des Wettbewerbs** restraint of trade; **~ der Zwangsvollstreckung** obstructing process;
sich einer ~ des Verkehrs strafbar machen to be guilty of obstruction.

Behörde authority, administrative body, administration, government department *(Br.)*, board, office, entity, agency *(US)*, *(Stadt)* council;
~n public authorities;
angegliederte ~ affiliated authority; **aufsichtsführende ~** supervising authority; **bescheinigende ~** certifying authority; **betreffende ~** relevant authority; **durchführende ~** executive agency; **eingesetzte (im Amt befindliche) ~n** constituted authorities; **einstufige ~** single-tier authority *(Br.)*; **Hohe ~** High Authority; **kommunale ~** municipal authority, local government; **maßgebende ~** appropriate authority; **nachgeordnete ~** ministerial office, accessorial agency, political subdivision; **politisch nachgeordnete ~** political subdivision; **säumige ~** default authority; **staatliche ~** governmental board (agency, *US*); **städtische ~n** civil (municipal) authorities; **unterstellte ~** subordinate authority; **unzuständige ~** incompetent authority; **vollziehende ~** executive branch of government; **Haushalt vorbereitende ~** budget-making agency *(US)*; **vorgesetzte ~** superior (higher) authority; **weisungsgebundene ~** ministerial office; **zivile ~** administrative authority; **zuständige ~** regulatory agency, competent (appropriate, proper) authority; **für Schankkonzessionen zuständige ~** licensing authority *(Br.)*;
Hohe ~ der Montan-Union High Authority of the European Coal and Steel Community; **~ für Umweltschutzfragen** environmental agency;
sich mit den ~n arrangieren to put o. s. right with the authorities; **~ auflösen** to dismantle an agency; **~n unterrichten (verständigen)** to give notice to the authorities; **bei einer ~ vorstellig werden** to apply to the authorities.

Behörden|anforderung authorization request; **~angestellter** salaried official; **~apparat** official machinery, administrative setup; **~aufbau** administrative structure; **~auflösung** dismantlement of an agency; **~eigenschaft** official capacity; **~etat** agency budget; **~fahrzeug** office car.

behördenfromm sein to be very humble towards one's superiors.

Behörden|frommheit blind deference to the authorities; **~kundschaft** institutional users; **~leiter** commissioner, agency head *(US)*, chief of an agency; **~parkplatz** office car park; **~sprache** officialese, gobbledygock *(US)*; **dreistufiges ~system** system of first, second and third tier authorities; **~vermittler** contact man; **~viertel** civic centre *(Br.)*; **~weg** official channels; **~weg genau einhalten** to go through the proper channels; **~wirtschaft** bureaucratic interference, red tape.

behördlich governmental, official, magisterial;
~ genehmigt approved by the authorities, licensed;
~e Anordnung administrative order; **~e Genehmigung** licence; **mit ~er Genehmigung** with the approval of the authorities; **~es Schreiben** official letter.

behördlicherseits officially.
behumpsen *(fam.)* to diddle, to welsh *(sl.)*.
behüte|n to protect, to shield;
er ~t sie wie seinen Augapfel she is the apple of his eye.
behutsam careful, cautious, wary;
~ anfassen to handle with care; **~ zu Werke gehen** to go about s. th. carefully; **~e Schritte machen** to proceed with caution; **~es Vorgehen** careful approach.
Behutsamkeit carefulness, heed.
Bei|akten subfolder, supplementary files, ancillary documents (papers); **~band** supplementary volume.
beibehalten to keep up, to maintain, to carry on;
Brauch ~ to preserve a custom; **Einrichtung ~** to retain an institution; **Geschwindigkeit ~** to maintain speed; **Kurs ~** to keep the course; **Kurs und Geschwindigkeit ~** to stand on; **hohes Niveau ~** to uphold high standards; **Preisbindung der zweiten Hand ~** to maintain fixed resale prices; **seine Staatsangehörigkeit ~** to retain one's nationality; **veraltetes Verfahren ~** to cling to an old-fashioned method.
Beibehaltung retention, maintenance;
unter ~ des früheren Firmennamens maintaining the original business name;
~ langjähriger Angestellter bei Entlassungen bumping *(US)*, backtracking *(US)*; **~ des angestammten Berufs** job retention; **~ der Beschlußfähigkeit** maintenance of a quorum; **~ der Staatsangehörigkeit** retention of nationality; **~ einer Zuständigkeit** retaining a cause *(Br.)*.
beibiegen, jem. etw. to drum into s. one's head.
Beiblatt supplementary sheet, rider, supplement;
~ mit Anzeigen advertising sheet.
Beiboot tender, longboat, dinghy, cockboat.
beibringen to adduce, to supply, *(Urkunden)* to produce, to furnish, to procure;
jem. etw. ~ to drum s. th. into s. one's head; **Beweis ~** to produce evidence, to furnish proof; **jem. die Flötentöne ~** to tell s. o. what is what; **Gift ~** to administer poison; **jem. Manieren ~** to teach s. o. manners; **jem. eine Niederlage ~** to downgrade (defeat) s. o.; **dem Feind eine Niederlage ~** to inflict defeat upon the enemy; **Referenzen ~** to furnish references; **jem. etw. schonend ~** to break the news gently to s. o.; **jem. eine Sprache ~** to teach s. o. a language; **dem Feind große Verluste ~** to inflict heavy losses on the enemy; **jem. Vernunft ~** to bring s. o. to reason; **Zeugen ~** to produce (bring forward) a witnesses.
Beibringung production, procurement;
gegen ~ eines ärztlichen Attestes on production of a medical certificate;
~ von Gift administering poison; **~ von Unterlagen** procurement (production) of documents; **~ von Zeugen** production of witness.
beiderseitig reciprocal, mutual, two-sided;
im ~en Einverständnis with mutual consent; **~e Verpflichtungen** reciprocal commitments; **zu ~em Vorteil** to mutual advantage.
beidrehen, Schiff to bring a ship in.
beieinander, dicht close together;
gut ~ sein to be as fit as a fiddle, to be in good shape; **nicht ganz ~ sein** not to be all there.
Beifahrer front-seat passenger, *(Lastwagen)* truck pilot, co-driver, truck-driver's helper, swamper *(sl.)*, *(Motorrad)* pillion passenger (rider), sidecar passenger;
~sitz passenger seat, *(Motorrad)* pillion seat.
Beifall applause, approval, approbation;
unter lautem ~ accompanied by loud cheers;
donnernder ~ thunderous applause; **frenetischer ~** frantic applause; **starker ~** loud applause; **uneingeschränkter ~** entire approval; **nicht enden wollender ~** round (no end) of applause; **einem Publikum ~ abringen** to draw applause from an audience; **Rede mit ~ aufnehmen** to greet a speech with cheers; **in ~ ausbrechen** to break into applause; **stürmischen ~ auslösen** to bring down the house; **großen ~ erhalten, reichen ~ ernten** to get a big hand, to bring down the house; **rasanten ~ erzielen** to panic (theater, *US sl.*); **~ der Kritiker finden** to win critical acclaim; **langanhaltenden ~ hervorrufen** to draw long applause; **~ klatschen** to applaud; **~ nicken** to nod approval; **tosend ~ rufen** to thunder applause; **geteilten ~ spenden** to accord a mixed reception; **im ~ untergehen** to be lost in applause; **allgemein mit ~ aufgenommen werden** to be met with general acclamation; **mit begeistertem ~ begrüßt werden** to be welcomed with enthusiastic applause.
beifällig approving, favo(u)rable;
~es Kopfnicken nod of approval.
Beifalls|äußerung, ~bezeugung sign of approval, acclamation; **~geschrei** loud cheers; **~getöse** thunder of applause; **~klatschen** applause; **~ruf** cry, cheer; **~sturm** burst (wildfire, hurricane) of applause.
Beifilm short [feature], supporting film (picture).
beifolgend enclosed, herewith.
Beifracht mariner's portage.
beifügen to inclose, to enclose, to adjoin, to attach, to annex, to add, to subjoin;
einem Bericht ein Dokument ~ to annex a document to a report; **einem Brief ~** to enclose with a letter; **einem Exposé eine Urkunde ~** to append a document to a dossier; **Muster ~** to attach a sample; **einem Testament ein Kodizill ~** to add a codicil to a will; **Urkunde einem Brief ~** to attach a document to a letter; **einem Vertrag eine Klausel ~** to put a clause into a contract.
Beifügung enclosure, attachment, apposition, addition, enclosing;
unter ~ eines Schecks enclosing a check *(US)* (cheque, *Br.*).
Beigabe addition, adjunct, extra;
als ~ into the bargain.
beigeben, Begleitschreiben to send a covering note; **als Begleitung ~** to delegate an escort; **klein ~** to sing small, to back down, to put one's pride in one's pocket, to have one's tail between one's legs, to take it lying down, to beat a parley, *(zu Kreuze kriechen)* to eat one's words, to backwater *(US)*, to strike sail *(fig.)*; **einem Minister einen Fachmann ~** to assign an expert as adviser to a minister.
beigefügt annexed, joined, appendant, hereby, by the presents;
~er Kuponabschnitt attached coupon sheet.
bei|geheftet, ~gelegt joined, subjoined.
beigeordnet associate, coordinate, assistant, deputy;
~er Bürgermeister deputy mayor; **~er Richter** assistant judge; **~er Satz** coordinate clause *(gram.)*.
Beigeordneter associate, *(Gericht)* assistant judge, *(städtische Verwaltung)* deputy [mayor], deputy, assistant.
beigeschlossen enclosed, attached, subjoined, under this cover.
Beigeschmack *(fig.)* smack, flavo(u)r, savo(u)r, spice, overtone;
romantischer ~ flavo(u)r of romance;
~ von Ironie tang of irony;
bitteren ~ haben to be tinged with bitterness; **~ des Gewöhnlichen haben** to smack of cheapness;
die Sache hat einen üblen ~ there's something fishy about it.
beigesellen, einem Ausschuß als Berater to attach to a committee as adviser.
beigetrieben *(Forderung)* collected, recovered, totted *(Br.)*;
nicht ~ unrecovered.
beiheften to adjoin, to subjoin, to attach.
Beihefter insert, tip-in.
Beihelfer principal in the second degree.
Beihilfe benefit, assistance, aid, help, *(Kommunen)* grants (appropriation) in aid, *(strafrechtlich)* aiding and abetting, abetment;
von einer Bedürftigkeitsprüfung abhängige ~ means-tested benefit *(Br.)*; **finanzielle ~** pecuniary aid; **nicht rückzahlbare ~** nonreturnable aid; **staatliche ~** subsidy, grant [-in-aid, *US*]; **staatliche ~ zum Studium** student aid, study grant;
~ in besonderen Fällen special hardship allowance; **~ für ein [unterstütztes] Familienmitglied** dependancy allowance; **~ zur Gefangenenbefreiung** aiding an escape; **~n für Luftpostbeförderung** air subsidies *(US)*; **~ bei einer Patentverletzung** contributory infringement;
~ von 200 DM bekommen to receive a grant of 200 DM; **~n gewähren** to grant aids; **~ leisten** to counsel and procure, *(Verbrechen)* to aid and abet;
~empfänger grantee, recipient of an allowance.
beikommen, jem. to get near s. o., to get at s. o. *(US)*.
Beiladung supplementary (additional) load.
Beilage inclosure, enclosure, subjunction, exhibit *(US)*, *(Anhang)* annex, appendix, *(Buch, Zeitung)* supplement, *(Gericht)* trimmings, *(Reklame)* stuffer *(US)*, inset, insertion, insert *(US)*;
~n trimmings;
gebundene ~ bound supplement; **gelieferte ~n** furnished inserts; **lose ~** loose inset;
~ zum amtlichen Kursbuch supplement list *(Br.)*;
~material stuffer; **~prospekt** insert.
beiläufig incidental, casual, in passing;
~ erwähnen to mention in passing, to remark casually;
~e Bemerkung machen to drop a remark.

beilegen to inclose, to enclose, to adjoin, to add, to annex, *(zuerkennen)* to attribute, to attach;
einem Brief Lichtbilder ~ to enclose photographs with a letter; **gütlich** ~ to arrange amicably, to adjust, to reconcile, to compromise; **Meinungsverschiedenheit** ~ to make up (settle) a difference; **schiedsgerichtlich** ~ to settle by arbitration; **sich einen Titel** ~ to assume a title; **Unterlagen** ~ to add supporting documents; **einer Sache Wichtigkeit** ~ to attach importance to s. th.; **einem Wort Bedeutung** ~ to attach a meaning to a word.
Beileger insert.
Beilegung settlement, adjustment, accommodation, reconcilement, reconciliation, arrangement;
außergerichtliche ~ settlement out of court; **friedliche** ~ peaceful settlement; **gütliche** ~ amicable settlement; **schiedsgerichtliche** ~ arbitral settlement;
~ **von Arbeitsstreitigkeiten** settling labo(u)r disputes; ~ **von Meinungsverschiedenheiten** settlement of differences; ~ **von Schwierigkeiten** adjustment of differences; ~ **von Streitigkeiten** settling of grievances; ~ **nachbarlicher Streitigkeiten** fence mending *(US)*; ~ **im Vergleichswege** settlement by compromise.
Beilegungsverfahren amicable composition.
Beileid condolence, sympathy;
aufrichtiges ~ hollow sympathy;
jem. sein ~ **aussprechen** to offer s. o. one's condolence, to express one's sympathy with s. o.
Beileids|besuch visit of condolence; ~**besuche verbeten** no visitors will be received; ~**bezeugung** expression of sympathy, condolences; ~**karte** condolence card; ~**schreiben** letter of sympathy; ~**telegramm** telegram of condolence.
beiliegen to be enclosed.
beiliegend under cover, enclosed, inclosed, subjoined, annexed, attached, herewith;
~ **erhalten Sie,** ~ **übersenden wir Ihnen** enclosed please find.
Beimengung admixture.
beimessen to attribute, to ascribe;
einem Ereignis Bedeutung ~ to attach importance to an event; **einer Nachricht Glauben** ~ to give credit to a piece of news; **einem Umstand großen Wert** ~ to attach great importance to a circumstance.
Beimessung attribution.
beimischen to admix.
Beimischung admixture, temper, tincture;
mit unzulässiger ~ **verpackt** falsely packed.
Bein, schon vor Tagesanbruch auf den ~**en** up and doing before day *(coll.)*; **wieder auf den** ~**en** out and about again;
sich die ~**e ablaufen** to be run off one's feet; **mit dem linken** ~ **zuerst aufstehen** to get out of bed on the wrong side; **sich kein** ~ **ausreißen** not to break one's neck; **sich ans** ~ **binden** to write off a bad debt; **j. einen Klotz ans** ~ **binden** to hamstring s. o.; **Sache auf die** ~**e bringen** to set a business on its legs; **Unternehmen wieder auf die** ~**e bringen** to put an enterprise on its feet again; **wieder auf die** ~**e fallen** to land on one's feet again; **seine** ~**e gebrauchen** to leg it; **etw. am** ~ **haben** to be saddled with s. th.; **jem. wieder auf die** ~**e helfen** to give s. o. a leg up, to help s. o. to pick up the pieces; **jem. finanziell wieder auf die** ~**e helfen** to set s. o. up again; **wieder auf die** ~**e kommen** to find one's legs, to recuperate, to recover; **jem.** ~**e machen** to keep s. o. on the trot, to have s. o. on the run; **sich auf die** ~**e machen** to stir one's stumps; **seine** ~**e unter den Arm (in die Hand) nehmen** to pick up one's heels, to take to one's legs *(fam.)*, to put one's best foot forward; **auf dem falschen** ~ **Hurra schreien** to come down on the wrong side of the hedge; **Stein und** ~ **schwören** to swear by all that's holy; **für sein Alter noch gut auf den** ~**en sein** to carry one's age well; **früh auf den** ~**en sein** to be an early riser; **immer auf den** ~**en sein** to go a steady trot, to be always on the run; **immer mit einem** ~ **im Gefängnis sein** to be in and out of prison; **wie ein Klotz am** ~ **sein** to be like a millstone round one's neck; **ganzen Tag auf den** ~**en gewesen sein** to have been on one's legs all day; **wieder auf den** ~**en sein** to be up and about (around, *US*) again; **immer noch die** ~**e unter Vaters Tisch stecken** to still live with one's parents, to be still under the paternal roof; **auf eigenen** ~**en stehen** to play off one's own bat, to be on one's own; **sich die** ~**e in den Bauch (Leib) stehen** to kick (cool) one's heels; **mit einem** ~ **im Grabe stehen** to have one foot in the grave; **auf schwachen** ~**en stehen** to be dotty on one's legs; **mit beiden** ~**en im Leben stehen** to have both feet on the ground; **jem. ein** ~ **stellen** to trip s. o. up, to pull a fast one on s. o. *(sl.)*; **auf die** ~**e stellen** to set on foot; **Heer auf die** ~**e stellen** to raise an army; **neue Organisation auf die** ~**e stellen** to call an organization into existence; **Werbekampagne auf die** ~**e stellen** to launch an advertising campaign; **über die eigenen** ~**e stolpern** to fall over one's own feet; **sich die** ~**e vertreten** to stretch one's legs, to go for a trot; **jem. einen Knüppel zwischen die** ~**e werfen** to put a spoke in s. one's wheel.
beinahe within an ace, near to.
Beinahe-Unfall a close call.
Beiname surname, cognomen.
Bein|amputierter basket case; ~**bruch** fracture of the leg; **das ist kein** ~**bruch** don't take it so serious.
beinhalten to contain, to cover, to comprise, to include, to imply.
beiordnen to adjoin;
jem. einen Anwalt ~ to assign a counsel to s. o.
Beiordnung eines Anwalts assignment of a counsel.
beipflichten to assent to, to agree, to concur;
einem Vorschlag ~ to agree to a proposal.
Beiprogramm supporting program(me), adjacencies, short subject.
Beirat advisory board (group), local board of directors, board of trustees, superintending committee, prudential committee *(US)*, *(Einzelperson)* counsel, adviser, advisor;
juristischer ~ legal adviser; **örtlicher** ~ local advisory board; **ständiger** ~ permanent advisory board; **wirtschaftlicher** ~ council of economic advisers; **wissenschaftlicher** ~ brains trust *(US)*;
j. als ~ **zuziehen** to consult s. o. as adviser.
Beirats|beschluß council decision; ~**empfehlung** council recommendation; ~**mitglied** member of a council; ~**sitzung** board (council) meeting.
beisammen|bleiben to remain together; **bis in die frühen Morgenstunden** ~**bleiben** to stay up until the small hours of the morning; **nicht alle** ~**haben** not to have all one's marbles *(sl.)*, to be three bricks (pickles) shy of a load (barrel), to have rocks in one's head *(sl.)*; **Geld schnell** ~**haben** to scratch together a few pounds quickly; **seine Ersparnisse** ~**halten** to be careful of one's small savings; **einträchtig** ~**leben** to dwell in unity.
Beisammensein togetherness, gathering, association;
geselliges ~ companionship, friendly gathering, informal reception; **informelles geselliges** ~ tunk *(sl.)*;
geselliges ~ **in Schwung bringen** to enliven a party.
beisammensein, nicht ganz not to feel very well.
Beisatz alloy.
Beischuß *(Buchhandel)* enclosure.
Beisein von Zeugen, im in the presence of witnesses.
beiseite bringen, Bankgelder to abstract the funds of a bank; **Geld** ~ to misappropriate funds; **Urkunde** ~ to suppress a document.
beiseite legen to lay off (by), to set apart, to shelve, to put (lay) aside, to throw into the discard;
Geld ~ to set aside money; **als unbrauchbar** ~ to discard.
beiseite nehmen, j. to draw s. o. aside.
beiseite schaffen to shuffle aside, to make away, to abstract, to clean up *(sl.)*;
Vermögensgegenstände ~ to remove property.
Beiseitebringung|von Urkunden abstraction of documents; ~ **von Vermögenswerten** abstraction of funds.
Beiseitelegen putting away.
Beiseitenehmen drawing apart.
Beiseiteschaffen *(Vermögensgegenstände)* abstraction, removal, misappropriation;
betrügerisches ~ surreptitious removal of goods;
~ **gepfändeter Gegenstände** pound breach of distraint goods; ~ **einer Leiche** removal of a corpse; ~ **zwecks Steuerhinterziehung** removal to avoid tax.
beisetzen to bury, to inter;
in der Familiengruft ~ to lay in the family vault.
Beisetzung funeral, burial, interment.
Beisetzungsfeier funeral [ceremony], obsequies.
Beisitzer puisne (associate, assistant, side) judge, assistant, assistor, auditor;
rechtskundiger ~ assessor; **sachverständiger** ~ expert (legal, *Br.*) assessor, *(Seeamt)* nautical assessor; **weiterer** ~ additional conferee.
Beispiel example, instance;
zum ~ for instance;
abschreckendes ~ deterrent; **eindrucksvolles** ~ object lesson; **klassisches** ~ classic example; **praktisches** ~ demonstration; **typisches** ~ representative example;
~ **anführen** to quote an instance; **mit** ~**en belegen** to exemplify; **jds.** ~ **folgen** to follow s. one's example, to follow suit, to take a leaf out of s. one's book; **praktisches** ~ **geben** to practise what one teaches; **sich an jem. ein** ~ **nehmen** to take a leaf out of s.

one's book, to pattern s. one's conduct; **mit gutem ~ vorangehen** to set a good example, to give s. o. a lead; **sich j. als ~ wählen** to take s. o. as a pattern.
beispiellos beyond example, unheard of, unprecedented; **~e Grausamkeit** unparalleled cruelty.
beispringen, jem. mit Geld to accommodate s. o. with money.
beißen, sich *(Farben)* to jar;
auf Granit ~ to meet with stiff resistance; **ins Gras ~** to bite the dust, to kick the bucket *(sl.)*;
den letzten ~ die Hunde the devil take the hindmost.
Beistand assistance, aid, aider, lift, support, *(Person)* coadjutant, assistant, helper;
ohne ~ unaided;
ärztlicher ~ medical attendance;
gerichtlich bestellter ~ für einen Minderjährigen guardian by appointment of the court; **~ in Steuersachen** fiscal cooperation;
sich des ~s eines Verteidigers bedienen to have a counsel for the defence; **jem. ~ leisten** to come to s. one's assistance.
Beistands|abkommen standby arrangement; **~kredit** standby credit; **neutralitätswidrige ~leistung** *(Völkerrecht)* hostile assistance; **~leistung in Seenot** salvage service; **~pakt** mutual assistance treaty, pact of mutual assistance.
beistehen to assist, to support, to back;
jem. in der Not ~ to roll a log for s. o. *(US)*; **mit Rat und Tat ~** to advise and assist.
beistehend assistant.
beistellen to attach, to add.
Beistell|teile accessory equipment, accessories; **~tisch** side table.
beisteuern to contribute, to subscribe, to kick in *(US sl.)*;
Artikel zu einer Festschrift ~ to contribute an article to a commemorative volume; **zur Deckung der Unkosten ~** to contribute towards the expenses; **neue Erkenntnisse zur Lösung eines wissenschaftlichen Problems ~** to contribute new information on a scientific problem; **Geldbetrag ~** to contribute a sum of money; **sein Scherflein ~** to give one's mite to a good cause.
beisteuernd contributive.
beistimmen to assent, to concur;
nicht ~ to withhold one's consent;
jds. Ansicht ~ to concur with s. o. in thinking; **einem Vorschlag ~** to agree to a proposal.
Beitrag contribution, *(Anteil)* share, quota, portion, scot, *(Mitglied)* subscription, [membership] dues *(US)*, *(Sammlung)* subscription, share, *(Umlage)* levy, assessment *(US)*, dues *(US)*, *(Versicherung)* premium, *(Zeitung)* contribution, article, *(Zuschuß)* allowance, supply;
auf die Sozialversicherung angerechneter ~ contribution credited; **anteilsmäßiger ~** prorata contribution; **berücksichtigungsfähiger ~** qualifying share; **eingesammelter ~** whip [-round]; **noch fälliger ~** contribution still due; **finanzieller ~** financial contribution; **freiwilliger ~** voluntary contribution; **jährlicher ~** annual subscription; **kritischer ~** critical essay; **laufender ~** periodical contribution; **steuerabzugsfähiger ~** deductible subscription, tax-deductible contribution; **wesentlicher ~** substantial contribution; **wissenschaftlicher ~** contribution to a paper;
~ zur Arbeitslosenversicherung unemployment insurance contribution; **einmaliger ~ auf Lebenszeit** life subscription; **wesentlicher ~ für die Öffentlichkeit** major public service; **~ zur Pensionskasse** superannuation contribution; **~ zur Produktionssteigerung** output contribution; **regelmäßiger ~ für eine mildtätige Stiftung** regular subscription to charity; **anteilsmäßiger ~ bei Versicherungsschäden** contribution in case of a loss; **~ für gemeinnützige (wohltätige) Zwecke** charitable (benevolent) contribution, contribution of alms;
seinen ~ bezahlen to pay one's subscription (scot, dues, *US*); **~ zu einer politischen Aktion einsammeln** to collect a political levy from its members; **~ in die Sozialversicherung einzahlen** to pay contributions into the scheme; **~ von zehn Pfund zur Pensionskasse erheben** to levy ten pounds for the pension fund; **~ durch Umlage erheben** to impose a contribution; **~ erhöhen** to raise the subscription; **~ leisten** to make a contribution; **seinen ~ leisten** to put up one's share, to pay one's contribution (share); **~ zur Pensionskasse leisten** to make contributions to the pension trust; **seinen ~ zu einer Sammlung leisten** to pay a subscription; **~ zu den Unterhaltskosten leisten** to make contributions towards the costs of maintenance; **~ zu einem Zweck leisten** to be instrumental to a purpose; **seinen ~ zahlen** to pay one's subscription (contribution, dues, *US*).
Beiträge contributions, dues *(US)*, *(Journalist)* correspondence; **noch ausstehende ~** contributions due; **freiwillige ~** voluntary contributions; **kritische ~** critical essays; **laufende ~** periodic dues *(US)*; **rückständige ~** *(Verein)* arrears;
~ zur Altersversorgung *(Bilanz)* contribution to pension trust; **~ für Berufsverbände** fees or subscriptions to professional societies (bodies); **~ zu Gewerbeverbänden** trade subscriptions; **~ aus dem Leserkreis** letters to the editor; **~ zu einer Pensionkasse** superannuation payments to pension fund, contributions to a trust scheme; **~ zur Sozialhilfe** social welfare contributions *(US)*; **~ zur Sozialversicherung** national insurance contributions *(Br.)*, social security contributions *(US)*; **~ für Zeitschriften** contributions to periodicals; **~ für politische Zwecke** political subscription; **~ zu wohltätigen Zwecken** charitable contributions;
durch ~ aufbringen to subscribe; **~ einsammeln** to collect contributions; **~ erheben** to collect dues; **~ zur Pensionskasse leisten** to make contributions to the pension trust; **schriftliche ~ liefern** *(für eine Zeitung)* to contribute to a newspaper, to write articles [for a paper]; **durch freiwillige ~ unterhalten werden** to be supported by voluntary contributions.
beitragen to contribute, to subscribe, to bear a charge in;
seinen Anteil ~ to contribute one's share, to pull one's weight; **voll zur Deckung des Gemeinkostenanteils ~** to absorb its full share of overheads; **zur Deckung der Unkosten ~** to contribute towards the expenses; **gleichmäßig zur abendlichen Entspannung ~** to contribute equally to the pleasure of the evening; **zu dem Erfolg ~** to contribute to the success; **zum Erfolg des Unternehmens ~** to conduce to the success of an enterprise; **sein Scherflein ~** to give one's mite to a good cause; **zu einer mildtätigen Stiftung ~** to subscribe to charity; **zu jds. Sturz ~** to help s. one's downfall; **seinen Teil ~** to pay one's share, to pull one's weight; **zu gleichen Teilen zu den Unkosten ~** to contribute equal shares to the expenses; **zum Untergang ~** to help down; **zum Unterhalt seiner Familie ~** to contribute to the family's keep; **nichts zu einer Unterhaltung ~** to take no share in a conversation; **wesentlich ~** to be instrumental; **zu einer Zeitung ~** to write for (contribute to) a newspaper.
Beitrags|abführung payment of dues; **~abrechnung** *(Sozialversicherung)* social insurance accounting; **~abschnitt** contribution period; **~abzug** deductions for insurance and pensions; **~anteil** share, subscription, quota; **~aufkommen** contributions received, *(Sozialversicherung)* social security revenue *(US)*; **~bedingungen, ~bestimmungen** contribution conditions; **~befreiung** *(Versicherung)* waiver of premium, *(Sozialversicherung)* relief from security payments *(US)*; **~bemessung** rating, assessment, tarifing *(US)*; **außerhalb der ~bemessungsgrenze liegen** *(Sozialversicherung)* to be relieved from social security payments *(US)*, to be outside the scope of the national insurance system *(Br.)*; **~bemessungsgrundlage** contributory basis; **~berechnung** premium statement; **automatische ~einhaltung** dues checkoff; **~einnahmen** subscription income; **~einnahmen der Lebensversicherungsgesellschaften** contributions received by life insurance companies; **~einziehung** collection of premiums; **~entrichtung** payment of dues, *(Lebensversicherung)* payment of premiums; **durch ~erhebung** by means of contribution; **~erhöhung** increased contributions, dues increase *(US)*; **~erhöhung vornehmen** to raise the subscription; **~ermäßigung** *(Versicherung)* premium rebate, discount; **~erstattung** contribution refund, *(Sozialversicherung)* refunding of social insurance contributions; **~fonds** contributory fund, contributing box; **~forderungen** outstanding dues, *(Sozialversicherung)* outstanding social security contributions.
beitragsfrei noncontributory;
~ sein *(Sozialversicherung)* to be relieved from social security payments *(US)*, to be outside the scope of the national insurance system *(Br.)*;
~e Leistungen noncontributory benefits; **~e Mitgliedschaft** free membership; **~es Pensionssystem** company-financed pension plan (scheme); **~e Versicherungspolice** paid-up insurance policy.
Beitrags|grenze, über der ~grenze liegen *(Sozialversicherung)* to be outside the social security payments *(US)*, to be outside the scope of the national insurance system *(Br.)*; **~grundlage** contributory basis; **~hinterziehung** *(Sozialversicherung)* evasion of social security contributions; **~höhe festsetzen** to assess the contribution; **~jahr** *(Sozialversicherung)* contribution year; **anrechnungsfähiges ~jahr** *(Sozialversicherung)* year of coverage; **~klasse** class of contributions, *(Sozialversicherung)* contribution scale; **~leistender** contributor.

Beitragsleistung subscription, payment of contributions, contribution dues *(US)*;
gestaffelte ~ graduated contribution; **soziale ~en** social contributions;
seine ~en einstellen to discontinue one's subscription; **j. zu ~en heranziehen** to collect dues from s. o.; **mit seinen ~en im Rückstand sein** to be in arrears with the payment of one's contributions.

Beitrags|marke subscription stamp; **~pflicht** liability to contribute, compulsory contribution.

beitragspflichtig contributory, liable for contribution, liable to contribute (subscription);
nicht ~ noncontributory;
~es Mitglied contributory [member]; **~e Pension** contributory pension; **~er Wert** contributory value.

Beitrags|pflichtiger contributory; **~quote** quota, share; **~rückerstattung** return of contribution, contribution refund, *(Lebensversicherung)* policy dividend; **~rückstände** contributions in arrears; **~satz** rate of contribution; **gestaffelter ~satz** graded contribution; **pauschaler ~satz** flat-rate contribution; **~sätze** contribution rates, rates of contribution; **~schlüssel** coefficient; **~staffel** contribution scale; **~staffelung** *(Versicherung)* scale (grading) of premiums, *(Lebensversicherung)* premium schedule; **~tabelle** contribution table; **~verfahren** contribution scheme; **~wert zur großen Havarie** general contributory value; **~woche** *(Sozialversicherung)* contribution week; **freiwilliger ~zahler** *(Krankenversicherung)* voluntary contributor; **~zahlung** payment of dues (contributions), subscription; **freiwillige ~zahlung** *(Krankenversicherung)* voluntary contribution; **von ~zahlungen abhängig sein** to be subject to contribution conditions; **anrechnungsfähige ~zeit** *(Sozialversicherung)* contribution record *(Br.)*, record of contribution *(Br.)*.

beitragzahlendes Mitglied subscribing member.

beitreibbar recoverable, collectible, exactable, *(gerichtlich)* enforceable;
nicht ~ irrecoverable, uncollectible, unrecoverable; **nicht gerichtlich ~** unenforceable.

beitreiben to collect, to recover, to intend, to get in, to ingather *(Scot.)*, *(Abgaben)* to requisition, to contribute, *(mil.)* to requisition, to commandeer;
Gebühren ~ to exact fees; **Schulden ~** to recover debts, to exact payment of debts; **Steuern ~** to collect taxes; **Zahlung gerichtlich ~** to enforce payment by legal proceedings.

Beitreibung recovery, collection, *(gerichtlich)* enforcement, exaction, *(mil.)* requisition;
unter Androhung der ~ under penalty of execution;
~ von Außenständen collection (recovery) of outstanding debts, debt collection; **~ einer Geldstrafe** recovery of a fine; **~ von Steuern** collection (exaction) of taxes.

Beitreibungs|kosten recovering expenses, collection charges; **~maßnahmen** collection activities; **~verfahren** collection proceedings (procedure).

beitreten to join, to become a member, *(Abkommen)* to accede;
einem internationalen Abkommen ~ to accede to an international agreement; **einem Bündnis ~** to enter into an alliance; **jds. Meinung ~** to fall in with (come round to) s. one's opinion; **einer Partei ~** to become a member of (adhere to) a party; **einem Prozeß ~** to join a lawsuit; **einem Verein ~** to join (subscribe to) a club, to become a member of a club.

Beitritt adhesion, adherence, *(Nebenintervention)* intervention, interpleader, *(Verein)* joining, enrolment, membership, *(Vertrag)* accedence, sign-up, accession;
freier ~ open membership; **freiwilliger ~** voluntary membership;
~ zu einem Abkommen adherence to a convention; **~ zu einem internationalen Abkommen** accession to an international agreement; **~ zu einem Bündnis** entering an alliance; **~ zum Gemeinsamen Markt** entry into the Common Market; **~ zu einer Partei** adherence to a party; **~ zu einem Rechtsstreit** intervention; **~ zu einem Verein** joining a club; **~ zu einem Vertrag** accession to a treaty;
seinen ~ erklären to give in one's adhesion; **seinen ~ zu einem Verein erklären** to declare one's membership of a club, to become a member of a club; **zum ~ offen stehen** to be open for adherence.

Beitritts|abkommen deed of accession; **~absicht** intention to enter; **~alter** *(Versicherung)* age at entry; **~antrag** application to join (for membership), membership application; **~bedingungen** conditions of membership; **~chance** chance of entry; **~erklärung** declaration of accession, *(Verein)* declaration of membership (enrolment); **~erklärung zu einem Vertrag** acceptance of an agreement; **~formular** application form; **~gesuch** application for admission, membership application; **~klausel** *(Abkommen)* clause of accession, association clause; **~pflicht** compulsory membership; **~protokoll** protocol; **~urkunde** deed of accession; **~verhandlungen** negotiations for an entry, entry negotiations, entry talks; **~vertrag** Treaty of Accession; **~zwang** compulsory membership; **~zwang nach Arbeitsanstellung in einem gewerkschaftlichen Betrieb** post-entry closed shop.

Beiwagen *(Motorrad)* side-car, *(Straßenbahn)* trailer.

Beiwerk accessory, decoration, trimmings;
modisches ~ accessories; **überflüssiges ~** *(Rede)* frills, padding.

beiwohnen to cohabit;
einem Ereignis ~ to witness an event; **einer Versammlung ~** to attend a meeting.

beiziehen, Sachverständigen to call in an expert.

Beiziehung|der Rückversicherungsbeträge reinsurance recovery;
~ von Unterlagen *(Gericht)* writ of certiorari; **~ öffentlicher Unterlagen** access to records.

bejahen to give an affirmative answer, to affirm, to say yes.

bejahend affirmative;
~e Lebenseinstellung haben to hold the affirmative attitude.

bejahendenfalls in case you agree.

bejahrt advanced in years;
schon ~ sein to be well on in years.

Bejahung affirmative answer;
~ des Lebens positive attitude towards life.

bejammern, sein Los to lament one's misfortunes.

bejammernswerter Zustand lamentable condition.

bekämpfen to fight against, to combat, to antagonize, *(Parteien)* to oppose, to contend;
Feuer ~ to fight a fire; **seine Gelüste ~** to curb one's desires; **Gesetzentwurf ~** to oppose a bill; **bis aufs Messer (mit allen Mitteln) ~** to fight tooth and nail; **Mißbräuche ~** to make a stand against abuses; **Schädlinge ~** to take action against pests; **Seuchen ~** to make war against diseases; **Vorurteil mit Erfolg ~** to outgrow a prejudice.

bekämpfende Parteien, sich opposing parties.

Bekämpfung|der Arbeitslosigkeit measures to cure unemployment; **~ subversiver Elemente** counterinsurgency war; **~ von Schädlingen** pest control; **~ von Seuchen** war against diseases.

bekannt known, *(angesehen)* renowned, famed, famous, noted, *(vertraut)* familiar;
allgemein ~ generally (widely) known; **einander seit langem ~** old-acquainted; **irgendwie ~** vaguely familiar; **miteinander ~** acquainted; **als Person ~** of known indentity; **weithin ~** well-known;
~ mit instructed in;
sich ~ anhören to have a familiar ring; **sich ~ machen** to make o. s. known, to make a name for o. s.; **mit jem. ~ machen** to introduce s. o.; **mit jem. ~ sein** to be acquainted with s. o.; **allgemein ~ sein** to be common property (a matter of common knowledge); **bald allgemein ~ sein** to soon gain currency; **für sein Benehmen ~ sein** to be notorious for one's goings-on; **mit etw. bestens ~ sein** to be thoroughly familiar with s. th.; **mit jem. flüchtig ~ sein** to be on nodding terms with s. o.; **miteinander gut ~ sein** to be on familiar terms; **wie ein bunter Hund ~ sein** to be known all over the place; **kaum ~ sein** to be little known; **für seine gute Küche ~ sein** *(Hotel)* to be renowned for its good cuisine; **unter dem Namen ... ~ sein** to go by the name ...; **jem. nur oberflächlich ~ sein** to have a nodding acquaintance with s. o.; **öffentlich ~ sein** to be a matter of public record; **jem. persönlich ~ sein** to know s. o. personally; **jem. vom Sehen ~ sein** to know s. o. by sight; **in einer Stadt bestens ~ sein** to know a town like the back of one's hand; **wenig ~ sein** to be in the shade; **einem irgendwie ~ vorkommen** to seem to strike a chord; **~ werden** to go out, to become public, to come into notice, to leak out; **mit jem. ~ werden** to become acquainted with s. o., to pick up (scrape an acquaintance) with s. o.; **allmählich ~ werden** to filter through; **schnell ~ werden** to fly abroad; **~ werden wollen** to seek publicity;
~e Leute well-known people; **~es Risiko** *(Versicherung)* known risk; **~er Schriftsteller** well-known writer; **~er Schwindler** notorious crook; **~er Treffpunkt** popular meeting place.

Bekannte|r acquaintance, friend, *(Mädchen)* boy friend, young man;
alter ~r crony;
zu ~n gehen to go to see some friends; **alte ~ sein** to have known each other for a long time.

Bekanntenkreis [circle of] acquaintances.

Bekanntgabe notice, notification, announcement, disclosure, *(Gesetz)* promulgation, *(Zeitung)* advertisement;
im Wege öffentlicher ~ by public announcement;
gerichtliche ~ court notice; **öffentliche** ~ official notification, public announcement, publication;
~ **über die Einlösung und Tilgung von Wertpapieren** notice of redemption, sinking-fund notice *(US)*; ~ **der Gewinner** publication of the winners; ~ **prozeßwichtiger Urkunden** discovery of documents; ~ **von Urkunden an die Gegenpartei** discovery upon oath *(Br.)*.

bekanntgeben to notify, to make known, to announce, to come out with, to give forth, to give out, to declare, to signify, *(durch Anschlag)* to post, *(verkünden)* to promulgate, to proclaim, *(in der Zeitung)* to advertise;
etw. allgemein ~ to give s. th. publicity; **amtlich** ~ to gazette, to bulletin; **durch Aushang** ~ to post up; **Einzelheiten** ~ to give details; **feierlich** ~ to proclaim; **formell** ~ to declare; **Gesetz** ~ to promulgate a law; **öffentlich** ~ to announce publicly, to publish, to bulletin, to make (a public notice) known to the public; **durch Rundfunk** ~ to broadcast; **Verlobung** ~ to announce an engagement; **Verordnung** ~ to publish a decree; **Wahlresultat** ~ to declare the poll, to return *(Br.)*.

bekanntgegeben divulged, made known.

bekanntgemacht, hiermit wird notice is hereby given that;
erstmalig ~ published for the first time.

Bekanntheitsgrad erreichen to rise to notice.

bekanntlich as is generally known.

bekanntmachen to make known (public), to notify, to announce, to give out, to enounce, to show forth, *(in der Zeitung)* to advertise;
sich ~ to make o. s. known; **sich mit jem.** ~ to introduce o. s. to (rub elbows with) s. o.; **amtlich** ~ to make an official announcement; **etw. allgemein** ~ to give s. th. publicity, to make public; **durch Anschlag** ~ to put up a notice, to post; **sich mit einer Materie** ~ to familiarize o. s. with a matter; **öffentlich** ~ to publish, to make known by public proclamation, to bulletin, to make a matter of public record, to publicize, to divulgate, *(Gesetz)* to promulgate; **Werk einer breiteren Öffentlichkeit** ~ to make a work known to a wider public; **j. mit den Tatsachen vorher** ~ to preacquaint s. o. with the facts; **in der Zeitung** ~ to advertise.

Bekanntmachung notification, intimation, *(Anschlag)* notice, poster, *(Gesetz)* promulgation, *(Verkündigung)* proclamation, promulgation, *(Verlautbarung)* communiqué, bulletin, divulgation, ban, *(Veröffentlichung)* announcement, publication, *(in der Zeitung)* advertisement;
im Wege öffentlicher ~ by public announcement;
amtliche ~ official publication (announcement, notice); **gerichtliche** ~ legal notice; **geschäftliche** ~ trade publication; **öffentliche** ~ public announcement (notice), notice by publication; **offizielle** ~ bulletin; **überraschende** ~ surprise announcement;
~ **über die Einlösung und Tilgung von Wertpapieren** notice of redemption, sinking-fund notice *(US)*; ~ **der Wahlergebnisse** declaration of the poll, return *(Br.)*; ~ **in der Zeitung** insertion of an announcement in a newspaper;
~ **anschlagen** to stick (put, pin) up a notice; **öffentliche** ~ **erlassen** to issue a proclamation, to give out a notice; ~ **verlesen** to read out an official announcement.

Bekanntmachungs|gebühr publication fee; ~**pflicht** duty to disclose; ~**tag** day of publication.

Bekanntschaft acquaintance, familiarity;
anrüchige ~**en** discreditable acquaintances; **flüchtige** ~ casual (speaking) acquaintance; **neueste** ~ recent acquaintance; **oberflächliche** ~ nodding acquaintance;
~ **und Verwandtschaft** kith and kin;
~ **erneuern** to renew an acquaintance; **bei näherer** ~ **gewinnen** to improve on acquaintance; **unangenehme** ~ **loswerden** to throw off a troublesome acquaintance; ~ **machen** to form (make) an acquaintance; **jds.** ~ **machen** to pick up with s. o.; **sich freuen, jds.** ~ **zu machen** to be pleased to meet s. o.; **jds.** ~ **pflegen** to push (cultivate) s. one's acquaintance; **mit jem.** ~ **schließen** to pluck up acquaintance with s. o.

Bekanntschaftsmoment acquaintance factor.

Bekanntwerden von Staatsgeheimnissen leakage of state secrets.

bekanntwerden to become known (public), to leak out;
gerüchteweise ~ to be rumo(u)red that.

bekehren to convert;
j. zu einer Meinung ~ to bring s. o. round to an opinion, to bring s. o. over.

Bekehrung conversion.

Bekehrungseifer missionary zeal.

bekennen to confess, to avow, to admit;
sich zu jem. ~ to stand up for s. o.; **Farbe** ~ to show one's hand, to come clean; **sich zum Kommunismus** ~ to profess o. s. a communist; **sich zu jds. Meinung** ~ to fall in with s. one's opinion; **sich schuldig** ~ to admit (plead) one's guilt, to confess o. s. guilty; **sich zu seiner Überzeugung** ~ to stand up for one's conviction.

Bekenntnis confession, avowal;
religiöses ~ denomination, religious belief;
~ **ablegen** to confess, to make a confession; **vollständiges** ~ **ablegen** to confess fully;
~**christ** professed Christian.

bekenntnisfreie Schule undenominational school.

Bekenntnis|freiheit religious freedom; ~**proporz** confessional equality; ~**schule** denominational (parochial, *US*) school.

beklagen to deplore, to lament, to grieve, to mourn;
sich über etw. ~ to complain about s. th.; **sich heftig** ~ to cry out; **sein Los** ~ to bewail one's lot; **sein Schicksal** ~ to deplore one's fate; **Tod eines Freundes** ~ to mourn the death of a friend; **Verlust** ~ to deplore a loss;
sich über j. nicht ~ **können** to have no quarrel with s. o.;
Menschenleben waren nicht zu ~ there was no loss of life.

beklagenswerter Unfall deplorable accident.

beklagt defendant;
~**e Gesellschaft (Partei)** defendant company (corporation), *(Ehescheidungsverfahren)* respondent.

Beklagte|r defendant, answerer, party sued, libellee, contestee, party to be charged, *(Ehescheidung)* respondent;
fiktiver ~**r** Richard Roe, otherwise troublesome; **gesamtschuldnerisch** ~ defendants jointly indebted;
~**r im Berufungsverfahren** respondent; ~**r im Revisionsverfahren** defendant in error;
als ~**r auftreten** to defend in a court of law; ~**n verurteilen** to find against the defendant; ~**n zur Zahlung der Prozeßkosten verurteilen** to condemn the defendant in costs.

beklatschen to applaud.

bekleben to paste (glue, stick) with, *(mit Etikett)* to label;
Mauer mit Plakaten ~ to placard a wall.

Beklebe|papier gummed paper; ~**zettel** [stick-on] label, gummed label.

bekleiden to cloth, to dress, to apparel *(US)*;
öffentliches Amt ~ to hold (be in) office, to fill (occupy) a position; **mit einem Amt** ~ to invest (endue) with an office; **Posten** ~ to occupy a post, to hold a position; **Stelle** ~ to fill a position.

bekleidet clothed, clad, dressed, *(mit Vollmachten)* vested;
~ **sein** to wear.

Bekleidung clothes, dress, *(mit einem Amt)* investiture;
unpassende ~ improper dress;
~ **eines Amtes** tenure of office;
j. für die ~ **eines Amtes als unfähig erklären** to disqualify s. o. from holding an office; **selbst für seine** ~ **sorgen müssen** to find o. s. in clothes.

Bekleidungs|gegenstände clothing, wearing apparel; ~**geschäft** clothing store *(US)*; ~**gewerbe** clothing manufacturers (trade); ~**haus** clothing store *(US)*; ~**industrie** clothing industry; ~**stücke** articles of dress (clothing); ~**vorschrift** *(mil.)* dress regulations.

bekloppt *(fam.)* crazy, cracked, nutty *(sl.)*, up the stick *(sl.)*.

bekohlen to coal, to bunker.

Bekohlung coaling.

Bekohlungsschiff coaling ship.

bekommen to get, to obtain;
jem. ~ to agree with s. o.; **es mit der Angst** ~ to get the wind up *(sl.)*; **seine Arbeit fertig** ~ to finish one's work; **Bescheid** ~ to be informed; **Entschädigung** ~ to be remunerated for s. th.; **Erkältung** ~ to catch a cold; **Erlaubnis** ~ to obtain leave; **Fieber** ~ to develop a fever; **Geschmack für etw.** ~ to come to like s. th.; **jem. glänzend** ~ to do s. o. a world of good; **Heimweh** ~ to grow homesick; **zehn Jahre** ~ to be sentenced to ten years of imprisonment; **Kind** ~ to be expecting (in the family way); **Korb** ~ to meet with a refusal; **Laufpaß** ~ to be given one's walking papers; **seinen verdienten Lohn** ~ to get one's deserts; **Lust zu etw.** ~ to feel inclined; **nicht** ~ *(Essen, Klima)* to disagree; **Orden** ~ to be awarded a decoration; **etw. mit der Post zugeschickt** ~ to receive s. th. with the mail; **Preis** ~ to win a prize; **ersten Preis** ~ to take the first prize; **Rückfall** ~ to relapse; **es satt** ~ to grow tired of; **Stellung** ~ to get a job; **wenig von jem. zu sehen** ~ to see little of s. o.;
nicht genug ~ **können** to be never satisfied.

bekömmliche Nahrungsmittel easily digestible food.
beköstigen to board, to feed;
sich selbst ~ to cook for o. s.
Beköstigung board[ing], *(Unterhalt)* alimentation;
bei freier ~ with free board;
volle ~ full board.
Beköstigungs|anweisung victualling note *(Br.)*; **~bon** meal ticket; **~geld** quarters allowance, allowance for board.
bekräftigen to affirm, to confirm, to strengthen, to vouch, to corroborate;
Aussage ~ to reinforce (corroborate s. one's) statement; **eidlich** ~ to take upon (affirm) one's oath; **in seiner Meinung** ~ to strengthen (endorse) s. one's opinion; **Zeugenaussage** ~ to corroborate a witness.
Bekräftigung affirmation, confirmation, corroboration;
zur ~ **seiner Argumente** in support of his arguments;
~ **einer Ansicht** endorsement of an opinion;
j. zur ~ **aufrufen** to vouch s. o. to warranty.
Bekräftigungseid asserty oath *(US)*.
bekriegen, einander to be at war with each another.
bekritteln to find fault with, to pick holes in.
bekritzeln to scribble, to scrawl.
bekümmern to trouble, to worry, to concern;
sich um jds. Angelegenheiten ~ to bother about s. one's affairs.
bekümmert worried about, concerned, troubled;
~ **sein** to be on the fret;
mit ~em Gesicht with a troubled face.
bekunden to manifest, to show, *(Zeuge)* to depose;
eidlich ~ to make a statement on oath; **seine Unwissenheit** ~ to show one's ignorance.
Bekundung demonstration, manifestation, testimony.
Beladefrist time for loading, loading time.
Beladen loading, lading;
~ **und Entladen** *(Schiff)* turn-round.
beladen to load, to lade, to cargo, to freight;
Fuhre ~ to load a cart; **j. mit Päckchen und Paketen** ~ to load down s. o. with parcels and packages; **Schiff** ~ to freight a ship, to take a ship to freight; **mit Stückgut** ~ to load in (freight by) parcels; **wieder** ~ to reload, to relade;
~ *(a.)* loaded, laden, weighted;
nicht ~ *(Schiff)* uncharged; **mit Schuld** ~ laden with guilt; **schwer** ~ heavily loaded; **mit Sorgen** ~ heavy with sorrows; **mit Speisen** ~ loaded with food; **tief** ~ laden to sink.
Beladeplan loading table.
Belader loader, stevedore, shipper, freighter.
Beladestation loading station.
Beladung loading, lading;
freie ~ free loading;
~ **eines Schiffes** ship loading, freighting; ~ **mit Stückgut** loading on the berth.
Beladungs|grenze load limit; **~kosten** loading costs.
Belag *(Brücke)* covering, *(Straße)* surface.
Belagerer beleaguerer.
belagern to besiege, to beleaguer, to invest.
belagert, von Jugendlichen mobbed by teenagers; **von Reportern** ~ besieged by newspaper reporters.
Belagerung siege, beleaguerment, investment;
~ **aufheben** to raise (break) a siege; ~ **einer Stadt beginnen** to sit down before a town; ~ **einer Stadt durchführen** to lay siege to a town; **einer** ~ **standhalten** to stand (withstand) a siege.
Belagerungs|heer besieging army; **~truppen** besieging force; **~zustand** siege, state of siege; **~zustand verhängen** to declare a state of siege.
Belang concern, matter, issue, concernment;
nichts von ~ nothing to write home about; **ohne** ~ irrelevant, of no account, quite out of the picture; **von** ~ of importance; **von großem** ~ **sein** to count for much.
belangbar indictable;
strafrechtlich ~ liable to criminal prosecution.
Belange interests, concerns;
gemeinsame ~ matters of common concern; **nationale** ~ national interests; **öffentliche** ~ public concern (interest); **wirtschaftliche** ~ trade concerns, economic interests;
kulturelle ~ **einer Stadt** cultural affairs of a town;
sich für die eigenen ~ **einsetzen** to stand up for o. s.; **jds.** ~ **vertreten** to represent s. one's interests; ~ **eines Landes vertreten** to represent a country.
belangen, j. disziplinarisch to take disciplinary measures against s. o.; **j. gerichtlich** ~ to sue s. o. at law, to go to law with (take legal steps against) s. o., to file an action against s. o., to bring s. o. to justice; **Gesellschaft** ~ to prosecute a company.
belanglos off the point, trifling, trivial, irrelevant, frivolous;
völlig ~ **sein** not to matter at all; **über ~e Dinge sprechen** to talk about trifles;
~e Sache featherweight.
belangt werden können, konkursrechtlich to be liable to be proceeded against under the bankruptcy law.
Belangung, strafrechtliche prosecution.
belassen to leave, to let rest;
j. in seinem Amt ~ to retain s. o. in office.
Belassung im Amt retention in office.
Belassungsquote permitted retention.
belastbar chargeable, debitable, *(techn.)* loadable;
hypothekarisch ~ mortgageable.
Belastbarkeit *(el.)* power rating, *(Körper)* maximum stress, *(techn.)* loading capacity;
am Ende seiner ~ **anlangen** to come to the end of one's endurance.
belasten *(anrechnen)* to charge, to debit, to count, to note down, to bill *(US)*, *(durch Aussage)* to incriminate, to charge, *(beladen)* to load, to lade, to burden, to put a load on;
j. ~ to place to s. one's debt; **j. mit zusätzlicher Arbeit** ~ to saddle s. o. with additional work; **Balken** ~ to load a beam; **Eisenbahnverkehr** ~ to make demands on the railway lines; **Etat mit etw.** ~ to burden the budget; **Etat der Gemeinden** ~ to burden the finances of the communities; **sein Gedächtnis mit unnützen Zahlen** ~ to burden (charge) one's memory with unnecessary figures; **sein Gewissen** ~ to weigh on one's conscience; **Grundstück mit einer Hypothek** ~ to mortgage (affect, *Scot.*) a piece of real estate, to charge one's land; **Grundstück zu Sicherheitszwecken** ~ to charge property as security; **Haushalt** ~ to burden the budget; **hypothekarisch** ~ to burden with a mortgage, to mortgage, to encumber; **jem. kaum** ~ to sit lightly upon s. o.; **Konto** ~ to charge (debit) an account, to pass (place) to the debit of an account, to enter s. th. to the debit side [of an account]; **jds. Konto** ~ to pass to s. one's debit, to make an entry against s. o.; **jds. Konto mit einem Betrag** ~ to charge an amount to s. one's account; **Konto mit sämtlichen Unkosten** ~ to charge an account with all the expenses; **Kreislauf** ~ to strain the circulation; **dem Kunden Porto** ~ to charge the postage to the customer; **seinen Magen** ~ to overload one's stomach; **mit übermäßiger Miete** ~ to rackrent *(Ireland)*; **nachträglich** ~ to make an additional charge; **jds. Nerven** ~ to tax s. one's nerves; **Posten** ~ to debit an item; **sich mit Schulden** ~ to encumber o. s. with (involve o. s. in) debts; **j. schwer** ~ to weigh on s. one's mind; **sich** ~ to take a load (burden) o. s., *(strafrechtlich)* to convict (incriminate) o. s.; **zu stark** ~ to overload; **mit Steinen** ~ to weigh down with stones; **mit Steuern** ~ to burden with taxes; **j. mit Verantwortung** ~ to saddle s. o. with responsibility; **zu viel** ~ to surcharge, to overcharge; **Waren mit Zoll** ~ to impose a tariff on goods; **zu wenig** ~ to undercharge; **mit unnützem Wissen** ~ to cram one's head with useless facts; **Zinsen** ~ to charge interest; **mit Zoll** ~ to impose a tariff; **zuviel** ~ to overcharge;
zu ~ **mit** chargeable.
belastend incriminatory, inculpatory;
~e Aussage incriminatory statement; **~es Material** incriminating evidence.
belastet weighted, *(Bankkonto)* charged with, debited, *(fig.)* burdened, saddled, charged, *(Grundstück)* encumbered, burdened, servient, *(Fahrzeug)* loaded, *(pol.)* incriminated, *(Telefonnetz)* busy, *(verpfändet)* bonded;
erblich ~ tainted; **hypothekarisch** ~ mortgaged; **nicht** ~ uncharged, not debited, *(Verdächtiger)* free of charge; **nicht hypothekarisch** ~ unmortgaged; **mit Schulden** ~ encumbered, incumbered, burdened with debts; **mit Sorgen** ~ heavily laden with worries; **zu stark** ~ overladen, overloaded; **steuerlich** ~ tax-laden (-burdened); **mit hohen Steuern** ~ heavily taxed; **voll** ~ fully loaded, *(Motor)* at full load; **weniger** ~ *(tel.)* less busy;
bei jem. ~ **sein** to be in s. one's debit; **mit etw.** ~ **sein** to have s. th. on one's hands; **abends am stärksten** ~ **sein** *(Straßen)* to have its peak hours in the evening; **erblich** ~ **sein** to have a hereditary disease; **politisch** ~ **sein** to be handicapped by one's political past; **mit Schulden** ~ **sein** to be burdened with debts; **hypothekarisch** ~ **werden** to become mortgaged;
hypothekarisch ~er Grundbesitz encumbered (burdened) estate; **~es Konto** debited account; **zu sehr ~es Leitungsnetz** overloaded network.
Belasteter incriminated person.
belästigen to disturb, to inconvenience, to trouble, to molest, to importune, to plague, to annoy, to pester, to worry, *(Prostituierte)* to solicit;

j. ~ to bother (badger) s. o., to make an intrusion upon s. o.; **j. mit Fragen** ~ to pester (plague) s. o. with questions; **j. mit Hilfsanforderungen** ~ to pester s. o. with requests of help; **j. mit seinen Paketen** ~ to embarrass s. o. with parcels.

belästigend annoying, troublesome.

belästigt, von Betrunkenen molested by drunken men.

Belästigung molestation, disturbance, importunity, trouble, nuisance, trial, *(Prostituierte)* solicitation;
anhaltende ~ continuing nuisance; **erhebliche** ~ material discomfort; **andauernde nachbarliche** ~ constant vexations from one's neighbo(u)rs; **nachbarrechtliche** ~ private nuisance; **rechtserhebliche** ~ actionable nuisance; **unbedeutende** ~ trivial nuisance;
~ **der Nachbarschaft** offence against (injury to) the neighbo(u)rhood; **Schikanen und** ~**en** annoyance and inconveniences.

Belastung weight, load, *(fig.)* charge, burden, drag, drain, incidence, handicap, *(Druck)* impact, *(gesundheitlich)* stress, *(Konto)* debiting, debit entry, charge, charging, *(Grundstück)* encumbrance, mortgage, *(strafrechtlich)* incrimination, charge, *(Tragkraft)* loading capacity;
außergewöhnliche ~ *(Einkommensteuer)* extraordinary expenses; **ausstehende** ~**en** *(Bilanz)* deferred charges; **betriebliche** ~ *(Eisenbahn)* engagement; **dauernde** ~ standing charge, *(Maschine)* permanent load; **dingliche** ~ encumbrance; **konkretisierte dingliche** ~ fixed charge *(Br.)*; **einkommensunabhängige** ~**en** non-income charges; **eintragungsfähige** ~ registrable charge; **erbliche** ~ hereditary disease (taint); **fest[stehend]e** ~ fixed charge; **finanzielle** ~ financial strain (drain, beating, burden, load), money charge; **schwere finanzielle** ~ great drain on the purse; **zu geringe** ~ underload; **geringste** ~ *(Maschine)* minimum load; **gleichbleibende** ~ fixed charge, *(Maschine)* constant load; **zu große** ~ overcharge; **höchstzulässige** ~ maximum useful load[ing]; **hypothekarische** ~ encumbrance, mortgage [charge], mortgage debt; **jährliche** ~ annual charges; **nachträgliche** ~**en** additional charges; **politische** ~ political incrimination; **zu starke politische** ~ overcommitment; **rückzahlbare** ~ redeemable charge; **ruhende** ~ dead load; **seelische** ~ mental strain; **steuerliche** ~ tax burden (load), charges for (burden of) taxation; **nicht abwälzbare steuerliche** ~ final (real) incidence; **übermäßige steuerliche** ~ overtaxation; **unausweichliche** ~ burden; **unmittelbare** ~ direct charge; **mit einem Legat verbundene** ~**en** charges falling on a legatee; **volle** ~ full load; **vorjährige** ~**en** prior years' charges; **wirtschaftliche** ~ economic handicap; **wissenschaftliche** ~ economic handicap; **zulässige** ~ safe (safety, work) load, allowable stress; **zusätzliche** ~ additional load;
~**en in Abteilung Eins des Grundbuchs** [etwa] Class A charges; ~ **in Abteilung Zwei des Grundbuchs** [etwa] covenants running with the land; ~ **des Arbeitsmarktes** pressure on the labo(u)r market; ~ **des landwirtschaftlichen Besitzes** agricultural charge *(Br.)*; ~ **der Bremsen** breaking load; ~ **der Devisenbilanz** pressure on the foreign exchange position; ~ **durch Eigengewicht** dead weight; ~ **je Flächeneinheit** unit load; ~ **des Fürsorgeetats** welfare load; **dingliche** ~ **einer Gesellschaft** corporate mortgage; ~ **seiner Gesundheit** tax on s. one's health; ~ **von Grundbesitz** land charge; ~ **mit einem Heimfallrecht** revertibility; ~**en des modernen Lebens** strain of modern life; ~ **durch eine Lehrfunktion** teaching load; ~ **durch Löhne und Gehälter** payload; ~ **eines Motors** load on a motor; ~ **des Naturhaushaltes** ecological pressure; ~ **ohne Nutzgewicht** dead load; ~ **durch Policenabtretung** existing indebtedness on a policy; ~ **in der Spitzenzeit** peak load; **große** ~ **der Staatsfinanzen** great drain on the country's resources; ~ **mit Steuern und Abgaben** fiscal charges;
~ **aushalten** to take the strain; **zu hohen** ~**en aussetzen** to overload; **Wirtschaft großen** ~**en aussetzen** to place great strains on the economy; ~ **für j. darstellen** to be an encumbrance (charge) on s. o.; **schwere finanzielle** ~ **für j. darstellen** to be a strain on s. one's resources; ~ **für das Geschäft darstellen** to be a dead weight (drain) on the business; ~**en des Schuldentilgungsdienstes erfüllen** to meet debt-service charges; ~**en ertragen** to sustain burdens; **von** ~**en freistellen** to disencumber; **große** ~ **für j. dargestellt haben** to have been a drag on s. o.; **ohne** ~ **laufen** *(Maschine)* to be running light; **sein Grundstück von** ~**en frei machen** to clear one's property of debts; **große** ~ **für j. sein** to be a charge (great strain) on s. o.; **starken finanziellen** ~**en ausgesetzt sein** to be under great handicap financially; **große** ~ **für seine Familie sein** to be a great trouble to one's family; **ein ganzes Leben lang für j. eine** ~ **sein** to be a drag on s. o. all his life; **den** ~**en des modernen Lebens nicht gewachsen sein** to suffer from the strain of modern life; **den** ~**en des Transportgewerbes gewachsen sein** to cope with the transportation burden.

Belastungs|änderung *(techn.)* load variation; ~**anweisung** debit ticket; ~**anzeige** advice of debit, debit note (advice, memorandum, *US*); ~**anzeigen auf einem Kundenkonto verbuchen** to post charges to customer's account; ~**aufgabe** debit advice (note); ~**dauer** load period; ~**fähigkeit** *(Maschine)* carrying capacity; ~**fähigkeit einer Brücke berechnen** to calculate the strains and stresses of a bridge; ~**faktor** load factor; ~**formular** *(Bankbuchhaltung)* debit (charge, *US*) ticket; ~**grenze** *(Grundstück)* limit of encumbrances, *(Last)* load limit; ~**höhe** extent of a charge; ~**kurve** load curve; ~**material** *(Strafverfahren)* evidence for the prosecution, incriminating documents (evidence); ~**mitteilung** notice of encumbrances; ~**nachweis** *(Grundbuch)* charge certificate; ~**probe** loading test; **jeder** ~**probe standhalten** to stand every test; ~**quote** load ratio; ~**register** register of charges *(Br.)*; ~**spitze** *(Bahn)* peak load; ~**tabelle** load (Gantt) chart; ~**urkunde** instrument of charge; ~**zettel** debit slip; ~**zeuge** witness for the prosecution, prosecuting witness, witness against s. o. (for the Crown, *Br.*), King's (Queen's, *Br.*, state's, *US*) evidence.

belaufen, sich to amount (come, mount up, run) to, to reach, to rise, to run into; **sich auf das Doppelte des Voranschlags** ~ to come to double the estimate; **sich auf 10.000 DM** ~ to foot up (figure out) to DM 10.000 debts; **sich auf etwa 100 £** ~ to reach approximately £ 100; **sich höher als 5000 DM** ~ to exceed DM 5000; **insgesamt** ~ to aggregate, to total; **sich ungefähr** ~ to come near to.

belauschen to eavesdrop, to overhear;
Gespräche Dritter ~ to listen in to other people's conversation.

beleben to animate, to encourage, to enliven, to kindle, to stimulate;
Absatz ~ to increase sales; **Diskussion** ~ to enliven a discussion; **Handel** ~ to reanimate (encourage) trade; **Konjunktur** ~ to enliven business, to stimulate business activity; **sich langsam** ~ to revive gradually; **Markt** ~ to stimulate the market; **neu** ~ to rekindle, to reanimate; **Produktion** ~ to stimulate (encourage) production; **Unterhaltung** ~ to animate the conversation.

belebend animating, stimulating, invigorating;
~**es Mittel** stimulant, restorative; ~**e Wirkung** restorative (stimulative) effect.

belebt *(Börse)* active, animated, brisk, *(Straße)* crowded;
in einer ~**en Straße wohnen** to live in a busy street.

Belebung *(Börse)* animation, stimulation, briskness, recovery, activity;
konjunkturelle ~ economic activity, stimulation of business activity; **plötzliche kurze** ~ flurry *(US)*;
~ **des Absatzes** increase in sales; ~ **des Arbeitsmarktes** reemployment; ~ **des Ausfuhrgeschäftes** growth in export, export increase; ~ **des Handels** reanimation of trade; ~ **der Konjunktur** economic recovery (revival), business recovery; ~ **des Marktes** stimulation of the market; ~ **der Produktion** stimulation of production; ~ **der Wirtschaft** stimulation of business activity, economic upswing; ~ **der Wirtschaft durch Anhebung des Preisniveaus** reflation.

Belebungs|komponenten stimulating factors; ~**mittel** stimulant, restorative; **wirtschaftliche** ~**mittel** means of stimulus; **konjunkturelle** ~**spritze** shot in the arm.

Beleg *(Akte)* record, *(Beispiel)* example, *(Beweisstück)* evidence, proof, *(für Buchung)* voucher, slip, *(für das Gericht)* exhibit, *(Quelle)* authority, source, *(Quittung)* receipt, *(Unterlage)* reference, *(Urkunde)* certificate, supporting document, documentary proof, warrant, *(für Wortgebrauch)* instance;
~ **anliegend** voucher attached;
abgestempelter ~ voucher stamp; **abgezeichneter** ~ chit *(Br.)*; **anerkannter** ~ approved voucher; **eigener** ~ internal voucher; **geprüfter und zur Zahlung angewiesener** ~ audited voucher, voucher payable;
~**e für die Portokasse** petty-cash voucher; ~**e für eine Rechnung** vouchers in support of an account; ~ **für eine These** authority for a thesis;
~ **abheften** to file a voucher; ~**e beibringen** to furnish evidence; ~**e einreichen** to present (submit) vouchers; ~**e in einem Buch geben** to give references in a book; ~**e kontieren** to code documents; **als** ~ **liefern** to furnish proof; ~**e überprüfen** to audit vouchers; ~**e vorlegen** to submit documentary material; **als** ~ **zitieren** to quote a passage;
~**ablage** voucher files; ~**abschnitt** voucher, *(am Scheck)* check *(US)* (cheque, *Br.*) voucher; ~**abzeichnung** expense bill (sheet); ~**artikel** tearsheet article.

belegbar provable, attestable;
durch Beispiele ~ exemplificative.

Beleg | bogen tear sheet; ~**buch** slip book; ~**buchhaltung** voucher system (bookkeeping), slip system; **vollständiges** ~**doppel,** ~**duplikat** complete voucher copy.

Belegen | von Frachtraum freight bookings; ~ **von Sendezeiten** time buying.

belegen to vouch, to make good;
mit Abgaben ~ to tax, to levy taxes (duties); **Abrechnung mit Quittungen** ~ to accompany an account with receipts; **Grube mit Arbeitern** ~ to man a mine; **Ausgaben** ~ to account for one's expenses, to voucher; **seine Aussage urkundlich** ~ to substantiate one's statement with documents; **durch Beispiele** ~ to exemplify, to illustrate with examples; **mit Beschlag** ~ to distress, to distrain, to levy a distraint; **Bett** ~ *(Krankenhaus)* to fill a bed; **Stadt mit Bomben** ~ to bomb a town; **Bremsen** ~ to line the brakes; **Boden mit Brettern** ~ to board the floor; **dokumentarisch** ~ to document, to support by vouchers; **mit Einquartierung** ~ to quarter, to billet; **im einzelnen** ~ to give specific reasons; **Fußboden mit Fliesen** ~ to flag the floor; **j. mit einem Fluch** ~ to lay a curse on s. o.; **Frachtraum** ~ to book freight; **Stadt mit einer Garnison** ~ to garrison a town; **j. mit einer Geldstrafe** ~ to [impose a] fine [on] s. o.; **Leitung** ~ to tie up a line; **mit einer Nachgebühr** ~ to surcharge; **Platz** ~ to retain a seat, to bag; **ersten Platz** ~ to take first place; **letzten Platz** ~ to be a tail-ender; **Platz im voraus** ~ **lassen** to reserve a seat, to book a seat in advance; **mit Rechnungen** ~ to verify with invoices; **Rückfahrt** ~ to book a return ticket; **j. mit Schimpfnamen** ~ to call s. o. names; **Sendezeit** ~ to buy time; **Sitz** ~ to occupy (secure, bag, *fam.*) a seat; **mit einer Sondersteuer** ~ to impose a surcharge; **Land mit Steuern** ~ to tax a country; **mit Strafe** ~ to inflict a penalty; **mit Teppichen** ~ to carpet; **Textstelle** ~ to quote one's authorities; **urkundlich** ~ to support by documents, to document, to record, to document one's claim; **seinen Anspruch urkundlich** ~ to document one's claim; **Vorlesung** ~ to subscribe to (enrol, register for, sign up for, *US*) a course of lectures;
~ *(a.)* situated, located;
~ **sein** to be located.

Belegenheit siting, situs, adjacency, location, situation, lie of the ground;
örtliche ~ local situation; **steuerliche** ~ taxable situs; **ungünstige** ~ ineligible location;
~ **von Betriebsvermögen** location of business assets; ~ **des eingetragenen Firmensitzes** situation of the registered office; **nahe** ~ **eines lauten Flugplatzes** neighbo(u)rhood of a noisy airport.

Belegenheits | gerichtsstand forum rei sitae; ~**land** country of domicile; ~**miete** situation rent; ~**nachteile** disadvantage of localization; ~**vorteil** locational advantage; ~**wechsel** change of the situation.

Beleg | exemplar checking (voucher, specimen) copy, tear sheet *US*), *(für öffentliche Bibliotheken)* deposit copy; **vollständiges** ~**exemplar** complete voucher copy *(Br.)*; ~**formular** voucher form; ~**inventur** cost voucher inventory; ~**material** documentary evidence; ~**nummer** checking copy, voucher number; ~**ordner** voucher register; ~**prüfung** examination of a long account, voucher audit; ~**quittung** accountable receipt; ~**sammlung** voucher register.

Belegschaft [shop] staff, workroom staff, workforce, working force, hands, employees, crew, [operating] personnel, labo(u)r force, [production] force *(US)*, operating (operational) staff *(US)*;
im Akkord arbeitende ~ task force; **gesamte** ~ total force of men employed; **gleichbleibende (ständige)** ~ permanent staff, stable force *(US)*; **ortsansässige** ~ local staff; **aus der Heimat stammende** ~ home-based staff;
~ **abbauen** to reduce the labo(u)r force; ~ **durchforsten** to slim the workforce; **seine gesamte** ~ **entlassen** to dismiss all one's hands; **zur** ~ **gehören** to be on the staff; ~ **reduzieren (verringern)** to pare the workforce, to lop the staff *(US)*.

Belegschafts | abbau personnel cutback, employees layoff; ~**abbau auf breiter Front** broad-scale workforce reduction; ~**abbau herbeiführen** to pare the workforce, to lop the staff *(US)*; ~**abgänge** labo(u)r-force dropouts; ~**aktien** staff employee shares *(Br.)*, employee stocks *(US)*; ~**aktienangebot** employee share offer; ~**aktienausschuß** employee stock purchase committee *(US)*; ~**aktiensystem** employees' shares (stock purchase, *US*) plan; ~**aktionär** staff shareholder *(Br.)*, holder of staff shares (employee stocks, *US*); ~**angehörige** staff, workforce, employees, personnel; ~**angehörige ohne Arbeitserlaubnis** unlicensed personnel *(US)*; ~**durchforstung** slimming of the workforce; ~**einrichtungen** staff amenities; ~**fluktuation** personnel mobility; ~**fonds** staff fund; ~**gehälter** salaries of staff; ~**hilfe** fringe benefits; ~**mitglied** staff member; **langjähriges** ~**mitglied** company old-timer; **zur mittleren Führungsschicht gehörige** ~**mitglieder** middle echelon staff members; ~**moral** staff morale; ~**nachrichten** employees' newsletter; ~**plan** employee roster; ~**raum** staff room; ~**reduzierung vornehmen** to cut back on the workforce, to lop the staff *(US)*; ~**rückgang** decline in manpower; ~**schulung** training of staff; ~**stärke** personnel strength, manpower strength; **tariflich vereinbarte** ~**stärke** personnel laid down in the agreement; ~**stärke in anderen Abteilungen abbauen** to reduce manning level in other departments; ~**tantieme** staff bonus; **völlige** ~**umschichtung** thorough turnover of the operational force; ~**wechsel** staff turnover; ~**zuwachs** accession.

Beleg | schein voucher; ~**seite** tear sheet (ticket, *US*); ~**sichtung** voucher audit, vouching; ~**stelle** quotation, instance, reference, passage, supporting authority; ~**stück** voucher (checking) copy, document in support, tear sheet (ticket, *US*); ~**system** voucher system.

belegt *(Krankenhaus)* occupied, *(Platz)* taken, booked, reserved *(US)*, *(Telefon)* engaged, busy *(US)*;
durch Tatsachen ~ documented; **urkundlich** ~ founded on documents, documented, authentic;
voll ~ **sein** *(Hotel)* to be fully booked;
~**es Bahngleis** occupied track; ~**er Platz** reserved seat *(US)*; ~**e Tatsache** matter of record.

Belegung *(Platz)* booking, reservation *(US)*;
urkundliche ~ documentation;
~ **durch Beispiele** exemplification; ~ **mit Bombenteppichen** saturation bombing; ~ **von Frachtraum** freight booking; ~ **einer Vorlesung** registration (enrolment) for a course of lectures (study).

Belegungszeit time used.

Beleg | versand sending of vouchers; ~**verzeichnis** [audit] voucher register; ~**zettel** voucher.

Belehnung enfeoffment.

belehren *(Geschworene)* to advise, to instruct;
j. eines Besseren ~ to enlighten s. o.; **j. über seine Rechte** ~ *(Strafrecht)* to warn s. o. of his rights; **j. über den wahren Sachverhalt** ~ to lay before s. o. all the facts of a case;
sich ~ **lassen** to listen to reason.

belehrend instructional, instructive.

belehrt werden, vom Gericht to be advised by the court.

Belehrung direction, instruction;
weitere ~ *(Geschworene)* further instructions.

beleidigen to insult, to offend, to give offence, to huff;
j. ~ to offer an insult to s. o., to call s. o. bad names, to utter a libel against s. o., to be offensive to s. o.; **grob** ~ to outrage; **öffentlich** ~ to offer an affront; **j. in seinem Stolz** ~ to injure s. one's pride; **j. tätlich** ~ to assault s. o.; **j. tödlich** ~ to sting s. o. to the quick; **j. zutiefst** ~ to hurt s. o. deeply, to insult s. o. to the last degree.

beleidigend slanderous, insulting, offensive, abusive;
offensichtlich ~ libel(l)ous per se;
in ~**er Absicht** with intend to offend; **keine** ~**e Absicht hegen** to mean no offence; ~**e Antwort geben** to give an offensive answer; ~**e Ausdrücke** insulting language; ~**e Äußerungen** defamatory statement; **in einem** ~**en Ton** in an offensive tone; ~**es Verhalten** insulting behavio(u)r; ~**e Worte** abusive language, offensive words.

beleidigt, leicht (sofort) easily offended; **tief** ~ deeply offended;
~ **sein** to take offence; **leicht** ~ **sein** to be quick to take offence;
sofort ~ **sein** to take offence at the slightest thing.

Beleidigter offended party.

Beleidigung offence, insult, abusive language, wound;
beabsichtigte ~ deliberate insult; **eingebildete** ~ supposed insult; **grobe** ~ gross insult; **grundlose** ~ gratuitous insult *(fam.)*; **öffentliche** ~ public affront; **persönliche** ~ personal insult; **schändliche** ~ outrageous insult; **schwere** ~ gross insult; **tätliche** ~ assault and battery; **tödliche** ~ mortal offence; **unverdiente** ~ gratuitous insult; **verleumderische** ~ libel, slander; **vorsätzliche** ~ studied insult; **wechselseitige** ~ mutual insult;
~ **des Gerichts** contempt of court;
mit ~**en attackieren** to fling out at s. o.; ~ **für das Auge darstellen** to offend the eye; ~**en einstecken (schlucken)** to swallow (put up with) an affront, to sit (lie down) under an insult; ~**en geduldig ertragen** to be patient of insults; ~

herunterschlucken to digest an insult *(coll.)*; ~ **ignorieren** to wink at an insult; ~ **einstecken müssen** to eat the leek; **sich für eine ~ rächen** to wipe out (avenge) an insult; ~ **übersehen** to ignore (pass over) an insult; **j. wegen ~ verklagen** to sue s. o. for libel, to serve s. o. with a writ for libel; **jem. ~en an den Kopf werfen** to give s. o. the rough edge of one's tongue; **jem. eine ~ zufügen** to be offensive to s. o., to utter a libel against.

Beleidigungs|klage libel action (writ), action for defamation (words, *Br.*), slander action; **jem. eine ~klage anhängen** to serve s. o. with a writ for libel; **~klage gegen eine Zeitung anstrengen** to sue a newspaper for libel; **~prozeß** libel suit (action); **~prozeß gegen j. anstrengen** to bring an action of libel against s. o.; **~- oder Verleumdungsverfahren** proceedings for libel or slander.

beleihbar pledgeable, *(Wertpapier)* eligible to serve as security (collateral).

Beleihbarkeit *(Wertpapiere)* eligibility to serve as collateral.

beleihen to lend, to [grant a] loan, to borrow, *(Grundstücke)* to hypothecate, to mortgage, to encumber;
Dokumente mit 10.000 Pfund ~ to lend £ 10.000 on the documents; **Effekten ~ [lassen]** to advance money on securities, to lodge stock as security *(US)*, to collateral securities *(US)*; **Grundstück bis zu 100% seines Wertes** ~ to borrow up to the value of the property; **Haus** ~ to raise a mortgage on (hypothecate) a house; **Haus zu 100% seines Wertes** ~ to lend up to 100 per cent of the valuation of a house; **kurzfristig** ~ to loan on short periods; **Police** ~ to borrow on a policy.

Beleihung lending, borrowing, granting a loan, *(Grundstück)* hypothecation;
~ **von Effekten** pledging of securities, hypothecation of securities for a loan *(US)*; ~ **einer Versicherung** policy loan.

Beleihungs|grenze, ~raum lending (borrowing) limit *(Br.)*, limit of credit *(Br.)*, credit line *(US)*; **~grundsätze** borrowing principles; **~höchstsatz** maximum advance; **~höchstwert** maximum loan value; **~objekt** collateral; **~satz** lending rate *(US)*; **~stopp** lending stop; **~wert** loan (collateral) value, *(mit Hypothek)* hypothecation (hypothecary) value *(US)*; **größter ~wert** maximum that may be advanced.

belesen studied, erudite, well-read;
sehr ~ deep-read.

Belesenheit, große wide reading.

beleuchten to illuminate, to light up, to lamp, *(fig.)* to shed light on;
Auto ~ to switch on the car lights; **Thema gründlich (von allen Seiten)** ~ to go over the ground thoroughly, to ring the changes.

Beleuchter *(Film, Theater)* lighting expert, electrician.

beleuchtet, elektrisch lighted by electricity; **mit Gas** ~ lit by gas;
schlaglichtartig ~ highlighted;
~e Straße lighted road.

Beleuchtung illumination, lighting;
elektrische ~ electric lighting; **festliche** ~ festive illumination; **indirekte** ~ indirect lighting; **künstliche** ~ artificial illumination (light); **städtische** ~ urban lighting;
~ **der Bühne** stage lighting; ~ **von Fahrzeugen** lighting of vehicles; ~ **durch Leuchtstoffröhren** fluorescent lighting; ~ **durch Röhrenlampen** tubular lighting;
~ **einschalten** to turn on the lights.

Beleuchtungs|anlage lighting [equipment], lighting plant; **~apparat** illuminating apparatus; **~effekt** illuminating effect; **~fachmann** lighting expert; **~industrie** lighting industries; **~ingenieur** illuminating (lighting) engineer; **~körper** lighting fixture; **~kosten** lighting expenses; **~probe** *(Theater)* light rehearsal; **~schirm** reflector; **neues ~system** new method of illumination; **~technik** illuminating engineering; **~techniker** electric-lighting engineer; **~verband** *(mil.)* merker unit; **~vorschriften** *(Auto)* lighting regulations; **~zeit** *(Auto)* lighting-up time.

beleumdet, gut of good reputation; **übel** ~ ill reputed, disreputable;
schlecht ~ sein to be in bad repute.

belichten to expose, *(Fotosatzmaschine)* to typeset;
zu kurz ~ to underexpose; **zu lange** ~ to overexpose.

belichtet, gut dense; **zu kurz** ~ underexposed; **zu lange** ~ overexposed.

Belichtung exposure [to light], exposition.

Belichtungs|angaben exposure data; **~armaturen** light fittings; **~automat** built-in automatic exposure control; **~befehl** *(Satzmaschine)* flash command; **~dauer** period of exposure; **~einstellung** exposure setting; **~messer** exposure meter; **elektrischer ~messer** photoelectric meter; **automatische ~schaltuhr** automatic interval timer; **~spielraum** latitude; **~tabelle** exposure table; **~zeit** period of exposure; **lange ~zeit erfordernd** slow.

Belieben discretion, convenience, choice, pleasure;
nach ~ at [upon] discretion, at pleasure; **nach deinem** ~ take it or leave it; **nach ~ des Gerichts** as the court may think fit; **ganz nach eigenem ~ handeln** to suit one's convenience, to suit o. s.; **in jds. ~ stehen** to be optional (rest) with s. o.; **in jds. ~ stellen** to leave it to s. one's discretion.

beliebig discretionary, optional, arbitrary, ad libitum;
~ **verwenden** to use freely;
~er Betrag any amount; **jede ~e Größe** any size desired; ~ **lange** for any length of time; **an einem ~en Ort** anywhere; **jede ~e Person** no matter who; **in ~ große Stücke schneiden** to cut into pieces of the desired size; **zu jeder ~en Zeit** at any time.

beliebt in request (favo(u)r, demand), *(Mode)* in vogue, fashionable, *(Person)* popular, fairhaired, *(Wertpapiere)* in demand;
sich bei jem. ~ machen to ingratiate o. s. (curry favo(u)r) with s. o.; ~ **sein** to be in great favo(u)r (demand); **allgemein ~ sein** to be a universal favo(u)rite; **beim Publikum ~ sein** to be favo(u)rite with the public; **sehr ~ sein** to be all the fashion; **überall ~ sein** to be a general favo(u)rite;
~er Artikel article very much in demand; **~e Redensart** stock phrase, tag line; **~er Schauspieler** popular actor.

Beliebtheit popularity, high favo(u)r, vogue;
sich kurzfristiger ~ erfreuen to have a short-lived vogue.

Beliebtheits|liste anführen to top the popularity poll; **~liste wieder anführen** to be back at the top of the popularity table; **~prozentzahl** public approval rating *(US)*; **~test, ~umfrage** popularity poll, *(Fernsehsendungen)* [television] ratings; **~wettbewerb** popularity test (contest, *US*).

beliefern to provide, to supply, to stock, to furnish, to serve, *(Lebensmittel)* to purvey, to cater;
nur Gaststätten ~ to cater for hotels and restaurants only; **Kunden** ~ to forward goods to a customer; **seine Kundschaft mit Fleisch** ~ to purvey meat to one's customers; **mit einem Sortiment** ~ to assort, to furnish with an assortment;
sich von A ~ lassen to obtain one's goods (supplies) from A.

beliefert, täglich supplied daily.

Belieferung supply, supplies, supplying, delivery;
bevorzugte ~ priority delivery;
~ **des Heeres** purveyance of supplies for the army; ~ **des Marktes** market supply;
~ **eines Händlers verweigern** to withhold supply from a dealer.

Belletristik elegant literature.

belobigen to command, *(mil.)* to mention in the dispatches;
j. für seine Verdienste ~ to notice s. o. services.

Belobigung commendation;
schriftliche ~ *(mil.)* certificate of merit;
~ **erhalten** *(Schule)* to be hono(u)rable mentioned.

Belobigungsschreiben letter of commendation.

belohnen to reward, to remunerate, to gratify, to recompense, to pay;
großzügig ~ to remunerate (reward) s. o. liberally; **j. für seine Mühewaltungen** ~ to remunerate s. o. for his trouble; **reich** ~ to reward richly; **j. mit Undank** ~ to repay s. o. with ingratitude; **geschäftliche Unehrlichkeit** ~ to put a premium on business dishonesty.

belohnt, reich amply rewarded.

Belohnung reward, rewarding, remuneration, award, gratification, pay, recompense, purse, prize, requital, *(Anreiz)* premium;
als ~ für as a reward for;
amtliche ~ official reward; **angemessene (entsprechende)** ~ due reward, adequate remuneration; **außergewöhnliche** ~ signal reward; **hohe** ~ rich reward; **schlechte** ~ poor return;
~ **mit einer Geldsumme** pecuniary reward;
~ **aussetzen** to hold out rewards, to advertise (offer) a reward; **~en austeilen** to mete [out] rewards; **jem. eine ~ gewähren** to confer a reward on s. o.; ~ **vereinbaren** to stipulate for a reward; **jem. eine ~ zuerkennen** to adjudge a price to s. o.

belüften to ventilate, to air, to aerate.

Belüftung ventilation.

Belüftungs|anlage airing plant, *(Auto)* ventilation system; **~klappe** *(Auto)* ventilator; **~schacht** ventilation shaft.

belügen, sich selbst to deceive o. s.

belustigen to amuse, to entertain;
sich über etw. ~ to make merry over s. th.

Belustigung amusement, entertainment, diversion;
~en im Freien outdoor diversions.

bemächtigen, sich to take hold of, to seize;
sich einer Sache widerrechtlich ~ to usurp s. th.; **sich des Throns** ~ to usurp the throne.
bemalt painted.
bemängeln, etw. to find fault with s. th.
Bemängelung fault-finding.
bemannen *(Schiff)* to man;
Schiff zu stark ~ to overman a ship.
bemannt, nicht voll light-handed;
~**e Raumfahrt** manned space travel; ~**er Torpedo** human torpedo.
Bemannung *(Schiff)* manning, crew, ship's company;
in voller ~ in full complement.
bemänteln to cloak, to daub, to disguise, to veil, to gloss over, to palliate;
seine Fehler ~ to cover up one's shortcomings.
Bemäntelung cloak, blind, gloss, disguise, palliation.
bemerkbar perceptible, noticeable, visible, discernible;
sich ~ **machen** to attract notice, to begin to show, *(Person)* to draw attention to o. s.; **sich unangenehm** ~ **machen** to be a nuisance.
bemerken to observe, to notice, to become aware of, *(äußern)* to remark, to point out;
sofort ~ to perceive (spot) at once; **Verschiedenes zu den Worten eines Redners** ~ to make several remarks in connection with what the speaker said.
bemerkenswert noticeable, remarkable, of note;
~**e Persönlichkeit** striking personality; ~**e Tatsache** noteworthy fact.
bemerkt, wie oben as stated above; **nebenbei** ~ incidentally, by the way.
Bemerkung remark, comment, observation, note, descant;
vom Thema abschweifende ~ wild remark; **abträgliche** ~ derogatory remarks; **beiläufige** ~ casual remark, obiter dictum; **einleitende** ~**en** introductory (preliminary, prefatory) remarks; **erläuternde** ~**en** explanatory remarks; **freche** ~ uncalled-for remark; **nicht zum Thema gehörige** ~ desultory remark; **geistlose** ~ inane remark; **gelegentliche** ~ incidental remark; **geringschätzige** ~ snide remark; **auf die Politiker gezielte** ~ hit at politicians; **hämische** ~**en** malicious remarks; **kritische** ~ critical comment; **sarkastische** ~ skit; **spitze** ~ sharp remark; **törichte** ~**en** imbecile remarks; **treffende** ~ clever remark; **übliche** ~**en** conventional remarks; **unangebrachte** ~**en** inopportune remarks; **unbedeutende** ~ mouthful *(sl.)*; **ungeschickte** ~ unhappy remark; **ungezogene** ~ vicious remark; **unpassende** ~ clanger; **unüberlegte** ~**en** impetuous (careless) remarks; **versteckte** ~ quiet dig; **vorausgehende** ~**en** precursory remarks; **witzige** ~ wisecrack, drive *(US)*; **zutreffende** ~ fitting remark;
~ **in Wahrnehmung berechtigter Interessen** fair comment on a matter of public interest; **scharfe** ~ **beim Weggehen** *(fig.)* Parthian shot; **kritische** ~**en über ein Werk** critical notes on a work;
~**en einflechten** to interpose a remark; ~ **einwerfen** to interject a remark; **kritische** ~**en von sich geben** to snap out one's criticism; ~ **fallen lassen** to plump out (drop) a remark; ~ **machen** to offer (pass) a remark; **abfällige** ~**en machen** to make derogatory remarks; **bissige** ~**en über j. machen** to give s. o. the rough edge of one's tongue; **heimliche** ~ **machen** to talk out of the corner of one's mouth; **herabsetzende** ~**en machen** to speak disparagingly, to make derogatory remarks; **nachteilige** ~**en über j. machen** to make snide remarks about s. o.; **nicht für die Öffentlichkeit bestimmte** ~ **machen** to speak off the record; **satirische** ~ **über j. machen** to have a sly hit at s. o.; ~ **riskieren** to hazard a remark; ~**en an den Rand schreiben** to make marginal notes; ~**en zurücknehmen** to eat one's words.
bemessen to rate, to assess, to measure, *(techn.)* to dimension, to size, to affeer, *(Strafe)* to award;
seine Ausgaben nach dem Einkommen ~ to proportion one's expenses to one's income; **zu knapp** ~ to scrimp; **Lohn nach der Leistung** ~ to pay according to the quality of the work; **sparsam** ~ to dole out; **Zeit genau** ~ to time it accurately; **Zeit knapp** ~ to cut it close *(coll.)*; **Zuteilung knappstens** ~ to cut an allocation as fine as possible.
Bemessung rating, assessment, valuation;
~ **einer Geldstrafe** assessment of a fine.
Bemessungsgrundlage basis of valuation (assessment).
Bemessungszeitraum *(Einkommenssteuer)* basic (assessment) period.
bemittelt well-to-do *(Br.)*, well off, of handsome property;
~**er Mann** man of means.
Bemühen endeavo(u)r, effort;
in dem ~ *(Abkommen)* anxious.
bemühen, sich to endeavo(u)r, to exert o. s., to [take] trouble; **j. um etw.** ~ to trouble s. o. for s. th.; **sich um j.** ~ to concern o. s. about (busy o. s. with) s. o.; **sich um ein Amt** ~ to try hard to obtain a position; **Anwalt** ~ to consult a lawyer; **Arzt** ~ to send for a doctor; **j. nicht mit Einzelheiten** ~ not to trouble s. o. with details; **sich hart um einen Erfolg** ~ to be striving hard to succeed; **sich erfolglos** ~ to beat the air; **sich um etw. ernsthaft** ~ to make a bold bid for s. th.; **sich** ~ **zu gefallen** to be anxious to please; **sich gemeinsam** ~ to club efforts; **sich um jds. Gunst** ~ to curry favo(u)r with s. o.; **sich um einen Kranken** ~ to nurse (attend to) a patient; **sich um seine Kundschaft** ~ to solicit one's custom; **sich persönlich** ~ to apply in person; **sich sehr** ~ to go to great lengths; **sich eifrig um eine Stelle** ~ to make every effort to get a job; **sich umsonst (vergeblich)** ~ to waste one's time; **sich zu Dutzenden um einen Verlagsvertrag für ein neues Buch** ~ to fall over each other for a new book.
Bemühung effort, trouble, endeavo(u)r, strain, exertion;
trotz aller ~**en** in spite of all his efforts;
ärztliche ~**en** medical attention (services); **fruchtlose** ~**en** unlucky efforts; **gemeinsame** ~**en** combined efforts; **nie nachlassende** ~**en** no letup in s. one's endeavo(u)rs; **rührende** ~**en** poor little efforts; **vergebliche (zwecklose)** ~**en** fruitless efforts; ~**en, seine Frau zufriedenzustellen** endeavo(u)rs to please one's wife;
j. für seine ~**en entschädigen** to remunerate (pay) s. o. for his trouble; **sich über jds.** ~**en hinwegsetzen** to flout s. one's attempt; **seine** ~**en konzentrieren** to concentrate one's efforts; **seine** ~**en verdoppeln** to redouble one's efforts.
bemüßigt fühlen, sich to feel obliged.
bemustern to pattern, to sample, to make up into samples.
Bemusterung sampling.
bemuttern to mother.
benachbart neighbo(u)ring, adjacent, adjoining, proximate, contiguous, vicinal;
~**e Fachgebiete** related fields; ~**e Familie** family next door; ~**es Grundstück** adjoining (adjacent) land; **im** ~**en Haus leben** to live next door; ~**es Städtchen** little town nearby.
benachrichtigen to let know, to advise, to send word, to inform, to notify, to notice, to acquaint, to communicate;
j. von etw. ~ to communicate s. th. to s. o., to give s. o. notice of s. th.; **Behörden** ~ to give notice to the authorities, to notify the authorities; **Polizei** ~ to notify (inform) the police; **j. regelmäßig** ~ to keep s. o. advised (posted); **sofort (umgehend)** ~ to give prompt notice, to let know at once; **j. telefonisch** ~ to inform s. o. by telephone; **im voraus** ~ to warn.
Benachrichtigung notice, notification, information, communication, message, *(Handelssprache)* advice [note], aviso;
mangels ~ for want of advice; **ohne vorherige** ~ without notice [given], unnotified; **ohne vorherige** ~ **zahlbar** payable on demand; **ohne weitere** ~ without further notice;
briefliche ~ mail advice; **ordnungsgemäße** ~ due and proper notice; **persönliche** ~ personal notice; **rechtzeitige** ~ due notice; **schriftliche** ~ notice in writing; **sofortige** ~ *(vom Eintritt des Versicherungsfalles)* immediate notice; **telefonische** ~ telephoned message; **unverbindliche** ~ advice without engagement; **unverzügliche** ~ immediate notice; **unzureichende** ~ inadequate notice; **ver[ab]säumte** ~ failure to give (omission to send) notice; **vorherige** ~ notice in advance;
~ **von Aktionären** notice of members; ~ **über die Anhängigkeit eines Schiedsverfahrens** notice of reference; **sofortige** ~ **vom Eintritt des Versicherungsfalles** immediate notice of the event insured; ~ **über einen Fristablauf** expiration notice; ~ **über die Ladebereitschaft** notice of readiness; ~ **über die Nichteinlösung** *(Wechsel)* notice of dishono(u)r; ~ **der Polizei** notification of the police; ~ **des Schuldners** notice of debtor; ~ **über die Terminfestsetzung** notice of issue; ~ **über Warenverlagerungen** *(Zoll)* cart note; ~ **über die Zahlungseinstellung** notice of suspension of payments; ~ **von der Geltendmachung des Zurückbehaltungsrechtes** notice of lien;
um ~ **bitten** to ask to be informed (notified); ~ **erhalten** to be informed.
Benachrichtigungs|form form of notice; ~**formular** notification form; ~**frist** time for giving notice; ~**gebühr** fee for notification; ~**muster** specimen form of notice; ~**schreiben** letter of advice, advice note; ~**verzicht** waiver of notice; ~**verzug** delay in giving notice; ~**wirkung** effect of [giving] notice; ~**zettel** *(Telefon)* notice, note.
benachteiligen to prejudice, to handicap, to injure, to aggrieve, to discriminate, to affect adversely (unfavo(u)rably);

j. zugunsten eines anderen Bewerbers ~ to discriminate s. o. against another candidate; **Gläubiger** ~ to prefer one creditor over the others; **j. bei internationalen Konferenzen** ~ to put s. o. at a disadvantage when attending international conferences.
benachteiligend discriminatory, detrimental, injurious;
sich ~ **auswirken** to be prejudicial;
~**e Zollsätze** discriminating duties.
benachteiligt handicapped, disadvantaged, adversely affected, *(geschädigt)* injured, damaged;
wirtschaftlich ~ underprivileged;
sich ~ **fühlen** to feel aggrieved (unfairly treated); ~ **sein** to be at a disadvantage; **schwer** ~ **sein** to be under a heavy handicap; **finanziell stark** ~ **sein** to be under a great handicap financially; ~ **werden** to be prejudiced, to suffer injury, to pay penalty; **bei einer Erbschaft** ~ **werden** to come off badly in a will; **wirtschaftlich** ~ **werden** to be shortchanged economically;
~**e Bevölkerungsschicht** underprivileged classes.
Benachteiligter prejudiced (injured) party, underdog, person injured.
Benachteiligung handicap, handicapping, disadvantage, damage, injury, *(Gläubiger)* prejudice, *(Zoll)* discrimination;
unter ~ **öffentlicher Interessen** to the disinterest of the public;
steuerliche ~ discriminatory taxation;
~ **im Berufsleben** job discrimination *(US)*; ~ **ausländischer Erzeugnisse** discrimination against goods from foreign countries; ~ **der Gläubiger** preference of one creditor over others, defrauding secured creditors *(US)*; ~ **der Minderheit** fraud on the minority.
benannt named, mentioned, nominated;
ausdrücklich ~ positively named.
Benannter nominee.
benebelt tipsy, hazy *(coll.)*;
~ **sein** to be fuddled.
Benehmen manners, behavio(u)r, conduct, deportment, walk, demeano(u)r, course, form, goings on *(coll.)*;
im ~ **mit** on consultation (agreement) with;
anständiges ~ decent behavio(u)r, common courtesy *(coll.)*; **bäuerisches** ~ rustic manners; **dämliches** ~ ignorant conduct; **empörendes** ~ outrageous behavio(u)r; **frostiges** ~ frost in s. one's manners *(coll.)*; **gutes** ~ mannerliness; **höfliches** ~ polite (soft) manners; **rüpelhaftes** ~ rowdiness; **schäbiges** ~ cheap conduct; **schlechtes** ~ bad conduct, misbehavio(u)r; **taktloses** ~ graceless behavio(u)r; **tölpelhaftes** ~ muff *(coll.)*; **überspanntes** ~ airs and graces; **unanständiges** ~ ungentlemanliness; **ungebührliches** ~ improper conduct; **ungehobeltes** ~ vulgar behavio(u)r; **ungehöriges** ~ misconduct, abusive (offensive) behavio(u)r, impropriety, improper conduct; **ungezwungenes** ~ ease of manner; **unwürdiges** ~ demerit; **verantwortungsloses** ~ irresponsible behavio(u)r;
~ **im Betrieb** business etiquette; ~ **wie in der Kneipe** pothouse manners; **unanständiges** ~ **in der Öffentlichkeit** public indecency;
für jds. gutes ~ **bürgen** to undertake for s. one's good behavio(u)r; **schlechtes** ~ **darstellen** to offend against good manners; **sich mit jem. ins** ~ **setzen** to get in touch with s. o., to hold consultation with (contact) s. o.
benehmen, sich to behave [o. s.]; **sich affektiert** ~ to affect; **sich anständig** ~ to behave; **sich auffällig** ~ to carry on, to cut a caper; **sich aufgeblasen** ~ to put on frills; **sich daneben (schlecht)** ~ to commit an act of misconduct, to blot one's copybook; **sich linkisch** ~ to have an awkward manner; **sich ordnungsgemäß** ~ to conduct o. s. in a proper manner; **sich richtig** ~ to conduct o. s. well, to behave well; **sich schlecht** ~ to misconduct o. s., to misbehave; **sich unschicklich** ~ to commit improprieties; **sich vorsichtig** ~ to be guarded in one's behavio(u)r; **sich würdevoll** ~ to comport o. s. with dignity; **sich völlig zwanglos** ~ to be free and easy, to behave with native ease;
sich zu ~ **wissen** to know how to behave.
Beneluxländer Benelux countries.
benennen to nominate, to name, to entitle, to denominate;
als Nachfolger ~ to designate as successor; **j. für einen Posten** ~ to nominate s. o. for a post; **Präsidentschaftskandidaten** ~ to nominate a man for the Presidency; **Preis** ~ to name a price; **Schiedsrichter** ~ to nominate an arbitrator; **Straße neu** ~ to give a new name to a street; **stückweise** ~ to specify; **Waren falsch** ~ to misbrand goods; **j. als Zeugen** ~ to call s. o. as witness.
Benennung nomination, appellation, naming, name, label, *(als Nachfolger)* designation, appointment, *(Wertpapier)* title, denomination, name;
falsche ~ misnomer; **gemeinsame** ~ joint designation;
~ **des Auftraggebers** disclosure of the name of the principal; ~ **für einen Posten** designation to a post; ~ **eines Zeugen** calling of a witness.
Benennungs|recht right to name; ~**system** nomenclature.
benommen stunned, stupefied, benumbed, dazed;
~ **sein** to be in a daze.
Benommenheit daze, numbness.
benoten *(Schule)* to score.
benötigen to require, to need, to want;
zusätzliche Arbeitskräfte ~ to require extra help; **etw. dringend** ~ to be in dire need (great want) of s. th., to be exigent of s. th.; **dringend neue Werkzeuge** ~ to be badly off for tools.
benötigte Mittel necessary funds.
Benotung marks, grades *(US)*.
Benotungsliste class list *(Br.)*.
benummern to number.
benutzbar usable;
nicht ~ *(Straße)* impassable.
benutzen to [make] use, *(verwenden)* to utilize, to employ, *(Verkehrsmittel)* to take, to go;
nur bei Feuersausbruch zu ~ for use only in case of fire; **seine Freizeit zur Fortbildung** ~ to improve one's leisure time for further education; **Gelegenheit** ~ to avail o. s. of an opportunity; **erstbeste Gelegenheit** ~ to leap at an opportunity, to take time by the forelock, to jump at a bargain; **gewinnbringend** ~ to turn to good account; **Küche gemeinsam** ~ to share a kitchen; **Lexikon viel** ~ to make great use of a dictionary; **Literatur** ~ to consult books; **jds. Namen** ~ to utilize s. o. name; **Patent** ~ to exploit (employ) a patent; **Rückfahrkarte nicht** ~ not to use the return ticket; **Straßenbahn** ~ to take the tram; **drei Stunden** ~ to occupy three hours; **Zimmer gemeinsam** ~ to share a room; **Zimmer im Winter nicht** ~ not to live in a room in the winter;
Bibliothek ~ **dürfen** to be welcome to the use of a library.
Benutzer user, exploiter, employer, *(Bibliothek)* borrower, reader;
außerbetrieblicher ~ *(öffentliche Bibliothek)* outside user; **beruflicher** ~ professional user; **gutgläubiger** ~ bona fide user; ~ **verbilligter Flugscheine** cheap-fare passenger; ~ **öffentlicher Verkehrsmittel** public transit passenger; ~ **eines Warenzeichens** user of a registered trademark;
~**karte** *(Bibliothek)* library ticket (card, *US*); ~**kreis** users.
benutzt used, employed;
einzeln ~ **werden können** to be used on a stand-alone basis;
~**e Literatur** books consulted.
Benutzung appropriation, usage, use, user, utilization, employment, occupancy;
bei ordnungsgemäßer ~ when properly used; **unter** ~ **von** with the aid of; **zur öffentlichen** ~ **freigegeben** open to the public; **ausschließliche** ~ exclusive use; **gemeinsame** ~ joint use; **gesetzwidrige** ~ illegal exploitation; **kostensparende** ~ cost-effective use; **mißbräuchliche** ~ abuse, adverse user; **unbefugte** ~ unauthorized use; **vorherige** ~ prior use; **vorübergehende** ~ transient occupancy; **zulässige** ~ permissive use, *(Urheberrecht)* fair usage;
~ **nur für Anlieger** residents only; ~ **und Aufenthaltsrecht** use and habitation; ~ **und Besitz** use and occupation; ~ **von Büchern** consultation of books; ~ **eines Dienstwagens** use of a company's car; ~ **einer Erfindung** exploitation of an invention; **unbefugte** ~ **eines Firmennamens** improper use of a firm's name; ~ **eines Geschäftslokals** occupation of business premises; ~ **noch nicht realisierter Gewinne zu neuen Spekulationen** pyramiding *(US)*; ~ **im öffentlichen Interesse** public use; **widerrechtliche** ~ **einer gepfändeten Sache** abuse of distress; ~ **durch den Staat** crown user *(Br.)*; ~ **einer Straße** use of a road; ~ **öffentlicher Unterlagen** access to records; **regelmäßige** ~ **öffentlicher Verkehrsmittel** commutation *(US)*; ~ **eines Warenzeichens** use of a trademark; **ungenaue** ~ **eines Wortes** lax use of a word;
nicht zur ~ **von Schnellzügen berechtigen** *(Fahrkarte)* to be unavailable for express trains; **für die öffentliche** ~ **freigeben** to throw open to the public; **einem Freund die** ~ **seiner Bibliothek gestatten** to give a friend the freedom of one's library; **bei der** ~ **an Wert gewinnen** to improve with use;
die ~ **ist nur Anliegern gestattet** residents only.
Benutzungs|dauer economic use; **Besitz- und** ~**einräumung** executed use; **ausdrückliche** ~**erlaubnis** *(Kraftfahrzeughalter)* express permission; ~**ermächtigung** notice of allowance; ~**gebühren** user fee (charge, tax), occupancy charge, facility fee, *(Autobahn)* toll revenue; ~**lizenz** licence to use.

Benutzungsrecht [right of] user, *(Grundstück)* licence;
alleiniges ~ sole use; **ausschließliches** ~ exclusive use; **aufschiebend bedingtes** ~ executory use; **gemeinsames** ~ common pasture;
~ **öffentlicher Gewässer** navigation servitude;
freies ~ **haben** to have the run (the freedom) of.

Benutzungs|zwang compulsory usage; ~**zweck** purpose of use.

Benzin petrol *(Br.)*, motor spirit, fuel, gas *(coll.)*, gasoline *(US)*, juice *(US sl.)*;
bleifreies ~ unleaded gasoline; **bleihaltiges** ~ lead petrol; **klopffestes** ~ high-octane petrol *(Br.)* (fuel, gasoline, *US*); **minderwertiges** ~ low-grade fuel, low-grade petrol *(Br.)*;
~ **im Reservekanister** extra gasoline *(US)*;
mit ~ **fahren** to run on gas *(coll.)* (petrol, *Br.*); **kein** ~ **mehr haben** to be short (out) of petrol *(Br.)*, to be at the end of one's petrol *(Br.)*, to run out of gasoline *(US)*; **nicht mehr genug** ~ **haben** to be low on fuel; ~ **nachfüllen** to fill up with petrol *(Br.)*, to refuel;
~**abgabepreis** pump price for petrol *(Br.)*; ~**anzeiger** fuel gauge; ~**behälter** petrol tank; ~**einfüllstutzen** gasoline (petrol) filler neck; ~**einspritzmotor** fuel injection engine; ~**einspritzung** direct injection; ~**filter** petrol filter *(Br.)*, fuel filter; ~**fresser** gas-guzzling car *(coll.)*, gas guzzler *(coll.)*; **schlechtes** ~**gemisch** *(Auto)* poor mixture; ~**gutschein** petrol coupon *(Br.)*, gas coupon *(US)*; ~**hahn** petrol tap *(Br.)*; ~**kanister** gasoline container (can) *(US)*, petrol can *(Br.)*; ~**kesselwagen** petrol bulk lorry *(Br.)*, gasoline truck *(US)*; ~**knappheit** petrol shortage *(Br.)*, gasoline shortage *(US)*; ~**kocher** petrol (gasoline, *US*) stove; ~**kosten** cost of petrol *(Br.)*; ~**kostenerhöhung** fuel cost increase; ~**lager** petrol store *(Br.)*, gasoline depot *(US)*; ~**leitung** fuel feed, fuel (gasoline, *US*) pipe; ~**marke** petrol ration coupon *(Br.)*; ~**motor** gasoline engine *(US)*, petrol motor (engine) *(Br.)*; ~**normalzuteilung** basic petrol ration *(Br.)*; ~**ofen** petrol heater *(Br.)*; ~**preis** petrol price *(Br.)*, fuel (gasoline, *US*) price; ~**preiserhöhung** fuel price hike; ~**preispolitik** fuel pricing; ~**pumpe** petrol pump, fuel (gasoline, *US*) pump; ~**rationierung** petrol rationing *(Br.)*; ~**rechnung** gas bill *(coll.)*; ~**reserve** fuel reserve; ~**schlucker** gas-guzzler *(coll.)*, gas-guzzling car *(coll.)*; ~**stand** gasoline *(US)* (petrol, *Br.*) level; ~**standsanzeiger** gasoline *(US)* (petrol, *Br.*) gauge; ~**steuer** petrol tax *(Br.)*, gasoline tax *(US)*, tax on gasoline *(US)*; ~**steuererhöhung** petrol tax increase *(Br.)*; ~**stoffzuleitung** fuel feed; ~**tank** petrol *(Br.)* (fuel, gas, *coll.*) tank; ~**uhr** fuel gauge, petrol *(Br.)* (gasoline, *US*) gauge; ~**verbrauch** petrol *(Br.)* (fuel, gasoline, *US*) consumption; **sparsamer** ~**verbrauch** petrol economy *(Br.)*, economy in fuel consumption; **verringerter** ~**verbrauch** slowdown in petrol consumption *(Br.)*; ~**verbrauchstest** fuel-consumption test (trial); ~**verbrauchszahlen** fuel-consumption figures; ~**versorgung** fuel allocation, fuel supply; ~**zufuhr** fuel feed; ~**zufuhr abstellen** to cut off the throttle; ~**zuschuß** petrol *(Br.)* (gasoline, *US*) allowance; ~**zuteilung** petrol allowance (ration) *(Br.)*, fuel allocation.

beobachten to observe, to keep under observation, to watch, *(Polizei)* to shadow;
mit Besorgnis ~ to view with concern; **feindliche Bewegungen** ~ to observe the enemy's movements; **strenge Diät** ~ to keep a strict diet; **Flugzeuge unbekannter Herkunft** ~ to spot unidentified objects; **Gang der Ereignisse** ~ to watch the progress of events; **alles genau** ~ to take stock of everything; **Haus** ~ to be watching outside the house; **Prozeß** ~ to watch a case; **Regel des Anstands** ~ to observe the proprieties; **j. auf Schritt und Tritt** ~ to dog s. one's footsteps; **etw. sorgfältig** ~ to make a study of s. th.; **Stillschweigen** ~ to preserve silence; **Vorschriften** ~ to comply with regulations; **Wahlen** ~ to watch elections;
j. ~ **lassen** to keep s. o. under observation; **j. heimlich** ~ **lassen** to set a watch upon s. o.

Beobachter observer, *(Flugzeug)* navigator, air scout, *(bei Wahlen)* watcher, *(Zuschauer)* spectator, looker-on, onlooker, bystander;
erfahrener ~ expert observer; **flüchtiger** ~ rude observer; **heimlicher** ~ Peeping Tom; **politischer** ~ political observer;
~ **aus Kreisen der Industrie** industry observer; ~ **der Vereinten Nationen** observer of the United Nations; **neugieriger** ~ **des Zeitgeschehens** keen observer of contemporary affairs;
für j. in einem Prozeß als ~ **fungieren** to watch a case (hold a watching brief) for s. o.; ~ **zulassen** to admit observers;
~**delegation** observers, observation team; ~**raum** cockpit; ~**status** observer status.

beobachtete Bevölkerungsgruppe *(Statistik)* observation sample.

Beobachtung observance, observation, watch;
unter ~ **aller Vorsichtsmaßregeln** taking every precaution;
Ja-Nein ~**en** sensitivity data;
~ **der Kaufgewohnheiten** purchase observation;
~**en anstellen** to make observations; **zur stationären** ~ **aufnehmen** to hospitalize for a period of observation *(US)*; **zur** ~ **ins Krankenhaus bringen** to take to hospital for observation; **der** ~ **entgehen** to escape observation; **Haus unter** ~ **halten** to keep a watch on a house; **unter** ~ **stellen** to place under observation.

Beobachtungs|abschnitt sector under observation; ~**auftrag** *(Anwalt)* watching brief; ~**bogen** *(Zeitstudie)* observation form; ~**fehler** *(Statistik)* ascertainment error, error of observation; **Korrektur der persönlichen** ~**fehler** personal equations; ~**fenster** *(Kino)* observation post; ~**gabe** outsight; **gute** ~**gabe** observing mind; ~**gruppe** observation team; ~**material** *(Statistik)* data; ~**methode** *(Marketing)* observational technique; ~**mine** observation mine; ~**posten** lookout [man]; ~**quarantäne** quarantine of observation; ~**satellit** earth-surveying satellite; ~**schlitz** observation slit, peep hole; ~**spiegel** *(U-Boot)* periscope; ~**station** observatory, *(Krankenhaus)* observation ward; ~**tätigkeit ausüben** *(Anwalt)* to hold a watching brief; ~**turm**, ~**warte** observation tower; ~**zeit** *(Zeitstudie)* attention time; ~**zeitraum** observation period; ~**zentrum** *(Jugendlicher Strafgefangener)* observation center.

beordern to commission, to order.

bepacken to pack, to burden.

bepackt loaded;
mit Geschenken ~ laden with gifts; **mit Koffern** ~ loaded with suitcases.

bepfeffern to pepper *(fig.)*.

bepflanzen to plant;
Straße mit Pappeln ~ to line a road with poplars.

bepflanzt, nicht unplanted.

bepflastern, Koffer mit Hotelaufklebern to plaster a trunk with hotel labels.

bequem convenient, comfortable, cosy, easy, easy-going, *(faul)* lazy, indolent;
~ **zu bewirtschaften** built for convenience; ~ **zu erreichen** easy to reach, within easy reach, convenient to reach; ~ **gelegen** conveniently situated; ~ **zu handhaben** easy to handle;
~ **den dritten Platz belegen** to come in an easy third; ~ **leben können** to be comfortably off; **es sich** ~ **machen** to make o. s. easy, to lay o. s. out, to make o. s. at home; ~ **wohnen** to be comfortably housed;
~**e Arbeit haben** to have a soft job; ~**es Leben führen** to live in comfort (easy circumstances); ~**er Lebensstandard** comfort standard; ~**e Lösung finden** to find a facile solution; ~**e Raten** easy terms; ~**e Reisemöglichkeit** comfortable ride; ~**e Schuhe** comfortable shoes; ~**er Sessel** easy chair; ~**e Stellung** fat job; ~**e Wohnung** comfortable flat; **mit** ~**en Zahlungsbedingungen** on convenient terms.

bequemen, sich to make an effort, to trouble o. s. to do.

Bequemlichkeit comfort, convenience, ease;
aus reiner ~ out of sheer laziness; **mit aller** ~ with all conveniences; **zur größeren** ~ **unserer Gäste** for the greater comfort of our guests;
häusliche ~**en** home comforts;
~ **während des Fluges** in-flight convenience;
für jds. ~ **sorgen** to attend (see to, provide for) s. one's comfort.

Bequemlichkeits|bedarf convenience goods *(US)*; **modernste** ~**bedürfnisse befriedigen** to be the last word in comfort and convenience.

berappen to plank down *(sl.)*, to pay the fiddler *(US sl.)*, to shell (fork) out, to pony up;
~ **müssen** to come across with *(sl.)*; **zusätzlichen Betrag** ~ **müssen** to come again *(sl.)*.

beraten to advise, to give advice, to counsel, to consult, *(beratschlagen)* to deliberate, to debate, to discuss;
sich mit jem. ~ to hold (take) counsel with s. o.; **über eine Angelegenheit** ~ to discuss a matter; **j. in einer Angelegenheit** ~ to advise s. o. on a matter; **sich mit einem Anwalt** ~ to consult a lawyer; **falsch** ~ to misadvise; **j. in einer Frage** ~ to advise s. o. on a question; **über eine Frage** ~ to deliberate upon a question; **sich mit seinen Freunden darüber** ~ to talk with one's friends about it; **über einen Gesetzentwurf** ~ to debate a bill; **j. gut** ~ to give s. o. a good piece of advice; **sich mit seinen Mitarbeitern** ~ to be in conference with one's colleagues; **sich miteinander** ~ to confer (take counsel) together; **nochmals** ~ to reconsider; **Sache** ~ to discuss a matter; **schlecht** ~ to misadvise; **sich vier Stunden** ~ to confer for four hours;

sich ~ lassen to take counsel, to seek advice; **sich von jem. ~ lassen** to ask s. one's opinion; **sich anwaltlich ~ lassen** to hire legal counsel *(Br.)*, to take legal advice; **sich fachmännisch ~ lassen** to take professional advice; **sich juristisch ~ lassen** to take legal advice, to hire legal counsel; **gut ~ sein** to be soundly advised; **schlecht ~ sein** to be ill advised; **noch ~ werden** *(Gesetz)* to be still under consideration.

beratend consultative, consultant, advisory;
dem Vorstand ~ zur Verfügung stehen to supply management advice;
~er Anwalt chamber counsel *(Br.)*, special pleader; **~er Ausschuß** advisory board (council, committee); **in ~er Eigenschaft** in an advisory capacity; **~e Funktion** deliberative (advisory) function; **~er Ingenieur** consulting engineer; **~e Körperschaft** deliberative body; **~e Stimme** deliberative voice; **~e Versammlung** deliberative assembly; **~e Versammlung des Europarates** Consultative Assembly of the Council of Europe.

Berater consultant, adviser, counsel, counsellor, guide, assessor, pilot, *(pol.)* adviser, aide;
außenpolitischer ~ advisor on foreign politics, foreign policy adviser; **fachmännischer ~** consultant; **innenpolitischer ~** domestic policy adviser; **juristischer ~** legal adviser, counsellor *(US)*; **landwirtschaftlicher ~** country agent; **persönlicher ~** *(Filmstar)* manager; **politischer ~** political consultant, policy adviser; **technischer ~** consulting engineer, technical adviser; **versicherungstechnischer ~** actuarial consultant; **wirtschaftlicher ~** economic consultant; **wirtschaftspolitischer ~** economic adviser, outside economist; **wissenschaftlicher ~** science (scientific) adviser;
freiberuflicher ~ in Absatzfragen marketing consultant; **~ der Geschäftsführung (Geschäftsleitung)** management adviser, consultant on business policy; **~ in Gewerkschaftsfragen** labo(u)r-relations consultant; **~ für Konjunkturfragen** economic adviser; **~ in Fragen der Öffentlichkeitsarbeit** public-relations consultant, (counsellor, adviser); **~ des Personalchefs** personnel counsellor; **~ für regionale Planungsvorhaben** regional planning consultant; **~ für Sparanlagen** savings specialist; **~ in Steuerfragen** tax consultant; **~ auf dem Gebiet der Steuervermeidung** adviser on tax avoidance; **~ in Verkehrsfragen** transportation consultant; **~ des Vorstands** staff officer, outside director *(US)*;
sich über seine ~ hinwegsetzen to override one's advisers; **sich von einem unbequemen ~ trennen** to drop a pilot; **j. als ~ zuziehen** to consult s. o.;
~gremium, ~gruppe consultative group, advisory board (group); **betriebliche ~gruppe** in-house consultant unit; **festangestellte ~gruppe** stable; **politische ~gruppe** policy-making cluster, kitchen cabinet *(US)*; **~position** advisory post; **~stab** council staff, brains trust; **~tätigkeit** advisory service; **~vertrag** advisory post; **dreijährigen ~vertrag bekommen** to be retained for three years as consultant.

beratschlagen to take counsel, to deliberate, to debate;
gemeinsam ~ to take counsel together.

Beratschlagung counsel, deliberation.

Beratung counsel *(US)*, council, consultation, *(Beratschlagung)* deliberation, meeting, conference, *(Gerichtshof)* discussion, *(Gesetzentwurf)* reading, *(von Kunden)* advice, counsel;
nach längerer ~ after due consideration; **ohne vorherige ~** without previous deliberation;
~en consultations, talks, proceedings;
anwaltliche ~ chamber counsel; **ärztliche ~** medical advice; **fachkundige ~** expert advice; **finanzielle ~** financial advice; **juristische ~** legal consultation (advice); **kostenlose ~** free counsel; **neutrale ~** independent advice; **nochmalige ~** reconsideration; **parlamentarische ~** parliamentary debate; **sachkundige ~** expert guidance; **schlechte ~** misguidance; **unparteiische ~** independent advice; **zwischenstaatliche ~en** intergovernmental consultations;
~ auf dem Anlagegebiet advice on investment; **~ und Aufklärung** *(Kunden)* clinic; **~ in Berufsfragen** vocational guidance; **~ in Devisenangelegenheiten** foreign-exchange advice; **~ in Einkommenssteuerfragen** income-tax service; **~ auf dem Finanzierungsgebiet** financial advice; **~ auf allen Gebieten** full service; **~ des Haushaltsplans** budget debate; **~ einer Körperschaft** vote of an assembly; **~ in Pensionsfragen** retirement counselling; **~ in Personalfragen** employee counselling; **~ beim Positionswechsel** outplacement; **~en auf Regierungsebene** consultations on cabinet level; **~ in Steuerangelegenheiten** tax service; **~ des Vorstands** management consultancy; **finanzielle ~ der gewerblichen Wirtschaft** corporate financial counseling *(US)*;
~ abhalten to hold a conference; **geheime ~ abhalten** to sit behind closed doors, *(Gericht)* to sit in camera; **fachkundige ~ durch geschultes Personal anbieten** to offer expert guidance through trained staff; **zur ~ anstehen** to be in agitation; **mit den ~en beginnen** to enter into consultations; **in ~en mit jem. eintreten** to enter into judgment with s. o.; **in die ~ einer Sache eintreten** to consult about (enter into deliberation of) a matter; **zur ~ kommen** to come under deliberation; **in ~ sein** to be under consideration; **zur ~ stellen** to bring up for discussion; **sich zu ~en zurückziehen** to retire to deliberate.

Beratungs|abteilung consultancy division; **~agentur** consulting outfit; **auf Finanzierungsfragen spezialisierte ~agentur** financial agency; **~anspruch** right to counsel.

Beratungsausschuß consultative (prudential, *US*) committee, advisory (deliberative) board, conference committee *(US)*, deliberative body;
politischer und wirtschaftlicher ~ brains trust;
~ für Verbraucherschutzfragen consumer protection advisory committee; **~ für Verkehrsbenutzer** Transport Users' Consultative Committee *(Br.)*;
~ einsetzen to establish an advisory committee.

Beratungsbefugnisse consultative powers, powers of deliberation.

Beratungsdienst counsel(l)ing, counsel(l)ing service, consulting (consultancy, advisory) service;
technischer ~ engineering consultancy;
~ für Kapitalanlagestellen institutional investor services; **~ in Vermögensfragen** investment management service;
seinen technischen ~ weltweit ausdehnen to expand its engineering consultation service on an international basis.

Beratungsfirma consulting (consultancy) organization;
~ für finanzielle Ausgabengebiete financial counsel(l)ing firm; **an eine ~ gegen Sonderhonorar vergeben** to farm out to a consulting organization.

Beratungs|gebiet consulting field; **~gebühr** fee for consultation, consultation (consultancy, consultant) fee; **~gegenstand** item on the agenda, subject matter, subject under discussion; **~gremium** advisory board (body); **~gremium des Vorstands** management advisory committee; **~kosten** consultation (consulting) fee, fee for consultation; **~organ** advisory board (body); **~position für Investitionsfragen** investment counsel(l)ing position *(US)*; **anwaltliche ~praxis** chamber practice *(Br.)*, office practice *(US)*; **~raum** conference room, *(Hotel)* customers' room; **~stadium** report stage; **~stadium einer Gesetzesvorlage** committee stage.

Beratungsstelle advisory board (body, office);
berufliche ~ vocational guidance center *(US)* (centre, *Br.*); **landwirtschaftliche ~** county farm bureau; **soziale ~** welfare center *(US)* (centre, *Br.*);
von der Gewerkschaft eingerichtete ~ Incorporated Labor Bureau *(US)*;
~, Schlichtungs- und Schiedsgerichtstelle Advisory, Conciliation and Arbitration Service *(Br.)*.

Beratungs|tätigkeit counsel(l)ing work, advisory service, consultancy [services]; **~vertrag** consultancy (consulting) agreement (contract); **dreijährigen ~vertrag bekommen** to be retained for three years as consultant; **~wesen** consulting field; **~zimmer** committee (conference) room, *(Hotel)* customers' room.

berauben to deprive, to denude, *(rauben)* to loot, to rob;
Betrunkenen ~ to roll s. o. *(US sl.)*; **sich eines Vergnügens ~** to deny o. s. a pleasure.

beraubt, aller Mittel destitute of all means; **eines Rechts ~** aggrieved.

Beraubung deprivation, *(Überfall)* robbery, spoliation.

berauschen to intoxicate, to make drunk;
Zuhörer ~ to carry away the audience.

berauschendes Getränk intoxicating (alcoholic) beverage.

berechenbar calculable, computable, countable.

Berechenbarkeit computability, calculability, countability.

berechnen *(abschätzen)* to estimate, to evaluate, to assess, to appraise, to rate, *(anrechnen)* to bring [in]to account, to charge, to bill, *(ansetzen)* to quote, *(rechnen)* to reckon, to compute, to calculate, to work out;
etw. ~ to make a computation of (charge for) s. th.; **nach der Abschreibungsmethode mit fallenden Quoten ~** to compute on the reducing instalment basis; **Besteck ~** *(Schiff)* to work out the ship's reckoning; **jem. einen Betrag ~** to charge s. o. a sum (a sum up to s. o.); **delcredere ~** to charge for delcredere; **auf drei Dezimalstellen ~** to calculate to three decimal places; **alles auf Effekt ~** to calculate everything for effect; **erneut ~** to

recompute, to recalculate; **falsch** ~ to miscompute, to miscalculate; **Faßinhalt** ~ to gauge the content of a barrel; **Fracht** ~ to charge freight; **Frist** ~ to compute a period; **Gebühr** ~ to charge a fee; **genau** ~ to calculate closely; **grob** ~ to calculate roughly; **Höhe eines Berges** ~ to gauge the height of a mountain; **etw. nach Jahren** ~ to date s. th. by years; **knapp** ~ to calculate closely; **Kosten** ~ to figure up (calculate) the costs; **Manuskript** ~ to cast off a manuscript; **Mietanteil in den Lebenshaltungskosten** ~ to reckon rent in the cost of living; **alle Möglichkeiten im voraus** ~ to allow for all possibilities; **zu niedrig** ~ to charge too little, to underbill; **bis auf den Pfennig genau** ~ to calculate to the last penny; **dem Kunden das Porto** ~ to put (charge) the postage to the customer; **früheren Preis** ~ to charge the old price; **niedrige Preise** ~ to ask moderate prices, to underquote; **Provision** ~ to charge commission; **Satzpreis** ~ to calculate the cost of setting; **Schaden** ~ to assess a loss, to value damage; **Selbstkosten** ~ to cost; **jem. etw. zum Selbstkostenpreis** ~ to let s. o. have s. th. at cost price; **sich** ~ to figure out (at, *US*), to work at; **Steuer** ~ to fix the amount of a tax; **stundenweise** ~ to charge by the hour; **pro Tag** ~ to charge a day; **Tara** ~ to rate the tare; **Unkosten** ~ to figure out the expenses; **Verkaufspreis** ~ to calculate the selling price; **Verlust** ~ to assess [the extent of] a loss; **seinen Verlust** ~ to reckon up one's losses; **für die Verpackung** ~ to charge for packing; **Wahlmöglichkeiten** ~ to gauge the voting strength; **zu wenig** ~ to undercharge; **Wert einer Arbeit in Zahlen** ~ to evaluate a work in material terms; **Wirkung einer Rede** ~ to estimate the effect of a speech; **Zinsen** ~ to compute (work out) the interest, *(belasten)* to charge interest; **Zinsen vierteljährlich** ~ to compound interest quarterly; **zuviel** ~ to overcharge;
sich nicht ~ **lassen** to be incalculable.

berechnend calculative, scheming.

Berechner reckoner, calculator, computer, *(Schaden)* assessor.

berechnet charged, billed, *(beabsichtigt)* intended, meant;
alles wohl ~ all things considered; **nur für Schüler** ~ intended only for school children; **Verpackung wird nicht** ~ no charge is made for packing; **wohl** ~ well-judged;
extra (gesondert) ~ **werden** to be charged for extra; **nach dem Tageskurs von ...** ~ **werden** to be calculated at the rate of exchange ruling on ...;
~**e Leistung** *(Motor)* rated load; **äußerst niedrig** ~**er Preis** rock-bottom price; **auf Basis von 360 Tagen** ~**e Zinsen** ordinary (exact) interest.

Berechnung reckoning, *(Belastung)* charge, charging, *(Besteck)* fixing, *(Fakturieren)* billing, invoicing, *(Preisstellung)* pricing, quotation, *(Rechnung)* calculation, computation, account, figuring out, *(Schätzung)* estimate, rate, valuation, assessment, *(Überschlag)* calculation, computation, account, estimate, rate, valuation, assessment, *(Umrechnung)* conversion, reduction;
außer aller ~ incalculable; **bei billigster (niedrigster)** ~ on most moderate terms, at the lowest price (calculation); **nach meiner** ~ according to my calculation; **nach ungefährer** ~ at a rough calculation (estimate); **nach untenstehender** ~ according to the statement below;
annähernde ~ approximation; **erneute** ~ recalculation; **falsche** ~ miscalculation, miscomputation; **flüchtige** ~ rough calculation; **genaue** ~ exact calculation; **pauschale** ~ flat calculation; **statische** ~ static calculation; **ungefähre** ~ dead reckoning; **vereinfachte** ~ short-cut computation; **vorsichtige** ~ conservative estimate;
~ **der Abschreibungsbeträge auf das Anlagevermögen** computation of the capital allowance *(Br.)*; ~ **des Aktienwertes** computation of share value; ~ **der Ausgleichspflicht** hotchpot calculation (computation); ~ **einer Belastung** computation of a charge; ~ **einer Frist** computation of a term; ~ **der Inlandskapitalrendite** domestic return-on-capital computation; ~ **der Kosten** calculation (computation) of expenses; ~ **des Manuskriptumfangs** cast off, casting off copy, character count *(Br.)*; ~ **des Möbelwertes** evaluation of the furniture; ~ **der Prämienreserve** *(Lebensversicherung)* calculation of reserves; ~ **der Produktionskosten** process costing; ~ **des Satzumfangs** cast off, character count *(Br.)*; ~ **der Selbstkosten (des Selbstkostenpreises)** costing, cost accounting; ~ **zu höheren Steuersätzen** higher rates calculation; ~ **von Zinsen** computation of interest;
~ **anstellen (vornehmen)** to make a calculation, to calculate, to work a sum; **genaue** ~ **anstellen** to make an exact calculation; **etw. mit** ~ **tun** to do s. th. for reasons of mere self-interest; **mit kühler** ~ **vorgehen** to act in a calculating manner; **seine** ~**en über den Haufen werfen** to disturb (upset) one's calculations.

Berechnungs|art method (manner) of calculation; ~**büro** engineering department; ~**einheit** work unit; ~**fehler** error of computing (calculation), computational error; ~**formel** formula of computation; ~**formel für Zinsen** formula for compound present value; ~**grundlage** basis of calculation, calculation basis, *(steuerlich)* basis of assessment; ~**methode** way of computing, method of computation, *(Preise)* pricing method, price formulation; ~**tabelle** calculator, *(Lebensversicherung)* experience table; ~**tafel** [calculation] chart, computation table, diagram; ~**weise** method (manner) of calculation; ~**zeitraum** period of computation, base period.

berechtigen *(bevollmächtigen)* to empower, to authorize, to enable, to warrant, *(Eignung geben)* to make eligible, to qualify, *(Recht geben)* to entitle, to give a right to, *(mit Vorrecht ausstatten)* to privilege;
zu der Annahme ~ to give good reason to believe; **zur Ausübung eines Berufs** ~ to qualify for a profession; **zum Bezug einer Altersrente** ~ to qualify for a pension under national insurance *(Br.)*; **j. zum Eintritt** ~ to admit s. o.; **zum Empfang einer Unterstützung** ~ to qualify for relief; **zu großen Hoffnungen** ~ to give rise to great hopes; **zu einer Pension** ~ to make eligible (qualify) for a pension; **zum Universitätsstudium** ~ to qualify for a university education.

berechtigt justified, rightful, justifiable, *(bevollmächtigt)* authorized, entitled, warrantable, *(geeignet)* qualified, eligible, *(lizensiert)* chartered, granted, *(zuständig)* competent;
nicht ~ not entitled (authorized), unauthorized; **voll** ~ fully entitled;
sich für ~ **halten** to consider o. s. competent (qualified); **sich nicht für** ~ **halten j. für eine Stellung zu empfehlen** not to see one's way clear to recommending s. o. for a job; ~ **sein** to be entitled (authorized), to have authority, *(Lizenz)* to be licensed; **zum Bezug von Dividende** ~ **sein** to be entitled for dividends; **zum Bezug einer Pension** ~ **sein** to be entitled to draw a pension; **zum Bezug von Sparprämien** ~ **sein** to be eligible for state savings premiums; **zur Unterschrift** ~ **sein** to be authorized to sign;
~**er Anspruch** legitimate (rightful) claim; ~**en Anspruch haben** to have a claim; ~**e Bemerkung** just remark; ~**e Beschwerde** justifiable complaint; ~**er Einwand** justifiable objection; ~**e Gründe** legitimate reasons; ~**e Hoffnung** legitimate hope; ~**es Interesse** lawful interest; ~**e Kritik** justified criticism; ~**e Schadensersatzansprüche** lawful damages; ~**e Schlußfolgerung** legitimate conclusion; ~**e Übersetzung** authorized translation; ~**e Zweifel** legitimate doubts.

Berechtigter claimant, party entitled, *(Bevollmächtigter)* proxy, attorney, *(Eigentümer)* rightful owner, proprietor, *(Lebensversicherung)* beneficiary, *(Lizenz)* permit holder, *(Scheck, Wechsel)* holder in due course.

Berechtigung justification, entitlement, *(Eignung)* qualification, *(Option)* option, *(Rechtsanspruch)* right, title, claim, validity, *(Vollmacht)* power, authority, warrant, *(Vorrecht)* priority, privilege;
~ **zum Bergwerksbetrieb** title to work a mine; ~ **zum freien Eintritt** free admission;
~ **einer Kritik anerkennen** to admit the justification of a criticism; ~ **eines Anspruchs bestreiten** to dispute the justice of a claim; **keine** ~ **haben** *(Gerücht)* to be unfounded; **keine** ~ **haben, sich einzumischen** to have no right to interfere; **volle** ~ **für etw. haben** to be fully entitled to do s. th.; ~ **zum Universitätsstudium haben** to be qualified for admission to the university; ~ **zur Unruhe haben** to justify alarm; **seine** ~ **zum Empfang einer Unterstützung nachweisen** to establish one's right to relief payments; **erneut seine** ~ **nachweisen** to requalify; ~ **einer Konkursforderung nachweisen** to prove a claim in bankruptcy; **mit einer gewissen** ~ **verlangen** to claim with some show of justice.

Berechtigungs|bestimmungen condition of entitlement; ~**erfordernisse** qualifications, requirements, *(Unterstützung)* eligibility requirements; ~**nachweis** qualification, certificate, licence; ~**nachweis für verteidigungsbedingte schnelle Abschreibungsmöglichkeiten** certificate of necessity *(US)*; ~**nachweis erbringen** to show a licence.

Berechtigungsschein voucher, written authorization, certificate, scrip, *(Dividende)* warrant, *(Lebensmittel)* coupon, *(Lebensversicherung)* benefit certificate;
~ **für spätere Dividendenleistungen** scrip dividend *(US)*; ~ **zum Erwerb (Bezug) neuer Aktien** subscription warrant *(Br.)*, stock allotment *(US)*, stock scrip *(US)*; ~ **zum Erwerb gestückelter neuer Aktien** fractional warrant *(Br.)*; ~ **auf bevorzugte Lieferung** certificate of priority.

bereden to discuss, to talk over, to confer;
j. ~ to persuade, to talk into; **sich mit jem.** ~ to talk s. th. over with s. o., to confer with s. o. about s. th.; **Angelegenheit** ~ to talk over a business; **j. zum Mitkommen** ~ to talk s. o. into coming along.

Beredsamkeit eloquence, readiness (fluency) of speech;
forensische ~ forensic oratory; **parlamentarische** ~ parliamentary oratory;
jds. ~ **Einhalt gebieten** to dam up s. one's eloquence.

beredt eloquent, fluent, *(bedeutsam)* expressive, meaningful;
~ **sein** to have a fluent tongue;
~**er Fürsprecher** eloquent advocate; ~**es Schweigen** meaningful silence; **mit** ~**er Zunge** with a glib tongue.

Beregnung, künstliche irrigation.

Beregnungsanlage irrigation plant, *(gegen Feuerschaden)* sprinkler irrigation.

Bereich reach, realm, precinct, beat, *(Einflußsphäre)* orbit, *(Gebiet)* sphere, field, domain, ambit, province, purview, territory, *(Gegend)* area, region, *(mil.)* zone, area, department, *(Reichweite)* range, *(Tätigkeit)* concern, scope;
außerhalb meines ~**s** outside my ken *(coll.)*; **im industriellen** ~ in the industrial field (sector); **im zivilen** ~ in the civil sector; **in allen anderen** ~**en** in all other respects;
im ~ **des Bauwesens** in the building trade; **im** ~ **der Fabel** in the realm of fiction; **im** ~ **der öffentlichen Hand** in the public sector; **im** ~ **des Möglichen** within the range (bounds) of possibility; **im** ~ **der Stadt** in the neighbo(u)rhood (precincts) of the town; **im** ~ **des menschlichen Verstandes** within the sweep of human intelligence; **im** ~ **der Wirtschaft** in the economic sphere;
analoger ~ *(Statistik)* similar region; **ausgedehnter** ~ wide range; **erfaßter** ~ *(Lautsprecher)* beam, *(Statistik)* coverage; **militärischer** ~ military area; **öffentlicher** ~ public sector; **privater (persönlicher)** ~ private sector;
gesamter ~ **der Finanzwirtschaft** all aspects of financial activities; **alle** ~**e des Marktes** all sections of the market; ~ **der Scheinwerfer** sweep of the searchlight; ~ **der Wirtschaft** economic domain;
im ~ **einer Hochdruckzone bleiben** to be influenced by an anticyclone; **größeren** ~ **erfassen** to ripple out into more sectors; **in jds.** ~ **fallen** to come (fall) within s. one's purview; **in den** ~ **der Naturwissenschaften fallen** to come within the province of natural science; **zu jds.** ~ **gehören** to be s. one's province (up s. one's street); **nicht in jds.** ~ **liegen** not to be s. one's department, to be out of s. one's line; **im professionellen** ~ **liegen** to be within the professional range; **im** ~ **des Innenministeriums liegen** to come within the purview of the Home Office *(Br.)*; **im** ~ **des Möglichen liegen** to lie within the scope of possible events; **nicht im** ~ **richterlicher Tätigkeit liegen** to be outside of the scope of the activities of a judge; **außerhalb des** ~**s des menschlichen Verstandes liegen** to be beyond the compass of human understanding; **jds.** ~ **sein** to come into s. one's domain.

bereichern to enrich, to make wealthy;
sich ~ to feather one's nest, to line one's pocket, to make one's pile; **sich auf Kosten anderer** ~ to batten upon others; **sich öffentlich** ~ to enrich o. s. from public office; **Sprache** ~ to add to a language; **seinen Wissensbereich** ~ to enlarge one's range of knowledge; **seinen Wortschatz** ~ to enlarge (increase) one's vocabulary.

Bereicherter benefited party.

Bereicherung enrichment;
ungerechtfertigte ~ unjust enrichment, unjustified benefit, *(Behauptung im Klagevortrag)* money had and received; **bedeutsame** ~ **eines Vereins** great acquisition to a club; ~ **des Wissens** extension of knowledge.

Bereicherungsklage action for money had and received *(Br.)*, trover.

Bereichs|abkommen area agreement; ~**leiter** area director; ~**umschaltung** *(Rundfunkgerät)* band selection.

bereifen to tyre *(Br.)*, to tire *(US)*;
Auto neu ~ to fit a new set of tyres (tires) on a car; **sich** ~ to cover with rime, to frost over.

bereift new-tyred *(Br.)*.

Bereifung tyres *(Br.)*, tires *(US)*;
doppelte ~ dual tyres (tires).

bereinigen to settle, to put straight, to clear, to clean up, to iron out, *(Statistik)* to adjust, *(Wertpapiere)* to revalidate, to reassess;
Anfangsschwierigkeiten ~ to iron out initial difficulties; **Angelegenheit** ~ to straighten out an affair; **Bilanz** ~ to verify (rectify) a balance sheet; **etw. endgültig mit jem.** ~ to have it out with s. o.; **Grenze** ~ to adjust a boundary; **Konten** ~ to square (correct) accounts; **Mißverständnis** ~ to clear up a misunderstanding; **Quoten** ~ to adjust quotas; **Register** ~ to rectify a register; **sein Sortiment** ~ to simplify one's product lines.

bereinigt adjusted, settled, *(Wertpapiere)* revalidated;
statistisch ~ statistically adjusted;
~**e Besteuerungsgrundlage** adjusted basis; ~**er Produktionsindex** adjusted production index; ~**er Selbstkostenpreis** adjusted cost basis.

Bereinigung settlement, regularization, reorganization, *(Bilanz)* verification, rectification, *(Konto)* correction, *(Statistik)* adjustment, *(Wertpapiere)* revalidation, reassessment;
~ **von Konten** squaring (correction) of accounts; ~ **und Neufassung eines Gesetzes** revision of a statute; ~ **eines Registers** rectification of a register; ~ **des Sortiments** product line simplification.

bereisen to travel, *(im Auto)* to tour, *(besichtigen)* to perambulate;
Bezirk ~ to work on (cover) a district; **Land** ~ to travel over a country; **Messen** ~ to frequent (tour) the fairs; **neue Strecke** ~ to travel over a new route; **Wahlkreis** ~ to canvass a constituency.

bereit in readiness, ready, prepared, willing, at (on) call, pat, on deck *(US)*, *(Schiff)* clear;
zum Aufbruch ~ ready for departure (to start); **zum sofortigen Gebrauch** ~ on tap; **zu Gegendiensten stets** ~ glad to reciprocate in similar kind; **zu Verhandlungen** ~ willing to enter into negotiations;
sich ~ **erklären** to express one's willingness; **Antwort** ~ **haben** to have one's answer pat; **Überraschung** ~ **haben** to have a surprise in store; **sich zu keinem Kompromiß** ~ **finden können** not to see one's way to a compromise; **zu allem** ~ **sein** to be easy, to stick at nothing, to be game for anything *(coll.)*; **zu Konzessionen** ~ **sein** to be willing to make concessions.

bereiten *(Mahlzeit)* to prepare, to get ready;
Arznei ~ to make up a medicine; **Boden für Verhandlungen** ~ to prepare the ground for negotiations; **jem. einen herzlichen Empfang** ~ to give s. o. a cordial reception; **einer Tratte guten Empfang** ~ to meet a bill with due hono(u)r; **einer Sache ein Ende** ~ to put an end to a matter; **jem. Enttäuschung** ~ to disappoint s. o.; **jem. eine kleine Freude** ~ to give s. o. a treat; **jem. Genugtuung** ~ to give s. o. satisfaction; **jem. ernsthafte Konkurrenz** ~ to expose s. o. to severe competition; **jem. Kummer** ~ to cause s. o. grief; **jem. schlaflose Nächte** ~ to cause s. o. sleepness nights; **der Familie Schande** ~ to be a reprobate of the family; **jem. Unannehmlichkeiten** ~ to put s. o. to inconveniences.

bereitgestellt *(Mittel)* earmarked;
~**es Material** reserved material.

bereithalten to keep ready, to hold in readiness;
für j. ~ to have in store for s. o.; **sich** ~ to hold o. s. in readiness, to stand by; **sich zum Angriff** ~ to lie ready to attack; **alles für einen frühen Aufbruch** ~ to have everything in readiness for an early start; **Entschuldigung** ~ to have an excuse pat; **Fahrkarten bitte** ~ have your tickets ready, please; **auf jede Frage eine Antwort** ~ to have always a ready answer; **Gold für ausländische Rechnungen** ~ to hold gold earmarked for foreign accounts; **immer ein paar Tricks** ~ to have always a few tricks up one's sleeve; **Zimmer für j.** ~ to hold a room in readiness for s. o.

bereitliegen, zur Abfahrt to be ready to depart (sail); **zur Abholung** ~ to be ready for collection.

bereitmachen, sich zur Abfahrt to make ready for departure.

Bereitschaft readiness, preparedness, preparation, willingness, *(Dienst)* attendance, *(mil.)* alert, stand-by, *(Polizei)* alert;
in ~ in waiting *(Br.)*, *(Arzt)* in attendance, *(mil.)* on the alert; **in ständiger** ~ *(Feuerwehr)* always on call, *(Polizei)* on the alert;
~ **zur Abnahme von Sonderangeboten** deal proneness; ~ **anderen zu helfen** readiness to help others; ~ **eine angemessene Arbeitsstelle anzutreten** availability for work; ~ **zur Aufnahme von Verhandlungen** willingness to enter into negotiations;
seine ~ **erklären** to express one's willingness; **in** ~ **halten** to hold in readiness (ready); **in** ~ **liegen** to lie ready; ~ **zur Diskussion zeigen** to show willingness to discuss.

Bereitschafts|arzt physician in attendance; ~**auftrag** *(Flugzeug)* air alert mission; ~**bataillon** stand-to battalion; ~**befehl** *(mil.)* stand-by order; ~**dienst** *(mil.)* emergency (standby) service, stand-by duty; **vierundzwanzigstündiger** ~**dienst** round-the-clock service, *(Luftwaffe)* air alert mission; ~**dienst haben**

(Apotheke, Arzt) to be on call, *(mil.)* to be on duty, to stand by; ~**erklärung** letter of intent *(US)*; ~**geld** *(Pilot)* half pilotage; ~**kredit** stand-by credit; ~**polizei** alert (riot) police, emergency squad; ~**raum** *(Flugplatz)* ready (briefing) room; ~**stufe** alert phase; ~**tasche** emergency (first-aid) kit, *(Fotoapparat)* ever-ready case.

bereitstehen to be ready (available), *(mil.)* to stand to, to be on the alert;
zur Abholung ~ to be ready for collection; **am Bahnhof** ~ to be waiting at the station; **zur Verschiffung** ~ to be ready for shipment.

bereitstehend|es Flugzeug waiting plane; ~**e Mittel** available funds.

bereitstellen to hold (keep) ready, to provide, to make available, to supply, *(Haushalt)* to place at disposal, to make available, *(sicherstellen)* to secure;
Arbeitskräfte ~ to allocate manpower; **Geld** ~ to provide (appropriate) money; **Geld für einen bestimmten Zweck** ~ to earmark funds; **bestimmten Geldbetrag für Forschungszwecke** ~ to earmark a sum of money for research; **Kaution** ~ to provide security; **Kisten zum Verladen** ~ to place the boxes ready for loading; **Luftlandetruppen** ~ to stage airborne troops; **Material** ~ to reserve material; **notwendige Mittel** ~ to make the necessary funds available; **für Steuern** ~ to allow (make provisions) for taxation; **notwendige Transportmittel** ~ to provide the necessary transport; **Truppen** ~ to assemble (concentrate, build-up) troops; **Zug** ~ to make up a train.

Bereitstellung setting apart, provision, procurement, supply, *(Gelder)* appropriation, provision, *(Haushaltsrecht)* allocation, provision, *(mil.)* deployment;
jährliche ~ annual provision; **mittelbare** ~ *(Waggon)* constructive placement; **tatsächliche** ~ actual placement;
~ **von Arbeitsgerät** provision of equipment; ~ **von Arbeitsplätzen** job availability; ~ **von Beträgen für eingegangene Verpflichtungen** commitment appropriations; ~ **für Einkommenssteuerzahlungen** provision for income tax; ~ **ausreichender postalischer Einrichtungen** running a decent postal system; **großzügige** ~ **von Essen und Trinken** liberal supply of food and drink; ~ **von Etatsmitteln** budgetary provision; ~ **von Fernsehprogrammen** television service; ~ **von Freizeiträumen** rest accommodation; ~ **von Geldbeträgen** appropriation of funds; ~ **von Geldbeträgen für bestimmte Zwecke** earmarking of funds; ~ **von Goldreserven** earmarking of gold; ~ **von Grundstücken zum Gemeingebrauch** appropriation of land; ~ **von Kapazitätsreserven** backup with reserve capacity; ~ **von Kapital** supply of capital; ~ **eines Kredits** granting of a loan; ~ **von Mitteln** appropriation of funds; ~ **von Notbetten** emergency bed service; ~ **der Tagesordnung** supply of the agenda paper; ~ **von Truppen** assembly (concentration, buildup) of troops; ~**en für Verluste** appropriations for losses; ~ **von Versorgungseinrichtungen** public service; ~ **von Wohnungen** provision of housing; ~ **eines Zuges** making up of a train.

Bereitstellungs|bescheid advance commitment; ~**fonds** available (earmarked) fund, appropriation fund *(US)*; ~**konto** appropriation (earmarked) account; ~**kosten** stand-by charges; ~**kredit** commitment credit; ~**liste** *(Fluglinie)* standby; ~**maßnahmen** earmarking transactions; ~**provision** commitment commission; ~**raum** *(Truppen)* assembly area, *(Luftlandetruppen)* marshal(l)ing (stage) area; ~**vereinbarung** *(Kreditlinie)* stand-by agreement; ~**zinsen** commitment interest.

bereitwillig ready, willing, unhesitating, *(dienstfertig)* obliging, with good grace.

Bereitwilligkeit readiness, willingness, promptitude, obligingness;
mit größter ~ most readily;
~ **einen Vorschlag anzunehmen** readiness to accept a proposal; **keine übergroße** ~ **zeigen** to be not too eager.

bereuen to be sorry, to regret;
Entscheidung ~ to regret a decision; **Tat aufrichtig** ~ to repent a deed sincerely.

Berg mountain, hill, peak;
über ~ **und Tal** up hill and down dale;
feuerspeiender ~ volcano; **goldene** ~**e** pie in the sky; **schneebedeckte** ~**e** snowcapped mountains;
~**e von Akten** pile of documents; ~**e von Büchern** heaps of books; ~**e von Geld** oceans of money; ~**e von Papier** mounds of paper; ~**e von Schulden** load (mountain) of debts; ~**e schmutziger Wäsche** piles of dirty washing;
~ **besteigen** to climb (ascend) a mountain, to mountaineer; ~**e von Arbeit bewältigen** to do a power of work; **im Urlaub in die** ~**e fahren** to spend one's holiday in the mountains; **mit seiner Meinung hinter dem** ~ **halten** to hold one's counsel; **mit seiner Meinung nicht hinter dem** ~ **halten** to speak one's mind; **sich einen** ~ **heraufquälen** to labo(u)r up a hill; **jem. die Haare zu** ~**e stehen lassen** to make s. one's hair stand on end; **über alle** ~**e sein** to be miles away, to be beyond reach; **über den** ~ **sein** to be over the hump, to have broken the back of the work, *(Kranker)* to have passed the crisis (turned the corner), *(Unternehmen)* to have come out of the red; **noch nicht über den** ~ **sein** to be not yet out of the wood, *(Betrieb)* to be still in the red *(US coll.)*; **wie der Ochs am** ~**e stehen** to be brought to a nonplus; **vor einem** ~ **von Schwierigkeiten stehen** to face insurmountable difficulties; ~**e versetzen** to move mountains; **jem. goldene** ~**e versprechen** to feed s. o. with empty promises, to promise miracles (the moon); ~**e von Kuchen vertilgen** to gobble up heaps of cake.

bergab *(auch fig.)* downward;
~ **fahren** to go downhill; ~ **gehen** *(Straße)* to descend;
mit ihm geht es ~ he is on the downgrade (going downhill), *(Kranker)* his sands are running out.

Berg|akademie mining academy; ~**amt** mining board; ~**anteil** mining share.

Bergarbeiter mineworker, coal miner, collier, pitman;
~**gewerkschaft** National Union of Mineworkers *(US)*; ~**kolonie** miner's housing estate; ~**sprache** pit talk; ~**streik** coal strike.

bergauf uphill, upward, up the hill.

Berg- und Talbahn switchback *(Br.)*, figure eight, big dipper, roller coaster *(US)*.

Bergbau mining, working of mines, mine work;
~ **im Tagebaubetrieb** strip mine *(US)*;
~ **betreiben** to be engaged in working mines, to work minerals; ~ **den Gesetzen der Marktwirtschaft entziehen** to isolate (insulate) the mining industry from the interplay of market forces;
~**berechtigung** location, mining claim *(US)*, mining licence; **enteigneter** ~**betrieb** expropriated mine; ~**bezirk**, ~**gebiet** mineral district, mining area, mining district, digging.

bergbaufähiges Land mineral land.

Berbau|industrie mining industry; ~**industrieller** mine-owner, mine operator; ~**ingenieur** mining engineer; ~**konzession** mining licence (concession), mineral claim; ~**produktion** mining output; ~**recht**, ~**regal** right to mine, mineral rights; ~**revier** mining area (district); ~**sachverständiger** mining expert; ~**sozialisierung** coal mines nationalization *(Br.)*; ~**vermögen** mining property.

Berg|besteigung ascent of a mountain; ~**bewohner** highlander, *(pl.)* hill folk; ~**dorf** mountain village.

Bergegeld salvage money, *(Bergbau)* dead rent.

bergehoch as high as mountains.

Berge|leistung civil salvage; ~**lohn** salvage money; **Höhe des** ~**lohns festsetzen** to assess the amount payable as salvage.

bergen to salvage, to rescue, to recover;
Bruchlandung ~ to make salvage of a shipwrecked cargo; **Ernte** ~ to get in the crop; **Ertrunkenen** ~ to recover the body of a drowned man; **Güter aus einem verunglückten Schiff** ~ to recover shipwrecked goods; **Ladung** ~ to save the cargo; **lebend** ~ to rescue alive; **Mannschaft eines untergehenden Schiffes** ~ to rescue the crew of a sinking ship; **aus den Trümmern** ~ to salvage from the debris.

bergeweise wholesale.

Berg|fahrt hill climbing; ~**führer** mountain (Alpine) guide; ~**gerechtigkeit** mining concession; ~**gipfel** peak, summit; ~**grundbuch** mining register; ~**hang** hillside, slope, incline, *(steil)* declivity; ~**hütte** mountain (Alpine) hut, refuge; **einfach zusammengeschlagene** ~**hütte** crude log cabin in the mountain; ~**ingenieur** mining engineer; ~**inspektor** surveyor of the mines, mine viewer; ~**kette** chain of mountains; ~**knappe** miner, pitman, collier; ~**land** hill country, highland, mountainous country; ~**landschaft** mountain scenery; ~**mann** miner, mineworker; ~**mannsprämie** workmen's compensation *(Br.)*; ~**paß** mountain pass; ~**recht** mining law; ~**regal** mining royalty, mineral rights; ~**regalabgabe** mineral rights duty *(Br.)*, dead (sleeping, fixed, outstroke) rent; ~**regalpacht** mining lease; ~**regalsteuer** mineral rights duty *(Br.)*; ~**rutsch** landslide; ~**spitze** pinnacle, hilltop; ~**steigefähigkeit** *(Auto)* hill-climbing capacity; ~**steiger** mountaineer, alpinist; **leichtsinnige** ~**steiger** mountain adventurer; ~**sturz** landslide; ~**tour machen** to go on an excursion to the mountains.

Bergung salvage, recovery, rescue;
~ **und Hilfeleistung** maritime assistance; ~ **einer Leiche** recovery of a dead body.

Bergungs|aktion recovery task; ~**arbeiten** salvage (rescue) operations; ~**arbeiter** salvage worker, salvager; ~**boot** salvage craft (boat); ~**dampfer** salvage ship, wrecker; ~**dienst** rescue service; ~**fahrzeug** salvage boat, hoveler, recovery vehicle, *(Flugplatz)* crash vehicle (truck), wrecker *(US)*; ~**gebühren** salvage dues; ~**gesellschaft** salvage company, rescue party (squad); ~**gut** salvage; **wiederverwertbares** ~**gut** recoverable salvage; ~**gut übernehmen** to take over the salvage; ~**hubschrauber** recovery helicopter; ~**kommando** salvage party (squad); ~**kosten** cost of salvage, salvage charge; ~**kran** breakdown (salvage) crane; ~**leiter** wreck commissioner *(Br.)*; ~**mannschaft** rescue party (squad); ~**maßnahmen** salvage operations; ~**schaden** salvage loss; ~**schiff** salvage vessel; ~**schlepper** salvage tug; ~**unternehmen** salvage company; ~**verpflichtung** salvage bond; ~**versuch** rescue bid; ~**vertrag** salvage agreement; ~**wert** salvage value.

Bergwacht rescue team;
~**station** mountain center *(US)* (centre, *Br.*).

Bergwerk mine, pit;
im Tagebau betriebenes ~ open mine; **eigengenutztes** ~ captive mine *(US)*;
im ~ **arbeiten** to work in the mines; ~ **auflassen** to shut a mine; ~ **ausbeuten (betreiben)** to work a mine at a profit; ~ **markscheiden** to measure out (survey) a mine; ~ **in Betrieb nehmen** to exploit a mine.

Bergwerks|abgabe mining royalty; **kapitalisierte** ~**abgabe** royalty value; ~**aktie**, ~**anteil** mining share (stock, *US*), *(Börse)* mines, coalers *(US)*; **eigengenutzte** ~**anlage** captive mine *(US)*; ~**- und Hüttenanlage** mining and foundry plant; ~**anteil** mining share (stock, *US*); ~**aufseher** mine viewer; ~**berechtigung** mining lease; ~**betrieb** mining works (company, concern); ~**eigentum** mining property; ~**eigentümer** mine owner; ~**gerechtigkeit** title to work a mine, mining concession; ~**gesellschaft** mining company (corporation, partnership, *US*), colliery company; ~**industrie** mining industry; ~**inspektor** surveyor of the mines; ~**interessen** mining interests; ~**konzession** mining concession (licence); ~**obligation** mining bond; ~**pacht** mining lease; ~**schäden** damage to a mine; ~**steuer** mineral rights duty *(Br.)*; ~**unglück** mining disaster; ~**unternehmen** mining venture; ~**verein** mining association; ~**verleihung** grant of minerals.

Bericht report, account, story, statement, notice, *(Abhandlung)* treatise, paper, *(Botschaft)* message, *(Chronik)* chronicle, page, *(Kommentar)* commentary, *(Protokoll)* record, minutes, *(Unterrichtung)* information;
laut ~ as per advice, as advised by; **mangels** ~**s** for want of advice, *(Wechselvermerk)* no advice; **ohne** ~ without advice;
abgehender ~ outgoing dispatch; **abgeschlossener** ~ completed report; **amtlicher** ~ official statement, return; **ausführlicher** ~ detailed statement (report), verbatim report; **authentischer** ~ authentic report; **begeisterter** ~ glowing account; **detaillierter** ~ circumstantial (detailed) account; **eingehender** ~ full and particular account, full particulars, detailed statement; **einleitender** ~ initial report; **entstellter** ~ garble; **nicht entstellter** ~ ungarbled report; ~ **erstattet von** report prepared by; **mündlich erstatteter** ~ verbatim (oral) report; **falscher** ~ misreport, false report; **farbiger** ~ colo(u)rful report; **gefälschter** ~ fabricated account; **gefärbter** ~ colo(u)red report; **gemeinsamer** ~ joint report; **genauer** ~ exact account; **genauer und sachlicher** ~ fair and accurate report; **sorgfältig geschriebener** ~ carefully written report; **günstiger** ~ favo(u)rable report; **irreführender** ~ misleading report; **jährlicher** ~ annual report (return); **kurzer** ~ summary; **langer** ~ Illiad; **laufender** ~ running commentary; **minutiöser** ~ minute report; **mündlicher** ~ oral (verbatim) report; **offizieller** ~ official bulletin; **offiziöser** ~ nonofficial report; **schriftlicher** ~ write-up; **schriftlicher eidesstattlicher** ~ *(der ordentlichen Generalversammlung)* statutory declaration; **statistischer** ~ statistical returns; **tendenziöser** ~ tendentious report; **ungenauer** ~ misreport; **gemeinsam verfasster** ~ joint report; **verleumderischer** ~ calumnious report; **vertraulicher** ~ confidential report; **vierteljährlicher** ~ quarterly statement; **vollständiger** ~ account given in full; **vorläufiger** ~ interim report; **widersprechender** ~ contradictory report; **einander widersprechende** ~**e** discrepant accounts; **wortgetreuer** ~ verbatim; **zusammenfassender** ~ survey, consolidated report; ~ **eines Arbeitsstabes** task-force report; ~ **einer Auskunftei** credit report; ~ **aus dem Ausland** report (advice) from abroad; ~ **der Autoindustrie** automotive report; ~ **eines Botschafters** disptach from an ambassador; ~ **der Buchprüfer** auditors' report; ~ **über die Einnahmen- und Ausgabenentwicklung** income and expenditure account; ~ **in zeitungsgeeigneter Form** rewrite *(US)*; **statistischer** ~ **über Geburten, Eheschließungen und Todesfälle** returns over births, deaths and marriages; **gesetzlich genehmigter** ~ **über ein Gerichtsverfahren** privileged report; **sachliche und genaue** ~**e von Gerichtsverhandlungen** fair and accurate reports of judicial proceedings; ~ **über das Geschäftsjahr** annual report; ~ **über die Konkursabwicklung** statement of proceedings; ~ **einer Kreditauskunftei** mercantile (agency business, *US*) report; ~ **zur Lage** commentary on the political situation; ~ **aus M.** dispatch from M.; ~ **der Minderheit** minority report; ~ **über den Notenumlauf** circulation statement *(US)*; ~ **über die Parlamentssitzungen** parliamentary reporting; ~ **über eine Reise** account of a voyage; ~ **eines Sachverständigen** expert's report; ~ **des Schatzmeisters** treasurer's report; ~ **des Schriftführers** secretary's report; ~ **über eine Sitzung** minutes of a meeting; ~ **des Treuhänders** trust report; ~ **über die Vermögenslage** financial report (statement, status), statement of affairs; ~ **des Wirtschaftsministeriums** Commerce Department Report *(US)*; ~ **des Wirtschaftsprüfers** auditor's report; **spaltenlange** ~**e in den Zeitungen** newspaper reports covering several columns; **täglicher** ~ **der Zollbehörde** customs bill of entry;
~ **abfassen** to prepare (draw up) a report; ~ **für j. anfertigen** to make a report for s. o.; ~ **anfordern** to request a report; ~ **annehmen** to adopt a report; **in einem** ~ **mit aufnehmen** to include in a report; ~ **ausarbeiten** to prepare a report; ~ **ausschmücken** to embroider a story; **einem** ~ **Unterlagen beifügen** to join documents to a report; ~ **bestätigen** to confirm a report; **frühere** ~**e anscheinend bestätigen** to lend credit to the earlier reports; ~ **einhellig billigen** to be unanimous in their approval of a report; ~ **auf den neusten Stand bringen** to bring a report up to date; ~ **zur Verlesung bringen** to read a report to the meeting; ~ **einreichen** to submit (file) a report; ~ **entgegennehmen** to hear a report; ~ **erstatten** to render an account, to give a report, to give account, to cover *(US)*; ~ **über eine Gesetzesvorlage erstatten** to report a bill; **schriftlichen** ~ **erstatten** to hand in a statement, to make (render) a report; **über ein Thema** ~ **erstatten** to cover a subject; **seinen** ~ **färben** to tinge one's report; ~ **formulieren** to frame a report; ~ **frisieren** to cook a report *(sl.)*; **detaillierten** ~ **geben** to go into particulars; **wahrheitsgemäßen** ~ **über die Tatsachen geben** to give a right account of the facts; **aus einem** ~ **hervorgehen** to appear from a report; **in einem** ~ **niederlegen** to mention in a report; **vollständigen** ~ **für eine Zeitung schreiben** to write up an affair for a paper; ~ **in Umlauf setzen** to give currency to a report; ~ **unterdrücken** to stifle a report; ~ **über eine Sportveranstaltung verfassen** to write off an account of a sports meeting; ~ **veröffentlichen** to issue (publish) a report; ~ **verstümmeln** to garble a report; ~ **vervielfältigen** to run off copies of a report; ~ **vervollständigen** to amplify an account; ~ **vorlegen** to submit a report.

berichten to tell, to [give a] report, to [render an] account, to come clean *(sl.)*, to narrate, *(unterrichten)* to advise, to inform, *(Zeitung)* to cover *(US)*;
amtlich ~ to lodge information; **jem. über den Stand seiner Arbeit** ~ to report progress to s. o.; **ausführlich** ~ to give a detailed account; **eingehend** ~ to make a detailed statement, to give full particulars, to write up, to go to town on; **jem. über die neuesten Ereignisse** ~ to inform s. o. of the latest events; **über nationale wie internationale Ereignisse gleichmäßig detailliert** ~ to offer a full diet of national and international coverage; **falsch** ~ to misinform; **in gedrängter Form** ~ to nutshell; **über eine Hauptversammlung** ~ to cover a meeting of shareholders *(US)*; **über eine Konferenz** ~ to cover a conference *(US)*; **über die Wiener Konferenz** ~ to cover the Vienna conference; **über die Rollendarstellung der Hauptschauspieler lobend** ~ to write up the acting of the leading players; **schriftlich** ~ to send in a written notice; **über die Sitzungen der Vereinten Nationen** ~ *(Zeitung)* to cover United Nations Sessions; **über eine Versammlung** ~ to give an account of a meeting; **das Wichtigste in Kürze** ~ to give a wrap-up of the news;
sich täglich ~ **lassen** to get a daily report.

berichtenswert newsworthy;
nicht ~ nothing to write home about.

Berichterstatter referendary, referee, rapporteur, teller, *(Gericht)* returning officer *(Br.)*, clerk of the court, recorder *(US)*, *(Gewährsmann)* informant, *(Rundfunk)* commentator, reporter, *(Zeitung)* [newspaper] correspondent, writer, pressworker, reporter, item man *(US)*, pressman *(sl.)*;
auswärtiger ~ foreign correspondent;
~ **des Parlaments** parliament rapporteur, floor manager;

als ~ arbeiten to cover *(US)*, to report; **als schlechtbezahlter ~ arbeiten** to penny-a-line; ~ **der „Times" sein** to report for the „Times"; **als ~ tätig sein** to report, to act as correspondent, to cover *(US)*.

Berichterstattung report, statement, notice, report preparation, *(für Zeitung)* reporting, presswork, journalism, coverage *(US)*; **zur ~** ad referendum; **zur ~ geeignet** reportable;
ausländische ~ foreign news report; **laufende ~** current accounts (reports); **lückenlose ~** full coverage; **unmittelbare ~** spot coverage; **unrichtige ~** misinformation; **unterlassene ~** failure to render a report; **voreingenommene ~** prejudicial (biassed) reporting; **zuverlässige ~** reliable reports;
~ **der Aktiengesellschaften** corporate reporting; ~ **über Gerichtsfälle** court reports *(US)*; ~ **in den Nachrichtenmitteln** media coverage; ~ **über Rechtsfälle** law reports; ~ **über Vorstadtereignisse** suburban coverage; ~ **über die Wahlen** election coverage;
Botschafter zur ~ zurückbeordern to recall an ambassador to report.

Berichterstattungs|aufgabe reporting rôle; ~**möglichkeiten** newsreporting facilities.

Berichterstellung report preparation.

berichtigen to rectify, to correct, to amend, to mend, to emend, *(ausgleichen)* to settle, *(Geschwindigkeitsanzeige)* to calibrate;
Buchstelle ~ to emend a passage in a book; **Buchung ~** to adjust (rectify) an entry; **Druckfehler ~** to correct a misprint; **Einkommensteuerveranlagung ~** to revise an assessment; **Erklärung ~** to correct a statement; **Grenze ~** to adjust a frontier; **Grundbuch ~** to rectify the register; **Grundkapital ~** to adjust the capital, to readjust the capital stock *(US)*; **Irrtum ~** to rectify an error; **Konto ~** to adjust an account; **Preisliste ~** to revise a price list; **Quoten ~** to adjust quotas; **Rechnung durch Nachrechnen (Rechnungsbetrag) ~** to correct an account; **Register ~** to rectify a register; **Text ~** to emend (amend) a text; **Vorjahresgewinn ~** to adjust prior year's profits.

berichtigende Buchung adjustment entry.

berichtigt adjusted, rectified;
~**e Rechnung** corrected invoice; ~**es Roheinkommen** adjusted gross income; ~**e Zahl** revised figure.

Berichtigung rectification, correction, *(Ausgleich)* settlement, *(Bilanz)* abatement, *(Buch)* corrigendum, *(Buchung)* adjustment, *(Streichung)* expurgation, *(Textverbesserung)* amendment, emendation, *(Verbesserung)* correction;
~**en vorbehalten** subject to correction; **zur ~ unserer Rechnung** to balance our account;
~**en** *(Buch)* errata;
steuerlich notwendige ~ adjustment for tax purposes; **rückwirkende ~** adjustment with retroactive effect;
~ **des Aktienkapitals** readjustment (rectification) of capital [stock, *US*]; ~ **einer Einkommensteuerveranlagung** revision of an assessment; ~ **eines Fehlers** correction of a mistake; ~ **einer Frachtrechnung** correction notice; ~ **des Gewinns** reconciliation of surplus; ~ **der Grenze** adjustment of a frontier; ~ **des Grundbuchs** rectification of the register; ~ **eines Irrtums** rectification of an error; ~ **des Kapitals** capital adjustment; ~ **des Klagevorbringens** amendment of a cause of action, amendment to a pleading, departure; ~ **eines Kontos** adjustment (correction) of an account; ~ **eines Patents** amendment of a patent; ~ **eines Preises** revision of a price, price change; ~ **eines Textes** emendation of a text; ~ **eines Urteils** amendment of a judgment; ~ **der Vorjahresbilanz** prior-year adjustment; ~ **der Vorjahresgewinne** adjustment of prior (previous) year's profits;
für ~en Vorsorge treffen to allow for readjustments; ~ **veröffentlichen** to publish a correction.

Berichtigungs|aktie scrip issue *(Br.)*, stock dividend *(US)*; ~**anzeige** notice of error; ~**bescheid** *(Patentrecht)* certificate of correction; ~**bilanz** rectified balance sheet; ~**buchung** adjustment entry, adjusting journal (correcting and adjusting, rectifying) entry; **durch die Revision veranlaßte ~buchung** audit adjustment; ~**eintrag** adjustment entry.

berichtigungsfähig rectifiable.

Berichtigungs|feststellung revision of an assessment; ~**fortschreibung** prior period adjustment; ~**konto** adjustment (reconciliation, suspense) account; ~**mitteilung** correction notice; ~**posten** adjustment (valuation) item, *(Bilanz)* deferred charges; ~**protokoll** protocol of amendment; ~**rücklage** qualifying reserve; ~**schein** *(Patentgesetz)* certificate of correction; ~**schreiben** rectifying letter; ~**spalte** adjustment column; ~**veranlagung** *(Steuern)* revision of an assessment, reassessment; ~**verfahren** rectification procedure.

Berichts|abfassung report writing; ~**auflagen** reporting requirements; ~**entwurf** draft report; ~**familie einer Haushaltsbefragung** household budget survey participant; ~**form** narrative form; ~**formular** reporting (statement) form; ~**jahr** year reported on, year under report (review, survey); **beträchtliche ~lücke** significant skip in an account; ~**monat** month under report (review); ~**periode** *(Revision)* audit period.

berichtspflichtig liable to render account.

Berichts|reihe periodical reports; ~**stadium** report stage; ~**woche** week under review; ~**zeitraum** given (covered) period, period under review.

beriechen, j. to size s. o. up; **Sache ~** to give s. th. the once-over *(US)*, to make a smell at s. th. *(US)*.

berieseln to water, to spray, *(Feld)* to irrigate;
Öffentlichkeit mit Reklame ~ to shower advertisements on the public.

Berieselung watering, irrigation.

Berieselungs|anlage irrigation plant; ~**feld** sewage farm.

Bersten, zum ~ voll crowded to overflowing, *(Bus)* packed to the door;
zum ~ gespannt sein *(Nerven)* to be at breaking point, to be all on edge.

bersten *(Eis)* to burst;
in zwei Teile ~ to break in two parts.

berüchtigt notorious, infamous, of ill fame;
~**es Hafenviertel** ill-famed dock area; ~**er Verbrecher** notorious criminal.

berückend captivating, enchanting, bewitching;
von ~er Schönheit of entrancing beauty.

berücksichtigen to take into account (consideration), to consult, to consider, to pay (have) regard to, to be regardful, *(Vorsorge treffen)* to make allowance for, to allow for;
j. ~ to take s. o. into account, to bear s. o. in mind; **Alter ~** *(Einkommensteuer)* to make allowance for age; **Antrag ~** to consider an application; **j. besonders ~** to give preferential treatment to s. o.; **Einwände nicht ~** to disregard objections; **Einzelheiten ~** to pay regard to details; **gebührend ~** to take due account, to give due consideration; **Kosten ~** to consider the expenses; **jds. Krankheit ~** to allow for s. one's being ill; **jds. Notlage ~** to make allowance for s. one's emergency; **Steuern ~** to make allowance for taxes; **neue Tatsachen ~** to take new circumstances into consideration.

Berücksichtigung consideration, regard;
bei ~ der Sonderausgaben allowing for special expenditure; **in ~ des ganzen Sachverhalts** taking all things into account; **in ~ dieses Umstands** in view of this; **in ~ seiner tadellosen Vergangenheit** in view of his unblemished record; **ohne ~ der Preiserhöhung** regardless of price increase; **unter ~ von** allowing for, with regard to; **unter ~ der Abnutzung** allowing for wear and tear; **unter voller ~ der wirtschaftlichen Interessen** full interest being given to the economic aspects; **unter ~ der Umstände** in view of the circumstances;
gebührende ~ due regard;
~ **des billigsten Angebots** allocation to the lowest tender; ~ **von Kosten** allowance for cost; ~ **von Werbungskosten** *(Einkommensteuer)* allowance for professional expenditure;
~ **finden** to receive attention, to be considered (taken into consideration); **besondere ~ finden** to be given special attention (notice, consideration).

Beruf profession [of business], occupation, job, *(Aufgabe)* function, office, duty, *(Berufung)* vocation, *(Fach)* line, department, *(Gewerbe)* trade, craft, walk, *(Geschäft)* business, shop, *(Geschäftskreis)* province, sphere of action, *(Laufbahn)* career, *(Stand)* calling, *(Stellung)* employment, position, post, situation, station, *(Tätigkeit)* pursuit, work;
in Ausübung meines ~es in pursuance of my vocation, in exercise of my calling; **keinem ~ angehörig** unprofessional; **ohne ~** no occupation, without a trade; **von ~** by profession, by trade, by occupation; **zum ~ gehörig** occupational;
akademischer ~ learned profession; **akademische ~e** the professions; **neu angefangener ~** entry-level job; **ausgefallener ~** godforsaken occupation; **gelegentlich ausgeübter ~** casual occupation; **hoch bezahlter ~** top-paying job; **bürgerliche ~e** civil employments, middle-class callings; **einträglicher ~** profitable profession; **erlernter ~** skilled trade; **fester ~** regular occupation; **freier ~** liberal profession, professional occupation; **freie und sonstige selbständige ~e** *(Einkommensteuer)* profession or vocation *(Br.)*; **gefährlicher ~** hazardous employment (occupation), dangerous occupation; **geistiger ~** intellectual pursuits (occupation); **gewerblicher ~** industrial occupation; **gleichartiger ~** similar job; **grafische ~e** printing

and allied trades; **handwerklicher** ~ handicraft pursuits, handicraft trade; **handwerkliche** ~e mechanical vocations; **hauswirtschaftlicher** ~ domestic calling; **höherer** ~ profession, higher-level job *(US)*; **juristischer** ~ legal profession; **kaufmännischer** ~ business occupation, mercantile profession; **landwirtschaftlicher** ~ agricultural occupation; **langweiliger** ~ dull occupation; **lebenswichtiger** ~ vitally important vocation, essential employment; **normaler** ~ usual vocation; **öffentlicher** ~ public calling (sector); **schwerer** ~ hard job; **soziale** ~e social work *(US)*; **ständiger** ~ regular occupation; **überfüllter (übersetzter)** ~ crowded profession, overcrowded vocation (profession); **unansehnlicher** ~ humble occupation; **unselbständiger** ~ wage-earning employment; **verwandte** ~e occupational families; **Durchsetzungskraft voraussetzender** ~ battling profession; **vordringlicher** ~ priority job;

~ **ohne Aufstiegsmöglichkeiten (Fortkommensmöglichkeiten, Zukunftsaussichten)** terminal (blind-alley) job; ~ **in der Bauindustrie** construction job; ~ **mit Fachausbilding** skilled trade; ~ **mit Lehrlingsausbildung** apprenticeable trade;

seinen ~ **angeben** to put down one's occupation; **in einem freien** ~ **arbeiten** to act as a free lance; **seinen** ~ **als Berufung auffassen** to think of one's vocation in terms of professional status; **in seinem** ~ **aufgehen** to be completely absorbed in one's work; ~ **ausüben** to carry (ply, follow) a trade, to pursue an occupation, to profess, to exercise a profession, to exercise a calling, to hold down a job *(US)*; **keinen festen** ~ **ausüben** to have no regular profession; **gleichen** ~ **ausüben** to practise (follow) the same profession; ~ **eines Journalisten ausüben** to be a journalist; **kriegswichtigen** ~ **ausüben** to be in a reserved occupation; **wirtschaftlich notwendigen** ~ **ausüben** to exercise a useful trade; **sich für einen** ~ **eignen** to be of professional calibre, to be fit for one's job; **sich für einen** ~ **nicht eignen** to be unfit for a job; ~ **ergreifen** to take up (go in for, enter) a profession, to choose an occupation, to go into trade; **anderen** ~ **ergreifen** to change one's vocation (profession); **kaufmännischen** ~ **ergreifen** to go into trade, to turn merchant; **neuen** ~ **ergreifen** to enter upon a new career; **Sport zum** ~ **erheben** to professionalize sport; **in seinem** ~ **keine Arbeit finden** to find no work in one's line; **in einen freien** ~ **gehen** to take up a profession; **sich an einen** ~ **gewöhnen** to shake down into a job; **für einen** ~ **gewinnen** to tag for a job; **an seinem** ~ **keine Freude haben** to have no heart in one's occupation; **in Ausübung seines** ~**s handeln** to act professionally; **sich nur für seinen** ~ **interessieren** to smell of the shop; **j. einen** ~ **erlernen lassen** to put s. o. to a trade; **j. für einen** ~ **als ungeeignet erscheinen lassen** to disqualify s. o. for a profession; **seinen neuen** ~ **schätzen lernen** to settle down to one's new job; **seinem** ~ **nachgehen** to pursue (follow) one's profession, to stick to one's job; **keinem bestimmten** ~ **nachgehen** to be without any particular profession; **neuen** ~ **planen** to map out a new career; **zwischen zwei** ~**en schwanken** to shuttle between two professions; **in einem** ~ **ausgebildet sein** to have learnt a trade (had vocational training); **in seinem** ~ **erfolgreich sein** to do one's job well; **ohne festen** ~ **sein** to be without any particular profession; **für seinen** ~ **ungeeignet sein** to be unfit for one's job; **Tischler von** ~ **sein** to be a joiner by trade; **j. für einen** ~ **trimmen** to groom s. o. for a job; **seinen** ~ **verfehlen** to miss (mistake) one's vocation; **sich einem** ~ **verschreiben** to embark on a career; **sich in einem neuen** ~ **versuchen** to take a fling at a new job; **sich auf einen** ~ **vorbereiten** to train for a career; **seinen** ~ **wechseln** to change one's vocation, to change one's profession, *(häufig)* to job-hop, to switch a job.

berufen to call, to appoint, to nominate, to convoke, to summon; **sich auf j.** ~ to refer to s. o., to mention s. one's name; **sich auf etw.** ~ to quote (cite) s. th.; **sich auf einen Artikel** ~ to invoke an article; **in einen Ausschuß** ~ to appoint to a committee; **sich auf eine frühere Entscheidung** ~ to rely upon a case, to quote a precedent; **j. zu seinem Erben** ~ to appoint s. o. one's heir *(US)*; **sich auf ähnliche Fälle** ~ to quote similar cases; **sich auf ein Gesetz** ~ to refer to an act; **sich auf seinen guten Glauben** ~ to plead one's good faith; **sich auf seinen Kollegen** ~ to refer to one's colleague; **auf einen Lehrstuhl** ~ to offer (call to) a chair; **sich auf Minderjährigkeit** ~ to plead infancy (the Baby Act, *US*); **j. zu seinem Nachfolger** ~ to designate s. o. as (for) one's successor; **sich auf verzögerte Postzustellung** ~ to plead postal delay; **sich auf einen Präzedenzfall** ~ to quote a precedent; **sich auf Unkenntnis des Gesetzes (Unwissenheit)** ~ to plead ignorance; **sich auf Verjährung** ~ to plead the Statute of Limitations; **als Vormund** ~ to appoint as guardian; **zum Vorsitzenden** ~ to appoint as chairman; **in den Vorstand** ~ to nominate a new director; **zum Lehramt** ~ **sein** to be called to the teaching profession; **zum Priester** ~ **sein** to be destined for the church; **auf einen Lehrstuhl** ~ **werden** to be offered a chair (professorship); **auf den Thron** ~ **werden** to be called to the throne;

~ *(a.)* authorized, entitled, *(befähigt)* qualified, *(zuständig)* competent;

aus ~**em Munde** from an authoritative source, straight from the horse's mouth; ~**er Vertreter seines Faches** qualified representative of one's field.

beruflich professional, occupational, vocational;

~ **geeignet** eligible for an occupation; ~ **ungeeignet** incompetent to do a (unfit for one's) job; ~ **verreist** away on business;

jem. ~ **fördern** to advance s. o. in his career; ~ **zu tun haben** to be on business; **j.** ~ **in Anspruch nehmen** to take professional advice from s. o.; ~ **ausgebildet sein** to have learnt a trade; ~ **nur bei einer Firma gewesen sein** to have spent one's working life with a company; ~ **tätig sein** to follow a trade, to exercise a profession; ~ **verhindert sein** to be detained by work; ~ **nach A verreisen** to be going to A on business; ~ **versagen** to fall down on the job *(coll.)*;

~**es Ansehen** professional reputation; ~**e Arbeit** professional work; ~**e Ausbildung** occupational training; ~**e Befriedigung** job satisfaction; ~**e Beweglichkeit** job mobility; ~**e Chancen** career chances; ~**e Diskriminierung** job discrimination; ~**e Eignung** occupational competence, qualification; ~**e Entwicklung** career development; ~**er Erfolg** career success; ~**e Förderung** career advancement; ~**e Fortbildung** adult education, advanced vocational training; ~**e Investition** vocational investment; ~**e Katastrophe** job disaster; ~**e Leistungsfähigkeit** job efficiency; ~**e Möglichkeiten** occupational opportunities; ~**e Position** job status; ~**e Schweigepflicht** professional secrecy; ~**e Schwierigkeiten** [on-the-job] quandaries; ~**e Sicherheit** job security; ~**e Stellung** business position; ~**e Tätigkeit** professional activity (employment), occupational duties; ~**e Tüchtigkeit** efficiency in one's work; ~**e Umgangsformen** job etiquette; ~**e Umwelt** job environment; ~**e Unabkömmlichkeit** occupational deferment; ~**e Unbeständigkeit** job instability; ~**e Vergangenheit** job record, business career; ~**e Weiterbildung** extended professional training; ~**er Werdegang** business career, career history, job record; ~**er Werdegang eines Bewerbers** candidate career; ~**e Zufriedenheit** job satisfaction.

Berufs|analyse vocational analysis, job analysis (breakdown, *US*), *(Zeitschriftenbezug)* occupational classification; ~**angabe** profession or vocation; ~**angaben** vocational data; **ohne** ~**angabe sein** to have not stated one's profession; ~**angehöriger** professional [man]; ~**anwärter** candidate; ~**arbeit** professional duties, *(in der Freizeit)* busman's holiday; ~**armee** professional army; ~**art** line of business; ~**aufgaben** *(Versicherter)* occupational (job) duties; ~**aufgliederung** functional classification.

Berufsausbildung vocational (professional) education (schooling, training), industrial (technical, vocational, occupational) training, pre-employment training, training for a calling, job training *(US)*, *(Einkommenssteuerformular)* training within industry, profession or vocation;

regelrechte ~ formal training; **weitere** ~ continuation training; ~ **am Arbeitsplatz** training within industry, on-the-job training *(US)*;

~ **haben** to be trained in a profession; **in der** ~ **sein** to be bound by indenture.

Berufsausbildungs|gesetz vocational education bill, Educational Act *(US)*, Industrial Training Act *(Br.)*; ~**kosten** cost of vocational education; ~**programm** vocational education program(me); ~**stätte** industrial training board *(Br.)*; ~**verhältnis** vocational training relationship; ~**vertrag** indenture.

Berufs|auslese selection on the basis of aptitude; ~**aussichten** professional (job) prospects; **gute** ~**aussichten für einen jungen Mann** fine openings for a young man; **jem. völlig neue** ~**aussichten eröffnen** to open up a new prospect to s. o.; ~**ausübung** exercise of profession, professional exertion (practice), professionalism; **regelmäßige** ~**ausübung** actual practice; **auf hohe ethische Grundsätze bei der** ~**ausübung bedacht sein** to maintain high professional standards; ~**beamte** established civil servants *(Br.)*; ~**beamtentum** professional government, civil service system *(Br.)*, career service (job) *(US)*, classified civil service *(US)*; ~**beamter** career *(US)* (established, *Br.*) civil servant; **hochqualifizierter** ~**beamter** high-career civil-service officer.

berufsbedingte Krankheit occupational disease.

Berufs|bedingungen job conditions; **~befähigung** professional qualification, occupational aptitude; **~begeisterung** job enthusiasm; **~beginn** job start; **~berater** vocational (professional) consultant (counselor, *US*, adviser), career master *(Br.)*, job counselor *(US)*, careers officer; **~beratung** vocational (job) counseling *(US)*.

Berufsberatungs|dienst placement service; **~gespräch** vocational counseling interview *(US)*; **~institut** vocational guidance clinic; **~stelle, ~zentrum** career-building (placement) bureau, career office, vocational guidance center *(US)* (centre, *Br.*); **~stelle für Jugendliche** juvenile employment bureau.

Berufs|beschränkung job reservation; **~bewertungsverfahren** job evaluation system, *(nach dem Punktsystem)* job rating system; **~bezeichnung** occupational name (title), job identification, business title, job title *(US)*; **als ~bezeichnung Journalist angeben** to set o. s. down as a journalist; **~bezeichnung eintragen** to put down one's occupation; **~bild** job analysis (breakdown, *US*).

berufsbildende Schule industrial (professional) school.

Berufs|chancen career chances (opportunities); **gleiche ~chancen** equal employment opportunities; **j. größere ~chancen gewähren** to help s. o. up the job ladder; **~diplomat** professional (career) diplomat (man), career minister *(US)*; **~diplomat sein** to follow diplomacy as a career; **~dünkel** professional pride; **~ehre** commercial morality; **~eignung** professional qualification (attainment), vocational aptitude, trade proficiency; **~eignungstest** vocational aptitude test; **~eingruppierung** job classification; **~einheit** job family; **~einkommen** employment income; **~einstellung** trade behavio(u)r; **~einstufung** job rating; **~entscheidung** choice of employment; **in der besten ~entwicklung stehen** to be in the prime of one's career.

Berufserfahrung work (professional, career) experience, professional skill;
ohne ~ young in one's job;
große ~en in etw. haben to be an old hand at it; **noch keine ~en haben** to be still green at one's job; **kostenlos ~en sammeln** to obtain beneficial experience in a profession.

Berufs|erfolg job success; **~erfordernisse** job requirements; **~erziehung** professional (vocational) education (training).

Berufsethik professional ethics;
ärztliche ~ medical etiquette; **schwindende ~** deterioration of professionalism;
~ der Anwälte legal etiquette.

berufsethisch professional, ethical;
~e Richtlinien festlegen to create standards of official conduct.

Berufs|ethos des Verkäufers sales etiquette; **dem ~ethos widersprechen** not to be considered ethical; **ins ~fach schlagend** of a professional nature; **~fachschule** technical (trade, *US*) school; **~fahrer** professional driver; **~feuerwehr** fire brigade (company, *US*); **~förderung** career advancement; **innerbetriebliche ~förderung** in-service training *(US)*; **~förderung leitender Angestellter** job economics training; **~fortbildung** advanced training; **~frage** professional problem; **~freiheit** occupational franchise.

berufsfremd nonoccupational;
auch bereit sein müssen, eine ~e Tätigkeit auszuüben to have to be prepared to accept employment of a different kind.

berufsgebunden incidental to employment.

Berufsgefahr occupational (job) hazard;
übliche ~ ordinary danger incident to employment, ordinary hazards of occupation.

Berufs|geheimnis professional secret (discretion, confidence), *(Anwalt)* privileged communication; **unter das ~geheimnis fallend** privileged; **~gemeinschaft** professional partnership; **~genossenschaft** professional partnership, professional corporation (association), vocational league, confraternity, *(Gewerkschaft)* trade union; **~gespräch** job interview; **~gewerkschaft** occupational union; **~gliederung** occupational distribution (classification); **~gruppe** occupational group (class, category), job class; **~gruppeneinteilung** vocational classification; **~gruppenindex** occupational (job classification, *US*) index; **~haftpflichtrisiko** risk incident to employment; **~haftpflichtversicherung** professional [risks indemnity] insurance *(Br.)*; **~handel** *(Börse)* professional trade *(US)*, floor brokers *(US)*, insider trading, insiders *(Br.)*; **~heer** regular army; **~hilfe** vocational rehabilitation; **seinen ~horizont als internationaler Bankier ausweiten** to broaden one's career as international banker; **~interesse** occupational (career) interest.

berufsinteressiert professional-minded.

Berufs|jargon jargon; **~kamerad** fellow worker, workmate, colleague; **~katalog** occupational characteristic check list; **~kategorie** occupational (professional) grouping; **~käufe** *(Börse)* shop buying; **~kenntnisse** job knowledge; **~kennzeichen** job characteristic; **~klassen** occupational (job) classes; **~klassifizierung** job classification; **~kleidung** habit, trade kit, business (professional, work, working) clothes; **~klima** climate of professionalism; **~kollege** professional colleague; **~kollegen** the professions; **~konkurrent** job competitor *(US)*; **~konsul** professional (career) consul, consul of career; **~körperschaft** professional body; **~krankheit** occupational disease *(Br.)*, trade (vocational, industrial, *Br.*) disease, prescribed industrial disease *(Br.)*; **höchste Aufmerksamkeit innerhalb der maßgebenden ~kreise erwecken** to receive top professional recognition; **~kunde** business administration; **~laufbahn** career, walk of life; **jds. ~laufbahn völlig beeinflussen** to determine the whole of s. one's career; **~leben** occupation, profession, work, professional (working) life; **ins ~leben eintreten** to start in life, to begin the world; **im ~leben stehen** to have a job, to be in work; **~leistung** job performance; **~leitfaden** career guide; **~lenkung** vocational guidance.

berufslos without occupation.

berufsmäßig vocational, in a professional way, professional, career *(US)*;
nicht ~ unprofessional, nonoccupational;
~ ausüben to professionalize.

Berufs|merkmal job characteristic; **~möglichkeiten** occupational opportunities, career potential; **freie ~möglichkeiten für leitende Angestellte** executive job mobility; **~moral** professional ethics; **~mörder** professional killer; **~neurose** occupational neurosis; **~niveau** occupational level; **~normung** job standardization; **~offizier** military officer, regular (career, professional, *US*) officer; **~organisation** professional agency; **erweiterte ~organisation** compound craft union; **~pendler** commuter *(US)*; **~pflicht** professional obligation; **~pläne** work plans; **~planung** career planning; **~politiker** professional (practical) politician; **~position** professional job, job slot *(US sl.)*; **übersehbare ~position** clearcut job; **~praxis** professional practice; **~psychologie** vocational psychology; **~pyramide** occupational pyramid; **~richter** professional judge, stipendiary magistrate *(Br.)*; **~risiko** occupational hazard (risk), job hazard, risk incident to employment; **übliches ~risiko** *(Lebensversicherung)* ordinary hazards of occupation, ordinary risk incident to employment; **~sachverständiger** vocational expert; **~schaden** industrial injury, professional injury (wrong), injury at work; **~schicht** profession, trade, occupational category; **führende ~schicht** management profession; **~schulausbildung** vocational education; **~schule** vocational (trade, *US*, training, *US*, day continuation) school.

Berufsschul|klasse vocational (technical) class; **~kursus** day release course; **~lehrer** vocational teacher; **~leiter** vocational director.

Berufsschulung training within industry.

Berufsschul|unterricht classroom instruction; **~wesen** vocational education.

Berufs|seminar career seminar; **~situation** job scene; **~soldat** professional (career) soldier, regular; **~solidarität** professionalism; **~sparte** category of occupation; **alle ~sparten** all walks of life; **~spekulant** *(Börse)* professional; **~spieler** professional [player], pigeon; **~spieler werden** to turn professional; **~sprache** vernacular, jargon; **~stand, ~status** profession[al] status, vocation, trade, professional category; **eigener ~stand** specialized vocation; **höhere ~stände** professional classes.

berufsständische Vertretung professional organization.

Berufs|start job start; **~statistik** occupational statistics, job analysis *(US)*; **~statistiker** trained statistician, job analyst *(US)*; **~stellung** business position, occupational category; **~sterblichkeit** occupational mortality; **internationale ~systematik** International Standard Classification of Occupations (ISCO); **~tarif** occupational rate.

berufstätig working, having a job, gainfully employed, occupied;
~ sein to work, to have a job;
~e Ehefrau working wife; **~e Frau** professional (career) woman.

Berufs|tätige working people; **~tätiger** professional worker; **~tätigkeit** professional activity (employment, business), work, occupation, job; **leitende ~tätigkeit** managerial occupation; **~thema** professional subject; **~tracht** working clothes; **~tüchtigkeit** occupational efficiency; **~umschulung** vocational rehabilitation, occupational retraining.

berufsunfähig disabled, incapable to work;
voll ~ wholly and permanently disabled.

Berufsunfähigkeit incapacity to work, disability, disablement.

Berufsunfall occupational (industrial) accident, occupational (industrial) injury;
~**rente** industrial injuries benefit *(Br.)*, workmen's compensation benefit *(US)*; ~**versicherung** industrial injuries insurance *(Br.)*, workmen's compensation insurance *(US)*; ~**versorgung** industrial injuries system *(Br.)*.

Berufs|verband functional (professional) organization, professional institution (body, society), vocational association, occupational group, *(Gewerkschaft)* craft union; **aus seinem** ~**verband ausgeschlossen** unfrocked *(sl.)*; ~**verbot** *(öffentliches Amt)* disqualification of a person for office, *(Richter)* disqualification of a judge; ~**verbrecher** professional (habitual) criminal; ~**verbrechertum** organized crime; ~**vereinigung** trade association, functional (professional) organization, professional institution (body, society); ~**vergehen** inconsistent conduct with the standards, *(Anwalt)* conduct discreditable to a barrister; ~**verhältnis** job relationship; ~**verkäufe** *(Börse)* shop selling; ~**verkehr** business (rush-hour) traffic, office-hour traffic, suburban (weekday) traffic, commuter traffic *(US)*, commuting *(US)*.

Berufsverkehrs|einrichtungen der Bahn commuter rail service *(US)*; ~**krise** commuter crisis; ~**netz** commuter lines *(US)*; ~**teilnehmer** suburban traveller, season-ticket holder *(Br.)*, commuter *(US)*; ~**verbindung** commuter line *(US)*; ~**zug** commuter train *(US)*.

Berufs|verlauf, nachweisbar erfolgreicher demonstrably effective track record; ~**verlust** job loss; ~**vertretung** professional representation (agency), trade association, occupational representation; ~**verzeichnis** dictionary of occupational titles, job dictionary; ~**vorbereitung** prevocational training; ~**vormund** guardian by appointment of court.

Berufswahl occupational decision, vocational (career) choice, choice of career (life);
freie ~ occupational choice, choice of job, free choice of profession; **richtige** ~ getting the right job;
~ **treffen** to choose an occupation; **richtige** ~ **treffen** to get the right job.

Berufswechsel occupational shift;
häufiger ~ job-hopping;
Arbeitskräfte zum ~ **verleiten** to lure labo(u)r into other jobs; **für einen** ~ **vorbereiten** to process for a new situation, to process out; ~ **vornehmen** to switch a job.

Berufs|welt professional world; ~**wertung nach Abteilungen** departmental ranking; ~**wettbewerb**, ~**wettkampf** job competition.

berufswidrig unprofessional;
~**es Verhalten** unethical conduct, malpractice.

Berufs|zählung occupational census; **mit zehnjähriger** ~**zeit** of ten years' standing; ~**zeitschrift** trade journal; ~**zentrum** occupational center *(US)* (centre, *Br.*); ~**ziel** occupation goal; ~**zugehörigkeit** professional (job, occupational) classification, occupational category; ~**zulassung** professional licence; ~**zusammensetzung** occupational distribution; ~**zuschlag** *(Lebensversicherung)* hazard bonus.

Berufszweig branch of trade, way of business, walk;
exklusiver ~ exclusive profession; **gesperrte** ~**e** closed professions; **überfüllter** ~ overcrowded vocation (profession).

Berufung *(Einsetzung)* appointment, nomination, call, *(Gericht)* appeal, *(Lehrstuhl)* call, appointment, *(Rechtsmittel)* appeal, *(Versammlung)* convocation, *(Verweisung)* reference;
nach seiner ~ **auf einen Lehrstuhl** after one's appointment as professor; **unter** ~ **auf** with reference to, referring to;
~ **ist unzulässig** without appeal, nonreversible; ~ **ist zulässig** with possible appeal;
innere ~ vocation; **zugelassene** ~ leave to appeal;
~ **im Armenrechtsverfahren** appeal in forma pauperis; ~ **auf einen Artikel** invocation of an article; ~ **auf die Ausschlußfrist** plea of lapse of time; ~ **auf eine Entscheidung** quotation of a case; ~ **als Erbe** appointment of an heir; ~ **auf früheren Freispruch** former acquittal; ~ **auf einen Lehrstuhl** teaching appointment, call to a heir; ~ **auf Minderjährigkeit** plea of infancy (the Baby Act); ~ **und Revision** appeal and error; ~ **in eine leitende Stellung** managerial appointment; ~ **in einer Strafsache** criminal appeal; ~ **eines Treuhänders** appointment of a trustee; ~ **auf Unzurechnungsfähigkeit** plea of insanity; ~ **gegen ein Urteil** appeal from (against) a judgment; ~ **in den Vorstand** board appointment; ~ **auf Wahrnehmung berechtigter Interessen** plea in justification;
~ **auf einen Lehrstuhl ablehnen** to refuse a chair (professorship); ~ **annehmen** to accept a chair (professorship); **sich einer** ~ **anschließen** to cross-appeal; **seinen Beruf als** ~ **auffassen** to think of one's vocation in terms of a professional status; ~ **auf einen Lehrstuhl ausschlagen** to refuse an appointment as professor; ~ **begründen** to state the reasons for an appeal; ~ **als zurückgezogen behandeln** to treat an appeal as abandoned; **über** ~**en beschließen** to hear and decide appeals; ~ **einlegen** to lodge an appeal against, to [give notice of an] appeal, *(gegen Strafmaß)* to appeal against a sentence (a case) *(US)*, to file an appeal, to reclaim *(Scot.)*; **erneute (weitere)** ~ **einlegen** to appeal to another court; **frist- und formgerecht** ~ **einlegen** to appeal in due form and time; **gegen das Urteil eines niederen Gerichts bei einem höheren** ~ **einlegen** to appeal from a lower court to a higher court; **gegen den Erlaß einer einstweilige Verfügung** ~ **einlegen** to appeal against an injunction; **einer** ~ **entgegenstehen** to negative an appeal; **über eine** ~ **entscheiden** to hear an appeal from a decision; ~ **auf einen Lehrstuhl erhalten** to be offered a chair; **seine** ~ **erkennen** to find o. s.; ~ **für zulässig erklären** to grant leave to appeal; **für die** ~ **zuständig sein** to have appellate jurisdiction; **der** ~ **stattgeben** to uphold a decision on (allow an) appeal; **der** ~ **unterliegen** to be subject to appeal; ~ **versagen** to refuse leave to appeal; ~ **verwerfen** to dismiss (negative) an appeal; ~ **zulassen** to allow (permit, grant leave to) an appeal, to give a case to the superior court; ~ **nicht zulassen** to refuse to take an appeal; ~ **zurücknehmen** to abandon (withdraw) an appeal; **jds.** ~ **zurückweisen** to dismiss (disallow) s. one's appeal.

Berufungs|abteilung appellate division; ~**abweisung** dismissal of an appeal; ~**akten** papers on appeal *(US)*; ~**antrag** [petition of] appeal; ~**antwort** respondent's answer on appeal; ~**ausführungen** brief on appeal; ~**ausschuß** appeal committee, *(Verwaltung)* review board *(US)*; ~**begründung** brief on (reasons for) appeal, assignment of error; ~**begründungsfrist** time limit for filing an appeal; ~**beklagter** appellee, respondent, defendant in court of appeal; ~**einlegung** lodging an appeal.

berufungsfähig appealable, appellate;
nicht ~ inappellable;
~ **sein** to be appealable.

Berufungs|fähigkeit appellability; ~**frist** time for appeal; ~**gebühren** cost of appeal; ~**gegner** appellee, respondent.

Berufungsgericht appellate (superior) court, court of appeal *(US)*, appeals court, court of review (of errors and appeals), High Court of Justice;
zeitweise eingesetztes ~ commission of appeal; **letztinstanzliches** ~ final court of appeal;
~ **für Arbeitsstreitigkeiten** Industrial Disputes Tribunal *(Br.)*, Industrial Court *(Br.)*; ~ **in Strafsachen** Court of Criminal Appeal *(Br.)*.

Berufungs|gerichtsbarkeit appellate jurisdiction; **kein** ~**grund sein** not to be available on appeal; ~**gründe** grounds (reasons) of appeal; **mehrere** ~**gründe als Erbe haben** to be a beneficiary under several provisions of a will.

Berufungsinstanz higher court, court of appeal *(US)*, second instance, reviewing authority;
in der ~ on appeal;
~ **in patentrechtlichen Streitigkeiten** court of patents appeal; **Entscheidung in der** ~ **aufheben** to squash a sentence on appeal, to reverse the decision of a lower court (a judgment on appeal); **Entscheidung als** ~ **bestätigen** to uphold a decision on appeal; **in der** ~ **freigesprochen werden** to be acquitted on appeal.

Berufungs|kammer court of appeal; ~**klage** appeal; ~**kläger** appealer, appellant, party appealing, plaintiff in appeal; ~**kosten** cost of appeal.

Berufungsmöglichkeit liberty to appeal;
beschränkte ~ limited appeal; **ohne** ~ without resort.

Berufungsrecht right of appeal;
ausschließliches ~ exclusive appointment;
von seinem ~ **keinen Gebrauch machen** to waive one's right of (abandon an) appeal.

Berufungs|richter court of appeal judge, appellate judge, Lord Justices of Appeal *(Br.)*; ~**sache** case on appeal, appealed case *(US)*, appeal matter, Court of Appeal case; ~**schriftsatz** reclaiming bill, instrument of appeal, statement of a ground of appeal; ~**stelle** board of appeal, *(Verwaltung)* review board *(US)*; ~**summe** sum involved in an appeal; **neuer** ~**termin** adjournment day in error; ~**urteil** judgment in error; ~**verfahren** appellate procedure *(Br.)*, appeals procedure; ~**verhandlung** hearing of an appeal; ~**verzicht** abandonment of appeal; ~**zulassung** leave to appeal.

beruhen to be based, to rest upon;
auf bloßen Annahmen ~ to be based on mere suppositions; **auf der Grundlage der Gegenseitigkeit** ~ to be on a basis of reciprocity; **auf gleichen Interessen** ~ to be founded on mutual interest; **auf einem Irrtum** ~ to be due to an error; **auf Tatsachen** ~ to be based on facts; **auf falschen Voraussetzungen** ~ to rest on false tenets; **auf gegenseitiger Zustimmung** ~ to be consensual;
etw. nicht auf sich ~ **lassen können** to have to do s. th. about it; **etw. auf sich** ~ **lassen** to leave a matter over, to let s. th. slide, to let a matter rest; **Beleidigung auf sich** ~ **lassen** to let an insult pass unnoticed; **Beleidigung nicht auf sich** ~ **lassen** not to be able to take an insult lying down.
beruhend, auf Tatsachen founded on facts; **nicht auf Tatsachen** ~ unreciprocated.
beruhigen to ease, to calm, to appease, to pacify, to quiet, to allay, to tranquillize, to cool down *(coll.)*;
j. ~ to set s. one's mind at ease (rest), to set s. one's heart at rest, to calm s. o. down; **sich** ~ to calm down, to compose one's mind, *(Börse)* to settle down, *(politische Lage)*, to become stable, to stabilize, to calm down, to quieten down, to ease, *(Sturm)* to calm down, to abate, to subside, to lull; **sich bei dem Gedanken** ~ to find comfort by the thought, to feel reassured thinking ...; **sein Gewissen** ~ to calm one's conscience; **weinendes Kind** ~ to hush a crying child; **Nerven** ~ to soothe the nerves; **sich nach den politischen Verwirrungen** ~ to quiet down after political disturbances;
sich nicht darüber ~ **können** not to be able to get over it; **sich nicht** ~ **lassen** to refuse to be notified;
in diesem Punkt kannst du dich ~ you may be quiet on that score.
beruhigend comforting, *(Mittel)* tranquillizing;
nicht gerade sehr ~ **sein** to be rather disquieting; ~ **wirken** *(Medizin)* to act soothingly;
~**en Einfluß auf j. ausüben** to exercise a calming influence on s. o.; ~**er Gedanke** reassuring thought; ~**es Mittel** sedative, tranquillizer; ~**e Nachrichten** heartening news.
beruhigt, sich ~ **fühlen** to feel reassured; **sich** ~ **haben** *(Markt)* to have found its feet again; **sich wieder völlig** ~ **haben** *(Lage)* to be back to normal.
Beruhigung appeasement, mollification, pacification, *(Börse)* settling down, *(Lage)* ease, *(Sturm)* abatement, lull, subsidence;
zu unserer großen ~ much to our relief; **zur** ~ **der Gemüter** to stop people talking; **zur** ~ **des Gewissens** for conscience sake; **große** ~ great comfort;
~ **des Arbeitsmarktes** employment stabilization;
zur ~ **der Nerven beitragen** to sooth the nerves; **große** ~ **für j. sein** to be very reassuring for s. o.
Beruhigungs|frist *(Arbeitsstreitigkeiten)* cooling-off period; ~**mittel** sedative, calmative, soothing syrup; **jem. eine** ~**pille geben** *(fig.)* to give a sop to Cerberus; ~**wirkung** calming effect; ~**zelle** pull pen *(US sl.)*.
berühmen, sich to arrogate, to jactitate.
berühmt prominent, famous, celebrated, renowned, eminent, *(berüchtigt)* notorious;
in der Geschichte ~ famous in history; **nicht gerade** ~ not up to much, nothing special;
Namen ~ **machen** to make a name famous; **für ihre Theater** ~ **sein** *(Stadt)* to be noted (famous) for its theaters; **noch nicht** ~ **sein** to be still unknown; ~ **werden** to come into prominence, to make o. s. famous; **früh** ~ **werden** to win early fame; **über Nacht** ~ **werden** to awake to find o. s. famous; **mit einem Schlage** ~ **werden** to leap into fame; ~ **werden wollen** to seek fame;
~**er Autor** prominent author.
Berühmtheit celebrity, person of note, lion, star, fame;
~**en** prominence, celebrities;
traurige ~ notoriety;
sich einer zweifelhaften ~ **erfreuen** to have a doubtful reputation; ~ **erlangen** to win fame; ~ **in seinem Fach sein** to have a great name in one's field.
Berühmtheitsgrad celebrity status.
Berühmung jactitation.
Berühren touch;
~ **verboten!** do not touch!
berühren *(angehen)* to affect, *(Interessen)* to converge, *(Straße)* to pass, to lead (go) through, to touch;
Bahnlinie ~ to touch a railway line; **einander** ~ *(el.)* to contact; **flüchtig** ~ to overrun; **Frage nur kurz** ~ to touch upon a question; **Frage in einer Rede kurz** ~ to mention a subject in a speech; **Hafen** ~ to call at a port; **wunden Punkt** ~ to touch a delicate matter; **j. schmerzlich** ~ to give s. o. pain; **j. seltsam** ~ to strike s. o. as very odd; **viele Städte** ~ to pass through many towns; **j. stärkstens** ~ to touch one's heart; **Thema nicht** ~ to keep off a subject; **ganze Welt** ~ to concern the whole world.
berührt touched, *(betroffen)* affected;
peinlich ~ embarrassed; **seltsam** ~ strangely affected;
von einer Sache nicht ~ **sein** to have no concern in a matter; **am stärksten** ~ **sein** to be most closely concerned; **unangenehm von etw.** ~ **sein** to make an unpleasant impression on s. o.
Berührung contact, touch;
bei der leichtesten ~ at the slightest touch;
~ **mit anderen Ladungen** contact with other cargos;
mit dem Feind in ~ **kommen** to make contact with the enemy; **miteinander in** ~ **kommen** to get into contact.
Berührungspunkt point of contact.
besagen to say, to purport, to imply;
nichts Näheres ~ to give no details; **nicht viel** ~ to amount to very little.
besagt aforesaid;
um auf den ~**en Hammel zurückzukommen** to return to our muttons; **in** ~**em Schreiben** in the document above.
besänftigen to appease, to calm, to quiet, to pacify, to disarm; **j.** ~ to calm s. o. down; **erregte Menge** ~ to calm an excited crowd; **jds. Zorn** ~ to smooth s. one's rumpled feathers, to soothe s. one's anger.
Besatzung personnel, *(Festung)* garrison, *(Flugzeug)* [flight] crew, *(mil.)* occupation [army], *(Schiff)* crew, complement;
zahlenmäßig geringe ~ weak crew; **volle** ~ full crew, full force of men (complement);
~ **abmustern** to pay off the crew; **einem Land** ~ **auferlegen** to keep occupation troops in a country; **einer** ~ **freien Abzug gewähren** to allow a garrison to leave free; ~ **in eine Stadt legen** to garrison a town; **mit der ganzen** ~ **untergehen** to be lost with all hands; ~ **einer Garnison verstärken** to reinforce a garrison.
Besatzungs|armee army of occupation, occupation army (troops); ~**behörde** occupation authority; ~**briefmarken** occupational stamps; ~**gebiet** occupation zone; ~**geld** occupation money, scrip dollar *(US)*; ~**kabine** crew compartment; ~**kosten** occupation costs; ~**macht** occupying power, occupational forces; ~**mitglied** *(Flugzeug)* aircrewman, *(Schiff)* member of the crew, crew member, crewman, hand; ~**schaden** occupation damage; ~**statut** occupation statute; ~**truppen** occupation troops (forces); ~**unterlagen** occupation records; ~**zone** occupied (occupation) zone.
besaufen, sich to get drunk (tight), to tank *(sl.)*.
beschädigen to damage, to damnify, to injure, to do an injury, to impair, to nip, *(Buchstaben)* to batter;
leicht zu ~ damageable;
Urkunde ~ to mutilate a document; **Verkaufsgegenstand** ~ to injure an article of merchandise.
beschädigt damaged, in a damaged state, defective, faulty, *(Lebensmittel)* spoilt, spoiled, *(Schiff)* averaged, disabled, *(Urkunde)* mutilated, *(Ware)* shopworn;
leicht ~ slightly damaged; **schwer** ~ seriously damaged, badly injured; **durch Seewasser** ~ damaged by sea water; **auf dem Transport** ~ damaged in transit; **unterwegs** ~ damaged in transit;
bei einem Luftangriff schwer ~ **werden** to be heavily damaged in an air attack;
~**er Buchstabe** battered (broken) letter, batter; ~**e Ware** damaged (spoilt) goods; ~**er Zustand** damaged condition.
Beschädigtenrente disablement pension (benefit, *Br.*).
Beschädigter party (person) injured, disabled [person].
Beschädigung damage, injury, hurt, *(Schiff)* average, *(Urkunde)* mutilation;
absichtliche ~ wilful damage; **böswillige** ~ malicious mischief; **finanziell gutzumachende** ~ reparable injury; **leichte** ~ slight damage; **mutwillige** ~ vandalism; **vorsätzliche** ~ positive waste;
~ **öffentlicher Anlagen** destruction of public property; ~ **eines Autos** damage to a car; ~ **von Denkmälern** malicious mischief of public monuments; ~ **eines Gebäudes** injury to a building; ~ **ausländischer Hoheitszeichen** violation of international emblemes; ~ **während des Transports** damage in transit; ~ **von Waren** injury suffered by goods;
über eine ~ **Verklarung einlegen** to enter a protest in case of damage; **für vorsätzliche** ~ **haften** *(Pächter)* to be liable for voluntary waste.
Beschädigungsschein certificate of damage.
beschaffen to procure, to provide, to supply, to acquire, *(Beweis)* to furnish, *(Geld)* to find, to raise, *(Wertpapiere)* to obtain, to procure;

Arbeit ~ to provide employment; **Arbeit für j.** ~ to procure employment for s. o., to find s. o. a job; **Deckung** ~ to provide cover; **Mittel** ~ to raise funds; **Urkunde** ~ to supply a document; **neuen Wohnraum** ~ to rehouse; **Wohnung** ~ to procure a flat *(Br.)* (an apartment, *US*);
schwer zu ~ difficult to get;
~ *(a.)* conditioned, qualified;
gut ~ in good condition; **schlecht** ~ ill-conditioned.
Beschaffenheit condition, state, make, *(innerer Aufbau)* structure, *(Eigenschaft)* property, quality, nature;
von guter ~ in good condition; **von vorzüglicher** ~ of superior quality;
bauliche ~ structural condition; **erstklassige** ~ *(Straße)* first-class state; **geistige** ~ composition; **mangelhafte** ~ disrepair; **normale** ~ merchantable quality; **schlechte** ~ damaged condition;
etwa gleiche ~ **und Güte** like grade and quality; **innere** ~ **und Inhalt unbekannt** inside and contents unknown;
~ **prüfen** *(Waren)* to condition.
Beschaffenheits|beschreibung quality description; ~**zeugnis** certificate of inspection.
Beschaffer procurer, provider.
Beschaffung procurement, procuring, provision, purchasing, acquisition, assembly, *(Akzept)* securing, *(Deckung)* providing, *(Kauf)* buying, acquisition;
örtliche ~ local purchase (procurement); **zentrale** ~ centralized purchasing;
~ **eines Darlehns** procuring (procurement of) a loan; ~ **von Geld** finding the means, supply of funds; ~ **der benötigten Geldmittel** raising the necessary funds; ~ **von Industrieerzeugnissen** industrial procurement; ~ **von Kreditunterlagen** provision of information for credit purposes; ~ **von Mitteln** procurement of funds; ~ **von Wertpapieren** acquisition of securities; ~ **von Wohnraum** housing accommodation.
Beschaffungs|abteilung store procurement division (department); ~**amt** supply office, procurement agency *(US)*; ~**auftrag zu von vornherein festgesetzten Preisen** total package procurement; ~**beamter** procurement officer; ~**behörde** supply office, procuring (procurement) agency *(US)*; ~**bindung** procurement tying; ~**ermächtigung**, ~**genehmigung** procurement (expenditure) authorization; ~**etat** procurement budget; ~**kosten** cost of acquisition, purchasing costs, original-cost standard; ~**liste** list of supplies.
beschaffungspolitische Maßnahmen des Staates government procurement policy.
Beschaffungs|preis supply price; **Stufen des** ~**prozesses** purchasing level; ~**stelle** source of supply, *(Amt)* procurement office (agency, *US*); ~**vergabe mit von Anfang an festgesetzten Pauschalpreisen** total package contracting; ~**vertrag** procurement contract; ~**weg** channels of supply; **normaler** ~**weg** normal channels of procurement; ~**wesen** system of supply, *(mil.)* defence procurement; **staatliches** ~**wesen** government procurement.
beschäftigen to employ, to occupy, to engage, to give employment, *(sich abgeben)* to deal, to concern;
j. ~ to give s. o. occupation (employment), to occupy (employ) s. o.; **sich** ~ to be busy, to work, to occupy o. s., to engage in, to sit over; **sich nur mit sich selbst** ~ to live within o. s.; **j. mit leichten Arbeiten** ~ to give s. o. an easy job to do; **sich flüchtig mit einem Autor** ~ to have a dip into an author; **sich intensiv mit seinen Briefmarken** ~ to busy o. s. with one's stamps; **sich mit anspruchsvollen Dingen** ~ to have a soul above material pleasure; **ganztägig** ~ to employ on a full-time basis; **j. gedanklich** ~ to fill s. one's mind; **seinen Geist** ~ to keep one's mind occupied; **j. kurzfristig** ~ to employ s. o. temporarily; **sich nebenher als ...** ~ to moonlight as ... *(US coll.)*; **sich oberflächlich mit etw.** ~ to dabble in s. th.; **sich oberflächlich mit Politik** ~ to dabble in politics; **sich mit einem Problem** ~ to concern o. s. with a problem; **j. als Sekretärin** ~ to employ s. o. as secretary; **tageweise** ~ hired by the day; **sich zu sehr mit der Vergangenheit** ~ to dwell too much upon one's past; **Vertreter** ~ to retain an agent; **voll** ~ to employ fully.
beschäftigt *(angestellt)* employed, in employment, engaged, *(tätig)* busy, occupied;
im Augenblick ~ busy at the moment; **ganzzeitig** ~ all-time, employed on a full-time basis; **gegen Entgelt (gewerblich)** ~ gainfully employed; **sehr** ~ throng; **nur mit sich selbst** ~ wedded to one's own opinion; **voll** ~fully occupied, *(Werk)* working to capacity;
~ **sein** to be in employment (employed, on the payroll), *(emsig sein)* to be busy (at work); **anderweitig** ~ **sein** to be tied up with other things; **bei jem.** ~ **sein** to be in s. one's employment; **nicht mehr bei jem.** ~ **sein** to be no longer on s. one's payroll; **in einer Branche** ~ **sein** to engage in a line of business; **mit einem Problem** ~ **sein** to roll a problem round in one's head; **mit Schreibarbeiten** ~ **sein** to be busy with writing; **sehr** ~ **sein** to be crowded for time; **mit der Übersetzung eines Romans** ~ **sein** to be occupied (engaged) in translating a novel; **voll** ~ **sein** to be busy, *(Arbeiter)* to be in full employment, *(Betrieb)* to operate at full strength, to work to capacity, to be operating at a high level.
Beschäftigte, abhängig wage and salary earners; **ständig** ~ permanently employed.
Beschäftigten|potential total manpower available; ~**stand** level of employment labo(u)r force; ~**stunde** output per hour; ~**zahl** number of [persons] employed, employment figure, labo(u)r force; ~**zentrum** employment center *(US)* (centre, *Br.*).
Beschäftigter employed person, employee;
in einem Dienstleistungsbetrieb ~ service worker; **im Freien** ~ outdoorman; **ganztägig** ~ whole (full) -timer; **in der Industrie** ~ industrial; **irregulär** ~ irregular; **kurzfristig** ~ short-term employee; **nebenberuflich** ~ sideliner; **auf Stundenlohnbasis** ~ hourly employee.
Beschäftigung employ[ment], engagement, appointment, *(Arbeit)* work, tread *(Scot.)*, play *(Scot.)*, *(Beruf)* vocation, occupation, job, pursuit, business, spell, lay *(sl.)*;
ohne ~ unemployed, out of work (employ); **ohne regelmäßige** ~ at a loose end;
abhängige ~ wage-earning employment; **Berufskrankheiten auslösende** ~ disease-breeding occupation; **außerberufliche** ~ outside activities; **berufliche** ~ business occupation; **einträgliche (entgeltliche)** ~ gainful occupation, profitable employment; **einzige** ~ exclusive employment (occupation); **fördernde** ~ nursery; **ganztätige** ~ full (whole) -time job (employment); **besonders gefährliche** ~ extra-hazardous employment; **geistlose** ~ routine business; **gelegentliche** ~ casual employment, employment of a casual nature; **geringfügige** ~ minor occupation; **gewinnbringende** ~ gainful occupation; **gewöhnliche** ~ usual occupation; **hauptamtliche** ~ full-time employment (job); **illegale** ~ underground employment; **irgendeine** ~ ordinary job; **kaufmännische** ~ commercial appointment; **leichte** ~ light occupation; **literarische** ~ desk work; **lohnsteuerpflichtige** ~ payroll employment *(US)*; **mangelnde** ~ underemployment; **nächtliche** ~ night work; **nebenberufliche** ~ occupation outside office work, part-time job (employment), minor occupation; **normale** ~ regular occupation; **probeweise** ~ probationary employment; **regelmäßige** ~ regular occupation; **saisonabhängige** ~ seasonal employment; **nicht selbständige** ~ wage-earning employment; **sitzende** ~ sedentary employment; **sozialversicherungsfreie** ~ employment outside the scope of national insurance *(Br.)* (relieved from security payments, *US*); **stundenweise** ~ part-time employment; **überwiegende** ~ *(Einkommensteuer)* paramount occupation; **übliche** ~ daily (usual) occupation, daily stint; **unbedeutende** ~ potty little job *(sl.)*; **ungleichmäßige** ~ unstable employment; **unregelmäßige** ~ irregular employment; **unselbständige** ~ wage-earning employment; **versicherungsfreie** ~ uninsured employment; **weibliche** ~ female occupation; **zeitweilige** ~ part-time employment; **zukunftsträchtige** ~ prospective employment; **zumutbare** ~ suitable employment; **zusagende** ~ suitable employment; **zusätzliche** ~ additional employment;
entgeltliche ~ **eines anderen** using the services of another for pay; ~ **älterer Arbeitnehmer** employment of elderly people; ~ **in der Bauindustrie** construction employment; ~ **auf der Baustelle** on-site employment; ~ **im industriellen Bereich** manufacturing employment; ~ **in der Dienstleistungsindustrie** service employment; ~ **von Gelegenheitsarbeitern** casualization; ~ **in der Industrie** factory employment, industrial occupation; ~ **von Jugendlichen** youth (juvenile) employment; ~ **von Kindern** child labo(u)r, employment of children; ~ **in Kurzarbeit** *(Arbeitsstreckung)* work sharing; ~ **mit Nichtigkeiten** shilly-shally; ~ **im Staatsdienst** government job, state employment; ~ **von Untervertretern** pyramid selling;
~ **zeitweise aussetzen** to suspend employment; ~ **ausüben** to carry on a business, to do a job; ~ **finden** to find employment; **untergeordnete** ~ **finden** to obtain menial tasks; **jem.** ~ **geben** to employ s. o.; **einträgliche** ~ **haben** to live on (be left to) one's purchases *(Scot.)*; **regelmäßige** ~ **haben** to have a regular job; **geregelter** ~ **nachgehen** to go about one's lawful business (occupation); **seiner täglichen** ~ **nachgehen** to go about one's usual work, to do one's daily stint; **um eine** ~ **nachsuchen** to

apply for a job; **seine ~ nicht ernst nehmen** to play around *(sl.)*; **ohne ~ sein** to be unemployed (out of a job); **ohne regelmäßige ~ sein** to be at a loose end; **sich nach einer geeigneten ~ umsehen** to look for occupation suited to one's abilities; **jem. eine ~ verschaffen** to find s. o. a job; **sich einer ~ widmen** to be engaged in an occupation.

Beschäftigungs|abfall decline in employment; **~anspruch** employment right; **~anstieg** pickup (leap) in employment; **~art** nature of employment, employment category; **~bedingungen** conditions of employment; **~beginn** commencing employment; **~bereich** area of employment; **~bescheinigung** certificate of employment, *(nach Entlassung)* discharge (walking, *coll.*) papers; **~bild** employment (labo(u)r) picture; **~dauer** period (length) of employment; **unterbrochene ~dauer** period of interruption of employment; **~einbruch** drop in employment; **~einheit** unit of employment; **~entwicklung** trend of employment, employment trend; **~genehmigung** labo(u)r permit; **~grad** level of employment, employment standard, employment rate, *(Industrie)* operating rate; **~index** business index; **~kategorie** employment category; **~kontinuität** continuity of employment; **~lage** state of employment, employment [possibilities] picture, labo(u)r situation; **~lage sichern** to preserve employment.

beschäftigungslos [thrown] out of employment, unemployed, inoccupied, without occupation (work, profession, job), jobless;
~ sein to be unemployed (out of work, workless); **~ werden** to be thrown out of employment.

Beschäftigungs|lose unemployed persons; **~losigkeit** unemployment, inoccupation, joblessness.

Beschäftigungsmöglichkeiten employment possibilities (opportunities);
verringerte ~ reduced employment; **zusätzliche ~** additional employment;
~ beschneiden to cut the employment potential; **~ eröffnen** to find jobs.

Beschäftigungs|nachweis employment bureau, *(Einzelperson)* employment records *(US)*, *(Statistik)* employment statistics; **~notlage** job pinch; **~optimum** maximum employment; **~ort** place of employment; **~politik** employment policies.

beschäftigungspolitisch, sehr zurückhaltende ~e Maßnahmen der öffentlichen Hand tight public sector employment policy.

Beschäftiguns|potential potential of employment, potential labo(u)r force, total manpower available; **~prämie** bonus; **~prozentsatz** employment rate; **~reserve** manpower reserve; **~rückgang** employment decline, paring of (fall in) employment; **~schwankungen** employment fluctuations; **~stabilität** employment stability; **~stand** employment picture (level); **~statistik** statistics of employment; **~struktur** employment pattern; **~therapie** occupational therapy; **~überblick, ~übersicht** employment possibilities.

beschäftigungsunfähig unemployable.

Beschäftigungs|unfähigkeit unemployability; **~verbot** prohibition of employment.

Beschäftigungsverhältnis employment, employ;
außerhalb des ~ses outside the scope of employment; **gemeinsames ~** common employment; **nicht pflichtversichertes ~** contracted-out employment; **sozialversicherungspflichtiges ~** insurable employment *(Br.)*; **nicht sozialversicherungspflichtiges ~** contracted-out employment, excepted employment *(Br.)*; **ständiges ~** continuous employment; **versicherungspflichtiges ~** insurable employment *(Br.)*;
~ der Ehefrau wife's employment;
~ beendigen to terminate employment; **~ eingehen** to take employment; **aus dem ~ herrühren** *(Beschädigung)* to arise out and in the course of employment; **~ ruhen lassen** to suspend employment; **in einem ständigen ~ stehen** to be continuously employed; **erstmals ein ~ suchen** to enter the labo(u)r market.

Beschäftigungs|volumen employment volume; **Gewerkschaftsmitgliedschaft als ~voraussetzung** maintenance of union membership; **~zahlen** employment data, employment figures; **~zeit** hours (period, length) of employment, appointive term; **unterbrochene ~zeit** interruption of employment; **verschiedene ~zeiten** different periods of employment; **~zentrum** occupational center *(US)* (centre, *Br.*); **~ziffern** employment figures; **lebenslängliche ~zusage** lifetime employment guarantee; **staatlicher ~zuschuß** employment subsidy; **~zwang** compulsory employment; **Berufskrankheiten auslösende ~zweige** disease-breeding occupations; **~zweige mit eigener Altersversorgung** nonparticipating employments *(Br.)*; **~zweige des Produktionsbereichs** secondary occupations.

beschämen to put out of face (to shame), to make s. o. feel ashamed, *(übertreffen)* to put s. o. in the shade;
j. durch seine Freundlichkeit ~ to overwhelm s. o. by one's kindness; **j. durch seine Güte ~** to heap coals on s. one's head.

beschämend disgraceful, shameful, humiliating;
~er Auftritt disgraceful scene; **~er Augenblick** humiliating moment; **~es Gefühl** humiliating feeling; **~es Verhalten** shameful conduct.

beschämt abashed, ashamed;
zutiefst ~ utterly disgraced;
tief ~ sein to be deeply ashamed.

beschatten *(Detektiv)* to shadow, to trail, to shade.

beschauliches Leben contemplative life;
~ führen to lead the life of Riley *(coll.)*.

Bescheid answer, reply, word, *(Anweisung)* instruction, direction, *(Auskunft)* information, *(Benachrichtigung)* advice, message, warning, *(Beschluß)* decree, decision, ruling, *(Schiedsgericht)* award;
bis auf weiteren ~ until further orders;
abschlägiger ~ refusal, rebuff, negative reply; **amtlicher ~** official reply; **endgültiger ~** final decision; **schriftlicher ~** notice in writing; **vorläufiger ~** provisional decision, preliminary answer; **zusagender ~** favo(u)rable reply;
~ bekommen to receive notice; **~ erhalten** to receive word, to be informed; **abschlägigen ~ erhalten** to get a rebuff; **so bald als möglich ~ erhalten** to be informed as soon as possible; **~ erteilen** to give a decision; **jds. ~ erwarten** to expect to hear from s. o.; **~ geben** to let s. o. know, to give notice to (inform) s. o.; **auf Fragen höflich ~ geben** to politely answer questions; **jem. rechtzeitig ~ geben** to let s. o. know in time; **umgehend ~ geben** to answer by return of post; **~ bekommen haben** to be on notice *(US)*; **jem. ~ hinterlassen** to leave word for s. o.; **jem. gehörig ~ sagen** to give s. o. a bit (piece) of one's mind; **jem. ~ stoßen** to turn down s. o. *(US sl.)*; **~ wissen** to know one's stuff, to know a thing or two, to understand about s. th.; **in seinem Fach gut ~ wissen** to know one's trade, to be well versed in a subject; **in einem Haus ~ wissen** to know one's way about a house; **in einer Sache genauesten ~ wissen** to know the ins and outs of a case; **sofort ~ wissen** to read while one runs; **in einer Stadt genauestens ~ wissen** to know a town like the back of one's hand.

bescheiden to inform [of a decision], to notify, to warn, to cite, *(zuteilen)* to assign, to award;
sich mit einer Antwort ~ to be satisfied with an answer; **endgültig ~** to give a final ruling; **Gesuch abfällig ~** to refuse (turn down) a request;
sich ~ to be satisfied (content); **j. vor Gericht ~** to summon s. o. to appear in court; **sich mit wenigem ~** to be content with very little;
~ *(a.)* modest, humble, unpretending, unassuring;
~ auftreten to do things on a humble scale *(fam.)*; **~ leben** to live in a small way;
aus ~en Anfängen from small beginnings; **~e Ansprüche stellen** to be modest in one's requirements; **~es Auftreten** unpretentious manners; **unter meinem ~en Dach** under my humble roof; **~e Forderungen** moderate claims; **mit einem ~en Gehalt auskommen** to manage on a modest salary; **~es Häuschen** humble cottage; **~es Mahl** frugal meal; **in ~em Maße** in a small way; **~e Mittel** limited means; **in ~en Verhältnissen leben** to live in a small way; **aus ~en Verhältnisses stammen** to spring from humble stock; **~es Vermögen** modest fortune; **~er werden** to change one's tune.

Bescheidenheit modesty, unpretentiousness;
mit der gehörigen ~ with all due modesty;
falsche ~ false modesty; **mädchenhafte ~** maiden modesty.

bescheinigen to attest, to warrant, to confirm in writing, *(durch Attest)* to certify;
amtlich ~ to authenticate; **Empfang ~** to [acknowledge] receipt.

bescheinigende Behörde certifying authority.

bescheinigt certified, attested;
amtlich ~ authenticated;
hiermit wird ~ this is to certify.

Bescheinigung certificate, certification, attestation, avouchment, assertion, bill, *(Beleg)* voucher, *(Bestätigung)* acknowledgement, *(Quittung)* receipt;
ohne amtliche ~ uncertificated;
amtliche ~ certificate, governmental authorization; **ärztliche ~** doctor's certificate; **behördliche ~** certificate by a public officer; **gefälschte ~** bogus certificate; **konsularische ~** consular certificate; **notarielle ~** notarial certificate; **offizielle ~**

acknowledgement; **staatliche** ~ national certificate; **mit Amtssiegel versehene** ~ certificate of acknowledgement; **vorgeschriebene** ~ qualifying certificate; **vorläufige** ~ provisional certificate; **zollamtliche** ~ customhouse certificate;
~ **über die Beschädigung an ausgeladenen Gütern** certificate of damage; ~ **daß kein Dumping betrieben wird** nondumping certificate; ~ **der Echtheit** authentication; ~ **des Konsulats** consular certificate; ~ **über einbehaltene Lohnsteuer** withholding statement; ~ **über die Prospektbefreiung** *(Aktienausgabe)* certificate of exemption; ~ **des Revisors** audit certificate; ~ **der Technischen Überwachungsstelle** obligatory test certificate; ~ **über abgabenfreie Verbringung ins Zollgebiet** duty-free entry certificate; ~ **über den Verkauf von Wertpapieren** ticket, certificate of transfer *(Br.)*; ~ **für zollfreie Wiederausfuhr** customhouse certificate;
~ **ausstellen** to certify, to [issue, write a] certificate; ~ **beibringen** to furnish a certificate; ~ **vorlegen** to produce a certificate.

Bescheinigungsvorlage presentation (production) of a certificate.

beschenken, j. to give a present to s. o.; **sich gegenseitig** ~ to exchange presents; **j. überreich** ~ to load s. o. with gifts, to shower gifts upon s. o.

Beschenkter donee, recipient of a gift.

bescheren, mit Glück to bless with fortune; **zu Weihnachten** ~ to give Christmas presents.

Bescherung, schöne nice state of affairs, a pretty kettle of fish *(US sl.)*.

beschicken, Märkte to supply a (send goods on the) market; **Messe** ~ to exhibit at a fair; **Tagung** ~ to send representatives to a meeting.

Beschickung | eines Marktes supply of a market; ~ **einer Messe** fairgoing.

beschießen to shoot, to fire, to bombard, to pill;
Festungsanlage mit schwerem Geschütz ~ to batter (cannonade) the fortifications with heavy artillery.

Beschießung bombardment, cannonade.

beschildern to signpost, *(Ausstellungsstücke)* to label;
Straße ~ to signpost a road.

Beschilderung road signs, signposts;
keine gute ~ **haben** to be inadequately signposted.

beschimpfen to insult, to slander, to abuse, to speak ill of, to give s. o. beans, to vituperate;
sich gegenseitig ~ to call each other names; **j. maßlos** ~ to pelt s. o. with abuses; **jds. guten Namen** ~ to drag s. one's name in the mud.

Beschimpfung indignity, insult, abuse of language, affront, invective;
grobe ~ gross affront;
~ **Verstorbener** disparaging the memory of the dead.

Beschimpfungen abusive language, offensive language, insulting names;
~ **ausstoßen** to hurl invectives; **j. mit** ~ **überhäufen** to load s. o. with abuse.

Beschlag fittings, *(jur.)* confiscation, seizure, attachment;
mit ~ **belegen** to attach, to distrain, to levy a distress, to lay attachment, to seize, to sequester, to arrest, to impound, to corral; **jds. Aufmerksamkeit völlig mit** ~ **belegen** to monopolize s. one's attention; **beste Plätze mit** ~ **belegen** to reserve (bag) the best seats; **Schiff mit** ~ **belegen** to arrest a ship, to lay an embargo on a ship, to condemn a ship as a lawful prize, to put a ship under stoppage; **Schmuggelware mit** ~ **belegen** to confiscate contraband goods; **Sitz im voraus mit** ~ **belegen** to preempt a seat; **Schuldnervermögen in** ~ **nehmen** to distrain upon a debtor.

beschlagen *(Fenster)* blurred, *(kenntnisreich)* proficient, studied, well-versed, proficient;
überall ~ allround;
~ *(v.)* *(Wände)* to sweat, *(Spiegel)* to mist over;
~ **sein** *(Fenster)* to steam up; **in Englisch sehr** ~ **sein** to have a sound knowledge of English; **in einem Fach gut** ~ **sein** to have a thorough knowledge of a subject, to be perfectly at home with a subject; **in Geschäftsdingen gut** ~ **sein** to be well versed in business matters.

Beschlagenheit proficiency, thorough knowledge;
~ **auf jedem Gebiet** allroundness.

Beschlagnahme arrest, arrestment, levy of distress, distraint, seizure, attachment, stoppage, *(Enteignung)* confiscation, trustee process *(US)*, *(Inanspruchnahme)* requisition, *(Schiff)* seizure, embargo, *(Seeschadensversicherung)* detainment, *(Völkerrecht)* sequestration, *(Zurückbehaltung)* retention, detention, *(Zwangsverwaltung)* sequestration;
unter ~ requisitioned, confiscated; **der** ~ **unterliegend** seizable; **generelle** ~ *(Völkerrecht)* general reprisal; **gerichtliche** ~ judicial sequestration, distress, distraint, impounding; **sofortige** ~ immediate extent; **unbeschränkte** ~ distress infinite; **vorläufige** ~ equitable levy; **vorübergehende** ~ *(Schiff)* embargo;
~ **beim Drittschuldner** garnishment; ~ **ausländischen Eigentums** foreign attachment; ~ **durch Eingriff von hoher Hand** restraint of princes and rulers; ~ **von Einkünften** *(Völkerrecht)* sequestration of income; ~ **der Ernte** seizure of the crop; ~ **von Forderungen** attachment (arrest) of debts, equitable garnishment, extent in aid; ~ **von Grundstücken (Immobilien)** seizure of real estate; ~ **eines Hauses** requisition of a house; ~ **und Inhaftierung** *(Völkerrecht)* positive reprisal; ~ **von Konterbande** impounding of contraband goods; ~ **eines Schiffes** arrest of a vessel; ~ **und Einbringung eines Schiffes** seizure of a ship; ~ **von Schmuggelware durch den Zoll** seizure of contraband by customs officers; ~ **durch Verfügungs-, Veräußerungsverbot** constructive seizure; ~ **eines Vermögens** attachment (seizure) of property; ~ **durch Wegnahme** actual seizure; ~ **einer Zeitung** suppression of a newspaper;
~ **anordnen (verfügen)** to levy an attachment order (a distress) *(US)*, to order the seizure of; ~ **eines Schiffes anordnen** to order the detention of a ship; ~ **eines Vermögens anordnen** to award sequestration of an estate; ~ **aufheben** to discharge (release, vacate, withdraw) an attachment, to loose an arrestment, to lift a seizure, to grant a replevin, *(Haus)* to derequisition *(Br.)*, *(Schiff)* to take off (remove) an embargo; **der** ~ **unterliegen** to be subject to attachment (seizure); ~ **vornehmen** to effect a seizure; ~ **durch einen Pfändungs- und Überweisungsbeschluß vornehmen** to institute garnishee proceedings;
~**anordnung**, ~**beschluß** [order of] sequestration, distress warrant, order of attachment, *(Haus)* requisition order; ~**antrag** petition for sequestration; ~**beschluß** warrant of attachment, attachment order.

beschlagnahmefähig seizable, attachable, distrainable, sequestrable, *(konfiszierbar)* confiscable.

beschlagnahmefrei exempt from seizure, not liable to confiscation, *(Grundstück)* off limits *(US)*, out of bounds *(Br.)*;
~ **sein** not to be liable to confiscation, to be exempt from seizure;
~**e Gegenstände** exemptions.

Beschlagnahme | freiheit exemption from seizure; ~**kosten** detention charges.

beschlagnahmen to attach, to arrest, to seize, to make seizure, to levy a distress, to distress, to distrain, to impound, to affect *(Scot., law)*, to appropriate, *(in Anspruch nehmen)* to [put in] requisition, to put a stop upon, *(konfiszieren)* to confiscate, to condemn, to vest *(US)*, *(Schiff)* to lay an embargo on;
Druckschriften ~ to confiscate printed papers; **Haus** ~ to requisition a house; **schlecht gewordene Lebensmittel** ~ to condemn defective provisions; **Leiche** ~ to take charge of a body; **die besten Plätze** ~ to bag the best seats; **Schmuggelwaren** ~ to confiscate contraband goods; **aufgrund gerichtlicher Verfügung** ~ to levy a distress; **das gesamte Vermögen** ~ to levy on the entire (take charge of) property; **Vorratslager** ~ to commandeer (condemn) stores (provisions); **Ware** ~ to confiscate goods; **Zeitung** ~ to suppress a newspaper; **aufgrund Zurückbehaltungsrechts** ~ to retain.

Beschlagnahme | protokoll sheriff's return, fieri feci; ~**recht** vesting powers; **vorbeugendes** ~**recht** *(Völkerrecht)* right of anticipated arrest; ~**risiko** risk of seizure; ~**risiko ausgeschlossen** free of capture and seizure; ~**verfügung** charging (confiscation) order, distress warrant, writ (warrant) of attachment, attachment order *(US)*, [writ of] execution, *(Inanspruchnahme)* requisition order, *(Konkursverfahren)* warrant in bankruptcy; **gerichtliche** ~**verfügung** attachment order, *(beim Drittschuldner)* garnishee order; **schriftliche** ~**verfügung** seizure note, requisition slip; ~**verlust** confiscation loss; ~**versicherung** insurance against capture and seizure; ~**vollmacht** *(Konkursverwalter)* receiver's certificate; ~**wert** condemnation value.

beschlagnahmt attached, condemned, seized, confiscated, sequestrated;
nicht ~ unattached; **vom Zoll** ~ confiscated by the customs authorities;
~ **sein** to be confiscated (under seizure), *(Schiff)* to be under an embargo.

beschleunigen to forward, to hasten, to quicken, to urge, to expedite, *(Auto)* to speed up, to accelerate, *(Zug)* to pick up speed;

seine Abreise ~ to accelerate one's departure; **seine Arbeit** ~ to hurry over a task, to speed up one's work; **Arbeitsverfahren** ~ to speed up a working process; **Ausschußberatungen** ~ to expedite the business of a committee; **Fahrt** ~ to gather (pick up) speed; **Pflanzenwachstum** ~ to expedite the growth of plants; **Plan** ~ to step up a scheme; **seine Schritte** ~ to quicken one's steps; **jds. Sturz** ~ to hasten s. one's fall; **Tempo** ~ to force the pace, to step on the accelerator, to speed up; **Verfahren** ~ to accelerate a procedure; **gerichtliches Verfahren** ~ to speed up judicial business.

beschleunigt accelerated;
~ **arbeiten** to expedite matters;
~**es Expressgut** accelerated express goods; ~**er Preisanstieg** price acceleration.

Beschleunigung expedition, urgency, *(Auto)* acceleration;
mit tunlichster ~ with the utmost dispatch;
gleichbleibende ~ uniform acceleration;
~ **der Geldvermehrung** acceleration of the increase in money supply; ~ **eines Verfahrens** speeding up a judicial business;
mit größtmöglicher ~ **arbeiten** to work with the greatest possible dispatch (at white heat).

Beschleunigungs | faktor *(Keynes)* coefficient of acceleration, acceleration factor; ~**gebühr** dispatch money; ~**kraft** accelerative force; ~**prinzip** acceleration principle; ~**vermögen** *(Auto)* zip.

beschließen to decide, to resolve *(US)*, to pass a resolution, *(Gericht)* to decree, to decide, to rule, to order, *(parl.)* to vote;
Antrag ~ to carry (adopt) a motion; **Dividende** ~ to declare a Dividend; **einstimmig** ~ to decide unanimously; **Geschäftsordnung** ~ to adopt the rules of procedure; **zusätzliche Mittel in Höhe von 150 Mio. Dollar** ~ to vote $ 150 million in extra money; **nochmals** ~ to repass; **seine Rede mit einem Zitat** ~ to wind up (conclude) one's speech with a quotation; **mit Stimmenmehrheit** ~ to decide by a majority of votes; **Streik** ~ to call out a strike; **seine Tage in Frieden** ~ to end one's days in peace; **Vertagung einer Versammlung** ~ to vote the adjournment of a meeting; **gemeinsames Vorgehen** ~ to decide on a concerted action; **Vorschlag einstimmig** ~ to accept a proposal with unanimous approval; **Zug** ~ to close the procession; **Zustimmung einer Versammlung** ~ to resolve that the meeting is in favor *(US)*.

Beschließer closer, custodian, keeper, turnkey.

beschlossen settled, fixed up;
einstimmig ~ unanimously decided; **vom Parlament** ~ parliamentary; ~ **und verkündet** ordered and pronounced as follows;
die Sache ist ~ the matter is settled; **es wurde** ~ resolved.

Beschluß *(Gericht)* decision, decree, act, [general] order, *(Ende)* conclusion, close, *(Entschließung)* determination, resolution, resolve *(US)*, *(parl.)* vote;
durch ~ by vote (resolution); **durch** ~ **des Ausschusses** in accordance with the committee's decision;
angefochtener ~ decision complained about, appealed decision; **außerordentlicher** ~ extraordinary resolution; **bindender** ~ binding order; **vorher festgelegter** ~ determinate decree; **gefaßter** ~ conclusion arrived at; **einstimmig gefaßter** ~ unanimous vote; **gerichtlicher** ~ order of the court, court order; **gleichlautender** ~ *(parl.)* concurrent resolution; **prozeßleitender** ~ preliminary measures; **qualifizierter** ~ special resolution; **rechtsgültiger** ~ valid resolution; **rechtskräftiger** ~ definite order, decree absolute, final ruling; **schriftlicher** ~ resolution in writing; **vorläufiger** ~ rule nisi; **zustimmender** ~ consent decree; **zwingender** ~ peremptory order;
~ **auf einseitigen Antrag** order ex parte; ~ **über die Aufhebung eines Haftbefehls** release on habeas corpus; ~ **über die Einleitung des Entmündigungsverfahrens** commission in lunacy; ~ **über die Eröffnung des Konkursverfahrens** order of adjudication, bankruptcy order; ~ **über die Nachlaßverteilung** decree of distribution; ~ **mit einfacher Stimmenmehrheit** ordinary resolution; ~ **des Vorstands** resolution of the board; ~ **über die Wiederaufnahme des Verfahrens** order of revivor *(Br.)*;
~ **ablehnen** to rescind (reject) a resolution; ~ **absetzen** to execute a decree; **durch** ~ **anordnen** to order and direct; ~ **aufheben** to discharge a rule, to rescind (reverse, annul) a decree, to set aside an order, to discharge a writ; ~ **in der Berufungsinstanz aufheben** to squash a sentence on appeal; ~ **ausfertigen** to execute a decree; ~ **aussetzen** to stay the execution of a decree; ~ **einbringen** to introduce (move) a resolution; **Antrag zum** ~ **erheben** to carry a motion; ~ **fassen** to arrive at a decision, to decide, *(Versammlung)* to pass a resolution, to resolve *(US)*; ~ **herbeiführen** to bring about a resolution; ~ **ergehen lassen** to issue a formal decree, to enter a decree; ~ **für nichtig erklären lassen** to rescind a decision; ~ **von einem Ausschuß genehmigen lassen** to get a resolution passed by a committee; **einem** ~ **Achtung verschaffen** to enforce respect for a decree;
es ergeht folgender ~ be it resolved;
~**abteilung** decision-making department; ~**annahme** adoption of a resolution; ~**aufhebung** recission of a resolution; ~**entwurf** draft resolution.

beschlußfähig sufficient in numbers, competent to make a decision;
~ **sein** to constitute (make) a quorum; **nicht** ~ **sein** to lack a quorum;
~**er Vorstand** director's quorum.

Beschlußfähigkeit quorum;
ausreichende ~ valid quorum; **mangelnde** ~ failure to muster a quorum, lack of quorum; **durch Eigeninteressen verhinderte** ~ disinterested quorum; **nicht vorhandene** ~ absence of quorum;
~ **aufrechterhalten** to maintain a quorum; ~ **ergeben** to constitute a quorum; ~ **feststellen** *(parl.)* to count out the House, to ascertain that there is a house; ~ **herbeiführen** to constitute (form) a quorum; ~ **durch Stimmenzählung feststellen lassen** to declare a count out; **auf die** ~ **ohne Einfluß sein** not to count towards a quorum; **bei der** ~ **mitgezählt werden** to be counted in a quorum.

Beschlußfassung resolution, conclusion arrived at, resolve *(US)*;
globale ~ omnibus resolution;
~ **durch Senat und Repräsentantenhaus** joint resolution; ~ **über die Vergütung des Vorstands** *(Generalversammlung)* voting of director's pay.

Beschluß | form form of resolution; ~**formular** order blank; **nicht ordnungsgemäß besetztes** ~**gremium** incompetent quorum; ~**protokoll** minutes of resolution.

beschlußreif ready to be voted on.

beschlußunfähig | sein to lack a quorum; ~ **geworden sein** to have ceased to constitute a quorum.

Beschlußunfähigkeit lack of quorum, failure to muster a quorum;
~ **feststellen** to find out that there is no quorum, to count out the house *(Br.)*; ~ **herbeiführen** to break a quorum.

Beschluß | verfahren, Sache im ~**verfahren entscheiden** to decide a case in chambers; ~**vorlage** draft resolution.

beschmeißen, mit faulen Eiern to rotten-egg.

beschmieren to smear, to coat, to cover, *(mit Farbe)* to daub;
mit Öl ~ to oil, to grease (lubricate) with oil;
Narrenhände ~ **Tisch und Wände** a white wall is a fool's writing paper.

beschmiert muddy;
mit Dreck ~ plastered with mud.

beschmutzen to soil, to spatter with mud, to foul, to daub, to defile, to spot, to muck up *(coll.)*;
sich die Finger ~ to dirty one's fingers, *(fig.)* to lower o. s.; **das eigene Nest** ~ to cry stinking fish, to foul one's own nest; **jds. guten Ruf** ~ to stain s. one's name, to tarnish s. one's reputation.

beschmutzt spotted.

Beschneiden | von Ausgaben expenditure cut, curtailment of expenses; ~ **des Spesenetats** expense account cutting, expenditure account cutback.

beschneiden *(Ausgaben)* to curtail, to scale down, to axe, to cut, to make cuts in;
Buch ~ to trim the edges of a book, to bleed a book; **jds. Einkommen** ~ to dock s. one's income; **jem. die Flügel** ~ to clip s. one's wings; **auf ein bestimmtes Format** ~ to cut to size; **Hecke** ~ to trim a hedge; **jds. Macht** ~ to restrict s. one's power; **jds. Monatswechsel** ~ to cut down (curtail) s. one's monthly allowance.

Beschneidung | von Ausgaben expenditure cut; ~ **des Spesenetats** expenditure account cutback.

beschnüffeln, sich gegenseitig to size each other up.

bescholten of blemished character, sullied.

Bescholtenheit stained reputation.

beschönigen to palliate, to gloss over, to whitewash;
ohne die Dinge zu ~ without mincing matters; **jds. Fehler** ~ to gloss (smooth) over s. one's faults; **jds. Handlungsweise (Verhalten)** ~ to put a varnish of legality upon s. one's actions *(coll.)*, to gloss s. one's conduct; **Wahrheit** ~ to put a gloss on the truth *(fam.)*.

beschönigt gilded.

Beschönigung palliation, gloss, varnish, extenuation.

beschottern to metal, to macadamize.

Beschotterung metalling, macadamization.

beschränkbar limitable, restrictable.
beschränken to confine, to limit, to restrict, to stint, to restrain, to bound;
sich ~ to narrow down, to confine o. s., to cut and contrive; **seine Ansprüche** ~ to take in sail, to modify one's demands; **Ausgabenwirtschaft** ~ to cut (limit) expenditure, to set a limit to the expenses; **sich auf einige Bemerkungen** ~ to confine one's remarks to specific points; **Freizügigkeit** ~ to restrict the freedom of movement; **Geschwindigkeit** ~ to limit the speed; **Handel** ~ to restrain trade; **Höchstgeschwindigkeit in geschlossenen Ortschaften auf 50 km** ~ to restrict to thirty miles an hour in built-up areas; **Kosten auf ein Minimum** ~ to cut costs to a minimum; **seine Kritik auf das Wichtigste** ~ to confine one's criticism to the essentials; **jds. Machtbefugnisse auf ein bestimmtes Gebiet** ~ to confine s. one's authority within certain limits; **sich lediglich auf zwei Punkte** ~ to restrict one's matter to two points; **Redezeit** ~ to limit the time allotted to each speaker; **sich in seinem Studium auf ein bestimmtes Gebiet** ~ to confine one's studies to one subject; **jds. Tätigkeitsfeld** ~ to restrain s. one's activities; **sich auf Tatsachen** ~ to confine o. s. to facts; **Teilnehmerzahl** ~ to limit the number of participants; **jds. Vollmachten** ~ to narrow s. one's powers; **jds. Vollmachten auf ein bestimmtes Gebiet** ~ to confine s. one's authority within certain limits; **Wettbewerb** ~ to restrict competition, to restrain trade.
beschränkend restrictive.
beschränkt limited, restricted, confined, qualified, *(Person)* narrow-minded, narrow, conditioned, of limited views (intelligence), dense-minded, dull;
~ **geschäftsfähig** of limited capacity; ~ **haftbar** with limited liability; **auf ein Land** ~ confined to one country; ~ **lieferbar** in short supply; ~ **steuerpflichtig** subject to limited taxation; **zeitlich** ~ limited in time;
~**e Absatzmöglichkeiten** limited (narrow) market; ~**e Annahme** conditional acceptance; ~**e Ansichten** narrow views; ~**e Anzahl** limited number; ~**e Auflage** limited edition; ~**es Fassungsvermögen** limited capacity; **Seuche auf ein bestimmtes Gebiet** ~ **halten** to localize a disease; ~**e Geschäftsfähigkeit** limited capacity; ~**es Giro** restrictive endorsement; ~**e Haftung** limited (limits of) liability; ~**er Horizont** restricted horizon; ~**e Intelligenz** limited intelligence; ~**e Konvertierbarkeit** limited convertibility; **in** ~**em Maße zutreffend** partially true; **nur** ~**e Mittel zur Verfügung haben** to have only limited resources; **nur eine** ~**e Personenzahl fassen** to hold only a limited number of people; ~**er Platz** confined space; **zeitlich** ~**e Revision** partial audit; ~**e Sicht** low visibility; ~**e Sitzzahl** limited seating capacity; ~**e Steuerpflicht** limited taxability (tax liability); ~ **Steuerpflichtiger** nonresident taxpayer; ~ **haftender Teilhaber** limited partner; ~**e Verhältnisse** narrow circumstances; **in** ~**en Verhältnissen leben** to live in a small way (straitened circumstances); ~**e Verkaufsmöglichkeiten** narrow market; ~**es Wahlrecht** limited suffrage; ~**er Wirkungskreis** limited sphere of activity.
Beschränktheit narrowness, narrow-mindedness, limited horizon, density, stupidity;
geistige ~ narrowness of mind.
Beschränkung limitation, restraining, restraint, restriction, confinement, *(Kürzung)* curtailment, cut;
keinen ~**en unterworfen** without restrictions; **ohne** ~ *(Seeversicherung)* with average;
finanzielle ~**en** financial restrictions; **gesetzliche** ~**en** statutory restrictions; **haushaltsrechtliche** ~**en** budgetary restraints; **mengenmäßige** ~**en** quantitative restrictions; **örtliche** ~ localization; **staatliche** ~ government restrictions; **verfassungsrechtliche** ~**en** constitutional limitations; **gegen das allgemeine Wohl verstoßende** ~ restrictions contrary to the public interest; **wirtschaftliche** ~ restriction on business; **zeitliche** ~ time limit;
~ **der Ausfuhr** restriction of export; ~**en der Ausgabenpolitik der öffentlichen Hände** cash limits on public spending; ~ **der Ausgabenwirtschaft** restraint in spending; ~**en der Devisenbewirtschaftung** currency (foreign-exchange) restrictions; ~ **der Einwechslungsverpflichtung** bank restriction; ~ **der Erbenhaftung** benefit of inventory; ~ **der persönlichen Freiheit** *(Südafrika)* banning order; ~ **auf bestimmte Gebiete** *(Wettbewerbsrecht)* territorial restriction; ~ **der Haftung** limitation of liabiltiy; ~ **der Haftung auf eigenes Verschulden** risk note; ~**en des Handels (Handelsverkehrs)** trade restrictions, restraint of foreign trade, felonious restraint *(US)*; ~ **der Konsumtivkreditgewährung** restriction of consumer credits; ~ **der Kontingente** quota restriction; ~ **des Schadensersatzanspruchs** abridgment of damages; ~ **einer Seuche auf ein bestimmtes Gebiet** localization of a disease; ~ **des Verteilerkreises** distribution classification; ~ **der Vollmachten** restraining powers, limit of authority; ~ **des Wettbewerbs** restraint of trade;
~**en abbauen** to delimitize; ~**en auferlegen** to impose restrictions; **jem.** ~**en auferlegen** to lay s. o. under restrictions (restraint), to put a restraint on s. one's activities; **sich** ~**en auferlegen** to restrain o. s.; **sich in den Ausgaben** ~**en auferlegen** to show spending forbearance; ~**en aufheben** to remove (abrogate, abolish, withdraw) restrictions, to remove controls, to lift a ban; **industrielle** ~**en aufheben** to scrap limitations on industry *(US)*; ~**en auf dem Abzahlungsgebiet aufheben** to lift restrictions on instalment buying; ~ **der Erbfolge aufheben** to cut off an entail *(US)*; ~**en befreien** to delimitize; ~**en beseitigen** to remove restrictions; ~**en festsetzen** to impose restrictions; ~**en handhaben** to administer restrictions; ~**en unterliegen** to be subject to restrictions; ~**en verschärfen** to intensify restrictions.
beschreibbar describable.
beschreiben to give a description, to describe, to set out, to paint;
ausführlich ~ to go into detail; **Kreis** ~ *(Flugzeug)* to circle; **Papier auf beiden Seiten** ~ to write on both sides of a paper; **seine Reise** ~ to give an account of one's journey; **auf der Rückseite** ~ to write on the back; **j. als unzulässig** ~ to characterize s. o. as unreliable;
nicht zu ~ to defy description.
beschreibendes Verzeichnis descriptive catalog(ue).
Beschreibung description, account, narration, *(für den Gebrauch)* instructions;
nach seiner eigenen ~ by his own account;
ausführliche ~ minute (particular, full) description; **endgültige** ~ *(Patent)* complete specification; **genaue** ~ faithful (correct) description, detailed (paricularized) account; **genaueste** ~ exact (detailed) description; **lebendige** ~ lively description; **ungefähre** ~ thumb-nail description; **ungenaue** ~ misdescription; **vorläufige** ~ *(Patent)* provisional specification;
~ **eines Autos** particulars of a car; **kurze** ~ **einer Erfindung** title of an invention (a patent); ~ **technischer Fertigkeiten** technography; ~ **des Inhalts** description of contents; ~ **eines Musters** design data; ~ **des Pachtgrundstücks** memorandum; ~ **eines Patents** patent specification; ~ **einer Reise** account (report) of a journey; ~ **eines Verbrechers** description of a criminal;
der ~ **entsprechen** to answer to description; ~ **geben** to give a description; **hastige** ~ **geben** to plunge headlong into a description; **jeder** ~ **spotten** to beggar (defy) every description; **mit der** ~ **übereinstimmen** to correspond to the description; ~ **eines Verbrechers veröffentlichen** to circulate a description of a criminal.
beschreiten, Rechtsweg to go to law, to take legal proceedings; **gefährlichen Weg** ~ to tread a dangerous path; **ganz neuen Weg** ~ to break new ground, to strike out untrodden paths.
beschrieben, ganz written all over.
beschriften *(Briefumschlag)* to superscribe, *(klassifizieren)* to classify, *(Listen)* to mark, *(Ware)* to label, to ticket, to letter, to docket;
Kiste ~ to mark a case.
Beschriftung inscription, direction, address, *(Kiste)* marking, *(Münze)* circumscription, *(Überschrift)* caption, heading;
~ **von Urkunden** classification of documents.
beschuldigen to charge, to bring a charge against, to accuse, to incriminate, to inculpate, to impeach, to allege, to impute, *(rügen)* to blame;
j. ~ to lay a charge at s. one's door; **alles und jeden** ~ to scatter accusations at large; **j. der Feigheit** ~ to accuse s. o. of cowardice; **j. der Nachlässigkeit** ~ to charge s. o. with negligence; **Richter der Bestechung** ~ to impeach a judge for taking bribes; **sich selbst** ~ to incriminate o. s.; **j. eines Verbrechens** ~ to impeach (indict) s. o. with a crime.
beschuldigend incriminatory, accusatory.
beschuldigt, des Diebstahls ~ charged with theft; **fälschlich** ~ wrongly accused; **der Mittäterschaft** ~ indicted on a charge of complicity.
Beschuldigter defendant, accused [person], person charged, culprit.
Beschuldigung criminal charge, accusation, indictment, crimination, incrimination, impeachment, imputation, appeal;
absurde ~ farcial accusation; **fälschliche** ~ false allegation; **verabscheuungswürdige** ~**en** abominable imputations; **verleumderische** ~ defamatory imputation;

sich ganz offen (freimütig) zu den vorgebrachten ~en äußern to make a direct answer to the charges brought against o. s.; ~ beweisen to make a charge stick; sich schweren ~en gegenübersehen to face serious charges; ~ auf den Kläger zurückfallen lassen to retaliate a charge on the accuser; ~ leugnen to deny a charge; ~en gegen j. vorbringen to bring a charge against s. o.; ~ zurückweisen to reject a charge.
beschummeln to diddle, to bamboozle, to trim *(coll.)*, to beat *(US sl.)*;
jem. ~ to take s. o. *(Br., sl.)*; **Zoll** ~ to cheat the customs.
Beschuß bombardment, cannonade, pounding;
unter ~ *(fig.)* under the gun, under fire, embattled;
unter ~ **nehmen** to barrage; **unter** ~ **stehen** to be under attack;
unter schwerem ~ **stehen** to take a pounding.
beschußsicher shelter-proof.
beschützen to protect, to shelter, to guard.
Beschützer paladin, knight;
~ **der Armen** father to the poor.
beschwatzen, j. to talk s. o. round; **j. zum Kauf von etw.** ~ to wheedle s. o. into buying s. o.
Beschwerde complaint, grievance, reclamation, bitch *(sl.)*, *(bei Gericht)* appeal, *(Protest)* remonstration;
auf die ~ **von** on complaint of;
~**n** inconveniences, complaints;
berechtigte ~ legitimate (justifiable) complaint; **eingebildete** ~**n** imaginary grievances; **eventuelle** ~**n** complaints, if any; **formelle** ~ formal complaint; **fortgesetzte** ~**n** continual complaints; **gemeinsame** ~ joint complaint; **redaktionelle** ~ editorial complaining; **sofortige** ~ fast bill of exceptions *(Georgia)*;
~**n des Alters** infirmities (inconveniences) of old age; ~**n der Angestellten** employee grievances; **die** ~**n des täglichen Lebens** the fret and fume of life; ~ **bei der Polizei** rumple *(sl.)*; ~**n über fahrlässiges Verhalten** negligence complaints;
einer ~ **abhelfen** to redress (remedy) a grievance, to silence (adjust) a complaint, to remove a cause of complaint, to remove a cause of (adjust, amend) a complaint; ~ **ablehnen** to disallow a complaint; ~**n abstellen** to remedy (redress) grievances; **sich mit einer** ~ **befassen** to look into a complaint; ~ **einlegen** to make (lay, lodge) a complaint; **bei jem.** ~ **einlegen** to give notice of appeal to s. o.; **gegen eine Entscheidung** ~ **einlegen** to appeal against a decision; **gegen einen Schiedsspruch** ~ **einlegen** to appeal against an award; **schriftlich** ~ **einlegen** to appeal in writing; ~ **einreichen** to file (lodge) a complaint; ~ **entgegennehmen** to receive a complaint; ~ **über j. erheben** to file a complaint against s. o.; ~ **führen** to state one's grievance, to appeal; **bei jem.** ~ **führen** to lodge a complaint with s. o.; **Grund zur** ~ **geben** to have cause to complain; **Grund zur** ~ **haben** to complain with good reason; **keinen Grund zur** ~ **haben** to have no cause for complaint; **etw. zum Gegenstand einer** ~ **machen** to make a grievance of s. th.; ~**n unterdrücken** to cushion complaints; **etw. gegen** ~**n verschreiben** *(Arzt)* to prescribe s. th. for a complaint; ~ **verwerfen** to refuse an appeal; ~ **vorbringen** to lodge (prefer) a complaint, to bring one's complaint to attention; **alte** ~**n von neuem vorbringen** to rake up old grievances; ~ **zulassen** to allow a complaint; ~ **zurückweisen** to dismiss (ignore) a complaint (s. one's appeal); ~**abfassung** filing of a complaint; ~**abhilfe** amendment of a complaint; ~**abteilung** complaints office, complaint department; ~**ausschuß** board of complaints, grievance (watchdog, appeals) committee, complaints commission (panel), *(Gewerkschaft)* union grievance committee; ~**ausschuß in Grundstücksbewertungsfällen** board of review; ~**begründung** sum and substance of a complaint; ~**berechtigter** aggrieved party (person); ~**brief** letter of complaint, appeal letter; ~**briefkasten** suggestion box; ~**buch** claims (request) book; ~**einlegung** appeal against a decision; ~**entscheidung** *(jur.)* determination of an appeal; ~**erledigung** processing of (dealing with) a complaint, reply to a complaint.
beschwerdefähig subject to appeal;
~ **sein** *(jur.)* to be removable by appeal.
Beschwerdefrist time for appeal.
beschwerdeführend, sich ~ **an jem. wenden** to lodge a complaint with s. o.; **sich** ~ **an das höhere Gericht wenden** to appeal to the court above;
~**e Partei** complaining party, complainant.
Beschwerde|führer person making a complaint, complainant, claimant, reclaimant, appealing party, appellant; ~**führung** complaint; ~**gegenstand** subject matter of complaint; ~**gegner** appellee *(US)*, respondent; ~**gericht** [circuit] court of appeal *(US)*, appellate court; ~**gerichtsbarkeit** appellate jurisdiction; ~**grund** grievance, cause to complain (of complaint), ground of (occasion for) complaint, gravamen, comeback *(US sl.)*, kick *(US sl.)*; **keinen** ~**grund haben** to have no cause for complaint; ~**instanz** complaints office, appellate court *(jur.)*; ~**instanz in Zoll- und Patentangelegenheiten** Court of Customs and Patent Appeal; **ausführliche** ~**liste** long list of complaints (grievances); ~**punkt** matter of complaint; ~**recht** right to complain; ~**rücknahme** withdrawal of appeal; ~**sache** appealed case *(US)*; **für** ~**sachen zuständig sein** to have appellate jurisdiction; ~**schreiben** letter of complaint, claim letter; ~**schrift** complaint, bill of complaint, notice to appeal, bill of exceptions (information, *US*); ~**schrift erledigen** to settle a bill of exceptions *(US)*; ~**stelle** complaints office (panel), *(Gericht)* appeals board; ~**verfahren** grievance (complaints, appeals) procedure; ~**vorbringen** lodgment of a complaint; ~**weg einschlagen** to lodge a complaint, to make complaints; ~**wert** civil debt; ~**zustellung** service of complaint.
beschweren to weigh, to load;
sich ~ to state one's grievance, to complain, to appeal, to sound off *(US sl.)*, to beef *(sl.)*, to bitch *(sl.)*; **sich bei jem.** ~ to lodge a complaint with s. o.; **sich über j.** ~ to make (lodge) a complaint against s. o.; **sich über das Essen** ~ to grumble about the food; **sein Gedächtnis mit unnützen Tatsachen** ~ to clog one's memory with useless facts; **jds. Gemüt** ~ to weigh upon s. one's mind; **sich gewaltig (lautstark)** ~ to be loud in one's complaints; **jem. Gewissen** ~ to lie on s. one's conscience; **sich über seinen Nachbar** ~ to lodge a complaint against one's neighbo(u)r; **sich mit gutem Recht** ~ to have good reason to complain; **Stapel Briefe** ~ to weigh down a pile of letters; **mit einem Vermächtnis** ~ to abate an inheritance with a legacy.
beschwerlich incommodious, wearisome, tedious, tiring;
jem. ~ **fallen** to inconvenience s. o., to be a burden for s. o.;
~**e Reise** tiring journey; ~**er Weg** arduous road.
Beschwernisse|einer Reise burden of travel;
von Polarforschern ausgehaltene ~ discomforts endured by explorers in the Arctic.
Beschwerter aggrieved person (party).
beschwichtigen to appease, to pacify, to calm, to soothe, to conciliate;
jds. Ärger ~ to soothe s. one's anger; **Gewissen** ~ to quiet the conscience; **aufständische Volksmenge** ~ to pacify the excited crowd.
beschwichtigender Einfluß soothing influence.
Beschwichtigung appeasement, pacification, placation;
zur ~ **des Gewissens** for conscience sake.
Beschwichtigungs|brief adjustment letter; ~**mittel** sop; ~**politik** policy of appeasement, adjustment (appeasement) policy, appeaser.
beschwindeln to swindle, to hoax, to cheat, to bamboozle;
j. um 100 DM ~ to diddle s. o. out of DM 100.
beschwingt cheerful, vivacious, gay, lively;
~ **ans Werk gehen** to set to work cheerfully; ~ **sein** to feel elevated, to be exhilarated;
~**e Melodien** lively tunes.
beschwipst muddled, mixed, tipsy, under the weather, merry, hazy, rosy *(sl.)*, well-oiled *(sl.)*, fresh *(sl.)*, mellow *(sl.)*;
leicht ~ happy *(coll.)*.
beschwören to take an oath on, to swear to, to adjure, *(anflehen)* to conjure;
j. ~ to implore (beseech, entreat) s. o.; **Aussage** ~ to make a deposit on oath; ~**, j. bezahlt zu haben** to swear to having paid s. o.; **alte Erinnerungen** ~ to conjure up old memories; **Geister** ~ to raise spirits;
ich könnte es ~ I would swear to it.
beschwörender Blick imploring (beseeching) look.
beschworene|Erklärung statutory declaration; ~ **Zeugenaussage** deposition on oath.
Beschwörung imploration, entreaty.
beseelt, von dem Wunsch inspired (filled) with the desire.
besehen, genau to examine closely; **etw. bei Licht** ~ to look at s. th. by daylight;
wie ~ with all faults.
beseitigen to remove, to clear (do) away, to liquidate, *(abschaffen)* to abolish, to lift, *(Fehler)* to cure, to eliminate, to polish off;
j. ~ to do away with (liquidate) s. o., to dispatch s. o.; **Armut** ~ to cure poverty; **Beeinträchtigung** ~ to abate a nuisance; **Beschränkungen** ~ to remove restrictions; **Buchungsunterlagen** ~ to dispose of books; **Embargo** ~ to remove an embargo; **Fehler in einem verdorbenen Text** ~ to make emendations in a corrupt text; **j. durch Gift** ~ to remove s. o. by poison;

Hindernis ~ to remove an obstacle; **Höchstpreise** ~ to remove price ceilings; **Krankheitsherd** ~ to remove the seat of a disease; **Mängel** ~ to remedy defects; **Mißstand** ~ to cure (remedy) an evil, to redress grievance, to abate a nuisance; **Mißverständnis** ~ to clear up (iron out) a misunderstanding; **Produktionsüberschüsse** ~ to trim excess production; **Rechtsmängel** ~ to remove clouds from title; **stilistische Schönheitsfehler** ~ to smooth out one's style; **Schwierigkeiten** ~ to smooth away (obviate) difficulties; **Spuren** ~ to remove traces; **Steuer** ~ to take off (abolish) a tax; **stillschweigend** ~ to quietly shunt aside; **Trümmer** ~ to remove (clear away) debris; **Ungeziefer** ~ to kill (get rid of) vermin; **Unklarheiten** ~ to remove any uncertainty; **Urkunde** ~ to suppress (abstract, conceal) a document; **letzte Zweifel** ~ to remove the last doubts.

Beseitigung removing, removal, liquidation, abolition, cancellation, elimination, *(Mord)* dispatch, murder, removal;
gewaltsame ~ *(Regierung)* subversion;
~ **radioaktiven Abfalls** disposal of radioactive waste material; ~ **von Beschränkungen** removal (abolition) of restrictions; ~ **der Buchungsunterlagen** disposal of books; ~ **sozialen Elends** remedy for social evils; ~ **von Elendsvierteln** redemption of slums, slum clearance; ~ **eines Embargos** removal of an embargo; ~ **eines Fehlers** correction (elimination) of a mistake; ~ **von Höchstpreisbestimmungen** removal of price ceilings; ~ **eines Mißstandes** abatement of (abating a) nuisance; ~ **von Rechtsmängeln** removing cloud from title; ~ **einer Schwierigkeit** disposal (removal) of a difficulty; ~ **einer Steuer** abolition of a tax; ~ **von Ungeziefer** destruction of vermin; ~ **von Urkunden** abstraction (suppression) of documents.

Besen, mit eisernem ~ kehren to rule with a rod of iron;
neue ~ kehren gut a new broom sweeps clean.

besessen obsessed, mad, *(rasend)* frantic, frenzied;
wie ~ like all possessed *(US)*;
von etw. ~ sein to become hooked on s. th. *(sl.)*; **von etw. völlig ~ sein** to become infatuated with s. th.; **von einer Idee ~ sein** to be possessed (obsessed) with an idea.

Besessener demon, maniac, demoniac;
sich wie ein ~ gebärden to behave like a madman.

Besessenheit madness;
seinen Plan mit einer wahren ~ verfolgen to show fanatical zeal for a cause.

besetzen to appoint, *(Land)* to occupy, *(Theater)* to cast;
falsch ~ *(Rolle)* to miscast; **Festung** ~ to man a fort; **feindliche Hauptstadt** ~ to occupy the enemy's capital; **Lehrstuhl** ~ to fill a chair; **neu** ~ *(Rolle)* to recast; **mit Pelz** ~ to trim with fur; **Platz im Zug** ~ to take a seat in a train; **Rathaus** ~ to take possession of the townhall; **Rolle** ~ *(Theater)* to fill a part; **Schützengräben** ~ to man trenches; **Stadt mit einer Garnison** ~ to garrison a town; **Stelle** ~ to fill a vacancy; **leere Stelle** ~ to fill a vacancy; **die Stelle eines Kassierers ist zu** ~ there is a vacancy for a cashier; **Stelle mit einer jüngeren Kraft** ~ to appoint a younger person to a post.

besetzt *(belegt)* occupied, taken, *(Hotel)* full, *(mil.)* occupied, *(Person)* busy, booked, *(Stellung)* filled, *(Straßenbahn, Bus)* packed, crammed, full up *(Br.)*, *(Taxe)* hired, *(Telefon)* engaged, busy *(US)*, *(Theater)* crowded to capacity, *(vorbestellt)* reserved, booked;
vom Feind ~ overrun by enemy troops; **gut** ~ well staffed; **nicht** ~ *(tel.)* disengaged; **mit Pelz** ~ furred; **schwach** ~ *(Theater)* thin; **mit köstlichen Speisen** ~ laden with delicious things; **voll** ~ *(Bus)* full up, crammed, packed to the door;
Land ~ halten to keep occupation troops in a country; **Telefonleitung für zwanzig Minuten ~ halten** to hold (tie up, engage) a line for twenty minutes; **noch ~ werden müssen** to remain to be filled; **gut ~ sein** *(Theaterstück)* to have a good cast; **schon ~ sein** *(Position)* to have been filled already; **stark ~ sein** *(Rennen)* to have many entries; **voll ~ sein** to be heavily booked; **[zeitlich] sehr ~ sein** to have many demands on one's time;
~es Gebiet occupied territory; **voll ~es Haus** crowded audience; **~e Leitung** engaged (busy, *US*) line; **voll ~es Orchester** fully manned orchestra; **~e Plätze** taken seats; **international ~es Rennen** international race; **mit Rubinen ~er Ring** ring set with rubies; **voll ~er Stundenplan** crowded timetable; **gut ~es Theater** full (crowded) house; **~e Zone** zone of occupation.

Besetztzeichen *(tel.)* circuit-busy *(US)* (engaged, *Br.*) signal, delayed-dial (engaged) tone.

Besetzung appointment, *(mil.)* occupation, *(Theater)* cast;
bei ~ eines Postens on conferring an employment; **in voller** ~ *(Gericht)* in banc; **erstklassige** ~ *(Theater)* excellent cast; **friedliche** ~ peaceful (pacific) occupation; **kriegerische** ~ belligerent occupation;
~ **feindlichen Gebiets** occupation of enemy territory; ~ **eines Rennens** entrants for a race; ~ **von Schlüsselpositionen** key appointments; ~ **von Stellen** filling in of vacancies; ~ **leitender Stellen aus dem eigenen Bereich** promoting from within;
~ **gewisser Stellen mit Ausländern nicht zulassen** to exclude aliens from posts.

Besetzungsrecht *(Behörde)* right of nomination.

besichern *(Kredit)* to furnish security, to collaterate *(US)*.

Besicherung furnishing security, collateral *(US)*.

Besicherungs|form form of collateral *(US)*; **zu ~zwecken verwenden** to pledge as collateral.

Besicht inspection, examination;
ohne ~ *(Grundstückskauf)* sight unseen;
auf ~ kaufen to buy subject to inspection.

besichtigen to go over, to inspect, to examine, to visit, to look round, *(Ferienreisender)* to sight-see, to tour, *(Schiff)* to survey;
bei uns zu ~ on show on our premises; **nur an Wochentagen zu** ~ open to the public on weekdays only;
Fabrik ~ to go over a factory; **Haus** ~ to look (go) over a house; **Land** ~ to make the tour of a country; **Land in zwei Wochen** ~ to do a country in a fortnight; **London** ~ to go sight-seeing in London; **Museum** ~ to visit a museum; **Regiment** ~ to inspect a regiment; **Schaden** ~ to inspect [the extent of] damage; **Schiff** ~ to survey a ship; **Stadt** ~ to make a town *(US)*; **Tatort des Verbrechens** ~ to visit the scene of a crime; **Truppen** ~ to review (hold an inspection of, visit, inspect) troops;
zu ~ sein to be on view (open to inspection).

besichtigend visiting.

Besichtigung inspection, examination, visit, visitation, view, *(Schiff)* survey;
bei ~ der Waren on examination of the goods; **bei näherer** ~ on closer examination; **ohne** ~ sight unseen; **ohne ~ zu verkaufen** on sale sight unseen *(US)*; ~ **vorbehalten** subject to inspection; **zur** ~ on show; **zur ~ freigegeben** exposed to view, open to inspection;
genaue ~ close inspection;
~ **einer Fabrik** trip through a factory; ~ **und Schadensschätzung beschädigter Fahrzeuge** damaged vehicle inspection service; ~ **durch geladene Gäste** private view; ~ **durch das Gericht** judicial survey; ~ **eines Grundstücks** viewing of land; ~ **des Mordschauplatzes** view of a scene of murder; ~ **eines Schiffes** survey of a ship; ~ **von Sehenswürdigkeiten** sight-seeing; ~ **von Truppen** inspection of troops; ~ **der Ware** inspection of goods;
~ **abhalten** *(mil.)* to hold an inspection; **zur ~ aufliegen** to be exposed (exhibited); ~ **an Ort und Stelle durchführen** to carry out an inspection on the spot; **zur ~ freigeben** to open for inspection; **jem. die ~ einer Fabrik gestatten** to let s. o. over a factory; **nach ~ kaufen** to buy after inspection; **dem Publikum zur ~ öffnen** to open to the public.

Besichtigungs|bericht *(Havarie)* report of survey, survey report; **~erlaubnis** order of review; **~fahrt** tour of inspection, inspection tour, *(Ferienreisende)* sight-seeing tour; **große ~fahrt** grand tour; **~gebühr** survey fee; **~genehmigung** order to view; **~genehmigung erteilen** to give an order to view; **~protokoll** certificate of survey; **~reise** tour of inspection, inspection tour, *(Tourist)* sight-seeing tour; **kostenlose ~reise** all-expense tour *(US)*; **~rundgang** tour of inspection, round; **~schein** inspecting order, survey certificate; **~tour** sight-seeing tour, organized tour; **~zeit** visiting hours; **~zeugnis** certificate of inspection, *(Schiff)* certificate of survey, survey certificate.

besiedeln to colonize, to settle, to plant, to people, to populate.

besiedelt populated;
dicht ~ densely populated; **dünn** ~ thinly peopled;
~ **werden** to become peopled.

Besiedlung colonization, settlement;
dichte ~ dense population; **dünne** ~ sparse population.

Besiedlungs|dichte density of population; **~gebiet** settlement area; **~plan** settlement project; **~politik** settlement policy; **~programm** land settlement scheme.

besiegeln to affix a seal;
Untergang eines Unternehmens ~ to sign the death warrant of an enterprise.

besiegen to defeat, to conquer, to overthrow;
Armee ~ to overthrow an army; **Feind** ~ to beat the enemy; **j. haushoch** ~ to beat s. o. hollow; **Land** ~ to conquer a country; **seine Leidenschaften** ~ to master one's passions; **j. spielend** ~ to beat s. o. into a fit *(coll.)*; **jds. Widerstand** ~ to overcome s. one's resistance.

besiegt defeated, beaten;
sich für ~ erklären to throw up the sponge, to throw in the towel; **~en Gegner schonen** to spare a defeated adversary.
Besinnen, nach kurzem after brief reflection.
besinnen, sich to consider, to think about, *(sich erinnern)* to remember; **sich anders ~** to alter (change) one's mind; **sich eines Besseren ~** to think better of it; **sich lange hin und her ~** to rack one's brains; **ohne sich lange zu ~** on the spur of the moment, without thinking twice; **sich auf seine Pflichten ~** to remember one's duty; **sich eine Weile ~** to think about it for a moment; **keine Zeit haben sich zu ~** to have no time to deliberate;
sich nicht auf jds. Namen ~ können not to be able to recall s. one's name.
Besitz possession, possessorship, hand, holding, occupancy, occupation, grasp, *(Effektenpaket)* holding, *(Gut)* estate, property, ownership, *(Habe)* havings, things, belongings, *(Reichtum)* wealth, *(Vermögen)* fortune, interests;
im ~ in possession; **im ~ angetroffen** found in; **in ausländischem ~** foreign-owned; **im ~ Ihres Briefes** in receipt of your letter; **in gemeinsamen ~** commonable, communal, held (owned) in common; **im ~ von Ländereien** possessed of land; **nicht im ~** not possessed; **im öffentlichen ~** state-owned; **in privatem ~** privately owned; **im staatlichen ~** state-owned; **im vollen ~ seiner geistigen Kräfte** with faculties unimpaired, of sound mind and memory *(US)*; **im ~ von Vermögen** possessed of property;
ansehnlicher (ausgedehnter) ~ large estate; **ausschließlicher ~** exclusive possession; **bedingter ~** estate upon (in) condition; **beschränkter ~** special property; **bestrittener ~** adverse possession; **jederzeit entziehbarer ~** precarious possession; **eigenmächtig erworbener ~** scrambling possession; **fiktiver ~** civil possession; **an Bedingungen gebundener ~** limited (qualified) fee; **erbrechtlich gebundener ~** settlement, settled property *(Br.)*; **gemeinsamer ~** community, common ownership, collective ownership, communion, plural tenure, concurrent possession; **gemeinschaftlicher ~** joint tenancy; **kostspieliger ~** white elephant; **erbrechtlich gebundener ~** settlement, settled property *(Br.)*; **landwirtschaftlicher (landwirtschaftlich genutzter) ~** peasant proprietary, agricultural holding *(US)*; **mittelbarer ~** constructive possession; **nutzungsberechtigter ~** beneficial interest in possession; **offenkundiger ~** notorious possession; **persönlicher ~** corporal possession; **mein persönlicher ~** my personal belongings; **rechtmäßiger ~** lawful possession; **rechtswidriger ~** adverse possession; **staatlicher ~** state property; **tatsächlicher ~** actual possession, manual (de facto) possession, *(ohne Rechtsanspruch)* naked possession; **treuhänderischer ~** fiduciary possession; **überschuldeter ~** embarrassed estate; **zeitlich unbegrenzter ~** perpetuity; **unbeschränkter ~** full possession; **ungestörter ~** full (peaceable) possession, *(Grundstück)* quiet enjoyment; **unmittelbarer ~** physical (actual, corporal, personal) possession; **unrechtmäßiger ~** adverse possession; **aller unser ~** all our worldly possessions; **unbeschränkt vererbbarer ~** tail general; **frei verfügbarer ~** one's own right; **gesetzlich vermuteter ~** constructive possession; **wertvoller ~** valued possession; **widerrechtlicher ~** hostile (faulty) possession; **wirtschaftlicher ~** constructive ownership; **wohlerworbener ~** vested rights;
~ von Aktien shareholding, stockholding *(US)*; **~ aufgrund eines Besitzmittlungsverhältnisses** derivative possession; **~ und scheinbares Eigentum** *(Konkursfall)* order and disposition *(Br.)*; **~ durch Ersitzung** adverse possession; **vereinter ~ von zwei Gerechtsamen** unity of possession; **~ der öffentlichen Hand** government ownership; **unerlaubter ~ von Handfeuerwaffen** illegal possession of firearms; **gegenwärtiger ~ und Nutznießung** present enjoyment, executed use; **~ nach Pachtablauf** holding over; **~ der Produktionsmittel** industrial ownership; **~ ohne Rechtstitel** naked possession; **~ von Staatsanleihen (Staatspapieren)** fundholding *(Br.)*, funded property; **unberechtigter ~ eines behördlichen Stempels** unlawful possession of an official stamp; **~ kraft rechtlicher Vermutung** apparent possession; **~ auf Zeit** terminal property; **~ seit unvordenklichen Zeiten** immemorial possession *(Louisiana)*;
seinen ganzen ~ abstoßen to sell off one's possessions, *(Wertpapiere)* to unload one's stock; **~ antreten** to come (enter) into (take) possession of an estate; **~ aufgeben** to surrender (part with) possession; **jds. ganzen ~ ausmachen** to constitute s. one's entire estate; **~ ausüben** to retain possession; **im ~ der Mietwohnung bleiben** to remain in possession of a flat *(Br.)* (rental apartment, *US*); **in ~ bringen** to reduce, to bring in possession; **etw. in seinen ~ bringen** to make o. s. master of s. th.; **wieder in den ~ einsetzen** to restore to possession; **j. in einen ~ wieder einsetzen** to reestablish (reintegrate) s. o. in his possession; **aus dem ~ entfernen** to oust, to evict; **~ entlasten** to clear an estate; **jem. den ~ entziehen** to divest (dispossess, expropriate) s. o. of s. th.; **jds. ~ erben** to be left heir to s. one's estate; **~ ergreifen** to take hold of, to lay hands on, to occupy, to take possession (seizin), to enter upon; **~ von etw. ergreifen** to lay hands on s. th.; **~ erlangen** to become possessed of; **seinen rechtmäßigen ~ erlangen** to come into one's own; **unmittelbaren ~ erlangen** to seize actual possession; **in den ~ von etw. gelangen** to become seized (come into possession) of s. th.; **im ~ haben** to hold, to possess, to occupy, to have in one's possession; **mit anderen gemeinsam als ungeteilten ~ haben** to have land by entireties; **kleinen ~ auf dem Lande haben** to have a small property in the country; **an seinem ~ hängen** to cling to one's possessions; **in ~ einer Sache kommen** to get possession of (get by) s. th.; **wieder in den ~ einer Sache kommen** to regain (resume) possession of a thing; **zu ~ kommen** to come into property; **jem. den ~ streitig machen** to dispute s. one's ownership; **in ~ nehmen** to take possession, to occupy, to lay hands on, to seize; **Stück Land in ~ nehmen** to appropriate a piece of land; **vorher in ~ nehmen** to prepossess; **widerrechtlich in ~ nehmen** to usurp; **etw. wieder in ~ nehmen** to reenter upon s. th., to resume possession of (recover, reseize) s. th.; **im ~ sein von** to be in receipt of; **überwiegend in ausländischem ~ sein** to be principally owned by foreign interest; **im ausschließlichen ~ von etw. sein** to be sole possessor of s. th.; **im ~ der Mietwohnung sein** to remain in possession of a flat *(Br.)* (rental apartment, *US*); **im ~ einer Sache sein** to own (possess, to be in possession of) s. th.; **im ~ von Vermögen sein** to be possessed of a property; **im ~ eines großen Vermögens sein** to be possessor of a large fortune; **aus dem ~ setzen** to evict, to oust; **in ~ setzen** to vest; **sich in den ~ von etw. setzen** to get possession of s. th.; **j. in den ~ einer Erbschaft setzen** to serve s. o. heir to a property; **wieder in den ~ setzen** to restore to possession; **im ausländischen ~ stehen** to be under foreign ownership; **j. in seinem ~ stören** to disturb s. one's lawful enjoyment, to interfere with s. one's possession; **~ in Stücke teilen** to sever, to estate; **aus dem ~ treiben** to eject, to oust; **in ~ übergehen** to vest in possession; **in jds. ~ übergehen** to pass (vest) into s. one's possession; **in ~ übernehmen** to receive in livery; **jem. einen ~ überlassen** to resign a property to s. o.; **seinen ~ auf seinen Sohn übertragen** to deliver over an estate to one's son; **im ~ verbleiben** to remain in possession; **~ verschaffen** to transfer possession, to put in possession; **sich ~ verschaffen** to secure possession; **mittelbaren ~ verschaffen** to constitute constructive delivery; **aus dem ~ vertreiben** to oust; **wieder in den ~ eingesetzt werden** to be restored to possession; **~ wiedererlangen** to resume possession, to recover possession by law; **~ zurückgeben** to render up possession.
besitzähnliches Verhältnis quasi possession.
Besitz|anspruch possessory claim (right, interest), claim to title; **seinen ~anspruch geltend machen** to assert one's claim to a property; **~antritt** taking possession, entry; **~anwartschaft** expectant estate; **~aufgabe** dereliction, surrender of possession; **mittelbare ~aufgabe** constructive abandonment; **~ausübung** enjoyment of possession; **~dauer** term of possession, tenure, *(Einkommensteuer)* holding period; **~diener** possessor's agent, underpossessor; **~einkommen** unearned income.
Besitzeinweisung delivery, livery of seizin;
gerichtliche ~ writ of possession, vesting order *(Br.)*.
Besitzeinweisungsbeschluß writ of assistance.
besitzen to possess, to be in possession, to occupy, to hold, to have and hold *(US)*;
Aktien ~ to hold shares (stocks, *US*); **als Eigentümer ~** to own, to possess in one's own right; **ausreichende Englischkenntnisse ~** to have a sufficient command of English; **die Frechheit ~** to have the cheek; **Gabe ~** to have a gift; **gemeinsam ~** to share, to hold in common, to possess jointly, to be joint owners; **Haus gemeinsam ~** to own a house jointly; **gute Nase für etw. ~** to have a good nose *(coll.)*; **nichts mehr ~** to be out of all; **als Pfandgläubiger ~** to hold as collateral; **Spezialgetriebe ~** to be equipped with a special transmission; **Tochtergesellschaft hundertprozentig ~** to own a subsidiary outright; **als Treuhänder ~** to hold in trust; **im Wege der Vergünstigung durch einen Dritten ~** to hold upon courtesy; **großes Vermögen ~** to be in possession of a large fortune; **jds. unbedingtes Vertrauen ~** to have s. one's complete confidence.
besitzend possessory;
~e Klassen propertied classes.

Besitzende und Proletariat the classes and the masses.
Besitzender occupant, have.
Besitzentsetzung ejectment, eviction, ouster;
widerrechtliche ~ disseizin.
Besitz|entsetzungsklage writ of ejectment; **~entziehung** dispossession, disvestment, disvestiture, disseizin, conversion, amotion of possession; **vollständiger ~entzug** total eviction.
Besitzer possessor, occupant, occupier, chief, master, *(Aktien)* holder, keeper, *(Eigentümer)* owner, proprietor, proprietary; **alleiniger ~** exclusive (sole) owner; **böswilliger ~** malafide holder, holder in bad faith; **ehrlicher (gutgläubiger) ~** bonafide owner (possessor), holder in due course (in good faith), innocent holder for value; **früherer ~** former proprietor; **gegenwärtiger ~** present owner; **nachfolgender ~** subsequent owner; **rechtmäßiger ~** legal possessor, rightful owner; **späterer ~** subsequent holder; **tatsächlicher ~** de facto owner; **tatsächlicher ~ ohne Rechtsanspruch** naked possessor; **treuhänderischer ~** holder on trust; **unberechtigter ~** adverse possessor; **unmittelbarer ~** actual possessor; **unredlicher ~** mala-fide holder; **wirklicher ~** true owner;
~ der Aktienmehrheit majority shareholder *(Br.)* (stockholder, *US*); **~ eines Autofriedhofs** car breaker; **~ eines eigenen Fuhrparks** own fleet operator; **~ von freiem Grundeigentum** freeholder *(Br.)*; **~ und Herausgeber** editor-publisher; **~ eines Hotels** proprietor of a hotel; **~ auf Lebenszeit** lifeholder; **~ des Nachbargrundstücks** abutting (adjoining) owner; **~ eines Schiffes** shipowner;
unmittelbarer ~ der Ware bleiben to retain possession of the goods; **~ wechseln** to change hands; **häufig den ~ wechseln** to pass through many hands.
Besitzergreifer occupant, occupier, *(widerrechtlich)* usurper.
Besitzergreifung [taking] possession, entry, occupancy, occupation, seizing, seizure;
gewaltsame und unerlaubte ~ forcible entry and detainer; **symbolische ~** seizin in law; **tatsächliche ~** actual (corporeal) possession; **unrechtmäßige ~** dispossession; **widerrechtliche ~** usurpation, duress of goods;
~ der Ernte perception of crops; **~ eines Grundstücks** seizin; **~ bei Vertragsbeendigung** occupation on completion.
Besitz|erlangung reduction into possession, occupation of realty; **~erlangung des Treuhandvermögens** reduction of the trust property into possession; **~erwerb** taking possession; **direkter ~erwerb** modus; **~gegenstand** possession; **in ungestörtem ~genuß sein** to enjoy quiet possession; **~klage** possessory action.
besitzlos abandoned, *(arm)* poor, unpropertied.
Besitz|losigkeit poverty; **~nachfolger** subsequent owner, assign, assignee; **~nachweis erbringen** to prove possession.
Besitznahme taking possession;
gesetzwidrige ~ intrusion; **offene ~** open possession.
Besitzpfandrecht possessory lien.
Besitzrecht possessory (possessive) right, estate, title;
mit unmittelbarem Nutzungs- und ~ vested in possession; **alleiniges ~** sole proprietorship; **zeitlich befristetes ~** estate for a term; **beschränktes ~** tail; **erbfolgemäßig festgelegtes ~** interest in tail, entailed interest; **strittiges ~** contentious possession; **ungestörtes ~** quiet possession; **unmittelbares ~** seizin in law; **nach Pachtablauf stillschweigend weitergewährtes ~** estate at sufferance *(US)*; **zukünftiges ~** future estate;
~ durch Aneignung title by occupance (abandonment); **~ mehrerer Erben** estate in corparcenary; **lebenslängliches ~ der Witwe an einem Drittel des beweglichen Nachlasses** estate in dower;
~ aufgeben to surrender an estate; **aufgrund behaupteten Rechtstitels das ~ ausüben** to hold possession under colo(u)r of title; **in jds. ~ eingreifen** to encroach [up]on s. one's land; **~recht an einer Sache erlangen (erwerben)** to gain possession of s. th.; **~e übertragen** to seize.
Besitzstand user, enjoyment of right, ownership, proprietary, *(Bilanz)* assets;
künftiger ~ estate in expectancy; **tatsächlicher ~** actual possession.
Besitz|steuer property (occupancy) tax; **~störer** trespasser, intruder.
Besitzstörung disturbance of possession, forcible detainer, ouster, illegitimite interference, prevention of enjoyment (possession), molestation, *(Grundstück)* forcible trespass, intrusion;
gemeinsam begangene ~ joint trespass; **dauernde ~** permanent nuisance;
~ beseitigen to abate a nuisance.
Besitzstörungs|fall case of trespass; **~klage** ejectment bill, action on the case, *(Grundstück)* action for trespass, possessory action *(US)*, forcible entry and detainer.
Besitztitel tenure, possessory title, instrument of title, *(Grundstück)* title deed;
präsumptiver ~ presumptive title.
Besitz|tum possession, property, estate; **~tumsstörung** civil nuisance; **tatsächlicher ~übergang** transfer of actual possession; **unmittelbarer ~übergang** actual change of possession; **~übertragung** livery of seizin.
Besitzung estate, [landed] property, having;
auswärtige ~en exterior (foreign) possessions; **große ~** big estate; **kleine ~en** small holdings;
seine ~en vergrößern to enlarge one's possessions.
Besitz|urkunde title deed, title to property; **~veränderung** transfer; **eingeschränktes ~verhältnis** special property; **~verhältnisse bestreiten** to discuss the possession of the ground; **~verlust** dispossession, disseizin; **~vermutung** derivative possession.
Besitzverschaffung tradition, livery of seizin, delivery of possession;
mittelbare ~ constructive (symbolical) delivery; **tatsächliche ~** actual delivery.
Besitz|versicherung occupancy insurance *(US)*; **~vertreibung** ouster, ejection; **~vorenthaltung** detinue, ouster; **~wechsel** change of hands (in ownership), *(Wechsel in der Bilanz)* bills (notes, *US*) receivable; **~wert** property value; **~zeit** *(Pacht)* term.
besoffen drunk, stiff, cock-eyed, under the table *(coll.)*, queer *(sl.)*;
sinnlos ~ inarticulate with drink; **~ wie eine Strandhaubitze** tight as a drum (lord, tick);
~es Zeug daherreden to talk through one's hat.
Besoffene|r drunk person;
~n vor die Tür setzen to pitch out a drunkard.
besolden to remunerate, to [pay a] salary.
besoldet salaried, stipendiary;
~ sein to receive a salary;
~e Stellung salaried position.
Besoldung salary, remuneration, stipend, *(Gehaltszahlung)* salary payment, *(mil.)* pay, *(Richter)* stipend;
~ des Personals remuneration of staff.
Besoldungs|dienstalter seniority; **~einstufung** salary classification; **~erhöhung** increase in pay, salary increase; **~gesetz** Classification Act *(US)*; **~gruppe** salary group (bracket, scale), pay bracket (grade); **~liste** salary list (roll); **~neuordnung** salary reclassification; **~niveau** pay level; **~ordnung** salary (pay) scale, pay plan *(US)*, Classification Act *(US)*; **~regelung** salary classification; **~rückstände** salary arrears; **~satz** salary rate; **~stufe** salary grade (bracket, class, group), pay level *(US)*; **~verbesserung** pay (salary) increase; **~verhältnisse** salary conditions; **~zulage** salary bonus, seniority allowance.
Besonderes something special (serious);
etw. ~ zum Abendessen something extra-special for dinner; **nichts ~ dabei finden** to think nothing of; **etw. ~ auf die Beine stellen** to put s. th. special on.
besonder|s separate, special, particular, peculiar, extra, extraordinary;
~e Abneigung pet aversion; **~e Anstrengungen machen** to take pains, to go all out; **~er Auftrag** special mission; **~e Ausstattung** extra equipment; **ohne ~e Begeisterung** without marked enthusiasm; **~e Eigenschaften** peculiar characteristics; **~e Eignung** special ability; **~e Erlaubnis haben** to have special permission; **~es Gebäude** separate building; **von ~em Interesse sein** to be of particular interest; **~e Kennzeichen** *(Paß)* characteristic signs; **~e wissenschaftliche Leistungen** outstanding scientific achievements; **ganz ~e Methode haben** to have a method of one's own; **~s hoher Preis** extra high price; **von ~er Qualität** of extraordinary quality; **von ~er Schönheit** of singular beauty; **~e Sorgfalt anwenden** to take extra (special) care; **~er Tarif** differential tariff; **in ~em Umschlag** under separate cover; **~e Umstände** particular circumstances; **~er Wunsch** special request; **~er Zweck** specific aim;
Wein wird ~s berechnet wine is extra.
Besonderheit peculiarity, speciality, special feature;
~en des Poststempels particulars on a postmark.
besonnen circumspect, prudent;
~ bleiben to cool it, to keep a cool head;
~er Kaufmann prudent business man.
Besonnenheit prudence, circumspection, discretion;
mit ~ handeln to act with circumspection; **politische ~ zeigen** to show political levelheadedness.

besorgen to provide, to procure, to supply, to undertake, *(kaufen)* to buy, to purchase, *(Sorge tragen)* to look after, to attend, to take care;
es jem. ~ to give s. o. hell; **für j. etw. ~** to go on errands for s. o.; **sich etw. ~** to furnish o. s. with s. th.; **das Abladen ~** to do (attend to) the unloading; **jds. Angelegenheiten ~** to attend to s. one's affairs; **Buchherausgabe ~** to prepare an edition; **Deckung ~** to provide funds; **Geld ~** to raise (find) money; **Gepäck ~** to see to the luggage *(Br.)* (baggage, *US*); **seine Geschäfte ~** to see (attend) to one's business; **es jem. gründlich ~** to pay s. o. back in his own coin; **jem. den Haushalt ~** to keep house for s. o.; **Inkasso eines Wechsels ~** to undertake the collection of a bill; **Ladengeschäft ~** to run a shop; **jem. eine Stelle ~** to find a job for s. o.; **einem Freund eine gute Stellung ~** to manoeuvre a friend into a good job; **jem. ein Taxi ~** to get s. o. a taxi; **Versicherung ~** to effect an insurance; **für j. Wege ~** to do errands for s. o.; **jem. ein Zimmer ~** to find (get) s. o. a room; **zur Zufriedenheit eines Kunden ~** to satisfy a customer; **viel zu ~ haben** to have a lot of shopping to do.
Besorgnis apprehension, fear, concern, doubt, disquiet;
kein Grund zur ~ no reason for concern; **mit tiefer ~** with deep concern;
Richter wegen ~ der Befangenheit ablehnen to challenge a judge; **in verschiedenen Hauptstädten erhebliche ~ auslösen** to cause considerable disquiet in some capitals; **Anlaß zur ~ geben** to give rise to anxiety (cause for apprehension).
besorgniserregend alarming, disquieting;
~ krank alarmingly ill.
besorgt worried, apprehensive, anxious, concerned, uneasy;
~ sein to have fears; **über jds. Gesundheitszustand ~ sein** to be worried about s. one's state of health; **um sein Leben ~ sein** to be in fear of one's life; **um jds. Sicherheit ~ sein** to be apprehensive for s. one's safety; **um jds. Wohlergehen ~ sein** to be solicitous for s. one's well-being; **sich über die politische Lage ~ zeigen** to show concern about the political situation.
Besorgung *(Auftrag)* commission, *(Beschaffung)* procurement, provision, *(Botengang)* errand, *(Einkauf)* purchase, *(Erledigung)* performance, handling;
~en shopping;
kleine ~en small commissions;
~ fremder Angelegenheit taking care of other people's business; **~ von Aufträgen** execution of orders; **~ von Geld** raising of money (funds); **~ des Haushalts** management of the household;
~en erledigen to do some shopping; **~en für j. erledigen** to go on errands for s. o.; **geschäftliche ~ erledigen** to attend to a matter of business; **seine ~en in Wohnungsnähe erledigen** to shop near one's home; **einige kleine ~en für j. zu erledigen haben** to have two or three commissions for s. o.; **j. eine ~ machen lassen** to send s. o. on an errand; **~en machen** to go shopping, to shop.
Besorgungs|gebühr handling fee, *(Buchhändler)* acquisition fee; **~geschäfte** procurement transactions; **~zettel** shopping list.
bespielen, Schallplatte to make a record.
bespieltes Tonband recorded tape.
bespitzeln, j. to spy on (watch upon) s. o., to set spies (narks) on s. o.
Bespitzelung spying.
bespötteln, jds. Schwächen to make derisive remarks about s. one's weak points.
Bespöttelung aussetzen, sich der to lay o. s. open to ridicule.
besprechen to talk over, to discuss, to argue;
mit jem. ~ to take up with s. o.; **sich ~** to confer, to hold a conference; **Angelegenheit ~** to discuss a matter, to talk a matter over; **ausführlich ~** to discuss at some length; **Buch ~** to review a book; **Buch positiv ~** to review a book favo(u)rably; **etw. gründlich ~** to talk things out; **Lage ~** to discuss the situation; **sich mit seinen Mitarbeitern ~** to be in conference with one's colleagues; **sich miteinander ~** to hold a consultation; **Sache ~** to talk a matter over; **Sache mit einem Anwalt ~** to consult a lawyer; **Sache ihrem wesentlichen Inhalt nach ~** to discuss s. th. on its merits; **Schallplatte ~** to record one's voice; **Tonband ~** to record a speech (on tape);
zu ~ under review.
Besprechung talk, meeting, conference, interview, *(Buch)* review, criticism, *(Diskussion)* discussion, debate, parley;
nach einer mehrstündigen ~ after a discussion lasting several hours;
einleitende ~en opening talks (discussions); **geschäftliche ~** business conference; **kritische ~** critique; **zwanglose ~** informal meeting; **zwischenstaatliche ~en** intergovernmental consultations;
~ unter vier Augen private conversation; **~ mit einem Anwalt** consultation of (briefing) a lawyer; **~ auf höchster Ebene** top-level conference; **~en auf höherer Ebene** high-level talks;
~ abhalten to hold (have) a conference; **~ der Wahlliste abhalten** to caucus; **politische ~en wieder aufnehmen** to resume political talks; **gute ~en bekommen** to have a good press; **schlechte ~en bekommen** to receive unfavo(u)rable criticism; **~ einberufen** to convene (convoke) a conference; **~en über Filme schreiben** to write reviews about films; **in einer ~ sein, an einer ~ teilnehmen** to sit (be) in a conference, to attend a meeting.
Besprechungs|exemplar press (review) copy; **~gebühr** *(Anwalt)* lawyer's fee; **~programm** agenda; **~teilnehmer** conferee *(US)*, conference member; **~zimmer** conference (briefing) room, *(Hotel)* commercial room; **reserviertes ~zimmer** *(Hotel)* private room.
bespritzt sein, von oben bis unten to be all in a muck.
besprochen werden müssen to be a matter of arrangement.
Besser, j. eines ~en belehren to disabuse s. o., to teach s. o. better; **eines ~en belehrt** undeceived; **sich eines ~en besinnen** to think better of it.
besser, erheblich a long sight better; **viel ~ in der Qualität** far superior in quality;
~ gehen to be improving; **es früher ~ gehabt haben** to have seen better days; **in jeder Hinsicht ~ dran sein** to have it all over; **sich ~ stehen** to be better off (better fixed financially); **~ verdienen** to earn more money; **~ werden** to change for better, to improve; **alles ~ wissen wollen** to be a know-all;
~er Artikel superior article; **aus ~er Familie kommen** to come from a respectable family; **~e Gegend** genteel neighbo(u)rhood; **meine ~e Hälfte** my better half; **~er Herr** gentleman, a toff *(fam.)*; **~es Hotel** better-class hotel; **~e Lebensbedingungen für die Armen herbeiführen** to improve the conditions of the poor; **~e Tage gesehen haben** to come down in the world; **wider ~es Wissen** against one's better judgment.
bessergestellt better off;
finanziell ~ sein to be better fixed financially;
~e Leute well-to-do people.
bessern to better, *(Landwirtschaft)* to meliorate;
sich ~ to improve, to take a turn for the better, to mend one's way, *(Kurse)* to improve, to make improvements, to rise, to advance, to go up, to gain;
die Geschäfte ~ sich things are improving (looking up); **die Preise ~ sich** prices are going up (rising, advancing).
Besserstellung, gesellschaftliche improvement in one's social conditions; **soziale ~** social improvement.
Besserung *(Konjunktur)* economic recovery, upturn, improvement, *(Krankheit)* mend, recovery, *(Kurse)* rise, advance, improvement, recovery, *(Landwirtschaft)* melioration, *(Strafe)* correction;
auf dem Wege zur ~ on the mend, improving;
deutliche (sichtliche) ~ pronounced (marked) improvement; **echte ~** *(Patient)* undoubted improvement; **leichte ~** moderate rise; **merkliche ~** marked improvement;
~ auf der gesamten Linie allround improvements; **~ im Pfundkurs** improvement in sterling exchange;
leichte ~ aufweisen to show signs of improvement; **nur geringe Hoffnung für eine ~ hegen** to hold little hope for recovery; **auf dem Wege der ~ sein** to be on the mend (way to recovery); **~ zeigen** to show signs of improvement; **weiterhin ~ zeigen** to continue to show improvement.
Besserungsanstalt reformatory [school], detention house, house of correction *(US)*, correctional institution, penitentiary *(Br.)*, approved school *(Br.)*, Borstal *(Br.)*, reform school *(US)*, industrial reformatory *(US)*, bridewell.
besserungsfähig improvable, *(Forderung)* reclaimable.
Besserungs|maßnahmen correction *(US)*; **~mittel** corrective.
Besserungsschein income and adjustment bond, debtor warrant; **~inhaber** income [bond]holder.
Besserungs|tendenz, leichte ~tendenz erkennen lassen to show a dash (signs) of improvement; **förmliches ~versprechen** *(Kartellrecht)* stipulation *(US)*.
Besserverdienende, zu den ~n zählen to be higher up in the income brackets.
Besser|wisser wiseacre, wise guy, faultfinder, back-seat driver, know-it-all *(US)*; **~wisserei** faultfinding.
bestallen to appoint, to nominate, to vest.
Bestallender appointer.
Bestallung appointment, nomination, investiture, instal(l)ment, patent;
verfahrenswidrige ~ irregularity of appointment;
~ eines Armenanwalts dock brief; **~ eines Arztes** licence to

practise as a doctor; ~ **als Nachlaßpfleger** letters testamentary; ~ **eines Vertreters** agency appointment; ~ **als Vormund** letters of guardianship.

Bestallungs|behörde appointor; ~**recht** power of appointment, vesting deed, investiture; ~**urkunde** letters patent, instrument (letter) of appointment, vesting deed, *(mil.)* commission; ~**urkunde erhalten** to take out a representation; ~**verfahren** mode of appointment.

Bestand *(Bank)* cash assets, *(Besitz)* possession, holdings, *(Beständigkeit)* permanence, *(Betrag)* amount, balance, *(Bilanz)* inventory, *(Effekten)* holdings, portfolio, *(Fortdauer)* continuance, permanence, *(Geldbeträge)* balance, funds, *(Kasse)* balance (cash) in hand, *(Rest)* remainder, rest, *(Vorräte)* supply, stores, *(Waren)* stock [in hand, inventory, trade, stockpile];

von kurzem ~ short-lived, *(Friede)* of short duration;

effektiver ~ actual amount; **eiserner** ~ base (permanent) stock, *(Geld)* permanent funds, funds on hand, iron ration *(fam.)*, *(mil.)* emergency (iron) ration; **fortdauernder** ~ perpetual succession; **gesamter** ~ total stock on hand; **geschlossener** ~ *(Abschreibungsmethode)* closed-end account; **höchstzulässiger** ~ maximum personal holding; **offener** ~ *(Abschreibungsmethode)* open-end account;

~ **an eigenen Aktien** common shares held in treasury, treasury shares, treasury stock *(US)*; ~ **an Arbeitskräften** manpower resources; ~ **an Aufträgen** orders (total work) on hand; ~ **an Bargeld** cash in hand, cash reserves; ~ **an abgeschlossenen Bausparverträgen** *(Bausparkasse)* business portfolio; ~ **an Devisen** foreign-exchange reserve; ~ **an Diskonten** discount holdings *(US)*, bills discounted; ~ **an Effekten** *(Bilanz)* securities in hand; ~ **an Fabrikaten** parts inventory; ~ **an Fabrikationsteilen** works inventory; ~ **an Fertigwaren** stock of finished goods, finished goods inventory; ~ **abgetretener Forderungen** *(Bilanz)* debts, outstanding receivables *(US)*, accounts discounted *(US)*; ~ **an Geld** cash balance (reserve); ~ **in Halbfabrikanten** *(Bilanz)* work in process inventory *(US)*; ~ **an Handelsbeteiligungen** commercial portfolio; ~ **an Holz** stock of timber; ~ **zum Jahresbeginn** initial inventory; ~ **zum Jahresende** closing inventory (stock); ~ **in der Kasse** cash, till money; ~ **an Lebensversicherungen** life insurance portfolio; ~ **am Monatsanfang** merchandise at the beginning of the month; **höchstzulässiger** ~ **pro Person** maximum personal holding *(Br.)*; ~ **der Staatskasse** treasury cash; ~ **an kampffähigen Truppen** effective strength; ~ **an lebendem Vieh** livestock; ~ **an Wechseln** portfolio of bills, bill holdings; ~ **an Wechseln, Schuldscheinen und Akzepten** *(Bilanz)* notes (bills) receivable *(US)*; ~ **an Wertpapieren** security holdings, investment portfolio; ~ **an eigenen Wertpapieren** treasury securities;

jem. seinen ganzen ~ **abkaufen** to empty s. one's shop; ~ **aufnehmen (feststellen)** to [take] inventory, to take stock; ~ **nicht mehr ergänzen** to withdraw from stock; **zum eisernen** ~ **eines Spielplans gehören** to be one of the stock plays; **keinen** ~ **haben** not to last long; ~ **von 500 Aktien haben** *(Makler)* to be long of 500 shares (stock, *US*); **rechtlichen** ~ **haben** to be valid in law; **von** ~ **sein** to be lasting (enduring); **über den** ~ **verkaufen** *(Börse)* to oversell.

Bestände stocked goods, stock, supply, inventory, holdings;

flottierende ~ float; **schwarze** ~ concealed assets; **unerschöpfliche** ~ inexhaustible supplies; **unsichtbare** ~ invisible supply; **unverkäufliche** ~ dead stock; **valutarische** ~ gold and foreign exchange holdings;

~ **zum Anschaffungs- oder niedrigerem Marktpreis angesetzt** inventories at the lower of cost or market; ~ **einer Bibliothek** holdings of a library; ~ **an Gold und Devisen** gold and foreign exchange holdings; ~ **im Einzug befindlicher Schecks** float of cheques (checks, *US*) in process of collection;

~ **abbauen** to run down stocks, to liquidate an inventory; **alte** ~ **abstoßen** to get rid of old stock; **seine** ~ **auffüllen** to replenish one's (lay in fresh) stock; **erhebliche** ~ **aufkaufen** to lay in stocks pretty heavily; **auf** ~**n festsitzen** to sit on stockpiles; ~ **freisetzen** to stockshed; **gute** ~ **an Wein haben** to have a good stock of wine; ~ **drastisch kürzen** to cut back drastically on stockpile; ~ **lockern** *(Forstwirtschaft)* to thin out; ~ **räumen** to clear shop; ~ **verschleudern** to slaughter stocks; ~ **zusammenlegen** to pool resources.

bestanden covered, *(Ufer)* lined, *(Prüfung)* passed, pass;

nicht ~ **haben** to be posted *(Br.)*.

beständig standing, continuous, permanent, fixed, constant, stationary, durable, firm, *(Börse)* steady, invariable, stable, *(Frieden)* lasting, enduring, eternal, *(zuverlässig)* reliable;

gegen Hitze ~ unaffected by heat;

~ **bleiben** to remain stationary; ~ **schneien** to snow consistently; **in seinen Bemühungen** ~ **sein** to be persevering in one's efforts; ~**er werden** *(Wetter)* to settle down;

~**er Frieden sein** to be a lasting (enduring) peace; **in** ~**er Furcht leben** to be in a permanent state of fear; ~**e Klagen** constant complaints; ~**e Nachfrage** steady demand; ~**es Wetter** stable weather.

Beständigkeit continuance, stability, *(fig.)* consistency, perseverance, *(Börse)* steadiness;

~ **des Wetters** stability of the weather.

Bestands|abbau inventory cut (cut-off); ~**abnahme** stock shrinkage; ~**abschreibung** inventory writedown; **Tempo der** ~**anreicherung erhöhen** to step up stockpiling pace; ~**auffüllung** stock replacement, inventory accumulation (buildup), stockpiling.

Bestandsaufnahme stocktaking, shop check, taking an inventory, inventory [taking], *(Bibliothek)* check;

belegmäßige ~ cost-voucher inventory; **körperliche (tatsächliche)** ~ actual stocktaking, physical inventory; **laufende** ~ book (continuous, perpetual) inventory; **räumliche** ~ regional survey;

~ **machen** to take stock, to [take] inventory, *(Bibliothek)* to check the books; ~ **überwachen** to observe an inventory.

Bestands|beleg stock voucher; ~**bewahrung** holding operation; ~**bewertung** stock evaluation, inventory pricing (valuation); ~**bewertungsmethoden** inventory valuation method; ~**buch** store book, inventory, warehouse book, *(Vieh)* stock book; ~**buchführung** stock accounting; ~**buchhaltung** stock record division; ~**dichte** *(Wald)* drop density; ~**dispositionen** stockpiling behavio(u)r; ~**eingruppierung** inventory classification; ~**fehlbetrag** inventory shortage; ~**finanzierung durch mittel- und langfristige Kredite** inventory loan; ~**freigabe** stockshedding; ~**größe** stock variable; ~**investitionen** inventory investments; ~**karte** stock ledger (record) card; **laufende** ~**kartei** perpetual inventory file *(US)*; ~**konto** asset (inventory, real) account; ~**kontrolle** inventory (stock) control, shop check; ~**liste** inventory, stock sheet; ~**lockerung** *(Forstwirtschaft)* thinning out; ~**masse** *(Forstwirtschaft)* stumpage; ~**meldung** stock report, return; ~**minderung** inventory decrease; ~**nachweis** inventory, stocktaking.

Bestandspolitik stockpiling policy;

vorsichtige ~ **betreiben** to keep down an inventory; ~ **völlig durcheinanderbringen** to knock the inventory picture out of focus.

Bestands|posten inventory item; ~**prüfung** inventory audit (verification); ~**prüfungsbescheinigung** certificate of inventory, inventory certificate; ~**schrumpfung** stock shakeout; ~**schwankungen** inventory fluctuations; ~**überwachung** inventory observation; ~**veränderung** inventory changes, *(Anlagegüter)* change in book value; ~**verlust** inventory shrinkage (loss); ~**vermehrung** increase in stocks; ~**verminderung** inventory reduction; ~**verzeichnis** inventory, inventory list (record, register, schedule); ~**verzeichnis anlegen** to draw up (make) an inventory; ~**wagnis** inventory risk; **verminderte** ~**werte** inventory price decline; ~**zahlen** inventory (stock) figures; ~**zunahme** inventory growth.

Bestandteil part, unit, ingredient, section, constituent, ingredient, *(Gebäude)* component, *(Zubehör)* material;

~e constituent parts, accessories;

elementarer ~ essence; **fakultative** ~**e** nonessentials, nonessential elements; **integrierender** ~ integral part; **konstituierende** ~**e** component parts; **unentbehrlicher** ~ necessary part; **unwesentliche** ~**e** nonessential elements, nonessentials; **verdrahtete** ~**e** *(Datenverarbeitung)* hardware; **wesentlicher** ~ integral (component, essential) part, part and parcel, *(Grundstück)* fixture;

wesentlicher ~ **eines anderen Stücks** part and parcel of another piece; **wesentlicher** ~ **eines Vertrages** integral part of a contract;

wesentlichen ~ **abgeben (bilden)** to be part and parcel of s. th.; ~ **eines Grundstücks bilden** to run with the land; **fester** ~ **werden** to become firmly established, *(Grundstück)* to become a fixture; **in seine** ~**e zerlegen** to unscramble.

bestärken to strengthen, to confirm, to encourage;

j. in seiner Ansicht ~ to strengthen s. one's opinions; **Richtigkeit einer Aussage** ~ to confirm s. one's words; **j. in seinem Vorsatz** ~ to fortify s. o. in a resolution.

bestätigen to confirm, to affirm, to vouch, to verify, to endorse, to countersign, *(bezeugen)* to warrant, to assure, *(genehmigen)* to approve, to ratify, to sanction, *(legalisieren)* to validate, to legalize, to homologate;

sich ~ to prove to be true (correct); **sich nicht** ~ to prove false; **amtlich** ~ to attest, to certify, to authenticate; **Auftrag** ~ to confirm an order; **jds. Aussage** ~ to corroborate s. one's statement; **Behauptung** ~ to bear out an assertion (a statement); **Bericht** ~ to verify (confirm) a report; **telefonische Bestellung** ~ to confirm a telephone order; **brieflich** ~ to confirm by letter (in writing); **Echtheit eines Manuskripts** ~ to authenticate a manuscript; **eidlich** ~ to verify [by oath] *(US)*; **jds. Eigentumsanspruch** ~ to confirm s. o. in a title; **Eingang eines Schreibens** ~ to acknowledge receipt of a letter; **Empfang** ~ to [acknowledge] receipt; **Entscheidung** ~ to uphold a decision; **Ernennung** ~ to approve [of] an appointment, to ratify a nomination; **Ernennung eines Gouverneurs** ~ to ratify a governor's nomination; **Gerücht** ~ to confirm a rumo(u)r; **Gültigkeit eines Testaments** ~ **lassen** to prove a will; **Identität** ~ to identify; **nicht** ~ to disaffirm; **notariell** ~ to notarize, to take acknowledgement of a deed, to acknowledge *(US)*; **Richtigkeit eines Kontoauszuges** ~ to verify an account; **bisherigen Schatzmeister** ~ to reappoint the retiring treasurer; **Scheck** ~ to confirm a cheque *(Br.)*, to certify a check *(US)*; **schriftliche** ~ to confirm (admit) in writing; **Testament** ~ to probate a will; **Übereinkommen** ~ to confirm an agreement; **telefonische Übermittlung brieflich** ~ to confirm a telephone message by letter; **Urteil** ~ to sustain (uphold) a judgment; **jds. Verdacht** ~ to confirm (verify) a suspicion; **Vertrag** ~ to ratify a contract; **vollinhaltlich** ~ to confirm full contents; **Wahlergebnis** ~ to validate an election; **Zeugenaussage** ~ to corrobate a witness.

bestätigend affirmative, confirmative, confirming;
~**er Beweis** corroborating evidence.

bestätigt confirmed, *(Vertrag)* ratified, sanctioned;
unterschriftlich ~ witness our hands;
erneut im Amt ~ **werden** to be continued in office;
unwiderruflich gültiges und ~**es Akkreditiv** irrevocable and confirmed letter of credit; ~**er Kredit** confirmed credit; **nicht** ~**e Nachrichten** unconfirmed reports (news); ~**er Scheck** marked cheque *(Br.)*, certified check *(US)*;
hiermit wird ~ this is to certify.

Bestätigung affirmation, certification, confirmation, endorsement, indorsement, establishment, affirmance, vouch, *(Bescheinigung)* certificate, *(Beurkundung)* legalization, witnessing, fiat, authorization, *(Genehmigung)* approval, ratification, sanction, *(Identität)* identification, *(Zeugenaussage)* corroboration;
gültig nur bei ~ subject to confirmation; **in** ~ **unseres Gesprächs** in confirmation of our conversation; **um** ~ **des Empfangs wird gebeten** please acknowledge receipt;
amtliche ~ attestation, certification, official indorsement; **eidliche** ~ confirmation by oath, verification *(US)*; **erneute** ~ reassurance, reinsurance; **feierliche** ~ ritual acknowledgement; **gerichtliche** ~ homologation, confirmation by a court of justice; **schriftliche** ~ confirmation in writing, written consent; **vorbehaltlose** ~ *(Prüfer)* positive confirmation; **Wort-für-Wort** ~ *(Telegramm)* verbatim confirmation;
~ **eines fernmündlichen gemachten Angebots** confirmation of a telephone offer; ~ **einer Anstellung** confirmation of an appointment; ~ **eines Auftrags** confirmation (acknowledgement) of an order, *(Spediteur)* confirmatory order; ~ **einer Aussage** corroboration of a statement; ~ **durch den Aussteller** drawer's verification; ~ **eines Bankauszugs** bank confirmation; ~ **eines Briefeinganges** acknowledgement of receipt of a letter; ~ **des Empfangs** acknowledgement, receipt; ~ **einer Ernennung** approval of a nomination; ~ **eines Gerüchtes** confirmation of a rumo(u)r; ~ **eines Kontoauszuges** verification of an account, confirmation of balance, bank confirmation; ~ **einer Konzession** confirmation of a grant; ~ **von Nachrichten** confirmation of news; ~ **durch die Öffentlichkeit** public sanction; ~ **der Reservierung** confirmation of a booking; ~ **der Richtigkeit** *(Prüfer)* verification; ~ **auf der Rückseite** endorsement; ~ **eines ungedeckten Schecks** marking *(Br.)*, overcertification *(US)*; ~ **eines Testaments** probate, proof of a will; ~ **eines ausländischen Testaments** ancillary grant *(Br.)*; ~ **eines Testamentsvollstreckers** confirmation of an executor; ~ **eines Vergleichs** confirmation of an arrangement; ~ **eines Wahlergebnisses** validation of an election; ~ **des Wareneingangs** delivery verification; ~ **einer Zeugenaussage** corroboration of a witness;
um ~ **des Empfangs wird gebeten** please acknowledge receipt; **von jds.** ~ **abhängen** to be subject to s. one's approval; ~ **finden** *(Gerücht)* to be confirmed, to prove true (correct); **offizielle** ~ **einer Meldung veröffentlichen** to publish an official confirmation of a report.

Bestätigungsbrief letter of acknowledgement, letter confirming an acceptance.

bestätigungsfähig confirmable, affirmable.

Bestätigungs|formular confirmation blank; ~**recht** power of appointment; ~**schreiben** confirmatory letter, confirmation [note], *(dipl.)* letter of credence; ~**siegel** seal of approval; ~**urkunde** confirmation [contract].

Bestätigungsvermerk notice of confirmation, *(Scheck)* certification, certifying of a check *(US)*, marking of a cheque *(Br.)*, *(Wirtschaftsprüfer)* audit (auditor's) certificate;
eingeschränkter ~ audit qualifications, negative confirmation, qualified certificate; **vorbehaltsloser** ~ positive confirmation;
~ **erteilen** *(Buchprüfer)* to certify a financial statement, to verify the accuracy of a balance sheet; ~ **verweigern** to refuse to certify a financial statement.

bestatten to bury, to inter;
auf dem Friedhof in A ~ to lay to rest in the cemetery at A; **auf hoher See** ~ to bury at sea.

Bestattung burial, funeral, interment, *(durch Verbrennung)* cremation;
feierliche ~ obsequies;
~ **auf hoher See** burial at sea.

Bestattungs|anstalt undertakers, funeral parlor *(US)*; ~**feierlichkeiten** funeral ceremonies, obsequies; ~**gebräuche** mortuary rites, sepulchral customs; ~**gebühren**, ~**kosten** funeral expenses (costs); ~**institut** undertakers, funeral home (parlor, *US*); ~**ort** resting (burial) place; ~**unternehmer** undertaker, funeral director *(US)*; ~**urkunde** warrant; ~**vorkehrungen** funeral arrangements.

Bestauftrag order at best, market order.

Beste, das plum, the pick, flower;
zu jds. ~**m bestimmt** designed for s. one's good;
das allgemeine ~ the common interest; **das** ~ **vom** ~**n** the pick of the basket (bunch); **der erste** ~ the next man;
sich das ~ **aussuchen** to take a fall out of s. th. *(US coll.)*; **sich als das** ~ **erweisen** to turn up trumps *(coll.)*; **j. zum** ~**n haben (halten)** to make (poke) fun at s. o., to have s. o. on, to play with (upon) s. o.; **das** ~ **herausholen (aus einer Sache machen)** to make the best of it, to get a fall out of s. th. *(US)*, to make the best of a bad business, to put a good face on; **sein** ~**s tun** to try one's best; ~**r werden** to come out top.

bestechen to bribe, to practise bribery, to corrupt, to gratify, to buy over, to graft *(US)*, to oil (grease) s. one's palm *(Br.)*, to smear *(sl.)*, to prime *(sl.)*, *(faszinieren)* to fascinate, to charm, to captivate;
j. ~ to get at s. o., to piece s. o. off *(sl.)*; **Beamten** ~ to bribe an official; **durch schlichte Eleganz** ~ to fascinate by virtue of simple elegance; **durch seine Liebenswürdigkeit** ~ to captivate with one's charm; **Zeugen** ~ to suborn (bribe) a witness;
sich ~ **lassen** to receive (take, accept) a bribe; **sich durch jds. Benehmen** ~ **lassen** to fall a victim to s. one's charm; **sich von beiden Seiten** ~ **lassen** to whipsaw; **sich nicht durch schöne Worte** ~ **lassen** not to be taken in by fine words.

bestechend captivating, charming, fascinating;
seine Gründe ~ **darlegen** to present one's reasons persuasively;
~**es Angebot** tempting offer; ~**e Leistung** brilliant performance; ~**e Liebenswürdigkeit** captivating charm; ~**e Manieren** engaging manner; ~**e Theorie** attractive theory.

Bestecher bribegiver, briber.

bestechlich corruptible, trading, open (accessible) to bribery, bribable, venal;
~ **sein** to have one's price;
~**e Presse** corrupt press; ~**e Staatsbeamte** corruptible government officials.

Bestechlichkeit corrupt practices, corruptibility, corruption, venality, gravy *(sl.)*, pie *(US sl.)*;
allgemeine ~ general corruption.

Bestechung bribe, bribery, subornation, corruption, corrupt practices, gratification, graft *(US)*, payoff *(sl.)*, palm greasing *(Br.)*, fix *(sl.)*;
der ~ **zugänglich** corruptible, open to bribery, bribable;
aktive ~ bribery, offering a bribe; **passive** ~ bribetaking, receiving a bribe, extortion; **schamlose** ~ unblushing corruption; **versuchte** ~ offering of bribes;
~ **durch die Geschäftswelt** *(Wirtschaft)* business (corporate) bribery; ~ **von Geschworenen** jury tampering, embracery; ~ **eines Zeugen** subornation (corruption) of (bribing) a witness;
~ **annehmen** to take a bribe; **j. durch** ~ **zum Schweigen bringen** to bribe s. o. to silence; **durch** ~ **gewinnen** to subsidize; **gegen** ~ **gefeit sein** to be proof against corruption; **wegen** ~ **zu einer Gefängnisstrafe verurteilen** to jail on a corruption charge.

Bestechungs|enthüllungen bribery revelations; ~**fonds** bribery (slush, *US*) fund; ~**geld** bribe, golden (silver) key, boodle, graft, sook *(US sl.)*, sweetener, baksheesh *(US)*, price, protection (hush) money, soap *(sl.)*, payola *(sl.)*, *(Schweigegeld)* slush fund *(US)*, hush money, palm oil (grease) *(Br.)*; **an die Polizei gezahltes ~geld** protection *(sl.)*; ~**gelder annehmen** to take bribes; **sich durch Annahme von ~geldern korrumpieren lassen** to lower o. s. by taking bribes; ~**geschenk** bribe, manche-present; ~**manöver,** ~**methode** handing out of bribes, corrupt practices, practice of bribery; ~**skandal** bribery (payoff, graft) scandal; ~**summe** price; ~**unwesen** bribery and corruption; ~**versuch** attempted bribery, embracery, attempt to bribe, offering of bribes; **wegen ~versuchs angeklagt sein** to be accused of attempted bribery.

Besteck plate, set, tableware, *(Schiff)* deal, reckoning, position; **ärztliches ~** surgical instruments; **gegißtes ~** dead reckoning; **silbernes ~** plate *(Br.)*;
drei ~e auflegen to lay the table for three; **komplettes silbernes ~ besitzen** to own a complete set of silver cutlery; **~ nehmen** to work out the ship's reckoning; **mit dem ~ voraus sein** to be ahead of one's reckoning;
~**aufnahme** working out of a reckoning, fix; ~**kasten** plate basket; ~**kommode** cutlery cabinet; ~**korb** plate basket *(Br.)*; ~**rechnung** dead reckoning.

Bestehen existence, *(Forderung)* insistence, persistence, *(Jubiläum)* anniversary;
nach ~ einer Prüfung having passed an examination; **seit ~ der Firma** since the firm was founded;
~ eines Examens (einer Prüfung) getting through (passing) an examination; **hartnäckiges ~ auf einem Punkt** pressing of one's point; **~ eines Rechtes** existence of a right;
50jähriges ~ feiern to celebrate its fiftieth anniversary; **hundertjähriges ~ feiern** to celebrate its centenary.

bestehen to exist, to be (have been) in existence, to last, *(Gültigkeit haben)* to be in force, to operate, *(Krise)* to weather, *(Prüfung)* to pass, to come (get) through, *(verlangen)* to insist, to persist;
auf etw. ~ to make a point of it, to insist on s. th.; **aus etw. ~** to be composed of, to consist of; **viele Abenteuer ~** to encounter many adventures; **im wesentlichem aus Aktien ~** *(Vermögen)* to consist mainly of shares; **auf einer sofortigen Antwort ~** to press for an immediate reply; **auf Bedingungen ~** to insist on conditions; **Bewährungsprobe ~** to stand (pass) the test, to go through times of trial; **auf Bezahlung ~** to press for payment; **Examen ~** to pass an examination, to get through; **auf seiner Forderung ~** to stand out for one's claims; **in einer Gefahr ~** to prove o. s. in a danger, to hold one's ground; **gerade noch ~** to get a bare pass; **hartnäckig darauf ~** to urge, to persist; **harten Kampf zu ~ haben** to have a hard battle to fight; **vor der Konkurrenz ~** to hold one's own in competitive markets; **vor jds. Kritik ~** to face s. one's criticism; **auf höheren Löhnen ~** to stand for more wages; **hartnäckig auf einer Lüge ~** to stick to a lie; **auf seiner Meinung ~** to stick to one's guns; **aus fünf Mitgliedern ~** to be composed of five members; **nebeneinander ~** to coexist; **noch ~** to subsist; **Prüfung ~** to pass an examination, to get through; **mündliche Prüfung ~** to pass the oral; **Prüfung mit Auszeichnung ~** to pass an examination with hono(u)rs; **Prüfung nicht ~** to fail in (flunk, *US*) an examination; **auf einem Punkt ~** to insist on a point; **zu Recht ~** to be justified; **auf seinen Rechten ~** to insist on one's rights; **ganz aus Rosenholz ~** to be made entirely of rosewood; **auf einer Sache ~** to be insistent on s. th.; **aus vielen Teilen ~** to be composed of many parts; **auf seiner Unschuld ~** to plead not guilty; **weiter ~** *(Firma)* to remain in existence; **auf Zahlung ~** to insist on payment;
zu ~ aufhören *(Firma)* to cease to exist.

bestehenbleiben *(Abmachung)* to hold good, to continue to exist, to remain in existence, *(Einspruch)* to hold, to stand;
auf einer Forderung ~ to persist in a demand, to keep up a claim.

bestehend existing, ruling;
seit langem ~ of long standing, old; **noch ~** still extant;
aus Wald und Weideland ~er Besitz estate composed of wood and meadow land; **aus einem Haus ~e Erbschaft** inheritance consisting of a house; **~es Gesetz** law in force; **bei den ~en Preisen** at current prices.

bestehlen, j. to steal from s. o., to rob (strip, relieve) s. o.

besteigen, Berg to climb (ascend) a mountain; **Fahrrad ~** to get on a bicycle; **Flugzeug ~** to enter (board) a plane; **Schaffot ~** to mount the scaffold; **Thron ~** to ascend (succeed to) the throne; **Zug ~** to board a train.

Besteigung des Throns accession to the throne.

Bestell|abschnitt order coupon; ~**abteilung** ordering department; ~**aufnahmeformular** order-acceptance form.

bestellbar deliverable, *(Feld)* tillable, cultivable, arable, *(Platz)* bookable, reservable *(US)*.

Bestell|bezirk postal district; ~**buch** book of commission, commission (order) book; ~**buchblatt** order-book sheet; ~**datum** date of order; ~**dienst** order service; ~**eingang** incoming (influx of) orders.

bestellen to [give an] order, to commission, to command, *(Botengänge erledigen)* to do errands (commissions), *(ernennen)* to appoint, to constitute, *(heranholen)* to send for, *(Hotelzimmer)* to book, to reserve *(US)*, to ask for a reservation, *(im Restaurant)* to order;
bei jem. etw. ~ to place an order with s. o., to order s. th. from s. o., to indent upon s. o. for s. th.; **j. [zu sich] ~** to ask s. o. to come, to send for (summon) s. o.; **jem. etw. ~** to deliver a message to s. o.; **jem. etw. ~ lassen** to have a message delivered to s. o.;
Anwalt ~ to engage the services of a lawyer, to brief (retain) a lawyer; **Artikel bei einer Firma ~** to place an order with a firm; **Aufgebot ~** to publish (put up) the banns; **j. zu seinem Bevollmächtigten ~** to give s. o. power of attorney; **seinen Boden im Rahmen einer ordnungsgemäßen Bewirtschaftung ~** to cultivate one's land in a good and husbandlike manner; **Briefe ~** to deliver letters; **j. zu seinem Erben ~** to appoint s. o. one's heir; **Fahrkarte ~** to order tickets, to book (reserve) seats; **Feld ~** to cultivate, to till; **Flasche Wein ~** to ask for (order) a bottle of wine; **Flugkarte ~** to book a flight; **schöne Grüße ~** to send one's kindest regards; **sein Haus ~** to put one's house in order; **Hypothek ~** to create a mortgage; **mündlich ~** to order orally; **laut Muster ~** to order goods from sample; **Pfand ~** to give a pawn; **Plätze ~** to book (engage, secure) seats; **Post ~** to deliver the mail; **j. in ein Restaurant ~** to ask s. o. to meet one in a restaurant; **j. zum Richter ~** to make s. o. a judge; **schriftlich ~** to write for; **Sicherheiten ~** to surrender (register) securities; **sofort ~** to place an order at once; **Taxi ~** to order (call) a taxi; **telefonisch ~** to order, to book by telephone; **telegrafisch ~** to order by cable; **Theaterplätze ~** to book seats for the theater; **Treuhänder ~** to appoint a custodian; **Verteidiger für den Angeklagten ~** *(Gericht)* to assign a counsel for the defendant; **j. zu seinem Vertreter ~** to appoint s. o. one's proxy; **im voraus ~** to book in advance (beforehand); **zum Vormund ~** to appoint a guardian; **Vorräte ~** to order in supplies; **unter Vorzugsbedingungen ~** to order on preferential terms; **Wagen für 9 Uhr ~** to order the car for nine o'clock; **Waren ~** to order goods, to put goods on order; **Zeitung ~** to subscribe (take in, *Br.*) a paper; **Zimmer [im voraus] ~** to book (reserve, *US*) a room.

Besteller orderer, committer, *(Käufer)* purchaser, buyer, *(Kunde)* client, customer, *(Zeitung)* subscriber.

Bestell|formular order form (sheet, slip), subscription, *(Einkäufer)* purchase order form; **genormtes ~formular** standard return form; ~**gang** errand, commission, *(Postbote)* circuit, postman's round *(Br.)*; ~**gebühr,** ~**geld** commission money, messenger's fee, *(Zeitung)* charge for delivery, delivery charge; ~**hinweise** ordering references; ~**index** index of orders booked; ~**karte** order card (form), want list *(US)*, *(Werbung)* return card; ~**kartei** order-card index; ~**kupon** reply coupon; ~**liste** docket *(Br.)*, order form (book), want list *(US)*, *(Bibliothek)* call slip *(US)*; ~**nummer** order (purchase, requisition, supply) number, *(Buch)* standard book number; ~**schein** order form (sheet, blank, *US*), subscription form, docket *(Br.)*, want slip *(US)*, *(Bibliothek)* call slip *(US)*; ~**zettel** order blank *(US)* (sheet, form).

bestellt on order, ordered, *(Einzelanfertigung)* made to order, custom *(US)*, *(Platz, Zimmer)* booked, reserved *(US)*;
~ und nicht abgeholt all dressed up and nowhere to go *(fam.)*; **ordnungsgemäß ~** duly appointed (designated); **nicht im voraus ~** unreserved;
sich etw. Kleines ~ haben to be in the family way; **~ sein** to have an (be here on) appointment, *(in Auftrag gegeben)* to be on order; **nicht gut um j. ~ sein** to be badly off;
schlecht ~er Acker badly cultivated field; **~e Felder** fields under cultivation; **schlecht ~e Felder** badly cultivated fields; **~e Waren** goods ordered;
es ist nicht gut um sein Geschäft ~ his business is in a bad way.

Bestellübermittlung, elektronische electronic order transmission.

Bestellung [purchase] order, ordering, commission, charge, line, *(Ernennung)* appointment, nomination, *(Feld)* tillage, cultivation, culture, *(Hotelzimmer)* booking, reservation *(US)*,

(Nachricht) message, *(Post)* postal delivery, *(Wertpapiere)* application, *(Zeitung)* subscription, subscription order, taking in *(Br.)*;
auf ~ to (on, against) order, as ordered, at command; **auf ~ angefertigt** turned out (made) to order, custom *(US)*, custom-made (built, *US*); **bei** ~ when ordering, on placing the order; **bis auf weitere** ~ until further notice (cancel(l)ed); **gegen ~ erhältlich** obtainable on order; **gemäß Ihrer** ~ according to your order; **laut** ~ as ordered, per order;
mündliche aufgegebene ~ verbal order; **telefonisch aufgegebene** ~ telephone order; **nicht ausgeführte ~en** unfilled orders; **bedeutende ~en** considerable orders; **dringende** ~ rush order; **feste** ~ firm order; **laufende** ~ standing order; **mündliche** ~ oral order; **neue** ~ repeat [order]; **schriftliche** ~ written order; **telegrafische** ~ cable order; **terminierte ~en** time ordering; **verbindliche** ~ binding order; **zusätzliche** ~ additional order; **~en auf Abruf** off-the-shelf order; ~ **eines Anwalts** briefing (retaining) a lawyer; ~ **eines Armenanwalts** dock brief; ~ **eines Bevollmächtigten** appointment of a proxy; ~ **zum Botschafter** ambassadorial appointment; ~ **von Briefen** delivery of letters; ~ **durch das Gericht** appointment by the court; ~ **einer Hypothek** creation of a mortgage contract; ~ **eines Konkursverwalters** appointment of a receiver; ~ **zur Lagerauffüllung** fill-in reorder; ~ **eines Nachlaßverwalters** letters testamentary; ~ **von Plätzen** booking of seats; ~ **der Revisoren** appointment of auditors; ~ **von Sicherheiten** surrender (registration) of securities; ~ **eines Treuhänders** appointment of a custodian; ~ **weiterer Treuhänder** assumption of new trustees; ~ **aus Übersee** overseas orders; ~ **im Verkaufsraum** ordering in salesroom; ~ **eines Verteidigers** assignment of a counsel; ~ **eines Vertreters** appointment of an agent, agency appointment; ~ **eines Vormunds** appointment of a guardian; ~ **zum Vorstandsmitglied** appointment as manager; ~ **ablehnen** to refuse (decline) an order; **auf ~ anfertigen** to make to order, to custom-build *(US)*, to customize *(US)*; ~ **annehmen** to take (book, accept) an order; ~ **annullieren** to cancel an order; **auf ~ arbeiten** to work to order; ~ **aufgeben** to [place an] order; ~ **auf Waren aufgeben** to put goods on order; ~ **aufnehmen** to book an order; ~ **ausführen** to deal with an order; **jem. eine ~ ausrichten** to deliver a message to s. o.; ~ **bearbeiten** to process an order; ~ **als vordringlich behandeln** to deal with an order as one of special urgency; ~ **schriftlich bestätigen** to confirm an order in writing; **Annahme einer ~ bestätigen** to acknowledge an order; **um ~ bitten** to send for orders; ~ **buchen** to book an order; **~en einholen** to call for orders; ~ **auf etw. erhalten** to take (be favo(u)red with) an order for s. th.; ~ **erneuern** to repeat an order; **viele ~en aufzugeben haben** to send away for many things; ~ **machen** to give (place) an order, *(Botengang)* to discharge an errand; ~ **rückgängig machen (stornieren)** to cancel an order; ~ **vorziehen** to give priority to an order, to predate an order; ~ **widerrufen** to countermand an order; ~ **eines Geschäftsführers widerrufen** to remove a manager.
Bestellungs|termin purchase date; **~zeiten** times of delivery.
Bestellzettel order form (sheet, slip, blank, *US*), requisition form *(Br.)*, *(Bibliothek)* call slip *(US)*.
bestens *(Börse)* at best, at the best price (figure), at the market *(US)*, *(Deviseneinkauf)* at the best possible rate, *(beim Kauf)* at the best possible bid, *(beim Verkauf)* at the best possible offer;
Auftrag ~ ausführen to execute an order at best.
Besten|auftrag, ~order order at best, market order *(US)*, *(bei Erreichen eines bestimmten Kurses wirksam)* stop [loss] order.
besteuerbar taxable, liable to taxation, chargeable, assessable, *(Gemeinde)* ratable.
Besteuerbarkeit taxableness, taxability.
besteuern to tax, to subject to taxes, to burden with taxes, to impose (levy) a tax on, to assess, *(Gemeinde)* to rate *(Br.)*, *(Verbrauchssteuer)* to excise, *(Zoll)* to impose duty on;
etw. ~ to put a tax on s. th.; **Einkommen an der Quelle** ~ to tax revenue at the source, to charge duty; **einkommensmäßig** ~ to levy by direct assessment; **im Ausland erzielte Einkünfte** ~ to tax foreign earnings; **geringer** ~ to reduce a tax; **Geschenke bis zwei Jahre vom Tode des Schenkers degressiv** ~ to levy tax on a declining scale on gifts made within two years of death; **Grundbesitz** ~ to levy on land; **zu hoch** ~ to overtax, to overrate; **indirekt** ~ to excise; **kräftig** ~ to rate heavily; **Luxusgüter** ~ to tax luxuries; **die Reichen kräftig** ~ to soak the rich; **übermäßig** ~ to grind down with taxes.
besteuert state-taxed, tax-burdened;
falsch ~ fortaxed; **hoch** ~ heavily taxed; **nicht** ~ untaxed, unlevied; **übermäßig** ~ ground down by taxation; ~ **sein (werden)** to be taxed; **mit Ausnahmesätzen ~ werden** to be subject to special income-tax rules; **als normales Einkommen ~ werden** to be taxable as ordinary income; **zum Grundtarif ~ werden** to suffer tax at the basic rate; **höher ~ werden** to be liable to a tax at a higher rate; **im unteren Proportionalbereich ~ werden** to be subject to the basic rate of personal income tax; **schwer ~ werden** to be heavily taxed.
Besteuerter taxpayer, assessed [person], *(Gemeinde)* ratepayer *(Br.)*.
Besteuerung taxation, tax, imposition of taxes, assessment, fiscalization, *(fam.)* Irish dividend, *(Gemeinde)* rating *(Br.)*;
von der ~ ausgenommen tax-exempt; **der ~ unterliegend** chargeable, taxable, ratable;
abgestufte ~ graduated taxation; **anteilsmäßige** ~ proportional taxation; **degressive** ~ graduated taxation; **direkte** ~ direct taxation; **einheitliche** ~ equal and uniform (uniformity) in taxation; **erträgliche** ~ reasonable taxation; **gegenseitige** ~ mutual taxation; **geringe** ~ light taxation; **gestaffelte** ~ graduated taxation; **gleichmäßige** ~ uniform[ity] taxation; **hohe** ~ harsh (heavy) taxation; **indirekte** ~ indirect taxation; **kommunale** ~ rating *(Br.)*; **konfiskatorische** ~ confiscatory taxation; **maßvolle** ~ commensurate taxation; **mehrfache** ~ multiple taxation; **pauschale** ~ flat-rate taxation; **progressive** ~ progressive taxation; **regressive** ~ regressive taxation; **rückbezügliche** ~ retroactive taxation; **übermäßige (übersetzte)** ~ excessive taxation, overtaxation; **unterschiedliche** ~ discriminatory taxation; **zusätzliche** ~ supplementary taxation;
~ **des Nutzungswertes des eigengenutzten Einfamilienhauses** landlord's property tax *(Br.)*; **beschränkte ~ ins Inland überwiesener Einkünfte** remittance basis *(Br.)*; ~ **von Körperschaften** corporate taxation *(Br.)*; ~ **einer Person** tax on s. o.; ~ **im unteren Proportionalbereich** marginal taxation, threshold tariff; ~ **an der Quelle** taxation at the source; ~ **von Veräußerungsgewinnen** capital-gain assessment; ~ **großer Vermögen** wealth tax; **verschärfte ~ größerer Vermögen** conscription of wealth;
für die ~ in Frage kommen to reach the taxable level; **der ~ unterliegen** to be taxable (ratable, *Br.*); **einer ~ unterwerfen** to levy (impose) a tax on; **größeren Teil des Erwerbseinkommens der normalen ~ unterwerfen** to shove more of the earned income into ordinary tax brackets.
Besteuerungs|art kind of taxation; **~befugnisse** revenue-raising powers; **~bestimmungen** taxing provisions.
besteuerungsfähig taxable, liable to be taxed, assessable, *(Gemeinde)* ratable *(Br.)*;
nicht ~ untaxable, unassessable, unratable *(Br.)*.
Besteuerungs|fähigkeit taxable capacity, taxability, taxableness; **~freigrenze** exemption; **~gebiet** area taxation; **~grenze** margin of taxation, tax limit; **aus ~gründen** for the purpose of taxation; **~grundlage** basis for apportionment (of taxation), tax base; **bereinigte ~grundlage** adjusted basis of taxation; **~prinzipien** canons of taxation; **~recht** taxing (taxation) power, power to tax; **kommunales ~recht** local tax power *(US)*, rating authority *(Br.)*; **~rechtsüberschneidung** overlap of taxing authority; **~satz** tax rate; **~system** taxation system; **~unterlagen** books of a tax receiver, tax digest; **~vollmachten** taxation powers; **~voraussetzungen schaffen** to bring within the orbit of taxation; **~vorschriften** tax regulations; **~verfahren** method of taxation; **~zeitraum** assessment (taxable) period; **~zweck** aims of taxation.
Bestfall optimum;
im ~ at best.
Bestform top condition.
bestgehend best selling.
bestgekleideter Mann best turned-out man.
bestialisch beastly, brutal, atrocious.
Bestialität brutality, atrocity.
Bestie in Menschengestalt beast of a fellow.
Bestsellerliste *(Buchhandel)* top-rating list.
bestimmen *(anordnen)* to direct, to order, to ordain, to rule, to will, *(ausbedingen)* to stipulate, *(ausersehen)* to mark, to select, *(bestellen)* to appoint, *(definieren)* to define, *(entscheiden)* to determine, to decide, to will, *(festlegen)* to ascertain, *(festsetzen)* to fix, to state, *(Gesetz)* to lay down, to destine, to say, to provide, *(Testament)* to direct, to dispose by will, *(veranlassen)* to dispose, to induce, *(vorsehen)* to provide, to designate, to name, to earmark, to schedule *(US)*, *(zuweisen)* to allocate, to assign, to appropriate, to set apart;
Bedingungen ~ to lay down conditions; **genaues Datum** ~ to fix a precise date; **j. zu seinem Erben** ~ to designate (appoint, *US*)

s. o. as one's heir; **Erbfolge** ~ to settle the succession; **Geldbeträge für einen Zweck** ~ to earmark funds for a purpose; **genauer** ~ to define more closely; **Güter für den Export** ~ to earmark goods for export; **j. zu einer strafbaren Handlung** ~ to move s. o. to commit an offence; **seinen Sohn zum Juristen** ~ to intend (design) one's son for the bar (legal profession); **jds. Laufbahn entscheidend** ~ to be decisive for s. one's career; **j. zu seinem Nachfolger** ~ to designate s. o. as (for) one's successor; **für Notfälle** ~ to provide for an eventuality; **Plätze für Ehrengäste** ~ to reserve seats for guests of hono(u)r; **Politik eines Landes** ~ to control the policy of a country; **Preis** ~ to fix (state) a price; **chemische Reaktionen** ~ to govern chemical reactions; **Schaden** ~ to assess damage; **jds. Schicksal** ~ to decide s. one's fate; **Schiffsort** ~ to fix the position of a ship; **Sitzungstermin** ~ to settle a day for a meeting; **Termin** ~ to decide upon a day, to fix a date; **in seinem Testament** ~ to provide in one's will; **Treffpunkt** ~ to determine a meeting place; **jds. Urteil** ~ to guide s. one's judgment; **sein ganzes Vermögen für wohltätige Zwecke** ~ to leave all one's money to (dispose of one's fortune in) charity; **zu seinem Vertreter** ~ to make s. o. one's deputy; **Volumen** ~ to work out the volume; **400 Millionen DM für den Wohnungsbau** ~ to allocate (appropriate) DM 400 millions for housing; **über seine Zeit frei** ~ to be master of one's time, to dispose of one's time at leisure; **für einen Zweck** ~ to design for a purpose;
j. dazu ~ seine Meinung zu ändern to induce s. o. to change his mind; **nichts zu ~ haben** to have no say; **über j. nicht ~ können** not to be able to anticipate s. one's wishes; **frei über etw. ~ können** to be entirely at s. one's disposal; **in einer Angelegenheit nicht ~ können** to have no voice in a matter; **über ein Vermögen frei ~ können** to have entire disposal of an estate; **sich zu sehr von seinen Gefühlen ~ lassen** to let one's feelings be influenced too much;
es ist schwer zu ~ it is difficult to ascertain.

bestimmend determinative, deciding;
für die Auswahl eines Vertreters ~ sein to govern the choice of a representative;
~er Faktor deciding factor.

bestimmt fixed, settled, *(deutlich)* clear, express, certain, *(entschlossen)* determinate, decided, explicit, *(festgestellt)* ascertained, *(vorgesehen)* specified;
durch seine Abneigung gegen j. ~ induced by one's dislike of s. o.; **von geheimen Beweggründen** ~ moved by secret motives; **für den Export** ~ intended for export; **für den Flugverkehr** ~ designed for air traffic; **gesetzlich** ~ prescribed by law, decreed; **hinreichend** ~ reasonably definite; **nur für Lehrer** ~ *(Buch)* for the use of teachers only; **satzungsgemäß (statutenmäßig)** ~ provided for by the articles [of association]; **sofern nicht anderweitig** ~ unless otherwise specified; **zum Verkauf** ~ to be sold; **nicht zur Veröffentlichung** ~ off the record *(US)*;
~ **nach** *(Schiff)* bound (destined) for;
~ **sein von (durch)** to be governed by; **für etw. ~ sein** to be marked down for s. th.; **nur für Sie ~ sein** to be intended for your sight only; **vom Angebot auf dem Markt ~ sein** to be determined by the amount on the market; **für einander ~ sein** to be made for each other; **von Kosten ~ sein** to be governed by costs; **von Angebot und Nachfrage ~ werden** to depend on supply and demand; **~ wissen** to know for certain (definitely);
~e Absicht special purpose, definite intention; **~e Bedingungen** certain conditions; **~er Betrag** given amount (sum); **~en Betrag von seinen Ersparnisse nehmen** to set so much out of one's savings; **~e Formel** set formula; **~en Geldbetrag für Forschungszwecke zur Verfügung stellen** to earmark a sum of money for research; **bis zu einem ~en Grade** to a certain degree; **genau ~e Grenzen** well-defined limits; **seine ~en Gründe für etw. haben** to have one's particular reasons for s. th.; **~e Pflichten zu erfüllen haben** to have to fulfil certain duties; **keine ~en Pläne haben** to have no particular plans; **vom Hersteller ~e Preise** prices laid down by the manufacturer; **~e Qualität** concrete (definite) quality; **am ~en Tag** on the appointed day; **~er Termin** fixed date; **in einem ~en Ton antworten** to reply in a decisive tone (determined manner); **zur Vernichtung ~e Urkunde** document to be destroyed; **~er Verdacht** definite suspicion; **~e Ware** specified goods; **zu einem ~en Zeitpunkt** at a given moment; **Gelder für einen ~en Zweck vorsehen** to earmark funds;
nicht für Dich ~ not meant for you.

Bestimmtheit definiteness, certainty;
mit genügender ~ beschreiben to describe with reasonable certainty; **mit ~ wissen** to know for certain;
~ **eines Tones** firmness of a voice; ~ **bei der Treuhandbestellung** certainty of the subject matter; ~ **beim Wechsel** certainty in a bill; ~ **von Worten** certainty of words.

Bestimmtheitskoeffizient *(Statistik)* coefficient of determination.

Bestimmung *(Begriff)* definition, determination, *(Berufung)* vocation, *(Ernennung)* appointment, nomination, designation, *(Festsetzung)* fixing, fixation, *(Feststellung)* ascertainment, *(Gesetz)* enactment, rule, *(Verfügung)* disposition, *(Verordnung)* regulation, ordinance, order, decree, *(Vertrag)* clause, stipulation, provision, condition, article, recital, *(Vorschrift)* direction, *(Zuweisung)* allocation, appropriation, assignation, assignment;
mit der ausdrücklichen ~ on the express stipulation;
auflösende ~ conditional clause; **ausdrückliche** ~ express condition; **ausdrückliche arbeitsvertragliche** ~ express statementt; **ausreichende** ~ satisfactory provision; **eingefügte** ~ inserted clause; **einleitende** ~ preamble; **einschränkende** ~ saving (restrictive, determinable) clause, proviso, *(Konkurrenzklausel)* restraining clause; **fakultative** ~ facultative clause; **gegenteilige** ~ provision (stipulation) to the contrary; **generelle** ~ blanket clause; **gesetzliche** ~ legislative enactment, rule *(US)*; **interne** ~ private statute; **lästige** ~ onerous clause; **nachträgliche** ~ *(Testament)* codicillary clause; **selbstverständliche** ~ understood clause; **testamentarische** ~ testamentary clause; **unabdingbare** ~ mandatory provision *(US)*; **unhaltbare** ~ clause which cannot be upheld; **wesentliche** ~ essential (material) provision; **zusätzliche** ~ additional clause; **zwingende** ~ mandatory provision *(US)*; **zwingende gesetzliche** ~ mandatory statutory provisions;
~ **über Barzahlung und Transport auf eigenen Schiffen** cash-and-carry clause *(US)*; ~ **eines Begünstigten** nomination of a beneficiary, *(Testament)* power of appointment; ~ **des Einzelhandelspreises** setting the retail price, retail-price determination (fixing, making); ~ **von 10 Millionen als Entwicklungshilfe** allocation of 10 million as development aid; ~ **des Erbberechtigten** institution (appointment, *US*) of an heir; ~ **des Gesellschaftszweckes** object clause; ~ **durch das Los** draw; ~ **eines Nachfolgers** designation of a successor; ~ **eines Termins** setting a date; ~ **eines Testaments** clause of a will; ~ **der Verkaufsrouten von Vertretern** routing of travel(l)ing; ~ **des Versicherungsumfanges** operative clause; ~ **über die Vertragsdauer** termination clause; ~ **eines Vertreters** appointment of an agent; ~ **einer Wortbedeutung** determination of the meaning of a word; ~ **eines Zeitpunkts** determination of a date; ~ **über die Zuständigkeit** jurisdictional clause;
am Ort seiner ~ ankommen to reach one's destination; ~ **annullieren** to make a clause void; ~ **anwenden** to apply a provision; ~ **weit auslegen** to construe a clause extensively; ~ **genau beachten** to adhere strictly to a clause; ~ **beibehalten** to retain a provision; ~ **erlassen** to lay down a regulation, to issue an order; **Ort seiner ~ nicht erreichen** to fail to reach its destination; **Einhaltung einer ~ erzwingen** to enforce [respect of] a law; **unter eine ~ fallen** to come within the scope of (be covered by) a clause, to fall within a definition; **sich unnachgiebig an eine ~ halten** to adhere strictly to a clause; ~ **nichtig machen** to make a clause void; **auf eine gesetzliche ~ Bezug nehmen** to count upon a statute; **keine ~ treffen** *(Vertrag)* to be silent; **Brücke ihrer ~ übergeben** to open a bridge; **Gebäude seiner ~ übergeben** to inaugurate a building; **Schiff seiner ~ als Schulschiff übergeben** to hand over a ship for its function as training ship; **sich seiner ~ unterwerfen** to mortgage o. s. to a clause; ~ **verletzten** to be in violation of a provision; **besondere ~ vorsehen** to make a special provision about.

Bestimmungen terms, conditions, provisions, regulations, rules;
auf Grund der ~ des Paragraphen 21 by the terms of article 21; **gemäß den nachfolgenden** ~ as hereinafter provided; **gemäß den vertraglichen** ~ according to (in accordance with) the provisions of the agreement; **laut steuerrechtlichen** ~ under tax laws; **mangels gegenteiliger** ~ in the absence of any provision to the contrary; **mit Ausnahme gegenteiliger (vorbehaltlich anderweitiger)** ~ save as otherwise provided; **nach den gesetzlichen** ~ under the provisions of the law; **nach den gültigen** ~ according to the present regulations; **nach den vertraglichen** ~ in accordance with (under) the articles; **den ~ zuwider** contrary to the rules;
allgemeine ~ general provisions; **amtliche** ~ official regulations; **ausdrückliche** ~ express terms; **bankgesetzliche** ~ provisions of the banking act; **bestehende** ~ prevailing regulations; **degressive** ~ *(Besteuerung)* tapering provisions;

durchzuführende ~ implemental clauses; **eingeschränkte** ~ modifying conditions; **einschlägige** ~ relevant provisions; **einschränkende** ~ restrictive (provisions, regulations) clauses; **elastische** ~ elastic rules; **engstirnige** ~ petty regulations; **dem Parteiwillen vermutlich entsprechende** ~ implied terms; **fakultative** ~ noncompulsory clauses; **formelle** ~ formal rules; **geltende** ~ current regulations, regulations in force; **gesetzliche** ~ clauses of a law; statutory (legal) provisions; **gewerbepolizeiliche** ~ inspection laws; **gleitende** ~ escalator clauses; **hauptsächliche** ~ major provisions; **haushaltsrechtliche** ~ budgetary regulations; **interne** ~ internal regulations; **konkursrechtliche** ~ bankrupt[cy] laws; **nachgiebige** ~ *(internationaler Güterverkehr)* deviation clause; **nähere** ~ specifications, specific regulations, particulars; **polizeiliche** ~ police regulations; **postalische** ~ postal regulations; **prozeßleitende** ~ directions *(Br.)*; **steuerrechtliche** ~ fiscal (tax-law) provisions; **nicht tarifgebundene** ~ nontariff provisions; **umsatzsteuerliche** ~ vat provisions; **unabdingbare** ~ mandatory provisions; **ungesetzliche** ~ illegal conditions; **unhaltbare** ~ clauses which cannot be held; **rechtlich unzulässige** ~ illegal conditions; **verfahrensrechtliche** ~ general (standing) rules of the court; **vertragliche** ~ articles of agreement (a contract); **vorstehende** ~ above provisions; **vorvertragliche** ~ precontractual terms; **wesentliche** ~ material terms; **zollamtliche** ~ customs regulations; **zusätzliche** ~ added (additional) clauses (provisions); **zwingende** ~ compulsory clauses;
~ **über die Altersversicherung** old-age provisions; ~ **über notwendige Arbeitsbereitschaft** work requirement provisions; ~ **über die Aufrechterhaltung der Versicherungsansprüche bei Verfall (Rückkauf) der Police** nonforfeiture provisions; ~ **des Ausbildungsvertrages** conditions of apprenticeship; ~ **für Ausnahmefälle** saving clauses; ~ **für den Autoexport** regulations for the export of cars; ~ **über Barzahlung und Transport auf eigenen Schiffen** cash-and-carry clause *(US)*; ~ **über die steuerliche Behandlung von Kapitalgewinn** *(Einkommensteuer)* capital gains provisions; ~ **über die steuerliche Behandlung von Kapitalverlusten** *(Einkommensteuer)* capital loss provisions; ~ **über die Bildung von Ausschüssen in Fragen des Industrieschutzes** safety committee regulations; ~ **über die Einbehaltung von Lohnsteuern** withholding regulations; ~ **über die Einberufung und Abhaltung von Hauptversammlungen** provisions as to notice and procedure at general meetings; ~ **des Einkommensteuergesetzes** income-tax regulations; ~ **über den Eisenbahngüterverkehr** railway company's regulations; ~ **im Falle sozial ungerechtfertigter Kündigung** unfair dismissal provisions; ~ **über das Führen von Telefongesprächen** telephone regulations; ~ **über die Führung von Andernkonten durch Rechtsanwälte** Solictors' Accounts Rules *(Br.)*; ~ **eines Gesetzentwurfs** provisions of a bill; ~ **über die Gewährung zusätzlicher Leistungen** fringe issues; ~ **einer Konvention** provisions of a convention; **einschränkende** ~ **für Lombardkredite** *(Börse)* margin rules *(US)*; ~ **über den Luftverkehr** rules of the air; ~ **gegen den Mißbrauch von Steuervergünstigungen** anti-avoiding provisions; ~ **über das Nettokapitalverhältnis** net capital rule; ~ **über das Postsparkassenwesen** Post Office Savings Bank Regulations; ~ **eines Testaments** clauses of a will; **einschränkende** ~ **aus Umweltschutzgründen** environmental restrictions; ~ **über übertarifliche Vergütungen** name in lights clauses; ~ **über den Versand von Standarddrucksachen** printed paper conditions; ~ **des Versicherungsaufsichtsamtes** state insurance regulations; ~ **einer Versicherungspolice** provisions of an insurance policy; **einleitende** ~ **eines Vertrages** preliminary articles of a treaty; ~ **im Zollverkehr** customs regulations;
die ~ **besagen** it says in the regulations;
auf Grund einzelner ~ **ablehnen** to give a qualified no; **durch vertragliche** ~ **absichern** to guard by clauses; ~ **anwenden** to apply provisions; ~ **aufheben** to abolish provisions; **einschränkende** ~ **aufheben** to deregulationize; **sich der** ~ **bedienen** to have recourse to the provisions; **sich auf gesetzliche** ~ **berufen** to invoke the provisions of a statute; **den** ~ **entsprechen** to comply with the terms; **unter die gesetzlichen** ~ **fallen** to come within the provisions (scope) of a law (provisions of an act); **unter die vertraglichen** ~ **fallen** to come within the terms of a contract; ~ **über die Beschlußfähigkeit festlegen** to fix the quorum; **keine** ~ **für einen derartigen Fall getroffen haben** to have made no provisions for a case of this kind; **gemäß den** ~ **handeln** to act in accordance with the rules; **in Übereinstimmung mit den** ~ **handeln** to conform with (to) provisions; ~ **eines Abkommens in Kraft setzen** to implement the provisions of a convention; **für einen Fall keine** ~ **treffen** to make no provisions for a case; **die notwendigen** ~ **treffen** to take the necessary steps; ~ **umgehen** to evade regulations, *(gesetzliche)* to dodge the law; **konkursrechtlichen** ~ **unterliegen** to be amenable to bankruptcy laws; ~ **verletzen** to wink at rules; ~ **verschärfen** to tighten restrictions; **gegen die elementarsten** ~ **verstoßen** to break the ground (basic) rules; **den** ~ **zuwiderhandeln** to contravene the terms.

Bestimmungsbahnhof station of destination.

bestimmungsgemäß in accordance with the regulations, according to the rules, *(Gesetz)* in compliance with the laws, *(Vertrag)* according to the terms;
~**e Mittelverwendung** due employment of funds.

Bestimmungs | hafen port of destination; ~**land** state (country) of destination, country of consignment.

Bestimmungsort goal, place (point) of destination;
endgültiger ~ final (ultimate) destination;
an seinem ~ **ankommen** to reach one's destination; **seinen** ~ **erreichen** to arrive (reach) one's destination.

Bestimmungspostamt office of destination *(Br.)*.

bestimmungswidrig contrary to the rules.

Bestimmungszweck intended purpose.

Bestleistung record performance;
neue ~ **aufstellen** to set up as a new record.

bestmöglich at the best price, *(Devisenkauf)* at the best possible rate;
Order ~**st ausführen** to execute an order at best;
~**es Ergebnis** best possible result; ~**e Verwertung** optimum use.

Bestmögliches tun, sein to do one's level best.

Bestochener bribetaker, bribee;
von beiden Seiten ~ ambidexter.

bestochener Zeuge suborned (corrupt, bribed) witness.

bestoßen *(drucktechn.)* to plane;
~**e Buchecken** damaged corners of a book.

Bestpreis highest (best) price;
zum ~ **verkaufen** to sell at the highest price (at best).

bestrafen to punish, to inflict punishment;
mit Arrest ~ *(mil.)* to confine to barracks; **mit vier Jahren Gefängnis** ~ to sentence to four years imprisonment; **mit Geldstrafe zu** ~ punishable by a fine; **j. mit einer Geldstrafe** ~ to fine s. o., to punish s. o. with a fine; **j. für ein Verbrechen** ~ to punish s. o. for a crime; **Verbrechen mit dem Tode** ~ to punish a crime with death; **Verbrecher schwer** ~ to inflict severe punishment on criminals.

bestraft werden to suffer penalty, to receive a sentence;
hart ~ to be severely punished; **für seine Verbrechen** ~ to be brought to punishment for one's crimes.

Bestrafung punishment;
abschreckende ~ exemplary punishment; **angemessene** ~ adequate punishment; **disziplinare** ~ discipline, disciplinary punishment; **grausame (harte)** ~ cruel and unusual punishment; **unzulässige** ~ prohibited punishment; **wirksame** ~ effective punishment;
erhöhte ~ **von Rückfalltätern** cumulative punishment;
von ~ **absehen** to refrain from punishment; **jem. eine** ~ **auferlegen** to inflict a punishment on s. o.; **sich der** ~ **aussetzen** to be liable to punishment; **der** ~ **entgehen** to escape punishment, to go unpunished (scot-free); **sich der** ~ **entziehen** to evade punishment; **seine** ~ **mannhaft hinnehmen** to stand one's punishment like a man *(fam.)*; **j. zur** ~ **melden** *(mil.)* to put s. o. on a charge; **angemessene** ~ **für ein Verbrechen vorsehen** to make the punishment fit the crime; ~ **nach sich ziehen** to carry a penalty.

Bestreben aspiration, endeavo(u)r, desire, attempt, effort;
in dem ~ *(Vertrag)* anxious, in the endeavo(u)r.

bestrebt solicitous, endeavo(u)ring;
stets ~, **Ihre Wünsche aufs beste zu erfüllen** it will be our constant endeavo(u)r to fulfil your orders; ~, **es allen recht zu machen** anxious to please everyone;
~ **sein** to have the will to do, to endeavo(u)r, to strive; **mit allen Mitteln** ~ **sein** to use one's best endeavo(u)rs.

Bestrebungen efforts, endeavo(u)rs, endeavo(u)rings, aims, movements;
auseinandergehende ~ struggle of wills; **staatsfeindliche** ~ subversive activities.

bestreichen, feindliche Stellungen mit Maschinengewehrfeuer to sweep the enemy position with machine-gun fire.

bestreiken to strike against, to black, to boycott;
aus Sympathie ~ to strike (walk out, *US*) in sympathy.

bestreikt strike-bound;
~**e Werften** shipyards affected by a strike.

Bestreikung strike, striking, blacking, boycott;
~ **eines nur mittelbar beteiligten Betriebes** secondary picketing.

bestreitbar traversable, impugnable, contestable, open to question, *(Kosten)* payable, defrayable;
nicht ~ unanswerable, incontestable, unquestionable.
Bestreiten denial, traverse, *(Beklagter)* defence, traverse;
allgemeines ~ *(Klageschrift)* common (general) traverse, traversing note, general issue (replication); **begründetes** ~ specific denial; **formelles** ~ negative avernment; **globales** ~ conjunctive denial; **restloses** ~ *(Klageschrift)* peremptory defence; **substantiiertes** ~ *(Klageschrift)* special traverse;
~ **der Aktivlegitimation** express colo(u)r; ~ **und Gegenvorbringen** special replication; **entscheidendes** ~ **eines Klagepunktes** negative plea; ~ **des gesamten Klagevorbringens** general denial (issue); ~ **der Kosten** defrayal of expenses; ~ **einzelner Punkte** special issue; ~ **der Schlüssigkeit der Klage** objection in point of law; ~ **einer Zeugenaussage** impugnment of a testimony;
sich das ~ **einer Sache gefallen lassen** to accept the denial of s. th.
bestreiten to contest, to contend, to challenge, to dispute, to disclaim, to defend, to traverse, to impugn, to controvert;
Anspruch ~ to contest (dispute) a claim; **Ausgaben** ~ to bear (defray) the expenses; **seine eigenen Ausgaben** ~ to support o. s.; **Behauptung** ~ to deny an assertion, to dispute (deny) a statement; **Besitzverhältnisse** ~ to dispute the possession of the ground; **Echtheit** ~ to put in a plea for forgery; **Echtheit seiner Unterschrift** ~ to deny one's signature; **Echtheit einer Urkunde** ~ to dispute (challenge) the validity of a document; **eidlich** ~ to forswear; **jds. Eigentumsrechte** ~ to dispute s. one's title; **energisch** ~ to deny stoutly; **jds. Erbfolgerecht** ~ to challenge s. one's succession; **Forderung** ~ to disallow a claim; **Gültigkeit** ~ to challenge the validity; **Gültigkeit eines Testaments** ~ to dispute a will; **Gültigkeit einer Wahl** ~ to contest an election; **Klagebehauptungen** ~ to defend an action; **Klagegrund** ~ to plead a demurrer; **Kosten** ~ to defray (bear, pay) the costs; **alle Kosten** ~ to meet all expenses; **Kosten eines Mittagessens** ~ to foot the bill of a luncheon; **jds. Lebensunterhalt** ~ to maintain (support) s. o.; **seinen Lebensunterhalt daraus** ~ to make a living out of it; **seinen Lebensunterhalt durch Stundengeben** ~ to earn one's livelihood by teaching; **das ganze Programm mit seinen eigenen Werken** ~ to fill the whole program(me) with one's own works; **jds. Recht** ~ to challenge s. one's right; **Rechtmäßigkeit eines Anspruchs** ~ to dispute (contest) a claim; **Rechtsanspruch** ~ to dispute (impugn) a claim; **seine Schuld** ~ *(Angeklagter)* to plead not guilty, to deny a charge; **Tatsache nicht** ~ to admit a fact; **großen Teil der Unterhaltung** ~ to contribute a large share of the conversation, to do most of the talking; **Unkosten** ~ to defray (meet) the expenses; **das gesamte Vorbringen** ~ to plead the general issue; **weiterhin nur ganz allgemein** ~ to plead over;
man kann die Tatsache nicht ~ there is no denying the fact.
Bestreitung | der Kosten defrayal of expenses; **zur** ~ **der Kosten beitragen** to contribute towards the costs; ~ **des Unterhalts** providing maintenance.
Bestresultat optimum result.
bestrichenes Gelände *(mil.)* area under fire, beaten zone.
bestricken, alle durch seine Liebenswürdigkeit to captivate everybody with one's charm.
bestritten controversial, in controversy;
nicht ~ unargued;
~ **werden** to be at issue;
~**es Eigentumsrecht** disputed title; ~**e Forderung** disputed claim; ~**e Frage** controversy.
Bestseller best seller;
~ **sein** to make the best-seller list.
bestücken *(mit Waffen)* to arm, *(mit Werkzeugen)* to equip.
bestückt equipped;
schwer ~**es Schiff** heavy-armed ship.
Bestückung equipment.
Bestuhlung seating.
bestürmen *(mil.)* to storm, to assail, to assault, to attack;
j. mit etw. ~ to ply (implore) s. o. with s. th.; **j. mit Bitten um Geld** ~ to press s. o. for money; **j. mit Fragen** ~ to pester (plague) s. o. with questions; **Stellung** ~ to make an assault on a position.
bestürzen to strike with consternation, to petrify, to stun, to dismay.
bestürzend dismaying, stunning;
~**e Gerüchte** bewildering, (consternating) rumo(u)rs.
bestürzt disconcerted, stunned, petrified, aghast;
von den Nachrichten ~ stunned by the news;
j. ~ **ansehen** to give s. o. a look of consternation, to look at s. o. in dismay; ~**es Gesicht machen** to look dismayed (nonplussed).
Bestürzung consternation, bewilderment, dismay, alarm, perturbation;
größte ~ **auslösen** to cause the greatest consternation; **mit** ~ **von einem Unglück erfahren** to be dismayed at the news of an accident; **Lager in** ~ **versetzen** to cast the camp into a state of alarm.
Best | verfahren model procedure; ~**wert** optimum.
Besuch visit, call, *(Besucherzahl)* attendance, *(längerer)* stay, sojourn;
beim ~ **des Museums** on visiting the museum;
förmlicher ~ set visit; **heruntergespielter** ~ low-key visit; **kurzer** ~ flying visit, run; **mehrstündiger** ~ visit of several hours; **nachfassender** ~ *(Vertreter)* follow-up visit; **offizieller** ~ formal call, visitation *(Br.)*; **nicht offizieller** ~ informal call; **persönlicher** ~ personal call; **regelmäßiger** ~ circuit, patronization; **schwacher** ~ poor attendance; **verschiedene** ~**e** number of calls; **vierzehntägiger** ~ a fortnight's stay; **willkommener** ~ welcome visit; **zweiter** ~ *(Vertreter)* callback;
~ **einer Ausstellung** visit to an exhibition; ~ **bei Freunden** visit to some friends; ~ **eines Geschäftsreisenden** call of a travel(l)er; ~ **von Sehenswürdigkeiten** sightseeing; ~ **einer Versammlung** attendance of an assembly; **regelmäßiger** ~ **von Vorlesungen** regular attendance of lectures; **starker** ~ **einer Vorstellung** good attendance at a performance;
~ **absagen** to cancel a visit; ~ **einer Gemäldegalerie absolvieren** to do a picture gallery; ~**e in der Nachbarschaft absolvieren** to pay calls near at hand; ~ **abstatten** to pay a visit, to make (pay) a call, *(Handelsvertreter)* to wait upon s. o.; **jem. einen formellen** ~ **abstatten** to pay a formal call on s. o.; **jem. einen kurzen** ~ **abstatten** to drop in on s. o.; **der Stadt einen kurzen** ~ **abstatten** to pop up to town; **jem. einen überraschenden** ~ **abstatten** to break in upon s. o.; **seinen** ~ **über Gebühr (ungebührlich) ausdehnen** to protract one's visit beyond measure, to overstay one's welcome; **seine** ~**e einstellen** to stop (discontinue) one's visits; **zu einem privaten** ~ **eintreffen** to arrive for a private visit; ~ **empfangen** to receive visitors; **jds.** ~ **erwidern** to return s. one's call; ~ **ins Auge fassen** to contemplate a visit; **viel** ~ **haben** to have a great deal of company; ~**e machen** to pay calls; **bei jem. einen** ~ **machen** to call on s. o.; **formlosen** ~ **machen** to go round; **kurzen** ~ **machen** to pay a flying visit, to go round to; **nur kurz zu** ~ **sein** to come for a brief call; **seinen** ~ **verlängern** to prolong one's visit; **j. von seinem beabsichtigten** ~ **verständigen** to notify s. o. of the day of one's visit; ~ **wiederholen** to call again.
Besuchemachen visiting, visitation.
besuchen to call, to visit, to go into, *(als Kunde)* to patronize, *(Vorlesung)* to attend;
j. ~ to [make a] call on s. o., to pay s. o. a call, to look s. o. up; **häufig** ~ to frequent, to patronize; **Kunden** ~ to call on a client; **Messen** ~ to frequent (visit) fairs; **noch** ~ *(Tourist)* to take in *(US)*; **Patienten** ~ to attend a patient; **regelmäßig** ~ to attend regularly; **Restaurant häufig** ~ to frequent (patronize) a restaurant; **Schule** ~ to go to (attend a) school; **j. auf einen Sprung** ~ to pay s. o. a flying visit.
Besucher visitor, caller, spectator, guest, *(Kunde)* customer, *(pl.)* turnout, *(Theater)* patron, *(Vorlesung)* attendant;
ausländischer ~ foreign visitor; **geschäftlicher** ~ invitee; **regelmäßiger** ~ frequenter; **ständiger** ~ habitué; **willkommener** ~ welcome guest;
häufiger ~ **eines Restaurants** patronizer of a restaurant; ~ **aus Übersee** overseas visitors;
~ **abweisen** to deny visitors; ~ **empfangen** to receive visitors; **ungehörige** ~ **aus dem Sitzungssaal entfernen lassen** to order the removal of disorderly persons; **häufiger** ~ **sein** to be a frequent visitor; **eifriger** ~ **von Kunstausstellungen sein** to eagerly frequent art exhibitions; **häufiger** ~ **eines Restaurants sein** to frequent (patronize) a restaurant;
ununterbrochene ~**folge** continuous succession of visitors; ~**gruppe** visiting group; ~**kreis** patronage *(coll.)*; ~**liste** visiting book; ~**paß** visitor passport; ~**rekord** attendance record, record attendance; ~**rückgang** decline in attendance; ~**strom** influx (stream) of visitors, flood of callers; ~**tag** visiting day; ~**tribüne** public (strangers') gallery; ~**visum** tourist visa; ~**zahl** number of participants, attendance, *(Sport)* gate; **geschätzte** ~**zahlen** anticipated visitors; **niedrige** ~**zahl** low attendance.
Besuchs | erlaubnis *(Gefängnis)* visitor's pass; ~**grund erfragen** *(Pförtner)* to demand s. one's business; ~**karte** visiting (calling, *US*) card; ~**liste** visiting book; **angemessene** ~**regelung** *(Kinder geschiedener Eltern)* reasonable access; ~**reise** visit; ~**tag** visiting day; ~**tour** round of visits, calling round; ~**verbot** no visitors!

besuchsweise as a visitor.
Besuchs|zeit *(Krankenhaus)* visiting hours; **~zimmer** spare (guest) room, *(Krankenhaus)* reception room.
besucht attended, visited, *(Gasthaus)* frequented;
stark ~ frequented, numerously attended; **wenig ~** unfrequented;
gut ~e Ausstellung exhibition which attracts many visitors; **stark ~er Ferienort** crowded holiday resort; **wenig ~er Ort** a spot visited by few, unfrequented spot; **gut ~e Versammlung** good attendance at a meeting; **gut ~e Vorstellung** well-attended performance.
besudeln to dirty, to stain, to defile, to spot, to muck up *(coll.)*; **jds. Ehre ~** to cast a stain on s. one's hono(u)r; **seine Hände mit Blut ~** to stain one's hands with blood; **jds. guten Namen ~** to drag s. one's name in the mud; **Tischtuch ~** to soil the tablecloth.
betagte Forderung deferred claim.
betanken to refuel, to tank up.
Betätigen der Bremsen operating the brakes.
betätigen to operate, to set in operation, to work;
sich aktiv ~ to take an active part; **sich als Aufpasser ~** to make the watchdog; **sich gelegentlich als Aushilfe ~** to potter at odd jobs; **Bremse ~** to apply (operate) the brake; **sich in den Sommerferien als Briefträger ~** to have a job as a postman in the holidays; **sich erfolgreich ~** to have a field day; **sich gewerblich ~** to engage in (carry on) a trade; **sich im Hause ~** to potter about the house; **Kupplung ~** to engage the clutch; **sich außerhalb seines Metiers ~** *(Künstler)* to go outside one's range; **sich nützlich ~** to make o. s. useful; **sich politisch ~** to take a hand (an interest, play, dabble) in politics, to politicize; **sich als Rechtsanwalt ~** to practise at the bar; **Sicherheitsvorrichtungen automatisch ~** to set a safety device automatically into motion.
Betätigung activity, participation, occupation, pursuit;
berufliche ~ professional pursuits; **geschäftliche ~** economic activity; **kaufmännische ~** commercial (mercantile) pursuit; **literarische ~** desk, literary pursuits; **nützliche ~** useful job; **politische ~** political activity; **wissenschaftliche ~** scientific (research) work;
~ als Winkelmakler outside broking;
jds. ~ einschränken to put a restraint on s. one's activities.
Betätigungs|drang verspüren to feel an urge to do s. th.; **~feld** range of activities, sphere of action; **sein ~feld ausdehnen** to extend the scope of one's activities; **~feld für seine kreative Anlagen suchen** to seek an outlet for one's creative instinct; **~freiheit behindern** to impede the liberty to work; **~hebel** control lever; **im Rahmen seines ~kreises liegen** to fall within the scope of one's work; **gewerkschaftliches ~recht** right to participate in trade-union activities; **~schalter** control switch; **~taste** operational key.
betäuben to stupefy, to narcotize, *(Geräusch)* to stun, to daze; **j. mit Chloroform ~** to chloroform s. o.; **seinen Kummer mit Alkohol ~** to drown one's sorrow in drink; **örtlich ~** *(med.)* to anaesthesize, to give s. o. a local anaesthetic; **sich durch Rauschgift ~** to drug (dope) o. s.; **j. durch einen Schlag ~** to knock s. o. out.
betäubender Lärm deafening (stunning) noise.
betäubt|vor Schreck in a stupor of dismay;
von einer Nachricht wie ~ sein to be stunned with the news.
Betäubung daze, stupefaction, stupor;
örtliche ~ local anaesthetization;
~ durch Chloroform chloroforming.
Betäubungsmittel palliative, anodyne, stupefying drug, painkiller, narcotic [drug], anaesthetic.
beteiligen, sich to take part, to participate, to share in, *(mitwirken)* to cooperate, to collaborate; **j. ~** give s. o. a share, to interest s. o.; **sich aktiv ~** to take an active part in an undertaking, to be an active member; **sich an einer Arbeit ~** to take one's part in a work; **sich an der Diskussion ~** to take a hand in the debate, to take a part (participate) in a discussion; **sich an der Filmindustrie ~** to break into the picture industry; **sich finanziell ~** to take up a financial participation, to become financially interested; **sich an einer Firma ~** to buy an interest in a firm; **gemeinsam ~** to share jointly; **j. an einem Geschäft ~** to make s. o. a partner; **sich an einem Geschenk ~** to contribute to a present; **sich an einem Gespräch lebhaft ~** to take much share in a conversation; **j. am Gewinn ~** to give s. o. a share in profits; **sich an einer strafbaren Handlung ~** to participate in committing an offence; **sich kapitalmäßig ~** to take a financial interest, to participate on an equity basis; **sich an den Kosten ~** to contribute towards the costs; **sich an einem Kuhhandel ~** to jockey a transaction; **sich an einem Rennen ~** to compete in a race; **sich an Rettungsarbeiten ~** to take part in the rescue work; **sich an einer Sache ~** to take a hand in the business; **j. an einer guten Sache ~** to let s. o. in on a good thing; **j. gegen Erstattung der Spesen ~** to let s. o. in for the expenses; **sich an der Unterhaltung ~** to join in a conversation; **j. an einem Unternehmen ~** to make s. o. a partner to an undertaking; **sich an einem Unternehmen finanziell ~** to take (buy) an interest in an enterprise, to invest one's money in a business enterprise; **sich mit jem. an einem Unternehmen ~** to share with s. o. in an undertaking; **sich an einem neugegründeten Unternehmen ~** to embark on a business undertaking; **sich mit Vermögenswerten an einem Unternehmen ~** to invest funds in a scheme; **sich an einer Verschwörung ~** to take part in a plot; **sich an einem Werk ~** to collaborate in a work; **sich an einem Wettbewerb ~** to take part in a competition; **sich am Wiederaufbau eines Hauses ~** to lend a helping hand with the rebuilding of a house;
sich ~ wollen to come in for a share.
beteiligt participating, involved, concerned, interested in, *(als Täter)* conjunct;
an einem Unfall ~ involved in an accident;
~ sein to have a hand in, to be concerned, to be sharer in, *(kapitalmäßig)* to participate, to take a share, to have an interest (a share); **mit 10% ~ sein** to hold a 10% interest; **an einer Bank ~ sein** to have a share in a bank; **an etw. ~ sein** to keep one's hand in at s. th.; **finanziell nicht ~ sein** to have no money interest in a concern; **an einer Firma hälftig ~ sein** to have a half interest in a firm; **an einem Geschäft ~ sein** to have an interest (a share) in a business; **an den Geschäftsverlusten zu gleichen Teilen ~ sein** to contribute equally towards the losses sustained by a firm; **mit 100.000 Dollar an einer Gesellschaft ~ sein** to have an interest in a company of $ 100.000; **am Gewinn ~ sein** to share in (partake of) profits, to have an interest in the profits; **am Gewinn und Verlust gleichmäßig ~ sein** to share and share alike; **am Kapital gleichmäßig ~ sein** to share equally in the capital; **an einem Konkurs als Gläubiger ~ sein** to enter into the rights of a creditor; **nicht ~ sein** not to be participating; **planend und ausführend an etw. ~ sein** to be art and part in s. th.; **an einer Sache ~ sein** to play a part in a business; **an einer Sache nicht ~ sein** to have no hand in an affair, to be unconcerned (have no share) in a business; **zu gleichen Teilen ~ sein** to participate equally in the profits, to go share and share alike *(Br.)*; **an einem Unternehmen [finanziell] ~ sein** to have a share in a business, to be financially interested in a firm, to have a concern in a business; **an einem Unternehmen finanziell nicht ~ sein** to have no money interest in a concern; **an einem Verbrechen ~ sein** to be a participator in a crime; **am Verlust ~ sein** to participate in a loss; **an einer Verschwörung ~ sein** to be concerned in a plot;
~e Interessen the interest at issue; **~e Personen** persons interested (concerned).
Beteiligte|r participant, party [interested, concerned], person involved, privy, *(Teilhaber)* partner;
die ~n those concerned (interested), concerned parties;
gemeinwirtschaftlich ~ privies; **gesellschaftsähnlich ~r** ostensible partner; **am Krieg ~** belligerent parties; **am Kuhhandel ~r** logroller *(US)*; **mittelbar ~r** remote party; **unmittelbar ~r** *(Wechselrecht)* immediate party;
~ eines Vertrages parties to an agreement;
~ laden to summon the parties; **~r an einer strafbaren Handlung sein** to be an accessory to a crime.
Beteiligtsein involvement, engagement, interestedness.
Beteiligung participation, sharing, *(Anlage)* investment, *(Anteil)* share, interest, *(an einem Buch)* piece, collaboration, *(Gesellschaftsanteil)* amount invested [in a company], contribution to capital, *(Mitwirkung)* cooperation, collaboration, *(Teilnehmerzahl)* attendance, *(Unterstützung)* support, contribution, *(bei Wahlen)* poll, turnout;
mit der Aussicht späterer ~ with a view to partnership; **mit ~ am Gewinn** participating; **unter zahlreicher ~ des Publikums** amid a large concourse of the public;
~en holdings, shareholdings, stockholdings *(US)*, *(Bilanz)* investments, equitable interest;
steuerlich absetzbare ~ tax-deductive share; **angemessene ~** fair share; **ausländische ~en** foreign interests, investments from abroad, foreign equity; **erstklassige ~** choice investment; **finanzielle ~** [financial] interest, financial holding (participation); **formale (nominelle) ~** nominal participation (interest); **geringe ~** thin attendance; **industrielle ~** industrial participation; **kommanditistische ~** limited partnership interest; **kurzfristige ~** temporary investment; **maßgebliche ~** control-

ling interest; **mehrheitliche** ~ controlling interest; **persönliche** ~ personal investment; **prozentuale** ~ quota; **staatliche** ~ government[al] participation (interest); **stille** ~ secret *(US)* (sleeping, *Br.*, dormant, silent, *Br.*) partnership; **tätige** ~ active partnership; **verschiedene ~en** *(Bilanz)* sundry investments and interests;
~en durch Aktienbesitz shareholdings *(Br.)*, stockholdings *(US)*; ~ **am staatlichen Altersversorgungswerk** contracting into the state pension scheme; ~ **der Angestellten (Belegschaft) am Aktienkapital** employee share ownership *(Br.)*, employee stock ownership *(US)*; ~ **der Arbeiter und Angestellten am Gewinn** industrial partnership, profit sharing; **~en im Ausland** foreign investments, investments abroad; **~en an Banken und Bankfirmen** shareholding stockholding *(US)*, interest in foreign banks; ~ **an einem Buch** collaboration on a book; **amerikanische ~en in Deutschland** American interests in Germany; ~ **an einem Dokumentengeschäft** negotiating a documentary credit; ~ **Dritter am Rechtsstreit** third-party notice; **~en an ausländischen Firmen** interests held in foreign companies; ~ **an der Geschäftsführung** management sharing *(US)*; **~en an Gesellschaften** *(Bilanz)* investment in companies (corporations, *US*); ~ **am Gewinn** share in profits, profit sharing, participation in earnings; **unmittelbare ~ am Gewinn** immediate participation; ~ **zur Hälfte** half interest; ~ **an einem Konsortium** underwriting participation; ~ **an den Kosten** shareholding (sharing) of costs; ~ **an der Patentverwertung** interest in the patent exploitation; ~ **der Pensionskasse** pension fund's holdings; ~ **am Stammkapital** equity participation; ~ **an Tochter- und Konzerngesellschaften** investments in subsidiaries and associated companies; ~ **von erheblichem Umfang** material interests; ~ **an einem Unternehmen** participation in an enterprise; ~ **an einem Verbrechen** complicity in a crime; ~ **am Verlust** sharing of loss; ~ **an einer Versammlung** attendance at a meeting; **starke ~ an einer Vorlesung** good attendance at a lecture; **gute (schlechte) ~ an der Wahl** heavy (small) poll; ~ **an einer Werbesendung** co-sponsoring; **~en und andere Wertpapiere** *(Bilanz)* bonds and other interests;
~ **abgeben** to realize an investment; **jem. eine ~ an seinem Geschäft anbieten** to offer s. o. an interest in one's business; **seine ~ aufgeben** to withdraw one's money from a business, to stand down; **mehrere ~en besitzen** to have holdings in several companies; ~ **der Arbeitnehmer am Gewinn einführen** to initiate a profit-sharing system; **Einkünfte aus einer ~ beziehen** to derive income from an investment; ~ **erwerben** to secure (purchase) an interest; ~ **durch Erlassen der Rückzahlung von Staatskrediten erwerben** to buy its way in by waiving repayment of state loans; ~ **an einer Firma erwerben** to buy an interest in a firm; **an einem Unternehmen in großzügiger Weise ~en erwerben** to launch a corporation on an acquisition drive; **seine ~ zu erkennen geben** to disclose one's interest; **mehrere ~en haben** to have holdings in several companies (corporations, *US*); **seine ~ den Steuerbehörden offenlegen** to reveal one's holdings to the tax authorities; ~ **realisieren** to realize an investment; **unter lebhafter ~ der Bevölkerung stattfinden** to be accompanied by demonstrations of public sympathy; **j. zur ~ an etw. veranlassen** to interest s. o. in s. th.; **seine ~ verkaufen** to dispose of one's interest in a firm, to sell out one's share of business (interest); **sich in immer größerem Ausmaß ~en zulegen** to play the acquisition game;
volle ~ zugesagt full interest admitted.
beteiligungsähnliche Ansprüche *(Bilanz)* interest in the nature of investments.
Beteiligungs|bank equity bank; **~bestand** investment in companies (corporations, *US*); **~betrag** amount invested; **~buchwerte** book value of a company's investments; **~darlehn** loan for the purpose of investment; **~dauer** life of partnership; **~erträge** investment earnings; **~erwerb** purchase of participations; **fünfzigprozentiger ~erwerb** acquisition of a 50 per cent interest; **~finanzierung** investment financing; **~firma** investment firm; **~fonds** investment fund; **~geschäft** transaction (deal) on joint account, joint venture; **~gesellschaft** holding (associated, affiliated) company, special partnership, joint venture, *(Konzern)* affiliate; **~gewinn** investment earnings; **~investitionen** portfolio investments; **~kapital** contribution to capital, investment capital; **ausländisches ~kapital** foreign equity capital; **~klausel** participation clause; **~konto** syndicate (participation, joint, *US*) account, *(Kapitalbeteiligung)* investment account; **~note** *(Versicherung)* insurance slip; **~papier** investment paper; **~prozentsatz** working interest; **~quote** interest, quota, share, contingent; **~recht** contribution to capital; **~schlüssel** distributive share; **~sparen** investment saving; **~syndikat** underwriting syndicate; **~system** profit sharing, industrial partnership, sharing plan *(US)*; **~umfang** size of holdings; **~umstellungen** shuffle of holdings; **~unternehmen** associated company *(Br.)*, affiliated corporation *(US)*; **~verhältnis** share, *(Gemeinschaftsunternehmen)* joint venture, *(Quote)* quota; **~vertrag** contract of partnership, partnership agreement, *(verschiedene Firmen)* joint venture agreement; **~zusage** commitment to participate.
beteuern to assure, to asseverate, to vouch, to declare;
seine Unschuld ~ to protest one's innocence.
Beteuerung asservation, protest[ation], assurance;
eidliche ~, ~ **unter Eid** oath of evidence, assertory oath *(US)*, verification *(US)*;
~ **seiner Unschuld** protestation of one's innocence.
betiteln to entitle, to designate, *(Artikel)* to head, to give a heading;
Buch ~ to title a book; **j. mit Lump** ~ to call s. o. a rogue; **j. mit Professor** ~ to address s. o. as professor.
betitelt headed, entitled, with the title.
Betitelung title.
Beton concrete;
armierter ~ reinforced concrete; **flüssiger** ~ chuted concrete; **hochwertiger** ~ high-quality concrete;
~ **mischen** to mix concrete;
~arbeiten concrete work; **~aufbereitung** concrete mixing; **~automat** concrete mixer; **~bau** concrete construction; **~bewehrung** concrete reinforcement; **~block** concrete block.
betonen *(gr.)* to accentuate, to stress, *(hervorheben)* to stress, to point out, to emphasize;
nachdrücklich ~ to urge, to insist, to emphasize, to underline; **Punkt** ~ to stress a point; **Tatsache** ~ to lay emphasis on a fact; **übermäßig** ~ to overemphasize; **Wert von Fremdsprachen** ~ to lay stress on foreign languages; **Wichtigkeit** ~ to emphasize the importance; **Wort falsch** ~ to stress a word wrongly; **Wort auf der ersten Silbe** ~ to stress a word on the first sylleable.
betonieren to concrete;
Mauer ~ to face a wall with concrete.
Beton|mauer concrete wall; **~mischer** concrete mixer.
Betonnung buoyage.
Beton|pfeiler concrete pile; **~pflaster** concrete pavement; **~plattform** concrete platform; **eingelassene ~schwelle** road bump; **~stahl** concrete steel; **~stein** concrete block (slab).
betont stressed, accentuated, *(fig.)* emphasized, pointed, pronounced;
j. ~ unhöflich behandeln to treat s. o. with marked incivility; **~er Optimismus** marked optimism; **~e Silbe** stressed (accentuated) syllable; **~es Zurschaustellen** emphatic display.
Betonung stress, accentuation, tone, *(fig.)* emphasis, stress;
zu starke ~ exaggeration.
Betonungsakzent stress mark.
betören to beguile, to captivate, to infatuate, to bewitch, to turn s. one's head;
j. durch Schmeicheleien ~ to deceive s. o. by flatteries;
sich ~ lassen to allow o. s. to be taken in.
betört bewitched, beguiled.
Betracht, außer ~ bleiben to be ruled (left) out of consideration, to be disregarded; **in ~ kommen** to come into consideration, to be possible; **als Bewerber in ~ kommen** to be a possible candidate; **nicht in ~ kommen** to be out of the question; **für eine Stellung nicht in ~ kommen** to be unsuitable for a post (out of the running); **außer ~ lassen** to disregard, to leave out of account (consideration); **alle Einzelheiten außer ~ lassen** to leave all details aside; **in ~ ziehen** to consider, to take into consideration (account), to contemplate; **Angebot in ~ ziehen** to consider an offer; **Gesuch in ~ ziehen** to attend to a request; **Gesuch wohlwollend in ~ ziehen** to take a request into favo(u)rable consideration; **jds. Krankheit in ~ ziehen** to make allowance for s. one's being ill; **Möglichkeit in ~ ziehen** to consider a possibility;
die in ~ kommenden Personen the persons concerned.
betrachten to look at, to see, *(erwägen)* to consider, to regard;
Problem mit anderen Augen ~ to look upon a problem in quite another light; **Angelegenheit mit den Augen des Steuerzahlers** ~ to view a matter from the taxpayer's standpoint; **alles durch eine rosarote Brille** ~ to see everything through rose-colo(u)red spectacles; **es als Ehre** ~ to deem it an hono(u)r; **seinen Eid nicht mehr als bindend** ~ to dispense with one's oath; **eingehend** ~ to examine closely; **etw. flüchtig** ~ to [take a] glance at s. th.; **j. als Freund** ~ to regard s. o. as friend; **nüchtern** ~ to exercise a sober judgment; **es als seine Pflicht** ~ to esteem it a duty; **alles positiv (optimistisch)** ~ to see the bright side of

things; **j. prüfend** ~ to look s. o. over; **Sache von allen Seiten** ~ to consider a matter from all angles; **etw. von der falschen Seite** ~ to see s. th. in a false light; **als selbstverständlich** ~ to take it for granted; **sorgfältig** ~ to examine carefully; **von einem anderen Standpunkt** ~ to take a different view; **etw. als ungesetzlich** ~ to regard s. th. as illegal; **j. verstohlen** ~ to watch s. o. from the tail of one's eye; **sein Werk wohlgefällig** ~ to be proud of one's work; **j. mit Wohlgefallen** ~ to be favo(u)rably disposed towards s. o.

Betrachter onlooker, observer, viewer, spectator.

betrachtet, an und für sich on its merits.

beträchtlich considerable, large, substantial, sizable, wide, material, pretty *(coll.)*, tidy (not small in size, *coll.*);
~er Ermessensspielraum large discretion; **~er Schaden** extensive (considerable) damage, serious loss; **~e Schulden** heavy (staggering) debts; **~e Steigerung** substantial increase; **~e Verbesserung** substantial improvement; **~es Vermögen** handsome (sizable) fortune.

Betrachtung consideration, speculation, reflection;
bei näherer ~ on closer examination (inspection); **bei oberflächlicher** ~ at a superficial glance;
nachdenkliche ~ contemplation;
~en über die Geschichte der Nachkriegszeit reflections upon the history of the post-war period;
~en anstellen to take into consideration, to consider, to mediate, to reflect on.

Betrachtungsweise mental outlook;
nüchterne ~ pragmatism, conservative view; **wissenschaftliche** ~ scientific approach.

Betrag amount, sum [of money], *(Buchungsposten)* item, *(Gesamtbetrag)* total, *(Satz)* rate, *(Wert)* value, *(Ziffer)* figure;
bis zum ~ **von** to the extent of, up to the amount of; **gut für jeden** ~ good for any amount; **im ~e von** amounting to, to the tune of *(coll.)*; **über den** ~ **von ...** good for...;
~ **erhalten** payment (amount) received, *(Wechsel)* for value received; ~ **bar erhalten** cash received;
abgebuchter ~ amount debited; **abgehobener** ~ draw; **von der Bank abgehobener** ~ sum withdrawn from the bank; **nicht abgehobener** ~ unexpended portion; **abgerundeter** ~ round sum, amount rounded off; **abgeschriebener** ~ amount written off; **abzugfähiger** ~ deductible amount, *(Einkommensteuer)* personal allowance *(Br.)* (credit, *US*); **angegebener** ~ indicated (stated) amount; **pro forma angelegter** ~ nominal amount; **mit 5% Zinsen angelegter** ~ sum invested at 5 per cent interest; **angezahlter** ~ amount paid on instalment (deposit); **anrechnungspflichtiger** ~ chargeable amount; **anteiliger** ~ pro rata amount; **ausgesetzter** ~ amount granted (allowed); **ausgezahlter** ~ amount paid on account, disbursement; **ausmachender** ~ final amount; **noch ausstehender** ~ balance due, amount owing; **beliebiger** ~ any amount; **benötigter** ~ amount required; **zuviel berechneter** ~ overcharge; **zu wenig berechneter** ~ undercharge; **bestimmbarer** ~ determinable amount; **bestimmter** ~ definite sum, specific amount, stated sum; **betroffener** ~ amount involved; **doppelter** ~ double the amount; **eingeforderter** ~ *(auf Aktien)* call; **eingeklagter** ~ amount indorsed; **eingeplanter** ~ budgeted amount; **eingesammelter** ~ whip round; **einzubehaltender** ~ amount to be withheld; **einem Kreditbrief entnommener** ~ amount withdrawn from a letter of credit; **entstandener, noch nicht fälliger** ~ amount accrued; **erheblicher** ~ substantial amount; **zu erwartender** ~ anticipated amount; **erzielter** ~ amount realized; **fakturierter** ~ invoiced charge; **fälliger** ~ amount (sum) due; **fehlender** ~ missing amount; **feststehender** ~ liquidated sum; **ganzer** ~ full amount, sum total; **doppelt gebuchter** ~ amount entered twice; **von der Versicherung gedeckter** ~ amount of insurance carried, amount covered; **genauer** ~ precise amount; **genehmigter** ~ amount allowed; **geringer** ~ small sum, petty amount; **gesamter** ~ total (aggregate) amount; **geschuldeter** ~ sum (amount) due (owing); **gesperrter** ~ blocked amount; **gewetteter** ~ bet; **zuviel gezahlter** ~ sum paid in excess; **gezeichneter** ~ subscribed amount, subscription; **gleicher** ~ equivalent (equal) amount; **gleichhoher** ~ equal sum of money; **gleichwertiger** ~ equivalence; **großer** ~ large sum; **auf Ertragskonto gutgeschriebener** ~ amount brought to credit of revenue account; **hinterlegter** ~ deposited amount; **als Sicherheit hinterlegter** ~ bail; **hübscher** ~ nice little sum; **kleiner** ~ small amount; **körperschaftssteuerfreier** ~ corporation tax relief *(Br.)*; **kreditierter** ~ amount advanced; **namhafter** ~ substantial amount; **pro forma angesetzter, sehr niedriger** ~ nominal sum (amount); **offenstehender** ~ uncovered amount; **realisierter** ~ amount realized; **restlicher** ~ remaining (residual) amount; **roher** ~ gross amount; **rückständiger** ~ arrears; **schwankender** ~ variable fee; **für die Dividendenausschüttung zur Verfügung stehender** ~ sum available for dividends; **noch zur Verfügung stehender** ~ unexpended balance; **steuerfreier** ~ exemption, credit *(US)*; **steuerpflichtiger** ~ taxable portion; **strittiger** ~ amount at issue (in dispute); **symbolischer** ~ token amount; **aus der Rücklage zu tragender** ~ sum chargeable to reserve; **überfälliger** ~ amount overdue; **überschießender** ~ amount (sum) in excess, exceeding amount, surplus, *(Saldo)* unpaid balance; **überwiesener** ~ amount remitted; **überzahlter** ~ excess amount; **überzogener** ~ overdraft; **unbedeutender** ~ miserable sum; **veranschlagter** ~ estimated amount; **vereinbarter** ~ amount agreed upon; **verfügbarer** ~ amount available; **für die Ausschüttung frei verfügbarer** ~ amount regarded as free for distribution; **für die Dividendenausschüttung verfügbarer** ~ sum available for dividends; **versicherter** ~ amount insured; **veruntreuter** ~ defalcation; **voller** ~ entire (full) amount; **vorausgezahlter** ~ amount paid in advance; **vorgetragener** ~ amount brought forward; **uns zustehender** ~ money owing to us;
~ **von etwa 4 Dollar** amount in the region (neighborhood, *US*) of 4 dollars; ~ **pro Einheit** unit amount; ~ **in bestimmter Höhe** definite and certain amount; **pro-Kopf** ~ capitation grant; ~ **in Worten** sum (amount) in words; ~ **in Zahlen** amount in figures;
~ **an j. abführen** to pay an amount to s. o.; ~ **abrunden** to make up an amount, to round off a sum; ~ **absetzen** to set aside an amount; **bestimmten** ~ **für Abnutzung absetzen** to write off so much for wear and tear; ~ **abziehen** to deduct an amount; ~ **abzweigen** to earmark an amount for a purpose; ~ **zu 6% anlegen** to invest a sum at 6 per cent interest; ~ **zur Zahlung anweisen** to authorize the payment of a sum; ~ **anzahlen** to pay an amount as deposit; **zum** ~ **von ... auflaufen** to mount up to the sum of ...; ~ **gleichmäßig aufteilen** to split a sum into equal shares, to prorate an amount; ~ **unter verschiedene Leute aufteilen** to allocate a sum amongst several people; **erheblichen** ~ **ausmachen** to run to a respectable figure; **fünfstelligen** ~ **ausmachen** to run into five figures; **Scheck über einen** ~ **von 1000 DM ausstellen** to write out a cheque *(Br.)* (check, *US*) for the amount of DM 1000; **j. mit einem** ~ **belasten** to charge an amount to s. one's account, to pass an amount to the debit of s. o.; **jds. Konto mit einem** ~ **belasten** to carry (place) a sum to s. one's debit; ~ **für etw. bestimmen** to allocate a sum to s. th.; **abstimmungsweise einen** ~ **bewilligen** to vote a sum; ~ **in Abrechnung bringen** to debit a sum; ~ **in Abzug bringen** to deduct a sum; ~ **als Ausgabe (im Soll) buchen** to enter [up] an amount in the expenditure; ~ **bei einer Bank einzahlen** to bank an amount, to pay an amount into the bank; ~ **auf jds. Konto einzahlen** to pay in a sum to s. one's credit; **Spenden zu jedem** ~ **entgegennehmen** to accept contributions of any size; **sich für den** ~ **seiner Spesen erholen** to recover expenses; **um den erforderlichen** ~ **zu erreichen** to make up the required sum; ~ **flüssigmachen** to realize an amount of money; ~ **von jem. fordern** to come upon s. o. for a sum; ~ **guthaben** to have a balance in one's favo(u)r; **jem. (jds. Konto) einen** ~ **gutschreiben** to place an amount to s. one's credit, to pass an amount (put a sum) to the credit of s. o.; **bedeutenden** ~ **verloren haben** to be a loser to a considerable amount; ~ **für etw. hinterlegen** to leave a deposit on s. th.; ~ **kündigen** to call in a sum; ~ **in einer Rechnung kürzen** ~ to reduce an item in an invoice; **bestimmten** ~ **von seinen Ersparnissen nehmen** to set apart so much out of one's savings; **für einen** ~ **gut sein** to be good for a sum; **jem. einen großen** ~ **schuldig sein** to be indebted to a large amount to s. o.; ~ **für Forschungszwecke zur Verfügung stellen** to earmark a sum of money for research; ~ **für wohltätige Zwecke zur Verfügung stellen** to subscribe a sum to charity; ~ **wieder zur Verfügung stellen** to refund an amount; **benötigten** ~ **überschreiten** to be in excess of the sum required; ~ **als Einnahme verbuchen** to put an amount in the receipts; ~ **unter verschiedene Leute [gleichmäßig] verteilen** to apportion a sum among several people; ~ **vorschießen** to advance an amount (a sum); ~ **zu Lasten eines Kontos vortragen** to charge a sum to the debit; ~ **auf neue Rechnung vortragen** to bring forward an amount; ~ **a conto zahlen** to make a downpayment; ~ **dem Reservefonds zuführen** to allocate an amount to the reserve fund;
~ **dankend erhalten** received with thanks.

Beträge, anfallende accruing amounts; **für politische Parteien aufgewendete** ~ subscriptions to political parties; **für Notfälle bereitgestellte** ~ emergency means; **im voraus eingegangene** ~ deferred revenue (income) *(US)*; **einzelne** ~ individual

amounts; **geringfügige** ~ petty cash; **Vertretern und Angestellten geschuldete** ~ *(Bilanz)* amounts due to vendors and employees; **kleinste** ~ the smallest amounts; **kreditierte** ~ credited amounts; **offenstehende** ~ open items; **nicht verbrauchte körperschaftssteuerfreie** ~ surplus [of] franked investment income *(Br.)*; **regelmäßig zahlbare** ~ money payable periodically;
steuerlich absetzbare ~ **für die Bewirtung von Geschäftsfreunden** travel and entertainment expense deductions; ~ **aus einer Vermögensverwaltung** settlement money; ~ **aus der Werbewirtschaft** advertiser money;
~ **bereitstellen (zweckbestimmen)** to earmark funds; **nach dem Verhältnis der** ~ **kürzen** to reduce pro rata; **kleinste** ~ **sparen** to save little by little; ~ **für wohltätige Zwecke zur Verfügung stellen** to subscribe a sum to charity; ~ **für die Pensionskasse zurückstellen** to deposit funds with a trustee.

Betragen behavio(u)r, conduct, course, walk, manners, demeano(u)r, deportment, bearing;
von musterhaftem ~ well-conducted, of good behavio(u)r; **anstößiges** ~ obnoxious conduct; **musterhaftes** ~ model behavio(u)r; **standes- und ehrenrühriges** ~ conduct unbecoming an officer and gentleman; **ungebührliches** ~ unbecoming conduct.

betragen to amount (come) to, to mount, to run up, to rise;
durchschnittlich ~ to average; **im ganzen** ~ to total [up to], to aggregate; **nur noch knapp 1/3 des 1980er Umfangs** ~ to run at less than a third of the early 1980s level; **sich** ~ *(Manieren)* to behave, to conduct o. s.; **sich mannhaft** ~ to play the man; **sich schlecht** ~ to behave badly; **30% des Verbrauchs** ~ to account for 30% of consumption.

betragsmäßig in figures.

betrauen to entrust (charge, commit) with;
j. mit einem Amt ~ to appoint s. o. to an office; **j. mit der Aufgabe** ~ to charge (entrust) s. o. with a task; **j. mit der Aufsicht über etw.** ~ to give s. o. the charge of s. th.; **j. mit der Führung eines Schiffes** ~ *(mil.)* to commission s. o.; **Angestellten mit Führungsaufgaben** ~ to entrust an employee with executive functions; **j. mit der Sorge für etw.** ~ to entrust the care of s. th. to s. o.; **j. mit dem Verkauf** ~ to entrust s. o. with the sale.

betrauern to mourn, to deplore, to bemoan;
jds. Schicksal ~ to deplore s. one's fate.

betraut commissioned;
mit etw. ~ **sein** to be in charge (have the care) of s. th.; **mit der Leitung eines Geschäftes** ~ **sein** to be in charge of a business.

Betreff angeben to quote a reference number.

betreff, in with respect to, *(Brief)* re, referring, subject.

betreffen to concern, to regard, to pertain, to appertain, to affect, to relate to, to respect;
jds. Amt nicht ~ not to pertain to s. one's office; **gestrigen Vorfall** ~ to refer to yesterday's incident.

betreffend regarding, concerning, pertaining, respecting;
~**e Behörde** relevant (competent) authority; ~**es Geschäft** business in question; ~**e Personen** parties concerned.

betreffs concerning, regarding, referring to.

Betreiben pursuit, prompting, *(Maschine)* operating, operation;
auf ~ **von** at the instigation (prompting) of;
~ **eines Geschäfts** prosecution of an undertaking; ~ **eines Gewerbes** prosecution of an industry; ~ **eines Ladengeschäfts** running of a shop; ~ **unreeller Maklergeschäfte** bucketing *(US)*; ~ **eines Planes** pursuit of a scheme; ~ **eines Prozesses** conduct of a case; ~ **eines Unternehmens** prosecution of an undertaking; ~ **der Zwangsvollstreckung** levying a distress, levy of execution, strict foreclosure.

betreiben to pursue, to carry on, to go in for, to prosecute, to practise, to conduct, *(Bergwerk)* to exploit, *(Fabrik)* to work, to run, to operate *(US)*, *(Maschine)* to work, to operate;
Angelegenheit eifrig ~ to urge on a piece of work; **seine eigenen Angelegenheiten** ~ to conduct one's private affairs; **Anlage mit Strom** ~ to operate a plant with electricity; **Anwaltspraxis** ~ to prosecute one's practice of the law; **Bankgeschäft** ~ to do business as a banker; **etw. berufsmäßig** ~ to do s. th. professionally, to pursue a profession; **eifrig** ~ to drive on; **Eisenbahnlinie** ~ to operate a railway line (railroad, *US*); **energisch** ~ to pep, to press, to push; **jds. Ernennung** ~ to work for s. one's appointment, to root for a candidate; **vier Fabriken** ~ to operate four factories; **alle Arten des Finanzierungsgeschäftes** ~ to diversify into the nonbanking fields; **Gastwirtschaft** ~ to keep an inn; **gemeinsam** ~ to run joint services; **Geschäft** ~ to carry on (operate, conduct) a business; **Gewerbe** ~ to follow (ply) a trade; **etw. gewerbsmäßig** ~ to make a business of s. th.; **Großhandelsgeschäft** ~ to do (run) a wholesale business; **kleinen Handel** ~ to have a small business; **Handwerk** ~ to ply (follow) a trade; **Kohlenbergwerk** ~ to operate a coal mine; **Ladengeschäft** ~ to operate (run) a shop; **Luftverkehrsunternehmen** ~ to operate an airline; **nachts** ~ to operate at night; **Omnibusunternehmen** ~ to run a bus company; **Pension** ~ to keep boarders; **abwartende Politik** ~ to wait and see; **Prozeß** ~ to prosecute an action, to carry on a lawsuit; **auf eigene Rechnung** ~ to operate for one's own account; **Sache eilfertig** ~ to hurry over a task; **seine Sache nachdrücklich** ~ to press one's case; **seine Studien mit Eifer** ~ to devote o. s. to one's studies; **Sturz der Regierung** ~ to work for the overthrow of the cabinet; **Unternehmen** ~ to operate an undertaking, to carry on an enterprise; **jds. Wahl** ~ to work for s. one's election, to root for a candidate; **etw. weiter** ~ to carry on with s. th., to push a matter.

betreibende Partei prosecuting party.

betretbar walkable, passable;
nicht ~ inaccessible.

Betreten entry, entering;
~ **verboten!** no trespassing, out of bounds *(Br.)*, off limits *(US)*!; ~ **bei Strafe verboten!** trespassers will be prosecuted!; **unbefugtes** ~ **eines Grundstücks** trespass, breaking the close *(US)*; **versehentliches** ~ **eines Grundstücks** innocent trespass; **Unbefugten ist das** ~ **der Bahnanlagen verboten!** no trespassing on railway property!

betreten to walk on, to enter, to set foot on;
Arena ~ to enter the arena; **englischen Boden zum ersten Mal** ~ to set foot on British soil for the first time; **Bühne** ~ to walk the boards; **jds. Grundstück** ~ to pass over s. one's land, *(unbefugt)* to trespass on s. one's property; **Haus** ~ to set foot in a house; **jds. Haus nicht mehr** ~ never to darken s. one's door again; **Zeugenstand** ~ to take the witness box;
bitte den Rasen nicht ~! do not tread on the grass!;
~ *(a.)* embarrassed, abashed;
~ **aussehen** to look self-conscious (disconcerted); **ziemlich** ~ **sein** to be rather taken aback;
~**e Gesichter machen** to look sheepishly; ~**es Schweigen** embarrassed silence; **selten** ~**er Weg** unfrequented path.

Betretungsrecht title of entry;
~ **blockieren** to toll the entry.

betreuen to have the care of, to look after, to maintain, *(Vertreter)* to cover;
j. ~ to take care of s. o.; **Flugplatz** ~ to maintain an airport; **Fremdenverkehr** ~ to cater for foreign tourists; **Gebiet** ~ to cover a territory; **Haus** ~ to look after a house; **Kleinanleger** ~ to cater for the small investors; **Kunden** ~ to serve customers.

Betreuer maintainer, caretaker.

Betreuung caretaking, care, *(Patient)* aftercare, *(Unterhaltung)* maintenance, *(Vertreter)* coverage;
ärztliche ~ medical care; **kostenlose ärztliche** ~ free medical facilities; **dauernde** ~ constant attendance; **gastronomische** ~ catering; **häusliche** ~ home care; **nachträgliche** ~ aftercare; **soziale** ~ social welfare;
~ **von Auslandsbesuchern** catering for foreign visitors; ~ **geistig Behinderter und Geisteskranker** mental health service; ~ **eines Bezirks** covering a district; **gastronomische** ~ **an Bord** catering service; ~ **des Fremdenverkehrs** catering for foreign tourists; **gastronomische** ~ **der Geschäftswelt** business catering; **außergewöhnliche** ~ **eines Invaliden** *(Einkommensteuer)* extraordinary services;
auf ärztliche ~ **verzichten** to dispense with the doctor's services.

Betreuungs|aufgaben service functions; ~**auftrag** *(Vertreter)* assignment for coverage; ~**ausschuß** catering committee; ~**firma** catering firm; ~**programm** program(me) for coverage; ~**stelle** welfare centre; ~**stelle für Mutter und Kind** maternity and child welfare centre *(Br.)*; ~**tätigkeit** custodial service, *(auf sozialem Gebiet)* welfare work.

Betrieb *(Arbeitsgang)* service, *(Betreiben)* working, running, operating, operation *(US)*, *(Betriebsamkeit)* activity, *(Betriebsanlage)* factory, [manufacturing] plant, works, mill *(Br.)*, *(Geschäftsführung)* management, *(Herstellungsgang)* manufacture, *(Maschine)* working, operation, running, *(auf Straßen)* traffic, bustle, rush, *(Trubel)* racket, stir, merry-making, goings-on, high jinks, *(Unternehmen)* firm, business [enterprise], commercial undertaking (establishment), [industrial] concern, company, corporation, *(Werkstatt)* workshop, shop *(Br.)*;
außer ~ standing idle, *(Bahn)* out of service (action), *(el.)* off, *(Fahrstuhl)* not working, out of order, *(Hotel)* not opening,

(Maschine) out of blast, idle, not operating, out of gear, *(nicht in Ordnung)* out of order, disabled, not working, defunct; **im ~** on the shopfloor; **im ~ stehengelassen** *(Gewinn)* retained in business; **in ~** operating, operative, in operation, in blast, at work, working, going, running; **in vollem ~** in full working order, in operation (action), going at full blast; **nicht im ~** inoperative, nonoperating;

aktiver ~ going concern; **arbeitender ~** going business (concern), operating property *(US)*; **billig arbeitender ~** low-cost plant; **für den Staat beschäftigter ~** government client; **auf Spezialitäten beschränkter ~** franchised unit; **bestreikter ~** struck shop; **dezentralisierter ~** departmentalized business (factory) *(US)*; **durcharbeitender ~** all-night service, *(ganze Woche)* seven-day operation; **durchgehender ~** continuous process, continuity of operations; **einschichtiger ~** single-shift operation; **einträglicher ~** profitable enterprise; **elektrischer ~** electric service; **ernährungswirtschaftlicher ~** food-processing industry; **an der Baustelle errichteter ~** on-site factory; **erstklassiger ~** top plant; **fahrplanmäßiger ~** scheduled operation *(US)*; **forstwirtschaftlicher ~** forestry company (industry); **an Preisabsprachen nicht gebundener ~** outsider; **gefährlicher ~** dangerous premises; **wissenschaftlich geführter ~** scientific management; **gemeinnütziger ~** nonprofit enterprise, public utility company (corporation, *US*), public service company *(Br.)* (corporation, *US*); **gemeinsamer ~** joint working; **gemischtwirtschaftlicher ~** mixed (semi-public) enterprise, quasi-public company, mixed ownership property *(US)*; **genossenschaftlicher ~** cooperative enterprise; **gesundheitsschädlicher ~** offensive trade; **gewerbepolizeipflichtiger ~** trade subject to licence; **gewerblicher ~** industrial enterprise (concern), manufacturing establishment; **gewerkschaftsfeindlicher ~** anti-union shop *(US)*; **gewerkschaftsfreier ~** nonunion shop, open shop *(US)*; **gewerkschaftsfreundlicher ~** preferential shop; **gewerkschaftspflichtiger ~** closed (agency, *Br.*) shop; **staatlich genehmigter gewerkschaftspflichtiger ~** approved closed shop *(Br.)*; **nicht gewerkschaftspflichtiger ~** open shop *(US)*; **grafischer ~** printing firm, commercial art company; **großbäuerlicher ~** large farm; **gutgehender ~** prosperous enterprise; **halbautomatischer ~** semi-automatic working; **handwerklicher ~** handicraft; **industrieller ~** industrial enterprise (concern); **kapitalintensiver ~** high-cost plant; **konzessionierter ~** licensed enterprise; **kriegswichtiger ~** essential industry; **landwirtschaftlicher ~** agricultural enterprise (undertaking), ranch, farm; **minderwertiger landwirtschaftlicher ~** submarginal farm; **nicht landwirtschaftlicher ~** nonagricultural enterprise (establishment); **laufender ~** going concern, current operation; **auf Hochturen laufender ~** drive; **reibungslos laufender ~** smooth-running entity; **lebenswichtiger ~** essential service, vitally important establishment; **lebhafter ~** brisk state of trade; **milchverarbeitender ~** milk-processing enterprise; **mittelbäuerlicher ~** medium-sized farm; **mittelgroßer (mittlerer) ~** medium-sized enterprise (business, *US*), small business *(US)*; **nahestehende ~e** affiliated enterprises; **öffentlicher ~** public enterprise; **voll gewerkschaftlich organisierter ~** closed (agency, *Br.*) shop; **produzierender ~** production unit; **rentabler ~** profitable enterprise, economic operation; **sparsamer ~** economic[al] operation; **staatlicher (staatseigener) ~** state-owned enterprise; **im Gemeineigentum stehender ~** publicly owned enterprise; **unter gewerkschaftlichem Einfluß stehender ~** unionized plant; **stillgelegter ~** mill out of work *(Br.)*, nonoperating property (factory) *(US)*; **störungsfreier ~** uninterrupted operation; **staatlich subventionierter ~** taxeater; **viel ~** merrymaking, goings-on, high jinks *(fam.)*; **volkseigener ~** socialized (nationalized, *Br.*) enterprise; **rationell wirtschaftender ~** efficiently run enterprise; **wirtschaftlicher ~** economic operation;

~ mit Akkordsystem contract shop *(US)*; **~ auf den Bahnhöfen** rush at the stations; **~ eines Bergwerkes** exploitation of a mine; **~ einer Eisenbahnlinie** operation of a railway (railroad, *US*) line; **~ mit Entlohnung nach dem Trucksystem** truck shop; **~ eines Geschäftes** operation of a business; **~ an der Grenze der Rentabilität** marginal producer (firm); **~ der öffentlichen Hand** government (state) enterprise; **~ mit begrenzter Kapazität** limited-capacity plant; **~ eines Ladengeschäfts** shopkeeping; **~ mit geringem Lohnniveau** low-wage unit; **~ eines Luftfahrzeugs** operation of an aircraft; **~ einer Omnibuslinie** publicly run bus; **~ eines Schiffes** operation of a ship; **~ mit Staatsaufträgen** government contractor; **viel ~ in der Stadt** rush of city life **~ eines Unternehmens** working of a business; **staatlicher ~ von Wirtschaftsunternehmen** governmental operation of business, quasi-public corporation;

im ~ seines Vaters arbeiten to work in one's father's firm; **~ aufnehmen** to begin working, to start running, *(Geschäft)* to open; **~ demnächst aufnehmen** *(Bahn)* to open a line shortly; **~ wieder aufnehmen** to resume work; **~ ausdehnen** to expand operations; **~ neu ausstatten** to equip a shop with new tools; **~ zum Erfolg bringen** to work up a business; **ganzen ~ kostenmäßig durchforsten** to cut costs throughout a company; **~ einstellen** to stop a factory (business), to cease (suspend) operations (working), to shut (close) down, *(Bahn)* to close a line; **~ vorübergehend einstellen** to close down temporarily; **~ eröffnen** to commence business; **großen ~ haben** to have a noisy party; **~ eingestellt haben** to have ceased running; **in ~ halten** to keep running (working); **Hochofen in ~ halten** to keep a furnace going; **~ aus den roten Zahlen herausbringen** to administer a company from red to black *(US coll.)*; **~ installieren** to equip a shop with tools; **~ anlaufen lassen** to put in (go into) operation, to begin working; **~ Fett ansetzen lassen** to beef up a plant *(sl.)*; **Fabrik in ~ setzen lassen** to give orders for the work to be started; **~ leiten** to manage a business, *(Werk)* to run a plant; **~ umsichtig leiten** to nurse a plant; **~ machen** to make merry, to liven up; **in ~ nehmen** to set going, to set (put) into operation, to operate; **automatisch in ~ nehmen** to press the button; **Bahnlinie in ~ nehmen** to open a line; **Omnibus in ~ nehmen** to put a bus on the road; **~ schließen** to close down; **~ infolge von Sparsamkeitsmaßnahmen schließen** to close its doors for reasons of economy; **~ vorübergehend schließen** to close temporarily; **außer ~ sein** *(Fabrik)* to be out of operation, *(Maschine)* to run idle, *(Rundfunkstation)* to be off the air; **billig im ~ sein** *(Auto)* to be run at small cost; **in ~ sein** *(Bahnlinie)* to be in operation (running), *(Fabrik)* to work, to be in operation, *(Hochofen)* to be in blast, *(Maschine)* to run, to operate, to be operating, to be worked, *(Omnibus)* to be on the road, *(Rundfunkstation)* to be on the air; **das ganze Jahr in ~ sein** *(Auto)* to be in commission all the year round; **nicht in ~ sein** to be out of work (at a standstill); **ständig in ~ sein** to run full time; **in vollem ~ sein** to hum with activity, to be going at full blast; **wieder in ~ sein** to be in regular work again, *(Hotel)* to be running (working) again; **aus dem ~ gezogen sein** *(Auto)* to be of service; **außer ~ setzen** *(Maschine)* to put out of operation, to throw out of gear; **Anlage außer ~ setzen** to discard an asset; **Bahnlinie außer ~ setzen** to close a line; **in ~ setzen** to put (set) into operation (action), to start [running (working)], to set to work, to prime; **wieder in ~ setzen** to reopen, to restart; **Eisenbahnstrecke in ~ setzen** to open a railway line; **~ stillegen** to close (shut) down; **~ völlig umkrempeln** to turn around a company; **auf elektrischen ~ umstellen** *(Bahn)* to electrify; **~ völlig auf Produkte für den Wohnungs- und Straßenbau umstellen** to aim a company at totally environmental products; **seinen ~ vergrößern** to enlarge one's business; **~ verlagern (verlegen)** to move a plant to another locality; **~ in Vorstadtgebiete verlagern** to go suburban; **~ in stark verkleinertem Umfang weiterführen** to operate on a drastically reduced scale; **in ~ genommen werden** to go into operation, *(Bahnlinie, Straße)* to be opened to traffic; **~ wiederaufnehmen** to resume activity; **in der Nähe des ~s wohnen** to live within a short distance of one's work; **aus dem ~ ziehen** to take out of service; **Flugzeug aus dem ~ ziehen** to ground a plane; **Omnibus aus dem ~ ziehen** to take a bus off the road.

betrieben operated;

auf kommerzieller Basis ~ commercially operated; **elektrisch ~** operated by electricity, electrically operated; **von einem einzigen Mann ~** one-man; **durch Maschinenkraft ~** power-operated; **staatlich ~** state-operated;

elektrisch ~ werden to work by electricity.

betrieblich operating, operative, operational, *(betriebsintern)* internal;

~e Altersversorgung self-administrated (company) pension scheme; **~e Anlagenplanung** plant layout; **~e Arbeitszeit** company time; **~e Aufwendungen** operating expenditure; **~es Ausbauprogramm** plant expansion program(me); **~e Eignungsprüfung** employment test; **~e Einrichtungen** plant facilities; **~e Erfordernisse** operational requirements; **~er Erweiterungsfonds** plant fund; **~e Finanzwirtschaft** business financing; **~e Förderung** inservice training; **~e Forschung** business research; **~er Gesundheitszustand** industrial health; **~e Gliederung** working organization; **~e Investitionen** investments; **~e Leistungsfähigkeit** plant capacity, operating efficiency; **~e Planung** business (operational) planning; **~e Produktivität** plant productivity; **~es Rechnungswesen** cost (manufacturing) accounting, costing; **~e Ruhegeldverpflich-**

tungen pension liabilities; ~**er Sozialfonds** employee benefit trust; ~**es Transportunternehmen** industrial carrier; ~**e Vergünstigungen** fringe benefits; ~**e Verlustquellen** operational deficiencies; ~**es Vorschlagswesen** suggestion system; ~**er Wettbewerb** works competition; ~**er Widerstand** shopfloor resistance.

Betriebs|abbau factory removal; ~**abgaben** taxes payable by a factory; ~**ablauf** operational procedure, sequence of operations; ~**abrechnung** manufacturing cost sheet, operational (shop) accounting, operating statement *(US)*; ~**abrechnungsbogen** master summary (expense distribution) sheet, operation sheet; ~**abschnitt** operational stage; ~**abstimmung** vote on the shopfloor.

Betriebsabteilung staff (business) department (division), branch, *(Eisenbahn)* operating department, *(Versicherungsgesellschaft)* business department;
kaufmännische ~ commercial department; **technische** ~ technical (engineering) department;
nach ~**en aufgliedern** to departmentalize.

Betriebs|abwicklung handling of a business; **interne** ~**abwicklung** back-office system; ~**aktiva** active assets, assets for use in the business.

betriebsam active, industrious, busy;
~**e Stadt** bustling town.

Betriebsamkeit activity, bustle, business, industry, stirabout.

Betriebs|amt *(Bahn)* traffic department; ~**analyse** operation analysis; ~**änderung** change of the object clause; ~**anforderungen** operating requirements; ~**angaben** shop data; ~**angehörige** work (working) force, personnel, staff; **neuen** ~**angehörigen einweisen (einarbeiten)** to sponsor a new employee *(US)*; ~**angehöriger** [shop] employee, company man (servant, official), staff member, worker.

Betriebsanlage factory, working plant, asset, facility, operating equipment, *(Betriebsaufbau)* plant layout, *(Betriebseinheit)* productive unit;
~**n** works, plant production facilites, industrial installations; **nur teilweise abgeschriebene** ~ only partially depreciated plant; **nicht ausgenutzte** ~**n** idle equipment; **festeingebaute** ~ fixed plant; **moderne** ~**n** works with modern equimpment; **stilliegende** ~ idle plant (facility);
~ **außer Dienst (Betrieb) setzen** to discard an asset;
~**buch** plant ledger; ~**werte** plant assets.

Betriebs|anleitung operating instructions, shop rules *(US)*; ~**anmeldung** registration of business; ~**anordnung** factory order, operating instructions; ~**anordnungen** operating instructions, shop rules *(US)*; ~**anteil** management share; ~**anweisung** operating (service) instructions, instruction manual, factory order, shop rules *(US)*, company ruling, *(Handbuch)* instruction manual; ~**anwesenheitslohn** portal-to-portal pay; ~**arbeiter** shopman, company man; ~**archiv** company archives; ~**arzt** company (plant) physician, factory doctor; ~**assistent** assistant to a manager; ~**atmosphäre** working atmosphere; ~**aufbau** corporate structure *(US)*; ~**aufgabe** closing down of a factory, plant closing, *(Bahn)* service abandonment; ~**aufnahme** going into operation, *(Statistik)* industrial census; ~**aufseher** works manager, supervisor [in a factory], *(Bahn)* traffic manager; ~**aufsicht** plant inspection, factory supervision; ~**aufstellung** working (operation, *US*) statement; ~**auftrag** service order; ~**aufwand** operating expenses, operational expenditure; ~**aufzeichnungen** company record; ~**ausbildung** industrial education (training), inservice training *(US)*; ~**ausbildungsausschuß** joint apprentice committee; ~**ausdehnung** business (plant) expansion; ~**ausfall** breakdown, *(Stillegung)* shutdown; ~**ausflug** works (staff) outing.

Betriebsausgaben expenses of operation, revenue (operating) expenditure;
abzugsfähige ~ deductible expenses; **allgemeine** ~ general operating (trading) expenses, overhead; **vorausbezahlte** ~ deferred charges to expense.

Betriebs|auslastung factory workload; ~**ausnutzung** plant utilization; ~**ausnutzungsfaktor** plant utilization factor; ~**ausrüstung** [factory] equipment, *(Bilanz)* investment in plant and equipment; ~**ausschuß** shop (works, factory) committee; **paritätisch besetzter** ~**ausschuß** joint industrial council *(Br.)*; ~**ausschuß für den Erwerb betriebseigener Aktien** employee stock purchase committee; ~**ausstattung** [factory] equipment, furniture and fixtures, *(Bilanz)* investment in plant and equipment; **vorgenommene** ~**ausstattungen** equipment investments; ~- **und Geschäftsausstattung** office equipment, *(Bilanz)* tools, furniture and fixtures; ~**ausweis** company identification card; ~**ausweitung** industrial expansion; ~**autorität** managerial authority; ~**bahn** industrial line; ~**bankett** company banquet.

betriebsbedingt operational;
~**e Notwendigkeiten** shopfloor necessities.

Betriebs|bedingungen shop conditions, *(techn.)* operating (working) conditions; **übliche** ~**bedingungen** normal working conditions; ~**bedürfnisse** operating requirements, corporate exigencies *(US)*; ~**belastung** *(el.)* working load; ~**belegenheit** plant location; ~**berater** management (business, *US*) consultant, accounting adviser, *(für den Personalchef)* industrial relations counsel(l)or; **selbständiger** ~**berater** business engineer *(US)*; ~**berater für den Vorstand** staff officer; ~**beratung** management consultancy; ~**beratungsfirma** management consulting firm; ~**beratungsgebühren** consultancy fees; ~**beratungsstelle** staff agency.

betriebsbereit serviceable, in running order, ready for operation.

Betriebs|bereitschaft readiness for service, serviceability; ~**bericht** operating (trading) report; ~**besichtigung** plant visit (tour), trip through a factory; ~**besichtigung gestatten** to permit to visit the works; ~**bestimmungen** operating instructions, company ruling, shop rules *(US)*; ~**besuch** factory visit; ~**bewertung** going-concern valuation; ~**bilanz** operating statement; **vergleichende** ~**bilanz** common size or percentage statement *(US)*; ~**blindheit** operational (plant) blindness; ~**buch** plant ledger, company ruling, *(Flugzeug)* log; ~**buchhalter** cost (company) accountant; ~**buchhaltung**, ~**buchführung** cost (manufacturing, industrial) accounting; ~**budget** operating budget; ~**büro** *(Bahn)* traffic department, *(Planungsabteilung)* planning department; ~**chemiker** industrial chemist; ~**daten** operating data; ~**dauer** operating period, *(Maschine)* service life; ~**defizit** operational (operating, plant) deficit; ~**delegation** representation of the workers; ~**dezernent** works (plant, *US*) manager; ~**dichte** density of distribution of firms; ~**diebstahl** employee theft; ~**dienst** technical service; ~**direktor** operations (plant, works) manager; ~**disziplin** industrial (shop) discipline; ~**drehzahl** normal speed, operational rate of revolutions; ~**düsenflugzeug** corporate (business) jet.

betriebseigen factory-owned, company-owned, in-house, internal;
~**es Geschäft** in-plant shop *(Br.)*, company store *(US)*; ~**er Prüfer** internal auditor.

Betriebs|eigentümer factory owner; ~**einheit** business entity, operating (business) unit; **dirigierbare** ~**einheit** manageable unit; **nichtselbständige** ~**einheit** dependent establishment; ~**einmischung** factory interference; ~**einnahmen** manufacturing income (earnings), net operating profit, company (operating) earnings, operating revenues (income), trading receipts, *(Bahn)* traffic receipts, railway (railroad, *US*) earnings; **konsolidierte** ~**einnahmen** consolidated income; ~**einrichtungen** [factory, operating, production] equipment, operational (plant) facilities, installations; **veraltete** ~**einrichtung** out-of-date plant; ~**einrichtung und** ~**ausstattung** *(Bilanz)* plant and equipment; ~**einrichtungen und Maschinen** *(Bilanz)* plant and machinery; ~**einschränkung** curtailment of production, *(verkürzte Arbeitszeit)* short-time working; ~**einstellung** suspension of operations, stoppage of business, plant closing (closure), closing down, shutdown; ~**einstellungskosten** shutdown costs; ~**eisenbahn** industrial line (railroad, *US*); ~**entscheidung** operating decision; ~**erfahrung** operating experience, *(praktische)* industrial know-how; ~**erfindung** employees' (works) invention; **seinem Arbeitgeber alle** ~**erfindungen zur Verfügung stellen** to pass on one's discoveries to one's employer; ~**erfolg** operating result; ~**erfordernisse** operational requirements, *(Bahn)* service requirements; **sich im Ernstfall den** ~**erfordernissen fügen** to knuckle down to factory muscle in the crunch; ~**ergebnis** operating (working, company, trading) result, company earnings; ~**ergebnisrechnung** operating *(US)* (performance income) statement, statement of operating results *(US)*; ~**ergebniszahlen** operating earnings figures; ~**erlaubnis** operating permission, licence to operate; ~**eröffnung** opening of a business; ~**errichtungskosten** quotations for plant; ~**erträge** business (working) proceeds, net operating profit, operating earnings, company earnings; ~**erweiterung** plant addition (expansion), factory extension; ~**erweiterungsfonds** plant fund; ~**erweiterungskosten** cost of plant addition; ~**erwerb** acquisition of a business enterprise; ~**erziehung** industrial education (training), in-service training *(US)*; ~**etat** operating budget; ~**expansion** business (plant) expansion; ~**fachmann** operating executive.

betriebsfähig operative, in operation, in working condition (order), in running order, fit for use, *(Bahn)* serviceable;
nicht ~ out of order, not working (operating);
voll ~ sein to be in good working order;
~**er Zustand** operating condition.

Betriebs|fähigkeit working (operating) condition; ~**fahrzeug** fleet car; ~**fahrzeuge** factory fleet; ~**faktoren** operating factors; ~**familie** corporate family; ~**fehlbetrag** operating deficit, plant deficiency; ~**ferien** works holidays, staff vacations; **wegen ~ferien geschlossen** shut (closed) down for holidays; ~**ferien machen** to close down for the holidays; ~**fernsehen** closed-circuit television.

betriebsfertig ready for operation (working, service), in running (working) order.

Betriebs|fest staff party; ~**finanzen** corporate finances *(US)*; ~**fläche** plant grounds, area of production *(US)*; **landwirtschaftliche ~fläche** farm land, farm real estate, agricultural area, acreage; ~**flotte** operating fleet; ~**flugzeug** company airplane, business aircraft; ~**fonds** business (working, company) fund; ~**form** type of business; ~**formular** company form; ~**forschung** operational *(Br.)* (operations, *US*) research.

betriebsfremd outside, extraneous;
~**e Einkünfte (Erträge)** nonoperating revenues; ~**e Mittel** outside capital.

Betriebsfremder outsider.

Betriebsführer works *(Br.)* (plant, business, industrial) manager, working manager *(US)*, managing director, business operator;
eigener ~ owner-manager; **hervorragender** ~ management engineer.

Betriebsführung operational (industrial, working, plant, *US*) management, conduct of operations;
landwirtschaftliche ~ farm management, farming business; **mehrstufige** ~ multiple management *(US)*; **oberste** ~ top management *(US)*; **ökonomische** ~ business administration; **paternalische** ~ paternalism; **schlechte** ~ bad management, mismanagement; **wirtschaftliche** ~ economic operation; **wissenschaftliche** ~ scientific management; **aus Nachwuchskräften zusammengesetzte** ~ management cabinet *(US)*;
~ **durch das Angebot von Variationsmöglichkeiten** management by alternatives; ~ **nur in Ausnahmefällen (nach Ausnahmeprinzipien)** management by exception *(US)*; ~ **durch die Belegschaft** worker management; ~ **durch Darlegung überzeugender Beweggründe** management by motivation; ~ **in partizipativem Führungsstil** management by delegation; ~ **durch Informierung und Anhörung der Mitarbeiter** management by communication and participation; ~ **und Mitarbeiter** line and staff; ~ **im autoritären Stil** management by direction and control; ~ **durch ständiges Streben nach Systemerneuerung** management by innovation; ~ **durch Systematisierung aller Leitungs- und Kontrolltätigkeiten** management by system; ~ **anhand eines Verhaltenskatalogs** management by decision rules; ~ **mittels weitgehender Weiterbildung** management by teaching; ~ **durch Zielvorgabe** management by objectives.

Betriebsführungs|fach management subject; ~**fragen** management problems; ~**funktion** management function; ~**gesellschaft** management company; ~**grundsätze** management principles; ~**lehre** management science; **raffinierte ~methoden** sophisticated management techniques; ~**politik** management policy (strategy); ~**praxis** management practice; ~**verfahren** management technique; ~**vertrag** management agreement; ~**wissenschaft** management science.

Betriebs|fürsorge industrial social work, personnel service *(US)*; ~**gas** fuel gas; ~**gebäude** company premises, factory building; ~**gebiet** operating area; ~**gefahr** operational risk (hazard); ~**gefüge** corporate structure; ~**gegenstand** object of an enterprise; ~**geheimnis** trade (industrial, manufacturing) secret; ~**geheimnisse verraten** to divulge trade secrets; ~**gelände** plant site (grounds, space), company premises; ~**gemeinkosten** indirect costs, factory overhead; ~**gemeinschaft** plant community, *(gemeinsamer Betrieb)* joint operation; ~**genehmigung** authorized operation, licence to operate, factory order; **landwirtschafliche ~genossenschaft** agricultural cooperation; ~**gesellschaft** operating company *(US)* (subsidiary); ~**gesundheit** industrial (shopcraft, company, *US*) health; ~**gewerkschaft** house union, puppet, industrial (shopcraft, company) union *(US)*; ~**gewicht** *(Fahrzeug)* dead weight.

Betriebsgewinn trading (operating) profit, profit from (on) operations, profits of the business, company's (operating) surplus *(US)*;
ausschüttungsfähiger ~ unappropriated earned surplus *(US)*; **den Rücklagen zugewiesener** ~ earned (appropriated) surplus.

Betriebs|gleis industrial line (track), house track; ~**gliederung** working organization; ~**größe** size of business, company size; **optimale ~größe** optimal size; ~**grundstück** business (factory) property, company property (premises), plant site; ~**grundstück in Besitz nehmen** to enter into occupation of premises; ~**gruppe** managerial group; ~**guthaben** *(ECU)* working balance.

Betriebshaftpflicht employer's liability;
~**gesetz** Employer's Liability Act *(US)*; ~**police** employer's liability policy; ~**versicherung** manufacturer's public liability (workmen's compensation, *US*) insurance, employers' liability insurance; ~**versicherungsgesellschaft** employers' liability assurance corporation *(Br.)*; ~**vorschläge** workers' compensation program(me).

Betriebs|handbuch employee handbook (manual); ~**handelsspanne** gross margin; ~**hauptbuch** property (factory) ledger; ~**haushaltsplan** operating budget; ~**hierarchie** management (business) hierarchy; ~**hygiene** industrial hygiene; ~**imperium** managerial state; ~**ingenieur** industrial (operation, production, plant, manufacturing, operating) engineer; ~**ingenieur für die Einführung von Elektronenrechenmaschinen** operations-research analyst *(US)*; ~**inhaber** factory owner; **mitarbeitender ~inhaber** working employer; ~**inspektion** factory inspection.

betriebsinterne|r Briefverkehr interoffice mail; ~ **Prüfung** internal auditing; ~ **Überwachung der Buchführung** accounting control.

Betriebs|inventar business (plant, factory) inventory, implements of trade; ~**investitionen** plant investment; **geplante ~investitionen** business investment intentions; ~ **und Maschinenparkinvestitionen** investment in plant and machinery; ~**investitionen erhöhen** to increase its spending on plant; ~**jahr** business (trading, operating, working, financial) year; ~**jargon** corporate parlance; ~**jubiläum** company anniversary; ~**justiz** industrial (shop) discipline; ~**kalkulation** costing, cost accounting (keeping); ~**kalkulation zu Marktpreisen** current cost accounting; ~**kalkulator** cost accountant (clerk), cost keeper; ~**kantine** industrial staff canteen, catering department; ~**kantineneinrichtung** employee food service; ~**kantinenwesen** industrial catering; ~**kapazität** operating competence (efficiency), plant (operating) capacity; ~**kapazität voll ausfahren** to work as flat out as plant permits; ~**kapazität beinahe voll ausnutzen** to operate close to capacity; **knapp 2/3 der ~kapazität ausnutzen** to operate at below two thirds of capacity; ~**kapazitätsausnutzung** full utilization of plant.

Betriebskapital current (net working, trading, circulating, business, liquid) capital, stock-in-trade, working fund, net quick assets, effective (floating) capital, *(Bank)* fund *(Br.)*, capital stock;
knappes ~ liquid capital shortage; **kurzfristiges** ~ short-time working capital; **notwendiges** ~ requisite capital;
~ **nach Abzug der Verbindlichkeiten** net working capital (current assets);
~ **verstärken** to beef up working capital;
~**erfordernisse** working-capital needs; ~**erhöhung** additions to working capital; ~**nachweis** working capital statement; ~**schmälerungen** deductions from working capital; ~**verhältnis** working capital ratio.

Betriebs|kasino company cafeteria (dining room), catering department; ~**kassenmittel** cash funds; ~**kennzahlen** operating figures; ~**kindergarten** factory nursery; ~**klima** working atmosphere; **angenehmes ~klima** pleasant office atmosphere; ~**klimauntersuchung** employee attitude measurement; ~**knigge** corporate etiquette; ~**koeffizient** operating ratio, working coefficient; ~**konkurse** business casualties; ~**kontingent** production quota; ~**konto** operating account (ledger), *(Handelsgesellschaft)* trading account; ~**kontrolle** working (plant) supervision, factory (operational) control, internal check; **gewerkschaftsfeindliche ~kontrolle** anti-union control of companies; ~**kontroverse** industrial dispute; ~**konzentration** business (industrial) concentration; ~**konzession** operating concession, licence to operate.

Betriebskosten operating (operational) costs (expenses), operating charges, cost of operation, working expense (cost, charges), factory cost (expense), dead charges, *(Eisenbahn)* expenses of running, running costs, *(Unterhaltungskosten)* carrying charges, overheads;
allgemeine ~ turnover costs; **laufende** ~ running expenses;
~ **für Fahrzeuge und Maschinen** equipment operation costs; ~ **bei voller Kapazitätsausnutzung** capacity costs; ~ **und Verwaltungskosten** expenses for management and administration; ~ **innerhalb eines Zeitraums** current expenditure;

~**ermittlung** cost accounting, costing; ~**koeffizient** ratio of working expenses; ~**kredite** *(Bankbilanz)* business lendings; ~**kreditziffern** working capital figures; ~**satz** operating cost ratio.

Betriebs|krankenkasse company sickness benefit fund; ~**kreislauf** operating cycle; ~**krise** operations crisis; ~**küche** industrial canteen; ~**kursus** shop course; ~**laden** inplant shop *(Br.)*, company store *(US)*; ~**lastwagen** business truck; ~**leistung** operating efficiency, performance under service conditions; **volle** ~**leistung** full operating capacity.

Betriebsleiter working (workshop) manager, works supervisor, operating (operations, plant, *US*, head, production) manager, plant superintendent *(US)*, boss *(fam.)*, *(Eisenbahn)* traffic manager;

oberster ~ top [-level] manager *(US)*; **technischer** ~ chief engineer;

j. vorübergehend als ~ **einsetzen** to put s. o. in temporary charge of a factory.

Betriebs|leiterin manageress; ~**leitung** [plant, *US*, shop, factory] management, *(Vorstand)* managerial staff, superintendence; ~**leitung einem Stab von Fachleuten übertragen** to entrust the working of an undertaking to a qualified staff; ~**lohnliste** industrial (factory) payroll; ~**loyalität** employee loyalty.

Betriebsmaterial stock-in-trade, factory supplies, working stock, *(Eisenbahn)* rolling stock, *(Spediteur)* company material;

unzureichendes ~ *(Bahn)* shortage of rolling stock.

Betriebs|materialien factory supplies; ~**medizin** industrial medicine; ~**mitteilung** company release.

Betriebsmittel employed funds, operating (working) fund, stock [in trade], trading capital, working assets (capital), floating assets, general cash, *(Anlagen)* production (plant) facilities, *(Eisenbahn)* rolling stock;

bare ~ corporate cash *(US)*; **landwirtschaftliche** ~ farm equipment; **umlaufende** ~ current assets; **vorhandene** ~ operating cash; **werbende** ~ revenue assets;

~ **für Kommunalzwecke** working-capital fund;

notwendige ~ **aufbringen** to raise corporate cash *(US)*; ~ **bereitstellen** to make the general cash available; **in den** ~**n sehr beschränkt sein** to be short of trading capital; ~ **zuweisen** to appropriate working funds;

~**anlagen** utilities; ~**bedarf** working capital needs; ~**bereitstellung** provision of operating funds; ~**defizit** working capital deficit; ~**fonds** operating (working) capital fund; ~**guthaben** working capital balance; ~**höhe** working capital figures; ~**kredit** working capital (operational, business) credit, loan advanced for use in business; ~**kredite** *(Bankbilanz)* business lendings; **sich** ~**kredit durch Debitorenabtretung verschaffen** to factor one's accounts; ~**reserve,** ~**rücklage** operating cash reserve; ~**rüstzeit** set-up time; ~**überschuß** working capital surplus; ~**überweisung** remittance of operating funds; ~**vorschüsse** working fund advances; ~**ziffern** working capital figures; ~**zuweisung** appropriation of operating funds; ~**zweck** working capital purpose.

Betriebs|moral employee morale; ~**nachkalkulation** subsequent revision of books; ~**netz** operational network; ~**normung** standardization of factories.

betriebsnotwendig operationally necessary;

~**es Kapital** fixed (permanent) working capital; ~**e Kassenmittel** cash funds required.

Betriebs|notwendigkeit operational necessity; ~**nudel** *(fam.)* hummer *(sl.)*; ~**oberingenieur** superintendent engineer; ~**obmann** works (shop, union, *US*) steward; ~**optimum** ideal capacity, optimum, pattern of production; ~**ordnung** working (shop) regulations, shop rules *(US)*; ~**organisation** industrial (management) organization; ~**organisator** management expert; ~**pachtvertrag** lease of business premises; ~**pause** rest pause (period); ~**pension** company-financed (occupational) pension; **beitragsfreie** ~**pension** noncontributory pension.

Betriebspensions|kasse employees' pension fund; ~**kasse auflösen** to wind up a pension scheme; ~**plan** company-financed pension plan; **am** ~**plan teilnehmen** to become eligible for company pension; **bei Versicherungen abgedecktes** ~**system** insured pension plan.

Betriebs|personal [shop (company)] staff, operating (shopfloor) staff, employees, company personnel, *(Eisenbahn)* maintenance team (staff), operating employees, *(aus der Heimat)* home-based staff; ~**personal einer Versicherungsgesellschaft** underwriting staff; ~**personal einsetzen** to assign operating personnel; **soziale** ~**pflege** personnel service *(US)*; ~**plan** operation schedule, *(Eisenbahn)* management; **mehrschichtiger** ~**plan** multiple-shift operation schedule; ~**planer** company planner; ~**planspiel** management game; ~**planung** management (operational) planning; **finanzielle** ~**planung** industrial budgetary control; ~**politik** management (business) policy, company [labo(u)r] policies; **langfristige** ~**politik** company strategy; ~**prämie** company bonus; ~**prämienwesen** company bonus plan; ~**probebilanz** trial balance; ~**problem** operating (operational) problem; ~**produkt** product, *(Handelsgesellschaft)* trading item; ~**programm** manufacturing program(me); ~**prüfer** public accountant, *(Revisionsabteilung)* [internal] auditor, *(Steuer)* income-tax investigator, tax inspector *(Br.)* (auditor, *US*); ~**prüferhaftung** legal liability; **[interne]** ~**prüfung** [internal] auditing; ~**prüfung durch das Finanzamt** tax inspection (audit, *US*, auditing, *US*); ~**prüfung haben** to have the auditors in; ~**prüfungsdienst** tax service; ~**psychologe** industrial psychologist; ~**psychologie** industrial psychology; ~**pyramide** corporate pyramid.

Betriebsrat factory (shop) committee, factory *(Br.)* (shop, *US*, employees', workers, staff) council, works committee (council), *(Einzelperson)* union steward (committeeman);

paritätischer ~ company council *(US)*.

Betriebs|rätegesetz shop council law *(US)*; ~**rationalisierung** plant rationalization.

Betriebsrats|forderungen shop stewards' demand; ~**mitglied** union steward (committeeman); ~**vereinigung** industrial union council; ~**versammlung** congress of factory councils *(US)*; ~**vorsitzender** shop chairman (deputy); ~**wahlen** election of the shop council *(US)*.

Betriebs|rechnung working (trading) account; ~**reingewinn** net operating income (profit, *US*), net profit from operations; ~**reklame** industrial advertising; ~**rentenkasse** occupational pension scheme; ~**reserve** operating (general, business) reserve; ~**revision** internal (staff) audit; ~**revisor** internal (staff, operational) auditor, company auditor, plant controller; ~**richtlinien** plant rules; ~**risiko** industrial hazard, operational risk (hazard); **heute** ~**ruhe** *(Hotel)* closed today; ~**satzung** operating by[e]-laws, shop rules; ~**schaden** industrial injury; ~**schadensrente** compensation benefit; ~**schalter** operating lever; ~**schema** operational setup; ~**schließung** [plant] shutdown (closing), closing down; **saisonbedingte** ~**schließung** seasonal shutdown; ~**schluß** closing hours; ~**schulden** business liabilities, company debts; ~**schutz** operational safety precautions; ~**schwankungen** industrial fluctuations; ~**schwierigkeiten** operational difficulties; ~**seminar** in-service seminar.

betriebssicher safe to operate, reliable in operation, *(Flugzeug, Maschine)* fool-proof.

Betriebs|sicherheit safety of operation (service), reliability of operation (service, working), industrial safety; ~**siedlung** company colony *(Br.)* (town, *US*); ~**sitz** headquarters, commercial domicile, seat of an enterprise; ~**sozialismus** industrial democracy, guild socialism; ~**soziologe** industrial sociologist; ~**soziologie** industrial sociology; ~**spaltung** separation of industrial units; ~**spannung** *(el.)* operating voltage; ~**sparen** industrial savings, contractual saving; ~**sparkasse** mutual benefit association; ~**sportplatz** company sports grounds; ~**stadium** operational stage; ~**standpunkt** operating standpoint; ~**statistik** business (operational) statistics, *(Eisenbahn)* traffic return; ~**stätte** permanent establishment, regular and established place of business, business premises, plant, factory, *(im Freien)* open-air premises; **unter Vollstreckungsschutz stehende landwirtschaftliche** ~**stätte** rural homestead *(US)*; ~**steuer** operating tax; ~**stillegung** closing down, close-down, suspension of operations, *(vorübergehende)* shutdown *(US)*; **umfassende** ~**stillegungen** plant-wide shutdowns *(US)*; ~**stillstandsversicherung** business interruption (use and occupancy, *US*) insurance; ~**stockung** shutdown, *(Eisenbahn)* breakdown [on a line], holdup.

Betriebsstoff fuel, petrol *(Br.)*, gasoline *(US)*;

~**e** factory supplies;

Hilfs- und ~**e** *(Bilanz)* operating supplies; **Roh-, Hilfs- und** ~**e** *(Bilanz)* raw materials and supplies;

~ **einnehmen** to fuel [up];

~**einnahme** fuelling; ~**lager** fuel yard; ~**verbrauch** fuel consumption; ~**versorgung** fuel supply.

Betriebs|störung interruption, shutdown, stoppage, *(Eisenbahn)* breakdown, holdup, *(Rundfunk)* jamming; ~**struktur** business (corporate) structure; ~**stunde** *(Arbeiter)* factory hour, *(Flugzeug)* flying hour, *(Maschine)* machine hour; ~**system** *(Datenverarbeitung)* operating system; ~**tagebuch** *(Flugzeug)* log; ~**tarifvereinbarung mit Beitragszwang** agency shop

agreement *(Br.)*; ~**tarifvertrag** shop (single-plant bargaining) agreement; ~**tätigkeit** operating activity, operation; ~**technik** industrial management (engineering), operational technique.
betriebstechnisch operational;
~**e Anforderungen** manufacturing requirements.
Betriebs|teil fixed-asset unit; ~**übergabe** surrender of a factory; ~**überlassungsvertrag** lease of a running concern; ~**übernahme durch den Staat** state takeover; ~**überschuß** earned (operating) surplus, net receipts; ~**überwachung** control of operations, factory inspection, plant supervision; ~**überwachungskosten** supervisory costs.
betriebsübliches Verfahren aufgeben to deviate from the corporate pattern *(US)*.
Betriebs|umfang scale of operations; ~**umfrage** employee attitude survey; ~**umstellung** shifting of a plant; **komplette** ~**umstellung** thorough turnover of the operating force.
betriebsunfähig out of order.
Betriebsunfall industrial (on-the-job) accident, industrial injury, injury at work;
zur Erwerbsunfähigkeit führender ~ disabling injury; **meldepflichtiger** ~ reportable accident in industry; **schadensersatzpflichtiger** ~ compensable injury;
~**entschädigung** workmen's compensation *(Br.)*; ~**fonds** accident fund; ~**gesetz** Workmen's Compensation Act *(Br.)*; ~**rente** industrial injury benefit *(Br.)*, pension for injury at work, workmen's compensation benefit *(US)*; ~**schutz** workmen's compensation; ~**verhütung** industrial accident prevention; ~**versicherung** industrial (injuries, *Br.*) accident insurance, workmen's compensation insurance *(US)*.
Betriebs|unglück corporate disaster *(US)*; ~**uniform** work uniform.
Betriebsunkosten operating cost (expenses), costs of operation, maintenance (operational, plant) costs, dead charges, overhead [expenses], *(Bahn)* running expenses;
allgemeine ~ factory overheads (cost, expense), turnover costs; **laufende** ~ current operating expenses.
Betriebsunterbrechung interruption of business.
Betriebsunterbrechungs|schaden use and occupancy loss *(US)*; ~**versicherung** use and occupancy (business interruption, *US*) insurance.
Betriebs|unterlagen plant (factory) records; ~**unternehmen besichtigen** to inspect a plant; ~**untersuchung** operation analysis; ~**untersuchungsverfahren** employee attitude measurement; ~**veranstaltung** staff party; ~**veräußerung** sale of plant; ~**verbesserungen** plant improvements; ~**vereinbarung** single-plant bargaining (shop, factory) agreement; ~**vereinheitlichung** standardization of factories; ~**verfahren** operating procedure, plant operations, trade process; ~**verfassung** shop rules; ~**verfassungsgesetz** [etwa] Labor-Management Relations Act *(US)*, works council bill *(Br.)*; ~**vergehen** shop infraction; ~**vergleich** interfirm (interfactory) comparative studies; ~**vergrößerung** plant extension; ~**verhältnisse** industrial relations, shop (operating, plant) conditions; ~**verlagerung** transfer (relocation) of a plant; ~**verlagerung durchführen** to move a plant to another locality; ~**verlagerung vorbereiten** to map a corporate move; ~**verlegung** relocation of a plant; **entschädigungspflichtige** ~**verletzung** compensable injury *(US)*; ~**verlust** loss of trade, operating deficit (loss), business (manufacturing, operational, trading) loss, plant deficiency; **vorgetragener** ~**verlust** trading loss carried forward, plant deficiency; ~**verlustversicherung** business insurance.
Betriebsvermögen working (operating, business) assets, regular working (trading, circulating) capital, *(AG)* company property;
landwirtschaftliches ~ farming stock; **notwendiges** ~ requisite capital; **produktives** ~ active assets.
Betriebs|verpflichtungen eingehen to make corporate commitments; ~**versammlung** meeting of workers, factory (shopfloor) meeting; ~**versammlung während der Arbeitszeit abhalten** to hold a meeting in company time; ~**versicherung** business insurance, *(für Angestellte)* group insurance; **kombinierte** ~**versicherung** trader's combined policy; ~**vertretung** employees' representation; ~**verwalter** estate manager; ~**verwaltung** management; ~**vollmacht** operating authority; ~**volumen** rate of operations; ~**voranschlag** operating budget; ~**vorrat** stock-in-trade, trading stock; ~**vorrichtungen** installations; ~**vorschriften** plant (working) regulations, operating (service) instructions, operating rules, *(Eisenbahn)* service regulations; **vertikales** ~**wachstum mit Angliederung einer nachgelagerten Produktionsstufe** forward integration; **vertikales** ~**wachstum mit Angliederung einer vorgelagerten Produktionsstufe** backward integration; ~**wahl** employee election; ~**weise** operating method; ~**welle** signal wave.
Betriebswert going [concern] value (worth), *(laufendes Geschäft)* tangible value, value of plant in successful operation (as a going concern);
~**e** *(Eisenbahn)* traffic data;
angemessener ~ fair value as a going concern.
Betriebs|wirksamkeit operational efficiency; ~**wirt** business administrator (economist, *Br.*); **graduierter** ~**wirt** master of business administration.
Betriebswirtschaft business administration *(US)* (economics, *Br.*), business management, industrial administration;
sich auf ~ **spezialisieren** to major in business administration *(US)*.
Betriebswirtschaftler business economist *(Br.)* (administrator).
betriebswirtschaftliche|Angaben business data; **erhebliche** ~ **Erfahrungen haben** to be heavy on managerial experience; ~ **Proportionen** management ratio; ~ **Technik** business management; ~ **Untersuchung** operation analysis.
Betriebs|wirtschaftlichkeit economy in operation; ~**wirtschaftlichkeitsquotient** operating ratio; ~**wirtschaftslehre** business administration *(US)* (economics, *Br.*); **allgemeine** ~**wirtschaftslehre** managerial economics; ~**wissenschaft** scientific management; ~**wohnung** company flat (dwelling, housing); ~**zahl** operating ratio; ~**zählung** industrial census; ~**zeit** working time, factory hours, *(Maschine)* service life; **während der** ~**zeit** in company time; ~**zeitraum** operating period; ~**zeitschrift** house organ, company magazine, personnel periodical; ~**zeitung** international (house, *US*) organ, employee (company) publication; ~**ziffern** business data; ~**zinsen** internal interest.
Betriebszugehörigkeit period of employment, company seniority;
stetige ~ continuity of service.
Betriebs|zugehörigkeitsdauer company seniority; ~**zusammenlegung** amalgamation of industries; ~**zuschuß** company contribution; ~**zustand** operating condition, *(Maschine)* working condition (order); **in gutem** ~**zustand sein** to be in good working order; ~**zweck** objects of a company, business use; ~**zweig** branch of industry; ~**zyklus** operating cycle.
betrifft *(im Brief)* Ref, re;
~ **Auftragsbestätigung** re confirmation of order;
was mich ~ as far as I am concerned.
betrinken, sich to get drunk (intoxicated, tight).
betroffen affected, concerned, *(bestürzt)* embarrassed, perplexed, taken aback;
vom Kriege schwer ~ hard hit by the war; **sichtlich von den Nachrichten** ~ visibly stunned by the news; **nachteilig** ~ injuriously affected; **persönlich** ~ personally involved; **von einem schweren Unglück** ~ befallen by a grave misfortune;
~ **sein** to be concerned; **von einer Sache nicht** ~ **sein** to have no concern in a matter; ~ **werden** to be affected; **von einem Gesetz** ~ **werden** to come under a law; **von einem Verlust** ~ **werden** to suffer a loss;
~**er Fall** case in question (referred to); **von der Flut** ~**e Gebiete** flood-stricken areas; ~**e Mienen** perplexed faces; **am schwersten vom Feuer** ~**e Stadtteile** districts worst affected by the fire.
Betroffener person concerned (afflicted, alluded to), sufferer.
Betroffenheit embarrassment, perplexity.
betrogen deceived, cheated, tricked, swindled;
um seine Ersparnisse ~ swindled out of one's savings; **um sein Geld** ~ done out of one's money;
in seinen Hoffnungen ~ **werden** to be disappointed in one's hopes;
~**er Ehemann** deceived husband; ~**er Käufer** defrauded purchaser.
Betrogener dupe, deceived person, victim.
betrüben to make sad, to grieve.
betrüblich saddening, distressing, deplorable, grievous.
betrübt sorry, distressed, miserable;
tief ~ deeply grieved; **zu Tode** ~ down at heart;
über etw. ~ **sein** to be sad (distressed) about s. th.;
mit ~**em Gesicht** with a sad face.
Betrug fraud in fact, deception, deceit, cheating, dishonesty, wilful misrepresentation, have *(Br., sl.)*, falsehood, fraud and wilful imposition *(Scot.)*, *(Hochstapelei)* imposition, imposture, *(Schein)* sham, *(Schwindel)* swindle;
auf ~ **beruhend** founded in fraud; **des** ~**es nicht fähig** incapable of deception; **durch** ~ fraudulently; **von Anfang an nichts als** ~ a do from the start;

ausgesprochener ~ a piece of deceit; **von vornherein beabsichtigter** ~ concealed fraud; **frommer** ~ pious fraud; **gemeiner** ~ plain cheating; **glatter** ~ clear case of fraud, clean shave *(Br.)*; **glaubhafter** ~ glossy deceit; **vollendeter** ~ actual (moral) fraud;
~ **des Finanzamtes** defraudation of the revenue;
jem. etw. durch einen ~ **abluchsen** to cheat s. o. out of s. th.; ~ **begehen** to commit a fraud, to obtain by false pretences, to practise deceit; ~ **entlarven** to show up a fraud; **etw. durch** ~ **erlangen** to obtain s. th. by a trick; **sich zum** ~ **hergeben** to descend to fraud; **sich eines** ~**es schuldig machen** to be guilty of fraud; **nach** ~ **riechen** to savo(u)r of deception; **sich durch** ~ **Geld verschaffen** to obtain money by fraud[ulent means] (false pretences).

betrügen to defraud, to deceive, to cheat, to beguile, to swindle, to take (let) in, to cozen, to delude, to do in, to shortchange *(US)*;
in der Absicht zu ~ with intent to defraud;
j. ~ to play s. o. false, to let s. o. in; **j. um etw.** ~ to swindle (trick) s. th. out of s. o.; **Finanzamt** ~ to defraud the tax authorities (revenue); **j. um sein Geld** ~ to jockey s. o. out of his money; **Gläubiger** ~ to defraud a creditor; **j. um seinen Lohn** ~ to trick s. o. out of his wages; **sich selbst** ~ to deceive o. s.; **beim Spiel** ~ to cheat at the game; **Zoll** ~ to cheat (defraud) the customs;
sich ~ **lassen** to allow o. s. to be cheated.

Betrüger fraudulent party, cheater, defrauder, deceiver, impostor, juggler, beguiler, tricker, confidence trickster, doer, counterfeiter, swindler, foul player, palterer, *(Verwalter fremden Eigentums)* maladministrator;
der betrogene ~ the biter bit; **raffinierter** ~ slicker; **routinierter** ~ spieler *(US sl.)*;
~ **beim Geldwechseln** shortchanger *(US)*.

Betrügerei fraud, fraudulency, imposture, imposition.

Betrügereien foul practices, trickery;
~ **begehen** to work a racket *(sl.)*; **bei der Buchung** ~ **begehen** to wangle accounts; **sorgfältig verborgene** ~ **ans Tageslicht bringen** to disclose skilfully concealed thefts; **sich** ~ **zuschulden kommen lassen** to commit a number of frauds; **von** ~ **leben** to live by trickery.

betrügerisch fraudulent, deceitful, swindling, surreptitious, on the crook *(sl.)*;
in ~**er Absicht** with intent to defraud, with fraudulent intent; **durch** ~**e Mittel** by fraudulent means; **in** ~**er Weise** fraudulently; **zu** ~**en Zwecken** for fraudulent purposes;
Falschgeld ~ **in Umlauf (in den Verkehr) bringen** to utter false notes, to palm off a bad coin on s. o.; ~ **erlangen** to obtain by fraud (false pretences); ~ **handeln** to deceive, to defraud;
~**e Ausstellung einer Urkunde** fraud in treaty; ~**er Bankrott** fraudulent bankruptcy; ~**er Bankrotteur** fraudulent (adjudicated) bankrupt; ~**e Geschäftsführung** fraudulent trading; ~**es Geschäftsgebaren** business fraud; ~ **erzielte Gewinne** fraudulent gains; ~**e Handlung** fraudulence of an action; **durch** ~**e Machenschaften** by fraudulent means; ~**er Nachdruck** fraudulent impression; ~**es Verhalten** fraud.

Betrugs|absicht intent to defraud; **in** ~**absicht** for fraudulent purposes; **in** ~**absicht handeln** to intend to fraud; ~**beteiligter** privy to a fraud; ~**charakter** fraudulent nature; ~**delikt** tort of fraud (deceit); ~**dezernat** *(Kriminalpolizei)* fraud department; ~**fall** fraud case; **glatter** ~**fall** clear case of fraud; ~**handlung** fraudulent or dishonest act; ~**klausel** fraudulent clause; ~**manöver** fraudulent dealing; ~**merkmal** essence of fraud; ~**möglichkeiten** opportunities for (possibilities of) fraud; ~**tatbestand erfüllen** to constitute fraud; ~**verfahren** action in deceit; ~**versuch** attempted fraud.

betrunken intoxicated, drunk, tight, the worse for liquor, in wine, knocked out, blind, plastered *(sl.)*, laid out *(sl.)*;
besinnungslos ~ drunk as a lord (to the light, *sl.*); **ganz schön** ~ three parts drunk *(fam.)*; **total** ~ stone blind *(sl.)*;
~ **wie eine Strandhaubitze** lit up like a Christmas tree (Times Square, a church) *(sl.)*;
~ **machen** to intoxicate; ~ **sein** to have an edge on *(US sl.)*; **leicht** ~ **sein** to have had a drop too much; **an jedem Löhnungstag** ~ **sein** to get tight every payday; **total** ~ **sein** not see a hole in a ladder, to be well primed with liquor *(coll.)*.

Betrunkener inebriate, drunken person, drunk.

Betrunkenheit state of intoxication, inebriation, drunkenness.

Bett bed, *(Bahn, Schiff)* berth, bunk *(fam.)*;
ans ~ **gefesselt** laid up; **ins** ~ between the sheets;
privat bezahltes ~ *(Krankenhaus)* pay bed *(Br.)*; **einschläfriges** ~ single bed; **oberes** ~ *(Schlafwagen)* upper;
für unerwartete Gäste ein ~ **auf dem Flur aufstellen** to make up a bed on the floor for unexpected guests; ~ **frisch beziehen** to put some clean sheets on a bed, to change a bed; **Kind zu** ~ **bringen** to pack a child off to bed; **zu** ~ **gehen** to turn in *(coll.)*; **krank zu** ~ **liegen** to be lying ill in bed; **wegen Grippe das** ~ **hüten müssen** to be down with the flu; **in getrennten** ~**en schlafen** to sleep in separate beds; **j. aus dem** ~ **schmeißen** to drag s. o. out of the bed; **an sein** ~ **gefesselt sein** to be a prisoner to one's bed; **durch eine Krankheit ans** ~ **gefesselt sein** to be taken to bed with an illness; **aus dem** ~ **steigen** to get out of bed, to show a leg *(fam.)*;
~**couch** studio couch, divan, put-you-up.

bettelarm dog-poor, destitute;
~ **machen** to pauperize.

Bettel|brief begging letter; ~**kinder** pauper children.

Betteln, Bettelei begging, beggary, mendicancy;
~ **und Hausieren verboten!** no canvassers! no hawkers! no circulars!;
~ **der Kinder** troublesomeness of the children;
sich durch ~ **ernähren** to live by begging; **sich aufs** ~ **verlegen** to resort to begging.

betteln to beg for alms, to panhandle *(US sl.)*, *(inständig bitten)* to implore, to entreat, *(schnorren)* to scrounge, to panhandle, to burn *(US)*, to cadge *(Br.)*;
um milde Gaben ~ to cadge handouts *(Br.)*; **auf der Straße** ~ to throw the hooks *(sl.)*;
~ **gehen** to go a-begging.

Bettelstab, j. an den ~ **bringen** to bring s. o. to beggary, to reduce s. o. to poverty (beggary), to beat s. o. all to nothing, to impoverish s. o.; **an den** ~ **gelangen** to come down to begging.

betten to bed;
j. zur letzten Ruhe ~ to lay s. o. to rest; **j. weich** ~ to find s. o. a cushy job; **sich weich** ~ to feather one's nest.

Bett|flasche hot-water bottle; ~**kammer** bedroom; ~**karte** berth ticket; ~**kasten** bed frame.

bettknüllen, bei jem. zwei Wochen to land on s. o. for a fortnight *(fam.)*.

bettlägerig sick-abed, laid up, bed-ridden, bedfast *(US)*;
~ **sein** to be confined to bed; **seit langem** ~ **sein** to have been bed-ridden for a long time.

Bettlägeriger cot case.

Bett|laken sheet; ~**lektüre** bedside books.

Bettler beggar, mendicant, panhandler *(US sl.)*;
zum ~ **machen** to reduce s. o. to poverty (beggary); ~ **zurückweisen** to turn away a beggar.

Bettler|ei beggary; ~**lohn** beggarly wage; ~**tum** beggary, beggardom, mendicity.

Bett|pfanne bed-pan; ~**platz** berth; ~**platz zuteilen** to berth; ~**platzverteilung** berthing; ~**ruhe** bed rest; ~**ruhe verordnen** to order to stay in bed; ~**schrank** wardrobe bed; ~**vorleger** rug; ~**wärmer** bed pan; ~**wäsche** bed-linen; ~**zeit** sack time *(sl.)*; ~**zeug** bedding, slop.

betucht, gut well-heeled *(US sl.)*, lace-curtain *(Irish, sl.)*.

betulich fussy, fussing, solicitous.

Beuge|haft coercive detention; ~**mittel** means of coercion.

beugen, Recht to pervert (warp) justice, to stretch a law.

Beule *(am Auto)* dent, bruise, bulge;
sich beim Zusammenstoß eine ~ **am Auto holen** to dent one's motorcar in a collision.

beunruhigen to trouble, to disturb, to agitate, to alarm, to make uneasy, to pester, to perturb, to disquiet, to distress;
j. ~ to disturb s. one's mind; **sich** ~ to worry o. s., to trouble o. s., to get uneasy; **sich nicht** ~ not to bother one's head; **Bevölkerung** ~ to alarm the population; **sich über jds. Gesundheitszustand** ~ to be concerned (anxious) about s. one's health; **sich über Nichts und wieder Nichts** ~ to worry about nothing.

beunruhigend disturbing, disquieting, alarming, worrying;
Angelegenheit immer noch ~ **finden** to keep worrying about a business; **Zukunft** ~ **finden** to be uneasy in one's mind about the future;
~ **hoher Fehlerprozentsatz** disquieting high percentage of errors.

beunruhigt concerned (anxious, worried, uneasy) about;
~ **aussehen** to have a worried look, to show signs of worry; **sich über etw.** ~ **fühlen** to feel concerned about s. th.; ~ **nach der Tür sehen** to look anxiously at the door; **ein bißchen** ~ **sein** to be a little disturbed; **sehr** ~ **sein** to be in troubled mind; **von schlechten Nachrichten** ~ **sein** to be troubled by bad news; **sich einigermaßen** ~ **zeigen** to show some perturbation;
~**e Börse** disturbed market.

Beunruhigung uneasiness, alarm, perturbation, vexation;
Nachrichten über jds. Krankheit mit ~ aufnehmen to be disturbed to hear the news of s. one's illness; **Angelegenheit mit ~ betrachten** to be under some apprehension about a matter; **~ hervorrufen** to cause disquiet.

beurkunden to acknowledge, to verify, *(Behörde)* to authenticate, to certify, to legalize, to witness, to [place on] record;
Geburt ~ to register a birth; **notariell ~** to notarize *(US)*, to attest, to prove; **Sterbefall ~** to register a death.

beurkundet *(in Verträgen)* witnessed;
amtlich ~ of record.

Beurkundung verification, *(Behörde)* authentication, legalization, certification, *(Zeuge)* witnessing, attestation;
zur ~ dieses in witness whereof;
gerichtliche ~ legalization; **notarielle ~** attestation, notarization;
~ einer Geburt registration of a birth; **~ des Personenstandes** civil registration, registration of births, marriages and deaths; **~ eines Sterbefalls** death registration.

Beurkundungs|befugnis authority to execute a deed; **~gebühren** notary's fees; **~vermerk** attestation clause.

beurlauben to give (grant) leave, to give time off, *(Beamten)* to suspend, *(Soldaten)* to furlough;
sich bei jem. ~ to take one's leave of s. o.; **Kassierer während der Untersuchung ~** to suspend a cashier during (pending) investigations; **kurz ~** to give time off; **auf unbestimmte Zeit ~** to suspend s. o. indefinitely;
sich ~ lassen to take one's leave, *(Beamten)* to apply for suspension.

beurlaubt on leave (furlough);
zeitweilig ~ on temporary leave, *(suspendiert)* suspended;
~ sein to be on leave [of absence]; **wegen Krankheit ~ sein** to be on sick leave.

Beurlaubtenstand *(mil.)* reserve status.

Beurlaubung granting leave, leave of absence, *(Beamter)* suspension from office, *(mil.)* furlough;
~ mit vollem Gehalt full-pay leave; **vorläufige ~ eines Kassierers** suspension of a cashier;
jds. zeitweilige ~ anordnen to order s. o. to be temporarily suspended; **Antrag auf ~ stellen** to apply (come in) for a leave.

beurteilen to judge, to pass judgment, to form an estimate, to give an opinion, to gauge, *(Leistungen)* to rate, to assess, *(Wert)* to assess, to estimate;
j. ~ to size up s. o.; **abfällig ~** to pass an adverse judgment; **für sich allein ~** to rest (stand) on its own merits; **andere nach sich ~** to measure others' feet by one's own last; **etw. völlig anders ~** to look upon s. th. from quite a different angle; **j. nach seinem Äußeren ~** to judge s. o. by his appearances; **erstklassig ~** to give star rating; **fachmännisch ~** to give expert advice; **falsch ~** to misjudge; **Geschehnisse anders ~** to take a different view of events; **gut ~** to give a good record; **Lage ernst ~** to take a grave view of a situation; **Lage falsch ~** to take a wrong view of the situation; **seine Mitmenschen nachsichtig ~** to judge other people with charity; **Sache positiv ~** to be friendly to a cause; **Sachlage richtig ~** to view a matter in the right light; **sachverständig ~** to survey; **Theaterstück ~** to review a play; **nicht ~ können** not to be competent to judge; **j. schlecht ~ können** to have a poor idea of s. one's abilities; **schwer zu ~ sein** to be a difficult man to place.

Beurteilender judge, rater.

beurteilt werden, günstig to receive favo(u)rable criticism.

Beurteilung judgment, view, opinion, *(Dienstzeugnis)* certificate, *(Leistungen)* appraisal, rating, *(in Personalakten)* confidential (efficiency) report (rating), *(Politik)* assessment;
dienstliche ~ confidental (efficiency) report; **falsche ~** error of judgment, misjudgment; **gegenseitige ~** *(Betriebsangehörige)* mutual rating *(US)*; **kontroverse ~** controversial opinions; **nachsichtige ~** charitable view; **negative ~** damaging report; **positive ~** approval rating;
~ von Angestellten employee (performance, merit, personnel) rating; **~ der leitenden Angestellten** executive evaluation; **~ der finanziellen Entwicklung** financial forecasting; **~ eines Kunden durch die Bank** customer's position at the bank, credit rating of a customer *(US)*; **~ der Leistung** efficiency rating; **~ von Personal** audit of personnel *(US)*; **~ eines Probeangestellten** progress report; **~ der Vermögenslage einer Kapitalgesellschaft** capital rating of a company (corporation) *(US)*;
sich positiv für die ~ auswirken to prove a personality bonus; **günstige ~ finden** to be viewed favo(u)rably; **in der ~ völlig einig sein** to be unanimous in a judgment; **jem. etw. zur ~ vorlegen** to submit s. th. to s. one's inspection.

Beurteilungs|ausschuß *(Angestellte)* rating committee; **~blatt** classification sheet; **~blatt eines Angestellten** employee rating chart; **~fehler** rating error; **~formular** rating form; **~grundlage** *(Angestellte)* basis of rating; **~merkmale** merits; **~methode** *(für Arbeitnehmer)* rating method, type of rating; **~programm für Arbeitnehmer** employee appraisal program *(US)*; **~programm für Gehaltseinstufung** rating program(me); **~skala** rating scale; **~system, ~verfahren** *(Personal)* assessment procedure, rating system; **~vermögen** discretion; **~zeitraum** *(für Gehaltseinstufungen)* rating period.

Beute booty, spoils, capture, captured property, loot, *(Dieb)* loot, haul, *(mar.)* prize;
fette ~ *(Politik)* pork *(US)*; **leichte ~** sitting duck, easy mark (meat) *(coll.)*, snack *(sl.)*;
auf ~ ausgehen to [go in search of] prey, *(fig.)* to go plundering; **an der ~ beteiligen** to cut s. o. in on the spoils *(sl.)*; **j. als leichte ~ betrachten** to mark (fasten on) s. o. as an easy prey; **plündernden Banden zur ~ fallen** to fall prey to marauding bandits; **mit reicher ~ heimkehren** to secure with a good bag; **~ machen** to loot, to pillage, to plunder; **fette ~ machen** to make a good hand; **gemeinsame ~ machen** to share the booty; **auf ~ aus sein** to go on the prowl; **für j. eine leichte ~ sein** to be an easy prey to s. o.; **leichte ~ für Schwindler sein** to be a fair game for swindlers; **sich gleichmäßig in die ~ teilen** to split even on the swag; **seinen Anteil an der ~ verlangen** to claim one's share of the booty; **~ verteilen** to piece up;
~anteil corner *(sl.)*; **sich seinen ~anteil gewaltsam sichern** to muscle in *(sl.)*.

Beutel bag, *(Geld)* purse, *(Tabak)* pouch;
voller ~ well-lined purse;
~ aufmachen to loosen the purse-strings; **an den ~ gehen** to cost a lot; **tief in den ~ greifen** to dive into one's pocket; **Daumen auf den ~ halten** to tighten the purse strings; **Loch in meinen ~ reißen** to make a hole in my pocket; **sich nach seinem ~ richten** to cut one's coat according to one's cloth; **seinen ~ ziehen** to cough up *(sl.)*; **seinen ~ zücken** to unstring one's purse, to cough up *(sl.)*; **seinen ~ zuhalten** to tighten the purse strings;
~schneider shaver, cutpurse, pickpocket; **~schneiderei** sharp practices, purse snatching.

beutelustig sein to be out for booty.

Beute|sammelstelle collecting point *(US)*; **~stücke** winnings, trophies; **~zug** forage, haul, find.

bevölkern to populate, to people, to settle;
sich ~ to become inhabitated, *(Straße)* to become peopled; **Gebiet planmäßig ~** to settle an area systematically; **Straßen ~** to throng the streets.

bevölkert peopled, populated;
dünn ~ sein to be thinly populated;
dicht ~ densely peopled, populous; **schwach ~** sparsely populated;
dicht ~e Gegend populous district; **von Touristen ~e Insel** island crowded with tourists.

Bevölkerung population, people, country, inhabitants;
aus allen Schichten der ~ from all walks of life;
absolute ~ total population **angelsächsische ~** the English-speaking world; **arbeitende (berufstätige) ~** working-class (employed) population, working classes; **arbeitsfähige ~** able-bodied people; **dichte ~** dense population; **einheimische ~** home population, natives; **fluktuierende ~** floating population; **gesamte ~** whole country; **dünn gesäte (geringe) ~** sparse population; **ortsansässige ~** permanent (resident) population; **relative ~** density of population; **schaffende ~** working classes; **schrumpfende ~** diminishing population; **seßhafte ~** settled population; **stationäre ~** stationary population; **überquellende ~** spillover; **nicht normal verteilte ~** *(Statistik)* nonnormal population; **wachsende ~** increasing population; **wahlberechtigte ~** constituent (voting) population; **arme weiße ~** white trash *(US)*; **werktätige ~** occupied (working-class) population; **zahlreiche ~** dense population;
~ ansiedeln to settle population; **überschüssige ~ in Übersee ansiedeln** to plant the surplus population abroad; **~ in einer Angelegenheit befragen** to poll a country on a question; **~ dezimieren** to thin out the population; **~ hinwegraffen** to wipe out a population; **~ auf 2 Millionen schätzen** to put a population at 2 millions.

Bevölkerungs|abnahme fall (decline) in population; **~abteilung** *(UN)* population division; **~abwanderung** exodus; **~anstieg** increase (swell) in population.

Bevölkerungsanteil part of the population;
fremdländischer ~ foreign population; **verheirateter ~** married population; **weiblicher ~** female section of the population.

Bevölkerungs|aufbau structure of population; ~**aufteilung** distribution of population; ~**austausch** population transfer; ~**bedürfnisse** population needs; ~**bewegung** population mobility (trend, movement); ~**bilanz** net population change, population census; ~**bombe** population bomb; ~**daten** census distribution; ~**dichte** population (employment) density, dense (density of) population, populousness; **geringe** ~**dichte** open (sparseness of) population; ~**druck** population pressure; ~**entwicklung** population trend, trend in the population; ~**entwicklung berechnen** to project the population trend; ~**explosion** population explosion (boom); ~**geschichte** demographic history; ~**gliederung** distribution of population; ~**größe** size of population **optimal günstige** ~**größe** optimum population; ~**gruppe** population class; **alle** ~**gruppen** great and small; ~**index** vital index; ~**kontrolle** population control; ~**kreise** sections of the population; ~**kunde** population theory, demography; ~**kurve** population curve; ~**lage** demographic situation; ~**mehrheit** greater part (bulk) of the population; ~**mittelpunkt** center *(US)* (centre, *Br.*) of population; ~**mobilität** population mobility; ~**optimum** optimum population; ~**politik** population policy, demography; ~**politiker** demographer, populationist.

bevölkerungspolitisch populational;
~**e Maßnahmen** demographic measures.

Bevölkerungs|problem population problem; ~**prognose** population forecast (projection); ~**pyramide** age (population) pyramid; ~**rückgang** population decline, fall (decrease) in population.

Bevölkerungsschicht population stratum, section of the population;
ärmere (benachteiligte) ~**n** underprivileged classes; **von der Krise betroffene** ~**en** people affected by the crisis; **demographisch definierte** ~ bracket; **einfache** ~**n** humble classes; **untere** ~**n** lower strata; **vornehme und einfache** ~**n** the gentle and simple classes.

Bevölkerungs|schichtung structure of the population; **ziviler** ~-**schutz** civil defence; ~**stand** level of population; ~**statistik** census (demographic) statistics, population statistics, demographical (popular, vital registration, *US*) demography.

bevölkerungsstatistisch demographic[al].

Bevölkerungs|strom population tide; ~**struktur** population (demographical) structure; ~**tabelle** census table.

Bevölkerungsteil part of the population;
abgewanderter ~ population overspill; **andersdenkende** ~**e** dissident population; **berufstätiger** ~ working population; **politisch einflußreicher** ~ silk-stocking district (ward) *(US)*; **im Gefängnis einsitzender** ~ prison population; **fremdländischer** ~ foreign population; **selbstversorgender** ~ farming section of the population; **nicht seßhafter** ~ floating population; **unterhaltsabhängiger** ~ dependent population; **wahlberechtigter** ~ constituent (voting-age) population; **wohlhabender** ~ leisure[d] classes.

Bevölkerungs|theorie population theory; ~**trend** demographic trend; ~**überführung** transfer of population; ~**überschuß** surplus (excess of) population; ~**umschichtungen** population changes; ~**verschiebung** population shift; ~**verteilung** distribution of population, *(Altersaufbau)* age pyramid; ~**vorausberechnung** population forecast; ~**wachstum** population growth; **natürliches** ~**wachstum** natural increase; ~**wissenschaft** demography.

bevölkerungswissenschaftlich demographic.

Bevölkerungszahl population figure;
geringe ~ small population; **gewachsene** ~ increased number of people; **gleichbleibende** ~ stationary population.

Bevölkerungs|zählung enumeration of the population, census; ~**zentrum** center *(US)* (centre, *Br.*) of population; **schwankende** ~**ziffer** floating population; **zugrundegelegte** ~**ziffer** sample, part of population.

Bevölkerungszunahme increase in (growth of) population, population increase (growth);
eingefrorene ~ zero population growth; **jährliche** ~ annual rate of population increase; **jährliche** ~ **in Prozenten** percentage rate of population growth per annum; **rapide** ~ upsurge in population; **starke** ~ population boom;
~**rate** population growth rate.

Bevölkerungszuwachs population increase.

bevollmächtigen to authorize, to give authority, to empower, to warrant, to constitute, to confer powers (authority), to fiat, *(beauftragen)* to commission, *(Gesandte)* to accredit;
jem. ~ to give s. o. (invest s. o. with) full power, to give s. o. power of attorney, to authorize (depute) s. o.; **schriftlich** ~ to authorize in writing; **j. uneingeschränkt** ~ to furnish s. o. with full powers; **j. zur Vertragsunterschrift** ~ to authorize s. o. to sign a contract.

bevollmächtigt duly authorized, authoritative, entitled, empowered, accredited, commissioned, commissional, delegatory;
nicht ~ unauthorized, not authorized, noncommissioned; **ordnungsgemäß** ~ duly authorized;
~ **sein** to have authority, to be authorized to act; **von jem.** ~ **sein** to hold a power of attorney for s. o.;
~**er Botschafter** minister plenipotentiary; ~**e Person** authorized agent; ~**er Vertreter** authorized agent (representative), proxy, *(Diplomat)* plenipotentiary.

Bevollmächtigte|r authorized person (commissioner), [authorized] agent, nominee, accredited person, deputy, proxy, *(Anwalt)* private attorney, attorney [in fact], *(Geschäftsführer)* managing clerk, *(Konkursfall)* assignee, doer *(Scot., law)*, *(im Prozeß)* procurator, *(Stellvertreter)* representative, delegate, deputy, proxy, *(Treuhänder)* trustee, *(Vertreter)* [authorized] agent, mandatary, mandatory;
als ~**r** per pro; **privatrechtlich** ~**r** attorney in fact;
~**r für den Verkauf von Aktien** transfer agent;
als ~**r auftreten** to act in the capacity of an agent; **sich als jds.** ~**r ausgeben** to proclaim o. s. agent for s. o.; ~**n bestellen** to appoint a proxy; **j. zu seinem** ~**n bestimmen (ernennen)** to appoint a proxy, to make s. o. one's proxy, to give s. o. power of attorney; **j. als** ~**n einsetzen** to give s. o. power of attorney, to authorize s. o.; **als** ~**r handeln** to act by procuration; **durch einen** ~**n abstimmen lassen** to vote by proxy; **jds.** ~**r sein** to hold power of attorney for s. o.

Bevollmächtigung authorization, empowerment, commission, [delegation of] authority, *(Vollmacht)* power of authority;
durch (aufgrund einer) ~ by proxy;
schriftliche ~ written authorization.

Bevollmächtigungs|recht, beschränktes limited power of appointment; ~**schreiben** letter of authorization (attorney), *(Hauptversammlung)* proxy statement; ~**urkunde** power of (instrument appointing an) attorney.

bevormunden to patronize, to tutor, to keep in tutelage;
j. ständig ~ to keep s. o. in leading-strings.

Bevormundung tutelage, wardship.

bevorraten to stockpile, to stock up, to assemble.

bevorratet *(Schiff)* found.

Bevorratung assembling, stockpiling.

bevorrechtigen to [grant a] privilege, *(im Konkurs)* to give a prior claim.

bevorrechtigt *(Forderung)* privileged, preferred, preferential, senior, *(Gläubiger)* preferred, secured, preferential;
nicht ~ unprivileged, unsecured;
~ **sein** to enjoy a privilege, to be privileged, *(Gläubiger)* to rank first, to have a prior claim (precedence);
~**e Forderung** priority of claim, privileged (preferential, preferred, *US*) debt; ~**er Gläubiger** preferential *(Br.)* (preferred, specialty, *US*) creditor; **nicht** ~**er Gläubiger** general creditor; ~**e Hypothek** first *(Br.)* (senior, *US*) mortgage; ~**e Konkursforderung** privileged (preferred, preferential) debt; ~**e Stände** privileged classes.

Bevorrechtigter exempt, privileged (preferred) person, priority holder.

Bevorrechtigung preference, preferment, privilege, priority.

bevorschussen to grant an advance, to advance money;
Kunden ~ to make advances to customers.

Bevorschussung advance, advancing;
~ **von Verladepapieren** advance against shipping documents; ~ **von Wertpapieren** loan against securities, collateral loan *(US)*.

Bevorstehen, nahes imminence.

bevorstehen to be in store (approaching, near), *(Krise)* to be impending (imminent), to impend;
jem. drohend ~ to hang over s. o.; **kurz** ~ to be at hand (near).

bevorstehend approaching, forthcoming, impending, *(Gefahr)* imminent;
in einiger Zeit ~ in the offing;
~**e Ankunft** forthcoming arrival; ~**e Konferenz** forthcoming conference; **drohend** ~**er Krieg** imminent war; **noch** ~**e Überraschungen** surprises yet to come; ~**e Wahlen** forthcoming elections.

bevorzugen to favo(u)r, to prefer, to give a preference, to privilege;
j. ~ to show partiality for s. o.; **Gläubiger** ~ to prefer one creditor over others; **Kunden** ~ to grant special favo(u)r to a customer; **Schüler** ~ to favo(u)r a pupil;
geneigt sein, j. zu ~ to be predisposed in s. one's favo(u)r.

bevorzugt *(Forderung)* privileged, preferred *(US)*, preferential *(Br.)*, senior;
j. ~ **behandeln** to show partiality towards s. o., to discriminate s. o. in favo(u)r of s. o. else, to privilege s. o.; **Angelegenheit ~ behandeln** to give priority to a matter; ~ **sein** to be given preference; **von jem. besonders ~ sein** to be the favo(u)rite of s. o.; ~ **abgefertigt (behandelt) werden** to enjoy (receive, be given) preference, to receive priority;
~**e Behandlung** preferential (priority, featherbed) treatment, discrimination; ~**e Behandlung erfahren** to be given preferential treatment; ~**e Forderung** preferential (preferred, *US*) debt; ~**er Gläubiger** preferential *(Br.)* (preferred, *US*) creditor; ~**e Marke** favo(u)rite brand; ~**e Stellung einnehmen** to have a privileged position; ~**e Zuteilung** allocation by priority.
Bevorzugung preference, preferment, featherbedding, discrimination in favo(u)r of;
unzulässige ~ eines Konkursgläubigers undue preference of a creditor *(Br.)*; ~ **von Nichtgewerkschaftsmitgliedern** discrimination in favo(u)r of nonunion men; ~ **durch den Verbraucher** consumer preference.
Bevorzugungsbereich *(Statistik)* zone of preference.
bewachen to guard, to set a guard on, to keep watch over, to watch;
Brücke ~ to set a guard on a bridge; **Gefangenen** ~ to guard a prisoner, to keep a prisoner under guard; **Gefangenen schärfer** ~ to keep a better watch over a prisoner; **scharf (streng)** ~ to keep a close (strict) watch over s. o.; **j. unauffällig** ~ to shadow s. o.;
Haus ~ lassen to set a guard on a house.
Bewacher guardian;
seinen ~n entkommen to elude the vigilance of one's guardians.
bewachsen covered, overgrown, *(Schiffsboden)* foul;
mit Moos ~ carpeted (covered) with moss; **mit Niederwald** ~ brush-covered.
bewacht guarded;
schwer (streng) ~ heavily guarded, close, confined;
~**er Parkplatz** car park with attendant.
Bewachung guard, custody, watch, escort, *(Überwachung)* surveillance;
unter ~ abführen to march off under guard; **j. unter strenger ~ halten** to keep s. o. under close guard.
Bewachungs|- und Beleuchtungsabgabe watch rate; ~**fahrzeug** escort vessel; ~**mannschaft** escort.
bewaffnen, sich to arm; **Truppen neu** ~ to rearm troops.
bewaffnet in arms, armed;
mit einem Gewehr ~ armed with a gun; **schlecht (unzureichend)** ~ underarmed, badly armed; **schwer** ~ heavily armed;
bis an die Zähne ~ sein to be armed to the teeth;
mit ~em Auge with a magnifying glass; ~**er Bandit** armed bandit; ~**e Demonstration** armed demonstration; ~**e Intervention** armed intervention; ~**er Konflikt** armed conflict; ~**e Macht** armed force; ~**e Neutralität** armed neutrality; ~**er Überfall** raid, armed attack; ~**en Widerstand leisten** to offer armed resistance.
Bewaffnung armament;
konventionelle ~ conventional armament.
bewahren to warrant, to guard, to keep, to preserve, to save;
jem. ein gutes Andenken ~ to treasure s. one's memory; **äußeren Anschein** ~ to keep up appearance; **seine Beherrschung (Fassung)** ~ to keep one's countenance; **Blumen vor Frost** ~ to protect flowers against frost; **seine Form** ~ to keep its shape; **Frieden** ~ to preserve peace; **etw. im Gedächtnis** ~ to treasure s. th. up in one's memory; **Geheimnis** ~ to keep a secret; **seinen Gleichmut** ~ to keep one's head; **alte Menschen vor der Verlassenheit des Alters** ~ to preserve old people from the loneliness of old age; **seinen guten Ruf** ~ to maintain one's reputation; **Stillschweigen** ~ to maintain silence; **Szene gut im Gedächtnis** ~ to retain a clear memory of a scene; **j. vor dem Tod des Ertrinkens** ~ to save s. o. from drowning; **jem. die Treue** ~ to remain faithful to s. o.
bewähren, sich to prove (give a good account of) o. s., *(Artikel)* to stand the strain (test), *(Grundsatz)* to hold good, *(Plan)* to turn out to be a success; **sich nicht** ~ to prove a failure; **sich als guter Arbeiter** ~ to prove to be a good worker; **sich gegen Erkältungskrankheiten** ~ to prove effective against colds; **sich in allen Lebenslagen** ~ to prove one's worth (to show one's mettle) in all situations; **sich als Rechtsanwalt nicht** ~ to be a failure as a lawyer;
j. sich ~ lassen to put s. o. on his mettle.
Bewahrer eines Geheimnisses counsel keeper.
bewahrheiten, sich to come true, to be verified; **sich nicht** ~ to prove false.
bewährt proven, reliable, time-tested, proved;
~**er Anwalt** experienced lawyer; ~**e Firma** reliable firm; ~**er Freund** tried friend; ~**e Freundschaft** well-established friendship; ~**er Grundsatz** established principle; ~**e Hilfsbereitschaft** usual readiness to help; ~**e Kraft einer Firma** old and trusted member of a firm; ~**es Material** reliable material; ~**e Methoden** approved methods; ~**es Mittel** proven remedy.
Bewahrung preservation, conservation;
~ **des Friedens** sustenation of peace; ~ **der Gesellschaftsordnung** conservation of social order; ~ **vor Mißbrauch** preservation from improper use.
Bewährung proof, trial, test, *(Strafrecht)* rehabilitation, probation, parole;
auf ~ [freigelassen] *(Häftling)* in probation, probationary;
zur ~ anstehen to be eligible for parole; **Strafe zur ~ aussetzen** to make an order for conditional discharge (probationary order), to put on parole; **aus der Strafhaft unter ~ entlassen** to release on probation, to parole *(US)*; **drei Jahre Gefängnis mit ~ erhalten** to get three years on probation; **Geldstrafe von 50 Pfund mit ~ erhalten** to be fined £ 50 with suspended execution of sentence; **auf ~ erkennen** to make a probation order; **j. auf ~ freilassen** to place s. o. on probation; ~ **gewähren** to bind over on probation; ~ **haben** to be out on ticket of leave; **auf ~ freigelassen sein** to be on parole; **unter ~ stellen** to place on probation; **Entscheidungen über Aussetzung der Strafe zur ~ mehr örtlichen Prüfungsausschüssen überlassen** to delegate more parole decisions to local review committees; **auf ~ entlassen werden** to be released on parole; **auf ~ ausgesetzte Strafe widerrufen** to revoke the parole.
Bewährungs|anwärter probationer, pro *(sl.)*; ~**auflage** terms of probation; **den ~auflagen zuwiderhandeln** to break the terms of probation, to break one's ticket of leave *(Br.)*; ~**aufsicht** parole supervision; ~**ausschuß für Strafgefangene** prison parole board; ~**bataillon** *(mil.)* rehabilitation battalion.
Bewährungsfrist probationary period, term of probation, probation period, transitional release *(US)*;
~ **bekommen** to be placed on probation; **jem. ~ zubilligen** to place s. o. on probation, to bind s. o. over on probation.
Bewährungs|gesetz Probation of Offenders Act *(Br.)*; ~**helfer** parole (probation, *US*) officer.
Bewährungshilfe parole administration, probation service *(US)*, ticket of leave *(Br.)*;
Voraussetzungen für die ~ erfüllen to be eligible for parole; ~ **versagen** to deny parole *(Br.)*; **unter ~ gestellt werden** to be placed under the supervision (care) of a probation officer.
Bewährungsprobe trial, acid test;
~ **bestehen** to stand (pass) the test; **j. auf eine ~ stellen** to put s. o. on his mettle.
Bewährungs|system probation system; ~**urteil** probation order; ~**voraussetzungen** parole eligibility; **zeit** [period of] probation, probationary (parole) term.
bewaldet woody, wooded, forested.
Bewaldung forest cover.
bewältigen to accomplish, to master, to manage, to cope with, to handle, to overcome;
Arbeit ~ to manage a piece of work; **seine Aufgabe** ~ to cope with one's task; **Fach** ~ to master a subject; **alle Hindernisse spielend** ~ to easily clear all obstacles; **Schwierigkeit** ~ to surmount a difficulty; **Strecke in 4 Stunden** ~ to cover a distance in four hours; **Thema** ~ to handle a subject; **Verkehr** ~ to cope with the traffic.
Bewältigung accomplishment, handling;
zur ~ dieser Aufgabe to accomplish this task;
~ **des Verkehrs** traffic handling.
bewandert versed, skilled, studied, proficient, perfect, conversant, experienced, well-informed;
in der Buchführung ~ proficient in bookkeeping; **in finanziellen Dingen** ~ conversant in finances;
in seinem Fach ~ sein to be perfectly at home with a subject; **in Geschäftssachen ~ sein** to be well versed in business matters; **nicht sehr ~ sein** not to be up to date.
Bewandtnis special circumstances;
damit hat es folgende ~ the case is as follows.
bewässerbar irrigable.
bewässern to water, *(künstlich)* to irrigate;
mit Hilfe kleiner Kanäle ~ to irrigate by means of water channels.
Bewässerung watering, irrigation;
künstliche ~ artificial irrigation; **natürliche** ~ water supply.

Bewässerungs|anlage irrigation plant (works); ~**bezirk** irrigation district; ~**gelände** irrigation terraces; ~**graben** irrigation canal (channel, ditch), drove *(Br.)*; ~**graben ziehen** to dig trenches for irrigation; ~**ingenieur** irrigation engineer; ~**kanal** irrigation canal (channel); ~**projekt,** ~**system** irrigation scheme (system); ~**pumpe** irrigation pump; ~**technik** irrigation engineering.

bewegen to move, to induce, to prompt, *(beschäftigen)* to occupy, to concern, *(Wasser)* to stir;
sich ~ to move, *(Preise)* to range (vary) from ... to ..., *(Satellit)* to travel, *(Temperatur)* to fluctuate; **sich abwärts** ~ to move down[wards], to be on the downgrade (skids, *US*); **sich um die eigene Achse** ~ to revolve about its own axis; **sich aufwärts** ~ *(Kurse, Preise)* to move up; **j. dazu** ~. **etw. zu tun** to prompt s. o. to do s. th.; **sich durch das Dorf** ~ *(Trauerzug)* to wind its way through the village; **sich fast einheitlich um die 20%** ~ to cluster around the 20 per cent mark; **sich dem Ende zu** ~ to be moving to the end; **sich in Extremen** ~ to move in extremities; **sich frei** ~ to move about freely; **die Gemüter lange Zeit** ~ to stir the country by deep emotion; **sich mit einer Geschwindigkeit von ...** ~ to travel at a speed of ...; **sich in der besten Gesellschaft** ~ to move in the best society; **sich zwischen 20 und 25 Grad** ~ to fluctuate between 20 and 25 degrees; **jds. Herz** ~ to move s. one's heart; **etw. im Herzen** ~ to ponder s. th. in one's heart; **sich dem Höhepunkt zu** ~ to near the climax; **sich in frischer Luft** ~ to go for a walk; **sich zwischen 20 und 30 Mark** ~ to range between 20 und 30 DM; **die Menschen eines Zeitalters** ~ to stir the people of an age; **j. zum Mitleid** ~ to stir s. o. to pity; **sich im Rahmen des Alltäglichen** ~ *(Gespräch)* to be confined to trivial matters; **sich in höheren Regionen** ~ to be in the clouds; **sich in der gleichen Richtung** ~ to tend in the same direction; **sich ruckweise** ~ to jog; **sich ruckweise vorwärts** ~ *(Auto)* to buck; **sich im Schneckentempo** ~ to move at a snail's pace; **die Seele** ~ to stir the soul; **sich sprunghaft nach oben** ~ to somersault up; **j. von der Stelle** ~ to make s. o. move; **sich südwärts** ~ to go south; **j. tief** ~ to move s. o. deeply; **Truppen** ~ to assemble troops; **sich verstohlen** ~ to worm; **sich wellenartig** ~ to wave; **j. zur Zustimmung** ~ to get s. o. to consent; **sich in Zweideutigkeiten** ~ to deal in ambiguities; **sich in einem Zylinder** ~ *(Kolben)* to reciprocate in a cylinder;
sich überhaupt nicht ~ **können** not to be able to stir a foot.

bewegende|Ansprache moving (stirring) speech; ~ **Erzählung** touching tale; ~**r Geist** moving spirit; ~ **Kraft** kinetic force.

Beweggrund drive, motive, ground, moving cause, spring, inducement;
verborgener ~ deep motive;
aus einem bestimmten ~ **handeln** to act from a given motive.

Beweggründe, eigennützige interested motives; **niedrige** ~ base motives; **tiefere** ~ ulterior motives; **wirtschaftliche** ~ economic motives;
Verbrechen aus politischen ~**n begehen** to commit a crime from a political motive; **menschliche** ~ **offenlegen** to unravel the skein of human motives; **von niedrigen und selbstsüchtigen** ~**n angetrieben sein** to be actuated by low and selfish motives; ~ **vorbringen** to motivate.

beweglich movable, mobile, flexible, travelling, ambulatory, *(Auto, Flugzeug, Schiff)* manoeuvrable, *(Geist)* versatile, agile, *(Vermögen)* personal, movable;
geistig ~ nimble;
geistig ~ **sein** to have an active mind; **noch sehr** ~ **sein** to be still very active;
~**es Arbeitszeitprogramm** flexible schedule; ~**e Bodenstelle** mobile surface station; ~**es Eigentum** [goods and] chattles, personal estate, movable property; ~**er Feiertag** movable holiday; ~**e Feste** movable feasts; ~**e Funkstelle** mobile radio station; ~**er Geist** supple mind, nimble (versatile) mind; ~**es Gerät** portable instrument; ~**e Güter** movable goods; ~**e Kosten** varying costs; ~**e Ladung** loose cargo; ~**e Lohnskala** sliding scale of wages; ~**er Maschinentisch** traversing machine table; ~**er Nachlaß** personal estate; ~**e Politik** pliable policy; ~**e Preise** flexible prices; ~**e Sandbank** shifting sand; ~**e Tarifskala** sliding scale of wages; ~**e Truppenteile** mobile units; ~**es Vermögen** movable property, movables, personalty, [goods and] chattels; ~**es und unbewegliches Vermögen** movables and immovables; ~**e Verteidigung** *(mil.)* mobile defence; ~**es Ziel** moving target.

Beweglichkeit mobility, *(Auto, Flugzeug, Schiff)* manoeuvrability, *(Politik)* suppleness, flexibility;
geistige ~ active mind, quickness; **leichte** ~ *(mil.)* mobility; ~ **eines Autos** manoeuvrability of a car *(Br.)*; ~ **bei der Festlegung von Bebauungsrichtlinien** flexible zoning *(US)*.

bewegt touched, *(Börse)* agitated, brisk, lively;
von Leidenschaften ~ stirred by passions; **vom Mitleid** ~ stirred to pity; **von den Nachrichten sehr** ~ stunned by the news;
~**e Diskussion** lively (animated, stormy) discussion; ~**es Leben führen** to lead a colo(u)rful life; ~**es Leben hinter sich haben** to have led an adventurous life; ~**e Schilderung** vivid description; ~**e See** troubled sea; **mit** ~**er Stimme** in a voice trembling with emotion; **leicht** ~**e Wasseroberfläche** rippling surface of water; **etw. mit** ~**en Worten schildern** to describe s. th. vividly; ~**e Zeiten** stirring (stormy) times.

Bewegung motion, movement, *(Preise, Kurse)* tendency, trend, movement, *(Rührung)* emotion, *(Unruhe)* agitation, stir;
in ständiger ~ on the fly; **nicht die geringste** ~ not a stir; **ohne die geringste** ~ **zu verraten** without showing the least emotion;
deflationistische ~ deflation; **körperliche** ~ physical exercise; **politische** ~ political movement; **erfolgreiche politische** ~ bandwaggon; **reaktionäre** ~ reaction; **rückgängige (rückläufige)** ~ *(Börse, Konjunktur)* downward (retrograde) movement; **soziale** ~ social movement; **staatsgefährdende** ~ subversive activities; **steigende** ~ *(Börse)* bullish performance; **ungeschickte** ~ clumsy movement; **volksverbundene politische** ~ grassroots political movement *(US)*; **wenig** ~ *(Börse)* little movement;
~ **des Anlagevermögens** changes in fixed assets; ~ **auf Bankkonten** fluctuation on bank accounts; **rückläufige** ~ **der industriellen Fertigung** decline in industry; ~**en der feindlichen Truppen** movements of the enemy troops; ~ **zur gewaltsamen Veränderung bestehender Wirtschaftsformen** criminal syndicalism;
aus der ~ **angreifen** *(mil.)* to attack from a marching column; **feindliche** ~**en beobachten** to observe the enemy's movements; **militärische** ~**en durchführen** to operate; **j. an einer frappanten** ~ **erkennen** to know s. o. by his knock; **in** ~ **halten** to keep going; **j. in** ~ **halten** to keep s. o. on the go; **seine** ~ **kaum verbergen können** to be hardly able to conceal one's emotion; **soziale** ~ **ins Leben rufen** to call a social movement into being; **in** ~ **sein** *(ganze Stadt)* to be up and about; **dauernd in** ~ **sein** to be always on the go; **in heftiger** ~ **sein** to be in a state of agitation; **in** ~ **setzen** to put into motion;; **alles in** ~ **setzen** to leave no stone unturned; **sich in** ~ **setzen** to start, to move [off], to make a move, *(Maschine)* to begin working; **Himmel und Erde in** ~ **setzen** to move (stir) heaven and earth *(fam.)*; **die Massen in** ~ **setzen** to stir up the people; **wenig** ~ **zeigen** *(Börse)* to be flat.

Bewegungs|ablauf physical equation; ~**bilanz** statement of application of funds (resources and their application), funds statement; ~**bild** trend; **saisonales** ~**bild** seasonal trend; ~**energie** kinetic energy.

Bewegungsfreiheit room for manoeuvre, freedom of movement, elbow room, latitude, rope, play;
große ~ ample scope; **uneingeschränkte** ~ full liberty of action; **jds.** ~ **einengen** to impose limitations upon s. one's liberty of action; **jem. jegliche** ~ **nehmen** to hedge s. o. with rules and regulations; **in seiner** ~ **durch Bestimmungen eingeengt sein** to be pegged down with regulations.

Bewegungskrieg open (mobile) warfare.

bewegungslos motionless, immobile;
~ **dastehen** to stand stock still.

Bewegungs|möglichkeit scope, leeway; **winziger** ~**raum** no room to swing a cat in; ~**studie** motion (time) study; ~**studio** motion study.

beweihräuchern, j. to fume (adulate) s. o.; **sich [selbst]** ~ to pat o. s. on the back, to toot one's own horn, to blow one's own trumpet, to sound one's own praises.

Beweihräucherung adulation, servile flattery.

Beweis proof, evidence, *(Beweisführung)* demonstration, *(Beweisgrund)* argument, *(Beweisstück)* piece of evidence, exhibit, *(Zeichen)* token, mark, sign;
als ~ as proof; **als** ~ **dienend** probatory *(US)*; **als** ~ **meiner Hochachtung** as a mark of my esteem; **bis zum** ~ **des Gegenteils** in the absence of proof to the contrary; **mangels** ~**es** for lack (in default) of evidence, failing proof; **nicht der Fetzen eines** ~**es** not one shred of evidence, no evidence on which you could hang a cat; **zum** ~ **von** in proof (as evidence, support, substantiation, token) of;
anderweitiger ~ extrinsic evidence; **angebotener** ~ evidence tendered; **angetretener** ~ indicative evidence, evidence adduced; **aufgenommener** ~ deposition; **ausreichender** ~ sufficient evidence; **für die Versicherungsgesellschaft ausreichender** ~ evidence satisfactory to the company; **ausschlaggebender** ~ decisive proof; **äußerer** ~ external evidence; **auf**

Indizien beruhender ~ circumstantial evidence; **nur auf Zeugenaussagen beruhender** ~ nude matter; **direkter** ~ direct evidence; **eindeutiger** ~ striking (positive) evidence, explicit proof; **einwandfreier** ~ absolute proof, clear evidence; **einwandfreier und klarer** ~ clear and convincing proof; **endgültiger** ~ positive evidence (proof); **entscheidender** ~ clinching argument; **faktischer** ~ factual proof; **formeller** ~ formal proof; **mit Originalurkunden geführter** ~ original evidence; **genaue** ~e chapter and verse; **glaubhafter** ~ prima facie evidence; **handfester** ~ solid evidence, tangible proof; **hinlänglicher (hinreichender)** ~ satisfactory (substantial) evidence; **indirekter** ~ indirect (circumstantial) evidence; **innerer** ~ internal evidence; **fast kein** ~ next to no evidence; **klarer** ~ tangible proof; **lückenhafter** ~ incomplete evidence; **lückenloser** ~ close argument; **mittelbarer** ~ secondary (circumstantial) evidence; **mündlicher** ~ oral evidence; **neuer** ~ fresh evidence; **primärer** ~ best evidence; **rechtserheblicher** ~ evidence sufficient in law; **sachdienlicher** ~ expert (relative, material) evidence; **scheinbarer** ~ sham (specious) proof; **schlagender** ~ convincing argument, striking (cast-iron) proof; **schlüssiger** ~ conclusive (decisive, substantial) proof; **schriftlicher** ~ written proof (evidence), evidence in writing; **selbständiger** ~ independent proof; **sicherer** ~ positive proof; **sichtbarer** ~ ocular proof (demonstration); **stichhaltige** ~e factual evidence; **triftiger** ~ valid proof; **überlieferter** ~ traditionary evidence; **überzeugender** ~ true indicator, clear and convincing proof, luculent testimony; **nicht überzeugender** ~ flimsy evidence; **umfassender** ~ full proof; **unmittelbarer** ~ direct evidence; **unwiderlegbarer** ~ incontrovertible proof; **urkundlicher** ~ documentary evidence (proof), proof by documents; **voller** ~ positive proof; **vollgültiger** ~ full proof, luculent testimony; **vorläufiger** ~ *(Versicherungsrecht)* preliminary proof; **zulässiger** ~ admissible evidence; **zwingender** ~ conclusive (cogent) evidence, strong argument;
~ **des ersten Anscheins** prima-facie evidence; ~ **durch Augenscheinsnahme** real evidence; ~ **für eine Behauptung** substantiation of a statement; ~ **aufgrund von Begleitumständen** circumstantiation; ~ **der Dankbarkeit** token of gratitude; ~ **der Echtheit** proof of authenticity; ~ **aus zweiter Hand** secondhand evidence; ~ **vom Hörensagen** secondhand (hearsay) evidence; ~ **aufgrund von Indizien** circumstantial evidence; ~ **eines Lehrsatzes** demonstration of a theorem; ~ **des Nichtvorhandenseins** negative evidence; ~ **durch Police allein** policy proof; ~ **durch Sachverständige** expert testimony; ~ **aufgrund eigener Wahrnehmung** direct evidence; ~ **guten Willens** mark of good will;
~ **anbieten** to offer proof, to tender (adduce) evidence; **als (zum)** ~ **anführen** to put in as evidence; ~ **antreten** to tender evidence (an averment in law), to adduce (introduce, produce) evidence, to lead proof *(Scot.)*; **Fall auf schwachen** ~**en aufbauen** to rest a case on slender evidence; ~ **aufnehmen** to take evidence; ~ **aufrechterhalten** to hold an argument; ~**e beibringen** to furnish (procure, present) evidence; **als** ~ **beibringen** to bring into court; **aufgrund magerer** ~**e entscheiden** to decide on inadequate grounds; ~ **erbringen** to aver, to adduce proof (evidence), to bring forward (exhibit) evidence, to discharge the onus of proof; **obliegenden** ~ **erbringen** to sustain the burden of proof; ~ **durch eine Aussage erhärten** to verify a statement; ~ **erheben** to hear (take) evidence; **nach einem** ~ **für jds. Schuld forschen** to seek for a demonstration of s. one's guilt; **als** ~ **gelten** *(Urkunde)* to be in evidence, to have full faith and credit *(US)*; **keine** ~**e gegen jem. haben** to have no case against s. o.; **jem. übermäßige** ~**e seiner Gunst zukommen lassen** to load s. o. with favo(u)rs; ~**e liefern** to furnish (produce) evidence, to prove; ~**e für eine Aussage liefern** to produce the proof of a statement; ~**e sammeln** to collect evidence; **lebender** ~ **von jds. Wohltätigkeit sein** to speak volumes of s. one's charity; **unter** ~ **stellen** to prove, to give proof of, to furnish evidence; **seinen Bürgersinn unter** ~ **stellen** to show o. s. public-spirited; ~ **vorbringen** to submit evidence; **als** ~ **vorbringen** to put in evidence; **dem Gericht als** ~ **vorliegen** to be in evidence; **aus Mangel an** ~**en freigesprochen werden** to be discharged on the ground of insufficient evidence; **durch** ~ **widerlegen** to rebut; ~ **würdigen** to weigh evidence; ~ **zerpflücken** to riddle an argument; **als** ~ **zulassen** to admit in evidence;
~**anerbieten** averment; ~**angebot für zulässig erklären** to rule that the evidence is admissible; ~**antrag** averment; ~**antrag ablehnen** to refuse to admit evidence; ~**antrag stellen** to offer to prove a plea; **sich seine** ~**anträge vorbehalten** to reserve one's defence.

Beweisantritt presentation of proof, defensive allegation, production of evidence, submission of evidence;
fehlender ~ failure of evidence;
~ **durch Urkunden** documentary evidence.

Beweisaufnahme hearing of evidence (of witnesses), taking evidence;
~ **für besondere Fälle** special argument;
~ **anordnen** to order evidence to be taken; ~ **unter Ausschluß der Öffentlichkeit durchführen** to take evidence in camera; **in die** ~ **eintreten** to hear evidence; ~ **schließen** to close (rest, *US*) a case; **zur** ~ **schreiten** to begin with the hearing of evidence.

Beweisausführungen factual argument.

beweisbar provable, demonstrable;
nicht ~ unprovable, incapable of proof.

Beweis|barkeit provableness, provability, demonstrability; ~**dokument** evidence, *(über Besitzwechsel)* common assurance, *(Zahlungsbefehl)* payment voucher; ~**einrede** demurrer to evidence.

beweisen to prove, to [furnish] evidence, to aver, to argue, to demonstrate, to make good, to verify;
durch beglaubigte Abschrift ~ to exemplify; **Anteilnahme** ~ to show interest; **Behauptung** ~ to substantiate a statement; **Unrichtigkeit einer Behauptung** ~ to disprove a statement; **das Gegenteil** ~ to prove the contrary; **klar** ~ to be evidentiary; **Lehrsatz** ~ to demonstrate a theory; ~, **daß man recht hat** to prove one's case; **etw. schlagend** ~ to be of striking evidence; **überzeugend** ~ to bring home; **jds. Unschuld** ~ to prove s. o. to be innocent; **unwiderlegbar** ~ to prove beyond doubt; **urkundlich** ~ to give documentary evidence, to evidence by documents;
Behauptung ~ **können** to give evidence for a statement; **sich leicht** ~ **lassen** to admit of an easy proof; **klar** ~ **müssen** to be put to strict proof.

Beweisergebnis evidence taken;
in Widerspruch zum ~ contrary to the evidence;
überwiegendes ~ fair preponderance;
~ **nicht anerkennen** to take exception to an evidence; ~ **zu jds. Ungunsten verfälschen** to arrange the evidence against s. o.; ~ **zusammenfassen** to sum up the (take summary of) evidence.

Beweiserhärtung corroboration of evidence.

beweiserheblich probative;
~**e Tatsachen** evidentiary facts.

Beweiserheblichkeit relevancy of evidence.

Beweiserhebung hearing (taking) of evidence;
gerichtliche ~ evidence in court; **mündliche** ~ parol[e] evidence; **vorläufige** ~ preliminary examination *(Br.)*;
aufgrund der ~ **feststehen** to be plain on the evidence.

Beweiserhebungsbeschluß noting brief.

beweisfähig susceptible (capable) of proof, provable.

Beweis|fähigkeit susceptibility of proof; ~**fälligkeit** failure of proof; ~**fälschung** cooking of evidence; **schriftlicher** ~**fragebogen** interrogatories; ~**führer** demonstrator.

Beweisführung argumentation, demonstration, line (marshal(l)ing) of arguments, reasoning;
außergerichtliche ~ extrajudicial evidence; **bündige (lückenlose)** ~ close reasoning; **gutachterliche** ~ opinion evidence; **negative** ~ negative testimony (evidence); **primäre** ~ primary evidence; **schriftliche** ~ written evidence, evidence in writing, literal proof; **spitzfindige** ~ wiredrawn argument; **tatsächliche** ~ real evidence; **umständliche** ~ tortuous argument; **zusammenfassende** ~ cumulative argumentation;
~ **aufgrund von Begleitumständen** circumstantiation;
sich jds. ~ **anschließen** to follow s. one's argument; ~ **unterstützen** to give point to an argument; **sich jds.** ~ **nicht verschließen** to yield to s. one's arguments.

Beweis|führungslast burden (onus) of proof; **fehlendes** ~**glied** link in a chain of evidence; ~**grund** proof, evidence, argument, reason; **vage** ~**gründe** intangible arguments; **verschiedene** ~**gründe anführen** to produce several arguments; **zwingende** ~**gründe anführen** to clinch an argument; ~**indiz** inferential proof; ~**kette** chain of evidence; ~**klassifizierung** classification of evidence; ~**komplex** body of evidence; ~**konflikt** conflicting evidence.

Beweiskraft effect of evidence, conclusiveness, conclusive (probatory, probative, *US*) force, demonstrative evidence;
in der Urkunde selbst liegende ~ internal evidence; **überzeugende** ~ strength of an argument; **zwingende** ~ mathematical evidence;
~ **einer Aussage** strength of a statement; ~ **eines Protokolls** minutes as evidence ~ **einer Zeugenaussage** validity of testimony;

über die gesetzliche ~ einer Urkunde entscheiden to decide whether a document is admissable as evidence; **~ haben** to have documentary authority; **keine ~ haben** to lack conclusive force.

beweiskräftig cogent, probative, conclusive, relevant;
nicht ~ not capable of proof.

Beweislast onus (burden) of proof;
dem Kläger die ~ auferlegen to cast the burden of proof upon the plaintiff; **~ umkehren** to shift the burden of proof; **~ zugunsten jds. umkehren** to give s. o. the benefit of the doubt; **ihm obliegt die ~** the burden of proof rests with him.

Beweis|lücke gap in an argument; **~mangel** lack of evidence.

Beweismaterial [supporting] evidence, proof;
hilfsweise angebotenes ~ substitutionary evidence; **ausreichendes ~** satisfactory evidence; **für die Urteilsfindung ausreichendes ~** legally sufficient evidence; **belastendes ~** state's *(US)* (King's, Queen's, *Br.*) evidence, evidence for the prosecution, incriminating documents; **besonderes ~** special matter; **bestätigendes ~** probative evidence; **einwandfreies ~** incontestable evidence; **entlastendes ~** evidence for the defence; **erdrückendes ~** damning evidence; **erhebliches ~** evidence having a bearing on the issue; **hinreichendes ~** substantive (satisfactory) evidence; **neuentdecktes ~** fresh evidence; **neues ~** fresh evidence; **originales ~** original evidence; **rechtserhebliches ~** evidence sufficient in law; **schriftliches ~** written evidence; **überwiegendes ~** preponderance of evidence; **überzeugendes ~** convincing evidence; **nicht überzeugendes ~** flimsy evidence; **umfangreiches ~** strong body of evidence; **unschlüssige ~** indecisive evidence; **unterstützendes ~** collateral (secondary) evidence; **unwiderlegbares ~** incontestable (unchallengeable) evidence; **unzulässiges ~** inadmissable evidence, fleet-book evidence; **urkundliches ~** documentary proof; **urteilstragendes ~** evidence to support the verdict; **weiteres ~** other evidence; **nicht widerlegbares ~** unchallengeable evidence; **widersprechendes ~** conflict of evidence; **widerspruchloses ~** clean evidence; **zugelassenes ~** legal (proper) evidence; **nicht zugelassenes ~** inadmissible (incompetent) evidence; **rechtlich zugelassenes ~** legal evidence; **zulässiges ~** competent evidence; **zusätzliches ~** corroborating evidence, cumulative evidence;
~ der Staatsanwaltschaft state's *(US)* (Kings's, Queen's, *Br.*) evidence;
~ nicht anerkennen to resist the evidence; **~ aufstöbern** to hunt up (out) evidence; **~ beibringen** to supply evidence; **~ gründlich durchleuchten** to probe the evidence; **~ fälschen** to cook up evidence; **mit ~ herausrücken** to come up with evidence; **über das ~ hinausgehen** to go outside the evidence; **belastendes ~ aus den Akten verschwinden lassen** to remove incriminating evidence from the files; **~ liefern** to lead (adduce) evidence; **~ sorgfältig prüfen** to sift evidence; **~ sammeln** to collect evidence; **aus dem ~ schließen** to gather from the evidence; **~ unterdrücken (unterschlagen)** to suppress (cover up) evidence; **~ verfälschen** to cook up evidence; **~ vorlegen** to satisfy production, to produce evidence; **neues ~ vorlegen** to bring forward some new evidence; **als ~ zulassen** to receive in evidence; **nicht als ~ zulassen** to bar as (resist) evidence; **~ zurückhalten** to withhold evidence; **~ zusammenstellen (zusammentragen)** to collect evidence, to build up a case.

Beweismittel judicial evidence, proof, supporting (source of, means of, instrument of) evidence, exhibit;
als ~ zugelassen admissible;
zufällig entstandenes ~ casual evidence; **fabrizierte ~** fabricated evidence; **gesetzliches ~** primary evidence; **indirekte ~** secondary evidence; **neue ~** fresh evidence; **primäres ~** best evidence; **zugelassene ~** legal (proper, admissable) evidence;
~ erster Ordnung primary evidence;
~ beibringen to present as evidence; **als ~beschlagnahmen** to impound as evidence; **als ~ zugelassen sein** to admit evidence, to be receivable in evidence; **~ unterdrücken** to suppress evidence; **~ vorlegen** to produce evidence, to satisfy production; **nicht als ~ zulassen** to bar as evidence; **~ zurückhalten** to withhold evidence.

Beweis|not failure of evidence (proof); **~pflicht für das Mitverschulden** *(Schiffskollision)* major and minor fault.

beweispflichtig sein to hold the affirmative burden of proof.

Beweis|protokoll record (transcript) of evidence; **~recht** law of evidence.

beweisrechtlich evidentiary.

Beweis|regeln rules of evidence (proof); **~sicherung** perpetuating (preservation of) testimony; **~stelle** quotation; **~stück** [piece of] evidence, record, exhibit, document, instrument, voucher, convincing object, corpus delicti, probatory term *(US)*; **belastende ~stücke** incriminating documents; **~stück ablehnen** to impugn a piece of evidence; **untergeordnete ~tatsache** minor fact; **~termin** hearing of evidence; **~thema** matter; **~umkehrung** shift of the burden of proof; **~unerheblichkeit** remoteness of evidence; **~unterlage** supporting record; **~unterschlagung** suppression of evidence; **~urkunde** [piece of] evidence, document, *(Schwurgericht)* test paper; **einseitige ~urkunde** unilateral record; **~verfahren** evidence; **abgeschlossenes ~verfahren** evidence completed; **~verfahren aufnehmen** to begin with the hearing of evidence; **~vernichtung** destruction of evidence; **~vorschrift** rule of evidence; **~wert** probative value; **~würdigung** consideration of evidence; **~würdigung vornehmen** to sum up (weigh) the evidence, to determine the value of evidence; **~zulässigkeit** admissibility of evidence.

bewenden lassen, es dabei to go no further into a matter, to let it go at that.

bewerben, sich to apply for, to stand as candidate, to run, to candidate, to seek, to contend, to go up *(Br.)*, *(um Lieferungen)* to make a bid for, to tender, *(um einen Preis)* to compete for, *(um Stimmen)* to solicit, to canvass;
sich um einen Abgeordnetensitz ~ to stand for Parliament *(Br.)*; **sich um ein Amt ~** to run (stand) for an office *(US)*; **sich um einen Auftrag ~** to make a tender; **sich um jds. Gunst ~** to court s. one's favo(u)r; **sich als Kandidat ~** to put o. s. forward, to stand for; **sich um ein Mädchen ~** to court a girl; **sich persönlich ~** to make a personal application; **sich um einen Posten ~** to compete for a job; **sich um eine Stelle ~** to apply (run) for a position, to seek employment, to put in for a post (job, *fam.*), to compete for a job; **sich um ein Stipendium ~** to compete for a scholarship; **sich um Staatsaufträge ~** to bid on government contracts.

Bewerber applicant, aspirant, candidate, comer, entrant, registrant *(US)*, job seeker *(US)*, *(Lieferungen)* bidder, tenderer, *(für Preis)* competitor;
ohne ~ unapplied for;
erfolgreicher ~ selected applicant; **ernsthafter ~** serious contender; **möglicher ~** prospect; **viele ~** wide choice of candidate; **zurückgewiesene ~** unsuccessful applicants;
~ um Stimmrechtsvollmachten proxy solicitor *(US)*;
~ ablehnen to turn down a candidate; **alle ~ ausprobieren** to take one's chance with all applicants for the job; **sich mit allen Mitteln für einen ~ einsetzen** to boom a candidate; **j. als geeigneten ~ ins Auge fassen** to look upon s. o. as a likely candidate; **als ~ in Betracht kommen** to be a possible candidate; **für einen ~ stimmen** to give one's vote to a candidate, to vote a candidate into office; **~ kräftig unterstützen** to boom a candidate; **j. gegen andere ~ zurücksetzen** to discriminate s. o. against other candidates; **~ideal** ideal candidate; **~liste** list of candidates, leet *(Scot.)*; **~schlange** queue of applicants.

Bewerbung application, competition, *(Gesuch)* petition, suit, *(Kandidatur)* candidateship, candidature *(Br.)*;
nur einzelne ~en only a few applicants; **ernsthafte ~** intent application; **handschriftliche ~** handwritten application; **schriftliche ~** application in writing, mailed application *(US)*; **bisher vorliegende ~en** applications received so far;
~ mit vollständigem Lebenslauf application with full career details; **~ um Stimmrechtsvollmachten** proxy solicitation *(US)*; **~ um eine Vertretung** agency application;
~ ablehnen to reject an application; **~ annehmen** to give one's hand to a suitor; **~ aufsetzen** to write an application; **jds. ~ befürworten** to back s. one's application; **~ einreichen** to send in an application; **Voraussetzungen einer ~ erfüllen** to qualify, to prove fit.

Bewerbungs|akten application files; **~antrag** employment application, application for employment; **~bogen** application form; **~datum** date of application; **~formular** application form, employment (application) blank *(US)*; **~frist** filing period, *(Ausschreibungen)* tender period; **~prüfung** competitive entrance examination; **~schreiben** [letter of] application, written application; **~schreiben verfassen** to write an application; **letzter ~termin** closing date for application, application close; **~unterlagen** application papers (files), application material, personal data and testimonials; **~verfahren** application procedure; **~vordruck** application form, employment (application) blank *(US)*.

bewerfen, jds. Namen mit Schmutz to sling mud at s. one's name.

bewerkstelligen to accomplish, to bring about, to manage, to perform, to engineer, to effect, to effectuate, to execute, to realize;

seinen Haushalt trotz jeden Monat steigender Preise ~ to contrive with prices rising every month; **seinen Umzug** ~ to have one's furniture removed; **Verkauf** ~ to effect a sale; **schwer zu** ~ **sein** to take a lot of doing; **irgendwie wird er es schon** ~ he will manage it somehow.

Bewerkstelligung accomplishment, performance, execution, realization, contrivance;

bewertbar appraisable, valuable, assessable.

Bewerten *(Marktuntersuchung)* weight.

bewerten to evaluate, to value, to appreciate, to judge, to price, *(Absatzuntersuchung)* to weigh, *(abschätzen)* to appraise, to estimate, *(Grundstück)* to extend, to assess, to valuate, *(klassifizieren)* to grade, to rate, *(schulische Leistungen)* to score, to mark, to grade *(US)*, *(steuerlich)* to assess, to rate; **mit 100%** ~ *(Bilanz)* to value at 100 per cent; **Aktie niedrig** ~ to set a low value on a stock; **Anlagegüter höher** ~ to appreciate fixed assets *(US)*; **Anlagen inm Licht des Liquidationstermins** ~ to value assets on a gone-concern basis; **Anspruch** ~ to assess a claim; **einzeln** ~ to value individually; **j. nach seinen Fähigkeiten** ~ to rate s. o.; **Film negativ** ~ to pass an unfavo(u)rable judgment on a film; **Forderungen** ~ to evaluate claims; **Gebäude für Versicherungszwecke** ~ to rate a building for insurance purposes; **Grundstück** ~ to estimate the value of land, to value a property; **immaterielle Güter bilanzmäßig mit nur einem Dollar** ~ to show their intangibles at one dollar; **etw. hoch** ~ to set a high value on s. th., to value s. th. at a high rate, to price s. th. high; **zu hoch** ~ to overrate, to overprice; **höher** ~ to inflate the value, to state higher, to rate higher; **jds. Leistung** ~ to rate s. one's performance; **Leistungsfähigkeit eines Angestellten** ~ to evaluate (rate) an employee; **zu Nachlaßsteuerzwecken** ~ to value for probate purposes; **Nettoinventar** ~ to value on a net asset basis; **neu** ~ to reprice, to transvalue; **niedrig** ~ to price low, to set a low valuation on; **zu niedrig** ~ to underrate; **niedriger** ~ to state lower, to deflate the value, to set a lower value on; **Patent** ~ to appraise a patent; **nach Punkten** ~ to rate on points; **j. unabhängig von seiner Stellung** ~ to dissociate s. o. from his position; **Verlust** ~ to estimate a loss; **Vermögen** ~ to assess property; **Waren** ~ to value goods; **Warenlager** ~ to appraise a stock of goods.

bewertet valued, assessed, rated, extended; **hoch** ~ high priced, high-priced; **zum Einstands- oder Marktpreis** ~ valued at the lower of cost or market; **nicht** ~ unvalued.

Bewertung estimate, valuation, evaluation, valuing, appraisal, appraisement, pricing, rating, *(Grundstück)* extent *(Br.)*, assessment, *(schulische Leistung)* score, marks, grades *(US)*; **erneute** ~ revaluation; **finanzielle** ~ capital rating *(US)*; **zu hohe** ~ overappraisal, overassessment; **marktgemäße** ~ market valuation; **niedrige** ~ reduced assessment; **zu niedrige** ~ underrate; **punktuelle** ~ rating by points; **steuerliche** ~ assessment, assessed valuation *(US)*; **vorsichtige** ~ conservative valuation; **zollamtliche** ~ official valuation; ~ **der Aktiva** valuation of assets; **höhere** ~ **von Anlagegütern** appreciation of fixed assets *(US)*; ~ **fester Anlagen** fixed asset valuation; ~ **eines Anspruches** claim assessment; ~ **einer Arbeit** job rating *(US)*; ~ **eines Betriebs** going-concern valuation; ~ **im Fall einer Liquidation** breakup valuation; ~ **von Fernsehsendungen durch das Publikum** television ratings; ~ **zur Festsetzung des Zolltarifs** valuation for duty purposes; ~ **von Forderungen** evaluation (valuation) of claims; ~ **der Forschungstätigkeit** research appraisal; ~ **von Führungskräften** executive evaluation; ~ **landwirtschaftlich genutzten Geländes** appraisal of agricultural land; ~ **eines Geschäftsgrundstücks** business property appraisal; ~ **eines Grundstücks** real-estate appraisal; ~ **von Grundvermögen** assessment of property; ~ **der Lagerbestände** stock evaluation, valuation of inventory; ~ **einer Leistung** efficiency (merit, *US*) rating; ~ **der Leistungsfähigkeit eines Angestellten** employee rating; ~ **für Nachlaßzwecke** valuation of probate; ~ **nach dem Nettowert der Prämien** net valuation; **berufliche** ~ **nach dem Punktsystem** job rating; ~ **zum Rechnungswert** costs method valuation; ~ **durch Sachverständige** expert appraisal, official appraisement; ~ **eines Schadens** assessment of a damage, ascertainment of a loss; ~ **gestellter Sicherheiten** valuation of securities; ~ **von Verbindlichkeiten** liability verification; ~ **zum Verkehrswert** [open] market valuation; ~ **des Verkehrswertes** fair valuation; ~ **zu Versicherungszwecken** appraisal for insurance purposes; ~ **des Vorratsvermögens zu Durchschnittspreisen** perodic average inventory plan; ~ **von Waren** evaluation of goods; ~ **anhand des Wirtschaftsindexes** index number valuation; ~ **zu einem früheren Zeitpunkt** retrospective appraisal; ~ **vornehmen** to make an appraisal, to value, to evaluate, to appraise; ~ **im Blitzverfahren vornehmen** to evaluate on a hurry-up basis; **zu hohe** ~ **eines Gebäudes vornehmen** to set too high a valuation on a building.

Bewertungs|abschlag reduction in stock valuation; ~**änderungen** changes in the valuation; ~**arten** types of valuation; ~**ausfall** valuation deficit; ~**ausschuß** *(Grundstücke)* assessment (appraisal) committee, valuation commission, *(Leistungen)* rating committee; ~**bereich** area of assessment; ~**bericht** valuation report; ~**buch** rating book *(US)*; ~**durchschnitt** weighted average; **zu verschiedenen** ~**ergebnissen gelangen** to arrive at different valuations; ~**fachmann** valuation expert; ~**fehler** ascertainment error; ~**firma** appraisal company; ~**formblatt** operation analysis chart; ~**formular** form of statement, qualification form; ~**fragebogen** appraisal questionnaire; ~**fragen** valuation matters; ~**freibetrag bei Ersatzbeschaffung für veraltete Wirtschaftsgüter** obsolescence allowance *(Br.)*; ~**freiheit** valuation privilege; ~**funktion** valuation function; ~**gesetz** assessment committee act; ~**gespräch** appraisal interview; ~**grad** *(Marktuntersuchung)* significance; ~**grundlage** valuation basis, basis of valuation, *(Rentabilitätsrechnung)* cost basis of accounting; ~**index** weighted index; ~**kommission** appraisement (appraisal, assessment) committee, commission of appraisement, valuation commission; ~**konto** valuation account; ~**liste** valuation list.

bewertungsmäßig valuational.

Bewertungsmaßstab valuation criterion, rate of assessment, *(Unternehmen)* price ratio *(US)*; **schwacher** ~ poor criterion; **vorsichtigen** ~ **zugrundelegen** to employ a more conservative estimate.

Bewertungs|maßstäbe evaluation techniques; ~**merkmal** *(Angestellte)* job factor; ~**methode** method of valuation, valuation method, *(Investmentfonds)* market appreciation; ~**möglichkeit** appreciation potentiality; ~**niveau** valuation level; ~**note einer Meinungsumfrage** public opinion poll rating; ~**programm** appraisal program(me); ~**punkt** rating point; ~**reserve** valuation reserve; ~**richtlinien** valuation rules, *(Steuer)* assessment principles; ~**skala** appraisal profile, *(Steuer, Versicherung)* scale of assessment; ~**standpunkt** valuation point of view; ~**stichtag** valuation date; ~**system** evaluation system, *(Effekten)* rating system *(US)*; ~**tabelle** cost process chart, *(Effekten)* rating table *(US)*; ~**tafel** rating table *(US)*; ~**unterlagen** rating book; ~**verfahren** valuation process, appraisal technique; ~**vorschriften** valuation rules, *(Steuer)* assessment principles.

bewettern *(Bergbau)* to ventilate.

Bewetterung *(Bergbau)* ventilation, circulation of the air.

bewiesen proved, in evidence; **unwiderlegbar** ~ proven beyond doubt.

bewilligen to grant, to allow, to accord, to afford, *(genehmigen)* to consent, to approve of, *(parl.)* to vote, to appropriate, *(zugestehen)* to concede; **jem. das Armenrecht** ~ to grant s. o. a legal aid certificate; **Audienz** ~ to grant an audience; **Aufwandsentschädigung** ~ to allow for special expenditure; **Betrag** ~ to allocate a sum; **Betrag abstimmungsweise** ~ to vote a sum; **Einstellung der Zwangsvollstreckung** ~ to grant a stay of execution; **Frist** ~ to allow time (a breathing space, *fam.*), to accord a respite; **Fristverlängerung** ~ to grant an extension of time; **Geldmittel** ~ to appropriate funds, *(Parlament)* to vote funds; **Gesuch anstandslos** ~ to grant an application without objection; **Haushalt (Haushaltsmittel, Haushaltsvoranschlag)** ~ to vote supplies (the appropriation, estimates); **jem. ein Interview** ~ to favo(u)r s. o. with an interview; **100.000 £ für die Katastrophengeschädigten (Unfallgeschädigten)** ~ to vote £ 100.000 for the sufferers of a flood; **Konzession** ~ to grant a commision (licence); **Kredit** ~ to allow a credit, to grant a loan (credit); **Kredit sukzessive** ~ to vote credits in instalments; **zusätzliche Mittel in Höhe von 150 Millionen Dollar** ~ to vote $ 150 million in extra money; **nachträglich** ~ to grant additionally; **Pension** ~ to grant (settle) a pension; **Provision** ~ to accord a commission; **Rabatt** ~ to allow a discount; **Rente** ~ to make an allowance; **Rücklagenzuführung** ~ to approve the amounts set aside to reserve; **900.000 DM für einen Schulneubau** to appropriate DM 900.000 for the new school building; **Sonderausgabe** ~ to allow a special item of expenditure; **jem. eine Unterredung** ~ to grant s. o. an interview; **Vorschuß** ~ to grant an advance; **Zahlungsaufschub** ~ to grant a respite; **Zuschuß** ~ to grant an allowance, to make a grant.

Bewilligender grantor.
bewilligt granted, allowed, concessionary;
nicht ~ ungranted;
jederzeit Pfundkredite ~ **bekommen** to get free access to sterling credit;
~**er Betrag von 100.000 Dollar für ein Vorhaben** vote of $ 100.000 for a project; ~**e Etatsätze (Haushaltsmittel)** budgetary appropriations; ~**er Werbeetat** advertising budget, advertising appropriation.
Bewilligung grant, granting, permission, allowance, allocation, *(Genehmigung)* consent, *(Konsession)* concession, licence, *(parl.)* vote, appropriation;
globale ~ block vote; **nachträgliche** ~ additional (supplementary) grant; **unverausgabte** ~**en** unspent appropriations; **vorläufige** ~ **eines Abschlages** vote of an account; ~ **des Armenrechts** legal aid (poor persons, *Br.*) certificate; ~ **einer Frist** granting of time; ~ **von Geldmitteln** grant of money appropriation of funds; **verzögerte** ~ **von Krediten** vote of credits subject to delay; ~ **eines Kredits** grant[ing] of a loan; ~ **durch das Parlament** parliamentary grant; ~ **einer Pension** settling a pension; ~ **eines Vorschusses** grant of an advance; **um die** ~ **eines Zuschusses einkommen** to put in a claim for a grant; **großzügige** ~**en vornehmen** *(parl.)* to vote on a liberal scale.
Bewilligungs | ausschuß allocation committee, *(parl.)* appropriation (budget) committee; ~**bescheid** licensing ordinance; ~**gesuch** petition for a grant-in-aid; ~**kontrollorgan** allocation control; ~**recht** appropriation privilege; ~**schreiben** letter of grant; ~**stelle** licensing authority *(Br.)*; ~**verfahren** licensing procedure.
bewirken to do, to effect, to cause, to implement, to bring to pass (about), to accomplish, to pull off *(fam.)*;
Heilung ~ to effect a cure; **Lieferung** ~ to make delivery; **Temperaturrückgang** ~ to cause a fall in temperature; **Veränderung** ~ to effect a change; **Zahlung** ~ to effect payment.
bewirkte Gegenleistung executed consideration.
Bewirkung effecting, accomplishment.
bewirten to entertain, to regale, to treat;
seine Freunde ~ to feast one's friends; **j. fürstlich** ~ to treat s. o. in a princely manner (like a lord); **j. großartig** ~ to do s. o. proud; **j. mit einem Kuchen** ~ to treat s. o. with a cake.
bewirtschaften to administer, to manage, *(Acker)* to till, to cultivate, *(zwangsweise)* to control, to ration, to allocate;
Boden intensiv ~ to cultivate the soil intensively; **Devisen** ~ to control foreign exchange; **Gut** ~ to manage an estate, to work a farm; **Hotel** ~ to run a hotel; **100 Morgen** ~ to farm a hundred acres; **Wohnungsmarkt** ~ to control housing;
staatlich ~ **lassen** to put under government control.
Bewirtschafter manager, *(Gut)* bailiff.
bewirtschaftet rationed, controlled, administered, restricted, *(Hof)* managed, *(Hotel)* open, *(Land)* cultivated, *(Waren)* on points;
nicht mehr ~ decontrolled, off the ration, unrationed; **schlecht** ~ ill-managed;
~ **sein** to be rationed (under allocation), to be (go) on points; **schlecht** ~**es Feld** badly cultivated field; ~**e Fläche** cultivated area; ~**e Waren** quota (rationed) goods; **nicht** ~**e Waren** commodities not under control; **nicht** ~**er Wohnraum** uncontrolled (unrestricted) dwelling; ~**er Wohnungsraum** controlled housing.
Bewirtschaftung management, planning, husbanding, *(Acker)* husbandry, tillage, cultivation, culture, farming, *(Kapital)* direction, *(Mangelwaren)* economic control, rationing;
extensive ~ extensive farming; **intensive** ~ intensive farming; **kollektive** ~ collective farming; **ordnungsgemäße** ~ proper management; **staatliche** ~ governmental planning (control); **schlechte** ~ **des Bodens** poor cultivation of the soil; ~ **von Devisen** foreign-exchange (currency, *US*) control, allocation of currency, rationing of foreign exchange; ~ **eines Gutes** working of a farm, farm management; ~ **von Lebensmitteln** food rationing; ~ **durch den Staat** government control; ~ **des Wohnungsmarktes** housing control;
kriegsbedingte ~ **aufheben** to dismantle wartime control; ~ **erleichtern** to facilitate housekeeping; **aus der** ~ **herausnehmen** to decontrol, to deration; **Wohnungen aus der** ~ **herausnehmen** to remove dwellings from control *(Br.)*; **unter** ~ **stellen** to put under government control.
Bewirtschaftungs | kosten administrative costs, costs of management; ~**maßnahmen** measures of control, rationing arrangements; ~**maßnahmen aufheben** to lift a control; **intensive** ~**methoden** intensive methods of agriculture; ~**plan** rationing scheme; ~**programm** rationing program(me); ~**stelle** ration board, ration-card agency, control office; ~**system**, ~**wesen** priority (control, allocation, rationing) system, *(Landwirtschaft)* farming system; **intensive** ~**systeme** intensive methods; ~**vorschriften** rationing regulations.
Bewirtung treat, treating, entertainment, hospitality;
festliche ~ celebration, treat;
~ **von Geschäftsfreunden** entertaining customers, business entertainment.
Bewirtungskosten entertainment allowance, entertaining expenses;
~ **für Geschäftsfreunde** cost of business entertainment.
bewohnbar habitable, inhabitable, fit for habitation (occupation).
Bewohnbarkeit [in]habitability.
Bewohnen eines Hauses occupation of a house.
bewohnen to inhabit, to dwell, to reside, *(Zimmer)* to occupy;
Erdgeschoß ~ to occupy the ground floor; **Haus** ~ to live in (occupy) a house; **Haus mietfrei** ~ to live in a house rent-free; **Zimmerflucht** ~ to occupy a suite of rooms.
Bewohner inmate, inhabitant, dweller, occupant, occupier, resident, *(Mieter)* tenant, lodger, roomer *(US)*;
~ **von Elendsgebieten** slum residents; ~ **einer Kolonie** colonial; ~ **einer Mietskaserne** cliff dweller *(US sl.)*.
Bewohnerschaft inhabitants, residents.
bewohnt inhabited, occupied, lived in;
kostenlos ~ occupied rent-free; **nachts** ~ occupied at night; ~**es Haus** inhabited house.
bewölken, sich to cloud, to become overcast.
bewölkt clouded, cloudy, overcast.
Bewölkung cloud formation, overcast;
aufgerissene ~ broken clouds; **starke** ~ heavy clouds; **strichweise** ~ scattered clouds.
Bewölkungsauflockerung dispersal of clouds.
bewuchert grown over, overgrown, overrun.
Bewuchs vegetation, *(Schiffsboden)* fouling, barnacles.
bewundern to admire;
j. ohne Gegenliebe zu finden ~ to carry a torch for s. o.
bewundernswerte Erfolge erzielen to succeed admirably.
Bewunderung admiration;
in ~ **zu jem. aufschauen** to stand in admiration before s. o.; **j. mit** ~ **erfüllen** to fill s. o. with admiration; ~ **erregen** to dazzle.
Bewunderungsschreie ausbrechen, in to cry out in admiration.
Bewurf rough coat.
bewußt conscious, aware, wittingly, *(absichtlich)* intentional, deliberate, knowingly, *(Klagevortrag)* well-knowing, *(zweckbetont)* purposeful;
j. ~ **irreführen** to mislead s. o. deliberately;
sich einer Gefahr ~ **sein** to be sensible of a danger; **sich der Geschehnisse nicht** ~ **sein** to be ignorant of what is happening; **sich keiner Schuld** ~ **sein** to have a clean conscience; **sich der Schwere seines Verbrechens völlig** ~ **sein** to be sensible of the enormity of one's crime; **sich der Tatsache** ~ **sein** to be sensible to the fact that; **sich voll** ~ **sein** to be well (fully) aware; **etw.** ~ **tun** to do s. th. on purpose; **sich** ~ **werden** to become aware; **sich seiner ausweglosen Lage** ~ **werden** to become conscious of one's hopeless situation;
~**e Absicht** deliberate intention; ~**e Angelegenheit** matter deferred to; ~**e Beleidigung** deliberate (studied) insult; ~ **falsche Darstellung** deliberate misrepresentation; ~**e Lüge** deliberate lie; ~**e Person** person in question; **zur** ~**en Stunde** at the time mentioned; **jds.** ~ **zur Schau gestellte Überlegenheit** s. one's conscious superiority; **sich zur** ~**en Zeit einfinden** to come at the time agreed upon.
bewußtlos unconscious, senseless;
j. ~ **schlagen** to knock s. o. senseless; ~ **werden** to become unconscious, to faint, to go off (lose consciousness), to black out *(fam.)*.
Bewußtlosigkeit unconsciousness;
Schallplatte bis zur ~ **spielen** to play a record endlessly; **in anhaltende** ~ **versinken** to lapse into a coma.
Bewußtsein conscience, awareness;
bei ~ conscious; **im** ~ **seiner Verantwortung** conscious of one's responsibility; **in dem** ~ *(Abkommen)* bearing in mind, aware, conscious;
moralisches ~ moral consciousness (conscience);
~ **nationaler Einheit** sense of nationhood;
allgemeines sittliches ~ **anheben** to improve the morals of a country; **zu** ~ **bringen** to drive home; **jem. zu** ~ **bringen** to make s. o. aware that, to bring s. o. round; **im vollen** ~ **der Folgen handeln** to act in full consciousness of the consequences; **jem.**

zum ~ kommen to occur to s. one's mind; **~ verlieren** to lose consciousness; **für kurze Zeit das ~ verlieren** to black out, to swoon, to faint; **~ wiedererlangen** to recover (regain) consciousness, to come to life.

Bewußtseins|ebene plane; **~grad** degree of awareness; **~lücke** blackout of consciousness, amnesia; **~schwelle** conscious level, margin of consciousness; **~spaltung** dissociation; **~störung** disturbance, confusion of the mind; **~trübung** clouding of consciousness.

Bezahlen, zum ~ dran sein to be one's turn to pay.

bezahlen to pay, to cash *(US)*, *(Betrag)* to subscribe, *(entlohnen)* to pay, to remunerate, *(entschädigen)*, to make good, to compensate, *(honorieren)* to fee, *(Scheck)* to hono(u)r, *(Schulden)* to discharge, to settle, to liquidate, to clear [off];
für j. ~ to pay for s. o., to pay s. o. from one's own pocket; **bei Ablieferung ~** to pay on delivery; **auf Abschlag ~** to pay in part; **anständig ~** to pay handsomely; **seinen Anteil an einer Rechnung ~** to pay one's own shot; **Apothekerpreis ~** to pay through the nose; **Arbeit ~** to remunerate labo(u)r; **Aufpreis ~** to pay extra; **Ausgaben ~** to defray expenses; **bar ~** to pay cash down (on the spot, [in] ready money); **Betrag in voller Höhe ~** to pay an amount in full; **j. für seine Dienste ~** to remunerate s. o. for his services; **Draufgeld für seine Lieferung ~** to pay a deposit on goods; **bei Eingang der Versandpapiere ~** to pay upon tender of shipping documents; **seinen Einstand ~** to pay one's footing; **Eintrittsgeld ~** to pay an entrance fee; **bei Erhalt ~** to pay on receipt; **aus laufenden Erträgen ~** to pay as you go; **aus dem städtischen Etat ~** to pay out of the town funds; **vollen Fahrpreis ~** to pay the full rate (fare); **vor Fälligkeit ~** to pay before maturity; **fristgemäß ~** to pay on the date agreed upon; **im ganzen ~** to pay in the lump; **im ganzen oder in Raten ~** to pay in full or in instalments; **Geldstrafe ~** to pay a fine; **gelegentlich ~** to pay at convenience; **Gepäckträger ~** to pay the porter; **getrennt ~** to pay for o. s., to go Dutch; **sein Glück teuer ~** to pay dearly for one's happiness; **alles auf Heller und Pfennig ~** to pay scot and lot; **Höchstpreise ~** to pay top prices; **Honorar an einen Anwalt ~** to fee a lawyer; **Jahresmiete im voraus ~** to pay the rent annually in advance; **Kosten ~** to bear (defray) the expenses; **Leistungslohn ~** to pay according to the quality of the work; **bei Lieferung ~** to pay on delivery; **in Monatsraten ~** to pay by monthly instalments; **nachträglich ~** to pay extra; **in Naturalien ~** to pay in kind; **nicht ~** to leave unpaid, to make default; **nochmals ~** to repay; **postnumerando ~** to pay on receipt; **pränumerando ~** to make payment in advance; **doppelten Preis ~** to pay double the price; **prompt ~** to pay cash (ready money, in ready cash); **pünktlich ~** to pay promptly; **in Raten ~** to pay by (in) instalments; **Rechnung ~** to pay an account, to pay (settle) a bill; **Reise ~** to pay for a trip; **Restbetrag ~** to pay the balance; **restlos ~** to pay in full; **Rückstand ~** to pay up arrears; **Runde ~** to stand a round; **in Sachwerten ~** to pay in kind; **mit Scheck ~** to pay by check (cheque, *Br.*); **schlecht ~** to underpay, to sweat; **seine Schuld auf Heller und Pfennig ~** to pay one's debt to the last penny (scot and lot); **seine Schulden ~** to settle (pay) one's debts, to get clear of debt; **alte Schulden ~** to pay off old scores; **für sich selbst ~** to pay one's own way; **[Teil des Wagnisses] selbst ~** to retent; **mit Skonto ~** to take cash discount; **sofort (auf der Stelle) ~** to pay cash down, to pay down (forthwith, on the nail); **seinen Spaß teuer ~** to pay for one's whistle; **Steuern ~** to return taxes to the revenue; **Steuerzuschlag ~** to pay extra duty; **Strafporto ~** to pay extra postage; **j. stundenweise ~** to pay s. o. by the hour; **j. aus der eigenen Tasche ~** to pay s. o. out of one's own pocket; **teilweise ~** to make a part payment; **teuer ~** to pay high; **zu teuer ~** to overpay; **etw. teuer ~ müssen** to pay the devil; **überreichlich ~** to outpay; **ungenügend ~** to underpay; **auf zwei Usi ~** to pay at two methods of trading; **jem. seinen Verdienstausfall ~** to compensate s. o. for his broken time; **viel für etw. ~** to give a long price for s. th.; **zu viel ~** to pay too much; **voll ~** to pay in full (up, twenty shillings in the pound); **im voraus ~** to prepay, to pay in advance (by anticipation, beforehand) to make payment in advance, to anticipate; **Wechsel [nicht] ~** to [dis]hono(u)r a bill; **mit einem Wechsel ~** to pay by means of a bill; **wochenweise (wöchentlich) ~** to pay by the week; **Wucherpreis ~** to pay through the nose; **Zeche ~** to foot the bill, to pay the piper (fiddler, *US sl.*); **Zoll für etw. ~** to pay duty on s. th., to pay the customs; **Zuschlag ~** to pay an extra charge;
Licht und Heizung sind extra zu ~ light and heating are extras.

bezahlt paid for, settled, payment received, *(besoldet)* stipendiary, salaried, *(Börse)* prices negotiated, done, *(gedungen)* hired, pensionary, *(Scheck, Wechsel)* hono(u)red;
Antwort ~ prepaid reply, reply paid; **in bar ~** paid out-of-pocket, paid in cash, cash-paid; **gering ~** low paid; **gut ~** well paid; **hoch ~** highly paid; **nicht ~** unpaid, undischarged; **schlecht ~** underpaid, ill remunerated, penny-a-line; **teuer ~** highly paid; **voll ~** paid in full;
~ erhalten contents received; **sich ~ machend** paying; **~ und quittiert** discharged and acquitted;
j. ~ haben to be clear of s. o.; **sich ~ machen** to yield, to pay in the long run, *(schadlos halten)* to make o. s. paid, to recoup; **sich nicht ~ machen** not to be worthwhile; **sich bei jem. ~ machen** to reimburse o. s. upon s. o.; **vollauf ~ sein** to be fully priced; **~ werden** to get paid; **angemessen ~ werden** to get a fair reward for one's labo(u)r; **monatlich ~ werden** to be paid monthly; **nicht rechtzeitig ~ werden** to lie over; **vierteljährlich ~ werden** to be paid by the quarter;
~e Arbeitskräfte paid labo(u)r; **~er Mörder** hired murderer; **~e Rechnungen** clear accounts; **~e Schuld** liquidated debt; **schlecht ~e Stelle** badly paid job; **~er Zeuge** bribed witness.

Bezahlt|meldung advice of fate; **~stempel** receipt stamp.

Bezahlung pay, payment, disbursement, *(Entschädigung)* compensation, *(Gehalt)* salary, *(Honorar)* fee, remuneration, *(Lohn)* wages, *(Scheck, Wechsel)* hono(u)ring, *(Schulden)* discharge, settlement, liquidation, satisfaction, quittance;
als ~ against payment; **als ~ für Ihre Dienste** as remuneration for your services; **bei ~** on payment; **bis zur endgültigen ~** until fully paid; **gegen ~** on (against) payment, remunerated; **gegen sofortige ~** for prompt cash, cash down; **nach ~ der Steuern** taxed paid;
angemessene ~ fair and reasonable compensation; **fristgerechte ~** due payment; **getrennte ~** Dutch treat; **irrtümliche ~** payment made in error; **langsame ~** dilatory payment; **nachträgliche ~** postpayment; **proratarische ~** progress payment; **pünktliche ~** readiness in payment; **schlechte ~** underpayment; **sofortige ~** prompt (short) payment, spot cash; **teilweise ~** part payment; **überdurchschnittliche ~** above-average compensation; **übermäßige ~** overpayment; **übertarifliche ~** payment over and above of wage scale (in excess of standard rates); **ungenügende ~** insufficient pay; **unzureichende ~** not enough pay; **verspätete ~** delayed payment; **volle ~** paying up; **vollständige ~** outright payment, payment (settlement) in full;
~ für den Anmarschweg deadheading pay; **~ für nicht wirklich geleistete Arbeit** featherbedding *(sl.)*; **~ bei Auftragserteilung** cash with order; **~ von Benzinlieferungen** money for fuel supplied; **~ von Dienstleistungen** remuneration of services; **ratenweise ~ der Erbschaftssteuer** instalment option; **~ nach Erfolg** payment by result; **~ der Kosten** defrayal of expenses; **~ einer Rechnung** payment (settlement) of an account; **~ gegen offene Rechnung** clean payment; **~ bei Rechnungsvorlage** payment on invoice; **~ von Schulden** settlement (payment) of debts; **~ der Sozialversicherungsbeiträge** social security tax payment; **~ unter Vorbehalt** payment on reserve; **~ in Waren** payment in goods, bartering, truck system *(Br.)*, store pay *(US)*; **~ bei Eingang der Waren** payment [must be made] on delivery; **~ eines Wechsels** protection of a bill;
~ ablehnen to decline (refuse) payment; **bei jem. die ~ des Mitgliedschaftsbeitrages anmahnen** to post s. o. for nonpayment of his dues; **~ annehmen** to accept payment; **Gäste gegen ~ aufnehmen** to take paying guests; **sich über schlechte ~ beklagen** to complain about bad pay; **auf ~ bestehen** to insist on payment; **auf sofortiger ~ bestehen** to demand prompt payment; **auf ~ drängen** to dun, to press for payment; **sich einer ~ entziehen** to elude payment; **angemessene ~ für seine Arbeit erhalten** to receive adequate remuneration for one's work; **~ eines Wechsels garantieren** to guarantee a bill of exchange; **mit der ~ hinhalten** to keep s. o. out of money; **mit der ~ dran sein** to be one's turn to pay; **gegen ~ verkaufen** to sell for value; **~ einer Schuld verlangen** to demand payment of a debt; **~ verweigern** to refuse payment; **Geld für die ~ von Schulden verwenden** to apply money to the payment of debts.

bezähmen, seine Neugier to restrain one's curiosity; **seine Wut ~** to suppress one's anger; **seine Zunge ~** to bridle one's tongue.

bezaubern to captivate, to charm, to bewitch;
j. ~ to lay s. o. under a spell; **alle durch seine Liebenswürdigkeit ~** to charm everybody by one's kindness.

bezaubernd charming, enchanting, captivating;
~e Frau witch; **~es Kleid** stunning dress; **~es Lächeln** charming smile.

bezeichnen to designate, to describe, to nominate, to indicate, to name, to denominate, *(kennzeichnen)* to indicate, to mark, *(Waren)* to label, to ticket, to mark, to brand;

sich als Arzt ~ to describe o. s. as a doctor; **j. als leichte Beute** ~ to mark s. o. for an easy prey; **kleine Büchersammlung euphemistisch mit Bibliothek** ~ to dignify a small collection of books by calling it a library; **genau** ~ to specify, to state in detail, to give precise details; **mit einem Kreuz** ~ to cross; **durch Leuchtbuchstaben** ~ to indicate by illuminated lettering; **in der beiliegenden Liste genauer** ~ to specify in the enclosed list; **j. als Lügner** ~ to call s. o. a liar; **j. als fähigen Mann** ~ to point out s. o. as a capable man; **Ort auf der Karte** ~ to mark a place on a map; **mit Punkten** ~ to mark by dots; **sich als Sachverständigen** ~ to call o. s. an expert; **Weg** ~ to mark out (to signpost) a path.

bezeichnend significant, indicative, symptomatic;
für jds. Einstellung ~ **sein** to be typical of s. one's attitude; ~**er Zug** characteristic feature.

bezeichnet marked;
nachstehend als ... ~ hereinafter called ...;
j. an der ~**en Stelle treffen** to meet s. o. at the appointed place; **schlecht** ~**e Straße** inadequately signposted road; **zur** ~**en Stunde** at the hour indicated; ~**er Wanderweg** marked-out path; **auf die** ~**e Weise** in the manner indicated.

Bezeichnung designation, description, signification, notation, denotation, *(Angabe)* indication, *(Ausdruck)* appellation, denomination, term, *(Fachbezeichnung)* termination, *(Name)* name, *(Titel)* title, style, *(Waren)* label, labelling, mark, marking, branding;
unter verschiedenen ~**en bekannt** known under several names; **amtliche** ~ official nomenclature; **falsche** ~ misnomer, *(Waren)* deceptive marking; **genaue** ~ detailed description; **geschützte** ~ proprietary name; **handelsübliche** ~ trade description; **herabwürdigende** ~ derogatory appellation; **irreführende** ~ misleading name; **kurze** ~ *(Abkommen)* short title; **mehrdeutige** ~ ambiguous description; **nähere** ~ detailed description, specification; **offizielle** ~ official nomenclature; **wissenschaftliche** ~ scientific term, book name;
~ **der Anlagegegenstände** fixed-asset classification; ~ **des Einkommensteuerzahlers** income unit; ~ **einer Erfindung** title of an invention; ~ **des Sachgebietes** subject label; **mißbräuchliche** ~ **von Waren als Markenartikel** misbranding of commodities, passing off one's goods as those of another make *(US)*;
verschiedene ~ **tragen** to be known under several designations.

Bezeichnungs|schild label, [tie-on] tag; ~**weise** nomenclature, terminology.

bezeigen to show, to display;
seine Dankbarkeit ~ to express one's gratitude; **seine Teilnahme** ~ to show one's sympathy.

bezetteln to label, to ticket, to tag.

bezeugen to [bear] witness, to certify, to testify, to depose, to attest, to warrant;
jds. Autorschaft ~ to attest that s. o. is the author; **eidlich** ~ to depose by oath; **jds. Fleiß** ~ to bear witness to s. one's industry; **gründliche Kenntnisse in einem Fachgebiet** ~ to testify to s. one's deep knowledge of a subject; **übereinstimmend das Gleiche** ~ to bear witness to the same point.

Bezeugung attestation, witnessing.

bezichtigen to charge, to accuse, to impute;
fälschlich ~ to accuse falsely; **j. der Feigheit** ~ to charge s. o. with cowardice; **j. des Hochverrats** ~ to charge s. o. with high treason; **j. der Nachlässigkeit** ~ to tax s. o. with neglect; **sich selbst** ~ to charge (to incriminate) o. s.; **j. der Undankbarkeit** ~ to tax s. o. with ingratitude; **j. eines Verbrechens** ~ to impute a crime to s. o.

bezichtigt werden to be under an imputation.

Bezichtigung accusation, charge, imputation, incrimination.

beziehbar obtainable, to be had, *(Haus)* ready to move in, inhabitable;
nur gegen bar ~ for cash only; **nur über den Großhandel** ~ obtainable through wholesalers only; **sofort** ~ immediate occupation, vacant possession.

Beziehen occupation;
~ **von Messen** fairgoing; ~ **einer Wohnung** move into a dwelling.

beziehen *(Aktien)* to subscribe, *(Geld)* to draw, *(Waren)* to obtain, to buy, to get, to procure;
direkt vom Verlag zu ~ obtainable direct from the publisher; **von allen Buchhandlungen zu** ~ stocked by all booksellers;
sich ~ *(Himmel)* to be clouding over; **sich auf etw.** ~ to relate (have reference) to s. th.; **sich auf j.** ~ to use s. one's name; **junge Aktien** ~ to exercise the right to subscribe to new shares (stock, *US*); **alles auf sich** ~ to take everything personally; **Arbeitslosenunterstützung** ~ to receive unemployment compensation, to draw the dole *(Br.)*; **bestimmten Artikel regelmäßig** ~ to have a standing order for an article; **sich auf jds. Aussage** ~ to refer to s. one's statement; **Bett frisch** ~ to change the bed-linen; **direkt** ~ to buy first hand; **regelmäßige Einkünfte** ~ to draw a regular income; **sich auf einen Gegenstand** ~ to refer to a subject; **Gehalt** ~ to draw a salary; **aus erster Hand** ~ to buy first hand; **Haus** ~ to move into (take possession of) a house; **Kapitaleinkünfte** ~ to derive income from an investment; **Kissen mit Seide** ~ to cover a cushion with silk; **Lager** ~ to encamp; **alle Lebensmittel in A** ~ to get all one's groceries in A; **Markt** ~ to frequent a market; **Messe** ~ to visit a fair; **nicht** ~ *(Aktien)* to nonsubscribe; **Polstermöbel neu** ~ to recover upholstered furniture; **Provision aus einem Geschäft** ~ to draw a commission from a transaction; **Prügel** ~ to get a hiding; **Rente** ~ to draw (receive) a pension; **sich auf ein Schreiben** ~ to refer to a letter; **Sozialhilfe** ~ to be on relief; **Stellung** ~ to move into a position; **gegen j. Stellung** ~ to take a stand against s. o.; **vorbereitete Stellungen** ~ to move into prepared positions; **Universität** ~ to go up to the university, to go to college; **sich auf eine Urkunde** ~ to refer to a document; **direkt beim Verlag** ~ to obtain from the publisher; **Wache** ~ to mount guard; **Waren** ~ to purchase (receive, procure, obtain) goods; **Waren aus dem Ausland** ~ to be supplied with goods (get commodities) from abroad; **Waren direkt von der Fabrik** ~ to obtain goods straight from the factory; **Wartestandsgeld** ~ to be on half-pay; **Winterquartier** ~ to go into winter quarters; **sein Wissen nur aus Büchern** ~ to obtain one's knowledge from books only; **Wohnung** ~ to move into a flat; **Wohnung erneut** ~ to reinstall o. s. in a flat; **Zeitung** ~ to take in *(Br.)* (subscribe to) a newspaper;
durch den Einzelhandel zu ~ stocked by all retailers.

Bezieher purchaser, buyer, *(Aktien)* allottee, *(Zeitung)* subscriber;
~ **einer Altersversorgung** old-age pensioner;
~**liste** list of subscribers; ~**zahl vergrößern** to swell the number of subscribers.

Beziehung respect, reference, regard, relation, connection, connexion *(Br.)*, contact, rapport;
in finanzieller ~ as to finance; **in gewisser** ~ in a way; **in jeder** ~ in every respect; **in jeder** ~ **tadellos** up to the mark; **in strategischer** ~ strategically; **mit** ~ **auf** referring, relating; **gegenseitige** ~ interrelationship; **geschäftliche** ~ business connection; **innere** ~ real understanding; **schuldrechtliche** ~ contractual relationship; **wechselseitige** ~ interrelation;
~ **zu etw. haben** to be related to s. th.; **in enger** ~ **stehen** to be intimately connected; **in keiner** ~ **stehen** to bear no relation to s. th.

Beziehungen relations, affinities, links, terms, dealings, bearings, pull, wires;
mit guten ~ well-connected;
ausgedehnte ~ widespread connections (connexions, *Br.*); **außereheliche** ~ extramarital relations; **auswärtige** ~ external relations, foreign connections; **eheliche** ~ marital relations; **ehewidrige** ~ adultery, intimacy; **enge** ~ close relations; **familiäre** ~ family relations; **freundschaftliche** ~ friendly relations, relationship, interrelations; **geschäftliche** ~ business relations (intercourse); **geschlechtliche** ~ sexual intercourse; **gespannte** ~ strained relations, bad terms; **gewohnte** ~ customary compliments; **gute** ~ good terms (understanding), *(Einfluß)* pull; **gut nachbarliche** ~ neighbo(u)rly relations; **intime** ~ intimate relations; **kaufmännische** ~ business connections; **landesverräterische** ~ treasonable relations; **langjährige angenehme** ~ pleasant business relations for many years; **menschliche** ~ human relations; **persönliche** ~ personal relationship; **politische** ~ political connections (affiliations, *US*); **staatliche** ~ policy; **vermögensrechtliche** ~ pecuniary relations; **weitreichende** ~ far-reaching connections; **wirtschaftliche** ~ economic relations; **zwischenmenschliche** ~ human relations; **zwischenstaatliche** ~ international (interstate) relations;
~ **zwischen leitenden Angestellten und dem Personalchef** staff relationship; ~ **zwischen Arbeitgebern und Arbeitnehmern** labo(u)r-management (industrial) relations; ~ **zu den Behörden** interests with the administration, governmental relations; ~ **zwischen dem Betrieb und überbetrieblichen Institutionen** industrial relations; ~ **zur Kundschaft** customer relations; **diplomatische** ~ **eines Landes** foreign (diplomatic) relations of a country;
~ **abbrechen** to break off connections, to sever relations; **alle** ~ **mit jem. abbrechen** to break off all relations with s. o., to drop s. o.; **geschäftliche** ~ **anknüpfen** to open up business relations;

~ **mit jem. aufnehmen** to come in rapport with s. o.; **diplomatische ~ aufnehmen** to establish diplomatic relations; **enge ~ zu j. aufnehmen** to establish close relations with s. o.; **geschäftliche ~ zu jem. aufnehmen** to contact s. o., to establish (make) contacts with s. o.; **mit jem. intime ~ aufnehmen** to become intimate with s. o.; **~ mit jem. aufrechterhalten** to continue relations with s. o.; **seine ~ ausnützen** to use one's influence; **~ einer Belastung aussetzen** to strain relations; **seine ~ für j. einsetzen** to use one's interest on s. one's behalf; **durch ~ erreichen** to work the oracle *(sl.)*; **in kompromittierende ~ geraten** to become entangled; **freundschaftliche ~ gestalten** to strengthen friendly relations; **~ haben** to have influential friends, to know the right people; **~ zu jem. haben** to have dealings (relations) with s. o.; **enge ~ haben** to have a strong bearing on; **gute ~ haben** to have influential friends, to be influentially connected, to have a friend at court, to have a lot of pull, to have good connections (influence); **gute ~ zu jem. haben** to be on a good footing (good terms) with s. o.; **weitreichende ~ haben** to have a long arm; **seine ~ spielen lassen** to pull wires (strings); **seine ~ zu jem. lösen** to drop s. one's acquaintance; **von seinen politischen ~ Gebrauch machen** to trade on one's political influence; **~ pflegen** to nurse a connection; **auswärtige ~ pflegen** to attend to foreign relations; **freundschaftliche ~ pflegen** to hold a correspondence; **~ zu seinen Verwandten pflegen** to cultivate one's relations; **mit jem. in guten ~ stehen** to be on friendly terms with s. o.; **mit jem. in ~ treten** to communicate with s. o.; **in geschäftliche ~ zu einer Firma treten** to open up a business connection with a firm; **mit jem. ~ unterhalten** to hold intercourse (entertain relations) with s. o.; **briefliche ~ unterhalten** to keep up a correspondence; **diplomatische ~ mit einem Land unterhalten** to maintain diplomatic relations with a country; **freundschaftliche ~ unterhalten** to sustain friendly relations; **gute ~ mit jem. unterhalten** to keep good relations with s. o.; **gutnachbarliche ~ unterhalten** to be on friendly terms with one's neighbo(u)rs; **seine nachbarlichen ~ verbessern** to mend one's fences *(US)*; **seine Stellung seinen ~ verdanken** to owe one's position to one's influence; **über gute ~ verfügen** to be well connected, to have influential friends; **über weitreichende ~ verfügen** to have far-reaching influence, to dispose over wide connections; **jem. aufgrund seiner ~ zu einem Amt verhelfen** to jockey s. o. into an office; **sich gute ~ verschaffen** to make useful social contacts; **diplomatische ~ wiederherstellen** to reestablish diplomatic relations.

Beziehungs|feld environment; ~**kauf** industrial (direct-to-customer) selling, direct purchase.

beziehungs|los unrelated, unconnected; ~**weise** respectively, relatively, with certain qualifications, and/or.

Beziehungszahl reference number, *(Statistik)* relative number.

bezifferbar quantifiable.

beziffern to [mark by a] number, to estimate;
sich ~ auf to amount (run up) to, to figure (work out) at; **sich auf mehrere Millionen DM ~** to amount to several million DM; **Umsatz auf 4 Millionen DM ~** to put the turnover at 4 million marks; **Verlust auf 100 Pfund ~** to put the loss at a hundred £.

beziffert figured at, *(Schadenersatz)* liquidated.

Bezifferung numbering, figuring.

Bezirk district, region, confine, zone, section, sector, division, area, land, side, *(amtlicher)* precinct, *(Bereich)* field, scope, sphere, domain, *(Gericht)* circuit, *(Stadt)* quarter, ward, *(Wahl)* constituency, borough, electoral district, precinct *(US)*;
im ~ wohnend resident; **zu einem ~ gehörig** regional;
abgegrenzter ~ specified territory; **äußerer ~** fringe, outskirts; **befriedete ~e** pacified areas; **ländlicher ~** rural (county, *Br.*) district; **postalischer ~** postal district; **städtischer ~** city (urban, *Br.*) district; **dem Gesundheitsamt unterstehender ~** urban sanitary district *(Br.)*; **ungenügend mit Arbeitskräften versorgter ~** labo(u)r-short area; **regional zurückgebliebener ~** underdeveloped area;
~ mit großer Arbeitslosigkeit distressed area *(Br.)*; **~ mit Ortsstatut** use district; **~ eines Vertreters** sales territory;
~ bearbeiten *(Vertreter)* to work a district (an area), to cover a territory; **ganzen ~ durchwandern** to walk the whole district; **in ~e einteilen** to district; **in neue ~e einteilen** to redistrict *(US)*; **Stadt in ~e einteilen** to divide a town in wards.

Bezirks|agent *(Börse)* district jobber; ~**agentur** regional agency, district office *(US)*; ~**amt** county office *(US)*; ~**amtmann** district constable *(US)*, county commissioner *(Br.)*; ~**arzt** medical officer; ~**aufsichtsbeamter** district surveyor; ~**ausgabe** local (regional, territorial) edition; ~**ausschuß** county *(Br.)* (district) council, district committee *(US)*; ~**außenstelle** *(Kommunalverwaltung)* divisional administration *(US)*; ~**beauftragter** regional commissioner, *(Gewerkschaft)* district organizer *(Br.)*; ~**behörde** area authority, Regional Board *(Br.)*; ~**bibliothek** county library; ~**bürgermeister** boroughholder, boroughhead, boroughmaster *(Br.)*; ~**büro** area (district, regional) office; ~**chef** marshal; ~**direktor** area (local, *Br.*) manager, regional director, *(Versicherung)* superintendent of agents; ~**gericht** county court *(Br.)*, district (divisional) court *(US)*, ward mote *(London)*; ~**geschäftsstelle** area headquarters; ~**geschäftsstelle des Nachlaßgerichts** district probate registry; ~**gliederung** regional organization; ~**grenze** regional boundary, district line; ~**haushalt** regional budget; ~**inspektor** district inspector; ~**karte** *(Bahn)* season ticket, commutation ticket *(US)*; ~**karte aufnehmen** to lay down a map of the district; ~**krankenhaus** district general hospital; ~**leiter** divisional (district, sales) manager, regional director, *(Gewerkschaft)* business agent; ~**leitung** area headquarters; ~**mandat** district seat; ~**ordnung** bye law *(Br.)*; ~**planungsstellen** regional authorities; ~**postamt** district post office; ~**rat** district (regional) council *(Br.)*; ~**regierung** regional government; ~**revisor** district auditor; ~**richter** district magistrate (judge, *US*); ~**schulze** rape reeve *(Br.)*; ~**stadt** county town (seat, *US*); ~**stelle** regional agency, *(Gesundheitsdienst)* area board; ~**streik** sectional strike; ~**tag** county (district) council; ~**tagung** district convention; ~**umlage** district rate, county rate *(Br.)*; ~**umsatz** district sales; ~**verband** regional association, county borough; ~**verbreitung** *(Zeitung)* city zone circulation; ~**verkaufsleiter** district [sales] (divisional sales, regional) manager; ~**verkehr** local traffic; ~**vermögen** county property (treasury); ~**versammlung** county (district) council, regional assembly; ~**vertreter** local agent, district (regional) representative, regional (district) salesman, distributor, *(Werbung)* special representative; ~**verwaltung** district authorities (committee, *US*); ~**verwaltungsstelle** district committee *(US)*; ~**vorsteher** county commissioner *(US)*; ~**wahlen** regional (local, *Br.*) elections.

bezirksweise by districts.

Bezirkszentrale area headquarters.

bezogen *(Bank)* drawn upon;
direkt ~ firsthand; **mit Wolken ~** clouded, cloudy;
~ werden können *(Wohnung)* ready to move in;
~e Bank drawee bank.

Bezogener drawee, acceptor, payer;
alternativ ~ alternative drawee.

Bezug relation, *(im Brief)* reference, regard, respect, *(Einkauf)* purchase, buying, *(Einzug)* moving in, occupation, *(Gehalt, Pension)* drawing of, *(Zeitungen)* subscription, taking in *(Br.)*;
bei ~ durch die Post if delivered by post; **bei regelmäßigem ~** with a standing order; **bei ~ von** when ordering; **bei ~ von 100 Stück Sonderrabatt** on orders for 100 special discount; **beim ~ dieser Waren** when buying these goods; **fertig zum ~** *(Haus)* ready to move in; **in ~ auf** with reference (respect) to, in respect of, in relation to, related to; **mit ~ auf Ihre Anfrage** regarding your enquiry; **ohne ~** unrelated; **während des ~es von Leistungen** while drawing benefits; **zum ~ angeboten** offered for sub-scription;
kostenloser ~ complimentary copy (subscription);
~ von jungen Aktien subscription to new shares (stock); **~ für ein Kissen** cushion cover; **~ mit Umtauschrecht** *(Buchhandel)* purchase with right to exchange; **~ von Waren** purchase (supply) of goods, ordering goods; **~ ausländischer Waren** importation of goods; **genossenschaftlicher ~ von Waren zu verbilligtem Preis** cooperative purchasing; **~ einer Zeitung** subscription to a newspaper;
Inhaber zum ~ berechtigen to entitle the holder to purchase; **~ erneuern** to renew a subscription; **bei ~ von 100 Stück 5% Rabatt gewähren** to allow a discount of 5% with orders of 100; **~ haben auf** to be pertinent (bear reference) to, to relate to; **~ nehmen auf** to refer to, to make reference to; **in ~ auf Intelligenz überlegen sein** to be superior in point of intelligence; **zum ~ einer Rente berechtigt sein** to be entitled to draw a pension.

Bezüge emoluments, earnings, income, *(Gehalt)* salary, remuneration, compensation, pay, *(Lieferungen)* supplies, imports;
angemessene ~ fair and reasonable compensation; **augenblickliche ~** present salary level; **einmalige ~** income of nonrecurring nature; **dem Verantwortungsbereich entsprechende ~** salary fully equated to the level of responsibility; **feste ~** stipend; **gesamte ~** remuneration package; **jährliche ~** annual earnings; **laufende ~** regular salary, fixed remuneration; **pfändbare ~** salaries subject to execution; **sonstige ~**

miscellaneous receipts; **steuerfreie** ~ income exempt from tax; **steuerpflichtige** ~ taxable emoluments; **überdurchschnittliche** ~ above-average compensation; **unpfändbare** ~ mace-proof salary *(US)*; **vereinbarte** ~ remuneration agreed upon; **übliche fünfstellige** ~ **für leitende Angestellte** normal senior remuneration into five figures; **satzungsmäßige** ~ **des Aufsichtsrats** statutory allowance to the board of directors; ~ **eines Aufsichtsratsvorsitzenden** emoluments of a chairman; ~ **im außertariflichen Bereich** salaries not covered by the salary scale; ~ **aus der öffentlichen Fürsorge** payments received by way of relief; **Gehalt und** ~ salary and other emoluments; ~ **eines Konsuls** consular salary; ~ **mit Pensionsberechtigung** pensionable emoluments; ~ **der Regierung** cabinet wage; ~ **aus der Sozialversicherung** income received from social insurance, social insurance benefits; ~ **eines Vorstandsmitglieds** director's emoluments, remuneration of a director;
angemessene ~ **erhalten** to receive an adequate remuneration for one's work; **jds.** ~ **herabsetzen** to cut s. one's salary; **mit gehobeneren** ~ **verbunden sein** to carry an attractive salary.

bezüglich re, relating, regarding, with regard to, referring in the matter of, concerning;
~ **Ihrer Anfrage** regarding your inquiry; ~ **Ihres Schreibens** referring to your letter.

Bezugnahme reference;
mit ~ **auf Ihr Schreiben** with reference to your letter; **unter** ~ **auf** referring to, with reference to; **unter weiterer** ~ **auf meinen Brief vom ...** with further reference to my letter of ...; **begriffliche** ~ conceptual framework; **lobende** ~ complimentary reference;
~ **auf Buchhaltungsbelege** folio reference.

bezugnehmend auf Ihr Schreiben referring to your letter.

Bezugs|aktien new shares (stock, *US*); **~angebot** *(Aktien)* rights issue *(Br.)*, subscription warrant *(US)*, stock right *(US)*; **~anweisung** delivery order; **~aufforderung** public offering; **mit ~aufforderungen belästigen** to persecute with requests for subscriptions; **einer ~aufforderung Folge leisten** to exercise one's subscription right; **~ausweis** buying permit; **~basis** basis of comparison, comparative basis; **~bedingungen** terms (conditions) of delivery (supply), *(Zeitungskopf)* business notice, *(Subskription)* terms of subscription.

bezugsberechtigt entitled to draw.

Bezugs|berechtigter *(Aktien)* allottee, allocatee, *(Rente)* beneficiary; **~berechtigter einer Versorgungsstiftung** beneficiary in a provident fund; **~berechtigung** *(Aktien)* subscription privilege *(US)* (right, *Br.*); **~berechtigungsschein** *(Aktien)* warrant [to stock owner] *(US)*, *(Waren)* purchasing permit; **~bescheinigung** allotment certificate *(US)*, subscription (stock allotment, *US*) warrant.

Bezugsdauer subscription period, period of subscription;
beschränkte ~ limited time.

Bezugserklärung declaration of option.

bezugsfertig *(Haus)* ready for occupancy (to move in);
sofort ~ with immediate possession, immediate occupation;
~ **zu vermieten** to be let with immediate possession.

Bezugs|formen forms of purchase; **~formular** order form (sheet, slip), *(Aktien)* subscription form (blank, *US*); **~frist** term of subscription; **~gebiet** supply area; **~gebühren, ~geld** subscription cost (fee); **~genehmigung** purchase permit; **~genossenschaft** cooperative purchasing association; **~größe** base; **~gruppe** reference group; **~jahr** basis year, year reported on, *(Sozialversicherung)* benefit year; **~kalkulation** costing, cost accounting; **~kosten** delivery cost (expenses), purchasing costs, *(Zeitung)* subscription cost; **~kurs** issue price; **~land** country of origin (delivery); **~liste** rights list; **~marke** coupon; **~menge** datum quantity; **~mitteilung** notice of rights; **~option** call [option]; **~patent** related patent; **~periode** subscription period, *(Statistik)* base period; **~position** reference position; **~prämie** call premium; **~preis** subscription, subscription price (money, rate), rate of subscription, *(Ausgabepreis)* issue price, *(EG)* reference price, *(für Lieferung)* price delivered, price of delivery, *(Stahleinfuhren)* trigger price, *(Zeitung)* advertised price; **~preis erhöhen** to raise the subscription; **~preissystem** *(EG)* reference price system; **~punkt** *(Vermessung)* datum point; **~quelle** market, source of supply, supplier, buying resource *(US)*; **~quellennachweis, ~verzeichnis** directory (classified list) of suppliers; **eingedruckter ~quellennachweis** dealer imprint; **~rahmen** *(Person)* frame.

Bezugsrecht *(Aktien)* subscription privilege *(US)* (right, *Br.*), right to subscribe *(Br.)*, rights issue *(Br.)*, preemptive right *(US)*, preemption *(US)*, [subscription] warrant *(US)*, stock right *(US)*, *(Option)* option;
auf Grund der Ausübung eines ~es on the exercise of an option; **mit ~en** with rights, cum subscription warrant *(US)*, rights on; **mit** ~ **auf junge Aktien** cum new; **ohne ~e** ex (exclusive subscription) rights; **ohne** ~ **auf neue Aktien** ex new;
~ **auf junge Aktien** share option *(Br.)*, option on new stock *(US)*; ~ **bei Anleiheumwandlung** subscription by conversion of securities;
~ **abtreten** to renounce an allotment letter; ~ **ausüben** to exercise rights, to take up an option; ~ **auf junge Aktien ausüben** to subscribe to (for) new shares (stock, *US*), to exercise the right to acquire new shares *(Br.)*; **~e handeln** to deal in rights; ~ **kaufen** to buy an option on stock *(US)*; **sein** ~ **auf der Börse verkaufen** to sell one's rights on the market; **~e im Inhaberauftrag verkaufen** to sell the rights on behalf of the holder.

Bezugsrechts|abschlag markdown of the right issue; **~angebot** rights offering (issue, *Br.*), subscription warrant *(US)*, stock right *(US)*; **~angebot in Höhe von 200 Mio £ zeitgerecht unterbringen** to slip in with a £ 200 m rights issue; **~ausgabe** rights issue; **~ausübung** exercise of subscription rights; **~ausübungsanträge zugunsten öffentlicher Beteiligung beschränken** to scale down applications to cut the public in; **~erlöse** proceeds from the sale of subscription rights; **~ersatz** substitute for a rights issue; **~formular** application form *(Br.)*; **~handel** rights dealing; **~mitteilung** allotment letter *(Br.)*, certificate of allotment *(US)*, rights letter, letter of allotment; **~obligation** option bond; **~schreiben** split letter; **~vereinbarung** option agreement; **~wert** subscription value.

Bezugsschein *(auf Aktien)* subscription (stock allotment, *US*) warrant, *(Auftrag)* delivery order, *(Berechtigungsschein)* scrip, *(Materialien)* materials requisition slip, *(mil.)* indent form, *(festverzinsliche Papiere)* talon, *(Waren)* purchasing permit, *(Warenbewirtschaftung)* ration card, coupon, docket, *(Zeitungsanzeige)* licence form;
~ **beantragen** to apply for a purchasing permit; ~ **einlösen** to cash a coupon;
~abschnitt unit; **~berechtigter** priority permit holder; **~besitzer** priority permit holder.

bezugsscheinfrei coupon-free, on free sale, off the ration.

Bezugsscheininhaber ration-book holder.

bezugsscheinpflichtig rationed.

Bezugsschein|stelle ration-card agency; **~system** rationing system.

Bezugs|spesen delivery cost (expenses); **~stoff** upholstery; **~system** frame of reference; **~tag** day of issue; **~termin** delivery date, *(Aktien)* date of issue; **~urkunde** relevant document; **~vereinigung** purchasing association; **~verhältnis von 1 : 2** *(junge Aktien)* proportion of one new share against every two old shares held; **~vertrag** supply contract (agreement) subscription; **~verträge vergeben** to award public supply contracts; **~wege für Bücher** book-purchase channels; **~wert** relative value, *(Statistik)* base; **~zeichen** reference mark; **~zeitraum** reference period.

bezuschußbar subsidizable.

bezwecken to aim at, to have in view;
nichts Böses ~ to mean no harm.

bezweifeln to doubt, to question, to dispute;
Wahrheit einer Geschichte ~ to doubt the truth of a story; **Wert einer Sache** ~ to question the value of s. th.

bezwingen to conquer, to overcome, to overpower, to vanquish;
sich ~ to master one's feelings (passions); **seine Angst** ~ to get the better of one's fear; **Festung** ~ to conquer a fortress; **Hindernis** ~ to overcome an obstacle; **seine schlechte Laune** ~ to control one's bad temper; **seine Neugier** ~ to fight down one's curiosity; **seine Wünsche** ~ to suppress one's wishes; **seinen Zorn** ~ to bottle up one's wrath.

Bibel|eid corporal oath; **~papier** Bible paper.

Bibliographie bibliography.

bibliographisch bibliographical;
~e Angaben bibliographic[al] data.

bibliophil bibliophile.

Bibliothek library, *(Bücherzimmer)* bookroom;
gut ausgestattete ~ well-stocked library; **kaufmännische** ~ businessman's library; **öffentliche** ~ free (lending, public) library; **umfassende** ~ comprehensive library; **nicht mehr unterzubringende** ~ overflow of a library;
~ **mit Büchern beliefern** to furnish a library with books.

Bibliothekar librarian, bibliothecary;
staatlich geprüfter ~ public librarian;
~beruf librarianship.

bibliothekarische Hilfskraft assistant librarian, sublibrarian.

Bibliotheks|ausgabe library edition; **~bestände** holdings of a library; **~buch** library book; **~direktor** director of a library; **~einband** library binding; **stabiler ~einband** particularly strong library binding; **~etat** library budget; **~gebäude** library; **~karte** library ticket (card, *US*); **~nachlaß** library rebate; **~nummer** class (call) number, pressmark; **mit einer ~nummer versehen** to pressmark; **~verwaltung** library management; **~wissenschaft** library science; **~zeichen** pressmark.

Bieberschwanzziegel plaintile.

bieder upright, honest, trustworthy;
~er Bürger simple-minded citizen; **~er Charakter** straightforward character.

Biegen, auf ~ und Brechen by hook or by crook, neck or nothing, sink or swim.

biegen *(Rohr)* to bend;
sich vor Lachen ~ to double up with laughter *(coll.)*; **sich nach Links ~** *(Straße)* to curve to the left; **das Recht ~** to stretch the law; **um eine Straßenecke ~** to turn round a street corner; **lügen, daß sich die Balken ~** to lie like a gas-meter (trooper).

biegsamer Bücherband limp binding.

Biegung turning, bend, wind, twist, wriggle;
U-förmige ~ hairpin bend;
~ machen to turn.

bienenfleißig as busy as a bee.

Bier beer;
abgestandenes ~ stale beer; **dunkles ~** brown (dark) ale, dark beer *(US)*; **helles ~** light ale, table beer *(Br.)*; **leichtes ~** light beer;
~ in Dosen canned beer *(US)*; **~ vom Faß** draught beer;
wie saures ~ anbieten to try to sell at a sacrifice; **ein ~ trinken gehen** to go to the pub; **~ zapfen** to draw beer;
das ist nicht mein ~ that's not my funeral (baby, *US*);
~ausschank pothouse, pub, alehouse, beerhouse *(Br.)*, beer hall *(US)*; **~bankpolitiker** armchair (holiday) politician; **~bauch** pot-belly; **~brauer** beer brewer; **schnell ein ~chen trinken** to have a quick one; **~deckel** beer mat; **mit wahrem ~eifer** brimming over with enthusiasm.

biereifrig over-zealous.

Bier|flasche beer bottle; **~garten** beer garden; **~glas** beer glass; **~hahn** spigot, tap, faucet; **~idee** crazy notion *(fam.)*; **~kasten** beer crate; **~keller** beer cellar; **~kneipe** pub; **~krug** beer mug; **~kutscher** drayman; **~lokal** tavern *(US)*, pub *(Br.)*, pothouse, porterhouse *(US)*; **~reise** drinking bout, pub crawl, binge *(sl.)*, bat *(US sl.)*; **auf eine ~reise gehen** to go on the (have a) binge, to go on the (have a) booze; **auf einer ~reise sein** to be off (on) a spree; **~restaurant** public house, pub *(fam.)*, beer house (hall, *US*), taproom, porterhouse *(US)*; **~ruhe** imperturbability; **~steuer** beer tax; **~stube** public house, pub *(Br.)*, tavern *(US)*, taproom; **~verbrauch, ~konsum** consumption of beer; **~verlag** beer depot (store); **~verleger** brewer's agent; **~wagen** dray; **~wirtschaft** public house, beer hall *(US)*, pub *(fam.)*.

Biest beast, creature;
kleines ~ bitch.

Bieten bidding;
verabredetes niedriges ~ chilling a sale;
~ zwecks Höhertreibung by-bidding.

bieten to offer, to tender, *(Auktion)* to [make a] bid;
jem. etw. ~ to give s. o. a whale of a time; **sich ~** to present itself; **lächerlichen Anblick ~** to make a sight of o. s.; **keine Angriffsfläche ~** to have no chink in one's armo(u)r, to be watertight *(fam.)*; **herrliche Aussicht ~** to command a magnificent view; **bis zu 400 $ ~** to go as high as $ 400; **fest ~** to offer firm; **gute Filme ~** to show good films; **gering ~** to bid low; **auf ein Haus ~** to bid for a house; **höher ~ als j.** to bid over s. o.; **mehr ~** to outbid; **jem. die Möglichkeit ~** to afford s. o. the opportunity; **Platz für 800 Personen ~** *(Saal)* to accommodate 800 people; **angemessenen Preis ~** to bid a fair price; **neues Programm ~** to show a new programme; **keine Schwierigkeiten ~** to present no difficulties; **jem. die Stirn ~** to bid defiance to s. o.; **einer Gefahr die Stirn ~** to face a danger; **gute Unterhaltung ~** *(Buch)* to make good reading; **weniger ~** to underbid; **zuerst ~** to make the first bid;
sich alles ~ lassen to put up with everything.

Bieter bidder.

Bietungs|absprache knockout agreement; **~garantie** guarantee of tender, performance (bid, proposal) bond *(US)*, participating guarantee.

Bigamie bigamy, bigamous marriage;
der ~ schuldig bigamous.

Bigamist bigamist.

Bijouterie[waren] trinkets, trinketry.

Bilanz balance [of accounts], *(Bilanzformular)* balance sheet, financial statement, statement [of assets and liabilities] *(US)*, overall statement *(US)*, statement of conditions *(US)*, *(Gesamtüberblick)* survey, review;
abgekürzte ~ condensed balance sheet, trial balance; **aktive ~** credit balance, *(Handelsbilanz)* favo(u)rable (credit) balance; **aufgestellte ~** balance sheet; **ausführliche ~** detailed balance sheet; **außenwirtschaftliche ~** visible (foreign-trade) balance; **berichtigte ~** post-closing balance sheet, closing trial balance, rectified balance sheet; **fiktive ~** proforma balance sheet (statement, *US*); **finanzwirtschaftliche ~** statement of application of funds *(US)*, source and disposition statement; **frisierte ~** window-dressed balance sheet; **gefälschte ~** false (faked, fraudulent) balance sheet; **vertikal gegliederte ~** vertical-form balance sheet; **geprüfte ~** certified balance, audited balance sheet; **jährliche ~** annual balance sheet; **konjunkturpolitische ~** appraisement of the cyclical trend; **konsolidierte ~** consolidated balance sheet; **nicht konsolidierte ~** unconsolidated balance sheet; **neueste ~** up-to-date balance sheet; **passive ~** adverse balance; **politische ~** political survey; **reine ~** final balance; **rohe ~** trial (rough) balance; **steuerliche ~** tax statement (status, report, balance sheet, *US*); **vergleichende ~** comparative balance sheet; **verschleierte ~** veiled (window-dressed) balance sheet; **versicherungstechnische ~** actuarial valuation; **vorläufige ~** tentative balance sheet; **zusammengefaßte ~** consolidated balance sheet;
~ einer Abrechnungsstelle clearinghouse statement; **~ einer Aktiengesellschaft** corporate balance sheet (statement, *US*); **~ ohne Aufwand und Ertrag** post-closing trial balance; **~ eines Einzelkaufmanns** sole trader's balance sheet; **~ eines Fonds** fund balance sheet; **~ des bisher Geleisteten** survey of what has been accomplished so far; **~ per 30. Juni** balance sheet as of 30th of June; **~ des langfristigen Kapitalverkehrs** long-term capital transactions; **~ einer OHG** partnership (sole trader's) balance sheet; **~ einer Vermögensverwaltung** fund balance sheet; **~ der gesamten Volkswirtschaft** net results of overall economic activity; **~ der Woche** outcome of the week;
~ abschließen to bring down a balance; **~ analysieren** to analyse (interpret, break down, *US*) a balance sheet; **in der ~ aufführen** to show in the balance; **in der ~ unter langfristigen Schulden aufführen** to place on the balance sheet among the long-term liabilities; **in die ~ aufnehmen** to include in the balance sheet; **~ aufstellen (erstellen)** to strike a balance sheet, to make up (get out, prepare, draw up) a balance sheet; **~ fälschen** to fake a balance sheet; **~ frisieren** to cook (doctor, fake) a balance sheet; **~ genehmigen** to approve [of] a balance sheet; **in der ~ positiv gestalten** to show up in black on the balance sheet *(US coll.)*; **~ lesen** to read the balance sheet; **~ machen** to balance; **~ überprüfen** to audit a balance sheet; **~ veröffentlichen** to make the balance sheet public; **~ verschleiern** to fake (cook, doctor) a balance sheet; **~ vorlegen** to submit a balance sheet; **~ zergliedern** to analyse (break down, *US*) a balance sheet; **~ ziehen** to balance the books, to strike a balance; **allgemeine ~ ziehen** to make a general survey of the situation; **~ seines Lebens ziehen** to take stock of one's life.

Bilanzabschluß financial statement;
~ genehmigen to approve a balance sheet;
~arbeiten closing of accounts; **~termin** accounting reference date.

Bilanz|abschnitt balance-sheet section; **~abschreibung** depreciation; **~abteilung** auditing department; **~analyse** analysis sheet, ratio (statement, *US*, analysis, breakdown, *US*, interpretation) of a balance sheet.

Bilanzangaben balance-sheet data;
~ über Forschungs- und Entwicklungskosten disclosure of research and development costs;
~ über Forschungs- und Entwicklungsaufwand machen to disclose research and development costs.

Bilanz|aufbereitung preparation of a balance sheet; **~aufsteller** balance maker; **~aufstellung** [making up a] balance sheet, statement of [financial] conditions *(US)*; **~ausdruck** balance-sheet term; **~ausgleich** balance-sheet equilibrium, balancing adjustment; **~ausgleichsposten** adjustment item; **wesentliche ~aussagen** balance-sheet highlights; **~ausweitung** expansion of the balance sheet; **~auszug** condensed (summarized) balance sheet, summary of assets and liabilities, statement of resources and liabilities *(US)*; **periodischer ~auszug** periodic summary; **~bericht** balance-sheet record; **~berichtigungen** debit and credit memoranda; **~bewertung** assessment of a balance sheet; **~bewertung vornehmen** to assess a balance sheet; **~bogen** balance sheet; **monatlicher ~bogen** monthly balance sheet;

~**buch** audit book; ~**buchhalter** balance clerk, accountant; ~**buchhaltung** auditing department; ~**delikt** financial juggle; ~**details** balance-sheet details; ~**duplikat einreichen** to send a copy of the balance sheet; ~**einzelheiten** balance-sheet items; ~**entwicklung** growth of balance sheet; ~**entwurf** tentative balance sheet.

Bilanzergebnis net result;
~ **positiv gestalten** to show up in black on the balance sheet *(US coll.)*; ~ **veröffentlichen** to make the balance sheet public.

Bilanz|erklärung making up a balance sheet, statement of application of funds *(US)*; **falsche** ~**erklärung** false financial statement; ~**erläuterungen** balance-sheet notes; ~**experte** accounting practitioner; ~**fachsprache** balance-sheet terminology; ~**fälschung** window dressing, falsification of a balance sheet; ~**frisur** tampering with a balance sheet, window dressing; ~**genehmigung** approval of a balance sheet; ~**gestaltung** balance-sheet layout; ~**gewinn** disposable profit, profit as shown in the balance (available for dividend), accounting profit, *(Notenbank)* rest *(Br.)*; ~**gleichung** balance-sheet equation; ~**gliederung** balance-sheet structure.

bilanzieren to prepare accounts, to make up a (show in the) balance.

Bilanzierung striking a balance, balancing of accounts, rest *(Br.)*.

Bilanzierungs|arbeiten accounting work; ~**fachmann** accounting practitioner; ~**grundsätze** accounting axioms; ~**kosten** balancing charges; ~**methode** reporting method; ~**periode** accounting period; ~**politik** balance-sheet policy; ~**richtlinien** accounting principles; ~**schema** sample balance sheet, statement heading *(US)*; ~**tag** balance-sheet (accounting, statement, *US*) date; ~**technik** accounting technique; ~**vorschriften** balancing requirements; **für** ~**zwecke** for balance-sheet purposes.

Bilanz|jahr financial (audit) year; ~**kennzahl** current position ratio; ~**kontinuität** continuity of a balance sheet; ~**konto** balance-[sheet] account; ~**kritik** ratio (statement, *US*) analysis; ~**lesen** reading a balance sheet; ~**liquidität** liquidity of balance sheet.

bilanzmäßig shown by the balance-sheet;
~**er Gegenposten** balance-sheet contra item.

Bilanzmuster sample balance [sheet].

bilanzneutral sein to have no effect on the balance sheet.

Bilanz|periode accounting period; ~**politik** accounting policy; ~**positionen** balance-sheet items; ~**positionen zu jederzeit realisierbaren Verkaufswerten aussetzen** to construct the balance sheet on a current market liquidation basis.

Bilanzposten heading of a balance sheet;
konsolidierte ~ consolidated balance-sheet items; **schnell realisierbare (äußerst liquide)** ~ quick items; **wesentlicher** ~ material item;
konsolidierte ~ **einer Konzerngesellschaft** intercompany items;
~ **unter verschiedenen Verpflichtungen verstecken** to tuck away under sundry liabilities.

Bilanz|projektion balance-sheet projection; ~**prüfer** chartered *(Br.)* (certified public, *US*) accountant, auditor.

Bilanzprüfung balance-sheet audit;
zum Jahresschluß durchgeführte ~ completed audit;
~ **vor Kreditgewährung** audit for credit purpose.

Bilanz|prüfungswesen auditing, accountancy service; ~**publizität von Aktiengesellschaften** corporate disclosure; ~**rechnung** balance account; ~**revision** auditing; ~**saldo** [capital] balance; ~**schema** sample balance sheet (statement heading, *US*).

bilanzsicherer Buchhalter accountant.

Bilanz|stichtag balance-sheet (accounting, statement, *US*) date; ~**struktur** balance-sheet structure; ~**summe** balance-sheet total; ~**tag** balance-sheet date; ~**transparenz** transparency in business practices; ~**überschuß** surplus of assets over liabilities; ~**untersuchung** ratio analysis, statement analysis *(US)*, breakdown of a balance sheet *(US)*; ~**verabschiedung** approval of a balance sheet; ~**veränderungen** balance-sheet changes; ~**vergleich** comparation of balance sheets; ~**verkürzung** contraction of the balance sheet; **ausgewiesener** ~**verlust** loss as shown in the balance sheet; ~**veröffentlichung** publication of a balance sheet; ~**verschleierung** window dressing, cooking of a balance sheet; ~**volumen** balance-sheet total (volume); ~**vorbereitungsbogen** worksheet form *(US)*; ~**vorlage**, ~**vorlegung** production (presentation) of balance sheet; ~**wachstum** balance-sheet growth; ~**wahrheit** truth in presentation of the annual balance; ~**wert** book (balance-sheet) value; ~**zahlen** balance-sheet figures (data); ~**zergliederung** analysis sheet, breakdown of a balance sheet *(US)*; ~**ziehung** balancing, striking a balance.

Bilanzziffern balance-sheet figures (data);
~ **in das übliche Bilanzformular übertragen** to rework statements into a standard form; ~ **veröffentlichen** to make the balance sheet public.

Bilanzzweck balance-sheet (statement, *US*) purpose.

bilateral bilateral, two-sided;
~**es Abkommen** bilateral agreement; ~**er Handel** bilateral trade.

Bild picture, image, likeness, *(Abbildung)* illustration, *(Fernsehen)* image, picture, *(Film)* shot, *(Foto)* view, snapshot, *(Idee)* conception, idea, *(Künstler)* painting, picture, portrait, *(Porträt)* portrait, photograph, exposure, *(Vorschau)* camera; **im** ~**e** informed, hep *(US sl.)*, in the know *(coll.)*, in the picture, next *(US)*, on *(US)*;
abgerundetes ~ rounded picture; **sprechend ähnliches** ~ speaking likeness; **eingeblendetes** ~ inset portrait; **geistiges** ~ *(Vorstellung)* picture, imagination; **günstigeres** ~ rosier picture; **latentes** ~ latent image; **lebende** ~**er** living pictures; **lebensgroßes** ~ full-length portrait; **unscharfes** ~ *(Fernsehen)* ghost; **verlaufendes** ~ *(Anzeige)* vignette; **wahres und richtiges** ~ *(Bilanz)* a true and fair view *(Br.)*;
~ **des Arbeitslosenmarktes** jobless picture; ~ **über die Beschäftigungsmöglichkeiten** employment possibilities picture; ~ **der Gesamtlage** overall picture; ~ **von einem Mädchen** peach of a girl *(fam.)*; ~ **und Schnitt** camera and cutting; ~ **der Zerstörung** scene of destruction;
~**er abhängen** to take down pictures from the wall; **wahres** ~ **der Liquiditätsverhältnisse aufzeigen** to imply true liquidity; **falsches** ~ **bekommen** to get a wrong impression; **uneinheitliches** ~ **bieten** *(Börse)* to make a mixed showing; ~ **von etw. entwerfen** to give a description of s. th.; **getreues** ~ **von etw. geben** to draw a faithful picture of s. th.; **kein klares** ~ **von etw. haben** to have no clear idea of s. th.; **sich ein** ~ **von etw. machen** to form a picture of s. th.; **sich ein klares** ~ **machen** to come to a true picture; ~ **malen** to paint a picture; **in** ~**ern reden** to speak metaphorically; **im** ~**e sein** to be in the picture (know), to know a thing or two; **über j. genauestens im** ~**e sein** to have s. o. on the tape *(sl.)*; **nicht im** ~**e sein** to be out of the picture; **ins** ~ **setzen** to put s. o. in the picture (wise, *US*); **j. im** ~**e verbrennen** to burn s. o. in effigy; **sich ein richtiges** ~ **verschaffen** to form a correct estimate; **sich ein wahres** ~ **verschaffen** to form a true notion; **richtiges** ~ **der Lage zeichnen** to give a just picture; **übertriebenes** ~ **zeichnen** to overpicture;
~ **abziehen lassen** to have a print made; ~ **vergrößern lassen** to have a picture enlarged;
das ~ **ist verwackelt** the picture is out of focus;
~**abtaster** scanning device, scanner; ~**abtastung** *(Fernsehen)* scanning, analysing of the picture; ~**abzug** photographic copy, photostat; ~**archiv** photographic archives; ~**aufbau** *(Fernsehen)* buildup; ~**aufklärer** *(mil.)* photoreconnaissance air-craft; ~**aufklärung** *(mil.)* photoreconnaissance; ~**auflösung** *(Fernsehen)* scan, resolution; ~**aufnahmegerät** vision pickup apparatus; ~**aufnahmeröhre** image pickup tube; ~**aufzeichnung** image recording; ~**ausschnitt** camera shot, detail; ~**ausschnitt reproduzieren** to reproduce a detail of a printing; ~**ausschnittsbestimmung** cropping; ~**auswerter** *(mil.)* photo-interpreter; ~**auswertung** *(mil.)* photographic interpretation; ~**band** film strip, book of plates; ~**beilage** illustrated supplement; ~**bericht** picture story, photographic report; ~**berichterstatter** press photographer, news cameraman (photographer); ~**berichterstattung** photo journalism; ~**beschreibung** iconography; ~**brief** teleautogram; ~**detektor** video detector; ~**diagramm** pictograph; ~**dokumentation** pictorial record; ~**einstellung** camera shot, focus[sing], *(Fernsehen)* framing, camera shot; ~**empfänger** television [receiver].

bilden to form, to shape, to compose, to constitute, to organize, *(Bildung verschaffen)* to broaden the mind;
sich ~ to come up, to develop, *(Bildung vergrößern)* to improve one's mind; **Ausnahme** ~ to be an exception; **Ausschuß** ~ to set up (form) a committee; **Beispiel** ~ to give an example; **jds. ganzen Besitz** ~ to constitute s. one's entire estate; **Charakter** ~ to mould a character, to form a mind; **ständige Gefahr** ~ to be a constant threat; **seinen Geschmack** ~ to cultivate one's taste; **Grenze** ~ to name the boundaries, to bound; **Hauptgesprächsthema** ~ to constitute the main topic of a conversation; **Hindernis für etw.** ~ to be an obstacle for s. th.; **Kapital** ~ to accumulate (amass) capital; **sich eine Meinung** ~ to form an opinion; **Nachhut** ~ to bring up the rear; **Regierung** ~ to form a government, to make up a cabinet; **Satz** ~ to construct a sentence; **Unterausschüsse** ~ to break up in subcommittees; **neue Wörter** ~ to coin new words, to neologize.

bildende|Künste the fine arts; ~ **Zeitschrift** educational magazine.
Bilder|band pictorial book; ~**bogen** sheet of prints and figures; ~**buch** picture book; ~**buchheirat** picture marriage; ~**dienst** *(Agentur)* picture service; ~**galerie** picture gallery; ~**geschichte** comic strip; **buntes** ~**heft** funny paper *(US)*; ~**katalog** illustrated price list; ~**nagel** pushpin; ~**rahmen** picture frame; ~**rätsel** pictorial puzzle, rebus.
bilderreich *(Stil)* flowery.
Bilder|sammlung collection of paintings; ~**schrift** pictographic inscription.
Bild|fahrplan graphic timetable; ~**feld** *(Fernsehen)* scanning field; ~**fenster** *(Fotoapparat)* picture gate; ~**fernschreiber** facsimile teletype.
Bildfläche picture plane, *(Fernsehen)* image area;
auf der ~ **erscheinen** to appear (arrive) on the scene; **plötzlich auf der** ~ **erscheinen** to streak on to the scene; **schlagartig auf der** ~ **erscheinen** to burst on the scene; **wieder auf der** ~ **erscheinen** to come round the track again; **elektronisch auf eine kleine** ~ **übertragen** to flash up on a small display face; **von der** ~ **verschwinden** to get out of sight.
Bild|folge sequence; ~**format** *(Fernsehen)* aspect ratio, size of image; ~**frequenz** camera speed, *(Fernsehen)* picture frequency; ~**frequenzkanal** video channel.
Bildfunk wireless picture telegraphy, picture transmission, radiophotography, television;
durch ~ **übertragen** to televise;
~**anlage** facsimile apparatus; ~**ausstattung** facsimile equipment; ~**dienst** facsimile transmission service; ~**gerät** facsimile apparatus; ~**telegraph** facsimile telegraph.
Bildgeschichte comic strip, strip cartoon.
bildhaft|er Stil pictiorial style; ~**e Schilderung** word picture.
Bild|helligkeit *(Fernsehen)* brightness; **vergrößerter** ~**hintergrund** background; ~**journalist** photo journalist; ~**kantenverhältnis** aspect ratio; ~**katalog** illustrated catalog(ue).
bildlich pictorial, graphic;
~ **gesprochen** figuratively;
~**e Darstellung** illustration.
Bild|linse picture-taking lens; ~**material** pictures; ~**montage** *(Foto)* photomontage, paste-up.
Bildnis image, *(Münze)* head, effigy;
~ **eines verstorbenen Freundes heraufbeschwören** to call up the image of a deceased friend.
Bild|plakat picture poster; ~**platte** picture disk; ~**projektor** slide projector; ~**punkt** picture element, spot *(fam.)*; ~**punktzahl** number of picture elements; ~**raster** scanning field; ~**rasterung** resolution of a picture; ~**redakteur** pictures editor; ~- **und Umbruchredakteur** art editor; ~**reportage** news picture, picture story; ~**reporter** news cameraman, press photographer; ~**röhre** television tube; ~**schärfe** picture resolution.
Bildschirm display (picture) screen, video terminal;
großflächiger ~ wide-screen television;
auf dem ~ **erscheinen** to come on;
~**format** aspect ratio; ~-**Terminal** Video Display Unit (VDU); ~**text** picture-screen text.
Bild|schreiber phototelegraph; ~**seite einer Münze** face (obverse) of a coin; ~**sendegerät**, ~**sender** video transmission set, facsimile transmitter.
bildsenden to transmit pictures.
Bild|signal picture (video, *US*) signal; ~**statistik** pictogram; ~**stelle** photographic service; ~**steuerung** picture (video, *US*) control; ~**streifen** film strip (track); ~**sucher** view finder; ~**telefon** video telephone, picturephone; ~**telefonkonferenzschaltung** conference via picturephone; ~**telefonverkehr** vision service; ~**telegraf** pantelegraph; ~**telegrafie** facsimile, phototelegraphy.
bildtelegrafisch phototelegraphic;
~ **übermitteln** to phototelegraph.
Bild|telegramm phototelegram, picture telegram; ~**telegramm absenden** to phototelegraph; ~**test** picture probe; **kurzer** ~**text** caption *(US)*; ~**träger** *(Fernsehen)* picture (video, *US*) carrier; ~**übermittlungsdienst** phototelegraph service; ~**übertragung** facsimile (picture) transmission; ~**übertragungsgerät** facsimile equipment; ~**umschlag** illustrated jacket.
Bildung formation, creation, *(Erziehung)* education, civility, culture, good breeding, learning, civility, *(Gründung)* foundation, formation, *(Kenntnisse)* knowledge, *(Organisation)* organization;
in der ~ **begriffen** in the course of formation; **mit akademischer** ~ college-trained; **ohne** ~ uneducated, uncultivated, unrefined;
akademische ~ college (scholastic) education, university training; **allgemeine** ~ good general education; **geistige** ~ literacy; **höhere** ~ secondary education; **humanistische** ~ classical education, humane learning; **umfassende** ~ allround education;
~ **eines Ausschusses** constitution of a committee; ~ **von Durchschnittsprämien** levelling of premiums; ~ **einer Gesamthypothek** consolidation of mortgages; ~ **von Kapital** accumulation of capital, new capital production; ~ **einer Regierung** formation (organization) of government, cabinet-making; ~ **von Rücklagen** creation of reserves, appropriation of surplus *(US)*; ~ **neuer Wörter** coinage of new words;
umfassende ~ **haben** to be a man of widest culture; **etw. für seine** ~ **tun** to improve one's mind.
Bildungs|anstalt educational establishment (institution); **höhere** ~**anstalt** secondary school, academy *(US)*; ~**arbeit** educational work; ~**aufwand** expenditure on education; ~**chancen** educational opportunities; ~**drang** thirst (hunger) for knowledge; ~**dünkel** intellectual conceit; ~**einrichtung** educational services (institution); ~**element des Kinos** educational side of the cinema.
bildungsfähig cultivable, developable;
~**er Verstand** plastic mind.
bildungsfeindlich hostile to education.
Bildungsfernsehen educational television.
Bildungsgang [course of] education, educational background;
zweiter ~ secondary education.
Bildungs|grad standard of knowledge; ~**ideal** ideal education; ~**investitionen** investment in human capital; **eintägiger** ~**kursus** day-release course.
Bildungslücke gap in one's knowledge, cultural lag;
seine ~**n schließen** to fill in the gaps in one's education.
Bildungsmangel illiteracy, unrefinement.
Bildungsmittelmittel educational medium, educator;
sich der Fotografie als ~ **bedienen** to enlist photography for educational purposes.
Bildungs|möglichkeiten educational facilities (opportunities); ~**monopol** monopoly of learning.
Bildungsniveau level of education (knowledge), educational level, academic rating;
allgemeines ~ general standard of education.
Bildungs|notstand cultural wilderness; ~**notstandsgebiet** educational priority area.
bildungspolitisches Ziel educational aim.
Bildungs|reform study reform; ~**reise** study tour.
Bildungsstand educational (cultural) level, level of education;
niedriger ~ low educational attainment;
seine ganze Freizeit verwenden, um seinen ~ **zu verbessern** to give all one's leisure time to study.
Bildungs|stätte educational establishment (center, *US*, centre, *Br.*); ~**struktur** pattern of education; ~**urlaub** study leave, day-release training; ~**voraussetzungen** educational requirements; ~**vorgang** formative process; ~**vorkehrungen** educational provisions; **zweiter** ~**weg** secondary education; **allgemeiner** ~**wert** general educative value; ~**wesen** education; ~**zentrum** educational center *(US)*, centre of learning *(Br.)*.
Bild|unterschrift caption *(US)*, legend; ~**verzerrung** *(Fernsehen)* picture distortion; ~**wähler** display selector; ~**wand** [projection] screen; ~**wandler** *(Fernseher)* picture (video, *US*) transformer; ~**warenzeichen** picture trademark; ~**werbung** illustrated advertisement *(Br.)*, pictorial advertising; ~**werfer** picture projector; ~**werferlampe** projection lantern; ~**wiedergabe** reproduction; ~**wiedergaberöhre** kinescope; ~**winkel** view; ~**wörterbuch** illustrated dictionary; ~**zeichen** pictorial trademark, figure; ~**zeile** *(Fernsehen)* scanning line; ~**zeitung** tabloid *(US)*, illustrated paper; ~**zerleger[röhre]** image dissector, sector tube; ~**zerlegung** scanning.
Billet note, ticket;
~**schalter** ticket (booking, *Br.*) office.
Billiarde a thousand billions *(Br.)*, quadrillion *(US)*.
Billiardzimmer billiard saloon *(Br.)*.
billig cheap, low-priced, inexpensive, low, at a low price, at little (small) cost, easy, at a moderate charge (low figure), cut-price, penny-a-line, twopenny, threepenny, twobit *(US)*, *(angemessen)* reasonable, fair, moderate, *(gerecht)* just, equitable, *(kümmerlich)* shoddy, cheap, *(Kurs)* at a cheap (low) rate;
anhaltend ~ steadily low-priced; **auffallend** ~ steadily low-priced; **außergewöhnlich** ~ extraordinarily cheap, dirt-cheap *(sl.)*; **so** ~ **wie möglich** with a fine pencil;
recht und ~ fair and equitable; ~ **zu verkaufen** *(Inserat)* offered for sale at a reasonable price;

enorm ~ **abgeben** to sell dirt cheap; ~ **aussehen** to look cheap; ~ **bestellen** to produce at low cost; **Waren im Ausland** ~ **auf den Markt bringen** to dump goods on a foreign market; ~ **davonkommen** to get off cheaply, to have a narrow squeak *(sl.)*; ~ **einkaufen** to buy cheap, to spend moderately; ~ **sein** *(Aktien)* to be in the dumps (down); **nicht mehr als** ~ **sein** to be only fair; ~ **zu haben sein** to be going cheap; ~ **weggehen** to go cheap; ~**e Arbeitskräfte** cheap labo(u)r; ~**e Ausgabe** cheap edition; ~**e Ausrede** poor (lame, paltry) excuse; ~**er Einkauf** bargain, cheap pennyworth *(Br.)*; ~**es Ermessen** discretion; ~**e Flugkarte** budget fare; ~**e Forderung** reasonable demand; ~**es Geld** easy (cheap) money; **für** ~**es Geld kaufen** to buy at a moderate price; ~**e Geldmarktsätze** easy money rates; ~**er Herstellungsbetrieb** low-cost producer; ~**es Hotelzimmer** low-priced room; ~**er Jakob** *(fam.)* cheap Jack; ~**er Kauf** bargain; ~**es Kleid** hand-me-down dress; ~**e Preise** low (moderate) prices; ~**er Trost** small consolation; ~**es Verlangen** reasonable demand; ~**e Waren** low-priced goods; ~**er Zinssatz** equitable rate of interest;
was dem einen recht ist, ist dem anderen ~ what is sauce for the goose, is sauce for the gander.

billigen to approve, to give approval, to consent, to authorize, *(nachträglich)* to sanction;
jds. Handlungsweise ~ to endorse s. one's action; **jds. Handlungsweise nicht** ~ to disapprove of s. one's conduct; **Rechnung** ~ to pass an invoice; **stillschweigend** ~ to acquiesce in.

billiger cheaper;
~ **im Verbrauch sein, je mehr man fährt** to get better mileage and save money every mile one drives; ~ **werden** to cheapen, to go down in price, *(Aktien)* to give way, *(Geld)* to loosen (ease) up;
~ **Preis** budget price; **äußerst** ~ **Preis** dead bargain.

billigerweise reasonably, equitably.

Billigflug|gesellschaft bargain airline; ~**karte** budget fare; ~**karte ohne Bordservice** rock-bottom, no amenities fare; ~**karten für Linienflugzeuge** budget fare on scheduled airlines *(US)*.

Billig|geschäft, ~**laden** cut-price shop, discount store *(US)*, thrift store, penny (dime, *US*) store.

Billigkeit justice, justness, equity, equitableness, fairness, *(niedriger Preis)* cheapness, moderateness, low price, *(verächtlich)* shoddiness;
aus Gründen der ~ for reasons of equity; **der** ~ **entsprechend** fair and equitable; **nach Recht und** ~ according to law and order; **einfachste Grundsätze der** ~ **verletzten** to contravene the first principles of equity.

Billigkeits|anspruch [claim in] equity, equity right; **stärkerer** ~**anspruch** paramount equity; ~**entscheidung** decision ex aequo et bono; ~**erwägungen** equitable rule; ~**flagge** flag of convenience; **aus** ~**gründen** for reasons of equity; ~**pfand** equitable lien; ~**recht** [law of] equity.

billigkeitsrechtlich equitable;
~**e Grundsätze** maxims of equity.

Billigkeits|sinn fair-mindedness; ~**wert** fair and equitable value.

Billigpreisländer low-price countries.

billigst at best, cheapest, at bottom;
~ **gestellt** at the lowest possible price.

Billigst|auftrag, ~**order** market order; ~**tarif** *(Fluglinie)* budget tariff.

Billigung approval, assent, approbation, consent, authorization, endorsement, sanction, allowance, applause;
mit allseitiger ~ by common consent;
gerichtliche ~ sanction of the court; **nachträgliche** ~ *(pol.)* indemnity; **stillschweigende** ~ acquiescence;
~ **eines Rechtsgeschäfts** adoption of a transaction;
~ **finden** to meet with approval, to meet with unanimous approval.

Billigwaren|geschäft penny (dime, *US*) store; ~**haus** cut-price shop, limited-price store *(US)*.

Billion billion *(Br.)*, trillion *(US)*.

bimetallisch bimetallic.

Bimetallismus bimetallism, double standard.

Bimetallist bimetallist.

Bimmelbahn *(fam.)* local line, parliamentary train *(Br.)*.

bimmeln *(tel.)* to ring.

Binde band, bandage, *(für Augen)* blindfold;
elastische ~ elastic bandage;
eins hinter die ~ **gießen** to wet one's whistle *(fam.)*; **Arm in der** ~ **tragen** to carry one's arm in a sling;
~**glied** link, tie, bond, connector; ~**mittel** fixing agent.

Binden eines Buches binding of a book.

binden to engage, to commit, to oblige, *(festbinden)* to fetter, to bind, *(Geldmittel)* to tie (lock, *Br.*) up, *(mil.)* to contain, *(für bestimmten Zweck)* to earmark;
sich ~ to commit s. o., to oblige o. s.; **Buch** ~ to bind a book; **Geldmittel** ~ to tie (lock, *Br.*) up money, *(für bestimmten Zweck)* to earmark funds; **j. an Händen und Füßen** ~ to bind s. o. hand and foot; **Korn** ~ to sheave corn; **Kurs des Pfundes an den Dollar** ~ to peg the value of the pound to the dollar; **jedem auf die Nase** ~ to broadcast a fact; **an einen Preis** ~ to limit to a price; **Preise** ~ to maintain retail prices; **sich an die Regeln** ~ to stick to the rules; **jem. etw. auf die Seele** ~ to impress s. th. on s. o.; **jem. ein Tuch vor die Augen** ~ to blindfold s. o.; **j.** ~ **vertraglich** ~ to tie s. o. down to a contract; **sich vertraglich** ~ to bind o. s. by contract.

bindend binding, obligatory, stringent, firm;
~ **für** valid for, binding on;
einseitig ~ unilaterally binding; **nicht** ~ noncommittal; **unbedingt** ~ *(Vertrag)* hard and fast; ~ **vorgeschrieben** mandatory;
Abmachung als ~ **ansehen** to regard an agreement as binding; **nicht** ~ **sein** to be of no binding force; **j.** ~ **zu etw. verpflichten** to bind s. o. over to do s. th.;
~**e Abmachungen** binding agreement; ~**es Angebot** firm offer; ~**er Beschluß** binding order; ~**e gesetzliche Bestimmung** mandatory statutory provision; ~**es Gesetz** binding law; ~**e Kraft** binding authority; **mit** ~**er Kraft** binding; ~**e Verpflichtung** binding commitment; **alle Vertragspartner** ~**e Verpflichtung** obligation binding on all parties; ~**e Wirkung** binding effect; **schnell** ~**er Zement** quick-setting cement.

Bindequote *(Buchhandel)* tie-up quota.

Bindestrich hyphen;
mit einem ~ **versehen** to hyphenate;
~**-Amerikaner** *(fam.)* hyphenated American *(US)*.

Bindfaden pack twine, string, cord, packthread;
~ **regnen** to be raining cats and dogs.

Bindung engagement, liability, obligation, commitment, bond, bondage, tie, link;
angesichts der eingegangenen ~**en** given the made commitments;
einseitige ~ naked bond; **gegenseitige** ~**en** mutual engagement; **kapitalmäßige** ~ financial relationship (connection, connexion, *Br.*); **örtliche** ~ local attachment; **persönliche** ~**en** personal ties; **zu starke politische** ~ overcommitment; **vertragliche** ~ contractual commitments; **wirtschaftliche** ~**en** business ties; **zwangswirtschaftliche** ~**en** public control;
~ **an den Börsenkurs** limited price; ~ **der Entwicklungshilfe** aid tying; ~ **von Feindkräften** containing action, holding attack *(mil.)*; ~ **von Geldbeträgen** freezing (immobilization) of funds; ~ **an das Gesetz** subordination to the law; ~ **an den Goldpreis** link to gold; ~ **an den Preis** price limit; ~ **der Preise** freezing of prices; ~ **von Truppenverbänden** immobilization of troops; ~ **einer Währung an den Dollar** link of a currency to the dollar; **jem.** ~**en auferlegen** to put s. o. under an obligation; ~**en eingehen** to enter into commitments; **vertragliche** ~**en eingehen** to enter into privity (engagements); **ohne** ~**en sein** to take (have) no roots.

Bindungsermächtigung commitment authorization.

Binnen|bedarf domestic (home) demand; ~**beziehung** internal relationship; ~**dock** inner dock; ~**entwässerung** interior drainage; ~**fischerei** fresh-water (river) fishing; ~**flughafen** domestic airport; ~**flugverkehr** inland (internal) air traffic; ~**frachtführer** inland carrier; ~**gebiet** inland; ~**geld** internal currency; ~**gewässer** territorial (internal) waters, inland waterways; ~**gewässer der USA** waters of the United States; ~**grenzen** *(EG)* internal frontiers; ~**hafen** close (inland) port, inner (landlocked) harbo(u)r, basin; ~**handel** country (home, interior, internal, inward, *US*) trade, domestic (interstate) commerce *(US)*, domestic trade *(US)*; ~**industrie** home industry; ~**klima** continental climate; ~**kolonie** back settlement; ~**konjunktur** domestic activity (state of business), internal economic trend (boom); **rückläufige** ~**konjunktur** domestic business slowdown; ~**konnossement** river bill of lading *(Br.)*, inland-waterway bill of lading; ~**konsum** domestic consumption; ~**land** interior, inland; **im** ~**land** inland; ~**länder** inlander.

binnenländisch interior, internal, inward, inland.

Binnen|luftverkehr domestic flights; ~**markt** home (inland, interior, domestic, *US*) market; ~**meer** landlocked (enclosed) sea; ~**monopol** internal monopoly; ~**nachfrage** internal (domestic, home) demand; ~**schiff** inland waterway craft, vessel of inland navigation; ~**schiffahrt** inland waters (internal) navigation *(US)*, inland shipping, inland waters navigation *(US)*, river navigation *(Br.)*.

Binnenschiffahrts|behörde River Board *(Br.)*; ~**gut** river freight *(Br.)*; ~**ordnung** Inland Rules of the Road *(US)*; ~**satz,** ~**tarif** river freight rate *(Br.)*, local tariff; ~**spediteur** waterway operator; ~**verkehr** inland waterways transport, inland water transportation (IWT) *(US)*; ~**versicherung** inland waterways insurance; ~**weg** inland waterway.

Binnen|schiffer waterman; ~**staat** landlock[ed state], inland state.

binnenstaatlicher Handel internal (domestic, *US*) trade.

Binnen|stadt interior town; ~**tarif** local tariff, inland rate.

Binnentransport inland transport, internal (inland) transportation *(US)*;
~**sachverständiger** internal transportation technician *(US)*; ~**system** inland transport *(Br.)*, internal transportation system *(US)*; ~**verkehr** inland communication (transport), inland (home) traffic, internal transportation *(US)*, intercity transport *(US)*; ~**versicherung** inland transportaion (marine, *US*) insurance; ~**wesen** inland transport *(Br.)* (internal transportation, *US*) system.

Binnen|verkehr inland communication (traffic, transport), internal transportation *(US)*, intercity transport *(US)*; ~**verkehrsausschuß** committee of inland transport; ~**verkehrsschadenversicherung** inland transportation insurance *(US)*; ~**währung** internal (domestic) currency; ~**wanderung** internal migration.

Binnenwasser|fahrzeug inland waterway craft; ~**straßen** inland waterways; ~**straßennetz** inland waterway system; **auf dem** ~**wege** by lake (river).

Binnen|wert domestic value; ~**wirtschaft** internal economy, domestic economy, home trade (economics) *(Br.)*.

binnenwirtschaftlich domestic, internal;
~ **orientiert** domestically orientated;
~**es Gleichgewicht** domestic equilibrium; ~**e Maßnahmen** domestic measures.

Binnenzoll inland (internal, inward, *Br.*) duty;
~**amt** inland customs office, interior customs post *(US)*.

Binsen gehen, völlig in die to go down the drain (to rack and ruin).

Binsenwahrheit commonplace, home (gospel) truth, truism;
ein paar ~**en einstecken müssen** to listen to a few home truths.

Bio|chemie biochemistry; ~**chemiker** biochemist; ~**graph** biographer.

Biographie biography;
~ **von jem. schreiben** to write s. one's life.

Birne *(el.)* bulb;
40-Watt ~**n einschrauben** to put forty-watt bulbs in; **weiche** ~ **haben** *(fam.)* to be weak in the upper storey.

bis auf weiteres until further notice.

bisher up to now, hitherto.

bisherig pre-existing, previous;
in meinem ~**en Leben** in my life so far; ~**er Minister** former minister; ~**er Präsident** retiring (outgoing) president; ~**er Rekord** previous record; ~**e Tätigkeit** past positions held; ~**e Verhandlungen** negotiations hitherto.

bißchen inch, morsel, bit, trace;
kein ~ not one jot or tittle; **kein** ~ **ängstlich** not a tick fleid *(Scot.)*; **kleines** ~ a tiny bit;
kein ~ **zu früh** not a moment too soon; **ein** ~ **spät** a bit late in the day *(fam.)*; **ein** ~ **voreilig** a little rash; **das** ~**, das ich weiß** the little I know;
ein ~ **bekloppt sein** to be a bit touched; **mit einem** ~ **vorliebnehmen** to be content with little;
~ *(a.)* little, a bit, somewhat;
kein ~ **Brot** not a morsel of bread; **ein** ~ **Englisch können** to have a smattering of English; **mein** ~ **Geld** that little money I have; **ein** ~ **Glück** a spot of luck; **mit ein** ~ **Menschenverstand** with a modicum of common sense; **ein** ~ **Wahrheit** a grain of truth.

Bissen bit, nibble, morsel;
fetter ~ piece of good luck;
jem. nicht den letzten ~ **gönnen** to take the bread out of s. one's mouth; **seit zwei Tagen keinen** ~ **angerührt haben** not to have touched food for two days; **heute noch keinen** ~ **gegessen haben** not to have had a bite all day; ~ **zu sich nehmen** to have a bit of s. th.; **kleinen** ~ **versuchen** to take a taste of s. th.; **jem. die** ~ **in den Mund zählen** to grudge s. o. the food he eats.

bissig biting, *(fig.)* mordant, pungent;
~**e Bemerkung** cutting remark; **Achtung!** ~**er Hund!** beware of the dog!; ~**er Kritiker** trenchant critic.

Bitte request, petition, solicitation, plea;
als ~ **formuliert** *(Testament)* in precatory words;
dringende ~ entreaty, instance, urgency, urgent request, adjuration; **letzte (letztwillige)** ~ dying request, precatory words; **spezifische** ~ special request;
~ **um Geld** request for money; ~ **um Kreditauskunft** credit inquiry *(US)*; ~ **um Regen** prayer for rain; ~ **um Rücksendung eines unbestellbaren Briefes** return request *(US)*;
jem. eine ~ **abschlagen** to turn down s. one's request; ~ **aussprechen** to ask for s. th.; **taub gegenüber allen** ~**n bleiben** to turn a deaf ear to s. one's entreaties; ~ **erfüllen** to grant a request; ~ **an j. richten** to petition s. o., to ask a favo(u)r of s. o.; **jem. eine** ~ **vortragen** to make a request to s. o.

bitten to beg, to request, to ask, to pray;
dringend ~ to entreat, to beseech; **j. um Entschuldigung** ~ to beg s. one's pardon; **um Erlaubnis** ~ to request (ask s. one's) permission; **j. um Feuer** ~ to trouble s. o. for a light; **um eine kurze Fristverlängerung** ~ to request a short delay; **j. um eine Gefälligkeit** ~ to ask a favo(u)r of s. o.; **um Geld** ~ to ask for money; **j. zu einem Glas Wein** ~ to invite s. o. to have a glass of wine; **um Gnade** ~ to plead for mercy; **inständig** ~ to adjure, to implore; **Mädchen um ihre Hand** ~ to propose to a girl; **um Spenden** ~ to solicit donations.

bitter|e Enttäuschung bitter disappointment; ~**e Erfahrungen** galling experience; ~**e Feinde** bitter enemies; ~**er Hunger** gnawing hunger; ~**e Ironie** biting irony; ~**e Kälte** bitter cold; **sich in** ~**er Not befinden** to be in dire need; ~**e Pille schlucken** to swallow the pill; ~**e Reue** bitter remorse; ~**es Unrecht** grievous wrong; **sich in** ~**er Verlegenheit befinden** to be in low straits; ~**e Vorwürfe** bitter reproach; **jem.** ~**e Vorwürfe machen** to reproach s. o. bitterly.

Bitterkeit bitterness, *(fig.)* sharpness, virulence;
die ~ **des Lebens** the gall of life;
~ **empfinden** to feel s. th. bitterly; ~ **bei jem. hinterlassen** to leave a gall in s. one's mind.

Bitt|gang approach; ~**gesuch** application for help.

Bittschrift petition, memorial, address;
~ **aufsetzen** to draw up a petition; ~ **einreichen** to put up a petition, to memorialize; **dem Gouverneur eine** ~ **überreichen** to present a petition to the Governor.

Bittsteller solicitor, solicitant, applicant, petitioner, supplicant, asker.

Bitumen bitumen, pitch, asphalt;
~**decke** asphalt surface; ~**pappe** tarred paper.

Biwak *(mil.)* bivouac.

biwakieren *(mil.)* to bivouac.

bizonal bizonal.

blamab|el humiliating, embarrassing, shameful, disgraceful;
für alle Beteiligte ~**le Geschichte** an action disgraceful to all concerned.

Blamage disgrace, stultification, humiliation;
absolute ~ absolute disgrace;
~ **erleiden** to make a laughingstock of o. s.

blamieren, sich to make a fool of o. s., to put one's foot in it, to make a gaffe (bloomer, blunder), to come a cropper *(coll.)*.

blank shining, shiny, bright, *(drucktechn.)* interlineal, interlinear, *(pleite)* broke;
völlig ~ **sein** to be stony-broke *(sl.)*, to be penniless; ~**ziehen** to draw one's sword;
auf dem ~**en Boden schlafen** to sleep on the bare ground; ~**es Eis** smooth ice; ~**e Fäuste** naked fists; **auf der** ~**en Haut** on the bare skin; ~**e Teile** *(Auto)* brightwork.

Blankett *(Formular)* blank form, *(Unterschrift)* [signature in] blank, *(Vollmacht)* carte blanche;
~ **ausfüllen** to fill in a blank;
~**ausfüllbefugnis** authorization to fill in (out, *US*) a blank; ~**ausfüllbefugnis zuerkennen** to authorize to fill in a blank; ~**ausstellung** making a blank *(US)*; ~**einkaufsauftrag** blanket purchase order; ~**gesetz** blanket act, enabling statute (act); ~**police** blank policy; ~**versicherungsschein** blanket position bond *(US)*, *(für Bankangestellte)* banker's blanket bond, *(gegen Versicherungsdelikte von Betriebsangehörigen)* commercial blanket bond *(US)*.

blanko blank, in blank, short, not filled in, *(Kredit)* uncovered, unsecured;
in ~ **giriert** indorsed in blank;
~ **abgeben** to bear *(Br.)*, to sell (go) short *(US)*; **in** ~ **akzeptieren** to accept in blank; ~ **ausstellen** to make out in blank; ~ **indossieren** to indorse in blank; ~ **trassieren** to draw in blank; ~ **übertragen** to assign in blank; ~ **unterzeichnen** to sign in blank; ~ **verkaufen** to sell ahead (a bear, short, *US*).

Blanko|abgabe bearish operation (sale) *(Br.)*, short sales *(US)*; **~abgaben** uncovered sales, short sale (selling) *(US)*, selling stocks short *(US)*; **~akzept** acceptance in blank, blank acceptance, inchoate instrument, uncovered acceptance *(US)*; **~auftrag** blank engagement (order), carte blanche order, *(Revision)* blank audit; **~barscheck** counter check *(US)*; **~formular** blank form, *(Brief)* skeleton letter; **~formular ausfüllen** to fill in a blank; **~geschäft** blank transaction, uncovered sale; **~girant** unqualified indorser; **~giro** assignment (indorsement) in blank, general endorsement, blank transfer *(Br.)*; **~indossament** assignment in blank, blank transfer *(Br.)*, blank (general) indorsement, indorsement in blank, fly power *(Br.)*; **mit ~indossament versehen** indorsed in blank.

Blankokredit blank credit, credit in blank, open *(US)* (unsecured) credit, uncovered loan, account opened without security, *(unbegrenzter Kredit)* unlimited credit;
kurzfristiger ~ unsecured short-term loan;
~e gewähren to lend money without security (collateral, *US*).

Blanko|obligationen blank bonds *(Scot.)*; **~offerte** offer in blank; **~papier** blank certificate (paper), paper signed in blank; **~police** blank policy; **~quittung** receipt in blank; **~scheck** blank cheque *(Br.)* (check, *US*); **~übertragung** blank transfer *(Br.)*; **~unterschrift** blank signature, signature in blank; **~verkäufe** bearish operations *(Br.)*, uncovered (open, short, *US*) sales, short selling *(US)*, selling short *(US)*; **~verkäufer** bear, short [seller] *(US)*; **~verpflichtung** blanket bond; **~vollmacht** full (blank) power of attorney, dormant warrant, unlimited powers (authority), carte blanche; **~vorlage, ~vorschuß** blank (unsecured, uncovered) advance; **~wechsel** blank bill; **~zertifikat** blank certificate; **~zession** assignment in blank, blank transfer *(Br.)*.

Blase bubble, *(med.)* blister, *(Gesindel)* gang, lot, crew;
die ganze ~ the whole lot;
sich eine ~ laufen to get a blister on one's foot; **~n ziehen** *(fig.)* to cause a sensation.

blasen to blow;
zum Angriff ~ to sound the charge; **jem. den Marsch ~** to give s. o. a dressing down; **jem. etw. in die Ohren ~** to whisper a word to s. o. (in s. one's ear); **zum Rückzug ~** to sound the retreat; **Trübsal ~** to have the blues *(coll.)*, to mope in solitude; **Zapfenstreich ~** to tatoo;
du kannst mir was ~ you can whistle for it.

blasiert blasé, smug;
~ sein to take an empty pride in s. th.

Blas|instrument wind instrument, pipe; **~musik** music of a brass (wind) band; **~orchester** wind band.

Blasphemie blasphemy, profane word.

blaß white, pale, pallid;
~ vor Neid green with envy; **~ wie der Tod** pale as death;
~ werden to grow (turn) pale; **in einer Rolle etw. ~ wirken** to seem somewhat colo(u)rless in a role;
von etw. nur eine ~e Ahnung haben to have only a foggy idea of s. th.; **nicht die ~este Ahnung haben** not to have the faintest idea; **~e Erinnerung** dim recollection.

Blatt leaf, *(Bandsäge)* band, *(Buch)* leaf, page, folio, *(Faltprospekt)* folder, *(Hubschrauber)* blade, *(Papier)* piece, sheet, *(Zeitung)* [news]paper, journal;
bekanntes ~ well-known paper; **führendes ~** leading newspaper; **gutes ~** *(Kartenspiel)* good hand; **loses ~** loose sheet; **unangesehenes ~** paper of no standing; **unbeschriebenes ~** *(fig.)* blank sheet (paper), dark horse, tabula rasa *(fig.)*;
neues ~ in der Geschichte new era of history; **neues ~ Papier** clean sheet of paper; **weißes ~ Papier** blank sheet of paper;
~ aus dem Schreibheft herausreißen to tear a page out of a notebook; **kein ~ vor den Mund nehmen** not to mince one's words, not to mince matters, not to put too fine an edge (point) on it, to be a plain-spoken man, to talk cold turkey *(US)*; **noch ein unbeschriebenes ~ sein** to be an unknown quantity; **alles auf ein ~ setzen** to put all one's eggs in one basket; **vom ~ spielen** to play from music; **auf einem ganz anderen ~ stehen** to be quite a different matter;
das ~ hat sich gewendet the tables are turned;
~breite width of page; **~drucker** page printing telegraph.

Blätter, grafische graphics; **lose ~** loose sheets (leaves); **öffentliche ~** public prints; **wöchentlich erscheinende ~** weekly prints.

blättern, in einem Buch to leaf (page, *US*) through a book.

Blatt|feder laminated spring; **~gold** gold leaf; **doppelseitige ~mitte** *(Anzeigen)* center *(US)* (centre, *Br.*) spread; **~schreiber** page printer; **~vergoldung** gilding; **~zahl** foliation; **~zinn** tin foil.

blau blue, *(betrunken)* tight;
total ~ as tight as an owl; **~ vor Wut** white with rage;
~ im Gesicht anlaufen to go black (blue) in the face; **sich grün und ~ ärgern** to be beside o. s. with anger, to be fit to be tied *(US)*; **~ machen** to cut, to pleasure *(coll.)*, to keep Saint Monday, *(Schule schwänzen)* to play truant (hooky, *US*); **Rest des Tages ~ machen** to tie it off *(sl.)*; **völlig ~ sein** to be as drunk as a lord;
~es Auge black eye; **mit einem ~en Auge davonkommen** to escape by the skin of one's teeth, to have a narrow squeak *(sl.)*; **das ~e Band** the blue ribbon; **~er Brief** mittimus, quietus; **jem. ~en Dunst vormachen** to pull the wool over (blow dust in) s. one's eyes; **~en Montag machen** to keep Saint Monday; **~e Stelle** bruise; **sein ~es Wunder erleben** to get the surprise of one's life.

blaublütig blue-blooded.

Blaubuch blue book *(Br.)*.

Blaue, ins cross-country;
das ~ vom Himmel herunterlügen to lie like a trooper (in one's throat); **das ~ vom Himmel herunterschwätzen** to talk the hind leg off a donkey *(fam.)*, to talk nineteen to the dozen *(Br.)*; **ins ~ hineinreden** to talk at random; **jem. das ~ vom Himmel versprechen** to promise s. o. the moon and stars.

Blauer blue man (bottle, *Br.*, *sl.*).

Blaues Kreuz temperance union.

Blau|feuer blue light; **~jacke** blue jacket; **~kreuzler** teetotaller; **~kreuzlerverein** temperance league (society), antisaloon league *(US)*; **~kreuzlerversammlung** teetotal meeting; **~licht** blue light; **~pause** blueprint, ozalide; **~pause machen** to blueprint; **~pauspapier** blueprint paper; **~stift** blue pencil; **~strumpf** bluestocking.

Blech sheet metal, tin plate;
verzinktes ~ galvanized sheet;
~ reden to talk rubbish;
~büchse, ~dose tin *(Br.)*, can *(US)*, tin cup (box) *(Br.)*; **~budenstadt** shanty town.

blechen to plunk down *(sl.)*, to pony up *(sl.)*, to cough (fork) up (out) *(sl.)*, to pay the fiddler *(US sl.)*, to shower down *(sl.)*;
j. ~ lassen to stick s. o. for the drinks; **schwer für etw. ~ müssen** to bleed for s. th., to come across with *(sl.)*.

Blech|geschirr tinware; **~instrument** brass instrument; **~kanne** tin [box] *(Br.)*, can *(US)*; **~napf** *(mil.)* dixie *(fam.)*; **~plakat** tinplate sign; **~rolladen** metal blind; **~schmied** tinsmith; **~topf** tin pot; **~walzwerk** sheet mill, plate-rolling mill; **~waren** tinware.

Blei lead;
in ~ fassen to lead; **~ an den Füßen haben** to have lead in one's pants *(sl.)*.

Bleibe lodge, lodging, tabernacle, accommodation, padhouse, pad *(sl.)*;
keine ~ haben to have no fixed abode.

bleiben to remain, to stay;
im Amt ~ to continue in office; **am Apparat ~** to hold the line; **an der Arbeit ~** to continue working; **bis zum letzten Augenblick ~** to sit it out; **bei seiner Aussage ~** to stick to one's statement; **bei der Behauptung ~, daß** to persist in maintaining that; **in Bewegung ~** to keep going; **auf dem Boden des Gesetzes ~** to be law-abiding, to keep within the bounds of the law; **für dauernd ~** to be here on keeps *(sl.)*; **bei seinem Entschluß ~** to abide by one's decision, to stand pat *(US)*; **zum Essen ~** to stay for dinner; **fest ~** *(Börse)* to keep firm, to remain steady, to maintain a firm attitude; **nicht ohne Folgen ~** to have its consequences; **länger als die anderen Gäste ~** to outsit the other guests; **im Gedächtnis haften ~** to ring in one's mind; **im Geschäft tätig ~** to remain active in business; **geschlossen ~** to be kept closed; **gültig (in Kraft) ~** to remain in force; **zu Hause ~** to stay (remain) at home; **weiter hoch ~** *(Kurse)* to keep up; **zu lange ~** to overstay one's welcome; **auf dem laufenden ~** to keep posted; **am Leben ~** to survive; **ledig ~** to remain single; **bei seiner Meinung ~** to stick to one's guns; **über Nacht ~** to stay overnight; **noch ~** to linger; **nüchtern ~** to stay sober; **an Ort und Stelle ~** to stay put; **ruhig ~** to keep calm; **bei der Sache ~** to stick to the point (one's text); **in der Schwebe ~** to be left in abeyance; **bei der Stange ~** to stick it out (to business); **beim Thema ~** to keep to the subject; **jem. überlassen ~** to rest with s. o.; **sich selbst überlassen ~** to be left to o. s.; **unbeachtet ~** to escape s. one's notice; **unbestraft ~** to go unpunished, to escape scot-free; **unentschieden ~** to play off a draw (tie); **ungenutzt ~** to hang by the wall; **unverkauft** to remain unsold; **wachsam ~** to sleep with one eye open; **bei der Wahrheit ~** to stick to the truth; **so lange ~ wie man will** to stay at one's pleasure; **ohne Wirkung ~** to be to no effect.

bleibend abiding, lasting, permanent;
~**e Eindrücke** lasting impressions; ~**er Wert** lasting value; ~**er Wohnsitz** permanent residence (abode).
bleibenlassen to leave (let) alone;
Rauchen ~ to stop (quit, *US*) smoking.
Bleibenzin lead gas (gasoline).
bleich white, pale, pallid;
~ **wie der Tod** as pale as death; ~ **wie die Wand** as white as chalk;
~ **werden** to turn pale.
bleibt *(drucktechn.)* stet.
bleiern leaden, plumbeous;
wie eine ~e Ente schwimmen to swim like a stone; ~**e Glieder** leaden limbs; ~**er Schlaf** leaden sleep.
Blei|fassung lead; **zulässiger ~gehalt** permissible lead content; ~**hütte** lead-works; ~**kabel** lead-covered cable; ~**lot** plummet; ~**sarg** lead coffin; ~**satz** metallic (hot) type.
Bleistift pencil;
~ **spitzen** to sharpen a pencil;
~**halter** portcrayon; ~**schale** pencil tray; ~**spitzer** [pencil] sharpener; ~**verlängerer** pencil holder; ~**zeichnung** pencil sketch (drawing).
Blende optical screen, diaphragm, *(Film)* bull's eye, *(mil.)* mask;
~ **einstellen** to set the diaphragm.
blenden to blind, to dazzle;
die Augen ~ to blink the eyes.
blendend glaring, dazzling, stunning, smashing, super, grand;
~ **miteinander auskommen** to hit it off with s. o.;
~**e Erscheinung** brilliant (magnificent) appearance; **von ~er Gesundheit sein** to be in the pink of health; ~**er Redner** brilliant speaker.
Blenden|einstellung diaphragm setting; ~**öffnung** diaphragm shutter (opening); ~**rechner** aperture computer.
Blender specious person, dazzler *(coll.)*.
Blend|fassade blind (dead) wall; ~**fenster** blind window; ~**lampe** dazzle lamp; ~**laterne** dark (police) lantern; ~**scheibe** *(Auto)* antidazzle shield, sun visor *(US)*; ~**schirm** eye shade, *(Fernsehen)* gobo.
Blendschutz|farbe *(Schiff)* dazzle paint; ~**lampe** antidazzle lamp; ~**scheibe** antidazzle screen, sun visor *(US)*; ~**vorrichtung** dimmer.
Blend|stein facing brick; ~**verschluß** diaphragm shutter; ~**werk** false front, phantasmagoria, glamo(u)r, trick; ~**werk des Teufels** snares of the devil.
Blick look, glance;
auf den ersten ~ at first blush (sight); **gleich beim ersten** ~ on the mere face of it; **mit einem flüchtigen** ~ at a cursory glance; **mit leerem** ~ with a vacant look; **mit neidischen ~en** with jealous eyes;
mit ~ **auf die Berge** with a view of the mountains;
abwesender ~ distant look; **ausdrucksloser** ~ vacant stare; **bedeutsamer** ~ knowing glance; **finsterer** ~ scowl; **flüchtiger** ~ transient glance, glimpse, glance; **lüsterne ~e** wanton looks; **mörderischer** ~ killing glance; **neidischer** ~ covetous eye; **schräger** ~ side-glance; **sehnsüchtiger** ~ lingering (longing) look; **verstohlener** ~ furtive glance; **verstörter** ~ wild look; **vielsagender** ~ look full of meaning;
~ **hinter die Kulissen** inside story; ~ **auf die Landschaft** peep of the scenery;
j. mit einem durchdringenden ~ **ansehen** to fix one's eye piercingly on s. o.; **j. mit einem vielsagenden** ~ **ansehen** to glance meaningly at s. o.; **den ~en entschwinden** to disappear from view; ~ **von etw. erhaschen** to catch a glimpse of s. th.; **jds. ~e fesseln** to arrest s. one's eyes; ~ **für etw. haben** to have an eye for s. th.; **bösen** ~ **haben** to have the evil eye; **seinen** ~ **durch das Zimmer schweifen lassen** to cast one's eye around the room; **sich den** ~ **nicht trüben lassen** to keep a clear head; ~**e auf sich lenken** to attract attention, to draw the eye; **den** ~ **ins Leere richten** to gaze into space; **etw. mit einem** ~ **sehen** to see s. th. with half an eye; ~ **senken** to lower one's eyes; **keinen** ~ **von jem. wenden** not to take one's eyes off s. o.; ~ **auf etw. werfen** to cast one's eye over s. th.; **flüchtigen** ~ **in ein Buch werfen** to have a dip into a book; **kurzen** ~ **auf etw. werfen** to have a squint at s. th.; **kurzen** ~ **auf einen Brief werfen** to glance over a letter; **kurzen** ~ **aus dem Fenster werfen** to have a peep through the window; **verliebte ~e auf j. werfen** to cast sheep's eyes at s. o.; **verstohlenen** ~ **auf etw. werfen** to steal a glance at s. th.; ~ **in die Zeitung werfen** to have a look into the newspaper; **jem. finstere ~e zuwerfen** to frown (scowl) at s. o.; **jem. einen fragenden** ~ **zuwerfen** to look a query to s. o. *(fam.)*; **jem. einen schäkernden** ~ **zuwerfen** to give s. o. the glad eye.

blicken to look;
finster ~ to wear an angry look, to frown, to scowl; **flüchtig auf etw.** ~ to glimpse upon s. th.; **herablassend auf etw.** ~ to look down one's nose at s. th.; **verstohlen auf j.** ~ to peep at s. o.; **sich** ~ **lassen** to show o. s., to let o. s. be seen; **sich selten** ~ **lassen** to make o. s. scarce;
lassen Sie sich hier nicht mehr ~ never darken my doors again; **das läßt tief** ~ that speaks volumes, it makes you think *(fam.)*.
Blick|fang, ~**fänger** eye appeal, eye catcher (stopper), hook, attention getter, *(Anzeige)* approach.
Blickfang|preis charm price; ~**wort** catchword; ~**zeile** headline.
Blickfeld purview, field of vision, sight;
in das ~ **geraten** to come into view; **ins öffentliche** ~ **geraten** to get into the public eye (limelight); **aus dem** ~ **verschwinden** to get out of sight.
Blickführungslinie *(Inserat)* leader.
Blickpunkt vision, focus, *(fig.)* point of view, side;
im ~ **der Interessen** in the center of interests;
im ~ **der Öffentlichkeit stehen** to be very much in the public eye, to be in the limelight (the target of all eyes).
Blick|richtung line of sight; ~**verlauf** *(Anzeige)* ad-page traffic; ~**weite** view; ~**winkel** view.
blind blind, *(Spiegel)* dull;
~ **in die Gegend schießen** to shoot at random; **auf einem Auge** ~ **sein** to be blind in one eye; ~ **gegen jds. Fehler sein** to be blind to s. one's faults; ~ **werden** to go blind, *(Glas)* to cloud, *(Metall)* to become tarnished;
~**er Alarm** false alarm; ~**es Fenster** blind window; ~**er Gehorsam** unquestioning (blind, unreasoning) obedience; ~**e Mauer** dead wall; ~**er Passagier** deadhead, blind baggage *(US sl.)*, *(auf Schiffen)* stowaway; ~**e Patrone** blank cartridge; ~**er Schacht** blind shaft; ~**er Schornstein** *(Schiff)* dummy funnel; ~**es Vertrauen** implicit confidence; ~**e Zeile** blank line; ~**er Zufall** blind (pure) chance.
Blind|abwurf *(mil.)* blind bombing; ~**anzeige** blind advertisement; ~**band** *(Buch)* dummy; ~**boden** dead floor.
blindbuchen *(Film)* to book in blocks.
Blind|buchung blind entry, *(Film)* block (blind) booking; ~**darmoperation** operation for appendicitis; ~**druck** blind blocking (tooling).
blinddrucken to blind-tool.
Blinden|anstalt home (asylum, institution) for the blind; ~**freibetrag** blind-person's allowance; ~**fürsorge** public care for the blind; ~**heim** asylum for the blind; ~**hilfe** aid to the blind; ~**hund** blind man's (seeing-eye, *US*) dog; ~**schreibmaschine** braille typewriter; ~**schrift** point alphabet, braille; ~**schriftsystem** string alphabet; ~**sendungen** literature for the blind.
Blinde|r blind man (person);
~**n führen** to lead a blind man; **wie ein ~r von der Farbe reden** to talk through one's hat.
Blinderinnerungstest *(Anzeigenwerbung)* blind product test.
Blindfliegen blind (instrument) flying.
blindfliegen to fly on instruments (blind), to fly by the seat of one's pants *(coll.)*.
Blindflug flying blind, blind (instrument) flying (flight);
~**plan** instrument flight plan.
Blindgänger blind shell, dud;
~**beseitigung** bomb clearance (disposal).
blindgeprägt *(Buchbinden)* antique.
Blindheit blindness;
mit ~ **geschlagen sein** to be struck blind.
Blind|landeeinrichtung radio approach (blind landing) system; ~**landung** blind approach (landing), instrument landing.
blindlings slapdash, headlong;
~ **drauflosschlagen** to lash out wildly; **sich** ~ **auf eine Auseinandersetzung einlassen** to plunge into an argument; ~ **ins Verderben rennen** to rush headlong to one's ruin.
Blind|material blank material, dead material; ~**muster** dummy [copy].
blindprägen to blind-stamp.
Blind|prägung blind tooling (blocking); ~**schreiben** touch typewriting.
blindschreiben to write (type) the ten-finger system, to touch-type.
blindschreibende Rechenmaschine blind calculator.
Blindverkehr blind traffic.
Blinkbake flashing beacon.
Blinken blink.
blinken to wink, to twinkle, *(Lichtzeichen geben)* to flash, to flicker.

Blinker winker, direction (flashing, traffic) indicator, *(Terminal)* cursor;
automatischer ~ self-cancelling traffic indicator;
verkehrswidrige ~**anzeige** improper signal(l)ing.
Blink|feuer blinker beacon, flashing (intermitting, revolving) light; ~**gerät** blinker apparatus, signal lamp (lantern); ~**leuchte,** ~**licht** blinker, winker, direction (flashing) indicator.
Blinklicht, gelbes flashing beacon *(Br.)*;
~ **für Fußgänger** pedestrian crossing lights, beacon;
~**anlage** traffic indicator lights, flashing red warning light, *(Bahnübergang)* flashing stop; ~**werbung** flashing sign.
Blinkzeichen geben to flash a signal.
Blinzeln wink, winking.
blinzeln to wink, to screw up one's eyes.
Blitz lightning, flash of lightning;
wie der ~ like winking; **wie ein geölter** ~ like greased lightning *(fam.)*;
~ **aus heiterem Himmel** bolt from the blue.
~**ableiter** lightning rod (conductor, *Br.*); ~**abstimmung** snap vote; ~**aktion** crash program(me); ~**antwort** condensed immediate reply.
Blitzbesuch flying visit.
blitzblank bright as a new pin.
Blitzdiät crash diet.
blitzen to flash, to sparkle.
Blitzentladung lightning discharge.
Blitzesschnelle lightning speed, flash;
mit ~ as quick as lightning, blue-streak.
Blitz|funktelegramm priority radiotelegram; ~**gerät** *(Fotoapparat)* flashgun; **mit** ~**geschwindigkeit** with lightning speed; ~**gespräch** *(tel.)* lightning call; ~**karriere machen** to leap up the ladder.
blitzkopieren to copyraid.
Blitz|krieg lightning war, blitzkrieg; ~**kursus** cram (crash) course; ~**lampe** photoflash.
Blitzlicht flashlight, [photo] flashlamp;
~**anschluß** flash socket (contact); ~**aufnahme** flashlight photography, photoflash picture; ~**birne** flash bulb; ~**fotografie** flashlight photography; ~**lampe** flash bulb (lamp); ~**röhre** flash valve (tube, *US*).
Blitz|meldung flash message; ~**programm** crash program(me); ~**reaktion** kickback; ~**reise** express journey.
blitzsauber as neat as a new pin, spanking clean *(sl.)*.
Blitzschaden lightning damage.
Blitzschlag [stroke of] lightning;
vom ~ **getroffen werden** to be struck by lightning;
~**klausel** lightning clause; ~**versicherung** lightning insurance.
blitzschnell like a streak of lightning, like a house on fire, as quick as lightning, at railway speed;
~ **reagieren** to take immediate action; **sich** ~ **verbreiten** to spread like wildfire;
~**er Entschluß** split-second decision.
Blitz|schutzvorrichtung lightning arrester; ~**strahl** flash of lightning, thunderbolt; **wie ein** ~**strahl aus heiterem Himmel** like a bolt from the blue; ~**telegramm** flash message, fast telegram; ~**test** *(Anzeigenwirksamkeit)* blind product test; ~**würfel** *(Fotoapparat)* flash cube; ~**zug** highspeed bullet train.
Block log, block, *(Briefmarkensammlung)* souvenir sheet, *(Fahrkarten)* book, *(Metall)* ingot, *(pol.)* bloc, *(Schreibblock)* pad, scribbling block;
im ~ **kaufen** to buy in blocks (in the lump);
~**abschnitt** *(Bahn)* block.
Blockade blockade, embargo, investment;
scharf durchgeführte ~ close blockade; **erfolgreiche** ~ effective blockade; **geistige** ~ intellectual blackout; **lokalisierte** ~ simple blockade; **völkerrechtlich notifizierte** ~ public blockade; **strenge** ~ close blockade; **unwirksame** ~ paper blockade; **wirkungsvolle** ~ effective blockade;
~ **aufheben** to raise (call off, remove, lift) a blockade; ~ **bekanntgeben** to notify a blockade; ~ **durchbrechen** to run the blockade; ~ **durchführen** to enforce a blockade, to lay an embargo on; **auch gegen Neutrale wirksame** ~ **durchführen** to render a blockade valid as against neutrals; ~ **lockern** to relax a blockade; ~ **verhängen** to embargo, to blockade; ~ **verschärfen (verstärken)** to tighten a blockade;
~**brecher** blockade runner; ~**durchbruch** blockade running; ~**erklärung** declaration of blockade; ~**freischein** navicert; ~**mannschaft** blockading force; ~**politik** embargo policy; ~**schiff** blockader; ~**streitmacht** blockading force; ~**verschärfung** tightening of a blockade; ~**zustand** state of blockade; ~**zustand über einen Hafen verhängen** to blockade a port.

Block|adresse block address; ~**bildung** *(pol.)* formation of blocs, alignment; ~**buch** block book; ~**buchung** block booking; ~**druck** block printing; ~**floaten** joint floating.
blockfreier Staat nonaligned (noncommitted) nation (state).
Block|freiheit nonalignment; ~**haus** blockhouse, log cabinet (hut); ~**heftmaschine** pointer's stitcher; ~**hütte** log hut.
blockieren to block [up], to jam, to blockade, to embargo, to obstruct, *(Druck)* to turn letters, *(Kapital)* to freeze, to lock (tie) up;
Annahme eines Gesetzes ~ to block the passage of a bill; **Fahrstrecke** ~ to block a line; **Konto** ~ to block (freeze) an account; **qualifizierten Mehrheitsbeschluß** ~ to block a special resolution; **Straße** ~ to shut (beset) a street, to obstruct (jam) a highway; **Verkehr** ~ to block the traffic.
blockiert *(Konto)* blocked, frozen;
~ **werden** *(Räder)* to lock;
~**e Devisen** blocked foreign exchange; ~**er Platz** blockaded place.
Blockierung *(Hafen)* blockade, *(geistig)* blackout, *(Konto)* stoppage, stopping payment, freeze;
~ **einer Straße** obstructing a highway.
Block|kalender tear-off (block) calendar; ~**police** block policy; ~**politik** bloc policy; ~**schaltung** single-unit circuit; ~**schokolade** slab chocolate; ~**schrift** block letters (type, writing); **halbfette** ~**schrift** clarendon; ~**signal** *(Bahn)* block signal; ~**stahl** ingot of steel; ~**station,** ~**stelle** *(Bahn)* signal box, blocked station; ~**straße** blooming mill train; ~**strecke** *(Bahn)* block; ~**system** *(Bahn)* block system; ~**verband** English bond; ~**wagen** box wagon, bogie *(Br.)*, boxcar *(US)*; ~**walzen** blooming *(US)*, cogging *(Br.)*; ~**wärter** *(Bahn)* signalman.
blöde *(schwachsinning)* feeble-minded, imbecile, half-witted, idiotic, *(ungeschickt)* stupid, foolish, silly;
~**r Fehler** silly mistake; ~**e Frage** stupid question; ~**r Kerl** silly fool; ~**e Situation** embarrassing situation.
blödeln to fool about (around).
Blödsinn muck, rubbish, nonsense, tommyrot;
höherer ~ utter nonsense;
~ **treiben** to be foolish, to skylark, to tomfool *(coll.)*.
blödsinnig imbecile, feeble-minded, mentally deficient;
von Geburt an ~ mentally retarded; ~ **teuer** shockingly expensive; **total** ~ absolutely ridiculous;
~**es Geschwätz** foolish talk.
bloß nude, naked, bare;
für das ~**e Auge sichtbar** visible to the naked eye; **auf der** ~**en Erde schlafen** to sleep on the bare ground; ~**e Formsache** mere formality; **mit** ~**en Füßen** barefooted; **der** ~**e Gedanke daran** the very thought of it; ~**e Kleinigkeit** mere trifle; ~**er Neid** sheer envy; ~ **zwei Pfund** only two pounds; **auf** ~**en Verdacht** on a mere suspicion.
Blöße, seine ~ **bedecken** to cover one's shame; **jem. eine** ~ **bieten** to show one's weak spot, to betray one's weak point; **sich eine** ~ **geben** to commit (expose) o. s.; **sich keine** ~ **geben** to have no chinks in one's armo(u)r.
bloßstellen to unmask, to compromise, to denounce;
sich ~ to expose o. s.; **j.** ~ to tip s. one's mitts *(US)*.
Bloßstellung denouncement, exposure;
~ **eines Verräters** denunciation of a traitor.
Blubbern *(Motorboot)* putt-putt.
blubbern to bubble, to gurgle, *(Mensch)* to gabble.
Bluff bluff.
blühen to flower, to flourish, to prosper, to thrive, to blossom, to bloom *(fig.)*.
blühend flourishing, prosperous, thriving, blooming, fresh;
im ~**en Alter sterben** to die in the flower of youth; ~**er Handel** flourishing trade; ~**e Handelsstädte** prosperous trading cities; **wie das** ~**e Leben aussehen** to look the picture of health; ~**er Unsinn** bare nonsense; ~**es Unternehmen** flourishing (prosperous) enterprise (concern).
blüht, sein Weizen his ship has come, he is in clover.
Blume flower, *(Wein)* bouquet, aroma;
durch die ~ sub rosa, in a roundabout way; **mit** ~**n geschmückt** decorated with flowers;
~ **abtrinken** *(Bier)* to take the top; **jem. etw. durch die** ~ **zu verstehen geben** to drop s. o. a gentle hint;
laßt ~**n sprechen** say it with flowers.
Blumen|arrangement spray of flowers, flower arrangement; ~**ausstellung** flower show; ~**beet** flower bed; ~**erde** garden mold (mould, *Br.*); ~**gebinde** wreath, garland; ~**händler** florist; ~**handlung** flower shop; ~**kinder** Flower People; ~**korb** flower basket; ~**korso** battle of flowers; ~**laden** flower shop; ~**markt** flower market; ~**muster** *(Kleid)* floral design.

blumenreiche Sprache flowery language.
Blumen|spenden sind nicht erwünscht no flowers by request; **~ständer** flower stand; **~strauß** bunch of flowers; **~stück** *(Malerei)* flower piece; **~topf** flower pot; **keinen ~topf gewonnen haben** to return without any success; **~verkäuferin** flower girl *(Br.)*; **~wagen** funeral car; **~zucht am Fenster** window gardening.
blümerant giddy, dizzy;
mir ist ganz ~ zumute my head is spinning.
Blut, mit ~ geschrieben written in blood;
blaues ~ blue blood; **böses ~** ill blood; **konserviertes ~** conserved blood;
j. bis auf ~ aussaugen to bleed s. o. white; **kaltes ~ bewahren** to keep one's head (one's shirt, hair) on *(sl.)*, to remain cool; **jds. ~ zum Sieden (Kochen) bringen** to make s. one's blood boil; **nach ~ dürsten** to thirst for blood; **heißes ~ haben** to be hot-headed; **j. bis aufs ~ hassen** to hate s. o. like poison (like the plague); **jds. ~ frieren lassen** to freeze s. one's blood; **im ~ liegen** to be inherent in the blood; **böses ~ machen** to stir the blood, to make bad blood between persons, to get all hot and bothered; **j. bis aufs ~ peinigen** to give s. o. hell; **j. bis aufs ~ reizen** to excite s. o. to the highest pitch; **im ~ schwimmen** to lie in a pool of blood; **~ und Wasser schwitzen** to sweat blood; **jem. im ~ stecken** to run in s. one's blood; **~ übertragen** to transfuse blood; **~ vergießen** to shed (spill) blood; **bis zum letzten Tropfen ~ verteidigen** to die in the last ditch; **einem Unternehmen frisches ~ zuführen** to put new life in an enterprise;
~ ist dicker als Wasser blood is thicker than water;
~alkoholgehalt blood-alcohol level; **~andrang zum Gehirn** congestion of the brain; **~armut** deficiency (poverty) of blood, anaemia; **~bad** slaughter, massacre, butchery; **~bank** blood bank; **~bild** blood picture; **~druck** blood pressure; **unter hohem ~druck leiden** to suffer from high blood pressure.
Blüte *(fig.)* prime, cream, elite, pride, *(Falschgeld)* snide, queery *(sl.)*;
in ~ in flower; **in der ~ der Jugend** in the first blush of youth; **in der ~ des Lebens** in the heyday of youth, in the prime of life, in one's prime;
~ der Jugend glow of youth; **~ der Nation** flower of the nation's manhood;
~n abfrieren lassen to pinch the blossom; **in höchster (voller) ~ stehen** to flower, to be in full bloom *(fig.)*, to have reached its peak.
bluten to bleed;
j. ~ lassen to sweat (leech) s. o.; **schwer für etw. ~ müssen** to pay through the nose, to have to fork out a lot of money, to bleed for s. th.
Blütenlese *(fig.)* gleanings, *(Literatur)* anthology.
Blutentnahme blood-letting, blood sample.
Blütezeit blossom, flower, *(fig.)* heyday, prime, *(Konjunktur)* boom, prosperity [era];
in der ~ des Lebens in one's prime, in the prime of life, in the heyday of youth;
konjunkturelle ~ boomtime; **wirtschaftliche ~** bonanza period of industrial development;
in der ~ seiner Laufbahn stehen to be in the prime of one's career; **in der ~ des Lebens stehen** to be in the flower of one's age.
Blut|geld blood money; **~gruppe** blood group (grouping, type); **~gruppe feststellen** to type blood; **~gruppenbestimmung** blood typing; **~gruppenuntersuchung** *(Vaterschaftsverfahren)* blood test.
blutig blood-stained, bloody;
~er Anfänger greenhorn, tyro, Johnny Raw; **~er Laie** complete layman; **~e Tränen vergießen** to shed bitter tears; **~e Zwischenfälle** bloody clashes.
blutjung green, in tender youth.
Blut|konserve unit of blood; **~kreislauf** blood circulation; **~lache** pool of blood; **einer Nation hohe ~opfer abverlangen** to take a heavy toll of a nation; **~paß** blood-group card; **~probe** blood test; **~rache** blood (deadly) feud; **~rausch** orgy of blood.
Bluts|bande blood bond, ties of blood; **~bruder** blood brother; **~brüderschaft** blood brotherhood.
Blut|sauger bloodsucker, leech; **~schande** incest; **~schänder** incestuous person.
blutschänderisch incestuous.
Blut|schuld blood-guiltiness; **~senkung** hypostasis; **~spende** blood donation; **~spender** blood donor; **fahrbare ~spendestelle** bloodmobile; **~spur** trail of blood, blood-stain.
blutsverwandt allied (related) by blood, cognate, consanguineous, kin, of kindred blood.
Blutsverwandte privies of blood;
~r cognate, blood relation, relative by blood;
nächste ~ one's next of skin.
Blutsverwandtschaft blood relationship, [proximity of] blood, natural cognation, line of consanguinity;
~ in gerader Linie lineal consanguinity; **~ in der Seitenlinie** collateral consanguinity.
Bluttat murder;
~ anrichten to massacre.
Blut|transfusion blood transfusion; **~untersuchung** blood test; **~vergießen** bloodshed; **als Vergeltungsmaßnahme gedachtes ~vergießen** retaliatory deaths; **~vergiftung** blood poisoning; **~zirkulation** blood stream.
Bö small gust, flaw, windfall, *(Luft)* air bump, squall.
Bock buck, he-goat, *(Gestell)* stand, rest, trestle, prop;
den ~ zum Gärtner machen to set the fox to keep the geese, to set a thief to catch a thief; **~ schießen** *(fig.)* to stumble, to make a blunder;
~bier double (bock) beer.
Bocken *(Kind)* kicking.
bocken to be obstinate, to grumble, to kick *(coll.)*.
Bockshorn jagen, ins to bulldoze, to bully, to brow-beat.
Bocksprünge machen to cut capers, to play one's pranks.
Boden ground, land, soil, *(Fußboden)* floor, *(Grundbesitz)* landed property, *(Dachboden)* loft, attic, *(Meer)* floor, bottom, *(Schiff)* bottom;
auf britischem ~ on British soil; **auf dem ~** in the loft; **auf dem ~ der Tatsachen** on the basis of facts;
nicht anbaufähiger ~ irreclaimable soil, barren land; **angeschwemmter ~** alluvial deposits; **armer ~** poor soil; **aufgeschütteter ~** made ground, embankment; **ausgelaugter ~** impoverished land; **doppelter ~** double (false) bottom; **ertragreicher ~** productive soil; **fruchtbarer ~** fat (rank, fertile) soil, rank land; **genutzter ~** seated land; **frisch gepflügter ~** newly ploughed land; **gesunder ~** sweet soil; **gewachsener ~** grown soil, natural ground; **jungfräulicher ~** unbroken ground, maiden soil; **lehmiger ~** heavy soil; **leichter (lockerer) ~** light (loose) soil; **marginaler ~** marginal land; **morastiger ~** marshy soil; **neutraler ~** neutral ground; **sandiger ~** sandy soil; **schwerer ~** heavy land; **steiniger ~** stony ground; **unebener ~** broken ground; **unergiebiger ~** poor soil; **ungenutzter ~** uncultivated (unseated, *US*) land;
Grund und ~ real estate, landed property; **schlüpfriger ~ der Politik** slipperiness of the political ground;
jem. ~ abgewinnen to gain on s. o.; **~ aufräumen** to turn out the attic; **dem Faß den ~ ausschlagen** to beat the band *(sl.)*; **~ für etw. bereiten** to prepare the ground for s. th.; **eigenen Grund und ~ besitzen** to own land; **~ bestellen** to till the soil; **gefährlichen ~ betreten** to be on slippery ground; **sich auf gefährlichem ~ bewegen** to be out of one's element, to be on dangerous ground *(coll.)*; **sich auf sicherem ~ bewegen** to be on sure ground; **~ bewirtschaften (bestellen)** to till the ground; **jem. den ~ ebnen** to smooth the way for s. o.; **~ einebnen** to smooth the soil; **jds. Behauptungen den ~ entziehen** to knock the bottom out of s. one's statement; **auf fruchtbaren ~ fallen** to fall on fertile ground; **gemeinsamen ~ für Verhandlungen finden** to find common ground for negotiations; **vom ~ freikommen** *(Flugzeug)* to become airborne; **an ~ gewinnen** to spread, to gain ground; **festen ~ gewinnen** to find one's feet, *(Unternehmen)* to get on its feet; **festen ~ unter den Füßen haben** to be on firm ground, to be within one's depth; **~ legen** to lay a floor; **j. in Grund und ~ reden** to talk s. o. down; **auf dem ~ des Meeres ruhen** to rest on the bottom of the sea; **aus dem ~ schießen** to mushroom, to pop up; **j. zu ~ schleudern** to fling s. o. to the ground; **am ~ zerstört sein** to be floored; **aus dem ~ stampfen** to throw up, to improvise, to conjure a rabbit out of a hat; **auf festem ~ stehen** to stand on firm ground; **auf dem ~ der Verfassung stehen** to be in accordance with the constitution; **sich auf den ~ des Gesetzes stellen** to keep within the bounds of [the] law; **sich auf den ~ der Tatsachen stellen** to take a realistic view, to face the music; **~ der Wirklichkeit verlassen** to climb out of touch with reality; **an ~ verlieren** to lose one's grip, to lose ground; **~ unter den Füßen verlieren** to get out of one's depth, to be all at sea, to be carried off one's feet; **Grund und ~ verstaatlichen** to nationalize land; **jem. den ~ unter den Füßen wegziehen** to cut the ground [from] under s. one's feet; **verlorenen ~ wiedergewinnen** to make up [for] lost ground; **in Grund und ~ wirtschaften** to bring to total ruin; **wieder auf den ~ der Wirklichkeit zurückkehren** to come back to earth, to come to one's senses;
das schlägt dem Faß den ~ aus that puts the lid on;

~**abstand** *(Auto, Flugzeug)* ground clearance; ~**analyse** soil analysis; ~**anlagen** *(Flugzeug)* ground facilities; ~**anleihe** land-grant bond; ~**anschwemmung** alluvion; ~**armut** poverty of soil; ~**auflockerung** loosening of the ground; ~**auslaugung** impoverishment of the soil; ~**bearbeitung** cultivation of the land; ~**belag** flooring *(Br.)*; ~**beleuchtung** ground lighting; ~**beschaffenheit** soil condition, quality of land, kind of soil, layer, ground; ~**beschaffungsplan** land acquisition program(m)e); ~**bestellung** tillage; ~**bewirtschaftung** husbandry, cultivation, management of land; **extensive** ~**bewirtschaftung** extensive cultivation; **intensive** ~**bewirtschaftung** high farming; ~-~**rakete** surface-to-surface missile; ~**dienst** *(mil.)* base services; ~**entwässerung** drainage; ~**erhebung** uplift, elevation, rising, eminence, up, rise in the ground; **vulkanische** ~**erhebung** upheaval; ~**erosion** soil erosion; ~**erschöpfung** impoverishment of the soil; ~**ertrag** farm (agricultural) produce, yield; ~**erzeugnisse** agricultural (farm) products; ~**fänger** *(drucktechn.)* taker-off *(Br.)*; ~**feuchte** soil moisture; ~**feuer** ground light, beacon; ~**fläche** acreage, *(Zimmer)* floor space; ~**freiheit** *(Auto)* clearance; ~**frost** ground frost; ~**früchte** fruits of the earth; ~**funkstelle** aeronautical station; ~**haftung** *(Auto)* road grip; ~**heizung** floor heating; ~**höhe** *(Haus)* ground level; ~**kammer** garret, attic; ~**klappe** trap door, *(Güterwagen)* drop bottom.

Bodenkredit mortgage loan, agricultural credit;
landwirtschaftliche ~**anstalt** mortgage bank, agricultural mortgage corporation limited *(Br.)*, federal land bank *(US)*; ~**bank** credit foncier; ~**institut** mortgage loan and investment company *(US)*, mortgage bank; ~**pfandbriefe** mortgage (real estate, land, *US*) bonds.

Bodenlandung alighting on earth.

bodenlos bottomless, fathomless, *(unerhört)* incredible, outrageous, indescribable;
~ **dumm** abysmally ignorant; ~**e Dummheit** crass stupidity; ~**e Frechheit (Unverschämtheit)** unbounded cheek; ~**e Gemeinheit** incredibly mean trick; ~**e Lügen verbreiten** to spread colossal lies; ~**e Tiefe** abyss, chasm; ~**e Ungerechtigkeit** outrageous injustice; ~**e Unwissenheit** utter ignorance.

Bodenlos, ins ~**e fallen** to go to the bottom;
die Kurse sind ins ~**e gesunken** the bottom has fallen out of the market.

Boden|-Luftrakete surface-to-air missile, ground-to-air missile; ~**luke** skylight, trapdoor; ~**mannschaft** ground crew; **mit** ~**markierungen versehen** to airmark; ~**nähe** *(Flugzeug)* flying (zero) altitude; ~**nebel** ground fog; ~**nutzung** cultivation, use of land, land use; ~**organisation** ground organization; ~**peilstelle** ground direction-finding station; ~**personal** *(Flugzeug)* ground staff (crew); ~**preis** price of land, land price; ~**probe** sample of the soil; ~**produkt** agricultural product, agricultural (farm) produce; ~**punkt** trigonometrical point; ~**rakete** land-based missile; ~**recht** land law; ~**rechtsreformgesetz** Law of Property Act *(Br.)*; ~**reform** agrarian (land) reform; ~**reformer** land reformer; ~**rente** ground rent; ~**satz der Arbeitslosen** hard core of the unemployed.

Bodenschätze natural (mineral) resources;
knappe ~ resource shortage; **unerschöpfliche** ~ inexhaustible resources;
~ **eines Landes ausbeuten** to exploit the natural resources of a country; ~ **nutzbar machen** to develop natural resources.

Boden|schätzung land appreciation; ~**schicht** layer; ~**senke** dip, downward slope, subsidence, depression; ~**spekulant** land jobber; ~**spekulation** land speculation, speculation in real estate *(US)*, real-estate venture *(US)*.

bodenständig native, permanent;
~**e Bevölkerung** autochthonous population; ~**es Brauchtum** local custom.

Boden|station *(Funk)* land station, *(mil.)* ground station; ~**strahl** direct ray; ~**streitkräfte** ground forces; ~**temperatur** soil temperature; ~**treppe** attic (garret) staircase; ~**truppen** ground troops; ~**untersuchung** exploration of the ground, soil analysis; ~**unterstützung** *(mil.)* close support; ~**verbände** ground troops; ~**verbesserung** [soil] improvement, improvement [of land], amelioration; ~**verhältnisse** ground conditions; ~**verkehr** property dealing, real-estate transactions; ~**verkehrsgenehmigung** permission to transact in real estate; ~**vermessung** surveying; ~**versetzung** displacement of the soil; ~**verteilung** distribution of land; ~**vorhersagekarte** surface forecast chart; ~**wärme** soil temperature; ~**welle** direct (earth) wave; ~**wert** land (site) value; ~**wetterkarte** surface map (chart); ~**zins** ground rent, land gabel; ~**zusammensetzung** composition of the soil.

Bodmerei bottomry, gross adventure;
~ **auf die Schiffsladung** respondentia loan;
auf ~ **geben** to lend (advance money on) on bottomry; **auf** ~ **nehmen** to take (borrow, raise) on bottomry;
~**brief** bottomry bond, bill of bottomry; ~**brief auf Schiff und Ladung** respondentia bond; ~**darlehen** maritime (marine) loan, bottomry money, gross adventure; ~**geber** lender on bottomry; ~**geld[er]** bottomry loan (money), loan on bottomry; ~**gläubiger** bottomry bondholders; ~**kredit** maritime loan; ~**kredit auf Schiff und Ladung** respondentia bond; ~**nehmer** borrower (taker) on bottomry; ~**prämie** bottomry interest, maritime profit; ~**schein** bottomry bond; ~**schuld** bottomry debt (loan); ~**schuldner** borrower (taker) on bottomry; ~**versicherung** bottomry insurance; ~**vertrag** bill of gross adventure, bottomry bond; ~**zins[en]** bottomry (marine, maritime) interest.

Böenfront squall front.

Bogen sheet, *(Kupon)* coupon sheet;
in Bausch und ~ wholesale, in the lump;
~ **Briefpapier** sheet of note paper; **neuer** ~ **Papier** fresh sheet of paper;
den ~ **bald herausbekommen** to learn the trick of it; **den** ~ **heraushaben** to have the knack of s. th.; **j. in hohem** ~ **hinauswerfen** to pitch s. o. out; ~ **machen** *(Straße)* to make a bend; ~ **um j. machen** to keep clear of s. o., to shun s. o.; **großen** ~ **um j. machen** to give s. o. a wide berth; ~ **überspannen** to carry things too far, to overdo it; **etw. in Bausch und** ~ **verkaufen** to sell s. th. wholesale (in the lump, in gross); ~ **eines Buches zusammentragen** to gather the pages of a book.

Bögen spucken, große to talk big, to draw the long bow.

Bogen|ableger layboy; ~**anschlag** bill posting; ~**anschlagsunternehmen** bill-posting agency, poster plant; ~**ausleger** fly; ~**erneuerung** renewal of coupon sheets; ~**fänger** taker-off *(Br.)*; ~**fenster** arched window; ~**format** sheet size; ~**licht** arc light; ~**zeichen** signature mark; ~**zirkel** bow (wing) compass.

Bohemien beatnik, Bohemian.

bohemienhafte Atmosphäre flavo(u)r of Bohemia.

Bohle plank;
mit ~**n belegen** to plank.

Bohlen|belag planking; ~**weg** plank way, boardwalk *(US)*.

böhmische Dörfer double-Dutch;
~ **für j. sein, jem. wie** ~ **vorkommen** to be all Dutch (Greek) to s. o.

Bohne bean;
nicht die ~ not a bit, not in the least; **nicht die** ~ **wert** not worth a fig;
blaue ~ pill *(mil., sl.)*;
nicht die ~ **davon verstehen** not to know the first thing about it.

Bohnenstange *(fig.)* bag of bones, thread paper.

Bohner|maschine floor polisher; ~**wachs** floor polish, polishing wax.

Bohr|anlage oil well; ~**apparat** portable drill, boring machine; ~**automat** automatiy boring machine.

bohren to bore, to drill;
Brunnen ~ to sink a well; **nach Öl** ~ to bore for oil; **Schiff in den Grund** ~ to send a ship to the bottom; **Tunnel** ~ to bore a tunnel; **in jds. Vergangenheit** ~ to dig into s. one's past; **nach Wasser** ~ to bore for water; **immer in der gleichen Wunde** ~ to have one's knife in s. o.

Bohrer borer, driller, bit.

Bohr|insel platform; ~**lizenz** exploration concession; ~**loch** *(Erdöl)* drill hole, wellhole, borehole; ~**löcher niederbringen** *(Bergbau)* to put down bore holes; ~**lochherstellung** well drilling; ~**maschine** boring machine, driller, drilling (perforating) machine; **elektrische** ~**maschine** power drill; ~**meißel** boring tool; ~**rechte** drilling rights; ~**schiff** drilling ship; ~**tätigkeit** exploration activity; ~**trupp** drilling team; ~**turm** oil rig, derrick of oil well.

Bohrung drilling;
fündige ~ productive drilling.

Bohr|versuch trial drilling; **auflösend bedingter** ~**vertrag** unless lease; ~**werkzeug** boring tool.

böig squally, gusty, bumpy.

Böigkeit bumpiness.

Boje, spitze conical buoy;
~**n auslegen** to put down buoys, to buoy; **an einer** ~ **festmachen** to make fast to a buoy; **an die** ~ **gehen** to pick up one's buoy; **durch** ~**n kennzeichnen** to buoy off; ~ **verankern** to put down a buoy.

Bojen|auslegung putting down a buoy; ~**legen** buoying; ~**system** buoyage.

Böllerschuß salute of guns.
Bollwerk stronghold, dike, dyke, bulwark, tower;
letztes ~ des Feindes last stronghold of the enemy; **~ der Freiheit** outpost of freedom.
Bolschewist Red, Bolshevik.
bolschewistisch bolshevist, red.
Bolzen bolt;
durchgehender ~ through bolt;
alle seine ~ verschossen haben to have nothing left to fall back on, to have shot one's last bolt.
Bombardement bombardment, bombing, shelling.
bombardieren to bombard, to bomb, to blitz, *(fig.)* to pepper;
j. mit Fragen ~ to put a rapid fire of questions on s. o., to pelt (bombard) s. o. with questions, to shoot questions at s. o.
Bombast fustian, bombast, pomposity.
bombastisch pompous, purple, tumid, mouth-filling;
~er Stil bombastic style.
Bombe bomb, *(Industrie)* oxygen bottle, gas cylinder, *(Schlager)* smash hit, wow *(sl.)*;
ferngesteuerte ~ razon bomb; **fliegende ~** flying bomb, doodle-bug; **selbstgesteuerte ~** robot bomb;
~ von 1000 Kilotonnen megaton bomb; **~n im Reihenwurf** stick of bombs; **~ mit Zeitzünder** time bomb; **~ für lebende Ziele** personnel bomb;
~n abwerfen to drop (release) bombs; **~n im Notfall abwerfen** to jettison one's bombs; **~n planlos abwerfen** to drop bombs at random; **mit ~n belegen** to bomb; **mit ~n und Granaten durchfallen** to be plucked *(Br.)*, to flunk in an examination *(US)*; **wie eine ~ einschlagen** to strike like a bombshell; **~ entschärfen** to defuse a bomb; **~ hochgehen lassen** to explode a bomb; **~n heimlich ins Flugzeug legen** to plant a bomb in an airplane; **Feind durch ~n aus seiner Stellung vertreiben** to bomb out the enemy;
die ~ ist geplatzt the balloon has gone up.
Bombenabwurf bomb dropping, bombing, bomb release;
gezielter ~ pinpoint bombing; **ungezielter ~** random bombing;
~ auf ein Flächenziel area bombing;
~gerät bomb-release gear; **~schacht** bomb bay.
Bomben|alarm bomb scare; **~anbringung in Gebäuden** property bombing; **~androhung** bomb threat; **~angriff** bombing raid; **~anschlag, ~attentat** bomb attack (outrage), bombing incident; **~auftrag** tall order; **~auslöser** bomb release.
bombenbeschädigt blitzed, bomb-damaged.
Bomben|beseitigung bomb clearance; **~besetzung** *(Film)* star cast; **~drohung** bomb threat; **~einschlag** bomb explosion (hit); **~entschärfer** bomb disposal expert; **~entschärfung** bomb disposal; **~entschärfungskommando** bomb squad; **~erfolg** huge success, smash hit *(sl.)*; **~erfolg sein** to go over big, to make a hit *(US)*; **~explosion** burst of a bomb, bomb explosion; **~fabrik** bomb factory.
bombenfest|machen *(mil.)* to blind;
das steht ~ it's a certainty, a sure thing.
Bomben|flächenwurf area bombing; **~flüchtling** evacuee; **~flug** bombing mission; **~flugzeug** bombing aeroplane, bomber, bomb plane; **~gehalt verdienen** to earn a packet of money; **~geld** big money.
bombengeschädigt bomb-damaged, blitzed.
Bomben|geschäft roaring (land-office, *US coll.*) business, gold mine; **~geschäfte machen** to drive a roaring trade; **~geschwader** bomber group (wing, *US*); **~krater** bomb crater; **~ladung** bomb load, *(für Reihenwurf)* stick; **~markierung** target indicator; **~neurose** shell-shock; **~punktzielwurf** precision (pin-point) bombing; **~räumtrupp** bomb-disposal squad; **~reihenwurf** pattern bombing; **~rolle** dream of a part; **~sache** stunner, smasher, raker *(sl.)*; **~schacht** bomb bay; **~schäden** air raid (bomb) damage; **~schütze** bomb-aimer, bombardier *(US)*.
bombensicher as sure as death (eggs is eggs), *(mil.)* bombproof;
~er Unterstand bombproof shelter, dugout.
Bomben|splitter bomb splinter; **~sprengkommando** bomb-disposal squad; **~stellung** dug-in job; **~stimmung** high jinks *(coll.)*, high spirits; **~teppich** bomb carpet; **mit einem ~teppich belegen** to pattern-bomb; **~teppichwurf** carpet bombing; **~tiefangriff** low-level bombing; **~träger** bomb carrier; **~treffer** bomb hit; **~trichter** bomb crater; **~visier** bomb sight; **~volltreffer** direct bomb hit; **~werfer** bomb thrower; **~ziel** target; **~zielanflug** run; **~zielvorrichtung** bomb-release gear.
Bomber|flotte, strategische strategic bomber force; **~geschwader** bomber group (wing, *US*); **~pilot** bomber pilot; **~staffel** bombardment (bomber) squadron; **~stützpunkt** bomber base; **feindlichen ~verband abfangen** to intercept the enemy's bombers.
bombig swell, smashing, stunning, fabulous.
Bon voucher, coupon, check, [club] chit, *(Gutschein)* credit slip.
Bonbon goody, sweet *(Br.)*, candy *(US)*;
~laden sweetshop *(Br.)*, candy store *(US)*.
Bonbonniere fancy sweet box, comfit box.
Bonbontüte bag of sweets *(Br.)* (candies, *US*).
Bonifikation compensation, allowance, *(Bankwesen)* rebate, commission, *(Wertpapier)* bonus;
jem. eine ~ von 15% gewähren to give s. o. a reduction of 15 per cent.
Bonifikations|abkommen bonus agreement; **~rückvergütung** commission rebate.
Bonität soundness, sound standing, solidity, credit solvency, credit standing (status), reliability, *(Grund und Boden)* grade of fertility, *(Warengüte)* superior quality.
Bonitäts|auskunft account solicitation service; **~liste** credit rating book *(US)*; **~prüfung** examination of soundness, credit rating *(US)*.
bonitieren to assess, to appraise, to classify.
Bonitierung valuation (assessment) of landed property.
Bonmot witticism, wisecrack.
Bonus bonus, premium, icing on the cake, *(Dividende)* additional (super, surplus, *US*) dividend, superdividend, plum *(US sl.)*;
größerer ~ melon *(US)*;
~ bei Schadensfreiheit *(Haftpflichtversicherung)* no-claim bonus *(Br.)*;
~system für Frühpensionierung job release scheme *(Br.)*; **nach einem ~system arbeiten** to work on a bonus system; **~zuteilung** bonus distribution.
Bonze bigwig, big shot (wheel, *US*), vip, tin god, boss, tycoon *(US)*.
Bonzentum bigwiggedness, boss rule *(US)*.
Boot boat, launch;
flaches ~ punt; **kleines ~** jolly boat, dinghy; **leichtes ~** walnut shell, light craft; **seetüchtiges ~** seagoing craft, seaworthy boat; **unsinkbares ~** compartment boat; **zusammenlegbares ~** collapsible boat;
~ mit voller Bemannung fully manned boat; **~ ohne Verdeck** open boat;
~ auspumpen to pump out a boat; **~ aussetzen** to launch (put out) a boat; **in einem ~ befördern** to boat; **~ zum Kentern bringen** to upset a boat; **~ fahren** to go boating; **~ herunterlassen** to lower a boat; **sich in die ~e retten** to take to the boats; **im selben (gleichen) ~ sitzen** *(fig.)* to row (be) in the same boat; **~ an Land ziehen** to pull a boat ashore.
Boots|ausrüstung boat equipment; **~ausstellung** boat show; **~bauer** boatbuilder; **~besitzer** boat owner; **~deck** boat deck; **~eigentümer** boat proprietor; **~fahren** boating; **~fahrerhotel** boatel; **~führer** boatman; **~haus** boathouse; **~industrie** boating industry; **~konstrukteur** boat-wright; **~körper** hull; **~ladung** boatloading; **~mann** waterman, boatman; **~mannspfeife** pipe; **~rennen** boat race; **~steg** landing stage; **~steuermann** coxswain; **~verkehr** boat traffic; **~verleih** boat hire; **~werft** boatyard.
Bord shelf, rack, stand, *(mar.)* board, *(Rand)* edge, border;
alle Mann an ~! all aboard!; **an ~** embarked, aboard, on board, shipboard, *(längsseits)* alongside; **an ~ gebracht und gestaut** free on board and trimmed; **frei [an] ~** delivered (free) on board, f.o.b.; **frei an ~ des Flugzeugs** free on aircraft; **frei ~ mittschiffs** free board amidships; **über ~** overboard;
an ~ bleiben to remain on-board ship; **an ~ bringen** to get aboard, to take on board; **Waren an ~ bringen** to deliver goods on board, to ship goods; **über ~ fallen** to go overboard; **an ~ gehen** to embark, to go (put) on board, to board (take) a ship; **über ~ gehen** to go overboard; **von ~ gehen** to leave the ship; **Fässer und Kisten an ~ hieven** to hoist casks and crates aboard; **frei an ~ zu liefern** to be delivered on board free of charge; **an ~ liegen** to lie alongside; **an ~ nehmen** to take shippings, to take on goods; **Passagiere an ~ nehmen** to ship passengers; **Waren an ~ nehmen** to take goods on board; **an ~ sein** to be on board; **über ~ spülen** to wash overboard; **an ~ verbringen** to place on board; **frei von ~ verkaufen** to sell free from board; **an ~ verladen** to ship on board; **über ~ gespült werden** to be washed overboard; **über ~ werfen** to dump overboard; **frühere Ansichten über ~ werfen** to discard old beliefs; **Ladung über ~ werfen** to jettison, to cargo; **Theorie über ~ werfen** to dismiss a theory; **alle Vorsicht über ~ werfen** to cast all prudence to the winds;
~aggregat marine set, *(Flugzeug)* airborne equipment; **~anlage** airborne equipment; **~antenne** ship's aerial, *(Flugzeug)* aircraft aerial; **~apotheke** medicine chest; **~aufklärer** shipboard

reconnaissance plane; ~**bescheinigung** mate's receipt; ~-**Boden** *(Flugabwehr)* air-ground; ~-**Boden Funkverkehr** air-to-ground radio; ~**buch** log, logbook, ship's journal, *(Flugzeug)* pilot's (flight) log; ~**dienst** *(Verkehrsflugzeug)* catering service.

Bordell brothel, disorderly (bawdy) house, whorehouse, house of ill fame, panel house *(US)*, case (sporting) house *(sl.)*, parlo(u)r house *(sl.)*;
~ **betreiben** to keep a disorderly house;
~**besitzer** keeper of a bawdy house; ~**viertel** red-light district, licensed quarter.

Bordempfangsschein board (mate's) receipt.

Bordereau memorandum, delivery note;
~**verzeichnis** bill of specie, specification.

Bord|fest ship's party; ~**flugzeug** carrier-borne (ship-borne) aircraft, shipplane; ~**funk** ship's radio, *(Flugzeug)* aircraft radio; ~**funkanlage** ship's wireless, *(Flugzeug)* airborne radio system; ~**funker** wireless operator; ~**funkgerät** aircraft radio; ~**funkstelle** wireless room; ~**gepäck** cabin luggage *(Br.)* (baggage, *US*); ~**geräte** *(Flugzeug)* flight instruments; ~**handbuch** flight manual; **nach** ~**instrumenten fliegen** to fly on instruments; ~**kanone** aircraft cannon; ~**kante** curb, kerb *(Br.)*; ~**karte** boarding pass (card), flight coupon; ~**kino** ship's cinema (theater, *US*); ~**konnossement** ship's bill, on-board (shipped) bill of lading; ~**küche** galley, pantry; ~**landefackel** landing flare; ~**linie** water line; ~**mechaniker**, ~**monteur** air mechanic, flight engineer; ~**papiere** ship's papers, *(Flugzeug)* plane's papers; ~**peilgerät** airborne direction finder; ~**personal** crew, *(Flugzeug)* flying personnel; ~**planken** planking, sheathing; ~**radargerät** Mickey; ~**rakete** airborne rocket; ~**scheinwerfer** landing lamp; ~**schütze** air gunner; ~**schwelle** kerb *(Br.)*, curb[stone] *(US)*; ~**seite** ship's side, side of a ship; ~**sender** airborne transmitter; ~**sprechanlage** intercommunication system, intercom *(coll.)*, interphone; ~**station** radio station, *(Flugzeug)* aircraft radio room; ~**stein** kerbstone *(Br.)*, curbstone *(US)*; ~**steward** cabin attendant; ~**telefon** intercom *(coll.)*; ~**uhr** chronometer.

Bordüre trimmings, braiding, *(drucktechn.)* ornamental border.

Bord|verpflegung flight rations; ~**wache** watch on deck; ~**waffen** aircraft armament; **mit** ~**waffen angreifen** to strafe; ~**waffenbeschuß** strafing; ~**wagen** *(Eisenbahn)* open goods wag(g)on, gondola car *(US)*; ~**wand** board, side of a ship; ~**wart** flight mechanic; ~**zeitung** ship's newspaper; ~**zentrale** central station; ~**zulage** hard-lying money *(Br.)*.

Borg *(fam.)* trust, tick *(Br.)*;
auf ~ **kaufen** to buy on tick *(Br.)* (on credit, on cuff, *US*); **auf** ~ **leben** to live on borrowed money (tick, *Br.*); **auf** ~ **nehmen** to take on credit.

Borgen borrowing;
~ **macht Sorgen** he who goes a-borrowing goes a-sorrowing.

borgen *(entleihen)* to borrow, *(verleihen)* to loan out, to lend, to [grant] credit, to loan *(US)*, to trust, *(vorschießen)* to advance; **erneut** ~ to reborrow; **fremde Gedanken** ~ to crib on the works of others; **auf Gefälligkeitswechsel** ~ to fly a kite *(Br.)*.

Borger borrower, *(Kreditgeber)* lender.

Born spring, well, fount, fountain;
unerschöpflicher ~ **der Weisheit** inexhaustible fountain of wisdom;
aus dem ~ **seiner Erfahrungen schöpfen** to draw on the fund of one's experiences.

borniert small-minded, narrow-minded, pigheaded;
~**e Ansichten** limited outlook.

Borniertheit small-mindedness, dense ignorance, narrow-mindedness, stupidity.

Börse [stock] exchange, [stock] market, *(Portemonnaie)* purse, [money] bag, leather;
an der ~ on the exchange, in the money market; **an der** ~ **[gehandelt]** obtainable on the market, [quoted] on the exchange, in the money market; **an der** ~ **zugelassen** quoted (listed, *US*) on the stock exchange; **auf der** ~ on change *(Br.)*; **auf der heutigen** ~ at today's market; **von** ~ **zu** ~ **gehandelt** interbourse;
abgeschwächte ~ down (sagging) market; **staatlich anerkannte** ~ recognized stock exchange; **angespannte** ~ stringent stock market; **beschränkt aufnahmefähige** ~ limited market; **wegen spekulativer Aufträge nicht mehr aufnahmefähige** ~ overbought market *(US)*; **bei fallenden Kursen nicht mehr aufnahmefähige** ~ oversold market *(US)*; **nicht sehr aufnahmefähige** ~ soft market, long market *(US)*; **bewegte** ~ disturbed market; **stürmisch bewegte** ~ greatly agitated market; **federführende** ~ leading stock exchange; **feste** ~ firm (strong, steady, buoyant, undepressed) market; **flaue** ~ dull exchange, stale (depressed, sick, *US*) market, dull stock market; **freundliche** ~ easy (cheerful) market; **gedrückte** ~ depressed (heavy) market; **äußerst gedrückte** ~ demoralized market; **[wohl]gefüllte** ~ well-lined purse; **inoffizielle** ~ curb (kerb, *Br.*) market, unofficial market; **lebhafte** ~ brisk (cheerful, active) market; **Londoner** ~ London Stock Exchange, The House *(Br.)*; **lustlose** ~ dull (dead, flat) market; **uneinheitliche und lustlose** ~ sick market *(US)*; **matte** ~ stagnant (lifeless) market; **New Yorker** ~ Consolidated Exchange, Big Board *(US)*; **Pariser** ~ Bourse; **empfindlich reagierende** ~ sensitive market; **regionale** ~ provincial *(US)* (local, *US*) stock exchange, out-of-town market *(US)*; **ruhige** ~ featureless market; **schwache** ~ weak (sagging) market; **auf umfangreiche Glattstellungen hin schwache** ~ liquidating market; **stagnierende** ~ depressed state of the market, stagnant market; **steigende** ~ buoyant market; **tonangebende** ~ leading (standard) market; **überregionale** ~ national security exchange; **umsatzlose** ~ flat (inactive) market; **fast umsatzlose** ~ nominal market; **unbelebte** ~ dull market; **wohlgespickte** ~ heavy (long, well-lined) purse;
~ **mit ausreichenden Umsätzen** liquid market;
Zulassung zur ~ **beantragen** to apply for official quotation *(Br.)*; **Zulassung neuer Stammaktien an der** ~ **beantragen** to make application to the council of the stock exchange for permission to deal in new ordinary shares; ~ **beeinflussen** to have an effect on the market; ~ **durch Konzertzeichnungen beeinflussen** to stag the market; ~ **beruhigen** to calm the market; ~ **besuchen** to attend the exchange; **an der** ~ **einführen (notieren)** to quote (list, *US*) on the stock exchange; **Verluste an der** ~ **erleiden** to meet with losses on the stock market; ~ **faszinieren** to mesmerize the market; **sich von der** ~ **fernhalten** to remain shy of the stock market; **der** ~ **Auftrieb geben** to give a fillip to the market; **auf die** ~ **gehen** to visit the stock exchange; **an der** ~ **sein** to be on the stock exchange; **zum Handel an der** ~ **zugelassen sein** to be accepted for trading (admitted for quotation, be listed, *US*) on the stock exchange; **an der** ~ **spekulieren** to gamble (operate) on the exchange, to play the stock market *(US)*, to dabble in stocks; **an der** ~ **steigen** to jump on the stock exchange; ~ **stützen** to peg the market; **an der** ~ **verkaufen** to sell on the stock exchange; **auf der** ~ **erörtert werden** to be rumo(u)red on the Street *(sl.)*; **an der** ~ **gehandelt werden** to be dealt in (quoted) on the stock exchange; **an der** ~ **notiert werden** to be quoted (listed, *US*) on the stock exchange; **auf der** ~ **für zahlungsunfähig erklärt werden** to be hammered on the exchange; **an der** ~ **zur amtlichen Notierung zulassen** to quote (list, *US*) on the stock exchange; **sich von der** ~ **zurückziehen** to waddle out of the alley *(Br., sl.)*.

Börsen|abkürzung stock-exchange (tape, ticker, *US*) abbreviation; ~**abrechnung** stock-exchange settlement; ~**abrechnungsstelle** stock-exchange clearing office; ~**abrechnungszettel** broker's ticket; ~**abschlüsse** transactions at the stock exchange, stock-exchange transactions; **tatsächlich getätigte** ~**abschlüsse** business done; ~**abschlußeinheit** regular (full, *US*) lot; ~**abteilung** bond trading department; ~**agent** stock-exchange broker; ~**aktivität** trading activity.

börsenamtlich under the rules.

Börsen|anfang opening of the market; ~**angestellter** stock-market worker; ~**anmeldung** application for quotation (listing, *US*) at the stock exchange; ~**anmeldung von Wertpapieren** registration of securities; ~**aufsicht** supervision of the stock exchange; ~**aufsichtsbehörde** Council of the Stock Exchange *(Br.)*, Securities and Exchange Commission *(US)*; **den Bestimmungen der** ~**aufsichtsbehörde genügen** to comply fully with the state security laws.

Börsenauftrag stock-exchange order;
sofort ausführbarer ~ immediate order; **für einen Monat geltender** ~ monthly order *(US)*; **nur einen Tag gültiger** ~ day order; **limitierter** ~ good order, limit[ed] order *(US)*, stop order; **unlimitierter** ~ unlimited (market, *US*) order;
~ **auf Wochenfrist** week order *(US)*;
limitierten ~ **geben** to stop a stock-exchange order.

Börsen|aufträge für den gleichzeitigen Kauf und Verkauf eines Wertpapiers matched orders; ~**auftragsnehmer** registered representative *(US)*; **erster** ~**auftritt** market debut; ~**ausdruck** stock-exchange committee (term); ~**ausschuß** stock-exchange committee; ~**barometer** market barometer; **bei** ~**beginn** at the opening, when the market opens; ~**bericht** stock-exchange news (account, report), market news, review of the market, exchange advice, market comment, official quotations, *(Zeitung)* city article, [money] market report; ~**berichterstatter** financial journalist; ~**bestimmungen für die Einführung von**

Wertpapieren listing requirements *(US)*; ~**besuch** attendance on the stock exchange; **vom ~besuch ausgeschlossen werden** to be excluded from membership of the stock exchange; ~**besucher** visitor of the stock exchange, *(Mitglied)* member of the stock exchange, stock-exchange member; ~**beurteilung** stock market judgment; ~**bewegung ohne bestimmte Gesamttendenz** sideways movement; ~**bewertung** bourse valuation; ~**blatt** financial paper, commercial newspaper, stock-exchange gazette, *(einer Zeitung)* financial section; ~**blatt für den Buchhandel** stationers' company gazette; ~**brauch** stock-exchange custom; ~**brief** market letter *(US)*; ~**coup** deal on the stock exchange, good speculation; ~**darlehn** *(an Makler)* stock-exchange loan; ~**diener** waiter *(Br.)*; ~**dilettant** dabbler on the stock exchange, market dabbler; ~**durchschnittswerte übertreffen** to outrun the market average; ~**effekten** securities admitted to the stock exchange, quoted (listed, *US*) securities; ~**einführung** stock market flotation, public offerings, admittance to (listing on, *US*) the stock exchange, introduction on the exchange *(Br.)*, stock-exchange introduction *(Br.)*; **bei der Börsenzulassungsstelle offizielle ~einführung beantragen** to make an application to the Council of the Stock Exchange to be admitted to the official list; **Antrag auf ~einführung stellen** to apply for admission on the stock exchange; ~**einführungsgebühr** stock-exchange admittance fee; ~**einführungskomitee** Secretary of the stock and loan department of the stock exchange *(Br.)*, Committee on stock list *(US)*; **nicht genehmigter ~einführungsprospekt** red-herring prospectus *(US)*; ~**engagement** stock-exchange commitment *(US)*; ~**entwicklung** tendencies of the stock market, stock-market trend; **Voraussage der ~entwicklung** stock-market prediction; **großer ~erfolg sein** to shoot up in the stock market; **überdurchschnittliche ~ergebnisse zeitigen** to out-perform the market; ~**erholung** recovery of the stock market; ~**eröffnung** opening of the market; ~**fachmann** stock-market observer, trading specialist.

börsenfähig admitted to (negotiable, quoted) on the stock exchange, on exchange, listed *(US)*, qualified to list *(US)*, on the board *(US)*;
nicht ~ unsalable, unlisted *(US)*;
~ **sein** to constitute a good delivery;
~**e Aktien** stock negotiable on the stock exchange, quoted (listed, *US*) stocks.

Börsen|fähigkeit negotiability; ~**feiertag** stock-exchange holiday; ~**fernschreiber** ticker, tape machine, quotation (stock) ticker *(US)*; ~**fernschreiberdienst** ticker service *(US)*; ~**flaute** dull stock market, dullness in the stock market; ~**freiverkehr** unofficial market *(Br.)*, curb (kerb, *Br.*, over-the-counter, *US*) market.

börsengängig [quoted] on exchange, listed on the stock exchange *(US)*, marketable;
~ **sein** to constitute a good delivery;
~**e Dividendenwerte** marketable equities; ~**e Effekten (Wertpapiere)** stock-exchange (listed, *US*) securities, marketable securities, quoted securities; ~**e Wertpapiere zum Anschaffungskurs** *(Bilanz)* quoted investment at cost.

Börsen|gebäude Exchange, *(London)* The Royal Exchange; ~**gebühren** dealing costs; **kurzfristiges ~geld** stock-exchange loan; **langfristiges ~geld** time money; **täglich fälliges ~geld** call money; ~**genehmigung** permission to deal on a stock exchange, stock-exchange approval; ~**gepflogenheiten** stock-exchange practices; ~**gerücht** market (stock-exchange) rumo(u)r.

Börsengeschäft [stock-]exchange business, stock (market) transaction, bargain;
~**e** operations on the stock exchange, stock [-exchange] operations, stock-exchange dealings (contracts), stock transactions;
abgeschlossenes ~ round transaction; **doppelte ~e** matched sales;
~ **mit Effekten** stock-exchange contract; ~ **zu verschiedenen Kursen** split transaction;
~**e machen** to deal on the stock exchange.

Börsen|geschehen stock-market activities, stock-exchange business; ~**gewinn** stock-market gain; **spekulationssteuerpflichtige ~gewinne** short-term capital gains; **ständig zunehmender ~gewinn** pyramid; ~**gewinne ausschütten** to distribute trading profits; ~**gläubiger** stock-exchange creditor; ~**halle** [board] room, exchange hall, floor; ~**handel** jobbing, stock-exchange dealings, stock transactions, stock brokerage (trading); ~**handel auf eigene Rechnung** on-floor trading *(US)*; **zum ~handel zulassen** to admit for quotation (list, *US*) on the stock exchange; ~**händler** stock[-exchange] operator, jobber; **zugelassener ~händler** floor trader *(US)*; ~**händlersystem** jobber system; ~**hausse** bull (bullish) market, market boom; ~**index** stock-exchange index, stock-price average; ~**information** stock-exchange news; ~**jahrbuch** Stock Exchange Year Book *(Br.)*; ~**jargon** stock-exchange slang; ~**jobber** stock-jobber; ~**journalist** financial journalist; ~**klima** tone (mood) of the market; ~**kollaps** stock-market collapse; ~**kommentar** financial commentary; ~**kommissar** exchange commissary; ~**kommission** stock-exchange committee.

Börsenkommissions|firma commission broker; ~**geschäft** stock-broking [transaction], stockbrokerage, broker's business, cross trade *(US)*, *(Auftrag)* stock transaction for third account, *(Firma)* [firm of] stockbrokers, ticker firm *(US)*.

Börsen|konsortium price ring, corner, pool, market syndicate; **beschränktes ~konto** restricted account; ~**krach** collapse of the market, crash, panic; **kurzfristiger ~kredit** stock-exchange loan; ~**kreise** financial (stock-exchange) circles; ~**krise** crisis in the stock market.

Börsenkurs [stock-exchange] quotation, quotation on the stock market, rate of exchange, market rate (price), exchange (city, share) price;
zum ~ at the present quotation, at the market *(US)*;
heute erzielte ~e rates obtained at today's market; **gestützte ~e** pegged market *(US)*; **letzter** ~ final quotation; **notierter** ~ quoted price; **sinkende ~e** stock market decline (slide);
~**e ungehindert fallenlassen** to put the market into a free fall; ~**e hochtreiben** to bull the market; **zum ~ kaufen** to buy at the price quoted; ~ **notieren** to quote a price; ~**e stützen** to peg (rescue) the market; **zum ~ verkaufen** to sell at the market *(US)*;
~**beobachter** tape watcher; **amtliches ~blatt** official (stock, *US*) list, stock-market report *(US)*; ~**schwankungen** fluctuations in the stock market [prices]; ~**wert** quoted value; ~**wiedergabegerät** desk-top terminal, stockmaster; ~**zettel** list of [market] quotations, market report, stock list.

Börsen|lage stock-market situation, condition on the stock exchange; ~**literatur** stock-market literature.

Börsenmakler [stock-]exchange broker, insider *(Br.)*, jobber, floor (specialist) broker *(US)*, ticker firm *(US)*, [stock]broker;
freier ~ **[einer Kapitalsammelstelle]** exempted dealer; **auf eigene Rechnung spekulierender (selbständiger)** ~ floor trader, floor broker *(US)*, room trader *(US)*; **unreeller** ~ bucketeer *(US)*; **zahlungsunfähiger** ~ declared defaulter; **zugelassener** ~ authorized clerk;
~**firma** commission house, ticker firm *(US)*; ~**geschäft** stockbroking; ~**verband** association of stock and share dealers, National Association of Securities Dealers *(US)*.

Börsen|manipulation manipulation on the stock exchange, market rigging; ~**mann** stockjobber.

Börsenmanöver stock-exchange manoeuvre, campaign, stock-jobbery, stockjobbing, rigging [the market], rig *(Br.)*, demonstration *(US)*, shaking out *(US)*;
~ **der Baissepartei** gunning for stocks *(US)*;
~ **durchführen** to wash sales of stock *(US)*; **viel Geld durch geschickte ~ verdienen** to make a lot of money by clever manipulations on the stock market.

börsenmäßig according to usance, under the rules;
~ **handelbar** negotiable on the stock exchange;
~ **gehandelte Buchwerte** inscribed stock *(Br.)*.

Börsenmitglied member of the stock exchange, exchange (floor) member;
auf eigene Rechnung spekulierendes ~ floor (room, *US*) trader;
zahlungsunfähiges ~ declared defaulter;
~ **der New Yorker Börse** specialist *(US)*;
~**schaft** stock-exchange seat.

Börsen|nachrichten financial (stock-exchange, business, city) news, stock-exchange intelligence *(Br.)*; ~**name** *(Wertpapier)* stock-exchange (nick) name.

börsennotiert quoted (listed, *US*) on the stock exchange;
~**e Werte** stock-exchange securities.

Börsennotierung market (exchange) quotation;
~**en** city prices;
amtliche ~ official list (quotation); **automatische ~en** automatic quotation service; **letzte** ~ last price; **zweite** ~ second call;
Aktien von der ~ absetzen to remove shares from the stock-exchange list *(Br.)*; ~ **aussetzen** to suspend a quotation; **zur ~ zulassen** to admit for quotation on the stock exchange, to quote (list, *US*) on the stock exchange.

Börsenorder [stock-exchange] order;
~ **gegen die Interessen des Auftraggebers ausführen** to sell out against a client.

Börsen|ordnung stock-exchange regulation, rules of the stock exchange; **~organe** stock-exchange authorities; **~panik** panic; **~papiere** stocks *(Br.)*, securities admitted to the stock exchange, listed securities *(US)*, stock exchange certificates *(US)*; **~papiere künstlich in die Höhe treiben** to balloon securities (stocks) *(US)*; **~platz** exchange center *(US)* (centre, *Br.*); **~preis** market rate, exchange price, House price *(Br.)*; **~preis haben** to be quoted (listed, *US*) on the stock exchange; **~prospekt** prospectus; **~prospekt herausgeben (lancieren)** to issue a prospectus; **~publikum** visitors of the stock exchange; **~reaktion** stock-market reaction; **~reform** reorganization of the stock exchange; **~register** official list; **~saal** [board] room, exchange hall, floor; **kleiner ~saal** garage *(US)*; **~scheingeschäft** matched sales, wash transactions *(US)*, washing *(US)*; **~scheinverkauf** wash sale *(US)*, washing *(US)*; **~schiedsgericht** stock arbitration.

Börsenschluß closing of the exchange, final hour of trading, *(Abschlußeinheit)* trading unit, full lot (board, *US*);
bei ~ when the market closes; **nach ~** after official hours, [done] in the street, street *(Br.)*;
gebrochener ~ *(weniger als 100 Aktien oder weniger als 1000 Obligationen)* odd lot *(US)*; **voller ~** even (full) lot;
bei ~ höher notieren to close dearer; **bei ~ 2 sh höher stehen** to close 2-up;
~kurs closing quotation.

Börsen|schwankungen exchange fluctuations, fluctuating market; **~schwindel** stockjobbery; **~schwindler** stock-exchange venturer, stag; **~sitz** [exchange] seat; **seinen ~sitz aufgeben** to drop one's exchange seat; **~sitzung** session; **schwerwiegender ~skandal** grave scandal on the stock exchange; **~spekulant** speculator, gambler, bargain hunter, stockjobber, stag, punter, operator; **unerfahrener ~spekulant** flunkey *(US)*; **~spekulation** stockjobbing, jobbery, gambling (speculation) on the [stock] exchange; **kurzfristige ~spekulationen durchführen** to be in and out of the market *(US)*; **~spiel** premium hunting, agiotage; **~spieler** manipulator, gambler; **~sprache** stock-exchange terminology, stock-exchange parlance *(sl.)*; **~stand** [trading] post, *(Weizenbörse)* pitch; **~stempel** stamp duty; **~stimmung** tone (mood) of the market, stock-market sentiment; **zuversichtliche ~stimmung** confident state of the market; **~strategie** stock-market tactics; **~strömung** tendency on the stock exchange, stock-market trend; **~stunden** official (stock-exchange) hours; **~sturz** market break; **~tag** trading (ticket, market) day, session.

börsentechnisch bedingt customary on the stock exchange.

Börsen|teil *(Zeitung)* city (commercial) news; **~telegraf** ticker, stock ticker (indicator, printer); **~tendenz** trend on the stock market, stock-market trend, tendencies of the market; **~terminauftrag auf Wochenfrist** week order; **~termingeschäft** option, trading in futures *(US)*, forward operation, futures deal *(US)*, transaction for the account *(Br.)*; **~terminologie** stock-market parlance; **~ticker** tape, ticker *(US)*; **~tickerabkürzungen** tape (ticker, *US*) abbreviations; **~tickernotierungen** tape (ticker, *US*) quotations; **~tiefstpunkt** bottom of the market; **~tip** stock tip, hint; **~tipgeber** tipster; **~titel** stock-exchange securities; **~transaktion** operation on the stock exchange, market transaction; **vollständig durchgeführte ~transaktion** turn *(US)*.

börsenübliche Stückzahl marketable parcels.

Börsenumsatz stockmarket turnover.

Börsenumsätze transactions at the stock exchange, stock-exchange transactions, trading;
bedeutende ~ important dealings; **mäßige ~** few dealings; **schwache ~** light trading.

Börsenumsatz|liste contract sheet; **~steuer** stock (securities, *US*) transfer tax, stock-exchange tax.

börsenumsatzsteuerfrei free of stamp.

Börsen|usancen stock usages (custom), market terms, stock-exchange practices; **~verein der Buchhändler** Stationers' Company *(Br.)*; **unsichere ~verhältnisse** unsettled state of the market; **~verlust** stock-market loss; **~versionen** stock-exchange rumo(u)rs; **~vertreter** stock-exchange agent, boardman; **~vertretung** market agency; **~viertel** the street, *(London)* square mile; **~vollmacht** stock power; **~vorschriften** stock-exchange rules; **~vorstand** stock-exchange committee, committee of the stock exchange, Council of the Stock Exchange *(Br.)*, Governing Committee of the Stock Exchange *(US)*; **~vorstand der Londoner Börse** Committee for General Purposes *(Br.)*; **~vorstand der New Yorker Börse** governing committee of the New York stock exchange *(US)*; **~wahrheit** market truth.

Börsenwert [stock-]exchange (market) value;
~e stock-exchange (quoted, listed, *US*) securities;
führende ~e market performers, leaders, representative stocks *(US)*.

Börsen|zeit trading (stock-exchange, official) hours; **~zeitung** financial paper, gazette *(Br.)*; **~zettel** stock-exchange list, list of [market] quotations, the list, Stock Exchange Daily Official List *(Br.)*; **~zulassung** admission to (listing on, *US*) the stock exchange, stock-exchange introduction, permission to deal on the stock exchange, stock-exchange approval; **~zulassung beantragen** to apply to the stock exchange for permission to deal, to qualify with the US Securities and Exchange Commission *(US)*.

Börsenzulassungs|antrag application to the stock exchange for permission to deal; **~ausschuß** commission of (council to, *Br.*) the stock exchange, quotations committee *(London)*; **~bescheid** official listing notice; **~prospekt** prospectus; **~stelle** committee on stock list *(US)*.

Börsenzusammenbruch stock-market crash, stock-market collapse, collapse of the market.

Börsianer [stock-exchange] operator, stag;
geprellter ~ fleece *(sl.)*; **gerissener ~** wolf.

Borte trimming, braiding.

bösartig vicious, malicious, iniquitous, ill-natured, ugly *(US coll.)*;
~en Charakter haben to be of a nasty nature; **~e Geschwulst** malignant tumor; **~e Krankheit** nasty illness, virulent disease; **~e Kritik** vicious criticism.

Bösartigkeit ill nature, malignity, viciousness.

Böschung slope, ramp, *(Bahn)* embankment, *(Fluß)* bank;
natürliche ~ slope of the ground;
~ mit Steinen verpacken to pitch a slope.

Böschungs|arbeiten embanking; **~mauer** revetment, revetment wall.

Böse evil, ill;
im ~n oder im Guten by fair means or foul;
jem. ~s antun to inflict an injury to (on) s. o.; **~s im Schilde führen (im Sinn haben)** to be bent on (get up to) mischief, to be up to no good; **nichts ~s im Sinn haben** to mean no harm; **jem. ~s nachreden** to speak ill of s. o., to run s. o. down; **nichts ~s darin sehen** to see no harm in s. th.; **das ~ vom Guten trennen** to know good from evil; **jem. ~s tun** to do s. o. harm; **~s mit Gutem vergelten** to return good for evil; **nichts ~s vorhaben** to intend no harm; **jem. nichts ~s wünschen** to wish s. o. no harm.

böse bad, foul, ill, perverse, *(wütend)* angry, annoyed, cross, offended;
~ aussehen to look bad; **j. ~ machen** to make s. o. angry; **jem. ~ mitspielen** to treat s. o. shabbily; **~ mit jem. sein** to be angry (cross, at outs, *US*) with s. o.;
in ~r Absicht with malice aforethought; **überall ~ Absichten vermuten** to look for an evil intention in everything; **~ Angelegenheit** nasty business; **~s Blut machen** to create ill feeling; **~n Einfluß ausüben** to have a pernicious influence; **~s Ende nehmen** to come to a bad end; **~ Erkältung haben** to have a bad cold; **~r Finger** sore finger; **in ~ Gesellschaft geraten** to get into bad company; **~ Gewohnheit** pernicious habit; **~r Glaube** bad faith; **~r kleiner Junge** naughty little boy; **~r Mensch** a bad lot (hat), wicked person; **~ Nachrichten** bad news, evil tidings; **gute Miene zum ~n Spiel machen** to put a good face on the matter, to make the best of a bad job; **jem. einen ~n Streich spielen** to do s. o. an ill turn, to play a nasty trick on s. o.; **in guten und ~n Tagen** through good and evil; **~r Traum** unpleasant dream, nightmare; **~ Vorahnungen haben** to have evil forebodings; **~s Wetter** nasty weather; **~ Zunge** evil tongue.

Bösewicht villain, scoundrel, rascal.

bösgläubig in bad faith, mala fide, fraudulent, dolose;
~er Besitzer holder in bad faith; **~er Erwerber** purchaser in bad faith.

Bösgläubigkeit bad faith, mala fides.

boshaft wicked, malicious;
~e Bemerkung spiteful remark; **~er Streich** shabby trick.

Boshaftigkeit wicked will.

Bosheit wicked will, wickedness, spitefulness;
aus reiner ~ out of pure mischief (malice).

Boß abgeben to be top dog, to boss it *(US)*, to run the show *(sl.)*.

böswillig fraudulent, dolose, wilful and malicious;
~ verlassen to desert one's wife;
in ~er Absicht with malice prepense; **~es Verlassen** wilful (obstinate) desertion, malicious abandonment; **~e Verleumdung** malevolent defamation.

Böswilligkeit malevolence, maliciousness, *(Schuldner)* malice.

Bote messenger, runner, delivery man, carrier, emissary, caddie, *(Hotel)* commissionaire *(Br.)*, *(Kurier)* messenger, express *(Br.)*, courier;
durch ~n by hand; **durch ~n abgegeben** delivered by hand; **beflügelter ~** wing-footed messenger; **flinker ~** expeditious messenger;
~n abfangen to intercept a messenger; **~n entsenden** to dispatch a messenger; **Brief durch ~n schicken** to send a letter by hand; **von einem ~n überbracht werden** to be delivered by hand.

Boten | dienst messenger service; **~dienste tun (versehen)** to run errands, to carry messages; **~gang** errand; **~gang erledigen** to discharge an errand; **~gänge für jem. erledigen** to deliver messages for s. o., to go (run) [on] errands for s. o.; **~gänger** errand goer, messenger, runner; **~inkassi** collection by hand, walk collections *(Br.)*, route items *(US)*; **~junge** messenger (delivery) boy; **~lohn** messenger's (bearer's) fee; **~zustellung** special delivery *(US)*, express delivery *(Br.)*.

Botin female messenger, womanpost.

Botmäßigkeit dominion, sway;
j. unter seine ~ bringen to bring s. o. under one's sway.

Botschaft message, word, post, mission, *(dipl.)* Embassy;
frohe ~ glad tidings, good news;
~ des Präsidenten presidential message *(US)*;
~ aufheben to close an embassy; **~ ausrichten** to deliver a message in cipher (cypher); **~ errichten** to create (establish) an embassy; **~ überbringen** to carry (present) a message; **jem. eine ~ übergeben** to give s. o. a message to deliver; **~ übermitteln** to transmit a message.

Botschafter ambassador;
in seiner Eigenschaft als ~ in his character of ambassador; **in Gegenwart des ~s** the ambassador will be pesent;
außerordentlicher ~ extraordinary ambassador; **außerordentlicher und bevollmächtigter ~** ambassador plenipotentiary; **fliegender ~** roving ambassador; **gemeinsamer ~** joint ambassador;
~-Stellvertreter ambassador's deputy; **~ guten Willens** goodwill ambassador;
j. als ~ entsenden to delegate s. o. as ambassador; **zum ~ ernannt werden** to be appointed ambassador; **~ zurückbeordern** to recall an ambassador to report;
~amt embassy; **auf ~ebene** on ambassador level; **~konferenz** ambassadorial conference, conference of ambassadors; **~lenkungsausschuß** Ambassadorial Group; **~posten** ambassadorial post, ambassadorship; **im ~rang** on ambassador level; **~stellvertreter** ambassador's deputy.

Botschafts | angehöriger embassy official; **~attaché** embassy attaché; **~fahrzeug** embassy car; **~gebäude** embassy building; **~gelände** embassy grounds; **~parkplatz** embassy car park; **~personal** embassy staff; **~rat** counsel(l)or of embassy, embassy counselor, diplomatic counsellor *(Br.)*; **~rat erster Klasse** counsel(l)or of embassy *(Br.)*, diplomatic counsellor *(Br.)*; **~sekretär** secretary of an embassy; **~sprecher** embassy spokesman.

Bottich tub.

Bottle Party shake, rent party.

Boulevard boulevard;
~blatt penny magazine *(Br.)*, tabloid *(US)*, yellow paper *(US)*; **~journalismus** claptrap journalism; **~presse** popular (tabloid, *US*) papers, penny *(Br.)* (gutter) press; **~restaurant** pavement café; **~zeitungen** the cheaper press, penny *(Br.)* (yellow, *US*) press; **volkstümlich aufgemachte nach rechts tendierende ~zeitung** popular right-wing tabloid *(US)*.

Bouquet flavo(u)r.

Boutique boutique.

Box *(Autorennen)* pit, *(Garage)* box, lockup *(Br.)*, *(Fotoapparat)* box camera, *(Tier)* stall.

Boxkampf, öffentlicher prize fight.

Boykott boycott;
durch besondere Anpreisung eigener Erzeugnisse durchgeführter ~ positive boycott; **mittelbarer ~** secondary boycott; **zwangsweise ausgeübter mittelbarer ~** compound boycott; **ökonomischer ~** economic boycott; **unmittelbarer ~** primary boycott;
~ durch Veröffentlichung einer schwarzen Liste negative boycott;
~ aufheben to call off a boycott; **~ über ein Hotel verhängen** to declare a hotel black;
~anwendung boycottage; **~druck** boycott pressure; **~durchführung** boycottism; **~feldzug** boycott campaign; **~forderungen** boycott demands; **~hetze** stirring up to boycott.

boykottieren to boycott, to black;
gesellschaftlich ~ to send to Coventry, to ostracize; **Laden ~** to put a shop under a boycott.

Boykottierer boycotter.

Boykottierung boycott, boycotting, blacking.

Boykott | liste black (stop) list, unfair list *(US)*; **sich der zentralgeleiteten ~politik anschließen** to toe the central boycott line; **~streik** secondary strike; **~unterstützung** boycott assistance; **~verbotsgesetzgebung** antiboycott legislation; **~ware** black *(Br., coll.)*.

Brachacker, Brache fallow [land].

Brachernte fallow crop.

Brachezeit fallowing season, *(Maschine)* down time, *(Zeitstudie)* idle time.

Brachfeld naked field.

Brachialgewalt, mit by brute force;
mit ~ angehen to go at it hammer and tongs.

Brachland fallow, waste land;
~ kultivieren to improve waste land.

brachliegen to lie idle (waste, dead upon one's hands), *(Feld)* to lie fallow, to vegetate;
~lassen to waste.

brachliegend unemployed, unused, dead-lying, [lying] idle, dormant, wasted, unemployed, unused, *(Feld)* fallow, *(Kapital)* idle, uninvested;
~e Gelder idle funds.

Brachliegenlassen noncultivation.

Branche branch [of industry], business line, line of business, line of commerce, trade, walk, department, lay *(sl.)*;
zukunftsträchtige ~ growth industry;
in einer ~ arbeiten to engage in a line of business; **in eine andere ~ hinüberwechseln** to cross over into a new industry; **in seiner ~ führend sein** to be leading in its line of business; **in einer ~ tätig sein** to engage (be employed) in a line of business, to deal in a line; **~ wechseln** to change over to a different line; **in der ~ anerkannt werden** to develop an influential position in the market.

Branchenadreßbuch classified (mercantile, trade, professional, commercial) directory.

branchenbedingt branch-conditioned.

Branchen | begabung, organisatorische line-organizing ability; **~bevollmächtigter** walking delegate; **~brauch** trade custom.

branchenerfahren well-up (versed) in a trade.

Branchenerfahrung experience (versedness) in trade.

branchenfremd inexperienced in a trade.

Branchen | fremdling poacher; **~handelsspanne** product line margin (markup), departmental markup; **~kenntnisse** experience in a business line, tricks of the trade; **~konjunktur** particular business trend.

branchenkundig well-up in a trade;
~ sein to be well versed in a trade.

branchenmäßig durchsetzen, sich to develop an influential position in the market.

Branchen | netz network of branches; **~tätigkeit** line activity; **~überziehungskredit** encashment credit.

branchenüblich customary.

Branchen | untersuchung investigation of a particular industry; **im ~vergleich** on a sectoral comparison; **~verzeichnis** trade (classified) directory, yellow pages *(Br.)*; **~werbung** trade advertising.

Brand fire, blaze;
bei ~ in case of fire; **in ~** burning, on fire;
ausgedehnter ~ conflagration, widespread fire; **um sich greifender ~** spreading fire; **verheerender ~** devastating fire;
~ eindämmen to localize a fire; **in ~ geraten** to catch fire; **~ löschen** to extinguish a fire; **seinen ~ löschen** to quench one's thirst; **~ schüren** to poke a fire; **in ~ stecken (setzen)** to fire, to set on fire; **in ~ stehen** to be on fire; **Land mit ~ verwüsten** to waste a country with fire and sword; **von einem ~ heimgesucht werden** to be ravaged by a fire; **durch ~ völlig zerstört werden** to burn down to the ground;
~bekämpfung fire fighting.

brandbeschädigt fire-damaged, damaged by fire.

Brand | beschädigung damage by fire; **~blase** blister; **~bombe** fire bomb, incendiary bomb; **~brief** *(fam.)* dunning letter; **~direktor** fire chief (marshal, *US*); **~eisen** branding iron.

branden to break, to surge, *(Verkehr)* to roar.

brandende See foaming sea.

Brand | fackel torch; **~flasche** Molotov cocktail; **~gasse** narrow lane; **~gefahr** fire risk; **~geruch** smell of burning; **~glocke** fire bell (alarm), tocsin; **~graben** fire lane; **~herd** seat of fire;

~**kasse** [etwa] board of fire underwriters, fire insurance office (fund) *(Br.)*; ~**kassenbeitrag** fire protection tax; ~**katastrophe** conflagration; ~**legung** arson, fire-raising *(Scot.)*; ~**mal** stigma, *(Vieh)* mark.
brandmarken to mark with a hot iron, *(fig.)* to denounce, to stigmatize;
gesellschaftlich ~ to ostracize, to send to Coventry.
Brandmarkung denouncement, stigmatization;
gesellschaftliche ~ ostracism.
Brand | material incendiary material; ~**mauer** fire (party) wall, common wall, fire[-proof] partition; ~**meister** fire inspector; ~**narbe** burn mark.
brandneu brand-new, spanking new *(sl.)*.
Brand | opfer burnt offering; ~**risiko** fire hazard (risk); ~**rolle** *(Schiffe)* fire bill; ~**satz** *(mil.)* incendiary composition; ~**schaden** loss by fire, fire damage, damage caused by fire; ~**schaden haben** to have suffered from fire.
brandschatzen to pillage, to plunder, to sack, to ravage;
Land ~ to lay a country under a contribution.
Brandschatzung pillage, plunder, ravage;
Land ~**en aussetzen** to put a country to fire and sword.
Brand | schätzer fire adjuster; ~**schneise** fire lane, firebreak; ~**schott** fireproof bulkhead; ~**schutz** fire protection; ~**stelle** scene of fire.
brandstiften to set (raise) fire.
Brandstifter incendiarist, arsonist, fire raiser *(Scot.)*, firebug *(US coll.)*, torch, firebug *(US coll.)*.
brandstifterisch incendiary.
Brandstiftung house-burning, fire-raising *(Scot.)*, incendiarism, arson;
einfache ~ simple arson;
~**stiftung begehen** to raise fire, to commit arson.
Brandstiftungstrieb pyromania.
Brandung surf, surge, breach, wash, breakers;
~ **des Verkehrs** roar of the traffic.
Brandungs | boot surf boat; ~**risiko** surf risk; ~**welle** breaker.
Brand | ursache source of fire; ~**verhütung** precautions against fire, fire prevention; ~**verhütungsdienst** fire-protection organization; ~**versicherung** fire insurance.
Brandversicherungs | gesellschaft fire insurance company; ~**police** fire policy *(Br.)*; ~**regulierung** fire insurance loss adjustment.
Brand | wache fire watch (warden, *US*), *(Forst)* fireguard; ~**wunde** burn.
Branntwein brandy, liquor, [distilled] spirits;
~**ausschank** sale of liquor; ~**brenner** distiller; ~**brennerei** distillery; ~**monopol** spirits (alcohol) monopoly; ~**schmuggel** bootlegging; ~**steuer** tax on liquors.
Braten, ein fetter a fat morsel;
~ **riechen** to smell the rat; **jem. den** ~ **versalzen** to spike s. one's guns.
braten to roast;
auf dem Rost ~ to grill; **in der Sonne** ~ to sunbathe, to bathe in the sun.
Bratrost gridiron, *(im Freien)* barbecue [grill].
Brauch custom, usage, use, observance, practice, routine, consuetude;
allgemeiner ~ general (common) usage; **althergebrachter** ~ time-hono(u)red (long) custom; **anerkannter** ~ convention; **eingefügter** ~ established custom; **entgegenstehender** ~ practice to the contrary; **örtlicher** ~ local usage; **ständiger** ~ established usage; **uralter** ~ immemorial usage;
~ **seit Menschengedenken** immemorial usage;
alten ~ **beibehalten** to retain an old custom.
brauchbar practical, practicable, useful, utilizable, serviceable, fit for use, *(Kleidungsstück)* wearable, *(Verfahren)* workable; ~**er Plan** plan that works; ~**e Vorschläge machen** to make useful suggestions.
Brauchbarkeit usefulness, use, serviceability;
praktische ~ practicability, feasibility.
Bräuche, frühere former customs;
alten ~**n anhängen** to keep up old customs, to be attached to old customs; **alte** ~ **aufgeben** to depart from old customs.
brauchen to use, to make use of, *(benötigen)* to require, to need, to want;
viel Benzin ~ to be heavy on fuel; **etw. dringend** ~ to want s. th. badly, to be in dire need of s. th.; **viel Geld** ~ to spend a lot of money; **vier Stunden** ~ to take four hours.
Brauchtum custom, folklore;
sein ~ **pflegen** to foster one's traditions.
Brauchwasser industrial water.
Brauerei | aktien breweries, brewery industry; ~**betrieb** brewery; ~**gerechtigkeit** brewing privilege; ~**gewerbe** brewing industry (business), the brewing interest; ~**wagen** beer truck; ~**werte** breweries, brewery stock *(US)*; ~**wirtschaft** brewing industry.
Braunkohle brown (soft) coal, lignite.
Braunkohlenbergbau brown (soft) coal mining.
Braut bride, fiancée;
~ **zuführen** to give away the bride;
~**ausstattung** bridal outfit, trousseau; ~**aussteuerversicherung** endowment insurance; ~**gemach** nuptial chamber; ~**geschenke** wedding presents, shower *(US)*.
Bräutigam bridegroom.
Braut | jungfer bridesmaid; ~**kleid** wedding dress; ~**leute** engaged couple; ~**paar** engaged couple; **auf die** ~**schau gehen** to go in quest of a wife.
Bravorufe cheers;
mit ~**n begrüßen** to cheer.
Bravourstück master stroke, stunt.
Brechen *(Wellen)* breach;
zum ~ **voll** crammed, crowded to capacity;
~ **eines Gesetzes** breach (transgression, violation) of a law;
auf Biegen oder ~ **zu erreichen versuchen** to try it by hook or crook;
es geht auf Biegen oder ~ neck or nothing.
brechen *(Gesetz)* to break, to transgress, *(Vertrag)* to break, to infringe, to violate, to infract *(US)*;
Bahn ~ to blaze a trail; **Blockade** ~ to run the blockade; **Damm** ~ to damage (breach) a dike; **Ehe** ~ to commit adultery; **jem. das Genick** ~ to break s. one's neck; **Gesetz** ~ to violate (infringe, break) a law; **mit einer Gewohnheit** ~ to break with a habit; **einer Flasche Wein den Hals** ~ to crack a bottle; **Sache übers Knie** ~ to rush into an affair; **Ladung** ~ to break bulk; **Lanze für j.** ~ to take up the cudgels for s. o., to go to bat for s. o. *(US)*; **mit seinem früheren Leben** ~ to break away from one's old life; **durch die feindlichen Linien** ~ to break through the enemy's lines; **Loch in die Mauer** ~ to make a hole in a wall; **Rekord** ~ to beat a record; **jem. das Rückgrat** ~ to break s. one's back; **sein Schweigen** ~ to break one's silence; **Stab über j.** ~ to condemn s. o. utterly; **Streik** ~ to break a strike; **mit der Tradition** ~ to break with tradition; **Vertrag** ~ to break (violate) a contract; **jds. Widerstand** ~ to break s. one's resistance; **sein Wort** ~ to break one's word; **Krieg vom Zaun** ~ to unleash a war; **Streit vom Zaun** ~ to trigger a strike;
nichts zu ~ **und zu beißen haben** not to have a crust to eat.
brechend voll jammed;
~ **sein** to be crowded to capacity.
Brecher water break, breaker;
~**linie** landwash.
Brech | koks unbroken (crushed) coke; ~**stange** lever; ~**walzwerk** crusher, crushing mill.
Brei, wie die Katze um den heißen ~ **herumgehen (um den heißen** ~ **herumreden)** to beat about the bush; **jem. zu** ~ **schlagen** to beat s. o. to a pulp.
breit broad, wide, *(drucktechn.)* extended;
~ **fundiert** broad-based; ~ **gestreut** diversified;
etw. weit und ~ **erklären** to explain s. th. at great length; ~**er machen** to widen; **weit und** ~ **bekannt sein** to be known all over the place;
~**en Buckel haben** to have a broad back; ~**e Darstellung** long-winded description; **Untersuchung auf** ~**er Grundlage durchführen** to make a broadly-based investigation; **die** ~**e Masse des Volkes** the general public; ~**es Publikum** large public; ~**es Publikum anlocken** to draw a large audience; ~**e Schichten der Bevölkerung** large sections of the population; ~**e Straße** wide road.
Breitband *(Film)* wide angle, *(Rundfunk)* broad band, *(Stahlwerk)* broad strip;
~**film** wide screen.
Breite breadth, width;
~ **der geäußerten Ansichten** diversity of opinions;
etw. der ~ **nach ausmessen** to measure s. th. breadthwise; **etw. in epischer** ~ **erzählen** to adopt an epic style; **in die** ~ **gehen** to fill out, to put on weight.
Breitengrad degree of latitude;
südlicher ~ south latitude.
Breitenkreis circle of latitude, parallel of latitude.
breitgefächertes Unternehmen diversified corporation.
breitlaufend *(Druck)* expanded.
Breitleinwand wide screen.
breit | machen, sich to spread o. s.; **j.** ~**schlagen** to talk s. o. into doing s. th.

Breit|seite *(Schiff)* broadside; **volle ~seite** *(mil.)* weight of weight; **~spur** *(Eisenbahn)* broad gauge, wide track.
breit|spurig broad-gauged; **etw. ~treten** to dwell on s. th., to labo(u)r a point.
Breitwagenmaschine long-carriage typewriter.
Breitwand|film wide-screen film; **~kino** wide-screen movie; **~-verfahren** wide-screen process.
Brems|abteil *(Bahn)* brake van *(Br.)*; **~anlagen** braking devices; **~backe** brake shoe; **~band** brake band; **~belag** brake lining; **~belag erneuern** to reline the brakes; **~belastung** brakeload; **plötzliche ~betätigung** jamming on a brake; **~block** brake block.
Bremse brake[s];
defekte ~n faulty (defective) brakes; **ausreichend funktionierende ~n** good and sufficient brakes; **selbstwirkende ~** power brake;
~ anziehen (betätigen) to operate (apply, pull up, put on) the brakes; **~ neu belegen** to reline the brakes; **~ lösen** to take off the brakes; **~ nachstellen** to adjust the brakes; **auf die ~ treten** to put on the brakes; **kräftig auf die ~ treten** to shove on the brakes.
Bremsen braking, *(fig.)* curb, restraint.
bremsen to apply (operate) the brake, to put on the brakes, to brake, *(Konjunktur)* to curb, to check;
Entwicklung ~ to slow down the development; **Fortschritt ~** to act as a brake upon progress; **mit voller Kraft ~** to jam on the brakes; **plötzlich ~** to brake suddenly; **jds. Tätigkeitsdrang ~** to restrain s. one's activities, to act as a brake on s. one's activities; **jds. Übermut ~** to curb s. one's exuberance.
Bremser brakesman, brakeman *(US)*, shack *(sl.)*.
Brems|fallschirm brake parachute, tail chute; **~flüssigkeit** brake fluid; **~flüssigkeitspegel** brake-fluid level; **~futter** facing of a brake; **~hebel** brake lever; **~leistung** brake horsepower; **~licht** brake (stop) light; **plötzliches ~manöver** emergency braking situation; **~pedal** brake pedal; **~rakete** retro-rocket; **~spur** skid marks; **~spuren hinterlassen** to leave a strip *(sl.)*; **~strecke, ~weg** stopping (braking) distance; **doppeltes ~system** dual braking; **~vorrichtung** *(Rad)* lock; **~weg** stopping distance.
brennbar combustible, inflammable, burnable;
nicht ~ uninflammable.
brennen to burn, to be on fire, to take fire, to be in flames, *(Porzellan)* to sinter, to fire, *(Sonne)* to be scorching, *(Straßenlampen)* to be lit;
jem. unter den Füßen ~ to be getting too hot for s. o.; **Gas ~** to use gas; **gut ~** *(Pfeife)* to smoke nicely; **Kohlen ~** to char (burn) coal; **lichterloh ~** to be ablaze; **nicht ~** *(Gas)* to be out; **jem. eins auf den Pelz ~** to singe s. one's hide; **Schnaps ~** to distil(l) alcohol; **unruhig ~** to flicker; **Vieh ~** to mark cattle; **Ziegel ~** to bake bricks; **wie Zunder ~** to burn like tinder;
zu ~ anfangen to catch fire; **darauf ~ etw. zu tun** to be all agog to do s. th.
Brenndauer *(Glühbirne)* lighting hours, *(Rakete)* period of combustion.
brennend *(Problem)* on the nail;
gut ~ quick; **~ heiß** roasting hot *(coll.)*;
es ~ nötig haben to be in dire need of s. th.; **~ interessiert sein** to be keenly interested; **etw. ~ wünschen** to burn with desire;
~er Durst parching thirst; **~e Frage** urgent (burning, pressing) question; **hell ~e Lampe** bright light; **~e Stadt** burning town; **~er Wunsch** fervent desire.
Brenner *(Alkohol)* distiller, *(Gasherd)* burner.
Brennerei distillery, still.
Brenn|gas combustible (fuel) gas; **~gemisch** mixture; **~herd** hearth.
Brennholz firewood, wood;
sich mit ~ eindecken to wood, to supply with wood;
~gerechtigkeit estovers; **~zuteilung** allotment of estovers.
Brenn|kammer firebox; **~material** firing fuel; **~ofen** hearth, tile kiln, tiler; **~öl** fuel oil.
Brennpunkt focus, nodal (focal) point;
~ der Ereignisse focal point of events; **~ des Interesses** focus of attention; **~e des Verkehrs** converging points of traffic;
in den ~ rücken to bring into focus.
Brennschluß *(Rakete)* burnout;
~ haben to burn out.
Brennspiegel concave mirror.
Brennstoff motor fuel, petrol *(Br.)*, gasoline *(US)*;
fester ~ solid fuel; **klopffester ~** antiknock fuel;
~ erneuern to refuel; **nicht mehr genug ~ haben** to be low on fuel; **viel (wenig) ~ verbrauchen** to be high (low) on fuel economy;
~aufnahme refuelling; **~bedarf** fuel requirements; **abwerfbarer ~behälter** slip fuel tank; **~düse** fuel nozzle; **~einsatz** fuel insert; **~ersparnis** fuel economy (saving); **~industrie** fuel industry (economy); **~knappheit** fuel shortage; **~kosten** fuel costs; **~krise** fuel crisis; **~lager** fuel yard (depot, dump); **~luftgemisch** gas-air mixture; **~rechnung** fuel bill; **~reserve** fuel reserve; **~technik** fuel engineering; **~verbrauch** fuel consumption; **~versorgung** supply of fuel, fuel supply (allocation); **~vorräte** fuel reserve; **~zufuhr** delivery of fuel; **~zuleitung** fuel feed.
Brennweite focal distance.
brenzlich smelling (tasting) of burning;
~e Angelegenheit matter of touch-and-go, precarious situation; **~er Geruch** smell of burn.
Bresche opening, *(mil.)* breach, gap;
~ in die feindlichen Linien schlagen to make a breach in the enemy's line; **für j. in die ~ springen** to help s. o. out of a tight corner.
Brett board, plank, deal, *(Regal)* shelf;
auf den ~ern, die die Welt bedeuten on the stage;
Schwarzes ~ notice *(Br.)* (bulletin, *US*) board, newsboard *(Br.)*; **verleimtes ~** glued board;
am Schwarzen ~ anschlagen to put up on the board; **~er aufklaftern** to pile up planks; **mit ~ern belegen** to plank, to floor; **~er erobern** to make a career on the stage; **100 mal über die ~er gehen** *(Theaterstück)* to have 100 performances; **ein ~ vor dem Kopf haben** to be slow in the uptake; **bei jem. einen Stein im ~ haben** to be in s. one's good books; **j. auf die ~er schicken** to knock s. o. down; **mit ~ern vernagelt sein** to be boarded up; **Waren mit ~ern vernageln** to crate goods.
Bretter|boden plank floor; **~bude** shack, shanty, shed, *(Markt)* stall, stand, booth; **morsche ~bude** decrepit shack; **~fußboden** boarded (plank) floor; **~gerüst** scaffolding; **~kiste** crate; **~verkleidung** plank revetment; **~verschlag** board partition, *(Warenkiste)* crate; **durch eine ~wand sehen können** to be able to see through a deal board (brick wall); **~zaun** hoarding, board fence *(US)*.
Brief letter, note, *(Börse)* paper, asked [price], sellers only, on offer;
~ angeboten *(Börse)* mainly sellers; **auf Ihren ~ bezugnehmend** referring to your letter; **~ folgt** letter to follow (following); **gehandelt und ~** sellers ahead; **in Beantwortung Ihres ~es** in reply to your letter; **in Besitz Ihres ~es** in receipt of your letter; **mit ~en überschwemmt** deluged with letters; **unter ~ und Siegel** under my hand and seal; **vorwiegend ~** *(Börse)* sellers over;
~e correspondence;
nicht abgeholter ~ unclaimed letter; **schlecht adressierter ~** blind letter, blind *(sl.)*; **anonymer ~** anonymous letter, poison-pen letter; **zu spät aufgegebener ~** late letter; **ausgleichender ~** adjustment letter; **auslaufender ~** outgoing letter (mail); **mit der Post beförderter ~** posted letter; **beiliegender ~** enclosed letter; **beleidigender ~** libellous letter; **fürs Ausland bestimmter ~** foreign (overseas) letter; **blauer ~** mittimus; **doppelter ~** double letter; **eigenhändiger ~** autograph letter; **eigentlicher ~** body of a letter; **einfacher ~** single-rate letter; **eingeschriebener ~** registered letter; **gut formulierter ~** well worded letter; **frankierter ~** [post]-paid (prepaid, stamped) letter; **ungenügend frankierter ~** short-paid letter; **unsere früheren ~e** our previous communications; **geharnischter ~** strongly worded letter; **gereizter ~** waspish letter; **geschäftlicher ~** business letter; **geschlossener ~** closed letter; **höflich geschriebener ~** letter written with courtesy; **die zwischen uns gewechselten ~e** letters that have passed between us; **gewöhnlicher ~** unregistered letter; **höflicher ~** polite letter; **Ihr ~ vom ...** your favo(u)r of ...; **kurzer ~** short letter, note, a few lines; **offener ~** open (published) letter; **persönlicher ~** personal (private) letter; **portofreier ~** letter exempt from postage, frank; **postlagernder ~** letter to be called for, caller's (post-office box) letter, poste restante; **privater ~** private letter; **unbefriedigender ~** unsatisfying letter; **unbehobener ~** unclaimed letter; **unbestellbarer ~** dead (blind) letter; **undatierter ~** letter of no date, undated letter; **unfrankierter ~** unpaid letter; **versiegelter ~** sealed letter; **vertraulicher ~** confidential (personal) letter; **vervielfältigte ~e** process letters; **vorhergehende ~e** previous letters; **vorliegender ~** letter in hand; **vorrangig zugestellte ~e** first-class letter post; **zurückgesandter ~** returned letter; **aus ausgeschnittenen Buchstaben zusammengesetzter ~** cut-out letter;
~ und Geld *(Börse)* sellers and buyers *(Br.)*, asked and bid; **mehr ~ als Geld** more buyers than sellers, buyer's market; **~ wegen Nichteinlösung eines Schecks** *(Bank)* reference slip; **~ und Siegel** sign and seal; **~ mit Wertangabe** insured letter *(Br.)*;

~ **abfangen** to intercept a letter; ~ **abheften** to file a letter away; ~ **abholen** to call for a letter; **seine ~e von der Post abholen** to collect (fetch) one's letters from the post office; ~**e alphabetisch ablegen** to file letters in alphabetical order; ~ **abschließen** to bring a letter to a close; ~ **wirkungsvoll abschließen** to round off a letter; ~ **absenden** to send off (dispatch) a letter; ~ **an j. adressieren** to cover a letter to s. o.; **alte ~e aufbewahren** to keep old letters; ~ **aufgeben** to post (dispatch, mail, *US*) a letter; ~ **stenografisch aufnehmen** to take down a letter; ~ **aufreißen** to break open a letter; ~ **aufsetzen** to draw up (build) a letter; ~ **ausfindig machen** to trace (track down) a letter; ~ **aushändigen** to hand s. o. a letter; ~**e aussortieren** to sort out letters; ~**e austauschen** to exchange letters, to correspond; ~ **austragen** to deliver a letter; ~ **beantworten** to answer to (reply, respond) a letter; ~ **beginnen** to head a letter; **j. mit einem ~ belästigen** to trouble s. o. with a letter; ~ **bestätigen** to acknowledge [receipt of] a letter, to confirm a letter; ~ **zur Post bringen** to take a letter to the post office; ~ **datieren** to date a letter; ~**e einordnen** to sort out letters; ~**e einsammeln** to collect the letters; ~ **einwerfen** to post a letter, to drop a letter into the mail box *(US)* (pillar box, *Br.*); ~ **vor Leerung der Briefkästen einwerfen** to catch the post; **einem ~ entnehmen** to understand from a letter; ~ **erhalten** to receive a letter; ~ **für unzustellbar erklären** to dead a letter; **Menge ~e erledigen** to do a lot of correspondence; ~ **expedieren** to get a letter off; ~ **fehlleiten** to misdirect a letter; ~ **freimachen (frankieren)** to pay the postage; ~ **zur Post geben** to take a letter to the post *(Br.)*, to post (mail, *US*) a letter; **jem. ~ und Siegel auf etw. geben** to give s. o. one's word, to assure s. o. of s. th.; **viele ~e zu erledigen haben** to have large correspondence; **aus einem ~ herauslesen** to read into a letter; ~ **auf der Schreibmaschine herunterrasseln** to run off a letter on the typewriter; ~ **herunterschreiben** to knock out a letter *(sl.)*; ~ **hinhauen** to scribble a letter; ~ **als persönlich kennzeichnen** to make a letter private; **seinem ~ einen Zahlungsbefehl folgen lassen** to follow up a letter with a summons; ~ **durch Boten überbringen lassen** to send a letter by hand; **in einen ~umschlag legen** to put a letter in an envelope; ~ **nicht in allen Einzelheiten mitbekommen** to lose a letter in detail; ~**e nachsenden** to forward letters to a new address; ~ **öffnen** to unseal a letter; ~ **unberechtigt öffnen** to break the seal of a letter; ~**e ordnen** to sort out letters; ~**e postieren** to take letters to the post, to post (mail, *US*) letters; ~ **an j. richten** to direct a letter to s. o.; ~ **an jds. Büroadresse schicken** to direct a letter to s. one's business address; ~ **als Eilbrief schicken** to express a letter; ~ **per Luftpost schicken** to send a letter by airmail; **jem. einen ~ schreiben** to write a letter to s. o.; **jem. einen beleidigenden ~ schreiben** to write s. o. a stinker; **jem. einen energischen ~ schreiben** to write in strong terms to s. o.; ~ **mit drei Durchschlägen schreiben** to make three carbon copies of a letter; ~ **in ansprechender Form schreiben** to give a letter an attractive look; ~ **mit verstellter Handschrift schreiben** to write a letter in a disguised hand; **sehr ausführlichen ~ nach Hause schreiben** to write a long epistle home; ~ **des Inhalts schreiben** to write a letter to the effect; **selten ~e schreiben** to be a bad correspondent; ~**e sortieren** to sort letters; **sich auf einen ~ stützen** to take one's stand on a letter; ~ **unterschlagen** to suppress a letter; ~ **verschließen** to seal a letter; ~ **vordatieren** to date a letter ahead; ~**e wechseln** to correspond; **mit ~en überschüttet werden** to be flooded with letters; ~ **zustellen** to deliver a letter;

~**abfertigung** postal delivery, dispatch of mail *(US)*, mail distribution *(US)*; ~**abholfach** letter box, post-office box, private box; ~**abholung** collection of letters; ~**ablage** letter file, filing of letters; **formeller ~abschluß** formal close; ~**abschrift** copy; ~**änderungen** changes in a letter; ~**anfang** opening of a letter; ~**annahme[stelle]** *(Post)* receiving counter, mail drop *(US)*; ~**- und Paketannahmestelle** receiving house; ~**anordnung** layout of a letter; ~**anschrift** postal address; ~**antwort** answer to a letter; ~**aufgabe** letter posting, posting (mailing, *US*) a letter; ~**aufgabe per Einschreiben** registration of a letter; ~**aufgabestempel** date stamp, postmark; ~**aufschneider** paper knife; ~**aufschrift** address of a letter; ~**ausgabe** postal delivery, delivery of letter; ~**ausgang** outgoing mail; ~**ausgangsbuch** letters dispatched book *(Br.)*; ~**beantwortung** answer to a letter; ~**beförderung** carriage of letters; ~**beilage** enclosure; ~**beileger** envelope stiffener; ~**beschwerer** letterweight, paperweight; ~**bestellung** mail order; ~**beutel** letter bag, mailbag; ~**block** [writing] pad; ~**bogen** note paper, sheet of paper; ~**bombe** letter bomb; ~**bote** letter messenger (carrier, *US*), postman *(Br.)*, mailman *(US)*; ~**boykott** mail boycott.

Briefchen short note;
~ **Streichhölzer** book of matches.

Brief|datum date of a letter; ~**drucksache** second-class letter, circular letter, surface printed papers *(Br.)*; ~**durchschlag behalten** to keep a copy of a letter; ~**eingang** incoming letters; ~**eingangsbuch** letters received book *(Br.)*; ~**einlauf** letters received; ~**einwurf** letter (pillar, *Br.*) box, *(Postamt)* mailbox *(US)*, letter drop; ~**empfang bestätigen** to acknowledge [the receipt of] a letter; ~**entwurf** draft [of a] letter; ~**fach** pigeonhole, post-office box; ~**faltmaschine** letter-folding machine; ~**form** style of a letter; **in ~form** by letter; ~**format** size of a letter; ~**frankiermaschine** franking machine; ~**freund** pen friend; ~**gebühr** postage (postal) rate; ~**geheimnis** secrecy of correspondence; ~**geheimnis verletzen** to break the secrecy of a letter; ~**grundschuld** [etwa] unregistered land charge *(Br.)*; ~**hülle** envelope, cover, wrapper; ~**hülle mit Breitbandklappe** open side; ~**hülle mit Schmalbandklappe** open end; ~**hypothek** [etwa] unregistered mortgage *(Br.)*; ~**inhalt** content (body) of a letter; ~**inhalt verstehen** to make out the meaning of a letter; ~**karte** letter *(Br.)* (folding, postal) card, correspondence card; ~**kassette** writing case.

Briefkasten letter box, drop box *(US)*, mailbox *(US)*, postbox *(Br.)*, post *(Br.)*, pillar box *(Br.)*, *(Vorschlagswesen)* suggestion box, *(Zeitung)* personal column;
toter ~ *(Spionage)* dead-letter box;
~ **leeren** to clear the letter box, to collect the mail *(US)*; **Brief in den ~ stecken** to drop a letter into the postbox (pillar box) *(Br.)*;
~**ecke** question and answer column; ~**firma** tramp (dummy, *US*) corporation, bubble company *(Br.)*, bogus company; ~**leerung** postal collection, collection (clearance) of letters; **sonntägliche ~leerung** Sunday collection; ~**system** *(Spionagewesen)* letter-box system.

Brief|klammer paper clip; ~**klappe** flap of an envelope; ~**kontrolle** censorship of the mail; ~**kopf** letterhead, notepaper heading, head of a letter, *(links oben)* corner card; ~**kopie** [carbon] copy; ~**kopie behalten** to keep a copy of a letter; ~**kopierbuch** letter book; ~**kopierpresse** letterpress, copying press; ~**korb** desk tray.

Briefkurs *(Börse)* asked price (rate, quotation), selling rate, offer (selling) price;
Geld und ~e closing bid and asked prices;
~ **für ausländische Valuta** posted rate *(US)*.

Briefkuvert envelope, cover, wrapper.

Briefleit|stelle letter-directing place; ~**verfahren** letter-directing scheme.

brieflich in writing, by letter (mail, *US*);
~ **bestätigen** to confirm by letter; ~ **überweisen** to remit by mail *(US)*; ~ **verkehren** to correspond;
~**e Anfrage** letter of inquiry; ~ **versandter Fragebogen** mail questionnaire *(US)*; ~**e Überweisung** letter remittance; ~**er Verkehr** correspondence, exchange of letters.

Briefmappe portfolio, writing case.

Briefmarke [postage] stamp;
aufgeklebte ~ affixed stamp; **eingedruckte ~** impressed stamp; **entwertete ~** defaced (cancelled) stamp; **falsche ~** bogus stamp; **gummierte ~** adhesive *(US)*; **nachgemachte ~** imitation stamp; **postfrische ~** mint stamp; **ungültige ~** spoilt stamp; ~**n in perforierten Bogen** coil stamps;
~ **aufkleben** to stick on (affix) a stamp; ~**n ausgeben** to issue stamps; ~**n einkleben** to mount stamps; ~**n am Tag der Ausgabe erwerben (kaufen)** to buy new stamps on the day of issue; ~**n sammeln** to collect stamps; **ausländische ~n tauschen** to swap foreign stamps.

Briefmarken|abtastvorrichtung stamp detection unit; ~**album** stamp album; ~**auktion** stamp auction; ~**ausgabe** issue of stamps; ~**ausstellung** exhibition of stamps; ~**automat** stamp-dispensing machine; ~**block** block of stamps; ~**entwertung** cancellation of stamps; ~**fälschung** imitation of stamps; ~**geschäft** stamp dealer; ~**handel** stamp dealing; ~**händler** stamp dealer; ~**hausse** stamp boom; ~**heft** book of stamps, stamp booklet; ~**katalog** stamp catalog(ue); ~**papier** stamp paper; ~**sammeln** stamp collecting; ~**sammler** stamp collector; ~**sammlung** collection of postage stamps, stamp collection; ~**serie** issue of stamps; ~**sonderausgabe** special stamp issue; ~**stempel** postage stamp, postmark; ~**versteigerung** stamp auction; ~**währung** postal currency.

Brief|muster form (model) letter; ~**notierung** *(Börse)* asked quotations; ~**öffner** envelope opener, letter opener; ~**öffnungsmaschine** letter cutter (opening machine); ~**ordner** letter file; ~**packen** pile of letters.

Briefpapier note (letter, writing) paper, stationery;
Bogen ~ sheet of note-paper; **dünnes** ~ light-weight stationery; **feines** ~ Bath paper (post); **geprägtes** ~ embossed note-paper; **hochwertiges** ~ bond paper;
~ **im Gewicht von 5 1/2 bis 10 Pfund per Ries** bank post; ~ **für Luftpostsendungen** airmail paper, onionskin; ~ **mit Trauerrand** mourning paper; ~ **mit dazupassenden Umschlägen** note-paper and envelopes to match;
~**kassette** fancy-boxed stationery.
Brief|partner correspondent; ~**porto** postage, letter rate *(Br.)*; **normales** ~**porto** penny post; **mit die niedrigsten** ~**portotarife in Europa besitzen** to maintain one's letter prices among the cheapest in Europe.
Briefpost letter post *(Br.)*, first mail *(US)*, mail matter *(US)*; **gewöhnliche (normale)** ~ penny post, surface letters *(Br.)*, first-class mail *(US)*; ~ **und Paketpost** postal matter;
beim Öffnen der ~ **anwesend sein** to superintend the opening of the letters;
~**sendungen** first-class matter *(US)*, surface mail *(Br.)*.
Brief|prospekt circular; ~**sammelstelle** letter-collecting place, mail distribution center *(US)*; ~**sammlung veröffentlichen** to edit a collection of letters; ~**schaften** correspondence, letters, papers; ~**schluß** end of a letter; ~**schreiber** letter writer, writer of a letter; **unzuverlässiger** ~**schreiber** remiss correspondent.
Briefschulden arrears of (outstanding) correspondence;
~ **aufarbeiten** to work off arrears of correspondence; ~ **haben** to fall behind (be in arrears) with one's correspondence; **bei jem. in** ~ **stehen** to owe s. o. a letter.
Brief|sendungen surface mail *(Br.)*, first-class matter *(US)*; ~-**und Paketsendungen** postal matter; ~**sortierer** letter sorter (carrier, *Br.*); **geschickter** ~**sortierer** expert mail sorter *(US)*; **automatische** ~**sortiereinrichtung** mechanical letter sorting; ~**sortiertisch** mailing table *(US)*; ~**sperre** suspension of mail; ~**ständer** letter rack; ~**steller** letter writer; ~**stempel** postmark, letter stamper, hand stamp; ~**stempel aufdrücken** to imprint a postmark with a letter *(Br.)*; ~**stempelmaschine** letter-stamping machine; ~**stil** epistolary, letter style; ~**tagebuch** letter book, daily mail ledger *(US)*; ~**tasche** wallet, letter (note) case, pocket book, billfold *(US)*, poke *(sl.)*, lizard *(sl.)*, leather *(sl.)*; **in die** ~**tasche greifen** to unclutch one's wallet; **seine** ~**tasche zücken** to cough up, to fork out; ~**taube** carrier pigeon, homer, homing pigeon; ~**taubennachricht** pigeongram; ~**taubenpost** pigeon post; ~**telegramm** letter (overnight) telegram, deferred telegram, telegram delivered by mail *(Br.)*, cable (day, night) letter *(US)*, lettergram *(US)*; ~**träger** postman *(Br.)*, mail carrier *(US)*, mailman *(US)*, postboy; ~**übergabe** delivery of a letter; ~**überweisung** postal [money]-order.
Briefumschlag envelope, cover, wrapper;
abgestempelter ~ postage envelope; **gummierter** ~ adhesive envelope; **offener** ~ unsealed envelope; **versiegelter** ~ sealed envelope;
~ **frei durch Ablösung** on Her Majesty's service *(Br.)*, O.H.M.S., penalty envelope *(US)*; ~ **ohne Adresse** blank cover; ~ **mit aufgedruckter Briefmarke** embossed envelope; ~ **für Urkunden** jacket;
~ **beschriften** to address an envelope.
Brief|unterschlagung mail theft *(US)*, theft of a letter; ~**verfasser** writer of a letter, letter writer; ~**verkehr** exchange of letters, correspondence; ~**versandunternehmen** envelope-addressing agency; ~**verschlußmaschine** letter-sealing machine, envelope sealer; ~**verteilanlage** mail-sorting machine; **automatisches** ~**verteilungssystem** automatic letter coding (sorting); ~**vorlage** model (specimen) letter; ~**waage** letter balance, letter scales *(US)*; ~**wahl** postal ballot, voting by post, vote by correspondence, mail ballot *(US)*, absent voting *(US)*; ~**wähler** outvoter *(Br.)*, absent voter *(US)*.
Briefwechsel correspondence, exchange of letters;
vertraulicher ~ close correspondence;
~ **mit Behörden** government correspondence;
~ **einleiten** to open a correspondence; ~ **einstellen** to drop a correspondence; ~ **führen** to maintain a correspondence; **geheimen** ~ **mit jem. führen** to keep up a secret correspondence with s. o.; **im** ~ **stehen** to correspond, to be in correspondence with; **mit jem. wieder in** ~ **treten** to resume correspondence with s. o.; ~ **unterhalten** to carry on (keep up) a correspondence.
Brief|zensur postal censorship, censorship of the mail *(US)*; ~**zusteller** postman, mailman *(US)*, mailcarrier *(US)*; ~**zustellung** delivery of letters, postal (letter) delivery; ~**zweck** aim (object) of a letter.

Brikett briquette;
~**fabrik** briquette works.
Brillant brilliant, cut diamond, sparkler *(sl.)*, *(drucktechn.)* excelsior;
mit ~**en besetzt** set with brilliants.
brillant brilliant, pyrotechnical, *(Stil)* purple;
~ **aussehen** to look splendid;
~**e Leistung** splendid performance; **in** ~**er Stimmung sein** to be in high spirits.
Brillant|feuerwerk cascade; ~**halsband**, ~**kollier** diamond necklace; ~**kollektion** parcel of diamonds; ~**ring** diamond ring; ~**schliff** diamond cutting.
Brille pair of glasses, [pair of] spectacles, eye glasses;
randlose ~ rimless glasses;
seine ~ **aufsetzen** to put on one's spectacles; **alles durch die eigene** ~ **sehen** to see all through one's own spectacles; **Welt durch eine rosarote** ~ **sehen** to see the world through pink-(rose-) colo(u)red spectacles; ~ **tragen** to wear spectacles.
Brillen|futteral spectacle case; ~**träger sein** to wear glasses.
brillieren to sparkle, to scintillate.
bringen to bring, to fetch, *(befördern)* to carry, to convey, *(Ertrag)* to yield, *(Rundfunk, Zeitung)* to present, to contain, to mention, *(Theater)* to present;
mit sich ~ to involve, to bring in its train, to carry with it; **j. auf etw.** ~ to put s. th. in s. one's hand; **j. dazu** ~, **etw. zu tun** to prevail on s. o. to do s. th.; **j. um 100 £** ~ to let s. o. down by £ 100; **in Abrechnung** ~ to deduct, to make a deduction; **zum Abschluß** ~ to make a deal (bargain); **zur Abstimmung** ~ to put to the vote; **in Abzug** ~ to make a deduction, to deduct; **in Anrechnung** ~ to take into consideration, to debit, to charge, to put to account; **es zu Ansehen** ~ to win a reputation; **in Anwendung** ~ to apply; **etw. zur Anzeige** ~ to bring before the authorities, to give notice, to denounce; **nichts als Ärger** ~ to cause nothing but annoyances; **zur Auktion** ~ to bring to the hammer; **zur Ausführung** ~ to execute; **j. im Auto nach A** ~ to drive s. o. to A; **j. zur Bahn** ~ to see s. o. off; **Bericht über etw.** ~ to print a report about s. th.; **etw. in seinen Besitz** ~ to make o. s. master of s. th.; **j. an den Bettelstab** ~ to reduce s. o. to beggary (poverty); **jem. etw. zu Bewußtsein** ~ to make s. o. realize; **Brief auf die Post** ~ to take a letter to the post; **auf die Bühne** ~ to stage; **Dividende** ~ to yield dividends; **j. um die Ecke** ~ to do s. o. in; **zu Ende** ~ to bring to a close; **auf den Erbteil in Anrechnung** ~ to bring (throw) into hotchpot; **in Erfahrung** ~ to find out, to learn; **jem. etw. in Erinnerung** ~ to remind s. o. of s. th.; **keinen Ertrag** ~ to yield no return; **jds. Fähigkeiten zur Entfaltung** ~ to develop s. one's powers; **Falschgeld in Umlauf** ~ to utter counterfeit notes; **j. aus der Fassung** ~ to disconcert s. o., to put s. o. out of face; **auf eine einfache Formel** ~ to reduce to a simple form; **in Gang** ~ to set going (in motion); **j. auf andere Gedanken** ~ to divert s. one's thoughts; **j. ins Gefängnis** ~ to land s. o. in prison *(fam.)*; **in Gegenrechnung** ~ to set off, to offset *(US)*; **Geld auf die Bank** ~ to deposit (put) money in the bank; **Geld unter die Leute** ~ to spend lavishly; **j. um sein letztes Geld** ~ to strip s. o. of his last penny; **j. vor Gericht** ~ to institute legal proceedings against s. o.; **Geschäft ins reine** ~ to clear a business; **Gewinn** ~ to be profitable; **j. ins Grab** ~ to be the nail to s. one's coffin; **etw. unter den Hammer** ~ to bring to the hammer; **in den Handel** ~ to bring into the market; **j. aus dem Häuschen** ~ to get s. one's shirt out *(sl.)*, to blow s. one's top; **j. nach Hause** ~ to see s. o. home, to escort s. o.; **etw. übers Herz** ~ to find it in one's heart; **es nicht übers Herz** ~ not to be able to bring o. s. to; **jem. Hilfe** ~ to aid s. o.; **etw. hinter sich** ~ to get s. th. over and done with; **Idee praktisch und wirksam zur Anwendung** ~ to put an idea into effective organizational action; **jem. etw. zur Kenntnis** ~ to call (bring) s. th. to s. one's notice; **Kind zur Welt** ~ to give birth to a child; **Koffer an Bord** ~ to carry the bags on board; **j. ins Krankenhaus** ~ to take s. o. to [the] hospital; **j. in eine schiefe Lage** ~ to land s. o. in an awkward position; **Leben in die Bude** ~ to make things hum, to put new life into an enterprise; **sein Leben zum Opfer** ~ to sacrifice one's life; **Licht in eine Sache** ~ to throw light upon a matter; **an den Mann** ~ to sell, to dispose of; **auf den Markt** ~ to [put on the] market; **es bis zum Minister** ~ to rise to be a minister; **in Mißkredit** ~ to [bring into] discredit; **in Mode** ~ to bring into fashion; **jem. eine Nachricht** ~ to take news to s. o.; **Nachricht unter die Leute** ~ to spread the news; **auf einen gemeinsamen Nenner** ~ to reduce to a common denominator; **es nicht über sich** ~ not to find it in one's heart; **jem. Nutzen** ~ to be of advantage to s. o.; **an die Öffentlichkeit** ~ to make known to the public; **in Ordnung** ~ to put right (in order), to straighten out; **j. auf die Palme** ~ to put s. one's

monkey up, to get s. one's goat; **zu Papier** ~ to put into writing; **Polizeikräfte auf ihre Sollstärke** ~ to bring the police force up to strength; **Post** ~ to deliver the mail; **j. an den Rand des Verderbens** ~ to bring s. o. to the brink of a disaster; **auf neue Rechnung** ~ to place to new account; **Redner aus dem Konzept** ~ to throw out an orator, to confuse a speaker with interruptions; **zur Reparatur** ~ to take to be repaired; **j. vor den Richter** ~ to take s. o. before the judge; **j. um seinen guten Ruf** ~ to damage s. one's reputation; **Sache zur Entscheidung** ~ to bring a matter to a head; **Satelliten auf eine Erdumlaufbahn** ~ to shoot a satellite into orbit; **Schiff ins Dock** ~ to bring a ship into dock; **j. zum Schweigen** ~ to snub (reduce) s. o. to silence; **Schwierigkeiten mit sich** ~ to entail trouble, to involve difficulties; **auf die Seite** ~ to make away with it, to put aside, to appropriate s. th.; **widerrechtlich zur Seite** ~ to appropriate unlawfully; **etw. in Sicherheit** ~ to put s. th. in a safe place; **auf den neuesten Stand** ~ to bring up to date; **jem. ein Ständchen** ~ to serenade s. o.; **j. um seine Stellung** ~ to cost s. o. his job; **sich um seine Stellung** ~ to lose one's job; **j. für eine Stellung in Vorschlag** ~ to offer s. o. for a post; **Streitigkeit vor Gericht** ~ to bring a case (dispute) before the court; **ans Tageslicht** ~ to bring forth; **aufs Tapet** ~ to bring upon the tapis; **j. aus dem Text** ~ to put s. o. out; **Thema zur Sprache** ~ to broach a subject; **auf die Titelseite** ~ to carry on the front page; **Tochter unter die Haube** ~ to marry off a daughter; **j. auf Touren** ~ to jack s. o. up; **jem. Trost** ~ to comfort (console) s. o.; **es über sich** ~ to find it in one's heart; **zur Überweisung** ~ to make remittance, to remit; **sich um etw.** ~ to rob o. s. of s. th.; **in Umlauf** ~ to circulate, to float; **Unglück über sich (sich ins Unglück)** ~ to bring misfortune upon o. s., to ruin o. s.; **große Unkosten mit sich** ~ to involve great expenses; **j. in Verdacht** ~ to lay s. o. open to suspicion; **Verhandlungen zum Abschluß** ~ to terminate negotiations; **in Verkehr** ~ to market, to sell; **j. in Verlegenheit** ~ to embarrass s. o.; **j. um sein Vermögen** ~ to cut s. o. out of his fortune; **zum Versand** ~ to post, to mail *(US)*, to dispatch; **in Verse** ~ to render into verses; **Versöhnung der Parteien zustande bringen** to bring the parties together; **j. um den Verstand** ~ to drive s. o. mad; **zur Versteigerung** ~ to put up for auction; **j. zur Verzweiflung** ~ to drive s. o. to despair; **nicht viel** ~ not to yield much profit; **es nie weiter als bis zum Vorarbeiter** ~ to never be more than a foreman; **in Vorschlag** ~ to put forward; **Wagen in die Garage** ~ to garage a car; **Wagen zum Halten** ~ to bring a car to a halt; **Wagen zu einer Werkstatt** ~ to take the car to a repair shop; **jem. Waren ins Haus** ~ to deliver goods to s. one's address; **Waren auf Lager** ~ to warehouse goods; **Waren außer Landes** ~ to take goods out of the country; **j. auf den richtigen Weg** ~ to get s. o. on the right way; **es weit** ~ to go far; **es nicht weit** ~ never come to much; **j. in Wut** ~ to get s. o. into a rage; **Zinsen** ~ to yield (bear, bring, produce) interest; **j. wieder zu sich** ~ to bring s. o. round; **Zwietracht in eine Familie** ~ to bring discord into a family; **seine Koffer zum Bahnhof** ~ **lassen** to have one's luggage *(Br.)*, (baggage, *US*) taken to the station.

Bringschuld debt by specialty (special contract), rent lying in prender *(Br.)*.

Brise breeze;
frische ~ fresh breeze; **leichte** ~ light breeze, flurry; **mäßige** ~ moderate breeze; **sanfte** ~ pleasant breeze; **schwache** ~ gentle breeze; **steife** ~ smacking breeze.

Brocken thick piece, lump, piece, bit, morsel, dump *(Br.)*, *(mil.)* shell, cookie;
ein harter ~ a tough job, tough guy (nut); **ein paar** ~ **Französisch** a few scraps of French; **meine paar** ~ my bits and pieces;
j. mit ein paar ~ **abspeisen** to give s. o. short shrift; **ein paar** ~ **des Gesprächs auffangen** to pick bits (overhear snatches of) a conversation; **jem. die besten** ~ **wegnehmen** to snatch the daintiest morsels from s. o.; **mit französischen** ~ **um sich werfen** to be fond of parading his few French words.

brockenweise bit by bit, little by little, piecemeal;
~ **antworten** to answer by fits and starts; **Bericht** ~ **aus j. herausbekommen** to drag a piece of news out of s. o. bit by bit.

brodeln to bubble;
im Volk ~ to be a seething unrest among the people.

Brokat brocade.

Bronze|medaille bronze medal; ~**papier** *(drucktechn.)* bronze paper; ~**waren** bronzes.

bronzieren to bronze.

Brosame crumb.

broschiert [wire-]stitched, unbound, in loose cover;
steif ~ in stiff cover (boards), bound in boards.

Broschur *(Buchhandel)* brochure.

Broschüre pamphlet, booklet, brochure, tract, folder, handout, leaflet;
kostenlose ~ free booklet;
~ **über postalische Abfertigungszeiten** posting time advice leaflet.

Broschüren|form booklet form; ~**schreiber** pamphleteer.

Brot, altbackenes stale (old) bread; **belegtes** ~ open sandwich; **ein** ~ a loaf [of bread]; **frisches** ~ new bread; **geröstetes** ~ toast; **selbstgebackenes** ~ home-made bread, household bread; **sein tägliches** ~ one's daily bread; **nicht mal ein Stück trockenes** ~ **zu Hause** not a pennyworth of food in the house; **sauer verdientes** ~ hard-earned money; **weiches** ~ soft tommy;
sich das ~ **vom Munde absparen** to stint o. s. of food; **Kampf ums tägliche** ~ **ausfechten** to scrabble for one's livelihood; **jem. um Lohn und** ~ **bringen** to deprive s. o. of his livelihood; **fremdes** ~ **essen** to work for other people; **jem. Lohn und** ~ **geben** to keep s. o. in one's pay; **sein gesichertes** ~ **haben** to have a steady income; **mehr als** ~ **essen können** to know a trick or two; ~**e machen** to make sandwiches; **jem. das** ~ **aus dem Munde nehmen** to take the bread out of s. one's mouth; ~ **rationieren** to ration [out] bread; **jem. dauernd aufs** ~ **schmieren** to rub it in, to ram s. th. into s. o.; **bei Wasser und** ~ **sitzen** to be on bread and water, to sit in clinc *(sl.)*; **sich als Schriftsteller sein** ~ **verdienen** to live by one's pen; **sein tägliches** ~ **verdienen** to win one's daily bread; **sein** ~ **ehrlich verdienen** to earn an honest penny; **sein** ~ **durch Nichtstun verdienen** to eat the bread of idleness; **sein** ~ **sauer (schwer) verdienen** to work hard for one's living; **sich sein** ~ **selbst verdienen** to earn one's bread and butter;
wessen ~ **ich esse, dessen Lied ich singe** he who pays the piper calls the tune;
~**beruf** bread-and-butter job; ~**beutel** tommybag, *(mil.)* haversack, field bag *(coll.)* tank.

Brötchen, belegtes canapé, savoury roll;
kleine ~ **backen** to live in a small way; **seine** ~ **verdienen** to earn one's bread and butter;
~**geber** employer, principal, boss; **von seinem** ~**geber positiv beurteilt werden** to find favo(u)r with one's employer.

Brot|erwerb breadwinning, making a living, gaining a livelihood; **als** ~**erwerb** as a trade, for a living; ~**getreide** bread stuffs, bread grain; ~**kasten** bread bin (box, *US*); ~**korb** bread basket; **jem. den** ~**korb höher hängen** to make s. o. tighten his belt, to put s. o. on short allowance; ~**krümchen** bread crumb; **jem. den letzten** ~**krumen wegfressen** to eat s. o. out of house and home; ~**lieferant** breadman.

brotlos *(arbeitslos)* unemployed, out of work, *(nicht einträglich)* unremunerative, not worthwhile;
j. ~ **machen** to throw s. o. out of work, to toss s. o. out of a job, to take the bread out of s. one's mouth, to put s. o. out of business.

Brot|marke bread coupon (unit, ticket, *Br.*); ~**röster** bread toaster; ~**schneidemaschine** bread cutter; **geröstete** ~**schnitte** toast; ~**schrift** *(drucktechn.)* body type; ~**verdiener** bread-earner, breadwinner; ~**verknappung** bread shortage; ~**zeit** teatime, coffee break.

Bruch breach, rupture, *(Arm)* fracture, *(Flugzeuglandung)* crash, crack-up *(US)*, prang *(Br., sl.)*, *(Gesetz)* nonobservance, violation, severance, *(math.)* broken number, fraction, *(Vertrag)* violation, infringement, *(Waren)* breakage, break;
frei von ~ free from breakage; **keine Gewähr für** ~ no risk for breakage;
echter ~ proper fraction; **gemeiner (gewöhnlicher)** ~ vulgar fraction; **gemischter** ~ mixed number; **komplizierter** ~ open fracture; **offener** ~ *(pol.)* open break; **unechter** ~ improper fraction;
~ **des Berufsgeheimnisses (der Amtsverschwiegenheit)** breach of professional secrecy; ~ **der Disziplin** departure from discipline; ~ **des Friedens** breach of peace; ~ **der Garantiehaftung** breach of warranty; ~ **des Gesetzes** breach (violation) of the law; ~ **in einer Kurve** jump in a curve; ~ **der getroffenen Vereinbarungen** violation of the covenant; ~ **der Verfassung** infringement of the constitution; ~ **eines Versprechens** breach of a promise; ~ **eines Vertrages** infringement (violation) of a contract; ~ **des Vertrauens** abuse of confidence;
Auto zu ~ **fahren** to smash a car; **zu** ~ **gehen** to go west, to come to naught, to go to pot *(fig.)*; **zum offenen** ~ **kommen** to break off a friendship; ~ **machen** to crack up, to crash, *(Flugzeug)* to pile up, to crash; ~ **vertiefen** to widen a breach;
~**bude** ramshackle old house, tumbledown; ~**festigkeit** breaking strength; ~**fläche** fault plane.

bruchfrei free from breakage.
Bruchgefahr risk of breakage.
brüchig full of cracks, cracked, *(Eis)* fragile, *(fehlerhaft)* flawy, weak, *(Metall)* brittle;
~**e Stelle** weak spot, flaw.
Bruch|klausel breakage clause; ~**kohle** broken coal.
bruchlanden to make a crash landing.
Bruchlandung crash [landing], smashup, prang *(Br., sl.)* crackup *(sl.)*;
zur ~ **führen** to ditch; ~ **machen** to pile up, to crash, to crash-land, to make a crash landing, to prang *(Br., sl.)*.
Bruch|last breaking load; ~**pilot** prune *(sl.)*; ~**probe** breaking test; ~**rechnung** fractional arithmetic; ~**risiko** risk of breakage.
Bruchschaden, frei von free of breakage;
für ~ **abziehen** to allow for breakage; ~ **ersetzen** to pay for breakage;
~**versicherung** insurance against breakage.
Bruch|schluß *(Börse)* broken (odd) lot; ~**schrift** grotesque *(Br.)*, Gothic *(US)*.
Bruch|stein quarry stone, rubble; ~**steinmauer** rubble walling; ~**steinmauerwerk** rubble masonry; ~**stelle** break, fracture, breaking point; ~**strich** fraction stroke.
Bruchstück fragment, [broken] piece, fraction, splinter, torso;
kleines ~ small particle;
~**e eines Briefes** scraps of a letter; ~**e eines Liedes** snatches of a song; ~**e einer Unterhaltung** snatches of a conversation;
um ~**e dem Tod entgehen** to escape death by a fraction of an inch.
bruchstück|artig, ~**haft** fragmentary; ~**weise** in fragments.
Bruchteil fraction, fractional part (amount), aliquot part;
im ~ **einer Sekunde** in a split second.
Bruchteils|aktie fractional share, fractional certificate *(Br.)*; ~**ansprüche** fractional interests, part ownership, severalty; ~**eigentum** part ownership, severalty, tenancy in common; ~**eigentümer** severalty owner, tenants in common; ~**gemeinschaft** common property; ~**veränderungen** *(Aktienkurs)* fractional changes; ~**vermögen** severalty; ~**wert** fractional value; ~**werte** fractional interests.
Bruch|waren fragile articles; ~**zahl** broken (fractional) number.
Brücke bridge, *(Teppich)* rug;
bewegliche ~ movable (opening) bridge; **fliegende** ~ flying bridge; **goldene** ~ golden bridge; **mautpflichtige** ~ toll bridge; **zweigeschossige** ~ double-level bridge;
~ **zur Vergangenheit** link with the past;
~ **abbrechen** to dismantle a bridge; **alle** ~**n hinter sich abbrechen** to burn one's boats (bridges) behind one; ~ **ausfahren** to open a bridge; ~ **bauen** to build a bridge; **jem. goldene** ~**n bauen** to hold out bright prospects to s. o.; ~ **fortreißen** to sweep away a bridge; ~ **fortspülen** to wash off a bridge; ~ **heben** to lift (raise) the bridge; ~ **konstruieren** to fabricate a bridge; ~ **schlagen** throw a bridge; ~ **senken** to lower the bridge.
Brücken|auffahrt rising of a bridge; ~**bahn** floor of a bridge; ~**bau** bridgebuilding, bridge construction; ~**bauauftrag annehmen** to contract to build a bridge; ~**bauer** bridgebuilder; ~- **und Straßenbauingenieur** bridge and road engineer; ~**baukommando** *(mil.)* bridging party; ~**belag,** ~**fahrbahn** floor of a bridge; ~**bock** trestle of a bridge; ~**boot** pontoon; ~**geld** bridge toll, pontage; ~**gerät** bridge equipment; ~**haus** pilothouse; ~**konstruktion** fabrication of a bridge; ~**kopf** *(mil.)* bridgehead, breachhead; ~**kopf jenseits des Flusses haben** to have a toehold across the river; ~**köpfe** heads of a bridge; ~**öffnung** opening of a bridge; ~**pfeiler** pier; ~**schlag** bridging; ~**spannung berechnen** to calculate the strains and stresses of a bridge; ~**überbau** superstructure of a bridge; ~**wärter** bridgemaster *(Br.)*; ~**zoll** toll charges.
Bruder brother, *(Freund)* friend, companion, *(Laie)* lay brother;
leiblicher ~ whole brother, own brother, brother german, german brother; **lustiger** ~ boon companion *(fam.)*; **sauberer** ~ bad egg; **warmer** ~ queer, pansy, fairy *(US coll.)*;
~ **Leichtfuß** happy-go-lucky fellow.
Brüder, unter ~**n** between you and me and the lamppost;
gleiche ~**, gleiche Kappen** birds of a feather flock together;
die ~ **werde ich mir kaufen** I'll tell them a thing or two.
Bruder|krieg fraternal fighting; ~**mord** fratricide; ~**schaft** fraternity, brotherhood.
Brüderschaft mit jem. schließen to make close friends with s. o.
Bruderschaftsversicherung fraternal insurance.
Brühe broth, stock, bouillon, *(schmutziges Wasser)* dirty water;
dünne ~ dishwater; **klare** ~ clear soup (broth), consommé;
j. in der ~ **sitzen lassen** to leave s. o. in the lurch; **in der** ~ **stecken** to be in the soup.

brühwarm erzählen, jem. to break the news hot to s. o.
Brummbär grumbler, growler, crosspatch *(coll.)*.
Brummen hum, growl, buzz, *(Verkehr)* drone.
brummen to hum, to buzz, to mumble, to grumble, to growl, *(einsitzen)* to do a stretch, *(Motor)* to drone, to buzz;
in seinen Bart ~ to mumble to o. s.
Brummer grumbler, growler, *(mil.)* heavy shell;
dicker ~ *(LKW)* juggernaut.
brummig sulky, surly, bad-tempered.
Brummschädel *(Kater)* hangover, thick head *(coll.)*;
~ **haben** to have a bad head *(sl.)*.
Brunnen [drinking] fountain, spring, well, waters;
~ **bohren** to sink a well; ~ **leerpumpen** to pump a well dry; ~ **senken** to drive (sink) a well; ~ **trinken** to take the waters; ~ **zudecken, wenn das Kind hereingefallen ist** to bolt the stable door after the horse has bolted;
~**anstalt** watering establishment; ~**bau,** ~**absenkung** well sinking; ~**bauer** well sinker; ~**becken** basin; ~**einfassung** curb of a well; ~**halle** well room; ~**häuschen** wellhead; ~**kammer** well house; ~**kur machen** to drink the waters; ~**vergiftung** well poisoning; ~**vergifter** calumniator; **moralische** ~**vergiftung** wholesale calumny; ~**wasser** well water.
brüsk brusque, rough, rude;
j. ~ **abfertigen** to be very short with s. o.;
~**es Anhalten** abrupt stop; ~**e Antwort** curt reply; ~**es Auftreten** rude manners.
brüskieren to snub, to brush off.
Brüskierung snub.
Brust, j. an seine ~ **drücken** to press s. o. to one's breast; **schwach auf der** ~ **sein** *(fig.)* to be short of money; **jem. eine Pistole auf die** ~ **setzen** to hold a pistol to s. one's head; **sich in die** ~ **werfen** to strike an attitude, to bridle up.
brüsten, sich to brag, to boast, to put on the dog; **sich mit etw.** ~ to pride o. s. on s. th., to plume o. s.; **sich mit fortschrittlichen Ansichten** ~ to flaunt advanced ideas; **sich mit seinen Kenntnissen** ~ to trot out one's knowledge.
Brust|fallschirm chest-pack parachute; ~**fernsprecher** portable telephone; ~**kind** nursing infant; **mit dem** ~**ton der Überzeugung** with a ring of conviction.
Brüstung breast, *(Balkon)* balustrade.
Brüstungsmauer breast (parapet) wall.
brutal brutal, beastly, bestial;
j. ~ **behandeln** to treat s. o. beastly;
~**e Gewalt** brute force; ~**er Mensch** beast; ~**es Verbrechen** brutal crime; ~**e Wahrheit** brutal truth.
Brutalität brutality, beastliness, bestiality.
brüten, über etw. to brood upon s. th.; **Rache** ~ to plan revenge, to brood over schemes of vengeance.
brütend|heiße Luft stifling hot air; ~**e Sonnenhitze** oppressive heat of the sun.
Brüter, schneller fast breeder.
Brut|hitze scorching heat; ~**reaktor** breeder reactor.
Brutstätte breeding place;
~ **der Krankheit** breeding ground of a disease; ~ **des Lasters** spawning-bed (hot-bed) of vice.
brutto [in the] gross, overall, *(Bilanz)* prior to deduction of taxes;
~ **erbringen** to gross up; **40.000 DM** ~ **verdienen** to have a gross income of DM 40.000; ~ **wiegen** to weigh in the gross.
Brutto|abrechnung grossing up computation; ~**absatz** gross sales; ~**anlageninvestitionen** gross investment in fixed assets; ~**anlagenkapitalbildung** gross fixed capital formation; ~**arbeitseinkommen** gross income from wages and salaries; ~**belastung** gross (total) load; ~**berechnung** grossing up [computation]; ~**bestand** gross total; ~**betrag** gross amount; **jährlicher** ~**betriebsertrag** *(Spediteur)* annual gross operating revenue; ~**betriebsgewinn** gross trading profit; ~**bezüge** gross pay; ~**bilanz** rough (trial) balance; ~**bodenertrag** gross production of the soil; ~**buchwert** gross book value; ~**dividende** gross dividend; ~**dividende als Teil des steuerpflichtigen Gesamteinkommens deklarieren** to include the gross dividend as part of one's statutory total income; ~**durchschnittsverdienst** gross average hourly earnings; ~**einfuhr** gross imports.
Bruttoeinkommen gross earnings (income), pretax income;
gewerbliches ~ gross income from business; **steuerpflichtiges** ~ gross earnings (income), pretax income, adjusted gross income *(US)*;
~ **aus unselbständiger Arbeit** gross income from wages and salaries; ~ **aus Unternehmertätigkeit** entrepreneurial income;
~ **aus Vermögen** property income;
~**steuer** gross income tax.

Brutto|einkünfte gross income; **~einkünfte vor Abschreibung** gross profits before depreciation; **~einlagen** gross deposits; **~einnahmen** gross receipts (earnings, takings), gross revenue returns; **~entlohnung** gross earnings before any deductions, gross pay before any stoppage *(Br.)*; **~entschädigung, ~entgelt** gross (total) compensation; **~erlös** gross profit sales; **~ersparnisse** gross savings; **~ertrag** gross proceeds (produce, profit, margin, receipts), *(Bilanz)* cashflow, *(Landwirtschaft)* gross yield; **~ertrag abwerfen** to gross up.
Bruttoertrags|analyse cashflow statement; **~kontrolle** cashflow control; **~vorschau** cashflow forecast; **~wert** *(Haus)* gross estimated rental; **~ziffern** gross earnings (cashflow) figures.
Brutto|fakturierungen gross billings; **~forderungen** *(Bilanz)* gross receivables *(US)*; **~fracht** gross freight; **~gegenwert** gross equivalent; **~gehalt** gross pay (salary), pay before stoppage *(Br.)*; **~geschäftsgewinn** gross trading profit; **~gewicht** gross (invoiced, tare) weight; **~gewicht feststellen** to weigh in gross.
Bruttogewinn gross profit (margin), variable gross margin, profit contribution, gross earnings;
~ erzielen to gross up;
~anstieg increase of net profits; **~marge, ~spanne** gross profit margin, gross markup; **~satz** gross merchandising margin; **~verhältnis** gross profit ratio; **~ziffern** gross profit figures; **~zuschlag** markup percentage *(US)*.
Brutto|handelsspanne gross margin, marginal income; **~inlandsinvestitionen** gross domestic investment; **~inlandsprodukt** gross domestic product, gross national income; **~investitionen** gross investment; **~investitionsquote** gross investment ratio; **~jahresertrag** gross annual value; **~jahresgehalt** gross annual income; **~kasseneinnahme** box-office gross; **~kleinhandelspreis** long price; **~ladefläche, ~ladefähigkeit** dead-weight capacity; **~lohn** gross wage (pay), pay before stoppage *(Br.)*; **~mehrwertsteuer** output tax *(Br.)*; **~meilentonne** gross ton mile; **~miete, ~mietertrag** gross rental; **~mietwert** gross annual value; **~nachlaß** gross estate; **~pacht** gross rental; **~pachtwert** gross annual value; **~prämie** gross premium; **~prämie einschließlich Verwaltungskostenzuschlag** office premium; **~preis** gross (long) price; **~prinzip** overall (gross) principle; **~provision** gross commission; **~rediskontlinien der dem Landeszentralbanksystem angeschlossenen Banken** net borrowed reserves of Federal Reserve member banks *(US)*; **~registertonne** gross registered ton; **~registertonnage** gross registered tonnage, GRT; **~reingewinn** gross trading surplus; **~rendite** gross yield; **~rente** gross rental; **~schaden** gross loss.
Bruttosozialaufwand gross national expenditure;
~ zu Faktorkosten gross national expenditure at factor cost; **~ zu Marktpreisen** gross national expenditure at market prices.
Bruttosozialprodukt gross national product, GNP, gross national expenditure (income);
~ zu Faktorkosten gross national product of factor cost; **~ zu Marktpreisen** gross domestic product (GDP);
mit dem ~ praktisch wieder gleichgezogen haben to be again moving broadly in line with the gross national product;
~anstieg gross national product recovery; **~schlüssel** gross national product key; **~ziffern** gross national product figures; **~zuwachsrate von etwa 6,4% aufweisen** to zip along at a yearly rate of increase of 6,4% of the gross national product.
Brutto|spanne gross margin; **~spanne ohne Skontoabzug** gross merchandising margin; **~stundenverdienste** gross hourly wages (earnings); **~tara** percentage tare; **~tarifpreis** *(Werbung)* gross; **~tonnage** gross tonnage; **~tonne** gross ton; **~tonnengehalt** gross tonnage; **~tragfähigkeit** gross carrying capacity; **~überschuß** gross surplus (balance); **~umsatz** gross sales (turnover); **~verbindlichkeit** gross liability *(US)*; **~verdienst** gross earnings (compensation), standard profit; **~verdienstspanne** gross merchandising margin; **~vergütung** total compensation, gross remuneration.
Bruttoverkaufs|gewinn gross profit on sales; **~summe** gross amount of sales; **~ziffer** cash throwoff.
Brutto|verleiheinnahme *(Film)* gross rental; **~verlust** gross loss; **~verlust an Einlagegeldern** disintermediation; **~vermögen** gross assets (estate); **~volkseinkommen** gross national income; **~warenumsatz** gross sales; **~wert** gross value; **~wochenverdienst** gross weekly earnings; **durchschnittlicher ~wochenverdienst** gross average weekly earnings; **~zinsen** gross interest.
Buch book, work, *(Band)* volume, *(24 Bogen)* quire, *(Exemplar)* copy, *(Hauptbuch)* ledger;
als ~ erschienen in book form; **nicht als ~ erschienen** not published in book form; **zu ~ stehend mit** at a book value of; **antiquarisches ~** secondhand book; **stets ausgeliehenes ~** *(Bibliothek)* book difficult to get hold of; **gut ausgestattetes ~** well-produced book; **broschiertes ~** paper-bound (-backed) book, paperback; **druckfähiges ~** printable book; **dünnes ~** slim volume; **fest eingebundenes ~** hard-cover printing; **erhebendes ~** elevating book; **auf das simpelste Niveau gebrachte ~** lowest-down-the-ladder book; **gebundenes ~** bound book, hardback copy; **meist gelesenes ~** most-read book; **noch nicht gelesenes ~** untasted book; **großformatiges ~** large volume; **grundlegendes ~** basic reading; **klassisches ~** class book; **langweiliges ~** dry book; **preisgebundenes ~** price-controlled book; **preisgekröntes ~** prize book; **seltenes ~** scarce book; **tiefschürfendes ~** profound book; **umstrittenes ~** controversial book; **ungebundenes ~** book in sheets; **uninteressantes ~** dull book; **vergriffenes ~** book out of point; **leicht verkäufliches ~** good seller; **viel verlangtes ~** best seller; **schwer verständliches ~** recondite book; **volkstümliches ~** popular book; **mit Tatsachen vollgestopftes ~** book as full of facts as an egg is full of meat; **wertvolles ~** worthwhile (sterling) book; **ganz zerlesenes ~** well-worn volume;
~ zum Einkleben von Zeitungsausschnitten scrap book; **~ im Folioformat** folio book; **~ der Geschichte** pages of history; **~ für Kochrezepte** recipe book; **~ in Loseblattform** looseleaf book; **~ Papier** quire; **~ mit sieben Siegeln** sealed book; **goldenes ~ einer Stadt** visitors' book of a town; **~ über die Verrechnung abgegebener Schecks** out-[clearing] book *(Br.)*;
~ anfangen to start on a book; **~ anzeigen** to announce a book; **~ aufschneiden** to cut a book [open]; **~ auswerten** to lay a book under contribution; **~ neu bearbeiten** to revise a book; **~ besprechen** to review a book; **in einem ~ blättern** to page through a book *(US)*; **~ ganz durchlesen** to read a book from cover to cover (right through); **sich in ein ~ einlesen** to get into a book; **in ein ~ eintragen** to enter in a book; **Schüler ins ~ eintragen** to give a pupil a black mark; **~ entstellen** to disfigure a book; **~ aus der Bibliothek entwenden** to filch a book out of a library; **sich nach einem ~ im Laden erkundigen** to inquire for a book at a shop; **~ führen über** to keep a (tally) record of; **über Ausgaben [genau] ~ führen** to keep an [a strict] account of expenses; **~ in Druck geben** to have a book printed; **neues ~ in Arbeit haben** to have a new book on the stocks; **~ herausbringen** to get (bring) out a book; **in einem ~ herumblättern** to page through a book; **~ konsultieren** to have recourse to a book; **~ abwertend kritisieren** to cut up a book; **~ unter seinem eigenen Namen erscheinen lassen** to publish a book under one's own name; **~ gegen unerlaubten Nachdruck registrieren lassen** to enter a book at Stationers' Company *(Br.)*; **~ ganz (von vorn nach hinten) lesen** to read a book right through; **in jem. wie in einem offenen ~ lesen** to read s. o. like an open book; **~ im Urtext lesen** to read a book in the original; **es sich mit einem guten ~ bequem machen** to curl up with a good book; **~ aus einem Regal nehmen** to remove a book from a shelf; **wie ein ~ reden** to speak (talk) like a book, to talk nineteen to the dozen *(Br.)* (like a blue streak, *US*); **~ rezensieren** to review a book; **zu ~ schlagen** to be profitable; **mit einem Herstellungswert von ... zu ~e schlagen** to stand at cost at ...; **~ schreiben** to write (to be writing) a book; **in einem ~ versunken (vertieft) sein** to be immersed (absorbed) in a book; **mit einem ~ fertig sein** to have finished a book; **ein ~ mit sieben Siegeln für j. sein** to be a sealed book to s. o.; **zu ~ stehen mit** to have a book value of; **bestimmte Stellen in einem ~ streichen** to expurgate a book; **~ überfliegen** to run (glance) through a book; **~ in der Bibliothek umstellen** to displace a book in the library; **~ in (bei) einem Verlag unterbringen** to plant a manuscript on a publisher; **~ im Subskriptionswege verkaufen** to subscribe a book; **~ verlegen** to undertake the publication of (publish) a book; **~ veröffentlichen** to publish a book, to bring out (produce) a book; **neues ~ veröffentlichen** to put forth a new book; **~ in einem Bezirk im Subskriptionswege vertreiben** to canvass a territory for a subscription book; **als ~ dringend benötigt werden** to be a great need for a book; **Blick in ein ~ werfen** to dip into a book; **jem. ein ~ widmen** to dedicate a book to s. o.; **~ aus dem Verkehr ziehen** to withdraw a book from circulation; **einem Autor ein ~ zuschreiben** to foist a book on an author;
Engländer wie er im ~e steht very model of an Englishman;
~abschluß closing (balancing) the books; **~ankündigung, ~anzeige** book notice; **~ankündigung vornehmen** to announce the publication of a book; **~aufdruck** lettering of a book cover; **~auflage** edition; **~ausgabe** *(Bibliothek)* loan desk; **von anstößigen Stellen gereinigte ~ausgabe** expurgated edition of a book; **~ausschnittsdienst** abstract service; **~ausstattung** getup (turnout) of a book; **~ausstellung** book exhibition; **~auszug** near-book excerpt, *(Konto)* abstract of account; **~auto** bookmobile; **~beleg** bookkeeping voucher; **~besprecher** critic.

Buchbesprechung book review.
gute ~ write-up; **kurze** ~ blurb;
~**en für Monatszeitschriften schreiben** to write reviews for monthly magazines.
Buch|bestellung book order; ~**binden** bookbinding.
Buchbinder bookbinder;
~**arbeiten** bookbinding.
Buchbinder|ei, ~**werkstatt** bookbindery *(US)*; ~**leim** bookbinding glue; ~**leinen,** ~**leinwand** book cloth; ~**pappe** millboard; ~**presse** screw (binding) press.
Buch|block inner book, cashier; ~**börse** Stationers Hall *(Br.)*; ~**decke** binding cover; ~**deckel** book cover, board; **überstehender** ~**deckel** extended cover.
Buchdruck book (letterpress) printing;
autografischer ~ autotypography.
Buchdrucker book printer, typographer.
Buchdrucker|ei printing establishment [office]; ~**kunst** typography.
Buchdruck|leiste border, headpiece; ~**maschine** printing machine, letterpress; ~**presse** printing press.
Bucheigentum registered property.
Bucheinband binding, book cover;
verstärkter ~ extra-strong binding;
~ **in Ganzleder** full-bound book;
~**rücken** book backing.
Buch|einlagen *(Bankwesen)* time deposits and saving accounts; ~**eintragung** [ledger] entry.
buchen to [bring to] book, to note down, to make an entry, to [place to] account, to record, to pass into the books, to tally *(Br.)*, *(ins Hauptbuch übertragen)* to post, *(ins Journal eintragen)* to journalize, *(reservieren)* to book, to reserve *(US)*; **Auftrag** ~ to book an order; **Betrag im Haben** ~ to put an amount in the receipts, to credit; **als Erfolg** ~ to count as success; **falsch** ~ to make a false (wrong) entry; **auf Gewinn- und Verlustkonto** ~ to pass to profit and loss account; **gleichlautend** ~ to book (enter, pass an entry) in conformity, to reciprocate an entry in the books; **im Haben** ~ to enter on the credit side; **irrtümlich buchen** to make a false (wrong) entry; **nachträglich** ~ to make a subsequent entry; **jeden Posten einzeln** ~ to post each entry singly; **rechtzeitig** ~ to make the booking early; **ins Soll** ~ to enter in the debit side, to debit; **als Verlust** ~ to put down to loss account.
Bücher books, accounts, business records;
bei Abschluß unserer ~ in closing (on balancing) our books; **mit Ihren** ~**n übereinstimmend** conformably to your books;
neu erschienene ~ new publications; **frisierte** ~ cooked accounts; **nachlässig (unordentlich) geführte** ~ slovenly kept books, books in disorder; **grundlegende** ~ basic reading; **lesenswerte** ~ books to read; **öffentliche** ~ public registers; **gesetzlich vorgeschriebene** ~ statutory books;
~ **und Geschäftspapiere** books and records;
~ **abschließen** to balance (close, make up) the books, to make up one's accounts; **alte** ~ **in einer Dachkammer abstellen** to house one's old books in an attic; ~ **abstimmen** to balance the books; **in die** ~ **aufnehmen** to put on the books; ~ **ausleihen** to lend [out] books; **in den** ~**n ausweisen** to carry in the books; ~ **in Ordnung befinden** to find accounts straight; **sich intensiv mit** ~**n beschäftigen** to converse with books; **nicht vorrätige** ~ **auf Wunsch bestellen** to obtain books to special order; ~ **auf den neuesten Stand bringen** to keep the books up to date; ~ **einsehen** to inspect the books; **in die** ~ **eintragen** to enter in (bring into) the books; ~ **aus einer Bibliothek entfernen** to take books out of a library; ~ **fälschen (frisieren)** to doctor (cook, manipulate) accounts; ~ **führen** to keep accounts, to maintain records; **getrennte** ~ **führen** to keep separate accounts; ~ **einer Firma führen** to keep the books of a firm; **ordnungsgemäß** ~ **führen** to keep books by double entry; ~ **in Bausch und Bogen kaufen** to buy a job lot of books; **in** ~**n nachschlagen** to consult books; ~ **prüfen** to audit the accounts (books), to examine the books; ~ **revidieren** to check the books; ~ **schließen** to close the books; ~ **ins reine schreiben** to post up the books; **über seinen** ~**n sitzen** to pore over one's books; ~ **in einer Bibliothek überprüfen** to sort out the books; ~ **übertragen** to post up the books; ~ **vergleichen** to compare the books; ~ **verramschen** to knock down books; ~ **zur Revision vorlegen** to produce accounts for inspection; **Umbuchung in den** ~**n vornehmen** to effect a transfer in the books; **seine** ~ **weglegen** to put away one's books;
~**abgabestelle** *(Bibliothek)* lending department, delivery station *(US)*; ~**abschluß** balancing (closing) the books, balancing of the accounts, rest, *(vor dem Jahresende)* interim closing; ~**abschluß vornehmen** to balance (close) the books; ~**auktion** trade sale; ~**ausgabe** *(Bibliothek)* issuing of books, lending desk *(US)*, lending department; ~**auszug** abstract of accounts; ~**beschreibung** bibliography; ~**bestand** book stock; ~**bestellzettel** *(Bibliothek)* book market order form, request slip; ~**bord,** ~**brett** bookboard, bookshelf; ~**bus** mobile library, bookmobile *(US)*.
Bücherei, städtische public library.
Bücher|einnahmen library earnings; ~**einsicht** inspection of books; **diplomierter** ~**experte** *(Schweiz)* certified public accountant *(US)* ~**fälschung** falsification of accounts (books); ~**freund** booklover, bibliophile; ~**gemeinschaft** book club; ~**gestell** bookcase, bookstack, bookrack; **drehbares** ~**gestell** revolving bookcase; ~**gutschein** book token *(Br.)*; ~**herstellung** bookmaking; ~**katalog** catalog(ue) of books; ~**kauf** book purchase; ~**kenner** bibliologist; ~**kunde** bibliography, bibliology; ~**laden** bookshop *(Br.)*, bookstore *(US)*; ~**leidenschaft** bibliomania; ~**liebhaber** booklover, bibliophile; ~**liste** book list, list of books; ~**macher** bookmaker, *(Vielschreiber)* hack writer; ~**mappe** briefcase, *(Schulranzen)* satchel; ~**marder** biblioklept; ~**markt** book market; ~**mensch** bookman; **reiner** ~**mensch sein** to live only for books; ~**nachweis** bibliography; ~**narr** bibliomaniac; ~**paket** packet of books; ~**regal** bookshelf, bookrack, bookcase, bookstack; **ganze** ~**reihe** whole series of books; ~**revision** examination of the books, auditing.
Bücherrevisor auditor, accountant;
beeidigter (öffentlicher, staatlich geprüfter) ~ chartered *(Br.)* (certified public, *US*, incorporated, *Br.*) accountant; **selbständiger** ~ professional auditor;
~ **zuziehen** to call in a chartered (certified) accountant.
Bücher|rezensent book reviewer; ~**rezension** book review (critic); **für** ~**rezensionen vorgesehen sein** to be devoted to book critics; ~**rückgabe** returning of books, *(Schalter)* handing-in counter; ~**saal** bookroom; ~**sammeln** book collecting; ~**sammelverkehr** book collective transport; ~**sammler** book collector; ~**sammlung** set (collection) of books; ~**schau** book exhibition; ~**schnitte marmorieren** to marble book edges; ~**schrank** bookcase, library case; ~**schreiber** bookmaker, bookwright; ~**sendung** packet (consignment) of books, *(Post)* book post (packet, *Br.*), printed papers at reduced rates; **neue** ~**sendung erhalten** to receive new supplies of books; ~**stand** bookstall, bookstand *(US)*; **drehbarer** ~**ständer** revolving bookcase; ~**stapel** pile of books; ~**stube** bookroom, reading room; ~**studium** bookwork; ~**stütze** book support, bookrest; ~**stützen** bookends; **drehbare** ~**stütze** swivel bookrest; ~**tasche** satchel; ~**tisch bei Tagungen** book table at conferences; ~**umschlag** dust jacket; ~**verbot** prohibition of books; ~**verbrennung** bookburning; ~**verkäufer** bookseller; ~**verleih** lending out of books.
Bücherverzeichnis catalog(ue), list of books;
alphabetisches ~ dictionary catalog(ue);
~ **anlegen** to list all one's books; **in ein** ~ **aufnehmen** to catalog(ue) books.
Bücher|vorrat stock of books; ~**wagen** book truck (wagon); ~**wagendienst** book car service; ~**wand** wall lined with book shelves; ~**weisheit** book learning, book[ish] knowledge; ~**wissen** book learning; ~**wurm** bookworm; ~**zensur** censorship of the press; ~**zettel** book slip.
Buch|exzerpte machen to copy notes; ~**forderung** book claim.
Buchforderungen *(Bilanz)* book accounts, accounts receivable *(US)*;
abgetretene ~ assigned book accounts; **entstandene** ~ accrued accounts receivable *(US)*;
~ **gegen Konzerngesellschaften** intercompany deposits.
Buchform, in in book form;
seine Vorlesungen in ~ **erscheinen lassen** to print one's lectures.
Buchformat book format (size).
buchführen to keep accounts.
Buchführer bookkeeper, accountant, *(Hauptbuch)* ledger clerk.
Buchführung accounting, the accounts, bookkeeping;
allgemeine ~ general accounting; **amerikanische** ~ columnar [system of] bookkeeping, tabular bookkeeping *(US)*; **betriebliche** ~ industrial (manufacturing) accounting; **doppelte** ~ double-entry (duplicate) bookkeeping, bookkeeping by double entry, double account system; **einfache** ~ single entry [bookkeeping], bookkeeping by single entry; **elektronische** ~ electronic bookkeeping; **kameralistische** ~ government accounting; **kaufmännische** ~ merchant's accounts; **kommunale** ~ municipal accounting; **ordnungsgemäße** ~ good accounting, consistently maintained sound accounting practice; **standardisierte** ~ uniform accounting;

~ **über die Einnahmen aus dem Linienverkehr** on-line revenue accounting; ~ **über in bar durchgeführte Geschäfte** cash basis; ~ **nach angefallenen Istkosten** historical accounting; ~ **einer Konzerngesellschaft** entity accounting; ~ **von Körperschaften** corporation accounting; ~ **mittels Lochkarten** punched-card accounting; ~ **in Loseblattform** loose-leaf ledger; ~ **einer Tochtergesellschaft** subsidiary company accounting;
~ **durcheinanderbringen** to muddle account books; ~ **einer Firma erledigen** to keep the books of a firm; **doppelte** ~ **haben** to keep books by double entry; **ordnungsgemäße** ~ **haben** to keep books of account, to keep books by double entry; **zur vollständigen** ~ **verpflichtet sein** to be required to keep full records, to be accountable; **ordentliche** ~ **unterhalten** to keep accounts, to keep books by double entry.

Buchführungs|angaben accounting information; ~**arbeit** bookkeeping work; ~**begriffe** accounting terms; ~**belege** accounting (bookkeeping) records; ~**daten** bookkeeping data; ~**dienst** accounting service; ~**eintrag** bookkeeping entry; ~**gebiet** accountancy field; ~**grundsätze** accounting principles; ~**kontrolle** auditing; ~**kosten** bookkeeping costs; ~**maschine** accounting machine; ~**methode** accounting method, principle (basis) of accounting; ~**methode für bestimmte Zeitabschnitte** accrual method; ~**mißbräuche** accounting abuses; ~**pflicht** compulsory bookkeeping; ~**sachverständiger** accounting expert.

Buchführungssystem accounting system, system of accounts;
einheitliches ~ uniform accounting system;
Einnahmen-Ausgaben-~ costs-book principle.

Buchführungs|technik accounting technique; ~**terminologie** accounting terminology; ~**unterlagen** [business] records, accounting records; ~**verfahren** accounting process; ~**vorgang** accounting process; ~**vorschriften** bookkeeping rules; ~**wesen** accountancy; **zu** ~**zwecken** for accounting purposes.

Buch|gattungen, alle all types of books; ~**geld** credit money (currency), fiduciary (fiat, *US*) money, money in account *(Br.)*, deposit currency *(US)* (money, *Br.*), bank money *(US)*; ~**gelehrsamkeit** book knowledge, letter learning; ~**gemeinschaft** book club; ~**gewerbe** book trade; ~**gewinn** book profit, *(aus Werterhöhungen)* surplus of appreciation; ~**gewinn aufgrund veränderter Lagerbestandsbewertung** book inventory profit; ~**gläubiger** book creditor; ~**großhändler** wholesale bookseller; ~**grundschuld** [etwa] registered land charge *(Br.)*; ~**guthaben** credit balance; ~**gutschein** book token.

Buchhalter bookkeeper, accountant, ledger (entry, entering, bookkeeping) clerk;
erster ~ chief clerk; **festangestellter** ~ established clerk; **leitender** ~ senior accountant; **zweiter** ~ junior clerk, assistant bookkeeper;
zum ~ **ausbilden** to train as a bookkeeper; ~ **entlassen** to dismiss a clerk; **versierter** ~ **sein** to be proficient in bookkeeping.

Buch|halterei accounting (bookkeeping) department; ~**halterin** lady bookkeeper.

buchhalterische|Ausbildung erfahren haben to have been trained as a bookkeeper; ~ **Belastung** accounting charge; ~ **Erfahrung haben** to have been trained as a bookkeeper.

Buchhalter|nachwuchs accountancy trainees; ~**posten** clerkship; ~**stelle** position as bookkeeper.

Buchhaltung bookkeeping, accountancy, accounting [set-up], *(Abteilung)* countinghouse, accounts (bookkeeping) department, accounting division (department);
zur Erleichterung der ~ for accounting convenience;
ordnungsgemäße ~ good accounting.

Buchhaltungs|abteilung accounting (bookkeeping) department (division), countinghouse *(Br.)*; **gut organisierte** ~**abteilung** well-arranged accounting organization; ~**aufwand** accounting cost; ~**ausdruck** bookkeeping term; ~**beleg** bookkeeping voucher; ~**chef** bookkeeping (accounting) supervisor, senior accountant; ~**fachmann** accountant, accounting expert; ~**grundsätze** accounting principles; **in eine andere** ~**kolonne übertragen** to extend into another column; ~**kosten** bookkeeping expense; ~**lehrling** accountancy student; ~**maschine** bookkeeping machine; ~**methoden** accounting methods; ~**nachweis** accounting evidence; ~**papier** ledger paper; ~**posten** clerkship; ~**unterlagen** bookkeeping (business) records, accounts; ~**unterlagen für selbständige Bilanzierung** self-balancing accounting records; ~**verfahren** accounting (bookkeeping) system; ~**vorgang** accounting (internal) transaction, accounting process; ~**vorstand** chief accountant, controller; ~**wesen** bookkeeping, accountancy.

Buchhandel bookselling, book trade;
im ~ **erhältlich sein** to be in print; **im** ~ **tätig sein** to be in the book line.

Buchhandels|kunde booktrade customer; ~**preis** trade price.

Buchhändler bookstall keeper, bookseller, bookdealer *(US)*;
fliegender ~ bookstall keeper, *(religiöse Schriften)* colporteur;
zugelassener ~ established bookseller;
~**abrechnungsgemeinschaft** booksellers' clearing company; ~**börse** Stationers' Hall *(Br.)*; ~**gepflogenheiten** customs of booksellers; ~**gewerbe** bookselling trade.

buchhändlerisch booksellerish;
~**er Abrechnungs- und Zahlungsverkehr** booksellers' clearing and payment system.

Buchhändler|knoten string easy to untie; ~**preis** bookseller's price; ~**rabatt** retail bookseller discount; ~**schule** bookseller's school of commerce; ~**tum** booksellerism; ~**vereinigung** booksellers association.

Buchhandlung bookshop, bookstall, bookstore *(US)*;
der Buchhändlervereinigung angeschlossene ~ charter group bookseller;
~ **mit Selbstbedienung** bookateria.

Buch|herausgabe publication of a book; ~**hülle** book (dust) jacket; ~**hypothek** recorded mortgage *(US)*; ~**inhalt neuverbrämt vorbringen** to dish up the contents of a book in another form; ~**inventur** book (record, perpetual, *US*) inventory; ~**klub** book club; ~**konten** book accounts; ~**korrektur** accountancy adjustment.

Buchkredit book credit;
laufender ~ open book credit; **offener** ~ open charge account; **offene** ~**e der Bundesnotenbank an die Regierung** ways and means advances *(Br.)*.

Buch|kritik book review; ~**kritiker** critic, book reviewer; ~**laden** bookshop, bookstall, bookstore *(US)*, *(für Restauflagenverkauf)* remainder shop; ~**laufkarte** book reference card.

Büchlein booklet.

Buchlizenzgeschäft trade in book rights.

Buchmacher bookmaker, bookie, ringman *(Br.)*, race track operator, turf commission agent;
die ~ the ring *(Br.)*;
betrügerischer ~ welcher *(Br.)*; **freier** ~ outside bookmaker;
größere Wetten teilweise bei anderen ~**n plazieren** to lay off part of heavy bets with colleagues;
~**wette** betting transaction *(US)*.

Buchmacherei bookmaking.

buchmäßig as shown by the books;
~**e Forderung** book claim; ~**er Gewinn** book profit; ~**e Haftung** *(Spediteur)* book liability; ~**e Mengenkontrolle** unit control; ~**er Überschuß** book surplus; ~**er Verlust** book loss; ~**er Wert** accounting value.

Buch|messe book fair (exhibition); ~**nummer** book number, *(Bibliothek)* call number; ~**papier** book paper; ~**passage ändern** to amend a passage in a book; ~**prämie** book prize; ~**preis auf die Hälfte herabsetzen** to mark a book down to half the price; ~**presse** letterpress.

Buchprüfer accountant, auditor;
beeidigter (öffentlich zugelassener) ~ chartered (incorporated) accountant *(Br.)*, certified public accountant *(US)*; **betriebseigener** ~ internal (operational) auditor; **konzessionierter** ~ chartered accountant *(Br.)*;
~ **ganztägig beschäftigen** to employ a private accountant on a full-time basis; ~ **zuziehen** to call in a certified accountant;
~**beruf** profession of accounting, auditing profession; ~**lehrgang** course of instruction in accounting; ~**tätigkeit** accounting practice.

Buchprüfung audit[ing];
bei der ~ when auditing the books;
abgekürzte ~ limited audit; **betriebseigene** ~ internal audit; **betriebsfremde** ~ external audit;
~ **und Betriebsprüfung** auditing service;
~ **aufgrund mitgenommener Belege** desk audit; **laufende** ~ **durch Betriebsbuchprüfer** continuous audit; ~ **und Betriebsprüfung** business auditing service; ~ **durch [betriebsfremde] Buchprüfer** external audit;
~ **abschließen** to conclude an audit; ~ **haben** to have the auditors in.

Buchprüfungs|abteilung audit department; ~**auftrag** audit engagement; ~**bericht** auditor's report; ~**dienst** accountancy (accounting) service; ~**gesellschaft** auditing firm; ~**kommission** audit commission; ~**kosten** auditing fee; ~**spezialist** accounting specialist; ~**termin** audit date; ~**unterlagen** audit notebook; ~**verfahren** accounting procedure; ~**vermerk** audit certificate.

Buch|revision audit[ing]; ~**rezensent** literary critic; ~**rücken** spine, back of a book; ~**sachverständiger** auditor, auditing expert; ~**sachverständigen zuziehen** to employ an expert accountant; ~**saldo** balance; ~**schlager** best seller; ~**schrift** book face.
Buchschuld book debt (account);
~ **löschen** to extinguish a book account.
Buchschulden ordinary debts, stated liabilities, accounts payable *(US)*;
entstandene ~ accrued accounts payable *(US)*;
~ **abzüglich Rückstellungen** accounts payable less reserve *(US)*.
Buchschuldner book debtor.
Buchse *(el.)* jack, socket.
Büchse tin *(Br.)*, can *(US)*;
in ~n einmachen to tin *(Br.)*, to can *(US)*.
Buchseite page;
auf der gegenüberliegenden ~ on the opposite page;
fehlende ~ missing page of a book;
~ **mit gerader Zahl** even page;
~ **herausnehmen** to tear a page out of a book; ~**n umblättern** to turn over the leaves of a book.
Büchsen|bier canned beer *(US)*; ~**fleisch** preserved meat; ~**gemüse** tinned (canned, *US*) vegetables; ~**macher** gunsmith; ~**milch** evaporated (tinned, canned, *US*) milk; ~**öffner** tin (can, *US*) opener, gadget for opening tins *(Br.)* (cans, *US*).
Buchstabe letter, character, *(Druckbuchstabe)* type;
am ~n des Gesetzes klebend letter-bound; **den ~n und dem Inhalt nach** by letter and spirit; **in ~n** in words; **in großen ~n** in large type;
beschädigter (lädierter) ~ batter, battered letter; **erhabener** ~ raised letter; **großer** ~ capital [letter]; **handkolorierter** ~ illuminated letter; **lateinischer** ~ Roman type; **verrutschter** ~ foul case; **verzierter** ~ ornamented letter;
~ **des Gesetzes** literal acceptation (letter) of the law; ~**n in roter Schrift** rubricated letters;
Auftrag bis auf den letzten ~n ausführen to carry out an order to the letter; **nach den ~n auslegen** to take s. th. literally; **mit ~n bezeichnen** to letter; **sich an den ~n des Gesetzes halten** to go by the letter of the law; **sich an den ~n eines Vertrages halten** to keep to the letter of an agreement; **am ~n kleben** to stick to the letter; **in großen ~n schreiben** to capitalize; ~**n zu setzen vergessen** to drop a letter.
Buchstaben|bezeichnung lettering, literal notation; ~**chiffre** substitution cipher.
buchstabengetreu|ausführen to carry out to the letter;
~**e Auslegung** literalist approach.
Buchstaben|glaube literalism; ~**gläubiger** literalist; ~**gläubigkeit** letter worship; ~**größe** size of a letter; ~**klauber** quibbler; ~**kombination** letter combination; ~**schloß** combination (puzzle) lock; ~**setzmaschine** typesetting machine.
Buchstabieren spelling.
buchstabieren to spell;
falsch ~ to misspell; **mühsam** ~ to spell over.
Buchstabierer speller.
Buchstabier|methode alphabetical method; ~**tafel** spelling table; ~**wörter** identification words.
buchstäblich to the letter, literally;
~ **in Stücke gerissen** literally cut to pieces;
~ **auslegen** to take in a literal sense, to literalize;
~**e Übersetzung** literal translation; ~**e Vernichtung** literal annihilation.
Buchstand bookstall.
Buchstelle piece out of a book;
~ **abschreiben** to copy out a passage from a book; ~ **streichen** to strike a passage out of a book, to expurgate a book.
Buchstütze bookend, bookrest.
Bucht bay, fleet, bight, inlet, *(Bus)* trans-in;
in eine ~ **eingeschlossen** embayed;
kleine ~ creek *(Br.)*, cove, inlet.
buchtige Küstenlinie indented coastline.
Buchtitel binder's title;
aufgeprägter ~ titling; **kurzer** ~ half title.
Buchumschlag book (dust) jacket, book wrapper.
Buchung booking [up], entering [up], posting, *(einzeln)* bookkeeping entry, item, *(Reservierung)* booking, reservation *(US)*;
abschließende ~ closing (balancing) entry; **berichtigende** ~ adjustment (adjusting) entry; **durchlaufende ~en** transit entries; **einfache** ~ single entry; **entsprechende** ~ corresponding entry; **falsche** ~ misentry, covering (wrong) entry; **feste** ~ firm reservation *(US)*; **fiktive** ~ imputed entry; **gleichlautende** ~ corresponding entry, entry in conformity; **irrtümliche** ~ entry made by mistake, erroneous entry; **maschinelle** ~ machine posting; **nachträgliche** ~ postentry, subsequent entry; **Promemoria-~** blind entry; **transitorische** ~ suspense entry; **umfangreiche ~en** heavy bookings; **unrichtige** ~ wrong entry, misentry; **für den Rückflug vorgenommene** ~ return place reservation *(US)*; **vorläufige** ~ suspense entry; **zusammengefaßte** ~ compound entry;
~ **auf einer Chartermaschine** charter booking; ~ **bereits verkaufter Flugplätze** *(Reisebüro)* sale and report system; ~ **ohne Gegenbuchung** unbalanced entry; **übliche** ~ **einer Geschäftstransaktion** entry in regular course of business;
~ **abändern** to rectify (alter) an entry; ~ **aufgeben** to book, to make a reservation *(US)*; ~ **berichtigen** to adjust an entry; ~ **bestätigen** to confirm a booking; ~ **festmachen** to nail down one's booking; ~ **rückgängig machen (stornieren)** to reverse (cancel) an entry (reservation); **falsche** ~ **streichen** to strike out a wrong entry; ~ **vornehmen** to make (effect, pass, post) an entry, to post an item; **gleichlautende** ~ **vornehmen** to effect a corresponding entry; **nachträgliche** ~ **vornehmen** to make a supplementary entry.
Buchungs|abschluß closing of the books (accounts); ~**agent** reservation agent *(US)*.
buchungsähnlicher Posten bookkeeping-type entry.
Buchungs|angaben particulars of an entry; ~**anzeige** *(Bank)* advice note; ~**arbeiten erledigen** to handle bookkeeping functions; ~**aufgabe** booking note; ~**aufgliederung** classification of entries; ~**ausweis** accounting statement; ~**automat** accounting (bookkeeping) machine; ~**beleg** bookkeeping (accounting) voucher, accounting (supporting) record, accountable receipt, recording medium, journal voucher, business paper, *(Hauptbuchübertragung)* posting medium; ~**bescheinigung über Aktienverkauf** stock receipt *(Br.)*; ~**bestätigung** confirmation of a booking, reconfirmation notice *(US)*, reconfirmation of reservation *(US)*; ~**betrag** amount booked; ~**fehler** bookkeeping error; ~**formular** bookkeeping form; ~**gang** recording routine; ~**gebühr** entry charge; ~**kreislauf** accounting cycle; ~**maschine** bookkeeping (accounting) machine; **vorbereitende ~maßnahmen** vouching; ~**methode** accounting method; ~**mittel** posting medium; ~**nachweis** accounting evidence; ~**nummer** number of entry.
Buchungsposten [booking] item, [bookkeeping] entry (item);
ausgesetzter ~ deferred entry;
~ **valutieren** to fix the value of an entry (item).
Buchungs|schluß closing of the books (accounts); ~**service** reservation service *(US)*; ~**stand** position of the accounts, accounting position; ~**stelle** accounting office, accountancy department; ~**stempel** entry stamp; ~**system** voucher system, set of accounts, *(Hotelwesen)* reservation system *(US)*; **computergesteuertes ~system** computer reservation network.
buchungstechnische Schwierigkeiten bookkeeping difficulties.
Buchungs|text narration of an entry; ~**unterlage** voucher, accounting record, posting medium; ~**unterlagen** bookkeeping (accounting, general) records, books of accounting; **inoffizielle ~unterlage** informal record; **die zur Erläuterung der Geschäftstransaktionen erforderlichen ~unterlagen aufheben** to keep accounting records sufficient to show and explain its transactions; ~**unterlagenverzeichnis** voucher register; ~**verfahren** bookkeeping method, posting operation, accounting system; **angreifbares ~verfahren** accounting manoeuvre; ~**vermerk** *(Flugzeug)* reconfirmation notice; ~**vorgang** accountable condition (event), posting operation; ~**wert** accounting value; ~**zeitraum** accounting (fiscal) period; ~**zyklus** bookkeeping cycle.
Buch|verkaufsstelle book sales agency (point); ~**verlag** [firm of] publishers, publishing firm (house); ~**verleih** lending library; ~**verlust** book loss, accounting (bookkeeping) loss; ~**veröffentlichung** publication of a book.
Buchwert book (accounting, carrying) value, book cost, *(Restwert)* depreciated cost;
~**e** book figures, nominal assets *(US)*;
börsenmäßig gehandelte ~e inscribed stocks *(Br.)*;
~ **nach Vornahme von Abschreibungen** net book value; ~ **vor Abschreibungen** gross book value; ~ **des Gesellschaftskapitals** book value of a company's resources;
~**e bei der Verwertung erzielen** to realize at book value; ~ **übersteigenden Erlös erzielen** to yield a profit over the book value; ~ **herabsetzen (heraufsetzen)** to write down (up) the book value; ~**e erheblich übersteigen** to be appreciably in excess of book values.
Buch|wissen book knowledge; ~**zeichen** bookmark, bookplate.

Buckel hump.
Bude hut, stall, shack *(US)*, hangout, cabin, den *(fam.)*, shebang *(US)*, *(Student)* digs *(Br., coll.)*, *(Verkaufsstand)* stand, stall, booth, kiosk;
elende ~ doghouse; **kümmerliche** ~ wretched little hole, doghouse; **verfallene alte** ~ old ramshackle house;
jem. die ~ **über dem Kopf anzünden** to set fire to s. one's house; **seine** ~ **aufgeben** to give up one's room (digs, *Br.*); **eigene** ~ **besitzen** to live in digs (diggings) *(Br.)*; **Leben in die** ~ **bringen** *(fam.)* to make things hum, to put life into an enterprise; **jem. die** ~ **einlaufen** to be never off s. one's doorstep *(fam.)*; **jem. wegen eines Buches die** ~ **einlaufen** to keep pestering s. o. for a book; ~ **haben** to dig *(Br., coll.)*; **jem. in die** ~ **regnen** to get into hot water; **jem. auf die** ~ **rücken** *(fam.)* to pay s. o. a surprise visit, to blow in on s. o. *(coll.)*; **jem. zu sehr auf die** ~ **rücken** to be overfamiliar with s. o.; ~ **auf den Kopf stellen** to turn a place upside down; ~ **zumachen** to shut up shop, to pack up.
Buden|angst claustrophobia; ~**besitzer** stallkeeper, stallman; ~**zauber veranstalten** to kick up a row, to make a night of it.
Budget budget, estimates *(Br.)*;
das ~ **betreffend** budgetary;
~ **ausgleichen** to set the budget on its feet again; ~ **einhalten** to keep to the budget; ~ **genehmigen** to vote the estimates *(Br.)*; ~ **vorlegen** to bring in the estimates *(Br.)*, to open (introduce) the budget; **im** ~ **vorsehen** to budget for;
~**abstrich** budget cut; ~**anforderungen beschneiden** to prune budget requests; ~**antrag** application request; ~**aufschlüsselung** breakdown of the budget *(US)*, allotment of appropriations; ~**aufstellung** budgeting, *(Privathaushalt)* income engineering *(US)*; ~**ausgleich** balancing of the budget, budget balancing; ~**ausschuß** budget commission (committee), budgetary commission (board), Committee of Ways and Means *(Br.)*; ~**beratung** debate on the budget; ~**buchführung** budgetary accounting; ~**debatte** budget debate; ~**defizit** deficit of the budget; ~**jahr** budget (fiscal) year; **ständige** ~**kommission** committee of supplies (ways and means, *Br.*); ~**kontrolle** budgetary control; ~**kürzung** budget cut; ~**maßnahmen** budgetary practices; ~**periode** budget (spending) period; ~**posten** budget item; ~**rechnungswesen** budgeting; ~**überschreitung** exceeding the budget; ~**überschuß** budget surplus; ~**voranschlag** budgetary estimate.
Budike pub *(Br.)*, saloon *(US)*, jerry *(Br., sl.)*.
Budiker publican *(Br.)*, saloonkeeper *(US)*.
Büffelei grind, sweat.
büffeln to dig away, to skull-drag, to sap *(Br., sl.)*, to mug up *(Br.)*, to bone up *(US)*, *(für die Schule)* to swot, to stew *(sl.)*, *(Student, sl.)* to pole;
für ein Examen ~ to cram for an examination.
Büffet refreshment room, bar, buffet;
kaltes ~ stand-up (cold) buffet; **warmes** ~ buffet supper;
~**dienst** take-away restaurant; ~**kellner** barman, bartender *(US)*.
Büffler plug, plodder, mothball, smug *(Br., sl.)*, dig *(US sl.)*, sap *(Br., sl.)*.
Bug *(Schiff)* bow, nose, *(Flugzeug)* nose, head;
jem. einen Schuß vor den ~ **verpassen** to sound a warning note to s. o.;
~**bewaffnung** *(Flugzeug)* front armament.
Bügel stirrup, *(Kleid)* coat hanger;
fest in den ~**n sitzen** to be firm in one's stirrups;
~**eisen** press (smoothing-) iron, flatiron; ~**falte** crease.
bügeln to iron;
Anzug ~ to press a suit.
Bug|fahrwerk landing gear; ~**fenster** nose window; ~**kanzel** cockpit.
buglastig nose-heavy.
Bug|landerad nose landing wheel; ~**licht** nose light.
Bugsieren towage.
bugsieren to tow, to warp.
Bugsier|kosten, ~**lohn** towage [charges]; ~**leine** warp; ~**schlepper** tugboat, towboat.
Bugspitze prow, head.
buhlen, um jds. Gunst to court s. one's favo(u)r; **um die Gunst der Öffentlichkeit** ~ to curry favo(u)r with the public.
Buhne breakwater.
Bühne room, *(Eisenbahn)* platform, *(Theater)* stage, boards;
auf der ~ on the boards; **für die** ~ **bearbeitet** dramatized; **hinter der** ~ off-stage, backstage, behind the scenes;
drehbare ~ revolving stage; **fliegende** ~ flying scaffold; **politische** ~ scene of politics, arena of politics, political stage; **provisorische** ~ fit-up *(Br.)*; **Städtische** ~**n** municipal theatre; **von der** ~ **abgehen** to make one's exit; **von der** ~ **abtreten** *(fig.)* to quit the scene; **auf der** ~ **auftreten** to act on the stage; **für die** ~ **bearbeiten** to adapt for the stage, to dramatize; **Roman für die** ~ **bearbeiten** to adapt a novel for the stage; **Stück auf die** ~ **bringen** to produce (stage) a play, to put a play on the stage; ~ **errichten** to build a platform; **auf der** ~ **erscheinen** to enter the stage; **über die** ~ **gehen** to be in progress; **erfolgreich über die** ~ **gehen** *(Stück)* to perform successfully; **[völlig] glatt über die** ~ **gehen** to go swimmingly; **zur** ~ **gehen** to take to the stage; **sich lange auf der** ~ **halten** to hold (keep) the stage; **politische** ~ **verlassen** to quit the stage of politics; **j. durch Zwischenrufe von der** ~ **vertreiben** to jeer s. o. off the stage; **sich von der** ~ **des öffentlichen Lebens zurückziehen** to retire in obscurity.
Bühnen|anweisung stage direction; ~**arbeiter** stage hand; ~**aufführung** stage production, theatrical performance; ~**auftritt** appearance; ~**ausbildung erhalten** to study for the stage; ~**ausgabe** action version; ~**ausstattung** scenery, set; ~**autor** playwright, theatrician; ~**bearbeitung** adaption for the stage; ~**bearbeitung eines Romans** dramatization of a novel; ~**beleuchtung** stage lighting; ~**bild** scenery, stage setting; **aufwendiges** ~**bild** elaborate set; **ständiges** ~**bild** permanent set; ~**bildner** stage setter; **hervorragender** ~**bildner sein** to manage the stage effects with great skill; ~**dekoration** decor, stage decoration; ~**eingang** stage door.
bühnenfähig sein to act.
Bühnenfassung acting version.
bühnengerecht actable, playable, stageworthy, dramatic;
nicht ~ unactable.
Bühnen|himmel cyclorama; ~**hintergrund** back of the stage; **im** ~**hintergrund** upstage; ~**jargon** stage slang; ~**kritiker** stage critic; ~**künstler** actor, performer; **über alle** ~**kunststücke verfügen** to learn all the tricks of the stage; ~**laufbahn** theatrical career, career on the stage; ~**leiter** stage manager; ~**leitung** stage management.
bühnenmäßig stagy.
Bühnen|musik incidental music; ~**name** stage name; ~**probe** rehearsal; ~**rechte** stage rights.
bühnenreif actable, playable.
Bühnen|requisiten stage property; ~**schaffen** dramatic works; ~**scheinwerfer** spotlight; ~**schriftsteller** dramatist, playright; ~**stück** stage play, piece; ~**stücke aufführen** to play; ~**technik** stagecraft.
bühnentechnische Anweisungen stage directions.
Bühnen|vordergrund front of the stage; **im** ~**vordergrund** downstage; ~**vorhang** curtain; ~**werk** theater, dramatic work.
bühnenwirksam dramaturgical;
~ **sein** to be good theater; **nicht** ~ **sein** not to stage well;
~**es Stück** play that is good theatre.
Bühnenwirkung stage effect.
Buhrufe booing, hissing.
Bulkladung bulk cargo.
Bullauge porthole, bull's-eye.
Bulldozer bulldozer, earthmoving machinery.
Bulle polyp *(fam.)*, long arm *(sl.)*, copper, bull *(US sl.)*.
Bullenhitze scorching heat.
Bulletin bulletin;
~ **herausgeben** to [issue (give out) a] bulletin.
Bummel stroll, razzle, spree, ramble;
gemächlicher ~ **über die Prachtstraßen** leisurely walk along the boulevards;
auf einem ~ on a jaunt;
auf den ~ **gehen,** ~ **machen** to be on a jag, to [go on a] spree, to go on a tear, to go on the razzle, to go on a pub crawl (for a stroll), to make whoopee *(US)*.
Bummelant lounger, saunterer, slowcoach, bum *(US)*.
Bummelantentum absenteeism.
Bummelleben führen to lead a dissipated life.
Bummeln loitering, lounging, loafing *(coll.)*;
~ **bei der Arbeit** goldbricking *(US)*.
bummeln to stroll, to be on the loaf, to linger, to loaf, to jaunt;
bei der Arbeit ~ to slack at one's work; **durch die Stadt** ~ to stroll through the town, to ramble about the streets; **durch die Straßen** ~ to go about the streets; **auf dem Wege** ~ to dawdle on the way;
~ **gehen** to [go on a] spree, to go pleasuring, to make whoopee *(US)*.
Bummel|streik work-to-rule strike, slowdown *(US)*, go-slow [strike] *(Br.)*; ~**zug** *(fam.)* omnibus (way, stopping, parliamentary, *Br.*, accommodation, *US*) train, peddler *(sl.)*.
Bummler gadabout, stroller, loafer, laggard, lounger, Johnny *(Br., sl.)*, slowpoke *(US)*, bum *(US)*.

Bums bang;
~**landung** pancake; ~**lokal** slap shop, joint *(sl.)*, penny gaff *(Br., sl.)*, dive, hash house *(US)*; ~**musik** oom-pah-pah.

Bund bond, union, federation, association, league, *(Band)* band, cord, *(Bündel)* bunch, *(Bundesregierung)* Federal Government, *(Bündnis)* alliance;
beim ~ *(coll.)* on active service; **vom** ~ **überwacht** federal-controlled;
~ **der Ehe** marriage tie, bond of marriage; ~ **Reisig** faglot of brushwood; ~ **Schlüssel** bunch of keys;
einem ~ **beitreten** to enter into an alliance; ~ **der Ehe (fürs Leben) schließen** to take the marriage vows; **sich den** ~ **enger schnallen** to tighten one's belt; **mit jem. im** ~**e sein** to be in league with s. o.; **Dritter im** ~**e sein** to make up the third in a trio.

Bündel bundle, bunch, pack, package, parcel, truss *(Br.)*;
~ **von Banknoten** wad (bundle) of banknotes, bankroll; ~ **von Briefen** packet of letters; ~ **internationaler Finanzleistungen** cash management; **ganzes** ~ **erneuter Inflationssteigerungsmaßnahmen** reflationary package; ~ **von Lichtstrahlen** beam of lights, pencil of light rays; ~ **energiepolitischer Maßnahmen** energy package; ~ **finanzpolitischer Maßnahmen** financing package; **ganzes** ~ **geldmarktpolitischer Maßnahmen** package of monetary relief; **ganzes** ~ **kreditverbürgender Maßnahmen** credit-guarantee package; ~ **von Maßnahmen zur Anhebung des Preisniveaus** reflationary package; ~ **von Notizen** sheaf of notes; ~ **von Reformvorschlägen** reform package; **für die Gesundung der Wirtschaft verordnetes** ~ **von Sanierungsvorschlägen** austerity package for the economy; ~ **von Sondervergünstigungen** batch of extras; ~ **von Sparmaßnahmen der öffentlichen Hand** austerity package for the economy; ~ **Stroh** truss of straw; **umfassendes** ~ **von zusätzlichen Vergünstigungen** substantial benefit package; ~ **handelspolitischer Vorschläge** trade package;
~ **von Vorschlägen zur Regelung der Beziehungen zwischen den Sozialpartnern ablehnen** to reject the industrial relations package; **wie ein** ~ **Elend dasitzen** to sit like a picture of misery; **in** ~**n packen** to make up in bundles; ~ **schnüren** to tie a bundle; **sein** ~ **schnüren** to pack up one's kit (things), to sling one's hook, to hook it; **zu einem** ~ **zusammenschnüren** to tie into a bundle;
~**durchschnitt** *(Fernsehen)* beam width.

bündeln to bundle, to make a bundle, *(Optik)* to focus, to beam, to concentrate;
Holz ~ to bundle wood; **Lichtstrahlen** ~ to concentrate rays of light; **Sonnenstrahlen mit einem Brennspiegel in etw.** ~ to focus the sun's rays on s. th. with a burning glass; **Stroh** ~ to truss straw.

Bündelpresse baling (packing) press.

Bündelung *(Licht)* focus[ing], concentration, *(Radar)* directivity.

bündelweise by bundles.

Bundes|amt, Statistisches Central Statistical Office *(Br.)*, National Bureau of Economic Research *(US)*; ~**angelegenheiten** federal matters *(US)*; ~**anleihen** government securities; ~**anstalt für Zivilschutz** Civil Defence Office; ~**anwalt** federal attorney *(US)*; ~**anzeiger** gazette *(Br.)*, Federal Register *(US)*; **im** ~**anzeiger bekanntgeben** to gazette *(Br.)*; ~**arbeitsgesetz** State Labor Law *(US)*; ~**archiv** Federal Record Center *(US)*; ~**aufgaben** functions of the Federal Government *(US)*.

Bundesaufsichtsamt|für das Bausparkassenwesen Federal Savings and Loan Insurance Corporation *(US)*; ~ **für das Kreditwesen** Credit Control Authority; ~ **für das Versicherungswesen** [etwa] State Insurance Commission, Industrial Insurance Commissioner *(Br.)*;
~**gesetz für das Versicherungswesen** Federal Union Act *(US)*.

Bundes|ausbildungsförderungsprogramm [etwa] Federal Insurance Loan Program *(US)*; ~**autobahn** motorway *(Br.)*, freeway *(US)*, express highway *(US)*; ~**bahn** railway, railroad *(US)*; ~**bahnpräsident** [etwa] director general of railroads *(US)*; ~**bank** Federal Reserve Bank *(US)*; ~**bankdirektorium** [etwa] Board of Governors of the Federal Reserve System *(US)*.

bundesbankfähig rediscountable at the federal bank *(US)*, [etwa] eligible to serve as special deposits for the Bank of England.

Bundes|bankgesetz Federal Reserve Act *(US)*; ~**bankpräsident** [etwa] Federal Reserve chairman; ~**beamter** federal officer *(US)*; ~**bediensteter** federal employee *(US)*; ~**behörde** federal agency *(US)*; ~**beihilfe** federal allowance *(US)*; ~**bürgschaft** government guarantee; ~**darlehnswohnungen** federal-financed low-cost housing *(US)*; ~**dienststelle** federal agency *(US)*; ~**druckerei** Government Printing Office *(US)*, Her Majesty's Stationery Office *(Br.)*; ~**durchschnitt** federal *(US)* (national) average; **auf** ~**ebene** at the federal level; ~**einkommen** [etwa] inland *(Br.)* (internal, *US*) revenue; ~**einkommensteuer** federal income tax *(US)*; ~**energiebehörde** Federal Energy Administration *(US)*; ~**ernährungsministerium** [etwa] Agricultural Department *(US)*, Board of Agriculture *(Br.)*; ~**etat** National Budget, Federal Budget *(US)*; ~**exekutive** White House *(US)*; ~**fernstraße** [etwa] long-distance road, multistrip highway *(US)*.

Bundesfinanz|behörde Commissioner of Inland Revenue *(Br.)*, Commissioner of Internal Revenue *(US)*; ~**hof** [etwa] Income Tax Appeal Tribunal; ~**minister** [etwa] Chancellor of the Exchequer *(Br.)*, Secretary of the Treasury Department *(US)*; ~**ministerium** [etwa] Commissioners of the Treasury *(Br.)*, Treasury Department *(US)*.

Bundes|fiskus [etwa] Queen's treasury *(Br.)*, crown *(Br.)*, Exchequer *(US)*; ~**flagge** national ensign; ~**forschungsamt** Nation Defense Research Council *(US)*; ~**forstverwaltung** Forest Service *(US)*; ~**gebiet** national territory; ~**genosse** confederate, ally, associate; ~**genossenschaft** confederation, alliance; ~**gericht** Federal Court *(US)*; ~**gerichtsbarkeit** federal jurisdiction *(US)*; ~**gerichtsentscheidung** decision of the Federal Court *(US)*.

Bundesgesetz federal law, Act of Congress *(US)*;
~**blatt** gazette *(Br.)*, Statutes at Large *(US)*; ~**gebung** federal legislation *(US)*; ~**sammlung** United States Code.

Bundes|gewalt federal power *(US)*; ~**grenzschutzangehöriger** border guard; ~**hauptkasse** [etwa] public treasury; ~**hauptstadt** federal city *(US)*; ~**haushalt** National (Federal, *US*) Budget; ~**hilfe** federal aid *(US)*; ~**hoheit** sovereignty; ~**justizminister** [etwa] High Chancellor *(Br.)*, Attorney General *(US)*; ~**justizministerium** Department of Justice *(US)*; ~**kanzler** Federal Chancellor; ~**kartellamt** [etwa] Registrar of Restrictive Trade Practices *(Br.)*, Antitrust Division *(US)*; ~**kasse** [etwa] Queen's treasury, crown *(Br.)*, Exchequer *(US)*; ~**kriminalamt** Federal Bureau of Investigation *(US)*; ~**land** state *(US)*; ~**luft- und Raumfahrtbehörde** National Aeronautic and Space Administration (NASA) *(US)*.

Bundesminister|für Arbeit Minister of Labour *(Br.)*, Secretary of State for Employment *(US)*; ~ **des Auswärtigen** Secretary of State *(US)*, Foreign Secretary *(Br.)*; ~ **für Energiewirtschaft** Minister of Power *(Br.)*; ~ **für Ernährung, Landwirtschaft und Forsten** Minister of Agriculture, Fisheries and Food *(Br.)*; ~ **für Familie, Jugend und Gesundheit** Minister of Health, Education and Welfare *(Br.)*; ~ **der Finanzen** Chancellor of the Exchequer *(Br.)*, Secretary of the Treasury Department *(US)*; ~ **für Forschung** Minister for Science and Technology *(Br.)*; ~ **mit besonderem Geschäftsbereich** [etwa] Minister without portfolio, Paymaster General *(Br.)*; ~ **des Inneren** Home Secretary *(Br.)*, Secretary of State Home Affairs *(US)*; ~ **für das Post- und Fernmeldewesen** Minister for Post and Telecommunications *(Br.)*; ~ **für Raumordnung, Bauwesen und Städtebau** Minister of Town and Country Planning *(Br.)*; ~ **für Verkehr** Minister of Transport *(Br.)*, Secretary of State for Transportation *(US)*; ~ **für Wirtschaft** Minister of Economic Affairs *(Br.)*; ~ **für Wohnungsbau** Minister of Housing and Local Government *(Br.)*; ~ **für wirtschaftliche Zusammenarbeit** Federal Minister for Economic Cooperation.

Bundes|ministerium für Verteidigung Ministry of Defence *(Br.)*; ~**mittel** federal funds; ~**nachrichtenstelle** [etwa] intelligence service, Counterintelligence Corps.

Bundesnotenbank [etwa] Federal Reserve Bank *(US)*, Bank of England, lender of last resort *(Br.)*;
~**ausweis** [etwa] Exchequer returns *(Br.)*; ~**präsident** chairman of the Federal Reserve Bank *(US)*.

Bundes|organ federal instrumentality *(US)*; ~**organisation** national organization *(US)*; ~**parlament** [etwa] parliament, House of commons *(Br.)*, Congress of the United States *(US)*; ~**parteitag** national convention *(US)*; ~**patentamt** Commissioner of Patents *(US)*; ~**post** Postal Service; ~**präsident** President of the Federal Republic; ~**rechnungshof** [etwa] Commissioner of Audits *(Br.)*, General Accounting Office *(US)*; ~**recht** federal law *(US)*; ~**rechtanwaltskammer** [etwa] Bar Council *(Br.)*, Faculty of Advocates *(Scot.)*; ~**rechtanwaltsordnung** [etwa] Solicitors Act *(Br.)*; ~**regierung** Federal Government *(US)*; ~**republik Deutschland** Federal Republic of Germany; ~**schatz** [etwa] public purse, coffers of the state; ~**schätze,** ~**schatzwechsel** [etwa] British savings bonds, United States note; ~**schatzmeister** [etwa] Register of the Treasury *(US)*; ~**schatzscheine** [etwa] British savings bonds; ~**schifffahrtsbehörde** Federal Maritime Commission *(US)*; ~**schlichter** Federal Mediator *(US)*; ~**schlichtungsausschuß** National

Mediation Board *(US)*; ~**schuld** federal (national) debt *(US)*, public (government) debt; ~**schuldbuch** National Debt Register; ~**schuldbuchforderungen** debt register claims; ~**schuldenverwaltung** [etwa] National Debt Commissioner *(Br.)*, Debt Management *(US)*; ~**schuldverschreibungen** [etwa] government (state) bonds *(US)*, funds *(Br.)*, public stocks; ~**siegel** Great Seal *(Br.)*; ~**sozialgericht** [etwa] Local Appeal Tribunal *(Br.)*; ~**sozialhilfegesetz** [etwa] Federal Insurance Contribution Act *(US)*, National Assistance Act *(Br.)*; ~**sparkassenverband** National Association of Savings Banks *(US)*; ~**staat** federal (federated) state *(US)*; **innerhalb eines ~staates** intrastate.

bundesstaatlich national, federal *(US)*;
~**es System** federal system.

Bundes|statistik government statistics; ~**statistiker** National Bureau economist *(US)*; ~**stelle für Außenhandelsinformationen** foreign-trade information office; ~**stelle für Wohnungsbau** Federal Housing Administration *(US)*; ~**steuer** federal tax *(US)*; ~**steuerverwaltung** Bureau of Internal Revenue *(US)*; ~**straße** highway; ~- **und Landesstraßen** A and B roads; **der ~straße 51 folgen** to pick up route 51; ~**straßennummer** road number; ~**tag** Parliament; ~**tagssitzung** parliamentary session; ~**tagswahlen** national elections; ~**unterstützung** federal aid *(US)*.

Bundesverband|der Börsenmakler National Association of Securities Dealers *(US)*; ~ **der Immobilienmakler** [etwa] National Association of Estate Agents; ~ **der Industrie** Confederation of Industry *(Br.)*; ~ **der Kapitalanlagegesellschaften** National Association of Investment Clubs *(Br.)*.

Bundes|vereinigung der Arbeitgeberverbände National Union of Manufacturers *(Br.)*; ~**verfassung** federal constitution *(US)*; ~**verfassungsgericht** Constitutional Court; ~**vermögen** public (crown, *Br.*) property; ~**versicherungsanstalt** Federal Security Agency *(US)*; ~**versicherungsanstalt für Krediteinlagensicherung** Federal Deposit Insurance Corporation *(US)*; ~**versorgungsgesetz** war pensions act *(Br.)*; ~**verteidigung** national defense *(US)* (defence, *Br.*); ~**verteidigungsminister** Minister of defence *(Br.)*; ~**verwaltung** federal administration; **unabhängige ~verwaltungsbehörde** independent agency *(US)*; ~**wehr** army, armed forces; ~**wehrangehöriger** member of the army; ~**wertpapiergesetz** Federal Securities Act *(US)*; ~**wirtschaftsrat** [etwa] National Economic Development Council *(Br.)*; ~**zuschuß** federal subsidy *(US)*, grant-in-aid *(US)*.

bündig succinct, to the point, concise, brief, *(ohne Einzug)* flush;
kurz und ~ sein to be brief and to the point;
~**er Stil** terse style.

Bündnis alliance, league, confederation, coalition, entente, combination, hookup;
militärisches ~ zur gegenseitigen Unterstützung abschließen to enter into a military alliance; ~**se auswechseln** to switch political alliances; ~ **eingehen** to engage in a confederation; **mit jem. ein enges ~ eingehen** to form a close alliance with s. o.; ~ **mit einem anderen Land eingehen** to contract an alliance with another country; ~ **schließen** to enter into an alliance; **von einem ~ abhängig sein** to hinge on an alliance; **sich zu einem ~ vereinigen** to federate;
~**austausch** switching political alliances.

bündnisfrei noncommitted, nonaligned;
~**es Land** uncommitted (nonaligned) nation.

Bündnis|freiheit nonalignment; ~**politik** alliance diplomacy; ~**system** system of alliances; ~**vertrag** pact.

Bundsteg back margin, *(drucktechn.)* gutter.

Bungalow[haus] bungalow, flat home;
mit ~s bebaut overbuilt with bungalows;
~**siedlung** bungalow town (estate).

Bunker bunker, *(mil.)* airraid shelter, pillbox, *(U-Boote)* pen;
~**kohle** bunker (steam) coal.

Bunkern bunkering.

bunkern to bunker, to fuel.

Bunker|preise in Heimathäfen bunker rate in home ports; ~**station** coaling station.

bunt colo(u)red, varied, multicolo(u)r;
~ **durcheinander liegen** to be in utter confusion; **wie ein ~er Hund bekannt sein** to be known all over the place; ~ **gekleidet sein** to be gaudily dressed; **es ~ treiben** to go the pace; **es zu ~ treiben** to carry matters too far; **jem. ~ vor den Augen werden** to make s. o. feel dizzy; **alles ~ durcheinander werfen** to throw down higgledy-piggledy;
~**er Abend** variety show; ~**e Blumen** bright flowers; ~**es Durcheinander** complete muddle; ~**e Farben** gay (bright) colo(u)rs; ~**es Gemisch** motley; ~**es Glas** stained glass; ~**es Leben führen** to lead a gay life; ~**e Menschenmenge** motley crowd; **zu ~es Muster** loud design; ~**e Platte** dish of various kinds of sliced meat; ~**es Programm** *(Fernsehen)* variety hour *(Br.)*, variety program(me); ~**e Reihe machen** to pair off; **in ~er Reihenfolge** in colo(u)rful succession; ~**e Unterhaltungsmusik** musical medley.

Bunt|bild colo(u)red picture; ~**druck** colo(u)red printing; ~**heit** variety.

buntkariert, mir ist ~ zumute my head is swimming.

Bunt|papier bright-colo(u)red paper; ~**stift** crayon, colo(u)red chalk; ~**waren** printed cotton goods.

Bunze *(drucktechn.)* counter.

Bürde load, burden, weight;
unter der ~ der Jahre under the weight of the years;
schwere ~ dead weight;
~ **des Alters** weight of age; ~ **der Verantwortung** strain of responsibility;
jem. eine ~ abnehmen to relieve s. o. of a burden; **von einer ~ befreien** to disburden; ~ **für j. sein** to be a charge (burden) on s. o.

Burg castle, stronghold, citadel, fortress.

Bürge bail, bailsman, surety, bond, bondsman, voucher, caution, cautioneer, *(für Einwanderer)* sponsor *(US)*, *(Garant)* guarantor, guarantee *(US)*, guaranty, warrantor;
als ~ guaranteed by; **wie ein ~** surety-like;
in Anspruch genommener ~ vouchee; **gesamtschuldnerische ~n** joint and several guarantors; **bedingt haftender ~** conditional guarantor; **leistender ~** paying surety; **selbstschuldnerischer ~** absolute guarantor, primary obligor *(US)*; **sicherer (tauglicher) ~** substantial surety; **solidarischer ~** joint guarantor; **unsicherer ~** straw bail;
~ **für eine Schuld** surety for a debt;
sich als ~ anbieten to come forward as a surety; **als ~ auftreten** to act (go) as bailsman; ~**n freistellen** to discharge a surety; **als ~ für j. haften** to stand bail (surety) for s. o.; **seinen ~n in Anspruch nehmen** to apply (resort) to one's surety; **sich als ~ qualifizieren** to justify; **für j. ~ sein** to go bail for s. o.; ~**n stellen** to find bail (surety), to furnish a surety, to fund bail, to put in a bailsman; **sich einen ~n verschaffen** to find bail; **als ~ zugelassen werden** to be admitted to bail.

bürgen to [stand] bail, to become surety, to vouch, *(für Einwanderer)* to sponsor, *(garantieren)* to guarantee, to be guarantee for, to warrant, to be answerable for, *(Rundfunkwerbung)* to sponsor;
für j. ~ to go (become) bail (answer) for s. o.; **für die Echtheit einer Ware ~** to guarantee the genuineness of goods; **für jds. Ehrlichkeit und Zuverlässigkeit ~** to warrant s. o. an honest and reliable person; **für den Eingang eines Betrages ~** to stand surety for payment of a sum; **für eine Schuld ~** to guarantee (answer for) a debt; **für jds. Verhalten ~** to vouch for s. one's good conduct; **für einen Wechsel ~** to guarantee [for the payment of] a bill *(Br.)*, to stand surety for the payment of a bill; **mit seinem Wort ~** to pledge one's word; **für jds. Zahlungsfähigkeit ~** to vouch for s. one's ability to pay.

Bürgen|gemeinschaft joint guarantors; ~**gestellung vor Pfändung** pledges to restore (foreign attachment, *Br.*); ~**haftung** surety's liability; ~**überprüfung** guarantor enquiry.

Bürger citizen, city dweller, civilian, commoner, freeman, *(Gesellschaftsschicht)* member of the middle class, *(Stadtbewohner)* townsman, resident, city dweller;
akademischer ~ student, gownsman, member of the university; **angesehener ~** respectable citizen; **einfacher ~** private citizen, commoner, commonalty; **freier ~** free citizen; **friedlicher ~** orderly citizen; **am schlechtesten gestellter ~** last-advantaged citizen; **prominente ~** civic headliners *(US)*; **stimmberechtigter ~** franchiser;
~ **einer Stadt werden** to get the freedom of a city;
~**ausschuß** citizens' committee; ~**gemeinschaft** community association (group); ~**gruppe** citizen group; ~**initiative** citizens' action group; ~**krieg** civil commotion (war), domestic warfare, internal (intestine) war; ~**kultur** civic culture; ~**kunde** civics.

bürgerlich civil, civic, *(nicht adlig)* untitled, *(einfach)* simple, plain, unpretentious, *(spießerhaft)* burgeois, philistine, *(Status)* middle-class, common;
~ **gekleidet** plainly dressed, in plain clothes; ~-**rechtlich** civil law;
~**er Beruf** civil employment; ~**e Ehe** civil marriage; ~**e Ehrenrechte** civic rights; ~**e Freiheit** civil liberty; ~**e Gesellschaft** civil society; ~**es Gesetzbuch** Civil Code; **aus ~em Hause sein** to come from a middle-class family; ~**er Haushalt**

middle-class family; ~es **Jahr** calendar (civil) year; ~e **Küche** plain cooking; ~e **Laufbahn** civil life; **im** ~en **Leben** in civilian life; ~e **Lebensweise** civil ways, plain living; ~e **Parteien** nonsocialist parties; ~es **Recht** civil law; ~er **Rechtsstreit** civil action (suit); ~er **Tod** civil death; ~e **Vorurteile haben** to have middle-class prejudices; ~e **Wohngegend** middle-class residential area.

Bürgermeister chief magistrate, mayor, town reeve *(Canada)*, magistrate *(Scot.)*;
berufsmäßiger ~ city manager; **früherer** ~ former mayor; **neuer** ~ incoming mayor; **SPD-**~ [etwa] Labour mayor *(Br.)*; **stellvertretender (zweiter)** ~ deputy mayor;
j. als ~ **einstellen** to appoint s. o. as mayor; **für das Amt des** ~s **kandidieren** to stand as mayor; ~ **sein** to serve as mayor;
~**amt** mayoralty, city hall; ~**frau** lady mayoress.

Bürgerpflichten civic (civil) duties, obligations of good citizenship.

Bürgerrecht citizenship, freedom of a city, franchise, citizen right *(US)*, political liberty, city freedom, burgesship;
~e personal (political) rights, privileges of citizens;
verfassungsmäßig garantiertes ~ civil liberty *(US)*; **Londoner** ~e the liberties of the City of London;
~**e und Pflichten** public (citizen, *US*) rights;
~**e besitzen** to be free of a city; **sich um** ~**e bewerben** to apply for registration as a citizen; ~**e erwerben** to take out one's freedom; ~ **haben** to rank as a citizen; **jem. das** ~ **verleihen** to enfranchise s. o., to make s. o. free of the city.

Bürgerrechts|bewegung Civil Rights Association; ~**gemeinschaft** citizens' action group; ~**gesetze** civil rights legislation; ~**initiative** citizen initiative; ~**programm** civil rights program(me).

Bürger|schaft citizens, citizenry, town council, town, townsfolk; ~- **und Studentenschaft** town and gown; ~**sinn** public spirit; **mangelnder** ~**sinn** incivism; ~**stand** the middle classes.

Bürgersteig pavement *(Br.)*, sidewalk *(US)*, banquette *(US)*, footway, footpath *(Australia)*;
auf dem ~ **zum Verkauf ausgelegt** peddled on the pavement; **fahrender** ~ moving sidewalk;
am ~ **anhalten** to pull up at the kerb; **auf den** ~ **zurückdrängen** to move back to the pavement;
~**seite** kerb- (near) side.

Bürger|steuer town (poll) tax; ~**tugend** civism; ~**tum** the middle classes; **gehobenes** ~**tum** upper middle classes; ~**vereinigung** civil league *(US)*; ~**versammlung** town meeting *(US)*; **jährliche** ~**versammlung** annual meeting of the parish.

Bürgerwehr militia, home guards *(Br.)*;
~**ausschuß** vigilance committee *(US)*; ~**mitglied** vigilante *(US)*.

Burg|friede party truce; ~**frieden mit jem. schließen** to make a truce with s. o.; ~**graben** moat; ~**hof** bailey.

Bürgschaft pledge, assurance, caution, cautionary, gage *(Br.)*, undertaking, *(Einwanderung)* sponsion, *(Garantie)* bond, guarantee, guaranty *(US)*, personal warranty, *(vor Gericht)* bail, surety, *(Rundfunkprogramm)* sponsorship, *(Sicherheit)* security, cover, collateral *(US)*, *(für Wechsel)* del credere *(Br.)*;
gegen ~ on security; **gegen** ~ **freigelassen** free on bail;
alleinige ~ sole guarantee; **auf einen Sonderfall beschränkte** ~ specific guarantee; **einwandfreie** ~ trustworthy guarantee *(Br.)*, *(für Wechsel)* del credere *(Br.)*; **gesamtschuldnerische** ~ joint and several guarantee (guaranty, *US*); **hohe** ~ ample bail; **kaufmännische** ~ commercial guarantee; **persönliche** ~ special guaranty, personal warranty; **selbstschuldnerische** ~ absolute guaranty *(US)*, guaranty of payment *(US)*; **sichere** ~ substantial (good) bail (surety), good security (surety); **solidarische** ~ collateral guaranty; **wechselseitige** ~ cross guarantee; **bei Aufforderung fällig werdende** ~ guarantee payable on demand;
~ **einer Bank** bank guarantee (guaranty, *US*); ~ **ohne Einrede der Vorausklage** absolute guaranty *(US)*, guaranty of payment *(US)*; ~ **für Erscheinen vor Gericht** common bail; ~ **für Qualität** quality warrant;
~ **aufbringen (beibringen)** to furnish a guarantee, to raise bail; ~ **eingehen** to enter into a suretyship; **gegen** ~ **freilassen** to release on bail; ~ **schießen lassen** to jump bail; ~ **leisten (stellen)** to bail, to give (furnish, stand) bail, to stand a guaranty, to put in a bailsman, *(garantieren)* to guarantee, to offer guarantee *(Br.)*, to warrant, *(Kaution)* to furnish (give) security, *(Schuld verbürgen)* to insure a debt, *(Wechsel)* to stand del credere *(Br.)*; **für j.** ~ **leisten** to become (stand) security (stand as guarantor) for s. o., *(Kaution stellen)* to go (become) bail for s. o.; **für die Schulden eines Dritten** ~ **leisten** to guarantee to pay (the payment of) a man's debt; **durch** ~ **verpflichtet sein** to be bound over; ~ **für j. stellen** to become bail for s. o.; ~ **übernehmen** to undertake (enter into) a guarantee, to go (stand, act as) surety, *(Rundfunkprogramm)* to sponsor; **für j.** ~ **übernehmen** to go guarantee (act as suretor) for s. o.; ~ **für pünktliche Lieferung übernehmen** to wage delivery; **selbstschuldnerische** ~ **übernehmen** to be liable as principal debtor (primary obligor, *US*); **durch** ~ **verpflichten** to bind over; **sich** ~ **verschaffen** to find bail; **Wechsel mit** ~ **versehen** to furnish a bill with surety; ~ **verstärken** to reinforce a guarantee.

bürgschaftsähnlich surety-like.

Bürgschafts|angebot offer of security (suretyship); ~**bedingungen** bail conditions; ~**brief** letter of indemnity; ~**empfänger** warrantee; ~**erklärung** declaration of guarantee (guaranty), surety warrant, guarantee *(Br.)*, guaranty *(US)*, surety [bond], warrant, warranty; **schriftliche** ~**erklärung** bail bond; ~**erklärung für Einwanderer** affidavit of support *(US)*.

bürgschaftsfähig bailable.

Bürgschafts|formular guarantee form; ~**formular einer Bank** standard form of bank guarantee; ~**girant** irregular indorser; ~**gläubiger** guarantee; ~**höhe** amount of guarantee, caution money *(Br.)*; ~**klauseln** guarantee clauses; ~**kredit** guaranteed credit; ~**leistung** bailment, surety, suretyship, guarantee *(Br.)*, guaranty *(US)*, *(Aktiengesellschaft)* corporate suretyship; ~**makler** security dealer; ~**nehmer** guarentee bailer; ~**provision** guarantee commission; ~**schein** deed of suretyship, security, security (bail) bond, warranty, surety, guarantee *(Br.)*, guaranty *(US)*, *(Strafrecht)* bail bond; **besonderer** ~**schein** special bond; ~**schuld** guarantee indebtedness *(Br.)*; ~**sicherheit** security, cover, collateral; ~**summe** amount of guarantee, caution money *(Br.)*, *(vor Gericht)* caution money, bail; ~**übernahme** giving bail; ~**urkunde** bail bond, warranty deed, cautionary *(Scot. law)*; ~**verhältnis** principal and surety.

Bürgschaftsverpflichtung guarantee, bondage, [obligation of] guaranty;
j. aus einer ~ **entlassen** to release s. o. from a bondage; **seinen** ~**en nachkommen** to pay under a guaranty.

Bürgschafts|versprechen, ~**vertrag** [contract of] suretyship, contract of guaranty, security (guarantee) contract, promise of guarantee or suretyship, collateral undertaking (promise), warrant;
einfaches (schriftliches) ~ guarantee under hand; **notarielles** ~ guarantee under seal; **vom Hauptschuldner unabhängiger** ~ suretyship contract; ~ **ohne Einrede der Vorausklage** contract of suretyship, surety contract.

Bürgschafts|volumen total guarantees; ~**wechsel** guaranteed bill of exchange; ~**wert** security value.

Büro office, store, bureau *(US)*, agency, *(Kontor)* countinghouse *(Br.)*;
fliegendes ~ airborne traffic; **kaufmännisches** ~ business office; **unser Londoner** ~ our London office; **ständiges** ~ permanent office; **technisches** ~ drawing office;
~ **für Auswanderungsfragen** emigration office; ~ **eines Freiverkehrsmaklers** bucket shop *(Br.)*; ~ **nach dem Raumgliederungssystem** open-plan office; ~ **für Reklamationen** complaints office; ~ **für unzustellbare Sendungen** dead-letter office;
im ~ **arbeiten** to work in an office, to clerk; **j. im** ~ **aufhalten** to keep s. o. in the office; **neues** ~ **errichten** to locate a new office; **ins** ~ **gehen** to go to the office, to clerk it; **kurz ins** ~ **hineinschauen** to look in at the office; **sich im** ~ **melden** to apply at the office; ~ **modernisieren** to bring an office up to date; **sein** ~ **mit jem. teilen** to share an office with s. o.; **sein** ~ **unterbringen** to locate one's office; ~ **unterhalten** to maintain an office; **eigene** ~**s in der ganzen Welt unterhalten** to operate own offices throughout the world; **auf jeden Fall pünktlich im** ~ **sein wollen** to be intent on getting to the office in time; **sich in sein** ~ **zurückziehen** to pen o. s. up in one's office;
~**adresse** business address, *(AG)* statutory office *(US)*; ~**angestellte** lady clerk, *(pl.)* blackcoated *(Br.)* (white-collar, *US*) classes, white-collared employees.

Büro|angestellter, ~**arbeiter** salaried (office) clerk, clerical worker (officer), employee, white-collar worker;
höherer ~ black-coated *(Br.)* (white-collar, *US*) worker;
als ~ **arbeiten (**~ **sein)** to clerk, to work in an office.

Büro|anschluß office telephone; ~**anschrift** official address.

Büroarbeit desk (office, clerical, secretariat) work;
~**en** paper work, clerical operations;
gehobene ~ black-coated *(Br.)* (white-collar, *US*) job; **gewöhnliche** ~ office routine;
mit allen ~**en vertraut sein** to be familiar with all office routine; ~ **verrichten** to do one's work in an office, to clerk.

Büro | artikel office supplies (appliances), stationery; ~**artikelmarkt** office-equipment market; ~**aufwand** office expenditure; ~**ausstattung** office appliances (layout, equipment), business equipment; ~**bauten** office buildings; ~**bautenkonjunktur** office-building boom; ~**bauvorhaben** nonresidential investment; ~**bedarf[sartikel]** stationery, office supplies (appliances), office requirements, clerical equipment *(US)*; ~**bedarfsfirma** office-equipment firm; ~**bedürfnisse** office requisites; ~**beschäftigung** clerical occupation; ~**betrieb** office routine (procedure), office operating; ~**chef** chief clerk, bureau chief; ~**diebstahl** office theft; ~**diener** office boy, messenger, commissionaire *(Br.)*; ~**dienst** clerical (secretarial) service; ~**einrichtung** office fittings (equipment), clerical equipment *(US)*, fixtures, office appliances (furnishing(s)), *(Bilanz)* furniture and office (business) equipment; ~**erfahrung** clerical routine, office-work experience; ~**fläche** office space; ~**gebäude** office building (block); **mehrstöckiges** ~**gebäude** multiple-story business building; **aus dem Geschäft der Errichtung von** ~**gebäuden aussteigen** to jump off one's office blocks; ~**gegenstände** office fixtures, stationery goods; ~**gehälter** salaries; ~**gehilfe** office boy, clerical assistant, writer *(US)*; ~**gemeinschaft** sharing office facilities; ~**gemeinschaft mit jem. unterhalten** to share an office with s. o.; ~**gerät** office model; ~**gestaltung** office planning; ~**grundstücke in Spitzenlage** top-quality office property; ~**hengst** pencil (pen) pusher *(sl.)*; ~**hilfe** junior clerk (desk), office boy (girl); ~**hilfskraft** clerical assistant; ~**hilfspersonal** back-office personnel; ~**hochhaus** office tower; ~**inventar** office fixtures; ~**klammer** paper clip; ~**klatsch** office gossip; ~**komplex** block of offices, office block; ~**kosten** office expenses (charges); **zu den** ~**kosten gehören** to come under office charges; ~**kraft** clerical worker, salaried clerk, office employee; ~**kräfte** office personnel (force), clerical force (staff).

Bürokrat red-tapist, bureaucrat;
aufgeblasener ~ jack-in-office, bureaucratist;
~**en der Europäischen Gemeinschaft** commission bureaucrats.

Bürokratie red-tape, officialdom, bureaucracy.

bürokratisch bureaucratic, red-tape[d];
~**e Unfähigkeit** bureaucratic bungling; ~**es Verhalten** bureaucratic behavio(u)r.

Büro | kratismus bureaucracy, red tape (tapism), red-tapedom (-tapery), bumbledom, officialism; ~**lampe** desk lamp; ~**leiter** office manager, managing clerk; ~**leitung** office management; ~**mädchen** office girl; ~**maschinen** business (office) machines; ~**material** stationery, office supplies; ~**miete** office rent; ~**mitbenutzung** secretarial facilities; ~**möbel**, ~**mobiliar** office furniture; ~**neubauten** office construction; ~**nutz[ungs]fläche** office floor space, office area; ~**organisation** office management; ~**organisation im Griff haben** to make for bureaucratic control; ~**personal** [office] personnel, clerical force (staff), office staff (force), hands; **untergeordnetes** ~**personal** junior office staff; ~**personal engagieren** to staff an office; ~**raum** office space; ~**raum zur Verfügung stellen** to furnish office room; ~**räume** office accommodation (premises), offices; **unvermietete** ~**räume** unlet office space; ~**räume mieten** to take offices; ~**raumgestalter** office planner; ~**schluß** closing time; ~**schrank mit Fächern** storage cabinet; ~**schreibmaschine** office typewriter; ~**stenotypist** office typist; ~**stuhl** office chair; ~**stunden** office (business) hours, hours of attendance; **seine** ~**stunden pünktlich einhalten** to be punctual in one's attendance (at one's office); ~**tätigkeit** secretarial (clerical) service, clerical occupation (work), desk work, office work (practice, services), *(gehobenere)* black-coated *(Br.)* (white-collar, *US*) job; ~**termin** *(Gericht)* hearing in chamber; ~**tratsch** chitchat; ~**unkosten** office expenses (expenditure), office-operating (clerical) costs; **generelle** ~**unkosten** office overheads; **zu** ~**unkosten gehören** to come under office charges; ~**unterbringung** office accommodation; ~**unterlagen** clerical records, files; ~**verwaltung** office management; ~**vorstand**, ~**vorsteher** head clerk, office keeper (manager), chief (head, senior) clerk, bureau manager, *(Anwaltsbüro)* senior (barrister's, counsel's, managing, *Br.*) clerk; ~**wand** office wall; ~**zeit** office hours, hours of attendance; **für** ~**zwecke** for office use.

Bursche lad, youth, dog, duck, guy *(US sl.)*;
aufgeblasener ~ swellhead; **durchtriebener** ~ deep card *(sl.)*; **gewitzter** ~ sharp lad; **hartgesottener** ~ hardened case, hard-boiled egg; **rüder** ~ slippery fellow; **toller** ~ shark *(US sl.)*; **tollkühner** ~ risk fellow; **übler** ~ bad egg (hat, lot).

burschikoser Zeitgenosse hail-fellow-well-met.

Bürstenabzug *(drucktechn.)* galley [stone] proof;
~ **machen** to beat a proof.

Bürsten | binder, wie ein ~**binder trinken** to drink like a fish; ~**binderware** brushware; ~**haarschnitt** crew cut.

Bus, mit Liegemöglichkeiten ausgestatteter rest-room equipped bus; **für den Pendelverkehr eingesetzter** ~ commuter (shuttle) bus; **gemieteter** ~ taxibus; **vollgestopfter** ~ crowded bus; **zweistöckiger** ~ double-decker;
~ **mit beschränkter Platzzahl** limited *(US)*;
aus dem ~ **aussteigen** to debus; ~ **benutzen** to ride on a bus; **mit dem** ~ **fahren** to go by bus; **2 Pence für den** ~ **kosten** to be a twopenny ride in the bus; ~ **in Betrieb nehmen** to put a bus on the road; **j. aus einem** ~ **schleudern** to tumble s. o. out of a bus; **aus dem** ~ **geschleudert werden** to be shot out of a coach; ~ **aus dem Verkehr ziehen** to take a bus off the road;
~**bahnhof** bus terminal *(Br.)*, bus pool *(US)*.

Busch bush, shrub;
hinter dem ~ **halten** to keep one's plans quiet; **auf den** ~ **klopfen** to beat about the bush.

Büschel Stroh wisp of straw.

Busch | krieg bush-fighting; ~**werk** shrubbery, underwood, undergrowth.

Busen bosom, breast;
Haß im ~ **nähren** to harbo(u)r hatred against s. o.; **Schlange an seinem** ~ **nähren** to nourish a viper in one's bosom; **Geheimnis tief in seinem** ~ **verschließen** to have a secret safely locked away in one's breast;
~**freund** bosom friend.

Bus | fahrer bus driver; ~**fahrkarte** [omni]bus ticket; ~**fahrplan** bus guide (schedule); ~**fahrt** bus ride; ~**geld** busfare; ~**haltelinie** priority (bus) lane; ~**halteplatz** bus area; ~**haltestelle** bus stop (station); **geschützte** ~**haltestelle**, ~**häuschen** bus shelter; ~**linie** bus line; **öffentlich betriebene** ~**linie** publicly run bus; ~**ruf** dial-a-bus; ~**schaffner** clippie.

Buße amend, *(Bußgeld, Geldstrafe)* exemplary damages, administrative fine, mulct, forfeit, *(Reugeld)* added (vindictive, punitive, *US*) damages, exemplary damages, atonement money;
~ **für Nichterfüllung eines Vertrages** liquidated damages;
~ **auferlegen** to fine; **j. mit einer** ~ **belegen** to impose a fine upon s. o.; ~ **bezahlen** to pay a fine; **jem. eine** ~ **erlassen** to let s. o. go unpunished; ~ **festsetzen** to assess a fine; ~ **tun** to penance, to repent; **zu einer** ~ **von 20 Dollar verurteilt werden** to be fined $ 20; ~ **zahlen** to atone;
~**angebot** tender of amends.

büßen, etw. mit seinem Leben to pay for s. th. with one's life;
schrecklich für seine Fehler ~ **müssen** to pay for it up to the hilt.

bußfertig penitent.

Bußgeld executory damages, atonement money;
~ **festsetzen** to assess a fine;
~**bescheid** penalty note; ~**katalog** fixed penalty code; ~**verfahren** summary proceedings.

Bußzahlung amercement, mulct, fine, cashlite.

Bus | transport von Schulkindern school bussing; **sich über die** ~**verbindungen vorher genauestens unterrichten** to assess bus connections efficiently; ~**verkehr** bus service; **stündlicher** ~**verkehr** hourly bus service.

Butangas bottle gas.

Bütte tub, vat, butt.

Büttel beadle, catchpoll, bum, bailiff *(Br.)*.

Bütten | papier hand-made paper; ~**rand** deckle-edge.

Butter butter;
in ~ *(fam.)* in apple-pie order, like lamb and salad, hunky *(US sl.)*;
sich nicht die ~ **vom Brot nehmen lassen** to stick up for one's rights, to know where one's bread is buttered; **wie** ~ **in der Sonne schmelzen** *(Geld)* to melt away; **in** ~ **sein** to be in apple-pie order; **weich wie** ~ **sein** to be as weak as water;
ein Gesicht machen, wie wenn einem die ~ **vom Brot gefallen wäre** to make a face as long as a fiddle;
ihm ist die ~ **vom Brot gefallen** he is down in the mouth;
~**berg** butter mountain.

Butterbrot | e bread and butter;
immer nur für ein ~ **arbeiten** to work all day and every day for a mere pittance; **für ein** ~ **bekommen** to pick up for a pittance, to get s. th. for a mere song; **dauernd aufs** ~ **schmieren** to rub it in, to ram s. th. into s. o.; ~ **streichen** to butter a slice of bread;
~**papier** greaseproof paper.

Butter | fach *(Kühlschrank)* butter compartment; ~**faß** tub for butter; ~**gebäck** cookies *(US)*.

buttern, Geld in etw. to put a lot of money into s. th.

Butterseite | des Lebens pleasant side of life;
immer auf die ~ **fallen** to always fall on one's feet again.

C

Cabriolet cabriolet, convertible.
Cafe coffee house, (shop, *US*), café.
Cafeteria cafeteria, snack bar.
Camping camping.
~**artikel** camping article; ~**ausrüstung** camping equipment; ~**bett** camping bed, cot; **schnelles** ~**fahrzeug** pickup camper; ~**führer** camping guide; ~**lager** camping ground; ~**platz** autocamp, camping place (ground), caravan site *(Br.)*, motor camp *(US)*; ~**tisch** folding table; ~**wagen** camper unit (vehicle).
caritativ charitable;
sich ~ **betätigen** to dispense charity;
~**e Einrichtung** charitable organization.
Carnet international customs pass, customs passbook, carnet.
Celsius celsius, centigrade;
35 Grad ~ **erreichen** to touch 35° C;
~**thermometer** centigrade thermometer.
Cent cent *(US)*.
Chaiselongue couch, lounge chair, *(Liegesofa)* divan.
Chalet chalet, country cottage.
Chance chance, opportunity, break, odds, opening, prospect, crack *(fam.)*, whack *(sl.)*;
ohne jede ~ out of court;
echte ~ fair field, even break; **nur eine** ~ bare (naked) possibility; **einmalige** ~ once-in-a-lifetime opportunity, chance in a thousand; **geringe** ~ off chance; **nicht die geringste** ~ not even a dog's chance, out of court; **gleiche** ~**n** close betting, *(Geschäft)* even break; **große** ~ big break; **reelle** ~**n** payoff opportunities; **mit Risiko verbundene** ~ sporting chance; **wirtschaftliche** ~**n** business prospects; **zukünftige** ~**n** future prospects;
~**n für den Einsatz von Risikokapital** risk capital opportunities; **geringe** ~ **bei starker Konkurrenz** no look-in with a strong competition; ~ **seines Lebens** chance of a lifetime;
die ~**n eines Abkommens abtasten** to feel one's way towards an agreement; **seine** ~ **abwarten** to watch one's time; ~ **beim Schopf ergreifen** to take time by the forelock, to leap at an opportunity; **jem. eine** ~ **geben** to give s. o. a break (the edge) *(coll.)*; **jem. keine** ~ **geben** to shut the door upon s. o.; ~**n haben** to have possibilities, to have fair prospects in life; **die besten** ~**n haben** to be well in on a deal *(fam.)*; **keine** ~ **haben** to have not a prayer *(sl.)*; **fast keine** ~ **haben** to be on the off chance; **keine** ~ **gegen seinen Gegner haben** to have no sight against one's opponents *(US)*; **nicht die geringste** ~ **haben** to have not an earthly chance; **mit gleichen** ~**n kämpfen** to meet on even ground; **nur geringe** ~**n für eine Besserung machen können** to hold out little hope for recovery; **sich eine** ~ **entgehen lassen** to miss (pass up, let slip) a chance (opportunity), to throw away an opportunity; ~ **fahren lassen** to omit an opportunity; ~ **ungenutzt lassen** to pass up a chance; ~ **vorbeigehen lassen** to gum up the works *(sl.)*; ~ **nutzen (zu nutzen wissen)** to improve the occasion, to avail o. s. of an opportunity, to make good use of an opportunity; **zu spät um eine** ~ **zu nutzen** the day after the fair; ~ **verpassen** to let an opportunity slip, to throw away a good opportunity, to miss the boat (bus, *sl.*); ~ **versäumen** to neglect an opportunity; **seine** ~ **verscherzen (vertun)** to blot one's copybook, to miss one's chance (the bus, *sl.*), to muddle away one's opportunities; **seine** ~**n wahrnehmen** to make the best of one's opportunities, to take one's chances, to grab at (seize upon) one's opportunities; ~ **nicht wahrnehmen** to waive a chance; **auf seine** ~ **warten** to watch (bide) one's time, *(auf einem Nebengleis)* to sit on the sidelines.
Chancengleichheit evenness (equality) of opportunities.
Chancengleichheitsprogramm Equal Opportunity Program *(US)*.
chancenreich *(Börse)* promising.
Chancenungleichheit im Wettbewerb imperfect competition.
Chaos chaos, snapu *(US sl.)*;
wirtschaftliches ~ economic chaos;
~ **in einem Zimmer anrichten** to make a litter in a room.
Charakter character, nature, mettle, colo(u)r, complexion;
amtlicher ~ officiality; **anständiger** ~ fine character; **despotischer** ~ domineering character; **fragwürdiger** ~ queer (doubtful) character; **freimütiger** ~ open character; **aus dem Leben genommener** ~ characters taken from life; **zwei grundverschiedene** ~**e** two characters stongly opposed; **konzernähnlicher** ~ quasi-trust character; **nachgiebiger** ~ pliable character; **niedriger** ~ vile character; **öffentlicher** ~ publicness; **offizieller** ~ officiality; **provisorischer** ~ provisionality; **staatlicher** ~ governmental character; **undurchsichtiger** ~ dubious character; **vornehmer** ~ noble spirit (mind); **zwingender** ~ compulsoriness;
~ **eines Professors (Dozenten)** status of a professor; **obligatorischer** ~ **eines Vertrages** obligatory scope of a contract;
jds. ~ **entscheidend beeinflussen** to determine s. one's character; ~ **beurteilen** to gauge a character; ~ **bilden** to form (mould) the character; ~ **eines Kindes bilden** to form a child's character; **dem Ergebnis den** ~ **einer Volksabstimmung geben** to put the plebiscite label on the outcome; **amtlichen** ~ **haben** to officialize; **vertraulichen** ~ **haben** to be of a confidential nature; **in jds.** ~ **liegen** to be part of s. one's nature; **nicht zu jds.** ~ **passen** to be foreign to s. one's nature, not to be in line with s. one's character; **vertraulichen** ~ **tragen** *(Besprechung)* to be of a confidential nature;
~**analyse** character analysis; ~**anlage** disposition, natural tendency; ~**beurteilung einer Person** estimate of a person's character; ~**beurteilung vornehmen** to gauge a character; ~**bild** character sketch (study).
charakterbildend character building (moulding).
Charakter|bildung character building; ~**darsteller** character actor; ~**eigenschaften** traits in character; ~**fehler** blot on the character, defect (flaw) in character.
charakterfest of strong character.
Charakterfestigkeit decision of character.
charakterisieren to characterize, to feature.
Charakterisierung characterization.
Charakteristik characterization, portrayal of character.
Charakteristikum characteristic feature, hallmark, touch, mark.
charakteristisch characteristic, distinctive, differential, representative, individual;
~ **für die oberen Klassen** U *(Br.)*;
~ **sein** to be typical; ~ **für ein Zeitalter sein** to mark an era;
~**es Merkmal** characteristic feature; **in** ~**er Weise** characteristically; ~**er Zug** touch, feature.
charakterlich moral;
~ **einwandfrei** of good moral character;
~**e Ausbildung** character moulding (building); ~**e Schwäche** weakness of character.
charakterlos characterless, unprincipled;
~**er Mensch** spineless creature.
Charakter|mangel bad character; ~**schulung** character building (moulding).
charakterschwach weak.
Charakter|schwäche weakness of character; ~**stärke** highness of character, force of character, strength of character, fibre *(fig.)*; ~**stück**, ~**studie** character sketch, character study.
charaktervoller Mann man of character.
Charakterzug, feiger yellow streak.
Charge *(mil.)* rank;
höhere ~**n** higher echelons;
~ **bekleiden** to hold a rank; **jem. eine** ~ **verleihen** to confer a rank on s. o.
Charité hospital.
charmant charming, engaging, winning, pleasant;
~**e Gesellschaft** pleasant society.
Charta charter, deed;
~ **der Vereinten Nationen** United Nations Charter.
Charter charter, *(Schiff)* charter, charterage;
~ **für eine ganze Reise** voyage charter; ~ **für die Hin- und Rückreise** round-trip charter; ~ **auf Zeit** time charter;
~**bedingungen** terms under which a ship (plane, bus) is chartered; ~**dienst** charter service; ~**flug** charter flight; ~**flüge durchführen** to operate charters.
Charterflug|geschäft nonsked business *(US)*; ~**gesellschaft** supplemental [carrier], air charterer; ~**passagier** charter passenger; ~**schein** charter fare; ~**zeug** hired aircraft, chartered plane, chartered aircraft; ~**zeug benutzen, mit dem** ~**zeug hinfliegen** to go on charter, to travel in a chartered aircraft, to airlift.
Charter|genehmigung für Touristenpauschalreisen inclusive tour charter; ~**geschäft** chartering business (operation); ~**gesellschaft** charter carrier (airline, operator), air charterer, supplemental [carrier]; ~**kapazität** charter capacity; ~**maschine** chartered (hired) aircraft; ~**maschine benutzen** to airlift, to fly on a nonscheduled trip *(US)*; ~**mietgebühr** charter hire.

Chartern charter, chartering;
~ **eines Schiffes** voyage charter.
chartern to [take on] charter.
Charter|partie charterparty; ~**preis** charter price; ~**satz** charter rate; ~**schiffahrt** chartering of ships; ~**unternehmen** charter operator; ~**verkehr** charter traffic; ~**vertrag** charterparty, charter agreement, contract of affreightment; ~**vertrag auf Zeit** time charter.
Chassis chassis, frame.
Chauffeur chauffeur, driver, carman;
guten ~ **auftreiben** to discover a good chauffeur *(coll.)*.
chauffieren to act as chauffeur, to drive.
Chaussee highroad, highway *(US)*;
~**graben** roadside ditch; **im** ~**graben landen** to be ditched; ~**schreck** spook.
Chauvinismus chauvinism, jingoism, *(fig.)* flagwaving, spread-eagleism *(US)*.
Chauvinist chauvinist, jingo, flagwaver *(coll.)*, spread-eagle *(US)*.
chauvinistisch chauvinist, jingoistic, flag-waving *(coll.)*, spread-eagle *(US)*;
~**e Partei** jingo (war) party.
Chef *(Prinzipal)* employer, head, chief, manager, principal, master, the old man, gaffer *(Br.)*, governor *(coll.)*, boss *(US)*, main squeeze *(sl.)*, *(Teilhaber)* senior [partner];
oberster ~ paramount chief;
~ **der Buchhaltungs[abteilung]** bookkeeping (accounting) supervisor; ~ **vom Dienst** desk (news, *US*) editor; ~ **des Generalstabes** *(mil.)* chief of staff; ~ **des Hauses** head of the firm, *(Hotel)* chef de cuisine; ~ **des Protokolls** head (chief, *US*) of protocol; ~ **der Verwaltung** chief magistrate;
~ **um Gehaltserhöhung angehen** to tackle the boss for a raise *(US)* (rise, *Br.*); **dem** ~ **täglich Bericht erstatten** to report daily to one's chief; **beim** ~ **schlecht angeschrieben sein** to be in bad with the boss *(US)*; ~ **vom Ganzen sein** to boss the show;
~**arzt** medical superintendant, head physician; ~**berater** copy chief; ~**bereich** bossdom; ~**delegierter** head of a delegation; ~**dolmetscher** chief interpreter; ~**ingenieur** chief engineer; ~**koch** head cook; ~**konstrukteur** chief designer; ~**pilot** test pilot; ~**redakteur** editor in chief *(US)*, managing editor; ~**schreibtisch** executive desk; ~**sekretärin** head secretary; ~**texter** copy chief (supervisor).
Chemie, gerichtliche forensic chemistry;
~**laborant** laboratory assistant; ~**markt** market for chemicals; ~**werte** chemicals, chemical issues.
Chemikalien chemicals.
chemisch chemical;
Anzug ~ **reinigen lassen** to have a suit dry-cleaned;
~**e Fabrik** chemical works; ~**er Krieg** chemical warfare; ~**e Produkte** chemicals; ~**er Prozeß** chemical operation; ~**e Reinigung** dry cleaning.
Chiffre cipher, key, character, *(Anzeige)* box-number;
unter der ~ under ciphers;
~**abteilung** ciphering service; ~**anschrift** code address; ~**anzeige** box- (key, keyed) number advertisement; ~**beamter** code clerk; ~**depesche** cipher telegram; ~**kode** cipher code; ~**nummer** *(Anzeige)* box (key) number; ~**schlüssel** cipher (key) code; ~**schrift** cipher writing; ~**telegramm** cipher telegram; ~**text entschlüsseln** to break a code; ~**werbung** keyed advertising, keying of advertisement; ~**zahl** code number.
Chiffreur code clerk.
chiffrieren to cipher, to code, to encipher, to encode;
Nachricht ~ to write a message in cipher; **Telegramm** ~ to code a telegram.
Chiffrier|gruppe code group; ~**kunst** coding, ciphering; ~**maschine** cipher machine, coder; **Telegramm ohne** ~**maschine verschlüsseln** to cipher telegrams by hand; ~**offizier** cipher officer; ~**raum** cipher room; ~**schlüssel** cipher key, cipher code; ~**schlüssel benutzen** to write a dispatch in code; ~**stelle** cipher office, code center *(US)* (centre, *Br.*).
chiffriert in code (cipher), *(Zeitungsanzeige)* keyed;
nicht ~ in plain language;
~**e Anzeige** keyed advertisement; ~**er Brief** coded letter; ~**e Meldung** ciphered message; ~**es Telegramm** code telegram.
Chiffriertext cipher text.
Chiffrierung coding, ciphering.
Chiffrier|unterlagen cryptographic keys, cipher documents; ~**verfahren** code system.
Chimäre pipe dream.
Chinesenviertel Chinatown.
Chinesische Mauer Great Wall.
Chirurg surgeon;
behandelnder ~ operating surgeon.
Chirurgie *(Krankenhausabteilung)* surgical department of a hospital, surgical ward;
kosmetische ~ cosmetic surgery.
chirurgische|Abteilung *(Krankenhaus)* surgical ward; ~ **Behandlung** operative treatment; ~**r Eingriff** operation; ~**n Eingriff vornehmen** to perform an operation.
Chor choir, chorus;
~ **einstudieren** to rehearse a chorus;
~**leiter** director of chorus.
Chose matter, business;
die ganze ~ caboodle, the works *(US coll.)*.
Christbaum Christmas tree, *(Leuchtbombe)* parachute flare.
Christlicher Verein Junger Männer Young Men's Christian Association.
Chrom chrome.
Chronik chronicle, page.
chronisch *(Krankheit)* chronic, confirmed;
~**e Arbeitslosigkeit** hard core of unemployment; **in** ~**en Geldschwierigkeiten stecken** to be constantly pushed for money; ~**e Krankheit** malady.
Chronist chronicler, annalist.
chronologisch chronological, in order of date;
~ **anordnen** to arrange in chronological order;
~**e Anordnung** chronology; ~**e Reihenfolge** chronological order.
Chronometer timepiece.
Cicero *(drucktechn.)* pica;
anderthalb ~ great primer;
kleine ~**schrift** small pica.
Cicerone guide, cicerone.
cif-Preis cif price.
circulus vitiosus vicious circle, merry-go-round.
Clan clan.
Clearing clearing;
auswärtige ~**s** out clearing *(US)*; **multilaterales** ~ multilateral clearing;
~ **im Finanzzentrum von London** town clearing *(Br.)*; ~ **zum Pariwert** par clearance *(US)*;
durch ~ **abrechnen** to clear;
~**abkommen** clearing agreement; ~**bank** clearing bank; ~**forderungen** clearing claims; ~**geschäft** clearing transaction; ~**guthaben** clearing assets.
Clearinghaus clearinghouse;
~**scheck** clearinghouse check *(US)*; ~**vereinigung** clearing-house association; ~**zertifikat** clearinghouse certificate *(US)*.
Clearing|konto clearing account; ~**kurs** settlement rate; ~**schuld** clearing debt; ~**stelle** clearinghouse; ~**system** clearing system; **starker** ~**verkehr** heavy clearing; ~**vertrag** clearing agreement; ~**vorschüsse** clearing advances.
Clique faction, clan, cabal, clique, coterie, set, junto;
zur ~ **gehören** to be one of the crowd.
Cliquen|mitglied *(Politik)* ringster; ~**wesen**, ~**wirtschaft** cliquism, partisanship.
Clown clown, *(Theater)* funny man.
Cockpit cockpit.
Cocktail cocktail;
~**empfang** cocktail reception; ~**empfang geben** to cocktail; ~**party** cocktail party.
Code code, cryptograph;
Nachricht in ~ **abfassen** to write a message in cipher (code);
~**adresse** code address; ~**buch** cipher key; ~**gruppe** code group; ~**raum** cipher room; ~**schlüssel** cipher code, cipher key; ~**system** code system; ~**text entschlüsseln** to break a code; ~**unterlagen** cipher documents, cryptographic keys; ~**wort** code word.
Collage collage.
College college;
im ~ **wohnend** internal;
in einem ~ **eingeschrieben sein** to be on the boards *(Br.)*; **in ein** ~ **aufgenommen werden** to be accepted at a college; **außerhalb des** ~ **wohnen** to live off campus.
Commerzbank commercial bank.
Compagnon companion, partner.
Computer computer, electronic brain;
mit ~**n ausgestattet** computerized;
~ **anwählen** to dial a computer; ~ **erstmalig in Betrieb nehmen** to initialize a computer; **mittels** ~ **telefonisch übertragen** to send by computer over a telephone line;

~**ausbildung** computer training; ~**ausbildungszentrum** computer training center *(US)* centre *(Br.)*; ~**ausdrücke** computer terms; ~**benutzer** computer user; ~**benutzung** computer use; ~**benutzungsgebühr** computer service fee; ~**einrichtung** computer installation; ~**einsatz** computer application; ~**ergebnis** computer output.

computergesteuert computer-controlled.

Computer|industrie computer industry; ~**ingenieur** computer engineer; ~**kauderwelsch** computer lingo; ~**krieg** electronic war; ~**layout** computerized layout; ~**markt** computer market; ~**mischmasch** computer double-talk (lingo); **zusammengeschaltetes** ~**netz** computer hookup; ~**programmierung** computer programming; ~**revision** computer auditing; ~**satz** computerized composition, computerized typesetting; ~**schlachtfeld** electronic battlefield; ~**sprache** computer language; **weltweiter** ~**verband** world-wide computer linkup; ~**verbundnetz** computer network; ~**vorhersage,** ~**vorschau** computerized (computer-assembled) forecast; ~**zeitalter** computer age; ~**zentrum** computing center *(US)* (centre, *Br.*).

Conférencier conferencier, announcer, compère *(Br.)*, M. C. *(Br.)*, emcee *(US sl.)*;
dem ~ Pointen zuspielen to stooge *(sl.)*.

Container container;
~**bahnhof** container terminal; ~**einrichtungen** container facilities; ~**expresszug** freightliner; ~**verkehr** container service (traffic); ~**wagen** container car.

conto, a for the account of.

Copyright copyright.

Corps Diplomatique diplomatic corps (body).

Couch couch, davenport *(US)*.

Coup coup, stroke, deal;
~ **landen** to pull off a coup, to make a scoop, to engineer a scheme; **jds. letzter ~ gewesen sein** to be s. one's last throw.

Coupé *(Auto)* coupé, *(Bahn)* compartment, *(Wagen)* brougham, coupé.

Couplet vaudeville song.

Coupon coupon, voucher *(Br.)*, *(Dividendenanteil)* dividend warrant;
~ **abtrennen** to detach a coupon;
~**abschlag einbringen** to recover the coupon; ~**kassierer** coupon collector; ~**konto** coupon book; ~**schneider** coupon clipper *(US)*; ~**steuer** coupon tax.

Cour, einer Dame die ~ machen (schneiden) to court (wait upon) a lady.

Courage courage, spirit, pluck *(coll.)*, pecker *(sl.)*;
jem. die ~ abkaufen to put s. o. out of courage; **Angst vor der eigenen ~ bekommen** to feel one has stuck one's neck out *(fam.)*; ~ **zu etw. haben** to have the courage to do s. th.

couragierter Mann courageous man.

Courtage brokerage, broker's fee (commission), turn, commission rate *(US)*.

courtagefrei free of brokerage.

Courtage|gebühr brokerage, broker's commission; ~**rechnung** brokerage account; ~**satz** commission rate; ~**tarif** scale of commission *(Br.)*, schedule of commission charges *(US)*.

Courtoisie courtesy;
internationale ~ comity of nations.

Couturier costume designer.

Couvert *(Kuvert)* envelope, *(Restaurant)* cover.

Cowboyfest rodeo *(US)*.

Credit credit;
Debet und ~ debtor and creditor.

Creme *(fig.)* elite, top, cream;
~ **der Gesellschaft** cream of society, top drawer.

Croupier croupier, stick.

cum laude with hono(u)rs (distinction, *US*).

D

D-Zug corridor (express, fast, long-distance, through, vestibule, *US*) train;
~ **mit Platzkarten** limited express, limited *(US)*.
da *(Zug)* in.
dabehalten to keep.
dabei | bleiben to stay with (persist in) it; **kein Geld ~haben** to have no money on one; **~sein** to be present (there); **nicht mit ~sein** to be out of it; **mit Leib und Seele ~sein** to throw o. s. body and soul into s. th.; **dicht ~stehen** to stand near.
Dach roof, housetop, *(Auto)* hood, roof;
alles unter einem ~ *(Einkaufen)* one-stop shopping; **mit aufklappbarem** ~ *(Auto)* convertible; **unter ~ und Fach** under shelter; **unter meinem bescheidenen** ~ under my humble roof; **unter dem väterlichen** ~ under the paternal roof;
abnehmbares ~ tuckaway roof; **flaches** ~ flat roof; **mit Stroh gedecktes** ~ thatched roof; **steiles** ~ steep (high-pitched) roof; **zurückschiebbares** ~ *(Auto)* sliding (folding) roof;
~ **abdecken** to unroof a house; ~ **abschrägen** to weather a roof; **eins aufs ~ bekommen** *(fam.)* to get a dressing-down, to get a crack on the nut, to get (catch) it in the neck *(sl.)*; **unter ~ und Fach bringen** to find backing for s. th., to finish with a piece of work; **Ernte unter ~ und Fach bringen** to bring in the harvest; **Haus unter ~ bringen** to roof a house; **durchs ~ durchkommen** *(Regen)* to work through the roof; **jem. eins aufs ~ geben** to give s. o. a crack on the head; **immer gleich Feuer im ~ haben** to fly off the handle instantly; **kein ~ über dem Kopf haben** to have nowhere to live; ~ **mittragen müssen** *(Balken)* to have to support the weight of the roof; **unter ~ und Fach sein** to be under cover; **im ~ nicht ganz richtig sein** to be wrong in the garret, to have bats in the belfry *(coll.)*; **jem. den roten Hahn aufs ~ setzen** to set s. one's house on fire; **jem. aufs ~ steigen** to jump down s. one's throat *(coll.)*, to sit upon s. o. *(sl.)*; **jem. gehörig aufs ~ steigen** to come down on s. o. like a ton of bricks; **mit jem. unter dem gleichen ~ wohnen** to live under the same roof with s. o.;
~antenne roof antenna (aerial, *Br.*), *(Auto)* overcar antenna; **~boden** loft, attic; **~decken** roofing, *(mit Ziegeln)* tiling; **~decker** roofer, *(mit Ziegeln)* tiler; **~deckerarbeiten** roofing; **~deckerhandwerk** roofing trade.
Dächer, die Spatzen pfeifen es schon von den ~n it is all over the town.
Dach | fenster skylight, dormer window; **~fonds** fund of funds; **~garage** rooftop garage; **~garten** roof garden; **~gaube** dormer window; **~gepäckträger** *(Auto)* roof rack; **~geschoß** attic storey (story, *US*); **~geschoßwohnung** attic apartment (flat), penthouse apartment; **~gesellschaft** controlling (holding, overhead, parent) establishment (enterprise), parent corporation (concern), stock trust *(US)*, umbrella company; **~gespärre** timberwork of a roof; **~gewerkschaft** parent union; **~kammer** attic, garret, boxroom; **mit Gerümpel angefüllte ~kammer** attic full of junk; **~kammerbewohner** garreteer; **~landeplatz** rooftop landing; **~luke** garret window; **~marke** family brand; **~neigung** slope of a roof; **~organisation** parent (umbrella, holding, overhead) organization; **~pappe** roofing paper; **~pfanne** pantile; **~pfette** purlin; **~restaurant** rooftop restaurant; **~rinne** gutter, rain [-water] pipe, waterspout; **~schaden** *(fam.)* mental injury; **leichten ~schaden haben** *(fam.)* to have a slate loose; **~schild** *(Werbung)* banner, streamer; **~schräge** slant (slope) of a roof; **~sparren** roof timbers; **~ständer** car rack; **~stübchen** sky garret; **nicht ganz richtig im ~stübchen sein** to be wrong in the garret, to have bats in the belfry; **~stube** garret; **~stuhl** roof timbers; **~traufe** eaves; **~unternehmen** parent enterprise; **~verband** umbrella organization; **~verband der britischen Gewerkschaften** Trades Union Congress *(Br.)*, (TUC); **~verschalung** roof planking; **~werbung** roof advertising; **ausgebaute ~wohnung** attic flat, *(Hochhaus)* penthouse; **~ziegel** tile.
Dafürhalten opinion, view.
dagegen against, *(Parlament)* not content;
~ **anführen** to counterplead; **etw. ~ haben** to have a kick against s. th.; ~ **sein** to be opposed to it; **grundsätzlich ~ sein** to refuse on principle; ~ **stimmen** to vote down.
dagewesen, noch nicht without precedent.
Daheim fireside.
daheimbleiben to stay at home.
dahin | dösen to drowse; **~fließen** *(Gespräch)* to flow; **~gehen** to pass by; **etw. ~gestellt lassen** to leave s. th. undecided (open, in the air); **nur noch ~kriechen** *(Verkehr)* to be reduced to a crawl; **unkontrolliert ~rasen** to run wild; **leicht ~reden** to talk in light terms; **~schleichen** *(Zeit)* to drag, to hang heavy on one's hands; **langsam ~schleichen** *(Verkehr)* to go at a crawl; **sich ~schleppen** to crawl, to plod along, *(Gespräch)* to drag on, *(Zeit)* to wear on; **~schmelzen** to melt away; **~schwinden** to pass (dwindle, ooze) away; **~siechen** to be wasting (waste) away; **an Kummer ~siechen** to consume away with grief.
dahinter | klemmen, sich to hold one's nose to the grindstone, to set to; **~kommen** to find out about it, to get at the truth about; **Dampf ~machen** to go at it full steam, to get things rolling; **sich ~setzen** to buckle to a task, to pull up one's socks *(Br., sl.)*; **seinen Anwalt ~setzen** to put one's solicitor on to it; **~stecken** to be behind it, to back it.
dahintrotten to go along at an easy jog.
Dakaporuf *(Theater)* encore, da capo.
Dalles sein, im to be hard up (stonebroke).
dalli, ein bißchen step on it, get a move on, make it snappy.
Dame, würdige alte dignified old lady; **vornehme** ~ gentlewoman;
~ **der Gesellschaft** society matron (lady);
ganz ~ sein to be a perfect lady; **die große ~ spielen** to play the fine lady.
Damen | begleitung female company; **~bekanntschaft** lady friend; **~friseur** haircutter, hairdresser; **~kränzchen** hen party *(coll.)*; **~oberbekleidung** women's outer wear; **~programm** ladies' program(me); **~salon** haircutting saloon; **~toilette** ladies cloakroom.
dämlich stupid, foolish, silly;
~es Glück gehabt haben to have had terrific luck; **sich dumm und ~ suchen** to search every nook and cranny.
Damm dam, mound, embankment, *(Deich)* dike, dyke, *(Hafendamm)* pier, jetty;
wieder auf dem ~ *(Patient)* up and about;
~ **aufwerfen (bauen)** to build a dyke (dam, an embankment; **j. auf den ~ bringen** to give s. o. a leg up; **einer Sache einen ~ entgegensetzen** to put an obstacle in the way; **auf dem ~ sein** to be on one's toes, to keep one's eye on the ball *(US sl.)*; **immer auf dem ~ sein** to know the score *(sl.)*; **nicht richtig auf dem ~ sein** to be out of sorts; **mit dem Festland durch einen ~ verbunden sein** to be connected to the mainland by a causeway; **wieder auf dem ~ sein** to be out and about again; ~ **unterspülen** to wash away the embankment;
~böschung slope of an embankment; **~bruch** breach in a dam, crevasse *(US)*.
Dämme, alle ~ brechen to break loose from all control.
dämmen to dam, to dike;
jds. Redefluß ~ to dam up the torrent of s. one's eloquence.
dämmerig dim, dark;
~er Kerzenschein faint light of candles.
Dämmerlicht dawn, *(abends)* dusk, twilight.
dämmern to dawn, *(abends)* to get dark (dusky);
bei jem. ~ to have a vague idea, to dawn on s. o.
Dämmer | schein first light, early dawn; **beim ~schein der Kerzen** in the faint light of the candles; **~schlaf** half-sleep; **~schoppen** sundowner; **~stunde** dusk hour, twilight.
Dämmerung twilight, dusk, *(morgens)* dawn;
bei Einbruch der ~ at dusk (nightfall).
Dämmerungs | wirkung night effect; **~zeit** lighting-up time.
Dämmer | zone twilight zone; **~zustand** twilight state.
Damm | grube *(Hochofen)* casting pit; **durch eine ~öffnung abfließen** to find a vent through the dykes.
Dämmplatte insulating board.
Damm | rutsch slip of an embankment; **~weg** causeway, causey.
Damoklesschwert sword of Damocles.
Dämon demon, devil;
wahrer ~ sein to be the devil incarnate; **von einem ~ besessen sein** to be possessed by a demon.
dämonische Leidenschaften demoniacal passions.
Dampf steam, vapo(u)r, *(Dunst)* mist, haze, *(Rauch)* smoke, fume;
~ **ablassen** to blow off steam, *(fig.)* to have kittens *(US sl.)*; ~ **absperren** to cut off steam; ~ **aufmachen** to raise (get up) steam; ~ **erzeugen** to generate steam; **mit halbem ~ fahren** to run half steam; ~ **haben** to get the wind up, to be in a blue funk; **jem. ~ machen** to chivvy s. o. about; ~ **dahinter machen** to put on steam; **unter ~ sein** to be under steam; **mit ~ angetrieben werden** to work by (run on) steam, to be steam-driven;

~antrieb steam drive; **~bad** vapo(u)r (Russian) bath; **~barkasse, ~beiboot** steam launch; **~druck** steam pressure, vapo(u)r pressure (tension).

dampfen to [emit] steam, *(Suppe)* to be steaming hot;
aus dem Hafen ~ to steam out of the harbo(u)r.

dämpfen to deaden, to muffle, *(Energieverbrauch)* to attenuate, *(Konjunktur)* to damp, to dampen, to curb, to cushion, *(Schmerzen)* to allay, to alleviate;
Auswirkungen ~ to cushion the effect; **jds. Begeisteung ~** to damp s. one's spirits; **allgemeine Begeisterung ~** to put a damper on the company, to damp the general high spirits; **Einfuhrbedürfnisse ~** to damp down import demands; **Licht ~** to soften (dim) the light; **jeden Schritt ~** to muffle every footfall; **Straßenlärm ~** to deaden street noises.

Dampfer steamer, steamship, steamboat;
mit dem ~ fahren to go by (sail on a) steamer, to travel by boat; **auf dem falschen ~ sitzen** *(fig.)* to be on the wrong tack (track).

Dämpfer damp[er], repression, wet blanket, soft pedal *(US sl.)*;
jem. einen ~ aufsetzen to take s. o. down a peg or two; **der Begeisterung einen ~ aufsetzen** to throw cold water on a plan (a wet blanket on s. th.), to put a damper on the company; **~ bekommen** to get a rap over the knuckles.

Dampfer|abfahrt sailing, departure; **~anlegestelle** landing stage (place, platform), jetty; **~fahrkarte** steamship ticket; **~fahrt** steamer voyage; **~linie** steamship line; **~route** steamship route; **~verbindung** steamship line; **regelmäßige ~verbindung einrichten** to establish a regular service; **~verkehr** steamship traffic (service).

Dampfheizung heating by steam, steam heating.

Dampfkessel steam boiler;
~anlage boiler plant; **~erprobung** proving of steam boilers; **~explosion** boiler explosion; **~überwachung** inspection of boilers; **~versicherung** boiler insurance.

dampfklar sein to be under steam.

Dampf|kochtopf pressure cooker; **~kraft** steam power; **~lokomotive** steam engine; **~maschine** steam engine; **~pumpe** steam (donkey) pump, pumping engine; **~roß** iron horse *(coll.)*; **~schiff** steam vessel; **~schiffahrt** steam navigation; **allgemeine ~schiffahrtsgesellschaft** general steamship navigation company; **~schiffahrtsroute** steamship route, trading voyage; **~strahlgebläse** steam jet blower; **~turbine** steam turbine.

Dämpfung *(el.)* attenuation, *(fig.)* curbing, check[ing], *(Geräusch)* deadening, *(Schmerzen)* alleviation, *(Stoßwirkung)* absorption;
~ der Inflation dampening down of inflation; **~ der Investitionstätigkeit** dampening of business spending; **~ der Konjunktur** curbing the boom, compensatory fiscal policy; **~ der Nachfrage** dampening of demand.

Dämpfungs|faktor cushion factor; **~glied** *(el.)* attenuator.

Dampfwalze steam roller.

Danaergeschenk Greek gift.

Danaidenfaß sisyphean labo(u)r.

daneben|benehmen, sich to misbehave; **~gehen** to go awry, to miss the mark, to misfire; **~greifen** *(fig.)* to drop a brick; **~hauen** to be wide of the mark, to make a mess of it; **völlig ~liegen** to be off the beam.

daniederliegen, mit Grippe to be laid up with influenza.

Dank thanks, gratitude, *(Anerkennung)* acknowledgement, recognition;
zum ~ für seine Dienste in recognition of his services;
herzlichen ~ warm thanks;
~ abstatten to render thanks; **seinen tiefempfundenen ~ aussprechen** to express one's heart-felt thanks; **wenig ~ ernten** to get more kicks than halfpence, to get small thanks; **jem. ~ schulden** to be indebted to s. o., to owe s. o. thanks; **jem. sehr zu ~ verpflichtet sein** to be greatly obliged to s. o.; **j. zu ~ verpflichten** to earn s. one's thanks; **jem. ~ zollen** to yield s. o. thanks;
~adresse vote of thanks.

dankbar *(einträglich)* profitable, paying, advantageous, *(verpflichtet)* obliged, grateful;
sich jem. gegenüber ~ erweisen to show gratitude to s. o.; **für eine schnelle Regelung ~ sein** to be obliged for an early settlement;
~e Arbeit rewarding task.

Dankbarkeit gratitude;
innige ~ deep gratitude; **überfließende (überschwengliche) ~** profuse gratitude;
jem. zur ~ verpflichtet sein to give s. o. a title to one's gratitude; **seiner ~ Ausdruck verleihen** to give expression to one's gratitude.

Dankbrief note of thanks, grateful letter, letter of acknowledgement (thanks), thank-you letter, *(für Einladungen)* roofer *(Br.)*.

dankend|ablehnen to decline with thanks; **~ erhalten** received with thanks.

Dankes|adresse *(Parlament)* address to the crown *(Br.)*; **~bezeugung** thank intimation of gratitude; **~rede halten** to propose a vote of thanks; **~schuld** debt of gratitude.

Dankgottesdienst harvest festival (thanksgiving).

Danksagung return (rendering) of thanks;
~ des Verfassers für Mitarbeit author's acknowledgement of assistance;
~ beschließen to pass a vote of thanks.

Danksagungsadresse vote of thanks;
jem. eine ~ übermitteln to tender s. o. a vote of thanks.

Danksagungs|brief congratulatory letter, thank-you note (letter); **~karte** thank-you card.

Dankschreiben letter of thanks.

daran|gehen to set to work; **alles ~setzen** to do one's level best, to go at it baldheaded.

daraufhin consequently, on the strength.

darben to be pinched (needy), to go without, to famish, to live in poverty;
freiwillig ~ to deprive o. s. of necessaries.

darbieten to offer, to present;
Volkstänze ~ to perform folk dances.

Darbietung presentation, show, offer, *(Anzeige)* exposure, *(Auslage)* display, *(Marketing)* exposition, *(Theater)* performance, *(Varieté)* act;
erstklassige ~ best performance; **musikalische ~en** musical performances; **verschiedenste ~en** all kinds of entertainment.

darbringen, als Opfer to sacrifice.

dareinfinden, sich to become resigned, to get reconciled.

darlegen to explain, to expound, to make clear, to manifest, to [re]present, to state, to set out (forth);
seine Ansichten ~ to state one's views; **seine politischen Ansichten öffentlich ~** to set forth one's political views in public; **ausführlich ~** to elaborate; **eingehend (im einzelnen) ~** to particularize, to explain (state) in detail, to specify; **seine Gründe ~** to state one's reasons; **seine Pläne ~** to expose one's plans; **Punkt für Punkt ~** to article; **seinen Standpunkt ~** to define one's position; **jem. seine Theorie ~** to expound one's theory to s. o.; **in Umrissen ~** to outline; **umständlich ~** to explain at great length.

Darlegung explanation, presentation, representation, statement, exposition, exposé;
~en speech, expositions;
schriftliche ~ written statement;
~ eines Falles statement of a case; **mündliche ~ des Tatbestandes** verbal statement; **~ seiner Vermögensverhältnisse** discovery of one's assets.

Darlegungsfähigkeit speaking ability.

Darlehn loan, credit, accommodation, *(Vorschuß)* advance;
bares ~ cash loan; **befristetes ~** time *(US)* (term) loan, loan on notice; **besichertes ~** covered advance, loan on collateral; **hypothekarisch besichertes ~** mortgage (real-estate) loan; **nachrangig besichertes ~** subordinated loan; **betriebliches ~** loan made to an employee; **billiges ~** equity loan; **dubioses ~** dead loan; **eingefrorenes ~** dead loan *(Br.)*, frozen credit (loan) *(US)*; **erststelliges ~** prior-lien loan; **auf einmal in voller Höhe fälliges ~** straight loan; **täglich fälliges ~ an Börsenmakler** day-to-day loan *(Br.)*; **gedecktes ~** covered (secured) advance; **durch verschiedene Sicherheiten gedecktes ~** mixed loan; **genehmigtes ~** authorized loan; **zur Instandsetzung der Wohnung gewährtes ~** home-improvement loan; **zu Liquiditätszwecken gewährtes ~** liquid loan; **gegen Sichtwechsel gewährtes ~** sight loan; **konzerninternes ~** intercompany loan; **kündbares ~** loan on notice (at call); **jederzeit (täglich) kündbares ~** precarious (demand, call) loan, loan on notice (at call), loan repayable on demand; **kommunalverbürgtes ~** loan guaranteed by local authorities *(Br.)*; **kurzfristiges ~** short[-term] loan; **landwirtschaftliches ~** agricultural loan; **langfristiges ~** long-sighted (long-period, time, *US*, term, fixed) loan; **offenes ~** advance; **preisverbilligtes ~** low-interest loan; **sofort rückzahlbares ~** call loan; **auf tägliche Anforderung rückzahlbares ~** loan repayable on demand; **unbefristetes ~** undated loan; **unbesichertes ~** unsecured loan; **unentgeltliches ~** free loan; **ungedecktes ~** uncovered loan; **ungesichertes ~** personal (unsecured) loan; **unkündbares ~** irredeemable loan; **unsicheres ~** unsafe loan; **unverzinsliches ~** interest-free loan; **wegen Nichtrückzahlung kurzfristig verlängertes ~** dead loan *(Br.)*; **verzinsliches ~** interest-bearing loan, loan bearing (at) interest;

wucherisches ~ loan at usurious interest; **zinsfreies** ~ free loan; **zinsloses** ~ noninterest (free) loan, advance free of (without) interest; **zweckgebundenes** ~ tied loan; **nicht zweckgebundenes** ~ untied loan;
~ **einer Bank** bank loan; **kurzfristiges** ~ **an Börsenmakler** stock-exchange (street, *US*) loan; ~ **zur Finanzierung der Viehwirtschaft** livestock loan *(US)*; ~ **in festgelegter Höhe** line-of-credit loan; ~ **der Landeszentralbank** reserve bank credit *(US)*; ~ **mit bestimmter Laufzeit** time loan *(US)*; ~ **gegen Pfandbestellung** loan against collateral; ~ **an erster Stelle** prior lien loan; ~ **mit Tilgungsplan** sinking-fund loan; ~ **der Tochter- an die Muttergesellschaft** upstream loan; ~ **aufgrund börsengängiger Wertpapiere** advance against marketable securities *(Br.)*, collateral loan *(US)*; ~ **mit wöchentlicher Zinszahlung** loan with payment of weekly interest;
jem. ein ~ **anbieten** to offer s. o. a loan; ~ **aufnehmen** to borrow money, to take up (negotiate, contract, raise) a loan; **hypothekarisch besichertes** ~ **aufnehmen** to raise a loan on an estate; ~ **für den gesamten Kaufpreis aufnehmen** to borrow the whole of the purchase price; ~ **gegen Lombardierung von Wertpapieren aufnehmen** to borrow on collateral securities *(US)*; ~ **zu erheblich verbilligten Zinssätzen aufnehmen** to borrow at a substantial negative rate of interest; **jem. mit einem** ~ **aushelfen** to oblige s. o. with a loan; ~ **ratenweise entsprechend den fertiggestellten Bauabschnitten auszahlen** to allow an advance to be taken as the various stages are completed; ~ **beantragen** to apply for a loan; ~ **beschaffen** to procure a loan; **beantragtes** ~ **erhalten** to obtain a loan of money by application; ~ **geben (gewähren)** to grant a loan, to lend, to make an advance, to loan [out] *(US)*; **als geschenktes** ~ **geben** to gift-loan; **besicherte** ~ **gewähren** to grant loans on security; **kurzfristiges** ~ **gewähren** to lend at short interest; ~ **gegen Hypothekenbestellung gewähren** to lend on mortgage; ~ **gegen Pfandbestellung gewähren** to lend on pawn; ~ **kündigen** to call in (recall) a loan; **Rückzahlung auf ein** ~ **leisten** to make payments on a loan; ~ **refinanzieren** to refinance a loan; ~ **tilgen** to amortize (redeem) a loan; ~ **zurückzahlen** to pay off (repay) a loan; ~ **vorzeitig zurückzahlen** to return a loan ahead of schedule.

Darlehns|abteilung credit department; ~**anfrage ablehnen** to turn thumbs down on a loan; ~**angebot** tender of a loan; **schriftliches** ~**angebot** letter offering a loan; ~**antrag** loan application, application for a loan.

Darlehnsaufnahme borrowing, taking up a loan;
gewerbliche ~ business borrowing;
~ **durch Kommunalbehörden** borrowing by local authorities; ~ **unter Zuwiderhandlung gegen die Satzung** ultra-vires borrowing.

Darlehns|bank loan bank; ~**beantragung** applying for a loan; ~**bearbeitungsgebühr** loan fee; ~**bedarf** loan demand, demand for borrowing; ~**bedingungen** terms of a loan; ~**beschaffung** procurement of a loan; ~**besicherung** security for borrowing; ~**bestimmungen** terms of a loan; ~**betrag** amount of a loan, loan (borrowed) money; ~**bewilligung** grant (granting) of a loan, lending; ~**dauer** life of a loan; ~**empfänger** recipient of a loan, borrower; ~**forderung** amount of a loan; ~**geber** loaner, [money] lender, advancer; ~**genehmigung** loan sanction; ~**geschäft** loan business, lending operations, lending business; ~**gesellschaft** credit corporation, remedial loan society *(Br.)*, finance (small-loan) company *(US)*; ~**gesuch** loan request.

Darlehnsgewährung granting (grant) of a loan, lending or loaning money on credit;
erneute ~ further advance;
~ **an Devisenausländer** lending to nonresidents; ~ **für fremde Rechnung** loan for account of offers; ~ **zum Zweck eines Eigenheimerwerbs** availability of loans for home purchase.

Darlehns|gläubiger loan creditor; ~**hilfe** loan assistance; ~**institut** lending institution; ~**interessent** would-be borrower; ~**kasse** loan association (office, society), loan bank; **genossenschaftliche** ~**kasse** remedial loan society, small-loan company *(US)*; **staatliche** ~**kasse** government lending agency; ~**kassenschein** treasury note *(US)*, loan certificate; ~**kassenverein** small loan company *(US)*, remedial loan society *(Br.)*; ~**kassenverein auf Gegenseitigkeit** mutual loan society; ~**konto** loan account; **alphabetisches** ~**konto** loan *(US)* (loans, *Br.*) ledger; **Entnahmen aus einem** ~**konto begrenzen** to stop a loan account; ~**makler** loan agent (broker), loanmonger; ~**mittel** loan funds, *(zur Lohnauszahlung gewährte)* advances for wages; **nicht in Anspruch genommene** ~**mittel** unused loan commitments; **von seinen** ~**möglichkeiten äußerst behutsam Gebrauch machen** to lock in one's loan commitments; ~**nehmer** borrower, loanee, receiver of a loan, *(gewerblicher)* business borrower; ~**nehmerin** *(Gesellschaft)* borrowing corporation; ~**programm** lending program(me); ~**quittung** receipt for a loan, loan receipt; ~**rückzahlung** loan repayment; ~**satz** loan rate; **am** ~**schalter Schlange stehen** to be waiting at the loan window; ~**schein** loan certificate; ~**schuldner** *(Bilanz)* loans payable *(US)*, debtors to a loan, borrowers; ~**sicherheit** loan backing, collateral, security; ~**stock** total lendings; ~**summe** borrowed money; **zurückgezahlte (rückfließende)** ~**summe** repaid loan; ~**system** loan system; ~**urkunde** loan certificate, bond; ~**usancen** lending practices; ~**valuta** borrowed money, sum advanced; ~**verein** credit (loan) society *(Br.)*, credit cooperative; ~**verhandlungen führen** to negotiate for a loan; ~**verlängerung** extension of a loan; ~**vermittler** loan agent (broker), loanmonger; ~**vermittlung** procurement of a loan; ~**verpflichtungen** loan commitments; ~**versprechen** standby credit; ~**vertrag** loan contract (agreement), contract of borrowing; ~**vorvertrag** preliminary loan agreement.

darlehnsweise as a loan.

Darlehns|wünsche äußern, wenig to have little appetite for advances; ~**zinsen** loan interest, interest on loan capital; **jährlich abgerechnete** ~**zinsen** annual rent; **vereinnahmte** ~**zinsen** loan interest received; ~**zinsforderung** loan-interest claim; ~**zinssatz** loan rate; ~**zusage** promise of a loan, standby credit, advance commitment; ~**zusage einer Bausparkasse** building society guarantee; ~**zweck** purpose of a loan.

Darniederliegen|des Handels [business] depression; ~ **der Landwirtschaft** agricultural depression.

darniederliegen to stagnate, to languish, to be at a stop (depressed);
hoffnungslos ~ to be past recovery; **völlig** ~ to be flat on its back.

darstellbar describable, portrayable, representable;
sehr schwer ~ *(Rolle)* very hard to play.

darstellen to [re]present, to produce, *(beschreiben)* to describe, to picture, *(Schauspieler)* to interpret, to play, to act;
schönen Anblick ~ to present a fine spectable to the eyes; **anschaulich** ~ to depict; **ausführlich** ~ to write up; **wichtigen Beitrag** ~ to constitute an important contribution; **bildlich** ~ to portray; **in einem Diagramm** ~ to plot a diagram; **Dinge deutlich** ~ to put things in clearer light; **Dinge so** ~ to put things in such a way; **wichtige Einnahmequelle** ~ to constitute an important source of income *(Br.)*; **im einzelnen** ~ to particularize; **Ereignis verzerrt** ~ to give a distorted picture of an event; **erschöpfend** ~ to give an exhaustive description; **als nicht existent** ~ to explain away; **jem. einen Fall in allen Einzelheiten** ~ to lay before s. o. all the facts of a case; **falsch** ~ to misrepresent; **genau** ~ to describe in detail; **als geringfügig** ~ to minimize; **grafisch** ~ to graph, to diagram, to plot, to chart, to represent graphically, to figure; **etw. günstig** ~ to put s. th. in a favo(u)rable light; **Kurve zeichnerisch** ~ to trace (plot) a curve; **Lage äußerst rosig** ~ to present a very rosy picture; **Sache völlig anders** ~ to give quite a different version of the affair; **Sachverhalt** ~ to state the facts; **schematisch** ~ to skeletonize; **sich in allen seinen Schwächen** ~ to betray all one's weak points; **übertrieben** ~ to exaggerate; **unrichtig** ~ to misrepresent, to misstate; **in großen Zügen** ~ to outline.

darstellend descriptive;
~**e Geometrie** descriptive geometry; ~**e Künste** interpretative arts.

Darsteller actor, enactor, performer, player, doer.

Darstellung presentation, [re]presentation, presentment, statement, account, story, description, *(Erklärung)* explanation, *(Parteivortrag)* recital, *(Theater)* performance, enactment, portrayal, presentation, interpretation;
nach seiner eigenen ~ according to his own words (story), on his own showing;
amtliche ~ official version; **anschauliche** ~ depiction; **ausführliche** ~ detailed description; **bildliche** ~ visual presentation, image, [textual] illustration; **erneute** ~ restatement; **bewußt falsche** ~ deliberate misrepresentation; **figürliche** ~ *(Statistik)* pictogram; **gedrängte** ~ précis; **genaue** ~ particularized account, detail; **geschickte** ~ hit-off *(sl.)*; **grafische** ~ graphic representation, diagram, graph, chart *(US)*; **individuelle** ~ version; **knappe** ~ succinct account; **kontenmäßige** ~ account-type representation; **logarithmische** ~ logarithmic chart; **mikrografische** ~ micrography; **symbolische** ~ image; **tabellarische** ~ tabulation; **technische** ~ technical description; **übertriebene** ~ high-colo(u)red description; **umfassende** ~ comprehensive report; **ungenaue** ~ inaccurate account; **zusammengefaßte** ~ summary;

[statistische] ~ **der Bevölkerungsdichte** control chart; ~ **ohne Effekthascherei** straight acting; ~ **eines Falles** presentation of a case; ~ **von Gewaltakten im Fernsehen** television violence; **listenmäßige** ~ **der Nachfrageentwicklung** demand schedule; **kurze** ~ **eines Rechtsfalls für den Prozeßanwalt** brief; ~ **in Romanform** novelization; ~ **des Sachverhalts (Tatbestands)** recital (statement, representation) of facts; **kurze** ~ **des Sachverhalts** summary of facts; ~ **in Umrissen** outline, condensed description; ~ **der Veränderungen im Gewinnvortrag** statement of earned surplus *(US)*;
anwaltliche ~ **entgegennehmen** to hear an argument by council; ~ **eidlich erhärten** to corroborate a statement by oath; **klare** ~ **geben** to give a clear account; **zusammenfassende** ~ **geben** to summarize; **jem. seine** ~ **eines Falles geben** to tell s. o. a story of one's own invention; ~ **des Sachverhalts geben** to recite facts; **betrügerische** ~ **seiner finanziellen Verhältnisse geben** to fraudulently misrepresent one's financial condition; ~ **mit Einzelheiten überladen** to overcharge a description with detail.
Darstellungs|art manner of representation; ~**einheit** *(el.)* display unit; **kleinste** ~**einheit** *(Datenverarbeitung)* bit; **konzentrierte** ~**form** *(Notizenanfertigung)* boiling-down technique; ~**verfahren** process of production; ~**weise** manner of representation; ~**zweck einer Firma** substratum of a company.
dartun to set forth, to demonstrate, to evidence, to prove.
Dasein existence, subsistence, life, presence, being;
jem. ein elendes ~ **bereiten** to make s. one's life miserable; **bequemes** ~ **fristen** to have an easy time; **jämmerliches** ~ **fristen** to lead a drab (drag on a miserable) existence, to live low; **das nackte** ~ **fristen** to earn a bare subsistence; **friedliches** ~ **führen** to live in peace and content; **vergnügtes** ~ **führen** to lead a happy existence.
dasein to be present, to attend;
noch nicht ganz wieder ~ to be not quite with it.
Daseins|bedingungen conditions of existence; ~**berechtigung** right to exist; ~**kampf** struggle for existence; ~**zweck** rational ground for existence, raison d'être.
dastehen, allein to stand alone; **einmalig** ~ to be unrivalled; **ohne Mittel** ~ to be without means, to be penniless; **stundenlang** ~ to stand there for hours and hours; **völlig geknickt** ~ to stand like a drooping lily *(coll.)*; **wie ein Ölgötze** ~ to stand there like a stuffed dummy; **wie ein begossener Pudel** ~ to stand there looking like a lost sheep; **wie versteinert** ~ to stand petrified.
Daten data, facts, *(Personalangaben)* particulars, details;
anfallende ~ available data; **einwandfreie** ~ reliable data; **statistische** ~ statistical data; **technische** ~ technical data, specifications; **zusammengefaßte** ~ integrated data; **technische** ~ **eines Autos** specification of a car;
~ **in einer international vergleichbaren Weise aufbereiten** to bring data to international comparable standards; ~ **erfassen** to collect data; ~ **verarbeiten** to process data;
~**abruf** polling; ~**aufzeichnung** data recording; ~**ausgabe** data output; ~**auswertung** interpretation of data; ~**bank** data bank; ~**behandlung** data handling; ~**eingabe** data input, *(Terminal)* keyboarding; ~**erfassung** data collection, acquisition; ~**fernübertragung** teleprocessing; **im** ~**fernverkehr monatlich bezogen werden können** to be available as monthly tape subscription; ~**fluß** data flow; ~**flußplan** flow chart.
datengesteuert computer-controlled.
Daten|menge file; ~**plan der Anzeigen** schedule of insertion, advertising schedule; ~**rückgewinnung** data retrieval; ~**schema** date plan, *(Anzeigen)* [space time] schedule; ~**schild** *(Maschine)* rating plate; ~**schutz** data protection; ~**sichtgerät** display screen; ~**speicher** data logger, memory unit; ~**speicherung** data storage; ~**speicherverfahren** data-gathering process; ~**stapel** data record; ~**steuerung** computer control; **ausgedruckter** ~**streifen** printout; ~**träger** medium, volume; ~**übermittler** data transmitter; ~**übermittlung** data communication; ~**übertragung** data transmission; ~**übertragungsgerät** modern; ~**übertragungssystem** data transmission system.
datenverarbeitend data-handling, data-processing.
Daten|verarbeiter data-processing machine *(Br.)*, data processor *(US)*, data set (processor); **kleiner** ~**verarbeiter** microprocessor *(US)*; ~**verarbeitung** data processing (handling), *(Terminal)* teleprocessing; **auf** ~**verarbeitung umstellen** to computerize.
Datenverarbeitungs|anlagen data-processing facilities; ~**gerät** data set (processor), computer equipment; ~**industrie** computing services industry; ~**kapazität** data-handling capacity; ~**kosten** data-processing costs; ~**maschine** data processor; ~**personal** operators; ~**schema** data-processing plan; ~**zentrum** computing service.
Datenwort item.
datierbar datable.
Datieren dating.
datieren to date;
falsch ~ to misdate; **später** ~ to postdate, to date forward.
datiert dated;
nicht ~ undated, without date;
~ **vom** bearing date of, dated as of; **aus London** ~ dated from London; **vom 1. d. M.** ~ under date of the 1st inst.;
~ **sein von** to bear date of.
Datierung dating.
dato, bis till now, up to the present; **nach** ~ after date, from this date;
drei Monate ~ three months after date.
Datowechsel dated bill, fixed (after-date) bill, time bill.
Datum date;
mit ~ **vom** hearing date of; **nach** ~ after date; **ohne** ~ undated, without date; **unter heutigem** ~ under this date; **zum festgesetzten** ~ on the appointed day;
gleichen ~**s** of same date; **heutigen** ~**s** of this date, today; **neueren** ~**s** of recent date;
angegebenes ~ stated date; **bei einer Durchschnittsberechnung angenommenes** ~ focal date; **falsches** ~ misdate; **fehlendes** ~ omission of date; **festes** ~ day certain; **gefälschtes** ~ false date; **irrtümliches** ~ wrong date; **späteres** ~ postdate; ~ **unvollständig** *(Wechsel)* date incomplete;
~ **der Antragstellung** date of application; ~ **der Ausfertigung einer Urkunde** date of execution of a document; ~ **der Einreichung** filing date; ~ **des Inkrafttretens** effective date; ~ **der Konkursanmeldung** time of bankruptcy; ~ **des Konkurseröffnungsbeschlusses** date of receiving order; ~ **des Poststempels** date of postmark, postal date; ~ **des Versands** mailing date, date of dispatch; ~ **der Wahl** day of election; ~ **der Zustellung** day of service;
~ **einsetzen** to fill in the date; **früheres** ~ **einsetzen** to set an early date; **frühes** ~ **eintragen** to predate; **durch Angabe des** ~**s entwerten** to date-cancel; ~ **festsetzen** to settle a date, to [fix a] date; **neuesten** ~**s sein** to be recent; **Brief mit** ~ **versehen** to date a letter; **mit späterem** ~ **versehen** to afterdate.
Datumsänderung alteration of a date.
Datumsangabe dating, date, *(Lebensmittelpackung)* code date;
falsche ~ misdating; **ohne** ~ without date;
~ **verifizieren** to verify dates.
Datums|anzeiger date box; ~**aufdruck** date mark; ~**grenze** date line.
datumsmäßig in order of date.
Datumsstempel dater, date stamp, *(Poststempel)* postmark;
mit dem ~ **entwerten** to date-cancel; **mit einem** ~ **versehen** to date-stamp.
Datumszeile *(Zeitung)* date line.
Dauer duration, [length of] time, length, period, term, *(Beständigkeit)* permanency, permanence, *(Fortdauer)* continuance, continuity;
auf die ~ for a continuance, permanently, in the long run; **auf die** ~ **von** for a period of; **auf** ~ **gearbeitet** made to last; **für die** ~ **von** for a period of; **für die** ~ **des Krieges** for the duration of the war; **für die** ~ **des Verfahrens** pending the action; **für unbestimmte** ~ for the duration; **von kurzer** ~ short-lived; **während der** ~ **der Konferenz** for the duration of the conference; **während der** ~ **des Rechtsstreits** pending the lawsuit; **während der** ~ **des Vertrages** during the term of the contract;
ununterbrochene ~ perpetuity; **vorgeschriebene** ~ prescribed date;
~ **der Arbeitsunfähigkeit** period of disability; ~ **einer Beteiligung** life of a partnership; ~ **einer Freiheitsstrafe** period of imprisonment; ~ **der Haftung** indemnity period; **durchschnittliche** ~ **eines eingeräumten Kundenkredits** average collection period; ~ **eines Mietvertrages** life of a lease; ~ **von drei Monaten** three-month period; ~ **des Notstands** emergency period; ~ **eines Patents** life (duration) of a patent; ~ **einer Rundfunksendung** length of a broadcast; ~ **des Treuhandverhältnisses** trust period; ~ **eines Vertrages** life of agreement;
keine ~ **haben** not to last; **auf die** ~ **nicht ertragen können** not to bear for any length of time; **von kurzer** ~ **sein** to flash in the pan, to be short-lived, not to last a long time; **für die** ~ **von 21 Jahren patentrechtlich geschützt sein** to be protected for a period of 21 years; **für die** ~ **von 4 Jahren gewählt werden** to be elected for a period of four years;
~**abkommen** lasting settlement; ~**abtastung** *(Radar)* continuous scanning; ~**abwesenheit** chronic absence; ~**akkreditiv**

permanent credit; ~**angestellte** established personnel; ~**angestellter** permanent (regular) employee; ~**anlage** long-term investment, permanent (investment) holdings (assets); ~**anleger** long-term investor; ~**anmeldung** *(tel.)* booked call; ~**anschlag in Verkehrsmitteln** car card advertising; ~**anstellung** regular employment; ~**arbeit** continuous chore; ~**arbeitsloser** hard-core worker, unemployable person, chronically unemployed; ~**arbeitslosigkeit** chronic (permanent, hard-core) unemployment; ~**arbeitsplatz** permanent post, stable position, place of permanent employment; ~**armut** pauperage; ~**arrest** imprisonment of no fixed duration; **erforderlicher** ~**aufenthalt** quasi-national domicile; ~**auftrag** permanent (standing) order, standing instructions; ~**auftrag an eine Bank** standing order on a bank; ~**auftragsüberweisung** standing order payment; ~**ausgaben** ordinary expenses; ~**ausschuß** standing committee; ~**ausstellung** continuous (permanent) exhibition; ~**ausstellungsstück** permanent exhibit; ~**ausweis** season ticket *(Br.)*, commutation ticket *(US)*; ~**beanspruchung** endurance stress (test); ~**behandlung** long-term treatment; ~**belästigung** continuing (standing) nuisance; ~**belastung** *(Maschine)* continuous rating, permanent (constant, *US*) load; **fiskalische** ~**belastungen** fiscal constituencies; ~**belegschaft** stable force; ~**beschäftigung** continuous (constant) employment, stable job, holding operation; ~**beschäftigung finden** to pick up a duration job; ~**beschuß** *(mil.)* sustained bombardment; ~**beschwerde** perpetual complaint; ~**besetzung** around-the-clock operation; ~**besitz** continuous possession, *(Wertpapiere)* permanent portfolio; ~**bestand** perpetual succession; ~**betrieb** continuous operation; ~**bewilligungen** *(durch das Parlament)* consolidated charges *(Br.)*; ~**brandofen** slow-burning stove; ~**bürgschaft** continuing security; ~**debatte** filibuster; ~**delikt** continuing crime; ~**einkommen** permanent income; ~**einladung** standing invitation; ~**einnahme** continuing revenue; ~**einrichtung** permanent institution; ~**erlaß** standing order; ~**erprobung** endurance test; ~**ertrag** sustained yield; ~**ertragsfähigkeit** long-time productivity (productiveness); **gesetzlich fingierte** ~**existenz** *(Körperschaft)* artificial succession; ~**fahrgast** regular passenger, season-ticket holder *(Br.)*, commutation passenger *(US)*, commuter *(US)*; ~**fahrkarte** season *(Br.)* (commutation, *US*) ticket; ~**fahrkarte benutzen** to commute *(US)*, to use a season *(Br.)* (communation, *US*) ticket; ~**fahrschein** [free] pass *(US)*; ~**fahrt** endurance run; ~**farbe** lasting colo(u)r; ~**festigkeit** fatigue limit (strength, *US*); ~**flamme** *(Gas)* pilot burner; ~**flug** endurance flight; ~**folgen einer Verletzung** continuing effects of an injury; ~**garantie** continuing (continuous) guarantee, (guaranty, *US*); ~**gast** *(Hotel)* resident at a hotel, fixture; ~**gemüse** dehydrated vegetables; ~**geschwindigkeit** cruising speed; ~**güter** durable manufactures, durables.

dauerhaft durable, lasting, serviceable, stable, standing, *(Farbe)* fast, *(Gebäude)* solid, stable;
~ **gebaut** solidly built; ~ **gemacht** made to last;
~**er Friede** enduring (lasting) peace; ~**e Konsumgüter** durable goods, durables.

Dauer|haftigkeit wear, *(Farbe)* fastness, *(Gebäude)* solidity, *(Lebensmittel)* durability; ~**inserat** rate holder *(US)*; ~**invalidität** permanent disability; ~**invaliditätsversicherung** permanent disability insurance; ~**kalender** perpetual calendar; ~**karte** season *(Br.)* (commutation, *US*) ticket, free pass *(US)*, subscriber's ticket; ~**karte nehmen** to take out a season *(Br.)* (commutation, *US*) ticket; ~**karteninhaber** season-ticket holder *(Br.)*, regular traveller, commutation passenger *(US)*, commuter *(US)*; ~**krankheit** permanent sickness; ~**kredit** continuous borrowing; ~**kunde** frequent (standing, regular) customer, *(Kreditnehmer)* continuous borrower, *(Werbung)* regular advertiser; ~**lasten** standing charges; ~**leistung** continuous service, *(el.)* continuous rating; ~**leser** regular reader; ~**lieferant** regular supplier; ~**magnet** permanent magnet; ~**mandat** general retainer; ~**miete** permanent tenancy; ~**mieter** permanent tenant; ~**mitglied** continuing member.

dauern to last, to go on, to continue;
von 8 - 13 Uhr ~ to run from 8 - 13; **zwei volle Stunden** ~ to take fully two hours.

dauernd lasting, permanent, enduring, regular, perpetual, abiding;
sich für ~ **niederlassen** to settle down for good; ~ **unterwegs sein** to be always on the move;
~**er Friede** lasting (enduring) peace; ~**e Gefahr** constant danger; ~**e Gegenleistung** continuing consideration; ~**e Grunddienstbarkeit** continuous easement; ~**e Klagen** perpetual complaints; ~**er Sitz** permanent seat; **in** ~**er Sorge** in a state of constant anxiety; ~**e Stellung** permanent position; ~**er Wohnsitz** permanent (fixed) abode, permanent residence.

Dauer|nutzungsrecht perpetual lease; ~**parken** all-day parking; ~**parker** all-day parker; ~**patient** long-stay patient; ~**pflegschaft** permanent curatorship; ~**plakat** permanent poster; ~**prüfung** *(Maschine)* endurance test; ~**prüfungsfahrt** endurance run; ~**redner** marathon speaker, perennial debater; ~**regelung** permanent regulation; ~**regen** incessant (continual) rain; ~**reisegeschwindigkeit** cruise (cruising) speed; ~**rente** perpetual annuity, permanent alimony; ~**schaden** constant loss, *(Person)* continuing (permanent) injury; **unmittelbarer** ~**schaden** *(Feuerversicherung)* direct loss; ~**schlaf** unbroken (protracted) sleep; ~**schuld** fixed debt (indebtedness); ~**schuldverhältnis** continuous obligation; ~**schuldverschreibung** perpetual debenture; ~**sitzung** permanent session; ~**speicher** *(Datenverarbeitung)* data logger, memory; ~**stellung** permanent position (appointment, assignment, *US*, employment, job, place, post, situation), long-term appointment, stable position, permanency; ~**stellung in einer Firma haben** to be permanently attached to a firm; **jem. zu einer** ~**stellung verhelfen** to establish s. o.; ~**störsender** continuous wave jammer; ~**straftat** continuing crime (offence); ~**strom** *(el.)* closed-circuit current; ~**ton** prolonged tone; ~**treuhand** perpetual trust; **unzulässige** ~**treuhandverwaltung** transgressive (perpetual) trust; ~**überweisungsauftrag** standing banker's order; ~**überziehungen** static overdrafts; ~**verfügung** permanent injunction; ~**verlust** constant loss; ~**verlust des rechten Arms** complete and permanent loss of the right arm; ~**verpflichtung** continuing covenant (obligation); ~**vertrag** running contract; ~**visum** permanent visa; ~**vollmacht** permanent power of attorney; ~**vorstand** permanent directors; ~**vorstellung** *(Kino)* continuous (nonstop) performance, grind show *(sl.)*; ~**wachposten** standing guard; ~**waren** durable goods, durables, *(Gastronomie)* nonperishable foodstuffs; ~**welle** permanent wave, perm *(Br.)*; **sich eine** ~**welle machen lassen** to have one's hair permed; ~**werbung** continuity in advertising; ~**wert** lasting value, *(Anlagegüter)* usefulness; ~**wettkampf** marathon; ~**wirkung** lasting (permanent) effect; ~**wohnrecht besitzen** to remain in a house during lifetime; ~**wohnsitz** fixed residence, permanent abode; ~**wohnung** permanent housing; ~**wurst** hard (dry, preserved) sausage; ~**zahlung** standing order payment; ~**zustand** permanency, perpetuity; ~**zustand daraus (aus etw.) machen** to make a habit of it.

Daumen thumb;
über den ~ **gepeilt** in the rough;
~ **drehen** to twiddle (twirl) one's thumbs; **jem. den** ~ **drücken (halten)** to keep one's fingers crossed for s. o.; **etw. über den** ~ **peilen** to give a rough estimate; **unter jds.** ~ **sein** to be under s. one's thumb; **jem. den** ~ **aufs Auge setzen** to put the screw on s. o., to clamp s. o. down;
~**abdruck** thumbmark; **um eine** ~**breite** by about an inch; ~**druckpapier** feather-weight; ~**index,** ~**register** *(Buch)* thumb index; **jem.** ~**schrauben anlegen (ansetzen)** to give s. o. another turn of the screw, to clamp down on s. o., to put the squeeze on s. o., to put on the fix *(US sl.)*.

Daunen|bett feather bed; ~**steppdecke** eiderdown [quilt].

davonkommen to get away;
mit einem blauen Auge (billig) ~ to escape with life and limb, to get away with a black eye, to get off cheaply, to have a narrow squeak *(sl.)*; **mit einer Geldstrafe** ~ to get off with a fine; **gerade noch (um Haaresbreite)** ~ to have a narrow (lucky) escape; **noch gut** ~ to get off lightly; **mit heiler Haut** ~ to save one's bacon, to get off with a whole skin; **mit knapper Mühe (Not)** ~ to have a narrow squeak *(sl.)*, to have a close shave; **ungeschoren** ~ to cop out, to break even; **ungestraft** ~ to get away with it;
~ **lassen** to let off.

Davonlaufen, zum punk *(sl.)*.

davonlaufen to make away (tracks, *US sl.*);
wütend ~ to go off in a huff.

davonlaufende Preise prices running away.

davonmachen, sich to cut away, to stir out *(US sl.)*; **sich eilends** ~ to run off, to take to one's heels; **sich heimlich** ~ to abscond.

davonstehlen, sich to slide *(sl.)*.

davonstürzen, ohne Aufwiedersehen zu sagen to dart off without saying goodbye.

davontragen, ersten Preis to carry (walk away with) the first prize; **dauernden Schaden** ~ to suffer permanent damage; **Verletzungen** ~ to receive injuries.

dazu in addition;
~**bringen** to persuade; ~**buttern** *(coll.)* to throw in; ~**geben** to throw into the bargain; ~**gehören** to belong to it, to be incidental, *(Person)* to be one of the party; **zu einem Amt ~gehören** to appertain to an office; ~**gehörig** appurtenant, appertaining, appropriate, attendant; **nicht ~gehörig** extrinsic; **mit der ~gehörigen Ausstattung** with the appropriate furnishing; **Zinsen ~schlagen** to add interest; **einige Zeilen ~schreiben** to add a few lines; **seine Unterschrift ~setzen** to add (append) one's signature; **das Seine ~tun** to pull one's weight, to do one's bit.
dazwischen|funken *(fam.)* to butt in; **energisch ~funken** to put one's foot down, to lay down the law; ~**kommen** to turn up, to interpose; ~**liegend** intermediate, intervenient, interjacent, mesne; ~**rufen** to interrupt the speaker; ~**schreiben** to interline.
Dazwischentreten interference, intervention, intermediation.
dazwischen|treten to intervene, to interfere, to intermediate, to have a go; **Bemerkung ~werfen** to throw in a remark.
Debatte debate, open discussion, parley, wrangle;
nach einer endlosen ~ after much debate;
allgemeine ~ full-dress debate; **außenpolitische ~** foreign-affairs debate; **bewegte ~** animated (lively) discussion; **endlose ~** gabfest *(US coll.)*; **entscheidende ~** crucial debate, field night *(Br.)*; **haushaltsrechtliche ~** debate on the budget; **heftige (hitzige) ~** heated (warm) debate; **innenpolitische ~** debate on home affairs; **langwierige ~** protracted debate; **lebhafte ~** lively debate; **öffentliche ~** open debate;
~ im Plenum full-dress debate; **~ über Wirtschaftsfragen** economic debate;
~ abkürzen to cut off a debate; **~ abwürgen** to prevent (guillotine, gag, *Br.*) a debate; **Schluß (Unterbrechnung) der ~ beantragen** to move to report progress *(Br.)*; **~ beenden** to close a debate; **sich an der ~ beteiligen** to take part in the debate; **~ zum Abschluß bringen** to closure *(Br.)*; **in eine ~ eingreifen** to join (take a hand in) a debate; **sich bei einer ~ erhitzen** to get hot over an argument; **~ für beendet erklären** to declare the discussion closed; **~ eröffnen** to open a debate, to open (begin) the discussion; **~ schließen** to apply the closure of (terminate) a debate, to close the discussion; **zur ~ stehen** to be on the carpet; **zur ~ stellen** to question; **Frage zur ~ stellen** to submit a question to the debate; **an einer ~ teilnehmen** to participate in a discussion; **j. bei einer ~ unterstützen** to back s. o. in an argument; **in die ~ werfen** to make a suggestion; **~ wiederaufnehmen** to renew a debate.
Debattenabkürzung mittels beschränkter Redezeit guillotined closure *(Br.)*.
debattieren to debate, to dispute, to discuss, to controvert;
mit der Regierungspartei ~ to debate across the floor; **über Zollfragen ~** to debate the tariff questions.
Debattier|klub debating society; ~**kunst** fence (readiness in debate).
Debet debit, debtor, *(fam.)* tick;
~ und Kredit debit and credit, debtor and creditor;
etw. ins ~ eines Kontos eintragen to enter s. th. to the debit side of an account; **im ~ stehen** to be on the debit (debtor) side;
~**anzeige** debit note (memorandum, *US*); ~**beleg** debit voucher (slip); ~**buch** debit book; ~**buchung** debit entry; ~**faktor** debit element; ~**konto** debit (debtor) account; ~**masse** bankrupt estate; ~**note** debit note (memorandum, *US*); ~**posten** debit entry (item), entry on the debit side; **als ~posten buchen** to debit.
Debetsaldo balance owing (due, payable), debit (debt, debtor) balance;
Ihr gegenwärtiger ~ balance standing to your debit; **schwankender ~** fluctuating advance;
~ abbuchen to wipe off a debit balance; **~ abdecken** to cover a short account; **~ aufweisen** to show a debit balance; **~ in Höhe von 100 £ aufweisen** to be overdrawn to the extent of £ 100; **~ stehenlassen** to leave a balance to one's debit.
Debet|seite debtor [side], debit [side], left hand side of an account, red; ~**spalte** debit column; ~**zinsen** interest on debit balances; ~**zinsen halbjährlich in Rechnung stellen** to add interest to the debt half-yearly; ~**zinssatz** debit interest rate; ~**zinszahlen** debit products *(Br.)*.
debitieren to debit, to charge;
jem. ~ to pass to s. one's debit, to charge against s. one's account; **j. mit einem Betrag ~** to pass (place) an amount to the debit of s. o.
Debitor debtor.
Debitoren *(Bilanz)* debtors, debts *(Br.)*, accounts (bills) receivable *(US)*, receivables *(US)*;
abgetretene ~ assigned debts, pledged accounts receivable *(US)*; **ausstehende ~** outstanding receivables *(US)*, outstanding debts *(Br.)*; **diverse ~** sundry debtors; **dubiose ~** doubtful (bad, *US*) debts; **noch nicht fällige ~** accrued receivable accounts *(US)*; **langfristige ~** long-term (uncollectible) receivables *(US)*, long-term debts *(Br.)*; **sichere ~** good debts; **sonstige ~** other accounts receivable *(US)*, sundry debtors *(Br.)*; **überfällige ~** past due (aging, extended) accounts receivable *(US)*; **uneinbringliche ~** irrecoverable debts; **verschiedene ~** sundry debtors *(Br.)*, other accounts receivable *(US)*;
~ aus Buchforderungen accounts receivable *(US)*; **~ am Ende eines Rechnungsabschnitts** period-end receivables *(US)*; **~ aus Schuldverschreibungen** bond subscription receivables *(US)*; **~ aus Wechselforderungen** draft receivables *(US)*.
Debitorenabtretung assignment of book debts, assignment of accounts receivable *(US)*;
offene ~ absolute assignment; **stille ~** equitable assignment;
~ in stiller Form vornehmen to operate on a nonnotification basis.
Debitoren|aufstellung nach Fälligkeit aging accounts receivable *(US)*; ~**auszug** accounts receivable statement *(US)*; **zedierter ~bestand** assigned debts, account receivables discounted *(US)*; ~**buch** accounts receivable *(US)* (customer's sales) ledger; ~**buchhalter** accounts receivable clerk *(US)*; ~**buchhaltung** accounts receivable department *(US)*; ~**buchhaltung mit einem Alarmsystem ausstatten** to flag the receivable records *(US)*; ~**fälligkeitstabelle** aging schedule; ~**geschäft** loan business, lending business; ~**guthaben** customer's credit balance, accounts receivable *(US)*; ~**konto** debit (trading) account, accounts receivable ledger *(US)*; ~**kredit** customer's loan, consumer credit, accounts receivable loan *(US)*; ~**laufzeit** average days in receivables *(US)*; ~**saldo** balance payable, debit balance; ~**sätze** lending (borrowing) rates; ~**umschlag** receivables turnover *(US)*; ~**umschlagsdauer** average days in receivables *(US)*; **[offener] ~verkauf** selling accounts receivable outright *(US)*, factoring; ~**versicherung** accounts receivable insurance *(US)*; ~**verzeichnis** schedule of accounts receivable *(US)*.
debitorisch|werden to run into debt;
~**e Konten** accounts having a debit balance, debit accounts; ~**e Posten** debts, receivables *(US)*, receivable items *(US)*.
Debüt first appearance, début;
sein ~ geben to make one's first appearance.
Debütant débutante.
debütieren to come out, to make one's first appearance.
dechiffrieren to decipher, to decode, to translate, to unscramble.
Dechiffrierung translation, decoding, decipherment.
Deck *(Bus)* top, *(Schiff)* deck, board;
auf ~ above (on) deck, topside; **unter ~** under hatches;
oberstes ~ upper deck;
auf dem ~ auf- und abgehen to walk the deck; **unter ~ schicken** to pipe away *(mar.)*; **~ schrubben** to wash the deck; **nicht ganz auf ~ sein** to be a bit off colo(u)r (out of sorts); **auf ~ spazierengehen** to promenade the deck; **an ~ verladen** to ship on deck;
~**adresse** code, accommodation, cover, arbitrary address, address of convenience; ~**anstrich** finishing coat, protecting varnish; ~**aufbauten** superstructure; ~**belastung** deckload; ~**bezeichnung** code name; ~**blatt** backer, flyleaf; ~**boot** boom boat; ~**dienst** duty on deck.
Decke blanket, cover, rug, *(Plane)* awning, *(Reifen)* outer cover, casing *(US)*, *(Steppdecke)* quilt, counterpane, *(Zimmer)* ceiling;
in fester ~ *(Straße)* hard-surfaced; **in fester ~ gebunden** case-(cloth) bound;
kassettierte ~ panelled (coffered) ceiling;
an die ~ gehen *(fig.)* to hit (fly at) the ceiling; **sich in eine ~ einwickeln** to wrap o. s. in a blanket; **~ in einen Raum einziehen** to ceil a room; **an der ~ hängen** to depend from the ceiling; **unter die ~ kriechen** to pull the blanket over one's head; **vor Freude an die ~ springen** to be in one's seventh heaven; **unter einer ~ stecken** to be in cahoots *(US sl.)*, to be in on the racket, to stand in (conspire) with; **sich nach der ~ strecken** to make both ends meet, to cut one's coat according to one's cloth.
Deckel lid, cover;
mit einem ~ verschlossen lidded;
jem. eins auf den ~ geben to give s. o. a good dressing-down; **~ hochstemmen** to prize a lid up; **eins auf den ~ kriegen** to get a crack on the nut;
Topf und ~ well-matched couple;
~**bezug** *(Buch)* covering; ~**korb** hamper; ~**krug** tankard.

decken to cover, *(abschirmen)* to shelter, to screen, to shield, to protect, *(rückerstatten)* to reimburse, *(sicherstellen)* to secure, to give security;
um sich zu ~ in order to be on the safe side;
Akzept ~ to provide for acceptance; **jds. Anordnungen** ~ to endorse s. one's orders; **Ausgaben** ~ to cover expenses; **Bedarf** ~ to meet (cover) the requirements, to meet the demand, to supply the needs; **Dach mit Ziegeln** ~ to tile a roof; **Defizit** ~ to make up a deficiency; **jem. Handlungen** ~ to assume personal responsibility for s. one's actions; **durch Hinterlegung einer Sicherheitssumme** ~ to margin; **j. mit dem eigenen Körper** ~ to shield s. o. with one's own body; **Kosten** ~ to defray (reimburse) the costs; **kaum die Kosten** ~ to cover barely the costs; **Landesbedarf** ~ to supply the needs of the country; **Leerabgaben einer Position** ~ to repurchase short sales *(US)*; **jds. Lügen** ~ to cover up s. one's lies; **Nachfrage** ~ to meet (satisfy) the demand; **Risiko** ~ to cover a risk; **jem. den Rücken** ~ to back s. o., to stand up for s. o.; **sich durch Rückversicherung** ~ to lay off a risk; **Rückzug der Armee** ~ to secure the retreat of an army; **Schaden** ~ to make good a loss (deficiency); **sich nach allen Seiten** ~ to hedge all bets; **sich** ~ *(Interessen)* to coincide; **sich nicht** ~ *(Interessen)* to differ; **sich teilweise** ~ to overlap one another; **sich zeitlich** ~ to coincide; **Tisch** ~ to lay (set) the table; **Untergebenen** ~ to shield a subordinate; **sich gegen einen Verdacht** ~ to shield o. s. against a suspicion; **Verlust** ~ to make good a loss; **sich gegen Verluste** ~ to take precautions against a loss; **Versicherung** ~ to cover an insurance; **Wechsel** ~ to meet (hono(u)r) a bill; **Zahlungsanweisung** ~ to remit cover.

Decken|beleuchtung overhead (ceiling) lights; **~hänger** *(Reklame)* dangler; **~heizung** overhead radiator heating; **~lampe** ceiling lamp, centre light; **~schild** ceiling panel; **~strahler** inverted lamp; **~träger** ceiling girder; **~ventilator** ceiling fan.

Deck|güter deck cargo; **~konto** fictitious account; **~ladung** deckload, deck cargo; **~landeflugzeug** carrier-borne aircraft, deck lander; **~liegestuhl** deck chair; **~mannschaft** deck hands.

Deckmantel cover, colo(u)r, cloak, stalking horse, mantle, veil;
unter dem ~ **der Freundschaft** under the guise of friendship;
etw. als ~ **benutzen** to use s. th. as a cloak.

Deck|material covering; **~name** pseudonym, assumed (cover, code, fictitious) name, *(Schriftsteller)* pen name, allonym;
unter einem ~namen reisen to travel under an alias; **~namensverzeichnis** list of code names; **~offizier** deck officer, machinist, warrant officer *(US)*; **~organisation** shadow (cover) organization.

Decksbelag deck flooring.

Deckschicht top layer (coat).

Decks|haus deckhouse; **~ladung** deck cargo; **~passage** deck passage; **~passagier** deck passenger.

Deckstein coping stone.

Deckung cover, covering, coverage, provision of funds, *(Banknoten)* backing, *(Barzahlung)* payment, *(Deckungsspanne)* margin, *(Geldsendung)* remittance, *(Kapital)* funds, provision, *(mil.)* shelter, protection, cover, *(Rückerstattung)* reimbursement, refund, *(Sicherheit)* security, collateral *(US)*, *(Tarnung)* concealment, camouflage, *(Währung)* cover, backing, *(Wechsel)* protecting, cover, hono(u)ring;
~ **angeschafft** cover overfloat (in transit); **mangels** ~ returned for want of funds, for want of cover, without cash; **ohne** ~ uncovered, unsecured, without cover (funds in hand), no effects; **zur** ~ **unserer Unkosten** to cover our expenses; **zur** ~ **verwendet** used as cover;
anteilige ~ *(Gruppenversicherung)* prorata distribution; **ausreichende** ~ sufficient security; **keine ausreichende** ~ not sufficient [funds] (n. s.), not provided for, *(Konto)* no funds, *(Scheckvermerk)* no effects; **automatische** ~ *(Versicherung)* automatic coverage; **bankmäßige** ~ collateral security *(US)*; **erforderliche** ~ requisite cover; **durch Rückversicherung beschaffte fehlende** ~ surplus coverage; **genügende (hinreichende)** ~ requisite cover, ample security, sufficient funds; **sehr knappe** ~ thin margin *(US)*; **mangelnde** ~ insufficiency of assets; **natürliche** ~ *(mil.)* accidental cover; **ungenügende** ~ insufficient funds; **völlig ungenügende** ~ *(Makler)* shoestring margin *(US)*; **volle** ~ full cover (coverage); **vorgeschriebene** ~ *(Lebensversicherung)* legal reserve; **vorläufige** ~ provisional cover; **weitere (zusätzliche)** ~ additional cover, collateral security *(US)*, surplus reserve *(US)*, *(Makler)* additional margin *(US)*;
~ **durch Aktiva** asset coverage; ~ **von Banknoten** backing of notes; ~ **des Bedarfs** supply, meeting the requirements; ~ **der öffentlichen Defizite** financing of the public deficits; ~ **gegen Fliegersicht** concealment from air observation; ~ **der Kosten** cost recovery; ~ **eines Risikos** covering a risk; ~ **eines Verlustes** covering a loss; ~ **erst bei Zahlungseingang** drawn against uncollected funds;
~ **ablehnen** *(Versicherung)* to disclaim liability; **als** ~ **annehmen** to take as reimbursement; ~ **anschaffen** to provide (furnish with) cover, to cover, to make (send, provide for) remittance, to provide (furnish with) funds, to provide payment, to remit, *(Makler)* to margin; **jem.** ~ **anschaffen** to furnish s. o. with cover, to supply s. o. with funds; ~ **in bar anschaffen** to deposit a margin in cash; ~ **für einen Wechsel anschaffen** to cover (give consideration for, provide for, make provision for cover of) a bill; **voll zur** ~ **des Gemeinkostenanteils beitragen** to absorb its full share of overhead; ~ **bieten** to afford shelter; **etw. in** ~ **bringen** to conceal s. th.; **als** ~ **dienen** to serve as cover (collateral, *US*); **Betrag als** ~ **einzahlen** to pay in an amount as deposit; **der** ~ **entgegensehen** to expect provision; ~ **gewähren** to provide cover; ~ **in Händen haben** to be covered, to hold security; **größere** ~ **hinterlegen** to put up more margin; **Aktien als** ~ **hinterlegen** to lodge stock as cover; ~ **nehmen** *(mil.)* to take shelter; **ohne** ~ **sein** to be uncovered (without funds in hand); **für** ~ **sorgen** to provide for payment (with funds); **für rechtzeitige** ~ **eines Betrages sorgen** to see that due provision for payment is made; **für die** ~ **eines Wechsels sorgen** to make provision for payment of a bill; **ohne kapitalmäßige** ~ **spekulieren** to overtrade; ~ **für Kursverluste stellen** *(Makler)* to margin up; **jem.** ~ **zur Verfügung stellen** to furnish s. o. with cover (funds); ~ **suchen** to take cover; ~ **gemeinsam übernehmen** to join the coverage; **ohne** ~ **verkaufen** *(Börse)* to sell a bear (short, *US*); ~ **verlangen** to want a security; ~ **verschaffen** to put under cover; **mit** ~ **versehen** to put in funds, to provide with cover; **Aktien als** ~ **verwenden** to apply shares as security (stock as collateral, *US*); ~ **vornehmen** to cover.

Deckungs|anschaffung providing cover; **~auflage** publisher's cost; **~auftrag** covering order, order to cover; **~ausschluß für Buchschulden** common memorandum *(Br.)*; **~austausch** shifting of funds; **~bedürfnis** need to cover, *(Börse)* short interest; **~beitrag** contribution, variable gross margin, profit contribution, marginal (variable gross) income; **~beitragsrechnung** contribution margin accounting, break-even analysis; **~bereich** *(Rundfunk, Fernsehen)* coverage; **~bescheid** covering note; **~bestände** *(Staatsbank)* cover of notes in circulation; **~betrag** margin, *(Versicherung)* amount insured, insured sum; **~einzahlung** payment to cover; **~erfordernisse** coverage requirements.

deckungsfähig eligible to serve as collateral *(US)*.

Deckungs|fähigkeit eligibility to serve as collateral *(US)*; **~fonds** unearned premium reserve; **~forderungen** covering claims, admitted assets; **~geschäft** hedge, hedging transaction; **~frist** period of coverage; **~geschäft unterbringen** to [place a] hedge; **~graben** *(mil.)* split trench; **~grad** cash ratio; **~grenze** legal limit, limit for cover, *(Versicherung)* office limit; **~höhe** insurance cover; **~kapital** legal capital, *(Bausparkasse)* guarantee stock, *(Versicherung)* unearned premium (actuarial insurance) reserve, insurance fund, *(Lebensversicherung)* net value.

Deckungskauf cover[ing] purchase, purchase of goods in replacement, *(Effekten)* buying in, short covering *(US)*;
~ **des Börsenvorstands** buying in under the rules;
~ **vornehmen** to buy goods in replacement.

Deckungskäufe purchases to cover, cover purchases;
~ **der Kontermine** bear[ish] covering;
plötzlich zu ~n gezwungen sein to be pinched; **zu ~n zwingen** *(Börse)* to squeeze the shorts (bears).

Deckungs|klausel savings clause; **~konto** fund account.

deckungslos *(Aktien)* short.

Deckungs|lücke *(Haushalt)* deficit; **~masse** general revenue fund, *(Hypothekenbanken)* guarantee fund.

Deckungsmittel cover, covering resources, funds, *(Haushalt)* ways and means;
ordentliche ~ *(Haushalt)* budgetary receipts; **ungeeignete** ~ *(Versicherung)* nonadmitted assets.

Deckungs|order covering order, order to cover; **~quote** cover (reserve, *US*) ratio; **~rücklage** *(Versicherung)* insurance (mathematical, unearned premium) reserve; **~satz** *(Bank)* cover ratio, reserve ratio *(US)*; **~schein** covering deed; **vorläufiger ~schein** memorandum of insurance *(Br.)*; **~schutz** insurance protection (cover); **~sicherheit** collateral security *(US)*; **~spanne** margin; **~stock** *(Bausparkasse)* guarantee stock, *(Versicherung)* premium stock, insurance fund, unearned premium (insurance, mathematical) reserve.

deckungsstockfähig eligible to serve as insurance reserve.
Deckungs|stockfähigkeit eligibility to serve as insurance reserve; **~summe** *(Versicherung)* amount covered; **~umfang der für den Betrieb abgeschlossenen Versicherungen** business insurance coverage; **~unterstand** foxhole *(mil.)*; **~verfügung** *(Staatsrechnungswesen)* covering warrant; **~verhältnis** *(Banknoten)* reserve (cover) ratio *(US)*; **gesetzlich vorgeschriebenes ~verhältnis** *(Banken)* legal reserve *(US)* (special deposits, *Br.*) requirements; **~verhältnistabelle** reserve ratio table *(US)*; **~verkauf** hedge selling, hedging sale; **~vorsorge** provision of funds; **~werte** admitted assets; **~zeit, ~zeitraum** period of coverage; **~zusage** *(Versicherung)* binding (conditional) receipt; **vorläufige ~zusage** *(Feuerversicherung)* covering (cover, *Br.*) note, provisional cover, slip *(Br.)*; **~zuschuß** additional cover.
Deckwort code word.
Dedikationsexemplar presentation copy.
Deduktion deduction.
deduktive Methode deductive method.
Defätismus defeatism.
Defätist defeatist.
defätistisch defeatist, negative *(US)*.
Defekt flaw, fault, defect, *(Buchstabe)* battered letter, batter, *(el.)* trouble;
angeborener ~ congenital defect; **geistiger ~** mental injury; **moralischer ~** moral insanity; **verborgener ~** hidden defect;
~ haben to break down; **geistigen ~ haben** to be mentally deficient.
defekt damaged, defective, out of order, faulty;
geistig ~ mentally deficient;
~ sein to be out of order;
~es Buch incomplete book; **~er Buchstabe** broken (battered) letter, batter.
Defekt|bogen defective (imperfect) sheet; **~buchstabe** broken (battered) letter, batter, imperfection; **~kasten** shell.
defensiv defensive;
sich ~ verhalten to stand on the defensive.
Defensivbündnis defensive alliance.
Defensive defensive;
j. in die ~ treiben to put s. o. on the defensive.
Defensiv|krieg defensive war; **~marke, ~zeichen** defensive trademark *(Br.)*; **~maßnahmen** defensive measures; **~streik** defence *(Br.)* (defense, *US*) (negative) strike; **~urteil** final judgment; **~waffe** defensive weapon.
Defilieren filing off, march-past.
defilieren *(mil.)* to march past, to defile, to pass by.
definierbar definable.
definieren to define, to give a definition, to circumscribe;
Wort ~ to define a word;
sich nicht ~ lassen to evade definition.
Definition definition;
genaue ~ precise definition;
~ als Diskussionsgrundlage working definition.
definitiv definitive, definite, final;
~ entscheiden to rule definitively;
~es Angebot final offer; **~er Bescheid** definite answer; **~er Titel** definitive bond.
Defizit deficit, deficiency, shortage, short, wantage, *(Bilanz)* adverse balance, red *(US coll.)*;
unbeabsichtigtes ~ casual deficit;
~ im Außenhandel foreign-trade (external) deficit; **~ am Gewicht** short[ness of] weight; **~ der öffentlichen Hände** public-sector deficit; **~ in der Handelsbilanz** deficit in the balance of trade; **~ in der Kasse** deficit in expense fund; **~ in der Leistungsbilanz** current account deficit; **~ der Pensionskasse** pension deficit; **~ der Post** postal deficit; **~ im Staatshaushalt** deficit in the budget, budgetary (fiscal) deficit; **~ im Steueraufkommen** deficit in taxes, tax deficit, shortfall in tax revenue; **~ durch Steuersatzsenkung** deficit without spending; **~ auf anderem als dem Warengebiet** deficit in the nonmerchandising field; **~ im Waren- und Dienstleistungsverkehr** deficit on trade and services; **~ in der Zahlungsbilanz** balance-of-payments deficit;
~ abdecken to cover a deficit; **mit einem ~ abschließen** to show (close with) a deficit; **mit ~ arbeiten** to operate on an income gap; **~ aufweisen** to show a deficit, to run red ink *(US)*; **~ ausgleichen (decken, ersetzen)** to make good a deficit, to supply (make good) the deficiency, to settle a deficit, to make up an amount; **schon bestehendes ~ erhöhen** to raise the accumulated red-ink figures *(US coll.)*; **mit dem ~ fertigwerden** to cope with the red ink *(US coll.)*; **ins ~ geraten** to slip into deficit; **immer tiefer ins ~ geraten** to plunge deeper in the red *(US coll.)*; **~ von 100 $ haben** to be $ 100 short; **~ im Staatshaushalt herbeiführen** to put the budget in the red *(US coll.)*; **aus dem ~ kommen** to get out of the red *(US coll.)*;
~finanzierung deficit budgeting, deficit spending *(US)*; **~haushalt** adverse budget, budget that shows a deficit; **~jahr** lean year; **~länder** deficit countries; **~vorschlag** deficit projection; **~wirtschaft** compensatory spending, deficit financing; **~wirtschaft betreiben** to spend one's way into deficit.
defizitär *(Bilanz)* adverse, in the deficit;
~e Handelsbilanz adverse balance of trade; **~er Haushalt** adverse budget.
Deflation deflation;
~ durchführen to deflate a currency.
deflationäre Maßnahmen deflationary measures.
deflationistisch deflationary;
~e Einflüsse deflationary influences; **~e Faktoren** deflationary factors; **seiner Zahlungsbilanzschwierigkeiten mittels ~er Maßnahmen Herr werden** to deflate its way out of its balance-of-payments difficulties; **~e Tendenz** deflationary tendency.
Deflations|anhänger deflationist; **~bewegung** deflationary movement; **~druck** deflationary pressure; **preislicher ~faktor** price deflator; **~krise** deflationary crisis; **~lücke** deflationary (output) gap; **~maßnahmen** deflationary measures; **~politik** deflationary policy; **~politik treiben** to deflate the currency; **~programm** deflationary program(me); **~prozeß** deflationary process; **~zeit** deflationary period.
deflatorische|Lücke deflation (deflationary) gap; **~ Währungspolitik** deflationary policy.
Defraudant defrauder, peculator, embezzler.
Defraudation fraud, peculation, embezzlement.
Degradation *(mil.)* degradation, demotion *(US)*.
degradieren *(mil.)* to degrade, to demote, to downgrade, to reduce to the ranks (a lower grade, *US*), to bust *(sl.)*.
degradiert *(mil.)* broken, reduced to the ranks;
~ werden to lose one's stripes.
Degradierung *(mil.)* demotion, reduction to the ranks (in rank, *Br.*, to a lower grade, *US*), downgrading.
Degression *(Steuer)* degression.
degressiv degressive, on a descending scale;
~e Abschreibung degressive depreciation; **~e Abschreibungsmethode** reducing-fraction method of depreciation; **~e Besteuerung** degressive taxation; **~e Steuer** degressive tax; **~er Tarif** sliding-scale tariff.
dehnbar elastic, flexible, tensile;
~es Gesetz flexible law; **~es Gewissen haben** to have an elastic conscience.
dehnen to stretch, to draw out, to extend, *(Zeit)* to drag on, to creep;
Besprechung in die Länge ~ to spin out a discussion.
Dehnfestigkeit tensile strength.
Deich dike, dyke, bank, embankment, dam;
~amt dike warden; **~arbeiter** diker; **~aufseher, ~hauptmann** dike grave, dike reeve *(Br.)*; **~bau** dike building; **~böschung** batter; **~bruch** bursting of a dike; **~land** innings; **~schleuse** floodgate.
deichseln to jockey, to engineer, to wangle, to manage.
Dekade decade.
Dekadenz decadence.
Dekan dean, faculty adviser.
dekartellisieren to decartelize.
Dekartellisierung decartelization.
Dekartellisierungsprogramm decartelization plan.
Deklaration proclamation, announcement, *(Zoll)* declaration, entry;
~ zur Einlagerung unter Zollverschluß warehousing entry; **~ für zollfreie Waren** entry for duty-free goods.
Deklarations|etikett declaration label; **~pflicht** liability to declare; **~schein** *(Zoll)* bill of entry *(Br.)*, declaration; **~wert** value at point of entry, declared value; **~zwang** compulsory declaration.
deklaratorisch *(jur.)* declaratory, adjudicative.
deklarieren to declare, to enter, to make a bill of entry, to report;
sein Einkommen ~ to file one's income-tax return; **zu hoch ~** to declare (value) too high; **zu wenig ~** to undervalue, to underbill *(US)*; **Waren zollamtlich ~** to enter goods at the customhouse; **Wert zollamtlich ~** to declare the value.
deklariert declared, entered;
nicht ~ unentered;
~er Wert registered (declared) value.

deklassieren to degrade, to lower the social position.
deklassiert werden to come down in the world.
Deklassierung degradation.
Deklinationskompaß variation compass.
Dekonzentration deconcentration;
~ **von Vermögenswerten** dispersal of assets.
Dekonzentrationsprogramm deconcentration program(me).
dekonzentrieren to deconcentrate.
Dekorateur decorator, *(Schaufenster)* window dresser, display man, *(Gardinen)* curtain fitter, *(Polsterer)* upholsterer, *(Theater)* scene painter.
Dekoration decoration, *(Schaufenster)* window display (dressing), *(Theater)* scene painting.
Dekorations|arbeit display work; ~**etikett** display sign; ~**farbe** display colo(u)r; ~**fenster** display window; ~**gestell** display stand; ~**karte** display card; ~**lager** *(Theater)* scenery store; ~**maler** scene painter; ~**malerei** *(Theater)* scene painting; ~**material** window display material, window decoration; ~**papier** fancy paper; ~**stoff** material for furnishing, drapery; ~**stück** set piece, ornament; ~**ware** goods displayed.
dekorativ decorative, ornamental.
dekorieren to decorate, *(im Fenster)* to display, to dress, *(mil.)*, to medal;
Fenster ~ to dress a window; **neu** ~ to redecorate; **Waren im Schaufenster** ~ to display goods in the window.
dekoriert decorated;
geschmackvoll mit Blumen ~ tastefully decorated with flowers.
Dekorierung decoration, decor, *(Schaufenster)* display.
Dekorum wahren to preserve appearances, to maintain one's decorum.
Dekret decree;
~ **erlassen** to decree.
dekretierbar decreeable.
dekretieren to decree.
Delegation delegation, delegacy, deputation, body of delegates, mission;
~ **leiten** to head a delegation.
Delegations|befugnis power of substitution; ~**chef** head of a delegation; ~**gruppe** block of delegates; ~**leiter** head of a delegation; ~**mitglied** member of a delegation.
delegierbar delegable.
delegieren to delegate, to deputize;
Verantwortlichkeit ~ to delegate responsibility; **seine Vollmacht** ~ to hand over one's authority.
delegiert delegate, deputy.
Delegierte|r delegate, deputy;
ständiger ~**r** permanent delegate;
als ~**n entsenden** to delegate, to deputize.
Delegierten|konferenz delegate conference; ~**versammlung** convention *(US)*.
Delegierung|von Amtsgewalt devolution of authority; ~ **von Pflichten** delegation of duty.
deliberalisieren to deliberalize.
Deliberalisierung deliberalization.
delikat delicate;
sehr ~**e Fragen behandeln** to tread on delicate ground *(coll.)*; ~**e Situation** delicate situation.
Delikatesse delicacy, dainty, delicatessen.
Delikatessengeschäft delicatessen shop.
Delikatesswarenhändler oilman *(US)*.
Delikt offence, tortious act, tort, delict, misfeasance, crime;
fortgesetztes ~ continued offence; **geringfügiges** ~ petty offence; **Polizeistrafen unterliegendes** ~ contravention;
~ **der unerlaubten Handlung** tort of conspiracy.
deliktfähig sein to be responsible for one's actions.
Delikts|anspruch tort claim; ~**haftung** tortious (tort) liability; ~**handlung** tortious act; ~**klage** tort action.
Delinquent delinquent, offender, misdemeanant.
Delkredere guarantee, surety, del credere *(Br.)*;
~ **anbieten** to offer guarantee; ~ **berechnen** to charge for del credere *(Br.)*; ~ **stehen** to stand surety, to insure a debt, to give (stand) guarantee; **für die Hälfte** ~ **stehen** to guarantee for the moiety; ~ **übernehmen** to stand del credere *(Br.)*, to give (stand) guarantee, to assure the credit risk;
~**agent** del-credere agent *(Br.)*; ~**fonds** contingent fund; ~**geschäft** del-credere business *(Br.)*; ~**haftung** del-credere responsibility *(Br.)*; ~**klausel** guarantee clause; ~**konto** contingent (contingency, reserve, del-credere, *Br.*) account; ~**provision** guarantee (del-credere, *Br.*) commission; ~**reserve** contingent fund; ~**risiko übernehmen** to act on a del-credere basis *(Br.)*; ~**rückstellung** contingency (del-credere, *Br.*) reserve, reserve for contingencies; ~**rückstellungen aus dem Reservefonds** reserve for surplus contingencies; ~**vereinbarung** del-credere agreement *(Br.)*; ~**versicherung** credit (commercial) insurance; ~**vertrag** del-credere agreement *(Br.)*; ~**vertretung** del-credere agency *(Br.)*.
Deltaflügel *(Flugzeug)* delta wing.
Demagoge demagogue, rabble rouser.
Demarche step, course of action;
offiziöse ~ informal step;
~ **unternehmen** to take the necessary steps.
Demarkation demarcation, delimitation.
Demarkationslinie line of demarcation, demarcation line.
demaskieren to unmask.
Demaskierung unmasking.
Dementi denial, disavowal, disclaimer, dementi;
abgeschwächtes ~ softened denial; **amtliches** ~ official denial; **formelles (offizielles)** ~ flat (formal) denial; **glattes** ~ outright (unqualified) denial; **uneingeschränktes** ~ unqualified denial; **formelles** ~ **abgeben** to give s. o. the lie direct; **einem** ~ **entgegentreten** to contravene a statement; ~ **geben** to give a formal denial; ~ **herausgeben** to issue a denial; **der Presse ein** ~ **zugehen lassen** to send a disclaimer to the press.
dementieren to deny, to disclaim;
etw. ~ to deny the truth of s. th.; **Behauptungen formell** ~ to give a formal denial to a statement; **glatt** ~ to give a flat denial.
Demission resignation, demission, vacating of office;
seine ~ **einreichen** to tender (send in) one's resignation.
demissionieren to leave (surrender one's) office, to tender one's resignation, to demit, to return the seals *(Br.)*, *(Minister)* to resign from the cabinet.
Demissionsangebot offer to resign.
Demoband demodisc.
demobilisieren *(mil.)* to demobilize.
Demobilmachung *(mil.)* demobilization, demob *(Br., coll.)*, general release.
Demographie demography.
demographische|Merkmale demographic characteristics; ~ **Struktur** audience composition.
Demokrat democrat;
kompromißloser ~ straight-out democrat; **unentwegter** ~ loyal (staunch) democrat.
Demokratie democracy;
autoritäre ~ democratic dictatorship; **parlamentarische** ~ parliamentary democracy; **plebiszitäre** ~ plebiscitary democracy; **representative** ~ representative democracy; **unmittelbare** ~ absolute (pure) democracy;
~ **mit aktiver Beteiligung der Staatsbürger** participatory democracy;
sich für die ~ **entscheiden** to choose the democratic road; **sich nur schwer mit der** ~ **abfinden können** to live uncomfortably with democracy.
demokratisch democratic;
~**e Regierungsform** democratic government; ~**e Spielregeln einhalten** to play the democratic rules.
demokratisieren to democratize.
Demokratisierung democratization, democratic process.
Demokratisierungsprozeß democratic process.
demolieren to demolish, to destroy, to destruct, to wreck.
Demolierung demolition, destruction.
demonetisieren to withdraw from circulation, to demonetize.
Demonstrant demonstrator;
~**en zerstreuen** to disperse demonstrators.
Demonstration demonstration, manifestation;
militärische ~ military demonstration;
~ **unzufriedener Arbeiter** demonstration by discontented workmen;
~ **durchführen (veranstalten)** to take part in (organize) a demonstration, *(mil.)* to demonstrate.
Demonstrations|blatt broadside; ~**film** demonstrational film; ~**flug** flying demonstration; ~**marsch** demonstration, protest march; ~**teilnehmer** demonstrator.
Demonstrationszug public procession, protest march;
~ **der Autonomistenbewegung** autonomist demonstration;
~ **umleiten** to re-route a procession; ~ **verbieten** to make an order prohibiting a public procession.
demonstrieren to demonstrate, to make a demonstration.
gegen die gestiegenen Lebenshaltungskosten ~ to demonstrate against the rising costs of living; **auf den Straßen** ~ to be out.
Demontage disassembling, dismantling, dismantlement, dismount;
wirtschaftliche ~ industrial dismantling;

~**arbeiten** dismantling operations; **während der ~arbeiten** during the process of dismantling; ~**liste** dismantling list; ~**programm** dismantling program(me); ~**verfahren** process of dismantling.
demontieren to take down, to disassemble, to dismantle, *(Maschine)* to knock down, to break up;
Fabrik ~ to pluck up a plant, to strip a factory.
demoralisieren to deprave, to demoralize.
demoralierende Wirkung demoralizing effect.
Demoralisierung demoralization, depravation.
Demoskop pollster.
Demoskopie public opinion research.
demoskopische Untersuchung public opinion poll.
demütig humble, lowly, meek.
demütigen to mortify, to humble, to abase, to cast down;
j. ~ to crop s. one's feathers; **sich** ~ to eat the humble pie; **sich vor jem.** ~ to prostrate o. s. before s. o.; **jds. Stolz** ~ to humble s. one's pride.
Demütigung mortification, abasement, humiliation, set-down;
alle ~en hinnehmen müssen to have to put up with every humiliation.
denkbar thinkable, intellectual, earthly *(coll.)*;
durchaus ~ easily possible;
sich die ~ **größte Mühe geben** to leave no stone unturned; ~ **leichte Sache** easiest thing imaginable; **in der** ~ **schönsten Umgebung** in the most beautiful surroundings; **in der** ~ **einfachsten Weise leben** to live in the simplest possible way.
Denken [way of] thinking, thought;
folgerichtiges ~ straight thinking; **genossenschaftliches** ~ cooperative spirit; **progressives** ~ forward thinking; **unternehmerisches** ~ management philosophy.
denken to think, to believe, to suppose, *(beabsichtigen)* to intend, *(überlegen)* to consider, to bear in mind;
antiquiert ~ to be a back number; **sich nichts Böses** ~ to mean no harm; **eingleisig** ~ to have a one-track mind; **Gedanken zu Ende** ~ to pursue a thought to the end; **kleinlich** ~ to be of a petty turn of mind; **an die Kosten** ~ to consider the expenses; **in einem Punkt anders** ~ to have a different view; **an das Schlimmste** ~ to expect the worst; **stets nur an sich** ~ to be a lump of selfishness; **im Stillen** ~ to think to o. s.; **an seine alten Tage** ~ to provide for one's old days; **sich seinen Teil** ~ to have an opinion about s. th.; **nicht im Traum daran** ~ not to dream of doing it; **nur an seinen eigenen Vorteil** ~ to take care of number one, to consult one's own advantage; **an eine größere Wohnung** ~ to want a larger apartment;
zu ~ **geben** to give food for thought; **dauernd an etw.** ~ **müssen** to get s. th. on the brain; **ohne sich dabei etw. zu** ~ without realizing the full implications.
Denker, freiheitlicher liberal thinker; **scharfsinniger** ~ deep thinker; **unselbständiger** ~ independent thinker.
Denk|fabrik think-tank; ~**fehler** false reasoning; ~**freiheit** liberty of thought.
Denkmal monument, memorial;
~ **aufstellen** to fix up a monument; ~ **enthüllen** to inaugurate a monument; ~ **errichten** to set up (rear) a monument; **jem. ein** ~ **errichten** to put up a statue in hono(u)r of s. o.
Denkmals|amt [etwa] Royal Commission on Historical Monuments *(Br.)*; ~**inschrift** monumental inscription; ~**pflege** preservation of monuments.
Denkmalsschutz architectural conversation;
unter ~ **gestellt sein** to be listed for preservation; **unter** ~ **stellen** to preserve as a historical site.
Denk|münze commemorative coin; ~**problem lösen** to work s. th. out; ~**prozeß** process of thought; ~**richtung** school of thought; ~**schema** pattern of thought; ~**schrift** memorandum, memorial, minute, address, exposé; ~**schrift einreichen** to present (submit) a memorial; ~**sportaufgabe** quiz, brain twister *(US)*; ~**sportecke** *(Zeitung)* puzzle corner; ~**spruch** maxim, motto; ~**tätigkeit** mental activity.
Denkungsart bent of mind.
Denkungsweise, provinzielle parochialism; **wissenschaftliche** ~ scientific thought;
allgemeine ~ **beeinflussen** to influence the current of thought.
Denk|vorgang process of the mind; ~**weise** line (way) of thinking; **schöpferische** ~**weise** creative thought.
denkwürdig memorable, noteworthy;
~**er Tag** red-letter day.
Denkzettel lesson, one in the eye;
tüchtigen ~ **bekommen** to get a thorough dressing down; **jem. einen** ~ **verpassen** to give s. o. snuff, to haul s. o. over the coals *(fam.)*, to give s. o. s. th. to tkink about.
Dentist dentist, dental mechanic.
Denunziant denunciator, denouncer, informant, common informer, nark, rat *(sl.)*, nightingale *(sl.)*, finger *(sl.)*, split *(sl.)*, stool pigeon *(sl.)*, stag *(sl.)*.
Denunziation information, denunciation, denouncement, delation, relation;
~**en gegen jem. vorbringen** to inform against s. o.
denunzieren to denounce, to delate, to inform, to grass *(sl.)*, to turn stag, to shop *(sl.)*, to fink *(sl.)*, to peach *(sl.)*;
j. ~ to round (split) on (inform against) s. o.; **j. bei der Polizei** ~ to denounce s o. to the police.
denunzierend denunciatory.
Dependance *(Hotel)* annex, dependency.
Depesche despatch, telegram, wire, cable;
über die Absendung von ~en entscheiden to control cable facilities.
Depeschen|anschrift telegraphic address; ~**boot** dispatch boat; ~**bote** telegraph messenger; ~**büro** dispatch agency; ~**formular** message (telegraph) form; ~**tasche** dispatch box; ~**wechsel** exchange of dispatches.
depeschieren to cable, to telegraph, to wire.
deplaziert misplaced, out-of-place, out of position;
sich ~ **fühlen** to feel out of place.
Deponent depositor, bailer, bailor.
Deponie dumping, tipping, rubbish dump, refuse disposal site;
geordnete ~ controlled tipping; **wilde** ~ fly dumping.
deponieren to deposit, to lodge, to bail, *(mil.)* to park;
Betrag für etw. ~ to leave a deposit on s. th.; **Geld bei einer Bank** ~ to deposit (lodge) money with a bank; **Waren** ~ to warehouse goods; **Wertpapiere** ~ to deposit securities for safe custody *(Br.)* (custodianship, *US*).
Deponierung deposit, depository, depositation, commitment, consignation, reposition, lodgment, bailment;
~ **von Geld** lodging of money.
Deport backwardation, under spot *(Br.)*, *(Terminhandel)* discount.
Deportation deportation.
Deportgeschäft backwardation business.
deportieren to deport, to send to penal servitude, to displace, to lag *(sl.)*;
Häftling ~ to transport a criminal.
deportiert displaced;
nach Australien ~ transported to Australia.
Deportierter deportee, transport, displaced (deported) person.
Deport|kurs, ~**satz** backwardation rate.
Depositar depositary, consignatory, bailee.
Depositen deposits, money on deposit, deposited funds;
befristete ~ time *(US)* (short-term) deposits; **sofort fällige** ~ demand *(US)* (call) deposits; **täglich fällige** ~ deposits on current account, current deposits, demand (sight) deposits *(US)*; **nicht in Anspruch genommene** ~ unclaimed deposits; **durch effektive Einlagen geschaffene** ~ primary deposits *(US)*; **für einen Lombardkredit hinterlegte** ~ derivative deposits; **jederzeit kündbare** ~ call (demand, *US*) deposits; **kurzfristige** ~ deposits at short notice; **zentralbankfähige** ~ eligible liabilities; ~ **zur Einziehung** deposits for collection; ~ **mit Kündigungsfrist** long-term (time, *US*) deposits;
~**abteilung** deposit department (division); ~**anstalt,** ~**bank** deposit bank, depositary [bank] *(US)*; ~**bankgeschäft** commercial banking; ~**buch** deposit book (passbook, *Br.*); ~**einlagen,** ~**gelder** consigned money, trust (deposit) money, deposit; **befristete** ~**gelder** deposits for a fixed period, deposit money *(Br.)*, term deposits, time deposits *(US)*; ~**geschäft** acceptance of deposits, deposit banking, depositing business; ~**guthaben** bank deposit, deposit in a bank; ~**inhaber** depositor; ~**kapital** deposited funds; ~**kasse** deposit and consignment office, *(Bankfiliale)* branch [office], deposit society *(Br.)*, neighbo(u)rhood bank branch *(US)*, suboffice; ~**konto** bank (deposit) account, depositors' ledger; ~**konto mit festgesetzter Fälligkeit** fixed deposit account; ~**konto mit vereinbarter Kündigungsfrist** deposit account at notice; ~**kunde** depositor; ~**posten** deposit item; ~**schein** certificate of deposit *(US)*, deposit certificate *(US)*, deposit receipt (slip, *US*), safe-custody receipt; **befristeter** ~**schein** time certificate of deposit; ~**stelle** branch [office]; ~**umlaufsmittel** deposit currency; ~**verbindlichkeit** [time] deposits; ~**versicherung** deposit (safe-deposit box) insurance, bank guarantee (guaranty, *US*); ~**volumen** total deposits; ~**zinsen** deposit rate; ~**zunahme** deposit growth.
depossidieren to dispossess, *(Monarch)* to dethrone.
Depossidierung dispossession.

Depot deposit[ory], *(Bank)* deposit of securities, security deposit, safe custody account *(Br.)*, custodianship account *(US)*, securities portfolio, *(Lagerplatz)* depot, dump, *(Lagerhaus)* store, depository, depot, storehouse, warehouse, *(Omnibus)* garage, *(Safe)* safe, strongroom, safe deposit *(US)*;
als ~ on deposit; **im ~ verwahrt** kept on deposit;
festes ~ special deposit; **gemeinschaftliches ~** alternate deposit; **geschlossenes ~** trust deposit; **gesperrtes ~** blocked (frozen, *US*) deposit; **lebendes ~** register of securities *(Br.)*, securities book *(Br.)* (register, *US*); **offenes ~** open deposit; **totes ~** securities ledger *(Br.)*; **gemeinschaftlich oder einzeln verfügbares ~** joint deposit; **verschlossenes ~** packed (vault, safe) deposit;
~ unter Streifband general (irregular) deposit; **~ für unverzollte Ware** bonded warehouse; **~ zu vermieten** deposit on lease;
im ~ aufbewahren to hold for safekeeping, to hold (keep) in safe custody; **Wertpapiere ins ~ einliefern** to deposit securities for safe custody *(Br.)* (custodianship, *US*); **~ errichten** to create a store; **etw. ins ~ geben** to place s. th. on deposit; **etw. bei einer Bank in ~ geben** to deposit s. th. with a bank; **Möbel ins ~ geben** to store furniture; **Wertpapiere ins ~ geben**to place securities into a deposit *(US)*, to deposit securities in safe custody *(Br.)*;
~s unterschlagen to embezzle trust funds;
~abteilung *(Bank)* safe-custody department *(Br.)*, securities department *(US)*; **~aufbewahrung** safe custody *(Br.)* (keeping); **~auszug** statement of deposited securities *(Br.)*, abstract of safe custody *(Br.)*, statement of custodianship account *(US)*.
Depotbank trustee *(Br.)*, deposit (depositary, *US*) bank, *(Kapitalanlagegesellschaft)* custodian bank, deposit company *(Br.)*;
~ mit Beschränkungen in der Annahme von Depots limited depositary *(US)*;
als ~ für eine Kapitalanlagegesellschaft fungieren to have safe custody of securities of a unit trust *(Br.)*.
Depot|bescheinigung safe-custody receipt *(Br.)*, deposit slip *(US)* (certificate), deposit receipt *(US)*; **~bestand** deposit holding.
Depotbuch securities ledger *(Br.)*, safe-deposit register *(US)*;
lebendes ~ securities book *(Br.)* (register, *US*);
~haltung securities department; **~handlung** depot bookstore.
Depot|einrichtungen einer Bank coffers of a bank; **~empfangsbescheinigung** safe-custody receipt (slip) *(Br.)*, deposit slip *(US)*; **~entgegennahme** acceptance of deposits; **~formular** form of proxy; **~garantie** depository bond; **~gebühr** safe-custody charges *(Br.)*, safe-deposit *(Br.)* (custodianship, *US*) fee; **~gegenstände** articles left for safe custody; **~geschäft** deposit banking, deposit[ing] business, safe-custody business *(Br.)*; **~geschäfte** safe-custody transactions *(Br.)*, custodianships *(US)*; **~gesetz** Protection of Depositors Act *(Br.)*; **~inhaber** depositor; **~konto** deposit (safekeeping, safe-custody, *Br.*) account, *(Kapitalanlagegesellschaft)* investment account, custodianship account *(US)*; **~miete** safe-deposit rent; **~mieter** renter of a safe; **~quittung, ~schein** balance ticket, certificate of deposit *(US)*, deposit slip, deposit receipt, safe-custody receipt *(Br.)*, custodianship receipt *(US)*, security deposit receipt *(US)*, deposit warrant, *(Lagerschein)* warehouse warrant; **~quittungskontrollabschnitt** safe-custody receipt counterfoil, *(Lagerschein)* warehouse warrant; **~rabattzuschlag** *(Buchhandel)* depot extra discount; **~schiff** storeship; **~stelle** safe custody department, depository for securities; **~steuer** bank deposit tax *(US)*; **~stimmrecht** proxy rights; **~stimmrechtsermächtigung** proxy power; **~stücke** safe-custody items; **~testament** will in custody; **~umbuchung** transfer of shares (stocks, *US*); **~unterlagen** deposit records; **~unterschlagung** embezzlement of trust money; **~verlust** forfeiture of deposit; **~verpfändung** pledging (hypothecation, *US*) of securities; **~versicherung** deposit (safe-deposit box) insurance; **~vertrag** safe-custody contract *(Br.)*, trust deed *(Br.)*, custodian agreement *(US)*.
depotverwahrt kept on deposit.
Depot|verwahrung safe custody of securities, securities custody, custodianship *(US)*; **~verwaltung** administration (service) of custodianship accounts *(US)*, *(Kapitalanlagegesellschaft)* portfolio management; **Aktien in ~verwaltung geben** to place shares in safe custody *(Br.)*; **~verwaltungsgebühren** safe-custody *(Br.)* (custodianship, *US*) charges; **~verwaltungsmethoden** safe-custody procedure; **~verzeichnis** memorandum of deposits *(US)*, safe-custody register *(Br.)*, deposit list *(US)*; **~wechsel** deposited (collateral, *US*) bill; **nur für ~zwecke** for deposit only.
Depression [business] depression, slump, slackness of business; **nervöse ~** nervous depression; **vorübergehende ~** spell of depression; **wirtschaftliche ~** economic depression;
unter ~en leiden to suffer from fits of depression, to have the pip *(sl.)*; **von der ~ betroffen werden** to feel the pinch.
Depressions|anfall pip *(Br., sl.)*; **~auswirkungen** effects of depression; **~jahr** depression (slump) year; **~periode, ~phase** period of depression, depression period (time, era, *US*); **~winkel** dip of the horizon; **~zeit** depression period (time).
depressiv|sein *(Konjunktur)* to show a depression; **~ veranlagt sein** to be easily depressed.
deprimieren to depress, to cast down the spirit, to deject.
deprimiert out of spirits, down in the mouth, in the doldrums, off colo(u)r;
~ sein to feel low, to be in low spirits, to feel down in spirits.
Deprimiertheit lowness of spirits.
Deputant tasker, sharecropper *(US)*.
Deputat allowance in kind;
~entlohnung product sharing.
Deputation deputation, delegation, body of representatives.
Deputat|kohle free coal; **~wohnung** company house, tied cottage *(Br.)*.
Deputierter delegate, deputee *(US)*, deputy, representative.
derangieren to derange.
dergleichen, nichts nothing of the kind.
Deroute *(Börse)* panic, collapse of the market, slump.
derzeitig for the time being.
Desaster calamity.
Deserteur *(mil.)* deserter, fugitive (runaround) soldier, *(pol.)* ratter.
desertieren *(mil.)* to quit the ranks, to desert one's colo(u)rs, to cut one's stick *(mar., sl.)*, *(in ein kommunistisches Land)* to defect, *(von seiner Partei)* to rat.
desertiert broken *(US)*.
Desertion *(mil.)* desertion.
Designationsrecht power of appointment.
designieren to designate;
j. zu seinem Nachfolger ~ to designate s. o. as successor.
designiert designate;
~er Botschafter ambassador designate.
Desinfektionsanstalt disinfecting station.
desinfizieren to disinfect.
Desintegrationsprozeß process of disintegration.
Desinteresse disinterestedness, detachment.
desinteressiert sein to take no further interest.
Desinvestition negative investment.
Desorganisation disorganization.
desorganisieren to disorganize.
Desperado desperado.
Despot despot, tyrant.
Despotie despotism, tyranny, arbitrary government.
despotisch despotic, tyrannical;
~ herrschen to domineer.
Dessert dessert.
Destillationsanlage distilling (distillation) plant.
Destille brandy shop, rum hole *(sl.)*.
destruktive Kritik destructive criticism.
Deszendent descendant.
Deszendenz descent, progeny, issue.
Detail detail, retail;
~s details, particulars;
praktische ~s nuts and bolts;
genauere ~s angeben to give exact details; **Schilderung mit ~s ausschmücken** to embellish a narrative with details; **Sache in allen ~s darlegen** to give full particulars of s. th.; **~s mitteilen** to give the items (full details); **im ~ verkaufen** to [sell by] retail;
~arbeit detail work; **~behandlung** detail; **~bericht** detailed statement, particularisation; **~geschäft** retail business, *(Firma)* retail house, *(Laden)* retail shop (store, *US*); **~handel** retail trade; **~händler** retail dealer (merchant), retailer.
detaillieren to detail, to particularize, to specify, to itemize *(US)*, *(einzeln verkaufen)* to [sell by] retail.
detailliert in detail, detailed, with full details, itemized, specified;
zu ~ niggling;
~e Aufstellung specification, itemized schedule *(US)*; **~e Auskunft** detailed information, full particulars; **~e Mittelzuweisung** segregate (itemized, *US*) appropriation; **~e Rechnung** specified (itemized, *US*) account.
Detaillierung particularization, itemization *(US)*.
Detaillist retailer.
Detail|preis retail price; **~schilderung** detailed description; **~verkauf** retailing, sale at retail; **~waren** retail goods; **~zeichnung** detailed drawing; **~zwischenhändler** retail middleman.
Detektei detective agency, firm of investigators.

Detektiv [police] detective, plain-clothes man, sleuth *(sl.)*, operative *(US)*, nab *(coll.)*, dick *(sl.)*, private eye *(sl.)*, gumshoe *(US sl.)*, slewfoot *(sl.)*, snowshoe *(sl.)*;
getarnter ~ undercover agent (man, officer);
als ~ tätig sein to detect;
~geschichte detective story; **~roman** detective story, crime fiction, mystery novel, thriller.
Detonation detonation, explosion.
detonieren to explode, to detonate.
Deut jot, tinker's dam, shuck, whit, rap, slit, mite, twopence;
kein ~ wahr not a grain of truth;
keinen ~ draufgeben to not to care a fig for it; **sich keinen ~ kümmern** not to care a stiver (whit); **um keinen ~ klüger sein** not to be a penny the wiser; **keinen ~ wert sein** not to be worth a brass farthing.
deuteln to split hairs, to quibble, to niggle.
deuten to explain, to interpret;
auf einen glücklichen Ausgang der Verhandlungen ~ to point to a happy issue of the negotiations; **mit dem Finger auf etw. ~** to point one's finger at s. th.; **Textstelle ~** to construe a passage; **auf den nahenden Winter ~** to indicate that winter is at hand.
deutlich clear, plain, explicit, distinct, conspicuous, obvious, manifest, sharp, pointed, precise, vivid, *(Sprache)* articulate;
sich ganz ~ über eine Sache äußern to be quite explicit about a matter; **~ sprechen** to speak clearly (distinctly); **einem noch ~ vor den Augen stehen** to be still fresh in one's memory; **ganz ~ werden** to be outspoken in one's remarks;
~e Anspielung obvious allusion; **~e Antwort** plain answer; **~er Beweis** clear and convincing evidence; **~e Erinnerung** clear recollection; **~e Handschrift** legible handwriting; **~e Handschrift schreiben** to write a clear hand.
Deutschland, in ~ hergestellt made in Germany;
~ausgabe special issue on Germany.
Deutung construction, interpretation.
Devalorisierung, Devalvation devalorization, devaluation.
devalvieren to depreciate, to devalue, to devaluate, to devalorize.
Devise motto, device;
~ London London exchange.
Devisen foreign currency (exchange, *Br.*), international exchange *(US)*, *(Wechsel in fremder Währung)* foreign bills;
in ~ zahlbar payable in currency;
bewirtschaftete ~ controlled currency; **blockierte (eingefrorene) ~** frozen (blocked) foreign exchange; **durch Verkauf eines außerhalb des Sterlingblocks gelegenen Grundstücks vereinnahmte ~** property currency *(Br.)*;
~ zu Tageskursen bills at the day's quotation;
~ anmelden to declare foreign exchange; **~ beantragen** to apply for foreign exchange; **~ für Auslandsinvestitionen über einen Dollar-Sonderfonds erwerben** to go through an investment currency pool *(Br.)*; **mit ~ eingedeckt sein** to be long of exchange *(US)*; **~ transferieren** to transfer foreign currency; **~ umrechnen** to reduce money; **~ zuteilen** to allocate exchange;
~abflüsse flow of foreign funds, foreign-exchange outflow; **~abführung** surrender of foreign currency; **~abgänge** foreign-exchange outflow; **~abkommen** foreign-exchange (offset) agreement, currency agreement, exchange clearing agreement; **~abrechnung** foreign-exchange statement (settlement); **~abrechnungsstelle** foreign-exchange clearing office; **~abschlüsse** foreign-exchange contracts; **~abteilung** foreign-exchange department (division); **~affäre** foreign-currency affair; **~anforderungen** currency demands, exchange requirements; **~ankauf** purchase of foreign currencies; **~ansammlung** accumulation of currency reserves; **~anspannung** foreign-exchange squeeze.
Devisenarbitrage arbitration of exchange, foreign-exchange arbitrage (arbitration), currency (exchange) arbitrage (arbitration);
indirekte ~ indirect arbitration;
~ in drei Währungen triangular arbitration.
Devisen|aufwand foreign-exchange costs (expenditure); **~ausgeber** spenders of foreign exchange; **~ausgleich** foreign-exchange offset.
Devisenausgleichs|abkommen [foreign-exchange] offset agreement; **~fonds** foreign-exchange equalization (stabilization) fund; **~konto** foreign-exchange equalization account; **~zahlungen** offset payments.
Devisenausländer resident outside the scheduled territories (sterling area) *(Br.)*, nonnational resident *(Br.)*, nonresident *(US)*;
begünstigter ~ nonresident beneficiary *(US)*;
~eigenschaft eines Kunden bezeugen to testify to the foreign residence of a customer; **~konto** nonresident account *(US)*.

Devisen|ausleihungen foreign-currency borrowings; **~bank** authorized depository (bank) *(Br.)*, exchange bank *(Br.)*; **~bedarf** need of foreign exchange; **~behörden** foreign-exchange authorities; **~belastung** foreign-exchange burden; **~berater** foreign-exchange adviser; **~beschaffung** procurement of foreign exchange; **~bescheinigung** foreign-exchange certificate (permit); **~beschränkungen** currency- (exchange-) control restrictions *(US)*; **~beschränkungen abbauen** to dismantle exchange controls.
Devisenbestände foreign-exchange funds (deposits, assets), currency (foreign-exchange) holdings, *(Bilanz)* foreign-currency items *(US)*;
nicht ausgenutzte ~ remaining foreign exchange; **blockierte ~** blocked foreign exchange;
Gold- und ~ gold and foreign-exchange holdings;
~ erwerben to purchase foreign-exchange facilities; **fast keine ~ mehr haben** to be almost drained of foreign-exchange reserves.
Devisen|bestimmungen currency (foreign-exchange) regulations; **~betrag** amount of foreign currency.
Devisenbeträge, nicht ausgenutzte remaining foreign exchange;
für Investitionen zur Verfügung stehende ~ investment currency *(Br.)*;
große ~ dem Fremdenverkehr verdanken to obtain large sums of foreign exchange from tourism.
devisenbewirtschaftetes Land, nicht free currency country.
Devisenbewirtschaftung control of foreign exchange, foreign-exchange (currency, *US*) control, currency (foreign-exchange) restrictions, rationing of foreign exchange, exchange management;
~ abbauen (aufheben) to dismantle (abandon) foreign-exchange control.
Devisenbewirtschaftungs|bestimmungen exchange-control regulations; **~gesetz** Exchange Control Act *(Br.)*; **~gesetzgebung** foreign-exchange legislation; **~vorschriften** foreign-exchange (currency, *US*) regulations.
Devisenbilanz balance of foreign-exchange payments, foreign-exchange position sheet, official financing account;
ausgeglichene ~ exchange balance in equilibrium.
Devisenbörse foreign-exchange market, currency exchange.
devisenbringend exchange-earning.
Devisen|bringer foreign-exchange earner; **~druck** foreign-exchange squeeze; **~eigenschaft nach seinem Wohnsitz festlegen** to determine s. one's residence for exchange-control purposes; **~einbringer** earners of foreign exchange; **~einfuhrkosten** foreign-exchange cost of import; **~einkünfte** foreign-exchange earnings; **~einnahmen** foreign-exchange proceeds; **~einnahmen aus Hartwährungsländern** hard-currency earnings (income); **~einzelkurs** single-exchange rate; **~engagements** foreign-exchange commitments; **~erfordernisse** foreign-exchange requirements; **~erklärung** currency declaration; **~erleichterungen** exchange facilities; **~erlös, ~ertrag** foreign-exchange proceeds (earnings); **~erwerb** purchase of foreign currency; **~forderung** foreign-currency claim; **~formular** currency form; **~freibetrag für Auslandsreisen (Ferienreisen)** travel allowance *(Br.)*; **~gebühren** exchange fees; **~genehmigung** foreign-exchange permit, exchange authorization, treasury licence.
Devisengeschäft transacting foreign business, *(einzelnes)* foreign-exchange transaction (dealings), currency transaction (dealing);
echtes ~ true exchange; **vierseitiges ~** quadrangular operation in exchange.
Devisen|gesetzgebung foreign-exchange control legislation, foreign-exchange legislation *(US)*; **~gewinn** foreign-exchange earnings; **~guthaben** foreign-exchange holdings, currency assets, foreign-exchange deposits (assets); **~handel** foreign-exchange dealings (business), foreign-currency trade (trading) *(US)*; **intervalutarischer ~handel** multilateral exchange dealings; **~händler** dealer in foreign exchange, foreign-exchange trader, cambist, currency (money) dealer *(US)*, authorized depository *(Br.)*; **~haushalt** foreign-exchange position; **~hoheit** monetary sovereignty; **~inländer** resident inside the sterling area *(Br.)*, resident *(US)*; **~inländereigenschaft verlieren** to cease to be resident *(US)*; **~inlandskonto** resident account *(US)*; **~investitionen** foreign-currency investment.
Devisenkassa|geschäft spot-exchange transaction, exchange for spot delivery; **~handel** foreign-exchange spot; **~kurs** spot-exchange rate.
devisenknapp short of foreign exchange.
Devisen|knappheit foreign-exchange (currency) shortage (stringency), shortage of foreign exchange (cash), scarcity of

currency; ~**kontingent** foreign-exchange quota; ~**kontingentierung** foreign-exchange control (rationing); ~**konto** foreign-currency account, external account *(Br.)*; **frei transferierbares ~konto** transferable account *(Br.)*; ~**kontrolle** currency (foreign-exchange) control; ~**kosten** foreign-exchange costs, exchange expenditure; ~**kredit** foreign-exchange credit; ~**kredite** foreign-currency borrowings; ~**krise** foreign-exchange crisis.

Devisenkurs [foreign] exchange rate, rate of exchange;
amtliche ~e official exchange rates; **freigegebener (frei veränderlicher) ~** floating exchange rate, free rate *(Br.)*; **künstlich gehaltene ~e** pegged exchange; **in Pence notierte ~e** direct rates *(Br.)*; **per Pfund notierte ~e** currency (indirect) rates *(Br.)*, uncertain quotations *(Br.)*;
~e auf dem schwarzen Markt black exchange rates; **~ für kurzfristige Wechsel** short rate; **~ für langfristige Wechsel** long rate;
~**zettel** foreign-exchange list, list of foreign exchanges.

Devisen|lage, schwierige exchange difficulties; ~**makler** exchange broker (dealer); ~**mangel** scarcity of currency.

Devisenmarkt foreign-exchange (currency) market;
internationaler ~ international exchange market;
~**interventionen** exchange-market interventions.

Devisen|notierung quotation of [foreign-] exchange [rates], foreign-exchange quotation; ~**plafond** foreign-exchange limit (ceiling); ~**politik** foreign-exchange policy; ~**polster** [foreign-] exchange reserve, foreign-exchange cushion; ~**portefeuille** holdings of foreign currency, foreign-exchange holdings; ~**position** foreign-exchange position sheet, currency option; ~**positionsmeldung** exchange position return; **ausländische ~quellen** nonresident sources; ~**quote** exchange allocation; ~**rationierung** foreign-exchange rationing; ~**rechnung** computation of exchange, exchange calculation.

devisenrechtlich|Ausländer sein to be resident for exchange-control purposes outside the Scheduled Territories *(Br.)*; **~e Beschränkungen** foreign-exchange restrictions; **~e Bestimmungen** foreign-exchange regulations.

Devisen|reserven foreign-exchange (currency, *US*) reserves; ~**restriktionen** exchange restrictions; ~**risiko** foreign-exchange risk; ~**rückfluß** foreign-exchange return; ~**rücklagen** currency *(US)* (foreign-exchange) reserves; ~**sache** foreign-exchange matter; ~**sätze** foreign-exchange rates; ~**schieber** currency (foreign-exchange) profiteer; ~**schiebung** currency racket, currency manipulation; ~**schmuggel** currency smuggling; **guten ~schnitt mitnehmen** to capture a nice bonus on foreign exchange.

devisenschwaches Land deficit nation, soft-currency nation.

Devisen|schwankungen fluctuations of the currency; ~**schwierigkeiten** exchange difficulties; ~**situation** currency position; ~**spekulation** speculation in foreign exchange; ~**spekulationsgewinne** profits on foreign exchange; ~**sperre** exchange embargo, blockade of exchange; ~**spielraum** margin of the exchange rate; ~**stabilisierungsfonds** exchange stabilization fund.

devisenstarkes Land hard-currency country.

Devisen|status foreign-exchange position sheet, *(Ausländer)* residential status for exchange-control purposes; ~**stelle** foreign-exchange control board *(US)*; ~**strom** currency flow; ~**swap** currency swap; ~**tausch** switch in foreign currencies.

Devisentermingeschäft forward exchange transaction *(US)*, forward exchange deal *(Br.)*, forward exchange operation *(US)*, exchange for forward (future, *US*) delivery, forwarded exchange dealings *(Br.)*;
~ mit vereinbartem Erfüllungstag outright forward *(Br.)*.

Devisentermin|handel forward exchange deals *(Br.)*, forward exchange operations *(US)*, future exchange *(US)*; ~**kurs** forward exchange rate; ~**markt** forward exchange market, foreign-exchange futures market *(US)*; ~**sätze** forward exchange rates.

Devisen|transaktion foreign-exchange operation (transaction), forwarded exchange deal *(Br.)*; ~**transfer** transfer of foreign exchange, foreign-exchange (currency) transfer; ~**überschuß** foreign-exchange surplus; ~**überwachung** foreign-exchange control; ~**verbindlichkeiten** currency liabilities; ~**vergehen** violation of currency, currency offence; ~**verkauf** foreign-exchange dealings, sale of foreign currencies; ~**verkehr** currency dealings; **freier ~verkehr** freedom of exchange operations; ~**verkehrsbeschränkungen** foreign-exchange restrictions *(US)*; ~**verlagerung** currency flow; ~**verlust** exchange (currency) loss, re-exchange *(Br.)*; ~**verpflichtungen** exchange commitments; ~**verrechnung** foreign-exchange clearing; ~**verrechnungskonto** foreign-exchange clearing account; ~**verrechnungssystem** multiple currency system; **~vorräte anhäufen** to accumulate reserves in foreign currencies; ~**vorschriften** currency (foreign-exchange) regulations, exchange rules; ~**währung** currency (exchange) standard, indirect foreign-exchange standard.

Devisenwechsel currency bill *(Br.)*;
kurzfristiger ~ short exchange *(Br.)*; **langfristiger ~** long exchange *(Br.)*.

Devisenwert currency (foreign-exchange) value;
~e [foreign-] exchange assets, foreign securities *(US)*;
~**berichtigungen** foreign-exchange adjustments.

Devisen|zahlung currency payment; ~**zuflüsse** inflow of foreign currency, foreign-exchange inflow; ~**zugänge** accrual of exchange, exchange accrual.

Devisenzuteilung currency allowance, foreign-exchange allotment *(Br.)* (allocation);
~en für private Auslandsreisen civilian allowances for foreign travel; **~ für Ferienreisen** travel allowance *(Br.)*; **jährliche ~ für Urlaubsreisen** annual holiday allowance in foreign currencies.

Devisen|zuwiderhandlung currency offence; ~**zwangswirtschaft** rationing of foreign exchanges, foreign-exchange (currency) control.

devot submissive, humble, cringing, abject.

Dezentralisation decentralization, regionalization, *(Betrieb)* departmentalization;
~ von Bundesbehörden decentralization of federal government departments.

Dezentralisationsidee brand of decentralization, regionalization concept.

dezentralisieren to decentralize, to regionalize, *(Betrieb)* to departmentalize.

Dezentralisierung decentralization, *(Betrieb)* departmentalization.

Dezentralisierungs|ausschuß decentralization committee; ~**idee** regionalization concept, brand of decentralization; ~**plan** decentralization program(me).

Dezentralismus decentralism, regionalism.

dezentralistisch decentralizing.

Dezernat department, division, section.

Dezernatsleiter section leader, *(Kommunalverwaltung)* group chief officer *(Br.)*.

Dezernent chief of branch, department head.

dezimal decimal.

Dezimal|bruch decimal fraction; ~**rechnung** decimal account; ~**stelle** decimal [place]; ~**system** decimal scales (system, numeration), metric system; ~**waage** weighbridge; ~**währung** decimal coinage (currency).

Dezimeterwelle ultra-short (ultra-high frequency) wave.

dezimieren, Bevölkerung to thin out (decimate) the population.

Dezimierung decimation.

Diabetiker diabetic;
~**kost** diabetic diet.

Diabibliothek photographic library.

Diagnose diagnosis.

diagnostizieren to diagnose.

diagonal on the bias, diagonal.

Diagonallesen skip reading.

Diagramm diagram, graph, chart *(US)*;
~ auswerten to analyse a graph *(US)*;
~**auswertung** analysis of a graph; ~**papier** graph paper.

Dialekt dialect, vernacular;
mit ausgeprägtem ~ broad.

Dialog dialogue.

Diamant diamond;
geschliffener ~ cut diamond; **glitzernde ~en** dazzling diamonds; **ungeschliffener ~** rough diamond;
~ reinsten Wassers diamond of the first water;
~en fassen to set diamonds;
~**druckausgabe** diamond edition.

Diamanten|ankauf, unerlaubter illicit diamond buying *(South Africa)*; ~**feld** diamond field; ~**mine** diamond mine.

diametral diametrical;
~ entgegengesetzt sein to be poles apart (diametrically opposed, opposite).

Diapositiv diapositive, filmslide, cinema slide *(Br.)*, transparency, lantern slide;
~**werbung** cinema (slide) advertising.

Diaprojektor slide projector.

Diät diet;
strenge ~ strict diet;
sich einer strengen ~ befleißigen to keep to a strict diet; **~ halten**

to diet; ~ **leben** to take a diet; **mit einer strengen ~ leben, streng nach ~ leben** to be a diet faddist, to follow a strict diet; **~änderung vornehmen** to vary one's diet.

Diäten *(Tagegeld)* per diem, daily (sessional expense) allowance, *(Abgeordnetenbezüge)* emoluments, parliamentary pay, *(Sitzungsgelder)* attendance fee;
~ **erhalten** to earn a salary.

Diät | küche diet kitchen; **sich einer ~kur unterziehen** to go on a diet; **~vorschrift** dietary rules, diet restrictions; **~zettel** dietary, diet sheet.

dicht thick, dense, *(Tank)* leak-proof;
~ **vor seiner Nase** right under his nose; ~ **am Ziel** near the end; **~besiedelt (bevölkert)** thickly (densely) populated; **~besiedeltes Gebiet** congested area; **~bevölkerte Gegend** densely populated region; **~bevölkerte Straßen** densely crowded streets; **~bewaldet** heavily wooded;
~ **halten** to be as tight as wax; **Laden ~ machen** *(fam.)* to shut up shop; **Schiff ~ machen** to caulk a ship; ~ **schließen** to shut tight; **mit Juwelen ~ besetzt sein** to be thickset with jewels; **jem. ~ auf den Fersen sein** to be hot on s. one's heels; ~ **vor dem Examen stehen** to be about to take one's examination;
in ~er Folge in rapid succession; **~e Hecke** thick (close-set) hedge; **~estes Menschengewühl** thick of the crowd; **~e Menschenmenge** dense crowd; **~er Nebel** dense fog; **in ~en Scharen** in crowds (hordes); **~er Verkehr** heavy traffic; **~ester Wert** *(Statistik)* mode.

Dichte *(Bevölkerung)* density, *(Verkehr)* density, frequency, heaviness;
soziale ~ social density.

dichten to write (compose) poems, *(techn.)* to make tight, to tighten;
Leck ~ to seal a leak.

Dichter *(Ausarbeitung von Reden)* speech writer.

dichterische Freiheit poetic licence.

dichtgedrängt packed;
~e Zuhörer densely (closely) packed audience.

dichthalten to be waterproof, *(fig.)* to keep one's mouth shut (mum about s. th.).

Dichtigkeit density, *(Foto)* intensity.

dichtmachen, Laden to shut up shop.

dichtschließende Fenster closely fitting windows.

Dichtung joint, jointing, gasket, packing, seal, *(Literatur)* imagination, fiction, poetry, literature;
~ **und Wahrheit miteinander vermischen** to interweave truth with fiction.

Dichtungs | leiste *(Fenster)* weather strip; **~material** packing; **~ring** packing ring.

dick thick, big, large, *(Person)* fat, heavy, stout, corpulent;
durch ~ und dünn through foul and fair (thick and thin); **jem. etw. ~ ankreiden** to nurse a grudge against s. o.; ~ **auftragen** to lay it on thick; **sich ~ und satt essen** to eat one's fill; **durch ~ und dünn mit jem. gehen** to go through thick and thin with s. o.; **es ~ haben** to be fed up with it; **~es Fell haben** to have a thick skin (hide); **es ~ hinter den Ohren haben** to look as if butter wouldn't melt in one's mouth; **~e Töne reden** to pile it on, to brag, to talk big; ~ **befreundet sein** to be very thick with s. o.;
~er Bauch paunch, big belly; **~er Baumstamm** big trunk; **~e Beziehungen haben** to have influential friends; **~er Brocken** hard nut to crack; **~es Buch** voluminous book; **~e Freunde** close (intimate) friends; **~er Geldbeutel** fat purse; **~e Gelder haben** to have money to burn; **~e Luft** *(fig.)* tense atmosphere; **bei jem. eine ~e Nummer haben** to be in s. one's good books; **~e Tränen vergießen** to shed large tears; **~es Wetter** *(Schiffahrt)* foggy weather.

Dickicht thicket, brushwood, shrubbery;
undurchdringliches ~ von Tatsachen tangled jungle of facts; **sich durch ein ~ winden** to writhe through a thicket.

Dickkopf mule, stubborn fellow.

dickköpfig headstrong, stubborn, pigheaded.

dickleibiger Wälzer fat tome.

Dickten | einstellung *(Terminal)* character spacing; **~reduzierung** width space reduction; **~stecker** *(Terminal)* width plug; **~wert** *(Terminal)* width value.

Dieb thief, larcener *(US)*, purloiner, *(Einbrecher)* housebreaker, burglar;
angeblicher ~ alleged thief; **gewerbsmäßiger ~** common thief; **kleiner ~** small-time thief, filcher, pilferer; **vermeintlicher ~** reputed thief;
~ **entlarven** to expose a thief; ~ **ergreifen** to capture a thief; **wie ein ~ in der Nacht kommen** to take s. o. unawares; ~ **beim Kragen nehmen** to collar a thief; ~ **verhaften** to arrest a thief; ~ **verscheuchen** to scare away a thief;
Gelegenheit macht ~e opportunity makes the thief.

Diebes | bande pack (set) of thieves, lay, push *(sl.)*; **~beute** tickle, game *(sl.)*; **~ehre** hono(u)r among thieves; **~falle** burglar alarm; **~finger haben** to be light-fingered.

Diebesgut stolen goods, booty, spoil, haul, swag;
weggeworfenes ~ waifs *(Br.)*;
~ **abliefern** to deliver up stolen goods; **mit ~ handeln** to fence *(sl.)*.

Diebes | handwerk thievery; **~nest** den of thieves; **~schlüssel** picklock.

diebessicher burglar- (thief-) proof.

Diebes | verdächtigen beschatten to dog a suspected thief; **~werkzeug** housebreaking instruments.

diebisch thievish, pilfering, light-fingered *(sl.)*;
sich ~ über etw. freuen to be as pleased as Punch.

Diebstahl theft *(Br.)*, larceny *(US)*, graft, stealing;
des ~s angeklagt arraigned on a charge of theft;
einfacher (leichter) ~ simple (common-law, petty, *US*) larceny; **räuberischer ~** robbery; **schwerer ~** compound (mixed, grand, aggravated) larceny *(US)*;
~ **und Abhandenkommen** theft, pilferage and nondelivery; ~ **geistigen Eigentums** literary piracy, plagiarism; ~ **einer Erfindung** piracy of an invention; ~ **im Rückfall** larceny recidivism; ~ **unter erschwerenden Umständen** compound larceny;
j. des ~s anklagen to accuse s. o. of theft; ~ **begehen** to commit larceny *(US)* (theft), to take by stealth, to thieve; **geistigen ~ begehen** to pick (suck) s. one's brains; **j. des ~s beschuldigen** to charge s. o. with theft (burglary); **sich des ~s schuldig machen** to be guilty of theft; **wegen ~s angeklagt werden** to be chargeable with (lie under a charge of) theft.

Diebstahls | begünstigung durch Nichtanzeige theft-bate; **~handlung** larcenous action; **~klausel** theft clause; **~risiko** theft risk; **~sicherung** theft prevention; **~unterdrückung** concealing theft.

Diebstahlsversicherung theft (burglary) insurance;
Haftpflicht- und ~ *(Auto)* comprehensive liability and property damage insurance;
vollgedeckte ~ full-coverage theft (burglary) insurance;
~ **offener Warenlager** mercantile open-stock insurance.

Diebstahlsvorsatz intent to steal, larcenous intent.

Diele hall, floor, parlo(u)r, table, *(Brett)* board, plank.

Dielenfußboden plank bottom, wooden floor[ing].

dienen to serve, to be of service, *(mil.)* to serve one's time;
aktiv ~ to be on active service, to serve with the colo(u)rs; **als Deckung ~** to serve as collateral; **als Freiwilliger ~** to volunteer; **beim Heer ~** to serve in the army; **von der Pike auf ~** to work one's way up, to rise from the ranks; **als gemeiner Soldat ~** to serve in the ranks; **als Vorwand einer Absage ~** to find a pretext for refusing; **jem. als Zielscheibe des Spottes ~** to be a butt of s. one's jokes; **privaten Zwecken ~** to serve some private ends.

dienend ancillary, subservient;
~es Grundstück servient tenement.

Diener servant, manservant, domestic [man], footman, man, groom, valet;
treu ergebener ~ man Friday; **Ihr ergebenster ~** your most humble servant; **livrierter ~** liveried servant, lackey, flunkey *(US)*; **stummer ~** dumb waiter, *(für Kleider)* valet;
Herr und ~ *(jur.)* master and servant; ~ **aus der alten Zeit** old-fashioned servant.

Dienerschaft servants, establishment, attendants, livery, flunkeydom *(US)*;
zur ~ gehörig menial.

dienlich instrumental, serviceable, useful, conducive, convenient, *(ratsam)* advisable, expedient;
der Gesundheit ~ wholesome, salutary;
nicht für ~ halten not to think it advisable; ~ **sein** to be of service (helpful); **jds. Zwecken ~ sein** to answer s. one's purpose;
~e Auskünfte useful information.

Dienlichkeit serviceableness, usefulness.

Dienst office, service, attendance, *(Amtsleistung)* duty, function, *(mil.)* service, duty, *(Stellung)* employ[ment], position, post, situation;
außer ~ out [of office], *(dienstfrei)* off-duty, *(im Ruhestand)* on half-pay, inactive, resigned, retired [from service], *(ohne Stellung)* without place, out of work; **im ~** on duty, orderly; **im aktiven ~** on the active list; **im ~ bewährt** with creditable records, time-tested; **im ~ ergraut** veteran; **im ~ von** in the

employment of; **im öffentlichen ~ [stehend]** public, in public employment; **in ~ gestellt** *(Schiff)* commissioned; **in Berücksichtigung Ihrer ~e für uns** in consideration of your services; **stets zu Ihren ~en** at your service at all times;
aktiver ~ service with the colo(u)rs, regular service; **anwaltliche ~e** professional services of a lawyer; **auswärtiger ~** diplomatic service, foreign service *(US)*; **einfacher ~** lower grade; **gehobener (höherer) ~** higher grade, executive class, classified service *(US)*; **geleistete ~e** services rendered, past services; **dem Staat geleistete ~e** service to the state; **gute ~e** *(Diplomatie)* good offices; **hervorragende ~e** conspicuous service; **höherer ~** administrative class *(Br.)*; **konsularischer ~** consular service; **langjährige ~e** veteran service; **mittlerer ~** second class *(Br.)*; **neutralitätswidrige ~e** partisan services; **niedrige ~e** menial offices; **öffentlicher ~** civil *(Br.)* (public, *US*) service, public employment; **schlechter ~** disservice; **schurkischer ~** villain services; **schwerer ~** hard service; **technischer ~** technical service; **treue ~e** faithful service; **turnusmäßiger ~** regular service; **unentgeltliche ~e** gratuitous service; **ungewöhnliche ~e** eminent services; **unterer ~** lower grade; **untergeordnete ~e** inferior (base) services; **wertvolle ~e** service of value, valuable service;
~e höherer Art qualified services; **~ am Kunden** after-sale service, prompt service to the customer; **~ nach Vorschrift** work-to-rule (according to the book, *US*), go-slow strike *(Br.)*; **jem. seine ~e anbieten** to offer (tender) one's service to s. o.; **seine guten ~e anbieten** to offer one's good offices; **seinen ~ antreten** to take up a position, to enter the employ of, to enter service (upon one's duty), to report for duty, *(Arbeit anfangen)* to start one's work (job), to punch the clock *(US)*; **seinen ~ baldmöglichst antreten** to take up duty as early as possible; **jem. den ~ aufkündigen** to refuse to serve s. o. any longer; **aus dem ~ ausscheiden** to leave office; **jds. ~e beanspruchen** to make use of s. one's services; **~ beenden** to go off duty; **seinen ~ um 10 Uhr beenden** to come off at ten o'clock; **~e belohnen** to pay for services; **vom ~ desertieren** to desert one's duty; **sich vom ~ drücken** to dodge the column; **in den diplomatischen ~ eintreten** to enter the diplomatic service; **wieder in jds. ~e eintreten** to reenter s. one's service; **aus dem ~ entfernen** to remove from office; **j. seines ~es entheben** to relieve s. o. of his post; **Kassierer während der Untersuchungen vorläufig vom ~ entheben** to suspend a cashier pending investigations; **aus dem ~ entlassen** to dismiss, to remove from office, to fire *(US)*, to turn out *(US)*; **j. für seine ~e entlohnen** to remunerate s. o. for his services; **im ~ ergrauen** to grow old (grey) in service; **~ erweisen** to render a service; **jem. einen großen ~ erweisen** to do s. o. a great favo(u)r; **j. einen guten ~ erweisen** to do s. o. a good turn; **jem. einen schlechten ~ erweisen** to deserve ill of s. o., to do s. o. a disservice, to do s. o. an ill turn; **dem ~ fernbleiben** to absent o. s. from work; **~ haben** to be on duty (in waiting); **jem. wesentliche ~e geleistet haben** to have been of a material service to s. o.; **in Ausübung seines ~es handeln** to act in one's official capacity; **~e hervorragender Fachleute in Anspruch nehmen können** to have recourse to the superior knowledge of specialists; **~ kündigen** to resign one's position; **~e leisten** to furnish services, to serve; **jem. einen guten ~ leisten** to do s. o. a good office; **hervorragende ~e leisten** to render eminent services; **sich zum ~ melden** *(mil.)* to report for duty; **in ~ nehmen** to engage, to take in one's employ, to hire *(US)*; **jds. ~e in Anspruch nehmen** to make use of s. one's services; **~e eines Anwalts in Anspruch nehmen** to engage the services of (retain) a lawyer; **~ quittieren** to quit one's job, to resign one's position; **aus dem ~ scheiden** to quit [work], to retire; **außer ~ sein** to be off duty; **im ~ sein** to be on duty, *(Schiff)* to lie up; **seit zwei Jahren nicht mehr im ~ sein** to have retired two years ago; **für den öffentlichen ~ qualifiziert sein** to qualify for a civil-service position; **im ~ stehen** to serve; **in jds. ~ stehen** to be in s. one's employ (service), to serve with s. o.; **im aktiven ~ stehen** to be on the active list; **außer ~ stellen** *(Schiff)* to decommission, to mothball; **in ~ stellen** to put in commission, *(Bahn)* to put into service; **sich in den ~ der Nation stellen** to offer one's services to one's country; **alle Kräfte in den ~ einer guten Sache stellen** to devote all one's strength to the service of a good cause; **Schiff in ~ stellen** to put a ship into commission; **Schiff außer ~ stellen** to take a ship off the active list, to disable (lay up, decommission, mothball) a ship; **jem. seine ~e zur Verfügung stellen** to place o. s. at s. one's service; **der Regierung seine ~e zur Verfügung stellen** to tender one's services to the government; **in ~ treten** to take on; **in jds. ~e treten** to enter [into] s. one's service, to take service with (engage o. s. to) s. o.; **~ tun** to be on duty, to serve [an office]; **im Ausland ~ tun** to serve overseas; **~ nach Vorschrift tun** to work to rule *(Br.)* (according to the book, *US*); **seinen ~ verrichten** to do one's work; **lediglich niedrige ~e verrichten** to fetch and carry; **untergeordnete ~e verrichten** to serve in a minor degree; **~ versagen** *(Motor)* to stop working; **sich der ~e jds. versichern** to enlist the services of s. o., to retain (secure) s. one's services; **~ verweigern** *(mil.)* to refuse duty; **vom ~ abgelöst werden** to be relieved of one's duties; **außer ~ gestellt werden** *(Schiff)* to be laid up in ordinary; **in ~ gestellt werden** to go (come) into service; **aus dem ~ entlassen werden** to be dismissed from one's post;
~ablauf office routine; **~ablösung** *(mil.)* relief; **~abteil** *(Bahn)* service compartment, caboose *(US)*, kitchen *(US sl.)*; **~abwesenheit** absence from duty; **~abzeichen** service mark, badge, insignia.

Dienstalter years (length) of service, job seniority *(US)*;
nach dem ~ in order of (by) seniority;
höheres ~ seniority; **pensionsfähiges ~** pensionable age;
nach dem ~ aufrücken to rise by seniority; **nach dem ~ befördert werden** to be promoted by seniority.

dienstälter senior.

Dienstalters|bestimmungen seniority rule; **~grenze** age of retirement; **~prinzip** seniority system; **~streifen** *(mil.)* service stripes *(US)*; **~stufe** grade of seniority; **~zulage** seniority pay (allowance, *US*).

Dienstältester *(mil.)* senior [officer].

Dienst|angebot, spontanes spontaneous offer of service; **~angelegenheit** official matter (business); **~anschluß** office telephone.

Dienstantritt entering upon service (one's duties), entrance to (assumption of) office, entry into service;
bei ~ on taking up one's duties; **frühestmöglicher ~** *(Anzeige)* when available to assume duty.

Dienst|anweisung instruction, manual, entertainment, official instruction, staff regulations; **ständige ~anweisung** *(mil.)* standing order; **~anzug** *(mil.)* service (official) uniform; **großer ~anzug** *(mil.)* dress uniform; **~art** *(mil.)* line of duty; **~aufsicht** service control, supervision; **~aufsicht führen** to be in charge.

Dienstaufsichts|behörde supervising (supervisory) authority, control office, regulatory body *(US)*; **~beschwerde** complaint; **~verfahren** disciplinary proceedings.

Dienst|aufwand service expense; **~aufwandsentschädigung** office (expense, entertainment) allowance; **~ausübung** discharge of duties; **~ausweis** pass; **~auszeichnung** decoration, *(mil.)* service medal; **~auto** office car, service vehicle.

dienstbar machen to subject;
sich jem. ~ to bring s. o. under one's rule.

Dienstbarkeit *(Grundbuch)* easement, servitude *(Scot., US)*;
im Einzelfall ausgeübte ~ discontinuing easement; **ununterbrochen ausgeübte ~** continuous easement; **zeitweilig ausgeübte ~** intermittent easement; **formlose ~** equitable easement; **negative ~** negative easement (servitude, *US*); **persönliche ~** personal servitude *(US)*; **beschränkt persönliche ~** personal servitude *(US)*, easement in gross; **positive ~** affirmative (positive) servitude *(US)*; **sichtbare ~** apparent easement (servitude, *US*); **städtische ~** urban servitude *(US)*; **völkerrechtliche ~en** state (international) servitudes *(US)*; **vorübergehende ~** noncontinuous easement;
~ ablösen to commute a right of user of an easement;
~ als Notrecht easement of necessity.

dienstbarkeitsähnliche Verpflichtung equitable easement.

Dienstbefehl *(Beamter)* official order, *(mil.)* service order.

dienstbeflissen officious, superserviceable, over-eager, anxious to please.

Dienst|beflissenheit officiousness; **~beginn** commencement of work; **~behinderung** obstructing an officer; **~bereich** province, competence, sphere of duties; **zugewiesener ~bereich** terms of reference.

dienstbereit at command, standing by, in waiting, *(Apotheke)* open.

Dienst|bereitschaft *(Apotheke)* service, *(mil.)* stand-by duty; **~beschädigung** disabling (industrial) injury; **~besprechnung** conference with one's colleagues.

Dienstbetrieb daily routine;
~ aufnehmen to come into service, to begin commercial service; **~ einschränken** to cut back service.

Dienstbezeichnung [occupational] title.

Dienstbezüge appointments, emoluments, perquisites, salary;
~ oder Arbeitseinkommen emoluments of office or employment;
ruhegehaltsfähige ~ pensionable emoluments.

Dienstbote servant, domestic, help *(US)*;
einem ~n kündigen to serve notice upon a servant.
Dienstboten|eingang service entrance; **~löhne** servant's wages; **~mangel** servant shortage; **zur ~tätigkeit verdammen** to put to wages; **~treppe** backstairs; **~vermittlung** employment bureau.
Dienst|buch *(Polizei)* police blotter *(US)*; **~bürgschaft** fidelity guaranty.
Diensteid official oath *(Br.)*, oath of allegiance (office *US)*;
einem Beamten den ~ abnehmen to swear in an official; **~ leisten** *(Beamter)* to be sworn in, to qualify *(US)*.
Diensteifer sequacious zeal.
diensteifrig zealous, *(übertrieben)* officious, busy.
Dienst|einkommen appointments, salary, emolument of office; **~einrichtung** service institution; **~einstufung** service rating; **~einteilung** *(mil.)* duty roster; **~enthebung** discharge from office, dismissal from service, removal, *(vorübergehende)* suspension; **vorläufige ~enthebung mit Einbehaltung der Dienstbezüge** suspension without salary; **~entlassung** dismissal, discharge, ejection (removal) from office; **~entlassungsentschädigung** dismissial compensation (pay, wage), severance (redundancy, *Br.*) pay; **~erfindung** employee invention.
dienstfähig able to earn, fit for duty (service).
Dienst|fahrplan *(Eisenbahn)* timetable, schedule *(US)*; **~fahrplan einhalten** to arrive right on schedule *(US)*; **~fahrt** official tour; **~fahrzeug** office car, service vehicle.
dienstfrei exempt from service, at leisure, off duty;
~er Tag blank day, day off; **~e Zeit** leisure time (hours).
Dienst|gebäude office building; **~geber** employer, master.
Dienstgebrauch official use;
nur für den ~ official use only, restricted *(Br.)*, restricted matter *(US)*, for official use only.
Dienst|gehalt salary, pay; **~geheimnis** official secret; **~gespräch** *(Telefon)* service (business) call; **~gewalt** authority.
Dienstgrad *(mil.)* rank, grade, character;
ohne ~ private;
untere ~e petty officers, people down the ladder;
~ mit Patent *(mil.)* substantive rank;
~ herabsetzen to demote;
~abzeichen badge; **~herabsetzung** degrading, demotion.
diensthabend in charge, on duty, *(mil.)* orderly;
~er Offizier officer on duty (in charge).
Dienst|handlung official function (act); **~herr** employer, master, principal, hirer *(US)*; **für seinen ~herrn tätig sein** to be about one's master's business; **~hund** *(Polizei)* police dog.
Dienstjahre years of service, years served;
an ~n in terms of service;
anzurechnende ~ reckonable service *(Br.)*;
viele ~ vorzuweisen haben to have seen much service.
Dienst|jubiläum jubilee; **~kleidung** uniform; **~kräfte** staff, personnel; **~kraftfahrzeug** service vehicle; **~laufbahn** career.
Dienstleistung rendering (rendition, performance of) services;
aktive ~en *(Dienstleistungsbilanz)* invisible exports; **althergebrachte ~en** *(Pächter)* customary services; **angemessene ~** adequacy of service; **ärztliche ~en** medical attendance; **nicht unter den Spediteurtarif fallende ~en** exempt services; **vertraglich festgelegte ~en** contract services; **freiberufliche ~en** professional services; **gelegentliche (kleine) ~en** odd jobs; **häusliche ~en** domestic services; **konzerninterne ~en** intergroup services; **kostenlose staatliche ~en** free government services; **öffentliche ~en** public utility services; **passive ~en** *(Dienstleistungsbilanz)* invisible imports; **pensionsanwartschaftsberechtigende ~en** pensionable services; **persönliche ~** personal service; **seemännische ~** maritime service; **städtische ~en** city services; **unsichtbare ~en** *(Dienstleistungsbilanz)* invisibles; **verwandte ~en** allied services; **werbende ~en** reproductive services; **zusätzliche ~en** additional (accessional, ancillary) services; **erwartete zusätzliche ~en** expected service;
~en bei der Abwicklung von Versicherungsansprüchen claims service provided; **~ der öffentlichen Hand** social services; **öffentliche Dienste und ~en im öffentlichen Interesse** services provided by public authorities; **~en öffentlicher Versorgungsbetriebe** public-utility services; **~ ohne Zwischenschaltung eines Produktionsbetriebes** direct service;
~ anbieten to market a service; **auf den einzelnen Kunden zugeschnittene ~en ausweiten** to extend tailor-made services; **jem. entsprechend dem Wert seiner ~en bezahlen** to pay for the value of s. one's services; **~en erbringen** to render services; **~ durch einen Erfüllungsgehilfen erbringen** to perform services vicariously; **~en honorieren** to pay for services; **neue ~en übernehmen** to launch new services; **~en der Post verbessern** to improve the postal services.

Dienstleistungs|abkommen service agreement; **~angebot** range of services, provision of services; **umfassendes ~angebot** comprehensive package of services; **~anlagen** service-yielding assets; **~bereich** service sector (field); **~beruf** service job; **~berufe** service occupations.
Dienstleistungsbetrieb public service (utility) company (corporation, enterprise, *US*), service business undertaking, service establishment;
auf Gäste eingestellter ~ guest-related service; **durch Steuern mitfinanzierter ~** tax-supported service; **städtische ~e** municipal services; **sich selbst tragender ~** self-supported service;
~ zu einer hundertprozentigen Leistungsfähigkeit bringen to build a service to a peak of efficiency.
Dienstleistungs|bilanz invisible balance, balance on current account (of service transactions), net position on services *(US)*; **Waren- und ~bilanz** balance of trade in goods and services; **~bündel** whole range of services; **~einrichtung** service institution; **~entzug** withdrawal of services; **~funktion** service office; **~gebiet** public utility field; **~gebühr** *(Agentur)* service fee (charge); **seine ~gebühr unabhängig festsetzen** to price one's service freely; **~geschäft** sale of services, personal service business *(US)*, *(Agentur)* agency services; **~geschäfte** service transactions; **~gewerbe** service industries, personal service business *(US)*; **~industrie** service industries (economy); **~kosten** cost of servicing, service costs; **~marke** service mark; **~potential** service potential; **~rabatt** *(Agentur)* service allowance; **~sektor** service sector, utilities area, public services; **~struktur** service pattern; **~system** service system; **~träger** service carrier; **~unternehmen** public service company, public utility company (corporation, *US*, establishment); **~verhältnisse** conditions of service; **~verkehr** service transactions, exchange of services, services, *(Zahlungsbilanz)* invisibles, invisible trade; **freier ~verkehr** free movements of services; **~vertrag** service (employment) contract; **persönlicher ~vertrag** contract of personal service; **bereits abgerechnete ~verträge** *(Bilanz)* deferred service contracts; **~wirtschaft** services industry; **~zeugnis** character, reference, testimonial; **~zeugnis ausstellen** to testimonialize, to hono(u)r.
Dienstleitung *(Telefon)* service line, official line.
dienstlich official, on official business, official capacity, functional, in the course of duty;
~ unterwegs sein to be out, to travel on official business; **~ verhindert sein** to be detained by business;
~e Angelegenheit official business (matter); **~er Befehl** official order, *(mil.)* service order; **in ~er Eigenschaft** while an officer; **in ~er Eigenschaft tätig werden** to act in one's official capacity; **~e Führung** conduct; **aus ~en Gründen** for official reasons; **~e Mitteilung** official communication; **~es Verschulden** malfeasance, official misconduct.
Dienst|liste roster; **~lohn** wages, pay; **~lokal** police station; **~mädchen** servant, waiting maid, maidservant, domestic, help *(US)*; **~mann** street porter, outporter *(Br.)*, jobber, messenger, expressman *(US)*, *(Hotel)* commissionaire *(Br.)*; **~marke** revenue stamp, service mark, fiscal; **~marke zücken** to flash a badge; **~medaille** service medal.
Dienstobliegenheiten official duties;
in Erfüllung seiner ~ in exercise of one's duties;
zu jds. ~ gehören to be part of s. one's official duties.
Dienst|ordnung official (service) regulations, *(mil.)* service regulations; **~ort** station, location; **~paß** official passport; **~personal** servants, service staff; **~personal einweisen** to give directions to servants.
Dienstpflicht official function, duty, service, *(mil.)* military service, conscription;
von seinen ~en entbinden to suspend s. o. from office; **seiner ~ genügen** to do one's military service; **seine ~ verletzen** to neglect one's duty.
dienstpflichtig liable to conscription;
in ~em Alter sein to be of military age.
Dienstpflichtiger *(mil.)* conscript, draft registrant *(US)*.
Dienstpflicht|verletzung neglect of duty; **~verweigerer** draft evader *(US)*; **~verweigerung** draft evasion *(US)*.
Dienst|plan *(mil.)* duty roster (list), rota; **~post** official business; **~prämie** step bonus, *(mil.)* gratuity.
Dienstrang service credit, *(Militär)* character, grade, rank;
im gleichen ~ of equal rank; **zeitweiliger ~** temporary rank; **~liste** seniority list.
Dienstraum office.
Dienstreise official tour (journey, trip), travel on official business, business trip;

sogenannte ~ **auf öffentliche Kosten unternehmen** to junket *(US)*;
~**ausweis** *(mil.)* travel pass; ~**vergütung** duty tour allowance.

Dienstsache official business, matter of official concern;
geheime ~ restricted matter *(US)*; **portofreie** ~ *(auf Briefen)* official communication, on Her Majesty's service *(Br.)*, O.H.M.S.

Dienstschluß closing hours;
nach ~ after hours (work);
5-Uhr-~klausel 5 o'clock quitting clause *(US)*.

Dienst|siegel *(Kommunalbehörde)* common seal, *(Notar)* notarial seal; ~**sitz** official residence, duty station, registered office.

Dienststelle bureau *(US)*, government agency, department, [government] office, entity, board;
ausführende ~ implementing agency; **mit besonderen Vollmachten ausgestattete** ~ extra-legal agency; **gleichgeordnete** ~ coordinate authority; **leitende** ~ executive office; **nachgeordnete** ~ subsidiary office; **staatliche** ~ government agency; **untergeordnete** ~ subordinate department; **zuständige** ~ proper department;
~**n abbauen** to axe agencies *(Br.)*; ~ **auflösen** to dismantle an agency; **sich bei einer** ~ **melden** to register at an office; **von der zuständigen** ~ **positiv aufgenommen werden** to be viewed favo(u)rably by the competent authorities.

Dienststellenleiter department head, chief of an agency *(US)*.

Dienststellung appointment, position;
gehobene ~ advanced position; **pensionsfähige** ~ pensionable office.

Dienststrafe disciplinary punishment.

Dienststraf|kammer disciplinary court; ~**ordnung** disciplinary regulations; ~**verfahren** disciplinary proceedings.

Dienststunden hours of attendance, office (official, business, working) hours;
regelmäßige ~ **einhalten** to keep regular hours.

Diensttätigkeit occupation, job.

diensttauglich able-bodied, *(mil.)* effective, fit for service;
für ~ **erklären** *(mil.)* to pass for military service.

Dienst|tauglichkeit fitness for active service; ~**telegramm** service telegram.

diensttuend in charge, on duty, *(Arzt)* in attendance, *(mil.)* orderly, in waiting, acting;
~**er Beamter** official in charge.

Dienstumschlag, frankierter penalty envelope *(US)*.

dienst|unfähig, ~**untauglich** invalid, disabled, *(aus Altersgründen)* superannuated, *(mil.)* unfit for service, reject, noneffective;
~ **machen** to disable.

Dienst|unfähiger invalid, disabled person; ~**unfähigkeit,** ~**untauglichkeit** disablement, disability, incapacity to work, *(mil.)* invalidity, disablement, unfitness for service; ~**unfall** industrial accident; ~**unterbrechung** interruption in working hours; ~**unterricht** *(mil.)* instruction; ~**vereinbarung** service agreement; ~**vergehen** malfeasance in office, neglect of duty, disciplinary offence.

Dienstverhältnis employment, existing employment contract *(US)*, master and servant relation;
ruhegehaltsfähiges ~ pensionable employment; **ständiges** ~ **und Anstellungsverhältnis** ordinary;
~ **eingehen** to take up an employment; ~ **fristlos kündigen** to terminate an employment contract without notice *(US)*; **im** ~ **stehen** to be under contract.

Dienst|verhältnisse employment conditions; **im** ~**verkehr** through official channels; ~**verletzung** injury sustained in the line of duty; **sich eine** ~**verletzung zuziehen** to be injured on duty; ~**vermerk** record; ~**vernachlässigung** dereliction of duty, neglect of one's duties.

dienstverpflichten to conscript, to draft, to impress.

dienstverpflichtet conscripted, drafted;
~**e Arbeitskräfte** conscript labo(u)r.

Dienstverpflichteter conscripted employee, enlisted specialist *(US)*.

Dienstverpflichtung conscription of labo(u)r, industrial (labo(u)r) conscription, *(Beschlagnahme)* requisitioning order;
gewaltsame ~ *(mil.)* impressment; **längere** ~ **verpflichtung** *(mil.)* long service.

Dienst|verpflichtungsvertrag *(Lehrling)* indenture; ~**verrichtung** official function (act); ~**versäumnis** neglect of duty; **zur** ~**verschwiegenheit verpflichtet sein** to be sworn to secrecy.

Dienstvertrag service (employment) agreement, contract of employment *(US)* (service), employment (labo[u]r) contract, hiring agreement *(US)*;
laufender ~ existing employment contract; **von Jahr zu Jahr laufender** ~ general hiring *(US)*;
~ **lösen** to terminate the contract of employment *(US)*.

Dienst|vertragsverhältnis master and servant relation, conditions of the employment contract; ~**verweigerung** refusal to work; ~**vorgesetzter** superior (ranking) officer, supervisor; **unmittelbarer** ~**vorgesetzter** first-level supervisor; ~**vorrang** seniority [in rank]; ~**vorschriften** service instructions, internal regulations, official regulations (instructions), *(mil.)* manual; ~**vorschriften der Kriegsmarine** navy regulations *(US)*; ~**vorschuß** imprest; ~**wagen** service vehicle, caboose [car] *(US)*; ~**wagenabteil** *(Bahn)* service compartment, caboose *(US)*, way car *(sl.)*.

Dienstweg official channels, routine;
auf dem ~ through official (authorized) channels;
~ **benutzen** to go through the proper channels; ~ **überspringen** to jump (ignore) channels.

dienstwidrig contrary to regulations, irregular.

Dienstwidrigkeit irregularity.

Dienstwohnung official dwelling, residence, *(Betrieb)* company dwelling (flat);
mietfreie ~ rent-free residence.

Dienstzeit period (length) of service, tenure in office, service period, service life, tenure of office, *(Dienststunden)* hours of attendance, official (office) hours;
in meiner langjährigen ~ during my long years in office;
[auf die Pension] anrechnungsfähige ~ contributing service, qualifying period of service; **gesetzliche** ~ statutory tenure *(US)*; **kürzere** ~ shorter record of service; **langjährige** ~ long service (years in office); **längste** ~ longest record of service;
~ **für Pensionsberechnung** service period for annuities;
seine zweijährige ~ **ableisten** to be called up for two years' military service; **etw. außerhalb der** ~ **erledigen** to do s. th. out of hours.

Dienst|zeugnis testimonial, clearance card, reference, *(Hausangestellte)* character; ~**zimmer** office; ~**zug** *(mil.)* wagon train *(US)*; ~**zulage** salary increase, *(Leistungszulage)* step bonus; ~**zwang** compulsory service.

Diesel|lokomotive diesel electric locomotive; ~**motor** diesel engine.

diesig hazy, misty.

Diesigkeit haziness.

Dietrich false (skeleton) key, picklock.

diffamieren, j. to blacken s. one's character, to bring s. o. into disrepute, to run s. o. down, to calumniate s. o.

diffamierend defamatory.

Diffamierung calumny, blackening of s. one's character.

Differential *(Motor)* differential;
~**achse** live axle; ~**fracht** discriminating freight; ~**getriebe** differential (compensating) gear; ~**gleichung** differential equation; ~**kostenspanne** cost differential; ~**kupplung** differential coupling; ~**lohnverfahren** differential piece-rate system; ~**quotient** differential quotient; ~**rechnung** differential calculus; ~**rente** economic surplus; ~**tarif** differential tariff; ~**zoll** differential (discriminating) duty, differential tariff.

Differenz difference, disagreement, margin, *(Kurse)* difference, spread *(US)*, *(Saldo)* balance, remainder, *(Überschuß)* surplus;
ungeklärte ~ *(Zahlungsbilanz)* residual error;
~ **zwischen Kassa- und Terminkurs** difference between cash and settlement price; ~ **zwischen Zahl und Wort** *(Scheck)* discrepancy in amounts;
~**en mit jem. haben** to disagree with s. o.; ~ **in seiner Rechnung haben** to have a discrepancy in one's account; ~ **von 100 DM in seiner Rechnung haben** to be 100 DM short in one's account (out in one's calculations); ~ **herauszahlen** to pay the difference; ~ **richtigstellen** to adjust a difference; **sich in die** ~ **teilen** to split the difference;
~**betrag** balance, residual quantity, *(in der Scheckverrechnung)* reclamation; ~**frachtsatz** distance (mil(e)age) rate.

Differenzgeschäft gambling in futures, margin business (transaction, trading, *US*), marginal trading *(US)*, time bargain;
~**e machen** to speculate for differences *(Br.)*, to stag the market *(Br.)*, to purchase on a margin basis *(US)*.

differenzieren to difference.

differenziert, geistig sophisticated.

Differenziertheit, geistige sophistication.

Differenzierung differentiation, variation;
branchenmäßige ~ inter-industry differential.

Differenz|konto over-and-short account; ~**zahlung** *(Börse)* marginal payment; ~**zoll** differential duty.

differieren to differ, to diverge.

Digital|rechenanlage, ~rechner digital calculator, dispatch (digital) computer; **~uhr** digital clock, digital watch.
Diktafon dictaphone, dictating machine.
Diktat dictation, dictate;
~ aufnehmen to take dictation; **nach jds. ~ schreiben** to write at (from) s. one's dictation; **~ auf die Schreibmaschine übertragen** to transcribe dictation;
~frieden dictated peace.
Diktator dictator;
~ in der Westentasche dictator on a small scale;
~eigenschaften qualities of a dictator.
Diktatorenherrschaft dictatorial rule, tyranny.
diktatorisch|es Auftreten haben to be dictatorial in one's manner; **~er Ton** authoritative tone.
Diktatschreiben dictation.
Diktatur dictatorship;
~ des Proletariats dictatorship of the proletariat;
zur ~ zurückkehren to revert to dictatorship.
diktaturähnlich near-dictatorial.
Diktatzeichen reference initials.
diktieren *(Brief)* to dictate a letter;
Friedensbedingungen ~ to dictate the terms of peace;
sich einen Brief ~ lassen to take a letter.
Diktier|gerät, ~maschine dictating machine, dictaphone.
Diktion diction, phraseology.
dilatorisch dilatory;
~e Behandlung dilatory policy; **~e Einrede** dilatory plea.
Dilemma dilemma, embarrassment;
in einem ~ between the devil and the deep blue sea;
sich in einem ~ befinden to be on the horns of a dilemma (in a quandary).
Dilettant dilettante, amateur.
dilettantisch dilettantish, amateurish;
~ arbeiten to work in a dilettante fashion.
Dilettantismus dilettantism, amateurism.
dilettieren, in etw. to do s. th. in an amateurish (dilettante) way;
in der Juristerei ~ to dabble in (at) law.
dimensional dimensional.
Dimensionen dimensions;
äußere ~ overall dimensions;
~ einer Maschine dimension figures of a machine;
erschreckende ~ annehmen to lose all sense of proportion; **Sache in den richtigen ~ sehen** to see a matter in its right perspective *(fam.)*; **auf die richtigen ~ zurückführen** to cut to size.
dimensionieren to dimension.
Ding thing, object, article, *(Diebessprache)* jump *(Br., sl.)*;
in finanziellen ~en erfahren conversant with finance, experienced in financial matters; **nach Lage der ~e** in the circumstances; **vor allen ~en** above all;
~e affairs, matters;
schöne ~e *(ironisch)* pretty mess; **tolles ~** whale of a thing; **unbelebte ~e** sticks and stones;
~ der Unmöglichkeit an impossibility;
unverrichteter ~e abziehen to return empty-handed; **Gang der ~e im nahen Osten beobachten** to watch the course of events in the Near East; **ein ~ drehen** to pull the job *(sl.)*; **sich in ~e einmischen, die einen nichts angehen** to interfere in what does not concern one; **den Weg aller ~e gehen** to go the way of all flesh; **den ~en ihren Lauf lassen** to let matters run their course; **die ~e so nehmen, wie sie sind** to take things in one's stride; **~e zu ernst nehmen** to take matters too seriously; **die ~e beim rechten Namen nennen** to call a spade a spade; **von erfreulichen ~en reden** to talk about s. th. more pleasant; **guter ~e sein** to be in high spirits; **in finanziellen ~en sehr pingelig (kleinlich) sein** to be rather mean over money matters; **jem. ein ~ verpassen** to play a trick upon s. o.;
das geht nicht mit rechten ~en zu there is s. th. fishy about it; **wie die ~e liegen** as matters stand.
dingen to employ, to hire *(US)*, to recruit *(US)*;
einheimische Arbeitskräfte ~ to farm native labo(u)r.
dingfest machen to run in, to put behind bars.
dinglich real, in rem;
~ belasten to encumber; **~ mit dem Grundstück verbunden sein** to run with the land;
~er Arrest attachment, distraint; **~ gesicherte Forderungen** debts covered by a security; **~e Klage** real action; **~es Recht** real right; **~e Sicherheit** real (underlying) security; **~er Vertrag** real contract.
Dingsbums, Dingsda *(fam.)* thingummy, thingumabob, thingumajig;
Herr ~ Mr. what's-his-name.

Dinner dinner [party];
ausgedehntes ~ elaborate dinner;
~ mit fünf Gängen five-course dinner.
Diplom diploma, degree, certificate, sheepskin *(coll.)*;
gefälschtes ~ shingle *(sl.)*; **volkswirtschaftliches ~** economics degree;
~ verleihen *(zuerkennen)* to [confer a] diploma;
~arbeit thesis.
Diplomat diplomat, diplomatist;
akkreditierter ~ resident diplomate; **höherer ~** public minister *(US)*;
~ der mittleren Rangklasse middle-grade diplomat;
~ sein to be in the diplomatic service.
Diplomaten|beruf diplomatic profession; **~gepäck** diplomatic pouch (box); **~ghetto** compound; **~leben** life in the diplomatic service, diplomatic life; **~pass** diplomatic passport; **~posten** [diplomatic] post; **~schreibtisch** pedestal writing table, kneehole writing desk; **~schule** Foreign Service Institute *(US)*; **~sprache** language of diplomacy, diplomatic language; **~tribüne** distinguished strangers' gallery; **~viertel** diplomatic quarter; **~visum** diplomatic visa; **~wohnsitz** diplomat's dwelling, residence.
diplomatisch diplomatic, politic;
sich gegenseitig ~ anerkennen to exchange diplomatic recognition; **es für ~ halten** to deem it policy; **~ sein** to be a good diplomat; **~ vorgehen** to act with (use a little) diplomacy;
~e Aktivität diplomatic activity; **~e Anerkennung** diplomatic recognition; **~e Antwort** diplomatic answer; **~es Asyl** diplomatic asylum; **~e Bedienstete** diplomatic personnel; **~er Beobachter** diplomatic observer; **~e Beziehungen** diplomatic (foreign) relations; **~e Beziehungen abbrechen** to sever diplomatic relations; **~e Beziehungen aufnehmen** to enter into diplomatic relations; **~e Beziehungen unterbrechen** to suspend diplomatic relations; **mit einem Land ~e Beziehungen unterhalten** to maintain diplomatic relations with a country; **~er Dienst** diplomatic (foreign, *US*) service; **in den ~en Dienst eintreten** to enter the diplomatic service; **auf ~er Ebene** at diplomatic level; **~e Gebräuche** diplomatic customs; **alteingebürgerte ~e Gepflogenheiten mißachten** to put a number of diplomatic noses out of joint; **~e Immunität** diplomatic immunity; **~e Kanäle** diplomatic channels; **~es Korps** diplomatic corps (body, *Br.*); **in ~en Kreisen** in diplomatic quarters; **~er Kurier** diplomatic courier; **~e Laufbahn** diplomatic career; **~e Mission** diplomatic mission; **~e Mitteilung** note; **~er Posten** diplomatic assignment; **~e Rangordnung** hierarchy of diplomatic agents; **~e Regelung** diplomatic management; **~er Schritt** diplomatic action; **~er Schutz** diplomatic protection; **~e Sondierung** diplomatic soundings; **~e Sprache** language of diplomacy; **~e Tätigkeit** diplomatic action; **~es Verfahren** diplomatic method; **~er Verkehr** diplomatic communications (intercourse); **~er Vertreter** envoy, diplomatic agent (representative); **~en Vertreter abberufen** to recall a diplomatic representative; **~en Vertreter ernennen** to appoint a diplomatic agent; **~e Vertretung** diplomatic representative (representation, mission, agency); **~e Vorrechte genießen** to be entitled to diplomatic privileges; **auf ~em Wege** through diplomatic channels; **auf ~em Wege an sein Ziel gelangen** to attain one's end by diplomacy.
Diplom|chemiker bachelor of science in chemistry; **~dolmetscher** certified interpreter.
Diplom|ingenieur certified (professional, graduate) engineer, bachelor of engineering *(Br.)*; **~inhaber** diploma holder; **~kaufmann** Bachelor of Commerce *(Br.)*; **~landwirt** bachelor of agriculture [science]; **~physiker** Bachelor of Science *(Br.)*; **~volkswirt** certified political economist, Bachelor of Economic Science; **~volkswirtszeugnis** Higher National Certificate in Business Studies.
direkt direct, immediate, proximate, *(Abstammung)* lineal, direct, *(Sendung)* live, *(völlig offen)* straightforward, pointblank, plainly;
~ ins Gesicht full in the face; **~ unter jds. Nase** under s. one's very nose;
~ beziehen to buy first hand, to obtain goods straight from the factory; **Waren an j. ~ zum Versand bringen** to ship goods to the consignation of s. o.; **~ von jem. hören** to have it straight from the horse's mouth; **~ aus M kommen** to come straight from M; **~ am Bahnhof liegen** to be immediately at the station; **sehr ~ sein** to be outspoken, to be a blunt man; **~ senden** *(Radio, Fernsehen)* to broadcast live; **sich ~ an j. wenden** to make personal contacts;

~er **Absatz** direct marketing (selling); **sehr ~e Antwort** plain answer; ~e **Besteuerung** direct taxation; **in ~er Beziehung zu etw. stehen** to have a close connection to s. th.; ~er **Bezug** direct buying (purchasing); ~e **Erhöhung der Inlandspreise** actual increase in domestic prices; ~e **Fahrkarte** through ticket; ~e **Fernsehsendung** live progam(me); ~e **Finanzierung** direct financing; ~e **Information** first-hand information; ~es **Interesse** personal interest; ~e **Kosten** direct cost (expense); ~er **östlicher Kurs** due east course; ~e **Linie** direct line; **von jem. in ~er Linie abstammen** to be a direct descendant of s. o.; ~e **Nachfrage** immediate demand; ~e **Rede** direct speech; ~er **Schaden** immediate injury; ~e **Steuer** direct (assessed) tax; ~e **Ursache** immediate cause; ~e **Verbindung** *(Bahn)* through connection; **in ~er Verbindung mit jem. stehen** to be in close touch with s. o.; ~er **Verkauf** direct sale; ~er **Verkehr** through traffic; ~er **Wagen** through carriage (coach), Pullman car *(US)*, transit (vestibule) car; ~er **Wahnsinn** sheer madness; ~er **Zug** through (vestibule, nonstop) train.

Direkt|abbuchung direct debiting; ~**absatz** direct marketing (selling); ~**aktion** *(pol.)* direct action; ~**aufnahme** *(Foto)* direct process, *(Rundfunk)* remote *(US)*; ~**besteuerung** direct taxation; ~**bezug**, ~**einkauf** direct buying (purchasing); ~**finanzierung** direct financing; ~**flug** direct flight; ~**flug durchführen** to fly nonstop; ~**flugzeug** through plane; ~**geschäfte zwischen Bankkunden** netting transaction among the clients; ~**handel** direct commerce; ~**investitionen** direct investments.

Direktion board, direction, directorate, management, *(Büro)* director's (manager's) office, head office, headquarters, *(Krankenhaus)* administration.

Direktions|assistent company (corporate) management secretary; ~**aufgaben** managerial duties; ~**ausschuß** managing (steering) committee; ~**beschluß** management (board) decision; ~**büro** director's (manager's, executive, *US*) office; ~**kollege** joint manager; ~**mitglied** board member, member of the board; ~**sekretär[in]** secretary of the managing director; ~**sitzung** board meeting, meeting of directors; ~**spesen** management expenses.

Direktive direction, instruction, orders;
~**n einer Partei** directives of a political party; ~**n zur Vermeidung von Steuerhinterziehungen** tax evasion directives; ~ **erhalten** to receive instructions.

Direkt|kauf von Gütern straightforward purchase of goods; ~**kredite der Wirtschaft** direct financing of the economy; ~**leitung** *(tel.)* direct line; ~**lieferung an die Haushaltungen** household delivery.

Direktor director, conductor, master, old man, boss *(coll.)*, *(AG)* officer, manager, *(Gefängnis)* governor, *(Schulleiter)* headmaster, head, schoolmaster, principal *(US)*, *(Vorsteher)* warden;
ausscheidender ~ retiring director; **erster** ~ president; **geschäftsführender** ~ acting director (manager), managing director, *(Weltwährungsfonds)* executive director; **kaufmännischer** ~ business (sales) manager; **stellvertretender** ~ assistant (vice) manager, assistant (associate) director, submanager; **technischer** ~ managing engineer, technical manager, technical director; **turnusmäßig zuständiger** ~ alternative director;
~ **der Finanzabteilung** finance manager, treasurer *(US)*; ~ **einer Niederlassung** branch manager; ~ **einer Privatschule** private schoolmaster; ~ **der Produktionsabteilung** production manager; ~ **der Verkaufsabteilung** sales manager.

Direktorat directorate, directorship.

Direktoren|gehälter, ~**honorar** directors' emoluments (fees); ~**kasino** executive dining room; ~**posten** directorate; **nicht besetzter ~posten** vacancy in the board of directors; ~**stelle** directorship, *(Schule)* principalship; ~**versammlung** board meeting, court of directors; ~**verzeichnis** register of directors; ~**wechsel** rotating of directors.

direktorial directorial, managerial;
~ **oder kollegial** one-man or committee (collegiate, *US*).

Direktorin schoolmistress, schooldame *(Br.)*, dame.

Direktorium board of directors (governors), executive directors, direction, directorate, governing body, managing board, *(EG)* Management Committee;
~ **eines Industrieunternehmens** management council of an industrial concern.

Direktoriumsmitglied member of directorate, board member, *(Weltwährungsfonds)* executive director.

Direktplazierung *(Wertpapiere)* direct placement.

Direktrice head saleswoman.

Direkt|schulden direct debts; ~**schuldner** direct debtor; ~**sendung** *(Rundfunk)* spot coverage, live broadcast (program[me]); ~**sucher** *(Foto)* direct vision finder; ~**transaktion** *(Makler)* put through; ~**übertragung** live transmission (broadcast), remote *(US)*, *(Fernsehen)* live vision, direct television coverage, camera reporting; ~**unterbringung** *(Wertpapiere)* direct placement; ~**verbindung zu A erhalten** *(Bahn)* to get nonstop to A.

Direktverkauf|an den Kunden direct sale (selling), direct-to-customer selling; ~ **durch Grossisten ohne eigenes Lager** drop shipment; ~ **an der Haustür (durch Vertreter)** house-to-house (door-to-door) selling.

Direkt|verkäufe industrial selling; ~**verkäufer** door-to-door seller, house-to-house salesman; ~**verkehr** direct traffic; ~**versand** direct shipment; ~**versicherung** direct insurance; ~**vertrieb** direct sale (selling); ~**wahl** *(pol.)* direct voting (election), *(tel.)* inward dialling system, distance dialling; ~**wählsystem** *(tel.)* direct dialling, group routing and charging equipment, Grace *(Br.)*; ~**werbedurchspruch** live announcement; ~**werbung durch die Post** direct-mail promotion (advertising shot); ~**zugriff** *(Computer)* random access.

Dirigent conductor, director.

dirigieren to direct, to give directions, to manage, to steer, to run, *(Verkehr)* to direct, to control, to route, *(Wirtschaft)* to control, *(Zeitung)* to write;
alle Einnahmen zu seinem Bankkonto ~ to divert all receipts into one's bank account; **Waren an ihren Bestimmungsort** ~ to dispatch goods to their destination; **j. zum Eingang** ~ to show s. o. the way to the entrance; **Passagiere zum Flugzeug** ~ to shepherd passengers to an airliner; **Orchester** ~ to conduct an orchestra; **in Richtung auf ...** ~ to shepherd toward ...

Dirigismus dirigism, statism;
staatlicher ~ planned economy.

dirigistisch planned, statist, state-controlled, dirigistic;
~e **Maßnahmen** planned measures.

Dirne prostitute, streetwalker, whore.

Dirnen|haus brothel; ~**wesen** prostitution, streetwalking.

Disagio disagio, discount;
mit ~ at a discount;
offenes ~ *(Anleihe)* true discount, arithmetical discount;
~ **auf Schatzwechsel** discount on treasury bills; ~ **auf Termindollars** discount on forward dollars;
mit ~ **kaufen** to buy at a discount; **mit** ~ **verkaufen** to sell at a discount; ~ **des Pfandbriefes über die Jahre verteilen** to spread bond discount over the years;
~**gewinn** unamortized debt (bond) discount; ~**konto** discount account; ~**notierung** discount quotation.

Diskjockey disc jockey, pancake turner *(sl.)*.

Diskont discount [rate], rate of discount (rediscount, *US*), bank rate *(Br.)*, rediscount rate *(US)*, *(Abzug)* deduction, discount, rebate;
ab[züglich] ~ less discount; **mit** ~ at a discount;
amtlicher ~ bank rate *(Br.)*, rediscount rate *(US)*; **einfacher** ~ simple discount; **nicht in Anspruch genommener** ~ discount lost; **übermäßiger** ~ shave *(US sl.)*; **üblicher** ~ discount;
~ **auf Zinseszins** compound discount;
~ **absetzen** to deduct the discount; **zum** ~ **bringen** to present for discount; ~ **erhöhen** to raise the bank rate *(Br.)*, to raise the discount (rediscount, *US*) rate; **Wechsel zum** ~ **geben** to have a bill discounted; ~ **gewähren** to allow a discount; ~ **herabsetzen** to cut the [rate of] discount (rediscount, *US*), to mark down (reduce) the discount rate; **Wechsel zum** ~ **hereinnehmen** to accept bills for discount; **in** ~ **nehmen** to take on discount; ~ **senken** to lower the bank *(Br.)* (discount, rediscount, *US*) rate; ~ **vergüten** to allow a discount; **zweiprozentigen** ~ **vornehmen** to strike off 2%;
~**abrechnung** discount note; ~**abzug** discount reduction; ~**änderung** discount (rediscount, *US*) rate change; ~**bank** acceptance house *(Br.)*, discount bank (corporation, *US*), merchant banker *(Br.)*; ~**basis** discount basis; ~**bestände** *(Bilanz)* discount holdings *(US)*; ~**bestimmungen** discount terms; ~**bewegungen** fluctuations of the bank *(Br.)* (discount, rediscount, *US*) rate; ~**einräumung** allowance of a discount.

Diskonten *(Wechsel)* discounts, investment bills, *(Wechsel in der Bilanz)* discounted bills, discount holdings *(US)*;
prima ~ fine papers, prime bills *(US)*.

Diskont|erhöhung discount rate rise, increase in the discount (bank, *Br.*, rediscount, *US*), raising of (rise in) the bank rate *(Br.)*; ~**erlös**, ~**erträge** discount earned, proceeds, net avails *(US)*; ~**ermäßigung** bank rate reduction *(Br.)*, lowering of (reduction in) the discount (rediscount, *US*) rate.

diskontfähig discountable, bankable *(Br.)*, eligible for discount (rediscount, *US*);
nicht ~ nondiscountable, net, ineligible *(US)*;
~**es Papier** eligible paper *(US)*.
Diskont|fähigkeit discountability, eligibility for discount (rediscount, *US*); ~**fuß** discount (bank, *Br.*, rediscount, *US*) rate; ~**geber** bill *(Br.)* (note, *US*) broker, discounter; ~**geschäft** *(Finanzierungswesen)* discount business, discount trading (transactions), discounting, discount transactions; ~**geschäftsbesitzer** discounter; ~**gesellschaft** discount company (corporation, *US*); ~**grenze** discount limit; ~**gutschrift** discount note; ~**haus** discount company (corporation, *US*), merchant bank *(Br.)*; ~**herabsetzung** bank-rate reduction *(Br.)*, lowering of the rate of rediscount *(US)*, reduction of the discount (bank, rediscount, *US*) rate.
diskontierbar discountable, bankable *(Br.)*, eligible for discount (rediscount, *US*);
nicht ~ nondiscountable, ineligible *(US)*.
Diskontierbarkeit discountability, eligibility for rediscount *(US)*.
Diskontieren discounting.
diskontieren to [take on] discount, to rediscount *(US)*;
begebbare Wertpapiere ~ to discount negotiable papers.
diskontiert discounted, rediscounted *(US)*;
~ **werden** to be discounted.
Diskontierung discounting;
~ **von Buchforderungen** assignment of accounts receivable *(US)*; ~ **einer Dokumententratte** negotiation of a commercial paper; ~ **von Nachrichten** *(Börse)* discounting news;
~ **in Anspruch nehmen** to take discount; ~ **eines Wechsels vornehmen** to undertake to discount a bill.
Diskontierungszeitraum discount period.
Diskont|kasse discount office; ~**kontingent** rediscount quota *(US)*; ~**kredit** discount (rediscount, *US*) credit; ~**makler** bill *(Br.)* (note, *US*, discount) broker; ~**markt** discount (commercial paper, bill, *Br.*, rediscount, *US*) market; ~**material** bills eligible for discount (rediscount, *US*); **seine** ~**möglichkeiten ausschöpfen** to take one's trade discount; ~**note** discount note; ~**politik** bank rate *(Br.)* (discount, rediscount, *US*) policy; ~**portefeuille** discount holdings; ~**provision** discount commission; ~**rechnung** discount note.
Diskontsatz discount, discount (bank, *Br.*) rate, minimum lending rate *(Br.)*, rate of discount (rediscount, *US*);
offizieller ~ official rate of discount;
~ **der Bank von England** bank rate *(Br.)*; ~ **der Londoner Banken und Wechselmakler** market rate *(Br.)*; ~ **der Bundesnotenbank** [etwa] bank *(Br.)* (rediscount, *US*) rate; ~ **der Federal Reserve Bank** Federal Reserve Rediscount Rate *(US)*; ~ **der Geschäftsbanken** private rate of discount *(Br.)*, bank minimum lending rate; ~ **der Landeszentralbank** Federal Reserve's rediscount rate *(US)*;
~ **erhöhen (heraufsetzen)** to raise (increase) the bank *(Br.)* (discount, rediscount, *US*) rate; ~ **herabsetzen (ermäßigen, senken)** to lower (cut, reduce, mark down) the discount (rediscount, *US*) rate, to lower (reduce) the bank rate *(Br.)*;
~**erhöhung** increase in the discount (rediscount, *US*) rate.
Diskont|senkung lowering (reduction) of (fall in) the bank *(Br.)* (discount, rediscount, *US*) rate; ~**senkung vornehmen** to lower the bank rate *(Br.)*, to mark down the discount (rediscount, *US*) rate; ~**spesen** discount charges; ~**tag** date of discount; ~**tage** discount days, terms of discount; **besondere** ~**tage** extra dating *(US)*; ~**umsatz** discount turnover; ~**verbindlichkeiten** *(Bilanz)* bills discounted, discounts, discounts payable *(US)*.
Diskontwechsel discounted (investment) bill, *(pl.)* discounts;
~ **zum Einzug hereinnehmen** to accept bills for collection (discount).
Diskont|wert discounted value; ~**zusage** discount promise.
Diskothek discotheque.
diskreditieren to discredit, to bring into disrepute, to disparage.
diskreditiert, in der Öffentlichkeit discredited in the public.
Diskreditionstage days of grace (respite).
Diskrepanz discrepancy, disparity, *(zwischen Anklage und Nachweis der Straftat)* variance;
zeitliche ~ time lag.
diskret discreet, unobtrusive;
~**e Farben** quiet colo(u)rs; ~**es Schweigen bewahren** to maintain a discreet silence.
Diskretion discretion, secrecy, confidence;
mit ~ **behandeln** to treat discreetly; **sich auf jds.** ~ **verlassen** to rely on s. one's secrecy; **j. zur äußersten** ~ **verpflichten** to enjoin strictest secrecy upon s. o.; **volle** ~ **wahren** to preserve strict confidence.
diskriminieren to discriminate, to differentiate;
j. ~ to deal unfairly with s. o.
diskriminierend discriminative, discriminatory;
~**e Behandlung** discriminating treatment; ~**e Handlungsweise** discriminatory action; ~**e Preisgestaltung** discriminatory prices; ~**e Vergeltungsmaßnahmen** discriminatory retaliation; ~**es Verhalten** discriminatory conduct; ~**e Zölle** discriminating duties (tariffs).
Diskriminierung discrimination, differentiation;
berufliche ~ job discrimination; **in das Steuersystem eingebaute** ~ built-in discrimination; **steuerliche** ~ tax discrimination, discriminatory taxation;
~ **durch eine Behörde** administrative discrimination; ~ **ausländischer Erzeugnisse** discrimination against goods from foreign countries; ~ **auf zollrechtlichem Gebiet** discrimination in customs duties; ~ **einer Prozeßpartei** discrimination of a party in interest;
~**en aufheben** to eliminate discriminations.
Diskriminierungsverbot prohibition of discrimination.
Diskussion discussion, debate, wrangle;
außerhalb jeder ~ **stehend** without dispute; **bevor wir in die** ~ **eintreten** prior to any discussion; **nach endlosen** ~**en** after much debate; **zur** ~ **stehend** under discussion, in dispute;
übermäßig ausgeweitete ~ long drawn-out discussion; **eifrige** ~ close (zealous) debate; **nicht enden wollende (ergebnislose)** ~ indeterminable debate; **endlose** ~ endless discussions; **fernsehübertragene** ~ televised debate, panel show *(US)*; **hitzige** ~ heated debate; **langanhaltende** ~ long debate; **öffentliche** ~ open (panel, *US*) discussion, forum *(US)*; **sachliche** ~ impersonal discussion; **überflüssige** ~ academic discussion;
~ **zu Dritt** three-cornered discussion; ~ **theoretisch möglicher Rechtsfälle** moot;
~ **aufnehmen** to pick up a discussion; ~ **wieder aufnehmen** to resume the debate; **Schluß der** ~ **beantragen** *(parl.)* to move the closure; **einer** ~ **bedürfen** to need discussion; ~ **beleben** to enliven a discussion; **sich an der** ~ **beteiligen** to take a hand in the debate, to engage in a discussion; ~ **wieder in Gang bringen** to reanimate the discussion; **in eine** ~ **eintreten** to enter into a discussion; ~ **für beendet erklären** to declare the discussion closed; ~ **eröffnen** to open a debate (the ball), to begin (open, start) a discussion; **zur** ~ **gelangen (kommen)** to come up for discussion; ~ **in Gang halten** to keep up a discussion; ~ **leiten** to conduct the proceedings, to hold a debate; **jede weitere** ~ **unmöglich machen** to close the door upon any discussion; **Thema der** ~ **zugänglich machen** to air a subject; **ohne weitere** ~ **nachgeben** to comply without arguing; ~ **schließen** to wind up the debate, to closure; **reif zur** ~ **im Plenum sein** to reach the report stage; **nicht mehr zur** ~ **stehen** to be off the map; **zur** ~ **stellen** to bring under deliberation, to invite to discuss, to moot; **moderne Ansicht zur** ~ **stellen** to set up a new opinion; **Frage zur** ~ **stellen** to submit a question to the debate; **sich in die** ~ **stürzen** to launch into a discussion; **an der** ~ **teilnehmen** to participate in a discussion, to take a hand in the debate; ~ **verschleppen** to protract a debate; **für die** ~ **vorsehen** to schedule up for discussion; **bei der** ~ **nicht weiterkommen** to argue in a circle; **zur** ~ **gestellt werden** to come up for discussion; ~ **wünschen** to invite discussion; **keine** ~ **über etw. zulassen** to allow no (shake off a) discussion on s. th.
Diskussions|basis basis for discussion; **zweiter** ~**beitrag** second speech; ~**beitrag leisten** to provide material for a discussion; **um** ~**beiträge bitten** to invite discussion.
diskussionsfähig open for discussion.
Diskussions|freiheit free discussion; ~**gegenstand** subject of discussion; ~**gegenstand abgeben** to provide matter for discussion; ~**grundlage** basis (agenda) for discussion; ~**gruppe** discussion group; ~**gruppen einrichten** *(Schule)* to hold classes for discussion; ~**kreis** discussion circle (session); **begrenzter** ~**kreis** narrow debate; ~**leiter** *(Fernsehen, Rundfunk)* moderator; **unparteiischer** ~**leiter** moderator; ~**objekt** subject of debate; ~**programm** discussion program(me); ~**problem** problem of discussion; ~**redner** speaker; ~**schluß** termination of a debate, closure; ~**stadium** discussion stage; ~**stoff abgeben** to provide material for discussion; ~**teilnehmer** *(Fernsehen)* panel member *(US)*; ~**thema** subject of a discussion; ~**veranstaltung** public (panel, *US*) meeting, forum *(US)*; **im** ~**verlauf** in the course of the discussion; ~**zeit** time for discussion; ~**zeit beschränken** to retrench discussion; ~**ziele abstecken** to specify the goals of a discussion.
diskutabel debatable, discussible.
diskutierbar discussible, debatable.

diskutieren to argue, to debate, to discuss, to dispute, to ventilate, to controvert, to question;
Problem ~ to air a subject; **Sache zu Ende** ~ to argue out a question.
diskutiert, heftig red-hot.
Dispache adjustment (settlement) of average, average statement;
~ **aufmachen** to adjust (state, make up) the average;
~**kosten** adjustment charges; ~**prüfungsstelle** average adjustment agency.
Dispacheur average adjuster (stater), adjustor, arbitrator of averages.
dispachieren to adjust (state the) average.
Disparität disparity.
Dispens dispensation, exemption;
jem. ~ **erteilen** to exempt s. o. from s. th., to dispense s. o.
dispensieren to dispense, to exempt, to excuse.
Disponent chief clerk, factor, managing clerk.
disponibel disposable, available.
Disponibilität availability, disposability.
disponible Ware disposable goods.
Disponieren disposal, placing of orders;
möglichst frühzeitiges ~ disposal at earliest possible date; **vorsichtiges** ~ caution in placing orders.
disponieren to dispose, to make over, *(Aufträge erteilen)* to place orders, *(Vorsorge treffen)* to arrange, to make arrangements, to plan ahead;
über etw. ~ to have s. th. at one's disposal; **über j.** ~ to dispose of s. o., to make arrangements on s. one's behalf; **Anzeige** ~ to place an advertisement; **entsprechend** ~ to make arrangements to the effect; **geschickt** ~ to arrange matters cleverly, to plan carefully; **über große Kapitalbeträge** ~ to dispose of a large capital, to have large capital at one's disposal; **knapp (vorsichtig)** ~ to show caution in placing orders; **über ein Konto** ~ to operate an account;
über große Geldbeträge ~ **können** to command great sums of money; **über seine Zeit** ~ **können** to be master of one's time.
disponiert, nicht indisposed;
sich heute nicht ~ **fühlen** not to be in the mood today; ~ **sein** to be disposed, to feel inclined; **gut** ~ **sein** to be in good form; **für bestimmte Krankheiten** ~ **sein** to be prone to certain diseases; **schlecht** ~ **sein** to be in bad form.
Disposition disposal, disposition, plan, preliminary arrangement, *(Auftragserteilung)* placing orders, *(Vorsorge)* arrangements, planning ahead;
laut ~ according to instructions; **mangels gegenseitiger** ~ unless otherwise instructed; **zu Ihrer** ~ at your disposal;
zur ~ **gestellt** *(Beamter)* on half pay;
abweichende ~**en** divergent instructions; **ausdrückliche** ~ express instruction; **der Bilanzpolitik zum Jahresschluß dienenden** ~**en** window-dressing at the end of the year; **im voraus erteilte** ~**en** ordering in advance; **längerfristige** ~ long-term planning; **saisonale** ~**en** seasonal preparations;
~**en des Handels** ordering by the trade; **freie** ~ **des Importhandels** free decision of the import trade; ~ **über ein Konto** operation of an account; **kurzfristige** ~**en der Kundschaft** hand-to-mouth orders of the public; ~**en öffentlicher Stellen** payment arrangements of government agencies;
zu jds. ~ **stehen** to be at s. one's disposal (service); **j. zur** ~ **stellen** *(mil.)* to put s. o. on half-pay, to send s. o. into temporary retirement; **Fonds zur** ~ **stellen** to make a fund (funds) available; **seine** ~**en treffen** to make arrangements, to plan ahead; **seine** ~**en umstoßen (umwerfen)** to make new arrangements; ~**en nur im Bedarfsfall vornehmen** to switch to a hand-to-mouth ordering pace; **alle** ~**en über den Haufen werfen** to upset (thwart) all plans.
Dispositions|befugnis disposing power; **prognostische** ~**beratung** advisory prognostics.
dispositionsfähig authorized.
Dispositions|fähigkeit *(für Geldbeträge)* spending power, *(Verfügungsberechtigung)* competence to dispose of property, authority; ~**fonds** general revenue fund; ~**fonds der Staatskasse** treasury chest fund *(Br.)*; ~**kredit** overdraft (drawing) credit; ~**möglichkeit** scope of spending; ~**recht** power of disposal; ~**reserve** general (operating) reserve.
dispositiv permissive, optional.
disproportionaler Gewinnpunkt leverage point.
Disproportionalität leverage.
disproportioniert out of proportion, disproportioned.
Disput dispute, controversy, contest.
disputieren, über eine Frage mit jem. to debate (argue) a question with s. o.

Disqualifikation disqualification.
disqualifizieren to disqualify, to incapacitate, to strike off the roll.
disqualifiziert disqualified, ineligible.
Disqualifizierung disqualification, ineligibility.
Dissens dissent, ambiguity;
offener ~ patent ambiguity; **versteckter** ~ latent ambiguity.
Dissertation dissertation, treatise;
~ **annehmen** to approve a dissertation; ~ **schreiben** to do a dissertation.
dissertieren, über etw. to deliver a dissertation (write a thesis) upon a subject.
Dissident dissident.
Dissidentengruppe group of dissidents.
Distanz distance;
~ **zu den Linksradikalen bewahren** to keep one's distance from the radical left; **auf** ~ **halten** to walk the tightrope; **j. auf** ~ **halten** to keep s. o. at a distance, to keep s. o. at arm's length; ~ **wahren** to keep one's place;
~**fahrt** long-distance (cross-country) race; ~**fracht** distance (pro rata, ratable) freight, freight pro rata; ~**geschäft** option business.
distanzieren, sich to backtrack, to take no part in, to stand aloof;
sich von etw. ~ to view s. th. with detachment; **sich von jds. Ansichten** ~ to dissociate o. s. from s. one's views; **sich deutlich** ~ to make a clean break.
distanziert distant, reserved, aloof, standoffish;
j. ~ **behandeln** to be distant to s. o.; **sich jem. gegenüber** ~ **verhalten** to be reserved with s. o.;
~**e Haltung** hands-off attitude; ~**e Haltung gegenüber der Regierung einnehmen** to stand aloof from the government; **mit** ~**er Höflichkeit** with reserved politeness.
Distanzierung standoffish air, standoff *(US)*.
Distanz|scheck out-of town check *(US)* (cheque, *Br.*); ~**tarif** proportional (distance) rate, reshipping rate; ~**wechsel** out-of-town bill *(Br.)*.
distinguiert grand, of higher rank;
~ **auftreten** to have quite a manner;
~**er Herr** very precise gentleman.
Disziplin discipline;
eiserne ~ iron discipline; **schlechte** ~ lax discipline; **strenge** ~ stern discipline;
strenger auf ~ **achten** to maintain discipline more strictly than others; ~ **aufrechterhalten** to keep discipline; **an** ~ **gewöhnen** to discipline; ~ **lockern** to loosen discipline; ~ **schwächen** to be an enemy to discipline; **für Aufrechterhaltung der** ~ **sorgen** to maintain discipline; ~ **einer Armee untergraben** to undermine (destroy) the discipline of the troops, to demoralize an army; ~ **der Truppen unterminieren** to undermine (destroy) the discipline of the troops.
Disziplinar|angelegenheit disciplinable offence, disciplinary case; **strenge Auffassungen in** ~**angelegenheiten vertreten** to be strict in the matter of discipline; ~**ausschuß** court of discipline, disciplinary committee *(Br.)*, disciplinary court, grievance committee; ~**befugnis** disciplinary power; ~**behörde** disciplinary authority; ~**bestimmungen** disciplinary regulations; ~**bestrafung** disciplinary punishment; ~**bücher** disciplinary records; ~**fall** disciplinary offence, disciplinary case; ~**gericht** court of discipline; ~**gerichtsbarkeit** disciplinary jurisdiction; ~**gewalt** disciplinary power; **aus** ~**gründen versetzen** to transfer for disciplinary reasons.
disziplinarisch disciplinarian, disciplinary;
j. ~ **belangen** to inflict disciplinary punishment on s. o., to take disciplinary action against s. o., to crack down on s. o. *(US coll.)*.
Disziplinar|kammer disciplinary court; ~**maßnahmen** disciplinary action (measures); ~**maßnahmen ergreifen** to take disciplinary measures; ~**ordnung** disciplinary regulations, code of ethics; ~**politik** disciplinary policy; ~**strafe** disciplinary fine (punishment, scourge), amercement royal *(Br.)*, *(mil.)* summary punishment; ~**strafe verhängen** to award a disciplinary punishment; ~**verfahren** disciplinary trial (proceedings), department trial *(US)*; **einem** ~**verfahren unterwerfen** to subject to a disciplinary action; ~**vergehen** official misconduct, disciplinary offence, misconduct in office by a public officer employee *(US)*; ~**vorgesetzter** disciplinarian, superior in rank; **auf dem** ~**weg** disciplinarily.
disziplinieren, sich to discipline o. s.;
Parteimitglieder ~ to bring party members under the whip.
diszipliniert patient;
sich sehr ~ **verhalten** to show perfect discipline.

Disziplinlosigkeit indiscipline.
Divergenz divergence;
~ **zweier Ergebnisse** divergence between two results.
divergieren to diverge.
divers varied, diverse, sundry;
~**e Angelegenheiten** several matters; ~**e Artikel** miscellaneous goods; ~**e Ausgaben** sundry expenses, sundries; ~**e Leute** various people.
Diverses miscellaneous, sundries, sundry goods, *(in Zeitung)* miscellaneous items.
Diversifizierung diversification.
Dividende dividend, share, *(Lebensversicherung)* bonus, dividend;
ausschließlich (ohne) ~ dividend off *(US)*, ex dividend *(Br.)*; **einschließlich (mit)** ~ cum dividend *(Br.)*, including dividend *(US)*, dividend on, yielding a dividend of;
abgehobene ~ collected dividend; **nicht abgehobene** ~ unclaimed dividend, dividend not yet collected; **mit Inkassoaufschlag abgehobene** ~**n** mandated dividends; **aufgelaufene** ~ accumulated (accrued) dividend; **ausgefallene** ~ omitted (passed, *US*) dividend; **ausgeschüttete** ~ distributed (declared, paid-out) dividend; **nach Zahlung der Körperschaftssteuer ausgeschüttete** ~**n** franked dividends *(Br.)*; **noch nicht ausgezahlte** ~ unpaid dividend; **ausländische** ~ foreign dividend; **außerordentliche** ~ bonus, extraordinary (special, surplus, *US*) dividend, superdividend, melon *(US)*, plum *(US)*; **noch ausstehende** ~ pending dividend; **nicht behobene** ~ uncalled (unclaimed) dividend; **bevorrechtigte** ~ preferential dividend; **noch nicht bezahlte** ~ accrued dividend; **einbehaltene** ~ retained dividend; **erklärte** ~ declared dividend; **ertragsorientierte** ~ earnings-related dividend; **fällige** ~ dividend due (payable), unpaid dividend; **später fällige** ~ deferred dividend; **festgesetzte** ~ declared dividend; **fiktive** ~ sham dividend; **garantierte** ~ guaranteed (fixed) dividend; **gewöhnliche** ~ noncumulative dividend; **anfangs gezahlte** ~ initial dividend; **aus dem Kapital gezahlte** ~ dividend paid out of capital, capital dividend; **durch Ausgabe von Schuldverschreibungen gezahlte** ~ liability dividend; **gleichbleibende** ~ stable dividend; **halbjährliche** ~ semiannual dividend; **kumulative** ~ cumulative dividend; **limitierte** ~ limited dividend; **normale** ~ regular dividend; **rückständige** ~ accumulated dividend, dividend in arrears; **satzungsmäßige** ~ statutory dividend; **steuerpflichtige** ~ taxable dividend; **unbehobene** ~ unclaimed dividend; **ungültige** ~ unauthorized dividend; **unvorhergesehene** ~ contingent dividend; **unzulässige** ~**n** unauthorized dividends; **beim Aktionär versteuerte** ~ consent dividend; **vierteljährliche** ~ quarterly dividend; **vorgeschlagene** ~ dividend proposed; **vorläufige** ~ interim dividend; **an festen Terminen zahlbare** ~ regular dividend; **zusätzliche** ~ cumulative (extra, additional, super) dividend, bonus;
~ **in Form von Aktien** stock dividend *(US)*, dividend in stock *(US)*; ~**n mit aufgeschobener Fälligkeit** deferred dividends; ~ **in bar oder in Form einer Gratisaktie** optional (stock, *US*) dividend; ~ **in Form von Gratisaktien anderer Aktiengesellschaften** property dividend, dividend in kind; ~ **in Form von Interimsscheinen** scrip dividend; ~ **in Form eigener Obligationen** bond dividend; ~ **abzüglich Steuern** dividend net *(Br.)*; ~**n in Streubesitz** dividends on portfolio investment; ~ **auf kumulative Vorzugsaktien** [ac]cumulative dividend;
~ **abheben** to collect a dividend; ~ **abwerfen** to yield a dividend; ~ **ausschütten** to declare (disburse, *US*, distribute, pay, strike) a dividend; **12%** ~ **ausschütten** to divide 12 per cent; **außerordentliche** ~ **ausschütten** to cut a melon *(US)*; **keine** ~ **ausschütten** to omit (pass, *US*) a dividend; **zusätzliche** ~ **ausschütten** to distribute an additional (supplementary) dividend; ~ **in Form eigener Aktien ausschütten** to declare a dividend in stock of the corporation *(US)*; ~**n beheben** to collect dividends; ~**n beziehen** to receive dividends, to collect dividends; ~ **von 14% bringen** to yield 14 per cent dividend; ~ **erhöhen** to raise the dividend; ~ **erklären (festsetzen)** to declare a dividend; ~ **in Form eigener Aktien festsetzen** to declare a stock dividend *(US)*; ~ **garantieren** to guarantee a dividend; **im Vorjahr 10%** ~ **gezahlt haben** to have paid 10 per cent dividend last year; ~ **herabsetzen** to cut its dividend; **seine** ~ **sich ansammeln lassen** to allow one's dividends to accumulate; ~ **ausfallen lassen** to default (omit, pass, *US*) a dividend; ~ **verteilen** to declare a dividend; **außerordentliche** ~ **verteilen** to cut a melon *(US)*; **zusätzliche** ~ **verteilen** to distribute an additional (supplementary) dividend; ~ **vorschlagen** to propose (recommend) a dividend; ~ **aus dem Kapital zahlen** to pay a dividend out of the capital.

Dividenden|abgabe dividend tax; ~**abschlag** reduction in dividends; ~**abschnitt** dividend warrant; ~**aktien** participating shares (stocks, *US*); ~**anfall** accrual of dividends; ~**ankündigung** notice of dividend, dividend announcement; ~**ansammlung** accumulation of dividends, dividend accumulation; ~**anspruch** right to a dividend; **fällige** ~**ansprüche** dividends payable (due); ~**ausfall** dividend omission, passing of a dividend *(US)*; ~**ausgleichskonto** dividend equalization account; ~**ausgleichsrücklage** dividend equalization reserve.
Dividendenausschüttung declaration (distribution, payment) of dividends, dividend disbursements (distribution, payment, payout) *(US)*;
[nicht] körperschaftssteuervorauszahlungspflichtige ~ [non]-qualifying distribution *(Br.)*; **steuerfreie** ~ tax-free distribution; **wiederangelegte** ~ dividend reinvestment;
~ **zuzüglich Abschreibung** cashflow, cash throwoff;
Geschäftsjahr ohne ~ **abschließen** to omit (pass, *US*) a dividend *(US)*; **schon im Juli an der** ~ **teilnehmen** to rank for July dividends *(Br.)*; **höhere** ~**en vornehmen** to distribute a higher dividend.
Dividenden|auszahlung dividend payout *(US)*; ~**auszahlungsanweisung** dividend order; ~**auszahlungsstelle** dividend disbursing agent; ~**begrenzungen** dividend restrictions, limitations on dividends; **gesetzliche** ~**begrenzungen** statutory dividend limitations *(Br.)*.
dividendenberechtigt entitled to (ranking for) a dividend;
~ **sein** to rank (qualify) for, to be entitled to a dividend.
Dividenden|berechtigung dividend rights, qualification for dividends; ~**berechtigter** recipient of dividends; ~**beschränkungen** limitation on dividends, dividend restrictions, dividend limitations; ~**besteuerung** dividend taxation; ~**beteiligung** participation in dividends.
dividendenbevorrechtigt sein to rank first in dividend rights *(Br.)*.
Dividenden|bevorrechtigung preference as to dividends; ~**bogen** coupon sheet; ~**bonus** bonus; ~**einkommen,** ~**einnahmen** dividend income; ~**empfänger** dividend receiver; ~**empfehlung** recommendation of dividends; ~**empfehlung geben** to recommend the amount of dividends; ~**erfordernisse** dividend requirements; ~**erhebung** collection of dividends; ~**erhöhung** dividend increase; ~**erhöhung vornehmen** to raise a dividend; ~**erklärung** declaration of dividends, dividend announcement (declaration, statement); ~**ertrag,** ~**erträgnisse** income from dividends, dividend income (yield); ~**erwartungstabelle** pending dividends timetable; ~**fähigkeit** dividend-paying ability; ~**festsetzung** declaration of dividends; ~**fonds** bonus (dividend) fund; ~**garantie** dividend guarantee; ~**garantiewerte** guaranteed stocks *(US)*; ~**guthaben** *(Lebensversicherung)* divisible (life insurance) surplus; ~**herabsetzung** reduction of dividends, dividend reduction; ~**inkasso** collection of dividends, bond coupon collection; ~**kontinuität** dividend continuity; ~**konto** dividend account; ~**kupon** dividend warrant, coupon, voucher for dividends; ~**kürzung** reduction in dividends, dividend reduction (remission, curb, cutting).
dividendenlos without dividend, dividend off *(US)*, ex dividend *(Br.)*.
Dividenden|nachzahlung payment of dividends accrued; ~**papiere** dividend-paying stocks, dividend payers *(US)*, equity (ownership) securities, equity shares, equities; ~**politik** dividend policy; **gleichbleibende** ~**politik** conformity in dividend politics; ~**pool** pooling of dividends; ~**rechte** dividend rights; **mit** ~**rechten ausgestattet sein** to rank with dividend rights; ~**rendite** dividend yield; ~**renditengrundlage** dividend yield basis; ~**renditeverhältnis** dividend yield ratio; ~**rückgang** dividend reduction; ~**rücklage** dividend provision, dividend reserve fund, *(Lebensversicherungsgesellschaft)* bonus reserve; ~**rückstände** dividends in arrear, dividend arrears; ~**satz** dividend rate; ~**scheck** dividend check *(US)* (cheque, *Br.*), dividend warrant; ~**schein** dividend warrant (coupon); ~**schluß** dividend date of record; ~**senkung** reduction of dividends, dividend cut; ~**steuer** withholding tax on dividends, dividends (coupon) tax; ~**stock** dividend reserve (bonus) fund; ~**stopp** curb on dividend rises; ~**strom** stream of dividends; ~**summe** total dividend payment; **mechanisches** ~**system** *(Versicherung)* arbitrary method of profit distribution; ~**termin** dividend day, record date [for payment of dividends]; ~**transfer** repatriation of dividends, dividend repatriation (remittance); ~**überweisungsauftrag** dividend mandate *(Br.)*; ~**umsätze** dividend returns; ~**verteilung** distribution (disbursement, *US*) of dividends, dividend distribution; ~**verzeichnis** dividend register, dividend list; ~**vorschlag** recommendation on dividends, dividend recommendation.

dividendenvorzugsberechtigt sein to rank first with dividend rights *(Br.)*.
Dividenden|werte, börsengängige dividend-paying securities, marketable securities, equities, equity securities (stock); ~**werte auf dem Markt unterbringen** to market equity securities; ~**zahlung** dividend payment (payout, *US*), payment of dividends; ~**zeitraum** dividend period.
dividieren to divide.
Division *(mil.)* division;
~ **auf Kriegsstärke auffüllen** to bring up a division to war establishment.
Divisions|abschnitt divisional sector; ~**artillerie** divisional artillery; ~**hauptquartier**, ~**stab** *(mil.)* divisional headquarters; ~**kalkulation** process cost accounting *(US)*; ~**zeichen** symbol of division, flash *(Br.)*.
Dock dock, quay, wharf, navy yard *(US)*;
im ~ **abgeliefert** delivered at docks;
einseitiges ~ offshore dock;
Schiff aus dem ~ **bringen** to take a ship out of dock; **Schiff ins** ~ **bringen** to put (bring) a ship into dock; **aus dem** ~ **gehen** to leave dock;
~**anlagen** dock (docking) facilities, docks, dockyard; ~**arbeiter** dock labo(u)rer, docker *(Br.)*, wharf porter (worker), cargo (quayside) worker, cargo man, docksman, longshoreman *(US)*; ~**arbeiterstreik** dock labo(u)rer strike; ~**becken** dock basin; ~**empfangsschein** dock receipt (warrant).
docken to [go into] dock.
Dock|gebiet docking area; ~**gebühren** dock rent, dock dues (charges), dockage, wharf dues; ~**geld** dock duty; ~**gesellschaft** dock company; ~**hafen** dock port; ~**lagermiete** dock rent; ~**lagerschein** dock warrant *(Br.)*; ~**lagerschein an Order** endorsable dock warranty *(Br.)*; ~**meister** dockmaster, dock inspector; ~**möglichkeiten** docking facilities; ~**schleuse** tide dock; ~**tor** dock gate; ~**wand** dockside.
Doggerboot dogger.
Dogma dogma;
~ **aufstellen** to dogmatize.
Dogmatismus dogmatism, close-mindedness.
Dogmen einer Partei party labels (platforms).
Doktor *(Arzt)* graduate doctor, physician, general practitioner, medical man;
~ **der Betriebswissenschaften** master of science in business administration degree; ~ **der Ingenieurwissenschaften** Doctor of Engineering Science; ~ **der Medizin** Doctor of Medicine; ~ **der Naturwissenschaften** Doctor of Natural Science; ~ **der Philosophie** Doctor of Philosophy; ~ **der Rechte** Doctor of Laws, Doctor of Civil Law *(Oxford)*; ~ **beider Rechte** Doctor of Civil and Canon Law; ~ **der Volkswirtschaft** [etwa] economics graduate;
~ **holen** to fetch (send for) the doctor; **seinen** ~ **machen** to take one's doctor's degree; **seinen** ~ **auf der Harvard Universität machen** to receive one's doctorate from Harvard; **zum** ~ **promoviert werden** to obtain a doctor's degree;
mit ~**abschluß** post-doctoral standard.
Doktorand doctorand, postgraduate *(US)*, candidate for scholastic hono(u)rs.
Doktoranden|kursus postgraduate course; ~**seminar abhalten** to teach a graduate course; ~**stipendium** postgraduate fellowship *(US)*.
Doktor|arbeit dissertation, thesis; ~**diplom** doctor's degree.
Doktorexamen promotional examination;
sein ~ **machen** to take one's doctor's degree; **ins** ~**examen steigen** *(fam.)* to go up for a degree; **sich auf das** ~ **vorbereiten** to be studying for a degree at a university.
Doktorgrad graduate degree, doctorate, doctor's (university) degree;
mit Auszeichnung erworbener ~ hono(u)rs degree *(Br.)*; **ehrenhalber verliehener** ~ honorary degree;
~ **der Literaturwissenschaften** degree of doctor of literature;
~ **erwerben** to take one's doctor's degree; ~ **verleihen** to confer a degree;
~**verleihung** degree granting.
Doktorhut doctoral hood.
Doktorierung commencement.
Doktor|promotion taking one's degree, promotion; ~**titel** doctorate, doctorship.
Doktorwürde doctorate, doctorship;
~ **vertreten** to propound a hypothesis.
Doktrin doctrine, hypothesis;
dem Volk eine neue politische ~ **oktroyieren** to instil a new doctrine on the people; ~ **vertreten** to propound a hypothesis.
doktrinär doctrinaire, doctrinal, dogmatic[al].
Dokument deed, document, instrument, paper, record title, voucher, writing, presents;
amtliches ~ official document; **authentisches** ~ authentic document; **begebbares** ~ negotiable instrument; **ergänzende** ~**e** supporting documents, documents in support; **gefälschtes** ~ forged document;
einem Bericht beigefügte ~**e** documents joined to a report;
~**e gegen Akzept** documents against acceptance; ~**e gegen Einlösung der Tratte** documents against payment; ~ **zum Handschriftenvergleich** test paper; ~ **über die erfolgte Hinterlegung von Inhaberpapieren** letter of charge *(Br.)*; ~ **der Schande** proof of ignominy; ~**e gegen Zahlung** documents against payment;
~ **abfassen (aufsetzen)** to draw up (execute) a deed, to execute a document; ~**e aufnehmen** to list documents; **seinen Anspruch mit** ~**en belegen** to document one's claim; **Echtheit eines** ~**s bestreiten** to dispute the validity of a document; ~ **durchpausen** to trace a copy from the original; ~ **fälschen** to forge a document; ~ **beglaubigen lassen** to have a document authenticated; **Aussage durch** ~**e stützen** to support a statement with documentary evidence; ~**e vorlegen** to tender documents.
Dokumentar|aufnahme documentary picture; ~**bericht** documentary [report]; ~**bericht im Fernsehen** television documentary; ~**film** actuality film, documentary; **gegenwartsnaher** ~**film** documentry film of topical interest.
dokumentarisch documentary;
~ **belegt** supported by documents, documentated;
~ **belegen** to document, to prove by documents;
~**er Beweis** documentary evidence.
Dokumentarsendung documentary.
Dokumentation documentation, documentary proof.
Dokumentationszentrum documentation center *(US)* (centre, *Br.*).
Dokumenten|akkreditiv documentary [letter of] credit; ~**akkreditivgeschäft** documentary credit operations; ~**geschäft tätigen** to negotiate a documentary credit; ~**inkasso** collection of bills (documents); ~**kette** series of documents; ~**kreditbrief** documentary letter of credit; ~**nachweis** documentary record; ~**ordner** file; ~**pfand** documentary pledge; ~**sammlung** archives; **vollständiger** ~**satz** full set of documents; ~**tasche** briefcase; ~**tratte** documentary (document) bill (draft), commodity paper *(Br.)*; ~**veröffentlichung** publication of documents; ~**vorlage** production (presentation) of documents; ~**wechsel** documentary (acceptance) bill (draft).
dokumentieren to prove by documents, to document, to show forth;
etw. öffentlich ~ to demonstrate s. th. publicly.
dokumentierte Geschichte recorded time.
Dolch knife, dagger;
~**stoß** stab; **jem. einen** ~**stoß versetzen** to knife s. o. *(US sl.)*.
Dollar dollar, buck *(sl.)*, smacker *(sl.)*, iron man *(sl.)*, bone *(sl.)*, wheel *(sl.)*;
außer einem ~ saving a dollar; **nicht mehr als insgesamt eine Million** ~ not exceeding in the aggregate one million dollars; **echter** ~ good dollar, *(unverfälschter)* clean dollar; **halber** ~ half-dollar *(US)*; **harter** ~ hard dollar;
~**s zum Ankauf von Überseebeteiligungen durch britische Staatsangehörige** investment of dollars *(Br.)*;
sich auf 100 ~ **belaufen** to come to $ 100; **zehn** ~ **zuwenig [in der Kasse] haben** to be $ 10 short; **mit vierhundert** ~ **auskommen können** to manage with $ 400; **höchstens zehn** ~ **kosten** to cost not more than $ 10; **in** ~ **rechnen** to calculate in dollars; **zehn** ~ **riskieren** to stand to lose $ 10; **täglich sechzehn** ~ **verdienen** to earn sixteen dollars a day; **100** ~ **verdienen** to make a profit of $ 100; **etwa 1000** ~ **verlieren** to lose a sum of approximately (in the neighbo(u)rhood of) $ 1000; **glatte 1000** ~ **verlieren** to lose a clear thousand dollars; **j. für vier** ~ **täglich verpflegen** to keep s. o. at four dollars a day; **auf 20.000** ~ **geschätzt werden** *(Forderungen)* to be returned at $ 20.000;
~**abfluß** dollar outflow; ~**abhebung** dollar drawings; ~**abwanderung** flight of the dollar; ~**abwertung** devaluation of the dollar, dollar depreciation; ~**abzüge** dollar drawings; ~**agio gegenüber dem Franken** premium of the dollar over the franc; ~**akzept** dollar acceptance; ~**anleihe** dollar loan (bonds); ~**bestände** dollar holdings; ~**betrag** dollar amount; ~**block** dollar area; ~**bonds** dollar bonds; ~**defizit** dollar deficit; ~**devisen** dollar exchange; ~**diplomatie** dollar diplomacy; ~**einkommen** dollar income; **vorsichtig zur** ~**finanzierung überreden** to steer gently towards dollar finance; ~**flucht** dollar

flight, flight of the dollar; ~**fluß** flow of dollars, dollar drain; ~**flut** flood of dollars; ~**guthaben** dollar balance (deposits), Eurocurrency; **für Auslandsinvestitionen verfügbare ~guthaben** investment dollars *(Br.)*; ~**imperialismus** dollar imperialism; ~**jagd** dollar hunt; ~**knappheit** dollar shortage, shortage of dollars; ~**könig** dollar king; ~**kredit** dollar credit; ~**kurs** dollar rate; ~**lücke** dollar gap; ~**notierung** dollar quotation; ~**notiz** dollar quotation; ~**obligationen** dollar debentures; ~**parität** dollar parity; ~**politik** dollar diplomacy; ~**raum** dollar area; **schwindende ~reserven** dwindling dollar resources; ~**rettung** dollar rescue; ~**scheck** dollar check; ~**schuldverschreibungen** dollar bonds; ~**schwäche** weakness of the dollar; ~**schwemme** flood of dollars; ~**schwund** dollar drain; ~**strom** flow (flood) of dollars; ~**sturz** fall of the dollar; ~**stützung** dollar support; ~**titel** dollar bonds; ~**überschuß** dollar surplus; ~**vorstoß** dollar drive; ~**währung** dollar exchange; **grüne ~währung** *(EG)* green currency; ~**wert von Geschäftsabschlüssen durch Vereinbarungen zukünftiger Kaufpreisbelegungen zu Goldpreisbedingungen sichern** to protect the dollar value of business transactions by asking for future payments in terms of the price of gold; ~**zinssätze am Euroanleihemarkt** eurodollar deposit rates.

Dolmetschanlage interpreting installation.

dolmetschen to act as interpreter, to interpret;
aus dem Englischen ins Deutsche ~ to translate from English into German.

Dolmetscher interpreter;
freiberuflicher ~ free-lance interpreter; **vereidigter ~** sworn interpreter; **bei Gerichten zugelassener ~** court interpreter; **als ~ fungieren** to act as (do the) interpreter, to interpret; **als ~ in einer Sitzung fungieren** to act as an interpreter to a meeting; **sich zum ~ einer Gruppe machen** to appoint o. s. spokesman of a group; **~ stellen** to supply an interpreter; **~ zuziehen** to call in an interpreter;
~**amt** interpretership; ~**prüfung** interpreter examination; ~**schule** interpreter school.

Dolus *(lat.)* malice.

Domäne demesne, Crown land *(Br.)*, domain, *(Sondergebiet)* domain, province;
staatliche ~ demesne of the state, Crown land *(Br.)*;
~ der Warenhäuser shop land *(fam.)*.

Domänen|besitz demesne lands of the Crown *(Br.)*, direct domain; ~**einnahmen** land revenue *(Br.)*; ~**land** demesne land, domain; ~**pächter** tenant of a domain; ~**verwalter** farm bailiff, land agent; ~**verwaltung** Crown Land Commissioners *(Br.)*.

dominieren to dominate, to predominate, to prevail.

dominierend dominant, dominating, prevailing, commanding;
~**e Lage über eine Stadt einnehmen** to dominate the town.

Dominiumsstatus dominion status.

Domino domino;
~**theorie** *(pol.)* domino theory; ~**wirkung**, ~**effekt** *(pol.)* domino effect.

Domizil *(Wohnsitz)* domicile, abode, residence, *(Zahlstelle)* paying agent;
sein ~ in A aufschlagen to settle in A;
~**akzept** domiciled acceptance; ~**angabe** domiciliation; **ohne ~angabe** not domiciled; ~**gebühr** domiciliation provision.

Domiziliat payee, paying agent.

domizilieren to domicile, to domiciliate, to be resident (located), to reside, *(Wechsel)* to domicile, to make payable.

domiziliert|es Akzept domiciled acceptance; ~**er Wechsel** domiciled bill of exchange.

Domizilierung domiciliation.

Domizil|provision commission for domicil[iat]ing; ~**wechsel** addressed (domiciled, domiciliary, domiciliated, indirect) bill, *(Wohnung)* change of residence.

Donner thunder, *(Geschütz, Wasserfall)* roar;
wie vom ~ gerührt dumbfounded, thunderstruck;
~ des Jüngsten Gerichts crack of doom.

Donnerbalken *(mil., sl.)* bog *(Br., sl.)*, privy *(US sl.)*.

donnern to thunder, *(Geschütz, Wasserfall)* to roar;
auf den Tisch ~ to pound on the table; **an die Tür ~** to hammer at the door.

donnernd thundering, roaring;
~ brechen to break with a roar; **~ über eine Brücke fahren** to thunder over a bridge; **~ zu Tal gehen** *(Lawine)* to thunder down;
~**er Beifall** thunderous applause; ~**es Gelächter** peals (roars) of laughter; ~**e Hochrufe** rousing cheers; **mit ~er Stimme** with a voice of thunder; ~**e Wellen** crashing (thundering) waves.

Donnerschlag thunderblast, thunderclap, clap of thunder;
j. wie einen ~ treffen to stun s. o.

Donnerwetter thunderstorm, thunder;
wie ein heiliges ~ dreinfahren to come down on s. o. like a ton of bricks; **ein ~ geben** to raise a stink (dust) *(fam.)*; **~ über sich ergehen lassen** to face the music; **sich auf ~ gefaßt machen** to look out for squalls.

Dontgeschäft trading in puts and calls, premium dealing *(Br.)*.

Doppel duplicate, double;
~**agent** double agent; ~**anspruch** double claim; ~**ausgabe** double issue; **koordinierte ~auswahl** *(Statistik)* method of overlapping maps.

doppelbahnig two-lane.

Doppel|band double volume; ~**belichtung** double exposure; ~**bereifung** dual (twin) tyres (tires, *US*); ~**beschäftigung** double employment; ~**besteuerung** double taxation; ~**besteuerungsabkommen** double-taxation agreement *(Br.)*, antidouble tax treaty *(US)*; ~**besteuerungsvergünstigung** double taxation relief; ~**bett** double bed; ~**bettcouch** studio couch, double divan; ~**bild** *(Fernsehen)* ghost; ~**bödigkeit** *(fig.)* ambiguity; ~**brief** overweight letter; ~**buchhaltung** bookkeeping by double entry; ~**buchstabe** compound letter; ~**deckerbus** two-tier bus, double-decker *(Br.)*.

doppeldeutig ambiguous, equivocal, misconstruable.

Doppel|druck mackle, blur; ~**ehe** bigamous marriage, bigamy; ~**eigentum** dual ownership; ~**eintrag** double entry; ~**erntewirtschaft** double cropping; ~**fenster** storm (twinlight) window; ~**funktion** dual function; ~**gänger** double; ~**garage** two-car garage; ~**gleis** *(Bahn)* double track.

doppelgleisig *(Bahn)* double-tracked;
~ fahren *(fig.)* to go off in different directions.

Doppel|haus two-family house, duplex house *(US)*; ~**heft** double issue; ~**hochzeit** double wedding; ~**leben führen** to lead a double life; ~**mandat** dual mandate; ~**mitgliedschaft** dual membership; ~**name** compound (hyphenated) name; ~**nummer** *(Zeitschrift)* combined issue; ~**patentierung** double patenting; ~**persönlichkeit** multiple personality; ~**prämie** compound (double) option (premium); ~**prämiengeschäft** compound option; ~**preissystem** dual pricing; ~**programm** two-feature program(me); ~**punkt** colon; ~**quittung** receipt in duplicate; ~**reifen** twin tire (tyre, *Br.*).

doppelreihiger Anzug double-breasted suit.

Doppel|schalter two-way switch; ~**scheibenwischer** tandem wiper; ~**schicht** double shift; ~**schnur** *(el.)* twin flex; ~**seite** double page; ~**seite-Blattmitte** center *(US)* (centre, *Br.*) page spread.

doppelseitig|e Anzeige double-page spread; **~ bespielte Schallplatte** two-sided record; ~**es Schuldverhältnis** mutual indebtedness.

Doppelsinn double meaning, ambiguity, equivocation.

doppelsinnig ambiguous, equivocal.

Doppel|sitzer *(Flugzeug)* two-seater, two-place aircraft *(US)*; ~**spiel treiben** to play a double game; ~**spuraufzeichnung** twintrack recording; ~**staatsangehörigkeit** dual nationality; ~**steckdose** two-way socket; ~**steuer** *(Flugzeug)* dual controls.

doppelstöckiges Bett two-bunk bed.

doppelt double, dual;
~ für einfach gültig receipted in duplicate;
~ ausfertigen to make out in duplicate; **Urkunde in ~er Ausfertigung ausstellen** to make out a document in duplicate; **~ soviel bezahlen** to pay twice as much; **~ setzen** *(drucktechn.)* to double; **~ überprüfen** to double-check; **~ verbucht werden** to be entered twice;
~**e Arbeit leisten** to do twice as much; **in ~er Ausfertigung** [delivered] in duplicate, in two copies; ~**er Betrag** double the amount; ~**er Boden** false (double) bottom; ~**e Buchführung** bookkeeping by double entry; **aus ~em Grunde** for two reasons; ~**e Haftung** *(Bankaktien)* double liability; ~**e Leistung bei Unfalltod** double accident benefit (indemnity, *US*); ~**er Preis** *(Anzeige)* double rate; ~**en Preis bezahlen** to pay double the price; ~**e Quittung** receipt in duplicate; ~**e Rechnungsausstellung** double-billing; ~**e Spesen in Rechnung stellen** to double-bill; ~**e Staatsbürgerschaft** dual nationality; ~**e Strafverfolgung** double jeopardy; **einem ~en Zweck dienen** to serve a dual purpose.

Doppeltarif maximum and minimum tariff.

Doppelte double;
das ~ bezahlen to pay twice as much, to pay double the value; **das ~ einbringen** to make double returns; **das ~ kosten** to cost double the amount; **um das ~ gestiegen sein** to have doubled.

Doppel|tür double (storm) door; ~**veranlagung** double assessment; ~**veranstaltung** doubleheader *(US)*; ~**verdiener** double earner, two-job worker (man, *US*), moonlighter *(US)*, dualist, pluralist; ~**verdienst** double pay; ~**verglasung** double glazing;

~**verkehr** *(Telefon)* two-way communication, duplex telephony; ~**vermietung** simultaneous letting; ~**versicherung** double insurance; ~**versicherungsklausel** double benefit (indemnity, *US*) clause; ~**währung** bimetallic (double) standard, gold-and-silver currency, bimetallism; ~**währungssystem** bimetallism; ~**wechsel** second of exchange; ~**wette** *(Pferderennen)* double; ~**wohnsitz** second domicile.

doppelzeilig *(Schreibmaschine)* double-spaced.

Doppel|zentner quintal; ~**zimmer** double room, two-bed room, room for two people *(US)*.

doppelzüngig sein to speak with forked tongue, to equivocate.

Doppelzüngigkeit double dealing, duplicity.

Dorf village, small town *(US)*;
auf dem ~**e** in the country;
aus dem ~ **jagen** to hunt from the village; **vom** ~**e sein** to be a country bumpkin; **auf dem** ~ **wohnen** to live in the country.

dorfähnlich villagey.

Dorfälteste village seniors.

Dorfanger village green;
seine Schafe auf dem ~ **weiden lassen** to pasture one's sheep on the village common.

Dorf|betrieb village industry; ~**bevölkerung** people in the village; **einfache** ~**bewohner** plain country folk.

Dörfchen, verschlafenes sleepy little village.

Dörfer, Potemkinsche facade, bluff;
auf die ~ **gehen** to barnstorm, to take a step down, to lower one's standards;
das sind spanische ~ **für mich** that's double Dutch, that's all Greek to me.

Dorf|erneuerung village renewal; ~**gasthaus** village inn (pub); ~**gemeinde** rural community; ~**gemeinderat** parish council; ~**gemeinschaft** village (farming, rural) council, village community; ~**gemeinschaftshaus** community center *(US)* (centre, *Br.*); ~**kneipe** local pub; ~**komödiant** strolling actor; ~**laden** village (country, *US*) store; ~**leben** country life; ~**postamt** village post-office; ~**sanierung** village renewal; ~**straße** local road; ~**tölpel**, ~**trottel** country bumpkin, joke of the village, village innocent, country jake *(US)*.

Dorn|im Auge thorn in one's flesh, eyesore;
ein ~ **im Auge für j. sein** to be an eyesore for s. o.; **auf** ~**en gebettet sein** to be on a bed of thorns.

dornenreich full of thorns;
~**es Leben** hard life.

Dornröschenschlaf hundred years sleep;
~ **schlafen** to live in a dream world; **j. aus seinem** ~ **wecken** to bring s. o. back to reality.

Dörrobst dried fruits.

Dose tin *(Br.)*, can *(US)*, *(Steckdose)* plug box, *(Schalldose)* pickup;
mit Diamanten besetzte ~ box set with diamonds;
auf ~ **aufgenommen** *(Rundfunk)* prerecorded, *(Fernsehen)* videotaped;
auf ~ **aufnehmen** *(Rundfunk)* to prerecord, *(Fernsehen)* to vidiotape; **in** ~**n einmachen** to can, to tin *(Br.)*; **jem. etw. in kleinen** ~**n verabreichen** to dose s. o. with small quantities of s. th., *(fig.)* to tell s. o. s. th. little by little.

dösen to doze, to drowse.

Dosen|bier tinned beer *(Br.)*, canned beer *(US)*; ~**konserven** canned *(US)* (tinned, *Br.*) food; ~**milch** evaporated (condensed) milk; ~**öffner** can (tin, *Br.*) opener.

dosieren to [administer a] dose;
Mittel zu gering ~ to underdose a drug; **Präparat** ~ to dose out a drug.

Dosierung dose, dosage;
tödliche ~ lethal dose; **zeitliche** ~ timing;
~ **für Erwachsene** adult dose.

Dosis dose, unit;
mit einer leichten ~ **von Ironie** with a dash of irony;
höchstzulässige ~ *(Strahlen)* maximum permissible dose; **zu schwache** ~ underdose; **tödliche** ~ lethal dose; **wirksame** ~ operative dose;
in kleiner ~ **verabreichen** to dose out; **über eine beträchtliche** ~ **von Selbstvertrauen verfügen** to have one's full share of self-confidence; ~ **verschreiben** to dose.

Dossier file, folder, dossier;
amtliches ~ official paper;
sich mit einem ~ **vertraut machen** to go through a dossier; ~ **redigieren** to brief a case;
~**information** credit report on file.

Dotalrecht dotal system.

Dotation dotation, endowment, allocation.

Dotationskapital endowment funds.

dotieren to endow, to allocate, to appropriate, to earmark, *(vergüten)* to remunerate;
Fonds ~ to endow a fund, to increase a reserve fund; **Konto** ~ to place an account in funds; **Rücklagen mit einem Betrag** ~ to appropriate to the reserve fund; **Rücklage aus dem Gewinn** ~ to build up a reserve fund out of the profit.

dotiert allocated, endowed;
gut ~ **sein** to have riches to spare; **sehr reichlich** ~ **sein** to be endowed with ample financial means;
gut ~**e Stelle** well-paid position; **reich** ~**e Stiftung** richly endowed foundation.

Dotierung dotation, endowment, *(Fonds)* allocation, appropriation, earmarking, *(Stellung)* pay, payment, remuneration;
~ **eines Kontos** alimentation (allocation) of an account; ~ **des Rücklagenfonds** allocation to the reserve fund.

Double *(Film)* double, stand-in *(US)*, stunt man *(US)*.

Doyen *(dipl.)* doyen, dean.

Dozent [university] lecturer, reader, fellow (college) assistant professor, instructor *(US)*;
~ **für Wirtschaftswissenschaften** lecturer in economics.

Dozenten|aufgaben lecturing duties; ~**schaft** university teachers; ~**stelle** teaching job, lectorship, teachership *(Br.)*; **dreijährige** ~**stellung** tour of three years as a lecturer; ~**tätigkeit** lecturing duties; ~**zimmer** common room.

Dozentin lecturess.

Dozentur readership, lectureship, teaching job (position) *(US)*;
~ **innehaben** to be a lecturer, to hold a lectureship.

dozieren to give lectures, to lecture, to profess *(Br.)*, *(dozierend sprechen)* to pontificate, to hold forth.

Drachenfliegen hang gliding.

Draht wire, *(Geld, coll.)* brass, gilt *(sl.)*, dough *(US)*, *(tel.)* telephone connection;
auf ~ *(coll.)* quick on the trigger, on one's toes (the beam, *sl.*);
heißer ~ *(internationale Politik)* hot line;
per ~ **antworten** to reply by wire; **direkten** ~ **zu j. haben** to have a direct connection to s. o.; **auf** ~ **sein** to be a live man (a quick one, up to scratch), to know how many beans make five, to be with it *(sl.)*; **nicht ganz auf** ~ **sein** not to feel quite up to the mark.

Drähte ziehen *(fig.)* to pull strings;
politische ~ to play at politics.

Draht|akzept telegraphic acceptance; ~**angaben** telegraphic quotation; ~**annahme** acceptance by wire, wire acceptance; ~**anschrift** cable address; ~**antwort** telegraphic answer, wire reply; ~**anweisung** cable transfer; ~**auskunft** cable (wire) report; ~**aviso** cable advice; ~**bericht** cable (wire) report; ~**bestätigung** cable confirmation; ~**blockheftung** wire block stitching; ~**einzäunung** wire fencing.

drahten to wire, to wireless, to cable, to telegraph.

drahtet ob bezahlt wire fate.

Draht|fernsehen wired television; ~**funk** wired wireless, wired radio *(US)*; ~**geflecht**, ~**gewebe** wire cloth, wirework; ~**gitter** wire, wire netting (mesh); ~**glas** reinforced (wired) glass; ~**hefter** *(Buchbinderei)* wiring machine; ~**heftung** *(Buchdruckerei)* saddel stitch, wire stitching; ~**hindernis** barbed-wire entanglement; ~**klammern** wire staples.

drahtlos wireless, radio *(US)*;
~**e Bildtelegrafie** facsimile; ~**es Fernsprechen** wireless telephony, radiotelephony *(US)*; ~**e Nachrichtenübermittlung** radio communication; ~**e Telegrafie** wireless (radio, *US*) telegraphy.

Draht|mitteilung telegraphic communication; ~**nachricht** cable information, message by telegraph, telegraphed message, telegram, wire; ~**offerte** telegraphic (cable) offer; ~**rückantwort** wire reply, telegraphic answer; ~**schutzmaske** face guard.

Drahtseil wire rope, *(Artist)* tightrope;
~**akrobat** tightrope acrobat, wire walker; ~**bahn** cable (funicular) railway, aerial cableway, ropeway; ~**brücke** wire bridge; ~**fähre** cable ferry.

Draht|stift wire nail; ~**überweisung** cable transfer; ~**verbindung** wire connection; ~**verhau** *(mil.)* barbed-wire entanglement; ~**zange** wire-tongs, wire cutter, pliers.

Drahtzaun wire fence;
elektrisch geladener ~ electric fence;
mit einem ~ **umgeben** wired.

Drahtzieher wiredrawer, *(fig.)* wirepuller, Mister Big *(sl.)*;
~ **sein** to wirepull, to pull the strings.

Draisine electric motor car (carriage), pop car *(US sl.)*, *(Eisenbahn)* inspection car, trolley *(Br.)*;
~ **mit Handbetrieb** handcar *(US)*.

drakonisch draconian, draconic, cruel;
~**e Maßnahmen** draconian measures.
Drall *(Geschoß)* twist, spin.
Drama drama, dramatic play;
zusammengebasteltes ~ nailed-up drama.
Dramatiker dramatist, playwright.
dramatisch dramatic;
um einen ~**en Effekt zu erzielen** with a view to dramatic effect; ~**er Konflikt** dramatic conflict; ~**e Schlußszene** drop scene; ~**e Veränderungen der internationalen Lage** dramatic changes in the international situation.
dramatisieren to dramatize;
sich gut ~ **lassen** to dramatize well.
Dramatisierung dramatization, stage adaptation.
Dramaturg dramatic adviser.
Dramenaufführung dramatic performance.
Dränage drainage [system], draining;
unterirdische ~ underdrainage;
durch ~ **trockenlegen** to well-drain;
~**behörde** drainage district; ~**graben** well drain; ~**rohr** drainage pipe; ~**system** drainage system.
dranbleiben to stick to it;
an jem. ~ to keep close to s. o.; **am Apparat** ~ to hold the line.
Drang urge, press, pressure, rush, impulse, stress, propulsion;
im ~ **des Augenblicks** on the spur of the moment; **im** ~ **der Geschäfte** in the hurry of business; **im** ~ **der Not** under the pressure of circumstances;
~ **nach Erfolg** eagerness to succeed; ~ **nach Freiheit** urge for freedom; ~ **der Geschäfte** pressure of business; ~ **in die Stadt** drift to the city;
einem augenblicklichen ~ **folgen** to act on the impulse of the moment; **unwiderstehlichen** ~ **haben, zu reisen** to have an irresistible urge to travel; ~ **verspüren** to feel an urge; **unwiderstehlichen** ~ **verspüren** to feel an irresistible impulse.
drangehen, mit Schwung to put a jerk in it *(sl.)*.
drängeln to jostle, to hustle;
j. ~ to badger (bother) s. o.; **sich mit jem. um etw.** ~ to jostle with s. o. for s. th.; **sich in einen Bus** ~ to thrust o. s. into a bus; **j. um Geld** ~ to pester s. o. for money; **sich an einem Regentag in die Kinos** ~ to be packing into the cinemas on a wet day; **j. zur Seite** ~ to push s. o. aside; **sich durch ein Tor** ~ to squash through a gate.
drängen to press, to urge, *(Zeit)* to be running short (pressing);
j. ~ to be urgent with s. o.; **sich** ~ to crowd, to press, to throng; **sich um j.** ~ to crowd round s. o.; **auf eine Antwort** ~ to press for an answer; **Arbeitstrupp zur Arbeit** ~ to urge on a gang of workmen; **zum Ausgang** ~ to throng towards the exit; **j. beiseite** ~ to push (shove, thrust) s. o. aside; **j. in eine Ecke** ~ to force s. o. into a corner; **zur Entscheidung** ~ to have to be decided immediately; **j. zu einer Entscheidung** ~ to hustle s. o. into a decision; **j. zum Handeln** ~ to urge s. o. to action; **zum Kauf** ~ to urge to buy; **seine Kunden mit der Begleichung der Rechnung** ~ to push one's clients to pay; **sich rücksichtslos durch die Menge** ~ to push (elbow) one's way through the crowd; **nicht** ~ not to be urgent; **Schuldner zur Zahlung** ~ to press a debtor for payment, to dun a debtor; **sich nach einer Stellung** ~ to rush for a job; **sich in den Straßen** ~ to throng in the streets; **sich in jds. Vertrauen** ~ to force one's way into s. one's confidence; **sich in den Vordergrund** ~ to get into the limelight; **nach vorn** ~ to crowd forward, to push one's way to the front; **auf Zahlung** ~ to press for payment.
drängend | er Gläubiger urgent creditor, dun; ~**e Menge** milling crowd.
drangsalieren to bully;
j. ~ to make s. one's life miserable, to harass s. o., to plague s. one's life out.
dran | halten, sich to hurry up, to hasten, to speed up, to hump; **noch zwei Stunden** ~**hängen** to add another two hours.
dränieren to drain.
Dräniergraben ditch.
dran | kommen to have one's turn; **j.** ~**kriegen** to get at s. o.; **sich** ~**machen** to set to; **j. zuerst** ~**nehmen** to take s. o. first; **nicht** ~**wollen** to fight shy of it.
drapieren to drape.
drastisch drastic, rigorous, radical;
~**e Maßnahmen** drastic measures; **mit** ~**en Worten schildern** to describe in vivid words.
Drauf | gabe boot (earnest) money; ~**gänger** wildcat (quick-tempered) person, dare-devil, pusher, go-getter *(coll.)*.
draufgängerisch foolhardy, dare-devil, reckless;
~**es Leben** rough-and-tumble life.
Draufgängertum daredevilry, foolhardiness, go-ahead, go-getting.
draufgeben to throw into the bargain;
jem. eines ~ to put s. o. in his place, to sit on s. o. *(fam.)*.
draufgegangen sein to have gone down the drain.
draufgehen to go west, to kick the bucket *(sl.)*, *(Vieh)* to die;
auf den Erwerb von Büchern ~ to go on books; **noch vor Langeweile** ~ to be bored to death; **auf Miete und Ernährung** ~ to go in rent and food.
Draufgeld bargain (forfeit) money (penny), earnest money, deposit.
drauf | hauen, jem. eins to land s. o. a blow; **100 DM** ~**knallen** to smack on DM 100 *(US sl.)*; **Geld** ~**legen** to lose money on it.
Drauflosarbeiten pegging away.
drauflosarbeiten to work away (like mad).
drauflosgehen to go off at scores;
wie der Teufel ~ to go at it hammer and tongs.
drauflos | quatschen to rattle on *(fam.)*, to shoot off one's mouth *(US sl.)*; ~**wirtschaften** to muddle on.
Draufsicht top (plan, *US*) view.
draußen outdoors, outside, out of doors, in the open [air].
Dreck mud, dirt, mire, filth, *(Kot)* mug, excrements, dung, *(Schund)* rubbish, trash, garbage;
alten ~ **aufrühren** to rake up old stories; **j. wie** ~ **behandeln** to treat s. o. like dirt; **j. wie den letzten** ~ **behandeln** to treat s. o. as a mere nobody; **j. mit** ~ **bewerfen** to sling mud at s. o., to pelt s. o. with mud; ~ **am Stecken haben** not to be without blemish; **sich einen** ~ **um etw. kümmern** not to care a dump (damn, hoots, pin); **sich um jeden** ~ **kümmern** to stick on trifles; **sich um seinen eigenen** ~ **kümmern** to peddle one's papers *(sl.)*; **sich einen** ~ **daraus machen** not to care a damn (two hoots); **aus dem größten** ~ **heraus sein** to be over the worst (nearly out of the wood); **einen** ~ **wert sein** not to be worth a damn *(coll.)*; **im** ~ **sitzen** to be in a mess (hard up, badly off); **seine Nase in jeden** ~ **stecken** to poke one's nose in everything; **im** ~ **steckenbleiben** to get stuck in the mud; **einen** ~ **von etw. verstehen** not to know a damn thing about it; **alles in den** ~ **ziehen** to disparage everything; **Karren aus dem** ~ **ziehen** to clear up a mess; **jds. Namen durch den** ~ **ziehen** to drag s. one's name through the mire;
~**arbeit** dirty work; ~**ecke** dirty place, stable *(sl.)*; ~**fink** dirty creature *(fam.)*.
dreckig dirty, soiled;
einem ziemlich ~ **gehen** to be in a bad way (tight spot);
~**e Bemerkung** nasty remark; **für** ~**e 20 DM** for a paltry DM 20; ~**e Wäsche** dirty (soiled) laundry; ~**er Witz** vulgar joke.
Drecksack guttersnipe.
Drecksbude, elende doghole;
in einer ~ **leben** to live in a slum.
Dreck | schleuder filthy tongue; ~**wetter** nasty (filthy) weather.
Dreh trick, gag, racket *(US sl.)*, *(Handgriff)* hang, knack;
einen ~ **finden** to set the ball rolling; ~ **heraushaben** to have the knack of it; ~ **bald heraushaben** to learn the trick of it; **auf einen** ~ **kommen** to strike upon an idea; **im** ~ **sein** to be in the swing.
Dreharbeiten *(Film)* shooting;
mit den ~ **beginnen** to start shooting.
Dreh | bank turning lathe; ~**bleistift** revolving (automatic, *US*) pencil; ~**brücke** swing (turn) bridge.
Drehbuch scenario, script, screenplay;
~ **mit genauen Regieanweisungen** continuity;
~ **schreiben** to script; **zu einem** ~ **verarbeiten** to scenarize;
~**autor** scenarist, continuity (scenario) writer; ~**bearbeitung** scenarization; ~**herstellung** screenwriting; ~**rechte** story rights.
Drehbühne revolving stage.
drehen *(Schiff)* to round;
an etw. ~ **und deuteln** to niggle and quibble about s. th.; **sich** ~ *(Börse)* to turn; **sich um ihre Achse** ~ *(Erde)* to rotate on its axis; **sich in den Angeln** ~ to swing on its hinges; **ein Ding** ~ to pull the job *(coll., sl.)*; **Film** ~ to shoot a film; **kleiner** ~ *(Gas)* to turn down; **sich im Kreis** ~ to go round in a circle; **Looping** ~ to loop the loop; **sein Mäntelchen nach dem Winde** ~ to trim one's sails to the wind; **jem. eine Nase** ~ to cock a snook at s. o.; **am Radio** ~ to twiddle the knobs; **jem. den Rücken** ~ to give s. o. the cold shoulder; **Runde** ~ to go for a stroll; **an einer Sache** ~ to give s. th. a twist; **Schiff um 180 Grad** ~ to turn a ship end for end; **auf der Stelle** ~ *(Schiff)* to pinwheel; **jem. einen Strick aus etw.** ~ to use s. th. to trip s. o. up; **sich nach Süden** ~ *(Wind)* to work round to the south; **Zigarette** ~ to roll a cigarette.
Dreh | feuer revolving lighthouse; ~**flügel** rotary wing, rotor; ~**flügelflugzeug** rotorplane, gyroplane, rotorcraft, rotary-

wing aircraft; ~**funkfeuer** omnidirectional radio beacon, rotating beacon; ~**knopf** knob; ~**knopfschloß** drawback lock; ~**kolbenmotor** rotary-piston engine; ~**kondensator** variable condensor; ~**kraft** torque; ~**kran** rotary (slewing) crane; ~**kreuz** *(für Fußgänger)* pay gate, turnstile; ~**leistung** torque; ~**orgel** street organ, hurdy gurdy; ~**ort** *(Film)* filming site, location lot; ~**plan** shooting script; ~**scheibe** *(Bahn)* turntable, turnplate, *(Telefon)* dial; ~**stift** propelling pencil; ~**strom** *(el.)* rotary (three-phase) current; ~**stromerzeuger** three-phase generator; ~**stuhl** swivel chair; ~**tür** swing door; ~**vervielfältiger** rotary duplicator.

Drehung turn, turning, twist, *(um Achse)* rotation, revolution, *(Börse)* turn, *(Rad)* rotation;
~ **im Uhrzeigersinn** clockwise rotation.

Drehzahl number of revolutions;
~**anzeiger** speed indicator; ~**messer** tachograph.

drei three;
ewig und ~ **Tage dauern** to take ages; **Hunger für** ~ **haben** to be as hungry as a bear; **sich j.** ~ **Schritt vom Leibe halten** to hold s. o. at arm's length; **etw. in** ~ **Worten sagen** to say it briefly; **nicht bis** ~ **zählen können** to be a fool (a perfect ass);
ehe man bis ~ **zählen kann** before you could say Jack Robinson; **so aussehen, als ob man nicht bis** ~ **zählen kann** to look as if butter wouldn't melt in one's mouth.

Dreiachser *(Auto)* six-wheeler.

drei|bahnig three-lane; ~**bändiges Werk** three-volume work.

Drei|bettkabine three-way shared room; ~**bogenplakat** *(Werbung)* three-sheet.

dreidimensional three-D.

Dreiecks|arbitrage triangular exchange; ~**geschäft** triangular transaction; ~**verhältnis** three-cornered relationship; ~**verkehr** triangular trade.

Dreier|ausschuß Committee of Three; ~**besprechung** triangular talk; ~**bündnis** tripartite alliance.

dreifach threefold;
in ~**er Ausfertigung** in triplicate.

Drei|fachschalter *(el.)* three-way switch; ~**farbendruck** three-colo(u)r printing, trichromatic process; ~**felderwirtschaft** open-field (three-course) system (rotation); ~**gangschaltung** three-gear shift; ~**gespann** troika.

dreigleisig three-rail.

Dreijahresfrist three-year period.

dreijährig triennial.

Dreikäsehoch whipper-snapper;
wie ein ~ pint-sized, knee-high to a grasshopper *(US coll.)*;
~ **sein** not to be the height of six pennyworth of coppers.

dreiköpfige Familie family of three.

Dreimächte|abkommen tripartite agreement; ~**konferenz** three-power conference.

dreimaliger Anstrich three-coat work.

Dreimeilen|grenze three-mile limit; ~**zone** three-mile zone (belt).

dreimonatlich quarterly.

Dreimonats|akzept three-months' paper; ~**einlagen** three-months deposit; ~**frist** period of three months; ~**geld** ninety days loan, three-months deposit (money); ~**papier,** ~**wechsel** three-months' draft (bill); **mit** ~**ziel** three months after date.

drein|finden, sich to put up with; **sich** ~**fügen** to take one's medicine; ~**reden** to put one's oar in.

Dreiphasenstrom three-phase current.

drei|phasig three-phase; ~**poliger Ausschalter** three-pole circuit breaker.

dreiprozentig bearing three per cent;
~**e Papiere** three-percents.

Drei|punktlandung three-point landing; ~**rad** tricycle; ~**radlieferwagen** tricar *(Br.)*; ~**satzrechnung** rule of three.

dreiseitig triangular, *(Abkommen)* trilateral;
~**e Handelsbeziehungen** three-cornered trade relations.

drei|spaltiger [Zeitungs]artikel three-column article; ~**sprachig** trilingual; ~**spurig** three-lane.

Dreißig|fach, zum ~**fachen des Jahresertrages** at thirty years' purchase; ~**ster** *(Witwen-Anteil)* widow's chamber.

dreist impudent, audacious, brazen, nervy *(sl.)*, off base *(sl.)*, *(unverschämt)* cheeky, saucy, fresh *(US coll.)*;
so ~ **sein, um ein Darlehn zu bitten** to have the neck to ask for a loan *(sl.)*;
~**e Bemerkung** bold remark; ~**er Bettler** importunate beggar; ~**er Diebstahl** daring robbery; ~**e Forderung** steep demand; ~**e Lüge** brazen (barefaced) lie.

dreistellig three-figure.

Dreistufenrakete three-stage rocket.

dreistündige Vorlesung three-hours' lecture.

Dreiviertel|mehrheit three-fourth majority; ~**verlustklausel** three-fourth loss clause; ~**wertklausel** three-fourth value clause.

drei|wöchiger Urlaub three-weeks holiday; ~**zehn Stück** baker's (printer's) dozen.

Dreizimmerwohnung three-room apartment (flat, *Br.*).

Dresche bekommen to get a thrashing (hiding).

Dreschen threshing.

dreschen *(Getreide)* to thresh;
Phrasen ~ to let off hot air; **leeres Stroh** ~ to plough the sand.

Drescher thresh.

Dreschmaschine threshing machine, thresher.

Dresseur animal trainer.

dressieren to train.

dressiertes Tier performing animal.

Dressur training.

Drill *(mil.)* drill.

drillen *(mil.)* to drill, to discipline.

Drillichanzug fatigue clothes (dress).

dringen to press, to urge, to insist;
bis zu jem. ~ *(Gerücht)* to reach s. o.; **in j.** ~ to press (plead with, be urgent with) s. o.; **auf Antwort** ~ to press for an answer; **auf sofortige Bezahlung** ~ to insist of being paid at once; **mit Bitten in j.** ~ to entreat s. o.; **darauf** ~**, daß etw. geschieht** to urge that s. th. should be done; **auf eine Entscheidung** ~ to press for a decision; **aus allen Fenstern** ~ *(Rauch)* to belch out of all the windows; **mit Fragen in j.** ~ to ply (pester) s. o. with questions; **bis auf die Haut** ~ *(Nässe)* to penetrate to one's skin, to soak to the skin; **in jds. Innerstes** ~ to move s. o. deeply; **durch die feindlichen Linien** ~ to penetrate through the enemy's lines; **jem. durch Mark und Bein** ~ to cut s. o. to the marrow, to pierce s. o. to the quick; **durch die Nacht** ~ *(Geschrei)* to ring through the night; **in die Öffentlichkeit** ~ to leak out, to get abroad, to reach the public; **durch alle Ritzen** ~ to be seeping through all the cracks; **auf Sparsamkeit** ~ to urge the need for economy; **auf Zahlung** ~ to press for (insist on) payment.

Dringend|es zuerst erledigen to attend to the most pressing thing first; **dem** ~**en den Vorrang geben** to put first things first.

dringend urgent, pressing, exigent;
äußerst ~ of the utmost urgency; ~ **verdächtig** highly suspicious;
Zahlung ~ **anmahnen** to press for payment; **etw.** ~ **benötigen** to want s. th. badly; **j.** ~ **um etw. bitten** to beseech (implore) s. o.; ~ **um Ruhe bitten** to insist on silence; ~ **empfehlen** to recommend strongly; ~ **benötigt werden** to be urgently required;
~**e Angelegenheit** pressing matter, matter of great urgency; ~**es Anraten** strong recommendation; ~**er Appell** urgent appeal; ~**es Bedürfnis** urgent need (want), urgency; ~**e Bestellung** rush order; ~**e Bitte** urgent request, adjuration; **jds.** ~**en Bitten willfahren** to yield to one's urgencies; ~**er Fall** urgent case, case of emergency; **zuerst die** ~**sten Fälle erledigen** to deal with the most urgent things first; ~**e Forderung** urgent request; ~**e Gefahr** imminent danger; ~**e Geschäfte** pressure of (pressing) business; ~**es Gespräch** *(tel.)* emergency (priority) call; ~**e Gründe** cogent (compelling) reasons; ~ **notwendige Maßnahme** measure of pressing necessity; ~**e Meldung** priority message; ~**e Nachfrage** pressing demand; ~**e Not** crying need; ~**e Notwendigkeit** dire (urgent) need (necessity); ~**e Postsendungen** urgent items; ~**es Telegramm** priority telegram; ~**er Verdacht** strong suspicion; **auf jds.** ~**e Vorstellungen** at s. one's urgent request; ~**e Zahlungsaufforderung** dunning letter.

dringlich pressing, urgent, exigent;
~ **behandeln** to give urgent attention; **als besonders** ~ **behandeln** to give high priority; ~ **sein** to brook no delay; **äußerst** ~ **sein** to be a matter of great urgency.

Dringlichkeit exigency, priority, urgency;
von höchster ~ of top priority;
größte ~ immediate urgency;
~ **eines Falles hervorheben** to urge the necessity of a case;
der ~ **ensprechend behandelt werden** to be dealt with in order of priority.

Dringlichkeits|antrag application for priority, *(parl.)* privileged motion, urgency *(Br.)*; ~**antrag stellen** to call for a vote of urgency; ~**auftrag** priority order; ~**bescheinigung** certificate of priority; ~**fall** urgent case, case of urgency; **über eine** ~**frage entscheiden** to establish priority; ~**grad** degree of urgency; ~**klausel** emergency clause; ~**liste** list of priorities, priority list; **persönliche** ~**liste** scale of preference; **am Ende der** ~**liste stehen** to be low on the priorities; ~**reparaturen** emergency repairs; ~**sache** case of emergency.

Dringlichkeitsstufe priority, degree of urgency;
höchste ~ besitzen to have the highest priority; **höchste ~ erhalten** to get top priority; **zur ersten ~ gehören** to come under priority; **hinsichtlich der Zuteilung höchste ~ zuerkennen** to give top priority in the allocation.
Dringlichkeits|verfahren summary procedure; **~vermerk** urgent note (memorandum); **~vermerk tragen** *(Parlament)* to be reported as urgent; **~vorhaben** emergency facilities; **~vorlage** application for priority, urgent case; **hohen ~wert zuerkennen** to put high in one's order of priority.
dritt|e Ausfertigung third [copy]; **aus ~er Hand** at third hand, third-hand; **~er Klasse** third class; **~es Land** *(EG)* outside country; **~e Person** third person (party); **Zahl in die ~e Potenz erheben** to cube a number; **von ~er Qualität** third-class (-rate); **~es Rad am Wagen** *(fig.)* third wheel; **von ~er Seite erfahren** to learn from another source; **an ~er Stelle stehen** to be placed third; **~e Wahl** third quality;
zum ersten, zum zweiten, zum ~en *(Auktion)* going, going, gone.
Dritt|anspruch third-party claim; **~ausfertigung** triplicate, third copy, *(Wechsel)* third of exchange; **~begünstigter** third-party (donee) beneficiary, *(Prozeß)* use plaintiff; **~berechtigter** third party; **~besitzer** third holder; **~beteiligter** third party.
Drittel|beteiligung one-third interest; **~seite** one-third page.
Dritt|er stranger, third [party (person)];
im Auftrag eines ~en by the order of a third party; **im Beisein ~er** before witnesses; **unbeschadet der Rechte ~er** without prejudice to the rights of third parties; **zugunsten eines ~en** for the benefit of a third party;
gutgläubiger ~er bona fide (innocent) third party, *(Wechsel)* holder in due course; **lachender ~er** tertius gaudens; **unbeteiligter ~er** *(Versicherung)* third party;
lachender ~er sein to play both ends against the middle; **bei einem ~en zahlbar stellen** to make payable by a third party; **gerade noch ~er werden** to run a poor third.
dritt|größt third-largest; **~klassig** tin-pot, third-class (-rate); **~klassige Waren** thirds.
Dritt|land third (outside) country; **~mitgliedsland** nonmember country.
drittrangig third-rate (-string).
Drittschuldner garnishee, third-party debtor, factor *(US)*, *(Absatzfinanzierung)* customer;
~ pfänden to garnish, to factorize *(US)*;
~pfändung garnishee proceedings.
Dritt|verwahrung escrow; **~widerspruch** third-party notice; **~widerspruchsklage** interpleader, third-party claim proceedings, third opposition *(Louisiana)*; **~widerspruchskläger** interpleader.
Droge drug, dope, medicine;
gefährliche ~ pernicious drug; **stimulierende ~** pot *(Br.)*;
mit ~n betäuben, ~n verschreiben to drug.
Drogen|aufklärung drug education; **~händler** drug trafficker; **~mißbrauch** drug abuse; **~sucht** drug habit (addiction); **~süchtiger** drug addict.
Drogerie chemist's shop *(Br.)*, drugstore *(US)*;
~waren pharmaceutical products.
Drogist druggist, apothecary, chemist *(Br.)*.
Drohbrief threatening (incendiary, *Scot.*) letter.
drohen to threaten;
jem. mit etw. ~ to hold s. th. over s. o.; **jem. mit der Faust ~** to shake one's fist at s. o.; **jem. mit dem Finger ~** to wag one's finger at s. o.; **mit Krieg ~** to menace war, to rattle the sabre; **einem Angestellten mit der Kündigung ~** to threaten an employee with dismissal; **jem. mit einem Prozeß ~** to threaten s. o. with legal proceedings;
fehlzuschlagen ~ to be in danger of breaking; **zusammenzubrechen ~** to be on the brink (verge) of collapse.
drohend threatening, imminent, menacing, impending;
j. ~ ansehen to give s. o. a lowering look; **~ am Himmel hängen** to hang louring on the sky;
~e Gefahr imminent (threatening) danger; **einer ~en Gefahr gegenübertreten** to counter a threat; **~e Haltung** threatening attitude; **~er Staatsstreich** threat of a coup; **mit ~er Stimme** in a voice of menace; **~en Ton anschlagen** to put a threatening tone in one's voice; **~es Unheil abwenden** to avert an impending disaster; **~es Verhalten** threatening behavio(u)r; **~er Verlust** danger of loss.
Drohne sluggard, drone, good-for-nothing, sponger, parasite, idler.
Drohnen|der Gesellschaft drones of society;
~dasein führen to drone one's life away.
Dröhnen *(Auto)* drone, *(Fabrikhalle)* vibration, *(Geschütze)* rumble, roar, roll, *(Maschinen)* hum, throb, roar, *(Stimme)* roar, boom;
entferntes ~ des Autobahnverkehrs drone of distant motorway traffic.
dröhnen *(Donner, Geschütz)* to rumble, to roar, to roll, *(Maschine)* to hum, to throb, to roar;
vom Lärm der Maschinen ~ to resound with the noise of the engines; **in jds. Ohren ~** to din in s. one's ears.
dröhnend resounding, roaring;
~es Gelächter roaring laughter; **~e Stimme** booming voice.
Drohung threat, compulsion, intimidation, menace;
bei Anwendung von ~en by threats;
leere ~en idle (empty) threats; **schreckliche ~** thunderbolt; **terroristische ~en** terroristic threats; **unbestimmte ~en** vague threats; **versteckte ~** hidden threat; **widerrechtliche ~** unlawful threat;
~ mit Gefahr für Leib und Leben threat to life and limb; **~ mit einem Prozeß** threat action;
~en ausstoßen to pour out (utter) threats; **durch ~en erzwingen** to concuss; **einer ~ nahekommen** to be in the nature of a threat; **~ wahrmachen** to carry out a threat; **j. auffordern, seine ~en wahrzumachen** to call s. one's bluff; **auf ~en hin zahlen** to pay under compulsion; **j. unter Anwendung von ~en zu etw. zwingen** to bully s. o. into doing s. th.
Droschke cab, hackney, hack *(US)*;
leere ~ crawler *(Br.)*.
Droschken|gaul cab horse; **~halteplatz** cab rank *(Br.)*, taxi stand *(US)* (rank), cabstand *(US)*, rank of cabs *(Br.)*.
Drossel *(Auto)* throttle, choke;
~klappe, ~ventil throttle valve.
drosseln to throttle, to choke, *(fig.)* to dampen, to curb, to curtail; **Ausgaben ~** to curb expenditure; **Dollarabfluß ~** to slow down the dollar outflow; **Einfuhr ~** to check back imports; **Geldversorgung ~** to tighten the supply of money; **Löhne ~** to curb wages; **Produktion ~** to restrain (curb, curtail) production, to throttle back the assembly line; **Zugang ~** to choke access.
Drosselung curbing, curb, restraint, checking, dampening;
~ der Ausgaben expenditure cut; **~ der kulturellen Betätigung** cultural dim-out; **~ der Betriebsausstattung** equipment curtailment; **~ der Einfuhr** curb on import; **~ des Geldangebots** monetary curbs, tightening of the money supply; **~ der Inflation** dampening of the inflation; **~ der Investitionstätigkeit** dampening of business spending; **~ des Konsums** curb on consumption; **~ der Produktion** production cut, dampening (curtailing) of production.
Druck pressure, force, squeeze, impact, heaviness, weight, *(Abzug)* impression, *(Beanspruchung)* load, *(Belastung)* stress, strain, *(Buchherstellung)* print[ing], impression, *(Kurse)* depressed state of the market, low level of prices, *(Notlage)* pinch, distress;
gut zum ~ press; **im ~** in course of printing, in print, on (in the) press; **in fettem ~** in bold type; **unter ~** under duress (constraint, compulsion); **unter dem ~ des linken Flügels** under left-wing pressure; **unter dem ~ der Verhältnisse** owing to the force (under the stress) of circumstances; **zum ~ gegeben** down; **anastatischer ~** anastatic printing; **angeschnittener ~** *(Anzeige)* bleed; **atmosphärischer ~** pressure of the atmosphere; **von den Gewerkschaften ausgeübter ~** union pressure; **hinter den Kulissen ausgeübter ~** backstage pressure; **bunter ~** colo(u)red print; **durchgeschlagener ~** blotted print; **finanzieller ~** financial squeeze (load); **fotografischer ~** photoprint; **großer ~** large print (type); **klarer ~** clear print; **kleiner ~** small print (type); **schwer lesbarer ~** print difficult to read; **moralischer ~** moral pressure; **nicht nachlassender ~** unrelenting pressure; **parteipolitischer ~** party whip *(US)*; **schlechter ~** poor print; **unbekannter ~** rare edition; **unreiner ~** slur; **unscharfer ~** unsharp impression; **verschwommener ~** blurred impression; **verwischter ~** mackle; **wirtschaftlicher ~** economic pressure; **zweiter ~** reimpression;
~ der Aktionäre shareholder pressure; **~ von außen** external force; **~ mit Blumenmuster** floral print; **~ von 5000 Exemplaren** run (edition) of 5000 copies; **~ mit Gummiklischee** flexographic printing; **~ der Herstellungskosten** cost-price squeeze; **~ auf die Preise** forcing down the prices; **~ und Satz** composition and presswork; **~ im Staatsauftrag** public printing; **~ auf die Tränendrüsen** sob stuff *(US sl.)*; **~ des Umweltschutzes** environmentalist pressure; **~ auf die Unternehmergewinne** squeeze on profits; **~ der Verhältnisse** pressure of circumstances;

~ **ausüben** to clamp down, to bring pressure to bear, to exert pressure; **wirtschaftlichen ~ ausüben** to exert economic pressure; ~ **auf den Geldmarkt ausüben (verursachen)** to place pressure on the money market; **keines besonderen ~s bedürfen** not to need much pressing; **sich im ~ befinden** to print, to be printing; **mit dem ~ beginnen** to start printing; ~ **dahintermachen** to step on it; **im ~ zuviel ergeben** to run over; **im ~ erscheinen** to appear in print (type), to be published; **Buch für den ~ fertigmachen** to get a book ready for the press; **in ~ geben** to [put into] print, to send to press; **schnellstens in ~ geben** to rush into print; **in ~ gehen** to go to press; ~ **nötig haben** to require pressing; **unter ~ handeln** to act under duress (pressure); **durch fetten ~ hervorheben** to print in bold type; **dem ~ nachgeben** to give way to pressure; **dem ~ der öffentlichen Meinung nachgeben** to yield to the pressure of public opinion; **dem ~ des Wassers nachgeben** to yield to the pressure of the water; ~ **von jem. nehmen** to make it easier on s. o.; **im ~ sein** to be printing; **finanziell im ~ sein** to be pinched for money; **mächtig im ~ sein** to be in a quandary; **nicht dem ~ der öffentlichen Meinung vor den Wahlen ausgesetzt sein** to be free of election-eve pressure; **schwer im ~ sein** to be in a quandary as to what to do next, to be hard up; **zeitlich schwer im ~ sein** to be hard pressed for time; **durch ~ auf einen Knopf in Betrieb setzen** to operate by pressing a button; **j. unter ~ setzen** to bring pressure to bear upon s. o., to put s. o. under constraint, to force s. one's hand, to squeeze s. o., to put the fix (bite, *US sl.*) on s. o., to exert undue influence on s. o., to put the squeeze on s. o., to pressure s. o. *(US)*; **Kessel unter ~ setzen** to get up steam; **j. kräftig unter ~ setzen** to lean hard on s. o. to do s. th.; **Vorstand unter ~ setzen** to put pressure on the management; ~ **in der Magengrube spüren** to have a sensation of pressure in the pit of one's stomach; **unter ~ stehen** to be under pressure; **von zwei Seiten her unter ~ stehen** to be between the upper and the nether millstone; ~ **eines Buches übernehmen** to undertake to print a book; ~ **überwachen** to supervise the printing; ~ **vermindern** to ease pressure; **unter ~ gesetzt werden** to be under pressure; **von seinen Gläubigern unter ~ gesetzt werden** to be pressed by one's creditors; **zum ~ freigegeben werden** to pass the proofs for press;

~**abfall** pressure drop; ~**änderungskarte** *(Wetter)* isobaric chart; ~**angabe** printer's imprint.

druckangeschnitten *(Anzeige)* bleed.

Druck|anstalt printing plant; ~**anwendung** pressure; ~**anzeiger** pressure gauge; ~**arbeiten** printing, presswork; **kleinere ~arbeiten** job printing; ~**auflage** print run; **sehr hohe ~auflage** immense printing; ~**auftrag** printing order; ~**ausfall** quality of prints; ~**ausgleich** pressure balance; **für ~ausgleich saisonaler Schwankungen sorgen** to ease seasonality pressures; ~**ausgleichskammer** decompression chamber; ~**ausübung** bringing pressure to bear; ~**beanspruchung** compressive stress; ~**beginn** start of printing; ~**behälter** pressure tank, vessel; ~**belüftung** *(Kabine)* pressurization; ~**berichtigung** correction of the press; ~**bewilligung** imprimatur, licence to print; ~**bleistift** propelling (automatic, *US*) pencil; ~**bogen** proof, news (printed) sheet; **noch unaufgeschnittener ~bogen** bolt; **vor Veröffentlichung zugesandte ~bogen** advance sheets; ~**bogen abziehen** to draw off a sheet; ~**buchstabe** block letter; **in ~buchstaben schreiben** to print, to write in typographical characters (block letters).

druckdicht|halten to pressurize;
~**e Kabine** pressurized cabin.

Drückeberger shirker, slacker, hedger, malingerer, skulker, embusque, quitter, picker *(US sl.)*, goldbrick *(US)*, crawfish *(US sl.)*, *(mil.)* dodger, skiver, scrimshanker *(Br.)*, draft evader *(US)*.

Drückebergerei dodging, shirking, flunk, soldiering *(sl.)*, get-off, skulk;
~ **vor dem Wehrdienst** draft evasion.

Drucken printing.

drucken to print, to imprint;
zu große Auflage ~ to overprint; **140 Blätter in der Minute ~** to run off 140 copies a minute; **Buch ~** to publish a book; **druckangeschnitten ~** to bleed; **Flugblätter ~** to print leaflets; **gesperrt ~** to space (blank) out; **kursiv ~** to print in italics; **Muster auf Stoff ~** to print material; **im Offsetverfahren ~** to offset; **zu schwach ~** to underprint; **5000 Stück ~** to strike (run) off 5000 copies; **unsauber ~** to print full of monks; **Zeitung ~** to print a newspaper;
~ **lassen** to bring out, to publish, to [put in] print.

drücken to press, to squeeze, *(Preise)* to bring (run) down, to lower, to bang, to depress;
sich ~ to back out, to goldbrick, to hedge, to duck, to skulk, to evade, to shirk, to wriggle out of, to take evasive action *(sl.)*, to play hookey *(US)*, to swing the lead *(Br., sl.)*, to funk out *(US)*, *(mil.)* to scrimshank *(Br.)*, to soldier *(sl.)*, to worm out of *(sl.)*; **sich in ein überfülltes Abteil ~** to squeeze one's way into an overcrowded compartment; **Anklagebank ~** to be in the dock; **sich vor der Arbeit ~** to shirk work; **sich vor der Beantwortung einer Frage ~** to shirk (dodge) a question; **sich ängstlich in die Ecke ~** to huddle frightened in a corner; **auf jds. Gewissen ~** to weigh on s. one's conscience; **jem. die Hand ~** to clasp s. one's hand; **Hebel nach unten ~** to push a lever downward; **Kleider in einen Koffer ~** to crush clothes in a suitcase; **auf den Knopf ~** to press the button; **Kurse ~** to run down prices; **Leistungen ~** to force down the standard of work; **Markt ~** to depress the market; **sich um den Militärdienst ~** to dodge military service; **auf die Preise ~** to force down the prices; **Rekord ~** to lower a record; **Schulbank ~** to go to school; **Siegel auf einen Brief ~** to impress a seal on a letter; **stark ~** *(Kurse)* to knock down *(coll.)*; **Stempel auf eine Urkunde ~** to stamp a document; **jds. Stimmung ~** to cast a gloom on s. o., to spoil s. one's day; **in der Menge zu Tode ~** to crush to death in the crowd; **auf die Tränendrüsen ~** to appeal to the emotions, to be a tearjerker *(US sl.)*; **auf die Tube ~** *(fam.)* to step on it, to step on the gas *(coll.)*; **sich vor der Verantwortung ~** to shirk the responsibility, to pass the buck *(US sl.)*; **j. an die Wand ~** to pin s. o. to the wall, to push s. o. aside.

drückend heavy, onerous, pressing, *(Luft)* stuffy, stifling, *(Stimmung)* gloomy, depressing, dismal;
sich ~ bemerkbar machen *(Steuer)* to press down heavily;
~**e Abgaben** oppressive taxes; ~**e Armut** pressure of poverty, dire need, grinding poverty; ~**e Bedingungen** onerous terms; ~**e Schulden** heavy-weighing debts; ~**es Schweigen** blank silence; ~**e Steuern** pressure of taxation; ~**es Wetter** sulky weather.

Drucker printer, printing worker, pressman, presser;
~ **ohne Gewerkschaftsausweis** rat *(sl.)*; ~ **und Verleger** printer and publisher;
~ **sein** to print.

Drücker push-button.

Druckerei printing establishment (office, shop, *US*), printery *(US)*, *(Raum)* pressroom;
kleine ~ job press;
in einer ~ arbeiten to work at a printer's; ~ **immer rechtzeitig beliefern** to keep neck and neck with the printers *(fam.)*;
~**besitzer** printer; ~**betrieb** printing establishment (plant), printer; ~**gehilfe** printer's devil; **ins ~geschäft einsteigen** to go into printing.

Drucker|gewerbe business of printing, printing trade (industry); ~**gewerkschaft** print union.

Druckerlaubnis imprimatur, privilege of printing a book, licence to print, printer's licence (permission);
~ **erteilen** to pass the proofs for press.

Druckerpresse letterpress, printing press *(Br.)*.

Drückerschloß thumb lock.

Drucker|schwärze printer's (printing) ink, colo(u)r; ~**zeichen** printer's mark.

druckfähig fit for printing, printable;
nicht ~ unprintable;
~ **sein** to be in type;
~**e Korrekturbogen** press revise (proof); ~**e Sache** press matter.

Druck|fahne galley proof, proof (advance) sheet, slip; ~**fahnenkorrektur** correction of proof sheets; ~**farbe** printer's ink.

Druckfehler printer's (literal, printing) error, error of the press, misprint, typographical error;
~ **feststellen** to note a misprint; ~ **übersehen** to overlook a printer's error;
~**teufel** printer's devil; ~**verzeichnis** corrigenda, errata.

druckfertig ready for (to go to) press, live, o. k. *(US)*, imprimatur;
für ~ erklären to sign for press, to okay to print *(US)*; ~ **sein** to be in type;
~**e Korrekturbogen** press revise (proof); ~**es Manuskript** fair copy; ~**er Satz** live matter.

druck|fest pressure-proof; ~**feucht** moist from press.

Druckform printing block, form;
~ **schließen** to quoin; ~ **stehenlassen** to keep the type standing.

Druck|formular printed form; ~**gang** run; **in einem ~gang** in one printing; ~**gefälle** pressure drop (gradient); ~**genehmigung** imprimatur, printer's licence; ~**gewerbe** printing trade; ~**größen** type sizes; ~**höhenmesser** pressure altimeter; ~**jahr** year of publication, date of impression; ~**kammer** pressure chamber; ~**kessel** pressure boiler.

Druckknopf push (press) button;
~**abstimmung** push-button tuning; ~**krieg** press-button war; ~**schaltung** push-button switching; ~**staat** push-button state; ~**steuerung** push-button control; ~**zugang** push-button access.
Druckkontakt *(el.)* press key.
Druckkosten printing expenses (cost, charges), costs of printing;
~**auftrag veranschlagen** to estimate a job of printing; ~**gebühr** *(Patent)* fee for printing; ~**rechnung decken** to offset the publisher's costs; ~**voranschlag** printing estimate.
Druckkugelschreiber ball-point pen.
Drucklegung going to press, printing;
während der ~ des Berichtes while the report was going to press;
~ **eines Buches überwachen** to see a work through the press.
Druck|legungsgebühr printing fee; ~**legungskosten** printing expenses (costs); ~**leiste** bearer; ~**leistung** printing capacity.
Druckluft compressed air;
mit ~ betätigt (betrieben) pneumatically (air-) operated;
~**anlage** pneumatic system; ~**behälter für eine Scheibenwaschanlage** windshield washer reservoir; ~**bremse** pneumatic brake; ~**einspritzung** air injection; ~**kabine** pressurized compartment; ~**messer** manometer.
Druck|maschine, vollautomatisierte ~- und Setzmaschine computerized press; ~**maschinen verlassen** to roll off the presses.
Druckmittel leverage, lever;
~ **gegen j. anwenden** to bring pressure to bear upon s. o.; **kein ~ gegen j. haben** to have nothing on s. o., to have no leverage to be able to bring to bear on s. o.
Druck|muster print; ~**ort** place of publication; ~**ortangabe** publisher's imprint; ~**papier** printing paper; **matt satiniertes ~papier** English finish; ~**platte** stereotype, printing plate (engraving), *(Banknoten)* bed piece; ~**platten herstellen** to plate.
Druckposten *(fig.)* soft (desk, cushy) job, snap, gravy train *(US sl.)*;
~ **erhalten** to board the gravy train *(US sl.)*; **seinen ~ verlieren** to fall off the gravy train *(US)*.
Druckpresse letterpress, printing press;
~ **aufstellen** to erect a printing press.
Druck|probe proof [sheet]; ~**pumpe** pressure pump; ~**punkt** pressure point; ~**regler** pressure regulator.
druckreif good (fit) for printing, ready for press, okay *(US)*, O. K. *(US)*;
~ **nach Korrektur** okay with corrections *(US)*;
für ~ erklären to sign for press, to okay to print *(US)*.
Druckrohr delivery pipe.
Drucksache printed matter (paper, *Br.*), insert, leaflet;
als ~ as printed paper, by bookpost *(Br.)*;
~**n** printed papers *(Br.)* (matter), literature, halfpenny post *(Br.)*, *(Zeitungen)* second-class mail *(US)*;
großformatige ~ broadsheet;
~ **zu ermäßigter Gebühr** printed papers at reduced rate;
als ~ verschicken to send by bookpost *(Br.)*.
Drucksachen|bezugspreis subscription rate by surface mail; ~**briefmarke** second-class stamp.
Drucksachengebühr printed papers reduced rate, book postage *(Br.)*;
normale ~ surface mail printed paper full rate;
~ **mit Luftpostzuschlag** air mail printed paper rate *(Br.)*.
Drucksachen|porto printed paper rate, rate for printed matter; ~**post** bookpost *(Br.)*, newspaper post, second- (third-) class mail *(US)*; ~**tarif** printed paper rate; ~**tarif für Zeitungen** newspaper rates; ~**werbung** printed (direct mail, *US*) advertising.
Drucksatz composition, matter, type, set;
~ **stehenlassen** to keep the type standing.
Druck|schleuse air lock; ~**schloß** latch; ~**schmierung** forced lubrication; ~**schraube** *(Flugzeug)* pusher airscrew (propeller, *US*).
Druckschrift printed matter, print, printscript, publication, *(Druckbuchstaben)* block letters;
geheftete ~ brochure; **öffentliche ~** printed publication;
Adresse in ~ schreiben to print an address; **seinen Namen in ~ schreiben** to print one's name.
druckschriftliche Veröffentlichung printed publication.
Druck|schwankungen variations of pressure; ~**seite** printed page; ~**seite abgeben** to make up a page of type.
drucksen, mit der Antwort to hum and haw before answering.
Druck|spalte column of type; ~**stift** push pencil; ~**stock** block *(Br.)*, engraving *(US)*, stereo plate, cliché; **ausgefräster ~stock** routed plate; ~**stoff** print cloth; ~**taste** press key; ~**tastenbedienung** push-button operation; ~**tasteneinteilung** push-button turning; ~**tastenwahl** *(Telefon)* push-button dialling; ~**turbine** pressure turbine; ~**type** type; **bestimmte ~typen nicht vorrätig haben** to be short of certain types; ~**unterlagen** copy, manuscript, artwork; ~**ventil** delivery valve; ~**verfahren** printing process (method); ~**vermerk** publisher's imprint, impressum, imprinting; ~**verzögerung** printing delay; ~**vorgang eines Buches überwachen** to supervise the printing of a book; ~**vorlage** manuscript, copy, artwork; ~**vorschrift** manual; ~**walze** mill, roller, printing roll; ~**waren** prints, printed goods; ~**wasserspeicher** hydraulic accumulator; ~**welle** pressure wave; ~**zeile** printline.
Drum und Dran, mit allem lock, stock and barrel; hook, line and sinker;
für das ganze ~ einer konventionellen Beerdigung zu zahlen haben to have to pay for all those top hats.
drunter und drüber upside down, topsy-turvy;
~ **gehen** to be at sixes and sevens.
Dschungelkrieg jungle warfare.
Dschunke junk.
Dübel treenail, plug, dowel.
dubiose|Forderung doubtful claim, bad debt *(Br.)*; ~**s Papier** unsafe paper.
Dubiosen bad *(US)* (doubtful, *Br.*) debts;
steuerlich anerkannte ~ debts written off as bad debts for tax purpose *(US)*;
~**konto** bad-debts account *(US)*; ~**rücklagen** bad-debt reserves *(US)*.
Dubleegold rolled gold.
Dublette duplicate, *(Juwelier)* doublet.
ducken, j. ~ to take s. o. down a peg or two, to soft-sell s. o. *(US sl.)*; **sich vor jem. ~** to cringe (humble o. s.) before s. o.; **sich vor einem Schlag ~** to duck to avoid a blow.
Duckmäuser cringer, servile person, goody-goody, yes-man.
Duckmäuserei cringing, servility, slyness, sneaking.
Dudelei drone, droning, *(Drehorgel)* grinding.
dudeln to drone, to hum.
Duell duel.
Duellant duellist.
duellieren, sich to fight a duel.
Duellpistolen duelling pistols.
Duft smell, odo(u)r, *(Zigarre)* perfume, fragrance, aroma.
duften to smell, to have a scent, to be fragant.
duftig *(Material)* filmy, foamy, gossamer.
Dukaten shiners *(sl.)*;
~**esel** [etwa] money spinner, cash coiner; ~**esel erfinden** to devise a scheme for making money.
dulden to put up with, to suffer, to endure, to tolerate, to bear;
keinen Aufschub ~ to brook no delay; **jds. Eigenarten ~** to put up with s. one's pecularities; **etw. stillschweigend ~** to shut one's eyes to s. th.; **keinen Widerspruch ~** not to bear contradiction.
Duldermiene martyred expression.
Duldung toleration, endurance, *(jur.)* sufferance;
stillschweigende ~ connivance, *(Landbenutzung)* implied dedication;
~ **des Rechtsscheins** holding out *(Br.)*.
Dumdumgeschoß dumdum bullet.
Dumm, der ~e sein to have to pay the piper, to be left holding the baby *(US)*; **den ~en spielen** to play the fool.
dumm stupid, silly, dense, thick, dumb *(US coll.)*;
~ **wie Bohnenstroh** as stupid as an owl (donkey, goose);
~ **ablaufen** to end badly; **sich ~ benehmen** to behave stupidly; **j. ~ und dämlich reden** to talk one's head off to s. o.; **unsagbar ~ sein** to be too silly for words; **sich ~ stellen** to play the idiot, to pretend ignorance, to achieve one's end; **j. für ~ verkaufen** to sell s. o. a packet *(coll.)*;
~**e Fragen stellen** to ask stupid questions; ~**e Geschichte** nasty business; ~**e Sache** awkward situation; **jem. einen ~en Streich spielen** to play s. o. up *(fam.)*; ~**en Unsinn reden** to talk double Dutch; ~**es Zeug** nonsense, rubbish, poppycock *(US coll.)*; ~**es Zeug reden** to talk nonsense, to be right of it *(sl.)*.
dummdreist saucy, cheeky.
dümmer sein als die Polizei erlaubt to be too stupid to come out in the rain.
Dummerchen little nilly.
Dummerjungenstreich schoolboy prank.
Dummheit stupidity, denseness, foolishness, dumbness *(US)*, *(Taktlosigkeit)* gaffe, faux pas, indiscretion;
entsetzliche ~ wretched stupidity; **hoffnungslose ~** dense ignorance;

~ **begehen** to put one's foot in it, to make a blunder; **j. vor ~en bewahren** to keep s. o. out of mischief; **nichts als ~en im Kopf haben** to play the fool all the time; ~ **machen** to do a stupid (foolish) thing; **jede nur mögliche ~ machen** to play all sorts of pranks; **grenzenlose ~ sein** to be the height of folly; **immer auf ~en aus sein** to be full of mischief; **der eigenen ~ zuzuschreiben sein** to pay for one's own folly; **seine ~ zur Schau stellen** to expose one's ignorance.

Dummkopf fool, ninny, nitwit, know-nothing, donkey, hash, blockhead, goose, thick *(sl.)*, jay *(sl.)*;
absoluter ~ positive fool; **alter** ~ silly old fool;
kein ~ sein to know a thing or two.

dumpf|dahinleben to lead a torpid existence;
~**e Ahnung haben** to have a vague feeling; **in ~es Brüten versinken** to lapse into brooding meditation; ~**es Gebrüll** low roaring; ~**es Geläut einer Glocke** muffled sound of a bell; ~**er Geschützdonner in der Ferne** rumble of guns in the distance; ~**e Gruft** damp vault; ~**e Kellerluft** musty air of the cellar; ~**es Rollen eines Wagens** rumble of carriage wheels; ~**er Schmerz** dull pain; ~**es Schweigen** heavy (gloomy) silence.

dumpfig musty, fusty;
~**er Keller** damp and musty cellar.

Dumping dumping, underselling;
verschleiertes ~ hidden dumping;
~ **betreiben** to dump;
~**bekämpfungszoll** antidumping tariff; ~**klage** dumping complaint; ~**klage erheben** to file a dumping complaint; ~**praktiken** dumping practices; ~**preis** dumping price; ~**spanne** margin of dumping; ~**verfahren** dumping charge, suit of dumping; ~**waren** dumped goods.

Düne dune, down.

Düngemittel manure, fertilizer;
künstliche ~ chemical (artificial) fertilizer;
~**industrie** fertilizer industry.

düngen to muck, to manure;
Boden ~ to fertilize (manure) the soil.

Dünger manure, fertilizer;
~**grube** manure (dung) pit.

Dunkel dark, shade;
in tiefes ~ gehüllt shrouded in darkness;
~ **der Nacht** darkness of the night;
im ~n bleiben *(Verbrechen)* to remain unsolved; **sich in geheimnisvolles ~ hüllen** to wrap o. s. in mystery; **im ~n lassen** to lurk in the dark; **alles im ~n lassen** to keep dark *(coll.)*; ~ **um einen Fall lichten** to clear up a mystery; **im ~ der Zukunft verborgen liegen** to be hidden in the future; **über jds. Pläne völlig im ~n gelassen sein** to be in complete darkness as to s. one's plans; **im ~n tappen** to be (grope) in the dark; **ins ~ zurücksinken** to sink into obscuritiy.

dunkel dark, dim, *(dubios)* sinister, fishy, shady, *(düster)* gloomy, dusky, dismal, somber *(US)*, sombre *(Br.)*, *(ungewiß)* dark, doubtful, uncertain, obscure, *(verschwommen)* dim, faint, murky;
~ **aussehen** *(Zukunft)* to be filled with gloom; **zu den ~sten Kapiteln der Geschichte gehören** to belong to the blackest chapters of history; **Zimmer ~ machen** to darken a flat; ~ **in Erinnerung sein** to be a blurred memory;.

Dünkel conceit, vanity, priggery, *(Arroganz)* presumption, arrogance;
jem. seinen ~ austreiben to do s. o. out of his vanity; **an seinem ~ fast ersticken** to be eaten up with self-conceit.

dünkelhaft proud, self-conceited, vain.

Dunkelheit dark, darkness, gloominess;
im Schutz der ~ by the help of the darkness; **in völliger** ~ in complete darkness; **unter dem Schutz der** ~ under cover of darkness.

Dunkelkammer darkroom, camera obscura;
~**ausrüstung** darkroom equipment; ~**lampe** safelight.

dunkle|Absichten deep designs; ~ **Absichten hegen** to harbo(u)r dark designs; ~ **Anspielungen** dark allusions; ~**r Begriff** unclear (vague) idea; ~**s Bier** dark (brown) beer; ~**r Ehrenmann** shady gentleman; ~**r Erdteil** Dark Continent; ~ **Erinnerung haben** to have a faint recollection; ~ **Existenz führen** to lead a mysterious life; ~**s Geheimnis** dark secret; ~ **Geschäfte** dubious dealings, shady transactions (business); **von ~r Hautfarbe sein** to be dark-skinned; **in ~r Nacht** in the darkness of the night; ~ **Pläne aushecken** to make sinister plans; ~**r Punkt in der Familie** skeleton in the cupboard; ~**r Sinn einer Rede** obscure meaning of a speech; ~ **Stimme** sombre voice; ~ **Textstelle** obscure passage; ~ **Vergangenheit** murky past *(coll.)*; ~ **Zimmerecke** dark corner of a room.

dünn thin, fine, delicate, flimsy, *(Person)* thin, lean, meagre, *(kümmerlich)* wishy-washy, weak, poor;
~ **bevölkert (besiedelt)** thin-peopled, thinly (sparsely) settled (populated); ~ **gesät** scarce, rare, few and far between;
~ **wie ein Faden** as thin as a lath;
sich ~e machen to hook (hop, *Br.*) it, to scram *(US)*, to light out *(sl.)*;
~**er Dunstschleier** fine haze; ~**e Entschuldigung** thin (paltry) excuse; ~**es Ergebnis** poor result; **an einem ~en Faden hängen** to hang by a thread; ~**er Kaffee** weak coffee; ~**er Stoff** fine fabric.

Dünndruck|ausgabe thin-paper (India paper) edition; ~**papier** thin printing paper, India paper.

Dunst mist, haze, vapo(u)r;
in ~ gehüllt enveloped in haze;
blauer ~ hot air; **nebliger** ~ foggy mist;
in Rauch und ~ aufgehen to end up in smoke; **sich in ~ auflösen** *(Wasser)* to dissolve in fine spray; **sich in blauen ~ auflösen** to vanish into thin air; **keinen blassen ~ davon haben** to have not the foggiest notion (faintest idea), not to know the first thing about it; **im ~ schwimmen** *(Berge)* to fade away in blue haze; **jem. blauen ~ vormachen** to blow (throw) dust in s. one's eyes, to gas s. o. *(sl.)*.

dünsten, auf kleiner Flamme to stew on low heat.

Dunstglocke smog.

dunstig hazy, misty;
~**e Waschküche** steamy washhouse; ~**es Wetter** misty (hazy) weather.

Dunstschleier haze.

Duodezfürst petty prince.

Duplexbetrieb duplex working.

Duplik rejoinder.

Duplikat tally, duplication, duplicate [copy], counterpart, double;
~ **anfertigen** to duplicate, to make out in duplicate; **Wechsel im ~ ausstellen** to draw bills in sets;
~**ätzung** duplicate block; ~**frachtbrief** duplicate consignment note; ~**quittung** receipt in duplicate, duplicate receipt; ~**rechnung** duplicate invoice.

duplizieren to make a rejoinder, to rejoin.

Duplizität duplicity;
~ **der Ereignisse** pair of similar occurences.

durch und durch out and out, first and last, throughgoing, to the backbone, straight *(US)*, from the ground up *(US)*;
~ **verdorben** rotten in the core;
~ **ein Engländer** British to the quirk; ~ **ein Gentleman** every inch a gentleman; ~ **Politiker** politician to the backbone;
London ~ kennen to know London like the back of one's hand;
~ **ein Egoist sein** to be a thoroughpaced egoist.

durchackern, etw. to plough through s. th.; **Buch** ~ to work through a book.

durcharbeiten to work without a break, *(sorgfältig prüfen)* to study thoroughly, to make a thorough study;
Akten ~ to study the files thoroughly; **sich bis zum Ausgang** ~ to work one's way through to the exit; **Buch sorgfältig** ~ to make a thorough study of a book; **sich mit Mühe** ~ to work round; **ganze Nacht** ~ to burn the midnight oil; **Woche** ~ to work out the week.

durcharbeitete Nacht night spent with work.

durchbeißen, sich to fight one's way through.

durchbekommen, Gesetz schnellstens to rattle a bill through the house *(Br.)*, to railroad a bill *(US)*.

durchberaten to discuss from point to point (thoroughly);
Gesetz ~ to read a bill; **Sache sorgfältig** ~ to go over and over the same ground; **Zolltarif** ~ to debate the tariff question.

durchbetteln, sich to beg one's way, to live by begging.

durchbeuteln, j. tüchtig to shake s. o. like a rat.

durchblättern to thumb through, to run over, to page through;
Buch ~ to leaf through a book *(US)*; **Buch flüchtig** ~ to ruffle a book; **etw. rasch** ~ to have a quick leaf-through.

Durchblick vista, view, perspective;
~ **durch eine Baumreihe** vista between a row of trees.

durchblicken to look (peep) through;
~ **lassen** to give to understand, to intimate, to hint.

Durchblutung blood circulation.

durchbohren to pierce, to bore;
j. mit seinen Augen ~ to pierce s. o. through and through; **Loch durch ein Brett** ~ to bore a hole through a board.

durchbohrend ansehen, j. to look s. o. in the face.

durchboxen, sich nach oben to jostle one's way to the front.

Durchbrechen|der Blockade running the blockade; ~ **der Schallmauer** breakthrough of the sound barrier.

durchbrechen to break through, to break free;
Absperrkette ~ to break through the barrier; **alle Anstandsregeln** ~ to violate all the rules of etiquette; **Blockade** ~ to run the blockade; **Damm** ~ to burst a dam; **feindliche Linien** ~ to pierce the enemy's lines; **Polizeikordon** ~ to break through a police cordon; **alle Regeln** ~ to ignore all rules; **Schallmauer** ~ to break through (crash) the sound barrier; **Verbindung zum Nebenhaus** ~ to cut a passage through to the next house; **Verbindungsstraße** ~ to open a thoroughfare; **Wand** ~ to break through a wall.

durchbrennen to make tracks *(US sl.)*, to welch, to run away, to vamoose *(US sl.)*, *(el.)* to burn out, to blow, to fuse *(Br.)*;
mit der Kasse ~ to make off with the money, to shoot the moon *(sl.)*; **mit seinem Liebhaber** ~ to elope with one's lover.

Durchbringen einer Gesetzesvorlage passage of a law, carriage of a bill *(US)*.

durchbringen *(Kandidat)* to run in;
sich ~ to manage; **sich ehrlich** ~ to make an honest living; **Antrag** ~ to carry a motion, to get a resolution adopted; **Geld** ~ to dissipate, to squander, to waste; **Gesetz** ~ to pass a law, to engineer a law through Congress *(US)*; **alle Kinder allein** ~ to rear one's children all by o. s.; **sich kümmerlich** ~ to scrape a living, to scruff; **Patienten** ~ to pull through a patient; **sein ganzes Vermögen** ~ to run through one's fortune.

durchbrochen *(Wolkendecke)* broken.

Durchbruch gap, opening, aperture, *(mil.)* breakthrough, *(Luft)* burst;
waffentechnischer ~ armo(u)red breakthrough;
~ **durch die Schallmauer** breaking of the sound barrier;
~ **erzielen** *(Autor)* to become known; **politischen** ~ **im ganzen Land erzielen** to achieve a breakthrough in national political terms; **zum** ~ **kommen** to become manifest; **einer Ansicht zum** ~ **verhelfen** to help propagate an idea.

Durchbruchstaktik shock tactics.

durch|buchen to book through; **Nacht** ~**bummeln** to make a night of it; ~**dacht** mature; ~**dachte Argumente** profound arguments; **Waren** ~**deklarieren** to enter goods as transit; ~**denken** to think over; ~**diskutieren** to thrash out.

durchdrängeln to push (force) one's way;
sich durch eine Menschenmenge ~ to bustle through the crowd; **sich rücksichtslos** ~ to push one's way through the crowd.

durchdrehen to go mad;
völlig ~ to have a nervous breakdown, to go clean off one's head, to crack up, to go to pieces, to get the screaming, abdabs *(fam.)*;
Motor ~ **lassen** to race the engine.

durchdringen to penetrate, to permeate, to pervade, *(Meinung)* to carry one's point, to prevail;
Finsternis ~ to pierce the darkness; **mit seiner Klage** ~ to win one's case; **feindliche Linien** ~ to penetrate the enemy's lines; **mit dem Verstand** ~ to grasp (fathom) with one's intellect; **mit einem Vorschlag** ~ to find acceptance for one's proposal.

durchdringend penetrating, penetrant, *(Verstand)* keen, percing, acute, incisive;
~**er Geruch** pungent smell; ~**e Kälte** piercing (biting) cold; ~**e Stimme** shrill (penetrating) voice.

Durchdringung penetration, infiltration, impregnation;
friedliche ~ peaceful penetration; **gegenseitige** ~ interpenetration; **wirtschaftliche** ~ economic penetration.

Durchdrücken des Gashebels full depression of the pedal.

durchdrücken to force, to hustle, to rush, *(Typen)* to come through;
Beschluß in wenigen Tagen ~ to rush an order [through] in a few days; **Beschlüsse in einer Versammlung** ~ to rush resolutions through an assembly; **Gashebel** ~ to open the throttle; **Gesetz** ~ to rattle a bill through Parliament *(Br.)*, to railroad a bill through Congress *(US)*; **sich durch eine Menschenmenge** ~ to force one's way through the crowd; **sich auf der anderen Seite** ~ *(Stempel)* to come through on the other side; **seinen Willen** ~ to get one's way.

Durcheinander helterskelter, topsy-turvy, muddle, mess, pie, hash, jumble, juggermugger, upset, clutter, tangle, puddle, mix-up, medley, litter, derangement, chaos, disarray, din, flap *(sl.)*, *(Verkehr)* dislocation of traffic;
großes ~ devil among the tailors; **heilloses** ~ utter confusion, snafu *(US sl.)*; **hoffnungsloses** ~ haywire *(US sl.)*; **ganz schönes** ~ pretty state of affairs; **wildes** ~ topsy-turvydom, shambles; **ziemliches** ~ a pretty kettle of fish;
~ **von Stimmen** hubbub of voices; **bürokratisches** ~ **und staatliche Überorganisation** muddle and waste of government departments;
~ **anrichten** to make a hash of it *(fam.)*; **riesiges** ~ **anrichten** to put everything out of order; **Ordnung in ein** ~ **bringen** to straighten out a muddle; **wüstes** ~ **darstellen** *(Zimmer)* to be in a state of utter confusion.

durcheinander topsy-turvy, higgledy-piggledy;
vollkommen ~ upside-down;
völlig ~ **geraten** to get into knots; **ganz** ~ **sein** to be at sixes and sevens; **ganz schön** ~ **sein** to be in a proper mess; **völlig** ~ **sein** to be struck (knocked) all of a heap *(coll.)*, to be in a muddle; **ziemlich** ~ **sein** to be in a fine fuss.

Durcheinanderbringen topsy-tursivication.

durcheinanderbringen to mix up, to pie, to muddle, to confuse, to turn topsy-turvy, to [throw into] disorder, to throw a monkey wrench into the machinery, to puzzle, to disarrange, to derange, to confound, to overset;
j. ~ to confuse s. o.; **alles** ~ to turn everything upside down; **Angelegenheit völlig** ~ to make a muddle of an affair; **Buchführung** to muddle account books; **Konten** ~ to confuse accounts; **Papiere auf einem Schreibtisch** ~ to disturb the papers on a desk; **Preise** ~ to put a crimp in prices *(US sl.)*; **etw. ganz schön** ~ to make a precious mess of s. th.; **Verkehr** ~ to dislocate the traffic; **etw. völlig** ~ to play havoc with s. th., to turn s. th. topsy-turvy; **sein Zimmer völlig** ~ to litter up one's room.

durcheinander|gekommen *(Preise)* out of line *(US)*; ~**geworfen** scrambled; **kunterbunt** ~**liegen** to be all in a tumble; ~**reden** to talk all at once.

durcheinanderwerfen to muddle (jumble) up, to make hay of;
alle Begriffe ~ to get everything mixed up; **Bücher** ~ to tumble books about.

durchfahren *(Auto)* to drive (pass) through, *(Schiff)* to sail through, *(Zug)* to go straight (right) through, to run with express speed (with few stops);
j. wie ein Blitz ~ to come over s. o. like a flash; **bei Gelb** ~ to run an amber *(Br.)* (yellow, *US*) light; **bis A. ohne Halt** ~ to go nonstop to A.; **Land auf dem kürzesten Wege** ~ to rush through a country; **ganze Nacht** ~ to travel all night; **bei Rot** ~ to run a red light.

Durchfahrt passage, thoroughfare, opening;
bloße ~ *(Völkerrecht)* simple passage; **enge** ~ narrow passage; **freie** ~ clear passage; **friedliche** ~ *(Völkerrecht)* innocent passage;
~ **verboten!** no passage (thoroughfare)!;
~ **durch den Kanal** passage through the canal;
~ **freihalten** don't block the passage (driveway, *US*); ~ **gestatten** to yield passage; **auf der** ~ **sein** to be passing through;
~**erlaubnis** transit pass.

Durchfahrtshöhe headroom, overhead clearance.

Durchfahrtsrecht right of passage;
vorrangiges ~ priority passage;
~ **auf öffentlichen Gewässern** public passage.

Durchfahrts|signal *(Bahn)* green light; ~**straße** through-road, thoroughfare; ~**verbot** no thoroughfare; ~**zoll** transit duty, toll.

Durchfallen *(Examen)* failure, fiasco, washout, plough, pluck *(Br.)*, *(Theaterstück)* flop.

durchfallen *(Antrag)* to be rejected (lost, turned down), *(Prüfling)* to break down, to fall through, to fail, to be plucked *(Br.)*, to be floored (knocked out), to make a boss shot *(sl.)*, *(Theaterstück)* to flop, to be rejected, *(Wahl)* to be defeated;
im Examen ~ to fail (flunk, *US*) in an examination, to be plucked *(Br.)*; **durch schwindelhafte Stimmenzählung** ~ to count out *(US sl.)*;
~ **lassen** *(Klubkandidat)* to pip *(Br., sl.)*; **Hälfte der Prüflinge** ~ **lassen** to pluck half the candidates *(Br.)*; **Stück** ~ **lassen** to damn a play; **bei der Wahl** ~ **lassen** to pill *(sl.)*.

durchfechten to wrestle out;
Sache ~ to carry one's point, to fight one's way through.

durch|feiern to feast away the night, to make a night of it; ~**finanzieren** to finance permanently.

Durchfinanzierung permanent financing.

durchfliegen *(im Examen)* to fail, to be ploughed (plucked, *Br.*), to flunk *(US)*, *(Flugzeug)* to fly through;
Buch ~ to skim through a book.

durchfließen to flow through.

Durchfluß flow;
~**menge** flow volume.

durchfluten, Straßen to flood the streets.

durchflutet, von Licht flooded with light, floodlight.

durchforschen to explore, to prospect, to research, to investigate;
Gebiet gründlich ~ to make a thorough enquiry into a subject.

durchforsten to thin out;
Betrieb ~ to weed the garden; **Regierungsstelle zwecks Einsparungen gründlich ~** to comb out a government department.
Durch|forstung *(Betrieb)* garden weeding; **~fracht** through shipment (rate) *(US)*, transit freight; **~frachtbrief** through bill of lading, waybill *(US)*.
durchfrachten to freight through.
Durchfracht|konnossement through bill of lading, waybill *(US)*; **~satz, ~tarif** combination (through, *US*) rate.
durchfressen *(Rost)* to corrode, to eat through;
sich durch ein Buch ~ to wade through a book; **sich auf Kosten seiner Freunde ~** to sponge upon one's friends.
durchfroren sein to be pinched with cold.
Durchfuhr transit, passage.
durchführbar feasible, performable, practicable, workable, contrivable;
nicht ~ impracticable; **praktisch ~** workable;
nicht ~ sein not to be practical politics.
Durchführbarkeit feasibility, practicability.
Durchfuhr|bescheinigung transit certificate (pass, permit); **~bewilligung** transit permit; **~deklaration** transit declaration.
durchführen to carry (put) through, to carry out, to execute, to proceed with, to enforce, to implement, to transact, *(Bahnlinie, Ölleitung)* to extend;
Abkommen ~ to implement an agreement; **durch eine Ausstellung ~** to show through an exhibition; **Blockade ~** to enforce a blockade; **Effektengeschäfte auf Provisionsbasis ~** to execute orders in listed securities on a commission basis; **Eisenbahnlinie bis nach A. ~** to extend the railway line to A.; **erfolgreich ~** to pull through, to make a go of, to swing *(US)*; **j. durch den Garten ~** to take s. o. through the garden; **Gesetz ~** to carry out (enforce) a law; **Kabel ~** to lead a cable; **Maßnahmen ~** to take measures; **Plan ~** to put a plan into execution; **praktisch ~** to put into practice; **Reform ~** to carry out (put through) a reform; **Reparaturen ~** to carry out repairs; **schrittweise ~** to implement step by step; **Unternehmen zu Ende ~** to go through with an undertaking; **Untersuchung ~** to conduct an investigation; **Untersuchung an Ort und Stelle ~** to make investigations on the spot; **Versuch ~** to conduct a test; **Vertrag ~** to fulfil (implement, perform) a contract; **Wahl ~** to hold an election.
Durchfuhr|erklärung transit entry; **~erlaubnis, ~genehmigung** transit permit (pass); **~gleis** through line; **~gut** goods in transit, transit goods; **~hafen** port of call; **~handel** transit trade; **~kosten** transit charges; **~lager** transit camp; **~land** transit country; **~recht** right of way (passage), transit privilege; **~schein** transit bill (pass), transit authorization certificate; **~spediteur** forwarding (transit) agent; **~spedition** forwarding agency; **~staat** transit country; **~stadium** transition period; **~tarif** transit (through) rate.
Durchführung accomplishment, completion, execution, performance, carrying out, handling, pursuit, transaction, *(Gesetz)* enforcement, operation, carriage, implementation;
in der ~ begriffen in course of execution;
mittels ~ eines Prozesses by going to law;
schrittweise ~ implementation step by step;
~ eines Abkommens execution of an agreement; **schnelle ~ einer Angelegenheit** dispatch of a matter; **~ seiner eigenen Angelegenheiten** conduct of one's own affairs; **~ von Aufgaben** performance of functions; **~ eines Auftrags** execution of an order; **~ einer Bahnlinie** extension of a railway line; **~ offener Baisseverkäufe** banging the market; **~ von Geschäften** transaction of business; **~ eines Gesetzes** enforcement of a law; **~ eines Kabels** lead-in of a cable; **~ von Reparaturen** completion of repairs; **~ von Rüstungsaufträgen** defence activities; **~ von Testverfahren** testing service; **~ einer Vereinbarung** satisfaction of an accord; **~ einer Verfügung** execution of an order; **~ eines Vertrages** fulfil(l)ment (implementation) of a contract; **~ einer Volkszählung** census taking; **~ von Zahlungsaufträgen von Kunden** making payments for customers; **~ der Zollvorschriften** customs enforcement;
~ einer Verordnung aussetzen to stop the execution of a decree; **zur ~ bringen** to carry into execution (effect); **~ erzwingen** to enforce a rule; **~ eines Auftrags vergeben** to place the contract for an enterprise; **~ eines Gesetzes verhindern** to interfere with the operation of a law.
Durchführungs|abkommen implementing agreement; **~anordnung** implementing order; **~aufgabe** regulatory job *(US)*; **~behörde** regulatory (implementing) agency *(US)*, enforcing authority; **~bereich** regulatory area; **~bericht** report of compliance; **~bestätigung** voucher.
Durchführungsbestimmungen rules and regulations, implementation clauses, implementing (administrative) regulations, enforcement provisions, regulative statutes, executive orders *(US)*;
wahrer Irrgarten von ~ regulatory maze;
~ eines Gesetzes provisions in execution of a law.
Durchführungs|etappen implementation stages; **~gesetz** executive act; **~kosten** cost of implementation; **~maßnahmen** regulatory measures; **~methoden** regulatory policies; **~organ** enforcement agency, executive department, regulatory (implementing) body *(US)*; **~plan** implementation plan.
durchführungsreif sein to be ripe for execution.
Durchführungs|rohr lead-in pipe; **~stelle** regulatory agency *(US)*; **~verordnung** implementing order, statutory instrument *(Br.)*, bylaw, regulation of an executive department, executive order *(US)*; **~zeitraum** period of implementation.
Durchfuhr|verbot transit embargo; **~verkehr** transit trade; **~waren** transit goods; **~zoll** transit duty.
durchfüttern to feed through the winter;
sich ~ lassen to sponge on s. o.
Durchgabe *(Eßzimmer)* hatch.
Durchgang gangway, lane, passage[way] *(Br.)*, pass, opening, thoroughfare, *(zwischen Sitzreihen)* aisle, gangway *(Br.)*, *(Waren)* transit;
freier ~ passage; **öffentlicher ~** public thoroughfare; **~ verboten!** no thoroughfare (passage)!
durchgängig general, universal, throughout, as a rule;
~ modern ausgestattet sein to have every modern convenience;
~e Ansicht universally held opinion.
Durchgangs|abgabe transit duty; **~amt** *(tel.)* tandem office; **~bahn** *(Satellit)* track; **~bahnhof** through (express, transit, way, *US*) station; **~fahrkarte** through ticket (fare); **~fernamt** trunk exchange *(Br.)*, zone center *(US)*; **~flughafen** transit (intermediate) airport.
Durchgangsfracht transit cargo (freight), through shipment *(US)*;
~brief through bill of lading, waybill *(US)*; **~gebühren** through freight charges; **~geschäft** through freight business; **~satz** transit (through) rate; **kombinierter ~satz** combination through rate.
Durchgangs|gebühr transit charges (costs); **~gespräch** *(tel.)* transit call; **~gleis** through line; **~gut** transit goods; **Waren als ~gut angeben** to enter goods as transit; **~halle** transit hall; **~handel** transit trade, transient business; **~hotel** commercial (transient, *US*) hotel; **~konnossement für das Ausland** uniform through export bill of lading; **~konto** transit account; **~ladung** through shipment, transit freight; **~lager** transit camp, *(Waren)* transit storehouse; **~land** transit country; **~passierschein** transit pass; **~personal** *(mil.)* casuals; **~platz** exchange (transit) point; **~posten** suspense (transitory) item, item (remittance) in transit; **~postverkehr** transit mail service *(US)*; **~recht** right of way, wayleave *(Br.)*; **~reisender** through passenger; **~satz** transit (through, *US*) rate; **~schein** transit bill (pass, certificate, permit); **~sendung** through shipment; **~stadium** transition period (stage); **~station** intermediate (through) station; **~stelle** transit point, checkpoint; **~straße** thoroughfare, throughroad, throughway *(US)*, cross-town route, transit route, through highway, arterial highway *(US)*; **~straßenbezeichnung** highway marker *(US)*; **~strecke** through route; **~tarif** transit (through, *US*) rate; **~telegramm** transmitted telegram; **~transport** transport in transit; **~verbindung** through route.
Durchgangsverkehr through traffic, transit, *(Telefon)* through communication, *(Post)* transit exchange of correspondence;
gesperrt für ~ road closed ahead, no thoroughfare;
im ~ abfertigen to convey goods in transit.
Durchgangs|verladung through shipment; **~visum** transit visa; **~wagen** corridor (through) carriage (coach, *Br.*), Pullman car *(US)*, transit car, through waggon, vestibule car *(US)*; **~waren** goods in transit, transit goods; **~weg** thoroughfare, throughroad, throughway *(US)*; **~zertifikat** transit certificate (pass); **~zoll** pass (transit) duty; **~zone** *(mil.)* staging area; **~zug** through (vestibule, *US*, nonstop) train, *(D-Zug)* corridor train.
durchgeben to pass on, to transmit, to circulate, *(Rundfunk)* to broadcast, to announce, to put on the air;
drahtlos ~ to [transmit by] radio; **Meldung telefonisch ~** to telephone a message; **Nachrichten ~** to read the news; **Telegramm telefonisch ~** to deliver a telegram by telephone; **Wetterbericht ~** to read the weather forecast.
durchgedreht all in, washed out, off one's head (rocker) *(sl.)*;
~ haben to be out of one's mind.

durch|gefallen *(Theaterstück)* flopped; ~**geführt** executed.
Durchgefallene|r fail, flunker *(US coll.)*;
auf die Liste der ~n setzen to post *(Br.)*.
durchgegangen *(Antrag)* passed, carried, *(Pferd)* bolted.
Durchgehen *(Gesetz)* passage;
nochmaliges ~ review.
durchgehen to go through, *(Antrag, Gesetz)* to get through, to be carried (adopted), to pass, *(prüfen)* to examine, to inspect, to review, *(Vorschlag)* to be adopted, *(Ware)* to be in transit, *(Zug)* to go right (straight) through, to go direct;
alte Akten ~ to examine old records; **Buch rasch** ~ to glance through (skim over) a book; **Faktura** ~ to check the invoice; **mit einer anderen Frau** ~ to run off with another woman; **etw. genau** ~ to examine s. th. thoroughly; **durch alle Instanzen** ~ to go through the usual channels; **mit der Kasse** ~ to make off (abscond) with the money, to shoot the moon *(sl.)*; **seine Konten (Rechnungen)** ~ to run (look) over one's accounts; **mit dem Liebhaber** ~ to elope (run off) with the lover; **Liste noch einmal** ~ to check a list once again; **Manuskript auf Schreibfehler** ~ to look through a manuscript in search of errors; **nicht** ~ *(Gesetz)* to lose; **Rolle noch einmal** ~ to go over a part again; **Sache flüchtig** ~ to course through a th.; **mitten durch die Stadt** ~ to run right through the center of the town; **Tatsachen noch einmal** ~ to recapitulate the facts;
etw. ~ **lassen** to overlook s. th., to let pass unnoticed; **jem. etw.** ~ **lassen** to let s. o. get away with s. th.
durchgehend passing, *(ohne Ausnahme)* without exception, universally, generally, *(Tragfläche)* one-piece, *(Verkehr)* transit, *(Wagen)* through, direct, *(zeitlich)* around-the-clock, *(Zug)* nonstop;
~ **geöffnet** open throughout (all day); ~ **schlecht** rotten to the core;
~ **vertretene Ansicht** universally held opinion; ~**e Arbeitszeit** continuous operation (process); ~**er Dienst** round-the-clock service, twenty-four-hour service *(US)*; ~**e Fahrkarte** through ticket; ~**e Fahrkarte lösen** to book through; ~**er Frachtbrief** through waybill *(US)*; ~**e Ladung** through shipment *(US)*; ~**e Linie** direct (through) line; ~**e Schlafwagenverbindung** daily through-sleeper service; ~**e Verbindung** through connection; ~**er Verkehr** through (transit) traffic; ~**e Waren** transit goods; ~**er Zug** nonstop (through) train.
durch|geistigte Gesichtszüge spiritual features; ~**gekreuzt** crossed; ~**geleiteter Kredit** loan passed on, transmitted credit; **viel ~gemacht haben** to have been through the mill (much trouble); ~**gesackte Stelle** sag; ~**geschlagener Druck** blotted print; **[nicht] ~gesehen** [un]revised; **sich ~gesetzt haben** to have authority in; ~**gestrichen** crossed.
durchgraben, sich to dig one's way through.
durchgreifen, hart to employ hard (take firm) measures, to crack down *(US coll.)*; **nicht scharf** ~ to raise the lid.
durchgreifend drastic, decisive, thorough, strong, effective;
~**e Änderung** radical change; ~**es Argument** conclusive argument; ~**e Maßnahmen** drastic (sweeping) measures; ~**e Verbesserungen** far-reaching improvements.
Durchgriffshaftung beim persönlichen Gesellschafter herbeiführen to pierce the corporate veil.
durchhaben *(Buch)* to have finished.
Durchhalteappell morale boosting.
Durchhalten von Aktien, langfristiges long-term holding of shares.
durchhalten to see a business through, to stick it out *(Br.)*, to stay the course, *(mil.)* to hold out against an attack;
bis zum Ende (Schluß) ~ to go the route, to keep one's end up, to hold out to the end; **mit der Lebensführung der Nachbarn** ~ to keep up with the Joneses; **Tempo** ~ to keep up the pace; **verzweifelt** ~ to hang on for dear life.
Durchhalte|politik die-hard policy, *(Wertpapiere)* buy- and hold approach; ~**rede** morale-boosting speech; ~**vermögen** survival powers, stamina; ~**vermögen vermissen lassen** to fail in perseverance.
durchhauen, j. to give s. o. a thrashing;
Holzklotz ~ to cleave a block of wood; **Gordischen Knoten** ~ to cut the Gordian Knot.
durchhecheln to gossip;
j. ~ to pick s. o. to pieces, to hatchel s. o.; **in der Presse** ~ to drag through the papers.
durch|helfen, sich to manage somehow; **sich ~hungern** to scrape a living.
durchkämmen to search, to comb, *(mil.)* to skirr, to mop;
feindliches Gebiet ~ to mop an area; **Wälder nach einem Verbrecher** ~ to comb the woods for a criminal.
durchkämpfen to fight it out.
Durchkartellisierung thorough cartelization.
durchkauen, immer wieder to go over and over again, to rehash.
Durchkommen passing through.
durchkommen to get on (through), to stand the racket, *(Antrag)* to be passed (carried), *(Charakterzug)* to become apparent, *(Patient)* to pull through, *(Prüfling)* to be successful, to come (get) through *(US)*, to pass an examination, *(Telefonanruf)* to come through;
bei jem. mit etw. nicht ~ to cut no ice with s. o.; **mit seinem Französisch ganz gut** ~ to manage (get along) quite well with one's French; **mit wenig Geld** ~ to manage with little money; **heil durch den Krieg** ~ to come safely through the war; **nur kümmerlich** ~ to eke out a [scanty] living, to scrape a living; **mit Lügen** ~ to get away with lies; **nicht** ~ *(Gesetz)* to fail to go through, to be defeated (rejected).
Durchkonnossement through bill of lading.
durchkosten, Freuden des Ruhmes to taste all the pleasures of fame.
durchkramen, seine Taschen to rummage through one's pockets.
durchkreuzen to frustrate, to baffle;
alle Meere ~ to sail the seven seas; **Pläne** ~ to interfere with s. one's plans, to run counter to (discomfit) a plan; **Scheck** ~ to cross a cheque *(Br.)*.
Durchkreuzung discomfiture, frustration, counteraction, *(Scheck)* crossing *(Br.)*.
Durchlaß opening, outlet, passage;
offener ~ open culvert;
jem. ~ **gewähren** to allow s. o. to pass.
durchlassen, j. to allow s. o. to pass; **j. durch ein Examen** ~ to let s. o. through an exam *(fam.)*; **Vorlage im Parlament** ~ to pass a bill through Parliament; **kein Wasser** ~ *(Stoff)* to be impermeable to water.
durchlässig pervious, permeable, *(Dach)* leaky, *(für Licht)* transparent.
Durchlaß|posten *(mil.)* examining point, checkpoint; ~**schein** permit, free pass, transire; **mit ~schein passieren** to have a permit for transire.
Durchlauf *(Lochkartensystem)* run;
unsteter ~ **eines Tonbandes** tape flutter; ~ **für Weidevieh** cattle pass.
durchlaufen to run through;
Aktenstücke ~ to run through the files; **durch eine Ausstellung** ~ to rush through an exhibition; **Bahn** ~ to describe an orbit; **mehrere Dienststellen** ~ to pass through various departments; **verschiedene Entwicklungsstadien** ~ to pass through various stages of development; **j. heiß** ~ to turn s. o. sick with fear; **Schule** ~ to pass through school; **ganze Stadt mit Windeseile** ~ *(Gerücht)* to spread through the whole town like wildfire; **unstet** ~ *(Tonband)* to flutter.
durchlaufend continuous, *(Buchhaltung)* transitory;
~**e Buchungen** transit entries; ~**er Kredit** transitory credit; ~**er Posten** transitory item.
Durchlauf|erhitzer flow heater; ~**konto** interim (transitory) account; ~**posten** transitory item, deposit in transit; ~**zeit** machining time.
durchlavieren, sich to pick one's way.
durchleben to go (live) through;
Schreckliches ~ to go through the most terrible experiences; **gute und schlechte Zeiten** ~ to see good days and bad.
durchleiten *(Kredit)* to pass on, to transmit.
Durchleitkredit loan passed on, transmitted credit.
Durchlesen perusal.
durchlesen to go over, to read through;
flüchtig ~ to skim (glance) over; **ganz zu Ende** ~ to read right through; **sorgfältig** ~ to peruse.
durchleuchten to test, *(Marketing)* to audit, *(med.)* to x-ray, to transilluminate, *(prüfen)* to investigate, to analize, to examine;
etw. gründlich ~ to probe deep into a matter; **j.** ~ *(fig.)* to screen s. o.; **jds. Vergangenheit** ~ to probe into (screen) s. one's past; **jds. dienstliches Verhalten** ~ to probe s. one's official conduct; **sich** ~ **lassen** to have a fluorescent examination.
Durchleuchtung investigation, screening, *(Marketing)* audit, *(med.)* x-ray examination, fluoroscope.
Durchleuchtungs|apparat fluoroscope; ~**schirm** fluorescent screen.
durchlochen to punch, to perforate.
durchlöchern, j. mit Kugeln to riddle s. o. with bullets; **Prinzip** ~ to undermine a principle; **Vorschriften** ~ to render regulations meaningless.
durchlöchert wie ein Sieb riddled like a sieve.

durchlüften to ventilate, to air thoroughly.
Durchlüftung ventilation, airing.
durchmachen to undergo, to endure, to suffer;
Ausbildungszeit (Lehre) ~ to serve one's apprenticeship; **Krise** ~ to go (pass) through a crisis; **ganze Nacht** ~ to make a night of it; **schwere Operation** ~ to undergo a serious operation; **Schreckliches** ~ to go through the most terrible experiences; **schwere Zeiten** ~ to go through hardships, to pass through hard times.
Durchmarsch march-through, *(med.)* diarrh(o)ea.
durchmarschieren to march through.
durchmessen to take the dimensions;
Strecke zu Fuß ~ to cover a distance; **Zimmer von einem zum anderen Ende** ~ to tread the room from end to end.
Durchmesser diameter.
durchmogeln, sich *(fam.)* to live by shifts, to pick one's way; **sich mit seinem Geld bis zur nächsten Gehaltszahlung** ~ to spin out until next pay day.
durchmustern to scan, to inspect closely, to examine one by one, to scrutinize, to look through closely.
Durchmusterung close examination, scrutiny.
durchnäßt, bis auf die Haut drenched to the skin; **völlig** ~ wringing wet;
~ **werden** to get a wetting; **bis auf die Haut** ~ **werden** to get wet to the skin.
durchnehmen, Thema mit einer Klasse to take a class through a subject.
durchnumerieren to number consecutively.
Durchnumerierung consecutive numbering.
durchpauken to ram through, to cram, to bone up on *(US sl.)*, to swot up *(Br., sl.)*;
Gesetz durchs Parlament ~ to railroad a bill through parliament *(US)*, to rattle (rush) a bill through the house *(Br.)*.
durch|pausen to trace; **Gesetz ~peitschen** to rattle (race) a bill through the house *(Br.)*, to jam (push, railroad) a bill through Congress *(US)*; **~proben** *(Theater)* to rehearse; **einzeln ~prüfen** to examine one by one; **j. ~prügeln** to dust s. one's jacket.
durchqueren to cross, to traverse;
Erdteil ~ to travel across a continent; **Fluß** ~ to ford (cross) a river; **Wüste** ~ to traverse a desert.
durchrasen to rush (dash) through;
Bahnhof ~ to race (tear) through the station.
durchrasseln to spin away *(sl.)*, to pluck *(Br., sl.)*.
Durchrationalisierung, gründliche thorough increase in efficiency.
durchrechnen to reckon (count) over, to recast, to check, *(berechnen)* to calculate;
Kalkulation noch einmal ~ to check a calculation.
durchregnen, durchs Dach to come through the roof; **ganze Nacht** ~ to be raining all through the night.
Durchreiche service hatch.
Durchreise passage, transit, way through;
auf der ~ on the way through;
jem. die ~ **gestatten** to allow s. o. transit;
~erlaubnis transit certificate (pass).
durchreisen to pass through, *(Auto)* to drive through;
ganz Europa ~ to tour all over Europe.
Durchreisender through passenger, passing traveller, transient [visitor] *(US)*, transient lodger.
Durchreise|sichtvermerk, ~visum transit visa.
durchringen, sich ~ **zu** to struggle to, to come round to doing s. th.; **sich zu einem Entschluß** ~ to finally make up one's mind.
Durchrutschen *(Prüfling)* shave.
durchsacken *(Flugzeug)* to sag, to stall;
~ **lassen** to pancake to the ground.
Durchsack|geschwindigkeit critical (stalling) speed; **~landung** pancake [landing].
Durchsage *(Rundfunk)* announcement, message, spot *(US)*;
[telefonische] ~ [telephone] message.
durchsagen *(Rundfunk)* to broadcast, to radio, to announce, to make an announcement;
Telegramm telefonisch ~ to deliver a telegram over the telephone, to telephone a wire.
durchschalten *(Auto)* to change up, *(tel.)* to put through.
durchschaubar perceptible, obvious, transparent;
schwer ~ puzzling, not easily seen through.
durchschauen, jds. seltsames Benehmen sofort to see at once what is behind s. one's peculiar behavio(u)r; **jds. Beweggründe** ~ to see through s. one's motives; **j. genau** ~ to read s. o. like a book, to see through s. o.; **jds. Maske** ~ to penetrate s. one's disguise; **jds. Spiel** ~ to see through s. one's little game.
durchschaut haben, j. to have s. one's number.
durchscheinen to show through, *(Charakterzug)* to become evident.
durchschießen *(drucktechn.)* to space out, to interline, to lead, to interleave;
Buch mit weißem Papier ~ to interleave a book.
durchschlafen, zwölf Stunden to sleep the clock round.
Durchschlag [carbon] copy, manifold, flimsy *(Br.)*, *(el.)* puncture, *(Geschoß)* penetration;
überflüssiger ~ surplus copy; **zusätzlicher** ~ blind carbon copy; ~ **für die Akten** file copy;
~ **erhalten haben** to have a copy of one's own; ~ **herstellen** to press-copy, to make a copy.
durchschlagen to go through, *(Charakteranlage)* to come through, to crop out, *(drucktechn.)* to strike (come) through, *(Rundfunksendung)* to break through, *(Sicherung)* to blow;
sich ~to make one's way, to shift for a living; **sich allein** ~ to fend for o. s., to fight one's own battle; **sich mit ein paar Brocken Englisch** ~ to manage one's way with a little bit of English; **nach zwei Generationen wieder** ~ *(Anlage)* to reappear after two generations; **sich gerade so** ~ to make both ends meet; **sich kümmerlich (mühsam)** ~ to pinch and scrape, to scrape (scratch) along, to eke out a [scanty] living; **auf die Ladenverkaufspreise** ~ to work through to prices in the shops; **sich durch die feindlichen Linien** ~ to fight one's way through the enemy's lines; **sich mit knapper Not** ~ to worry along; **Panzerung** ~ to pierce through armo(u)r; **direkt auf die Preise** ~ to feed straight through into the prices; **sich recht und schlecht** ~ to rub through the world; **glatt die Tür** ~ *(Geschoß)* to go clean through the door; **Wand** ~ to knock a hole in the wall.
durchschlagend striking, sweeping, smashing;
~e Wirkung haben to have the desired effect.
Durchschlagpapier onionskin, flimsy, carbon (bank, copying) paper.
Durchschlagskraft punch, *(Beweis)* convincing power, *(Geschoß)* percussive force;
~ **eines Arguments** vigo(u)r (force) of an argument; ~ **einer Werbung** advertising impact.
durchschlängeln, sich to wind about, to twist one's way through.
durchschleppen, j. mit sich to drag s. o. along.
durchschleusen *(Schiff)* to pass through a lock, *(Truppen)* to marshal;
j. ~ to pass s. o., to process s. o. *(US)*; **j. durch eine Prüfung** ~ to push s. o. through an examination.
Durchschlupf hole, way out.
durchschlüpfen, durch den Stacheldraht to slip through the barbed wire.
durchschmelzen *(Sicherung)* to fuse.
durchschmuggeln to smuggle through the customs.
durchschneiden, Band *(Straßeneinweihung)* to cut the tape; **jem. die Kehle** ~ to cut s. one's throat; **das ganze Land** ~ *(Kanäle)* to intersect the entire country.
Durchschnitt average, standard, *(Menschen)* ordinary run, *(Statistik)* arithmetic mean;
im ~ on an average, in the lump; **über (unter) dem** ~ above (below) standard;
annähernder ~ rough average; **gewogener** ~ weighted mean; **gleitender vierwöchiger** ~ moving average; **guter** ~ fair average; **provisorischer** ~ *(Statistik)* working mean; **ungefährer** ~ rough average;
~ **der Bevölkerung** cross-section of the people; **der große** ~ **der Bevölkerung** the majority (common run) of the people; ~ **der Käufer** ordinary run of buyers;
~ **berechnen** to find the average; **sich über den** ~ **erheben** to rise out of the ruck; ~ **erreichen** to be up to the average; ~ **von 400 Dollar am Tag erreichen** to average $ 400 a day; **im** ~ **erzielen** to average; **erwarteten** ~ **erzielen** to average as expected; **zum guten** ~ **gehören** to keep up a good average; **über dem** ~ **liegen** to be above average; ~ **nehmen** to strike (find) the average; **nur** ~ **sein** to have only average abilities; **unter dem** ~ **sein** to be below the mark; **im** ~ **verkaufen** to sell on an average; **Gebäude im** ~ **zeichnen** to draw a building in section.
durchschnittlich average, normal, mean, overhead, on a par *(Br.)*, *(gewöhnlich)* common, ordinary, *(mittelmäßig)* middling, second-rate, medium;
~ **betragen** to average; ~ **ergeben** to rough in the average;
~es Alter average age; **~e Einnahmen** normal proceeds; **~es Ergebnis nehmen** to take an average of results; **von ~er Größe** medium-sized; **~es Heiratsalter** average marrying age; **von ~er Intelligenz** of ordinary intelligence; **~e Kursentwicklung** market average; **~e Laufzeit** equated period; **~e Lebensdauer**

average duration of life, *(Versicherung)* standard life; ~**e Qualität** medium (ordinary) quality; ~**e Zahlungsfrist** average collection period.

Durchschnitts|alter average age; ~**anteil** average proportion; ~**arbeiter** average workman, normal operator *(US)*; ~**auflage** *(Zeitung)* average circulation; ~**aufwand** average cost; ~**baumwollqualität** cotton standard; ~**beförderungsentgelt** average transport charges; ~**beitragssatz** average contribution; ~**belegschaft** average working force; ~**bestand eines Warenlagers** average holding of the goods in store; ~**besteuerung** income averaging; ~**betrag** average amount; **jährlicher** ~**bruttoumsatz** average annual gross sales; ~**bürger** average citizen, commonplace kind of man; ~**dauer eines eingeräumten Kredits** average collection period; ~**einkommen** average income (earnings), *(dreijährig)* statutory income; ~**einkünfte pro Beförderungsziffer** average revenue per passenger mile; ~**einnahme** average revenue; ~**entgelt** average remuneration; ~**ertrag** average return (yield); **geschätzter** ~**ertrag** estimated running yield; ~**erzeugnis** average production; **einfaches** ~**erzeugnis** run of mill, run-of-the-mill line; ~**erzeugung** average production; ~**fachmann** *(Patentrecht)* average mechanic skilled in the art; ~**fahrer** average driver; ~**filme** run-of-the-mill film; ~**firma** representative firm; ~**gäste** run-of-the line (mill) guests; ~**geldbeutel** average pocket; ~**gemeinkostensatz** average burden rate.

Durchschnittsgeschwindigkeit average speed;
~ **beibehalten** to maintain a speed; ~ **von 120 km erzielen** to average 80 miles an hour.

Durchschnitts|gestehungspreis average cost price; ~**gewinn** average (normal) profit; ~**größe** medium size; ~**guthaben** average balance; ~**kandidat** passman; ~**kapazität** average (mean) capacity; ~**kapital** average capital; ~**klasse** common run.

Durchschnittskosten, langfristige long-run average costs;
~ **pro Einheit** average unit cost;
~ **vermindern** *(Börse)* to average down (up);
~**methode** cost averaging; ~**verminderung** *(Börse)* averaging down (up).

Durchschnitts|kunde average customer; ~**kurs** average price, market average, mean rate of exchange, *(Devisen)* average rate; **zu einem** ~**kurs weiterverkaufen** to sell on a scale; ~**laufzeit** equated period; ~**leistung** mean efficiency (output), average performance; ~**leser** general (ordinary) reader; ~**lohn** average wage, straight-time pay; ~**menge** average quantity.

Durchschnittsmensch average person (mind), common run of man, reasonable man, man in the street;
normaler ~ ordinary prudent person;
einfacher ~ **sein** to be just an ordinary man.

Durchschnitts|miete average rent; ~**niveau** average standard; **hohe** ~**note** high-grade average; ~**notierung** average quotation; ~**prämie** average premium; ~**preis** medium price, market average, *(Milch)* blended price; ~**produktion** average output, standard production; ~**produktivität** average productivity; ~**prozentsatz** average percentage; **gute** ~**qualität** fair average (standard) quality; **mittlere** ~**qualität** run of the mill; ~**rechnung** *(Münzwesen)* alligation medial; ~**rendite** average yield; ~**saldenliste** average book; ~**satz** average rate; ~**steuersatz** average rate, *(Umsatzsteuer)* composite rate; ~**stundenlohn** average (straight-time) hourly earnings, common labo(u)r rate; ~**stundenverdienst** average hourly earnings; ~**summe** average sum; ~**tagessaldo** *(Zinsberechnung)* average daily balance; ~**talent** man (woman) of average ability; ~**tara** average (computed, mean) tare; ~**temperatur** mean temperature; ~**termin** average date; ~**transportkosten** average haul; ~**umsatz** average turnover, average sales; ~**valuta** *(Wertstellung)* average value date; ~**verbrauch** average consumption; ~**verbraucher** average consumer; ~**verdienst** average earnings (earned rate); ~**verfalltag** average due date; ~**verfallzeit** average [term of] maturity; ~**verhältnis** average ratio; ~**verkaufsauflage** average net paid; ~**verladegewicht** average shipping weight; ~**wähler** middle-of-the-road voter, middle roader, ordinary voter; ~**ware** articles of average quality; ~**wert** average (mean, standard) value; ~**zahl** average figure (number), mean number; ~**zahl der Beträge ermitteln** to average the amounts; ~**zinsen** average interest.

durchschossen, doppelt double-leaded;
~**e Bände** interleaved volumes; ~**er Satz** leaded matter.

Durchschreibe|bestellbuch carbon-copy order book; ~**block** carbon-copy pad; ~**buch** manifold book; ~**buchführung** multiple-copy (duplicating bookkeeping, mechanical) system, manual mechanical bookkeeping.

durchschreiben to make a carbon copy.

Durchschreibe|stift carbon pencil; ~**verfahren** duplicating.

Durchschreib|papier copying (carbon) paper; ~**satz** typing batch.

durchschreiten to walk (stride) through;
Zimmer mehrere Male ~ to pace through the room.

Durchschrift carbon copy.

Durchschuß *(drucktechn.)* white (interlineal, interlinear) space, blank material, lead, slugs, *(Buchbinden)* interleaf;
mit weitem ~ loose-leaded; **ohne** ~ solid;
~**linie** white line, interline; ~**material** leads, spaces.

durchschütteln, j. to jog s. o. up and down.

durchschwimmen to swim across.

durchsehen to look through, to examine, to check, *(Druckbogen)* to revise, to read;
durch etw. ~ to grasp the meaning of s. th.; **Akten noch einmal** ~ to examine the files once more; **Brief flüchtig** ~ to glance over a letter; **Bücher** ~ to inspect the books; **flüchtig** ~ to run over; **gründlich** ~ to peruse; **Manuskript** ~ to go through a manuscript; **seine Post** ~ to run through one's mail, to go through one's correspondence; **seine Rechnungen** ~ to examine (look over) one's accounts, to go through one's bills; **seinen Schreibtisch** ~ to search one's desk; **seine Unterlagen** ~ to search through one's papers;
nicht mehr ~ **können** not to be able to make head or tail of it.

durchsetzbar enforceable;
nicht ~ unenforceable, imperfect; **vor Gericht** ~ enforceable by legal proceedings.

durchsetzen to carry (put) through, to accomplish, to enforce;
sich ~ to get one's own way, to come into one's own, to come to the top, to gain ground, to assert o. s., to win through, to come into vogue, *(Erzeugnis)* to prevail on the market, *(Künstler)* to win recognition, *(Mode)* to come into vogue; **sich bei jem.** ~ to work one's will upon s. o.; **bei jem. etw.** ~ to prevail upon s. o. to consent; **sich auf einem Absatzmarkt** ~ to penetrate a market; **sich mit seiner Ansicht** ~ to gain one's point; **Anspruch** ~ to enforce a claim; **sich beruflich** ~ to establish o. s. in a job; **sich bei allen Bevölkerungssparten** ~ to take on among all classes; **sich in einer Diskussion gegen j.** ~ to get the better of s. o. in an argument; **sich erneut** ~ to make a comeback; **sich im Leben** ~ to make one's way; **Maßnahmen bei jem.** ~ to enforce a course of action upon s. o.; **sich mehr und mehr** ~ *(Ansichten)* to be gradually gaining ground; **seine Meinung** ~ to carry one's point; **seine Pläne mit Gewalt** ~ to force one's plans through; **seine Rechte** ~ to enforce one's rights; **sich überall** ~ to get the better of people; **alles beim Vater** ~ to get anything one likes out of one's father; **seinen Willen** ~ to get one's way; **seinen Willen bei jem.** ~ to enforce one's will on s. o.; **seine Ziele** ~ to achieve one's objects.

Durchsetzung accomplishment, realization, enforcement;
gemeinsame ~ collective enforcement; **gerichtliche** ~ enforcement through a court;
~ **eines Anspruches** enforcement of a claim; ~ **der Autorität** flow of authority; ~ **von Bedingungen** enforcement of conditions; ~ **von Lohnforderungen** wage push; ~ **eines Rechtsanspruchs** enforcement of a right; ~ **ausländischer Schiedsansprüche** enforcement of foreign awards.

Durchsetzungs|anspruch right to enforce; **über genügend** ~**vermögen verfügen** to have enough muscle.

durchseucht contaminated, infected.

Durchsicht going through, looking over, auditing, examination, inspection, check, *(Korrekturen)* revise, revisal, *(Text)* revision, recension;
bei nochmaliger ~ on second inspection; **bei** ~ **unserer Bücher** on looking over our books, upon consulting (in reviewing) our records; **bei** ~ **meiner Korrespondenz** when looking through my letters; **bei** ~ **der Sendung** on checking the consignment; **zur gefälligen** ~ for your kind inspection;
nochmalige ~ re-examination; **redaktionelle** ~ editorial revision; **repräsentative** ~ cross section; **sorgfältige** ~ perusal;
~ **der Schulhefte** correction of exercises;
einer genaueren (sorgfältigen) ~ **unterziehen** to examine carefully, to give s. th. a careful perusal.

durchsichtig transparent, *(Bilanz)* visible;
~**es Papier** flimsy.

Durchsichtigkeit transparency.

Durchsickern *(mil.)* infiltration, *(Nachricht)* leakage;
~ **eines Geheimnisses** oozing out of a secret; ~ **von Staatsgeheimnissen** leakage of state secrets.

durchsickern *(Nachricht)* to leak (seep) out, to begin to spread, to filter through, to ooze out, to permeate, to leach;

allmählich ~ to leak out gradually; **durch die feindlichen Linien** ~ to infiltrate the enemy lines;
~ **lassen** to trickle through.
durchsieben to screen, to filter.
durchsprechen, am Telefon to discuss on the telephone.
Durchstarten, sofortiges *(Konjunkturpolitik)* rushing the economy back to full employment levels.
durchstarten, sofort wieder *(Konjunkturpolitik)* to rush the economy back to full employment levels.
durchstechen to prick.
Durchstechereien bribery and corruption, corrupt practices;
kommunale ~ municipal jobbery;
~ **in der Beamtenschaft** abuses in the civil service.
durchstehen to endure, to go through, to see through, to stick it out *(Br.)*;
Affäre mannhaft ~ to go gamely through an affair.
Durchstehvermögen *(mil.)* holding power.
durchstellen *(tel.)* to put through, to transfer;
sofort ~ to put through at once.
Durchstich excavation, cutting.
durchstöbern, Schreibtischschublade to rummage in a desk drawer; **Wörterbuch nach einem passenden Wort** ~ to rummage a dictionary for a satisfactory word.
Durchstoß *(mil.)* break-through.
durchstoßen *(mil.)* to break through;
durch die Wolkendecke ~ to fly through the overcast.
Durchstoßlandung descent-through-cloud landing.
Durchstreichen deletion, cancellation, crossing out.
durchstreichen to delete, to cross (strike, blot) out, to cancel;
Wort ~ to put one's pen through a word.
Durchstreichung cancelling, crossing out.
durchsuchen to search, to ransack, *(Gepäck)* to go through, *(Person)* to shake down *(US sl.)*, *(Völkerrecht)* to visit and search;
genau ~ to rifle for *(fam.)*; **jds. Gepäck** ~ to search s. one's trunks; **Haus** ~ to search a house; **ganze Stadt** ~ to comb the whole city; **seine Taschen** ~ to ransack one's pockets, to turn one's pockets inside out; **Verbrecher** ~ to search a criminal; **j. nach Waffen** ~ to search (frisk, *sl.*) s. o. for weapons; **zollamtlich** ~ to search, to rummage *(Br.)*.
durchsucht, nicht unsearched.
Durchsuchung visitation, search, frisk *(sl.)*, *(Völkerrecht)* visit and search;
der ~ **unterliegen** visitable;
unberechtigte ~ unlawful search; **zollamtliche** ~ rummage *(US)*, search;
~ **und Beschlagnahme** search and seizure;
einer sorgfältigen ~ **unterziehen** to examine carefully; ~ **in einem Haus vornehmen** to search a house.
Durchsuchungs|beamter des Zolls customhouse searcher; **~befehl** search warrant; **~recht** right of visitation; **~recht auf hoher** See right of visit and search.
Durchtarif *(Seeschiffahrt)* through tariff (rate).
durchtrainiert in top form.
durchtränkt soaked, saturated, steeped;
mit Öl ~er Lappen oil-soaked rag.
durchtrieben cunning, wily, artful, tricky;
~es Bürschchen a downy bird *(fam.)*, slippery customer.
Durchtriebener, ein ganz a deep one *(sl.)*.
Durchtriebenheit cunning policy.
durchuntersuchen to examine thoroughly, to overhaul.
durchuntersucht overhauled.
Durchuntersuchung visit, overhaul.
durchverbinden *(tel.)* to put through, to transfer a call.
durchwachen, ganze Nacht to sit up all night.
durchwachte Nacht sleepless night.
Durchwahl *(tel.)* direct (trunk, *Br.*) dial(l)ing;
~apparat direct-dial telephone; **~apparat mit Badezimmeranschluß** direct-dial telephone with bathroom extension; **~betrieb** dial (direct dial(l)ing) system.
durchwählen to dial through (direct).
Durchwahl|fernverkehr direct distance (toll-line) dial(l)ing; **~nummer** direct dial number; **~system** direct dial(l)ing system; **internationaler ~verkehr** international subscriber dial(l)ing.
durch|wandern to perambulate; **~wegs** throughout, altogether, without exception; **~weicht** soaked, drenched, soggy, wet.
durchwinden, sich to wriggle (meander) through; **sich durch Schwierigkeiten** ~ to wriggle out of a difficulty.
durchwühlen to rummage, to ransack;
Papiere ~ to forage among papers; **Schreibtischschublade** ~ to rummage in a desk drawer.
durchwursteln to muddle through;
sich irgendwie ~ to jog along somehow.
durchzählen to count.
durchzechen, Nacht to feast away the night.
Durchzeichenpapier detail (tracing) paper.
durchzeichnen to trace.
durchziehen to pass through, *(Truppen)* to march through;
sich wie ein roter Faden durch ein ganzes Werk ~ to run through a work like a red thread; **Gebäude** ~ *(Geruch)* to penetrate a building; **Gesetzesvorlage** ~ to push a bill through.
durchzogen, von Kanälen traversed by canals.
Durchzug *(mil.)* marching through;
~ **machen** to ventilate a room, to let in fresh air.
Durchzugsrecht right of passage (to march through).
durchzwängen, sich to squash o. s.; **sich durch eine Menschenmenge** ~ to thread one's way through a crowd.
dürftig indigent, needy, poor, slim, wretched, *(Einkommen)* meagre, paltry, scanty;
~er Beweis slim evidence; **~e Entschuldigung** lame (paltry, threadbare) excuse; **~er Ersatz** poor substitute; **~e Kenntnisse** scanty (sketchy) knowledge; **in ~en Verhältnissen** in narrow straits; **in ~en Verhältnissen leben** to be poorly off, to be in needy circumstances, to live in wretched poverty; ~ **besuchter Vortrag** poorly attended lecture.
Dürftigkeit indigence, necessity, poverty;
~ **einer Entschuldigung** paltriness of an excuse.
Dürftigkeitseinrede plea of insufficient assets.
dürr dry, dried up, dead, *(Land)* barren, infertile, arid, parched;
~es Gestell *(fam.)* beanstalk, maypole; **kleines ~es Männchen** little dried-up man; **~er Sommer** summer of drought; **mit ~en Worten** bluntly, without mincing matters.
Dürre drought, dryness, aridity, parchedness;
~gebiet dryland; **~periode** drought, dry period; **~region** drought region, dust bowl *(US)*; **~zeit** drought tide.
Durst thirst;
brennender ~ raging (burning) thirst;
einen über den ~ **getrunken haben** to have taken a drop too much (had one over the eight, *Br., coll.*); **seinen** ~ **löschen** to quench one's thirst; **seinen** ~ **stillen** to cool one's coppers.
dürsten to be (feel) thirsty;
nach Anerkennung ~ to hunger after praise *(fam.)*; **nach Lob** ~ to have a craving for praise; **nach Rache** ~ to thirst for revenge; **nach Regen** ~ to be thirsty for rain.
durstig thirsty;
~e Kehle haben to have a parched throat.
durstlöschende Getränke thirst-quenchers *(fam.)*.
Dusche shower [bath];
kalte ~ *(fig.)* wet blanket, cold pig *(sl.)*;
jem. eine kalte ~ **geben** to poor cold water on s. one's enthusiasm, to bring s. o. back to earth; **wie eine eiskalte** ~ **wirken** to be like a wet blanket.
Dusch|ecke shower cubicle; **~gelegenheit** shower facility; **~kabine** shower cabinet; **~raum** shower room; **~vorhang** shower curtain.
Düse nozzle, jet.
Dusel luck, fluke;
großen ~ **haben** to hit the jack pot.
Düsenantrieb jet propulsion;
mit ~ jet-propelled.
düsenartig jet-style.
Düsen|bomber jet bomber; **~einstellung** injection timing; **~flugschein** jet fare; **~flugverkehr** jet service.
Düsenflugzeug jet [plane], jet propulsion plane, jetliner, jet aircraft (airliner), straight jet;
betriebseigenes ~ company (corporative, *US*) jet; **konventionelles** ~ regular jet;
~ **des Linienflugdienstes mit 120 - 160 Sitzen** 120 - 160 seat civil jet airliner;
täglich im ~ **zum Büro fliegen** to jet-commute;
~flotte jet fleet; **~hafen** jet port; **~motor** jet-aircraft engine; **~pendler** jet commuter; **~rundreise** roundtrip jet; **~verkehr** jet service.
Düsenfracht jet freightage;
~flugzeug jet cargo plane, jet freighter; **~gut** jet freight.
Düsen|hubschrauber jet helicopter; **~jäger** jet fighter; **~kampfflugzeug** jet fighter, lightning rod *(sl.)*; **~kopf** *(Auto)* nozzle head; **~maschine** jet transport; **~motor** jet engine; **~pilot** jet pilot (jockey, *sl.*); **~transportflugzeug** jet transport (freighter); **~treibstoff** jet fuel; **~triebwerk** jet engine; **~vergaser** jet carburettor; **~verkehrsflugzeug** jet liner (plane), jet airliner, commercial jet aircraft, turboliner; **~zeitalter** jet age.

Dussel sap, simpleton, nincompoop, dope *(US sl.)*.
dusselig silly, drowsy, sleepy.
düster gloomy, sombre, dark;
~ **aussehen** to look gloomy (blank); **alles ganz ~ sehen** to see the gloomy side of things;
~**es Bild von etw. entwerfen** to paint a gloomy picture of s. th.; ~**er Blick** sullen look; ~**e Farben** sombre colo(u)rs; **Zukunft in ~en Farben malen** to take a gloomy view of the future; ~**e Gedanken** melancholic thoughts; ~**er Lichtschein** dim light; ~**e Nacht** murky night; **mit ~er Stimme** in a sepulchral voice; ~**e Stimmung** dismal mood; ~**e Stimmung hervorrufen** to throw a gloom over the company; ~**e Vorahnungen** dark forebodings; ~**es Wetter** gloomy weather.
Düsternis gloom.
Dutzend dozen;
im ~ billiger cheaper by the dozen; **im ~ verkauft** sold by the dozen;
genau ein ~ an even dozen; **großes ~** long dozen; **knappes ~** a bare dozen; **volles ~** a round dozen;
pro ~ einen Dollar verlangen to ask a dollar a dozen;
~**erscheinung** very ordinary kind of man, mediocrity.
dutzendmal dozens and dozens of times.
Dutzend|mensch commonplace kind of man, mediocrity; ~**preis** price by the dozen; ~**ware** articles sold by the dozen, *(Menschen)* commonplace people.
dutzendweise by the dozen.
Duzfreundschaft [etwa] intimate friendship.
Dynamik dynamic.
dynamische|Persönlichkeit dynamic (forceful) personality; ~ **Rente** index-linked pension.
Dynamit, politisches political dynamite;
mit ~ sprengen to blow up with dynamite;
~**ladung** dynamite charge; ~**patrone** dynamite cartridge; ~**sprengung** dynamiting; ~**stange** stick of dynamite.
Dynamo, handbetriebener hand dynamo.
Dynast dynast.
Dynastie dynasty, house.
dynastisch dynastic.

E

E-Werk electricity works, electric company;
am ~ angeschlossen sein to take one's power from the mains.
Ebbe ebb, *(in der Kasse)* low water (tide);
wirtschaftliche ~ recession, slump;
~ und Flut ebb and flow, tide;
mit der ~ auslaufen to go out with the tide.
eben even, flat, level, plain, flush;
~er Boden flat bottom; **zu ~er Erde wohnen** to live on the ground (first, *US*) floor; **~es Land** flat country; **~e Straße** level road.
Ebenbild image, likeness;
absolutes ~ express image; **das ganze (genaue) ~** the living image, the very spit of;
~ seines Vaters picture (image, very spit) of one's father.
ebenbürtig of equal birth (rank);
j. den großen Schriftstellern für ~ halten to rank s. o. among the great writers; **jem. ~ sein** to be the equal of s. o., to be on a par with (match) s. o.;
ein mir geistig ~er Mensch a man of my own level.
Ebenbürtiger peer.
Ebenbürtigkeit equality of birth (rank, status).
Ebene plane, plain, flat, level [ground];
auf allen ~n at all levels; **auf gleicher ~** on a level; **auf höchster ~** top-level, at top level, on the highest level; **auf privater ~** privately; **auf staatlicher ~** at government level; **auf umfassender ~** on a wider plane; **über zwei ~n gebaut** split-level; **ausgedörrte ~** torrid plain; **handelspolitische ~** trade-policy level; **höhere gesellschaftliche ~** higher social level; **horizontale ~** horizontal plane; **schiefe ~** inclined plane; **staatliche ~** government level; **zweite staatliche ~** intermediate level of government;
~ für Personalentscheidungen manning level;
Gespräche auf höchster ~ führen to hold high-level talks; **auf die schiefe ~ geraten** to go to the bad, to be on the downgrade *(US)*; **auf eine höhere ~ heben** to lift; **auf der gleichen ~ stehen** to be on a (the same) level.
ebenerdig on the ground (first, *US*) floor;
~es Fenster ground-floor window; **~e Kreuzung** grade *(US)* (level, *Br.*) crossing.
ebenmäßige Gesichtszüge regular features.
ebnen to even [up], to plane, to make plane (even), to level;
jem. den Weg ~ to smooth (pave) the way for s. o.; **Verhandlungen den Weg ~** to clear (prepare) the ground for negotiations.
Echo echo;
~ finden to meet with a response; **in der ganzen Stadt ein ~ finden** to be the talk of the town; **lebhaftes ~ finden** to meet with lively approval; **starkes ~ finden** to create a big stir; **weltweites ~ finden** to excite world-wide interest; **~ in einem Gebirgstal hervorrufen** to wake echoes in a mountain valley; **weltweites ~ hervorrufen** to cause world-wide repercussions;
~lot sonic depth finder, *(mit Ultraschall)* echo sounder; **~lotung** echo sounding, radiolocation; **~zeichen** *(Radar)* blip.
echt genuine, bona fide, real, true, *(rechtmäßig)* legitimate, lawful, *(rein)* pure, *(unverfälscht)* unadulterated, *(Urkunde)* authentic[al], *(verbürgt)* warranted;
~es Anliegen matter of real concern; **~er Bruch** *(math.)* proper fraction; **~er Diskont** true discount; **~er Dollar** clean dollar; **~e Ersparnisse** genuine savings; **~e Farbe** fast colo(u)r; **~er Franzose** typical (true-born) Frenchman; **~e Freude** unmixed joy; **~e Freundschaft** true friendship; **~es Gold** real gold; **~er Kurs** true rate; **~es Leder** genuine leather; **~e Perlen** real pearls; **~er Perser[teppich]** real Persian carpet; **~er Rembrandt** genuine Rembrandt; **von ~em Schrot und Korn sein** to be a man of the old stamp; **~es Silber** sterling silver.
Echtheit genuineness, authenticity, *(Charakter)* sincerity, *(Farbe)* fastness, *(Rechtmäßigkeit)* legitimacy, *(Reinheit)* sterling quality;
~ der Unterschrift genuineness (authenticity) of a signature; **~ bestreiten** to put in a plea of forgery; **~ einer Urkunde bestreiten** to dispute the validity of a document; **~ feststellen** to authenticate; **für die ~ eines Artikels garantieren** to guarantee a thing as genuine; **berechtigte Zweifel an der ~ einer Unterschrift haben** to have reason to doubt the genuineness of a signature; **~ eines Diamanten prüfen** to test whether a diamond is real; **~ eines Textes verbürgen** to warrant the genuineness of a text; **mit dem Stempel der ~ versehen** to hallmark.
Echtheits|bescheinigung certificate of authenticity, authentication; **~beweis** proof of authenticity; **~beweis für etw. antreten** to prove the authenticity of s. th., to prove s. th. to be genuine; **~bürgschaft** warranty of genuineness; **~probe** forge test; **~zeugnis** certificate of authenticity.
Echtzeit *(Datenverarbeitung)* real time.
Ecke corner, *(Nische)* nook, recess;
in allen ~n und Winkeln in every hole and corner (nook and cranny); **mit abgerundeten ~n** round-cornered;
gefährliche ~ dangerous corner (intersection, crossing); **gemütliche ~** snug corner; **linke ~** left-hand corner; **obere ~** upper corner; **scharfe ~** sharp corner; **noch eine ziemliche ~** quite a distance;
alle ~n und Winkel eines Hauses the ins and outs of a house; **j. um die ~ bringen** to bump s. o. off, to do s. o. in *(sl.)*, to make away with s. o.; **Geld um die ~ bringen** to squander money; **j. in die ~ drängen** to back s. o. into a corner; **um die ~ fahren** to turn the corner; **jem. an allen ~n und Enden fehlen** to be quite lost without s. th.; **sich die ~n und Kanten abgestoßen haben** to have acquired polish; **aus allen ~n und Enden kommen** to come from all quarters (corners of the world); **~ mitnehmen** *(Auto)* to shave a corner; **um eine ~ sausen** to swing round a corner; **um die ~ herum mit jem. verwandt sein** to be distantly related to s. o.; **an allen ~n und Enden sparen** to save at a high rate; **etw. in die ~ stellen** *(fig.)* to shelve (pigeonhole) s. th.; **etw. in allen ~n suchen** to search for s. th. in every nook and cranny, to search high and low for s. th.; **jem. nicht um die ~ trauen** not to trust s. o. out of sight; **Geschäft an der ~ übernehmen** to take a corner shop; **um die ~ wohnen** to live round the corner (next door).
Ecken|steher corner man, loiterer, loafer; **~verstärkung** *(Buch)* corner.
Eck|fenster corner window; **~grundstück** open lot; **~haus** corner house.
eckig square, angular, *(ungeschickt)* clumsy, jerky, stiff;
sich ~ bewegen to move awkwardly;
~e Klammern square brackets.
Eck|laden corner shop (grocery, *US*); **~lohn[tarif]** basic wage (hourly rate), basic rate of pay, base pay (wage rate); **~lohnregelung** basic rate settlement; **~platz** corner seat; **oberer ~platz der Titelseite** box on the right of the masthead; **~pfeiler** corner post (pillar), *(fig.)* cornerstone; **~stein** cornerstone, headstone; **~stein der Zivilisation** cornerstone of civilization; **~stützen** *(Buch)* book ends; **~tisch** corner table; **~zimmer** corner room; **~zins** standard interest.
ed|el noble, aristocratic;
von ~ler Abstammung of noble birth; **~len Zweck verfolgen** to pursue a high purpose.
Edel|holz ornamental (fancy) wood; **~mann** noble.
Edelmetall precious metal;
ungemünztes ~ bullion;
~gewicht troy weight; **~handel** bullion trade; **~händler** bullion dealer; **~makler** bullion broker; **~prüfer** assayer.
edelmütig erweisen, sich to show o. s. magnanimous.
Edelstahl special (refined) steel.
Edelstein precious stone, gem, jewel;
ungeschliffener ~ uncut (rough) stone;
~imitation imitation jewelry; **~schleifer** cutter.
Edikt edict, law, enactment.
Effeff, etw. aus dem ~ verstehen to know one's stuff (onions), to be perfectly at home with s. th.
Effekt effect, result;
auf ~ berechnet calculated for effect; **ohne ~** ineffective, without avail; **zu diesem ~** to this end, to this purpose;
dramatische ~e scenic effects; **kurzfristiger ~** near-term effect; **typografischer ~ zur Führung des Lesers** bridge;
alles auf ~ berechnen to calculate everything for effect; **gewünschten ~ erzielen** to have the desired effect; **keinen ~ haben** to be of no effect; **nach ~ haschen** to play to the gallery (grandstand, *US*); **auf ~ aus sein** to grandstand *(US sl.)*.
Effekten papers, securities, negotiable instruments, effects, property, *(Aktien)* shares, stocks *(US)*, *(Obligationen)* debenture bonds, funds;
abhanden gekommene ~ lost securities; **ausländische ~** foreign securities; **beleihbare ~** securities eligible as collateral; **börsengängige ~** marketable securities (stocks, *US*); **an der Börse eingeführte ~** securities quoted at the stock exchange *(Br.)*, listed securities *(US)*; **alle an der Börse eingeführten ~** the

list *(US)*; **erstklassige** ~ high-grade (gilt-edged, *Br.*) securities, blue chips *(US)*; **festverzinsliche** ~ fixed-interest bearing securities; **fungible** ~ marketable securities; **international gehandelte** ~ international (interbourse, *Br.*) securities; **lebhaft gehandelte** ~ active securities; **in Report genommene** ~ stock taken in *(Br.)*; **aus dem allgemeinen Rahmen der Börsentendenz herausfallende** ~ market spots *(US)*; **hinterlegte** ~ securities deposited; **hochspekulative** ~ wildcat securities; **hochwertige** ~ high-grade (gilt-edged, *Br.*) securities, blue chips *(US)*; **lieferbare** ~ good delivery securities; **lombardierte** ~ pledged (pawned) securities, securities held in pledge (as collateral, *US*), stocks loaned *(US)*, pawned stocks *(US)*; **marktfähige (marktgängige)** ~ marketable securities (stocks, *US*), negotiable securities; **mündelsichere** ~ gilt-edged securities *(Br.)*, legal (trust) investments, trustee securities (investments) *(Br.)*; **nicht an der Börse notierte** ~ unlisted stock *(US)*, nonadmitted securities; **persönliche** ~ personal effects (belongings); **plazierte** ~ digested securities *(US)*; **nicht plazierte** ~ undigested securities *(US)*; **zur Börsennotierung zugelassene** ~ securities admitted to (listed at, *US*) the stock exchange;
~ **aus eigenen Beständen** long sale; ~ **mit Dividendenberechtigung** securities entitled to a dividend; ~ **mit Sonderbewegungen** market stocks *(US)*; ~ **mit geringen Umsätzen** inactive securities; ~ **mit täglichen Umsätzen** active securities, heavily traded shares;
zur Besicherung (in Kost) gegebene ~ **auswechseln** to commute securities; ~ **beleihen** to advance (lend) money on securities, to hypothecate securities *(US)*; ~ **an der Börse einführen** to introduce (list, *US*, market) securities on the stock exchange; ~ **an der Londoner Börse einführen** to obtain quotations of securities on the London stock exchange *(Br.)*; ~ **an der New Yorker Börse einführen** to list securities on the New York stock exchange *(US)*; **mit** ~ **festsitzen (festgefahren sein)** to be loaded up with securities; ~ **hinterlegen** to deposit securities; ~ **beleihen lassen** to borrow on (collaterate, *US*) securities; ~ **lombardieren lassen** to borrow on securities, to have securities hypothecated *(US)*; ~ **bei einer Bank lombardieren lassen** to pledge securities with a bank for payment of a loan; **als Pfand erhaltene** ~ **lombardieren lassen** to have securities rehypothecated *(US)*; ~ **lombardieren** to advance (lend, borrow) money on securities, to collaterate (hypothecate) securities *(US)*; **hochwertige** ~ **lombardieren** to sweeten a loan *(US)*; ~ **aus dem Depot nehmen** to withdraw securities from a deposit; ~ **ins Depot nehmen** to receive securities for safe custody *(Br.)* (safekeeping, *US*); **mit** ~ **hinreichend eingedeckt sein** to be long of the market *(US)*; **mit** ~ **sehr stark eingedeckt sein** to be loaded up with securities; ~ **verpfänden** to pledge securities; ~ **im Depot verwahren** to hold securities for safekeeping *(US)* (safe custody, *Br.*); ~ **vortragen** to carry over stock *(US)*;
~**abrechnung** stock account; ~**abrechnung erteilen** to pass a name; ~**abrechnungsstelle** clearinghouse; ~**absatz** marketing of securities; ~**abteilung** securities department (division), stock office *(US)*; ~**agio** premium on shares, stock discount *(US)*; ~**angebot** securities offerings; **gleichzeitiger** ~**ankauf und** ~**verkauf auf Terminbasis** straddling the market *(US)*; **spekulativer** ~**ankauf** *(während einer Baisse)* accumulation of securities.

Effektenanlage investment in securities;
risikoärmere, risikoschwächere ~ *(Kapitalanlagegesellschaft)* defensive portion; **risikoreichere** ~ *(Kapitalanlagegesellschaft)* aggressive portion *(US)*;
als ~ **für lange Sicht gelten** to be a purchase for the long pull *(US)*;
~**berater** investment adviser (counsel(l)or).

Effekten|arbitrage arbitrage in securities (funds), stock arbitrage (arbitration, *US*); ~**aufstellung** statement of securities; ~**auftrag** stock order; ~**ausführungsbuch** securities sales book (blotter, *US*); ~**austausch** portfolio switch; ~**auswahl** diversification of securities *(US)*; ~**bank** issuing house *(Br.)*, investment bank (banker) *(US)*, trust company *(US)*, security floating company *(US)*; ~**bankgeschäft** investment banking; ~**beleihung** advances on (against) securities, hypothecation of securities for a loan *(US)*; ~**berater** investment adviser (counsel(l)or), security research (stock, *US*) analyst, *(eines Maklers)* customer's man; ~**beratung** security advice; ~**beratung andienen** to offer security advice; ~**beratungstätigkeit** investment services; ~**bescheinigung** register certificate *(Br.)*; ~**besitz** paper holdings, stockholdings *(US)*, stock ownership *(US)*; ~**besitzer** security holder, shareholder, stockholder *(US)*, stockowner *(US)*.

Effektenbestand, Effektenbestände stocks in hand, security holdings, investment portfolio;
risikoärmerer ~ defensive portion; **risikoreicherer** ~**bestand** aggressive portion.

Effekten|bewertung securities rating *(US)*; ~**börse** stock exchange, stock market; ~**buch** stock ledger (market, *Br.*, transfer) book; ~**bündel** unit; ~**büro** securities department (division).

Effektendepot security *(US)* (safe custody, *Br.*) account, security register *(Br.)*, deposit of securities, stock deposit *(Br.)*, portfolio of securities;
~ **zum Taxwert** investment at valuation;
~**abteilung** safe custody *(Br.)* (custodianship, *US*) department; ~**gebühr** safe deposit *(Br.)* (custodianship, *US*) fee; ~**verwaltung** safe custody of securities *(Br.)*, portfolio management.

Effektendifferenzgeschäft marginal trading, margin business (buying, trading, *US*), buying on margin;
einzelnes ~ margin transaction.

Effekteneinführung quoting (marketing, listing, *US*) of securities.

Effektenemission securities (underwriting, capital) issue, issue of securities;
~ **garantieren (übernehmen)** to underwrite.

Effektenemissions|bank issuing house *(Br.)*, investment bank[er] *(US)*, trust company *(US)*; ~**geschäft** underwriting business; ~**konsortium** underwriting syndicate; ~**provision** underwriting commission; ~**vertrag** underwriting contract.

Effektenengagements [stock-exchange] commitments;
bis über den Hals in ~ **stecken** to be loaded up with securities; ~ **umstellen** to switch commitments.

Effekten|erfahrung stockbroking experience; ~**erwerb** purchase of securities; ~**finanzierungsgesellschaft** investment trust; ~**garantie** underwriting guarantee; ~**gattung** description (class) of securities.

Effektengeschäft dealing in stocks *(Br.)*, stock-exchange (securities) business, stockbroking [transaction], [stock]brokerage, stockjobbing, stockjobbery *(Br.)*;
~**e** securities dealings;
einzelnes ~ security (stock-exchange) transaction;
~**e auf Provisionsbasis durchführen** to execute orders in quoted (listed, *US*) securities on commission basis; **ins** ~ **gegangen sein** to have taken up stockbroking.

Effektengesellschaft mit festgelegtem Bestand fixed investment trust.

Effektengiro transfer of securities, marked transfer *(Br.)*, transferring of stock;
~**bank** clearinghouse; ~**verkauf** securities transaction through a clearinghouse.

Effekten|gruppe class of securities; ~**guthaben** portfolio of securities.

Effektenhandel stockbrokerage, stockbroking, brokerage, [stock]jobbing, stockjobbery *(Br.)*, security trading, securities dealings, stock trading *(US)*, dealing in stocks *(Br.)*;
außerbörslicher ~ over-the-counter business (trade) *(US)*;
~ **im Druckknopfverfahren** pushbutton trading; ~ **mit Hinweis auf die Erfolgsgeschichte des Unternehmens** jobbing backwards.

Effekten|händler securities (investment) dealer, jobber *(Br.)*, dealer in stocks, dealer in securities, [stock]broker, stockjobber *(Br.)*, trader *(US)*; ~**hausse** stock-market boom; ~**index** securities index, Dow John index *(US)*; ~**inhaber** holder of securities, stockowner *(US)*, stockholder *(Br.)*, bondholder; ~**kassierer** securities teller; ~**kauf** purchase of securities; ~**kauf mit Sicherungsleistung** margin system *(US)*; ~**käufer** taker; ~**kommission** underwriting commission; ~**kommissionsgeschäft** stock-exchange transaction; ~**konto** stock account, *(lebendes Depotkonto)* securities book *(Br.)* (register, *US*), *(totes Depotkonto)* securities ledger.

Effektenkredit advance on securities, collateral loan *(US)*;
~**anstalt** credit mobilier *(US)*.

Effekten|kundschaft investing public; ~**kurs** stock quotation, price of securities, security (market) price; ~**kurs jeder Gesellschaft widerspiegeln** to display quotations for each security; ~**kursniveau** stock-market level; ~**liquidationsbüro** settlement department *(Br.)*, clearinghouse *(US)*; ~**lombard** loan on security (upon collateral security, *US*); ~**lombardierung** pledging of securities, borrowing on collateral security *(US)*; ~**lombardkredit** share (stock, *US*) loan, collateral advance (loan) *(US)*; ~**makler** stockbroker, stockjobber, securities broker, salesman *(US)*; ~**maklerverband** securities industry association *(US)*.

Effektenmarkt stock (security) market, market for stocks *(Br.)*; **außerbörslicher** ~ over-the-counter securities market *(US)*; ~ **à la Baisse** bear market *(Br.)*; ~ **bis in seine Grundfesten erschüttern** to rock the securities market to its foundations.

Effekten|notierungen [securities] quotations; ~**order** stock order.

Effektenpaket block [of shares (bonds)], lot *(US)*; ~ **unter 1000 Dollar Nominalwert** broken lot *(US)*; ~ **billig abstoßen** to dump a block of shares.

Effekten|parität parity of stocks; ~**plazierung** placing of securities with the public; **direkte** ~**plazierung** private placing *(Br.)*.

Effektenportefeuille securities on hand, holdings, investment (security) portfolio; **eigenes** ~ securities owned by the bank; **gestreutes** ~ diversified portfolio; **optimal zusammengestelltes** ~ portfolio selection; **sein** ~ **am Börsentiefstpunkt abstoßen** to liquidate one's portfolio at the bottom of the market.

Effekten|posten lot; ~**preise** security prices; ~**provision** stock-exchange commission; ~**quittung** stock receipt *(Br.)*; ~**rechnung** stock *(Br.)* (security) account; ~**register** securities ledger *(Br.)*; ~**rendite** security (dividend) yield; ~**reserven** stock in reserve; ~**sammeldepot** omnibus deposit; ~**schalter** bargain counter; ~**sparen** investment saving; ~**spekulant** stock adventurer *(Br.)*, [stock]jobber; ~**spekulation** stock-market speculation, bargain hunting, stock adventure *(Br.)*; ~**spekulationen auf lange Sicht** long pull *(US)*; ~**stempel** stamp duty (tax), consideration money *(Br.)*, *(Schlußnotenstempel)* contract (transfer, *US*) stamp; ~**strazze** securities journal *(Br.)* (blotter, *US*); ~**termingeschäfte** forward operations (transactions) in securities, trading in security futures; ~**transaktionen** stockbroking [transactions], security (market, stockbroking) transactions; **spekulative** ~**transaktion durchführen** to take a flier *(US)*; ~**transaktion glattstellen** to undo a bargain *(Br.)*; ~**übernahmegesellschaft** underwriter; ~**übertragung** transfer of securities; ~**umsatz** transaction in securities.

Effektenverkauf, freihändiger over-the-counter trading *(US)*, direct sale to the public; ~ **aus eigenen Beständen** long sale; ~ **an Kapitalsammelstellen** institutional selling.

Effekten|verkäufe sale of securities, security sales; ~**verkäufer** giver, securities salesman; ~**verkaufsauftrag geben** to authorize the sale of stocks *(US)*; ~**verkaufsbefugnis** stock power *(US)*; ~**verkehr** stockbroking, stock-brokerage, stock and share business, market trading; **stückeloser** ~**verkehr** stock-market trading without transfer *(US)*; **außerbörslicher** ~**verkehr mit Kapitalsammelstellen** institutional trading; **ausgewogen angelegtes** ~**vermögen** balanced portfolio of assets; ~**vermögen einer Bank** bank portefeuille; ~**verwahrung** safekeeping *(US)* (safe custody, *Br.*) of securities; ~**verwalter** portfolio manager; ~**verwaltung** *(Banken)* safe deposit (custody of securities, *Br.*), custodianship *(US)*, management of securities, *(Kapitalanlagegesellschaft)* portfolio management; ~**verwertungsgesellschaft** securities company *(US)*; ~**verzeichnis** statement of securities, securities register *(US)*, deposit list *(US)*, memorandum of deposits *(US)*; ~**verzinsung** current yield; **ausmachender** ~**wert** cost of securities; ~**zinsen** interest on securities.

Effekthascherei showmanship, gallery play, histrionics, flamboyance, grandstand *(US)*, grandstand play *(US)*.

effektiv effective, real, actual; ~ **gesehen** in practical terms; ~ **zu hoch** definitively too high; ~ **im Besitz befindliche Aktien** real shares (stock, *US*); ~ **ausgegebenes Aktienkapital** issued stock *(US)*; ~**er Bedarf** actual demand; ~**er Bestand** actual amount, realized assets; ~**e Blockade** effective blockade; ~**es Einkommen** real income; ~**es Gehalt** effective pay rate; ~**e Kaufkraft** real purchasing power; ~**er Kontrast** effective contrast; ~**e Kosten** actual cost, actual price; ~**e Leistung** effective power; ~**er Markt** present market; ~**er Nettolohn** real take-home pay; ~**er Notenumlauf** active circulation; ~**er Preis** actual price; ~**e Stücke** actual bonds; ~**e Vertragserfüllung** specific performance; ~**e Verzinsung** *(Wertpapiere)* effective rate of interest, net (effective interest) yield; ~**e Waren** goods ready for immediate delivery; ~**er Wert** effective (actual, real) value; ~**e Wertminderung** actual depreciation; ~**er Zinssatz** effective rate.

Effektiv|bestand actual amount (balance), realizable assets; ~**bezüge** salaries actually earned; ~**einkommen** real income (earnings); ~**einnahmen** actual receipts; ~**geld** *(Versicherungspolice)* cash value; ~**geschäft** cash sale (transaction), spot transaction; ~**gewinn** actual profit; ~**händler** service wholesaler; ~**klausel** *(Wechsel)* currency clause; ~**kosten** actual costs; ~**kraft** effective force; ~**leistung** effective power; ~**lohn** net earnings (wage), take-home pay (package, income, wage); ~**preis** cash price; ~**stärke** *(mil.)* effective.

Effektivverzinsung effective interest yield, *(Wertpapier)* current [true] yield, net yield; ~ **bei rückkaufbaren Vorzugsaktien** effective rate of interest; ~ **von 7% bringen** to yield an effective sum equivalent to 7 per cent.

Effektiv|wert cash value, *(Versicherung)* actual cash value; ~**zahl** actual number; ~**zins** effective rate.

Effektmusik *(Film)* sound effects.

effektuieren to accomplish, to effect, to execute, to carry out.

Effektuierung eines Auftrages execution of an order.

effektvoll effective, purple.

Effizienz des Mitteleinsatzes cost effectiveness.

egal all the same, *(gleichartig)* alike, equal, uniform; **jem.** ~ **sein** to make no difference to s. o., not to matter with s. o.; **nicht** ~ **sein** not to match.

egalisieren to equalize, to adjust.

Egge farrow.

Egoismus egoism, egotism, selfishness, dissociality.

Egoist durch und durch thoroughpaced egoist.

egoistisch egoistic, selfish, asocial, self-seeking.

egozentrisch self-centered.

Ehe marriage, matrimony, wedlock; **aus erster** ~ from the first marriage; **die** ~ **betreffend** nuptial; **nicht voll anerkannte** ~ irregular marriage; **anfechtbare** ~ voidable marriage; **vom Schwiegervater erzwungene** ~ shotgun wedding; **freie** ~ common-law marriage; **gemischte** ~ mixed marriage; **gescheiterte** ~ marriage failure; **geschiedene** ~ divorced marriage; **im Ausland geschlossene** ~ foreign marriage; **mündlich geschlossene** ~ consensual marriage; **glückliche** ~ happy union; **gültige** ~ lawful marriage; **heimliche** ~ secret marriage; **kaputte** ~ broken home; **morganatische** ~ morganatic marriage; **nachfolgende** ~ subsequent marriage; **nichtige** ~ void marriage; **rechtsgültige** ~ regular (legal, valid) marriage; **ungültige** ~ void marriage; **vollzogene** ~ consummated marriage; **wilde** ~ compassionate marriage, cohabitation in state of adultery, concubinage; **zerbrochene** ~ broken home; **zerrüttete** ~ irretrievably broken-down marriage; ~ **anfechten** to contest the validity of a marriage; ~ **aufheben** to annul (dissolve, evacuate) a marriage; ~ **brechen** to commit adultery; ~ **eingehen** to contract a marriage, to get married; **mit jem. die** ~ **eingehen** to take s. one's hand in marriage; **zweite** ~ **eingehen** to marry again, to marry a second time, to remarry; **sich in eine** ~ **einmischen** to meddle in a marriage; ~ **für nichtig erklären** to declare a marriage invalid, to annul a marriage; **im Hafen der** ~ **landen** to get hitched *(coll.)*; ~ **für nichtig erklären lassen** to have a marriage nullified by decree of court; **in glücklicher** ~ **leben** to be happily married; **in wilder** ~ **leben** to live in [open] sin, to cohabit; ~ **scheiden** to grant a divorce, to divorce a couple; ~ **schließen** to marry, to celebrate a marriage, to get married; **gemischte** ~ **schließen** to intermarry; **in den heiligen Stand der** ~ **treten** to be joined in holy matrimony; ~**anbahnung** marriage brokerage, matchmaking; ~**anbahnungsinstitut** matrimonial agency; ~**anerkennung** *(Fremdstaat)* recognition of a marriage; ~**anfechtbarkeit** contestability of a marriage; ~**anfechtungsklage** action for annulment, suit of nullity of marriage; ~**aufgebot** banns; ~**aufhebung** annulment (dissolution) of a marriage; ~**aufhebungsklage** nullity suit, suit of nullity of marriage; ~**auflösung** absolute dovorce, dissolution of marriage; ~**auflösungsklage** nullity suit; ~**band** marital bond, marriage tie, band of matrimony; ~**berater** matrimonial adviser, marriage guidance counsellor; ~**beratung** marriage guidance; ~**beratungsstelle** marriage guidance council (relations clinic), family agency *(US)*; ~**betrug** marriage under false pretences.

ehebrechen to commit adultery.

Ehebrecher adulterer.

ehebrecherisch adulterous, adulterate; ~**er Umgang** adulterous intercourse.

Ehebruch adultery, criminal conversation, conjugal infidelity; ~ **begehen** to commit adultery.

ehebrüchig werden to become an adulterer.

Ehe|bund marriage bond; ~**bund eingehen** to be joined in marriage; ~**dispens** marriage dispensation; ~**drachen** battle-axe *(sl.)*; ~**erlaubnis** marriage lines *(Br.)* (licence, *US*).

ehefähig marriageable, nubile.

Ehefähigkeitszeugnis certificate of nubility.

Ehefrau wife, spouse, married woman, feme covert;
rechtmäßig angetraute ~ lawful [wedded] wife; **berufstätige** ~ working wife; **getrennt lebende** ~ wife living apart, grass widow; **[nicht] mitarbeitende** ~ [non]working wife; **perfekte** ~ pattern wife; **verlassene** ~ neglected wife;
~ **finden** to win a wife; **ohne** ~ **kommen** to come stag; **seine** ~ **verlassen** to leave one's wife; **seine** ~ **böswillig verlassen** to desert one's wife without cause.

Ehegatte husband, spouse, consort, marital partner, mate;
geschiedene ~**n** divorced couple (parties); **getrennt lebender** ~ separated marital partner; **überlebender** ~ surviving spouse (partner);
~**n hintergehen** to be false to one's husband.

Ehegatten|anteil in einem Heiratsvertrag contribution of each party in a marriage settlement; ~**besteuerung** taxation of spouses; ~**freibetrag** *(Einkommensteuer)* marriage allowance; ~**straftat** crime against the other; ~**unterhalt** matrimonial maintenance *(Br.)*.

Ehe|gelöbnis vow; ~**gemeinschaft** conjugal consortium; ~**genehmigung** marriage licence *(US)* (lines, *Br.*); ~**gesetz** Marriage Act; ~**güterrecht** regime.

Ehehindernis civil disability, bar (impediment) to marriage;
~**se** impedimenta;
absolutes ~ absolute impediment; **kirchliches** ~ canonical disability; **relatives** ~ relative impediment; **trennendes (unheilbares)** ~ diriment impediment.

Ehe|jahr year of matrimony; ~**joch** matrimonial yoke; **sich ins** ~**joch begeben** to put one's head in the marriage noose; ~**kandidat** marrying man; ~**konsens** marriage licence; ~**leben** married (wedded, conjugal) life.

Eheleute husband and wife, married couple (people), conjoints, spouses;
wie ~ **zusammenleben** to live and cohabit as husband and wife.

ehelich connubial, conjugal, matrimonial, marital, nuptial, *(Kind)* legitimate, trueborn;
~ **geboren** born in wedlock; ~ **verbunden** yoked in marriage; **für** ~ **erklären** to legitimate, to legitimize;
von ~**er Abstammung** to legitimate descent; ~**e Bande** marriage ties; ~**e Differenzen** matrimonial differences; ~**e Gemeinschaft** conjugal community, married life; ~**e Gemeinschaft aufheben** to separate from bed and board; ~**e Gemeinschaft wiederherstellen** to restitute conjugal rights; ~**e Gewalt** marital powers; ~**e Gütergemeinschaft** communion of goods; ~**es Kind** legitimate child; ~**es Leben** wedded (married) life; ~**e Lebensgemeinschaft** conjugal consortium; ~**e Nachkommen** legitimate issue; ~**e Nutznießung** apronstring tenure; ~**e Pflichten** marital (conjugal) duties, matrimonial obligations; ~**e Rechte** conjugal (marital) rights; ~**e Schwierigkeiten** matrimonial troubles; ~**er Status** status of legitimacy; ~**er Unterhalt** matrimonial maintenance; ~**e Untreue** conjugal infidelity; ~**e Verbindung** matrimony, marriage; ~**e Verbindung eingehen** to contract a marriage; ~**er Verkehr** marital relations; ~**er Wohnsitz** matrimonial domicile; **der** ~**en Zuneigung entfremden** to alienate affection; ~**es Zusammenleben** matrimonial cohabitation.

ehelichen to marry, to take in marriage.

Ehelichkeit legitimacy;
~ **anfechten** to contest legitimacy.

Ehelichkeitserklärung legitimation.

ehelos unmarried, single.

Ehelosigkeit unmarried (unwedded) state, disgrace, celibacy.

Ehemakler matchmaker.

ehemalig late, ex, former, one-time, old, *(außer Betrieb)* defunct;
~**er Bürgermeister** late burgomaster (mayor); ~**er Minister** ex-minister; ~**er Präsident** former president; ~**er Schüler** former pupil, old boy *(Br.)*, alumnus *(US)*; **in unserer** ~**en Wohnung** in our old flat.

Ehemann husband, married man;
bedachter ~ prudent husband;
~ **ergattern** to hook a husband *(coll.)*; **sich von seinem** ~ **scheiden lassen** to divorce one's husband; **sich jem. als** ~ **schnappen** to land s. o. for a husband.

ehemännlich marital;
~**e Genehmigung** husband's authorization.

ehemündig of marriageable age, nubile.

Ehe|mündigkeit legal age to consent marriage, nubility, marriageableness; ~**name** married name; ~**nichtigkeit** nullity of marriage, diriment impediment.

Ehenichtigkeits|antrag suit of nullity of marriage, nullity suit; ~**erklärung** decree of nullity; ~**grund** diriment impediment; ~**urteil** annulment of marriage.

Ehe|paar married couple; ~**paar ohne Verpflichtungen** married couple without encumberment; ~**partner** spouse; ~**problem** matrimonial problem; ~**prozeß** matrimonial course, divorce suit; ~**recht** law of marriage, matrimonial law; ~**ring** marriage ring; ~**sache** matrimonial action (cause).

Ehescheidung judicial divorce, dissolution of marriage;
endgültige ~ decree absolute;
~ **im gegenseitigen Einverständnis** divorce by mutual consent;
~ **beantragen, auf** ~ **klagen** to sue for a divorce, to petition for divorce.

Ehescheidungs|gericht Court for Divorce and Matrimonial Causes, divorce court; ~**gesetz** divorce law; ~**grund** ground for divorce; ~**klage** petition for divorce, divorce suit; ~**klage einleiten** to start (take) divorce proceedings; ~**prozeß** divorce suit; ~**recht** law of divorce; ~**reform** divorce law reform; ~**sache** divorce suit (case); ~**urteil** divorce decree, decree of nullity; ~**verfahren** divorce proceedings.

Eheschließender party contracting marriage.

Eheschließung marriage [ceremony], contraction (celebration) of marriage;
formlose ~ Scotch marriage; **gültige** ~ valid marriage; **heimliche** ~ clandestine marriage; **standesamtliche** ~ commonlaw (civil) marriage; **zweite** ~ deuterogamy;
~ **zur linken Hand** left-hand marriage; ~**en pro Kopf der Bevölkerung** marriage rate;
~ **anzeigen** to announce a marriage; ~ **legitimieren** to acknowledge a secret marriage.

Eheschließungs|akt marriage ceremony; ~**feierlichkeit** marriage ceremony; ~**urkunde** marriage certificate.

Ehestand marital status, married life (state), matrimony, wedlock, connubiality;
heiliger ~ holy state of matrimony;
in den ~ **treten** to contract a marriage, to get married.

Ehestands|beihilfe marriage grant; ~**darlehn** marriage loan.

Ehe|stifter matchmaker; ~**streitigkeit** matrimonial cause.

ehetauglich marrigeable.

Ehetauglichkeit marriageabilitiy, marrigeableness.

Ehetauglichkeitszeugnis marriage certificate.

Ehe|trennung separation from bed and board; ~**unbedenklichkeitsbescheinigung** marriage certificate (lines, *Br.*).

eheunmündig not of marrigeable age.

Ehe|urkunde marriage certificate; ~**verbot** restraint of marriage, marriage barrier, prohibitive impediment; ~**verfehlung** matrimonial offence; ~**verlöbnis** engagement; ~**vermittlung** marriage brokerage, matchmaking; ~**vermittlungsvertrag** marriage brokerage contract; ~**versprechen** marriage promise.

Ehevertrag marriage settlement, marriage (civil) contract, covenant of marriage;
nach der Eheschließung abgeschlossener ~ antenuptial (postnuptial) settlement; **vorläufiger** ~ marriage articles.

ehewidrig|e Beziehungen extramarital relations, intimacy; ~**es Verhalten** matrimonial offence, constructive desertion; ~**es Verhältnis** extramarital relationship.

Ehe|widrigkeit matrimonial offence; ~**wohnung** matrimonial home (domicile); ~**zerrüttung** irretrievable breakdown of marriage; ~**zwistigkeiten** matrimonial differences.

Ehrabschneidung defamation of character, calumnination.

ehrbar honest, respectable, esteemed, worthy.

Ehrbarkeit honesty, respectability.

Ehre hono(u)r, escutcheon, glory, distinction;
bei meiner ~ upon my word; **um der** ~ **zu genügen** for hono(u)r's sake; **zu jds.** ~ to s. one's hono(u)r;
akademische ~**n** academic hono(u)rs; **zweifelhafte** ~**n** dubious hono(u)rs;
jem. die ~ **abschneiden** to blacken s. one's reputation; **jem. etw. zur** ~ **anrechnen** to give s. o. credit for s. th.; **dem Essen alle** ~ **antun** to do justice to a meal; **etw. als** ~ **betrachten** to consider it an hono(u)r; **um die** ~ **von jds. Besuch bitten** to request the hono(u)r of s. one's company; **j. um seine** ~ **bringen** to dishono(u)r s. o.; **Brauch wieder zu** ~**n bringen** to bring a custom into hono(u)r; **seine** ~ **dareinsetzen** to make it a point of hono(u)r; **jem.** ~ **einbringen (zur** ~ **gereichen)** to do s. o. credit; **j. mit allen ihm gebührenden** ~**n empfangen** to receive s. o. with all due hono(u)rs; **jem.** ~ **erweisen** to do s. o. the hono(u)r, to pay homage to s. o.; **jem. die letzte** ~ **erweisen** to pay the last hono(u)rs (final respects) to (perform the last offices for) s. o., to follow s. o. to his grave (to the grave-side); **jem. militärische** ~**n erweisen** to grant s. o. military hono(u)rs; **sich in seiner** ~ **gekränkt fühlen** to feel wounded in one's hono(u)r; **sich die** ~ **geben, j. einzuladen** to request the pleasure of s. one's company; **zu jds.** ~**n ein Essen geben** to tender s. o. a

complimentary dinner; **jds. in ~n gedenken** to hono(u)r the memory of s. o.; **seiner ~ verlustig gehen** to forfeit one's hono(u)r; **zu den höchsten ~n gelangen** to attain the highest hono(u)rs; **jem. zur ~ gereichen** to reflect credit on s. o.; **Fleck auf seiner ~ haben** to have a blot on one's escutcheon; **keine ~ im Leib haben** to have no sense of hono(u)r; **j. in hohen ~n halten** to hold s. o. in high esteem; **Bankett zu jds. ~n halten** to give a testimonial dinner for s. o.; **jds. ~ herabsetzen** to impeach s. one's hono(u)r; **mit ~n aus einer Sache hervorgehen** to come out of an affair with hono(u)r; **plötzlich zu ~n kommen** to strike into reputation; **Geld in ~n nicht annehmen können** not to be able in hono(u)r to accept the money; **jds. Mut alle ~ machen** to speak well for s. one's courage; **seinem Lande ~ machen** to do credit to one's country; **seiner Schule alle ~ machen** to be a credit to one's school; **j. bei der ~ packen** to appeal to s. one's hono(u)r, to put s. o. on his mettle; **auf seine ~ pfeifen** to fling away one's hono(u)r; **in ~n ergraut sein** to have reached a venerable old age; **auf dem Feld der ~ gefallen sein** to have died for one's country (on the field of hono(u)r); **die ~ in Person sein** to be the soul of hono(u)r; **seiner ~ schuldig sein** to be bound in hono(u)r; **seine ~ aufs Spiel setzen** to stake one's hono(u)r; **seine ~ höher stellen als Reichtum** to put hono(u)r before riches; **seine ~ in den Staub treten** to fling away one's hono(u)r; **j. mit ~n überschütten** to shower s. o. with hono(u)rs; **jds. ~ verletzen** to cast a slur on s. one's reputation; **seine ~ verpfänden** to pledge one's hono(u)r; **auf ~ und Gewissen versichern** to state on one's hono(u)r; **seine ~ wahren** to guard one's good name; **seine ~ wegwerfen** to fling away one's hono(u)r;

~ **wem ~ gebührt** hono(u)r to whom hono(u)r is due.

ehren, auszeichnen to hono(u)r, to dignify.

Ehren|abordnung guard of hono(u)r; ~**abzeichen** medal, decoration; ~**akzept** collateral acceptance, acceptance for (upon) hono(u)r *(Br.)* (supra protest, *US*); ~**akzeptant** acceptor for hono(u)r; ~**amt** honorary appointment, office of hono(u)r, honorary office (function, position), unpaid position; ~**amt bekleiden** to hold an honorary office.

ehrenamtlich honorary, in an honorary capacity, unsalaried, unpaid;

~ **tätig sein** to serve in an honorary capacity;

~**e Funktion** honorary duties; ~**er Präsident** honorary president; ~**e Tätigkeit** honorary service; ~ **tätiger Treuhänder** honorary trustee; ~**er Vertreter** unpaid agent.

Ehren|angelegenheit affair of hono(u)r; ~**annahme** act of hono(u)r, collateral acceptance, acceptance for (upon) hono(u)r *(Br.)* (supra protest, *US*); ~**bankett** testimonial (complimentary) dinner; ~**beleidigung** insult; ~**bezeigung** *(mil.)* salute.

Ehrenbürger freeman of a city, honorary freeman;

~ **einer Stadt werden, zum ~ ernannt werden** to be admitted as freeman of a city;

~**recht** freedom of a city; ~**recht verliehen erhalten** to be admitted as freeman of a city.

ehrend|es Andenken bewahren, jem. ein to hono(u)r (pay tribute to) s. one's memory; ~**e Anerkennung** hono(u)rable mention.

Ehren|denkmal honorary monument; **jem. den letzten ~dienst erweisen** to pay the last hono(u)rs (final respects) to s. o.; ~**doktor** honorary degree; ~**doktorwürde** honorary doctorate; ~**eintritt** act of hono(u)r; **notariell beurkundeter ~eintritt** notarial act of hono(u)r; ~**erklärung** satisfaction, amende honorable; ~**formation abschreiten** to inspect the guard of hono(u)r; ~**friedhof** memorial cemetery; ~**gabe** testimonial; ~**garde** guard of hono(u)r; ~**gast** guest of hono(u)r; ~**gehalt** honorarium; ~**geleit** escort; ~**gericht** court of hono(u)r, *(Anwaltskammer)* disciplinary committee; **ärztliches ~gericht** Medical Council.

ehrengerichtliches Verfahren disciplinary proceedings.

Ehrengerichts|barkeit disciplinary jurisdiction; ~**verfahren** disciplinary proceedings.

ehrenhaft honorable, respectable, worthy;

~ **im Heeresbericht erwähnt werden** *(Soldat)* to be mentioned in the dispatches;

auf ~e Art und Weise honestly; ~**e Bedingungen** honorable terms; ~**es Leben führen** to lead a respectable life.

ehrenhalber for hono(u)r's sake;

~ **verliehener Grad** honorary degree; ~ **verliehener Rang** honorary rank.

Ehren|halle pantheon; ~**intervention** intervention supra protest; ~**karte** complimentary ticket; ~**kodex** code of hono(u)r; **journalistischer ~kodex** press code; **sich an den ungeschriebenen ~kodex halten** to play the game; ~**komitee** committee of hono(u)r; ~**kompanie abschreiten** to inspect the guard of hono(u)r; ~**kränkung** slander, defamation, insult to s. one's hono(u)r, affront; ~**mahl** complimentary dinner; ~**mal** war memorial; ~**mann** gentleman; **durch und durch ein ~mann sein** to be the soul of hono(u)r; ~**medaille** medal; **mit einer ~medaille auszeichnen** to award a medal; ~**mitglied** honorary member; ~**mitgliedschaft** honorary membership; ~**patenschaft** honorary sponsorship; ~**platz** complimentary seat, seat of hono(u)r; ~**platz einnehmen** to occupy the seat of hono(u)r; ~**platz in der Ruhmeshalle einnehmen** to have a niche in the temple of fame; ~**präsident** honorary chairman; ~**preis** prize; ~**preis gewähren** to award a prize of hono(u)r; ~**preis gewinnen** to carry off the first prize; ~**punkt** punctilio of hono(u)r.

Ehrenrechte, bürgerliche civil (civic) rights;

der bürgerlichen ~ verlustig infamous;

jem. die bürgerlichen ~ aberkennen, zum Verlust der bürgerlichen ~ verurteilen to deprive (dispossess) s. o. of civil rights.

Ehren|rechtsverlust loss of civil (civic) rights; ~**redner** guest speaker; ~**retter** apologizer; ~**rettung** rehabilitation, whitewash *(Br.)*; **zu jds. ~rettung** in vindication of s. one's conduct.

ehrenrührig dishono(u)rable, discreditable, disgraceful, slanderous, libellous, defamatory;

~**e Behauptungen** defamatory matter; ~**e Dinge verbreiten** to publish (exhibit) intentionally libellous matter.

Ehrensache *(Strafgericht)* libelsuit;

jem. eine ~ anhängen to bring an action of slander against s. o.; **etw. als ~ ansehen (betrachten)** to make (regard) it a point of hono(u)r.

Ehren|salut schießen to sound the last post; ~**schuld** honorary debt; ~**sitz** place of hono(u)r, chair; ~**sold** honorary pay; ~**tafel** memorial tablet, roll of hono(u)r; ~**tag** great day; **an seinem ~tag** on his birthday; ~**tage** *(Wechsel)* days of grace; ~**titel** courtesy (honorary) title; ~**tribüne** tribune of hono(u)r; ~**urkunde** certificate of hono(u)r; ~**veranstaltung** testimonial *(US)*; ~**verleihungen** hono(u)rs *(Br.)*.

ehrenvoll|er Abschied honorable discharge; ~**en Abzug aus einer Festung erhalten** to leave a fortress with all the hono(u)rs of war.

Ehren|vorsitzender honorary president (chairman); ~**wache** guard of hono(u)r; ~**wache abschreiten** to inspect the guard of hono(u)r.

ehrenwert esteemed, respected, worthy;

äußerst ~ up and up *(sl.)*.

Ehrenwort parole, word of hono(u)r;

auf ~ upon my hono(u)r;

sein ~ brechen to break one's parole; **Gefangene auf ~ entlassen** to put a prisoner on parole; **sein ~ geben (verpfänden)** to pledge one's word; **auf ~ freigelassen sein** to be on parole; **jem. auf sein ~ hin trauen** to put s. o. on his hono(u)r.

ehrenwörtlich|verpflichtet sein to be on one's hono(u)r;

~**es Versprechen** solemn promise.

Ehren|zahler *(Wechsel)* payer for hono(u)r; ~**zahlung nach Protest** payment for hono(u)r supra protest; ~**zeichen** distinction, decoration, medal; **mit allen Orden und ~zeichen** beribboned and bemedalled.

ehrerbietig respectful, deferential.

Ehrerbietung hono(u)r, respect, deference, homage, obeissance;

jem. ~ erweisen to pay reverence to s. o., to lay one's homage at s. one's feet.

Ehrfurcht veneration, reverence, awe;

~ **vor etw. empfinden** to feel respect for s. th.; **jds. in ~ gedenken** to treasure s. one's memory.

ehrfürchtiges Schweigen reverent silence.

Ehrgefühl sense of hono(u)r;

jds. ~ verletzen to hurt s. one's pride.

Ehrgeiz, vom ~ angestachelt (angetrieben) spurred by ambition, for the sake of kudos;

brennender ~ fire on one's belt; **gesellschaftlicher ~** tufthunting; **grenzenloser (hemmungsloser) ~** limitless (unbound) ambition; **höchster ~** top of s. one's ambition; **krankhafter ~** morbid ambition;

~ **anspornen** to wake ambition; **jds. ~ anstacheln** to pander to s. one's ambition, to put s. o. on his mettle; **seinen ~ fahren lassen** to lay aside all ambitions; **vom ~ besessen sein** to be possessed with ambition.

ehrgeizig ambitious, high-flying.

Ehrgeizling highflier, pusher;

gesellschaftlicher ~ tufthunter.

ehrlich honest, straight from the shoulder, aboveboard, sincere, candid, transparent, clean-fingered, on the square *(coll.)*, on the level, up-and-down *(US coll.)*, white *(US coll.)*;

sich ~ bemühen to try to the best of one's ability; **~ glauben** to truly believe; **es ganz ~ meinen** to be quite honest about it; **~ mit jem. sein** to be frank (open) with s. o.; **um ganz ~ zu sein** to be perfectly candid; **offen und ~ zugehen** to be open and aboveboard;
~e Absichten honorable intentions; **~e Antwort** frank answer; **auf ~e Art und Weise** honestly; **~er Bericht** candid account; **sein ~es Brot verdienen** to earn an honest penny; **~en Charakter haben** to be an upright character; **~er Geschäftsmann** straight man of business; **~es Gewerbe** honest trade; **~e Gewinne** honest profits; **~er Handel** square deal; **~e Haut** honest nature, soul of hono(u)r; **~e Leute** honest people; **seine ~e Meinung sagen** to speak one's mind; **~es Mitgefühl** sincere sympathy; **in ~er Sorge** the devil to pay; **auf ~e Weise** by fair means;
~ währt am längsten honesty is the best policy.

Ehrlichkeit truth, sincerity, honesty, truthfulness, fairness;
übertriebene ~ hypersincerity;
jds. ~ in Frage stellen to question the honesty of s. o.;
~ zahlt sich aus honesty pays.

ehrlos dishonourable, disreputable, infamo(u)s.

Ehrlosigkeit infamy.

Ehrungen, akademische academic hono(u)rs;
~ anläßlich des Neuen Jahres New Year's hono(u)rs;
jem. mit ~ überhäufen to load s. o. with hono(u)rs; **auf ~ verzichten** to waive hono(u)rs.

Ehrverletzung real injury, defamation.

ehrwürdig venerable, hoary.

Ei egg, *(Kugel)* pill *(sl.)*;
wie aus dem ~ gepellt as sweet as nuts, spick and span; **wie ein ~ den anderen ähnlich** like two peas [in a pod];
faules ~ rotten egg;
~ des Kolumbus it is simplicity itself;
j. wie ein rohes ~ behandeln to handle s. o. with kid gloves, to step gingerly around s. o.; **für einen Apfel und ein ~ bekommen** to get it for a mere song; **mit faulen ~ern bewerfen** to rotten-egg; **wie auf ~ern gehen** to mind one's P's and Q's *(coll.)*; **wie ein ~ dem anderen gleichen** to be as like as two peas; **sich nicht um ungelegte ~er kümmern** not to cross one's bridges before one comes to them *(fam.)*; **das ~ will klüger als die Henne sein** go and try to teach your grandmother to suck eggs.

Eichamt, staatliches Office of Weights and Measures *(Br.)*, Bureau of Standards *(US)*, gauging office.

Eiche, fest wie eine ~ stehen to stand as firm as a rock.

Eichen, Eichung standardization, calibration, gauging.

eichen to gauge *(Br.)*, to calibrate, to standardize, to gage *(US)*, to measure, *(Gewicht)* to adjust.

Eich|gewicht standard weight; **~maß** gauge; **~meister** public weigher, surveyor of weights and measures *(Br.)*, gauger; **~schein** gauger's certificate, *(Schiff)* certificate of measurement; **~stab** gauging rod.

Eichung gauging, standardization, rectification, admeasurement.

Eid oath;
an ~es Statt in lieu of an affidavit (oath); **unter ~** by (on, upon, under) oath;
vom Richter abgenommener (vor Gericht abgelegter, gerichtlich auferlegter) ~ judicial oath, oath in supplement; **außergerichtlicher ~** extrajudicial oath; **beschränkter ~** qualified oath; **falscher ~** false oath; **wissentlich falscher ~** perjury; **feierlicher ~** solemn (corporal) oath; **nicht gebrochener ~** unbroken oath; **unverbrüchlicher ~** ironclad oath; **zugeschobener ~** decisive (decisory) oath;
~ auf die Bibel gospel oath;
~ ablegen to take an oath upon, to execute an oath; **~ auf die Verfassung ablegen** to swear to uphold and to defend the constitution; **jem. einen ~ abnehmen** to administer (tender) an oath to s. o.; **~ auferlegen** to impose an oath; **unter ~ aussagen (bezeugen)** to testify under oath; **als Zeuge unter ~ aussagen** to make oath and depose; **unter ~ bestätigen** to affeer; **unter ~ bezeugen** to testify under oath; **seinen ~ brechen** to violate one's oath; **j. seines ~es entbinden** to release s. o. from (relieve s. o. of) his oath; **unter ~ erklären** to state on oath; **an ~es Statt erklären (versichern)** to execute an affidavit, to make an affirmation; **~ leisten** to swear (make, take) an oath; **~ nachsprechen** to repeat the oath; **etw. auf seinen ~ nehmen** to take it on one's oath; **falschen ~ schwören** to commit perjury, to perjure o. s.; **tausend ~e schwören** to swear by all that is holy; **durch einen ~ gebunden sein** to be under (on one's) oath; **unter ~ verneinen** to forswear; **~ verweigern** to refuse to take on the oath; **jem. den ~ zurückschieben** to tender back an oath to s. o.; **jem. den ~ zuschieben** to put s. o. on his (give s. o. the) oath.

Eidbruch perjury, violation (breach) of an oath, oath-breaking.

eidbrüchig forsworn, perjured;
~ werden to break one's oath.

Eides|ablegung, ~leistung taking an oath; **~abnahme** administration of an oath, juration.

eidesfähig oathworthy.

Eidesfähigkeit oathworthiness.

Eidesformel wording (text) of an oath;
vorgeschriebene ~ set form of an oath.

Eidesleiter taker of an oath, oathmaker, deponent, affiant *(US)*.

Eidesleistung swearing, taking of an oath, *(Rekruten)* attestation *(Br.)*;
nach der ~ after the administration of an oath;
feierliche ~ solemn oath.

Eidespflicht verletzen to violate the sanctity of an oath.

eidesstattlich versichern to affirm *(US)*, to depose on oath.

eidesstattliche Erklärung (Versicherung) statutory declaration *(Br.)*, affidavit, testimony under oath.
verjährte ~ stale affidavit;
~ abgeben to file a statutory declaration *(Br.)* (an affidavit); **~ entgegennehmen** to take an affidavit.

Eides|verletzung violation of an oath; **~verweigerer** nonjuror; **~verweigerung** refusal to take the oath.

eidlich [up]on (under) oath, juratory;
~ verpflichtet oath-bound, by (on, upon, under) oath;
~ bestreiten to forswear; **~ erhärten** to confirm by oath; **~ gebunden sein** to be on one's oath; **jem. ~ vernehmen** to tender (examine) s. o. on oath; **jem. ~ verpflichten** to take the oath of s. o., to bind s. o. by oath;
~e Aussage sworn deposition, statement on oath; **~e Erklärung** affidavit, statutory declaration; **~e Zeugenaussagen machen** to make oath and depose.

Eidschwur, durch by (on, upon, under) oath.

Eier|briketts ovoids; **~handgranate** egg-shaped hand-grenade, pineapple *(sl.)*; **~händler** egg dealer (man); **~kiste** egg box; **~landung** three-point landing; **einer Henne das ~legen beibringen wollen** to teach one's grandmother to suck eggs; **~schalen ablegen** to come of age; **~schalen noch nicht abgelegt haben** to be still wet behind the ears; **~tanz aufführen** to walk on eggshells.

Eifer eagerness, zeal, fervour, diligence;
im ~ des Gefechts in the heat of the moment; **mit übertriebenem ~** overzealously;
blinder ~ blind enthusiasm; **unermüdlicher ~** unflagging enthusiasm;
mit ~ an die Arbeit gehen to put one's heart and soul into one's work; **voller ~ sein, vor ~ sprühen** to glow with zeal, to kindle with eagerness;
blinder ~ schadet nur haste makes waste.

eifern, gegen alles to campaign against everything; **mit jem. um die Wette ~** to compete (vie) with s. o.

Eifersucht green-eyed monster, jealousy;
vor ~ verzehrt werden to be affected by the fumes of jealousy.

Eifersüchteleien, ewige constant jealousy.

eifersüchtig jealous, yellow.

eifrig earnest, eager, zealous, enthusiastic, ardent, fervent;
~ ergeben hand and foot;
sich ~ bemühen to put one's best foot forward; **~ lernen** to be an eager pupil; **~ bei der Arbeit sein** to be busy at (have a keen interest in one's) work; **~ darauf bedacht sein, zu gefallen** to be anxious to please; **~ bei der Sache sein** to show keen interest in; **~er Anhänger sein** strong partisan, heeler *(coll.)*; **~er Anhänger der neuen Bewegung** ardent supporter of the new movement; **~er Leser** avid reader.

eigen [of one's] own, to one's name;
zu ~ haben to own; **sich jds. Ansicht zu ~ machen** to agree with s. one's opinion; **sehr ~ in seiner Kleidung sein** to be fussy about one's clothes;
~e Aktien reacquired bonds, own shares *(Br.)*, treasury stock *(US)*; **~es Akzept** promissory note; **nach ~en Angaben** according to one's own statement; **aus ~em Antrieb** on one's own account; **~er Bedarf** personal requirements; **~er Bericht** *(Zeitung)* from our own correspondent; **~er Besitz** private property; **aus ~er Erfahrung sprechen** to speak from personal experience; **nach ~em Ermessen handeln** to use one's own discretion; **unser ~es Fabrikat** our own make; **sich ins ~e Fleisch schneiden** to cut off one's nose to spite one's face; **sein ~ Fleisch und Blut** one's own flesh and blood; **auf ~en Füßen stehen** to be on one's own (one's own master); **~er Garten** home garden; **auf ~e Gefahr** *(Transport)* at owner's risk; **~es Geld besitzen** to have money of one's own; **dem Empfänger zu**

~en Händen abzugeben to be delivered to the addressee in person; sein ~er Herr sein to be one's own master; keine ~en Kenntnisse von einem Ereignis haben to get news secondhand; etw. am ~en Leibe erfahren to taste it o. s.; ~e Mittel resources of one's own; im ~en Namen under one's own name; das ~e Nest beschmutzen to cry stinking fish; ~e Note *(Veranstaltung)* special flavo(u)r; ~e Order my [own] order; für ~e Rechnung for one's own account; für ~e Rechnung arbeiten to work on one's own; auf ~es Risiko at one's own risk; kümmere Dich um Deine ~en Sachen mind your own business; mit der ihm ~en Sorgfalt with the care characteristic of him; aus der ~en Tasche bezahlen to pay one's own way; auf ~e Verantwortung on one's own account; ~er Verbrauch personal consumption; ~es Vermögen independent means; über kein ~es Vermögen verfügen to have no resources of one's own; auf seinen ~en Vorteil bedacht sein to take care of number one; j. mit seinen ~en Waffen schlagen to beat s. o. at his own game; ~er Wagen *(Bahn)* home car; seinen ~en Wagen fahren to have one's own car; ~er Wechsel note of hand, promissory note; ~e Wohnung residential flat, individual apartment; seine ~en Worte his very words; ~es Zimmer separate room.

Eigen|akzept promissory note; **mit ~antrieb** self-driven (-powered); **~anzeige** *(Verleger)* house ad *(US)*; **~art** trait, peculiarity, characteristic feature; **~arten einer Stadt** individuality of a town.

eigenartig peculiar, odd, queer, strange, singular, rum *(Br., sl.)*; **~es Benehmen** strange (odd) behavio(u)r; **~e Schönheit** peculiar beauty.

Eigen|aufwand *(für Gerät und Kleidung)* personal expense; **~bau** self-construction.

Eigenbedarf personal requirements, personal use, *(eines Landes)* home requirements;
nur für den ~ for domestic use, for one's own needs, captive *(US)*;
~ für eine Wohnung anmelden to establish one's need of the property as the sole residence of o. s. or an adult member of one's family *(Br.)*; **~ selbst decken** to supply one's personal needs.

Eigenbehalt *(Versicherung)* self-retention; **~belastung** dead load; **~beleg** internal (intermediate) voucher; **~benutzung** occupation for s. o.; **~bericht unserer Zeitung** from our own correspondent; **~besitz** proprietary possession, proprietorship, exclusive (proprietary) possession, *(Grundstück)* [legal] freehold, demesne; **~besitzer** proprietary possessor.

Eigenbetrieb own factory, *(Landwirtschaft)* owner-operator; **kommunaler ~** owner-operated municipal enterprise; **landwirtschaftlicher ~** home (owner-operated, *US*) farm.

Eigen|bewertung akzeptieren, jds. hohe to take s. o. at his own valuation; **~bewirtschaftung** owner-operator; **~brötler** recluse, queer character; **~brötler sein** to keep o. s. to o. s.; **~erzeugung** domestic production; **~fabrikat** own make, self-produced article; **~fertigung** company-produced assets; **~finanzierung** independent financing, self-financing.

eigengebaut home-grown.

Eigen|gebrauch personal use; **~gefahr** *(Feuerversicherung)* individual risk.

eigengenutzt owner-occupied.

Eigen|geschäft business for one's own account, one's own business; **~geschwindigkeit** *(Flugzeug)* true airspeed; **maritime ~gewässer** national (inland) waters; **~gewicht** net (stamped, dead) weight, dead load, *(Eisenbahn)* tare weight, *(Flugzeug)* empty weight, *(Kraftfahrzeug)* empty; **~gut** fee simple, freehold; **~haftung** *(Kraftfahrer)* collision damage responsibility; **~handel** private trade, trade for one's own account; **~handelsvereinbarung** exclusive dealer arrangement *(US)*.

eigenhändig by (of, with) one's own hand, *(Brief)* autographic, handwritten, *(persönlich)* personally;
~ von mir unterschrieben given under my hand and seal;
etw. ~ schreiben to write s. th. in one's own hand; **Brief ~ schreiben** to write a letter in one's own hand; **jem. ~ übergeben** to deliver into s. one's hands; **~ unterschreiben** to sign personally;
~er Brief autograph letter; **~es Manuskript** autograph; **~ geschriebenes Testament** holographic will; **~e Unterschrift** autographic (one's own) signature.

Eigenhändler principal, distributor, *(Börse)* jobber *(Br.)*, floor trader *(US)*.

Eigenheim own home, owner-occupied house *(Br.)*, homecroft *(Br.)*, homestead *(US)*;
gewerblich genutztes ~ mit Viehzucht stock-raising homestead *(US)*;
~ erwerben to buy one's own house, to buy a home of one's own, to homestead *(US)*; **Erwerb eines ~s für Normalverbraucher unerschwinglich machen** to push home prices out of reach of ordinary people;
~anteil residential segment; **~ausstellung** home exhibition; **nachlassende ~baukonjunktur** slump in home building; **~besitz** owner-occupied housing, home ownership *(US)*; **~besitzer** home dweller (builder), owner occupier, homecrofter *(Br.)*, homeowner *(US)*, homesteader *(US)*; **~besitzer sein** to own one's home; **~errichtung** home building; **~erwerb** home purchase (buying), purchase of a home; **~erwerber** home buyer; **~finanzierung** financing of a new home, residential (home) financing; **~garage** home garage; **~grundstück** home site, single-family ground, residential estate; **~hypothek** residential (home, private house) mortgage; **~interessent** home seeker; **~mitglied** home-owning member; **betriebliches ~system** cottage system *(Br.)*; **~versicherungsgesellschaft** home insurer.

Eigen|heit feature, peculiarity; **~interesse** self-serving interest; **seine ~interessen fördern** to advance one's interests.

Eigenkapital equity [capital], owned (ownership) capital, proprietary capital, proprietor's stake, *(AG)* stockholder's (shareholder's) equity, net worth *(US)*, *(Bank)* capital resources, *(in der Bilanz)* capital and reserves, capital ownership;
zu niedrig bemessenes ~ low-geared capital; **festgesetztes ~** capital value; **verfügbares ~** disposable capital; **in den Rücklagen steckendes zusätzliches ~** capital surplus *(US)*;
~ einer Aktiengesellschaft shareholder's equity, equity of stockholders *(US)*, corporate net worth *(US)*;
~ ansparen to build equity;
~ausstattung equity equipment; **~bildung** equity accumulation; **~erhöhung** increase in equity; **bei Darlehnsvergabe ausgehandelter ~erwerb** equity kicker; **~koeffizient, ~quote** equity ratio; **~konto** proprietary account; **~verhältnisse** equity position; **~verzinsung** return on common equity (net worth, *US*).

Eigen|kontrolle ausüben to self-regulate; **~kosten** primary costs; **~leben** privacy; **~leistung** *(Anlagegüter)* self-construction, *(Warenbestand)* self-production; **aktivierte ~leistungen** company-manufactured capitalized items; **~liquidation** *(Hauptversammlung)* member's voluntary liquidation; **verbotene ~macht** unlawful act, illegitimate interference, private nuisance, *(Land)* deforcement, unlawful act, *(Grundstück)* forcible entry.

eigenmächtig arbitrary, unauthorized, usurpingly, high-handed;
etw. ~ tun to do s. th. off one's own bat; **~ vorgehen** to take the law into one's own hands;
~e Entscheidung arbitrary decision; **~es Handeln** unauthorized act.

Eigenmächtigkeit arbitrary action, high-handedness.

Eigen|marke private (house, own) brand; **~markenausstattung** private label(l)ing; **kostenlos beförderte ~materialien** nonrevenue freight; **~mittel** own resources, own funds, *(Bauherr)* building capital; **liquide und fast liquide ~mittel** cash and near-cash resources; **~mittel [ver]stärken** to strengthen its own funds; **~name** proper (family) name; **~nutz** self-interest, selfishness.

eigennützig selfish, self-interested.

Eigen|nutzung self-interest, *(Hauseigentümer)* owner occupation, occupation for o. s.; **~nutzungswert** *(Hauseigentümer)* imputed rent; **~persönlichkeit** personality; **~produktion** self-production; **auf ~rechnung** for one's own account.

eigens expressly, purposely;
~ dafür bestimmte Mittel earmarked funds.

Eigenschaft capacity, quality, appanage, *(Eigentümlichkeit)* peculiarity, *(jur.)* legal status, *(Merkmal)* property, attitude, nature, feature, characteristic;
in behördlicher ~ in its governmental capacity; **in beratender ~** in consultative capacity; **in dienstlicher ~** while an officer; **in der ~ als** in the capacity as; **ohne die erforderlichen ~en** ill-qualified; **in seiner ~ als Anwalt** as an advocate; **in seiner ~ als Richter** in his judicial capacity;
amtliche ~ official position; **berufliche ~** professional capacity; **geforderte berufliche ~en** qualities required for a post; **besondere ~en** personal (peculiar) characteristics; **charakteristische ~** attribute; **erworbene ~en** acquired characteristics; **gewertete ~** quality rated; **hervorragende ~en** sterling qualities; **kaufmännische ~** trading ability; **notwendige ~** essential quality; **persönliche ~en** personal characteristics; **physikalische ~en** physical properties; **unternehmerische ~en** executive skills; **wertvolle ~** asset; **wesentliche ~** essential quality, essentiality;

wichtige ~ key quality; **zuerkannte** ~ attribution; **zufällige** ~ accidental quality; **zugesicherte** ~ warranted quality;
~ **der Begebbarkeit** negotiability;
charakteristische ~ **von seinem Vater erben** to inherit a characteristic from one's father; **in amtlicher** ~ **handeln (tätig werden)** to act in virtue of one's office; **in doppelter** ~ **handeln** to occupy a dual capacity; **in seiner** ~ **als Vormund handeln** to act in one's capacity as guardian; **mit einer** ~ **ausgestattet sein** to be possessed of a quality; **über die gleiche** ~ **verfügen** to share an attribute; **über viele gute** ~**en verfügen** to have many good qualities.

Eigenschafts|beurteilung qualification rating *(US)*; ~**wort** adjective.

Eigensinn obstinacy, stubbornness.

eigensinnig wilful, obstinate, stubborn.

eigenstaatlich sovereign, national, autonomous.

Eigenstaatlichkeit sovereignty, statehood, autonomy.

eigenständig in one's own right, on one's own.

eigensüchtig selfish, egoistic.

eigentlich real, actual, true;
~**e Feier** ceremony itself; ~**er Grund dafür** original reason for; **im** ~**en Sinn des Wortes** in the strict sense of the word; ~**er Wert** intrinsic value.

Eigentor zur Folge haben to be self-defeating.

eigentrassierter Wechsel house bill.

Eigentum property, proprietorship, ownership, title, *(Besitz)* havings, own, hand, possession, *(Vermögen)* faculty, estate;
im ~ owned; **im gemeinsamen** ~ jointly owned; **im öffentlichen** ~ publicly owned; **in ausländischem** ~ foreign-owned;
im ~ **des Arbeitgebers** employer-owned; **im** ~ **von Ausländern** foreign-owned;
absolutes ~ absolute property; **später anfallendes** ~ contingent estate; **anfechtbares** ~ flaw in a title; **ausländisches** ~ foreign-owned property; **ausschließliches** ~ exclusive (sole) ownership; **bedingtes** ~ conditional estate, qualified title; **aufschiebend bedingtes** ~ imperfect title; **belastetes** ~ imperfect ownership, property charged, mortgaged property, remainder; **beschränktes** ~ special ownership (property), restricted (limited) ownership; **erbrechtlich beschränktes** ~ estate in tail, fee-tail settled property *(Br.)*; **besitzloses** ~ mere right; **bewegliches** ~ goods and chattels, personal property, personal estate (goods), personalty, movables; **doppeltes** ~ duality of ownership; **einwandfreies** ~ clear title of record; **entgeltlich erworbenes** ~ onerous title; **in Einzelrechtsnachfolge erworbenes** ~ singular title; **durch Ersitzung erworbenes** ~ prescriptive title; **nach der Heirat erworbenes** ~ *(Ehefrau)* after-acquired property; **rechtsgeschäftlich erworbenes** ~ estate by purchase; **feindliches** ~ alien (enemy) property; **fiskalisches** ~ government (crown, *Br.*) property; **freies** ~ freehold property; **fremdes** ~ *(Strafrecht)* property of another *(US)*; **geistiges** ~ intellectual (literary) property, copyright, brainchild; **gemeinsames** ~ joint property (ownership); **gesamthänderisches** ~ joint tenancy, *(von Eheleuten an Grundbesitz)* estate in entirety; **gewerbliches** ~ proprietary rights, industrial property; **herrenloses** ~ abandoned (disclaimed) property; **juristisches** ~ legal ownership; **konkursfreies (pfändungsfreies)** ~ exempt property; **lastenfreies** ~ unencumbered estate; **literarisches** ~ literary property; **materielles** ~ beneficial ownership; **nachlaßfähiges** ~ estate of inheritance *(US)*; **nutznießerisches** ~ beneficial ownership; **öffentliches** ~ state property; **persönliches** ~ personal property (effects, belongings), personalty; **rechtmäßiges** ~ lawful title, rightful property; **rechtsmängelfreies** ~ clear record title; **soziales** ~ social ownership; **städtisches** ~ municipal (city) property, property of a corporation (city); **treuhänderisches** ~ equitable lien, beneficial interest; **zur Sicherheit überlassenes** ~ pledged property; **unbelastetes** ~ clear title; **unbeschränktes** ~ absolute title (ownership), unlimited (perfect, *US*) ownership, general property, ownership in fee *(US)*; **unbestreitbares** ~ good title; **unbewegliches** ~ real estate, landed property, immovables; **untergegangenes** ~ extinct title; **unumschränktes** ~ absolute ownership (estate); **unvollständiges** ~ imperfect title; **unbeschränkt vererbliches** ~ property held in fee simple; **vermutliches** ~ reputed ownership; **volles** ~ good title; **vorläufiges** ~ equitable (imperfect) title; **wirtschaftliches** ~ business (beneficial, equitable) ownership; **zukünftiges** ~ future-acquired property;
~ **und Besitz** full right; ~ **nach Bruchteilen** severalty; ~ **der Ehefrau** married woman's property; ~ **an Früchten** title by increase; ~ **der Gesellschaft** company (corporate) property; ~ **zur gesamten Hand** undivided property, joint title (ownership), tenancy in common, coparcenary; ~ **der öffentlichen Hand** public property; ~ **auf Lebenszeit** freehold for life; ~ **und Nießbrauch** fee and life rent; ~ **an Waren** title to (property in the) goods;
sich unberechtigt ~ **aneignen** to convert property; ~ **an einen Grundstückskäufer auflassen** to convey land to a purchaser; **sein** ~ **aus der Konkursmasse aussondern** to take as true owner goods out of the bankrupt's possession; ~ **beanspruchen** to claim a title; **Diebstahl an öffentlichem** ~ **begehen** to steal public property; ~ **am Grundstück behalten** to retain the property (ownership) in one's estate; ~ **belasten** to charge (encumber) property; ~ **beschlagnahmen** to seize property; **zu** ~ **besitzen** to hold property, to own, to possess in one's own right; **sein** ~ **in die Gütergemeinschaft einbringen** to bring one's property into the communal estate; **fehlerfreies** ~ **erlangen** to acquire a good title; ~ **erwerben** to acquire property (ownership), to take title, to purchase for value; **aus jds.** ~ **gehen** to pass out of s. one's hands; **jem. zu** ~ **gehören** to be owned by s. o.; ~ **haben** to own, to hold property; ~ **an Waren haben** to hold the title [to goods]; **sein** ~ **herausverlangen** to claim one's own; ~ **kennzeichnen** to define property; ~ **konkretisieren** to appropriate goods to the contract; ~ **übergehen lassen** to convey property, to pass title; ~ **wieder in Besitz nehmen** to reverse property; **jds.** ~ **pfänden** to distrain upon s. one's belongings; ~ **schaffen** to constitute title; **in jds.** ~ **stehen** to be owned by s. o.; **teilweise in ausländischem** ~ **stehen** to be partially owned by foreign capital; **im gemeinsamen** ~ **stehen** to be jointly owned; **in öffentlichem** ~ **stehen** to be under public ownership (publicly owned); **jds. geistiges** ~ **stehlen** to pick s. one's brains; ~ **übernehmen** to take the property, to assume ownership; ~ **übertragen** to transfer ownership (property), to pass title (into ownership); **sein** ~ **auf den Konkursverwalter übertragen** to make an assignment for the benefit of one's creditors; **mit fremdem** ~ **leichtsinnig umgehen** to play pitch and toss with s. one's property; **im** ~ **des Lieferanten verbleiben** to remain the property of the seller; **sich am geistigen** ~ **anderer vergehen** to pirate; **sich an fremdem** ~ **vergreifen** to steal; **jds.** ~ **verletzen** to infringe s. one's property; **treuhänderisches** ~ **verschaffen** to deliver in trust; ~ **an einem Grundstück verschaffen** to vest with title and possession of an estate; **treuhänderisch** ~ **verwalten** to hold in trust; **sich das** ~ **vorbehalten** to reserve the right of property, to reserve one's proprietary rights, to retain (reserve) title; **sein** ~ **wiedererlangen** to recover title; **jds.** ~ **zurückbehalten** to withhold s. one's property; ~ **zurückübertragen** to reinvest property, to transfer a title back.

Eigentümer [general] owner, proprietor, proprietary, master, *(Effekten)* holder;
vom ~ **bewohnt** owner-occupied;
alleinverfügungsberechtigter ~ *(Feuerversicherung)* sole and unconditional owner; **augenscheinlicher** ~ reputed owner; **vernünftig denkender** ~ reasonably minded owner; **derzeitiger** ~ owner for the time being; **eingetragener** ~ record (registered, *US*) owner; **formeller** ~ legal owner; **früherer** ~ previous owner; **gegenwärtiger** ~ present owner; **gutgläubiger** ~ bona-fide owner, bona-fide holder (purchaser) for value; **jeweiliger** ~ owner for the time being; **lebenslänglicher** ~ life owner; **materieller** ~ beneficial owner; **mutmaßlicher** ~ reputed owner; **nachfolgender** ~ successor in title; **neuer** ~ alienee, new owner; **rechtmäßiger** ~ lawful (true, legitimate) owner, legal possessor (owner), *(Effekten)* holder in due course; **späterer** ~ subsequent owner; **tatsächlicher** ~ equitable owner; **treuhänderischer** ~ trustee; **unumschränkter** ~ absolute owner; **unumstrittener** ~ uncontested owner; **vermutlicher** ~ reputed owner; **vorheriger** ~ predecessor in title; **vorübergehender** ~ special owner; **wirklicher** ~ real (true) owner; **wirtschaftlicher** ~ equitable owner;
~ **zu Bruchteilen** severalty owners; ~ **eines Grundstücks** property owner, property (title) holder; ~ **des belasteten Grundstücks** servient owner; ~ **des herrschenden Grundstücks** dominant owner; ~ **zur gesamten Hand** coparcener, joint owner, *(Grundstück)* tenants in common; ~ **eines Hotels** hotel proprietor; ~ **einer geborgenen Ladung** salvagee; ~ **eines Landwirtschaftsbetriebes** rural property holder; ~ **auf Lebenszeit** life owner; ~ **einers Schiffes** shipowner; ~ **eines Werbemittels** medium owner;
als ~ **auftreten** to claim to be the owner; **Grundstückseintragung als** ~ **beantragen** to apply to be registered as proprietor; **als** ~ **besitzen** to possess in one's own right; **enteigneten** ~ **entschädigen** to indemnify the owner of property taken for public use; **rechtmäßiger** ~ **sein** to hold property (title [to

goods]); **als ~ verfügen** to dispose of property; **dem rechtmäßigen ~ zurückgeben** to return property to its rightful owner; **zum ursprünglichen ~ zurückkehren** to return to its original owner; **~ zurückübertragen** to reinvest property, to transfer a title back;
~haftpflicht owner's liability, liability of the owner; **~haftpflichtversicherung** owner's [public] liability insurance; **~rechte ausüben** to exercise ownership powers; **namentliches ~verzeichnis** register of names of owners, *(Grundbuch)* proprietorship register *(Br.)*.

eigentümlich peculiar, singular, *(im Eigentum stehend)* proprietary;
~er Geschmack odd flavo(u)r; **mit der ihm ~en Sorgfalt** with the care characteristic of him.

Eigentümlichkeit trick, peculiarity, characteristic, oddness, quirk;
~ einer Sprache peculiarity of a language.

Eigentumsanspruch property right, title, interest in property; **augenscheinlicher ~** colo(u)r of title; **gerichtlich festgestellter ~** marketable title [to land]; **unzureichender ~** colo(u)rable title; **~ erneuern** to renew a title; **~ haben** to have colo(u)r of title to s. th.; **seinen ~ nachweisen** to show one's right.

Eigentums|anteil stake in ownership, ownership interest, ownership share; **25%iger ~anteil** 25% share in the ownership; **~anwartschaft** equitable title; **~aufgabe** dereliction; **~ausübung** enjoyment of property; **~beeinträchtigung** actionable nuisance; **~belastung** charge on property; **~benutzer** owner-user; **~bescheinigung** certificate of title *(US)*; **~beschränkungen** restriction on title; **~bildung** creation of ownership, wealth creation (formation); **~delikt** property crime *(US)*, offence against property; **~erschleichung** theft by false pretext.

Eigentumserwerb ownership purchase, acquisition of property (title);
abgeleiteter ~ derivative acquisition; **originärer ~** original acquisition;
~ durch Anwachsung title by accession; **~ durch Erbgang** title by descent; **~ durch Ersitzung** title by adverse possession, positive prescription; **~ durch Kauf** title by purchase; **~ durch Schenkung** title by gift; **~ durch (im Wege der) Verarbeitung** right by specification; **~ im Wege der Verjährung** title by prescription; **~ im Vermächtniswege** title by devise; **~ durch Vermischung** title by accession, adjunction.

Eigentums|feststellungsklage action to quiet title, declarator *(Scot.)*; **~feststellungsverfahren** quiet title proceedings; **~folge** devolution of title; **~gefüge** property structure; **~grundsatz** rule of property; **~herausgabeanspruch** revindication; **~herausgabeklage** revindication (petitory, *Scot.*) action, writ of replevin *(US)*; **~klage** claim of ownership, right and title; **~konkretisierung** appropriation; **~konzentration** concentration of ownership; **~nachweis** property qualification, brief (abstract, evidence) of title, report on title, search, statement of ownership, property qualification, *(urkundlich)* root of title.

Eigentumsnachweis, vollständiger ~ aufgrund von Urkunden chain of title;
~ für ein Grundstück document of title to land;
~bericht report on title.

Eigentums|nutzung use of property; **~papiere** documents of title.

Eigentumsrecht ownership, title, proprietary interest, proprietorship, property right *(Scot.)*;
mit dem ~ verbunden running with the reversion;
absolutes ~ absolute ownership; **abstraktes ~** mere right; **ausgeübtes ~** estate in possession; **bedingtes ~** determinable estate, qualified property (title), *(an einem Grundstück)* determinable life interest; **nur auf dem Papier bestehendes ~** paper title; **bestrittenes ~** disputed title; **bloßes ~** bare ownership; **dingliches ~** absolute title, legal estate; **fehlendes ~** bad title; **formelles ~** legal title; **originäres ~** original estate; **unbeschränktes ~** absolute ownership; **wohlerworbenes ~** vested estate;
~ am Grundstück freehold estate; **~ an Waren** title to goods; **jds. ~e beeinträchtigen** to trench upon s. one's property; **volles ~ besitzen** to own outright; **jds. ~ bestätigen** to confirm s. o. in a title; **jds. ~ bestreiten** to dispute s. one's title; **in ~e eintreten** to assume ownership; **~ erwerben** to acquire the title; **~e an einem Depot erwerben** to take title by a deposit; **befristetes ~ gewähren** to limit an estate; **~ geltend machen** to claim to be the owner; **~ sicherstellen** to secure an estate; **~ vorbehalten** to reserve the right of property, to reserve (retain) title, to reserve one's proprietary rights.

Eigentums|schutz protection of property; **~streuung** disposal of ownership; **~titel** title [deed], instrument of title, title of ownership; **rechtsmängel- und lastenfreier ~titel** good and clear record title free from encumbrances; **~übergabe** delivery.

Eigentumsübergang devolution (passage) of title, transfer of title, passing of property (title);
unentgeltlicher ~ *(Grundstück)* voluntary conveyance;
~ kraft Gesetzes title by operation of law; **~ von Todes wegen** transfer on death, devolution upon death;
über den ~ einig sein to have and to hold.

Eigentumsübertragung transfer of ownership (property, title), devolution of property, translation, settlement, bargain and sale, *(Grundstück)* conveyance of property;
unentgeltliche ~ *(Grundstück)* voluntary conveyance (settlement);
~ zur Umgehung der Einkommensteuer transfer to avoid income tax; **~ eines Grundstücks** conveyance of land; **~ von Schuldnervermögen zum Zweck der Gläubigerbenachteiligung** fraudulent transfer of property; **~ von Todes wegen** transfer on death; **~ aufgrund einer letztwilligen Verfügung** transfer by will; **~ vornehmen** to transfer title (property).

Eigentums|übertragungsurkunde deed of conveyance; **~umschreibung zugunsten der Gläubiger** transfer for the benefit of creditors; **~urkunde** title deed, document of title, *(über ein Grundstück)* conveyance, certificate of ownership (title, *US*); **~urkunden überprüfen** to peruse title deeds; **~urkundenkette** progress of title *(Scot.)*; **~verbotsklausel** *(Spediteur)* commodities clause; **~verfügung** disposition of property; **~vergehen** offence against property, property crime *(US)*.

Eigentumsverhältnis [status of] ownership;
grundbuchlich nachgewiesenes ~ record ownership; **ungeklärtes ~** uncertain ownership;
~se einer Gesellschaft untersuchen to investigate ownership of a company.

Eigentums|verletzung damage to property, *(Grundstück)* trespass; **~verlust** loss of property; **~vermutung** reputed ownership, presumption of ownership; **~vermutungsklausel** *(Konkurs)* order and disposition clause; **~verschaffungspflicht** duty to pass good title; **~verteilung** ownership distribution; **~verzeichnis** register of names of owners, proprietorship register *(Br.)*; **~verzicht** renunciation of title, relinquishment of property.

Eigentumsvorbehalt reservation of ownership, title retention, retention of title, *(Spediteur)* shipper's order, *(Verkäufer)* vendor's (secret) lien;
geheimer ~ secret lien; **schriftlicher ~** [title] retaining note *(US)*;
~ machen to reserve one's proprietary rights; **einem ~ unterliegen** to be subject to an unpaid seller's right of lien.

Eigentums|vorbehaltsklausel retention-of-title clause, commodity clause *(US)*; **~wechsel** shift of ownership, change of hands, translation; **~wert** property value.

Eigentumswohnung owner-occupied flat, freehold flat *(Br.)*, condominium residence *(US)*, condominium apartment *(US)*; **eigengenutzte ~** owner-occupied flat (apartment, *US*);
~ zur Vermietung an Feriengäste erwerben to purchase a flat to let for holiday purposes.

Eigentums|zeichen earmark, mark; **~zurückbehaltungsrecht ausüben** to retain in exercise of one's lien.

Eigen|verbrauch home (private, own, personal, self-) consumption, office use; **~vermögen** *(der Ehefrau)* separate property; **nicht ins Gewicht fallendes ~verschulden** supervening negligence; **~versicherung** self-insurance; **~versorgung** national self-sufficiency; **~verwaltung haushaltsfreier Mittel** appropriation-in-aid; **~vorteil** self-benefit; **~wechsel** promissory note; **~werbung** institutional advertising, *(Agentur)* house advertising, self-advertising; **~werbung betreiben** to self-advertise; **~wert** *(Unternehmen)* intrinsic value.

eigenwillig highly individual, *(bockig)* obstinate, headstrong;
~er Stil style of one's own.

Eigenwirtschaft, kleine landwirtschaftliche small holding *(Br.)*.

eignen, sich to qualify, to be suitable (qualified); **sich für etw. nicht ~** to be unsuitable for (unable to do) s. th.; **sich für eine Aufgabe hervorragend ~** to be cut out for a job; **sich für eine Aufgabe schlecht ~** to be badly qualified for a task; **sich für einen Beruf ~** to be of professional calibre, to be fit for one's job; **sich zur Bestellung ~** to lend itself to cultivation; **sich gut für ein Büro ~** to do for an office; **sich zur Kapitalanlage ~** to be suitable for investment; **sich zum Lehrer nicht ~** not to be made to be a teacher; **sich für eine Stellung nicht ~** not to be fit for a position; **sich für jds. Zwecke vorzüglich ~** to suit s. one's purposes perfectly.

Eigner proprietor, owner.

Eignung qualification, ability, aptitude, vocation, fitness, eligibility, *(Brauchbarkeit)* usability, suitability, applicability;
berufliche ~ professional aptitude, vocational equipment; **besondere** ~ special ability, fitness for a particular purpose; **erforderliche** ~ necessary qualification; **fachliche** ~ professional qualification; **mangelnde** ~ lack of ability; **mangelnde** ~ **für ein Amt** insufficiency for an office; ~ **eines Bewerbers für eine Stellung** suitability of a candidate for a post; ~ **zur bedingten Entlassung** *(Strafgefangener)* parole eligibility; ~ **als Leiter** executive ability; ~ **für Wohnzwecke** fitness for habitation;
sich eine Meinung über jds. ~ **bilden** to form an estimate of s. one's abilities; **seine körperliche** ~ **nachweisen** to prove one's physical fitness.
Eignungs|auslese selection on the basis of aptitude; ~**bericht** service report; ~**garantie** warranty of fitness *(US)*; ~**karte** *(Betrieb)* qualification card.
Eignungsprüfung qualifying examination, probation, aptitude (screening, *US*, qualification) test;
berufliche ~ job (trade, vocational) test; **betriebliche** ~ employees test; **schriftliche** ~ competitive examination;
~ **für den Film** film test.
Eignungs|untersuchung fitness test; ~**wert** service value.
Eil|abfertigung speedy dispatch; ~**auftrag** rush job (order); ~**bedarf** urgent requirement.
eilbedürftig *(jur.)* urgent;
~ **sein** to require immediate attention, to have priority.
Eil|bedürftigkeit, aus Gründen der for the sake of expedition; ~**beförderung** express *(Br.)*, special delivery *(US)*, express forwarding *(Br.)*, *(Pakete)* expressage; ~**bericht** rush report; ~**bestelldienst** special delivery service *(US)*; ~**bestellung** urgent (rush) order, *(Post)* express *(Br.)*, special delivery *(US)*, *(Paket)* expressage, special handling *(US)*.
Eilbote express [messenger] *(Br.)*, special messenger *(US)*, expressman *(US)*, *(Kurier)* courier, poster;
~ **bezahlt** express paid *(Br.)*; **durch** ~**n** by special delivery *(US)*, [by] express *(Br.)*, by express messenger *(Br.)*; **per Luftpost** ~**n** per express airmail *(Br.)*;
Brief per ~**n schicken** to express a letter *(Br.)*; **per** ~**n senden** to [send by] express *(Br.)* (special delivery, *US*).
Eilboten|sendung express delivery *(Br.)*, special delivery service *(US)*; ~**zustellung** high-speed delivery service.
Eilbrief express *(Br.)* (special delivery, *US*) letter, express *(Br.)*, speedy *(sl.)*;
~! *(auf Umschlag)* express!, urgent!, special delivery! *(US)*; ~**sendungen** special delivery mail *(US)*, express items *(Br.)*; ~**umschlag** special delivery envelope *(US)*; ~**zustellung** express delivery *(Br.)*, special delivery service *(US)*.
Eildienst expedited service.
Eile hurry, haste, expedition, dispatch;
in aller ~ in great haste; **in fürchterlicher** ~ in hot haste; **in großer** ~ in a hurry, posthaste; **in überstürzter** ~ in breathless haste; **mit äußerster** ~ with utmost precipitance, with the utmost expedition;
fieberhafte ~ white heat; **größte** ~ tearing down; **übertriebene** ~ undue haste;
~ **mit Weile** more haste less speed, haste makes waste;
j. zur ~ **antreiben** to hurry s. o. up, to hasten s. o.; **keine** ~ **haben** to be in no hurry; **immer in** ~ **sein** to be always in a hurry; **etw. in der** ~ **vergessen** to forget s. th. in the rush; **sein Mittagessen in größter** ~ **verzehren** to take a hurried luncheon;
es hat keine ~ there is no hurry with it.
eilen to hasten, to hurry, to rush;
sich ~ to make haste; **nach Hause** ~ to go home as quickly as possible; **jem. zu Hilfe** ~ to run to s. one's aid; **an jds. Krankenlager** ~ to hasten to s. one's sickbed; **sehr** ~ to be very urgent.
Eilfracht express (dispatch, fast) goods *(Br.)*, fast (express) freight *(US)*, expressage *(US)*;
als ~ by fast freight train *(US)*.
Eilfrachter express cargo liner (freighter, *US*).
Eilgebühr express *(Br.)*, expressage *(US)*;
~ **bezahlt** express paid *(Br.)*.
Eilgeld dispatch money *(Br.)*;
~ **nur im Ladehafen** dispatch loading only; ~ **in Höhe des halben Liegegeldes** dispatch half demurrage all time saved; ~ **in Höhe des halben Liegegeldes für die gesamte gesparte Zeit** dispatch half demurrage all time saved; ~ **in Höhe des halben Liegegeldes für die gesparte Arbeitszeit** dispatch half demurrage working time saved; ~ **nur im Löschhafen** dispatch discharging only.
Eilgut railway express *(Br.)*, fast (express) freight *(US)*, express *(Br.)*, dispatch (fast, speed) goods *(Br.)*;
per ~ by express (fast goods, *Br.*, fast freight, *US*) train, [by] express *(Br.)*;
beschleunigtes ~ accelerated express goods *(Br.)*;
als ~ **befördern** to [forward by] express *(Br.)*, to ship by express [train] *(US)*, to send goods by fast train *(Br.)*;
~**abfertigung** dispatch of fast goods *(Br.)*; ~**beförderung** express carriage; ~**beförderungsgesellschaft** express company *(US)*.
Eilgüter|bahnhof fast goods station *(Br.)*; ~**schiff** express cargo liner (freighter, *US*); ~**wagen** express car (wag(g)on) *(US)*; ~**zug** fast goods *(Br.)* (express) train, express freight train *(US)*.
Eilgut|fracht express (fast) goods *(Br.)*, dispatch goods *(Br.)*, express freight *(US)*, expressage *(US)*; ~**gesellschaft** express company *(US)*; ~**ladeschein** express bill of lading *(Br.)*; ~**sendung** express items *(Br.)*; ~**tarif** express (fast goods, *Br.*) tariff; ~**verkehr** express business *(US)*, special delivery service *(US)*, fast goods traffic *(Br.)*; ~**wagen** express wag(g)on (van) *(US)*; ~**zustellungsgebühr** expressage *(Br.)*, special delivery fee *(US)*.
eilig urgent, pressing, quick, hasty;
~ **aufbrechen** to go out in a hurry; **etw.** ~ **erledigen** to do s. th. in haste; **es** ~ **haben** to be in haste, to be in a hurry; **es mit seinem Aufbruch nicht besonders** ~ **haben** to be in no hurry to leave; **es fürchterlich** ~ **haben** to be in a devilish hurry; **es mit dem Geldverdienen äußerst** ~ **haben** to be in too great a hurry to make money; **es ungebührlich** ~ **haben** to crowd the mourners *(US sl.)*; ~ **aus dem Zimmer stürzen** to tear out of the room; ~**e Besichtigung** hurried inspection; ~**er Brief** urgent letter; ~**er Fall** urgent case; ~**e Schritte** quick steps; **ein paar** ~**e Worte** a few hurried words;
es ist sehr ~ there is no time to lose.
eiligst with dispatch;
~**e Sachen zuerst erledigen** to do first things first.
Eil|kurier express messenger *(Br.)*, courier; ~**marsch** forced march.
Eilpaket express parcel *(Br.)* (package, *US*);
mit ~ by express parcel post *(Br.)*;
als ~ **aufgeben** to send a parcel [by] express *(Br.)*.
Eilpost express *(Br.)*, special delivery *(US)*;
durch ~ by express messenger *(Br.)* (special delivery *US*);
~**sendungen** express *(Br.)*, express items *(Br.)*, special delivery mail *(US)*; ~**zusteller** express messenger *(Br.)*, special delivery mailman *(US)*; ~**zustellung** express delivery *(Br.)*, special delivery service *(US)*.
Eilsache urgency;
~**n sofort erledigen** to dispatch current business.
Eil|tempo, im at high speed, hurriedly, at a gallop; ~**verfahren** summary proceedings; ~**zug** express, express (fast freight, *US*) train; **im** ~**zugstempo** at express speed; ~**zugswagen** express car (wag(g)on) *(US)*; ~**zuschlag** *(telegrafische Geldüberweisung)* urgent rate; ~**zuschrift** immediate reply, reply by express mail; ~**zustellgebühr** expressage *(Br.)*, special delivery fee *(US)*; ~**zustellung** express (special, *US*) delivery.
Eilzustellungs|bezirk express delivery limits; ~**dienst** express *(Br.)* (special delivery, *US*) service; ~**gebühr** express *(Br.)* (special, *US*) delivery fee, *(Pakete)* expressage *(Br.)*, special handling postage charge *(US)*.
Eimer bucket, pail;
im ~ *(coll.)* in the soup, up the spout, down the drain;
in den ~ **gucken** to be left in the cold; **wie mit** ~**n schütten** to be raining cats and dogs (in buckets, sheets, torrents); **total im** ~ **sein** to be down the drain (up the spout);
~**kette** pitch (bucket) chain.
eimerweise in buckets (bucketfuls);
~ **Briefe erhalten** to be showered with letters.
ein|und alles, jds. the apple of s. one's eye;
bei jem. ~ **und aus gehen** to have the run of the house; **jds.** ~ **und alles sein** to be everything to s. o.; **weder** ~ **noch aus wissen** to hold the wolf by the ears, to be at one's wit's end.
Einachser two-wheeler, single-axle trailer.
einachsig two-wheeled, single-axled.
Einakter curtain raiser.
einarbeiten to initiate, to instruct, to train;
jem. ~ to train s. o. [for a job]; **sich** ~ to acquaint (familiarize) o. s. with a new job, to get the hang of (become familiar with) s. th.; **Artikel** ~ to insert a new paragraph in an essay; **letzte Entdeckungen in ein Buch** ~ to incorporate the most recent discoveries into a book; **sich in ein Geschäft** ~ to get to know the details of a business; **jem. langsam** ~ to ease s. o. in his

work; **Neueingestellten** ~ to be sponsor for a new employee *(US)*; **sich schnell in etw.** ~ to acquaint o. s. quickly with a job; **sich in einer neuen Stellung** ~ to settle down in a new job.
Einarbeitung vocational adjustment.
Einarbeitungszeit break-in period, period of vocational (professional) adjustment, familiarization period.
einäschern to incinerate, to reduce to ashes, *(Leiche)* to cremate; **Stadt** ~ to reduce a town to ashes.
Einäscherung incineration, cremation.
Einäscherungshalle crematorium.
Einbahnbetrieb single-track line.
einbahnig *(Bahn)* single-line, *(Straße)* one-way.
Einbahn|schnellweg mit wechselnder Verkehrsrichtung reversible express lane; ~**straße** one-way street (only, *Br.*); ~**straße in falscher Richtung befahren** to drive the wrong way in an one-way street; ~**strecke** *(Eisenbahn)* single track; ~**verkehr** one-way traffic.
Einband binding, book cover;
mit festem ~ hard-cover;
flexibler ~ flexible binding;
~**arten** types of binding; ~**decke** book cover, case; ~**entwurf** bookbinding design.
einbändig one-volume.
Einbandvorschriften binding specifications.
Einbau installation, instal(l)ment, fitting, mounting;
beim ~ **des Flugzeugmotors** when instal(l)ing the engine in an aircraft;
~ **von Abhörvorrichtungen** bugging *(sl.)*; ~ **verfassungsrechtlicher Schutzklauseln** entrenchment of constitutional clauses;
~ **einer Zentralheizung** installation of central heating;
~**antenne** built-in aerial (antenna); ~**badewanne** built-in bath.
einbauen to build in, to instal(l), to mount;
Abhörvorrichtungen ~ to conceal microphone recording devices, to bug *(sl.)*; **neuen Motor in ein Auto** ~ to fit (instal) a new engine in a car.
einbaufertig ready to be fitted.
Einbau|kosten installation cost; ~**küche** kitchen unit; ~**möbel** unit furniture, built-in furniture, built-ins; ~**schrank** unit cupboard; ~**teil** package.
Einbauten, gewerbliche trade fixtures; **im Handel unverwendbare** ~ nondetachable facilities;
~ **der Pächter** agricultural fixtures; ~ **und Zubehör des Mieters** fixtures and fittings.
Einbauvorschriften assembly instructions.
einbegreifen to include, to involve, to implicate.
einbegriffen inclusive, included, involved;
nicht mit ~ not included; **stillschweigend** ~ implicit;
Frühstück ist im Preis ~ the terms are inclusive of breakfast;
der Kundendienst ist im Kaufpreis ~ service is included in the price.
einbehalten to keep (hold) back, to retain, *(Steuer)* to deduct, to withhold, *(Teilbetrag)* to recoup;
etw. ~ to take toll of s. th.; **Betrag vom Lohn** ~ to retain an amount out of pay, to keep back s. th. from s. one's wages;
Gewinne ~ to retain earnings (profits); **soundsoviel von jds. Lohn** ~ to withhold so much out of s. one's pay; **Lohnsteuer** ~ to withhold a tax from wage payment (income tax, *US*); **10 Prozent** ~ to keep back ten per cent; **Steuern zu Unrecht** ~ to deduct taxes wrongfully; **Teil des Geldes** ~ to retain part of the money;
~**e Garantiesumme** retention money *(Br.)*; ~**e Gewinne** retained earnings.
Einbehaltung retention, *(Steuern)* deduction, withholding, *(Teilbeträge)* recoupment;
~ **von Beiträgen zur Pensionskasse** deduction of superannuation contributions; **vereinbarte** ~ **von Gewerkschaftsbeiträgen** voluntary checkoff of union dues *(US)*; **zwangsweise** ~ **von Gewerkschaftsbeiträgen durch den Arbeitgeber** compulsory checkoff of union dues *(US)*; ~ **von Legaten** subtraction of legacies; ~ **des Lohns** stoppage of pay, deduction (detention) from wages, retention of earnings; ~ **der Lohnsteuer** withholding of tax from wage payment (income tax) *(US)*;
automatische ~ **eines Sparbetrags** save-as-you-earn; ~ **von Steuern** deduction of taxes.
Einbehaltungsbestimmungen *(Lohn)* withholding regulations *(US)*.
einbehaltungsfähig retainable.
Einbehaltungszeit time for withholding.
Einbelichtungskamera one-shot camera.
einberufen to call in, to convene, to convoke, *(mil.)* to conscribe, to conscript, to call up, to draft *(US)*, to induct *(US)*; **Aktionäre zur Hauptversammlung** ~ to summon shareholders; **Delegierte** ~ to assemble delegates; **mit Fristverkürzung** ~ to call a meeting at short notice; **Gläubigerversammlung** ~ to summon creditors; **zum Heeresdienst** ~ to call to the colo(u)rs, to draft *(US)*, to induct *(US)*; **Parlament** ~ to convene (summon, convoke) Parliament; **Parlament wieder** ~ to recall Parliament; **Reservisten** ~ to conscript (summon, call up, draft, *US*) reservists; **satzungsgemäß** ~ to convene properly; **Sitzung** ~ to convoke a meeting; **Sitzung auf zwölf Uhr** ~ to fix a meeting for twelve o'clock; **Tagung (Versammlung)** ~ to convene (call) a meeting;
~ **werden** to join the colo(u)rs;
~ *(a.)* conscript, enlisted, drafted *(US)*.
einberufene Soldaten conscript soldiers.
Einberufener *(mil.)* conscript, serviceman, enlisted man *(US)*, enlistee *(US)*, inductee *(US)*, selectee *(US)*, draftee *(US)*.
Einberufer convener, convocator, assembler.
Einberufung convention, calling, summoning, convocation, *(mil.)* conscription, call-up, call to arms, calling [out], enlistment, draft [call] *(US)*, induction *(US)*;
besondere ~ *(Hauptversammlung)* special notice;
~ **der Gläubiger** summoning of creditors; ~ **der Hauptversammlung** notice of meeting, call meeting *(US)*; ~ **des Parlaments** convening of Parliament; ~ **des Plenums** quorum call; ~ **der Reserven** calling of the reserves; ~ **von Truppen** call of troops; ~ **einer Versammlung** notice (convention) of a meeting; **ordnungsgemäße** ~ **einer Versammlung** due calling of a meeting; **unkorrekte** ~ **einer Versammlung** failure properly to convene a meeting;
auf seine ~ **warten** to wait for one's conscription (draft, *US*).
Einberufungs|befehl conscription (draft, induction, *US*) order; ~**gesetz** draft law *(US)*; ~**ort** induction station *(US)*; ~**schreiben** notice of a meeting; ~**vollmacht** authority to convene.
einbetonieren to embed (set) in concrete.
Ein|bettkabine single-berth cabin, stateroom *(US)*; ~**bettzimmer** single bedroom.
einbeulen, Konjunkturkurve to put a big dent in the economy.
Einbeulung *(Kotflügel)* dent.
einbezahlt paid in.
einbeziehen to include, to comprehend, to comprise, to incorporate, *(in Fürsorge)* to cover;
alle Familienmitglieder ~ *(Versicherung)* to cover all members of a family.
Einbeziehung inclusion, incorporation;
~ **in die Arbeitslosenfürsorge** coverage by unemployment relief; ~ **von Einzelstraftatbeständen** joinder of offences; ~ **von Vorausempfängen bei der Nachlaßverteilung** hotchpot.
einbezogen, Frühstück ist im Preis the terms are inclusive of breakfast.
einbiegen to turn into;
in eine andere Straße ~ to take another road.
Einbiegeverkehr traffic turning the corner.
einbilden, sich to imagine, to think, to suppose, to fancy; **sich dauernd etw.** ~ to fancy all kinds of things; **sich** ~, **Fußtritte gehört zu haben** to fancy to having heard footsteps; **sich maßlos viel** ~ to be eaten up with conceit; **sich nicht** ~, **etw. von der Malerei zu verstehen** not to profess to understand anything about painting; **sich auf eine Sache etw.** ~ to make a merit of s. th.; **sich steif und fest** ~ to be firmly convinced; **sich viel auf sich** ~ to be terribly conceited, to think no small beer of o. s.; **sich viel auf sein Englisch** ~ to have too good an opinion of one's English; **sich viel auf seine rednerischen Fähigkeiten** ~ to fancy o. s. as a speaker; **sich viel auf seine Klugheit** ~ to flatter o. s. on one's cleverness; **sich zu viel auf sich** ~ to think a precious sight too much of o. s. *(coll.)*.
Einbildung imagination, fancy, *(Dünkel)* conceit, self-esteem, *(Trugbild)* illusion, delusion, hallucination;
reine ~ mere imagination;
nur in jds. ~ **existieren** to be only an idea of s. o.; **seiner** ~ **Raum geben** to give full play to one's imagination; **dauernd** ~**en haben** to imagine all sorts of things; **an** ~**en leiden** to suffer from hallucinations; **nur in der** ~ **vorhanden** imaginary.
Einbildungskraft imagination, phantasy, fantasy.
einbinden to bind;
in Leder ~ to bind in leather.
einblasen, jem. etw. to whisper s. th. to s. o., to make flattering remarks to s. o.
einblenden *(Film, Fernsehen)* to fade in;
eine Farbe in eine andere ~ to blend one colo(u)r with another.
Einblendung fade-in, fading in.

einbleuen, jem. etw. to whip (drum) s. th. into s. o., to ram s. th. into s. one's head; **jem. Kenntnisse** ~ to thump knowledge into s. o.; **jem. etw. Vernunft** ~ to thwack some sense into s. one's head; **einem Prüfling Wissen** ~ to pump knowledge into a candidate;
jem. ~, was er sagen soll to prime s. o. with a speech.

Einblick insight;
~ **in etw. gewinnen** to gain insight into s. th.; **tieferen** ~ **in etw. gewinnen** to get a deeper insight into a matter; **in Akten** ~ **nehmen** to consult official documents; ~ **in die Bücher einer Firma nehmen** to have access to the books of a company; ~ **in eine Sache nehmen** to look into a matter.

einbooten, sich to embark, to go aboard.

einbrechen to break in, to break and enter, to commit burglary, to burglarize *(US)*, *(einstürzen)* to collapse, to give way;
ins Eis ~ to break (go) through the ice; **in ein Haus** ~ to burgle (burglarize) a house; **in die feindlichen Linien** ~ to penetrate the enemy's lines, to break in upon the enemy.

einbrechend|e Dunkelheit dusk; **bei ~er Nacht** at nightfall, when night sets in.

Einbrecher burglar, housebreaker;
richtiger ~ real live burglar;
~ **auf frischer Tat ertappen** to surprise a burglar in the act; ~ **verfolgen** to go gunning for a burglar;
~alarm burglar alarm; **~bande** gang of burglars; **~syndikat** ring of burglars.

einbringen to bring in, to contribute, *(abwerfen)* to return, to yield, to recoup, to gain, to fetch, to gather in *(fam.)*;
Abänderungsantrag ~ to move an amendment; **viel Anerkennung** ~ to win recognition; **parlamentarische Anfrage schriftlich** ~ to table a question; **Antrag** ~ to put a motion to the vote, to table a motion *(Br.)*; **seine Arbeitskraft** ~ to contribute one's services; **das Doppelte** ~ to make double return; **in die Ehe** ~ to bring as a dowry; **jem. Ehre** ~ to add to s. one's reputation; **Entschließung** ~ to put a resolution to the meeting, to propose; **Ernte** ~ to get in the crop, to harvest; **jem. Freunde** ~ to win s. o. friends; **Gesetzesvorlage** ~ to introduce (table, *Br.*) a bill; **schönen Gewinn** ~ to yield a handsome profit; **Kapital** ~ to contribute capital; **Klage** ~ to prefer a suit, to lodge a claim; **Mißtrauensvotum** ~ to introduce a motion of censure; **nicht viel** ~ not to pay; **nichts** ~ not to pan out well; **Nutzen** ~ to benefit; **Reingewinn von DM 10.000** ~ to net 10.000 DM; **Resolution** ~ to put a resolution to the meeting; **Ruf eines Geizkragens** ~ to gain the reputation of a miser; **jem. Ruhm** ~ to reflect credit on s. o.; **Schiff in den Hafen** ~ to put the ship into port; **Schiff sicher in den Hafen** ~ to reach port safely; **Verlust** ~ to make up for a loss; **Vorteil** ~ to bring advantage; **verlorene Zeit** ~ to make up for lost time; **Zinsen** ~ to yield interest.

einbringlich paying, profitable, lucrative;
~es Geschäft lucrative business.

Einbringung contribution;
~ **eines Antrages** proposal of a motion; ~ **seiner Arbeitskraft** contribution of one's services; ~ **der Ernte** harvesting; ~ **eines Gesetzentwurfes** introduction (presentation, tabling, *Br.*) of a bill; ~ **von Kapital** contribution to capital; ~ **verschiedener Klagen über ein- und denselben Streitgegenstand** multiplicity of action; ~ **eines Mißtrauensvotums** introduction of a motion of censure; ~ **nach Prisenrecht** military salvage; ~ **einer Resolution** filing of a resolution; ~ **von Sachwerten** contribution in kind.

Einbringungskapital capital invested.

einbrocken, jem. etw. to let s. o. in for (land s. o. with) s. th., to bring s. th. about s. one's ears; **sich etw. [Schönes]** ~ to get o. s. into trouble (in a mess, fix), to land o. s. in a nice pickle.

Einbruch breaking and entering, housebreaking, breach of close *(Br.)*, burst *(sl.)*, *(Feind)* incursion, invasion, *(geologisch)* subsidence, *(Kälte)* setting in, invasion, *(Kursniveau)* setback, slump, drop, fall, break, *(nachts)* burglary, *(Straße)* washout; **bei** ~ **der Dunkelheit** at nightfall (dusk); **bei** ~ **der Nacht** when night sets in;
bewaffneter ~ armed burglary; **feindlicher** ~ enemy incursion; **konjunktureller** ~ cyclical downswing (downturn); **saisonbedingter** ~ seasonal slump;
scharfer ~ **der Baumwollpreise** heavy slump of cotton prices; ~ **in die Front** breach in the enemy's lines; ~ **in ein Schiff** shipbreaking *(Scot.)*;
~ **begehen** to housebreak, to commit burglary, to burglarize *(US)*.

Einbruchsabsicht, mit burglariously.

einbruchsähnliche Tatbestände constructive breaking into a house.

Einbruchsdiebstahl burglary, housebreaking *(Br.)*;
~ **begehen** to housebreak, to burglarize.

Einbruchsdiebstahlspolice burglary policy.

Einbruchsdiebstahlsversicherung residence and outside theft (burglary) insurance;
gewerbliche ~ office burglary insurance;
~ **für Waren und Wertpapiere in Safes von Geschäftsunternehmen** mercantile safe insurance; ~ **von Warenlagern** mercantile open stock insurance.

Einbruchsgebiet depression, sinking area.

einbruchssicher burglar-proof.

Einbruchs|sicherung antiburglar device; **~stelle** *(mil.)* breach; **~versicherungsschutz** residential theft coverage; **~versuch** burglarious attempt, attempted burglary; **~werkzeuge** housebreaking tools (instruments).

einbuchen *(Scheck)* to give the value date.

einbuchten *(fam.)* to lock up, to jug *(sl.)*;
j. ohne Verfahren ~ to railroad s. o. *(sl.)*.

Einbuchtung indentation, bay.

einbürgern to naturalize, to nationalize *(Br.)*, to citizenize, to domesticate;
sich ~ to come to stay, to become established, to take root; **ausländische Sitte** ~ to domesticate a foreign custom; **teilweise** ~ to denizen; **neues Wort** ~ to familiarize a new word; **Wörter** ~ to vernacularize;
sich ~ **lassen** to take out naturalization papers.

Einbürgerung naturalization, nationalization *(Br.)*, denization *(Br.)*, indenization *(Br.)*, domestication;
~ **von Wörtern** vernacularization;
~ **erreichen** to take out citizen papers *(US)*.

Einbürgerungs|antrag petition for nationalization; **~antrag stellen** to petition for naturalization; **~bedingungen** qualification for naturalization; **~fähigkeit** eligibility for naturalization; **~unfähigkeit** ineligibility for naturalization; **~urkunde** certificate of registry, certificate (letter) of naturalization, naturalization papers, citizen (first) papers *(US)*; **~verfahren** naturalization proceedings; **~voraussetzungen erfüllen** to be eligible for naturalization.

Einbuße sacrifice, damage, forfeiture, loss, *(Erträge)* dent;
unter ~ **seines gesamten Vermögens** at the expense of one's property;
~ **an Kundschaft** loss of custom;
empfindliche ~ **erleiden** to suffer a severe loss; ~ **in seiner gesellschaftlichen Stellung hinnehmen müssen** to sink in the social scale; **jds. Beliebtheit keine** ~ **zufügen** not to detract from s. one's popularity; **dem Wildbestand große ~n zufügen** to cause great damage to the wildlife.

einbüßen to lose, to sustain a loss, to forfeit;
sein Ansehen ~ to lose face; **bei einem Geschäft viel Geld** ~ to drop a lot of money on a deal; **Kursverlust** ~ to suffer a decline; **Stimmen** ~ to lose votes.

Einbüßung loss, forfeiture.

eindämmen to embank, to dam, to stem, to dike, to curb, *(fig.)* to check, to restrain, *(pol.)* to contain;
Kreditexpansion ~ to curb credit expansion; **Seuche** ~ to stem an epidemic; **Waldbrand** ~ to check a forest fire.

Eindämmung embankment, dike, *(fig.)* curb[ing], restraint, *(pol.)* containment;
~ **der Inflation** curbing of inflation; ~ **der stetig steigenden Krankenhauskosten** hospital cost containment; ~ **politischer Stimmungen** containment of political movements.

Eindämmungspolitik policy of containment.

eindecken to provide, *(Börse)* to rebuy, to buy back, to cover;
sich ~ to provide o. s. with, to stock up, to buy heavily (in), to lay in stock, *(Baissier)* to cover; **j. mit Arbeit** ~ to load s. o. with work; **sich gut mit Büchern** ~ to lay in a good stock of books; **Dach mit Ziegeln** ~ to tile a roof; **sich kräftig** ~ to lay in stocks pretty heavily; **sich für einen Notfall** ~ to provide for an emergency; **sich mit Vorräten** ~ to replenish one's stock; **sich mit Vorräten für den Winter** ~ to lay in stores (stock up) for the winter; **sich mit Waren** ~ to supply o. s. with goods; **sich mit Weihnachtsartikeln** ~ to stock o. s. up for the Christmas trade; **zwangsweise** ~ *(Börse)* to buy in under the rule *(US)* (against s. o., *Br.*).

Eindecker monoplane, *(mar.)* single-deck aeroplane, single-decker.

Eindeckung provision, supply, replenishment of stocks, *(Börse)* buying back (short, *US*), covering;
zwangsweise ~ **von Effekten** buying in against *(Br.)*, buying in under the rule *(US)*.

Eindeckungswelle purchasing boom.

eindeichen to embank.
Eindeichung embankment.
eindeutig evident, plain, decided, univocal, unequivocal;
ganz ~ zu verstehen geben to intimate quite unmistakably; **ganz ~ sein** to be perfectly clear;
~e Antwort unambiguous response; **~er Beweis** definite proof; **~er Fall von Bestechung** clear case of bribery; **~e Handbewegung** unmistakable gesture.
eindeutschen to germanize.
Eindeutschung germanization.
eindocken, Schiff to take a ship into dock, to dock a ship.
Eindollarmann dollar-a-year man.
eindosen to pack, to can, to tin.
eindösen to doze off.
eindrängen to penetrate, to make one's way;
sich bei jem. ~ to intrude (force) o. s. upon s. o.; **sich in die Geschäfte anderer ~** to interlope with the business of others; **sich in eine Versammlung ~** to force one's way into a meeting.
eindrillen, jem. etw. to ram s. th. into s. one's head.
Eindringen inroad, *(pol.)* infiltration;
gewaltsames ~ forcible entry into a house; **strafbares ~** criminal trespass *(US)*; **unerlaubtes ~** surreptitious entry;
~ in fremde Räume forcible entry into enclosed premises.
eindringen to enter, to invade, to intrude, to penetrate, to force one's way, *(mil.)* to invade, *(pol.)* infiltrate, *(Volksmenge)* to throng (surge) into, *(Wasser)* to rush into;
auf j. ~ to attack (mob, *fam.*) s. o.; **allmählich ~** to work one's way in gradually; **mit Bitten auf j. ~** to plead with s. o.; **in den Boden ~** *(Regen)* to soak into the ground; **auf den Feind ~** to make an assault (charge, attack) on the enemy; **mit Fragen auf jem. ~** to ply (entreat) s. o. with questions; **in ein Gebäude ~** to invade a building, *(Einbrecher)* to break into a house; **in ein Geheimnis ~** to fathom a mystery; **in den Geist einer Sprache ~** to grasp the spirit of a language; **in die feindlichen Linien ~** to penetrate into the enemy's lines; **tief in eine Materie ~** to get to the very bottom of a matter; **mit einem Messer auf j. ~** to close in on s. o. with a knife; **in die Nahrungsmittelindustrie ~** to diversify into foods; **tief in die Probleme ~** to study the problems of a matter closely, to go deeply into a problem; **durch alle Ritzen ~** *(Feuchtigkeit)* to be seeping in through all the cracks; **in eine Sprache ~** *(Fremdwörter)* to infiltrate into a language; **in eine Stadt ~** to enter into a town; **unberechtigt ~** to encroach; **bei jem. ungebeten ~** to intrude upon s. o.
eindringlich urgent, pressing;
~ empfehlen to advise strongly;
~e Rede halten to make a powerful speech; **mit ~en Worten** insistently, with moving words.
Eindringling intruder, invader, gatecrasher, incursionist.
Eindruck impression, *(drucktechn.)* printing, imprint;
bleibender ~ lasting impression; **finanzieller ~** financial showing; **tiefer ~** skin-deep impression; **visueller ~** visual impression;
verwischter ~ eines Fußes flurred footprint; **~ des Niedergangs** sense of decline;
den ~ erwecken to come through *(US)*; **~ einer Autobiographie erwecken** to purport to be an autobiography; **~ bei jem. hinterlassen** to leave an impression (one's mark) on s. one's mind; **im Parlament einen großen ~ hinterlassen** to leave a strong impression on the House; **schlechten ~ hinterlassen** to create a bad impression; **ungünstigen ~ bei jem. hinterlassen** to impress s. o. unfavo(u)rably; **~ auf j. machen** to impress s. o.; **nicht den geringsten ~ auf j. machen** to cut no ice with s. o. *(coll.)*; **großen ~ machen** *(Rede)* to be most impressive, to go home *(coll.)*; **möglichst guten ~ machen** to put one's best foot forward; **keinen ~ machen** to fall flat, to cut no ice, not to register with, to be lost upon; **schlechten ~ auf j. machen** to impress s. o. unfavo(u)rably; **tiefen ~ machen** to make a deep impression, to go home; **um ~ zu schinden** for show; **unter dem ~ eines Unfalls stehen** to be under the spell of an accident; **lange unter dem ~ eines Unglücks stehen** to be greatly affected for a long time by a terrible disaster; **~ vermitteln** to create the impression; **~ bei jem. zurücklassen** to leave an impression on s. one's mind.
eindrucken to print, to imprint.
eindrücken *(einbeulen)* to dent, to indent;
Fensterscheibe ~ to press (break) a window pane; **feindliche Front ~** to make a breach in the enemy's line; **Kotflügel ~** to make a dent in the fender (mudguard, *Br.*); **Kühler ~** to stave in the radiator; **Schiffsseite ~** to smash (stave in) the side of a ship; **Siegel ins Wachs ~** to press the seal into the wax; **Tür ~** to push in the door.

Eindruck|schinden name-dropping; **~schinder** name-dropper.
eindrucksvoll impressive, effective, striking;
~es Beispiel striking example; **~e Erscheinung** imposing figure; **~e Rede** powerful speech; **~e Stille** impressive silence.
einebnen *(Baugrundstück)* to level;
Stadt völlig ~ to raze a town to the ground; **soziale Unterschiede ~** to level social distinctions.
Einehe monogamy.
einengen to narrow, to restrict, to inclose, to pinch;
Gewerbefreiheit ~ to restrict the freedom of trade; **Gewinnspanne ~** to narrow the profit margin; **jds. Tätigkeitsfeld ~** to restrict s. one's sphere of activity; **jds. Vollmacht ~** to narrow down s. one's power.
Einengung restriction, confinement, limitation;
~ eines Gesetzes restriction of a law; **~ der Gewinnspannen** narrowing of profit margins.
Einer oner *(coll.)*;
~ausschuß committee of one.
Einerlei, tägliches the daily grind, routine work.
Einerzelt one-man tent.
einfach single, singular, *(Fahrkarte)* single, one-way *(US)*, *(Mensch)* plain, ordinary, common, *(schlicht)* homely, homespun, *(nicht schwer)* simple, easy, *(ungekünstelt)* unsophisticated;
etw. als ~ hinstellen to simplify s. th.;
~e Aufgabe simple task; **~e Breite eines Stoffes** single width of a material; **~e Buchführung** bookkeeping by single entry; **~er Diebstahl** simple larceny; **~es Essen** homely dinner; **~e Fahrkarte** single [ticket], one-way ticket *(US)*; **~er Fahrpreis** single fare; **~e Gebrauchsgüter** utility goods; **~e Havarie** particular (simple) average; **~e Konstruktion** straightforward design; **~e Kost** simple diet, plain fare; **~es Landvolk** plain country folk; **~es Leben führen** to lead a simple life; **~e Lebensweise** plain living; **~e Leute** plain homely people; **~eine Lüge** a downright lie; **der ~e Mann** the man on the street; **~e Mehrheit** simple (bare) majority; **um es auf den ~sten Nenner zu bringen** to put it in a nutshell; **~es Porto** ordinary postage; **~er Schalter** one-way switch; **~er Soldat** regular soldier, private; **~ unmöglich** simply impossible; **~ Wahnsinn** sheer madness; **~e Wahrheit** unadorned truth; **~ Zeitverschwendung** pure waste of time.
Einfach|arbitrage direct arbitration (arbitrage) *(Br.)*, simple arbitration *(Br.)*; **der ~heit halber** for the sake of simplicity; **~leitung** *(tel.)* single line; **~telegrafie** simplex telegraphy.
einfädeln *(fig.)* to manage, to jockey, to engineer, to wangle, to frame up *(coll.)*;
Sache ~ to set the ball rolling; **schlau ~** to go about a matter subtly; **von einer Spur in die andere ~** to change from one lane into another; **sich in den Verkehr ~** to cut (filter) in the traffic.
Einfädelung cutting in.
Einfahren *(Auto)* road test, *(Bergbau)* descent, *(Zug)* entry.
einfahren to drive into, *(Auto)* to run (break, *US*) in, *(Fahrgestell, Sehrohr)* to retract, *(Schiff)* to enter, to sail into, *(Zug)* to come into;
sich ~ to get used to driving; **in den Bahnhof ~** to enter (pull in into) the station; **500 Millionen Devisen ~** *(Handelsflotte)* to be able to earn DM 500 millions of foreign exchange; **Ernte ~** to bring in the crop, to harvest; **in eine Grube ~** to go down a shaft, to descend into a mine; **sicher in den Hafen ~** to reach the port safely; **jem. den Kühler ~** to stave in s. one's radiator; **pünktlich ~** to come in on time (on schedule, *US*); **Schwimmbrücke ~** to float pontoons into place; **Zaun ~** to knock down a fence.
Einfahr|gleis arrival track; **~signal** home signal.
Einfahrt entry, *(Auto)* running in, driving in, *(Autobahn)* entry point, *(Gebäude)* gateway, carriage, entrance, drive, way in, driveway *(US)*, *(Hafen)* mouth, *(in Schacht)* descent, *(Tunnel)* mouth, *(Verkehrsschild)* entrance, way in;
keine ~! no entry!;
~ in den Bahnhof entering the station; **~ in eine Grube** descent into a pit;
~ auf Gleis 4 haben to come into platform 4;
der Zug hat ~ the signal is at green;
bitte die ~ freihalten! please keep entrance clear!
Einfahrts|bahnsteig arrival platform; **~boje** entrance buoy; **~geschwindigkeit** running-in *(US)* (breaking-in, *Br.*) speed; **~gleis** arrival track (line); **~schleuse** entrance lock; **~signal** *(Bahn)* home signal; **~straße** access road; **~tonne** entrance buoy; **~weg** approach, drive, driveway *(US)*.
Einfahr|vorschriften running-in *(US)* (breaking-in, *Br.*) instructions; **~zeit** *(Auto)* running-in (breaking-in, *US*) period.

Einfall *(Einsturz)* downfall, collapse, *(Idee)* idea, notion, hit, conceit, imagination, *(mil.)* raid, invasion, inroad, incursion; **besonderer** ~ gag; **feindlicher** ~ descent upon the enemy; **launischer** ~ whim, caprice; **merkwürdiger** ~ queer notion; **phantasievoller** ~ fancy; **plötzlicher** ~ inspiration, freak, sudden whim; **räuberischer** ~ predatory excursion; **seltsamer** ~ passing whim; **verrückter** ~ brain storm;
~ **in ein Gebiet** invasion of (incursion into) a territory; **zum** ~ **bringen** to cause to collapse; **einem plötzlichen** ~ **folgen** to act on the impulse of the moment; **auf einen** ~ **kommen** to strike upon an idea.
Einfälle, voll witziger full of jest.
einfallen *(Gebäude)* to fall (tumble) down, to collapse, to decay, *(mil.)* to fall in, to invade;
jem. ~ to occur to s. o. (s. one's mind); **bei jem.** ~ to drop in on s. o.; **während des Erdbebens** ~ to collapse during the earthquake; **jem. gerade** ~ to strike s. one's mind; **in ein Land** ~ to invade (make a raid into, overrun) a country; **scharenweise** ~ to overrun; **in jds. Wehklagen** ~ to chime in with s. one's lamentations; **jem. wieder** ~ to enter s. one's head;
sich etw. Besseres ~ **lassen** to think of s. th. better;
es würde mir nicht im Traum ~ I wouldn't dream of it.
einfallende Wetter intake air.
einfalls|los shiftless, lacking in ideas; ~**reich** full of ideas, imaginative.
Einfallsreichtum ingenuity, wealth of ideas.
Einfallstraße access road.
einfältig simpleminded, simple, dupable, *(leichtgläubig)* credulous, gullible, *(töricht)* silly, foolish, stupid;
~**e Bemerkungen** silly remarks; ~**er Mensch** simple soul; ~**es Zeug reden** to talk rubbish.
Einfaltspinsel simpleton, ninny, mug *(Br.)*, dupe, oaf, flat *(sl.)*, pigeon *(sl.)*.
Einfamilien|haus self-contained house, single-family home, single residence *(US)*; ~**wohnung** single (one-family) dwelling; ~**wohnungseinheit** single-family dwelling unit.
einfangen to capture, to seize;
sich einen Ehemann ~ to hook a husband; **Leben mit Stift und Farbe** ~ to translate life into line and colo(u)r; **Verbrecher wieder** ~ to recapture a criminal.
einfarbig single-colo(u)red, unicolo(u)red, self-colo(u)r, plain.
einfassen to border, to edge, to line, *(Edelstein)* to set, to mount, *(Satz)* to frame, to box in;
mit einer Hecke ~ to hedge in; **Quelle** ~ to kerb (curb) a well.
Einfassung border, lining, edge, framing, *(drucktechn.)* border.
Einfassungsmauer surrounding wall.
einfetten to lubricate, to grease, to oil, *(Haut)* to cream.
einfinden, sich to appear, to turn up, to collect; **sich an einem Ort** ~ to come to a place; **sich zu einer Sitzung** ~ to meet for a session; **sich pünktlich um 12 Uhr** ~ to turn up punctually at twelve o'clock; **sich zur verabredeten Zeit** ~ to arrive on time, to present o. s. at the appointed time.
einflicken *(im Text)* to interpolate.
einfliegen to airlift, *(Einflieger)* to test-fly, to fly in;
in ein feindliches Gebiet ~ to fly into enemy country; **Maschine** ~ to test-fly an aircraft; **Truppen** ~ to fly in troops.
einfließen lassen to give to understand;
einige bissige Bemerkungen ~ to insert some biting words.
einflößen, jem. etw. to pour into s. one's mouth, to feed s. o. with s. th.; **jem. ein Getränk mit Gewalt** ~ to force a drink down s. one's throat; **jem. gesunde Grundsätze** ~ to instil good principles into s. o.; **jem. Mitleid** ~ to fill s. o. with pity; **jem. Mut** ~ to import courage to s. o., to encourage s. o.; **jem. Verdacht** ~ to arouse s. one's suspicion; **jem. Vertrauen** ~ to inspire s. one's confidence.
Einflug|punkt point of entry; ~**schneise** flying lane, flight path, air corridor; ~**zeichen** marker; ~**zone** entrance zone.
Einfluß influence, hold, pull, sway, grip, weight, bearing, prestige, drag *(US)*, wires, authority, heft *(US)*, *(Druckmittel)* leverage, *(Macht)* power control, influence, sway;
unter dem ~ **von** influenced by, under the sway of; **unter dem** ~ **von Alkohol** under the influence of alcohol;
ansteckender ~ contagion; **beherrschender** ~ ascendary; **belebender** ~ ozone; **bestimmter** ~ drift; **immer gegenwärtiger** ~ pervasive influence; **geheimer** ~ secret influence; **günstiger** ~ favo(u)rable influence; **maßgeblicher** ~ controlling vote; **negativer (zersetzender)** ~ poison; **positiver** ~ influence for good; **schädlicher** ~ blight, rust, blast; **schlechter** ~ infection; **schlimmer** ~ evil eye; **sichtbarer spanischer** ~ traces of Spanish influence; **störender** ~ disturbance; **weitreichender** ~ far-reaching influence; **herzlich wenig** ~ fat lot of influence;
seinen ganzen ~ **aufbieten** to pull all strings *(coll.)*; ~ **ausüben** to exercise influence; **auf j.** ~ **ausüben** to take a grip on s. o.; **ausschlaggebenden** ~ **ausüben** to control; **großen** ~ **auf j. ausüben** to have a strong pull with s. o.; **großen internationalen** ~ **ausüben** to be an international force; **guten** ~ **ausüben** to become a power for good; **langanhaltenden** ~ **ausüben** to cast a shadow; ~ **auf die Preise ausüben** to influence prices; **ungehörigen** ~ **auf j. bei der Testamentsabfassung ausüben** to use undue influence with the maker of a will; **verhängnisvollen** ~ **auf j. ausüben** to have a fatal influence over s. o.; ~ **bekämpfen** to counteract an influence; **j. unter seinen** ~ **bekommen** to get a hold on s. o.; **jds.** ~ **brechen** to set s. one's influence at nought; **um den** ~ **bringen** *(Politik)* to scalp *(US)*; **seinen** ~ **zur Geltung bringen** to make one's influence felt; **seinen** ~ **für j. einsetzen** to use one's influence on behalf (in favo(u)r of) s. o.; **sich einem** ~ **entziehen** to resist an influence; ~ **über j. erlangen** to win upon s. o.; **unter jds.** ~ **geraten** to come under the influence of s. o.; **steigenden** ~ **bei jem. gewinnen** to grow (gain increasing influence) on s. o.; **bestimmenden** ~ **auf ein Land gewinnen** to gain ascendancy over a country; ~ **haben** to pull strings, to have a voice, to carry weight; ~ **am Hofe haben** to have interest (influence) at court; **großen** ~ **bei jem. haben** to have great credit with s. o.; **großen** ~ **im Parlament haben** to have great sway in the House; **keinen** ~ **bei jem. haben** to have no power over s. o.; **keinen** ~ **auf die politische Entwicklung haben** to have no effect on the political situation; **in einer Sache keinen** ~ **haben** to have no say in a matter; **maßgeblichen** ~ **haben** to have a controlling vote; ~ **auf die Wahlen haben** to sway the elections; **wenig** ~ **haben** to have little weight; **an** ~ **verloren haben** to be on the ebb *(fam.)*; **unter dem** ~ **eines Irrtums handeln** to labo(u)r under a delusion; **außerhalb jds.** ~**es liegen** to be beyond s. one's control; **sich von jds.** ~ **frei machen** to break free from s. one's influence; **seinen** ~ **geltend machen** to work, to interpose (exercise) one's authority, to pull, to throw one's weight about; **seinen** ~ **bei jem. geltend machen** to bring influence to bear on s. o.; **seinen** ~ **zu jds. Gunsten geltend machen** to exercise (use) one's influence on behalf (in favo(u)r) of s. o.; ~ **eines Landes im Ausland schwächen** to water down a country's influence abroad; **unter jds.** ~ **stehen** to be under the influence (ruled by) s. o.; **ausländischem** ~ **unterliegen** to be controlled by foreign interests; **seinen** ~ **verstärken** to consolidate one's influence;
~**bereich** orbit, range (sphere) of influence; **j. in seinen** ~**bereich zurückführen** to lure s. o. back into one's sphere of influence; **sozialpolitische** ~**faktoren** business environments; ~**gebiet** incidence, sphere of influence, *(Planet)* orb; **marktunabhängige** ~**größen** nonmarket forces.
einflußlos without influence;
~**e politische Minderheit** political minority without influence.
Einflußlosigkeit lack of influence.
Einflußnahme auf die Gesetzgebung influencing legislation.
einflußreich influential, weighty, powerful;
sehr ~ **sein** to cast a long shadow, to have a strong pull; **über** ~**e Beziehungen verfügen** to have far-reaching influence; ~**e Freunde haben** to have friends at court (influential friends); **sich Vorteile bei** ~**en Leuten verschaffen** to make up to influential people; ~**e Persönlichkeit sein** to be a man with sway; ~**er Politiker** influential politician; ~**e Stellung** post of authority.
Einfluß|sphäre, ~**zone** orbit, circle, reach, sweep, *(Völkerrecht)* sphere of influence; ~**zone** radius, zone of influence.
einflüstern, jem. etw. to whisper s. th. to s. o., *(fig.)* to put s. th. into s. one's head; **auf j.** ~ to prompt s. o. to s. th.
Einflüsterungen insinuation, whispered temptations;
~ **von Untreue** insinuation of infidelity;
bösartige ~ **vornehmen** to insinuate s. th. nasty.
einfordern to call in, to claim, to demand;
Außenstände ~ to collect outstanding debts; **Einzahlung auf Aktien** ~ to make a call on shares; **Kapital** ~ to call in funds; **Nachschuß** ~ to call for an additional payment (cover); **Steuern** ~ to collect taxes.
Einforderung calling in, *(Steuern)* collection.
einfrieden to enclose, to close in, to fence, to discommon;
mit einer Hecke ~ to hedge in.
Einfriedung enclosure, ring, fence, *(mit Mauer)* wall.
Einfriedungs|hecke surrounding hedge; ~**recht** right of enclosure.
Einfrieren freezing, immobilization, blocking;
~ **ausländischer Guthaben** freezing of foreign assets; ~ **von Konten** freezing (blocking) of accounts; ~ **der Unfallversicherungsprämien** disability freeze.

einfrieren *(Kapital)* to freeze, to be blocked, *(Kühler)* to freeze up, *(Schiff)* to become icebound, *(Verhandlungen)* to reach a deadlock;
Nahrungsmittel ~ to deep-freeze food;
~ **lassen** *(Konto)* to block.
einfügen to insert, to embody, to interpolate, to write in;
Bemerkung ~ to throw in a word; **Klausel** ~ to insert (embody) a clause; **sich in jds. Plan** ~ to fit into s. one's plan; **sich gut in das Stadtbild** ~ to fit well into the general aspect of the town; **Stein in eine Mauer** ~ to set (fit) a stone into a wall; **sich seiner neuen Umgebung** ~ to adapt o. s. to one's new surroundings; **zwischen den Zeilen** ~ to interline.
Einfügsel fill-in.
Einfügung insertion, embodiment, interpolation;
~ **in einen Text** insertion into a text; ~ **in eine neue Umgebung** adaptation to new surroundings.
einfühlen, sich in j. to empathize with s. o.; **sich in einen Dichter** ~ to enter the spirit of a poet; **sich in die Seele eines Kindes** ~ to project o. s. into the mind of a child.
Einfühlungsvermögen intuitive power, intuition;
psychologisches ~ insight into human character; **technisches** ~ mechanical sensitivity.
Einfuhr import[ation], imports, import trade;
bei der ~ when imported; **vorübergehend zur** ~ **zugelassen** passed for temporary importation;
~**en** goods imported;
ausländische ~**en** imports from abroad; **billige** ~**en** low- (cut-) priced imports; **freie** ~ free import of goods; **gewerbliche** ~**en** commercial and industrial imports; **hochwertige** ~**en** higher-quality imports; **kontingentierte** ~**en** quota imports; **nicht kontingentierte** ~ nonquota imports; **kreditabhängige** ~**en** credit-based imports; **liberalisierte** ~ liberalized imports; **sichtbare** ~ visible imports; **symbolische** ~ token imports; **übermäßige** ~ overimportation; **unentgeltliche** ~ imports free of payment; **unerlaubte** ~ clandestine imports; **unmittelbare** ~**en** direct imports; **unsichtbare** ~ invisible imports; **zeitweilige zollfreie** ~ temporary admission; **zollermäßigte** ~ tariff-reduced imports; **zollfreie** ~ free import, free entry;
~ **und Ausfuhr** imports and exports; **sichtbare** ~ **und Ausfuhr** visible items of trade; ~ **zum eigenen Gebrauch** home-use entry; **freie** ~ **zum sofortigen persönlichen Gebrauch bestimmter Waren** free consumption entry; ~ **in handelsüblichen Mindestmengen** importation of goods in minimum commercial quantities; ~ **auf Partizipationsrechnung** import on joint account; ~ **unter Zollvermerkschein** entry under bond; ~ **unter Zollverschluß** importation in bond; ~ **im Zollvormerkverfahren** temporary import;
~**en begünstigen** to encourage imports; ~ **beschränken** to reduce imports; ~ **drosseln** to curb (choke back, slow down, restrict) imports; ~ **erhöhen** to increase imports; ~ **kontingentieren** to fix import quotas; ~ **lenken** to steer imports; ~ **liberalisieren** to decontrol imports; **Kontrollbestimmungen bei der** ~ **vereinfachen** to simplify import inspection requirements; **zur zollfreien** ~ **zulassen** to grant duty-free importation;
~**abgabe** levy on imports, import levy (charges), surcharge on imports, countervailing excise (import) duty; ~**abgaben endgültig aufheben** to liquidate import duty; ~**agent** import agent, importer; ~**anschlußlieferungen** follow-up imports; ~**anstieg** increase of imports; **plötzlicher (rasanter)** ~**anstieg** jump (upsurge) in imports; ~**antrag** import application; ~**artikel** articles of importation, imported articles, importations; **[nicht] kontingentierte** ~**artikel** [non]quota imports; ~**aufschlag** import markup; ~-**Ausfuhrbank** Export-Import Bank of Washington; ~**ausgleichsabgabe,** ~**ausgleichssteuer** import equalization fee (tax, *US*); ~**ausnahmetarif** protective tariff.
Einfuhr|bedarf, ~**bedürfnisse** import requirements; ~**bedürfnisse dämpfen** to damp down import demands; ~**beglaubigung** documentation of imports; ~**begrenzung** import limitation; ~**begrenzungsabkommen** import limitation agreement; ~**begünstigung** encouragement of imports; ~**belebung** uptrend in imports; ~**berechtigungskonto** import entitlement account; ~**bescheinigung** import clearance, clearance inward.
Einfuhrbeschränkungen limitation of imports, import restrictions (restraints), curbs on imports;
gezielte ~ selective import restrictions; **mengenmäßige** ~ quantitative restrictions of imports;
in Krisenzeiten einzelne Positionen mit ~ **belegen** *(EEC)* to slap emergency restrictions on some items; ~ **einführen** to put on import restrictions.
Einfuhrbestimmungen import regulations;
verschärfte ~ **erlassen** to tighten import regulations.
Einfuhr|bewilligung import licence (authorization, permit); ~**bewilligungsantrag** import application; ~**deklaration** bill of entry *(Br.)*, entry (declaration, *Br.*) inwards; ~**drosselung** curb on imports; ~**einheit** unit of imported goods; ~**embargo** embargo on imports.
einführen *(Einrichtungen)* to establish, to set up, to institute, to install, to initiate, *(j. empfehlen)* to recommend, *(j. vorstellen)* to introduce, to present, *(Waren)* to import, to bring in;
in ein Amt ~ to install into (induct, establish in) an office; **an der Börse** ~ to obtain quotation *(Br.)*, to list on the stock exchange *(US)*; **feierlich** ~ to herald in; **Geschwindigkeitsbegrenzung für eine Straße** ~ to restrict a road; **in die Gesellschaft** ~ to bring out, to knock down *(US sl.)*; **Gesetz** ~ to institute a law; **Kabel in ein Haus** ~ to lead a cable into a house; **in einen Klub** ~ to initiate into a club; **auf dem Markt** ~ to launch on the market; **neue Methode** ~ to adopt new methods; **Minister in sein Amt** ~ to install a minister in a new charge; **Mode** ~ to set (introduce) a fashion; **Neuerungen in einem Geschäft** ~ to introduce new ideas into a business; **Präsidenten der Vereinigten Staaten in sein Amt** ~ to inaugurate the President of the United States; **Reformen** ~ to carry out reforms; **schrittweise** ~ to establish by steps; **neues System** ~ to inaugurate a new system; **Tabaksteuer** ~ to establish a tax on tobacco; **ungehindert** ~ to import freely; **Verbesserungen** ~ to adopt improvements; **Waren in ein Land** ~ to import goods into a country; **Waren zum freien Verkehr** ~ to enter goods for consumption; **wieder** ~ to reimport; **Zölle** ~ to introduce customs duties; **zollfrei** ~ to import duty-free.
einführend introductory, initiatory;
~**es Kapitel** introductory chapter; ~**e Worte** introductory remarks.
Einfuhr|erklärung bill of entry *(Br.)*, entry (declaration, *Br.*) inwards, import declaration *(US)*; ~**erlaubnis,** ~**freigabe,** ~**genehmigung** import licence (permit), import certificate; ~**erleichterungen** import facilities; ~**erleichterungspolitik** policy of easing imports; ~**finanzierung** financing of imports; ~**finanzierungskredit** advance to finance imports; ~**firma** import house, importer; ~**flut** import tide; ~**genehmigungsverfahren** import licensing; ~**geschäft** import transaction; ~**geschäfte** import trade; ~**güter** imported goods, imports; ~**hafen** port of entry, import (inward) port; ~**hahn zudrehen** to switch off the import tap; ~**handel** import (passive, inward) trade; ~**händler** importer, import merchant (dealer); ~**hemmnis** import handicap; ~**hindernis** import bar; ~**hinterlegungssumme** import deposit *(Br.)*; ~**kommissionär** import commission agent, importer; ~**konnossement** inward bill of lading.
Einfuhrkontingent import quota;
~**e für Weine** *(EG)* wine import quotas;
~**e festsetzen** to fix quotas for import; ~**e verteilen** to fix quotas for import.
Einfuhr|kontingentierung fixing of import quotas; ~**kontrolle** import control; ~**kredit** advance for imports, import (domestic, *US*) credit; ~**kreditbrief** import letter of credit; ~**kurve** trend in imports; ~**kürzungen** import cuts (cutbacks); ~**land** country of importation (purchase), importing country; ~**liberalisierung** decontrol (liberalization) of imports; ~**lieferungen** import shipments; ~**liste** list of arrivals; ~**liste zollfreier Gegenstände** import free list; **größere** ~**mengen hereinlassen** to open the door to more imports; ~**monopol** import monopoly; **lebhafte** ~**nachfrage** rush of imports; ~**nachteile** import damage; ~**plafond** import ceiling; ~**prämie** bounty on importation; ~**preis** import price; ~**preisindex** price index of imports; ~**prognose abgeben** to forecast the course of imports; ~**quote** import quota; **überhöhte** ~**rechnungen ausstellen** to overinvoice imports; ~**regelung** import arrangement; ~**rückgang** turndown (decrease, fall-off) in imports, import reduction; ~**schein** bill of entry, import certificate (clearance); ~**sicherungsprogramm** program(me) of anticipating imports; **inflatorisch bedingter** ~**sog** inflation-induced pull of imports; ~**sonderzoll** surcharge on imports; ~**sperre** embargo on imports; ~**statistik** import statistics; ~**steigerung** increased (increases in) imports; ~**stelle** import agency; ~- **und Vorratsstelle für landwirtschaftliche Erzeugnisse** intervention board for agricultural produce; ~**steuer** import excise tax *(US)*; ~**stopp** embargo on (cessation of) imports; ~**tarif** import rate (tariff); ~**tempo verlangsamen** to slow down imports; ~**tief** low level of imports; ~**überschuß** import surplus, excess of imports over exports; ~**unbedenklichkeitsbescheinigung** import certificate (clearance).

Einführung introduction, grounding, send-in *(sl.)*, *(in Betrieb)* orientation, induction, *(an der Börse)* introduction, listing *(US)*, *(Einrichtung)* installation, establishment, *(Gesetz)* adoption, establishment, *(Neuerungen)* innovation, *(von Personen)* introduction, recommendation, *(in Verein)* initiation, introduction, *(Vorwort)* preface, introduction, foreword, *(Versicherung)* lead;
als ~ by way of introduction;
feierliche ~ inauguration; **gesellschaftliche ~** debut, knockdown *(US sl.)*;
~ in ein Amt installation (initiation, instalment, *Br.*, induction) into an office; **~ neuer Artikel** new-product introduction; **~ von Beschränkungen** institution of restrictions; **~ an der Börse** admission *(Br.)* (listing, *US*) on the stock exchange; **~ einer Geschwindigkeitsbegrenzung** restriction of a road; **~ in die englische Literatur** introduction (guide) to English literature; **~ auf dem Markt** launching on the market; **~ der Sommerzeit** alteration to summer time; **~ einer neuen Steuer** establishment of a new tax; **~ in eine Vereinigung** initiation into a society; **~ von Vorschriften** institution of rules; **~ in eine Wissenschaft** initiation into a science; **schrittweise ~ eines gemeinsamen Zolltarifs** progressive introduction of a common customs tariff;
~ von Einfuhrbeschränkungen beabsichtigen to plan restrictions on imports; **jem. eine ~ für j. mitgeben** to give s. o. an introduction to s. o.

Einführungs|abend *(Studentenverbindung)* hell night; **~antrag an der Börse** application for official quotation *(Br.)* (listing, *US*) on the stock exchange; **~anzeige** launch ad *(US)*; **~auftrag** initial order; **~bericht** introductory report; **~brief** letter of introduction, recommendatory letter; **~draht** lead-in; **~feierlichkeiten** inaugural ceremonies; **~feldzug** initial (announcement) campaign; **~feldzug starten** to launch an advertising campaign; **~formel eines Gesetzes** enacting clause of an act; **~geschenk** introductory gift; **~gesetz** introductory law; **~heft** *(Zeitschrift)* introductory (inaugural) number; **~kabel** lead-in cable; **~kampagne** *(Werbung)* initial (introductory, announcement) campaign; **~konsortium** underwriting syndicate; **~kurs** opening price (quotation, rate), rate of issue; **~kursus, ~lehrgang** course of training, survey (link) course; **~preis** introduction (placing) price, early-bird price, *(Zeitschrift)* introductory rate; **~reklame** advertising campaign; **großangelegte ~reklame für etw. aufziehen** to launch s. th. on the market; **~schreiben** introductory (recommendatory) letter, letter of introduction; **~tarif** introductory rate; **~unterricht** preliminary instruction, preparatory school; **~werbung** introductory campaign, original (launch, *US*) advertising, original advertisement; **~worte** opening remarks; **~zeit** lead time; **~zeremonien** initiation (inaugural) ceremony.

Einfuhr|verbot prohibition of imports, import prohibition (ban), embargo; **~verbrauchsabgabe** import excise tax *(US)*; **~verfahren** import procedure; **~verlagerung** shifting of imports; **~volumen** volume of imports; **~waren** imported goods (commodities), import merchandise, articles of import, imports, importations; **kontingentfreie ~waren** free goods; **~welle** import wave; **~wert** value of import, import value; **~ziffern** import figures.

Einfuhrzoll customs inwards, import duty (rate), duty on importation *(US)*, external taxes, impost;
etw. mit ~ belegen to clap import duties on s. th.; **~ für ein Schiff deklarieren** to enter a ship inwards; **~ erheben** to levy a duty on goods, to place duties on imports;
~erklärung duty-paid entry; **~schein** bill of entry; **~tarif** revenue tariff; **~zuschuß** bounty on importation; **~zuteilung** import allocation.

einfüllen to fill (pour) in;
in Fässer ~ to cask, to tun; **in Flaschen ~** to bottle.

Einfüll|öffnung inlet; **~stutzen** tank inlet, filler neck; **~trichter** funnel, hopper.

Eingabe petition, presentation, address, request, application, memorial, paper filed, submission, *(Datenverarbeitung)* input; **schriftliche ~** *(Klageantrag)* exhibit;
~ abschlägig bescheiden to refuse a petition; **~ beim Bürgermeisteramt einreichen** to petition the mayor; **~ machen** to file a petition, to present (submit) a memorial; **einer ~ stattgeben** to grant a petition;
~daten *(Datenverarbeitung)* input data; **~frist** time limit; **~information** *(Datenverarbeitung)* input; **~kartei** input file; **~tastatur** entry keyboard; **~termin** closing date.

Eingang entrance, gate[way], door[way], way in *(Br.)*, *(Aktenkorb)* in-file, *(Beginn)* threshold, *(Durchgang)* passage, opening, *(Hafen, Tunnel)* mouth, *(Einnahmen)* receipts, taking in, takings, *(Eintritt)* entering, entry, admittance, *(Gelder)* accrual, *(Schulden)* recovery, payment, *(Waren)* coming in, arrival, entry, goods received;
am ~ des vorigen Jahrhunderts at the beginning (treshold) of the last century; **bei ~ des Wechsels** on receipt of the draft; **in der Reihenfolge des ~s** in strict rotation; **nach ~** when in cash (paid), on payment, when cashed, *(Lieferung)* on (against) receipt; **nach ~ Ihres Briefes** on receipt of your letter; **noch als ~ zu erwarten** receivable; **vorbehaltlich des richtigen ~s** reserving due payment;
kein ~! no admittance (entrance)!; **rechtzeitiger ~** payment in due time, provided due payment; **verbotener ~!** no entry!;
~ von Aufträgen incoming orders; **langsamer ~ von Außenständen** delay in receipt of outstanding debts; **~ eines Berichts** arrival of a report; **~ einer bereits als Verlust abgebuchten Forderung** realization of a retired debt, capital recovery *(US)*; **~ von Geldern** receipt of money; **~ für Lieferanten** tradesmen's entrance;
~ eines Briefes bestätigen to acknowledge [the] receipt of a letter; **sich den ~ erzwingen** to force one's way in; **~ finden** to gain admission, *(Waren)* to find favo(u)r (favo(u)rable acceptance); **im Ausland ~ finden** to find a market abroad; **~ in ein Land finden** to make its way into a country; **~ beim Publikum finden** to be well received by the public, to meet with favo(u)rable reception from the public; **sich ~ verschaffen** to gain admission, to force one's way in; **jem. ~ verschaffen** to pave the way for s. o.; **jem. ~ in eine Gesellschaft verschaffen** to obtain access for s. o. to a society; **sich in ein Haus gewaltsam ~ verschaffen** to force an entrance into a house; **sich mit Lug und Trug ~ verschaffen** to force one's way in under false pretences; **allen möglichen Mißbräuchen ~ verschaffen** to open the door to all sorts of abuses; **vor dem ~ auf jem. warten** to wait for s. o. at the doorway;
~ bitte freihalten! keep clear of the entrance!; **Unbefugten ist der ~ verboten!** no admittance except on business!

Eingänge *(Briefkorb)* in, *(von Kunden)* receipts from customers, *(von Waren)* arrivals, incoming goods, incomings, deliveries, *(von Zahlungen)* inward payments, proceeds, payments received, incomings;
nach Maßgabe der ~ in conformity with the receipts;
schleppende ~ slow collections; **tägliche ~** daily receipts;
~ und Ausgänge incomings and outgoings, *(finanziell)* income and expense; **~ aus Zöllen und Verbrauchssteuern** revenue from customs and excise;
~ buchen to book the receipts.

Eingangs|abfertigung *(Zoll)* clearance inwards; **~abgabe** duty on importation, import duty; **~abteilung** receiving department; **~anzeige** notice of arrival, *(Gutschrift)* credit advice, *(Zahlung)* acknowledgement of receipt; **~beleg der Portokasse** petty-cash receipt; **~benachrichtigung, ~bestätigung** notice of arrival, arrival notice, acknowledgement of receipt; **~besteuerung** marginal taxation, treshold; **~buch** *(Zahlungen)* book of entries (receipts); **~datum** date of receipt, *(Scheck)* value date *(Br.)*, availability date *(US)*; **~deklaration** bill of entry, clearance inwards, jerquing *(Br.)*, *(eidesstattliche)* oath of entry; **~fakturenbuch** invoice book; **~formel** preamble, caption, *(Gesetz)* enacting clause, *(Vertrag)* title; **~formel einer Urkunde** lien of a covenant; **~fracht** inward freight, freight-in; **~gespräch** initial interview; **~gewicht,** weight delivered, fallway; **~hafen** port of entry; **~halle** entrance hall; **~journal** book of original entries, purchase journal; **~komplex** entrance complex; **~körbchen** in-file; **~meldung** receiving report, *(ohne Mengenangabe)* blind receiving report; **~mitteilung** notice of arrival, *(Eisenbahn)* notification; **~nummer** receipt number; **~pforte zum Ruhm** gateway to fame; **~preis** *(EG)* threshold price; **~quittung** deposit receipt; **~rede** opening speech; **~stelle** *(für Klageschriften)* seal office *(Br.)*; **~stempel** receipt (received) stamp, *(Post)* date stamp, *(für Besucher)* time clock; **~steuersatz** *(Einkommensteuer)* standard rate of income tax, marginal tax rate, treshold tariff; **~steuersätze senken** to cut marginal taxation at the bottom; **~tag** date of receipt; **~tag eines Gerichtsantrags** seal day *(Br.)*; **~tarif** threshold tariff; **~tor** gate, portal, gateway; **~tür** front door; **~vermerk** file mark; **mit ~vermerk versehen** to file; **~wert** *(Programmierung)* input; **~worte** opening words; **~zoll** duty of entry, entrance (inward, *Br.*) duty; **~zollschein** jerque note *(Br.)*.

eingebaut built-in, installed;
~e Flexibilität *(Konjunkturpolitik)* built-in flexibility; **fest ~e Maschinenanlagen** trade fixtures; **~er Wandschrank** built-in wardrobe.

eingeben *(Bittschrift)* to hand in, to present, to submit, *(Computer)* to feed (key) in, to enter;
jem. Arznei ~ to administer a medicine, *(tropfenweise)* to instil(l) a medicine; **für eine Beförderung** ~ to put forward for a promotion; **einem Elektronenrechner Daten zur Speicherung** ~ to feed a computer with data; **Informationen über Wählscheiben** ~ to set up dimensional data on dials.
eingebeulter Kotflügel dented mudguard.
eingebildet conceited, arrogant, priggish, proud, notial;
auf seinen Reichtum ~ purse-proud;
jem. ~ **machen** to give s. o. a swelled head; ~ **sein** to think no small beer of o. s.; **maßlos** ~ **sein** to suffer from a swollen head *(coll.)*; **ganz schön auf sich** ~ **sein** to think a precious sight too much of o. s.;
~**er Affe** conceited (puppy) ass; ~**e Krankheit** imaginary illness.
eingeblendet faded-in;
~**e Szene** fade-in; ~**e Werbesendung** integrated commercial; ~**er Werbespot** tie-in advertising.
eingeboren native, indigenous;
~**es Gerechtigkeitsgefühl** inborn sense of justice.
Eingeborene natives, indigene.
Eingeborenen|aufstand native rising; ~**bräuche** native customs; ~**reservat** native settlement, reserve; ~**sprache** aboriginal language; ~**stamm** native tribe.
eingebracht *(Ehefrau)* dotal;
~**es Gut der Ehefrau** marriage portion; ~**es Kapital** capital invested, assets brought in; ~**e Sachen des Mieters** personal property of a tenant.
eingebuchtet locked up, on the peg *(US sl.)*.
Eingebung inspiration, fancy;
einer plötzlichen ~ **folgen** to act on the spur (impulse) of a moment; **der** ~ **seines Herzens folgen** to follow the dictates of one's heart; **plötzliche** ~ **haben** to have a sudden inspiration, to have a intuition.
eingebürgert naturalized;
~ **sein** *(Brauch)* to have taken root; ~ **werden** to become naturalized, to be admitted to citizenship by naturalization *(Br.)*;
~**e Waren** well-introduced articles.
Eingebürgerter naturalized citizen.
eingedämmt confined by dikes.
eingedeckt stocked, provided, *(Börse)* long, covered, bought back;
zu hoch ~ overstocked;
~ **sein** *(Börse)* to be long; **mit etw.** ~ **sein** to be sufficiently provided with, to have enough; **mit Aktien** ~ **sein** to be long of stock; **mit Devisen** ~ **sein** to be long of exchange; **gut** ~ **sein** to be well stocked (provided); **mit Kohlen** ~ **sein** to have a sufficient stock of coal; **nicht** ~ **sein** *(Börse)* to be short; **mit Vorräten gut** ~ **sein** to have laid in a good stock of provisions.
eingedenk *(Abkommen)* conscious of;
~ **der Tatsache** in view of the fact; ~ **der Toten** in memory of the dead;
einer Sache ~ **bleiben** to be mindful of a thing.
ein|gedruckte Adresse embossed address; ~**gedrückte Fensterscheibe** broken window; **in ein Problem überhaupt nicht** ~**gedrungen sein** to have touched only the fringe of a question.
eingefahren *(Auto)* run-in *(Br.)*, broken in *(US)*;
wird ~ running in;
sich in ein ~**en Geleisen bewegen** to get into a rut, to keep to the beaten track.
eingefleischt confirmed, dyed-in-the-wood, staunch;
~**e Abneigung** deep-rooted dislike; ~**er Junggeselle** confirmed bachelor; ~**er Kommunist** staunch communist, communist to the core (backbone); ~**er Reaktionär** diehard; ~**e Vorurteile** deep-rooted (ingrained) prejudices.
ein|geflüstert, vom Teufel prompted by the devil; ~**gefordertes Kapital** called capital; ~**gefressen** *(Säure)* corroded, pitted; ~**gefriedet** enclosed.
eingefroren frozen, blocked, *(Schiff)* locked in the ice, icebound;
~**e Forderungen** frozen debts; ~**e Gelder** frozen money, blocked funds; ~**e Guthaben** frozen assets; ~**es Konto** blocked account; ~**er Kredit** frozen credit; ~**e Preise** price rigidity, frozen prices; ~**e Vermögenswerte** blocked property.
ein|gefuchst sein to be drummed into; ~**gefügt** by the present.
eingeführt initiated, *(importiert)* imported;
an der Börse ~ quoted *(Br.)* (listed, *US*) on the stock exchange; **aus England** ~ imported from England; **in die Gesellschaft** ~ out; **neu** ~ new-fashioned; **nicht** ~ *(Börse)* not quoted *(Br.)* (listed, *US*) on the stock exchange *(Br.)*;
gut ~ **sein** to be well established, to have a good reputation on the market; **gesellschaftlich** ~ **werden** to be introduced to society;
neu ~**e Artikel** novelties; **gut** ~**es Geschäft** well-established business; **gut** ~**e Waren** well-introduced articles.
eingegangen received, *(Kleid)* shrunk;
in die Geschichte ~ storied;
in die Gemeinsprache ~ **sein** to have entered the common language;
~**e Beträge** amounts collected; ~**e Gelder** receipts, takings; ~**e Spenden** contributions which came in; ~**e Verpflichtungen** obligations assumed; ~**e Zeitung** defunct paper.
eingegliedert incorporated, affiliated;
nicht ~ unaffiliated;
~**e Versorgungsbetriebe** integrated public utility system.
Eingehen *(Aufhören)* discontinuance, cessation, extinction, closing down, *(Auflösung)* dissolution, *(von Geldern)* receipt, *(Schulden)* realization, *(von Waren)* arrival, coming in, *(Zustimmung)* acceptance, consent, agreement;
~ **auf ein Angebot** accepting an offer; ~ **auf Bedingungen** consent to conditions; ~ **einer Ehe** conclusion of a marriage; ~ **abgeschriebener Forderungen** capital recovery; ~ **eines Risikos** taking a risk; ~ **von Schulden** incurrence of debts; ~ **einer Verbindlichkeit** incurring a liability; ~ **eines Vertrages** entering an agreement; ~ **auf einen Vorschlag** acceptance of a proposal; ~ **einer Zeitschrift** cessation of a publication.
eingehen *(Aufträge)* to come in (to hand), to drop in, *(einwilligen)* to comply (agree) with, to submit to, *(Firma)* to go under, to close down, to cease to exist, to become extinct, to fizzle out, to pack up *(coll.)*, *(Geld)* to be paid (received), to come in (to hand), *(Spenden)* to come (flow, pour) in, *(Vieh)* to perish, to die, *(beim Waschen)* to shrink, *(Waren)* to arrive, *(Zeitung)* to perish, to cease to appear [publication];
jem. ~ to sink into s. one's mind; **auf ein Angebot** ~ to accept an offer; **bei jem. aus- und** ~ to be a frequent visitor to s. o., to have the run of the house with s. o.; **auf Bedingungen** ~ to yield (agree, submit) to conditions; **auf eine Bitte** ~ to fall in with a request; **Bürgschaft** ~ to stand surety; **Ehe** ~ to contract (celebrate) a marriage; **auf Einzelheiten** ~ to go into details; **auf jds. Entschuldigungen nicht** ~ not to listen to s. one's apologies; **Geldheirat** ~ to marry money; **in die Geschichte** ~ to go down in history; **jem. glatt** ~ to lap it up *(fam.)*; **Gläubigervergleich** ~ to compound with one's creditors; **Kosten** ~ to incur expenses; **vor Langeweile beinahe** ~ to nearly die of boredom; **jem. leicht** ~ to grasp s. th. easily; **auf einen Plan** ~ to consent to a plan; **auf eine Preisherabsetzung** ~ to consent to a reduction of the price; **rasch** ~ to pour in; **Risiko** ~ to undertake (run, incur) a risk, to take a chance *(US)*; **kein Risiko** ~ to play for safety; **auf eine Sache** ~ to go closely into a matter; **schleppend** ~ to come in slowly; **Schulden** ~ to assume (incur) debts; **Sozietät** ~ to enter into partnership; **in die Unsterblichkeit** ~ to attain immortality; **Verbindlichkeiten** ~ to contract liabilities; **eheliche Verbindung mit jem.** ~ to be joined with s. o. in matrimony, to contract a marriage with s. o.; **Vergleich** ~ to come to terms (an arrangement), to reach an agreement, to enter into an arrangement, *(mit Gläubigern)* to compound; **auf Verhandlungen** ~ to enter into negotiations; **Verpflichtung** ~ to enter into a commitment (an obligation), to incur a liability, to commit o. s.; **bindende Verpflichtung** ~ to enter into a binding agreement; **Vertrag** ~ to enter into an agreement; **auf einen Vorschlag näher** ~ to consider the details of a proposal; **Wette** ~ to take up a wager; **auf einen Wunsch** ~ to comply with a wish;
Filiale ~ **lassen** to close down (give up) a branch office; **Zeitschrift** ~ **lassen** to stop publishing a magazine.
eingehend full, in detail, circumstantial, profound, comprehensive, *(Geld, Ware)* incoming, *(gründlich)* detailed, thorough;
nicht ~ *(Stoff)* shrink-proof;
~ **begründen** to give full reasons; ~ **behandeln** to detail, to particularize, **sich** ~ **mit einer Sache beschäftigen** to go closely into a matter; ~ **beschreiben** to give a detailed description; **Frage** ~ **diskutieren** to discuss a question thoroughly; **sich** ~ **nach jem. erkundigen** to inquire at length about s. o.; ~ **prüfen** to examine thoroughly;
~**e Begründung** full reasons; ~**er Bericht** circumstantial account, detailed report; ~**e Beschreibung** detailed description; ~**e Darstellung** detailed account; ~**e Gelder** receipts, takings, money coming in; ~**es Gewicht** weight delivered; ~**e Kenntnisse** thorough knowledge; ~**e Post** incoming (arriving) mail; ~**e Prüfung** close (careful) examination; ~**e Rechnungen** inward invoices; ~**e Schilderung** detailed description; ~**es**

Studium comprehensive (close) study; **nach ~er Überlegung** after careful consideration; ~e **Untersuchung** thorough inquiry; ~e **Waren** arrivals; ~e **Zahlungen** receipts, takings.
eingekauft purchased;
am teuersten ~, zuerst verbraucht highest-in, first-out.
eingekeilt sandwiched, squeezed in;
in eine Menschenmenge ~ sein to be wedged in a crowd.
eingekesselt, von feindlichen Kräften encircled by enemy forces.
eingeklagt sued for;
~e **Forderung** litigious right.
ein|geklammert in brackets, bracketed; **nur ~geklinkt** on the latch.
eingeladen|sein to be asked out (invited);
nicht ~ out of it.
eingelagert|sein to be stored in a warehouse;
~e **Waren** goods in storage, stored (warehouse) goods.
eingelassen *(Edelstein)* mounted.
eingelegt salted, pickled;
mit Perlmutter ~ inlaid with mother-of-pearl.
ein|geleitet brought, initiated; ~**gelocht sein** to be in jug.
eingelöst discharged, paid, redeemed;
nicht ~ unredeemed, unpaid, *(Wechsel)* dishono(u)red.
eingemacht preserved, *(in Dosen)* canned *(US)*, tinned *(Br.)*.
Eingemachte|s preserves;
ans ~ gehen to attack vested rights.
eingemauert walled-in.
eingemeinden to incorporate into a parish (town), to communalize, to municipalize, to suburbanize.
eingemeindet incorporated.
Eingemeindung communalization, municipalization, suburbanization.
eingemottet *(mil.)* in mothballs;
~e **Gegenstände einsatzbereit machen** to demothball.
eingenommen, von sich full of o. s.;
für j. ~ sein to be prepossessed (biassed) in s. one's favo(u)r; **leidenschaftlich für etw. ~ sein** to be deeply prejudiced in favo(u)r of s. th.; **gegen j. ~ sein** to be prepossessed (prejudiced) against s. th., to have a bias against s. o., to be ill-disposed towards s. o.; **völlig ~ sein** to be wrapped up; **sehr von jem. ~ sein** to be infatuated with s. o.; **von etw. ~ sein** to be captivated (intrigued) by s. th.; **sehr von sich ~ sein** to think o. s. no small potatoes (no small beer of o. s.), to think no end of o. s., to be full of one's importance; **sehr von etw. ~ sein** to be heart and soul for s. th.
Eingenommenheit bias, prejudice, partiality, prepossession.
eingepaukt drilled-in.
eingeprägt, ins Gedächtnis engraved on the memory.
eingerechnet inclusive;
alles ~ all things considered; **nicht** ~ exclusive, *(Verpackung)* not to be allowed for; **Frühstück ist nicht** ~ breakfast is not included; **Verpackung ist nicht** ~ package is not allowed for.
eingerichtet *(Wohnung)* furnished;
elegant ~ elegantly furnished;
auf etw. ~ sein to be prepared; **bequem in einer neuen Wohnung ~ sein** to be comfortably installed in a new home;
zweckmäßig ~er Arbeitsraum efficiently arranged working room.
eingerostet rusty.
eingerückte Zeile indented line.
Eingerückter *(mil.)* conscript, inductee *(US)*, draftee *(US)*.
Eingesandt *(Zeitung)* letter to the editor.
eingeschaltet intermediate, *(el.)* live, switched (turned) on, *(Rundfunk)* on;
~**er Tag** intercalary day; ~**er Zustand** on position.
eingeschenkt, gut stiff.
eingeschlagen under cover;
in Papier ~ wrapped in paper.
eingeschlossen locked in, *(beigefügt)* subjoined, under cover, *(abgeschlossen)* isolated, secluded, close;
vom Eis ~ icebound; **in einer Grube** ~ trapped in a pit.
eingeschmuggelte Waren smuggled goods.
eingeschnappt sore, peeved, offended;
leicht ~ easily offended, very touchy, thin-skinned;
~ **sein** to have the sulks *(coll.)*.
eingeschneit snowed under;
mehrere Tage ~ sein to be snowed up for several days;
~**es Dorf** snowbound village.
eingeschoben run-in;
~**er Satz** interpolated clause.
eingeschossenes Kapital contribution to capital.
eingeschossig single-storey.
eingeschränkt conditioned, qualified, limited, restricted;
nicht ~ unlimited, unrestricted;
in seiner Bewegungsfreiheit ~ sein to be restricted in one's freedom of movement;
~**e Annahme** qualified acceptance; ~**e Lebensweise** straightened circumstances; ~**er Prüfungsvermerk** qualified approval;
~**e Stimmberechtigung** contingent voting power.
eingeschrieben *(Brief)* registered, special handling *(US)*;
Brief ~ schicken to register a letter.
eingesessen resident, domiciled, long-established.
Eingesessener resident.
eingesetzt institutional, appointed;
~ **sein** to be stationed;
~**es Aktivvermögen** assets employed.
eingesperrt locked up, confined;
~ **werden** to be placed behind prison bars.
eingespielt, gut well-established;
gut ~ sein to work hand in glove, to show perfect teamwork.
eingestandenermaßen confessedly, avowedly.
Eingeständnis confession, admission, acknowledgement;
glattes ~ naked confession; **ungewolltes** ~ incidental admission;
~ **eines Diebstahls** admission of a theft.
eingestehen to confess, to admit, to acknowledge;
seine Schuld ~ to admit one's guilt; **Verbrechen** ~ to confess a crime.
eingestellt engaged, hired *(US)*, *(adjustiert)* adapted, adjusted, *(Gerät)* tuned in, *(Optik)* focussed;
ganz auf seine Arbeit ~ centered on one's job; **falsch** ~ out of tune; **feindselig** ~ at odds with; **fortschrittlich** ~ progressive; **freundlich für j.** ~ well disposed towards s. o.; **nicht auf Gäste** ~ not prepared to take visitors; **glänzend aufeinander** ~ hand in glove; **ganz aufs Heiraten** ~ all thoughts centered on marriage; **materialistisch** ~ bread-and-butter minded; **praktisch** ~ practically minded; **scharf** ~ *(Foto)* in focus; **unscharf** ~ *(Radio)* broadly tuned;
auf etw. ~ sein to be adapted to s. th.; **gegen j. ~ sein** to be against s. o.; **großzügig ~ sein** to be generously minded; **konservativ ~ sein** to be conservative, to have conservative leanings; **auf das moderne Leben ~ sein** to be attuned to modern life; **materialistisch ~ sein** to be a materialist; ~ **werden** to cease, to get the nod, *(Zahlungen)* to stop, to be discontinued;
auf die modernen Entwicklungen ~e Gesetze laws attuned to the tendencies of the day; **fortschrittlich ~er Mensch** liberal.
eingestimmt, aufeinander attuned to each other.
eingeteilt, in Absätze paragraphical.
eingetragen registered, booked, on record, inscribed *(Br.)*, *(Aktiengesellschaft)* incorporated;
amtlich ~ incorporate; **gerichtlich** ~ on record; **handelsgerichtlich** ~ registered, incorporated; **nicht** ~ unregistered, unrecorded, *(Aktiengesellschaft)* unincorporated;
~ **sein** to be written (registered); **auf jds. Namen ~ sein** *(Haus)* to stand in s. one's name;
~**er Aktionär** holder of record *(US)*, registered shareholder *(Br.)*; ~**e Effekten** registered securities; **im Grundbuch ~er Eigentümer** registered proprietor; ~**es Gebrauchsmuster** registered design; **handelsgerichtlich ~e Gesellschaft** registered (incorporated, *US*) company; ~**es Kapital** registered (authorized) capital; ~**es Mitglied** enrolled member; ~**e Reallast** registered charge *(Br.)*; ~**e Schutzmarke** registered trademark; ~**er Verein** registered club *(Br.)*, incorporated association *(US)*, registered *(Br.)* (incorporated, *US*) society, membership corporation *(US)*; ~**es Warenzeichen** registered trademark; ~**er Warenzeichenbenutzer** registered user.
eingewandert immigrant.
Eingewanderter immigrant;
außerhalb des Kontingents ~ nonquota immigrant *(US)*.
eingeweiht initiated, in the know;
~**e Kreise** well-informed quarters, *(Börse)* insiders;
~ **sein** to be privy (in the secret, in the know), to know the ropes; **in das Geheimnis ~ sein** to be in the secret; **in eine Verschwörung ~ sein** to be let into the plot.
Eingeweihten spielen to assume a knowing air.
eingewiesen let in, briefed;
besonders ~ sein to have special briefings.
eingewöhnen, sich to acclimatize o. s., to settle down, to become acclimatized, to get accustomed; **sich in seinen Beruf** ~ to familiarize with one's job.
eingewöhnt haben, sich völlig to feel quite at home, to have settled down; **sich in seine neue Umgebung** ~ to have adapted o. s. to one's new surroundings.

Eingewöhnung acclimatization, familiarization, breaking in.
Eingewöhnungszeit settling-in period.
eingeworfen *(Brief)* posted;
nicht in den Briefkasten ~ unposted.
eingewurzelt, tief deep-rooted, old established;
~**er Brauch** deeply rooted custom.
eingezahlt, bei der Bank paid into the bank; **teilweise** ~ partly paid; **voll** ~ fully paid, paid up;
voll ~**e Aktie** [fully] paid-up share; ~**es Kapital** paid-up capital; **noch nicht** ~**es Kapital** uncalled (unpaid) capital.
eingezogen moved in, *(drucktechn.)* indented, *(konfisziert)* confiscated, seized, forfeited, *(Soldat)* conscript, enlisted in the army, drafted *(US)*;
zum Militärdienst ~ **werden** to be called to the colo(u)rs (drafted, *US*);
~**e Erkundigungen** information obtained; ~**er Gegenstand** forfeiture.
Eingezogener *(mil.)* conscript, enlisted man, draftee *(US)*, inductee *(US)*.
ein|gipsen to bed in plaster; ~**glasen** to glaze.
eingleisig single-line (-track, -rail);
~**er Betrieb** single-track working; ~**e Strecke** single[-track] line.
eingliedern to incorporate, to integrate, *(Gebiet)* to annex, *(klassifizieren)* to classify;
sich ~ to fit in; **j. in den Arbeitsprozeß** ~ to find employment for s. o.; **ein Land in ein anderes** ~ to incorporate one state into another; **in eine Organisation** ~ to incorporate into an organization; **Truppen in das atlantische Verteidigungssystem** ~ to integrate troops into the Atlantic defence system; **wieder** ~ to resettle.
Eingliederung incorporation, integration, *(Annektion)* annexation, *(Klassifizierung)* classification;
horizontale ~ horizontal integration; **schrittweise** ~ progressive integration; **wirtschaftliche** ~ economic integration;
~ **neuer Kräfte in den Arbeitsprozeß** absorption of new workers into the labo(u)r force; ~ **fremden Staatsgebietes** incorporation of a territory.
Eingliederungs|prozeß integration process; ~**zeitraum** integration period.
eingraben to bury;
sich ~ *(mil.)* to entrench o. s., to dig o. s. in; **Pfahl in die Erde** ~ to sink a pile into the ground.
eingravieren to engrave.
Eingreifdivision counterattack division.
Eingreifen interference;
bewaffnetes ~ armed intervention;
~ **des Staates** state intervention;
~ **erforderlich machen** to necessitate action.
eingreifen to interfere, to step in, to take action, to intervene;
in jds. Befugnisse ~ to encroach upon s. one's functions; **in eine Debatte** ~ to take a hand in a debate; **in den Gang der Ereignisse** ~ to influence the course of events; **ineinander** ~ to interlock; **in den Kampf** ~ to join the battle; **in die Privatwirtschaft** ~ to interfere with private business; **in jds. Rechte** ~ to encroach (entrench) upon s. one's rights; **in fremde Rechte** ~ to trespass on the rights of others; **in eine Unterhaltung** ~ to cut in on the conversation; **in ein schwebendes Verfahren** ~ to interfere with a pending lawsuit; **widerrechtlich** ~ to impinge, to trespass.
eingreifend incisive, drastic;
von ~**er Bedeutung sein** to be of decisive importance; ~**e Folgen** far-reaching consequences; ~**e Maßnahmen** drastic (strong) measures.
Eingreif|geschwader flying squadron; ~- **und Unterstützungskräfte** *(Nato)* strike force; **strategische** ~**reserve** rapid deployment force; ~**verband** striking force.
eingrenzen to enclose, *(Vollmacht)* to delimit, to narrow;
Epidemie ~ to localize an epidemic.
Eingrenzung der Wechselkursrisiken management of exchange risks.
Eingriff encroachment, trespass, infringement, inroad, entrenchment, *(Intervention)* interference, intervention, *(med.)* operation;
operativer ~ operation; **staatlicher** ~ state interference, government regulation; **störender** ~ disturbance; **verbotener** ~ illegal operation; **widerrechtlicher** ~ trespass, impingement; **wirtschaftspolitischer** ~ economic intervention;
~ **in jds. Rechte** encroachment upon (entrenchment upon, infringement, invasion of) s. one's rights; **gerichtlicher** ~ **in die Verwaltung** judicial interference; **staatlicher** ~ **in die Wirtschaft** direct intervention in the economy;
staatliche ~**e auf ein Minimum beschränken** to keep state interference at a minimum; ~**e machen in** to encroach upon; **operativen** ~ **vornehmen** to perform an operation; ~ **in jds. Intimsphäre vornehmen** to disturb s. one's privacy.
eingruppieren to group, to classify, to regiment, to class, to label.
Eingruppierung grouping, regimentation, classification, grading.
einhaken to cut (hook) in, *(Fensterläden)* to fasten;
Sicherheitskette ~ to put the chain on.
Einhalt curb, stop, brake;
~ **gebieten** to call a halt to, to put a check on; **einer Sache** ~ **gebieten** to put a brake on s. th.
einhalten to keep, *(Bestimmungen)* to conform with, to observe, to adhere, *(Lohn)* to deduct;
Abmachung ~ to abide by an agreement; **Bedingungen** ~ to observe conditions, to adhere to terms; **Bestimmung genau** ~ to adhere strictly to a clause; **Bestimmungen** ~ to comply with the rules; **Fahrplan** ~ to stick to a timetable; **Frist** ~ to keep within time, to comply with (observe) a time limit, to meet the deadline *(US)*; **Frist nicht** ~ to exceed a period of time; **Gesellschaftsstatuten** ~ to observe the articles of association; **Kündigungsfrist** ~ to observe the terms of notice; **Lieferfrist** ~ to deliver on schedule; **Limit** ~ to keep within the limit, to observe a price limit; **Richtung** ~ to follow the same direction; **Spielregeln** ~ to obey the rules of a game; **Termin** ~ to observe (keep to) a time limit; **Termin nicht** ~ to let the appointed time pass; **Verabredung** ~ to keep an appointment; **Verabredung nicht** ~ to break an appointment; **Verfahrensregeln** ~ to comply with the rules; **Verpflichtung** ~ to fulfil (perform) an obligation; **seine Verpflichtungen** ~ to meet (keep) one's commitments, to keep one's engagements; **Vertrag** ~ to abide by a contract; **Vertragsbestimmung** ~ to comply with a condition (clause) of a contract; **Vorschriften** ~ to adhere to instructions; **Zahlungen** ~ to be prompt in payment; **Zeit** ~ to be punctual; **Zeitplan** ~ to stick to a timetable, to run on schedule *(US)*.
Einhaltung compliance, observance, adherence;
unter ~ **einer Frist von zwei Wochen** subject to a term of two weeks;
genaue ~ strict observance;
~ **der Arbeitsstunden** job attendance; ~ **der gesetzlichen Formalitäten** compliance with legal formalities; ~ **einer Frist** observance of a term, meeting the deadline *(US)*; ~ **der Tagesordnung** preservation of order of business; ~ **eines Vertrages** adherence to a contract; ~ **von Wiederverkaufspreisen** maintaining resale prices, resale price maintenance; ~ **von Zahlungsverpflichtungen** promptness in payments;
nicht auf der ~ **eines Versprechens bestehen** to dispense with a promise; ~ **einer Bestimmung erzwingen** to enforce a rule.
einhämmern, jem. etw. to din s. th. into s. o., to burn s. th. into the mind of s. o., to hammer an idea into s. one's head, to drum s. th. into s. o.; **der Masse Schlagwörter** ~ to hammer slogans into the minds of the public.
einhandeln to barter, to trade in;
etw. mit ~ to get s. th. as a (into the) bargain; **sich etw. Schönes** ~ to land o. s. in a nice fix *(coll.)*; **billig** ~ to buy cheaply.
einhändigen to surrender, to hand (turn) in, to deliver.
Ein|händigung delivery, surrender; ~**hängetasche** suspension file.
einhängen *(Anhänger)* to hitch on, *(Wagen)* to couple on;
sich bei jem. ~ to take s. one's arm; **Buchblock in die Buchdecke** ~ to attach the book to its cover; **Fenster** ~ to put a window on its hings; **Hörer** ~ to replace (hang up) the receiver; **Tür** ~ to hang a door.
einhauen *(Tür)* to break down;
tüchtig ~ to tuck in.
einheften to file away.
einheimisch inland, native, national, domestic, home[grown], home-made, home-produced, homebred;
~**e Arbeitskräfte** native labo(u)r; ~**er Bedarf** domestic (home) demand; ~**e Bevölkerung** local population, inhabitants, natives; ~**e Erzeugnisse** home (inland) produce, home manufacture, native products; ~**es Fabrikat** home (inland, native) product; ~**e Industrie** home (native) industry; ~**er Markt** domestic market; ~**er Verbrauch** home consumption; ~**e Waren** inland commodities, domestic (homemade) goods; ~**e Wertpapiere** home descriptions *(Br.)*; ~**e Wirtschaftsgüter** domestic goods.
Einheimischer native, indigene.
einheimsen to pocket, *(sl.)* to clean up;
Ruhm für sich ~ to take the glory for o. s., to win laurels; **hübsche Summe Geldes** ~ to rake in a pretty penny.

Einheiraten marriage into a family.
einheiraten to marry into a family;
in ein Geschäft ~ to marry into a business.
Einheit unit, unity, *(Börse)* unit of trade, full (board, even) lot *(US)*, *(mil.)* outfit *(US)*, unit;
in sich abgeschlossene ~ self-contained unit; **nationale** ~ national unity; **organisatorische** ~ organizational unity; **politische** ~ political unity; **selbständige** ~ separate unit; **erfaßte statistische** ~ census information; **strategische** ~ *(mil.)* strategical unit; **taktische** ~ *(mil.)* tactical unit; **wirtschaftliche** ~ economic entity (whole); **wirtschaftspolitische** ~ politico-economic entity;
~ **der ersten Auswahlstufe** primary (first-stage) unit; ~ **der zweiten Auswahlstufe** secondary (second-stage) unit; ~ **bei Kursschwankungen** point in exchange fluctuations; ~ **des Ortes, der Zeit und der Handlung** unities of place, time and action; ~ **der Partei** party unity; ~ **der Stichprobenauswahl** *(Bevölkerungsstatistik)* unit of sampling; ~ **der Zeitdauer** unity of time;
sich zu seiner ~ **begeben** to join one's unit; ~ **bilden** to be as one; **Einzelteile zu einer** ~ **verschmelzen** to weld the parts into a homogeneous whole; **Bevölkerung zu einer** ~ **zusammenschließen** to unify the population.
einheitlich uniform, unitary, standard, flat, *(Börse)* regular, *(genormt)* standardized, *(homogen)* homogeneous, integrated, *(pol.)* unionist, *(ungeteilt)* undivided;
nicht ~ *(Börse)* divided, uneven, irregular;
nicht ~ **sein** *(Börse)* to make an irregular showing; ~ **vorgehen** to act jointly;
~**er Auftrag** standard order; ~**e Besteuerung** uniformity in taxation; ~**es Buchführungssystem** uniform accounting system; ~**e Front bilden** to form a united front; ~**e Gestaltung** unity of form; ~**e Größenregelung** standardization of sizes; ~**e Kleidung** uniform (utility) clothes; ~**e Kleidung tragen** to be dressed alike; ~**e Maßstäbe anwenden** to apply uniform standards; ~**e Methode** consistent method; ~**er Plan** coherent (concerted) plan; ~**e Prämie** flat rate; ~**er Preis** standard price; ~**er Rechtsgrund** unity of title; ~**e Richtlinien** uniform rules; ~**er Satz** flat rate; ~**es Vorgehen** concerted action; ~**er Wert** uniform value.
Einheitlichkeit uniformity, *(Kurs)* regularity, *(System)* homogeneity.
Einheits|beitrag *(Sozialversicherung)* flat-rate contribution; ~**bestrebung** unitary action (tendency); ~**bewegung** unitary movement; ~**bilanzformular** standard balance sheet; ~**buchführung** job order cost accounting; ~**dividende** uniform (standard) dividend; ~**dividendensatz** standard dividend rate; ~**erzeugnis** standardized product; ~**fabrikation** standard production; **fünfköpfige** ~**familie** family-of-five unit *(US)*; ~**fertigung** standardized production; ~**feuerversicherungspolice** standard fire [insurance] policy; ~**form** standard form; ~**format** standard size; ~**formular** standard [type of] form; ~**formular für die Anmeldung von Entschädigungsansprüchen** standard form for presentation of loss and damage claims; ~**fracht** standard freight; ~**front** united front, bloc; ~**gebühr** uniform (flat, standard) rate; ~**gehalt** straight salary; ~**gesellschaft** unit company; ~**gewerkschaft** industrial union; **fachliche** ~**gewerkschaft** horizontal union; ~**gewicht** standard weight; ~**größe** standard size; ~**gründung** single-step foundation; ~**kabel** coaxial cable; ~**kleidung** uniform (utility) clothes; ~**konnossement** uniform bill of lading; ~**kontenrahmen** uniform system of accounts; ~**konto** standard account; ~**kontoblatt** standard account form; ~**kosten** unit (standard) cost; ~**kurs** standard (uniform) quotation; ~**liste** *(Wahl)* single list; ~**lohn** single rate, union (standard) wage; ~**lohnsatz** standard rate of wages; ~**mietvertrag** standard form of rent agreement; ~**munition** fixed ammunition; ~**muster** standard (pattern) sample; ~**organisation** standard organization; ~**police** standard policy, *(Arbeitsunfallversicherung)* Universal Standard Workmen's Compensation Policy *(US)*, *(Feuerversicherung)* standard fire policy; ~**prämie** *(Lebensversicherung)* single premium.
Einheitspreis flat price (rate), uniform (unit, all-at-one, blanket) price, price line *(US)*, *(Auktion)* reserve price;
zum ~ all at one price;
vom Lieferort unabhängiger ~ uniform delivered price *(US)*;
~ **für eine Zone** zone price;
~**auszeichnung** unit-price labelling; ~**erzeugnis** dimestore product *(US)*; ~**festsetzung** unit pricing; ~**geschäft** chain *(Br.)* (one-price, *US*, fixed-price) shop, limited price (five and dime, single-price) store *(US)*, unit-pricing store *(US)*; **billige** ~**konsumgüter** low unit-priced consumer goods; ~**lage** price line; ~**politik** one-price (open-price) policy; ~**system** standard cost system, single-price policy; ~**ware** one-price articles, dime-store products *(US)*.
Einheits|qualität standard (merchant) quality, standard [quality] grade; ~**rechnung** *(Kostenrechnung)* job order cost system; ~**regierung** unified (unitary) government; **nationale** ~**regierung** national unity government; ~**sachen** utility goods; ~**satz** flat (standard, uniform) rate, *(Feuerversicherung)* basic rate; ~**schule** comprehensive school *(Br.)*; ~**schule einrichten** to comprehensivize *(Br.)*; ~**sorte** uniform (standard) grade; ~**staat** unitary state; ~**steuer** specific (unit) tax; ~**strecke** standard distance; ~**stücklohn** standard piece rate; ~**tarif** single-schedule (general, flat, unilinear) tariff, blank (block, group) rate, *(Bahn)* zone price, *(el.)* flat rate, *(Lohn)* flat (standard wage) rate, *(Nahverkehr)* flat fare; ~**tarifvertrag** standard agreement; ~**unterstützungssatz** standard benefit; ~**versicherung** all-risks (standard) insurance, *(Lagerhaus)* omnium policy; ~**vertrag** standard form contract; ~**vordruck** standard form; ~**währung** standard currency; ~**waren** utility (standardized) goods, utilities, standard articles.
Einheitswert standard value, *(Grundstück)* basic (site, assessed, ratable, *Br.*, taxable) value;
~ **eines Gebäudes zu hoch ansetzen** to set too high a valuation on a building; ~**e in einer Gemeinde festlegen** to survey and value a parish; ~ **eines Grundstücks festsetzen** to assess (value) a building (an estate); ~ **eines Grundstücks neu feststellen** to assess property for improvements; ~ **eines Hauses herabsetzen** to reduce the assessment on a building; ~ **eines Gebäudes für Versicherungszwecke schätzen lassen** to rate a building for insurance purposes;
~**angleichung** equalization of assessments; ~**bescheid** tax assessment note; ~**tabelle** valuation list *(Br.)*.
Einheits|wortzahl folio; ~**zahlungsbestimmungen** standard payment clauses; ~**zeit** standard time; ~**zoll** uniform duty; ~**zolltarif** single-schedule tariff.
einheizen to fire (heat) a room;
jem. tüchtig ~ to give it hot to (make it hot, make things lively for) s. o., to give s. o. hell.
einhellig concordant, unanimous;
~ **beschließen** to decide by common consent;
~**e Meinung** common consent, unanimous opinion; ~**e Zustimmung finden** to meet with unanimous approval.
einherstolzieren to stalk about (along), to strut.
einholen to get, to procure, *(Genehmigung)* to apply for, *(Verluste)* to recover, to recoup;
j. ~ to catch (draw, meet, *US*) up (draw level) with s. o.; **Akzept** ~ to present for (procure) acceptance; **Auskunft** ~ to gather (ask for) information; **Auskünfte über j.** ~ to make inquiries about s. o.; **Auto** ~ to catch up with another car; **Bestellungen** ~ to call for orders; **Erkundigungen über j.** ~ to make inquiries about s. o.; **jds. Erlaubnis** ~ to ask s. one's permission; **Fahne** ~ to lower the flag; **j. feierlich** ~ to escort s. o. home; **jds. Genehmigung** ~ to seek s. one's approval; **Instruktionen** ~ to ask (apply) for instructions; **Rat** ~ to seek advice, to consult s. o.; **Rechtsgutachten** ~ to take counsel's opinion; **Sachverständigengutachten** ~ to obtain an expert opinion; **Verspätung (verlorene Zeit)** ~ to make up for (recover) lost time; **jds. Vorsprung** ~ to catch up with s. o.; **Zustimmung** ~ to secure agreement;
~ **gehen** to go shopping.
Einholung|eines Akzepts procuring acceptance; ~ **von Auskünften** gathering of information; ~ **der Fahne** lowering of the flag; ~ **eines Gutachtens** request for an opinion; ~ **von Nachrichten** collection of news.
einhüllen to wrap up, *(ummanteln)* to sheathe;
sich in eine Decke ~ to wrap o. s. in a blanket; **Fluß** ~ *(Nebel)* to envelop the river; **Leiche in ein Leichentuch** ~ to shroud a corpse.
einig|sein to be of one mind, to be of the same opinion;
sich mit jem. ~ **sein** to be of s. one's opinion, to be in agreement (agree) with s. o.; **sich über die Bedingungen** ~ **sein** to be agreed on the conditions; **sich in der Fachwelt über etw.** ~ **sein** to reach a consensus among the experts; **sich nicht** ~ **sein** to differ, to disagree; **sich über einen Preis** ~ **sein** to have settled on a price; **in einem Punkt alle** ~ **sein** to be unanimous on a point; **sich selbst nicht** ~ **sein** not to be able to make up one's mind; **im wesentlichen** ~ **sein** to be in substantial agreement; **[sich]** ~ **werden** to agree, to come to terms, to come to an agreement; **die Gelehrten sind sich hierüber noch nicht** ~ authorities still differ on this point.

einige some, several, a few;
~**s Aufsehen erregen** to cause quite a sensation; **aus** ~**r Entfernung** from a distance; **über** ~ **Erfahrung verfügen** to have a little experience; ~**s auf einem Gebiet verstehen** to know quite a lot in a field; **über** ~**s Geld verfügen** to have some money of one's own; ~ **Zeit dauern** to take some time.

einigeln, sich to roll up like a hedgehog.

einigen to unite, to unify;
sich ~ to go together, to agree, to come to terms (an understanding, an agreement), to settle an issue *(Br.)*; **sich außergerichtlich** ~ to settle out of court; **sich mit seinen Gläubigern** ~ to compound with one's creditors; **sich über die Grundsätze** ~ to agree on principle; **sich auf die Gründung einer Gesellschaft** ~ to agree to form a company; **sich gütlich** ~ to settle a matter amicably, to come to an amicable arrangement; **Land** ~ to unify a country; **sich nachträglich** ~ to agree subsequently; **sich auf einen bestimmten Preis** ~ to agree on a certain price; **sich vergleichsweise** ~ to reach a settlement.

einigermaßen to some degree, to a certain extent;
~ **richtig sein** to be fairly important; ~ **Bescheid wissen** to have some idea.

einiggehen, mit jem. to agree (be in agreement) with s. o., to be of s. one's opinion in a matter.

Einigkeit unity, union, *(Ansichten)* unanimity, accord;
in völliger ~ **leben** to live in perfect harmony.

Einigung agreement, arrangement, settlement, understanding, *(pol.)* union, unification, *(Schuldrecht)* mutual assent, *(Übereinstimmung)* harmony, concord, accord, *(Versöhnung)* reconciliation;
mangels einer ~ failing an agreement;
außergerichtliche ~ consent (settlement) out of court; **gütliche** ~ amicable (friendly) arrangement, amicable (private) agreement; **mangelnde** ~ lack of consent, *(Irrtum)* mutual mistake; **tatsächliche** ~ reality of consent;
~ **über den Sachverhalt im Prozeß** case agreed on; ~ **über eine Wahl im Betrieb** consent election;
~ **zustande bringen** to reach an understanding, to bring about a reconciliation; ~ **mit jem. erzielen** to make terms with s. o.; **in allen Fragen** ~ **erzielen** to reach an agreement on all issues; **keine** ~ **erzielen** *(Geschworene)* to hang; **zu einer** ~ **gelangen** to arrive at an ageement, to come to an agreement (terms).

Einigungs|amt arbitration board (tribunal); ~**bewegung** unification movement; ~**formel** working agreement, modus vivendi; ~**mangel** lack of consent; ~**modalitäten** lines on which an understanding can be reached; ~**verfahren** stipulation (conciliation) proceedings *(US)*; ~**versuch** attempt at reconciliation; ~**vorschlag** recommendation, conciliatory proposal; ~**werk** unification work.

einimpfen, jem. etw. to implant s. th. in s. o., to indoctrinate s. o. with s. th.

einjagen, jem. Schrecken to frighten (terrify, scare) s. o.

einjährig|e Dienstzeit a year's military service; **nach** ~**er Tätigkeit** after working a year.

Einjähriges [etwa] ordinary certificate of education *(Br.)*.

einkalkulieren to take into account, to discount.

einkalkuliert, im Preis included in the price.

Einkalkulierung|eventueller Entlassungen *(Altersversorgungsplan)* discounting for severance; ~ **von Fehlerquellen** allowance of a margin for errors.

Einkammersystem *(parl.)* unicameral (single-chamber) system, unicameralism.

einkapseln, sich völlig to retire into one's shell.

einkassierbar encashable, collectible.

einkassieren to encash, to cash, *(Schulden, Wechsel)* to collect, to call in;
Beiträge monatlich ~ to collect contributions monthly; **Hälfte des Gewinns** ~ to pocket half the profit; **Scheck** ~ to cash a check *(US)* (cheque, *Br.*); **ausstehende Schulden** ~ to recover outstanding debts.

Einkassierung encashment, cashing, *(Wechsel)* collection;
~ **ausstehender Schulden** recovery of outstanding debts.

Einkauf buying, purchase, purchasing, *(Abteilung)* purchasing department, *(gekaufter Gegenstand)* buy, acquisition, *(Hausfrau)* shopping;
beim ~ **von Lebensmitteln** when buying food;
billiger ~ good pennyworth *(Br.)*, bargain; **en gros** ~ wholesale purchase; **genossenschaftlicher** ~ cooperative buying; **täglicher** ~ daily shopping; **zu Kontrollzwecken vorgenommener** ~ comparison shopping; **zentraler** ~ central buying, centralized purchasing;
~ **unter einem Dach** one-stop shopping; ~ **zollfreier Gegenstände** duty-free shopping; ~ **beim Konkurrenzbetrieb** comparison shopping; ~ **zu Sonderpreisen** cut-price buying; ~ **und Verkauf** buying and selling, purchase and sale;
j. mit dem ~ **von etw. beauftragen** to commission s. o. to buy s. th.; **über den** ~ **entscheiden** to make a buying decision; ~ **tätigen** to make a purchase.

Einkäufe, auf Grund plötzlicher Überlegung zustande gekommene impulse buying;
~ **per Auto** car shopping; ~ **zu sofortiger Verwendung** hand-to-mouth buying;
seine ~ **bar bezahlen** to make one's purchases on a cash basis; ~ **eines Kunden einpacken** to parcel a customer's purchases; **einige** ~ **erledigen** to do some shopping, to make some purchases; **seine** ~ **in der Stadt erledigen** to do one's shopping in town; ~ **machen (tätigen)** to go shopping, to shop, to do one's marketing, to make purchases.

Einkaufen shopping;
regelmäßiges ~ patronage.

einkaufen to buy, to purchase, to make purchases, to shop, to go shopping, to market;
sich ~ to buy-in **sich in ein Altersheim** ~ to buy a place in a home for the aged; **auf Ausverkäufen** ~ to sale; **bar** ~ to purchase for cash; **bestens** ~ to buy at best; **billig** ~ to buy low (cheap, at a cheap rate); **en gros (zum Großhandelspreis)** ~ to buy wholesale; **sich in eine Gesellschaft** ~ to become a member of a society by redemption; **im kleinen** ~ to buy [at] retail; **regelmäßig in einem Laden** ~ to patronize a shop, to trade with a shop *(US)*; **in einem Laden zum ersten Mal** ~ to buy in a shop for the first time; **in einem Laden in Zukunft nicht mehr** ~ to withdraw one's custom from a shop; **sich in eine Lebensversicherung** ~ to take out a life insurance policy; **auf Rechnung in einem Geschäft** ~ to run an account with a shop; **sich in eine Sterbeversicherung** ~ to pay premiums on a burial insurance; **nur stückweise** ~ to buy only piecemeal; **teuer** ~ to buy at a high figure; **neue Vorräte** ~ to lay in fresh stock;
~ **gehen** to go shopping; **jem.** ~ **schicken** to send s. o. down to the shops.

Einkäufer buyer for a firm, purchasing (buying) agent, *(Käufer)* buyer, customer, shopper, merchant *(Br.)*;
im Ausland ansässiger ~ nonresident buyer; **erfahrener** ~ senior buyer; **erster** ~ head buyer; **ortsansässiger** ~ resident buyer; **regelmäßige** ~ *(pl.)* patronage *(coll.)*;
~ **für die Betriebsmitglieder** plant shopper; ~ **von Firmenwagen** fleet buyer; ~ **für die Industrie** industrial buyer; ~ **für ein Warenhaus** departmental buyer.

Einkaufs|abrechnung *(Einkaufskommissionär)* account purchases; ~**abschluß** buying contract; ~**abteilung** purchasing department, buying office; ~- **und Verkaufsabteilung** buying and sales department; ~**agent** market representative; ~**angebot** purchase tender; ~**anweisung** purchase requisition; ~**ausschuß** purchasing (merchandise) committee; ~**bedingungen** buying conditions, purchase (merchandise) terms; ~**beleg** purchase voucher (record); ~**beutel** shopping bag; ~**buch** bought (invoice, register, purchase, record) book, purchase journal, voucher register; ~**budget** purchase budget; ~**bummel** buying spree; ~**büro** buying (purchasing) office; **gemeinsames** ~**büro** associated buying office; ~**delegation** buying mission; ~**disposition** purchasing decision; **richtige** ~**disposition** purchase planning; ~**erforschung** purchase observation; **telefonische** ~**erledigung** shop-by-phone; ~**erleichterung** shopping facility; ~**ermächtigung** commission to buy, purchasing permit; ~**etat** purchase budget; ~**fahrt** buying trip; ~**folge** purchasing frequencies; ~**gebiet** purchase area; ~**gegend** buying location; ~**gemeinschaft** purchasing combine (group, pool); ~**genehmigung** purchasing permit, docket *(Br.)*; ~**genossenschaft** cooperative buying society *(Br.)*, *(Einzelhandel)* retail co-ops, *(Großeinkauf)* cooperative wholesale society (buying association), wholesale purchasing cooperative; **staatliches** ~**geschäft** state-run shop; ~**gesellschaft** trading company, buying association, purchasing agency (association); **staatliche** ~**gesellschaft** state-buying organization; ~**gewohnheiten** buying habits; **freie** ~**grenze** *(im Einzelhandel)* open-to-buy allowance *(US)*; ~**häufigkeit** purchasing frequencies; ~**hinweis** shopping note; ~**journal** purchase journal; ~**kartell** purchasing cartel; ~**kommission** purchasing commission, buying committee; ~**kommissionär** buying (purchasing) agent, commission buyer; ~**kontingent** buying (purchase) quota; ~**konto** buying (purchase) account; ~**kontor** buying agency; ~**korb** shopping basket; ~**kosten abzüglich Warenskonto** merchandise cost; ~**kraft einer Familie** family buying power; ~**kredit** purchase-money loan; ~**land**

country of purchase; ~**leiter** *(Einkaufsabteilung)* purchasing manager, purchasing officer, chief buyer; ~**liste** shopping list; ~**möglichkeit** opportunity to buy; **zollfreie** ~**möglichkeit** duty-free facilities; **staatliches** ~**monopol** state-buying monopoly; ~**netz** string bag, marketing net; ~**order** buying order, indent; ~**organisation** buying organization; ~**orgie** shopping spree; ~**ort** point of purchase.

Einkaufspreis cost (purchase, buying, original, first, invoice, base, sterling) price, sterling (prime) cost;
unter dem ~ below (at less than) cost; **zum** ~ at first cost; **zum** ~ **verkaufen** to sell at [prime] cost;
~**liste** cost book.

Einkaufs|programm buying plan; ~**provision** buying commission, commission on purchase; ~**psychologie** buying psychology; ~**quelle** source; ~**rabatt** purchase discount; ~**rechnung** purchase invoice, *(Einkaufskommissionär)* account purchases; ~**rechnungspreis** invoice cost; ~**retouren** purchase returns; ~**retourenjournal** purchase returns journal; ~**sachbearbeiter** purchasing agent; ~**sammelbuch** traveller *(US)*; ~**spesen** purchasing costs; ~**stadt** business town; **staatliche** ~**stelle** state-buying agency; ~**straße** shopping promenade; ~**tag** shopping day; ~**tasche** shopping basket (bag); ~**tätigkeit** buying activity, purchasing business; ~**tour** buying trip (spree); **billige** ~**tour** cheap excursion; ~**tüchtigkeit** buying ability; ~**verband** buying group (combine), purchasing association (combine); ~**vereinigung** buying association (combine), voluntary group; ~**verfahren** purchasing pattern; **zurückhaltendes** ~**verhalten** go-slow buying pattern; ~**verhalten bei Haushaltsanschaffungen** household purchasing behavio(u)r; ~**verhältnisse** buying conditions; ~**vertrag** buying contract; ~**vertreter** buying (purchasing) agent; **im Ausland ansässiger** ~**vertreter** resident buyer; ~**vertretung** buying agency, market representation; ~**vollmacht** authority to purchase; ~**wägelchen** basket (shopping) cart, trolley; ~**wert** value at cost, cost value, purchasing value, acquisition cost; **zum** ~**wert einsetzen** to value at cost; ~**zeit** shopping hours; ~**zentrum** discount department store *(US)*, discount house *(Br.)*, shopping center (mall, precinct), *(außerhalb der Stadt)* exurban shopping center *(US)* (centre, *Br.*), array of shops, shop array, supermarket; ~**zentrum mit begrenztem Warenangebot** limited-range discounter; ~**zettel** shopping list; ~**zwischenlandung** shopping stopover.

einkehren, in einem Gasthaus to stop (put up, stay) at an inn, to bait *(Br.)*.

einkellern to store, to cellar.

Einkellerung storage, cellarage.

einkerkern to confine, to immure, to incarcerate, to dungeon up.

Einkerkerung confinement, duress.

einkesseln *(mil.)* to encircle, to pocket.

Einkesselung *(mil.)* encirclement, pocketing.

einklagbar enforceable, claimable, actionable, suable *(US)*, demandable, recoverable by law;
nicht ~ unimpeachable, unenforceable; **selbständig** ~ actionable per se;
~ **sein** to be enforceable at law;
nicht ~**e Forderung** debt dead in law.

Einklagbarkeit enforceability, suability *(US)*.

Einklagen|einer Forderung enforcement (prosecution) of a claim, suit for a debt; ~ **eines Teilbetrags** splitting a cause of action.

einklagen to sue out, to file a suit;
seine Gebühren ~ to sue for one's fees; **sein vertraglich vereinbartes Gehalt** ~ to sue for one's salary under a contract; **Forderung** ~ to take legal proceedings for the recovery of a debt; **Teilbetrag** ~ to split an action; **angemessenen Teilbetrag** ~ to sue on a quantum meruit.

Einklagung taking legal action, suing *(US)*.

einklammern to put in parenthesis, to parenthesize, to enclose;
Wort ~ to put a word in brackets, to bracket a word.

Einklang agreement, accordance, harmony;
im ~ **mit** in step (keeping) with, consistent with, in accord with;
in ~ **bringen** to bring into line, to harmonize, to reconcile; **im vollkommenen** ~ **mit seiner Umwelt leben** to live in complete harmony with one's environment; **mit der Welt im** ~ **sein** to be square with all the world; **im** ~ **stehen** to be in keeping, to comply with, to harmonize, to jibe *(US coll.)*; **mit jem. im** ~ **stehen** to be of one mind with s. o., to be of s. one's opinion (mind); **mit der öffentlichen Meinung im** ~ **stehen** to be in harmony with public opinion.

einklarieren to enter, to invoice from a country, *(Schiff)* to clear in (inwards).

Einklarierung entry, import clearance, *(Schiff)* clearance inwards.

Einklarierungstag day of entry.

Einklebebuch scrapbook.

Einkleben von Beilagen sticking in of insets.

einkleben to stick into;
Briefmarken ~ to put in stamps; **Fotografien in ein Album** ~ to stick photographs in an album.

einkleiden to vest, to clothe;
j. neu ~ to fit s. o. out with a new set of clothes; **sich völlig neu** ~ **müssen** to have to renew one's wardrobe.

Einkleidung clothing, *(mil.)* fitting out.

Einkleidungsgeld *(mil.)* outfit allowance.

einklemmen, Auto zwischen zwei Lastwagen to wedge in a car between two trucks.

einklinken *(Tür)* to latch;
Schleppseil ~ to attach the towing cable.

Einknopfbedienung one-knob tuning.

Einkommen income, revenue, penny, rent, *(Einkünfte)* emoluments, perquisites, *(Ertrágnisse)* earnings, *(Gewinne)* gainings, gains *(US)*, *(Mittel)* means, *(Rente)* rent;
ohne ~ without income;
abgeleitetes ~ derived income; **in England anfallendes** ~ income arising in the United Kingdom; **im Rechnungsabschnitt anfallendes** ~ current income; **für längeren Zeitraum in einem Steuerjahr anfallendes** ~ bunched income; **angemessenes** ~ fair income; **antizipatorisches** ~ deferred income *(US)*; **bei der Steuererklärung nicht aufgeführtes** ~ omitted income; **ausreichendes** ~ sufficient income; **steuerlich begünstigtes** ~ preference income; **beitragspflichtiges** ~ income liable to subscription; **berufliches** ~ professional earnings; **besteuerungsfähiges** ~ taxable income; **die Lebensbedürfnisse deckendes** ~ income commensurate with one's needs; **effektives** ~ real income; **erarbeitetes** ~ earned income; **tatsächlich erzieltes** ~ actual income; **festes** ~ regular (settled, permanent, steady, stable, assured, fixed) income; **freiberufliches** ~ earned income, income from a profession or vocation; **freies** ~ income above the living wage; **fundiertes** ~ unearned income (revenue); **fünfstelliges** ~ five-figure income; **garantiertes** ~ guaranteed income; **gebundenes** ~ living wage; **gemeinsames** ~ *(Ehepaar)* combined income; **geringes** ~ small income; **geschätztes** ~ estimated income, estimated earnings; **gesichertes** ~ settled (secured) income, income security; **gewerbliches** ~ industrial (business) income; **gutes** ~ considerable (comfortable) income; **höheres** ~ fairly large income; **hohes** ~ large (high, big) income; **jährliches** ~ annual income, annuity; **knappes** ~ scanty income; **pro Kopf** ~ income per capita, individual earnings; **körperschaftssteuerpflichtiges** ~ income chargeable with (liable to) corporation tax; **lebenslängliches** ~ life income; **mäßiges** ~ small income; **mittleres** ~ middle-bracket (median, *US*) income; **niedriges** ~ low income; **nominales** ~ nominal income; **persönliches** ~ personal income; **reales** ~ actual pay; **ruhegehaltsfähiges** ~ pensionable emoluments; **sicheres** ~ assured (dependable) income; **sonstiges** ~ other income (revenue); **sozialversicherungspflichtiges** ~ income inside the scope of the national insurance system; **spärliches** ~ pittance; **ständiges** ~ regular (fixed) income; **zur freien Verfügung stehendes** ~ spendable (disposable, *US*) income; **rasch steigendes** ~ fast-mounting income; **steuerfreies** ~ tax-exempt *(US)* (nontaxable, untaxable) income, income exempt from taxation; **steuerpflichtiges** ~ income liable to tax, taxable (chargeable, assessable, *US*) income; **voll steuerpflichtiges** ~ income wholly liable to tax; **tatsächliches** ~ real income; **transitorisches** ~ transitory income; **unregelmäßiges** ~ nonrecurring revenue (income); **unselbständiges** ~ income from wages (work, employment), income arising from any office or employment of profit; **unversteuertes** ~ income before taxes, pretax income; **veranlagungspflichtiges** ~ assessable income *(US)*; **tatsächlich verbrauchtes** ~ realized income; **verfügbares** ~ spendable (disposable, *US*) income; **frei verfügbares** ~ *(Volkswirtschaft)* disposable *(US)* (discretionary) income; **verläßliches** ~ dependable income; **zu versteuerndes** ~ taxable (assessable, *US*) income, income liable to tax; **versteuertes** ~ taxed income; **vorweggenommenes** ~ deferred income; **wertbeständiges** ~ stable income; **wirkliches** ~ real income; **zusätzliches** ~ additional income;
~ **nach Abzug der Steuern** income after taxes; ~ **vor Abzug der Steuern** pretax income; ~ **von Aktiengesellschaften** corporate income *(US)*; ~ **aus selbständiger Arbeit** income arising from any office or employment of profit; ~ **aus unselbständiger Ar-**

beit wage income; ~ **aus Arbeit und Kapital** mixed income; ~ **verschiedenster Art** miscellaneous income; ~ **aus freier Berufstätigkeit** professional earnings; ~ **zwischen 15.000 und 20.000 Dollar** income in the $ 15.000 - 20.000 brackets *(US)*; **freies** ~ **über dem Existenzminimum** income above the living wage, surplus value; ~ **aus Gewerbebetrieb** industrial income (earnings), profits from trade or business *(Br.)*, business income; ~ **aus Grundbesitz** income derived from land (landed property), property income; ~ **aus Kapitalvermögen** unearned income, investment income; ~ **pro Kopf der Bevölkerung** per capita income; ~ **von Körperschaften** corporate income; ~ **auf Lebenszeit** income for life; ~ **aus Publikationen (Anzeigen)** advertising revenue; ~ **der mittleren Steuerklasse** middle-bracket income *(US)*; **frei verfügbares** ~ **nach Steuern** disposable income *(US)*; ~ **aus Vermögen[sanlage]** unearned (investment) income, income property; ~ **aus unbeweglichem Vermögen** income from real property; ~ **aus Wertpapierbeständen** income from securities *(Br.)*, investment income;
sein ~ **angeben** to make an income-tax statement *(US)*; **sein** ~ **zu niedrig angeben** to understate one's income; ~ **angleichen** to equalize income; **sein ganzes** ~ **ausgeben** to live up to one's income; **mit seinem** ~ **auskommen** to live within one's income, to suit one's expenditure to one's means, to make both ends meet; **als in diesem Jahr angefallenes** ~ **behandeln** to report as income for the year; ~ **besteuern** to tax income; ~ **an der Quelle besteuern** to tax revenue at the source; ~ **beziehen** to draw (derive) income; **steuerpflichtiges** ~ **darstellen** to constitute taxable income; ~ **steuerlich an der Quelle erfassen** to tax income at source; **sein** ~ **erhöhen** to make up (augment) one's income; ~ **ermitteln** to determine an income; **gutes** ~ **erzielen** to make a good income; **geringes** ~ **[zu versteuern] haben** to be in low income brackets *(US)*; **gutes** ~ **haben** to have a good income; **hohes** ~ **[zu versteuern] haben** to be in high income brackets *(US)*; **40.000 Dollar** ~ **im Jahr haben** to have an income of $ 40.000 a year; **vierstelliges** ~ **haben** to have an income of four figures; **von seinem** ~ **leben** to live off one's income; ~ **zur Besteuerungsgrundlage nehmen** to base taxation on the income; **jds.** ~ **auf jährlich 8000 Pfund schätzen** to put s. one's income at £ 8000 a year; **als normales** ~ **versteuerbar sein** to be taxable as ordinary income; **dem** ~ **zuzurechnen sein** to be of a revenue nature; **zum** ~ **in keinem Verhältnis stehen** to be out of proportion to one's income; ~ **für die Steuerveranlagung mit größeren Sätzen veranschlagen** to compute the income for assessment at higher rates; **sein** ~ **im voraus verbrauchen** to anticipate one's income; **sein** ~ **verdoppeln** to double one's income; **über ein** ~ **verfügen** to have an income in one's own right; **sein** ~ **vermehren** to augment one's income; **als** ~ **versteuern** to report as taxable income; **50.000 Dollar an** ~ **versteuern** to return one's income at $ 50.000; ~ **aus Steuergründen über die Jahre verteilen** to spread out income; **steuerlich als** ~ **behandelt werden** to be attributed to revenue; **aus dem laufenden** ~ **bezahlt werden** to be paid out of income; **vom laufenden** ~ **gespeist werden** to come from current income; **mit dem** ~ **verrechnet werden** to be chargeable against income; **Teil seines** ~**s zurücklegen** to set aside a part of one's income.

einkommen *(Beträge)* to come in, to be paid;
um etw. ~ to petition (apply, make an application for) s. th.; **um seinen Abschied** ~ to tender one's resignation; **um eine Gehaltserhöhung** ~ to apply for an increase in salary, to tackle the boss for a rise *(Br.)*; **um Urlaub** ~ *(mil.)* to ask for leave.

Einkommens|abstand income gap; ~**angleichung** adjustment of incomes; ~**anstieg** revenue increase, earnings advancement, upgrading (growth) of income; **sprunghafter** ~**anstieg** jump in incomes; ~**anteil** portion (part) of income; **zur persönlichen Verfügung stehender (frei verfügbarer)** ~**anteil** personal disposable income *(US)*; ~**arten** types of income; ~**aufstellung** income (earnings) statement, income sheet; ~**aufteilung** *(Steuererklärung)* split, income-splitting; ~**ausfall** loss of income; ~**ausgleich** income hotchpot; **höchstmöglicher** ~**ausgleichseffekt** *(Steuersystem)* maximum social advantage; ~**begünstigter** income beneficiary; ~**belastungen** charges on income; **konzerninterne** ~**belastungen** intercompany charges on income; **gewinnübersteigende** ~**belastungen** excess charges on income; ~**berechnungen** computation of income.

einkommensberechtigt sein to be eligible for income.

Einkommens|bereich range of income; **unterer** ~**bereich** lower income brackets, treshold; ~**beschlagnahme** *(Völkerrecht)* sequestration of income; ~**besteuerung** personal taxation, taxation on income; **getrennte** ~**besteuerung beantragen** to make a claim for separate assessment; **der** ~**besteuerung gänzlich entgehen** to escape the income-tax net; ~**betrag** amount of income; ~**bezieher** income earner *(US)*; **hohe** ~**bezieher** high-income people; ~**bildung** production of income.

einkommenschaffender Faktor income-producing factor.

Einkommens|defizit revenue deficit; ~**effekt** income effect; ~**elastizität der Nachfrage** income elasticity; ~**empfänger** recipient of income, income receiver; ~**entwicklung** earnings record, growth of income; ~**erhöhung** growth of income; ~**erklärung** income-tax return (statement, *US*); ~**ermittlung** income determination; ~**ertrag** income yield; ~**faktor** income-producing factor, income factor, revenue earner; **übliches** ~**formular** reducing-balance form; ~**garantie** income guarantee; ~**gefälle** income differential; **höhere** ~**gegend einer Stadt** upper-income section of a city; **niedrige** ~**gegend** low-income neighbo(u)rhood; ~**gewinn** income benefit; ~**gliederung** distribution of incomes; ~**grenze** income limit, margin of income.

Einkommensgruppe income group (class, bracket, *US*);
betroffene ~ range of earnings affected; **höhere** ~**n** higher income brackets *(US)*; **mittlere** ~**n** middle income classes; **niedrige** ~ lower [income] class;
zu den hohen ~**n gehören** to be in high income brackets *(US)*.

Einkommens|höhe level of income, income level (floor); ~**index** earnings index.

Einkommensklasse income group (class, bracket, *US*);
niedrige ~ lower [income] class; **untere** ~**n** working classes.

Einkommens|konto revenue account; ~**kontrolle** income control; ~**modell** income expenditure model; ~**nachholbedarf** earnings lag; ~**neuverteilung** redistribution of income; ~**niveau** level of income, income level; ~**pfändung** garnishment of earnings; ~**politik** incomes policy *(Br.)*; ~- **und Preispolitik** policy for prices and income; **steuerlich begünstigte** ~**positionen** tax preference items; ~**prozentsatz** percentage of income; ~**quelle** source of income (earnings), revenue; **zusätzliche** ~**quelle** subsidiary source of income; ~**quellenbesteuerung** taxation at the source, *(Lohnsteuer)* withholding tax principle *(US)*; **staatliche** ~**regulierung** statutory control of incomes; ~**rückgang** decline of income; ~**rücklage** unspent income; ~**schätzung** estimate of income; ~**schicht** income group (class); **mittlere** ~**schichten** middle-income classes, middle-income earners; ~**schwelle** threshold; ~**sicherung** income maintenance; ~**stand** income level; ~**steigerung** increase (rise) of income, income increment; ~**streuung** distribution of income.

Einkommensteil income element;
lohnunabhängige ~**e** fringe benefits *(US)*; **steuerpflichtiger** ~ *(Stiftung)* unrelated business income;
großen ~ **verschlingen** to take heavy tolls of one's income; ~**e zurücklegen** to set aside part of one's income.

Einkommenstendenz earnings trend.

Einkommensteuer [federal] income tax, personal income tax *(US)*, tax on income, normal tax *(US)*;
bei der Veranlagung der ~ in levying income tax;
zum Grundtarif anfallende ~ basic-rate income tax; **mit einem höheren Tarif anfallende** ~ higher-rate income tax; **fällige** ~ income tax accrued; **gestaffelte (progressive)** ~ graduated income tax; **gesamt gezahlte** ~ gross income tax; **hinterzogene** ~ evaded income tax; **nachgezahlte** ~ conscience money; **negative** ~ negative (reserve) income tax; **progressive** ~ progressive income tax; **veranlagte** ~ assessed (individual, *US*) income tax; **zurückgestellte** ~**n** deferred national taxes on income;
~ **auf das selbstgenutzte Eigenheim** schedule tax on owner-occupied house; **zusätzliche** ~ **auf Einkommen über 4000 £** surtax *(Br.)*; ~ **auf ausgeschüttete Gewinne** income tax on profit distributed; ~ **für natürliche Personen** income tax on individuals *(US)*; ~ **im unteren Proportionalbereich** basic rate income tax; ~ **und Vermögenssteuer** taxes on income and property;
~ **durch Steuerabzug abgelten** to settle income tax by deduction at the source; **von der** ~ **befreien** to exempt from income tax; ~ **einbehalten** to withhold income-tax; **der** ~ **gänzlich entgehen** to escape the income tax net; ~ **erheben** to tax income; ~ **festsetzen** to value an income; ~ **hinterziehen** to cheat on one's income tax; **der** ~ **unterliegen** to be liable to income tax; **zur** ~ **veranlagen** to levy by direct assessment, to make an income-tax assessment; **zehnprozentige Erhöhung der** ~ **vornehmen** to increase income tax by 10 per cent; **völlig von der** ~ **freigestellt werden** to be removed from the income-tax rolls entirely;
~**abgabe** income-tax preparation; ~**abteilung** income-tax division *(US)*, inland revenue section *(Br.)*; ~**abzug** income-tax deduction.

einkommensteuerabzugsfähig deductible from income tax.

Einkommensteuer|änderung income-tax amendment, income tax changes; ~**aufkommen** income-tax receipts, income-tax yield, internal revenue *(US)*; ~**aufstellung** income sheet *(US)*; ~**ausfall** income-tax deficiency, failure in revenue; ~**bearbeiter** income-tax collector.

einkommensteuerbegünstigt sein to rank for income-tax relief *(Br.)*.

Einkommensteuer|behandlung income-tax treatment; ~**behörde** income-tax collector (authority), Internal Revenue Service *(Br.)*, Internal Revenue Office *(US)*; ~**belastung** income-tax load; ~**bemessungsgrundlage** income-tax base; ~**beratung** income-tax service; ~**berechnung** income-tax computation, income-tax calculation; ~**berichtigung** amended return; ~**bescheid** income-tax (assessment, *US*) bill; ~**bestimmungen** income-tax regulations; ~**bezirk** collection district; ~**buchführung,** ~**buchhaltung** income-tax accounting, accounting for income tax; ~**durchführungsverordnung** tax implementation ordinance; ~**erhebung** collection of income tax; ~**erhöhung** income-tax increase.

Einkommensteuererklärung income-tax return (statement, *US*), return (declaration, *Br.*) of income, income-tax declaration *(Br.)*;
berichtigte ~ corrected return; **gemeinsame** ~ joint income tax return; **getrennte** ~ separate return; **unrichtige** ~ false return; ~ **im Konzernverband** consolidated income-tax return;
seine ~ **abgeben** to file one's income-tax return (statement, *US*), to complete a return of income, to declare one's income *(Br.)*, to declare to a tax inspector *(Br.)*; **detaillierte** ~ **abgeben** to return the details of one's income; **gemeinsame** ~ **abgeben** *(Ehepaar)* to file a joint return; **getrennte** ~**en abgeben** to file separate returns; **keine** ~ **abgeben** to fail to file an income-tax return; ~ **aufsetzen (ausfüllen, bearbeiten)** to prepare an income-tax return (statement, *US*); **bei der** ~ **betrügen** to fiddle an income-tax return *(sl.)*; ~ **fertigen** to make an income-tax statement *(US)*; **seine** ~ **machen** to make one's income-tax return; **der Finanzverwaltung eine** ~ **vorlegen** to furnish a return to the Commissioners of Inland Revenue *(Br.)*; ~ **in notarieller Form vornehmen** to notarize an income-tax declaration *(Br.)*.

Einkommensteuer|erlaß abatement of income tax; ~**erleichterung** income-tax credit *(US)* (relief, *Br.*); **mit** ~**erleichterungen verbunden sein** to be eligible for income-tax relief *(Br.)*; ~**ermäßigung** allowance of income tax, income-tax reduction; ~**erstattung** refunding (refund) of income tax; ~**festsetzung** income-tax computation; **Bargeld oder Wertpapiere mit** ~**forderungen verrechnen** to set off cash or securities against the income-tax accrual.

Einkommensteuerformular income-tax form (return, blank, *US*), form of return, tax return form, income tax return form, income sheet *(US)*, schedule *(US)*;
bearbeitetes ~ processed return;
~ **zusenden** to issue a return form.

einkommensteuerfrei tax-exempt, free of income-tax;
~ **und kapitalgewinnsteuerfrei** free of all income tax and capital gains tax;
~ **machen** to exempt from income tax; ~ **ausbezahlt (vereinnahmt) werden** to be paid out (received) without deduction of income tax.

Einkommensteuerfreibetrag tax-exempt amount *(US)*, income-tax credit *(US)*, income-tax allowance, income-tax relief *(Br.)*; **persönlicher** ~ personal income-tax exemption *(US)*;
~ **für Berufstätige** earned income relief (allowance) *(Br.)*; ~ **für die erwerbstätige Ehefrau** wife's earned income allowance *(Br.)*; ~ **für Einkünfte im unteren Proportionalbereich** small-income allowance *(Br.)*.

Einkommensteuer|freigrenze income limit; **altersbedingte** ~**freigrenze** income-tax age exemption; ~**freiheit** exemption from income tax; ~**fuß** income-tax rate; ~**gesetz** Income Tax Act *(Br.)*, Internal Revenue Code *(US)*; ~- **und Körperschaftssteuergesetz** Income and Corporations Taxes Act *(Br.)*; ~**gesetzgebung** income-tax legislation; ~**gesichtspunkt** income-tax angle; **aus** ~**gründen** for income-tax purposes; ~**grundsätze** income-tax principles; **zwecks Sicherstellung des** ~**grundtarifs** for basic-rate income-tax purposes; ~**gruppe** income class, income [tax] bracket *(US)*; ~**herabsetzung** income-tax cut; ~**herabsetzungen finanzieren** to fund reductions in income tax; ~**hinterzieher** income-tax dodger; ~**hinterziehung** income-tax evasion, evasion of income tax, defraudation of the revenue; ~**höchstsatz** top rate of income tax; ~**indexierung** income-tax indexation; ~**jahr** income-tax year; ~**klasse** income group (bracket, *US*, schedule, *Br.*), income class, income group; **in der höheren** ~**klasse** upper bracket *(US)*; **mittlere** ~**klassen** middle-income brackets *(US)*; ~**konto** income-tax account.

einkommensteuerliche| Aufgabe (Tätigkeit) personal income-tax job; ~ **Vorsichtsmaßnahmen** income-tax safeguards.

Einkommensteuer|nachlaß rebate for income tax; ~**novelle** income-tax amendment; ~**nummer** income-tax reference number.

Einkommensteuerpflicht income-tax liability.

einkommensteuerpflichtig sein to be liable for income tax.

Einkommensteuer|pflichtiger income-tax payer; **buchführender** ~**pflichtiger sein** to be required to keep full records; **langfristige** ~**politik** long-range tax strategy; ~**progression** income-tax progression; ~**prüfer** income-tax investigator; ~**recht** income-tax law; ~**reform** income-tax reform; ~**richtlinien** income-tax rules (directives); ~**richtlinien erlassen** to fix the income tax; ~**rückerstattung** refunding of (refund on) income tax, income-tax rebate; **einem** ~**rückstand nachgeordnet sein** to be subordinated to a claim of the Inland Revenue; ~**rückstellungen** reserve for income tax; ~**sache** income-tax case.

Einkommensteuersatz [personal] income-tax rate;
höchster ~ top earned tax rate, highest marginal rate of income tax;
~ **im unteren Proportionalbereich** basic rate income tax;
nur den halben ~ **auslösen** to attract income tax on only 50%; **mit dem höchsten** ~ **konfrontiert sein** to face the highest marginal tax rate; **10ige% Erhöhung des** ~**es vornehmen** to increase income tax by 10 per cent; **nur mit dem halben** ~ **versteuert werden** to be eligible for the earned-income ceiling rate of 50%.

Einkommensteuersätze|erhöhen to scale up income tax; ~ **in der Höhe von 28% festlegen** to fix the income tax at 28%; ~ **um 10% heraufsetzen** to increase (scale up) income tax 10 per cent; **zu niedrigen** ~**n veranlagt werden** to be taxed at lower income rates; **normale** ~ **zahlen** to pay tax at the basic rate.

Einkommensteuer|schuld income-tax liability, income-tax obligation; ~**senkung** income-tax reduction, income-tax cut, cut in income tax; ~**stufe** income level, income group (class, -tax, *US*, bracket); **hohe** ~**stufen** high income brackets *(US)*; **einer niedrigen** ~**stufe angehören** to be in low income brackets *(US)*; ~**system** income-tax system; ~**tabelle** income-tax schedule, income-tax scale; ~**tarif** revenue tariff, taxpayer's code, [personal] income rate; ~**überzahlung** excess payment of income tax.

Einkommensteuerveranlagung income-tax assessment, income-tax bill *(US)*; **sofortige** ~ jeopardy assessment;
Einspruch gegen eine ~ **einlegen** to appeal against an income-tax assessment; **Fehler oder Irrtümer bei der** ~ **feststellen** to discover some error or mistake in an income-tax assessment.

Einkommensteuer|veranlagungskommission assessors of income tax; ~**verfahren** income-tax litigation; ~**vergünstigung** income-tax credit *(US)* (relief, *Br.*); **altersbedingte** ~**vergünstigung** age relief *(Br.)*; **zu** ~**vergünstigungen berechtigen (berechtigt sein)** to qualify for income-tax relief *(Br.)*, to be entitled to relief from income tax *(Br.)*; ~**verordnung** income-tax directive; ~**verpflichtung** income-tax liability, income-tax obligation; ~**verwaltung** administration of income tax, *(Behörde)* Internal Revenue Service *(US)*, Inland Revenue Authorities (Office) *(Br.)*; ~**vorauszahlung** advance payments of income tax, tax instalment *(US)*; ~**vorschriften** income-tax regulations; ~**zahler** income-tax payer; ~**zahler in den oberen Steuerstufen** high-bracket people *(US)*; ~**zahlung** income-tax payment; ~**zuschlag** income-tax surcharge (surtax), additional income tax *(Br.)*; ~**zuwachs** revenue raiser; **für** ~**zwecke** for income-tax purposes.

Einkommens|träger taxpayer; ~**überschuß** revenue, income surplus; ~**übertragung** transfer of income, transfer payments; ~**umschichtung,** ~**umverteilung** redistribution of income, income redistribution; ~**ungleichheit** inequalities of income; ~**unterschiede** income differences; ~**unterstützungszahlung** income maintenance payment; ~**veränderungen** variations in income, income changes; ~**vergrößerung** accession to one's income; ~**verlagerung** shifting of income; ~**verlust** loss of income; ~**verschiebung,** ~**verteilung** redistribution (apportionment) of income, income distribution; **funktionale** ~**verteilung** functional distribution of income; ~**verteilung auf mehrere Jahre** income averaging; ~**ziffern** income figures; ~**zunahme** jump in incomes; ~**zusatzsteuer** tax surcharge; ~**zuwachs** growth of income, income gain (growth); ~**zuwachsrate** rate of income growth, income growth rate.

einkopieren to superimpose.

Einkreisempfänger one-circuit set.
einkreisen to encircle, to isolate.
Einkreisung encirclement, isolation.
Einkreisungs|manöver encircling manoeuvre; ~**politik** policy of encirclement.
Einkünfte emoluments, revenue, income, incomings, earnings, receipts, takings, gains, gainings, usance, *(Wohlfahrtsorganisation)* proceeds;
im Rechnungsabschnitt anfallende ~ current revenues; **anrechnungsfähige** ~ *(Sozialversicherung)* reckonable earnings; **auf die Pension anrechnungsfähige** ~ pensionable earnings; **bei der Steuererklärung nicht aufgeführte** ~ omitted income; **ausländische** ~ foreign income; **außerbetriebliche** ~ nonoperating revenues; **außerordentliche** ~ extraordinary income; **steuerlich begünstigte** ~ [tax] preference income; **pauschal besteuerte** ~ income taxed at a flat rate; **betriebliche** ~ operating income; **einkommensähnliche** ~ receipts of an income nature; **einkommensteuerfreie** ~ net-of-tax income; **entgangene** ~ lost profits; **entstandene, noch nicht fällige** ~ accrued income (revenue); **feste** ~ fixed income, stable revenue; **zu Steuerzwecken festgesetzte** ~ relevant income; **feststehende** ~ fixed income; **freiberufliche** ~ earned income, income from a profession or vocation *(Br.)*, professional earnings, remuneration from a profession; **gemeinsame steuerpflichtige eheliche** ~ joint taxable earnings of husband and wife; **gewerbliche** ~ business income, industrial earnings, profits from trade; **im Ausland erzielte gewerbliche** ~ income derived from trading abroad; **nicht gewerbliche** ~ nontrading (nonbusiness) income; **grundsteuerpflichtige** ~ income from ownership of land *(US)*; **inländische** ~ domestic income; **jährliche** ~ annual revenue; **kapitalähnliche** ~ receipt of a capital nature; **nebenberufliche** ~ spare-time earnings; **regelmäßige** ~ steady income, regular income; **rückständige** ~ income in arrears; **sonstige** ~ *(Bilanz)* other income (receipts), miscellaneous revenues, *(Einkommensteuerformular)* income not charged under any other heading *(Br.)*; **ständige** ~ permanent income; **steuerfreie** ~ income exempt from tax, tax-exempt income, exclusions from gross income; **steuerpflichtige** ~ taxable income, taxable emoluments, emoluments subject to tax; **tatsächliche** ~ actual income; **thesaurierte** ~ *(Stiftung)* accumulated income; **überseeische** ~ overseas income; **alle übrigen** ~ *(Einkommenssteuerformular)* all other earnings; **den Devisenbestimmungen unterliegende** ~ income subject to exchange control; **der Quellenbesteuerung unterliegende** ~ income received under deduction of tax at source; **vermischte** ~ *(Bilanz)* miscellaneous income; **zu versteuernde** ~ taxable income; **nicht vorgesehene** ~ windfall receipts; **wiederkehrende** ~ regular (recurring) income; **nicht wiederkehrende** ~ nonrecurring income; **dem Gemeinschuldner zustehende** ~ income due to a bankrupt;
~ **aus Abzahlungsgeschäften** income from instalment sales; ~ **aus Aktienbesitz** income from securities; ~ **aus nichtselbständiger Arbeit** wage income, income from employment; ~ **aus selbständiger Arbeit** income from a profession or vocation, self-employment (earned) income; ~ **aus selbständiger und nichtselbständiger Arbeit** mixed income; ~ **für in mehreren Jahren geleistete Arbeit** long-term compensation; ~ **im Ausland** foreign income; ~ **einer Behörde** departmental earnings; ~ **der Ehefrau** income of the wife, wife's income; ~ **aus Eigentum an Grund und Boden** issue of an estate, income from rents and profits of land; ~ **aus Eigentum in Land- und Forstwirtschaft** income from real property; ~ **aus selbständiger Erwerbstätigkeit** self-employment (-earned) income; ~ **aus unsichtbaren Geschäftstransaktionen** invisible earnings; ~ **aus Gewerbebetrieb** industrial income (earnings, profits), business (trading) income, business gains, business profits, commercial profits, profits from trade or business *(Br.)*; ~ **aus Grundbesitz** income issuing out of land, estate income, rents, issues and profits (rents and profits) from land; ~ **der öffentlichen Hand** public revenue; ~ **aus Kapital- und Gewinnanteilen einer Gesellschaft** income arising from participation in the capital and profits of a company; ~ **aus Kapitalvermögen** income from interest (capital, securities, *Br.*), unearned income (revenue), income from investment *(US)*, investment income *(US)*, revenue from income; ~ **aus Land- und Forstwirtschaft** income derived from landed (real) property, property (farm, estate, *Br.*) income; **besondere** ~ **auf Grund vorzüglicher Leistungen** economic (net, pure, true) rent; ~ **aus Miete und Pacht** rental, rentroll; ~ **aus dem Passagierverkehr** passenger revenue; ~ **natürlicher Personen** personal income; ~ **aus dem Schiffsverkehr** shipping earnings; ~ **aus wohltätigen Spenden** charitable income; ~ **aus einer Stiftung** settlement income; ~ **aus einem Stipendium** income from scholarship; ~ **aus freiberuflicher Tätigkeit** professional (occupational, business) income, professional earnings, income from a profession or vocation, remuneration from a profession, profits of profession or vocation, personal earnings; ~ **aus gewerblicher Tätigkeit** business income, earned income *(Br.)*; ~ **aus nichtselbständiger Tätigkeit** income from wages, income from employment (work); ~ **aus schriftstellerischer Tätigkeit** author's royalties; ~ **aus selbständiger Tätigkeit** income from a profession or vocation, income from self-employment *(Br.)*, self-employment income *(Br.)*; ~ **aus dem Überseegeschäft** overseas earnings; ~ **aus der Vermietung von Garagenplätzen** income from a garage; ~ **aus Vermietung und Verpachtung** income from rents and profits of land, rental revenue, rentroll; **gewerbliche** ~ **und solche aus Vermögensnutzung** income from business and property; ~ **aus Warenlieferungen** commodity income; ~ **aus auswärtigen Wertpapierbeständen** income from foreign securities; ~ **aus Wertpapieren** income from securities; ~ **aus Wertpapiervermögen** income from securities; ~ **aus [nicht] möblierten Wohnungen** rents from [un]furnished lettings;
seine ~ **durch das Verfassen von Kurzgeschichten aufbessern** to augment one's income by writing short stories; ~ **mit den Sätzen des unteren Proportionalbereichs besteuern** to charge income at the basic rate; ~ **beziehen** to derive income (revenue) from; ~ **an der Quelle steuerlich erfassen** to tax income at the source; **regelmäßige** ~ **haben** to have a steady income; ~ **zur Verfügung haben** to enjoy income; ~ **entstehen lassen** to generate earnings; ~ **der Ehefrau steuerlich getrennt veranlagen lassen** to have a wife's earnings treated separately; **von seinen ~n leben** to live on one's income; **von den ~n seiner Ehefrau leben** to live on one's wife; **seine** ~ **durch journalistische Beiträge verbessern** to supplement one's income by journalism; **seine** ~ **über mehrere Jahre verteilen** to average one's income; **auf zustehende** ~ **verzichten** to disclaim one's right to income.
Einkunfts|arten classes of revenue (income); ~**quelle** source of income.
einkuppeln to [let in the] clutch, to throw into gear.
einkuscheln, sich ins Bett to snuggle down in one's bed.
Einladebahnhof loading station.
Einladen und Ausladen loading and unloading.
einladen *(Gast)* to invite, to ask, *(beladen)* to load, to freight, *(Flugzeug)* to emplane, *(Lastkraftwagen)* to entruck, *(Schiff)* to ship, to lade, to embark, to load, to take in [cargo], to put cargo on board;
j. ~ *(freihalten)* to pay for s. o., to take s. o. out; **j. zum Abendessen** ~ to request the favo(u)r of s. one's company to dinner; **Aktionäre zur Zeichnung** ~ to invite shareholders to subscribe capital; **Freunde zum Abendessen** ~ to entertain friends to dinner; **j. zu einem Glas Wein** ~ to treat s. o. to a glass of wine; **zu Mißbräuchen** ~ to be asking for trouble; **j. zum Mittagessen** ~ to ask (invite) s. o. for lunch; **Pakete in einen Waggon** ~ to load parcels in a luggage van *(Br.)* (baggage car, *US*); **zu einer Sitzung** ~ to convene (call) a meeting; **zu viel Teilnehmer zu einer Sitzung** ~ to overstaff a meeting; **j. für das Wochenende** ~ to ask s. o. for the weekend.
einladend inviting, alluring;
nicht sehr ~ **aussehen** not to be very inviting;
mit einer ~en Handbewegung with a sweeping gesture; ~**es Land** inviting country; ~**es Wetter** tempting weather.
Einladung invitation, treat, party, *(Gastfreundschaft)* hospitality, entertainment, bid, engagement;
schon lange ausgesprochene ~ long-standing invitation; **eilige** ~ pressing invitation; **formelle** ~ stiff card *(sl.)*; **königliche** ~ command *(Br.)*; **schriftliche** ~ written invitation;
~ **zum Mittagessen** invitation to lunch; ~ **zur Zeichnung** subscription offer;
~ **ablehnen** to refuse (decline) an invitation; ~ **aussprechen** to extend an invitation; **sich um eine** ~ **bemühen** to angle for an invitation to a party; **jem. für eine** ~ **danken** to thank s. o. for his hospitality; ~ **nicht gut absagen können** to be bad taste to refuse an invitation; **einer** ~ **Folge leisten** to hono(u)r an invitation, to come at s. one's invitation; **jem. eine** ~ **schicken** to send s. o. an invitation; **j. mit ~en überschütten** to pelt s. o. with invitations; ~**en verschicken** to mail out invitations; **massenweise ~en verschicken** to send out invitations wholesale; ~ **versenden** to send out an invitation; ~ **zurückziehen** to cancel an invitation, to put off one's guests.
Einladungs|karte invitation card; ~**liste** invitation list; ~**schreiben** letter of invitation.

Einlage *(Anlage)* enclosure, inclosure, *(Bankkonto)* deposit, *(Beilage)* inset, insert, *(Geldanlage)* investment, capital invested, *(Gesellschaftsanteil)* stock, initial share, *(Kapital)* put-in (contribution to) capital, capital contribution, advanced capital, money (sum) paid in, assets brought in, stake, *(einmalige Prämie)* single payment, *(Programm)* turn *(Br.)*, *(in Straße)* iron mesh reinforcement, *(Theater)* intermezzo, interlude, *(Wette)* stake, *(Zwischengang)* side dish, entree;
auf die ~ beschränkt limited by shares;
jederzeit abrufbare ~ call deposit; **befristete ~** time (demand) deposit *(US)*, fixed deposit; **erste ~** initial share, original investment; **feste ~** fixed deposit; **gemeinschaftliche ~** joint deposit; **kleine ~** small deposit; **kurzfristige kündbare ~** money at short notice; **kurzfristige ~** short-term deposit, deposit at short notice; **langfristige ~** deposit on deposit account, deposit at long notice, time (long-term) deposit; **leicht liquidierbare ~** near money *(US)*; **musikalische ~** musical interlude; **unversicherte ~** uninsured deposit; **per Scheck verfügbare ~** demand deposit subject to check *(US)* (cheque, *Br.*);
~ bei einer Bank deposit in a bank; **~ auf Depositenkonto** fixed (time, *US*) deposit;
etw. als ~ einbringen to bring in s. th; **~ machen** to make a deposit *(US)*; **~ in gleicher Höhe machen** to pay in an equal sum; **seine ~ zurückziehen** to withdraw one's capital;
~blatt loose leaf; **~brett** *(Tisch)* leaf; **~buch** passbook, deposit book, bank book; **~kapital** paid-in (invested, advanced, deposit) capital, contribution, *(Anfangskapital)* initial (opening) capital, original investment; **~karton** card insertion; **~konto** deposit *(US)* (investment) account, *(Sparkasse)* savings account; **~konto mit sofortiger Scheck- und Wechselgutschrift** immediate credit account *(US)*.

Einlagen deposits;
ausstehende ~ unpaid capital; **ausstehende ~ auf das Grundkapital** subscribed capital stock, uncalled capital; **aus öffentlichen Geldern bestehende ~** public deposits *(Br.)*; **effektive ~** primary deposits *(US)*; **täglich fällige (jederzeit kündbare, kurzfristige) ~** short (demand, current) deposits *(US)*, sight deposits *(US)*, deposits at short notice, deposits on current accounts; **gebietsfremde ~** nonresident deposits; **kommunale ~** deposits by local authorities; **längerfristige ~** time and savings deposits; **langfristige ~** deposits at long notice, deposits on deposit account, fixed deposits; **leicht liquidierbare ~** near money *(US)*; **mindestreservepflichtige ~** safety fund *(US)*, special deposits with the Bank of England *(Br.)*; **öffentliche ~** public deposits; **gegen Kündigung rückzahlbare ~** money at short notice, demand (sight) deposits *(US)*; **unverzinsliche ~** noninterest-bearing deposits; **per Scheck verfügbare ~** demand deposits subject to check *(US)* (cheque, *Br.*); **verzinsliche ~** interest-bearing deposits;
~ in Form beweglicher oder unbeweglicher Sachen contribution (assets brought in) in kind; **ausstehende ~ auf das Grundkapital** subscribed capital stock, uncalled capital; **~ im Kontokorrentverkehr** deposits on current account; **~ mit 7tägiger Kündigung** deposits subject to (at) seven days notice; **~ mit Kündigungsfrist** deposits at short notice, deposits for a fixed period, fixed (time, *US*) deposits; **~ mit besonders vereinbarter Kündigungsfrist** availability items *(US)*; **~ mit fester Laufzeit** fixed (time, *US*) deposits; **~ mit sechsmonatlicher Laufzeit** deposits with maturities of six months; **~ auf gebührenfreie Rechnung** *(Bankbilanz)* current deposits; **~ auf gebührenfreie Rechnung und sonstige Gläubiger** *(Bankbilanz)* current account deposits and other accounts; **~ auf Sicht** sight deposits *(US)*, demand deposits *(US)*;
~ entgegennehmen to accept deposits; **öffentliche ~ entgegennehmen** to take deposits from the general public; **~ verzinsen** to pay interest on deposits; **~ mit 4% verzinsen** to allow 4% on deposits;
~ansturm abstoppen to stop a run on deposits; **~bestand** deposits in a bank; **~buch** passbook; **~entwicklung** development of deposits; **~garantie** bank guaranty *(US)*; **~geschäft** deposit banking (business); **~kündigung** notice of withdrawal of funds; **~politik** deposit policy; **~rückstand** unpaid calls; **landeszentralbankfreie ~summe** reserve-free base figure *(US)*; **~versicherung** Federal Deposit Insurance *(US)*; **~versicherungsfonds** Permanent Insurance Fund *(US)*; **~verzinsung mit 4%** allowance of 4% interest on deposits; **~werbung** advertisement for deposits *(Br.)*; **~zuwachs** increase of deposits.

Einlagern storage, storing, warehousing *(US)*, stockpiling.

einlagern to put in store, to store [in, away], to [deposit in a] warehouse *(US)*, to stockpile;
für Rechnung der Bank ~ to warehouse in the bank's name *(US)*; **in den Keller ~** to cellar; **Möbel ~** to warehouse furniture *(US)*; **Vorräte ~** to lay in provisions, to restock; **Wintervorräte ~** to store goods for the winter; **unter Zollverschluß ~** to bond, to warehouse *(US)*.

Einlagerung storage, storing, warehousing *(US)*, stockpiling;
~ von Durchgangsgütern transit warehousing *(US)*; **~ unter Zollverschluß** bonding, warehousing *(US)*.

Einlagerungs|gebühren storage, warehouse charges *(US)*; **~kapazität** storage capacity; **~kredit** storage credit, warehouse loan *(US)*; **~maßnahmen** storage arrangements; **~schein** warehouse receipt *(US)* (keeper's certificate, *Br.*); **~wechsel** warehouse bill *(US)*.

Einlagezinsen interest on deposits.

Einlaß admission, admittance, access, letting in;
~ nur aufgrund besonderer Einladung admission by invitation only; **~ ins Theater** admission to the theater *(US)* (theatre, *Br.*);
~ 1/2 Stunde vor der Vorstellung early door;
~ begehren to knock in *(sl., Br.)*; **~ finden** to be admitted, to gain admission; **jem. ~ gewähren** to let s. o. in; **sich ~ verschaffen** to gain admission, *(mit Gewalt)* to force one's way in; **~ verwehren** to deny access;
der ~ für die Theaterbesucher beginnt um 19 Uhr doors open to the public at 7 p. m.

Einlassen letting in.

einlassen to let in, to admit;
sich auf etw. ~ to let o. s. in on s. th., to become entangled (engage) in s. th.; **sich unüberlegt auf etw. ~** to go off at the deep end *(US)*; **sich mit jem. ~** to get mixed up with s. o.; **Besucher einzeln ~** to admit visitors one at a time; **sich mit einem Drücker ~** to let o. s. in with a latch-key; **sich auf ein Geschäft ~** to embark upon a business; **sich auf ein Gespräch ~** to enter into a conversation, to get o. s. involved in a discussion; **sich zur Hauptsache ~** to join issue; **in ein Haus ~** to admit into a house; **sich auf eine Klage ~** to enter an appearance, to defend an action; **sich auf Politik ~** to get mixed up in politics; **sich auf eine unangenehme Sache ~** to get involved in a nasty business; **sich auf leere Versprechnungen ~** to be satisfied with empty promises; **Wasser in die Badewanne ~** to run water into the bath.

Einlaß|geld door (gate) money, entrance fee; **~karte** admission card (ticket), ticket, access card, *(für Ersatzveranstaltungen)* rain check *(US)*; **~rohr** inlet pipe; **~schein** entry permit, order *(Br.)*; **nur gegen besonderen ~schein** by ticket only, by special order *(Br.)*; **~stutzen** *(Benzintank)* neck.

Einlassung *(bei Gericht)* appearance, defence *(Br.)*, defense *(US)*, normal issue;
bedingte ~ conditional appearance; **vorbehaltslose ~** general appearance;
~ auf die Anklage pleading to the charge; **~ des Beklagten** entry of appearance; **~ zur Hauptsache** joinder of issue.

Einlassungs|erklärung memorandum of appearance *(Br.)*; **~frist** notice to plead, time for entering an appearance; **~termin** appearance day.

Einlaßventil inlet (admission) valve, intake valve.

Einlauf *(Briefe)* letters received, incoming mail;
bei ~ des Zuges on arrival of the train;
in der Reihenfolge des ~s in order of receipt;
freier ~ und Auslauf free ingress and egress.

Einlaufen *(Schiff)* entry [into harbo(u)r], *(Textilien)* shrinkage, *(Waren)* arrival, coming in;
~ und Auslaufen eines Schiffes entry and departure of a vessel;
~ eines Schiffes in den Hafen entrance of a ship into (a) port.

einlaufen to arrive, to come (get) in, *(Aufträge)* to drop (come) in, *(Beträge)* to come in (to hand), *(Spenden)* to flow (pour) in, *(Textilien)* to shrink;
sich ~ to warm up, *(Motor)* to run in, to be broken in *(US)*; **in den Bahnhof ~** to enter (pull into) the station; **fahrplanmäßig ~** to arrive on time (as scheduled, *US*); **in den Hafen ~** to enter harbo(u)r, to put into port; **zur Vornahme von Reparaturen in den Hafen ~** to put into port for repair; **pünktlich ~** *(Zug)* to get in up to time (as scheduled, *US*); **jem. das Haus ~** to live on s. one's doorstep.

einlaufend incoming;
nicht ~ unshrinkable, shrink-resistent;
~e Bestellungen incoming orders, orders received; **~e Briefe** incoming mail *(US)*; **~e Gelder** receipts; **~e Post** incoming mail *(US)* (post); **~e Rechnungen** inward invoices; **~e Waren** incoming goods.

Einlauf|gleis arrival track; **auf ~kurs liegen** to stand for the shore; **~leitung** inlet pipe; **~rohr** inlet pipe.

einleben, sich to acclimatize (accustom) o. s., to strike root, to become accustomed; **sich in einen Beruf** ~ to settle into a job; **sich gut** ~ to settle down well, to feel quite at home; **sich schwer** ~ to have difficulties in getting acclimatized.

Einlege|apparat feeder; ~**arbeit** inlay, inlaid work; ~**blatt** loose leaf; ~**brett eines Tisches** leaf of a table.

einlegen *(in Bank)* to deposit, to pay into, to put in, *(in Brief)* to enclose, to inclose, *(in Zeitung)* to insert;
Anschlußberufung ~ to cross-appeal; **Berufung** ~ to appeal against a judgment; **weitere Berufung** ~ to appeal to another court; **Beschwerde** ~ to lodge a complaint; **Blatt in ein Ringbuch** ~ to insert a leaf into a ring-clip file; **mit etw. Ehre** ~ to bring hono(u)r upon o. s.; **Einspruch** ~ to lodge an objection; **Film** ~ to load (slip in) a new film; **Gang** ~ *(Auto)* to engage a gear; **Geld in einen Brief** ~ to enclose money in a letter; **Kapital** ~ to contribute capital; **Löschpapier** ~ to insert blotting paper between the sheets; **Möbelstück mit Rosenholz** ~ to inlay a piece of furniture with rosewood; **Papier in die Schreibmaschine** ~ to feed paper into the typewriter; **Pause** ~ to make a break (pause); **Protest** ~ to enter protest; **Quittung in einen Brief** ~ to enclose a receipt with a letter; **Rechtsmittel** ~ to lodge an appeal; **Revision** ~ to appeal to the Supreme Court; **Sonderzüge** ~ to put on extra trains; **Verwahrung** ~ to enter a protest; **Veto** ~ to veto; **Vorräte** ~ to store (stock) provisions; **Waren** ~ to lay in goods; **Widerspruch** ~ to raise an objection; **bei jem. ein gutes Wort** ~ to put in a good word for (intercede with) s. o.

Einleger [bank] depositor, *(Kapital)* investor, contributor.

Einlegung lodging, filing;
~ **einer Berufung** appealing, notice of appeal, lodging an appeal; ~ **eines Rechtsmittels** lodging an appeal; ~ **eines Widerspruchs** raising an objection;
~ **ankündigen** to give notice of appeal.

einleiten to initiate, to introduce, to start, to commence, *(anfangen)* to begin, to prelude;
militärische Aktionen ~ to commence operations; **neue wirtschaftliche Blütezeit** ~ to usher in a new period of prosperity; **Buch** ~ to write an introduction to a book, to preface a book; **Katastrophe** ~ to prelude a catastrophe; **Maßnahmen** ~ to adopt (take) measures; **Rede mit etw.** ~ to begin a speech; **Schritte** ~ to take steps; **Strafverfahren** ~ to institute (take) criminal proceedings; **Tagung mit einer Podiumsdiskussion** ~ to start a conference with a panel discussion; **Untersuchung** ~ to set up an enquiry; **Verfahren gegen j.** ~ to order proceedings to be taken against s. o.; **gerichtliches Verfahren** ~ to initiate legal proceedings; **Verhandlungen** ~ to open (initiate, enter into) negotiations; **neues Zeitalter** ~ to inaugurate a new era.

einleitend introductory, preliminary, opening, initiatory;
~**e Bemerkungen** introductory remarks; ~**e Erklärung** opening statement; ~**e Maßnahmen** preliminaries, prelude; ~**e Schritte** preliminary steps; ~**er Teil eines Vertrages** lien of a covenant.

Einleitung initiation, institution, preliminary, prelude, *(im Buch)* introduction, preface, prologue, *(Präambel)* preamble, *(Verhandlung)* preliminary;
langatmige ~ long-winded opening; **kurz zusammenfassende** ~ lead;
~ **und Abwicklung multinationaler Finanzierungsgeschäfte** initiating and structuring of multinational financing; ~ **eines Konkursverfahrens** institution of bankruptcy proceedings; ~ **des Liquidationsverfahrens** institution of winding-up proceedings; ~ **eines Prozesses** raising an action; ~ **gerichtlicher Schritte** institution of legal proceedings; ~ **eines Strafverfahrens** commencement of criminal proceedings, criminal letters *(Scot.)*; ~ **einer Untersuchung** institution of an inquiry; ~ **eines gerichtlichen Verfahrens** institution of legal proceedings; ~ **von Verhandlungen** opening of negotiations;
~ **eines Konkursverfahrens beantragen** to make application for receivership *(Br.)*, to petition for the appointment of a receiver *(US)*; **als** ~ **dienen** to serve as an introduction; ~ **schreiben** to write an introduction.

Einleitungs|beschluß *(Konkurs)* receiving order; ~**formel** *(Urkunde)* caption, heading, protocol, *(Entschließung)* resolving clause; ~**kapitel** opening chapter; ~**rede** introductory discourse; ~**satz** opening paragraph; ~**sätze** premises; ~**worte** recital, preamble.

einlenken to show o. s. conciliatory, to give in.

einlesen, sich in ein Buch to get into a book; **sich in jds. Handschrift** ~ to get to know s. one's handwriting.

einleuchten to be plain (evident, obvious, clear);
jedem ~ to be evident to everyone.

einleuchtend obvious, clear, evident;
aus ~**en Gründen** for plausible reasons.

einliefern to hand in, to submit, *(Briefe)* to post, to mail *(US)*, *(Effekten)* to deliver, to deposit;
Brief als Drucksache ~ to send a letter as printed matter; **ins Gefängnis** ~ to commit to prison; **in ein Krankenhaus** ~ to take to a hospital, to hospitalize *(US)*; **Paket** ~ to dispatch (send off) a parcel; **Wertpapiere ins Depot** ~ to deposit securities for safe custody *(Br.)* (custodianship, *US*).

Einlieferung *(Briefe)* posting, mailing *(US)*, *(Effekten)* delivery, deposit;
~ **ins Gefängnis** commitment (committal) to prison; ~ **ins Krankenhaus** admittance to hospital, hospitalization *(US)*; ~ **von Postsendungen** posting of items *(Br.)*.

Einlieferungs|befehl committal order, warrant of commitment *(US)*; ~**schein** certificate of posting, [postal] receipt, *(Effekten)* deposit slip; ~**zeit** time of delivery.

einliegen *(in Briefen)* to be enclosed.

einliegend enclosed (inclosed) [herewith].

Einlieger lodger;
~**wohnung** separate flat (apartment).

einlochen to lodge s. o. in gaol (jail), to put away *(sl.)*, to put in jug *(fam.)*.

einlogieren, sich bei jem. to lodge with s. o., to establish o. s. in s. one's house; **sich in einem Hotel** ~ to put up in (take rooms at) a hotel.

einlösbar *(einziehbar)* collectible, *(fällig)* due, *(Papiergeld)* convertible, *(rückzahlbar)* redeemable, *(umtauschfähig)* convertible, *(zahlbar)* payable;
auf Verlangen ~ redeemable on demand; **nicht** ~ irredeemable, inconvertible; **zum Nennwert** ~ redeemable at par;
[in Gold] ~**es Papiergeld** convertible paper currency, convertible money.

Einlösbarkeit redeemableness, redeemability.

Einlösegebühr *(entlaufenes Vieh)* poundage.

einlösen *(Akzept, Wechsel)* to meet, *(eintauschen)* to convert, *(Rechnungen)* to pay, to discharge, *(Sichtwechsel, Schecks)* to hono(u)r, to turn into cash, *(tilgen)* to redeem, *(aus dem Verkehr ziehen)* to withdraw from circulation;
seine Akzepte ~ to meet one's drafts; **Banknoten** ~ to cash (redeem) bank notes; **sein Gepäck** ~ to collect one's luggage *(Br.)*; **Kupons** ~ to cash coupons; **Nachnahme** ~ to pay a cash on delivery; **nicht** ~ to refuse payment; **Obligationen** ~ to pay off bonds, to redeem a pledge; **Pfand** ~ to take out of pawn, to redeem a pledge; **Police** ~ to pay (take up) a policy; **Scheck** ~ to cash (collect) a check (cheque, *Br.*); **Scheck bei einer Bank** ~ to get a check (cheque, *Br.*) cashed at a bank; **Scheck nicht** ~ to reject a check (cheque, *Br.*); **seine Verpflichtungen** ~ to meet one's engagements (commitments); **Versprechen** ~ to make good (keep) a promise, to carry out one's promise; **Wechsel** ~ to remit (hono(u)r, redeem, meet, discharge) a bill; **Wechsel in bar** ~ to encash a bill; **Wechsel bei Fälligkeit** ~ to take up a draft when due; **Wechsel vor Fälligkeit** ~ to anticipate a bill; **Wechsel nicht** ~ to dishono(u)r a bill; **Wechsel bei Verfall** ~ to protect a bill at maturity; **Wertpapiere** ~ to convert securities; **Zinsscheine** ~ to pay interest coupons.

Einlöser paying agent.

Einlösung *(Akzept)* discharge, *(Banknoten)* withdrawal, *(Bankzahlung)* payment, *(Konvertierung)* conversion, *(Pfand)* redemption, *(Police)* payment, *(Scheck)* cashing, *(Tilgung)* redemption, *(Wechsel)* taking up, hono(u)ring;
vertraglich vereinbarte ~ solicited redemption; **vorzeitige** ~ previous redemption;
~ **von Banknoten** redemption of bank notes; ~ **vor Fälligkeit** anticipated repayment; ~ **von Investmentanteilen** repurchase of units *(Br.)*; ~ **von Kupons** payment of interest coupons; ~ **zum Nennwert** redemption at par; ~ **eines Pfands** redemption of a pledge; ~ **eines Schecks** cashing of a check, check *(US)* (cheque, *Br.*) cashing; ~ **bei Verfall** redemption at maturity; ~ **vor Verfall** mandatory redemption; ~ **eines Versprechens** performance of (keeping) a promise; ~ **eines Wechsels** protection (discharge) of a bill, retiral;
zur ~ **aufrufen** to call for redemption; **zur** ~ **auslosen** to draw for redemption; ~ **eines Schecks auf einen bestimmten Empfänger beschränken** to specialize a check *(US)* (cheque, *Br.*); ~ **garantieren** to guarantee payment; **zur** ~ **vorlegen** to present for payment; **einer Bank einen Scheck zur** ~ **vorlegen** to cash a check *(US)* (cheque, *Br.*) at a bank.

Einlösungs|abschnitt redemption warrant; ~**auftrag** encashment (collection) order; ~**bestimmungen** redemption provisions; ~**betrag** redemption capital; ~**ermächtigung** authority to pay;

~fonds redemption (sinking, amortization) fund; **~form** redemption (call) feature; **~frist** time of redemption; **~frist abgelaufen** *(Scheck)* out of date *(Br.)*; **~kasse** redemption office; **~klausel** redemption clause; **~kosten** redemption fee; **~kurs** rate of redemption, redemption rate (price, *US*); **gesetzliche ~pflicht** convertibility, redeemability; **~prämie** redemption premium; **~recht** right (equity) of redemption; **sein ~recht verkaufen** to release one's equity of redemption; **~schein** redemption of voucher; **~stelle** redemption office, *(Bank)* paying department; **~termin** date of maturity, *(Effekten)* date of redemption, redemption date; **~verfahren** redemption proceedings; **~vorbehalt** proviso for redemption; **~vorschriften** redemption provisions; **~wert** redemption (surrender) value.

einlotsen to pilot.

einlullen, allmählich to ease in gradually; **j. mit falschen Hoffnungen ~** to lull s. o. with false hopes; **jds. Verdacht ~** to lull s. one's suspicion.

Einmachapparat fruit preserver.

einmachen to conserve, to preserve.

einmal, auf all at once, at one jerk, *(Zahlung)* in one amount; **alles auf ~** all of a lump; **zunächst ~** for one thing;
nur ~ gesicherter Gläubiger single creditor.

Einmalbehälter disposable (one-way) container.

Einmaleins multiplication table.

einmalig single, nonrecurring, one-shot, nonrecurrent, unique; **~e Abfindung** lump-sum payment; **~e Ausgaben** nonrecurring expenses; **nach ~em Durchlesen** after reading it once; **~es Gastspiel** one-night stand *(US)*; **~e Gelegenheit** unique opportunity, a chance in a thousand; **~es Versehen** single mistake; **~e Zahlung** single payment.

Einmal|packung disposable (one-way) package; **~prämie** single premium; **~tarif** *(Werbung)* one-time rate.

Einmann|betrieb one-man establishment (outfit, show, stage, business); **~firma** one-man outfit (business); **~führung** one-man leadership; **~gesellschaft** one-man company, corporation sole *(US)*; **~gummiboot** parachute boat; **~liste** *(parl.)* straight ticket; **~zelt** pup tent *(sl.)*.

Einmarsch marching in, entry.

einmarschieren, in ein Gebiet to enter (march into) a territory.

ein|mauern to immure, to wall in, *(Urkunde)* to enclose in a wall; **Namen in ein Grabmal ~meißeln** to inscribe a tomb with a name.

einmengen, sich to interfere, to intervene; **sich unberufen ~** to shove an oar in *(coll.)*.

einmieten to lodge o. s., to take lodgings, *(Landwirt)* to pit.

einmischen, sich to intervene, to interfere, to meddle, to thrust (poke) one's nose in, to barge in *(fam.)*, to stick (put in) one's oar, to mix in *(US)*, to screw o. s. into s. th.; **sich in jds. Angelegenheiten ~** to interfere in s. one's affairs, to mix into s. one's business *(US)*; **sich in die Angelegenheiten eines Landes ~** to intervene in the affairs of a country; **sich in Dinge ~, die einen nichts angehen** to intermeddle with what does not concern one; **sich in Familienstreitigkeiten ~** to interfere in family quarrels; **sich in ein Gespräch ~** to join a conversation, *(störend)* to butt in on a conversation; **sich in etw. nicht ~** to leave s. th. alone; **sich in jds. Sachen ~** to intrude o. s. into s. one's business, to poke one's nose into others' affairs; **sich überall ~** to have an oar in every man's boat; **sich unberechtigt (unbefugt) ~** to intromit *(Scot.)*, to interlope, to mess in *(US)*.

Einmischung interference, intermeddling, *(Intimsphäre)* intrusion, *(unberechtigt)* intromission, *(Völkerrecht)* intervention; **~ in anderer Leute Sachen** interference in the business of others, intrusion on other's privacy; **staatliche ~ in die Wirtschaft** direct intervention in the economy;
~ auf ein Mindestmaß beschränken to keep interference at a minimum; **keine ~ dulden** to brook no interference.

Einmischungspolitik policy of intervention, interventionism.

ein|motorig single-engined; **~motten** *(mil.)* to mothball, to cocoon; **sich in eine Decke ~mummen** to wrap o. s. in a blanket.

einmünden, in den Marktplatz to lead into the market place; **in die See ~** to flow into (enter) the sea.

Einmündung *(Fluß)* mouth, *(Straßen)* junction.

einmütig with one consent (assert), unanimous, solid *(US)*;
~ beschließen to decide by common consent; **~en Beifall finden** to meet with unanimous approval; **~ protestieren** to protest with one voice; **~ hinter j. stehen** to stand solidly behind s. o.

Einmütigkeit unanimity, concord, unity of sentiment.

Einnahme receipts, return(s), takings, drawings, *(aus einem Amt)* emoluments, *(Einkommen)* income, revenue, *(mil.)* capture, *(Theater)* take, taking in, *(Verdienst)* earnings;
~ in bar receipt in cash; **~ einer Stadt** seizure (capture) of a town; **~ von Steuern** collection of taxes;
in ~ bringen to enter as receipt, to book as received;
steuerlicher ~faktor revenue producer; **~kasse** cash-receiving office; **~konto** revenue account.

Einnahmen receipts, takings, earnings, income, incomings, revenue, returns, *(Erlöse)* proceeds;
aufzeichnungspflichtige ~ receipts as per profit and loss account; **außerordentliche ~** extraordinary income; **außerplanmäßige ~** unbudgeted income; **bare ~** cash receipts; **betriebsfremde ~** nonoperating revenues; **effektive ~** actual receipts; **im voraus eingegangene [zunächst als Verbindlichkeiten behandelte] ~** deferred liabilities; **einmalige ~** nonrecurring receipts; **entgangene ~** missed proceeds; **gelegentliche ~** casual emoluments; **nicht aus Steuereingängen herrührende ~** nontax revenues; **jährliche ~** annual receipts, yearly revenue; **laufende ~** current receipts; **öffentliche ~** public (national, *US*) revenue; **ordentliche ~** *(Staat)* ordinary receipts *(US)*; **passivierte ~** deferred liabilities; **sonstige ~** *(Bilanz)* other receipts; **städtische ~** revenues of the city council; **steigende ~** receipts on the increase; **tägliche ~** daily receipts; **nicht veranlagungspflichtige ~** receipts not assessable; **verminderte ~** diminished receipts; **verschiedene ~** *(Bilanz)* sundry receipts; **zu versteuernde ~** fiscal earnings; **voraussichtliche ~** dependencies *(Br.)*, assets likely to accrue; **wirkliche ~** actuals; **zweckgebundene ~** restricted (earmarked) receipts;
~ und Ausgaben income and expenditure, incomings and outgoings, *(parl.)* receipts and expenditures; **~ der Bauwirtschaft** construction earnings; **~ nach Einstellung eines Gewerbebetriebs** post-cessation receipts; **~ im außerordentlichen Etat** nonrevenue receipts; **~ aus dem Fremdenverkehr** tourist receipts; **~ aus dem Güterverkehr** goods traffic *(Br.)*; **~ aus laufender Rechnung** current receipts; **~ in harter Währung** hard-currency earnings;
Betrag aus seinen ~ abzweigen to take a sum out of one's income; **~ zur Bank bringen** to bank the takings; **einmalige ~ steuerlich über drei Jahre verteilen** to spread a lump sum over three years; **~ verwenden** to disburse revenues;
~anstieg increase in revenue, revenue raising; **~aufgliederung** revenue classification; **~aufstellung einer Vorverkaufskasse** note of box-office receipts; **~ausfall** revenue shortfall; **unvorhergesehener ~ausfall** casual deficiency of revenue; **~buch** receipts book; **~- und Ausgabenbuch** receipts and expenses (expenditures); **~-Ausgaben-Buchführungssystem** costbook principle; **~defizit** deficit in revenue; **~- und Ausgabenplan** cash budget; **~- und Ausgabenrechnung** income and expenditure account, bill of receipts and expenditures; **~rückgang** drop in takings, decrease of receipts, reduction in revenue, decline in revenue; **~schätzung** revenue calculation; **~seite** revenue side, *(Gewinn- und Verlustrechnung)* income account; **~steuer** receipt tax; **~verbuchung** revenue realization; **~verwendung** disbursement of revenues.

Einnahme|politik revenue policy; **~posten** item in the revenue, income (revenue) item, sum received; **in der Bilanz noch nicht in Erscheinung tretende ~posten** unrealized revenue; **~quelle** source of revenue (income); **wichtigste ~quelle** chief asset; **~rückgang** decline (shortfall) in revenue; **~rückstände** receipts in arrear; **~schmälerung** revenue deduction; **~struktur** revenue pattern; **~tag** date of receipt; **~überschuß** surplus receipts (revenue), excess of receipts over expenditure, excess of income; **~übertragung** assignment of revenue; **~verlust** loss of income.

einnebeln *(mil.)* to lay a smoke screen;
sich ~ to fog.

Einnehmen intake.

einnehmen *(Geld)* to receive, to collect, to take, *(mil.)* to conquer, *(verdienen)* to earn, to have as income, *(Ware)* to ship, to take in, to load;
j. für etw. ~ to prejudice s. o. in favo(u)r of s. th.; **j. für sich ~** to win s. o. over, to prepossess s. o. in one's favo(u)r, to captivate s. o., to gain s. one's favo(u)r; **j. zugunsten eines Dritten ~** to prejudice s. o. in favo(u)r of s. o.; **Festung ~** to capture (take, seize) a fortress; **j. günstig für sich ~** to arouse (favo(u)rable) feelings for o. s.; **feindliche Hauptstadt ~** to occupy the enemy's capital; **100.000 DM im Jahr ~** to have an annual income of DM 100.000; **Ladung ~** to take in (embark) cargo; **volle Ladung ~** to take in the full complement of cargo; **Mahlzeiten im Hotel ~** to take one's meals in the hotel; **j. gegen einen Plan ~** to prejudice s. o. against a plan; **seinen Platz ~** to take one's seat, to station o. s., *(vorher)* to prepossess one's place; **seinen Platz wieder ~** to repossess o. s. of a place; **zu viel Platz ~** to occupy

too much room; **Posten** ~ to hold (fill) a position; **großen Raum in jds. Forschungsarbeiten** ~ to occupy a large part of s. one's research work; **vier Spalten** ~ *(Zeitungsartikel)* to take up (go over) four columns; **jds. Stelle** ~ to replace s. o., to take (fill) s. one's place, to step into s. one's shoes *(coll.)*; **erste Stelle** ~ to hold the first place, to rank first; **hervorragende Stelle** ~ to rank high; **führende Stellung** ~ to hold a high-level position; **hohe Stellung in der Gesellschaft** ~ to occupy a high position in society; **Steuern** ~ to collect (receive) taxes; **Wasser** ~ *(Schiff)* to take in water.

einnehmend prepossessing, fetching, captivating, *(fesselnd)* engaging;
~**es Wesen haben** to have taking (engaging) manners.

Einnehmer receiver, taker, *(Steuer)* tax collector (gatherer).

einnicken to nod (doze) off.

einnisten, sich to nest; **sich bei jem.** ~ to live on s. o., to park o. s. on s. o. *(US coll.)*.

Einöde desert, wilderness, solitude.

Einödhof isolated farm.

einölen, sich to oil one's skin.

einordnen to arrange, to range, to rank, *(Akten)* to [place on] file, *(integrieren)* to integrate, to incorporate, *(klassifizieren)* to classify, *(Konkursforderungen)* to marshal;
sich ~ to fall into line, *(Auto)* to get into the correct traffic lane, to filter in *(Br.)*, *(Schlange)* to take one's place in a queue (line); **Briefe** ~ to file letters; **Buch unter die Romane** ~ to class a book as a novel; **sich in die Landschaft** ~ to fit perfectly into the landscape; **sich rechts** ~ to move into the right traffic lane; **in alphabetischer Reihenfolge** ~ to file in alphabetical order; **etw. an der falschen Stelle** ~ to put s. th. in the wrong place; **in eine Tarifposition** ~ to classify under a tariff item; **Tatsachen** ~ to pigeonhole facts; **sich in den Verkehrsstrom** ~ to filter into the road (streaming) traffic *(Br.)*;
sich schwer ~ **lassen** to be difficult to place.

Einordnung arrangement, *(Klassifizierung)* classification;
~ **von Briefen** filing of letters; ~ **von Konkursforderungen** marshalling of a bankrupt's debts; ~ **in den Verkehrsstrom** filtering into the streaming traffic.

Einordnungsstreifen *(Verkehr)* approach lane.

Einpacken packing.

einpacken to bundle [up], to pack, to parcel, to put up, *(einwickeln)* to wrap up, *(Waren)* to box, to embale;
sich fest in seine Decke ~ to wrap o. s. in one's blanket; **in Kisten** ~ to case; **Paket** ~ to roll up a parcel; **Patienten** ~ to pack a patient; **seine Sachen** ~ to pack up one's things; **Waren in Ballen** ~ to make up in bales;
~ **können** to be at the end of one's tether.

Einpacker packer, wrapper *(US)*.

Einpackpapier packing (wrapping, brown) paper, packing sheet.

einparken, in eine Parklücke to pull into a parking space.

Einparteien|herrschaft one-party dictatorship; ~**staat** one-party state; ~**system** one-party system.

Einpassieren *(Schiff)* inward passage.

einpassieren, in den Hafen to enter the harbo(u)r; **in die Kaserne** ~ to return to barracks.

Einpauken coaching, quiz *(US)*.

einpauken to coach, to ram, to hammer (knock, drum) into, to quiz *(US)*;
sich etw. ~ to grind away on s. th., to bone up on s. th. *(US)*; **jem. etw.** ~ to drum s. th. into s. o.; **sich auf ein Fach** ~ to mug up a subject; **Kandidaten** ~ to cram (prime) a candidate; **jem. eine Lektion** ~ to cram (hammer, drum) a lesson into s. one's head; **sich auf ein Thema** ~ to cram up a subject.

Einpauker coach, tutor, crammer, driller, grinder *(Br., sl.)*;
als ~ **tätig sein** to coach.

Einpaukerei cram, coaching.

Einpeitscher party whip *(Br.)*, floor leader *(US)*.

einpendeln, sich *(Kurse)* to even out, to settle down.

einpferchen to cram, to pen up, to crowd;
Flüchtlinge in einen Raum ~ to crowd refugees into a room.

Einphasen|steuer one-stage tax; ~**strom** single-phase current; ~**umsatzsteuer** single-stage turnover tax.

einplanen to program(me), to plan ahead, to schedule, to include in a plan;
Kredite ~ to schedule credits; **mögliche Verzögerung** ~ to take a possible delay into account.

einplanieren to level, to even up.

Einplanung planning, making provisions.

Einplanungsliste planning schedule.

einpökeln to salt [down], to brine;
Du kannst Dich ~ **lassen** you can go and hang yourself.

einprägen to imprint, to impress, to implant;
sich etw. ~ to fix s. th. in one's memory; **jem. etw. fest** ~ to stamp (print) s. th. on s. one's mind; **sich Daten** ~ to fix dates in one's mind; **ins Gedächtnis** ~ to imprint (fix) s. th. on (into) the memory; **sich in die Seele** ~ to engrave itself on s. one's mind.

Einprägung impression, imprint, stamp.

einquartieren to lodge, *(mil.)* to quarter, to billet;
sich bei jem. ~ to take up one's quarters with (quarter o. s. on) s. o., to come to stay with s. o.

einquartiert sein to have lodgings with, *(mil.)* to be quartered (billeted).

Einquartierung lodging, *(mil.)* accommodation, quartering, billeting.

Einquartierungsschein billet of residence.

einquetschen, sich den Finger to squeeze (pinch) one's finger; **j. zwischen zwei Menschen** ~ to sandwich (wedge) s. o. between two people.

einrahmen to frame, *(drucktechn.)* to box, to border.

Einrahmung *(drucktechn.)* border, frame, framing.

einrangieren to fit in, to range, to classify, to put in its place;
Buch wieder ~ to return a book to its place.

Einrangierung classification.

einrasten to click into place.

einräumen to grant, to allow, to accord, *(verstauen)* to put away (in its place), to stow away, to store, *(zugestehen)* to make concessions, to concede, to own, to acknowledge, to admit;
Bücher in ein Regal ~ to place books on a shelf; **Diskont** ~ to allow a discount; ~, **einen Fehler gemacht zu haben** to own up to having made a mistake; **einem Flüchtling ein Zimmer** ~ to let a refugee have a room; **finanziellen Fragen Vorrang** ~ to give precedence to financial matters; **Frist** ~ to grant (accord) a respite; **Kommission** ~ to accord (grant) a commission; **jem. einen Kredit** ~ to allow (grant) s. o. a credit; **sich einen Kredit** ~ **lassen** to open a credit account with s. o.; **Möbel in ein Zimmer** ~ to put the furniture into a room; **jem. seinen Platz** ~ to give up one's place to s. o.; **jem. einen Preisabschlag** ~ to allow a reduced price to s. o.; **finanziellen Problemen den Vorrang** ~ to give preference to financial matters; **jem. den Vorrang** ~ to yield precedence to s. o.; **jem. ein Vorrecht** ~ to concede (grant) a privilege to s. o.; **gewisse Vorteile** ~ to grant certain facilities; **jem. eine Wochenfrist** ~ to give s. o. a week.

Einräumung allowance, grant, granting, *(Zugeständnis)* admission, concession, allowance;
~ **einer Dienstbarkeit** grant of an easement; ~ **eines beschränkten Eigentumsrechtes** limitation of a lesser estate; ~ **einer Erwiderungsfrist** imparlance; ~ **einer Frist** allowance of time, *(für Zahlungen)* respite, delay of payment; ~ **eines Kredits** granting (opening) of a credit [account]; ~ **eines Nießbrauchsrechtes für die Witwe** establishment of dower; ~ **eines Tarifvorrechtes** tariff concession; ~ **eines Vorrechts** granting of a privilege.

einrechnen to include, to reckon in, to count in, *(einkalkulieren)* to take into account, to allow for, to include in one's calculations;
Kosten einer Taxifahrt mit ~ to reckon in the cost of a taxi; **Möglichkeit von Verspätung** ~ to allow for possible delays; **Vorauszahlungen** ~ to allow for sums paid in advance.

Einrechnung inclusion;
unter ~ **der Spesen** including the expenses.

Einrede plea, bar, defence, defense *(US)*, exception, traverse;
absolute ~ peremptory plea; **aufschiebende** ~ dilatory exception; **begründete** ~ good defence; **besondere** ~ special plea; **dilatorische** ~ dilatory plea; **negatorische** ~ negative plea (averment); **neue** ~ special plea; **peremptorische** ~ peremptory exception, peremptory (defense) plea; **prozeßhindernde** ~ nonissuable plea, demurrer in action, preliminary objection, absolute bar, defence in bar; **prozessuale** ~ affirmative defense, plea in abatement; **rechtsvernichtende** ~ peremptory plea, plea in bar *(US)*; **unbegründete** ~ bad plea; **unzulässige** ~ defence not available; **ursprüngliche** ~ original defense;
~ **der mangelnden Aktivlegitimation** plea of incapacity to sue; ~ **des höheren Befehls** *(Völkerrecht)* plea of superior order; ~ **mehrerer vorhandener Bürgen** benefit of division; ~ **der Dürftigkeit des Nachlasses** plene administravit; ~ **der Erfüllung des Klageanspruchs** plea in discharge; ~ **der Erschöpfung des Nachlasses** fully administered; ~ **mit Gegenvorbringen** plea in reconvention; ~ **der mangelnden Geschäftsfähigkeit wegen Geisteskrankheit** plea of insanity; ~ **ohne Klageleugnung** confession and avoidance; ~ **des unschlüssigen Klagevorbringens** general exception; ~ **sachlicher Kritik** plea for fair comment; ~ **der Minderjährigkeit** plea for infancy; ~ **eines**

Prozeßmangels plea in abatement; ~ **der Prozeßunfähigkeit** nonability [to sue]; ~ **der erfolgten Rechnungslegung** plene computavit; ~ **der Rechtshängigkeit** another action pending; ~ **der inneren Rechtskraft** estoppel by verdict; ~ **der rechtskräftig entschiedenen Sache** plea of res judicata, *(Strafrecht)* plea of autrefois convict; ~ **der mangelnden Substantiierung** common bar; ~ **der Unschlüssigkeit einer Klage** speaking demurrer, exception of no cause of action; ~ **der Unzulässigkeit des Rechtweges** defence of equitable estoppel; ~ **der Unzurechnungsfähigkeit** plea of insanity; ~ **der Unzuständigkeit** foreign plea *(US)*, plea in abatement, objection (plea as) to jurisdiction; ~ **des eigenen fahrlässigen Verhaltens** estoppel by negligence; ~ **des eigenen schuldhaften Verhaltens** estoppel by matter in pais; ~ **der Verjährung** defence under the statute of limitations, plea of lapse of time; ~ **mangelnder Verpflichtung** nonassumpsit; ~ **des erfüllten Vertrages** plea in discharge; ~ **des nicht erfüllten Vertrages** equitable defence (defense, *US*), plea of equitable lien; ~ **der Vorausklage** benefit of discussion, right of discussion *(Scot.)*;

~ **abschneiden** to bar a defense; **j. mit einer ~ ausschließen** to estop s. o.; ~ **erheben** to demur, to traverse, to enter (tender, offer) a plea; ~ **geltend machen** to set up (bring forward) a defence; ~ **der Verjährung geltend machen** to plead the statute of limitations (lapse of time); ~ **vorbringen** to enter a plea, to plead as a (set up à) defence; **prozeßbehindernde ~ vorbringen** to estop; ~ **der Unzurechnungsfähigkeit vorbringen** to enter (put forward) a plea of insanity; **mit einer ~ ausgeschlossen werden** to be precluded; **durch eine ~ gehindert werden** to be estopped; ~ **zurückweisen** to overrule an objection.

einreden, jem. etw. to make s. o. believe, to talk s. o. into believing that; **auf j. ~** to fast-talk s. o., to buttonhole s. o.; **eine halbe Stunde auf j. ~** to keep onto s. o. for full half-hour; **sich etw. ~** to persuade o. s. of s. th., to get s. th. into one's head.

einredeweise by way of defence.

einreichen to hand (give, put, turn) in, to file with, to present, to send in, to submit, to exhibit;

sein Abschiedsgesuch ~ to tender one's resignation, *(mil.)* to send in one's papers; **Angebot ~** to lodge a tender; **Antrag ~** to file an application; **Baugesuch beim Stadtbauamt ~** to submit a plan to the city council; **Belege ~** to present vouchers; **Beschwerde ~** to lodge a complaint; **Bewerbung ~** to send in an application; **Bilanz ~** to submit a balance sheet; **Bittschrift ~** to make a petition; **seine Entlassung ~** to tender one's resignation, *(mil.)* to send in one's papers; **Forderung ~** to lodge a claim; **bei Gericht ~** to put in court; **Gesuch ~** to [present a] petition; **Klage gegen j. ~** to bring an action against s. o.; **Kupons ~** to present coupons; **Patentanmeldung ~** to file an application for a patent; **Rechnungen bei einer Versicherung ~** to send in bills to an insurance office; **Scheck zur Bezahlung ~** to present a check *(US)* (cheque, *Br.*) for payment; **Scheck zur Gutschrift ~** to deposit a check *(US)* (cheque, *Br.*); **Scheidungsklage ~** to petition for divorce; **Spesenbelege ~** to submit expense accounts; **seine Spielmarken [beim Kassierer] ~** to hand (cash, pass) in one's checks; **seine Unterlagen ~** to send in one's papers; **dreitägigen Urlaub ~** to put in for three days' leave (holiday); **Voranschlag ~** to put in an estimate; **Wechsel zum Diskont ~** to remit (present, offer) a bill for discount.

Einreicher exhibitor, *(Wechsel)* presenter;

erster ~ first person to file;

~ **einer verspäteten Steuererklärung** delinquent filer *(US)*.

Einreichung presentation, filing, handing in, submittal, exhibition, *(Offerte)* tender, delivery, *(Wechsel)* presentment, presentation;

bei ~ on submission;

~ **zum Akzept** presentation for acceptance; ~ **eines Antrags** filing of an application; ~ **einer Beschwerde** lodgement of a complaint; ~ **einer Bilanz** presentation of a balance sheet; ~ **einer Bittschrift** putting up a petition; ~ **des Ehescheidungsantrages** filing of the petition; ~ **einer Klage** entering (filing of) an action; ~ **der Klagebeantwortung** delivery of defence; ~ **eines Konkursantrages** filing of a bankruptcy petition, presentation of a petition; ~ **eines Liquidationsantrages** presentation of a petition for winding-up; ~ **einer Patentklage** suing s. o. for infringement; ~ **von Schriftsätzen** delivery of pleadings; ~ **einer Strafanzeige** bringing a charge, reporting; ~ **eines Testaments** insinuation of a will; ~ **von Urkunden** exhibition (putting forward) of documents; **rechtzeitige ~ eines Wechsels** due presentment of a bill of exchange.

Einreichungs|datum closing date, deadline *(US)*, *(Konkursantrag)* filing date; **~frist** filing term, tender period; **~termin** *(Konkursantrag)* filing date, *(Patent)* date of patent.

einreihen to incorporate, to place, to range, to classify, *(Urkunden)* to file;

sich ~ to take s. one's place in a queue, *(mit dem Auto)* to filter in *(Br.)*; **j. in die höchste Dringlichkeitsstufe ~** to give s. o. top priority; **Karteikarten ~** to file index cards; **neue Kräfte in den Arbeitsprozeß ~** to absorb new workers in the labo(u)r force; **sich in eine Marschkolonne ~** to fall into line; **sich in eine Organisation ~** to join an organization; **sich in die Schlange der Wartenden ~** to line (queue, *Br.*) up; **j. unter die großen Schriftsteller ~** to place (rank) s. o. among the great writers; **in eine Tarifposition ~** to classify under a tariff item.

Einreiher single-breasted suit.

einreihig *(Anzug)* single-breasted.

Einreise entry;

~ **und Ausreise** travel to and from home, entering and leaving the country;

jem. die ~ verweigern to refuse s. o. admission, to refuse s. o. entry into a country;

~bedingungen conditions of entry; **~bewilligung, ~erlaubnis, ~genehmigung** entry permit, visa; **~flughafen** airport of entry; **~genehmigung erteilen** to visa; **~sichtvermerk** entrance (entry) visa; **~verbot für Ausländer** exclusion of aliens; **~visum** entrance (entry) visa.

einreisen to enter a country.

einreißen to tear, *(Haus)* to knock (break) down, to demolish, to dilapidate, to pull (tear) down, *(Unsitte)* to spread, to become a habit, to gain ground;

etw. nicht ~ lassen to stop a habit.

einrenken, Sache wieder to straighten things out.

einrennen, jem. die Bude to live on s. one's doorstep; **sich den Schädel ~** to crack one's skull, *(fig.)* to beat one's head against a brick wall; **offene Türen ~** to flog a dead horse.

einrichten to institute, to regulate, to adjust, to establish, to install, to appoint, *(arrangieren)* to arrange, to adjust, to organize, to manage, to dispose, *(ausrüsten)* to equip, to fit out, to get (set) up, *(Druckmaschine)* to make ready;

sich ~ to furnish one's home, *(anpassen)* to accommodate o. s. to circumstances, *(sparen)* to make both ends meet *(coll.)*; **sich auf etw. ~** to make arrangements (preparations) for s. th.; **neue Buslinie ~** to establish a new bus line; **Fabrik ~** to tool a factory, to equip a shop with tools; **sich auf Gäste ~** to be prepared for guests; **sich mit wenig Geld ~** to manage with little money; **Geschäft ~** to fit out a shop; **seinem Sohn ein Geschäft ~** to set up one's son in a trade; **sich geschmackvoll ~** to furnish one's home with taste; **sich bei jem. häuslich ~** to sponge on s. o.; **Konto ~** to open an account; **neuen Lehrstuhl ~** to establish (found) a new chair; **sich neu ~** to refurnish o. s.; **sehr schlau ~** to manage it very cleverly; **neue Schule ~** to set up a new school; **Stipendium ~** to fund (establish) a scholarship; **Vertretung ~** to establish an agency; **sich einen Waschsalon ~** to set up a laundry; **Werkstatt ~** to fit out (equip) a workshop; **Wohnung ~** to furnish (fit out) an apartment; **Zimmer als Büro ~** to adapt (convert) a room to office use;

es zeitlich so ~ to time it so that.

Einrichter setup man, machine setter.

Einrichtezeit setting-up (setup, *US*) time.

Einrichtung *(Anlage)* plant, installation, *(Anordnung)* arrangement, disposition, setup *(US)*, *(Anstalt)* establishment, institution, *(Ausrüstung)* outfit, equipment, installation, *(Haus)* furniture, appointments, *(Justierung)* adjustment, justification, *(Laden)* fittings, *(Organisation)* organization, institute, institution, *(Vorrichtung)* appliance, apparatus, device, contrivance, gadget *(US)*;

~en facilities, appliances, services;

arbeitsparende ~en labo(u)r-saving appliances; **nicht für Wohnzwecke bestimmte ~en** nonresidential premises; **bleibende ~** permanent establishment; **feste ~** fixed base; **feststehende ~** permanent institution; **gemeinnützige ~** nonprofit corporation, public utility, charitable institution, nonprofitmaking institution; **gebührenfreie gemeinnützige ~** pure charity; **gewerbliche ~en** commercial and industrial buildings; **gewerkschaftliche ~en** union institutions; **karitative ~** charitable institution; **militärische ~en** military installations; **moderne ~** modern equipment; **neumodische ~en** newfangled ideas; **öffentliche ~en** public institutions (accommodations, utilities), collective goods; **postalische ~en** postal facilities; **regionale ~** regional agency; **sanitäre ~en** sanitary conveniences (facilities), sanitary arrangements (installations); **schadensverhütende ~en** safety devices; **soziale ~** welfare organization, charitable (nonprofitmaking, *US*) institution; **staatliche ~** governmental institution; **staatliche ~en** govern-

mental (state, *US*) facilities; **städtische ~en** municipal services; **ständige ~** regular process; **technische ~** engineering facilities; **wohlbekannte ~** well-known institution; **zwischenstaatliche ~** intergovernmental agency;
~en für Datenverarbeitungen data-processing equipment; **~ der Gesundheitspflege** health services *(Br.)*; **~ eines Hauses** furniture of a house; **~ für erste Hilfe** first-aid equipment; **~ eines Kontos** opening an account; **~ einer Küche** equipment of a kitchen; **~ eines neuen Lehrstuhls** establishment of a new chair; **~en eines Luftfrachthafens** air-cargo terminal facilities; **zweckmäßige ~ einer Werkstatt** practical layout of a workshop;
um ~ eines Kontos nachsuchen to solicit for an account; **postalische ~en verbessern** to improve the postal services; **feste ~ werden** to become a fixture.

Einrichtungs|gegenstände fixtures, equipment, appointments, fitments, fittings, furnishings, *(Haushalt)* household stuff, furniture; **~haus** furniture shop (store, *US*); **~konto** equipment account; **~kosten** setting cost, cost of installation, *(Firma)* initial capital expenditure; **steuerbegünstigter ~kredit** qualifying loan *(Br.)*.

einrosten *(fig.)* to rust;
seine Englischkenntnisse ~ lassen to allow one's knowledge of English to rust *(fam.)*.

Einrücken *(Zeile)* indention, indentation, *(Soldat)* joining the colo(u)rs, induction *(US)*;
~ einer Anzeige putting in of an advertisement, insertion of an advertisement; **~ in die Kaserne** return to barracks; **~ von Truppen** entry of troops.

einrücken *(drucktechn.)* to indent, *(technisch)* to shift, to engage, to throw into gear, *(Truppen)* to enter, to march in[to];
in die öffentlichen Blätter ~ to insert, to print s. th. publicly; **in die Kaserne ~** to return to barracks; **zum Militär ~** to join the army (the ranks), to be called up; **in die Stadt ~** to enter (march into) the town; **in jds. Stelle ~** to supplant (succeed) s. o., to take s. one's place; **in eine höhere Stelle ~** to move up to an executive position; **bei jedem Absatz die erste Zeile ~** to indent the first line of each paragraph;
~ lassen *(Anzeige)* to insert, to advertise.

Einrückung *(Anzeige)* insertion, publication, *(Zeile)* indent, indentation.

Einrückungs|befehl call-up (induction, *US*) order; **~kosten** advertising expenses; **~tarif** advertising rate.

einrühren, sich eine böse Suppe to get o. s. into a mess (into a nice pickle), to land s. o. into a nice fix.

Eins *(Schule, Universität)* first *(Br.)*, alpha *(US)*, oner *(coll.)*;
im Fach für neuere Sprachen bei der Prüfung mit ~ abschließen to get a first in modern languages; **Prüfung mit ~ bestehen** to get a first (full marks), to make a grade *(US)*; **eine ~ schreiben** to get full marks *(Br.)* (an alpha, *US*) for an essay.

eins, Nummer number one;
jem. ~ auswischen to play s. o. a dirty trick.

einsacken to [pack in a] sack, to bag, *(einkassieren)* to pocket;
hübsche Summe Geldes ~ to rake in a pretty penny.

einsam lonely, lonesome, solitary, *(zurückgezogen)* retired, secluded;
~ und verlassen forlorn, forsaken;
~e Gegend lonely place; **~es Leben führen** to live in seclusion, to lead a secluded life; **durch ~e Straßen wandern** to walk through deserted streets.

Einsamkeit loneliness, solitude;
unter ~ leiden to suffer from loneliness.

Einsammeln gathering, collection, collecting.

einsammeln to collect, to gather, to glean;
Geldbeträge ~ to collect contributions; **Mieten ~** to collect the rents.

Einsammler taker.

einsargen, seine Hoffnungn to bury one's hopes;
Du kannst Dich ~ lassen go and shoot yourself.

Einsatz *(Anzeige)* insertion, *(Anteil)* share, *(Arbeitsverwendung)* use, employment, appointment, assignment, *(eingesetztes Stück)* inset, *(Einsetzen)* mobilization, *(im Filter)* element, cartridge, *(Flugzeug)* sortie, mission, *(von Kapital)* employment, *(mil.)* action, operation, [operational] mission, engagement, *(Pfand)* pledge, deposit, *(Rohrstück)* adapter, *(Spiel)* table stake, *(Tisch)* extension leaf, *(Wagnis)* risk, venture, *(Wette)* stake [money], wager, pool;
beim ~ when in action, under operational conditions, at operational level; **durch ~ von** by using; **im ~** on active service, *(mil.)* in action; **im regelmäßigen ~** in commercial service; **in besonderem ~** on special mission; **in vollem ~** *(Maschine)* in full operation; **unter ~ des Lebens** at the risk of one's life; **unter ~ aller zur Verfügung stehenden Mittel** make using of all means at one's disposal; **zum ~ bereit** ready for action;
anderweitiger ~ *(mil.)* redeployment; **bestmöglicher ~** optimum utilization; **freiwilliger ~** voluntary service; **ein zu hoher ~** too high a stake; **kleiner ~** chicken stake *(Br.)*; **militärischer ~** military operations;
~ von Arbeitskräften assignment of labo(u)r; **~ gegen Erdziele** surface mission; **~ von Führungspersonal** management input; **~ aller Kräfte** exertion of all one's strength; **gemeinsamer ~ von Kräften** pooling of efforts; **~ von Mitteln** employment of funds; **unberechtigter ~ von Mitteln** misdirection of funds; **~ der Schiffahrt** disposition of shippings; **~ von Truppen** employment (use) of troops;
zum ~ bringen to employ, to use, *(Maschinen)* to put into operation; **Flugzeuge zum ~ bringen** to put aircraft into action; **~ erhöhen** to double the stakes; **im ~ fallen** to be killed in action; **~ fliegen** to fly a sortie; **als Bankkredit zum ~ gelangen** to be made available in the form of a bank credit; **große Beträge bei einem Unternehmen im ~ haben** to have large sums at stake in an enterprise; **zum ~ kommen** to be brought into action; **in überschlagendem ~ vorgehen lassen** to leapfrog; **größeren ~ machen** to lay long odds; **seinen ~ machen** to put down one's stake; **um einen hohen ~ spielen** to play for high stakes, to play high; **im ~ stehen** *(Krankenschwester)* to be on duty; **zwölf Stunden pausenlos im ~ stehen** to be in action for twelve hours on end; **seinen ~ verdoppeln** to double one's stake; **seinen ~ verpassen** *(Schauspieler)* to miss one's entry; **erstmaligen ~ von Verkehrsflugzeugen vorsehen** to plan the first commercial flight; **~ zurückhalten** to draw stakes; **seinen ~ zurückziehen** to withdraw one's stake;
~anweisung, ~auftrag *(mil.)* operational direction, mission, *(Flugzeug)* sortie; **~befehl** operation order; **~bereich** field of application.

einsatzbereit *(betriebsfertig)* ready [for service (use)], operationally fit, fit for duty (service), ready for working (use), *(Flugzeug)* operational, ready to take off, *(mil.)* effective, ready for action, at command;
nicht ~ unready;
sich ~ halten to stand by, to be ready for action; **~ machen** *(mil.)* to demothball; **jederzeit ~ sein** to have one's finger on the trigger;
~e Maschine machine in operating condition.

Einsatzbereitschaft readiness for service (use), willingness to serve, *(Luftwaffe)* alert, *(mil.)* operational readiness;
mangelnde ~ unreadiness;
~ der Truppen erhöhen to increase the fighting efficiency of the troops.

Einsatz|bericht mission report; **~besprechnung** *(Flugzeug)* [de]-briefing, brief; **~dienst** emergency service; **~erfolg analysieren** to debrief.

einsatzfähig available, employable, usable, *(Flugzeug)* serviceable, operational, ready to take off, *(mil.)* under arms, *(Person)* fit, able-bodied.

Einsatz|fähigkeit availableness, fitness for use, *(mil.)* able-bodiedness; **~fahrzeug** *(Feuerwehr)* fire-fighting vehicle, fire engine; **~flughöhe** operational height; **~flugplatz** advance aerodrome; **~flugzeug** operational aircraft; **~form** *(Kapital)* method of employment.

einsatzfreudig dynamic.

Einsatz|freudigkeit drive; **~gebiet** field of application, *(mil.)* operational area, area of operation; **~gruppe** task force; **~hafen** base of operations, *(Flugzeug)* operational aerodrome; **~halter** stakeholder; **~kommando** emergency squad; **~kräfte der UNO** United Nations Emergency Forces; **besondere ~kräfte** units combined for operational purposes; **~leiter** director of operations, control officer, *(Polizei)* squad leader; **~menge** *(Programmierung)* input; **~methode** method of operation; **~möglichkeit** field of application, serviceability; **~ort** *(Diplomat)* post; **~plan** employee roster; **~preis** reserve price, *(Auktion)* starting (upset) price; **~raum** operational area, area of operation.

einsatzreif ready to go into operation.

Einsatz|stab staff headquarters; **~truppe** task force; **~verpflegung** composite (field, *US*) rations; **~wagen** *(Polizei)* squad car, *(Straßenbahn)* special streetcar (tramcar, *Br.*); **~wert** book (assessed) value; **~zug** relief train.

einsaugen to suck (soak) up, to absorb;
etw. mit der Muttermilch ~ to suck in s. th. with one's mother's milk, to cut one's teeth on it; **jds. Worte gierig in sich ~** to suck in s. one's words.

Einschaltblatt inset.
einschalten *(Kalendertag)* to intercalate, *(Klausel)* to interpolate, to insert, to switch on, *(el.)* to cut in, *(Motor)* to engage, to start, *(Radio)* to turn (switch) on, to tune in;
sich ~ to intervene, to step in; **sich in Auseinandersetzungen** ~ to intervene in a dispute; **örtliches Bankgeschäft** ~ to employ (interpolate) a local bank; **sich in die Diskussion** ~ to join in the discussion, to take a hand in the debate; **ersten Gang** ~ to go into (throw in the) first (bottom) gear; **kleineren Gang** ~ to shift to low speed; **sich in ein Gespräch** ~ to join a conversation; **Hebel** ~ to shift a lever in position; **Kondensator in einen Stromkreis** ~ to insert a condenser into a circuit; **Kupplung** ~ to let in the clutch; **Rechtsanwalt** ~ to engage the services of a lawyer; **j. in die Verhandlungen** ~ to call s. o. in on the negotiations; **j. als Vermittler** ~ to call s. o. in as a mediator.
Einschalter *(el.)* circuit closer, contactor, switch.
Einschalt|hebel starting lever; ~**knopf** push button; ~**motor** starting motor; ~**plan** *(Anzeiger)* advertising schedule; ~**quote** *(Fernsehen)* ratings; ~**stellung** on-position; ~**strom** starting current.
Einschaltung insertion, interpolation, parenthesis, *(el.)* switch, *(Kalendertag)* intercalation, *(in Verhandlungen)* intervention;
~ **einer Anzeige** insertion of an advertisement; ~ **einer Bank am Platze** employment (interpolation) of a local bank; ~ **eines Motors** starting an engine.
Einschaltungszeichen *(drucktechn.)* caret, insertion mark.
Einschalt|vorrichtung switch hook; ~**zeit für die Straßenbeleuchtung** lighting-up time.
einschätzen to value, to estimate, to appraise, to size up, *(Steuer)* to assess, to rate *(Br.)*;
j. ~ to take s. one's measure; **jds. Fähigkeiten zu hoch** ~ to overrate s. one's abilities; **etw. hoch** ~ to set a high value on s. th.; **j. hoch** ~ to rate s. o. high; **zu hoch** ~ to overestimate; **Lage völlig falsch** ~ to misjudge the situation entirely; **neu (nochmals)** ~ to re-assess; **zu niedrig** ~ to underrate, to value at a low rate *(US)*; **richtig** ~ to form a true estimate; **sich selbst** ~ to make a self-assessment; **Steueraufkommen** ~ to forecast the tax revenue.
Einschätzung estimation, estimate, appraisal, valuation, *(Patent)* appraisal, *(Steuern)* assessment, rating *(Br.)*;
zu hohe ~ overassessment, overestimation; **zu niedrige** ~ underestimation;
~ **der Kreditfähigkeit** rating assessment, credit rating *(US)*; ~ **des Risikos** assessment of a risk; **falsche** ~ **seiner Umwelt** false valuation of one's environment.
Einschätzungskommission assessment committee, assessors of taxes.
einschenken, jem. ein Glas to fill s. one's glass; **jem. reinen Wein** ~ to come out into the open, to tell s. o. the unvarnished truth.
einschichtig single-shift.
einschicken to send in (up), *(Geld)* to remit.
einschieben to interpolate, *(Kalendertag)* to intercalate;
Papier in die Maschine ~ to feed the paper into the machine; **Sonderzug** ~ to put on an extra train; **Vorlesung** ~ to put in an extra lecture.
Einschiebesatz parenthetical clause.
Einschiebsel run-in, interpolation.
Einschiebung interpolation, *(Kalendertag)* intercalation.
Einschienenbahn monorail;
~**verbindung** monorail connections.
Einschienenhängebahn overhead monorail.
einschießen *(Kapital)* to contribute, to invest, to put (pay) in, *(Teilzahlung auf Aktien)* to pay a call;
sich auf j. ~ to zero in on s. o.; **Geld in ein Unternehmen** ~ to invest money in a business.
einschiffen, sich to embark, to get (go) aboard, to join one's ship, to go (put) on board, to take ship; **sich in B.** ~ to board a ship at B.; **sich nach New York** ~ to take one's passage to New York; **sich wieder** ~ to reembark.
Einschiffung embarkation, embarkment.
Einschiffungs|erlaubnis embarkation permit; ~**hafen** port of embarkation; ~**karte** embarkation card; ~**offizier** embarkation officer; ~**tag** date of entry.
Einschlafen am Steuer falling asleep whilst driving (at the wheel).
einschlafen to fall asleep, to drop (dose) off, *(Bein)* to have got pins and needles, *(Beziehungen)* to be dropped, to cease gradually, *(Brauch)* to die out, to fall into disuse, *(Gerücht)* to die, *(Konversation)* to flag;
über einem Buch ~ to fall asleep over a book; **am Steuer** ~ to fall asleep whilst driving (at the wheel);
Angelegenheit ~ **lassen**to let an affair peter out.
einschläfern to lull to sleep, to make drowsy;
sein Gewissen ~ to salve one's conscience; **j. durch falsche Hoffnungen** ~ to lull s. o. with false hopes; **jds. Verdacht** ~ to allay s. one's suspicion.
einschläfernd soporific, somnolent;
~**e Lektüre** soporific reading; ~**es Mittel** narcotic; ~**er Trank** sleeping (soporific) draught; ~**e Wirkung haben** to have a soporific effect.
Einschläferung mercy killing, euthanasia.
Einschläferungsmittel soporific, sleep-inducing drug, narcotic.
einschläfriges Bett single bed.
Einschlag *(Blitz)* stroke, *(Geschoß)* impact, *(Merkmal)* touch, element, *(Textilien)* woof, weft, *(Wald)* felling rate;
mit stark religiösem ~ with a strong element of religion; **maurischer** ~ Moorish element; **negroider** ~ infusion of negro blood; **vollständiger** ~ **der Vorderräder** complete steering lock.
einschlagen *(Artikel)* to be a success (hit), to catch on, *(einpacken)* to wrap into, to fold, *(Erfolg haben)* to come home, *(Film)* to take, *(Geschoß)* to strike, to hit, *(Pflanzen)* to cover with earth;
auf j. ~ to thrash (strike at) s. o.; **Abkürzungsweg** ~ to take a short cut; **Auto nach links** ~ to pull the wheel over to the left; **Blatt in einem Buch** ~ to turn down a page in a book; **Boden eines Fasses** ~ to stave in the bottom of a cask; **wie eine Bombe** ~ to come like a bombshell, to cause a sensation; **Fenster** ~ to break (smash) a window; **in jds. Hand** ~ to clasp s. one's hand; **in ein Haus** ~ *(Blitz)* to strike a house; **Laufbahn** ~ to enter upon a career; **Nagel** ~ to drive a nail into; **jem. die Nase** ~ to flatten s. one's nose; **in Papier** ~ to wrap up in paper; **Richtung nach dem Dorf** ~ to take the path towards the village; **jem. den Schädel** ~ to bash in s. one's head in; **schnelleren Schritt** ~ to quicken one's pace; **sofort** ~ to be an immediate success; **Tür** ~ to batter down a door; **anderen Weg** ~ *(fig.)* to adopt another method; **falschen (verkehrten) Weg** ~ to take the wrong track; **völlig neue Wege** ~ to strike out untrodden paths.
einschlagend salable, marketable;
nicht ~ unsalable;
~**e Artikel** salable articles, hit.
einschlägig pertinent, relevant [in point], material;
~ **vorbestraft** previously convicted;
alle ~**en Artikel** the whole range of articles; ~**e Behörden** competent authorities; ~**es Beispiel** case in point; ~**e Bestimmungen** governing regulations; ~**er Fall** precedent; ~**es Geschäft** speciality shop, limited-line retailer *(US)*, stockist *(Br.)*; **in allen** ~**en Geschäften zu haben** obtainable from all stockists *(Br.)*; ~**e Literatur** relevant literature, books pertinent to a question.
Einschlag|papier wrapping (brown) paper; ~**tuch** wrapping cloth; ~**winkel** *(Auto)* angle of steering.
einschleichen, sich to twist o. s. (steal) into, *(Agent)* to infiltrate, *(Fehler)* to creep in; **sich in jds. Gunst** ~ to worm one's way (creep) into s. one's favo(u)r; **sich in eine Übersetzung** ~ *(Fehler)* to creep into a translation; **sich in jds. Vertrauen** ~ to worm o. s. into s. one's confidence.
einschleppen to tow in;
ansteckende Krankheit ~ to introduce a contagious disease.
einschleusen to let (channel) in, to infiltrate, *(in Arbeitsprozeß)* to direct, *(Schiff)* to lock in, *(Spion)* to feed, to infiltrate;
Flüchtlinge in ein Lager ~ to channel refugees into a camp; **Geld in den Wirtschaftskreislauf** ~ to put money into circulation, to pump money into the economy; **in eine Organisation** ~ to infiltrate into an organization; **Schiff in ein Dock** ~ to pass a ship into a dock.
Einschleusung|von Flüchtlingen channel(l)ing of refugees; ~ **von Spionen** infiltration of spies.
Einschleusungspreis *(EG)* sluice-gate price.
einschließen to lock (shut) up, *(einfrieden)* to close in, to imply, *(Gefangenen)* to put in prison, *(mil.)* to encircle, to pocket, *(umfassen)* to include, to involve, to comprise;
sich ~ to lock o. s. in, to shut o. s. in, to immure o. s.; **alle Bedeutungen** ~ *(Begriff)* to include all meanings; **Festung** ~ to surround (invest) a fort; **Garten mit einer Hecke** ~ to hedge in a garden; **j. in sein Gebet** ~ to remember s. o. in one's prayers; **in den Handel** ~ to include in the bargain; **sechs europäische Hauptstädte** ~ *(Autotour)* to take in six European capitals; **im Preis** ~ to include in the price; **Provision** ~ to include the commission; **Schiff im Nebel** ~ to envelop a ship in mist; **seinen Schmuck im Safe** ~ to shut up one's jewels in a safe; **fremdes Staatsgebiet** ~ to enclave alien territory; **Stadt** ~ to invest (encircle, blockade) a town; **Wort in Klammern** ~ to bracket a word; **j. in seinem Zimmer** ~ to shut s. o. up in a room.

einschließlich inclusive, to ... including, included;
~ **allem** overall; ~ **und bis zu** up to and including, through *(US)*; ~ **Bedienung** inclusive of service; ~ **Dividende** cum dividend, dividend on *(US)*; ~ **Kosten, Versicherung und Fracht** cif (cost, insurance, freight); ~ **Porto** postage included; ~ **der Spesen** adding (including) charges; ~ **Verpackung** package (packing, *Br.*) included.

Einschließung inclusion, confinement;
~ **einer Stadt** encirclement of a town.

einschlummern to doze off, *(sterben)* to pass away.

Einschluß enclosure, *(Bergbau)* inclusion, pocket, *(mil.)* encirclement;
mit ~ including, inclusive; **mit** ~ **der Bedienung** inclusive of service; **unter** ~ **sämtlicher Kosten** all costs (expenses) included; **unter** ~ **der Spesen** including the expenses;
~ **eines Gebiets** enclavement of a territory;
~**gebiet** enclave; ~**zeichen** *(drucktechn.)* bracket, parenthesis.

einschmeicheln, sich to curry favo(u)r, to ingratiate o. s.; **sich bei jem.** ~ to creep into s. one's favo(u)r, to wind o. s. into s. one's affection, to fawn on s. o.

einschmeichelndes Wesen ingratiating (insinuating) manners.

Einschmeichelung insinuation, ingratiation.

einschmeißen, jem. die Fenster to smash (break) s. one's windows.

einschmelzen to melt down, *(fig.)* to amalgamate, to fuse.

einschmiegen, sich in ein Tal *(Dorf)* to nestle in a valley.

einschmieren to grease, to oil, to smear.

einschmuggeln to smuggle into;
sich ~ to sneak in; **sich in ein Land** ~ to enter a country illegally; **sich in eine Versammlung** ~ to gate-crash (crash, *US*) a meeting.

einschnappen to snap, to click, to close, *(fig.)* to have the sulks *(fam.)*.

einschneiden to cut, *(Kerbe)* to notch, *(Namen)* to carve in;
tief in das Wirtschaftsleben ~ to control the economic life of a region.

einschneidend drastic, radical, trenchant, rigorous;
~**e Maßnahmen** drastic (rigorous) measures; ~**e Wirkungen haben** to have far-reaching consequences; ~**e Wirkungen auf die Konjunktur haben** to take a bigger bite out of the economy.

einschneien to be snowed up, to become snowbound.

Einschnitt notch, nick, *(Bahn)* excavation, *(Küste)* breach, *(ins Leben)* break, hiatus, turning point, *(Reifengummi)* cut;
~ **in jds. Leben** turning point of s. one's life;
großen ~ **in jds. Leben darstellen** to have far-reaching consequences for s. one's life.

einschnüren, Pakete to tie up parcels.

einschränkbar qualificatory, confinable, modifiable.

einschränken *(Ausgaben)* to diminish, to reduce, to economize, to retrench, to cut down, to cut back, to curb, to scant, *(Behauptung)* to qualify, *(beschränken)* to restrain, to restrict, to confine, to limit, to modify, *(kürzen)* to curtail, to retrench, to cut (pare) down;
sich ~ to economize, to reduce one's standard of living, to tighten one's belt, to retrench (limit, curtail) one's expenses, to reef one's sails, to pull back, to stint o. s.; **sich sehr** ~ to tighten one's belt, to reduce one's standard of living; **seine Ausgaben** ~ to curtail (reduce) one's expenses; **seine Ausgaben auf ein vernünftiges Maß** ~ to keep one's expenditure within reasonable limits; **private Banktätigkeit** ~ to curb private banking operations; **Bedingungen eines Testaments durch eine Klausel** ~ to qualify the terms of a will by means of a clause; **jds. Betätigungsfeld** ~ to put a restraint on s. one's activities; **sich in vielen Dingen** ~ to cut down on a lot; **Erklärung** ~ to make a reserved statement; **Freizügigkeit** ~ to restrict the freedom of movement; **seinen Lebensstandard** ~ to reduce one's standard of living; **jds. Machtbefugnisse auf ein bestimmtes Gebiet** ~ to confine s. one's authority within certain limits; **Personal** ~ to reduce the establishment (staff); **Pfandauslösungsrecht** ~ to clog on the equity of redemption; **Produktion** ~ to curb production, to restrain production; **Redezeit** ~ to limit the time allowed to each speaker; **jds. Tätigkeitsbereich** ~ to restrain s. one's activities; **Verbrauch auf das Allernotwendigste** ~ to reduce consumption to bare necessities; **jds. Vollmachten** ~ to narrow down (place restrictions) on s. one's powers; **Wettbewerb** ~ to restrict (restrain) competition; **seinen Zigarettenverbrauch** ~ to cut down one's cigarettes;
sich sehr ~ **müssen** to live in narrow circumstances.

einschränkend restrictive, modifying, qualifying;
~ **auslegen** to put a restrictive interpretation on;
~**e Behauptung** qualifying statement; ~**e Bestimmungen** restrictive (restraining) clauses; ~**es Konnossement** restrictive endorsement; ~**e Maßnahmen** restrictive measures.

Einschränkung *(Beschränkung)* restriction, restraint, diminution, limitation, *(Einsparung)* retrenchment, stint, cutback *(US)*, lid *(US)*, *(Kürzung)* cut, curtailment, reduction, *(Modifizierung)* modification, qualification, *(Revision)* qualification, *(Vorbehalt)* reserve, reservation;
mit ~**en** in a qualified sense, qualified; **mit dieser** ~ with this reservation; **mit gewissen** ~**en** with a grain of salt; **nach Jahren voller** ~**en und Entbehrungen** after years of scraping and self-denial; **ohne** ~ without reservation, unreservedly; **ohne jede** ~ without any qualification, unreservedly, without reservation (reserve);
ausdrückliche ~ express reservation; **mengenmäßige** ~**en** quantitative restrictions; **unerläßliche** ~ must reservation; **wirtschaftliche** ~**en** restrictions on business, retrenchment, austerity;
~ **des Absatzes** sales restrictions; ~ **der Abzahlungsgeschäfte** hire-purchase (instalment) restrictions; ~ **eines Angebots** qualification of an offer; ~ **von Ausgaben** cutting down of expenses, retrenchment, expenditure cut; ~ **der Ausgabenwirtschaft** restraint in spending; ~ **der öffentlichen Ausgabenwirtschaft** public spending curb; ~**en der Einfuhr** import restrictions; ~ **des Energieverbrauchs** restriction in the use of power, energy conservation; ~**en und Entbehrungen** scrimping and pinching; ~ **des Erteilungsverfahrens** *(Patentrecht)* file wrapper estoppel; ~ **der Geldmenge** monetary contraction; ~ **der Haftung** limitation of liability; ~ **der Investitionen** cutback in investments; ~ **des Konsums** cut in consumption; ~ **des Notenumlaufs** contraction of the currency; ~**en im Personalbereich** retrenchment of employees; ~ **des Pfandauslösungsrechtes** clog on the equity of redemption; ~ **der Pressefreiheit** restriction of the freedom of the press; ~ **des Spesenaufwands** expense account restrictions, expenditure account cutback; ~ **des Staatshaushalts** budget cut, retrenchment of budgetary expenditure; ~ **des Wehretats** defence cuts; ~ **des freien Wettbewerbs** restraint of trade; ~ **der Zuständigkeit** limitation of jurisdiction;
ohne ~**en annehmen** to accept without reservation (qualification); **sich** ~**en auferlegen** to impose limits on one's expenditure, to make retrenchments; ~**en aufheben** to abolish a reserve; ~**en enthalten** *(Testat des Wirtschaftsprüfers)* to contain qualifications; ~ **machen** to make a reserve; **mit** ~**en abgesichert sein** to be hedged about with qualifications; ~ **unterliegen** to be subject to restrictions; **zu strengen** ~**en unterwerfen** to overgovern; **einem Plan mit bestimmten** ~**en zustimmen** to agree to a plan with certain reservations.

Einschränkungs|klausel, territoriale *(Versicherung)* restrictive travel clause; ~**maßnahmen** economy (austerity) measures; ~**maßnahmen aufheben** to derestrict, to decontrol restrictions.

einschrauben, Glühbirne to screw in an electric bulb.

Einschreibe|brief registered letter; ~**gebühr** registration (entrance, enrolment, booking) fee, *(Post)* registration (registry, *US*) fee.

Einschreiben registration, registered!, special handling *(US)*, by registered mail *(US)*;
Briefaufgabe per ~ registration of a letter;
Brief per ~ **schicken** to send a letter by registered post *(Br.)*, to send a letter by special handling *(US)*.

einschreiben to write in, to put down, to inscribe, *(Brief)* to register, *(buchen)* to enter, to record, *(eintragen)* to enter, to register, to sign on, *(als Mitglied)* to enrol(l);
sich ~ to enter one's name; **Brief** ~ **lassen** to have a letter registered, to send a letter by registered post (special handling, *US*); **in ein Buch** ~ to inscribe in a book; **Kind** ~ to enter a child for *(Br.)* (enrol a child in a, *US*) school; **in eine Liste** ~ to add to (enrol(l), enter in) a list; **sich in eine Liste** ~ to put down one's name on a list; **seinen Namen ins Gästebuch** ~ to enter one's name in the visitors' book; **sich bei einer Universität** ~ to put one's papers in, to matriculate, to enrol(l), to incorporate, to register *(US)*; **sich für eine Vorlesung** ~ to enrol(l) for a course of lectures; **Widmung in ein Buch** ~ to dedicate a book.

Einschreibe|gebühr registration fee; ~**päckchen** registered parcel (package, *Br.*); ~**paket** registered parcel (packet, *Br.*); ~**quittung** post-office receipt; ~**sendung** registered letter (item, mail, *US*); ~**zettel** registration label.

Einschreibung *(Universität)* matriculation, enrolment, registration *(US)*.

Einschreiten interference, intervention;
polizeiliches ~ police intervention.

einschreiten to intervene, to interfere, to step in, to take measures (steps);
gegen Demonstranten ~ to take action against (disperse) demonstrators; **energisch gegen etw.** ~ to take drastic measures; **gegen j. gerichtlich** ~ to take legal proceedings against (go to law with) s. o., to proceed against s. o., to prosecute (sue) s. o., to take s. o. to court; **mit Waffengewalt** ~ to employ force.
Einschub parenthesis, interpolation, insertion.
einschüchtern to intimidate, to daunt, to bully, to browbeat, to bluff, to terrorize, *(Zeugen)* to intimidate;
durch befehlhaberisches Auftreten ~ to outhector; **j. komplett** ~ to overawe s. o. into submission.
Einschüchterung intimidation, terrorization, *(Zeugen)* undue influence, intimidation;
Wähler durch ~en von der Wahl abhalten to keep voters from the polls by intimidation; **~en nachgeben** to surrender to intimidation.
Einschüchterungs|politik system of intimidation; **~versuch** bluff, *(pol.)* attempt to intimidate; **~versuch machen** to bluff.
einschulen to school, to train;
Kind ~ lassen to send a child to school.
Einschulung training, *(Kind)* enrolment.
Einschuß *(Anflug)* touch, tinge, stroke, *(Differenzgeschäft)* margin, *(Kapital)* capital invested, share, stake, investment, contribution to capital, *(Kugel)* bullet hole;
~ **von Ironie** tinge of irony;
~ **leisten** to pay down (on account), *(Differenzgeschäft)* to [put up a] margin, *(Kapital)* to satisfy a call;
~aufforderung call; **~bedarf im Effektendifferenzgeschäft** margin requirements; **Gewinnspanne lassendes ~konto** marginal (margin) account *(US)*; **~pflicht** margin borrowing *(US)*; **~zahlung leisten** to [put up a] margin.
einschütten, Koks in den Hochofen to charge the blast furnace.
einschwärzen *(drucktechn.)* to ink.
einschwatzen, jem. etw. to put s. th. into s. one's head.
einschwenken to come round, *(Film)* to move in, *(Gerät)* to swivel;
auf eine neue Linie ~ to swing into a new line; **in eine Seitenstraße** ~ to turn into a sidestreet.
einsegnen to consecrate, *(konfirmieren)* to confirm.
Einsegnung confirmation.
Einsehen sense, understanding;
ein ~ haben to have some sense, to be reasonable.
einsehen to look at, to examine, to inspect;
etw. ~ to realize, to understand; **Akten** ~ to have access to files; **Bücher** ~ to inspect the books, to examine the books; **Fachliteratur** ~ to study the relevant (special) literature; **seine Fehler nicht** ~ to shut one's eyes to one's faults; **Grund** ~ to see the reason; **Grundbuch** ~ to search the title, to inspect the land register *(Br.)*; **seinen Irrtum** ~ to see the error of one's ways, to own one was wrong; **Manuskript** ~ to get a look at a manuscript; **Muster** ~ to have a look at the patterns; **jds. Papiere** ~ to look through s. one's papers; **einschlägige Texte** ~ to read through the relevant texts; **Urkunde** ~ to consult a document;
Straße ~ können to be able to observe a street.
einseifen, j. to softsoap s. o., to fleece s. o., to take s. o. in.
einseitig unilateral, one-sided, *(ausschließlich)* exclusive, *(parteiisch)* partial, biassed, *(Stoff)* nonreversible, *(Verkehr)* one-way;
~ **bedruckt** not backed; ~ **beschrieben** written on one side; **Thema ~ behandeln** to be biassed in one's treatment of a subject; ~ **sein** to be onesided, to have a one-track mind;
~er Antrag ex-parte application; **~e Behauptung** partial statement; **~e Erklärung** unilateral declaration; **~e Ernährung** unbalanced nutrition; **~e Information** one-sided information; **~er Irrtum** unilateral mistake; **~er Mensch** single-track mind; **~e Parteiverhandlung** ex-parte hearing; **~es Rechtsgeschäft** unilateral transaction; ~ **eingestellter Richter** partial judge; **~e Überlebensrente** reversionary annuity; **~e Verpflichtung** unilateral obligation, naked bond; ~ **bindender Vertrag** unilateral (nude, naked) contract; **~e Verzichtserklärung** renunciation by one party.
Einseitigkeit one-sidedness, *(Vorurteil)* bias, prejudice.
einsenden to send in, to forward, to transmit, *(an Zeitung)* to contribute;
Geld ~ to remit money; **Rechnung** ~ to send in a bill; **Zeitungsartikel** ~ to submit an article to a newspaper.
Einsender sender, *(Geldbetrag)* remitter, *(Zeitung)* contributor; **~kartei** card file of writers; **~termin** copy date.
Einsendeschluß closing day, deadline *(US)*.
Einsendung sending, submission, *(Geld)* transmittal, remittance, *(an Zeitung)* contribution;
gegen ~ von on receipt (remittance) of.
einsetzbar suitable, applicable, *(austauschbar)* interchangeable, replaceable.
Einsetzen der Flut flow of the tide.
einsetzen *(anwenden)* to employ, to apply, to use, *(bestallen)* to invest, to constitute, to inaugurate, to institute, to install, to nominate, to vest, *(Edelstein)* to mount, *(einschieben)* to interpolate, *(ernennen)* to install, to appoint, to establish, *(Flut)* to set in, to be on the flow (tide), *(Geld)* to stake, to bet, to wager, *(stiften)* to institute, *(in die Zeitung)* to insert, to advertise;
sich für etw. ~ to speak in support of s. th., to stand up (to be counted, *US*) for s. th., to make a plea for s. th., to climb aboard the bandwaggon; **sich für j.** ~ to take a stand in favo(u)r of (put a good word in for) s. o., to intercede for s. o.; **sich sehr für j.** ~ to do a great deal for s. o.; **sich für j. bei einem anderen** ~ to plead with (intercede, speak, stick up, stand up) for s. o.; **j. in ein Amt** ~ to install (induct) s. o. in an office; **j. feierlich in ein Amt** ~ to inaugurate s. o. in an office; **Annonce** ~ to run (put in) an advertisement; **schwere Artillerie** ~ to bring up heavy artillery; **Ausschuß** ~ to appoint (set up) a committee; **sich bis zum Äußersten** ~ to go all out *(sl.)*; **bei Bedarf in kürzester Zeit wieder** ~ to take out of mothballs in a jiffy; **Begünstigten** ~ *(Lebensversicherung)* to nominate a beneficiary; **Bischof in sein Amt** ~ to enthrone a bishop; **j. in der Buchführung** ~ to assign s. o. to the accounting department; **j. als Bürgermeister** ~ to appoint s. o. as mayor; **j. als Direktor** ~ to make s. o. a director; **seinen Einfluß für j.** ~ to use one's influence on behalf of s. o.; **seinen ganzen Einfluß** ~ to throw one's weight about; **sich energisch für etw.** ~ to push hard for s. th.; **j. zu seinem Erben** ~ to constitute (institute, appoint, *US*) s. o. one's heir; **Ersatzteil** ~ to fix a spare part; **Fensterscheibe** ~ to pane a window; **neuen Film** ~ to put in a new film; **Fische in einen Teich** ~ to stock a pond with fish; **Flüchtlingsausschuß** ~ to set up a commission for the investigation of the refugee problem; **Flugzeug** ~ to bring aircraft into action; **Geld in die Lotterie** ~ to have a stake in the lottery; **j. als Hilfskraft** ~ to employ s. o. on a temporary basis; **seine Hilfsquellen** ~ to use one's resources; **höher** ~ *(Bilanz)* to write up; **sich für eine Idee** ~ to support an idea; **sich intensiv für etw.** ~ to go all out for s. th.; **sich intensiv für j.** ~ to work hard for s. o.; **sich für jds. Interessen** ~ to safeguard s. one's interests; **sich für einen Kandidaten** ~ to support a candidate, to groom a candidate for office *(US)*; **Klausel in einen Vertrag** ~ to insert a clause in a contract; **seine ganze Kraft** ~ to leave no stone unturned; **Kräfte gemeinsam** ~ to pool one's forces; **sein Leben** ~ to risk one's life; **sein ganzes Leben für etw.** ~ to dedicate one's life to s. th.; **sich bis zum Letzten** ~ to do one's utmost; **Liquidator** ~ to appoint a liquidator; **sich für Lohnerhöhungen** ~ to stand up for higher wages; **sich für eine elastische Lohnpolitik** ~ to advocate a more flexible wage policy; **modernste Maschinen** ~ to use the most modern machinery; **Miliz** ~ to call out militia; **Motor** ~ to install an engine; **Nachfolger** ~ to designate a successor; **zusätzlichen Omnibus** ~ to put on a relief bus; **als Pfand** ~ to pledge, to pawn; **Polizei gegen Demonstranten** ~ to call in the police against demonstrators; **j. wieder in seine Rechte** ~ to reestablish (reinstate, restore) s. o. in his rights; **neue Regierung** ~ to establish a new government; **sich für eine Sache** ~ to champion a cause; **Sonderzüge** ~ to run extra trains; **an Stelle eines Wortes ein anderes** ~ to substitute a word; **sich für niedrigere Steuern** ~ to fight for lower taxes; **Testamentsvollstrecker** ~ *(Erblasser)* to nominate an executor, *(Nachlaßgericht)* to grant letters of administration; **Treuhänder** ~ to appoint a trustee (custodian); **Truppen** ~ to mobilize troops; **über das ganze Unternehmen verteilt** ~ to redistribute throughout the company; **Untersuchungsausschuß** ~ to set up a court of inquiry; **Vermögenswerte eines Unternehmens anderweitig** ~ to redeploy the assets of a company; **Vertreter** ~ to appoint (employ) an agent; **sich voll** ~ to do one's utmost, to use one's best endeavo(u)rs; **wieder** ~ to reinstall, to reinstate, to replant, to reseat, *(Spekulation)* to revive; **wirksam** ~ to use to good effect; **sich wirksam für j.** ~ to give s. o. effectual support; **Zug** ~ to start a train; **neues Zugpaar auf einer Strecke** ~ to put a new service on a line.
Einsetzung appointment, nomination, installation, induction, *(Einrichtung)* establishment;
gemeinsame ~ joint appointment; **testamentarische** ~ appointment by will;

~ **von Arbeitskräften** deployment of labo(u)r; **kriegsbedingte** ~ **von Arbeitskräften** essential work orders *(Br.)*; ~ **eines Ausschusses** constitution of (appointment, setting up) of a committee; ~ **eines Begünstigten** *(Lebensversicherung)* nomination of a beneficiary; ~ **eines Erben** institution (appointment, *US*) of an heir; ~ **eines Ersatzerbens** substitution of an heir; ~ **eines Gerichts** constitution of a court; ~ **eines Geschworenengerichts** array of a jury, panel(l)ation; ~ **eines Gouverneurs** appointment of a governor; ~ **einer Klausel in einen Vertrag** insertion of a clause in a contract; ~ **eines Liquidators** appointment of a liquidator; ~ **eines Nachfolgers** designation of a successor; ~ **eines Testamentsvollstreckers** appointment of an executor; ~ **eines Treuhänders** appointment of a trustee; ~ **eines Vertreters** appointment of an agent.

Einsicht insight, wisdom, understanding, *(Prüfung)* examination, inspection consultation, *(Verständnis)* discernment, understanding;
gegen meine bessere ~ against my better judgment; **nach dem Maß seiner** ~ according to his lights; **zur** ~ for perusal (inspection);
mangelnde ~ lack of discernment; **mangelnde politische** ~ lack of political vision; **zu späte** ~ hindsight; **jedermann zugängliche** ~ public inspection;
~ **in die Akten** access to files, inspection of documents; ~ **in die Bücher** inspection of the books; ~ **ins Grundbuch** search of title;
zur öffentlichen ~ **ausliegen** to be open to (available for) inspection; ~ **gestatten** to grant inspection; ~ **in etw. gewinnen** to gain an insight in s. th.; ~ **nehmen** to inspect, to consult; ~ **ins Grundbuch nehmen** [etwa] to make requisitions as to title; ~ **in Urkunden nehmen** to consult documents; **zur** ~ **zur Verfügung stehen** to be available for inspection; ~ **in einen Garten verhindern** to obstruct the view into a garden; **jem.** ~ **in etw. verschaffen** to give s. o. insight into s. th.; **jem. die Bücher zur** ~ **vorlegen** to show s. o. the books; ~ **in die Schwächen anderer zeigen** to show insight into human character.

einsichtig discerning, understanding;
~**er Mann** man of insight.

Einsichtnahme inspection, perusal, examination, vidimus;
gegen ~ on sight; **nach** ~ after perusal; **zur** ~ for your attention (perusal);
amtliche ~ official search;
~ **in die Geschäftsbücher** inspection of the books; ~ **ins Grundbuch** search of (requisition on) title; ~ **in Rechnungsbücher und Konten** access to books and accounts; ~ **in Urkunden** consultation of documents;
jem. zur gefälligen ~ **übersenden** to submit for s. one's kind inspection.

Einsichts|formular search form; ~**losigkeit** lack of discernment; ~**recht** right to inspect; ~**recht in die Bücher haben** to have access to the books.

einsichtsvoll judicious, reasonable.

einsickern to soak in, to ooze, to trickle, *(fig.)* to infiltrate;
langsam ~ to advance by infiltration; **in die feindlichen Linien** ~ to infiltrate into the enemy's lines; **durch eine Ritze im Dach** ~ to trickle (seep) in through a crack in the roof.

Einsickerung *(mil.)* infiltration.

Einsiedler hermit, anchorite, recluse;
wie ein ~ **leben** to live the life of a recluse (like a hermit);
~**leben** [life of a] recluse, seclusion.

einsilbige Antworten monosyllabic answers.

einsinken to sink, *(Gebäude)* to subside, to cave in, to give way;
im Schlamm ~ to sink into the mud.

Einsitzer single-seater.

einsortieren, alphabetisch to arrange in alphabetical order.

Einspaltentarif unilinear (single-column) tarif.

einspaltig one-column;
~**er Satz** composition to full measure.

einspannen *(Pferd)* to harness, *(technisch)* to fix, to mount;
j. für sich ~ to enlist s. one's help; **j. für eine Arbeit** ~ to rope s. o. in for a job; **Papier in die Schreibmaschine** ~ to feed the paper into the typewriter; **Zeitung** ~ *(Leseraum)* to fix a newspaper into the holder.

Einspänner one-horse carriage.

einspännig one-horse.

einsparen to economize, to make economies, to cut down, to save, to retrench, to reduce expenses;
Arbeitskräfte ~ to save labo(u)r; **größere Beträge** ~ to make greater economies; **kleine Beträge** ~ to save little by little; **Stelle** ~ to abolish (dispense with) an office; **Zeile** ~ to save a line.

Einsparung saving, economy;
erzwungene ~**en** compulsory savings; **finanzielle** ~ saving of cash, financial economies; **größere** ~**en** major economies; **technische** ~**en** technical economies; **verwaltungsmäßige** ~**en** managerial economies;
~ **an Arbeitskräften** saving of labo(u)r, manpower savings, labo(u)r saving; ~ **von Benzin** savings in fuel; ~**en auf dem Energiesektor** energy savings; ~**en im Staatshaushalt** budget restrictions, retrenchment of budgetary expenditure; ~**en durch erhöhte Übernahme eigenen Risikos** risk-bearing economies; ~**en durch Verbesserungen des Absatzsystems** marketing economies; ~ **in der öffentlichen Verwaltung** civil service cut; ~**en auf dem Verwaltungssektor** economies in administration;
~**en vornehmen** to make economies, to retrench one's expenses; ~ **im Staatshaushalt zugunsten privater Investitionen vornehmen** to trim government's own budget to make room for private investments.

Einsparungs|ausschuß paring-down committee; ~**feldzug** cost-cutting drive; ~**maßnahmen** economy measures; **von** ~**maßnahmen betroffen werden** to fall victim to a cost-reduction (retrenchment) program(me); ~**politik** policy of retrenchment.

einsperren to put in jail, to confine, to imprison, to incarcerate, to clap by the heels;
Gefangenen ~ to run in (shut up) a prisoner; **Kind in seinem Zimmer** ~ to confine a child to its room.

Einspiegeln *(Redakteur)* copy fitting.

einspiegeln *(Redakteur)* to copy-fit.

einspielen *(Film)* to take, to bring in;
sich ~ to get into full swing, to get going; **sich aufeinander** ~ to team up with s. o., *(fam.)* to get used to each other's ways; **brutto** ~ to gross up; **eine Million Dollar** ~ to gross a million dollars; **sich nach marktwirtschaftlichen Regeln aufeinander** ~ to work together according to the rules of market economy; **sich in eine Rolle** ~ to get under the skin of a part.

Einspielergebnis trade shown;
hervorragendes ~ box-office success.

einspinnen, sich in Studien to wrap o. s. up in one's studies.

einspringen to help out, to lend a helping hand;
für j. ~ to substitute for s. o., to step in (deputize) for s. o., to take s. one's place, to pinch-hit for s. o. *(US coll.)*; **für den Hauptdarsteller** ~ to understudy the lead.

Einspritzdüse injection nozzle.

einspritzen to inject;
jem. etw. ~ to give s. o. an injection.

Einspritz|motor fuel-injection engine; ~**pumpe** priming pump.

Einspritzung *(Motor)* injection, priming.

Einspritzvergaser jet carburettor.

Einspruch objection, veto, caveat, protest[ation], exception, appeal, *(Beschwerde)* reclamation, *(Einrede)* demurrer, *(Patentrecht)* opposition;
im Fall eines ~**s** in case of opposition;
begründeter ~ well-founded objection; **örtlicher** ~ local veto; ~ **gegen eine Einkommenssteuerveranlagung** income-tax appeal; ~ **gegen zu hohe Einschätzung** *(Firmenwert)* rating appeal; ~ **gegen die Entlastung des Gemeinschuldners** opposition in bankruptcy law; ~ **gegen eine Patentanmeldung (Patenterneuerung)** notice of opposition, caveat; ~ **gegen einen Schiedsrichter** objection to an arbitrator; **komplizierter** ~ **gegen eine Steuerfestsetzung** highly technical appeal against assessment; ~ **gegen eine Wahl** election petition; ~ **gegen einen Zeugen** exception to a witness;
~ **gegen ein Patent anmelden** to lodge an opposition to a patent; ~ **aufrechterhalten** to sustain a demurrer; ~ **nicht beachten** to take no notice of an objection; ~ **einlegen** to [enter (put) in a] caveat, to interpose an (offer) objection, to enter (lodge, raise) a protest; ~ **gegen die Entlastung eines Gemeinschuldners einlegen** to file an objection to a bankrupt's discharge; **gegen eine Entscheidung des Finanzamtes** ~ **einlegen** to appeal against a decision of the Inland Revenue; ~ **beim Finanzamt gegen zu hohe Veranlagung einlegen** to make representations to the Inspector of Taxes about an excessive assessment; ~ **gegen eine Patentanmeldung einlegen** to oppose an application; **gegen einen Plan** ~ **einlegen** to veto a plan; ~ **gegen einen Steuerbescheid einlegen** to appeal against a tax assessment; **gegen einen Zeugen** ~ **einlegen** to protest a witness; ~ **entgegennehmen** to receive a protest; ~ **erheben** to raise (lodge, interpose, enter) a protest (an objection, an appeal), to protest, to object, to interpose (impose) one's veto, to oppose an action, to take defence, to make a plea; **schriftlichen** ~ **erheben** to make a written protest; **gegen die Eheschließung** ~ **erheben** to

forbid the banns; ~ **gegen eine Entscheidung erheben** to appeal against a decision; ~ **für unbegründet halten** to regard an appeall as being without merits; ~ **nicht gelten lassen** to overrule an objection; **einem ~ stattgeben** to uphold (allow) an objection; ~ **übergehen** to override a veto, to brush aside an objection; **über einen ~ gegen eine Einkommensteuererklärung verhandeln** to hear an appeal against an income-tax assessment; ~ **verwerfen** to disapprove (disallow) an objection; ~ **zurücknehmen** to withdraw an opposition (objection); ~ **zurückweisen** to overrule an objection.

Einspruchs | begründung *(Patentrecht)* grounds of opposition; ~**einlegender** *(Patentverfahren)* caveator; ~**einlegung** *(Patentrecht)* notice of opposition; ~**entscheidung** *(Patentamt)* ruling of the commissioner of patents *(US)*; ~**erhebender** demurrant, objector; ~**erhebung** intervention, protest[ation]; ~**frist** period for objection, time of appealing, term of preclusion, *(Patentrecht)* period of entering an opposition, opposition period, *(Urteil)* time of appealing; ~**gebühr** *(Patentrecht)* opposition fee *(US)*; ~**partei** *(Patent)* opponent; ~**patent** opposition patent; ~**recht** right to veto, right of representation, *(Einkommenssteuerveranlagung)* right of appeal; ~**rücknahme** *(Kartellrecht)* negative clearance *(US)*, *(Patent)* withdrawal of objection; ~**stelle gegen zu hohe Einheitsbewertung** local valuation court *(Br.)*; ~**verfahren** *(Patent)* opposition (interference) proceedings, public use proceedings *(US)*, *(Steuerrecht)* procedure on appeals, appeals procedure (hearing); ~**verfahren einleiten** *(Patentrecht)* to give notice of opposition; **für ~zwecke ausliegen** *(Patent)* to lie open to opposition.

einspurig single-line (-track, -rail).

einstampfen *(Akten)* to pulp.

Einstampf | maschine pulper; ~**papier** wastepaper.

Einstand entrance, footing, *(neue Wohnung)* housewarming party;
seinen ~ bezahlen to pay one's footing; **seinen ~ feiern** to give a housewarming party.

Einstands | bedingungen initial terms; ~**berechnung** cost accounting; ~**fest** housewarming [party]; ~**geld** entrance money, footing; ~**geschenk** handsel; ~**kosten** initial (prime) costs; ~**preis** cost (delivery) price; ~**preis der Waren** cost of goods purchased; ~**recht** right of preemption.

Einstandswert cost base (value);
bewertet zum ~ oder Marktwert *(Bilanz)* valued at the lower of cost or market.

einstanzen to impress, to imprint, *(Nummer)* to stamp.

einstecken to put in, *(el.)* to plug in;
j. ~ to be one better; **Beleidigung** ~ to pocket (swallow) an insult; **Briefe in den Briefkasten** ~ to drop letters into the letter box; **Gewinne** ~ to pocket gains; **j. leicht** ~ to be more than a match for s. o.; **etw. nicht** ~ not to take s. th. lying down *(coll.)*; **Schlüssel ins Schloß** ~ to insert the key in the lock; **viel** ~ to take a lot;
genug Geld ~ haben to have enough money on one.

Einsteckschloß mortise lock.

einstehen to be responsible (answerable), to go bail;
für j. ~ to go bail (be surety) for s. o.; **für etw.** ~ to pledge o. s. (be answerable) for s. th., *(geradestehen)* to stand up for s. th., *(garantieren)* to vouch for s. th.; **für die Folgen** ~ to answer for the consequences; **für einen Kredit** ~ to respond (answer) for a debtor; **für einen Schaden** ~ to be answerable for the damage done (for a loss); **für seine Überzeugung** ~ to stand up for one's convictions;
für die Schulden seiner Frau ~ müssen to be liable for debts incured by one's wife.

Einsteige | dieb cat burglar, porch climber *(sl.)*; ~**diebstahl** cat burglary.

einsteigen *(Auto, Bus, Zug)* to get in, to enter;
in eine Branche ~ to get into a line of business; **in einen Bus** ~ to get into a bus; **durch ein Fenster** ~ to climb through a window; **in ein Flugzeug** ~ to board a plane; **in ein Geschäft** ~ to become a partner of a firm, to embark on a business undertaking; **gründlich in etw.** ~ to go deeply into s. th.; **in ein Projekt** ~ to participate in a project; **bei einer Sache** ~ to get into s. th. (in on the act); **gründlich in eine Sache** ~ to thoroughly examine a matter; **in ein Schiff** ~ to board (embark) a ship, to go aboard (on board);
~! all-aboard! *(US)*.

einsteigern, selbst to bid (buy) in.

Einsteigerung buying in [at an auction].

Einsteig | loch, ~**luke** manhole, *(Flugzeug)* access hatch, *(Tank)* doorway.

einstellbar adjustable.

einstellen *(Arbeiter)* to engage, to enlist, to take on, to employ, to recruit *(US)*, to hire *(US)*, *(aufgeben)* to give up, to leave off, to drop, *(aufhören)* to discontinue, to stay, to suspend, to put a stop to, *(Betrieb)* to shut down, to stop operations, *(Empfangsgerät)* to tune in, to switch on, *(Zünder)* to time;
j. bei sich ~ to give s. o. a job in one's business; **etw. bei jem.** ~ to leave s. th. at s. one's house; **sich** ~ to appear, to occur, to set in, *(Aufträge, Bedarf)* to arise, *(Person)* to appear, to turn up, to show up *(fam.)*, *(Schwierigkeiten)* to crop up; **achsgerade** ~ to align; **Arbeit** ~ to stop working, to leave off, *(streiken)* to [come out on] strike, to lay down tools, to walk out *(US)*; **zusätzlich 200 Arbeiter** ~ to take on 200 extra hands; **Arbeitskräfte** ~ to enrol(l) workers, to recruit labor *(US)*; **als erster wieder früher entlassene Arbeitskräfte** ~ to be the first to reinstate redundant workers; **unnötige Arbeitskräfte** ~ to featherbed; **zusätzliche Arbeitskräfte** ~ to take on extra workers; **sich im richtigen Augenblick** ~ to turn up at the right moment; **Auto** ~ to put the car away, to garage the car; **seine Beitragsleistungen** ~ to discontinue one's subscription; **Betrieb** ~ to shut down, to suspend operations, to stop business (a factory); **Betrieb vorübergehend** ~ to close temporarily; **Briefverkehr** ~ to drop a correspondence; **Bücher** ~ *(Bibliothekar)* to shelve books; **Dienst** ~ to hive off a service; **sich elektrisch ~ lassen** to adjust electrically by push-button; **sich auf Energieeinsparungen** ~ to switch over to energy saving; **Entfernung** ~ *(Fotoapparat)* to focus the camera; **Erscheinen** ~ to cease to appear, to discontinue publication; **Feindseligkeiten** ~ to cease fire; **als Freiwilligen** ~ to enlist s. o. as a volunteer; **sich ganz auf j.** ~ to bestow one's attention upon s. o.; **j. in seinem Geschäft** ~ to give s. o. employment (a job); **sich häufig** ~ to frequent; **sich im Haus eines Freundes** ~ to present o. s. at a friend's house; **Instrument** ~ to adjust an instrument; **Konkursverfahren mangels Masse** ~ to stop bankruptcy proceedings for lack of assets; **sein Leben ganz auf Arbeit** ~ to center one's whole life on work; **seine Möbel bei jem.** ~ to store one's furniture with s .o.; **Omnibuslinie** ~ to abandon a bus line; **Pensionszahlung an j.** ~ to take away a pension from s. o.; **sich plötzlich** ~ to supervene; **Prozeß** ~ to abate (dismiss) an action, to discontinue a lawsuit; **sich auf sein Publikum** ~ to adapt o. s. to an audience; **Rekord** ~ to equal a record; **in die freien Rücklagen** ~ to allocate to reserve fund, to appropriate to free reserve; **in die offenen Rücklagen** ~ to allocate (transfer) to published (declared) reserves; **Rundfunksender** ~ to tune in on a radio station; **sich später** ~ *(Folgen)* to make themselves felt later; **Strafverfahren** ~ to dismiss a charge [on indictment]; **Tätigkeit** ~ to hive off a service; **sich auf die Umstände** ~ to adapt (accommodate) o. s. to circumstances; **auf unendlich** ~ to focus on (for) infinity; **Verfahren** ~ to abate (discontinue, stop the) proceedings; **Verkauf** ~ to discontinue selling; **Verkehr** ~ to break off relations; **seinen Vortrag auf das niedrigere Niveau seines Publikums** ~ to talk down to an audience; **auf eine bestimmte Wellenlänge** ~ to tune in to the frequency of a transmitting station; **wieder** ~ to rehire *(US)*; **sich wieder** ~ to return, to reappear; **Zahlungen** ~ to suspend (stop) payment, to fail; **sich auf schwere Zeiten** ~ to be prepared for the worst; **Zwangsvollstreckung** ~ to stay execution;
sich ~ lassen to sign on.

Einstellhebel adjusting lever.

einstellige Zahl one-digit number.

Einstell | knopf knob; ~**lohn** entrance rate; ~**lupe** focusing magnifier; ~**marke** adjusting mark; ~**ring** *(Fotoapparat)* focusing ring; ~**schraube** adjusting screw, *(Foto)* focusing glass.

Einstellung *(Arbeitskräfte)* engagement, enlistment, employment, placement, signing on, hire *(US)*, hiring *(US)*, recruitment *(US)*, recruiting *(US)*, *(Beendigung)* cessation, stoppage, discontinuance, *(Betrieb)* shutdown, stoppage, discontinuance, suspension of operations, *(Gerät)* adjustment, regulation, *(Kamera)* focus, *(mil.)* enrolment, *(Motor)* adjustment, *(Rundfunkgerät)* tuning, *(inneres Verhältnis)* attitude, behavio(u)r, *(Verkauf, Verkehr)* discontinuance;
gut abgestimmte ~ well-orchestrated sentiment; **bevorzugte** ~ preferential hiring *(US)*; **bürokratische** ~ bureaucratism, redtapism; **einstweilige** ~ *(Verfahren)* temporary suspension; **fatalistische** ~ fatalistic attitude; **freundliche** ~ goodwill; **gewerkschaftsfeindliche** ~ anti-union attitude; **industriefeindliche** ~ anti-industry stance; **kapitalistische** ~ capitalistic spirit; **kriegsbedingte** ~**en** war hirings *(US)*; **kritische** ~ critical attitude; **liberale** ~ broad-mindedness; **persönliche** ~ personal attitude; **politische** ~ political opinion (attitude); **provinzielle** ~

provincial attitude of mind; **richtige ~** *(Instrument)* rectification; **überwundene ~** outworn attitude; **von möglichen Repressalien unbeeinflußte ~** damn-the-torpedo approach; **unkonventionelle ~** fresh approach; **vorläufige ~** suspension; **~ eines leitenden Angestellten** senior appointment; **~ der Arbeit** suspension of (cessation from) work, stoppage, *(Streik)* strike, walkout *(US)*; **~ zur Arbeit** work attitude, attitude towards work; **~ ungelernter Arbeiter** dilution of labo(u)r; **~ älterer Arbeitnehmer** employment of elderly people; **~ von Arbeitskräften** recruitment of labo(u)r; **~ der Atomwaffenversuche** suspension of nuclear tests; **~ der Auslandshilfe** cutoff of foreign aid; **~ der Bautätigkeit** construction work stoppage; **~ des Betriebes** suspension of operations; **~ des Buchungsverkehrs für Revisionszwecke** cutoff of posting operations for auditing purposes; **~ des Ermittlungsverfahrens** nolle prosequi; **~ der Feindseligkeiten** cease-fire, cessation of hostilities, suspension of arms; **~ einer Fertigung (bestimmter Fertigungszweige)** line shutup, cutoff of production divisions *(US)*; **~ des Feuers** cease-fire; **~ des Flugverkehrs** suspension of air service; **~ eines Gerichtsverfahrens** abatement of action; **~ wegen Geringfügigkeit** *(Verfahren)* prosequi; **~ des Geschäftsbetriebes (der Geschäftstätigkeit)** suspension (discontinuance) of business, cessation of trade; **bevorzugte ~ von Gewerkschaftsmitgliedern** preferential hiring of union members *(US)*; **~ aus dem Jahresüberschuß** allocation from the net earnings; **~ der Kampfhandlungen** cessation of hostilities, suspension of military operations; **~ des Konkursverfahrens** closing of bankruptcy proceedings; **~ des Konsumenten** consumer attitude; **~ dem Leben gegenüber** outlook of life; **~ von Lehrlingen** employment of apprentices; **~ der Lieferung** cessation of delivery, disconnection of service; **~ von Minderheitsangehörigen** minority hiring *(US)*; **~ der Öffentlichkeit** public attitude; **günstige ~ der Öffentlichkeit** favo(u)rable attitude of the public; **~ einer Omnibuslinie** discontinuance of a bus line; **~ in die Pauschalwertberichtigung von Forderungen** general reserves for accounts receivables *(US)*; **~ von Personal** recruitment of staff; **~ auf Probe** probationary appointment; **~ eines Prozesses** abatement of an action; **~ des Reiseverkehrs** discontinuance of travel; **~ in freie Rücklagen** allocation to reserve fund; **~ in die offenen Rücklagen** *(Bilanz)* allocation to declared (published) reserves, transfers to surplus reserves; **~en in Sonderposten mit Rücklageanteil** transfer to special reserves; **~ eines Strafverfahrens** withdrawal of a charge, dismissal of a criminal case, nolle prosequi; **~en während einer Streikperiode** hiring during a strike; **~ der Tätigkeit aller öffentlichen Dienste** total suspension of all public services; **~ eines Teilbetriebes** cessation of a branch; **~ des Verbrauchers** consumer attitude; **~ des Verfahrens** stay, discontinuance of proceedings, abatement of action; **~ des Verkehrs** abandonment of lines; **~ der Zahlungen** stoppage, suspension of payments, failure; **~ auf unbekannte Zeit** indefinite appointment, hiring at will *(US)*; **~ der Zündung** ignition timing; **~ der Zwangsvollstreckung** stay of execution; **~ des Zwangsvollstreckungsverfahrens** stay of foreclosure;
seine ~ ändern to shift in one's mind (ground); **~ des Verfahrens anordnen** to enter a nolle prosequi; **jds. ~ für eine Stelle durchsetzen** to obtain s. one's appointment for a post; **feindselige ~ gegen j. haben** to assume an attitude of hostility against s. o.; **~ eines Strafverfahrens veranlassen** to drop a charge.

Einstellungs|alter hiring age *(US)*; **~änderung** attitude change; **~antrag** *(Zwangsvollstreckungsverfahren)* application for stay of proceedings; **~anweisung** *(Strafverfahren)* letters of abolition; **~bedingungen** conditions of employment, outline specification, hiring conditions *(US)*; **~befragung** *(Betrieb)* main interview; **~befugnis** disposition of an appointment; **~beschluß** *(Zwangsvollstreckung)* stay of execution; **~büro** employment office, recruiting gang (firm) *(US)*; **motorisiertes ~büro** motorized recruiting squad *(US)*; **~gespräch** employment interview; **~gesuch** letter of application; **~grenzen** employment (hiring, *US*) limits; **~kampagne** recruitment campaign *(US)*; **~kosten** setting costs; **~leiter** recruiter *(US)*; **~liste** list of nominees; **~methoden** recruiting methods *(US)*; **~politik** recruitment policy *(US)*; **~prämie** premium; **~programm** recruitment program *(US)*; **~programm für Dauerarbeitslose** hard-core hiring program *(US)*; **~prüfung** entrance (competitive) examination, qualifying test; **~quote, ~rate** accession (employment) rate, hiring quota (rate) *(US)*; **~skala** *(Interviews)* opinion scale; **~sperre** recruitment ban *(US)*; **~stab** recruiting staff *(US)*; **~stopp verfügen** to put a freeze on employment (hirings, *US*); **zentralisiertes ~system** centralized employment (hiring, *US*); **~termin** starting date; **~verbot** recruitment ban *(US)*; **~verfahren** employment procedure, recruitment technique *(US)*; **~verfügung** writ of supersedeas, *(an unteres Gericht)* writ of prohibition *(US)*; **~versuch** recruiting attempt *(US)*; **~vertrag** employment contract; **~voraussetzungen** eligibility for appointment; **~zeit** recruiting season *(US)*, employment period; **~zusage** recruitment obligation; **~zuschuß** employment grant, hiring subsidy *(US)*.

Einstieg *(Bus)* entrance, *(Flugzeug)* boarding;
~luke manhole, *(Panzer)* access hatch.

Einstiegsposition *(Flugzeug)* boarding position.

einstimmig unanimous, with one voice, with one assent, by common consent, consentaneous, with no-one dissenting, without dissent, in a joint and corporate voice;
~ angenommen agreed unanimously; **~ gewählt** unanimously elected;
etw. ~ annehmen to vote solidly for s. th.; **Vorschlag ~ annehmen** to carry a vote unanimously; **~ beschließen** to vote unanimously; **sich ~ weigern** to refuse with one voice;
~er Beschluß unanimous vote.

Einstimmigkeit unanimity, unanimous vote;
~ in allen Punkten agreement on all points; **~ eines Votums** solidarity of a vote;
~ erzielen to achieve unanimity; **Beschluß mit ~ fassen** to adopt a resolution unanimously.

einstöckig one-storied (-storeyed);
~e Bauweise single-storey construction; **~es Haus** one-storey house, bungalow.

Einstrahlung insolation.

einstreichen, Dividenden to rake in dividends; **ganzen Gewinn ~** to sweep the board; **Provision ~** to pocket a commission.

einstreuen, Zitate to interlard with quotations.

Einströmen *(Luft)* entrainment.

einströmen *(Luft)* to entrain, *(Wasser)* to pour in.

einstudieren to make a thorough study, *(Theater)* to rehearse, to produce;
Rolle ~ to learn a role; **mit jem. eine Rolle ~** to coach s. o. in a part.

einstudiert, nicht unstudied;
~ werden to be in rehearsal.

Einstudierung *(Aufführung)* staging, production, *(Rolle)* study.

einstufen to scale, to classify, to group, to grade, to categorize, to label, to place in a category, *(steuerlich)* to graduate, to assess, to rate;
hoch ~ to rate high; **j. höher ~** *(Versicherung)* to rate s. o. up, to upgrade s. o.; **neu ~** to reclassify; **gehaltlich neu ~** to regrade; **tariflich niedriger ~** to downgrade, to demote; **j. in eine höhere Steuerklasse ~** to put s. o. in higher tax brackets; **Waren nach Güteklassen ~** to grade goods.

Einstufung categorization, classification, *(Angestellte)* employee rating *(US)*, grading, *(steuerlich)* assessment, rating, graduation;
berufliche ~ job grading, service rating; **höhere ~** promotional classification; **niedrigere ~** *(Tarif)* downgrading, demotion; **preisliche ~** graduation of prices;
~ nach Güteklassen grading of commodities; **~ nach der Leistungsfähigkeit** performance rating; **~ in eine höhere Lohngruppe** promotional classification change; **~ in eine niedrigere Lohngruppe** demotional classification change; **niedrige ~ ohne Lohnkürzung** ingrade classification change;
~en vornehmen to make classifications.

Einstufungs|abänderungsantrag application for changes in the classification; **~ausschuß** *(Steuer)* classification committee; **~fehler** rating error *(US)*; **~gruppe** class, grade; **~programm** rating program(me); **~skala** *(Angestellte)* rating scale *(US)*; **~system** grading practice, rating system *(US)*; **~tabelle** classification schedule, *(Angestellte)* rating scale *(US)*; **~test** grading test; **~verfahren, ~vorgang** rating process *(US)*.

einstündig one-hour.

einstürmen, mit Fragen auf j. to pester (assail, bombard) s. o. with questions.

Einsturz *(Gebäude)* fall, collapse, crash;
durch ein Erdbeben zum ~ gebracht thrown down by an earthquake;
kurz vor dem ~ stehen to be about to collapse.

einstürzen *(Ereignisse auf j.)* to crowd in, *(Gebäude)* to collapse, to tumble down, to fall [down];
wie ein Kartenhaus ~ to collapse like a house of cards.

Einsturz|gefahr!, Vorsicht! danger! building unsafe!; **~klausel** *(Versicherung)* fallen-building clause.

einstweilig provisional, provisory, temporary, in the interim, interlocutory;
~**e Anordnung** provisional arrangement (remedy); ~**e Lösung** provisional solution; ~**e Regelung** interim solution; ~**er Ruhestand** half-pay; ~**er Schriftführer** secretary for the time being; ~**e Verfügung** restraining (interlocutory) order, provisional injunction, extent; ~**e Verfügung aufheben** to dissolve an injunction; **Weg der** ~**en Verfügung beschreiten** to use an injunctive route; ~**es Verfügungsverfahren** injunctive process.
eintägig lasting one day, ephemeral.
Ein|tagsfliege mayfly, passing fad, *(fig.)* ephemera; ~**tänzer** gigolo.
eintasten to key in, *(Computer)* to feed.
Eintausch exchange, barter, truck, trucking, swap *(coll.)*, trade-in *(US coll.)*;
im ~ gegen in return (exchange) for.
eintauschbar convertible;
nicht ~ inconvertible.
eintauschen to barter, to [receive in] exchange, to truck, to swap, to swop *(coll.)*, *(in Zahlung geben)* to trade in *(US)*;
alte Aktien in neue ~ to exchange old shares (stocks, *US*) for new ones; **ausländische Briefmarken** ~ to swop foreign stamps *(coll.)*.
Eintauschwagen trade-in car *(US)*.
einteilen to divide, *(zur Arbeit)* to detail, to assign, *(einklassifizieren)* to grade, to class, to classify, *(Meßinstrument)* to graduate, *(verteilen)* to distribute, to parcel out;
sich etw. ~ to make s. th. last; **j. zu einer Arbeit** ~ to detail (tell off) s. o. for a particular service; **seine Arbeit** ~ to plan (organize) one's work; **Beamte in neun Klassen** ~ to classify officers in nine grades; **Bevölkerung nach Einkommensklassen** ~ to grade the population according to income; **Buch in Kapitel** ~ to divide a book into chapters; **sein Geld** ~ to husband one's money, to suit one's expenditure; **in Gruppen** ~ to group; **in Klassen** ~ to classify, to class, to grade; **Meßinstrument** ~ to calibrate an instrument; **in Phasen** ~ to phase; **Stadt in Bezirke** ~ to divide a town into wards; **seinen ganzen Tag genau** ~ to plan (schedule, *US*) one's day in detail; **seine Vorräte für die ganze Woche** ~ to deal out one's provisions for the whole week; **zum Wachdienst** ~ to detail for guard duty; **seine Zeit** ~ to budget one's time;
nicht ~ **können** to be a bad manager.
einteilig one-piece.
Einteilung division, distribution, regimentation, *(Anordnung)* disposition, arrangement, *(Klassifizierung)* graduation, scale, classification, grouping;
~ **der Arbeit** planning (organization) of one's work; ~ **der Außenstände nach Fälligkeit** aging accounts; ~ **der Erde in Breitengrade** division of the earth into latitudes; ~ **in Frachttarifzonen** freight classification; ~ **in Gefahrenklassen** *(Versicherung)* classification of risks; ~ **nach Güteklassen** grading of commodities; ~ **der Waggons nach Klassen** classification of cars; **willkürliche** ~ **in Wahlbezirke** gerrymander *(US)*; ~ **von Waren in Zolltarife** classification of goods in custom tariffs; ~ **der Zeit** time budget (management), scheduling one's time *(US)*, timing; ~ **in Zonen** zoning, zonation;
keine ~ **haben** to have no sense of planning, *(in finanziellen Dingen)* to be a bad manager; ~ **nach Klassen vornehmen** to make a classification.
Einteilungssystem system of classification.
eintönig monotonous, humdrum;
~**e Arbeit** tedious (dull) work; ~**es Leben** dull life.
Eintonner one-ton truck.
Eintopfgericht stew, hotpot, hodgepodge, hotchpotch.
Eintracht concord, unity, union, harmony;
in völliger ~ **leben** to live in perfect union.
Eintrag entering, entry, registration, register, *(Buchungsposten)* entry, item;
berichtigender ~ adjusting entry; **falscher** ~ misentry, wrong (fraudulent) entry; **kein** ~ *(Vorstrafenliste)* no previous conviction; **nachträglicher** ~ postentry;
~ **einer Gegenbuchung** reversing of entry; ~ **ohne Gegenbuchung** single entry;
~ **ins Klassenbuch erhalten** to get a black mark; ~ **vornehmen** to make an entry.
eintragen *(amtlich)* to register, to incorporate, to list, to docket, to record, *(buchen)* to book, to enter, to post, to make an entry, to pass into the books, to record, *(Bücher in Katalog)* to accession *(US)*, *(einfügen)* to insert, to write in, *(einschreiben)* to write (put) down, to enter, *(Gewinn)* to yield, to bring in, to return, to fetch, *(in eine Liste)* to inscribe, to list, to item, *(ins Logbuch)* to log, *(als Mitglied)* to enrol(l), *(in Wahliste)* to poll, to register, *(Wetterkarte)* to plot;
sich ~ to enter one's name, to put o. s. down, to register o. s.; **als AG** ~ to incorporate *(US)*; **amtlich** ~ to make an official entry; **falsch** ~ to mis-enter, to make a wrong entry; **Firma handelsgerichtlich** ~ to register (incorporate, *US*) a company; **auf dem Führerschein** ~ to endorse a licence; **sich ins Gästebuch** ~ *(Hotel)* to sign the visitors' book; **Geschworenen in die Schöffenliste** ~ to empanel (impanel) a juror; **hohen Gewinn** ~ to pay well, to be profitable; **sich als Journalist** ~ to put o. s. down as a journalist; **in eine Liste** ~ to [enter in a] list; **sich in eine Liste** ~ to give in one's name, to put one's name down; **seinen Namen** ~ to register one's name; **neu** ~ to reincorporate; **in sein Notizbuch** ~ to enter in one's notebook; **Ordinate eines Punktes** ~ to plot the ordinates of a point; **j. polizeilich** ~ to lodge s. o. in the registry; **Posten ins Hauptbuch** ~ to enter an item into the ledger; **rein** ~ to net; **jem. Ruhm** ~ to bring s. o. fame; **j. in die Schöffenliste** ~ to empanel a juror; **Schutzmarke** ~ to register a trademark; **Sperrvermerk im Grundbuch** ~ to vacate a registration; **viel** ~ *(Geschäft)* to be paying (a lucrative business), to pay well; **nicht viel** ~ to be unremunerative, to yield little; **sich in die Wählerliste** ~ to register o. s. in the voting list; **wieder** ~ to reregister, to replace on the register;
sich ~ **lassen** to give one's name; **Geburt eines Kindes** ~ **lassen** to have a child's birth registered; **gerichtlich** ~ **lassen** to file with the court; **sich im Gesellschaftsregister** ~ **lassen** to file accounts with the Registrar of Companies *(Br.)*; **sich als Grundstückserwerber** ~ **lassen** to enter land *(US)*; **Hypothek ins Grundbuch** ~ **lassen** to register (record, *US*) a mortgage; **Verein** ~ **lassen** to incorporate a club.
einträglich remunerative, profitable, gainful, paying, lucrative, revenue-earning, yielding, fat, beneficial to business;
nicht ~ gainless, unremunerative;
~ **beschäftigt** gainfully employed (occupied);
~ **sein** to bring grist to the mill;
~**es Amt** lucrative office (business); ~**e Beschäftigung** gainful occupation; ~**es Geschäft** paying (profitable) business.
Einträglichkeit profitableness, profitability, lucrativeness, remunerativeness.
Eintragung posting, *(amtlich)* registry, register, registration, incorporation, recording *(US)*, docketing, *(Buchung)* entering [up], entry, recording, booking, posting, *(Buchungsposten)* item, entry, *(Einfügung)* inscription, insertion, *(als Mitglied)* enrolment;
laut ~ as per entry; **mangels** ~ for want of record;
falsche ~ mis-entry; **fehlerhafte** ~ erroneous entry, improper registration; **handelsgerichtliche** ~ registration of business name (company, corporation), incorporation *(US)*; **nachträgliche** ~ postentry, subsequent entry; **periodische** ~ periodic entry; **unrichtige** ~ false entry; **zollamtliche** ~**en** customs entries; **zusammengefaßte** ~ *(Journalbuchung)* compound journal entry;
~ **einer Geburt** registration of a birth; ~ **ohne Gegenbuchung** single entry; ~ **eines Geschmacksmusters** registration of a design; ~ **in die Geschworenenliste** impanelment; ~ **einer Gesellschaft ins Handelsregister** partnership registration *(Br.)*, incorporation of a company *(US)*; ~ **von Grundbesitz** land registration; ~ **ins Grundbuch** recording of title, entry made in the register, land registration *(Br.)*; ~ **von Grundbuchbelastungen** registration of [land] charges; ~ **einer kommunalen Grundstückslast** registration of notice; ~ **einer Handelsgesellschaft** registration of a company *(Br.)*; ~ **ins Handelsregister** registration of business name, incorporation *(US)*; ~ **einer Hypothek** registration of a mortgage, recording of a mortgage *(US)*; ~ **ins Journal** journalization; ~ **auf einer Liste** listing; ~ **eines Patents (in die Patentrolle)** registration (issue) of a patent; ~ **im Schiffsregister** registry of a ship, marine registry *(Br.)*; ~ **einer Vormerkung** lodging of a caution; ~ **in die Wählerliste** registration of voters, general registration; ~ **eines Warenzeichens (in die Warenzeichenrolle)** registration of a trademark, trademark registration;
~**en abändern (berichtigen)** to rectify entries; **keine** ~ **enthalten** to record no mention; ~ **löschen** to expunge a registration, to cancel an entry, to vacate an entry of record; ~**en im Buch löschen** to strike off (delete) entries, to cancel registrations; ~ **eines Warenzeichens löschen** to expunge the registration of a trademark; ~ **machen** to pass an entry; **nach einer bestimmten** ~ **suchen** to search for a particular registration; ~ **im Personenstandsregister unterzeichnen** to sign the register *(Br.)*;

einer Firma die handelsgerichtliche ~ **versagen** to refuse to register a business; **falsche** ~ **vornehmen** to make a wrong entry, to mis-enter; ~ **auf dem Führerschein vornehmen** to endorse a licence; ~ **verbindlich vorschreiben** to make registration compulsory.

Eintragungs|anspruch registration privilege *(US)*; ~**antrag** application for registration; ~**antrag zurückweisen** to deny a registration; ~**bedingungen** registration requirements; ~**bescheinigung** certificate of registry, registration certificate; ~**beschluß** decree of registration; ~**bewilligung** *(Grundbuch)* recording consent *(US)*; ~**buch** entry book, register; ~**datum** date of registration; ~**dauer** registration period; ~**erfordernisse** recording requirements *(US)*.

eintragungsfähig registrable, capable of being registered, eligible for registration, recordable;
nur dem Kapital nach ~ registrable as to principal only.

Eintragungs|fähigkeit registrability; ~**gebühr** booking (filing, recording, *US*, registration, incorporation) fee, expenses of registration; ~- **und Umschreibegebühr** registration and transfer fee; ~**genehmigung** *(Grundbuch)* recording consent *(US)*; ~**hindernisse** obstacles to registration; ~**kosten** booking fees, posting (entry) costs, expenses of registration, recording fees *(US)*; ~**nummer** registered (registration) number; **von der** ~**pflicht ausnehmen** to provide an exemption from registration.

eintragungspflichtig subject to registration;
~ **sein** to require one's registration.

Eintragungs|stelle registry; ~**system** *(Grundbuch)* recording system *(US)*; ~**system nach zeitlichen Präferenzen** *(Grundbuch)* race-type statute *(US)*; ~**termin** date of inscription (registration); ~**unterlagen** registration statement *(US)*; ~**urkunde** registration certificate; ~**verbot** *(Grundbuch)* inhibition *(Br.)*; ~**verfahren** registration proceedings; ~**verlauf** recording routine; ~**vermerk** memorandum of registration, registration, note of entry; ~**voraussetzungen** recording requirements, essentials to registration; ~**vorgang** recording act; ~**wirkung** effect of registration; ~**zwang** compulsory registration.

eintränken, es jem. to make s. o. smart for it, to play s. o. a dirty trick.

einträufeln to infuse, to instil drops.

Eintreffen arrival, incoming;
bis zum ~ **weiterer Nachrichten** pending further news.

eintreffen to arrive, to come to hand (in), *(Prophezeiung)* to come true;
bei jem. ~ to reach s. o.; **rechtzeitig am Bestimmungsort** ~ to reach one's destination in good time; **absolut pünktlich** ~ to arrive at the minute; **stoßweise** ~ to arrive in batches; **um neun Uhr** ~ **sollen** to be due at nine o'clock; **völlig rechtzeitig** ~ to arrive in plenty of time; **in gutem Zustand** ~ to arrive in good condition.

eintreibbar collectable, exactable, exigible, recoverable, *(auf gesetzlichem Wege)* exigible, enforceable;
nicht ~ not enforceable, unenforceable, judgment-proof *(US)*; **schwer** ~ difficult to collect.

Eintreibbarkeit recoverableness, *(gerichtlich)* enforceableness.

eintreiben to collect, to call in, to recover, *(auf gesetzlichem Wege)* to exact, to enforce, to levy;
Außenstände (Schulden) ~ to make collections, to recover (call in) debts; **Schulden beschleunigt** ~ to speed up collection of debts; **Steuer** ~ to collect (exact, levy) a tax; **Zahlungen gerichtlich** ~ to enforce payments.

Eintreibung recovery, collection, levy;
gerichtliche ~ enforcement;
~ **von Forderungen** collection of debts; ~ **ausstehender Schulden** recovery of amounts outstanding; ~ **von Steuern** exaction (levy) of taxes.

Eintreibungskosten collection (recovering) charges.

Eintreten entry, entrance, *(für j.)* intercession, advocacy, espousal;
unvermutetes ~ supervention;
~ **für besondere Interessen** special pleading *(US)*.

eintreten to enter, to make one's entrance, to come in, *(Dunkelheit)* to fall, *(gesetzliche Folgen)* to attach, *(Haftpflicht)* to accrue, *(Kälte)* to set in, *(Notwendigkeit)* to arise, to crop up, *(als Partner)* to join, to come in, to associate, *(Risiko)* to attach, *(Schwierigkeit)* to crop up, *(vorkommen)* to occur, to take place, to happen, to come to pass;
für etw. ~ to stand for (support, stick up, stand up, speak up for) s. th.; **für j.** ~ to speak in s. one's favo(u)r, to stand up for s. o., to go to bat for s. o., to intercede for s. o., to take up the cudgels for s. o., *(als Ersatz)* to deputize for s. o., to fill s. one's position; **bei jem. für j.** ~ to use one's influence with s. o. on s. one's behalf, to plead s. one's cause with s. o.; **in Beratungen** ~ to enter into consultations; **in die Beweisaufnahme** ~ to take evidence; **in jds. Dienste** ~ to enter into s. one's service; **in eine Erbfolge** ~ to succeed to an inheritance; **in eine Firma** ~ to go in a firm; **in eine Firma als Teilhaber** ~ to enter into partnership, to join a firm as partner; **als Freiwilliger** ~ to volunteer; **in das Geschäft seines Vaters** ~ to join one's father's firm; **für einen Grundsatz** ~ to champion a principle; **häufig** ~ to be a frequent occurrence; **in das Heer** ~ to join the army (ranks); **für eine Idee** ~ to support an idea; **in den Krieg** ~ to enter the war; **für gleichen Lohn** ~ to advocate equal pay; **neu** ~ to join a society; **offen für j.** ~ to speak up for s. o.; **in eine Partei** ~ to join a party; **in jds. Pflichten** ~ to take over s. one's obligations; **in eine neue Phase** ~ to enter a new phase; **wieder in die Plenarsitzung** ~ to resume the session; **plötzlich** ~ to come suddenly; **für seine Rechte** ~ to stand on one's rights; **in jds. Rechte (als Rechtsnachfolger)** ~ to succeed to s. one's rights; **für die Rentner** ~ to plead the case of the old-age pensioners; **für eine Sache** ~ to support a cause, to become an advocate of a cause; **für einen Schaden** ~ to answer for a loss; **als Schuldner** ~ to assume a debt; **sofort** ~ to be instantaneous; **in ein kritisches Stadium** ~ to reach a turning point; **in einen Streik** ~ to come out on strike, to walk out *(US)*; **in die Tagesordnung** ~ to proceed to the order of the day; **für seine Überzeugung** ~ to act up to one's convictions; **unerwartet** ~ to chance; **in einen Verein** ~ to join an association, to enter a club; **in die Verhandlung** ~ to open the proceedings; **in Verhandlungen** ~ to enter into negotiations; **für ein Volksbegehren** ~ to advocate a referendum.

eintretend, bei ~**em Bedarf** if required; **bei** ~**em Frost** if frost sets in.

eintretendenfalls should the case occur, in case of need.

Eintretender entrant, *(Verein)* new member.

eintrichtern, jem. etw. to grind (drum, hammer, cram) s. th. into s. o. (s. one's head).

Eintritt entrance, entry, entering, entrée, *(Anfang)* beginning, *(Ereignis)* coming, *(Zulassung)* admittance, admission, access, *(Zutritt)* ingress;
bei ~ **einer Bedingung** upon the happening of a condition; **bei** ~ **der Dunkelheit** after dark; **bei** ~ **des Erbfalls** upon devolution of the estate; **bei** ~ **des Todes** upon death; **beim** ~ **eines Schadensfalles** at the time (upon the occurrence) of a loss; **beim** ~ **ins Zimmer** on entering the room; **nach** ~ **des Schadensfalles** after loss; **nach** ~ **der Volljährigkeit** after majority; **seit** ~ **des Klageanspruchs** from the accrual of the cause of action; **vor** ~ **des Tauwetters** before the thaw sets in;
~ **frei** admission free, no charge for admission, open door; ~ **verboten!** no admittance!, private!; **Kinder haben freien** ~ children [are] admitted free;
freier ~ admission free, free admission;
~ **einer Bedingung** fulfilment of a condition; ~ **in einen Bundesstaat** accession to a confederacy; ~ **in die Bundeswehr** [etwa] entry into the forces; ~ **nur auf Grund besonderer Einladung** admission by invitation only; ~ **in eine Erbfolge** succession to an inheritance; ~ **des den Klageanspruch begründenden Ereignisses** accrual of a cause of action; ~ **in ein Geschäft** initiation into a business, joining of a firm; ~ **eines Landes in den Krieg** entering of a country into the war; ~ **in eine Laufbahn** entering upon a career; ~ **ins Leben** launch into life; ~ **in eine Partei** joining a party; ~ **in Rechte** subrogation of rights; ~ **in die Regierung** entrance upon a ministerial office; ~ **in die Tagesordnung** proceeding to the order of the day; ~ **eines Teilhabers** joining a firm as (admission of a) partner; ~ **in einen Verein** initiation into a society; ~ **des Versicherungsfalles** occurrence of the event insured against, occurrence of loss; ~ **der Volljährigkeit** coming of age;
~ **erlangen** to get admission to; **sich den** ~ **erschleichen** to gateerash, to rug-cut *(sl.)*; **möglichen** ~ **eines Ereignisses erwägen** to consider the possibility of an event; **jem. den** ~ **in einen Klub nicht gestatten** to blackball s. o. from a club; **freien** ~ **haben** to have free entrance, to be admitted gratis; ~ **verlangen** to charge admission; **sich gewaltsam** ~ **verschaffen** to force one's entry; ~ **verwehren** to deny access;
Unbefugten ist der ~ **verboten!** no entrance (admittance) except on business!, no unauthorized entry!

Eintritts|alter entry age, age-at-entry; ~**bescheinigung** entrance certificate; ~**datum** entry point; ~**erlaubnis** entrance, admission; ~**examen** entrance (competitive) examination; ~**gebühr** [entrance] fee, charge of admission (admittance), door money, *(Verein)* initiation fee *(US)*; ~**geld** entrance (entry, door, gate) money, entrance fee, admission [fee], admission charge; **sein ~geld bezahlen** to pay one's entrance; **~hafen** port of entry; **~karte** admission card (ticket), voucher, entry card, pass check *(US)*, paste-board *(sl.)*; **teuerste ~karte** top ticket; **verbilligte ~karte** throwaway, reduced ticket; **~kasse** box office; **~phase** *(Raumschiff)* reentry; **~preis** admission [fee], price of admission, cost of entry, entrance fee, admission, entrance price; **~prüfung** entrance (competitive) examination; **~prüfung bestehen** to pass the entrance examination; **~recht** right of preemption; **befristetes ~recht** option; **~termin** date of admission; **~verpflichtung** pledge; **~voraussetzungen** entrance requirements; **~voraussetzungen für eine Vereinsmitgliedschaft erfüllen** to be eligible for membership in a society.

eintrüben, sich to become dull.

Eintrübung dull weather.

eintüten to put into paper bags.

einüben to practise, to study;
mit jem. etw. ~ to coach s. o. in a part.

einverleiben to incorporate, to embody, to annex, to nationalize *(Br.)*;
sich ~ to put into one's system; **sich ein anderes Gebiet ~** to annex another territory; **ein Stück seiner Sammlung ~** to add a piece to one's collection.

einverleibt incorporate.

Einverleibung incorporation, embodiment, nationalization *(Br.)*, *(Annektion)* annexation;
~ in seine Sammlung addition to one's collection; **~ fremden Staatsgebiets** incorporation of territory.

Einvernahme hearing, interrogation.

Einvernehmen understanding, agreement, harmony, concord;
im ~ mit in accordance, in concert (agreement) with, after consultation; **im gegenseitigen ~** by agreement between themselves, by mutual agreement; **im ~ mit seinen Kollegen** working in concert with one's colleagues; **in gutem ~** on friendly terms;
gegenseitiges ~ mutual arrangement; **geheimes ~** secret understanding; **gutes ~** good understanding, amity; **gütliches ~** friendly understanding; **stillschweigendes ~** tacit understanding;
gutes ~ unter den Nationen comity of nations;
in bestem ~ leben to live in perfect harmony; **sich mit jem. ins ~ setzen** to come to an understanding with s. o.; **mit der Gegenpartei in ~ treten** *(Anwalt)* to prevaricate.

einvernehmen, j. to to interrogate (examine) s. o.; **Zeugen ~** to examine a witness.

einvernehmlich with (by mutual) consent.

Einvernehmlichkeitserklärung statement of understanding.

einverstanden|! agreed!, okay! *(US sl.)*, *(Politik)* content *(Br.)*;
sich mit etw. ~ erklären to express one's approval with s. th.; **~ sein** to agree, to accept, to assent, to consent; **mit jem. ~ sein** to be in agreement with s. o.; **nicht ~ sein** to disagree, to disapprove; **mit jem. nicht ~ sein** to disapprove of s. o., to be at variance with s. o.; **mit jds. Bedingungen ~ sein** to assent to s. one's conditions; **mit einem Preis ~ sein** to be willing to pay a price; **mit einem Vorschlag ~ sein** to be in agreement with a proposal.

einverständlich by mutual consent;
~ von etw. Kenntnis nehmen to understand and agree;
~e Vertragsbeendigung discharge by agreement.

Einverständnis consent, assent, accord, agreement, understanding, concurrence;
im ~ mit in suit with; **im strafbaren ~ mit** done with the connivance of; **in gegenseitigem ~** by mutual consent; **von jds. ~ abhängig** subject of s. one's approval;
geheimes (heimliches) ~ connivance, collusion, secret understanding; **mündliches ~** verbal agreement; **schriftliches ~** written consent; **stillschweigendes ~** tacit understanding, acquiescence, implied consent;
~ mit einem Antrag consent to a request;
wenn kein ~ erreicht wird failing agreement;
sein ~ erklären to express one's approval; **~ über etw. erzielen** to come to an understanding; **sein ~ geben** to approve of; **sein ~ mit einem Plan zu verstehen geben** to intimate one's approval of a plan; **im ~ mit jem. handeln** to act in agreement with s. o.; **stets in gegenseitigem ~ handeln** to hunt in couples; **im geheimen ~ mit jem. handeln** to collude (act in collusion) with s. o.; **mit jem. im geheimen ~ stehen** to be in connivance with s. o., to connive with s. o.; **im geheimen ~ mit dem Feinde stehen** to aid and comfort the enemy;
~erklärung mit den allgemeinen Geschäftsbedingungen *(Bankwesen)* [budget] charge agreement.

Einwand reclamation, objection, *(jur.)* defence, defense *(US)*, plea, demurrer, *(Vorwand)* pretext;
formeller ~ technical traverse; **auf Formfehler gestützter ~** special demurrer; **klageleugnender ~** preemptory exception; **persönlicher ~** personal defence; **rechtshemmender ~** estoppel; **schikanöser ~** frivolous plea; **schlüssiger ~** available plea; **unerheblicher ~** immaterial objection; **unwesentlicher ~** immaterial issue; **unzulässiger ~** inadmissible defence (defense, *US*); **wesentlicher ~** material issue;
~ der fehlenden Beweiserheblichkeit demurrer to evidence; **~ der Genehmigung des Grundstückseigentümers** leave and licence; **~ der Minderjährigkeit** plea of infancy (the Baby Act, *US*); **~ der Nichtigkeit** plea of nullity; **~ der mangelnden Passivlegitimation** interpleader; **~ der Rechtskraftswirkung** estoppel by judgment; **~ des seinerzeitigen Stands der Technik** *(Patentrecht)* state of the art defence; **~ der Unschlüssigkeit** general demurrer; **~ der Unzuständigkeit** jurisdictional (foreign) plea, plea as to jurisdiction; **~ der Vorausklage** *(Bürge)* benefit of discussion; **~ der geleisteten Zahlung** plea of payment; **~ gegen die Zuständigkeit** jurisdictional plea;
~ nicht anerkennen to ignore an objection; **~ entkräften** to refute an objection; **~ erheben** to raise a query (objection); **~ der Ausländereigenschaft erheben** to put in a plea of alienism; **~ der Fälschung erheben** to put in a plea of forgery; **~ der Minderjährigkeit erheben** to plead the Baby Act *(US)* (infancy); **~ der Nichterrichtung einer Urkunde erheben** to raise a plea of non est factum; **~ der Prozeßunfähigkeit erheben** to declare to have no right of action; **rechtshemmenden ~ erheben** to estop; **~ der Unzurechnungsfähigkeit erheben** to plead insanity; **~ der Unzuständigkeit erheben** to enter a plea in bar of trial; **sich über einen ~ hinwegsetzen** to override an argument; **keinen weiteren ~ machen** to raise no further objection; **einem ~ stattgeben** to sustain an objection; **~ übergehen** to foreclose an objection; **~ vorbringen** to present a plea; **Einwand der Unkenntnis vorbringen** to plead ignorance; **~ der Verjährung vorbringen** to plead the statute of limitations; **~ widerlegen** to refute an objection; **~ zurückweisen** to overrule an objection;
dem ~ wird nicht stattgegeben objection overruled.

Einwände, trotz der notwithstanding the objections;
~ erheben to make objections; **keine ~ erheben** to make no demurrer; **stichhaltige ~ gegen einen Plan erheben** to raise valid objections to a scheme; **alle ~ überkommen** to face down all objections; **~ vorwegnehmen** to preclude objections; **jds. ~n zuvorkommen** to obviate s. one's objections.

Einwanderer immigrant, new chum *(Australia, sl.)*;
illegaler ~ wetback *(sl.)*;
europäische ~ assimilieren to assimilate people from European countries;
~zahl immigration figures.

einwandern to migrate to a country, to immigrate.

Einwanderung immigration;
~ zulassen to admit immigrants.

Einwanderungs|abteilung immigration department; **~beamter** immigration officer; **~behörde** immigration office (authorities); **von den ~behörden festgehalten werden** to be held up by the immigration authorities; **~beschränkungen** immigration restrictions; **~bestimmungen** immigration regulations; **~erlaubnis** immigration permit; **~frage** immigration issue; **~gesetz** Race Relations Act *(Br.)*, Immigration and Nationality Act *(US)*; **~kontingent** immigration quota; **~kontrolle** immigration control; **~land** immigration country; **~papiere** immigration papers; **~politik** immigration policy; **~projekt** immigration scheme; **~quote** immigration quota; **~recht** immigration law, quota law *(US)*; **~sperre** ban on immigration; **~sperre beschließen** to slam the door on new immigrants; **~steuer** head tax *(US)*; **~stopp** moratorium on immigration, immigration bar; **~stopp erlassen** to exclude immigrants from the country; **~verbot** ban of immigration; **~verfahren** immigration proceedings; **~visum** immigration visa.

einwandfrei faultless, flawless, correct, accurate, above board, unobjectionable, perfectly satisfactory, irreproachable, *(Bilanz)* uncooked, *(Leumund)* spotless, unblemished, immaculate, *(unanfechtbar)* incontestable;
charakterlich ~ of good moral character; **juristisch ~** watertight; **moralisch ~** decent, unimpeachable; **nicht ~** faulty, objectionable, shady;
für ~ befinden to clear; **sich ~ benehmen** to behave irreproachably; **~ feststehen** to be beyond question; **für ~ halten** to deem fit and proper; **~ laufen** *(Motor)* to run perfectly; **etw. ~ nachweisen** to establish s. th. beyond doubt;

~es **Alibi** perfect alibi; ~e **Beweise** incontestable proof; ~e **Führung** irreproachable conduct; **nicht ganz** ~es **Geschäft** shady transaction; ~er **Pachtvertrag** watertight lease; ~es **Patent** clean patent; **aus völlig** ~er **Quelle** from an unimpeachable source; ~e **Vergangenheit** clean record; ~er **Wechsel** clean (approved) bill; **in** ~em **Zustand** in perfect condition.

einwechseln to change, to [give in] exchange, *(Banknoten)* to convert, *(einlösen)* to cash;
ausländisches Geld ~ to change foreign currency.

Einwechselung exchange, change, *(Banknoten)* conversion.

einwecken to preserve.

Einweckglas preserve jar.

Einweg|behälter one-trip container *(US)*; ~**erzeugnis** one-trip product; ~**flasche** nonreturnable (nondeposit, *US*) bottle; ~**güter** disposables; ~**miete** *(Autovermietung)* one-way rental; ~**packung** one-way (nonreturnable, expendable) package; ~**schalter** one-way switch.

einweihen to inaugurate, to dedicate *(US)*;
Denkmal ~ to inaugurate a monument; **jem. in ein Geheimnis** ~ to let (initiate) s. o. into a secret; **Kleid** ~ to wear a dress for the first time; **Schiffahrtskanal** ~ to inaugurate a ship canal; **in eine Verschwörung** ~ to let into a plot; **Wohnung** ~ to give a house-warming party.

Einweihung inauguration, dedication *(US)*.

Einweihungs|feierlichkeiten inaugural (dedication, *US*) ceremonies; ~**fest** *(Haus)* flat-warming, house-warming party; ~**rede** inaugural (inauguration) address; ~**zeremonien** initiatory ceremonies.

einweisen to direct, to instruct, to install, *(Angestellten in Betrieb)* to escort, to brief, *(mit Radar)* to vector;
j. in sein Amt ~ to install s. o. in (escort s. o. into) his office, to introduce s. o. in his duties; **Angestellten in die Buchführung** ~ to instruct a clerk in bookkeeping; **in den Besitz** ~ to vest in possession; **j. in den Besitz einer Erbschaft** ~ to serve s. o. heir to a property; **neuen Betriebsangehörigen** ~ to be sponsor for a new employee; **Flugzeug** ~ to direct an aircraft; **in eine Heil- und Pflegeanstalt** ~ to remand to a mental hospital *(US)*; **j. in ein Krankenhaus** ~ to commit s. o. to a hospital, to hospitalize s. o. *(US)*; **j. in ein Lager** ~ to send s. o. to a camp; **j. in eine Parklücke** ~ to direct s. o. into a parking space; **j. in eine Wohnung** ~ to assign quarters (a flat) to s. o.

Einweisung instruction, direction, *(in Amt)* installation, *(in Betrieb)* introduction, escort, briefing, committal, *(in Wohnung)* assignment;
~ **in den Besitz** vesting order; ~ **in eine Erziehungsanstalt** detention in a reformatory; ~ **in eine Heil- und Pflegeanstalt** admission to a mental hospital; ~ **in ein Krankenhaus** committal to a hospital, hospitalization *(US)*; **vorläufige** ~ **in eine Nervenheilanstalt** summary reception order.

Einweisungs|anordnung commitment to prison, order of commitment; ~**beschluß in eine Irrenanstalt** certificate of lunacy; ~**schema** *(Betrieb)* escort plan; ~**vollmacht** *(Gericht)* vesting power.

einwenden to object, to raise an objection, to protest, *(jur.)* to plead, to set up;
~, **daß** ... to submit the plea that ...; **Bedürftigkeit** ~ to plead poverty; **Minderjährigkeit** ~ to plead infancy (the Baby Act, *US*); **Unzurechnungsfähigkeit** ~ to plead insanity, to enter (put forward) a plea of insanity; **Unzuständigkeit** ~ to enter a plea in bar of trial; **Verjährung** ~ to plead the Statute of Limitations; ~, **in Wahrung gerechtfertigter Interessen gehandelt zu haben** to plead justification and privilege; **verspätete Zustellung** ~ to plead postal delay.

Einwendung objection, protest, challenge, *(jur.)* plea, defence, defense *(US)*, exception *(US)*, demurrer;
berechtigte ~ good defence; **auf bestimmte Wechselinhaber beschränkte** ~en personal defence; **gestaffelte** ~en *(Leumundsprozeß)* rolled-up plea; **alle nur möglichen** ~en full defence; **persönliche** ~ equitable defence; **prozessuale** ~ special demurrer; **rechtserhebliche** ~ valid objection; **rechtshindernde** ~ plea of confession and avoidance; **rechtsvernichtende** ~ affirmative plea, traverse; **sachliche** ~ issuable defence, plea; **schikanöse** ~en pettifogging objections; **unzulässige** ~ defence not available; **zusätzliche** ~ supplemental plea;
~ **der unzulässigen Anspruchshäufung** double plea; ~ **mittels Gegenvorbringen** colo(u)rable pleading; ~ **höherer Gewalt** commercial frustration; ~ **formaler Unzulässigkeit** action of a writ; ~ **verspäteter Zustellung** plea of postal delay;
~**en erheben** to enter (lodge, raise) a protest, to demur, to except, to object, to interpose a demurrer, *(gegen Wahlergebnis)* to challenge *(US)*; **keine** ~**en erheben** to make no objection, to give way without protest; ~**en machen** to start an objection, to take exception against, to demur; **auf die Geltendmachung von** ~**en verzichten** to waive a defence; **sich** ~**en vorbehalten** to reserve defence; ~**en vorbringen** to show cause; **übertriebene** ~**en vorbringen** to cavil; ~**en zurückweisen** to overrule objections.

einwerfen, Brief to post (mail, *US*) a letter; **Fensterscheiben** ~ to smash (break) window panes; **Münze in einen Automaten** ~ to insert a coin in a slot machine.

einwickeln, j. to run rings around s. o.; **sich in eine Decke** ~ to wind a blanket round o. s.; **in Papier** ~ to wrap up in paper.

Einwickelpapier wrapping (brown, *Br.*, kraft, *US*) paper.

einwiegen, j. mit falschen Hoffnungen to lull s. o. with false hopes.

einwilligen to comply, to consent, to agree, to accede, to allow, to assent to, to say yes;
in ein Angebot ~ to be open to an offer; **in jds. Bedingungen** ~ to accept s. one's conditions; **in die festgelegten Bedingungen** ~ to agree as to certain conditions; **in eine Preisherabsetzung** ~ to consent to a reduction of price; **in jds. Vorschläge** ~ to consent to s. one's proposals; **widerstandslos** ~ to acquiesce.

Einwilligung agreement, assent, consent, allowance, compliance, authorization, sufferance, leaven;
elterliche ~ parental consent; **fehlende** ~ lack of consent; **schriftliche** ~ written assent; **stillschweigende** ~ acquiescence; ~ **in eine Preisherabsetzung** consent to a reduction of price; **jds.** ~ **erhalten** to obtain s. one's consent; **seine** ~ **erteilen** to give one's consent; **jds.** ~ **sicher sein** to be sure of s. one's compliance; **seine** ~ **vorenthalten** to withhold one's consent.

einwirken to [exert (exercise)] influence;
auf j. ~ to work (exercise one's influence) on s. o.; **beschwichtigend auf j.** ~ to exert a soothing influence on s. o.; **günstig auf j.** ~ to have a favo(u)rable effect on s. o.; **wechselseitig aufeinander** ~ to act upon each other, to interact; ~ **lassen** to bring to bear upon; **etw. auf sich** ~ **lassen** to succumb to the spell of s. th.

Einwirkung effect, influence, impact;
unter der ~ **von Alkohol** under the influence of alcohol; **liquiditätspolitische** ~en liquidity-creating effect; **notenbankpolitische** ~en central bank policy; **schädliche** ~ *(auf Nachbargrundstück)* nuisance; **wechselseitige** ~ interaction; **jds. persönliche** ~ **erkennen lassen** to carry the personal stamp of s. o.

Einwohner inhabitant, resident, citizen, *(pl.)* country, people, land, resident, population;
~**kartei** parish book (register); ~**meldeamt** population (general, *Br.*) register, registration office; ~**meldepflicht** compulsory registration; ~**schaft** inhabitants, people, [resident] population, resident community; ~**steuer** inhabitant (poll) tax, resident tax; ~**verzeichnis** directory; ~**zahl** number of inhabitants, *(Land)* population.

Einwurf objection, interjection, *(Briefe)* slit, *(Münzen)* slot;
~ **vorbringen** to make an interjection, to object.

einwurzeln to take root.

Einzahl singular.

einzahlbar payable.

einzahlen to pay in, to [pay a] deposit *(Br.)*, to consign;
Aktien voll ~ to pay up shares; **bei der Bank** ~ to pay into the bank; **eingeforderten Betrag auf Aktien** ~ to pay a call on shares; **Betrag als Deckung** ~ to pay in an amount as a deposit; **zur Gutschrift** ~ to pay in for credit; **Kapital** ~ to pay in capital; **auf ein Konto** ~ to pay into an account; **bei der Post** ~ to pay at the post office; **20 $ per Postanweisung** ~ to take out a postoffice order for $ 20 *(US)*; **wieder** ~ to redeposit.

Einzahler payer, depositor;
~ **einer Zahlungsanweisung** sender of a money order.

Einzahlung payment, paying in, inpayment, lodgment, consignation, *(eingezahlter Betrag)* deposit;
~en money paid in, payments-in, cash items;
nicht belegte ~en unrecorded deposits; **erste** ~ *(auf Aktien)* application call; **teilweise** ~ part payment, payment in part, instal(l)ment;
~**en und Abhebungen** deposits and drawings, *(Bank)* cash paid and received; ~ **auf Aktien** payment (call) on shares; **erste** ~ **auf Aktien** application call; ~**en und Auszahlungen** receipts and payments; ~ **bei der Bank** payment into the bank; ~ **bei Gericht** payment into court; ~ **auf das Grundkapital** assessment of stock; ~ **auf abgerufene Kapitalanteile** payment of calls; ~ **auf ein Konto** payment into an account; ~**en in die Pensionskasse** pension deposits; ~ **auf das eigene Postscheckkonto** payment in holder's own giro account *(Br.)*;

zur ~ auffordern to request payment; **Kapital zur ~ aufrufen** to make a call for capital; **neue ~ auf Aktien ausschreiben** to make a fresh call on shares; **~en entgegennehmen** to receive payments; **~ leisten** to [make a] deposit *(US)*, to pay a deposit *(Br.)*; **~ auf Aktien leisten** to pay a call on shares; **~ machen** to pay money in, to make a deposit *(US)* to pay a deposit *(Br.)*; **~ auf Aktien verlangen** to make a call on shares; **~ vornehmen** to make a deposit, to effect payment.

Einzahlungs|anordnung *(Staatsrechnungswesen)* covering warrant; **~aufforderung** call on shares, notice of call, call letter; **~beleg** credit voucher, credit memorandum *(US)*, paying-in slip *(Br.)*, pay-in slip *(Br.)*, depositary certificate, deposit slip *(US)*, deposit receipt (ticket, *US*); **~beleg, ~durchschlag** duplicate deposit slip; **~bescheinigung** pay-in slip *(Br.)*, deposit receipt (slip, *US*); **bei Sicht ausfolgbare ~bescheinigung einer Bank** demand certificate of deposit *(US)*; **~buch** passbook, bankbook *(US)*, paying-in book *(Br.)*; **~durchschlag** duplicate deposit slip; **~formular** application (paying-in) form; **~kasse** receiving teller's department *(US)*; **~kassierer** receiving cashier (teller, *US*); **~quittung** deposit receipt; **~schalter** collection (paying-in, deposit, *US*) window; **~schein** pay-in (credit) slip, deposit slip (receipt) certificate of deposit *(US)*; **~tag** day of payment; **~termin** date of payment; **~überschuß** *(Sparvorgang)* excess of new savings; **~verpflichtungen** depository obligations, *(auf Aktien)* call-in obligations, *(Bilanz)* liabilities for possible calls on shares; **von weiteren ~verpflichtungen freistellen** to discharge from all calls due; **~zettel** pay-in (credit) slip, deposit slip (receipt) *(US)*.

einzäunen to fence (hedge) in, to enclose, to picket.

Einzäunung enclosure, fence, fencing.

einzeichnen to inscribe, to enter *(Lageplan)* to plot, to line in, to mark on;
sich ~ to enter one's name [on a list], to put o. s. down to subscribe.

Einzeichnung inscription, entry, subscription.

einzeilig one-line, single-line, *(Schreibmaschinentext)* single-spaced.

Einzel|abkommen *(mit Gläubigern)* separate compromise; **~abnehmer** individual purchaser; **~abrede** special arrangement; **~abstimmung** voting by roll-call; **~abteil** single compartment; **~akkord** individual piecework; **~akkordsatz** individual rate; **~aktionär** single shareholder (stockholder, *US*); **~anfertigung** individual (single-part) production, individual output, job work, job shop operation *(US)*, manufacture to customer's specification; **~anfertigungsbetrieb** job shop *(US)*; **~angaben** specification, particulars, detailed information, detail, isolated data; **~anleger** individual investor; **~anschluß** *(Telefon)* single line; **~aufführung** detailed statement, itemization *(US)*, *(Theaterrollen)* credit; **~aufhängung** independent suspension; **~aufstellung** specification, detailed statement, itemized schedule *(US)*; **~auftrag** individual (piecemeal) contract; **~aufzählung** enumeration, itemization *(US)*; **~ausbildung** individual training; **gültige ~ausfuhrgenehmigung** individually validated export licence; **~ausgabe** *(Buchhandel)* separate edition; **~aussteller** individual exhibitor; **unabhängige ~bank** unit bank *(US)*; **~bankwesen** unit banking *(US)*; **~bedingung** single condition; **~befragung der Geschworenen** polling the jury; **~beispiel** isolated instance; **~belüftung** individual air outlet; **in ~beratungen eintreten** *(parl.)* to go into committee; **~bereich** individual area; **~bericht** detailed report; **~beschäftigung** one-man job; **~beschreibung** detailed description; **unrentable ~besorgungen** *(Buchhandlung)* unprofitable individual acquisitions; **~besprechungen** separate discussions, detailed negotiations; **~besteuerung** personal taxation; **~bestimmungen eines Geschäftsabschlusses** details of a business contract; **~betrag** single item, individual amount; **~betreuung** casework; **~betrieb** single plant; **~bett** single bed; **~bewertung** unit (individual) valuation; **~bilanz** individual statement *(US)*; **~bild** *(Film)* frame, still; **~bürge** several guarantor; **~bürgschaft** specific *(US)* (several) guarantee; **~darstellung** monograph; **~depot** custody held for sole depositor, special (specific) deposit *(US)*; **~eigentum** individual proprietorship *(US)*; **~einsatz** *(mil.)* sortie; **~erbfolge** singular succession; **~erfinder** sole inventor; **~erscheinung** isolated instance; **~ersparnisse** individual (personal) savings; **~erzeuger** individual producer; **~etat** separate budget; **~examen** unassembled examination; **~exemplar** odd piece, *(Buch)* single volume; **~exemplarpreis** cover price; **~fabrikation** individual (job) production.

Einzelfahr|karte single [fare], one-way ticket; **~preis** single fare; **~schein** single ticket.

Einzelfall concrete (particular) case, isolated instance (case);
in einem ~ in a given instance; **in jedem ~** in each specific case.

Einzel|fällen, in on particular occasions; **in vergleichbaren ~fällen** in cases of similar nature; **~fallhilfe** social casework; **~fertigung** job production, individual construction *(US)*; **~firma** single firm, sole business (proprietor) *(US)*, single proprietorship *(US)*, individual firm *(US)*, one-man business, individual proprietorship (enterprise) *(US)*; **~flug** *(mil.)* sortie; **feindliches ~flugzeug** intruder; **~frage** point; **~gänger** outsider, individualist, mugrump, lone wolf *(sl.)*, *(Politik)* maverick; **~gängertum** mugrumpery; **~garage** one-car garage; **~garantie** *(Völkerrecht)* individual guarantee; **~genehmigung** special permit, exclusive licence; **~geschäft** retail store, sole proprietorship *(US)*; **~gesellschafter** individual partner; **~gewerbetreibender** sole trader (proprietor, *US*); **~gewerkschaft** union branch, craft union *(US)*; **~haft** solitary (separate) confinement, reclusion; **~haftung** single (several) liability.

Einzelhandel retail[ing], retail[ing] trade, retailing;
im Groß- und ~ wholesale and retail; **vom ~ gefördert** retailer-sponsored;
ungebundener ~ independent retail trade;
~ durch Aufgabe von Rabattmarken zum Schwanken bringen to rock the retail trade by dropping trade stamps; **im ~ führend sein** to lead the retail sector; **Waren im ~ verkaufen** to sell goods [by] retail.

Einzelhandels|abteilung retail department; **~artikel** retail goods; **~artikel außerhalb des Nahrungsmittelsektors** nonfoods; **~artikel auszeichnen** to mark retail merchandise; **~bedürfnisse** retail demands; **~betrieb** retail enterprise (establishment, operation); **~betrieb mit Sonderrabatt** discount house; **~erhebung** dealer survey; **~fachgeschäft** single-line retail store *(US)*, stockist *(Br.)*; **~firma** retail enterprise (establishment, firm); **~funktion** retail function.

Einzelhandelsgeschäft retail shop *(Br.)* (store, *US*, line, house, business), marketing (retail) outlet *(US)*;
selbständiges ~ independent store (outlet) *(US)*;
~ für die landwirtschaftliche Bevölkerung country store;
~e besuchen to make retail calls; **~ betreiben** to retail; **ins ~ einsteigen** to go into retailing; **~ eröffnen** to set up shop.

Einzelhandels|gesellschaft retailing company; **~gewerbe** retail industry (trade); **~gewinnspanne** retail margin; **~höchstpreis** retail ceiling price; **~index** retail price index; **~industrie** retail industry; **~kaufmann** retail trader (dealer); **~kette** retail chain, chain (retailing) organization; **~konjunktur** retail spending boom; **~konkurrenz** retail competitors; **~konzession** retail licence; **~kredit** retail credit; **~kreditauskunftei** retail credit bureau; **~kunde** retail customer (account); **~kunden Warenkredit einräumen** to make sales on credit to retail customers; **~kundschaft** retail clientèle; **~laden mit Rabattsystem** discount shop (store, house, *US*), cut-price shop; **~lizenz** retail licence; **~markt** retail (merchandise) market, retail outlet; **~märkte** retail outlets; **~mindestpreis** minimum resale price; **~mitglied** retail member; **~nettoverdienst** retail net profit; **~organisation** retail sales organization.

einzelhandelsorientiert retailer-affiliated.

Einzelhandels|preis retail [selling] (resale) price, consumer price; **~preisindex** general index of retail prices, index of commodity prices in retail markets; **~rabatt** retail discount; **~reklame** retail advertising; **~richtpreis** recommended retail price; **~spanne** retail margin; **~steuer** retail sales (retailers' excise) tax; **~struktur** retail structure; **~umsatz** retail [trade] turnover, retail sales; **~umsätze** retail-store sales *(US)*; **~umsatzsteuer** retail sales tax; **~unternehmen** retail enterprise (establishment, operation); **~verkauf** sale by retail, retail sale, retail issue (shop selling), retailing; **~verkaufsorganisation** retail sales organization; **~versandgeschäft** mail-order retailer *(US)*; **~verteilung** retail distribution; **~verteilungsstelle** retail distribution agency; **~vertrieb** sale at retail, retail sale; **~volumen** volume of retail sales; **~werbung** retail advertising; **~wert** retail value; **~wettbewerb** retail competition; **~zweig** retail line.

Einzelhändler retailer, retail dealer (merchant), small business man, dealer *(US)*;
selbständiger ~ independent (single-store, *US*) retailer, retail trader;
~ sein to be in trade *(Br.)*;
~befragung retailer survey; **~einkaufsgenossenschaft** retailer cooperative *(US)*; **~lager** dealer inventory; **~rabatt** retail dealer's discount; **~sortiment** retail line; **~vereinigung** retail association *(US)*.

Einzel|handlungsvollmacht sole (single) procuration; ~**haus** detached house; ~**heft** single copy; ~**heftpreis** single-copy price; ~**heit** detail, item, particular.

Einzelheiten details, data, particulars, ins and outs;
~ **sind anzugeben!** be specific!;
alle ~ full particulars; **genaue** ~ full details (particulars); **modische** ~ fashion details; **nähere** ~ further particulars; **technische** ~ technical details, technicalities; **unbedeutende** ~ minor (petty) details; **wichtige** ~ key details;
~ **über die finanziellen Abmachungen** financial details; ~ **der Anklage** particulars of a criminal charge; **alle** ~ **einer Sache** ins and outs of a matter; ~ **der Schriftsätze** particulars of pleadings; **alle** ~ **eines Werbemittels** media details;
nähere ~ **anführen** to give full particulars; ~ **angeben** to furnish particulars; **sich mit** ~ **befassen** to go into details; **auf** ~ **eingehen** to particularize, to enter (go) into details; **in weitere** ~ **eintreten** to go into further details; ~ **erfragen** to ask for detailed information; **nähere** ~ **erfragen** to ask for further particulars; **in allen** ~ **erzählen** to give a circumstantial account, to discuss a matter in detail; **in** ~ **gehen** to go into particulars; **Sache in allen** ~ **kennen** to know the ins and outs of a matter; **sich um alle** ~ **kümmern** to be a stickler for detail(s); **alle nur möglichen** ~ **mitteilen** to give all possible details; ~ **nachtragen** to fill in an outline; **in allen** ~ **schildern** to write at large; **in** ~ **schwelgen** to luxuriate in details; ~ **übergehen** to pass over the details; ~ **in Fußnoten unterbringen** to relegate details to footnotes; **sich in** ~ **verlieren** to get lost in the (dwell at too great length on) details; **sich** ~ **versagen** to forbear to go into details; ~ **weglassen** to leave out the details; **überflüssige** ~ **weglassen** to cut out superfluous details.

Einzel|hof isolated farm; ~**inhaber** sole proprietor *(US)*; ~**inhaberschaft** sole proprietorship *(US)*; ~**inserat aufgeben** to run an advertisement only once; ~**insertionstarif** transient rate; ~**kabine** roomette *(US)*; ~**kabine in der ersten Klasse** single first-class cabin; ~**kalkulation** unit calculation; ~**kalkulationsaufschlag** individual markup *(US)*; ~**kampf** *(mil.)* dogfight *(coll.)*; ~**käufer** individual purchaser; ~**kaufmann** sole (single, *Br.*) trader, sole proprietor *(US)*; **selbständiger** ~**kaufmann** independent retailer; ~**kind** only child; ~**konto** individual (personal, separate) account; ~**konzession** exclusive licence; ~**körperschaft** corporation sole; ~**kosten** individual (itemized, specific, direct, prime, *US*) cost; ~**kosten einer Abteilung** departmental charges; ~**kredit** personal loan; ~**kreditnehmer** single borrower; ~**kunde** retail customer; ~**ladenpreis** retail price; ~**lehrer** individual tutor; ~**leistung** individual achievement, one-man show; ~**liquidator** special manager; ~**liste** *(Produktion)* sectional price list; ~**lizenz** individual licence; ~**lizenzkosten** production-oriented licence fees; ~**lohn** individual wage; ~**mensch** individual; ~**mieter** sole tenant; ~**mietverhältnis** several tenancy; ~**mitglied** private (individual) member, *(Krankenkasse)* individual subscriber; ~**mitgliedschaft** individual membership.

einzeln single, singular, solitary, parcelled, odd, several, *(abgetrennt)* detached, separate, *(für sich allein)* individual, isolated, lone, *(besonders)* special, particular;
im ~**en** in detail, with full details; **bis ins** ~**e** in every detail;
~ **aufführen** to particularize, to specify; **im** ~**en auf etw. eingehen** to go into the details of s. th.; **Besucher** ~ **einlassen** to admit visitors one at a time; **j.** ~ **erwähnen** to give individual mention to s. o.; **ins** ~**e gehen** to go into details (particulars), to detail; ~ **verkaufen** to sell separately;
~**e Abrechnungsposten** particulars of an account; ~**er Band** separate volume; **nur** ~**e Bewerbungen** only a few applications; ~**er Fall** individual case; ~**es Haus** detached house; ~**e Mitgliedstaaten** various member states; ~**e Punkte in einem Bericht gesondert behandeln** to treat a few points in a report separately; **Maschine in** ~**e Teile zerlegen** to take a machine to pieces.

Einzelnachweis specification.

einzelnstehend isolated, solitary, detached.

Einzel|nummer *(Zeitschrift)* odd number, single copy; ~**objekt** individual property; ~**pächter** sole tenant; ~**pachtverhältnis** severalty tenancy; ~**patent** single patent; ~**person** individual, single (individual) person; ~**plan** *(Etat)* departmental budget; ~**police** specific policy; ~**posten** item; ~**prämie** individual rate; ~**preis** unit price; ~**produktion** individual output (production); ~**projekt** single project; ~**prokura** single (sole) procuration; ~**prokurist** signing clerk; ~**prospekt** sectional price list; ~**punkt** point, item; ~**radaufhängung** independent suspension; ~**rechtsnachfolge** single succession; ~**rechtsnachfolger** singular successor *(US)*; ~**reisender** individual passenger.

Einzelrichter sole (single) judge, examiner, recorder *(US)*, official referee *(Br.)*;
als ~ **tätig sein (verhandeln)** to sit in chambers *(Br.)* (camera), to hear a case in private (in camera, in chambers, *Br.*);
~ **in Ehesachen** commissioner for matrimonial causes;
~**beschluß auf Antrag** summons and order *(Br.)*.

Einzel|schichtbetrieb single-shift operation *(US)*; ~**schiedsvertrag** special agreement; ~**schuld** several debt; ~**schulden** *(Teilhaber)* individual debts; ~**schuldner** sole (several) debtor; ~**schuldverhältnis** several obligation; ~**schuldverschreibung** single debenture; ~**sendung** retail consignment; ~**spalte** single column; ~**staat** constituent member, member state, state of the Union *(US)*.

einzelstaatlich *(EG)* national.

Einzel|straftat instantaneous crime; ~**stück** odd piece, oddment.

Einzeltarif *(mit der Gewerkschaft)* sole bargaining contract, *(Luftfracht)* commodity rate *(US)*;
~**abschluß** site bargaining; ~**verhandlung**, ~**vertrag** single-plant (employer, individual) bargaining, agency shop (sole bargaining) agreement; ~**vertragspartner** sole bargaining agency.

Einzelteil component [part], section, single part;
~**fertigung** manufacture of single parts; ~**lager** parts inventory.

Einzel|thema, wichtiges most important single topic; ~**transport** individual shipment *(US)*; ~**treuhänder** sole trustee; ~**unfallversicherung** personal accident insurance; ~**unternehmen** single enterprise, one-man business *(US)*, sole (single, individual) proprietorship *(US)*; ~**unternehmen in eine Gesellschaft umwandeln** to turn the business of a sole proprietor into a partnership *(US)*; ~**unternehmer** individual entrepreneur, sole (individual) proprietor *(US)*; ~**unterricht** private lessons; ~**unterricht durch Tutoren** tutorial system; ~**unterschrift** single signature; ~**urkunde** individual document; ~**verbraucher** individual consumer; ~**verkauf** retail sale (trade), *(Zeitung)* boy sales; ~**verkäufer** individual vendor; ~**verkaufspreis** retail [selling] price; ~**verkaufssteuer** retail sales tax *(US)*; ~**vermächtnis** specific bequest (device), special (specific) legacy; ~**vermächtnisnehmer** specific legatee; ~**vernehmung** *(Ehefrau)* separate examination; ~**veröffentlichung eines Gesetzes** slip law *(US)*; ~**verpackung** unit (individual) packing; ~**verpflichtung** several covenant (debt); ~**versand** single shipment; ~**versicherer** individual insurer, underwriting member; ~**versicherung** individual insurance; ~**versicherungspolice** specific policy; ~**versicherungsunternehmen** private underwriter *(US)*; ~**versteuerung** separate assessment; ~**vertrag** separate (individual, several) contract; ~**vertretungsmacht** special agency; ~**verwahrung** regular (special, *US*) deposit; ~**vollmacht** single (sole) procuration, specific power of attorney; ~**vormund** general guardian; ~**vorstand** governing (sole, individual) director; ~**wahl** uninominal voting; ~**währung** monometallism; ~**werbung** direct (individual) advertising; ~**werbung durch die Post** direct mail advertising *(US)*; ~**wertberichtigung** adjustment of value, value adjustment; ~**wesen** individual, person; ~**wirkungsgrad** efficiency per unit; ~**zeichnung** detail drawing; ~**zeitverfahren** repetitive timing, snapback method; ~**zelle** single cell, cubicle; ~**zimmer** separate room, *(Hotel)* single bedroom, *(Krankenhaus)* private room; ~**zimmerreservierung** single-room accommodation.

einziehbar cashable, recoverable, collectable, *(beschlagnahmefähig)* seizable, confiscable, *(verwirkbar)* forfeitable.

Einziehen moving in, *(Druckzeile)* indentation;
~ **des Fahrgestells** *(Flugzeug)* retraction of the undercarriage;
im ~ **begriffen sein** to be on the move.

einziehen to draw (take) in, *(beschlagnahmen)* to confiscate, to seize, to forfeit, to condemn, *(Kapital)* to call in, *(mil.)* to conscribe, to recruit, to call up, to induct *(US)*, to muster in *(US)*, *(Münzen)* to demonetize, *(Schulden)* to encash, to collect, to ingather *(Scot.)*, *(Steuern)* to collect, *(aus dem Verkehr ziehen)* to withdraw from circulation, to recall, *(Wechsel)* to retire, *(Winter)* to draw on, *(in Wohnung)* to move in, to take lodgings, *(Zeile)* to indent;
bei jem. ~ to take lodging with s. o., to move into s. one's house; **Aktien** ~ to recall shares; **Anker** ~ to take the anchor aboard; **Auskünfte** ~ to make inquiries; **Außenstände** ~ to collect money due, to make collections, to pull in the cash; **Banknoten** ~ to withdraw [bank] notes; **Beiträge** ~ to collect dues; **jds. Besitz** ~ to confiscate s. one's property; **Betrag** ~ to recover an amount; **in den trockenen Boden** ~ to penetrate into the dry ground; **in den Bundestag** ~ to become a member of parliament; **Decke in ein Haus** ~ to put up a ceiling in a house;

Erkundigungen ~ to make inquiries, to gather information; **Fahrgestell** ~ to retract the undercarriage; **Falschgeld** ~ to confiscate counterfeit money; **Flagge** ~ to haul down the flag; **jds. Führerschein** ~ to withdraw s. one's driving licence; **schlechtes Geld** ~ to call in base money; **Jahrgang** ~ to draft on age group; **Kabel** ~ to haul in a cable; **Mieten** ~ to collect rents; **Münzen** ~ to withdraw coins from circulation, to immobilize coins; **Paß** ~ to withdraw a passport; **Pfandbriefe** ~ to redeem bonds; **Rekruten** ~ to enlist recruits; **Scheck** ~ to collect a check *(US)* (cheque, *Br.*); **aufgebrachtes Schiff und Ladegut prisengerichtlich** ~ to condemn a captured vessel and her cargo; **Schmuggelware** ~ to seize contraband; **in eine Stadt** ~ to make one's entry into a town; **Stelle** ~ to abolish a post; **Steuern** ~ to collect taxes; **Vermögen** ~ to confiscate property; **Wechsel** ~ to cash a bill.

Einziehschacht downcast.

Einziehung *(Außenstände)* collecting, collection, retirement, *(Banknoten)* calling in, withdrawal, *(Beschlagnahme)* seizure, condemnation, confiscation, *(Druckzeile)* indentation, *(von Geld)* immobilization, *(Kapital)* calling in, *(Völkerrecht)* sequestration, *(mil.)* calling up, recruitment, drafting *(US)*, induction *(US)*, *(durch Strafkammer)* forfeiture, *(Wechsel)* cashing, retirement;
in der ~ **befindlich** in process of collection; **zur** ~ for collection; **zwecks** ~ **und Überweisung** for collections and returns;
prisengerichtliche ~ condemnation;
~ **von Auskünften** making inquiries; ~ **von Außenständen** collection of outstanding debts; ~ **von Banknoten** withdrawal of bank notes; ~ **von Erkundigungen** collecting information; ~ **von Falschgeld** confiscation of counterfeit money; ~ **von Forderungen** collection of debts (claims); ~ **des Führerscheins** withdrawal of the driving licence, forfeiture of licence *(Br.)*, revocation of the driver's licence *(US)*, driving ban *(Br.)*; ~ **der Gebühren** collection of fees; ~ **von Gewerkschaftsbeiträgen durch den Betrieb** maintenance of union dues; ~ **von Liegenschaften** escheat of lands; ~ **der Miete** rent collection; ~ **von Münzen** immobilization of coins; ~ **eines Passes** withdrawal of a passport; ~ **von Pfandbriefen** redemption of bonds; ~ **eines aufgebrachten Schiffes und seiner Ladung** capture of a condemned ship and her cargo; ~ **von Schmuggelware durch den Zoll** seizure of contraband by customs officers; ~ **von Schulden** encashment (collection) of debts; ~ **durch den Staat** forfeiture, seizure, confiscation; ~ **einer Stelle** abolishment of a post; ~ **von Steuern** collection of taxes; ~ **einer Straße** abondonment of a road; ~ **des Vermögens** seizure (confiscation) of property;
~ **von Erbschaftssteuern beschleunigen** to speed up the collection of estate taxes *(US)*; ~ **eines Wechsels besorgen** to encash a bill; ~ **des Vermögens zur Folge haben** to involve the forfeiture of property; **zur** ~ **übersenden** to remit for collection.

Einziehungs|anzeige advice of collection; ~**auftrag** collection order; ~**befugnis** power to collect; ~**benachrichtigung** advice of collection; ~**bescheid** *(mil.)* draft card *(US)*; ~**beschluß** sequestration; ~**gebühr** collection fee; ~**kosten** collection expense, cost of collection, recovering charges (expenses), walking charges *(Br.)*; ~**provision** commission for collecting, collecting commission; ~**recht** right to collect; ~**schwierigkeiten** collection troubles; ~**spesen** collection (walking, *Br.*) charges; ~**stelle** *(mil.)* draft board; ~**verfahren** collection proceedings; ~**vollmacht** power to collect, collecting power; ~**weg** channels of collection.

einzig only, single, sole;
kein ~**er** not one, none whatever;
~ **und allein davon abhängen** to depend entirely on whether; ~ **dastehen** to be unique; ~ **auf seinem Gebiet sein** to be without equal;
~**er Erbe** sole heir; ~**es Kind** one and only child; **kein** ~**er Mensch** not a single person; **das** ~ **Richtige** just the thing; ~**er Überlebender** only survivor; ~ **möglicher Weg** sole way possible.

einzigartig unique, singular, alphaplus;
~**e Gelegenheit** chance in a thousand.

Einzimmerapartment one-room flat.

einzudecken haben, noch Aktien to be short of stock *(US)*.

Einzug entry, entrance, *(drucktechn.)* indentation, *(Gelder)* collecting, collection, encashment, *(in Haus)* moving in, *(Zeile)* indent;
ohne ~ *(Druckzeile)* flush;
~ **sofort** *(Wohnungsanzeige)* immediate occupancy;
~ **von Forderungen** collection of claims (debts); ~ **in eine neue Wohnung** moving into a new flat;
~ **in die neue Wohnung feiern** to give housewarming party; **seinen** ~ **halten** to make one's entry; **Wechsel zum** ~ **hereinnehmen** to accept bills for collection.

Einzugs|auftrag collection order; ~**bedingungen** terms of collection; ~**bereich** commuter belt; ~**feier,** ~**fest** housewarming party; ~**gebiet** trading (buying) area, shopping hinterland, *(Arbeitskräfte)* labo(u)r market area, commuter zone (belt), *(Fluß)* catchment area (basin), drainage area *(US)*, watershed *(Br.)*; ~**gebühren** collecting charges; ~**geschäft** collection business; ~**kosten** collecting charges, collection costs; ~**posten** items for collection; ~**provision** commission for collecting, collecting commission; ~**spesen** collection (collecting, encashment) charges, costs of collection; **zuzüglich** ~**spesen** with exchange *(US)*; ~**stelle** collection agency; ~**tag** *(in Haus)* moving day; ~**verfahren** collection system (proceedings); **beschleunigtes** ~**verfahren** collection speedup; ~**verkehr** collecting (collection) business; ~**wechsel** short (country) bill, bill for collection; ~**werte** items received for collection.

einzurangieren sein, schwer to be difficult to place.

einzuwenden haben, nichts to have no objections.

Einzweckflugzeug single-purpose aircraft.

einzylindrig one-cylinder.

Eis, mit ~ **bedeckt** frozen; **vom** ~ **eingeschlossen** nipped (detained) by ice, icebound;
brüchiges ~ unsound ice; **fahrbares** ~ open ice; **gemischtes** ~ mixed ice cream; **trügerisches** ~ treacherous ice;
~ **am Stiel** ice lollipop *(Br.)*;
sich mit ~ **bedecken** to cover with ice, to frost [over]; ~ **vorsichtig betreten** to tread cautiously on the ice; **im** ~ **festsitzen** to be locked in ice; **j. aufs** ~ **führen** to lead s. o. up the garden path; **Lebensmittel auf** ~ **legen** to keep food on ice; **Sache auf** ~ **legen** to table *(US)* (pigeonhole) s. th., to put into cold storage; **völlig vom** ~ **eingeschlossen sein** to be completely iced up; **sich auf dünnes** ~ **wagen** to skate on thin ice;
~**bahn** skating rink; ~**becher** carton, *(mit Früchten)* sundae; ~**berg** iceberg, floating island; ~**bericht** *(Meteorologie)* ice report; ~**beutel** *(med.)* ice pack; ~**block** block of ice.

Eisblumen ice-ferns, frostwork;
~ **an einem Fenster** tracery on a frosted window;
mit ~ **überziehen** to frost over;
~**muster** frost pattern.

Eis|bombe ice pudding; ~**brecher** *(Brücke)* ice apron, *(Schiff)* ice breaker; ~**creme** ice cream; ~**decke** ice cap; ~**diele** ice parlo(u)r.

Eisen iron;
aus ~ made of iron; **zum alten** ~ **geworfen** on the shelf;
geschmiedetes ~ wrought iron; **heißes** ~ *(fig.)* sore subject, delicate matter, hot potato;
heißes ~ **anfassen** to play with fire, to tread on delicate ground *(coll.)*; **zum alten** ~ **gehören** to be no longer any use; **mehrere** ~ **im Feuer haben** to have a few more irons in the fire (more than one string to one's bow), to have two strings to one's bow; **zu viele** ~ **im Feuer haben** to have too many irons in the fire; **Gesundheit wie aus** ~ **haben** to have an iron constitution; **Mann in** ~ **legen** to put a man in fetters (irons); **heißes** ~ **sein** to be a tricky business; **zum alten** ~ **geworfen sein** to be on the shelf; **zum alten** ~ **werfen** to throw on the scrap-heap, to discard as worthless , to junk *(US sl.)*;
Not bricht ~ necessity knows no law;
das ~ **schmieden solange es heiß ist** to strike while the iron is hot, to make hay while the sun shines;
~**abfall** scrap iron; ~**arbeit** ironwork.

Eisenbahn railway *(Br.)*, railroad *(US)*;
auf der ~ on the railway, in the train; **frei** ~ free on rail; **in der** ~ on the train; **per** ~ by rail (freight, *US*);
einspurige ~ single-line (-track) railway (railroad, *US*); **elektrische** ~ electric railway, *(Spielzeug)* toy railway; **stillgelegte** ~ defunct railway; **zweigleisige** ~ double-track railway;
bei der ~ **arbeiten** to work for the railway, to railroad *(US)*; ~**en in einem Land bauen** to railroad a country *(US)*; **mit der** ~ **befördern** to send (consign, forward) by rail, to railroad *(US)*; ~ **benutzen** to go by train; **mit der** ~ **fahren** to travel by train, to railway, to railroad *(US)*; **bei der** ~ **beschäftigt sein** to work on the railway, to [be employed on a] railroad *(US)*; ~ **verstaatlichen** to take over the railways;
es ist höchste ~ there is no time to lose;
~**abkommen** railroad agreement *(US)*; ~**abonnement** season ticket *(Br.)*, commutation ticket *(US)*; ~**abrechnungsstelle** railway clearinghouse; ~**abstellgleis** siding; ~**abteil** compartment, railroad division *(US)*; ~**aktien** railway shares *(Br.)*, rails

(Br.), railroads *(US)*, railroad stocks *(US)*; **amerikanische ~aktien** Yankees *(Br.)*; **hochstehende ~aktien** heavy lines *(Br.)*; **~angestellter** railway (railroad, *US*) official (employee), railroader *(US)*; **~anlage** railway installation; **~anlagen** railway (railroad, *US*) facilities; **~anleihe** railway (railroad, *US*) loan; **hypothekarisch auf Teilstrecken gesicherte ~anleihe** divisional bond *(US)*; **~anschluß** siding, sidetrack, *(Verbindung)* junction; **~arbeiter** railway (railroad, *US*) worker; **~ausbau** railway development; **~ausbesserungswagen** repair truck; **~ausbesserungswerk** railway repair (railroad, *US*) shop, carshop; **~ausrüstungsteile** railroad equipment *(US)*; **~avis** railway (railroad, *US*) advice; **~bau** railway engineering (making), construction of a railway line, railroading *(US)*; **Kanal- und ~bauten** internal improvements *(US)*; **~bauunternehmer** railway contractor; **~beamter** railway official (company's servant), railroad official (employee) *(US)*; **~beförderung** rail transport; **~behälterverkehr** train container service; **~benutzer** railway traveller; **~betrieb** train (railroad, *US*) services, railway undertaking, railroad operation *(US)*.

Eisenbahnbetriebs|einnahmen railway (railroad, *US*) earnings; **~leiter** operating director; **~leitung** rail way head office *(Br.)*, railroad division *(US)*; **~material, ~mittel** rolling stock.

Eisenbahn|brücke railway (railroad, *US*) bridge, viaduct; **~damm** railway embankment; **~defizit** railway's deficit; **~dienststellen** railway authorities; **~direktion** railway head office *(Br.)*, railroad division *(US)*; **~durchgangsverkehr** rail transit system; **~endstation** railhead terminus.

Eisenbahner railway man, railroadman *(US)*, railroader *(US)*; **~gewerkschaft** National Union of Railwaymen *(Br.)*; **~streik** railway (railroad, *US*) strike.

Eisenbahn|fähre train (car) ferry, ferry bridge; **~fahrkarte** [train] ticket, railway ticket *(Br.)*, railroad ticket *(US)*, railway fare *(Br.)*, railroad fare *(US)*; **unbegrenzt gültige ~fahrkarte** unlimited railway ticket; **~fahrplan** timetable of trains, railway timetable (guide, *Br.*), train sheet, schedule of trains *(US)*.

Eisenbahnfahrt train journey;
vierstündige ~ a four hours' train trip;
~ über eine weite Entfernung long-distance rail travel.

Eisenbahnfracht railway (railroad, *US*) freight;
~brief railway (railroad, *US*) bill, waybill *(US)*; **~einnahmen** railway freight revenue; **~gut** railway parcels; **~kosten** railway charges, carrying cost; **~linie** railway (railroad, *US*) freight line; **~tarif** railway (railroad, *US*) freight charge; **~tarifsatz** rail freight rate; **~verkehr** railway (railroad, *US*) freight traffic (transportation, *US*), rail freight traffic.

Eisenbahn|fusion railroad merger *(US)*; **~gelände** railway property; **~geschichte** railroading history *(US)*; **~gesellschaft** railway company, railroad corporation *(US)*, line; **gemeinsam verwaltete ~gesellschaften** family lines; **einer ~gesellschaft Korporationsrechte verleihen** to incorporate a railway (railroad) company; **~gesetz** Railway Act *(Br.)*.

Eisenbahngleis railway (railroad, *US*) line (track), rail track;
normalspuriges ~ standard-gauge track; **privates ~** private siding.

Eisenbahn|gut- und Expressgutverkehr express (fast flight, *US*) service; **~güterverkehr** railway (goods) traffic *(Br.)*, freight traffic *(US)*, rail transportation *(US)*, transport by rail *(Br.)*; **~hafen** railway port; **~hotel** terminus hotel; **~ingenieur** railway (railroad, *US*) engineer; **~karte** railway sheet; **~kartell** railway pool *(Br.)*; **~katastrophe** railway disaster; **~kilometer** train milage; **~knotenpunkt** [railway (railroad, *US*)] junction, meet; **~konnossement** railway (railroad, *US*) bill of lading; **~konstrukteur** railway maker; **~konzession** railway concession.

eisenbahnkrank carsick.

Eisenbahn|krankheit railway (railroad, *US*) sickness; **~kreuzung** cross-over; **~kursbuch** railway (railroad, *US*) guide, schedule *(US)*, Appleton *(US)*; **alphabetisches ~kursbuch** ABC *(Br.)*.

Eisenbahnlinie [railway (rail)] line, railroad line *(US)*;
gerade ~ straight shoot *(US)*;
~ ausbauen to extend a railway (railroad, *US*); **~ bauen** to lay down a railway, to build a railroad *(US)*; **~ betreiben** to operate a railway line (railroad, *US*); **~ finanzieren** to finance a railroad *(US)* (railway, *Br.*); **~ dem Verkehr übergeben** to submit a railway to traffic, to give traffic to a railroad *(US)*; **~ für den öffentlichen Verkehr unterhalten** to maintain a railroad *(US)*.

Eisenbahn|netz railway network, railway system *(Br.)*, network (system) of railways (railroads, *US*), railroad net *(US)*, railway system, rail network *(Br.)*; **~oberbau** permanent way *(Br.)*, roadbed, superstructure.

Eisenbahnobligationen railway bonds (debentures, *Br.*), terminal bonds, rail (railroad) bonds *(US)*;
hypothekarisch gesicherte ~ land grant bonds *(US)*; **später auch hypothekarisch gesicherte ~** extension bonds *(US)*; **auf einer Einzelstrecke hypothekarisch gesicherte ~** divisional bonds *(US)*;
~ zur Finanzierung eines Bahnhofs terminal bonds *(US)*.

Eisenbahn|papiere heavy rails *(Br.)*; **~passagier** railway passenger *(Br.)*; **~personenverkehr** passenger transport *(Br.)* (transportation, *US*); **~plakat** railroad showing *(US)*; **~projekt** railroad plan *(US)*; **~reklame** railroad advertising *(US)*; **~reise** train journey; **~schaffner** railway guard *(Br.)*, railroad conductor *(US)*; **~schienen** rails, metals; **~schnellweg** high-speed rail corridor; **~schuldverschreibungen** railway bonds, rail bonds *(US)*; **~schwelle** crosstie *(Br.)*, tie *(US)*, sleeper *(Br.)*; **~spediteur** [railway] carrier, shipper *(US)*; **~spurweite** gauge; **~station** railway station *(Br.)*, [railroad, *US*] station, depot *(US)*; **~stillegung** rail tie-up; **~strecke** road, [railway (railroad, *US*)] line; **Betrieb auf einer ~strecke einstellen** to close a line; **unrentable ~strecken stillegen** to eliminate unprofitable lines; **~streckenführung** railway (rail) line, railroad routing *(US)*; **~subventionen** railway subsidies; **~system** railway system *(Br.)*, railroad system *(US)*, road *(US)*; **~tarif** rate (schedule) of fares, railway (railroad, *US*) rates, tariff; **für mehrere Linien geltender ~tarif** multilinear tariff; **~transport** conveyance (carriage, transport) by rail, railway carriage, rail transportation *(US)*; **~transportbericht** shipping report *(US)*; **~trassenland** place lands; **~überführung** railway *(Br.)* (railroad, *US*) bridge over a line; **~übergang** grade (level, *US*) crossing; **~übersichtskarte** railway map; **~unfall** railway (railroad, *US*) accident; **~unfallversicherung** railway passenger (rail transportation, *US*) insurance; **~unglück** railway crash, railway (train, railroad, *US*) accident; **~unterhaltung** maintenance of way; **~unternehmer** railway contractor; **~unterstützungsfonds** railroad relief fund *(US)*; **~verbindung** railway (train) connection; **gute ~- und Omnibusverbindungen** good train and bus connections; **schlechte ~verbindungen** poor railroad service *(US)*; **~verkehr** railway (railroad, *US*) traffic, railway (train) service *(Br.)*; **~verkehrsordnung** railway traffic regulations; **~versand** transport by railway, shipping by rail *(US)*; **~verwaltung** Railway Executive *(Br.)*, railway authorities, management of a railroad *(US)*; **~verwaltungsrat** railway committee *(Br.)*; **~viadukt** trestle bridge, viaduct.

Eisenbahnwagen railway carriage *(Br.)*, coach *(US)*, [railway] car *(Br.)*, passenger car;
gemischter ~ composite carriage; **vorbestellter ~** private car *(Br.)*;
~ dritter Klasse third-class carriage.

Eisenbahnwaggon railroad freight car *(US)*, [railway] carriage *(Br.)*, railway truck (waggon) *(Br.)*, goods van *(Br.)*, car *(US)*, boxcar *(US)*;
~ für Schüttgut gondola car *(US)*;
~knappheit scarcity of rolling stock.

Eisenbahn|wärter linekeeper; **~werbung** railway (railroad, *US*) advertising.

Eisenbahnwerte carriage shares, railway (railroad, *US*) stocks, rails *(Br.)*, railways *(Br.)*, railroads *(US)*, roads *(US)*;
ausländische ~ foreign rails *(Br.)*; **einheimische ~** home rails *(Br.)*; **erstklassige ~** old line rails *(Br.)*.

Eisenbahn|wesen railway (railroad, *US*) matters, railroading *(US)*; **~zentrum** railway centre *(Br.)*, railroad center *(US)*; **~zubehör** railway (railroad, *US*) equipment;
~zug train; **~zug mit Kücheneinrichtung** train with dining car, lunch counter car; **~zulieferer** railway supplier; **~zusammenstoß** train (railway) collision; **~zustellung** railway delivery; **~zustellungskosten** hauling costs; **für ~zwecke enteignen** to condemn land for a railway.

eisenbewehrt reinforced.

Eisen|blech sheet iron; **mittelstarkes ~blech** tank iron; **verzinktes ~blech** tin plate; **~draht** iron wire; **~erz** iron ore; **~erzbergbau** iron-ore mining; **~erzgrube** ore mine; **~erzeugung** iron production; **~- und Nichteisenmetallerzeugung** iron and nonferrous metals production; **~fresser** *(fig.)* fire-eater; **~gießerei** iron foundry; **~handel** hardware business; **~händler** hardwareman, ironmonger *(Br.)*; **~hütte** ironworks; **~hüttenbesitzer** ironmaster *(Br.)*; **~industrie** iron industry; **die ~industrie** *(Börse)* the iron interest; **~- und Stahlindustrie** iron and steel industry; **~konstruktion** ironwork.

eisenschaffende Industrie iron-and-steel producing industry.

Eisenwaren hardware, ironmongery *(Br.)*;
~- und Metallwarenbranche hardware trade; **~händler** hard-

wareman, ironmonger *(Br.)*; ~**handlung** ironmonger's shop *(Br.)*, hardware store *(US)*; ~- **und Stahlvereinigung** Iron and Steel Federation *(Br.)*;
~, **Blech- und Metallwaren** base metal goods.
eisern iron, *(Fleiß)* indefatigable, unremitting, tireless;
mit ~em Besen auskehren to make a clean sweep of it; ~**er Bestand** reserve (permanent) stock (fund), funds on hand; ~**e Disziplin** strict (stern, cast-iron) discipline; **j. mit ~er Faust niederhalten** to hold s. o. in a grip of iron; ~**es Gesetz der Notwendigkeit** iron law of necessity; ~**e Gesundheit** iron constitution; **mit ~em Griff** with a grip of iron; ~**e Grundsätze** cast-iron principles; **mit ~er Hand regieren** to rule with a rod of iron; ~**es Lohngesetz** iron law of wages; ~**e Lunge** iron lung; ~**en Magen haben** to have the digestion of an ostrich; **mit ~er Miene** with a strong look; ~**e Nerven haben** to have iron nerves, to have nerves of steel; ~**e Notwendigkeit** dire necessity; ~**e Ration** iron (emergency, *US*) ration; **mit ~er Ruhe regieren** to act with the utmost composure; ~**es Sparen** compulsory saving; ~**e Sparsamkeit** rigid (strict) economy; **mit ~er Stirn** brazen-faced, with a brazen face; ~**es Tor** iron gate; ~**er Vorhang** fireproof curtain, *(pol.)* iron curtain; ~**er Wille** will of iron.
Eis|fabrik ice-manufacturing plant; ~**feld** ice field.
eisfrei *(Schiffahrtslinie)* free of ice, ice-free.
Eisgang breaking up of the ice, ice drift.
eisgekühlt ice-cooled, iced;
~**es Getränk** ice drink.
Eis|glätte icy surface; ~**grenze** glacial limit; ~**gürtel** ice belt; ~**herstellung** ice making.
eisig icy, cold as ice;
~**er Empfang** icy welcome; ~**e Höflichkeit** chilly politeness.
Eiskaffee iced coffee.
eiskalt ice-cold, icy, freezing;
~ **sein** *(Mensch)* to play it cool, *(Zimmer)* to be like ice; **j. ~ überlaufen** to give s. o. the creeps.
Eis|kappe *(Nordpol)* ice cap; ~**kasten** ice safe; ~**keller** icehouse; ~**klumpen** lump of ice; **meine Füße sind wie ein ~klumpen** my feet are like ice; **dünne ~kruste** thin crust of ice; **mit einer ~kruste bedeckt** crusted over with ice; ~**laufbahn** skating rink; ~**lotse** ice pilot; ~**mann** ice dealer, iceman *(US)*; ~**maschine** ice machine, ice-cream freezer; ~**meldedienst** Ice Patrol; ~**nebel** arctic smoke; ~**niederschlag** *(Flugzeug)* airfrost; ~**papier** frosted paper; ~**regen** glazed frost, icestorm *(US)*; ~**revue** ice show, ice pantomine; ~**schicht** ice [layer]; **mit einer ~schicht bedeckt** frozen over; ~**scholle** ice field, pancake ice; **kleine ~scholle** patch ; **treibende ~scholle** pan; ~**schrank** refrigerator, icebox *(US)*, fridge *(fam.)*; ~**stoß** ice jam; ~**treiben** ice drift; ~**verkäufer** ice dealer, iceman *(US)*; ~**versorgung** *(Kühlwaggon)* icing; ~**versorgungsgebühr** icing charge; ~**waggon** ice car; ~**warndienst** Ice Patrol; ~**würfel** ice cube; ~**zeit** ice age.
eitel vain, windy, gassy, boastful;
~ **wie ein Pfau** as vain as a peacock;
das Leben ist nicht ~ Freud und Sonnenschein life is not all beer and skittles.
Eitelkeit vanity, vainness;
jds. ~ schmeicheln to flatter (tickle) s. one's vanity.
eit|ler Affe dandy, coxcomb, fancy pants *(US sl.)*; ~**les Geschwätz** empty words, idle gossip; ~**ler Sonnenschein** sunshine all the way; ~**ler Tand** vanities; ~**le Versuche** futile attempts.
Ekel disgust, loathing for, toad, *(widerlicher Mensch)* loathsome (nasty) fellow, beast, stinker;
bis zum ~ ad nauseam, to satiety;
~ **empfinden** to be overcome with nausea; ~ **vor etw. haben** to have an aversion to s. th., to feel disgust at s. th.
ekelhaft disgusting, offensive, repulsive, nauseating;
~ **heiß** terribly hot; ~ **kalt** bitter cold;
j. ~ behandeln to be nasty to s. o.; **sich ~ benehmen** to behave nastily; ~ **riechen** to smell offensively; ~ **weh tun** to hurt like hell;
~**e Arbeit** nasty job; ~**en Geschmack zurücklassen** to leave a nasty taste in the mouth; ~**er Kerl** nasty fellow; ~**e Speisen** revolting food; ~**es Wetter** wretched (nasty, beastly) weather; ~**es Zeug** vile stuff.
ekeln, sich to be disgusted, to loathe it, to have an aversion to, to feel repugnance.
eklig repulsive, disgusting, offensive;
sich ~ benehmen to behave abominably; ~ **zu jem. sein** to be nasty to s. o.
Ekstase ecstasy, rapture, transport;
in ~ geraten to go into raptures; **j. in ~ versetzen** to throw s. o. into ecstasy.

elaborieren to elaborate.
Elan pep, go, spirit, vigo(u)r, drive, rush, verve, impetus, vim;
mehr ~ dahintersetzen to put more vim into it; **mit ~ an die Arbeit gehen** to go at it vigourously, to roll up one's sleeves, to hitch up to a job; **einer Sache den ~ nehmen** to take the pep out of s. th.; **über genügend ~ verfügen** to have plenty of push.
elastisch elastic, flexible, resilient, *(biegsam)* pliable, *(Markt)* buoyant;
sich den veränderten Umständen ~ anpassen to adapt o. s. easily to changed circumstances; **Verordnung ~ handhaben** to apply a regulation very loosely;
~**e Außenpolitik** flexible foreign policy; ~**er Bedarf** elastic demand; ~**e Bestimmungen** flexible provisions, elastic rules; ~**er Etat** flexible budget; ~**e Geldmarktsteuerung** flexible control of the money market; ~**es Gewissen haben** to have an elastic conscience; ~**e Handhabung** flexible use, elastic demand; ~**er Mensch** agile mind; ~**e Währung** elastic (flexible) currency; ~**er Wirkungsgrad** resilience.
Elastizität elasticity, flexibility, give, tone, *(Biegsamkeit)* pliability, ductibility, *(Markt)* buoyancy;
~ **des Angebots** overall elasticity of supply; ~ **des Geldmarktes** elasticity of the money market; ~ **der Nachfrage** elasticity of demand; ~ **der Preise** flexibility of prices.
Elefant *(fig.)* clumsy person, baby elephant *(fam.)*;
~ **im Porzellanladen** bull in a China shop;
aus einer Mücke einen ~en machen to make mountains out of a molehill, to chronicle small beer.
Elefantenhaut haben to be thick-skinned.
elegant elegant, genteel, smart, fashionable, well-rounded, chic;
~ **gekleidet** elegantly dressed;
~**es Auto** smart car; ~**er Herr** polished gentleman; ~**e Lösung finden** to find a smart solution; ~**er Treffpunkt** tuxedo junction; ~**es Viertel** genteel suburb; **in einem ~en Viertel wohnen** to live in a fashionable quarter.
Elegantestes vom Eleganten pink of elegance.
Eleganz elegance, smartness, chic *(coll.)*, *(Stil)* gracefulness, neatness;
von schlichter ~ neat;
auffällige ~ swank; **schlichte ~** neatness; **unaufdringliche ~ eines Zimmers** tone of quiet elegance of a room; **verblichene ~** shabby gentility.
elegisch elegiac, melancholy.
elektrifizieren to electrify.
elektrifiziert electrified.
Elektrifizierung electrification.
elektrisch electric;
sich ~ einstellen lassen *(Autositz)* to adjust electrically by push-button; ~ **betrieben werden** to be electrically operated, to go by electricity;
mit ~em Antrieb electrically driven; ~**e Eisenbahn** electric railway; ~**e Geräte** electrical goods; ~**er Heizofen** electric heater; ~**e Leitung** electric circuit (wire); ~**e Leitungen in einem Haus verlegen** to wire a house; ~**es Licht** electric light; ~**er Schlag** electric shock; ~**er Strom** electric current; ~**er Stuhl** electric chair, hot seat *(US)*; ~**e Taschenlampe** electric torch.
Elektrische electric *(coll.)*.
elektrisieren, sich to get an electric shock; **j. ~** to strike sparks from s. o.
Elektrizität electricity;
~ **erzeugen** to generate electricity; ~ **leiten** to transmit electricity; **Stadt mit ~ versorgen** to supply a town with electricity.
Elektrizitäts|aktien electricals, electrical issues; ~**arbeiter** power worker; ~**bedarf** demand for electricity; ~**erzeugung** production of electricity, electricity generation; ~**gesellschaft** electric power company; ~**industrie** electricity industry; ~**leitung** power line, electric cable; ~**netz** electricity grid; ~**unternehmen** electric utility; ~**verbrauch** electric power (current) consumption; ~**verbundsnetz** electricity grid; ~**versorgung** electricity (current) supply; ~**versorgungsbetrieb** electricity supply undertaking; ~**versorgungswirtschaft** electricity supply industry; ~**werk** power station (works), electricity works, powerhouse, electric power plant; **herkömmliches ~werk** conventional power station; ~**werte** electricals, electrical issues; ~**wirtschaft** electrical engineering industry; ~**wirtschaftsgesetz** Electricity Act *(Br.)*; ~**zähler** electric meter.
Elektro|akkustik electroacoustics; ~**aktien** electricals; ~**anlage** electric plant; ~**antrieb** electrical drive; ~**aufnahme** electrical transcription; ~**ausstattung eines Autos** electrical equipment of a motor car.
Elektrodenspannung electrode potential.

elektrodynamischer Lautsprecher electrodynamic loudspeaker.

Elektro|gerät electric appliance; ~**gerätehersteller** electrical appliances manufacturer; ~**geschäft,** ~**händler** electric outfitter; ~**industrie** electricity (electrical engineering) industry, electrotechnics, electrical engineering; ~**ingenieur** electrical engineer; ~**installateur** electrician; ~**lok** electric locomotive; ~**meister** electrician; ~**messe** electric goods fair; ~**mobil** electric automobile (motor car); ~**monteur** electrical fitter; ~**motor** electric motor.

Elektronen|blitz flashlight, speedflash *(US)*; ~**blitzgerät** electronic flash unit, speedlight *(US)*; ~**buchführung** electronic accounting; ~**gehirn** electronic computer (brain), thinking machine, devil box; ~**industrie** electronics industry; ~**rechner** electronic computer (calculator); ~**röhre** thermionic valve, valve *(US)*.

elektronisch|es Feld electric field; ~**e Musik** electronic music; ~**e Steuerung** electronic control system.

Elektro|technik electrotechnics, electrical engineering; ~**techniker** electrical engineer, electrician; ~**wagen** electric car; ~**werte** electricity shares.

Element *(Bauteil)* component, member agent, structural part, *(el.)* element, *(Grundbegriff)* elements, rudiments, grounding; **in seinem** ~ in one's element, at home;
asoziale ~**e** antisocial elements; **entfesselte** ~**e** raging elements; **galvanisches** ~ galvanic (primary) cell; **lichtscheue** ~**e** shady characters; **radioaktives** ~ radioactive element; **werbewirksames** ~ feature;
germanische ~**e im Englischen** germanic components in the English language;
in seinem ~ **sein** to be in one's element; **nicht in seinem** ~ **sein** to be like a fish out of water; **das treibende** ~ **sein** to be the life and soul (prime mover) of it; **unerfreuliches** ~ **sein** to be a most undesirable acquaintance; **den** ~**en trotzen** to brave the elements; **j. in den** ~**en der Wissenschaft unterrichten** to give s. o. a grounding in science.

elementar elementary, elemental, *(grundlegend)* basic, rudimentary, fundamental;
von ~**er Bedeutung** of fundamental importance; ~**e Begriffe der Buchführung** fundamentals of bookkeeping; ~**e Größe** elemental grandeur; ~**e Kraft** elemental force; ~**e Leidenschaften** overpowering passions; ~**e Mathematik** elementary mathematics; ~**e Menschenrechte** basic human rights; ~**e Pflichten gegenüber der Gemeinschaft** fundamental duties towards the community; ~**e Wahrheiten** elemental truth.

Elementar|begriff basic (fundamental) idea; ~**bildung** elementary education; ~**buch** form-book, primer; ~**ereignis** Act of God; ~**faktoren** production factors; ~**geist** elemental spirit; ~**gewalt eines Sturms** elemental fury of a storm; ~**kenntnisse** rudimentary knowledge; ~**schaden** damage by the elements, emergency loss; ~**schadensversicherung** hazardous insurance; ~**schulbildung** primary education; ~**schule** elementary (primary, grade, *US*) school; ~**stufen** primary grades *(US)*; ~**teilchen** elementary particle, corpuscle; ~**unterricht** elementary teaching; ~**zeitbestimmungssystem** method-time measurement; ~**zeiten** standard elemental times.

Elend misery, destitution, distress, squalor, gripe;
aus tiefstem ~ from the depth of misery;
menschliches ~ human misery; **soziales** ~ social evil; **unbeschreibliches** ~ untold squalor;
Not und ~ destitution and misery;
~ **des Krieges** calamities of war;
das heulende ~ **bekommen** to get the blues (maudlin), to have the dismals; ~ **über j. bringen** to inflict misery on s. o.; **wie ein Häufchen** ~ **dasitzen** to sit there looking a picture of misery; **ins** ~ **geraten** to be reduced to poverty; **sein** ~ **herunterspülen** to sluice the worries; **im tiefsten** ~ **leben** to be utterly destitute; **j. ins** ~ **stürzen** to plunge s. o. into poverty, to render s. o. destitute; **im** ~ **umkommen** to die a dog's death.

elend poor, poverty-stricken, wretched, distressed, desolate, miserable;
~ **aussehen** to look very ill; **sich** ~ **fühlen** to feel wretched; ~ **dran sein** to be in a pitiable state;
~**e Baracke** shack, shanty, hovel; ~**e Behausungen** squalid dwellings; **jem. ein** ~**es Dasein bereiten** to make s. one's life a misery; ~**e Flüchtlingsexistenzen** miserable lives of refugees; ~**es Gesindel** *(fam.)* bunch; **jds.** ~**e Lage beseitigen** to put s. o. out of his misery; ~**es Nest** wretched hole, miserable place; ~**e Schinderei** sheer drudgery; ~**er Schurke** despisable creature, wretch; **in** ~**en Verhältnissen leben** to live in dire (wretched) poverty (distressed circumstances); ~**es Wetter** wretchedness of the (wretched) weather.

Elends|beseitigung remedy for social evils; ~**bezirk,** ~**gebiet** slum (distressed, *Br.*) area; ~**gebiete beseitigen** to clear insanitary areas; ~**quartier** hovel, slum house, substandard dwelling, substandard housing, hole, shanty; ~**viertel** slums.

Eleve apprentice, pupil.

eliminieren to eliminate.

Eliminierung elimination.

Elite best set, élite, pick, cream, flower;
~ **der Armee** pick of the army;
~**einheit zur Bekämpfung von Terroristen** crack antiguerilla unit; ~**status** elite status; ~**truppen** crack troops, élite, first line.

Elle yard.

Ellbogen elbow;
j. mit dem ~ **anstoßen** to nudge s. o.; **seine** ~ **gebrauchen** to elbow one's way; **keine** ~ **haben** to have no push.

Ellenbogenfreiheit elbow room.

ellenlang|er Bericht long-winded report; ~**e Geschichte** endless story; ~**e Zahlenkolonne** string of figures a yard long.

Ellenmaß yard-stick.

Elmsfeuer St. Elm's fire, jack-o-lantern.

Eloge praise, compliment;
jem. ~**n sagen** to give s. o. a pat on the back, to be warm in s. one's praise.

Eloquenz eloquence.

Elster, geschwätzig wie eine ~ **sein** to talk nineteen to the dozen.

elterlich parental, parent;
zu den ~**en Aufgaben gehören** to be the part of parents; ~**es Erbteil** patrimony; ~**e Gewalt** parental (paternal) authority, tutorship by nature; ~**e Pflichten** parental duties.

Eltern parents;
von gleichen ~ **abstammend** whole blood;
an ~ **Statt** in loco parentis; ~ **und Verwandte** parents and relations;
von seinen ~ **unabhängig sein** to be independent of one's parents; **von den** ~ **nicht versorgt werden** to lack parental care;
~**abend** parents' evening; ~**beirat** *(Schule)* Parent-Teacher Association (P.T.A.) *(US)*; ~**haus verlassen** to leave home; ~**liebe** parental affection; ~**mord** parenticide; ~**schaft** parenthood; ~**schlafzimmer** master bedroom; ~**teil** parent; **angeheirateter** ~**teil** parent-in-law; **sorgeberechtigter** ~**teil** guardian for nurture; ~**vereinigung** parents' association; ~**versammlung** parents' assembly.

Emailleschild enamel sign.

Emanzipation emancipation.

Emanzipationsbewegung emancipation movement.

emanzipiert emancipated;
~**e Frau** emancipated woman.

Emballage cover, package.

emballieren to bale.

Embargo embargo, restraint of rulers and princes;
völkerrechtliches ~ hostile embargo;
~ **auf Gold** gold embargo; **totales** ~ **auf den Handelsverkehr** outright economic embargo, interdiction of commerce (commercial intercourse); ~ **auf eigene Schiffe** civil embargo;
~ **auf feindliche Schiffe** hostile embargo;
~ **auferlegen** to slap on an embargo; ~ **aufheben** to lift (remove) an embargo; ~ **erlassen** to impose an embargo; ~ **legen** to place an embargo; **mit** ~ **belegt sein** to be under an embargo; ~ **verhängen** to [impose an] embargo, to lay an embargo on;
~**beseitigung** removal of embargo; ~**bestimmungen erlassen** to put an embargo on; ~**debatte** embargo debate; ~**empfehlung** embargo recommendation; ~**frage** embargo issue; ~**gesetz** Embargo Act; ~**liste** embargo list; ~**politik** embargo policy.

Emblem emblem, symbol, *(ausgestanzt)* die-cut.

emeritieren to retire from active duty, to receive emeritus status.

emeritiert *(Professor)* emeritus.

Emigrant refugee, emigrant, exile, émigré.

Emigranten|regierung refugee government; ~**tum** emigration.

Emigration emigration;
innere ~ passive resistance;
in die ~ **gehen** to emigrate; **in der** ~ **leben** to live in exile.

emigrieren to emigrate, to expatriate o. s., to exile.

eminent eminent, outstanding, prominent.

Emission emission, *(Banknoten)* emission, issue;
~**en** capital floatations (flotations);
alte ~ senior stock; **bevorrechtigte** ~ privileged issue; **junge** ~ junior stock; **öffentliche** ~ public issue; **ursprüngliche** ~ first allotment;
~ **einer Aktiengesellschaft** corporate issue *(US)*; ~**en zur Finanzierung öffentlicher Einrichtungen** issue of utility shares (stocks, *US*); ~ **von Obligationen** bond (debenture) issue,

floating of bonds; ~ **über Pari** issue above par; ~ **von Schuldverschreibungen** debenture (bond) issue; ~ **in Serien** serial issue of bonds;
~ **begeben** to dispose of an issue; ~ **en bloc begeben** to sell an issue en bloc; **Übernahme einer** ~ **garantieren** to underwrite a loan; **zur** ~ **kommen** to be issued; ~ **plazieren** to place an issue; **fällige** ~**en zurückkaufen** to retire outstanding issues.
Emissions|abteilung [capital] issue department; ~**angebot** issues on offer; ~**bank** issuing house (banker), bank of issue, security-floating company *(US)*, securities underwriter; ~**bedingungen** terms [and conditions] of an issue; ~**betrag** declared value; ~**betrieb** nuisance industry; ~**ergebnis** issuing result; ~**erlös** proceeds of an issue.
emissionsfähig issuable.
Emissions|firma securities underwriter, underwriting company (house), investment banking house *(US)*; ~**garantie** underwriting guarantee; ~**garantiesystem** underwriting system; ~**genehmigung erhalten** to qualify a stock issue *(US)*; ~**geschäft** investment banking [business], security issuing [business], *(einzelnes)* issuing transaction; ~**gesellschaft** issuing company, security floating company *(US)*; ~**gewinn** contributed surplus, paid-in surplus.
Emissionshaus issuing house *(Br.)* (company), securities underwriter, overrider *(Br.)*, investment banker (banking house, *US*), investment underwriter *(US)*, underwriter;
auf Provinzplätze beschränktes ~ local underwriter;
~ **für einheimische Werte** national underwriter.
Emissions|jahr year of issue; ~**kapital** issued capital *(Br.)*, stock capital *(US)*; ~**konsortialvertrag** underwriting agreement; ~**konsortium** underwriting group (syndicate), underwriter purchase (distributing, issuing, selling) syndicate; ~**kosten** stock-issue costs, underwriting costs, issuing expenses; ~**kurs** issue price, rate of issue; ~**land** issuing country; ~**markt** capital (new issue) market; ~**modalitäten** terms [and conditions] of an issue; ~**ort** issuing place; ~**pause für Inlandsanleihen** freeze on new domestic bond issues; ~**politik** capital market policy; ~**prospekt** underwriting prospectus; ~**provision** underwriting commission; ~**rationierung** quota restriction of security issue; ~**reife** readiness for capital issues; ~**reserve** potential stock; ~**satz** *(öffentliche Anleihe)* tender rate *(Br.)*; ~**sperre** capital issue restrictions; **unverkaufte** ~**spitze** unsold portion of an issue; ~**stelle** issuing agency (office); ~**stempel,** ~**steuer** stamp (capital) duty *(Br.)*, stamp tax *(US)*; ~**tag** date of issue, issuing date; ~**tätigkeit** capital issues, issuing activity; ~**termin** date of issue; ~**überhang** excess of capital issues; ~**übernahmegeschäft** underwriting business; ~**vergütung** underwriting commission; ~**vertrag** underwriting contract (agreement); ~**volumen** issue volume; ~**vorhaben** issue project; ~**währung** bond issue currency; ~**welle** spate of new issues; ~**wert** declared value.
Emittent issuer, emitter.
Emittentengruppe issuing group.
emittieren to issue, to emit;
Wertpapiere über Pari ~ to issue securities at a premium; **Wertpapiere unter Pari** ~ to issue securities at a discount.
emittiert issued;
nicht ~ unissued.
Emotion emotion, incitement;
an ~**en appellieren** to appeal to the emotion; ~**en hervorrufen** to occasion emotion.
emotionell veranlagt sein to be emotional.
Empfang receipt, receiving, acceptance, welcome, *(Aufnahme)* reception, *(gesellschaftliches Ereignis)* reception, society function, *(Hotel)* receptionist, reception [desk], *(Rundfunkgerät)* receiving;
bei ~ on receipt of, *(Waren)* on delivery; **durch einen** ~ **eingeleitet** preceded by a reception; **nach** ~ when received; **zahlbar bei** ~ payable on receipt, cash on delivery;
begeisterter ~ enthusiastic welcome; **eiskalter** ~ frosty reception *(coll.)*; **formeller** ~ formal reception, drawing room *(Br.)*; **frostiger** ~ cold (frosty, chill) reception; **herzlicher** ~ warm welcome, open-armed reception; **kühler** ~ cold (cool) reception; **offizieller** ~ formal reception, official display; **rauschender** ~ rousing reception; **saftiger** ~ warm reception; **schlechter** ~ *(Rundfunkgerät)* poor reception; **steifer** ~ stiff reception; **störungsfreier** ~ reception without interference; **unfreundlicher** ~ rough welcome;
~ **eines Fernsehprogramms** reception of a television program(me); ~ **durch die Stadtverwaltung** civil reception *(Br.)*; ~ **anzeigen** to acknowledge receipt; **jem. einen herzlichen** ~ **bereiten** to give s. o. a cordial reception; **jem. einen kümmerlichen** ~ **bereiten** to give s. o. a poor reception; **einer Tratte guten** ~ **bereiten** to meet a bill with due hono(u)r; ~ **bescheinigen** to respond, to receipt a bill; ~ **eines Geldbetrages bescheinigen** to receipt a bill, to make out a receipt; ~ **bestätigen** to [acknowledge] receipt; **auf** ~ **bleiben** *(Funker)* to stay on the beam, *(Radio)* to stand by; ~ **geben** to hold a reception (drawing room, *Br.*); **in** ~ **nehmen** to receive, to take receipt of, to accept, *(Waren)* to take delivery; ~ **der Waren quittieren** to acknowledge receipt of the goods; **mit einem kühlen** ~ **rechnen** to be prepared to be coolly received; **an einem großen** ~ **teilnehmen** to take part in a big do *(fam.)*; **gesellschaftlichen** ~ **veranstalten** to give a party; ~ **verbessern** *(Antenne)* to make for better reception; ~ **frühzeitig verlassen** to get away early from a reception.
empfangen to receive, *(Frau)* to become pregnant, *(auf Quittung)* paid;
in Gegenrechnung ~ received on account; **Wert** ~ value received;
j. mit offenen Armen ~ to welcome s. o. with open arms; **Auszeichnung** ~ to receive a distinction; **j. am Bahnhof** ~ to meet s. o. at the station; **Gäste** ~ to welcome guests; **Gehalt** ~ to draw a salary; **heute niemanden** ~ not to be at home today; **Sender** ~ to get a station; **als voraus** ~ to receive an advance; **offiziell** ~ **worden sein** to have the receiving line; **in Audienz** ~ **werden** to be received in audience; **begeistert** ~ **werden** to be received with enthusiasm; **mit allen Ehren** ~ **werden** to enjoy a full red-carpet treatment; **kühl** ~ **werden** to meet with a cool reception.
Empfänger getter, receiver, recipient, party receiving, *(Brief)* addressee, *(Erwerber von Wertpapieren)* transferee, *(Rundfunkgerät)* receiver, receiving set, *(Telegraf)* receiving station, *(Waren)* consignee, *(Wechsel)* payee;
~ **bezahlt** cash *(Br.)* (collect, *US*) on delivery;
am Wohnsitz des ~**s zahlbar** payable at address of payee;
eingeschaltete ~ sets in use; ~ **unbekannt** addressee unknown;
~ **von Arbeitslosenunterstützung** recipient of unemployment relief, dole drawer *(Br.)*; ~ **einer Effektenzuteilung** allottee; ~ **einer Geldsendung** remittee, benificiary; ~ **eines Vermächtnisses** legatee; ~ **einer Zuwendung** gratuitant;
persönliche ~**benachrichtigung** personal notice; ~**bildschirm** recipient's screen; ~**land** recipient (donee) country, receiving nation; **alphabetisches** ~**verzeichnis** voucher index.
empfänglich receptive, susceptible, *(für Krankheiten)* prone;
für neue Ideen ~ receptive to new ideas; **für Kritik sehr** ~ sensitive to criticism; **für Schmeicheleien** ~ susceptible to flattery;
für böse Einflüsse ~ **sein** to be an easy prey for bad influences; **für Trinkgelder immer** ~ **sein** to be always welcome to a tip.
Empfangnahme receiving, receipt, *(von Waren)* taking delivery;
bei ~ upon receipt (delivery).
Empfängnis|verhütung conception control; ~**verhütungsmittel** birth control aids; ~**verhütungspille** birth-control pill; ~**zeit** period of possible conception.
Empfangs|abteilung receiving department (division); ~**anlage** receiving set; ~**anzeige** notice of receipt; **unter** ~**anzeige** under advice; ~**apparat** receiver, receiving set; ~**bahnhof** receiving yard, destination.
empfangsberechtigt authorized to receive.
Empfangs|berechtigter [authorized] recipient, party entitled to receive, authorized (rightful) beneficiary; ~**berechtigung** authorization to receive; ~**bereich** *(Rundfunkgerät)* reception area.
empfangsbereit *(Rundfunkgerät)* tuned in;
~ **sein** to be open to receive guests.
Empfangsbescheinigung receipt form (voucher), certificate (notice, acknowledgement) of receipt, receipt, *(Zustellungsurkunde)* acceptance of service;
amtliche ~ official receipt; **schriftliche** ~ written receipt slip.
Empfangs|bestätigung acknowledgement, receipt; **vorbehaltlose** ~**bestätigung** clean receipt; ~**bevollmächtigter** resident agent, party entitled to receive; ~**büro** reception [desk], reception office; ~**chef** receptionist, reception (room, *US*) clerk, *(Laden)* shopwalker *(Br.)*, floorwalker *(US)*, *(Hotel)* [reception] desk, hotel clerk; ~**dame** hostess, receptionist, desk *(fam.)*; ~**datum** date of receipt; ~**frequenz** receiving frequency; ~**gebäude** station building; ~**gerät** receiving set, receiver; ~**halle** reception area; ~**komitee** reception committee; ~**loch** *(Rundfunkempfang)* blind spot; ~**ort** receiving place; ~**postamt** receiving office; ~**prämie** *(Börse)* premium of receipt; ~**quittung** [accountable] receipt; ~**raum** reception (receiving, desk) room, reception area; ~**räume** receiving area, public rooms; ~**saal** presence chamber (room) *(Br.)*; ~**salon** reception

(drawing, *Br.*) room; ~**schalter** reception desk; ~**schein** receipt, receiving sheet, *(Post)* return receipt; **gegen ~schein** against receipt; **doppelt ausgefertigter ~schein** receipt in duplicate; ~**spediteur** terminal carrier; ~**staat** *(Völkerrecht)* receiving state; ~**station** receiving yard (station), point of destination; ~**stempel** receipt stamp; ~**störung** *(Feindsender)* jamming, interference, *(durch Wetter)* atmospherics *(Br.)*, static *(US)*; ~**tag** regular (calling) day; **bestimmter ~tag** fixed day, at-home, jour fixe; ~**zeit** time of delivery; ~**zimmer** reception (drawing) room, parlo(u)r, audience, audience chamber, salon.

empfehlen to recommend, to commend, to advise;
j. besonders ~ to recommend s. o. highly; **sich ~** to take one's leave, to say goodbye; **sich jem. ~** to give (present, send) one's respects to s. o.; **sich unauffällig ~** to walk one's chalks *(sl.)*, to take French leave;
Bewerber ~ recommend a candidate; **Richtpreis ~** to recommend a price; **warm ~** recommend strongly (warmly);
sich jem. ~ lassen to give one's compliments to s. o.

empfehlend recommendatory.

empfehlenswert [re]commendable, advisable;
nicht ~ inadvisable.

Empfehlung recommendation, reference, introduction, suggestion, plug *(coll.)*, *(Rat)* advice;
auf ~ upon the recommendation; **mit den besten ~en** yours truly; **mit den besten ~en des Verfassers** with the compliments of the author;
~en compliments, respects, greetings, references;
geschäftliche ~ business reference; **persönliche ~** personal reference; **unverbindliche ~** noncommittal recommendation;
~ aussprechen to make a recommendation; **~en beschließen** *(Völkerrecht)* to decide; **etw. auf ~ eines Freundes erwerben** to buy s. th. on the recommendation of a friend; **gute ~en haben** to be highly recommended; **jem. für seinen Arbeitgeber eine ~ mitgeben** to commend a man to his employers; **auf jds. ~ schreiben** to write in recommendation of s. o. (on s. one's recommendation); **~ an den Ausschuß zurückverweisen** to refer back a recommendation to the committee.

Empfehlungs|brief letter of commendation (introduction), letter recommendatory, commendatory letter; **~brief der Partei für einen Kandidaten** party ticket; **~karte** business card; **~liste** recommended list, list of recommendations; **~schreiben** letter of recommendation (introduction), testimonial, credentials, *(geschäftliches)* reference, trade card.

Empfinden mind, opinion;
künstlerisches ~ artistic sense;
ethisches ~ eines Volkes moral consciousness of a nation.

empfinden to feel, to perceive;
mit jem. ~ to feel for s. o.; **Argwohn ~** to be suspicious; **Groll gegen j. ~** to nourish a grudge against s. o.; **Mitleid ~** to feel pity; **keine Reue ~** to have no regrets.

empfindlich sensitive, susceptible;
gegen Schmerz ~ susceptible to pain;
~ auf Konjunkturschwankungen reagieren to be sensitive to business movements; **~ auf politische Unruhen reagieren** to be sensitive to political disturbances; **Handel ~ schädigen** to affect trade seriously; **gegen Kälte ~ sein** to feel the (be sensitive to) cold; **j. ~ treffen** to touch s. o. to the quick (on a tender place);
~ reagierende Börse sensitive market; **~e Lücke** noticeable gap; **~es Material** delicate material; **~ wie eine Mimose** hypersensitive; **~er Schaden** serious damage; **jem. einen ~en Schlag versetzen** to deal s. o. a heavy blow; **~e Stelle** tender (sore) spot; **j. an seiner ~en Stelle treffen** to touch s. o. on the raw, to tread on s. one's pet corn *(fam.)*; **~e Strafe** severe punishment; **~e Verluste erleiden** to sustain heavy losses.

Empfindlichkeit gegen Konjunktureinflüsse sensitivity to economic fluctuations.

empfindsamer Mensch sentimentalist.

Empfindung feeling, sentiment, *(Sinneswahrnehmung)* sensation;
aus seinen ~en kein Hehl machen not to conceal one's feelings;
subjektive ~ eines Betrachters widerspiegeln to lie in the eye of the beholder.

empfohlen durch introduced by.

empfohlener|Listenpreis suggested list price; **~ Preis** recommended (reference) price.

emporarbeiten, sich to work one's way up, to win one's way from poverty.

empören, j. to fill s. o. with indignation; **sich ~** to rise [in insurrection] to rebel, to revolt, *(mil.)* to mutiny; **sich über etw. ~** to be angry (indignant) at s. th.; **sich über sein Schicksal ~** to rebel against one's fate.

empörend shocking, infuriating;
~e Zumutung outrageous suggestion.

Empörer insurgent, rebel *(mil.)* mutineer.

emporgekommen upstart.

emporkommen to rise in the world.

Emporkommen advancement, rise [in social position].

Emporkömmling new man, arrivé, parvenu, pushing man, up, upstart, cocktail *(Br.)*, shoddy *(US)*, beggar on horseback;
als ~ behandeln to treat s. o. as an upstart.

emporschießen, wie Pilze to mushroom.

emporschlängeln, sich am Berghang *(Straße)* to wind up the hillside.

Emporschnellen, sprunghaftes jump, skyrocketing *(US)*;
~ der Kurse market upsurge.

emporschnellen *(Kurse)* to jump [up], to surge upward, to soar, to shoot up, to skyrocket *(US)*.

Empörung indignation, *(Aufstand)* insurgence, revolt, insurrection, *(mil.)* mutiny;
weltweite ~ world vituperation.

emporzüngeln, am Dach *(Feuer)* to lick the roof.

emsig expeditious, diligent, industrious;
~ wie eine Biene as busy as a bee;
ganzen Tag ~ gearbeitet haben to have been busy all day.

End|abnehmer ultimate buyer; **~abrechnung** final account, closing statement; **~abstimmung** final vote; **~alter** *(Versicherung)* age at expiry, maturity age; **~aufteilung** final partition; **~ausführung einer Zeichnung** finished drawing; **~bahnhof** terminus *(Br.)*, terminal station; **~bearbeitung** finishing process; **~bescheid** definite answer, final information given, final decision; **~bestand** final (closing) inventory; **~betrag** final amount.

Ende *(Ablauf)* expiration, *(Ausgang)* end, issue, closure, *(Bedingung)* termination, winding up, windup, *(Radiotelefonie)* over, *(Pacht)* determination, expiration, *(Schluß)* close, conclusion, *(Ziel)* finish, goal;
am anderen ~ des Dorfes at the other end of the village; **am ~ des Jahres** at the close of the year; **am ~ der Rechnungsperiode** at the close of the financial period; **am ~ der Straße** at the bottom at the road; **am ~ des Zuges** at the rear of the train; **an allen Ecken und ~n** here, there and everywhere; **bis zum bitteren ~** to the end of the chapter, to the very (bitter) end; **bis zum ~ aller Tage** to the end of time; **bis ans ~ der Welt** to the world's end; **gegen ~ des Monats** towards the end of the month; **gegen ~ des Sommers** in late summer;
letzten ~s when all is said and done; **von allen ~n** from all quarters; **von Anfang bis zum ~** from beginning to end; **von einem ~ bis zum anderen** from end to end; **zu ~** up;
das dicke ~ the thick end of the wedge; **glückliches ~** happy end;
~ des Betriebsabschnittes period end; **~ eines Buches** conclusion of a book; **~ der Lebensmittelkartenzeit** end of the ration-book era; **das ~ vom Lied** the upshot of all; **~ des laufenden Monats** the last instant; **~ einer Prozession** tail end of a procession; **~ einer Rede** termination of a speech; **~ einer Seite** foot of a page; **~ des Zitats** unquote;
das ~ absehen to foresee the end; **j. bis zum ~ anhören** to hear s. o. out; **am falschen ~ anfangen (anfassen)** to begin (start) at the wrong end, to put the cart before the horse, to go (do s. th. in) the wrong way, to start off on the wrong foot; **das ~ von jds. Plänen bedeuten** to be fatal to s. one's plans; **einer Sache ein ~ bereiten** to put an end to s. th.; **zu ~ bringen** to bring to a close; **Sache zum guten ~ bringen** to drive the nail home; **in das ~ eines Zuges einsteigen** to get in at the rear end of a train; **sein ~ finden** *(Vertrag)* to run out; **schlimmes ~ finden** to come to a bad end; **tragisches ~ finden** to meet with a tragic death; **jem. bis ans ~ der Welt folgen** to follow s. o. to the ends of the earth; **Unternehmen zu ~ führen** to go through with an undertaking; **zum glücklichen ~ führen** to bring to a happy issue; **zu ~ gehen** *(Jahr)* to go out, *(Urlaub)* to be over, *(Vorräte)* to run short (low); **allmählich zu ~ gehen** to wind down to a close; **langsam zu ~ gehen** to wear to an end; **bis zum bitteren ~ kämpfen** to die in the last ditch; **zum ~ kommen** to draw to a close; **um zu einem ~ zu kommen** in order to end the matter; **Brief zu ~ lesen** to finish reading a letter; **seinem Leben ein ~ machen** to commit suicide; **einer Sache ein ~ machen** to make an end of s. th.; **sich dem ~ nähern** to move towards its end, to draw to an end (close), *(Fonds)* to be running low; **ein schlimmes ~ nehmen** to come to a sticky end; **am ~ sein** to be on one's last end, to be at the end of one's resources (tether); **seinem ~ nahe sein** to be near one's last; **mit seiner Kunst (seinem Latein) am ~ sein** to be at one's wit's end, to come to the end of one's tether; **mit dem**

Öl am ~ sein to be out of heating oil; **einer Sache ein ~ setzen** to put paid to s. th. *(sl.)*; **bis zum bitteren ~ standhalten** to die in the last ditch; **vor seinem ~ stehen** to face the final curtain; **letzten ~s tun** to end (wind) up doing; **am anderen ~ der Welt wohnen** to live at the back of beyond; **dem ~ zugehen** to draw to an end; **langsam dem ~ zugehen** to be draining away; **sich dem ~ zuneigen** to draw to a (to wear towards its) close;
das dicke ~ kommt noch the sting is in the tail;
~ gut, alles gut all's well that ends well.
Endeffekt, im to all intents and purposes, in the long run, in the upshot.
enden to cease, to finish, to [come to an] end, to turn out (end up), *(Versammlung)* to break up, to terminate, *(Vertrag)* to expire;
abrupt ~ to come to an abrupt ending;
am Galgen ~ werden to be heading straight for the gallows; **im Gefängnis ~** to wind up in prison; **mit einer Schlägerei ~** to finish with a brawl; **tragisch ~** to have a tragic ending; **unentschieden ~** to result in a draw; **auf schreckliche Weise ~** to meet with a terrible death; **mit den Worten ~** to wind up by saying.
End|entscheidung final order, *(Statistik)* terminal decision; **~ergebnis** final result, upshot; **im ~ergebnis** in the long run; **~erzeugnis** final (finished) product, end-product.
Endesunterzeichner undersigned.
End|fabrikat final product; **~fertigung** finishing process; **~finanzierung** permanent financing; **~gehalt** final salary; **~gerät** *(Datenverarbeitung)* terminal; **~geschwindigkeit** terminal (final) velocity.
endgültig final, definitive, definite, for good and all, peremptory, for keeps *(US coll.)*, *(Beweis)* conclusive, *(rechtskräftig)* final, absolute, irrevocable;
~ entscheiden to deliver a final judgment; **Sache ~ erledigen** to settle a matter for good; **~ feststehen** to be certain, to be established without doubt; **~ regeln** to clinch;
j. seine ~e Absicht wissen lassen to give s. o. definite information as to one's intentions; **~er Andruck** final pull; **~e Antwort** definite answer; **~e Auflage** definitive edition; **~er Bestimmungsort** final (ultimate) destination; **~e Entscheidung** ultimate decision; **~er Entschluß** final resolution; **~e Obligation** terminal bond; **~e Regelung** clinch; **~es Scheidungsurteil** final decree, decree absolute; **zu einer ~en Vereinbarung gelangen** to come to a definite understanding.
Endgültigkeit finality, definitiveness.
End|hafen final (home) port; **~haltestelle** terminus; **packender ~kampf** grandstand finish; **in den ~kampf kommen** to be in at the finish; **~kosten** terminal costs; **~kreditnehmer** ultimate borrower.
endlich finality, at length;
schließlich und ~ after all;
~e Größe finite magnitude; **~e Reihe** terminating series.
endlos endless, unending, never ending, boundless, infinite;
~ lange dauern to go on for hours on end;
~e Autoschlange never-ending string of cars; **~e Beschwerden** unending complaints; **~e Diskussion** endless discussion; **~e Geduld** patience of Job.
Endlos|band endless band; **~druck** continuous printing; **~formular** continuous form; **~kabel** endless cable; **~lochstreifen** continuous tape.
End|lösung final solution; **~montage** final assembly; **~montageprodukt** final assembled product; **~nachfragestruktur** pattern of final consumption, final consumption pattern; **~preis** final price, price to consumer; **~produkt** end-product, final (finished) goods, end-item; **~punkt** *(Fahrtziel)* point of destination, terminus; **~saldo** closing balance, final balance; **~sieg** ultimate victory; **~siegwaffe** last-ditch weapon; **zum ~spurt ansetzen** to put on a spurt; **~station** terminus, railhead, final stopping point, jumping-off place, terminal *(US)*, *(Flughafen)* town air terminus, *(Nebenlinie)* bay; **~stationsanlagen** terminal facilities; **~stecker** *(el.)* terminal; **~stufe** final stage; **~summe** grand total, count; **~termin** final date, dies ad quem; **~termin für die Frachtannahme festsetzen** to close for cargo.
Endurteil definitive (final) judgment, final decision (sentence), *(Ehescheidung)* decree absolute, final decree;
bedingtes ~ conditional judgment, decree nisi; **obsiegendes ~** final recovery *(US)*;
~ der Geschworenen general verdict; **~ in der Hauptsache** decree absolute.
Endverbrauch ultimate consumption.
Endverbraucher ultimate (final, marginal, last) consumer;
~erzeugnis end-use certificate; **~preis** ultimate consumer (fixed retail) price; **~werbung** consumer advertising.
End|verschluß *(Kabel)* end sleeve; **~version** full-scale version; **~verstärker** power amplifier; **~verteilung** final distribution.
Endwert final amount, tailhead, accumulated value, *(Kapital mit aufgelaufenen Zinseszinsen)* compound amount;
~ einer Rente amount of annuity; **~ einer nachschüssigen Rente** amount of ordinary annuity; **~ einer vorschüssigen Rente** amount of annuity due.
End|zahl count; **~ziel** ultimate goal, *(Reise)* end; **~zinssatz** debtor interest rate; **~zweck** final aim.
Energie *(el.)* energy, power, *(fig.)* energy, vigo(u)r, drive, push, team, go, pep, kick, nerve, getup *(US)*, starch *(US sl.)*;
voller ~ hard as nails;
elektrische ~ electric energy; **ungenutzte ~** waste energy; **zugeführte ~** input of energy;
sich mit aller ~ dransetzen to give all one's whole energies to a task, to put one's back into it; **keine ~ haben** to lack energy, to have no drive; **~ vermissen lassen** to be lacking drive; **seine ganze ~ an etw. setzen** to fling all one's energy into s. th.; **~ sparen** to reduce energy consumption; **voller ~ stecken** to have plenty (be full) of go; **über keine ~ verfügen** to have no go;
~abgabe energy output; **~anlagen** power installations; **~anleihe** electricity loan; **~aufwand** expenditure of energy; **~ausgleich** power balance; **~ausschuß der Regierung** cabinet committee on energy *(Br.)*; **~austausch** trade-off of energy; **~bedarf** demand for energy, power demand (requirements, consumption); **~berater** energy overseer; **~bereich** energy sector; **~bündel** *(fig.)* powerhouse; **~bündel sein** to be real live wire *(fam.)*; **gestiegene ~einfuhren** hike in energy imports; **~einsatz** input; **~einsparung** energy conservation (savings).
Energieeinsparungs|maßnahmen energy conservation measures; **umfassende ~maßnahmen** energy package; **~möglichkeiten** energy-saving potential.
Energieexport energy export.
energiegeladen full of pep, vigorous.
Energie|haushalt power economy; **~knappheit** power (energy) shortage; **~kommission** power commission; **steigende ~kosten** rising costs of energy; **~krise** energy crisis; **~leistung** power (energy) production.
energielos sein to have no drive.
Energie|lücke energy gap; **~minister** Energy Secretary *(Br.)*; **~ministerium** Ministry of Fuel and Power *(Br.)*; **~nachfrage** demand for energy; **~politik** energy (electricity) policy; **~potential** potential energy; **~produktion** energy output, power (energy) production; **~protz** hot sketch *(sl.)*; **~quelle** source of power, energy source (resources); **~reserve** store of energy; **keine ~reserven mehr haben** *(fig.)* to run out of steam; **~sektor** energy area; **~sparprogramm** energy conservation program(me); **~speicherung** accumulation of energy; **~träger** source of energy; **~überschuß** surplus energy; **~übertragung** power transmission; **~verbrauch** power (energy) consumption; **~verbrauch einschränken** to reduce energy consumption; **~verknappung** energy shortage; **~verlust** power loss; **~verschwendung** waste of energy; **~versorgung** electric[al] power (energy) supply; **~versorgungsgesellschaft** energy supply company; **~wesen** energy field; **~wirtschaft** electric power industry, power economy (supply industry), energy business; **~wirtschaftsgesetz** energy bill; **~wirtschaftsunternehmen** [electric] power plant; **~zuteilung** power allocation.
energisch energetic, full of go, resolute, vigorous, firm, without gloves, high-pressure;
~ bestreiten to deny stoutly (emphatically); **~ erledigen** to snap into it; **~ ans Werk gehen** to go at it vigorously; **~ protestieren** to protest loudly; **~ mit jem. verfahren** to deal firmly with s. o.; **~ vorantreiben** to push forward vigorously; **~ vorgehen** to take a strong line; **~ werden** to put one's foot down;
~e Anstrengungen unternehmen to make great strides; **~es Auftreten** swagger; **~e Maßnahmen** strong measures; **~er Mensch** energetic man, go-getter *(coll.)*, zipper; **~e Rede** forceful speech; **in ~em Ton** in a resolute tone.
eng close, narrow, confined, cramped, rowded, *(fig.)* parochial, *(Gewinnspanne)* narrow;
~ verbunden closely connected;
Bestimmung ~ auslegen to construe a clause narrowly; **sich ~ an das Original halten** to keep close to the original; **sich ~ an den Text halten** to stick to the text; **~ schreiben** to cramp one's writing; **~ befreundet sein** to be bosom friends; **auf dem Deck ~ zusammengedrängt sein** to be huddled together on the deck; **~er werden** *(Straße)* to narrow;

~e **Auslegung** narrow construction; ~**erer Ausschuß** select committee; **nur die ~sten Freunde einladen** to ask only intimate friends; ~**e Freundschaft** intimate friendship; **in ~en Grenzen** within narrow limits; ~**er Horizont** restricted horizon, parochial point of view; ~**er Kontakt** close contract; **im ~en Kreis der Familie** in the family circle; ~**ster Mitarbeiter** closest colleague; **auf ~stem Raum** in a cramped space; **auf ~em Raum zusammenleben** to live in close quarters; ~ **beschriebene Seiten** closely written pages; **im ~eren Sinne** strictly speaking; **in ~en Verhältnissen leben** to live in a small way (cramped conditions, narrow circumstances); ~**e Wahl** short list; **in die ~ere Wahl kommen** to be put on the short list; ~**en Wirkungskreis haben** to have a restricted sphere of action; ~**ere Zusammenarbeit** close cooperation.

Engagement engagement, employment, undertaking, *(Börse)* commitment *(US)*, *(Verpflichtung)* obligation;
besonderes ~ fine edge of interest; **fehlendes** ~ lack of commitment; **persönliches** ~ personal commitment; **prozentuales** ~ percentage commitment;
~**s der Baissepartei** bear accounts (engagements) *(Br.)*, short interests *(US)*; ~ **der Belegschaft** commitment of employees; ~**s der Haussepartei** bull accounts (engagements) *(Br.)*, long accounts (interests) *(US)*; ~ **für die Menschenrechte** human rights drive;
sein ~ abbauen to run down one's involvement; ~ **durchhalten** to overstay a position; ~ **eingehen** to enter into a commitment, to commit o. s.; **festes ~ haben** *(Schauspieler)* to have a permanent engagement; ~**s lösen** to cancel an obligation, *(Börse)* to lighten the commitments *(US)*; **ohne ~ sein** to be out of a job, to be disengaged;
~**bereitschaft** readiness to commit o. s.

engagieren to take on, to engage, to enlist, to employ, to hire *(US)*, to recruit *(US)*, *(Kapital)* to tie (lock, *Br.*) up, to invest;
sich ~ to commit o. s.; **sich für j.** ~ to put o. s. out for s. o.; **sich für nichts und wieder nichts** ~ to win the porcelain hairnet *(sl.)*; **sich politisch** ~ to make the political scene *(sl.)*; **als Sekretärin** ~ to engage as secretary; **sich unüberlegt** ~ to step off at the deep end.

engagiert engaged, *(bereit)* dedicated, committed;
persönlich ~ personally involved;
~**es Kapital** locked-up (tied-up, *Br.*) capital.

Enge narrowness, narrow way (place, space), *(Bedrängnis)* straits, tight corner;
in die ~ getrieben up against a wall, cornered;
geistige ~ narrowmindedness;
~ **des Marktes** narrowness of the market;
in fürchterlicher ~ leben to live in cramped conditions; **in die ~ getrieben sein** to be put on the spot (in a tight corner); **in die ~ treiben** to [drive into a] corner, to push to the wall, to nonplus, to stalemate, to squeeze; **j. in die ~ treiben** to tree s. o. *(coll.)*, to put s. o. in a hole, to pinch s. o.

Engelszungen, mit ~ reden to speak honeyed words.

engherzig hidebound, petty.

Engländern English stitching.

england|feindlich anglophobe, anti-British; ~**freundlich** anglophile, pro-British.

Englisch, reines Queen's English *(Br.)*;
ins ~e übersetzen to translate into English.

englische Erzeugnisse English products.

Englisch|kenntnisse command of English; ~**lehrer** English master, master in English *(Br.)*.

englischsprechende Völker English-speaking nations.

Englischunterricht, hervorragenden ~ erhalten to receive thorough instruction in English.

Engpaß *(geogr.)* pass, passway, road narrow *(US)*, defile, *(Produktion)* bottleneck, shortage, squeeze;
~ **in der Produktion** production bottleneck, bottleneck in production;
~ **schnell sichtbar machen** to run fast into a bottleneck; **in einen ~ geraten sein** to be in a tight corner, *(Produktion)* to have reached a bottleneck;
~**beseitigung** removal of a bottleneck.

engros [by] wholesale;
~ **bezogen** bulk-purchased;
~ **verkaufen** to wholesale, to sell in [the] gross.

Engros|abnehmer wholesale buyer (receiver, *US*); ~**abteilung** *(Warenhaus)* contract department; ~**bezug** bulk buying, wholesale purchase; ~**firma** wholesale firm (house).

Engrosgeschäft wholesale business, *(Firma)* wholesalehouse (firm), *(Laden)* wholesale store, *(Tabak)* loose-leaf warehouse;
~ **betreiben** to conduct a wholesale business.

Engroshandel wholesale [trade].

Engroshändler wholesale dealer, wholesaler;
~ **ohne eigenes Lager** wholesale peddler, waggon (truck) distributor *(US)*, truck wholesaler *(US)*.

Engros|kauf wholesale purchase; ~**käufer** wholesale purchaser; ~**kaufmann** wholesale merchant (dealer); ~**kosten** volume cost; ~**preis** wholesale price (cost), trade (merchant's) price; ~**rabatt** trade discount; ~**sortimenter** cash-and-carry wholesaler; ~**verkauf** [selling by] wholesale, *(Tabakgeschäft)* loose-leaf sale; ~**verkäufer** wholesale salesman; ~**vertreter** functional wholesaler; ~**zwischenhändler** wholesale middleman.

engstirnig small- (narrow-) minded, suburban, parochial, hidebound, insular.

Engstirnigkeit narrow-mindedness, parochialism, insularity of outlook *(Br.)*.

Enklave enclave, self-enclosed area;
zeitlose ~ timeless pocket.

enorm enormous, smashing, tremendous[ly], stupendous.

Enquete official inquiry, *(parl.)* select (joint) House *(Br.)*, Senate *(US)*, committee;
königliche ~ Royal commission *(Br.)*.

Ensemble *(Theater)* ensemble, company, troupe;
ständiges ~ stock company;
~**mitglied** trouper.

entarten to degenerate, to deteriorate;
sittlich ~ to become decadent.

Entartung degeneration, deterioration, depravation;
literarische ~ vice of a literary style;
~ **der Sitten** deterioration in morals; ~ **einer Sprache** corruption of a language.

entäußern, sich allen Besitzes to give up all one possesses; **sich seiner Rechte** ~ to forgo one's rights; **sich einer Sache** ~ to alienate s. th.

Entäußerung alienation.

entbehren to go (do) without, to spare, to dispense, to spare, to lack, to miss;
der Begründung ~ to be void of reasons; **Buch** ~ to spare a book; **jds. Dienste nicht ~ können** not to be able to dispense with s. one's services; **jeder Grundlage** ~ to be without any foundation whatsoever, to be absolutely unfounded; **Kraftfahrzeug leicht ~ können** to do easily without a car; **nicht mehr ~ können** not to be able to do without it; **nichts** ~ to lack nothing; **einer Sache** ~ to be empty of s. th.;

entbehrlich dispensable, superfluous;
~ **sein** to be no great miss.

Entbehrung privation, deprivation, destitution;
~**en der Kriegszeit** privations of wartime;
sich zahlreiche ~en auferlegen müssen to suffer many small privations; ~ **nicht gewohnt sein** to be unaccustomed to hardships.

entbieten, jem. seinen Gruß to present one's compliments to s. o.

entbinden to disengage, to dispense, to release, to exonerate, *(Arzt)* to deliver of a child;
j. von etw. ~ to dispense s. o. from s. th.; **j. von einem Eid** ~ to release s. o. from (discharge s. o. of) an oath; **j. von einem Gelöbnis** ~ to absolve s. o. from a pledge; **j. von einer Verpflichtung** ~ to release (exonerate) s. o. from an obligation.

Entbindung childbirth, birth, delivery, accouchement, confinement, *(Befreiung)* disengagement, discharge, exoneration, exemption, *(vom Eid)* release.

Entbindungs|abteilung maternity ward; ~**anstalt** maternity home (hospital); ~**beihilfe** maternity relief, confinement grant; ~**fürsorge** maternity care; ~**geld** maternity benefit (fee); ~**heim** maternity hospital (home); ~**station** maternity ward; ~**urlaub** maternity leave.

entblößen to denude;
sich ~ to take one's clothes off, to strip; **Flanke** ~ *(mil.)* to expose one's flank; **j. von allen Mitteln** ~ to strip s. o. of his money, to deprive s. o. off all his means; ~ **von Truppen** to withdraw troops from.

entblößt bare, naked, nude;
von allen Mitteln ~ destitute of all means.

Entblößung, öffentliche indecent exposure;
~ **eines Landes von Truppen** withdrawal of troops from a country.

entbrennen to kindle;
von neuem ~ *(Kampf)* to break out again.

entbunden werden to be delivered of a child.

Entbürokratisierung debureaucratization.

entdecken to discover, to find out, to detect, to expose;
ganzes Ausmaß einer Verschwörung ~ to make a discovery of

the whole plot; **jds. wahren Charakter** ~ to find s. o. out; **Fehler** ~ to detect a mistake; **frühzeitig** ~ to detect at an early stage; **Gasaustritt** ~ to detect an escape of gas; **Geheimnis** ~ to disclose (divulge, reveal) a secret; **Kontinent** ~ to discover a continent; **Krankheitsursache** ~ to discover the cause for an illness; **wertvolle Manuskripte in einem Altwarenladen** ~ to unearth valuable manuscripts in a junk shop; **j. in der Menge** ~ to spot s. o. in a crowd; **Ölquelle** ~ to strike oil; **Schiff am Horizont** ~ to discern a ship on the horizon; **Verbrechen** ~ to bring a crime to light, to detect a crime; **Verschwörung** ~ to uncover a plot; **etw. durch Zufall** ~ to stumble across (upon) s. th.

Entdecker discoverer, *(Forscher)* explorer.

Entdeckung discovery, find, detection;
neue physikalische ~ new departure in physics;
~ **eines Betrugs** disclosure of a fraud; ~ **eines Geheimnisses** revelation of a secret; ~ **einer Verschwörung** discovery of a plot;
alle neuesten ~en berücksichtigen to incorporate all the latest discoveries; **der ~ entgehen** to escape (evade) detection, to go unnoticed; **zu einer ~ führen** to lead to a discovery; ~ **machen** to make a discovery.

Entdeckungsreise [exploration, exploratory] expedition, voyage of exploration, exploratory voyage;
auf ~ gehen to go exploring, to launch out on a voyage of discovery.

Entdeckungsreisender explorer.

Ente *(fig.)* hoax, canard, grapevine;
lahme ~ lame duck;
wie eine bleierne ~ schwimmen to swim like a stone (millstone, a tailor's goose).

entehren to degrade, to disgrace, to dishonour, *(Frau)* to ravish, to violate, *(Jungfrau)* to deflower;
seine Familie ~ to bring dishono(u)r to one's family.

entehrend degrading, disgraceful, dishono(u)rable;
~e Strafe degrading punishment.

Entehrung degradation.

enteignen to expropriate, to disappropriate, to condemn *(US)*, to purchase compulsorily *(Br.)*;
für den öffentlichen Bedarf ~ to take for public use; **Privatgrundstück** ~ to expropriate *(Br.)* (condemn, *US*) private property, to take land by eminent domain *(US)*.

Enteigner dispossessor.

enteignet condemned, expropriated;
~er Bergbaubetrieb expropriated (condemned, *US*) mine; **~e Gesellschaft** condemned *(US)* (dispossessed) company; **~es Grundstück** expropriated (condemned, *US*) property.

Enteignung eminent domain *(US)*, compulsory surrender (sale, purchase, *Br.*), expropriation, condemnation *(US)*, disappropriation, public taking of private property, recapture *(US)*;
entschädigungslose ~ expropriation without compensation; **unberechtigte** ~ excess condemnation *(US)*;
~ **im öffentlichen Interesse** expropriation for public purpose; ~ **ausländischen Vermögens** expropriation of alien property.

Enteignungs|akt expropriation act; **~ausschuß** lands tribunal; **~beschluß** vesting order *(Br.)* condemnation award *(US)*; **~betrag** condemnation money *(US)*; **~entschädigung** indemnity for expropriation, special benefit, land damages *(Br.)*, compensation money *(US)*; **~gesetz** expropriation act, Land Clauses Act *(Br.)*; **~maßnahmen** forms of expropriation; **~recht des Staates** eminent domain *(US)*; **vom ~recht Gebrauch machen** to exercise the power of eminent domain *(US)*; **~taxe** condemnation appraisal *(US)*; **~verfahren** eminent domain (condemnation) proceedings *(US)*, expropriation.

enteisen to deice, to defrost.

Enteisungs|anlage de-icer, defroster; **~flüssigkeit** de-icing fluid.

Enten|flugzeug tailfirst plane, canard-type aircraft; **~schnabel** panhandle *(US)*.

Entente entente.

enterbar *(Schiff)* boardable.

enterben to cut off from an estate, to disinherit *(US)*, to exheredate;
vollständig ~ to cut off with a shilling.

Enterbung disherison, exheredation, disinheritance *(US)*, abdication.

Enterhaken *(mar.)* grapnet.

Entern *(mil.)* boarding.

entern *(mil.)* to board.

entfachen, Diskussion to provoke a discussion; **Feuer** ~ to kindle (light) the fire; **Leidenschaften** ~ to fan passions into flame; **Streit** ~ to stir up a contest.

entfallen *(nicht anwendbar sein)* not to apply, to be inapplicable, *(Anteil)* to be apportioned (allotted), *(Kosten)* to fall upon;
auf jds. Anteil ~ to fall to s. one's share; **jem. im Augenblick** ~ to escape s. o. for the moment; **auf Einzelhändler** ~ to be allotted to retailers; **auf die Erben der väterlichen Seite** ~ to fall to the heirs of the paternal side; **jds. Gedächtnis** ~ to slip s. one's memory.

entfallendes Einkommen attributable income.

entfällt *(Formular)* not applicable.

entfalten to develop, *(mil.)* to deploy;
große Ausdauer ~ to exhibit great powers of endurance; **j. seine Fähigkeiten ~ lassen** to give s. o. scope for his abilities; **unerwartete Kühnheit** ~ to show unexpected daring; **ungeheure Pracht** ~ to surround o. s. with great splendo(u)r; **großen Prunk** ~ to make a great display; **angestrengte Tätigkeit** ~ to display great activity; **Zeitung** ~ to unfold a newspaper;
sich voll ~ können to have free (full) scope to act.

Entfaltung development, *(mil.)* deployment;
~ **der Persönlichkeit** pursuit of happiness;
jds. Fähigkeiten zur ~ bringen to develop s. one's powers; **durch eine große Familie an seiner ~ gehindert sein** to be encumbered with a large family.

Entfaltungsmöglichkeiten beschneiden, jds. to cramp s. one's style.

entfernbar *(Zubehör)* removable.

Entfernen, heimliches *(Mietsachen)* fraudulent removal.

entfernen to remove, to take away, to withdraw;
sich ~ to go away, to leave, to pull out *(US)*; **aus dem Amt** ~ to remove from office; **Beamten aus dem Dienst** ~ to dismiss an official; **ungehörige Besucher aus dem Sitzungssaal ~ lassen** to order the removal of disorderly persons; **Flecken** ~ to take out a stain; **j. aus dem Haus** ~ to throw s. o. out; **sich heimlich** ~ to take French leave; **Hindernis** ~ to clear away an obstacle; **Kind von einer Schule** ~ to expel a child from school; **Namen von einer Liste** ~ to strike a name off a list; **Offizier aus dem Heer** ~ to dismiss an officer ignominiously; **sich vom Original** ~ to depart from the original; **Siegel** ~ to remove (take off) the seals; **sich weit vom Thema** ~ to deviate (wander) from the subject; **sich unerlaubt** ~ *(mil.)* to be absent without leave, to go awol; **widerrechtlich** ~ *(Mieter, Pächter)* to strip; **zwangsweise aus dem Besitz** ~ to oust, to eject.

entfernt remote, distant, far away, off;
nicht weit ~ a short way off, not a great way away;
fünf Kilometer vom Bahnhof ~ liegen to be three miles distant from the station; **weit ~ sein** to be a long way off, *(fig.)* to be a far cry from; **sehr weit von der nächsten Ortschaft ~ sein** to be far away from the next village; ~ **miteinander verwandt sein** to be remotedly related to one another; **aus einer Versammlung ~ werden** to get chucked out of a meeting;
~e Ähnlichkeit remote (faint) resemblance; **~e Möglichkeit** remote possibility.

entferntest ultimate, farthest;
nicht im ~en not in the least, not at all;
ich habe nicht im ~en daran gedacht it never occurred to me.

Entfernung distance, way, *(Reichweite)* range, *(aus einer Stellung)* removal, discharge;
gerichtlich angeordnete ~ *(aus dem Protokoll)* striking out; **geringe** ~ short distance; **große** ~ Sunday run *(sl.)*; **totale** ~ *(Beamte)* bulk removal; **unerlaubte** ~ absence without leave; **zurückgelegte** ~ distance covered; **zwangsweise** ~ mandatory removal, *(Mieter)* ejection, ouster;
~ **aus dem Amt** ejection (removal) from an office, ouster, dismissal from a post; ~ **aus dem Heer** dishono(u)rable discharge; ~ **in der Luftlinie** airline distance; ~ **von Zubehör** removal of fixtures;
~ **abschätzen** to judge a distance; ~ **auf einer Karte abstecken** to mark the distance on a map; **keine ~ darstellen** to be no distance at all; ~ **einstellen** *(Kamera)* to focus.

Entfernungs|anzeiger range indicator; **~einstellung** *(Artillerie)* range setting, *(Foto)* [zone] focussing; **~fehler** *(Artillerie)* range error; **~messer** [optical] range finder, odometer; **~messung vornehmen** to measure the distance; **~skala** focussing (distance) scale; **~staffel** mileage rate.

entfesseln to set loose, to unleash;
stürmischen Beifall ~ to bring down the house; **Krieg** ~ to unleash a war; **Sturm der Entrüstung** ~ to raise a storm of indignation.

entfesselt raging, unleashed;
den ~en Elementen preisgegeben sein to be exposed to the fury of the elements; **~e Leidenschaften** uncontrolled passions.

Entfettungskur reducing (starvation, slimming) diet.

entflammbar inflammable;
leicht ~ easily set on fire, *(fig.)* easily kindled.
entflammen to inflame, to ignite, *(fig.)* to kindle;
j. für eine neue Idee ~ to rouse s. one's interest for a new idea; **für j. in Liebe** ~ to fall in love with s. o.
entflechten *(Kartell)* to disentangle, to decartelize, to decentralize, to deconcentrate, to dissolve *(US)*, to break up;
Konzern ~ to unscramble a business concern.
Entflechtung *(Kartell)* disentanglement, disengagement, deconcentration, decartelization, decentralization, dissolution *(US)*, divorcement *(US)*, divestiture *(US)*, trust-busting *(US sl.)*.
Entflechtungs|abkommen disengagement agreement; **~abteilung** decartelization branch; **~behörde** decartelization agency; **~gesetz** deconcentration (decartelization) law; **~maßnahmen** dissolution, divestiture and divorcement *(US)*; **~plan, ~programm** deconcentration (decentralization) plan, decartelization (deconcentration) program(me).
entfliehen to escape, to fly from;
aus dem Gefängnis ~ to escape from prison; **seinem Schicksal** ~ to escape one's fate.
entflohen fugitive;
~er Gefangener escaped prisoner, fugitive, escapee.
entfremden to alienate, to estrange, to antagonize *(US)*;
sich jem. ~ to turn s. o. away from o. s.; **seine Freunde** ~ to estrange o. s. from one's friends; **Mittel dem vorgesehenen Zweck** ~ to alienate funds from their natural channels; **Wohnung ihrem Zweck** ~ to convert rooms to office use.
Entfremdung alienation, estrangement, antagonise *(US)*;
~ **ehelicher Zuneigung** alienation of affection;
vorübergehende ~ temporary estrangement;
zu einer ~ **zwischen alten Freunden führen** to cause estrangement between old friends; ~ **verursachen** to come between.
entführen to kidnap, to snatch, to sneeze *(sl.)*, *(Minderjährigen)* to abduct;
j. ~ to put the snatch on s. o. *(sl.)*; **Flugzeug** ~ to highjack an airplane;
sich ~ **lassen** to run away (elope) with s. o.
Entführer kidnapper, abductor, *(Flugzeug)* hi[gh]jacker.
Entführung kidnapping, snatch *(sl.)*, sneeze *(sl.)*, *(Flugzeug)* highjacking;
mißglückte ~ kidnap attempt;
~ **zwecks unerlaubter Eheschließung** elopement; ~ **eines Mündels zwecks unerlaubter Eheschließung** ravishment of ward;
ohne ~en sein to be kidnap-free.
Entführungs|fall case of kidnapping; **~heirat** runaway marriage; **~versicherung** snatch insurance; **~versuch** kidnap attempt.
entfusionieren to demerge.
Entfusionierung demerger.
entgangener Gewinn *(jur.)* lost profit, ceasing gain.
entgasen *(mil.)* to decontaminate, to degas.
entgegenarbeiten, jds. Plänen to counter (thwart, interfere with) s. one's plans.
entgegenbringen, seiner Arbeit Interesse to show interest in one's work; **einer Sache Verständnis** ~ to have a great understanding for s. th.; **jem. Vertrauen** ~ to repose confidence in s. o.
entgegenführen, glücklichen Zeiten to lead to a happy future.
entgegengehen, jem. to go to meet s. o.; **dem Ende** ~ to draw to a close; **seinem Ende** ~ to be nearing one's end; **glücklichen Zeiten** ~ to be heading for a happy future.
entgegengesetzt opposite, opposed, contrary, counter, reverse;
diametral ~ diametrically opposed;
~ **dem Sinn des Uhrzeigers** counterclockwise, anticlockwise;
~ **sein** to be still poles apart;
~e Interessen conflicting interests; **~er Rat** counter advice; **in ~er Richtung** in the opposite direction.
entgegenhalten to reply, *(Patentverfahren)* to cite, *(Verhandlung)* to rebut;
einem Anspruch ~ to set up as a bar to a claim.
Entgegenhaltung replication, rejoinder, rebuttal.
Entgegenkommen obligingness, courtesy, compliance, complaisance, comity, indulgence, concession;
~ **zeigen** to be accommodating (obliging);
aus reinem ~ for accommodation merely; **dank seinem freundlichen** ~ thanks to his kindness;
einem Gast bezeigtes ~ indulgence to a guest;
~ **auf halbem Wege** meeting s. o. half way, halfway house; ~ **in der Wohnungsmiete** rent concession;
einem Schuldner ~ **bezeigen** to indulge a debtor.
entgegenkommen to come from the opposite direction, *(Fahrzeug)* to approach, *(fig.)* to oblige, to be obliging, to accommodate, to indulge, to be complaisant;
jem. am Gartentor ~ to welcome s. o. at the garden gate; **jds. Geschmack** ~ to suit s. one's taste; **den Kundenwünschen** ~ to cater for the needs of the customer; **jem. auf halbem Wege** ~ to meet s. o. half way; **jds. Wünschen** ~ to oblige s. o., to comply with s. one's wishes.
entgegenkommend obliging, compliant, accommodating, forthcoming, *(Fahrzeug)* approaching, oncoming;
nicht ~ unfriendly;
sich ~ **verhalten** to show o. s. accommodating;
sehr ~er Mann very obliging man; **~er Verkehr** oncoming traffic.
entgegenkommenderweise accommodatingly.
entgegenlaufen *(Tendenz)* to run counter.
entgegenlaufende Interessen opposite (counter) interests.
Entgegennahme receipt, acceptance;
~ **eines Auftrags** taking an order; ~ **eines Berichtes** taking of account; ~ **einer Beschwerde** acknowledgement of a complaint; ~ **von Beweisen** reception of evidence; ~ **von Kontokorrenteinlagen** acceptance of money on current account; ~ **der Mietzahlung** acceptance of rent; ~ **einer Zustellungsurkunde** acceptance of service.
entgegennehmen to receive, to accept, to take;
einen Auftrag ~ to take (receive, accept) an order; **Beschwerde** ~ to receive a complaint; **Gesuch** ~ to receive a petition; **Glückwünsche** ~ to receive congratulations; **Versicherungsantrag** ~ to secure an application; **Zustellung** ~ to accept service.
entgegensehen to await, to look forward;
Aufträgen ~ to await (look forward to an) order; **mit gemischten Gefühlen** ~ to await with mixed feelings; **einer Sache mutig** ~ to brace o. s. for s. th.; **dem Tod ruhig** ~ to face death calmly.
entgegensehend, einer baldigen Antwort in anticipation of an early reply; **Ihrem Auftrag** ~ awaiting your order;
entgegensetzen to set up, to counter;
Widerstand ~ to offer resistance; **dem feindlichen Vorrücken Widerstand** ~ to resist an advance of the enemy.
entgegenstehen *(ausschließen)* to bar, to preclude, to be an obstacle;
jem. ~ to stand in s. one's way; **jds. Ansichten** ~ to come into conflict with s. one's opinion; **falls nicht Ansprüche Dritter** ~ unless barred by adverse third-party claims; **einem Antrag** ~ to defeat a motion; **den mageren Ergebnissen** ~ *(Kosten)* to be in marked contrast with; **einer Sache** ~ to be opposed to s. th.
entgegenstehend adverse, contending, conflicting, contradictory;
~e Bestimmungen regulations to the contrary; **~e Rechte** conflicting rights.
entgegenstellen, sich jem. to confront s. o.; **sich einer Sache mutig** ~ to breast o. s. to s. th.; **sich Vorschlägen energisch** ~ to oppose proposals vigorously.
entgegentreten to oppose, to offer resistance;
einer Behauptung ~ to contradict a statement; **dem Feind** ~ to confront the enemy; **Forderungen** ~ to reject demands; **einer Gefahr** ~ to face (confront) a danger; **einem Gerücht** ~ to deny a rumo(u)r; **einem Projekt** ~ to oppose a scheme.
entgegenwirken to counteract, to work against, to antagonize.
entgegnen to answer, to reply, to rejoin;
jem. höflich ~ to give s. o. a polite answer; **nichts** ~ to make no reply.
Entgegnung answer, reply, replication, rejoinder;
kräftige ~ *(fig.)* counterblast; **scharfe** ~ sharp reply; **schlagfertige** ~ retort;
zwei Seiten lange ~ **schreiben** to write a two-page reply.
entgehen to avoid, to evade;
jds. Aufmerksamkeit ~ to escape s. one's attention; **einer peinlichen Situation** ~ to avoid an embarrassing situation; **sich eine Gelegenheit** ~ **lassen** to miss (let slip) an opportunity; **sich kein Wort** ~ **lassen** not to miss a word.
entgeistert flabbergasted, petrified, dumbfounded.
Entgelt payment, pay, fee, reward, *(Belohnung)* remuneration, reward, *(Ersatz)* recompense, *(Honorar)* fee, *(Vertragsleistung)* consideration, price, *(gleicher Wert)* equivalent, *(Wiedergutmachung)* compensation, indemnification;
als ~ for reward; **als** ~ **für Ihre Dienste (Tätigkeit)** as payment (in return) for your services; **als** ~ **für Ihre Mühewaltung** as recompense for your trouble; **gegen** ~ subject to payment, for reward (valuable consideration, value); **gegen ein geringes** ~ for a small fee; **ohne** ~ free of charge, gratuitously, gratis, without remuneration, for nothing;

abzugsfähiges ~ deductible remuneration for services rendered; **angemessenes** ~ onerous cause, adequate consideration (remuneration); **ausreichendes** ~ onerous cause; **umsatzsteuerpflichtige** ~e receipts liable to turnover tax; **vereinbartes** ~ remuneration agreed upon;
kostendeckendes ~ **für Leistungen** remunerative rate; ~ **für angerichtete Schäden** compensation for damage;
ohne ~ **behandeln** to treat free of charge; **angemessenes** ~ **erhalten** to receive an adequate remuneration for one's work, to get a fair reward for one's labo(u)r; **gutgläubig gegen** ~ **erwerben** to acquire for value without notice.

entgelten to remunerate, to compensate, to indemnify, *(bezahlen)* to pay;
j. etw. ~ **lassen** to make s. o. pay for s. th.

entgeltlich for valuable consideration, for value, against payment, fee-charging;
Wertpapier ~ **erwerben** to take an instrument for value *(US)*; ~ **erworbenes Eigentum** onerous title; ~**er Vertrag** onerous contract; ~**e Verwahrung** lucrative bailment.

Entgeltklausel consideration clause.

Entgeltlichkeit remunerativeness.

Entgeltvereinbarung compensation agreement.

entgiften to decontaminate.

Entgiftung decontamination, cleanup.

Entgiftungstrupp decontamination squad.

Entgleisen jumping off the metals, derailment.

entgleisen to go (run) off (jump) the rails, to derail, to leave the rails, to run off the metals *(Br.)*, to jump (leave) the track, to ditch *(US)*, *(fig.)* to make a slip;
moralisch ~ to lapse from virtue into vice.

Entgleisung lapse, slip, gaffe;
gesellschaftliche ~ offence against good manners; **moralische** ~ lapse from virtue;
Zug zur ~ **bringen** to derail a train.

entglorifizieren to debunk *(sl.)*.

Entglorifizierung debunking *(sl.)*.

enthaften to disencumber.

enthalten to forbear, *(umfassen)* to cover, to embody, to comprise, to comprehend, to contain, to include;
im Preis nicht ~ not included in the price;
sich ~ to restrain, to refrain; **sich des Alkoholgenusses** ~ to abstain from beer and wine; **folgende Bestimmungen** ~ to embody the following regulations; **sich einer Frage** ~ to refrain from asking a question; **sich feindseliger Handlungen** ~ to refrain from hostile actions; **Körnchen Wahrheit** ~ to contain a grain of truth; **sich weiterer Schritte** ~ to refrain from further action; **sich der Stimme** ~ to abstain (refrain) from voting;
Frühstück ist im Preis nicht ~ breakfast is not included in the price.

enthaltsam abstinent, abstemious, *(mäßig)* moderate, temperate.

Enthaltsamkeit temperateness, abstention, continence;
gänzliche ~ teetotalism;
Leben der ~ **führen** to live continently (in complete chastity);
sich zur ~ **verpflichten** to sign the pledge.

Enthaltsamkeits|verpflichtung, ~**gelübde** the pledge.

Enthaltung forbearance, *(Stimmabgabe)* abstention [from voting].

enthaupten to decapitate, to behead.

Enthauptung decapitation, beheading.

entheben to discharge, to dismiss, to oust, to eject, to remove, to relieve, to release;
j. seines Amtes ~ to dismiss s. o. from (relieve, remove s. o. of) his post; **j. vorläufig seines Amtes** ~ to suspend s. o. from office; **j. der Mühe** ~ to save s. o. the trouble; **j. der Notwendigkeit** ~ **noch arbeiten zu müssen** to relieve s. o. of the necessity of working; **j. jedweder Verantwortung** ~ to relieve s. o. of all responsibility.

Enthebung dismissal, removal, relief from office, exemption;
vorläufige ~ suspension; **zwangsweise** ~ mandatory removal; ~ **von einer Verpflichtung** discharge of (from) an engagement.

entheiligen to profane, to desecrate.

Entheiligung profanation.

Enthemmung disinhibition.

enthoben, seines Amtes dismissed from service, deprived of one's office.

enthüllen to disclose, to divulge, to divulgate, to reveal, to bring to light;
Denkmal ~ to unveil a monument; **seine geheimsten Gedanken** ~ to unbosom one's thoughts; **jem. seine innersten Gefühle** ~ to reveal one's innermost feelings to s. o.

Enthüller debunker.

enthüllt|sein to be out; ~ **werden** to come to light.

Enthüllung discovery, divulgation, revelation, exposure, disclosure, denouncement;
sensationelle ~**en** sensational disclosures;
~ **eines Denkmals** unveiling of a monument; ~ **der tatsächlichen Machtmittel** showdown *(US)*;
jem. mit ~**en drohen** to threaten s. o. with exposure; ~**en machen** to make revelations.

Enthüllungsfeier unveiling ceremony.

enthusiasmieren to send into ecstasy;
sich ~ to go into raptures, to enthuse.

Enthusiasmus enthusiasm.

entindustrialisieren to de-industrialize.

Entindustrialisierung de-industrialization.

entjungfern to deflower.

Entjungferung defloration.

entkartellisieren to decartelize.

Entkartellisierung decartelization, cartel disposal, breaking-up of cartels, trust busting *(US sl.)*.

Entkartellisierungsgesetz decartelization law.

entkeimen to sterilize, *(Milch)* to pasteurize.

entkleiden to undress, *(vom Amt)* to divest;
sich ~ to undress, to take one's clothes off.

Entkleidungsnummer striptease.

Entkommen getaway, evasion, escape, slip;
geglücktes ~ lucky miss; **knappes** ~ narrow squeak, near escape (touch), close call (shave), a near toucher; **äußerst knappes** ~ hairbreadth escape.

entkommen to get away (free), to come off, to escape;
jem. ~ to give s. o. the slip; **seinen Bewachern** ~ to escape from one's warders; **aus dem Gefängnis** ~ to escape from prison; **um Haaresbreite** ~ to have a hairbreadth escape; **mit Hilfe seiner Freunde** ~ to escape by the contrivances of one's friends.

entkoppeln *(Radio)* to decouple.

entkräften to invalidate, to weaken, to debilitate, to disprove;
Argument ~ to weaken (invalidate) an argument; **Behauptung** ~ to refute a statement.

entkräftet, durch eine lange Krankheit weakened by a long illness.

Entkräftung weakness, debility;
in einem Zustand völliger ~ in a state of complete collapse;
~ **eines Beweises** invalidation of evidence;
vor ~ **sterben** to die of exhaustion.

Entlade|beginn breaking bulk; ~**dauer** time of discharge, unloading time; ~**dock** unloading dock; ~**erlaubnis** discharging permit; ~**frist** unloading time (period), free time; ~**gebühr** unloading charge, discharging expenses; ~**gerät** unloading equipment; ~**gewinn** *(durch sofortige Löschung)* dispatch earnings; ~**gleis** team track; ~**hafen** port of discharge; ~**kosten** discharging fees (expenses), unloading charges; ~**mannschaft** unloading party, *(Schiff)* dock crew.

Entladen unloading, discharge, turnround, offloading *(South Africa)*;
mit dem ~ **beginnen** to break bulk; ~ **besorgen** to do the unloading.

entladen to unload, to discharge a cargo, *(Batterie)* to discharge, *(Flugzeug)* to deplane, *(Schiff)* to unlade, to discharge, *(Schüttgut)* to dump;
sich ~ to give vent to one's anger; **sich über der Stadt** ~ *(Gewitter)* to break over the town;
~ *(a.) (Batterie)* run down.

Entladeplatz unloading place, *(Schiff)* unloading berth.

Entlader discharger, unloader, stevedore, *(Wagen)* dump car.

Entlade|rampe ramp, unloading, platform; ~**risiko** unloading risk; ~**station** unloading station; ~**stelle** unloading point, discharging place (berth); ~**tage** *(Schiff)* ship's days; ~**vorrichtung** unloading unit, discharging gear, tipple *(US)*; ~**zeit** unloading time (period); **befristete** ~**zeit** expiration of free time.

Entladung discharge, unloading, *(Funken)* stroke, *(Gewitter)* burst;
plötzliche ~ disruptive discharge;
~ **einer Batterie** discharge of a battery.

Entladungs|gewinn *(durch sofortige Löschung)* dispatch earning; ~**kosten** discharging expenses (fees).

entlang|segeln, in Küstensichtweite to lie along the shore; **Straße** ~**marschieren** to walk up the road; ~**trotten** to dodge (plod) along.

entlarven to expose, to lay open, to unmask, to detect;
Betrüger ~ to expose (show up) an impostor; **Dieb** ~ to expose a thief; **etw. als Schwindel** ~ to prick the bubble; **Verräter** ~ to unmask a traitor.

Entlarver debunker.
Entlarvung exposure, detection, unmasking;
~ **eines Diebes** detection of a thief.
entlassen to dismiss, to send off, *(Arbeiter)* to discharge, to pay off, to lay off, to put out, to throw out of employment, to sack *(fam.)*, to drop, to fire *(US)*, to swap *(sl.)*, to put to pasture *(coll.)*, *(Beamte)* to remove, to separate, *(mil.)* to demobilize, to disband, to muster out *(US)*;
j. ~ to write s. one's ticket, to turn s. o. out of his job, to give s. o. the chuck *(Br.)*, to give s. o. his marching orders *(fam.)*; **j. aus dem Amt** ~ to relieve s. o. of his office; **Arbeiter** ~ to discharge a workman; **Arbeiter vorübergehend** ~ to lay off workers; **Arbeiter in Zeiten wirtschaftlicher Depression vorübergehend** ~ to lay off workmen during a business depression; **j. als nicht mehr benötigte Arbeitskraft** ~ to make s. o. redundant *(Br.)*, to dismiss for redundancy *(Br.)*; **Beamten aus dem Dienst** ~ to relieve an official of his post; **Beamten wegen Pflichtversäumnisse** ~ to dismiss an officer from the service for neglect of duty; **auf Bewährung** ~ to release on probation; **j. aus einer Bürgschaftsverpflichtung** ~ to release s. o. from a bondage; **Dienstboten** ~ to dismiss a servant, to give a servant the sack *(fam.)*; **fristlos** ~ to dismiss without notice (immediately, summarily); **aus einer Garantieverpflichtung** ~ to release from a guarantee; **Geschworene** ~ to discharge the jury; **aus berechtigten Gründen** ~ to discharge for a just cause; **j. aus gesundheitlichen Gründen** ~ to free s. o. for health reasons; **j. aus der Haft** ~ to release s. o. from custody; **j. kurzerhand** ~ to send s. o. to the right about; **kurzfristig** ~ to lay off at short notice; **Mannschaft** ~ to pay off (discharge) the crew; **Offizier** ~ to put an officer on half-pay; **mit Pension** ~ to pension off; **plötzlich** ~ to decapitate; **j. sofort** ~ to dismiss summarily (without notice); **Soldaten** ~ to cast a soldier; **aus dem Staatsangehörigkeitsverhältnis** ~ to release from nationality; **Strafgefangenen bedingt** ~ to discharge s. o. on licence *(Br.)*, to put s. o. on parole *(US)*; **Truppen** ~ to disband an army; **Überhang an Angestellten** ~ to remove excess white-collar jobs; **unberechtigt** ~ to dismiss without justification; **unehrenhaft** ~ to cashier; **j. in Ungnade** ~ to disgrace s. o.; **j. aus vertraglichen Verpflichtungen** ~ to release s. o. from a contract; **vorübergehend** ~ to stand (lay) off; **aus dem Wehrdienstverhältnis** ~ to separate from the service *(US)*;
~ *(a.)* dismissed, discharged;
leicht zu ~ easily sackable *(fam.)*;
sich ~ **lassen** to take one's discharge *(mil.)*; ~ **sein** to be off the payroll *(US)*; ~ **werden** to be (get) dismissed, to receive notice, to get sacked (the sack) *(fam.)* (the boots, cards, ticket, *sl.*), to get the axe *(US)*, *(Schüler)* to leave school; **bedingt** ~ **werden** to be released on parole *(US)* (on licence, *Br.*); **fristlos** ~ **werden** to get the chop *(fam.)*; **wegen Unredlichkeit** ~ **werden** to be dismissed for being dishonest; **aus einer Verpflichtung** ~ **werden** to obtain a release from an obligation.
Entlassenenfürsorge aftercare for discharged prisoners.
Entlassener *(mil.)* discharge;
bedingt ~ *(Strafgefangener)* probationer, ticket-of-leave man *(Br.)*, man on parole *(US)*.
Entlassung discharge, dismissal, discard, dismission, sack *(Br., fam.)*, close out, firing *(coll.)*, chuck *(Br., sl.)*, sack *(sl.)*, gate *(US)*, *(Beamter)* removal, decapitation *(US)*, *(aus Gefängnis)* release, letting out, *(Pensionierung)* retirement, *(Truppen)* break-up, demobilization;
ohne vorzeitige ~ with no day suspended;
automatische ~ mandatory removal; **bedingte** ~ *(Strafgefangener)* conditional release (discharge) *(Br.)*, discharge on parole *(US)*; **bedingungslose** ~ *(Gefangener)* absolute (unconditional, *Br.*) discharge; **begründete** ~ discharge for cause; **ehrenhafte** ~ hono(u)rable discharge; **endgültige** ~ *(Konkursschuldner)* full discharge, *(Strafgefangener)* discharge from parole *(US)*; **vom Angestellten erzwungene** ~ constructive discharge; **fristlose** ~ removal, summary (instant) dismissal, dismissal (removal) without notice, kick-off *(US sl.)*; **grundlose** ~ discharge without cause; **plötzliche** ~ shock sacking, boot *(sl.)*, bounce *(US sl.)*; **rezessionsbedingte** ~**en** recession layoffs; **saisonbedingte** ~**en** seasonal layoffs; **sofortige** ~ instant (summary) dismissal; **unberechtigte** ~ removal without proper cause, unjust discharge; **unehrenhafte** ~ cashierment, cashiering, dishono(u)rable discharge; **sozial ungerechtfertigte** ~ unfair dismissal *(Br.)*; **vorläufige (vorübergehende)** ~ suspension from office, *(Arbeitskräfte)* layoff; **vorzeitige** ~ *(Häftling)* premature release; **widerrechtliche fristlose** ~ unlawful dismissal, removal without proper cause; **zwangsweise** ~ mandatory removal;
~ **aus dem Amt** discharge (removal) from office; ~ **eines Angestellten** discharge of an employee; ~ **eines Arbeiters** discharge of a worker; ~ **von Arbeitskräften** labo(u)r separation; ~ **nicht mehr benötigter Arbeitskräfte** dismissal on grounds of redundancy *(Br.)*; ~ **der Geschworenen** dismission (discharge) of a jury; ~ **aus dem Heer** discharge from the army; ~ **gegen Kaution** *(Häftling)* release (remand) on bail, bailment; ~ **aus dem Krankenhaus** discharge from hospital; ~ **und Abstellung zur Reserve** discharge without allowance; ~ **in Rezessionsperioden** firing in times of recession *(coll.)*; ~**en bei Rüstungsbetrieben** defense layoffs *(US)*; ~ **aus der Schule** leaving school; ~ **von Spitzenkräften** top-level dismissal; ~ **aus dem Staatsangehörigkeitsverhältnis** release from nationality; **vorübergehende** ~**en bei der Stahlindustrie** steel layoffs; ~ **von Streikführern** victimization; ~ **wegen mangelnder Tauglichkeit** *(mil.)* discharge for unfitness; ~ **von Truppen** dismission, disbandment of troops; ~**en während der Urlaubszeit** holiday layoffs; ~ **wegen ungehörigen Verhaltens** dismissal for misconduct; ~ **aus dem Wehrdienstverhältnis** separation from the service *(US)*; ~ **wegen Wehrunwürdigkeit** dishono(u)rable discharge;
~ **eines Häftlings anordnen** to order s. one's release from prison; **seine** ~ **beantragen** to ask for one's discharge; **ernsthaft seine** ~ **befürchten** to stand in great fear of dimissal; **zur fristlosen** ~ **aus wichtigem Grunde berechtigen** to justify summary dismissal; **auf jds.** ~ **bestehen** to insist on s. one's dismissal; **um seine** ~ **bitten** to hand in (tender) one's resignation; **jem. mit der** ~ **drohen** to threaten s. o. with the sack *(fam.)*; **seine** ~ **einreichen** to surrender one's office, to send (hand) in (tender, submit) one's resignation, *(mil.)* to send in one's papers; **seine** ~ **erhalten** to receive notice, *(mil.)* to be dismissed from service; **Einwand sozial ungerechtfertigter** ~ **erheben** to claim unfair dismissal *(Br.)*; ~ **eines Häftlings gegen Kaution erwirken** to bail a prisoner; **für die bedingte** ~ **in Frage kommen** *(Strafgefangener)* to be eligible for release on parole *(US)*; **anderen Arbeitern bei der** ~ **vorgehen** to bump other workers *(US)*; **willkürlich zur** ~ **bei Überangebot von Arbeitskräften vorgesehen werden** to be selected for redundancy on an arbitrary basis *(Br.)*; **bedingte** ~ **widerrufen** *(Strafgefangener)* to revoke the parole *(US)*.
Entlassungs|abfindung severance *(US)* (dismissal) pay, golden handshake, redundancy payment *(Br.)*, terminal wage *(US)*; **gekürzte** ~**abfindung** reduced layoff pay; ~**alter** *(Schüler)* school-leaving age, age for leaving school; ~**anordnung** discharge, *(Häftling)* order for release from prison; ~**ausgleich** dismissal (severance) pay (wage, compensation), redundancy pay *(Br.)*; ~**bescheid** notice of dismissal; ~**bescheid zustellen** to issue dismissal notice; ~**bescheinigung** discharge slip; ~**beschluß** *(Strafgefangener)* order of release; ~**beschränkungen** restrictions on discharge; **bedingter** ~**dienst außerhalb der Strafanstalt** field parole service *(US)*; ~**entschädigung** dismissal compensation (wage), layoff benefit (pay), redundancy pay *(Br.)*.
entlassungsfähig dischargeable.
Entlassungs|fall discharge case; ~**feier** school-leaving ceremony; ~**gehalt** dismissal pay (compensation, wage); ~**geld** severance wage *(US)*, dismissal pay (payment), compensation pay *(US)*; ~**gesuch** tender of resignation; **sein** ~**gesuch einreichen** to hand in one's resignation; ~**grund** reason for dismissal, grounds for removal (discharge); **berechtigter** ~**grund** good (sufficient) cause; ~**lager** *(mil.)* separation center *(US)*; **auf der** ~**liste stehen** to be due for the chop *(coll.)*; ~**papiere** walking *(US)* (discharge) papers, walking ticket *(US)*, pink slip *(sl.)*; **um die** ~**papiere bitten** to ask for one's cards; ~**schein** discharge papers, certificate of discharge, *(Soldat)* ticket of leave, discharge certificate, ticket *(Br., sl.)*; ~**schreiben** notice (letter) of dismissal, dismissal letter; ~**stelle** *(mil.)* demobilization center *(US)* (centre, *Br.*); ~**tag** date of dismissal; ~**urlaub** terminal leave (vacation, *US*); **betriebliche** ~**vereinbarung** private redundancy agreement *(Br.)*; ~**verfahren** dismissal procedure; ~**verfahren nach der Anziennität** last-in, first-out basis; ~**verfügung** *(Häftling)* discharge; ~**warnung** valentine *(sl.)*; ~**zahlung** dismissal wage; ~**zentrum** *(mil.)* separation center *(US)* (centre, *Br.*); ~**zeugnis** testimonial, certificate of discharge.
entlasten to relieve, to discharge, to credit, to exonerate, *(von Anklage)* to release, to exculpate, to exonerate, to clear, *(Geldmarkt)* to ease, *(Grundstück)* to disencumber;
sich ~ to clear o. s.; **Arbeitsmarkt** ~ to improve the labo(u)r market; **Aufsichtsrat** ~ to ratify the board of directors' acts; **j. für einen Betrag** ~ to credit s. one's account with an amount;

Eisenbahn ~ to relieve the railway; **j. finanziell** ~ to ease s. one's financial burden; **sein Gedächtnis** ~ to aid (unburden one's) memory; **sein Gewissen** ~ to ease one's conscience; **Hauptschuldner** ~ to release the principal debtor; **Konkursschuldner** ~ to discharge a bankrupt; **Markt** ~ to relieve the market; **Schatzmeister** ~ to accept (pass) the treasurer's account; **Staat finanziell** ~ to be a relief for the state; **j. für eine Summe** ~ to credit s. o. (a sum to s. one's account) for an amount; **Treuhänder** ~ to discharge a trustee; **j. von einer Verantwortung** ~ to relieve s. o. from his responsibilities; **Verkehr** ~ to ease traffic; **j. von einer Verpflichtung** ~ to exonerate s. o. from an obligation; **Vorstand** ~ to approve the executive committee's acts.

entlastend exculpatory, infirmative;
~**es Beweismaterial** material evidence; ~**e Tatsachen** exculpatory facts; ~**e Zeugenaussage** exonerating evidence.

entlastet *(Konkursschuldner)* discharged, whitewashed;
nicht ~ undischarged.

Entlasteter releasee.

entlasteter Konkursschuldner discharged bankrupt.

Entlastung discharge, release, credit, relief, approval, *(Entschuldung)* disencumbrance, *(Freispruch)* acquittal, clearing [from charge], *(am Geldmarkt)* ease, easing, *(Rechtfertigung)* exoneration, exculpation;
zu unserer ~ to our discharge; **zur** ~ **meines Kontos** to reduce my debit account;
endgültige ~ *(Gemeinschuldner)* full discharge; **finanzielle** ~ financial ease; **liquiditätsmäßige** ~ ease in money rates; **steuerliche** ~ tax relief; **verweigerte** ~ *(Konkursverfahren)* opposition, *(Revisor)* disallowance; **vollkommene** ~ general release, *(Konkursschuldner)* absolute discharge;
~ **des Arbeitsmarktes** improvement of the labo(u)r market; ~ **des Aufsichtsrates** ratification of the board of directors' acts; ~ **eines Bürgen** release of surety; ~ **des Gemeinschuldners** grant of discharge, discharge of a debtor; ~ **des Kapitalmarktes** easing of the capital market; ~ **der Leistungsbilanz** easing the pressure on the current-account balance; ~ **des Liquidators** release of liquidator; ~ **des Schatzmeisters** acceptance of the treasurer's account; ~ **eines Treuhänders** discharge of a trustee; ~ **des Vorstands** approval of the executive committee's acts;
Einspruch gegen die ~ **eines Gemeinschuldners einlegen** to file an objection to a bankrupt's discharge; ~ **erteilen** to give relief, to relieve, to grant a discharge; **[un]eingeschränkte** ~ **erteilen** to grant a discharge [un]conditionally; **dem Aufsichtsrat** ~ **erteilen** to approve of the acts of the directors; **dem Vorstand** ~ **erteilen** to approve the executive committee's acts; ~ **verlangen** *(Treuhänder)* to demand a release; ~ **verweigern** to withold release.

Entlastungs|angriff *(mil.)* diverting (relief, *US*) attack; ~**antrag** *(Gemeinschuldner)* petition of discharge; ~**anzeige** credit note; ~**bahn für den Güterverkehr** relief freight railway line; ~**bericht** *(Konkursverfahren)* record of release; ~**beschluß** vote of approval; ~**beweis** evidence for the defence, exonerating evidence; ~**erteilung** *(Aufsichtsrat, Vorstand)* approval, ratification; ~**gebiet** overspill area; ~**kanal** spill channel; ~**klausel** relieving clause, *(Treuhänder)* exculpatory clause; ~**klausel für Steueranwälte** tax lawyer's relief clause; ~**material** *(Strafverfahren)* material evidence, evidence for the defence; ~**ort** *(Raumplanung)* expanded (new) town; ~**punkt** *(Beweisverfahren)* infirmative consideration; ~**straße** ancillary road, bypass; ~**ventil** relief valve; ~**verfügung eines Treuhänders** order discharging a trustee; ~**verweigerung** *(Konkurs)* opposition, *(Prüfer)* disallowance; ~**zeuge** attesting witness, witness for the defence; ~**zeugnis** *(für Gemeinschuldner)* duplicate relief, certificate of discharge; ~**zug** extra (relief) train.

Entlaufen elopement.

entlaufen to run away.

entlaufener|Soldat deserter; ~ **Sträfling** runaway convict.

Entlausungsanstalt *(mil.)* delousing station.

entledigen, sich to rid o. s., to get rid of, to free o. s.; **sich eines Angestellten** ~ to rid o. s. of an employee; **sich einer Aufgabe glänzend** ~ to tackle a job marvelously; **sich eines Auftrags** ~ to carry out (execute) a commission; **sich seiner Konkurrenz** ~ to get rid of a rival; **sich seiner Pflichten** ~ to fulfil one's obligations, to discharge one's duties; **sich einer Sache** ~ to acquit o. s. successfully, to relieve o. s. of s. th.; **sich seiner Schulden** ~ to free o. s. from debts.

entleeren *(Faß, Tank)* to drain, to empty.

Entleerung *(Tank)* drainage.

Entleerungs|hahn drain cock; ~**leitung** drain pipe.

entlegen remote, out of the way (map), distant, secluded;
sehr ~ **sein** to lie remote from the road;
an einem ~**en Ort** at a remote place.

Entlegenheit remoteness, seclusion, isolation.

entlehnen, Idee to borrow an idea.

entleihen to borrow;
Buch aus einer Bibliothek ~ to borrow (take out) a book from a lending library.

Entleiher borrower.

entliberalisieren to deliberalize.

Entliberalisierung deliberalization.

entloben, sich to break off one's engagement, to disengage o. s.

Entlobung disengagement.

entlocken, jem. etw. to extract (elicit, coax) s. th. from s. o.; **jem. eine Antwort** ~ to elicit a reply from s. o.; **jem. ein Geheimnis** ~ to worm a secret out of s. o.; **jem. sein Geld** ~ to wheedle s. o. out of his money; **jem. eine Genehmigung** ~ to elicit an admission from s. o.

entlohnen to pay off, to compensate, *(in Waren)* to truck;
Arbeiter mit Waren ~ to truck labo(u)rers; **j. für seine Dienste** ~ to remunerate s. o. for his services; **schlecht** ~ to underpay; **wochenweise** ~ to pay by the week.

entlohnt paid;
schlecht ~ underpaid;
angemessen ~ **werden** to get a fair reward for one's labo(u)r; **für harte Arbeit und Mühewaltung kümmerlich** ~ **werden** to work hard and get very little for one's pain.

Entlohnung payment, paying off, pay, remuneration, emolument, compensation *(US)*;
gegen ~ for a consideration;
angemessene ~ adequate remuneration; **tägliche** ~ per diem pay;
doppelte ~ **für Arbeit an gesetzlichen Feiertagen** holiday pay; ~ **in bar** payment in cash; ~ **im Bereich der öffentlichen Hand** public sector pay; ~ **für Notstandsarbeiten** relief payment; ~ **in Sachwerten** payment in kind, store pay *(US)*.

Entlohnungssatz wage rate.

entlüften to ventilate, to vent, to air.

Entlüfter ventilator, *(Druckluftbremse)* bleeder.

Entlüftung ventilation, *(Industrie)* de-aeration;
mangelhafte ~ defective ventilation.

Entlüftungs|anlage aerator, ventilation system; ~**hahn** air relief cock; ~**öffnung** vent hole; ~**rohr** air vent, breather.

entmachten to deprive of power;
vollständig ~ to strip totally of any power.

Entmachtung, politische deprivation of political rights.

entmannen to sterilize, to unman.

Entmannter castrate, spado.

Entmannung sterilization.

entmasten to dismast, to unmast.

entmaterialisieren to dematerialize.

entmenscht brutalized, inhuman.

entmilitarisieren to demilitarize.

Entmilitarisierung demilitarization.

entminen to sweep mines.

Entminung mine sweeping.

entmotten *(mil.)* to demothball;
Schiff ~ to recommission a ship.

entmündigen to incapacitate, to put under tutelage, to place (put) under guardianship;
Geisteskranken ~ to certify a lunatic *(Br.)*;
jem. ~ **lassen** to have s. o. declared incapable of managing his own affairs.

entmündigt under control, declared incapable of managing one's own affairs, incapacitated;
~ **werden** to be put under restraint.

Entmündigter incapacitated person, *(wegen Verschwendungssucht)* prodigal.

Entmündigung incapacitation, interdiction;
~ **eines Geisteskranken** certifying of a lunatic *(Br.)*, interdiction of lunacy.

Entmündigungs|antrag petition in lunacy (for mental incompetency); ~**ausschuß** commission of (in) lunacy; ~**bericht** state of facts and proposals *(Br.)*; ~**beschluß** reception order; ~**gesetz** Mental Health Act *(Br.)*; ~**sachen** mental cases; ~**verfahren** inquisition (inquest) of lunacy, lunacy proceedings *(Br.)*.

entmutigen to discourage, to throw cold water on, to cast a damper (gloom) on, to depress, to demoralize, to wet-blanket;
sich leicht ~ **lassen** to get easily discouraged.

entmutigend discouraging.

Entmutigung discouragement;
tiefe ~ despondency.
Entnahme *(Borgen)* borrowing, *(Gas, Strom)* use, *(Konto)* taking off, withdrawal, drawing on an account *(Br.)*;
bei ~ on taking;
~**n** drawings, withdrawals;
~**n des Firmeninhabers** proprietor's drawings; ~ **aus freien Rücklagen** *(Bilanz)* drawing on free reserves; ~**n aus offenen Rücklagen** *(Bilanz)* transfers from surplus reserves; ~ **von Stichproben** random sampling; **widerrechtliche** ~ **von Strom** illegal use of electricity;
~**n aus einem Debetkonto begrenzen** to stop a loan account; **mehrere** ~**n bei einem anderen Autor machen** to take several passages from an author; **durch** ~ **von Mustern prüfen** to sample;
~**konto** drawing (personal) account; ~**recht** prendre; ~**satz** *(Konto)* rate of withdrawal; ~**schein** stock requisition.
entnehmen *(aus Buch zitieren)* to quote, to cite, *(vom Konto)* to withdraw, *(Kredit)* to borrow, *(Vorrat)* to take from, *(durch Wechsel)* to draw from;
aus etw. ~ to deduce (conclude) from, to draw an inference from; **aus einem Artikel** ~ to learn from an article; **einem amtlichen Bericht** ~ to gather from an official report; **aus einem Brief** ~ to learn (understand) from a letter; **der Brieftasche ein Schriftstück** ~ to draw a document from one's wallet; **Geld aus der Ladenkasse** ~ to take money from the till; **Proben** ~ to draw samples; **Stelle aus einem anderen Buch** ~ to lift a passage from a book; **elektrischen Strom** ~ to use electricity; **elektrischen Strom widerrechtlich** ~ to steal electricity; **Summe von jem.** ~ to draw a sum on s. o.; **einer Zeitung** ~ to see from a newspaper.
Entnehmer drawer, taker, *(elektrischer Strom)* user.
entnervendes Klima enervating climate.
entnervt unnerved;
durch ein ungesundes Klima ~ sapped by an unhealthy climate.
entnommen withdrawn, taken, *(Zitat)* borrowed, quoted;
nicht ~ undistributed, retained *(US)*;
~**er Gewinn** distributed profit.
entpersönlichen, j. to strip s. o. of his personality (individuality).
entpersönlicht werden to lose one's individuality.
entpflichten to release, to relieve of duties.
Entpflichtung eines Treuhänders release of trustee.
entpolitisieren to depoliticize.
Entpolitisierung depoliticization.
entproletarisieren to deproletarize.
Entproletarisierung deproletarization.
entpuppen, sich als etw. to reveal o. s., to show o. s.; **sich als Schwindler** ~ to turn out to be a swindler.
entraten müssen, etw. to have to do without s. th.
enträtseln, Brief to puzzle out a letter; **Geheimnis** ~ to solve a mystery; **Schrift** ~ to decipher a handwriting.
entrechten to deprive of a right;
Volk politisch ~ to deprive a people of its political rights.
entrechtet underprivileged.
Entrechteter pariah.
Entrechtung, politische deprivation of political rights.
entreißen, jem. to wrest from s. o.; **dem Meer** ~ to snatch from the sea; **etw. der Vergangenheit** ~ to rescue s. th. from oblivion.
Entrepot bonded store (warehouse, *US*).
entrichten to discharge, to pay;
jährliche Abgaben ~ to render annual dues; **in bar** ~ to pay cash; **Schulden** ~ to discharge debts; **Steuern** ~ to pay taxes; **im voraus** ~ to pay in advance; **Zoll auf etw.** ~ to pay duty on s. th.
Entrichtung payment, discharge;
~ **von Schulden** discharge of debts.
entriegeln to unbolt, to unlock.
entringen, jem. ein Geständnis to ring (extort) a confession from s. o.
Entrinnen, knappes near escape.
entrinnen to escape, *(Zeit)* to fly by;
dem Tod um Haaresbreite ~ to escape death by a hair's breath; **seinen Verfolgern** ~ to escape from one's pursuers.
entrollen to reveal, to unfold;
Bild menschlicher Gemeinheit ~ *(Bericht)* to reveal a dreadful picture of human depravity; **Flagge** ~ to unfurl a flag; **Karte** ~ to unroll a map.
entrosten to remove the rust.
entrücken, der Wirklichkeit to remove from reality.
entrückt lost in thought, *(entzückt)* enraptured, entranced;
dem Gesichtskreis ~ **sein** to be beyond s. one's scope.
entrümpeln to clear of rubbish, to dejunk.
Entrümpelung clearance of rubbish.
Entrümpelungsaktion rubbish clearance.
entrüsten, sich to be full of indignation; **sich über etw.** ~ to be shocked (scandalized) at s. th.; **sich über j.** ~ to cry shame on s. o.; **sich moralisch** ~ to feel moral indignation.
entrüstet indignant, shocked, scandalized;
über etw. ~ **sein** to be scandalized at s. th., to be full of indignation about s. th.
Entrüstung indignation;
Vorschlag mit ~ **ablehnen** to turn down a proposal indignantly; **allgemeine** ~ **hervorrufen** to provoke general indignation.
Entrüstungs|geschrei outcry of indignation; ~**schreie** shrieks of outrage; ~**sturm** wave of indignation, storm of anger.
entsagen to renounce, to give up, to forswear, to abstain, to abjure;
dem Alkohol für immer ~ to swear off drinking, to take (sign) the pledge; **einem Anspruch** ~ to waive (renounce) a claim; **seinem Besitz** ~ to dispose of one's possessions; **dem Thron** ~ to renounce (abdicate) the throne.
Entsagung, feierliche abjuration;
~ **eines Anspruchs** renouncement (waiving) of a claim;
sich ~**en auferlegen** to deny o. s.; **ein Leben der** ~ **führen** to lead a life of constant self-denial.
Entsalzungsanlage desalination station.
entsandt werden, zu j. to be sent on a mission to s. o.
Entsatz relief, rescue, succo(u)r;
~ **einer Festung** relief of a fortress;
~**heer** relief [army], relieving army; ~**schiff** relief vessel; ~**truppen** relieving troops (force).
entschädigen to compensate, to indemnify, to make amends (up for), to redeem, to recoup, *(zurückerstatten)* to reimburse, to recompense, to repay;
j. ~ to make good the damage [done] to s. o.; **sich für etw.** ~ to recover one's loss, to reimburse (recoup) o. s.; **j. für seine Bemühungen** ~ to pay (recompense, remunerate) s. o. for his trouble; **j. für seine Dienste** ~ to remunerate s. o. for his services; **enteigneten Eigentümer** ~ to indemnify the owner of property taken for public use; **zu reichlich** ~ to overpay; **j. für einen Verdienstausfall** ~ to compensate s. o. for his broken time; **j. für einen Verlust** ~ to compensate (indemnify, recoup, recompense) s. o. for a loss; **j. voll** ~ to pay full indemnity to s. o.
entschädigend compensatory, compensative, compensating.
Entschädiger indemnitor.
entschädigt werden to obtain (recover) damages, to get an indemnity.
Entschädigter receiver of an indemnity.
Entschädigung indemnification, indemnity, compensation, consideration [money], reparation, compensatory damages, pay, recompense, recoupment, amends, recourse, making up, *(Abfindung)* dismissal compensation, *(Vergütung)* remuneration, allowance, *(Zurückerlangung)* reimbursement, recoupment;
als ~ **für** by way of compensation; **als** ~ **für Ihre Mühewaltung** as recompense for your trouble; **gegen** ~ for a consideration; **ohne** ~ uncompensated; **zur** ~ by way of requital;
angemessene ~ fair and reasonable compensation, single recovery; **besondere** ~ additional damages (compensation); **dürftige** ~ scanty compensation; **den Verletzungen entsprechende** ~ compensation proportional to the injuries; **im Schiedsverfahren festgesetzte** ~ compensation award; **finanzielle** ~ financial compensation, pecuniary damages; **freiwillige** ~ ex-gratia payment; **geschuldete** ~ compensation payable; **großzügige** ~ fair damages (indemnity), fair and reasonable compensation; **über den verursachten Schaden hinausgehende** ~ exemplary (added) damages; **unzumutbar niedrige** ~ gross inadequacy; **staatliche** ~ governmental indemnification; **überdurchschnittliche** ~ above-average compensation; **vertraglich vereinbarte** ~ compensation agreed upon, liquidated damages; **volle** ~ due compensation, full indemnity; **zuerkannte und fällige** ~ accrued compensation; **gesetzlich zustehende** ~ legal compensation;
~ **in bar** compensation in cash; ~ **für durchgeführte Enteignungen** damage (indemnity) for expropriation of dispossessed owners; ~ **für Erwerbsunfähigkeit** disability allowance; ~ **für entgangenen Gewinn** consequential damages; ~ **für gestiegene Lebenshaltungskosten** allowance for cost of living; ~ **für Opfer von Gewaltverbrechen** criminal injuries compensation *(Br.)*; ~ **für Verdienstausfall** allowance for loss of trade (broken time); ~ **für den Verlust eines Vorstandspostens** compensation for loss of office; ~ **im Wege der Widerklage** compensation by reconvention;

als ~ beanspruchen (beantragen) to claim as compensation (damages), to put in a claim for compensation; **gegen ~ beilegen** to compound; **für seine Verluste keine ~ erhalten** to get no redress for one's losses; **~ festsetzen** to fix damages, to assess compensation; **~ fordern** to claim damages; **~ gewähren** to pay compensation, to indemnify, to compensate; **keine ~ gewähren** to disallow compensation; **~ für Sonderaufwand gewähren** to allow for special expenditure; **auf ~ klagen** to sue for damages; **etw. gegen eine ~ tun** to do it for a consideration; **~ vereinbaren** to settle the amount of compensation; **~ verlangen** to claim damages, to demand (claim as) compensation; **von der Versicherung ~ verlangen** to call upon the insurance office; **~ zahlen** to pay compensation; **~ zuerkennen** to award compensation.

Entschädigungs|anspruch claim to loss (damages), compensation claim (demand), right of indemnity (recovery); **~antrag** action for damages; **~ausgleich** compensating adjustment.

entschädigungsberechtigt entitled to damages.

Entschädigungs|berechtigter indemnitee *(US)*; **~bestimmungen** compensation provisions; **~betrag** indemnity, amount of damages (compensation), sum granted as recompense, *(bei Enteignung)* condemnation money *(US)*; **geforderter ~betrag** amount of compensation demanded; **~festsetzung** assessment of damages; **~fonds** relief fund; **~fonds für freigesetzte Arbeitskräfte** redundancy payment fund *(Br.)*; **~formel** compensation formula; **~grenze** limit of compensation; **~grundlage** basis of remuneration; **~grundstück** land indemnity; **~höchstsumme** indemnity limit; **~kasse** indemnity fund; **~klage** action for damages; **~leistung** compensation, indemnification; **freiwillige ~leistung** ex gratia payment.

entschädigungslos without compensation.

Entschädigungspflicht liability for damages.

entschädigungspflichtig liable to pay damages.

Entschädigungs|prämie für automatisationsbedingte Arbeitszeitverkürzung lonely pay; **~rente** *(Betrieb)* pension for injury at work.

Entschädigungssumme amount of damages, indemnity, compensatory damages, *(Angestellter)* dismissal pay (compensation);

über den verursachten Schaden hinausgehende ~ smart money, consequential damages; **höchste ~** indemnity limit;

~ bestimmen (festsetzen) to assess [the amount of] damages.

Entschädigungs|vereinbarung recourse agreement; **unbefristete ~vereinbarung** open-end agreement; **~verfahren** *(Enteignung)* condemnation *(US)* (expropriation) proceedings; **stillschweigend übernommene ~verpflichtung** implied indemnity; **jem. etw. im ~wege zahlen** to pay s. o. a sum by way of indemnification; **~zahlung** compensatory payment; **~zahlungen einer Versicherungsgesellschaft** insurance proceeds; **~zeitraum** compensation period.

entschärfen *(Buch)* to bowdlerize, *(Sprengkörper)* to defuse, to neutralize, to deactivate;

sich ~ *(Lage)* to ease, to mitigate; **Lage ~** to ease the crisis (tension).

Entscheid answer, decision, *(amtlich)* decree, ruling;

gerichtlicher ~ legal decision; **schiedsgerichtlicher ~** [arbitration (arbitrator's)] award, arbitrament;

~ über die Zulässigkeit einzelner Vernehmungsfragen settling interrogation;

gegen einen ~ Beschwerde einlegen to appeal against a decision.

entscheiden to decide, to determine, *(Entschluß fassen)* to resolve, *(Gericht)* to adjudge, to hold, to find, to rule, to render (pass) judgment, to decree;

sich ~ to make up one's mind, to elect, to come to a decision; **sich für etw. ~** to resolve (decide) upon s. th., to judge in favo(u)r of s. th.; **durch Abstimmung ~** to take a vote; **nach Aktenlage ~** to decide on the record; **Angelegenheit ~** to resolve a matter; **nach Anhörung ~** to hear and determine *(US)*; **nach dem äußeren Anschein ~** to judge by appearances; **sich für eine Arbeitsmethode ~** to decide upon a method of work; **zugunsten des Beklagten ~** to find for the defendant; **zuungunsten des Beklagten ~** to resolve an issue against the defendant; **endgültig ~** to clinch an argument, to settle; **Fall richterlich ~** to give a decision on a case; **Fall schriftlich ~** to do business in chambers; **Fall allein aufgrund der ihm innewohnenden Umstände ~** to judge a case on its merits; **von Fall zu Fall ~** to decide on the merits of each particular case; **Frage ~** *(Gericht)* to rule on a point, to adjudicate, to settle a question; **gegen j. ~** to give it against s. o.; **gerichtlich ~** to adjudicate, to pass on *(US)*; **zu jds. Gunsten ~** to rule (give a decision) in s. one's favo(u)r; **in der Hauptsache ~** to give judgment on its merits; **in erster Instanz ~** to deliver a judgment in the first instance; **zugunsten des Klägers ~** to go for the plaintiff, to find for the defendant; **über die Kosten ~** *(Urteil)* to carry costs; **durchs Los ~** to settle by lot; **sich für die liberale Partei ~** to join the side of the liberals *(Br.)*; **Prozeß zu jds. Gunsten ~** to give judgment in favo(u)r of s. o.; **Rechtsfrage ~** to decide a point of law; **richterlich ~** to judge, to hear and determine *(US)*; **in einer Sache ~** to decide (cognosce) a case, to rule on an matter; **als Schiedsrichter ~** to arbitrate, to award, to adjudge; **vorab ~** to give a preliminary ruling; **über die Zuständigkeitsfrage ~** to decide the point;

völlig frei ~ können to be master in one's own house; **sich nicht ~ können** to waver between two opinions, to shift, to shilly-shally; **Zufall ~ lassen** to leave things to chance.

entscheidend decisive, deciding, sentential, leading, vital, essential, *(schicksalsschwer)* fatal;

jds. Laufbahn ~ beeinflussen to determine s. one' career;

~e Antwort definite answer; **im ~en Augenblick** at the critical moment; **von ~er Bedeutung** of vital importance; **~er Beweis** conclusive (decisive) evidence; **~en Fehler machen** to make a fatal mistake; **~e Frage** crucial question (point); **~es Mitspracherecht haben** to be closely involved with decisions; **~er Punkt** crucial point; **~e Schlacht** decisive battle; **~e Schritte tun** to take the decisive steps (plunge, *fam.*); **~e Schwäche des Aktienmarktes** essential weakness of the market; **~e Stimme** casting vote; **~e Wahl** runoff vote.

Entscheidung decision, determination, clinch, *(Krise)* head, *(Urteil)* verdict, judgment, sentence, finding, *(Verfügung)* ruling, decree;

auf richterlicher ~ beruhend judge-made; **solange die richterliche ~ aussteht** pending a decision of the court;

~en speeches *(Br.)*;

ablehnende ~ judgment of dismissal; **abschließende ~** final decision; **abweichende ~** dissenting opinion; **abweisende ~** judgment of dismissal; **alternative ~** alternative decision; **angefochtene ~** decision complained of, appealed decision; **anstehende ~** issuable matter, cause at issue; **[durch Rechtsmittelinstanz] aufgehobene ~** decision set aside; **bedeutsame ~** key decision; **auf einem Prozeßvergleich beruhende ~** consent judgment; **bindende ~** decision binding on all parties; **nicht bindende ~** persuasive precedent; **einschlägige ~** a case in point; **endgültige ~** final determination (judgment), ultimate decision, settlement, rule absolute *(Br.)*; **erstinstanzliche ~** ruling of a lower court; **frühere ~** previous decision; **gerechte und billige ~** just and lawful decision; **gerichtliche ~** decision of a court, court (judicial) decision, ruling of a court, judicial act, adjudication; **auf höherer Ebene getroffene ~** top-level management decision; **gleichlautende ~** concurrent sentence; **grundsätzliche ~** leading decision; **herausstehende ~** landmark decision; **hochpolitische ~** decision of highly political importance; **höchstrichterliche ~** decision of the superior court; **industriefreundliche ~** favo(u)rable-to-industry ruling; **klare ~** flat decision; **maßgebliche ~en** ruling cases, precedents; **rechtskräftige ~** final decision (judgment); **nicht rechtsmittelfähige ~** nonappealable decision; **richterliche ~** judicial (court) decision, adjudication, consideration, sentence, decision of a judge, judgment; **sachliche ~** decision on the merits; **schiedsrichterliche ~** arbitration, arbitrator's award, arbitrament; **sofortige ~** prompt decision; **unanfechtbare ~** rule absolute *(Br.)*; **unbillige ~en** hard cases; **unüberlegte ~** headlong decision; **unwiderrufliche ~** irrevocable decision; **mit Gründen versehene ~** reasoned decision; **voreilige ~** premature decision; **vorläufige ~** interlocutory decree, rule nisi; **widerrechtliche richterliche ~** iniquity *(Scot., law)*; **zustimmende ~** affirmative determination;

~ für j. adjudication in s. one's favo(u)r; **~ des Berufungsgerichtes** appeal court decision; **~ auf höchster Ebene** top-level management decision; **~ des Gerichts** ruling of the court; **~ nach Gutdünken** arbitrary decision; **~ in der Hauptsache** judgment on its merits; **~ über die Kosten** order to pay cost premature; **~ nach Lage der Akten** decision on the merits; **~ einer Rechtsfrage** declaration; **~ eines Rechtsstreites** decision of a suit; **~ am grünen Tisch** armchair decision; **~ von politischer Tragweite** policy decision; **~ unter Vorbehalt** point reserved; **ausdrückliche ~ für eine alternative Zuwendung** express election;

~ abändern to revise a decision; **~ der unteren Instanz abändern** to overrule the decision of a lower court; **sich mit einer ~ abfinden** to submit to a decision; **von seinen eigenen ~en abgehen** to overrule one's own holdings *(US)*; **durch gerichtliche ~ anerkennen** to adjudge; **~ anfechten** to appeal against a decision; ~ **anführen** to quote a case; **Begründung für seine** ~ **angeben** to state one's reasons for a decision; ~ **angreifen** to dispute a decision; **sich jds.** ~ **anschließen** to endorse s. one's view; **auf** ~ **antragen** to ask for a stated case; ~ **aufheben** to quash (rescind) a decision; **jds.** ~ **wieder aufheben** to overrule s. o.; **seine** ~ **aufheben** to reverse one's decision; **frühere** ~ **aufheben** to reverse an earlier decision; ~ **einer unteren Instanz aufheben** to disaffirm the judgment of an inferior court, to overrule a lower court; ~ **aufrechterhalten** to uphold (abide by) a decision; ~ **aussetzen** to adjourn a decision; **gerichtliche** ~ **beantragen** to sue for a court order; ~ **beeinflussen** to prejudice a decision; ~ **auf dem Verwaltungswege bekanntgeben** to inform the administration of a decision; ~ **in zweiter Instanz bestätigen** to uphold a decision; ~ **billigen** to endorse a decision; **bei seiner** ~ **bleiben** to hold by one's decision; **zur** ~ **bringen** to bring to a head (an issue); **auf eine** ~ **drängen** to press for a decision to be made; **schiedsrichterliche** ~ **einholen** to go to arbitration; **gegen eine** ~ **Berufung einlegen** to appeal against a judgment; **maßgeblich auf die gerichtliche** ~ **einwirken** to affect the findings; **Frage einer neuen** ~ **entgegenführen** to place a question on a new issue; ~ **erlassen** to give a ruling, to grant a rule, to render judgment; ~ **erzwingen** to force an issue, to bring matters to a head; ~ **fällen** to render judgment, to pass a decision, to make a ruling; ~ **zu jds. Gunsten fällen** to give a ruling in favo(u)r of s. o.; ~ **zugunsten des Beklagten (Klägers) fällen** to find for the defendant (plaintiff); **zu einer** ~ **gelangen** to arrive at a decision; **sich an eine** ~ **halten** to abide by a decision; ~ **herbeiführen** to bring about a decision; **gerichtliche** ~ **herbeiführen** to submit a case to the court; ~ **bei einer Abstimmung herbeiführen** to swing a key vote; ~ **mit Gewalt herbeiführen** to force a decision, to bring a matter to a head; **zu einer** ~ **kommen** to reach (arrive at) a decision (conclusion); ~ **nachprüfen** to review a decision; **schiedsrichterliche** ~ **in Anspruch nehmen** to resort to arbitration; **an** ~**en gebunden sein** to be bound by precedents; **vor einer schwierigen** ~ **stehen** to be confronted with (face) a difficult decision; **j. vor eine** ~ **stellen** to bring s. o. to the scratch; ~ **treffen** *(Gericht)* to rule, to come to a decision, to decide; **endgültige** ~ **treffen** to make a final decision; ~ **über die Kosten treffen** *(Urteil)* to carry costs; **rasche** ~**en bei der Kreditgewährung oder der Einräumung von Überziehungskrediten treffen** to make quick decisions on loans and overdrafts; ~ **umstoßen** to overrule (quash) a decision; ~ **durch ein Schiedsgericht vereinbaren** to agree to submit a dispute to arbitration; ~ **mit Gründen versehen** to state one's reasons for a decision; ~ **vertagen** to postpone a decision; **sich die** ~ **vorbehalten** to reserve one's decision; ~**en des Gerichts zur Veröffentlichung vorbereiten** to report; **zur** ~ **vorlegen** to submit for decision; **jem. eine Frage zur** ~ **vorlegen** to refer a question to s. one's decision; **Fall dem Gericht zur** ~ **vorlegen** to submit the case to the court; ~ **zurückstellen** to defer making a decision; **durch gerichtliche** ~ **zusprechen** to adjudge, to adjudicate.

Entscheidungsbefugnis competence, power (allocation) of decision, jurisdiction;
keine ~ **in einer Sache haben** to have no voice in a matter.

Entscheidungsbildung decision making.

entscheidungserhebliche Tatsachen ultimate facts.

Entscheidungs|fähigkeit judgment; ~**findung** decision making; ~**forschung** operational *(Br.)* (operations, *US*) research; ~**freiheit** freedom of choice; ~**gewalt** competence, jurisdiction, say-so; ~**gründe** grounds for a decision, reason stated, merits of a case, opinion; ~**gründe des Berufungsgerichts** rescript *(US)*; ~**hilfe beim Einkauf** purchase decision aid; ~**instanz** decision-making unit; ~**kampf** decisive battle, showdown *(US)*; ~**merkmal** criterion; ~**modell** target (decision) model; ~**prozeß** decision-making process; ~**punkt** critical point; **zeitlicher** ~**rahmen** time horizon; ~**raum** *(Statistik)* decision space.

entscheidungsreif ripe for judgment.

Entscheidungs|richter judicial officer; ~**sammlung** law reports, case book *(US)*, table of cases, Session of Cases *(Scot.)*; **höchstrichterliche** ~**sammlung** summary of leading cases and decisions; ~**schlacht** decisive battle; ~**spielraum** freedom of choice; ~**stunde** critical hour; ~**träger** decision maker.

entschieden decided, *(Rechtssache)* held;
längst ~ cut and dried; **noch nicht** ~ not yet settled, open, *(Rechtsfall)* sub judice; **noch nicht höchstrichterlich** ~ without precedent;
~ **der Beste** undeniably the best;
sich ~ **dagegen aussprechen** to pronounce in strong terms against s. th.; **auf seiner Behauptung** ~ **beharren** to insist firmly on one's claim; ~ **bestreiten** to deny categorically; ~ **für etw. eintreten** to come out strongly in favo(u)r of it; **sich noch nicht** ~ **haben** to straddle; ~ **dagegen sein** to be firmly (strong, dead, *fam.*) against it; ~ **verrückt sein** to be positively mad; **in der letzten Instanz** ~ **werden** to be in the last stage of appeal;
~**er Fortschritt** marked improvement; ~**er Gegner** declared enemy; ~**e Haltung** uncompromising attitude; ~**es Nein** categorical no; ~ **zu hohe Preise** definitely too high prices; ~**er Ton** firm (resolute) tone; ~**e Wendung zum Besseren** definite turn for the better.

Entschiedenheit resoluteness, determination;
mit aller ~ **bestreiten** to deny categorically; **sich mit** ~ **für etw. einsetzen** to advocate s. th. strongly.

entschlafen, sanft to pass away (die) peacefully.

Entschlafener deceased.

entschleiern, Geheimnis to reveal (unveil) a secret.

entschließen, sich to determine, to decide, to come to a decision, to make up one's mind, to resolve, to elect; **sich anders** ~ to change one's mind; **sich zum Ankauf eines Autos** ~ to decide on the purchase of a car; **sich zu einem kleinen Bungalowhaus** ~ to fix upon a little bungalow; **sich endlich** ~ to make up one's mind at last; **sich langsam** ~ to be slow to make up one's mind; **sich schnell** ~ not to be long in making up one's mind; **sich nur schwer zu einer Zustimmung** ~ to agree reluctantly.

Entschließung resolution, resolve *(US)*, *(Entscheidung)* ruling, order, decision;
einstimmige ~ unanimous resolution; **gemeinsame** ~ joint (concurrent, *US*) resolution; **nachstehende** ~ following resolution; **mit Stimmenmehrheit verabschiedete** ~ majority resolution;
~ **ablehnen** to reject a resolution; **über eine** ~ **abstimmen** to vote on a resolution; ~ **annehmen** to pass (adopt, carry) a resolution; **sich für eine** ~ **aussprechen** to support a resolution; ~ **einbringen** to move (put) a resolution [to the meeting]; ~ **zur Abstimmung vorlegen** to put a resolution to the vote.

Entschließungs|entwurf draft resolution; ~**entwurf vorbereiten** to draft a resolution; ~**freiheit** free determination.

entschlossen resolute, determined, determinate, firm, unfaltering, without gloves, bound and determined *(US coll.)*;
fest ~ resolved; **kurz** ~ on the spur of the moment, without thinking twice; **schnell** ~ quick to make up one's mind;
~ **auftreten** to have a resolute manner; ~ **handeln** to act resolutely; **fest** ~ **sein** to be all set to do *(fam.)*; **mehr denn je** ~ **sein** to be more determined than ever; **ziemlich fest zu etw.** ~ **sein** to have a good mind to do s. th., to be quite decided about s. th.; **zu allem** ~ **sein** to be equal to anything;
~**en Eindruck machen** to seem quite determined; ~**e Haltung einnehmen** to adopt (preserve) a firm attitude, to take a firm stand; ~**e Miene** air of purpose; ~**e Miene aufsetzen** to assume an air of determination.

Entschlossenheit determination, determinatedness, firmness;
unbeugsame ~ grim determination.

entschlüpfen to slip away, to escape;
sich eine Gelegenheit ~ **lassen** to let an opportunity pass (slip); **der Polizei** ~ to give the police the slip.

Entschluß determination, decision, resolution, resolve *(US)*, purpose;
aus eigenem (freiem) ~ on one's own initiative, voluntarily; **fester** ~ settled intention, stern resolve *(US)*; **konjunkturpolitischer** ~ anti-cyclical policy resolution;
von einem ~ **abgehen** to reverse a decision; ~ **aufgeben** to retract from a resolve *(US)*; **bei seinem** ~ **bleiben** to abide by one's decision, to stand pat; ~ **fassen** to come to a determination, to determine, to make up one's mind, to reach a decision, to decide; **festen** ~ **fassen** to make a dead set; **an einem** ~ **festhalten** to stick to a resolve *(US)*; **zu einem** ~ **kommen** to make up one's mind; **j. in seinem** ~ **wankend machen** to shake s. one's determination; ~ **vertagen** to postpone a decision; **in einem** ~ **wankend werden** to weaken.

Entschlüsse, einsame top-of-the-head thinking.

Entschlüsseler cipher clerk, cryptographer, decoder.

entschlüsseln to decode, to decipher, to unscramble, to break a code.

Entschlüsselung cipher breaking, decoding, deciphering, decryptment *(US)*.

Entschlußfreiheit free determination.

Entschlußkraft determination, determinatedness, strength of purpose;
mangelnde ~ lack of resolution; **ohne** ~ weak of purpose;
von schneller ~ **sein** not to be long in making up one's mind.

entschlußlos irresolute, undecided.
entschuldbar excusable.
entschulden to disencumber, to free of debts;
Besitz ~ to clear an estate; **Grundstück** ~ to free a property from mortgages.
entschuldet free from encumbrances.
entschuldigen, sich to apologize, to make an apology, to excuse o. s.; **sich für seine Abwesenheit** ~ to ask to be excused from attendance, to send regrets *(US)*; **sich mit Arbeit** ~ to make work one's excuse; **jds. Fernbleiben** ~ to excuse s. one's absence; **sich für Nichteinhaltung einer Zusage** ~ to call off an engagement; **sich mit Unwissenheit** ~ to plead ignorance.
entschuldigend excusatory;
mit einem ~en Lächeln with an apologetic smile.
entschuldigt excused;
nicht ausreichend ~ **fehlen** to stay away without good cause.
Entschuldigung excuse, exculpation, apology;
als ~ by way of excuse; **ohne ausreichende** ~ without good cause;
ausreichende ~ reasonable excuse; **fadenscheinige** ~ paltry (thin) excuse; **aus den Fingern gesogene** ~ trumped-up excuse; **erste greifbare** ~ the first excuse to hand; **absolut natürliche** ~ built-in valid excuse; **schriftliche** ~ written justification; **schwache** ~ poor excuse; **wenig überzeugende** ~ slim excuse; **ungenügende** ~ blind excuse; **unzählige ~en** a thousand apologies; **unzureichende** ~ lame excuse;
seine ~ **anbieten** to offer an apology; **irgendeine** ~ **auftischen** to dish up some excuse or other *(coll.)*; **um** ~ **bitten** to offer an apology; ~ **erfinden** to feign an excuse; ~ **parat halten** to have one's excuse pat; **kaum eine** ~ **finden können** to be hard up for an excuse; **jem. eine** ~ **schreiben** to write a note of excuse to s. o.; ~ **stammeln** to blunder out an apology, to falter an excuse; ~ **stottern** to stumble through an apology; **nach einer** ~ **suchen** to cast about for an excuse; **seine** ~ **vorbringen** to tender one's apologies; **schriftliche** ~ **vorlegen** to send a written excuse.
Entschuldigungs|brief letter of apology, written apology, exculpatory letter; **~grund** excuse; **ohne triftigen ~grund** without good cause; **etw. als ~grund angeben** to offer s. th. as an excuse; **~schreiben** letter of regret; **~zettel** *(Schule)* note of excuse.
Entschuldung redemption of debts, sinking of debts, *(Grundstück)* disencumberment, disencumbrance.
entschwinden to disappear, to vanish;
wie im Flug ~ *(Zeit)* to seem to fly; **dem Gedächtnis** ~ to fade (slip) from memory; **aus dem Gesichtskreis** ~ to vanish from sight.
entsenden to send;
j. als Bevollmächtigten ~ to delegate s. o.; **Boten** ~ to dispatch a messenger.
Entsendestaat sending state.
Entsendung delegation, deputation, sending;
~ **von Truppen** dispatch of troops.
Entsetzen horror, fright, dismay, panic;
vor ~ **starr** horror-stricken, paralysed with horror;
Nachricht mit ~ **aufnehmen** to be shocked to hear a news report; **vor** ~ **stumm sein** to be dumbfounded with terror.
entsetzen *(aus dem Besitz)* to dispossess, to eject, to evict, to oust, *(mil.)* to rescue;
j. seines Amtes ~ to remove s. o. from his post; **sich über etw.** ~ to be horrified (frightened, terrified, shocked) about s. th.; **belagerte Stadt** ~ to relieve a town; **j. des Thrones** ~ to dethrone s. o.
entsetzlich horrible, horrifying, terrible, awful, dreadful, frightful, *(grausam)* atrocious, cruel;
~ **gefährlich** terribly dangerous;
j. ~ **finden** not to be able to stand s. o., to be an abomination to s. o.; **jem.** ~ **auf die Nerven gehen** to get under s. one's skin; **~er Anblick** ghastly sight; **~e Angst haben** to be dreadfully (terribly) frightened; **~en Hunger haben** to be awfully hungry; **~er Lärm** frightful (terrible) noise; **mit ~en Schmerzen sterben** to die in agony; **~es Verbrechen** detestable (atrocious) crime; **~es Wetter** dreadful (terrible, abominable) weather.
entsetzt horrified, horror-stricken, appalled, frightened, terrified;
zu Tode ~ shocked to death;
ganz ~ **sein** to be quite appalled; ~ **zurückweichen** to recoil in horror;
~er Aufschrei frightened scream; **in ~em Schweigen** in a silence full of horror.
Entsetzung *(vom Amt)* dismissal, removal, *(aus Besitz)* ouster, ejection, dispossession, *(mil.)* relief, rescue.
entseuchen to decontaminate.
Entseuchung decontamination.
entsiegeln to unseal, to break (take off) the seal.
Entsiegelung taking off the seals.
entsinnen, sich to remember, to recall.
entspannen to relax, to slacken, *(Krise)* to ease off;
sich ~ to find relaxation, to unbrace o. s., *(Geldmarkt)* to ease, *(politische Lage)* to ease up (off), to ease, to become a little easier; **Konjunktur** ~ to ease the economic situation; **Lage** ~ to ease (relieve, relax) the tension; **Nerven** ~ to have a soothing effect on the nerves; **sich eine Stunde** ~ to relax for an hour.
entspannend recreative, relaxing;
~e Lektüre relaxing reading, escape literature; **~e Wirkung haben** to be a relaxation for the mind.
entspannt relaxed, at ease;
die Lage hat sich ~ the situation has eased;
~e Atmosphäre relaxed atmosphere.
Entspannung escape, relaxation, remission, resource, remission, *(pol.)* relaxation, alleviation of tension, ease, detente;
zur ~ as a relaxation;
~ **am Geldmarkt** ease in money rates; ~ **des Kapitalmarktes** easing of the capital market; ~ **der Konjunktur** easing of cyclical conditions; ~ **der Lage** relief (relaxation, easing) of the tension; ~ **am Markt für kurzfristige Geldmarktpapiere** easing of short-term rates;
zur ~ **beitragen** to reduce tension; **zur** ~ **der politischen Lage beitragen** to contribute to the easing of the political situation; **zur** ~ **lesen** to seek relaxation in books; ~ **verschaffen** to ease.
Entspannungs|lektüre escape literature; **~mittel** relaxant, surfactant *(US)*; **~offensive** *(pol.)* offensive of detente; **~politik** policy of detente; **~therapie** release therapy.
entsperren, Konto to deblock (unblock) an account.
Entsperrung unblocking.
entsprechen to answer, to conform, to correspond, *(statistische Angaben)* to be correlative to;
einem Abkommen ~ to conform with an arrangement; **den Anforderungen** ~ to answer (meet) the requirements; **seinen Berechnungen nicht** ~ not to accord to one's calculations; **den Bestimmungen** ~ to comply with the terms; **den Erwartungen** ~ to come up to scratch, to answer expectations; **den Erwartungen nicht** ~ to fall short of expectations; **den Formalitäten** ~ to comply with the formalities; **dem Geist eines Vertrages** ~ to correspond to the spirit of a treaty; **einem Gesuch** ~ to grant a request; **dem Muster** ~ to correspond to sample; **einer Personenbeschreibung** ~ to answer a description; **seinen Prinzipien nicht** ~ not to accord to one's principles; **den Tatsachen** ~ to be in accordance with the facts; **den Tatsachen nicht** ~ not to be consistent with the facts; **der zwischenstaatlichen Übung** ~ to conform to international standards; **den Vorschriften** ~ to conform to the provisions; **jds. Wünschen** ~ to comply (conform, fall in) with s. one's wishes; **Wünschen einer neuen Publikumsschicht** ~ to cater to a new public; **dem Zweck** ~ to serve a purpose; **dem Zweck nicht** ~ to be inadequate to a purpose.
entsprechend *(angemessen)* adequate, *(beiderseitig)* reciprocal, *(gleichwertig)* equivalent, comparable, *(passend)* suitable, *(sinngemäß)* analogous, *(Statistik)* correlative, *(übereinstimmend)* answering, according, corresponding, *(verhältnismäßig)* proportional, commensurate;
Ihren Anforderungen ~ in compliance with your instructions; **den Bestimmungen** ~ in accordance with the regulations; **dem Gesetz** ~ according to law; **nicht der Jahreszeit** ~ unseasonable; **dem Muster** ~ up to sample; **den Vorschriften** ~ in accordance with the regulations;
seine Pläne ~ **ändern** to alter one's plans accordingly; **j.** ~ **belohnen** to reward s. o. adequately; **sich seinem Alter** ~ **benehmen** to behave as befits one's age; **sich** ~ **einleben** to get acclimatized appropriately; ~ **sein** to correspond, to come up, to tally;
~e Anwendung analogical application; **~e Anwendung finden** to apply analogically; **~er deutscher Ausdruck** equivalent expression in German; **~e Belohnung** adequate reward; **~e Buchung** corresponding entry; **ein der Stellung ~es Gehalt** salary appropriate to an office; **~e Kleidung** appropriate (proper) clothes; **~e Mittel** adequate means; **sich bei der ~en Stelle erkundigen** to inquire at the appropriate quarter; **~er Vermerk in den Akten** corresponding entry in the files.
entspringen *(Fluß)* to have its source, to rise;
einem Mißverständnis ~ to spring from a misunderstanding.
entsprungener Sträfling runaway convict.
entstaatlichen to denationalize.
Entstaatlichung denationalization.

entstammen to issue, to come of;
einem vornehmen Geschlecht ~ to be of noble descent; **einem gemeinsamen Vorfahren** ~ to originate from a common ancestor; **einer gemeinsamen Wurzel** ~ to derive from a common root.
entstanden *(Zinsen)* accrued;
~ **sein** *(Anspruch)* to have been perfected;
~**e Kosten** costs incurred (accrued); ~**er Schaden** resulting damage; ~**e Unkosten** expenses incurred.
Entstaubung dust removal.
Entstaubungsanlage smoke filter.
Entstauungskosten cost of breaking the stowage.
entstehen to arise, to come into being, to originate, to grow out, to be borne, *(Anspruch)* to arise, *(Feuer)* to break out, *(Gewohnheit)* to grow up, *(Industrie)* to spring up, *(Kosten)* to result, *(Risiko)* to attach, *(Schwierigkeit)* to emerge, to arise, *(Verlust)* to occur, *(Zinsen)* to accrue;
aus falscher Ernährung ~ to be due to a wrong diet; **langsam** ~ to emerge gradually; **aus einem Mißverständnis** ~ to originate in (ensue from) a misunderstanding; **durch die Unachtsamkeit eines Angestellten** ~ to be caused by the negligence of an employee;
~ **lassen** to give birth to.
entstehend incoming, accruing, *(Risiko)* attaching;
daraus ~**e Folgen** resulting consequences; **daraus** ~**e Kosten** costs arising from it; **möglicherweise** ~**e Schwierigkeiten** potential difficulties; **neu** ~**e Staaten** emergent countries; ~**e Zinsen** accruing interest.
Entstehung coming into being, rise, *(Staat)* emergence, *(Ursprung)* origin, origination, birth, *(Zinsen)* accrual;
in der ~ in the making (embryo);
~ **der Anlagebereitschaft** investment commitment process; ~ **eines Anspruchs** arisal of a claim; ~ **neuer Ideen** birth of new ideas; ~ **neuer Industrien** coming into being of new industries; ~ **eines Klageanspruchs** accrual of a case of action; ~ **einer Legende** origin of a legend; ~ **eines Rechts** accrual of a right; ~ **eines Risikos** attachment of a risk; ~ **eines Streites** origin of a quarrel; ~ **eines Unternehmens** inception of an enterprise;
zur ~ **gelangen** to accrue.
Entstehungs|datum date of origin, accrual date; ~**herd einer Krankheit ausfindig machen** to locate the seat of a disease; ~**ort** place of origin; ~**rechnung des Sozialprodukts** calculation of the national income; ~**termin einer Steuerschuld** lien date; ~**zeit** days of creation, *(Forderung)* time of inception; ~**zeit eines Manuskriptes in das zehnte Jahrhundert legen** to place a manuscript not later than the tenth century; ~**zeitpunkt einer Hypothek** date of a mortgage.
entstellen to distort, to disfigure, to mutilate, to deface, to deform, to blemish, *(fig.)* to pervert, to twist, *(Telegrammtext)* to corrupt;
Bericht ~ to garble an account; **Buch** ~ to disfigure a book; **körperlich** ~ to disfigure; **Landschaft** ~ to disfigure (mar) a landscape; **Sinn eines Textes** ~ to distort the meaning of a text; **Stadtbild** ~ to spoil the beauty of a town; **Tatsachen** ~ to misrepresent (distort) the facts; **Telegramm** ~ to corrupt a telegram; **Textstelle** ~ to warp the sense of a passage; **Wahrheit** ~ to pervert the truth.
entstellende| Narbe disfiguring scar; ~ **Zeitungsberichte** distorted newspaper accounts.
entstellt disfigured, distorted, *(Landschaft)* spoiled, marred;
~**er Bericht** garbled account; ~**er Text** *(Telegramm)* corrupt text.
Entstellung distortion, disfigurement, mutilation, misinterpretation, deformation, defacement, *(Landschaft)* marring, spoiling;
körperliche ~ disfigurement;
~ **der Tatsachen** distortion of the facts; ~ **eines Textes** corruption of a text; ~ **einer Textstelle** warping the sense of a passage; ~ **der Wahrheit** perversion of the truth.
entstören *(el.)* to suppress interferences, *(Telefon)* to clear, to dejam;
Gerät ~ to remove defects in an apparatus; **Motor** ~ to fit a suppressor to an electric motor.
Entstörgerät suppressor.
entstört noise-suppressed.
Entstörung *(el.)* suppression.
Entstörungs| kondensator suppressor; ~**vorrichtung** noise eliminator.
enttäuschen to disappoint, to disillusion;
j. ~ to let s. o. down, to lower s. one's spirits *(fam.)*.
enttäuschende Aufführung disappointing performance.
enttäuscht, angenehm apreeably disappointed;
~ **und verbittert** disillusioned and bitter;
~ **in sich zusammensacken** to slump in disappointment;
~**er Ehrgeiz** disappointed ambition.
Enttäuschung disappointment, disillusion;
schwere ~ deep disappointment; **zahlreiche** ~**en** numerous frustrations;
jem. ~ **bereiten** to disappoint s. o.
entthronen to dethrone, to depose.
Entthronung dethronement, deposition.
enttrümmern, Stadt to clear away the debris from a town.
Enttrümmerung rubble clearance.
entvölkern to dispeople, to depopulate, to unpeople, to desolate.
entvölkert unpeopled, unmanned, depopulated;
~**e Stadt** deserted town.
entwachsen, den Kinderschuhen to emerge from childhood, to be past a boy (girl); **seinen Kleidern** ~ to outgrow one's clothes.
entwaffnen to disarm.
entwaffnendes Lächeln disarming smile.
Entwaffnung disarmament.
entwalden to deforest, to disforest, to disafforest.
Entwaldung deforestation, disafforestation, forest liquidation.
entwarnen to sound the all-clear.
Entwarnung off-signal, all-clear.
Entwarnungssignal all clear (raiders past) signal;
~ **auslösen** to sound the all-clear.
entwässern top ditch, to well-drain;
Gebiet ~ to drain an area.
Entwässerung drainage.
Entwässerungs|anlage drainage system; ~**behörde** catchment board; ~**brunnen** drainage well; ~**gebiet** catchment (drainage, *US*) area; ~**gebühr** drainage rate; ~**graben** drain, lode *(Br.)*; **schmaler** ~**graben** drove; ~**hahn** drain cock; ~**kanal** drainage canal; ~**netz** system of drainage; ~**pumpe** drainage pump; ~**rohr** drainage pipe, drainpipe; ~**schacht** drainage shaft (tunnel); ~**system** drainage system; ~**ventil** drain valve.
Entweder-Oder alternative, take it or leave it.
Entweichen *(Gas)* escape, leak.
entweichen *(Gas)* to escape, to leak;
aus dem Gefängnis ~ to escape from prison.
Entweichenlassen, fahrlässiges negligent escape;
~ **von Gefangenen** gaol delivery.
entweihen to profane, to desecrate.
Entweihung profanation, desecration;
~ **einer Kirche** violation of a church.
entwenden to embezzle, to abstract, to misappropriate, *(Kleinigkeiten)* to pilfer;
jem. etw. ~ to steal s th. from s. o.;
Buch aus der Bibliothek ~ to filch a book out of a library.
Entwendung embezzlement, abstraction, misappropriation.
Entwerfen *(Vertrag)* composition, draft.
entwerfen to project, to outline, *(Konstruktion, Muster)* to construe, to design, *(Programm)* to scheme, to chart, *(Verfassung)* to frame, *(Vertrag)* to draft, to draw up, to minute, to compose, to prepare;
anschauliches Bild der Lage von etw. ~ to give a graphic picture of the situation; **Bucheinband** ~ to design a book binding; **flüchtig** ~ to sketch, to make a rough draft; **Haus** ~ to make a sketch of a house; **neu** ~ to redraft; **Plan** ~ to make a plan, to outline a scheme; **Pläne für eine neu anzulegende Straße** ~ to sketch out proposals for a new road; **mit wenigen Strichen** ~ to touch; **Urkunde** ~ to draft (draw up) a document.
entwerten to reduce in value, to disable, to impair in worth, *(abwerten)* to devalue, to devaluate, to reduce in value, to depreciate, to debase, *(Briefmarken)* to date-cancel, to obliterate, *(Geld)* to call in, to demonetize, to inflate, *(Stempelmarken)* to cancel, to deface, to obliterate;
Aussage stark ~ to diminish the value of an evidence; **mit dem Datumsstempel** ~ to date-cancel; **Pfund** ~ to depreciate (devaluate) the pound; **völlig** ~ to render valueless; **Währung** ~ to debase a currency.
entwertet depreciated, devalued, *(abgestempelt)* cancelled, defaced, obliterated;
nicht ~ undepreciated, uncancelled, undebased, not devalued;
~ **werden** to fall in value;
~**e Briefmarke** used stamp.
Entwertung reduction in value, *(Abwertung)* depreciation, devaluation, *(Anlagegut)* lost usefulness, *(Außerkurssetzung)* withdrawal, demonetization *(Br.)*, *(Briefmarken)* obliteration, *(Geld)* inflation, *(Stempel)* obliteration, cancellation, defacement;

tatsächliche ~ physical depreciation; **unvorhergesehene** ~ loss of useful value *(Br.)*;
~ **des Pfundes** devaluation of the pound.

Entwertungs|klausel depreciation clause; ~**marke** cancellation mark, postmark; ~**rücklage** allowance (reserve, provision) for depreciation, depreciation reserve (allowance); ~**satz** depreciation rate; ~**stempel** cancelling (obliterating, postmarking, nonvalidating, *US*) stamp, postmark, canceller *(Br.)*; ~**zeichen** cancellation mark.

entwickelbar *(Film)* developable.

entwickeln to develop, to work up, *(Foto)* to develop, *(fördern)* to promote, to further, *(Gedanken)* to elaborate, to enlarge, to work out, *(Handel)* to grow up, *(mil.)* to deploy;
sich ~ to expand; **sich bedenklich** ~ to grow into an awkward position; **seine Fähigkeiten** ~ to develop one's faculties; **Film** ~ to develop a film; **Gedanken weiter** ~ to enlarge an idea; **sich günstig** ~ to take a favo(u)rable turn; **sich gut** ~ to shape well, *(Kind)* to frame well; **sich zu einem Industriestaat** ~ to become an industrial nation; **Industriezweig** ~ to expand a branch of industry; **sich langsam** ~ to develop gradually (slowly), to move slowly; **sich lebhaft** ~ *(Geschäft)* to rush; **ungeahnten Mut** ~ to display unexpected courage; **Plan** ~ to form a plan; **jem. seine Pläne** ~ to unfold one's plans to s. o.; **sich programmgemäß** ~ to come off all right; **sich schnell** ~ *(Konjunktur)* to advance with a rush, to boom; **sich zu einer unangenehmen Situation** ~ to grow into a awkward situation; **sich in einer Stellung** ~ to improve one's position; **lebhafte Tätigkeit** ~ to display great activity; **sich ungünstig** ~ to go to the bad, *(Kind)* to frame badly; **sich weiter** ~ to climb upward; **sich zufriedenstellend** ~ to be shaping well;
die Dinge sich ~ **lassen** to let matters take their course, to let things develop.

entwickelt developed;
geistig ~ mature; **hoch** ~ sophisticated; **voll** ~ full-blown; **sich äußerst angenehm** ~ **haben** to have been all sweetness and light; **sich unglücklich** ~ **haben** to have come to a sad pass.

Entwickler *(Foto)* developer;
~**bottich** *(Foto)* developing tank; ~**schale** *(Foto)* developing tray.

Entwicklung development, progress, growth, devolution, *(Bildung)* formation, *(Foto)* development, *(mil.)* deployment, *(Tendenz)* trend, tendency;
in der ~ **begriffen** in process of development; **noch in der** ~ in the shell, in its infancy;
allgemeine ~ general tendency; **berufliche** ~ professional growth, career development; **betriebliche** ~ organization development; **binnenwirtschaftliche** ~ trends in the domestic economy; **defizitäre** ~ trend towards a deficit; **exportbedingte** ~ export-led growth; **fortschrittliche** ~ march of progress; **industrielle** ~ industry trend; **kassenmäßige** ~ cash position; **konjunkturelle** ~ cyclical (economic) trend, development of business tendencies; **zurückgebliebene kulturelle** ~ cultural lag; **langanhaltende** ~ secular trend; **längerfristige** ~ long-term development; **marktbestimmende** ~**en** governing market trends; **natürliche** ~ outgrowth; **persönliche** ~ personal progress; **rückläufige** ~ recession, *(Börse)* downward trend; **sofortige** ~ instantaneous exposure; **soziale** ~ social evolution; **städtebauliche** ~ urban development, town planning *(US)*; **technische** ~ engineering development; **technologische** ~ technological progress, development of technology; **volkswirtschaftliche** ~ economic process; **vorauszusehende** ~ parameter; **wirtschaftliche** ~ commercial (economic, industrial) development, economic growth; **zollpolitische** ~ tariff development; **zukünftige** ~ future trend;
~ **des Außenhandels** development of foreign trade; ~**en des Bankwesens** trends in banking; ~ **der Börse** stock-market trend; ~ **des Einkommens** growth in income; ~ **der Einlagen** development of deposits; ~ **fotografischer Filme** development of photographic films; ~ **des Fremdenverkehrs** tourist development; ~ **der Geburtenziffer** trend of births; ~ **von Gedanken** progress of thoughts; ~ **des Geldmarktes** tendency of the money market; ~ **eines Geschäfts** growth of a business; ~ **einer Idee** enlargement of an idea; ~ **der Infrastruktur** infrastructure development; ~ **der Kosten** cost trend; ~ **der Kurse** tendency on the stock market; **generelle** ~ **der politischen Lage** general drift of political affairs; ~ **der Landwirtschaft** rural development; ~ **der Löhne** wage development; ~ **der Preispolitik** pricing policy formation; ~ **eines Produkts im Markt** product history; ~ **der Rücklagen** development of reserves; **industrielle** ~ **einer Stadt** urban economics; **rapide** ~ **einer Stadt** boom of a town; ~ **eines Unternehmens** company progress; ~ **neuer Verkaufsmöglichkeiten** development selling; ~ **der Volkswirtschaft** economic growth (performance); ~ **der Wirtschaft** economic development; ~ **zur Wohngegend** residential development; ~ **des Wohnungsbaus** housing development; **rückwärtige** ~ **der Zinsgefälle** downturn (trend) in interest rates;
~ **der Ereignisse abwarten** to wait for the cat to jump; **sich in kumulierender Weise negativ auf die konjunkturelle** ~ **auswirken** to exert cumulative downward pressure on economic activity; **Gang der** ~ **beobachten** to wait and see; **der allgemeinen** ~ **der Konjunktur nicht folgen** to buck the trend; **mit der modernen** ~ **Schritt halten** to keep pace with modern invention; **mit der allgemeinen** ~ **der Volkswirtschaft nicht Schritt halten** to be out of phase with the national economy; ~ **der öffentlichen Meinung erkennen lasssen** to mark the trend of public opinion; **Grund für eine spätere** ~ **legen** to lay the foundation of one's career; **in der** ~ **sein** to be in a stage of development (developmental stage); **in der** ~ **zurückgeblieben sein** to be mentally retarded; ~ **stören** to arrest development, to interfere with the development; **die inflationelle** ~ **vorantreiben** to make inflation worse; **zukünftige** ~**en voraussagen** to predict future developments; ~ **des Wohnungsmarktes vorherbestimmen** to take the measure of the housing market.

Entwicklungs|ablauf evolution; ~**abschnitt** phase of a man's career; ~**alter** developmental age; ~**anleihe** development loan; ~**anleihefonds** development loan fund; ~**arbeiten** development (developmental, design) work, work of development; **neues Kapitel zur Finanzierung von** ~**aufträgen aufbringen** to raise growth capital; ~**ausgaben** development costs; ~**ausschuß** committee for development aid; ~**aussichten** economic prospects; ~**bad** *(Foto)* developing bath; ~**bank für die lateinamerikanischen Länder** Inter-American Development Bank; ~**banken** development banks.

entwicklungsbedingte Wachstumsrate des Bruttosozialproduktes trend rate of the national product growth.

Entwicklungs|bedingungen der Konjunktur trend-setting development; ~**bedürfnisse** developmental requirements; ~**behörde** Development Commissioner; ~**behörde für Zonenrandgebiete** Development Board *(Br.)*; ~**bericht** progress report; ~**büro** engineering firm; ~**darlehn** development loan; ~**diagramm** progress chart; ~**einrichtung** development organization; ~**etappe** phase (stage) of development; ~**etat** development budget; ~**fachmann** development expert.

entwicklungsfähig developable, viable, susceptible of development, *(vielversprechend)* promising.

Entwicklungsfonds für die überseeischen Gebiete development fund for overseas territories.

entwicklungsfreudig developmental.

Entwicklungs|gang course of evolution, *(beruflich)* career; ~**gebiet** less developed (developing, development) area *(Br.)*, growth area; **auf dem** ~**gebiet** in the field of development; ~**gerät für Mikrofilme** microfilm processor; ~**gesellschaft** development company (corporation), Overseas Private Investment Corporation *(US)*; ~**gruppe** development team; ~**helfer** volunteer, aid official, development-aid man.

Entwicklungshilfe development assistance (aid work), foreign aid;
amerikanische ~ US-financed foreign aid; **private und öffentliche** ~ composite flow; **projektgebundene** ~ tied aid; ~**gesetz** Foreign Aid Appropriation Act *(US)*; ~**programm** foreign-aid program *(US)*.

Entwicklungs|ingenieur development engineer; ~**jahre eines Kindes** formative years of a child; ~**jahrzehnt** decade of development; ~**kosten** development expenses (costs), costs of development, costs of construction; ~**kredit** development loan; ~**land** undeveloped (less developed) country; ~**länder** developing (undeveloped, less developed) countries, developing (the third) world; ~**linie** trend, tendency.

entwicklungsmäßig developmental;
~ **bedingte Arbeitslosigkeit** technological unemployment.

Entwicklungs|minister Economic Cooperation Minister; ~**möglichkeiten** development potentialities, way, room to advance; **geschäftliche** ~**möglichkeiten** business development possibilities; ~**niveau** development level; ~**papier** developing paper; ~**phase** stage, phase of a man's career; ~**planer** development planning economist, aid planner; ~**planung** development planning; **kommunale** ~**planung** corporate planning; ~**prioritäten** development priorities; ~**problem** development problem; ~**programm** development program(me); ~**projekt** development (aid) project; ~**raum** developing room; ~**reihe** *(Statistik)* series; ~**richtung** tendency, trend; ~**schale** developing dish;

~**schema** pattern of development; ~**schwerpunkt** growth point; ~**skala** developmental sweep; ~**stadien** phases of a man's career; ~**stadium** stage (phase) of development, *(Jugendlicher)* formative stage, pilot (juvenile) stage; **geschichtliches ~stadium** phase of history; **noch nicht aus dem ~stadium heraus sein** to have never got beyond the shell stage; ~**stand** stage of development; **Internationale ~stelle** International Development Agency; ~**störung** *(med.)* arrest of development; ~**stufe** stage (phase) of development; ~**tätigkeit** development work; ~**techniker** development engineer; ~**tendenz** future trend; **wirtschaftliche ~tendenz** trends in the economy, economic trend.

entwicklungsträchtig ripe for development.

Entwicklungs|unkostenkonto development account; **konjunktureller ~verlauf** economic trend; ~**vermögen** capacity for growth; ~**voraussetzung** prerequisite for development; ~**vorhaben** development project (operation, scheme); ~**vorhersage** prognostic of developments; ~**zeit** development time, period of development, *(Foto)* developing time, *(Krankheit)* incubation period; ~**ziel** planning target; **räumliches ~ziel** environmental goal.

entwidmen, Straße to reclassify a road.

entwinden, sich jds. Griff to wrench o. s. from s. one's grasp.

entwirren to unravel, to unsnarl.

entwischen, jem. to give s. o. the slip.

entwöhnen, j. von etw. to break (disaccustom) s. o. of a habit; **Süchtigen** ~ to wean an addict; **Trinker** ~ to rescue a drunkard.

entwöhnt disaccustomed.

Entwöhnungskur dry-out.

entwürdigen to degrade, to abase, to debase.

entwürdigend degrading, disgraceful;

für alle Beteiligten ~ sein to constitute an act disgraceful to all concerned;

~**es Benehmen** disgraceful behavio(u)r; ~**e Zumutung** degrading suggestion.

Entwürdigung degradation, debasement.

Entwurf *(Gestaltung)* design, outline, *(Konzept)* draft, draught *(Br.)*, drawing, foul (rough) copy, skeleton, sketch, minute, *(Modezeichnung)* cartoon, style, design, *(Plan)* plan, scheme, model, project, device, blueprint *(US)*, *(Skizze)* outline; **abgeänderter** ~ amended draft; **ausgearbeiteter** ~ plan; **endgültiger** ~ final project; **erster** ~ first (rough) draft, first (rough) sketch, *(unfertiger)* scribble; **flüchtiger** ~ rough sketch; **kurzer** ~ minute, short; **neuer** ~ redraft; **schriftlicher** ~ composition, draft; **vorgeschlagener** ~ draft proposal; **zweiter** ~ redraft;

~ **und Ausführung** art and part; ~ **eines Briefes** draft of a letter; ~ **einer Erklärung** draft statement; ~ **eines Gesetzes** bill; ~ **des Haushaltsplans** estimates, proposed budget; ~ **für eine Rede** draft for a speech; ~ **eines Vertrages** draft agreement;

~ **anfertigen** to make a draft; ~ **einer Rede anfertigen** to work out the plan of a speech; **detaillierten ~ ausarbeiten** to blueprint *(US)*; **über das Stadium des ~s nicht hinauskommen** never to pass the planning stage; **neuen ~ machen** to redraw; **im ~ sein** to be in the planning stage; **im ~ fertig sein (vorliegen)** to be finished in the outline; **Anregungen in einem ~ verarbeiten** to incorporate suggestions in a plan; ~ **vorlegen** to submit a plan.

Entwürfe|für ein Kleid designs for a dress;

~ **ausarbeiten** to work up designs.

Entwurfs|ausschuß drafting committee; ~**form** draft form; ~**grafiker** layout man, layouter; ~**ingenieur** project engineer; ~**skizze** sketch design; ~**skizze einer Werbesendung** story board; ~**stadium** planning (blueprint, *US*) stage; **über das ~stadium nie herausgekommen sein** to have never passed the planning stage; ~**zeichner** draftsman, draughtsman *(Br.)*.

entwurzeln to disroot, to uproot.

entwurzelt *(fig.)* uprooted.

entzerren to counteract, to correct, to equalize, *(el.)* to attenuate.

Entzerrer antidistortion device, *(el.)* attenuator.

Entzerrung correction, compensation, equalization, *(el.)* attenuation.

Entzerrungsgerät *(Foto)* rectifier.

entziehen to deprive, to withdraw, to dock, to table away, *(Besitz)* to dispossess, to evict, to oust, *(Staatsangehörigkeit)* to denaturalize, *(Wahlrecht)* to disfranchise;

sich ~ to evade, to back out; **sich jem.** ~ to hold aloof from s. o.; **sich der Beantwortung einer Frage** ~ to shirk a question; **sich der Begriffsbestimmung** ~ to elude definition; **sich allen Berechnungen** ~ to baffle all calculations; **Besitz** ~ to divest of s. th., to dispossess; **sich jds. Beurteilung** ~ to be beyond s. one's judgment; **sich der Bezahlung seiner Schulden** ~ to evade paying one's debts; **den Blicken** ~ to hide from view; **sich einer Diskussion** ~ to back out of a discussion; **sich seinen Feinden** ~ to elude one's enemies; **sich der Festnahme durch die Flucht** ~ to abscond; **jem. den Führerschein** ~ to disqualify s. o. from holding (revoke) a driving licence *(Br.)*; **sich dem Gericht** ~ to flee from justice; **einem Gerücht die Grundlage** ~ to knock the bottom out of a rumo(u)r; **sich seinen Gläubigern** ~ to evade one's creditors; **sich jds. Kenntnis** ~ to be beyond s. one's knowledge; **einem Kind zur Strafe das Taschengeld** ~ to cut off a child's pocket money as a punishment; **Konzession** ~ to revoke (cancel) a licence; **Kredit** ~ to withdraw a credit; **Legat** ~ to revoke a legacy; **Lizenz** ~ to revoke a licence; **jem. das Mandat** ~ to unseat s. o.; **sich dem Militärdienst** ~ to dodge military service; **sich den Nachforschungen der Polizei** ~ to hide from the police; **jem. die Nahrung** ~ to cut off s. one's food; **jem. die Pension** ~ to dock s. one's pension; **j. jds. Rache** ~ to protect s. o. from s. one's wrath; **jem. seine Rente** ~ to cancel s. one's pension; **jem. die Staatsangehörigkeit** ~ to deprive s. o. of his citizenship; **sich einer Strafe** ~ to evade punishment, to cheat justice (the gallows); **sich der Unterhaltspflicht** ~ to evade one's liability to provide maintenance (legal obligation to support); **sich der Verantwortung** ~ to withdraw from a responsibility; **sich der strafrechtlichen Verfolgung** ~ to evade (flee from) justice; **sich einer Verpflichtung** ~ to shirk duty, to elude (back out of) an obligation; **jem. sein Vertrauen** ~ to withdraw one's confidence from s. o.; **jem. seine Vollmachten** ~ to divest (strip) s. o. of his powers, to revoke s. one's powers; **Wahlrecht** ~ to disfranchise; **jem. das Wort** ~ to rule s. o. out of order, to closure s. o.; **sich einer Zahlung** ~ to elude payment; **sich jds. Zugriff** ~ to put s. th. out of s. one's reach.

Entziehung deprivation, privation, cancellation, revocation, revoking;

~ **des Besitzes** dispossession, eviction, ouster; ~ **der bürgerlichen Ehrenrechte** civic degradation; ~ **von Elektrizität** abstraction of electric power; ~ **des Führerscheins** forfeiture (disqualification) of s. one's driving licence *(Br.)*; ~ **einer Konzession (Lizenz)** revocation of a licence; ~ **des Kredits** withdrawal of credit; ~ **verfassungsmäßig zustehender Rechte** deprivation of constitutional rights *(US)*; ~ **des Ruhegehalts** deprivation of a pension; ~ **der Staatsangehörigkeit** forfeiture (deprivation) of citizenship, denaturalization, expatriation; ~ **der Vollmacht** revocation of power; ~ **des Wahlrechts** disfranchisement.

Entziehungs|anstalt inebriate asylum; **staatliche ~anstalt** state inebriate reformatory; ~**erscheinungen** withdrawal symptoms; ~**klinik** treatment center; ~**kur** corrective training, cure of addiction, dry-out; ~**kur bei jem. durchführen** to cure an addict; ~**kur machen** to dry; ~**recht** power of revocation; ~**vermutung** *(Rückerstattung)* presumption of confiscation.

entzifferbar decipherable, *(Funkspruch)* to decode.

entziffern to decipher, to decode, to cryptanalyze;

verschlüsselten Funkspruch ~ to work out a coded message; **Brief nicht ~ können** not to be able to read a letter.

Entzifferung deciphering, *(Funkspruch)* decoding.

Entzücken delight, joy;

in ~ geraten to be carried away; **j. in ~ versetzen** to send s. o. into raptures.

entzücken to captivate, to charm, to enrapture, to enchant.

entzückend delightful, charming, enchanting, ravishing;

~ **aussehen** to look charming;

~**er Hut** fetching hat; ~**e kleine Wohnung** delightful little flat.

entzückt charmed, enchanted, delighted;

~ **sein** to be filled with delight; **über etw. hellauf ~ sein** to be in raptures (crazy) about s. th.

Entzug|der bürgerlichen Ehrenrechte deprivation of civil rights; ~ **des Führerscheins** forfeiture (disqualification) of s. one's driving licence *(Br.)*, driving ban *(Br.)*; ~ **der Schlüsselgewalt** inhibition against a wife; ~ **des Wahlrechts** disfranchisement.

entzündbar combustible, ignitable.

entzünden, sich to kindle, to ignite, to inflame, *(Wunde)* to become inflamed; **sich von selbst** ~ to catch fire spontaneously; **alle Herzen** ~ to fire all hearts; **wilde Leidenschaft** ~ to rise violent passion; **Streichholz** ~ to strike a match.

entzündete Augen inflamed eyes.

entzündlich ignitable, inflammable;

leicht ~e Stoffe inflammables.

Entzündung ignition, inflammation.

Entzündungsgemisch ignition mixture.

entzweien to disunite;

sich ~ to quarrel, to fall out, to split; **Volk** ~ to turn the people against each other, to divide a people.

entzwei|gehen to fall asunder; ~**schneiden** to cut into pieces.
entzweit, sich mit jem. ~ **haben** to be on bad terms (at loggerheads) with s. o.;
~**es Volk** divided people.
Enzyklopädie encyclopaedia.
Epaulette epaulet, knot.
Epidemie epidemic [disease];
~**ausbruch** outbreak of an epidemic.
Episode episode, incident, *(Novelle)* underplot.
Epistel, jem. gehörig die ~ **lesen** to give s. o. a good dressing down; **lange** ~ **nach Hause schreiben** to write a screed.
Epoche era, epoch, date;
~ **einleiten** to mark an era.
epochemachend epoch-making (-marking), revolutionary.
erachten to consider, to deem, to think, to believe;
als notwendig ~ to think it necessary; **es als seine Pflicht** ~ to deem it one's duty.
Erachtens, meines in my opinion, in my view.
erarbeiten to obtain by labo(u)r;
mühsam ~ to eke out, to work hard for.
erarbeitet, schwer ~**er Reichtum** hard-won fortune.
Erb|abfindung forisfamiliation of a child; ~**anfall** hereditary succession, [devolution of] inheritance, accruer, reversion of an estate; ~**anfall an den Staat** irregular succession, esheat; ~**anspruch** title (claim) to inheritance *(US)*; **bedingter** ~**anspruch** contingent remainder; ~**ansprüche geltend machen** to claim to be the rightful heir; **auf weitere** ~**ansprüche verzichten** to forisfamiliate; ~**anteil** portion, share in an inheritance *(US)*; **gesetzlicher** ~**anteil** distributive share *(US)*; **ohne** ~**anteil** portionless.
erbanteilsberechtigt sein to have an interest in an estate.
Erb|antritt succession to an estate; ~**anwachs** portion accruing to each heir; ~**anwärter** expectant heir, claimant, heir apparent; **nächster gesetzlicher** ~**anwärter** presumptive heir; **übergangener** ~**anwärter** pretermitted heir; ~**anwartschaft** estate in expectancy, expectant (contingent) estate.
Erbarmen pity, mercy, compassion;
kein ~ **kennen** to know no mercy; **zum** ~ **singen** to sing miserably (deplorably).
erbärmlich miserable, little, pitiable, pitiful, poor-spirited;
sich ~ **benehmen** to behave wretchedly; ~ **frieren** to be miserably cold;
~**e Auswahl** poor variety; ~**e Hütte** wretched hovel; **in einer** ~**en Lage sein** to be in a sorry (sad) plight; ~**es Leben führen** to live in wretched poverty; ~**e Leistung** miserable performance; ~**e Qualität** bottom quality; ~**er Schriftsteller** very poor writer; ~ **kleines Stück** not more than a morsel; ~**es Wetter** abominable (awful) weather; ~**er Wicht** despicable wretch; **in einem** ~**en Zustand sein** to be in a wretched plight (pitiable state).
erbarmungslos pitiless, merciless, with a heavy hand;
~ **verfolgt werden** to be subject to relentless persecution;
~**er Mann** man of iron.
erbarmungswürdig pitiable, lamentable, wretched;
in einem ~**em Zustand** to be in a sad plight.
erbauen to build, to construct, to erect;
sich an etw. ~ to be edified (uplifted) by s. th.
Erbauer constructor, builder, erector, architect.
Erb|auseinandersetzung division (distribution) of a deceased's estate; ~**auseinandersetzung durchführen** to distribute an estate; ~**auseinandersetzungsanspruch** distributive share *(US)*; ~**auseinandersetzungsvertrag** family settlement (contract); ~**ausgleich** [putting in (bringing into)] hotchpot; ~**ausschlagung** disclaimer of an estate (inheritance, *US*), refusal to accept an estate, renunciation (relinquishment, renouncement) of an inheritanc (succession, *US*); ~**ausschließung** exclusion from inheritance; ~**aussichten bei einer Tante haben** to have expectations from an aunt.
Erbauungs|buch devotional book; ~**literatur** books for moral improvement.
Erbbau|berechtigter leaseholder, superficiary; ~**recht,** ~**vertrag** building lease *(Br.)*, rental right *(Br.)*, mixed estate *(US)*, lease in perpetuity; **99jähriges** ~**recht an einem Bürogrundstück erwerben** to purchase a 99-year lease of office premises; ~**vertrag** building lease *(Br.)*; ~**vertrag über 99 Jahre abschließen** to take on 99 years lease.
Erbbegräbnis family grave (vault).
erbberechtigt entitled (qualified) to inherit;
~ **sein** to have an interest (be entitled to a share) in an estate, to inherit; ~ **werden** to fall in for;
~**e Abkömmlinge** inheritable descendants; ~**er Personenkreis** testamentary class.
Erbberechtigte|r heir, inheritor, devisee, successor;
lebende ~ living heirs; **nächster** ~**r** next devisee; **nächster männlicher** ~**r** first male heir; **die normalen** ~**n** natural object of testator's bounty;
~ **bestimmen** to appoint the persons to enjoy an estate.
Erb|berechtigung right of inheritance *(US)* (to succeed), heirship; ~**beschränkung aufheben** to cut off an entail; ~**besitz** inheritance *(US)*, hereditament.
Erbe heir, inheritor, natural (real) representative, *(Erbschaft)* heirdom, heritage, inheritance *(US)*, hereditament, legacy;
ohne ~**n** heirless;
alleiniger ~ sole (universal) heir; **treuhänderisch besitzender** ~ special occupant *(US)*; **testamentarisch bestimmter** ~ testamentary (appointed) heir *(US)*, heir by device; **auf den Restnachlaß eingesetzter** ~ residuary beneficiary; **ungeduldig erwartetes** ~ dead men's shoes; **falscher** ~ suppositious heir; **gesetzlicher** ~ legal (statutory, *US*, rightful, *Br.*) heir, heir apparent *(Br.)*, heir-at-law *(US)*, intestate successor, lawful issue; **nach Inventarerrichtung beschränkt haftender** ~ beneficiary heir; **künftiger** ~ heir apparent *(Br.)*; **legitime** ~**n** legitimate heirs; **leiblicher** ~ bodily heir, heir of one's body; **letzter** ~ last heir *(Br.)*; **männlicher** ~ male heir; **mutmaßlicher** ~ heir presumptive *(Br.)*; **nächster** ~ immediate heir; **pflichtteilsberechtigter** ~ forced heir *(US)*; **rechtmäßiger** ~ legal (lawful, right, rightful) heir; **aus der Seitenlinie stammender** ~ collateral heir; **testamentarischer** ~ heir testamentary, heir by device, devisee *(US)*; **zukünftiger** ~ heir apparent;
~ **mit Beschränkung auf das Nachlaßverzeichnis** beneficiary heir; ~ **aufgrund eines Erbvertrages** conventional heir; ~ **durch Geburtsrecht** natural heir; ~ **in gerader Linie (erster Ordnung)** heir of line; **in gerader Linie mit dem Erblasser verwandte** ~**n** lineal (natural) heirs; ~ **mit dem Recht der Nacherbenbestimmung** appointer; ~ **in der Seitenlinie (dritter Ordnung)** heir collateral; ~ **des beweglichen Vermögens** heir to personal estate; ~ **aufgrund von Verwandtschaft** heir of the blood;
j. als rechtmäßigen ~**n anerkennen** to own as heir, to recognize s. o. as a lawful heir; ~**n nicht anerkennen** to disown an heir; **sein** ~ **antreten** to step into the shoes of s. o., to take possession of an estate; **sein Vermögen unter seine** ~**n aufteilen** to share one's estate among one's heirs; **sich als** ~ **benennen** to declare o. s. an heir; ~**n bestimmen** to designate (design) an heir; **j. zu seinem** ~**n bestimmen** to make s. o. one's heir; **j. zu seinem** ~**n einsetzen** to constitute (appoint, institute, *US*) s. o. as one's heir; **zum** ~**n erklären** to serve *(Scot.)*; **an die gesetzlichen** ~**n fallen** to go by intestacy; **keine** ~**n hinterlassen** to leave no issue; **jds.** ~ **sein** to be s. one's heir; **auf den** ~**n übergehen** to devolve upon (pass to) the heir; **auf den gesetzlichen** ~**n übergehen** to vest in the heir-at-law; **sein väterliches** ~ **vergeuden** to squander one's estate (patrimony); **auf sein** ~ **verzichten** to renounce an inheritance; **den** ~**n zufallen** to inure to the heirs.
erbeben *(Erde)* to shake, *(Stimme)* to tremble;
unter unseren Füßen ~ to quake under one's feet; **Häuser** ~ **lassen** *(Detonation)* to shake the houses.
erbeingesessene Familie long-established family.
Erbeinheit gene.
Erbeinsetzung institution (appointment) of an heir *(US)*;
gegenseitige ~ double will;
~ **auf den beweglichen Nachlaß** indefinite legacy.
Erbeinsetzungsvertrag family settlement.
erben to inherit, to be heir to, to take by inheritance *(US)*, to succeed to, to fall (come) in for;
etw. von jem. ~ to inherit s. th. from s. o.; **Besitz** ~ to come into a property; **gemeinsam** ~ to inherit jointly; **Grundstück** ~ to inherit a plot of land; **Gut** ~ to succeed to an estate; **zu gleichen Teilen** ~ to inherit equally; **Vermögen** ~ to fall heir to a property, to come into money, to drop into a fortune; **zusammen** ~ to inherit jointly (conjointly).
Erben|eigenschaft heirship; ~**gemeinschaft** privity of estate, estate in comparcenary, community of heirs *(US)*, *(Grundstück)* estate in common; ~**haftung** liability of an heir.
erbenlos heirless.
Erbenlosigkeit dying without issue, failure of issue, escheat, default of heirs.
Erbeserbe reversioner.
erbetteln to beg;
Geld von jem. ~ to wheedle money out of s. o.
erbeuten to seize, to capture, to carry off;
wertvolle Kette ~ *(Einbrecher)* to get away with a valuable necklace *(coll.)*.
erbfähig hereditable, inheritable, qualified (able, competent) to inherit.

Erb|fähigkeit heritability, ability to inherit; **~faktor** *(biol.)* factor; **~fall** devolution upon death, succession; **~fallschulden** debts accruing from an inheritance; **~feind** hereditary enemy; **~feindschaft** secular rivalry.

Erbfolge [hereditary] succession, devolution upon death, descent *(US)*, *(Grundeigentum)* entail;
aufgrund testamentarischer oder gesetzlicher ~ by device or by descent; **durch** ~ **übertragbar** [in]heritable, hereditary; **im Wege der** ~ by way of succession;
auf einzelne Erben beschränkte ~ tail special; **auf die leiblichen Nachkommen beschränkte** ~ tail general; **auf männliche Nachkommen beschränkte** ~ tail male; **auf die weiblichen Nachkommen beschränkte** ~ tail female; **gesetzliche** ~ intestate (legal, hereditary, *US*) succession, statute of distribution *(US)*; **gewillkürte** ~ testamentary succession; **legitime** ~ inheritable blood; **lineare** ~ linear inheritance; **mittelbare** ~ mediate descent; **natürliche** ~ natural succession; **testamentarische** ~ testamentary succession; **unbekannte** ~ vacant succession;
~ **an den Jüngsten** ultimogeniture; ~ **in gerader Linie** linear succession; ~ **in der Seitenlinie** collateral succession; ~ **nach Stämmen** representation, inheriting per stirpes;
~ **aufheben** to dock the entail; **von der** ~ **ausschließen** to bar from succession, to exclude from inheritance *(US)*; **von einer festgelegten** ~ **befreien** to disentail; **jds.** ~ **bestreiten** to challenge s. one's succession; **aufgrund gesetzlicher** ~ **erben** to take by descent, to acquire by inheritance *(US)*;
~beschränkung special tail; ~ **gesetz** law of decedent's estate *(US)*; **~ordnung** canons of descent, statute of distribution (descent), [order of] succession; **~recht** law of decedent's estate *(US)*, right of succession *(Br.)*.

Erbgang devolution of inheritance (upon death);
im ~ by inheritance; **im** ~ **übertragbar** hereditable, [in]heritable;
im ~ **anfallen** to accrue by way of succession.

Erb|gesundheit eugenics; **~gut** entail, inheritance *(US)*, hereditament, heritage, demesne, *(Allodialgut)* fee simple; **~hof** ancestral estate, fee tail.

erbieten, sich to offer to do.

Erbin female heir, heiress, inheritress;
gesetzliche ~ heiress-at-law.

erbitten to ask, to solicit, to request;
sich Bedenkzeit ~ to ask for respite; **Rat** ~ to ask for advice; **sich** ~ **lassen** to yield to entreaties.

erbittern, j. to make s. o. feel bitter, to fill s. o. with bitterness.

erbittert|er Kampf stubborn battle; **~er Konkurrenzkampf** cutthroat competition; **~en Widerstand leisten** to offer stubborn resistance.

Erbkrankheit hereditary disease.

erblassen to become (turn) pale;
jem. vor Neid ~ **lassen** to make s. o. green with envy.

Erblasser testator, bequeather, deceased [person], predecessor, ancestor, decedent *(US)*, *(von Grundbesitz)* devisor;
eigenhändig vom ~ **geschrieben** entirely written by the hand of the testator.

Erblasserin testatrix.

erblasserisch legatorial.

Erblasserschulden ancestral debts.

Erblehn entail;
Unveräußerlichkeit eines ~s aufheben to break the entail; ~ **veräußern** to bar (dock) an entail.

erblich inheritable, hereditable, hereditary, by inheritance *(US)*, heritable *(Scot.)*;
~ **belastet sein** to suffer from a hereditary discase;
~e Belastung hereditary taint; **~e Monarchie** hereditary monarchy.

Erblichkeit heritability, hereditability.

erblicken, j. to catch sight of s. o.; **Licht der Welt** ~ to see the light; **j. in einer Menschenmenge** ~ to spot s. o. in a crowd; **großen Vorteil in etw.** ~ to see a great advantage in s. th.

erblinden to go (become) blind, to lose one's eyesight.

erblindet blind.

Erblinie line of succession.

erblühen to bloom, to blossom.

erblüht|e Blume full-blown flower;
zu voller Schönheit ~ **sein** to grow into a beauty.

Erb|masse *(Erbanlagen)* heredity, *(Nachlaß)* genetic endowment; **~monarchie** hereditary monarchy; **~nachfolge** hereditary succession.

erbosen, sich to get cross (angry, infuriated).

erbost annoyed, vexed, furious.

erbötig zeigen, sich to be willing (ready).

Erbpacht copyhold, fee farm, leasehold estate, socage tenure, term of years absolute *(Br.)*, building lease *(Br.)*, lease in perpetuity, rental right *(Br.)*;
befristete ~ determinable fee; **99jährige** ~ ninety-nine years building lease *(Br.)*, mixed estate *(US)*;
~ **auf Lebenszeit eines Dritten** lease for life;
in ~ **vergeben sein** to be leased for a long term;
~besitzer customary tenant, rentaler *(Br.)*, kindly tenant *(Scot.)*.

Erbpächter fee farmer, copyholder *(Br.)*.

Erbpacht|grundstück vermachen to devise land held in socage; **~gut** customary freehold; **~vertrag** building lease; **~zins** annual, fee-farm (ground, *Br.*) rent.

Erbquote share of an estate.

Erbrechen vomit, sickness.

erbrechen, sich to vomit, to throw up.

Erbrecht law of succession (decedent's estate, *US*), right of inheritance *(US)*, heirship *(US)*, *(Witwe)* dower, dowry;
gesetzliches ~ intestate succession *(Fiskus)* esheat; **unzweifelhaftes** ~ heir apparency;
~ **antreten** to come into an inheritance *(US)*; ~ **der Witwe festsetzen** to admeasure a dower; **gesetzliches** ~ **geltend machen** to claim under intestacy.

erbrechtlich begrenzt tail.

Erbrechtsfestsetzung appointment of a person to enjoy an estate;
~ **der Witwe** admeasurement of dowry.

Erbregelung, ohne ~ **sterben** to die intestate.

erbringen, Beweis to adduce evidence; **nichts** ~ to come to nothing.

Erbringer von Dienstleistungen supplier of services.

Erbringung von Beweisen adduction (production) of evidence.

Erbschaft deceased estate, inheritance *(US)*, heritage, hereditament, heirdom, *(Vermächtnis)* legacy;
von der ~ **ausgeschlossen** debarred from succeeding;
noch nicht angetretene ~ estate in abeyance; **dem Staat anheimgefallene** ~ escheat; **annehmbare** ~ fair heritage; **aus einem Hause bestehende** ~ inheritance consisting of a house; **rechtlich einwandfreie** ~ rightful inheritance; **gemeinsame** ~ coinheritance; **herrenlose** ~ vacant succession; **noch nicht regulierte** ~ unsettled estate; **ruhende** ~ inheritance in abeyance *(US)*; **jem. überkommene** ~ estate developed upon s. o.; **unerwartete** ~ landfall; **verschuldete** ~ estate encumbered with debts;
~ **von der Seitenlinie** collateral inheritance *(US)*;
jem. durch ~ **anfallen** to devolve upon s. o.; ~ **antreten** to enter upon a property (an inheritance, *US*), to accede to an estate, to step into a dead man's shoes, to come (enter) into (take) possession of an estate, to assume a succession, to come into an heirdom, to fall into title; ~ **ausschlagen** to disclaim (renounce, resign) an inheritance (one's interest in an estate), to resign an inheritance; ~ **zur Verteilung bringen** to partition an estate among the heirs; **j. in eine** ~ **einweisen** to put s. o. in possession of (vest s. o. with) an inheritance; **sich eine** ~ **erschleichen** to obtain an estate by false pretences; **größere** ~ **zu erwarten haben** to have great expectations; ~ **hinterlassen** to leave an estate; ~ **machen** to come in for a fortune (an inheritance, estate, money), to inherit an estate, to drop into a fortune; ~ **verteilen** to parcel out an inheritance *(US)*, to partition an estate among the heirs; **auf eine** ~ **verzichten** to relinquish (renounce) an inheritance *(US)* (one's interest in an estate); **auf eine** ~ **warten** to wait for a dead man's shoes; **bei einer** ~ **benachteiligt werden** to come off badly in a will; **durch** ~ **zufallen** to descend.

Erbschafts|anfall devolution of an inheritance *(US)*, reversion (accrual) of an estate; **~anfall an den Staat** escheatage; **~angelegenheiten** probate matters; **~annahme** entering upon an inheritance; **~anspruch** claim to (right of) inheritance *(US)*; **gleicher ~anteil** coparceny, share of an estate (inheritance); **~antritt** entrance upon an inheritance *(US)*, accession to an estate; **~anwärter** heir in expectancy, expectant heir; **~aufteilung** partition of an estate (succession); **~ausschlagung** disclaimer of an estate, relinquishment (renouncement) of a succession, renunciation of an inheritance *(US)*; **~aussichten haben** to have good prospects; **~besitzer** hereditary proprietor, heritor; **~besteuerung** taxation of an estate; **~erschleichung** subreption of a legacy, legacy hunting; **~erwartung** remainder, expectancy of an inheritance *(US)*; **~erwartung vorwegnehmen** to discount an expected inheritance; **bewegliche ~gegenstände** corporal hereditaments; **~gläubiger** creditor of an estate; **~inventar** inventory; **~masse** estate, inherited property, assets; **~sachen** probate matters; **~schulden** ancestral debts.

Erbschaftssteuer duty payable on death, death duty *(Br.)*, duty on inheritance *(US)*, transfer (inheritance, death) tax *(US)*, *(Vermächtnis von Gegenständen)* legacy duty, *(für bewegliches Vermögen)* probate duty *(Br.)*, succession duty *(Br.)*, estate tax *(US)* (duty, *Br.*);
verminderte ~ transfer-tax mitigation;
~ **[auf den beweglichen Nachlaß)** legacy duty *(Br.)*; ~ **für Nachlässe aus der Seitenlinie** collateral inheritance tax *(US)*; ~ **und Schenkungssteuer** capital transfer tax *(Br.)*; ~ **für unbewegliches Vermögen** succession duty *(Br.)*;
völlig von der ~ befreien to exempt completely from estate tax; **gesonderter ~ unterliegen** to be exempt from aggregation; **zur ~ veranlagen (veranschlagen)** to assess death duties, to charge estate duty *(Br.)*; ~ **vermeiden** to avoid estate duty *(Br.)*;
zulässige ~abzüge allowable deductions for estate duty *(Br.)*; **~aufwand** estate-tax outlay *(US)*; **~befreiung** exemption from estate duty *(Br.)*; **~belastung** charge to estate duty *(Br.)*, estate-duty charge *(Br.)*; **~berechnung** estate-duty computation *(Br.)*; **~betrag** estate-duty value *(Br.)*; **berichtigte ~erklärung** corrective affidavit; **~ersparnis** estate-duty saving *(Br.)*, estate-tax savings *(US)*; **~festsetzung** charging estate duty *(Br.)* (tax, *US*); **~formular** Inland Revenue Affidavit *(Br.)*; **~freibetrag** lifetime (inheritance) exemption *(US)*, exemption from inheritance tax *(US)*, estate-duty credit (allowance, *Br.*); **~freibetrag der überlebenden Ehefrau** surviving spouse exemption; **~freibetrag für bestimmte Wertpapiere beantragen** to claim exemption for particular stocks *(US)*; **~freibetragsgrenze** estate-duty exemption limit *(Br.)*; **~freigrenze** estate-duty exemption limit *(Br.)*; **~gesetzgebung** estate-duty legislation *(Br.)*.

erbschaftssteuerliche Tragweite estate-duty implication *(Br.)*.

Erbschaftssteuer|milderung estate-duty mitigation *(US)*; **~nachlaß auf landwirtschaftliche Betriebsflächen** agricultural value relief; **~nachlaß auf Maschinen und maschinelle Anlagen** machinery and plant relief.

erbschaftssteuerpflichtig subject to death duties *(US)*;
~ **werden** to become liable to estate duty *(Br.)*.

Erbschaftssteuer|richtlinien estate-duty regulations *(Br.)*; **~recht** estate-duty law *(Br.)*; **~sätze** rates of estate duty *(Br.)*, estate-duty rates *(Br.)*; **~schätzung** estate-duty valuation *(Br.)*; **~schuld** charge to estate duty, estate-duty liability *(Br.)*; **~situation** estate-duty position *(Br.)*; **~tabelle** table of estate-duty rates *(Br.)*; **~tarif** rates of estate duty *(Br.)*; **allgemeiner ~tarif** general scale of estate duty *(Br.)*; **~umgehung** avoidance of estate duty; **~veranlagung** charge to estate duty, assessing death duties *(US)*; **~veranschlagung** estate-duty valuation *(Br.)*; **~vorteil** estate-duty advantage *(Br.)*; **~wesen** inheritance taxation *(US)*; **~zahlung** inheritance tax payment *(US)*; **~zinsen** interest on estate duty *(Br.)*, estate-duty interest *(Br.)*; **für ~zwecke** for estate-duty purposes *(Br.)*.

Erbschafts|teilung division of an estate, partition of a succession *(US)*; **~teilung vornehmen** to partition (parcel) an inheritance; **~vermögen** estate property, adventitious property; **~verteilung** distribution of an estate; **~verteilung vornehmen** to parcel out an inheritance; **~vertrag** contract concerning the leaving of property by will; **~verwalter** personal representative;
~verwaltung administration of an estate; **~verzicht** disclaimer of estate (inheritance, *US*).

Erbschein heir's certificate *(US)*, [etwa] probate of a will, *(Testamentsvollstrecker)* letters testamentary;
aufgrund eines Testaments einen ~ ausstellen to grant (take out) probate of a will; ~ **einziehen** to revoke probate of a will; ~ **erteilen** to grant probate of a will;
~ausfertigung retour of service *(Scot.)*.

Erbscheins|einziehung revocation of probate; **~erbe** irregular heir; **~erteilung, ~verfahren** [etwa] probate of a will.

Erbschleicher legacy hunter (monger), captator, inveigler.

Erbschleicherei legacy hunting, captation, inveiglement.

Erbsensuppe *(Flugwesen)* pea soup *(sl.)*.

Erbskohle pea coal.

Erb|staat hereditary state; **~stück** heirloom.

Erbteil portion, distributive share, appanage, share in an estate (inheritance, *US*), *(Witwe)* dower, dowry;
elterliches ~ patrimony; **zu erwartendes** ~ possession in expectation; **gesetzliches** ~ lawful (legal, distributive, heriditary, *US*) share, statutory portion (share) *(US)*, legitimate (legal, *US*), portion, share under an intestacy, forced heirship; **jedem Erben zukommendes** ~ portion accruing to each heir;
auf das ~ anrechnen (in Anrechnung bringen) to bring into hotchpot; ~ **aushändigen** to forisfamiliate.

Erbteilsanspruch des Ehemannes am Vorbehaltsgut der Ehefrau right of courtesy.

Erbteilung distribution of an estate, partition of an inheritance.

Erbübergang auf den jüngsten Sohn junior right *(Br.)*.

erbunfähig incapable of succeeding to an estate.

Erb|unfähigkeit incapacity to inherit, incompetence to succeed, inability of succeeding to an estate; **~vergleich** family settlement; **dem ~verpächter zufallen** to revert to the lessor; **~vertrag** family arrangement (settlement), testamentary contract; **~verzicht** disclaimer of an estate (an inheritance, *US*), relinquishment of a succession, release of expectancy *(US)*.

Erbvoraus advancement;
~ **in Form von Kapitalbeträgen** capital advancement;
~ **erhalten** to receive an advance of inheritance; **einem Kind einen ~ gewähren** to advance a child;
~vermutung presumption of advancement.

Erbwege, im by inheritance *(US)*; **im ~ übertragbar** hereditary, [in]heritable;
jem. im ~ anfallen to devolve upon s. o.

Erbzins ground *(Br.)* (quit) rent, rent charge *(Br.)*, canon, reprise *(Br.)*;
~berechtigter owner of a rent charge *(Br.)*, rent owner *(Br.)*; **~obligationen** rent charge bonds.

Erdabfuhr site clearance.

erdacht|er Charakter imaginary (invented) character; **~e Geschichte** fictitious story.

Erd|anschluß *(el.)* ground, earth; **~anziehungskraft** force of gravity; **~anziehungskraft überwinden** to escape from earth; **~arbeiten** earthworks, excavation; **~arbeiter** groundman, excavator, navvy *(Br.)*; **wieder in die ~atmosphäre eintauchen** to dive back into the earth's atmosphere; **~aufklärung** *(mil.)* ground reconnaissance; **~aufschüttung** filling with earth; **erforderlichen ~aushub vornehmen** to take out the quantities; **~ball** earth, terrestrial globe; **~ball umkreisen** to circle the globe; **~ballen** ball of soil.

Erdbeben earthquake, shake *(US coll.)*;
unterseeisches ~ submarine earthquake;
von einem ~ zerstört sein to be thrown down (destroyed) by an earthquake; **bei einem ~ umkommen** to perish in an earthquake.

erdbebenfrei earthquake-free.

Erdbeben|gebiet earthquake district (region), disturbed area; **~geschädigter** victim of an earthquake; **~herd** seismic focus, center of an earthquake; **~hilfe** earthquake relief; **~karte** seismic (earthquake) map; **~katastrophe** earthquake disaster; **~klausel** *(Versicherung)* earthquake clause; **~opfer** earthquake victim; **~registrierung** seismography; **~risiko** earthquake hazard; **~schock** earthquake shock; **~tätigkeit** earthquake activity; **~versicherung** earthquake insurance; **~warte** seismological station.

Erd|bewegungen earthworks; **~bewohner** terrestrial, earthling.

Erdboden soil, ground, earth;
dem ~ gleichmachen to [make] level with the ground; **Stadt dem ~ gleichmachen** to raze a town to the ground; **etw. aus dem ~ stampfen** to produce s. th. out of a hat, to conjure s. th. up.

Erddamm embankment, dam.

Erde earth, world, *(el.)* ground;
auf der ganzen ~ in the whole world; **über der** ~ above ground; **zu ebener** ~ at ground level; **zwischen Himmel und** ~ between heaven and earth;
lockere ~ mold, mould *(Br.)*, dirt; **sandige** ~ sandy soil; **verbrannte** ~ scorched earth;
Grube mit ~ auffüllen to fill a pit with earth; **j. unter die ~ bringen** to bring s. o. to the grave; **um die ~ kreisen** to orbit; **in fremder ~ begraben sein** to be buried in a foreign land; **Himmel und ~ in Bewegung setzen** to stir heaven and earth; **mit beiden Beinen auf der ~ stehen** to have both feet on the ground; **mit der ~ verbinden** *(el.)* to earth, to ground; **zu ebener ~ wohnen** to live on the ground (first, *US*) floor.

erden *(el.)* to earth, to ground.

Erdenbürger mortal, earthling;
neuer kleiner ~ new addition to the human race.

erdenkbar conceivable.

Erdenkbare, alles nur the devil and all *(coll.)*.

erdenken to think (make) up;
Lügen ~ to fabricate lies.

erdenklich conceivable, imaginable, thinkable;
sich alle ~e Mühe geben to leave no stone unturned, to spare no pains.

Erdenleben natural life, earthly existence.

Erd|entfernung orbital distance; ~**erschütterung** earth tremor.
Erdgas natural gas;
~**einkünfte** gas revenues; ~**erzeuger** gas producer; ~**fund** natural-gas discovery; ~**industrie** natural-gas industry; ~**knappheit** gas shortage; ~**lagerstätten** natural-gas deposits; ~**leitung** natural-gas pipeline; ~**vorkommen** gasfield.
Erdgeschoß ground floor *(Br.)*, first floor *(US)*;
im ~ wohnen to occupy the ground (first, *US*) floor;
~**höhe** ground level.
Erd|hälfte hemisphere; ~**hügel** mound, hillock, butte *(US)*.
erdichten to feign, to think (make) up, to invent, to fabricate.
erdichtet drummed up, concocted, cooked-up;
~**es Lügengewebe** cock-and-bull story, string *(US sl.)*.
Erd|inneres interior (bowels) of the earth; ~**kabel** earth (underground) cable; ~**kampfflugzeug** ground attack fighter; ~**kern** core of the earth; ~**klumpen** lump of earth, clod; ~**kreis** world; ~**kreisparkraum** orbital parking space; ~**krieg** ground warfare; ~**krümmung** curvature of the earth; ~**kugel** globe, earth; ~**kunde** geography; ~**leitung** *(el.)* earth wire, ground wire *(US)*; ~**loch** *(mil.)* foxhole, dugout; **große ~massen** masses (tons) of earth; **in ~nähe** *(Mond)* in perigee; ~**oberfläche** surface of the earth, upper world.
Erdöl mineral (crude) oil, petroleum, kerosene *(US)*;
~ im Küstenvorland onshore oil;
auf ~ stoßen to strike oil;
~**aktien** oil shares (stocks, *US*); ~**ausfuhrland** oil-exporting country; ~**bedarf** oil demand; ~**bohrungen** oil explorations.
erdolchen to stab;
j. mit seinen Blicken ~ to look daggers at s. o., to give s. o. a withering look.
Erdöl|defizit oil deficit; ~**einfuhren** oil imports; ~**erzeuger** oil producer.
erdölexportierende Länder oil exporters.
Erdöl|fazilitäten *(Weltwährungsfonds)* oil facilities; ~**feld** oil field; ~**förderländer** oil-producing countries; ~**förderung** oil production; ~**fund** oil discovery; ~**gebiet** oil field (territory); ~**gelder** oil money; ~**gesellschaft** oil company; ~**gewinnung** oil (petroleum) production.
erdölhaltig petroliferous.
Erdöl|industrie oil (petroleum) industry; ~**kartell** petroleum cartel; ~**konzession** oil concession rights; ~**lager** oil deposit; ~**land** oil-producting (-exporting) state; ~**leitung** pipeline; ~**markt** oil market; ~**politik** oil policy; **eingefrorener ~preis** frozen oil price; **von der OPEC festgelegter ~preis** Opec-fixed oil price; ~**produkt** oil product; ~**produzent** oil producer; ~**quelle** oil well (spring); ~**reserven** oil reserves; ~**steuereinkünfte** oil tax revenue; ~**sucher** oil prospector; ~**überfluß** oil affluence; ~**überschußland** oil-surplus land; ~**überschwemmung** oil glut; ~**verarbeitung** oil refining; ~**verknappung** oil shortage; ~**vorkommen** oil occurrence (incidence, deposit, basin, field); ~**werte** oils; ~**zone** oil belt.
Erd|pol pole; ~**reich** soil, dirt, loose earth.
erdreisten, sich to have the audacity (impudence, nerve, *US*, cheek).
erdröhnen to roar, to resound;
aus dem Lautsprecher ~ to boom out from the loudspeaker.
erdrosseln to throttle, to strangle, to garotte.
Erdrosselung strangulation, garotte.
erdrücken to crush, to death, *(fig.)* to overwhelm, to overpower, to overcome.
erdrückend crushing, overwhelming;
~**e Beweise** overwhelming evidence; ~**e Mehrheit** overwhelming majority; ~**e Übermacht** overwhelming superiority.
erdrückt crushed to death;
von Kummer ~ weighted down with grief; **von seinen Sorgen ~** overwhelmed by one's worries; **von Steuern ~** crushed by taxation;
von der Schuldenlast fast ~ sein to be nearly crippled with debts; **von der Last der Arbeit ~ werden** to be snowed under (up to one's eyes in) work.
Erd|rutsch *(pol.)* landslide; ~**rutschsieg** runaway victory; ~**satellit** earth satellite, bird, Explorer *(US)*; ~**schluß** *(sl.)* earth, ground; ~**stoß** earth tremor, earthquake shock; ~**strom** *(el.)* earth current; ~**teil** continent; ~**umkreisung** orbital flight.
Erdumlaufbahn orbit;
auf einer ~ orbiting;
in eine ~ katapultieren to blast into orbit.
Erdung *(el.)* ground (earth) connection.
Erd|verbindung *(el.)* earth; ~**wall** earthwork, bank, mound, earthworks.
ereignen, sich to occur, to happen, to take place, to come about.
Ereignis event, occurrence, incident, happening;
falls keine unvorhergesehenen ~se eintreten barring unforeseen developments; **von unsicheren ~sen abhängig** eventual;
alltägliches ~ common event; **bedauerliches ~** lamentable occurrence; **besonderes ~** quite an event; **bevorstehendes ~** fixture; **denkwürdiges ~** notable event; **unerwartet eintretendes oder außergewöhnliches ~** unlooked for mishap or untoward event; **nie eintretendes ~** blue moon; **wahrscheinlich eintretendes ~** probable event; **im Mittelpunkt stehendes festliches ~** focal celebration; **großes ~** great occasion; **herausragendes ~** outstanding event; **historisches ~** historic event, classic event; **kriegerische ~e** hostilities; **rechtsbegründendes ~** law-creating event; **singuläres ~** singular occurrence; **unabwendbares ~** Act of God; **ungewisses ~** contingent event, contingency; **unglückliches ~** unfortunate occurrence; **Kausalzusammenhang unterbrechendes ~** *(Haftung)* superseding cause; **unvermeidliches ~** inevitable accident; **unvorhergesehenes ~** unforeseen event, accident, contingency; **unvorhersehbares ~** fortuitous event; **verkaufsförderndes ~** sales event; **voraussehbares ~** foreseeable event; **zufälliges ~** fortuitous event, chance; **noch nicht lange zurückliegende ~se** recent events;
große ~se auf dem Balkan great doings in the Balkans;
~ begießen to wet a bargain *(sl.)*; **kommende ~se am Markt im voraus berücksichtigen** to discount the market; **~ feiern** to celebrate the occasion; **~ auf einem Gemälde festhalten** to picture an incident; **auf neuere ~se zu sprechen kommen** to descend to more recent events; **von den ~sen überholt sein** to be outdated by [the] events; **politische ~se verfolgen** to keep track of current events; **künftige ~se voraussagen** to forecast future events;
große ~se werfen ihre Schatten voraus coming events cast their shadows before.
Eremit hermit, anchorite, recluse;
wie ein ~ leben to live the life of a recluse.
ererbt inherited, patrimonial;
~**es Vermögen** estate of inheritance *(US)*.
Ererbtes inherited property.
erfahren to hear, to learn, to come to know, *(durchmachen)* to undergo;
etw. über j. ~ to hear s. th. about s. o.; **Demütigung ~** to be humiliated; **etw. unter der Hand ~** to hear on the quiet; **Kritik ~** to meet with criticism; **Kurssteigerung ~** to experience a rise (an advance); **Niederlage ~** to suffer a defeat; **aus zuverlässiger Quelle ~** to have it on good authority (from a reliable source); **erneuten Rückgang ~** to experience a fresh decline; **etw. unmittelbar ~** to learn s. th. first hand; **Verlust ~** to meet with (sustain) a loss; **Wertminderung ~** to suffer a depreciation;
~ *(a.)* expert, versed, experienced, proficient, practised, conversant;
in der Buchhaltung ~ proficient in bookkeeping; **in finanziellen Dingen ~** conversant with finance; **in geschäftlichen Dingen ~** experienced in business;
im Leben viel Undank ~ haben to have met with a great deal of ingratitude during one's lifetime; **etw. am eigenen Leibe ~ haben** to know s. th. from experience; **in Gelddingen wenig ~ sein** to have little experience in money matters; **im Geschäftsleben ~ sein** to be well versed in business;
~**er Buchhalter** senior accountant.
erfährt, man *(Presse)* it is learned.
Erfahrung experience, practice, skill, knowledge;
auf dem Wege der ~ by trial and error; **auf ~en gegründet** based on experience; **aufgrund eigener ~** from one's own experience; **aus Mangel an ~** from lack of experience; **nach herkömmlichen ~en** conventional wisdom says; **ohne ~en** unexperienced; **soweit ich aus persönlicher ~ beurteilen kann** as far as my experience goes; **um eine ~ reicher** wise after the event;
angenehme ~ delightful experiences; **teuer bezahlte ~en** hard-bought experience; **bittere ~** gall; **geschäftliche ~en** experience in business, business experience, versedness in trade; **große ~** wide experience; **jahrelange ~en** long personal experience; **kaufmännische ~** commercial knowledge; **langjährige ~** grey experience, years of practice; **langjährige ~en erforderlich** *(Anzeige)* long experience essential; **nachgewiesene ~en** qualifying experience; **nachweisbare (praktische) ~** practical knowledge, practical (field) experience, know-how; **nützliche ~en** wholesome experience; **reiche ~en** ample experience; **technische ~en** know-how;
~**en im Anlagengeschäft** investment experience; **~ im Außendienst** field experience; ~**en im Bankgeschäft** knowledge of banking; ~**en in der Buchhaltung** bookkeeping experience;

~en im Exportgeschäft export business experience; ~en auf dem Forschungsgebiet research experience; ~ in der Führung des Hauptbuches ledger experience; ~en auf dem Gebiet der Exzedentenschadensversicherung excess of loss background; ~en auf dem Gebiet der Gelddispositionen cash management experience; ~en in mehreren Industriezweigen multiindustry experience; ~ als Lektor tutoring experience; ~ mit faulen Schuldnern bad-debt experience; ~ in Steuersachen tax experience; ~ in Strafsachen trial experience; ~en als Universitätslehrer university teaching experience;
jahrelange ~en benötigen to take years of practice; in ~ bringen to learn, to find out; etw. über j. in ~ bringen to learn s. th. about s. o.; schmerzliche ~en hinter sich bringen to go through painful experiences; bittere ~en gemacht haben to know from bitter experience; erste ~en mit den Kunden hinter sich haben to have had its initial fling with the customers; reiche ~en im Umgang mit Menschen haben to have a wide experience with men; alle bisher gesammelten ~en außer acht lassen to throw the lessons of the past to the winds; aus ~ lernen to profit by experience; böse ~en machen to catch (get) it in the neck *(coll.)*; seine ~en machen to see life, to pay one's dues *(US sl.)*; schlechte ~en mit jem. machen to fare badly with s. o.; seine ~en teuer bezahlen müssen to pay dearly for one's experience; schlechte ~en machen müssen to go through painful experience; ~en sammeln to gather experience; um eine ~ reicher sein to have become wiser; über erhebliche ~en als Geschäftsmann verfügen to be well versed in business matters; über genügende ~en im Geschäftsleben verfügen to have enough business experience; über große ~en verfügen to have much experience; über langjährige ~en verfügen to have a long track record; über langjährige diplomatische ~en verfügen to be old in diplomacy; über zu wenig ~en verfügen to lack experience; durch ~en klug werden to profit by experience, to go through the mill, to cut one's wisdom teeth; etw. aus ~ wissen to know s. th. by experience.

Erfahrungs|austausch exchange (sharing) of experience; ~**bericht** progress report, case history.

erfahrungsgemäß according to (from previous) experience.

Erfahrungs|methode rule of thumb; ~**richtsatz** *(Invalidenversicherung)* experience rate; ~**satz** maxim; ~**schatz** wealth of experience; ~**tatsachen** facts within s. one's experience; ~**wert** empirical value; **technisches ~wissen** technical know-how.

erfaßbar *(Statistik)* recordable, registrable, ascertainable;
steuerlich ~ taxable; **zahlenmäßig ~** calculable.

Erfassen des Signals *(Raumfahrt)* acquisition of signal.

erfassen to comprehend, to comprise, to grasp, to understand, *(Arbeitslosenfürsorge)* to cover *(US)*, *(beschlagnahmen)* to requisition, *(einschließen)* to include, to comprise, to cover, *(statistisch)* to cover, to register, to record, *(Vermögen des Gemeinschuldners)* to marshal, *(Ziel)* to pick up, to detect;
Altersgruppe statistisch ~ to make a statistical survey of an age group; **amtlich ~** to register; **Bedeutung von etw. ~** to make out the meaning of s. th., to grasp the importance of s. th.; **selbst entlegene Dörfer ~** to include even the most isolated villages; **einheitlich ~** to organize into a uniform system; **Einkünfte an der Quelle ~** to tax income at the source; **Feindflugzeuge mit Scheinwerfern ~** to pick out enemy planes by searchlights; **Fußgänger ~** *(Auto)* to knock down a pedestrian; **genau ~** to assimilate property; **gewerkschaftlich ~** to organize into a trade union; **karteimäßig ~** to card-index; **listenmäßig ~** to catalog(ue); **ganzen Markt ~** to blanket the entire market; **radarmäßig ~** to pick up (scan) by radar installations; **statistisch ~** to take a census; **steuerlich ~** to tax, to make taxable; **alle Steuerpflichtigen ~** to apply to all persons liable to tax; **für den Wehrdienst ~** to call to the colo(u)rs; **zahlenmäßig ~** to count.

erfaßt, von Furcht overcome by fear; **vom Schwindel ~** seized with dizziness;
es ~ haben to have got it; **Problem voll ~ haben** to have a thorough grasp of a problem; **[nicht] ~ sein** [not] to be on the register; **von Mitleid ~ werden** to be moved to pity; **steuerlich ~ werden** to become taxable; **von einer Untersuchung ~ werden** to be covered by a survey;
~**er Bereich** *(Statistik)* coverage.

Erfassung *(amtlich)* registration, *(Arbeitslosenfürsorge)* coverage, *(Beschlagnahme)* requisition, *(Radar)* pickup, acquisition, *(Statistik)* registration, survey, *(Vermögen des Gemeinschuldners)* marshalling, *(Wehrpflichtige)* call-up;
karteimäßige ~ card-indexing; **listenmäßige ~** listing; **statistische ~** census enumeration; **steuerliche ~** taxation, assessment;
~ der Inflationsentwicklung inflation accounting; **~ von Konkursverfahren** registration of bankruptcy proceedings; **~ des Leserkreises** audience measurement; **~ der Rangordnung von Pfandobjekten** marshalling of liens.

Erfassungs|bereich scope of application; **geschlossene ~gruppe** *(Statistik)* cluster; ~**klausel** overreaching clause; ~**radar** acquisition radar; ~**stelle** registration office, *(mil.)* requisitioning authority, collecting center *(US)*.

erfinden to invent, to devise, to contrive;
Entschuldigung ~ to trump up an excuse; **Geschichte ~** to fabricate (weave, make up) a story; **Lügen über j. ~** to invent calumnies about s. o.; **neues Wort ~** to coin a new word.

Erfinder inventor, orginator, discoverer, deviser;
alleiniger ~ sole inventor; **angestellter ~** employee inventor; **eigentlicher ~** original inventor; **wahrer ~** true and first inventor;
von vornherein auf alle ~ansprüche verzichten to sign away all rights to any invention; ~**anteil** royalty; ~**ausstellung** inventions exhibition; ~**eigenschaft** inventive faculty (skill); ~**geist** creative conception; ~**gemeinschaft** joint inventors; ~**prämie** award to inventor, *(Angestellter)* technical bonus; ~**recht** inventor's (patent) right; ~**schutz** protection of inventions.

erfinderisch inventive, ingenious;
Not macht ~ necessity is the mother of invention.

Erfindung invention, origination, *(Fälschung)* fabrication, *(Patent)* patent, *(Vorrichtung)* gadget, device;
ältere ~ prior invention; **zum Patent angemeldete ~** invention sought to be patented; **bahnbrechende ~** epoch-making invention; **menschliche Arbeitskraft einsparende ~** labo(u)r-saving invention; **fertige ~** perfect machine; **gebrauchsmusterfähige ~** discovery; **gemeinsame ~** joint invention; **gleiche ~** same invention, identity of invention; **kollidierende ~en** interfering inventions; **neueste ~** latest invention; **äußerst nützliche ~** most useful invention; **patentfähige ~** patentable invention; **patentierte ~** patented invention; **technische ~** technical discovery; **umwälzende ~** revolutionary invention; **verwandte ~en** cognate inventions; **vollendete ~** perfect machine; **zusätzliche ~** additional invention;
~ eines Angestellten invention made by an employee;
~ zum Patent anmelden to apply for a patent; **~ ausnutzen** to work a patent; **~ ausprobieren** to try out an invention; **Umfang einer ~ begrenzen** to define the scope of an invention; **neue ~ allgemein zur Anwendung bringen** to generalize the use of a new invention; **~ auf den neuesten Stand bringen** to perfect an invention; **Widerspruch gegen eine zum Patent angemeldete ~ einlegen** to lodge an opposition to a patent; **Umfang einer ~ erweitern** to enlarge the scope of an invention; **Gegenstand einer ~ herstellen** to produce an invention; **~ fallen lassen** to abandon an invention; **~ patentieren lassen** to take out a patent for an invention; **~ machen** to invent; **~ nutzen** to exploit an invention; **~ patentieren** to patent an invention; **~ prüfen** *(Patentamt)* to examine an invention; **~ unter Geheimschutz stellen** to impose secrecy on an invention; **Patent auf eine ~ stützen** to base a patent on a discovery; **~ eines anderen vervollkommnen (vervollständigen)** to refine upon another's invention; **~ [praktisch, gewerblich] verwerten** to exploit an invention, to reduce an invention to practice.

Erfindungs|gabe inventive faculty (skill), ingenuity; ~**gedanke** *(Patentrecht)* inventive idea; ~**gegenstand** invention; ~**gegenstand herstellen** to produce an invention.

Erfindungshöhe *(Patentrecht)* amount of invention, level of invention, inventiveness, inventive merit (level);
unzureichende ~ insufficient subject matter;
~ bestreiten *(Patentrecht)* to deny the inventive level; **~ erreichen** to amount to invention; **~ verneinen** to deny the inventive step.

Erfindungs|patent patent for invention, letters patent *(Br.)*; ~**priorität** priority of invention.

Erfolg success, victory, do, hit *(US)*, *(Artikel)* vogue, *(Ausgang)* end, issue, *(Ergebnis)* result, outcome;
mit nachweisbaren ~en with a proper record of success; **ohne ~** without success, in vain; **ohne bleibenden ~** without lasting effect; **von ~ gekrönt sein** crowned with success;
außergewöhnlicher ~ eminent success; **beispielloser ~** unexampled success; **bisherige ~e** track records; **durchschlagender ~** telling effect; **fast ein ~** a near miss; **finanzieller ~** financial success; **geschäftlicher ~** business success (winner), money winner, *(Unternehmen)* company's success; **glänzender ~** capital go; **kaufmännischer ~** commercial success; **kolossaler ~** howling success; **moralischer ~** moral victory; **nachgewiese-**

ner beruflicher ~ proven track record; **revolutionärer** ~ breakthrough; **viel** ~! more power to your elbow! *(coll.)*; **voller** ~ complete success;
~ **unserer Bemühungen** outcome of our labo(u)r; ~ **auf dem Büchermarkt** best seller; **einziger** ~ **des Streikes** the only effect of the strike; ~ **als Unternehmer** managerial success;
mit gutem ~ **arbeiten** to work with good results; **erstaunliche** ~**e aufweisen** to make a very strong showing; **zu dem** ~ **beitragen** to contribute (cooperate) to the success; ~ **einer Schlacht bestimmen** to decide a battle; ~ **erringen** to score a success; ~ **haben** to come to much, to make one's way in the world, to succeed, to make the grade, to do well, to come to the top, to go to town *(sl.)*, to pull off, to make out *(US)*, to bring home the bacon *(sl.)*, *(Waren)* to go off well, to come through *(US)*; **mit seiner Arbeit keinen** ~ **haben** to labo(u)r in vain; **durchschlagenden** ~ **haben** to carry the world before one, to strike twelve; **gewünschten** ~ **haben** to have the desired effect; **gleich zu Anfang** ~ **haben** to succeed the very first time; **kaum** ~ **haben** to be to little purpose; **keinen** ~ **haben** *(Nachforschungen)* not to produce the desired result, *(Theaterstück)* to fall flat; **überall** ~ **haben** to be successful all along the line; **wahrscheinlich** ~ **haben** to bid to succeed; **etw. zu einem** ~ **machen** to make a go of s. th.; **glänzenden** ~ **in Anspruch nehmen** to claim a triumph; **mit einem** ~ **rechnen** to figure on a success *(US)*; **von** ~ **zu** ~ **schreiten** to have one success after the other; ~ **sein** *(Theaterstück)* to make a hit, to be a box-office success *(US)*; **dem** ~ **zum Greifen nahe sein** to have success within one's grasp; **großer** ~ **sein** to be a go; **von vollem** ~ **begleitet sein** to be entirely successful; **sich seines** ~**es sicher sein** to feel confident of success; ~ **verbürgen** to ensure success; ~ **versprechen** to promise well; **unbedingt** ~ **haben wollen** to be anxious to succeed; **durchschlagenden** ~ **zeitigen** *(Rede)* to go a long way; **seinen** ~ **harter Arbeit zuschreiben** to attribute one's success to hard work.

erfolglos unsuccessful, futile, vain, ineffective;
sich ~ **um eine Stelle bewerben** to have no success in competing for a job; ~ **bleiben** to come to nothing; ~ **protestieren** to protest in vain;
~**e Bemühungen** vain efforts; ~**er Bewerber** unsuccessful candidate.

Erfolglosigkeit failure, ill success, futility;
~ **auf dem Vollstreckungsbefehl vermerken** to make a return of nulla bona to the writ of fiere facias.

erfolgreich prosperous, successful;
auf allen Gebieten ~ free-ranging;
~ **abschließen** to crown, to wrap it up; **Examen** ~ **bestehen** to succeed in passing an examination; **sich** ~ **entwickeln** to turn out a success; **Aufgabe** ~ **erledigen** to deal successfully with a task; **sich für** ~ **halten** to value o. s. on being successful; ~ **sein** to win out *(US coll.)*; **gesellschaftlich** ~ **sein** to get a lift up in the world; **hundertprozentig** ~ **sein** to work like a charm; **im Leben** ~ **sein** to make one's way in life; **trotz zahlreicher Schwierigkeiten** ~ **sein** to succeed in the face of many difficulties;
~**er Kandidat** successful candidate; ~**es Unternehmen** prosperous enterprise.

erfolgsabhängig dependent upon success.

Erfolgs|aktie performer; **überdurchschnittliche** ~**aktie** high performer; ~**analyse** profit analysis; ~**anteil** royalty, production bonus; ~**anteilskonto** detailed profit and loss account; ~**anteilssystem** bonus (profit-sharing) system; ~**aussichten** prospects of success; **nur geringe** ~**aussichten haben** to have but a poor chance of success; ~**ausweis** trading report; **auf** ~**basis** on a contingent basis.

erfolgsbedingt dependent upon success.

Erfolgs|bedingung condition of success; ~**beitrag** contribution to profit; ~**bereich eines Unternehmens** profit center; ~**bericht** success story; ~**beteiligung** profit sharing; ~**beteiligung am Produktivitätszuwachs** progress sharing; ~**bilanz** operating *(US)* (surplus) statement *(US)*, statement of surplus *(US)*; ~**buch** best seller.

Erfolgschance prospects of success, *(eines Kandidaten)* availability *(US)*;
geringe ~**n** slim chances of success; **gute** ~ fair chance of success;
~**n eines Vorhabens abtasten** to feel out the possibilities of a scheme; **große** ~**n für einen Plan sehen** to see great possibilities in a scheme; **sich** ~**n vorgaukeln** to flatter o. s. with hopes of success.

Erfolgs|ermittlung income determination, ascertainment of returns; **im** ~**fall** in the event of success; **durchschlagender** ~**film** smash hit; ~**haftung** strict liability; ~**hascherei** playing to the gallery; ~**honorar** contingent (contingency, *US*, success, result, *Br.*) fee, quota litis *(US)*, *(Autor)* royalty; **Übernahme gegen** ~**honorar** champerty *(US)*; ~**honorarvereinbarung** contingent fee contract, champertous contract *(US)*; ~**jahr** bonanza year; ~**konto** profit (nominal, income statement) account; ~**kontrolle** *(Werbung)* result testing; **innerbetriebliche** ~**kontrolle** internal control; ~**kontrollstelle** *(Werbung)* ad-checking bureau *(US)*; ~**leiter** avenue to (ladder of) success; ~**leiter emporschnellen** to be on the way to success; **j. die** ~**leiter wieder herunterfallen lassen** to bring s. o. back down the ladder; ~**lohn** result (incentive) wage, payment by results; ~**mandat** *(Anwalt)* result fee *(Br.)*, champerty *(US)*; ~**maßstab** indicator of success; ~**mensch** careerist, hustler, go-getter *(US)*; ~**mensch sein** to make one's way in the world, to go to town; ~**messung** *(Anzeigenwesen)* activation research, feedback score *(US)*; ~**nachweis** evidence of success; **langfristige** ~**planung** long-range profit planning; ~**posten** item; ~**prämie** efficiency bonus; ~**provision** profit commission; ~**rechnung** profit account (statement); **kurzfristige** ~**rechnung** cursory income statement; **volkswirtschaftliche** ~**rechnung** national income accounting; ~**regulierungsposten** deferred item.

erfolgssicher sure of succeeding, surefire *(US)*.

Erfolgs|strategie game plan *(US)*; ~**stück** smash hit; ~**sucht,** ~**streben** eagerness to succeed; ~**tag** *(Börse)* break-even day; ~**träger** profit-yielding product.

erfolgstrunken flushed with (inebriated by) success.

Erfolgs|unternehmen performer; ~**voraussetzungen** requirements for success; ~**weg** key avenue; **sicherer** ~**weg** highroad to success.

erfolgswirksam affecting the operating result.

Erfolgswünsche, herzliche devout wishes for your success.

erfolgversprechendes Unternehmen promising undertaking.

erforderlich requisite, required, needed, necessary;
falls ~ if required, in case of need; **nicht** ~ unnecessary, not required; **nicht unbedingt** ~ not compulsory;
es ~ **machen** to make it necessary, to necessitate; **weitere Nachforschungen** ~ **machen** to necessitate further inquiries;
~**es Alter** required age; ~**e Deckung** requisite cover; ~**es Kapital** capital required, requisite capital; ~**e Maßnahmen treffen** to take the necessary steps; ~**e Mittel haben** to have the money required; **mit der** ~**en Sorgfalt** with due care.

Erforderliche, alles ~ **veranlassen** to make all necessary arrangements, to take appropriate measures; **das** ~ **veranlassen** to do the needful.

erfordern to require, to demand, to take;
sorgfältige Behandlung ~ to need to be dealt with carefully; **viel Geld** ~ to require a great deal of money; **Hilfe** ~ to demand assistance; **sofortige Operation** ~ to call for an immediate operation; **viel Sorgfalt** ~ to need much care; **Takt** ~ to need tactful handling; **Zeit** ~ to take time; **viel Zeit** ~ to cost much time.

Erfordernis condition, requirement, demand, *(Befähigung)* qualification;
dringendes ~ exigency, necessity, pressing demand; **unbedingtes** ~ a must.

Erfordernisse requirements, needs, formalities;
fakultative ~ nonessential elements, nonessentials; **gesetzliche** ~ legal formalities; **handels- und wirtschaftspolitische** ~ exigencies of commercial and economic policy; **unwesentliche** ~ nonessentials, nonessential elements; **wesentliche** ~ essential elements, essentials;
~ **eines Schecks** requisites for a valid check *(US)* (cheque, *Br.*); ~ **des Verkehrs** traffic requirements;
den ~**n genügen** to meet the requirements; **den gesetzlichen** ~**n genügen** to fulfil(l) the requirements of the law; **den** ~**n einer Stellung Genüge leisten** to have the necessary qualifications for a post; **gesetzliche** ~ **als erfüllt nachweisen** to prove out *(US)*.

erforschen to explore, *(untersuchen)* to investigate, to try to find out, to get to the bottom of, *(Wissensgebiet)* to study, to research;
sein Gewissen ~ to search one's conscience; **Hintergründe eines Falles** ~ to go behind a case; **Land** ~ to explore a country; **genauen Sachverhalt** ~ to find out the precise facts.

Erforschung|der Einkaufsgewohnheiten purchase observation; ~ **der Meerestiefen** exploration of the ocean depths; ~ **der öffentlichen Meinung** public opinion poll; ~ **des Weltraums** space exploration.

erfragen, bei Herrn N. zu apply to Mr. N.; **im Büro zu** ~ inquire at the office.

erfrechen, sich to have the cheek (nerve, *US*).

erfreuen to please, to delight;
sich großer Beliebtheit ~ to be in great favo(u)r, *(Politiker)* to top the popularity poll *(US)*; **j. mit einem Geschenk** ~ to please s. o. with a gift; **sich bester Gesundheit** ~ to be in the peak of health; **sich eines guten Rufes** ~ to enjoy the highest reputation; **sich guten Zuspruchs** ~ *(Restaurant)* to be frequented.
erfreulich pleasing, pleasant;
~**e Absatzzunahme** gratifying increase in sales; ~**er Anblick** a sight that pleases the eye; ~**e Nachrichten** good (pleasant) news, glad tidings.
erfreut glad, delighted;
~**, Sie kennen zu lernen** pleased to meet you *(Br.)*, glad to know you *(US)*.
erfrieren to die of exposure, to freeze to death.
Erfrierungen injuries through frostbite;
~ **zweiten Grades** second-degree frostbite;
sich ~ **zuziehen** to suffer frostbite.
Erfrierungserscheinung frostbite.
erfrischen to refresh, to revive;
sich mit einem Getränk ~ to refresh o. s. with a drink.
erfrischend|es Getränk refresher, refreshment; ~**e Naivität** refreshing innocence; ~**er Schlaf** refreshing sleep.
Erfrischung refreshment, refresher, refection, beverage;
kostenlose ~**en** snacks available free of charge; **leichte** ~**en** light refreshments, eleven plus *(Scot.)*;
~**en reichen** to serve refreshments.
Erfrischungs|bude refreshment stand; ~**getränk** refreshment, refresher; ~**kiosk** refreshment stand (booth); ~**pause** bait; ~**raum** refreshment room; ~**stand** refreshment stand, canteen.
erfroren frostbitten, *(tot)* frozen to death;
~**e Füße haben** to have frostbite in one's feet.
erfüllbar capable of performance;
teilweise ~ partially executory.
erfüllen to discharge, to perform, to satisfy, *(abzahlen)* to acquit, *(Verpflichtung)* to carry out, *(Vertrag)* to perform, to execute, to fulfil *(Br.)*, to fulfill *(US)*, to complete, to implement, *(verwirklichen)* to realize;
nicht ~ to default; **sich** ~ to materialize, *(Prophezeiung)* to come true;
Bedingung ~ to answer (meet) a condition; **Bedingungen nicht** ~ to fail to comply with conditions; **mit Bewunderung** ~ to fill with admiration; **Bitte** ~ to grant a request; **Erwartungen nicht** ~ to fall short of expectations; **Forderung** ~ to satisfy a claim; **Forderung des Klägers** ~ to satisfy a claimant; **alle vorgeschriebenen Formalitäten** ~ to comply with all the necessary formalities; **fristgemäß** ~ to carry out within a given time; **seine Pflicht** ~ to perform (do) one's duty; **Satzung** ~ to comply with the rules; **mit großer Trauer** ~ to fill with great sadness; **Verpflichtungen** ~ to meet liabilities; **Versprechen** ~ to keep a promise; **sein Versprechen nicht** ~ to go back on one's promise; **Vertrag** ~ to perform (fulfil(l), execute, satisfy) a contract; **Vertragsbedingung** ~ to comply with a clause in a contract; **Voraussetzungen** ~ to meet the requirements; **Zweck** ~ to serve a purpose.
erfüllt fulfilled, performed;
~ **von Dankbarkeit** full of gratitude; **von dem Gedanken** ~ possessed with the idea; **von seiner eigenen Wichtigkeit** ~ **sein** to think no small beer of o. s.;
~**er Vertrag** satisfied contract; **beiderseits** ~**er Vertrag** executed agreement (contract).
Erfüllung *(Bestimmungen)* compliance, *(Verpflichtung)* discharge, feasance, acquittal, *(Vertrag)* fulfil(l)ment, performance, completion, accomplishment, accomplished delivery, satisfaction, implementation, consummation, *(Verwirklichung)* realization;
an ~**s Statt** in lieu of [specific] performance; **in** ~ **Ihrer Anordnungen** in compliance with your orders; **in** ~ **seiner Dienstobliegenheiten** in exercise of his duties; **in** ~ **seiner Pflicht** in discharge of his duty; **in** ~ **einer übernommenen Verpflichtung** in fulfil(l)ment of a pledge; **nach** ~ **des Vertrages** on completion of contract;
effektive ~ specific performance; **unmöglich gewordene** ~ frustration of contract; **mangelhafte** ~ *(Vertrag)* failure to perform, defective performance (compliance); **sofortige** ~ prompt delivery; **sorgsame** ~ due diligence; **teilweise** ~ part performance; **unmögliche** ~ impossibility of performance; **vergleichsweise** ~ accord and satisfaction; **vertragsgemäße** ~ specific performance; **vertragstreue** ~ faithful performance; **im wesentlichen vertragstreue** ~ substantial performance; **verzögerte** ~ delayed performance;
~ **eines Abkommens** carrying out an agreement; ~ **einer Amtspflicht** performance of a duty; ~ **einer Aufgabe** accomplishment of an enterprise; ~ **der Aufnahmebedingungen** eligibility for admission; ~ **in bar** payment in cash; ~ **einer Bedingung** satisfaction (compliance, fulfilment) of a condition; ~ **seines Ehrgeizes** consummation of one's ambition; ~ **einer Forderung** settlement of a claim; ~ **von Formalitäten** compliance with formalities; ~ **einer Garantiepflicht** implementation of a guarantee; ~ **des Kaufvertrages** completion of sale and purchase *(Br.)*; ~ **einer Leistung** discharge by performance; ~ **in natura** specific performance; ~ **eines Schenkungsversprechens** manual delivery; ~ **eines Traums** realization of a dream; ~ **einer Verpflichtung** discharge of an obligation; ~ **eines Vertrages** implementation (performance, fulfilment) of a contract; ~ **einer Vertragsklausel** compliance with a clause in a contract; ~ **Zug um Zug** contemporaneous (simultaneous) performance;
~ **anbieten** to tender performance; ~ **von Lieferungsverträgen aussetzen** to defer fulfil(l)ment of supply contracts; ~ **seines Lebens im Kloster finden** to find satisfaction in a monastic life; **auf** ~ **klagen** to sue for specific performance.
Erfüllungs|angebot offer to deliver; ~**annahme** acceptance in fulfilment; ~**anspruch** right to performance.
erfüllungsberechtigt entitled to performance.
Erfüllungs|eid suppletory oath; ~**gegenstand** subject matter; ~**gehilfe** vicarious agent; **übergeordneter** ~**gehilfe** superior fellow servant; **für den** ~**gehilfen haftbar sein (haften)** to be vicariously liable; ~**geschäft** delivery.
erfüllungshalber in fulfil(l)ment.
Erfüllungs|interesse general damages; ~**klage** action to claim specific performance of contract, action for assumpsit; ~**mangel** failure to perform (of performance), want of delivery; ~**ort** *(Börse)* settling place, *(Lieferort)* delivery place, place of delivery (performance), to be delivered at, *(Wechsel)* domicile; ~**ort für Geschäftsschulden** location of debts; ~**tag** date of payment, *(Börse)* settling (settlement, name) day, payday *(Br.)*; ~**vereitelung** obstructing performance; ~**verpflichtung** obligation to perform; ~**verweigerung** repudiation; **angekündigte** ~**verweigerung** anticipatory breach of contract; ~**zeit** time of performance.
erfunden invented, devised;
von A bis Z ~ pure invention;
das Pulver nicht ~ **haben** not to have set the Thames on fire;
~**e Geschichte** made-up story; ~**e Person** fictitious character.
ergänzen *(auffüllen)* to fill up, to piece out, *(ersetzen)* to replace, *(hinzufügen)* to supplement, *(Lager)* to replenish, to assort, *(Summe)* to make up, *(vervollständigen)* to complement, to complete, to supplement, to fill;
sich ~ to be complementary (recruited from); **Fehlendes** ~ to make up a deficiency; **Investitionsgüter** ~ to replace capital goods; **sein Lager (Lagerbestände)** ~ to replenish one's inventory (stock), to refill (replace) the stock; **seine Sammlung** ~ to complete one's collection; **Schiffsvorräte** ~ to replenish ship's stores; **fehlende Summe** ~ to make up the requisite sum; **Urteil** ~ to amend a judgment; **Vorräte** ~ to complete with provisions; **fehlende Worte** ~ to add the missing words.
ergänzend complementary, ancillary, supplemental, subsidiary, novel;
~ **abändern** to amend;
~**er Schriftsatz** supplemental answer.
Ergänzung completion, complement, supplement, supplementation, *(Gesetz)* amendment, *(Lagerauffüllung)* replenishment, *(Wiederherstellung)* restoration;
als ~ supplementary; **ohne** ~**en** unamended; **zur späteren** ~ *(Gesetz)* ad referendum;
~**en** addenda;
personelle ~ recruitment *(US)*;
~ **abgenützter Einzelteile** replacement of worn-out parts; ~ **einer Erklärung** additional explanation; ~ **des Lagers** replacement (replenishment) of inventory; ~ **der gestellten Sicherheiten** replenishment of a loan; ~ **eines Urteils** amendment of a judgment; ~ **der Vorräte** replenishment of supplies;
in jem. seine ~ **finden** to find one's complement in s. o.; ~ **vornehmen** to supply an omission; ~**en des Lagers vornehmen** to replenish one's inventory.
Ergänzungs|abgabe special levy, surtax, personal tax *(Br.)*; ~**abkommen** supplementray agreement, additional agreement (convention); ~**antrag** application to amend, *(Gesetz)* supplemental bill; ~**artikel** amending (additional) article; ~**band** supplement, supplementary volume; **jährlicher** ~**band** reference annual; ~**batterie** buffer (booster) battery.

ergänzungsbedürftig sein, nicht *(Gesetz)* to be complete in itself.
Ergänzungs|bericht supplementary report; ~**bestellung** replenishment order; ~**bestimmungen** supplementary (additional) provisions; ~**bilanz** supplementary statement; ~**etat** supplementary budget (estimates).
ergänzungsfähig *(Gesetz)* amendable;
nicht ~ unamendable.
Ergänzungs|gesetz supplemental (amending) act; ~**haushalt** supplementary budget (estimates); ~**heft** supplementary issue, supplement; ~**information** supplementary information; ~**kredit** supplementary credit; ~**kredit gewähren** to supplement a loan; ~**kursus** supplementary course; ~**lager** replenishing stock; ~**police** supplementary policy; ~**prämie** additional premium; ~**protokoll** supplementary protocol; ~**richter** substitute judge; ~**statut** bye-law; ~**steuer** additional tax; ~**stück** complement; ~**verfahren fehlender Werte** *(Statistik)* missing plot technique; ~**versicherung** complementary insurance; ~**vertrag** supplementary contract; ~**vorlage** supplementary estimates; ~**vorschlag** amendment; ~**vorschriften** complementary rules, supplementary regulations; ~**wahl** supplemental (bye-, *Br.*, special, *US*) election; ~**werbung** supplementary (accessory) advertising; ~**zuweisung** additional grant.
ergattern to make a snatch, to sponge, to grab;
etw. endlich ~ to latch onto s. th. *(sl.)*; **alte Buchausgabe** ~ to unearth an early edition; **Ehemann** ~ to hook a husband; **Sitzplatz** ~ to get hold of a seat; **letztes Stück Kuchen** ~ to grab the last piece of cake.
ergaunern to graft, to sharp, to get on the crook, to trick out of, to touch *(sl.)*;
etw. von jem. ~ to string s. o. for s. th.; **1000 DM von jem.** ~ to chisel s. o. out of DM 1000.
ergeben *(abwerfen)* to produce, to recoup, to yield, *(betragen)* to total, to amount, to work out at;
sich ~ to ensue, to arise out of, to follow, to result, *(der Polizei)* to hold up one's hands; **Defizit** ~ to show a deficit; **im Durchschnitt** ~ to average; **gute Ernten** ~ to yield (produce) good crops; **Gewinn** ~ to yield (leave) a profit; **sich auf Gnade und Ungnade (bedingungslos)** ~ to surrender unconditionally; **Resultate** ~ to show (yield) results; **sich ganz einer Sache** ~ to devote o. s.; **sich in sein Schicksal** ~ to resign to fate; **sich dem Trunk** ~ to become addicted to drink; **Verlust** ~ to result in (show) a loss; **siebenprozentige Verzinsung** ~ to yield an effective sum equivalent to 7 per cent;
~ *(a.)* obedient, thick and thin;
völlig in sein Schicksal ~ completely resigned to one's fate; **dem Suff** ~ addicted to the bottle;
Ihr ~**er** yours sincerely *(Br.)*, yours [very] truly;
jem. ~ **dienen** to serve s. o. loyally; **alles** ~ **über sich ergehen lassen** to submit to everything;
~**er Freund** loyal friend.
Ergebenheit devotion, loyalty;
geheuchelte ~ lip service.
ergebenst [most] respectfully [yours];
~**er Diener** obedient servant.
Ergebnis issue, result, outcome, fruit, *(Ertrag)* returns, receipts, yield, *(Erzeugnis)* product, *(Produktionsmenge)* output, progeny, *(Untersuchung)* findings, *(Waage)* return, *(Wirkung)* effect;
buchmäßiges ~ book profit (loss); **finanzielles** ~ financial result; **greifbare** ~**se** tangible results; **günstiges** ~ favo(u)rable result; **interne** ~**se** inside data; **kümmerliche** ~**se** drab (poor) results; **praktisches** ~ physical result; **annähernd richtiges** ~ approximate result; **wissenschaftliche** ~**se** scientific results, findings; **zusätzliches** ~ by-result;
~ **fünfjähriger Arbeit** product of five years' work; ~ **unserer Bemühungen** effect of our labo(u)r; ~**se der Bevölkerungszählung** census findings; ~ **der Beweisaufnahme** summary of evidence; ~ **der durchgeführten Ermittlungen** result of an investigation; ~ **des Geschäftsjahres** result of the business year; ~**se einer Leserumfrage** readership ratings; ~ **eines Unfalls** result of an accident; ~ **der Volksabstimmung** referendum vote; ~ **einer Wahl** result (returns) of an election;
mit einem besseren ~ **abschließen** to close with a better result; **gute** ~**se aufweisen** to show good results; ~**se bekanntgeben** to give out (announce) the results; ~**se der Wahl bekanntgeben** to declare the poll; **positive** ~**se nicht vor 1984 erwarten** not to expect to evaluate results until well into calendar 1984; **zu einem** ~ **kommen** to arrive at a conclusion; **durchschnittliches** ~ **nehmen** to take an average of results; ~ **zeitigen** to return (yield) a result, to bear fruit;
~**abführungsvertrag** surrender of profits agreement; ~**aufstellung** earnings statement; ~**beeinflussung durch die Befrager** interviewer bias; ~**beteiligung** profit sharing, participation in profit; ~**genauigkeit** *(Datenverarbeitung)* accuracy.
ergebnislos without result, unsuccessful, fruitless, vain;
Suche ~ **abbrechen** to abandon a search; ~ **sein** to be in vain; ~ **verlaufen** to come to nothing, to fail;
~**e Bemühungen** fruitless efforts; ~**er Versuch** vain attempt.
ergebnisneutral behandeln to be neutral as regards operating income.
Ergebnis|rechnung profit and loss account, earnings statement, statement of operating results *(US)*; ~**rechnung auf der Basis variabler Kosten** marginal income statement; ~**übernahmevertrag** surrender-of-profits agreement.
ergehen *(Gesetz)* to be published (issued), *(Urteil)* to be pronounced;
sich in feierlichen Beteuerungen seiner Unschuld ~ to make a solemn protestation that one is innocent; **sich in Dankesbezeugungen** ~ to be profuse in one's gratitude; **sich im Garten** ~ to take a stroll in the garden; **gegen den Kläger** ~ to go against the plaintiff; **sich des längeren über etw.** ~ to hold forth on s. th.; **sich in Lobpreisung** ~ to be profuse in one's praise; **sich in langen Reden über ein Thema** ~ to dwell on a subject; **sich in begeisterten Schilderungen** ~ to give an enthusiastic description; **sich in Schmähungen** ~ to break out into a stream of abuse; **sich in Vermutungen** ~ to indulge in supposition;
etw. über sich ~ **lassen** to suffer, to bear, to endure; **Aufruf an die Bevölkerung** ~ **lassen** to make an appeal to the population; **Beschluß** ~ **lassen** to issue a formal decree; **Einladung an j.** ~ **lassen** to send an invitation to s. o.; **Gnade vor Recht** ~ **lassen** to show clemency; **jds. Redeschwall über sich** ~ **lassen** to submit to the torrent of s. one's words; **einen Ruf an j.** ~ **lassen** to offer s. o. a professorship (chair); **Verordnung** ~ **lassen** to issue a decree; **Versäumnisurteil gegen sich** ~ **lassen** to suffer default.
ergiebig *(ertragreich)* paying, profitable, lucrative, remunerative, *(Land)* yielding, rich, fertile, fat, fruitful, *(produktiv)* productive, *(reich)* abundant;
~ **sein** to yield, to pan out *(US sl.)*;
~**e Ernte** rich harvest; ~**e Geldquelle** plentiful source of money; ~**es Mahl** substantial meal; ~**e Mine** productive mine, bonanza *(US)*; **auf eine** ~**e Ölquelle stoßen** to strike it rich; ~**es Thema** broad subject.
Ergiebigkeit *(Einträglichkeit)* lucrativeness, profitableness, profitability, *(Fruchtbarkeit)* prolificness, *(Produktivität)* productiveness, productivity, *(Überfluß)* abundance, richness.
ergießen, sich to gush, to pour, to flow.
erglühen *(Gesicht)* to blush, to flush;
in Liebe für j. ~ to fall passionately in love with s. o.
Ergonomie human engineering.
Ergötzen delectation, delight, amusement.
ergötzen to entertain, to delight, to divert, to amuse;
Zuschauer ~ to amuse the audience.
Ergötzung, der ~ **Halbgebildeter dienen** to be suitable for the delectation of half-educated people.
ergrauen to turn gray (grey, *Br.*);
im Dienst ~ to grow old in service.
ergreifen to seize, to grasp, to take hold of, to gripe, *(überkommen)* to touch, to move, to stir;
jem. beim Arm ~ to grasp s. one's arm; **Beruf** ~ to enter a profession; **Besitz** ~ to take possession; **Dieb** ~ to seize (capture) a thief; **Flucht** ~ to take to one's heels; **Gelegenheit** ~ to avail o. s. of an opportunity; **Gelegenheit beim Schopf** ~ to take time by the forelock; **jds. Hand** ~ to take hold of s. one's hand; **Hasenpanier** ~ to take to one's heels; **Macht** ~ to seize power; **Maßnahmen** ~ to adopt (take) measures; **Nachbargebäude** ~ *(Flammen)* to spread to the next house; **jds. Partei** ~ to side with (stick up, stand up for) s. o.; **gerichtliche Schritte gegen j.** ~ to take legal steps against s. o.; **Seemannsberuf** ~ to use the sea; **Verbrecher** ~ to capture (arrest, apprehend) a criminal; **das Wort** ~ to make a speech, to take the floor; **Zügel der Regierung** ~ to take up the reins of government.
ergreifende Worte moving (touching) words.
Ergreifung seizure, *(Dieb)* apprehension, arrest;
~ **der Macht** assumption (usurption, seizure) of power; ~ **von Maßnahmen** adoption of measures; ~ **eines Verbrechers** capture of a criminal.
ergriffen touched, moved, *(Verbrecher)* arrested, seized, captured;
von Angst ~ overcome with fear; **nicht** ~ unapprehended; **von Panik** ~ panic-stricken; **sehr** ~ deeply moved, touched to the heart;

~ **sein** to be touched (moved), to be overcome with emotion; **von einem Anblick sehr ~ sein** to be much affected at the sight of s. th.; **von einer tiefen Bewegung ~ sein** to be stirred by a deep emotion; **von einer Geschichte sehr ~ sein** to be deeply moved by a story; **von einem Taumel der Begeisterung ~ sein** to be seized by a whirl of enthusiasm.

Erguß discharge, *(fig.)* flow, flood, torrent, outburst.

Ergüsse, jds. ~ über sich ergehen lassen to submit to the flow of s. one's words.

erhaben elevated, raised, *(Gefühl)* lofty, sublime, elevated, *(großartig)* magnificent, grand;
über jede Kritik ~ above criticism; **über alles Lob ~** beyond all praise;
sich über etw. ~ dünken to fancy o. s. to be above s. th.; **über Schmeicheleien ~ sein** to be superior to flattery; **über jeden Verdacht ~ sein** to be above suspicion (beyond reproach);
~er Anblick magnificent sight; **~e Arbeit** embossed work; **~es Gefühl** feeling of exhaltation.

Erhabenheit des Geistes elevation of the mind.

erhalten to obtain, to get, to receive, *(bewahren)* to preserve, to save;
j. ~ to keep (support) s. o.; **sich selbst ~** to maintain o. s.; **Bauwerk ~** to take care (maintain) a building; **Bescheid ~** to be informed; **Besuch ~** to have a visitor; **Brief ~ haben** to be in receipt of (receive) a letter; **Erlaubnis ~** to obtain permission; **Frau und sieben Kinder ~** to support a wife and seven children; **Frieden ~** to preserve peace; **Gehalt ~** to draw a salary; **sich gesund ~** to keep o. s. in good health; **Haus in gutem Zustand ~** to keep a house in good repair; **j. bei guter Laune ~** to keep s. o. in good mood; **j. am Leben ~** to keep s. o. alive; **größeren Marktanteil ~** to get a bigger foot in the market; **Preis ~** to be awarded a prize; **besseren Preis ~** to fetch a higher price; **vier Tage Urlaub ~** to be granted four days [of] leave; **sein Teil ~** to get one's share; **Vitamine in Speisen ~** to preserve the vitamins in food; **Zutritt ~** to gain access;
~, was einem zusteht to come into one's own;
~ *(a.)* received;
Betrag ~ payment received; **Betrag bar ~** cash received; **dankend ~** received with thanks; **gut ~** incorrupt, *(Ware)* well preserved, incorrupt, *(Münze)* in mint condition; **richtig ~** duly received; **schwarz zu ~** black; **Wert ~** *(auf Wechseln)* value received;
~ bleiben *(Gebäude)* to remain undamaged, *(überleben)* to survive; **sich bis heute ~ haben** *(Brauch)* to be still alive; **gut ~ sein** to be in good condition, *(Gebäude)* to be in good repair; **schlecht ~ sein** to be in poor condition, *(Gebäude)* to be in bad repair;
gut ~e Statuen well-preserved statues; **in gut ~em Zustand** in good condition.

erhältlich available, obtainable, procurable;
gegen Bestellung ~ obtainable on order; **frei ~** freely obtainable; **in allen Größen ~** available in all sizes; **im Handel ~** by way of trade, on the market; **noch ~** *(Buch)* still in print; **Prospekte hier ~** prospectuses sold here; **Schuhe hier ~** shoes stocked here;
~ sein *(Börse)* to be on the way, *(Buch)* to be in print, *(Ware)* to knock about; **in allen Fachgeschäften ~ sein** to be obtainable from all stockists; **nicht mehr im Handel ~ sein** to be off the market; **leicht ~ sein** to be easy to obtain; **auf dem Markt ~ sein** to be sold commercially, to be on the market; **nicht ~ sein** not to be had; **nicht mehr ~ sein** to be no more available; **schwer ~ sein** to be difficult to obtain (get);
schwer ~er Artikel article difficult to get at;
Fahrpläne sind am Schalter ~ timetables can be obtained at the counter; **Karten sind im Vorverkauf ~** tickets can be booked in advance.

Erhaltung conservation, preservation, maintenance, support;
zur ~ des Friedens in order to preserve peace;
~ des gegenwärtigen Abschlußniveaus maintenance selling; **~ eines alten Brauches** retention of an old custom; **~ einer Familie** support (maintenance) of a family; **~ eines Gebäudes** building maintenance, preservation (upkeep) of a building; **~ von Vermögenswerten** conservation of assets;
etw. zur ~ seiner Gesundheit tun to do s. th. for one's health.

Erhaltungs|aufwand maintenance cost (charges), maintaining expenses, expenses of maintenance, cost of maintenance, routine maintenance; **~aufwand für landwirtschaftlich genutzte Gebäude bestreiten** to incur expenditure on agricultural buildings; **~kosten** maintenance charges, expenses of upkeep; **kombinierte Abschreibungs- und ~methode** combined depreciation and maintenance method; **~pacht** tenant-repairing lease.

erhaltungspflichtig maintainable.

Erhaltungswerbung maintenance advertising.

Erhaltungszustand state of preservation (repair);
in schlechtem ~ out of repair;
einwandfreier ~ tenantable repair; **ordnungsgemäßer ~** proper state of repair; **schlechter ~** nonrepair.

Erhängen hanging.

erhängen, sich to hang o. s.

erhärten to strengthen, to reinforce, to confirm, to corroborate;
sich ~ *(Zement)* to harden, to set; **eidlich ~** to affirm (confirm) by oath; **seine Meinung durch Tatsachen ~** to substantiate one's opinion by facts; **Theorie ~** to bear out a theory; **durch Urkunde ~** to vouch by documents.

Erhärtung confirmation, corroboration, substantiation.

erhaschen, Blick von jem. to catch s. one's eye.

erheben *(Beitrag)* to collect, to levy, *(erfassen)* to record, *(ermitteln)* to ascertain, *(Steuern)* to collect, to exact, to impose, to levy;
sich ~ *(aufstehen)* to rise [to one's feet], to uprise, to get up, to stand up, to get on one's legs, *(Frage)* to spring up, *(Volk)* to rise against, to rise in insurrection, to revolt;
Abgaben ~ to levy taxes; **Anspruch ~ auf** to lay (lodge) claim to; **Beanstandungen ~** to raise objections; **Bedenken ~** to raise doubts; **falsche Beschuldigungen ~** to bring a false accusation; **Beweis ~** to take (hear) evidence; **Einspruch ~** to lodge a protest; **keinen Einspruch ~** to take no objection against; **keine Eintrittsgebühr ~** to charge no entrance fee; **Einwand ~** to enter a plea; **Einwendungen ~** to raise objections; **sich früh ~** to rise early; **Gebühr ~** to charge a fee; **großes Geschrei ~** to set up a loud shout; **zum Gesetz ~** to make into law, to enact; **sein Glas ~** to raise one's glass; **sein Glas auf jds. Wohl ~** to drink s. one's health; **Hand gegen j. ~** to lift one's hand against s. o.; **j. in den Himmel ~** to sing the praises of s. o., to laud (praise) s. o. to the skies; **sich hoch ~** to tower; **Klage gegen j. ~** to bring an action against s. o.; **sich Mann für Mann ~** to rise bodily; **per Nachnahme ~** to collect on delivery; **Parkplatzgebühr ~** to lay a charge upon the use of a carpark; **Protest ~** to enter (lodge) a protest; **ins Quadrat ~** to square; **j. in einen höheren Rang ~** to raise s. o. to a higher rank; **Steuern ~** to levy taxes; **Steuern an der Quelle ~** to levy tax at the source, to withhold a tax; **seine Stimme für j. ~** to speak up for s. o.; **etw. zum System ~** to reduce s. th. to a system; **auf den Thron ~** to seat s. o. on the throne; **sich gegen den Tyrannen ~** to rise against the tyrant; **Vorschlag zum Beschluß ~** to adopt a resolution; **Wechselprotest ~** to protest a bill; **Widerspruch ~** to make objections, to oppose; **Zahl zur dritten Potenz ~** to cube a number; **Zinsen ~** to charge interest.

erhebend|er Anblick edifying sight; **~e Feier** solemn ceremony; **~es Gefühl** feeling of exhaltation.

Erheber eines Patentwiderspruchs opposer *(US)*.

erheblich considerable, substantial, material, relevant, grave;
~ gestiegen sein to have risen considerably; **nicht ~ sein** to be of no importance;
von ~er Bedeutung of considerable importance; **~er Beitrag** substantial contribution; **~e Geldsumme** handsome sum of money; **~er Gewinn** substantial gain; **~e Menge** large quantity; **~es Risiko** substantial risk; **~er Schaden** serious (heavy, considerable) loss; **~e Schulden** heavy (staggering) debts; **~e Unkosten** considerable expenses; **~e Verbesserungen** substantial improvements; **~es Vermögen** sizable (handsome) fortune.

Erhebung *(Aufstand)* insurrection, revolt, uprising, upheaval, *(Erdboden)* rise, hill, height, rising, eminence, elevation, *(Gelder)* collection, gathering, *(Statistik)* statistics, census, survey, poll, *(Untersuchung)* investigation, survey, inquiry, inquest, research;
~en enquiries, data collected;
amtliche ~ official inquiry; **bankstatistische ~en** banking statistics; **stichprobenartig durchgeführte ~en** sample statistics; **nur teilweise durchgeführte ~** incomplete census; **statistische ~en** statistical inquiries (investigations), collection of statistics; **unvollständige ~** incomplete census;
~ einer Abgabe levy of a duty; **~ eines Anspruchs** lodging a claim; **~en innerhalb der Betriebe** industrial census; **~ übermäßiger Gebühren** collection of illegal fees; **~ zum Gesetz** enactment; **~ von Kampfzöllen** fiscal retaliation; **~ einer Klage** bringing (filing) of an action; **~ per Nachnahme** collection *(US)* (cash, *Br.*) on delivery; **~en auf dem Postwege** mail survey; **~ in die zweite Potenz** squaring; **~ in die dritte Potenz** cubing; **~ an der Quelle** *(Steuer)* withholding at source; **~ zur kreisfreien Stadt** incorporation of a town; **~ von Steuern** collection (imposition) of taxes; **~ von Zöllen** levy of duties;

~**en anstellen** to investigate, to make inquiries; **statistische ~en anstellen (durchführen)** to investigate s. th. statistically, to take a census; ~**en an Ort und Stelle durchführen** to make investigations on the spot; **zu einer nationalen ~ führen** to touch off a national uproar; **einheimische Industrie durch ~ von Zöllen schützen** to protect domestic products from foreign competition.

Erhebungs|angaben census (statistical) data; ~**auswahl** sample; ~**bogen** census form; ~**einheit** statistical unit; ~**fehler** *(Statistik)* ascertainment error; **systematischer ~fehler** procedural bias; ~**gebiet** collection district; ~**grundlage** *(Statistik)* frame; ~**jahr** census year; ~**kosten** charges for recovering, collection charges; ~**plan** *(Statistik)* survey design; ~**stichtag** statistical reference date; ~**termin** *(Steuer)* tax payment date; ~**verfahren** taxation system; ~**zeitraum** *(Statistik)* period under survey, *(Steuer)* period of collection, *(EG)* reference period.

erheitern to amuse, to entertain.

Erheiterung amusement, entertainment;
~ **der Volksmenge** entertainment of the crowd.

erhellen to illuminate, to light up;
sich ~ *(Himmel)* to brighten, to clear up.

erhitzen to heat;
sich ~ to hot up, to fly into a temper; **auf 70° C** ~ to rise to 70° C; **Gemüter** ~ to make feelings run high, to stir up the minds; **sich an einem Thema** ~ to warm on a subject.

erhitzt heated, excited, stirred up, *(Gesicht)* warm, hot;
leicht ~ sein to be easily excited;
~**e Auseinandersetzung** fierce argument; ~**e Debatte** heated debate; ~**e Gemüter** excited minds, hot-heads; ~**e Wangen** flushed cheeks.

Erhitzung warming;
~ **der Gemüter** excitement of feelings.

erhoben raised, *(Steuer)* collected;
noch nicht ~ uncollected.

erhoffen to hope (wish) for.

erhofft hoped-for, expected;
weit mehr ~ haben to have expected much more.

erhöhen to advance, to increase, to raise, to heighten, *(Geschwindigkeit)* to accelerate, to put (speed) up, *(Kurse)* to increase, to key up, *(Preise)* to enhance, to advance, to raise, to lift, to mark up *(US)*, to up, to jack up *(coll.)*;
sich ~ to be increased, *(Kurse)* to advance, to increase, to rise, to go up, *(Spannung)* to grow, to be increased; **in Anspruch genommene Kredite** ~ to increase the borrowings; **Ausgaben** ~ to increase the expenditure; **Diskontsatz** ~ to raise the bank *(Br.)* (discount, rediscount, *US*) rate; **um das Doppelte** ~ to double; **Fahrt auf 20 Knoten** ~ to increase speed to twenty knots; **jds. Gehalt** ~ to increase (raise) s. one's salary, to give s. o. a rise; **Geschwindigkeit** ~ to increase the speed; **Grundkapital** ~ to increase the share capital *(US)* (capital stock, *US*); **Haus um zwei Stockwerke** ~ to raise a house two stories (storeys); **Leistung** ~ *(Motor)* to tune up; **Limit** ~ to extend (raise) the limit; **Löhne** ~ to put up (increase, lead up) wages; **Mindestreserven** ~ to increase the special deposits with the Bank of England *(Br.)* (minimum reserve requirements, *US*); **Preise sprunghaft** ~ to jump prices; **Produktion** ~ to increase (raise) step up production; **j. im Rang** ~ to elevate (raise) s. o. to a higher rank, to carbonize s. o. *(sl.)*; **Scheck in betrügerischer Absicht** ~ to raise a cheque *(Br.)* (check, *US*); **Sicherheitsleistung** ~ to enlarge bail; **Spannung eines Dramas** ~ to intensify the action of a drama; **Steuern** ~ to increase (raise) taxes; **Tarif** ~ to raise a tariff; **jds. Verstimmung** ~ to deepen s. one's resentment; **Warenpreise** ~ to enhance the prices of goods; **Wert** ~ to improve the value; **Zinsfuß von 8 auf 8 1/2%** ~ to raise the rate of interest from 8 to 8 1/2 per cent.

erhöht increased, raised, added;
um das Doppelte ~ doubled;
~**er Blutdruck** increased blood pressure; ~**e Geschwindigkeit** accelerated (increased) speed; ~**er Grundpreis** raised standard rate; ~**e Lebenshaltungskosten** advanced (increased) cost of living; ~**er Lohn** higher wages (pay); **in ~em Maße** to a higher degree; ~**er Preis** higher (increased, enhanced) price; ~**es Risiko** aggravated (added) risk; ~**e Sorgfalt** increased care; ~**e Temperatur** raised temperature; ~**e Temperatur haben** to have (run) a temperature; ~**e Tribüne** raised platform, advancement; ~**er Umsatz** increased turnover; ~**e Zinsen** increased interest.

Erhöhung advance, increase, rise, step-up, increment, *(Anhöhe)* elevation, rising, *(Gehälter)* raise *(US)*, rise *(Br.)*, stepup *(US)*, level (l)ing up, *(Preise)* enhancement, *(Wert)* improvement;
nach Abrechnung der inflationsbedingten ~ after inflation retention;
erhoffte ~ hoped-for increase; **pauschale** ~ flat increase; **saisonbedingte** ~ seasonal increase; **spürbare** ~ appreciable increase;
~ **der industriellen Abschreibungsbeträge** increase in depreciation allowances for industry; ~ **des Aktienkapitals** increase of share capital; ~ **der Aktienkurse** improvement in stocks; ~ **des Bahntarifs** raising of railway rates *(Br.)*; ~ **des Banknotenumlaufs** increase of notes in circulation; ~ **des Diskontsatzes** increase in the discount (bank, *Br.*, rediscount, *US*) rate; ~ **des Eigenkapitals** increase in equity; ~ **des Einkommensteuerfreibetrages** income-tax allowance increase; ~ **der Eisenbahntarife** raising of railway rates *(Br.)* (railroad, rates, *US*); ~ **der Freibetragsgrenze** *(Einkommensteuer)* personal exemption increase; ~ **der Fremdkapitalintensität** high gearing; **bereits vereinbarte ~ der Gehälter** rises already agreed *(Br.)*; ~ **der Geschwindigkeit** acceleration; ~ **der Golddeckung der Währung** increase in the gold backing for the currency; ~ **des Kapitals** increase of share capital, capital increase, increase in capital; **lohnseitig bedingte ~ der Kosten** wage-induced rise in costs; ~ **des Kredits** increase of credit; ~ **der Kreditvolumen** increase in the amount of bank credit; ~ **der Landegebühren** increase in landing fees; ~ **des Lebensstandards** rise in the standard of living; ~ **der Löhne** rise (raise, *US*) in wages, wage increase (increment, *Br.*); ~ **der Mieten** increase (raising) of rents; ~ **der Mindestreserven bei der Landeszentralbank** increase of [their] special deposits with the Bank of England *(Br.)* (required minimum reserves, *US*); ~ **der Pension** pension increment; ~ **um 3500 Pfund** £ 3500 plus increase; ~ **der Portogebühren** increase in (rise of) postal charges, postal increase, rise of postal charges *(Br.)*; ~ **der Preise** rise in prices; **sprunghafte ~ der Preise** rapid enhancement of prices; ~ **der Produktion** increase of production; ~ **um einen Punkt** one-point rise; ~ **im Rang** elevation in rank, advancement; ~ **des Risikos** increase of the risk; ~ **der Sondervergünstigungen** fringe increase; **zur Arbeitsbeschaffung vorgenommene ~ der Staatsausgaben** make-work increase in government spending; ~ **des Steueraufkommens** revenue increase (raising); ~ **des Steuerfreibetrages** exemption increase *(US)*; ~ **der persönlichen Steuerfreibeträge** raising personal allowances; ~ **der indirekten Steuern** indirect tax increase; ~ **des Umsatzes** rise in sales; ~ **des Wertes** increase (improvement of) value; ~ **des Zahlungsmittelumlaufs** monetization of the debt *(US)*;
~ **aufweisen** to show an increase; ~ **der Staatsverschuldung auslösen (herbeiführen)** to involve a great increase in the national debt; ~ **des Verteidigungsetats beantragen** to ask for more money for defence (defense, *US*); ~ **im Kurs erfahren** to experience a rise in prices; ~ **der Kosten teilweise selbst tragen** to absorb part of the cost increase.

Erhöhungs|basis, prozentuale percentage increase basis; ~**tendenz** rising tendency.

erholen, sich to recreate, to convalesce, to recuperate, to pick up, *(Kurse)* to be making good progress, to look (pick, prick) up, to recover, to revive, to rally, to rise, to improve, *(Mensch)* to pick up (recover) strength, to come round *(coll.)*, *(sich schadlos halten)* to make up for one's losses, to repay (reimburse, recoup) o. s., to be making good progress, to take a rest, to relax; **sich bei jem.** ~ to draw (reimburse o. s.) upon s. o.; **sich bis auf 490** ~ *(Kurs)* to rise to 490, *(Kurse)* to make good recoveries; ~ **von seiner Arbeit** ~ to rest from one's labo(u)r; **sich für den Betrag seiner Spesen** ~ to recover expenses; **sich von einem geschäftlichen Fehlschlag** ~ to recover from a business setback; **sich beim Giranten** ~ to have recourse to the endorser of a note; **sich gut** ~ to be doing (mending) nicely; **sich von einer Krankheit** ~ to recover from an illness; **sich auf dem Lande** ~ to seek relaxation in the country; **sich von den Nachwirkungen des Krieges** ~ to recover from the effects of the war; **sich von einem geschäftlichen Rückschlag** ~ to recover after a business setback; **sich bei den Schlußkursen** ~ to be improving at the close; **sich schnell** ~ to recover quickly, *(Kurse)* to brisk up; **sich wieder** ~ to work round, *(Kurse)* to be picking up again, to experience a recovery; **sich finanziell wieder** ~ to recover one's strength (financially), to recuperate; **sich für eine Zahlung** ~ to cover (recoup) o. s.

erholend recreative.

erholsam recreative, restful, relaxing, *(Schlaf)* refreshing.

erholt recovered, rested;
gut ~ aussehen to look fit again; **sich völlig ~ haben** to feel quite strong again; **sich wieder ~ haben** to be on one's feet, to be on one's hind legs.

Erholung recourse, distraction, play, *(Arbeitsruhe)* recreation, relaxation, *(Ferien)* holiday, vacation *(US)*, *(nach Krankeit)* convalescence, recovery, recuperation of health, *(Markt)* improvement, recovery, recuperation, revival, pick-up *(US coll.)*;
durchgreifende ~ all-round recovery; **finanzielle** ~ financial recovery; **gemeinsame** ~ collective recreation; **rasche** ~ speedy (quick) recovery; **schnelle** ~ *(Kurse)* rally; **wirtschaftliche** ~ economic recuperation;
~ **der Aktienkurse** improvement in stocks; ~ **der Konjunktur** revival in business; **konsumbedingte** ~ **der Konjunktur** consumer-led recovery; ~ **der Kurse** recovery of (comeback, rally in) prices; ~ **der Weltwirtschaft** world economic recovery; **dringend** ~ **brauchen** to badly need a rest; **zur** ~ **fahren** to go on a vacation; ~ **an der See suchen** to seek relaxation at the seaside; **an einer nachfolgenden** ~ **teilhaben** to share in a subsequent recovery.

Erholungs|anlagen facilities for recreation, recreational facilities, pleasure grounds *(Br.)*; ~**aufenthalt** holiday, rest cure, vacation *(US)*.

erholungsbedürftig in need of a rest, run down.

Erholungs|bedürftiger person needing a rest; ~**beihilfe** vacation allowance.

erholungsfähig *(Markt)* buoyant.

Erholungs|fähigkeit *(Markt)* buoyance; ~**flächen** pleasure grounds *(Br.)*; ~**gebiet** recreation area; **förderungswürdiges** ~**gebiet** country park *(Br.)*; ~**gebiete im Riesenmaßstab errichten** to build resorts on a monster scale; ~**gelände** *(Werk)* recreation center (ground, site), pleasure grounds *(Br.)*; ~**heim** sanatorium, holiday camp, rest center *(US)* (centre, *Br.*), *(mil.)* convalescent hospital (home); ~**kur** rest cure; ~**möglichkeiten** recreational facilities (amenities); ~**ort** health (pleasure) resort, spa; ~**pause** recreation time, rest period, allowed time, breather; ~**programm** recreational program(me); ~**reise** pleasure trip; ~**reise machen** to travel for one's health; ~**stätte** recreation ground (center, *US*, centre, *Br.*), rest center *(US)* (centre, *Br.*); ~**stunde** an hour's remission, leisure hour; ~**suchender** holidaymaker, holidayer, vacationist *(US)*, vacationer *(US)*; ~**urlaub** holiday, vacation *(US)*, *(Krankheitsurlaub)* sick leave; ~**urlaub machen** to [go on a] holiday; ~**verkehr** recreational traffic; ~**wert** recreational value; ~**zeit** recreation time, *(Urlaub)* holiday (vacation, *US*) time, vacancy, convalescence; ~**zentrum** rest center *(US)* (centre, *Br.*); ~**zuschlag** fatigue allowance.

erinnerlich sein, jem. nicht to have slipped (escaped) s. one's memory.

erinnern to remind, to put in mind;
sich ~ to call to mind; **j. an etw.** ~ to put s. o. in mind of s. th.; **sich an etw.** ~ to remember (recall) s. th.; **sich gern an j.** ~ to have a pleasant memory of s. o.; **sich gut** ~ to remember well; **sich an j. nicht** ~ **können** not to be able to place s. o.; **soweit ich mich** ~ **kann** to the best of my recollection, as far as I recollect, to the best of my memory.

Erinnerung remembrance, memory, *(Mahnung)* reminder;
aus meinen frühesten ~**en** from my earliest memories; **in** ~ **vieler Lebender** within living memory;
bleibende ~ lasting memory; **deutliche** ~ lively (distinct) recollection; **nebelhafte** ~ blur in one's memory; **schwache** ~ distant recollection; **überkommende** ~ ancestral memory; **verschwommene** ~ vague memory, dreamy recollection;
~ **aus der Kindheit** reminiscences of one's youth, childhood memories; **schwache** ~**en an die Kindheit** dim recollections of childhood; ~ **gegen Pfändungsbeschluß** action of replevin; **als** ~ **an eine Reise** as a souvenir of a trip; **vage** ~ **an vergangene Zeiten** vistas of bygone times;
~**en austauschen** to exchange reminiscences; **etw. in deutlicher** ~ **behalten** to have a clear recollection of s. th.; **j. in freundlicher** ~ **behalten** to remember s. o. kindly; **jem. etw. in** ~ **bringen** to remind s. o. of s. th.; ~ **einlegen** to raise an objection; **über eine** ~ **gegen einen Kostenfestsetzungsbeschluß entscheiden** to review taxation; **dunkle** ~ **haben** to be a blurred memory; **noch gut in** ~ **haben** to be fresh in one's memory; **klare** ~ **an etw. behalten haben** to retain a clear memory of s. th.; **in der** ~ **haften** to stick in s. one's memory; **alte** ~**en wachrufen** to call up old memories, to bring many recollections to s. one's mind; ~**en wecken** *(fam.)* to ring a bell.

Erinnerungs|anzeige reminder advertisement, repeat; ~**bild** visual memory; ~**brief** reminder (follow-up) letter; ~**fähigkeit** memory, power of recognition; ~**fehler** memory error; ~**geschenk** token, souvenir; ~**hilfe** remembrance, *(Werbung)* aided recall; ~**lücke** gap in one's memory; ~**medaille** campaign medal; ~**münze** commemorative coin; ~**posten** *(Buchführung)* promemoria figure, reminder (nominal) value; ~**postwurfsendung** follow-up mailings *(US)*; ~**schreiben** monitory (reminder, follow-up, *US*) letter; ~**spange** *(mil.)* battle clasp; ~**stück** remembrance, token; ~**tafel** memorial tablet; ~**täuschung** amnestic delusion; ~**test** *(Anzeige)* aided-recall (recognition) test; ~**test nach einer Aktion** post interview recall; ~**testmethode** recall method; ~**verlust** loss of memory, amnesia; ~**vermögen** auditory memory span; ~**vorstellung** memory image; ~**werbung** reminder (follow-up, institutional) advertising; ~**wert** memory value, *(Bilanz)* promemoria figure, reminder (nominal, *US*) value; ~**zeichen** trophy.

erkalten to grow cold, *(Lava)* to cool down.

erkälten, sich to catch a cold (chill).

erkältet sein to have a cold (chill).

erkaltete Leidenschaft dead passion.

Erkältung cold, chill;
hartnäckige ~ obstinate cold;
~ **auskurieren** to nurse a cold; ~ **bekämpfen** to fight off a cold; **sich gegen eine** ~ **schützen** to fortify o. s. against a cold; **sich eine** ~ **zuziehen** to catch a cold (chill); **sich eine schwere** ~ **zuziehen** to bring on a bad cold; **sich leicht** ~**en zuziehen** to have a natural disposition to catch cold.

erkämpfen, sich einen Erfolg schwer ~ **müssen** to have to struggle hard for one's success.

erkannt *(Gericht)* held, *(Konto)* credited.

erkaufen, jds. Stillschweigen durch Bestechung to square s. o. to hold his tongue.

erkauft, teuer ~**er Sieg** dearly bought victory.

erkennbar recognizable, discernible, perceptible, perceivable;
deutlich ~ pronounced, distinct.

erkennen to discern, to distinguish, to recognize, to perceive, *(Gericht)* to find, to pass a sentence (judgment), to hold, *(herausfinden)* to make out, to detect, *(Krankheit)* to diagnose; **antragsgemäß** ~ to find for the plaintiff; **j. als Ausländer** ~ to spot s. o. as a foreigner; **Autonummer** ~ to read (make out) a licence number; **als Bekannten** ~ to recognize an old acquaintance; **j. mit einem Betrag** ~ to credit s. o. with an amount; **auf Einziehung** ~ to order confiscation; **seine Fehler** ~ to see the error of one's ways; **auf Freispruch** ~ to acquit; **Gefahr** ~ to realize a danger; **auf eine Geldstrafe** ~ to impose a fine; **j. als den Gesuchten** ~ to identify s. o. as the person wanted; **zu jds. Gunsten** ~ to find for (give judgment in favo(u)r of) s. o.; **Kirchturmspitze in der Ferne** ~ to make out the spire in the distance; **zugunsten des Klägers** ~ to find for the plaintiff; **Konto** ~ to credit an account, to enter on the credit side of an account; **jds. Konto** ~ to place an amount to s. one's account; **j. in einer Menschenmenge** ~ to distinguish s. o. in a crowd; **auf einen Monat Gefängnis** ~ to pass sentence of one month's imprisonment; **für Recht** ~ to find, to decide; **über eine Sache** ~ to pass sentence of s. th., to cognose a case; **auf Schadensersatz** ~ to award damages; **j. für schuldig** ~ to find s. o. guilty; **sich selbst** ~ to come at a true knowledge of o. s.; **sofort** ~ to perceive at once; **auf eine Strafe** ~ to award a sentence; **auf Todesstrafe** ~ to pronounce a death sentence; **j. völlig** ~ to see through s. o.; **Wahrheit** ~ to discern the truth;
sich zu ~ **geben** to disclose one's identity; **seine Absicht zu** ~ **geben** to show one's intention.

erkenntlich grateful, obliged;
sich ~ **zeigen** to show one's gratitude.

Erkenntlichkeit gratitude, appreciation.

Erkenntnis discovery, perception, knowledge, understanding, recognition, realization;
in der ~ *(Vertragsformel)* aware of;
allerneueste ~**se** up-to-the-minute knowledge; **gut verarbeitete** ~**se** well-digested knowledge; **wissenschaftliche** ~**se** scientific information;
~ **einer Gefahr** realization of a danger; ~**se des Gerichts** findings of the court; ~**se eines langen Lebens** accumulated experience of a long life (lifetime);
wertvolle ~**se ergeben** to shed valuable insights into; **zu der** ~ **gelangen** to come to the conclusion (realize); **neue** ~**se über etw. gewonnen haben** to have new lights upon s. th.; **jenseits menschlicher** ~**se liegen** to be beyond the boundary of human knowledge;
~**kräfte** knowing faculties; ~**vermögen** intellectual capacity, cognition; ~**wert** informative value.

Erkennung recognition, perception, identification.

Erkennungs|dienst *(Polizei)* records department, criminal investigation department *(Br.)*; ~**karte** identity card; ~**kartei** identification register; ~**marke** identity disk (tag), *(Soldat)* identification tag (disk, *US*), dog tag *(US sl.)*; ~**melodie** *(Rundfunkstation)* signature tune; ~**merkmal** distinguishing mark; ~**signal** *(mil.)* recognition signal; ~**vermögen** cognition; ~**verzögerung** recognition lag; ~**wort** test word, *(mil.)* password, watchword; ~**zahl** key number; ~**zeichen** identification mark, *(Flugzeug)* markings; **gegenseitiges** ~**zeichen** sign and countersign; **polizeiliches** ~**zeichen** *(Auto)* registration (identification) plate.

Erker oriel, bay;
~**fenster** bay window.

erklären to explain, to explicate, to give an explanation, *(auslegen)* to interpret, to expound, *(darlegen)* to state, to declare, to represent, to expose, to put over, to put out, *(zollamtlich deklarieren)* to declare, to enter at the customs;
etw. ~ to give an explanation of s. th.; **sich** ~ to make a statement, *(Differenzgeschäft)* to declare options; **sich für etw.** ~ to pronounce o. s. in favo(u)r of s. th.; **Angelegenheit** ~ to clear up a matter; **ausdrücklich** ~ to state expressively; **seinen Austritt aus der Regierung** ~ to leave the Cabinet; **j. bankrott** ~ to adjudge s. o. bankrupt, to declare s. o. at the exchange, to hammer a defaulter *(Br.)*; **sich für befangen** ~ to plead partiality; **sich für befriedigt** ~ to profess o. s. satisfied; **durch ein Beispiel** ~ to illustrate by an example; **seinen Beitritt zu einem Verein** ~ to declare one's membership of a club; **sich bereit** ~ to declare one's willingness, to undertake, to offer; **mit Bestimmtheit** ~ to state positively; **etw. deutlich und präzise** ~ to explain s. th. in plain and precise terms; **Dividende** ~ to declare a dividend; **unter Eid (eidlich)** ~ to state under (depose on) oath, to declare (make a statement) on oath, to make (swear) an affidavit; **sich einverstanden (sein Einverständnis)** ~ to [give one's] consent, to agree; **sich zum Erben** ~ to declare o. s. heir; **für eröffnet** ~ to declare open; **für fällig** ~ to declare due; **falsch** ~ to misinterpret; **feierlich** ~ to asseverate; **j. für geisteskrank** ~ to declare s. o. a lunatic, to certify s. one's insanity; **Hypothek für verfallen** ~ to foreclose a mortgage; **Klage für zulässig** ~ to declare an action admissible; **Kriegszustand** ~ to declare a state of war; **einem Land den Krieg** ~ to declare war on a country; **sich zum Nachfolger** ~ to declare o. s. the successor; **näher** ~ to specify; **für null und nichtig** ~ to declare null and void; **öffentlich** ~ to profess, to avow; **etw. offiziell** ~ to put s. th. on record; **Prämie** ~ to declare an option; **für gute Prise** ~ to declare a lawful prize; **für rechtsgültig** ~ to validate, to make valid; **für rechtmäßig** ~ to legitimate, to legitimize; **Richter für befangen** ~ to challenge a judge; **seinen Rücktritt** ~ to hand in one's resignation; **Schiff für seeuntüchtig** ~ to condemn a ship; **sich von selbst** ~ to be self-explanatory; **Text** ~ to interpret a text; **j. für tot** ~ **lassen** to allege s. o. to be (declare s. o. legally) dead; **für unehelich** ~ to bastardize; **für ungültig** ~ abrogate, to annul, to cancel, to override, to declare void; **sich für unschuldig** ~ *(Angeklagter)* to plead not guilty; **Unterschrift für gefälscht** ~ to pronounce a signature to be a forgery; **j. für unzurechnungsfähig** ~ to declare s. o. irresponsible; **seinen Vereinsaustritt** ~ to resign from a club; **sein Verhalten** ~ to explain one's conduct; **Vertrag für ungültig** ~ to invalidate an agreement; **j. für vogelfrei** ~ to outlaw s. o.; **j. für volljährig** ~ to declare s. o. to be of age; **Wahl für nichtig** ~ to declare an election void; **sich für zahlungsunfähig** ~ to declare o. s. insolvent (a bankrupt), to fill a petition in bankruptcy; **seine Zustimmung schriftlich** ~ to signify one's consent.

erklärend declaratory, illustrative, explanatory;
~ **hinzufügen** to add by way of explanation;
~**e Anmerkung** explanatory notes; ~**e Feststellung** explanatory statement.

Erklärender declarant, affirmant.

Erklärer demonstrator.

erklärlich explainable, explicable, understandable;
aus leicht ~**en Gründen** for obvious reasons.

erklärt professed, open, avowed;
~**er Gegner** declared enemy; ~**er Publikumsliebling** acknowledged favo(u)rite of the public; ~**er Sozialist** avowed socialist; ~**er Weiberfeind** professed woman-hater; ~**er Wert** *(Postsendung)* insured value.

Erklärung declaration, statement, representation, demonstration, pronouncement, *(Auslegung)* interpretation, *(Aussage)* deposition, testimony, explication, *(Erläuterung)* explanation, *(Definition)* definition, legend, comment, exposition, definition, *(Gründe)* reasons, *(Veranschaulichung)* illustration;
nach seinen eigenen ~**en** according to his own statement;
in Erfüllung rechtlicher, moralischer oder sozialer Pflichten abgegebene ~ statements made in discharge of a legal, moral or social duty; **im Laufe der Verhandlung abgegebene** ~ statement made during the course of negotiations; **aus freien Stücken (freiem Willen) abgegebene** ~ voluntary statement; **amtliche** ~ official statement; **ärgerniserregende** ~ scandalous statement; **ausdrückliche** ~ specific statement; **ordnungsgemäß beglaubigte** ~ duly attested declaration; **belastende** ~ incriminatory statement; **berichtigende** ~ qualifying statement; **bindende** ~ binding declaration; **deklaratorische** ~ declaratory statement; **deutliche** ~ lucid explanation; **eidesstattliche** ~ assertory oath, affirmation, declaration in lieu of oath *(Br.)*, affidavit, statutory declaration *(Br.)*; **gegenteilige eidesstattliche** ~ counteraffidavit; **verjährte eidesstattliche** ~ stale affidavit; **eidliche** ~ declaration (statement) on oath, sworn statement, exhibit; **einleitende** ~**en** opening statement; **einleuchtende** ~ luculent explanation; **einseitige** ~ unilateral declaration; **erläuternde** ~ explanatory declaration; **falsche** ~ inaccurate statement, false demonstration, misrepresentation; **feierliche** ~ solemn declaration, protest; **formelle** ~ explicit declaration; **freiwillige** ~ voluntary statement; **gemeinsame** ~ joint statement; **genaue** ~ correct statement; **irrtümliche** ~ mistaken statement; **keine** ~ no statement; **mündliche** ~ verbal statement, parol; **öffentliche** ~ public statement; **offizielle** ~ official statement, declaration; **persönliche** ~ personal explanation *(parl.)*; **rechtserhebliche** ~ material statement; **rechtsunerhebliche** ~ immaterial statement; **schriftliche** ~ written statement; **selbstbelastende** ~ declaration against interest; **umfassende** ~ full statement; **umständliche** ~ roundabout explanation; **rechtlich unbedeutende** ~**en** mere representations; **unberechtigte** ~ illegitimate (unauthorized) statement; **rechtlich unerhebliche** ~ immaterial statement; **unerhörte** ~ outrageous statement; **unrichtige** ~ false demonstration; **unwiderrufliche** ~ irrevocable statement; **verleumderische** ~**en** libellous statements; **vorvertragliche** ~ representation; **widersprechende** ~**en** conflicting statements; **wohlbegründete** ~ well-reasoned statement;
mündliche ~ **unter Anwesenden** speaking to those present; ~ **über die Beendigung eines Treuhandverhältnisses** deed of discharge; ~ **des Börsenvorstands über den Konkurs eines Börsenmitglieds** declaration of default *(Br.)*; ~ **der üblichen Dividende** regular dividend announcement; ~ **an Eides Statt** affirmation, statutory declaration; ~ **über die Entwicklung des Eigenkapitals** statement of investment, statement of stockholders' equity; **schriftliche eidesstattliche** ~ **der ordentlichen Generalversammlung** statutory declaration; ~ **vor Gericht** judicial declaration; ~ **über das ausgewiesene Grundkapital** statement of nominal capital; **allgemeine** ~ **der Menschenrechte** universal declaration of human rights; ~ **des Präsidenten** pronouncement of the President; ~ **an die Presse** statement to the press; ~ **der Regierung** announcement by the government; ~ **auf dem Sterbebett** dying declaration, deathbed deed; ~ **eines Textes** commentation of a text; **eidesstattliche** ~ **über Urkundenechtheit** affidavit of verification; ~ **des Vorstands über dem Prüfer zur Verfügung gestellte Unterlagen** liability certificate *(US)*; ~ **über die Wahlausgaben** *(parl.)* declaration as to election expense; ~ **in Wahrnehmung berechtigter Interessen** statement on a privileged occasion *(Br.)*; ~ **des letzten Willens** publication;
~ **abändern** to modify a statement; ~ **abgeben** to declare, to give (make) a declaration, to make a statement, to announce; **amtliche** ~ **abgeben** to make an official statement; **eidesstattliche** ~ **abgeben** to depose on oath, to affirm *(US)*; **einschränkende** ~ **abgeben** to qualify a statement; **wissentlich falsche** ~ **abgeben** to make knowingly false statements; **feierliche** ~ **abgeben** to make a solemn declaration; **langatmige** ~**en abgeben** to enter into long explanations, to go into a lengthy explanation; **persönliche** ~ **abgeben** to make a personal statement; **unmißverständliche** ~ **abgeben** to be more explicit in one's statements; ~ **unter Eid abgeben** to make a statement on oath (statutory declaration, *Br.*); ~ **für sein Verhalten abgeben** to give explanations for one's conduct; ~ **in Wahrnehmung berechtigter Interessen abgeben** to make a statement on a privileged occasion; **eidesstattliche** ~ **abnehmen** to administer an affirmation; ~ **aufsetzen** to draw up a statement; **keiner** ~ **bedürfen** to need no explanation; ~ **bestätigen** to bear out (verify) a statement; **durch eidesstattliche** ~ **bestätigen** to verify by affidavit; ~ **dementieren** to deny a statement; **eidesstattliche** ~ **entgegennehmen** to take an affidavit; ~ **finden** to come with an answer; **sich in** ~**en flüchten** to launch out into explanations; ~ **zu Protokoll geben** to read a statement into the minutes; ~ **für sein Verhalten geben** to give explanations for one's conduct; ~ **gutheißen** to justify a statement; **offizielle** ~ **herausgeben** to

issue a formal statement; **von einer ~ Kenntnis nehmen** to take note of a declaration; **~ durch Zeugenaussagen untermauern** to produce testimony of a statement; **~ von jem. verlangen** to have s. o. down for an explanation; **befriedigende ~ verlangen** to want satisfactory reasons; **~ veröffentlichen** to publish a statement; **auf die eidesstattliche ~ eines Zeugen verzichten** to dispense with the signature of a witness; **~ widerrufen** to retract a statement; **jds. ~ in Zweifel ziehen** to call s. one's statement into question;
zu einem Thema keine ~en abgeben dürfen not to be competent to speak on a matter; **~ wortwörtlich wiedergeben können** to have a good verbal memory.

erklärungsbedürftig sein to need an explanation.

Erklärungs|empfänger authorized recipient; **~pflicht** obligation to disclose; **~tag** *(Börse)* contango (carrying over, making-up, option, *Br.*) day, *(Dividende)* date of declaration; **~versuch** attempt at explanation.

erklecklich considerable, substantial, respectable;
~es Sümmchen substantial amount, tidy money.

erklimmen, Gipfel to climb to (go up to) the top of a hill; **Gipfel der Macht ~** to reach the summit of power.

erklingen to sound, to resound, to ring out;
Fensterscheiben ~ lassen to make the window rattle; **Gläser ~ lassen** to clink the glasses.

erkranken to fall ill (sick), to sicken, to come down with *(coll.)*; **an Gelbsucht ~** to develop jaundice.

erkrankt diseased, ill;
lebensgefährlich ~ dangerously ill;
~ sein to be ill (down); **lebensgefährlich ~ sein** to be on the danger list.

Erkrankung affection, *(Unpäßlichkeit)* indisposition;
leichte ~ slight indisposition; **schwere ~** severe illness; **schwere ~ der Nieren** serious affection of the kidneys.

Erkrankungs|fall, im in case of illness, in the event of sickness; **~häufigkeit** morbidity rate; **~ziffer** illness frequency rate, morbidity.

erkühnen, sich to make so bold as to, to have the audacity, to dare.

erkunden to explore, *(mil.)* to reconnoitre, to scout;
Gelände ~ to reconnoitre the ground; **Lage ~** to see how the land lies.

erkundigen, sich to ask, to inquire, to make inquiries, to find out;
sich nach jds. Befinden ~ to inquire after s. one's health; **sich in einem Laden nach einem Buch ~** to inquire for a book in a shop; **sich nach dem Preis ~** to ask (inquire) about the price, **sich eingehend nach jds. Verhältnissen ~** to inquire into s. one's position; **sich nach dem Weg ~** to ask s. o. the way.

Erkundigung inquiry, information, query;
weitere ~en further inquiry;
eingehende ~en nach etw. anstellen to inquire into s. th.; **~en über jem. einholen** to go in quest of information about s. o.; **~ einziehen** to collect information, to inquire into, to make inquiries.

Erkundung exploration, investigation, *(mil.)* reconnaissance;
gewaltsame ~ reconnaissance in force;
~ der Arktis vornehmen to explore the Arctic region.

Erkundungs|auftrag reconnaissance mission; **~fahrzeug** scout vehicle (car); **~flug** reconnaissance flight; **~flugzeug** scout plane, reconnaissance aircraft; **~trupp** reconnaissance detachment.

erlahmen to grow weary, to tire, to fail.

erlangbar procurable, obtainable, attainable.

erlangen to obtain, to acquire, to achieve, to get, to reach, to procure, to attain;
große Bedeutung ~ to gain great importance; **Besitz ~** to come into possession; **Rechtskraft ~** to obtain legal force; **Schadensersatz ~** to obtain (recover) damages; **unter Vorspiegelung falscher Tatsachen ~** to obtain by fraud; **Kenntnis von einem Vorfall ~** to hear of an incident; **Vorteile ~** to obtain advantages.

Erlangung obtainment, acquisition, attainment, recovery;
nach ~ des Pensionsalters after attaining retiring age;
~ des Besitzes entering possession; **~ durch Betrug** obtaining by false representation, obreption; **~ eines Patentes** taking out a patent; **~ von Schadensersatz** recovery of damages; **~ der Volljährigkeit** coming of age.

Erlaß *(Rabatt)* reduction, deduction, *(Schulden)* release, remission, cancellation, *(Steuer)* abatement, remission, *(Strafe)* remission, letoff, acquittal, *(Verordnung)* act, decree, order, ordinance, issue, issuance, rescript, ukase, enactment, mandate;
amtlicher ~ authority, decree, writ; **förmlicher ~** release under seal; **ministerieller ~** ministerial act (order), departmental order; **oben zitierter ~** the above decree;
~ einer Amnestie issuing an amnesty; **~ der Einkommensteuer** exemption from income tax; **~ eines Examens** exemption from examination; **~ einer Forderung** release of a claim; **~ von Gebühren** remission of charges (fees); **~ eines Gesetzes** promulgation (enactment, issuance, *US*) of a law; **~ einer Schuld** release of a claim, remission (release) of a debt, acquittance, acquittal; **formeller ~ einer Schuld** express release, conventional remission; **freiwilliger ~ einer geringfügigen Schuld** acceptilation; **stillschweigender ~ einer Schuld** tacit remission; **~ einer Steuer** remission of a tax; **teilweiser ~ einer Strafe** remission of part of a sentence; **~ eines Urteils** pronouncement (passing, delivery) of a judgment, rendition; **~ einer Verfügung** issue (issuance) of an order (decree); **~ einer einstweiligen Verfügung** granting an injunction; **~ von Zinsen** waiver of interest;
~ aufheben to annul (rescind, reserve) a decree; **Durchführung eines ~es aussetzen** to stop the execution of a decree; **um ~ der mündlichen Prüfung bitten** to ask for an exemption from the oral examination; **~ unterschreiben** to fill out a writ; **~ zurückziehen** to recall a decree.

erlassen *(Rabatt gewähren)* to make an allowance, to abate, to deduct, *(Schuld)* to remit, to release, *(Strafe)* to forgive, to remit, *(Verordnung)* to issue, to enact, to order, to decree;
jem. etw. ~ to release s. o. (let s. o. off) from s. th.; **Amnestie ~** to issue an amnesty; **Anordnung ~** to issue an order; **jem. die Antwort ~** to excuse s. o. from answering; **Aufruf ~** to launch an appeal; **jem. die Einkommensteuer ~** to exempt s. o. from income tax; **Entscheidung ~** to enter a decree; **Gebühren ~** to waive (cancel) charges; **Geldstrafe ~** to remit a fine; **Gesetz ~** to enact (promulgate) a law; **Haftbefehl ~** to issue a warrant of arrest; **Pfändungsbeschluß ~** to levy an attachment order; **jem. eine Prüfung ~** to dispense (absolve) s. o. from an examination; **Richtlinien ~** to adopt rules; **jem. eine Schuld ~** to forgive s. o. a debt; **Schulden ~** to release (waive) debts; **Steuer ~** to remit (abate) a tax; **jem. eine Steuer ~** to exempt s. o. from a tax; **Strafe ~** to remit a penalty; **Urteil ~** to pass (render, deliver) a judgment; **Verfügung ~** to issue an order; **einstweilige Verfügung ~** to grant (award) an injunction; **einstweilige Verfügung ohne mündliche Verhandlung ~** to grant an injunction ex parte; **Verordnung ~** to pass (issue) a decree; **jem. eine Verpflichtung ~** to absolve s. o. from an obligation; **Versäumnisurteil ~** to deliver judgment by default;
~ sein *(Haftbefehl)* to be out.

erlauben to allow, to permit, to license;
wenn es die Umstände ~ if circumstances permit;
mehrere Auslegungen ~ to admit of several interpretations; **sich Extravaganzen ~** to indulge in extravagancies; **sich Freiheiten ~** to take liberties; **sich mit jem. einen Scherz ~** to play a joke on s. o.; **sich einen unverschämten Ton ~** to adopt a tone of insolence; **sich jem. gegenüber Vertraulichkeiten ~** to become too familiar with s. o.; **keine Verzögerung ~** to permit of no delay;
sich etw. nicht ~ können not to be able to afford an expense.

Erlaubnis licence, permit, permission, leave, allowance, grant *(US)*, *(Ermächtigung)* authorization, faculty;
mit amtlicher ~ gedruckt printed under authority; **mit gerichtlicher ~** by leave of court; **mit Ihrer gütlichen ~** with your kind permission; **mit obrigkeitlicher ~** by authority; **ohne ~ gedruckt** unlicensed; **ohne auch nur um ~ zu fragen** without even asking permission;
allgemeine ~ omnibus permit; **behördliche ~** official permit, licence, license *(US)*; **besondere ~** special licence; **gerichtliche ~** leave of court; **offizielle ~** green light; **schriftliche ~** permission in writing; **staatliche ~** government permission; **uneingeschränkte ~** plenary licence; **jederzeit widerrufliche ~** simple licence;
~ zum Betrieb einer Druckerei printer's licence; **~ des Eigentümers** owner's permission; **~ zollfreier Warenausfuhr von Hafen zu Hafen** bill of sufferance;
~ ausstellen to issue a permit; **~ bekommen** to obtain permission; **um ~ bitten** to request permission; **~ erhalten** to obtain permission, to be granted a licence; **~ erteilen** to grant permission, to grant (give) leave, to permit; **fest mit einer ~ rechnen** to take a permission for granted;
~erteilung granting a permission.

Erlaubnisschein licence, permit, permission, pass;
~ für den Geschäftsbeginn certificate to commence (permission to transact) business;

~ **beschaffen** to take out a licence (license, *US*); ~ **verlängern** to extend a permit;
~**inhaber** permit holder.
erlaubt permissible, permitted, allowed;
gesetzlich ~ warrantable (permitted) by law, lawful;
~**e Abweichung** permissible deviation; ~**e Grenzen überschreiten** to break bounds.
Erlaubte | s, gesellschaftlich ~**s und Verbotenes** do's and don'ts of society; **jenseits der Grenzen des** ~**n** beyond the pale; **sich hart an der Grenze des** ~**n bewegen** to sail close to the wind.
erläutern to expound, to explain, to interpret, to exemplify, *(mit Bildern)* to illustrate, *(kommentieren)* to comment, to annotate;
an Beispielen ~ to exemplify; **schwierige Buchstelle** ~ to eludicate a difficult passage in a book.
erläuternd illustrative, commentarial, explanatory, descriptive;
~**e Anmerkungen** explanatory annotations (notes); ~**er Zusatz** commentory.
Erläuterung explanation, comment, explanatory statement, explication, exemplification, illustration, interpretation, elucidation, *(Kommentar)* commentary, annotation;
mit ~**en** with explanatory notes;
juristische ~ general instruction;
~ **anhand von Beispielen** explanation with illustrative examples, exemplification; ~ **eines Textes** commentation of a text;
langatmige ~ **abgeben** to enter into long explanations; **einer** ~ **bedürfen** to come in for an explanation; **mit** ~**en versehen** to annotate; **Text mit** ~**en versehen** to make a commentary on a text.
Erläuterungs | bericht explanatory statement; ~**beschluß** speaking order; ~**bestimmung** declaratory clause; ~**gesetz** expository statute.
erleben to live up to, *(erfahren)* to experience;
zehn Auflagen ~ to reach (run up) to ten editions; **großen Aufschwung** ~ to experience a boom; **viele Enttäuschungen** ~ to suffer many disappointments; **etw. gemeinsam** ~ to share s. th. together; **etw. Seltsames** ~ to have a strange experience; **große Überraschung** ~ to be taken by surprise; **viel Unglück in seinem Leben** ~ to see a good deal of trouble in one's life; **sein blaues Wunder** ~ to get the surprise of one's life; **Zeit des Friedens** ~ to go through a time of peace; **schlechte Zeiten** ~ to come on bad times.
Erlebensfall, im in case of survival;
~**versicherung** endowment insurance *(US)*, pure endowment assurance *(Br.)*.
Erlebens | wahrscheinlichkeit probability of survival; ~**zeit** *(Versicherung)* endowment period.
Erlebnis experience, occurrence, event, *(Abenteuer)* adventure;
aufregendes ~ thrill; **schreckliches** ~ terrifying experience;
über seine ~**se berichten** to relate one's experiences; **widerliches** ~ **haben** *(fam.)* to have a nasty experience; **jem. das größte** ~ **seines Lebens vermitteln** to give s. o. the thrill of one's lifetime.
erlebt | e Geschichten true stories;
selbst ~ **haben** to know from experience; **bessere Zeiten** ~ **haben** to have seen better days.
erledigen to execute, to settle, to finish, to adjust, to arrange, to effect, to deal, to complete, to discharge, to handle, to attend to, to dispose of, to put in order, to carry through, to fix (wind) up, to polish off, to dish *(sl.)*;
sich ~ to settle itself, *(Posten)* to fall vacant; **etw.** ~ to deal with s. th., to get s. th. out of the way; **etw. für j.** ~ to go on a message (an errand) for s. o.; **j.** ~ to settle s. one's hash *(fam.)*, *(umbringen)* to dispose of s. o., to do s. o. in *(sl.)*, to rub s. o. out; **Anfrage** ~ to answer an inquiry; **jds. Angelegenheiten** ~ to attend to s. one's affairs; **Angelegenheit außergerichtlich** ~ to settle a matter without going to law; **Angelegenheit endgültig** ~ to drive the nail home; **Angelegenheit schnell** ~ to give a matter prompt attention, to attend promptly, to make short work of it, to knock s. th. off; **Angelegenheit so schnell wie möglich** ~ to deal with s. th. as soon as possible; **seine Arbeit** ~ to finish with a piece of work; **Arbeitsrückstände** ~ to clear off arrears of work; **Auftrag** ~ to carry out (execute) an order; **Auftrag selbst** ~ to see to an order o. s.; **Beschwerde** ~ to adjust a complaint; **Botengang** ~ to discharge an errand; **seine Einkäufe** ~ to do one's shopping; **Fall** ~ to dispose of (handle) a case; **Fall in der Hauptsache** ~ to deal with a case on its merits; **j. finanziell** ~ to do one's business for s. o. *(coll.)*; **Formalitäten** ~ to comply with formalities; **Gegner** ~ to extinguish an adversary; **Geschäft** ~ to dispatch a business; **Geschäfte aller Art** ~ to handle any sort of business; **zuerst das Geschäftliche** ~ to get through business first; **auf rein geschäftsmäßige Weise** ~ to do it in a business-like way, to deal with at arm's length; **etw. geschickt** ~ to make a good job of it; **Gesuch** ~ to deal with an application; **gleich morgen früh** ~ to see to it first thing in the morning; **nach Großmütterchens Art** ~ to do s. th. in a leisurely fashion; **etw. gut** ~ to make a good job of s. th.; **seine Korrespondenz** ~ to attend to one's correspondence; **seine Post** ~ to dispose of the mail; **alte Rechnungen** ~ to wipe off old accounts; **Reparaturen** ~ to carry out repairs; **Sache endlich** ~ to see the last of a job; **Sache glatt** ~ to see a business through; **viele Sachen gleichzeitig** ~ to handle a lot of business; **Sache schiedsgerichtlich** ~ to settle a case by arbitration; **etw. nicht besonders sorgfältig** ~ to take no particular care over doing s. th.; **summarisch** ~ to dispose of a case summarily; **etw. in weniger als zwei Tagen** ~ to do s. th. inside of two days *(US)*; **durch Vergleich** ~ to settle by compromise; **Prozeß durch Vergleich** ~ to settle a lawsuit amicably; **j. mit ein paar Zeitungsartikeln völlig** ~ to settle s. one's hash in a couple of articles; **Zollformalitäten** ~ to clear the customs; **letzte Zweifel** ~ to dispel every doubt;
etw. zu ~ **haben** to be on an errand, to have s. th. to attend to; **etw. für jem. zu** ~ **haben** to have a little job to do for s. o.; **einige Sachen in der Stadt zu** ~ **haben** to have some errands to run in the town.
erledigt settled, dealt with, done, *(Person)* exhausted, finished, out on one's feet, ready to drop, done with *(coll.)*, *(ruiniert)* under hatches, washed-out (-up, *sl.*), finished, out the window *(sl.)*;
absolut ~ whacked; **definitiv** ~ *(Amt)* vacant; **endgültig** ~ finally disposed of; **ganz** ~ all to pieces, all-in *(sl.)*; **gänzlich** ~ wholly finished, *(erschöpft)* dead-tired; **noch nicht** ~ outstanding; **total** ~ used up by one's toil; **völlig** ~ all-out, dead;
j. ~ **haben** to have cooked s. one's goose; ~ **sein** to be done up (dead-beat, bushed, *US*), to be a has-been; **für j.** ~ **sein** to be through with s. o.; **völlig** ~ **sein** to be reduced to a pulp (at the end of one's tether);
~**er Mann** has-been; ~**e Rechnung** settled account; ~**e Stelle** vacant position, vacancy.
Erledigung disposal, dispatch, discharge, handling, settlement, execution, finishing off;
bis zur ~ pending arrangement; **in** ~ **dienstlicher Angelegenheiten** in discharge of official duty; **in** ~ **Ihres Auftrags** as concerns your order; **nach** ~ on completion;
außergerichtliche ~ settlement out of court; **endgültige** ~ final disposition; **erneute** ~ redoing; **förmliche** ~ solemnization; **gütliche** ~ amicable arrangement; **prompte** ~ prompt discharge (attention); **rasche** ~ quick way of doing; **schiedsrichterliche** ~ submission to arbitration; **schnelle** ~ speedy dispatch; **sofortige** ~ prompt attention; **umgehende** ~ immediate attention; **zügige** ~ swift fashion;
~ **eines Amtes** vacancy of an office; ~ **einer [geschäftlichen] Angelegenheit** dispatch (settlement) of a matter, disposal of a piece of business; ~ **eigener Angelegenheiten** conduct of one's own affairs; ~ **eines Auftrags** execution of an order; ~ **einer Beschwerde** adjustment of a complaint; ~ **von Formalitäten** compliance with formalities; ~ **einer Frage** disposal of a question; ~ **von Geschäftsvorgängen** disposal of business affairs; **schnelle** ~ **eines Gesuchs** dispatch of a petition; ~ **der Hauptsache** judgment on the merits; **selbständige** ~ **eines Nutzungsrechtes** special limitation; ~ **einer Rechnung** settlement of an account, payment of a bill; ~ **eiliger Sachen** dispatch of current business; ~ **der Schulaufgabe** learning of lessons;
Sache zur ~ **bringen** to settle a matter; ~ **von Sachen in die Hand nehmen** to assume the management of affairs; **Angelegenheit schiedsrichterlicher** ~ **überlassen** to leave a matter to arbitration; **jem. eine Sache zur** ~ **übertragen** to put (place) a matter into s. one's hands; ~ **einer Sache verschleppen** to pigeonhole a matter.
Erledigungsschein release, quitclaim.
Erlegung, gegen on payment.
erleichtern to facilitate, to ease, to make easy (easier), to lighten, to alleviate, *(klauen)* to steal, to pinch *(US sl.)*;
jem. etw. ~ to grant s. o. facilities; **jds. Aufgabe** ~ to lighten s. one's task; **Aufnahme von Kredit** ~ to make credit easier, to shade credit standards; **jds. Geldbeutel** ~ to ease s. o. of his purse; **sein Gepäck** ~ to travel light; **sein Gewissen** ~ to lighten one's conscience; **Hausarbeit** ~ to facilitate housework; **sein Herz** ~ to unburden one's troubles, to disburden one's heart; **jds. Los** ~ to alleviate s. one's fate; **Zahlung** ~ to facilitate payment.

erleichterte | Geldmarktbeziehungen easier money circumstances; ~ **Patentverwertungsmöglichkeiten** easing the flow of patents; ~ **Versilberung** ease of realization; ~ **Vollstreckungsmöglichkeiten** ease of enforcement; ~ **Zulassungsbedingungen** easing of admission requirements.

Erleichterung facilitation, easing, easement, *(Notlage)* relief, alleviation, *(Strafe)* relaxation;
finanzielle ~en pecuniary ease; **geldmarkttechnische ~en** easing of monetary policy; **kreditpolitische ~en** easing in credit; **sofortige ~** instant relief; **steuerliche ~en** tax relief measures; ~ **bei Auslandsinvestitionen** easing up in foreign investments; ~ **am Geldmarkt** ease (easing) in (relaxation of) money rates; ~ **des Handels zwischen zwei Ländern** facilitation of trade between two countries; **steuerliche ~en für Investitionen** investment tax credit; **~en für den Kapitalmarkt** easing of the capital market; **~en für das Kreditgeschäft** easing up (ease) in credit; **steuerliche ~en bei der Schaffung von Arbeitsplätzen** job-creation palliative; ~ **der kreditpolitischen Situation** ease (relaxation) in credit (of credit squeeze); ~ **der Staatslast** lightening of the burden of the state; ~ **der Zahlungsbedingungen** payment facilities, facilitation of payment;
Seufzer der ~ ausstoßen to heave (breathe) a sigh of relief; **~en auf dem Steuergebiet bringen** to lighten taxes; **um ~en in den Reparationszahlungen einkommen** to ask for a relaxation in the matter of reparations; **sich für ~en des Geldverkehrs einsetzen** to favo(u)r easier money; **Tendenz in der ~ der Geldmarktpolitik fortsetzen** to continue one's run toward ease in money rates; **jem. jegliche ~en gewähren** to afford s. o. every facility; **kreditpolitische ~en gewähren** to ease credit controls; **jem. ~en verschaffen** to give s. o. ease; **einem Kranken ~ verschaffen** to ease a patient.

erleiden to suffer, to sustain, to endure;
Arbeitsunfall ~ to sustain an industrial injury; **starken Einbruch ~** *(Börse)* to break sharply; **Kurseinbuße bis zu 10% ~** to suffer a loss in exchange up to 10 per cent; **Nervenzusammenbruch ~** to have a nervous breakdown; **leichten Rückgang ~** *(Börse)* to suffer a slight decline; **geschäftlichen Rückschlag ~** to suffer a setback in one's business; **schwere Schäden ~** *(Maschine)* to be severely damaged; **Schiffbruch ~** to be ship-wrecked; **im Leben Schiffbruch ~** to make shipwreck of one's life; **Schmerzen ~** to endure pains; **Tod ~** to suffer (meet with) death; **Unfall ~** to meet with an accident; **Veränderungen ~** *(Preise)* to undergo changes; **Verlust ~** to sustain (incur, suffer) a loss; **Verzögerungen ~** to be delayed.

Erlernen learning;
beim ~ einer Sprache keine große Schwierigkeiten haben to find a language to present little difficulty.

erlernen to learn, to get hold of *(coll.)*;
Fremdsprache ~ to learn (acquire) a foreign language; **Handwerk ~** to learn from a master.

erlesen excellent, choice, selected, exquisite, dainty;
~e Genüsse exquisite enjoyment; **~e Gesellschaft** select company; **~e Kostbarkeiten** precious things; **~e Leckerbissen** dainties; **~e Qualität** choicest quality.

erleuchten to lighten, to illuminate;
j. ~ to enlighten (inspire) s. one's mind; **Raum ~** to light up a room.

Erleuchtung lightening, illumination, crosslight;
plötzliche ~ flash of wit, inspiration, brain storm *(US)*.

Erliegen, zum ~ bringen to bring to a standstill; **zum ~ kommen** *(Bergbaubetrieb)* to be worked out, *(Handel)* to be at an absolute standstill; **zum ~ gekommen sein** *(Verkehr)* to be paralyzed (brought to a standstill); **vollständig zum ~ gekommen sein** *(Verhandlungen)* to be at an absolute standstill, to have reached a deadlock.

erliegen, jds. Charme to fall victim to s. one's charm; **seinem Gegner ~** to be defeated by one's opponent; **einem Irrtum ~** to run into error; **einer Krankheit ~** to be carried off by a disease; **einer Propaganda ~** to fall a victim of propaganda; **der Übermacht ~** to be overcome by superiority; **einem Verkehrsunfall ~** to be the victim of a motor accident; **seinen Verletzungen ~** to die from one's injuries; **der Versuchung ~** to succumb to temptation.

erlogen false, made-up, trumped-up;
von A - Z ~ not a grain of truth in it, completely made up; **~er Bericht** false report; **~e Geschichte** trumped-up story.

Erlös proceeds, returns, earnings, issue, net profit, avails *(US)*, *(Reingewinn)* net profits;
bei der Liquidation erzielter ~ proceeds of a liquidation; **im Liquidationszeitraum erzielte ~e** profits arising during a winding-up; **beim Zwangsverkauf erzielter ~** forced-sale value; **tatsächlicher ~** actual earnings; **verminderter ~** diminished proceeds;
~e aus Abfallverwertung proceeds from utilization of waste material; **~e einer Auktion** proceeds of an auction; **~e von Auslandstöchtern** foreign earnings; ~ **aus Diskontierung** net avails *(US)*; ~ **einer Erfindung** benefit of an invention; **~e aus dem Exportgeschäft** proceeds from exports; ~ **aus Konzerntransaktionen** intercompany profits; ~ **per Lagereinheit** earnings per stock unit; **~e aus Monopolen** profits from patents and secret processes; ~ **für begebene Obligationen** debenture capital; ~ **einer Transaktion** profit on a transaction; **~e aus Veräußerungen** profit sales, sales returns; **~e aus dem Verkauf von Anlagegütern** *(Investitionsgütern)* profits on the sale of fixed assets, capital profits; ~ **pro Verkaufseinheit** profit per unit; **~e aus einer Versteigerung** proceeds of an auction, avails of a sale by auction *(US)*;
einen den Buchwert übersteigenden ~ abwerfen to yield a profit over the book value; **sich aus dem ~ befriedigen** to pay o. s. out of the profit; **jds. Konto mit dem ~ erkennen** to place the profits to s. one's account; ~ **verteilen** to distribute the proceeds;
~anteil profit share; **~bild** earnings picture.

erloschen expired, forfeited, *(Dienstbarkeit, Feuer)* extinguished, *(Firma)* extinct, *(Police)* lapsed, expired, extinct, spent, dead;
völlig ~ stone dead;
~ **sein** *(Firma)* to have ceased to exist;
~e Firma extinct (dissolved) firm; **~e Konzession** expired licence; **~es Patent** expired patent; **~es Urheberrecht** lapsed copyright.

Erlöschen expiration, expiry, *(Firma)* extinction, *(Prokura)* discontinuance, cessation, *(Schuld)* extinguishment, extinction, *(Versicherung)* expiration, lapse;
bei ~ on expiry, at the time of expiration;
~ **eines Anspruchs (einer Forderung)** extinction of a claim; ~ **einer Firma im Handelsregister** extinction of a firm, cancellation of a firm in the register of business names; ~ **einer Grunddienstbarkeit** extinguishment of an easement; ~ **einer Hypothek** discharge of a mortgage, cancellation of a mortgage *(US)*; ~ **der Mitgliedschaft** termination of membership; ~ **eines Pachtvertrages** expiry of a lease; ~ **eines Patents** expiry (lapse, expiration date) of a patent; ~ **eines Pfandrechtes** extinguishment of a lien; ~ **eines Rechtes** extinguishment of a right; ~ **eines Schuldverhältnisses** discharge of an obligation, cancellation of a debt; ~ **eines Urheberrechtes** extinguishment (lapse) of a copyright; ~ **von Verbindlichkeiten** discharge of liabilities; ~ **einer Versicherungspolice** expiration (lapse) of policy; ~ **eines Vertrages** lapse (expiry) of contract; ~ **der Vollmacht** termination (superannuation) of authority, termination of a power of attorney; ~ **eines Warenzeichens** lapse of a trademark; ~ **einer Wechselverbindlichkeit** discharge of a bill; ~ **von Wegerechten** extinguishment of ways;
Feuer zum ~ bringen to extinguish a fire.

erlöschen to expire, to abate, to become extinct, *(Angebot)* to terminate, *(Familie)* to become extinct, to die out, *(Feuer)* to die down, *(Firma)* to cease to exist, to go out, *(Grunddienstbarkeit)* to be extinguished, *(Licht)* to go out, *(Paß)* to expire, *(Versicherung)* to lapse, to become void, *(Vollmacht)* to superannuate;
Recht ~ lassen to forfeit a right.

erlöschend fading;
mit ~er Kraft with failing strength; **mit ~er Stimme** with a feeble voice.

Erlös | deckung earnings cover; **~druck** pinch on profits, earnings squeeze; **~einbruch** profit slump; **~einbuße** shortfall in profits.

erlösen to releasee, to free, to liberate;
Gefangenen ~ to liberate a prisoner; **j. von seinem Leiden ~** to deliver s. o. from his suffering; **aus einer peinlichen Situation ~** to rescue s. o. from an embarrassing situation; **von einer Sorge ~** to free s. o. of a burden.

erlösendes Wort sprechen to break the ice.

Erlös | erträge earnings, yields; **~erwartungen** earnings expectations; **~faktor** profit maker; **~konto** profit (income) account; **~lage** profit situation.

erlösmindernd profit-reducing.

Erlös | rückgang profit dip (drop), earnings drop, shrivel(l)ing profits; **~schmälerungen** nonoperating expense, income deducts, *(kommunales Rechnungswesen)* revenue deductions; **~schrumpfung** profit shrinkage; **~situation** profit situation; **~situation rapide verschlechtern** to send earnings into a dive; **~spanne** profit margin; **~stabilisierung** earnings stabilization; **~steigerung** earnings increase (growth).

erlöst relieved;
von einer schweren Last ~ relieved of a great weight;
~ **aufatmen** to heave a sigh of relief; **nach langem Leiden** ~ **werden** to die after a long period of suffering;
aus einer Auktion ~**es Geld** proceeds (avails, *US*) of an auction.

Erlös|tendenz profit (earnings) trend; ~**verbesserung** profit (earnings) improvement; ~**verknappung** earnings (profit) pinch; ~**verwendung** distribution of proceeds.

ermächtigen to empower, to authorize, to give authorization, to commission, to enable, to license;
j. ~ to vest s. o. with powers.

ermächtigt empowered, authorized, entitled, intra vires;
nicht ~ unauthorized; **ordnungsgemäß** ~ duly authorized;
~ **sein** to have authority, to be empowered.

Ermächtigung faculty, delegated power, authority, authorization, empowerment, fiat, *(Urkunde)* warrant, warranty, *(Vollmacht)* power [of attorney];
im Rahmen seiner ~ within the scope of one's authority; **ohne** ~ unlicensed, unauthorized, ultra vires;
ausdrückliche ~ special authorization; **mir erteilte** ~ powers conferred on one; **gesetzliche** ~ statutory authority; **richterliche** ~ judicial authority; **satzungsgemäße** ~ corporate powers; **schriftliche** ~ written authorization; **staatliche** ~ authority from the state *(US)*; **übertragene** ~ delegated authority; **uneingeschränkte** ~ unlimited authority;
~ **zur Abhebung** drawing authorization; ~ **zum Ankauf** *(Bank)* authority to negotiate; ~ **zur Anwendung außerordentlicher Maßnahmen** emergency power; ~, **Dokumententratten auf den Käufer zu ziehen** drawing authorization; ~ **der Einkaufsabteilung** purchase requisition; ~ **zum Einzug der Versicherungssumme** *(Hypothekengläubiger)* open mortgage clause; ~ **zur Kreditaufnahme** borrowing authorization, lending power; **satzungsgemäße** ~ **zur Kreditaufnahme** statutory power to borrow; ~ **zur Tätigung von Ausgaben** spending power;
jem. ~ **erteilen** to authorize s. o.; ~ **für etw. haben** to be qualified (authorized) to do s. th.; **in Überschreitung seiner** ~ **handeln** to act ultra vires; **nur im Rahmen gesetzlicher** ~ **tätig werden** to carry out functions only under statutory authority.

Ermächtigungs|depot authorized deposit; ~**gesetz** enabling statute *(US)*; ~**indossament** restrictive indorsement; ~**schreiben** letter of authorization (delegation).

ermahnen to admonish, to exhort, *(Schule)* to give a reprimand;
Untergebenen ~ to rebuke an subordinate; **j. zur Vorsicht** ~ to urge s. o. to be careful.

Ermahnung admonition, exhortation, *(Tadel)* rebuke.

ermangeln, einer Sache to be lacking s. th.

Ermangelung, in in the absence of, in default of, failing;
in ~ **besonderer Absprachen** failing special agreement; **in** ~ **genauer Anweisungen** for want of definite instructions; **in** ~ **von Beweisen** in the absence of evidence (proof).

ermannen, sich to pluck up courage, to pull o. s. together, to pluck up (take) heart.

ermäßigen to reduce, to mark down, to allow, to abate, to diminish, to lower, to cut (bring) down;
Buchpreis auf die Hälfte ~ to mark a book down to half price; **Diskontsatz** ~ to lower (mark down, reduce) the discount (bank, *Br.*, rediscount, *US*) rate; **Forderung** ~ to reduce a claim; **Gebühr** ~ to abate (reduce) a fee; **Grundsteuer** ~ to reduce the tax on a house; **um die Hälfte** ~ to reduce by half; **Kaufpreis** ~ to abate the purchase price; **Miete** ~ to lower the rent; **Preis eines Artikels** ~ to reduce (lower, abate, cut, cut down, *US*) the price of an article; **Preise stark** ~ to slash prices; **Steuer** ~ to reduce (abate, cut down, *US*) a tax; **Warenpreis** ~ to mark down (reduce) the price of an article, to cut down the price of an article *(US)*; **Zinssatz** ~ to lower the rate of interest; **Zollsätze** ~ to reduce the customs duties.

ermäßigt reduced, cut, cut-rate *(US)*;
~**er Anzeigenpreis** reduced (short) rate; **zu** ~**em Fahrpreis** at a reduced rate; **zu einem** ~**en Preis** at a lower rate; **zu** ~**en Preisen** at reduced (cut) prices; **stark** ~**e Preise** greatly reduced prices; ~**er Tarif** reduced rate.

Ermäßigung reduction, allowance, abatement, discount, cut *(US)*, *(Steuer)* relief, remission, *(Steuerfreibetrag)* allowance, credit;
25%ige ~ discount (reduction) of 25%; **starke** ~ great reduction, big cut;
~ **bei Belegen mehrerer Regionalausgaben desselben Blattes** combined edition discount; ~ **des Diskontsatzes** lowering of the rediscount *(US)* (bank, *Br.*) rate; ~ **der Einkommenssteuersätze** abatement of income tax; ~ **der Eisenbahnfahrpreise** cut in railway fares, reduction of fares; ~ **des Fahrpreises** reduction in fares; ~ **einer Forderung** reduction of a claim; ~ **der Frachtsätze** reduction in the freight rate; ~ **von Gebühren** abatement of fees, reduction of charges; ~ **der Geldmarktsätze** relaxation of (ease in) money rates; ~ **des Kaufpreises** abatement of the purchase price; ~ **der Kommunalabgaben** rate rebate *(Br.)*; ~ **bei Mengenabnahme** quantity discount (rebate, reduction), space (volume, frequency) discount; ~ **eines Preises** diminution of a (reduction in) price; ~ **bei Serienbelegung** *(Anzeigen)* frequency discount; ~ **einer Steuer** reduction (abatement) of a tax; ~ **des Steuersatzes für Kinder** tax allowance for dependants; ~ **der Zinssätze** cut in interest rates; ~ **der Zollsätze** reduction in the rate of duty;
~ **gewähren** to allow a discount (reduction); ~ **eintreten lassen** to grant (make) a reduction; **mit einer** ~ **verkaufen** to sell at a discount.

Ermäßigungs|antrag application for a reduction; ~**grenze** *(Einkommensteuer)* abatement limit.

ermatten to grow weaker, to tire;
in seinem Eifer ~ to flag in one's zeal.

ermattet exhausted, tired, weary, spent;
von der Hitze ~ limp with the heat.

Ermessen discretion, opinion, judgment;
im freien ~ **des Gerichts** within the discretion of the court; **dem** ~ **anheimgegeben, in das** ~ **gestellt** discretionary, arbitrary, facultative; **nach billigem** ~ discretionary; **nach eigenem** ~ at one's [own] discretion; **nach meinem** ~ in my view;
freies ~ absolute discretion; **gerichtliches (richterliches)** ~ breast of the court, judicial (legal) discretion;
~ **des Gerichts** discretion of a court; ~ **der Verwaltungsbehörde** administrative discretion; ~ **des Vorstands** discretion of the directors;
nach freiem ~ **entscheiden** to be vested with discretion; **nach bestem** ~ **handeln** to use one's best judgment, to use one's discretion, to take one's own course; **nach eigenem** ~ **handeln** to act independently, to take one's own course, to use one's discretion; **sein** ~ **mißbrauchen** to abuse one's discretion; **jds.** ~ **anheimgestellt sein** to be at s. one's discretion; **dem richterlichen** ~ **überlassen sein** to be left to the discretion of the judge; **in jds.** ~ **stellen** to leave it to s. one's discretion, to submit to s. one's judgment; **in jds. freies** ~ **stellen** to leave s. th. entirely with s. o. to judge.

ermessen to calculate, to measure, to estimate, to judge, *(begreifen)* to conceive, to understand;
Schaden ~ to assess damages; **in seiner ganzen Tragweite** ~ to realize the full significance.

Ermessens|akt discretion, facultative enactment; ~**akte der Verwaltung nachprüfen** to review administrative actions judicially; ~**ansprüche** discretionary claims; ~**ausmaß** degree of discretion; ~**ausübung** exercise of discretion; ~**befugnis** discretionary (facultative, arbitrary) power, special proxy; **unbeschränkte** ~**befugnis** arbitrary power; ~**behelf** discretionary remedy; ~**bereich** scope of discretion; ~**bereich der Verwaltung** administrative discretion; ~**entscheidung** arbitrary (discretionary) decision, decision ex aequo et bono; ~**fehler** abuse of discretion; ~**frage** matter of discretion; ~**freiheit** discretionary powers; **vernünftiger Gebrauch der richterlichen** ~**freiheit** sound judicial discretion; ~**gebrauch** exercise of judgment, *(Richter)* exercise of judicial discretion; ~**handlung** discretionary action; ~**irrtum** error of judgment; ~**mißbrauch** abuse of discretion; ~**nachprüfung von Verwaltungsakten** judicial review of administrative actions; ~**recht** discretionary power; **von seinem** ~**recht Gebrauch machen** to use one's discretion; ~**sache** discretionary matter; ~**schaden** discretionary damages; **erheblicher** ~**spielraum** large discretion; ~**spielraum des Strafrichters herabsetzen** to reduce a judge's sentencing discretion; ~**spielraum mißbrauchen (überschreiten)** to exceed one's discretionary powers; ~**überschreitung** abuse of discretionary powers; ~**umfang** scope of discretion; **besondere** ~**zahlung** extra discretionary payment.

ermitteln to trace, to find out, to discover, to determine, *(Aufenthaltsort)* to locate, to trace, *(Sachverhalt)* to ascertain, to establish, *(untersuchen)* to investigate, to inquire;
jds. Adresse ~ to find out s. one's address; **Aufenthalt** ~ to trace the whereabouts; **Einkommen** ~ to determine an income; **in einem Fall** ~ to make an inquiry into a case; **nicht gründlich genug** ~ to fail to make a reasonable investigation; **Kosten** ~ to ascertain the costs; **Sachverhalt** ~ to establish (find out, ascertain) the facts; **Schaden** ~ to assess the damage; **Täter** ~ to discover the culprit; **wegen eines Verbrechens** ~ to investigate a crime; **Wert** ~ to ascertain the value;
zu ~ ascertainable; **Adressat nicht zu** ~ addressee unknown.

ermittelt ascertained;
nicht ~ unascertained.
Ermittler investigator, investigating officer.
Ermittlung ascertainment, detection, discovery, *(Aufenthaltsort)* location, *(Berechnung)* computation, calculation, *(Schadensabschätzung)* valuation, appraisal, ascertainment, appraisement, *(Untersuchung)* inquiry, investigation;
~ **der Bürozeit** clerical work measurement; ~ **der Einkünfte** determination of the income; ~ **des Gewinns** ascertainment of profit; ~ **der Kosten** ascertainment of costs.
Ermittlungen inquiries, *(Feststellungen)* findings, facts, ascertainments;
nach den angestellten ~ according to the findings; **während der weiteren** ~ pending further investigations;
amtliche ~ official inquiry; **von Amts wegen angestellte** ~ ex officio inquiries; **sich über mehrere Jahre erstreckende** ~ inquiries extending over several years; **polizeiliche** ~ investigations by the police; **staatsanwaltliche** ~ criminal investigations; **umfangreiche** ~ extensive investigations;
~ **der Kosten** ascertainment of the costs; ~ **der Kriminalpolizei** criminal investigations; ~ **an Ort und Stelle** investigations on the spot;
~ **anstellen (einleiten)** to institute investigations, to investigate, to make inquiries, to inquire into; ~ **durchführen** to conduct an inquiry (investigations); ~ **einstellen** to drop investigations; ~ **leiten** to have an investigation in charge; ~ **veranlassen** to order an inquiry; **Fall zwecks weiterer** ~ **zurückweisen** to remand a case for further inquiry.
Ermittlungs|akten investigation records; ~**ausschuß** fact-finding (investigating) committee; ~**beamter** investigator, investigating officer, *(Steuerfahndung)* tax ferret; ~**befugnisse** power to investigate; ~**behörde** investigating authority (agency); ~**ergebnis** result of an investigation; ~**fehler** *(Statistik)* ascertainment error; ~**kosten** investigation cost; ~**maßnahmen** preliminary measures; ~**methoden** methods of investigation; ~**richter** committing (examining, investigating) magistrate, examining judge; ~**sache** investigative matter; **sich im** ~**stadium befinden** to be under investigation; ~**tätigkeit** investigating activity, investigative work; ~**verfahren** procedure before trial, preliminary examination (procedure), judicial inquiry, investigative process, *(wissenschaftlich)* detection method; ~**verfahren einleiten** to hold a judicial inquiry; ~**verfahren vor sich haben** to be under investigation; ~**zeitraum** investigating period.
ermöglichen to make possible, to afford;
jem. etw. ~ to enable (allow) s. o. to do s. th.; **reibungslosen Ablauf der Veranstaltung** ~ to make possible for a function to go off smoothly; **jem. eine Auslandsreise** ~ to afford s. o. a trip abroad; **keine Diskussion** ~ to allow no discussion; **jem. die frühzeitige Pensionierung** ~ to enable s. o. to retire early; **heute nicht gerade viel** ~ not go very far nowadays.
ermorden to murder, to assassinate, to slay.
Ermordeter person murdered.
Ermordung murdering, assassination.
ermüden to fatigue, to tire, to grow tired (weary);
seine Augen durch zu vieles Lesen ~ to strain one's eyes by reading too much; **leicht** ~ to get tired easily.
ermüdend exhausting, tiring, tedious, fatiguing, weariful;
auf den größten Teil der Zuschauer ~ **wirken** to pall upon most of the listeners.
Ermüdung tiredness, weariness, fatigue, *(techn.)* fatigue of metal;
vor ~ **umfallen** to drop with fatigue.
ermüdungsbeständig antifatigue.
Ermüdungs|bruch fatigue fracture; **erste** ~**erscheinungen zeigen** to show first signs of fatigue; ~**festigkeit** *(Metall)* fatigue strength; ~**grenze** endurance limit; ~**kurve** work (fatigue, *US*) curve.
ermuntern to encourage, to incite, to animate, *(beleben)* to invigorate, to put new life into;
j. ~ to cheer (buck, *fam.*) s. o. up; **j. zur Arbeit** ~ to incite s. o. to work.
ermunternd|er Brief cheerful letter; ~**e Zurufe** shouts of encouragement.
ermuntert werden müssen to need pluck.
Ermunterung encouragement, cheer.
ermutigen to hearten, to inspire;
j. ~ to put s. o. in good heart, to encourage (hearten) s. o.; **zu größeren Anstrengungen** ~ to stimulate s. o. to greater efforts.
ermutigende Nachrichten encouraging (heartening) news.
ermutigt, sich ~ **fühlen** to feel encouraged; **sich nicht gerade** ~ **sehen** to receive little encouragement.
Ermutigung encouragement.
ernähren to nourish, to feed, *(unterhalten)* to support, to make provision, to maintain;
j. ~ to supply s. one's needs; **sich** ~ to live on, to subsist; **sich selbst** ~ to make one's own living, to earn one's keep; **sich von seiner Hände Arbeit** ~ to live by the sweat of one's brow; **seine Familie** ~ to maintain one's family; **sich größtenteils von Fisch** ~ to live mainly on fish; **gewaltsam (zwangsweise)** ~ to force-feed; **sich von pflanzlicher Kost** ~ to be a vegetarian; **j. künstlich** ~ to feed s. o. artificially; **sich eine Zeit lang nur von Milch** ~ to go on a milk diet;
Frau und sieben Kinder zu ~ **haben** to have a wife and seven children to support; **sich von seiner Frau** ~ **lassen** to live on one's wife's income.
Ernährer breadwinner, breadearner;
alleiniger ~ **seiner Familie sein** to be one's family's sole support.
ernährt, gut well-fed; **schlecht** ~ undernourished.
Ernährung food, nourishment, nutrition, nurture;
einfache ~ plain food; **falsche** ~ wrong diet; **intravenöse** ~ intravenous feeding; **künstliche** ~ artificial feeding; **richtige** ~ correct diet; **schlechte** ~ malnutrition; **ungenügende** ~ undernourishment, malnutrition;
~ **einer Familie** maintenance (support) of a family;
für die menschliche ~ **als ungeeignet erklären** to condemn as unfit for human consumption.
Ernährungs|amt food office *(Br.)*; ~**aufwand** amount spent on food; ~**fachmann** nutrition expert, nutritionist; ~**güter** food [stuffs]; ~**industrie** food-processing industry; ~**lage** food conditions, food situation; ~**minister** Minister of Supply (of Agriculture, Fisheries and Food, *Br.*); ~**ministerium** Ministry of Food *(Br.)*; ~**niveau** nutrition level; ~**- und Landwirtschaftsorganisation** *(FAO)* Food and Agricultural Organization; ~**politik** food policy; ~**sektor** food sector; ~**standard** standard of nutrition; ~**störung** dystrophy; ~**therapie** dietetic therapy; ~**weise** diet; ~**wirtschaft** food-processing industry, food production; ~**wissenschaft** food (nutrition) science; ~**wissenschaftler** nutrionist; ~**zustand** standard of nutrition, nutritional status.
ernannt appointed, nominated, designate;
neu ~**er Minister** newly appointed minister.
Ernannter appointed, nominee, appointee *(US)*.
ernennen to nominate, to put in nomination, to appoint, to name, to call;
Bevollmächtigten ~ to appoint a proxy; **j. zum Direktor** ~ to make s. o. a director, to nominate s. o. as a new director; **zum Nachfolger** ~ to designate a successor; **j. zum Professor** ~ to appoint s. o. to a professorship; **zum Vorsitzenden** ~ to appoint as chairman; **zum Vorstandsmitglied** ~ to nominate a new director; **wieder** ~ to reappoint.
Ernennung nomination, appointment, designation, call, preferment, *(Diplomat)* posting;
vor seiner ~ prior to his appointment;
umstrittene ~ controversial appointment; **vorläufige** ~ pre-appointment;
~ **auf Lebenszeit** appointment for life; ~ **eines Nachfolgers** designation of a successor; ~ **zum Professor** professorial appointment; ~ **zweier weiterer Richter** creation of two additional judges; ~ **eines Vertreters** agency appointment; ~ **zum Vorstandsmitglied** appointment as manager (of a director); ~ **auf Widerruf** temporary appointment;
~ **bestätigen** to confirm an appointment, to ratify s. one's nomination; **jds.** ~ **für eine Stelle durchsetzen** to obtain s. one's appointment for a post; **seine** ~ **als Minister erhalten** to receive one's appointment as minister; **zur** ~ **als Schatzmeister vorsehen** to slate for nomination as treasurer.
Ernennungs|ausschuß nominations committee; ~**befugnis** power of appointment; ~**befugnis weiterer Vermögensverwalter** power of appointing new trustees; **im Rahmen ministerieller** ~**befugnisse liegen** to lie within the power (in the gift) of a minister; ~**recht** power of appointment; ~**schreiben** *(Konsul)* commission; ~**tag** day of nomination, date of appointment; ~**termin** nominating time; ~**urkunde** letter of appointment, letters patent, diploma, *(Offizier)* officer's papers, letters patent, commission, *(Treuhänder)* decree dative; **seine** ~**urkunde als Minister erhalten** to receive one's appointment as minister; ~**vorschlag** nomination for an appointment.
erneuen, sich to be renewed.
erneuerbar renewable.
erneuern *(ausbessern)* to repair, to mend, to renovate, to restore, *(ersetzen)* to replace, *(Patentrecht, Vertrag)* to renew, to revive;

sein Abonnement ~ to renew one's subscription; **Anlagen** ~ to replace fixed asstes; **Auftrag** ~ to repeat an order, to reorder; **Batterie** ~ to replace a battery; **Bekanntschaft** ~ to renew an acquaintance; **Betriebsausstattung** ~ to replace antiquated equipment; **Bezug eines Sessels** ~ to re-cover an armchair; **Dach** ~ to put a new roof on a house; **Eigentumsanspruch** ~ to renew a title; **Feindseligkeiten** ~ to resume hostilities; **Freundschaft** ~ to revive a friendship; **Gemälde** ~ to renovate (touch up) a painting; **Laufzeit eines Vertrages** ~ to prolong a contract; **Maschine** ~ to overhaul a machine; **seine Mitgliedschaft** ~ to renew one's membership; **Öl** ~ to change the oil; **Paß** ~ to renew a passport; **Patent** ~ to renew a patent, to extend the terms of a patent, to reissue a patent *(US)*; **sich periodisch** ~ *(Lagerbestände)* to revolve; **seine Reifen** ~ to renew one's tyres; **Straßenbelag** ~ to resurface a road; **Versicherungspolice** ~ to renew a policy; **Vertrag** ~ to renew a contract; **Vorräte** ~ to replenish with fresh supplies.

erneuerte Anlage replaced unit.

Erneuerung renovation, *(Ausbesserung)* restoration, repair, *(Maschine)* replacement, *(Vertrag)* renewal, revival, prolongation;
laufende ~en subsequent renewals; **unbedingt notwendige** ~ emergency repairs; **stillschweigende** ~ tacit renewal;
~ **des Abonnements** renewal of subscription; ~ **von Anlagen** replacement of fixed assets; ~ **eines Auftrages** renewal of an order; ~ **alten Brauchtums** revival of an old custom; ~ **eines Eigentumsanspruchs** renewal of title; ~ **einer Freundschaft** revival of a friendship; ~ **des Hausanstrichs** repainting of a house; ~ **einer Kraftfahrzeugversicherung** motor insurance renewal; ~ **des Maschinenparks** machinery replacement; ~ **des Öls** change of oil; **stillschweigende** ~ **des Pachtvertrages** tacit relocation; ~ **eines Patents** renewal (reissue) of a patent *(US)*; ~ **eine Schuldverhältnisses** novation; ~ **des Verfahrens** return of process; ~ **der Verlagsrechte** renewal of copyright; ~ **eines Versicherungsvertrages** reinstatement of an insurance; ~ **eines Versprechens** repetition of a promise; ~ **eines Vertrages** renewal of an agreement (contract); ~ **eines Wechsels** renewal of a bill of exchange;
an einem Hause ~en durchführen to repair (renovate) a house.

Erneuerungs|anspruch *(Lebensversicherung)* right of reinstatement; **~antrag für ein Patent** application for the renewal of a patent; **~arbeiten** repair activity (work); **kostspielige ~arbeiten** costly renovations; **soziale ~arbeiten** social renewal work; **~- und Unterhaltungsarbeiten** renewal and maintenance work; **~auftrag** reorder, renewal (repeat) order; **~aufwand** replacement outlay; **~bedarf** replacement demand; **~bedingungen** terms of renewal.

erneuerungs|bedürftig in need of repair; **~fähig** renewable.

Erneuerungs|fonds renewal (replacement) fund, *(Staatsrechnungswesen)* revolving fund *(US)*; **~gebühr** *(Patentrecht)* renewal fee; **~kommission** *(Versicherung)* renewal commission; **~konto** renewal (depreciation reserve) account; **~kosten** renewal costs; **~kostenberechnung** physical valuation; **~maßnahmen in großem Stil** large-scale restorations; **~plan** renovation scheme; **~police** continuation (renewal) policy; **~prämie** renewal premium; **~provision** renewal commission; **~quittung** renewal receipt; **~rate** renewal rate; **~rechnung** renewal invoice; **~rücklage** reserve for renewals and replacements, renewal fund, reserve for additions, betterments and improvements; **~schein** renewal certificate, talon, coupon sheet; **~tag**, **~termin** renewal date; **~verfahren** *(Versicherung)* renewal procedure; **~vertrag** renewal procedure; **~vorhaben** renovation scheme; **~wert** physical (replacement) value.

erneut|in die Verhandlung eintreten to rehear a case; ~ **darauf hinweisen** to point out again; **seine Beschwerde** ~ **vorbringen** to renew one's complaint;
~e Angriffe fresh attacks; **~en Angriff starten** to renew an attack; **~e Kämpfe** new fighting; **~e Tätigkeit** renewed activity; **~e Verhandlung** rehearing, new trial.

erniedrigen to diminish, to lower, to reduce;
sich ~ to degrade (abase, humiliate, humble) o. s., to join the mob; **j. vor seinen Freunden** ~ to humiliate s. o. in front of his friends; **Preis eines Artikels** ~ to reduce (lower) the price of an article; **j. zu einem Sklaven** ~ to degrade a man to the level of a slave; **j. soweit** ~ to abase s. o. so far; **sich soweit** ~ **etw. zu tun** to lower (debase) o. s. so far as to do s. th.; **j. zutiefst** ~ to humble s. o. in the dust.

erniedrigend degrading, humiliating, humbling.

Erniedrigung *(Preise)* lowering, reduction, degradation, humiliation, abasement;
Leben der ~ **führen** to live a life of degradation; **jeder Art von ~en ausgesetzt sein** to suffer all sorts of humiliations.

Ernst earnest, seriousness, gravity, solemnity;
angesichts des ~es der Lage in view of the gravity of the situation; **in vollem** ~ in good earnest;
blutiger ~ deadly earnest;
~ **des Lebens** serious side of life;
mit dem ~ **des Lebens wieder anfangen** to go back to the grindstone; **mit einer Drohung** ~ **machen** to do what one has threatened to do; **mit seinen Plänen** ~ **machen** to put one's plans into practice.

ernst serious, grave, earnest, solemn, *(aufrichtig)* genuine, sincere, *(bedrohlich)* serious, critical, dangerous, grave;
~ **aussehen** to look grave; **es nicht so** ~ **gemeint haben** to be only half in earnest; **es** ~ **meinen** *(fam.)* to mean business; **es wirklich** ~ **meinen** to be in real earnest; **Frage nicht** ~ **nehmen** to palter with a question; **j.** ~ **nehmen** to take s. o. seriously; **nicht** ~ **gemeint sein** not to be meant in earnest;
~es Gesicht grave face; **~e Lage** critical situation; **mit ~er Miene** with an earnest air; **~e Miene aufsetzen** to put on a solemn face; **~e Musik** classical music; **~e Nachrichten** grave news; **~en Ton anschlagen** to speak in a serious tone; **~es Wort mit jem. sprechen** to speak to s. o. in earnest (seriously to s. o.).

Ernstfall, im in case of emergency, *(mil.)* in case of war;
mit dem ~ **rechnen** to be prepared for anything.

ernstgemeint earnest, genuine;
~es Angebot serious offer; **~e Drohungen** no empty threats.

ernsthaft earnest, serious-minded, solemn, dingdong;
ganz ~ **bleiben** to keep a straight face; **sich** ~ **an die Arbeit machen** to set to work in earnest; **es völlig** ~ **meinen** to be dead serious; ~ **dagegen sein** to be dead against it;
~e Absichten haben to have hono(u)rable intentions, to be serious *(sl.)*; **~e Angelegenheit** serious matter, no joke; **~e Anstrengung** earnest effort; **~er Käufer** genuine buyer; **~e Zweifel** serious doubts.

Ernsthaftigkeit seriousness, gravity.

ernstlich|erkrankt seriously ill; ~ **verletzt** badly injured;
jds. Interessen ~ **gefährden** to jeopardize s. one's interests; ~ **zweifeln** to be in serious doubt;
~e Bedenken serious doubts; **in ~er Gefahr einzustürzen** in grave danger of collapse; **in ~er Verlegenheit sein** to be in low straits; **mein ~er Wunsch** my sincere wish.

ernstzunehmender|Gegner dangerous opponent; ~ **Politiker** serious politician.

Ernte harvest, crop, yield, *(Weinkarte)* vintage;
während der ~ at harvest time;
erste ~ main crop; **frühe** ~ forward crop; **gute** ~ generous harvest; **hervorragende** ~ heavy crop; **knappe** ~ crop shortage; **magere** ~ small harvest; **nach Pachtablauf reifende** ~ waygoing crop; **schlechte** ~ poor harvest; **gut stehende** ~ thriving crop; **überreiche** ~ bountiful (liberal, overflowing) harvest; **verhagelte** ~ crop ruined by hail;
~ **auf dem Halm** standing (growing) crop, outstanding (off-going) crop;
~ **einbringen** to take (gather) in (win, store) the harvest, to harvest, to get the crop in, to carry corn; **reiche** ~ **einbringen** to produce heavy crops, to crop heavily; **reiche** ~ **halten** *(Tod)* to take a heavy toll; ~ **tragen** to crop; ~ **auf dem Halm verkaufen** to sell the crop standing;
wie die Saat so die ~ as you sow you reap;
~arbeit harvest work, harvesting; **~arbeiter** harvester, harvest worker, harvestman, straw-cat *(sl.)*; **~ausfall** crop failure; **~aussichten** crop (harvest) prospects, prospect of the harvest; **~bericht** harvest report; **~berieselung zur Insektenbekämpfung** crop dusting; **~beurteilung** crop forecast; **~dankfest** harvest thanksgiving (home), Thanksgiving Day *(US)*, Turkey Day *(US coll.)*; **~einbringung** harvesting, gathering in of the crop, harvest collection, harvesting; **~einlagerung** storage of crop; **~ergebnis**, **~ertrag** crop yield; **~ertragsschwankungen** harvest fluctuations; **~erzeugnisse** agricultural products; **~fest** harvest home (festival); **~finanzierungskredit** loan for harvesting expenses, crop (agricultural, *US*) loan; **~helfer** volunteer harvester *(US)*; **~hervorbringung** production of crops; **~index** crop index; **~jahr** crop year; **hervorragendes ~jahr** banner year for crops; **~kredit** crop loan; **~maschine** harvester.

ernten to harvest, to gather, to reap;
reichen Beifall ~ to earn a big hand, to bring down the house; **Früchte seiner Arbeit** ~ to reap the harvest of one's work; **Getreide** ~ to reap the corn; **Lorbeeren** ~ to carry off the bag, to win laurels; **nichts als Undank** ~ to reap ingratitude; **Wein** ~ to vintage grapes.

Ernte|pfandrecht agricultural lien; ~**recht des gekündigten Pächters** waygoing crop; **unverwertbarer ~rest** crop residues; ~**schäden** crop damage; ~**schätzung** crop forecast (estimate); ~**segen** rich harvest; ~**überschluß**, ~**übertrag** carryover; ~**verfahren** harvesting method; ~**versicherung** crop insurance; ~**vorschau** crop forecast; ~**wagen** harvesting waggon; ~**zeit** harvesting period, harvest time.
ernüchtern to [make] sober, *(fig.)* to disillusion, to disenchant;
j. ~ to sober s. o.
ernüchternd down-to-earth;
~**e Wirkung** sobering effect.
ernüchtert, völlig in a state of complete disillusionment.
Ernüchterung disillusion, disenchantment, disillusionment.
Eroberer conqueror.
erobern to conquer, to capture;
j. ~ to make a conquest of s. o.; **neue Märkte** ~ to open up new markets; **Publikum im Sturm** ~ to take the audience by storm; **Stadt stückchenweise (in Etappen)** ~ to take a town piecemeal.
erobertes Gebiet conquered territory.
Eroberung conquest, capture;
neue ~ **machen** *(fig.)* to make a conquest; ~**en auf dem Exportmarkt machen** to make inroads in the export market; **auf** ~**en aus sein** *(fam.)* to be out to kill.
Eroberungs|drang determination to conquer; ~**krieg** war of conquest.
erodieren to erode, to eat away.
erodiert, von den Wellen worn by the waves.
eröffnen to open, *(einweihen)* to inaugurate, to dedicate *(coll.)*, *(förmlich)* to notify;
jem. etw. ~ to notify (disclose) s. th. to s. o., to break a matter to s. o.; **sich jem.** ~ to open o. s. (one's heart) to s. o., to open out to s. o.; **leicht abgeschwächt** ~ *(Börse)* to open at a slight discount; **Akkreditiv** ~ to open a letter of credit; **Anwaltsbüro** ~ to hang out one's shingle; **Aufstiegschancen** ~ to offer good prospects; **Betrieb** ~ to commence business; **Buchhandlung** ~ to establish o. s. as a bookseller; **Debatte** ~ to open the debate (discussion); **feierlich** ~ to dedicate; **Feindseligkeiten** ~ to start hostilities; **fest** ~ *(Börse)* to open firm (steady); **Festspiele** ~ to inaugurate the festival; **Feuer** ~ to open fire; **Filiale** ~ to open a new branch, to establish a branch office; **Fluglinie** ~ to inaugurate an air service; **sich einem Freund** ~ to disburden one's mind to a friend; **Geschäft** ~ to establish o. s., to set up shop, to open a business; **Gespräch** ~ to start a conversation; **Hauptverfahren** ~ to indict, to arraign, to find a true bill; **Konkurrenzbetrieb** ~ to set up a business in competition; **Konkursverfahren** ~ to institute bankruptcy proceedings; **Konto** ~ to set up an account; **Konto bei einer Bank** ~ to open an account with a bank; **Konto zu jds. Gunsten** ~ to open an account with a bank in s. one's favo(u)r; **Kredit zu jds. Gunsten** ~ to lodge a credit in favo(u)r of s. o.; **Kreditlinie** ~ to open a credit line *(US)*; **Laden** ~ to start a shop; **neue Möglichkeiten** ~ to open (offer) new prospects; **Parlament** ~ to open Parliament; **den Reigen** ~ to open the ball; **ruhig** ~ *(Börse)* to open quietly; **Sitzung** ~ to open a meeting, *(Gericht)* to open a court; **Spielzeit** ~ *(Theater)* to open; **neue Straße dem Verkehr** ~ to open up a new road to traffic, to dedicate a highway; **Testament** ~ to read a will; **Testament** ~ **und bestätigen lassen** to probate a will; **um 10 Uhr** ~ to open at ten o'clock; **uneinheitlich** ~ *(Börse)* to open irregularly; **Verfahren** ~ to open the proceedings; **Verhandlungen** ~ to start negotiations, to set negotiations on foot; **öffentliche Versammlung** ~ to open a public meeting; **wieder** ~ to reopen; **Zweigstelle** ~ to set up a branch.
Eröffnung *(Börse, Konto)* opening, *(Diskussion)* gambit, *(Einweihung)* inauguration, dedication, *(Gründung)* institution, establishing, *(Überraschung)* announcement, disclosure *(US)*, overture;
feierliche ~ formal opening; **lebhafte** ~ *(Börse)* active opening; **offizielle** ~ official opening;
~ **eines Akkreditives** opening (issue of) a letter of credit; ~ **eines Geschäftes** opening of a (starting up) a business, setting up shop; ~ **des Hauptverfahrens** arraignment, indictment, true bill; ~ **der Hauptversammlung** call to order; ~ **eines Hotels** opening of a hotel; ~ **eines Konkursverfahrens** adjudication of bankruptcy, institution of bankruptcy proceedings, winding up *(Br.)*; ~ **eines Kontos** opening of an account; ~ **eines Kredits** opening of a credit; ~ **eines neuen Ladens** new store opening *(US)*; ~ **eines Testaments** probate (reading) of a will; ~ **des Vergleichsverfahrens** decree of insolvency; ~ **einer Verhandlung** opening of a case; ~ **von Verhandlungen** opening of negotiations; ~ **einer Zweigstelle** opening of a new branch;
~ **des Hauptverfahrens ablehnen** to quash the indictment, to dimiss a charge of indictment; ~ **des Konkursverfahrens ablehnen** to dismiss a petition in bankruptcy; **jem. eine** ~ **machen** to notify (disclose) s. th. to s. o., to break the news to s. o.; **nach fester** ~ **schwach werden** *(Börse)* to turn weak after a firm opening.
Eröffnungs|ansprache inaugural address, opening speech (address, statement), ~**beschluß** *(Konkursverfahren)* adjudication of bankruptcy, receiving order *(Br.)*, *(Strafverfahren)* true bill, indictment; **Antrag auf einen** ~**beschluß stellen** to make application for receivership *(US)*, to file a petition in bankruptcy; **jem. einen gerichtlichen** ~**beschluß zustellen** to serve a process on s. o.; ~**bestand** opening stock (inventory), initial stock; ~**bilanz** initial (opening) balance sheet, registration statement; ~**buchung** opening entry; ~**fahrt** inaugural run; ~**feier** opening ceremony; ~**feierlichkeiten** inaugural ceremonies, opening exercises; ~**flug** inaugural flight; ~**gebot** opening bid; ~**inventar** original (opening) inventory; ~**jahr** opening year; ~**kurs** starting (opening) price, opening quotation (rate); **stark voneinander abweichende** ~**kurse** wide (split, *US*) opening; ~**masche** opener; ~**notierung** opening quotation; ~**notierung mit stark abweichenden Kursen** wide (split, *US*) opening; ~**nummer** *(Zeitschrift)* inaugural issue; ~**preis** opening price (quotation, rate); ~**rede** opening speech, inaugural address; ~**runde** opening round; ~**sitzung** initial meeting, formal opening sitting, *(parl.)* opening session; ~**spiel** *(Sport)* opener; ~**tag** *(parl.)* opening [day] session, *(Schule)* inauguration day; ~**verhandlung** *(Nachlaßgericht)* probate proceedings; ~**vorsitzender** temporary chairman; ~**vorstellung** *(Theater)* opening, first night; ~**zeit** hours for opening, opening hours (time).
erörtern to consider, to argue, to discuss, to debate, to ventilate; **Angelegenheit mündlich** ~ to discuss a matter personally; **ausführlich (eingehend)** ~ to discuss in great detail (at some length); **Fall** ~ *(Gericht)* to break a case; **das Für und Wider einer Sache** ~ to go into the merits of a case; **gründlich** ~ to examine thoroughly; **Rechtsfrage** ~ to argue a point of law; **alle Seiten einer Frage** ~ to consider all angles of a question; **Thema** ~ to debate a subject; **Thema ausführlich** ~ to deal at length with a subject; **Vorschlag näher** ~ to consider the details of a proposal.
Erörterung consideration, argument, ventilation, discussion, debate;
nach längeren ~**en** after much dicussion; **nach sorgfältiger** ~ after careful consideration;
gründliche ~ thorough discussion; **juristische** ~ legal argument;
~ **eines Falles** *(Gericht)* breaking a case;
zur ~ **kommen** to come up for discussion; ~ **einer Angelegenheit bis zur nächsten Sitzung zurückstellen** to remit the consideration until the next session.
Erosion erosion, eating away.
Erosionsbasis base level.
erpicht eager, keen;
auf Gewinn ~ greedy of gain (profits); **auf Ruhm** ~ eager for fame; **sehr** ~ as keen as mustard;
auf etw. ~ **sein** to have set one's heart on s. th.; **aufs Geldverdienen** ~ **sein** to be dead set (keen) on moneymaking; **auf Neuigkeiten** ~ **sein** to be eager for news.
Erpressen einer Aussage extortion of a statement.
erpressen to blackmail, to extort;
j. ~ to levy blackmail on s. o.; **Geld von jem.** ~ to bleed money from (squeeze money out of) s. o.; **Geständnis** ~ to extort a confession; **Lösegeld von jem.** ~ to exact a ransom from s. o.
Erpresser blackmailer, extortioner, wringer, suckegg, highbinder, racketeer *(US)*;
~**brief** blackmailing letter.
erpresserisch extorsive, extortionary;
~**e Methoden** extortionary methods; ~**e Wegnahme** extorsively taking; **auf** ~**e Weise** extorsively.
Erpressertrick blackmail racket *(US)*.
erpreßtes Geständnis extorted confession.
Erpressung exortion, blackmail, blackmailing, squeeze, squeezing, racket *(US)*;
förmliche ~ literary blackmail; **nukleare** ~ nuclear blackmail; **politische** ~ political duress;
~ **unter Gewaltandrohung** protection racket;
wegen ~ **anklagen** to indict for extortion.
Erpressungs|manöver *(Politik)* strike *(US sl.)*; ~**verfahren** indictment for extortion; ~**versuch** attempted blackmail (extortion); ~**versuch begehen** to levy blackmail.

erproben to prove, to try out, to test;
neue Methode ~ to try out a new method; **jds. Mut** ~ to put s. one's courage to the test; **praktisch** ~ to put to the test of experience, to reduce to practice.
erprobt approved, proved, *(zuverlässig)* reliable.
Erprobung proof, test, tryout, trial;
~ **auf dem Prüfstand** shop trial.
Erprobungs|flug test (trial) flight; ~**gebiet** testing area.
erquicken to refresh, to revive, to reinvigorate.
erquickend|er Anblick refreshing sight; ~**es Getränk** refresher, refreshment; ~**e Luft** reinvigorating air; ~**er Schlaf** refreshing sleep.
erraten to guess.
errechnen to compute, to calculate;
Zinsen ~ to work out the interest; **Zylinderinhalt** ~ to work out the capacity of a cylinder.
errechnet|e Summe sum arrived at; ~**er Wert** computed value.
Errechnung computation, calculation;
~ **des Barwertes** computation of cash value; ~ **des Fondswertes** *(Kapitalanlagegesellschaft)* validation of fund *(Br.)*; ~ **der Rücklagen** valuation of reserves; ~ **der Zinsen** working out the interest.
erregbar, leicht impulsive, easily excited.
erregen to excite, to stir up, to arouse;
sich über etw. ~ to feel strongly about s. th.; **Ärgernis** ~ to give rise to a scandal, to scandalize; **Aufsehen** ~ to attract publicity, to make a splash; **Bewunderung** ~ to call forth admiration; **Eifersucht** ~ to arouse jealousy; **j. geschlechtlich** ~ to rouse s. o.; **heftig** ~ to heat; **jds. Mißfallen** ~ to incur s. one's displeasure; **öffentliches Mitleid** ~ to excite public pity; **Neid** ~ to excite envy; **jds. Neugier** ~ to excite s. one's curiosity; **jds. Verdacht** ~ to incur s. one's suspicion.
erregend|es Mittel stimulant, excitant; ~**e Nachricht** sensational piece of news.
Erreger *(el.)* exciting agent, *(med.)* bacillus, pathogen;
~ **öffentlichen Ärgernisses** disorderly person.
erregt excited, in great excitement, agitated, heated, disturbed, up;
~ **antworten** to make a heated reply; ~ **sein** to be keyed up; **leicht** ~ **sein** to be hot-headed (quick to flare up);
~**e Antwort geben** to make a heated reply; ~**e Auseinandersetzung** fierce argument; ~**e Debatte** heated debate; ~**e Gemüter** heated minds; ~**e Menge** excited crowd; **mit** ~**er Stimme** in a voice quivering with emotion; ~**e Worte** heated words.
Erregtheit heat, excitement, agitation.
Erregung emotion, incitement, affect, tumult, provocation;
aus höchster ~ out of a white heat of emotion;
heftige ~ boil; **seelische** ~ disturbance; **wilde** ~ wild excitement; ~ **öffentlichen Ärgernisses** indecent exposure, disorderliness in a public place, scandalization, disorderly conduct;
sich in höchster ~ **befinden** to be wound up to a high pitch of excitement; **sich zur größten** ~ **steigern** to work o. s. up into a white heat; **j. in höchste** ~ **versetzen** to wind up one's temper to a pitch; **seiner** ~ **Herr werden** to govern one's temper.
Erregungszustände, emotional bedingte emotional disturbances.
erreichbar derivable, within reach, reachable, approachable, obtainable, available, get-at-able, achievable, come-at-able *(coll.)*;
zu Fuß ~ within walking distance; **leicht** ~ handy, within easy reach; **schwer** ~ difficult of attainment; **Tag und Nacht** ~ available day and night;
etw. für j. ~ **machen** to put s. th. on the map for s. o.; **telefonisch** ~ **sein** to be on the telephone.
Erreichbarkeit get-at-ability.
Erreichen reaching, attainment;
bei ~ **der Altersgrenze** upon reaching the age limit; **bei** ~ **der Volljährigkeit** on coming of age.
erreichen to reach, to get, to obtain, to attain, to achieve, to come it *(coll.)*, to hit *(US)*;
j. ~ to get hold of s. o.; **bei jem. etw.** ~ to have success with s. o.; **Abhilfe** ~ to obtain redress; **seine Absicht** ~ to attain one's end; **hohes Alter** ~ to live to an old age; **Altersgrenze** ~ to reach (attain) the age limit; **seinen Anschluß** ~ to get (make) one's connexion; **sechs Auflagen** ~ to reach (run up) to 6th editions; **Aufschub** ~ to obtain an adjournment; **vom Bahnhof leicht zu** ~ within easy reach of the station; **fast** ~ to approximate; **Hafen** ~ to fetch the harbo(u)r; **100 km pro Stunde** ~ to touch 60; **etw. nicht** ~ to fall short of s. th.; **Pensionsalter** ~ to superannuate, to be due to retire; **Preis** ~ to reach a price; **sein Reiseziel** ~ to arrive at (reach) one's destination; **j. telefonisch** ~ to get s. o. on the (in touch with s. o. by) telephone [line]; **Volljährigkeit** ~ to come of age; **durch seine Maßnahmen wenig** ~ to take little by an action; **Zahlungsaufschub** ~ to obtain a delay of payment; **sein Ziel** ~ to attain one's end; **Zug** ~ to catch (make, *US*) a train; **jds. Zustimmung** ~ to prevail upon s. o. to consent; **seinen Zweck** ~ to succeed in (attain) one's object, to achieve a purpose.
Erreichung attainment;
bei ~ **des 65. Lebensjahres** on reaching one's 65th year.
Errichten building, erection, construction, institution.
errichten to build, to erect, to raise, to put (set) up, to plant, to fabricate, *(gründen)* to establish, to ground, to found;
Fabrikationsbetrieb ~ to set up a manufactory; **Fonds** ~ to raise a fund; **Gebäude** ~ to erect (construct) a building; **Geschäft** ~ to set up shop, to establish a business; **auf festem Grund** ~ to build on firm ground; **Inventar** ~ to [take an] inventory, to take stock; **Konto** ~ to open an account; **Lehrstuhl** ~ to establish (found) a new chair; **Majorat** ~ to found an entail; **Montagewerk** ~ to set up an assembly plant; **Schreckensherrschaft** ~ to set up a reign of terror; **Stiftsschule** ~ to found a school; **Testament** ~ to make a will; **Treuhandvermögen** ~ to create a trust; **Zweigstelle** ~ to set up a new branch.
Errichter eines Treuhandverhältnisses trust maker.
errichtet, neu new-built;
~ **werden** to go up.
Errichtung construction, erection, building, fabrication, *(Geschäft)* setting-up, *(Gründung)* foundation, establishment, institution;
für die ~ **von Einfamilienhäusern bestimmt** zoned residential - A *(US)*;
schrittweise ~ progressive establishment;
~ **einer Behörde** establishment of an agency *(US)*; ~ **in gehöriger Form** *(Testament)* due execution; ~ **eines Gebäudes** erection (construction) of a building; ~ **eines Inventars** inventory taking, stocktaking; ~ **eines Kontos** opening of an account; ~ **eines Lehrstuhls** establishment of a new chair; ~ **einer Mauer** building of a wall; ~ **eines Miethauses** foundation of a block of flats; ~ **einer Pensionskasse** funding of a pension plan; ~ **einer Stiftung** creation of a trust; ~ **eines Testaments** making a will; ~ **eines Treuhandvermögens** strict settlement; **testamentarische** ~ **eines Treuhandvermögens** settlement created by will; ~ **von Wohnungen** creation of dwellings; ~ **von Wohnungen mit Mitteln des sozialen Wohnungsbaus** council housebuilding *(Br.)*;
für die ~ **von Einfamilienhäusern vorsehen** to zone for one-family residence *(US)*.
Errichtungskosten cost of construction, erection (construction) costs.
erringen to achieve, to gain, to win;
Preis ~ to carry off a prize; **Stipendium** ~ to win a scholarship.
Erringung achievement, acquisition;
~ **von mehr als der Hälfte der Wahlstimmen** polling over half the votes.
Erröten blushing, blush;
j. zum ~ **bringen** to bring blushes to s. one's cheeks.
erröten to redden, to blush;
bei dem bloßen Gedanken ~ to blush by the mere thought; **über und über** ~ to blush to the roots of one's hair; **vor Scham** ~ to blush for shame.
Errungenschaft acquisition, achievement, stroke, spoil, *(Eherecht)* acquired property;
letzte ~ latest acquisition; **die sogenannten** ~**en** the so-called improvements; **sozialistische** ~**en** socialistic achievements; **technische** ~**en** technical advances (feats); **wissenschaftliche** ~**en** scientific developments (achievements);
~**en der Forschung** scientific achievements; ~ **der modernen Technik** modern technical devices.
Errungenschaftsgemeinschaft community property *(US)*.
Ersatz replacing, replacement, substitution, *(Alternative)* equivalent, alternation, *(Ersatzmittel)* surrogate, substitute, stopgap, ersatz, *(Gegenwert)* equivalent, *(Person)* substitute, spare hand, *(Rückerstattung)* refund, restitution, *(Schadloshaltung)* compensation, indemnification, damages, reimbursement, recompense, amends, *(Wiedergutmachung)* reparation, *(Wiederherstellung)* reparation, redress, replacement;
als ~ in exchange, in return for, spare, *(Entschädigung für)* by way of compensation; **als** ~ **beschädigter Waren** as a setoff for damaged goods;
behelfsmäßiger ~ makeshift; **gleichwertiger** ~ adequate substitute;
~ **menschlicher Arbeitskraft durch Maschinen** displacement of human labo(u)r by machines; ~ **für werterhöhende Aufwendun-**

gen compensation for improvements; ~ **von Auslagen** compensation (reimbursement) for outlay incurred; ~ **von Betriebseinrichtungen** equipment replacement; ~ **des Drittschadens** civil damages *(US)*; ~ **abgenutzter Einzelteile** replacement of worn-out parts; ~ **in Geld** monetary indemnity; ~ **der Reisespesen** substitute for travel, refund of travel expenses; ~ **des gesamten Schadens** necessary damages; ~ **für nicht wieder gutzumachenden Schaden** irreparable damages; ~ **immateriellen Schadens** special damages; ~ **des mittelbaren Schadens** constructive damages; ~ **des tatsächlichen Schadens** compensatory damages; ~ **des unmittelbaren Schadens** prospective (direct, proximate) damages; ~ **für zeitweise erlittenen Schaden** temporary damages; ~ **der üblichen Schäden** general damages; ~ **aller Schadensfolgen** necessary damages; ~ **der Spesen** reimbursement for expenses incurred; ~ **für Streikfälle** strike replacement; ~ **des Substanzschadens** *(Grundstück)* fee damages; ~ **bis zu 3/4 der versicherten Werte** three-fourth value clause;
~ **für den zugefügten Schaden anbieten** to offer an equivalent for damage; **als ~ für j. einspringen** to step in as a substitute for s. o.; ~ **erhalten** to recover; ~ **für Havarie erhalten** to recover average; ~ **fordern** to claim damages; ~ **gewähren** to satisfy; ~ **herausgeben** to turn over a compensation; ~ **leisten** to compensate, to make restitutions (amends), to recoup, to restitute, to repay, to recompense, to indemnify, to atone; **zum ~ verpflichtet sein** to be liable for damages; ~ **verlangen** to claim compensation; ~ **des unmittelbaren Schadens verlangen** to claim constructive damages; **sich ~ verschaffen** to recover; ~**abteilung** *(mil.)* home battalion, depot *(Br.)*; ~**angebot** alternative tender; ~**anlage** emergency set; ~**anschaffungen** replacements, replaced equipment.

Ersatzanspruch [claim for] damages, damages (compensation) claim, recourse;
entstandener ~ damages sustained; **erlittenen Schaden übersteigender ~** added (punitive, *US*, exemplary) damages; ~ **für Transportverzögerung** claim for delay in transit; **auf einen ~ verzichten** to waive a claim to indemnity.

Ersatz|ansprüche, auf psychische Berufsschäden gegründete mental injury claims; ~**antenne** artificial antenna; ~**anzeige** make-good, stopgap advertisement, repeat, replacement ad *(US)*; ~**arbeiter** relief worker; ~**arbeitsplatz anbieten** to offer another job in substitution; ~**artikel** substitute articles; ~**aufwand**, ~**aufwendungen** replacement expenditure (outlay); ~**ausrüstung**, ~**ausstattung** replacement equipment; ~**bataillon** *(mil.)* home battalion, depot *(Br.)*; ~**batterie** spare battery; ~**bedarf** replacement needs (demand).

ersatzberechtigt entitled to damages.

Ersatz|bereifung spare tyres *(Br.)* (tires, *US*); ~**beschaffung** replacement; ~**beschaffungsmethode** replacement method; **angemessene ~beschäftigung** suitable alternative employment; ~**betrag** substituted amount; ~**bezirk** *(mil.)* recruiting district; ~**deckung** substitute cover; ~**delegierter** substitute delegate; ~**dienst** special duties; **sich für den ~dienst entscheiden** to opt for alternative service; ~**dienststelle** *(mil.)* recruiting center *(US)* (centre, *Br.*); ~**einheit** replacement unit; ~**einlagen für Ringbücher** filler paper; ~**einsetzung** *(Erde)* destination *(Scot.)*.

Ersatzerbe substituted *(US)* (alternative, representative) heir, substitute *(Scot.)*;
~**en bestimmen (bestellen)** to substitute an heir; **als ~ berufen sein** to inherit by right of representation.

Ersatz|erbfolge reversionary succession; ~**erzeugnis** substitute; ~**exemplar** replacement copy; ~**fahrzeug** replacement car; ~**flugzeug** replacement aircraft; ~**forderung** damage claim; ~**füllung** refill; ~**geld** token money; ~**geldstrafe** option of a fine; ~**gerät** *(Raumfahrt)* back-up; ~**geschworener** talesman; ~**güter** replacement goods; ~**grundstück** *(Bahn)* indemnity land, *(Enteignung)* lieu land; ~**heer** the reserve; ~**investition** replacement investment, replacement capital assets; ~**konnossement** exchange bill of lading; ~**kosten** replacement costs; ~**kräfte für Streikfälle** strike replacement; ~**krankenkasse** [etwa] provident association *(Br.)*; ~**ladung** substitute cargo; ~**leistender** compounder; ~**leistung** substitute performance, replacement, *(Schadenersatz)* indemnification, compensation; ~**lieferung** replacement delivery, delivery of substitute; ~**lieferung verlangen** to ask for delivery of other goods, to require goods in replacement; ~**lösung** alternative solution.

Ersatzmann emergency (spare) man, spare hand, odd hand (man), pinch hitter *(US)*;
als ~ anlernen to train a replacement; **als ~ einstudieren** to understudy; **als ~ fungieren** to substitute, to act as substitute, to come as a stopgap.

Ersatz|mannschaft reserve team, *(mil.)* replacements, *(Raumfahrt)* back up; ~**mine** *(Bleistift)* refill; ~**mitglied** alternative (alternate, *US*) member; ~**mitglied eines Ausschusses** assistant member of a committee; ~**mittel** substitute, surrogate; **als ~mittel verwenden** to surrogate; ~**pfändung** ancillary attachment; ~**pflicht** liability to pay damages.

ersatzpflichtig liable to pay damages.

Ersatz|programm senden to fill in a program(me); ~**rad** spare wheel; ~**reifen** spare tyre (tire, *US*); **sich zu einer ~religion entwickeln** to pan out as a new kind of religion; ~**schiff** replacement ship; ~**schlüssel für die Eingangstür anfertigen lassen** to duplicate keys for the front door; ~**schöffe** talesman; ~**schuldverschreibungen** rescission bonds; **anerkannte ~schule** controlled school; ~**sicherheit** substitute cover; ~**sprengstoff** replacement warhead; ~**steuer** lien tax; ~**stoff** substitute commodity; ~**stück** spare part, replacement copy.

Ersatzteil spare [part], reserve part (unit, piece), replaced part, bit;
immer neue ~e einsetzen to go on replacing with spares; ~**dienst** spare-part service; ~**knappheit** parts shortage; ~**lager** depot for spares, stock of spare parts, spare parts warehouse, parts depot; ~**nummer** spare-part number; ~**sendung** shipment of spare parts; ~**versorgung** parts supply.

Ersatz|testamentvollstrecker executor by substitution, substituted (substitutionary) executor, administrator de bonis non; ~**tonnage** replacement tonnage; ~**treuhänder** successive trustee; ~**truppenteil** home battalion, depot *(Br.)*; ~**universität** red-brick university *(Br.)*; ~**unterbringung** alternative accommodation; ~**urkunde** duplicate; ~**veranlagung** assessment subsequent; ~**verbindlichkeit** secondary obligation; ~**- und Austauschverfahren** unit replacement; ~**vermächtnis** substituted legacy, substitutional gift; ~**vermächtnisklausel** shifting clause; ~**vermächtnisnehmer** substituted legatee; ~**verpflichtung** secondary obligation; ~**vertrag** replacement contract; ~**vornahme** substitute performance; ~**vornahmen anordnen** *(Kommunalverwaltung)* to exercise default power *(Br.)*; ~**vorschlag** alternative proposal; ~**wache** waiting guard *(mil.)*; ~**wahl** by-election *(Br.)*, special election *(US)*; ~**währung** alternative currency (standard); ~**ware** replacement goods, substitute articles; ~**wechsel** replacement draft.

ersatzweise alternatively, as makeshift, in substitution for.

Ersatz|werbedurchspruch make-good; ~**werkstoff** alternative material; ~**wert** replacement (reproduction cost) value, *(Versicherung)* full value; ~**wesen** *(mil.)* recruiting and replacement; ~**wohnung** replacement housing; **geeignete ~wohnung** suitable alternative accommodation; ~**zustellung** constructive (substituted, *Br.*) service of process; **angenommene ~zustellung** accepted service.

ersaufen to be (get) drowned, *(Bergwerk)* to be flooded.

ersäufen, seinen Kummer in Alkohol to drown one's sorrow in drink.

erschaffen to create, to make.

erschallen to resound, *(Gelächter)* to ring out.

erschaudern to shudder, to tremble, to quiver;
vor Entsetzen ~ to be thrilled with horror.

erschauern to shiver, to shudder;
vor Ehrfurcht ~ to be awestruck;
j. ~ lassen to make s. one's flesh creep.

Erscheinen appearance, attendance, *(Briefmarken)* issue, *(Buch)* publication, appearance, coming out;
bei ~ *(Börse)* when issued; **im ~ begriffen** forthcoming; **sofort nach ~** as soon as published;
äußeres ~ outward appearance; **persönlich freigestelltes ~** voluntary appearance; **persönliches ~** personal appearance; **gerichtlich angeordnetes persönliches ~** compulsory appearance; **tägliches ~** *(Zeitung)* daily publication; **vorbehaltsloses ~** general appearance; **zwangsweises ~** compulsory attendance; ~ **auf dem Fernsehbildschirm** appearance on television, television appearance, screening; ~ **vor Gericht** entering an appearance, forthcoming *(Scot.)*; ~ **eines Landes auf der weltpolitischen Bühne** entry of a country into world politics; **persönliches ~ unter Vorbehalt** corporal appearance; ~ **eines Zeugen** attendance of a witness;
~ **einstellen** to cease (discontinue) publication, to be discontinued; **Briefmarken am Tag des ~s kaufen** to buy new stamps on the day of issue; **Buch bei ~ lesen** to read a book on first publication; **vom ~ befreit sein** to be excused from attendance; **am ~ verhindert sein** to be unfit to attend; **auf das ~ eines Zeugen verzichten** to dispense with the calling of a witness; ~ **wiederaufnehmen** *(Zeitung)* to resume publication; **sein ~ zusagen** to agree to come.

erscheinen *(Börse)* to be issued, *(Briefmarken)* to be issued, *(Buch)* to come out, to be published, to appear in print, *(kommen)* to appear, to come on the scene, to come out, *(Posten)* to appear, *(sichtbar werden)* to become visible, to outcrop, *(Wort)* to occur;
kann ~ *(Anzeige)* to be announced;
auf der Bildfläche ~ to appear on the scene; **zum ersten Mal auf der Bühne ~** to make one's debut on the stage; **demnächst ~** to be published shortly; **vor Gericht ~** to put in (enter) an appearance, to come (appear) before the court, to compear before a court of justice *(Scot.)*; **in Lieferungen ~** to be published in instal(l)ments; **im rechten Moment ~** to appear just at the right moment; **nicht ~** *(bei Gericht)* to fail to appear, to default; **aus dem Nichts ~** to appear out of the blue; **in der Öffentlichkeit ~** to appear in public; **auf der Passivseite der Bilanz ~** to appear on the debit side of the balance sheet; **persönlich ~** to appear in person, to put in an appearance; **persönlich vor Gericht ~** to attend personally in court; **plötzlich ~** to pop up; **zu einer Prüfung ~** to present o. s. for an examination; **als Prozeßbevollmächtigter für den Beklagten (Kläger) ~** to appear for the defendant (the defence, the plaintiff); **pünktlich zur Untersuchung ~** to present o. s. punctually for an examination; **unvermutet ~** to come unsought; **vernünftig ~** to seem good sense; **vertraut ~** to seem familiar; **vierteljährlich ~** to appear quarterly; **weiterhin ~** *(Zeitung)* to keep publishing;
Angelegenheit in anderem Licht ~ lassen to throw a different light on a matter; **Buch ~ lassen** to publish (bring out) a book; **Buch unter seinem eigenen Namen ~ lassen** publish a book under one's own name; **in Fortsetzungen ~ lassen** to serialize; **seine Vorlesungen in Buchform ~ lassen** to print one's lectures; **nur um sich zu zeigen ~** to attend for the sake of appearance.
erscheinend, demnächst *(Buch)* out soon, to be published shortly.
Erscheinung aspect, appearance, *(Geist)* ghost, spectre, phantom, *(Vorkommnis)* occurrence, event, phenomenon;
alltägliche ~ everyday occurrence; **äußere ~** outside [appearance], facies; **bedeutende ~** distinguished figure, somebody; **kurzlebige ~** flash in the pan; **merkwürdige ~** curious-looking object; **singuläre ~** singular occurrence; **unbedeutende ~** no bargain *(sl.)*; **weit verbreitete ~** wide-spread phenomenon; **verstaubte ~** back number;
~ der Nachkriegszeit symptom of postwar times; **bedeutendste ~ seines Zeitalters** greatest figure of one's era;
glänzende ~ sein to cut a fine figure; **in ~ treten** to appear, to show up, *(Wirkung)* to make itself felt, to come into the picture; **deutlich in ~ treten** to be clearly seen; **gern groß in ~ treten** to be fond of display; **fast überhaupt nicht in ~ treten** to keep very much in the background.
Erscheinungsbild, äußeres outward appearance (state), cut of s. one's jig;
~ in der Öffentlichkeit public image;
sein äußeres ~ vernachlässigen to be neglectful of one's appearance.
Erscheinungs|datum *(Buch)* publication date, *(Zeitschrift)* date of issue; **geplantes ~datum** publication goal; **wirtschaftliche ~form** economic phenomenon; **~intervall** *(Anzeigen)* interval of publication; **~jahr** year of publication; **~plan** *(Anzeige)* advertising schedule; **~tag** day (date) of publication, publication date, *(Briefmarke, Wertpapiere)* day of issue; **~termin** publication date, *(Anleihe)* issue date; **periodisch wiederkehrende ~termine** cycle issue dates; **~vermerk** imprint; **~weise** frequency of publication, publication schedule.
erschienen *(Buch)* published, out, in print;
gerade ~ *(Buch)* just out; **in unserem Verlag ~** brought out by our firm; **nicht ~** absent; **noch nicht ~** not yet out (published, in print); **noch nicht ~, Bestellung ist vorgemerkt** not yet published, order noted; **soeben ~** just published (out), new.
Erschienener person appearing, *(beim Notar)* deponent;
nicht ~ défaulter.
Erschießen shooting.
erschießen to shoot dead (to death, *US*), to fusilade;
sich ~ to shoot o. s., to blow one's brains out *(fam.)*; **j. mit dem Revolver ~** to shoot s. o. with a revolver;
j. standrechtlich ~ lassen to have s. o. court-martialled and shot.
Erschießung execution, shooting;
standrechtliche ~ military execution.
Erschießungs|befehl order to execute; **~kommando** firing squad.
erschlaffen *(Interesse)* to languish, to flag, to abate, to slacken.
erschlafft, durch die Hitze exhausted by the heat.
erschlagen to kill, to slay;
Korn ~ *(Regen)* to beat down the corn;
vom Blitz ~ sein to be struck by lightening;
~ *(a.)* tired, beat, exhausted, washed out, whacked, bushed *(US)*, *(überrascht)* dumbfounded, flabbergasted;
von einer Nachricht völlig ~ sein to be dumbfounded (flabbergasted) at the news.
Erschleichen obtaining under false pretences;
~ freien Eintritts gate-crashing; **~ einer Erbschaft** legacy hunting, subreption of a legacy *(Scot.)*; **betrügerisches ~ der Gläubigerzustimmung** obtaining by fraud the consent of creditors; **~ eines Vermögens mittels vorsätzlicher Täuschung** obtaining property by false representation.
erschleichen, betrügerisch to obtain by fraud, to obtain by false pretences (surreptitiously); **sich freien Eintritt ~** to gatecrash; **sich jds. Gunst ~** to creep into s. one's favo(u)r, to curry favo(u)r with s. o.; **sich jds. Vertrauen ~** to worm o. s. into s. one's confidence, to creep into s. one's good favo(u)r.
Erschleichung, betrügerische der Gläubigerzustimmung obtaining by fraud the consent of creditors.
erschlichen surreptitious, subreptitious.
erschließbar developable.
erschließen to open up, to develop, to plan, to tap, to improve; **neue Absatzmärkte ~** to find new outlets, to open up new markets; **Bauland ~** to develop ground (building lots, land); **Bergwerk ~** to open up (exploit) a coal mine; **neue Energiequellen ~** to tap new sources of energy; **für den Fremdenverkehr ~** to open up to the tourist trade; **Gebiet ~** to develop a district; **Gelände ~** to open up; **Geldquelle ~** to strike a lead (it rich, oil, *US*); **Grundstück baulich ~** to develop a property; **jem. sein Herz ~** to open one's heart (reveal one's soul) to s. o.; **neue Hilfsquellen ~** to tap (create) new resources; **Inneres eines Kontinents ~** to make the interior of a continent accessible; **Kohlenschätze eines Landes ~** to develop a coal area; **neue Kreditquellen ~** to tap alternative sources of credit; **Land ~** to exploit (develop) a country; **Land dem Handel ~** to open up a country to trade; **Markt ~** to tap a market; **weitere Märkte ~** to carve out wider (open new) markets; **jem. neue Möglichkeiten ~** to open new prospects to s. o.; **Neuland ~** to break new ground, to open up new frontiers; **Park dem Publikum ~** to open a park to the public; **Schloß dem Publikumsverkehr ~** to throw a castle open to the public; **neue Straße dem Verkehr ~** to open up a new road to traffic; **neue Wege ~** to strike out a new line.
Erschließung developing, development, opening [up], *(Grundstück)* planning;
in der ~ begriffen in process of develoment;
industrielle ~ industrial development; **kommunale ~** corporate planning; **regionale ~** regional planning; **wirtschaftliche ~** economic development;
~ neuer Absatzgebiete opening-up of new outlets; **~ von Baugelände** land development, development of building ground; **~ eines Bergwerks** exploitation of a mine; **~ von Bodenschätzen** tapping of natural resources; **~ zurückgebliebener Gemeindegrundstücke** community development; **~ von Geschäftsgrundstücken** development of commercial business; **~ neuer Hilfsquellen** creation (tapping) of new resources; **~ eines Landes** exploitation of a country; **~ küstennaher Ölvorkommen** offshore oil development.
Erschließungs|abgabe development land tax *(Br.)*; **~aufwand** development expenditure (costs), costs of improvement; **~ausschuß** development committee; **~beitrag** local improvement assessment, development fee.
erschließungsberechtigt entitled to develop.
Erschließungs|bezirk improvement district *(Br.)*; **~- und Bauentwicklungserlaubnis** planning permission *(Br.)*; **~fonds** planning fund; **~gebiet** planning (developing, development, *Br.*) area; **~gebühr** *(Regionalplanung)* development charge *(Br.)*; **~gelände** development site (land); **industrielle ~genehmigung** industrial development certificate *(Br.)*, permission to develop; **~gesellschaft** [industrial] development company, development agency; **~gewinn** development gain; **~grundstück** development land (site); **~kosten** property development expenses; **allgemein geplante ~maßnahmen** general improvements; **~plan** development plan *(Br.)*; **vorläufiger ~plan** interim development *(Br.)*; **vordringliches ~programm** action area plan *(Br.)*; **~vorhaben** real-estate development, development project (scheme), planning scheme; **~wert** development value inherent in the land.
erschlossen opened up, ripe for development;
~es Gelände developed tract of land.

erschöpfen to exhaust, to use up, to wear out, to tire, to deplete, *(Bodenschätze)* to drain, to pump out, *(ermüden)* to sap;
sich ~ *(Vorräte)* to run dry (low); **sich in unnützen Anstrengungen** ~ to exhaust o. s. in useless efforts; **Boden** ~ to impoverish the soil; **jds. Geduld** ~ to wear out (exhaust) s. one's patience; **Kontingent** ~ to use up a quota; **seine Mittel** ~ to exhaust one's resources; **Rechtsmittelweg** ~ to exhaust the remedies; **Silbermine** ~ to work out a silver mine; **Staatskasse** ~ to deplete the treasury; **Wohlstand eines Landes** ~ to drain a country of its wealth.
erschöpfend exhaustive, full;
Thema ~ **behandeln** to treat a subject exhaustively, to exhaust a subject; ~ **erlernen** to outlearn;
~**e Aufzählung** complete enumeration; ~**e Auskunft** exhaustive information.
erschöpft exhausted, *(Person)* worn out, dead-beat, pumped out, played out, prostrate, at an end, languid, fagged out, fatigued, spent, done up *(coll.)*, *(Vorräte)* running low (out);
völlig ~ outspent, worn out;
sich völlig ~ **fühlen** to feel washed out; ~ **sein** to be worn out (exhausted); **bald** ~ **sein** *(Fonds)* to be running low; **beinahe** ~ **sein** to be getting short; **völlig** ~ **sein** to be done in; **durch die viele Arbeit völlig** ~ **sein** to be worn out by all this work; ~ **werden** *(Kredit)* to run out; ~ **zusammensinken** to droop;
~**e Batterie** run-down battery; ~**en Eindruck machen** to look tired.
Erschöpfung fatigue, distress, distressed state, *(Bodenschätze)* depletion, exhaustion, *(Lager)* depletion;
geistige ~ impoverishment of the mind, brainfag; **nervöse** ~ nervous exhaustion;
~ **des Bodens** impoverishment of the soil; ~ **der natürlichen Hilfsquellen** depletion of resources; ~ **der Kontingente** using up quotas; **allmähliche** ~ **der Petroleumvorräte** gradual exhaustion of mineral oil; ~ **der innerstaatlichen Rechtsmittel** exhaustion of local remedies; ~ **der verwaltungsmäßigen Rechtsmittel** exhaustion of administrative remedies; ~ **der Reserven** exhaustion of reserves;
sich in einem Zustand völliger ~ **befinden** to be in a state of complete exhaustion; **vor** ~ **beinahe umfallen** to be ready to drop with exhaustion; ~ **der Bodenschätze verlangsamen** to slow down the depletion of resources.
Erschöpfungsanzeichen signs of distress.
Erschöpfungszustand state of exhaustion;
allgemeiner ~ general debility;
in einem völligen ~ **sein** to be in a state of exhaustion.
Erschrecken fright, alarm, scare.
erschecken to alarm, to frighten, to scare;
sich über etw. ~ to be frightened (scared, terrified); **j. entsetzlich** ~ to scare s. o. stiff *(coll.)*; **sich furchtbar** ~ to be frightened out of one's wits; **beim geringsten Geräusch** ~ to be scared at the slightest noise; **j. zu Tode** ~ to frighten s. o. to death (s. o. out of his wits).
erschreckend alarming, frightening, terrifying;
~**e Ausmaße annehmen** to assume appalling proportions; ~**es Bild bieten** to offer a terrible sight; ~**e Nachrichten** startling news.
erschrocken frightened, terrified;
zu Tode ~ startled out of one's wits;
zu Tode ~ **sein** to be scared to death (stiff, *coll.*);
mit ~**er Stimme** with a voice trembling with fright.
erschüttern to shake, to make quiver, to totter, to rock, *(Kredit)* to shake, to affect;
j. ~ to shock (ruffle) s. o., to ruffle s. one's feelings; **Boot** ~ *(See)* to make a boat shudder; **j. gewaltig** ~ to give s. o. a dreadful shock; **Grundlagen der Gesellschaft** ~ to shake the foundations of society; **Haus** ~ *(Erdbeben)* to rock a house; **das ganze Haus** ~ to upset everything in a house, *(Maschine)* to jar up the whole house; **Öffentlichkeit** ~ to shock the public; **Publikum** ~ to convulse an audience; **Stabilität der Währung** ~ to upset the stability of the currency; **seine eigene Stellung** ~ to do s. th. derogatory to one's position; **tief** ~ to disturb profoundly, to move deeply; **jds. Vertrauen** ~ to shake s. one's faith; **Wasseroberfläche** ~ to ruffle the surface of the water; **Zeugenaussage** ~ to shake the witness's evidence;
j. nicht ~ **können** to leave s. o. cold; **leicht zu** ~ **sein** to be easily upset emotionally.
erschütternd touching, moving, shocking, soul-stirring;
~**e Erzählung** touching tale; ~**e Nachrichten** shocking news.
Erschütterndes, etw. ~ **erlebt haben** to have had a terrible upset.
erschüttert agitated, upset, staggered;
nicht leicht ~ not easily shocked; **sichtlich** ~ visibly moved;
von einem Anblick ~ **sein** to be shocked at a sight; **ziemlich** ~ **sein** to be quite upset about it;
~**e Börse** disturbed market; ~**e Stellung** *(coll.)* shaky position.
Erschütterung percussion, tremor, vibration, thrill, *(fig.)* shock;
durch ein Erdbeben ausgelöste ~**en** earthquake shocks; **politische** ~**en** political convulsions; **seelische** ~ traumatizing shock; **einem Erdbeben vorausgehende** ~**en** preliminary tremor;
~**en auf dem Geldmarkt** tottering state of the money market; ~**en eines Motorrads** jars of a motor cycle; ~**en durch die Straße** road shocks;
Gebäude gegen ~**en abdichten** to insulate the foundations of a building against vibrations; **sich von dem durch die Haushaltsvorlage ausgelösten** ~**en erholen** to recover from the shock of the budget.
erschütterungsfest shock-proof.
Erschütterungs|gebiet disturbed area; ~**welle** earthquake wave.
erschweren to hamper, to hinder, to obstruct, to impede, to aggravate, *(Verbrechen)* to handicap;
Außenhandel ~ to be an impediment to foreign trade; **jem. die Ausübung seiner Pflichten** ~ to obstruct s. o. in the execution of his duty; **wirtschaftlichen Fortschritt** ~ to hamper the progress of business; **Lage** ~ to complicate the situation; **Suche nach den Verunglückten** ~ to hamper the search for the victims; **Verhandlungen** ~ to make negotiations more difficult.
erschwerende Umstände aggravating circumstances.
Erschwernis handicap, impediment, hindrance, burden.
erschwerte Bedingungen less favo(u)rable conditions.
Erschwerung handicap, impediment, hindrance, complication, aggravation.
erschwindeln to sharp, to swindle;
etw. von jem. ~ to chisel (cheat) s. th. out of s. o.; **Geld von jem.** ~ to swindle money out of s. o.
erschwindelt, alles pure fabrication.
erschwingen to afford;
nicht ~ **können** to be beyond one's purse.
erschwinglich *(Preis)* reasonable, agreeable;
finanziell ~ within the reach of everybody's pocket[book];
für j. nicht ~ **sein** to be beyond s. one's means.
ersehen to learn, to understand, to see;
aus einem Brief ~ to learn from a letter; **aus dem Beweismaterial** ~ to gather from the evidence;
daraus ist zu ~**, daß** hence it appears that.
ersehnen to long, to yearn, to wish;
Frieden ~ to long for peace.
ersehnt, lang ~**e Gelegenheit** long-desired opportunity.
ersetzbar fungible, replaceable, reparable, repairable, substitutable, *(Kosten)* reimbursable, refundable;
~**er Verlust** retrievable loss.
ersetzen to replace, to substitute, *(Auslagen)* to repay, to refund, to reimburse, *(Schadenersatz leisten)* to make good (up), to pay compensation, to recoup, to recompensate, to make amends, to compensate, *(wiedergutmachen)* to restitute, to repair;
j. ~ to supersede (supplant) s. o., to fill s. one's place, to replace s. o., to substitute s. o. [in his shoes]; **drei Arbeitskräfte** ~ *(Maschine)* to do the work of three men; **menschliche Arbeitskraft durch Maschinen** ~ to displace human labo(u)r by machinery; **jem. alle Auslagen** ~ to refund (reimburse) s. o. for all his expenses; **alte Betriebsausstattung** ~ to replace antiquated equipment; **Defizit** ~ to make up a deficiency; **Freiwillige durch Berufssoldaten** ~ to displace volunteers by a professional army; **j. stehenden Fußes** ~ to replace s. o. without a moment's notice; **unterschlagenes Geld** ~ to replace stolen money; **Investitionsgüter** ~ to replace capital goods; **gewöhnliche Landstraßen** ~ to supersede ordinary roads; **alte Maschine** ~ to supersede an old machine; **jem. die Spesen** ~ to reimburse s. o. for his costs; **jem. seinen Verdienstausfall** ~ to compensate s. o. for his broken time; **Verlust** ~ to make good (compensate for, recompense) a loss; **alle Verluste** ~ to cover all losses; **durch einen neuen Vertrag** ~ to supersede by a new contract.
ersetzt, Schaden ~ **bekommen** to recover damages; **von jem.** ~ **werden** to give place to s. o.
Ersetzung replacement, substitution, supersession, renewal;
~ **der menschlichen Arbeitskraft** labo(u)r displacement.
ersichtlich apparent, manifest, obvious, evident;
~**er Vorteil** obvious advantage;
wie aus dem Zusammenhang ~ as can be seen from the context.
ersinnen to contrive, to concoct, to weave, to think up;
Ausrede ~ to concoct an excuse; **Geschichte um einen Unfall** ~ to weave a story round an accident.

ersitzbar prescribable.
ersitzen to acquire by prescription, to have a hold, to usucapt, to acquire by adverse possession;
Recht ~ to prescribe a right.
Ersitzer adverse possessor.
Ersitzung adverse possession, usucaption, acquisitive (positive) prescription *(US)*;
Recht aufgrund von ~ beanspruchen to claim a right by prescription.
Ersitzungs|frist *(Grundstück)* period of prescription; **~recht geltend machen** to prescribe.
erspähen to descry, to catch sight;
j. in der Menschenmenge ~ to notice (spot) s. o. in the crowd; **neue Möglichkeiten ~** to see new vistas.
ersparen to save, to spare, to economize;
sich eine Bemerkung ~ to keep a remark to o. s.; **sich Geld ~** to save money, to make economies; **sich Kummer ~** to spare o. s. grief; **sich die Mühe ~** not to bother; **jem. die Mühe ~ etw. zu tun** to save s. o. the trouble of doing s. th.; **jem. nichts ~** to call s. o. hard names.
Ersparnis economy, *(beim Beamtenkörper)* retrenchment;
~ an Zeit saving of time;
aus ~gründen for economy's sake.
Ersparnisse savings, economies;
der ~ halber for economy's sake;
noch nicht wieder angelegte ~ fluid savings; **betriebliche ~** business savings; **gesamtwirtschaftliche ~** savings proportion; **geschäftliche ~** business savings; **größere ~** savings amounting to a large sum; **inflationssichere ~** index-linked savings; **private ~** personal savings;
~ beim Erwerb einer Flugkarte air-fare savings; **~ auf dem Postsparkassenbuch** postal savings; **~ auf dem Sachkostengebiet** savings of material cost;
seine ~ abheben to draw on one's savings; **~ angreifen** to dip into one's savings; **seine ~ zur Schuldenbezahlung angreifen** to dip into one's savings to pay current debts; **j. um seine ~ bringen** to cheat s. o. out of his savings; **seine ~ in einem Geschäft investieren** to invest one's savings in a business enterprise; **auf ~ zurückgreifen können** to have a sum put by to fall back upon; **von seinen ~n leben** to live on one's savings; **~ machen** to save, to make savings, to economize; **größere ~ machen** to save at higher rates; **Loch in seine ~ reißen** to make a large hole in (inroads upon) one's savings; **seine ~ in ein Geschäftsunternehmen stecken** to invest one's savings in a business enterprise; **auf seine ~ zurückgreifen** to draw on one's savings;
~ gestattender Lohn saving wage.
Ersparnisverwendung offsets of savings.
Erspartes spare money.
erspartes Geld savings, money put aside.
ersprießlich profitable, fruitful, beneficial.
erst|es Anrecht first refusal; **nach dem ~en Anschein** at the first blush; **beim ~en Blick** at the first sight; **~er Entwurf** rough draft, first (rough) sketch; **~e Etage** first (second, *US*) floor; **~e Familie in der Stadt** first family in the town; **~e Fassung** original version; **~er Gang** *(Auto)* first (bottom) gear, first speed *(Br.)*; **~es Gebot** *(Auktion)* opening bid; **~e Geige spielen** to play the first fiddle; **bei ~er Gelegenheit** at your earliest convenience; **~e Güte** finest (top-grade) quality; **aus ~er Hand** first-hand; **~e Hilfe** first aid; **jem. ~e Hilfe leisten** to apply first aid to s. o.; **~e Hypothek** senior (first, *Br.*) mortgage; **~e Instanz** first instance; **~e Klasse** *(Bahn)* first class, *(Grundschule)* first form (grade, *US*); **~er Klasse reisen** to travel first (Pullman, *US*); **~e Kontaktaufnahme** initial contact; **~er Korrekturabzug** first proof; **in ~en Kreisen verkehren** to move in the leading circles; **~er Kurs** *(Börse)* opening price; **~e Lesung** *(Gesetz)* first reading; **in ~er Linie** first and foremost, first of all; **das ~e Mal in der Stadt sein** to be fresh from the country; **zum ~en Male in einem Laden einkaufen** to buy in a shop for the first time; **~es Modehaus** leading fashion house; **~e Post** morning mail; **~e Qualität** firsts, prime, first-rate (top) quality; **von ~er Qualität** of prime quality, first-class; **~er Rang** *(Theater)* dress circle; **~e Rate** first instalment; **~e berufliche Schritte** first steps in one's career; **~es Schuljahr** first year at school; **auf der ~en Seite** first-page; **an ~er Stelle stehen** to be the first consideration; **~es Stockwerk** first *(Br.)* (ground, *US*) floor; **~es Versicherungsjahr** *(Selbstmordklausel)* first policy year; **~e Wahl** top-grade (choice) quality; **~er Weltkrieg** World War I;
zum ~en, zum zweiten, zum dritten! going, going, gone!;
~ die Arbeit dann das Spiel business before pleasure.

Erst|absatz initial sales; **~absatz von Wertpapieren** initial placing of securities; **~abschreibung** initial capital allowance; **~angebot** bidding prices; **~anlage** original investment; **~anmelder** *(Patent)* first applicant; **~anmeldung** *(Patent)* initial (original) application; **~anmeldung beanspruchen** *(Patentrecht)* to claim priority for an application.
erstarken to regain strength;
wirtschaftlich ~ to recover.
Erstarkung, wirtschaftliche economic recovery.
erstarren *(Stahl)* to solidify;
in den Adern ~ *(Blut)* to freeze in the veins; **vor Entsetzen ~** to be petrified (paralysed); **in Konventionen ~** to ossify; **zu einer Maske ~** to have set in a mask.
erstarrt *(Leiche)* rigid, stiff;
wie zur Salzsäule ~ rooted to the ground (spot);
~e Finger fingers stiff with cold; **in ~en Formen der Tradition** in an ironbound tradition; **~e Glieder** rigid limbs.
erstatten to reimburse, to compensate, to recompense, to refund, *(zurückgeben)* to return, to restore;
Anzeige gegen j. ~ to give (lay) information against s. o.; **Auslagen ~** to reimburse (refund) expenses; **Bericht ~** to report, to make (give) a report; **Gebühr ~** to rebate a charge; **zuviel gezahltes Geld ~** to return an overpaid amount; **Gutachten ~** to render an opinion; **Portospesen ~** to reimburse for postage incurred, to refund the cost of postage; **überzahlte Steuer ~** to refund an excess of tax.
Erstattung remission, compensation, *(Kosten)* reimbursement, repayment, compensation, *(Rückgabe)* return, restitution, *(Steuern)* refunding;
gegen ~ der baren Unkosten for reimbursement of out-of-pocket expense(s);
~ einer Anzeige reporting to (informing) the police, filing a declaration; **~ bei Ausfuhr in Drittländer** *(EG)* refund on export to nonmember countries; **~ von Auslagen** compensation (reimbursement) for expenses incurred; **~ gezahlter Beiträge** contribution refund, return of contribution; **~ eines Berichts** rendering a report; **~ zuviel gezahlter Einkommensteuer** refund of income tax; **~ von Frachtkosten** refund of freight charge; **~ von Gebühren** reimbursement of fees; **~ des Kaufpreises** refund of purchase price; **~ von Kosten** compensation of outlay incurred; **~ der Reisekosten** refund of travel expenses; **~ überzahlter Telefongebühren** return of charges;
~ beantragen to claim repayment; **auf ~ der Kosten gegenseitig verzichten** to waive all claims of costs; **~ vornehmen** to make restitution, to reimburse.
Erstattungs|anspruch reimbursement (refunding) claim, *(für Aufwendungen während der Pachtzeit)* tenant's right, *(Steuerzahler)* claim to repayment, *(Versicherungsnehmer)* insurance claim; **~anspruch geltend machen** to claim repayment; **~antrag** application for reimbursement; **~berechtigter** claimant; **~bescheid** notice of restitution; **~beschluß** restitution order *(Br.)*; **~betrag** amount of compensation, refunded amount.
erstattungsfähig liable to reimbursement, recoverable, repayable;
nicht ~ nonreimbursable;
~e Anwaltskosten party-and-party costs.
Erstattungspflicht obligation to repay, taxability.
erstattungspflichtig liable to repay (reimbursement), taxable, reimbursable;
nicht ~ nonreimbursable.
Erstattungsverfahren restitution proceedings, *(Steuern)* tax refund proceedings.
Erst|aufführung first performance, opening (first) night, premiere; **~aufführungstheater** first-run theater; **~auflage von 5000 Stück** first impression of 5000 copies; **~auflage von 5000 Stück drucken** to run off first printing of 5000 copies; **~auftrag** initial order; **einem ~auftrag gern entgegensehen** to look forward to the pleasure of a first order.
Erstaunen astonishment, surprise, amazement;
zu meinem großen ~ to my great (much to my) surprise;
einiges ~ hervorrufen to cause some raised eyebrows; **j. in ~ versetzen** to take s. o. by surprise.
erstaunen to surprise, to astonish, to amaze.
erstaunlich astonishing, astounding, amazing, surprising;
~e Geldsumme prodigious sum of money; **~e Geschichte** amazing story; **~e Geschicklichkeit** amazing dexterity; **~e Leistung** stupendous feat; **~ Mengen vertilgen** to devour enormous quantities.
erstaunt astonished, amazed;
über etw. ~ sein to be surprised (astounded) at s. th.;
~es Gesicht machen to look surprised (mystified).

Erst|ausbildung initial training; ~**ausfertigung** engrossed document, original; ~**ausführung** prototype; ~**ausgabe** first (original) edition, *(phil.)* first; ~**ausgabepreis** *(Emission)* issue price; ~**ausrüstung** *(mil.)* initial equipment; ~**ausstattung** initial equipment, *(Auto)* original equipment, *(Firma)* initial capitalization, *(nach Währungsreform)* initial allocation; ~**begebung** *(Scheck)* first delivery; ~**begünstigter** primary beneficiary; ~**begünstigung** primary insurance benefit; ~**benutzer** original user; ~**berechtigter** *(Erbrecht)* institute [heir]; ~**bezieher von Aktien** subscriber to the memorandum; ~**bezug von Aktien** subscribing to the memorandum.

erstechen, j. to stab s. o. to death.

erstehen to purchase, to buy, to acquire, *(entstehen)* to spring up, to arise, to result from;
billig ~ to get cheap; **bei der Versteigerung** ~ to buy at auction.

Ersteher purchaser, buyer, *(Auktion)* last and highest bidder.

Erstehung purchase, acquisition.

ersteigen to climb, to get up;
Gipfel ~ to climb a peak; **nächste Stufe der gesellschaftlichen Leiter** ~ to climb a rung of the social ladder.

Ersteigerer purchaser, auction buyer, last and highest bidder;
zahlungspflichtiger ~ responsible bidder.

ersteigern to buy (purchase) at *(US)* (by, *Br.*) auction;
selbst ~ to buy in.

Ersteigerung purchase by *(Br.)* (at, *US*) auction.

Erst|einlage starting rate, original investment; ~**einstufung** initial placing; ~**eintragung** first registration.

erstellen to erect, to construe, to build;
Gutachten ~ to render (deliver) an opinion; **Rohbilanz** ~ to prepare a trial balance; **Sozialwohnungen** ~ to subsidize house building.

Erstellung erection, construction, building;
~ **kommunaler Anlagen** municipal engineering; ~ **eines Gutachtens** rendering an opinion; ~ **von Sozialwohnungen** subsidized house-building; ~ **von Terminplänen** scheduling *(US)*; ~ **eines Testamentsnachtrags** execution of a codicil.

Erstellungskosten cost (expenses) of construction.

erstens first, in the first place, for one thing.

Erster first, firstcomer;
einmal ~ **nach M und zurück** first-class return to M;
~ **sein** to be [at the] top of one's class.

ersterben *(Geräusch)* to die away, to fade;
vor Ehrfurcht ~ to be awestruck.

Ersterfinder prior (original) inventor.

ersterwähnt first mentioned.

Erst|erwerb original acquisition, initial (original) purchase; ~**erwerber** first (original) purchaser, original subscriber, perquisitor; ~**erwerber eines Hauses** first-time house purchaser; ~**finanzierung** new financing; ~**flug** maiden trip.

erstgeboren first-born.

Erstgebot first (opening) bid.

erstgenannt of the first part.

Erst|girant principal endorser; ~**hypothek** first *(Br.)* (senior, *US*, legal) mortgage.

Ersticken suffocation, asphyxia;
zum ~ **heiß** stifling hot;
~ **eines Aufruhrs** stifling a revolt; ~ **eines Gefühls** suppression of a feeling;
dem ~ **nahe sein** to be nearly suffocating.

ersticken to suffocate, to choke, to stifle, *(Gefühl)* to suppress;
j. ~ to throttle s. o., to choke the life out of s. o.; **in seiner Arbeit** ~ to be up to the neck in (snowed under with) work; **Aufruhr** ~ to stifle (smother, quell) a rebellion; **im eigenen Fett** ~ to be as fat as a pig *(sl.)*; **Feuer** ~ to smother (quench, extinguish) a fire; **an giftigen Gasen** ~ to be suffocated by poisonous gas; **im Gelde bald** ~ to be rolling in money *(sl.)*; **Geräusch** ~ to muffle a sound; **vor Hitze fast** ~ to be stifled by the heat; **im Keim** ~ to nip in the bud; **vor Lachen** ~ to choke with laughter; **im Rauch fast** ~ to get choked up with smoke; **Skandal** ~ to smother up (suppress) a scandal; **Streit** ~ to burke an issue; **jeden Widerstand** ~ to snuff out all opposition; **vor Wut** ~ to choke with anger;
Feuerwehrmänner fast ~ **lassen** to almost stifle the firemen.

erstickend suffocating;
~**e Hitze** stifling heat; ~**er Kampfstoff** asphyxiant; ~**e Wetter** *(Bergbau)* choke damp.

erstickt stifled, choked, suffocated;
von Tränen ~ choked with tears;
mit halb ~**er Stimme** in a strangled (stifled) voice.

Erstickungstod sterben to die from suffocation.

Erstimpfung primary vaccination.

erstinstanzlich at first instance;
~ **tätig sein** to have original jurisdiction;
~**es Gericht** court of first instance; ~**e Gerichtsbarkeit** original jurisdiction.

Erst|investitionen initial investments; ~**kauf** initial purchase.

erstklassig top, topflight, crack, classic, tiptop, excellent, first-rate, first grade, first chop *(Br.)*, high-grade (-class), of the first order, of first rate (make), star, prizeworthy, on top of the world, classy *(sl.)*, boss *(US sl.)*, *(Schiff)* A 1, *(Wertpapier)* first-class (-rate), gilt-edged *(Br.)*, prime *(US)*;
sich ein ~**es Abendessen einverleiben** to get outside of a good dinner *(sl.)*; ~**e Anlage** high-grade investment; ~**e Arbeit** excellent piece of work; ~**es Bankakzept** prime banker's acceptance; ~**e Bedingungen** top conditions; ~**er Handelswechsel** prime trade bill; ~**es Hotel** first-class hotel; ~**e Kapitalanlage** gilt-edged *(Br.)* (high-grade, choice) investment; ~**e Obligationen** prime bonds; ~**es Papier** gilt-edged (fine) paper *(Br.)*, prime paper *(US)*; ~**e Sekretärin** first-rate secretary; ~**es Unternehmen** first-class firm; ~**e Waren** first-rate goods, superior (good-class) articles; ~**er Wechsel** first-rate (fine, *Br.*, prime, *US*) bill; ~**e Wertpapiere** gilt-edged stocks *(Br.)*, blue chips *(US)*.

Erst|klassigkeit distinction; ~**konzession** original charter.

Erstlings|arbeit first product; ~**rede** maiden speech; ~**roman** first novel; ~**versuch** debut.

erstmalig new, novel, unprecedented;
~**e Aufführung** *(bei Abschreibungen)* first return; ~**er Rechtsfall** first impression.

erstmals entstanden first accrued.

Erst|meldung *(Zeitung)* exclusive story, scoop *(sl.)*, beat *(US)*; ~**montage** green assembly; ~**plazierte** front ranks, first strings *(US sl.)*; ~**plazierung** initial placing; ~**prämie** first premium.

erstrahlen to shine, to sparkle, to gleam;
vor Freude ~ to light up with joy.

erstrangig ranking first, first-ranking, top-rate, overriding, *(Hypothek)* first-mortgage, prior;
~ **sein** to rank first;
~**e Hypothek** first *(Br.)* (senior, *US*) mortgage; ~**e Pfandbriefe** first debentures.

erstreben to aspire to, to strive after;
absolute Herrschaft ~ to aim at absolute power; **Ruhm** ~ to aspire to fame.

erstrebenswert worthwhile, desirable.

erstrecken, sich to extend, to stretch, *(Küste)* to trend, *(umfassen)* to include, to comprise, to embrace; **sich bis zum Fluß** ~ to extend as far as the river; **seine Forschungstätigkeit nur auf ein bestimmtes Gebiet** ~ to confine one's studies to one subject; **sich über die Grenzen seines Heimatlandes** ~ *(Einfluß)* to reach far beyond the frontiers of one's own country; **sich kilometerweit** ~ to stretch for miles; **sich tief ins Land** ~ to splash out into the countryside; **sich über mehrere Monate** ~ *(Verhandlungen)* to spread over several months; **sich nach Norden** ~ to verge to the north; **sich auf alle Rentenempfänger** ~ *(Gesetz)* to apply to all pensioners; **sich über einen Zeitraum von 30 Jahren** ~ to cover a period of thirty years.

Erstreckungsklausel *(Treuhänder)* overreaching clause.

erstreiten, im Prozeß to recover in one's lawsuit.

Erst|richter trial judge; ~**risikoversicherung** first-loss insurance; ~**schrift** original; ~**schuldner** principal debtor; ~**schürfrecht** ore-leave; ~**semester** freshman, frosh *(US)*, rat *(sl.)*.

erststellige Hypothek first (legal, *Br.*, senior, *US*) mortgage.

Erst|stimme first vote; ~**tagsmarke** *(phil.)* first-day cover; ~**täter** first offender *(US)*, stooge *(sl.)*.

erstunken und erlogen a pack of lies.

Erstürmen *(mil.)* seizure, capture, storm, assault, forcing.

erstürmen to [take by] storm;
Festung ~ to storm (escalade) a fortress.

Erst|verarbeiter primary processor; ~**veröffentlichung** first publication; ~**versicherer** direct (original) insurer, leading (principal) underwriter, direct-working carrier, ceding company (office); ~**versicherung** direct insurance; ~**zeichner** original subscriber; ~**zeichnung** initial subscription.

Ersuchen request, demand, petition, application, solicitation, instance, entreaty;
auf ~ on application, at the request of;
behördliches ~ official request; **dringendes** ~ urgent request; **gerichtliches** ~ requisition, commission *(US)*;
~ **zur Feststellung der Gültigkeit eines Anspruchs** claim tracer;
~ **um Rechtshilfe** letters rogatory.

ersuchen to ask, to petition, to pray, to beseech;
um Genehmigung ~ to apply for consent; **j. um eine Gütigkeit** ~

to ask a favo(u)r of s. o.; **um eine Unterredung** ~ to ask for an interview; **um eine Verlängerung der Aufenthaltsgenehmigung** ~ to apply for an extension of one's residence permit.
ersuchend precatory.
ertappen, j. to catch s. o. unawares; **j. bei einer Lüge** ~ to find s. o. out in a lie; **auf frischer Tat** ~ to catch s. o. in the very act ([in] flagrante delicto, red-handed).
ertappt, auf frischer Tat caught red-handed.
erteilen, Abrechnung to render an account; **Antwort** ~ to reply, to answer; **Anweisungen** ~ to give instructions; **Auflassungsgenehmigung** ~ to grant bargain and sell; **Auftrag** ~ to [place an] order, *(Behörde)* to confer (award) a contract; **jem. einen Auftrag** ~ to entrust s. o. with a commission; **Auskunft** ~ to give information; **jem. einen Befehl** ~ to give s. o. an order; **Belastung** ~ to debit; **Bescheinigung** ~ to issue a certificate; **Bewilligung** ~ to grant permission; **Entlastung** ~ to relieve, to grant discharge; **dem Vorstand Entlastung** ~ to approve the acts of directors, to approve the executive committee's acts; **Erlaubnis** ~ to grant permission, to approbate; **Faktura** ~ to [make out an] invoice; **Gutschrift** ~ to credit; **jem. eine Lektion** ~ to teach s. o. manners, to read s. o. a lesson; **Lizenz** ~ to [grant a] licence; **jem. ein Lob** ~ to praise s. o.; **Ordnungsruf** ~ to call to order, to name a member *(Br.)*; **Patent** ~ to grant a patent; **Prokura** ~ to authorize to sign, to confer powers of attorney on; **Quittung** ~ to [give a] receipt; **jem. einen Rat** ~ to give s. o. [a piece of] advice, to counsel s. o.; **Rechnung** ~ to render account; **Richtigbefund** ~ to verify an account; **einem Untergebenen eine scharfe Rüge** ~ to rebuke a subordinate; **Unterricht** ~ to instruct, to teach, to give a lesson; **jem. einen Verweis** ~ to reprimand s. o.; **jem. Vollmacht** ~ to authorize s. o., to bestow (grant) power of attorney; **jem. das Wort** ~ to give s. o. the floor; **Zuschlag** ~ to allocate, to adjudicate; **dem Meistbietenden den Zuschlag** ~ to allot to the highest bidder.
erteilt *(Patent)* granted.
Erteilung | einer vollstreckbaren Ausfertigung final process; ~ **von Auskünften** supply of information; ~ **eines Befehls** giving an order; ~ **eines Ordnungsrufes** naming of a member *(parl., Br.)*; ~ **von Parallellizenzen an mehrere Lizenznehmer** multiple licensing *(US)*; ~ **eines Patents** grant of a patent; ~ **einer Vollmacht** authorization; ~ **des Zuschlags an den Meistbietenden** allocation to the highest bidder.
Erteilungstermin date of granting.
Ertrag *(Bergbau)* output, get *(Br.)*, *(Einkünfte)* earnings, receipts, gainings, *(Ernte)* harvest, yield, outturn, *(aus Geldanlage)* investment, profit, revenue, usance, *(aus einem Geschäft)* returns, *(Gewinn)* gain, profit, proceeds, issue, avails *(US)*, *(Produktionsergebnis)* yield, produce, *(aus Rente)* revenue;
mangels ~ failing yield;
abnehmender ~ diminishing return; **angemessener** ~ reasonable return; **barer** ~ net proceeds (profit, earnings, returns); **betriebsbedingter** ~ operating profit; **betriebsfremder** ~ nonoperating profit; **pekuniär bewerteter** ~ pecuniary return; **durchschnittlicher** ~ average yield; **laufender** ~ current yield; **nicht realisierter** ~ unrealized profit; **reiner** ~ net yield; **risikofreier** ~ basic yield; **sinkender** ~ decreasing returns; **zur Ausschüttung zur Verfügung stehender** ~ profit available for appropriation; **steuerfreier** ~ tax-free return, tax-exempt income; **steuerpflichtiger** ~ taxable profit; **unversteuerter** ~ untaxed earnings;
~ **vor Abzug der Steuern** income before income taxes, *(Gewinn- und Verlustrechnung)* profits before taxation; ~ **unserer Arbeit** fruits of our labo(u)r; ~ **des investierten Kapitals** return on investment; ~ **pro Morgen** yield per acre, acre produce; ~ **nach Steuern** after-tax earnings (profits); ~ **vor Vornahme der Abschreibungen** profit before depreciation;
guten ~ **abgeben** to bring a fair return; ~ **abwerfen** to yield a profit; **guten** ~ **abwerfen** to pay well; **reichen** ~ **abwerfen** to yield high returns; ~ **aufweisen** to show a profit; **aus dem laufenden** ~ **bezahlen** to pay as you go; ~ **bringen** to yield [profit], to produce, to pan out *(US sl.)*; **keinen** ~ **bringen** to yield no return; **reichen** ~ **einbringen** to bring in good profits, to crop heavily; **seinen** ~ **steigern** to increase one's profit.
ertragbringend productive, lucrative;
~**e Aktiva** earning assets.
Erträge proceeds, earnings, *(Kapitalanlagegesellschaft)* income, profits, gains;
ähnliche ~ similar income; **anfallende** ~ incoming profits; **im Rechnungsjahr anfallende** ~ current income; **in neuen Kapitalanteilscheinen angelegte** ~ income reinvested in units; **antizipative** ~ *(Bilanz)* accrued income; **künstlich aufgeblähte** ~ artificially swollen profits; **nicht ausgeschüttete** ~ undistributed profits; **ausgewiesene** ~ reported earnings; **ausschüttungsfähige** ~ distributable earnings; **außerordentliche (außergewöhnliche)** ~ extraordinary (extra) profits, income of nonrecurring nature *(Br.)*, nonrecurrent income (profits) *(Br.)*; **außerordentliche und betriebsfremde** ~ extraordinary and outside (nonoperating) income (revenue); **steuerlich begünstigte** ~ preference income; **für örtliche Wohltätigkeitseinrichtungen bestimmte** ~ proceeds to go to local charities; **einbehaltene** ~ retained earnings *(US)*; **im voraus eingegangene** ~ *(Bilanz)* deferred [credits to] (unearned) income *(US)*, deferred revenue *(US)*; **einmalige** ~ nonrecurrent receipts (income, *Br.*); **entgangene** ~ missed proceeds; **geringfügige** ~ drab earnings; **gewerbliche** ~ income from trade and industry, business income, industrial earnings; **nicht gewerbsmäßige** ~ nontrading income; **industrielle** ~ fruits of industry; **jährliche** ~ annual income; **kapitalähnliche** ~ receipts of an income nature; **zur Ausschüttung kommende** ~ distributable income; **körperschaftssteuerfreie** ~ net-of-tax income; **laufende** ~ current revenues, *(Betrieb)* operating earnings; **periodenfremde** ~ *(Bilanz)* periodic income; **private** ~ internal effects; **rückläufige** ~ decreasing returns; **sonstige** ~ *(Bilanz)* other income (revenue); **nicht überwiesene** ~ unremitted earnings; **der Quellenbesteuerung unterliegende** ~ income received under deduction of tax at source; **unversteuerte** ~ pretax income; **verschiedene** ~ *(Bilanz)* miscellaneous income; **wiederangelegte** ~ reinvested earnings; **zukünftige** ~ future earnings; **zunehmende** ~ increasing return;
~ **aus dem Abgang von Gegenständen des Anlagevermögens** gains from sale of plant property; ~ **des Amortisationsfonds** sinking-fund income; ~ **aus der Auflösung von Sonderposten mit Rücklageanteil** transfers from special reserves; ~ **aus Beteiligungen** *(Bilanz)* income from investments (affilitates), investment profit; ~ **aus Dienstleistungen** income from service transactions; ~ **aus dem Dienstleistungsgeschäft** earnings on services, service earnings; ~ **aus anderen Finanzanlagen** income from other investments; ~ **aus Gewinnabführungsverträgen** income from profit-transfer agreements; ~ **gemäß Gewinn- und Verlustrechnung** receipts as per profit and loss account; ~ **aus Grundstücksanlagen** issues and profits; ~ **aus vorgenommenen Investitionen** investment revenue *(Br.)*; ~ **aus auswärtigen Investitionsvorhaben** earnings on investments abroad; ~ **aus Kapitalanlagen** yield on invested funds, profits from capital, revenue from income; ~ **von Rentenpapieren** bond market yields; ~ **vor Steuern** income before income tax; ~ **von Tochtergesellschaften** income from affiliates; ~ **nach der Trennung** fruit fallen; ~ **aus dem Warengeschäft** merchandise earnings; **laufende** ~ **aus Wertpapieren** current receipts from securities; ~ **von auswärtigen Wertpapieren** income from foreign securities; ~ **aus Zuschreibungen auf Gegenstände des Anlagevermögens** *(Bilanz)* valuation adjustment of plant property and investment;
gute ~ **abwerfen** to yield well; **den Buchwert übersteigende** ~ **abwerfen** to yield a profit over the book value; ~ **nicht entnehmen und im Geschäft wieder anlegen** to plough (plow, *US*) earnings back into the business, to retain in the business *(US)*; ~ **nachteilig beeinflussen** to hurt profits; **weiterhin gute** ~ **erwirtschaften** to maintain its good earnings position; **im nächsten Geschäftsjahr nur mit Mühe** ~ **erwirtschaften** to run into more earning troubles next year; ~ **in Staatsbetrieben erwirtschaften** to run state enterprises on an economic basis; ~ **erzielen** to draw profits; ~ **lediglich buchungstechnisch erzielen** to show earnings by mere bookkeeping devices; **langfristige Kapitalsicherheit mit hohen** ~**n kombinieren** to combine a high income with capital security in the long term; ~ **ansteigen lassen** to boost earnings; ~ **der Privatwirtschaft enorm zurückgehen lassen** to plunge private industry into pitifully low earnings; ~ **aus Kapitalanlagen lediglich der Körperschaftssteuer unterwerfen** to charge unfranked income to corporation tax only *(Br.)*; ~ **aus Wertpapieranlagen kapitalertragssteuerfrei vereinnahmen** to receive income from securities without deduction of income tax; ~ **aus seiner Kommanditbeteiligung als persönliches Einkommen versteuern** to report one's prorata share of a limited partnership as one's own income.
ertragen to endure, to sustain, to bear, to stand;
Belastungen ~ to sustain burdens; **jds. Launen geduldig** ~ to bear patiently with s. one's moods; **Schmerzen geduldig** ~ to bear one's pains patiently; **Unglück** ~ to endure misfortune; **jds. Unverschämtheiten** ~ to tolerate s. one's impudence; **Verlust** ~ to bear (stand) a loss;
j. nicht ~ **können** not to be able to abide s. o.; **jds. Benehmen nicht mehr** ~ **können** to be unable to tolerate s. one's

behavio(u)r any longer; **nicht mehr länger zu ~ sein** to become unbearable; **für seine Familie kaum zu ~ sein** to be a big knock to one's family *(sl.)*.
erträglich tolerable, endurable, bearable, *(mittelmäßig)* bearable, fair to middling *(coll.)*, possible *(coll.)*, *(Wetter)* passable; **einem ganz ~ gehen** to be tolerably well; **ganz ~ sein** not to be too bad; **nicht mehr ~ sein** to be no longer bearable;
~es Auskommen haben to have a sufficiency; **~es Einkommen** tolerable income.
ertraglos nonproductive, unproductive, rentless, unprofitable, *(Aktie)* nonpaying.
Ertrāgnis return.
Erträgnisse earnings, proceeds, profits, returns, *(Kapitalanlagegesellschaft)* income;
abnehmende ~ decreasing (diminishing) returns; **betriebsfremde ~** *(Bilanz)* nonoperating income (revenue); **im voraus eingegangene ~** *(Bilanz)* prepaid income; **einmalige ~** *(Bilanz)* nonrecurring income; **geringfügige ~** drab (poor) earnings; **sonstige ~** *(Bilanz)* other income, nonoperating revenue (income); **nicht aus dem Geschäftsbetrieb stammende ~** nonoperating revenue;
~ des Amortisationsfonds sinking-fund income; **~ aus Beteiligungen** investment profit, profit due from participations, income from subsidiaries; **~ einer Fluggesellschaft** airline earnings; **~ aus Kapitalanlagen (Vermögensanlagen)** income from investment; **der Körperschaftssteuer unterliegende ~ aus Kapitalanlagen** unfranked investment income *(Br.)*; **körperschaftssteuerfreie ~ aus Kapitalanlagen** franked investment income *(Br.)*; **~ aus Kapitalanlagen vor Steuerabzug** nonfranked income *(Br.)*; **~ aus Monopolen** *(Bilanz)* profits from patents and secret processes *(US)*; **~ aus dem Verkauf von Anlagegütern** profits on the sale of fixed assets; **~ aus Zuschreibungen auf Gegenstände des Anlagevermögens** *(Bilanz)* gains from valuation adjustments;
sich sofort in ~n niederschlagen to give rise to immediate income.
ertragreich profit-yielding, [rent-] paying, rent-producing, productive, payable, pay, profitable, lucrative;
nicht ~ nonremunerative;
~ sein *(Geschäft)* to show a good profit;
~er Boden fruitful soil; **~es Erz** pay ore.
Ertrags|abnahme diminishing returns; **~aktivierung** capitalization of earnings; **~analyse** profit analysis; **~anstieg** earnings rise (advancement); **rasanter ~anstieg** surge in earnings; **sprunghafter ~anstieg** jump in earnings; **~anteil** share of earnings, portion of a gain, royalty; **~aufbesserung** earnings recovery; **~aufstellung** earnings statement; **~aufteilung** apportionment of the profit; **~aufwand** profit costs; **~ausfall** loss of earnings (profit); **~ausschüttung** *(Investmentfond)* distribution of income *(Br.)*; **~aussichten** earning prospects, earnings projection, profit outlook; **unter Berücksichtigung der ~aussichten Absatz finden** to sell on a yield basis; **~begrenzung** ceiling on earnings; **~berechnung** calculation of earning power; **~beschränkung** restriction of output; **~besserung** recovery in profits; **~besteuerung** taxation on income; **~beteiligung** profit sharing; **~bilanz** balance of payments on current account; **~bild** profit picture; **verzerrtes ~bild** earnings distortion; **~chancen** profit-earning possibilities, earnings opportunities; **~chancen durch Investitionen auf bisher vernachlässigten Gebieten verbessern** to generate additional earnings through investments in special undervalued situations; **~deckung** *(Maklergeschäft)* earnings coverage; **~denken** profit-seeking motive; **~einbruch** profit shrinkage; **~einbuße** dent in earnings, shave-off profit, loss of profits; **~einkommen** produce income; **~entwicklung** profit trend; **progressive ~entwicklung** earnings progress; **~ergebnis** earnings yield; **~erwartungen** earnings expectations.
ertragsfähig productive, profitable;
~ machen to put on a profitable track.
Ertragsfähigkeit profit-earning (productive, yield) capacity, earnings quality, earning power, productivity, productiveness;
an der Grenze der Rentabilität liegende ~ marginal productivity;
~ einer Gesellschaft herstellen to turn a company into a winner.
Ertrags|faktor revenue earner, profit maker; **~gesetz** law of variable proportions; **~grenze** margin of profit, profit margin; **verhältnismäßig sichere ~grundlage** hard core of relatively stable earnings; **~inflation** earnings inflation; **~konto** revenue account; **~kosten** profit cost; **~kraft** earnings performance, earnings capacity (power), *(Frachtflugzeug)* pay[ing] load; **normale ~kraft** earning-capacity standard; **~kurve** earnings (productivity) curve; **~lage** earnings base (potential, power), profit situation; **gesunde ~lage** health of earnings; **gleichbleibende ~lage** earnings stability; **~leistung** earnings performance, *(Angestellter)* earnings record; **~leiter** earnings ladder; **~losigkeit** unproductivity; **~lücke** yield gap; **~miete** break-even rent.
ertragsmindernd profit-reducing.
Ertrags|minderung decline in earnings; **Kurs- und ~multiplikator** price-earnings multiple; **~niveau** level of earnings; **~planziel** earnings target; **~position** earnings base (potential, power); **~- und Aufwandsposten** income and expense items; **als antizipatives Passivum gebuchter ~posten** deferred profit; **~prüfung** profits review; **~rechnung** profit-and-loss (income) account, *(Gesellschaft)* corporate earnings report *(US)*, earnings statement; **~- und Aufwandsrechnung** income and expenditure account; **in die ~rechnung einsetzen** to put down to profit and loss; **~rückgang** decline in earnings, earnings slide (dip, drop), drop in earnings (profits), reduction in revenues, diminishing returns, shrivel(l)ing profits; **beträchtlichen ~rückgang aufweisen** to show considerable profit diminution; **~rücklage** revenue reserve *(Br.)*; **~schätzung** calculation of earning power; **~schein** dividend warrant, coupon; **~schwankungen auffangen (ausgleichen)** to even out fluctuations in earning power; **~schwelle** break-even point, payoff stage; **~schwelle wieder erreichen** to get back into profit; **~situation** profit situation, earnings base; **~situation rapide verschlechtern** to send earnings into a dive; **~spitze** peak yield; **~stabilisierung** earnings stabilization; **wiederauflebende ~stärke** resurgence in earnings; **~steigerung** increased earnings, earnings increase, earnings growth, increase in profits; **nicht produktionsgekoppelte ~steigerung** nonoutput-linked income rise; **~steuer** tax on earnings, profits tax *(Br.)*; **~tendenz** profitable (earnings) trend; **nicht vorkalkulierte ~überschüsse** unappropriated income; **~umdispositionen** coupon switching; **~verbesserungen** earnings (profit) improvement; **~vergleich** earnings comparison, comparison of yields; **Kurs-~-Verhältnis** earnings-to-sales ratio; **~verlust** loss of profits (earnings); **~vorschau** earnings projection (prospects, estimate); **~wachstum** growth in earnings, income growth.
Ertragswert income value, earning-capacity value, capitalized earning power (value);
jährlicher ~ net annual value *(Br.)*; **voraussichtlicher ~** expectation value; **zwischenzeitliche ~e** interim profit figures;
~ eines Betriebes going-concern value (worth);
~abschätzung income property appraisal; **~analyse** income analysis; **~berechnung** revenue principle; **~eignung** capacity to earn rental returns.
Ertrags|zahlen earnings figures, *(Geschäftsbericht)* trading figures; **~ziel aufgrund nachträglich errechneter Selbstkosten** historic-cost profit target; **~zunahme** earnings gains, growth of income (earnings); **~zunahmeaussichten** earnings growth expectation; **~zuwachs** earnings growth.
ertränken, seinen Kummer in Alkohol to down one's sorrows in drink.
erträumen to dream of, to imagine, to see in one's imaginations.
erträumt dreamed of, imaginary;
nie ~es Glück undreamed-of happiness.
Ertrinken, j. vor dem ~ retten to save s. o. from drowning.
ertrinken to drown, to be drowned, to perish by drowning, to go to Davy Jones's locker;
in Bestellungen ~ to be swamped with orders; **in Briefen ~** to be flooded with letters; **in einer Flut von Einladungen ~** to be snowed under with invitations.
Ertrinkender drowning person.
ertrotzen to obtain by sheer stubbornness.
Ertrunkener drowned man (person).
Ertüchtigung, körperliche physical training.
erübrigen *(Geld)* to save, to put aside;
sich ~ to be unnecessary (superfluous); **Stunde für j. ~** to spare s. o. an hour; **große Summen ~** to save large sums.
erübrigt haben to have left over;
keinen Pfennig ~ to have not a penny left.
Erwachen, beim on waking;
böses ~ rude awakening;
Tote zum ~ bringen *(Geräusch)* to waken the dead.
erwachen to wake up, to awaken, *(Neugier)* to be aroused;
aus einer Illusion ~ to awake from an illusion; **aus tiefem Schlaf ~** to awake out of a deep sleep; **plötzlich ~** to wake up with a start; **vom Tode ~** to come back to life.

erwachsen to result, to grow out, *(Kosten)* to arise, *(Zinsen)* to accrue;
aus dem Arbeitsverhältnis ~ to arise out of the employment; **aus handelspolitischen Erwägungen** ~ to grow out of commercial considerations;
~ *(a.)* grown up, full-grown, adult.
erwachsend incoming, accruing;
~**e Unkosten** expenses incurred, accruing costs; **aus einer Vereinbarung** ~**e Vorteile** advantages accruing from an agreement.
Erwachsenen | alter adult age; ~**fahrkarte** adult fare; ~**fortbildung** adult education, university extension; ~**lehrgang für Ortsansässige** residential course *(Br.)*; ~**schule** adult school.
Erwachsene | r adult [person], grown-up person;
nur für ~ adults only.
Erwachsensein adulthood.
erwägen to consider, to weigh, to ponder, to contemplate, to deliberate, to think over, to take into account;
Angelegenheit sorgfältig ~ to give a matter careful consideration; **Besuch** ~ to contemplate a visit; **ernstlich** ~ to consider seriously; **Folgen einer Handlung** ~ to weigh up the consequences of an action; **Für und Wider** ~ to weigh (study) the pros and cons; **nochmals** ~ to reconsider; **Vorschlag** ~ to deliberate a proposal.
erwägenswert worth considering.
Erwägung consideration, deliberation, reflection, contemplation, thought;
in der ~ whereas; **nach abermaliger** ~ after (upon) reconsideration; **nach ernsthafter** ~ after serious thought; **nach reiflicher** ~ after due consideration (second thought); **nach sorgfältigen** ~**en** after mature consideration (long deliberation); **von der** ~ **geleitet** *(Präambel)* considering;
finanzielle ~**en** pecuniary considerations; **kluge** ~**en** prudentials; **nochmalige** ~ reconsideration; **steuerliche** ~**en** tax considerations; **wirtschaftliche** ~**en** economic policy;
der ~ **wert sein** to be worth considering; **Ankauf eines Wagens in** ~ **ziehen** to consider buying a car; **Gesuch in wohlwollende** ~ **ziehen** to take a request into favo(u)rable consideration, to accord sympathetic consideration.
erwählen to choose, to elect.
erwähnen to [make] mention, to refer to;
j. einzeln ~ to give individual mention to s. o.; **j. lobend** ~ to commend s. o., to speak in praise of s. o.; **j. im Kriegsbericht lobend** ~ to give s. o. mention in dispatches *(Br.)*; **etw. überhaupt nicht** ~ not to speak a word of it; **Tatsache** ~ to refer to a fact; **j. in seinem Testament** ~ to mention s. o. in one's will; **das Wichtigste** ~ to touch the high spots *(US)*.
erwähnenswert worth mentioning, mentionable;
nicht ~ not worth mentioning, unmentionable.
erwähnt mentioned;
oben ~ above-mentioned; **unten** ~ noted below, undermentioned; **vorher** ~ said.
Erwähnung mention, reference to;
ehrenvolle ~ hono(u)rable mention, *(mil.)* citation;
ehrenhafte ~ **im Heeresbericht** mention in dispatches; ~ **in der Zeitung** mention in a newspaper, scratch *(sl.)*;
nicht der ~ **wert sein** not to be worth mentioning.
erwärmen to warm (heat) up;
sich für j. ~ to warm up to s. o.; **j. für etw.** ~ to arouse s. one's interest for s. th.; **sich für einen Plan** ~ to warm up to a plan; **sich um 5%** ~ *(Luft)* to rise (warm up) by 5%;
sich für etw. nicht ~ **können** to feel no enthusiasm about s. th.
Erwärmung warming [up], heating;
geringe ~ slight warming up;
~ **um 8%** a rise in temperature of 8%.
Erwarten, wider contrary to anticipation (expectation).
erwarten to expect, to await;
j. am Bahnhof ~ to wait for s. o. at the station; **Besuch** ~ to expect visitors; **größere Erbschaft zu** ~ **haben** to have great expectations.
Erwartung expectation, prospect;
brennend vor ~ on tiptoe with expectation; **entgegen allen** ~**en** contrary to expectations; **in angenehmer** ~ in pleasant anticipation; **in** ~ **Ihrer Antwort** awaiting your reply; **in** ~ **Ihres geschätzten Auftrags** looking forward to the pleasure of your instructions; **in freudiger** ~ **Ihres Besuches** looking forward to seeing you;
mathematische ~ mathematical expectation;
jds. ~**en entsprechen** to come up to s. one's expectations, to be equal to s. one's expectations; **den** ~**en nicht entsprechen** to fall short of (to be contrary to) expectations; **seine** ~**en herunterschrauben** to scale down one's expectations; **in gespannter** ~ **sein** to be tense with expectancy (on tenterhooks); **seine** ~**en zu hoch spannen** to pitch one's aspirations too high; **jds.** ~**en übertreffen** to exceed s. one's expectations.
erwartungsgemäß according to expectations.
Erwartungs | größe *(Wahrscheinlichkeitstheorie)* anticipation term; ~**kauf** sale by expectancy; ~**parameter** expectational cycle; ~**struktur** *(Marketing)* anticipation.
erwartungstreu *(Statistik)* unbiassed.
erwartungsvoll expectant;
j. ~ **ansehen** to gaze at s. o. expectantly;
~**es Schweigen** electric silence.
Erwartungswert expectation, expected value, *(Wahrscheinlichkeitstheorie)* anticipation term.
erwecken, den Anschein ~ **als ob** to create the impression that; **neues Bedürfnis** ~ to create a new want; **Erinnerungen** ~ to bring back memories; **Furcht** ~ to give rise to anxiety; **Hoffnungen wieder zum Leben** ~ to revive hopes; **Kundeninteresse** ~ to excite a customer's interest; **jds. Mitleid** ~ to stir s. o. to pity; **jds. Neugier** ~ to excite s. one's curiosity; **j. aus dem Schlaf** ~ to arouse s. o. from sleep; **j. vom Tode** ~ to raise s. o. from the dead; **Verdacht** ~ to arouse (be looked upon with) suspicion; **Vertrauen** ~ to inspire confidence.
erwehren, sich jds. to ward off s. o., to keep s. o. at bay;
sich nicht des Eindrucks ~ **können** not to be able to help feeling; **sich jds. Zudringlichkeiten nicht** ~ **können** to be helpless against s. one's insistence.
erweichen, j. to soften (move, touch) s. o.; **jds. Herz** ~ to melt s. one's heart;
sich ~ **lassen** to relent; **sich nicht** ~ **lassen** to keep a stiff upper lip.
Erweis für etw. erbringen to produce proof of s. th.
erweisen, sich to prove; **jem. Achtung** ~ to pay deference to s. o.; **sich dankbar** ~ to show o. s. grateful; **jem. einen Dienst** ~ to render a service to s. o.; **jem. einen schlechten Dienst** ~ to do s. o. a bad turn; **jem. die letzten Ehren** ~ to pay the last hono(u)rs (one's last respects) to s. o.; **sich als Fälschung** ~ to prove (turn out) to be a forgery; **sich als Feigling** ~ to show o. s. [to be] a coward; **sich freigebig** ~ to come out handsomely; **jem. einen Gefallen (eine Gunst)** ~ to do (grant) s. o. a favo(u)r; **sich nachsichtig** ~ to extend indulgence; **sich als nützlich** ~ to prove useful; **sich als Trugschluß** ~ to prove to be a fallacy; **sich als Vorteil** ~ to turn out to be an advantage; **sich als wahr** ~ to prove to be true; **sich seines guten Rufes würdig** ~ to live up to one's reputation; **jem. Wohltaten** ~ to confer benefits upon s. o.
erweislich provable, demonstrable, verifiable.
erweitern to extend, to expand, to enlarge, to widen, to aggrandize;
Anlagen ~ to expand its plant; **seinen Bekanntenkreis** ~ to enlarge one's circle of acquaintances; **gesetzliche Bestimmungen** ~ to widen the terms of a law; **sich beträchtlich** ~ to grow considerably; **Bruch** ~ to reduce a fraction to higher terms; **Fabrikgelände** ~ to extend the works; **sein Geschäft** ~ to expand (extend, enlarge) one's business; **seinen Gesichtskreis** ~ to enlarge one's view; **Klageantrag** ~ to extend the action; **seine Kenntnisse** ~ to improve one's stock of learning, to extend one's knowledge; **Machtbereich eines Staates** ~ to aggrandize a state; **Mündung eines Flusses** ~ to open out the mouth of a river; **sein Produktionsprogramm** ~ to broaden its line of production; **Satzungsbefugnisse** ~ to extend a charter; **sein Sortiment auf breiter Basis** ~ to hold the widest possible range of stock; **Stadtgrenzen** ~ to extend the city boundaries; **Umfang einer Erfindung** ~ to enlarge the scope of an invention; **seinen Wirkungskreis** ~ to extend one's sphere of activities; **seinen Wissensstand** ~ to enlarge one's knowledge.
erweitert enlarged.
Erweiterung enlargement, expansion, extension, continuation, aggrandizement, amplification;
territoriale ~ territorial aggrandizement;
~ **eines Auftrages** extension of an order; ~ **des Betriebes** plant addition, factory expansion; ~ **seines Geschäfts** expansion (enlargement) of one's business; ~ **des Gesichtskreises** enlargement of the mind; ~ **der Kenntnisse** improvement of one's stock of learning, increase of (accession to) knowledge; ~ **des Klageantrags** extending the action; ~ **der Produktenpalette** diversification of products; ~ **des unteren Proportionalbereiches** *(Einkommensteuer)* threshold increase; ~ **der Staatsbefugnisse** state expansion; ~ **des Vorstands** addition to the management;

~en auf dem Fabrikgelände vornehmen to extend the works; ~ seines Wirkungskreises vornehmen to extend one's sphere of activities.

Erweiterungs|bau expansion, extension, annex, addition to building; ~**bau zu einem Krankenhaus errichten** to build an extension to a hospital; ~**bauten** enlargements; ~**gesetz** enlarging statute; ~**investitionen** increase in capital investments, capital widening; ~**kosten** cost of addition, expansion cost; ~**mitteilung** expansion announcement; ~**plan**, ~**programm**, ~**projekt** expansion plan (scheme); ~**rücklagen** reserve for extension.

Erwerb acquisition, purchase, buy, acquest, obtainment, *(Unterhalt)* living, livelihood, *(Verdienst)* earnings, gains *(US)*, getting, income, profit;
auf ~ gerichtet acquisitive, profitable; **nicht auf ~ gerichtet** nonprofit;
abgeleiteter (nicht originärer) ~ derivative acquisition; **bedingter ~** conditional purchase; **gemeinschaftlicher ~** joint purchase; **gutgläubiger ~** innocent (bona-fide) purchase for value without notice, bona-fide transaction (acquisition); **originärer ~** original acquisition; **steuerpflichtiger ~** chargeable (taxable) gain; **unentgeltlicher ~** gratuitous transfer; **vorteilhafter ~** lucrative succession *(Scot.)*;
~ **von Aktien** acquisition of shares (stocks); ~ **von Anlagegütern im Leasingverfahren** sale-lease back *(US)*; ~ **von Anlagepapieren in großem Umfang** giant-scale buying of securities; ~ **übriggebliebenen Anzeigenraums** remnant buying; ~ **von Ausrüstungsgegenständen** equipment purchase; ~ **einer 50%igen Beteiligung** acquisition of a 50 per-cent interest; ~ **unter Eigentumsvorbehalt** acquisition with reservation of title; ~ **des Führerscheins** driving test; ~ **durch Geburt** *(Staatsangehörigkeit)* acquisition at birth; ~ **eines Grundstücks** purchase of real estate (land); ~ **aus zweiter Hand** secondhand purchase; ~ **eines Heimfallrechts** purchase of reversion; ~ **in fremdem Namen** purchase in the name of another; ~ **der Staatsangehörigkeit** acquisition of nationality; ~ **in der verkaufsarmen Zeit** off-season buy;
seinem ~ nachgehen to earn one's living.

erwerbbar acquirable.

erwerben to acquire, to make an acquisition, to get, to obtain, to procure, to gain, to secure, *(kaufen)* to purchase, to buy, *(verdienen)* to earn, to win, to make;
auf Abzahlung ~ to buy on the instalment (deferred payment, *US*) system; **lediglich die Anlagen eines Betriebes ~** to acquire only the assets of another business; **antiquarisch ~** to purchase at secondhand; **auf einer Auktion ~** to buy by *(Br.)* (at, *US*) auction; **Beteiligung ~** to secure an interest; **Beteiligung durch Erlaß der Rückzahlung von Staatskrediten ~** to buy its way in by waiving repayment of state loans; **betrügerisch ~** to obtain by fraud; **billig ~** to buy at a low figure (cheap); **sich sein Brot sauer ~** to work by the sweat of one's brow; **Eigentum ~** to acquire the title, to take title to property *(US)*; **durch eine Erbschaft ~** to take under a will; **Fachkenntnisse ~** to gain expert knowledge; **sich viele Freunde ~** to make many friends; **Führerschein ~** to pass one's driving test; **zum Großhandelspreis ~** to buy wholesale (bulk); **Grundstück ~** to buy a piece of (some) land; **gutgläubig ~** to purchase in good faith, to acquire bona fide, to acquire for value without notice; **Kapitalmehrheit eines Unternehmens ~** to acquire a controlling interest in a concern; **käuflich ~** to purchase for value, to acquire (take) by purchase; **Patent ~** to procure a patent; **etw. zu herabgesetzten Preisen ~** to buy s. th. on the cheap; **rechtmäßig ~** to obtain lawfully; **Rentenwerte ~** to buy funds; **sich einen guten Ruf ~** to win a reputation for o. s.; **Staatsangehörigkeit ~** to acquire nationality (citizenship); **britische Staatsbürgerschaft ~** to become a British subject (great); **Urheberrecht ~** to obtain the copyright; **sich große Verdienste um das Vaterland ~** to deserve well of one's country; **Verlagsrechte für ein Buch ~** to copyright a book; **Vermögen ~** to make (gain) a fortune; **jds. Vertrauen ~** to obtain s. one's confidence; **im Wege der gesetzlichen Erbfolge ~** to acquire by inheritance.

Erwerber acquirer, acquisitor, purchaser, purchasing party, buyer, vendee *(US)*, alienee, transferee;
bösgläubiger ~ purchaser in bad faith, mala-fide purchaser, bad-faith taker, *(Nachlaß)* fraudulent alienee; **erster ~** first (original) purchaser, perquisitor; **gutgläubiger ~** bona-fide holder (purchaser) for value, innocent purchaser, good-faith taker; **gutgläubiger entgeltlicher ~** innocent purchaser for value; **steuerpflichtiger ~** taxable transferee;
~ **aus zweiter Hand** secondary market trader; ~ **aufgrund eines Vorkaufsrechtes** preemptor.

erwerbs|behindert, ~**beschränkt** partially disabled, incapacitated.

Erwerbs|beschränktheit partial disablement; ~**beschränkungen** job reservations; ~**betrieb** business enterprise; ~**datum** purchase date.

Erwerbseinkommen wage (professional) income, income from wages, business (earned, *Br.*) income;
auf ~ gerichtet gainful;
~ **der Ehefrau** wife's earned income;
~ **milder besteuern** to tax earned income more leniently; ~ **der Ehefrau aus Steuergründen getrennt veranlagen** to deal with wife's earnings entirely separately for tax purposes.

Erwerbseinkünfte business income.

erwerbsfähig able to earn a livelihood, capable of making (earning) one's living, fit for work;
nicht ~ unemployable; **nur bedingt ~** nondescript; **voll ~** of full earning capacity; **vorübergehend nicht ~** temporarily incapacitated;
in ~em Alter of employable age.

Erwerbs|fähiger earner; ~**fähigkeit** ability to earn one's livelihood, earning power (capacity); **verminderte ~fähigkeit** decreased earning (reduced working) capacity; ~**genossenschaft** provident society *(Br.)*, buying association, industrial society *(US)*, cooperative association *(US)*; ~**- und Wirtschaftsgenossenschaft** industrial and provident (cooperative purchasing) society *(Br.)*; ~**- und Wirtschaftsgenossenschaftsgesetz** Industrial and Provident Society Act *(Br.)*; ~**geschäft** *(Doppelbesteuerungsabkommen)* trade or business carried on for purpose of profit; ~**gesellschaft** moneyed (business, *US*) corporation, trading company; ~**grundlage** means of livelihood (living); **jem. seine ~grundlage entziehen** to deprive s. o. of his livelihood; ~**kapital** working (acquisitive) capital; ~**kosten** original (acquisition) costs, purchase price; **Ausgabenzuschlag zuzüglich ~kosten** *(Investmentgesellschaft)* loading; ~**kraft** earning power; ~**leben** business (working) life, gainful employment (occupation).

erwerbslos unemployed, nonemployed, unoccupied, out [of work], out of employ, idle, jobless *(US)*;
j. ~ machen to toss s. o. out of a job; ~ **sein** to be out of employment; ~ **werden** to lose one's job, to become unemployed.

Erwerbslosen|fürsorge unemployment relief; ~**quote** unemployment ratio.

Erwerbslosenunterstützung unemployment benefit (relief, compensation, *US*), dole *(Br.)*;
~ **beziehen** to be on the dole *(Br.)* (unemployment rolls, *US*); **sich zur ~ melden** to go on the dole *(Br.)* (unemployment rolls, *US*).

Erwerbslosen|versicherung unemployment insurance; ~**ziffer** unemployment figure.

Erwerbs|loser unemployed, nonemployed person; ~**losigkeit** unemployment, redundancy *(Br.)*; ~**minderung** reduced working capacity, reduction in earning capacity; ~**möglichkeit** job opportunity; ~**pension** working pension; ~**person** gainfully employed person, wage earner; **unselbständige ~personen** wage and salary earners; ~**personen nach Wirtschaftsbetrieben und Stellung im Beruf** distribution of labo(u)r according to occupation; ~**preis** purchase (acquisitive) price, actual cost; **zum ~preis** at cost; ~**quelle** source of income, means of living (livelihood); **reine ~quelle** potboiler; **unsichere ~quelle** precarious living; ~**quote** activity rate; ~**sinn** business sense; ~**steuer** profit tax.

erwerbssteuerfrei sein to be exempted from purchase tax *(Br.)*.

erwerbstätig gainfully employed (occupied), *(selbständig)* self-employed.

Erwerbstätigenquote participation rate.

Erwerbstätiger gainfully employed person, employee, gainful worker, earner;
selbständiger ~ self-employer, self-employed person.

Erwerbstätigkeit gainful occupation (employment);
selbständige ~ self-employment; **unselbständige ~** paid occupation; **vorübergehende ~** temporary employment;
~ **mit örtlicher Bedeutung** basic employment; ~ **mit überörtlicher Bedeutung** nonbasic employment; ~ **beider Ehegatten** joint industry of husband and wife;
~ **ausüben** to pursue a gainful occupation, to earn a living.

Erwerbstrieb acquisitiveness, business sense.

erwerbstüchtig acquisitive.

erwerbsunfähig disabled, incapable to work, incapacitated, unemployable, unable to earn (make) one's living;
dauernd ~ permanent invalid;

~ **machen** to disable; **dauernd ~ sein** to be permanently disabled; **dauernd ~ werden** to become permanently incapacitated.

Erwerbsunfähiger disabled [person], incapacitated worker.

Erwerbsunfähigkeit physical disability, disablement, incapability to support o. s., incapacity for employment (to work); **auf Krankheit beruhende ~** sickness disability; **dauernde ~** permanent disability (incapacity); **vollständige ~** total disability (incapacity); **vorübergehende (zeitweilige) ~** temporary disability (disablement), incapacity.

Erwerbsunfähigkeitsrente industrial disablement benefit *(Br.)*, disability pension *(Br.)*, disability insurance benefit *(US)*, invalidity allowance *(US)*.

Erwerbs|urkunde title (purchase) deed; **~verhältnisse** economic (working) conditions; **~vermögen** productive property, earning assets; **~wert** purchase (cost, acquisition) value; **zum ~wert** at cost; **~wirtschaft** free enterprise; **zu ~zwecken** for purpose of gain; **~zweig** profession, trade, line of business (trade), branch of industry (trade).

Erwerbung acquisition, acquirement, purchase, procurement.

erwidern to reply, to answer, to retort;
Besuch ~ to return a visit; **Böses mit Gutem ~** to return good for evil; **nichts ~** to make no reply; **auf eine Replik ~** to rejoin.

Erwiderung answer, reply, response, return, *(Replik)* rejoinder, answer;
in ~ Ihres Briefes in reply to your letter.
scharfe ~ retort; **offensichtlich unhaltbare ~** frivolous reply; **~ des Beklagten** rejoinder; **~ des Klägers** replication.

Erwiderungsfrist time to reply.

erwiesen established, proven, demonstrated;
klar ~ clearly proved;
als ~ ansehen to take for granted; **eindeutig ~ sein** to be beyond doubt.

erwirken to effect, to bring about, to obtain, to get;
Aufschub ~ to obtain a postponement; **Beschluß ~** to bring about a reduction; **Freispruch ~** to obtain an acquittal; **Gerichtsbeschluß ~** to sue out a writ; **Haftbefehl ~** to take out a warrant against s. o.; **Patent ~** to take out (procure) a patent; **Scheidungsurteil ~** to obtain a divorce; **Urteil ~** to procure (obtain) a judgment; **Urteil gegen den Beklagten ~** to recover judgment against the defendant; **einstweilige Verfügung ~** to obtain an injunction; **Visaverlängerung ~** to succeed in obtaining an extension of visa.

Erwirkung eines Urteils procurement of a judgment.

erwirtschaften, Profite durch maximale Auftragsgrößenordnungen to reap economies of scale; **gute Rendite ~** to get a good return on an investment; **Überschuß ~** to make a surplus.

erwischen to catch, to collar *(coll.)*;
j. ~ to get hold of s. o.; **Dieb ~** to catch (cop, nab, pinch) a thief; **guten Sitzplatz ~** to get a good seat; **auf frischer Tat ~** to catch red-handed (flat-footed, *US*); **Zug gerade noch ~** to just manage to catch a train;
j. ~, wenn er guter Laune ist to catch s. o. in one of his good moods; **schwer zu ~** hard to come by.

erwischt, von der Polizei nabbed by the police.

Erwischtwerden, auf frischer Tat a fair cop.

erwogen, reichlich mature;
~ werden to be under consideration.

erworben, kürzlich recently acquired; **unrechtmäßig ~** ill-gotten.

erwünscht welcome, desired, most opportune;
~e Wirkung desired effect;
Besucher nicht ~! no visitors, please!; **praktische Erfahrungen ~** practical experience required; **Kurzschrift ~, aber nicht Bedingung** shorthand is an advantage but not essential; **persönliche Vorstellung ~** applications should be made in person.

Erwürgen strangulation.

erwürgen to throttle, to strangle, to choke to death, to burke;
Gefangenen ~ to garotte a prisoner.

Erz ore;
geringwertiges ~ low-grade ore; **gewaschenes ~** pulp;
~ aufbereiten to dress (prepare) ore; **wie aus ~ gegossen dastehen** to stand like a statue *(fam.)*;
~abbau ore winning (mining); **~abfall** tailings; **~ader** mineral lode (vein); **blinde ~ader** blind vein.

Erzählen story-telling, narration.

erzählen to tell, to narrate, to dish out;
j. alles ~ to tell s. o. all one's business; **jem. etw. ~** *(ihn tadeln)* to give s. o. a piece of one's mind; **ausführlich ~** to recount in detail, to give a detailed account of a happening; **seinen Freunden alles ~** to keep nothing back from one's friends; **gern aus seinem Leben ~** to like to talk of one's life; **Neuigkeit im ganzen Dorf ~** to tell the news to everybody in the village; **das kannst du deiner Großmutter ~** tell that to the marines *(coll.)*; **Ich werde Dir etw. ~!** I'll tell you what!;
etw. zu ~ haben to have seen a great deal.

erzählend|e Literatur fiction; **~er Teil** narrative part.

erzählenswert worth telling (recounting).

Erzähler narrator;
~talent literary artist.

Erzählung narration, account, report, story;
anschauliche ~ descriptive narration; **kleine ~** storiette; **zusammenfassende ~** consecutive narration;
~en und Märchen stories and fairy tales;
~ bestätigen to verify a narrative; **~ mit Einzelheiten überladen** to lumber a story with details.

Erzählungsweise, breitangelegte broad canvass.

Erz|aufbereitung dressing of ore, preparation of ores, ore preparation; **~bergbau** ore mining; **~bergwerk** ore mine; **~betrüger** arch deceiver.

erzeigen, sich dankbar to show o. s. grateful.

erzeugen to manufacture, to fabricate, to produce, to make, to be productive, *(Landwirtschaft)* to grow, *(Wirkung)* to engender, to create;
Elektrizität ~ to generate (produce) electricity; **Kapitalgüter ~** to create capital goods.

Erzeuger manufacturer, maker, producer, outputter *(US)*, *(Vater)* progenitor, father;
inländischer ~ inland (domestic) producer;
Kartoffeln direkt vom ~ beziehen to obtain potatoes straight from the producer;
~genossenschaft producer cooperative; **~großmarkt** central market; **~grundpreis** basic production price; **~gruppe** manufacturing group; **~industrie** manufacturing industry; **~kosten** cost of production; **~land** producer (producing) country, country of origin; **~monopol** production monopoly; **~preis** producer cost, producer (factory) price; **industrieller ~preis** industrial producer price; **landwirtschaftliche ~preise** farm-product (-produce) prices; **staatliche ~preisstützung** valorization *(US)*; **~richtpreis** standard production price; **~risiko** producer's risk; **~stufe** producer stage; **~verband** producer organization, combine of producers; **~vertrag** producer's contract.

Erzeugnis product, produce, production, manufacture, article, merchandise, turnout, make, work;
~se wares, goods, merchandise;
vom Einkommen des Durchschnittsverbrauchers abhängige ~se responsive products; **schwer abzusetzende ~se** products difficult to sell; **ausländische ~se** foreign-made products, articles of foreign manufacture; **zum Verkauf bereitstehende ~se** products available for sale; **deutsches ~** manufactured (made) in Germany; **unser eigenes ~** our own make; **einheimisches ~** domestic (home) produce, domestic product, inland produce; **einziges ~** sole product; **englische ~se** goods of British production; **erlösgünstige ~se** profit-yielding products; **erstklassiges ~** first-rate make; **fertiges ~** finished product; **forstwirtschaftliche ~se** forest products; **freie ~se** natural products; **fremdländische ~se** goods of foreign origin; **geistiges ~** brain child; **gewerbliches ~** factory (industrial, manufactured) product, industrial manufacture; **gleiche oder gleichartige ~se** identical or similar products; **halbfertiges ~** semimanufactured product; **halbfertige ~se** *(Bilanz)* work in process *(Br.)* (progress, *US*); **halbfertige und fertige ~se** *(Bilanz)* work in process and finished goods; **maschinell hergestellte ~se** machine-made products; **hochqualifizierte ~se** high-quality (-class) goods, high-quality products, big ticket items; **hochwertige ~se** high-value (-quality) goods; **industrielles ~** industrial product, manufacture, manufactured article; **inländische ~se** home products (manufacture), domestics; **kriegswichtige ~se** war goods; **ladeneigenes ~** store-brand item *(US)*; **landwirtschaftliche ~se** agricultural commodities (produce), farm produce; **leichtverderbliche ~se** perishable goods; **literarische ~se** literary production; **markenpflichtige ~se** coupon goods; **milchwirtschaftliche ~se** dairy products; **minderwertige ~se** poor quality goods; **nichtstrategische ~se** nondefense products *(US)*; **patentiertes ~** patented article (product); **preisgebundene ~se** price-bound (-fixed) merchandise; **preisstabile ~se** price-maintained products (articles); **nicht sortierte ~se** nongraded products; **steuerpflichtige ~se** taxable products; **teures ~** high-priced line; **tiefgekühlte ~se** frozen foods; **veredelte ~se** improved goods, finished products; **schwer verkäufliches ~** hard-to-move product;

vermietete ~se products on lease; **mit falschen Warenzeichen versehene** ~se misbranded products *(US)*; **versicherte** ~se insured goods; **weggeworfene** ~se throwaway products; **weiterverarbeitete** ~se processed products; **strategisch wichtige** ~se strategic goods (items); **zollempfindliche** ~se sensitive products;
~se **aller Art** goods, wares and merchandise; ~se **eines bestreikten Betriebes** hot cargo; ~se **in der Fabrikation** *(Bilanz)* work in progress *(US)* (process, *Br.*); ~se **der besten Güteklasse** firsts; ~se **französischer Herkunft** goods of French origin; ~se **eines Landes** products (produce) of a country; ~se **der Leichtindustrie** light products; ~se **mit gleichbleibenden Preisen** price-maintained goods (articles); ~se, **die keiner Produktionssteuerung bedürfen** nonbasic commodities; ~se **der ersten Verarbeitungsstufe** products of first processing stage; ~se **der Weiterverarbeitung** processing products;
seine ~se **billig abgeben** to sell one's wares cheaply; ~se **absetzen** to market products; ~se **in großen Mengen billig auf den Markt bringen** to dump goods; ~ **fördern** to merchandise; ~se **aller Preisklassen führen** to carry a full-price range; **lizenzpflichtige** ~se **herstellen** to manufacture under licence; ~se **verschiedenster Qualität herstellen** to manufacture goods in various qualities; ~se **unberechtigt als Markenartikel verkaufen** to palm off goods as those of another make; **für seine** ~se **werben** to advertise one's wares;
~**kostenrechnung** product cost accounting.
erzeugt, im Lande home-grown.
Erzeugung production, manufacture, making, output;
fortlaufende ~ constant production; **gewerbliche (industrielle)** ~ economic (industrial) production; **kontinuierliche** ~ constant production; **landwirtschaftliche** ~ farm production (produce); **mengenmäßige** ~ output in volume; **rückläufige** ~ falling production; **ungenügende** ~ underproduction;
~ **von Dienstleistungen** production of services; ~ **von Elektrizität** generation (production) of electricity; ~ **für den Handel** production for commerce *(US)*; ~ **von Massenartikeln** mass production, large-scale manufacture; ~ **landwirtschaftlicher Produkte** agriculture production, agricultural produce;
~ **beschränken** to curtail production.
Erzeugungs|beschränkung output restriction; ~**einheit** unit of production; ~**gebiet** production area; ~**kosten** production (prime) cost, manufacturing expenses; ~**kraft** production capacity; ~**land** producer country; ~**menge** output; ~**ort** place of production; ~**quote** production quota; ~**stätte** factory; ~**steigerung** growth of production; ~**vorhaben** production scheme.
Erz|feind archfiend, arch-enemy; ~**gang** course of ore; ~**gauner** double-dyed villain, archrogue; ~**gewinnung** ore winning.
erziehen to educate, to school, to instruct, to train, to tutor, *(Kinder)* to bring up, to rear, to raise *(US)*;
seinen Sohn zum Juristen ~ to educate one's son for the bar; **j. zur Pünktlichkeit** ~ to train s. o. to be punctual; **j. zur Selbständigkeit** ~ to bring s. o. up to be independent; **mit dem Struwwelpeter** ~ to bring up on Bill Hunter; **Kinder zu guten Staatsbürgern** ~ to train children to be good citizens.
Erzieher educator, instructor, educationalist, *(Internat)* tutor.
Erzieherin governess.
erzieherisch educational, disciplinal, disciplinary, pedagogic;
auf j. ~ **einwirken** to have an educational influence upon s. o.; ~**e Maßnahmen** instructive measures; **aus** ~**en Zwecken** for educational purposes.
Erziehung education, upbringing, cultivation, *(Ausbildung)* training, instruction, *(Internat)* tutoring;
nur auf den Broterwerb abgestellte ~ bread-and-butter education; **akademische** ~ university (academical) training; **allgemeinbildende** ~ liberal education; **gute** ~ good breeding (upbringing); **schlechte** ~ ill breeding; **sorgfältige** ~ careful upbringing; **vorschulische** ~ preschool education;
gemeinsame ~ **von Knaben und Mädchen** co-education;
seine ~ **abschließen** to complete one's education; **gute** ~ **genießen** to receive a good education; **gute** ~ **genossen haben** to be well educated (approved, *Br.*), to have had a good education; **seinem Kind eine miserable** ~ **angedeihen lassen** to drag up a child.
Erziehungs|alter educational age; ~**anstalt** educational establishment (institution); ~**anstalt für verwahrloste Kinder** industrial (training) school *(US)*, reformatory school *(Br.)*; ~**ausschuß** educational panel; ~**behörde** education authority; ~**beihilfe** education[al] allowance, education grant; ~**berechtigter** parent, legal guardian; **in** ~**fragen** in matters educational.
Erziehungsgewalt parental authority (power, *US*);
in der ~ **des Vaters bleiben** to remain in the custody of the father; ~ **entziehen** to take the custody of a child away from s. o.; ~ **zugesprochen erhalten** to be awarded custody of the children.
Erziehungs|gremium educational body; ~**heim** reform school *(US)*, community home *(Br.)*, approved school *(Br.)*; ~**kosten** cost of upbringing; ~**maßregelungen** disciplinary measures for juvenile delinquents; **neumodische** ~**methoden** newfangled ideas about education; ~**minister** Education Secretary *(Br.)*; ~**ministerium** Department of Education; ~**pflicht** parental duty; ~**recht** custody of the children; ~**system** educational system; ~**wesen** educational system (matters); ~**wissenschaft** pedagogy; ~**zoll** educational tariff; ~**zulage** education[al] allowance.
erzielen to reach, to achieve, to obtain, to arrive at, *(Kurs)* to obtain;
Abkommen ~ to reach an agreement; **Abschluß** ~ to conclude a bargain; **Buchwerte bei der Verwertung** ~ to realize at book value; **Einigung** ~ to arrive at an agrrement; **Erfolg bei der Nachwahl** ~ to score a success in the by-election; **gute Fortschritte** ~ to get along well; **Gewinne** ~ to realize (make, secure) profits; **in rascher Steigerung neue Höchstkurse** ~ to shoot into new high ground; **Höchstpreis** ~ to secure the best value; **Kursgewinn** ~ to score an advance; **nur geringen Nutzen** ~ to get only a small profit; **hohen Preis** ~ to fetch (realize) a good (high) price; **höhere Preise** ~ to secure (obtain) higher prices; **als Reingewinn** ~ to clear a profit, to net; **keinen Reingewinn** ~ to leave a zero net; **Übereinkommen** ~ to reach an agreement; **Verständigung** ~ to come to (reach) an understanding; **Wirkung** ~ to tell upon.
erzielter Gewinn profit made, realized profit.
Erzielung achievement, obtainment;
~ **eines Gewinns** making (realization) of profits, profitmaking.
erzittern to tremble, to shake, to quiver, *(Brücke)* to vibrate, *(Erde)* to quake;
bei jds. Anblick ~ to tremble before s. o.
erzkonservativ ultraconservative, unreconstructed *(US)*, spread-eagle *(US)*.
Erzkonservativer old fog(e)y, spread-eagle *(US)*, ultraconservative.
Erz|lagerstätte mineral deposit, ore bed; ~**nest** pocket.
erzogen, gut well-bred, well brought up; **schlecht** ~ unmannered, vulgar, unrefined.
Erz|reaktionär reactionary blimp, spread-eagle *(US)*; ~**schurke** unredeemed blackguard, precious rascal; ~**schwindel** rank swindle.
erzürnen, j. to make s. o. angry, to irritate; **sich über jds. Benehmen** ~ to get annoyed about s. one's behaviour.
erzwingbar enforceable.
erzwingen to obtain by force;
Aussage ~ to wring (wrest) a confession; **sich den Eintritt in ein Haus** ~ to force one's way into a house; **Entscheidung** ~ to force an issue; **Geständnis** ~ to extort a confession; **jds. Rücktritt** ~ to force s. o. to resign; **Versprechen von jem.** ~ to wring a promise from s. o.; **Vertragsleistungen** ~ to enforce a contract; **Zahlung** ~ to enforce payment; **Zugeständnis von jem.** ~ to wring a concession of s. o.
Erzwingung der Gesetzesanwendung law enforcement.
Erzwingungs|geld administrative fine; ~**haft** punitive retention; ~**recht** compulsory powers.
erzwungen forced;
~**es Geständnis** forced confession; ~**es Lächeln** artificial (unnatural) smile; ~**er Rücktritt** involuntary resignation.
Esel donkey, ass, *(fig.)* duffer, fool, goose;
bepackt wie ein ~ loaded like a donkey; **dumm wie ein** ~ as stupid as an ass; **störrisch wie ein** ~ stubborn (obstinate) as a mule;
sich wie ein ~ **aufführen** to make an ass of o. s.;
den ~ **führt man nur einmal aufs Eis** once bitten twice shy; **ein** ~ **schimpft den anderen Langohr** the pot calls the kettle black; **wenn man den** ~ **nennt, kommt er schon gerennt** talk of the devil and he will appear.
Esels|brücke *(sl.)* mule, trot, crib *(Br.)*, pony *(US)*, horse *(US sl.)*; ~**brücke benutzen** to side a pony *(sl.)*; ~**ohr** dog's ear, crease; ~**ohr in eine Seite machen** to fold down a corner of a page, to dogs-ear a page; ~**rücken** *(Bahn)* hump; **jem. einen** ~**tritt geben** to hit a man when he is down.
Eskadron *(mil.)* squadron.
Eskalation escalation;
~ **der Kosten** escalation of costs.

Eskalationsdrohung escalation threat.
eskalieren to escalate;
konventionellen Krieg in einen Atomkrieg ~ lassen to escalate conventional war into nuclear warfare.
eskalierende Reglementierung der Wirtschaft escalating business regulation.
Eskalierung der Verteidigungslasten escalation of defense (defence, *Br.*) costs.
Eskompt discount.
Eskorte escort, convoy;
~fahrer outrider.
eskortieren to escort, to convoy.
Esprit wit, sprightliness, salt, esprit;
~ haben to have a ready wit.
Essay essay.
eßbar fit to eat, eatable, edible.
Eßbares finden, etw. to find s. th. to eat.
Eßbesteck table cutlery, flatware *(US)*.
Esse chimney, flue.
Eßecke dining alcove (recess).
Essen food, victuals, fare, grub, *(Festessen)* banquet, complimentary (gala) dinner;
nach dem ~ post-prandial; **zum ~ eingeladen** asked out for dinner;
kostenlos ausgegebenes ~ welfare meal; **gutes ~** good food; **kümmerliches ~** meagre meal; **miserables ~** lousy dinner *(coll.)*; **offizielles ~** formal dinner; **schickes ~** fine dinner; **vorzügliches ~** slap-up dinner;
~ à la carte table d'hôte lunch;
~ über Spesen abrechnen to justify a lunch as business expense; **~ mit Kaffee abschließen** to top off a dinner with coffee; **das ~ auftragen** to dish up the dinner; **zum ~ ausführen** to ask (take) out to dinner; **j. zu einem feudalen ~ ausführen** to take s. o. to a swell dinner party; **kostenlos ~ ausgeben** to furnish meals without charge; **j. zum ~ dabehalten** to keep s. o. for dinner; **jem. zum ~ einladen** to invite (treat) s. o. to dinner; **~ im Kreis der Familie einnehmen** to dine in private; **~ fassen** *(mil.)* to join the chow line *(US)*, to queue up for one's meal *(Br.)*; **~ fertigmachen** to prepare the dinner; **~ geben** to give a dinner; **anläßlich jds. Anwesenheit ein ~ geben** to hold a banquet in hono(u)r of s. one's arrival; **zu jds. Ehren ein ~ geben** to give s. o. a testimonial dinner; **zum ~ gehen** to proceed to the dining room; **nicht genug zum ~ haben** not to have enough to eat, to be on short commons *(Br.)*; **an seinem ~ herumnörgeln** to grumble about one's food; **im ~ herumstochern** to nibble (pick) at one's food; **auf das ~ Wert legen** to keep a good table; **am ~ sparen** to stint o. s. in food; **Ansprüche an sein ~ stellen** to be dainty about one's food; **sein ~ rasch vertilgen** to soon dispatch one's dinner; **~ vorbereiten** to make preparations for a meal; **mit jds. ~ vorliebnehmen** to take pot-luck with s. o.; **mit einem kümmerlichen ~ vorliebnehmen** to put up with a bad fare; **nach dem ~ einzunehmen** to be taken after meals;
nach dem ~ sollst Du ruhn oder tausend Schritte tun after dinner sit a while, after supper walk a while.
essen to eat;
zu Abend ~ to have supper; **im Abonnement ~** to buy meal tickets (luncheon vouchers); **auswärts ~** to eat (board, dine) out; **Diät ~ müssen** to be on a diet; **sich dick und rund ~** to eat one's fill; **gern und reichlich ~** to play a good knife and fork; **gierig ~** to gobble (shovel) one's food; **gut ~** to have a good feed; **jem. die Haare vom Kopf ~** to eat s. o. out of house and home; **einen Happen ~** to have a quick meal; **nach der Karte ~** to eat à la carte; **Kleinigkeit ~** to have a bite; **mit dem großen Löffel ~** to eat high on the hog; **zu Mittag ~** to [have] lunch; **fast nichts ~** to eat next to nothing; **im Restaurant ~** to take one's meals in a restaurant; **wie ein Scheunendrescher ~** to eat one's head off *(coll.)*; **Teller leer ~** to clear one's plate; **tüchtig ~** to eat heartily; **umsonst ~** to grub for nix; **ununterbrochen ~** to be always on the eat *(fam.)*; **vorzüglich ~** to feed at the high table; **warm ~** to have a warm meal; **wie ein Wolf ~** to eat like a wolf;
nicht genug zu ~ haben to be on short commons; **nicht allein ~ können** to be helpless to feed o. s.
Essenholer *(mil.)* ration carrier.
Essens|aufzug dinner (service) lift, plate hoist; **~ausgabe** distribution of rations; **~bon** food stamp benefit; **~entzug** deprivation of food; **solide ~grundlage** square (solid) meal; **~korb** hamper; **~kübel** food bucket; **~marke** meal (bread, *US*) ticket, meal (luncheon) voucher; **~pause** lunch break; **~träger** dining bucket (pail, *US*); **~zuschuß** meal (lunch) allowance.
Essenz eines Buches essence of a book.
Esser eater;
schlechter ~ poor knife; **starker ~** big feeder;
schwacher ~ sein to eat lightly.
Eß|geschirr plates and dishes, table ware, *(mil.)* mess gear; **~gewohnheiten** appetites.
Essig vinegar;
mit unseren Plänen ist es jetzt ~ our plans are ending in smoke.
Eß|lokal eatery, eating house; **~möglichkeiten** eating facilities; **~napf** *(mil.)* messtin; **~paket** food package; **~raum** dining room; **~tisch** dining table; **~waren** provisions, victuals, eatables, food, comestibles.
Eßzimmer dining room;
~schrank sideboard; **~stuhl** dining chair; **~tisch** dining table.
Estrade estrade, dais.
Estrich rubble floor.
etablieren, sich to establish o. s., to set up shop for o. s., to start a business; **j. ~** to start s. o. in business, to set up s. o. in trade; **sich in einem Zimmer ~** to settle down in a room.
etabliert, fest entrenched;
sich im neuen Haus gut ~ haben to be comfortably established in one's new house; **~ sein** to belong to the establishment.
Etablierung establishment, setting-up, setup, settlement.
Etablissement joint *(US sl.)*, penny gaff *(Br.)*, dive;
anrüchiges ~ house of ill fame.
Etage floor, flat, story storey;
erste ~ first floor *(Br.)*, second story *(US)*; **obere ~** upper storey *(Br.)*;
erste ~ bewohnen to live on the first (second, *US*) floor; **j. auf der obersten ~ unterbringen** to perch s. o. at the top of the house.
Etagen|heizung multiple heating; **~leiter** *(Kaufhaus)* shopwalker; **~miete** apartment rent *(US)*; **~schlüssel** latchkey; **~wohnhaus** block of flats *(Br.)*, apartment building; **~wohnung** [self-contained] flat *(Br.)*, apartment *(US)*; **kleine ~wohnung** maisonette; **~wohnung mit Bedienung** service flat *(Br.)*.
Etappe phase, period, *(mil.)* rear, base, lines of communication, communication zone, *(Teilstrecke)* stage;
in der ~ leben to be behind the lines; **in bequemen ~n reisen** to travel by easy stages; **Verletzte in die ~ zurückbringen** to remove casualties into the rear; **Strecke in ~n zurücklegen** to cover a distance in stages.
Etappen|gebiet line of communications area, communications zone; **~lazarett** base hospital, clearing station; **~ort** field base; **~schwein** base wallah *(Br., sl.)*.
etappenweise by stages.
Etat budget, estimates, supplies;
außer ~ extra-budgetary; **in den ~ eingestellt, im ~ vorgesehen** provided for in the budget, budgeted; **zum (nicht zum) ordentlichen ~ gehörig** above (below) the line *(Br.)*;
den Produktionsschwankungen angepaßter ~ variable budget; **für mehrere Jahre aufgestellter (festgelegter) ~** fixed budget; **ausgeglichener ~** balanced budget; **nicht ausgeglichener ~** adverse (unbalanced) budget; **ausgeweiteter ~** expansionary budget; **außerordentlicher ~** extraordinary (double) budget; **mit Wahlgeschenken belasteter ~** give-away budget; **beweglicher ~** supplies-approved budget; **bewilligter ~** supplies *(Br.)*; **defizitärer ~** adverse budget; **elastischer ~** flexible budget; **für mehrere Jahre festgesetzter ~** fixed budget; **durch regelmäßige Einnahmen gedeckter ~** balanced budget; **genehmigter ~** approved budget; **Ist-~** performance (program(me)) budget; **knapper ~** tight budget; **leichtgewichtiger ~** easy budget; **normaler ~** business-as-usual budget; **ordentlicher ~** ordinary budget; **städtischer ~** city budget; **starrer ~** static budget; **unausgeglichener ~** adverse (unbalanced) budget; **unzureichender ~** shoestring budget; **veränderlicher ~** sliding budget; **veranschlagter ~** estimates, proposed budget; **vorläufiger ~** tentative budget;
~ der Europäischen Gemeinschaft community budget; **zusammengesetzte ~s einer Gesellschaft** overall company budgets;
gesamten ~ ablehnen to throw out the whole budget; **~ annehmen** to pass the budget; **~ anreichern (auffüllen)** to fatten a budget; **~ aufstellen** to draw up (prepare) the budget, to make a statement (budget), to prepare (make up) the estimates *(Br.)*; **regelrechten ~ aufstellen und danach leben** to keep an actual budget; **~ ausgleichen** to balance the budget; **~ wieder ausgleichen** to set the budget on its feet again; **~ der Gemeinden belasten** to burden the finances of the communities; **~ beraten** to debate on the budget; **~ beschneiden** to prune a budget; **~ bewilligen** to vote the appropriation (supplies, estimates, *Br.*); **aus dem städtischen ~ bezahlen** to pay out of the town's funds;

ganzen ~ **durcheinanderbringen** to throw a budget out of gear; ~ **einbringen** to introduce (present) the budget, to bring in the estimates *(Br.)*; **für Verabschiedung des ~s eintreten** to vote that the budget be accepted; **angespannten ~ entlasten** to ease the stress on the budget; ~ **festsetzen** to fix the budget; ~ **genehmigen** to vote the appropriation, to vote the budget (the estimates, *Br.*); ~ **ausgeglichen halten** to keep the budget in line; ~ **das ganze Jahr kontrollieren** to work around the year on the budget; **übersetzten ~ kürzen** to trim fat from one's budget; **mit einem knappen ~ auskommen müssen** to run a tight budget, to work on a shoestring budget; **für den ~ verantwortlich sein** to run the nation's budget; ~ **auf Streichungsmöglichkeiten überprüfen** to scan a budget for possible cutbacks; ~ **überschreiten** to exceed (break) one's budget, to exceed one's estimate; **festgesetzten ~ nicht überschreiten, seinen ~ nicht überziehen** to hold the budget line, to live within one's budget; **seinen ~ vergrößern** to increase one's expenses; **in einem ~ verstecken** to bury in a budget; ~ **verwalten** to have charge of a budget; ~ **vorlegen** to introduce (present) the budget, to bring in the estimates *(Br.)*; **Einsparungen im ~ zugunsten privater Investitionen vornehmen** to trim government's own budget, to make room for private investments; ~ **zurückführen** to rein back a budget; ~ **zusammenstreichen** to slash a budget.

etatisieren to budget for, to include in the budget;
Posten ~ to enter an amount in the budget.

etatisiert provided for in the budget;
nicht ~ not included in the budget.

Etatisierung budgeting.

Etatisierungs|methode budgeting method; **~verfahren** budgeting procedure; **~verfahren vom Ausgangspunkt** zero-base budgeting process.

Etats|abstrich budget cut; **~abweichung** budget variance; **~änderung** budget changes; **~anforderung** budget request; **~anforderungen beschneiden** to prune budget requests; **~annahme** budget grant; **~ansatz** draft budget, forward projection budget, budget estimates; **in die Zukunft projektierter ~ansatz** forward projection budget; **~ansatz zurückführen** to rein back a budget; **~ansätze nicht erreichen** to fall below budget figures; **~anteil** slice of a budget; **nicht verbrauchte ~anteile** continuing appropriation; **~aufschlüsselung** breakdown of a budget; **~aufstellung** making up (preparation of) a budget; **~ausgleich** budgetary balance, balancing of the budget, budget balancing (equilibrium, *Br.*); **antizyklischer ~ausgleich** cyclical budgeting; **~aussichten** budget outlook; **wöchentlicher ~ausweis** week's budget statement; **~ausweitung** budget busting; **~bedürfnisse** budget (budgetary) needs; **beträchtliche ~belastung** heavy burden on the budget; **~beratung** budget debate (session, trading, *US*), budgetary negotiations; **~beschränkungen** budgetary restraints; **~bewilligung** budget grant, budgetary appropriation, voting the estimates *(Br.)*; **monatliche ~bewilligung** monthly supply vote.

etatsbewußt budget-minded.

Etats|bewußtsein budget-mindedness; **~debatte durchführen** to debate on the budget.

Etatsdefizit adverse budget, budget (budgetary) deficit;
aus der Vollbeschäftigungspolitik entstandene ~e full employment budget deficits;
~ **ausgleichen** to balance an adverse budget; ~ **herbeiführen** to put the budget in the red *(coll.)*; **sich ein großes ~ leisten** to run a large budget deficit.

Etats|druck budget squeeze; **~einnahmen** budgetary receipts; **~einsparungen** budget savings, budgetary economies; **~entwurf** budgetary estimates, proposed budget; **~erfahrung** budgetary experience; **ausweitende ~ergänzung** budget-busting addition; **~fachmann** budget analyst; **~fehlbetrag** fiscal (budgetary) deficit, adverse budget; **~frage** budgetary question; **~genehmigung** budget approval; **~höchstgrenze festsetzen** to fix an extreme limit for a budget; **~jahr** budget[ary] year, *(Statistik)* fiscal (financial) year; **~kontrolle** budgetary control; **~kosten** budgetary costs; **~kürzung** budget cut[ting] (slash); **~kürzung vornehmen** to prune a budget; **~lage** budgetary position.

etatsmäßig budgetary, according to the budget, in accordance with the estimates, *(Beamtenstelle)* established, permanent;
nicht ~ extrabudgetary.

Etats|maßnahmen budgetary practices; **~mißbrauch** budget dissavings.

Etatsmittel budgetary means, voted (budget) funds;
noch nicht ausgegebene und noch nicht verplante ~ unencumbered allotment; **noch nicht ausgegebene, jedoch verplante ~** unexpended appropriation; **bewilligte ~** budget grant, budgetary appropriations; **noch zur Verfügung stehende (nicht verbrauchte) ~** unallotted appropriations, surplus fund; **nicht verbrauchte ~** surplus fund; **frei verfügbare ~** unapplied cash;
~ **nicht voll ausschöpfen** to underspend on the budget; ~ **zuteilen** to apportion budget funds;
~bereitstellung budgetary appropriation.

Etats|nachtrag supplementary budget (estimate, *Br.*); **~planung** budget estimates, budgeting; **antizyklische ~planung** cyclical budgeting.

Etatspolitik, langfristige long-range budgeting; **restriktive ~** restrictive budget policy; **jeden Einzelposten grundsätzlich zur Diskussion stellende ~** zero-base budgeting approach;
die bisher expansionsbedingte ~ auf einen scharf restriktiven Kurs umstellen to change government's budgetary policies sharply from the expansive to the restrictive.

Etats|posten item included in the budget, budgetary item; **ordentlicher ~posten** item above the line *(Br.)*; **Inlandsausgaben im ~rahmen halten** to hold domestic spending within the budgetary plan; **~recht** budget law *(US)*.

etatsrechtlich budgetary;
~ **genehmigt sein** to fall within the budget;
~e Bestimmungen budgetary regulations.

Etats|rede budget speech (message, statement); **~rede halten** to open the budget; **~schwierigkeiten** budget (budgetary) difficulties (troubles); **~spezialist** budget man (specialist) budgeteer; **~streichungen** budget slashing; **~streichungen durchführen** to cut public expenditures; **~stärke** *(mil.)* authorized strength; **~summe** total [sum] of a statement, *(Werbung)* billing; **~system** budgetary system; **mittelfristiges ~system** medium-term budgetary framework.

Etatstitel budget item (heading);
~ **zur Zahlung anweisen** to pass an account for payment; ~ **auflösen** to deobligate.

Etats|überschreitung excess of the budget estimates *(Br.)*; **~überschreitung vermeiden** to hold the budget line; **~überschuß** budget surplus, carryover funds; **noch nicht ausgegebener, jedoch bereits verplanter ~überschuß** unexpended balance; **~umfang endgültig festlegen** to wrench a budget into final shape; **~verabschiedung** budget resolution; **~veränderung** budget shift; **~verschiebungen** budgetary operations; **~verwalter** budget keeper; **~verwaltung** budget keeping; **~voranschlag** budgetary estimate, budget worksheet *(US)*; **~voranschlag vornehmen** to approve (pass) the budget, to vote the estimates *(Br.)*; **~vorbereitung** budgetary preparation; **~vorlage** application request; **~vorschlag** budget proposal; **~vorschlag annehmen** to approve the budget; **~ziel** budget[ary] target; **~zuweisung** budget[ary] allocation.

etepetete namby-pamby, niminy-piminy, very particular.

Ethik morals, moral science, morality.

ethisch|e Erziehungsgrundlage ethical basis for education; **~e Grundsätze** ethics; **~e Werbung** ethical advertising.

Ethos moral sense;
hohes ~ haben to rise to a higher ethical standard.

Etikett label, tally, ticket, docket, *(Anhänger)* tag, *(Preiszettel)* price tag, *(Warenzeichen)* trademark, stamp, brand;
~ **zum Aufkleben** adhesive label;
gummiertes ~ stick-on label, sticker *(US)*;
mit ~ versehen to label, to ticket, to docket, to tag.

Etikette etiquette, decorum, ceremonial;
streng nach der ~ de rigueur;
auf ~ halten to stand on ceremony; **gegen die ~ verstoßen** to commit a breach of etiquette.

Etikethalter tag fastener.

etikettieren to label, to ticket, to tag, to tally, to docket;
neu ~ to relabel.

Etikettiermaschine labelling machine.

Etikettierung labelling;
aufklärende ~ informative labelling; **übliche ~** descriptive labelling.

etwa about, approximately, nearly, perchance.

etwas entfernt some way off.

etymologische Bedeutung von Wörtern studieren to study the derivation of words.

Eugenik eugenics.

Eulen nach Athen tragen to carry coals to Newcastle, to throw water into the Thames, to hold a candle to the sun.

euphorisch zu werden beginnen to take off on a visionary cloud.

Euroanleihemarkt Eurobond market;
seine ersten Einsichten in den ~ weiter vertiefen to develop its initial penetration of the primary Eurobond Market.

Eurodollar Eurodollar;
~**anleihe** Eurodollar bond, Eurocurrency loan; ~**finanzierung** Eurocurrency finance; ~**markt** Eurocurrency (Eurodollar) market; ~**marktsätze** Eurocurrency money market rates; ~**verschuldung** Eurodollar borrowings.
Eurogeldmarkt Eurocurrencies;
~**geschäfte** Eurocurrency transactions (business); ~**zinssatz** interbank rate.
Euro|kapitalmarkt Eurobond market; ~**kommunismus** Eurocommunism; ~**konsortialgeschäft** syndicated Eurocredit sector; ~**krat** Eurocrat; ~**kredit** Eurocredit; ~**kreditgeschäft** Eurocredit business; ~**kreditmarkt** Eurocredit market.
Europa, in ~ stationiert European-based;
~**gedanke** European idea; ~**handel** continental trade *(Br.)*.
Europäisch|es Atomforschungszentrum European Nuclear Research Centre; ~**e Atomgemeinschaft** European Atomic Energy Community; ~**er Ausrüstungs- und Garantiefonds für die Landwirtschaft** European Agricultural Equipment and Guarantee Fund; ~**e Binnentransportorganisation** Central Inland Transport Organization; ~**e Bodenkarte** European Soil Charter; ~**er Börsenindex** Eurosyndicate index; ~**er Entwicklungsfonds** European Development Fund; ~**e Exekutive** European executive bodies; ~**e Firmentransportorganisation** European Central Inland Transport Organization; ~**er Fonds** European Fund (EF); ~**er Fonds für währungspolitische Zusammenarbeit** European Monetary Cooperation Fund; ~**es Forschungsinstitut für Raumordnung und Städteplanung** European Research Institute for Regional and Urban Planning; ~**e Freihandelszone** European Free Trade Association, EFTA; ~**es Fürsorgeabkommen** European Convention on Social and Medical Assistance; ~**e Gemeinschaft** European Community; ~**e Gemeinschaft für Kohle und Stahl** European Coal and Steel Community; **der ~en Gemeinschaftsorganisation angehören** to enter into the European Communities; ~**e Gemeinschaftsregion** Common Market territory; ~**er Gerichtshof** European Court of Justice; ~**er Gerichtshof für Menschenrechte** European Court of Human Rights; ~**e Gesellschaft für die Finanzierung von Eisenbahnmaterial** European Company for the Financing of Railway Rolling Stock; ~**es Gleichgewicht** European balance of power; ~**e Investitionsbank** European Investment Bank; ~**es Jugendzentrum** European Youth Center; ~**e Kernenergieagentur** European Nuclear Energy Agency (ENEA); ~**es Komitee für Normung** European Committee for Coordination of Standards; ~**e Kommission** European Commission; ~**e Kommission für Menschenrechte** European Commission for Human Rights; ~**e Kommunalkonferenz** European Conference of Local Authorities; ~**es Kulturabkommen** European Cultural Convention; ~**e Marktordnung** European Market regulations; ~**e Menschenrechtskommission** European Convention on Human Rights; ~**es Niederlassungsabkommen** European Convention on Establishment; ~**e Organisation für Kernforschung** European Organization for Nuclear Research; ~**e Organisation von Marktforschungsinstituten** European Society for Opinion and Marketing Research (ESOMAR); ~**e Organisation für Raumforschung** European Space Research Organization (ESTEC); ~**e Organisation zur Sicherung der Luftfahrt** European Organization for the Safety of Air Navigation; ~**e Organisation für Wirtschaftliche Zusammenarbeit** Organization for European Economic Cooperation (OEEC); ~**es Parlament** European Parliament; ~**e Patentorganisation** European Patent Organization; ~**es Patentregister** European Register of Patents; ~**es Patentübereinkommen** European Patent Convention; ~**e Produktivitätszentrale** European Productivity Agency; ~**e Raumordnungsministerkonferenz** European Conference of Regional Planning Ministers; ~**e Rechnungseinheit** European Unit of Account; ~**es Rundfunkabkommen** European Broadcasting Agreement; ~**er Sozialfonds** European Social Fund; ~**e Transportministerkonferenz** European Conference of Ministers of Transport; ~**es Übereinkommen über die obligatorische Haftpflichtversicherung für Kraftfahrzeuge** European Convention on compulsory insurance against civil liability in respect of motor vehicles; ~**es Übereinkommen über den Personenverkehr** European Agreement on the Movement of Persons; ~**e Verkehrsministerkonferenz** European Conference of Ministers of Transport; ~**e Verteidigungsgemeinschaft** European Defence Community; ~**es Währungsabkommen** European Monetary Agreement; **künstliche ~e Währungseinheit** European Monetary Combined Unit (EURCO); ~**es Währungssystem** European Monetary System; ~**er Währungsverbund** European currency float; ~**e Weltraumorganisation** European Space Agency; ~**es Wiederaufbauprogramm** European Recovery Program(me) (ERP); ~**e Wirtschaftsgemeinschaft** European Economic Community, Euromarket, European Common Market *(Br.)*; ~**e Wirtschaftskommission** Economic Commission for Europe; ~**er Wirtschaftsrat** European Economic Council; ~**e Wirtschafts- und Währungsunion** European Economic and Monetary Union; ~**e Zahlungsunion** European Payments Union (ECMU); ~**es Zentrum für Weltraumtechnik** European Space Technology Centre; ~**es Zentrum für mittelfristige Wettervorhersage** European Centre for Medium-Range Weather Forecasts; ~**e Zivilluftfahrtorganisation** European Civil Aviation Conference; ~**e Zollunion** European Customs Union.
europäisches Zukunftsbild entwerfen to envisage a Europe of the future.
europäisieren to Europeanize, to westernize.
Europäisierung Europeanization, westernization.
Europa|parlament European Assembly; ~**politik** European policy; ~**rat** Council of Europe; ~**recht** European law; ~**reise** tour of the continent; **längere ~reise** extended trip to Europe (continental tour, *Br.*); ~**reise machen** to travel on the Continent *(Br.)*; ~**union** European Union.
Euroscheck Eurocheque *(Br.)*;
~**karte** Eurocard, check guarantee card *(US)*; ~**system** Eurocheque scheme; ~**verrechnungszentrale** Eurocheque clearing centre.
Eurovisionssendung Eurovision transmission.
Euthanasie euthanasia, mercy killing.
evakuieren, Kinder aufs Land to evacuate children to the country; **Stadt ~** to evacuate a town.
evakuiert displaced, evacuated.
Evakuierter evacuee, displaced person.
Evakuierung evacuation.
Evakuierungs|gebiet evacuation zone (area); ~**plan** evacuation plan; ~**probe** evacuation test.
evangelisch protestant.
Evangelium *(fig.)* gospel.
Eventual|anspruch contingent claim; ~**antrag** secondary motion; ~**fall** contingency; **für jeden ~fall gerüstet sein** to be ready for all eventualities; ~**fonds** contingency fund; ~**forderung** contingent claim; ~**haftung** contingent liability.
Eventualität possible event, eventuality, contingency;
für alle ~en gerüstet provided for all eventualities;
alle ~en berücksichtigen to allow for all possibilities; **für alle ~en Vorsorge treffen** to provide for emergency.
Eventual|kosten contingent charge (cost); ~**reserve** contingent (contingency) reserve; ~**verbindlichkeiten** *(Bilanz)* contingencies, [reserve for] contingent liabilities *(Br.)*, contingent (indirect, secondary, *US*) liabilities; ~**verpflichtung** cautionary obligation, contingent (secondary, *US*) liability.
eventuell contingent, possible, *(notfalls)* if necessary, should the occasion arise;
~**e Änderungen** possible changes; **gegen ~e Unfälle versichern** to insure against possible accidents; ~**e Verluste** possible losses.
EWG Vertrag Treaty of Rome.
ewig eternal, lasting, timeless, never-ending;
~ **gestrig** ultrareactionary, unreconstructed *(US)*;
~ **seine Meinung ändern** to be always chopping and changing;
~ **dauern** to take ages; ~ **fortleben** to last for ever; ~ **jammern** to be ever grumbling; **jem. ~ dankbar sein** to be eternally grateful to s. o.; ~ **schade sein** to be too bad; **jem. ~ leid tun** to be terrible sorry for it;
~**e Beschwerden** everlasting complaints; ~**es Einerlei** unending monotony; ~**e Freundschaft** eternal friendship; ~**er Friede** perpetual peace; ~**es Geschwätz** eternal chatter *(coll.)*; **in die ~en Jagdgründe eingehen** to go west; ~**er Kalender** perpetual calendar; ~**es Leben** eternal life; ~**e Neutralität** perpetual neutrality; ~**e Rente** perpetual annuity, perpetuity; **zur ~en Ruhe eingehen** to be laid to rest; ~**er Student** perpetual student; ~ **und drei Tage** for ever and a day; **seit ~en Zeiten** from time immemorial.
Ewiggestriger ultrareactionary.
Ewigkeit eternity, perpetuity;
seit einer ~ for donkey's years *(Br., fam.)*;
~ **dauern** to take ages; **j. eine ~ warten lassen** to keep s. o. waiting for an eternity.
exakt exact, accurate, by the square;
~**e Beschreibung** precise description; ~**e Übersetzung** close (accurate) translation.

Exaktheit exactness, accuracy.
exaltiert eccentric, exalted, uplifted, extravagant;
~ **über etw. sprechen** to gush about s. th., to talk extravagantly; ~**es Benehmen** exalted behavio(u)r.
Examen examination, exam *(fam.)*;
mit abgeschlossenem ~ graduated;
geradezu lächerliches ~ farcial examination; **mündliches** ~ oral (viva voce) examination; **nachgeholtes** ~ make-up *(US)*; **schriftliches** ~ written examination; **schweres** ~ hard examination; **ziemlich schweres** ~ stiffish examination; **unerwartetes** ~ pot test *(sl.)*;
~ **abhalten** to hold an examination; ~ **ablegen** to go in (sit for) an examination; **sein** ~ **mit Eins abschließen** to obtain first-class hono(u)rs; **sein** ~ **bestehen** to pass one's examination, to get through; ~ **mit Auszeichnung bestehen** to get a double first; ~ **glänzend bestehen** to do brilliantly at an examination, to floor a paper *(Br., fam.)*; ~ **nicht bestehen** to fail (flunk, *US*) in an examination; **schriftliches** ~ **bestehen** to pass the written examination; **für ein** ~ **büffeln (ochsen)** to mug up for an examination *(Br.)*; **in einem** ~ **durchfallen** to fail, to go down (flunk, *US*) in an examination; **bei einem** ~ **gerade noch durchrutschen** to shave through an examination; **ins** ~ **gehen** to go in (sit for) an examination, to go up for one's examination *(Br.)*; **sich zu einem** ~ **melden** to apply for admission to (enter for) an examination; **sich erneut zu einem** ~ **melden** to reenter an examination; **in einem** ~ **pfuschen** to copy during an examination, to cheat in an examination; **vor einem** ~ **stehen** to be in for an examination; **in ein** ~ **steigen, sich einem** ~ **unterziehen** to go in for an examination; ~ **um ein Jahr verschieben** to degrade *(Cambridge University)*; **sich auf ein** ~ **vorbereiten** to study (prepare, read) for an examination; **zu einem** ~ **zugelassen werden** to be admitted to sit for an examination.
Examensangst exam fever.
Examensarbeit paper;
gerade noch durchgehende ~ paper just on the line;
seine ~ **abgeben** to give in one's paper;
bei ~**en grundsätzlich betrügen** to make a practice of cheating at examinations.
Examens|aufgabe paper, test; ~**aufgaben bekanntgeben** to give out the examination papers; ~**ausschuß** board of examiners, examining body; ~**ergebnis** examination result; ~**fächer** examination schools; ~**frage** examination question; **alle** ~**fragen beantworten** *(fam.)* to clear (floor, *Br., fam.*) a paper; ~**gebühr** examination fee; **Prüfling von den** ~**gebühren befreien** to remit a candidate's examination fees; ~**kandidat** examinee, finalist; ~**leistungen** examination performance; ~**leiter** chief examiner; ~**methode** examination technique; ~**nachweis** examination qualification; ~**noten** examination marks; **gute** ~**note erhalten** to get a passing grade; ~**semester** term for examination; ~**versuch riskieren** to have a shy at an examination; ~**voraussetzungen** qualification for an examination; ~**vorschriften** examination requirements.
examinieren to examine, to scrutinize, to investigate;
j. ~ to question s. o. closely.
exekutieren *(Börse)* to sell out against, to execute under the rules, *(Schuldner)* to distrain upon, *(Verbrecher)* to execute.
Exekution execution, *(Börse)* buying in, selling out, forced realization.
Exekutions|befehl death warrant; ~**kauf** *(Börse)* forced realization, buying in *(Br.)*, buying in (under the rules *US*); ~**kommando** firing squad (party); **dem** ~**kommando überstellen** to deliver over to execution; ~**verkauf** forced sale, selling out; ~**verkauf gegen j. durchführen** to sell out against s. o.
exekutiv executory.
Exekutiv|aufgaben, ~**funktionen** executive functions; ~**ausschuß** executive committee.
Exekutive Executive [Branch], executive authority (power), law enforcement.
Exekutiv|gewalt executive power; ~**organ** executive body, law enforcement officer; ~**rat** *(EG)* executive council.
Exempel example;
~ **an jem. statuieren** to make an example of s. o.
Exemplar *(Buch)* copy, exemplar, *(Muster)* pattern, sample, specimen, *(Urkunde)* set, *(Zeitung)* number;
altes ~ back number; **maßgebliches** ~ master copy; **nichtverkaufte** ~**e** returns, unsold copies, dead stock; **seltenes** ~ rare specimen; **mit dem Original genau übereinstimmendes** ~ diplomatic copy; **überschüssige** ~**e** overrun; **unverkaufte** ~**e** unsold copies, dead stock; **noch vorhandene** ~**e** copies still on hand;
~ **in Großformat** bulky copy; ~ **minderer Qualität** poor copy; **schönstes** ~ **in einer Sammlung** finest piece in a collection; **nur 1000** ~**e drucken** to print only 1000 copies of a book; **in drei** ~**en ausgestellt sein** *(Wechsel)* to be drawn in sets of three.
exemplarisch exemplary, standard, model;
~**e Strafe** exemplary punishment.
Exequatur exequatur;
~ **erteilen** to grant the exequatur; ~ **zurückziehen** to revoke the exequatur.
Exerzieren drill.
exerzieren to drill.
Exerzier|munition dummy ammunition; ~**patrone** dummy cartridge; ~**platz** parade ground, the square *(fam.)*; ~**reglement** drill regulations (book); ~**schritt** goose step.
Exhibitionismus exhibitionism, indecent exposure.
Exhibitionist exhibitionist.
exhumieren to exhume, to disentomb, to disinter, to unbury, to unearth.
Exhumierung disentombment, disinterment, exhumation.
Exhumierungserlaubnis permission to dispose of a body.
Exil exile, banishment;
ins ~ **gehen** to go into exile, to go into banishment; **ins** ~ **schicken** to exile;
~**regierung** government in exile, exile government; ~**regierung bilden** to set up a government in exile.
existent in being.
Existenz existence, being, subsistence, living, livelihood;
bedauernswerte ~ wretch; **bescheidene** ~ modicum; **dunkle** ~**en** shady individuals; **gescheiterte** ~**en** failures, wreckage; **gesicherte** ~ secure existence; **nackte** ~ bare life; **unsichere** ~ hand-to-mouth existence; **verkrachte** ~ shipwrecked person, failure in life; **zweifelhafte** ~**en** shady individuals (characters); **sich eine** ~ **aufbauen** to build up an existence; **jds.** ~ **bedrohen** to threaten s. one's very existence; **kümmerliche** ~ **fristen** to make a bare living, to eke out a scanty living; **trostlose** ~ **führen** to live in wretched poverty, to lead a miserable existence; **unsichere** ~ **führen** to make a precarious living; **auskömmliche** ~ **haben** to earn one's livelihood, to have enough to live on; **unsichere** ~ **haben** to make a precarious living; **sich um seine** ~ **Sorgen machen** to fear for one's livelihood; **jem. zu einer** ~ **verhelfen** to start s. o. in business;
~**angst** fear of life; ~**aufbauhilfe** financial rehabilitation; ~**bedingungen** living conditions; ~**berechtigung** right to exist; ~**chance** possibility to exist.
existenzfähig able to exist, *(Betrieb)* paying.
Existenz|frage matter of life and death, matter of subsistence for man; ~**grenzbereich** margin of subsistence.
Existenzgrundlage basis of existence, livelihood;
jem. um seine ~ **bringen** to deprive s. o. of his livelihood; **seine ganze** ~ **verlieren** to lose one's entire subsistence.
Existenz|kampf struggle for existence; ~**lohn** subsistence (living) wages.
Existenzminimum minimum of existence, subsistence level, bread line, living wage;
unter dem ~ below poverty level;
wöchentliches ~ minimum weekly budget;
~ **für eine Familie** family minimum subsistence;
~ **nicht erreichen** to live below the bread line; **nahe am** ~ **leben** to lead a hand-to-mouth existence; ~ **sicherstellen** to procure the bare necessities; ~ **unterschreiten** to live below the minimum standard, to live below the poverty line;
~**zuschuß** family income supplement *(Br.)*.
Existenz|mittel means of existence (support); ~**möglichkeit** possibility to exist; ~**stufe** level of existence; ~**unsicherheit** job insecurity.
existieren to exist, to subsist, to live;
früher ~ to preexist; **gerade so** ~ to earn a bare subsistence; **in jämmerlichen (schrecklichen) Verhältnissen** ~ to live in wretched poverty (circumstances); **knapp** ~ to pick up a scanty livelihood, to earn a bare living; **nicht mehr** ~ to be no more.
existierend existing, living;
nicht mehr ~ off the map *(sl.)*.
exklusiv exclusive, select, *(Wertpapiere)* ex;
~ **berichten** to carry an exclusive story;
~**er Berufszweig** exclusive profession; ~**e Gesellschaft** exclusive social circles, select party; **in** ~**en Gesellschaftskreisen verkehren** to move in exclusive circles; ~**e Veröffentlichung** class publication; ~**e Wohngegend** select part of a city, affluent area, silkstocking ward *(US)*.
Exklusiv|bericht exclusive [report]; ~**bestimmung** exclusive clause; ~**film** exclusive film; ~**interview** exclusive interview.

Exklusivität exclusivity.
Exklusiv|meldung scoop; ~**modell** exclusive model; ~**nachricht** exclusive news; ~**recht** exclusive right; ~**rechte für die Verfilmung** exclusive moving-picture rights; ~**vereinbarung** exclusive dealing; ~**verkauf** exclusive sale; ~**verkaufsrecht** dealer franchise; ~**vertrag** exclusive agreement (contract), tying contract, *(Händler)* exclusive dealer arrangement.
Ex|kommunikation excommunication, curse; ~**kulpation** exculpation.
exkulpieren, sich to exculpate o. s.
Ex|kursion, wissenschaftliche scientific excursion; ~**kursionsteilnehmer** excursionist; ~**libris** bookplate; ~**matrikulation** removal from the register.
exmatrikulieren lassen, sich to take one's name off the books *(Br.)*, to go down.
Ex|minister late minister; ~**mission** evictment, eviction, ejectment, ouster.
Exmissions|auftrag dispossess warrant; ~**verfahren** dispossess proceedings.
exmittieren to eject, to evict, to turn out, to dispossess, to oust, to dislodge, to unlodge.
Exmittierung eviction, ejection, ouster;
faktische ~ constructive eviction;
~ **aus einzelnen Räumen** partial eviction.
exogene Einflüsse extraneous influence.
expandieren to expand, to extend;
langsamer ~ to expand at lower rate.
Expansion expansion, extension, growth;
nicht inflationsbedingte ~ noninflationary growth; **konsumbedingte** ~ consumer expansion; **übermäßige** ~ overexpansion; **wirtschaftliche** ~ business (industrial) expansion;
~ **eines Geschäfts** expansion of a business, company growth; ~ **der Volkswirtschaft** economic growth;
~ **der Wirtschaft fordern** to promote economic expansion.
expansionsbedingt expansionary.
Expansions|bestrebungen expansionist tendencies; ~**bremse** expansion curb.
expansionsdämpfende Politik betreiben to check economic expansion.
Expansions|drang expansionism, expansionist tendencies; ~**engpaß** expansion bottleneck; ~**gebiete** areas for expansion, growth fields; ~**gelände** expansion site; ~**grenze erreicht haben** to come to the end of the growth line; ~**grundlage** basis for expansion; ~**kosten** expansion costs; ~**kraft** expansionary force; **Politik auf einen kräftigen** ~**kurs umstellen** to switch policy to a strongly expansionary line; ~**kurve** expansion path; ~**möglichkeiten** growth potentialities; ~**phase** expansionary phase; ~**politik** expansionism, expansionary (expansionist) policy, policy of expansion; ~**politiker** expansionist; ~**prognose** expansion forecast; ~**programm** expansion program(me); ~**prozeß** process of expansion; ~**rate** rate of expansion, growth rate; ~**tempo** pace of expansion; ~**tendenz** expansionist tendency.
expansiv expansive, expansionist, reflationary;
~**e Geldpolitik** expansive monetary policy.
expatriieren to deprive of citizenship, to expatriate, to exile.
Expatriierung expatriation, deprivation of citizenship.
Expedient copying (forwarding, dispatch, dispatching, shipping, *US*, cargo, *US*) clerk, [post] dispatcher.
expedieren to expedite, to dispatch, to forward, to send [off], to ship *(US)*;
Briefe ~ to send off letters; **j. an einen anderen Ort** ~ to whisk s. o. along to another place.
Expedition expediting, dispatching, forwarding, shipping *(US)*, *(Abteilung)* dispatching office, outward mail (shipping) department, outward mail department *(US)*, *(Forschungsreise)* expedition, progress, *(Zeitung)* office, bureau;
militärische ~ military expedition; **vom Unglück verfolgte** ~ unfortunate expedition; **verhängnisvolle** ~ unlucky expedition;
~ **ausrüsten** to furnish (prepare) an expedition; ~ **leiten** to lead an expedition; **an einer** ~ **teilnehmen** to go on an expedition; ~ **unternehmen** to make an expedition.
Expeditions|abteilung forwarding (mailing, dispatch, shipping, *US*) department; ~**führer sein** to head an expedition; ~**gebühren** forwarding (mailing, shipping, *US*) charges; ~**korps**, ~**kräfte** *(mil.)* expeditionary forces; ~**leiter** conductor of an expedition; ~**truppen** expeditionary forces.
Experiment experiment, test;
gewagtes ~ bold experiment;
~ **durchführen** to [make (try, carry out) an] experiment.
Experimentalfilm experimental film.
experimentell experimental;
~ **bewiesen** proved by experiment;
~ **gewonnene Erkenntnisse** empirical knowledge.
experimentieren to experiment, to experimentalize.
Experimentiertheater fringe theater.
Experte expert, pundit, dabster *(Br.)*, dab;
nach Ansicht der ~**n** according to the experts;
landwirtschaftlicher ~ agricultural expert; **nautischer** ~ marine surveyor; **wissenschaftlicher** ~ professionalist, back-room boy *(coll.)*;
~ **in Steuerfragen** tax expert;
~**n zur Konsultation hinzuziehen** to take expert advice, to call in an expert; ~**e auf einem Gebiet sein** to be an expert on a subject.
Experten|arbeit back-room work; ~**eigenschaft** expert capacity; ~**gremium**, ~**gruppe** panel of experts, learned committee; **hochqualifizierte** ~**gruppe** brains trust; ~**kommission** fact-finding mission; ~**rat** brains trust; ~**stab** professional staff; ~**tum** professionalism.
Expertise expertise, expert's report, survey;
~ **machen** to carry through a survey.
explodieren to explode, to detonate, to blow, to burst, *(fig.)* to blow one's mind, to explode;
vor Wut ~ to explode with rage.
Explosion|des Verkehrswesens traffic explosion; ~ **der Warenpreise** commodity price explosion;
zur ~ **bringen** to explode.
explosionsartiges Ansteigen der Mietpreise rental explosion.
Explosions|druck explosion pressure; ~**gefahr** explosive hazard, *(Erzeugnis)* liability to explode; ~**gemisch** explosive mixture; ~**mittel** exploder; ~**motor** explosion *(Br.)* (internal combustion) engine; ~**pilz** *(Atombombe)* mushroom; ~**schaden** explosion damage.
explosionssicher explosion-proof.
Explosions|versicherung explosion insurance; ~**welle** explosive wave; ~**wirkung** explosive effect.
explosiv explosive.
Explosivstoff, politischer political explosive.
Exponate exhibit goods, exhibits.
Exponent exponent, advocate, champion;
~ **des Kaufwertes** exponent of exchangeable value.
exponieren, sich to lay o. s. open (expose o. s.) to criticism; **sich zu weit** ~ to stick one's neck out *(coll.)*.
exponiert exposed;
in ~**er Lage** in an exposed position, in a precarious situation.
Export exportation, export [trade];
für den ~ **bestimmt** earmarked for exportation;
zur Begleichung von Auslandsschulden dienende ~**e** unrequited exports; **gesteigerte** ~**e** increased exports; **[in]direkte** ~**e** [in]direct exports; **kontingentierte** ~**e** rationed exports; **primärer** ~ primary export; **staatlich subventionierte** ~**e** bounty-fed exports;
~ **drosseln** to curb exports; ~**e erhöhen** to increase (step up) exports; ~ **fördern** to subsidize exports; ~ **kontingentieren** to allocate (fix) export quotas; **für den** ~ **bestimmt sein** to be intended for export (earmarked for exportation); ~ **steigern** to increase exports;
~**abfertigung** export clearance; ~**abgabe** export duty (tax), export levy, tax (levy) on exports.
exportabhängig export-dependent.
Export|abhängigkeit dependence on exports (of foreign trade); ~**absatz** export market; ~**abschluß** export transaction; ~**abschwächung** downtrend of exports; ~**absprache** *(Kartellgesetz)* export agreement; **eingegliederte** ~**abteilung** built-in export department; ~**abwicklungskonto** export settlement account; ~**agent** export broker (agent); ~**akkreditiv** export letter of credit; ~**angebot** exports tender (offer); ~**ankurbelung** boosting of exports; ~**anstieg** rise in exports; **plötzlicher** ~**anstieg** jump in exports; **nachlassende** ~**anstrengungen** weakening export performance; ~**anteil** exports, export share (ratio, content); ~**antrag** application for export; ~**artikel** goods intended for export, exported article (item), *(pl.)* exports; **industrielle** ~**artikel** manufactured exports; ~**auflagen** export requirements; ~**aufstellung** statement of exports; ~**auftrag** export order; ~**auftragsformular** export order form; ~**ausführung** export model; ~**ausgangsquote** initial export quota; ~**aussichten** export prospects; ~**ausstellung** export exhibition; ~**ausweitung** export expansion; ~**-Import-Bank** Export-Import Bank of Washington; **regionaler** ~**basiskoeffizient** economic base ratio; ~**bedarf** export requirements; ~**bedingungen** terms of export, export terms; ~**bedürfnisse** export demands; **freiwilliges** ~**begrenzungsabkommen** volun-

tary export restraint agreement; ~**beihilfe** export bonus; ~**beratungsstelle** export service division; ~**bescheinigung** certificate of clearance outward; ~**beschränkungen** export restrictions; **freiwillige** ~**beschränkungen** voluntary freeze on export; ~**bestimmungen** export regulations; ~**bewilligung** export licence (permit), transire *(Br.)*.

exportbewußt export-inclined (-minded).

Export|bonus export bounty, premium for export; ~**bonusbescheinigung** export bounty certificate; ~**dämpfung** slowdown of exports; ~**daten** export data; ~**defizit** export deficit; ~**deklaration** entry (declaration) outwards *(Br.)*, export declaration *(US)*; ~**devisen** export exchange; ~**dokumente** export documents; ~**einnahmen** export receipts (revenue); ~**embargo** embargo on exports; ~**entwicklung** export trend; **rückläufige** ~**entwicklung** declining exports; ~**erfahrung** export business experience; ~**erfolge** export achievement; **unerwartet hoher** ~**erfolg** export bonanza; ~**erhöhung** rise in exports; ~**erklärung** export declaration *(US)*; ~**erlaubnis** export permit (licence); ~**erleichterungen** export facilities; ~**erlös** proceeds from exports, export income (earnings); ~**erlösverlust** loss on export income; ~**erträge stabil halten** to stabilize export earnings; ~**erweiterung** expansion of exports; ~**erzeugnis** export product.

Exporteur exporter, export merchant;
europäischer ~ indent merchant;
~ **für mehrere Warengattungen** general exporter.

Exportfabrikant direct exporter.

exportfähig exportable.

Export|faktor export earner; ~**feldzug** export drive; ~**finanzierung** export financing (finance), finance of foreign trade.

Exportfinanzierungs|gesellschaft export-financing concern; ~-**instrument** export credit instrument; ~**kredit** advance to finance exports, export financing loan.

Exportfirma export house (firm, company, merchant), exporter, exporting firm;
selbständige ~ export subsidiary.

exportfördernd export-promoting.

Exportförderung export promotion (drive, subsidy), boost to exports.

Exportförderungs|ausschuß export-promotion committee; ~-**gremium** export council; ~**programm** export promotion program(me).

exportfreudig export-minded.

Export|freudigkeit export mindedness; ~**garantie** export guarantee; ~**gemeinschaft** export association *(US)*; ~**gemeinschaften** mixed export groups; ~**genehmigung** export licence (permit, authorization); ~**genehmigung erteilen** to pass (grant) an export licence.

Exportgeschäft export house (merchant), *(einzelnes)* export transaction (business);
für das ~ **herstellen** to produce for export; ~**e machen** to engage in foreign trade; **im** ~ **tätig sein** to be engaged in export; **ein bißchen vom** ~ **verstehen** to have some idea of the export business.

Export|gesellschaft export company (house, merchant); ~**gewinnspanne** export profit margin; ~**großhändler** customer agent; ~**gut**, ~**güter** exports, exported commodities, merchandise intended for export; ~**hafen** port of exportation; ~**handel** export (active) trade; ~**händler** exporter, export dealer, merchant shipper *(Br.)*; **selbständiger** ~**händler** combination export manager *(US)*; ~**haus** export house; ~**hindernis** export bar.

exportieren to export, to sell abroad.

exportindiziertes Wachstum export-led growth.

Export|industrie export industry; ~**intensität** export ratio; ~**interesse** export incentive.

exportinteressiert export-minded.

Export|investitionen investments undertaken to promote exports; ~**kampagne** export drive; ~**kapazität** export capacity; ~**kartell** export cartel; ~**katalog** export catalog(ue); ~**kaufmann** export (indent) merchant, exporter; ~**kaution** export bond; ~**kolli** export packages; ~**kommissionär** export commission house; ~**konjunktur** export boom (trend); ~**konnossement** outward bill of lading; ~**kontingent** export quota; ~**kontingentierung** allocation of export quotas; ~**kontrolle** export control.

Exportkredit export (exporter's) credit, export loan;
festverzinslicher ~ fixed export credit; **über ein halbes Jahr finanzierter** ~ extended credit *(Br.)*;
~**brief** export letter of credit; ~**garantie** export credit guarantee; ~**versicherung** export credit insurance.

Export|land exporting country; ~**lastigkeit** predominance of exports; ~**leistung** export performance; ~**leiter** export manager; ~**lenkung** controlled exports, export control; ~**lieferungen** export shipments (consignments); ~**liste** export list; ~**lizenz** licence outward, federal export licence *(US)*, transire; ~**makler** export broker.

Exportmarkt export market;
auf dem ~ **konkurrenzfähig bleiben** to face world competition for export markets; **Eroberungen auf dem** ~ **machen** to make inroads in the export market.

Export|messe export exhibition; ~**modell** export model; ~**möglichkeit** export possibilities (potential); ~**monopol** export monopoly, foreign staple; ~**müdigkeit** reluctance to export; ~**multiplikator** foreign-trade multiplier; ~**musterlager** export sample store; ~**nachrichten** export intelligence *(Br.)*; ~**neigung** propensity to export; ~**offerte** export tender.

exportorientiert export-oriented;
~ **sein** to be geared to export.

Export|papiere export (shipping) documents; ~**politik** export policy; ~**prämie** export bounty, bonus; ~**prämienschein** export bounty certificate; ~**preis** export price; ~**preisfestsetzung** export pricing; ~**preisindex** price index of exports; **regionale** ~**produktion** base activity; ~**programm** export program(me); ~**publizität** export publicity; ~**quote** export quota (content); **marginale** ~**quote** marginal propensity to export; ~**rechnung** export invoice; **staatliche** ~**regelung** control of exports; ~**rückgang** decline (cut) in exports, fall in exports, export fall, export shortfall, shrinkage of the export trade, drop in export orders; ~**sachbearbeiter** export clerk; ~**schema** export pattern; ~**schlacht** export drive; ~**schrumpfung** shrinkage in the export trade; ~**sendung** export consignment (shipment); **beim Zoll vorzulegende** ~**sendung** manifest freight; ~**sperre** embargo on exports, export ban (prohibition); ~**statistik** export statistics; ~**steigerung** increased exports, rise in exports, export increase; **forcierte** ~**steigerung** export drive; **sich allein auf** ~**steigerungen versteifen** to hitch a ride on exports; ~**steuer** export tax (duty), duty on exports, export subsidy; ~**subvention** subsidy to exports, export subsidy, bounty; ~**subventionierung** subsidizing of exports; ~**tarif** export rates; ~**tonnage** export tonnage.

exportträchtig export-promoting.

Export|tratte export draft; ~**überschuß** exports in excess of imports, export surplus, overbalance of exports; **bilateraler** ~**überschuß** unrequited exports; ~**überschußfaktor** export earner; ~**verband** export association *(US)*; ~**verbot** prohibition of (embargo on) exports; ~**vergünstigung** export incentive; ~**vergütung** refund of duty, bounty on exportation, drawback; ~**verkaufsleiter** export sales executive; ~**verkaufsrechnung** export sales note; ~**vermittler** manufacturer's export agent *(US)*; ~**verpackung** export packing; ~**verpflichtungen** export obligations; ~**vertrag** export contract; ~**vertreter** export agent; ~**vertreter mit Sitz im Käuferland** cif agent; ~**verweigerung** nonexportation *(US)*; ~**volumen** export volume; ~**wachstum** export growth; ~**waren** export commodity (commodities); ~**werbung** export advertising, export publicity; ~**wert** export value; ~**werterklärung** declaration of export value; ~**wirtschaft** export industry (trade); ~**ziffern** export figures; ~**zoll** export duty (tariff), customs outward, exitus.

exportzoll|frei free of export duty; ~**pflichtig** liable to export duty.

Export|zunahme growth of exports, export increase; ~**zuteilung** export allocation.

Exposé exposé, memorandum;
beigefügtes ~ annexed memorandum.

Expreß express [train];
per ~ **[versandt]** shipped by express, express *(Br.)*;
Waren per ~ **schicken** to express goods, to send goods by fast train (freight, *US*); **per** ~ **zustellen** to send by express delivery *(Br.)* (special delivery, *US*).

expreß by fast goods service, by express messenger *(Br.)*;
Brief ~ **schicken** to send a letter express (by special delivery).

Expreß|beförderung express (special, *US*) delivery; ~**bote** express messenger, special messenger *(US)*; ~**brief** express *(Br.)* (special delivery, *US*) letter; ~**gebühr** express, expressage.

Expreßgut [railway] express, expedite[d] freight, fast freight *(US)*;
als ~ by express goods train *(Br.)*;
~**dienst** express freight service, special delivery *(US)*; ~**gesellschaft** express company *(US)*; ~**paket** express parcel *(Br.)*, express package *(US)*, special handling parcel *(US)*; ~**paket aufgeben** to send a parcel express; ~**spedition** express business; ~**verkehr** express *(Br.)* (special, *US*) delivery service.

Expressionismus expressionism.
Expreß|zug express [train], flier; ~**zustellung** express *(Br.)* (special, *US*) delivery.
Expreßzustellungs|bezirk express delivery limits *(Br.)*; ~**gebühr** expressage *(Br.)*, express delivery fee *(Br.)*, special delivery fee *(US)*.
expropriieren to expropriate.
Expropriierung expropriation.
exquisit exquisite, select, choice, dainty.
extempore sprechen to speak extempore (off the cuff).
extemporieren to speak extempore (off the cuff).
Extensitätsgrenze extensive margin.
extensive|Auslegung extensive interpretation; ~ **Wirtschaft** extensive farming (cultivation).
extern outside, extern, *(Student)* outcollege, nonresident.
Externat dayschool.
Externer extern, nonresident pupil, day-scholar (boy).
Externspeicher *(Datenverarbeitung)* external memory.
exterritorial exterritorial;
~**e Vorrechte** exterritorial privileges and rights.
Exterritorialität exterritoriality, diplomatic privilege;
~ **genießen** to possess exterritoriality status.
Exterritorialitätsrechte exterritorial privileges and rights;
~ **genießen** to possess exterritorial status.
extra extra, separately, apart, *(zusätzlich)* extra, in addition, over and above;
~ **angefertigt** custom-built *(US)*, made to measure; ~ **bezahlen** to pay separately; **es** ~ **getan haben** to have done it on purpose; **etw.** ~ **verdienen** to make a little money on the side;
Getränke werden ~ **berechnet** drinks are charged separately.
Extra|aufgeld overagio *(Br.)*; ~**ausgabe** extra *(Br.)*, *(Buch)* special edition; ~**ausgaben** sundry expenses, sundries; ~**ausstattung** *(Auto)* optional equipment; ~**blatt** special [edition], extra [special] *(Br.)*; ~**bogen** supplementary sheet; **als** ~**bonbon** thrown in as a bonus; ~**dividende** super dividend, bonus, plum *(US)*, melon *(US)*; ~**exemplar** over.
extrafein superfine, of special quality;
~**e Qualität** superior quality.
extragalaktisch extragalactic.
Extra|gebühr extra fee; ~**gutgewicht** extra draft.
extrahieren to [make an] extract, *(Buchhalter)* to make an abstract.
Extra|honorar refresher *(Br.)*, champerty *(US)*; ~**kosten** extra (additional) costs, sundry expenses, sundries, overruns *(US)*.
Extrakt *(Buch)* extract, abstract, summary;
~ **eines Buches anfertigen** to make extracts from a book.
Extra|leistungen, keine no frills; ~**liegetage** days of demurrage, extra lay-days; ~**ordinariat** readership *(Br.)*, associate professorship *(US)*; ~**ordinarius** reader *(Br.)*, associate professor *(US)*; ~**porto für spät aufgelieferte Briefe** late fee; ~**prämie** special bonus, overagio *(Br.)*; ~**rabatt** extra discount, special rebate; ~**risiko** special risk.
Extras frills *(US)*.
Extra|steuer supertax; ~**stück** spare; ~**stunden** overtime; ~**territorialität** extraterritoriality.
extravagant wild;
sich in ~**e Ausgaben stürzen** to launch out into extravagance; ~**er Geschmack** extravagant taste; ~**e Person** highflyer.
Extravaganz extravagance, splurge;
sich ~**en leisten** to indulge in extravaganc(i)es.
Extra|vergütung special allowance; ~**versicherung** additional insurance; ~**wurst haben wollen** to want jam on it *(fam.)*; ~**zeile** line by itself; ~**zoll auf von Ausländern eingeführte Waren** petty customs; ~**zug** extra-fare train, special train.
Extrem extreme, pole;
von einem ~ **ins andere fallen** to go from one extreme to the other; **ins entgegengesetzte** ~ **verfallen** to fly to the opposite extreme.
extrem extreme, utmost;
~**e Ansichten vertreten** to hold extreme views; **die** ~**e Rechte** extreme right; **einer** ~**en Richtung angehören** to belong to an extreme school of thought.
Extremfall extreme case.
Extremismus extremism.
Extremist extremist.
Extremwert extreme value.
Exzedenten|rückversicherung excess reinsurance; ~**versicherung** excess insurance; ~**vertrag** *(Rückversicherung)* excess of loss treaty.
Exzentriker eccentric, oddball *(sl.)*, *(Theater)* grotesque comedy artist.
exzentrisch eccentric, queer, peculiar;
~**es Benehmen** eccentric behavio(u)r, excentricity; ~**er Mensch** queer fellow.
exzerpieren to excerpt, to make excerpts.
Exzerpt excerpt, extract.
Exzeß excess, outrage, immoderation;
bis zum ~ excessively, immoderately;
alkoholischer ~ excessive drunkenness; **von den Truppen verübte** ~**e** excesses committed by the troops;
~**e begehen** to commit excesses; **für seine** ~**e bekannt sein** to be known for one's loose living.

F

F, nach Schema as a matter of routine, according to pattern, stereotyped;
alle Mahnbriefe nach Schema ~ schreiben to write all reminders according to a set formula.

Fabel fable, tale, fiction, fabulous story, myth legend, *(Grundhandlung)* plot, story;
im Bereich der ~ in the realm of fiction;
Äsop's ~n Aesop's fables;
jem. eine ~ auftischen to tell s. o. a fable (fib); **hübsche ~n erzählen** to invent beautiful tales; **ins Reich der ~ gehören** to be a pure fabrication;
~buch book of fables; **~dichter** fable writer, fabulist; **~erzähler** fable teller.

fabelhaft fabulous, marvel(l)ous, wonderful, peachy *(sl.)*, *(erstaunlich)* amazing, astonishing, *(sehr groß)* prodigious, immense, enormous;
~ viel Geld ausgeben to spend an incredible sum of money; **~ aussehen** to look splendid; **~ funktionieren** to work wonderfully;
~e Abendgesellschaft swell dinner party; **~er Arzt** marvelous doctor; **~es Essen** scrumptious food *(coll.)*; **~e Geschicklichkeit** amazing dexterity; **~er Kerl sein** to be a regular brick *(sl.)* (great guy, *US*); **~es Namensgedächtnis** phenomenal (wonderful) memory for names; **~e Rede halten** to make a capital speech; **~er Reichtum** fabulous wealth; **~e Toilette** stunning getup.

Fabel|land fableland; **~reich** realm (region) of fable; **~tier** fabulous creature; **~welt** realms of fancy.

Fabrik factory, [manufacturing] plant, works, shop, workshop, mill *(Br.)*;
ab ~ ex (loco) factory (works, mill, *Br.*), [direct] from factory *(US)*; **in der ~** at the works;
billig arbeitende ~ low-cost plant; **mit Verlust arbeitende ~** plant working with a deficit; **voll automatisierte ~** fully automated plant; **bestreikte ~** strike-bound (struck) factory; **chemische ~** chemical works; **an der Baustelle errichtete ~** on-site factory; **auf eigenem Grund und Boden errichtete ~** freehold factory; **in staatlicher Regie geführte ~** government-operated (nationalized, *Br.*) factory; **neu in Betrieb genommene ~** newly established plant; **keramische ~** pottery; **stillgelegte ~** nonoperating factory, mill out of work *(Br.)*; **unterirdische ~** underground factory;
~ mit sehr schlechten Arbeitsbedingungen sweatshop *(sl.)*; **~ vom Fließband** ready-built factory; **~ zur Verarbeitung von Waren unter Zollaufsicht** bonded factory; **~ oder Werkstatt** industrial hereditaments; **~ mit Zubehör** factory together with plant complete;
~ anlegen to set up a factory; **in einer ~ arbeiten** to work in a factory (mill, *Br.*); **in einer ~ mit Verlust arbeiten** to run a factory at a loss; **~ ausrüsten** to fit a workshop; **~ mit den notwendigen Maschinen ausstatten** to tool a factory; **~ bauen** to erect a factory; **~ bestreiken** to strike a work; **~ betreiben (besitzen)** to operate (run) a factory; **~ gründen** to set up a factory; **ab ~ kaufen** to buy on ex work's terms; **~ leiten** to manage a factory; **~ in Betrieb nehmen** to open a factory; **neue ~ in Betrieb nehmen** to commission a new factory; **~ stillegen** to tie up (close down) a factory; **~ wegen Stahlmangels stillegen** to close down a factory because of steel shortage; **~ in einen Vorort verlegen** to transfer (relocate) the works to a suburb;
~abgabepreis industrial (factory) price, price at works; **~absatz** direct sale to the public; **~abwässer** trade effluent; **~angestellter** industrial employee, factory worker.

Fabrikanlage factory, works, installation, manufacturing establishment, [manufacturing] plant, industrial plant, *(Anlegung)* plant layout;
stilliegende ~ idle plant;
~n besichtigen dürfen to be permitted to visit the works.

Fabrikant manufacturer, maker, industrial producer, fabricant, fabricator, *(Inhaber)* factory owner, millowner *(Br.)*;
direkt absetzender ~ direct-selling manufacturer.

Fabrik|arbeit factory work, factory job, shopfloor job, millwork *(Br.)*, *(im Gegensatz zur Handarbeit)* manufactured goods;
~arbeit leisten to work in a factory; **~arbeiter** industrial worker (labo(u)rer), shopfloor worker, factory hand (worker, operative, mill hand, *Br.*), blue-collar worker *(US)*, *(pl.)* factory people; **~arbeiterin** factory woman, work (factory) girl.

Fabrikat make, product, manufacture[d article];
ausländisches ~ foreign product (make); **bestes ~** best make (product); **eigenes ~** own make; **einheimisches ~** domestic (inland, home) manufacture, inland home-produced goods; **erstklassiges ~** first-class brand, first-rate make; **minderwertiges ~** inferior make, common make of goods;
~e unterschiedlicher Größe articles of various sizes.

Fabrikation production, manufacture, manufacturing, fabrication, making, make run, output;
eigene ~ own make;
~ aufnehmen to go into production; **~ drosseln (einschränken)** to curb (curtail) production; **~ künstlich einschränken** to ca'canny; **~ erhöhen** to increase production; **in die ~ geben** to put into production; **~ in Gang halten** to keep production wheels humming.

Fabrikations|abfall waste; **~ablauf** manufacturing process; **~abteilung** manufacturing division, production department; **~anlagen** producing (production) facilities, plant facilities, productive equipment; **~auftrag** factory (production, manufacturing, special, job) order; **~auftrag erteilen** to award a contract; **~auftragsnummer** job-order number; **~ausstoß** factory output; **~ausstoß erhöhen** to step up production.

Fabrikationsbetrieb manufacturing enterprise (establishment, company, *Br.*) (corporation, plant, operation, *US*);
billiger ~ lower-cost manufacturer;
~ einrichten to set up a manufactory; **~ umstellen** to adapt a factory to the production of other products.

Fabrikations|buch factory ledger; **~dauer** production period; **~einrichtungen** productive (plant) equipment, producing facilities; **~erfahrung** productive experience; **~ertrag** production output.

Fabrikationsfehler manufacturing defect, flaw;
~ bei der Flugzeugherstellung aircraft defect;
~ beseitigen to supply (remedy) a defect in a manufacture; **~ haben** to be faulty in its manufacture.

Fabrikations|gang course of manufacture, *(Verarbeitung)* processing, manufacturing process; **~geheimnis** secrecy of manufacture, trade (manufacturing) secret.

Fabrikationsgemeinkosten factory overheads, production overhead charges;
~konto factory overhead account; **~satz** factory overhead rate.

Fabrikations|genehmigung production permit; **~gesellschaft** manufacturing establishment (company, corporation, enterprise); **~gewerbe** manufacturing trade; **~gewinn** manufacturing (trade) profit, factory profit; **~halle** factory building; **~jahr** year of manufacture; **~kapazität** manufacturing (production) capacity; **~kenntnisse** manufacturing knowledge, know-how; **~konto** production (factory, manufacturing, process) account; **~kontrolle** production control; **~kosten** cost of production (manufacture, manufacturing, goods manufactured), manufacturing (processing) cost, factory expenses (costs); **~kostenaufstellung** manufacturing cost sheet; **~leiter** production manager; **~lizenz** production (manufacturing) permit, licence to manufacture; **~löhne** direct labo(u)r cost; **~methode** manufacturing process (method), method of operation; **kostensparende ~methoden** cost-saving production methods; **~monopol** production (manufacturing) monopoly; **~name** style name; **~nummer** manufacturer's (serial) number; **~ort** place of manufacture, manufacturing place; **~partie** job lot; **~plan** production plan, manufacturing schedule; **~preis** production cost (price), manufacturing (manufacturer's cost) price, *(Selbstkosten)* prime cost, cost price; **~programm** production plan (range), working scheme, manufacturing schedule (program(me)); **sein ~programm abrunden** to round off one's production; **~projekt** manufacturing project; **~prozeß** manufacturing process; **~rechte** manufacturing (shop) rights.

fabrikationsreif ready to go into production.

Fabrikations|reife finished-product stage; **~risiko** risk of production; **~rückgang** production decline; **~sammelkonto** manufacturing summary account; **~stadium** manufactured stage; **~stätte** factory, production (manufacturing) establishment, manufacturing place, workshop; **industrielle ~stätten** operative side of an industry; **~studie** manufacturing study; **~system** manufacturing process, production system; **~tätigkeit** productive (manufacturing) activity; **~teil** production (manufacturing) part; ~**überwachung** production supervision; ~**unkosten** factory expense (overheads), cost of production; ~**unkostenkonto** factory overhead account; ~**unternehmen** manufacturing establishment (plant); ~**verbot** production prohibition; ~**verfahren** manufacturing method (process), method of operation; **rationalisiertes** ~**verfahren** production rationalization; ~**volumen** manufacturing volume; ~**vorhaben** manufacturing project; ~**vorschriften** production prescriptions; ~**zeit** individual production time; ~**zentrum** manufacturing zone; **für** ~**zwecke** for manufacturing purposes; ~**zweig** [line of] manufacture, manufacturing branch, producing line; **einzelne** ~**zweige stillegen** to halt certain production lines.

fabrikatorisch manufacturing.

Fabrikats|preis manufacturing price, production cost; ~**steuer** fabrication (manufacturer's excise, *US*) tax.

Fabrik|auftrag manufacturing order; ~**ausbau** factory extension; ~**auslieferungen** factory deliveries; ~**ausstattung** production equipment; ~**ausstoß** manufacturing output; ~**ausweitung** plant (factory) expansion; ~**bahn** factory (works) railway; ~**beschädigung** damage to a factory; ~**besichtigung** trip through a factory; **jdm. eine** ~**besichtigung gestatten** to let s. o. over the factory; ~**besitz** factory property; ~**besitzer** manufacturer, owner of a factory, factory owner, occupier of a factory, factory's occupier, millowner *(Br.)*; ~**betrieb** factory, works, industrial unit, plant, mill *(Br.)*; **staatlich ausgerüsteter** ~**betrieb** government-furnished plant; ~**betrieb umstellen** to convert a factory; ~**bevölkerung** industrial population; ~**bezirk** industrial (manufacturing) district; ~**buchhaltung** factory accounting; ~**direktor** factory (plant) manager, managing director; ~**einrichtung** factory equipment; ~**errichtung** factory construction; ~**errichtung auf der grünen Wiese** exurbia; ~**erzeugnis** manufactured article, product.

fabrikfertig factory-built.

Fabrik|gebäude manufactory, factory building (premises), plant premises, factory; **für** ~**gebiete vorgesehen sein** to be zoned for manufacturing enterprises *(US)*; ~**gegend** manufacturing district, industrial district (area); ~**gelände** factory site (area), works (factory) area, plant grounds; ~**gleis** factory rails, industrial line, siding, sidetrack *(US)*; ~**grundstück** factory (industrial) property, factory plot (premises), industrial site; **in der** ~**halle** on the floor; ~**handel** direct-marketing manufacture; ~**herr** manufacturer, millowner *(Br.)*; ~**hof** factory yard; ~**inspektion** factory inspection; ~**inventar** factory (industrial) inventory; ~**komplex** manufacturing complex; ~**kosten** shop cost; ~**lage** plant location; ~**lager** factory (industrial) inventory, factory stores; ~**leiter** works (factory, plant, *US*) manager; ~**leitung** factory (plant, *US*) management (supervision); ~**mädchen** workgirl; ~**marke** trademark, brand, manufacturer's mark, manufacturer's brand; **notwendige** ~**maschinen aufstellen** to tool up a plant.

fabrikmäßig|hergestellt factored, factory-made, mass-produced, manufactured;

~ **herstellen** to mass-produce; ~ **hergestellt sein** to be manufactured wholesale;

~**e Herstellung** manufacturing, serial manufacture, mass production.

Fabrik|nähe vicinity of a factory; ~**name** style, brand.

fabrikneu brand-new.

Fabrik|niederlage sales office; ~**nummer** factory (serial, maker's) number; ~**ordnung** shop rules; ~**ort** manufacturing place; ~**packung** original packing; ~**planung** planning of a factory; ~**posten** plant job; ~**preis** factory cost (price), industrial (manufacturing cost) price, price at works, cost-plus price; ~**projekt** manufacturing (factory) project; ~**räume** workshop; ~**schließung** plant (mill, *Br.*) shutdown; ~**schornstein** factory smokestack, factory chimney; ~**schutzmarke** trademark; ~**sirene** factory hooter, hoot *(Br.)*; ~**stadt** factory (manufacturing, mill, *Br.*) town, industrial city; ~**straße** factory roadway; ~**tor** factory (plant) gate; ~**unfall** industrial accident; **tödlicher** ~**unfall** industrial fatality; ~**unterlagen** factory records; ~**verlagerung** transfer of a factory; ~**vertreter** manufacturer's agent (representative); ~**viertel** manufacturing quarter; ~**ware** manufactured articles (goods, items, commodities), machine-made goods, factory-produced (-made) articles (goods), manufactures, factory products; ~**werkstätte** manufacturing establishment (shop, plant); ~**wesen** factory system; ~**zeichen** brand, certification mark, style, manufacturer's sign, trademark; **eingetragenes** ~**zeichen** registered trademark; ~**zeichenschutz** protection of trademarks; ~**zentrum** manufacturing center *(US)* (centre, *Br.*); ~**zufahrt** access road.

fabrizieren to make, to manufacture, to produce, to fabricate; **billige Romane** ~ to turn out cheap novels.

fabulieren to tell tales, to make up (fabricate) stories.

Facette *(Diamant)* facet.

Fach *(Abteil)* compartment, section, partition, division, *(Arbeitsgebiet)* field, department, line, sphere of business (action), province, beat, *(Berufszweig)* trade, profession, branch, business, walk, shop, racket *(sl.)*, *(Bücherschrank)* shelf, *(drucktechn.)* box, *(Schreibtisch)* drawer, pigeonhole, *(Schriftkasten)* box, *(Spezialgebiet)* special line (subject), special(i)ty, bailiewick, major subject *(US)*, *(im Unterricht)* subject;

in meinem ~ in my profession; **ins** ~ **schlagend** of a professional nature;

geheimes ~ secret drawer; **kaufmännisches** ~ commercial line; **oberstes** ~ top shelf; **wahlfreies** ~ optional subject, elective *(US)*;

sein ~ **beherrschen** to know a subject inside out (one's stuff), to have a good grasp of a subject, to master a subject; **sein** ~ **völlig beherrschen** to know one's onions (oil, oats); **sich auf ein bestimmtes** ~ **beschränken** to specialize, to become a specialist in s. th.; **in jds.** ~ **fallen** to be s. one's province; **nicht in jds.** ~ **fallen (gehören)** not to fall (lie) in s. one's way, to be outside s. one's field, not to be within s. one's province, to be off s. one's beat *(coll.)*; **in jedem** ~ **gute Noten haben** to have good marks in all subjects; **in ein** ~ **legen** to pigeonhole; **in jds.** ~ **schlagen** to lie (be) in s. one's line; **nicht in jds.** ~ **schlagen** to be out of s. one's line; **vom** ~ **sein** to be in the line; **nicht vom** ~ **sein** not to be a member of the profession; **sich in einem** ~ **spezialisieren** to specialize (major, *US*) in a subject; **über umfassende Kenntnisse in seinem** ~ **verfügen** to know s. th. perfectly; **sein** ~ **verstehen** to be skilled in one's profession; **in einem** ~ **geprüft werden** to be examined in a subject; **in seinem** ~ **gut Bescheid wissen** to be well up in one's subject;

~**abteilung** special branch, functional department, *(Klinik)* ward; ~**akademie** technical college; ~**angaben** technical data; ~**anwalt für Grundstückssachen** conveyancing lawyer; ~**anwalt für Steuerrecht** tax lawyer; ~**arbeit** skilled work, expert workmanship; ~**arbeit auswählen** to set a paper.

Facharbeiter skilled (qualified) worker (operative), expert (skilled) workman, skilled craftsman, technician, specialist, *(pl.)* skilled labo(u)r;

angelernter ~ semi-skilled worker; **hochqualifizierter** ~ key worker;

~**beruf** skilled factory job; ~**lohn** occupational wage; ~**mangel** shortage of skilled manpower; ~**nachweis** certificate of proficiency.

Facharzt medical specialist (expert, consultant);

~ **für Berufskrankheiten** occupational therapist; ~ **für Hals-, Nasen- und Ohrenkrankheiten** ear-nose-and-throat specialist, otolaryngologist; ~ **für innere Krankheiten** internist.

fachärztlich|untersuchen lassen, sich to be examined by a specialist;

~**e Behandlung** specialist treatment.

Fach|aufsicht supervisory power; ~**aufsichtsbehörde** supervisory authority.

Fachausbildung industrial (occupational, professional, vocational, special) training, technical (vocational, professional) education;

~ **in Kurzlehrgängen** short-course training;

~ **genossen haben** to be trained in a profession, to have learnt a trade.

Fachausbildungs|lehrgang vocational course; ~**stelle** industrial training board *(Br.)*.

Fachausdruck technical term (expression), word (term) of art, *(Technik)* technicality;

juristischer ~ forensic (legal) term; **wissenschaftlicher** ~ scientific term.

Fach|ausdrücke der Versicherungssprache actuarial terms; ~**ausschuß** panel (committee) of experts, functional commission, technical (blue-ribbon) committee; ~**ausschuß für Wirtschaftsfragen** economic committee; ~**ausstellung** trade exhibition; ~**ausübung** professionalism; ~**autor** writer scholar; ~**beauftragter** supervisor; ~**berater** counselling specialist, technical adviser, special consultant; ~**beratung** technical advice; **nicht zu jds.** ~**bereich gehören** to be outside s. one's range; ~**bericht** expert's report; ~**beruf** skilled occupation; ~**bezeichnung** technical term (expression); ~**blatt** trade journal (publication); **landwirtschaftliches** ~**blatt** farm publication; ~**buch** technical book, textbook; ~**bücherei** specialized (technical) library; ~**buchhandlung für Wirtschaftsliteratur** economics bookshop; ~**buchinteressenten** prospective purchasers of technical textbooks; ~**diplom** diploma; ~**eignung** special ability; ~**einkäufer** specialist buyer; ~**eintrag** *(Bibliothek)* form entry; ~**einzelhändler** dealer, stockist *(Br.)*, limited-line retailer *(US)*.

Fächer fan, range, scope, compass;
in ~ aufgeteilt partioned off, sectioned;
breiter ~ wide range;
breiter ~ des Fabrikationsprogrammes diversified product lines; **breiter ~ von Warenangeboten** large array (range) of goods offered;
seinen Kunden den ganzen ~ eines Speditionsunternehmens anbieten to package transportation services for its customers;
gesamten ~ des Darlehnsgeschäfts zur Verfügung stellen to engage in a wide variety of lending activities;
~**antenne** fan (umbrella) aerial; ~**aufklärung** *(mil.)* fanwise reconnaissance.

fächerförmig fan-shaped;
sich ~ ausbreiten to fan out.

Fachgebiet field, line, province, department, subject, special branch [of study], speciality, bailiwick, major subject *(US)*, metier, *(Patentrecht)* art;
für Gasthörer eingerichtetes ~ extramural department *(Br.)*;
~ beherrschen to profess, to know what's what (one's onions);
sich über ein ~ informieren to read up a subject; **auf einem ~ erfahren sein** *(Patentrecht)* to be skilled in an art; **in verschiedenen ~en unterrichten** to teach several trades.

Fach|gebietsleiter line manager; ~**gelehrter** expert, specialist.

fachgemäß, fachgerecht expert, professional, workmanlike;
etw. ~ ausführen to make a professional job of s. th.

Fachgemeinschaft, wissenschaftliche scientific community.

Fachgeschäft speciality shop (store), one-line shop (business), dealer, stockist *(Br.)*, limited-line retailer *(US)*;
~ für Haushaltswaren hardware shop; **~ für Radio und Fernsehen** radio and television specialist;
in allen ~en zu haben obtainable from all stockists.

Fachgespräch shoptalk.

Fachgewerkschaft amalgamated craft (vertical, horizontal) union;
örtliche ~ local industrial union; **unabhängige ~** independent union *(US)*; **vereinigte ~** amalgamated craft union *(US)*.

Fach|gewerkschaftsmitglied craft unionist; ~**gremium** technical (professional) body; ~**größe** authority; ~**gruppe** subbranch, industrial division, trade (professional) group, *(Schule)* subject section; ~**handel** dealers, specialized (single-line retail) trade; ~**händler** dealer, stockist *(Br.)*, limited-line retailer *(US)*; ~**hochschule** technical (specialist) college, professional school *(US)*, college; ~**idiot** one-track mind (specialist) *(sl.)*; ~**ingenieur** engineering specialist; ~**ingenieur für Tiefbau** civil engineer; ~**jargon** occupational jargon, lingo, *(jur.)* legalese *(US sl.)*; ~**katalog** subject index, *(Bibliothek)* form catalog(ue).

Fachkenntnisse special (specialized, technical, expert) knowledge, *(Patentrecht)* art;
besondere ~ know-how; **gediegene ~** in-depth knowledge of a subject; **erforderliche ~** *(Inserat)* technical knowledge required;
~ erwerben to gain expert knowledge; **über umfassende ~ verfügen** to have a thorough knowledge in a field; **über ~ in Struktur-, Steuer-, und Preisproblemen spezialisierter Märkte für Investitionspapiere verfügen** to be knowledgeable in the structure, taxation and pricing in particular financial markets;
besondere ~ sind nicht erforderlich *(Inserat)* special knowledge not required.

Fach|kollege colleague; ~**kommission** expert (blue-ribbon, *US*) commission; ~**können** specialized skill; ~**kraft** qualified person, skilled worker, *(im Büro)* specialized clerk; **leitende ~kraft** head clerk.

Fachkräfte skilled labo(u)r, trained men, technical manpower, technical personnel, specialist staff;
erste ~ highly skilled workers; **qualifizierte ~ mit praktischen Erfahrungen** qualified experts with practical experience;
~ erfordern to demand professional standards.

Fachkreise experts, specialist circles, specialists;
in ~n among experts;
höchste Anerkennung innerhalb der maßgebenden ~ erfahren to receive top professional recognition.

fachkundig expert, specialized, competent, skilled, functional in a professional manner.

Fachkundiger authority.

fachkundlich professional, specialist;
~**e Ausbildung** technical (specialized) training.

Fach|lehrer specialist teacher; ~**lehrgang** technical course.

Fachleute, von zahlreichen ~n behandelt treated by numerous experts;
führende ~ men of light and leading;
Dienste hervorragender ~ in Anspruch nehmen können to have recourse to the knowledge of specialists; **Unternehmensführung einem Stab von ~ übertragen** to entrust the working of an undertaking to a qualified staff.

fachlich technical, professional, functional, expert, competent;
~ ausgebildet sein to be skilled in business (professionally trained), to have learnt a trade; **~ qualifiziert sein** to be qualified in one's subject; **sich ~ spezialisieren** to specialize in a subject;
~**es Ansehen** professional reputation; **~ ausgebildete Arbeitskräfte** skilled labo(u)r (manpower); ~**e Ausbildung** technical (professional) training; ~**e Eignung** professional qualification (aptitude); **in ~er Hinsicht** technically speaking; ~**e Vertretung** functional representation; ~**e Vorschriften** technical regulations; ~**e Weiterbildung** extended professional training.

Fachliteratur trade (specialized) literature, literature of a subject, literary tools;
~ einsehen to study the relevant literature.

Fachmann master hand, practitioner, expert, specialist, professional man, technician, authority, judge, connoisseur;
mit dem Auge des ~s with an expert's eye;
alter (erfahrener) ~ old hand (timer); **ausgebildeter ~** career professional; **hochqualifizierter und überzeugender ~** professional of high calibre and potential;
~ auf dem Buchprüfungsgebiet accounting specialist; **~ für Fragen der Absatzförderung** marketing consultant (expert); **~ in militärischen Angelegenheiten** militarist; **anerkannter ~ auf seinem Gebiet** recognized authority in one's field; **~ auf dem Gebiet des Verfassungsrechts** constitutional expert; **~ in Kartellrechtsfragen** expert on anti-trust law; **~ für Umweltfragen** environment man, environmentalist;
sich als ~ ausgeben to pose as an expert; **~ befragen** to consult an expert; **~ hinzuziehen** to take expert advice; **sich von einem ~ beraten lassen** to take expert advice; **~ auf einem Gebiet sein** to be an authority on a subject; **kein ~ sein** to be no judge.

fachmännisch expert, professional, workmanlike, specialized, specialistic;
nicht ~ nonprofessional, unprofessional, lay;
etw. ~ ausführen to do s. th. professionally; **j. ~ beraten** to give s. o. expert advice; **etw. ~ erledigen** to do s. th. in a workmanlike manner;
~**e Arbeit** professional job; ~**e Ausführung** expert workmanship; ~**es Geschick** professional skill; ~**es Gutachten** expert's report, expertise; ~**e Leitung** professional management; ~**en Rat einholen** to take professional advice on a matter; ~**es Thema** professional subject; ~**e Überprüfung** expert examination; ~**es Urteil** expert opinion.

Fach|messe trade exhibition, trade fair *(Br.)*, dealer show, specialized fair; ~**minister** minister with portfolio, departmental minister; ~**ministerium** competent ministry, government department; ~**mitglied** trade member; ~**normen** engineering standards; ~**normenausschuß** standardization committee; ~**organ** trade (business) paper; ~**organisation** technical organization, professional (special) agency.

fachorientiert specialized.

Fach|personal skilled (specialized, technical, trained) staff (personnel); ~**planung** sector planning; ~**presse** technical (trade) press; ~**prüfung** subject (qualifying, professional) examination; ~**redakteur** special editor; ~**referat** functional department, *(Vortrag)* technical lecture; ~**richtung** field of major professional interest, specialization, *(Schule)* stream; ~**schaft** trade association, occupational group, guild, *(Universität)* faculty; ~**schriftsteller** expert writer; ~**schulbildung** technical (vocational, professional) training; ~**schule** vocational (technical, technical high, *US*, industrial, trade, professional) school; **landwirtschaftliche ~schule** agricultural college; **technische ~schule** polytechnic; **landwirtschaftliches ~schulwesen** agricultural education; ~**seminar** special seminar; ~**simpelei** shoptalk, shoppy talk; **nach ~simpelei klingen** to smell of the shop.

fachsimpeln to talk shop.

Fach|sprache technical language, occupational jargon, vernacular, cant, terminology, nomenclature; **medizinische ~sprache** medical language; ~**stelle** technical office; ~**studium** specialized studies (training), professional training; ~**tabelle** professional chart; ~**tagung** specialist course, *(auf dem Wirtschaftsgebiet)* trade conference; ~**terminologie** technical language; ~**übersetzer** technical translater; ~**übersetzung**

technical translation; ~**unternehmen** professional firm; ~**unterricht** expert tuition, technical instruction; ~**verband** subassociation, professional body, industrial *(US)* (trade) association, technical organization; ~**verbandsverzeichnis** trade-association directory; ~**verlag** specialist publishing house; ~**vertreter** special representative; ~**virtuosität** professional skill.

Fachwelt trade, the experts, professionalists, specialist circles;
in der ~ among experts;
in der ~ **allgemeine Anerkennung finden** to meet with general approval among experts; **in der** ~ **anerkannt sein** to be generally acknowledged in one's trade; **in der** ~ **wenig bekannt sein** to be little known among experts.

Fachwerk framework, panelwork, baywork, *(Skelettbau)* skeleton structure;
~**haus** frame house *(US)*, half-timbered house; ~**rumpf** *(Flugzeug)* framework body; ~**träger** trussed girder.

Fach|wissen technical knowledge; ~**wissen haben** to profess; ~**wissenschaft** special branch of knowledge; **juristische** ~**wissenschaft** science of law; ~**wort** technical term (word); ~**wörterbestand** inventory of technical terms; ~**wörterbuch** special (professional, technical, subject) dictionary; ~**wortkartei** card file of terms; ~**zeitschrift** trade (business) paper, technical publication, trade magazine, professional journal (magazine); **industrielle** ~**zeitschrift** industrial magazine; ~**zeitschriftenwerbung** trade-paper advertising; ~**zulage** technical inducement.

Fackel torch, link, lighted brand, firebrand;
~ **der Zwietracht** torch of discord;
~ **des Krieges anzünden** to light the fires of war; ~ **des Wissens weitergeben** to hand on the torch of knowledge, to pass on the lamp.

Fackeln lohnt sich nicht it's no use shilly-shallying.

fackeln to shilly-shally;
nicht lange ~ not to think twice, to lose no time.

Fackel|schein torchlight; ~**träger** torchbearer; ~**zug** torchlight procession.

fade inanimate, inane, uninspired, wishy-washy, *(Buch)* heavy, stuffy, without savo(u)r, *(geschmacklos)* tasteless, flavo(u)rless;
~**n Geschmack im Munde haben** to be left with a nasty taste in one's mouth; ~ **schmecken** to taste insipid;
~**r Kerl** dull (boring) person, a bore.

Faden thread, string, strand, *(Buch)* clue, *(el.)* filament, *(Thermometer)* column;
um ~**s Breite** by a hair's breadth;
~ **der Geschichte wieder aufnehmen** to pick up the thread of a story; ~ **seiner Rede wieder aufnehmen** to get back to one's muttons, to resume the thread of one's discourse; **keinen trockenen** ~ **am Leib haben** to have no dry stitch (thread) on o. s.; **an einem dünnen (seidenen)** ~ **hängen** to hang by a (single) thread (by the eyelids), to hang by a hair; **keinen guten** ~ **an einem Autor lassen** to pull an author to pieces; **keinen guten** ~ **an jem. lassen** to tear s. one's reputation to shreds; **den** ~ **verlieren** to lose the thread of one's discourse; **sich wie ein roter** ~ **durch das ganze Werk ziehen** to run like a red thread through the whole work.

Fäden, geheime wires;
~ **in der Hand halten** to pull the strings; ~ **der Regierung in der Hand halten** to hold the reins of government; **seine** ~ **über ein weites Gebiet spannen** to spread one's influence over a wide field; ~ **einer Geschichte miteinander verknüpfen** to gather up the threads of a story; ~ **der Unterhaltung verlieren** to lose the threads of one's discourse; ~ **wiederaufnehmen** to pick up (resume) the threads.

Faden|heftmaschine book-sewing machine; ~**heftung** thread stitching; ~**kreuz** reticule, cross hair.

fadenloses Bindeverfahren perfect binding.

fadenscheinig threadbare, flimsy, worn-out;
~ **werden** to wear thin;
~**e Entschuldigung** paltry (threadbare) excuse; ~**e Geschichte** threadbare story; ~**er Grund** poor reason; ~**e Moral** trite morality.

Fadentransistor filamentary transistor.

Fading *(Radio)* fading;
~**ausgleich** automatic volume control.

fähig able, capable, competent, apt;
zur Arbeit ~ **sein** fit for work;
sich für ~ **halten** to consider o. s. qualified; **verschiedener Deutungen** ~ **sein** to admit of various interpretations; **jedes Verbrechens** ~ **sein** to be capable of any crime;
~**er Arbeiter** able worker; ~**er Kopf sein** to be a man of parts, to have a good head on one's shoulders.

Fähigkeit ability, aptitude, capacity, power, competence, *(Anlage)* faculty, talent, gift, bump, *(Befähigung)* qualification;
berufliche ~ occupational competence; **durchschnittliche** ~**en** reasonable skill; **geistige** ~**en** mental power, intellectual faculties; **verminderte geistige** ~ mental deficiency; **handwerkliche** ~**en** mechanical skill; **journalistische** ~**en** journalistic skills; **latente** ~ latent abilities; **unbedingt notwendige** ~ survival skill; **organisatorische** ~ organizing (administrative) ability; **unternehmerische** ~**en** executive potential;
~ **zur selbständigen Arbeit** ability to work independently; ~ **seine Gedanken schriftlich zu formulieren** ability to express ideas in writing; ~ **zum Richteramt** eligibility to discharge judicial functions; ~ **im Umgang mit Menschen** communication skills; ~ **Verbindlichkeiten einzugehen** capacity to incur liability; ~ **besitzen Vertrauen auszustrahlen** to have the quality of inspiring confidence;
seine ~ **gegenüber der Konkurrenz ausprobieren** to measure one's skill with a rival; **ungewöhnliche** ~**en besitzen** to be possessed of unusual qualities (highly gifted); **jds.** ~ **bezweifeln** to doubt s. one's abilities; **jds.** ~ **zur Entfaltung bringen** to develop s. one's powers; **seine** ~ **unter Beweis stellen** to show one's capacity.

Fähigkeitenverzeichnis employee skills inventory.

fahl pale, palid, wan;
~**e Beleuchtung** lurid light; ~**er Himmel** pallid sky.

Fähnchen pennant, pennon, *(Kleid)* flimsy dress, cheap frock.

fahnden to search, to look for, to hunt, to pursue;
nach einem Verbrecher ~ to hunt a criminal.

Fahndung search [for a fugitive].

Fahndungs|abteilung investigative unit, tracing and search department; ~**auftrag** tracing order; ~**ausschreibung** hue and cry *(London)*; ~**beamter** *(Steuer)* tax ferret; ~**behörde** investigative agency; ~**blatt** police gazette; ~**buch** wanted-person file; ~**dienst** *(Zoll)* preventive service; ~**gesuch** search warrant; ~**liste** wanted-persons file; **auf der** ~**liste** wanted by the police white hot *(sl.)*; ~**stelle** investigative unit.

Fahne flag, banner, standard, *(Abzug)* slip, galley proof, *(Regiment)* colo(u)rs;
erbeutete ~**n** captured colo(u)rs; **erste** ~ *(drucktechn.)* pull; **weiße** ~ white flag, flag of truce;
~**n aufhängen** to hang out flags; ~ **aufrollen** to unfurl a flag; ~ **aufziehen** to hoist (run up) the flag; ~ **nach dem Winde drehen** to swim with the tide (stream), to sail with every shift of wind; ~ **haben** *(fam.)* to reek of alcohol; **Sieg an seine** ~ **heften** to gain a victory; ~ **hochhalten** *(fam.)* to keep the flag flying, to stand one's ground; ~**en lesen** *(drucktechn.)* to proofread; ~ **niederholen** to lower the flag; **sich um jds.** ~ **scharen** to join s. one's party; **mit** ~**n schmücken** to drape with flags; **Freihandel auf seine** ~ **schreiben** to raise the standard of free trade; ~ **schwenken** to flourish (brandish) a flag; **unter der** ~ **sein** to be with the colo(u)rs; ~ **senken** to dip the flag (one's ensigns); **mit fliegenden** ~**n übergehen** to change sides; **mit fliegenden** ~**n untergehen** to go down fighting; **zu den** ~**n einberufen werden** to be called to the colo(u)rs.

Fahnen|abordnung *(mil.)* colo(u)r guard; ~**abzieher** proof puller; ~**abzug** slip (first, galley) proof; ~**eid** oath of allegiance; ~**eid schwören** to be sworn in *(US fam.)*.

Fahnenflucht desertion;
j. zur ~ **anstiften** to procure s. o. to desert; ~ **begehen** to desert the colo(u)rs.

fahnenflüchtig deserting, over the hills *(US sl.)*;
~ **werden** to desert the colo(u)rs, to quit the ranks.

Fahnen|flüchtiger deserter; ~**junker** cornet, ensign; ~**korrektur** galley (slip) proof; ~**mast** flagpole; ~**parade abnehmen** to troop the colo(u)rs *(Br.)*; ~**träger** standard bearer, flagman.

Fahr|abteilung factory fleet, *(mil.)* transport unit; ~**auftrag** driving order.

Fahrausweis travel voucher, ticket;
ohne gültigen ~ without a [valid] ticket;
übertragbarer ~ transferable ticket.

Fahrbahn lane of traffic, roadway, runway, trackway, pavement *(US)*, carriageway, driveway *(US)*, *(Gleise)* road, *(Straßenseite)* lane;
auf der ~ on the road; **mit drei** ~**en** three-lane;
äußere ~ outside (offside) lane; **doppelte** ~ dual carriageway, dual highway *(US)*; **innere** ~ inside lane; **linke** ~ left-hand traffic lane; **mittlere** ~ central lane; **verengte** ~ narrow road, *(Straßenschild)* road narrows; **zweigeteilte** ~ divided highway *(US)*;

~ **einer Brücke** road of a bridge; ~ **für Langsamfahrzeuge** deceleration lane; ~ **für Linksabbieger** filter lane;
~ **begrenzen** to edge the road; ~ **freigeben** to authorize vehicles to proceed; **auf der** ~ **parken** to park on the carriageway; ~ **überschreiten** to cross the road; ~ **wechseln** to change from one lane to another, *(vorschriftswidrig)* to straddle the lane;
ohne ~begrenzungslinie nonedgelined; **~benutzer** road user; **falsche ~benutzung** improper lane usage; **~breite** width of a carriageway; **gesamte ~breite ausnutzen** to take advantage of the full width of a carriageway; **~disziplin** lane discipline; **eigene ~hälfte** near side; **~markierung** lane (surface) marking; **~rand** edge of a road; **~randbegrenzungslinie** edgelining; **~seite** roadside; **~verengung** *(Schild)* road narrows; **vorschriftswidriger ~wechsel** lane straddling; **~wechsel vornehmen** to change from one lane to another, *(verboten)* to straddle the line.

fahrbar movable, travelling, *(befahrbar)* practicable, passable;
~er Arbeitstisch travelling table; **~e Bücherei** mobile library *(Br.)*, travelling library, bookmobile *(US)*; **~er Kran** travel(l)ing crane; **~es Montagegestell** dolly; **~es Postamt** travelling post office; **~e Straße** road passable for vehicles; **~e Treppe** moving staircase, mobile gangway; **~er Untersatz** *(fam.)* conveyance, vehicle; **~e Verkaufsstelle** mobile shop; **~e Werkstatt** travelling workshop; **~e Zahnklinik** travelling dental clinic.

Fahr|barkeit practicability, passableness; **~befehl** *(mil.)* trip (work, *Br.*) ticket; **~bereich** cruising range, travel(l)ing distance.

fahrbereit roadworthy, road-ready, ready to drive, *(mil.)* in running order, *(Schiff)* ready to sail;
nicht ~ unroadworthy;
~er Zustand *(Schiff)* efficient state.

Fahrbereitschaft roadworthiness, *(Betrieb)* factory fleet, motor pool, carpool *(US)*.

Fähr|betrieb ferry service; **~betriebsmittel** *(Bahn)* rolling stock; **~boot** ferry craft, ferryboat; **~bootsverkehr** ferry service.

Fahrbrücke flying scaffold.

Fährbrücke aerial ferry.

Fahrdamm road[way], carriageway, *(Bahn)* permanent way *(Br.)*, railway embankment;
mitten auf dem ~ **gehen** to walk in the middle of the road.

Fähr|dampfer ferry steamer; **~dienst versehen** to ferry, to ply.

Fahrdienst|leiter [train] dispatcher, starter, traffic manager (superintendent), station master *(Br.)*; **~leiterraum** signal-control room; **~personal** train crew (staff); **~vorschriften** operating regulations; **~zimmer** station office.

Fähre ferry, ferryboat;
fliegende ~ trail ferry; **öffentliche** ~ public ferry;
~ **benutzen** to take the ferry; **Auto mit der** ~ **übersetzen** to ferry a car across.

Fahreigenschaften *(Auto)* handling qualities, roadability.

Fahren driving, riding, travel(l)ing;
angenehmes ~ smooth driving; **fahrlässiges (leichtfertiges)** ~ careless driving; **zu schnelles** ~ speeding; **unfallfreies** ~ accident-free driving record;
~ **auf der Autobahn** motorway driving; ~ **ohne Führerschein** driving without licence; ~ **trotz eingezogenen Führerscheins** driving while disqualified; ~ **ohne Haftpflichtversicherung** driving while uninsured; ~ **auf der Landstraße** roading *(US)*; ~ **ohne Licht** driving without lights; ~ **zur See** seafaring; ~ **in betrunkenem Zustand** driving while intoxicated *(US)* (under the influence of drink, *Br.*);
öffentliche Sicherheit beim ~ **gefährden** to drive to the public danger; **jem. wegen rücksichtslosen ~s einen Strafzettel verpassen** to book s. o. for reckless driving.

fahren to go, *(im Auto)* to drive, to motor, to wheel, *(befördern)* to carry, to convey, to ship *(US)*, *(mit Fahrrad)* to cycle, *(Kamera)* to pan, *(in Verkehrsmitteln)* to travel, to ride, to go, *(Zug)* to run;
mit dem Aufzug ~ to go by lift (elevator, *US*); **ins Ausland** ~ to travel abroad; **mit dem Auto** ~ to go by car, to motor; **Auto in die Garage** ~ to run a car into the garage; **j. zum Bahnhof** ~ to drive s. o. to the station; **aus dem Bett** ~ to jump out of bed; **über eine Brücke** ~ to cross a bridge; **in einem Bus zum Bahnhof** ~ to convey to the station in a bus; **mit dem Dampfer** ~ to travel by boat; **mit Dieselkraftstoff** ~ to be diesel-driven; **um die Ecke** ~ to turn a corner; **in eine Einbahnstraße** ~ to turn into a one-way street; **mit der Eisenbahn** ~ to travel by rail[way], to go by train, to railroad *(US)*; **elektrisch** ~ to operate on batteries; **in der Fahrtrichtung** ~ to sit facing the engine; **mit dem Rücken zur Fahrtrichtung** ~ to sit with one's back to the engine, *(im Bus)* to face backwards; **j. über den Fluß** ~ to row s. o. across the river; **auf Fracht** ~ to sail on freight; **ohne Führerschein** ~ to drive without a licence; **trotz eingezogenen Führerscheins** ~ to drive while disqualified; **im höchsten Gang** ~ to drive in top gear; **Gepäck zum Bahnhof** ~ to run the luggage *(Br.)* (baggage, *US*) to the station; **im Geschäftsinteresse** ~ to drive on one's master's business; **mit höchster Geschwindigkeit** ~ to be going at top speed; **mit hoher Geschwindigkeit** ~ to travel (get on) at high speed; **mit einer Geschwindigkeit von 100 Stundenkilometern** ~ to cruise at a speed of sixty miles an hour; **jem. in die Glieder** ~ to give s. o. a shock; **in eine Grube** ~ descend into a mine; **gut mit etw.** ~ to fare well with s. th.; **gut mit jem.** ~ to cotton on with s. o.; **einander in die Haare** ~ to go for one another, to fall foul of each other; **aus dem Hafen** ~ to leave port; **ohne gültige Haftpflichtversicherung** ~ to drive while uninsured; **j. über den Haufen** ~ to run s. o. over (down); **j. mit dem Auto nach Hause** ~ to motor s. o. home; **aus der Haut** ~ to jump out of one's skin, to go off the handle; **über den Kanal** ~ to cross the Channel; **nach der Karte** ~ to drive by the map; **Karren** ~ to push a wheelbarrow; **erster Klasse** ~ to go first [class], to travel Pullman *(US)*; **jem. an die Kehle** ~ to jump down s. one's throat; **20 Knoten** ~ to be sailing at twenty knots; **Kohlen** ~ to carry coals; **bestellte Waren zu den Kunden** ~ to deliver the ordered goods to the customers; **aufs Land** ~ to go down to the country; **über Land** ~ to travel over a the country; **Langsam** ~! Drive with caution!; **langsam** ~ to drive slowly, to proceed at a moderate speed; **langsamer** ~ to slow down; **im Leerlauf** ~ to coast; **ohne Licht** ~ to drive without lights; **mit dem Auto gegen eine Mauer** ~ to run one's car against a wall; **übers Meer** ~ to cross the sea; **ohne Motor** ~ to coast; **Motorrad** ~ to ride a motor-cycle; **jem. über den Mund** ~ to jump down s. one's throat, to put s. o. in his place, to reduce s. o. to silence; **nebeneinander** ~ to drive side by side; **mit dem Omnibus** ~ to go by (ride on a) bus; **jem. in die Parade** ~ to snap off s. one's nose; **rechts** ~ to drive on the right side of the road; **Roller** ~ to scooter; **rücksichtslos** ~ to drive recklessly, to road-hog; **rückwärts** ~ to reverse; **mit dem Schiff** ~ to sail; **schlecht** ~ *(fig.)* to fare badly; **viel zu schnell** ~ to drive much to fast; **Schritt** ~ to drive at walking speed, to crawl; **zur See** ~ to go to sea; **durch eine Stadt** ~ to motor through a town; **in die Stadt** ~ to go to town; **mit der Straßenbahn** ~ to go by tram; **mit der Straßenbahn zur Arbeit** ~ to ride to work on a streetcar *(US)* (tramcar, *Br.*); **auf der falschen Straßenseite** ~ to drive on the wrong side of the road; **Strecke in zwei Stunden** ~ to cover a distance in two hours; **80 Stundenkilometer** ~ to go at fifty miles an hour; **täglich** ~ *(Züge)* to run every day; **zu Tal** ~ to go downstream; **mit dem Taxi** ~ to take a taxi; **umsonst** ~ to ride free; **unfallfrei** ~ to drive accident-free; **auf Urlaub** ~ to go for a holiday *(Br.)* (on vacation, *US*); **in geschlossenem Verband** ~ to sail under convoy; **zum Vergnügen** ~ to travel for pleasure, to joy-ride; **entgegen dem Verkehrsstrom** ~ to travel against the traffic; **unter Verletzung der öffentlichen Sicherheitsvorschriften** ~ to drive to the public danger; **zu Verwandten** ~ to visit relatives; **vorsichtig** ~ to drive with caution; **seinen eigenen Wagen** ~ to drive one's own car; **wie wahnsinnig** ~ to drive like mad; **zweimal wöchentlich** ~ *(Bus, Zug)* to run twice a week; **in betrunkenem Zustand** ~ to drive while intoxicated *(US)* (under the influence of drink, *Br.*);
noch 5 Kilometer zu ~ **haben** to be still three miles from one's destination; **gut** ~ **können** to be good at driving; **sich leicht** ~ **lassen** to be easily handled; ~ **lernen** to take driving lessons.

fahrend travelling, itinerant, vagrant;
langsam ~es Fahrzeug slow-moving vehicle; **~er Geselle** travelling journeyman; **~e Habe** goods and chattels, movables; **~es Postamt** travelling post office; **~e Schauspielertruppe** touring (fit-up, road, *US*) company; **~es Volk** vagabonds, vagrants; **~er Zug** moving train.

fahrenlassen, alle Hoffnung to abandon all hope.

Fahrer driver *(Br.)*, motorist, runner *(US)*, *(Chauffeur)* chauffeur, driver, *(Fahrrad)* cyclist, rider, *(Motorrad)* rider;
rücksichtsloser ~ road hog, reckless driver, spook; **schlechter** ~ poor driver; **unerwünschte** ~ *(Autoversicherung)* undesirable risks; **unfallflüchtiger** ~ hit-and-run driver, hit-and-run motorist; **unfallhäufiger** ~ undesirable risk; **pflichtwidrig unversicherter** ~ insurance dodger; **zuverlässiger** ~ safe driver;
~ **eines Fluchtautos** wheelman *(sl.)*; ~ **ohne Verkehrserfahrung** unexperienced driver;
guter ~ **sein** to be good at driving;
~ausbildung driver training.

Fahrerei, ewige long trek *(fam.)*.

Fahrerflucht hit-and-run driving (offence);
~ **nach einem Unfall** hit-and-run accident;

~ **begehen** to be a hit-and-run driver; **wegen ~ angeklagt sein** to be prosecuted on a hit-and-run charge;
~**opfer** hit-and-run victim; ~**vergehen** hit-and-run offence.
Fahrerhaus driver's cabin.
Fahrerin woman driver.
fahrerische Leistung driving performance.
Fahrerlaubnis driving licence *(Br.)*, driver's license *(US)*, licence to operate a motor vehicle, pink *(sl.)*;
~ **entziehen** to disqualify from driving;
~**entziehung** disqualification from driving.
Fahrer|sitz driver's (driving) seat, *(LKW)* dickey box, *(Motorrad)* saddle; ~**unfallflucht** hit-and-run accident.
Fahrfläche tread.
Fahrgast passenger, *(Taxi)* fare;
stehender ~ straphanger;
~ **auf Abruf** standby passenger; ~ **ohne Sitzplatz** standing passenger;
~ **absetzen** to drop a passenger; ~ **aufnehmen** to load a passenger; ~ **unterbringen** to seat a passenger;
~**bedürfnisse** passenger requirements; ~**fluß** stream of passengers; ~**kapazität** transport capacity; ~**raum** passenger space, *(Flugzeug)* cabin; ~**schiff** passenger boat (ship), liner; **auf ~suche** *(Taxi)* cruising; **auf ~suche herumfahren** to ply for hire.
Fahrgefühl driving sensation, sense of balance, road sense *(Br.)*.
Fahrgeld passage, fare, *(Auto)* carfare *(US)*, *(Boot)* boatage, *(Schiff)* passage money;
~ **für Hin- und Rückfahrt** round trip (return, *Br.*) fare;
~ **abgezählt bereithalten** please tender [the] exact fare; ~ **veruntreuen** to knock down appropriate railroad fares *(US sl.)*.
Fährgeld ferry dues, fare, ferriage.
Fahr- und Wegegelder fare payments.
Fahrgeld|erstattung reimbursement of transportation expenses; ~**hinterziehung** obtaining transport by fraud; ~**vergütung**, ~**zuschuß** transport allowance, assisted passage.
Fahrgelegenheit transport facilities, [means of] conveyance, *(Anhalter)* lift;
~ **zu abgelegenen Plätzen außerhalb der Spitzenzeit des Verkehrs sicherstellen** to provide off-peak services to isolated villages; **mit ~ versenden** to send by land.
Fahrgemeinschaft carpool *(US)*.
Fährgerechtigkeit ferry licence, ferry franchise.
Fahrgeschwindigkeit travelling (cruising) speed;
mit einer ~ von 12 Knoten at a rate of twelve knots;
übermäßige ~ excessive speed;
höchstzulässige ~ für Kraftfahrzeuge motor-vehicle speed limit.
Fahrgestell *(Auto)* chassis, *(Flugzeug)* landing gear, undercarriage, carriage;
einziehbares ~ retractible landing gear, contractible carriage;
~ **einziehen** to retract the undercarriage;
~**nummer** chassis number.
Fahrgleis track, line, *(Straßenbahn)* tramline.
Fährhaus ferryhouse.
fahrig fidgety, dithery, nervous.
Fahrkabine lift, cable car.
Fahrkarte [passenger] ticket, *(Eisenbahn)* [railway (railroad, *US*)] ticket, pasteboard *(sl.)*, *(mil.)* washout;
nicht benutzte ~ unused ticket; **billige ~** low-cost fare; **direkte (durchgehende) ~** through ticket; **einfache ~** single (one-way, *US*) ticket; **ermäßigte ~** reduced fare; **unbenutzte ~** unused ticket; **ungültige ~** invalid ticket; **verbilligte ~** limited (cheap, bargain-tour) ticket; **stark verbilligte ~** cut-rate fare; **verfallene ~** out-of-date ticket; **verlorengegangene ~** lost ticket; **durch Magnetcode verschlüsselte ~** magnetically coded fare ticket;
~ **für die Ausreise** outward ticket; ~ **zum vollen Fahrpreis** full fare; ~ **mit beschränkter Gültigkeit** limited ticket; ~ **hin und zurück** round-trip *(US)* (return, *Br.*) ticket; ~ **erster Klasse** first-class (Pullman, *US*) ticket; ~ **zweiter Klasse** second-class ticket; ~ **zum halben Preis** half-fare ticket; ~ **zum vollen Preis** full-fare ticket; ~ **zum zurückgesetzten Preis** cheap ticket;
seine ~ bei der Sperre abgeben to turn (hand) in one's railway ticket; ~**n abnehmen** to collect the tickets; **sich für ~ anstellen** to queue up to buy tickets *(Br.)*; ~**n ausgeben** to issue tickets; ~**n aushändigen** to ticket *(US)*; **Zug ohne ~ benutzen** to jump a train *(US)*, to steal a ride; ~ **auf jds. Namen bestellen** to book a ticket in s. one's name; **seine ~ bezahlen** to pay one's fare; ~**n datieren** to date tickets; **ohne ~ fahren** to steal a ride; ~ **lochen** to punch a ticket; ~ **lösen** to buy (book, *Br.*, take) a ticket; **direkte ~ nach A nehmen** to book through to A.; ~ **schießen** *(mil.)* to miss the target; ~**n vorzeigen!** all fares, please!; **seine ~ vorzeigen** to produce (show) one's ticket; **seine ~ bei der Sperre [auf Verlangen] vorzeigen** to produce one's railway ticket at the station [on request];
~ **bereithalten!** tickets ready!
Fahrkarten|abnehmer ticket collector; ~**abschnitt für die Hinfahrt** outward half; ~**ausgabe** ticket office (counter), booking office *(Br.)*; ~**automat** ticket machine; ~**block** book of tickets; ~**büro** ticket agent; ~**drucker** ticket printer; ~**heft** book of tickets; ~**inhaber** ticket holder; ~**kontrolle** ticket control (inspection, *US*); ~**kontrolleur** ticket inspector *(US)* (collector, puncher), checkman *(Br.)*; ~**locher** ticket punch; ~**prüfung** ticket control (inspection, *US*); ~**schalter** booking *(Br.)* (ticket, *US*) office (window); ~**schalterbeamter** passenger agent; ~**sperre** ticket gate; ~**steuer** passenger duty; ~**tasche** ticket envelope; ~**umsatz** ticket sales; ~**verkauf** ticket sales (booking, *Br.*); ~**verkauf im Omnibus** entrance platform of a bus; ~**verkäufer** ticket clerk (seller, *US*), booking clerk *(Br.)*, paperweight *(Eisenbahn, sl.)*; ~**verkaufsstelle** ticket agent *(US)*; ~**zange** ticket nipper.
Fahrkomfort riding comfort.
Fährkonzession ferry franchise.
Fahrkorb *(Seilbahn)* cage.
Fahrkosten travelling expenses;
sich an den ~ beteiligen to split the expense of a carriage, to share a ride;
~**aufwand** *(Berufsverkehr)* commuting costs *(US)*; ~**zuschuß** transportation (travel) allowance.
Fahr|kran travelling crane; ~**künste** driving performance; ~**ladeschaffner** luggage guard, baggage man *(US)*.
fahrlässig negligent, careless, by negligence;
grob ~ reckless, grossly negligent;
~ **handeln** to act carelessly, to constitute negligence; **sich ~ über Verkehrsbestimmungen hinwegsetzen** to be negligent of traffic rules;
~**er Bankrott** reckless bankruptcy; ~**es Entweichenlassen** negligent escape; ~**er Falscheid** false swearing; ~**es Handeln** active negligence, negligent (careless) act, negligent care, action of negligence; ~ **begangene unerlaubte Handlung** negligence in tort; ~**e Körperverletzung** bodily injury caused by negligence; ~**e Straftat** negligent offence; ~**e Unkenntnis** constructive notice; ~**es Unterlassen** passive negligence; ~**e Verletzung eines Gesetzes** negligent violation of a statute; ~**er Vertragsabschluß** negligence in contract.
Fahrlässigkeit want of care, carelessness, negligence, neglect, fault;
durch ~ through want of care;
bewußte ~ wilful negligence *(US)*; **grobe ~** recklessness, gross fault (carelessness, negligence); **bewußte grobe ~** wanton (wilful, crash) negligence *(US)*; **strafbare grobe ~** criminal gross negligence; **leichte ~** slight fault (negligence, *US*), ordinary negligence *(US)*; **reine ~** negligence without fault; **rechtserhebliche ~** actionable negligence; **strafbare ~** culpable (criminal) negligence; **gesetzlich vermutete ~** negligence per se; **zum Schadenersatz verpflichtende ~** actionable negligence, negligence in law; **zu vertretende ~** imputed negligence *(US)*; **zugerechnete ~ Dritter** imputed negligence *(US)*; **mitwirkende ~ des Verletzten** contributory negligence;
Tatbestand der ~ erfüllen to constitute negligence; **auf jds. ~ zurückzuführen sein** to be due to s. one's negligence; **sich den Vorwurf der ~ zuziehen** to be chargeable with negligence.
Fahrlässigkeits|delikt tort of negligence, negligent offence; ~**haftung ohne Nachweis der Schuld** negligence per se *(US)*.
Fahr|lehrer driving instructor; ~**leistung** covered distance, mileage, *(Auto)* road performance; ~**leitung** *(Straßenbahn)* conductor (third) rail; ~**leitungsomnibus** trolley bus.
Fährmann ferryman.
Fahrneuling learner driver.
Fahrnis goods and chattels, chose in possession, personal property, personalty, movables;
~**gemeinschaft** *(jur.)* conventional community; ~**pfändung** seizure of property; ~**versicherung** insurance of property.
Fahr|pelz driving fur; ~**personal** train crew (staff) *(US)*.
Fahrplan timetable, time bill *(Br.)*, list of trains, railway guide, train sheet, schedule of trains *(US)*, [train] schedule *(US)*, *(Flughafen)* flight list, *(Bus)* bus guide, *(Schiff)* sailing list;
ungültig gewordener ~ timetable that is no longer valid; **grafischer ~** train diagram;
~ **ändern** to rearrange the timetable, to change the schedule *(US)*, to alter the working of trains; **neuen Zug in den ~ aufnehmen** to schedule a new train *(US)*, to introduce into the regular service; ~ **aufstellen** to compile a timetable; ~ **einhalten**

to maintain a schedule *(US)*, to stick to a timetable; **in den ~ aufgenommen werden** to be introduced into regular train service; **neuen ~ zusammenstellen** to make up a new railway guide;
~**änderung** rearrangement of the timetable, schedule change *(US)*; ~**änderung vornehmen** to alter the working of trains; ~**einhaltung** timetable (schedule, *US*) maintenance; ~**einschränkung** reduction in train schedules *(US)*.
fahrplanmäßig regular, on time, according to schedule *(US)*, as scheduled *(US)*;
nicht ~ nonscheduled *(US)*, not as scheduled *(US)*, wildcat; ~ **abfahren** to start on (according to) schedule *(US)*; ~ **mittags ankommen** to be scheduled to arrive at noon *(US)*; ~ **auslaufen** to sail to schedule *(US)*; ~ **einlaufen (eintreffen)** to arrive on time (right on schedule, *US*); **nicht ~ laufen** to be running behind time (schedule, *US*); ~ **ankommen müssen** to be due to arrive; ~ **verkehren** to run to a fixed schedule *(US)*;
~**e Abfahrt[szeit]** scheduled time (departure, *US*); ~**e Ankunftszeit** schedule time *(US)*; ~**e Geschwindigkeit** scheduled speed *(US)*; ~**er Luftverkehrsdienst** regular (scheduled, *US*) airline service; ~**es Schiff** scheduled ship *(US)*; ~**er Zug** regular (ordinary, scheduled, *US*) train.
Fahr|planzeit ziemlich genau einhalten to run pretty well on time; ~**praktiken** driving habits; ~**praxis** driving experience.
Fahrpreis passage, [rate of] fare, railroad fare *(US)*, *(Bus)* carfare *(US)*;
zu ermäßigtem ~ at a reduced fare;
einfacher ~ single fare; **ermäßigter** ~ cheap fare; **gesetzlich festgelegter** ~ legal fare; **halber** ~ half fare; **verbilligter** ~ bargain-tour fare, *(außerhalb der Saison)* low seasonal fare; **voller** ~ full rate, full fare;
~ **für die Hin- und Rückfahrt** return *(Br.)* (round-trip, *US*) fare; ~ **per Meile** mil(e)age rate;
vollen ~ bezahlen to pay full fare; **billige ~e haben** to run cheaply;
~**anzeiger** fare schedule *(Br.)*, clock, taximeter; ~**bestimmungen** tariff; ~**differenz** differential; ~**erhöhung** fare hike *(US)* (increase); ~**ermäßigung** fare reduction, reduction in (lowering of) fares, reduced fares; ~**gefüge** fare structure; ~**kategorie** fare category; ~**tabelle**, ~**verzeichnis** tariff, register (schedule) of fares; ~**zone** fare stage *(Br.)*; ~**zuschlag** excess (supplementary) fare; ~**zuschlag bezahlen** to pay the excess [on one's ticket].
Fahrprüfung driving (driver's, *US*) test;
~ **bestehen** to pass one's driving test *(Br.)*.
Fahrrad bicycle, cycle, bike *(fam.)*, wheel *(US)*;
~ **mit Hilfsmotor** autocycle; ~ **mit zwei Sitzen hintereinander** tandem bicycle;
vom ~ absteigen to dismount from a bicycle; **sein ~ aufpumpen** to pump up one's bike;
~**anhänger** cycle trailer; ~**aufbewahrung** cycle depot, storage of cycles; ~**benutzer**, ~**fahrer** bicyclist; ~**bereifung** bicycle tyres *(Br.)* (tires, *US*); ~**fabrik** bicycle plant; ~**fahrer** push cyclist *(fam.)*; ~**geschäft** cycle trade; ~**händler** cycle dealer; ~**industrie** bicycle industry; ~**karte** *(Bahn)* bicycle ticket; ~**kette** bicycle chain; ~**lampe** bicycle lamp; ~**produktion einstellen** to cease making bicycles; ~**pumpe** bicycle pump; ~**schlauch** bicycle tube; ~**schlauchventil** valve of a bicycle tyre; ~**schloß** cycle padlock; ~**stand** bicycle stand; ~**ständer** bicycle holder; ~**versicherung** pedal-cycle insurance; ~**weg** cycle (bicycle) track.
Fahr|regeln sailing rules; ~**rinne** navigable channel, track, *(durch Eis)* water lane, fairway, waterway; ~**schacht** manway.
Fahrschein [passenger] ticket;
ungültiger ~ ticket no longer valid; **vergünstigter** ~ privilege ticket;
~ **zweiter Klasse** tourist-class fare *(US)*;
~**ausgabe** ticket counter; ~**ausstellung** ticketing, booking; ~**automat** ticket-vending (-slot) machine; ~**heft** ticket book, coupon ticket, book of mileage tickets; ~**heft für Bahn, Bus und Schiff** combined ticket; ~**inhaber** ticket holder; ~**verkaufsstelle** ticket centre *(Br.)* (office, *US*); ~**werbung** ticket advertising; ~**wesen** fare system.
Fährschein ferry ticket.
Fahrschiene *(Kran)* rail.
Fährschiff train ferry, ferryboat;
~**werbung** ferryboat advertising.
Fahr|schule motor (driving) school; ~**schüler** learner-driver, driving-school customer *(Br.)*, *(Schule)* day boy *(Br.)*, day scholar; ~**schülerzeichen** L plate; **elementare ~schulung** *(mil.)* basic driving; ~**schulunterricht** driving-school instruction.
fahrsicher *(Schule)* roadworthy.
Fahr|sicherheit safe driving, *(Fahrzeug)* roadworthiness; ~**signal** *(Bahn)* line-clear signal.
Fahrspur lane of traffic, [traffic] lane;
~**en** tracks;
~**markierung** lane marking; ~**system** tracking system.
Fahr|stativ *(Filmkamera)* dolly; ~**straße** driveway, roadway, highway; **vierbahnige ~straße** four-lane carriageway; ~**strecke** route, tour, itinerary, road, distance covered; **billigste ~strecke benutzen** to travel by the cheapest route; ~**streifen** traffic lane *(Br.)*; **seitlicher ~streifen** side lane.
Fahrstuhl lift *(Br.)*, elevator *(US)*, *(Rollstuhl)* wheel (bath) chair; **mit dem ~ herunterfahren** to ride down in a lift *(Br.)*; **mit dem ~ hinauffahren** to go up by lift *(Br.)* (elevator, *US*); ~ **zum 20. Stock nehmen** to take the lift to the twentieth floor *(Br.)*;
~**druckknopf** lift *(Br.)* (elevator, *US*) starter; ~**führer** lift attendant (boy) *(Br.)*, elevator conductor *(US)*, elevator man (operator) *(US)*; ~**gesellschaft** lift (elevator, *US*) company; ~**kabine** cage, elevator car *(US)*; ~**rufanlage** elevator signal *(US)*; ~**schacht** lift (elevator, *US*) shaft; ~**versicherung** elevator insurance *(US)*.
Fahrstunde driving lesson;
eine ~ entfernt an hour's drive.
Fahrt drive, driving, ride *(US)*, run, *(Bahnsignal)* clear, *(Fahrkarte)* fare, *(Flugzeug)* airspeed, *(Geschwindigkeit)* speed, *(Reise)* journey, tour, trip, *(Schiff)* speed, way, *(Tempo)* speed, *(Überfahrt)* voyage, passage, crossing, cruise;
auf ~ *(Schiff)* under way; **auf der ~ nach A** on the way to A; **bei zu schneller** ~ when speeding; **in** ~ *(Kraftfahrzeug)* in motion, *(Schiff)* under way; **nach drei Stunden** ~ after a journey of three hours;
einfache ~ one-way (single, *Br.*) fair; **freie** ~ green light, road clear *(US)*; **große** ~ *(Schiff)* foreign trade, ocean voyage; **halbe** ~ half speed; **kleine** ~ *(Schiff)* home trade; **private** ~ nonwork journey; **volle ~ voraus** full speed ahead;
~ **achteraus** sternway; ~ **zur Arbeit (zum Arbeitsplatz)** work journey, travelling to work; ~ **ins Blaue** mystery tour; ~ **über Grund** *(Flugzeug)* ground speed; ~ **ins Grüne** summer outing; ~ **auf U-Bahn und Bus** combined tube and bus journey; ~ **voraus** seaway, headway;
~ **antreten** to set out on a journey; ~ **aufnehmen** *(Schiff)* to gather way; **während der ~ auf einen Zug aufspringen** to jump onto a moving train; **j. in ~ bringen** to jack up s. o., to get s. o. going; **freie ~ für ein Vorhaben erhalten** to receive the go-ahead for a project; **seine ~ fortsetzen** to proceed on one's journey, *(Schiff)* to proceed on the voyage; **freie ~ geben** to signal the traffic to advance, *(Bahn)* to clear the line; **auf ~ gehen** *(Pfadfinder)* to hike about the country; **freie ~ gewähren** to frank; **freie ~ haben** to have green light (free pass); ~ **halten** to maintain speed; **in ~ kommen** to get up speed, *(Schiff)* to get under way, *(in Schwung kommen)* to get going, to warm up, to get one's hand in, to get into full swing, *(wütend werden)* to fly off the handle (into a temper); **richtig in ~ kommen** to hit one's stride; ~ **machen** to make way (headway); **wenig ~ machen** to sail at reduced speed; ~ **ins Gebirge machen** to take a trip to the mountains; **auf ~ sein** *(Pfadfinder)* to be on the hike, to hike it; **in ~ sein** to be under way, to have way on, *(auf dem Kriegspfad)* to be on the warpath, *(tüchtig arbeiten)* to be hard at it; **in voller ~ sein** to be going at top speed; ~ **unterbrechen** to break one's journey, to stop over *(US)*; ~ **unternehmen** to go for a drive, to joy-ride; ~ **verlieren** *(Schiff)* to lose headway, to lose way; ~ **vermehren** to increase speed; ~ **vermindern** to slacken (reduce) speed; **Schiff aus der ~ ziehen** to lay up a ship;
~**antritt** departure, *(Schiff)* embarkation; ~**anweisungen** sailing instructions; ~**anzeige** *(Flugzeug)* indicated air speed.
fahrtauglich able to drive, *(Fahrzeug)* roadworthy.
Fahrt|auslagen travelling expenses; ~**ausweis** ticket, *(Führerschein)* driving (driver's, *US*) licence; ~**bericht** *(Bahn)* journal; ~**dauer** length of journey.
Fährte trail, track, trace, scent, foil *(Br.)*;
auf der falschen ~ off the trail;
falsche ~ false trail, red herring; **frische** ~ hot trail; **kalte** ~ cold scent;
j. falsch informieren und von der ~ abbringen to throw s. o. off the scent; **von der ~ abkommen** to be thrown off the scent; **j. auf die falsche ~ bringen (setzen)** to throw s. o. off the scent, to put s. o. on a false scent; **auf der falschen ~ sein** to be on the wrong (off the) track, to bark up the wrong tree; **auf der richtigen ~ sein** to be on the right track (scent).
Fahrtechnik driving technique.
Fahrten|buch, ~**nachweis** logbook *(US)*; ~**schreiber** speed recorder.

Fahrt|entschädigung mil(e)age; ~**geber** air-speed head; ~**geschwindigkeit** speed; ~**geschwindigkeit vermindern** to slow down, to slacken speed.

Fahrtkosten travelling expenses, transportation costs;
tägliche ~ commuting costs;
sich in die ~ **teilen** to go halves in (split) the expenses of a carriage, to share a ride;
~**entschädigung** commuting allowance.

Fahrt|messer *(Auto)* speedometer, *(Flugzeug)* air-speed head, *(Schiff)* log; ~**messeranzeige** indicated airspeed; **unfallfreier** ~**rekord** accident-free driving record.

Fahrtrichtung line of travel, *(Schiff)* course;
vorgeschriebene ~ direction to be followed;
~ **freigeben** to signal the traffic to advance; **gegen die** ~ **sitzen** to face backwards; **in** ~ **sitzen** to face forward.

Fahrt|richtungsänderung change of direction; ~**richtungsanzeiger** direction (traffic) indicatior, blinker; ~**route** *(Schiff)* lane, trade route; **von der üblichen** ~**route abziehen** to take off its usual run; ~**signal** *(Bahn)* clear signal, highball *(US)*; ~**teilnehmer** passenger; **als** ~**teilnehmer eintragen** to ticket *(US)*; ~**übertretung** motoring offence *(Br.)*.

fahrtüchtig fit to drive, *(Fahrzeug)* roadworthy;
kaum ~ barely mobile.

Fahrtüchtigkeit fitness to drive, *(Fahrzeug)* roadworthiness.

Fahrtunterbrechung break, stopover *(US)*, *(Flugbesatzung)* layover;
mit beliebiger ~ with option of breaks of journey.

Fahrunterricht driving lessons (instruction);
~ **nehmen** to take driving lessons.

fahruntüchtig unfit to drive, *(Wagen)* unroadworthy.

Fahr|untüchtigkeit unfitness to drive, *(Wagen)* unroadworthiness; ~**verbot** driving ban *(Br.)*; **vorübergehendes** ~**verbot** suspension of a driver's licence *(US)*; ~**verhalten** driving performance; ~**vorschriften** traffic regulations.

Fahrwasser navigable water, *(fig.)* element;
offenes ~ clear water;
ins politische ~ **geraten** to take a politic turn; **aus dem** ~ **kommen** to be put off one's stroke; **im richtigen** ~ **sein** to be in one's element (in the groove, *US*); **in ein ruhiges** ~ **zurückbringen** to put back on an even keel;
~**bezeichnung** channel markings; ~**boje** fairway buoy; **nicht ausreichende** ~**tiefe** lack of depth of a river.

Fahrweg [carriage] road, roadway, concourse *(US)*, trackway, carriageway, *(Park)* drive, driveway *(US)*.

Fahrweise, leichtfertige careless driving; **rücksichtslose** ~ reckless driving; **verkehrsgefährdende** ~ wanton and furious driving; **vernünftige** ~ proper lookout;
auf leichtsinnige ~ **zurückzuführen sein** to be due to careless driving.

Fahrwerk *(Auto)* chassis, *(Flugzeug)* carriage, undercarriage, landing (running) gear *(Br.)*;
einziehbares ~ retractable landing gear; **festes** ~ fixed landing gear;
~ **einziehen** to retract the landing gear.

Fahr|widerstand tractive resistance, *(Windwiderstand)* wind resistance; ~**wind** airstream, *(Flugzeug)* slipstream; ~**zeit** running time.

Fahrzeug conveyance, vehicle, machine, motor car (vehicle), *(Schiff)* vessel, ship, craft;
per ~ by road;
gesperrt für ~**e aller Art** no entry, closed to traffic; **gesperrt für** ~**e über 5 t Gesamtgewicht** weight limit 5 tons;
angemietetes ~ contract (for-hire) vehicle; **ausgedientes** ~ old crock; **ausländisches** ~ foreign-made vehicle; **in Reparatur befindliches** ~ deadline vehicle; **bei einem Zusammenstoß schwer beschädigtes** ~ motor-car badly dented in a collision; **den Sicherheitsbestimmungen voll entsprechendes** ~ safety vehicle; **ferngesteuertes** ~ *(mil.)* drone; **geländegängiges** ~ all-terrain (cross-country, *Br.*) vehicle; **gemietetes** ~ for-hire vehicle; **teils geschäftlich teils privat genutztes** ~ car used partly during employment and partly private; **gewerblich genutztes** ~ commercial vehicle; **landwirtschaftlich genutztes** ~ agricultural vehicle; **gepanzertes** ~ armo(u)red vehicle (car); **nicht gepanzertes** ~ soft-skinned vehicle; **motorisiertes** ~ motor vehicle; **plombiertes** ~ sealed vehicle; **überholendes** ~ overtaking vehicle; **zugelassenes** ~ legally operating automobile *(US)*; **für die öffentliche Personenbeförderung zugelassenes** ~ livery conveyance;
erstes ~ **in einer Kolonne** front door *(US sl.)*; ~**e der Polizei** vehicles belonging to the police; ~ **der öffentlichen Verkehrsbetriebe** public vehicle;
~ **nicht ordnungsgemäß abstellen** to leave a vehicle in a dangerous position; ~ **anhalten** to stop a car; ~ **zum Mitfahren anhalten** to hitchhike, to thumb a lift, to knock it *(sl.)*; ~ **anmelden** to register a motor vehicle; ~ **von der Zulassungspflicht befreien** to exempt a vehicle from the obligation of being registered; **jds.** ~ **benutzen** to operate s. one's automobile *(US)*; ~ **im Zustand der Trunkenheit fahren** to drive a car while intoxicated; ~ **lenken** to drive; ~ **künftig nur noch privat nutzen** to transfer a car from business to private use; **für** ~**e gesperrt sein** to be closed for (to) vehicular traffic; ~**e für den Transport zum Flugplatz stellen** to provide door-to-airport limousine service;
~**abnahme** auto trial; ~**anhäufung** knot of vehicles; ~**anleitungen** driving hints; ~**ausstoß** vehicle output; ~**bau** vehicle building, construction of vehicles, car manufacturing, *(Industriesparte)* motor (automotive) industry; ~**beleuchtung** lighting of a vehicle; ~**benutzer** vehicle user; ~**bestand** car park, number of vehicles registered; ~**dichte** traffic density; ~**einsatz** running of a fleet; ~**erneuerung** vehicle replacement; ~**führer** driver of a car *(Br.)*, operator of a car *(US)*; ~**geschwindigkeit** road speed; ~**halle** vehicle bay; ~**halter** motorist, car (motor-vehicle) owner; ~**halter sein** to own (use) a motor vehicle; ~**händler** dealer in motor vehicles, motorcar dealer *(US)*; ~**hersteller** motorcar manufacturer *(US)*; ~**industrie** motor industry, vehicle business; ~**insasse** occupant of a vehicle; ~**klasse** class of a vehicle; ~**kolonne** column of motor vehicles, fleet (string) of cars, line of moving traffic, convoy, motorcade *(US)*; ~**konto** delivery equipment account; ~**mechaniker** motor fitter (mechanic); ~**motor** motor-vehicle engine; ~**nummer** number (licence, *US*) plate; ~**papiere** registration papers, claim check *(US)*, vehicle registration certificate *(US)*; ~**park** fleet of trucks (cars); ~**produktion** vehicle production; ~**reparaturwerkstätte** motor-vehicle repair shop, motor repairs; ~**schäden** vehicle damage; ~**schlange** queue of cars; ~**steuer** vehicle tax; ~**tank** vehicle tank; ~**tunnel** vehicular tunnel; ~**überprüfung** testing of vehicles; **unangenehmer** ~**unfall** bad turnover in a carriage; ~**unterhaltung** auto (motorcar, *US*) maintenance; ~**unterhaltungskosten** automobile (motorcar) operating costs *(US)*; ~**verkehr** vehicular (vehicle) traffic; ~**versicherung** vehicle insurance *(US)*; **kombinierte** ~- **und Kaskoversicherung** comprehensive cover *(US)*; ~**versicherung mit DM 300 Selbstbehalt** DM 300 deductible comprehensive insurance; ~**versicherung unterhalten** to carry a public liability motor insurance; ~**werte** *(Börse)* motor shares; ~**zubehör** automobile accessories; ~**zulassung** vehicle registration (licence), licensing of a motor vehicle, road licence *(Br.)*; ~**zulassungsgebühr** vehicle licence duty; ~**zuschuß** car allowance.

Faible soft spot;
~ **für j. haben** to have a liking (a soft place in one's heart) for s. o.

fairer Wettbewerb fair competition.

Fairness equity, fairness.

Faksimile facsimile, *(Wertpapiere)* specimen;
~ **herstellen** to [make a] facsimile;
~**abschrift** copy in facsimile, facsimile document; ~**ausgabe** facsimile edition; ~**druck** facsimile print; ~**stempel** signature (facsimile) stamp; ~**telegraph** facsimile telegraph; ~**übertragung** facsimile transmission; ~**unterschrift** facsimile signature.

faksimilieren to facsimile.

faksimilierte Unterschrift facsimile signature.

Fakten, wissenschaftliche scientific data.

Faktion *(pol.)* faction.

faktisch factual, effective, real, actual, virtual, practical;
etw. ~ **beweisen** to prove s. th. by facts; ~ **unmöglich sein** to be in fact impossible;
~**e Anerkennung** de facto recognition; ~**er Beweis** factual (real) proof; ~**er Inhaber** actual owner.

Faktor factor, element, coefficient, *(Verwalter)* departmental manager, factor, taker-in, steward, *(Werkmeister)* foreman, overseer;
außerbetriebliche ~**en** external factors; **bestimmender** ~ determinant; **deflationistische** ~**en** deflationary factors; **entscheidender** ~ decisive (determining) factor; **drei gesetzgebende** ~**en** the three Estates of the Realm *(Br.)*; **konjunktureller** ~ cyclical factor; **menschlicher** ~ human factor; **persönlicher** ~ personal element; **preisbildender** ~ rate-making factor; **preiserhöhender** ~ price-raising factor; **veränderliche** ~**en** variables; **wertsteigernder** ~ *(Grundstück)* corner influence; **wichtiger** ~ asset;
entscheidender ~ **beim Vertragsabschluß** deal clinch;

alle ~en berücksichtigen to consider all factors involved; **~analyse** factor analysis; **~bewertung** *(Statistik)* factor loading.
Faktorei agency, factory, factoring (trading) company, foreign trading station;
~handel agency business; **~system** factory system.
Faktorgebühr factor's fee.
Faktoring|gesellschaft factoring company, factor *(US)*; **~gruppe** factoring group; **~kette** factoring chain.
faktorisieren to factorize.
Faktor|kosten *(Volkswirtschaft)* factor cost; **~mobilität** horizontal mobility; **~wanderung** factor movement.
Faktotum do-all, Jack-of-all-trades, handyman, man of all work, factotum.
Faktura invoice, bill, account, bill of parcels;
beim Durchgehen Ihrer ~ on examining (checking) your invoice; **bei Übersendung der ~** on transmitting the invoice; **laut ~** as per invoice (as invoiced);
beglaubigte ~ legalized invoice; **fingierte ~** proforma invoice; **spezifizierte ~** itemized invoice; **mit Preisen versehene ~** priced invoice;
~ ausstellen to [make out an] invoice; **~ beglaubigen** to legalize an invoice; **~ erteilen** to [make out an] invoice;
~betrag invoiced amount; **~buch** invoice book, book of invoices; **~duplikat** duplicate of invoice; **~preis** invoice[d] price; **~stempel** invoice stamp; **~wert** invoice value.
Fakturen|abteilung billing (invoice) department; **~betrag** invoiced amount; **~buch** invoice book (register); **~datum** date of invoice, billing date *(US)*; **~handbuch** billing guidebook.
Fakturieren billing, invoicing of goods.
fakturieren to bill, to invoice.
Fakturiermaschine billing (invoicing) machine.
fakturiert|er Preis invoice[d] price; **~e Ware** invoiced goods.
Fakturierung billing;
~ von Halbfabrikaten progress billing *(US)*.
Fakturierungs|arbeiten invoice work; **~fehler** billing error; **~methode** billing method.
Fakturist invoice (billing, accounts, parcels) clerk.
Fakultät faculty, school;
juristische ~ faculty of law, law faculty, law school *(US)*; **medizinische ~** faculty of medicine; **philosophische ~** faculty of letters, Department of Liberal Arts *(US)*; **volkswirtschaftliche ~** faculty of economics;
~ einer Universität faculty of a university.
fakultativ facultative, optional, voluntary, permissive, permissible, *(Studienfach)* facultative, elective;
~e Erfordernisse nonessentials, nonessential elements; **~e Fächer** optional subjects, electives *(US)*; **~e Studienfächer** optional studies; **~e Versicherung** optional insurance.
Fakulativ|fach optional, facultative, (extra) subject, elective; **~klausel** *(Völkerrecht)* optional clause.
Fakultäts|angelegenheiten faculty business *(US)*; **~ausschuß** faculty committee, board of study; **~mitglied** faculty member; **~sitzung** faculty meeting; **~streik** student-faculty strike *(US)*; **~verzeichnis** faculty list *(US)*.
Falke *(politische Richtung)* falcon.
Falkenaugen, mit eagle-eyed.
Fall event, case, matter, occurrence, occasion, affair, *(Börsenkurs)* decline, fall, *(Preise)* decline, decrease, fall, *(Rechtsfall)* case, precedent, *(Regierung)* fall, downfall, *(Staat)* decline, collapse, *(Sturz)* fall, tumble, plunk, plunge;
auf jeden ~ at any rate, in any case, by fair means or foul; **auf keinen ~** in no circumstances; **auf Knall und ~** on the spot; **für den ~, daß** should the case arise; **gesetzt den ~, das Gerücht stimmt** supposing, the rumo(u)r were true; **im ~e** in the event of; **im allerschlimmsten ~** at its very worst; **im vorliegenden ~** in the present case; **im zweiten ~** in the second instance; **im ~ einer Betriebsstillegung** in the event of a shutdown; **im ~e eines ~es** if need be; **im ~ eines Krieges** in the event of war; **im ~ eines Unfalls** in case of an accident; **im ~ der Unzustellbarkeit** in case of nondelivery; **im ~ des Verzuges** in the event of default; **in jedem ~** at all events; **je nach Lage des ~es** as the case may be; **von ~ zu ~** as the case may be selective; **wenn der ~ eintritt** should the occasion arise;
abgeschlossener ~ shut case; **zur Entscheidung anstehender ~** case at bar, case on the cause list; **außergewöhnlicher ~** unusual (extreme) case; **äußerster ~** push; **betreffender ~** case in point; **dringender ~** pressing case, case of emergency, exigency, urgency; **dumpfer ~** dump; **einschlägiger ~** case in point, precedent; **einzelner ~** individual case; **gleichgelagerter ~** similar case; **grundlegender ~** landmark case; **heftiger ~** plump; **hoffnungsloser ~** gone case, goner; **hypothetischer ~** hypothetical case; **interessanter ~** interesting case; **klarer ~** plain sailing, pipe *(sl.)*; **konkreter ~** concrete case; **besonders krasser ~** blatant example; **innerhalb der Zuständigkeit liegender ~** case within the purview; **nicht mein ~** not my dish, not my cup of tea; **möglicher ~** contingency; **völlig neuer ~** case of first impression; **plötzlicher ~** *(Börse)* drop, plunge; **schwebender ~** matter, case in point; **schwieriger ~** case difficult to deal with; **seerechtlicher ~** maritime claim; **streitiger (strittiger) ~** case under dispute, case at issue, matter in dispute; **totsicherer ~** airtight case; **typischer ~** a case in point; **unerledigter ~** remanet; **unvorhergesehener ~** unforeseen event; **vereinzelter ~** isolated case (instance); **dem Obergericht zur Entscheidung vorgelegter ~** certified case; **in den Bestimmungen nicht vorgesehener ~** case unprovided for by the rules; **vorgetragener ~** case stated *(Br.)*; **vorliegender ~** individual (instant) case, case in question;
einwandfreier ~ von Betrug clear case of fraud (cheating); **~ von Fahrlässigkeit** negligence case; **~ einer Festung** downfall of a fortress; **~ von Geisteskrankheit** mental case; **~ absoluter Notwendigkeit** case of absolute necessity; **~ flagranter Ungerechtigkeit** flagrant piece of injustice;
seinen ~ abschwächen to break one's fall; **~ absetzen** to strike an action off the roll; **seinen ~ auf Treu und Glauben abstellen** to rest one's case on equity; **konkreten ~ annehmen** to take a concrete case; **~ aufgreifen** to move into a case; **~ erneut aufrollen** to reopen a case; **~ bearbeiten** to handle (deal with) a case; **j. mit einem ~ beauftragen** to put s. o. on a case; **~ im Schnellverfahren behandeln** to dispose of a case summarily; **j. zu ~ bringen** to topple s. o., to trip s. o. up, to knock s. o. off his prim *(coll.)*; **Antrag zu ~ bringen** to defeat a motion; **~ vor Gericht bringen** to take a case to court; **Gesetzentwurf zu ~ bringen** to defeat (kill) a bill; **Klage zu ~ bringen** to quash an action; **jds. Pläne zu ~ bringen** to thwart s. one's plans; **Regierung zu ~ bringen** to overthrow a government; **j. wirtschaftlich zu ~ bringen** to ruin s. o.; **~ vor Gericht darlegen** to submit a case to the court; **~ schriftlich darlegen** to submit a written statement of a case; **~ einmotten** to put a case in mothballs; **~ nicht einschließen** *(Bestimmung)* not to reach a case; **von ~ zu ~ entscheiden** to decide on the merits of each particular case; **~ richterlich entscheiden** to give a decision on a case; **~ allein auf Grund der ihm innewohnenden Umstände entscheiden** to decide (judge) a case on its merits; **~ erledigen** to dispose of a case; **Für und Wider eines ~es erörtern** to go into the merits of a case; **auf jeden ~ Entschädigungsansprüche haben** to have at any rate a right to indemnity; **moralisch zu ~ kommen** to lapse from virtue into vice; **schwer zu ~ kommen** to have a nasty fall, to come a cropper; **~ komplett vortragen können** to be given a full hearing; **~ durch einen Sachverständigen begutachten lassen** to appoint an expert to report on a case; **Schlüssigkeit eines ~es prüfen** to examine the merits of a claim; **nicht gerade jds. ~ sein** not to be s. one's cup of tea; **hoffnungsloser ~ sein** to be past all hope (redemption); **~ noch einmal überprüfen** to review a case; **~ genauestens untersuchen** to look closely into an affair; **~ verhandeln** to sit in judgment on a case; **~ erneut verhandeln** to retry a case; **~ vor Gericht verhandeln** to try (hear) a case; **etw. auf jeden ~ versuchen** to attempt s. th., hit or miss; **~ vor Gericht vertreten** to present a case; **~ dem Gericht zur Entscheidung vorlegen** to submit a case to the court; **~ vortragen** to state (submit, plead) a case, to present one's brief; **~ schlüssig vortragen** to state a case; **auf jeden ~ verkauft werden** to be sold without reserve; **analogen ~ zitieren** to quote a case in point (precedent); **~ zur Rechtsmittelhilfe zurückverweisen** to throw a case back for remedy;
~beil guillotine; **~bö** air hole (pocket), white squall.
Falle trap, mantrap, snare, deadfall, pit, *(mil.)* decoy;
in einer ~ fangen to trap; **in die ~ gehen** to turn in, to kip down *(Br., sl.)*, to hit the sack *(US)*, *(fam.)* to go between the sheets; **in eine ~ gehen** to be decoyed, to fall (walk) into a trap, to put one's head into a noose, to take the bait; **in die von der Polizei gestellte ~ gehen** to be caught in the net of the police; **in eine ~ geraten** to fall into a trap; **wie die Ratte in der ~ sitzen** to be like a rat in a hole; **~ stellen** to lay a trap, to dig a pit; **j. eine ~ stellen** to set a trap (snare) for s. o.; **in eine ~ gelockt werden** to be lured into a trap.
Fälle, auf alle on the safe side; **für besondere ~** for special occasions;
bürgschaftsähnliche ~ cases analogous to suretyship;
zuerst die dringendsten ~ erledigen to deal with the most urgent things first; **in drei ~n zu mehreren Jahren Gefängnis verurteilen**

to sentence on three counts to several years of penal servitude; **alle ~ in einer einzigen Formel zusammenfassen** to embrace all the cases in a single formula.

Fallen *(Barometer)* fall, *(Flut)* abatement, recession, fall, *(Kurse)* fall, decline, drop, slump, sinking, easing off, *(Politiker)* downfall, *(Preise)* decline, downward movement, depression, *(Temperatur)* drop, descent;

plötzliches ~ der Preise break, slump *(Br.)*, smash *(US)*; **~ und Steigen der Preise** fluctuation of prices; **~ des Vorhangs** fall of a curtain;

im ~ begriffen sein to be on the decline (wane); **auf das ~ spekulieren** to speculate for a fall.

fallen to fall, *(Barometer)* to fall, to lapse, to drop, to sink, *(Entscheidung)* to be reached, *(Fieber)* to subside, to go down, to fall, *(Gelände)* to descend, to decline, to slope, *(Hochwasser)* to recede, to sink, to go down, to fall, *(Kurse)* to drop, to fall, to decline, to decrease, to go down (flat), to relapse, to recede, to experience a depression, to sink, to plummet, to slip back, to ease, *(Preise)* to be on the decline (fall, on the downgrade), to sag, to come down, to skid, to get low, to sink, to depreciate in value, to experience a depression, *(Regierung)* to be overthrown;

auf j. ~ *(Verdacht)* to fall on s. o.; **etw. ~** *(Kurse)* to ease off; **jem. in den Arm ~** to stay s. one's hand; **in jds. Aufgabenbereich ~** to come within s. one's province; **unter den Begriff ~** to come under the heading; **in den Bereich eines Abkommens ~** to fall within the ambit of an agreement; **unter eine Bestimmung ~** to fall within a definition; **in Bewußtlosigkeit ~** to become unconscious; **ins Bodenlose ~** to go to the bottom; **im Einsatz ~** to be killed in action, to bite the dust; **durch Erbübergang an j. ~** to devolve on (pass to) s. o.; **einem Fieber zum Opfer ~** to succumb to a fever; **auf einen Freitag ~** to fall on a Friday; **immer auf die Füße ~** to land on one's feet in any case; **über die eigenen Füße ~** to trip over one's own feet; **nicht in jds. Gebiet ~** not to be within s. one's province; **der Gemeinde zur Last ~** to come upon the parish; **unter ein Gesetz ~** to come within the scope of a law; **ins Gewicht ~** to be of consequence, to carry weight; **jem. um den Hals ~** to fling one's arms around s. one's neck; **kämpfend ~** to die in battle; **auf die Knie ~** to fall on one's knees; **im Kurs ~** to sag in price; **der Länge lang auf den Teppich ~** to measure one's length on the carpet; **jem. zur Last ~** to be thrown upon s. one's resources, to become a burden on s. o.; **auf die Nase ~** to fall on one's face; **in Ohnmacht ~** to faint; **plötzlich [im Wert] ~** to plunge, to slump *(Br.)*, to toboggan, to tumble *(US)*; **der Propaganda zum Opfer ~** to fall victim to propaganda; **nur um 5/8 Prozent ~** to drop a meagre 5/8 *(Br.)*; **durch eine Prüfung ~** to fail (flunk, *US*) in an examination; **um mehrere Punkte ~** *(Thermometer)* to drop several degrees; **um zwei Punkte auf 480 ~** to drop two points to 480; **aus dem Rahmen ~** to be out of place (line, *US*); **rapide ~** to nosedive; **unter die Räuber ~** to fall among thieves; **aus der Rolle ~** to drop a brick; **jem. in den Rücken ~** to stab s. o. in the back, to attack s. o. from the rear; **in einen tiefen Schlaf ~** to fall soundly asleep; **jem. in den Schoß ~** to fall into s. one's lap; **in einen schnelleren Schritt ~** to quicken one's step (pace); **stark ~** to descend steeply; **steigen und ~** to rise and fall, to fluctuate; **immer tiefer ~** *(fig.)* to go downhill; **unter den Tisch ~** to be dropped, to go to the board; **jem. mit der Tür ins Haus ~** to spring a surprise on s. o.; **in Ungnade ~** to fall out of favo(u)r; **unter einen Vertrag ~** to be covered by (fall within) an agreement; **ins Wasser ~** *(fig.)* to fall through, to end up in smoke; **im Wert ~** to depreciate; **aus allen Wolken ~** have the surprise of one's life; **jem. ins Wort ~** to interrupt s. o., to cut s. o. short.

fällen, Schiedsspruch to [make an] award; **Urteil ~** to pronounce (pass) judgment.

fallend falling, declining, receding, on the downgrade, *(Barometer)* falling, declining, *(Kurse)* falling, sagging, bearish, bear;

~e Blätter falling leaves; **~e Kosten** decreasing costs; **~e Kurse (Preise)** falling prices; **~e Tendenz** downward (bearish) tendency.

Fallenlassen|einer Erfindung abandonment of an invention; **~ eines Patents** abandonment of a patent.

fallenlassen to drop, to discard;

j. ~ to drop s. one's acquaintance, to give s. o. the wind *(sl.)*; **Anker ~** to drop (let go) the anchor; **Anspielung ~** to make an allusion; **Anspruch ~** to waive (abandon, drop) a claim; **Bekannten ~** to drop an acquaintance; **nachteilige Bemerkung über j. ~** to make snide remarks about s. o.; **Bombe ~** to drop a bomb; **Forderung ~** to drop a demand, to waive (relinquish) a claim; **alte Freunde ~** to discard old friends; **alle Hemmungen ~** to let down the bars; **Idee ~** to relinquish an idea; **etw. wie eine heiße Kartoffel ~** to drop s. th. like a hot potato (chestnut); **Klage ~** to withdraw (relinquish) an action; **Maske ~** to throw off one's mask; **Patent ~** to abandon a patent; **Plan völlig ~** to throw a scheme overboard; **Sache ~** to let a matter drop; **Thema ~** to drop a subject; **Vorhang ~** to ring down the curtain; **kein Wort ~** to keep one's mouth shut.

Fallen|stellen snaring, trapping; **~steller** trapper.

Fällestudium case study.

Fall|fenster sash window; **~gatter** portcullis; **~grube** pitfall; **~grube ausheben** to dig a pit.

Fallieren failure, bankruptcy, insolvency.

fallieren to break down, to fail, to turn (become) bankrupt, to smash, to fold up *(Br.)*.

fällig mature, matured, due, *(Kupon)* collectible, *(zahlbar)* payable, dischargeable, outstanding;

~ am with a maturity of; **am längsten ~** longest outstanding; **am 15. ~** payable on the 15th prox.; **bei Lieferung ~** payable on delivery; **bei Sicht ~** *(Wechsel)* payable on demand; **jederzeit ~** on demand, due at call; **längst ~** overdue; **noch nicht ~** not yet due, undue, unmatured, immature[d]; **täglich ~** due at call; **wenn ~** at maturity; **~ werdend** accruing;

für ~ erklären to declare due; **~ sein** to be due; **seit einem Monat ~ sein** to be outstanding for one month; **~ stellen** to fix a due date; **~ werden** to grow (become, fall) due, to run, to come around, *(Bezugsrecht)* to expire, *(Obligationen)* to mature, *(Wechsel)* to run off, to mature, *(Zinsen)* to accrue; **am 15. ~ werden** to mature on the 15th;

~er Betrag amount due; **~es Darlehn** straight loan; **~e Gebühren** fees due; **täglich ~es Geld** money at call, call money; **sofort ~e Rente** immediate annuity; **~e Schuld** existing debt, debt due; **noch nicht ~e Schuld** future debt; **~e Steuern** matured taxes; **~e Wechsel** bills to mature, expired bills; **~e Zinsen** interest due.

Fälligkeit maturity, due date (day), payability, *(Bezugsrecht)* expiration;

bei ~ at (on) maturity; **mit kurzer ~** short-dated; **vor [Eintritt der] ~** prior to maturity, before falling due, anticipated; **zahlbar bei ~** cash at maturity;

~ drei Monate nach Ausgabedatum maturity three months after date of issue; **~ bei Sicht** maturity on demand; **~ eines Wechsels** date of a bill;

auf monatliche ~ abstellen to calculate maturity on a monthly basis; **~ aufschieben** to defer (delay) maturity; **vor ~ bezahlen** to prepay, to pay before maturity; **Wechsel vor ~ bezahlen** to anticipate a bill; **Wechsel bei ~ einlösen** to take up a draft when due; **~ hinausschieben** to prolong; **~ über mehrere Jahre verteilen** to space payment over several years; **vor ~ zahlen** to pay in advance (anticipation), to anticipate payment.

Fälligkeits|analyse age analysis; **~anspruch** maturity claim; **~aufstellung** aging statement; **~avis** reminder of due date; **~basis** accrual basis; **~betrag** amount due at maturity; **~buchführung** accrual accounting; **~datum** due (accrual, maturity) date, date of maturity; **~gliederung** spacing of payments; **~jahr** year of maturity; **~klausel** *(Abzahlungsvertrag)* acceleration clause; **~liste, ~tabelle** aging schedule, expiration list, maturity tickler *(US)*, *(für Schecks)* deposit list; **~tag** due (accrual, maturity) date, day of payment, date of maturity, settlement date, season *(US)*; **nach dem ~tag** post claim; **~termin** due (accrual, maturity) date, day of payment, *(Wechsel)* average due date; **~wert** maturity value.

Fällig|stellung, frühzeitige acceleration of maturity; **~werden** expiration.

Fallissement failure, bankruptcy, insolvency.

fallit broken, bankrupt, bust, sold up.

Fall|klappe *(Telefonvermittlung)* call (drop) indicator; **~methode** case method; **~recht** case law; **~reep** accommodation ladder, gangway, gangway ladder; **~rohr** downcomer, gutter (rain) pipe; **~sammlung** table of cases.

Fallschirm parachute;

mit dem ~ absetzen (abwerfen) to paradrop, to drop by parachute, to airdrop; **mit dem ~ abspringen** to parachute, to descend, to bale (bail, *US*) out;

~absetzung airdrop; **~absprung** parachutism, descent, jump; **~abwurf** paradrop, airdrop; **~boot** parachute boat; **~drachen** parakite; **~einheiten** parachute detachments; **~fangleine** rigging line.

fallschirmgelandet paraborne.

Fallschirm|gurt parachute harness; **~jäger** parachuter; **~jäger mit Zielobjektauftrag** paraspotter; **~sack** parachute container;

~**seide** parachute silk; ~**springen** parachuting, parachute jumping; ~**springer** skyman, parachuter; ~**traube** cluster of parachuters; ~**truppen** parachute troops, paratroops; ~**truppen absetzen** to hang out the laundry *(sl.)*.

Fallsonde dropsound.

Fallstrick snare, trap, pitfall, noose;
~**e des Gesetzes** *(fam.)* pitfalls of the law;
in die ~e einer Verschwörung geraten to be ensnared in a plot; **sich in den ~en des Gesetzes verfangen haben** to be caught in the tails of the law.

Fall|stromvergaser downcraft carburettor; ~**studie** case study; ~**tank** gravity tank; ~**tür** trap door; ~**wind** downwind.

falsch *(gefälscht)* forged, falsified, feigned, fraudulent, *(Münze)* false, base, *(nachgemacht)* counterfeit, *(unecht)* spurious, bogus, mock, artificial, sham, fake *(US)*, *(unehrlich)* double-crossing, two-faced, perfidious, deceitful, treacherous, two-tongued, *(ungenau)* inaccurate, erroneous, *(unrichtig)* incorrect, false, mistaken, untrue, *(verkehrt)* wrong;
~ **adressiert** incorrectly addressed; ~ **ausgesprochen** ~ markedly wrong; ~ **ausgestellt** *(Scheckvermerk)* irregularly drawn; ~ **unterrichtet** wrongfully informed; ~ **verbunden** wrong number (connection);
~ **abbiegen** to take a wrong turning; ~ **ablegen** *(drucktechn.)* to distribute the letters into wrong boxes; ~ **adressieren** to misaddress a letter; ~ **anwenden** to misapply; ~ **auslegen** to misconstrue, to misinterpret; **Gesetz ~ auslegen** to misread a law; **jds. Worte ~ auslegen** to put a wrong construction on s. one's words; ~ **aussagen** to give false evidence; ~ **berechnen** to miscalculate; ~ **datieren** to misdate; ~ **eintragen** to misenter, to make a wrong entry; ~ **gehen** to go wrong; **völlig ~ liegen** to be dead wrong; ~ **plädieren** to misplead; ~ **schwören** to forswear; ~ **unterrichtet sein** to be misinformed; ~ **übersetzen** to translate incorrectly; **j. ~ verstehen** to misunderstand s. o.; **Wort ~ verstehen** to take a word in the wrong sense; ~ **wählen** *(Telefon)* to dial a wrong number; **Geschichte ~ wiedergeben** to falsify a story;
~**e Adresse** wrong address; **an die ~e Adresse geraten** to come to the wrong shop; ~**e Angaben** false statement (accounts); ~**e Angaben in Subskriptionsanzeigen** misstatement in a prospectus; ~**e Anklage erheben** to fabricate an accusation; ~**e Anschuldigung** trumped-up charge; ~**e Anwendung** misapplication, misemployment; ~**e Auskunft** wrong information; ~**e Auslegung** misinterpretation, misconstruction; ~**e Auslegung vornehmen** to put a false interpretation on s. th.; ~**e Aussprache** mispronunciation; **frühzeitig auf die ~e Bahn geraten** to go wrong in early life; ~**e Banknote** forged (counterfeit, spurious, bad, dud) note, bogus money; **mit dem ~en Bein zuerst aufstehen** to get out of bed on the wrong side; ~**e Berechnung** miscalculation; ~**e Bescheidenheit** misplaced (mock) modesty; ~**e Bezeichnung** misnomer; ~**e Bilanzerklärung** false financial statement; ~**es Bild** wrong impression; ~**e Buchung** misentry, wrong entry; **auf dem ~en Dampfer sitzen** to be on the wrong track; ~**es Datum** wrong date; ~**e Datumsangabe** misdating; **etw. am ~en Ende anfassen** to put the cart before the horse; ~**e Erklärung** inaccurate (mistaken) statement, false demonstration; ~**e Fassade** false front; **unter ~er Flagge segeln** to sail under false colo(u)rs; ~**er Gebrauch eines Wortes** improper use of a word; ~**es Geld** counterfeit (bogus) money; ~**es Geldstück** false (bad) coin; ~**e Gewichtsangabe** false billing; **etw. in den ~en Hals bekommen** to get hold of the wrong end of the stick, to go down s. one's Sunday throat *(US)*; **in die ~e Kehle geraten** to go the wrong way *(coll.)*; **bewußt ~es Klagevorbringen** false answer; **Sache in ~em Licht erscheinen lassen** to throw a false light on a matter; ~**e Maße und Gewichte** false weights and measurements; ~**e Meinung** mistaken opinion; ~**e Meldung** false alarm; ~**er Mensch** perfidious person; ~**e Münze** spurious (fake) coin; ~**e Nachrichten** false news; ~**e Nachricht aufbringen** to forge news; ~**er Name** assumed (fictitious) name; ~**e Namensführung** false impersonation; ~**e Nummer wählen** to dial a wrong number; **am ~en Platz sein** to be in the wrong place, to be a square peg in a round hole; ~**er Prophet** false prophet; ~**e Rechnung** miscalculation; ~**e Schiffspapiere** false papers; ~**e Schlange** snake in the grass; ~**er Schmuck** imitation jewellery; ~**en Schritt tun** to take a wrong step; **auf der ~en Seite aus der Straßenbahn aussteigen** to get out at the wrong side of a tram; **auf der ~en Seite stehen** to ply a losing game; ~**es Spiel** double-dealing, misplay *(US)*; ~**es Spiel mit jem. treiben** to play s. o. false, to double-cross s. o. *(sl.)*; ~**e Spur hinterlassen** to draw a red herring over a trail; **an der ~en Stelle lachen** to laugh at the wrong place; **auf der ~en Straßenseite fahren** to drive on the wrong side of the road; ~**e Tatsachen vorspiegeln** to misrepresent fraudulently; **Kredit unter Vorspiegelung ~er Tatsachen erhalten** to obtain money by false pretences; ~**e Telefonverbindung** wrong connexion; ~**er Titel** bogus title; ~**en Ton anschlagen** to strike a false note; ~**e Übersetzung** wrong translation; **auf ~en Voraussetzungen beruhen** to rest on erroneous premises; ~**e Vorstellung** misconception, wrong idea; ~**en Weg einschlagen** to take the wrong way (road); ~ **angesetzte Werbung** misplaced advertising; ~**er Würfel** loaded die; **mit ~en Würfeln spielen** to cog; ~**es Zeugnis ablegen** to bear false witness, to give false evidence; ~**es Zitat** misquotation; ~**er Zug** wrong move.

Falsch|angaben, gravierende actionable misrepresentation; ~**anschuldigung** false accusation; ~**anzeige** misrepresentation; ~**aussage** false evidence, false witness, mentition; ~**bekundung** falsification; ~**beurkundung** falsification of a registry; ~**bezeichnung von Waren** misbranding of goods; ~**buchung** false (fraudulent, wrong) entry, misentry; ~**darstellung** misstatement; **unbeabsichtigte ~darstellung** innocent misrepresentation.

Falsche, genau das ~ tun to do the wrong thing in the wrong place.

Falscheid false oath (swearing);
~ **schwören** to forswear, to commit perjury.

Falschen, an den ~ geraten to catch a tartar.

fälschen to falsify, to feign, *(Geld)* to fabricate, to counterfeit, *(Nachrichten)* to slant, *(Nahrungsmittel)* to adulterate, *(Spielkarte)* to mark, to nick, *(Urkunde)* to forge, to falsify, to doctor, to fake *(US)*, *(verdrehen)* to distort, *(Würfel)* to load, to cog;
Abrechnungen ~ to falsify the accounts; **Banknoten ~** to forge bank notes; **Bilanz ~** to cook (fake, doctor, tamper) a balance sheet; **Bücher ~** to falsify the accounts; **Geschäftsbericht ~** to fake a business report; **Nahrungsmittel ~** to adulterate food; **Rechnungsposten ~** to falsify an item in an amount; **Scheck ~** to alter (forge, raise, *US*) a check; **Testament ~** to fabricate (forge) a will; **Unterschrift ~** to counterfeit (forge) a signature; **Urkunde ~** to forge a document; **Wahlergebnis ~** to manipulate the election returns; **Wechsel ~** to forge a bill (promissary note).

Fälscher counterfeiter, forger, fabricator, imitator, faker *(coll.)*, falsificator, falsifier, adulterer, adulterator;
~**bande** counterfeiting ring; ~**werkstatt** coiner's den, forger's shop, bogus press *(US)*; ~**zentrale** counterfeiting ring.

falschgehen *(Uhr)* to go wrong;
in seiner Vermutung ~ to be wrong in one's surmise.

Falschgeld counterfeit (bad, *Br.*, base, forged, white, adulterated, bogus, *US*, queer, *US*) money, bogus bill *(US)*, base (false) coin, counterfeit, snide, queery *(sl.)*, queer *(sl.)*, sinker *(US sl.)*, wallpaper *(sl.)*;
~ **anfertigen** to counterfeit money; ~ **in Umlauf bringen (setzen)** to pass (publish) counterfeit money (forged coins), to put forged notes (false money) in circulation, to utter forged money, to push *(sl.)*, to shove the queer *(sl.)*; ~ **loswerden (unterbringen)** to put (get) off a counterfeit note (false coin); ~ **bei jem. loswerden** to palm off a bad coin on s. o.;
~**druckerei** bogus *(US)* (forging) press; ~**note** counterfeit note; ~**scheine** spurious bills; ~**verbreiter** paper pusher; ~**verbreitung** uttering false notes; ~**verteiler** dropper.

Falschheit falsehood, falsity, insincerity, deceit;
keiner ~ fähig sein to be incapable of deceit.

fälschlich mistaken, wrong, incorrect, erroneous;
~ **beschuldigt** wrongly accused;
sich ~ als Arzt ausgeben to pretend to be a doctor; **j. ~ verdächtigen** to hold s. o. wrongly suspicion;
von ~en Voraussetzungen ausgehen to proceed on wrong assumptions.

Falschlieferung wrong shipment.

Falschmeldung false news (report), *(Zeitung)* canard, hoax;
~ **verbreiten** to spread (circulate) false news, to disseminate a false report.

falschmünzen to forge coins, to counterfeit.

Falschmünzer [false] coiner *(Br.)*, counterfeiter, falsifier, forger of coins, adulterator, queery-bit maker *(sl.)*;
~**bande** counterfeiting ring.

Falschmünzerei counterfeiting, false coining;
~ **betreiben** to counterfeit (forge) coins, to coin base money.

Falschmünzwerkstatt coiner's den.

falschspielen to cheat at cards.

Falschspieler foul player, card sharper, blackleg *(coll.)*.

Fälschung falsification, false making (forgery), imitation, counterfeiting, adulteration, fabrication, fake, phony *(US sl.)*,

mock, *(Banknote)* counterfeit, dud *(sl.)*, *(Entstellung)* distortion, *(Gemälde)* fake picture, *(Nahrungsmittel)* adulteration, *(Urkunden)* forgery;
~ **eines Arbeitszeugnisses** false character *(Br.)*; ~ **von Banknoten** forgery of bank notes; ~ **einer Bilanz** falsification (window dressing) of a balance sheet; ~ **von Geschäftsunterlagen** falsification of accounts; ~ **eines Passes** forgery of a passport; ~ **von Postwertzeichen** forgery of postal stamps; ~ **von Rechnungsbüchern** falsification of accounts; ~ **eines Schecks** alteration (raising, *US*) of a check; ~ **der Wahlergebnisse** manipulation of the election returns; ~ **von Warenzeichen** imitation of trademarks; ~ **eines Wechsels** forgery of a bill;
~ **anfertigen** to falsify; ~ **begehen** to commit forgery; ~ **einwenden** to put in a plea of forgery; **sich als ~ herausstellen** to prove to be a forgery; ~ **sein** to be a fake; **~en in den Geschäftsbüchern vornehmen** to falsify business records; **der ~ für schuldig befunden werden** to be found guilty of forgery.
Fälschungs | einwand erheben to put in a plea of forgery; **~mittel** adulterant; **~versuch** attempted forgery.
Falschurkunde forged instrument (document);
~ **in Umlauf setzen** to utter a forged document.
Falsifikat counterfeit, falsification, *(Banknote)* forged note, forgery, dud *(Br., sl.)*.
faltbarer Stuhl collapsible chair.
Falt | bett folding (camp) bed; **~blatt, ~prospekt** leaflet, pull-out, folder *(US)*; **großes ~blatt** broadside; **~boot** collapsible boat.
Fältchen um die Augen wrinkles round the eyes.
Faltdach *(Auto)* collapsible top.
Falte fold, *(Hose)* crease, *(Papier)* bite, *(Stirn)* pucker, wrinkle;
in den geheimsten ~n seines Herzens in the innermost recess of one's soul;
im Rücken ~n werfen *(Rock)* to pucker at the back; **seine Stirn in ~n ziehen** to wrinkle (pucker up) one's forehead (brow).
falten, Blatt Papier to fold a sheet of paper; **Hände im Schoß ~** to sit on one's hands.
faltenlose Stirn smooth brow.
Faltenrock pleated skirt.
faltiges Gesicht wrinkled (lined) face.
Falt | schachtel folding box, collapsible carton; **~stuhl** collapsible chair; **~tür** folding door.
Falz *(Buchbinden)* lap.
falzen, Papier to fold (crease) paper.
Falzmaschine folding machine.
familiär familiar, *(ungezwungen)* free and easy, informal;
~ **miteinander verkehren** to be on familiar terms;
~er Ausdruck colloquialism, informal expression; **~e Beziehungen** intimate relations; **aus ~en Gründen** for family reasons; **~er Umgang** familiarity.
Familie family, folk *(Br.)*, folks *(US)*, *(Abkunft)* stock, lineage, house, name, *(Haushalt)* household;
aus guter ~ good-class, from a good family; **im Schoße der ~** in the bosom of the family; **nicht zu einer bekannten ~ gehörend** of no special family;
angesehene ~ respectable family; **benachbarte ~** family next door; **Sozialhilfe beziehende ~** public-aid (needy, *US*) family, family on relief; **engste ~** immediate family; **erbeingesessene ~** long-established family; **fünfköpfige ~** family of five; **fürsorgebedürftige ~** needy family; **gute ~** gentle family; **kinderreiche ~** large family; **meine ~** my people; **umquartierte ~** rehoused family; **unterhaltsberechtigte ~** family dependent upon s. o. for support; **von der Gemeinde unterstützte ~** family on relief, public-aid family; **unterstützungsbedürftige ~** needy family *(US)*, public-aid family; **zerrüttete ~** broken home;
~ **mit in der Ausbildung befindlichen Kindern** family with dependent children; ~ **mit höherem Einkommen** upper-income family;
von einer puritanischen ~ abstammen to come of Puritan stock; **ganz in seiner ~ aufgehen** to have no life apart from one's family; **j. in seine ~ aufnehmen** to receive s. o. into one's family; ~ **auseinanderreißen** to disrupt a family; **seine ~ der Gefahr des Notstandes aussetzen** to utterly neglect one's family; **in eine ~ einheiraten** to marry into a family; ~ **ernähren** to maintain (raise) a family; **zur ~ gehören** to be one of the household; **zu einer angesehenen ~ gehören** to belong to a family of good standing; ~ **gründen** to found a family; **seine ~ auf die Fürsorge angewiesen sein lassen** to force one's family on the town *(US)*; **bei seiner ~ leben** to live with one's people; **in der ~ liegen** to run in the blood (family); **nur für seine ~ da sein** to be a family man; **Lebensunterhalt einer ~ sicherstellen** to support a family; **aus einer adligen ~ stammen** to descend from a noble family; **aus einer guten ~ stammen** to come (stem) from a good line (family, stock, kin), to issue from a good family; ~ **unterhalten** to support (supply, maintain, sustain) a family; **große ~ unterhalten** to provide for a large family; **an die ~ zurückfallen** to return to the family.
Familien | abkommen domestic agreement, family arrangement (compact, settlement); **~abzüge** *(Einkommensteuer)* allowance (credit) for dependants, personal allowance; **~ähnlichkeit** family likeness (resemblance); **~angehörige** kinsfolk; **~angehöriger** family member, kinsman, *(Einkommensteuer)* dependant relative; **abhängige ~angehörige** dependence; **~angehörigkeit** family relationship; **~angelegenheit** family affair, private concern of a family; **dringende ~angelegenheit** *(Urlaubsgrund)* emergency visit; **mit ~anschluß** as one of the family; **~anwalt** family lawyer; **~anzeige** personal announcement; **~archiv** family archives; **~ausgabe** household edition; **~ausgleichskasse** family equalization fund; **~auto** family sedan; **~bad** mixed bathing; **~bande** family ties; **~bedürfnisse** family needs; **kostenlose ~beförderung** free family passage; **~beihilfe** family allowance (benefit); **betriebliche ~beihilfe** company family allowance; **~beihilfeprogramm** family assistance programme; **~besitz** family estate; **im ~besitz** family-owned; **im ~besitz sein** to be in possession of a family; **~betreuung** family service; **~betrieb** family-owned business (enterprise), family firm; **landwirtschaftlicher ~betrieb** agricultural family enterprise, family-sized farm *(US)*; **~beziehungen** family relations; **~bild** family photograph; **~bindung** family ties; **~buch** register of marriages; **~budget** *(fam.)* family budget; **~dynastie** family dynasty.
familieneigene Kräfte family labo(u)r.
Familien | eigenschaft sein to run in the family; **~einheit** family unit; **~erbstück** family inheritance, heirloom; **~ereignis** family situation; **~ermäßigung** family reduction (rates, *US*); **~fahrschein** family ticket; **~faktotum** old family retainer; **~feier, ~fest** family do; **~fideikommiß** entailed estate; **~forschung** genealogy.
familienfreundlich family-orien[ta]ted.
Familien | fürsorge family casework (care, welfare); **~geist** familiar spirit; **~gemeinschaft** household; **in ~gemeinschaft leben** to share s. o.'s household; **~gericht** family court *(Br.)*; **~geschichte** family history; **~gesellschaft** family company, family corporation, close company *(Br.)* (corporation, *US*), exempt private company; **~grab** family grave, family plot *(US)*; **~größe** family size; **in der ~gruft beisetzen** to lay in the family vault; **~gründung** foundation of a family; **~gut** entailed (family) estate, family seat; **~haupt** head of the family, family head; **~haushalt** family household; **~haushaltsplan** household (family) budget; **~haushaltsrechnung** family accounting; **~heim und Mobiliar** matrimonial home and contents *(Br.)*; **~herkunft** family background; **~hilfe** family assistance; **~hotel** family (residential) hotel; **~kaufkraft** family buying power; **~krach** family row, family jar; **~krankheiten** family medical history; **~- und eigene Krankheiten** family and personal history; **~kreis** family circle; **~kutsche** family automobile (sedan), family coach; **siebensitzige ~kutsche** seven-seater-saloon, family sedan; **~leben** family (home, domestic) life; **~leben pflegen** to rock a cradle; **~lektüre** family reading; **sich zur ~lektüre nicht eignen** to be unfit for family reading; **~mitglied** family member; **als mithelfendes ~mitglied tätig sein** to be family-employed; **~mitglieder** home-folk; **sich den Wünschen der älteren ~mitglieder fügen** to defer to one's elders; **~nachrichten** *(Zeitung)* birth, marriages and deaths; **~name** family (last, *US*) name, surname *(Br.)*, cognomen; **~namen entehren** to disgrace the family name; **~oberhaupt** family head, pater familias; **~packung** *(Waren)* family size, giant package; **hochwertige ~pauschalversicherung** comprehensive high-ticket family policy; **~pension** residential (family) hotel; **~pfründe** family living *(Br.)*; **~planung** birth control, family planning; **bei der ~planung mit Rat und Tat zur Seite stehen** to provide family planning service and advice; **~prämie** family premium; **~rat** family meeting (council); **~recht** family law, law of domestic relations *(US)*; **Gesetz zur Reform des ~rechtes** Family Law Reform Act *(Br.)*; **~roman** family saga; **~schande** skeleton in the cupboard, family skeleton; **~schmuck** family jewels; **~sinn** familiar spirit; **~sitz** family estate (seat); **~stamm** stirpes; **~stammbaum** family tree, genealogical table, stirpes, lineage; **~stammbaum zurückverfolgen** to trace back one's family line; **~stand** family (personal, marital) status; **~stand der Ehefrau** coverture; **~standslohn** family wage; **~stiftung** personal (private) trust, family pool; **~streit** family row, family argument; **~szene** domestic scene; **~treffen** family gathering; **~übereinkommen** family arrangement (compact,

contract); ~**überführung** family passage; ~**unternehmen** family partnership, family firm (enterprise), family-run concern, family-owned enterprise; ~**unterhalt** upkeep of a family; ~**unterstützung** family allowance (assistance, benefit); ~**unterstützungsprogramm** family assistance program(me); ~**vater** breadwinner, breadearner, *(typischer)* family man; ~**verhältnisse** family background; **in geordneten ~verhältnissen leben** to have a normal home life; ~**vermögen** family estate (property); ~**verpflichtungen** family commitments; ~**versicherung** family insurance; ~**versorgung** family protection; ~**vertrag** family contract; ~**vorstand** head of a family; ~**wappen** family crest, [household] coat, armour *(Br.)*; ~**wohnung** family dwelling (living accommodation); ~**zeitschrift** family magazine; ~**zulage** family allowance (benefit); ~**zusammenführung** family reunion; ~**zusammenkunft** family gathering; ~**zusammensetzung** family composition; ~**zuschlag** family allowance *(Br.)* (benefit); ~**zuwachs** addition to the family.

famos wonderful, marvel(l)ous, splendid, nailing *(sl.)*, swell *(US)*;
~**e Idee** marvel(l)ous idea; ~**er Kerl** jolly good fellow, a regular brick *(fam.)*, swell guy *(US)*.

famulieren, in der Klinik to walk the wards.

Fan fanatical supporter, fan *(coll.)*, buff *(US fam.)*.

Fanal *(fig.)* beacon, torch.

Fanatiker extremist, fanatic, zealot, hound *(US sl.)*, gold buck *(US sl.)*.

fanatisch|er Anhänger fanatical (zealous) supporter; ~**e Sekte** fanatic sect.

Fanatismus fanaticism, zealotry.

Fang *(fig.)* bargain, catch, haul, draught, draw, *(Fischer)* catchings, *(Jäger)* bag, kill, take;
guten ~ machen to get a fine (make a good) haul, to make a scoop (bargain);
~**beschränkung** fishing limitation.

Fänge, in seinen ~n halten to hold in one's clutches.

fangen to catch, *(fesseln)* to captivate, to fascinate;
sich ~ to regain possession of, to pull o. s. together *(fam.)*, *(Flugzeug)* to flatten (straighten out); **Feuer ~** to catch fire; **leicht Feuer ~** to be easily smitten; **Fische im Netz ~** to net fish; **Kunden ~** to tout customers; **Ohrfeige ~** to get a box on the ear; **sich in der eigenen Schlinge ~** to be caught in (fall into) one's own trap; **sich in einem Staubecken ~** *(Wasser)* to collect in a basin; **Stimmen ~** to catch votes; **Tier in einer Falle ~** to catch a beast in a trap; **Tier mit der Schlinge ~** to snare (noose) an animal; **Verbrecher ~** to catch a criminal; **sich wieder ~** to find its feet again, to get o. s. back into shape, to pull up one's socks *(Br., coll.)*; **Zeugen durch geschickte Fragen ~** to trip a witness by skilful practices.

Fang|frage catch question; ~**gebiet**, ~**gründe** fishing area (ground); ~- **und Schongebiete** open and close areas; ~**geräte** fishing tackle; ~**grube** pitfall; ~**netz** *(Polizei)* dragnet, *(Straßenbahn)* tray *(Br.)*; ~**platz** fishing grounds; ~**schuß** coup de grace.

Fanklub fan club.

Farb|abstufungen, verschiedene graded tints; ~**abweichung** colo(u)r distortion; ~**andruck** colo(u)r (progressive) proof; ~**anstrich** coat of paint; ~**anzeige** colo(u)r advertising (unit); ~**aufnahme** colo(u)r photo (shot); ~**ballen** *(Druckerei)* dab.

Farbband copying (inking, typewriter, *Br.*) ribbon;
~**einsteller** ribbon switch; ~**transport** ribbon feed; ~**umstellung** ribbon reverse.

Farb|beilage colo(u)r supplement; ~**diapositiv** colo(u)r slide; ~**drehbleistift** propelling pencil with colo(u)red leads; ~**druck** colo(u)red impression, colo(u)r print; **fotografischer ~druck** carbon bromide, carbro.

Farbe colo(u)r, shade, paint, hue, *(Farbton)* tinge, tint, hue, shade;
in allen ~n erhältlich obtainable in all shades; **in allen ~n schillernd** rainbow-hued;
auffallende ~ striking colo(u)r; **ausgewaschene ~** washy colo(u)r; **sich beißende ~n** jarring colo(u)rs; **bunte ~n** vivid colo(u)rs; **gedämpfte ~** subdued colo(u)r; **grelle ~n** hard colo(u)rs; **leuchtende ~** bright colo(u)r; **licht- und waschechte ~** fast colo(u)r; **schreiende ~n** glaring colo(u)rs; **undefinierbare ~** nondescript colo(u)r; **unechte ~n** fugitive colo(u)rs; **zusammengesetzte ~n** secondary colo(u)rs;
~ auftragen to lay on colo(u)rs; **~ dick auftragen** *(fig.)* to lay it on thick *(fam.)*; **~ bekennen** to show one's hand, to lay one's cards on the table, to come clean, to own up; **gesunde ~n haben** to have a healthy complexion; **in düsteren ~n malen** to have a gloomy outlook; **etw. in kräftigen ~n schildern** to paint s. th. in bright colo(u)rs; **alles in rosigen ~n schildern** to paint everything in rosy colo(u)rs; **in schwarzen ~n schildern** to paint black; **alles in rosigen ~n sehen** to see everything through rose-colo(u)red spectacles; **einer Geschichte ~ verleihen** to lend colo(u)r to a story.

farbecht colo(u)r-fast, nonfading.

Farb|effekt colo(u)r effect; **automatisch justierte ~einstellungskontrolle** keyed automatic colo(u)r gain control.

Färbemittel colo(u)ring agent.

farbempfindlich colo(u)r-sensitive.

färben to colo(u)r, to dye, to tinge;
sich ~ *(Gesicht)* to get red, to blush; **waschecht ~** *(Wolle)* to dye in the grain.

Farben|auswahl choice of colo(u)rs; ~**bevorzugung des Konsumenten** consumer colo(u)r preference.

farbenblind colo(u)r-blind.

Farben|blindheit colo(u)r blindness; ~**fabrik** paint-manufacturing firm.

farbenfreudig bright, vivid.

Farben|geschäft paint shop (store, *US*); ~**händler** paint dealer, colo(u)rman; ~**industrie** paint and varnish industry; ~**kunstdruck** colo(u)red plate; ~**lichtdruck** collotype; ~**reichtum** wealth of colo(u)r; ~**skala** colo(u)r chart; ~**sortiment** set of colo(u)rs; ~**spiel** play of colo(u)rs; ~**steindruck** cromolithography; ~**trennung** colo(u)r separation; **vollkommene ~übereinstimmung** perfect match of colo(u)rs; ~**zusammenstellung** scheme of colo(u)rs, colo(u)r scheme.

Färberei dye works;
etw. in die ~ geben to send s. th. to be dyed;
~**gewerbe** dyeing trade.

Farb|fehler colo(u)r defect; ~**fernsehen** colo(u)r television; ~**fernseherröhre** colo(u)r-picture tube; ~**fernsehgerät**, ~**fernseher** colo(u)r television receiver (set); ~**fernsehsendung** colo(u)r television broadcasting, colo(u)rcast; ~**fernsehsystem** colo(u)r television system.

Farbfilm colo(u)r film;
~**aufnahme** filter shot; ~**verfahren** technicolo(u)r.

Farb|filter *(Foto)* colo(u)r filter; ~**fotodiapositiv** dye transfer; ~**fotografie** colo(u)r photography, photochromy; ~**gebung** colo(u)ring, tinting.

farbig colo(u)red, polychrome;
mit ~en Abbildungen with colo(u)red reproductions; ~**e Arbeitskräfte** colo(u)red labour; ~**er Bericht** colo(u)rful report; ~**e Kacheln** colo(u)r-glazed tiles; ~**e Schilderung** lively description; ~**e Schreibe** colo(u)rful style of writing.

Farbige colo(u)red people;
~**r** gentleman of colo(u)r, colo(u)red man.

Farb|kamera colo(u)r camera; ~**klischee** colo(u)r engraving (block, *Br.*); ~**komposition** colo(u)r composition; **greller ~kontrast** violent contrast of colo(u)rs; ~**kopie** colo(u)r print; ~**kunstdruck** colo(u)red plate; ~**läufer** *(drucktechn.)* rubber.

farblich aufeinander abgestimmt harmonized in colo(u)r.

farblos uncolo(u)red, colo(u)rless, *(fig.)* drab;
völlig ~ sein *(Rede)* to have no guts in it;
~**es Dasein führen** to lead a colo(u)rless existence; ~**e Schilderung** dull description; ~**er Stil** colo(u)rless style.

Farb|losigkeit *(fig.)* drab; ~**lösung** staining dip; ~**mine** colo(u)red cartridge; ~**muster** *(Werbung)* swatch; **nicht ganz dem ~muster entsprechend** off shade; ~**nuancen** touches of colo(u)r; ~**satz** set of colo(u)r plates; ~**satzskala** progressive proofs; ~**schattierung** colo(u)r gradation, hue; ~**skala** range of colo(u)rs; ~**stift** colo(u)red pencil; ~**stoff** dye, dyestuff; ~**tafel** colo(u)r chart; ~**ton** shade, tint; ~**tönung** colo(u)r gradation; ~**überzug** washing.

Färbung colo(u)r, *(Beeinflussung)* bias, *(Färben)* dyeing process;
politische ~ einer Zeitung political colo(u)r of a journal;
Politiker aller ~en antreffen to meet politicians of all shades.

Farbwalze inking roller;
schwingende ~ vibrator.

Farb|wiedergabe *(Foto)* colo(u)r rendering; **kombinierte ~wirkung** interplay of colo(u)rs; ~**zusatz** colo(u)ring agent.

Farce farce, *(Theater)* mockery;
Prozeß zu einer ~ machen to make a farce of a trial.

Farm farm, ranch.

Farmer farmer, rancher, ranger;
nicht einseitig kündbare ~kredite nonrecourse loans *(US)*.

Farmhaus farmhouse.

Fasching carnival.

Faschings|dienstag Shrove (Pancake) Tuesday, Mardi Gras *(US)*; ~**fest** carnival ball; ~**kostüm** carnival dress; ~**teilnehmer** carnivaler.

Faselei rigmarole, slobber, waffle.
Faselhans fabler, blatherer, rambler.
faselig scatterbrained, harum-scarum.
faseln to piffle, to drivel, to talk through one's hat *(sl.)*, to rot, to tripe, to blather, to waffle;
dummes Zeug ~ to talk nonsense (tommy rot, *sl.*), to be right of it *(sl.)*.
Faser thread, vein;
keine trockene ~ **mehr am Leibe haben** to be soaked to the skin, not to have a dry stitch on o. s.; **mit allen ~n seines Herzens an etw. hängen** to have one's heart in s. th.;
schweres ~papier cover stock; **~richtung** fibre direction; **~stoff** fibre, textile; **~zeichen** *(Banknote)* thread mark.
Faß cask, vat, tun, tub *(Br.)*, barrel;
vom ~ drawn from the wood, *(Bier)* on tap;
frisch angestochenes (angezapftes) ~ fresh tap; **sehr großes** ~ hogshead;
~ **ohne Boden** the bottomless pit; ~ **Wein** piece of wine;
aus einem ~ **abfüllen** to tap off from a barrel; ~ **anstechen** to tap (broach) a barrel; **dem** ~ **den Boden ausschlagen** to take the cake (biscuit); **in ein** ~ **füllen** to vat; ~ **kippen** to tilt a cask; ~ **ohne Boden sein** to swallow up more than one's earnings.
Fassade façade, front, face, shell;
ausgebrannte ~n burnt-out shells; **falsche** ~ false (put-up) front;
~ **erneuern** to reface; **hinter die** ~ **schauen** to see behind the curtain.
Fassaden|beleuchtung floodlighting; **~kletterer** cat burglar, porch climber *(US)*.
Faß|bier draught beer; **~boden** head of a cask; **~butter** tub butter.
Fäßchen tub.
Faßdaube stave.
fassen to grasp, to seize, to grab, to lay hold, *(Anker)* to bite, *(ausdrücken)* to express, to formulate, to put, *(beinhalten)* to contain, to hold, *(begreifen)* to conceive, to grasp, to understand, to comprehend, to believe, *(Bremsen)* to grip, to hold, *(jur.)* to draft, to draw up, to word, *(Quelle)* to curb, *(Treibstoff)* to fuel, to refill, *(Verbrecher)* to apprehend, to catch;
sich ~ to pull o. s. together, to find one's tongue; **etw. ins Auge** ~ to envisage s. th.; **Bandenführer** ~ to catch the leader of the gang; **Bericht streng wissenschaftlich** ~ to couch a report in scientific terms; **Beschluß** ~ to adopt a resolution, to resolve *(US)*; **j. bei seiner Ehre** ~ to appeal to s. one's hono(u)r; **Entschluß** ~ to make up one's mind, to reach a decision; **Essen** ~ *(mil.)* to draw rations; **Fuß** ~ to gain a foothold, to strike root; **seine Gedanken in Worte** ~ to formulate one's thoughts; **sich in Geduld** ~ to possess one's soul in patience; **sein Glück kaum** ~ to hardly believe one's luck; **j. an der Gurgel** ~ to pin s. o. by the throat; **sich ein Herz** ~ to pluck up courage; **Kohlen** ~ to recoal, to bunker; **j. am Kragen** ~ to grab s. o. by the collar, to collar s. o.; **sich kurz** ~ to be brief, to express o. s. briefly; **um es kurz zu** ~ to make it brief; **Mut** ~ to summon up one's courage; **sich an die eigene Nase** ~ to sweep before one's own door; **neu** ~ to reword, to re-write; **2000 Personen** ~ *(Saal)* to have a seating capacity for 2000 people; **sich rasch** ~ to recover quickly; **Schreiben kurz** ~ to keep a letter brief; **j. an seiner schwachen Seite** ~ to get at s. one's weak side; **j. auf frischer Tat** ~ to catch s. o. red-handed; **Tritt** ~ to fall into step; **Vertrauen zu jem.** ~ to have confidence in s. o.; **sich wieder** ~ to rally one's spirits; **in Worte** ~ to word, to voice; **in andere Worte** ~ to make s. th. read differently; **Wurzel** ~ to strike root; **Zuneigung zu jem.** ~ to begin to like (take a liking to) s. o.;
j. zu ~ **bekommen** to get hold of s. o.; **j. nicht** ~ **können** not to be able to pin s. o. down; **sich vor Glück nicht** ~ **können** to be beside o. s. with happiness; **Perlen neu** ~ **lassen** to have pearls reset.
Fässer, Wein auf ~ **füllen** to cask (barrel) wine; ~ **und Kisten an Bord hieven** to hoist casks and crates aboard.
fässerweise by the barrel (cask);
~ **kaufen** to buy by the barrel.
Faß|hahn tap; **~inhalt** volume of a cask, contents of a cask; **~inhalt berechnen** to gauge the contents of a barrel; **~ladung** barrel cargo; **~lager** gantry, stilling, stillion.
faßlich, schwer difficult to understand.
Fasson shape, cut, make, form;
aus der ~ **geraten** to lose one's presence of mind, to go haywire, *(dick werden)* to lose one's figure; **nach seiner eigenen** ~ **leben** to live up to one's principles; **aus der** ~ **gegangen sein** *(Hut)* to have lost its shape.
Faßreifen hoop.
Fassung tenor, text, version, wording, draft, drafting, formulation, *(Juwelen)* setting, *(Lampe)* lamp holder, socket, *(Stil)* make;
außer ~ upset; **in der** ~ **vom** *(Gesetz)* as amended on; **nicht im geringsten aus der** ~ **gebracht** not in the least perturbed (disconcerted), with no skirt button out of place; **ungültig wegen unklarer** ~ void for uncertainty;
abgeänderte (berichtigte) ~ amended version; **abgeschwächte** ~ watered-down version; **auf Band aufgenommene** ~ tape-recorded version; **englische** ~ English version; **ergänzte** ~ amended version; **erste** ~ first draft; **gekürzte** ~ abridged version; **maßgebende** ~ authentic text, authorized version; **revidierte** ~ revised version;
~ **für Erwachsene** adult version; ~ **eines Gesetzentwurfes** drafting of a bill;
seine ~ **bewahren** to keep one's balance; **jdm. aus der** ~ **bringen** to put s. o. out of his play (face), to discomfit (discompose, disconcert, upset, stump, unhinge) s. o., to put (stare) s. o. out of countenance; **in eine gemeinverständliche** ~ **bringen** to couch in popular style; **nicht leicht aus der** ~ **zu bringen** not easily disconcerted; **aus der** ~ **geraten** to lose control of o. s.; **aus der** ~ **nehmen** *(Schmuckstück)* to dismount; **ganz aus der** ~ **sein** to be badly shaken; ~ **verlieren** to lose one's balance (one's hair); **seine** ~ **wiedergewinnen** to regain one's composure.
Fassungskraft comprehension, mental capacity, reach, grasp, grip;
jds. ~ **übersteigen** to be beyond s. o. *(fam.)*.
fassungslos disconcerted, shaken, bewildered, thunderstruck, nonplussed, rattled, perplexed;
~ **vor Empörung** speechless with indignation;
j. ~ **ansehen** to give s. o. a disconcerted look; ~ **sein** to be beside o. s.; ~ **weinen** to weep uncontrollably.
Fassungslosigkeit discomposure, bewilderment.
Fassungsvermögen comprehensive (mental) faculty, *(Fahrzeug)* loading (holding) capacity, *(Saal)* seating capacity, *(Tank)* tankage;
~ **eines Eisenbahnzuges** train capacity, trainload;
über jds. ~ **gehen** to be beyond s. o. *(fam.)*; ~ **von 50.000 Zuschauern haben** to hold 50.000 spectators.
Faßwaren barrelled goods, barrels.
faßweise by the barrel.
fast next to, almost, nearly, close to;
~ **gar nichts** hardly anything; ~ **nie** hardly ever, practically never; ~ **niemand** hardly anybody, almost no one *(US)*; ~ **unmöglich** next to (all but) impossible.
fasten to fast, to starve *(fam.)*, to go without food.
Fastenkur fasting cure, *(streng)* hunger cure.
Fastnachtszug carnival procession.
Faszikel fascicle, *(Veröffentlichung)* instal(l)ment.
Faszination spell, fascination.
faszinieren to fascinate, to enthrall, to enrapture, to captivate, to spellbind.
faszinierend fascinating, captivating, enchanting, magnetic, bewitching.
fasziniert, j. ~ **anstarren** to gaze at s. o. in fascination; ~ **sein** to knock o. s. out *(sl.)*; **von jdm.** ~ **sein** to be under the spell of s. o.
Fata Morgana mirage.
fatal disastrous, fatal, calamitious;
~e Angelegenheit awkward (embarrassing) situation; **~e Auswirkungen** disastrous consequences; **~er Irrtum** ghastly mistake; **~es Lächeln** ominous smile; **in einer ~en Lage sein** to be in a precarious situation.
Fatalismus fatalism.
fauchen to spit, to snap.
faul idle, lazy, inert, afraid of hard work, *(Firma)* unsound, *(Fisch)* rotten, stinking, tainted, putrid, *(Frucht)* rotten, bad, decayed, *(Kunde)* bad, phony *(US sl.)*, *(Moral)* rotten, *(Wasser)* foul, *(windig)* phony, dubious, shady, fishy;
durch und durch ~ rotten to the core; **nicht** ~ prompt, smart;
~ **aussehen** to look suspicious; ~ **wie die Sünde sein** to be a lazybones; **jem. reichlich** ~ **vorkommen** to smell a rat;
~e Ausrede lame (paltry) excuse; **~er Boden** *(Schiff)* foul bottom; **mit ~en Eiern beschmeißen** to rotten-egg; **~es Fleisch** tainted meat; **~er Friede** hollow peace; **~es Geschäft** shady business, equivocal (illicit) transaction; **~er Geschmack** filthy taste; **auf der ~en Haut liegen** to lie down on the job; **~er Hund** lazy dog, layabout, idler, lazy good-for-nothing; **~es Leben führen** to eat the bread of idleness; **~e Redensarten** hollow pretext; **~e Sache** bad egg, fishy (nasty) business; **~er Scheck** dud check (cheque, *Br.*); **~e Schulden** bad (doubtful) debts; **~er Schuldner** bad debtor; **~er Strick** idler, good-for-nothing; **~er**

Wechsel query (worthless) bill; ~**er Zahler** slow payer; ~**er Zauber** monkey business, eyewash, humbug, mumbo-jumbo, hogwash *(US)*.
faulen to decay, to rot, to go bad, *(Wasser)* to putrefy, to become putrid.
faulendes Wasser putrid water.
Faulenzen lounge, lounging, idleness, no-work.
faulenzen to be lazy (idle), to idle, to [be on the] loaf, to drone, to lollygag *(sl.)*;
auf jds. Kosten ~ to loaf on s. o.
Faulenzer loafer, lazybones, sluggard, do-nothing, idler, lounger, truant, loaf *(coll.)*.
Faulenzerei idleness, no-work, lounging.
Faulenzerleben führen to eat the bread of idleness.
Faulfracht dead freight.
Faulheit laziness, idleness, sloth;
glatte ~ pure and simple laziness;
sich die ~ **angewöhnen** to acquire idle habits; ~ **belohnen** to put a premium on laziness; **Anwandlung von** ~ **haben** to have a lazy fit; **vor** ~ **stinken** to be bone-idle (-lazy).
Faulpelz sluggard, idler, idle fellow, lazybones, lazy-boots, crawler, do-nothing.
Faust, auf eigene on one's own hat (hook, *US coll.*), off one's own bat;
geballte ~ clenched fist;
~ **in der Tasche ballen** to bottle up one's rage; **jem. mit der** ~ **drohen** to shake one's fist at s. o.; **aus der** ~ **essen** to eat with one's fingers; **auf eigene** ~ **handeln** to do s. th. off one's own bat (hook, *US coll.*), to go it alone; **wie die** ~ **aufs Auge passen** to fit exactly; **mit eiserner** ~ **regieren** to rule with a rod of iron; **mit der** ~ **auf den Tisch schlagen** to bang one's fist on the table, to put one's foot down, to get tough about it; ~ **des Diktators im Nacken spüren** to be under the heel of a dictator; **auf eigene** ~ **vorgehen** to play a lone hand on s. th.
Fäustchen, sich ins ~ **lachen** to laugh up one's sleeve.
faustdick|e Lüge whopper, whopping (whacking) lie;
etw. ~ **auftragen** to lay it on with a trowel (thick); **es** ~ **hinter den Ohren haben** to know the ropes, to be pretty fly *(Br., sl.)*;
es kommt immer gleich ~ it never rains but it pours.
Fäuste, grobe clumsy hands;
mit den bloßen ~**n kämpfen** to fight with naked fists.
Faust|feuerwaffe small firearm; ~**formel** approximate formula; ~**handschuh** mitten; ~**kampf** pugilism, boxing [match]; ~**pfand** pawn, dead pledge; ~**recht** law of the jungle, lynch (club, fist) law; ~**recht üben** to take the law into one's own hands; ~**regel** rule-of-thumb; ~**schlag** punch, sock *(sl.)*; ~**skizze** rough (first) sketch.
Fauteuil armchair, easy chair.
Fautfracht dead freight, forfeit.
Fauxpas slip, gaffe, bad break;
~ **begehen** to make a blunder.
Favorit favo(u)rite, minion;
~ **an Stelle eines anderen werden** to put s. one's nose out of joint.
Favoriten *(Börsenwerte)* standard (special, *US*) stocks, seasoned securities, *(Börse)* leaders, glamor stocks *(US)*;
~ **im Schallplattengeschäft** top-selling records;
jem. nicht mehr zum ~**kreis zählen** to count o. s. out of the race.
Faxen silly jokes, nonsense, buffoonery, tomfoolery;
~ **machen** to play the fool, to lark about; ~ **schneiden** to pull faces;
~**macher** buffoon, wag, grimacer.
Fazilitäten facilities.
Fazit final issue, upshot, total;
~ **ziehen** to total up, to strike a balance.
FD-Zug long-distance train, limited express *(US)*.
fechten *(schnorren)* to cadge, to sponge, to panhandle *(sl.)*.
Feder *(Bett)* spring, *(Schreibfeder)* pen, quill, *(Vogel)* feather, plume;
mit eilender ~ in all haste; **mit fremden** ~**n** in borrowed plumes;
mit der ~ **in der Hand** quill in hand;
gewandte ~ ready pen;
~ **am Hut** feather in one's cap;
etw. der ~ **anvertrauen** to put down in writing; ~ **ergreifen** to put one's (set) pen to paper; **geschickte** ~ **führen** to wield a skilful pen; **scharfe** ~ **führen** to have a scathing pen; **zur** ~ **greifen** to put (set) one's pen to paper; **gewandte** ~ **haben (gute** ~ **schreiben)** to be a ready writer, to have a facile pen; **einige** ~**n gelassen haben** to have been mauled by the critics; **aus den** ~**n kriechen** to tumble out; **in die** ~**n kriechen** to turn in; **seiner** ~ **freien Lauf lassen** to write without restraint; **bei einer Diskussion** ~**n lassen müssen** to have to concede a few points in a discussion; **sich mit fremden** ~**n schmücken** to steal s. one's thunder, to strut in borrowed plumes; **zum ersten Mal die** ~ **üben** to flesh one's pen; **etw. mit Nut und** ~ **versehen** to tongue and groove s. th.;
den Vogel erkennt man bei den ~**n** you can tell a leopard by its spots;
~**aufhängung** spring suspension; ~**barometer** aneroid barometer; ~**bett** eiderdown-quilt, feather-bed; ~**bolzen** spring bolt; ~**fuchser** scribbler, quill driver, pencil pusher *(sl.)*; ~**fuchserei** quill driving.
federführend initiating, leading, in charge;
~ **sein** to lead a syndicate;
~**e Bank** syndicate manager, leading underwriter; ~**e Gesellschaft** pilot company.
Feder|führung syndicate management *(Konsortialgeschäft)* leading underwriter; ~**führung haben** to lead a syndicate; ~**halter** penholder; ~**kasten** pencil box; ~**kernmatratze** spring mattress; ~**kontakt** spring contact; **nicht viel** ~**lesens machen** to make no bones about it; **nicht viel** ~**lesens mit jem. machen** to give s. o. short shrift; ~**messer** penknife.
federn to be resilient (springy), *(Tischler)* to tongue;
Fahrzeug ~ to spring a vehicle; **gut** ~ *(Wagen)* to have good springs; **nicht** ~ *(Matratze)* not to give.
federnd|e Aufhängung spring (cushioned) suspension; ~**es Lager** flexible bearing; **mit** ~**en Schritten** with a springy step.
Feder|schloß spring lock; ~**strich** dash, stroke of the pen; **mit einem** ~**strich** with a stroke of the pen.
Federung *(Auto)* spring suspension, *(Biegsamkeit)* flexibility, *(Lager)* resilience;
gute ~ **haben** to have good springs.
Feder|vieh fowl, poultry; ~**wild** game birds; ~**wolke** spindrift cloud, cirrus; ~**zeichnung** pen-and-ink sketch, line drawing; ~**zirkel** bow compasses, spring dividers; ~**zug** stroke of the pen.
Fegefeuer purgatory.
fegen to sweep, *(Schnee)* to clear away;
über die Ebene ~ *(Schneestürme)* to rage across the plain; **um eine Ecke** ~ *(Auto)* to whisk round a corner; **Papiere vom Tisch** ~ to sweep papers from the table; **durch alle Ritzen** ~ *(Wind)* to rush through all the cracks; **Schmutz in die Ecke** ~ to sweep dirt into a corner; **vor seiner eigenen Tür** ~ to mind one's own business; **in ein Zimmer** ~ to sail into a room.
Fehde feud, warfare;
literarische ~ paper war;
in offener ~ **mit jem. leben** to be in open feud with s. o., to be at daggers drawn with s. o., to be on fighting terms;
~**handschuh aufnehmen** to take up the glove; **jem. den** ~**handschuh hinwerfen** to throw down the gauntlet (glove) to s. o.
Fehl, ohne without fault, faultless, flawless; **ohne** ~ **und Tadel** without blemish.
fehl am Platze out of place, wide of the mark;
~ **sein** to be in the wrong box, to be a square peg in a round hole; **mit seiner Bemerkung** ~ **sein** to be talking out of turn.
Fehl|ablieferung *(Brief)* misdelivery; ~**abschluß** deficit balance; ~**abzüge** shorts; ~**alarm** false call; ~**alarmprozentsatz** false call rate; ~**anflug** missed approach; ~**anlage** misemployment; ~**anpassung** *(el.)* mismatch, *(Soziologie)* maladjustment; ~**anruf** lost call, wrong connection; ~**anzeige** negative report, *(falsche Angabe)* false declaration, no entry, *(Computer)* error indicator, *(auf Fragebogen)* nil, *(mil.)* nil return; ~**anzeige erforderlich** nil return requested; ~**auslegung** misinterpretation; ~**bedarf** shortfall, deficit, uncovered demand; ~**belichtung** incorrect exposure; ~**benennung** misnomer; ~**berechnung** miscalculation; ~**besetzung** mistaken appointment, *(Theater)* miscasting; ~**bestand** deficiency, shortage, short[fall] *(US)*, *(Lager)* inventory deficiency.
Fehlbetrag missing (deficient) amount, deficit, deficiency, shortage, *(Kasse)* cash deficit, shortage in the cash;
jährlicher ~ annual debit;
~ **im Staatshaushalt** deficit of the budget, budget[ary] (fiscal) deficit;
mit einem ~ **abschließen** to close with a deficit; ~ **aufweisen** to show a deficit; ~ **ausgleichen (decken)** to make up a shortage (the deficit), to supply a deficiency.
Fehl|beträge, Überschüsse und shorts and overs; ~**beurteilung** mistake of judgment; ~**bezeichnung** misnomer, *(Testament)* false words; ~**bitte** vain request; ~**bitte tun** to meet with a refusal; ~**bohrung** dry hole; ~**buchung** erroneous entry; ~**deutung** misinterpretation; ~**diagnose stellen** to make a

diagnostic error; ~**disposition** misplanning; ~**druck** freak, foul proof, spoilt sheet, *(Briefmarke)* error, *(Philatelie)* misprint, error.
fehldrucken to misprint.
Fehleinsatz misdirection.
Fehlen lack, failing, failure, *(Abwesenheit)* absence;
unentschuldigtes ~ absence without leave; **dauerndes unentschuldigtes** ~ chronic unexcused absence;
häufiges ~ **am Arbeitsplatz** absenteeism; ~ **eines Testamentes** intestacy.
fehlen to be absent (missing), to fail, to want, to miss, *(Geld)* to be short, to lack;
an allen Ecken und Enden ~ to be short of everything; **entschuldigt** ~ to be absent with leave, to be on a leave of absence; **an der nötigen Erfahrung** ~ to lack the necessary experience; **jem. an Mut** ~ to lack the courage; **es an nichts** ~ **haben** to lack for nothing; **in der Schule** ~ to be absent from school; **unentschuldigt** ~ to be absent without good excuse; **in Vorlesungen** ~ to cut lectures.
fehlend missing, lacking, null;
~**er Beweisantritt** failure of evidence; ~**es Engagement** lack of commitment; ~**e Gegenleistung** want (failure) of consideration; ~**es Giro** lack of endorsement; ~**es Glied** missing link; ~**es Kapital** lack of capital, want of funds; ~**e Mitglieder** missing members; ~**e Stellungnahme** no comment; ~**e Transportmöglichkeiten** lack of transport; ~**e Unterlagen** missing documents; ~**es Vertrauen** mistrust; ~**e Vertretungsmacht** lack of authority; ~**e Waren** missing goods; ~**e Zustimmung** want of assent.
Fehlentscheidung wrong decision, misjudgment;
politische ~ political mistake.
Fehlentwicklung des Bedarfs misdirected demand.
Fehler defect, fault, blunder, balk *(Br.)*, flaw, trip, *(Datenverarbeitung)* trouble, fault, *(im Edelstein)* cloud, flaw, *(Haken)* drawback, *(Lapsus)* lapse, *(Makel)* blemish, *(Recht und Statistik)* error, mistake, *(beim Schießen)* bad (boss, *coll.*) shot, *(Störung)* trouble, *(Ware)* flaw, imperfection;
mit den gleichen ~**n** tarred with the same brush *(fig.)*; **mit allen seinen** ~**n** with all his failings; **mit allen Mängeln und sonstigen** ~**n** with all faults and imperfections; **voller** ~ full of mistakes; **absoluter** ~ *(Statistik)* absolute error; **durchschnittlicher absoluter** ~ mean absolute error; **ausgleichungsfähiger** ~ *(Statistik)* compensating error; **belangloser** ~ trifling error; **charakterlicher** ~ defect (flaw) in character; **bei Anfragen entstandene** ~ interviewer errors; **äußerlich erkennbarer** ~ apparent defect; **aus dem Protokoll ersichtlicher** ~ error apparent of record; **fundamentaler** ~ fundamental mistake, radical error; **grammatischer** ~ grammatical error (mistake); **grober** ~ gross (clumsy) mistake, blunder; **innerer** ~ inherent vice; **körperlicher** ~ physical defect; **lächerlicher** ~ howler *(coll.)*; **leichter** ~ slip, slight mistake; **materiellrechtlicher** ~ defect of substance; **offenbarer** ~ error apparent of record; **offener** ~ patent defect; **offensichtlicher** ~ apparent defect; **orthographischer** ~ fault of spelling, spelling mistake, misspelling; **riesengroßer** ~ glaring blunder; **statistischer** ~ *(Statistik)* probable error; **stichprobenfremder** ~ nonsampling error; **verzerrender systematischer** ~ bias; **taktischer** ~ tactical error; **unbeabsichtigter** ~ unconscious mistake; **unbedeutende** ~ petty faults; **unverzerrter** ~ unbias(s)ed error; **verhängnisvoller** ~ fatal mistake; **versteckter** ~ latent defect; **wahrscheinlicher** ~ *(Statistik)* probable error;
~ **bei der Abfassung einer Urkunde** faulty drafting of a document; ~ **vom Amt** *(coll.)* dud; ~ **in der Beweisführung** flaw in the argument; ~ **eines Buches** shortcomings of a book; **systematischer** ~ **bei der Erhebung** procedural bias; ~ **des Materials** faulty material; **wahrscheinlicher** ~ **statistischer Mittelwerte** probable error; ~ **erster Ordnung** error of first kind; ~ **ersten Ranges** blunder of the first magnitude; ~ **bei der Umfrage** interviewer errors;
seine ~ **ablegen** to mend one's ways; **jem. einen** ~ **anlasten** to impute a fault to s. o.; ~ **anstreichen** to mark mistakes; **einige** ~ **aufweisen** to offer a few flaws; ~ **ausgleichen** to be an offset to a fault; ~ **begehen** to make a mistake, to commit an error; **schweren** ~ **begehen** to blunder; ~ **berichtigen** to correct an error, to repair a mistake; ~ **beschönigen (bemänteln)** to smooth over a fault, to gloss over s. one's faults; ~ **beseitigen** to supply a defect, to correct a mistake; ~ **eingrenzen** to locate a fault; **mögliche** ~ **einkalkulieren** to allow a margin for mistakes; **seine** ~ **einsehen** to see the error of (to mend) one's ways; ~ **entdecken** to detect a mistake; **zu** ~**n führen** to speed (lead to) failures; ~ **gutmachen** to redeem an error; ~ **in einer Arbeit heraussuchen** to pick up the mistakes in a work; **sich vor** ~**n hüten** to watch one's step; **jem. einen** ~ **zur Last legen** to lay a mistake to s. one's charge, to lay the blame at s. one's door; **aus seinen** ~**n lernen** to learn from one's mistakes; ~ **machen** to commit a fault, to slip; **auf** ~ **aufmerksam machen** to warn of defects; **niemals einen** ~ **machen** never to put a foot wrong; **null** ~ **machen** to get a naught; **schlimmen** ~ **machen** to make a bad break; **mehrere** ~ **nachweisen** to detect several mistakes; ~ **offenlegen** to reveal a defect; **von den** ~**n der Konkurrenz profitieren** to capitalize on the errors of a rival firm; **von** ~**n strotzen** to teem with mistakes; ~ **übersehen** to overlook shortcomings; ~ **verbessern** to correct a mistake; **j. zu einem** ~ **verleiten** to lead s. o. into an error; ~ **wiedergutmachen** to make atonement for a fault; **dummen** ~ **wiederholen** to blunder again; **von** ~**n wimmeln** to be teeming with mistakes; ~ **zugeben** to avow a fault, to stand corrected, to acknowledge one's mistake (the corn, *coll.*);
~**anhäufung** mass of mistakes; ~**anzeige** *(Computer)* error indicator, *(Datengerät)* flag; ~**behebung** *(Datenverarbeitung)* debugging; ~**berechnung** calculation of an error; ~**bereich** *(Statistik)* error band; ~**beseitigung** elimination of errors; ~**eingrenzung** localization of a fault.
fehlerfrei sound, clean, faultless, flawless, clear from faults, free from defects, *(genau)* correct, accurate, *(Ware)* sound, faultless;
~ **schreiben** to write without making spelling mistakes;
~**es Buch** immaculate book; ~**er Diamant** clean diamond; ~**es Holz** clean timber; ~**es Stück** effective unit; ~**e Ware** goods in sound condition.
Fehlergrenze margin of error, tolerance, *(math.)* approximation.
fehlerhaft bad, false, faulty, defective, deficient, full of mistakes, all abroad, incorrect, imperfect, inexact, unsound, vicious, *(beschädigt)* damaged;
~ **besitzen** to be in adverse possession;
~**er Abdruck** inaccurate copy; ~**e Ablesung** *(Stromzähler)* error in reading off; ~**e Auslegung** misconstruance, misconstruction; ~**e Aussprache** incorrect pronunciation, mispronunciation; ~**e Besetzung eines Gerichts** defective constitution of a court; ~**er Besitz** adverse possession; ~**er Besitzer** adverse possessor; ~**er Bogen** spoilt sheet; ~**e Bremsen** faulty brakes; ~**er Eigentumstitel** imperfect title; ~**e Eintragung** erroneous entry; ~**es Fernsehbild** faulty image; ~ **errichtete Gesellschaft** defective company; ~**e Isolierung** *(el.)* fault; ~**e Konstruktion** defect in construction; ~**e Lieferung** deficient delivery; ~**e Peilung** spurious bearing; ~**es Prozeßverfahren** mistrial; ~**er Rechnungsauszug** faulty statement; ~**er Schriftsatz** mispleading; ~**e Stelle** flaw, *(Holz)* burl; ~**e Stenogrammübertragung** mistranscription in shorthand; ~**es Stück** defective unit; **zugelassene** ~**e Stücke** allowable defects; ~**e Textstelle** incorrect text, corrupt passage in a text; ~**es Verfahren** mistrial; ~**e Verpackung** faulty packing; ~**er Vertrag** defective contract; ~**e Verwaltungshandlung** failure to act; ~**e Ware** faulty goods.
Fehler|haftigkeit faultiness, incorrectness, inaccuracy; ~**häufigkeit** mass of mistakes; ~**korrekturprogramm** *(Computer)* error-correcting program(me); **normale** ~**kurve** normal error curve.
fehlerlos faultless, flawless, correct, perfect, untainted, *(Text)* incorrupt.
Fehlernährung false nutrition.
Fehlernte crop failure;
~ **ergeben** to yield a bad crop.
Fehler|ortsbestimmung localization of a fault; **beunruhigend hoher** ~**prozentsatz** disquietingly high percentage of errors; ~**quelle mit einkalkulieren** to allow a margin for errors; ~**rechnung** *(Statistik)* calculus of error; ~**risiko** risk of error; ~**spanne**, ~**spielraum** margin of error, error margin; ~**stelle** *(Text)* corrupt passage; ~**suche** *(Computer, el.)* trouble shooting, *(Datenverarbeitung)* debugging; ~**tabelle** accuracy table; ~**verbesserung** correction, rectification; ~**verzeichnis** *(Buch)* corrigenda, errata; ~**wahrscheinlichkeit** error probability.
Fehl|fabrikat defective article; ~**farbe** off-shade; ~**fracht** dead freight, forfeit; ~**geburt** miscarriage, abortion; ~**geburt haben** to miscarry.
fehlgehen to be mistaken.
Fehlgeld *(Kassierer)* risk money, allowance for errors;
~**entschädigung** cash indemnity.
fehlgeleitet misdirected;
~ **werden** to miscarry;
~**e Sendung** misrouted freight.
fehlgeschlagener Versuch abortive attempt.

Fehlgewicht deficiency in weight, underweight.
fehlgreifen to miss one's hold;
in der Wahl seiner Mittel ~ to take faulty measures.
Fehl | grenze *(Münze)* maximum [of] deficiency; ~**griff** slip of the hand, mistake, *(Taktlosigkeit)* faux pas; ~**griff tun** to make a false movement, *(Irrtum begehen)* to make a wrong choice; ~**handlung** blunder, faux pas; ~**information** misinformation, misinterpretation.
Fehlinvestition misemployment, investment failure, misappropriated capital, misconceived capital project, false (mistaken, negative, *US*) investments, misinvestment;
volkswirtschaftliche ~**en** national misdirected investments;
sich als ~ **herausstellen** to turn sour; ~ **vornehmen** to lose money by bad investment.
Fehl | jahr bad (off, fail, *US*) year; ~**kalkulation** wrong calculation, miscalculation, miscomputation, miscount; ~**konstruktion** faulty construction (design); ~**landung** faulty (balked, *US*) landing; ~**leistung** poor performance, *(Psychologie)* slip, lapse; **menschliche** ~**leistung** human slip.
fehlleiten to mislead, to misdirect;
Brief ~ to misdirect a letter; **Kapital** ~ to misdirect capital, to misappropriate (misapply) funds; **Zug** ~ to misroute a train.
Fehlleitung failure, lapse, miscarriage, misdirection;
~ **eines Briefes** misdirection of a letter; ~ **von Kapitalien** misappropriation (misapplication, misdirection) of funds, disinvestment.
Fehl | lenkung von Kapital misapplication of funds; ~**liste** *(Büchersammler)* desiderata list, *(phil.)* wants list; ~**meldung** false report; ~**menge** deficit, deficiency, shortage; **bei Schiffsankunft festgestellte** ~**menge** shortlanded cargo; ~**planung** bad planning; ~**produkt** faulty product; ~**rechnung** miscasting, miscalculation, wrong calculation; ~**schaltung** wrong connection (connexion, *Br.*); ~**schätzung** wrong estimate, misestimation; ~**schicht** dropped (missed) shift; ~**schichten** absenteeism.
fehlschießen to miss the target *(fig.)*, to be wide of the mark (far out).
Fehlschlag *(fig.)* failure, setback, washout *(sl.)*;
sich als wirtschaftlicher ~ **erweisen** to prove an abortion, to be proving unproductive.
fehlschlagen to prove a failure, to fail, to miscarry, to fall flat, to backfire, to come to nought, to go wrong, to founder.
Fehl | schluß wrong (false) conclusion; ~**spekulation** wrong (unlucky, bad) speculation, misconjecture; ~**start** *(Flugzeug)* false takeoff, unsuccessful take-up; **nach einigen** ~**starts** after several false starts; ~**stelle** *(mil.)* vacancy; ~**steuerung von Kapital** misdirection of capital; **zugelassene** ~**stücke** allowable defects; ~**stunden** hours absent.
Fehlt *(Marktbericht)* not to be had, nothing offered.
Fehl | treffer *(mil.)* washout; ~**tritt** side slip, misstep, stumble, trip-up; ~**tritt begehen** *(fig.)* to commit a fault; ~**tritt tun** to take a false step; ~**urteil** failure of justice, error of (fault in) judgment, erroneous (false) judgment, misjudgment, perverse verdict, miscarriage of justice; ~**urteil verkünden** to rule a mistrial; ~**verbindung** *(tel.)* wrong connection (connexion, *Br.*); ~**verhalten** misapplication, misconduct, *(Schuldrecht)* miscarriage; **schwerwiegendes** ~**verhalten** gross misconduct; **vorsätzliches** ~**verhalten** wilful misconduct; ~**versuch** abortive attempt; ~**weisung** compass error.
fehlzünden to misfire, to backfire, to balk *(US)*.
Fehlzündung *(Motor)* backfire, backflash, misfire.
Feier ceremony, celebration, festivity, society function, do *(Br., coll.)*, exercises *(US)*;
zur ~ **des Tages** to celebrate the occasion;
kleine ~ small party;
~ **zum fünfundzwanzigen Jubiläum** silver anniversary ceremony;
an einer ~ **teilnehmen** to attend a ceremony.
Feierabend time to knock off, knocking-off time, knock-off *(US coll.)*, *(Freizeit)* time off, leisure time;
nach ~ in one's spare time, after hours;
seinen ~ **genießen** to enjoy some leisure; ~ **machen** to call it quits (a day, *US coll.*), to leave off work, to cease working, to knock off *(coll.)*, to shut up shop.
feierlich ceremonial, solemn, festive, gala;
Ereignis ~ **begehen** to celebrate an event; **vor Zeugen** ~ **erklären** to declare before witnesses; ~ **eröffnen** to open with due ceremony;
~**er Anlaß** ceremonial occasion; ~**er Augenblick** solemn moment; ~**es Begräbnis** solemn burial, obsequies; ~**er Eid** solemn oath; ~**er Empfang** formal reception; ~**e Erklärung** solemn declaration; ~**e Eröffnung** ceremonial opening; ~**e Handlung** ceremony; ~**e Miene aufsetzen** to straighten one's face; ~**er Protest** solemn protest; ~**e Versicherung** solemn assertion.
Feierlichkeit ceremony, celebration, festivity, active event, *(Würde)* gravity;
~ **stören** to disturb a ceremony; **an einer** ~ **teilnehmen** to be present at a ceremony.
feiern to celebrate, to make merry, to carouse, *(ausruhen)* to rest, *(Arbeit einstellen)* to leave work, to be idle, to walk out *(US)*, *(ehren)* to commemorate, to honour;
seinen Geburtstag ~ to celebrate one's birthday; **Hochzeit** ~ to have a wedding party; **krank** ~ to be idle, to malinger; **ersten Mai** ~ to keep May Day; **Orgien** ~ to hold orgies; **Triumphe** ~ to have great success; **Weihnachten zu Hause** ~ to spend Christmas at home;
j. als großen Schauspieler ~ to acclaim s. o. as a great actor;
~ **müssen** *(Arbeiter)* to be laid off.
Feierschicht dropped shift, *(Bergbau)* idle shift;
~**en** absenteeism;
~**en einlegen (verfahren)** to drop shifts.
Feierstunde ceremony, celebration, function.
Feiertag holiday, festival, day, feast;
~**e** festive season;
gesetzlicher ~ bank (official, public, statutory, national) holiday, day of obligation, red-letter day; **gesetzlich geschützter** ~ recognized holiday; **kirchlicher** ~ church festival; **öffentlicher** ~ public (general, legal, *US*) holiday; **zweiter** ~ *(Weihnachten)* Boxing Day, *(Ostern)* Easter Monday;
Sonn- und ~ nonbusiness day;
~ **begehen** to make holiday; **Tag zum** ~ **erklären** to appoint a day as holiday; ~ **zum Nationalfeiertag machen** to nationalize a holiday.
feiertags on holidays.
Feiertags | kleidung Sunday clothes, go-to-meeting garments *(US)*, best bib and tucker; ~**ruhe** Sunday closing (observance); ~**zuschlag** holiday pay.
feige cowardly, poor-spirited;
sich ~ **benehmen** to behave cowardly;
~**s Benehmen** cowardly behavio(u)r; ~**s Verbrechen** dastardly crime.
Feigheit vor dem Feind cowardice in the face of the enemy.
Feigling coward, craven, pudding heart;
j. als ~ **anprangern** to post s. o. as a coward.
feil for (on) sale, *(bestechlich)* venal, vendible, hireling.
feilbieten to offer (put up) for sale.
feilen, an einem Satz sorgfältig to file a sentence carefully *(coll.)*.
Feilhalten von Waren keeping (issue) for sale.
feilhalten to keep for sale;
an einem Stand ~ to keep a stall; **billige Waren** ~ to show a cheap line of goods.
Feilhaltung pitching.
Feilschen haggling, [bazaar] bargaining, chaffer, dicker *(US)*.
feilschen to bargain, to barter, to chaffer, to huckster, to dicker *(US)*, to haggle;
mit jem. um etw. ~ to palter with s. o. about s. th.; **um den Preis** ~ to haggle over the price.
Feilscher bargainer, bargainor, haggler.
fein fine, refined, high-grade, choice, of the best quality, *(tadellos)* splendid, great, swell *(US coll.)*, posh *(Br., sl.)*, *(vornehm)* genteel, elegant;
sich zu ~ **dünken, einer Partei beizutreten** to be too proud to join a party; ~ **einstellen** to tune in sharply; **sich** ~ **machen** to put on one's best bib and tucker; ~ **angezogen sein** to be elegantly dressed; ~ **heraus sein** to strike it lucky *(US coll.)*; **sich für etw. zu** ~ **vorkommen** to think s. th. beneath o. s.;
~**e Backwaren** fancy cakes; ~**e Bedeutungsnuancen** nice shades of meaning; ~**e Beobachtungsgabe** sensitive power of observation; ~**e Dame** elegant lady; ~**e Familie** genteel family; ~**es Gehör haben** to have a delicate ear; ~**er Geschmack** discriminating taste; ~**es Gold** pure (fine) gold; ~**e Ironie** subtle irony; ~**er Kerl** nice chap (fellow); ~**e Küche** high-class cooking, haute cuisine; ~**es Lächeln** faint smile; ~**er Laden** fashionable shop; ~**es Leder** soft leather; ~**e Manieren** refined manners; ~**e Marke** prime quality; ~**er Nebel** thin mist; ~**er Pinkel** slicker, toff *(Br., sl.)*, swell *(US sl.)*; ~**ste Qualität** finest quality; ~**e Sache sein** to be smashing; ~**ste Sorte** choicest quality, top grade; ~**er Unterschied** subtle distinction; ~**e Wäsche** dainty lingerie; ~**er Wechsel** first-class paper, prime bill; ~**er Wein** exquisite wine; ~**e Züge** delicate features.
Feinablesegerät vernier scale.

Feinabstimmung precision adjustment, *(Radio)* fine tuning;
~en bei einer auf vollen Touren laufenden Wirtschaft vornehmen to fine-tune an economy already at full capacity.

feinbearbeiten to finish.

Feinblech thin metal plate, sheet metal.

Feind enemy, foe, *(Gegner)* adversary, opponent, antagonist;
von ~en umringt hemmed in by enemies;
geheimer ~ snake in the grass; **heimlicher ~** underminer; **radikaler ~** deep enemy;
~ abwehren to hold off the enemy; **~ heftig bedrängen** to press the enemy hard; **dem ~ die Stirn bieten** to face the enemy; **dicht am ~ bleiben** to keep in touch with the enemy; **dem ~ tüchtig einheizen** to give the enemy hell; **sich seinen ~en entziehen** to evade one's enemies; **vor dem ~ fallen** to be killed in action; **~ fesseln** to pin down the enemy; **dem fliehenden ~ auf dem Fuße folgen** to follow hotfoot on the heels of the retreating enemy; **mit dem ~ halten** to range o. s. with the enemy; **auf den ~ losstürmen** to make a dash at the enemy; **sich j. zum ~ machen** to make an enemy of s. o.; **~ in die Flucht schlagen** to put the enemy to flight; **~ vernichtend schlagen** to cut the enemy to pieces; **sich selbst der ärgste ~ sein** to be one's own (worst) enemy; **~ jedes Fortschritts sein** to be opposed to any form of progress; **sich auf den ~ stürzen** to dive down on the enemy; **~ überfallen** to make inroads upon the enemy; **Stellung dem ~ überlassen** to abandon a position to the enemy; **~ in hochverräterischer Weise unterstützen** to collaborate; **~ aus dem Lande vertreiben** to drive the enemy out of the country; **~ aus einer Stellung vertreiben** to dislodge the enemy from a position; **dem ~ eine offene Flanke zeigen** to offer one's flank to the enemy; **~ zurückwerfen** to fling back the enemy; **~ zur Schlacht zwingen** to force an action on the enemy;
~begünstigung aiding and comforting the enemy; **~begünstigung begehen** to aid and comfort the enemy, to act in aid of the enemy; **~beobachtung** observation of the enemy; **~berührung** contact with the enemy; **~bewegungen stören** to impede the enemy's movements; **~einflug** enemy incursion; **~einwirkung** enemy action.

Feindes|gebiet enemy-occupied territory, hostile territory; **~gewalt** act of the King's (Queen's) enemy *(Br.)*; **in ~hand fallen** to fall into the hands of the enemy; **~land** enemy country, hostile territory.

Feind|flug sortie, mission; **~flugzeug** enemy (hostile, raiding) aircraft.

feindfrei clear of the enemy.

Feind|fühlung nehmen to feel for the enemy; **~gebiet** hostile territory; **~handlung** hostile act; **~kräfte** enemy forces.

feindlich adverse, hostile, inimical, enemy, opposed;
jem. fortgesetzt ~ begegnen to show persistent hostility towards s. o.; **jem. ~ gesinnt sein** to be hostile to s. o., to entertain hostile intentions regarding s. o.;
~er Angriff enemy attack; **~e Armee** hostile army; **~es Ausland** enemy countries; **~er Ausländer** enemy alien; **~e Einstellung** hostile feelings; **~e Flagge** enemy flag; **~e Flotte** enemy fleet; **~e Front** enemy front; **ins ~e Lager übergehen** to go over to the enemy; **~e Linien** enemy's lines; **~e Mächte** hostile powers; **~e Regierung** enemy government; **~e Truppen** enemy troops; **~e Umwelt** enemy world.

Feind|macht hostile power; **ausgewertete ~nachrichten** military intelligence; **in unmittelbarer ~nähe** in the immediate vicinity of the enemy; **~propaganda** enemy propaganda.

Feindschaft enmity, ill blood;
alte ~en begraben to bury the hatchet; **keine ~ gegen j. hegen** to feel no hostility towards s. o., to bear no grudge against s. o.; **mit jem. in ~ leben** to be in enmity (at feud, with loggerheads) with s. o.; **in offener ~ mit jem. leben** to live in open defience with s. o.; **seine ~ mit angeblicher Freundschaft tarnen** to mask one's enmity under an appearance (a guise) of friendship.

feindselig inimical, hostile, malevolent;
~e Gesinnung hostile feelings; **~e Handlung** hostile act; **~e Menge** hostile crowd.

Feindseligkeit hostility, animosity, antagonism, ill will.

Feindseligkeiten hostilities;
beim Ausbruch der ~ at the outbreak of hostilities;
offene ~ open hostilities; **unterschwellige ~** undertone of hostility;
mit den ~ beginnen to start the fight, to take arms; **~ einstellen** to cease (suspend) hostilities; **~ eröffnen** to start (begin, open) hostilities; **~ fortsetzen** to continue hostilities; **~ wiederaufnehmen** to resume hostilities.

Feind|staat enemy state; **~unterstützung** relief of the enemy; **~unterstützung begehen** to relieve the enemy; **~vermögen** enemy property; **~vermögen beschlagnahmen** to alienate enemy property; **~vermögensverwalter** alien property custodian.

Feineinstellung fine (precision) adjustment, master touch, *(Radio)* fine tuning.

Feineinstellungsskala vernier scale.

Feingefühl delicacy, sensitivity;
~ besitzen to be sensitive; **jds. ~ verletzen** to outrage s. one's delicacy.

Feingehalt assayed value, alloy;
gesetzlicher ~ standard of fineness;
~ feststellen to assay.

Feingehalts|einheit standard of fineness; **~stempel** hallmark, standard mark, touch; **mit einem ~stempel versehen** to hallmark, to touch; **~wert** assay office value.

feingerastert with fine screen.

Feingewicht standard, precision weight.

Feingold fine (pure) gold;
~gehalt weight of fine gold; **~klausel** fine-gold clause.

Feinheit fineness, choiceness, nicety, delicacy, *(Qualität)* fineness, superior quality;
~en niceties, ins and outs;
finanztechnische ~en financial niceties; **letzte ~en** finishing touches;
~en der Politik subleties of policy; **~en der Sprache** niceties of a language.

Feinheits|grad *(Textilien)* count; **~grad von Gold** fineness of gold.

Fein|korn *(Foto)* fine grain; **~kornfilm** fine-grain film; **~kost** delicatessen, table delicacies; **~kosthändler, ~kosthandlung** delicatessen shop.

feinmachen, sich to put on one's Sunday clothes (best bib and tucker), to spruce up *(sl.)*.

feinmaschig fine-meshed.

Fein|mechanik [high-] precision engineering; **~mechanik und Optik** precision and optical goods; **~mechaniker** precision toolmaker.

feinmechanische Industrie precision engineering.

Fein|meßgerät precision instrument; **~putz** hard finish; **~schmeckerkost** gourmet fare; **~silber** fine silver.

feinsinnig subtle, sensitive.

Feinstbearbeitung superfinishing.

Fein|straße sheet rolling; **~wäsche** fine laundering; **~waschmittel** light-duty detergent.

feixen to smirk, to grin from one ear to the other.

Feld field, open country, *(Arbeitsgebiet)* field, domain, province, sphere, *(mil.)* [battle] field, *(Tabelle)* column;
~er grounds;
auf freiem ~ in open country; **im ~** *(mil.)* at the front, out, in the field;
ausgekohltes Feld worked section; **bestelltes ~** tilled (cultivated) field; **schlecht bestelltes ~** badly cultivated field; **magnetisches ~** magnetic field; **gut stehende ~er** thriving crops; **unbestelltes ~** unlabo(u)red field;
~ abbauen *(Bergbau)* to exploit a face; **~ absammeln** to glean a field; **~ bebauen (bestellen)** to till (cultivate) the ground; **~ behaupten** to remain in possession of (hold) the field, to stand one's ground; **~ mit Weizen bestellen** to put a field under wheat; **das ~ betreten** to enter the arena; **jem. ein weites ~ zur Entwicklung bieten** to open up a fine field of action for s. o.; **~ düngen** to distribute manure over a field; **sich über ein weites ~ erstrecken** to range over a wide field; **seine Gründe ins ~ führen** to marshal one's arguments; **Heer ins ~ führen** to lead an army into battle; **übers ~ gehen** to go across country; **freies ~ haben** to have full scope (free rein); **noch im weiten ~ liegen** to be still unsettled; **an der Spitze des ~es liegen** to lead the field; **einem Rivalen das ~ streitig machen** to enter into rivalry with s. o.; **~ pflügen** to plough a field; **~ räumen** to beat a retreat, to yield the palm; **~ für j. räumen** to leave s. o. in possession of the field; **Gegner aus dem ~e schlagen** to knock an opponent out of the ring; **im ~ geblieben sein** to have been killed in action; **im ~ stehen** to be at the front; **ins ~ ziehen** to go to the front; **gegen j. zu ~e ziehen** to draw one's sword (campaign) against s. o.; **gegen die Büchergemeinschaft zu ~e ziehen** to buck the book clubs;
~, Wald oder Wiesen common or garden *(fam.)*;
~ansteuerung *(Computer)* field selection; **~anzug** *(mil.)* battle dress; **~arbeit** farm work, *(Soziologie)* fieldwork; **~arbeiter** agricultural labo(u)rer, farmhand *(US)*; **leichte ~artillerie** light field artillery; **~arzt** field surgeon; **~ausrüstung** field equipment; **~bahn** narrow-gauge railway; **~bau** agriculture,

cultivation, tillage; ~**becher** canteen cup; ~**befestigung** *(mil.)* fieldwork, field fortification, intrenchment; ~**bestellung** cultivation, tillage; ~**bett** camp (tent) bed, *(mil.)* cot; ~**binde** *(mil.)* sash; ~**dienst** *(mil.)* field service.

felddienstfähig fit for active service.

Feld|dienstordnung field manual; ~**dienstübung** field training (manoeuvre); ~**einheit** unit; ~**fernsprecher** *(mil.)* field telephone; ~**flasche** water bottle; ~**flugplatz** field airport, satellite (auxiliary) airfield; ~**fruchtanbau** growing of crops; ~**früchte** field crops; ~**funksprechgerät** walkie-talkie *(coll.)*; ~**gendarmerie** military police; ~**gepäck** [battle] kit *(Br.)*, field pack *(US)*; **mit vollständigem** ~**gepäck** in full battle order; ~**geschrei** battle cry; ~**geschütz** fieldpiece, field gun; ~**gottesdienst** drumhead service; ~**herr** commander-in-chief, general; ~**herrnmiene** air of authority; ~**hüter** field driver *(US)*; ~**jägerkommandant** provost marshal; ~**jägertruppe** military police; ~**kabel** assault cable (wire); ~**kiste** *(mil.)* foot locker; ~**kommandantur** area command; ~**küche** field (rolling) kitchen, *(mil.)* canteen; ~**lazarett** field hospital, casualty clearing station *(Br.)*, hospital station *(US)*; ~**lazarettgehilfe** hospital orderly; ~**markung** field boundary, landmark; ~**marschall** field marshal.

feldmarschmäßig in full marching order, in battle dress and full kit *(US)*;
~**e Ausrüstung** field equipment.

Feld|messer surveyor, measurer; ~**messung** land measuring, surveying; ~**mütze** forage (garrison, *US*) cap; ~**polizei** army patrol.

Feldpost military post *(Br.)*;
~**amt** army post office; ~**karte** army postcard; ~**nummer** army post office number.

Feld|schaden crop damage; ~**schanze** intrenched camp; ~**scheune** barn, *(offen)* Dutch barn; **offene** ~**schlacht** pitched battle; ~**stärke** *(el.)* field strength; ~**stecher** field glass, pair of binoculars; **angrenzendes** ~**stück** adjoining field; ~**verbandsplatz** advanced dressing station, collecting station *(US)*; ~**verpflegung** field ration.

feldverwendungsfähig fit for active service, fit for service in the field.

Feld|wache outlying picket, outguard; ~**webel** sergeant; ~**weg** farm (cart, dirt, *US*) road, lane, track, path, community highway *(US)*; ~**zelt** dog tent *(mil., sl.)*; ~**zeugpark** ordnance park; ~**zeugwesen** ordnance.

Feldzug campaign, drive, military expedition;
~ **zur Abschaffung der Sklaverei** movement to abolish slavery; ~ **für Straßensicherheit (Verkehrssicherheit)** campaign for road safety; ~ **für Tarifvertragsfreiheit** free collective bargaining crusade;
~ **für günstigere Steuersätze führen** to campaign for more favo(u)rable tax treatment; ~ **mitmachen** to campaign.

Feldzugs|plan operational plan, plan of operations; ~**pläne entwerfen** to plan out a military campaign.

Felge rim of a wheel.

Fell skin, pelt, coat, fur;
~ **abziehen** to skin; **jem. das** ~ **gerben** to tan s. one's hide, to give s. o. a good thrashing; **dickes** ~ **haben** to be thick-skinned; **j. beim** ~ **packen** to get hold of s. o. by the scruff of the neck; **das** ~ **des Bären verkaufen, bevor er erlegt ist** to count one's chickens before they are hatched; **jem. das** ~ **versohlen** to trim s. one's jacket; **jem. das** ~ **über die Ohren ziehen** to fleece s. o. of his money.

Felsabhang precipice, declivity.

Felsen rock;
senkrecht abfallender ~ vertical cliff; **gewachsener** ~ living rock;
auf ~ **bauen** to build on a firm foundation.

felsenfest firm as a rock;
~ **behaupten** to declare firmly; ~ **feststehen** to be as sure as eggs; ~ **überzeugt sein** to be absolutely convinced; **sich** ~ **auf j. verlassen** to rely steadfastly on s. o.;
~**e Überzeugung** deep-rooted conviction; ~**es Vertrauen** unshaken confidence.

Felsformation rock formation.

felsige Küste rocky shore.

Felswand rockface, wall of rock.

Fender *(mar.)* fender.

Fenster window, *(Glasscheibe)* glazing, windowpane, *(Ladenfenster)* shop window, *(Oberlicht)* skylight, *(Projektor)* gate aperture;
mit ~**n versehen** windowed; **zum** ~ **heraus** down the drain; **blindes** ~ mock (blind) window; **mit Vorhängen versehene (zugezogene)** ~ curtained windows; **automatisch versenkbares Fenster** *(Auto)* roll-down power window; **zweiflügeliges** ~ two-sashed window;
~ **einsetzen** to window; **jem. die** ~ **einwerfen** to smash s. one's windows; **Geld zum** ~ **herauswerfen** to play ducks and drakes with one's money, to throw one's money down the drain; **zum** ~ **hereinklettern** to climb in at the window; **zum** ~ **hinausreden** to talk to a brick wall; **im** ~ **liegen** to lean over the window-sill; ~ **zumauern** to wall up a window;
~**anordnung** fenestration; ~**aufkleber** *(Werbung)* window streamer; ~**bank** window sill; ~**brett** window board, elbow board; ~**briefumschlag** window (panel) envelope; ~**feststeller** skylight stay; ~**flügel** casement; ~**futter** case; ~**gitter** grille; ~**gitter anbringen** to fit a grille on to a window; ~**glas** windowpane, window glass, glazing; ~**glasversicherung** plate-glass insurance; ~**heber** sash lift, *(Auto)* window regulator; ~**klebeplakat** window sticker.

Fensterladen [window] shutter;
klappbarer ~ box shutter;
~ **anbringen** to shutter; ~ **streichen** to paint shutters on a wall.

Fenster|öffnung window opening; ~**putzer** window cleaner; ~**rahmen** window frame (sash); ~**recht** ancient lights.

Fensterscheibe windowpane, window glass;
bereifte ~**n** frosted windowpanes;
zerbrochene ~ **reparieren** to mend a broken window; ~ **zerbrechen** to break a window.

Fenster|sims window ledge; ~**sitz** window seat; ~**sprosse** window bar; ~**stock** window box; ~**sturz** window head; ~**umschlag** visible (window) envelope; ~**vorhang** blind.

Ferien holiday(s), vacation *(US)*, vac *(Br., coll.)*, leave, *(parl., US)* recess;
große ~ summer holidays *(Br.)*, long vacation;
~ **an der See** seaside holiday;
seine ~ **genießen** to enjoy one's holiday; ~ **haben** to have a holiday; **große** ~ **haben** to be on long leave; ~ **dringend nötig haben** to want a holiday; ~ **machen** to take (go for) a holiday, to [be on] vacation *(US)*, to go vacationing *(US)*, *(parl.)* to be up, *(Schule)* to break up; ~ **auf dem Lande machen** to be at grass; **in den** ~ **sein** to be on one's holidays, to go vacationing *(US)*, *(parl.)* to be in recess; **Teil seiner** ~ **streichen** to curtail one's holidays; **seine** ~ **im Ausland verbringen** to spend one's holidays (vacation, *US*) abroad; **in den** ~ **verreisen** to get away for the holiday;
~**adresse** holiday (vacation, *US*) address; ~**andrang** holiday rush; **billiges** ~**angebot** saving holiday package; ~**anschrift** holiday (vacation, *US*) address; ~**anwalt** vacation barrister *(US)*; ~**anzug** holiday clothes; ~**arbeit** holiday (vacation, *US*) work; ~**aufenthalt** holiday stay (resort); ~**aufgabe** *(Schule)* holiday task; ~**aufwand** holiday (vacation, *US*) expense; ~**ausschuß** *(parl.)* recess (intersessional) committee; ~**austausch** holiday exchange.

ferienbedingte Schließung holiday (vacation, *US*) shutdown.

Ferien|beratungsdienst vacation information service *(US)*; ~**beruf**, ~**beschäftigung** vacation job *(US)*, holiday (vacation, *US*) post; ~**billet** excursion ticket; ~**billet mit einem Mindestaufenthalt von zwei Wochen** excursion fare with minimum 14-day stay; ~**budget** holiday (vacation, *US*) budget; ~**dorf** holiday (vacation, *US*) village; ~**eigentumswohnung** vacation condominium *(US)*; ~**einrichtungen** holiday (vacation, *US*) facilities; **deutliche** ~**erinnerungen** vivid recollections of a holiday; ~**erlebnis** vacation adventure *(US)*; ~**fahrkarte** holiday ticket; ~**foto** holiday snap; ~**gast** vacationist *(US)*, paying guest; ~**gebiet** holiday region (ground); ~**gegend** holiday ground; ~**geld** holiday pay, vacation payment *(US)*; ~**gewerbe** holiday trade; ~**handbuch** holiday guide; ~**haus**, ~**heim** holiday (vacation, *US*) home, holiday chalet, weekend cottage, crib; ~**hotel** resort hotel; ~**industrie** holiday trade; ~**kammer** *(Gericht)* vacation court *(US)*; ~**karte** tourist ticket; **in** ~**kluft** in holiday attire (array); ~**kolonie** holiday camp; ~**kursus** holiday course, summer school, vacation school *(US)*; ~**lager** holiday camp; **modebedingter** ~**lagerfimmel** modern craze of a holiday camp; ~**land** vacation land *(US)*; ~**lektüre** holiday reading; ~**möglichkeiten** vacation facilities *(US)*; ~**ordnung** holiday (vacation, *US*) schedule.

Ferienort holiday (vacation, *US*) spot, summer resort;
eleganter ~ fashionable summer resort; **überlaufener** ~ crowded holiday resort;
sich über den diesjährigen ~ **schlüssig werden** to determine where one is going to spend one's holiday.

Ferien|paradies holiday paradise, tourist haven; ~**plakat** holiday poster; ~**plan** vacation schedule *(US)*.

Ferienpläne | durcheinanderbringen to derange plans for a holiday; **andere ~ haben** to have other views for the holidays; **dieses Jahr spanische ~ haben** to have some thoughts of going to Spain this summer; **~ machen** to lay down a plan for the holidays.

Ferien | planer vacation planner *(US)*; **~platz** holiday (vacation, *US*) spot; **~projekt** resort project; **~quartier** holiday accommodation.

Ferienreise holiday (vacation, *US*) travel, holiday tour; **billige ~** low-cost vacation tour *(US)*; **kleine ~** short holiday; **~ mit eigenem Reisebegleiter** personally conducted tour; **~ über ein Reisebüro buchen** to go on holiday through a travel agency; **sich nicht zu einer ~ entschließen** to decide against a holiday; **sich eine ~ leisten** to run a holiday; **keine ~ machen** to go without a holiday; **~kosten** holiday visit passage.

Ferien | reisender holidaymaker, holidayer, vacationist *(US)*, vacationer *(US)*; **~reisender mit kleiner Brieftasche** low-budget vacationer *(US)*; **~reisezug** car-sleeper express; **~reservierung** holiday booking, vacation reservation *(US)*; **von alterprobtem ~rhythmus abweichen** to break one's long-standing holiday arrangements; **~richter** vacation judge *(Br.)*; **~sache** *(Gericht)* vacation business; **~saison** holiday season, vacation time *(US)*; **~schließung** holiday (vacation, *US*) shutdown; **~siedlung** holiday camp; **~sitz** vacation site *(US)*; **~sitzungen** sittings after term; **~stellung**, **~tätigkeit** vacation job; **in ~stimmung** in holiday mood; **~tag** holiday; **bezahlte ~tage** days of paid vacation *(US)*; **~tag genießen** to appreciate a holiday.

Ferientarif *(Fluglinie)* holiday tariff, holiday specials; **45 Tage vorausbezahlter ~** advanced purchasing excursion (open) tariff; **billiger vorauszuzahlender ~** *(Fluglinie)* super-Apex tariff; **~ mit Vorausbuchung** advanced purchase excursion fares (Apex).

Ferien | transportvergütung holiday visit passage; **~unterbringung**, **~unterkunft** holiday accommodation; **~vergütung** holiday remuneration (pay), vacation pay *(US)*; **~verkehr** holiday traffic; **~versicherung** holiday insurance; **~vertreter** vacation barrister *(US)*; **~vertretung** holiday (vacation, *US*) replacement; **~vertretung übernehmen** to take over the duties of a post in the interim; **ideales ~wetter** ideal weather for a holiday; **~wetterversicherung** weather insurance; **~wohnung** holiday residence; **~zeit** holiday time (season), vacation period (season, time) *(US)*; **die ganze ~zeit genießen** to enjoy every minute of one's holiday; **~zeitplan** vacation schedule *(US)*; **~zug** excursion train; **~zulage**, **~zuschlag** vacation bonus (time allotment, *US*).

Ferkel piglet, piggy, *(schmutziges Kind)* piggy-wiggy, mucky pup *(Br.)*.

Ferkelei smut, *(Zote)* obscenity, smutty joke.

fern far [away], distant, remote; **von nah und ~** from far and near.

Fernamt long-distance operator, trunk exchange *(Br.)* toll office, trunks *(Br.)*, long distance *(US)*, *(Nahverkehrsamt)* toll exchange; **~anmeldung** long-distance operator *(US)*.

Fern | anzeige remote indication; **~anzeigegerät** distant-reading instrument; **~aufklärer** *(mil.)* reconnaissance aircraft; **~aufklärung** *(mil.)* distance reconnaissance; **~aufnahme** distant shot, telephotograph, telephoto, long shot; **~auskunft** trunk enquiries *(Br.)*; **~auslöser** remote-control release; **~barometer** telebarometer.

fernbedienen to radio-control.

fernbedient remote- (radio-) controlled.

Fern | bedienung remote (radio) control; **~bedienungsgerät** remote-control device; **~beförderung** long-distance transport *(US)*.

fernbetätigen to operate by remote control.

Fernbleiben absence, nonappearance, nonattendance, *(Schule)* truancy; **unentschuldigtes ~** absenteeism, absent (absence) without leave.

fernbleiben to absent o. s., to stay away; **unentschuldigt (unerlaubt) ~** to be absent without leave, *(Schüler)* to play truant; **wegen Krankheit der Arbeit ~** to be out on account of illness; **einer Sitzung ~** to stay away from a meeting; **ein paar Tage ~** to keep away for a few days.

Fern | blick distant view, vista; **~bomber** long-range bomber; **~druck** teletypesetting; **~drucker** teleprinter, ticker; **~-D-Zug** long-distance train, limited express *(US)*.

Ferne distance, remoteness; **in weiter ~ liegen** to lie in the distant future.

Fern | empfang long-distance reception; **~empfangszone** sky-wave service area.

Ferner Osten Far East.

ferner, in ~ Vergangenheit in ages past and gone; **in ~ Zukunft** in the distant future.

Fern | fahrer lorry *(Br.)* (long-distance, truck) driver, trucker, truckman; **~fahrerraststätte** transport café, truck stop *(US)*; **~funk** long-range broadcast; **~gang** *(Auto)* overdrive; **~gas** town (commercial) gas; **~gasversorgung** commercial gas supply.

ferngehalten prevented.

ferngelenkt remote-controlled; **~es Geschoß** guided missile.

Ferngeschoß long-range missile.

Ferngespräch trunk call *(Br.)*, long-distance [telephone] call *(US)*, *(im Nahverkehr)* toll call; **abgehendes ~** outgoing long-distance call; **ankommendes ~** incoming long-distance call; **~e abhören** to tap telephone calls (wires); **~ [zu jem.] anmelden** to give in a call, to book a trunk call *(Br.)*, to call s. o. long-distance *(US)*, to book a long-distance call *(US)*; **~ bezahlen** to pay for a call; **~ führen** to telephone, to long-distance *(US)*; **kostenloses ~ führen** to call a toll-free number; **~ herstellen** to put a call through; **~e mithören** to tap telephone wires.

Ferngesprächs | gebühr tariff charge for calls, long-distance charge, toll; **~verbindung** trunk connection.

ferngesteuert remote-controlled (guided); **~es Aufklärungsflugzeug** reconnaissance drone.

ferngetraut proxy-wedded.

Fern | glas binoculars, spyglass; **~güterzug** long-distance freight train.

fernhalten to keep away, to hold off, *(ausschließen)* to exclude; **sich ~** to steer (keep) clear of, to estrange o. s.; **sich von jem. ~** to fight shy of s. o.; **etw. von jem. ~** to keep s. th. from s. one's knowledge; **Ärger ~** to stave off troubles; **Besucher ~** to ward off visitors; **sich von der Politik ~** to keep o. s. aloof from politics.

Fern | heizung district heating; **~hörer** *(tel.)* receiver; **~kabel** trunk (long-distance, *US*) cable; **~kabelnetz** long-distance cable system *(US)*; **~kampfwaffe** long-range weapon (armament); **~kurs** correspondence course; **~laster** long-distance truck, long-distance road train *(US)*, industrial long-haul truck *(US)*, juggernaut.

Fernlast | fahrer long-haul *(Br.)* (truck) driver, trucker *(US)*, truckman *(US)*, long-distance lorry driver *(Br.)*; **~fahrerhalteplatz** transport café, truck stop *(US)*; **~unternehmen** haulage-contracting business; **~verkehr** long-distance road traffic *(US)* (haulage, *Br.*), long haulage, long-haul transport *(US)*; **~verkehrsgewerbe** long-distance road-haulage services; **~wagen** industrial (long-haul, highway, *US*) truck, long-distance road train.

Fernlehr | anstalt correspondence college; **~gang** correspondence course; **~institut** correspondence school.

Fernleitung trunk *(Br.)* (long-distance, toll, *US*) line, *(Ölleitung)* pipe line; **gemietete ~** leased line.

Fernleitungs | kabel toll cable *(US)*; **~netz** trunk-line system (network) *(Br.)*, toll system (network) *(US)*; **~verkehr** trunk (toll, *US*) telephone (line) service; **~wahl** long-distance (toll-line, *US*) dialling; **~wähler** long-distance connector, trunk offering *(Br.)* (toll, *US*) final selector; **~wesen** trunk telephone service *(Br.)*.

Fernlenkboot radio-controlled boat.

fernlenken to steer by remote control.

Fernlenk | flugkörper remotely piloted missile; **~flugzeug** remote- (tele-) controlled aircraft, drone *(US)*, queen bee *(fam.)*; **~geschoß**, **~waffe** guided weapon (missile); **~pult** control desk.

Fernlenkung remote (radio, *US*) control, telecontrol.

Fernlicht *(Auto)* distance light, headlight; **abgeblendetes ~** dipped headlight; **aufgeblendetes ~** glaring headlight; **~ abblenden** to dim the headlights.

fernliegen to be far from.

Fernlinie *(tel.)* trunk (toll, long-distance, *US*) line.

Fernmelde | amt Federal Communication Administration *(US)*; **~anlage** telecommunication installation (facilities); **~ausstattung** communications equipment; **~dienst** telecommunication service, *(Heer)* signal service, *(Marine)* communications branch; **~einheit** telecommunication division; **~einrichtungen**

telecommunication facilities; ~**geschäft** telecommunications business; ~**gesetz** Federal Communication Act *(US)*; ~**industrie** communications industry; ~**ingenieur** telephone (communication) engineer; ~**mittel** means of communication; ~**netz** telecommunication network; **computergesteuertes elektronisches ~netz** computer-controlled electronic communications network; ~**offizier** signal officer; ~**satellit** telecommunication satellite; ~**sektor** telecommunication side; ~**stelle** *(mil.)* communication center *(US)* (centre, *Br.*); ~**technik** communication engineering, telecommunications; ~**technologie** telecommunications technology; ~**truppe** signal corps, Royal Corps of Signals *(Br.)*; ~**verbindungen** telecommunications, *(mil.)* signal communications; ~**verkehr** telecommunications, telecommunication traffic; **Internationaler ~vertrag** International Telecommunication Treaty; ~**wesen** telecommunications, telecommunication traffic, *(mil.)* signal communications; ~**wirtschaft** telecommunications business; ~**zentrale** *(mil.)* communication center *(US)* (centre, *Br.*).

Fernmeß|anlage telemeteorograph; ~**daten** telemetry data; ~**gerät** telemeter; ~**technik** telemetry.

Fernmessung telemetry.

fernmündlich telephonic, by telephone;
j. ~ benachrichtigen to inform s. o. by telephone;
~**e Antwort** answer by telephone; ~**e Mitteilung** telephone message; ~ **zugestelltes Telegramm** telephoned telegram; ~**e Unterredung** telephone conversation.

Fernobjektiv *(Fotoapparat)* telephoto lens.

Fernost Far East;
~**politik** Far-Eastern policy; ~**korrespondent** Far-Eastern correspondent.

fernöstliche Handelsbeziehungen Far-Eastern trade relations.

Fern|rakete long-range rocket; ~**rechnen** *(EDV)* teleprocessing; ~**registrierung** remote recording; ~**rohr** telescope; ~**ruf** [telephone] call, *(auf Briefbogen)* telephone; ~**schalter** remote-controlled switch; ~**schnellzug** express train, long-distance train, limited express *(US)*.

Fernschreib|anlage teleprinter (teletype, telex, *US*) connection, teletype terminal; ~**anschluß** teleprinter (teletype, *US*) connection; ~**dienst** teleprinter (teletype, telex, *US*) service.

Fernschreiben teletype, telex [message];
~ **schicken** to [send a] telex.

fernschreiben to teleprint, to teletype, to telex.

Fernschreiber *(Gerät)* simplex printer, type-writing (printing) telegraph, telewriter, [tele]-printer *(Br.)*, teletyper *(US)*, *(Person)* teleprinter, teletype (telex) operator *(US)*;
durch ~ übermitteln to teletype, to teleprint, to telex *(US)*.

Fernschreib|gebühr telex call charge, line cost; ~**grundgebühr** telex rental; ~**kanal** teletype (teleprinter) channel; ~**leitung** teleprinter (teletype, telex, *US*) line; ~**lochstreifen** wire service tape; ~**maschine** typewriting telegraph, simplex printer, typewriter, teleprinter, teletyper *(US)*; ~**mietgebühr** line cost; ~**nachricht** telex message *(US)*; ~**netz** teleprinter network, teletype (telex, *US*) network; ~**nummer** telex number *(US)*; ~**stelle** teleprinter (teletype, telex, *US*) unit; ~**teilnehmer** teleprinter, teletype (telex, *US*) user; ~**teilnehmernetz** teleprinter network, teletype (telex, *US*) network; ~**verbindung** teletype link *(US)*; **direkte ~verbindung** direct printer (teleprinter) link; **hergestellte ~verbindung** telex call; ~**verkehr** teleprinter (teletype, telex, *US*) communication; ~**vermittlung** telex exchange.

fernschriftlich by teleprinter (teletype, telex, *US*);
~**e Übermittlung** teleprinter transmission.

Fernseh|abtaster scanner; ~**ansager[in]** television (video, *US*) announcer; ~**ansprache** televised speech, television address; ~**ansprache halten** to speak on television; ~**anstalt** television organization; ~**antenne** television mast (antenna).

Fernsehapparat television receiver (set);
mit einem ~ ausgestattet *(Hotelzimmer)* equipped with television;
~ **abschalten** to switch the television off; ~ **aufstellen** to install a television set; ~ **einschalten** to switch the television on.

Fernsehaufnahme, ~aufzeichnung television pick-up (take, recording), telerecording;
für ~n sehr geeignet telegenic;
~**raum** television studio; ~**röhre** television pick-up tube; ~**wagen** television pickup van, video truck *(US)*.

Fernseh|auftritt appearance on television, television appearance, living room gig *(sl.)*; **seine ~auftritte verringern** to cut down one's television appearance; ~**aufzeichnung** telerecording, television recording; ~**auge** television eye; ~**autor** scriptwriter, scripter, screen writer *(US)*.

Fernsehband television (video tape, *US*) band;
~**aufnahme** videotape recording *(US)*; ~**gerät** home video, video-tape recorder *(US)*; ~**material** recorded television material.

Fernseh|bearbeitung television adaptation; ~**bedienungsgerät** slave arm; ~**beliebtheitstest** television ratings; ~**berichterstattung über den Wahlkampf** television coverage of the election campaign; ~**beteiligung** television interests.

Fernsehbild television picture (image), teleimage, *(im Kontrollraum)* monitor;
fehlerhaftes ~ faulty image;
gut sichtbares ~ aufweisen to be viewable;
~**berichterstatter** television cameraman; ~**fläche** image, aspect ratio; ~**röhre** television tube; ~**schirm** [television] screen; ~**sender** picture (visual) transmitter.

Fernseh|buchungsbüro television booking office; ~**diskussion** television debate, panel discussion; **an einer ~diskussion teilnehmen** to panelize; **auf ~dose aufnehmen** to video-tape; ~**drahtfunk** wired (piped) television.

fernseheigene Produktion production commissioned for television.

Fernseh|empfang television reception; ~**empfänger** television set; **gemeinschaftliche ~empfangsanlage** covision.

Fernsehen television, video *(US)*;
zum ~ gehörig video;
direktes ~ direct pickup; **drahtloses ~** radiovision; **farbiges ~** colo(u)r television; **innerbetriebliches ~** closed-circuit television; **kommerzielles ~** commercial (independent) television, commercial scene; **öffentliches ~** open-circuit television;
im ~ auftreten to go on television; **Nachrichten weitgehend nur vom staatlich kontrollierten ~ beziehen** to depend mainly on government-controlled television for news; **im ~ bringen** to televise, to screen; **im ~ erscheinen** to appear on television; ~ **haben** to have television; **wie gebannt vor dem ~ sitzen** to be riveted to the screen; **im ~ sprechen** to go on television; **im ~ übertragen** to broadcast on television, to televise, to telecast; **im ~ übertragen werden** to be televised.

fernsehen to teleview, to watch (look at the) television, to watch a television program(me).

fernsehentstört suppressed for television.

Fernseher television set, box *(Br.)*, *(Person)* televiewer.

Fernseh|experte television expert; ~**fachsprache** video vernacular *(US)*; ~**fanatiker** television addict.

Fernsehfilm television film, telefilm;
dokumentarischer ~ television documentary;
~**kassette** video cartridge *(US)*; ~**produzent** television producer; ~**verleihvertrieb** television rental company.

Fernseh|frequenz television (video, *US*) frequency; ~**gebühr** television licence; ~**genehmigung** television licence.

Fernsehgerät television set, box *(Br.)*;
tragbares ~ portable television;
~ **im Westentaschenformat** pocket-sized television set;
~ **ohne Gebühr benutzen** to crash television; ~ **mit halbjährigem Kundendienst kaufen** to buy a television with service for six months.

Fernsehgeräte|fabrik television factory; ~**geschäft** television-set dealer; ~**hersteller** television manufacturer.

fernsehgerecht tailored for television.

Fernseh|gesellschaft television company; **kommerzielle ~gesellschaft** associated television company *(Br.)*, independent television contractor; ~**heft** viewing guide; ~**industrie** television (video, *US*) industry; ~**industrieanlage** closed-circuit television; ~**ingenieur** television engineer; ~**inszenierung** television production; ~**interviews** television interviews; **mit jem. ein ~interview machen** to interview s. o. on television; ~**kabel** television cable; ~**kamera** television camera; ~**kanal** television (video, *US*) channel; ~**kanalzuweisung** allocation of channels; ~**kassette** [electronic] video recording cartridge *(US)*, video cassette; ~**kassette für das Heimkino** home television cartridge.

Fernsehkassetten|aufnahmen video cassette recording *(US)*; ~**filmband mit einstündiger Spieldauer** cartrivision one-hour tape; ~**gerät** video [tape] recorder.

Fernseh|koffergerät portable television, pocket-sized television; ~**kommentator** television commentator (announcer, *US*) network commentator; **bekannter ~kommentator** television personality; ~**konferenz** television conference; ~**konserve** canned television item; ~**konzession** television franchise; ~**kritik** television criticism; ~**kritiker** television critic; ~**kursus**, ~**lehrgang** television course, telecourse; ~**lehrgang abhalten** to teleteach; ~**leitung** television broadcasting circuit; ~**mann-**

schaft television crew; ~**manuskript** television script; ~**mast** television mast; ~**mechaniker** projectionist; ~**nachrichtendienst auf Sonderleitungen** teletext service; ~**netz** television network; **innerbetriebliches** ~**netz** closed-circuit system; ~**plauderei** televised chat; ~**pressekonferenz** television press conference; ~**produktion** television production; **unabhängige** ~**produktionsgesellschaft** independent television contractor *(Br.)*; ~**produzent** program(me) producer.

Fernsehprogramm television program(me) (schedule, network); **vom Publikum abgewertetes** ~ rating flop; **beliebtes** ~ high-rated program(me);
~ **anschauen** to watch a television program(me); **sich das abendliche** ~ **ansehen** to listen in tonight; ~ **auf Band aufnehmen** to record a television program(me) off the air;
~**auswahl** television viewing.

Fernseh|programmierer television programmer; ~**publikum** television (viewing) audience; ~**publikum während des Tages** daytime audience; ~**publizität** publicity on television; ~**raster** scanning device; ~**rechte** television rights; ~**redakteur** television editor, television interviewer; ~**regisseur** television director *(US)*; ~**reklame** television advertising; ~**relaisstation** television relay station; ~**reportage** out-side broadcast, television coverage; ~**reporter** outside broadcast commentator; ~**röhre** television (picture) tube; ~**schau** television show; ~**schauspieler** screen actor, telecaster; ~**schirm** television screen, telescreen; **großflächiger** ~**schirm** wide-screen television; **vor dem** ~**schirm sitzen** to sit before the screen; ~**schüler** student of television; ~**sender** television station (transmitter); **tragbarer** ~**sender** walkie-pushie; ~**sendergruppe** network television; ~**sendeturm** television tower; **vorrangige** ~**sendezeit** prime television time.

Fernsehsendung television broadcasting, video[cast] *(US)*, telecast *(US)*;
für ~**en besonders geeignet** telegenic;
gemeinsam ausgestrahlte ~ television linkup; **betriebliche** ~ closed-circuit telecast; **günstig gelegene** ~ prime-time television show; **kurze** ~ television short; **sehenswerte** ~ viewable television show;
~ **mit Niveau** viewable television show; ~ **mit Zuschauerabteilung** giveaway show.

Fernseh|serie television serial; **rührselige** ~**serie** soap opera *(US)*; **großangelegtes** ~**sonderprogramm**, ~**sonderserie** television special; ~**souffleur** teleprompter; ~**spiel** tele-play; ~**sprechdienst** video telephone service *(US)*; ~**sprecher** television announcer; ~**sprechsystem** talk-back television system; ~**star** screen star; ~**station** television station, telestation; ~**störung** television interference, bugs in television; ~**stück** television play, screen play; ~**studio** television studio, floor; **privates** ~**system** television network *(US)*; ~**technik** television engineering, video technique *(US)*; ~**techniker** television engineer; ~**teilnehmer** [tele]viewer, looker-in, television looker; ~**telefon** video telephone *(US)*, picturephone; ~**telefonie** video telephony *(US)*; ~**teleskop** telescope camera; ~**tonbandgerät** videotape recorder *(US)*; ~**truhe** television cabinet; ~**turm** television tower.

Fernsehübertragung television transmission, telecast *(US)*;
direkte ~ live television coverage;
einer ~ **beiwohnen** to televiewr; ~ **bringen** to telecast.

Fernseh|überwachung television monitoring; **hauseigene** ~**überwachungskamera** closed-circuit television camera; ~**universität** Open University; ~**verbot** television ban; **transatlantischer** ~**verkehr** transatlantic television; **auf Kassette aufgenommene** ~**vorlesung** videotaped lecture *(US)*; ~**vortrag** television lecture.

Fernsehwerbe|einheit time slot; ~**einnahmen** television ad revenues *(US)*; ~**gesellschaft** television advertiser, commercial television company.

Fernsehwerber pitchman *(sl.)*.

Fernsehwerbe|sendung television commercial; ~**sendung für Versandartikel** package goods commercial; ~**spot** television spot; ~**verbot** television ad ban *(US)*; ~**zeit** television commercial time, airtime.

Fernsehwerbung television advertising, *(kurze)* blurb;
~ **in Plakatform** billboard commercial;
~ **mit einbeziehen** to add television to its media.

Fernseh|zeit television watching hour; **gebührenfreie** ~**zeit** free time on television; ~**zensur** television censorship; ~**zuhörerschaft** television audience; ~**zusatzgerät** television-set accessory; ~**zuschauer** television viewer (looker); **kein regelmäßiger** ~**zuschauer sein** to not ordinarily watch television; ~**zuschüsse** television grants.

Fern|setzmaschine teletypesetter; ~**sicht** view, prospect, perspective, *(Wetterkunde)* visibility; ~**spediteur** long-distance mover, land (long-haul) carrier, road haulage firm *(Br.)*, haulage contractor *(US)*.

Fernsprech|alphabet telephone alphabet, list of spellers; ~**amt** [telephone] exchange, central *(US)*; ~**anlage** telephone installation (facilities); ~**ansagedienst** telephone enquiries (information, *US*) service, mass announcement exchange; ~**anschluß** subscriber's line, telephone extension, telephone connection (connexion, *Br.*); ~**anschluß auf dem Zimmer** *(Hotel)* room telephone; ~**anschluß haben** to be on the telephone; **mit zu wenig** ~**anschlüssen ausgestattet** telephone-starved; ~**anschlußgebühr** subscriber's rental; ~**apparat** telephone; ~**aufnahmegerät** automatic telephone recording machine; ~**auftragsdienst** automatic telephone answering service; ~**auskunftsdienst** telephone enquiries (information, *US*) service; ~**auslandsdienst** Overseas Telephone Service *(Br.)*; ~**automat** telephone booth (kiosk), public call box *(Br.)*, pay station *(US)*; ~**beamter** telephone operator; ~**bedienung** telephone attendant; ~**buch** telephone book *(US)* (directory, *Br.*); ~**dienst** telephone service; ~**einrichtungen** telephone equipment (facilities).

Fernsprecher telephone;
durch (mittels) ~ on the telephone, telephonic;
öffentlicher ~ telephone booth (kiosk), public telephone, public call box *(Br.)*, pay station *(US)*.

Fernsprech|gebühr tariff charge on calls, telephone charge, phone rate; ~**gebührenrechnung** telephone bill; ~**grundgebühr** line charge; ~**häuschen** telephone booth (kiosk), public call box *(Br.)*, pay station *(US)*; ~**kabel** telephone cable; ~**kabine** telephone booth (kiosk), public call box *(Br.)*, pay station *(US)*; ~**kanal** telephone channel; ~**leitung** telephone (long-distance) line, telephone circuit; **normale** ~**leitungen benutzen** to operate over ordinary phone lines; ~**linie** telephone line; ~**nebenstelle** telephone extension; ~**netz** telephone system, [telephone] network; ~**nummer** telephone (call) number; ~**sammelnummer** party line, multiple telephone number *(US)*; ~**säule** *(Verkehrswacht)* roadside telephone; ~**schrank** telephone switchboard; ~**sonderdienst** special telephone service; **öffentliche** ~**stelle** public telephone, telephone booth (kiosk), public call box *(Br.)*, pay station *(US)*; ~**tarif** telephone rates.

Fernsprechteilnehmer telephone subscriber;
~ **sein** to be on the telephone; **zwei** ~ **miteinander verbinden** to connect two subscribers;
~**verzeichnis** telephone directory (book, *US*).

Fernsprech|verbindung telephone connection; ~**verbindung herstellen** to put through (complete) a call; ~**verkehr** telephone service; ~**vermittlung** [telephone] exchange, central *(US)*; ~**vermittlung mit Handbetrieb** *(tel.)* manual exchange; ~**verzeichnis** directory (book); ~**wesen** telephony; ~**zelle** public telephone, [public] call box *(Br.)*, [telephone] booth *(US)*, telephone call-box *(Br.)*, pay station *(US)*; ~**zentrale** telephone switchboard (desk exchange, chief operator).

Fernspruch telephone message, *(Bahn, mil.)* signal.

fernstehen, einer Sache to have no personal connection with s. th.

Fernstehender outsider, onlooker.

Fernsteueranlage remote-control installation.

fernsteuern to operate (steer) by remote control.

Fernsteuerung remote control, teleautomatics, *(Flugzeug)* telearchics;
mechanische ~ telemechanics.

Fernstraße classified (trunk) road *(Br.)*, highway *(US)*;
sechsbahnige ~ six-lane highway *(US)*;
als ~ **einstufen** to class as a trunk road *(Br.)*.

Fernstraßen|bezirk highway parish *(US)*; ~**gesetz** Trunk Roads Act *(Br.)*, Highway Law *(US)*; ~**netz** network of highways *(US)*, highway network *(US)*, trunk-road scheme *(Br.)*; **fertiggestelltes** ~**netz** new trunk-road scheme *(Br.)*; ~**programm** highway program *(US)*; ~**projekt** highway project *(US)*; ~**verkehrsnetz** highway network *(US)*, trunk-road scheme *(Br.)*; ~**verkehrsschild** route (highway, *US*) marker.

Fern|strecke main line, trunk line; ~**student** correspondence-course student; ~**studium** correspondence course; ~**thermometer** distant-reading thermometer, telethermometer; ~**transport** long-distance *(US)* (overland) transport, haul transport; ~**trauung** marriage by proxy.

fernübertragen to transmit over a long distance.

Fern|überwachung remote monitoring; ~**universität** open university, learn-by-mail school; ~**unterricht** correspondence class (study); ~**unterrichtsstelle** correspondence (learn-by-mail) school; ~**verbindung** *(Telefon)* long-lines communication, trunk connection (line) *(Br.)*, long-distance communication *(US)*, toll call *(Br.)*, *(Verkehr)* long-distance route; ~**verbindungen** *(Nachrichtenverkehr)* telecommunications; ~**verbindungsstrecke** grand route; ~**verkehr** long-distance (-hauls) transport (traffic), *(tel.)* trunk (toll-, *US*) line service, trunk traffic *(Br.)*.

Fernverkehrs|bereich *(tel.)* trunk zone *(Br.)*; ~**düsenflugzeug** long-haul jet; ~**flugzeug** long-range aircraft; ~**lastwagen** freight truck; ~**linie** long-distance route; ~**omnibus** cross-country *(Br.)* (long-distance) bus, motor coach; ~**schild** highway *(US)* (route) marker.

Fernverkehrsstraße arterial road, arterial highway *(US)*, trunk road *(Br.)*;
durch mehrere Bundesstaaten führende ~ interstate highway *(US)*; **plankreuzungsfreie** ~ freeway *(US)*, motorway *(Br.)*, superhighway *(US)*; **sechsbahnige** ~ six-lane highway *(US)*; ~ **mit Parallelbahnen** dual carriageway *(Br.)*, multistrip highway *(US)*.

Fernverkehrsstraßen|gesetz Trunk Roads Act *(Br.)*; ~**programm** highway program *(US)*.

Fern|vermittlung long-distance telephone connection; ~**versorgung** long-distance supply; ~**waffe** longe-range weapon; ~**wahl** *(Telefon)* subscriber-trunk *(Br.)* (direct, long-distance, toll-line, *US*) dialling; ~**wärmenetz** long-distance heating system; ~**wasserversorgung** long-distance water supply; ~**wirkung** long-range effect, distant action; ~**zähler** telecounter; ~**ziel** distant goal, ultimate object; ~**-D-Zug** extra-fare train.

Ferse heel;
dicht auf den ~**n** on the track, upon s. one's heels;
jem. dicht auf den ~**n bleiben** to dog s. one's footsteps, to be hot on s. one's heels; **Polizei dicht auf den** ~**n haben** to have the police on one's tail; **sich an jds.** ~**n heften** to heel; **jem. dicht auf den** ~**n sein** to follow hard upon s. one's heels, to be on s. one's tail, to be hot on the trace of s. o.

Fersengeld geben to turn tail, to show a clean pair of heels, to give leg bail.

fertig ready, ready-made, finished, accomplished, through, *(körperlich erledigt)* exhausted, worn-out, dead-beat, *(fabriziert)* manufactured, *(finanziell ruiniert)* broke, ruined, *(Kleidung)* ready-made, ready to wear, reach-me-down *(Br.)*, *(Speisen)* precooked, prepared, cooked, *(vollendet)* finished, completed, done, through, *(vorgefertigt)* prefabricated;
auf die Plätze! ~**!** on your marks!;
fast ~ near completion; **restlos** ~ dead-beat, *(betrunken)* tight; ~ **zum Aufbruch** ready to start;
~ **bearbeiten** to finish; ~ **kaufen** to buy ready-made; **mit jem.** ~ **sein** to have done with s. o.; **mit einer Arbeit** ~ **sein** to be through with a job; **mit einem Buch** ~ **sein** to have finished a book; **rechtzeitig** ~ **sein** to be finished in time; **mit einer Sache** ~ **sein** to have finished (done) with; **völlig** ~ **sein** to be exhausted (worn-out, dead-beat, all in), *(total betrunken)* to be completely drunk; ~ **werden** to be nearing completion; **mit etw.** ~ **werden** to cope with s. th.; **praktisch mit allem** ~ **werden** to be able to turn one's hand to anything; **mit einer Sache** ~ **werden** to be able to tackle it; **mit einer Sache endlich** ~ **werden** to see the last of a job; **mit einem Schicksalsschlag** ~ **werden** to get over a blow; **mit allen Schwierigkeiten** ~ **werden** to fight through all the troubles; **spielend mit jem.** ~ **werden** to put s. o. into one's pocket;
~**e Zeichnung** finished drawing.

Fertig|anzug ready-made suit, *(fam.)* hand- (reach-) me-down; ~**bau** prefabricated building, prefab; ~**bauteil** prefabricated unit, *(Beton)* precast part; ~**bauweise** prefabricated construction.

fertigbearbeiten to finish.

Fertig|bearbeitung finishing [operation], finish, master touch; ~**beton** ready-mixed concrete.

fertigbringen to achieve, to bring about, to manage, *(übers Herz bringen)* to have the (find it in one's) heart to do;
es glatt ~ to be mean (low) enough to do; **es nicht** ~ not to bring o. s. to do.

fertigen to make manufacture, to produce, to fabricate, to machine.

Fertig|erzeugnisse, ~**fabrikate** finished products (goods), manufactured (wrought) goods; ~**fabrikatingenieur** product engineer *(US)*.

fertiggepackt packaged.

Fertig|gericht package food, ready-to-serve dish, pre-packaged food; ~**gerichtelieferant** [industrial] caterer, catering establishment.

fertiggestellt made up, completed;
noch nicht ~ **sein** to be in the making;
~**e Waren** fully manufactured goods.

Fertig|gewicht finished weight; ~**haus** prefabricated (precut) house (building), prefab *(Br., coll.)*; ~**hausbetrieb** prefabricator; ~**hausteile** prefabricated units; ~**industrie** finishing industry; ~**keit** skill, craft, hand, knack, facility, *(Begabung)* accomplishment, talent, *(manuell)* dexterity, craft; **große** ~**keit haben** to be highly proficient; ~**keiten** attainments, perfections; ~**kleidung** ready-to-wear, ready-made clothes, off-the-peg clothes; ~**kleidungsbetrieb** ready-to wear textile firm.

fertigmachen to complete, to finish, *(Standpauke halten)* to tell off, to dress down, to skunk *(US sl.)*;
j. ~ to tell s. o. what is what, to make s. o. sing small; **Arbeit** ~ to finish (complete) a piece of work; **jem. in einer Artikelserie** ~ to dispose of s. o. in a couple of articles; **Buch** ~ to finish the binding; **Gästezimmer** ~ to get a room ready for guests; **jds. Rechnung** ~ to get s. one's bill ready; **sich für eine Reise** ~ to get ready for a journey; **j. restlos (total)** ~ to slaughter an opponent *(US)*, to sew up s. o. *(sl.)*, to knock s. o. into a cocked hat *(sl.)*, to have s. o. on the ropes; **j. völlig** ~ to finish s. o. off.

Fertig|mahlzeit take-away meal; ~**montage** final assembly; ~**produkte** finished products, manufactured articles.

fertigstellen to accomplish, to complete, to get ready, to prepare, *(Produktionsvorgang)* to finish, to process.

Fertigstellung accomplishment, completion, perfection, finishing, *(Produktionsvorgang)* finishing, processing;
fristgemäße ~ completion on schedule;
~ **von Einzelteilen** perfection of detail; ~ **einer Steuerveranlagung** issue of assessment; ~ **einer Straße** opening of a new street;
kurz vor der ~ **sein** to near completion.

Fertigstellungs|klausel readiness clause; ~**termin** date of completion, completion date; **fünf Jahre nach dem** ~**termin eröffnen** to open five years behind schedule.

Fertig|straße *(Metallverarbeitung)* rolling (finishing) mill train; ~**suppe** industrially made soup; ~**teil** *(Haus)* manufactured building (prefabricated) part.

Fertigung making, manufacture, manufacturing, production, output;
bedarfsorientierte ~ demand-oriented production; **eigene** ~ own make; **handelsübliche** ~ commercial production;
~ **aufnehmen, in die** ~ **gehen** to go into production (on stream, *US*); **wesentlichen Teil der** ~ **ausmachen** to form the bulk of the production; ~ **drosseln** to curb (restrict) production; ~ **einstellen** to hold, to discontinue the manufacture; ~ **in Gang halten** to keep production wheels humming; ~ **programmieren** to scale production; ~ **stillegen** to halt production lines.

Fertigungs|abfall production slump; ~**ablauf** production flow (run); ~**ablauf festigen** to schedule production *(US)*; ~**abteilung** manufacturing (production) department; ~**anlage** factory, plant, works, manufacturing establishment; **mengenmäßiger** ~**anstieg** increase in the volume of production; ~**anteil** share of production; ~**aufgabe** line shutup; ~**aufnahme** going into production; ~**auftrag** production order; ~**auftrag erst nach positiv verlaufenen Modellversuchen erteilen** to fly before you buy; ~**ausfall** loss of production; ~**auslastung** working to capacity; ~**ausstoß erhöhen** to step up production; ~**ausweitung** expansion of production; ~**bedingungen** manufacturing conditions; ~**bereich** product line; ~**beruf** production job; ~**beschränkung** restriction (curtailment) of production; ~**betrieb** factory, manufacturing establishment, manufacturing enterprise (plant); ~**betrieb für transportable Häuser** mobile home plant; ~**büro** production office; ~**dauer** production (manufacturing) time; ~**diagramm** process chart; ~**einheit** production unit, unit of output, assembly; ~**einleitung** starting up of production; ~**einrichtungen** production facilities (equipment), manufacturing facilities; ~**engpaß** bottleneck in production; ~**fehler** defect due to workmanship; **normaler** ~**gang** regular course of manufacture; **unrentable** ~**gebiete aufgeben** to eliminate unprofitable operations.

Fertigungsgemeinkosten indirect (supplementary) cost, overhead costs, overheads, factory overhead [expenses];
~**konto** factory overhead account; ~**mehranfall** under-absorbed indirect cost; ~**satz** factory overhead rate.

Fertigungs|gruppe production unit; ~**industrie** manufacturing industry; ~**ingenieur** production (product, *US*) engineer; ~**jahr** year of manufacture; ~**kapazität** production capacity; ~**kontrolle** production control, supervision of manufacture.

Fertigungskosten direct material costs, cost of production, manufacturing expenses;

~ **teilweise übernehmen** to contribute in part to the expense of production;
~**kontrolle** manufacturing cost control; ~**rechnung** manufacturing cost sheet; ~**senkung** manufacturing economics; ~**stelle** productive burden center *(US)* (centre, *Br.*).

Fertigungs|leiter production manager; ~**löhne** direct labo(u)r [cost], productive wages (labo(u)r); ~**lohnkosten** direct labo(u)r cost; ~**lohnstunde** direct labo(u)r hour; ~**material** direct material; ~**methode** production method, operating procedure; ~**modell** production model; ~**phase** processing stage; ~**plan** production plan, manufacturing schedule; ~**planer** planning engineer; ~**planung** production planning, production scheduling *(US)*; **endgültige** ~**planung** final manufacturing estimates.

Fertigungsprogramm production (manufacturing) program(me);
gemischtes ~ product mix;
~**e von entscheidender Bedeutung** key-product lines;
als Interessent für das gesamte ~ **auftreten** to bid for the whole package; ~ **in verschiedene Industriebezirke ausdehnen** to diversify into different industries.

fertigungsreif ready to go into production.

Fertigungs|sektor secondary sector; ~**serie** line, run; ~**sortiment** production mix; ~**stand** state of production; ~**stätte** manufacturing establishment (plant), production unit factory, workshop; **betriebseigene** ~**stätten** own facilities; ~**stätten unterhalten** to manufacture; ~**stelle** production center *(US)* (centre, *Br.*), producing unit, manufacturing establishment; ~**steuerung** industrial *(US)* (product) engineering, production control; ~**straße** production (assembly) line, conveyor system; ~**stufe** stage of production, production step; ~**technik** production (product) engineering; ~**teil** production part; ~**tempo** tempo of production, production rate; ~**überwachung** production control; ~**vereinfachung** product simplification; ~**verfahren** production (manufacturing) method; **rationelles** ~**verfahren** efficient manufacturing process, product rationalization; ~**vorbereitung** preparatory work, process engineering, production scheduling; ~**vorgang** job operation, productive (manufacturing) process; ~**zahlen** output (production) figures; ~**zeit** production (manufacturing) time; **auftragsloser** ~**zweig** empty production line; **einzelne** ~**zweige zum Zweck der Liquiditätsverbesserung aufgeben** to sell production divisions to raise cash.

fertigverpackt prepacked.

Fertigwaren finished goods (products), end products, manufactures;
gewerbliche ~ industrial manufactures;
zu ~ **verarbeiten** to convert into finished products;
~**anstieg** increase in finished goods; ~**bestand** finished-goods inventory; ~**industrie** manufacturing industry; ~**journal** finished-goods journal; ~**konto** finished-goods account; ~**lager** stock of finished goods, finished-goods inventory.

fertigwerden to cope (deal) with, to manage, to get along.

Fertigzeitung final artwork.

fesch posh *(fam.)*, nifty *(US sl.)*;
äußerst ~ quite the thing.

Fessel fetter, cord, hamper, tie *(coll.)*.

Fesselballon captive (barrage, kite observation) balloon;
~**schutz** balloon apron.

Fesseln fetters, chains;
in ~ in bonds;
~ **der Knechtschaft abstreifen** to throw off the yoke; **jem.** ~ **anlegen** to put a man in irons; **seine** ~ **sprengen** to burst one's fetters.

fesseln to fetter, to shackle, to manacle, to handcuff *(fig.)*, to intrigue, to grip, to hold s. one's attention;
Zuhörer ~ to hold one's audience spell-bound.

fesselnd engaging, magnetic.

Fest feast, festivity, celebration, function, *(Gesellschaft)* party;
ausgelassene ~**e** rollickings; **unbewegliche** ~**e** immovable feasts;
~ **feiern** to keep a feast, to feast, to celebrate, to make holiday; ~ **aus der Taufe heben** to inaugurate a fête; ~ **für j. sein** to be a treat for s. o.

fest *(Börse)* firm, stiff, *(dauerhaft)* durable, *(endgültig)* definitely, for certain, *(entschlossen)* determinate, tough, *(Gesundheit)* sound, robust, *(Kurs)* firm, *(Kosten)* fixed, *(sicher)* fast, fixed, *(ortsfest)* stationary, *(solide)* firm, solid, *(Stellung)* fixed, permanent, *(unveränderlich)* stable, steady, *(verbindlich)* binding, firm, *(zuverlässig)* unfailing;
~ **abgemacht** definitely agreed upon, for sure; ~ **angelegt** *(Kapital)* tied (locked, *Br.*) up; ~ **angestellt** permanently appointed, on the establishment; ~ **eingeplant** all planned; **etw.** ~**er** *(Börse)* cheerful; **nicht** ~ unstable; **sehr** ~ *(Börse)* strong, buoyant;
~ **mit Remmissionsrecht** outright purchase with right to return; ~ **abmachen** to fix up, to settle finally; ~ **abschließen** to make a bargain, to finalize a deal; ~ **anbieten** to offer firm; **Kapital** ~ **anlegen** to lock *(Br.)* (tie up) capital; **j.** ~ **anstellen** to put s. o. on the establishment; **Schrauben** ~ **anziehen** to tighten screws; ~ **bleiben** to stand firm, to stick to one's guns, *(Börse)* to maintain a firm attitude, to keep (remain) steady; **weiterhin** ~ **bleiben** *(Börse)* to continue to rule high; ~ **bei seiner Meinung bleiben** to stand one's ground, to stick to one's guns; ~ **eröffnen** *(Börse)* to open steady; ~ **kaufen** to buy outright; ~ **mit der Unterstützung eines Ausschusses rechnen können** to be solid with a committee; ~ **offerieren** to offer firm; ~ **schließen** *(Börse)* to close firm, to show a good tone; **jem.** ~ **in die Augen sehen** to look s. o. straight in the eye; **sehr** ~ **sein** *(Börse)* to be strong; ~ **angestellt sein** to be in regular work, to be on the establishment, to draw a fixed salary, to be permanently appointed; **in einem Fach** ~ **sein** to be well versed (up, *US*) on a subject; ~ **im Sattel sitzen** to be in the saddle; ~ **verkaufen** to sell outright (firm); **sich** ~ **auf j. verlassen** to place reliance upon s. o.; **Flasche** ~ **verschließen** to seal a bottle; ~ **versprechen** to give a solemn promise; ~ **werden** *(Börse)* to stiffen, to harden, to [turn] firm, to become firm; ~**er werden** *(Kurse)* to firm up, to move up; ~ **zupacken** to be hard at it; ~ **zusammenhalten** to stick together; ~ **zuschlagen** to strike hard;
~**e Abmachung** binding agreement; ~**er Abschluß** firm deal; ~**e Absicht** declared intention; ~**er Akkordlohnsatz** permanent piece rate; ~**es Angebot** firm offer (bid), positive offer; **in** ~**em Angestelltenverhältnis stehen** to be on the regular staff (establishment); ~**e Anlagen** fixed assets, fixtures, permanent (slow) assets; ~**e Ansichten** settled opinions; ~**e Anstellung** permanent position (appointment, employment); ~**er Anteil** stated proportion; ~**e Arbeit** steady work; **ohne** ~**en Aufenthalt** without fixed abode; ~**er Auftrag** standing (definite) order; ~**e Bandbreiten** *(Wechselkurs)* fixed limits (margins of exchange); **ohne** ~**e Beschäftigung** without a permanent occupation; **in** ~**em Besitz sein** to be unlikely to change hands; ~**en Boden unter den Füßen haben** to be on firm ground; ~**e Börse** firm (steady) market; ~**es Börsentermingeschäft** time bargain, future deal; ~**er Einband** stiff cover; **mit** ~**em Einband** hardcover; ~**es Einkommen,** ~**e Einkünfte** stable (regular, permanent, settled) income; ~**e Einrichtung** fixed base; ~**er Entschluß** settled intention, firm resolution; ~**es Fahrwerk** fixed landing gear; **einer Sache eine** ~**e Form geben** to give shape to s. th.; ~**en Freund haben** to go (be going) steady; ~**e Freundschaft** lasting friendship; ~**e Funkstelle** fixed station; ~**en Fuß fassen** to gain a foothold; ~**es Gebot** firm bid; ~**e Gebühren** fixed dues; ~**es Gehalt** fixed (straight) salary; ~**es Geld** time money, fixed deposit, time deposit *(US)*; ~ **angelegtes Geld** tied (locked-up, *Br.*) money; ~**e Gestalt annehmen** to be taking definite shape; ~**er Gewahrsam** safe custody; **auf** ~**em Grund bauen** to build on firm ground; ~**e Grundsätze** strong principles; ~**e Haltung** *(Börse)* firmness; ~**e Haltung einnehmen** to adopt a firm attitude; **in** ~**en Händen sein** to be unlikely to change hands; ~**es Honorar** general retainer; ~**e Hypothekenzusage** firm commitment *(US)*; ~**e Kapitalanlage** fixed investment; ~**es Kaufangebot** *(Makler)* firm bid; ~**er Knoten** tight knot; ~**e Kosten** fixed charges, overhead expenses, overheads; ~**e Kundschaft** regular (steady) customers; ~**er Kurs** fixed (steady) price; ~**es Lager** fortified camp; ~**e Meinung** settled conviction; ~ **eingebaute Möbel** fixed furniture; ~**e Nahrung** solid food; **keine** ~**en Pläne haben** to have no definite plans; ~**er Platz** stronghold; ~**er Preis** firm (standing) price, fixed (flat) fee; ~**es Preisgefüge** stable price structure; ~**e Preisgrenzen** firm limits; ~**e Preise** *(Schaufenster)* no reductions (abatement, discount); **auf** ~**e Rechnung kaufen** to buy outright; **keine** ~**e Regel** no hard-and-fast rule; **zu** ~**en Sätzen** at fixed rates; ~**en Schlaf haben** to be a sound sleeper; ~**er Schluß** *(Börse)* steady closing; ~ **eingebauter Schrank** built-in cupboard; ~**e Stadt** fortified town; ~**e Stellung** permanent position, perch; **mit** ~**er Stimme** in a steady voice; ~**er Termin** fixed date; ~**er Treibstoff** solid fuel; ~**e Übernahme** *(Konsortium)* underwriting guarantee; ~**er Umrechnungskurs** direct exchange; **auf** ~**em Untergrund errichten** to build on firm ground; ~**er Verkauf** firm sale; ~**es Verteilungsverhältnis** fixed ratio; ~**er Vertrag** standing agreement; ~**e Vorstellung haben** to have a clear conception; **ganz** ~**e Vorstellungen über seine Verwendungsmöglichkeiten haben** to be vocal about one's

assignments; ~e **Währung** hard (stable) currency; ~e **Wechselkurse** fixed exchange rates; ~er **Wohnsitz** settled abode, permanent abode (residence); **ohne** ~en **Wohnsitz** of no fixed abode; ~es **Zeitungsabonnement** standing order for a newspaper.

Fest|akt solemn ceremony; ~akt **durch seine Anwesenheit auszeichnen** to hono(u)r a ceremony with one's presence; ~**angebot** binding (firm) offer; ~**angestellter** fixture, jobholder, permanent employee; ~**anlage** time money, fixed deposit, time deposit *(US)*; ~**ansprache** ceremonial address; ~**antenne** fixed antenna; ~**aufführung** gala performance; ~**aufmarsch** celebration parade; ~**auftrag** standing (firm) order; ~**auftrag auf eine bestimmte Zeit** fixed-period order; ~**ausgabe** souvenir edition; ~**ausschuß** festival committee; ~**bankett** complimentary (testimonial) dinner, junket, banquet.

festbegründet vested.

Festbeilage commemorative supplement.

festbeißen, sich in seiner Arbeit to be engrossed in one's work; **sich in einem Buch** ~ to be absorbed in a book.

Festbeleuchtung gala illumination.

festbesoldet salaried;
~ **sein** to draw a fixed salary.

festbezahlter Autor staff writer.

Fest|bezug *(Buchhandel)* outright purchase; ~**bezüge** emoluments.

festbinden to tie [up], to cord.

festbleiben to remain firm, to stick to one's guns.

Festbrennstoff solid fuel.

Fest|dekoration festive decoration; ~**dividende** fixed dividend.

Feste tower, stronghold.

festeingefügt embedded.

Festessen banquet, feast, gala (solemn, state, complimentary) dinner.

festfahren *(Schiff)* to run aground;
sich ~ *(Auto)* to stall, to bog down, *(Examenskandidat)* to be at the end of one's tether, *(Verhandlungen)* to come to a standstill; **Fahrzeug im Schlamm** ~ to get a vehicle stuck in the mud; **Schiff** ~ to run a ship aground; **sich völlig** ~ *(Verhandlungen)* to come to a deadlock.

Festfeuer fixed light.

fest|fressen, sich *(Kolben)* to stick, to jam, *(Lager)* to seize, to jam, *(Rost)* to eat into; ~**frieren** *(Schiff)* to become icebound.

Festgabe commemorative edition, memory publication.

festgefahren *(Auto)* got stuck, stuck in the mud, bogged down, *(fig.)* at a dead set;
~ **sein** *(Schiff)* to be stranded (aground), *(Verhandlungen)* to rest in deadlock, to have come to a standstill (deadlock);
~e **Schneedecke** packed-down snow; ~e **Verhandlungen** deadlocked negotiations.

festgefügt tight.

Festgehalt fixed (regular) salary.

festgehalten, als Geisel kept as hostage; **durch Nebel** ~fogbound; **von der Polizei** ~ held by the police.

Festgeld consolidated money, fixed loan (deposit) *(Br.)*, time (fixed-term) deposit *(US)*;
~**bescheinigung** deposit certificate *(US)*; ~**einlagen** deposits on deposit account *(US)*; ~**guthaben** balance at bank deposit account; ~**hypothek** mortgage for a fixed sum, fixed (closed, standing) mortgage; ~**konto** fixed deposit *(Br.)*, time deposit *(US)*, deposit account *(US)*; ~**quittung** deposit certificate *(US)*; ~**zinseinnahmen** time interest earned.

festgelegt in set terms, fixed, determinate, determined, *(Kapital)* tied (locked, *Br.*) up, hung up *(US)*, *(Politik)* committed, aligned;
gesetzlich ~ legally determined; **vorher** ~ preordained;
sich ~ **haben [auf]** to be committed to, to be nailed down (in for it, *sl.*); **auf etw.** ~ **sein** to be fixed on s. th.;
in der im folgenden rechtlich ~**en Form** in the form hereinafter set forth; ~e **Grenze** defined frontier; **nicht genau** ~e **Grenze** no definite border; **künstlich** ~er **Preis** administered price; **in** ~en **Raten** by stated instalments; **genau** ~e **Rechte** definite rights; ~er **Wortlaut** set wording.

fest|gemacht *(Schiff)* in; **wie an den Erdboden** ~**genagelt** nailed to the ground; **von der Polizei** ~**genommen** arrested (pulled up) by the police.

Festgenommener person under arrest, arrested (attached) person.

festgesetzt fixed, settled, set, determined, determinate, assigned, vested, *(vertraglich)* stipulated;
~e **Bedingungen** conditions agreed upon; **amtlich** ~er **Höchstpreis** ceiling price; ~er **Preis** stated (fixed, upset) price; **amtlich** ~er **Preis** administered (controlled) price, price as fixed by the authorities; **vertraglich** ~er **Preis** fixed contract price; **zur** ~en **Stunde** at the appointed time; ~er **Termin** appointed time; **zur** ~en **Zeit** at the stated time; ~er **Zeitraum** definite period.

festgestellt stated, established, *(Schaden, Schuldbetrag)* liquidated;
amtlich ~ on record; **nicht** ~ *(Schaden)* unliquidated; **urteilsmäßig** ~ **sein** to be reduced to judgment;
~er **Schaden** observed (ascertained) damage; ~er **Schadensersatzanspruch** proven damages; ~e **Tatsache** ascertained fact; ~er **Wert** assessed value.

festhaken, Abschleppseil an einem Auto to hitch a tow rope to a car; **Fenster** ~ to hook up a window.

Festhalle hall, auditorium *(US)*, banqueting hall.

Festhalten adherence, *(Gefangener)* detention;
~ **an einer Berufsstellung** jobholding; ~ **an seinen Grundsätzen** fidelity to one's principles; ~ **an einer Politik** adhesion to a policy.

festhalten to adhere, *(ergreifen)* to gripe, to hold on, *(Polizei)* to arrest, to detain, to nail *(sl.)*;
j. ~ to arrest (apprehend) s. o.; **sich** ~ to hang on, to adhere; **sich an jem.** ~ to cling to (rely on) s. o.; **an einer Absprache** ~ to abide by an agreement; **am Alten** ~ to stand in the ancient ways; **zäh an einer Ansicht** ~ to hug an opinion; **an einer Aufgabe** ~ to stick to a task; **Aussage** ~ to put a statement on record; **an seiner Aussage** ~ to stick to one's statement; **an seinem Beruf** ~ to hold a job down *(coll.)*; **Dieb** ~ to stop a thief; **j. unter der Bezichtigung des Diebstahls** ~ to hold s. o. on charge of theft *(US)*; **im Gedächtnis** ~ to keep in one's mind; **im Gefängnis** ~ to detain in prison; **sich gegenseitig** ~ to cling to each other; **als Geisel** ~ to keep as a hostage; **sich am Geländer** ~ to hold on to the railing; **an einer Gewohnheit** ~ to cling to a habit; **an seinem Glauben** ~ to hold firm to one's belief; **an der Grenze** ~ to hold up at the frontier; **etw. krampfhaft** ~ to clutch at s. th.; **j. bis zur Zahlung eines Lösegeldes** ~ to hold s. o. for ransom; **an einer Meinung** ~ to cling to an (persist on one's) opinion; **für die Nachwelt** ~ to deliver to posterity; **an einer Politik** ~ to adhere to a policy; **an seinen Prinzipien** ~ to be steadfast in one's principles; **an einer Regel** ~ to observe a rule; **schriftlich** ~ to put down in writing, to commit to paper, to place on record; **auf Tonband** ~ to tape-record; **an einem Vertrag** ~ to abide by a contract; **unnachgiebig an einer Vertragsbestimmung** ~ to adhere strictly to a clause.

Festhypothek standing (closed, fixed) mortgage.

festigen to strengthen;
sich ~ *(Börse, Preise, Kurse)* to firm, to become firm, to steady, to stiffen, to strengthen, to harden, to stabilize, *(Gesundheit)* to improve, *(Verhältnisse)* to consolidate; **Charakter** ~ to fortify a character; **Dollarkurs** ~ to strengthen the dollar price; **Frieden** ~ to consolidate peace; **seine Stellung** ~ to strengthen one's position, to solidify one's place; **jds. Stellung** ~ to assure s. one's position; **Stellung der Regierung** ~ to strengthen the hands of the government; **Währung** ~ to stabilize the currency.

Festigkeit *(Börse)* strength, *(Charakter)* heart, granite, *(Faden)* strength, *(Gewebe)* closeness, *(Markt)* firmness, steadiness, *(Material)* resistance, fastness, *(Währung)* stability, *(Widerstandsfähigkeit)* resistance;
~ **der Börse** firmness of the market; ~ **der Sätze für tägliches Geld** firmness in calls;
zur ~ **neigen** *(Börse)* to incline to rise.

Festigkeits|berechnung calculation of strength; ~**grad** tensile strength; ~**grenze** breaking point.

Festigung strengthening, *(Verhältnisse)* consolidation, *(Währung)* stabilization;
~ **der Börse** hardening (stiffening, strengthening, recovery) of the market; ~ **eines Bündnisses** consolidation of an alliance; ~ **des Dollarkurses** strengthening of the dollar price; ~ **der Gesundheit** improvement in health; ~ **der Kurse** firming up (stiffening) of prices; ~ **des Marktes** consolidation (firmness) of the market; ~ **der Rohstoffpreise** stabilization of raw-material prices; ~ **seiner Stellung** consolidation of one's position.

Festival festival.

Festkauf firm purchase.

festklammern *(Büroklammer)* to clip on, *(Wäsche)* to peg, to fasten;
sich ~ to hang on; **sich an einer Hoffnung** ~ to cling to a hope; **sich an einem Strohhalm** ~ to clutch at a straw; **sich an dem Text** ~ to stick to the text.

festkleben, an etw. to stick (glue, gum) to s. th.

Fest|kleid gala dress, one's best bib and tucker; ~**kleidung** gala; ~**komitee** festival committee; ~**komma** *(Datenvererarbeitung)* fixed point; ~**konto** time (fixed-term) deposit *(US)*, deposit account *(US)*, fixed deposit *(Br.)*; ~**körper** solid; ~**kosten** fixed charges, overhead expenses, overheads; ~**kraftstoff** solid fuel; ~**kurs** fixed rate; ~**land** main[land], earth, continent; ~**land betreffend** continental *(Br.)*.

festländisch continental.

Festlands|auftrag continental order *(Br.)*; ~**börse** continental bourse *(Br.)*; ~**gespräch** continental call *(Br.)*; ~**hoch** continental high; ~**presse** continental press *(Br.)*; ~**reise** continental tour *(Br.)*; ~**sockel** continental shelf; ~**wechsel** continental bill *(Br.)*.

festlegen to set (lay) down, to state, *(anteilig)* to apportion, to allocate, *(bestimmen)* to assign, to fix, to determine, to locate, to schedule *(US)*, *(Kapital)* to sink, to tie (lock, *Br.*) up, *(Kurs)* to plot;
j. auf etw. ~ to pin (nail) s. o. down to s. th.; **sich auf etw.** ~ to commit (bind) o. s. to do s. th.; **ausdrücklich** ~ to stipulate (state) expressly; **j. auf seine Aussage** ~ to pin s. o. down to what he said; **Bankgelder** ~ to immobilize bank funds; **Bedingungen** ~ to lay down (stipulate) conditions; **Erbfolge** ~ to settle the succession; **erneut** ~ to reschedule; **sich feierlich auf etw.** ~ to swear to a cause; **Frachtsendungen** ~ to route shipments; **sein Geld in Grundstücken** ~ to tie up one's money in land; **enormen Geldbetrag** ~ to nail down an enormous amount of money; **gesetzlich** ~ to regularize, to regulate; **Grenzen** ~ to fix, to determine (mark out, define) boundaries; **Grenzen einer Bergwerkskonzession** ~ to locate a mining claim; **Grundsatz** ~ to lay down a principle; **Grundstücksgrenzen** ~ to locate the lines of a property *(US)*; **Guthaben auf zwei Monate** ~ to fix a deposit for two months; **haargenau** ~ to pinpoint; **sich auf eine bestimmte Handlungsweise** ~ to plump for a course of action *(fam.)*; **Kapitalbeträge** ~ to tie (lock, *Br.*) up the capital; **Leitweg** ~ to route; **Lizenzgebühr** ~ to fix a royalty; **sich auf eine Methode** ~ to commit o. s. to a method; **sich auf ein Muster** ~ to decide on a pattern; **Nacherbschaft** ~ to settle property; **sich nicht** ~ to play the field, *(Politiker)* to float; **sich ja nicht** ~ to pussyfoot *(US sl.)*; **sich noch nicht** ~ to keep one's option open; **örtlich** ~ to locate, to localize *(US)*; **gemeinsame Politik** ~ to define a common policy; **j. politisch** ~ to keep s. o. to a line of policy; **Preis** ~ to fix (determine) a price; **Produktionsablauf** ~ to schedule production *(US)*; **Quote** ~ to fix a quota; **Regeln** ~ to lay down rules; **sich in einer Sache** ~ to nail one's colo(u)rs to the mast; **Schiff** ~ to make a ship fast, to moor a ship; **Signal** ~ *(Bahn)* to lock a signal; **Sitzungstermin** ~ to settle (determine) a day for a meeting; **Streckenführung einer Eisenbahnlinie** ~ to locate a railroad *(US)*; **Termin** ~ to appoint a time; **Treffpunkt** ~ to fix a meeting place; **sich ungern** ~ to be reluctant to commit o. s.; **Vermögen** ~ to tie up an estate; **sein ganzes Vermögen in Grundstücken** ~ to lock up all one's capital in land; **vertraglich** ~ to stipulate by contract; **Vertragsbedingungen** ~ to settle (stipulate) the terms (set forth the conditions) of a contract; **Vollmachten** ~ to prescribe powers; **alles im voraus** ~ to plan everything ahead; **vierteljährliche Zahlungen** ~ to stipulate that payment should be quarterly; **sich zeitlich** ~ to tie o. s. down as to time;
sich nicht ~ **wollen** *(Zeuge)* to hedge.

festlegend, sich nicht noncommittal, pussyfoot *(US sl.)*.

Festlegung assignment, fixing, determination, stipulation, *(Bindung)* commitment;
örtliche ~ localization *(US)*;
~ **von Bankgeldern** immobilization of bank funds; ~ **von Bedingungen** stipulation of conditions; ~ **von Fernsehkanälen** allocation of television channels; ~ **der Firmenpolitik** policy formation; ~ **von für das Verfahren wesentlichen Fragen** settling issues *(Br.)*; ~ **einer Grenze** determination of a frontier; ~ **der Höchsttarife** rate regulation; ~ **von Kapitalbeiträgen** accumulation of capital, lockup of capital *(Br.)*; ~ **des Leitweges** routing; ~ **der Media** media strategy; ~ **der Parität** expression of par value; ~ **der Reihenfolge der Arbeitsabläufe** routing sheet; ~ **des strittigen Sachverhalts** joinder in pleading; ~ **einer Steuer** assessment (determination) of a tax; ~ **eines Verantwortungsbereichs** assignment of responsibilities; ~ **der Verkaufstournee** routing plan; ~ **des Versicherungsumfangs** insuring clause; ~ **der Vertragsbedingungen** stipulation of the terms of an agreement; ~ **der Vertretergebiete** routing of salesmen; **parteiliche** ~ **auf Zollsenkungen** a party's commitment to tariff reduction.

festlesen, sich in einem Buch to, become engrossed (absorbed) in a book.

festlich festive, gala;
~ **bewirtet** lavishly entertained; ~ **geschmückt** festively decorated;
Ereignis ~ **begehen** to celebrate an event with due ceremony; **gesamte Familie** ~ **bewirten** to feast one's entire family;
~**er Anlaß** festal occasion; ~**e Eröffnung einer Tagung** ceremonial opening of a congress; ~**e Gewänder** festive robes; ~**e Stimmung** festive mood, festivity; ~**e Veranstaltung** festivity, festive event (affair).

Festlichkeit gala, festival, festivity, function, treat, do *(Br., coll.)*;
~**en stören** to mar the festivities.

festliegen *(Börse)* to firm up, to be a hard spot, *(Grenze)* to be determined, *(Kapital)* to be locked *(Br.)* (tied) up, to be frozen, *(Preise)* to be fixed (settled), *(Schiff)* to be stranded (aground, grounded), *(Termin)* to be fixed (scheduled, *US*), *(Vertragsbedingungen)* to be settled (laid down), *(Zeit)* to be fixed;
wegen Benzinmangels ~ to be stranded through lack of petrol; **bereits** ~ to have been stipulated already; **auf Käufe hin** ~ to be firm (steady) on account of buying orders; **mit Maschinenschaden im Hafen** ~ to be held up in port with engine trouble; **noch nicht** ~ *(Termin)* not yet have been fixed.

festliegend tied (locked, *Br.*) up, *(Schiff)* grounded, stranded;
~**es Kapital** frozen capital, lockup *(Br.)*; ~**e Mittel** tied-up funds; ~**e Route** route laid down.

Festmache|boje mooring buoy; ~**leine** mooring line.

festmachen to fasten, to fix, to tie, to attach, to hitch, *(vereinbaren)* to arrange, to settle;
Anhänger am Koffer ~ to tie a label to one's suitcase; **an einer Boje** ~ to make fast to a buoy; **Boot am Ufer** ~ to tie up a boat to a post; **Bücherbrett an der Wand** ~ to fix a bookshelf to the wall; **schlagenden Fensterladen** ~ to fasten a banging shutter; **Handel** ~ to conclude (close) a bargain; **Schiff** ~ to make a ship fast, to moor a ship; **an einem Seil** ~ to tail on a rope.

Festmeter *(Holz)* cubic meter.

festnageln, j. to tag s. o. all right; **seinen Gegner auf einen Punkt** ~ to pin one's opponent down to a point; **jem. mit einer Lüge** ~ to nail a lie to the counter (barn); **j. auf sein Versprechen** ~ to pin s. o. down (keep s. o. to) his promise.

Festnahme arrest, arrestment *(Scot.)*, detention, apprehension, pinch *(sl.)*, trip to prison *(sl.)*;
vorläufige ~ investigative (provisional) arrest, seizure; **widerrechtliche** ~ false imprisonment, malicious arrest;
~ **eines Reisenden** stoppage of a passenger; ~ **eines Verbrechers** capture of a criminal;
sich der ~ **widersetzen** to resist arrest;
~**befugnis** power of arrest; ~**gruppe** arrest squad.

festnehmen to arrest, to apprehend, to detain, to take in charge, to capture, to lay fast, to pinch *(sl.)*, to snatch;
Demonstranten ~ to take demonstrators into custody; **sofort** ~ to arrest on the spot; **j. wegen des Verdachts finanzieller Unregelmäßigkeiten** ~ to take s. o. into custody on suspicion of financial impropriety; **vorläufig** ~ to arrest immediately without warrant.

festnehmender Beamter arresting officier.

Fest|order firm order, limit; ~**ordner** steward, marshal; ~**platz** fairground.

Festpreis fixed (set, firm, one-) price, price fixed by the government;
nur zu ~**en verkaufen** to sell goods only at fixed prices;
~**auftrag** straight (fixed) -price contract *(US)*; ~**auftrag mit Neufestsetzung des Preises** fixed-price contract with provision for redetermination of price *(US)*; ~**vereinbarung** fixed-price policy; ~**vertrag** fixed-price contract; ~**vertrag mit Leistungszuschlägen** fixed-price incentive fee contract.

Fest|programm program(me); ~**punkt** *(Vermessung)* bench mark; ~**rede** ceremonial address; ~**redner** [official] speaker; ~**saal** banquet room, banqueting hall; ~**satzkredit** fixed-interest credit; ~**schmaus** treat; ~**schmuck** festive decoration.

festschnallen to buckle on, to fasten on;
sich ~ to fasten one's seat-belt; **Koffer auf dem Gepäckträger** ~ to fasten a suitcase down on the luggage rack; **sich mit dem Sicherheitsgurt** ~ to fasten o. s. with a safety belt.

Festschrift memorial publication, commemorative issue.

festsetzbar determinable.

festsetzen *(arrestieren)* to lay fast, to arrest, *(ausbedingen)* to stipulate, to lay down, *(bestimmen)* to fix, to determine, to decide, to name, to state, to provide, *(Gesetz)* to rule, *(konstituieren)* to constitute, to establish, *(Normen)* to standardize, *(Termin)* to appoint, to assign, to set, to fix, to settle, to schedule *(US)*, *(verordnen)* to decree, *(vorschreiben)* to regulate, to prescribe;

j. ~ to put s. o. in prison, to arrest s. o.; **sich** ~ to settle; **seine Abreise** ~ to fix one's departure; **anteilsmäßig** ~ to prorate; **Bedingungen** ~ to lay down (settle) conditions; **Bußgeld** ~ to assess a fine; **Dividende** ~ to declare a dividend; **Einkommensteuersätze mit 28%** ~ to fix the income tax at 28%; **in gegenseitigem Einvernehmen** ~ to agree upon; **Entschädigungssumme** ~ to assess the amount of (fix) damages; **Erbfolge** ~ to settle the succession; **sich in einer Festung** ~ to establish o. s. in a citadel; **Frist** ~ to set a period of time, to lay down a time limit; **Gehalt für eine Stellung** ~ to assign a salary to an office; **Gerichtskosten** ~ to tax the costs; **Geschwindigkeitsbegrenzung für eine Straße** ~ to restrict a road; **sich in den feindlichen Gräben** ~ to lodge o. s. in the enemy's trenches; **Höchstbeträge** ~ to fix a limit; **Hochzeitstag** ~ to name the wedding day; **Kontingent** ~ to fix a quota; **Kosten** ~ to fix (determine) the costs; **Lieferfrist** ~ to stipulate a time for delivery; **Limit** ~ to set (fix) a limit; **Lizenzgebühr** ~ to fix a royalty; **Mietpreis** ~ to fix a rent; **Preis** ~ to lay down (determine, establish, fix, settle) a price; **Preis für ein neues Modell** ~ to fix the price of a new model; **Prozeßkosten** ~ to tax the bill of costs; **Quote** ~ to fix a quota; **Reiseroute** ~ to fix a route; **Schadensersatz** ~ to assess (ascertain, award) damages; **Sitzung für 10 Uhr** ~ to fix (schedule, *US*) a meeting for ten o'clock; **Sitzungstermin auf den 15.** ~ to set down a meeting for the 15th; **neue Steuer** ~ to establish a new tax; **Steuern** ~ to assess (graduate) taxes; **Strafe** ~ to award a sentence; **Tarif** ~ to fix a tariff; **Termin** ~ to appoint a time, to decide upon a day; **Verhandlungstermin** ~ to assign a day for a hearing in court; **Vertragsbedingungen** ~ to stipulate the terms of a contract; **Vorstellungsbeginn auf 20 Uhr** ~ to schedule a performance to begin at 8 o'clock; **Wert** ~ to assess a value; **Witwengeld** ~ to assign a dower; **vierteljährliche Zahlungen** ~ to stipulate that the payment should be quarterly; **Zeit und Ort für die nächste Sitzung** ~ to arrange (determine) time and place for the next meeting.

Festsetzung fixing, determination, establishment, appointment, assignment, arrangement, *(Abmachung)* stipulation, condition, settlement, *(Regelung)* regulation, *(Verhaftung)* imprisonment, arrest;
anteilsmäßige ~ assessment, allocation; **wirtschaftliche** ~ trade foothold;
~ **von Bedingungen** stipulation of conditions; ~ **der Dividende** declaration of dividend; ~ **der Dringlichkeit** priority rating; ~ **des Einzelhandelspreises** retail-price determination; ~ **der Eisenbahntarife** railway rating; ~ **einer Entschädigung** assessment of damages; ~ **von Erschließungskosten entsprechend den Grunderwerbskosten** block-to-block rule; ~ **von Exportpreisen** export pricing; ~ **von Feuerversicherungsprämien für öffentliche Speicher** rating of warehouses; ~ **des Fluchtlinienplanes** zoning *(US)*; ~ **der Gerichtskosten** taxing of costs; ~ **einer Geschwindigkeitsgrenze** restriction of a road; ~ **des Goldpreises** gold fixing; ~ **von Höchstbeträgen** fixing of a limit; ~ **von Konkurrenztarifen** competitive rating; ~ **der Kosten** assessment of costs, *(Gericht)* taxing of costs; ~ **erstattungsfähiger Kosten** *(Gericht)* taxation of party-to-party costs; ~ **des Pflichtteilsanspruchs der Witwe** assignment of dower; ~ **höherer Prämien** rating up; ~ **der Prämienhöhe** rating measures; ~ **eines Preises** price determination; ~ **von Quoten** fixing of quotas; ~ **des Rückkaufswertes** *(Lebensversicherung)* insurance valuation; ~ **von Schadenersatz** assessment of damages; ~ **der Steuer** tax assessment, taxing, determination of a tax; ~ **einer neuen Steuer** establishment of a new tax; ~ **eines Tarifes** rating; ~ **einer Vergütung** assessment of remuneration; ~ **eines Verhandlungstermins** assigning a day for a hearing in court; ~ **einer Vertragsstrafe** penalty clause.

Festsetzungs | ausschuß rating committee; ~**bescheid** tax assessment.

festsitzen *(Fahrzeug)* to be stuck (bogged down), *(Schiff)* to be fast aground, to be stranded (aground), *(Verband)* to be tight;
im Eis ~ to be icebound; **im Schlamm** ~ to be stuck in the mud.

Festspiele festival.

Festspiel | haus festival theatre; ~**woche** festival, gala week.

feststecken to pin, to fasten;
Preisetikett ~ to pin on a price ticket; **im Schlamm** ~ to be stuck in the mud.

feststehen *(Anspruch)* to be established, *(gewiß sein)* to be a fact, to be certain (beyond doubt), *(Programm)* to be fixed (scheduled, appointed, arranged), *(Tatsache)* to be an established fact;
einwandfrei ~ to be an undisputed fact.

feststehend stationary, fixed, steady, set, positive, *(Film)* still, *(Ventil)* seated;
~**e Abschreibungssätze** fixed depreciation; ~**er Anlageposten** fixed-assets unit; ~**e Einrichtung** permanent institution; ~**e Gebühren** fixed dues; ~**e Geschäftsordnung** standing orders; ~**e Redewendungen** set phrases; ~**e Tatsache** established fact, settled thing; ~**e Unkosten** assured costs.

feststellbar ascertainable, detectable, traceable, determinable, *(Person)* identifiable, *(Sachen)* ascertainable;
nicht ~ unascertainable, *(Person)* untraceable; **sicher** ~ certifiable;
~**es Risiko** perceivable risk; ~**e Tatsache** discoverable fact.

Feststellbremse *(Auto)* parking (emergency, *US*) brake.

feststellen to establish, *(bestimmen)* to determine, *(erklären)* to state, to declare, to assert, to be declaratory, *(ermitteln)* to discover, to make (find) out, to ascertain, to trace, *(Fehler)* to locate, to localize, *(zur Feststellung gelangen)* to realize, *(Patent)* to find out;
Adresse ~ to find out an address; **aktenmäßig** ~ to place (take) on record; **Aktiva** ~ *(Konkurs)* to marshal the assets; **etw. amtlich** ~ to give official notice of s. th.; **jds. Aufenthalt** ~ to trace s. one's whereabouts; **ausdrücklich** ~ to state expressly; **Beschlußfähigkeit** ~ to ascertain that there is a quorum; **Einheitswert** ~ to assess a building; **Einheitswert eines Grundstücks neu** ~ to assess a property for improvements; **Entstehungsherd einer Seuche** ~ to locate the seat of an epidemic disease; **Fehler und Irrtümer bei der Einkommenssteuererklärung** ~ to discover some error or mistake in a return of income; **Gasaustritt** ~ to detect an escape of gas; **gerichtlich** ~ to establish in court; **jds. Identität** ~ to establish s. one's identity; **Jahresabschluß** ~ to establish statement of accounts, to make a balance; **Krebs** ~ to diagnose cancer; **durch Kursvergleich** ~ to arbitrate; **Materialfehler** ~ to find a flaw in the material; **Mietwert** ~ to ascertain the rental value; **Nichteignung** ~ to disqualify; **in aller Öffentlichkeit** ~ to declare in public; **jds. Personalien** ~ to identify s. o., to establish s. one's identity; **plötzlich** ~, **daß es für den Zug zu spät war** to suddenly discover that it was too late to catch the train; **Quelle eines Gerüchts** ~ to trace back a rumo(u)r; **genauen Sachverhalt** ~ to find out the precise facts; **Schaden** ~ to ascertain (assess) the damage; **Täter** ~ to discover the culprit; **Tod** ~ to record the death; **genauen Todestag** ~ to determine the exact day of a death; **Todesursache** ~ to state the cause of death; **am Ton einer Antwort** ~, **daß** to tell by the tone of an answer that; **Unterschied** ~ to perceive a difference; **Valutierung** ~ to fix a value date; **Zahl der Anwesenden** ~ to count the house; **Zulässigkeit einer Klage** ~ to declare an action admissible.

feststellend declaratory.

Feststeller *(Schreibmaschine)* shift lock.

Feststellung establishment, *(Behauptung)* declaration, assertion, statement, *(Bestimmung)* determination, *(Ermittlung)* ascertainment, discovery, *(Schätzung)* appraisement, appraisal, assessment, *(Vertrag)* retical, *(Wahrnehmung)* perception, observation;
nach den letzten ~**en** according to the findings;
abschließende ~ final statement; **aktenmäßige** ~ placing on record; **ausdrückliche** ~ positive finding; **bewiesene** ~ certified statement; **einheitliche** ~ uniformity of assessment; **erklärende** ~ explanatory statement; **maßgebende** ~ authoritative statement; **rechtskräftige** ~ final decision; **richterliche** ~**en** finding of the court; **tatsächliche** ~**en** finding (statement) of facts; **wahre** ~ just statement;
~ **der Aktiva** marshalling the assets; ~ **des Alkoholgehalts** determination of alcoholic strength; ~ **von jds. Aufenthaltsort** establishment of s. one's whereabouts; ~ **der Echtheit** verification, authentication; ~**en des Gerichts** findings of the court; ~ **eines Gewinns** ascertainment of profits; **einfache** ~ **der Gültigkeit eines Testaments** common form of probate; ~ **der Heimstätteneigenschaft eines Grundstücks** declaration of homestead *(US)*; ~ **der Hörerschaft zur Werbeerfolgskontrolle** audience measurement; ~ **der Hypothekenrestschuld** deficiency decree; ~ **des Jahresabschlusses** adoption of the annual statement; ~ **der Kollision von Patentansprüchen** *(Patentamt)* interference ruling; ~ **der Konkursbilanz** filing of a schedule; ~ **einer Konkursforderung** allowance of a claim provable in bankruptcy; ~ **durch Kursvergleich** arbitration of exchange; ~ **der Nichteignung** disqualification; ~ **der Personalien** identification; ~ **eines Rechts** proof of a right; ~ **des Rechtes auf abgesonderte Befriedigung** declaration of charge; ~ **des Sachverhaltes** finding of facts; ~ **des Schadens** ascertainment of damage; ~ **eines Schadens** ascertainment of a loss; ~ **des Schadensersatzes** assessment of damages; ~ **einer Steuerschuld**

tax assessment note *(Br.)* (notice, *US*); ~ **der Vaterschaft** affiliation order; ~ **des mittleren Zahlungstermins** equation of payments; ~ **eines Zeitpunktes** determination of a date;
~ **als Beleidigung auffassen** to read a statement as an insult; **grundsätzliche** ~ **der Verpflichtung zum Schadensersatz beantragen** to sue for damages at large; **sich mit der** ~ **begnügen** to be content to state; **zur** ~ **gelangen** to realize; ~ **machen** to remark; **die zur** ~ **seiner Person erforderlichen Angaben machen** to identify o. s.; ~**en treffen** to make findings.
Feststellungs|beamter loss assessor, adjuster; ~**befund** finding; ~**behörde** assessment office; ~**bescheid** [notice of] assessment; ~**beschluß** declaratory decree; ~**gesetz** Assessment Committee Act.
Feststellungsklage declaratory action, bill of peace, rescissory action *(Scot.)*;
negative ~ action in jactitation of title, action of jactitation; ~ **auf unwirksame Kündigung** action for wrongful dismissal; ~ **auf Vorliegen eines Treuhandverhältnisses** declarator of trust; ~ **auf Unechtheit einer Urkunde** improbation *(Scot., law)*;
~ **erheben** to seek declaratory action; **negative** ~ **erheben** to appeal to a court for exemption from responsibility.
Feststellungsurteil decree of constitution, declaratory judgment; ~ **zugunsten des Klägers** declaration of plaintiff's rights;
~ **ergehen lassen** to declare a right.
Feststellungsverfahren detection method, *(Gericht)* declaratory proceedings.
Feststimmung holiday mood.
Feststoff solid [matter];
~**rakete** solid-fuelled rocket.
Festtafel festive board.
Festtag festival, holiday, high day, red-letter day;
~**e** festive season.
festtäglich festive;
~ **gekleidet** in one's best bib and tucker.
Festung fortress, fort, stronghold;
geheime ~ underground fortress; **praktisch uneinnehmbare** ~ virtually impregnable fortress;
~ **aufgeben** to yield a fortress; **Stadt zur** ~ **ausbauen** to embattle a city; ~ **erobern** to seize a fortress, to win; **sich in einer** ~ **festsetzen** to establish o. s. in a citadel; ~ **im Sturm nehmen** to assault a fortress; ~ **schleifen** to dismantle a fortress; ~ **dem Feind übergeben** to deliver a fortress to the enemy.
Festungs|anlagen fortifications, defences, works; ~**artillerie** siege artillery; ~**bauten** fortified buildings; ~**besatzung** garrison; ~**front** front of fortifications; ~**gebiet** fortified area; ~**graben** ditch, moat; ~**gürtel** cordon of forts; ~**haft** confinement in a fortress; ~**mauer** counterscarp wall; ~**stadt** fortress town; ~**übergabe** delivery of a fortress; ~**wall** rampart; **Stadt mit** ~**wällen umgeben** to fence a town with walls; ~**werk** works, fortification; **mit** ~**werken schützen** to fortify.
Festveranstaltung gala performance.
festverzinslich fixed-interest bearing;
~**e Werte** fixed-income investment.
Festwagen float, waggon.
festwalzen to roll.
Fest|wert standard (fixed) value, *(Mathematik)* constant; ~**wiese** fairground; ~**woche** festival, gala week.
festwurzeln to take (strike) root.
Fest|zeichen *(Radar)* permanent echo; ~**zeitgespräch** fixed-time call; ~**zeitgesprächsvermittler** telephone reservation agent.
festziehen to tighten, to pull;
Bremse ~ to put the hand brake on.
Festzug procession, parade.
Fett fat, grease, *(Schmalz)* lard;
sein ~ **abkriegen (bekommen)** to catch it, to get it hot, to be hauled over the coals; ~ **abschöpfen** *(fig.)* to skim off the cream; ~ **ansetzen** to put on weight; **im eigenen** ~ **braten** to fry in its own grease; **mit** ~ **einschmieren** to grease; **jem. sein** ~ **geben** to settle s. one's hash, to give s. o. the works; **j. im eigenen** ~ **schmoren lassen** to let s. o. stew in his own juice; **im** ~ **schwimmen (sitzen)** to live on the fat of the land (in clover), to live in plenty; **von seinem** ~ **zehren** to live on one's hump *(fam.)*.
fett *(Benzingemisch)* rich, *(Boden)* rich, fat, *(drucktechn.)* bold, full-faced, *(Erbschaft)* lucrative, profitable;
~ **drucken** to print in bold (heavy) type; **sich dick und** ~ **essen** to eat one's fill; **sich an jem.** ~ **machen** to turn and rend s. o.; **dick und** ~ **werden** to grow fat;
~**e Beute** pork *(US sl.)*; ~**er Kunde** big customer; ~**e Milch** rich milk; ~**e Pfründe** fat living; ~**e Schrift** boldface; ~**es Schwein** fat pig (swine); ~**e Umrandung** heavy frame; ~**e Zeiten** times of plenty.
Fettansatz corpulence.
fett|arm low in fat; ~**dichtes Papier** greaseproof paper.
Fettdruck heavy type, boldface, thick print, extrabold [print].
fetten to grease, to oil.
Fettfleck grease mark.
fettgedruckt boldface.
fettig *(Wolle)* greasy, oily.
Fett|kohle fat coal; **ins** ~**näpfchen treten** to drop a clanger, to drop a brick *(coll., Br.)*, to put one's foot in it; ~**polster** *(Rücklagen)* guaranty fund; ~**stift** grease pencil.
Fetzen shred, scrap, piece, tatter, frazzle, ribbon *(US)*;
alte ~ old rags;
nicht der ~ **eines Beweises** not one shred of evidence;
~ **Papier** scrap of paper;
arbeiten, daß die ~ **fliegen** to work at white heat; **in** ~ **gehen** to fall to pieces; **jem. in** ~ **um den Leib hängen** to hang round s. o. in rags and tatters; **in** ~ **herumlaufen** to go around in rags; **Brief in** ~ **reißen** to tear a letter to tatters (in shreds).
feucht *(Klima)* damp, moist, humid;
noch ~ **vom Druck** moist from ink; **noch** ~ **hinter den Ohren** still wet behind the ears;
~**e Angelegenheit** drinking bout, spree, binge *(sl.)*; ~**e Augen** watery eyes, eyes moist with tears; **in einem** ~**en Bett schlafen** to sleep in a damp bed; **j. einen** ~**en Dreck angehen** to be none of s. one's business; ~**es Grab finden** to find a watery grave; ~**es Gras** wet grass; ~**e Hitze** damp (humid) heat; ~**er Keller** damp cellar; ~**e Luft** humid air.
feuchtfröhlich jolly, merry, convivial;
~**er Abend** spree, drinking bout, binge *(sl.)*, bender *(US)*; ~**e Fahrt** boozy trip.
Feuchtigkeit *(Klima)* damp[ness], moisture;
vor ~ **schützen!** keep dry!
Feuchtigkeitsanzeiger hydroscope.
feuchtigkeitsbeständig moisture-proof.
Feuchtigkeits|gehalt moisture content, humidity; **hoher** ~**grad** high percentage of moisture; ~**schaden** damage due to moisture.
feudal sumptuous, magnificent, grand, swanky, posh, swell, plush;
~ **bewirten** to entertain sumptuously; ~ **leben** to live like a lord; ~**es Essen** gourmet meal, swanky dinner; **j. zu einem** ~**en Essen ausführen** to take s. o. to a swell dinner party; ~**e Geschenke** top-of-the-line gifts; ~**e Gesellschaft** aristocratic society; ~ **eingerichtetes Haus** luxuriously furnished house; ~**er Klub** plushery *(sl.)*; ~**ster Laden in der Stadt** poshest shop in town; ~**e Lebensführung** sumptuous living; ~**e Wohnung** luxury flat (apartment).
Feudal|herrschaft seigniory; ~**ismus** feudalism; ~**staat** feudal state.
Feuer fire, flame, *(Begeisterung)* enthusiasm, ardo(u)r, fervo(u)r, torch, *(Edelstein)* fire, glow, *(Feuerbrand)* blaze, conflagration, *(Wein)* body, vigo(u)r;
im ersten ~ **der Begeisterung** in the first flush of enthusiasm; **vom** ~ **zerstört** devastated by fire; **wie** ~ **und Wasser** oil and vinegar; **zwischen zwei** ~**n** between the devil and the deep blue sea;
vorsätzlich angelegtes ~ intentional fire; **bengalisches** ~ blue fire, Bengal light; **festes** ~ beacon, fixed light; **konzentriertes** ~ concentrated fire; **offenes** ~ open fire; **olympisches** ~ Olympic flame;
~ **durch Brandstiftung** incendiary fire; ~ **und Flamme** as keen as mustard; ~ **und Schwert** fire and sword;
~ **anfachen** to fan a fire; ~ **anmachen** to kindle fire; ~ **austreten** to tread a fire out, to beat out a fire; ~ **bekämpfen** to fight a fire; ~ **auf etw. dirigieren** to play the guns on s. th.; ~ **einstellen** to cease fire *(mil.)*; ~ **eröffnen** to fire, to open fire; **dem** ~ **zum Opfer fallen** to be destroyed by fire; ~ **fangen** to catch (take) fire, to kindle, *(fig.)* to become enthusiastic; **leicht** ~ **fangen** *(fig.)* to be easily smitten, to be easily carried away; **jem.** ~ **geben** to give s. o. a light; **für j. durchs** ~ **gehen** to go through fire and water (go down the line) for s. o.; **Öl ins** ~ **gießen** to add fuel to the flames; ~ **gefangen haben** to be smitten with a girl; **Kastanien aus dem** ~ **holen** to pull the chestnuts out of the fire; **etw. bei schwachem** ~ **kochen** to cook s. th. on a slow fire; ~ **konzentrieren** to concentrate the firing; ~ **ausgehen lassen** to let the fire die down; **seine Hand für etw. ins** ~ **legen** to stake one's oath (life) on it; ~ **an ein Haus legen** to set a house on fire; **unter feindlichem** ~ **liegen** to come under the fire of the enemy; ~ **löschen** to put out a fire; ~ **machen** to make fire; ~ **im Garten machen** to make a bonfire in the garden; **Stellung unter** ~ **nehmen** to bring the enemy position under fire; **das** ~ **schüren** to

mend (nurse, poke) the fire, to add fuel to the flames, to fan the flames; ~ **und Flamme für etw. sein** to be heart and soul for s. th., to take to s. th. like ducks to water; ~ **und Flamme für j. sein** to fall for s. o.; **wie ~ und Wasser sein** to be as like as chalk and cheese; **beim ~ sitzen** to sit by the fireside; ~ **speien** *(Vulkan)* to spit fire, to erupt; **mit dem ~ spielen** to play with edged tools (with fire), to bell the cat, to court disaster; **Land durch ~ und Schwert verheeren** to put a country to fire and sword; **sich am ~ wärmen** to warm o. s. at the fire; **feindliches ~ auf sich ziehen** to draw the enemy's fire;
wo Rauch ist, ist auch ~ there's no smoke without fire;
~alarm fire alarm; **~alarmübung** fire drill; **~anzünder** firelighter; **~assekuranz** fire insurance; **~ausbruch** outbreak of fire; **~ausbruchstelle** fire area; **~bake** beacon; **~ball** fireball; **~befehl** command to open fire; **~bekämpfung** fire fighting; **~bekämpfungsmittel** means for fighting fire; **~bereich** fire area *(mil.)* fire zone.

feuer|beschädigt touched from the fire, damaged by fire, fire-damaged; **~beständig** fire-resisting, fireproof.

Feuer|beständigkeit fire resistance; **~bestattungsanstalt** crematorium; **~bestattungsurne** cinerary urn; **~brand** blaze, conflagration; **~eifer** enthusiasm; **mit ~eifer darangehen** to show a lot of zeal; **~einstellung** *(mil.)* cease-fire, cessation of hostilities.

feuerfest fireproof, flame-proof, fire-resisting, heat-proof (-resisting);
~er Geldschrank fireproof strongbox; **~es Geschirr** ovenware; **~es Material** fire material; **~er Stahlschrank** fire-resisting steel cabinet; **~e Tür** fire door; **~er Ziegel** refractory brick, firebrick.

Feuergarbe cone of fire.

feuergefährdetes Gebäude fire trap.

feuergefährlich liable to catch fire, inflammable;
~e Ladung inflammable cargo.

Feuer|gefährlichkeit inflammability; **~gefecht** shooting, shoot-up; **~glocke** fire bell, tocsin; **~gürtel** fire belt; **~hahn** fire hydrant; **jem. den ~hahn aufs Dach setzen** to set s. one's house on fire; **~haken** fire hook; **~holz** fire wood; **~hydrant** fire plug; **~kraft** *(mil.)* fire-power; **~leitanlage** *(mil.)* fire-control system; **~leiter** fire escape; **~leitradar** fire control radar; **~leitstellung** command post; **~leitung** *(mil.)* fire direction.

Feuerlösch|anlage fire-extinguishing apparatus; **~apparat** fire-fighting machine; **~boot** fire-fighting craft, monitor, *(mar.)* fireboat; **~dienst** fire-fighting service; **~eimer** fire bucket.

Feuerlöscher fire extinguisher.

Feuerlösch|fahrzeug fire-fighting vehicle; **~gerät** fire extinguisher; **~kommando** fire company *(US)*; **~mannschaft** fire party; **~pumpe** fire pump; **~station** *(Schiff)* fire station; **~teich** static water tank; **~übung** fire drill; **~wagen** fire-fighting machine; **~zug** set of fire-fighting vehicles.

Feuer|meer sea of flame; **~meldeanlage** fire-alarm system; **~melder** fire alarm, *(automatisch)* fire detector;

Feuermelde|stelle fire-alarm point; **~system** fire-alarm system.

Feuern *(mil.)* firing.

feuern to fire;
j. ~ to sack (fire, *sl.*) s. o., to give s. o. his cards (the order of the boot), to brush s. o. off *(US sl.)*, to can (rif) s. o. *(US sl.)*; **auf jem. ~** to shoot at (fire upon) s. o.; **jem. eine ~** to land s. o. a blow in the face;
wegen gewerkschaftlicher Betätigung ~ to sack for union activities; **vor den Bug ~** to fire across the bow; **in die Ecke ~** to hurl in the corner; **mit Holz ~** to burn with wood; **j. kurzerhand ~** to give s. o. his running shoes *(sl.)*; **Salve ~** to volley; **Schmelzofen ~** to stoke a furnace.

Feuer|pause break in firing; **~polizei** fire police.

feuerpolizeiliches Zeugnis fire certificate.

Feuerprobe crucial (acid) test, ordeal by fire;
seine ~ bestehen to go through one's facings; **~ bestanden haben** to have gone through the fire; **j. auf die ~ stellen** to put s. o. through an ordeal.

Feuer|risiko fire hazard (risk); **~rost** fire grate; **~säule** column (pillar, *Br.*) of fire.

Feuersbrunst blaze, conflagration.

Feuerschaden loss (damage caused) by fire, fire loss, fire waste;
unmittelbarer ~ direct loss by fire;
~ abschätzen to appraise a loss by fire; **gegen ~ versichert sein** to be insured against fire.

Feuer|schadensabteilung *(Versicherungsgesellschaft)* fire department *(Br.)*; **~schein** firelight; **~schiff** lightship; **~schirm** fire screen; **kurzer ~schlag** *(mil.)* burst; **~schneise** fire lane, firebreak *(US)*; **~schott** *(Schiff)* fireproof bulkhead.

Feuerschutz fire prevention (protection), *(mil.)* fire support, covering fire;
~ geben to deliver covering fire;
~abgabe fire prevention levy; **~abteilung** *(Versicherung)* protective department; **~anstrich** fire-retardent paint; **~behörde** fire authority; **~dienst** fire protection organization; **~steuer** fire protective tax; **~verband** Fire Protection Association *(Br.)*; **~vorkehrungen** fire precautions.

Feuersgefahr fire risk (hazard), risk of fire;
allgemeine ~ common hazard.

feuersicher *(Safe)* fireproof;
~er Schacht fire tower; **~er Vorhang** fire curtain.

Feuersog vortex.

feuerspeiender Berg volcano.

Feuer|spritze fire engine; **~stätte, ~stelle** fireplace, hearth; **~stein** flint; **~stellung** *(mil.)* gun (fire, firing) position; **Geschütze in ~stellung bringen** to bring the guns into firing position; **~stoß** *(mil.)* burst of fire; **~strahl** jet of fire; **~sturm** fire storm; **~taufe** *(mil.)* baptism of fire; **~treppe** fire escape; **~tür** *(Ofen)* fire door; **~überfall** gunfire attack.

Feuerung firing, heating, *(Kesselanlage)* stoking.

Feuer|unterstützung *(mil.)* fire support; **~vereinigung** *(mil.)* concentration of fire.

feuervergoldet fire-gilt.

Feuer|verhütung fire prevention; **~verhütungsmaßnahmen** fire precautions; **~verlust** loss (damage caused) by fire.

feuerversichert sein to be insured against fire.

Feuerversicherung fire insurance;
gleichzeitige ~ des gleichen Objekts bei mehreren Gesellschaften concurrent fire insurance;
~ abschließen to take out a fire insurance.

Feuerversicherungs|anstalt, ~gesellschaft fire office *(Br.)* (underwriter), fire insurance company, fire-casualty insurer, fire insurer; **~police** fire [insurance] policy; **auf Grund periodisch zu erstattender Wertangabe ausgestellte ~police** reporting (declaration) policy *(US)*; **~prämie** fire-insurance premium; **~risiko** fire-insurance risk; **~tarif** fire insurance rates; **~träger** fire underwriter; **~verband** National Board of Fire Underwriters *(US)*.

feuerverzinkt hot-galvanized.

Feuer|vorhang *(mil.)* curtain of fire; **~wache** fire watch, fire picket (station, *US*), *(Forst)* fire warden *(US)*; **~waffe** firearm, gun; **~walze** *(mil.)* rolling (creeping) barrage; **~wand** wall of fire; **~warnanlage** fire-call system.

Feuerwehr fire brigade *(Br.)* (company, *US*, department, *US*);
wie die ~ like a flash;
örtliche freiwillige ~ fire brigade *(US)*;
~ alarmieren to call out the fire brigade; **wie die ~ fahren** to drive like mad (blazes);
~auto fire engine; **~bezirk** fire district; **~fahrzeug** fire-fighting vehicle, fire engine; **~hauptmann** fire fighter, fire marshal *(US)*; **~leiter** fire (aerial) ladder; **~mann** fireman; **~mannschaft** fire-brigade team *(Br.)*; **~schlauch** fire hose; **~übung** fire drill; **~wagen** fire engine.

Feuerwerk fireworks, pyrotechnic display, sparkler;
~ geistreicher Einfälle firework of witty ideas;
~ abbrennen (veranstalten) to let off fireworks.

feuerwerkartig pyrotechnical.

Feuerwerker fireworker, display hand, pyrotechnist, firework-maker.

Feuerwerks|körper petard, squib *(Br.)*; **~rakete** shell; **~veranstaltung** display of fireworks, firework display.

Feuer|zange fire tongs; **etw. nicht mal mit der ~zange anfassen** not to touch s. th. with a barge-pole; **~zangenbowle** burnt punch; **~zeug** lighter; **~zone** firing zone.

Feuilleton feuilleton, middle [article] *(Br.)*;
~abteilung column *(US)*.

Feuilletonist feuilletonist, serial writer, columnist.

feuilletonistisch feuilletonistic, belletristic.

Feuilletonredakteur literary editor.

feurig fiery, red-hot, *(Edelstein)* sparkling, *(leidenschaftlich)* ardent, ferrid, fervent, fiery, passionate;
~e Augen flashing (burning) eyes; **~e Kohlen auf jds. Haupt sammeln** to heap coals of fire on s. one's head; **~er Liebhaber** passionate (ardent) lover; **~e Rede halten** to make a fiery speech; **~er Redner** fervid orator.

Fex faddist.

Fiaker cab, cabcart, hackney.

Fiasko fiasco, dead failure, fizzle, washout *(sl.)*;
komplettes ~ dead failure;
mit einem ~ enden to be a fiasco (flop).

Fibel first reader, primer, speller *(US)*.
Fiber fibre;
mit jeder ~ seines Herzens an etw. hängen to have one's whole heart in s. th.
Fideikommiß fee tail, entailed estate, conditional fee, entail, settled land;
zeitlich beschränktes ~ contingent limitation;
geteiltes ~ für zwei Stämme several tail;
~ ablösen to disentail an estate; **~ aufgeben** to discontinue an estate; **~ aufheben** to cut off an entail; **als ~ besitzen** to hold in trust; **~ errichten** to make over one's estate in fee; **als ~ vererben** to entail an estate.
fideikommißähnliche Bestimmung quasi entail.
Fideikommiß | aufgebungsvertrag disentailing deed; **~begründung** strict settlement; **~begünstigung** strict settlement; **~bestimmungen verletzen** to contravene; **~eigentum** estate tail; **~eigentümer** tenant in tail; **~erbe** heir special, feoffee in (of) trust, fidei commissary; **~gesetz** Settled Land Act *(Br.)*; **~verbot** rule against perpetuities, perpetuity rule.
fidel cheerful, merry, jolly;
sehr ~ sein to be in high spirits, to have one's tails up;
~es Haus jolly fellow; **~e Korona** merry crew;
es ging ~ zu everything went with a swing.
Fidibus wisp of paper.
fiduziäre Notenausgabe fiduciary issue.
fiduziarisch fiduciary;
~er Erbe fiduciary heir; **~es Rechtsgeschäft** fiduciary contract, trust transaction; **~e Übereignung** trust receipt *(US)*; **~e Zuwendung** voluntary trust.
Fieber temperature, fever;
eintägiges ~ diary fever; **starkes ~** high fever;
im ~ phantasieren to be delirious;
~anfall attack of fever; **kurzer ~anfall** touch of fever.
fieberhaft | arbeiten to work at white heat;
~e Aufregung fever of excitement.
Fieber | hitze *(med.)* heat; **~kurve** temperature chart.
fiebern to run a temperature;
nach etw. ~ to crave for s. th.; **vor Erwartung ~** to be on tenterhooks.
Fieber | phantasie hallucination, wandering; **~phantasien haben** to be delirious with fever; **~thermometer** clinical (fever) thermometer; **~zustand** febrile state, fever.
Fiedel fiddle;
gespannt wie ein ~bogen sein to be on tenterhooks.
Figur figure, form;
beherrschende ~ dominating figure; **gute ~** neat figure **kümmerliche ~** third-rater; **zentrale ~** *(Drama)* central figure; **ganz gute ~ abgeben** to be in pretty good shape; **jämmerliche (schlechte) ~ abgeben** to cut a poor (sorry) figure; **gute ~ machen** to make a good show, to cut a fine figure, to cut a dash; **eine lächerliche ~ machen** to make an exhibition of o. s.; **auf ~ gearbeitet sein** to be sharply tailored.
figurieren to figure, *(im Konto)* to appear.
figürlicher Teil *(Markenname)* trade character.
Fiktion, gesetzliche fiction in law;
~ des Kennens imputed knowledge; **~ der Umwandlung von Grundvermögen in flüssige Mittel** doctrine of conversion.
fiktiv fictitious, imaginary, feigned, proforma;
~es Angebot feigned bid; **~e Bilanz** proforma balance sheet; **~er Kauf** feigned (fictitious) purchase; **~es Konto** fictitious (proforma) account; **~e Kreditoren** fictitious liabilities; **~er Preis** fictitious price; **~e Übergabe** symbolic delivery; **~er Umsatz** fictitious turnover; **~er Verkauf** sham (fictitious) sale; **~er Vertrag** sham contract; **~er Wechsel** accommodation bill; **~er Wert** apparent (fictitious) value; **~e Zahlung** feigned (fictitious) payment; **~er Zahlungsempfänger** fictitious payee.
Filial | abschlüsse branch transactions; **~abteilung** branch office; **~aufwand** branch expenses; **~avis** branch advice.
Filialbank branch bank;
~system branch (group, chain, *US*) banking; **~tätigkeit** branch-banking activities; **~wesen** branch (chain, group) banking, branch banking system.
Filialbelegschaft branch staff.
Filialbetrieb ancillary undertaking, branch establishment, chain of shops, *(Einzelhandel)* multiple *(Br.)*, chain (integrated, *US*) store;
~ sein to be chain-operated.
Filial | bilanz branch balance sheet (statement, *US*); **~buchführung** branch accounting (ledger); **~büro** branch premises, branch (affiliate) office; **~direktor** branch manager, *(Bank)* bank agent.
Filiale branch [house], local branch, branch establishment (office), *(Bank)* agency, branch bank, *(Kettenladen)* multiple [shop], branch (chain, *US*) store;
kleine ~ branchlet; **überseeische ~** overseas branch;
neue ~ aufmachen (eröffnen) to establish (open) a new branch; **~ errichten (gründen)** to establish a branch office; **~n im ganzen Land unterhalten** to operate a state-wide (nation-wide) system of branches.
Filial | erträge branch profits; **~gebäude** branch building; **~geschäft** branch [office], branch shop, multiple shop, chain (integrated) store *(US)*, chain drugstore *(US)*, *(Abschlüsse)* branch activity, *(Bank)* branch bank; **~gewinne** branch profits; **~gründung** establishment of a branch, founding of affiliates, formation of a subsidiary firm; **~gründungen vornehmen** to set up branches; **~inventar** branch inventory; **~konto** branch account; **~leiter** manager of a branch office, branch manager, *(Bank)* bank agent; **~netz** network of branches, branch network; **sich über das ganze Land erstreckendes ~netz** state-wide (nation-wide) system of branches; **~tätigkeit** branch activities; **~unkosten** branch expenses; **~unternehmen** branch shop (establishment), ancillary undertaking, *(Einzelhandel)* multiple chain, multiple *(Br.)*; **~verwaltung** branch administration; **~vorsteher** branch manager; **~wechsel** house bill.
Film film, *(Lichtspielfilm)* motion (moving) pictures, film, picture play, movie *(US)*, the screen, pix *(sl.)*, flickers *(sl.)*, *(für Offset)* offset transparency;
beim ~ on the films (screen);
abendfüllender ~ full-length (feature) film, full-length picture; **aktueller ~** topical film, topic; **wieder aufgeführter ~** rerun movie; **avantgardistischer ~** free film; **nicht brennbarer ~** acetal; **dreidimensionaler ~** three-dimensional film, movie in the round; **noch nicht entwickelter ~** *(Foto)* film stock; **gehaltvoller ~** quality film; **während des Fluges gezeigter ~** in-flight movie; **niedrig kalkulierter ~** low-budget film; **besonders lichtempfindlicher ~** *(Foto)* fast film; **synchronisierter ~** synchronized sound film; **tragischer ~** photodrama; **unbelichteter ~** unexposed film; **ungekürzter ~** uncut film; **wiederaufgeführter ~** rerun; **billiger (schnell zusammengestoppelter) ~** quickie;
~ in Fortsetzungen serial film;
sich einen ~ ansehen to go to the pictures (films); **~ belichten** to expose a film; **~ drehen** to shoot a film; **sich gut für den ~ eignen** to screen well; **~ einlegen** to thread a film; **~ entwickeln** to expose a film; **~ zum Verleih freigeben** to release a film; **zum ~ gehen** to break into pictures; **~ abgedreht haben** to have a film in the can; **~ herstellen** to produce a film; **in einen ~ investieren** to sink into a film; **~ ablaufen lassen** to unreel a film; **~ zur Veröffentlichung fertig machen** to edit a motion picture; **in einem ~ mitspielen** to play in a film; **~ schneiden** to cut a film; **beim ~ sein** to be in the film (motion picture, *US*) business; **~ umspulen** to rewind a film; **~ verleihen** to distribute a film; **~ mit Text versehen** to cut in titles in a motion picture; **~ mit Unterschrift versehen** to subtitle; **~ vorführen** to show a film, to exhibit pictures; **~ weiterdrehen** *(Fotoapparat)* to wind a film; **~ zulassen** to release a film;
~abfälle cuttings; **~abtastung** film scanning; **~archiv** film library; **~archivmaterial** stock shots; **~atelier** film (motion picture, *US*) studio; **~aufnahme** shooting, take, filming; **~aufnahmeleiter** film (motion picture, *US*) director; **~aufnahmen machen** to shoot a film; **~aufnahmen im Freien machen** to shoot on location; **charakteristischer ~auftakt** establishing shot; **großformatiger ~ausschnitt** spectacular; **~autor** film author, scriptwriter, scripter, screenwriter *(US)*; **~band** reel, film strip; **~bauten** film (motion picture, *US*) sets; **~bearbeitung** film (screen, *US*) adaptation; **~besucher** cinema (picture, movie, *US*) goer, filmgoer; **~bewertungsausschuß** film censorship committee; **~bezugsvertrag** distribution agreement; **~bibliothek** photographic library; **~börse** film exchange; **~boß** movie mogul; **in der ~branche sein** to be in the film business; **~breite** film gauge; **~dekoration** film set; **~diva** film (screen, *US*) actress; **~drama** photodrama; **~einnahmen** film receipts.
filmen to film, to shoot, to picture, to take, to screen, to reel.
Film | entwicklung film processing; **~erzeugnisse** films, motion pictures *(US)*; **~export** export of films; **~fachmann** screen technician; **~fan[atiker]** cinema (film) addict, picture-goer *(Br.)*; **~fassung** screen edition; **~fassung auf möglichst niedriges Niveau bringen** to pitch a screen version; **~fenster** *(Foto)* film gate; **~festspiele** film festival; **~finanzierung** film finance, film (movie, *US*) financing; **~förderungsanstalt** film-subsidy board; **~führungsrolle** *(Fotoapparat)* film take-up spool; **~geschäft**

cinema business; ~**geschmack** cinematic taste; ~**gesellschaft** film (motion-picture, movie, *US*) company, newsreel company; ~**gestalt** character on the screen; ~**hersteller** filmmaker; ~**herstellung** film production, filmmaking, moviemaking *(US)*; ~**industrie** film (motion-picture, movie, *US*) industry, the films, pix *(sl.)*; ~**journalist** film journalist; ~**kamera** film (motion-picture, movie, *US*) camera; **fahrbare** ~**kamera** dolly camera; **versteckte** ~**kamera** hidden camera; ~**kassette** film magazine, *(Film)* movie cartridge; ~**klammer** film clip; ~**klebemittel** *(Foto)* film cement; ~**klebestreifen** cellophane tape; **freiwillige** ~**kontrolle** film-review board; ~**kopie** film copy; ~**kopieranstalt** film-processing firm; ~**kopierwerk und Versand** mail-order film processing firm; ~**kritik** film critic; ~**länge** footage of a film; ~**leinwand** silver screen; **hochziehbare** ~**leinwand** roll-up map; ~**manuskript** film script; ~**musical** tuner *(sl.)*; ~**musik** incidental music to a film; ~**narr** film addict (freak), cinema adict; ~**pack** pack of films, film pack; ~**patrone** cartridge; ~**plakat** film spectacular; **inoffizielle** ~**präsentation** sneak preview; ~**preis** Oscar; ~**premiere** first run of a film, film premiere; ~**produktion** motion-picture production, film production, movie-making *(US)*; **teilweise im Aufnahmegelände hergestellte** ~**produktion** part-location production; ~**produktionszentrum** film-producing centre; ~**produzent** filmmaker, film producer, motion-picture producer, moviemaker *(US)*; ~**programm** movie program *(US)*; ~**projektor** film (motion-picture, movie, *US*) projector; ~**prüfstelle** film-review board, British Board of Film Censors *(Br.)*; ~**publikum** film audience, filmgoers, movie public *(US)*; ~**rechte** screen (film, cinema) rights; **an den** ~**rechten eines Buches interessiert sein** to ask for an option of the film rights of a book; ~**regisseur** film director, film producer; ~**reklame** moving-picture (screen) advertising; ~**rohfassung** film rush; ~**rolle** *(Fotoapparat)* spool *(US)* (roll, *Br.*) of film, film spool, *(Schauspieler)* film part; ~**satz** filmsetting, phototypography; ~**schaffende** motion picture staff; ~**schauspieler** film (screen, movie, *US*) actor; **ausgeliehener** ~**schauspieler** loan out *(sl.)*; ~**schnitt** cut; ~**schönheit** professional beauty; ~**schwank** slapstick picture; ~**selbstkontrolle** film review board; ~**spule** film reel; ~**star** film (motion-picture, movie, *US*) star, cinema actor (actress); **als** ~**star herausgebracht** starred; **herausgeschnittene** ~**stellen** cuts in a film; ~**sternchen** starlet; ~**stoff** screen story; ~**streifen** reel, movie; ~**streifenmarkierung** key; ~**studio** film (motion-picture, movie, *US*) studio; ~**szene** take; ~**test** screen test; ~**theater** picture theater, cinema palace (theatre), movie house *(US)*, picturedrome; ~**titel** fim (motion-picture, *US*) title; ~**unterstützung** film aid; ~**uraufführung** film premiere; ~**verleih** distribution of a film, film distribution (exchange), film trade, *(Unternehmer)* renter, distributor; ~**verleiher** distributor; ~**verleihgeschäft** film-distributing business; ~**verwertungsrechte** film rights; ~**voranzeige** trailer.

Filmvorführ|anlage projector; ~**apparat** vitascope *(US)*, film (motion-picture, movie, *US*) projector.

Filmvorführer projectionist, cinema operator.

Filmvorführ|kabine film projection booth; ~**raum** film projection room.

Filmvorführung film performance, exhibition (showing) of a film, cinema (picture) show;
kostenlose ~**en im Hotel** free in-house movies; ~ **vor der Uraufführung** pre-review, preview, prevue *(US)*;
~ **veranstalten** to run a film show.

Film|vorlage, Roman als ~**vorlage nehmen** to put a novel on the film; ~**vorschau** prereviews, preview, prevue *(US)*; ~**vorschub** film advance; ~**vorstellung** cinema (picture) show, film performance; ~**welt** screenland *(US)*; ~**werbung** cinema (motion-picture, screen, movie, *US*) advertising; ~**wesen** cinema (motion-picture, *US*) industry; ~**wirtschaft** film (motion-picture) industry, moviedom; ~**zähler** footage counter; ~**zeitschrift** movie magazine *(US)*; ~**zensur** censorship of a film, film censorship; ~**zensurbehörde** Board of Film Censors; ~**zuschuß** film aid.

Filter *(Foto)* optical screen;
~**kaffee** drip coffee; ~**mundstück** filter tip.

filtern *(Kaffee)* to filter, to percolate.

Filter|papier filter paper; ~**zigarette** filter-tipped cigarette.

Filz felt, *(Geizkragen)* miser, skinflint, niggard, piker *(sl.)*.

Filzen frisk *(US sl.)*.

filzen *(fam.)* to shake down *(US sl.)*, to frisk *(US sl.)*.

filzig *(geizig)* niggardly, parsimonious, penurious, miserly.

Filz|pantoffel felt slipper; ~**schreiber** felt-tip pen; ~**tuch** silence cloth; ~**unterlage** felt pad.

Fimmel craze, craziness, brain crack;
~ **haben** to be crazy (nuts, *US*).

Finanz|abkommen financial agreement, monetary convention; ~**abteilung** finance department (division), financial department, financial (fiscal, *US*) division.

Finanzamt tax and revenue office, inland revenue office *(Br.)*, tax (fiscal, internal revenue, *US*) office, income-tax authority (office), treasury board;
~ **betrügen** to defraud the authorities (revenue); **aufs** ~ **gehen** to go to the tax office.

Finanzamts|bescheid tax demand *(US)* (notice); ~**leiter** commissioner (collector) of internal revenue *(US)*, inspector of taxes *(Br.)*.

Finanz|analyse financial analysis; ~**analytiker** financial analyst; ~**angelegenheiten** financial affairs (concerns, matters); ~**angelegenheiten verwalten** to manage the finances; ~**anlagen** *(Bilanz)* investments; ~**anschlag** estimate, budget; ~**anzeige** financial advertisement; ~**apparat** financial machinery; ~**aufgaben** treasury functions; ~**aufkommen** budgetary receipts, inland *(Br.)* (internal, *US*) revenue; ~**aufstellung** financial statement *(US)*; **gefälschte** ~**aufstellung** false financial statement; ~**aufwand** revenue expenditure; ~**ausdruck** financial term; ~**ausgleich** tax (revenue) sharing *(US)*, Exchequer Equalization Grant *(Br.)*; ~**ausgleichsformel** tax-sharing formula *(US)*; ~**ausgleichstelle** Board of Equalization; **kommunale** ~**ausgleichszuweisung** rate support grant *(Br.)*; ~**auskunft** status report; ~**auskunftei** status enquiry agency; ~**ausschuß** finance committee, financial commission, *(Parlament)* Committee of Ways and Means *(Br.)*, appropriation committee *(US)*; ~**ausweis** financial statement (status) *(US)*; ~**autonomie** financial autonomy; ~**beamter** assessor of taxes, tax assessor (official), Inland Revenue Official *(Br.)*, revenue officer *(US)*; **örtlich zuständiger** ~**beamter** district collector *(US)*; ~**bedarf** financial (monetary) requirements, financial needs (demand), pecuniary wants.

finanzbedingte Hemmnisse financial handicaps.

Finanz|behörde fiscal agency, revenue (fiscal, treasury) authority; **oberste** ~**behörde** Board of Inland Revenue *(Br.)*, Internal Revenue Office *(US)*; ~**beihilfe** financial aid; ~**beitrag** *(EG)* financial contribution; ~**berater** financial adviser (analyst, consultant); ~**beratung** financial advice (counselling); ~**bericht** financial return, *(Zeitung)* city article *(Br.)*; ~**beschaffung** financing; ~**besprechungen** financial talks; ~**boykott** boycott of finance; ~**buchhalter** financial (general) accountant; ~**buchhaltung** financial accounting, general accounting department; ~**chef,** ~**direktor** director of finance, treasurer *(US)*; **knappe** ~**decke** shortage of finance; ~**defizit** deficit in the financial accounts; ~**direktor** director of finance, treasurer *(US)*; ~**direktor eines Konzerns** group treasurer.

Finanzen finance, financial policy;
für die ~ **verantwortlich** in charge of finance;
gesunde ~ sound finances; **kommunale** ~ local (municipal) finances; **meine kümmerlichen** ~ *(fam.)* the impoverished state of my exchequer; **öffentliche** ~ public finances, home finance *(Br.)*; **zerrüttete** ~ disordered (shattered) finances;
~ **einer Firma** exchequer of a firm;
jds. ~ **in Ordnung bringen** to put s. one's finances on a healthy basis; ~ **eines Landes in Ordnung bringen** to purge the finances of a country; **mit seinen** ~ **durcheinanderkommen** to get one's sums wrong; **seine** ~ **regeln** to adjust one's finances; ~ **einer Gesellschaft sanieren** to rehabilitate a company financially.

Finanz|ergebnis financial result; **sehr gute** ~**ergebnisse zeitigen** to do very nicely financially; ~**erträge** financial income; ~**experte** financier, financial analyst (expert); ~**fachmann** financial specialist (analyst, executive), financier; **führender** ~**fachmann** top financial expert; ~**fachmann sein** to be versed in questions of finance; ~**fachsprache** financial terminology; ~**faktor** financial factor; ~**flußrechnung** cashflow (funds) statement; ~**frage** financial question; ~**gebaren** finance, financial policy (dealings, management, measures, performance); **betriebliche** ~**gebarung** business finance; **gesunde** ~**gebarung** sound finance, financial health; **unkorrekte** ~**gebarung** financial wrong-doing; ~**gebiet** field of finance, financial field; ~**genie** financial wizard; ~**genie sein** to have a genius for finance; ~**gericht** tax (fiscal) court; ~**gerichtsbarkeit** fiscal jurisdiction; ~**geschäfte** financial affairs (transactions); **erfolgreiche** ~**geschäfte auf allen Gebieten abwickeln** to function in all financial fields; ~**gesetz** Finance Act *(Br.)*; ~**gesetzesvorlage** Finance Bill; ~**gesetzgebung** financial legislation; **örtliche** ~**größen** local financial opinions; ~**gruppe** finance group, monetary organization, syndicate; ~**haushalt** financial budget;

~hilfe financial aid; staatliche ~hilfe government aid; ~hof fiscal (tax) court, Court of Exchequer *(Br.)*, Court of Claims *(US)*; ~hofverfahren tax-court case; ~hoheit financial sovereignty (privilege), fiscal prerogative.

finanziell financial, fiscal, pecuniary, *(währungspolitisch)* monetary;
~ **gesichert** above water; ~ **gestellt** financially situated; ~ **schlecht gestellt** financially depressed; ~ **gesund** [financially] sound, financially strong; ~ **haftbar** liable, financially responsible; ~ **intakt** [financially] sound; ~ **leistungsfähig** financially able; ~ **selbständig (unabhängig)** financially independent; ~ **überlastet** top-heavy; ~ **verantwortlich** in charge of finance; ~ **wohlfundiert** [financially] sound;
sich ~ auszahlen to make financial sense; **sich an einem Unternehmen ~ beteiligen** to participate financially in an enterprise; ~ **besser dastehen** to be better fixed financially; ~ **unter die Arme greifen** to tide s. o. over; ~ **gut dran sein** to be in funds (well off, fixed, *US*); ~ **schlecht gestellt sein** to be badly situated (in a poor, weak financial situation, in low water); ~ **so gestellt sein** to have one's finances in such a shape; ~ **interessiert sein** to be financially interested in; ~ **besser stehen** to be better fixed financially; **j. ~ unterstützen** to back s. o. with money, to help s. o. financially; **sich ~ verbessern** to get a raise *(US)* (rise, *Br.*); **sich ~ diszipliniert verhalten** to observe financial discipline; ~ **anstehende Fragen übersichtlich vortragen** to develop financial reporting; ~ **unterstützt werden** to receive financial support;
~e **Aktivitäten** financial activities; ~e **Angaben** financial data; **seine ~en Angelegenheiten selbst erledigen** to handle one's own financing; ~e **Anreize** financial incentives; ~e **Ansprüche** money claims; ~e **Ausblutung** financial bleeding; ~er **Aufgabenbereich** finance functions; ~e **Basis verstärken** to give financial muscle; ~e **Bedürfnisse** pecuniary wants; ~er **Beistandsfonds** *(OECD)* financial support fund; ~e **Belange** moneyed (pecuniary) interests; ~e **Belastung** financial burden (drain, beating, drag); ~e **Beratung** financial advice (counselling); ~e **Beteiligung** financial interest; ~er **Druck** money (financial) squeeze; ~e **Durchhaltekraft** financial staying power; ~er **Eindruck** financial showing; ~e **Entschädigung** financial compensation; ~e **Entwicklung** financial position; ~er **Erfolg** financial success; ~es **Ergebnis** financial result; ~e **Ersparnisse** financial savings; ~es **Gebiet** financial field; **aus ~en Gründen** for financial reasons; **auf eine gesündere ~e Grundlage stellen** to put on a better financial footing; ~e **Haftung** financial responsibility *(US)*; ~e **Hilfeleistung** pecuniary (moneyed) assistance; **in ~er Hinsicht** financially; ~e **Inanspruchnahme** financial drain; ~es **Interesse**, ~e **Interessen** moneyed interest, pecuniary interests (conditions); ~e **Katastrophe** financial disaster; ~e **Lage** pecuniary circumstances, financial condition, financial standing (statement), financial position, financial status *(US)*, *(Börse, Markt)* financial situation, *(des Ehemannes bei der Ehescheidung)* faculty; **gute ~e Lage** strong finances; **in mißlicher ~er Lage sein** to be in financial difficulties (straits); ~e **Leistungsfähigkeit** financial capacity (power); ~e **Maßnahmen** financial measures; ~e **Misere** financial hardship (plight); ~e **Mittel** financial means; **im Bereich der ~en Möglichkeiten von jem. liegen** to be within the pocket of s. o.; ~es **Opfer** financial sacrifice; ~es **Risiko** financial risk; ~er **Rückhalt** financial backing; ~er **Ruin** financial undoing; ~er **Schaden** pecuniary loss; ~e **Schwierigkeiten** pecuniary (fiscal) difficulties; **in ernsthafte ~e Schwierigkeiten geraten** to slide into deep financial troubles; **weiterhin in ~en Schwierigkeiten sein** to continue in financial straits; ~e **Stärke** financial strength (muscle); ~er **Status** financial rating (status, *US*); ~e **Überlegungen** pecuniary considerations; ~e **Unabhängigkeit** comfortable independence; ~e **Unterlagen** financial records; ~e **Unterstützung** subvention, subsidy, financial backing (help), pecuniary (financial) assistance, pecuniary aid; ~e **Unterstützung gewähren** to extend financial aid; ~er **Verantwortungssinn** financial responsibility; ~e **Vergünstigungen gewähren** to distribute financial favo(u)rs; ~e **Vergütung** monetary reward; ~e **Verhältnisse** financial situation; **in guten ~en Verhältnissen sein** to be in good financial circumstances; ~e **Verhandlungen** financial talks; ~er **Verlust** pecuniary loss; **schwer unter ~en Verlusten leiden** to be hard hit by one's financial losses; ~e **Verpflichtungen** financial responsibilities (obligations); **sich ~en Verpflichtungen entziehen** to repudiate financial obligations; ~er **Zusammenbruch** financial collapse (failure); ~er **Zuschuß** financial contribution; ~e **Zuwendung** financial benefit.

Finanzier financier, moneylender, money broker; **zweifelhafter** ~ shady financier.

finanzieren to [furnish with] finance, to financier, to conduct financial operations, to bankroll *(US)*, to fund, *(Anleihe)* to float, *(Bergbau)* to habilitate *(US)*, *(unterstützen)* to subsidize; **etw.** ~ to supply the capital for s. th.;
seine Bekleidung selbst ~ to find o. s. in clothes; **aus Bruttoerträgen** ~ to finance out of cashflow; **mit Fremdmitteln** ~ to trade on the equity; **bis zu 75 %** ~ to finance up to 75%; **mit kurzfristigen Geldmitteln** ~ to finance with short-term money; **gemeinsam** ~ to join wallets for; **Geschäft** ~ to finance a business; **Rundfunkprogramm** ~ to sponsor a radio program(me).

finanziert financed;
auf privater Basis (frei) ~ privately financed; **vom Bund** ~ federally financed; **staatlich** ~ state-financed, state-paid, bounty-fed.

Finanzierung financing, funding, *(von Anleihen)* floating, *(Bergbau)* habilitation *(US)*, *(Unterstützung)* subsidizing;
bei ~ und Verleih in financing and distributing;
anteilige ~ proportional financing; **ausgleichende** ~ compensatory financing; **bankmäßige** ~ financing through banks; **kurzfristige** ~ short-term financing; **langfristige** ~ long-term financing; **mittelfristige** ~ medium-range financing; **ungenügende** ~ insufficient capitalization;
~ **durch Abtretung der Debitoren (mittels Forderungsabtretung)** debt (accounts receivable, *US*) financing; ~ **von Abzahlungsgeschäften** instalment finance, hire-purchase finance *(Br.)*, financing of hire-purchase transactions *(Br.)*; ~ **von Aktiengesellschaften** financing of joint-stock companies, corporation finance *(US)*; ~**en jeglicher Art** every type of financing; ~ **von Ausfuhrschwankungen** *(Weltwährungsfonds)* compensatory financing of export fluctuations; ~ **durch Ausgabe von Wandelschuldverschreibungen** convertible financing; ~ **von Ausgabenspitzen langfristiger Projekte durch Anleihen** pay as you use principle; ~ **des Außenhandels** foreign-trade financing; ~ **durch eine Bank** bank finance; ~ **von Eigenheimen** financing of new homes; ~ **durch Einräumung eines Erbbaurechts** leasehold financing; ~ **auf dem Eurodollarmarkt** Eurocurrency financing; ~ **von Exportgeschäften** export finance; ~ **durch Fremdmittel** outside financing, trading on the equity, equity trading; ~ **von Großprojekten** large-scale financing; ~ **des Haushalts** budgeting; ~ **von Investitionen** investment financing; ~ **durch unmittelbare Kapitalmarktunterbringung** direct placement financing; ~ **von Miethäusern** leasehold financing; **privatwirtschaftliche** ~ **von Rundfunkprogrammen** commercial sponsoring of program(me)s; ~ **der Staatsausgaben** government financing; ~ **eines Wahlfeldzuges** campaign financing; ~ **von Warenforderungen** debt (accounts receivable, *US*) financing; ~ **von Wohnungen** financing of housing, home financing;
Kapitalgeber wegen der ~ **eines Unternehmens ansprechen** to sound a capitalist with regard to a proposed investment; ~ **eines Unternehmens durchführen** to finance a scheme (an enterprise); **für die** ~ **eines Projektes geradestehen** to underwrite the cost of a project; **größeren Unternehmen mit langfristigen Obligationen eine direkte** ~ **gewähren** to lend long-term bond finance direct to major companies; ~ **sicherstellen** to wrap up financing; ~ **einer Reise sicherstellen** to find the money for a journey; ~ **eines Rundfunkprogramms übernehmen** to sponsor a radio program(me); ~ **eines Unternehmens übernehmen** to finance an enterprise.

Finanzierungs|abkommen financing (financial) agreement; **entgegenkommendes ~angebot** soft finance package; **gebündeltes ~angebot** financing package; **~anleihen mit Chartereinnahmen zurückzahlen** to pay back its loans from the ship's charter earnings; **~anteil** share of the finance; **~art** type of financing; **~aufschlag** financing charge; **~aufwand** financial expenditure; **~bank** issuing (financial) house; **~basis** financial basis; **~bedarf** financial requirements; **~bedingungen** terms of financing; **günstige ~bedingungen anbieten** to offer favo(u)rable finance; **~bedürfnisse** financing requirements; **~beitrag** financial contribution; **~besprechungen** finance talks; **~darlehn** financing loan; **~dienst** financing service; **~erleichterungen** financing facilities; **~etat** finance budget; **~form** method of financing; **~frage** question of financing; **in ~fragen beraten** to furnish financial counsel; **~garantie** standby financing; **~gebühr** finance charges; **~gemeinschaft** financial community; **~genehmigung** financing approval; **~geschäft** financial transaction (operation), *(durch Effektenemission)* investment banking.

Finanzierungsgesellschaft commercial credit (sale finance) company, financial service company, commercial finance company, financing company (agency), financial company (house) *(Br.)*, financial institution, finance subsidiary, consumer credit agency;
~ **für Auslandstöchter** base company; ~ **für Eisenbahnbedarf** car (equipment) trust *(US)*; ~ **für Grundstücksmeliorationen** land-improvement company; ~ **für Industriebedarf** industrial trust *(US)*; ~ **für Kleinkredite** personal finance (consumer loan, *US*) company.

Finanzierungs|hilfe pecuniary (financing) assistance; ~**institut** financing institution, financial enterprise (organization), commercial finance company, finance house *(Br.)*; ~**institut für die Industrie** Finance Corporation for Industry *(Br.)*; **komplettes** ~**instrument** financing package; ~**investitionen** investment in securities; ~**konzept** financing concept; ~**kosten** cost of financing, financing costs, financing (financial) expenses, finance charge, *(Gesellschaftsgründung)* promotion expense (money); ~**last** burden of financing; ~**leistung** financing service; ~**leistungen an finanzschwache Gemeinden** Exchequer Equalization *(Br.)* (rate deficiency, *US*) grants; ~**lücke** financial (money) gap; **angespannter** ~**markt** tight financing; ~**methoden** methods of financing; **modebedingte** ~**methoden** fashions in financing.

Finanzierungsmittel financial means, source of refinancing, credit instrument;
erwirtschaftete ~ cashflow; **längerfristige** ~ longer-range financing; **langfristige** ~ long-term lendings (financing);
fremde ~ **einsetzen** to be trading on the equity; ~ **revolvierend einsetzen** to make finance available on a receiving and reducing basis.

Finanzierungs|modalitäten financing arrangements (terms); ~**möglichkeiten** financing capabilities; **günstige** ~**möglichkeiten beschaffen** to find favo(u)rable financing; ~**möglichkeiten schaffen** to structure financing vehicles; ~**nachweis** *(pol. Partei)* financing statement *(US)*; ~**plan** financial plan[ning] (scheme, program(me)), financing plan; ~**polster** financial cushion; ~**projekt** financial project; ~**provision** finder's fee; ~**quelle** source of financing, financial resources; **industrielle** ~**quelle** industrial paymaster; **kurzfristige** ~**quellen** short-term financing sources; **letzte** ~**quelle** lender of last resort; **gesamtwirtschaftliche** ~**rechnung** flow-of-funds system; **sich anderweitig** ~**rückhalt beschaffen** to switch financing; ~**saldo** net financial investment; ~**schema** financing scheme; ~**schwierigkeiten** financial difficulties; ~**schwindler** shady financier; ~**sektor** *(volkswirtschaftliche Gesamtrechnung)* financing sector; ~**spezialist** financial specialist; ~**stelle für Kommunalinvestitionen** public works loan board *(Br.)*; ~**system** financing scheme; **neues** ~**system erfinden** to strike out a new plan of finance; ~**titel** finance paper; ~**träger** financial backer, commercial finance company; ~**übersicht** financial planning, financing scheme; **hoher** ~**umfang** high scale of financing; ~**vereinbarung** financing agreement; ~**verfahren** financing plan; ~**vermittler** money broker; ~**vertrag** financing agreement; ~**vorschlag** financing proposal; ~**wechsel** finance bill; ~**weise** method of financing; ~**zusage** standby financing, promise to finance; **öffentliche** ~**zuschüsse** governmental grants, grants-in-aid *(US)*.

Finanz|institut financial enterprise (house institution), financial institution; ~**interessen** financial interest; ~**jahr** financial year *(Br.)*, fiscal year *(US)*, budgetary year; ~**kapital** moneyed capital; ~**kasse** revenue office, Exchequer *(Br.)*, treasury; ~**kommissar** *(EG)* finance commissioner; ~**kompetenz** financial responsibility; ~**konferenz** financial conference; ~**konsortium** financial syndicate; ~**kontrolle** controlled finance, budgetary (financial) control; ~**kosten** financial expenses; ~**kraft** financial strength (capacity, power, muscle, resources); ~**kraft einer Bank in Frage stellen** to put a bank's financial health in question.

finanzkräftig financially strong, well-heeled.

Finanz|kreise financial circles (quarters); **örtliche** ~**kreise** local financial opinions; **weltweite** ~**krise** world-wide financial crisis; **mit einer** ~**krise fertig werden** to ride out a financial crisis.

Finanzlage financial standing (rating, condition, position, status, *US*, state), finances, *(Staat)* fiscal situation;
angespannte ~ tight money, money squeeze; **gesunde** ~ sound financial position; **gute** ~ strong finance; **mißliche** ~ precarious finances; **schlechte** ~ financial embarrassment; **ungesunde** ~ unsound financial conditions;
seine ~ **gefährden** to jeopardize one's finances.

Finanz|last financial burden; ~**leute** financial world; **führende** ~**leute** finance leaders; **führende** ~**leute am Platz** top local financial people; ~**magnat** magnate of finance; ~**makler** loan agent, loanmonger, money (investment) broker, moneylender; ~**mann** financier, city man *(Br.)*; **führender** ~**mann** financial leader; **erfahrener** ~**mann sein** to be versed in questions of (understand) finance; ~**markt** financial (finance) market, *(Schweiz)* money market; ~**masse** total revenue; ~**mathematik** mathematics of finance; ~**mathematiker** financial economist; ~**miete beweglicher Wirtschaftsgüter** finance equipment leasing; ~**minister** Minister of Finance, Finance Minister, Chancellor of the Exchequer *(Br.)*, Secretary of the Treasury Department *(US)*, Treasury Secretary *(US)*, Treasurer *(Australien)*, revenue minister *(Canada)*; ~**ministerium** Finance Ministry, Ministry of Finance, Lords (Commissioners) of the Treasury *(Br.)*, Board of Exchequer *(Br.)*, Treasury [Department] *(US)*.

Finanzmittel financial means, funds;
~**aufbringung** raising of the necessary funds; ~**bindung** earmarking of funds; ~**verwendung** application of funds.

Finanz|monopol financial (fiscal) monopoly; **aus seinen** ~**nöten herauskommen** to get out of one's financial difficulties; ~**operationen** monetary transactions, financial operations; ~**organisation** financial organization; ~**periode** fiscal (budgetary) period; ~**plan** budget, financial program(me); ~**planung** financial planning (management), budgetary accounting, budgeting; **mittelfristige** ~**planung** medium-term revenue plan; ~**platz** financial center *(US)* (centre, *Br.*); ~**politik** financial (fiscal) policy; **extrem defizitäre** ~**politik** high-deficit financial policy.

finanzpolitisch|gesehen from a financial point of view;
~**e Abteilung** financial policy department; ~**e Maßnahmen** measures of fiscal policy; ~**es Programm** financial program(me).

Finanz|prognose financial forecasting; ~**programm** financial program(me); ~**projekt** financial project; ~**prüfungsabteilung** auditing department; ~**quellen erschließen** to tap financial sources; ~**recht** budget law *(US)*; ~**reform** fiscal reform; ~**ressort** finance office; ~**richter** tax-court judge; ~**sachverständiger** financial expert; ~**sachverständiger sein** to be versed in questions of finance.

finanzschwach financially weak.

Finanz|schwierigkeiten pecuniary (financial) difficulties; ~**schwindel** financial juggle; ~**sektor** financial field; **für den gesamten** ~**sektor mit dem Schwerpunkt langfristiger Vorausplanungen verantwortlich sein** to run the complete financial function with emphasis on long-term financial planning; ~**skandal** financial scandal.

finanzstark financially strong.

Finanzstärke financial power (muscle, strength);
~ **einer Bank in Frage stellen** to put a bank's financial health in question.

Finanzstatistik financial statistics (data).

Finanzstatus financial condition (statement, rating, status, *US*), list of assets and liabilities, statement of financial position *(US)*;
disproportionaler ~ financial leverage; **zukünftiger** ~ projected financial statement;
~ **für besondere Zwecke** special-purpose financial statement.

Finanz|stromrechnung flow of fund accounts; ~**struktur** financial structure; ~**system** financial system; ~**tarif** tariff of revenue, revenue tariff; ~**tätigkeit** fiscal service.

finanztechnisch financial, fiscal;
~**e Feinheiten** financial niceties.

Finanz|teil *(Zeitung)* financial page (columns); ~**theorie** financial theory; ~**transaktion** financial dealing (transaction), monetary transaction (operation), fiscal operation (transaction); **langfristige** ~**transaktion** long-term transactions; ~**transaktionen durchführen** to conduct financial transactions, to finance, to financier; **erläuternde** ~**übersicht** descriptive financial statement; ~**unkosten** financial expense; ~**unterlagen** financial records; ~**unternehmen** financial enterprise; ~**vereinbarung** financing agreement; ~**verfassung** financial system; ~**verflechtung** financial interrelation.

Finanzverhältnisse financial conditions (position), financials;
gesunde ~ sound [financial] position; **günstige** ~ favo(u)rable financial conditions; **zerrüttete** ~ disordered finances;
sich in bedrängten ~**n befinden** to suffer financial hardship.

Finanz|vermögen financial assets; ~**verwaltung** *(Firma)* money management, finance (fiscal) administration, *(Staat)* [Inland] Revenue Department *(Br.)*, Inland Revenue Authorities *(Br.)*,

Bureau of Internal Revenue *(US)*, taxes management; ~**verwaltungsressort** Chamberlain's Department *(Scot.)*; ~**vorlage** *(parl.)* money *(US)* (revenue) bill, Finance Bill *(Br.)*; ~**vorschau** financial forecast; ~**vorstand** finance officer, financial executive (manager), treasurer of a corporation *(US)*, corporate treasurer *(US)*; ~**wechsel** accommodation (finance, *US*) bill; **kurzfristige behördliche** ~**wechsel** revenue bonds *(US)*; ~**welt** financial world (community, circles), moneyed interests; ~**wesen** financial affairs; **öffentliches** ~**wesen** public finances, system of national finances; ~**wirrwarr** financial maze.

Finanzwirtschaft financial economy (policy, system, market);
staatliche ~ **finances;**
~ **von Körperschaften** corporate finance;
seine ~ **in Ordnung bringen** to put one's financial house in order; ~ **zerrütten** to shatter finances.

finanzwirtschaftlich financial;
sich beruflich nur mit ~**en Fragen beschäftigen** to spend one's entire career on the financial side;
~**e Kennziffern** financial ratios.

Finanz|wirtschaftspolitik fiscal policy; ~**wissenschaft** public finances; ~**zentrum** financial district, financial (money) center *(US)* (centre, *Br.*), hub of the financial world; ~**zoll** financial duty, tariff revenue, revenue tariff (duty), fiscal tax, duty of a fiscal nature; ~**zolltarif** tariff of revenue only; ~**zuweisung** allocation of funds, grant-in-aid *(US)*; ~**zuweisungen verweigern** to withhold grants.

Findelkind foundling, parish boy.

finden *(jur.)* to find;
Absatz ~ to meet with a ready market; **Anerkennung** ~ to meet with approval; **Anwendung** ~ to be applied; **Arbeit** ~ to find a job; **kühle Aufnahme** ~ to win a cool reception; **keinen Ausweg** ~ to find no way out; **Beifall** ~ to meet with applause; **Berücksichtigung** ~ to be taken into consideration, to be considered; **nichts Böses dabei** ~ to see no harm in it; **Deckung** ~ to get cover; **einen Dreh** ~ to pull the trick *(US)*; **Eingang** ~ to find favo(u)r; **kein Ende** ~ *(Redner)* never come to an end; **sein Ende** ~ *(Vertrag)* to run out; **sein Fortkommen** ~ to make a living; **Freude an etw.** ~ to take pleasure in s. th.; **ebenbürtigen Gegner** ~ to find one's equal; **aufmerksames Gehör** ~ to find an attentive audience; **rechtliches Gehör** ~ to gain a hearing; **Geschmack an etw.** ~ to come to like s. th.; **Gnade vor jds. Augen** ~ to find favo(u)r with s. o.; **sich bei Goethe** ~ *(Zitat)* to occur in (come from) Goethe; **etw. höchst interessant** ~ to get a kick out of s. th.; **Lösung** ~ to hit upon a solution; **seinen Meister in jem.** ~ to meet more than one's match; **keinen Mieter für sein Haus** ~ not to get a tenant for one's house; **Mittel und Wege** ~ to contrive ways and means; **taube Ohren** ~ to fall on deaf ears; **früh in die Politik** ~ to begin one's political activities early; **verborgenen Schatz** ~ to turn up a buried treasure; **sich in sein Schicksal** ~ to resign o. s. to one's fate; **j. an der bezeichneten Stelle** ~ to meet s. o. at the appointed place; **Stellung im Ausland** ~ to find a situation abroad; **bei einem Unfall den Tod** ~ to be killed in an accident; **es unmöglich** ~ to think it impossible; **Widerstand** ~ to encounter opposition; **keine Worte dafür** ~ to stand speechless, to be at a loss for words; **das rechte Wort** ~ to say the right thing; **zufällig** ~ to come across; **Zustimmung** ~ to meet with approval;
das wird sich noch ~ that remains to be seen, time will tell.

Finder finder;
~ **belohnen** to reward a finder;
~**lohn** finder's reward.

Findling foundling.

Findlingsheim foundling hospital.

Finesse finesse, subtlety;
alle ~**n kennen** to know the tricks of the trade.

Finger, mit dem kleinen with a wet finger, with a feather;
warnender ~ warning finger;
der ~ **Gottes** the finger of God;
sich alle zehn ~ **danach ablecken** to jump to it; **Ausstellungsbesucher an den** ~**n abzählen** to count the visitors of an exhibition on one's fingers; **etw. mit spitzen** ~**n anfassen** to set about s. th. gingerly; **nur die** ~ **danach ausstrecken** only to lift the little finger; **etw. in die** ~ **bekommen** to get one's hands on s. th.; **mit dem kleinen** ~ **alles bekommen** to win everything hands down; **jem. mit dem** ~ **drohen** to wag one's finger at s. o.; **sich die** ~ **in der Tür einklemmen** to pinch one's fingers in the doorway; **einem durch die** ~ **gleiten** to slip through one's fingers; **klebrige** ~ **haben** to be given to pilfering; **etw. im kleinen** ~ **haben** to have s. th. at the tip of one's fingers, to have it at one's finger tips; **seine** ~ **im Spiel haben** to have a finger in the pie (a hand in); **seine** ~ **überall drin haben** to have a finger in every pie (an oar in every man's boat); **j. auf die** ~ **klopfen** to give s. o. a rap on (over) the knuckles; ~ **von etw. lassen** to keep one's hands off, to let s. th. well alone; ~ **in die Wunde legen** to put (lay) one's finger on the evil, to put one's finger on s. one's weak spot; **etw. mit dem kleinen** ~ **machen** to do s. th. standing on one's head; **lange (krumme)** ~ **machen** to pilfer, to be light-fingered; **keinen** ~ **rühren** not do a hand's turn, not to move hand or foot, not to stir a peg *(sl.)*, not to do a link of work *(US)*; **keinen** ~ **für j. rühren** not to turn a hand to help s. o.; **sich aus den** ~**n saugen** to trump up; **sich eine Geschichte aus den** ~**n saugen** to cook up a story; **sich in den** ~ **schneiden** to cut one's finger, *(fig.)* to make a blunder; **sich die** ~ **wund schreiben** to write until one's fingers ache; **jem. durch die** ~ **sehen** to turn a blind eye to s. o.; **j. scharf auf die** ~ **sehen** to keep a sharp eye on s. o.; **sich die** ~ **verbrennen** to burn one's fingers, to singe one's feathers, to stub one's toe; **j. um den kleinen** ~ **wickeln** to twist (wind) s. o. round one's little finger; **mit dem** ~ **auf j. zeigen** to point one's finger at s. o.; **mit** ~**n auf j. zeigen** to point the finger of scorn at s. o.; **einem zwischen den** ~**n zerrinnen** to burn a hole in one's pockets; **das kann man sich an den** ~**n abzählen** that's as clear as daylight; **mein kleiner** ~ **sagt mir** a little bird told me; **wenn man ihm den kleinen** ~ **gibt, nimmt er gleich die ganze Hand** give him an inch and he'll take an ell;
~**abdruck** fingerprint, finger mark, dactylogram.

Fingerabdrücke, voller finger-marked;
jds. ~ **nehmen** to fingerprint s. o., to take s. one's fingerprints, to print s. o. *(sl.)*; ~ **untersuchen** to check fingerprints.

Finger|abdruckverfahren fingerprint identification; ~**alphabet** finger (manual) alphabet; ~**anschlag** *(Schreibmaschine)* finger stop.

Fingerbreit, keinen ~ **von gegebenen Anweisungen abweichen** not to depart an inch from s. one's orders; **keinen** ~ **nachgeben** not to budge an inch;
~**e** breadth of a finger.

fingerdick|auftragen to lay it on thick (with a trowel); **Butter** ~ **aufs Brot streichen** to spread butter lavishly on the bread.

Finger|druck, sich mit einem ~ **bedienen lassen** to work at the touch of a finger; ~**ling** finger-stall.

fingern, etw. schon to manage somehow.

Finger|spitze finger tip; ~**spitzengefühl** intuition, finesse; ~**spitzengefühl haben** to show great tact in dealing with people; ~**sprache** deaf-and-dumb language; ~**zeig** index, tip-off, leak, hint, clue, indication, pointer *(US)*.

fingieren to simulate, to feign, to sham.

fingiert feigned, fictitious, sham, phony, dummy, colo(u)rable, straw, assumed, imaginary, simulated, *(jur.)* constructive;
~**er Anspruch** fictitious claim; ~**e Dividende** sham dividend; ~**es Geschäft** sham (fictitious) transaction; ~**e Kreditoren** fictitious liabilities; ~**er Name** fictitious (feigned) name; ~**er Preis** fictitious price; ~**e Rechnung** proforma (fictitious) account; ~**er Remittent** fictitious payee; ~**er Schaden** constructive injury; ~**e Umsätze** fictitious sales; ~**e Vermögenswerte** fictitiuous assets; ~**er Vertrag** fictitious (sham) contract; ~**er Wechsel** bogus bill; ~**er Wert** apparent (fictitious) value; ~**e Zahlung** fictitiuous payment.

finster pitch-dark, sombre, gloomy, murky;
j. ~ **ansehen** to frown (scowl) at s. o.; ~ **aussehen** *(Lage)* to look bad;
Zeitungsartikel in ~**er Absicht schreiben** to write an article with a sinister purpose; ~**e Angelegenheit** sinister (shady) affair, murky business; ~**er Bursche** a man of sinister countenance; ~**es Gesicht machen** to have a sullen face; ~**e Kneipe** low dive; ~**es Lächeln** grim smile; **in** ~**er Nacht aufbrechen** to start in the dead of night; ~**er Plan** evil plan; **mit** ~**er Stirn** with a worried brow; ~**e Wege wandeln** to live a shady life.

Finstern, im ~ **tappen** to grope in the dark.

Finsternis darkness, gloom, murkiness, *(Astrologie)* eclipse;
partielle ~ partial eclipse;
~ **durchdringen** to pierce the darkness.

Finte manoeuvre, red herring, false attack, feint;
~**n jem. gegenüber gebrauchen** to practise deceit on s. o.; **auf eine** ~ **hereinfallen** to walk into a trap; **durch eine** ~ **täuschen** to feint, to trick.

Firma firm, business, concern, commercial (business) house, enterprise, establishment, company, *(Firmenname)* style, business, [trade] name;
unter der ~ under the firm (style) of;
abonnierende ~ subscriber firm; **abwickelnde** ~ firm in liquidation; **alte** ~ old trading house; **alteingesessene** ~ old (well) -established firm; **angeschriebene** ~ addressee firm;

angesehene ~ renowned firm, house of good standing; **bedeutende** ~ leading (important) firm (house); **im Familienbesitz befindliche** ~ family-held company; **in Liquidation befindliche** ~ firm in liquidation; **befreundete** ~ business connection (correspondent); **weltweit bekannte** ~ world-renowned firm; **Geschäftswerbung betreibende** ~ business advertiser; **Rundfunkwerbung betreibende** ~ commercial sponsor, radio advertiser; **bezogene** ~ drawee; **gut eingeführte** ~ well-established house; **unternehmerisch eingestellte** ~ enterprising business firm; **handelsgerichtlich eingetragene** ~ registered (incorporated, *Br.*) company; **nicht eingetragene** ~ unincorporated business; **erloschene** ~ dissolved (defunct) firm; **erstklassige** ~ first-class (-rate) firm; **frühere** ~ old firm; **führende** ~ leading firm; **gut fundierte** ~ sound business house (firm); **im Handelsregister gelöschte** ~ extinct firm; **Ihre geschätzte** ~ your esteemed firm; **gutgehende** ~ flourishing concern; **kreditaufnehmende** ~ corporate borrower; **mittelgroße** ~ medium-sized business; **notleidende** ~ ailing firm; **preisunterbietende** ~ price cutter; **reelle** ~ reliable (respectable) firm; **gut renommierte** ~ firm of good repute; **selbständige** ~ independent firm; **solide** ~ reliable firm, solid business, sound business house; **überprüfte** ~ surveyed firm; **unabhängige** ~ independent firm; **unsolide** ~ firm of speculators; **untersuchte** ~ surveyed firm; **unzuverlässige** ~ shaky firm; **vertrauenswürdige** ~ reliable firm; **weltbekannte** ~ universally known (world-renowned) firm; **zahlungsunfähige** ~ failed firm *(US)*;
~ **mit breitgestreutem Produktionsprogramm** multiple product firm; ~ **mit zugelassenem Werksverkehr** C-firm *(Br.)*;
bei einer ~ **ankommen** to find employment with a firm; **Geschäftsbeziehungen zu einer** ~ **aufnehmen** to get in with a firm; **unter eigener** ~ **auftreten** to carry on the business under one's own name; **aus einer** ~ **ausscheiden** to retire from a firm, to withdraw from a company; **Inkassodienst für eine** ~ **besorgen** to effect the collection of a firm; **sich an einer** ~ **beteiligen** to take an interest in a firm; ~ **unter seinem eigenen Namen betreiben** to trade under one's own name; **neue Ideen in einer** ~ **zum Tragen bringen** to introduce new ideas into a business; **in eine** ~ **als Teilhaber eintreten** to enter a firm as partner, to join a firm as an associate (a partner); ~ **fortführen** to carry on a business; ~ **führen** to trade under the style; **Artikel bei einer** ~ **in Auftrag geben** to place an order for an article with a firm; ~ **gründen** to bring a firm into existence; **neue** ~ **gründen** to set up a new firm; **dreißig Jahre nur für eine** ~ **gearbeitet haben** to have worked for a firm for thirty years, man and boy; ~ **aus den roten Zahlen herausführen** to administer a company from red to black *(US coll.)*; ~ **herunterwirtschaften** to let a firm down; ~ **mit der Kundschaft kaufen** to buy the goodwill of a house; **unter seiner** ~ **klagen** to sue in its corporate name; ~ **handelsgerichtlich eintragen lassen** to have a firm entered in the register of companies, to register a company; ~ **leiten** to manage a firm; ~ **liquidieren** to liquidate (wind up) a company; ~ **im Handelsregister löschen** to take a company off the books; ~ **gewinnträchtiger machen** to put a company on a more profitable road; ~ **sanieren** to rehabilitate a company financially, to reorganize a company; **an einer** ~ **hälftig beteiligt sein** to have a half interest in a firm; **mit einer anderen** ~ **geschäftlich verbunden sein** to be tied up with another company; **unter einer** ~ **Handel treiben** to trade under the name (style) of; ~ **übernehmen** to take over a business; ~ **in eine Aktiengesellschaft umwandeln** to turn a firm into a joint stock company; ~ **durch Zeichnung des Firmennamens verpflichten** to bind a firm by signing the firm's name; ~ **vertreten** to travel for (represent) a firm, to agent; ~ **weiterführen** to carry on a business; **für eine** ~ **zeichnen** to sign on behalf of a firm.

Firmen zusammenschließen to consolidate business companies.

Firmen|absatz company sales, sales effort of a company; ~**abschreibung** corporate depreciation *(US)*; ~**akten** company files; ~**aktien** company stock; ~**aktiven** assets; ~**änderung** change of trade name (style); ~**angabe** business (trade) name; ~**angehöriger** servant of a company, company official (employee, man); ~**angelegenheit** corporate business *(US)*; ~**angestellter** company's servant (official), employee, company man; **unmittelbar mit den leitenden** ~**angestellten verhandeln** to deal directly with the senior corporate officers; ~**anmeldung** registration of business; ~**anschaffung** corporate acquisition; ~**anschrift** company (business) address; ~**anteil** share in a business, business (partnership) interest; ~**anwalt** company lawyer; ~**anwerber** company recruiter; ~**archiv** company archives, records of a corporation *(US)*; ~**aufdruck** *(Brief)* letterhead; ~**auflösung** dissolution of partnership; ~**aufwand** corporate expenditure *(US)*; ~**aufwendungen** corporate spending *(US)*; ~**ausschuß** business committee; ~**austritt** withdrawal of a partner; ~**ausweis** company-identification card; ~**bankrott** bankruptcy of a firm, company (firm's) bankruptcy; **Hilfsmaßnahmen für einen** ~**bankrott einleiten** to rescue a bankrupt company; ~**besitzer** proprietor of a firm; ~**besprechung** company meeting; ~**besteuerung** company taxation; ~**beteiligung** firm participation; ~**bevollmächtigter** company's nominee; ~**bewertung** business evaluation, corporate analysis *(US)*; ~**bezeichnung** firm (business, trade) name, style; ~**bilanz** partnership balance sheet, company statement, company balance sheet; ~**briefbogen** company stationery; ~**buchführung** partnership (company) accounts, enterprise accounting; ~**buchhaltung** company bookkeeping; ~**budget** business budget; ~**bürgschaft** company guarantee; **psychologische** ~**charakterisierung** corporate image; ~**chef** principal of a firm, company president; ~**depot** custody held for a partnership, commercial deposit; ~**disziplin** discipline in a company.

firmeneigen company-owned;
~**er Wagen** company (business) car.

Firmen|eigentum company (corporate, *US*) ownership, corporate assets (property) *(US)*; ~**eigentümer** company owner; ~**eindruck** corner card; **alle** ~**einnahmen auf ein Konto einzahlen** to pay in all one's trading credits in an account; ~**eintragung** registration of a company; ~**elite** corporate elite *(US)*; ~**entwicklung** corporate development *(US)*; ~**erfordernisse** corporate requirements *(US)*; ~**erwerb** company buying; ~**erzeugnis** manufacturer's product; ~**fahrzeug** company car; ~**finanzen** company (corporation, corporate, *US*) finances; ~**flugzeug** business aircraft (airplane), company plane, corporate aircraft *(US)*; ~**forderung** *(Bilanz)* debt owed to us; ~**fortführung** carrying on (continuation) of business; ~**garantie** company's guarantee; ~**gebäude** business premises; **unbefugter** ~**gebrauch** improper use of a firm's name; ~**gelände** company property (premises); ~**geschäfte im erforderlichen Ausmaß einstweilig weiterführen** to carry on the company's business as far as is necessary; ~**geschichte** company history; ~**gewinn** company's surplus, corporate profit *(US)*; ~**gläubiger** creditor of a firm (partnership), company (partnership) creditor; ~**größe** company size; ~**gründer** founder (promoter) of a business, company promoter; ~**grundstück** partnership land; ~**gründung** company promotion, organization of a business; ~**gruppe** group of companies; ~**guthaben** commercial; ~**haftung** partnership (corporate, *US*) liability; ~**hauptquartier** corporate headquarters *(US)*; ~**image** business (corporate, *US*) image; ~**indossament** indorsement of a firm; ~**inhaber** owner (head, member) of a firm, company head, principal of a firm, senior partner, proprietor of a business; ~**inventar** business inventory; ~**investitionen** corporate investment *(US)*; ~**jahr** company's financial year; ~**kapital** [firm's] (company's) capital; ~**kauf** company buying; ~**konkurs** bankruptcy of a partnership, partnership bankruptcy, corporate bankruptcy *(US)*; ~**konsortium** consortium of companies; ~**konto** partnership (company) account, corporate account *(US)*; **betroffener** ~**kreis** range of companies covered; ~**kunde** company customer, business client, trading customer, corporate client (customer) *(US)*; ~**kundschaft** corporate customers *(US)*; ~**leitung** management of a firm, company management, corporate management *(US)*; ~**lieferant** company supplier; ~**liquidation** liquidation of a company; **außergerichtliche** ~**liquidation** creditors' voluntary winding up; ~**liquidität** corporate liquidity *(US)*; ~**löschung** taking a company off the books; ~**makler** *(Börse)* board man *(US)*; ~**mängel** corporate sickness *(US)*; ~**mantel** shell; ~**marke** trademark; ~**mitglied** senior officer *(US)*; ~**mitteilung** company release; ~**mittel** company (corporate, *US*) funds; ~**nachfolger** subsequent owner of a firm.

Firmenname [name of a] firm, firm (business, company's, corporate, *US*, trade) name, name of a company (firm), style of a business firm;
unter dem ~**n** doing business as *(US)*;
eingetragener ~ registered name;
im ~**n klagen** to sue in the firm's (its corporate, *US*) name; ~**n tragen (führen)** to go under the name (style) of.

Firmen|netz corporate network; ~**neugründungen** new entrants; ~**pensionär** company pensioner; ~**politik** company strategy, corporate policy *(US)*; ~**praktikant** industrial (on-the-job, *US*) trainee; ~**rechte** trade rights; ~**register** register of companies *(Br.)* (corporations, *US*), register general, Registrar of business names *(Br.)*, Companies Registration Office; ~**registrierung** business incorporation; ~**reingewinn** corporate surplus *(US)*; ~**rendite erzielen** to put a company in the black *(US coll.)*; ~**reorganisation,** ~**sanierung** reconstruction of a company *(Br.)*, company reconstruction *(Br.)*, corporate reorganization *(US)*, business (corporate, *US*) reorganization; ~**satzung** constitution of a firm, memorandum (articles) of association, articles of incorporation *(US)*; ~**scheck** company check (cheque, *Br.*); ~**schild** facia, signboard, name plate, shingle *(US)*; ~**schriftzug** logotype, signature; ~**schulden** company liabilities, company debts, partnership debts, corporation debts *(US)*, *(Bilanz)* debts owed by us; ~**schutz** protection of trade names; ~**siedlung** company town; ~**siegel** common seal *(Br.)*, corporate seal *(US)*; ~**sitz** commercial domicile, company's registered office; ~**sprecher** company spokesman; ~**status** company financial statement; ~**stempel** firm stamp; ~**syndikat** consortium of companies; ~**syndikus** company (corporation, *US*) lawyer; ~**tradition** company tradition; ~**übergang** transfer of a business; ~**umsatz** company sales; ~**unkosten** corporate expenditure *(US)*; ~**unterschrift** signature of a firm, corporate signature *(US)*; ~**urkunden** records of a corporation *(US)*; ~**veranlagung** company rating (assessment, *US*); ~**verbindlichkeiten** company obligations, corporate liabilities *(US)*; ~**verfall** corporate deterioration *(US)*; ~**vergrößerung** expansion of a firm; ~**vergütung** company reimbursement; ~**verkaufskonto** trading account; ~**verlust** partnership (corporate, *US*) loss; ~**vermögen** firm property (assets), assets of a business, partnership estate, partnership (company) property, corporate estate *(US)*, corporate property *(US)*; ~**vermögen nach Abzug aller Verbindlichkeiten** corporate equity *(US)*; ~**verpflichtungen** partnership obligations, corporate liabilities *(US)*; ~**verschmelzung** consolidation of firms; ~**vertreter** firm's traveller, manufacturer's (corporate, *US*) agent; ~**verzeichnis** [trade] directory; ~**vorstand** board of directors; ~**wagen** business (company) car; ~**wechsel** company note; **langfristige** ~**werbung** institutional (corporate, *US*) advertising; ~**wert** goodwill, value of plant in successful operation, enterprise value, intangible property; ~**wert eines Konzerns** consolidated goodwill; ~**wertkonto** goodwill account; ~**zeichen** brand, stamp, trade[mark] name, logotype; **mit** ~**zeichen versehen** to brand; ~**zeichnung** signature of a firm, corporate signature *(US)*; ~**zusammenschluß** coming together of firms, business combination, merger; ~**zuschuß** company contribution.

firmieren to do business under the name, to trade under the style, *(Firma zeichnen)* to sign a firm.

Firmierung trading under the name.

Firnis varnish, *(äußerer Schein)* veneer;
fertiges Gemälde mit ~ **überziehen** to varnish a finished printing.

Fisch, frisch wie ein as fresh as paint *(coll.)*, as sound as a bell; **fröhlich wie ein** ~ **im Wasser** as merry as a cricket; **so kalt wie ein** ~ as cool as ice; **stumm wie ein** ~ mute as a fish;
weder ~ **noch Fleisch** neither fish, flesh nor good red herring;
wie ein ~ **auf dem Trockenen** like a fish out of water;
faule ~**e** putrid (bad) fish, *(fig.)* hollow pretexts; **großer** ~ *(fig.)* bigwig, big noise *(sl.)*; **kleine** ~**e** easy proposition, small fry, mere nothing, small potatoes *(US)*, pipe *(sl.)*;
~**e mit dem Schleppnetz fangen** to trawl; **sich wohl wie ein** ~ **im Wasser fühlen** to be in one's element; ~**e füttern** *(seekrank sein)* to be seasick, to feed the fishes *(sl.)*;
~**dampfer** fisherman, trawler; ~**distrikt** fishing grounds.

fischen, in einem Fluß to fish in a river; **sich die besten Brocken aus der Suppe** ~ to take the best for o. s.; **im Trüben** ~ to fish in troubled waters.

Fischer fisherman.

Fischerboot fishing boat (craft, vessel).

Fischerei fishing, fishery;
für die ~ **bestimmt** piscatorial;
~**abkommen** fishing agreement, common fishery; ~**aufseher** water bailiff; ~**berechtigung** fishing rights, piscary; ~**beschränkungen** fishing restrictions; ~**distrikt** fishing ground; ~**erlaubnis** fishing licence; ~**erzeugnisse** fish products; ~**fahrzeug** fishing boat (vessel); ~**flotte** fishing fleet; ~**gebiet** fishing ground; ~**gerechtsame** free (common) fishery, common of piscary; ~**gesetze** fishery laws; **flache** ~**gewässer** fishing banks; ~**grenzen** fishing limits; ~**hafen** fishing port; ~**recht** right of fish, fishery, piscary; **selbständiges** ~**recht** several fishery; ~**schein** fishing permit *(US)* (licence, *Br.*); ~**schutz** fishery protection; ~**schutzfahrzeug** fishery protection vessel; ~**schutzzone** conservation zone; ~**wirtschaft** fisheries economics; ~**zone** fishing zone.

Fischfahrzeug fishing vessel.

Fischfang draught, fishery, fishing;
vom ~ **leben** to earn one's living by fishing;
~**gebiet** fishing grounds, fishing ground (area), piscary; ~**industrie** trawling industry, fishing industry; **gemeinsame** ~**polizei** *(EG)* common fisheries police; ~**rechte** fishing rights, piscary; ~**stelle** piscary, fishing place.

Fisch|gericht weglassen to miss out the fish course; ~**geschäft** fish (fishmonger's) shop; ~**grätenmuster** herring-bone; ~**gründe** fishing grounds, piscary; ~**haken** gaff; ~**halle** fishhouse; ~**handel** fish trade; ~**händler** fishmonger; ~**händlerin** fishwife; ~**handlung** fish (fishmonger's) shop; ~**kasten** *(im Boot)* fish well; ~**konserve** preserved (canned, tinned, *Br.*) fish; ~**lagerstätte** fishyard; ~**markt** fish market; ~**netz** fishing (fish) net; ~**reichtum** abundance of fish; ~**restaurant** fish restaurant; ~**revier** fish preserve, piscary, fishing place; ~**schoner** fishing schooner; ~**stäbchen** fish sticks.

Fischteich fishpool, fishpond, vivary *(Br.)*;
persönlicher ~ private pond;
~ **besetzen** to stock a pond with fish.

Fisch|verarbeitung fish processing; ~**verarbeitungsschiff** factory vessel; ~**wagen** fish carrier, *(Bahn)* fish car; ~**wilderei** fish poaching; ~**wirtschaft** fishing industry; ~**zucht** fish culture, pisciculture, fish breeding; ~**zuchtbeauftragter** fish commissioner *(US)*; ~**züchter** fish breeder, pisciculturist.

Fischzug haul, draught;
reicher ~ good haul of fish, *(fig.)* good haul;
~ **machen** to get a good haul, to make a payday *(sl.)*.

Fisimatenten ado, hanky-panky, *(Ausflüchte)* hollow pretexts;
~ **machen** to make (kick up) a fuss.

Fiskalgelder tax money.

fiskalisch fiscal, financial;
~**es Eigentum** government property; ~**e Gebühr** tariff revenue; **aus** ~**en Gründen** for purpose of revenue; ~**e Kontrolle** fiscal control; ~**e Politik** fiscal policy; ~**es Vermögen** state property, King's (Queen's) Treasury *(Br.)*; ~**e Verwaltung** administration by the Crown *(Br.)*.

Fiskalismus fiscalism.

Fiskal|jahr fiscal year; ~**lasten** fiscal charges; ~**politik** fiscal policy; **geändertes** ~**verhalten** shift in fiscal attitudes.

Fiskus fisc, King's (Queen's) Treasury *(Br.)*, Inland Revenue *(Br.)*, crown *(Br.)*, Exchequer *(US)*;
an den ~ **fallen** to revert by escheat;
~**gebühren** fiscal dues (fees); ~**vertreter** fiscal agent.

Fistelstimme falsetto [voice].

Fittiche, j. unter seine ~ **nehmen** to take s. o. under one's wing.

fitzen to work hastily.

fix fixed, set, *(flott)* nimble, agile, bright, *(im Rechnen)* quick;
~ **und fertig** *(Zimmer)* all clear; ~ **und fertig angezogen** completely dressed;
~ **auffassen** to be quick in the uptake; **Programm** ~ **und fertig ausarbeiten** to work out a program(me) to the last detail; **j.** ~ **und fertig machen** to make s. o. sing small, to tell s. o. what is what; ~ **und fertig sein** to be all in (dead-beat, bushed, *US*), *(ruiniert sein)* to be completely ruined (smashed up); **mit jem.** ~ **und fertig sein** to have done with s. o.; **mit seiner Arbeit** ~ **und fertig sein** to have completely finished one's work; **Vertrag** ~ **und fertig vorlegen** to submit a contract all cut and dried;
~**e Anlagen** fixed assets; ~**es Gehalt** fixed salary; ~**e Idee** obsession, bee in one's bonnet; **an** ~**en Ideen leiden** to suffer from obsessions; ~**er Junge** bright lad, quick-witted (smart) fellow; ~**e Kosten** fixed charges, overhead expenses, overheads; **Geschäfte auf** ~**e Lieferung tätigen** to effect future deals.

Fixauftrag firm order.

Fixen selling stocks short *(US)* (a bear, *Br.*), short selling *(US)*.

fixen *(Börse)* to sell short *(US)*, to [sell a] bear *(Br.)*, to buy on (operate for) a fall.

Fixer *(Börse)* speculator for a fall, bear *(Br.)*, short [seller] *(US)*.

Fixgeschäft time bargain, futures deal *(US)*, operation for a fall, short sales (selling) *(US)*, selling stocks short *(US)*;
~**e abdecken** to cover short sales *(US)*.

Fixierbad *(Foto)* fixer, fixative (fixing) bath.

Fixieren eines Films fixation of a photographic film.

fixieren to fix, to settle, to determine, *(Preis, Valuta)* to fix;
j. ~ to fix one's eyes upon s. o., to give s. o. a stare; **etw. mit den Augen** ~ to nail one's eyes on s. th. *(fam.)*; **Bedingungen** ~ to lay down conditions; **Bedingungen eines Vertrages** ~ to stipulate the terms of a contract; **etw. schriftlich** ~ to set down in (reduce to) writing; **verfassungsmäßig** ~ to institutionalize.

Fixiermittel fixing agent.

Fixierung von Bedingungen stipulation of conditions.

Fixigkeit brightness, agility, nimbleness;
~ **im Kopfrechnen** speed in mental arithmetic.
Fix|kauf time purchase, futures deal *(US)*; ~**klausel** fixed-date clause; ~**kosten** fixed costs, fixed charges, overheads; ~- **und Gemeinkosten** supplementary costs; ~**stern** fixed star.
Fixum basic salary, fixed allowance.
flach flat, even, level, *(oberflächlich)* trivial, superficial, shallow, *(Schuh)* flat-heeled;
~ **wie ein Pfannkuchen** as flat as a pancake;
~ **auf die Erde fallen** to fall flat on one's face; ~ **liegen** *(fig.)* to be in narrow straits;
~**es Gebäude** low building; ~**e Gewässer** shallow water, shallows, shoal; **auf der** ~**en Hand liegen** to be as plain as daylight; ~**er Kopf sein** to be a shallow-headed individual; ~**e Küste** flat shore; **auf dem** ~**en Lande** in the depth of the country; ~**e Stirn** flat forehead; ~**es Tiefdruckgebiet** shallow depression; ~**e Unterhaltung** shallow talk.
Flach|ablage flat-top (horizontal) filing; ~**bahn** *(Flugbahn)* flat trajectory; ~**bau** low building; ~**dach** flat roof.
Flachdruck surface (flat-bed, level, straight) printing;
~**abzug** flat proof; ~**presse** flat-bed press; ~**verfahren** planography.
Fläche plain, plane, level, flat, surface, *(Anschlagstelle)* site, *(Gebiet)* area, space;
bebaute (angebaute) ~ *(Landwirtschaft)* enclosed ground, area under cultivation, *(Stadt)* built-up area; **bedeckte** ~ floor space; **freie** ~ open space; **forstwirtschaftlich genutzte** ~ forested land; **kultivierte** ~ enclosed ground; **öde** ~ waste; **spiegelglatte** ~ mirror-smooth surface; **zu Vermietungszwecken zur Verfügung stehende** ~ rental space; **tragende** ~ *(Flugzeug)* wing area; **vermietete** ~ rental space;
~ **für Plakatanschlag** stand *(US)*, hoarding *(Br.)*.
Flächen|antenne flat-top antenna (aerial); ~**aufteilung** local planning, zoning *(US)*; ~**aufteilungsplan zugunsten wirtschaftlicher Nutzung abändern** to rezone for corporate business *(US)*; ~**bedarf** floor space required, *(Landwirtschaft)* land requirements; ~**berechnung** planimetry, measuration of plane surfaces.
flächenbezogen site-specific.
Flächen|blitz sheet lightning; ~**bombardierung** pattern (area) bombing, bombing of target areas; ~**brand** conflagration; ~**denken** area thinking; ~**druck** relief (flat-bed) printing; ~**einheit** square unit; ~**gesteller** owner of a site.
flächengetreu *(Karte)* of equal area.
Flächen|heizung panel heating; ~**inhalt** floor space; ~**klassifikation** site classification; ~**maß** square measure; ~**nutzung** land use (development); ~**nutzungsplan** local plan *(Br.)*, [etwa] structure plan *(Br.)*, development plan, zoning ordinance *(US)*, plan for zoning *(US)*; ~**nutzungsplan ändern** to rezone *(US)*; ~**nutzungsplan aufstellen** to plan a city, to zone *(US)*; ~**stichprobe** *(Statistik)* area sample; ~**stichprobenverfahren** area sampling; ~**winkel** plane angle; ~**ziel** *(mil.)* target area.
flachfallen to fall flat, to come to nothing.
Flachheiten superficialities, trivialities.
Flach|kopf shallow-minded person; ~**küste** flat shore; ~**land** plain, flat [country], lowland; ~**landbewohner** lowlander, plainsman.
flachsen to be joking, to put s. o. on *(US)*.
Flach|wagen flatcar *(US)*, platform car; ~**wagen für den Huckepackverkehr** piggyback flatcar *(US)*; ~**wähler** *(tel.)* panel selector; ~**ziegel** flat (plain) tile.
Flackerlampe flickering lamp, *(Telefon)* busy signal.
flackern to flicker, to twinkle, to flash *(US)*.
flackernd verlöschen to flicker out.
Flackerzeichen flashing signal.
Flagge flag, *(mil.)* colo(u)rs, *(Schiff)* flag, ensign;
unter falscher ~ under false colo(u)rs;
billige ~ flag of convenience; **feindliche** ~ enemy flag;
~ **der Handelsmarine** merchant flag, Red Ensign *(Br.)*;
~ **aushängen** to put out one's flag; ~ **dippen** to dip the flag; ~ **einholen** to lower one's flag; ~ **einziehen** to haul down a flag; **mit der roten** ~ **einem Zug entgegengehen** to wave a red flag to stop a train; ~ **entrollen** to unfurl a flag; **unter der** ~ **von ... fahren** to fly the flag of ...; ~ **hissen** to hoist (run up) a flag, to show one's colo(u)rs; **unter der** ~ **der Freiheit kämpfen** to fight under the banner of freedom; **Schiff unter falscher** ~ **laufen lassen** to mask a ship under neutral flag; ~ **niederholen** to lower (haul down) a flag; **unter falscher** ~ **segeln** to sail under false colo(u)rs; ~ **auf halbmast setzen** to fly the flag at half-mast; ~ **streichen** to lower (strike) one's colo(u)rs; ~ **zeigen** *(Schiff)* to show (display) one's flag, to display one's colo(u)rs.
flaggen to hang out flags, *(Schiff)* to put out one's flags, to fly a flag;
halbmast ~ to half-mast a flag.
Flaggen|attest certificate of registry; ~**buch** flag book; ~**diskriminierung** flag discrimination; ~**ehrung** salute of the colo(u)r, color *(US)*; ~**entfaltung** display of the flag; ~**gruß** flag salute; ~**kontrolle** visit; ~**mast** flagpoll, flagstaff; ~**mißbrauch** misuse of flag; **tägliche** ~**parade** salute of the colo(u)r, color *(US)*; ~**prüfung** verification of a flag; ~**recht** law of the flag; ~**signal** flag signal; ~**signalsystem** code of signals, International Signal Code; ~**stock** staff, flagstaff; **durch** ~**zeichen warnen** to flag; ~**zeugnis** certificate of registry.
Flagg|offizier flag officer; ~**schiff** flagship.
flagrante Ungerechtigkeit outrageous injustice.
flagranti, in red-handed, in flagrante delicto.
Flak anti-aircraft gun (artillery), A. A. gun, archie *(Br., sl.)*;
~**batterie** anti-aircraft battery; ~**feuer** anti-aircraft fire, aerial barrage; ~**geschütz** anti-aircraft (ack-ack, *sl.*) gun.
Flakon perfume bottle.
Flak|sperrgürtel ring defence *(US)*; ~**stellung** anti-aircraft position; ~**waffenlenkgeschoß** surface-to-air missile.
Flamme flame, *(fig.)* torch, *(Freundin)* sweetheart, flame, *(Gas)* burner;
den ~**n zum Opfer gefallen** destroyed by flames;
alte ~ old flame; **auflodernde** ~**n** leaping flames; **flackernde** ~ flicker; **olympische** ~ Olympic torch;
~**n der Leidenschaft** fire of passion;
~**n des Hasses schüren** to fan the flames of hatred; **in** ~**n stehen** to be in flames, to be in a blaze.
Flammenausbruch burst of flame.
flammender Protest fiery protest.
Flammen|meer sea of fire; ~**sog** vortex of flames; ~**werfer** flame projector (thrower).
Flanell flannel.
Flaneur saunterer, stroller.
Flanieren sauntering, stroll, no-work.
flanieren to saunter, to stroll.
Flanke *(mil.)* flank;
Gegner in der ~ **angreifen** to attack the enemy in the flank; **in die offene** ~ **des Gegners einbrechen** to attack the uncovered flank of the enemy.
Flanken|angriff flank attack; ~**bewegung** flank movement; ~**deckung** flank guard; ~**feuer** flank fire; ~**manöver gegen den Feind durchführen** to attack the enemy in the flank; ~**schutz** flank defence.
flankieren, Wagen to flank the car.
flankierend|es Feuer enfilade, flanking fire; ~**e Maßnahmen** flanking measures.
Flasche bottle, *(fig.)* washout, nitwit, no-good;
in ~**n abgefüllt** bottled;
auf ~ **abfüllen (ziehen)** to bottle; **bei seiner** ~ **Wein sitzen bleiben** to linger over one's cups; **einer** ~ **Wein den Hals brechen** to crack a bottle of wine; **der** ~ **frönen** to have a partiality for the bottle; **auf** ~**n füllen** to bottle up; ~ **Wein kosten** *(hum.)* to discuss a bottle; ~ **kreisen lassen** to make the bottle go round; **sich eine** ~ **Wein leisten** to treat o. s. to a bottle of wine; **mit jem. eine** ~ **Wein trinken** to join s. o. in a bottle of wine; **der** ~ **eifrig zusprechen** to ply (partake freely of) the bottle.
Flaschen|abzug bottling; ~**bier** bottled beer; ~**füllmaschine** bottle filler; ~**füllung** bottle filling; ~**gas** bottle (cylinder) gas; ~**gestell** bottle stand (rack); ~**hals** neck of a bottle; ~**kind** child brought up on the bottle; ~**nahrung** bottle feeding; ~**öffner** bottle opener; ~**pfand** bottle deposit; ~**post** bottle post, drift bottle; ~**spülmaschine** bottle washer; ~**verschluß** seal of a bottle.
flaschenweise verkaufen to sell by the bottle.
Flaschenzug block and pulley (tackle);
~**seil** hoisting cable.
Flattergeist fickle person.
flatterhaft capricious, fickle, unsteadfast;
~ **sein** to whiffle;
~**es Ding** flibbertigibbet; ~**er Mensch** harum-scarum; ~**es Wesen** whiffling turn of mind.
Flattermarke *(drucktechn.)* collating mark.
Flattern *(Film)* flutter, *(Rundfunkempfang)* fading, *(Ventil)* bounce.
flattern to flutter, *(Fahnen)* to stream, to fly, *(fig.)* to wave, *(Mittelwelle)* to fade, *(Steuerrad)* to judder, *(Ventil)* to bounce;
jem. auf den Schreibtisch ~ to alight on s. one's desk; **den Steuerzahlern ins Haus** ~ to flop on the mat of the taxpayers.
Flattersatz unjustified composition, ragged copy.

flau *(Börse)* dull, dead, lifeless, sluggish, slack, stagnant, depressed, quiet, inactive, inanimate, languid, heavy, featureless, bear, off, flat *(Br.)*, *(Geschäft)* slow, slow-moving; **sich ~ fühlen** to have butterflies in one's stomach; **~ liegen** to hold weak; **~ schließen** to leave off flat; **~ sein** to stagnate; **anfangs ~ sein** to open flat *(Br.)*; **~ werden** to slacken, to turn dull;
~e Geschäftszeit slack period (season); **~e Stimmung auf dem Aktienmarkt** dull tone (dullness) in the stock market; **~e Zeit** slack (dull) time, slack season, dullness, flatness *(Br.)*.
Flauheit *(Börse)* dullness, stagnancy, stagnation, slackness, flatness *(Br.)*.
Flaumacher scaremonger, killjoy, wet blanket.
Flausch tuft.
Flause fib, whim, funny idea;
jem. die ~n schon austreiben to knock stupid ideas out of s. o.; **~n im Kopf haben** to have a bee in one's bonnet; **nichts als ~n im Kopf haben** to be swayed by (full of) whims; **~n machen** to tell fibs; **jem. ~n in den Kopf setzen** to put ideas into s. one's head.
Flausen|macher fibber, windbag; **~macherei** taradiddle.
Flaute *(Börse)* dullness, deadness, dead calm, stagnation, dull (inactive) market, inanimateness, lifelessness, slackness of the market, slack market (season, times), bearish tone, dull time, lull, flatness *(Br.)*, *(Handel)* depression, flat season, downturn, inactivity, *(auf See)* dead calm, lull in the wind;
in einer ~ in the doldrums, off;
geschäftliche ~ slack time in business, slackness of trade; **konjunkturelle ~** cyclical stagnation, economic downturn; **plötzliche ~** letdown; **sommerliche ~** seasonal slack; **wirtschaftliche ~** business depression;
~ durchmachen to be stagnant; **unter einer ~ leiden** to be on the wane; **richtige ~ durchstehen müssen** to be locked in the doldrums; **~ überwinden** to take up the slack.
Flautezeit period of sluggishness, times of depression;
geschäftliche ~ lull in business; **konjunkturelle ~** economic downturn, cyclical stagnation.
flechten, Körbe to weave baskets.
Fleckchen speckle, fleck;
~ Erde spot of land.
Fleck[en] stain, mark, spot, blot, *(im Diamant)* cloud, flaw, blemish, taint, blur, *(kleiner Ort)* hamlet, townlet, *(Spritzer)* splash;
blauer ~ blue mark, bruise; **kleiner ~** speckle, fleck; **nasser ~** slop;
ungenutzter ~ eines Baulandes undeveloped piece of building land; **weißer ~ auf der Landkarte** white (unexplored) area on the map; **~ auf der weißen Weste** scar (stain) upon one's reputation, blot on the escutcheon, hole in one's coat;
~ aufsetzen to put a patch on a garment; **sich nicht vom ~ bewegen** not to budge an inch; **überall blaue ~ haben** to be a mass of bruises *(coll.)*; **Herz auf dem rechten ~ haben** to have one's heart in the right place; **~ auf seiner weißen Weste haben** to have blotted one's copybook; **Mädchen vom ~ weg heiraten** to marry a girl out of hand; **vom ~ kommen** *(Verhandlungen)* to make progress; **nicht vom ~ kommen** to mark time, to be a deadlock; **mit der Arbeit nicht vom ~ kommen** to make no headway in one's work; **sich einen ~ aufs Hemd machen** *(fig.)* to be finicky; **sich nicht vom ~ rühren** to stay put; **vom ~ weg verhaften** to arrest on the spot.
fleckenlos unstained, untainted, spotless, *(Charakter)* fair, flawless, faultless;
~ aus einer Sache hervorgehen to come out of a business without a stain (smirch) on one's character;
~er Ruf spotless (stainless) reputation; **~e Weste** clean slate; **~e Weste haben** to be without a spot on one's reputation.
Fleckentfernungsmittel stain remover.
Fleckfieber spotted fever.
fleddern, Leichen to rob corps.
Flegel bully, lout, boor, tough guy *(US)*, rude fellow;
kleiner ~ little rascal.
Flegelei rudeness, hooliganism;
sich ~en erlauben to behave rudely.
flegelhaft boorish, loutish, saucy, insolent;
sich ~ benehmen to behave rudely.
Flegeljahre awkward age.
flehen to implore, to beseech;
um Frieden ~ to pray for peace; **um Gnade ~** to beg for mercy.
flehend supplicant, beseeching;
j. ~ ansehen to look at s. o. imploringly;
~er Blick imploring look.
flehentlich beseeching, imploring, supplicatory.

Fleisch flesh, meat, *(drucktechn.)* shoulder, white space;
verdorbenes ~ tainted meat;
sein eigenes ~ und Blut one's own flesh and blood, kith and kin *(Br.)*; **~ in Dosen** canned meat;
vom ~ fallen to lose much weight; **sich ins eigene ~ schneiden** to cut off one's nose to spite one's face; **Pfahl in jds. ~ sein** to be a thorn in s. one's flesh; **jem. in ~ und Blut übergegangen sein** to have become second nature with s. o.;
der Geist ist willig, aber das ~ ist schwach the spirit is willing but the flesh is weak;
~beschau meat inspection; **~beschauer** food inspector; **~brühe** broth, beef tea, consommé; **~dauerwaren** preserved meat goods.
Fleischer butcher.
Fleisch|fabrik preserved-meat factory; **~gericht** meat dish; **~gewerbe** butchery; **~hackermethode** meat-axe approach.
Fleischkonserven preserved (canned, tinned) meat;
~fabrik preserved-meat factory; **~industrie** meat-packing industry.
fleischliche Lüste carnal desire, lusts of the flesh.
fleischloser Tag meatless day.
Fleisch|marke meat coupon; **~platte** meat dish; **~ration ausgeben** to issue a provision of meat; **sich nach den ~töpfen seiner Mutter zurücksehnen** to long for the flesh pots of Egypt; **~verarbeitung** meat packing; **~verarbeitungsbetrieb** meat packer, meatworks, meat-packing establishment; **~waren** meat products; **~wolf** meat chopper (mincer); **j. durch den ~wolf drehen** to put s. o. through the mill.
Fleiß diligence, industry, assiduity, sedulity;
mit unermüdlichem ~ with unremitting industry;
großen ~ anwenden to take great pains; **seinen ganzen ~ aufbieten** to do one's utmost; **~ erfordern** to require hard work; **etw. mit allem ~ erledigen** to be sedulous in doing s. th.;
ohne ~ kein Preis no pains no gains, no sweet without sweat.
fleißig diligent, industrious, hard-working, assiduous, *(sorgsam)* painstaking, careful;
~ wie eine Biene as busy as a bee;
~ arbeiten to work diligently; **etw. ~ benutzen** to make good use of s. th.; **~ seinen Geschäften nachgehen** to be diligent in one's business; **sehr ~ sein** to be very industrious; **~ spazierengehen** to do plenty of walking;
~er Arbeiter hard worker; **~er Briefmarkensammler** enthusiastic stamp collector; **~er Schuljunge** painstaking schoolboy; **~er Theaterbesucher** frequent theatre-goer; **~es Volk** hard-working people.
flexibel flexible, *(anpassungsfähig)* adaptable, pliable, *(Preis)* flexible.
Flexibilität, eingebaute *(Konjunkturpolitik)* built-in flexibility;
~ der Preise flexibility of prices.
flexible|r Einband flexible (limp) binding; **~ Handhabung** *(Vorschrift)* flexible use; **~r Tarif** flexible tariff; **~r Wechselkurs** flexible exchange rate (parity).
Flickarbeit patchery, patchwork.
Flicken patch, *(Ausbessern)* mending;
aufgesetzter ~ vamp.
flicken to patch, to mend, to vamp up, to piece;
Kessel ~ to tinker (repair) a kettle; **j. etw. am Zeuge ~** to find fault with s. o.
Flicken|decke patchwork (crazy, *US*) quilt; **~teppich** rag rug.
Flick|korb mending basket; **~schneider** jobbing tailor; **~schuster** cobbler, shoe repairman *(US)*, vamper; **~stelle** mend; **elendes ~werk** miserable hotch-potch; **zusammengestückeltes ~werk** patchwork, patchery, vamp; **~werk sein** to be patchy; **~wort** filler, wasteword, expletive.
Fliege fly;
mit ~n angeln to fly-fish; **sich matt wie eine ~ fühlen** to feel like a limp rag; **keiner ~ etw. zuleide tun können** not to be able to say boo to a goose; **so aussehen, als ob man keiner ~ ein Leid tun könnte** to look as if butter wouldn't melt in one's mouth; **zwei ~n mit einer Klappe schlagen** to kill two birds with one stone; **wie die ~n sterben** to die like flies;
in der Not frißt der Teufel ~n beggars can't be choosers.
Fliegen flying, flight, fly;
~ im Verband formation flying.
fliegen to fly, to go (travel) by air, to take a flight, to airplane, *(entlassen werden)* to get the sack (boot) *(sl.)*, *(Puls)* to be racing;
auf j. ~ to go for s. o.; **auf etw. ~** to be crazy (wild) about s. th.; **über den Atlantik ~** to fly the Atlantic; **blind ~** to fly by instruments; **mit dem Düsenflugzeug ~** to travel by jet; **von Düsseldorf nach München ~** to go by air from Düsseldorf to

Munich; **Flugzeug** ~ to fly (pilot) an airplane; **ins Gefängnis** ~ to be thrown in clink *(sl.)*; **aufs Gesicht** ~ to smack on one's face; **jem. um den Hals** ~ to throw one's arms around s. one's neck; **Handelsgüter** ~ to carry goods by air; **hoch** ~ to fly high; **am ganzen Körper** ~ to be trembling all over; **Kurs** ~ to fly a course; **im Liniendienst** ~ to fly commercially; **in die Luft** ~ to blow up; **unter 300 m** ~ to fly a zero; **Nachteinsätze** ~ to fly night-time sorties; **auf die Nase** ~ *(fig.)* to strike a bad patch; **von Ort zu Ort** ~ *(Nachricht)* to spread like wildfire; **mit einer Reisegeschwindigkeit von 800 km in der Stunde** ~ to have a cruising speed of 800 km an hour; **von der Schule** ~ to be kicked out, to get the axe *(US)*; **zwei Stunden** ~ to be in the air for two hours; **tief** ~ to hedgehop *(sl.)*; **Truppen ins Kampfgebiet** ~ to fly troops into a combat area; **umsonst** ~ to fly free; **von der Universität** ~ to be sent down *(Br.)* (rusticated); **im Wind** ~ *(Fahne)* to stream in the wind; **mit dem Wind** ~ to fly with tail wind;
Modellflugzeug ~ **lassen** to fly a model airplane.

fliegend flying, *(wehend)* streaming;
in ~er Eile in a hurry; **~e Festung** flying fortress; **~er Gerichtsstand** itinerant tribunal, circuit court *(Br.)*; **mit ~en Händen** with trembling hands; **~er Händler** pedlar, street trader, door-to-door trader, itinerant dealer; **~e Hitze** hot flushes; **~es Laboratorium** flying laboratory; **~es Lazarett** field hospital; **~es Personal** flying (flight) personnel, aircrew; **~es Postamt** travelling post office; **~er Start** flying start; **~er Teppich** magic carpet; **~e Untertasse** flying saucer; **~er Verband** flying unit; **~e Vermessung** *(Küste)* running survey.

Fliegen|falle flycatcher; **~fenster** window screen; **~gitter** wire mesh (screening); **~klappe** flapper; **~kopf** *(drucktechn.)* turned letter, turn; **~schrank** meat safe.

Flieger pilot, aeronaut, flyer, flying man, airman, aviator, *(mil.)* aircraftsman second class *(Br.)*, basic airman *(US)*;
~abwehrfeuer anti-aircraft fire; **~abzeichen** aviation badge *(US)*; **~alarm** air alert, airraid alarm (warning); **~anzug** flying suit; **~ausbildung** flying training; **~ausrüstung** flying equipment; **~beschuß** strafing; **~bombe** drop bomb, egg *(sl.)*; **~deckung** cover from air attack.

Fliegerei flying, aviation.

Flieger|geschwader group *(Br.)*, wing *(US)*; **~horst** air base.

fliegerisch aerial;
~es Ereignis flying event; **~e Leistung** flying feat; **~e Vorführung** aerial performance.

Flieger|karte aviation chart; **~klub** flying club; **~kombination** flying suit; **~leit- und Flugmeldedienst** control and reporting; **~leutnant** pilot officer *(Br.)*; **in ~marschbreite** *(mil.)* dispersed in width; **~notsignal** aircraft distress signal; **~schule** flying (aviation) school; **~sichtstreifen** marking panel; **~staffel** flying (flight, *US*) squadron; **~suchaktion** aerial search; **~tätigkeit** flying activities; **~warndienst** airraid warning service; **~zulage** flying allowane.

fliehen to flee, to fly, to escape, to take to flight;
völlig aufgelöst ~ to flee in disorder; **ins Ausland** ~ to escape abroad; **vor einer Gefahr** ~ to run away from a danger; **über die Grenze** ~ to escape across the border; **aus dem Lande** ~ to flee (skip) the country; **aus der Öffentlichkeit** ~ to shun publicity.

fliehend fugitive;
~es Kinn retreating chin.

Fliehkraft centrifugal force.

Fliese floor tile, flag;
mit ~n auslegen to tile the floor.

Fließarbeit serial (flow, standardized, mass) production, flow process, progressive operations, work on the assembly line.

Fließband band (belt) conveyor (conveyer), assembly line;
am ~ **arbeiten** to stand at a conveyor belt; ~ **verlassen** to come off the production line, to roll (rumble) off the assembly line;
~anlernling assembly trainee; **~arbeit** work on the assembly line, assembly-line work, flow (conveyor-belt) production; **~arbeiter** worker on the assembly line, assembly-line worker, assembly-line operator; **~bauten** industrialized building; **~einrichtungen** automatic assembly facilities; **~fabrik** ready-built factory; **~fertigung** belt system of production, assembly-line (conveyor-belt) production, flow system (production), conveyor-line production; **~montage** conveyor-line assembly, conveyor (assembly, *US*) line, progressive assembly *(US)*; **~prinzip** conveyor-belt system; **~produktion** assembly-line (flow) production, assembly-line technique; **~produktion von Fertighäusern** factory production of homes; **~satz** solid matter, undisplay *(US)*; **~stadt** assembly-line town, conveyor-belt city; **~streik** skippy strike *(sl.)*; **~system** conveyor system; **~vorarbeiter** assembly-line foreman.

Fließ|bild flow sheet; **~diagramm** flow chart.

fließen to flow, to go, *(Tantiemen)* to come in, *(Verkehr)* to flow, to run smoothly;
ins Meer ~ to flow into the sea; **über den Rand** ~ to overflow the brim; **reichlich** ~ *(Gaben)* to come in freely; **von der Stirn** ~ to pour from the brow; **stoßweise** ~ *(Ölquelle)* to flow by heads; **in die eigene Tasche** ~ to go into one's own pockets.

fließend *(Sprachbeherrschung)* fluent, with great fluency;
sich ~ **abwickeln** *(Verkehr)* to flow smoothly; ~ **Englisch sprechen** to speak fluent English;
~er Verkehr moving traffic; **~es Wasser** running water.

Fließ|heck hatchback; **~papier** absorbent (blotting) paper; **~satz** area composition; **~zustand** *(Börse)* state of flux.

Flimmerkiste *(fam.)* [goggle] box, flicks, telly *(Br.)*.

Flimmern glimmer, glitter, *(Fernsehen)* snow, flicker, *(Sterne)* twinkle.

flimmern to glitter, to scintillate, *(Luft)* to shimmer, *(Fernsehbild)* to flicker, *(Sterne)* to twinkle, to glimmer.

flimmernde|Hitze shimmering heat; ~ **Leinwand** cinema (silver, movie, *US*) screen.

flimmert, es ~ **mir vor den Augen** my head is swimming.

flink nimble, agile, quick, lively, like the wind, *(aufgeweckt)* bright, smart, swift;
~ **bei der Hand** ready to help, on the spot;
~ **arbeiten** to be a quick worker; ~ **zum Kolonialwarengeschäft gehen** to pop over to the grocer; ~ **wie ein Wiesel laufen** to run like a hare (blazes, the devil); ~ **auf den Beinen sein** to be quick on one's pins;
~e Finger light (nimble) fingers; **~es Mundwerk haben** to have a glib tongue; **~en Verstand haben** to be swift of wit.

Flinte gun, rifle;
~ **ins Korn werfen** to throw (chuck) up the sponge *(sl.)*, to throw the helve after the hatchet.

Flirt flirt, girl (boy) friend, flame, crush *(sl.)*.

Flittchen tart, floozy, tramp *(coll.)*.

Flitter spangles, *(Tand)* tawdry, tinsel, gingerbread.

Flitterwochen honeymoon;
~ **verbringen** to honeymoon.

Flitzbogen, gespannt wie ein on tenterhooks.

flitzen to flash, to fleet, to pop, to nip *(sl.)*;
schnell zum Bäcker ~ to pop over to the baker; **um die Ecke** ~ to whisk (whip) round the corner.

Flitzer snappy little car, peppy *(US)*.

Flitztour run.

Floaten *(Wechselkursfreigabe)* floating;
sauberes ~ clean floating; **schmutziges** ~ dirty floating (float).

Floh| ins Ohr gesetzt bekommen to see the red light *(fam.)*; ~ **im Ohr haben** to have bats in the belfry; **jem. einen** ~ **ins Ohr setzen** to put a flea in s. one's ear *(US sl.)*, to put things into s. one's head;
~kiste flea bag *(sl.)*; **~leiter** *(Strumpf)* ladder, run *(US)*; **~markt** flea market.

Flor tissue, *(Trauerflor)* mourning band.

florieren to flourish, to prosper, to thrive.

florierend flourishing;
~es Geschäft rattling trade, thriving business.

floskelhaft flowery, meaningless, empty.

Floskeln flourish, embellishment, empty phrases;
einleitende ~ *(pol.)* protocol;
~ **gebrauchen** to flourish; **nichts als** ~ **sein** to be mere words (empty phrases).

Floß float, raft.

flößbar floatable.

Floßbrücke float bridge.

Flosse *(Flugzeug)* stabilizer, *(Luftschiff, Rakete)* fin.

Flößer raftsman, rafter, riverman, river driver *(US)*.

Flöte, nach jds. ~ **tanzen** to dance to s. one's tune.

flöten *(affektiert sprechen)* to say in a honeyed voice;
~gehen *(Geld)* to go down the drain;
das ganze Vermögen ist ~gegangen the whole fortune has slipped through his hands.

Flötentöne beibringen, jem. to tell s. o. what is what.

flott quick, brisk, fast, *(Auftreten)* crisp, *(Geschäftsgang)* brisk, lively, *(schick)* snappy, stylish, smart, chic, *(Schiff)* afloat;
~ **gekleidet** smartly dressed;
~ **maschineschreiben** to be a quick typist; ~ **sein** to be a quick one; **wieder** ~ **sein** to be on its feet again, *(bei Kasse)* to be flush;
~ **vorangehen** *(Arbeit)* to go without a hitch; **gleich wieder** ~ **werden** *(Schiff)* to touch and go;
~er Umsatz quick sale.

flottantes Material *(Börse)* floating supply.

Flotte fleet, navy, naval establishment;
feindliche ~ enemy fleet; **hochseegängige** ~ ocean-going fleet; ~ **in Heimatgewässern** home fleet *(Br.)*.
Flotten|abkommen naval agreement; ~**bewegung** naval manoeuvre; ~**demonstration** demonstration of the fleet; ~**einheit** naval unit; ~**gericht** naval courts-martial; ~**kommando** naval command; ~**parade** naval review, review of the fleet; ~**police** fleet policy; ~**stützpunkt** naval base (station); ~**vertrag** navy bill *(Br.)*; ~**vorlage** Naval Estimates.
flott|er Arbeiter quick workman; ~**er Fahrer** speedy driver; ~**es Geschäft** roaring business; ~**er Geschäftsgang** brisk state of trade; ~**e Kellnerin** efficient waitress; ~**es Mädchen** quite a girl; ~**er junger Mann** dashing young man; ~ **geschriebener Roman** novel written in a brisk style; ~**er Tänzer** excellent dancer; **in** ~**em Tempo** at a quick pace; ~**e Unterhaltung** animated (snappy) conversation.
flottgehend flourishing, thriving.
Flottille flotilla.
Flottillenführer flotilla leader.
flottmachen *(mar.)* to float, to refloat;
Auto wieder ~ to get a car going again; **Schiff** ~ to refloat a ship; **Unternehmen wieder** ~ to put an enterprise on its feet again.
flottwerden, wieder *(Geschäft)* to get on its feet again, *(Schiff)* to be refloated; **gleich wieder** ~ *(Schiff)* to touch and go.
Flöz seam, lode, reef, vein.
Fluch curse, malediction;
~ **ausstoßen** to utter a curse; **j. mit einem** ~ **belegen** to call down curses from heaven upon s. o.; **unter einem** ~ **stehen** to lie under a curse.
fluchen to utter a curse (profanities), to use bad language, to cuss *(sl.)*;
wie ein Landsknecht ~ to swear like a trooper (porter, bargee).
Flucht flight, escape, run, evasion, getaway, *(Baulinie)* straight (building) line;
auf der ~ on the run, on the lam *(sl.)*;
panikartige ~ headlong flight; **panikartige** ~ **zum Ausgang** stampede for the door; **überstürzte** ~ precipitated flight;
~ **nach Kautionsgestellung** absconding in bail cases; ~ **in Sachwerte** conversion into property; ~ **vor der Verantwortung** evasion of responsibility; ~ **aus der Währung** flight from the currency;
~ **in die Öffentlichkeit antreten** to resort to publicity (the press); ~ **nach vorn antreten** to take the bull by the horns; ~ **begünstigen** to aid the escape; **in wilder** ~ **davonstürzen** to run away panic-stricken, to flee in panic; **jds.** ~ **stillschweigend dulden** to connive at s. one's escape; ~ **ergreifen** to flee, to take to one's heels; **Feind in die** ~ **schlagen** to put the enemy to flight; **auf der** ~ **sein** to be on the run; **der** ~ **verdächtig sein** to be under suspicion of intending to escape; **sein Heil in der** ~ **suchen** to seek safety in flight, to take to one's heels; **jds.** ~ **vereiteln** to foil s. one's escape; **jem. zur** ~ **verhelfen** to help s. o. to escape.
fluchtartig precipitous, hasty, rash, headlong;
~ **verlassen** to beat a hasty retreat; **Lokal** ~ **verlassen** to blow a place *(US sl.)*.
Fluchtauto would-be-get-away vehicle.
flüchten to flee, to take to flight, to run away, to escape, *(Schuldner)* to abscond;
aus dem Gefängnis ~ to escape from prison; **über die Grenze** ~ to escape across the border; **in ein Haus** ~ to take shelter in a house; **aus einem Land (außer Landes)** ~ to flee from a (run the) country; **in ein Land** ~ to take refuge in a country; **in eine Lüge** ~ to resort (fall back upon) a lie; **in die Öffentlichkeit** ~ to resort to publicity (the press); **sich in eine Traumwelt** ~ to take refuge in a dream world; **sich in die Wälder** ~ to take to the woods; ~ **und einige Wertsachen mitnehmen** to go off with some treasured possessions; **vor der Wirklichkeit** ~ to run away from reality.
Flucht|gefahr, wegen ~**gefahr verhaftet** arrested on suspicion; ~**geld,** ~**kapital** flight (refugee) capital, hot (crisis) money; ~**geschwindigkeit** *(Raumschiff)* escape velocity; ~**helfer** escape agent; ~**hilfe** aiding and abetting an escape.
flüchtig fugitive, absconding, on the run, fleeing, unapprehended, runaround, *(eilig)* in a hurry, hurriedly, hastily, *(Fahrer)* hit-and-run, *(fahrig)* fickle, *(kurz)* cursory, brief, short, *(kurzlebig)* short-lived, momentary, *(oberflächlich)* superficial;
immer noch ~ still on the run;
Schlagzeilen ~ **ansehen** to glance at the headlines; **Formular** ~ **ausfüllen** to fill in a form carelessly; ~ **begrüßen** to greet s. o. in passing; **Thema** ~ **behandeln** to treat a subject cursorily; **etw. nur** ~ **zu sehen bekommen** to catch a glimpse of s. th.; **Zeitung** ~ **durchsehen** to skim through a newspaper; **seine Arbeit** ~ **erledigen** to do one's work slapdash, to scurry through one's work; **j.** ~ **kennen** to have a nodding acquaintance with s. o.; ~ **niederschreiben** to jot down; ~ **sein** *(Schuldner)* to have absconded, *(Verbrecher)* to be on the run (at large); ~ **streifen** to glance briefly on; ~ **werden** to escape, to flee from justice, to abscond;
~**er Arbeiter** slapdash worker; ~**er Autofahrer** hit-and-run driver; ~**e Bekanntschaft** casual (nodding) acquaintance; ~**e Berechnung** rough calculation; ~**er Besuch** flying (fleeting, brief) visit; ~**er Blick** transient (quick) glance; ~**en Blick auf eine Urkunde werfen** to glance at a document; ~**e Durchsicht** superficial investigation, cursory inspection, once-over; ~**er Eindruck** vague (hazy) impression; ~**er Entwurf** rough sketch; **Vorschlag mit einer** ~**en Handbewegung ablehnen** to dismiss a suggestion with a flick of the hand; ~**e Kenntnisse** sketchy knowledge; ~**es Öl** volatile oil; ~**er Rechtsbrecher** fugitive from justice; ~**er Ruhm** transient (short-lived) fame; ~**er Schuldner** absconding debtor; ~**e Skizze** rough sketch; ~**e Unterhaltung** brief conversation; ~**e Untersuchung** cursory inspection; ~**er Verbrecher** fugitive offender, escaped prisoner; ~**e Vorstellung von etw. haben** to have a vague idea.
Flüchtigkeitsfehler oversight, slip, slip-up *(coll.)*.
Fluchtkapital flight capital, fugitive fund.
Flüchtling fugitive, runaway, escapee, abscondee, *(Ausgewiesener)* displaced person (DP), expellee, *(Evakuierter)*, evacuee;
politischer ~ political refugee; **im Lager untergebrachter** ~ camp refugee;
einem ~ **Herberge geben** to give shelter to a fugitive; **als** ~ **anerkannt sein** to be recognized as a refugee; ~**e unterstützen** to provide relief for refugees.
Flüchtlings|ausweis refugee's identity card; ~**eingliederung** refugee resettling; ~**gruppe** band of fugitives; ~**hilfe** refugee relief, assistance to (relief for) refugees; ~**hilfsfonds** *(US)* Refugees' fund; ~**kommissar** *(UNO)* United Nations High Commissioner for Refugees; ~**lager** refugee camp; ~**mentalität** refugee mentality; ~**probleme** refugee problems; ~**psychose** evacuosis; ~**siedlung** refugee settlement; ~**status** refugee status; ~**strom** flow of emigration, stream of refugees.
Fluchtlinie *(Gebäude)* building (straight) line, *(Perspektive)* vanishing line.
Fluchtlinien|ausschuß building board, zoning board *(US)*; ~**bestimmungen** local building regulations *(Br.)*, zoning regulations *(US)*; ~**plan** building code *(Br.)*, zoning ordinance *(US)*; ~**plan durchsetzen** to enforce zoning *(US)*; ~**tafel** alignment chart; ~**verfahren** zoning practices *(US)*.
Flucht|route escape route; ~**stab** pole; **j. wegen** ~**verdachts verhaften** to detain (arrest) s. o. on suspicion.
fluchtverdächtig sein to be believed to be a fugitive from justice.
Fluchtversuch attempt to escape (at escaping), attempted escape, escape attempt, break;
~ **unternehmen** to attempt a flight, to make a break for liberty; **erfolgreichen** ~ **unternehmen** to make one's escape.
Flucht|wagen getaway van; ~**weg** way of escape, escape route; **kein** ~**weg** no means of escape.
Flug flight, fly, flying, air travel (trip, passage);
im ~**e** on the wing; **während des** ~**es** *(Versicherungsrecht)* engaged in aviation;
aufgehobener ~ flight cut down; **kurz vor Reiseantritt gebuchter** ~ walk-on daily flight; **im voraus gebuchter** ~ advanced booking flight; **an der Rentabilitätsgrenze liegender** ~ borderline flight; **planmäßiger** ~ regular (scheduled, *US*) flight; **überzogener** ~ stall; **unbemannter** ~ unmanned flight; **verbilligter** ~ thrift flight;
~ **mit Bodensicht** visual (contact) flying, visual flight; ~ **in der Touristenklasse** economy-class travel; ~ **um die Welt** round-the-world flight; ~ **ohne Zwischenlandung** nonstop flight;
seinen ~ **antreten** to embark on one's flight; ~ **aufrufen** to call a flight; **ruhigen** ~ **haben** to have a smooth flight; **zu einem** ~ **starten** to take off; **im** ~ **tanken** to refuel in midair; ~ **unternehmen** to fly;
~**abfertigung** airport reception, handling of flights; **sich bei der** ~**abfertigung melden** to check in; ~**abfertigungsstelle** check-in desk; ~**abschnitt** flight coupon.
Flugabwehr antiaircraft (air) defense *(US)* (defence, *Br.*);
~**anlagen** antiaircraft equipment; ~**geschütz** antiaircraft gun; **halbautomatisches** ~**netz** semi-automatic air-defence network; ~**rakete** antiaircraft rocket; ~**raketeneinheit** antiaircraft rocket unit.

Flug | anschluß flight connection; ~**anweisung** flight instructions, brief; ~**anweisungen erhalten** to receive one's brief; ~**apparat** flying machine; ~**asche** quick ash; ~**aufklärung** air reconnaissance; ~**aufnahme** airscape; ~**ausbildung** flying instruction; ~**bahn** flight path, *(Rakete)* trajectory, *(Satellit)* track, orbit; ~**bahnbild** *(Rakete)* trajectory chart; ~**bahnhof** air terminal; ~**basis** air base *(US)*; ~**bedingungen** flying conditions.
flugbegeistert air-minded.
Flug | begeisterung air-mindedness; ~**begleiter** flight attendant, steward; ~**begleiterin** stewardess; ~**beratung** briefing, flying information; ~**bereich** flying range, area of operation.
flugbereit ready to take off.
Flug | besprechung briefing, pre-flight conference; ~**betrieb** air traffic, aircraft operations, flying, aviation; ~**betriebsbereich** flight segment; ~**blatt** throwaway, leaflet, fly (loose) sheet, flyleaf, handbill, pamphlet, broadsheet, flier *(US)*; ~**blätter verteilen** to give out (scatter) handbills; ~**blattverteilung** handbill distribution; ~**boot** flying boat, sea plane, *(transatlantisch)* clipper; ~**buch** logbook; ~**büro** airline office; ~**dauer** duration of flight; ~**deck** flying deck; ~**dienst** airline (air) service; ~**eigenschaften** flying qualities.
Flügel *(Gebäude)* wing, annex, aisle, *(mil.)* wing, flank, *(Musik)* grand [piano];
linker ~ *(pol.)* left wing;
~ **der Phantasie** wings of phantasy;
neuen ~ **anbauen** to throw out a new wing to a building; ~ **hängen lassen** *(fig.)* to look down in the mouth; **jem. die** ~ **stutzen** to cramp s. one's style, to clip s. one's wings; **jem.** ~ **verleihen** to lend wings to s. o.
Flügelklappe *(Flugzeug)* wing clap.
flügellahm *(fig.)* lame, without pep.
Flügel | mann flanker, marker; ~**mauer** wing wall; ~**schraube** thumbscrew; ~**spanne** wing span; ~**tür** folding door.
Flug | entfernung flight, air distance; ~**erfahrung** flying (aviation) experience; ~**erprobung** flight test; ~**feld** flying (landing) field, airfield, aerodrome; ~**formation** flight formation; ~**frequenz** flight frequency; ~**funkdienst** air radio service; ~**funkgerät** aircraft radio.
Fluggast airline (air) passenger, airline traveller (customer);
beim Abflug nicht erschienener ~ no-show *(US sl.)*;
~ **einer Chartermaschine** charter passenger; ~ **einer Linienmaschine** regularly scheduled passenger *(US)*; ~ **in der Touristenklasse** economy-class passenger; ~ **auf der Warteliste** standby passenger;
~**annahme** [passenger] check-in; ~**betreuung** passenger handling; ~**gebühr** airport (passenger) service charge; ~**kabine** passenger cabin; ~**kapazität** passenger capacity; ~**kilometer** airplane passenger kilometer (kilometre, *Br.*); ~**versicherung** air passenger insurance.
flügge fully-fledged;
~ **sein** to stand on one's own feet; ~ **werden** to leave the family nest.
Fluggelände flying ground.
Fluggepäck passenger luggage *(Br.)* (baggage, *US*);
~**abschnitt** baggage check *(US)*.
Flug | gerät flight artefact; ~**geschwindigkeit** air (cruising) speed, *(mit Belastung)* flying speed; **berichtigte** ~**geschwindigkeit** calibrated air speed.
Fluggesellschaft airline [company, corporation], carrier;
nicht fahrplanmäßig fliegende ~ nonscheduled airline *(US)*; **internationale** ~ international carrier; **nationale** ~ flag carrier; **im Nahverkehr operierende** ~ commuter airline *(US)*; **auf Nebenstrecken (im Chartergeschäft) zugelassene** ~ supplemental airline;
~ **mit festem Fahrplan** scheduled airline *(US)*;
~ **betreiben** to operate an airline; **unmittelbar bei der** ~ **buchen** to make one's reservation direct with the airline; ~ **zum Luftverkehr zulassen** to license an airline.
Fluggewicht flying weight, all-up weight.
Flughafen airport, airdrome *(US)*, airfield, aerodrome *(Br.)*;
häufig angeflogener ~ heavy-traffic airport; **aufgelassener** ~ phased-out airport; **zweitrangiger** ~ secondary airport;
~ **anfliegen** to call at a port; **für die Instandhaltung eines** ~**s Sorge tragen** to maintain an airport; **in einem** ~ **unterbringen** to aerodrome; **den Lärmvorschriften bei Benutzung eines** ~**s gerecht werden** to meet airport noise rules;
~**ausbau** airport development; ~**befeuerung** airport lights (lighting); ~**bereich** airport location; ~**gebäude** terminal building, air (airport) terminal; ~**gebühr** airport service charge; ~**gelände** premises of an airport, airport property (location); ~**hotel** airport inn; ~**planung** terminal design; ~**polizei** airport police; ~**restaurant** airport restaurant; ~**verwaltung** airport operator; ~**zollstelle** airport customs; ~**zubringer** airport feeder; ~**zubringerdienst** airport feeder service.
Flug | handbuch flight manual; ~**höhe** flying height, altitude; **maximale** ~**höhe** *(Satellit)* height of apogee; ~**höhe über Grund** absolute altitude; ~**informationen weiterleiten** to process flight information; ~**insel** seadrome; ~**instrumente** flying instruments; ~**kapitän** flight captain; ~**karte** aeroplane (airline) ticket, air fare (ticket), airline fare, flight coupon; **seine** ~**karte lösen** to book one's passage; **gebündeltes** ~**kartenangebot** fares package; **ungebundener** ~**kartenverkauf** free-sale system; ~**kilometer** aircraft kilometer.
flugklar ready to take off.
Flug | komfort in-flight convenience; ~**kommandant** airline pilot; ~**körper** flight artefact, flying object, missile; **nachfolgender** ~**körper** backup mission; **unbekannter** ~**körper** unidentified flying object, UFO; ~**krankheit** air sickness; ~**kunststück** stunt; ~**kunststücke vorführen** to stunt an airplane; ~**lage** attitude of flight; **in überzogene** ~**lage geraten** to stall; ~**lärm** air-traffic noise; ~**lehrer** flying (flight, pilot) instructor; ~**leistung** flight performance; ~**leitung** flight control.
Fluglinie airline, airway, route, straight short *(US)*, *(Fluggesellschaft)* airline company (corporation), carrier, *(Rakete)* trajectory;
festgelegte ~ air corridor (tunnel);
~ **mit fahrplanmäßigem Dienst** scheduled airline *(US)*; ~ **mit hoher Verkehrsdichte** high-density route;
~ **abstecken** to charter a route; ~ **neu festlegen** to reroute.
Fluglinien | antrag route application; ~**festlegung** route planning; ~**karte** route map; ~**verkehr** air service, airline traffic; ~**verkehr aufnehmen** to inaugurate air service; ~**zuteilung** route award.
Flug | lizenz air carrier permit; ~**lotse** air-traffic controller; ~**lotsen** flight-control personnel, air-traffic control staff; ~**maschine** flying machine; ~**mechaniker** flight (aircraft) mechanic; ~**meldedienst** airraid warning service; ~**meldeposten,** ~**melder** spotter *(Br.)*; ~**meldezentrale** filter center *(US)* (centre, *Br.*); ~**modell** flying model; ~**möglichkeit** availibility of flights; ~**motor** air motor (engine); ~**motorenherstellung** aeroengine production; ~**nachrichtenstelle** airways station; ~**nachrichtenverkehr** aircraft communications; ~**navigation** air navigation, avigation *(US)*; ~**netz** network of air routes; ~**novize** dodo *(sl.)*; ~**nummer** flight number; ~**objekt** flying object; **unbekanntes** ~**objekt** unidentified flying object, UFO; ~**ordnung** flying formation; ~**parade** fly past; ~**passagier** air[line] passenger; ~**personal** air staff, airmen, flying personnel; ~**pionier** aviation pioneer; ~**plan** airline timetable (table), schedule [of plans] *(US)*, flying schedule *(US)*.
Flugplatz airport, airfield, aerodrome *(Br.)*, airdrome *(US)*, airline seat;
häufig angeflogener ~ heavy-traffic airport; **aufgelockert angelegter** ~ dispersed airport; **aufgelassener** ~ phased-out airport; **kleiner** ~ flying field; **zweitrangiger** ~ secondary airport;
~ **anfliegen** *(Fluggesellschaft)* to head for an airport, to serve an airport; ~ **im Linienverkehr anfliegen** to serve an airport commercially; ~ **bestellen** to book a seat on an aeroplane; **von der Fabrik zum** ~ **fliegen** to ferry; **für die Instandhaltung eines** ~**es Sorge tragen** to maintain an airport; **j. am** ~ **verabschieden** to see s. o. off at the airport;
~**abholdienst** door-to-airport limousine service; ~**ausbau** airport development; ~**bahnhof** terminus station; ~**befeuerung** airport lights (lighting); ~**gelände** airport location, terminal area; ~**hotel** hotel at an airport, airport inn; ~**kommission** airport commission; ~**nähe** access to airport; **reservierte** ~**nummer** flight seat number; ~**planung** airport planning; ~**reservierung** flight (plane) reservation; ~**rollbahn** airport runway; ~**schließung** airport shutdown; ~**versicherung** airport liability insurance; ~**verwaltung** airport operator; ~**wettervorhersage** terminal (aerodrome, *Br.*) forecast; ~**zentrale anfunken** to call the control station of an airport.
Flug | praxis flying experience; ~**preis** plane (airline) fare, airline charge; **gegen Nachnahme des** ~**preises** on charges collect basis; ~**preissenkung** reduction of airline fares; ~**prüfung** flying examination; ~**radius eines Flugzeuges** flying range of an aircraft; ~**reise** journey by air, air passage; **geschäftliche** ~**reise** commercial flight, air trip; ~**reisebüro** air-travel bureau; ~**reisender** air travel(l)er (tourist); ~**reservierung** flight (plane) reservation; ~**reservierungen billiger Flugscheine in der Reihenfolge des Eintreffens auf dem Flugplatz** first-come, first-

served booking at the airport; ~**richtung** direction of flight, *(Kurs)* heading, course; ~**risiko** flying risk; ~**route** air route, flight route (track), aircraft route, flight path, airway; **vereinbarte** ~**route** agreed route; ~**route einer königlichen Maschine** purple airway; ~**sand** drifting sand; ~**schau** air (aircraft) display, air circus (show).

Flugschein [air-plane] ticket, air fare (ticket), aeroplane ticket, flight coupon;
stark verbilligter ~ cut-rate air fare; **kurz vor dem Abflug angebotener verbilligter** ~ standby fare; **21 Tage voraus gebuchter verbilligter** ~ budget fare;
~**gebühr** airline ticket tax *(US)*; ~**verkauf ohne festgelegtes Flugdatum** standby ticket sale; ~**verkaufsstelle** airline ticket center *(US)* (centre, *Br.*).

Flug|schneise air lane, flying lane (corridor); ~**schrauber** gyrodyne, autogiro; ~**schreiber** flight recorder; ~**schrift** brochure, broadsheet, leaflet, pamphlet; **verbotene** ~**schrift** clandestine tract; ~**schrift herausgeben** to [put out a] pamphlet, to pampleteer; ~**schule** flying school; ~**schüler** trainee pilot, stooge, pilot trainee, dodo *(sl.)*; ~**sicherheit** flying (air) safety, airline security; ~**sicherheitsbehörde** civil aeronautics board; ~**sicherheitsexperte** air-safety expert; ~**sicherung** air-traffic control.

Flugsicherungs|beamter air-traffic controller; ~**behörde** Federal Aviation Agency *(US)*, Civil Aeronautics Board; **internationale** ~**behörde** Eurocontrol; ~**bestimmungen** state aviation rules; ~**dienst** air-traffic control service; ~**informationsgebiet** flight information region; ~**kontrollbezirk** air-traffic control area; ~**personal** air-traffic control staff, flight control personnel; ~**turm** control tower; ~**zentrale** air-traffic control center *(US)* (centre, *Br.*); ~**zwecke** air-traffic control purposes.

Flug|sicht flight visibility; **verstellbarer** ~**sitzplatz** regulation airplane seat;~**speditionsvertreter** ramp agent; ~**sport** aviation; ~**steig** apron, gate, channel; ~**stewardessen** cabin staff; ~**stornierung** flight cancellation; ~**straße** airway, air corridor; ~**strecke** [flight] route, airline, airway, air (aircraft) route; ~**streckenbefeuerung** airway beacon; ~**stunde** flying hour; **vier** ~**stunden** 4 hours flying; ~**stützpunkt** air base; **schwimmender** ~**stützpunkt** seaplane tender; ~**tag** flying meeting; ~**tagebuch** logbook; ~**tasche** flight bag; ~**tätigkeit** flying activities.

flug|tauglich, ~**tüchtig** airworthy.

Flug|tauglichkeit airworthiness; ~**tauglichkeitszeugnis** certification of an aircraft; ~**taxe,** ~**taxi** taxi aircraft, taxiplane; ~**technik** aviation, aeronautics, *(Pilot)* airmanship; ~**techniker** aeronautical engineer.

flugtechnisch aeronautical, flying;
~ **erproben** to flight-test.

Flug|termin flight date; ~**test** flight test.

Flugticket air[-plane] ticket, flight coupon;
auf einheitlicher Berechnungsbasis ausgestellte ~**s für Gesellschaftsreisen** tour basing fares; **im Vorverkauf erworbenes** ~ budget fare; **längerfristig vorausgebuchtes** ~ advance-purchased ticket;
mit an Charterpreisen angenäherten ~**s Geschäfte machen** to make money with fares close to charter levels.

Flug|tourimus air tourism; ~**tüchtigkeit** airworthiness; ~**überwachung** flying (flight) surveillance, *(Flugplatz)* air-traffic control.

Flugüberwachungs|instrumente flying instruments, air controls; ~**pult** display board; ~**zone** surveillance zone.

Flug|unfall flying accident; ~**unkosten** costs of flying; ~**unterbrechung** stopover; ~**unterhaltungskosten** operating costs; ~**unterricht** flying instruction; ~**veranstaltung** air show (display, circus); ~**verband** flying unit; ~**verbindung** connection by air, air connection, connecting flight; ~**verbindungsnetz** flight network; ~**verbot** grounding; **unter** ~**verbot stehen** to be grounded.

Flugverkehr aviation, air traffic (transport), *(Warnschild)* low-flying aircraft;
betrieblicher ~ corporate air travel *(US)*; **verbilligter** ~ **ohne Extraleistungen** no-frills cheap air service.

Flugverkehrs|einrichtungen, private contract flying service; **spezielles** ~**gebiet** aviation bailiwick; ~**gesellschaft zulassen** to license an airline; ~**industrie** airline industry; ~**linie** airline, air route; **fahrplanmäßige** ~**linie** regular (scheduled, *US*) airline service; ~**netz** network of air routes, airline network; ~**plan** airline timetable, [flight] schedule *(US)*; ~**risiko** aviation risk; ~**sicherheit** air-traffic safety; ~**tarif** airline rates; ~**vorschriften** air-traffic regulations.

Flug|vorführung flying demonstration; ~**wache** air lookout post; ~**warndienst** airraid warning service; ~**warnung** air alert, airraid warning; ~**warte** aeronautical weather station; ~**weg** airway, air lane, flight path; ~**werk** skeleton; ~**wesen** aeronautics, aviation, flying; ~**wettbewerb** flying competition.

Flugwetter flying (flyable) weather;
kein ~ unflyable weather;
~**dienst** aeronautical weather service, route forecast; ~**überwachungsstelle** meteorological watch office; ~**vorhersage** flight forecast.

Flug|woche flying meeting; ~**zeit** flight (flying) time; **gering belegte** ~**zeiten** off-peak flights; ~**zentrum** flying center *(US)* (centre, *Br.*); ~**zettel** flysheet, handbill, leaflet.

Flugzeug aircraft, airliner, aeroplane, plane, airplane, flier, ship; **frei** ~ free on aircraft; **per** ~ by air;
abgestürztes ~ writeoff *(sl.)*; **angreifendes** ~ airraider; **atomangetriebenes** ~ nuclear aircraft; **mit elektronischen Einrichtungen voll ausgestattetes** ~ electronics-loaded aircraft; **in der Planung befindliches** ~ projected aircraft; **nicht eingesetztes** ~ idle plane; **im Frühwarnsystem eingesetztes** ~ early-warning aeroplane; **im Linienverkehr eingesetztes** ~ commercial airliner; **im Pendelverkehr eingesetztes** ~ commuter aircraft *(US)*; **entführtes** ~ hi(gh)jacked plane; **feindliches** ~ hostile aircraft; **ferngesteuertes** ~ drone; **mit Unterschallgeschwindigkeit fliegendes** ~ subsonic airliner; **automatisch gesteuertes** ~ pilotless plane; **technisch hochgezüchtetes** ~ sophisticated airplane; **hochleistungsfähiges** ~ high-performance plane; **schwanzgesteuertes** ~ tail-steering plane; **senkrecht startendes und landendes** ~ vertical takeoff and landing aircraft; **unbemanntes** ~ pilotless aircraft, drone; **undefinierbares** ~ bogie *(sl.)*;
~ **mit Druckschraube** pusher airplane; ~ **des Düsenzeitalters** jet-age aircraft; ~ **mit Strahlantrieb** jet-propelled aircraft; ~ **mit Turbinenbetrieb** turbine-powered aircraft; ~**e auf Wartebahn** stack;
~ **durch Heckfallschirm abbremsen** to power-brake an airplane; ~ **abfertigen** to handle a flight; ~ **abschießen** to bring (shoot) down (kill) an aeroplane; ~ **als verunglückt abschreiben** to write off an aircraft as lost; ~ **mit Radar anpeilen** to radiolocate an airplane; ~ **benutzen** to ride an aeroplane; ~**e einsetzen** to bring aircraft into action; **in ein** ~ **einsteigen** to board (embark) a plane, to emplane; ~ **entführen** to hi[gh]jack a plane; ~ **mit dem Scheinwerfer erfassen** to pick out a plane by searchlight; ~ **fliegen** to fly an airplane, to pilot an aircraft, to aviate, to avigate *(US)*; ~ **für den Linienverkehr freigeben** to allow a plane into revenue service; ~ **kapern** to hi[gh]jack an airplane; ~**e konstruieren** to design aircraft; ~ **landen** to down a plane; ~ **sicher landen** to land an airliner safely; **im Aktionsbereich eines** ~**s liegen** to be within an aircraft's range; ~ **startbereit machen** to tune up an airplane; **per** ~ **reisen** to travel (go) by air (airplane), to aeroplane; **aus dem** ~ **springen** to bail out; ~ **stabilisieren** to stabilize an airplane; ~ **starten** to pull the plane off the ground; ~ **steuern** to pilot an aircraft, to fly an airplane, to avigate *(US)*; **mit dem** ~ **transportieren** to transport by airplane, to flight-deliver *(US)*; ~ **auf dem Radarschirm verfolgen** to follow the flight of an aircraft by radar; ~ **in die normale Lage zurückbringen** to redress an airplane;
~**abstellplatz** aircraft parking, hardstand; ~**absturz** aircraft crash; ~**abwehr** antiaircraft defense *(US)* (defence, *Br.*); ~**abwehrgeschütz** antiaircraft gun; ~**aktien** aviation shares; ~**angriff** airraid; **schwerer** ~**angriff** blitz; ~**ankunft** airliner's arrival; ~**anschluß erreichen** to catch a plane; ~**aufnahme** aerial view; ~**auftrag** aircraft contract; ~**bake** aviation beacon; ~**bau** aeronautical (aircraft) engineering; ~**bauer** aircraft manufacturer, *(Ingenieur)* aircraft designer; ~**bauingenieur** aeronautical engineer; ~**behälter** flying safe-deposit box; ~**behälterversand** flying safe-deposit system; ~**benzin** aviation fuel; ~**beobachter** spotter; ~**besatzung** aircrew, flight crew (personnel); ~**entführer** hi[gh]jacker, skyjacker; ~**entführung** hi[gh]-jacking, aeroplane highjack, aerial piracy, skyjacking; ~**entwicklung** aircraft development; ~**erkennungsdienst** aircraft recognition service; ~**export** aircraft export; ~**fabrik** aircraft factory (works); ~**fabrikant** aircraft maker; ~**fahrgestell** landing gear, undercarriage; ~**firma** aircraft company; ~**führer** pilot, aviator; **zweiter** ~**führer** co-pilot; ~**führerschein** pilot's licence; ~**führerstand** cockpit; ~**geräusch** aircraft noise; ~**gerippe** skeleton; ~**geschwader** aircraft formation, fleet of airplanes; **staatliche** ~**gesellschaft**state-owned airline; ~**halle** hangar; ~**hersteller** aircraft manufacturer; ~**herstellung** aircraft manufacture; ~**industrie** aircraft industry (manufacturers), air (airline, aviation) industry, aircraft business; **nicht zur** ~**industrie gehörige Geschäftssparte** nonaviation business;

~**ingenieur** aircraft (aeronautical) engineer; ~**kabine** cabin; ~**kapitän** airline pilot; ~**katastrophe** aircraft disaster; ~**kommandant** airline pilot, pilot in command *(US)*; ~**konstrukteur** aircraft designer; ~**ladung** plane load, bellyload; **sichere ~landung durchführen** to land an airliner safely; ~**markt** aircraft market; ~**mechaniker,** ~**monteur** flight (aircraft) mechanic, aeromechanic, rigger, grease monkey *(US sl.)*; ~**miete** charter money; ~**modell** model of an aircraft; ~**motor** air engine (motor), aircraft engine; ~**motorenfabrik** aircraft engine plant; ~**motorenhersteller** builder of aircraft engines; ~**muster** aircraft type; ~**mutterschiff** seaplane tender; ~**nachrichtenverkehr** aircraft communication; ~**nahverkehr** commuter airlines *(US)*; ~**nahverkehrslinie** commuter airline; ~**ortung** aircraft direction finding; ~**park** aircraft fleet; ~**passagier** air travel(l)er, airline (air) passenger; ~**peilgerät** airborne direction-finding equipment; ~**produktion** aircraft production (manufacture); ~**programm** aircraft program(me); ~**propeller** airscrew, propeller; ~**rallye** aviation rally; ~**reise** airline travel; ~**reparatur** aircraft repair; ~**risiko** air hazard; ~**rumpf** fuselage; ~**sabotage** air sabotage; ~**schlepp** aerotow flight; ~**schleuder** launcher, catapult; ~**schuppen** aeroplane hangar, airplane hangar (shed); ~**sitz** airline (airplane) seat; ~**sporn** skid; ~**staffel** squadron; ~**start** takeoff; ~**steuergerät** automatic flight control; ~**stützpunkt** air base; ~**torpedo** aerial torpedo; ~**träger** aircraft (airplane) carrier, flattop *(US sl.)*; **atomgetriebener ~träger** nuclear[-powered] carrier; **kleiner ~träger** aircraft escort; ~**treibstoff** aviation spirit (fuel); ~**trimmung** trim; ~**trümmer** wreckage of an aircraft; ~**typ** aircraft type; ~**unfall** airline accident; **schwerer ~unfall** crackup *(sl.)*; ~**unglück** air accident, air[craft] (airplane) crash, airplane (flying) accident, stack-up *(sl.)*; ~**verband** flight formation; **täglicher ~verkehr** daily emplanement; ~**versicherer** aviation insurer; ~**versicherung** aviation (aircraft) insurance; ~**wart** aircraft mechanic; ~**wartung** servicing aircraft, aircraft maintenance; ~**werte** *(Börse)* aircrafts; ~**zeitalter** air age; ~**zelle** bag.

Flug | ziel destination; ~**zustand** flight (flying) condition; **überzogener ~zustand** stall.

Fluidum atmosphere, air, aura.

Fluktuation flow, fluctuation, *(Arbeitskräfte)* turnover;
~ **der halben Belegschaft innerhalb eines Jahres** fluctuation of fifty percent in a year; ~ **der Devisenkurse** exchange fluctuations.

Fluktuations | arbeitslosigkeit frictional unemployment; ~**bestand** frictional float; **zulässige ~breite** permissible margin of fluctuation; ~**quote** *(Angestellte)* rate of turnover (fluctuation), turnover by the labo(u)r force.

Fluktuieren fluctuation;
~ **der Preise** price fluctuations.

fluktuieren to fluctuate, to flow;
frei ~ können to be free to fluctuate on the market.

fluktierender Bevölkerungsteil floating population.

Flunkerei fib, fibbing, taletelling, hoax, taradiddle, string *(US sl.)*.

Flunkerer fibber, story teller, taleteller.

flunkern to draw the long bow.

Flunsch ziehen to pout.

Flur field, plain, farm land, farm real estate, *(Hausflur)* entry, entrance hall, vestibule, corridor, passage *(Br.)*;
Wald und ~ woods and meadows;
allein auf weiter ~ stehen to stand alone;
~**bereich** cadastral map; ~**bereinigung** land consolidation; ~**bereinigungsverfahren** land consolidation procedure; ~**buch** field book, cadastral map (plan, survey), lot book, terrier; ~**buchauszug** cadastral extract; ~**buchnummer** cadastral number; ~**garderobe** clothes rack, hall tree *(US)*; ~**karte** field (cadastral) map (plan); ~**lampe** corridor lamp; ~**name** name of a field; ~**schaden** field damage; ~**stück** plot, lot *(US)*; ~**zersplitterung** parcellation of farm holdings; ~**zwang** open-field system.

Fluß river, stream, *(Geld)* flow, flux, *(Verkehr)* flow;
unmittelbar am ~ right on the river;
träge dahinfließender ~ lazy river; **internationalisierter ~** internationalized river; **kleiner ~** brook, streamlet, creek *(US)*; **reißender ~** rapid-flowing river; **schiffbarer ~** navigable river (stream), open river; **vom Fabrikabfall verschmutzter ~** river defiled by waste from factories;
~ **heißen Geldes** hot money outflow; ~ **einer Rede** fluency of a speech;
an einen ~ angrenzen to touch a river; **j. über den ~ bringen** to put s. o. over the river; **Unterhaltung wieder in ~ bringen** to get the conversation under way again; **festgefahrene Verhandlungen wieder in ~ bringen** to overcome a deadlock in the negotiations; **in einen ~ einmünden** to join a river; **sich am ~ hinziehen** *(Grenze)* to run along the river; **in ~ kommen** to get under way; **richtig in ~ kommen** *(Arbeit)* to hit one's stride, *(Unterhaltung)* to warm up; **unmittelbar am ~ liegen** to stand right on the river; **in ständigem ~ sein** to be in a state of flux; **noch im ~ sein** to be in a state of flux; ~ **überqueren** to pass (cross) a river; ~ **überspannen** *(Brücke)* to traverse a river; ~ **umleiten** to divert the course of a river; ~ **seiner Gedanken unterbrechen** to break s. one's train of thought; **auf dem ~ verkehren** *(Fähre)* to ply the river.

Flußablagerung river deposit.

flußabwärts downstream, down.

Flußanlieger riparian owner, riverain;
~**rechte** riparian rights; ~**staaten** riparian nations.

Flußarm branch of a river.

flußaufwärts up the river.

Fluß | bauamt, ~**behörde** conservator of rivers *(Br.)*, conservancy *(Br.)*, River Board; ~**bett** river bed, channel, ditch; ~**bettkarte zeichnen** to map the basin of a river; **flachgehendes ~boot** punt *(Br.)*; ~**dampfer** river steamer; ~**deich** embankment, level *(US)*, riverbank; ~**delta** delta; ~**diagramm** flow chart; **binäres ~diagramm** binary flow chart; ~**einzugsgebiet** river (drainage) basin; ~**fahrzeug** river craft; ~**frachtgut** river freight; ~**frachtsatz** river freight rate; ~**gebiet** river basin, drainage area; ~**größe** flow item; ~**grundstück** waterfront property; ~**hafen** river port.

flüssig fluid, *(Bank, Firma)* liquid, cash-rich, financial, solvent, fluid *(US)*, ready, *(Geldmarkt)* easy, *(Kapital)* available, *(Stil)* fluent, flowing;
nicht ~ frozen, not liquid; **sehr ~** highly liquid, cash-heavy;
~ **ablaufen** *(Verkehr)* to run smoothly; **Ersparnisse ~ angelegt haben** to hold savings in liquid form; ~ **lesen** to read fluently; ~ **machen** to realize, to set free, to bank; ~ **reden** to speak fluently; ~ **sein** to be financially sound (long on cash); **nicht ~ sein** to be short of liquid assets, to lack liquidity; **wieder ~ sein** *(Geldmarkt)* to be easy again; ~ **werden** to melt; **wieder ~ werden** to replenish one's funds;
~**es Anlagekapital** money[ed] capital; ~**e Anlagen** quick (liquid, fluid) assets; ~**e Barmittel** available cash; ~**e Gelder (Mittel)** cash, ready money, available funds, liquid resources, funds in hand, spare capital; ~**er Geldmarkt** easy money market; ~**e Grenzen** not clearly defined lines; **über ~e Mittel verfügen** to be liquid (in funds); ~**e Nahrung** liquid food; ~**er Stil** easy (smooth) style; ~**es Vermögen** liquid (fluid, *US*) assets.

Flüssigkeit fluid, *(Bank)* cash (current) position, *(Bilanz)* liquidity, liquid position, *(Geldmarkt)* ease of money rates, *(Nachlaß)* solvency;
mangelnde ~ shortage in money accounts, liquidity shortage; ~ **der Bilanz** liquid position; ~ **auf dem Geldmarkt** easiness on the money market;
für ausreichende ~ sorgen to establish enough liquidity.

Flüssigkeits | behälter tank, reservoir; ~**druck** hydraulic pressure; ~**erfordernisse** commercial standards of solvency; ~**getriebe** *(Auto)* fluid drive; ~**grad** degree of liquidity; ~**koeffizient** current position ratio, *(Zentralbank)* reserve ratio *(US)*; ~**kupplung** fluid drive (coupling); ~**maß** liquid measure; ~**pegel** fluid level; ~**position** liquid position; ~**stoßdämpfer** hydraulic shock absorber; ~**verhältnis** *(Bilanz)* current position (liquidity, acid test, quick assets, *US*) ratio; ~**verlust im Faß** ullage.

Flüssigmachen setting free, convertibility into cash, realization, liquidation;
~ **von Kapital** mobilization (liberation) of funds, liquidation of assets.

flüssigmachen to mobilize, to realize, to convert into cash;
Aktien ~ to liquidate shares; **Geld ~** to mobilize money; **Obligationen kurzfristig ~** to realize bonds at short notice.

Fluß | kraftwerk river power station; ~**ladeschein,** ~**konnossement** river (inland) bill of lading; ~**linie** flood-mark; ~**mitte** middle of the river; ~**mündung** river mouth, entry; ~**polizei** riverside police; ~**polizist** river policeman; ~**regulierung** correction of a river; ~**risiko** dangers of a river; ~**schiffahrt** river navigation (traffic); ~**spediteur** water carrier; ~**stahl** ingot iron; ~**übergang** river crossing, *(Furt)* ford; ~**ufer** riverbank, riverside, watersite; ~**umleitung** diversion of a stream; ~**verkehr** river traffic; ~**verlauf** course of a river; ~**verschmutzung** pollution of rivers; ~**versicherung** river insurance; **normaler ~wasserstand** riparian water.

Flüstergalerie whispering gallery.
Flüstern whisper.
flüstern to whisper, *(tuscheln)* to buzz.
Flüster|propaganda whispering campaign, grapevine *(US)*, grapevine telegraph *(Australia)*; **im ~ton** in a whisper, under one's breath; **fast im ~ton** in a near whisper; **~tüte** *(fam.)* speaking trumpet, megaphone.
Flut [flood] tide, *(Überschwemmung)* flood, inundation, overflow, waters (flood), *(fig.)* stream, torrent, spate, volley, sweep, volume;
hohe ~ spring tide; **zurückgehende ~** outgoing tide;
Ebbe und ~ ebb and flow;
~ von Aufträgen flush of orders; **~ von Beschimpfungen** flood of abuse; **~ von Beschwerden** ocean of complaints; **~ von Briefen** shower (avalanche, volume) of letters; **~ von Forderungen** deluge of claims; **~ von Licht** flood of light; **~ von Protesten** stream (torrent) of protests; **~ gesellschaftlicher Veranstaltungen** vortex of social life; **~ von Verbrechen** wave of crimes; **~ von Verwünschungen** torrent (stream, flood) of abuse;
~ von Empfindungen auslösen to unlock a flood of emotions; **~ von Verwünschungen ausstoßen** to let loose a hurricane of abuse *(fam.)*; **von der ~ fortgerissen werden** to be swept away by the flood; **mit einer ~ von Briefen überschwemmt werden** to be flooded (deluged) with letters;
~becken wet dock.
fluten to stream, to flood, to flow, *(Verkehr)* to surge;
in einen Saal ~ to pour into a hall; **Schleuse ~** to flood a sluice.
flutender Verkehr surging traffic.
Flut|gebiet tide waters; **~grenze** tidal limit; **~hafen** tidal harbo(u)r; **~höhe** tidal range; **~kammer** float chamber; **~katastrophe** flood disaster; **~kraftwerk** tidal power station; **~licht** floodlight; **mit ~licht anstrahlen** to floodlight; **~lichtanlage**, **~beleuchtung** floodlighting; **~lichtscheinwerfer** floodlight projector; **~linie** high-water mark; **~marke** high watermark.
flutschen *(Arbeit)* to go swimmingly;
durch die Finger ~ *(Geld)* to slip through one's fingers.
Flut|schleuse tide lock; **~tank** ballast tank; **~tor** flood gate; **~ventil** flooding valve; **~welle** tidal wave; **~zeit** flood tide.
fob free on board (f. o. b.).
Fobklausel free-on-board clause.
Föderalismus federalism.
Föderalist federalist, federal.
föderalistisch federalist, federal.
Föderation federation, federacy.
föderativ federative.
föderiert federated.
Föhn wind in Switzerland, hot blast, foehn;
~welle mountain wave.
Folge result, outcome, effect, consequence, run, cycle, train, *(Datenverarbeitung)* sequence, *(Fortsetzung)* continuation, instalment;
für die ~ in the future; **in rascher ~** hand over hand, in rapid succession; **mit weitreichenden ~n** of heavy (far-reaching) consequences;
sich ergebende ~n ensuing consequences; **mittelbare ~n** remote consequences; **neue ~** new series; **schlimme ~n** bad consequences; **schwerwiegende ~n** serious consequences; **unangenehme ~n** unpleasant consequences; **unmittelbare ~** proximate result; **unvermeidliche ~** necessary consequence;
~ von Ereignissen chain of events; **Fortsetzung in der nächsten ~** *(Zeitung)* to be continued; **~ einer Krankheit** after-effects of a disease; **~ eines Krieges** consequences (aftermath) of war; **~ von Unglücksfällen** series of disasters; **verheerende ~n eines Wirbelsturms** devastating effects of a hurricane;
~ bedenken to count the cost; **in ungezwungener ~ erscheinen** *(Bücher)* to be published in no particular order; **zur ~ haben** to result in, to entail; **Kosten zur ~ haben** to involve expense; **Krieg zur ~ haben** to result in a war; **~n seiner Dummheit zu tragen haben** to pay the penalty of one's foolishness; **Anweisungen ~ leisten** to act upon instructions; **einer Aufforderung ~ leisten** to comply with a request; **einem Befehl ~ leisten** to obey an order; **einer Einladung ~ leisten** to accept an invitation; **einer Vorladung ~ leisten** to answer a summons; **den Weisungen seines Auftraggebers ~ leisten** to comply with one's principal's instructions; **~n auf sich nehmen** to abide by (bear) the consequences, to face the music; **in chronologischer ~ ordnen** to arrange in chronological order; **die ~n tragen** to stand the racket, to face the music; **~n zeitigen** to be pregnant with consequences; **unangenehme ~n nach sich ziehen** to bring trouble in its wake;
die ~n sind nicht abzusehen the consequences cannot be foreseen;
~aufnahme follow shot; **~brief** follow-up letter; **~erscheinung** subsequency, sequel, corollary, resulting phenomenon, consequence; **~kosten** resulting (consequential) costs; **~kosten bei Verteidigungsanlagen** defence-induced costs.
folgen to follow;
jds. Ausführungen nicht ~ können not to understand what s. o. is saying; **einem Befehl ~** to obey an order; **jds. Beispiel ~** to follow suit; **einem Brief einen Zahlungsbefehl ~ lassen** to follow a letter with a summons; **dicht aufeinander ~** to tread on each other's heels; **einer Einladung ~** to accept an invitation; **der falschen Fährte ~** to be on the wrong track; **jem. auf den Fersen ~** to be hot on s. one's heels; **dem Rat eines Freundes ~** to act in accordance with a friend's advice; **dem Ruf einer Universität ~** to accept a chair; **jem. auf Schritt und Tritt ~** to dog s. one's footsteps; **jem. auf dem Thron ~** to succeed s. o. to the throne; **einem flüchtigen Verbrecher ~** to pursue a fugitive from justice; **einer Vorladung ~** to answer a summons; **aufs Wort ~** to obey to the letter.
folgend following, next;
dicht ~ fast upon.
folgendermaßen as follows.
folgen|reich full of consequences; **~schwer** weighty, momentous, of serious consequences.
Folge|prämie renewal (current) premium; **~prüfung** *(Statistik)* sequential test; **~recht** right of stoppage [in transitu].
folgerichtig consequential, logical, consistent.
Folgerichtigkeit consistency.
folgern to conclude, to gather, to draw a conclusion.
Folgerückversicherung retrocession.
Folgerung conclusion, deduction, consequence, implication;
juristische ~ implication of law; **natürliche ~** natural presumption; **sachliche ~** material consequence;
~en ziehen to draw conclusions.
Folge|schaden consequential damages (loss); **~schadenversicherung** consequential loss (damage) insurance, loss-of-profit insurance; **~schätzung** *(Statistik)* sequential estimation; **~verzug** consequential delay.
folgewidrig inconsequent, inconsistent.
Folgewidrigkeit inconsequence, inconsistency.
Folgewirkung|en consequential effects;
finanzielle ~ financial involvement; **vermutliche ~** probable consequence;
~en eines Unfalls results of an accident; **~en einer Verletzung** effects of an injury.
Folgezeit, in der in the sequel.
folgsam obedient, manageable.
Foliant tome, folio volume.
Folie foil.
Folien|druck foil printing; **~papier** foil paper.
foliieren to folio, to foliate.
Folio folio, page;
~band folio volume; **~blatt** folio; **~format** folio [size].
Folter torture, torment;
auf die ~ gespannt on the rack;
gewöhnliche ~ common question;
durch ~ erpressen to sweat s. th. out *(sl.)*; **j. auf die ~ spannen** to put s. o. on the rack, to torture s. o. *(fig.)*, to keep s. o. on tenterhooks; **j. der ~ unterwerfen** to subject (put) s. o. to torture;
~beschuldigung torture charge; **~knecht** torturer.
foltern to torture, to put to the question.
Folterqualen erleiden to endure agonies.
Folterung torture, torment, heat *(US)*;
jem. durch ~en ein Geständnis abpressen to torture s. o. into making him confess s. th.; **~en ertragen** to undergo torture.
Folterverhör third-degree practices;
Gefangenen einem ~ unterwerfen to put a prisoner through the third degree.
Fön *(Gerät)* hair-dryer.
Fonds fund, box, pool, *(Kapital)* capital, funds, purse, *(Kapitalanlagegesellschaft)* investment fund, unit trust *(Br.)*, *(Staatspapiere)* government stocks *(Br.)* (bonds, *US*), public funds *(Br.)*, *(Stiftung)* foundation, donation;
amerikanische ~ United States bonds; **sich automatisch auffüllender ~** revolving fund; **englische ~** British funds; **sich stets erneuernder ~** *(Staatsrechnungswesen)* revolving fund; **gemeinsam von Industrie und Gewerkschaften errichteter ~** joint union-industry fund; **in Krisenzeiten für Makler gebildeter ~** money pool; **aus Sonderveranlagungen gebildeter**

~ special-assessment fund; **gemeinsamer** ~ community fund, stock, purse, pool; **gemischter** ~ mixed fund; **getrennter** ~ separate fund; **konsolidierte** ~ consols; **liquider** ~ cash-heavy fund; **politischer** ~ political fund; **schwarzer** ~ secret (slush, *US*) fund; **thesaurierender** ~ cumulative (accumulative, restricted, nonexpendable) fund; **durch Mitgliederwerbung ständig vergrößerter** ~ snowball *(Br.)*; **nach bestimmten Richtlinien zu verwaltender** ~ directory trust; **vom Staat zu verwaltender** ~ state-operated fund; **von einer Treuhandstelle verwalteter** ~ trust and agency fund;
~ **für soziale Abfindungen** Redundancy Fund *(Br.)*; ~ **für unvorhergesehene Ausgaben** contingency fund; ~ **zur Finanzierung von Sonderaufgaben** special revenue fund; ~ **für Kommunalbetriebszwecke** working-capital fund; ~ **im Rahmen der Sonderziehungsrechte** *(Weltwährungsfonds)* special drawing account;
~ **alimentieren** to endow a fund; ~ **anderweitig anlegen** to convert funds to another purpose; ~ **Treuhändern anvertrauen** to commit a fund to the care of trustees; ~ **auffüllen** to reestablish a fund; ~ **auflösen** to liquidate a fund; **zu einem** ~ **beisteuern** to pay into a fund; ~ **bewilligen** to vote a fund; ~ **bilden** to create a fund; ~ **dotieren** to endow a fund; **Geldbeträge aus einem** ~ **entnehmen** to take money out of a fund; ~ **gründen** to launch a fund; ~ **für seine privaten Zwecke mißbrauchen** to funnel funds to one's own use; ~ **zur Disposition stellen** to make a fund available; ~ **übertreffen** to outperform a fund; **einem besonderen** ~ **zufließen** to be placed in a special fund; ~ **zweckentfremden** to divert a fund;
~**anlage** fund investment; ~**anteil** share in a fund, *(Kapitalanlagegesellschaft)* share *(US)*, unit *(Br.)*; **überwiegender** ~**anteil** bulk of a fund; ~**anteilseigner** shareholder *(US)*, unitholder *(Br.)*; ~**auflösung** liquidation of a fund; ~**ausstattung** allocation of a fund; ~**beiträge** contributions to a fund; ~**bericht** stock-exchange news; ~**besitzer** stockholder, fundholder *(Br.)*; ~**bestände** stockholdings, fundholdings *(Br.)*; ~**börse** stock exchange (market); ~**erträge** income of a fund; ~**finanzierung** fund financing; ~**geschäft** stock-exchange business; ~**händler** stockbroker, jobber in securities *(Br.)*, *(pl.)* bond crowd *(US)*; ~**konto** fund account; ~**makler** stockbroker, stockjobber, jobber *(Br.)*, bond broker *(US)*, *(pl.)* bond crowd *(US)*; ~**markt** stock exchange (market); ~**spekulant** stock adventurer *(Br.)*, floor trader *(US)*; ~**spekulation** stock adventure *(Br.)*, stock-exchange speculation; ~**überschuß** fund surplus; ~**vereinigung** consolidation of funds; ~**vermögen** fund (trust) assets, assets of a fund, *(Kapitalanlagegesellschaft)* asset value; ~**vermögen anderweitig anlegen** to convert a fund to another purpose; ~**verpflichtung** fund liability (obligation); ~**verwalter** fund manager (administrator); ~**verwaltung** fund management, *(Pensionsplan)* deposit administration; ~**verwaltungsgesellschaft** management company *(Br.)*; ~**wert** trust asset value; ~**werte eines Investmenttrustes** investment trust securities; ~**zugänge** accruals to a fund.

Foppen tease, teasing, hoax, bamboozlement, legpull *(sl.)*.

foppen to tease, to fool, to hoax, to kid, to rig, to bamboozle.

Fopper teaser, kidder, chaffer, legpuller *(sl.)*.

forcieren *(beschleunigen)* to accelerate, to speed up, *(Markt)* to force, to strain, to push;
Arbeitstempo ~ to step up the rate of work; **Exportgeschäft** ~ to push exports; **Produktion** ~ to step (ginger) up production; **Projekt** ~ to push up a project (scheme); **Tempo** ~ to speed up.

forciert strained, unnatural.

Förder|abgaben mining royalties; ~**anlage** conveyer, conveyor, conveying plant, *(Bergwerk)* hauling plant; ~**ausfall** decline in production; ~**bahn** waggonway, roadway, *(Bergbau)* tramway; ~**band** conveyor belt, band (belt) conveyor, production line; ~**bandstrecke** belt conveyer road; ~**beitrag** *(Parteiwesen)* political contribution; ~**eimer** bucket.

Förderer furtherer, fosterer, booster *(coll.)*, patron, promoter, protector, friend, favo(u)rer, *(Rundfunk)* sponsor, *(technisch)* conveyor, transporter;
~ **der schönen Künste** patron of the fine arts.

Förder|ergebnis production [mining] output; ~**gebiet** development area (district) *(Br.)*, special area *(Br.)*; ~**geleise** haulage track; ~**gemeinschaft** [etwa] benefit society *(Br.)*; ~**gerät** conveyer, conveyor; ~**gerüst** headgear, pithead; ~**geschwindigkeit** conveying speed; ~**gremium** sponsoring body; ~**kapazität** production capacity; ~**kette** conveyor chain; ~**klasse** [etwa] remedial class; ~**kohle** run of mine coal; ~**korb** cage; ~**kreis für A.** group for the common cause of A.; ~**kübel** conveyer bucket; ~**leistung** conveying capacity, [delivery] output, production.

förderlich wholesome, advantageous, conducive;
jds. Interessen ~ **sein** to be beneficial to s. one's interests.

Fördermaschine winder.

Fördermenge flow, mass, delivery volume, *(Bergbau)* output, tonnage;
vereinbarte ~ miner's weight.

fordern to claim, to demand, to request, to require, to call, to exact, to arrogate;
j. ~ to challenge s. o.; **Entschädigung** ~ to claim compensation; **schnelle Entscheidungen** ~ to call for quick decisions; **Erklärung** ~ to demand an explanation; **kurze Fristverlängerung** ~ to request a short delay; **Gehorsam** ~ to exact obedience; **Lohnerhöhung** ~ to stand (stick out) for higher wages; **Preis** ~ to charge (ask) a price; **zu hohen Preis von jem.** ~ to ask too much of s. o.; **von jem. Rechenschaft** ~ to call s. o. to account; **sein Recht** ~ to claim one's right; **Schadensersatz** ~ to demand damages, to claim compensation for a loss; **zusätzlich** ~ to demand in addition ([as] extra); **zuviel** ~ to overcharge.

fördern to further, to promote, to encourage, to bring forward, to advance, to develop, to foment, to push, to patron, to patronize, to boost, to foster, to help, *(Bergbau)* to haul, to mine, to produce, to win, to extract, *(beschleunigen)* to speed up, to accelerate, to expedite, *(Rundfunksendung)* to sponsor, *(technisch)* to convey, to deliver;
Absatz ~ to increase (promote) the sale of goods, to push one's business; **jds. Aufstieg mit allen Mitteln** ~ to groom s. o. for advancement; **Ausfuhr** ~ to boost exports; **jds. Bestrebungen** ~ to encourage s. one's endeavo(u)rs; **Beziehungen zwischen zwei Staaten** ~ to promote good feelings (cultivate the friendship) between two states; **Entstehung der Schwerindustrie** ~ to foster the growth of heavy industries; **Freundschaft** ~ to foster friendship; **Gesundheit** ~ to be conducive to health; **Handelsverkehr** ~ to facilitate trade; **Idee** ~ to advocate an idea; **Industrie** ~ to encourage industry; **jds. Interessen** ~ to further s. one's interests; **Investitionsvorhaben** ~ to promote investments; **völlig unbekannten Kandidaten** ~ to promote s. o. from the shadows; **j. in seiner beruflichen Laufbahn** ~ to advance s. o. in his career; **Monopol** ~ to foster a monopoly; **Plan** ~ to promote a scheme; **jds. Pläne** ~ to forward s. one's plans; **Projekt** ~ to push up a scheme; **Sache des Friedens** ~ to further the cause of peace; **steuerlich** ~ to assist by fiscal policy; **j. durch ein Stipendium** ~ to put s. o. on a foundation; **Studenten** ~ to make a grant to a student; **jds. Studien** ~ to encourage s. one's studies; **Tourismus** ~ to promote tourism; **Unternehmen** ~ to encourage an enterprise; **zutage** ~ to bring to light.

fördernd promotive, promotional;
~**es Mitglied** paying member; ~**e Saisontendenz** upward seasonal trend.

Förder|plattform oil platform; ~**schacht** hoisting shaft; ~**schicht** production shift; ~**schranke** conveyer; ~**seil** hoisting cable, hauling rope; ~**sohle** winding level, plane, roadway; ~**stollen** adit; ~**strecke** haulage way, roadway, plane; ~**tätigkeit** sponsorship; ~**turm** winding tower, hoist frame, hoisting gear, headgear.

Forderung call, demand, postulation, requirement, *(Anspruch)* claim, title, debt, *(Bedingung)* stipulation, *(mil.)* requisition, *(Preisforderung)* charge;
abgetretene ~ assigned claim (debt); **ältere** ~ anterior claim; **anerkannte** ~ acknowledged (allowed) claim, debt by special contract, *(Versicherungsgesellschaft)* admitted claim; **im Feststellungsverfahren anerkannte** ~ debt on record, judgment debt; **im Konkursverfahren anerkannte** ~ proved debt; **angebliche** ~ pretended claim; **anmeldefähige** ~ provable claim (debt); **im Konkurs anmeldefähige** ~ debt provable in bankruptcy; **ausgeklagte** ~ judgement debt; **aussonderungsfähige** ~ colo(u)rable claim, claim of exemption *(US)*; **bedingte** ~ contingent claim; **bevorzugt zu befriedigende** ~ preferential (preferred) debt (claim); **befristete** ~ deferred claim; **ziffernmäßig nicht begrenzte** ~ unlimited claim; **begründete** ~ legitimate (sound) claim; **vertraglich begründete** ~ debt founded on contract (upon a written instrument), simple debt; **nicht beitreibbare** ~ unenforceable claim; **berechtigte** ~ legal demand, equitable (rightful) claim; **dinglich besicherte** ~ debt covered by a security; **bestrittene** ~ disputed claim; **bevorrechtigte** ~ *(Konkursverfahren)* secured (preferential, preferred) debt, prior (preference, preferential, priority) claim, claim entitled to priority, *(Nachlaßverfahren)* privileged debt; **nicht bevorrechtigte** ~ simple (unsecured, ordinary) debt, nonprovable claim; **bezifferte** ~ liquidated demand; **billige** ~ reasonable demand, equity; **blockierte** ~ blocked debt;

buchmäßige ~ book claim; nicht durchgesetzte ~ dormant claim; eingefrorene ~ frozen (blocked) debt; einklagbare ~ legal debt, debt at law, recoverable claim; nicht einklagbare ~ debt dead in law; vertraglich entstandene ~ simple debt; durch betrügerische Machenschaften entstandene ~ fraudulent debt; erdichtete ~ fictitious claim, simulated debt; erfundene ~ bogus claim; leichtfertig erhobene ~ frivolous claim; erloschene ~ extinct claim; stets erneuerte ~ continual claim; fällige ~ pure debt, debt due, existing debt, matured claim; sofort fällige ~ liquid debt; festgestellte ~ liquidated demand, (durch Gericht) judgment debt, debt of record, (Konkurs) proved debt; fingierte ~ simulated debt, bogus claim; gegenwertige und künftige ~ debt owing and accruing; geldähnliche ~ near money (US sl.), quasi money (US); geldwerte ~ monetary claim; gepfändete ~ garnished debt; gesicherte ~ secured debt (claim), money secured; durch Grundpfandrecht gesicherte ~ hypothecary debt; hypothekarisch gesicherte ~ mortgage claim; gesperrte ~ blocked debt; getilgte ~ debt paid; gewöhnliche ~ (im Konkurs) simple debt; gültige ~ existing debt; hartnäckige ~ persistent demand; hochgeschraubte ~ exaggerated demand; hypothekarische ~ mortgage claim, hypothecary debt; kurzfristige ~ short-term debt; laufende ~ current account; im Range nachgehende ~ subordinated debt; nachgewiesene ~ (Konkurs) proved debt; [noch] nicht nachgewiesene ~ unsubstantiated claim; nachweisbare ~ provable debt; nicht nachweisbare ~ nonprovable claim (debt); privilegierte ~ preferential (preferred) debt, (Nachlaßverfahren) privileged debt; jederzeit realisierbare ~ solvent debt; rückständige ~ debt in arrears; sichere ~ good debt; sichergestellte ~ secured debt; strittige ~ disputed claim; [noch] nicht substantiierte ~ unsubstantiated claim; territoriale ~ revindication; nicht übertragbare ~ nonassignable claim; übertriebene ~ exaggerated demand (exaction); unbedingte ~ noncontingent claim; unbegründete ~ false claim, nonprovable debt; unberechtigte ~ unfounded claim; der Höhe nach unbestimmte ~ unliquidated demand; uneinbringliche ~ bad debt, desperate debt, irrecoverable claim; ungedeckte ~ unsecured debt; ungesicherte ~ unsecured claim; unklare ~ vague demand; unmäßige ~ exorbitant (unreasonable) demand; unsichere ~ doubtful (bad, US) debt; unverschämte ~ steep demand; unverzinsliche ~ passive (noninterest-bearing) debt; notariell verbriefte ~ debt by special contract, specialty (bonded) debt; verjährte ~ debt barred by the Statute of Limitations, statute-barred claim, outlawed obligation (claim, US); fast verjährte ~ stale debt (demand, US); verzinsliche ~ interest-bearing debt, active debt; vollstreckbare ~ judgment debt, enforceable claim; vorrangige ~ preferred (preferential) debt, claim entitled to priority; wucherische ~ excessive charge; zukünftige ~ future debt; zulässige ~ allowable claim; hinsichtlich des Rechtsanspruchs zweifelhafte ~ doubtful (Br.) (bad, US) debt;

~ für geleistete Dienste service charge; ~ der Gerechtigkeit call of justice; ~ nach Lohnerhöhung wage demand; ~ auf angemessene Vergütung quantum meruit claim;

~ abbuchen to wipe off a debit balance; ~ abgeben to discharge a debt; ~ ablehnen to run down a claim; uneinbringliche ~ abschreiben to charge off a debt; zweifelhafte ~ abschreiben to write off a doubtful claim (Br.) (bad debt, US); von einer ~ abstehen to renounce a claim; ~ abtreten to assign a claim (debt), to cede (make over) a debt; ~ abweisen to disallow a claim; ~ anerkennen to admit (allow) a claim; ~ nicht anerkennen to disallow a claim; jds. ~ widerspruchslos anerkennen to allow s. one's claim without question; ~ anmelden to lodge a proof of (report a) debt, to lodge (prove, file) a claim; ~ beim Konkursverwalter (zur Konkurstabelle) anmelden to lodge a proof of debt with the official receiver, to lodge a proof in bankruptcy; ~ aufgeben to abandon a claim; ~ aufstellen to set a requirement; ~ beanstanden to demur to a claim; ~ befriedigen to pay (satisfy) a claim; ~ belegen to prove a debt; auf einer ~ bestehen to press a claim, to stand by one's (persist in a) demand; unbarmherzig auf seiner ~ bestehen to have one's pound of flesh; ~ bestreiten to put a claim in issue, to impugn (disallow, contest) a claim; [Gültigkeit seiner] ~ beweisen to support (make good) one's claim, to prove a debt; unverschämte ~ darstellen to be highway robbery; ~ durchsetzen to enforce a demand, to settle a claim; ~ einklagen to litigate (prosecute) a claim, to take legal proceedings for the recovery of a debt, to file a claim in court; ~ im eigenen Namen einklagen to sue on a debt in one's own name; ~ einreichen to make (enter) a claim, to lay (lodge) claim to; ~ beim Konkursverwalter einreichen to lodge a proof of debt with the official receiver; ~ eintreiben to collect a claim; ~ erfüllen to answer (satisfy) a claim; ~ erheben to lodge (raise, vindicate) a claim; ~ auf etw. erheben to lay claim to (set up a claim for) s. th.; Verjährungseinwand gegen eine ~ erheben to bar a debt by the Statute of Limitations; ~ erlassen to release (remit) a claim; ~ in bestimmte Redewendungen kleiden to couch a demand in certain terms; ~ fallen lassen to drop a demand, to abandon a claim; ~ verjähren lassen to outlaw a debt; ~ gegen j. geltend machen to claim s. th. from (prefer a claim against) s. o.; ~ gerichtlich geltend machen to file a claim in court; ~ nachlassen to remit (reduce) a claim; ~nachweisen to prove a debt (claim); ~ im Gesellschaftskonkurs nachweisen to prove a debt in liquidation; von einer ~ Abstand nehmen to relinquish a claim; ~ pfänden to arrest (attach) a debt, to trustee (US); ~ beim Drittschuldner pfänden [lassen] to garnish, to institute garnishee proceedings; ~ reduzieren to reduce a claim; ~ regulieren to settle a claim; jds. ~ in Abrede stellen to repudiate s. one's claim; ~ substantiieren to qualify a claim, to substantiate a charge; ~ auf j. übertragen to transfer a claim upon s. o.; ~ umreißen to stake out a claim; auf eine ~ verzichten to resign (quit, renounce) a claim, to recede from a demand; jem. eine ~ über £ 5000 vorlegen to lodge with s. o. a claim for £ 5000; ~ zulassen to admit (allow) a claim; ~ zurückweisen to turn down a claim.

Forderungen (Bilanz) debts (Br.), debtors (Br.), accounts receivable (US), receivables (US);

zum Ausgleich aller ~ in full settlement;

abgetretene ~ (Bilanz) pledged accounts receivables (US); ausstehende ~ active (outstanding) debts, arrears, accounts receivable (US); bedingte ~ contingent receivables (US); nicht bevorrechtigte ~ ordinary debts; buchmäßige ~ book debts; diverse ~ (Bilanz) sundry debtors, sundries; dubiose ~ doubtful (Br.) (bad, US) debts (notes and accounts, US), doubtful accounts; eingefrorene ~ frozen debts; eingegangene, schon abgeschriebene ~ bad debts collected (US); im Nebenprozeß eingeklagte ~ debts on mesne process; entstandene, aber noch nicht fällige ~ accrued income (receivable accounts, US), accruals receivable (US); durch betrügerische Machenschaften entstandene ~ fraudulent debts; fällige ~ debts due; täglich fällige ~ claims payable on demand; gegenseitige ~ mutual debts (demands); gegenwärtige und zukünftige ~ debts owing or accruing; dinglich gesicherte ~ debts covered by a security; hypothekarisch gesicherte ~ mortgage receivables (US); hartnäckige ~ importunate claims; hochgeschraubte ~ exaggerated claims; künftige, noch nicht fällige ~ deferred accounts receivable (US); kurzfristige ~ (Bilanz) liquid (current) assets; lohnfremde ~ nonwage demands; maßlose ~ unreasonable demands; rückständige ~ arrears; sonstige ~ (Bilanz) sundry debtors, other accounts receivable (US); übertriebene ~ exaggerated claims; uneinbringliche ~ irrecoverable (bad, US) debts, uncollectible receivables (US); ungewisse ~ contingent receivables (US); verschiedene ~ (Bilanz) sundry debtors, sundries; vorrangige ~ debts having priority; zweifelhafte ~ (Bilanzkonto) reserve for bad debts;

~ am Ende eines Rechnungsabschnittes period-end receivables (US); ~ an Konzernunternehmen due from affiliates; ~ an Kreditinstitute claims on credit institutions; ~ aus gewährten Krediten accounts receivable resulting from loans (US); ~ an Kunden (Bankbilanz) receivables from customers (US), trade-account receivables (US), uncollected debts; ~ aus Lieferungen und Leistungen accounts receivable for sales and services (US); ~ der Mehrheit majority demand; ~ gegen einen Nachlaß demands on an estate; unsinnige ~ im Rahmen eines Manteltarifvertrages blue-sky bargaining; ~ aus laufender Rechnung debts founded on open account; ~ an verbundene Unternehmen accounts receivable from affiliates (US); ~ und Verbindlichkeiten (Bilanz) debtors and creditors, receivables and payables (US); ~ aufgrund von Warenlieferungen (Bilanz) debts founded on merchantable goods, trade accounts receivable (US), trade debtors;

von seinen ~ abgehen to withdraw one's claims; staatliche ~ ablehnen to balk government demands; uneinbringliche ~ abschreiben to charge (write) off doubtful (Br.) (bad, US) debts; gegenseitige ~ ausgleichen to set off claims; ~ bewerten to evaluate claims; ~ einklagen to sue for debts; ~ eintreiben to pull in cash; seine ~ zu Recht erheben to act within one's rights by claiming; seine ~ ermäßigen to moderate one's claims; ~ herunterschrauben (mäßigen) to modify (moderate) one's demands; seine ~ geltend machen to enforce one's claims; ~ nachgeben to give in to demands; groteske ~ stellen to set up ridiculous pretensions; massive ~ an j. stellen to put a bomb on

s. o.; **übertriebene ~ stellen** to exaggerate one's claims; **gegenseitige ~ verrechnen** to set off claims; **seine ~ schriftlich vorbringen** to put down one's demands in writing; **~ der Opposition vorwegnehmen** to preempt opposition demands; **in seinen ~ radikaler werden** to become more insistant in one's demands; **~ zedieren** to assign claims.

Förderung promotion, furtherance, patronage, advancement, development, facilitation, encouragement, fosterage, boost, aid, *(Fördermenge)* mining output, production, *(Güter)* conveyance, haulage, *(Unterstützung)* support, assistance, aid, *(Zuschuß)* grant;
berufliche ~ career advancement (development); **betriebliche ~** corporate promotion *(US)*, in-service training; **staatliche ~** government promotion, grant;
~ des Absatzes sales promotion; **~ der Auswanderung** encouragement of emigration; **staatliche ~ der Bedürftigen** public (social) assistance to needy persons; **~ des Bildungswesens** advancement of education; **~ der Ersparnisbildung** promotion of savings; **~ des Exports** boost to exports, boosting of exports, export promotion; **~ der Forschung** research assistance; **~ der Freundschaft zwischen zwei Staaten** cultivation of friendship between two states; **~ des Führungsnachwuchses** promotion of prospective managers; **~ zurückgebliebener Gemeindegrundstücke** community development; **~ von Handel und Verkehr** promotion of trade and transport; **~ des Handelsverkehrs** facilitation of trade; **~ der Industrie** encouragement of industries; **~ von Investitionsvorhaben** investment promotion; **~ eines Kohlenbergwerks** output of a colliery; **~ der schönen Künste** encouragement of the arts; **~ eines Künstlers** sponsorship of an artist; **~ des Nachwuchses** promotion of prospective managers; **~ des Tourismus** promotion of tourism; **~ des Verkaufs** commercial development; **~ der Wirtschaft** promotion of industries; **~ der Wissenschaften** promotion of science; **~ des Wohnungsbaus** development of housing;
~ den Absatzmöglichkeiten anpassen to match output to the absorption; **~ beantragen** to put in a claim for a grant; **zur ~ der Wissenschaft beitragen** to contribute to the advancement of science; **staatliche ~ erfahren** to be state-sponsored; **~ von seiten seiner Vorgesetzten erfahren** to receive encouragement from one's superiors; **~ steigern** to increase the production (output); **~ verdienen** to merit promotion.

Forderungsabtretung assignation (assignment) of claim, assignment of choses in action, assignment of accounts receivable *(US)*;
formlose ~ equitable assignment; **offene ~** absolute assignment; **stille ~** equitable assignment, nonnotification plan;
~ in stiller Form equitable assignment, nonnotification plan; **~ offenlegen** to operate on a notification basis; **~ in stiller Form vornehmen** to operate on a nonnotification basis.

Forderungs|abschreibung writing off of doubtful *(Br.)* (bad, *US*) debts; **~abtretungsvertrag** assignment agreement; **~anerkennung** allowance of a claim; **~ankauf mit bis zur Fälligkeit aufgeschobener Auszahlung** maturity factoring.

Forderungsanmeldung filing of claim, *(im Konkursverfahren)* proof of claim (debts);
zur ~ eine Frist setzen to limit time to make proof of claim.

Forderungsaufkauf purchase of accounts receivable *(US)*.

Förderungsausbildung advanced training.

Forderungsbefriedigung settlement of an account, satisfaction of a claim;
vergleichsweise ~ compounding of claims.

forderungsberechtigt entitled to a claim;
als ~ aufgeführt werden to rank as creditor.

Forderungs|berechtigter claimant, creditor, obligee, *(Versicherungspolice)* beneficiary; **~bestand** amount of claims, *(Bilanz)* debts *(Br.)*, accounts receivable *(US)*; **~betrag** amount to be claimed; **~einziehung, ~einzug** collection of debts (of a claim).

Förderungsgemeinschaft syndicate.

Forderungsinhaber holder of a debt (claim);
gutgläubiger ~ bona-fide holder.

Förderungs|kauf purchase of accounts receivable *(US)*; **~kontingent** output quota; **~kredit** reconstruction credit, rehabilitation loan, pump-priming credit *(US)*; **~kursus** upgrading course; **~maßnahmen** promotional activities (measures), support measures; **energische ~maßnahmen** promotional push; **öffentliche ~maßnahme** government promotion; **~mittel revolvierend einsetzen** to recycle aid; **~nachweis** proving (proof, statement of) debts, claim check; **~nachweis im Konkursverfahren** proof in bankruptcy; **~pfandgläubiger** garnisher.

Forderungspfändung garnishment, garnishee execution, order of attachment, extent in aid, arrest (attachment) of a debt, trustee process *(US)*;
~ durchführen to garnish, to trustee *(US)*.

Forderungspfändungs|beschluß garnishee order; **~verfahren** garnishee proceedings, trustee process *(US)*.

Förderungs|plan *(Produktion)* target; **~prämie für Ausfuhren in den Dollarraum** dollar premium *(Br.)*; **~programm** promotional program(me), program(me) of achievement; **~quantum** *(Bergbau)* rate of extraction.

Forderungsrecht chose in action, legal claim;
gesetzliche ~e lawful (legal) things in action.

Förderungssystem promotional system.

Forderungs|teilbetrag portion of a claim; **~tilgung** settlement of a claim.

Forderungsübergang assignment (transmission) of claim;
automatischer ~ automatic assignment; **gesetzlicher ~** statutory (legal) assignment, legal subrogation;
~ kraft Gesetzes legal subrogation, assignment by operation of law, involuntary transfer; **~ auf den Konkursverwalter** assignment in bankruptcy; **~ im Todesfall** assignment on death.

Forderungsübernehmer assignee in law, assign.

Forderungsübertragung assignment (assignation) of claim;
gesetzliche ~ transfer by operation of law;
~ auf den Konkursverwalter assignment for the benefit of creditors.

Forderungs|umschlag accounts receivables turnover *(US)*; **~umschlagziffer** collection ratio; **~untergang kraft Gesetzes** release by operation of law; **~verzeichnis** *(Konkursmasse)* schedule of a bankrupt's estate; **~verzicht** remission of a claim.

Förderungswille beneficial intention.

förderungswürdig sein to deserve promotion.

Forderungs|zessionar equitable assignee; **~zinsen** interest earned.

Förderungszuschlag incentive bonus.

Förder|unterricht remedial instruction; **~wagen** *(Bergbau)* tram, truck, lorry, mine car, tub; **~ziffer** production figure.

Form form, design, mode, fashion, figure, *(drucktechn.)* mould, mold *(US)*, *(Förmlichkeit)* formality, *(Gestalt)* shape, frame, *(Modell)* model, type, *(Umgangsformen)* manners, behavio(u)r;
in ~ in good fettle; **in abgekürzter ~** in abridged form, abridged; **in der im folgenden rechtlich festgelegten ~** in the form hereinafter set forth; **in gehöriger (gültiger) ~** in due form, formal; **in konzentrierter ~** in tabloid form; **in mündlicher ~** orally, by word of mouth, verbally; **in neuzeitlicher ~** *(Möbel)* in contemporary designs; **in notarieller ~** before a notary; **in rechtsgültiger ~** in due form [of law]; **nicht der allgemein anerkannten ~ entsprechend** nonstandard; **nicht ganz in ~** a little off form; **nicht in vorgeschriebener ~ abgefaßt** informal, irregular;
feierliche ~ solemn form; **gängige ~** conventional design; **gehörige ~** requisite form; **gesellschaftliche ~** form; **gesetzliche ~** solemn form; **vorgeschriebene ~** formality; **gesetzlich vorgeschriebene ~** statutory (legal) form, form required by law;
~en des Anstandes proprieties; **neue ~en des Familienlebens** new patterns of family life; **teuerste ~ der Kreditaufnahme** peak cost of borrowing; **~ einer gerichtlichen Verfügung** frame of a writ;
Einkommensteuer in notarieller ~ abgeben to notarize an income tax declaration; **in notarieller ~ abschließen** to notarize; **allmählich ~ annehmen** to begin to take shape; **feste ~en annehmen** to crystal(l)ize; **gefährliche ~en annehmen** to assume a dangerous character; **in verschiedenen ~en auftreten** to appear in various forms; **in aller ~ benachrichtigen** to give due notice; **sich in aller ~ bewerben** to file an application with full career details; **j. in aller ~ um Entschuldigung bitten** to make a formal apology to s. o.; **Bruch auf die einfachste ~ bringen** to reduce a fraction to its lowest terms; **in die richtige ~ bringen** to lick into shape; **schriftliche ~ erfordern** to require written evidence; **konkrete ~ geben** to embody; **einer Sache feste ~ geben** to give shape to s. th.; **gewinnende ~en haben** to have winning manners; **sehr auf ~en halten** to be very observant of form; **um der ~ zu genügen handeln** to do s. th. for form's safe; **sich über alle ~en hinwegsetzen** to defy conventions; **an ~en kleben** to be a slave to convention; **zu sehr auf ~en Wert legen** to pay too much attention to form; **~ schließen** to lock up a form; **in guter und gehöriger ~ sein** to be in good and due form; **nicht in ~ sein** to be not up to the mark;

schwer in ~ (in blendender ~) sein to be at one's best, to be in capital (crashing, *US*) form; **die ~en wahren** to observe the proprieties; **in notarieller ~ abgeschlossen werden** to be concluded before a notary; **in kürzester ~ zusammenfassen** to put it in a nutshell.

formal formal;
nur ~ on paper;
~e Ausbildung *(mil.)* drill; **~er Einwand** technical objection; **in ~er Hinsicht** formally; **~e Unterschiede** differences in form; **~er Verfahrensverstoß** legal irregularity.

Formal|antrag formal motion; **~beleidigung** defamatory per se, verbal injury, abusive language; **~delikt** technical offence; **~einwand** technical traverse, special exception.

Formalien formalities.

Formalist formalist, stickler for etiquette.

formalistisch formalistic.

Formalität formality, form;
ohne ~ free and easy, shirt-sleeve;
~en circumstances, formalities;
bedeutungslose ~ empty formality, mere form; **gerichtliche ~en** forms of a court; **gesetzliche ~en** legal formalities; **leere ~en** dead forms; **reine ~en** empty formalities, mere forms; **vom Zoll vorgeschriebene ~en** customs formalities;
nicht auf ~en bestehen to be no stickler for formalities; **vorgeschriebene ~en erfüllen** to comply with all necessary formalities; **auf ~en verzichten** to dispense with formalities.

formalrechtlich in accordance with the letter of the law.

Formal|rüge *(Prozeß)* special exception; **~vertrag** formal (standard) contract.

Format format, size, *(fig.)* caliber, calibre *(Br.)*;
auf ~ geschnitten cut to size; **von internationalem ~** of international calibre; **von mittlerem ~** medium-sized; **ungewöhnliches ~** unusual size;
~ haben to be a man of caliber (calibre, *Br.*); **Schriftsteller von internationalem ~ sein** to be a writer of international distinction; **nicht über das ~ verfügen** to be short of stature;
~änderung *(Werbung)* rescale.

Formation *(mil.)* formation, unit;
aufgelockerte ~ *(mil.)* dispersed formation.

Formationsflug formation flight (flying), fly-over.

formbedürftiger Vertrag specialty (formal) contract.

formbeständig shape-retaining.

Form|blatt [printed] form, blank *(US)*, schedule; **~einrichtung** imposition.

Formel form, formula;
rettende ~ saving formula; **stereotype ~n** hackneyed formulas; **~ für Lohnerhöhungen** loan increase formula;
auf eine ~ bringen to formulate; **eine für alle Beteiligten annehmbare ~ finden** to find a formula acceptable to all parties;
~buch formulary.

formelhafte Wendungen set phrases.

formell formal, full-dress, trig;
~ und materiell gültig valid in form and fact;
Behauptung ~ dementieren to give a formal denial to a statement; **sehr ~ sein** to stand on one's dignity (on ceremony); **sehr ~ empfangen werden** to get a stiff reception; **Behauptung ~ zurückziehen** to retract a statement;
~er Antrag formal application; **~er Besuch** formal call; **~er Briefabschluß** formal close; **~es Dementi** formal denial; **aus ~en Gründen** as a matter of form, for the sake of formality; **~e Quittung** formal receipt; **~es Recht** adjective law.

Formelsammlung formulary, collection of formulas.

formen to put into shape, to shape out, to compose, to form, to mould, to mold *(US)*, *(Worte)* to frame;
jds. Charakter ~ to mould (form) s. one's character; **junge Menschen ~** to mould young people; **nach einem Vorbild ~** to form from a model.

Formen|erfordernisse formal requirements; **~kram** formalities; **~mensch** formalist, stickler for formalities; **reiner ~mensch sein** to be a slave to convention; **~reichtum** abundance (wealth) of forms; **~vereinheitlichung** standardization of forms; **~wesen** formalism.

Formfehler defect of form, flaw, formal defect, irregularity, *(fig.)* blunder, faux pas, *(Wechsel)* irregularity, informality;
wegen eines ~s im Giro on account of an irregularity in the indorsement;
~ in der Ausstellung irregularly drawn;
~ einer Urkunde durch Gerichtsbeschluß abändern lassen to reform a deed; **~ im Beschlußwege heilen** to vote to waive an irregularity.

Formfrage matter of form.

formfrei informal;
~er Vertrag informal contract.

Formfreiheit informality.

Formgebung, gewerbliche (industrielle) industrial design, styling.

Formgebungsausschuß Council of Industrial Designs *(Br.)*.

formgerecht in due (the proper) form, duly.

Formgestalter industrial designer, designer of patterns.

formgewandt polished, refined, urbane.

formidabel terrific, tremendous.

formieren *(drucktechn.)* to make up in pages, *(mil.)* to troop;
sich ~ *(Menschenmenge)* to form up, to form into rank, *(mil.)* to form (draw) up, to fall (form) into line.

formierte Gesellschaft aligned society.

Formkasten moulding box;
im ~ festmachen to lock up.

förmlich conventional, formal, ceremonious, ceremonial, official, *(pedantisch)* punctilious, *(Vertrag)* in due form, *(vorgeschrieben)* formulary;
j. ~ begrüßen to welcome s. o. ceremoniously; **~ dementieren** to issue a formal denial; **Zeitung dem Verkäufer ~ aus der Hand reißen** to tear a newspaper virtually out of a newsdealer's hand; **~ zu etw. gezwungen sein** to be literally forced to do s. th.; **~ auf etw. versessen sein** to be absolutely set on (crazy for) s. th.;
~er Anlaß ceremonial occasion; **~er Aufstand** regular row; **~er Empfang** stiff reception; **~e Eröffnungssitzung** formal opening sitting; **~e Erpressung** literary (tantamount to) blackmail; **~e Ladung** summons; **~e Quittung** formal receipt; **~er Vertrag** specialty contract; **~er Wahnsinn sein** to be sheer madness; **~e Zustellung** service of process; **~e Zustimmung geben** to give one's consent.

Förmlichkeit formality, form, primness, *(Feierlichkeit)* solemnity, *(Pedanterie)* punctiliousness, circumstance;
in aller ~ in due and proper form; **ohne ~** without fuss;
bloße ~ mere formality;
~en eines Verfahrens legal technicalities;
sehr auf ~en aus sein to be a stickler for formalities; **auf ~en verzichten** to dispense with formalities.

formlos formless, without shape or form, *(Antrag)* not specific, *(nicht feierlich)* unsolemn, informal, unceremonious, *(unkonventionell)* casual, unconventional;
~e Abendgesellschaft quiet dinner party; **~er Vertrag** agreement under hand, parole agreement.

Formlosigkeit lack of form, informality.

Formmangel informality, irregularity, want of form, lack of form, formal defect;
~ heilen to cure a defect of form;
~heilung *(Hypothekenbestellung)* graft.

Formrahmen *(drucktechn.)* chase.

Formsache formality, matter of form, routine;
reine (lediglich eine) ~ a mere matter of form, merely a formality;
reine ~ sein to be only routine.

formschön beautifully designed, stylish.

Form|stahl structural steel; **~strenge** strict observance of form.

Formular [set] form, printed form, blank *(US)*, schedule;
gedrucktes ~ printed form; **unausgefülltes ~** blank, printed form, *(Wechsel)* skeleton bill; **vorgeschriebenes ~** regulation form;
~ für die Einkommensteuererklärung income-tax return blank *(US)*; **~ für gleichzeitige Ein- und Auszahlungen** exchange slip *(Br.)*;
~ ausfüllen to fill in *(Br.)* (up, to complete, to execute) a form, to fill out a blank *(US)*;
~ausfüllung completion of form, form filling; **~brief** form letter; **~buch** paper (precedent) book, formulary.

formularmäßig according to printed form.

Formular|muster specimen form; **~sammlung** book of [printed] forms; **~satz** set of forms, *(Setzen)* forms composition; **vollständiger ~satz** *(Konnossement)* complete set; **~streifen** *(Bankwesen)* slip; **~unwesen** paper war; **~vertrag** standard contract; **~wesen** paperwork.

formulieren to formulate, to formularize, to word, to draft, to verbalize, to couch, to phrase;
etw. anders ~ to put it differently; **Antwort unverschämt ~** to couch a reply in insolent terms; **Erklärung ~** to shape a statement; **seine Gedanken ~** to formulate one's thoughts; **knapp ~** to word precisely; **Passage neu ~** to reword a passage; **Satz ~** to frame a sentence; **sorgfältig ~** to phrase (word) carefully; **Textstelle neu ~** to reword a passage; **Vertrag ~** to

draw up a contract; **Vorbehalt** ~ to make reservations, to stipulate a reserve; **Vorschrift neu** ~ to reword a regulation; **seine Worte klar** ~ to enunciate one's words clearly.

formuliert, geschickt well-turned.

Formulierung formulation, [form of] wording, drafting, drawing up, stipulation, embodiment, verbalization, stipulation;
anerkannte ~ common form; **kristallklare** ~ crystal-clear formulation; **letztwillige** ~**en** precatory expressions; **ungenaue** ~ uncertainty of words; **unklare** ~ obscure formulation; **unpräzise** ~ loose wording; **zutreffende** ~ apt words;
~ **eines Absatzes** drafting of a section; ~ **eines Entschließungsentwurfs** draft of a resolution; ~ **eines Grundsatzes** enunciation of a doctrine; ~ **eines Vertrages** wording of a contract; ~ **eines Vorbehalts** stipulation of a reserve;
für alle annehmbare ~ **finden** to find a formula acceptable for all parties.

Formulierungs|ausschuß commission to codify; ~**fehler** faulty drafting; ~**kunst** draftsmanship, draughtsmanship.

formvollendet *(Stil)* well-rounded, of perfect shape, perfectly shaped;
sich ~ **verbeugen** to bow with perfect elegance.

Formvordruck blank form.

Formvorschrift formality, formal requirement (rule);
~**en eines Pachtvertrages** formalities of a lease;
gesetzliche ~**en** legal requirements.

formwidrig informal, contrary to form, irregular.

Formzwang mandatary clause *(US)*.

forsch vigorous, energetic, robust, *(schneidig)* smart, dashing;
Sache ~ **angehen** to go at it vigorously; ~ **auftreten** to go it, to show plenty of dash;
~**er Fahrer** peppy driver *(US)*; ~**er Kerl** dashing fellow.

forschen to research, to do research work;
in alten Papieren ~ to rummage among old papers; **in alten Urkunden** ~ to search through old records; **nach jds. Verbleib** ~ to inquire about s. one's whereabouts.

forschender Blick scrutinizing (searching) look.

Forscher research worker, researcher;
als ~ **tätig sein** to be engaged in research;
~**gruppe** research unit.

Forschung research, science, exploration, advanced study;
angewandte ~ applied research; **außerbetriebliche** ~ external research; **betriebswissenschaftliche** ~ business research; **mit Verteidigungsaufträgen finanzierte** ~ defence-funded research; **wissenschaftliche** ~ scientific research; **zweckfreie** ~ pure research;
~ **für Vorhaben im großen Stil** big science;
in die ~ **gehen** to do research work.

Forschungs|abteilung research (experimental) department, research arm *(US)*; ~**amt** Committee for Scientific and Industrial Research *(Br.)*; ~- **und Archivamt** research and documentation center *(US)* (centre, *Br.*); ~**anlagen** research facilities; ~**anstalt** research establishment; ~**arbeit** research work, field study; ~**arbeit auf dem gleichen Gebiet** research work on parallel lines; **wissenschaftliche** ~**arbeit betreiben** to study and research; ~**arbeiten** exploration work; ~**aufgabe** research assignment; ~**aufgaben auf dem Verteidigungssektor** defence research; **sich an den** ~**aufgaben aktiv beteiligen** to take an active part in the research program(me); ~**auftrag** research assignment (contract); ~**aufwand** spending on research, cost of exploration, research expenditure (effort); ~**ausgaben** research expenditure; ~**basis** scientific outpost; ~**beihilfe** research grant; ~**bericht** research report; ~**dienst** research service; ~**einrichtungen** research organization; ~**ergebnisse** research material (findings); ~**etat** research budget; ~**gebiet** area of research, field of study; ~**gemeinschaft,** ~**gesellschaft** research association; ~**gruppe** research group (team); ~**hilfe** aid for research; ~**ingenieur** research (experimental) engineer; ~**institut** research institute (establishment); ~**institut für Verbraucherfragen** Research Institute for Consumers' Affairs; **in einem** ~**institut tätig sein** to be engaged in research work; ~**kosten** research expenditure; ~**kredit** fellowship; ~**laboratorium** research laboratory; ~**leiter** director of research; ~**minister** research minister, Minister of Science and Technology *(Br.)*; ~**ministerium** [etwa] Ministry of Technology (*Br.*, abolished 1970); ~**objekt** research base; ~**organisation** research organization; ~**programm** scientific research program(me); ~**projekt** research project; ~**rat** Council of Scientific and Industrial Research *(Br.)*, National Research Development Corporation *(US)*; ~**reaktor** research reactor; ~**reise** exploring expedition, exploratory voyage, voyage of exploration; ~**satellit** research satellite; ~**stätte** research establishment; ~**stelle** research unit (secretariat, center, *US*, centre, *Br.*); ~**stipendium** [research] scholarship, research studentship *(Br.)*; ~**tätigkeit** exploration work, research effort; **eigene** ~**tätigkeit** original research; ~**tätigkeit im Bereich der Betriebsführung** management science research; ~**unternehmen** research project; **gemeinsames** ~**unternehmen** joint research; ~**vorhaben** research project; ~**vorhaben auf dem Gebiet der Sonnenenergie** solar energy research; ~**wissenschaftler** research scientist; ~**zentrum** research center *(US)* (centre, *Br.*).

Forst forest, woodland;
~**akademie** forest (forestry) school; ~**amt** Commissioner of Woods and Forests; ~**amtmann** forest warden; ~**arbeit** forestcraft; ~**aufseher** woodreve *(Br.)*, forestkeeper, gamekeeper *(Br.)*, verderer, verderor *(Br.)*; ~**beamter** forest officer, forester; **landwirtschaftlicher** ~- **oder Fischereibetrieb** carrying out of agriculture, forestry or fishing operations; ~**bezirk** forest range beat.

Förster forester, gamekeeper *(Br.)*, forest officer (ranger, *US*).

Forst|erhaltung conservancy; ~**ertrag** yield of a forest; ~**fach** forestry; ~**fachmann** forester; ~**fahrzeug** forestry vehicle; ~**frevel** rape of the forest; ~**gebäude** forestry; ~**gericht** forest court, justice of the forest *(Br.)*, justice seat *(Br.)*, court of attachments; ~**gesetz** ordinance of the forest *(Br.)*; ~**polizei** forest sheriff.

forstpolizeiliche Bestimmungen forest regulations.

Forst|produkt forest product; ~**recht** forest laws; ~**schaden** forest damage; ~**schule** forest school; ~**schutz** forest protection; ~**schutzbeamter** forest guard; ~**verwalter** keeper of the forest; ~**verwaltung** forest administration (management); ~**wart** forest keeper (ranger, *US*), gamekeeper *(Br.)*; ~**wirtschaft** forest economics.

forstwirtschaftlicher Betrieb forestry industry, forestry company.

Forstwirtschaftsbetrieb forestry company.

fortan henceforth, henceforward, from this time onwards.

Fortbestand continued existence, continuance;
~ **einer Firma** continuance (continuation) of a business (firm);
~ **eines Staates** continuity of a state.

fortbestehen to continue, to subsist, to endure, *(Firma)* to be still in existence;
eigenständig ~ to survive on one's own.

fortbestehend standing;
~**es Interesse** continued interest.

fortbewegen to move;
sich auf Krücken ~ to go about on crutches; **sich langsam** ~ *(Verkehr)* to be reduced to a crawl; **sich im Schneckentempo** ~ to move at a snail's pace; **sich schwerfällig** ~ to lumber; **sich auf allen Vieren** ~ to walk on all fours; **sich nicht einen Zoll** ~ not to budge an inch.

Fortbewegung im Bodenverkehr transportation at ground.

Fortbewegungs|methode method of transport; ~**mittel** motive transport, vehicle.

fortbilden, sich to continue one's education, to improve one's knowledge; **sich in Abendkursen** ~ to attend evening classes; **sich in den Abendstunden** ~ to burn the midnight oil.

Fortbildung continued education, continuation schooling, advanced training, further education *(Br.)*;
berufliche ~ adult education, advanced vocational training, continuation of education (training); **betriebliche** ~ in-plant (-service) training, *(Führungskräfte)* executive training; **eigene** ~ self-development.

Fortbildungs|einrichtungen development service; ~**klasse** continuation class; ~**kosten** advancement costs; ~**kursus** extension (advanced training, placement, improvement) course, further education course *(Br.)*, *(Abendschule)* evening classes, *(für Lehrkräfte)* refresher course; **außerbetrieblicher** ~**kursus** out-of-company course; ~**lehrgang** continuation course; ~**möglichkeiten in der Freizeit** leisure education.

Fortbildungsprogramm development program(me);
betriebliches ~ manpower development program(me); **persönliches** ~ program(me) of personal development.

Fortbildungs|schule continuation (finishing, evening, night, *Br.*, county, part-time) school, college of further education, institution for higher education; ~**seminar** additional training seminar; ~**studium** postgraduate course; ~**unterricht** further education *(Br.)*; ~**unterricht besuchen** to join evening classes; ~**verein** mutual improvement society; **[berufliches]** ~**wesen** extension work.

Fortbleiben nonattendance.

fortbleiben to stay away;
von der Schule ~ to play truant.

fortbringen to take away, to bring off;
sich kümmerlich ~ to eke out a scanty living.
Fortdauer continuance, continuation, duration;
~ **des veränderlichen Wetters** *(Wetterbericht)* the weather will continue changeable.
fortdauern to continue, to last, to go on;
hartnäckig ~ to persist in going on.
fortdauernd constant, continual, continuous, lasting;
~**e Ausgaben** recurrent expenses; ~**e Regenfälle** continuous rainfall.
fortentwickeln to develop.
Fortentwicklung growth;
~ **einzelner Erzeugnisse** product development.
fortfahren to depart, to leave, to go away, *(tr.)* to drive (carry) away, *(weitermachen)* to go along (ahead), to resume;
mit seiner Arbeit ~ to proceed with one's work; **mit dem Auto** ~ to drive away; **mit einer Erzählung** ~ to continue one's story; **morgen** ~ to be leaving tomorrow; **in seiner Rede** ~ to resume (proceed with) one's speech; **damit** ~, **j. zu schikanieren** to keep on at s. o. *(fam.)*.
Fortfall cessation, discontinuance, *(Paragraph)* omission;
~ **von Wegerechten** extinguishment of ways; ~ **von Zahlungen** discontinuance of payments; ~ **eines Zuges** cancellation of a train;
in ~ **kommen** *(Bestimmungen)* to be abolished (dropped), *(Zahlungen)* to be dropped (discontinued).
fortfallen *(Bestimmungen)* to be abolished (dropped), *(Nachteil)* to disappear, *(Paragraph)* to be omitted, *(Schwierigkeit)* to be removed, *(Zahlungen)* to cease, to be discontinued, *(Zug)* to be cancelled.
fortführen to pursue, to continue, to keep up, *(Krieg, Prozeß)* to carry on;
j. ~ to lead s. o. away; **Geschäft** ~ to continue (carry on) a business; **Unterhaltung** ~ to go on with a conversation; **Verhandlungen** ~ to continue negotiations.
Fortführung continuation, pursuance, pursuit;
~ **eines Geschäftes** carrying on (continuation of a) business.
Fortgang progress, process, run, *(Weggang)* departure, leaving;
nach seinem ~ **von der Universität** after he had left the university;
~ **einer Arbeit** progress of a work;
über den ~ **berichten** to report progress; **über den** ~ **eines Unternehmens berichten** to present a report on a plan; **guten** ~ **nehmen** to make [good] progress; **schnellen** ~ **nehmen** to progress rapidly.
fortgehen to depart, to take one's departure, to leave, to go away, to get off, to pull out *(US)*;
ohne Abschied ~ to take French leave; **schrittweise** ~ to proceed by stages.
fort|gelaufen runaway; **von einer tückischen Krankheit** ~**gerafft** carried off by a malignant disease; ~**gerissen von jds. Beredsamkeit** enraptured with s. one's eloquence.
fortgeschritten advanced, forward, proficient;
weit ~ far gone;
weit ~ **sein** to be well up;
~**es Krankheitsstadium** advanced stage of an illness; **in** ~**en Lebensjahren** advanced in years; ~**es Studium** advanced studies; **zu einer** ~**en Stunde** at a late hour, late (well on) in the night.
Fortgeschritten|enkurs advanced course; ~**er** advanced student.
fortgesetzt continued, continuing;
~ **reden** to talk nineteen to the dozen;
~**es Studium** continuous studies.
forthelfen, jem. to assist s. o.
fortjagen, j. to turn s. o. out, to chase s. o. away, to sack s. o., to kick s. o. out, to give s. o. the boot.
Fortkommen *(Existenz)* livelihood, subsistence, competency, living;
berufliches ~ getting on in one's career;
jds. berufliches ~ **im Auge behalten** to follow s. one's progress; **sein** ~ **finden** to make a living; **sich selbst um sein** ~ **kümmern** to intend one's advancement.
fortkommen to get on, to make progress;
im Leben ~ to make one's way.
fortlassen, j. to allow s. o. to go; **Buchstaben** ~ to leave out (omit) a letter.
fortlaufen to run away;
ohne Absatz ~ *(drucktechn.)* to run on; **von zu Hause** ~ to run away from home; **mit einem Liebhaber** ~ to elope with a lover; **vor einer Verantwortung** ~ to run away from (shirk) a responsibility.
fortlaufend uninterrupted, consecutive, continuous, running, constant;
~ **numerieren** to number consecutively; ~ **gefragt werden** to continue in demand; ~ **notiert werden** *(Börse)* to be quoted (listed, *US*) consecutively;
~ **geführte Akte** continuous record; ~**es Einkommen** regular income; ~**e Kosten** overheads; ~**er Kurs** currently adjusted rate; ~**e Notierung** consecutive quotation (listing, *US*); ~**e Numerierung** consecutive numbering; ~**e Nummern** serial (successive) numbers; ~**er Werbeeinsatz** continuity in advertising.
fort|leben to live on, to survive, to linger; **sich heimlich** ~**machen** to steal away, to make away (off).
fortpflanzen, sich to propagate, *(Gerücht)* to spread; **sich von Generation zu Generation** ~ to be handed down from generation to generation; **sich mit großer Geschwindigkeit** ~ *(Epidemie)* to spread rapidly; **sich schneller als der Schall** ~ to travel faster than sound.
Fortpflanzung propagation, reproduction;
~ **des Lichts** transmission of light.
Fortpflanzungsgeschwindigkeit transmission speed.
fortreißen to tear away, *(Flut)* to sweep away;
Publikum mit sich ~ to sweep one's audience before one;
sich von seinen Gefühlen ~ **lassen** to be carried away by one's feelings.
Fortschaffen removal;
widerrechtliches ~ asportation.
fortschaffen to carry away (off), to remove, to clear away (off), to bring off;
altes Mobiliar ~ to get rid of old furniture; **widerrechtlich** ~ to asport.
fort|scheuchen to scare away; ~**schicken** to send away (off), to turn away, to dismiss, *(Briefe)* to dispatch letters; **sich** ~**schleichen** to sneak (steal, lurk, slip) away; ~**schleppen** to drag away; ~**schreiben** *(Grundstückswert)* to adjust, *(Statistik)* to extrapolate.
Fortschreibung *(Statistik)* extrapolation;
~ **des Grundstückswerts** adjustment of real-estate value.
Fortschreiten, allmähliches *(Krankheit)* encroachment.
fortschreiten *(Verhandlungen)* to make progress, *(Zeit)* to march on;
langsam ~ to make slow progress.
fortschreitend progressive;
~**e Industrialisierung** growing industrialization.
Fortschritt advance, evolution, course, progress, step forward, improvement;
entschiedener ~ marked improvement; **erzielte** ~**e** progress achieved; **gewerblicher** ~ *(Patentrecht)* advance in the art; **langsame** ~**e** tardy progress; **merkliche** ~**e** marked progress; **rasanter** ~ lightning progress *(fam.)*; **sozialer** ~ social progress; **ständiger** ~ progressive advance, the up and up; **technischer** ~ engineering progress, *(Patentrecht)* advance in the art; **investitionsabhängiger technischer** ~ built-in technical progress; **vom Kapitaleinsatz unabhängiger technischer** ~ disembodied technical progress; **technologischer** ~ technological progress; **unzweifelhafter** ~ decided step forward; **wirtschaftlicher** ~ economic progress (advancement); **wissenschaftlicher** ~ scientific advance;
~ **der Technik** technical (technological) progress; ~ **der Wissenschaften** advance of knowledge; ~**e im Wohnungsbau** improvements in housebuilding;
~ **abschätzen** to gauge the progress made; ~ **aufhalten** to stop progress; **großen** ~ **bedeuten** to mark a great improvement; **über** ~**e berichten** to report progress; ~ **darstellen** to be an improvement; **technischen** ~ **darstellen** to constitute a technical improvement; **von den** ~**en in der Krebsforschung handeln (berichten)** to treat of the progress of cancer research (article); ~**e machen** to [make] progress, to make headway, to improve, to get on, to advance, to go forward, *(mil.)* to gain ground; **gute** ~**e machen** to get along well; **rasche** ~**e machen** to make great strides; **dem** ~ **im Wege stehen** to impede progress.
Fortschrittler progressionist.
fortschrittlich progressive, forward, *(Einrichtung)* up-to-date, modern;
~ **gesinnt** progressive-minded; **nicht** ~ stick-in-the-mud;
~ **denken** to think on advanced lines;
~**e Erziehungsmethoden** progressive education; ~**e Ideen** advanced ideas; ~ **eingestellter Mensch** progressive, progressionist; ~**er Parteiflügel** progressive wing of a party; ~**e Politik** progressive policy; ~**e Strömungen** progressive tendencies; ~**es Unternehmen** forward-looking company.

Fortschrittlichkeit progressiveness.
Fortschritts|anhänger sein to be progressive; **~beteiligung** progress sharing.
fortschrittsfeindlich antiprogressive.
Fortschritts|gegner foe to progress; **~partei** progressive party; **~rate** rate of development (progress); **~zeitverfahren** continuous timing method.
fort|schwemmen to sweep away; **~sein** to be away.
fortsetzen to pursue, to continue, to sustain, to proceed, *(Geschäft)* to carry on, to continue, to pursue;
Gerichtsverhandlung ~ to proceed with the trial; **Gesellschaftsverhältnis ~** to carry on a business partnership; **Pachtverhältnis ~** to renew a lease; **seine Reise ~** to proceed on (continue) one's journey; **sein Studium ~** to resume (continue) one's studies; **sein Studium nach der Schulentlassung ~** to pursue one's studies after leaving school; **Tradition ~** to carry on a tradition; **Unterricht ~** to proceed with the lesson; **Verhandlungen ~** to continue negotiations; **seinen Weg ~** to proceed on one's way; **weltweit ~** to continue on a global scale.
Fortsetzung continuation, prosecution, pursuit, *(Veröffentlichung)* instal(l)ment;
~ folgt *(Zeitung)* to be continued [in our next issue]; **in sieben ~en** in seven instalments;
~ einer Geschichte continuation of a story; **~ eines Gesellschaftsverhältnisses** carrying on (continuance) of a partnership business; **~ des Mietverhältnisses** attornment of tenancy; **~ in unserer nächsten Nummer** to be continued in our next issue; **fünfte ~ eines Romans** fifth instalment of a novel; **~ und Schluß** *(Fortsetzungsgeschichte)* concluded; **~ von Seite 14** continued from page 14; **~ siehe nächste Spalte** continued in next column; **~ des Studiums** continuation of study; **~ eines ruhenden Verfahrens** revival of an action; **~ des Versicherungsverhältnisses** renewal of an insurance;
Roman in ~en drucken to serialize a novel; **in ~en erscheinen** to appear in parts (instalments); **~ des Arbeitsverhältnisses nicht zumutbar erscheinen lassen** to prevent further satisfactory continuance of the relationship; **~ eines Buches schreiben** to write a sequel; **Roman in ~en veröffentlichen** to serialize a novel; **in ~en veröffentlicht werden** to be published in instal(l)ments.
Fortsetzungs|anzeige following-on; **~blatt** continuation sheet; **~delikt** continuing offence; **~geschichte** serial story; **~roman** serialized novel; **aufregende ~serie** cliffhanger; **~werbeprogramm** soap opera *(US)*; **~werk** work published in parts, *(Bibliothek)* continuation.
fort|spinnen, Gedanken to pursue a train of thought; **Thema ~spinnen** to elaborate a subject; **~spülen** to wash away; **~stellen** to sneak away; **~tragen** to carry away, to carry off; **Boot vom Ufer ~treiben** to force a boat away from the shore.
fortwährend without intermission (end), enduring, lasting;
~e Beschwerden constant complaints; **~es Steigen der Preise** continual increase of prices.
fortwirkender Einfluß influence still felt today.
Fortwirkung after effect.
fort|wursteln to muddle on; **~ziehen** to move on (out), to leave.
Fortzug move, departure.
Forum forum, platform, panel;
~ der öffentlichen Meinung tribunal of public opinion *(fam.)*.
Forums|diskussion panel (round table) discussion; **~teilnehmer** panelist.
Foto[grafie] photo[graph], picture, snapshot.
Foto|abzug, vollendeter master print; **~album** photographic album, album of views; **~apparat** photographic apparatus, camera; **sich seinen ~apparat schnappen** to jump one's camera; **~artikel** photographic goods; **~ausrüstung** photo equipment; **~druck** photogelatine; **~einrichtungen** photographic facilities.
fotogen sein to be photogenic, to have a film face, to always come out well.
Foto|geschäft photographic goods shop; **~graf** photographer; **~graf werden** to go in for photography; **~grafie** photography, snapshot; **~grafie einrahmen** to frame a photograph.
Fotografieren photography;
sich in der Freizeit mit ~ beschäftigen to take up photography.
fotografieren to photograph, to take a photo (picture, snapshot), to photo;
mit Blitzlicht ~ to flashlight; **stereografisch ~** to stereograph; **sich ~ lassen** to have one's photograph (likeness) taken.
fotografisch photographic.
Fotokopie photocopy, photoprint, photostat, photostatic (photographic) copy, xerox;
beglaubigte ~ certified photocopy.
fotokopieren to photostat, to xerox.
Fotokopiergerät photocopying machine, photocopier.
fotokopiert photocopied.
Foto|laborarbeiten photofinishing; **~lampe** photoflood lamp.
fotomechanisch photomechanical;
~es Druckverfahren photoprocess.
Foto|modell auf der ersten Seite cover girl; **~montage** photomontage, stripping; **~satz** computer-based typesetting, cold type, filmsetting, phototypography; **im ~satz herstellen** to filmset; **~thek** photograph collection, *(Bücher)* photo library; **~zeitschrift** photographic periodical; **~zelle** photocell, electric eye; **~zubehör** photographic materials.
Foyer foyer, lounge, lobby, crush room, *(Theater)* lobby of a theater.
Fracht freight, cargo, charge, *(Güter)* goods, *(Kosten)* freightage, portage, carriage, cartage, rate, *(Ladung)* load, loading, lading, freight, shipment *(US)*;
als ~ by goods train *(Br.)*; **franko ~** free of freight; **in gewöhnlicher ~** paying freight as customary; **ohne ~** without freight; **unter Vorauszahlung der ~** carriage prepaid (free), freight free (paid);
abgehende ~ outward freight (cargo); **anteilsmäßige ~** prorata freight; **ausgehende und eingehende ~** freight back and forth; **unterwegs befindliche ~** floating cargo; **von mehreren Spediteuren beförderte ~** interline freight; **zu Vorzugsbedingungen beförderte ~** preference freight; **zu viel berechnete ~** overcharge of freight; **nicht deklarierte ~** undeclared cargo; **durchgehende ~** through freight; **zuviel erhobene ~** freight overcharge; **ermäßigte (vertraglich vereinbarte) ~** contract freight; **ganze ~** gross freight; **gemischte ~** mixed freight; **gestundete ~en** respited freights; **in Raten gezahlte ~** time freight; **nicht lohnende ~** unremunerative freight; **pauschale ~** lump-sum freight; **tote ~** *(Schiff)* dead freight; **unvorhergesehene ~** back freight; **verlorene ~** lost (wrecked) freight; **volle ~** full cargo; **vorausbezahlte ~** advance[d] (prepaid) freight; **im Ausland zahlbare ~** freight payable abroad; **zahlende ~** revenue (paying) freight *(US)*;
~ und Auslagen freight and disbursements; **~ bezahlt** freight paid; **Kosten, Versicherung und ~** cost, insurance and freight, cif;
~ zahlbar am Bestimmungsort freight payable at destination; **~ laut Charterpartie** chartered freight, freight as in charterparty; **~ bezahlt der Empfänger (gegen Nachnahme)** freight *(US)* (carriage, *Br.*) forward, freight collect *(US)*; **~ für die ganze Reise** voyage freight; **~ zu ermäßigtem Tarif** released freight; **~ im voraus bezahlt** freight prepaid; **~ zu herabgesetztem Wert** released freight;
~ eines Schiffes bei der Ausfahrt anmelden to enter outwards; **~ eines Schiffes bei der Einfahrt anmelden** to enter inwards; **~ bedingen** to settle the terms of a (engage the) freight; **~ befördern** to carry cargo, to carry goods; **~ berechnen** to charge freight; **~ im voraus zu bezahlen** freight to be prepaid; **~ einnehmen** to take a lading; **~ auf Leichter entladen** to discharge cargo overside; **auf ~ fahren** to sail (trade) on freight; **~ führen** to carry goods; **~ nachnehmen** to freight upon delivery; **Schiff in ~ nehmen** to charter a ship; **etw. mit der ~ schicken** to send s. th. by freight, to send by goods train *(Br.)*;
~abfertigung freight office; **~abnahme** acceptance of freight (shipment); **kollektive ~absatzberechnung** multiple basing point system *(US)*; **~abschluß** freight fixing; **~abteil** cargo section; **~angebot** freight offered; **~ankunftsbenachrichtigung** landing (arrival) notice; **~annahme** receiving (goods, *Br.*) office; **Endtermin für die ~annahme festsetzen** to close for cargo; **~annahmeschein** shipping note *(Br.)*; **~annahmestelle** freight *(US)* (goods, *Br.*) office; **~anspruch** freight claim; **~anteil** amount of freight, share in a freight, cargo share, primage; **~anteile festlegen** to fix cargo shares; **~aufschlag** additional freight, surcharge, extra carriage freight *(US)*; **kleiner ~aufschlag** average; **~aufseher** *(Schiff)* supercargo; **~auftrag** shipping order *(US)*; **~ausgangspunktsystem** single basing point system *(US)*; **~ausgleich** freight equalization *(US)*, equalization of freight rates *(US)*; **~basis** port equalization; **~bedingungen** terms of freight; **~behälter** [freight] container; **~benachrichtigung** arrival (landing) notice; **~berechnung** calculation of freight; **~berechnungsgrundlage** rate basis; **differenziertes ~bescheinigungssystem** charging what the traffic will bear; **~betrieb** shipment operation; **~bezahlung bei Warenankunft** freight forward.
Frachtbrief waybill *(US)*, bill of freight (lading) *(US)*, freight bill *(US)* (note, *Br.*), consignment note, letter (bill, *US*) of consignment;

durchgehender ~ through waybill *(US)*; **erloschener** ~ spent bill of lading *(US)*; **internationaler** ~ international consignment note;
~ **ausstellen** to make out a consignment note; ~ **einlösen** to receipt a consignment note;
~**duplikat**, ~**doppel** counterfoil waybill *(US)*, duplicate [of] waybill *(US)*, duplicate consignment note; ~**nummer** freight bill number *(US)*, waybill number *(US)*; ~**original** original waybill *(US)*.

Fracht|buch book of cargo (loading), cargo book; ~**buchung** freight booking; ~**büro** freight office; ~**dampfer** freight steamer, cargo boat (steamer), freighter; **zusätzliche** ~**dekkungsklausel** institute cargo clause *(Br.)*; ~**defizit** freight deficit; ~**dienst** cargo (freight, shipping, *US*) service; ~**differenz** freight differential; ~**dokumente** forwarding documents; ~**duplikat** duplicate of waybill *(US)*, duplicate consignment note; ~**einkünfte** freight (cargo) revenue; **zu erwartende** ~**einnahmen** anticipated freight; ~**empfänger** consignee.

Frachten|annahme acceptance of freight (shipment, *US*); ~**ausgleich** equalization of freight rates, freight equalization; ~**ausschuß** committee for merchandise traffic, *(Schiffseigentümer)* conference; ~**börse** freight market, shipping exchange *(US)*; ~**inkasso** collection of freight charges; ~**makler** freight canvasser (broker, salesman, agent), chartering broker, ship broker *(US)*; ~**maklergeschäft** ship brokerage *(US)*; ~**markt** freight market, shipping exchange *(US)*; **gemeinsames** ~**rechnungswesen** connecting line accounting; ~**verrechnungsabkommen** pooling of freights *(US)*; ~**versicherer** cargo underwriter.

Frachter [transport] freighter, cargo boat (vessel), transport ship (vessel), *(Verfrachter)* freighter, shipper *(US)*;
~ **umleiten** to divert a cargo vessel.

Fracht|erhöhung increase in freight rates; ~**erlaß** freight release; ~**ermäßigung** reduction in the freight rate, freight reduction; ~**erträgnisse** freight (cargo) revenue; **erwartete** ~**erträgnisse** anticipated freight; ~**flug** cargo flight; ~**flughafen** freight airport; ~**flugverkehr** air freight service; ~**flugzeug** freight airplane (aircraft), airfreighter, heavy transport (cargo) aeroplane, freight plane (carrier); ~**forderung** freight claim.

frachtfrei free of freight, carriage prepaid (paid), carriage-free, freight free (paid);
~ **bis zur Grenze** carriage (freight) paid to border; ~ **und spesenfrei** freight and charges prepaid; ~ **verzollt** free of freight and duty;
~**e Sendung** carriage-paid consignment.

Frachtfreigabe freight authorization.

Frachtführer carrier [by land], *(Rollfuhrunternehmer)* freighter, haulage contractor, [freight] hauler;
gewerbsmäßiger ~ common carrier;
~**pfandrecht** carrier's (cargo) lien; ~**pfandrecht besitzen** to have a lien upon a cargo.

Frachtfuhr|unternehmen carrier's business; ~**unternehmer** [common] carrier, haulage contractor, [freight] hauler, waggoner.

Frachtgebühr cartage, carriage [charges], cost of carriage, freight, freight rates (charges, expense), freightage, *(Eisenbahn)* railway toll, *(Schiff)* boatage;
ausgehandelte ~**en** agreed charge *(Br.)*; **zuviel erhobene** ~ freight overcharge; **in Raten gezahlte** ~ time freight; **vorausbezahlte** ~ advance[d] freight.

Fracht|geld freight[age], cartage, carriage; ~- **und Liegegeld** freight and demurrage; ~**genehmigung** freight authorization; ~**geschäft** carriage of goods, carrying trade (business), *(See)* chartering business; ~**gewicht** waybilling (shipment, *US*) weight; ~**gleichstellung** freight equalization *(US)*.

Frachtgut cargo, freight [commodities], load, package, slow (shipped, *US*) goods, shipment *(US)*, goods to be shipped *(US)*;
als (per) ~ by freight (goods, *Br.*) train; **als** ~ **registriert** received in shipment *(US)*;
leicht verderbliches ~ perishable freight;
~ **befördern** to carry cargo, to haul freight, to freight *(US)*; **etw. als** ~ **schicken** to send s. th. by freight (goods, *Br.*) train;
~**beförderung** transmission of freight; ~**meldeformular** *(Hafenamt)* dock loading account *(Br.)*; ~**sendung** consignment; ~**verkehr** freight traffic, slow-goods traffic *(Br.)*.

Fracht|inkasso collection of freight charges; ~**kahn** barge; ~**kalkulation** calculation of freight; ~**kilometer** freight mile; ~**klausel** long-and-short haul clause *(US)*; ~**knotenpunkt** junction point; ~**konjunktur** trend in freights; ~**kontrakt** freight contract, *(Schiff)* charterparty; ~**kontrolleur** tally clerk.

Frachtkosten freight[age], cost of carriage, carriage [expenses], carriage charges, charges for freight, freight charges (expenses), charge of carriage, cartage, portage;
~ **zahlt der Empfänger** charges forward; ~ **per Nachnahme** carriage forward *(Br.)*, freight forward (collect) *(US)*; ~ **für ausgehende Waren** freight outward *(US)*; ~ **für eingehende Waren** freight inward *(US)*;
~ **berechnen** to charge for carriage (freight); ~ **bezahlen** to commute freight charges; ~ **um 20% kürzen** to wash 20% out costs in freight; ~ **übernehmen** to absorb freight charge(s); **erhöhte** ~ **zahlen** to absorb the excess freight;
alle ~ **bis zum Ankunftshafen vom Verkäufer bezahlt** cost and freight;
~**ausgleich** freight equalization *(US)*, equalization of freight rates *(US)*; ~**ersparnis** saving in freight; ~**erstattung** refund of freight charges; ~**nachnahme** carriage forward; ~**übernahme [durch den Verkäufer]** freight absorption.

Fracht|kursnotierung quotation of freight rates, freight quotation; **genormte** ~**lademenge** carlot *(US)*, truckload *(Br.)*, bulk load; ~**leistung** transportation service; ~**leiter** freight handler; ~**linie** freight [line]; ~**liste** package list, memorandum note, [cargo] manifest; ~**lohn** [charges of] carriage, cartage, freightage; ~**makler** freight (ship, *US*) broker; ~**maklergebühr** freight (ship, *US*) brokerage; ~**maklergeschäft** freight broking; **günstige** ~**möglichkeiten** freight (shipping, *US*) facilities; ~**nachlaß** freight absorption, rebate of freight; ~**nachlaß gewähren** to absorb freight charges; ~**nachnahme** carriage forward, freight collect, collect shipment *(US)*, memorandum collection; ~**nachnahmenummer** memorandum collection number; ~**niederlage** depot; ~**note** freight bill *(US)* (note, *Br.*); ~**notierung,** ~**notiz** freight quotation, quotation of freight rates; ~**papiere** forwarding documents, shipping documents *(US)*; ~**parität** freight parity; ~**police** cargo (freight) policy; ~**quittung** freight receipt.

Frachtrabatt freight absorption, rebate[ment];
~ **für regelmäßige Verlader** deferred rebate[ment];
~ **gewähren** to rebate;
~**system** rebate[ment] system.

Frachtrate carriage (freight) rate;
~**n nach regulären Bedingungen [Bedingungen des Linienverkehrs]** *(Charterflug)* liner's rates.

Frachtraum freight, freight space (room), freight capacity, cargo (shipping, *US*) space, *(Schiff)* [freight] tonnage, [cargo] hold;
freier ~ surplus cargo space;
~ **belegen** to book freight;
~**belegung** freight booking; ~**fähigkeit** freight capacity (tonnage); ~**verkaufsleiter** cargo sales executive.

Frachtrechnung freight bill (note, *Br.*), freight (carriage) account, revenue waybill *(US)*;
~ **in mehrfacher Ausfertigung** multipart freight bill.

Frachtrechnungswesen, gemeinsames connecting line accounting.

Frachtsatz freight (transportation, shipping, *US*) rate;
angemessener ~ reasonable rate; **anwendbarer** ~ applicable rate; **einheitlicher** ~ basing tariff; **erhöhter** ~ advanced rate; **gleichmäßiger** ~ freight-of-all-kinds rate;
~ **für Ladungen unter 50 kg** through rate *(Br.)*; **verbilligter** ~ **für Leergut** returned freight (shipment, *US*) rate; ~ **für Waggonladungen** carload rate *(US)*, truckload rate *(Br.)*;
~**anzeiger** schedule of freights.

Frachtsätze, vorausbezahlte previous prepays;
~ **angleichen** to adjust freight rates; ~ **für Waggonladungen zur Anwendung bringen** to handle a shipment as a carload *(US)* (truckload, *Br.*).

Frachtschaden damage to cargo.

Frachtschiff cargo boat (carrier, steamer, vessel, ship), freighter, freight steamer (vessel), general ship, transport ship (vessel);
~ **in der Linienfahrt** cargo liner;
~ **chartern** to charter, to affreight.

Fracht|segler wherry *(Br.)*; ~**sendung** consignment; **teure** ~**sendungen in Spitzenzeiten** high-cost peak shipments *(US)*; ~**sendungen dirigieren** to route shipments *(US)*; ~**senkung** reduction in the freight rate, freight reduction; ~**spediteur** freight forwarder (shipper), carrier, cargo (freight) agent, carloading company *(US)*; ~**spesen** freightage, freight (shipping, *US*) expenses, carriage [inwards], freight outward *(US)*, cartage; ~**strecke** freight line, route; ~**stück** package, parcel, bale; ~**stundung** respited freight; ~**tabelle** transportation schedule.

Frachttarif freight rates (tariff, *US*), freight revenue tariff, transportation rate, cargo tariff, rate of shipping *(US)*, schedule of rates *(US)*, *(Eisenbahn)* railway tariff;

nach Kilometern berechneter ~ freight mil(e)age; **einheitlicher** ~ basing tariff; **ermäßigter** ~ all-commodity rate, schedule (less-than-carload) rate *(US)*; **geltender** ~ freight rates in force; **gemeinsamer** ~ joint freight rate; **behördlich genehmigter** ~ official rate; **gestaffelter** ~ freight rate scale *(US)*; **gleichmäßiger** ~ freight-of-all-kinds rate; **kombinierter** ~ combination mil(e)age and rate prorate *(US)*;
verbilligter ~ **für Durchgangsgüter** transit rate; ~ **für Expreßversand** spot rate; ~ **mit ausgeschlossenem Risiko** conditional rate;
~**erhöhung** freight-rate increase; **durchgehende** ~**erhöhung** general increase in freight (transportation) rates; ~**senkung** rate cutting, reduction of rates.

Fracht | tonne freight (shipping, *US*) ton; ~**transport** transport of goods, freight transportation *(US)*; ~**umschlag** freight handling; ~**unkosten** transportation cost; ~**unterbietung** rate cutting; ~**unternehmen** trucking company, haulage firm, carriers, shipping agency *(US)*, freight corporation *(US)*; ~**unternehmer** carrier, freight forwarder, haulage contractor, carloading company *(US)*; ~**unterschied** freight differential; ~**urkunde** consignment note, cargo manifest, waybill *(US)*, shipping document *(US)*; ~**vergünstigung** cargo preference; ~**vergütung** reimbursement of freight; ~**verkehr** goods *(Br.)* (cargo, freight, shipping, *US*) traffic; **integrierter** ~**verkehr** integrated freight system *(Br.)*; **auf Mittelbetriebe zugeschnittener** ~**verkehr** lorry-size freight service *(Br.)*, speedlink *(Br.)*; ~**versender** consigner, consignor, freight forwarder, shipper *(US)*; ~**versicherer** cargo underwriter; ~**versicherung** insurance on cargo, freight insurance; ~**versicherungspolice** cargo (freight) policy; ~**verstauung** trimming freight; ~**vertrag** contract of carriage (affreightment), freight (shipping, *US*) contract, *(Schiff)* charterparty; ~**vorschuß** advance[d] freight; ~**waggon** goods (box, covered) waggon *(Br.)*, freight wagon *(US)*, boxcar *(US)*; **schwerer** ~**waggon** heavy-duty freight wagon *(US)*; **ungewöhnlich hoher** ~**wert** extraordinary value; ~**wesen** freight system; ~**zettel** waybill, freight (dispatch) bill *(US)*, freight note *(Br.)*; ~**zone** freight area; ~**zusätze** adoption supplements; ~**zuschlag** additional (extra) carriage, privilege, additional (excess, extra, *US*) freight, primage, *(bei Güterstau)* congestion charge; ~**zuschuß** freight subsidy; ~**zustellgebühr** terminal (carriers) charges, cartage; ~**zustellung** freight delivery.

Frack swallow-tail coat, tails;
jem. den ~ **vollhauen** to dust s. one's jacket;
~**anzug** dress suit, tails; ~**zwang** *(auf Einladung)* „tails", „white tie".

Frage question, query, *(Problem)* problem;
nicht in ~ **gestellt** undoubted;
rein akademische ~ academic question; **aktuelle** ~**n** questions of present interest, live questions, living causes; **anstehende** ~ question that is on the nail; **immer wieder auftretende** ~ recurring question; **frei beantwortbare** ~ open-ended question; **mit Ja oder Nein zu beantwortende** ~ categorical question; **für die Entscheidung bedeutsame** ~ material issue; **entscheidende** ~ key (crucial) question, fundamental issue; **nach Bundesrecht zu entscheidende** ~ federal question *(US)*; **vom Gericht zu entscheidende** ~ judicial question; **erledigte** ~ closed issue; **gerichtliche** ~ interrogatory; **heikle (delikate)** ~ nice (delicate) question; **hypothetische** ~ hypothetical question; **indirekte** ~ indirect (oblique) question; **interessante** ~ point of interest; **mehrere Abteilungen interessierende** ~ inter-departmental business; **korrespondierende** ~ interlocking question; **lebenswichtige** ~ pivotal question; **materiellrechtliche** ~ matter of substance; **nebensächliche** ~ subordinate question; **offene** ~ *(Erhebung)* free-response question; **noch offene** ~ moot point; **politische** ~ political question; **prozeßrechtliche** ~ matter of remedy; **rhetorische** ~ rhetorical question; **schwebende** ~ unsolved (undecided) question; **soziale** ~ social problem; **zur Diskussion stehende** ~ question under debate (discussion); **strittige** ~ question in dispute, vexed question; **unentschiedene** ~ open question; **zusätzliche ungezwungene** ~**n** qualitative interview; **verfahrensrechtliche** ~ procedural (technical) question; **verkehrsrechtliche** ~**n** traffic policies; **währungspolitische** ~**n** questions of currency; **wesentliche** ~ matter of substance; **wirtschaftliche** ~ economic issue (question); **zweitrangige** ~ question of minor interest;
~ **mit vorgegebener Antwortmöglichkeit** closed-end question; ~ **von Bedeutung** question of substance; ~**n von allgemeiner Bedeutung** question of public interest; ~ **von zweitrangiger (nebensächlicher) Bedeutung** question of minor interest, sideshow; ~ **von allgemeinem Interesse** question of common concern; ~**n von öffentlichem Interesse** questions of public interest; ~**n, bei denen es um Leben und Tod geht** life-and-death matters; ~ **der Moral** moral question;
~ **anschneiden** to broach (raise) a question; ~ **aufwerfen** to raise an issue (question), to state an issue, to agitate (state, throw out) a question, to toss up a question; **einer** ~ **ausweichen** to fence with (blink) a question, to straddle an issue; **alle** ~**n beantworten** *(Examen)* to dispose (floor) a paper; **sich intensiver mit einer** ~ **befassen** to go further into a question; ~ **sofort mit allen Einzelheiten behandeln** to deal with the whole of a subject matter; ~ **von allen Seiten beleuchten** to view a question from all sides; **über eine** ~ **beraten** to deliberate upon a question; **sich mit einer** ~ **beschäftigen** to sit on a question; **in allen** ~**n voll bestehen** *(Prüfung)* to obtain full marks; ~ **als nicht zur Tagesordnung gehörig bezeichnen** to rule a question out of order; ~ **zur Sprache bringen** to raise a question; ~ **diskutieren** to be at issue on a question; **über politische** ~**n diskutieren** to argue political issues; **tiefer in eine** ~ **eindringen** to go further into a question; **Untersuchungsausschuß zur Lösung einer** ~ **einsetzen** to launch an inquiry on a question; ~ **entscheiden** to resolve a question; **sich der Beantwortung einer** ~ **entziehen** to shirk a question; ~ **erledigen** to dispose of a question; ~ **erörtern** to raise a subject; ~ **neu formulieren** to restate a question; **einer** ~ **aufgeschlossen gegenüberstehen** to maintain an open mind on a question; ~ **herunterspielen** to play down an issue; **als Kandidat in** ~ **kommen** to be a possible candidate; **nicht in** ~ **kommen** to be out of question; **für eine Stellung nicht in** ~ **kommen** to be unsuitable for a post; ~ **offen (ungeklärt) lassen** to leave a question unanswered (an issue up in the air); ~ **unentschieden lassen** to leave a subject at large; **schwebende** ~**n lösen** to solve a pending problem; **bei einer** ~ **mitreden** to strike in on a problem; ~ **in ihrem ganzen Zusammenhang prüfen** to examine a question in its entirety; ~ **auf die Tagesordnung setzen** to place a question on the agenda; **j. mit einer** ~ **in Verlegenheit setzen** to puzzle s. o. with a question; **zu einer** ~ **stehen** to stand on an issue; ~ **stellen** to ask a question; **jem. eine** ~ **stellen** to put s. o. a question; **in** ~ **stellen** to impeach, to query; **während der Debatte eine** ~ **stellen** to interrupt the debate with a question; **jds. Ehrlichkeit in** ~ **stellen** to question s. one's honesty; **Haufen von** ~**n stellen** to ask a lot of questions; **schriftliche** ~**n an die gegnerische Prozeßpartei stellen** to deliver interrogatories; **j. mit einer** ~ **überrumpeln** to bump into s. o. with a question; **mit** ~**n überschütten** to overwhelm with questions; ~ **ventilieren** to raise a question; ~**n miteinander verbinden** to link up one question with another; ~ **auf einen späteren Zeitpunkt der Sitzung verschieben** to postpone a question until later in the meeting; ~ **dem Gericht vorlegen** to submit a question to the court; ~ **nicht zulassen** *(Gericht)* to rule that a question is out of order;
einzig in ~ **kommende Lösung** only feasible solution.

Fragebogen [inquiry] form, question form, questionary, questionnaire, *(Statistik)* schedule, *(Versicherung)* survey [sheet];
beruflicher ~ job questionnaire; **statistischer** ~ census questionnaire; **brieflich versandter** ~ mail questionnaire; **mit der Post zurückgeschickter** ~ mailback form;
~ **mit vorgedruckten Antworten** aided-recall survey; ~ **für Meinungsforschung** opinionaire *(US)*;
~ **ausfüllen** to complete (fill in, *Br.*) a questionnaire;
~**aktion** survey; ~**fälschung** falsification of a questionnaire; ~**prüfung** piloting.

Fragekasten *(Zeitung)* letters to the editor.

fragen to question, to ask, to put a question, *(sich erkundigen)* to inquire;
einen Dreck danach ~ not to care a damn about it *(coll.)*; **j. um Erlaubnis** ~ to ask s. one's permission; **Lexikon um Rat** ~ to consult a dictionary; **jem. ein Loch in den Bauch** ~ to pester s. o. with questions; **j. plötzlich** ~ to up and ask s. o.; **nach dem Preis** ~ to inquire about (as to) the price; **j. um Rat** ~ to consult s. o., to seek s. one's advice; **sich durch die Stadt** ~ to ask one's way through the town; **nach den Ursachen** ~ to inquire about the causes.

Fragenbeantwortung, intelligente (kluge) intelligent answers to questions.

fragend ansehen, j. to look at s. o. inquiringly.

Fragen | folge *(Interviewer)* continuity of questions; **alle** ~**gebiete berühren** to discuss outside subjects; ~**komplex** group of questions; ~**kreis zusammen mit der zuständigen Abteilung lösen** to solve a problem between the departments concerned; ~**strom** string of questions.

Frager asker, questioner.

Frage | steller interrogator, questioner, interviewer, puller of a question, pollster *(US)*; ~**stellung** formulation of a question, interrogation, *(parl.)* putting the question *(Br.)*; **jem. mit einer ~stellung überraschen** to jump a question on s. o.; ~**stunde** *(parl.)* question time *(Br.)* (period, *US*); ~- **und Antwort-Spiel** quiz program(me); ~- **und Antwort-Treffen** question and answer session; ~**zeichen** query; **mit einem ~zeichen versehen** to take with a grain of salt.
fraglich questionable, disputable;
~**e Angelegenheit** matter in question.
fraglos unquestionable, beyond (without) controversy.
Fragment fragment, scrap.
fragmentarisch fragmentary, unfinished;
~**er Bericht** fragmentary report; ~**er Punkt** point in question.
fragwürdig questionable, doubtful, *(Geschäft)* suspicious, shady, queer;
~**e Behauptung** questionabe assertion; ~**er Charakter** doubtful (dubious) character; ~**es Geschäft** shady business; ~**e Geschäfte** equivocal transaction; ~**es Subjekt** suspect person.
Fraktion *(parl.)* [parliamentary] group;
technische ~ coalition group;
j. aus der ~ ausschließen to remove the whip from s. o. *(Br.)*.
Fraktions | anweisung whip *(Br.)*; ~**beschluß** party resolution; ~**disziplin** party discipline *(Br.)*; ~**disziplin wahren** to heel to the party whip; ~**führer** leader of a parliamentary group, chief whip *(Br.)*, floor leader *(US)*; ~**führer der Parlamentsmehrheit** majority whip; ~**geschäftsführer** chief whip *(Br.)*.
fraktionslos independent.
Fraktions | mitglied group member; ~**sitzung** meeting of a parliament group; ~**vorsitzender** parliamentary leader of a party *(US)*, chief whip *(Br.)*, floor leader *(US)*; ~**wechsel** defection, changing sides, ratting.
Fraktionszwang party whip *(Br.)*, whipping system *(Br.)*;
unter ~ abstimmen to vote by the whip *(Br.)*; ~ **aufheben** to take off the whip *(Br.)*; ~ **nicht einhalten** to break the whip; **sich dem ~ fügen** to follow the party roll book; **dem ~ unterliegen** to be under the party whip *(Br.)*; **nicht dem ~ unterliegen** to be free.
Frakturschrift black letter, Old English, Gothic.
Franken | aufwerten to raise the value of the franc; ~ **stützen** to give support to the franc;
~**zone** zone of the franc.
Frankierautomat franking (mailing) machine, mailer *(US)*.
frankieren to prepay, to pay the postage, to send post paid, to frank, to stamp;
Paket ~ to pay carriage for a parcel.
Frankiermaschine postage meter (machine, *US*), franking (stamping) machine, mailer.
frankiert prepaid, stamped, postage paid, postage-free, post-paid;
nicht genügend (ungenügend) ~ more to pay, insufficiently stamped (paid), postage underpaid;
~**er Brief** prepaid letter, stamped envelope.
Frankierung prepayment of postage, stamping;
wegen ungenügender ~ zurückgehalten held for postage matter *(US)*;
ungenügende ~ insufficient prepayment.
Frankierungs | maschine franking (stamping) machine, postage meter (machine, *US*), mailer; ~**zwang** compulsory prepayment.
franko postage free, post-paid, prepaid, [delivered] free of charge, *(frei Bord)* free on board, *(Fracht bezahlt)* carriage paid *(Br.)*, freight free (paid), flat *(US)*, *(zollfrei)* duty-free;
~ **ab** ... delivered at ...; ~ **Bahnhof** free station; ~ **Berlin (Bestimmungsort)** delivered free Berlin (destination); ~ **Bord** free on board (f. o. b.); ~ **Courtage** free of broker's commission; ~ **Fracht und Zoll** carriage and duty prepaid; ~ **Löschung** landed terms; ~ **Provision** free of commission (charge); ~ **Schiene** free on rail; ~ **Valuta** free of value, franco *(Br.)*; ~ **Waggon** free on rail; ~ **Zinsen** flat, including interest.
Franko | umschlag stamped envelope; ~**vermerk** frank, note of prepayment.
Franse fringe;
in ~n sein to be in shreds.
fransig reden, sich den Mund to talk one's head off.
Franzband binding in calf, calf binding.
französisch, sich auf ~ empfehlen to take French leave, to walk one's chalks *(sl.)*; **fließend ~ sprechen** to speak fluent French.
frappieren, j. to take s. o. aback.
frappierendes Benehmen striking behavio(u)r.
frappiert astonished, surprised, struck.
Fraß grub, muck, chow *(US sl.)*;
den Geiern zum ~ dienen to serve as food for the vultures.

fraternisieren to fraternize.
Fraternisierung fraternization.
Fraternisierungsverbot nonfraternization.
Frau woman, feme, female;
alleinstehende ~ feme sole; **ausgehaltene** ~ kept woman; **berufstätige** ~ employed woman, professional (career, *US*) woman; **emanzipierte** ~ liberated woman; **geschiedene** ~ divorced woman, feme discovert, divorcee; **gnädige** ~ *(Briefanfang)* madam; **ledige** ~ feme sole; **unbescholtene** ~ innocent woman; **unverheiratete** ~ single woman, feme sole, spinster; **junge unverheiratete** ~ maiden; **verheiratete** ~ feme covert; **volljährige** ~ woman of full age;
~ **des Hauses** lady of the house; ~ **mit Vergangenheit** woman with a history; ~ **von Welt** woman of the world;
seine Tochter zur ~ geben to give one's daughter in marriage; ~ **und Kinder haben** to have a wife and children; ~ **und Kinder zu unterhalten haben** to have a wife and family to keep; **sich von seiner ~ scheiden lassen** to divorce one's wife.
Frauen | angelegenheiten things feminine; ~**arbeit** female occupation; ~**beilage** ladies' supplement; ~**bekanntschaft** female acquaintance; ~**beruf** feminine trade; ~**bewegung** woman's movement, feminism; ~**emanzipation** emancipation of women; ~**feind** woman hater; ~**funk** woman's program(me); ~**jäger** skirt-chaser, wolf *(fam.)*; ~**kleidung** woman's wear; ~**rechte** woman's rights; ~**rechtlerin** feminist, suffragette; ~**seite** *(Zeitung)* women's (ladies) page; ~**stimmen** women's vote; ~**wahlrecht** woman (female) suffrage; ~**zeitschrift** woman's magazine; **ausgehaltenes ~zimmer** kept woman; **liederliches ~zimmer** wanton woman.
fraulich womanlike, womanly, female.
frech brazen, bold, daring, *(unverschämt)* impudent, impertinent;
~ **gegen j. sein** to be cheeky (saucy) with s. o.; **so ~ sein** to have the insolence;
~**e Antwort** saucy answer, back-talk *(US)*; ~**e Bemerkung** impertinent remark; ~**er Kerl** insolent fellow; ~**e Lüge** barefaced lie; **mit ~er Stirn** brazenly; ~**es Stück** hussy, minx.
Frechdachs cheeky (saucy) devil, *(Kind)* naughty child, cheeky little nipper.
Frechheit insolence, impudence, cheekiness, sauciness, freshness *(US coll.)*, nerve *(coll.)*;
bodenlose ~ incredible piece of impudence;
gute Portion ~ besitzen to have a great deal of cheek; **sich ~en herausnehmen** to take liberties; ~**en an den Kopf werfen** to hurl insolent remarks at s. o.
Fregatte frigate, *(aufgetakeltes Frauenzimmer)* woman dressed up to the nines.
Fregattenkapitän commander.
frei free, immune, quit, *(Ansichten)* liberal, broad, free, *(nicht arbeitsmäßig verplant)* leisured, *(Benehmen)* emancipated, free and easy, unconventional, *(Eisenbahn)* free on rail, *(franko)* prepaid, postfree, *(freiwillig)* voluntary, *(Leitung)* disengaged, not busy *(US)*, *(ohne Manuskript)* off the cuff, *(offen)* outspoken, frank, candid, straightforward, *(Paket)* carriage-paid, *(von Steuern)* exempt, *(Straße)* clear, *(Taxi)* for hire, *(umsonst)* gratis, gratuitous, *(unabhängig)* independent, without restraint, unbound, *(unbehindert)* unhampered, *(unbeschäftigt)* unoccupied, not engaged, *(unbeschrieben)* blank, *(unbesetzt)* vacant, open, void, *(unbewirtschaftet)* without control, unrationed, *(unbewirtschaftet, Miete)* decontrolled, *(unbewohnt)* void, vacant;
~ **ab hier** delivered here; ~ **Abgangsbahnhof** free station of departure; ~ **durch Ablösung** on Her (His) Majesty's Service *(Br.)*, franking privilege *(US)*; ~ **von Abzügen** free from all deductions; ~ **für Anlieger** open to residents only; ~ **von Aufbringung und Beschlagnahme** free of capture and seizure; ~ **Bahnhof** free station; ~ **Bahnwagen** free on rail; ~ **Baustelle** free at building site; ~ **von Belastungen** free from encumbrances; ~ **von Beschlagnahme als Strandgut** wreck-free; ~ **Bestimmungsbahnhof** free station of destination; ~ **an Bord** free on board, fob, free on steamer; ~ **an Bord des Flugzeugs** free on aircraft, free on plane; ~ **an Bord und gestaut** free on board and trimmed; ~ **von Bruch und Beschädigung** free from break and damage; ~ **durch den Bund** franking privilege *(US)*; ~ **Eisenbahngleis** free on platform; ~ **bis zur Entladung** free overside; ~ **erfunden** fictitious; ~ **erhältlich** freely obtainable; ~ **finanziert** privately financed; ~ **Flugzeug** free on aircraft; ~ **geliefert** free delivered; ~ **ein und aus und gestaut** free in and out and stowed; ~ **[ins] Haus** free to the door, carriage-free, delivery-free, no charge for delivery; ~ **von Havarie** free of average; ~ **Kai (Ufer)** free docks, free on quay; ~ **für Kinder**

(Film) suitable for children; ~ **konvertierbar** convertible; ~ **von allen Kosten** cost-free; ~ **LKW ab Lager** free on truck; ~ **gegen Lieferschein** free against documents; ~ **einschließlich Löschung im Ankunftshafen** free overside; ~ **von Rechten Dritter** *(Nachlaß)* free and clear; ~ **Schiff** free on steamer, free overside (overboard); ~ **längsseitig Schiff** free alongside ship (vessel); ~ **von Schulden** clear (free) of debt, unencumbered; ~ **von Sentimentalität** devoid of sentimentality; ~ **von Teilhavarie** free from particular average; ~ **und unbelastet** *(Grundstück)* free and clear; ~ **und ungebunden** free and easy, fancy-free; ~ **von jedem Verdacht** clear of any suspicion; ~ **verfügbar** freely disposable; ~ **von Vergütung für gesparte Ladezeit** free dispatch; ~ **verkäuflich** for sale without restrictions; ~ **Waggon** free on rail; ~ **Warenhaus** delivered in store; ~ **zugänglich** easy of access; ~ **von Zusätzen** without admixtures;
~ **ausgehen** to get off scot-free; **seine Meinung** ~ **äußern** to speak one's mind; **Tag** ~ **geben** to give a day off; ~ **haben** to have a holiday, to be off duty; **keinen Augenblick** ~ **haben** not to have a moment to spare; **20 Pfund Gepäck** ~ **haben** to be allowed 20 pounds luggage *(Br.)* (baggage, *US*); **sich einen Tag** ~ **halten** to keep a day open; ~ **herumlaufen** *(Hund)* to be at large; **über sein Vermögen** ~ **verfügen können** to have entire disposal of one's estate; ~ **lassen** to leave blank (void); **sich einen Tag** ~ **geben lassen** to take a day off; **Arbeitsplätze** ~ **machen** to release jobs; **Eingang** ~ **machen** to clear the entrance; **sich eine Woche** ~ **machen** to take a week off; **Wohnung** ~ **machen** to vacate an apartment; **sich** ~ **nehmen** to take time off; ~ **und offen reden** to speak candidly; ~ **sein** to be off duty, to have finished work (knocked off), *(Buch)* to be out of copyright; **morgen abend** ~ **sein** to have nothing on tomorrow evening; ~ **sprechen** to speak without notes (off the cuff, *US*); ~ **stehen** *(Haus)* to be detached; **über seine Zeit** ~ **verfügen** to dispose of one's time; ~ **werden** *(Posten)* to fall void (vacant); ~ **Bahnsteig geliefert werden** to be delivered free railway station; **von der Haftung** ~ **werden** to be exonerated;
~**e Ansichten** liberal views; ~**e Aussicht** unhampered view; **nach** ~**em Belieben** at liberty; ~**er Beruf** liberal profession; ~**er Bürger** free citizen; ~**e Ehe** free love; ~**e Einfuhr** free import; ~ **verfügbares Einkommen** spendable income, discretionary income; ~**er Eintritt** free admission, open door; **nach** ~**em Ermessen** at one's own discretion; ~**er Frachtraum** surplus cargo space; **j. auf** ~**em Fuße lassen** to leave s. o. at liberty; ~**er Geldumlauf** free circulation of money; ~**es Geleit** safe conduct; ~**es Gespräch** heart-to-heart talk; ~**er Grenzübertritt** free entry; ~**er Grundbesitz** freehold; ~ **verfügbare Guthaben** available (free) assets; ~**e Hand** free scope, *(ungebunden)* noncommittal; ~**e Hand lassen** to give free run, to allow s. o. free rein; **im** ~**en Handel** in the shops; **etw.** ~ **Haus liefern** to deliver s. th. at s. one's house; **sein** ~**er Herr sein** to be one's own master; **unter** ~**em Himmel** in the open air; ~**er Journalist** free-lance writer; ~**e Kapazität** spare capacity; ~ **verfügbare Kaufkraft** discretionary buying power; ~**es Kontingent** free quota; ~**e Kost und Station** board and lodging; ~**e Künste** liberal arts; ~**en Lauf lassen** to give free rein (scope, full swing); ~**es Leben führen** to lead the life of Riley *(US coll.)*; ~**e Liegezeit** free time; ~**er Makler** outside (street, *Br.*) broker; ~**er Markt** open market, *(Börse)* outside (unofficial, open, street, *Br.*, curb, kerb, *Br.*) market; ~**er Marktpreis** open price; ~**e Marktwirtschaft** free-enterprise system, free market [economy], laissez-faire economy; ~**er Marktzugang für jeden Anbieter** freedom of entry into the market; ~**es Meer** open sea; ~**e Meinungsäußerung** free speech; ~**e Mieten** decontrolled rents; ~**er Mitarbeiter** *(Werbung)* outside artist, *(Zeitung)* freelance[r]; ~ **verfügbare Mittel** loose funds; ~**er Nachmittag** half holiday, afternoon off; ~**er Personen-, Dienst- und Kapitalverkehr** *(EG)* free movement of persons, services and capital; ~**er Platz** open space; ~**en Platz lassen** to leave a blank; ~**e Presse** free press; ~**er Raum** blank space; ~**e Rücklagen** available (voluntary, free) reserve, reserve at disposal, discretionary appropriations *(US)*, *(Versicherung)* free surplus; ~ **vereinbarte Schiedsgerichtsbarkeit** voluntary arbitration; ~**e Seite** blank page; ~**er Sender** independent broadcasting station; ~**e Stadt** free city; ~**e Station** free board and lodging; ~**e Stelle** vacancy, vacant office (post); ~**e Stelle ausschreiben** to advertise a vacancy; ~**e Stelle besetzen** to fill a vacancy; **sich um eine** ~**e Stelle bewerben** to apply for a vacant position; ~**e Strecke** *(Bahn)* open track; ~**e Stücke** *(Börse)* negotiable securities; **aus** ~**en Stücken** of one's own accord, voluntarily; ~**er Stuhl** unoccupied seat; ~**er Tag** holiday, day off, open (free) day; ~**e Übersetzung** free (loose) translation; ~**es Unternehmertum** free enterprise; **im Wege** ~**er Vereinbarung** by private treaty; ~**e Verfügbarkeit** *(Anzeige)* vacant possession; **jem. zur** ~**en Verfügung stehen** to be at s. one's disposal; ~**es Verfügungsrecht** right to dispose; ~**er Verkehr** open market; ~**es Vermögen** unencumbered assets; ~ **verfügbarer Vermögensanteil** *(Erblasser)* disposable portion of property; ~ **verfügbare Vermögenswerte** liquid assets; ~**e Wahl** free choice; ~**e Wahl haben** to have the liberty of choice; ~**e Wahlen** free elections; ~**e Wählergemeinschaft wählen** to vote for the independents; ~ **konvertierbare Währung** freely convertible currency; ~**er Währungsraum** free-currency area; ~ **eingeführte Waren** freely imported goods; ~**e Wareneinfuhr** free import of goods; ~**e Wechselkurse** fluctuating exchange rates; ~**er Wettbewerb** free (freedom of, open) competition; **jem. seinen** ~**en Willen lassen** to let s. o. have his own way; ~**e Wirtschaft** uncontrolled economy; ~**er Wohnraum** unrestricted (uncontrolled) dwelling space; ~**e Wohnung** free accommodation; ~ **finanzierter Wohnungsbau** privately financed dwellings; ~**e Zeit** leisure time; **Zimmer** ~ rooms to let *(Br.)* (rent, *US*); ~**er Zugang für den Handel** open door; ~**e Zustellung** delivery free; ~**en Zutritt zu etw. haben** to be made free of s. th.; ~**en Zutritt zur Bibliothek haben** to have the run of the library.

Frei|aktie stock dividend, bonus stock *(US)*; ~**antenne** outdoor aerial; ~**antwort** *(Post)* prepaid reply; ~**aushang** free posting; ~**bad** open-air (outdoor) swimming pool; ~**ballon** free balloon.

freibekommen, Tag to get a day off.

Freiberufler self-employer;
ganztägig tätiger ~ full-time professional.

freiberuflich professional, self-employed, *(Journalist)* free-lance; ~ **arbeiten** to [act as a] free-lance;
~**e Arbeitskraft** professional worker; ~**e Einkünfte** independent income; ~**er Mitarbeiter** free-lance contributor; ~**e Tätigkeit** profession, occupation of a professional nature, professional occupation; **in** ~**er Tätigkeit** in an independent capacity.

Freibetrag *(Einkommensteuer)* [income tax] relief *(Br.)* (credit, *US*), tax exemption *(US)*, *(Lohnsteuer)* withholding exemption *(Br.)*, *(Steuer)* exempted (tax-exempt) amount, tax allowance *(Br.)*, basic abatement *(US)*;
altersbedingter ~ income-tax age exemption; **rechnerisch angenommener** ~ notional allowance; **allgemein gewährter** ~ outright exemption *(US)*; **sonst gewährter** ~ allowance given against other income; **kein** ~ allowances nil; **pauschaler** ~ *(Einkommensteuer)* basic abatement, flat exemption *(US)*, standard tax deduction *(US)*; **pensionsbezogener** ~ allowance given against a pension; **persönlicher** ~ *(Pfandgegenstand)* personal allowance *(Br.)*, *(Steuer)* single allowance *(Br.)*, personal relief *(Br.)* (exemption, *US*); **üblicher persönlicher** ~ ordinary personal allowance *(Br.)*; **zusätzlicher persönlicher** ~ additional personal allowance *(Br.)*; **gesetzlich zugestandener** ~ coding allowance *(Br.)*;
~ **für weitab wohnende Arbeitnehmer** mobility allowance *(Br.)*; **steuerlich anerkannter** ~ **für Berufskleidung** deduction for special clothing; ~ **für Berufstätige** earned-income relief (allowance) *(Br.)*; ~ **für Beschäftigung einer Haushaltshilfe** housekeeper relief (allowance) *(Br.)*; ~ **für Blinde** blind person's allowance *(Br.)*; ~ **für das Büro im eigenen Haus** office-at-home deduction; ~ **für die Ehefrau** *(Schenkungs- und Erbschaftssteuer)* marital deduction; ~ **für Ehegatten und Kinder** personal allowance *(Br.)* (exemption, *US*), credit for dependents *(US)*; ~ **für niedriges Einkommen** small-income allowance (relief) *(Br.)*; ~ **für Einkünfte aus freiberuflicher Tätigkeit** earned-income allowance *(Br.)* (credit, *US*); ~ **für Erbschaftssteuern** *(Ehefrau)* surviving spouse exemption *(US)*; ~ **für das Erwerbseinkommen der Ehefrau** wife's earned income (earnings) allowance *(Br.)*; **steuerlicher** ~ **für Familienangehörige** personal allowance *(Br.)*, dependency exemption *(US)*, credit for dependents *(US)*; ~ **für unterstützte Familienangehörige** child dependency allowance; ~ **für unterstützungsbedürftige Familienangehörige** dependent relatives allowance *(Br.)*; ~ **für ungewisse Forderungen** *(Einkommensteuer)* bad-debts reduction *(US)*; ~ **für über 65jährige** age relief *(Br.)*, old-age exemption *(US)*; ~ **für Grubenuntersuchungen** mining works allowance; ~ **für Investitionen** investment allowance; ~ **für ein in der Ausbildung befindliches Kind** child dependency allowance *(Br.)*; ~ **für Kinder** children's exemption *(US)*; ~ **für Lebensversicherungsprämien** life-insurance relief (allowance) *(Br.)*; ~ **für Ledige** single allowance *(Br.)*; ~ **für die Pflege eines Schwerbeschädigten** invalid care allowance *(Br.)*; ~ **für die Tätigkeit als Vormund** guardian's allowance *(Br.)*; ~ **für die im**

Haushalt mitarbeitende Tochter daughter's services allowance *(Br.)*; ~ **für die Unterstützung abhängiger Verwandter** dependent-relative relief *(Br.)*; ~ **für Verheiratete** marriage (married, *Br.*) allowance; ~ **für Versicherungsprämien und Pensionsbeiträge** deductions from pay for insurance and pension; ~ **bei der Wertzuwachssteuer** stock appreciation relief *(Br.)*; ~ **für einen doppelten Wohnsitz** temporary living-quarters allowance *(Br.)*; ~ **für karikative Zuwendungen** deductions allowed for gifts to charity; ~ **für wohltätige Zwecke** exemption (deduction) for charitable purposes;
~ **aufteilen** to split an allowance *(Br.)*; ~ **für ein auswärts studierendes Kind beantragen** to claim the allowance available in respect of a student on a full-time course *(Br.)*; ~ **bei der Wertzuwachssteuer auf ausländische Sorten gewähren** to grant stock appreciation relief on its holding of foreign currency notes *(Br.)*; **Anspruch auf einen ~ haben** to be eligible (qualify) for exemption *(US)*.

Freibetrags|abzüge, in die Lohnsteuertabelle eingearbeitete coding deductions from allowances *(Br.)*; **~änderungen** *(Steuer)* changes in allowances *(Br.)* (deductions, *US*); **~aufteilung** splitting the allowance *(Br.)*; **~belastung** bite into exemptions *(US)*.

freibetragsberechtigt sein to qualify for an exemption *(US)*, to be eligible for relief *(Br.)*.

Freibetrags|erhöhung increase in allowance *(Br.)*, exemption increase *(US)*; **~grenze** deduction (exemption, *US*) limit; **~höhe** amount of an allowance *(Br.)*; **~kürzung** cut in the exemption *(US)*; **~voraussetzungen erfüllen** to qualify for an exemption *(US)*, to be eligible for relief *(Br.)*.

Frei|beuter freebooter, buccaneer, filibuster; **~beuterei** freebootery; **~bezirk** *(Hafen)* franchise, free zone; **~bier erhalten** to have one on the house.

freibleibend without engagement (obligation), conditional, subject to prior sale, *(Änderungen vorbehalten)* subject to alterations (change) without notice;
~ **anbieten** to offer without engagement; **Preise ~ aufgeben** to quote prices conditionally;
~es Angebot conditional quotation (offer), quotation without obligation; **~er Auftrag** conditional order.

Freibörse curb [market] *(US)*, kerb [market] *(Br.)*.

Freibrief blank charter, carte blanche, full (discretionary) power;
~ **für weitere Ausschreitungen** free ticket for further offences; **jem. einen ~ ausstellen** to give s. o. carte blanche.

Freidenker freethinker.

Freien, im in the open [air], under the open sky, in the fresh air, out-of-doors, outdoors;
im ~ übernachten to camp, to sleep out of doors (in the open).

Freiersfüßen, auf ~ gehen to be a-wooing.

Frei|exemplar presentation (gratis, free) copy, free sample, complimentary subscription (copy), *(Anzeigenkunde)* voucher copy; **per Post versandte ~exemplare** free distribution by mail; **~exemplarliste** complimentary list, controlled circulation *(US)*; **~fahrkarte, ~fahrschein** free [admission] (complimentary) ticket, free pass *(US)*; **~fahrschein haben** to have a free ticket, to deadhead *(US)*; **~fahrscheinausgabe nur an Betriebsangehörige** free transportation *(US)*; **~fahrscheininhaber** deadhead *(US)*; **~fahrt** free ride; **~fahrtsignal** *(Bahn)* clear signal, highball *(US)*; **~fallschirm** drop-type parachute; **~flächen und Grünanlagen** open-space areas; **~flug** free ride, gratuitous flight; **~flughafen** customs-free airport.

Freigabe release, *(Bewirtschaftung)* decontrol, *(Flugzeug)* clearance, *(mil.)* clearance, derequisition, *(Konto)* unblocking, *(Wohnraumbewirtschaftung)* derequisition, decontrol of rents; **technische ~** engineering release;
~ **eines Buches** release of a book; ~ **von Depotstücken** release of custody items; ~ **eines Films** release of a film; ~ **eines gepfändeten Gegenstands** replevin; ~ **von Geheimmaterial** declassification *(US)*; ~ **von gehortetem Gold** release of hoarded gold; ~ **eines gesperrten Kontos** release of a blocked account; ~ **von Mitteln** release of funds; ~ **der Preise** price decontrol; ~ **für die Presse** press release; ~ **von Sicherheiten** release of security; ~ **einer Straße für den Verkehr** opening of a road to traffic; ~ **durch den Treuhänder** trust release; ~ **für den Verleih** release of a film; ~ **zur Veröffentlichung** press release; ~ **der Wechselkurse** floating of the exchange rate;
~ **anordnen** *(Pfand)* to discharge (release, vacate) an attachment, to vacate a judgment; ~ **erlangen** to replevy, to replevin;
~antrag *(Pfandgegenstand)* replevin; **~datum** release date; **~erklärung** *(mil.)* clearance certificate, *(Foto)* model release; **~garantie** indemnification guarantee; **~klausel** exemption clause; **~nummer** release number; **~signal** *(Bahn)* clear signal, highball *(US)*; **~verfügung** replevy, replevin.

freigeben to release, to license, *(im Betrieb)* to give time off, *(Bewirtschaftung aufheben)* to decontrol, to free, *(Konto)* to unblock, to deblock, to release, *(mil.)* to release, to derequisition, *(Wechselkurse)* to float, *(Wohnraumbewirtschaftung)* to derequisition, *(Zensur)* to lift, to pass;
j. ~ to let s. o. off from his engagement; **Bauarbeiten ~** to give the go-ahead for construction work; **Eingang ~** to move out of (clear) an entrance; **Film ~** to release (pass) a film; **Flugzeug zum Start ~** to clear an aircraft for take-off; **gepfändeten Gegenstand ~** to replevy, to replevin; **Geheimmaterial ~** to declassify; **Kreuzung für Fußgänger ~** to signal to the pedestrians to proceed over a crossing; **Mieten ~** to decontrol rents; **gesperrte Mittel ~** to release funds; **jem. den Nachmittag ~** to give s. o. the afternoon off; **für die Presse ~** to release for the press; **Start für die Produktion ~** to start production; **Startbahn ~** to clear a number; **für den öffentlichen Verkehr ~** to open to traffic; **zur Veröffentlichung ~** to release for publication; **aus der treuhänderischen Verwahrung ~** to release from custody; **Waren gegen Zahlung ~** to release goods against payment;
sich ~ lassen to arrange to have time off.

freigebig liberal, lavish, free, openhanded, handsome, with open hands, magnanimous, munificent, free-handed, profuse, generous, large-handed;
~ **sein** to spend freely, to give generously, to be generous with one's money; **äußerst ~ sein** to be extensive in one's charity.

Freigebigkeit generosity, liberality, largesse, bounty, openhandedness, munificence.

freigegeben *(Geheimmaterial)* declassified *(US)*;
für Kinder ~ *(Film)* suitable for children; **redaktionell ~** ready for press;
~e Fahrbahn clear lane; **für Jugendliche nicht ~er Film** X film; **~er Pfundkurs** floating pound; **~e Waren** derationed goods; **~e Wechselkurse** floating exchange rates.

freigehalten werden to have all expenses paid, to have free quarters.

Freigehege open-air enclosure.

Freigelände open ground (-air site), *(Film)* lot;
ungenutztes ~ open-use area.

freigelassen free, at liberty, released;
bedingt ~ probationary; **gegen Bürgschaft ~** out on bail; **bedingt ~ sein** to be on parole; **bedingt ~ werden** to be released on parole.

Freigelassener *(historisch)* freeman;
bedingt ~ probationer.

freigemacht prepaid, postage paid, postage-free, stamped;
nicht ~ unpaid;
nicht ~e Sendung underpaid packet.

freigenommen, für den morgigen Tag ~ haben to have leave to stay away from the office tomorrow.

Freigepäck free luggage *(Br.)* (baggage, *US*).

Freigepäcksgrenze *(Flugzeug)* free-luggage *(Br.)* (-baggage, *US*) allowance.

freigesprochen discharged and acquitted;
im Berufungsverfahren ~ acquitted on appeal.

freigestellt facultative, optional, *(mil.)* exempt from military service, draft-exempt *(US)*;
jem. ~ sein to be left to s. one's option.

Freigewicht weight allowed free, baggage allowance *(US)*, free luggage allowance *(Br.)*.

freigeworden *(Posten)* vacant, void, free.

Frei|grenze free quota, *(Steuer)* exemption limit *(US)*, basic (personal) allowance *(Br.)*, *(für Versicherer)* franchise; **~gut** bonded manifest, charter load, *(Lehnswesen)* fee simple, freehold, *(Zoll)* goods free of duty, duty-free goods.

Freihafen free (bonded, open) port, sufferance wharf;
~gebiet free zone *(US)*, free port area; **~niederlage** sufferance wharf, free port store.

freihalten, j. to pay for s. o. (s. one's expenses), to stand up (the shot for) s. o., to treat s. o. to s. th.; **jem. einen Platz ~** to keep a seat for s. o.; **sich von einem Schiff ~** to bear off from a vessel.

Freihandel free trade;
im ~ verkauft by private contract, privately, over-the-counter; **sich für den ~ aussprechen** to go on record as a free trader; **Anhänger des ~s sein** to stand for free trade.

Freihandels|anhänger free trader, tariff reformer *(US)*; **~anhänger sein** to stand for free trade; **Europäische ~gemeinschaft** European Free Trade Association (EFTA); **~lehre** Cobdenism, free-trade teaching; **überzeugter Anhänger der ~lehre sein** to nail one's colo(u)rs to the mast of free trade; **~politik** mercantilism, free-trade policy; **~politiker** free trader, tariff reformer *(US)*; **~system** free trade; **~vereinbarung** free-trade agreement; **~verkauf** sale in the open market; **~versprechen** free trade pledge; **~zone** zone of free trade, free-trade area, foreign trade zone *(US)*; **kleine ~zone** European Free Trade Association (EFTA); **~zonengemeinschaft** free-trade area community.

freihändig by private contract, privately, over-the-counter *(US)*;
~ schießen to shoot offhand; **~ verkaufen** to sell by private contract (privately, over-the-counter, off-hand, *US*); **~ zeichnen** to draw freehand;
~er Verkauf voluntary sale, sale in the open market, *(Effekten)* sale in the open market, over-the-counter trade *(US)*; **~e Zeichnung** freehand drawing.

Freihändler mercantilist, free trader, independent dealer, *(Börse)* jobber.

freihändlerisch free-trading.

Freihandverkauf sale by private contract (in the open market), over-the-counter (off-hand) sale *(US)*.

freihängende Decke suspended ceiling.

Freiheit freedom, liberty, franchise;
akademische ~ academic freedom; **bürgerliche ~** civil liberty; **dichterische ~** poetic licence; **geistige ~** freedom of thought; **von der Verfassung gewährleistete ~** constitutional liberty; **persönliche ~** personal liberty; **staatsbürgerliche ~** political freedom;
~ wirtschaftlicher Betätigung freedom of trade; **~ des Luftraums** freedom of the air; **~ der Meere** freedom of the seas; **~ der Meinungsäußerung** freedom of speech; **~ der Person** natural liberty; **~ der Presse** freedom (liberty) of the press; **~ des Wettbewerbs** free competition;
j. der ~ berauben to rob s. o. of his freedom; **seine ~ fordern** to postulate to be free; **~ in vollen Zügen genießen** to taste the joys of freedom; **jem. genügend ~en gewähren** to give s. o. line enough; **jem. große ~en gewähren** to allow s. o. great latitude; **sich jem. gegenüber ~en herausnehmen** to take liberties with s. o.; **jem. vollkommene ~ lassen** to leave s. o. free to do what he wants; **sich die ~ nehmen** to take the liberty; **jem. die ~ schenken** to bestow freedom on s. o.; **einem Gefangenen die ~ schenken** to set a prisoner at large (free, at liberty); **j. wieder in ~ setzen** to remit s. o. to liberty; **seine ~ verschachern** to bargain away one's freedom; **auf seine ~ verzichten** to surrender one's liberty; **seine ~ wiedererlangen** to retrieve (regain) one's freedom; **j. die ~ wiedergeben** to restore s. o. to liberty.

freiheitlich liberal;
~ gesinnt liberal-minded;
~e Wirtschaftsordnung free economic system.

Freiheits|beraubung unlawful detention, unlawful (forcible) detainer, false arrest, duress of imprisonment, false imprisonment, wrongous imprisonment *(Scot.)*; **~beraubung im Amt** malicious arrest; **~beschränkung** restraint upon liberty; **der ~bewegung einen Schlag versetzen** to deliver a blow to the cause of freedom; **~entziehung** unlawful detention, incarceration, imprisonment; **rechtmäßige ~entziehung** lawful detainer; **~kampf** struggle for liberty; **~kämpfer** freedom fighter; **~krieg** war of liberation; **~marsch** freedom march; **~statue** Statue of Liberty.

Freiheitsstrafe imprisonment, prison sentence;
kurze ~ short-term imprisonment; **lebenslängliche ~** imprisonment for life, life imprisonment (sentence), lifer; **übliche ~** ordinary term *(US)*;
~ mit unbestimmter Dauer indeterminate sentence; **~ ohne Geldersatzstrafe** imprisonment without the option of a fine; **auf eine verlängerte ~ erkennen** to impose a sentence of imprisonment for an extended term *(US)*; **~ verbüßen** to serve a prison term; **seine ~ verbüßen** to serve one's time of imprisonment.

Frei|jahr year of grace; **~karte** free ticket (pass), order *(Br.)*, *(Theater)* complimentary (free) ticket, pass, paper *(sl.)*.

Freikarten|verteilen *(Theater)* to paper *(sl.)*;
~inhaber deadhead *(US)*; **Theater durch ~verteilung für die Premiere füllen** to paper a theatre for an opening night *(sl.)*.

Frei|kauf *(Geisel)* ransom; **~kirche** free church; **~klausel** *(Versicherung)* franchise clause *(Br.)*.

freikommen *(Flugzeug)* to become airborne.

Frei|konvertierbarkeit für das englische Pfund nonresident convertibility *(Br.)*; **~konzert** free concert; **~körperkultus** nudism; **~korps** volunteer corps; **~kuvert** stamped (addressed, return, business, reply, *US*) envelope; **~kux** free share; **~ladeverkehr** full truck traffic; **~lager** bonded warehouse *(US)* (store, *Br.*); **~lagerung** open-air storage; **~land** open land; **~landzucht** outdoor culture.

freilassen to release, to set free, to enlarge *(US)*;
j. bedingt ~ to put s. o. on parole *(US)*; **Gefangenen ~** to free a prisoner; **Häftlinge nach Verbüßung der Hälfte der Strafe ~** to release prisoners halfway through their terms; **gegen Kaution ~** to release on bail.

Freilassung liberation, discharge;
bedingte ~ conditional release *(Br.)*, parole *(US)*; **sofortige ~** quick-fire release; **widerrechtliche ~** illegal release;
~ gegen Bürgschaftsleistung (Kautionsgestellung) bailment, release (remand) on bail; **~ nach richterlicher Haftprüfung** release on habeas corpus;
j. ~ anordnen to order s. one's release from prison; **~ eines Untersuchungsgefangenen erreichen** to bail out a prisoner; **~ widerrufen** to revoke the parole.

Freilassungs|anordnung prerogative writ; **~beschluß** release order.

Freilauf *(Fahrrad)* freewheel;
~bremse freewheel *(US)* coaster brake; **~kupplung** freewheel clutch.

freilegen, Leitung to uncover a cable.

Frei|leitung *(Telefon)* open (overhead) line.

Freileitungs|kabel overhead cable; **~mast** pylon.

Freilicht|aufführung open-air performance; **~aufnahme** exterior shot; **~bühne** open-air theater *(US)* (theatre, *Br.*), straw hat *(US sl.)*; **~kino** open-air cinema *(Br.)*, drive-in, ozoner *(US)*.

Freiliste *(zollfreier Gegenstände)* free list.

Freilos free ticket;
~ ziehen to draw a bye.

Freiluft|kur open-air cure; **~schule** open-air school.

freimachen to prepay, to frank, to stamp;
sich ~ to win free (loose); **sich von einem Einfluß ~** to free o. s. from s. one's grasp, to fling off a restraining influence; **sich von den persönlichen Gefühlen völlig ~** to dismiss any personal feeling; **Platz ~** to vacate a seat; **Straße ~** to clear the street.

Freimachung prepayment of postage, stamping, franking;
ungenügende ~ underpaid postage.

Freimachungs|gebühr postage, prepayment fee; **~maschine** franking (mailing) machine, mailer; **~prinzip** franking of letters; **~zwang** compulsory prepayment; **Einschreibsendungen unterliegen dem ~zwang** registered packets must be prepaid.

Freimarke postage stamp;
nicht benutzte ~ unused stamp.

Freimarken|automat mailer; **~heftchen** book of stamps; **~stempel** impressed postage stamp.

Freimaurer freemason;
~ sein to be on the square.

Freimaurerei freemasonry.

Freimaurer|grad Masonic degree; **~loge** freemasons' lodge; **~orden** Free and Accepted Masons; **~sitzung** communication.

freimütig frank, free-hearted;
~ für j. eintreten to stand up for s. o.; **~ gestehen** to confess quite frankly; **~ seine Meinung sagen** to speak one's mind;
~e Bemerkungen outspoken comments.

Freimütigkeit frankness, unreserve.

freinehmen, sich einen Tag vom Büro to arrange to take a day off, to get away from the office for a day.

Freiplatz *(Stipendium)* foundation, prize, scholarship, *(Theater)* free seat, paper *(sl.)*;
~ erhalten to gain (win) a scholarship;
~inhaber scholar, free placer *(Br.)*, foundationer *(Br.)*.

Frei|quartier free quarters; **~raum** *(Seeversicherung)* free space; **~raumklausel** clear (free) space clause.

freischaffend free-lance, freelance.

Freischaffender freelance[r].

Freischärler guerilla, irregular, partisan;
~bewegung guerilla movement; **~gruppe** guerilla group.

Frei|schicht extra shift; **~schule** free [public] school; **~schüler** foundationer *(Br.)*, exhibitioner.

freisetzen *(Energie)* to release;
überschüssige Arbeitskräfte ~ to shed (release) surplus labo(u)r; **Kapital ~** to unlock capital.

Freisetzung|von Arbeitskräften durch Maschinen displacement of human labo(u)r by machinery; **~ überschüssiger Arbeitskräfte** shedding (release) of surplus labo(u)r.

freisprechen to bring in a verdict of not guilty, to pronounce an acquittal, to exonerate, to discharge, to clear;
Angeklagten in allen Punkten ~ to discharge the accused on every count; **j. von einer Anklage ~** acquit s. o. of a charge, to

find s. o. not guilty; **j. mangels Beweises** ~ to give s. o. a bare acquittal; **Lehrling** ~ to release an apprentice from his articles; **Minister von der Anschuldigung der Überschreitung seiner Befugnisse** ~ to indemnify a minister; **von Schuld** ~ to justify, to pronounce free from guilt.

Freisprechung discharge, exoneration, acquittal, absolution, *(Lehrlinge)* release.

Freispruch acquittal, verdict of not guilty, discharge;
bedingter ~ conditional discharge; **teilweiser** ~ partial verdict; **voller** ~ absolute discharge;
~ **mangels Beweises** charge not proven *(Scot.)*; ~ **aus tatsächlichen Gründen** acquittal in fact; ~ **aus Rechtsgründen** acquittal in law; ~ **wegen erwiesener Unschuld** verdict of not guilty, hono(u)rable acquittal; ~ **wegen Unzurechnungsfähigkeit** verdict of guilty but insane;
~ **beantragen** to plead not guilty; **gegen einen** ~ **Berufung einlegen** to appeal against an acquittal; **auf** ~ **erkennen** to bring in a finding against; **für** ~ **plädieren** *(Gericht)* to cast a vote of acquittal; ~ **verkünden** to bring in a verdict of not guilty, to pronounce an acquittal.

Freistaat free state;
Stadt als ~ **errichten** to establish a city as free city.

Freistätte asylum, sanctuary, refuge, haven, franchise;
~ **gewähren** to grant asylum.

freistehen to be open, *(Haus)* to be unoccupied, to stand empty; **jem.** ~, **zu widersprechen** to be open to s. o. to object.

freistehend|sein to stand on one's own;
~**er Glockenturm** campanile; ~**es Haus** detached (unoccupied, empty, vacant) house; ~**e Zeile** line by itself.

Freistelle foundation, prize, scholarship, free place *(Br.)*, *(Altersheim)* free quarters.

freistellen to release, *(vom Militär)* to defer *(US)*, to exempt; **es jem.** ~ to leave to one's choice (option), to be optional with s. o. *(US)*; **j. von der Bezahlung der Sozialversicherungsbeiträge** ~ to exempt s. o. from social security payments; **von der Haftung** ~ to indemnify against liability; **vom Schöffendienst** ~ to exempt from jury duty; **von einer Steuer** ~ to exempt from a tax; **jem. die Teilnahme** ~ to give s. o. the option of participating; **j. von einer Verpflichtung** ~ to release s. o. from an obligation; **j. für vier Wochen** ~ to give s. o. four weeks leave.

Freistellen|inhaber foundationer *(Br.)*, free placer *(Br.)*; ~**wesen** *(Schule)* free place system *(Br.)*.

Freistellung release;
völlige ~ *(Schuldner)* unconditional release;
~ **von etwaigen Ansprüchen gegen den Käufer** special warranty; ~ **eines Bürgen** release of surety; ~ **zur beruflichen Fortbildung** day release; ~ **von Haftung** indemnity against liability; ~ **vom Militärdienst** discharge from draft, deferment (exemption) from military service *(US)*; ~ **von Rechten Dritter für alle Zeit** general warranty; ~ **von den Sozialversicherungsbeiträgen** exemption from social security payments; ~ **von der Steuer** exemption from a tax.

Freistellungs|anspruch exemption privilege, right of indemnity, *(Rückgriffsrecht)* right of recourse; ~**bescheid** *(Steuer)* notice of exemption; ~**bestimmungen** exemption provisions; ~**erklärung** deed of release; ~**garantie** indemnification bond; ~**klausel** exemption clause *(Br.)*; ~**verfahren** exemption proceedings.

freistempeln to frank.

Frei|stempler postage meter *(US)*, *(mit werblichem Aufdruck)* franking machine; ~**stück** free copy; ~**stunde** loose (off) hour; ~**tisch** free meals; ~**tod** suicide; **durch** ~**tod sterben** to take one's own life, to commit suicide.

freitragend|er Balken cantilever; ~**es Dach** single-span roof construction; ~**e Treppe** cantilever steps.

Frei|treppe perron, grand staircase; ~**umschlag** stamped (addressed, return, business, reply, *US*) envelope; ~**verkauf** voluntary sale.

Freiverkehr *(Börse)* inofficial dealings, curb (kerb, *Br.*) market, open (outside, free, street, *Br.*, unofficial, *Br.*) market, listless trading *(US)*, over-the-counter market *(US)*;
im ~ in the open (on the curb) market, street, over-the-counter *(US)*;
im ~ **handeln** to sell over the counter *(US)*.

Freiverkehrs|börse, ~**handel** curb *(US)* (kerb, *Br.*) exchange, unofficial market *(Br.)*, outside (over-the-counter, *US*) market; **New Yorker** ~**börse** New York Curb Exchange; ~**händler** dealer in outside (unlisted, *US*) securities; ~**kurs** sidewalk *(US)* (kerb[stone], *Br.*, street [market], *Br.*) price, curb [market] price *(US)*, free-market price; ~**makler** outside (unofficial) stockbroker, outsider, street *(Br.)* (kerb[stone], *Br.*, curb[stone], *US*) broker, dealer in unlisted securities *(US)*, curbstoner *(US coll.)*; ~**markt** outside (unofficial, free, kerb, *Br.*) market, curb (over-the-counter) market *(US)*; ~**notierung** unquoted list *(Br.)*, unlisted quotation *(US)*; ~**system** free market price system; ~**umsätze** outside transactions; ~**verkauf** voluntary sale, over-the-counter sale *(US)*, unofficial dealings *(Br.)*; ~**werte** outside *(Br.)* (unlisted, *US*) securities, over-the-counter stock *(US)*, curb stocks *(US)*.

Frei|vermerk prepaid notice, frank; ~**wache** *(Schiff)* watch below; ~**werden** avoidance, vacancy, vacation of office, voidance.

freiwerdend falling vacant, *(Anzeige)* with immediate possession.

Freiwild fair game;
~ **für j. sein** to be fair game for s. o.

freiwillig voluntary, on a voluntary basis, of one's own accord, willingly, optional, spontaneous, unsolicited;
sich ~ **melden** to volunteer; ~ **aus dem Leben scheiden** to take one's own life; **sich** ~ **zur Verfügung stellen** to volunteer; ~ **an einem Feldzug teilnehmen** to volunteer for a campaign;
~ **übernommene Arbeit** voluntary work; ~**e Beitragszahlung** voluntary contribution; ~**es Exportbegrenzungsabkommen** voluntary export-restraint agreement; ~**e Gerichtsbarkeit** voluntary (noncontentious) jurisdiction; ~**es Geständnis** voluntary confession; **auf** ~**er Grundlage** on a voluntary basis; ~**er Helfer** voluntary helper; ~**er Hilfsdienst** voluntary service; ~**e Hilfsorganisation** voluntary agency; ~**e Klagerücknahme** voluntary discontinuance; ~**e Liquidation** voluntary liquidation, winding up by agreement; ~**er Rücktritt** voluntary resignation (quit); ~**e Sozialleistungen** voluntary social contributions *(US)*; ~**e Vermögensübertragung auf den Konkursverwalter** voluntary assignment; ~**e Verpflichtung** voluntary undertaking; ~ **Versicherter** voluntary contributor; ~**e Versicherung** optional (voluntary) insurance; ~**e Versteigerung** private auction; ~**e Weiterversicherung** voluntary continued insurance; ~**e Zahlung** voluntary payment; ~**er Zuschuß** voluntary contribution.

Freiwillige|r volunteer;
als ~**r eintreten (dienen)** to volunteer; ~ **durch Berufssoldaten ersetzen** to displace volunteers by a professional army.

Freiwilligen|ausschuß volunteer committee; ~**korps** volunteer corps; ~**verband** volunteer unit.

Freiwilligkeits|grundlage voluntary basis; ~**prinzip** voluntarism.

Freizeichen *(Telefon)* dial (ringing) tone.

freizeichnen, sich to contract out, to exempt o. s. from a liability.

Freizeichnung exoneration, *(Haftungsausschluß)* nonliability;
~ **der Inkassobank** statutory protection; ~ **für bestimmte Schadensursachen** *(Versicherung)* excepted perils.

Freizeichnungsklausel exoneration clause, *(Abrechnung)* saving errors and omissions (S.E.A.O.), *(Dokumenten-Akkreditiv)* disclaimer clause, *(Garantie)* nonwarranty clause, *(Havarie)* average clause, *(Seetransportversicherung)* memorandum (excepted perils) clause, *(Treuhänder)* exculpatory clause, *(Völkerrecht)* contracting-out clause;
~ **für Fahrlässigkeit** negligence clause.

Freizeit leisure (free, off, spare) time, leisure hours, playtime, vacancy, time off, spell *(Australia)*;
in seiner ~ at one's leisure;
absolute ~ discretionary time; **bezahlte** ~ paid (dead) time; **persönliche** ~ *(Arbeitnehmer)* personal allowance;
sich seine ~ **einteilen** to employ one's spare time; **seine** ~ **genießen** to enjoy some leisure; **seine** ~ **gestalten** to spend (organize) one's leisure time; **jem. nur geringe** ~ **lassen** to scant s. o. in leisure; **jem. viel** ~ **lassen** to leave a lot of spare off-duty time on s. one's hands; **in seiner** ~ **malen** to paint as a hobby; **seine** ~ **verbringen** to spend one's leisure time; **seine** ~ **vergeuden** to throw away one's leisure time;
~**angebot** *(Touristik)* leisure package; ~**anlagen** leisure facility; ~**arrest** *(Jugendstrafe)* attendance centre *(Br.)*; ~**artikel** leisure items (products); ~**ausgaben** spending leisure; ~**bedürfnisse** leisure-time needs; ~**beratung** recreation guidance; ~**bereich** leisure activities.

Freizeitbeschäftigung leisure pursuit, spare-time job, recreational (spare-time) activities;
bevorzugte ~**en** favo(u)rite diversions; **unterhaltsame** ~ entertaining pursuit;
etw. als ~ **betreiben** to do s. th. at one's leisure.

Freizeit|dienstleistungen leisure-time service; ~**einrichtungen** recreation facilities; ~**erzeugnisse** leisure products (items); ~**fahrzeug** recreational vehicle; ~**gärtner** amateur gardener; ~**gebiet**, ~**gelände** leisure (recreation) area, recreation site, *(leitende Angestellte)* executive retreat; **Landschafts- und ~gelände** scenneric and recreational property; **~geräte** recreational equipment; **~gestalter** recreation director, physical culturist; **~gestaltung** spending of leisure time, leisure[-time] activities; **~heim** retreat house, recreational centre; **~industrie** leisure industry (business), recreation market; **~interessen** leisure interests; **~kleidung** leisure wear; **~klub** recreation club; **~komplex** leisure complex; **~lager** holiday (vacation, *US*) camp; **~leiter** recreation director; **~markt** leisure-time market; **betriebliches ~programm** company recreational program(me); **~reisen** spare-time travel; **~tätigkeit** off-the-job (recreational) activities; **kostspieliges ~vergnügen** expensive hobby; **~wert** recreational value; **~wesen** recreation field; **~zentrum** amenities (recreation) center *(US)* (centre, *Br.*); **~zimmer** family room *(US)*; **~- und Erholungszweck** amenity purpose.

Freizone free zone.

freizügig unrestricted, at large, liberal.

Freizügigkeit personal liberty, liberty of movement, liberty to come and go, free movement;
 ~ der Arbeitnehmer *(EG)* free movement of workers; **~ des Devisenverkehrs** freedom of exchange operations;
 jds. ~ behindern to obstruct s. one's movements; **jds. ~ einschränken** to tie s. o. down; **~ genießen** to move about freely.

Freizügigkeits|bedingungen für Einwohner der EWG-Länder European Economic Community obligations; **~beschränkung von Fürsorgeempfängern** settlement of paupers.

fremd foreign, alien, extraneous, continental *(Br.)*, *(reserviert)* distant, reserved, *(unbekannt)* unknown;
 ~ anmuten to strike as queer; **~ gehen** to be unfaithful to (two-time, *US*) one's wife; **in einer Stadt ~ sein** to be a stranger to a town; **sich ~ werden** to become estranged;
 sich in ~e Angelegenheiten einmischen to meddle in other people's affairs; **~es Eigentum** *(Strafrecht)* property of another; **mit ~en Federn** in borrowed plumes; **~e Gelder** trust money, third-party funds; **in ~e Hände übergehen** to change hands; **~e Hilfe** extraneous help; **~es Kapital** outside (borrowed) capital; **~es Land** foreign country; **~e Mittel** outside (borrowed) funds; **~er Name** assumed (adopted) name, pseudonym; **unter ~em Namen reisen** to travel under an alias; **nicht für ~e Ohren bestimmt** not meant for anyone else; **für ~e Rechnung** for third account; **in ~e Rechte eingreifen** to infringe s. one's rights; **~e Umgebung** strange surroundings; **sich in einer ~en Umgebung schnell eingelebt haben** to feel quite at home in one's surroundings; **~e Währung** foreign currency.

Fremd|anleihesteuer loan capital duty *(Br.)*; **~anzeige** third-party deposit notice; **~arbeiter** foreign labo(u)rer (worker), alien employee.

fremdartig extraneous, foreign, strange, *(seltsam)* odd, queer, eccentric.

Fremd|aufwendungen extraneous (extraordinary) expenses; **~beeinflussung** heterosuggestion; **~begünstigung** aiding and abetting **~beleg** external voucher; **zufällig erlangter ~besitz** involuntary bailment.

Fremde strange parts;
 in der ~ leben to live away from home, to live abroad.

Fremdeinfluß foreign influence.

Fremden|ausweis certificate of registration; **~bett** tourist bed; **~buch** visitors' book *(Br.)*, book of arrival, hotel register; **sich in das ~buch eintragen** to register with a hotel, to enter one's name in the visitors' book *(Br.)*; **~feind** xenophobe.

fremdenfeindlich xenophobic.

Fremden|feindlichkeit xenophobia; **~führer** tourist guide, *(Buch)* guidebook; **~haß** xenophobia; **~heim** guesthouse, boarding (lodging) house; **~invasion** invasion of tourists; **~legion** foreign legion; **~legionär** legionary; **~liste** list of arrivals; **abgesonderte ~niederlassung** settlement, *(Diplomaten)* compound; **~paß** alien's passport; **~pension** boardinghouse, guesthouse, private hotel, pension; **~polizei** aliens' department (registration office); **~steuer** visitor's (nonresident) tax; **~übernachtungen** overnight reservations.

Fremdenverkehr tourism, tourist trade (traffic);
 Gebiet für den ~ erschließen to open up an area for the tourist trade; **~ heben** to attract foreign visitors; **vom ~ leben** to be dependent on tourism for one's living; **große Beträge dem ~ verdanken** to obtain large sums from foreign tourism.

Fremdenverkehrs|abgabe nonresident (tourist) tax; **~amt** tourist board (bureau), British Tourist Authority *(Br.)*; **~angestellter** tourist officer; **unausgeglichene ~bilanz** tourist imbalance; **~büro** tourist agency, tourist office *(Br.)*; **~defizit** tourist deficit; **~einnahmen** tourist receipts; **~förderung** promotion of tourism (touristic traffic), tourist promotion; **~gebiet** tourist area (center, *US*, centre, *Br.*); **~gewerbe, ~industrie** tourist trade (industry); **~möglichkeiten** tourism facilities; **~ort** tourist center *(US)* (centre, *Br.*), tourist resort; **~prospekt** tourist prospectus; **~statistik** tourist-trade statistics; **~steuer** tourist tax; **~verband** tourist association, Tourist Board *(Br.)*; **~werbung** tourism (tourist) advertising, tourist traffic propaganda; **~wesen** tourism business; **~wirtschaft** tourist trade; **~zentrum** tourist center *(US)* (centre, *Br.*); **~zunahme** touristic growth.

Fremdenzimmer guestchamber, spare room;
 ~ zu vermieten rooms to let.

Fremdenzustrom influx of aliens.

Fremder stranger, foreigner, alien, *(Hotel)* guest, *(Urlauber)* tourist.

Fremd|erträge extraneous (extraordinary) income; **~erzeugnis, ~fabrikat** outside product; **~finanzierung** outside (debt) financing, trading on the equity, equity trading; **hohen ~finanzierungsgrad aufweisen** to be highly leveraged; **~finanzierungsquote** leverage factor; **~geld** borrowed money, third-party funds, deposits by customers; **~geschäft** transactions for third account; **~gruppe** *(Soziologie)* out group; **~herrschaft** foreign domination (rule), alien rule; **treuhänderisch gehaltene ~hypothek** party mortgage.

Fremdkapital outside (borrowed) capital (funds), loan capital *(Br.)*;
 hohes ~ high-geared capital; **kurzfristiges ~** *(Bilanz)* current liabilities;
 mit ~ finanzieren to trade on the equity;
 erhöhte ~intensität high gearing; **~wirkung auf die Eigenkapitalrentabilität** income gearing, financial gearing (leverage).

Fremd|konto third-party account; **~körper** foreign body, alien element, cuckoo in the nest.

fremdländische|Beteiligung foreign equity (interests); **~r Bevölkerungsteil** foreign population.

Fremd|leistung outside service; **~ling** newcomer, stranger; **~löhne** wages paid to outside labo(u)r; **~mittel** outside resources, borrowed money (funds); **sonstige ~mittel** *(Bilanz)* other borrowings; **~mittelfinanzierung** trading on the equity; **~personalkosten** outside personnel costs; **~posten** extraordinary item; **~reparaturen** cost of repair work carried out by outside contractors; **~scheck** third-party check.

Fremdsprache foreign language;
 ~ leicht aufschnappen *(fam.)* to pick up a language; **sich in einer ~ ausreichend verständigen können** to have a working knowledge of a foreign language; **~n studieren** to study languages.

Fremdsprachen|ausbildung language training; **~begabung** foreign-language capability; **~institut** foreign-language institute; **~korrespondent** foreign correspondent; **~sekretärin** foreign-correspondence secretary; **~unterricht** foreign-language tuition.

Fremdsprachler linguist.

fremdsprachlich in a foreign language, linguistic;
 ~er Unterricht foreign-language tuition.

Fremd|umsatz *(Konzernbilanz)* external (outside) sales; **~- zu Eigenkapitalverhältnis** leverage factor; **~versicherung** third-party insurance; **~währung** foreign currency.

Fremdwährungs|anleihe currency (external) loan; **~konto** [foreign] currency account; **~kredit** foreign-exchange (currency) credit; **~mittel für Auslandsinvestitionen** investment currency; **~schuld** foreign-currency debt; **~schuldverschreibungen** foreign-exchange bonds, foreign-currency bonds *(US)*; **~wechsel** foreign-exchange (currency) bill.

Fremdwerte foreign assets, *(Bank)* deposits.

Fremdwort foreign word;
 gerade in die Sprache neu aufgenommenes ~ foreign word of recent introduction;
 ~ in die Landessprache aufnehmen to domesticate a word.

frequentieren to frequent, to go into, *(Gaststätte)* to patronize.

Frequenz *(el., Zugverkehr)* frequency, *(Besucher)* number, *(Schule)* attendance;
 ~en zuteilen to allocate frequencies;
 ~abstimmung syntonization; **~band** *(Radio)* [communication] band, wave (frequency) band; **großes ~band** broad band; **~bandbreite** bandwidth; **~bereich** range of frequency, frequency range; **~filter** wave filter; **~liste** attendance sheet; **~messer** wave meter; **~messung** measurement of frequency; **~schwankungen** swinging, fading; **~verteilung, ~zuteilung** allocation of frequencies.

Freßbeutel nose-bag.

Fresse, große ~ haben *(sl.)* to have a big mouth; **jem. eins in die ~ hauen** to give s. o. a sock in the kisser.
Fressen *(Tiere)* food;
zum ~ sein to be perfectly sweet; **gefundenes ~ für j. sein** to bring grist to s. one's mill, to play into s. one's hands.
fressen to eat greedily, to gobble, *(Brandung)* to erode, *(Vieh)* to feed;
an jem. ~ to prey on s. one's mind; **an etw. ~** *(Säure)* to corrode; **einen Besen ~** to eat one's hat; **j. mit den Blicken ~** to devo(u)r s. o. with one's eyes; **ein Drittel des Etats ~** to eat up a third of the annual budget; **sich dudeldick ~** to eat one's fill; **viel Geld ~** to cost a pretty penny; **Geschichte glatt ~** to swallow it hook, line and sinker; **jem. die Haare vom Kopf ~** to eat s. o. out of house and home; **jem. aus der Hand ~** to eat out of s. one's hand; **Kilometer ~** to eat up a distance; **viel Öl ~** *(Motor)* to be heavy on (consume a lot of) oil; **wie ein Scheunendrescher ~** to eat one's head off (like a horse); **auf der Weide ~** to graze on the meadow; **Weisheit mit Löffeln ~** to be a paragon of wisdom.
Fresserei *(fam.)* spread, feast, blow-out, tuck-in *(Br., sl.)*.
Fress|gier greediness; **~korb** hamper, gift basket; **~paket** food parcel; **~sack** glutton, greedy-guts.
Freud und Leid des Lebens sweet and sour of life.
Freude glee, joy, gladness, pleasure;
bar jeder ~ empty of joy; **voller ~** with great pleasure, full of joy; **vor ~ außer sich** transported with joy; **zu meiner großen ~** to my great delight;
diabolische ~ gloating; **diebische ~** malicious joy;
~ am Fahren driving pleasure; **~ des Familienlebens** home joys; **~ bereiten** to please; **jem. große ~ bereiten** to please s. o. greatly; **seine ~ haben** to pleasure; **~ an seiner Arbeit haben** to enjoy one's work; **~ an Blumen haben** to be fond of flowers; **herrlich und in ~n leben** to live in the lap of luxury; **aus ~ einen Luftsprung machen** to jump for joy; **vor ~ außer sich sein** to be beside o. s.; **jem. die ~ verderben** to spoil s. one's fun; **seiner ~ Ausdruck verleihen** to give expression to one's pleasure; **in ~ und Leid zusammenhalten** to stick together through thick and thin.
Freuden|ausbruch outburst of joy; **~botschaft** glad tidings; **~fest** bean feast; **~fest veranstalten** to make whoopee; **~feuer** bonfire; **~haus** brothel, house of ill fame, bawdy house, whorehouse; **~tag** red-letter day; **~tränen vergießen** to shed tears of joy.
freudetrunken drunk with joy;
~ sein to be flushed with.
freudig cheerful, joyful, *(bereitwillig)* ready, willing;
j. ~ begrüßen to give s. o. a warm welcome;
~es Ereignis happy event; **einem ~en Ereignis entgegensehen** to be expecting a baby (in the family way); **in ~er Erregung** in a state of happy excitement; **~e Gesichter** happy faces; **~en Herzens** cheerfully; **~e Stimmung** high spirits.
freuen, j. to delight s. o., to give s. o. pleasure; **sich ~** to be glad (happy, pleased); **sich auf etw. ~** to look forward to s. th.; **sich über etw. ~** to rejoice at (over) s. th.; **sich zu früh ~** to count one's chickens before they are hatched; **sich seines Lebens ~** to lead a life of pleasure; **sich wie ein Schneekönig ~** to be as pleased as Punch.
Freund friend, crony, pal, chum, mate;
bewährter ~ approved friend; **dicke ~e** close friends, great pals; **ehemaliger ~** quondam friend; **einflußreicher ~** friend at court; **enger ~** familiar friend; **intimer ~** near (close, particular) friend, chum; **rücksichtsvoller ~** thoughtful friend; **unzuverlässiger ~** fair-weather friend; **zuverlässiger ~** tried friend; **konsequenter ~ der arbeitenden Bevölkerung** consistent friend of the working classes; **~ der schönen Künste** lover of fine arts; **sich als wahrer ~ erweisen** to prove a good friend; **j. zum ~ gewinnen** to win s. one's friendship; **festen ~ haben** to be going steady; **alte ~e fallen lassen** to discard old friends; **j. alle ~e verlieren lassen** to estrange all one's friends; **sich j. zum ~ machen** to make friends with s. o.; **~ der Musik sein** to be fond of music; **kein ~ von vielen Worten sein** to be a man of few words; **~ verlieren** to be widowed of a friend; **seine ~e um sich versammeln** to gather one's friends together; **j. zu seinen ~en zählen** to include s. o. among one's friends;
ein ~ in der Not ist ein ~ in der Tat a friend in need is a friend indeed.
Freundchen laddie *(Br.)*, buddy *(US)*.
Freundesdienst, jem. einen ~ leisten to do s. o. a friendly turn.
Freundeskreis circle of friends;
enger ~ knot of friends;
seinen ~ erweitern to make new friends; **über einen großen ~ verfügen** to have a large circle of friends.
Freundin girl friend, sweetheart;
alte ~ old flame;
feste ~ haben to be going steady.
freundlich genial, friendly, kind, gentle, well, *(Börse)* cheerful, bright, *(coll.)* nice, *(Wetter)* pleasant, mild;
j. ~ aufnehmen to give s. o. a friendly (kind) reception; **Gäste ~ aufnehmen** to make o. s. pleasant to visitors; **Vorschlag ~ aufnehmen** to give a proposal a kind reception; **jem. ~ begegnen** to show kindness to s. o.; **Zimmer ~ machen** to brighten up a room; **jem. ~ gesinnt sein** to be well (kindly) disposed towards s. o.; **jem. ~ stimmen** to disarm s. o., to put s. o. in a pleasant mood; **~ aufgenommen werden** to meet with a kindly reception; **~e Aufnahme** friendly reception; **~e Beziehungen unterhalten** to maintain friendly relations; **~er Empfang** warm reception; **etw. in ~en Farben malen** to paint a happy picture of s. th.; **von ~en Gefühlen bewegt** prompted by feelings of kindness; **mit ~er Genehmigung** with kind permission, by courtesy of; **~e Grüße** kind regards; **~e Miene machen** to look cheerful; **~e Note** happy touch; **sich von seiner ~sten Seite zeigen** to make fair weather; **~es Wesen** friendliness; **~es Wort** kind word.
Freundlichkeit friendliness, kindness;
beabsichtigte ~ would-be kindness; **falsche ~** hypocritical friendliness;
jem. eine ~ erweisen to do s. o. a kindness; **sich jds. ~ bewußt sein** not to be insensible of s. one's kindness; **mit ~ überhäufen** to kill with kindness.
Freundschaft friendship;
aus angeblicher ~ under the guise of friendship;
enge ~ close (intimate) friendship; **falsche ~** hollow friendship; **leichtfertig geschlossene ~** promiscuous friendship; **vorübergehende ~** surface friendship;
in aller ~ auseinandergehen to part good friends; **jem. ~ bewahren** to hold in with s. o.; **jds. ~ hoch einschätzen** to treasure s. one's friendship; **mit jem. in guter ~ leben** to be on friendly terms with s. o.; **~ pflegen** to cultivate a friendship; **~ mit jem. schließen** to become friends, to make friends with s. o.; **~en zu schließen wissen** to have a genius for making friends.
freundschaftlich friendly, amicable;
Angelegenheit ~ beilegen to settle a matter amicably; **jem. ~ gesinnt sein** to have friendly feelings towards s. o.; **~ miteinander verkehren** to be on friendly terms with s. o.;
~e Beziehungen unterhalten to maintain friendly relations; **mit jem. auf ~em Fuß stehen** to be on friendly terms with s. o.; **~er Ratschlag** friendly piece of advice; **~es Verhältnis** friendly footing.
Freundschafts|abkommen treaty of friendship; **~bande** ties of friendship; **~besuch** goodwill mission; **feierliche ~beteuerungen** solemn protestations of friendship; **~dienst** good turn, good offices; **~fahrt, ~reise** goodwill cruise; **~ring** token ring; **~spiel** friendly game (match); **~vertrag** treaty of friendship, friendship treaty; **~-, Handels- und Schiffsvertrag** Treaty of Friendship, Commerce and Navigation *(US)*; **~wechsel** accommodation bill *(Br.)* (note, *US*).
Frevel sacrilege, blasphemy, outrage;
~ begehen to commit an outrage.
frevelhaft outrageous, iniquitous, wicked.
freveln to [commit an] outrage;
gegen das Gesetz ~ to violate the law.
Freveltat outrage, crime.
Frieden, im tiefsten deep in peace; **um des lieben ~s willen** for the sake of peace and quietness;
dauerhafter ~ lasting (enduring) peace; **ehrenvoller ~** hono(u)rable peace, peace with hono(u)r; **fauler ~** hollow truce; **kollektiver ~** collective peace; **sozialer ~** industrial peace; **unehrenhafter ~** ignoble peace; **ununterbrochener ~** unbroken peace; **zusammengestoppelter ~** patched-up peace, patchwork peace;
~ seiner Asche peace to his memory; **~ um jeden Preis** peace at any price;
~ bewahren to preserve peace; **einem Land ~ bringen** to bring peace to a country; **~ festigen** to strengthen (settle, consolidate) peace; **~ gefährden** to endanger (threaten) the peace; **~ gewährleisten** to ensure peace; **j. in ~ lassen** to leave s. o. alone; **in ~ leben** to live unmolested; **mit seinen Nachbarn in ~ leben** to be at peace with the neighbo(u)ring states; **mit seiner Umwelt in ~ leben** to be in charity with one's neighbo(u)rs; **~ schließen** to conclude peace, to bury the tomahawk (hatchet); **~ mit einem Land schließen** to make peace with a country; **~ stiften** to establish peace; **~ stören** to trouble the waters; **wegen des ~s verhandeln** to treat for peace; **~ vermitteln** to mediate a peace; **~ wiederherstellen** to restore peace.

Friedens|abordnung peace delegation; ~**absprache** peace accord; ~**aktion** peace-keeping operation; ~**angebot** proffer of peace, peace offer (bid, overture); ~**appell** appeal for peace; ~**aussichten** prospects of peace; ~**bedarf** peacetime consumption (needs, requirements); ~**bedingungen** peace terms; ~**bedingungen aushandeln** to negotiate terms of peace; **einem geschlagenen Feind ~bedingungen diktieren** to dictate terms to a defeated enemy; ~**bedrohung** threat (danger) to peace; ~**bemühungen** peace-keeping operations, efforts to maintain peace, peace efforts, peace search; ~**betrieb** peacetime operation; ~**bewegung** peace movement; ~**blockade** pacific blockade; ~**brecher** peacebreaker, disturber of the peace; ~**bruch** breach of the peace; ~**delegation** peace delegation; ~**diktat** dictated peace; ~**diplomatie** peace-making diplomacy; ~**emblem** emblem of peace; ~**erklärung** declaration of peace; ~**etat** peacetime budget; ~**feldzug** peace drive; ~**fühler ausstrecken** to put out peace feelers, to make a tentative peace approach; ~**gefährdung** threat to peace; ~**gesellschaft** peace society; ~**gespräch** peace talk; ~**initiative** peace initiative; ~**kämpfer** partisan of peace; ~**konferenz** peace conference; ~**korps** Peace Corps *(US)*; ~**lager** peace camp; ~**marsch** peace demonstration.

friedensmäßig peacetime;
~**e Preise** prices at peacetime level; ~**e Qualität** pre-war quality.

Friedens|miete pre-war rent; **normale ~miete [per 3. 8. 1914]** standard rent *(Br.)*; ~**mission** peace mission; ~**offensive** peace offensive; ~**pakt** peace pact; ~**parität** peacetime (pre-war) parity; ~**partei** *(pol.)* doves; ~**pfeife mit jem. rauchen** to smoke the pipe of peace with s. o.; ~**plan** peace plan; ~**politik** peaceful (pacific) policy; ~**preise** pre-war prices; ~**produktion** peacetime production; **Wirtschaft wieder auf ~produktion umstellen** to reconvert industry; ~**programm** peace program(me); ~**regelung** peace settlement; ~**resolution** peace resolution, peace rally.

Friedensrichter stipendiary magistrate *(US)*, Justice of the Peace *(Br.)*, city judge *(US)*, country commissioner *(US)*;
~ **sein** to be in the commission of the peace *(US)*; **zum ~ ernannt werden** to be sworn as justice of the peace *(Br.)*;
~**amt** commission of the peace *(US)*.

Friedens|schluß conclusion of peace, truce; ~**stärke** *(mil.)* peace establishment, peace footing; ~**stifter** peacemaker, pacificator; ~**taube** dove of peace; ~**truppen** peacekeeping force; ~**unterhändler** peace negotiator; ~**verbrauch** peacetime consumption; ~**verhandlungen** peace negotiations; ~**verhandlungen führen** to negotiate the peace, to treat with the enemy for peace; ~**verrat** betrayal of peace; ~**vertrag** peace treaty; ~**vertrag unter Druck abschließen** to sign a treaty of peace under compulsion; ~**verwendung** peacetime application; ~**vorschlag** proposal for peace; ~**ware** pre-war goods; ~**wert** pre-war value; ~**wille** will for peace; ~**wirtschaft** peacetime commerce (economy); ~**zahlen** peacetime figures; ~**zeit** peacetime; **kurze ~zeit** brief peace; **im ~zustand** at peace.

friedfertige Natur pacific nature.

Friedhof burial (burying) ground, churchyard, graveyard, cemetery, memorial park *(US)*.

Friedhofs|kapelle funeral chapel; ~**ruhe** graveyard peace; ~**stille** deathlike (deadly) silence; ~**verwaltung** Cemetery Board.

friedlich peaceable, peace-loving, quiet;
Auseinandersetzung ~ beilegen to settle a dispute amicably; **j. ~ stimmen** to mollify s. o.;
~**er Abend** peaceful evening; ~**e Durchdringung** peaceful penetration; ~**e Lösung** peaceful solution; ~**e Methoden** nonviolent methods; ~**e Nutzung der Atomenergie** peaceful use of atomic energy; ~**er Tod** peaceful death; ~**e Veränderung** peaceful change; ~**es Zusammenleben** *(pol.)* coexistence.

Friedrich Wilhelm *(Unterschrift)* John Hancock.

frieren to freeze, to become frozen, *(Mensch)* to be (feel) cold;
wie ein Schneider ~ to be frozen stiff; **Stein und Bein ~** to be freezing hard;
jds. Blut ~ lassen to freeze s. one's blood.

frisch fresh, *(Gesichtsfarbe)* rosy, healthy, ruddy, *(Ware)* incorrupt, *(Wind)* chilly;
~ **gestrichen!** wet paint! fresh paint! *(US)*; ~ **von der Leber weg** from one's heart; ~ **und munter** alive and kicking; **nicht mehr ~** stale;
~ **von der Presse** hot news; ~ **von der Schule** new from school; ~ **von der Universität** straight from the university;
~ **drauflosreden** to talk nineteen to the dozen; **gleich immer ~ ans Werk gehen** not to let the grass grow under one's feet; ~ **halten** to preserve, to conserve; **sich ~ machen** to freshen up;
~**e Brise** fresh breeze; ~**e Brötchen** fresh rolls; ~ **gebackener Ehemann** newly married husband; ~**e Eier** new-laid eggs; **noch in ~er Erinnerung sein** to be still fresh in one's memory; ~**e Farben** gay (cheerful) colo(u)rs; ~**es Faß anstechen** to broach (tap) a new barrel; ~**es Gemüse** fresh vegetables; **mit ~en Kräften** with renewed strength; ~**e Laken** clean sheets; **j. an die ~e Luft setzen** to chuck s. o. out; ~**er Schnee** newly fallen snow; ~**e Spur** warm scent; ~**e Spur verfolgen** to be hot on the trail; **j. auf ~er Tat ertappen** to catch s. o. red-handed; ~**e Truppen** fresh troops; ~**e Vorräte** new stock, fresh supplies; ~**e Wäsche anziehen** to put on clean underwear.

Frische *(Stil)* snap, *(Wind)* chilliness;
in der ~ der Jugend in the vigo(u)r of youth;
geistige ~ mental alertness.

Frisch|ei new-laid egg; ~**fleisch** carcass meat; ~**gemüse** fresh vegetables; ~**haltebeutel** airtight bag; ~**haltepackung** airtight packet; **in ~haltepackung** vacuum-packed; ~**haltung** conservation, preservation; ~**luftanhänger** fresh-air fanatic; ~**luftzuführung** fresh-air inlet; ~**milch** fresh milk; ~**produktenmarkt** fresh market; ~**wasser** fresh water; ~**wassertank** fresh-water tank.

Friseur haircutter, hairdresser, *(für Herren)* barber;
~**laden,** ~**geschäft** hairdressing business; ~**salon** hairdresser's salon.

Friseuse hairdresser.

Frisieren *(Bilanz)* window dressing.

frisieren *(fig.)* to fake up, to doctor, to cook, to juggle, to manipulate;
j. ~ to comb (dress) s. one's hair; **Abrechnung ~** to cook the accounts; **Auto ~** to tune (soup, *US*, doll, hot) up a car; **Bilanz ~** to fake (cook, doctor) a balance sheet; **Einkommensteuererklärung ~** to fiddle an income-tax return; **Jahresabschluß ~** to dress up the year-end books; **Konten ~** to wangle accounts; **Nachrichten ~** to slant (angle) news; **auf neu ~** to rehash.

Frisier|kommode dressing table, dresser; ~**mantel** dressing jacket.

frisiert *(fig.)* cooked, faked;
nicht ~ uncooked;
~**es Auto** junked (tuned, souped, *US*) -up car; ~**e Bilanz** faked (cooked, doctored) balance sheet; ~**e Bücher** cooked accounts; ~**es Konto** wangled account; ~**er Motor** junketed engine, specially tuned engine.

Frisier|toilette, ~**tisch** toilet table, vanity table *(US)*.

Frist period [of time], time [allowed], prescribed period, definite period, *(Aufschub)* extension, prolongation, *(Kündigungsfrist)* notice, *(Termin)* time limit, terminal date, [set, fixed] term, fixed day, deadline *(US)*, *(Zahlungsaufschub)* delay, respite, grace, extension;
auf kurze ~ *(Kredit)* on short terms; **bei Ablauf dieser ~** after the expiry of this period; **in angemessener ~** within a reasonable period of time; **in kürzester ~** at a minute's warning (very short notice), within the shortest possible time; **in der vorgeschriebenen ~** within the required time (prescribed time); **in einer ~ von zwei Monaten** in a period of (within) two months; **innerhalb der ~** not later than; **innerhalb der gesetzlichen ~** within the time allowed (prescribed) by the law; **innerhalb der vorgeschriebenen ~** within the required time; **nach Ablauf dieser ~** after expiration of this period; **unter Einhaltung einer ~** keeping within a period of;
abgelaufene ~ elapsed time, expired term; **achttägige ~** eight days' period; **angegebene ~** stated period; **angemessene ~** reasonable length of time; **äußerste ~** final date, deadline *(US)*; **bestimmte ~** specific period; **dreimonatige ~** period of three months; **eingeräumte ~** time granted; **festgesetzte ~** fixed time; **gesetzliche ~** statutory period, the law's delays; **zusätzlich gewährte ~** additional time; **kurze ~** short notice (date, delay); **laufende ~** running period; **letzte ~** final respite; **peremptorische ~** peremptory day; **richterliche ~** regular term; **vereinbarte ~** specific period; **vertraglich vereinbarte ~** term agreed upon; **nicht verlängerungsfähige ~** nonrenewable term; **vorgeschriebene ~** limitation; **zusätzliche ~** extension of time; ~ **zur Beweiserhebung** probationary term *(US)*; ~ **zum Erbantritt** general charge *(Scot., law)*; ~ **zur Klagebeantwortung** time for entering an appearance; ~ **zur Klageerhebung** notice to plead; ~ **für die Kündigung** term of notice; ~ **von einer Stunde** an hour's delay;
~ **abkürzen** to shorten a period; **auf kurze ~ ausleihen** to loan for a short period; ~ **berechnen** to compute a period; ~ **bewilligen** to grant time; ~ **einhalten** to adhere to (comply with) the time, to observe (comply with) a time limit, to meet the deadline *(US)*; ~**en und Kostenvoranschläge einhalten** to be on

time and on budget; ~ **einräumen** to allow time (a breathing space, *fam.*), to accord (grant) a respite; ~ **erbitten** to ask for time; **zwei Monate ~ zur Schuldenbegleichung erhalten** to be given two months to pay one's debts; ~ **festsetzen** to set a period of time; ~ **gewähren** to allow grace, to accord (grant) a respite, to grant time, to [allow] time; **dem Schuldner eine ~ von einer Woche gewähren** to give a debtor a week's grace; **einen Tag ~ gewähren** to grant (give) a day's grace; **für eine Tratte noch einen Monat ~ gewähren** to extend (prolong) a draft for another month; **Lauf einer ~ hemmen** to suspend the running of a time; **j. mit einer ~ von einem Monat kündigen** to give s. o. a month's notice (warning); ~ **verstreichen lassen** to let the appointed time pass; ~ **setzen** to fix a period, to set a time, to set a term, to lay down a time limit, to fix a deadline *(US)*; ~ **zur Forderungsanmeldung setzen** to limit time to make proof of one's claims; ~ **von sechs Monaten setzen** to give six months notice; ~ **überschreiten** to exceed the prescribed period, to exceed a time limit; ~ **verkürzen** to abridge a time, to shorten a term; ~ **verlängern** to extend a period (the time); ~ **zur Abgabe einer Erklärung verlängern** to extend the time for filing an answer; ~ **versäumen** to fail to comply with a term; ~ **vorsehen** to provide a time limit; ~ **wahren** to observe a term, to adhere to (comply); ~ **zugestehen** to accord a respite;
die ~ beginnt the time begins to run; **die ~ läuft** the time runs; ~**ablauf** expiration (expiry) of a period, end of a term, elapsed time, lapse of time, deadline *(US)*; **bei ~ablauf** upon expiry of the time; **ohne ~angabe** without day; ~**beginn** inception of a period, dies a quo; ~**berechnung** calculation of (computing) time, computation of a term (period); **bei der ~berechnung** in reckoning time; ~**bestimmungsfehler** metachronism; ~**bewilligung** granting of time; **unangemessene ~dauer** unreasonable length of time; ~**einhaltung** observance of a time limit, meeting the deadline *(US)*; ~**einlagen** term (time, *US*) deposits.
fristen, sein Leben to eke out (scrape) a scanty living.
Fristende end of term, dies ad quem.
fristgemäß within the set period (prescribed time), in due time (course);
~ **ausführen** to carry out within the given time.
fristgerecht in due time, in due course, timely, on the appointed day, in season;
nicht ~ out of time.
Frist|gesuch petition for respite, dilatory plea; ~**gewährung** *(für Zahlungen)* allowance of time, respite, delay of payment; ~**hemmung** interruption of a period; ~**kalender** tickler, follow-up calendar.
fristlos at a minute's warning, without notice;
jem. ~ kündigen to dismiss s. o. without notice, to fire s. o. on the spot; ~ **entlassen werden** to be dismissed without notice; ~**e Entlassung** dismissal without notice, instant dismissal; ~**e Kündigung** summary termination.
Frist|setzung appointment of a date; ~**überschreitung** non-compliance with a time limit, failure to meet the time limit (deadline, *US*); ~**unterbrechung** interruption of a period; ~**verkürzung** abridgement of time, shortening of a term.
Fristverlängerung extension of time, *(schriftlich)* letter of licence, *(Zahlungsaufschub)* prolongation, delay in payment, dating, respite;
um eine kurze ~ einkommen to request a brief delay; ~ **erreichen** to get an extension of time; ~ **zugestehen** to grant an extension of time, to grant a delay for payment.
Frist|verlängerungsantrag petition for respite, request for extension of time; ~**versäumnis** failure to comply with the time limit (deadline, *US*), *(bei Gericht)* default; ~**wahrung** observance of the time limit.
frivol frivolous, flippant;
~**e Bemerkung** frivolous remark; ~**es Benehmen** flippant behavio(u)r; ~**es Prozessieren** frivolous or vexatious action; ~**er Witz** indecent joke.
Frivolität frivolousness, flippancy, *(Sprache)* indecency.
froh happy, cheerful, joyful;
seines Lebens ~ sein to be glad to be alive; ~ **stimmen** to fill with joy;
~**es Beisammensein** happy gathering; ~**e Botschaft** glad tidings; ~**e Gesichter** happy faces; ~**en Mutes sein** to be cheerful; ~**e Weihnachten** merry (happy, *US*) Christmas.
frohgelaunt in a happy mood.
fröhlich gay, merry, cheerful;
~ **werden** to cheer up;
~**es Leben führen** to lead a merry life; ~**e Stimmung** high spirits; ~**es Treiben** merrymaking.
Fröhlichkeit mirth, cheerfulness.
frohlocken to rejoice, to gloat, to be exultant, to jubilate;
zu früh ~ to count one's chickens before they are hatched.
frohlockende Menge exultant crowd.
Froh|natur happy disposition; ~**sinn** cheerfulness, light-heartedness, mirth.
fromm pious, devout, *(bigott)* hypocritical, canting;
~ **wie ein Lamm** docile as a lamb;
~ **werden** to get religion;
mit einem ~en Augenaufschlag with innocently up-cast eyes; ~**er Betrug** pious fraud; ~**es Getue** sanctimoniousness; ~**e Literatur** pious literature; ~**e Lüge** white lie; **j. mit ~en Sprüchen abspeisen** to pay s. o. in empty words; ~**e Wünsche** wishful thinking.
Frömmler devotionalist.
Fronde conspiracy, rebellion;
~ **anführen** to head the faction.
Frondeur *(pol.)* malcontent, conspirator.
Frondienst gavel work, statute labo(u)r.
frönen to indulge, to gratify, to pamper;
dem Alkohol ~ to be addicted to the bottle; **seinen Leidenschaften ~** to give free rein to one's passions; **der Mode ~** to be a slave to fashion; **seiner Neigung ~** to indulge one's taste.
Fronpflichtiger bondsman.
Front *(Haus)* front, fore, face, *(mil.)* front;
hinter der ~ behind the lines; **in vorderster ~** in the first flight; **feindliche ~** enemy line; **gemeinsame ~** united front; **grüne ~** *(parl.)* agricultural (farm) bloc; **intakte ~** *(mil.)* unbroken front; **verhärtete ~en** hardened fronts;
~ **abschreiten** to pass down the ranks, to review the troops, *(Ehrenkompanie)* to take the salute; ~ **aufrollen** to roll up the front; **geschlossene ~ gegen die Arbeitgeber bilden** to form a united front against the employers; **an die ~ gehen** to go to the front (up the line), to go into the front lines; **an zwei ~en kämpfen** to fight on two fronts; **in ~ liegen** to be ahead; **mit der ~ nach Süden liegen** *(Haus)* to face south; **gegen etw. ~ machen** to stand up against s. th.; **hinter der ~ Aufstellung nehmen** to take post in the rear; **an der ~ stehen** to be at the front; **im Kampf für das Wahlrecht an vorderster ~ stehen** to be always in the forefront of the battle for voting rights; **Truppen an die ~ werfen** to hurry soldiers to the front; ~ **zurücknehmen** to pull back the front;
~**abschnitt** frontage, sector.
frontal frontal, head-on;
~ **zusammenstoßen** to collide head-on.
Frontal|angriff frontal (head-on) attack; ~**zusammenstoß** *(Auto)* head-on crash, head-on (frontal) collision.
Front|ansicht front view; ~**antrieb** front-wheel drive; **Auto mit ~antrieb kaufen** to buy a front-wheel drive car; ~**ausbuchtung** bulge; ~**ausdehnung** front; ~**bericht** report from the front; ~**berichterstatter** front-line correspondent; ~**berichtigung** correction of the front; ~**bogen** salient; ~**breite** *(Haus)* frontage; ~**dienst** operation duties, service at the front, active (field) service; **zum ~dienst kommen** to go into action; ~**durchgang** *(Wetter)* passage of a front; ~**einsatz** action in the front service.
Frontenwechsel change of sides, turnround, about-face.
Front|erfahrung field experience; ~**flug** combat sortie; ~**flugzeug** battle plane; ~**gebiet** front; ~**geschütz** front-line artillery piece; ~**länge** *(Haus)* frontage; **Baugelände mit einer ~länge von ... kaufen** to buy land at so much per foot of frontage.
frontlastig *(Flugzeug)* nose-heavy.
Frontlinie front line;
intakte ~ bilden to present an unbroken front.
frontnah, im ~en Bereich in the forward area.
Front|offizier line officer; ~**richtung** front; ~**scheibe aus Verbundglas** safety-laminated windscreen; ~**soldat** front-line soldier; **ehemaliger ~soldat** ex-service man, veteran; ~**triebwagen** front-wheel drive car; ~**truppen** regular troops of an army, front-line troops; ~**urlaub antreten** to go home on furlough; ~**verkürzung** pulling back of the front; ~**verlauf** front line; ~**wechsel** *(fig.)* turnabout, change of sides, about-face, *(mil.)* conversion; ~**wechsel durchführen** to execute a change of front, to change front, *(fig.)* to perform an about-face; ~**zulage** active service (action, field) allowance, combat pay.
Frosch *(Eisenbahn)* frog, *(Feuerwerk)* cracker, firecracker, squib;
aufgeblasen wie ein ~ puffed up with pride;
~ **im Hals haben** to have a frog in one's throat;
sei kein ~ don't be a spoilsport;
~**aufnahme** *(Foto)* low-angle shot; ~**augen** protruding eyes; ~**hüpfen** leapfrog; ~**mann** frogman; ~**perspektive** perspective from below; ~**test** frog test.

Frost frost, *(Kältegefühl)* chill, coldness;
bei eintretendem ~ when frost sets in; **vom ~ beschädigt** nipped by the frost;
anhaltender ~ freeze; **beißender (klirrender) ~** hard (sharp, black) frost; **leichter ~** slight frost; **strenger ~** hard frost;
~aufbrüche *(Straßenschild)* road damaged by frost.
frostbeschädigt touched by the frost.
Frost|beschädigung nip; **~beschlag** silver thaw.
frostbeständig frostproof.
Frost|beule frostbite, chilblain; **aufgesprungene ~beule** kibe; **~brand** nip; **~einbruch** onset of frost; **bei ~einbruch** when frost sets in.
Frösteln sudden chill, shiverness, shiver.
frösteln to shiver, to feel shivery;
j. ~ machen to make s. o. shiver.
frost|empfindlich *(Pflanze)* frost-tender; **~frei** frost-free.
Frost|gefahr danger of frost; **~grenze** frost limit (line, *US*).
frostig frosty, *(fig.)* chilly, cool;
~ empfangen to receive coldly;
~es Benehmen frost in one's manner; **~er Empfang** frostiness of a reception; **mit ~er Höflichkeit** with chilly politeness; **~es Lächeln** icy smile.
Frostigkeit frostiness.
Frost|nebel frost smoke, ice mist; **~periode** frost period; **~riß** frost crack (cleft); **~schaden** frost damage; **~schäden** *(Straßenschild)* road damaged by frost; **~schutz** frost protection, anti-freeze; **~schutzmittel** anti-freeze agent (fluid, solution); **~schutzscheibe** screen (windshield, *US*) defroster.
frostsicher frost-proof.
Frost|ventil frost valve; **~versicherung** frost insurance; **~warnung** frost signal; **~wetter** frosty weather.
frotzeln, j. to pull s. one's leg, to tease s. o.
Frucht fruit, result, *(biologisch)* progeny;
~ der Liebe love child;
~ abtreiben to induce abortion, to cause a miscarriage; **reiche ~ tragen** to bear a rich crop, to crop heavily; **~ auf dem Halm verkaufen** to sell the crop standing.
fruchtbar fruitful, fertile, fecund, prolific, rich, productive, rank, *(fig.)* pregnant;
auf ~en Boden fallen to find a ready acceptance; **~e Ehe** fruitful marriage; **~e Phantasie** fertile imagination.
Fruchtbarkeit prolificness, fertility;
~ des Bodens productive power of the soil, soil fertility.
Fruchtbarkeits|rückgang fall in fertility; **~ziffer** fertility rate.
Fruchtbonbon jujube, fruit candy, boiled sweet *(Br.)*, sour drop.
Früchtchen scamp, young rascal, pickle *(coll.)*;
sauberes ~ bad egg (lot).
Früchte, getrocknete dried fruit; **gezogene ~** gathered fruits; **ungeerntete ~** unharvested crop;
~ seiner Arbeit products (fruits) of one's labo(u)r; **~ einer Erfindung** produce of an invention; **~ auf dem Halm** standing crop, emblements; **~ des Krieges** progeny of war; **~ einer Sache** natural products; **~ der Saison** products of the season;
~ ernten to reap the fruits; **~ harter Arbeit ernten** to reap the harvest of one's hard work; **~ tragen** *(fig.)* to bear fruit; **zahlreiche ~ tragen** to produce a large quantity of fruit; **verbotene ~ schmecken am besten** forbidden fruit is sweetest.
Fruchteis fruit-flavo(u)red ice-cream.
fruchten, wenig to be of no purpose (effect).
früchtereiches Jahr plentiful year.
Frucht|folge rotation of crops; **~genuß** usufruct.
fruchtlos of no effect, fruitless, futile;
~ sein to be of no avail;
~e Pfändung nulla bona, unsatisfied execution *(US)*.
Frucht|presse juice liquidizer; **~saft** fruit juice, squash; **~wechsel** rotation (succession) of crops, crop rotation; **im ~wechsel anbauen** to rotate crops.
früh, nicht eine Minute zu not a minute too soon; **so ~ wie möglich** as early as possible; **von ~ bis spät** from morning till night; **zu ~ sterben** to die before one's time; **~ in den Ruhestand treten** to retire early;
bis in den ~en Morgen into the small hours; **~es Stadium** early stage; **~er Tod** premature (untimely) death; **zu einer schrecklich ~en Zeit** at an ungodly (unearthly) hour.
Früh|alarm *(mil.)* early warning; **~aufstehen** early rising; **~aufsteher** early bird (riser); **~ausgabe** *(Zeitung)* early-bird issue *(US)*; **~beet** hotbed; **~bezugsrabatt** seasonal allowance; **~diagnose** early diagnosis; **~dienst** morning shift.
Frühe early part;
in aller ~ at an early hour; **in der ~ des Lebens** in the morning of life.

früher earlier, prior, anteceding, *(ehemalig)* former, ex, late, *(einstmals)* in former times, formerly;
~ oder später sooner or later, first or last;
~e Abmachungen previous arrangements; **~er Anmelder** *(Patentrecht)* prior applicant; **~ Arbeitsschluß** early-closing day; **~e Ausgabe** earlier edition; **~e Bräuche** former customs; **~er Bürgermeister** ex-mayor; **~er Eigentümer** previous owner; **~e Firma** old firm; **~e Generation** previous (former) generation; **~er Inhaber** prior holder; **~ Ladenschluß** early-closing day; **~es Modell** former model; **~es Patent** prior patent; **~er Präsident** former president; **~e Schuld** antecedent debt; **~es Urteil** prior judgment; **~e Verabredung** previous engagement; **~e Vereinbarung** prior engagement; **unsere ~e Wohnung** the flat we used to live in; **in ~en Zeiten** in bygone days; **~er Zustand** original state.
frühest *(Kultur)* primitive.
Früh|geburt premature birth; **~gemüse** early vegetables.
Frühindikator foreshadowing indicator;
zukunftssensibler ~ sensitive indicator.
Frühinvalidität disablement before retiring age.
Frühjahrs|artikel spring merchandise; **~bestellung** spring cultivation; **~einkauf** spring shopping; **~müdigkeit** spring fever *(coll.)*; **~muster** spring samples; **~putz** spring cleaning; **~umsatz** spring sales.
Frühkapitalismus early capitalism.
Frühling spring time, prime of the year.
Frühlings|bedarf spring goods; **~beginn** early spring; **~zeit** springtime, springtide.
Früh|nachrichten *(Rundfunk)* morning news; **~nebel** early mist; **~pensionierung** early retirement.
Frühpost morning (general) post *(Br.)*, first (morning) mail *(US)*;
~ bearbeiten to dispose of the morning post (mail, *US*); **mit der ~ zugestellt werden** to come by the first delivery.
frühreifes Kind precocious child.
Früh|schicht morning shift; **~schoppen** morning glass, eye opener *(Br., coll.)*.
Frühstück breakfast;
ausgedehntes ~ brunch; **dürftiges ~** poor breakfast; **einfaches ~** continental breakfast *(Br.)*.
Frühstücks|beutel tommybag; **~brot** packed lunch; **~pause** tea break *(Br.)*, coffee break *(US)*; **~tisch decken** to lay the table for breakfast; **~zimmer, ~raum** *(Hotel)* breakfast (morning) room, coffee room (shop) *(US)*.
Frühvorstellung *(Film)* first house.
Frühwarn|anlage *(mil.)* early-warning system; **fliegendes ~gerät** *(mil.)* airborne early warning; **~satellit** early-warning satellite; **~signal** early-warning signal; **~station** early-warning station; **~system** early-warning system; **fliegendes ~- und Kontrollsystem** airborne warning and control system (Awacs); **~system gegen Luftangriffe installieren** to provide for early warning of air attack.
Früh|warnung distant early warning; **~zeit** early period (stage), youth.
frühzeitig at an early age;
~ erfolgte Kündigung long notice; **~er Tod** untimely death.
Früh|zug early (morning) train; **~zündung** preignition, spark advance; **~zustellung** early-morning delivery.
Frustration frustration.
frustriert frustrated, stalled, through the mill *(coll.)*.
Fuchs knowing card, *(Studentenverbindung)* freshman;
alter ~ sly dog; **schlauer ~** old file;
wo sich ~ und Hase gute Nacht sagen at the back of beyond.
fuchsen to vex, to rile, to gripe *(US)*, to make wild.
fuchsteufelswild hopping mad;
~ machen to annoy s. o. to blazes, to bum up *(US sl.)*.
Fuchtel, j. unter seiner ~ haben to have s. o. under one's thumb, to have the whip hand of s. o., to get s. o. by the short hairs *(sl.)*; **j. unter die ~ nehmen** to crack down on s. o. *(US)*.
fuchtig, j. ~ machen to drive s. o. mad; **~ werden** to get one's monkey up *(sl.)*.
Fuder load, cartload.
fuderweise by cartloads.
Fug und Recht, mit with good reason.
Fuge join, joint, gap;
aus den ~n out of joint, off the hinges; **wegen des Nebels völlig aus den ~n** disorganized by the fog;
aus allen ~n geraten to be knocked off balance; **aus allen ~n geraten sein** to be in a state of a chaos.
fügen, sich to accommodate o. s.; **sich in etw. ~** to submit to (acquiesce into) s. th.; **sich in eine Entscheidung ~** to bow to a decision.

fügsam pliant, facile, compliant, ductile, tractile.
Fügsamkeit conformation, pliancy, tractability.
Fügung providence;
durch eine besondere ~ by a special providence;
glückliche ~ stroke of luck;
~ **der Vorsehung** dispensation of providence.
fühlbar tangible, noticeable, perceptible;
~**e Lücke** noticeable gap; ~**er Unterschied** perceptible difference; ~**er Verlust** serious loss.
fühlen, mit jem. to sympathize with s. o.; **sich** ~ *(wichtig vorkommen)* to fancy o. s.; **sich ganz anders als früher** ~ to feel a different man; **sich ausgezeichnet** ~ to feel perfectly well; **sich ganz benommen** ~ to feel queer all over; **sich unendlich besser** ~ to feel miles (heaps) better; **sich total betrogen** ~ to feel absolutely done in; **sich heimisch** ~ to feel at home; **sich als Herr im Hause** ~ to regard o. s. as master of the house; **sich ganz klein** ~ to be humbled; **sich lausig** ~ to be off colo(u)r, to be tenpence to the bob; **sich wie neugeboren** ~ to feel a new man; **sich phantastisch** ~ to feel on top of the world; **sich unbehaglich** ~ to be out of one's element, to be uneasy in one's mind; **Nachwirkungen eines Unfalls** ~ to feel the effects of an accident; **sich unwohl** ~ to feel shaky; **sich wichtig** ~ to feel one's oats; **sich nicht besonders wohl** ~ to feel not quite the thing, to be feeling only middling, to feel below par *(fam.)*; **sich heute gar nicht wohl** ~ to be rather poorly this morning *(coll.)*; **jem. auf den Zahn** ~ to sound s. o. about s. th.
Fühler tentacle, feeler;
~ **ausstrecken** to throw out a feeler.
Fühlung contact;
~ **aufnehmen** to get into touch, to establish contact; **mit dem Feind** ~ **aufnehmen** to make contact with the enemy; **mit einem Kunden** ~ **aufnehmen** to approach a customer (purchaser); **persönliche** ~ **aufnehmen** to make personal contacts; **enge** ~ **mit jem. haben** to be in close contact with s. o.; **mit jem. in** ~ **stehen** to be in touch with s. o.; ~ **mit jem. verlieren** to lose touch with s. o.
Fühlungnahme [taking] contact, consultation, approach, *(pol.)* rapprochement;
durch ~ **mit den zuständigen Stellen** by approaching (contacting) the competent authorities;
erste ~ initial contact; **persönliche** ~ face-to-face (personal) contact;
mit jem. in ~ **sein** to be in contact with s. o.
Fuhre cartload, waggonload, truckload, *(Taxi)* fare.
Führen management, control, guidance;
unberechtigtes ~ **eines Amtstitels** unauthorized use of an official title; ~ **eines Kraftfahrzeuges** driving of a motor car, operating of a motor vehicle *(US)*.
führen to lead, to conduct, to direct, to guide, to master, *(leiten)* to manage, to operate *(US)*;
jem. auf Abwege ~ to lead s. o. astray; **Angelegenheit zu einem guten Ende** ~ to carry a matter through, to bring a matter to a successful issue; **zu der Annahme** ~ to lead to the conclusion; **Argumente ins Feld** ~ to put forward arguments; **Artikel** ~ to have (keep) an article in stock, to deal in an article; **Artikel nicht** ~ not to stock (be out of) an article; **Aufsicht** ~ to supervise, to superintend; **Auto- und Fußgängerverkehr getrennt** ~ to segregate vehicular traffic from pedestrians; **Besprechungen** ~ to hold a conference; **Beweis** ~ to furnish proof, to produce evidence; **verschiedenste Bezeichnungen** ~ to go under a variety of names; **zu einer konjunkturellen Blütezeit** ~ to usher in a period of prosperity; **Böses im Schilde** ~ to be up to no good; **Briefwechsel** ~ to correspond, to carry on a correspondence; **Bücher** ~ to keep the books; **in den Büchern** ~ to carry in the books; **Dame zu Tisch** ~ to take a lady in to dinner; **glückliche Ehe** ~ to be happily married; **zu Ende** ~ to bring to an end; **j. zu der Erkenntnis** ~ to make s. o. realize; **j. durch die Fabrik** ~ to show s. o. over the factory; **Fahne** ~ to fly a flag; **Fahrzeug** ~ to drive a car, to operate a motor vehicle *(US)*; **Feldzug** ~ to conduct a campaign; **Fracht** ~ to carry goods, to freight; **am Gängelband** ~ to conduct in leading strings; **Gepäck mit sich** ~ to carry luggage *(Br.)* (baggage, *US*) with o. s.; **Geschäft** ~ to carry on (ply) a trade, to run a shop; **jds. Geschäfte** ~ to manage s. one's affairs; **j. aufs Glatteis** ~ to lead s. o. up the garden path; **Haushalt** ~ to keep the house, to run s. one's house; **Hochwasser** ~ to be in spate; **zum dramatischen Höhepunkt** ~ to lead up to the final event of a drama; **Kasse** ~ to be in charge of the cash, to bear the bag, to hold the purse; **Kennzeichen** ~ to carry a registration number; **Klassenaufsicht** ~ to be in charge of a class; **Konten** ~ to keep accounts; **Konto bei einer Bank** ~ to have an account with a bank; **Korrespondenz** ~ to conduct a correspondence; **Krieg** ~ to wage war; **zum Krieg** ~ to lead up to war; **Krieg defensiv** ~ to fight a defensive war; **zu Kurssteigerungen** ~ to carry to higher prices (levels); **ehrbares Leben** ~ to walk the chalk line; **Luxusleben** ~ to live a life of luxury; **zu Mißverständnissen** ~ to bring about misunderstandings; **j. durch ein Museum** ~ to show s. o. round a museum; **Nachweis** ~ to furnish proof; **Namen** ~ to bear a name; **zu nichts** ~ to come to nothing, to end in smoke, to lead nowhere; **Partei in den Wahlkampf** ~ to lead a party into the election campaign; **seinen Paß mit sich** ~ to carry one's passport; **j. zu seinem Platz** ~ to show (guide, usher) s. o. to his place; **Polizei durch Sprechfunk** ~ to guide police by radio telephone; **Protokoll** ~ to keep the minutes; **Prozeß** ~ to carry on a lawsuit, to maintain an action; **Rechnungsbücher** ~ to keep accounts; **lose Reden** ~ to engage in loose talks; **nur in der Regenzeit Wasser** ~ *(Fluß)* to flow only in the rainy season; **jds. Sache** ~ to plead s. one's cause; **entscheidenden Schlag** ~ to deal a decisive blow; **Selbstgespräche** ~ to talk to o. s., to hold a monologue; **auf eine falsche Spur** ~ to put on the wrong track; **j. über die Straße** ~ to take s. o. across the street; **Titel** ~ to bear a title; **keine Übergrößen** ~ not to stock outsizes; **Verhandlungen** ~ to carry on (conduct) negotiations; **j. in Versuchung** ~ to lead s. o. into temptation; **Verzeichnis** ~ to keep a list; **Vorsitz** ~ to be in the (fill the speaker's) chair, to preside; **durch einen Wald** ~ *(Weg)* to lie through a forest; **Ware** ~ to have goods on stock, to stock goods; **zu weit** ~ to take things too far; **das große Wort** ~ to monopolize (engross) a conversation; **nicht zum Ziel** ~ to be unsuccessful; **j. zu seinem Zimmer** ~ to take s. o. to his room.
führend leading, prominent, [top-] ranking, in the van of progress, *(erstklassig)* standard, first-rate, *(leitend)* managerial;
~ **sein** to be leading (at the top), to rank first; **auf seinem Gebiet** ~ **sein** to be a leader in the field; **auf dem Markt** ~ **sein** to be leading in its line of business; **in der Mode** ~ **sein** to lead the fashion; **an** ~**er Stelle sein** to occupy a prominent position;
~**e Bank** leading bank; ~**e Berufsschicht** management profession; ~**e Börsenwerte** market performers, representative stocks *(US)*; ~**er Finanzfachmann** top financial expert; ~**e Geschäftsleute** key businessmen; ~**es Haus** leading firm; ~**er Industrieller** captain of industry, top industrialist, tycoon *(US)*; **in** ~**en Kreisen** in the leadership ranks; ~**e Leute im Betrieb** key company people; ~**er Modesalon** leading fashion house; ~**e Persönlichkeit** dominant leader, leading man; ~**e Persönlichkeiten des Finanz- und Wirtschaftslebens** leading figures in finance, industry and trade; ~**e Position in der Welt einnehmen** to lead the world; ~**e Rolle** leadership, *(Theater)* leading part; ~**e Rolle spielen** to hold a leading position, to play a key role; **im Leben der Stadt eine** ~**e Rolle spielen** to play a prominent part in civil life; ~**e Schicht** leading class; ~**e Stellung** position of authority, leading position; **in einer** ~**en Stelle sein,** ~**e Stellung einnehmen** to occupy a prominent position, to hold a high-level position; ~**e Tagespolitiker** leading men of the day; **seit je** ~**e Werte** traditional leaders on prices; ~**e Zeitung** leading (key) paper.
Führer leader, chief, boss, headman, *(Handbuch)* manual, guidebook, *(Fremdenführer)* guide, tour conductor, vademecum, cicerone, *(Kran)* operator;
amtlicher ~ official guide; **zuverlässiger** ~ safe guide;
~ **für Einkäufer** buyer's guide; ~ **eines Fahrzeuges** driver (operator, *US*) of a vehicle; ~ **durch London** guide to London; ~ **im Taschenbuchformat** pocket guide; ~ **eines öffentlichen Verkehrsfahrzeugs** public service vehicle driver;
zum ~ **des Unterhauses ernannt werden** to be appointed to the leadership of the House of Commons; **zu den** ~**n gerechnet werden** to reckon among the leaders;
~**eigenschaften** executive abilities, leadership qualities; **seine** ~**eigenschaften ausprobieren** to flex one's leadership muscles; ~**gondel** *(Luftschiff)* control car; ~**haus** driver's cabin; ~**kabine,** ~**kanzel** pilot's cockpit; ~**kollektiv** collective leadership; ~**korb** *(Kran)* cabin, cage.
führerlos headless, *(Fahrzeug)* driverless, without a driver, *(Flugzeug)* pilotless, *(fig.)* unpiloted, *(Partei)* leaderless, without a leader.
Führer|natur born leader; ~**natur sein** to have the makings of (be cut out for) a leader; ~**persönlichkeit** dominant leader; ~**prinzip** leader principle; ~**raum** *(Flugzeug)* cockpit; ~**schaft** leadership, bossdom *(US)*; ~**schaftsimage** brand of leadership.
Führerschein driving licence *(Br.)*, driver's license *(US)*, licence (license, *US*) to drive a car;
internationaler ~ international driving permit;
~ **vorübergehend abnehmen** to suspend a driving licence *(Br.)*; ~

bekommen to take out a driving licence *(Br.)*; ~ **entzogen bekommen** to forfeit one's driving licence *(Br.)*; ~ **einziehen (entziehen)** to withdraw a driving licence *(Br.)*, to disqualify from driving *(Br.)*, to suspend the driver's (operator's) license *(US)*; ~ **zeitweilig entziehen** to suspend a licence; ~ **für ein Jahr erwerben** to take out a licence for a year *(Br.)*; ~ **machen** to pass one's driving test *(Br.)*; **Eintragung auf dem ~ machen** to endorse a motorist's licence *(Br.)*, to endorse a driver's license *(US)*; **eingezogenen ~ zurückgeben** to remove the disqualification on a driving licence *(Br.)*;
~**alter** driving age; ~**ausgabestelle** driver's license bureau *(US)*; ~**eintragung** endorsement of licence; ~**entzug** driving ban *(Br.)*, disqualification (forfeiture) of licence *(Br.)*, driving disqualification, revocation of the driver's license *(US)*; **vorübergehender ~entzug** suspension of a driving (driver's) licence; ~**inhaber** possessor of a driving *(Br.)* (driver's, *US*) licence.

führerscheinpflichtig sein to require a driving licence.

Führerschein|prüfung driving test; ~**prüfung bestehen** to pass one's driving test; ~**rückgabe** removal of a disqualification.

Führer|sitz driver's seat; ~**stand** *(Lokomotive)* driver's cab; **tarifpolitische ~stellung** wage leadership; ~**talent** executive talent.

Fuhr|geld carriage, cartage; ~**geschäft** carriage, haulage; ~**lohn** [charges of] carriage, cartage, wag(g)onage, freight charges (expenses); ~**mann** wag(g)oner, carrier, carriage operator, hauler, carter, driver.

Fuhrpark transport (car) park, carpool *(US)*, motor pool *(US)*, fleet of trucks, truck fleet, *(für Kundendienst)* delivery equipment;
~**ankauf** fleet buying *(US)*; ~**besitzer** fleet owner *(US)*; ~**konto** delivery truck account; ~**leiter** fleet manager *(US)*; **eigenes ~unternehmen betreiben** to run one's own vehicle operation.

Führung lead, leading, leadership, directing, guidance, direction, government, helm, *(Benehmen)* conduct, behavio(u)r, *(Besichtigung)* guided tour, *(Geschäft)* management, running, *(mil.)* command, control, *(Verwaltung)* administration;
unter ~ under the leadership; **unter ~ des Wirtschaftsministers** headed by the Minister of Economics;
gute ~ *(Strafgefangener)* good conduct; **höhere ~** higher command *(Br.)*; **kollektive ~** collective leadership; **oberste ~** top management; **schlechte ~** mismanagement, *(Benehmen)* misbehavio(u)r, bad behavio(u)r, ill conduct, *(mil.)* misconduct; **strategische ~** strategic planning;
~ **der Bücher** accounting, bookkeeping; **ordnungsgemäße ~ der Geschäfte** proper conduct of business; ~ **eines Landwirtschaftsbetriebs** farm operation (management) *(US)*; ~ **eines Produktionsbetriebes** production management; ~ **des Protokolls** keeping the minutes; ~ **eines Prozesses** conduct of a lawsuit; ~ **eines Titels** use of a title; ~ **eines Urkundenbeweises** proof by documentary evidence; ~ **von Verhandlungen** conduct of negotiations; ~ **durch Vorgabe von Zielen** management by objectives;
sich einer ~ anschließen to join a conducted party; **sich jds. ~ anvertrauen** to resign o. s. to s. one's guidance; **sich gern fremder ~ anvertrauen** to lean upon others for guidance; **jds. ~ entgleiten** to slip out of s. one's hands; **Beamten wegen schlechter ~ entlassen** to dismiss an official for unsatisfactory conduct; **jem. die ~ entreißen** to remove s. o. from the helm; ~ **innehaben** to have the lead (command); **an einer ~ durch ein Museum teilnehmen** to take part in a tour of the museum; ~ **übernehmen** to take the lead (head, running), *(Börse)* to forge ahead; ~ **eines Unternehmens übernehmen** to get operational responsibilities; **für gute ~ ausgezeichnet werden** to be awarded a prize for good conduct; **wegen guter ~ vorzeitig entlassen werden** *(Strafgefangener)* to get a couple of years remission for good conduct; **der ~ einer immer breiter gefächerten Unternehmensgruppe gerecht werden** to manage increased diversity.

Führungs|abteilung operations department; ~**akademie** *(mil.)* staff college; ~**anspruch** claim to leadership; ~**apparat modernisieren** to update its management techniques; ~**aufgaben** executive duties (functions); **Angestellten mit ~aufgaben betrauen** to entrust an employee with executive functions; ~**befähigung** management talent, managerial qualities; ~**befugnisse** managerial authority; ~**buch** conduct book.

Führungsebene management (managerial) level;
mittlere ~ middle management *(US)*.

Führungseigenschaften managerial qualities;
seine ~ ausprobieren to flex one's leadership muscles; **seine ~ unter Beweis stellen** to exercise one's skill of leadership.

Führungsfunktionen managerial functions, executive nature.

Führungsgremium leadership forum, governing body, *(Partei)* machines;
erstklassiges ~ blue-chip roster of partners *(US)*; **zweistufiges ~** two-tier board;
~ **aus leitenden Angestellten** inside board *(US)*;
~ **von Grund auf umstrukturieren** to structure one's management from scratch.

Führungs|größe management level; ~**grundsatz** management principle; ~**gruppe** top executive (management) team, management (leading) group; ~**hierarchie** management hierarchy; **sein ~instrumentarium umrüsten** to retool one's management knowledge; ~**kollektiv** collective leadership.

Führungskraft executive [employee, officer] *(US)*;
Rangunterschiede beachtende ~ echelon-oriented executive; **betriebliche ~** business executive; **erfahrene ~** senior executive; **fachliche ~** functional manager; **an den Arbeitsplatz gebundene ~** deskbound executive; **junge ~** freshman executive; **kaufmännische ~** business executive; **mittlere ~** middle-management executive; **oberste ~** top-level manager; **ortsansässige ~** resident executive; **im Ausland stationierte ~** foreign-based executive; **tantiemeberechtigte ~** fringe executive; **technische ~** technical executive; **unterstellte ~** managerial subordinate; **für Geschäftsrisiken verantwortliche ~** risk manager;
~ **im Außendienst** field executive; ~ **für den Verkauf** sales executive (manager); ~ **einer Versicherungsgesellschaft** underwriting executive.

Führungskräfte management (high-level, top, *US*) executives, management personnel, executive officers (personnel, *US*), managerial staff, leadership personnel;
auf dem Gebiet der mittleren ~ on middle management level; **nicht zu den ~n zählend** rank and file;
mittlere ~ middle management (lower echelon) executive; **oberste ~** top management;
~ **mit hohem Einkommensniveau** high-income management people; ~ **eines Landes** leaders of a country; ~ **aller Rangklassen** all-level executives;
ausgebildete ~ erfordern to demand professional management standards;
~**bedarf** executive requirements.

Führungs|kreisen, in in the leadership ranks; ~**krise** crisis of leadership; ~**kunst** management expertise; ~**liste** *(Vorstrafenregister)* police record.

führungslos *(Auto, Bahn)* without a driver, driverless, *(Flugzeug)* without a pilot, pilotless, *(mil.)* without commanders, *(Partei)* without a leader.

Führungs|mannschaft management team; ~**methoden** managerial techniques; **bewegliche ~methoden** management flexibility; ~**nachwuchs** *(Industrie)* management trainees, prospective managers; ~**nachwuchsgruppe** management reserve group; ~**niveau** management level, level of management; ~**note** mark of conduct.

Führungsposition management (managerial) position;
gehobene ~ senior executive position; **verantwortliche ~** line position;
~**en aus den eigenen Reihen besetzen** to fill senior positions from one's own staff.

Führungs|posten executive (management) post; ~**potential** leadership potential; ~**problem** managerial (entrepreneurial) problem; **stetig nachlassende ~qualifikationen** management decline; ~**qualitäten** good executive abilities, management abilities (talent), management skills; **keine ~qualitäten besitzen** to lack leadership; ~**rolle** leading role; ~**rolle beanspruchen** to claim leadership; ~**schicht** leadership community, establishment; **mittlere ~schicht** advanced (middle) management *(US)*; ~**schiene** tongue, guide rail; ~**schwelle** management level.

Führungsspitze higher echelons, top management *(US)*;
oberste ~ Chief Executive *(US)*.

Führungs|stab top executive team (staff), *(mil.)* operational headquarters (staff); **gemeinsamer ~stab** joint operation center *(US)*; ~**stellung** leadership position; ~**stil** management style; ~**struktur** management structure; ~**stufe** management level, *(mil.)* level of command; **die höheren ~stufen** the higher echelons; ~**tätigkeit** management functions; ~**unterlagen** *(mil.)* tactical and intelligence information; ~**wechsel** change in leadership, change in the management; ~**wirksamkeit** management perfection; ~**zeugnis** good-conduct certificate, certificate of character (good behavio(u)r), *(mil.)* service record, *(Polizei)* clearance certificate; **gutes ~zeugnis vorlegen** to deliver a certificate of good character.

Fuhr|unternehmen carrier, carter, trucking (carloading) company *(US)*, haulage-contracting business, hauler; ~**unternehmer** carrier, carter, haulage (cartage) contractor, teamster *(US)*, hauler *(US)*, *(Möbelspediteur)* mover *(US)*; ~**werk** cart, wag(g)on, conveyance, vehicle; ~**wesen** wag(g)on traffic, conveyance, trucking.

Füll|anzeige stopgap advertising (advertisement), filler; **später auszuwechselnder ~artikel** bogus *(US sl.)*; ~**auftrag** fill-in order; ~**bleistift** refilling (mechanical, *US*) pencil.

Fülle abundance, wealth, amplitude, exuberance, store, flood, plenty, luxuriance;
körperliche ~ corpulence, stoutness, ample figure;
~ **von Aufträgen** spate of orders; ~ **des Ausdrucks** richness of expression; ~ **von Beispielen** wealth of examples; ~ **von Besuchern** flood of callers; ~ **von Beweisen** mass of evidence; ~ **von Briefen** flood (mass, shower, volume) of letters; ~ **neuer Bücher** spate of new books; ~ **der Details** wealth of details; ~ **von Erfahrungen** wealth of experience; ~ **von Fragen** host (shower, crop) of questions; ~ **meines Glücks** depth of my happiness; ~ **von Ideen** host of ideas; ~ **von Nachrichten** lots of news; ~ **von Tatsachen** large body of facts; ~ **gesellschaftlicher Veranstaltungen** vortex of social life;
~ **von Versprechungen abgeben** to make promises in profusion; ~ **von Gerüchten auslösen** to touch off a spate of rumo(u)rs; **etw. in Hülle und ~ haben** to have plenty of s. th.; **Geld in Hülle und ~ haben** to have money to burn, to be rolling in money; **mit einer ~ von Begabungen ausgestattet sein** to have riches to spare; **eine ~ interessanter Menschen treffen** to meet no end of interesting people.

füllen to fill, *(Kissen)* to stuff;
sich den Bauch ~ to eat one's fill; **jds. Glas ~** to fill s. one's glass; **seinen Kopf mit unnützem Wissen ~** to stuff one's head with unnecessary facts; **sich langsam ~** *(Saal)* to begin to fill up slowly; **Lücke ~** to stop a gap; **in Säcke ~** to sack; **drei Seiten ~** *(Artikel)* to cover (take up) three pages; **Tank ~** to fill a tank; **sich die Taschen ~** to line one's pockets; **Wein in Fässer ~** to barrel wine; **Wein auf Flaschen ~** to bottle wine.

Füller fountain pen, *(Anzeige)* stopgap advertising, filler, *(Artikel)* fill, filler, quadder, *(Puffersendung)* cushion.

Füllfederhalter fountain pen;
~**ständer** pen desk set.

Füll|gas *(Ballon)* lifting gas; ~**horn** horn of plenty, cornucopia.

füllig plump, ample;
~ **werden** to fill out.

Füllmaterial filling, stuffing, *(drucktechn.)* blank material, stuffing *(sl.)*.

Füllsel *(Zeitung)* filler, quadder.

Füllung filling, stuffing.

Füllwort expletive, wasteword.

fulminante|Erscheinung dashing figure, striking appearance; ~ **Rede** brilliant speech.

fummeln to fumble, to fiddle, to tinker;
Stunde an seinem Rundfunkgerät ~ to have an hour's tinker at one's radio; **an einem Schlüsselloch ~** to fumble at a lock.

Fund find, object found, lost property, finding, haul;
~ **verheimlichen** to conceal a find;
~**abteilung** lost-property office.

Fundament fundament, foundation, base, substructure, *(Druckpresse)* bed, *(fig.)* basis, foundation, bedrock;
auf sicherem ~ on a steady foundation;
~ **der modernen Gesellschaft** foundations of modern society; ~ **für ein Gebäude errichten** to lay the foundations of a building; ~ **seiner Einkunftsmöglichkeiten erweitern** to widen one's revenue base.

fundamental fundamental, basic.

Fundamentblock foundation block.

Fund|büro lost-property *(Br.)* (and found, *US*) office; ~**gegenstand** object found, find, finding, lost property.

Fundgrube mine, bonanza, treasure house (trove), quarry;
~ **von Anekdoten** hoard of anecdotes; ~ **für Informationen** treasury (mine) of information.

fundieren to consolidate, to fund, *(Haus)* to lay the foundation;
Anleihe neu ~ to refund a loan; **Behauptung ~** to establish the truth of an assertion; **Schuld ~** to fund a debt, to convert a floating debt; **Staatsschuld ~** to consolidate the public debt.

fundiert funded, well-grounded, *(Anleihe)* consolidated, bonded, *(Firma)* sound, solid;
nicht ~ unfunded; **schlecht ~** poor, without reserves;
~**es Einkommen** unearned income; **gut ~es Geschäft** well-established business; ~**e Kenntnisse** thorough knowledge; ~**e Schuld** funded (consolidated, bonded, permanent) debt; ~**e Staatspapiere** funds, consols *(Br.)*; ~**es Wissen** thorough knowledge.

Fundierung foundation, *(Anleihe)* funding, consolidation;
~ **der Altersversorgungskosten** aggregate funding; ~ **einer Anleihe** consolidation of a loan; ~ **einer schwebenden Schuld** conversion of a floating debt.

Fundierungs|anleihe consolidation loan; ~**anreiz** inducement to fund; ~**schuldverschreibungen** funding bonds; ~**transaktion** funding operation.

fündig *(Lagerstätte)* rich;
~ **werden** to strike oil, *(fig.)* to touch bottom, to get at the root.

Fund|objekt finding; ~**ort** find place (spot), *(Bergbau)* strike, *(Mineralien)* locality, *(zool.)* habitat; ~**sache** object found, lost property; ~**stätte**, ~**stelle** find, place, habitat, ~**stellenverzeichnis** list of references; ~**unterschlagung** larceny by bailee.

Fundus *(Theater)* equipment, *(Wissen)* resources.

fünf, so aussehen, als ob man nicht bis ~ zählen kann to look as if butter would not melt in one's mouth; **sich an den ~ Fingern abzählen können** to be as plain as a pikestaff; ~ **gerade sein lassen** to turn a blind eye on s. th.; **sich auf seine ~ Buchstaben setzen** to park one's backside; **seine ~ Sinne zusammennehmen** to pull o. s. together;
~**te Kolonne** *(pol.)* fifth column.

Fünf|centstück nickel; ~**dollarnote** five.

Fünfer|alphabet five-unit code; ~**gruppe** five-letter group.

fünffach *(Urkunde)* in quintuplicate.

Fünfjahres|frist quinquennial period; ~**plan** five-year (fifth economic) plan.

fünfjährig quinquennial.

Fünfpfundnote fiver *(Br.)*.

fünfprozentig [bearing] five per cent;
~**e Papiere** five-percents.

fünfstellig|sein to run into five figures;
~**es Einkommen** five-figure income.

Fünf|sternehotel five-star hotel; ~**stufenrakete** five-stage rocket; ~**tagewoche** five-day week; ~**uhrtee** five-o'-clock tea; ~**undzwanzigdollaraktie** quarter stock *(US)*.

Fünfzig|dollaraktie half stock *(US)*; **falscher ~er sein** to be full of guile, to be phony *(US)*.

fünfzigprozentige Preiserhöhung fifty per cent price increase.

Fünfzimmerwohnung five-roomed flat.

fungibel fungible, interchangeable.

Fungibilität fungibility.

fungieren to function, to officiate, to serve, to act as;
als Hausfrau ~ to play the role of the housewife; **als Standesbeamter ~** to officiate as registrar; **als Stellvertreter ~** to act as deputy, to deputize; **als Verbindungsmann ~** to liaise; **als Vertreter ~** to deputize; **als Vorsitzender ~** to officiate as chairman, to chair.

Funk wireless, radio *(US)*;
Stück für den ~ bearbeiten to adapt a play for broadcasting; **mit ~ ausgerüstet sein** to be equipped with radio; **durch ~ miteinander in Verbindung stehen** to be in radio contact; **Mitteilung durch ~ übermitteln** to transmit a message by radio (wireless);
~**amateur** wireless amateur, radio ham; ~**anlage** radio (wireless) installation; ~**antenne auf einen Sender einstellen** to direct the aerial towards a station; ~**aufklärung** radio intelligence; ~**ausrüstung** wireless (radio) equipment; ~**ausstellung** radio and television exhibition, wireless exhibition; ~**autor** scriptwriter, scripter; ~**bake** [radio] beacon, radio beam (marker); ~**bastler** radio amateur (ham); ~**bearbeitung** radio adaptation, adaptation for broadcasting; ~**befehl** radioed order; ~**bereitschaft** *(mil.)* listening service; ~**bericht** broadcast account; ~**berichterstatter** commentator; ~**betrieb** wireless service; ~**bild** radio picture, photoradiogram, radiophotograph.

Fünkchen element, trace, spark, ounce, scrap, particle;
kein ~ Humor not a trace of humo(u)r; **kein ~ von Intelligenz** not the least glimmer of intelligence; **kein ~ gesunden Menschenverstands** not an ounce of common sense; ~ **Wahrheit** element (ray) of truth; **kein ~ Wahrheit** not a vestige of truth.

Funkeinrichtung wireless installation.

Funkeln eines Brillanten fire of a diamond.

funkeln to sparkle, *(Stern)* to twinkle;
zornig ~ to glitter with rage.

funkelnagelneu brand (sparkling, span-) new, spick and span, neat as a new pin, *(Münze)* in mint condition, mint.

Funk|empfang wireless reception; ~**empfänger** radio (wireless) receiver.

Funken spark, *(fig.)* ounce, flicker;
elektrischer ~ spark of electricity;
kein ~ **eines Beweises** not a sliver (glimmer) of evidence; **kein** ~ **Hoffnung** not a ray of hope; ~ **gesunden Menschenverstandes** ounce of common sense;
~ **auslösen** to produce a spark; **arbeiten, daß die** ~ **fliegen** to work at white-hot speed; **keinen** ~ **Anstand im Leibe haben** to have no spark of generosity; ~ **schlagen** to strike fire; **zündender** ~ **für einen Aufstand sein** to spark off the uprising; ~ **sprühen** to sparkle, to flash.
funken to wireless, to radio, to transmit;
Meldung ~ to transmit a message by radio; SOS ~ to transmit a distress signal.
Funken|bildung sparking; ~**entladung** spark discharge; ~**fänger** *(Lokomotive)* spark arrester; ~**flug** flying sparks.
Funkentelegrafie wireless telegraphy.
funkentelegrafisch by wireless.
funkentstört suppressed for radio.
Funkentstörung noise suppression;
~ **einbauen** to fit a suppressor to an electric motor.
Funker wireless (radio) operator, telegraphist, telegrapher, *(mil.)* signalman, lid *(sl.)*, sparks *(sl.)*;
~**kabine** wireless room.
Funk|erlaubnis radio licence; ~**fassung** adaptation for broadcasting.
funkferngesteuert radio- (wireless) controlled.
Funkfern|peilung long-range direction finding; ~**schreiber** teletypewriter *(US)*, radio teletyper; ~**sehen** radiovision; ~**sprecher** radiotelephone, wireless telephone.
Funk|feuer radio beam (marker), [radio] beacon; **ungerichtetes** ~**feuer** nondirectional beacon; ~**frequenz** radio-frequency; ~**gerät** wireless transmitter; **gegen** ~**störungen unempfindliches (entstörtes)** ~**gerät** jam-resistant radio; ~**gespräch** radiotelephone conversation; ~**haus** broadcasting station; ~**kanal** radio channel; ~**kennung** radio beacon signal; ~**kompaß** radio compass; ~**kontakt haben** to be in radio contact.
Funkleit|station homing station; ~**strahl** radio beam, beam rider guidance, *(Flugzeug)* localizer; **mit** ~**strahl führen** to beam; ~**strahlsystem** beam-rider guidance; ~**weg** glider path.
Funk|lenksystem *(Raumfahrt)* radio guidance system; ~**lotterie** radio lottery; ~**manuskript** script, scenario; ~**meßanlage**, ~**meßgerät**, ~**meßstation** radar installation, radar (radiolocation) station; ~**meßtechnik** radiolocation; ~**meßwesen** electronics; ~**netz** radio network; ~**notsignal** distress (emergency) signal; ~**offizier** wireless officer; ~**ortung** radio navigation (direction finding), radiolocation; ~**ortungsgerät**, ~**peiler**, ~**peilgerät** radiolocator, position (direction) finder, radio compass, huff-duff; ~**peilung** radio bearing, direction finding, [radar] bearing; ~**raum** wireless room; ~- **und Fernsehreferent** *(Agentur)* time buyer; ~**richtstrahl** radio beam; ~**rufzeichen** code signal; ~**schatten** blind area, dead spot, shadow region; ~**sender** wireless transmitter; ~**signal** signal; **undeutliches** ~**signal** mud; ~**sonde** radiosonde.
Funksprech|anlage ausgestattet, mit radioequipped; ~**gerät** radiophone, radio telephone; **tragbares** ~**gerät** walkie-talkie, peepie-creepie *(sl.)*; ~**kanal** radio telephone channel; ~**verbindung** radio link; ~**verkehr** radiotelephony.
Funkspruch wireless (radio) message, radiogram, radiotelegram, *(mil.)* signal, aerogram;
abgefangener ~ intercept;
~ **abfangen** to intercept a radiotelegram; ~ **absetzen** to send a message by radio (a wireless message).
Funk|sprüche, sich durch ~**sprüche verständigen** to talk by exchange of wireless messages; ~**station** wireless station; **bewegliche** ~**stelle** mobile radio station; **feste** ~**stelle** fixed radio station.
funksteuern to radio-control.
Funk|steuerung radio control (navigation); ~**stille** wireless silence, dead air; ~**stille ansagen** to sign off *(US)*; ~**störung** radio interference, *(Störsender)* jamming; ~**strahl** radio beam, beacon; ~**streife** squad *(US)* (police, radio patrol) car, cruise (prowl) car *(US)*, cruiser *(US)*, mobile patrol; ~**streifeneinsatzkräfte** patrol force; ~**streifenwagen** radio patrol (squad, *US*, police) car; ~**tagebuch** radio log; ~**taxi** radio taxi, call car; ~**technik** radio engineering; ~**telefon** radiotelephone, transceiver; ~**telefonie** wireless telephony, radiotelephony.
funktelefonisch übermitteln to radiotelephone.
Funktelegrafie wireless telegraphy, radiotelegraphy.
funktelegrafisch radiotelegraphic.
Funktelegramm radiogram, wireless message;
~ **senden** to radiotelegraph.
Funktion function, office, role, duty;
in seiner ~ **als Magistratsbeauftragter** in his function as magistrate; **mit schiedsrichterlicher** ~ **ausgestattet** arbitrative; **voneinander abhängige** ~**en** interdependent functions; **amtliche** ~**en** official functions; **außergewöhnliche** ~ offbeat role; **beratende** ~ advisory function; **betriebsleitende** ~**en** managerial functions; **ehrenamtliche** ~**en** honorary duties; **einstweilige** ~**en** provisional duties; **grundsätzliche** ~**en** basic functions; **hoheitsrechtliche** ~**en** sovereign powers; **lebenswichtige** ~**en** vital functions; **richterähnliche** ~**en** quasi-judicial functions; **richterliche** ~**en** functions of a judge; **staatliche** ~**en** governmental functions; **treuhänderische** ~ fiduciary duty; **vollziehende** ~**en** ministerial functions;
~ **eines Beamten** function of an officer of state;
~ **des Gesetzgebers abschaffen** to destroy a legislative function;
~ **ausüben** to occupy a position, to carry out (exercise) a function, to play a role; **richterliche** ~**en ausüben** to act the part of a judge; ~**en auf j. übertragen** to devolve duties upon s. o.; ~**en auf einen Ausschuß übertragen** to put an office into commission.
funktionale|Kontenrechnung functional accounting; ~ **Kostenentscheidung** functional statement.
Funktionär functionary, office bearer, officeholder *(US)*;
~**e** *(Politik)* machines *(US)*;
staatlicher ~ magistrate *(US)*;
~ **auf Besuchsreise** *(Gewerkschaft)* walking delegate.
funktionell functional;
~**e Kostenaufgliederung** functional division of expenses; ~**e Trennung** functional partition.
Funktionieren efficient working, action, *(Maschine)* running, working;
reibungsloses ~ smooth functioning;
~ **des Gewissens** workings of conscience; ~ **der Volkswirtschaft** functioning of the economy.
funktionieren to function, to work, *(Maschine)* to be working, to run, to operate, to be in operation, to go, to operate;
gerade noch ~ to tick over; **gut** ~ to be in good working order, to work well; **nicht** ~ to go wrong, to become deranged; **nicht mehr** ~ to get out of order, to break down; **reibungslos** ~ to run smoothly, to function without friction; **immer noch reibungslos** ~ to be still going like the clappers *(fam.)*.
funktionierend working, running, operating, in operation, *(in gebrauchsfähigem Zustand)* in commission;
gut ~ efficient; **nicht** ~ not working, out of whack *(coll.)*.
Funktions|anspruch functional claim; ~**dauer** term (period) of office.
funktionsfähig *(Plan)* workable, efficient.
Funktions|gliederung functional distribution; ~**leiter** *(Statistik)* nomographic scale; ~**mangel** functional deficiency; ~**prüfung** operational test; ~**rabatt** functional discount; ~**raum** functional (nodal) region; ~**schädigung** lesion; ~**störung** malfunction, functional disease (disorder); ~**stufe** functional grade.
funktionsunfähig broken down, unworkable, ramshackle *(sl.)*.
Funktions|unfähigkeit unworkability; ~**verhältnis** functional relationship; ~**zulage** special allowance.
Funk|trupp radio section; ~**turm** radio tower; ~**übertragung** radio relay; ~**überwachung** monitoring; ~**verbindung** radio contact (communication, link); ~**verbindung aufnehmen** to establish radio contact; ~**verkehr** radio communications, wireless communication; ~**wagen** radio car, radio patrol (squad, *US*) car, cruise (prowl) car *(US)*, cruiser *(US)*; **auf dem** ~**wege** by radio (wireless); ~**welle** air (radio) wave; ~**werbung** broadcast (radio) advertising; **schwerpunktartige** ~**werbung** spot radio; ~**werbungsmengenrabatt** time discount; ~**wetterdienst** radio weather service; ~**zeitung** radio periodical.
Funzel loose thread;
alte ~ ugly old woman.
Für und Wider pros and cons;
das ~ **erörtern** to go into the details of a case.
Fürbitte intercession, plea;
durch seine ~ through his mediation;
~ **für j. einlegen** to intercede with s. o. for s. o.
Furche furrow, trough.
Furcht fear, alarm, dread, *(Bestürzung)* dismay, alarm;
von ~ **beherrscht** possessed of fear, awestruck;
jem. ~ **einflößen (einjagen)** to inject fear into s. o., to scare s. o.; **in** ~ **und Unruhe geraten** to be running scared; **von ständiger** ~ **geplagt sein** to labo(u)r under a constant anxiety; ~ **und Schrecken verbreiten** to spread fear and terror; **seine** ~ **deutlich zeigen** to show the white feather; **vor** ~ **zittern** to tremble with fear.

furchtbar terrible, dreadful, frightful, vicious *(coll.)*;
~ **lachen** to laugh till one's sides ache; **sich ~ wichtig vorkommen** to think no small beer of o. s.;
~**es Englisch sprechen** to speak a ghastly English; ~**e Folgen** dire consequences; ~**er Geizhals** dreadful miser; ~**er Mensch** awful person; ~**es Schicksal** terrible fate; ~**es Verbrechen** appalling crime.

furchteinflößend frightening, fearsome.

fürchten to fear, to be afraid (frightened, scared);
Arbeit ~ to fight shy of work; **Schande ~** to be afraid of disgrace.

fürchterlich terrible, dreadful, vicious *(coll.)*.

furchtlos dauntless, intrepid, fearless;
ganz ~ sein to be wholly void of fear.

furchtsam timid, shy.

Furie hell cat, a devil in petticoats;
wie von ~n gehetzt like all possessed;
~**n** dire sisters.

Furnier veneer, inlay.

furnieren to veneer, to inlay.

Furnierholz veneer, fancy woods, inlay.

furniert veneered.

Furore great stir, hit, splash, rage;
~ **machen** to make a splash, to create a sensation, *(Mode)* to be all the rage.

Fürsorge provident care, [provisory] care, custody, *(Wohlfahrt)* [poor] relief *(Br.)*, welfare work, plug *(coll.)*;
ärztliche ~ medical care; **gemeinbezogene ~** parochial charity; **geschlossene ~** indoor relief, institutional care; **liebevolle ~** tender care; **öffentliche ~** poor relief *(Br.)*, public welfare work; **private ~** charity; **soziale ~** national *(Br.)* (public, *US*) assistance, public relief *(Br.)*, social welfare (service); **staatliche ~** supplementary benefits *(Br.)*; **väterliche ~** paternal care; **zärtliche ~** tender care;
~ **für die Armen** maintenance of the poor; ~ **für die ganze Familie** family provision *(Br.)*; ~ **für die Lebensbedürfnisse** provision for the necessities of life; ~ **für Mutter und Kind** maternity welfare; ~ **für Strafentlassene** aftercare for discharged prisoners;
der öffentlichen ~ zur Last fallen to be put on public assistance rolls *(US)*, to come upon the parish (rates, town, *US*); **schließlich der ~ zur Last fallen** to end up on the welfare rolls; ~ **angedeihen lassen** to administer relief; **von der ~ leben** to be a public charge; **in der ~ tätig sein** to do welfare work; **jds. ~ übergeben** to commit to s. one's care; **von der ~ unterstützt werden** to receive national *(Br.)* (public, *US*) assistance, to be on welfare rolls;
~**abteilung** welfare department; ~**amt** National *(Br.)* (Public, *US*) Assistance Authority, overseer of the poor *(Br.)*, welfare agency (center) *(US)*, relieving office; ~**anspruch** eligibility for public relief; ~**anstalt** reformatory, correctional institution, approved school *(Br.)*; ~**arzt** medical officer; ~**aufwand**, ~**ausgaben** social service expenditure (spending), welfare expenditure; ~**ausschuß** national *(Br.)* (public, *US*) assistance committee *(US)*, welfare committee; ~**beamter** welfare worker (officer, *US*), guardian (reliever) of the poor *(Br.)*, poor-law guardian *(Br.)*, relieving officer *(Br.)*, *(für Kinder)* probation officer *(US)*, *(für Straffällige)* probation officer, prob *(fam.)*.

fürsorgebedürftig in need of assistance *(Br.)*.

Fürsorge|bedürftiger needy person; ~**behörde** poor-law board, Supplementary Benefits Commission *(Br.)*, National Assistance Board *(Br.)*, welfare agency (branch) *(US)*; **sich an die ~behörde wenden** to apply to the union house *(Br.)*.

fürsorgeberechtigt eligible for relief (welfare).

Fürsorge|berechtigung eligibility for relief; ~**bestimmungen** welfare-service provisions; ~**bezirk** new (poor-law, *Br.*) parish; ~**einrichtungen** welfare facilities (institutions, center), social service; ~**empfänger** welfare recipient (beneficiary, client), public charge, assisted person *(Br.)*, recipient of relief; **nicht ortsansässiger ~empfänger** casual pauper *(Br.)*; ~**empfängerliste** national *(Br.)* (public, *US*) assistance roll; ~**erziehung** reformatory school *(US)*, approved school system *(Br.)*; ~**experte** welfare expert; **zu bearbeitende ~fälle** case load; ~**familie** welfare family; ~**funktionen** welfare functions; ~**funktionen der gewerblichen Wirtschaft** industrial responsibility; ~**gesetz für Mutter und Kind** Maternity and Child Welfare Act *(Br.)*; ~**gesetzgebung** welfare legislation; ~**heim** rescue home, Borstal Institution *(Br.)*; **in ein ~heim kommen** to be put into care; ~**helfer** welfare assistant; ~**internat** approved school *(Br.)*, community home *(Br.)*; ~**kasse** public welfare (assistance, *US*) provident fund; ~**lasten** welfare costs (expenditure); ~**leistungen** welfare (public, assistance, *US*) benefits; ~**leistungen [aus der Sozialhilfe]** social security benefits *(Br.)*, social welfare benefits *(US)*; ~**liste** welfare roll; ~**merkmale** welfare features; ~**organisation** charity organization; ~**patient** rate-aided patient; ~**pflicht** obligation to provide welfare maintenance; ~**politik** public assistance policy *(US)*, welfare policies; ~**programm** welfare program(me).

Fürsorger reliever of the poor *(Br.)*, welfare worker, welfare (relieving) officer, *(für Straffällige)* probationer.

Fürsorge|recht poor laws *(Br.)*; ~**rente** provident benefit, national *(Br.)* (public, *US*) assistance, welfare check; ~**richtlinien** welfare rules; ~**richtsätze** standard national *(Br.)* (public, *US*) assistance rates.

fürsorgerisch, sich ~ betätigen to do welfare work;
~**e Tätigkeit** welfare work.

Fürsorge|staat welfare state; ~**stelle** poor-law parish *(Br.)*, welfare agency (center) *(US)*; ~**system** welfarism, welfare system (statism); ~**tätigkeit** casework, social work *(US)*, welfare work *(US)*; ~**unternehmen** charitable undertaking.

Fürsorgeunterstützung welfare check (payment) *(US)*, provident benefit, parish (charity) relief *(Br.)*, out[door] relief *(Br.)*, outrelief *(Br.)*, national assistance *(Br.)*, public (social) assistance *(US)*, public relief *(US)*, supplementary benefits *(Br.)*;
auf ~ angewiesen on the parish *(Br.)*, on relief *(US)*; ~ **beziehen (empfangen)** to be on local public relief *(US)* (the parish, *Br.*), to be in receipt of national *(Br.)* (public, *US*) assistance, to be on welfare *(US)*, to go on relief rolls, to receive state relief *(US)*, to obtain relief *(US)*.

Fürsorgeunterstützungs|berechtigung eligibility for relief; ~**empfänger** welfare recipient (client, beneficiary), public charge, assisted person *(Br.)*; **auf die Liste der ~empfänger setzen** to put on welfare (public assistance, *US*) rolls.

Fürsorge|verband, ~**verein** welfare association (organization), poor-law union *(Br.)*, relief association; ~**vorkehrungen** welfare provisions; ~**wesen** welfare system, welfarism, district visiting; **öffentliches ~wesen** social service scheme, poor-law administration *(Br.)*; ~**zögling** ward.

fürsorglich thoughtful, solicitous.

Fürsprache intercession, interposition, mediation, plea;
~ **für j. einlegen** to intercede for s. o.; **jds. ~ in Anspruch nehmen** to make use of s. one's good offices.

Fürsprecher intercessor, advocate, booster, advocate;
für j. als ~ auftreten to intercede for s. o.; **einflußreiche ~ haben** to have friends at court; **sich zum ~ der Armen machen** to make o. s. the voice of the poor.

Fürst ruler, sovereign, prince;
wie ein ~ leben to live like a lord.

Fürstentum principality, princedom.

fürstlich royal, magnificent, sumptuous;
j. ~ belohnen to reward s. o. royally; **j. ~ bewirten** to entertain s. o. lavishly; ~ **leben** to live in lavish style;
~**es Mahl** opulent meal; ~**es Trinkgeld** princely tip.

Furt ford, passing, passage.

Fusel rotgut *(sl.)*, tape *(sl.)* moonshine *(sl.)*.

füsilieren to fusilade, to execute [by firing squad].

Fusion merger, merging, fusion, tie-up, absorption, amalgamation, consolidation *(US)*, *(jur.)* confusion of rights *(US)*;
staatlich geförderte ~ government-aided merger; **komplette ~** full-fledged merger; **multinationale ~** multinational merger; **vertikale ~** vertical merger;
~ **von Aktiengesellschaften** consolidation of corporations, corporate consolidation, corporate merger *(US)*; ~ **durch Aktienübernahme** amalgamation by share purchase; ~ **von Banken** bank merger; ~ **von Eisenbahngesellschaften** consolidation of railway lines; ~ **von Konkurrenzunternehmen** horizontal merger; ~ **der Mutter- mit der Tochtergesellschaft** downstairs merger; ~ **branchenfremder Unternehmen** conglomerate merger;
~ **rückgängig machen** to undo a merger; **einer ~ im Wege stehen** to block a merger.

fusionieren to merge, to combine, to amalgamate, to fuse, to consolidate *(US)*;
mit anderen ~ to incorporate with others.

fusionierende Gesellschaft merger company, consolidated corporation *(US)*.

fusioniert, teilweise half merged.

Fusionierung merger, fusion, amalgamation, consolidation.

Fusions|abkommen merger arrangement; ~**angebot** merger offer (bid); ~**anhänger** fusionist; ~**antrag** merger application; ~**bedingungen** terms for merger; ~**beschluß** merger decision;

~beschluß inhibieren to freeze action on merger; ~bewegung merger movement; ~bilanz consolidation (consolidated) balance sheet; ~druck merger pressure; ~erklärung merger statement; ~fieber merger fever; ~front merger front; ~genehmigung merger clearance *(US)*; für ~genehmigungen zuständig sein to rule on mergers; im ~geschäft den Ton angeben to dominate in the merger scene; ~gesellschaft merger company, consolidated corporation *(US)*; ~gespräche merger talks; ~gewinn consolidation profit (excess); ~kandidat merger candidate; ~kontrolle merger control; ~kosten consolidation expenditure; vorausgehende ~mitteilung premerger notification *(US)*; ~möglichkeiten merger possibilities; ~neigung inclination (urge) to merge; ~partner merger partner; ~projekt merger plan; sich an dem ~spiel beteiligen to play the merger game; ~tendenz merger trend; ~überschuß negative goodwill, consolidation excess; ~vereinbarung merger accord (agreement); ~verhandlungen merger talks; ~vertrag agreement of consolidation, deed of amalgamation, merger agreement; ~vorschlag proposed merger.

Fuß foot, *(Damm)* toe, *(Klischee)* base, mount, *(Scheinwerfer)* socket, *(Seite)* bottom;
eilenden ~es hot-foot; **leichten ~es** lightly; **schwankenden ~es** with faltering steps; **stehenden ~es** at once, without delay, on the spot, immediately;
am ~ der Schloßmauer under the castle wall; **auf freiem ~ befindlich** at liberty (large); **auf großem ~e** in a grand manner; **auf vertrautem ~** hand in glove; **von Kopf bis ~** from top to toe; **zu ~** on foot;
mit dem linken ~ aufstehen to get out of bed on the wrong side; **~ fassen** to gain a foothold; **festen ~ fassen** to obtain a firm plant on the ground; **gesellschaftlich ~ fassen** to get a footing in society; **in einem anderen Industriebereich ~ fassen** to gain a foothold in another industry; **wieder ~ fassen** to get on one's legs (feet) again; **jem. auf dem ~e folgen** to follow at (tread) s. one's heels, to dog s. one's footsteps, to hang on s. one's rear; **den Entdeckern auf dem ~e folgen** to come in the wake of explorers; **zu ~ gehen** to stump it *(sl.)*; **trockenen ~es nach Hause kommen** to get home without getting wet; **auf großem ~e leben** to live in grand (great) style (on a large scale, expensively); **auf gespanntem ~ mit jem. leben** to live a daggers drawn with s. o.; **zu ~ reisen** to tramp it; **noch auf freiem ~e sein** to be still at large; **gut zu ~ sein** to be a good walker; **zu ~ [bequem] zu erreichen sein** to be within [easy] walking distance; **auf freien ~ setzen** to set free, to disimprison; **keinen ~ mehr über jds. Schwelle setzen** not to darken s. one's door; **auf freundschaftlichem ~ stehen** to be on a friendly footing (on friendly terms); **immer mit einem ~ im Gefängnis stehen** to be always on the shady side of the law; **mit jem. auf gespanntem ~ stehen** to live in a state of tension with s. o.; **Gewehr bei ~ stehen** *(fig.)* to be ready to intervene; **mit einem ~ im Grabe stehen** to have one foot in the grave; **auf vertrautem ~ stehen** to be on terms of intimacy (on intimate terms) with s. o., to be hand in glove with s. o., to be cozy with s. o.; **mit jedermann auf vertrautem ~ stehen** to be hail fellow well met with everyone; **von einem ~ auf den anderen treten** to shift from one foot to the other;
~abblendschalter foot-operated dip switch; ~abdruck trace; ~abstreifer footscraper, door scraper; ~angel mantrap, *(fig.)* trap door, pitfall; ~antrieb pedal drive.

Fußball|platz football ground; ~spiel football match; ~toto football pools.

Fuß|bank footrest; ~bekleidung footwear, footgear.

Fußboden pavement;
~belag flooring, floorcloth; ~fliese paving tile; ~heizung underfloor heating.

Fußbreit width of a foot, *(fig.)* inch;
um jeden ~ des Bodens kämpfen to dispute every inch of the ground; **keinen ~ weichen** not to yield (give way) an inch.

Fuß|bremse foot (pedal) brake; ~bremspedal brake pedal.

Füße, sich die ~ nach etw. ablaufen to run off one's feet; **kalte ~ bekommen** *(fig.)* to get the wind up; **immer auf die ~ fallen** *(fig.)* to fall on one's feet; **auf eigenen ~n stehen** to stand on one's own feet; **auf schwachen ~n stehen** to be built on sand, to lack a sound basis, *(Argument)* to rest on weak premises, *(Unternehmen)* to be financially weak; **mit beiden ~n auf der Erde stehen** to have a down-to-earth outlook; **über die eigenen ~ stolpern** to trip o. s.; **j. mit ~n treten** to treat s. o. like a dog, to walk over s. o. *(US)*, to put the boot into s. o.; **etw. mit ~n treten** to treat s. th. with contempt; **Boden unter den ~n verlieren** to loose one's footing, to get out of depth, to be all at sea; **sich die ~ vertreten** to stretch one's legs; **jem. den Boden unter den ~n wegziehen** to cut the ground from under s. o.; **sich jem. zu ~n werfen** to throw o. s. on s. one's mercy; **jem. das Geld vor die ~ werfen** to throw the money into s. one's face; **jem. den ganzen Kram vor die ~ werfen** to chuck up the whole thing.

Fußeisen trap, mantrap.

fusselig fuzzy, linty *(US)*;
sich den Mund ~ reden to talk one's head off.

fußen|auf to rely (rest) on, to take as a base; **auf bloßen Annahmen ~** to be based on mere suppositions.

Fußgänger pedestrian, foot passenger, road user on foot;
einzelner ~ solitary pedestrian; **entgegenkommender ~** oncoming pedestrian; **unachtsamer ~** jaywalker;
~ anfahren to knock down a pedestrian;
~ampel [traffic] beacon *(Br.)*, pedestrian crossing light; ~bereich pedestrian zone (precinct); ~brücke footbridge; ~insel safety island; ~promenade pedestrian mall; ~reservat pedestrian island; ~steg footbridge; ~steig catwalk; ~streifen zebra crossing; **~tour zur Stadtbesichtigung** conducted walk; ~tunnel subway *(Br.)*, underpass *(US)*; ~überweg crosswalk, pedestrian crossing (platform, lines), zebra crossing; ~unterführung pedestrian subway, underpass *(US)*; ~verkehr pedestrian traffic; ~weg pedestrian street (platform); **mobiler ~weg** speedwalk; **öffentlicher ~weg** travelled part of highway (way); ~zone [car-free] pedestrian zone, safety lane.

Fußhebel pedal, foot lever.

fußhoch ankle-deep.

Fußhöhe, in above floor level.

fußkrank footsore.

Fuß|leiste baseboard, skirting board *(Br.)*; ~licht footlight; ~marsch march; ~matte door mat; ~note footnote; **als ~noten drucken** to print notes at the bottom of a page; **auf eine ~note verweisen** to refer to a footnote; ~notenverweis footnote reference; ~pfad footpath, footway; ~platte floor tile; ~raste footrest; ~reise tramp; ~schalter foot switch; ~schaltung pedal control; ~spur footprint, foottracks; ~spuren footsteps, footmarks; **seine ~spuren im Sand hinterlassen** to print one's footsteps on the sand; **in jds. ~stapfen** in the wake of s. o., to tread in s. one's footsteps, to step into s. one's shoes, to follow s. one's track; **in die ~stapfen seines Vaters treten** to follow one's father's profession; ~steg footpath; ~steig pavement, walk, sidewalk *(US)*, *(Flugplatz)* apron; ~tritt footstep, step; **j. mit einem ~tritt hinausbefördern** to kick s. o. out; ~volk infantry; **~volk einer Partei** rank and file of a party; ~wanderung hike, walking tour *(Br.)*; ~weg foot road, footpath, *(erhöht)* banquette.

futsch spoiled, ruined, *(kaputt)* broken, bust;
~ sein to have gone, to have had it *(fam.)*.

Futter food, fodder, forage, feed, peck *(Br., sl.)*;
sich ~ suchen to gather fodder.

Futteral covering, case.

Futteralien nosh, provender, grub *(sl.)*, eats *(US)*, chow *(US sl.)*.

Futter|automat automatic feeder, self-feeder *(US)*; ~behälter feed container, silo; ~getreide coarse (feed) grain; ~krippe pie counter, *(pol.)* gravy train *(US sl.)*; **an der ~krippe sitzen** to have a soft job.

Futterkrippen|politiker spoilsman *(US)*, placeman *(Br.)*; ~wirtschaft placemanship *(Br.)*, spoils system *(US)*, old-boy net *(Br.)*.

Futter|mangel lack of feed; ~mauer breast (retaining) wall.

Futtermittel fodder, forage;
~handlung feed store *(US)*.

Futtern forage;
j. in der Küche beim ~ antreffen to find s. o. on a forage in the kitchen *(coll.)*.

futtern to tuck away, to peck *(Br., coll.)*.

füttern to feed, *(drucktechn.)* to key;
Mantel mit Pelz ~ to line a coat with fur; **mit Vokabeln ~** to cram with words.

Futterneid *(fig.)* professional jealousy.

Fütterung feeding;
~ auf dem Transport feeding in transit.

Futurologe futurologist.

Futurologie futurology.

G

Gabe gift, donation, distribution, contribution, handout *(US sl.)*, *(Fähigkeit)* talent, faculty, gift, talent;
freiwillige ~n voluntary contributions; **mildtätige ~** gift to charity, charitable distribution, distribution of money in charity, eleemosynary gift;
~ der Beredsamkeit gift of the gab *(coll.)*;
um milde ~n bitten to ask for alms; **glückliche ~ besitzen, stets das Richtige zu sagen** to have the happy knack of saying the right thing; **milde ~n sammeln** to make up a basket; **milde ~n verteilen** to dispense charity.
Gabel *(Telefonapparat)* receiver rest, cradle;
~frühstück brunch, elevenses *(Br., coll.)*.
gabeln, sich *(Straße)* to branch, to bifurcate; **sich einen Ehemann ~** to pick up a husband; **nach etw. ~** to fish for s. th.
Gabelung *(Straße)* fork of a road, forking, bifurcation.
Gabentisch gift table.
gaffen to gaze, to gape, to rubberneck *(US sl.)*.
gaffend open-mouthed, gaping, staring.
Gag gag, gimmick, wheeze *(sl.)*.
Gage salary, pay;
einmalige ~ honorarium.
gähnen to yawn.
gähnend|er Abgrund gaping chasm; **~e Langeweile** utter boredom; **~e Leere** yawning emptiness.
Gala gala, gala dress, *(mil.)* review order, wampum *(US sl.)*;
in ~ with bells on;
sich in ~ werfen to dress up, to put on one's best bib and tucker; **~anzug** gala dress (clothes), state clothes, full dress; **~aufführung** gala (special) performance; **~dinner** gala (banquet) dinner; **~kleidung** trim, gala dress; **~kutsche** state coach.
Galan gallant, beau.
galant gallant, polite, chivalrous;
~es Abenteuer love affair; **~e Krankheit** venereal disease.
Galanterie gallantry, gallant manners;
~arbeit imitation jewellery; **~waren** fancy goods, notions *(US)*.
Gala|tag field day; **~uniform** gala dress; **~veranstaltung** dress affair; **~vorführung** gala performance.
Galerie gallery, loft, *(Theater)* upper circle, gallery;
obere ~ family circle *(US)*;
~ schöner Frauen bevy of beauties;
für die ~ spielen to play to the gallery (grandstand, *US*);
~besucher gallerite; **~direktor** gallery director.
Galgen gallows, gibbet, *(Film)* boom;
j. an den ~ bringen to hang s. o., to send s. o. to the gallows; **am ~ enden** to end on the gallows; **mit knapper Not dem ~ entgehen** to slip one's head out of the hangman's noose; **für den ~ bestimmt sein** to be destined for the gallows;
~frist short shrift; **~gesicht** gallows look; **~gesicht haben** to have the gallows in one's face, to have the look of a gallows bird; **~humor** grim humo(u)r; **~vogel** goal bird, gallows bird, lab.
Galle verspritzen to dip one's pen in gall.
Gallionsfigur fiddlehead, *(fig.)* figurehead.
Gallupumfrage gallup poll.
Galopp gallop;
im ~ at a gallop, in double-quick time;
seine Arbeit im ~ erledigen to gallop through one's work; **wie im ~ gehen** to be going at breakneck speed; **im ~ durch die Kinderstube geritten sein** to have no manners, to be badly brought up.
galvanisch|e Batterie voltaic battery; **~er Strom** voltaic current.
galvanisieren to galvanize.
Galvano electro.
Gamaschen gaiters, leggings, *(kurze)* spats;
~ vor etw. haben to be in a blue funk, to have the wind up.
Gang way, go, *(Ader)* lode, *(Auto)* gear, *(Bewegung)* motion, *(Bote)* errand, commission, *(Gericht)* course, *(Haus)* corridor, hall, passage *(Br.)*, *(Maschine)* running, operating, working, action, *(Schraube)* turn, *(Schritt)* walk, tread, *(zwischen Sitzreihen)* gangway *(Br.)*, aisle *(US)*, *(Verlauf)* course, *(Zug)* corridor;
im ~ going, at work; **im ersten ~** in low gear; **im höchsten ~** in full (top) gear; **in einem schnellen ~** in high gear; **in vollem ~** in full activity (play, progress, swing);
dritter ~ *(Auto)* third gear; **erster ~** *(Auto)* first (low, bottom) gear, first *(Br.)*, *(Menü)* first course; **höchster ~** *(Auto)* top gear; **langer ~** vista; **der letzte ~** last journey; **niedriger ~** low gear; **regelmäßiger ~** rota *(Br.)*; **schleppender ~** shuffle; **unterirdischer ~** underground passage; **vergeblicher ~** fruitless journey, fool's errand; **würdevoller ~** stalk; **zweiter ~** second [gear]; **der übliche ~ der Dinge** the normal run of things; **~ der Ereignisse** course (march, progress, tendency, run) of events; **~ der Gerechtigkeit** working of justice; **täglicher ~ in die Stadt** daily walk into town;
~ der Ereignisse abwarten to await the issue of events; **j. auf seinem letzten ~ begleiten** to follow s. o. to the graveside; **seinen ~ beschleunigen** to quicken one's pace; **in ~ bringen** to put into play, to get in motion (going, train), to work, to wind up; **Angelegenheit in ~ bringen** to get s. th. under way, to set an undertaking on its feet; **Gespräch in ~ bringen** to start the ball rolling *(coll.)*; **Sache richtig in ~ bringen** to give a favo(u)rable turn to a business; **in den ~ der Rechtspflege eingreifen** to impede the course of justice; **höheren ~ einschalten** to shift into high gear; **seinen höchsten ~ einschalten** *(fig.)* to shake a leg *(sl.)*; **~ eines Seemanns haben** to have sea-legs; **in ~ halten** to keep going (working, running, thriving), to operate; **Dinge in ~ halten** to keep things ticking over; **Gespräch in ~ halten** to keep the ball rolling; **~ herausnehmen** to shift the gear into neutral; **in ~ kommen** to swing into action, to get under way; **langsam in ~ kommen** to be off to a slow start; **richtig in ~ kommen** to hit one's stride; **ruckweise in ~ kommen** to jerk into action; **~ einer Maschine regeln** to regulate the working of a machine; **in den zweiten ~ schalten** to change into (engage) the second gear; **außer ~ sein** *(Auto)* to be out of (run in neutral) gear; **im ~e sein** *(Projekt)* to be on foot (in progress, process, going on), *(Maschine)* to be running (working); **in ~ sein** *(Maschine)* to be working (running); **in vollem ~ sein** to be in full swing; **in ~ setzen** to set afloat (in operation), to put in motion; **Gespräch in ~ setzen** to start the ball rolling; **Maschine außer ~ setzen** to stop a machine; **~ wechseln** to change (shift, *US*) gears;
es ist etw. im ~e there is s. th. in the wind.
gang und gäbe geworden sein to have become the usual thing.
Ganganordnung *(Auto)* gearshift.
gangbar feasible, practicable, passable, workable, *(Münze)* current, *(Ware)* salable, marketable, easy to sell, merchantable, vendible, *(Weg)* passable, practicable.
Gangbarkeit practicableness, workableness, feasibility, *(Münze)* currency, *(Ware)* salableness, salability, marketability, merchantableness, vendibility;
allgemeine ~ currency, general acceptance.
Gänge für j. erledigen to run errands for s. o.
Gängelband leading strings;
am ~ seiner Ehefrau tied to one's wife's apronstrings;
am ~ führen to conduct in leading strings, to lead s. o. by the nose, to have on a string, to ride on the snaffle.
Gängelei leading-strings.
gängeln, j. to lead s. o. by the nose.
gängig common, current, prevalent, *(Absatz)* selling, salable, vendible, merchantable, *(Aktie)* marketable, active;
~ sein to sell readily; **hauptsächlich im Sommer ~ sein** to sell mostly in the summer;
~er Ausdruck common expression; **~e Münze** current coin; **~er Typ** salable type; **~e Waren** salable (marketable) goods; **~e Ware darstellen** to find a ready sale; **~er Wert** fair market value.
Gängigkeit vendibility, salability, marketability.
Gang|ordnung *(Auto)* gearshift; **~schalter** gear lever; **~schaltung** gear change.
Gangster gangster, mobsman, racketeer *(US)*, hood *(US sl.)*;
~bande gang of criminals; **~braut** gun moll *(sl.)*; **~tum** gangsterism, racketeering *(US)*.
Ganove crook, hustler *(US sl.)*.
Gans, dumme silly thing;
wie eine ~ schnattern to cackle; **~ töten, die goldene Eier legt** to kill the goose that lays the golden eggs.
Gänschen ninny *(coll.)*.
Gänse|füßchen inverted commas, quotation marks; **~haut** creeps, goose pimples, *(fig.)* creeping sensation, shivers, gooseflesh; **jem. eine ~haut einjagen** to make s. one's flesh crawl; **~marsch** single (Indian) file; **im ~marsch abmarschieren** to file off, to walk in Indian file; **~wein** Adam's ale.
ganz all, whole, entire, full, round, undivided, complete, total;
~ und gar out and out, neck and crop, down to the ground, to

the backbone, from the ground up *(US)*, up to the hub *(US)*; ~ **und gar nicht** not a bit; ~ **und gar verrückt** as mad as a hatter; ~ **unter uns** between you and me and the lamppost;
~ **im Gegenteil** on the contrary, just the opposite; ~ **oder teilweise** in whole or in parts, wholly or partly; ~ **unmöglich** well nigh impossible; ~ **der Vater** the dead spit (spitting image, *US*) of his father;
~ **bezahlen** to pay in full; **Buch** ~ **durchlesen** to read a book from cover to cover; ~ **und gar versagt haben** to have been a complete (down the line, *US*) failure; ~ **lassen** to leave intact; **etw.** ~ **machen** to mend s. th.; ~ **und gar dafür sein** to be all for it; **jem.** ~ **egal sein** to be all the same to s. o.; **nicht** ~ **richtig im Kopf sein** to have lost a button; ~ **in Ordnung sein** to be in apple-pie order; **etw.** ~ **allein tun** to do s. th. entirely on one's own; **sich erneut** ~ **dem Geschäft widmen** to devote o. s. anew to business; ~**e Arbeit leisten** to make a thorough job of it, to go the whole hog; ~**e Aufmerksamkeit** undivided attention; **meine** ~**e Barschaft** all the money I have; ~**er Betrag** full (total) amount; ~**e Familie** whole family; **sein** ~**es Geld in Büchern anlegen** to spend a small fortune on books; **von** ~**em Herzen** wholeheartedly; ~**es Jahr** full year; **das** ~**e Jahr hindurch** throughout the year; **seine** ~**e Kraft aufbieten** to do one's utmost; **durch das** ~**e Land** throughout the country; **in** ~**er Länge** full-length; **auf der** ~**en Linie** all along the line; **ein** ~**er Mann** every inch a man; ~ **armer Mann** very poor man; ~ **Ohr sein** to be all ears; ~**es Problem** entire problem; ~ **andere Sache** s. th. altogether different; **den** ~**en Staat betreffend** nation-wide; **die** ~**e Stadt** the whole town; **sein** ~**er Stolz** the apple of one 's eye; **zwei** ~**e Stunden warten** to wait two hours on end; ~**e Summe** total (full) amount; **den** ~**en Tag** all day [long]; ~ **großes Tier** a big shot; ~ **kleine Unterschiede** minute differences; **mein** ~**es Vermögen** my entire fortune; **während des** ~**en Winters** throughout the winter.

Ganzaufnahme full-length portrait (picture), stand-up.

Ganze whole, total, entirety, gross;
im ~**n** in *(US)* (by the, *Br.*) bulk; **im** ~**n berechnet** reckoned all together; **im** ~**n gesehen** on balance; **im großen** ~**n** first and last; **Aufs-**~**-Gehen** whole hoggism;
aufs ~ **gehen** to go the whole length (the whole hog); **ums** ~ **gehen** to be neck or nothing; **im** ~**n kaufen** to buy in bulk (wholesale, in the lump).

Ganz|fabrikat finished product, wholly manufactured article; ~**gewebeband** full fabric binding; ~**holzbauweise** all-wood construction.

ganzjährig [all-the-]year round;
~**er Lehrgang** full year's course.

Ganzleder, in full-bound; ~**ledereinband** full-leather binding; ~**leinen** full cloth; ~**leinenband** cloth (full) binding.

gänzlich outright, complete, whole, entire, neck and crop;
~ **verschiedene Charaktere** entirely different characters; ~**e Hilflosigkeit** utter helplessness; ~**e Unwissenheit** absolute ignorance.

Ganz|metallbauweise all-metal construction; ~**sache** *(philat.)* entire, cover; ~**seiteninserat** full-page newspaper advertisement.

ganzseitig|e Abbildung full-page illustration; ~**e Anzeige** full-page advertisement; ~**er Bericht** report covering a whole page.

Ganzstahl, aus ~ **bestehend** all-steel;
~**bauweise** all-steel construction; ~**karosserie** all-steel body.

Ganzstelle *(Anzeige)* solus site.

ganztägig all day [long], full-time;
~ **arbeiten** to work full time;
~**e Beschäftigung** full-time job (employment).

Ganztags|beschäftigung full-time job (employment); **sich zu einer** ~**beschäftigung entwickeln** to grow into a full-time employment; ~**student** full-time student; ~**tätigkeit** full-time role; ~**unterricht** full-time attendance at school.

Garage [automobile] garage, car shed;
in einer ~ **abgestellt** garaged; **mit angebauter** ~ with a garage attached;
schwimmende ~ floating garage; **umgebaute** ~**n** mews *(Br.)*;
in eine ~ **einstellen, Auto in die** ~ **fahren** to garage a car; **Auto rückwärts aus der** ~ **fahren** to back a car out of a garage; ~ **nur teilweise gewerblich nutzen** to use a garage half for business.

Garagen|arbeiter garageman; ~**besitzer** garage keeper (proprietor); ~**besitzerhaftpflichtversicherung** garage keeper's liability; ~**einfahrt** drive *(Br.)*, driveway *(US)*; ~**firma** garage company; ~**haftpflichtversicherung** garage keeper's liability insurance; ~**halle** open garage; ~**miete** garage rent; ~**schlüssel** garage key; **sich automatisch öffnende** ~**tür** remote-controlled garage door; ~**wärter** garage attendant.

Gäranlage fermentation plant.

Garant guarantor, guarantee *(Br.)*, guaranty *(US)*, warrantor, surety, *(Effektenemission)* underwriter;
~ **des Friedens** guarantor of peace.

Garantie guarantee *(Br.)*, guaranty *(US)*, *(Bürgschaft)* surety-[ship], *(Haftbarkeit)* responsibility, engagement, *(Sicherheit)* security, *(des Verkäufers)* warranty, *(Zusicherung)* undertaking, pledge;
als ~ **für** in security for; **mit** ~ warranted; **mit dreijähriger** ~ warranted for three years; **ohne** ~ no guarantee, without guaranty *(US)*, for what it is worth;
abgelaufene ~ expired guarantee *(Br.)*; **in die Verfassung eingebaute** ~**n** constitutional guarantees; **gesetzliche** ~ surety created by operation of law; **stillschweigend gewährte** ~ implied warranty; **kollektive** ~**n** *(Völkerrecht)* collective guarantee *(Br.)*; **sichere** ~ reliable guarantee; **ausdrücklich übernommene** ~ express warranty; **unbeschränkte** ~ unlimited guarantee *(Br.)*; **verfallene** ~ expired guarantee *(Br.)*; **vertragliche (vertraglich zugesicherte)** ~ warranty in the contract;
~ **einer Bank** bank guarantee *(Br.)* (guaranty, *US*); ~ **eines Bauunternehmers** construction bond; ~ **des Direktabsatzes** *(Emissionskonsortium)* standby guarantee *(Br.)*; ~ **der Durchschnittsqualität** warranty of merchantibility *(US)*; ~ **von Effektenemissionen** underwriting; ~ **der Geldrückgabe bei Nichtgefallen** money-back guarantee; ~ **der unmittelbaren Gewinnbeteiligung** immediate participation agreement; ~ **der Herstellerfirma** maintenance bond *(coll.)*, warranty for fitness; ~ **für gerade auf den Markt gebrachte Erzeugnisse** new-product guarantee *(Br.)*; ~ **gegen Preisrückgang** decline guarantee *(Br.)*; ~ **auf Schadloshaltung** indemnity bond; ~ **von dritter Seite** third-party guarantee *(Br.)*;
~ **annullieren** to cancel a guarantee *(Br.)*; ~ **ausfüllen** to implement a guarantee *(Br.)*; ~ **einschränken** to limit a guarantee *(Br.)*; ~**n erhalten** to obtain safeguards; ~ **fordern** to stipulate for a guaranty *(US)*; **jem.** ~ **geben** to give s. o. security; **ein Jahr** ~ **haben** to be guaranteed for one year *(Br.)*; ~ **leisten** to guarantee *(Br.)*, to furnish (give) security; ~ **in Anspruch nehmen** to call up a guarantee *(Br.)*, to raise claims under a guarantee *(Br.)*; ~ **für jem. stellen** to stand security for s. o.; ~ **übernehmen** to guarantee, to warrant; **persönlich für etw.** ~ **übernehmen** to enter into one's own recognizance; **für jds. Verhalten** ~ **übernehmen** to vouch for s. one's good conduct; ~ **verlangen** to ask for a guaranty *(US)* (guarantee, *Br.*);
~**abkommen** guarantee agreement *(Br.)*, covenant of warranty; ~**abteilung** fidelity department, *(Emissionsbank)* underwriting department; ~**aktie** deposit stock; ~**änderung** variation of guarantee *(Br.)*; ~**angebot** guarantee offer *(Br.)*, offer of indemnity; ~**angebot an unbestimmte Gläubiger** general guaranty *(US)*.

Garantieansprüche warranty claims;
~ **durchsetzen** to make a guarantee stick *(Br.)*; ~ **erfüllen** to fill the warranty; ~ **erheben** to raise a claim (claims) under a guarantee *(Br.)*; **seiner** ~ **verlustig gehen** to lose one's rights under a guarantee *(Br.)*.

Garantie|arbeiten warranty work; ~**ausschluß** exclusion of warranty; ~**begünstigter** beneficiary under a guarantee *(Br.)*; ~**bestimmungen** terms of a guarantee *(Br.)*, warranty rules; ~**betrag** amount guaranteed, caution money *(Br.)*; ~**deckungskonto** guarantee security account; ~**depot** collateral security (guaranty); ~**durchschrift** copy of guarantee *(Br.)*; ~**einschränkungen** *(auf Formular)* fine print; ~**empfänger** guarantee *(Br.)*, warrantee; ~**erklärung** guarantee *(Br.)*, guarantee bond *(Br.)*, guaranty *(US)*, warranty, *(Freistellung)* bond, *(Scheck)* certification *(US)*; ~**erklärungen** *(vertragliche Zusicherungen)* representations; **schriftliche** ~**erklärung** guaranteed bond *(Br.)*, *(gegen Transportschaden)* letter of indemnity; ~**fonds** *(Bankwesen)* guarantee *(Br.)* (guaranty, *US*) fund, contingency fund; **besser (lieber) einen** ~**fonds errichten** to be preferable to establish a guarantee fund; ~**fondszeichner** underwriter; ~**frist** term (period) of a guarantee *(Br.)*, guaranteed period *(Br.)*; ~**geber** guarantor, warrantor; ~**gemeinschaft** joint guarantors; ~**gesellschaft** surety company *(US)*, guarantee association *(Br.)*, guaranty company *(US)*; ~**gewährung** granting a guarantee *(Br.)*; ~**haftung** guarantee *(Br.)*, guaranty, guarantee liability *(Br.)*; **Verletzung der** ~**haftung** breach of warranty; ~**höhe** amount guaranteed, caution money *(Br.)*; ~**inanspruchnahme** service under a guarantee *(Br.)*; ~**kapital** capital resources; ~**klausel** clause of warranty, warranty clause; ~**klausel für versteckte Mängel** latent-defect clause; ~**konsor-**

tium underwriters, underwriting syndicate, underwriting consortium; ~**kosten** warranty costs; ~**leistung** guarantee *(Br.)*, guaranty *(US)*, surety, suretyship; ~**lohn** guaranteed wage; ~**mittel** guarantee fund; ~**nehmer** guarantee *(Br.)*, warrant creditor; **einer ~pflicht nachkommen** to implement a guarantee *(Br.)*.

garantiepflichtig sein to be subject to security.

Garantie|preis guaranteed price; ~**provision** underwriting (surety) commission, guarantee commission *(Br.)*; ~**rahmen** extent of warranty.

garantieren to guarantee, to guaranty, to warrant, to undertake, to furnish (give) security, to insure, to ensure, to avouch, *(Effektenemission)* to underwrite;
für j. ~ to vouch (act as guaranty) for s. o.; **für etw.** ~ to make for s. th.; **für erstklassige Arbeit** ~ to guarantee the finest workmanship; **für die Bezahlung einer Schuld** ~ to guarantee payment; **für die Echtheit einer Ware** ~ to guarantee the genuineness of goods (s. th. as genuine); **Erfolg einer Arbeit** ~ to assure the success of one's work; **für pünktliche Lieferung** ~ to warrant punctual delivery; **Minderheitsaktionären eine Dividende** ~ to guarantee a dividend to minority stockholders; **Wechsel** ~ to guarantee a bill of exchange.

Garantiereparaturen *(Autohändler)* warranty work.

garantiert guaranteed, warranted;
~ **echt** warranted genuine; ~ **ladebereit** guaranted for cargo; ~**e Dividende** guaranteed dividend; ~**es Grundgehalt** guaranteed rate, base pay; ~**er Jahreslohn** guaranteed annual wage; ~**e Mindestauflage** guaranteed minimum circulation; ~**e Mindestbeschäftigung** guaranteed employment; ~**er absoluter Mindestlohn** guaranteed minimum wage for all trades; ~**e Plazierung** *(Anzeige)* guaranteed position; ~**er Stundenlohntarif** guaranteed hourly rate; ~**er Tageslohnsatz** guaranteed day rate; ~**e briefliche Überweisung** guaranted mail transfer; ~**er Wochenlohn** guaranteed week.

Garantierücklage general purpose contingency reserve.

Garantieschein [guarantee] bond, guaranty *(US)*, del credere, bond *(Br.)*, certificate of guarantee (suretyship) *(Br.)*, surety bond *(US)*, *(für Effekten)* letter of indemnity *(Br.)*, indemnity bond *(US)*, *(Verkäufer)* warrant of fitness, quality warrant, guarantee registration card, warrant letter *(US)*;
kaufmännischer ~ maintenance bond *(US)*, warrant of merchantability *(US)*.

Garantie|schreiben letter of indemnity *(Br.)*, warrant letter *(US)*; ~**sicherheitskonto** warranty reserve; ~**summe** amount guaranteed, caution money *(Br.)*; ~**umfang** extent of warranty; ~**unkosten** warranty cost; ~**unterschrift** guarantee signature *(Br.)*; ~**urkunde** surety bond; ~**verband** underwriters, underwriting syndicate; ~**vereinbarung** indemnity contract, del credere agreement *(Br.)*; ~**verletzung** breach of warranty.

Garantieverpflichtung guarantee liability, [security] bond, quality warranty *(US)*, warranty of fitness (quality) *(US)*, bond of indemnity *(Br.)*, indemnity bond *(Br.)*;
staatliche ~**en** government bonds *(Br.)*;
~ **für Durchschnittsqualität** warrant of merchantability *(US)*; ~ **eingehen** to enter into a surety bond; ~ **gegenüber den Zollbehörden eingehen** to enter into a bond with the customs authorities; ~ **nicht einhalten** to break a warranty; **seinen** ~**en nachkommen** to pay up under one's guarantee.

Garantieversicherung guaranty (fidelity) insurance, fidelity guarantee *(Br.)*, commercial insurance.

Garantieversicherungs|gesellschaft guarantee company (society) *(Br.)*, guarantee insurance association *(US)*, surety company *(US)*, *(für Eigentumsnachweis)* title insurance company; **betrieblicher** ~**schein [anhand einer Personalaufstellung]** schedule bond *(US)*.

Garantieversprechen guarantee undertaking, warranty promise (deed), contract of indemnity, indemnity contract, security contract, contract of suretyship *(Br.)* (warranty, *US*);
gegenseitiges ~ mutual guarantee; **schriftliches** ~ guarantee in writing;
~ **einlösen** to stand behind a guarantee *(Br.)*, to stand back of a guaranty *(US)*; ~ **ungültig erklären** to cancel a guarantee, to rescind a guaranty *(US)*.

Garantievertrag contract of indemnity (suretyship, *Br.*), indemnity contract, security contract, guaranty [agreement (contract, *US*)], contract of warranty *(US)*, warranty deed.

Garantie|vertragsformular indemnity form; ~**vertragsverletzung** breach of warranty; ~**vertreter** *(Kommissionär)* del credere agent *(Br.)*; ~**verzicht** renunciation of guarantee *(Br.)*; ~**wechsel** security bill, bill of security; ~**wert** security value; ~**zeit** [period of] guarantee, guaranteed period.

Garantiezusage guarantee undertaking;
betriebliche ~**n** factory guaranty policies;
~ **für den Nichtverkauf von Aktien** investment letter *(US)*;
~ **aufheben** to cancel a guarantee *(Br.)*, to rescind a guaranty *(US)*; ~ **erfüllen** to hono(u)r a guaranty *(US)*, to fill a warranty.

Garaus machen, jem. den to settle s. one's hash, to do s. one's business, to give s. o. the finishing stroke, to cook s. one's goose *(sl.)*, to finish (knock, *US*) s. o. off, to do s. o. in *(Br.)*; **einer Sache den** ~ to deal a deathblow to s. th. *(coll.)*, to put the kibosh on s. th.

Garbe *(Getreide)* sheaf.

Garde the guards;
zur alten ~ **gehören** to be an old-timer, to belong to the old school;
~**kavallerie** Horse Guards.

Garderobe cloakroom *(Br.)*, checkroom *(US)*, *(Kleidung)* wardrobe, *(Theater)* tiring room;
seine ~ **abgeben** to leave one's things in the cloakroom *(Br.)* (checkroom, *US*), to check one's things *(US)*; **in der** ~ **hängen** to be on the coatrack.

Garderoben|abgabe cloakroom *(Br.)*, checkroom *(US)*; ~**aufbewahrung** cloakroom *(Br.)*, checkroom *(US)*; ~**frau** cloakroom attendant *(Br.)*, checkroom woman *(US)*; ~**gebühr** cloakroom *(Br.)* (checkroom, *US*) fee; ~**marke**, ~**schein** cloakroom ticket *(Br.)*, checkroom ticket *(US)*, voucher check *(US)*; ~**nummer** cloakroom (checkroom, *US*) ticket number; **eingebauter** ~**schrank** built-in wardrobe; ~**ständer** clothes rack (tree), hall stand, coatrack, hall tree *(US)*.

Garderobiere cloakroom attendant *(Br.)*, checkroom woman *(US)*.

Gardetruppen household troops.

Gardine curtain;
hinter schwedischen ~**n sitzen** to be behind prison bars; ~**n vorziehen** to draw the curtains.

Gardinenpredigt curtain lecture, jaw *(sl.)*;
j. eine ~ **halten** to talk to s. o. like a Dutch uncle; **jem. eine ausführliche** ~ **halten** to lecture s. o. at great length.

gär|en to ferment;
es ~**te im ganzen Volk** the whole population was in a turmoil.

Garmondschrift long primer.

Garn yarn;
~ **für j. auslegen** to set a snare for s. o.; **jem. ins** ~ **gehen** to fall into s. one's snare; ~ **spinnen** to pull *(fam.)* (put up, *sl.*) a yarn.

garnieren to garnish, to trim, to dress.

Garnierung garnishment, trimming.

Garnison garrison;
~ **von Truppen entblößen** to deplete a garrison of troops; **in einer Stadt in** ~ **liegen** to keep garrison in a town.

Garnisons|ältester garrison commander; ~**dienst** garrison duty; ~**stadt** garrison town; ~**stadt aufheben** to civilianize.

Garnitur set, suit[e], *(Ausrüstung)* outfit, *(drucktechn.)* furniture, *(mil.)* complete uniform, *(Mode)* trimmings, *(Unterwäsche)* set of underwear;
vollständige ~ full set;
sich zur ersten ~ **emporarbeiten** *(Schauspieler)* to work o. s. up to the top-rank actors; **zur zweiten** ~ **gehören** *(fig.)* to be a second string.

garstig nasty, loathsome, *(Kind)* naughty;
~**es Wetter** beastly (wretched) weather.

Garten garden, yard *(US)*;
botanischer ~ botanical garden; **nach hinten heraus gelegener** ~ backyard *(US)*;
~ **anlegen** to lay out a garden, to make a garden; **im** ~ **arbeiten** to garden;
~**anlage** garden, grounds; **j. mit** ~**arbeiten beschäftigen** to employ a man to look after the garden; ~**architekt** landscape gardener, landscaper; ~**bank** garden seat.

Gartenbau garden designing, gardening, horticulture;
~ **treiben** to garden;
~**amt** parks department; ~**ausstellung** horticultural show; ~**erzeugnis** garden stuff (truck, *US*), horticultural product; ~**gestaltung** landscape gardening.

gartenbaulich horticultural.

Garten|blume garden flower; ~**erde** humus, mould *(Br.)*, mold; ~**erzeugnisse** garden stuff (produce, truck, *US*), horticultural products; ~**fest** garden party; ~**gemüse** garden truck; ~**geräte** gardening tools (implements); ~**grundstück** garden plot, *(vom Gartenarchitekten angelegt)* landscaped lot; ~**haus**, ~**laube** arbo(u)r, summerhouse; ~**land** garden plot; ~**lokal**, ~**restaurant** open-air restaurant, beer (tea-) garden; ~**mauer** garden wall; ~**pflanzen** open-air plants; ~**pflege** gardening services;

~**plage** garden pest; ~**schlauch** garden hose; ~**stadt** garden city; ~**stuhl** garden chair; ~**tür** garden gate; ~**vorstadt** garden suburb *(Br.)*.

Gärtner gardener.

Gärtnerei market (truck, *US*) garden, *(Baumschule)* nursery.

gärtnerisch horticultural.

Gärung fermentation;
die ganze Bevölkerung war in ~ the whole population was in a turmoil.

Gas gas, *(Benzin)* petrol;
mit ~ **betrieben** gas-operated;
~ **abdrehen (abstellen)** to cut (turn) off the gas; **jem. das** ~ **abdrehen** *(fig.)* to settle s. one's hash, to cook s. one's goose *(sl.)*; ~ **aufdrehen** to turn on the gas; ~ **geben** *(Auto)* to step on the accelerator (gas pedal), to step on the juice *(coll.)*; **kräftig** ~ **geben** to open out the throttle; **Zimmer mit** ~ **heizen** to heat a room with gas; ~ **auf Sparflamme stellen** to turn down the gas to a pinpoint; **aufs** ~ **treten** to pour on the coal *(sl.)*; **mit** ~ **töten** *(mil.)* to gas; **mit** ~ **versorgen** to gas; ~ **wegnehmen** to throttle down;
~**ableser** gasman; ~**angriff** *(mil.)* gas attack; ~- **und elektrische Anlagen** gas and electric light fittings; ~**anlasser** *(Flugzeug)* gas starter; ~**anschluß** gas main; ~**anstalt** gasworks; ~**anzünder** gaslighter; ~**arbeiter** gas fitter, gasman; ~**austritt** escape of gas, gas leakage; ~**austritt feststellen** to detect an escape of gas; ~**automat** gas-slot machine; ~**badeofen** geyser; ~**behälter** gas tank, gasometer.

gasbeheizt gas-heated.

Gas|beleuchtung gaslighting; ~**beton** aerated concrete; ~**brenner** gas burner; ~**dichtung** gas check; ~**druck** gas pressure; ~**erzeugung** gas generation; ~**fabrik** gasworks; ~**fachmann** gas engineer; ~**feuerung** gas heating; ~**flamme** gas jet; ~**flasche** gas cylinder, gasholder; **leere** ~**flasche** depleted gasbag; ~**gemisch** gas compound; ~**geruch** smell of gas; ~**gesellschaft** gas company; ~**hahn** cock, gas tap *(Br.)*; ~**hebel** *(Auto)* throttle lever; **durch Verwertung von Müllrückständen betriebene** ~**heizung** garbage gas heating; ~**industrie** gas industry; ~**installateur** gasman, gas fitter; ~**installation** gas installation; ~**kammer** gas chamber; ~**kampfstoffe** war chemicals; ~**koks** gas coke; ~**krieg** gas warfare; ~**lampe** gaslight; ~**laterne** gas lamp; ~**leitung** gaspipe, gas pipeline, gas main, plumbing; ~**leitung legen** to lay on the gas; ~**leitungsnetz** gas pipelines network; ~**licht** gaslight; ~**lieferungsvertrag** gas deal; ~**mann** gasman; ~**maske** *(mil.)* gas mask; ~**messer** gas meter; ~**motor** gas engine; ~**ofen** gas fire, gas oven.

Gaspedal gas pedal, throttle lever, accelerator;
~ **blockieren** to press a pedal home; ~ **durchtreten** to press the pedal down, to press down the accelerator (gas) pedal, to open out the throttle; ~ **ganz durchtreten** to depress the pedal fully.

Gas|pistole gas pistol; ~**rohr** gas pipe.

Gasse lane, passage, bystreet, alley, alleyway, *(Setzersaal)* row;
auf der ~ in the street;
sich eine ~ **bahnen** to elbow one's way through the crowd; ~ **bilden** to form a lane; **auf allen** ~**n zu hören sein** to be in everybody's mouth.

Gassen|hauer popular song, hit; ~**junge** street arab (boy, *Br.*), city Arab *(Br., sl.)*; ~**kehrer** scavenger, street sweeper; ~**kind** gutter child.

Gasspürgerät gas detector.

Gast guest, visitor, caller, stranger, *(Fremdenheim)* boarder, guest, *(Hotel)* travel(l)er, lodger, tourist, *(Theater)* star, *(Wirtshaus)* customer, patron;
als erster aufbrechender ~ party pooper *(sl.)*; **kostenlos beförderter** ~ free-loading guest; **hoher** ~ distinguished guest; **regelmäßiger** ~ regular [customer], frequenter; **seltener** ~ infrequent visitor; **ungebetener** ~ intruder, gate-crasher; **umsonst wohnender** ~ deadhead *(US)*; **zahlender** ~ paying guest, lodger;
~ **des Hauses** house guest, guest of the management; ~ **auf halbe Pension** day boarder;
j. zu ~ **haben** to entertain s. o.; **abends einen** ~ **eingeladen haben** to have s. o. in for dinner; ~ **links liegen lassen** to slight a guest; **bei jem. zu** ~ **sein** to stay with (be invited by) s. o.; ~ **des Hauses sein** to be a guest of the management.

Gastarbeiter foreign (immigrant) worker, foreign labo(u)r, alien employee;
ausgebeuteter ~ exploited foreign worker;
~**land** labo(u)r-importing country; ~**lohn** immigrant wage.

Gastarif gas tariff.

Gast|auftritt *(Theater)* guest appearance; ~**dirigent** guest conductor; ~**dozentur** visiting appointment.

Gäste *(Gastwirt)* customers, patrons;
Parken nur für ~ *(Schild)* for patrons only;
preisempfindliche ~ price-finicky customers;
~ **aufnehmen** to sign in guests; ~ **gegen Bezahlung aufnehmen** to take paying guests; ~ **freundlich aufnehmen** to make o. s. pleasant to visitors; **sich bemühen, seinen** ~**n das Beste zu bieten** to endeavo(u)r to offer the best service to one's customers; ~ **höflich bitten** *(Hotelier)* to request the patrons kindly; ~ **in seinem Klub einführen** to extend guest privileges; ~ **erwarten** to expect company; ~ **haben** to entertain company; ~ **zum Abendbrot haben** to have a party to dinner; **vornehme** ~ **haben** *(Gastronomie)* to have a select patronage; **sich um seine** ~ **kümmern** to be attentive to [the needs of] one's guests;
~**abend** *(Klub)* guest night; ~**bett** spare bed; ~**buch** visitors' book; **kein** ~**empfang** not at home; **vor** ~**empfängen einen Horror haben** not to feel equal to receiving visitors; ~**haus** guesthouse; ~**heim** boarding house; ~**ordnung** hotel regulations; ~**zimmer** guestchamber, spare room (bedroom), *(Hotel)* guest room.

gastfrei, gastfreundlich open-doored;
äußerst ~ **sein** to entertain in a large way (a great deal).

Gastfreundschaft hospitality, entertainment, open house;
großzügige ~ large hospitality;
~ **gegenüber jedermann** promiscuous hospitability;
jds. ~ **genießen** to cut mutton with s. o.; **jem.** ~ **gewähren** to show hospitality to s. o.; **jds.** ~ **in Anspruch nehmen** to eat s. one's salt; **für** ~ **berühmt sein** to be big on hospitality; ~ **üben** to entertain, to keep open door.

gastgebend|e Stadt host town; ~**es Vereinsmitglied** host member.

Gastgeber host, entertainer;
~ **im Büro** office host;
dem ~ **assistieren** to cohost; **sich als** ~ **aufspielen** to play the hospitality act; **als** ~ **fungieren** to act as host, to do the hono(u)rs; **als** ~ **bei einem Abendessen fungieren** to officiate as host at a dinner party;
~**funktion** office of host; ~**gemeinschaft** host community.

Gastgeber|in hostess; ~**staat** host nation.

Gast|geschenk gift; ~**gewerbe** hotel and restaurant business.

Gasthaus public eating house, tavern, saloon *(US)*, restaurant, refreshment house *(Br.)*, stop, *(Hotel)* inn, boarding house, hotel, *(Rasthaus)* roadhouse;
auf halbem Weg gelegenes ~ halfway house; **miserables** ~ wretched inn;
~ **an der Landstraße** road-side inn, wayside inn, roadhouse; **in einem** ~ **absteigen** to put up at an inn; **in einem** ~ **sehr gut unterkommen** to find excellent quarters at an inn; **in einem** ~ **verkehren** to frequent an inn;
~**besitzer** eating-house keeper, landlord; ~**schild** signboard.

Gasthof tavern, [common] inn;
~**besitzer** innkeeper, landlord.

Gasthörer extramural student *(Br.)*, auditor *(US)*;
als ~ **eine Vorlesung besuchen** to audit a lecture *(US)*;
~**vorlesung** extramural teaching.

gastieren to star, to barnstorm *(US)*;
auswärts ~ to take to the road; **in der Provinz** ~ to tour the province.

Gastland host country (state, government);
nicht den Gesetzen des ~**es unterworfen** extraterritorial.

gastlich hospitable;
~ **aufnehmen** to sign in guests, to show s. o. hospitality, to entertain.

Gastlichkeit hospitability.

Gast|professor guest (visiting, exchange) professor; ~**regierung** host government.

Gastrolle, in einer ~ **auftreten** to appear as a guest; **nur eine** ~ **geben** to be a bird of passage; **kurze** ~ **geben** to play a flying visit.

Gastronomielieferant mobile catering company.

gastronomische Betreuung catering.

Gastschauspieler, als ~ **auftreten** to star, to barnstorm *(US)*.

Gastspiel guest performance;
einmaliges ~ one night stand *(US)*;
~**dauer** stand; ~**gebiet** road *(US)*; ~**reise** starring tour; ~**reise unternehmen** to take the road (a company on tour); ~**reise mit einem Ensemble unternehmen** to take a company on tour; ~**truppe** road company, barnstormers *(US)*; **feste** ~**vorführungen geben** to travel over a regular circuit.

Gaststätte public *(Br.)* (eating) house, inn, victual(l)ing house, eatery, refreshment house *(Br.)*, tavern, saloon *(US)*, tearoom, restaurant, place *(coll.)*;
brauereigebundene ~ tied house.

Gaststätten|angestellter restaurant worker; ~**besitzer** restaurant owner, publican *(Br.)*, saloonkeeper *(US)*, innkeeper; ~**betrieb**, ~**einrichtung** catering establishment, caterer; ~**gesetz** Licensing Act *(Br.)*; ~**gewerbe** catering trade (industry, market), business of innkeepers, hotel and restaurant business; **im** ~**gewerbe tätig sein** to be in the public line *(coll., Br.)*; ~**lieferant** catering firm, caterer; ~**marken** meal tickets; ~**sektor** catering field; ~**versorgung von Flugplätzen** airport catering; ~**wesen** catering [industry], hotel and restaurants industry.
Gaststube parlo(u)r, bar room, taproom.
Gasturbine gas turbine.
Gast|vorlesung guest lecture, extramural teaching *(Br.)*; ~**vorlesung besuchen** to audit a lecture *(US)*; ~**vorrechte** guest privileges; ~**vorstellung** guest performance.
Gastwirt innkeeper, landlord, hotelkeeper, restaurant keeper (proprietor), common victualler, host, publican *(Br.)*, saloonkeeper *(US)*;
auf Kosten des ~**s** on the house;
konzessionierter ~ licensed victualler *(Br.)*.
Gastwirtschaft public *(Br.)* (eating) house, inn, restaurant, catering establishment, tavern, saloon *(US)*;
brauereiabhängige ~ tied house; **brauereiunabhängige** ~ free house;
~ **betreiben** to keep an inn (saloon, *US*).
Gastwirts|haftung liability of an innkeeper, liability towards guests, innkeeper's liability; ~**haftung beschränken** to restrict unlimited liability towards guests; **jem. eine** ~**konzession erteilen** to license s. o. to keep an inn; ~**pfandrecht** innkeeper's lien.
Gastzimmer guest (spare) room, spare bedroom.
Gas|uhr gas (wet, dry) meter; ~**uhr ablesen** to read the gas meter; ~**verbrauch** gas consumption; ~**vergiftung** gas poisoning; **städtische** ~**versorgung** town gas, gas service; ~**werk** gas plant, gasworks; ~**werksgesellschaft** gas company; ~**wirtschaft** gas-supply industry; ~**zähler** gas meter; ~**zähler ablesen** to inspect the gas meter; ~**zentralheizung** gas central heating.
Gatte husband, consort.
Gatter lattice door, railing, fence, trellis.
Gattin wife, spouse, consort.
Gattung kind, type, sort, cast, species, description, quality, class.
Gattungs|anspruch generic claim; ~**begriff** generic term; ~**kauf** quantity contract, sale of unascertained goods, purchase (sale) by description; ~**merkmal** generic character; ~**name** specific (common, appellative) name; ~**nummer** type number; ~**sachen** fungible things, nonspecified (unascertained) goods; ~**schuld** indeterminate obligation; ~**vermächtnis** indefinite (general) legacy; **beschränktes** ~**vermächtnis** demonstrative legacy; ~**waren** unascertained (nonspecified) goods; ~**wort** *(Grammatik)* common noun.
Gaukel|bild phantasmagoria; ~**spiel** jugglery, mountebankery, legerdemain, *(Täuschung)* delusion; **sein** ~**spiel mit jem. treiben** to delude s. o. [with vain promises].
Gaukler juggler, conjuror, mountebank, legerdemainist, charlatan, knockabout comedian;
~**trick** juggler's trick.
Gaul [cab] horse, *(verächtlich)* jade, nag;
~ **beim Schwanz aufzäumen** to put the cart before the horse; **einem geschenkten** ~ **sieht man nicht ins Maul** never look a gift horse in the mouth.
Gaumen kitzeln to tickle the palate.
Gauner crook, kite, trickster, twister, wangler, shark, rascal, sharper, swindler, blackleg *(coll.)*, whipster *(Br.)*;
abgefeimter ~ consummate scoundrel; **kleiner** ~ punk, packrat *(sl.)*;
~**bande** gang, set of crooks.
Gaunerei sharp practices, roguery, trickings, piece of knavery, racket, cross.
Gauner|sprache flash language, argot, cant, thieves' Latin; ~**trick** hocus-pocus, take-in, do, roguery, knavish trick; ~**volk** flash people.
geachtet reputable.
geächtet under a ban, outlawed.
Geächteter outlaw, outcast, lawless man.
geartet natured, disposed;
besonders ~**er Fall** particular case.
Gebäck baker's ware;
feines ~ pastries, fancy cakes.
Gebälk timberwork, framework;
es knistert im ~ there are signs of an impending catastrophe.
geballte Ladung concentrated charge.
gebannt, wie spellbound, fascinated.
Gebärde gesture.
gebärden, sich wie ein Verrückter to behave like a madman, to fly off the handle.
Gebärdenspiel gesticulation;
stummes ~ pantomime.
Gebaren behavio(u)r, conduct, demeano(u)r.
Gebäude building, house, construction, structure, edifice, architecture, fabric, *(Geschäftshaus)* premises;
abgerissenes ~ wrecked building; **abschreibungsfähiges** ~ qualifying building; **nicht abschreibungsfähiges** ~ nonqualifying structure; **groß angelegtes** ~ building of great dimensions; **angrenzendes** ~ adjoining building; **bankeigenes** ~ bank's premises; **baufälliges** ~ dilapidated building; **bewohntes** ~ occupied building; **gut erhaltenes** ~ building in good repair (preservation); **feuergefährdetes** ~ fire trap; **gewerblich genutztes** ~ industrial (commercial) building, building in use for the purpose of trade; **nicht für die Produktion genutztes** ~ nonproductive building; **standardisiertes gewerbliches** ~ advance factory *(Br.)*; **imposantes** ~ noble building; **landwirtschaftliches** ~ farm building; **leerstehendes** ~ building standing empty; **öffentliches** ~ public building; **städtisches** ~ municipal building; **symmetrisches** ~ regular building; **vermietetes** ~ let property;
~ **nach Abschreibungen** *(Bilanz)* buildings less depreciation; **Grundstücke und** ~ *(Bilanz)* land and buildings; **das ganze** ~ **von jds. Hoffnungen** the whole edifice of s. one's hopes;
das ~ **ist versichert** building is covered;
~ **abreißen** to take (pull) down a building; ~ **abschätzen** to assess a building; ~ **aufstocken** to raise a building; ~ **im Submissionsweg ausschreiben** to invite tenders for a building; ~ **zu hoch bewerten** to set too high a valuation on a building; ~ **niedriger bewerten** to reduce the assessment of a building; ~ **in gutem Zustand erhalten** to keep a building in good repair; ~ **errichten** to erect (set up) a building; ~ **schnell errichten (hochziehen)** to run up a building; ~ **zu bewachen haben** to have the care of a building; **j. in ein** ~ **hineinlassen** to let s. o. into a building; ~ **für Versicherungszwecke schätzen lassen** to rate a building for insurance purposes; ~ **wetterfest machen** to weatherize a building; ~ **niederreißen** to destroy a building; ~ **schätzen** to assess a building; ~ **seiner Bestimmung übergeben** to inaugurate a building; ~ **unterhalten** to keep a building in repair; ~ **untersuchen** to examine a building; **gewerblich** ~ **vermieten** to carry on a trade of plant hire; ~ **mit technischen Neuerungen versehen** to modernize a building; ~ **wiederherstellen** to restore a ruined building; ~ **maßstabsgerecht zeichnen** to scale a building;
~**abnahme** final architect's certificate; ~**abnutzung** depreciation of buildings; ~**abnutzungsfonds** premises redemption fund; ~**abschätzer** building (quantity, *Br.*) surveyor; ~**abschätzung** assessment of a building, quantity surveying *(Br.)*; ~**abschreibung** depreciation of buildings; ~**aufführung** building construction; ~**aufwand** building outlay; ~**ausbesserung** repair to a building; ~**ausgaben** building outlay; ~**bewertung** assessment of a building, building survey *(Br.)*; **zu hohe** ~**bewertung vornehmen** to set too high a value on a building; ~**dekoration** building display; ~**eigentümer** owner of a building; ~**einsturz** collapse of a building; ~**erhaltung** maintenance of structure, *(Kirche)* fabric; ~**erhaltungsauflage** preservation order; ~**erneuerung** renewal of a building; ~**errichtung**, ~**erstellung** housebuilding, construction of a building; ~**ertragswert** annual value of a building; ~**erweiterung** expansion of a building, extension to a house; ~**fläche** floor area; ~**flügel** wing; ~**front** front of a building; **zurückgesetzte** ~**front** setback; **zusammenhängende** ~**gruppe** solid row of buildings; ~**haftung** houseowner's liability; ~**hauptbuch** building ledger; ~**heizung** heating of a building; ~**herstellungskosten** cost of construction; ~**höhe** building height; ~**inneres** interior of a building; ~**instandhaltung** maintenance of a building; ~**instandsetzung** repairs to (restoration of) a building; ~**komplex** mass (group) of buildings, pile; ~**konto** building account; **verschwommene** ~**konturen** dim outlines of buildings; ~**miete** rent of a structure; ~**nutzfläche** useful area of a building; ~**plan** plans of a house; ~**planung** architectural planning; ~**reparaturen** building repairs, repairs of structure; ~**reparaturrücklage** provision for building repairs; ~**sanierung** restoration project; ~**schaden** injury to a building, structural damage; **auf Nässe zurückzuführende** ~**schäden** injuries to a building due to the wet; ~**schätzung** assessment of a building, building survey *(Br.)*; ~**steuer** habitation tax, house duty (tax, *Br.*);

zurückgesetzter ~teil retreating part of a building; **allgemein zugängliche ~teile** common parts of a building; **~unterhaltung** building (property) maintenance; **wertsteigernde ~verbesserung** beneficial improvement; **~versicherung** insurance of structure, *(Wohngebäude)* residence insurance; **~- und Mobiliarversicherung** insurance of structure and contents; **~verwalter** property manager, janitor *(US)*; **~verwaltung** building management; **~wert** property value; **~werterhöhung** improvement of buildings *(US)*, appreciation of a building; **~zugang** building approach.

gebaut built;
unsolide ~ jerry-built;
~ werden to go up.

gebefreudig generous, open-handed, beneficent, bountiful.

Geben und Nehmen *(Prämiengeschäft)* put and call *(Br.)*, straddle *(US)*, spread *(US)*.

geben to give, to present, to furnish, *(aufführen)* to represent, to stage, *(Optionsgeld)* to put, *(zuteilen)* to allot, to apportion;
es jem. ~ to give s. o. beans;
jem. den Abschied ~ to dismiss (discharge) s. o.; **Almosen ~** to bestow alms; **sich ein Ansehen ~** to give o. s. airs; **in Auftrag ~** to order; **Ausschlag zu jds. Gunsten ~** to turn the scales in favo(u)r of s. o.; **Beispiel ~** to set an example; **viel auf gutes Benehmen ~** to attach great importance to good manners; **Bescheid ~** to give word, to inform; **sich eine Blöße ~** to expose o. s.; **Brief auf die Post ~** to post (mail) a letter; **Buch in Druck ~** to have a book printed; **jem. zu denken ~** to make s. o. think; **sich die Ehre ~** to do o. s. the hono(u)r; **sich zu erkennen ~** to reveal one's identity; **guten Ertrag ~** to yield well; **Fersengeld ~** to show a clean pair of heels; **jem. einen Freibrief ~** to give s. o. carte-blanche; **Geld auf Zinsen ~** to put money out at interest; **jem. den Gnadenstoß ~** to administer the coup de grace (give the finishing stroke) to s. o.; **jem. Grund zur Besorgnis ~** to give s. o. cause for concern; **jem. etw. fest an die Hand ~** to make a firm offer to s. o.; **jem. neue Hoffnung ~** to fill s. o. with new hope; **Interview ~** to grant an interview; **Jungen in die Lehre ~** to apprentice a boy; **Kind in Pflege ~** to farm out a child; **Kredit ~** to grant a credit; **auf Kredit ~** to give upon trust, to chalk up; **jem. den Laufpaß ~** to give s. o. his walking papers; **nichts auf etw. ~** to think nothing of s. th.; **jem. eine Ohrfeige ~** to box s. one's ears, to fetch s. o. one *(fam.)*; **in Pension ~** to place in a boarding school, to put out to board; **als Pfand ~** to give as a pledge; **keinen Pfifferling darauf ~** not to care a tinker's damn; **in Prolongation ~** *(Prämiengeschäft)* to give on stock *(Br.)*; **Quittung ~** to receipt a bill; **Rabatt ~** to allow discount; **jem. Recht ~** to admit that s. o. is right; **jem. Saures ~** to give s. o. hell (the works, *US*); **jem. die Schuld ~** to lay the blame at s. one's door; **Stoff zum Nachdenken ~** to provide food for thought; **Stunden ~** to give lessons; **jem. einen Tag frei ~** to give a holiday; **es jem. tüchtig ~** to give it hot to s. o.; **Unterricht ~** to teach, to give lessons (tuition); **jem. etw. zu verstehen ~** to intimate s. th. to s. o.; **jem. einen Verweis ~** to reprimand (rebuke) s. o.; **auf etw. viel ~** to set a great store by s. th.; **viel dafür ~ zu erfahren** to give a lot to know; **Vorprämie ~** *(Dontprämiengeschäft)* to give for the call of a stock *(Br.)*; **seinen Wagen in Zahlung ~** to trade-in one's car *(US)*; **Waren in Kommission ~** to supply goods on a commission basis, to send goods on return; **Wink ~** to drop a hint; **sein Wort ~** to pledge one's word; **in Zahlung ~** to offer as (deliver in) payment, to trade in *(US)*; **Zahlungsaufschub ~** to [grant a] respite, to grant an extension of time; **sich zufrieden ~** to acquiesce in.

Geber giver, donor, *(Verkäufer)* seller;
~ und Nehmer *(Börse)* sellers and buyers;
~land donor country; **~laune** generous mood.

gebessert *(Kurse)* improved;
~ sein to show improvement.

Gebet, inbrünstiges earnest prayer;
j. ins ~ nehmen to question s. o. closely, to have s. o. on the carpet, to give s. o. a going over *(US)*.

Gebetsteppich prayer rug.

Gebiet district, area, ground, region, territory, *(Fluß)* basin, *(Landstrich)* tract, country, circuit, *(mil.)* zone, *(Thema)* subject, *(Wirkungskreis)* field, domain, province, line, sphere of business, range, scope, realm, *(Zuständigkeit)* jurisdiction;
auf deutschem ~ on German ground (territory); **auf landwirtschaftlichem ~** in the area of agriculture; **auf politischem ~** in the range of politics; **auf sozialem ~** in the social field; **auf wirtschaftlichem ~** in the economic sphere, in economic matters;
auf dem ~ der mittleren Führungskräfte on middle management level;
abgetretenes ~ ceded territory; **abhängiges ~** dependency, appanage; **annektiertes ~** annexed territory; **ausschlaggebendes ~** key area; **[nicht] autonomes ~** [non]self-governing territory; **bebautes ~** built-up area; **befriedetes ~** pacified territory; **begrenztes ~** *(fig.)* pale; **von den Gewerkschaften beherrschtes ~** heavily-unionized area; **benachbartes ~** adjacent land; **besetztes ~** occupied area; **ungenügend mit Arbeitskräften besetztes ~** labo(u)r-short area; **von Kommunisten besetztes ~** communist-occupied area; **besiedeltes ~** settled area; **dicht besiedeltes ~** built-up (congested) area; **dünn besiedeltes ~** sparsely settled area, thinly populated region; **vom Krieg betroffenes ~** war-stricken area; **bewaldetes ~** wooded tract; **entlegene ~e** outlying districts; **entmilitarisiertes ~** demilitarized zone; **erschlossenes ~** developed land; **im Wege des Planfeststellungsverfahrens festgelegtes ~** zone *(US)*; **von Baubeschränkungen freies ~** architectural-freedom zone *(US)*; **im Stadtzentrum gelegenes ~** midtown area; **landwirtschaftlich genutztes ~** agricultural (rural) area; **geräumtes ~** evacuated area; **gewachsene ~e** natural areas; **zum Ödland gewordenes ~** derelict land; **großes ~** *(fig.)* wide domain; **zu statistischen Zwecken herausgesuchtes ~** census tract *(US)*; **rein industrielles ~** district devoted to industry; **katastrophengefährdetes ~** disaster-prone area; **50-km-~** restricted area, slow-drive zone *(US)*; **kohlenreiches ~** area rich in coal; **ländliches ~** rural area (district), landward area *(Scotland)*; **rein landwirtschaftliches ~** purely agricultural district; **luftgefährdetes ~** target area; **neutrales ~** neutral territory; **ölträchtiges ~** proven territory; **politisches ~** field of politics; **störanfälliges ~** *(Auto)* trouble area; **assoziierte überseeische ~e** *(EG)* associated overseas territories; **übervölkertes ~** overspill area; **überwachtes ~** controlled area; **umstrittenes ~** no man's (debatable) land; **unbekanntes ~** unknown country *(fig.)*; **unbewohntes ~** deserted region, uninhabited area; **unerforschtes ~** unchartered territory; **unerschlossenes ~** undeveloped land (country); **unklares ~** grey area; **unterentwickelte ~e** undeveloped (developing) areas; **unterversorgtes ~** area of multiple deprivation; **Bebauungsbeschränkungen unterworfenes ~** restricted zone (area); **verbotenes ~** touch-me-not; **von Arbeiterunruhen verschontes ~** district free of labo(u)r troubles; **verstädtertes ~** urbanized area; **verwandte ~e** allied subjects, related fields; **zur Entlastung vorgesehenes ~** overspill area; **weites ~** wide domain; **wirtschaftliches ~** economic field; **zugehöriges ~** constituent territory, appendant; **zurückgebliebenes ~** *(Regionalplanung)* underdeveloped (backward) area; **~ mit Anbauverbot** no-grow area; **~ mit erhöhter Arbeitslosigkeit** green area; **~ mit hoher Arbeitslosigkeit** pockets of unemployment, distressed area *(Br.)*, development district *(Br.)*; **~ mit geringen Baubeschränkungen** unrestricted zone; **~e für kurzfristige Kapitalanlagen** short-term capital areas; **~ der schönen Künste** field of art; **~e ohne Selbstregierung** nonself-governing territories; **~ mit absolutem Sendeverbot** radio quiet zone; **~ mit niedriger Sterblichkeit** low-mortality area; **~ unter Treuhandverwaltung** trust territory; **~ der öffentlichen Versorgungsbetriebe** public utility field;
~ abfliegen to patrol an area; **~ abriegeln** to seal off an area; **~ abtreten** to cede a territory; **auf ein bestimmtes ~ beschränken** to specialize; **~ höher bewerten** to upgrade an area; **~ in Bezirke einteilen** to district an area; **in ein ~ fallen** to fall under a subject; **nicht in jds. ~ fallen** not to be within (outside) s. one's province, not to be s. one's shop, not to come within the purview of s. o., to lie outside s. one's sphere; **~ räumen** to abandon a territory; **Fachmann auf einem ~ sein** to be an authority on a subject; **~ sperren** to forbid an area; **sich auf einem ~ spezialisieren** to specialize one's studies, to major in a subject *(US)*; **~ überfliegen** to fly over a territory; **sein ~ vergrößern** to extend one's territory.

gebieten to command, to order, to direct;
jem. Schweigen ~ to impose silence upon s. o.; **über ein Volk ~** to rule over a nation; **über einen großen Wortschatz ~** to have a large vocabulary at one's command.

Gebieter lord, ruler, governor.

Gebieterin mistress.

gebieterisch imperative, imperious, domineering;
~ auftreten to have domineering ways;
in ~er Art und Weise in a dictatorial manner; **mit ~er Stimme** in a peremptory voice.

Gebiets|abgrenzung demarcation, zoning *(US)*; **~abkommen** regional arrangement; **~abtretung** cession of a territory; **~änderung** territorial change; **~ansässiger** person resident in a territory, resident; **~anspruch** territorial (zonal) claim; **~ansprüche geltend machen** to put forward territorial claims;

~**aufteilung** territory (territorial) assignment, repartition, *(Zerteilung)* regional dismemberment; ~**ausschuß** regional (local) committee; ~**austausch** exchange of territory; ~**beauftragter** *(Gewerkschaft)* divisional officer *(Br.)*; ~**bereinigung** rectification of boundaries; ~**beschränkungen** *(Kartellrecht)* territorial restrictions *(US)*; ~**einheit** subarea; ~**entwicklungsplan** regional planning program(me); ~**erweiterung** expansion of territories, territorial expansion; ~**erwerb** acquisition of territory; ~**forderungen** territorial claims; ~**fremder** person not resident in a territory, nonresident person, nonresident; ~**garantie** territorial guarantee; ~**grundsatz** territorial principle; ~**herrschaft,** ~**hoheit** territorial sovereignty (jurisdiction); ~**kartell** localized cartel; ~**körperschaft** body politic, governmental (administrative) unit, political corporation (subdivision, *US*), local corporation *(US)*; **kommunale** ~**körperschaft** local authority *(Br.)*, municipal corporation *(US)*; ~**leiter** district manager, *(Gewerkschaft)* area organizer; ~**provision** overriding commission *(Br.)*; ~**reform** regional reorganization; ~**streifen** zone; ~**tarif** territorial rating; ~**teilung** division of territory; ~**übertragung** transfer of territory; ~**veränderungen** border (territorial) changes; ~**vergrößerung** territorial expansion; ~**verletzung** violation of the border; ~**verlust** territorial loss; ~**vertreter** distributing agent; ~**wettervorhersage** area forecast; ~**zentrum** regional center *(US)* (centre, *Br.*).

Gebilde entity, shape, frame, form, structure;
~ **von Menschenhand** creation of man.

gebildet accomplished, educated, refined, civilized, polite, polished, true-bred, *(belesen)* well-read (-grounded), lettered;
akademisch ~ with a university education;
~ **sein** to be well educated; **vielseitig** ~ **sein** to be a man of general information, to have a wide education;
~**er Mensch** educated man; ~**es Publikum** educated people.

Gebildeten, die the educated classes.

Gebildetsein literacy.

gebilligt, von der Regierung federally approved *(US)*;
~ **werden** to meet with approval.

Gebimmel tinkle, tinklings, jingle;
~ **des Telefons** ringing of the telephone.

Gebinde package, bundle, cask;
in ~**n** in barrels (packages).

Gebirge mountains, highland;
festes ~ solid rock; **taubes** ~ gangue.

Gebirgs|bach mountain stream; ~**bahn** mountain railway (railroad, *US*); ~**bewohner** mountain dweller, highlander; **abgelegenes** ~**dorf** long-mountain village; ~**gegend** mountainous district; ~**kamm** crest; ~**kessel** range of mountains, corrie, cirque; ~**kette** range of mountains; ~**klima** highland climate; ~**kurort** mountain resort; ~**landschaft** mountainous country, mountain scenery; **zur** ~**marine gehören** *(hum.)* to be in the horse marines; ~**rücken** crest, ridge; ~**schlucht** ravine, gorge; ~**truppen** mountain troops; ~**volk** hill folk.

geblieben, auf Lager left on hand.

geblümt *(Stoff)* flowered.

geboren, im Ausland foreign-born; **außerehelich** ~ illegitimate, born out of wedlock; **lebend** ~ born alive; **neu** ~ new-born; ~**er Amerikaner** true-born American; ~**er Engländer** British by birth; ~**er Geschäftsmann** born businessman; ~**er Geschäftsmann sein** to be cut out for business.

geborene *(Frau)* née.

geborgen fühlen, sich to feel safe and secure.

geborgt borrowed.

Gebot offer, call, command, *(Befehl)* order, *(Versteigerung)* bid, bidding;
ohne ~**e** no offers;
erstes ~ opening (first) bid; **festes** ~ firm bid; **geringstes** ~ lowest bid, put-up price; **höheres** ~ higher (further) bid, advance; **letztes** ~ last (closing) bid; **niedrigstes** ~ lowest bid; **die zehn** ~**e** the Ten Commandments, the tables of the law; **das** ~ **des Gewissens** the dictates of conscience; ~ **für Kraftfahrzeuge** motor vehicles only; **zehn** ~**e zum Telefonieren** ten telephone commandments; **höheres** ~ **zur Wiederaufnahme der Versteigerung** upset bid;
~ **abgeben** to bid; **erstes** ~ **abgeben** to make the first bid, to start the price; ~ **machen** to bid; **höheres** ~ **machen** to bid over s. o.; **stets oberstes** ~ **sein** to always come first; **jem. zu** ~**e stehen** to be at s. one's disposal; **gegen ein** ~ **verstoßen** to break a rule; **Not kennt kein** ~ necessity knows no law.

geboten required, necessary, *(Auktion)* bid;
~**e Möglichkeit** option; **mit** ~**er Vorsicht** with due care.

Gebots|gesetz affirmative statute; ~**zeichen** *(Verkehr)* mandatory sign.

Gebrabbel mumbling.

gebracht brought.

Gebrandmarkter marked man.

Gebrauch use, usage, employment, application, exercise;
außer ~ disused, out of use, obsolete; **bei ordnungsgemäßem** ~ under proper use; **durch häufigen** ~ **abgenutzt** worn with frequent use; **für den einheimischen** ~ for home consumption; **nach örtlichem** ~ according to local habit; **nur zum eigenen** ~ for private use, captive *(US)*; **sparsam im** ~ economical; **zum** ~ **fertig** ready for use; **zum innerlichen** ~ *(med.)* for oral use; **zum persönlichen** ~ for personal use; **zum täglichen** ~ for daily use; **zum** ~ **oder Verbrauch** for use or consumption;
allgemeiner ~ general usage; **angemessener** ~ *(Urheberrecht)* fair usage; **gesetzlich berechtigter** ~ executed use; **bestimmungsmäßiger** ~ contractual use; **dauernder** ~ constant use; **gewöhnlicher** ~ ordinary use; **mißbräuchlicher** ~ adverse user; **redlicher** ~ *(Urheberrecht)* fair usage; **sachgemäßer** ~ proper use; **unberechtigter** ~ unauthorized use; **unzulässiger** ~ improper use; **zugelassener** ~ permissive use;
vernünftiger ~ **der richterlichen Ermessensfreiheit** sound juridical discretion; ~ **und Innehabung** use and occupancy; **betrügerischer** ~ **einer Vollmacht** frauds on a power;
etw. zum eigenen ~ **behalten** to keep s. th. for one's own spending; **zum öffentlichen** ~ **bestimmen** to devote to the public use, to dedicate *(US)*; **außer** ~ **kommen** to fall into disuse, to go out of use, to become a dead letter; **von etw.** ~ **machen** to make use of s. th.; **von Äußerungen keinen** ~ **machen** to treat a matter off the record; **keinen gewerblichen** ~ **von etw. machen** not to use for any purposes connected with business; **intensiven** ~ **von etw. machen** to make the most of s. th.; **von den vorhandenen Möglichkeiten zu wenig konzentrierten** ~ **machen** to spread a thing's use too thinly; **von einem Recht** ~ **machen** to avail o. s. of a right; **schlechten** ~ **machen** to abuse; **vorsichtigen** ~ **machen** to use with discretion; **außer** ~ **sein** to be out of usage; **außer** ~ **setzen** to invalidate.

Gebräuche, menschliche man-made customs;
Landessitten und ~ manners and customs of a country.

gebrauchen to employ, to [make] use, to apply, to work;
Arzt ~ to take medical advice; **äußerlich zu** ~ *(Medizin)* for external application; **gewohnheitsmäßig** ~ to use; **zum ersten Mal** ~ to handsel; **alle Mittel** ~ to leave no stone unturned; **nicht zu** ~ no earthly use; **seinen Verstand** ~ to use one's brains; **j. als Werkzeug** ~ to make a tool of s. o.; **Wort falsch** ~ to misuse a word;
etw. gut ~ **können** to put s. th. to good use; **praktisch zu allem zu** ~ **sein** to turn one's hand to most jobs; **für nichts zu** ~ **sein** to be good for nothing.

gebräuchlich usual, in use, customary, ordinary, common;
allgemein ~ in common use, set; **nicht mehr** ~ no longer in use; **noch nicht** ~ new;
allgemein ~ **sein** to be in current (general) use; **nicht mehr** ~ **sein** to be out of usage; ~ **werden** to come into use;
~**es Wort** word in general use.

Gebrauchs|abnahme *(Gebäude)* final architect's certificate; ~**abnutzung** wear and tear; ~**abschreibung** physical depreciation, depreciation for wear and tear; ~**abweichung** variance; ~**änderung** change of use; **wesentliche** ~**änderung** *(Gebäude)* material change of use *(Br.)*; ~**anforderung** requirement; ~**anmaßung** unauthorized use; ~**anweisung** directions for use, instruction booklet, fly sheet, *(Maschine)* maintenance instructions; ~**artikel** article, commodity, consumer item, *(pl.)* consumer goods; **persönliche** ~**artikel** personal effects; **einfache** ~**ausführung** utility type; ~**beschränkung** restraint of use; ~**eignung** usability, serviceableness; ~**einheit** service unit; ~**entzug** loss of use.

gebrauchsfähig serviceable, fit for use, utilizable.

Gebrauchs|fähigkeit usability, serviceableness; ~**fahrzeug** commercial vehicle.

gebrauchsfertig ready-made, ready for use, *(drucktechn.)* live.

Gebrauchs|garantie warranty of fitness; ~**gegenstand** artifact, utensil, requisite, functional object; **täglicher** ~**gegenstand** article of everyday use; **kleinere** ~**gegenstände** smalls; **persönliche** ~**gegenstände** personal effects; ~**geschirr** crockery; ~**gestattung** permission to use; ~**grafik** applied (commercial) art, industrial design; ~**grafiker** industrial artist.

Gebrauchsgüter utility goods (commodities), consumer durables, durable goods, *(mil.)* nonexpendable supplies, hardgoods *(US)*;
einfache ~ utility goods (commodities); **hochwertige** ~ major consumable goods; **langlebige** ~ consumer durables, durable goods; **persönliche** ~ convenience goods.

Gebrauchskategorien *(Städteplanung)* zoning classes *(US)*.
Gebrauchsmuster registered pattern, design (utility, petty, *US*) patent, utility model *(US)*, *(Änderung)* deviation, *(Modell)* sample;
eingetragenes ~ registered design *(Br.)*;
~ **kopieren** to pirate designs;
~**gesetz** Protection of Inventions Act *(US)*; **eingetragener** ~**inhaber** registered proprietor; ~**rolle** register of designs; ~**schutz** protection of registered designs *(Br.)* (of inventions, *US*).
Gebrauchs|porzellan crockery; **uneingeschränktes** ~**recht** full right of user; ~**überlassung** loan for use, productive use.
gebrauchsunfähig unserviceable, unusable;
Gebäude für ~ **erklären** to condemn a building.
Gebrauchsvorschrift directions for use.
Gebrauchswert value in use, use (going, function, amenity, service) value;
augenblicklicher ~ present value; **festgelegter** ~ established use value.
Gebrauchszweck, normaler normal purpose.
gebraucht used, [at] secondhand;
nicht ~ unused;
etw. ~ **kaufen** to buy s. th. secondhand;
~**e Artikel** secondhand (used) articles; ~**e Marke** used stamp; ~**e Möbel** secondhand furniture; ~**e Sachen** secondhand goods.
Gebrauchtwagen used (secondhand, utility) car;
wenig gefahrener ~ used car with small mil(e)age;
~**geschäft** business in used cars; ~**händler** dealer in used cars, used-car dealer; ~**umsatz** used-car sales; ~**verkauf** used-car lot.
Gebrauchtwarenmarkt secondhand market.
Gebrechen constitutional vice;
körperliches ~ physical defect (deficiency);
~ **des Alters** infirmities of old age.
gebrechlich invalid, infirm, disabled, frail, weak, out of health.
Gebrechlicher invalid, disabled person.
Gebrechlichkeit infirmity, invalidity, disability.
Gebrechlichkeitspfleger [etwa] special guardian.
gebrochen|es Bein broken (fractured) leg; ~**es Englisch sprechen** to speak broken English; ~**e Zahl** fractional number.
Gebrochener, restlos down-and-outer.
Gebrüll roar[ing], *(Geschrei)* howl, crying.
gebucht booked, reserved, *(im Hauptbuch)* posted, entered, written down;
nicht ~ unentered.
gebückt bowed;
in ~**er Haltung** with a stoop.
Gebühr charge, fee, duty, indirect tax *(US)*, subscription, *(Anwalt)* retainer, *(Gericht)* six and eightpence, *(Lizenz)* royalty, *(Postanweisung)* poundage *(Br.)*, *(Provision)* commission, *(Straßenbenutzung)* toll, turnpike money, road tax *(Br.)*, *(Tarif)* rate scale, *(Telefon)* charge, toll *(US)*, *(Unterricht)* tuition fee, *(Zoll)* duty;
für eine ~ **von** at a charge of; **gegen eine geringe** ~ for a small fee; **nach** ~ duly, properly; **über** ~ excessively, unduly, immoderately, to excess; **zu ermäßigter** ~ at reduced rate; **zu einer herabgesetzten** ~ at a modified rate (fee);
zuviel berechnete ~ surcharge; ~ **bezahlt** postage paid; **doppelte** ~ double rate; **einmalige** ~ *(Kapitalanlagegesellschaft)* initial charge; **entsprechende** ~ appropriate rate; **ermäßigte** ~ reduced charge; **feste** ~ fixed fee, specific duty; **fiskalische** ~ revenue duty, fiscal due (fee); **notarielle** ~ notarial charge (fee); **prozentuale** ~ percentage; **standesamtliche** ~ marriage fees; **statistische** ~ statistical fees; **stramme** ~ stiff fee; **übermäßige** ~ excessive charge; **übliche** ~ usual charge; **mit einem Eigentumsrecht verbundene** ~ fee incident to a title;
~ **für bevorzugte Abfertigung** priority fee; ~ **pro Einheit** unit charge; ~ **für Nachfrageschreiben** inquiry fee; ~ **für die Rechtstitelüberprüfung** search fee; ~ **für Standardbriefdrucksachen** surface mail printed paper full rate;
j. nach ~ **belohnen** to reward s. o. suitably; ~ **berechnen** to charge a fee, to lay a charge (levy a fee) on; ~ **einziehen** to collect a fee; ~ **entrichten** to pay (charge) a fee, to pay a levy on; ~ **erheben** to charge a fee, to levy (lay) a charge; ~ **erhöhen** to raise a fee; ~ **erlassen** to remit a fee; ~ **ermäßigen** to reduce (abate) a fee; **jds. Dienste über** ~ **in Anspruch nehmen** to make excessive use of s. one's services; ~ **rückvergüten** to refund a fee.
Gebühren charges, fees, dues, emoluments, *(Tarif)* rates, *(Universität)* pension *(Br.)*;
gegen Zahlung der ~ upon payment of charges;
amtliche ~ official fees; **letzthin angefallene** ~ fees as lately accumulated; **erhobene** ~ charges levied; **fällige** ~ fees due, fees payable; **feste** ~ fixed dues; **gesetzliche** ~ legal charges; **städtische** ~ city taxes, rates; **statistische** ~ statistical fees; **übertriebene** ~ excessive charges; **veränderliche** ~ variable dues; **volle** ~ full rates; **zurückzuerstattende** ~ returnable fees;
~ **und Abgaben** rates and taxes; ~ **für freiberufliche Beratung** professional charges; ~ **für die Erteilung eines Patents** fees incurred in obtaining a patent; ~ **für Luftpostdrucksachen** all-up newspaper rates; ~ **für Privatkonten** personal account charges; **keine besonderen** ~ **für fehlgeleitete Sendungen** free astray; **Steuern und** ~ taxes and fees; **höhere** ~ **für wertvollere Versandgüter** what the traffic will bear; ~ **der öffentlichen Versorgungsbetriebe** public-utility charges (rates);
Unterlagen nach Zahlung der ~ **aushändigen** to hand out the papers on payment of fees; ~ **entrichten** to pay the fees; ~ **für Ferngespräche erhöhen** to raise the fees for trunk calls; ~ **erstatten** to refund fees; **unstatthafte** ~ **fordern** to extort fees; ~ **niederschlagen** to abate fees; ~ **senken** to cut rates;
~ **zahlt der Empfänger** postage to be collected, *(Telefon)* reverse charge.
gebühren, jem. to be due to s. o.
Gebühren|abkommen free arrangement; ~**anhebung** fee (rate) increase, increase in charges; ~**ansage** *(Telefon)* advice duration and charge call; ~**ansatz** assessment of a fee; ~**anstieg** fee increase (hike, *US*); ~**anteil** portion of fees; ~**anzeiger** charge indicator *(Br.)*, toll charge meter *(US)*, *(Taxi)* taximeter; ~**aufschlag** extra charge, excess fee; ~**aufstellung** table (account) of charges; ~**aufteilung** fee splitting; ~**befreiung** remission of (exemption from) charges; ~**begleichung** payment of a fee; ~**berechnung** calculation of fees; ~**betrag** rate.
gebührend due, adequate, appropriate, proper, fit, befitting, suitable;
mit ~**er Sorgfalt** with due care.
Gebühren|einheit tariff unit, *(tel.)* unit charge, telephone call per unit, chargeable time; ~**einnehmer** *(Straße)* turnpike man; ~**entrichtung** payment of fees; ~**erhebung** collection (levying) of charges, *(Autobahn)* toll; **übermäßige** ~**erhebung** collection of illegal fees; **unstatthafte** ~**erhebung** extortion of fees; ~**erhöhung** fee (rate) increase, increase in charges, *(Zoll)* increases in duty; ~**erlaß** remission of (abatement in, waiver of) fees; ~**ermäßigung** reduction (abatement of) fees; ~**errechnung** calculation of fees; ~**erstattung** reimbursement of fees (charges), *(Telefon)* return of a charge; ~**ertrag** fee income; ~**festsetzung** assessment of a fee, rate making; ~**fonds** fee fund.
gebührenfrei free of charge, all charges paid, *(steuerfrei)* tax-exempt (-free, *US*), exempt from taxes (taxation), *(tel.)* toll-free, *(zollfrei)* duty-free;
~ **sein** to be exempt from charges;
~**e Dienstsache** official communication, on Her Majesty's service *(Br.)*; ~**e Lizenz** royalty-free licence.
Gebühren|freiheit remission (exemption) of fees, exemption from taxes (charges); ~**freiheit genießen** to be exempt from charges; ~**herabsetzung** reduction of charges, fee cut; ~**hinterziehung** evasion of taxes; ~**kommission** tariff commission; ~**kürzung** limitation of fees; ~**marke** revenue stamp; ~**melder** *(Telefon)* charge indicator; ~**minuten** *(Telefon)* chargeable time; ~**nachlaß** reduction of fees; ~**ordnung** scale of charges (fees), schedule of commissions (fees) *(US)*, tariff.
gebührenpflichtig taxable, liable to charges, subject to a fee, chargeable, *(Post)* subject to postage, postage to be paid, *(Zoll)* customable;
~**er Anruf** chargeable call, toll call *(US)*; ~**e Straße** turnpike (toll, *US*) road; ~**e Verwarnung** parking ticket *(US)*, warning and fee *(Br.)*; ~**e Verwarnung wegen falschen Parkens** parking fine.
Gebühren|rahmen scale of fees; ~**rechnung** note of fees, fee note (sheet) *(Br.)*, bill of charges *(US)*, *(Anwalt)* bill of costs (charges, *US*); ~**rechnung überprüfen und anerkennen** to tax the costs *(Br.)*; ~**rückerstattung** reimbursement of charges, return of duties; ~**satz** [tariff] rate; ~**sätze** scales of fees; **amtliche** ~**sätze** official scales of fees; **höchste** ~**sätze** costs on the highest scale; ~**schutz** rate protection; ~**senkung** cut in rates, reduction of charges, fee cut; ~**staffel** tariff (fee) scale; **verbindliche** ~**staffel** compulsory fee scale; ~**stempel** tax (revenue) stamp; **festes** ~**system** *(Agenturgeschäft)* fee system; ~**tabelle** scale of charges, schedule (table) of fees; ~**tarif** tariff, *(tel.)* phone rate; ~**teilung** fee splitting, *(Spediteur)* division of rates; ~**überhebung** overcharge, overcharging; ~**übernahme** absorption of charges; **nochmalige** ~**überprüfung** review of

taxation *(Br.)*; ~**überweisung** remittance of fees; ~**vereinbarung** *(Anwalt)* fee arrangement, champerty *(US)*; ~**vereinbarung treffen** to operate on a fee basis; ~**vereinheitlichung** *(Post)* postalization; ~**verzeichnis** tariff, table of charges, *(Gericht)* cost book, *(Telefon)* charge book; ~**vorschuß** fees paid in advance, advance offered, *(Anwalt)* retainer, retaining fee; ~**zahler** dues (fee) payer; ~**zahlung** payment of fees; ~**zone** zone *(US)*, *(Telefon)* tariff area; ~**zuschlag** additional charge, excess fee (charge), surcharge.

gebührlich befitting, suitable, proper.

Gebührnisse öffentlicher Betriebe public-utility rates.

gebündeltes|Kreditangebot loan package; ~ **Übereinkommen** package settlement.

gebunden bound, subject to, *(durch Abmachungen)* committed, bound, engaged, *(gelenkt)* controlled, directed, *(Kapital)* tied [up], locked up *(Br.)*, *(Politik)* committed *(Br.)*, *(verpflichtet)* obliged, *(zweckgebunden)* earmarked;

in Halbfranz ~ half-bound; **in der ersten Hand** ~ *(Preise)* price-controlled (maintained); **an einen Index** ~ index-tied; **in Leder** ~ bound in leather, wholebound; **in Leinen** ~ cloth-bound; **nicht** ~ untied, *(Politik)* uncommitted *(US)*; **vertraglich** ~ bound in treaty (by indenture);

sich ~ **haben** to be committed; **sich an eine Abmachung** ~ **halten** to hold to an agreement; ~ **sein** to underlie; **anderweitig** ~ **sein** to be tied up with other things; **an sein Angebot** ~ **sein** to be bound by one's offer; **an eine andere Firma geschäftlich** ~ **sein** to be tied up with another company; **nicht** ~ **sein** *(Buch)* to be in sheets, *(pol.)* to float; **an feste Termine** ~ **sein** to be made on fixed dates; **vertraglich** ~ **sein** to be bound by indentures; **vollkommen** ~ **sein** to be tied hand and foot;

vertraglich ~**e Arbeitskräfte** indentured labo(u)r; ~**er Besitz** settlement, settled property *(Br.)*; **an eine Brauerei** ~**e Gaststätte** tied house; ~**e Preise** maintained (controlled) prices; **in** ~**er Rede** in metrical language; ~**e Währung** controlled currency; **in** ~**em Zahlungsverkehr** *(ECU)* through clearing channels; ~**e Zinssätze** amounts of interest set aside.

Geburt [child] birth, nativity, *(Abstimmung)* birth, descent;

kurz vor der ~ confined;

eheliche ~ legitimacy; **schwere** ~ *(fig.)* tough job; **uneheliche** ~ illegitimacy, bastardy *(US)*; **vorzeitige** ~ premature;

~ **[beim Standesamt] anmelden** to notify (register) a birth; **von** ~ **Engländer sein** to be British by birth; **bei der** ~ **sterben** to die in childbed.

Geburten|abnahme fall in the birth rate; ~**ausfall** falling birth rate; ~**beihilfe** maternity benefit; ~**beschränkung** restriction of the birth rate, birth control; **für** ~**beschränkung eintreten** to stand for birth control; ~**buch** register of births; ~**eintragung** registration of birth; ~**explosion** populartion explosion; ~**häufigkeit** birth rate; ~**kontrolle** birth (population) control; ~**planung** planned parenthood; **rückläufige** ~**rate** declining birth rate; ~**regelung** family planning, birth control; ~**register** register of births; ~**registrierung** birth registration; ~**regulierung** birth regulation; ~**rückgang** fall in the (falling) birth rate, birth-rate decline; ~**rückgang erzielen** to bring down the birth rate.

geburten|schwach with a low birth rate; ~**stark** with a high birth rate.

Geburten|statistik vital statistics; ~**sterblichkeitsziffer** natal death rate; ~**tafel** table of births; ~**überschuß** excess (surplus) of births over deaths.

Geburtenziffer birth rate, natality;

nicht aufgegliederte ~ crude birth rate; **fallende** ~ falling birth rate; **niedrige** ~ low birth rate.

gebürtig native, born;

aus A ~ **sein** to hail from A;

~**er Amerikaner** true American by birth.

Geburts|anmeldung notification of birth; ~**anzeige** announcement of birth, *(Zeitung)* birth column; ~**anzeige vornehmen** to announce a birth; ~**ausfall** falling birth rate; ~**beihilfe** maternity benefit; ~**datum** birth date; ~**fehler** congenital deformity; ~**haus** birthplace; ~**helfer** obstetrician, man midwife; ~**jahr** birth year; ~**land** native (mother) country, birthland, country of one's birth, fatherland; ~**mal** birthmark; ~**monat** birth month; ~**name** birth name, *(Ehefrau)* maiden name; ~**ort** place of birth, birthplace, native place; ~**recht** birthright; ~**register** register of births; ~**schein** birth certificate, certificate of birth; ~**stadt** birthplace, native (home, *US*) town; ~**stunde** birth hour; ~**tag** birthday; ~**tagsfest**, ~**tagsfeier** birthday party; ~**tagsgeschenk** birthday gift (present); ~**urkunde** birth certificate, certificate of birth; ~**wohnsitz** [etwa] domicile of origin.

Gebüsch brush, bush, brushwood, *(Dickicht)* thicket.

Geck dandy, jackanapes, buck, dude, nut, fashionist, attitudinizer, sport *(US coll.)*, high-hat *(US sl.)*;

junger ~ whippersnapper, puppy.

geckenhaft dandyish, foppish, dudish *(US sl.)*.

gedachte Größe imagined quantity.

Gedächtnis remembrance, memory, mind;

aus dem ~ from memory, without books, off the cuff *(US)*; **ins** ~ **eingegraben** branded (embedded) in one's memory, indelibly engraved on the mind;

geschultes ~ well-stocked memory; **gutes** ~ good memory; **schlechtes** ~ defective (poor) memory; **unzuverlässiges** ~ treacherous (elusive) memory, leaky memory; **visuelles** ~ photographic memory; **weitreichendes** ~ long memory; **zuverlässiges** ~ exact memory;

sein ~ **auffrischen** to refresh one's memory; **jds.** ~ **auffrischen** to give s. one's memory a jog, to keep s. one's memory green, to jog s. one's memory; **im** ~ **behalten** to bear in mind, to retain in one's mind; **sein** ~ **belasten** to task one's memory; **sein** ~ **mit sinnlosen Einzelheiten belasten** to clog (burden) one's memory with useless facts; **sein** ~ **bemühen** to draw upon one's memory; **im** ~ **bewahren** to treasure up in one's memory; **im** ~ **haften bleiben** to ring in one's mind; **in jds.** ~ **haften bleiben** to dwell in s. one's memory; **in jds.** ~ **einprägen** to inseminate in s. one's mind; **seinem** ~ **einprägen** to embed (imprint) in one's memory, to infix in the mind; **seinem** ~ **unauslöschlich einprägen** to brand on one's mind, to imprint in (on) one's memory; **dem** ~ **entfallen (entgleiten)** to slip (escape) one's memory; **schwaches** ~ **haben** to have a weak memory; ~ **wie ein Sieb haben** to have a memory like a sieve; **sich ins** ~ **rufen** to call s. th. back to mind; **sein** ~ **strapazieren** to task one's memory; ~ **stützen** to aid memory; **aus dem** ~ **tilgen** to erase from one's memory, to pass the sponge over; **unliebsame Begebenheiten der Vergangenheit aus dem** ~ **tilgen** to efface unpleasant memories of the past; **sein** ~ **überfordern** to trust one's memory too much; **sich auf sein** ~ **verlassen** to trust one's memory; **sein** ~ **verlieren** to lose one's memory; **ins** ~ **zurückkehren** to come back; **sich ins** ~ **zurückrufen** to call to mind (memory);

~**auffrischung** refreshing one's memory; ~**ausfall** lapse of memory; ~**briefmarke** commemorative stamp; ~**fehler** lapse (slip) of memory; ~**gottesdienst** memorial service; ~**hilfe** assistance to memory, memory aid; ~**kunst** mnemonics; ~**protokoll** memorandum; ~**rede** memorial address; ~**säule** monument; ~**schwäche** failure (defect, shortness) of memory; ~**schwund** amnesia, blackout *(sl.)*; ~**skizze** memory sketch; ~**speicherung** memory retention; ~**stätte** memorial; ~**störung** partial amnesia; ~**stütze** aid (help) to memory, memorandum, *(Werbung)* aided recall; ~**übung** exercise of memory; ~**verlust** amnesia; ~**vermögen** memory retention; ~**versagen** lapse of memory.

gedämpft muffled, dull, deadened, *(Farbe, Licht)* subdued;

mit ~**er Stimme** in an undertone; ~**e Unterhaltung** hushed conversation.

Gedanke thought, idea, imagination, conception, notion;

in ~**n versunken (vertieft)** deep in thought, in a brown study, in the clouds; **in seinen verborgensten** ~**n** at the back of one's mind;

flüchtiger ~ random thought; **kluger** ~ wise idea; **konfuse** ~**n** scattered thoughts; **schöpferischer** ~ creative idea; **selbständiger** ~ self-supporting idea; **späterer** ~ afterthought; **unschuldige** ~**n** pure thoughts; **wirre** ~**n** wooly thoughts;

zwei Seelen, ein ~ two minds with but a single thought;

~**n über einen neuen Roman anstellen** to have a new novel in contemplation; ~**n austauschen** to compare notes; **sich mit einem** ~**n befreunden** to resign o. s. to an idea; **jds.** ~**n begreifen** to grasp s. one's intentions; **seine** ~ **nicht beisammenhaben** to be absent-minded; **seine** ~**n beisammenhalten** to have one's wits about one; **j. auf** ~**n bringen** to put ideas into s. one's head; **auf jds.** ~**n eingehen** to understand what is in s. one's mind; **nur** ~**n für eine Sache haben** to have s. th. on the brain; **gemeine** ~**n hegen** to think bad thoughts; **auf den** ~**n kommen** to hit upon the idea, to fall into the motion; ~**n aufkommen lassen** to invite reflection; **sich von dem** ~**n leiten lassen** to be guided by the idea; **jds.** ~**n lesen** to read s. one's mind, to read s. one's thoughts; **sich über etw.** ~**n machen** to be uneasy (worry) about s. th.; **jem. seine** ~**n mitteilen** to open one's mind to s. o.; **seinen** ~**n nachhängen** to be lost in thought; **sich in** ~**n schon als Anwalt sehen** to fancy o. s. as a lawyer; **in** ~**n sündigen** to entertain sinful thoughts; **sich mit einem** ~**n tragen** to have in mind, to entertain an idea; **seinen** ~**n Ausdruck verleihen** to give mouth to one's thoughts.

Gedanken|armut poverty of ideas; ~**austausch** exchange of ideas (views), communication; ~**blitz** brilliant idea, brain child *(coll.)*; ~**entwicklung** progress of thought; ~**freiheit** freedom (latitude) of thought; ~**fülle** wealth of ideas; ~**gang** tenor, train of thoughts (ideas); ~**gang eines Arguments verstehen** to get the drift of an argument; ~**gut** stock of ideas, ideology; ~**kette** line of thought; ~**lesen** mind reading; ~**leser** mind (thought) reader.

gedankenlos thoughtless, lightheaded, *(leichtsinnig)* dizzy;
~ **vor sich hinstarren** to have a vacant look.

Gedankenlosigkeit want of thought, vacancy.

gedankenreiche Abhandlung thoughtful essay.

Gedanken|richtung trend of thought; ~**spiel** intellectual exercise; ~**splitter** aphorism; ~**sprung** inconsistency; ~**strich** dash, pause, break; ~**tiefe** *(Buch)* depth of thought; ~**übertragung** mental telepathy, thought transmission; ~**verbindung** association of ideas, overtones; ~**verlorenheit** brown study; ~**vorbehalt** mental reservation.

gedanklich, rein notional;
~ **lösen** to brainstorm *(US)*; **sich ~ mit jem. völlig eins wissen** to live in intellectual fellowship with s. o.;
~**e Anstrengung** mental effort.

Gedeck cover, plate, cutlery, *(Gebühr hierfür)* cover charge;
trockenes ~ restaurant meal without drinks;
~ **auflegen** to lay a place.

gedeckt covered, *(sichergestellt)* secured, *(Versicherung)* held covered, *(Wechsel)* protected;
nicht ~ *(Wechsel)* unprotected, refer to drawer; **voll** ~ *(Versicherung)* fully covered;
~ **sein** to be held covered, *(im Konkurs)* to hold security; **gegen einen Verlust ~ sein** to be insured against a loss; **durch Versandpapiere ~ sein** to be secured by shipping documents;
~**es Konto** secured account; ~**er Kredit** collateral credit.

Gedeih und Verderb, auf neck or nothing, come what may, sink or swim, for better or worse, for good or evil, win or lose, at all costs;
jem. auf ~ ausgeliefert sein to be left to s. one's mercy; **sich mit jem. auf ~ verbinden** to throw in one's lot with s. o.

Gedeihen prosperity, *(Verhandlungen)* [good] progress.

gedeihen to prosper, to be prosperous, to flourish, to thrive, *(Verhandlungen)* to make progress;
prächtig ~ to develop splendidly; **bis zu einem bestimmten Punkt** ~ to reach a certain stage.

gedeihlich prosperous, thriving.

gedemütigt, bis ins letzte humiliated to the dust.

Gedenk|ausgabe commemorative issue; ~**block** *(Philatelie)* souvenir block.

Gedenken, zum in memory (remembrance).

gedenken, jds. in einer Rede to make mention of s. o. in a speech; **jener glücklichen Tage** ~ to call back those happy days; **jds. in seinem Testament** ~ to remember (mention) s. one in one's will.

Gedenk|feier memorial ceremony, commemoration, anniversary; ~**feier abhalten** to memorialize; ~**kranz** memorial wreath; ~**marke** commemorative stamp; ~**minute** a minute's silence; ~**münze** commemorative coin; ~**platte** memorial tablet; ~**rede** memorial address; ~**stätte** memorial; ~**stein** memorial stone, tombstone; ~**stunde** memorial service; ~**tafel** mural tablet; ~**tag** anniversary.

Gedicht poem;
~ **von einem Hut** a peach of a hat;
~ **für sein eigenes ausgeben** to work off a poem as one's own *(sl.)*; **ein ~ sein** to be just lovely.

gediegen true, genuine, *(massiv)* solid, sterling;
~**e Arbeit** solid workmanship, able work; ~**er Charakter** sterling character; ~**e Firma** sound business house, solid business firm; ~**es Gold** native (solid) gold; ~**e Kenntnisse** thorough knowledge; ~**e Möbel** furniture of quality and distinction; ~**e Waren** sterling goods.

Gediegenheit solidity, thoroughness, *(min.)* genuineness.

gediehen, so weit ~ sein, daß to be at such at point that.

Gedinge piecework, contract system;
im ~ arbeiten to work by the job;
~**arbeit** piecework, job (contract) work; ~**arbeiter** pieceworker; ~**lohn** piece wage; ~**wesen** contracting.

gedopt snowed up *(sl.)*.

Gedränge throng, crowd, hustle, jam, cram *(coll.)*, crush;
~ **und Gehetze** hustle and bustle;
furchtbares ~ frightful crush; **hektisches** ~ stampede;
ins ~ geraten to get into a crowd, *(zeitlich)* to cut (run) it fine; **erheblich ins ~ kommen** *(finanziell)* to be reduced to great straits; **sich im ~ verlieren** to get lost in the crowd.

Gedrängel squash, jostle, jostling;
~ **nach den besten Plätzen** scramble for the best seats.

gedrängt crowded, packed, crammed, *(Stil)* succinct, terse;
~ **voll** crowded to capacity;
~**e Übersicht** summary statement, condensed account, digest.

Gedrängtheit succinctness.

gedrechselt *(Stil)* stilted.

gedreht werden, gerade *(Film)* to be in production.

gedruckt in print (type), off the press, in black and white;
auffallend ~ displaced; **gesperrt** ~ spaced; **halbfett** ~ boldfaced; **kursiv** ~ in italics; **schlecht** ~ ill-set; ~ **vorliegend** in print; **zweispaltig** ~ printed in double columns;
sich gern ~ sehen to like to see o. s. in print; ~ **sein (vorliegen)** to come from the press, to be in print; ~ **werden** to go to press, to appear in print;
~**es Antragsformular** printed application form.

gedrückt *(Börse)* depressed, heavy, low, *(Geldmarkt)* stringent;
auf Verkäufe hin ~ liegen to be under selling pressure;
~**e Börse** stringent stock market.

Gedrucktes print, printing.

Gedrücktheit depression, depressed state, *(Geldmarkt)* stringency;
~ **der Kurse** low level of prices; ~ **des Marktes** heaviness of the market.

Geduld patience;
außergewöhnliche ~ extreme patience; **unendliche** ~ patience of Job; **unermüdliche** ~ unfailing patience;
jds. ~ erschöpfen to exhaust s. one's patience; **mit jem. keine ~ mehr haben** to be out of patience with s. o.; **jds. ~ auf die Probe stellen** to prove the patience of s. o.; **jds. ~ strapazieren** to tax (try) s. one's patience; **jds. ~ aufs äußerste strapazieren** to stretch s. one's patience to its limits; **sich in ~ üben** to possess one's soul in patience; **seine ~ verlieren** to get out of (lose one's) patience.

gedulden, sich to possess one's soul in patience.

geduldet sein, in bestimmten Kreisen to pass in certain circles.

geduldig patient;
~ **wie ein Lamm** as patient as Job;
alles ~ über sich ergehen lassen to put up with everything;
Papier ist ~ paper won't blush *(coll.)*.

Gedulds|probe, eine a fiddling job; **j. auf eine harte ~probe stellen** to try (tax) s. one's patience; ~**spiel** puzzle.

gedungen mercenary, hired, pensionary.

geeicht calibrated, standardized.

geeignet *(Person)* qualified, capable, apt, eligible, fit, *(Sache)* appropriate, applicable, convenient, convenable, fitted, suitable, proper;
für einen Beruf ~ fit for a job, eligible for an occupation; **zur Kapitalanlage** ~ suitable for investment; **nicht** ~ ill qualified, nonapplicable; **für meine Zwecke** ~ suitable for my purposes; **für eine Stellung nicht ~ sein** not to be fitted for a position;
im ~en Augenblick at the right moment; ~**er Kandidat** eligible candidate; ~**e Maßnahmen** appropriate measures; ~**en Zeitpunkt feststellen** to decide on a fit time.

Geeignetheit qualification, suitability.

geerbtes Haus ancestral home.

Gefahr danger, peril, distress, *(Risiko)* risk, hazard, jeopardy;
angesichts der ~ in the presence (in the face) of danger; **außer** ~ out of danger;
auf ~ des Absenders at consignor's (sender's) risk; **auf ~ der Bahn** at company's risk; **auf ~ des Empfängers** at receiver's risk; **auf eigene Rechnung und** ~ at one's own risk, at owner's risk; **gegen alle ~en** against all risks (A.A.R.); **in der größten** ~ in the utmost danger; **mit ~ verbunden** risky, aleatory;
akute ~ imminent danger; **augenscheinliche** ~ apparent danger; **ausgeschlossene ~en** hazards not covered; **durch den Arbeitgeber verursachte außergewöhnliche** ~ extraordinary risk; **äußerste** ~ extreme danger; **berufsfremde** ~ *(Angestellter)* extraterritorial risk; **besondere** ~ extraneous peril; **unmittelbar bevorstehende** ~ clear and present danger, emergent (imminent) danger; **dauernde** ~ constant danger; **drohende** ~ overhanging danger, menace, imminent peril; **eingebildete** ~ a lion in the way; **erhöhte** ~ aggravated risk; **erkennbare** ~ perceivable risk, obvious danger; **gedeckte ~en** *(Versicherung)* risks and perils, perils insured against; **gegenwärtige** ~ present danger; **gemeinsame** ~ common danger; **inflationistische ~en** risks of inflation; **mögliche** ~ potential menace; **offensichtliche** ~ obvious risk; **reiseübliche ~en** dangers incident to travel; **übernommene** ~ subscribed risk; **übersehbare** ~ perceivable risk; **unabwendbare ~en** *(Transportversicherung)* unavoidable dangers [of the rivers]; **ungewöhnliche** ~ *(Arbeitnehmer)*

extraordinary danger; **verborgene** ~ snake in the grass; **versicherte** ~ risk run, risk subscribed, peril insured against; **versicherungsfähige** ~ insurable risk;
~ **beim Absender** consignor's risk; ~ **des Einsturzes** danger of collapse; ~ **des Fortgespültwerdens** risk of being washed away by the sea; ~ **für Leib und Leben** danger to life and limb, extreme danger; ~ **für die Menschheit** threat to mankind; ~ **für die Öffentlichkeit** public danger; **sämtliche ~en der Schiffsreise** risks and perils of the sea; **~en der Seefahrt** dangers of navigation; ~ **für die Staatssicherheit** danger to national security; **~en im Straßenverkehr** perils of the street; ~ **des schlechten Straßenzustands** dangers of the road; ~ **des Verfrachters** shipper's risk; ~ **des Verlustes** risk of loss; ~ **der zufälligen Verschlechterung** danger of deterioration; ~ **einer erneuten Verurteilung** double jeopardy; ~ **der Verurteilung zu einer schweren Strafe** jeopardy of life and limb; ~ **im Verzug** delays are dangerous, imminence, periculum in mora; **mehrere ~en des Wohnungsinhabers** homeowners' multiple peril;
versicherte ~ in eine andere abändern to vary the risk; **sich einer ~ aussetzen** to incur a danger, to endanger o. s., to give hostages to fortune; **sich aus einer ~ befreien** to extricate o. s. from a danger; **sich Hals über Kopf in ~ begeben** to thrust o. s. into peril; **ernsthafte ~en für die Störung der öffentlichen Ruhe beschwören** to create a serious risk for public disorder; **~en bestehen** to overcome dangers; **~en mit sich bringen** to involve a risk; **jds. Interessen in ~ bringen** to jeopardize s. one's interests; **ernste ~ darstellen** to pose a serious threat; ~ **beim Autofahren darstellen** to constitute a driving hazard; ~ **für die öffentliche Sicherheit darstellen** to be dangerous to the public; **alle ~en decken** to cover all risks; **einer drohenden ~ gegenübertreten** to counter a threat; **~en heraufbeschwören** to pose hazards; ~ **laufen** to run a risk; **~en auf die leichte Schulter nehmen** to make light of dangers; **j. vor ~ schützen** to guard s. o. against danger; **einer ~ ins Auge sehen** to face up to a danger, to do s. th. with one's eyes open; **mit ~ verbunden sein** to include risks; **allen ~en standhalten** to wash in all dangers; ~ **tragen** to bear the risk; **den größten ~en trotzen** to go through fire and water; **etw. auf eigene ~ tun** to do s. th. at one's own risk (peril); ~ **übernehmen** to take a risk; ~ **wittern** to have a feeling of (to sense) danger; **sich angesichts einer gemeinsamen ~ zusammentun** to make common cause in the face of common danger;
~änderung alteration in risk.

gefahrbringend dangerous.

gefährden to endanger, to jeopardize, to imperil, to risk;
sich ~ to expose o. s. to danger; **Aufrechterhaltung der öffentlichen Sicherheit** ~ to endanger the maintenance of public order; **jds. Interessen** ~ to jeopardize s. one's interests; **jds. Ruf** ~ to compromise (risk) s. one's reputation; **Staatssicherheit** ~ to imperil national security; **Unternehmen** ~ to endanger an undertaking.

gefährdet, sich als ~ erweisen to prove vulnerable; **j. für moralisch ~ halten** to judge s. o. to be a risk; **besonders ~ sein** to be particularly at risk; **sittlich ~ sein** to be in moral danger;
~es Vermögen impaired (precarious) fortune.

Gefährdeter *(Strafrecht)* predelinquent person.

Gefährdung endangering, danger, *(Versicherung)* risk, jeopardy;
zusätzliche ~ additional danger;
~ **der Allgemeinheit** public danger; ~ **der Aufrechterhaltung der öffentlichen Ordnung** endangering the maintenance of public order; **vorsätzliche ~ Dritter** wilful interference in the safety of others; ~ **von Gläubigerinteressen** jeopardizing a creditor's interest.

Gefährdungshaftung strict (absolute, full) liability.

Gefahren|abwendung prevention of accidents; **~änderung** alteration in the risk insured; **~anzeige** *(Versicherung)* representation; **~bereich** danger area (zone); **~einteilung** *(Versicherung)* classification of risks; **~erhöhung** increase of risk (hazard); **~geld** danger money; **~grenze** critical point; **~häufung** accumulation of risks; **~herd** *(pol.)* storm center *(US)* (centre, *Br.*), trouble spot; **~höhe** degree of risk; **~industrie** hazardous industry; **~klasse** class (category) of risk, accident branch; **~klassifizierung** classification of risks, hazard classification; **~klausel** emergency clause; **~lage** *(Fahrzeug)* situation of danger; **~meldeanlage** alarm system; **~meldung** danger warning; **~merkmale** particulars of a risk; **~minderung** decrease in risk; **~mitte** *(Flugwesen)* point of no return; **~prämie** risk premium; **~punkt** danger spot (point).

Gefahrenquelle unusual danger, source of danger;
ständige ~ permanent nuisance;
~ **für Kinder** attractive nuisance *(US)*; ~ **für die Schiffahrt** danger to shipping.

Gefahren|rücklage *(Versicherung)* catastrophe reserve; **~schutz** *(Industrie)* factory protection; **~signal** danger signal, *(Bahn)* danger position, *(Schiffahrt)* distress signal; **mit einer ~situation konfrontiert werden** to be confronted by an emergency; **~stelle** dangerous place, danger (accident, black) spot; **~tarif** special risk rate **~träger** risk taker (bearer); **~tragung** risk of loss; **~übernahme** risk taking, assumption of risk; **~übertragung** transfer of risk; **~umfang** degree of risk; **versicherte ~umstände detailliert festlegen** to set out the circumstances in which the insurance is operative; **~verteilung** diversification (spread) of risk; **~zeichen** *(Straßenschild)* warning sign; **~zone** danger zone, danger area; **~zulage** *(Angestellter)* hazard (danger zone, hazardous work) bonus, danger money, *(Versicherung)* penalty rates *(US)*; **~zulage bei Gebäudeversicherungen** builder's risk policy; **~zustand** dangerous state.

Gefahrgüter dangerous articles, hazardous goods.

gefährlich dangerous, risky, insecure, wild, warm, disagreeable, touch-and-go, *(Küste)* foul, *(unsicher)* insecure, precarious, unsafe, *(Versicherung)* hazardous, risky;
von Natur aus ~ dangerous per se;
für j. ~ werden to become a danger for s. o.
~e Angelegenheit risky business; **~er Arbeitsplatz** hazardous situation; **~er Beruf** hazardous employment (occupation); **~e Betriebe** dangerous premises; **sich auf ~em Boden bewegen** to be on dangerous ground; **~es Ereignis** dangerous occurrence; **~er Fehler** serious mistake; **~es Geschäft** touch-and-go business; **~es Gewerbe** dangerous trade; **~e Güter** hazardous goods, dangerous articles; **~e Ladung** dangerous cargo; **sich in einer ~en Lage befinden** to be in an insecure position, to be a touch-and-go situation; **~es Spiel treiben** to skate on thin ice; **~es Unternehmen** risky undertaking; **sich in ~em Zustand befinden** *(Patient)* to be in a critical situation.

Gefährlichkeit dangerous nature, insecurity.

gefahrlos safe, *(Versicherung)* riskless;
~es Unternehmen safe undertaking.

Gefahrlosigkeit safety.

Gefährt vehicle, carriage, conveyance, cart.

Gefährte companion, attendant, attender, fellow, mate.

Gefahr|tragung risk of loss, risk taking; **~übergang** passing of risk.

Gefälle slope, ascent, grade *(US)*, [downward] gradient, incline, pitch, fall, downgrade, *(Löhne)* differential, *(Preise)* price gap, *(Steuer)* revenues, imposts, *(Zins)* margin;
kulturelles ~ difference in cultural level; **starkes** ~ drop, inclination, *(Straßenschild)* steep gradient;
~ **einer Kurve** slope of a curve;
starkes ~ haben *(Fluß)* to fall sharply.

Gefallen favo(u)r, kindness, pleasure, liking, palate, fancy;
persönlicher ~ personal favo(u)r;
um einen ~ bitten to ask a favo(u)r; ~ **erweisen** to do a favo(u)r; **um jem. einen ~ zu erweisen** to please s. o.; **einem Freund einen ~ erweisen** to oblige a friend; ~ **an etw. finden** to take a fancy to s. th., to take pleasure in doing; ~ **an jem. finden** to take a liking for (fancy, shine to, *US*) s. o., to become fond of s. o.; ~ **an einer Sache finden** to be pleased with an idea; **jem. zu ~ sein** to oblige s. o., to do s. o. a favo(u)r, to be accommodating to s. o.

gefallen *(Kurs)* down;
im Krieg ~ killed (died) in action;
jem. ~ to please (suit) s. o.; **sich in Anspielungen** ~ to indulge in allusions; **sich in der Rolle eines Beschützers** ~ to fancy o. s. as protector;
sich alles ~ lassen to put up with everything; **sich nichts ~ lassen** to take (have) no nonsense; ~ **sein** *(Preise)* to have dropped; **plötzlich ~ sein** to have come down with a run.

Gefallenen|denkmal war memorial; **~ehrung** memorial service; **~friedhof** war cemetery.

gefällig pleasing, pleasant, obliging, complaisant, good-natured, accommodating, fair, agreeable;
~ **und zuvorkommend** kind and obliging;
~ **sein** to be accommodating; **jem. ~ sein** to oblige s. o., to do s. o. a good turn;
~e Antwort kind answer; **~e Aufmachung** nice getup; **~es Benehmen** easy manners; **zur ~en Kenntnisnahme** for your kind attention, with compliments; **~e Melodie** attractive tune; **Ihr ~es Schreiben** your favo(u)r; **~er Wein** pleasant wine;
um ~e Antwort wird gebeten the favo(u)r of an answer is requested.

Gefälligkeit kindness, favo(u)r, facility, compliance, obligingness, accommodation, good turn, courtesy, pleasure, goodwill, complaisance, neatness;

aus [reiner] ~ as a favo(u)r, for accommodation only; **nur aus** ~ **für Sie** only to please you;
gewohnte ~ usual complaisance;
j. um eine ~ **bitten** to solicit a favo(u)r of. s. o.; **jem. eine** ~ **erweisen** to confer a favo(u)r on s. o., to oblige s. o., to do s. o. a service (pleasure).
Gefälligkeits|adresse accommodation address; **~akzept** accommodation acceptance (bill, paper, note, *US*); **~aussteller** accommodation maker; **~brief** introductory letter; **~girant** accommodation endorser (indorser); **~giro, ~indossament** accommodation (collateral) endorsement (indorsement); **~papier** accommodation paper; **~partei** accommodation party; **~stempel** *(Philatelie)* cancellation by request; **~unterschrift** bogus signature; **~wechsel** accommodation (proforma, nonvalue) bill, accommodation note, windbill *(Br.)*, windmill *(Br.)*, kite *(Br.)*, financial paper *(US)*; **~wechsel ziehen** to fly a kite *(Br.)*; **unverbindliche ~zusage** gentlemen's agreement.
Gefällstrecke incline, grade, gradient.
gefälscht false, fake, faked up, phony, forged, counterfeit[ed];
~e Banknote falsified (dud, *sl.*) note; **~e Bilanz** cooked (doctored, faked) balance sheet; **~es Geld** counterfeit coin (money), counterfeits, bad (base, *Br.*) money; **~er Scheck** forged check *(US)* (cheque, *Br.*); **~e Unterschrift** forged signature; **~e Urkunde** forged document; **~er Wechsel** forged (counterfeited) bill.
gefangen captive;
in einer Falle ~ trapped; **mit einem Netz** ~ netted;
sich ~ **geben** to yield o. s. prisoner.
Gefangene|r prisoner, captive, *(mil.)* prisoner of war;
als ~r festgehalten detained in captivity;
ausgebrochener ~r rabbitfoot *(sl.)*; **streng bewachter ~r** close prisoner; **entlaufener ~r** escapee; **politischer ~r** political prisoner, prisoner of state; **verzweifelter ~r** despondent prisoner;
~r mit dem höchsten Sicherheitsrisiko maximum security prisoner;
~n abführen to remove (escort) a prisoner; ~ **austauschen** to exchange prisoners; **~n befreien** to make a rescue; **~n bewachen** to keep a prisoner under guard, to guard a prisoner; **Haftentlassung eines ~n bewirken** to bail a prisoner; **~n einsperren** to lock up a prisoner; **~n gegen Kautionsgestellung aus der Haft entlassen** to remand a prisoner on bail; ~ **nach Verbüßung der Hälfte ihrer Strafzeit entlassen** to release prisoners halfway through their terms; **~n fesseln** to chain a prisoner; **~n freilassen** to release (free) a prisoner, to set a prisoner at liberty; **~n bedingt freilassen** to put a prisoner on parole; **einem entsprungenen ~n Unterschlupf gewähren** to harbo(u)r an escaped prisoner; **fünfhundert** ~ **machen** to capture 500 of the enemy; ~ **mißhandeln** to abuse prisoners; **~n in Untersuchungshaft nehmen** to commit a prisoner for trial; ~ **repatriieren** to get prisoners back to their homes; **~n unter Bewachung transportieren** to conduct a prisoner under escort; **~n überstellen** to surrender a prisoner.
Gefangenen|anstalt prison; **~arbeit** prison labo(u)r (work), convict labo(u)r; **~arbeit für Aufgaben im öffentlichen Interesse** public works and wages system; **~arbeitssystem** lease (state account, state-use, US) system; **~aufseher** turnkey, warden of a prison *(US)*, warder *(Br.)*, guard, keeper, gaoler; **~aufstand** prison riot; **~ausbruch** prison escape; **~aussage** prisoner's statement, statement of a prisoner; **~austausch** exchange of prisoners of war; **~befreiung** delivery of a captive; **gewaltsame ~befreiung** jail delivery; **~begünstigung bei der Flucht** voluntary escape; **~beschäftigung** occupation of prisoners; **~eskorte durchführen** to conduct a prisoner under escort; **~flucht** escape from prison; **~fürsorge** prison welfare, discharge prisoner's aid *(Br.)*; **~fürsorgeverein** Discharged Prisoner's Aid Society *(Br.)*; **~hilfe** discharged prisoner's aid; **~lager** compound; **geheimes ~lager** secret detention centre; **~meuterei** prison revolt; **~produktion** prison production; **~revolte** prison riot; **~transport** convoy of prisoners; **~transportwagen** Black Maria *(coll.)*, booby hatch, paddy wag(g)on *(US)*; **~verhör, ~vernehmung** examination of a prisoner; **~verlegung** transfer of prisoners; **~vernehmung** interrogation of prisoners; **~ware** prison-made goods; **~wärter** turnkey, warder *(Br.)*, guard, keeper, gaoler; **~zug** prison train.
gefangengehalten werden to be held prisoner (under duress).
gefangenhalten to imprison, to hold s. o. a prisoner, to keep confined (a prisoner), to detain.
Gefangen|haltung detention, imprisonment; **~nahme** arrest, seizure, apprehension, *(mil.)* capture.
gefangennehmen to arrest, to seize, to apprehend, *(mil.)* to capture;
sich ~ **lassen** to give o. s. up as a prisoner.
Gefangenschaft captivity, fetters;
in ~ detained in captivity;
j. aus der ~ **befreien** to deliver s. o. from captivity; **in** ~ **geraten** to be taken prisoner (captured); **aus der** ~ **heimkehren** to return from captivity; **in** ~ **sein** to be a prisoner of war.
gefangensetzen to apprehend, to imprison, to prison.
Gefängnis prison, prison house, hold, pound, cage, condemned ward, gaol, jail, jailhouse *(US)*, penitentiary *(US)*, reception center *(New York)*, booby hatch *(sl.)*, mill *(sl.)*, hell *(sl.)*, *(Strafe)* imprisonment;
von der Polizei ins ~ **verbracht** commited in presence of an officer;
lebenslängliches ~ life imprisonment; **offenes** ~ prison without walls; **provisorisches** ~ lockup house;
~ **mit Bewährung** suspended execution of sentence; ~ **bis zu fünf Jahren** *(Strafrahmen)* imprisonment for a term not exceeding five years;
ins ~ **abführen** to carry (take, hale) off to prison; **jds. Entlassung aus dem** ~ **anordnen** to order s. one's release from prison; **aus dem** ~ **ausbrechen** to break prison; **ins** ~ **einliefern** to commit to prison; **ins** ~ **einweisen** to mittimus *(US)*, to send s. o. to prison; **im** ~ **enden** to wind up in prison; **aus dem** ~ **entkommen** to escape from prison; **aus dem** ~ **entlassen** to release (discharge) from prison; **auf** ~ **erkennen** to inflict (condemn to) imprisonment; **ohne Anklageerhebung im** ~ **festsetzen** to hold in jail without formal charge; **aus dem** ~ **fliehen** to escape from prison; **ins** ~ **kommen** to go to prison (gaol); **j. im** ~ **enden lassen** to land s. o. in prison *(fam.)*; **aus dem** ~ **loseisen** to spring *(sl.)*; **im** ~ **schmachten** to rot in jail, to languish in prison; **im** ~ **sitzen** to be (sit) in prison, to be imprisoned, to be in gaol, to enjoy Her Majesty's hospitality *(fam.)*; **im** ~ **stecken** to lay by the heels; **mit** ~ **bestraft werden** *(Straftat)* to be liable for imprisonment; **aus dem** ~ **entlassen werden** to be released from prison; **zu drei Jahren** ~ **verurteilt werden** to be sentenced to three years' imprisonment, to get three years; **j. ins** ~ **werfen** to put (clap, throw) s. o. in prison, to clap up (jail, *US*) s. o.; **sich im** ~ **wiederfinden** to end up in prison, to wind up behind bars;
~abteilung prison ward; **~anstalt** prison building; **~aufgaben** prison functions; **~aufseher** prison warden *(US)*, jailer *(US)*, warder *(Br.)*, warden of a prison *(US)*; **~ausbruch** prison breach, prison breaking, jailbreaking *(US)*, prison breakout, escape from (breach of) prison, actual escape; **~ausbruch mit Einverständnis der Wärter** voluntary escape; **~beamter** prison officer; **~behörde** prison commissioners; **~bereich** gaol (jail) limits; **~direktor** prison governor, (director, warden, *US*); **~einweisung** sending to prison, mittimus *(US)*; **~gebäude** prison; **~hof** prison yard; **~insasse** prison inmate, collegian *(Br., sl.)*; **~jahre** time *(coll.)*; **~kleidung** prison uniform (garb); **~krankenhaus** prison hospital (clinic); **~ordnung** prison rules; **~reform** prison reform; **~revolte** prison riot.
Gefängnisstrafe prison terms, [penalty of] imprisonment, jail sentence *(US)*, vacation *(sl.)*;
bei einer ~ **von** under pain of imprisonment;
aufgegliederte ~ split-level prison sentence *(Br.)*; **auf Bewährung ausgesetzte** ~ suspended [prison] sentence; **einjährige** ~ one-spot *(sl.)*;
~ **ohne Geldersatzstrafe** imprisonment without the option of a fine;
~ **abbüßen (absitzen)** to serve a term of imprisonment, to do one's time; ~ **für andere Verbrechen absitzen** to be in gaol (jail) *(US)* on convictions for other crimes; ~ **antreten** to go behind bars; **sich einer** ~ **aussetzen** to be liable for imprisonment; ~ **zur Bewährung aussetzen** to suspend a prison sentence; **mit knapper Not einer** ~ **entgehen** to escape prison; **zehnjährige** ~ **erhalten** to get ten years; **auf eine** ~ **erkennen** to inflict imprisonment; ~ **verdient haben** to deserve to be sent to prison; **einer** ~ **unterliegen** to be liable to imprisonment; ~ **verbüßen** to undergo a prison sentence; **zu einer** ~ **verurteilen** to send up *(sl.)*; **Dieb zu einer** ~ **von einem halben Jahr verurteilen** to sentence a thief to six months imprisonment; **zu einer** ~ **verurteilt werden** to draw jail terms.
Gefängnis|system penitentiary system; **~wagen** prison (patrol, *US*) van, Black Maria *(coll.)*, paddy wag(g)on *(US)*, booby hatch *(sl.)*; **~wärter** prison guard (warden, *US*), warder *(Br.)*, prison guard, gaoler *(Br.)*, turnkey, screw *(sl.)*; **~werkstatt** prison workshop; **~zelle** hole, pen, prison cell; **schmutzige ~zelle** foul prison cell.

gefärbt painted;
in der Wolle ~ *(fig.)* dyed in the wool;
~**e Ansichten** biassed opinions.
Gefasel drivel, twaddle.
Gefäß vessel, jar.
gefaßt *(fig.)* collected, composed, calm, *(Edelstein)* mounted, *(Vertrag)* worded;
sich auf etw. ~ **machen müssen** to be in for it; **aufs schlimmste** ~ **sein** to be prepared for the worst.
Gefecht *(mil.)* engagement, encounter, fight, combat, rencontre, action;
durch eine Lungenentzündung außer ~ **gesetzt** down with pneumonia; **in der Hitze des** ~**s** in the heat (warmth) of the debate;
hinhaltendes ~ delaying action; **kurzes** ~ affray; **laufendes** ~ running fight;
~ **abbrechen** to break off an engagement; **klar zum** ~ **blasen** to beat to quarters *(mar.)*; **Argumente ins** ~ **führen** to bring arguments into play; ~ **herbeiführen** to bring about an engagement; **Schiff klar zum** ~ **machen** to clear a ship for action; **j. außer** ~ **setzen** to put s. o. out of action, to disable s. o.; **feindliche Stellung außer** ~ **setzen** *(Artillerie)* to silence the battery of an enemy; **an einem** ~ **teilnehmen** to take part in an action; **Feind in ein** ~ **verwickeln** to engage the enemy.
Gefechts|aufstellung array; ~**auftrag** objective; ~**ausbildung** combat training; ~**befehl** combat order; ~**bereich** battle area, combat zone *(US)*; ~**bereitschaft** combat readiness; **erhöhte** ~**bereitschaft** standby alert *(US)*; **erhöhte** ~**bereitschaft anordnen** to place on full alert; ~**breite** frontage; ~**dienst** field training; ~**einheit** fighting (combat) unit; ~**einsatz** combat service; ~**feldwaffen** theatre *(Br.)* (theater, *US*) weapons.
gefechtsklar machen to clear for action.
Gefechts|kopf *(Rakete)* warhead, *(Torpedo)* war nose; **blinder** ~**kopf** dummy warhead; ~**kraft** fighting strength; ~**landeplatz** advanced landing ground, landing field *(US)*; ~**lärm** din of battle; ~**laterne** battle lantern; ~**linie** fighting line; **in** ~**linie übergehen** to deploy; ~**meldung** situation report; ~**pause** lull in the fighting; ~**stand** command post; **vorgeschobener** ~**stand** headquarters, advanced command post; ~**stärke** fighting strength; **auf** ~**station gehen** to go into action; ~**streifen** battle area, combat zone *(US)*; ~**turm** turret; ~**übung** field exercise, combat exercise; ~**vorposten** outpost; ~**ziel** objective.
Gefeilsche haggle, haggling, chaffer.
gefeit proof, immune;
gegen beruflichen Ärger ~ **sein** to have become immune to the drawbacks of one's job; **gegen alle Krankheiten** ~ **sein** to be proof against disease.
gefestigt consolidated;
sich ~ **haben** *(Kurse)* to show greater strength.
gefeuert werden to get the sack *(coll.)*, to get the boot *(sl.)*, to be fired *(US sl.)*, to be given the air *(sl.)*, to go down the line *(US)*, to catch (get) it in the neck *(sl.)*.
Gefeuertwerden sack *(coll.)*, firing *(coll.)*, boot *(sl.)*, letout *(sl.)*.
Gefilde countryside, landscape;
sich in vertrauten ~**n befinden** to be on familiar ground, to be in surroundings one knows.
geflissentlich intentional, wilful, deliberate;
j. ~ **übersehen** to overlook s. o. on purpose;
~**e Auslassung** wilful omission.
Geflügel poultry, fowl;
~**ausstellung** poultry show; ~**farm** poultry farm; ~**halter** poultry keeper; ~**haltung** poultry keeping; ~**laden** poultry shop.
geflügelte Worte standard quotations.
Geflügel|wirtschaft poultry husbandry; ~**zucht** poultry farming (culture, raising); ~**züchter** poultryman.
Geflüster whisper.
Gefolge following, retinue, attendance, train, attendants;
im ~ in the wake, as a result;
journalistisches ~ tail of journalists; **ziviles** ~ civilian component;
zu jds. ~ **gehören** to be part of s. one's train; **im** ~ **haben** to have in its train; **Nahrungsmittelknappheit im** ~ **haben** to lead to food shortages; **in jds.** ~ **sein** to be among s. one's followers.
Gefolgschaft *(Anhänger)* adherents, followers, partisans, *(Betrieb)* personnel, workers, employees, staff *(Br.)*;
große ~ **haben** to have a numerous following; **einer Partei treue** ~ **leisten** to give one's full allegiance to a party.
Gefolgschafts|abbau reduction of staff; ~**fürsorge** staff welfare management; ~**mitglied** employee; ~**siedlung** company colony; ~**treue** allegiance; ~**unterstützung** staff welfare.
Gefolgsmann adherent, attendant, fellower, henchman;
skrupelloser ~ myrmidon.
gefördert sponsored, promoted;
staatlich ~ government-sponsored, state-aided, subsidized.
gefragt in request (demand, favo(u)r), asked for, sought after, inquired for;
am meisten ~ hottest selling; **nicht** ~ dull, unquestioned; **nicht mehr** ~ *(Waren)* out of favo(u)r; **sehr** ~ in great demand; **wenig** ~ not much required, in little request, *(Börse)* neglected;
~ **sein** to sell well, to have a ready market; **von Anfang an** ~ **sein** *(Aktien)* to open active; **fortlaufend** ~ **sein** to continue in demand; **sehr** ~ **sein** to have the call, to be all the rage (vogue), to have a considerable run; **wenig** ~ **sein** to be in little demand, *(Börse)* to be neglected.
gefressen haben, j. to get one's knife into s. o.
Gefrier|anlage refrigerating plant; ~**apparat** ice machine, refrigerator.
gefrieren to freeze;
jds. Blut in den Adern ~ **lassen** to make s. one's blood run cold.
Gefrier|fach freezing box, freezer; ~**fleisch** chilled (frozen) meat; ~**kühlschiff** cold-storage vessel; ~**ladung** frozen cargo; ~**maschine** freezer, deep freeze; ~**punkt** freezing point; **am** ~**punkt** freezing; ~**raum** refrigerating room, chillroom; ~**schutzmittel** antifreeze; ~**temperatur** freezing temperature; ~**verfahren** freezing process.
Gefüge structure, fabric, frame, framework, pattern, edifice, system;
soziales ~ the whole fabric of society, social fabric (structure, framework, organism);
staatliches ~ **einer Demokratie** political system of a democracy.
gefügig compliant, amenable, manageable;
j. ~ **machen** to bend s. one's will; **sich Menschen** ~ **machen** to work men to one's will; **jem. völlig** ~ **sein** to be wax in s. one's hand;
~**er Charakter** pliant character.
Gefühl feeling, feel, touch;
im Überschwang der ~**e** carried away by one's emotions; **mit gemischten** ~**en** with mingled feelings; **von seinen** ~**en fortgerissen** swayed by one's feelings; **von persönlichen** ~**en nicht völlig frei** not altogether disinterested;
edle ~**e** noble sentiments; **erhabene** ~**e** high-pitched emotions; **gemischte** ~ mixed feelings; **gruseliges** ~ creeping sensation; **innerste** ~**e** heartstrings; **instinktives** ~ instinct, intuition; **unbehagliches** ~ uneasy feeling; **ungutes** ~ uncomfortable feeling, misgivings; **widerstreitende** ~**e** conflicting emotions; **das höchste der** ~**e** an earthly paradise; ~ **der Sicherheit** sense of security; **samtartiges** ~ **eines Stoffes** velvety touch of a fabric; ~ **der Verunsicherung** sense of bewilderment;
~ **ansprechen** to touch a string; **an jds.** ~ **appellieren** to appeal to s. one's emotions; **an das** ~ **der Zuhörer appellieren** to appeal to the feelings of one's audience; **jem. freundschaftliche** ~**e entgegenbringen** to entertain a kindly feeling for s. o.; **seinen** ~**en beredten Ausdruck geben (verleihen)** to give eloquent expression to one's feelings, to give the measure of one's feelings; **gegen jds.** ~ **gehen** to go against s. one's better judgment; **im** ~ **haben** to feel it in one's bones, to know instinctively; **kein** ~ **für die Regeln des Anstands haben** to have no sense of propriety; ~ **des Unrechts haben** to labo(u)r under a sense of wrong; **vages** ~ **haben** to have a dim feeling; **seine** ~**e im Zaun halten** to contain one's feelings; ~ **hegen** to nourish a feeling; **seinen** ~**en freien Lauf lassen** to give vent (utterance) to one's feelings, to have kittens *(US sl.)*; **seinen** ~**en Luft machen** to open the sluices of one's feelings; **seine** ~**e offen zur Schau stellen** to wear one's heart on one's sleeve; **jds.** ~**e mit Füßen treten** to outrage s. one's feelings; **seine** ~**e unterdrücken** to bottle up one's feelings; **seine wahren** ~**e verbergen** to dissemble one's emotions, to sail under false colo(u)rs; **sich auf sein** ~ **verlassen** to rely on one's intuition; **seinen** ~**en Ausdruck verleihen** to give utterance to one's feelings; **jds.** ~**e verletzen** to hurt (harrow, do an injury to) s. one's feelings, to jar on (lacerate) s. one's feelings, to tread on s. one's kibes; **von seinen** ~**en fortgerissen (überwältigt) werden** to be swayed by one's feelings (overcome by the force of one's emotions).
gefühllos heartless, callo(u)s, *(gegen Schmerzen)* numb, insensible;
völlig ~ **werden** to become callo(u)s to the sufferings of others.
Gefühls|abstumpfung stupefaction; ~**anwandlung** emotion; **sich seinen** ~**aufwallungen überlassen** to indulge in high-flown sentiment, to give way to one's emotions; ~**ausbruch** emotional outburst.

gefühlsbeherrscht impulsive.
Gefühls|bewegung emotion; **an die ~drüsen appellieren** to touch the right chord; **~duselei** emotionalism, mushy sentimentality, slush gush.
gefühlsduselig mawkish, maudlin, sloppy, mushy;
~er Mensch soft slob.
Gefühls|eindruck feel; **~kälte** frigidity.
gefühlsmäßig, Publikum ~ ansprechen to appeal to the feelings of an audience; **~ das Richtige tun** to have an instinct for doing the right thing; **~ wissen** to know by intuition;
~e Reaktion emotional reaction.
Gefühls|mensch creature of impulse, emotionalist; **~regung** emotion; **keine ~regung erkennen lassen** to display no signs of emotion; **~sache** matter of instinct.
gefühlsselig mawkish, maudlin.
Gefühls|skala, gesamte the whole gamut of feelings; **~überschwang** exuberance of feeling; **in ihrem ~überschwang** carried away by her emotions; **~wert** feeling (sentimental) value.
geführt *(Artikel)* stocked;
gut ~ well-conducted; **vom Lehrer ~** preceded by a teacher.
gegangen werden to be retired.
gegeben given, *(passend)* proper;
jem. ~ sein to be s. one's nature;
innerhalb einer ~en Frist within a specified time; **~e Größe** given quantity; **unter den ~en Umständen** under the prevailing conditions; **zur ~en Zeit** at the proper time.
gegebenenfalls in case of need, if the occasion should arise, in the appropriate circumstances, if [it should prove] necessary.
Gegebenheit condition, reality, factor, actual fact;
~en given facts;
soziale ~ social structure;
sich mit den ~en abfinden to face the facts of life.
gegen against, contrary, versus, *(als Entgelt)* in exchange (return), *(etwa)* in the neighbo(u)rhood, around *(US)*, *(örtlich)* towards, *(Prozeß)* re;
~ Austausch von in exchange for; **~ bar** for cash (ready money); **~ Entgelt** in exchange (return); **~ Nachnahme** cash (collect, *US*) on delivery; **~ Quittung** on receipt.
Gegen|abdruck counterproof; **~abdruck machen** to counterprove; **~abschreckung** *(mil.)* counterdeterrence; **~abzug** counterproof; **~akkreditiv** countervailing (secondary, *US*, back-to-back, *US*, dos-a-dos, *US*) credit; **~aktion** *(pol.)* counteraction; **~angebot** competitive bid, counteroffer; **~angriff** *(mil.)* recharge, counterattack; **~anordnung** counternotice; **~anschaffung** return remittance; **durch einen ~anschlag vereiteln** to countermine; **~ansprüche geltend machen (stellen)** to crossclaim, to counterclaim.
Gegenantrag cross motion (petition), counterpetition, alternative proposal, counterproposal, *(parl.)* countermotion;
~ einbringen to table an amendment, to crosspetition; **~ stellen** to counterpetition; **~ unterstützen** to speak against a motion;
~steller counterpetitioner.
Gegen|antwort reply; **~anwalt** opposing counsel *(Br.)*, adverse solicitor *(Br.)*; **~argument** counterargument; **~aufstellung** counterstatement; **~auftrag** counterorder, countermandate; **~aussage** statement to the contrary; **~äußerung** answer, reply; **~bedingung** counterstipulation; **~befehl** counterorder, countermand; **~behauptung** counterstatement; **~beleidigung** counterinsult; **~berichtigungskonto** contra account; **~beschuldigung** counteraccusation, countercharge, recrimination; **~beschuldigungen vorbringen** to recriminate; **~beschwerde** countercomplaint; **~bestätigung** confirmation; **~bestrebung** countertendency; **~besuch** return visit (party); **~besuch machen** to return a call; **~bewegung** countermovement, *(mil.)* countermanoeuvre.
Gegenbeweis proof to the contrary, counterevidence, rebuttal, rebutting evidence;
~ führen to rebut, to traverse, to produce proof to (prove) the contrary.
Gegen|beziehung reciprocal relationship; **~bieter** competitive bidder.
Gegenblockade counterblockade;
~ verhängen to counterblockade.
Gegenbuch *(Bank)* passbook, *(Kunde)* tally.
gegenbuchen to make a counterentry (cross entry).
Gegenbuchhalter checking clerk.
Gegenbuchung counterentry, cross (contra, offsetting, *Br.*) entry, reversing entry, reversal, *(Posten)* counteritem, setoff *(Br.)*, offset *(US)*;
als ~ einzutragen per contra;
~ vornehmen to make a cross (reverse an) entry.
Gegenbürgschaft countersecurity, countersurety *(Br.)*.
Gegend area, quarter, region, district, countryside, ground, land, direction, *(Wohngegend)* neighbo(u)rhood, residential quarter, vicinity, environs, surroundings, way;
aus allen ~en from all quarters; **in dieser ~** in this locality; **in der ~ des Bahnhofs** in the railway-station area;
attraktive ~ field of attraction; **benachbarte ~** surrounding area; **dicht besiedelte (bevölkerte) ~** densely populated region; **dünn besiedelte ~** sparsely settled area; **viel besuchte ~** much travelled part of the world; **einsame ~** lonely spot; **völlig entlegene ~** four corners of the earth; **feine ~** fashionable neighbo(u)rhood; **fruchtbare ~** fertile region; **gefährliche ~** danger area; **rein landwirtschaftliche ~** purely agricultural district; **unbesiedelte ~** unsettled region; **unsere ~** our neighbo(u)rhood; **verfallene ~** blighted area; **verkehrsdichte ~** high-density area; **verrufene ~** tough neighbo(u)rhood; **hoch versicherte ~** high-risk neighbo(u)rhood;
entlegendste ~en der Welt four corners of the world;
ganze ~ nach etw. abklappern to scour the whole district; **in einer schönen ~ liegen** to be beautifully situated; **sich in einer ~ niederlassen** to settle down in a locality *(US)*; **nicht aus dieser ~ sein** not to come from these parts; **aus derselben (der gleichen) ~ stammen** to have the same regional background, to hail from the same place; **~ auf das Vorhandensein von Lagerstätten untersuchen** to prospect a district; **~ verlassen** to jump a locality *(US)*; **in einer guten ~ wohnen** to live at a good address; **in einer ruhigen ~ wohnen** to live in a quiet neighbo(u)rhood; **in einer vornehmen ~ wohnen** to live in a fashionable part of a town; **in eine andere ~ ziehen** to shift (change) one's quarters; **aus allen ~en zusammenströmen** to flock in from all quarters.
Gegen|darstellung counterstatement; **~deckung** countersecurity, counterremittance, *(Börse)* hedge, hedging; **~dementi abgeben (veröffentlichen)** to return a denial, to contradict a statement; **~demonstration** counterdemonstration; **~dienst** return (reciprocal) service; **~dienst leisten** to reciprocate, to render a service in return; **zu ~diensten gern bereit sein** to be glad to reciprocate in similar kind; **~druck** counterpressure; **~eintrag** reverse entry, reversal; **~einwand** counterplea; **~entwurf** alternative draft; **~erklärung** counterdeclaration, answer, reply, disclaimer; **~fahrbahn** opposite side of the road; **~fehler** *(in der Rechnung)* compensating (corresponding) error; **~feuer** backfire.
Gegenforderung cross demand, cross claim, counter claim, claim in return, counterdemand, setoff *(Br.)*, offset *(US)*;
als ~ per contra;
als ~ benutzen to take as setoff *(Br.)*; **~ erheben (geltend machen)** to [set up a] counterclaim, to deliver a counterclaim, to crossclaim.
Gegen|frage counterquestion; **selbstsicher mit einer ~frage antworten** to counter blandly; **~funkstelle** answering station; **~gebot** counter bid, counteroffer; **erstes ~gebot** bidding price; **~geschäft** barter, *(Versicherung)* return business, *(Börse)* hedge; **~geschäft unterbringen** *(Börse)* to [place a] hedge; **~geschenk** present in return; **~gewerkschaft** dual union; **~gewicht** balance, counterbalance, counterpoise; **~gewicht bilden** to counterweigh, to weigh against; **~gift, ~mittel** antidote; **~gutachten** opposing opinion; **~kampagne auf dem PR-Gebiet aufziehen** to mount a counteroffensive public relations campaign.
Gegenkandidat running (rival, opposing) candidate, opponent;
ohne ~ unopposed;
als jds. ~ auftreten to run against s. o.; **~en schlagen** to defeat an opposing candidate; **in einer Wahl ohne ~ gewählt werden** to be returned unopposed.
Gegenklage cross action (bill), countersuit, countercharge;
~ anstrengen to cross-sue.
Gegen|kläger counterclaimant; **~koalition** opposition league; **~kompliment machen** to return a compliment; **~konto** control (duplicate) account, *(Wertberichtigung)* contra (offset, *US*) account; **~kontrahent** other party; **~konzessionen machen** to give concessions in return; **~kräfte** counteracting forces; **~kreuzverhör eines Zeugen** reexamination of a witness; **~kundgebung** counterdemonstration; **~kündigung** *(Mieter)* counternotice; **~kurs** back course; **~kurs einschlagen** to go on an opposite course; **Schiff auf einem ~kurs passieren** to pass a ship on an opposite course; **~läufigkeit** opposite movement.
Gegenleistung consideration, value, *(Gegenwert)* equivalent;
als ~ in exchange (return), per contra; **auf einer ~ beruhend** founded on a consideration; **mangels ~** for want of consideration; **ohne ~** nude, gratuitous, without consideration; **unter Bedingung einer ~** on reciprocal terms;

abschätzbare ~ valuable consideration; **angemessene** ~ fair (adequate) consideration, reasonable reward; **ausreichende** ~ good consideration; **moralisch bedingte** ~ good consideration; **auf einer Anstandspflicht beruhende** ~ meritorious consideration; **bewirkte** ~ executed consideration; **entgeltliche** ~ valuable consideration; **dem Geldwert entsprechende** ~ money (pecuniary) consideration; **ernstgemeinte** ~ solid consideration; **vertraglich erwähnte** ~ express consideration; **fällige** ~ consideration due; **fehlende** ~ lack (absence, failure, want) of consideration; **feste (ausdrücklich festgelegte)** ~ fixed consideration; **formale** ~ nominal consideration; **fortdauernde** ~ continuing consideration; **geldwerte** ~ valuable (pecuniary) consideration; **im voraus gewährte** ~ antecedent valuable consideration; **gleichwertige** ~ adequate consideration; **gleichzeitige** ~ concurrent consideration; **mangelnde** ~ failure (want) of consideration; **rechtswirksame** ~ valid consideration; **sittenwidrige** ~ immoral consideration; **symbolische** ~ nominal consideration; **unbestimmte** ~ vague consideration; **ungesetzliche (unerlaubte)** ~ illegal consideration; **rechtlich unzulässige** ~ illegal consideration; **vereinbarte** ~ consideration bargained for; **vollwertige** ~ fair and valuable consideration; **zukünftige** ~ executory consideration; **rechtlich zulässige** ~ legal consideration;
~ **erbringen** to give value for; **als** ~ **gewähren** to pay in return; **jem. eine** ~ **schulden** to owe s. o. some return.

Gegenlicht | aufnahme exposure against the sun; ~**blende** lens hood, lens screen, sky shade.

Gegen | liebe, keine unrequited love; **für seinen Vorschlag keine ~liebe finden** to meet with no enthusiasm from the other side; ~**lizenz** cross licence; ~**lizenz ausstellen** to cross-license; ~**maßnahmen** counteraction, preventive measures, contermeasure; **rechtzeitige** ~**maßnahme** counterpreparation; ~**mine legen** *(Börse)* to make a market; ~**mine vortreiben** *(mil.)* to countermine; ~**mittel gegen die Inflation** inflation antidote; ~**note** *(dipl.)* counternote; ~**offensive** counteroffensive; ~**offerte** counteroffer, counterorder.

Gegenpartei adverse (opposing) party, opponent, the other side, *(Prozeßpartei)* opposite party;
sich mit der ~ **einigen** to settle an issue; ~ **ergreifen** to take the other side; **zur** ~ **übergehen** to cross the floor, to rat.

Gegen | pol opposite pole; ~**posten** contra, counterentry, contra entry *(Br.)*, *(Bilanz)* contra asset, setoff *(Br.)*, offset *(US)*; ~**probe** check (control) test; ~**probe machen** to countercheck, to work the sum round the other way; ~**propaganda** counterpropaganda; ~**quittung** receipt in return; ~**reaktion** counteraction.

Gegenrechnung counterreckoning, check *(Br.)* (controlling, *US*) account, compensation, *(Gegenforderung)* counterclaim, setoff *(Br.)*, offset *(US)*;
in ~ **empfangen** received on account; ~ **saldiert** balanced in account;
~ **aufmachen** to make out a contra account; **durch** ~ **ausgleichen** to counterbalance; **in** ~ **bringen** to bring to opposite account, to set off *(Br.)*, to offset *(US)*; **in** ~ **stehen** to have mutual accounts; **jem. die** ~ **vorlegen** to present one's account in one's turn.

Gegen | rechnungsbuch customer's book; ~**rede** rejoinder; **Rede und** ~**rede** dialogue; ~**referat** coreport; ~**regierung** opposite government, government in exile; ~**revolution** counterrevolution; ~**rimesse** return remittance; ~**saldo** counterbalance.

Gegensatz opposition, antithesis;
im ~ contrary (in opposition) to; **im** ~ **zu mir** unlike me; **im** ~ **zu unseren Erwartungen** contrary to our expectations; **in offenem** ~ in direct contradiction;
scharfer ~ marked antagonism;
mit seiner eignenen Meinung im starken ~ **stehen** to contrast strongly with one's own opinions; **sich in** ~ **zur herrschenden Meinung stellen** to place o. s. in opposition to the prevailing opinion.

Gegensätze überbrücken to smooth out differences.

gegensätzlich opposite, opposed, contrary;
~**e Begriffe** antonyms; **zwei** ~**e Charaktere** two characters strongly opposed; ~**e Vorschriften** conflicting regulations; ~**e Ziele** cross purposes.

Gegensätzlichkeit antagonism.

Gegenschlag counterplot, counterblow;
begrenzter ~ *(mil.)* controlled response; **wohlabgewogener** ~ *(mil.)* flexible response;
~ **tun** to counter.

Gegen | schriftsatz answer [to a charge], counterpleading; ~**schuld** counterobligation.

Gegenseite opposite (other) side, opponent, *(Münze)* reverse (obverse) side;
zur ~ **übergehen** to go over to the other side, to rat, *(Abgeordneter)* to cross the floor of the House *(Br.)*.

gegenseitig reciprocal, mutual, opposite;
sich ~ **ausschließen** to be mutually exclusive; **sich** ~ **beziehen** to counterdraw; **sich** ~ **Vorwürfe machen** to reproach each others; ~**e Abhängigkeit** interdependence; ~**e Ansicht** opposite opinion; ~**e Bankguthaben** interbank deposits; ~**e Beziehung** interrelation; ~**e Durchdringung** interpenetration; **im** ~**en Einverständnis** by mutual consent; ~**e Forderungen** mutual debts; ~**e Forderungen ausgleichen** to counterbalance; ~**e Gutschriften** mutual credits; ~**e Hilfe** mutual aid; ~**es Interesse** mutual interest; ~**e Lebensversicherung** mutual life insurance (assurance, *Br.*); ~**er Schutz von Kapitalanlagen** reciprocal protection of investments; ~**es Testament** reciprocal (double, mutual) will; **in** ~**er Übereinkunft** by mutual consent; ~**e Unterstützung** mutual assistance (aid); ~**er Vertrag** reciprocal (mutual, bilateral) contract; ~**e Wirkung** interaction, interplay; ~**e Zugeständnisse** mutual concessions.

Gegenseitigkeit reciprocity, mutuality, *(Völkerrecht)* mutual principle;
auf ~ on mutual terms; **auf der Grundlage der** ~ on the basis of (based upon) reciprocity; **nicht auf** ~ **beruhend** unreciprocated; **unter Voraussetzung der** ~ subject to reciprocity;
~ **der Zolltarife** reciprocity in trade;
~ **gewähren** to grant reciprocal treatment; **auf** ~ **gründen** to found on mutual interest; **Geschäft auf der Grundlage der** ~ **vorbereiten** to arrange a transaction on a mutual principle; ~ **zusichern** to guarantee reciprocity.

Gegenseitigkeits | abkommen reciprocal trade, offset agreement; ~**geschäfte** barter transactions, reciprocity dealings; ~**klausel** *(Handelsabkommen)* reciprocity clause (stipulation); ~**konto** mutual account; ~**pakt** mutual assistance treaty; ~**prinzip** reciprocity principle; ~**verein** mutual aid (relief) association, mutual benefit society *(US)*; ~**verein mit gleichhohen Prämiensätzen** deposit premium company; ~**vereinbarung** mutual aid agreement, reciprocal understanding; ~**verhältnis schaffen** to mutualize; ~**verpflichtung** mutual promise; ~**versicherung** reciprocal insurance, *(Geschäftspartner)* partnership insurance; ~**vertrag** reciprocity treaty.

Gegen | sicherheit counterbond; ~**sicherheit leisten** to put up a counterbond; ~**siegel** counterseal; ~**spekulant** market maker; ~**spekulation** market making; ~**spieler** opposite number, antagonist; ~**spieler von X sein** *(Film)* to play opposite X; ~**spionage** counterespionage, counterintelligence, military intelligence *(Br.)*; ~**sprechanlage** duplex (intercom) system; ~**sprechtelegrafie** duplex telegraphy; ~**sprechverkehr** duplex communication.

Gegenstand object, article, item, thing, matter, kind, *(Rede)* text; **[in der Urkunde] ausgenommener** ~ exceptive, specific clause in a contract; **ausgestellter** ~ exhibit; **behandelter** ~ subject matter; **besprochener** ~ subject under discussion; **gefälschter** ~ privy token; **zum Nachlaß gehöriger** ~ object belonging to the inheritance; **gekaufter** ~ buy, purchase; **gepfändeter** ~ distress, object seized; **patentrechtlich geschützter** ~ patented article; **mechanisch gleichwerter** ~ *(Patentrecht)* mechanical equivalent; **lebensgefährlicher** ~ imminently dangerous article; **patentfähiger** ~ subject matter of patent; **sicherungsübereigneter** ~ equitable lien; **spottbilliger** ~ exceptionally cheap article; **steuerpflichtiger** ~ taxable object; **streitbefangener** ~ matter in issue; **transportabler** ~ chose transitory; **unbedeutender** ~ trifle; **verfallener** ~ forfeit; **verpfändeter** ~ pawn, pledge; **versicherter** ~ insured matter, subject matter insured, risk, *(Feuerversicherung)* the premises insured; **vom Kunden vorausbezahlter und für ihn zurückgelegter** ~ will-call or layaway *(US)*; **weggeworfener** ~ discarded property; **zerlegbarer** ~ knockdown;
~ **einer Abhandlung** substance of an essay; ~ **des täglichen Bedarfs** article of prime necessity; ~ **der Bewunderung** object of admiration; ~ **der Diskussion** subject under debate; ~ **der Erfindung** subject matter of invention; ~ **allgemeinen Gelächters** laughing stock of everyone; ~ **einer Gesellschaft** object of a company, partnership purpose, corporate object; ~ **öffentlichen Interesses** matter of public concern; ~ **der Klage** subject matter (object) of the action, matter in dispute (controversy); ~ **der vereinbarten Lieferung** article to be supplied; ~ **des Mitleids** object of pity; ~ **des Sachanlagevermögens** fixed capital asset; ~ **der Unterhaltung** topic of a conversation; ~ **eines Unternehmens** object of a company; **[erneuter]** ~ **von Verhandlungen** subject of [renewed]

negotiations; ~ **der Versicherung** subject matter insured; ~ **des Vertrages** subject matter of the agreement; ~ **des Vertretungsverhältnisses** subject matter of the agency;
vom ~ abkommen to wander from the subject; **jeden ~ abschätzen** to value each object; **sich mit einem ~ befassen** to deal with a subject; **zum ~ haben** to treat of; **wichtiges Thema zum ~ haben** to deal with an important problem; ~ **der Erfindung herstellen** to produce an invention; **etw. zum ~ eines Prozesses machen** to make s. th. the subject of a lawsuit; ~ **von Verhandlungen sein** to be in issue; **jeden ~ einzeln taxieren** to value each object; **zum ~ allgemeinen Spottes werden** to be the target of popular ridicule.
Gegenstände, vom Versicherungsschutz ausgeschlossene memorandum articles; **zum persönlichen Gebrauch bestimmte** ~ chattels personal, personal effects; **bewegliche** ~ movable things; **bei der Straftat erlangte** ~ fruits of crime; **gepfändete** ~ goods taken in execution; **fabrikmäßig hergestellte** ~ manufactured articles; **immaterielle** ~ incorporeal things; **körperliche** ~ things in possession, things corporeal, corporeal property; **kunsthandwerkliche** ~ arts-and-crafts items; **unkörperliche** ~ intangibles; **unpfändbare** ~ exempt property; **vererbliche** ~ corporeal hereditaments; **verlorene** ~ lost property; **verschiedene** ~ odds and ends; **versicherte** ~ *(Feuerversicherung)* premises insured;
~ **des täglichen Bedarfs** articles of prime necessity, necessaries of life; ~ **des persönlichen Gebrauchs** personal effects, chattels personal; **eingebaute** ~ **des Pächters** tenant's fixtures; ~ **von geringem Wert** truck.
gegenständlich objective, concrete.
gegenstandslos irrelevant, invalid, groundless, abortive, nugatory, *(Kunst)* nonfigurative;
~ **geworden sein** to have lost all significance, *(Vertrag)* to be no longer valid; ~ **werden** *(Angebot)* to lapse.
Gegenstandsloswerden eines Angebots lapse of offer.
Gegen|standswort *(Grammatik)* noun; ~**stelle bedienen** to be working the machine at the other end.
gegensteuern *(Auto)* to drive into a skid.
Gegenstimme dissenting (dissident) voice, blackball, *(Parlament)* no;
mit einer ~ with one dissenting (dissentient) voice; **mit fünf ~n** with five votes against; **ohne** ~ unanimously, unopposed; **ohne ~n gewählt werden** to be returned unopposed.
Gegen|strömung countercurrent, crosscurrent, underset; **geheime ~strömung** undercurrent; ~**stück** counterpiece, counterpart, match, tally, companion piece; ~**stück bilden** to form a pendant; ~**taktschaltung** push-pull circuit.
Gegenteil contrary, opposite, converse;
bis zum Beweis des ~s failing proof to the contrary; **im** ~ on the contrary;
das genaue ~ the exact opposite, direct contrary, quite the reverse, the clear contrary;
das ~ von Lob praise over the left *(sl.)*;
~ **behaupten** to maintain the contrary; ~ **bewirken** to have the opposite effect; ~ **raten** to counsel to the contrary; **Äußerung ins ~ verkehren** to twist the meaning.
gegenteilig opposite, contrary;
~**e Anordnungen** instructions to the contrary; ~**er Ansicht sein** to take a different view; ~**e Berichte** reports to the contrary; ~**e Wirkung** opposite effect.
Gegen|tendenz countertrend, countertendency; ~**transaktion** *(Börse)* hedge, straddle *(US)*; ~**treuhänder** joint trustee, cotrustee.
gegenüber|liegen to confront; ~**liegend** opposite; **sich Schwierigkeiten ~sehen** to be confronted with difficulties; **jem. ~sitzen** to sit opposite s. o.
gegenüberstehen to face;
ablehnend ~ to oppose; **sich feindlich** ~ to be at enmity with s. o.; **einer Frage aufgeschlossen** ~ to maintain an open mind to a question; **dem Nichts** ~ to be faced with ruin; **einem Plan skeptisch** ~ to frown upon a plan; **jds. Plan wohlwollend** ~ to take a favo(u)rable view of s. one's plan; **einer Situation hilflos** ~ to be helpless in face of a situation.
gegenüberstehend opposite, contending.
gegenüberstellen to front, to confront;
Personen einander ~ to bring persons face to face; **Vor- und Nachteile** ~ to oppose advantages and disadvantages; **zwei Zeugen einander** ~ to confront two witnesses.
Gegenüberstellung comparison, *(Zeugen)* confrontation, identification parade;
durch ~ von Tatsachen by comparing facts.
Gegenübertext *(Werbung)* facing text matter.
gegenübertreten, einer Gefahr to face a danger.
Gegen|unterschrift countersignature; ~**verfügung** counternotice; ~**verkauf** countersale, sale in return; ~**verkehr** oncoming (cross, two-way) traffic; ~**verkehrsstraße** two-way road; ~**verordnung** counterstatute; ~**verpflichtung** counterobligation; ~**verschreibung** counterbond; ~**versicherung** mutual (reciprocal) insurance, counterassurance *(Br.)*, *(Rückversicherung)* reinsurance; ~**versuch** control experiment, check test.
Gegenvorbringen affirmative defence, plea in reconvention;
leichtfertiges ~ frivolous defence; **neues** ~ affirmative defence; **spontanes** ~ voluntary answer; **substantiiertes** ~ special plea; **unbegründetes** ~ sham defence; **offensichtlich unschlüssiges** ~ frivolous answer (pleading); **verspätetes** ~ pretermitted defence; **verzögerndes** ~ false plea;
~ **widerlegen** to rebut a defence.
Gegenvormund deputy (joint) guardian, concurator, undertutor *(Louisiana)*;
gerichtlich ernannter ~ surrogate guardian.
Gegenvormundschaft joint guardianship.
Gegenvorschlag alternative proposal, counterproposal;
mit einem ~ antworten to counter a proposal with one of one's own.
Gegenvorstellung remonstration, remonstrance;
~**en erheben** to remonstrate.
Gegenwart presence, present time, nowadays;
bis auf die ~ down to our times; **in jds.** ~ in s. one's hearing; **in ~ des Botschafters** the Ambassador will be present; **in ~ fremder Personen** in the hearing of strangers; **in ~ von Zeugen** in the presence of witnesses;
für die ~ schreiben to write for one's contemporaries.
gegenwärtig current, actual, present, attendant, at present (the present) time;
~**e Bedeutung** present-day significance; ~**er Besitz und Nutznießung** present enjoyment; ~**e Gefahr** imminent danger; ~**e Kurse** current (ruling, *US*) prices; ~**e Lage** present state of affairs; ~**e Regierung** present cabinet (government); ~**er Stand der Dinge** present state of affairs; **unter den ~en Umständen** under the prevailing circumstances.
gegenwartsfern remote.
Gegenwarts|geschehen contemporary events; ~**geschichte** contemporarian history.
gegenwartsnah topical;
~**er Dokumentarfilm** documentary film of topical interest.
Gegenwarts|nähe einer Zeitschrift topical quality of a magazine; ~**präferenz** time preference; ~**wert** present (actual) value.
Gegen|wechsel counterbill, cross bill; **trotz verzweifelter ~wehr** in spite of desperate resistance.
Gegenwert worth, equivalent, value, valuable consideration, countervalue, *(Ausgleich)* compensation, setoff *(Br.)*, offset *(US)*, *(Ausgleichsposten)* balancing entry, *(Erlös)* proceeds, net avails *(US)*;
als ~ for value received;
angemessener ~ fair equivalent; **entsprechender** ~ adequate (valuable) consideration; **geldeswerter** ~ valuable consideration; **hinreichender** ~ sufficient consideration;
~ **in Geld** money equivalent, equivalent in money, consideration money, pecuniary consideration; ~ **für sein Geld** run for one's money; ~ **eines Gewichtes Feingold in Münzen** mint par of bullion (price of gold, *US*); ~ **in Pfunden** sterling equivalent; ~ **für einen Wechsel** consideration for a bill of exchange;
~ **für den zugefügten Schaden anbieten** to offer an equivalent for damage done; ~ **anschaffen** to remit the proceeds; **jem. den ~ gutschreiben** to place the proceeds to the credit of s. o.; ~ **zur Verfügung der Firma ... halten** to hold the proceeds at the disposal of Messrs ...; **entsprechenden ~ leisten** to give value for; ~ **überweisen** to transmit the return;
~**konto** *(ECA)* counterpart account *(US)*; ~**mittel** *(ECA)* counterpart funds *(US)*.
Gegen|wind head (foul) wind, cross wind, upwind; ~**wirkung** countereffect.
Gegenzeichen countersign, countermark;
mit ~ versehen to countermark.
gegenzeichnen to countersign, to countermark, *(indossieren)* to back.
Gegen|zeichnender countersigning party; ~**zeuge** adverse witness, counterwitness; ~**zug** corresponding train, *(Eisenbahn)* opposite train, *(fig.)* countermove.
geglaubt werden *(Geschichte)* to go down.
gegliedert constructed, planned;
architektonisch schlecht ~ sein to be poor in design.

Gegner opponent, opposer, objector, adversary, foe, *(mil.)* enemy;
ebenbürtiger ~ worthy adversary; **entschiedener** ~ declared enemy; **furchterregender** ~ formidable opponent; **grundsätzlicher** ~ opponent on principle; **hartnäckiger** ~ stiff adversary; **kümmerlicher** ~ meat *(sl.)*; **politischer** ~ political opponent; **nicht zu unterschätzender** ~ no mean foe; **unversöhnliche** ~ irreconcilable enemies;
~ **des Kommunismus** anticommunist;
~ **erledigen** to floor an opponent; **ebenbürtigen** ~ **finden** to find one's equal *(coll.)*; **besiegten** ~ **schonen** to spare a defeated adversary; **zum** ~ **überlaufen** to go over to the other side, to rat; **dem** ~ **unterliegen** to succumb to one's adversary; ~ **zermürben** to soften up an enemy.
gegnerisch adverse, opposing;
~**er Anwalt** opposing counsel *(Br.)*, adverse solicitor *(Br.)*; ~**e Flotte** enemy fleet; ~**es Heer** hostile army; ~**e Kräfte** adverse forces; ~**es Lager** enemy camp; ~**e Partei** adverse party; ~**es Plädoyer** adversary's speech.
Gegnerschaft hostility, antagonism;
aus der ~ **zweier Stämme herrühren** to originate in the rivalry of two tribes.
gegründet established.
Gehacktes mincemeat.
Gehalt salary, earnings, pay, compensation, emoluments, remuneration, stipend, screw *(Br., sl.)*, *(Fassungsvermögen)* capacity, volume, *(Inhalt)* content(s), percentage, *(Metall)* grade, *(Münze)* alloy, *(Qualität)* quality, *(Schiff)* tonnage, *(Wert)* intrinsic value;
mit einem hohen ~ high-salaried; **mit Angabe des** ~**s** *(Anzeige)* stating salary; **ohne tieferen** ~ *(Buch)* superficial; **zu einem** ~ **von** at a wage of;
festes ~ **beziehend** salaried;
anständiges ~ remunerative salary; **augenblickliches** ~ salary to date; **ausgezahltes** ~ spendable earnings; **außertarifliches** ~ payment over and above; **dickes** ~ *(fam.)* fat salary; **dreizehntes** ~ [etwa] end-of-tax-year bonus; **dem Verantwortungsbereich entsprechendes** ~ salary fully equated to the level of responsibility; **festes** ~ **[ohne Beteiligung]** standing wages, straight (fixed, stated, regular) salary; **gefordertes** ~ salary requested; **hohes** ~ high salary; **lächerliches** ~ miserable salary; **lohnsteuerfreies** ~ tax-free pay; **lohnsteuerpflichtiges** ~ taxable pay; **nachgezahltes** ~ call-in pay; **rückständiges** ~ overdue pay; **staatliches** ~ government salary; **steigendes** ~ increasing salary; **steuerfreies** ~ tax-free salary; **tarifliches** ~ flat rate of pay; **tatsächliches** ~ effective pay rate; **mit einer Stellung verbundenes** ~ salary appendant to a position; **vereinbartes** ~ salary agreed upon; **vergleichbares** ~ competitive salary; **volles** ~ full pay;
~ **an Alkohol** alcoholic strength; ~ **und andere Bezüge** salary and other emoluments; ~ **an Feuchtigkeit** moisture content, degree of humidity; ~ **und Gestalt** matter and manner; ~ **eines Konsuls** consular salary; ~ **Nebensache** *(Anzeige)* salary is of secondary consideration (no object); ~ **nach Vereinbarung** salary by arrangement; ~ **ist Verhandlungssache** salary open; **sein** ~ **abheben** to draw one's salary; ~ **und Lebensunterhalt für ein Jahr anbieten** to offer a salary and support for a year; ~ **aufbessern** to raise (increase) a salary; **mit seinem knappen** ~ **auskommen** to manage on one's small salary; ~ **auswerfen** to appoint (fix) a salary; **sein monatliches** ~ **bekommen** to receive one's monthly pay; ~ **bezahlen** to salary; ~ **beziehen** to draw a salary (one's pay), to be in a salaried position, to receive a salary; **anständiges** ~ **beziehen** to be adequately paid; **Teil des** ~**s einbehalten** to retain an amount of the pay; **Zahlung eines 13.** ~**s zwangsweise wieder einführen** to restore the compulsory annual bonus of one's monthly salary; ~ **erhöhen** to raise (increase) a salary; ~ **für ein Amt festsetzen** to assign a salary for an office; **schönes** ~ **haben** to earn good wages, to earn a good salary; **wenig** ~ **haben** *(Buch)* to be of little substance, *(Wein)* to have not much body; **jds.** ~ **herabsetzen** to cut s. one's salary; **bescheidenes** ~ **durch sparsame Lebensweise kompensieren** to offset a small salary by living economically; ~ **kürzen** to cut a salary; **von seinem** ~ **leben** to live on one's salary; **von kleinem** ~ **leben** to live on a small salary; **auf sein** ~ **angewiesen sein** to depend on one's salary; **mit seinem augenblicklichen** ~ **zufrieden sein** to be content with one's present salary; **gutes** ~ **verdienen** to earn a good salary; **sein** ~ **weiterbeziehen** to be kept on the payroll; **mit vollem** ~ **pensioniert werden** to be retired on full pay; **jem.** ~ **zahlen** to give s. o. a salary; **am** ~ **zulegen** to increase a salary; **jem. ein bestimmtes** ~ **zusichern** to assure s. o. a definite salary.

gehalten | sein *(Kurse)* to be maintained, to maintain their level; **gut** ~ **sein** to maintain a good tone; **für fest** ~ **werden** to be held firm.
Gehälter, fällige *(Bilanz)* accrued payrolls;
~ **leitender Angestellter** wages of management;
~ **kürzen** to whittle down salaries;
~**anstieg** earnings rise; ~**experte** compensation expert; ~**fachmann** compensation expert *(US)*; ~**fonds** salary (payroll) fund; ~**index** earnings index; ~**liste** payroll [records], pay (payment) *(Br.)* sheet, salary roll; ~**niveau** pay level; ~**stabilisierung** pay stabilization; ~**unkosten** salary expense.
gehaltlos thin, null to nothing, *(Nahrung)* with no food value, *(Wein)* of no body.
Gehaltsabbau reduction of salary, salary reduction.
gehaltsabhängig earnings-related.
Gehalts | abrechnung payroll *(US)*, payroll accounting *(US)*, salary roll; ~**abteilung** payroll department (division, *US*); ~**abtretung** assignment of salary; ~**abzug** reduction (deduction, *US*) from (retrenchment of) salary, payroll deduction *(US)*, stoppage *(Br.)*; ~**änderung** change in salary; ~**angabe** *(Anzeige)* stating salary, *(Lohnliste)* payroll data; ~**angebot** pay offer; **gebündeltes** ~**angebot** salary package; ~**angebot machen** to offer a salary; ~**angleichung** salary adjustment; ~**anspruch** salary demand (claim), pay claim; ~**ansprüche** *(Anzeige)* salary required (expected, requirements), stating salary; **mit gehobeneren** ~**ansprüchen verbunden sein** to carry an attractive salary.
Gehaltsanstieg pay boost;
automatischer ~ automatic salary increase; **einheitlicher zehnprozentiger** ~ horizontal increase in salaries of ten per cent *(US)*; **starker** ~ pay jump.
Gehalts | anteil salary proportion; ~**aufbesserung** addition to s. one's salary, supplementation of salaries, salary increase (rise, increment, boost, *US*), additional pay, raise *(US)*, *(anläßlich einer Beförderung)* promotional raise *(US)*; ~**aufbesserungen** improvements in pay; ~**aufbesserung erfahren** to receive an increase, to get a raise *(US)*; ~**aufwandposten** salary expense item; ~**auszahlung** wage paying, payroll servicing (disbursement); ~**basis** salaried basis; **reine** ~**basis** straight salary; ~**bescheinigung mit Angabe der Lohnsteuereinbehaltung** certificate of pay and tax deducted; ~**bestimmung** *(Metallurgie)* assay; ~**bezüge** emoluments; ~**bogen** pay schedule; ~**diskriminierung** pay discrimination; ~**einbehaltung** detention (retention) of wages; ~**eingruppierung** salary classification; ~**einnahmen** wage earnings; **Lohn- und** ~**einnahmen** wage and salary receipts; ~**einschränkung** pay curb; ~**einstufung** salary classification; ~**einstufungsverfahren** rating procedure.
Gehaltsempfänger salary (wage) earner, salaried employee (worker), payroller *(US)*, wage-earning man, stipendiary, *(pl.)* salaried personnel (class), salaried staff;
~ **sein** to receive a salary.
Gehaltsentwicklung salary progression (promotion), salary evolution (history), compensation history;
auf den neuesten Stand gebrachte ~ salary progression to date.
Gehaltserhöhung salary advance (hike, increase, increment), increase (augmentation) of salary (pay), raising of salaries, pay increase (rise, *Br.*, raise, *US*), addition to s. one's salary, salary rise, rise *(Br.)* (raise, *US*) in (of) wages;
altersbedingte ~ longevity pay; **automatische** ~ automatic salary increase; **laufbahnmäßige** ~**en** within-grade salary advancements; **steuerfreie** ~ tax-free raise *(US)* (rise, *Br.*); **mit einer Beförderung verbundene** ~ promotional salary increase; **bereits vereinbarte** ~**en** rises already agreed *(Br.)*;
seinen Arbeitgeber auf ~ **ansprechen** to approach (ask) one's employer about an increase in salary (for a raise, *US*); **um** ~ **einkommen** to apply for a boost *(US)* (an increase, a rise) in salary; **jem. eine** ~ **gewähren** to increase s. one's salary; **auf** ~ **hoffen** to count upon an increase in one's salary; ~ **jährlich prüfen** to review a salary annually.
Gehalts | erhöhungsprogramm pay increase program(m)e; **Lohn und** ~**etat** labo(u)r budget; ~**festsetzung** assignment of a salary, wage fixing; ~**festsetzung vornehmen** to set the compensation *(US)*; ~**forderung** salary demand (claim), pay claim; ~**forderungen** salary requirements; ~**fortzahlung im Krankheitsfall** payment during illness; **Lohn- und** ~**fortzahlungen im Krankheitsfall** *(Krankenkasse)* short-term disability benefits; ~**frage** salary problem; ~**gefüge** pay structure; **oberste** ~**grenze** maximum salary; **unterste** ~**grenze** minimum salary; ~**gruppe** salary group (bracket, class, range, scale, grade, *Br.*), pay level *(US)*; ~**gutschrift** pay credit; ~**hälfte zur Bank tragen** to bank half one's salary; ~**herabsetzung** salary

(pay) cut, salary reduction; ~**höhe** size of salary; **leistungsabhängige ~höchstgrenze** efficiency bar; ~**inflation** salary inflation; ~**klasse** salary bracket (group, class, grade, *Br.*); ~**konto** salary (payroll, *US*) account; **Lohn- und ~kontrolle** wage and salary control.

Gehaltskürzung salary decrease (cut), reduction (retrenchment) of salary, pay cut;
~ **infolge anderer Tarifeinstufung** demotional salary decrease; **10%ige ~ durchführen** to cut the payroll by ten per cent; ~ **erfahren** to have one's salary docked; ~**en rückgängig machen** to roll back the pay cuts; ~ **bei jem. vornehmen** to cut down s. one's salary.

Gehaltsliste payroll [ledger] *(US)*, list of salaries, salaries list (roll), paysheet *(Br.)*;
~ **von Rüstungsbetrieben** defence payroll;
~ **aufstellen** to make out a payroll; **j. auf die ~ setzen** to put s. o. on the payroll; **nicht mehr auf der ~ stehen** to be off the payroll.

Gehalts|nachweis salary record; ~**nachzahlung** back pay; ~**niveau** earnings level; **niedriges ~niveau** low scale of pay; ~**ordnung** scale of salaries; ~**periode** pay (payroll, *US*) period; ~**pfändung** attachment of earnings *(Br.)*, garnishment of wages; ~**posten** labo(u)r item *(US)*; ~**prämie** bonus; **im Arbeitsvertrag nicht abgesicherte ~prämie** noncontractual bonus; ~**progressionen** salary progression; ~**rahmen** salary range (indicator, structure); **üblicher ~rahmen** ordinary scale of remuneration; ~**rahmen festlegen** to fix the level of pay; **zusätzliche ~regelungen** pay supplements; **mit seiner ~regelung nicht zufrieden** dissatisfied with one's salary; ~**rückstand,** ~**rückstände** salary arrears, accrued salaries, back pay; ~**satz** salary rate, rate of pay *(US)*; ~**sätze** salary (pay) scale; ~**scheck** pay (salary) check *(US)* (cheque, *Br.*); ~**senkung** reduction of salary, salary reduction; ~**skala** salary (pay, *US*) scale, scale of salaries; ~**stabilisierung** pay stabilization; ~**staffelung** scale of salaries; ~**staffelung für Dozenten** lecturer scale; ~**steigerung** salary increase, raise *(US)*; **jährliche ~steigerung** yearly (annual) increment; ~**steigerungstabelle** increment scale; ~**steigerungsverfahren** pay increase procedure; ~**streifen** salary (pay) slip; ~**stufe** step, salary bracket (group, grade), pay level *(US)*; **höhere ~stufen** upper pay brackets (scale); **in eine niedrigere ~stufe zurückversetzen** to employ a demotional classification change; ~**system** salary system; ~**tabelle** pay schedule (scale, *US*), salary scale; ~**tarif** scale of salaries, pay schedule; **auf ein ~teil zugunsten eines Verwandten verzichten** to allot a portion of pay to a relative; ~**tüte** pay envelope; ~**überweisung** transfer of salaries; ~**unterschied** pay gap; ~**veränderung** change in salary; ~**verbesserung** salary increase, raise in wages *(US)*; **Lohn- und ~verwaltung** wage and salary administration; ~**verzeichnis** payroll; **teilweiser ~verzicht** allotment of pay; ~**vorgriff** anticipation of salary; ~**vorschuß** advance[d] salary, advance of (on) salary, salary advance, advance pay; ~**vorschuß bekommen** to receive advance payments on one's salary, to receive part of one's salary in advance, to anticipate one's salary; ~**wesen** compensation field; ~**wünsche** desired salary, *(Anzeige)* salary expected (required), stating salary; ~**zahlung** salary payment; **13. ~zahlung zwangsweise wieder einführen** to restore the compulsory annual bonus of one month's salary; ~**ziffern** salary figures.

Gehaltszulage addition to one's salary, additional (extra) pay, pay supplement, increase of salary, [salary] bonus, raise *(US)*, wage supplement;
~**n für erschwerte Arbeitsbedingungen** salary differential;
~ **beantragen** to apply for an increase in salary; ~ **bekommen** to get a raise *(US)* (rise, *Br.*); ~ **gewähren** to raise a salary.

Gehaltszuschlag pay supplement;
~ **für Auslandstätigkeit** expatriate inducement (allowance).

Gehaltszuschüsse durchs Hintertürchen back-door pay supplements.

gehaltvoll substantial, meaty, *(Wein)* full-bodied;
~**es Buch** profound book.

gehandelt *(Börse)* done, traded, quoted (listed, *US*) on the stock exchange;
~ **und Brief** *(Börse)* sellers ahead *(US)*;
~ **werden** to change hands, to be obtainable at; **an der Börse ~ werden** to be dealt in on the stock exchange; **im Telefonverkehr ~ werden** to be dealt in after hours *(Br.)*; **wenig ~ werden** to have a narrow market.

gehängt werden to come to the gallows.

geharnischt ironclad;
~**e Antwort** sharp reply; ~**er Brief** strongly worded letter; ~**er Protest** sharp protest.

gehässig malicious, spiteful;
~ **über j. reden** to backbite (vilify) s. o., to run s. o. down; ~**e Bemerkung** spiteful remark; ~**e Kritik** venomous criticism; ~**e Vorwürfe** rancorous reproaches.

Gehäuse *(Radio)* cabinet, case.

geheftet wire-stitched, in sheets.

Gehege enclosure, warren, *(Wild)* preserve;
jem. ins ~ kommen to poach on s. one's preserve; **einander ins ~ kommen** to jostle each other.

geheim secret, hidden, private, closed, clandestine, dormant, covert, latent, under one's hat, mystic *(US)*, intrinsic, under cover, *(mil.)* classified, *(pol.)* underground, *(vertraulich)* confidential;
nicht ~ unclassified; **nicht ~ gehalten** open skies; **streng ~** in strict secrecy, top secret;
~ **abstimmen** to [take a] ballot; **etw. äußerst ~ betreiben** to do s. th. with great secrecy; ~ **tagen** to meet secretly; ~ **verhandelt werden** to be tried in closed session (camera, *Br.*);
~**e Absprache** collusion; ~**e Abstimmung** ballot[ing]; ~**e Akten** confidential documents; ~**er Bote** emissary; ~**en Briefwechsel mit jem. führen** to keep a secret correspondence with s. o.; ~**e Dienstsache** classified *(US)* (restricted) matter; ~**e Drohung** covert threat; ~**e Eheschließung** clandestine marriage; ~**er Eigentumsvorbehalt** secret lien; ~**es Einvernehmen** secret understanding, collusion; **im ~en Einvernehmen handeln** to act in collusion; ~**es Fach** secret drawer; ~**ste Gedanken** innermost thoughts; ~**es Gefangenenlager** secret detention center; ~**es Herstellungsverfahren** secret [manufacturing] process; ~**e Kommandosache** *(mil.)* top secret, cosmic *(US)*; ~**er Kreditgeber** confidential creditor; ~**er Mangel** latent defect; **in ~er Mission** on a secret mission; ~**er Rat** privy council; ~**e Tätigkeit** underground activity; ~**es Testament** closed will; ~**er Verführer** hidden persuader; ~**er Vorbehalt** mental reservation; ~**e Wahl** secret ballot (voting); ~**e Zusammenkunft** clandestine meeting.

Geheim|abkommen secret treaty, secret agreement; ~**agent** secret (intelligence) agent, undercover man (agent), intelligencer; ~**akten** confidential documents; ~**anschluß** exdirectory (unlisted, *US*) telephone; ~**archiv** secret archives; ~**auftrag** undercover mission; ~**ausschuß** secret committee; ~**ausschuß des Parlaments** secret house committee; ~**befehl** secret order, sealed orders; ~**bericht** confidential (classified, *US*) report *(US)*; ~**besprechung abhalten** to sit in conclave; ~**besprechungen mit jem. führen** to go into a huddle with s. o.; ~**bestimmung** secret clause; ~**bücher** private books; ~**bund** secret society; **in einen ~bund aufgenommen werden** to ride the goat *(US)*; ~**bündelei** underground dealings; ~**bündnis** secret alliance.

Geheimdienst secret (intelligence) service, Central Intelligence Agency *(US)*, military intelligence, *(Marine)* Naval Intelligence Division;
~**beamter** intelligence officer (operative), spook *(US sl.)*; ~**experte** intelligence expert.

Geheimdienstler intelligence operative, intelligencer.

Geheimdienst|organisation intelligence setup; ~**stelle** intelligence agency.

Geheim|diplomatie subterranean (secret) diplomacy; ~**dokument** secret document; ~**druckerei** clandestine printing; ~**einstufung** security grading *(Br.)* (classification, *US*); ~**fonds** secret [service] fund, slush fund *(US)*.

geheimgehalten undisclosed, undivulged;
~**er Anspruch** secret equity.

Geheimgesellschaft secret society;
j. in eine ~ aufnehmen to initiate s. o. into a secret society; **in eine ~ aufgenommen werden** to ride the goat *(US)*.

geheimhalten to hush up, camouflage;
etw. vor seiner Familie ~ to keep s. th. secret from one's family.

Geheimhaltung concealment, secrecy, *(Zensur)* wrap;
zur ~ verpflichtet under a vow of silence;
~ **von Erfindungen** secrecy of inventions;
strengste ~ utmost secrecy;
strikte ~ bewahren to maintain strictest secrecy; **zur ~ verpflichtet sein** to be sworn to secrecy; **j. zur ~ verpflichten** to bind s. o. to secrecy; **seine Zuhörer zur ~ verpflichten** to pledge one's hearers to secrecy; **mit größter ~ behandelt werden** to rate top-secret treatment.

Geheimhaltungs|anlage *(Telefon)* scrambler; **auf seine ~ansprüche verzichten** to waive one's right of privacy.

Geheimhaltungsbestimmungen classification curtain *(Br.)*;
unter strengen ~ arbeiten to work in tight security; ~ **aufheben** to declassify restricted data *(US)*; **in zu hohe ~ einstufen** to overclassify.

Geheimhaltungs|einstufung security rating (grading, *Br.*, classification, *US*); ~**lücke** confidentiality gap; ~**pflicht** duty of secrecy.
Geheimhaltungsstufe, erhöhte hush-hush;
~ **aufheben** to declassify *(US)*; **in die falsche ~ einordnen** to misclassify; ~ **eines Schriftstücks heraufsetzen (herabsetzen)** to upgrade (downgrade) the security classification *(US)* (grading, *Br.*) of a document; **mit ~ versehen** to classify.
Geheimhaltungs|system security system; ~**verpflichtung** pledge to secrecy; ~**versprechen** promise of secrecy.
Geheim|information classified information *(US)*, secret information; ~**informationen haben** to have secret channels of information; ~**instruktion** secret order; ~**kabinett** privy chamber; ~**klausel** secret clause; ~**konferenz** secret session; ~**konto** private (secret) account; ~**kult** mystery religion, occultism; ~**kurier** intelligence courier; ~**material** *(mil.)* classified material; ~**material freigeben** to declassify restricted data *(US)*; ~**mittel** patent medicine, nostrum; ~**nachrichten** secret intelligence.
Geheimnis secret, mystery;
dunkles ~ dark secret; **streng gehütetes** ~ skeleton in the cupboard; **offenes** ~ open (nobody's) secret; **unergründliches** ~ impenetrable secret; **ungelöstes** ~ unsolved mystery;
~ **des Lebens** facts of life;
jem. ein ~ anvertrauen to tell s. o. a secret; ~ **aufdecken** to get hold of a secret; ~ **ausplaudern** to blab out (give away) a secret, to let the cat out of the bag, to have a loose tongue; ~ **ausquatschen** to blurt (babble out) a secret; ~ **bewahren** to keep a secret, to keep s. th. dark, to button up one's lips *(sl.)*; ~ **schlagartig zum Vorschein bringen** to flash a sudden light upon a mystery; ~ **durchschauen** to pierce a mystery; **j. in ein ~ einweihen** to let s. o. into a secret; ~ **entdecken** to ferret a secret out; ~ **enthüllen** to disclose (reveal) a secret, to unseal a mystery; **seinen Freunden ein ~ enthüllen** to discover a secret to one's friends; **jem. ein ~ entlocken** to get (fish) a secret out of s. o.; **jem. ein ~ entreißen** to pump a secret out of s. o. *(fam.)*; ~ **ergründen** to penetrate into a secret; ~ **versehentlich herauslassen** to tip one's mitt *(sl.)*; **hinter ein ~ kommen** to get at the bottom of a mystery; ~ **loswerden** to unburden a secret, to disburden one's heart of a secret; ~ **aus etw. machen** to make a mystery of s. th.; ~ **preisgeben** to disclose (reveal) a secret; **von ~sen umgeben sein** to be wrapped in (be in a shroud of) mystery; **auf ein ~ stoßen** to drop on to a secret; ~ **verraten** to betray a secret, to spill (reveal) a secret; ~ **in seinem Herzen vertiefen** to hide away a secret in one's heart;
~**krämer** secretmonger; ~**krämerei**, ~**tuerei** mystery, secretmongering, pig's whisper, secreteveness.
geheimnisumwittert wrapped in mystery.
Geheimnis|verletzung violation of a secret; ~**verrat** betrayal of secrets.
geheimnisvoll mysterious, cryptic, obscure.
Geheim|nummer *(Telefon)* ex-directory (unlisted, *US*) number; ~**organisation** secret society (organization); ~**papiere** secret papers, classified material *(US)*; ~**patent** secret patent; ~**plan haben** to have a card up one's sleeve; ~**polizei** secret police force; ~**polizist** detective, plain-clothes (secret-service) man, gumshoe man, sleuth *(coll.)*; ~**projekt** hush project; ~**protokoll** secret protocol; ~**rat** privy counsellor; ~**ratsecken haben** to be balding at the temples *(US)*; ~**sache** classified matter *(US)*, restricted data *(US)*, security matter; ~**sachen** confidential books; ~**schloß** combination lock.
Geheimschrift cipher, code, secret (cipher) writing;
in ~ geschrieben cryptogrammic;
in ~ schreiben to code;
~**analyse** cryptanalysis.
Geheim|schublade secret drawer; **Erfindung unter ~schutz stellen** to impose secrecy on an invention; **unter ~schutz stehende Angaben** classified information, restricted data *(US)*; ~**sender** secret (clandestine) transmitter; ~**siegel** privy seal *(Br.)*; ~**sitzung** secret session; ~**sitzung abhalten** to go into [a] secret session; ~**sphäre** private sphere; ~**sprache** code language; ~**telefon** scrambler [telephone]; ~**tinte** invisible (sympathetic) ink; ~**tip** tip; ~**treppe** concealed staircase; ~**tür** secret door; ~**verbindung** secret society; **mit einem Parteiführer ~vereinbarungen treffen** to deal with a party leader; ~**verfahren** *(Produktion)* secret process, letters of secret; ~**verhandlungen** clandestine talks, private (secret) negotiations; ~**versammlung** secret (clandestine) meeting, secret assembly; ~**vertrag** secret agreement (treaty); ~**waffe** secret weapon; ~**wissenschaft** occult sciences; ~**wissenschaftler** boffin *(sl.)*; ~**zeichen** secret sign, character, key; ~**zimmer** cabinet.

geheimzuhalten *(mil.)* restricted, classified.
Geheiß bidding, order.
geheizt heated.
gehemmt frustrated, uneasy, awkward, *(Verjährungsfrist)* suspended;
~ **sein** *(Recht)* to be estopped.
Gehen walking;
freies Kommen und ~ free issue and entry, run of the house; **ständiges Kommen und ~** comings and goings;
Maschine zum ~ bringen to set a machine going.
gehen to go, to walk, *(Angestellter)* to leave, to quit, *(Artikel)* to sell, to be in good demand, *(Erbschaft)* to fall to, *(erlaubt sein)* to be permitted, *(Gerücht)* to have it, *(Klingel)* to ring, *(Maschine)* to run, to operate, to go, to function, to work, *(Radio)* to be on, *(Schiff)* to depart, to sail, *(Zug)* to go, to leave, to depart;
nach A ~ *(Schiff)* to be bound for A; **von A ab ~** *(Zug)* to run from A; **über X ~** *(Brief)* to be routed via X; **Abkürzung ~** to take a shortcut; **an alle ~** *(Aufruf)* to be intended for everyone; **jem. über alles ~** to paramount with s. o.; **vor Anker ~** to cast anchor; **auf Arbeit ~** to go out (take) to work; **ins Ausland ~** to go abroad; **bis zu 10.000 DM ~** to go as high as DM 10.000; **auf dem Bahnsteig auf und ab ~** to walk up and down the railway platform; **bankrott ~** to fail, to flutter, to smash; **jem. um den Bart ~** to flatter (wheedle) s. o.; **über jds. Begriff ~** to be beyond s. o.; **über alle Begriffe ~** to beat everything; **betteln ~** to go a begging; **in die Binsen ~** to come to naught; **an Bord ~** to go on board, to board a ship; **wie die Katze um den heißen Brei ~** to beat about the bush; **zur Bühne ~** to become an actor (actress); **nach Canossa ~** to go to Canossa; **drunter und drüber ~** to become topsy-turvy; **wie auf Eiern ~** to proceed gingerly; **einkaufen ~** to go shopping; **in Einzelheiten ~** to go into details; **einer Entscheidung aus dem Wege ~** to sidestep an issue; **in Erfüllung ~** to become true; **ins Examen ~** to go up for one's examination; **mitten auf dem Fahrdamm ~** to walk in the middle of the road; **durch die ganze Familie ~** *(Charakterzug)* to run in the blood; **zum Finanzamt ~** to go to the tax office; **flau ~** to drag; **an die Front ~** to go into the line; **aus den Fugen ~** to get out of joint; **jem. ins Garn ~** to let o. s. be hoodwinked; **ins Geld ~** to run into money *(coll.)*; **gewaltig ins Geld ~** to make a big hole in one's capital; **sehr gemächlich ~** to go at a crawl; **gemütlich ~** to stroll; **genau ~** *(Uhr)* to keep good time; **mit jem. streng zu Gericht ~** to take s. o. to task; **wie geschmiert ~** to go like clockwork; **viel in Gesellschaft ~** to go out frequently; **glänzend ~** to be booming, to sell like hot cakes (dogs) *(US)*; **einer Sache auf den Grund ~** to get to the bottom of s. th.; **gut ~** to be selling well, to find a ready market; **gerade noch gut ~** to be a near go; **jem. an die Hand ~** to give s. o. a helping hand; **durch jds. Hände ~** to pass through s. one's hands; **von Haus zu Haus ~** to canvass from door to door; **hin und her ~** *(Briefe)* to pass; **hoch ~** *(See)* to run high; **sprunghaft in die Höhe ~** *(Preise)* to skyrocket; **in die Hose ~** to go haywire, to turn out crabs; **vor die Hunde ~** to go to the dogs; **in die Hunderte ~** to run into the hundreds; **ins vierte Jahr ~** to enter the fourth year; **kaputt ~** to break in pieces, to bust, to get smashed, *(Röhre)* to phut; **zur Konkurrenz ~** to go to the other side; **jem. durch den Kopf ~** to cross s. one's mind; **jem. nicht aus dem Kopf ~** to keep running through one's head; **jem. an den Kragen ~** to cost s. o. his neck; **auf Krücken ~** to walk on crutches; **aufs Land ~** to go into the countryside; **außer Landes ~** to leave the country, to go abroad; **auf Leben und Tod ~** to be a matter of life and death; **über Leichen ~** to have no regard for human life, to ride (run) rough-shod; **jem. auf den Leim ~** to fall into s. one's trap; **in die Luft ~** to fly off the handle *(US sl.)*; **miteinander ~** to go steady (together), to keep company with s. o. *(sl.)*; **auf Mitternacht ~** to be nearly midnight; **mit der Mode ~** to follow the fashion; **mühsam ~** to plod; **von Mund zu Mund ~** to spread from mouth to mouth; **immer der Nase nach ~** to follow one's nose; **auf die Neige ~** to draw to a close, to run low; **jem. auf die Nerven ~** to be a trial to s. o., to get on s. one's nerves (under s. one's skin); **mit großen Plänen schwanger ~** to fly high; **mit sich zu Rate ~** to deliberate; **richtig ~** *(Uhr)* to keep correct time; **alle Stunden seine Runde ~** to make one's round every hour; **jem. schlecht ~** to be in a bad way, *(finanziell)* to be badly off; **zur Schule ~** to go to school; **schwer ~** *(Maschine)* to pull heavily; **an die See ~** to go to the seaside; **in See ~** to put out to sea; **zur See ~** to follow (use) the sea; **wie warme Semmeln ~** to sell like hot cakes (dogs); **unter die Soldaten ~** to join the army, to join the colo(u)rs; **in den Staatsdienst ~** to become a civil servant; **stiften ~** to take to one's heels; **nach der Straße ~** to face (overlook) the street; **auf den Strich ~** to walk

the streets; **jem. gegen den Strich** ~ to upset s. one's plans; **in die Tausende** ~ to run up into thousands; **ans Theater** ~ to become an actor (actress); **zu Tisch** ~ to sit down to table; **in Trauer** ~ to go into mourning; **auf die Universität** ~ to go up to the university *(Br.)*; **auf allen Vieren** ~ to walk on all fours; **neue Wege** ~ to strike out untrodden paths; **zu weit** ~ to go too far, to overshoot the mark; **ans Werk** ~ to set to work; **behutsam zu Werke** ~ to go it carefully; **in die Wirtschaft** ~ to enter private business; **mit der Zeit** ~ to go with the times, to keep pace with modern invention;
jederzeit kommen und ~ **dürfen** to have the run of the house; **es sich gut~ lassen** to do o. s. well *(fam.)*; **sich durch den Kopf** ~ **lassen** to think it over; **es sich wohl~ lassen** to have the time of one's life; ~ **müssen** to walk the plank; **gerade** ~ **wollen** to be on the point of leaving.
gehend, gut prosperous, flourishing, thriving.
gehenlassen, sich to let down one's hair, to cut loose, to be lax in one's conduct; **sich allzusehr** ~ to be overfree in one's conduct; **sich in seinem Äußeren** ~ to neglect one's appearance.
Gehentfernung walking distance.
gehetzt hurried, rushed;
von seinen Gläubigern ~ hounded by one's creditors.
geheuer, nicht uncanny, spooky;
jem. nicht ganz ~ **sein** to feel uneasy about it;
an der Sache ist etw. nicht ~ there is s. th. fishy about it.
Geheul howl.
Gehilfe hand, aid, aider, subworker, assistant, helper, accomplice, adjunct, coadjutor, underling, subsidiary, [help]-mate journeyman;
~**n und Anstifter** aiders and abettors; ~ **eines Flugkontrolleurs** assistant air traffic controller.
Gehilfen|löhne journeymen's wages; ~**prüfung** final examination.
Gehirn brain, mind, intelligence;
menschliches ~ little grey cells *(sl.)*;
sein ~ **anstrengen** to rack one's brains, to use one's head *(coll.)*; ~ **mit nutzlosem Wissen belasten** to encumber a mind with useless learning; **sein** ~ **strapazieren** to exercise one's mind; **sich das** ~ **zermartern** to beat (cudgel) one's brain;
~**akrobatik** whetstone; ~**erschütterung** concussion of the brain; ~**erweichung** softening of the brain; ~**kasten** cranium, skull; **nichts im** ~**kasten haben** to have got nothing upstairs *(sl.)*; ~**schaden** brain damage; ~**schmalz** *(fam.)* brain sweat; ~**trust** brains trust; ~**wäsche** *(Politik)* brainwashing, menticide.
gehoben|ere Ansprüche higher pretensions; ~**e Bedarfsgüter** luxuries and semiluxuries; ~**e Sprache** literary (lofty) language; ~**ere Stellung** elevated position; **in** ~**er Stimmung sein** to be in high spirits.
Gehöft farmstead, wick, steading *(Br.)*.
Gehör hearing;
feines ~ quick ear; **rechtliches** ~ audience, due process of law; **einwandfreies rechtliches** ~ fair hearing;
aufmerksames ~ **finden** to find an attentive audience; **der Vernunft** ~ **geben** to listen to reason; **jem.** ~ **gewähren** to lend an ear to s. o.; **den Parteien rechtliches** ~ **gewähren** to hear the parties; **ausgezeichnetes** ~ **haben** to have a keen sense of hearing; **jem.** ~ **schenken** to listen to s. one's words, to lend an ear to s. o., to give s. o. a hearing; **jds. Bitten kein** ~ **schenken** to turn a deaf ear to s. o.; **sich** ~ **verschaffen** to gain a hearing.
gehorchen to obey, to be obedient;
dem Gesetz ~ to obey the law; **nicht** ~ to disobey; **der Not** ~ to bow to the inevitable; **dem Ruder** ~ *(Schiff)* to obey (respond to) the helm; **widerspruchslos** ~ to obey without question; **jem. auf den leisesten Wink** ~ to be at s. one's back and call.
gehören to belong (appertain) to, to pertain;
~ **zu** *(Anspruch)* to vest with, to be incidental, *(Teil bilden)* to form part, *(zählen zu)* to rank;
sich ~ to be suitable (proper); **sich nicht** ~ not to be the ticket; **zu einem Amt** ~ to be attached (appertain) to an office; **zu jds. Arbeit** ~ to be part of s. one's job; **zu einem Ausschuß** ~ to sit in a committee; **zur Bundesrepublik** ~ to form a part of the German Republic; **zu den Bürounkosten** ~ to come under office charge; **zu Deutschland** ~ to form part of Germany; **zu Eigentum** ~ to be owned by s. o. (s. one's property); **seiner Frau** ~ to belong to one's wife; **zu den Großmächten** ~ to rank among the Great Powers; **zum Haus** ~ to go with the house; **nicht zu etw.** ~ to be extraneous to s. th.; **nicht hierher** ~ to be beside the point; **nirgendwohin** ~ to be nondescript; **zum ständigen Repertoire** ~ to be a stock play; **unter eine andere Rubrik** ~ to fall under a different heading; **ganz und gar nicht zur Sache** ~ to be wide of the mark (beside the point); **vor ein Schiedsgericht** ~ to come within the jurisdiction of an arbitration court; **dem Staat** ~ to be state- (government-) owned; **nicht zum Thema** ~ not to be pertinent to the subject; **zum guten Ton** ~ to be the proper thing.
gehörend owned;
nicht dazu ~ extrinsic.
Gehörfehler defect in hearing.
gehörig belonging (appertaining) to, owned, *(Anspruch)* incident, just, *(korrekt)* fitting, suitable, proper, in due form;
dem Besitzer nur beschränkt ~ particular; **zur Sache** ~ relevant, pertinent, to the point; **nicht zur Sache** ~ not to (off) the point, not relevant, irrelevant, incompetent;
sich ~ **entschuldigen** to apologize in due form; **es jem.** ~ **gegeben haben** to have given s. o. a piece of one's mind; ~ **hereinfallen** to be done brown; **jem.** ~ **die Meinung sagen** to tell s. o. a few home-truths; ~ **hereingelegt worden sein** to have really been taken in;
in ~**er Form** to due form; **zur Familie** ~**e Personen** persons belonging to the family; **über eine** ~**e Portion Frechheit verfügen** to have a great deal of cheek; ~**en Respekt vor jem. haben** to have a healthy respect before s. o.; **mit dem** ~**en Respekt von jem. reden** to speak of s. o. with due reverence; ~**er Schluck** hearty (deep) draught; ~**en Schluck tun** to take a swig at the bottle; ~**e Strafe** stiff (severe) punishment; ~**e Tracht Prügel bekommen** to get a sound thrashing.
gehorsam obedient.
Gehorsam, absoluter implicit obedience; **blinder** ~ blind (unquestioning) obedience, nonresistance; **sklavischer** ~ servile obedience; **unbedingter** ~ implicit obedience;
~ **gegen das Gesetz** obedience to the law;
~ **erzwingen** to exact obedience; ~ **fordern** to insist on obedience; **unbedingten** ~ **leisten** to obey to the letter; **jem.** ~ **schulden** to owe allegiance to s. o.; ~ **von jem. verlangen** to compel obedience from s. o.; **j. zum** ~ **zwingen** to reduce s. o. to obedience *(fam.)*; **durch Einschüchterung zum** ~ **zwingen** to cow into obedience.
Gehorsamsverweigerung [act of] disobedience, insubordinate conduct, insubordination.
Gehörsinn auditory sense.
Geh|steig, ~**weg** footpath, curb, banquette, pavement *(Br.)*, sidewalk *(US)*, walkway *(US)*;
gepflasterter ~ flagging; **überdachter** ~ covered walkway.
Gehudel slipshod (botched piece of) work.
gehupft wie gesprungen as broad as long.
Geier, hol's der confound (hang) it; **hol dich der** ~ devil take you.
Geifer *(Wut)* spleen, ranco(u)r, venom, spite;
seinen ~ **gegen j. verspritzen** to be perpetually vituperating against s. o.
geifern, vor Wut to be foaming with rage.
Geige, die erste ~ **spielen** to play the first fiddle; **nur die zweite** ~ **spielen** to be a second string, to play second fiddle.
geigen, jem. gründlich die Meinung to tell s. o. what is what, to give s. o. a piece of one's mind.
Geiger, erster concertmaster.
Geisel hostage;
als ~ **festgehalten** held in hostage;
als ~ **behalten** to keep as hostage; ~**n nehmen** to take hostages; ~**n stellen** to hostage;
~**erschießung** execution of hostages; ~**gestellung** delivery of hostages; ~**nahme** hostage taking; ~**nahmeaktion** hostage-taking operation.
Geißel whip, scourge, plague.
geißeln to flagellate.
Geist spirit, intellect, mind, wit, genius, *(Phantom)* specter, spectre *(Br.)*, *(Wein)* body;
im ~ in imagination, within o. s.; **nach dem** ~ **des Gesetzes** according to the spirit of the law;
anpassungsfähiger ~ versatile mind; **einfallsreicher** ~ pregnant mind; **sein guter** ~ one's good genius; **kleiner** ~ small pot *(sl.)*; **der menschliche** ~ the human mind; **schöpferischer** ~ creative mind; **skeptischer** ~ mind prone to doubt; **sondierender** ~ probing mind; **unbeugsamer** ~ unbroken spirit;
~ **des Gesetzes** spirit of the law; ~ **und Materie** mind and matter; ~ **der Toleranz** spirit of tolerance; ~ **der Verfassung** spirit of the constitution;
~ **anregen** to provide food for the mind; **seinen** ~ **anstrengen** to use one's wits; **seinen** ~ **aufgeben** to breath one's last; **sich im** ~**e ausmalen** to picture; ~ **eines Gesetzes und nicht seine Buchstaben befolgen** to obey the spirit not the letter of a law; **seinen** ~ **bilden** to cultivate one's mind; **jds.** ~ **erleuchten** to penetrate s. one's mind; **lebhaften** ~ **haben** to be quick-witted;

jem. im ~ verbunden sein to be in spirit with s. o.; **vor ~ sprühen** to sparkle with wit; **gegen den ~ eines Gesetzes verstoßen** to circumvent the spirit of a law; **sich im ~ vorstellen** to figure o. s.; **sich im ~ zurückversetzen** to cast one's mind back.
Geister, erlesene choice spirits; **kleine ~** little minds; **große ~ eines Zeitalters** intellects (leading minds) of an age; **seine müden ~ auffrischen** to revive drooping spirits; **~ beschwören** to conjure spirits; **einer der größten ~ seiner Zeit sein** to be one of the most excellent spirits of one's time; **von allen guten ~n verlassen sein** to have lost one's senses; **~bahn** *(Rummelplatz)* ghost train; **~bild** *(Fernsehen)* ghost, echo; **~reich** shadowland; **~schiff** phantom ship; **~stadt** ghost town.
geistesabwesend absent-minded, vacant.
Geistes | abwesenheit absent-mindedness, vacancy; **~anstrengung** mental effort; **~arbeit** brain work; **~arbeiter** professional man, brainworker, black-coated worker *(Br.)*, white-collar worker *(US)*; **~blitz** flash of wit, stroke of genius, sally, brain storm *(US)*, brain wave; **~frische** freshness of mind; **~gaben** mental, faculty talent, gift; **~gegenwart** readiness (presence) of mind.
geistesgestört mentally deranged, brainsick, lunatic, insane, demented, unbalanced of mind, crazy;
nachgewiesenermaßen ~ certifiably insane; **unheilbar ~** incurably insane;
j. amtlich für ~ erklären to declare s. o. insane, to certify s. one's insanity; **~ sein** to suffer from mental disorder, to be of unsound mind.
Geistes | gestörter lunatic, mentally unbalanced person, mental defective *(Br.)*, person of unsound mind *(US)*, mental patient *(Br.)*; **~gestörtheit** brainsickness, alienation of mind, insanity, mental disorder (alienation), lunacy, derangement; **~größe** master mind; **~gut** intellectual products; **~haltung** mentality, attitude (state) of mind; **~kraft** mental power, vigo(u)r.
geisteskrank insane, brainsick, disordered, mentally ill (disordered, incompetent, *US*), of unsound mind *(US)*, non compos mentis *(lat.)*;
nachgewiesenermaßen ~ certifiably insane; **unheilbar ~** of incurably unsound mind;
j. für ~ erklären to declare s. o. insane, to certify s. one's insanity; **~ werden** to become insane; **nach amtlicher Untersuchung für ~ befunden werden** to be found lunatic by inquisition *(Br.)*.
Geisteskranke | r insane person, lunatic, defective, mentally disordered person, mental case, unfortunate *(Irish)*, person of unsound mind *(US)*, madman;
entmündigter ~r certified lunatic (insane); **mittelloser ~r** indigent insane person; **unheilbarer ~r** perfect idiot;
~n entmündigen to put a lunatic under restraint.
Geisteskrankheit brainsickness, lunacy, mental disease (illness, disorder, defectiveness), insanity;
angeborene ~ idiophatic insanity; **unheilbare ~** incurable insanity (unsoundness of mind, *US*); **völlige ~** essential insanity;
~ infolge chronischen Alkoholismus settled insanity;
~ bestätigen to certify s. one's insanity.
Geistes | leben intellectual life; **~produkt** brain child *(coll.)*; **~richtung** turn (cast) of mind; **neue ~richtung** new mental outlook; **~riese** mastermind; **~schärfe** acuteness of mind, perspicacity; **~schöpfung** intellectual product, conception.
geistesschwach feeble-minded, idiotic, weak-minded, weak in mind, imbecile, infirm, mentally defective, mentally incompetent *(US)*, lunatic.
Geistes | schwäche mental deficiency (infirmity, defect), feeble-mindedness, weakness of mind, weak-mindedness, imbecility, touch in the brain, *(wegen Alters)* decline of intellectual power; **~schwacher** mental defective, imbecile, feeble-minded person, lunatic, idiot; **~störung** mental alienation (disorder, defect), mental derangement, aberration, derangement of the mind, craze.
Geistestätigkeit brainwork;
Störung der ~ mental deficiency (aberration, defect), unbalanced mind; **vorübergehende Störung der ~** temporary insanity.
Geistesträgheit mental indolence.
Geistesverfassung mental health, mental condition, habit (state) of mind;
durchschnittliche ~ normal mind; **in der richtigen ~** all set.
geistesverwandt congenial.
Geistes | verwandtschaft spiritual affinity, congeniality; **~verwirrung** mental aberration; **~wissenschaften** humanities, liberal arts; **~wissenschaftler** humanist, professional.
geisteswissenschaftlich academic, humane;
~e Abteilung humanities department.
Geisteszerrüttung aberration, disorder of the mind.
Geisteszustand mental state, state of a man's mind;
normaler ~ soundness of the mind, sanity;
j. zur Überprüfung seines ~s in eine Anstalt einweisen to place s. o. in an institution for defectives for examination; **j. auf seinen ~ untersuchen** to give s. o. a mental examination.
geistig mental, intellectual, spiritual, unmaterial, inner;
~ anspruchslos low-brow; **~ anspruchsvoll** high-brow; **~ beschränkt** narrow-minded, stupid; **~ beweglich** flexible in thinking; **~ krank** mentally ill; **~ normal** of sound mind, sane; **~ umnachtet** insane, brainsick, disordered, mentally ill, of unsound mind *(US)*; **~ zurückgeblieben** mentally retarded;
~ zurechnungsfähig sein to be mentally competent;
~e Anlagen natural gifts; **~e Anregung** intellectual stimulus; **~e Arbeit** brainwork, mental work, headwork; **~er Arbeiter** brainworker, black-coated *(Br.)* (white-collar, *US*) worker; **~e Armut** poverty of intellect; **~e Aufgeschlossenheit** open-mindedness; **~e Behinderung** mental disablement; **~er Beruf** intellectual pursuits; **~er Defekt** mental deficiency (injury); **~en Diebstahl begehen** to commit plagiarism, to plagiarize, to pick s. one's brains; **~e Eigenschaften** intellectual qualities; **~es Eigentum** literary (intellectual) property; **~e Einstellung** mental set; **~e Elite** intellectual elite; **~e Fähigkeiten** intellectual powers (faculties); **~e Getränke** spirituous liquors, alcoholic beverages, spirits; **~ und körperlich behinderte Kinder** mentally and physically handicapped children; **~es Leben eines Landes** intellectual activity of a country; **~er Mittelpunkt** spiritual centre; **~e Nahrung** pabulum; **in den ~en Stand eintreten** to take holy orders; **~e Störung** derangement, mental alienation (deficiency); **~e Substanz** spiritual substance; **~e Umnachtung** mental derangement, unsoundness of mind *(US)*; **~er Urheber** author; **~er Vater** spiritual father; **~e Veranlagung** mental disposition; **~e Verfassung** morale; **~e Verwandtschaft** spiritual relationship; **~e Vorstellung** mental image; **~es Zentrum eines Landes** spiritual center *(US)* (centre, *Br.*) of a country.
geistlich | e und weltliche Angelegenheiten matters spiritual and temporal; **~e Besitztümer** church lands; **~e Gerichtsbarkeit** ecclesiastical jurisdiction.
Geistlicher clergyman, parson, priest, minister.
Geistlichkeit clergy, churchmen.
geistlos flat, inane, insipid, dull;
~e Bemerkung inane remark, platitude; **~e Beschäftigung** soulless occupation; **~e Komplimente** insipid compliments; **~e Unterhaltung** vapid conversation.
Geistlosigkeit lack of spirit, dullness;
aus lauter ~en bestehen *(Rede)* to be a mere string of platitudes.
geistreich witty, sparkling, *(Buch)* stimulating;
sehr ~ sein to have a great fund of wit;
~e Bemerkung witty remark, quip, wisecrack *(sl.)*; **~er Einfall** witty idea, happy thought; **~e Konversation** sparkling conversation; **~es Theaterstück** sophisticated play.
geist | sprühend sparkling; **~tötende Beschäftigung** monotonous occupation.
Geiz parsimony, stinginess, niggardliness, tightness, closeness.
geizen to be miserly (niggardly);
mit seinem Geld ~ to be stinting with one's money; **mit seinem Geld nicht ~** to spend money without stint; **mit seinem Lob ~** to be grudging (sparing) of praise; **mit seinem Lob nicht ~** to be unstinting in one's praise; **mit seinen Worten ~** to be chary of one's words; **mit seiner Zeit ~** to be anxious not to waste a single minute.
Geiz | hals, ~kragen miser, skinner, skinflint, niggard, scrapepenny, pinchfist, muckworm, screw *(sl.)*;
als ~ verschrien sein to have gained the character of a miser.
geizig avaricious, close-fisted, tight-fisted, miserly, stingy, parsimonious, penny-pinching;
~ sein to skin a flint, to be a screw *(sl.)* (tightwad, *US*).
Geizkragen miser, skinflint, skin, flint, scrapepenny *(Br.)*, scratchpenny, pinchfist, screw, tightwad *(US sl.)*, money-grubber, Scotchman, cheap skate *(US sl.)*;
fürchterlicher ~ sein to be mean beyond expression; **sprichwörtlicher ~ sein** to be a proverb for meanness.
Gejammer lamentation, moaning and groaning, bellyaching;
pausenloses ~ unending grumble.
Gejohle bawling, shouting, caterwauling.
gekauft bought;
nicht ~ unbought;
auf der Auktion ~ auction-bought.

Gekeife scolding, squawk *(sl.)*.
gekennzeichnet marked, labelled, under earmark;
nicht ~ unlabelled, unmarked.
Gekicher giggling, tittering.
Gekläff yelping.
Geklapper rattle, chattering.
gekleidet dressed;
auffallend ~ **sein** to come on flashy.
Geklimper jingle, clink, tinkling.
Geklingel tinkle, tinkling, jingle, *(Telefon)* ringing.
Geknister crackling.
gekonnt accomplished, masterful.
Gekrakel scrawl, scribble.
gekränkt sore, offended;
leicht ~ **sein** to be easily touched; **tief** ~ **sein** to be hurt to the quick;
mit ~**er Miene** with a hurt expression; ~**er Stolz** wounded pride.
Gekreisch screaming, shrieking.
gekreuzt *(Scheck)* crossed.
Gekritzel scribble, scrawl, scratch, doodle.
gekühlt, tief refrigerated.
gekündigt *(Anleihe)* called;
ordnungsgemäß ~ duly determined by notice to quit;
~ **zwecks Aushandlung einer Folgeprämie** *(Versicherung)* cancelled at renewal;
~ **sein** to be under notice to quit; ~ **werden** to receive one's notice, to get sacked *(sl.)*, to be fired *(US)*.
gekünstelt unnatural, sophisticated, theatrical, prim.
gekürzt abridged, condensed, *(Film)* shortened, cut-down.
Gelächter laughter, laugh;
brüllendes ~ roars of laughter;
in ein schallendes ~ **ausbrechen** to burst out into a peal of laughter; **sich dem** ~ **der Menge aussetzen** to make an ass (an exhibition) of o. s.; **j. zum** ~ **machen** to make a laughingstock (butt) of s. o.; **im allgemeinen** ~ **untergehen** to be drowned (lost) in the general laughter.
gelackmeiert sein *(fam.)* to be the sucker.
geladen *(el.)* live, charged, *(wütend)* furious;
ganz schön ~ loaded (drunk, *sl.*);
mit Spannung ~ **sein** to tingle with interest.
Geladener person summoned.
Gelage banquet, spread, binge, carouse, wassail, high time, booze *(coll.)*;
~ **halten** to have a drinking bout (binge), to hold a feast.
gelagert, verschieden diversified.
gelähmt, vor Schreck paralysed with terror.
Gelände [piece of] ground, lot *(US)*, terrain, tract of land, area, yard *(US)*, *(Grundstück)* site, plot, lot *(US)*;
abfallendes ~ falling slope; **ansteigendes** ~ rising ground; **bebautes** ~ built-up area; **ebenes** ~ level ground; **nicht einsehbares** ~ hidden ground; **erschlossenes** ~ development, developed (seated) land, improved site; **freies** ~ open country; **militärisch genutztes** ~ defence land; **für stark gepanzerte Fahrzeuge schwer passierbares** ~ difficult terrain for heavy armo(u)red vehicles; **riesiges** ~ vast extent of ground; **unbebautes** ~ idle (undeveloped) land, open spaces *(Br.)*; **wellenförmiges** ~ undulating land;
~ **ausbauen** to build up an area; **sich auf vertrautem** ~ **befinden** to be in surroundings one knows; **sich auf bekanntem** ~ **bewegen** to travel over old ground; ~ **erschließen** to develop building lots; ~ **gewinnen** to gain ground; ~ **sondieren** to make a reconnaissance; ~ **verlieren** to lose ground; **verlorenes** ~ **wiedergewinnen** to make up lost ground;
~**abschnitt** sector, area; ~**anpassung** *(mil.)* camouflage; ~**antrieb** *(Auto)* all-wheel drive; ~**aufbereitung** site preparation; ~**auffüllung** landfill, fill; ~**aufnahme** topographic survey, surveying; ~**aufnahme aus der Luft** aerial photography; ~**ausbildung** *(mil.)* field training; ~**beschaffenheit** nature of the ground; ~**besprechung** *(mil.)* staff walk, tactical exercise without troops; ~**dienst** *(mil.)* field training; ~**erkundung** *(mil.)* reconnaissance; ~**erschließung** [land] development; ~**fahrt** cross-country drive; ~**fahrzeug** off-road (cross-country) vehicle; ~**gang** *(Auto)* auxiliary (booster, *US*) gear, high [gear].
geländegängig cross-country;
~**es Fahrzeug** cross-country (off-road) vehicle, jeep.
Gelände|gängigkeit cross-country mobility; ~**gewinn** *(mil.)* territorial gains; ~**hindernis** natural obstacle; ~**karte** general map; ~**marke** landmark; ~**profilreifen** off-the-road tyre, tractor tire *(US)*; ~**punkt** bench mark, landmark; ~**punkte** *(Urkunde)* locative calls.
Geländer handrail, rail, *(Balkon)* balustrade, *(Schiff)* railing.
Gelände|rennen point-to-point race; ~**spiel** scouting game; ~**streifen** strip of land, *(mil.)* sector; **vom Staat beanspruchter** ~**streifen** right of way; ~**überwachung** observation of the ground; ~**übung** *(mil.)* field exercise, field training; ~**verhältnisse** ground conditions; ~**verlust** *(mil.)* loss of ground; ~**vermessung** [land] surveying, site survey; ~**wagen** cross-country car, jeep; ~**winkel** *(Artillerie)* angle of site.
gelangen, zum Abschluß to reach an understanding, to come to an agreement, to get a settlement; **zur Anrechnung** ~ to be taken into account; **zu Ansehen** ~ to gain reputation; **zur Aufführung** ~ to be put on the stage, to be performed; **zur Ausführung** ~ to become effective; **in den Besitz von etw.** ~ to come into possession of s. th.; **an seinen Bestimmungsort** ~ to reach one's destination; **zu der Erkenntnis** ~ to come to a conclusion; **in den Hafen** ~ to reach port; **in andere Hände** ~ to change hands; **in die Hände eines Erpressers** ~ to fall into the hands of a blackmailer; **an die Macht** ~ to come to power; **zu Macht und Ansehen** ~ to reach a position of influence; **zu Reichtum** ~ to make a fortune, to come to wealth; **zum Versand** ~ to be dispatched; **ans Ziel** ~ to attain one's end.
gelangweilt dreinschauen to look bored.
gelassen composed, calm, tranquil, even-tempered, with unconcern;
Nachricht ~ **aufnehmen** to receive the news calmly;
~ **bleiben** to retain one's composure; **immer** ~ **bleiben** to never get ruffled, to never turn a hair; **scheinbar** ~ **bleiben** to betray no emotion; **äußerst** ~ **vorgehen** to act with the utmost composure;
in ~**em Ton sprechen** to speak calmly.
Gelassenheit composure, calmness, quietness, tranquillity;
jds. ~ **durchbrechen** to disturb s. one's equanimity; **etw. mit** ~ **tragen** to bear s. th. lightly; **seine** ~ **wiedergewinnen** to regain one's composure, to recover one's equanimity.
Gelatinepapier bromide paper.
geläufig flowing, fluent, fluid, common;
~ **sein** to be familiar to (conversant with); ~ **Englisch sprechen** to speak English fluently;
~**er Ausdruck** common expression; ~**e Redensart** common saying, current phrase; ~**e Zunge haben** to have a glib tongue.
Geläufigkeit fluency.
gelaunt disposed;
schlecht ~ ill-tempered, in a bad temper, in a pet;
glänzend ~ **sein** to be as fit as a fiddle.
Geläut ringing of bells, chiming.
gelb|vor Neid green with envy;
j. ~ **und grün schlagen** to beat s. o. black and blue;
es wurde ihm ~ **und grün vor den Augen** his head was swimming;
~**es Fieber** yellow fever (jack); ~**es Licht überfahren** to shoot the amber; ~**e Presse** yellow (stunt) press, sensational newspapers, tabloid journalism.
Gelb|buch *(pol.)* Blue Book; **aufsteckbarer** ~**filter** attachable yellow filter; ~**kreuz** *(mil.)* mustard gas; ~**licht** *(Verkehrsampel)* amber-light signal.
Geld money, furniture of one's pocket *(coll.)*, gold, dimes, scales *(US)*, *(Bargeld)* cash, *(Börse)* buyers, bid, prices negotiated, *(Hartgeld)* coin, *(Kleingeld)* small change, *(Papiergeld)* paper money (currency, notes), *(Wechselgeld)* change;
für ~ mercenarily; **gegen bares** ~ for cash; **hinter dem** ~ **her** on the make, on the pitch *(sl.)*; **in** ~ **ausgedrückt** in cash terms; **in gutem** ~ in good money; **keinen Pfennig** ~ not a shot in the locker; **knapp an** ~ low in cash, short of money; **mit** ~ **ausgerüstet** heeled *(sl.)*; **mit** ~ **wohl versehen** amply supplied with money, moneyed, flush of money; **nur mit wenig** ~ **versehen** scant of money; **ohne** ~ moneyless, out of funds, without means; **ohne jedes** ~ out of cash, penniless, broke *(sl.)*; **so gut wie bares** ~ as good as (equal to) cash; **solange das** ~ **reicht** while the money lasts; **Unmenge** ~ lump of money; **viel** ~ **verschlingend** money-guzzling;
auf ~ **wird nicht gesehen** *(Anzeige)* money is no object; ~ **gesucht** *(Kurszettel)* wanted, inquired matter; ~ **spielt keine Rolle** money is no object; **nicht für** ~ **und gute Worte** for neither love nor money;
abgenutztes ~ worn currency; **angelegtes** ~ money put up, funds (money) invested, investment; **fest angelegtes** ~ tied-up (locked-up, *Br.*) money, lockup *(Br.)*, deposit account *(US)*; **mit Kündigungsfrist angelegtes** ~ term (time, *US*) deposit; **nicht angelegtes** ~ unemployed money; **sicher angelegtes** ~ money safely invested; **auf einem Sparkonto angelegtes** ~ money on deposit account; **anvertrautes** ~ consigned money, money held on trust, trust fund; **in den Ferien ausgegebenes** ~ holiday

expense; **ausgelegte ~er** money advanced; **ausgeliehenes ~** money lent; **ausgezahltes ~** cash disbursements; **ausstehendes ~** money due, outstanding money, outstandings; **bares ~** cash, cash money *(US)*, present (dry, ready) money, ready coin (cash), specie, money down *(sl.)*; **auf dem Transport (unterwegs) befindliches ~** bullion in transit, money in the post *(Br.)* (mail, *US*); **im Verkehr befindliches ~** current money; **bereitliegendes ~** cash in hand; **billiges ~** cheap (light, easy, easy-terms) money; **ein bißchen ~** a little money; **brachliegendes ~** dead money, money paying no interest (lying idle); **disponibles ~** funds available; **echtes ~** good money; **eigenes ~** own money; **eingefrorenes ~** frozen money; **eingegangenes ~** cash receipts; **eingesammeltes ~** purse; **mittels Zwangsvollstreckung eingetriebenes ~** money made; **eingezahltes ~** deposit; **einzelnes ~** loose change (money); **erspartes (erübrigtes) ~** savings, spare money; **fakultatives ~** facultative money; **täglich fälliges ~** money at (on) call *(Br.)*, money at short notice, call money *(Br.)*, day-to-day money *(Br.)*, money on current account, demand deposit *(US)*; **falsches ~** counterfeit coin (money), adulterated money, bad *(Br.)* (bogus, base, *Br.*) money; **festes ~** time loan *(US)* (money), deposit account *(US)*, fixed (time) deposit *(US)*; **festgelegtes ~** immobilized money; **flüssiges ~** funds in hand, ready money, liquid funds; **fremdes ~** foreign money; **gangbares ~** current (good) money; **mein ganzes ~** the whole of my money; **gefundenes ~** windfall; **gehortetes ~** inactive money; **geliehenes ~** borrowed money; **gemünztes ~** coin, specie, metallic currency; **geprägtes ~** coinage; **gepumptes ~** touch *(sl.)*; **außer Kurs gesetztes ~** money withdrawn from circulation; **aus dem Verkehr gezogenes ~** money withdrawn from circulation; **hartes ~** hard currency; **heißes ~** hot money, refugee capital; **herausgegebenes ~** change, small coin; **hinausgeworfenes ~** money down the drain, wasted money; **gerichtlich hinterlegtes ~** cash under the control of the (money in) court; **investiertes ~** capital invested; **irreguläres ~** nonstandard money; **kleines ~** change; **knappes ~** dear (close, tight) money; **konvertierbares ~** convertible money; **frei konvertierbares ~** hard money; **kurzfristig kündbares ~** money on (at) short notice; **kursierendes ~** current money; **kurzfristiges ~** money at short notice *(Br.)*, short loan *(Br.)*, short-term loan *(US)*; **langfristiges ~** time money (loan, deposit, *US*), call (long-term, *US*) money, street (demand, *US*) loan; **leichteres ~** easier money; **eine Masse ~** a powerful lot of money; **minderwertiges ~** debased currency; **gerade passendes ~** even money; **privates ~** private funds; **restliches ~** odd money; **schwarzes ~** black money; **tägliches ~** demand loan (deposit, money) *(US)*, call loan (money, *Br.*), overnight credit, day-to-day money *(Br.)*; **teures ~** dear (close, tight, high, *US*) money; **überschüssiges ~** surplus money; **postalisch überwiesenes ~** postal money; **telegrafisch überwiesenes ~** telegraphic money; **übriges ~** loose money, spare cash; **umlaufendes ~** current (effective) money, currency; **ungemünztes ~** heavy money; **ungültiges ~** money that is no longer current; **leicht verdientes ~** easy money, money easily earned, money for jam (old rope), soft *(sl.)*; **sauer (schwer) verdientes ~** hard earnings, hard-earned money, tough buck *(sl.)*; **schnell verdientes ~** fast buck *(US sl.)*, turkey *(sl.)*; **vereinnahmtes und verausgabtes ~** money received and expended; **verfügbares ~** disposible funds; **tatsächlich verfügbares ~** effective money supply; **treuhänderisch verwaltetes (verwahrtes) ~** money held on trust, trust funds; **viel ~** good deal of money, plenty of money; **sehr viel ~** no end of money; **vollwertiges ~** sterling money; **testamentarisch zum Ankauf von Grundstücken vorgesehenes ~** money land; **weggeworfenes ~** money thrown away; **wertbeständiges ~** store-of-value money; **wöchentliches ~** weekly fixtures; **restlos zurückgezahltes ~** money refunded in full;
Brief und ~ *(Börse)* bills and money, bid and asked, bids and offers, sellers and buyers; **mehr ~ als Brief** *(Kursbericht)* more buyers than sellers, buyer's market (over, *Br.*);
~ auf Abruf (auf tägliche Kündigung) call loan (money, *Br.*), day-to-day loan (money) *(Br.)*, street (demand, *US*) loan; **~ wie Heu (Mist)** oodles of money; **~ in der Ladenkasse** till money; **~ auf lange Sicht** time deposit; **~ und sofort fällige Staatsbankguthaben** treasury cash; **~ der Steuerzahler** taxpayer's money; **~ in der Tasche** shot in the locker; **~ mit gleichbleibendem Wert** stable money; **~ auf eine Woche** weekly fixtures; **~ mit Zwangskurs** legal tender, lawful money *(US)*; **~-aus-der-Tasche-ziehen** shakedown *(US sl.)*;
~ abheben to withdraw money; **~ von der Bank abheben** to draw money from the bank; **~ mittels Scheck abheben** to check out *(US)*; **jem. ~ abknöpfen** to sting s. o. for money, to squeeze money out of s. o.; **~ beim Schatzamt abliefern** to cover money into the Treasury *(US)*; **jem. sein ~ bis zum letzten Heller abnehmen** to fleece s. o. of every halfpenny; **~ abzweigen** to divert money; **jem. ~ anbieten** to offer s. o. money; **j. um ~ angehen** to draw on s. o. for money; **j. fortlaufend um ~ angehen** to keep at s. o. with appeals for money; **j. um ~ anhauen** *(fam.)* to touch s. o. *(sl.)*; **~ anlegen** to embark (put out) money, to invest funds, to make an investment; **sein ~ in Aktien anlegen** to invest one's money in stocks and shares; **sein ganzes ~ in Büchern anlegen** to spend a small fortune on books; **sein ~ falsch anlegen** to misemploy one's money; **~ fest anlegen** to place money on deposit; **sein ~ in Grundstücken anlegen** to invest one's money (make investments) in real estate; **sein ~ gut anlegen** to invest one's money to good account, to get good value for one's money; **~ im Hausbesitz anlegen** to put money into houses; **sein ~ klug anlegen** to bestow one's money wisely; **sein ~ nutzbringend anlegen** to lay out one's money profitably; **sein ~ in mündelsicheren Papieren anlegen** to invest one's money in a safe stock; **~ in Rentenwerten anlegen** to sink money in an annuity; **sein ~ schlecht anlegen** to make bad use of one's money; **~ auf Sparkonten anlegen** to place money in savings accounts; **~ spekulativ anlegen** to venture money in a speculation; **~ in Staatspapieren anlegen** to fund *(Br.)*; **~ vernünftig anlegen** to put money to good use; **~ verzinslich anlegen** to put one's money out at interest; **sein ~ vorteilhaft anlegen** to lay out one's money to advantage; **~ zinsbringend anlegen** to place money on interest; **um ~ anpumpen** *(fam.)* to touch (pump) for money *(sl.)*; **sein ~ einer Bank anvertrauen** to give money to the bank for safe-keeping; **~ anweisen** to remit money; **~ aufbringen** to put up funds, to put up (borrow, raise, procure, take up) money, to raise cash, to finance; **~ für einen Prozeß aufbringen** to invest money in a lawsuit; **~ für ein Unternehmen aufbringen** to put up (find) the money for an undertaking; **~ durch Zeichnung aufbringen** to raise funds by subscriptions; **~ aufnehmen** to borrow (raise, take up) money, to take the rate; **~ auf ein Grundstück aufnehmen** to raise money on an estate; **~ gegen hypothekarische Sicherheiten aufnehmen** to borrow on a mortgage; **~ gegen Verpfändung der Anlagenwerte aufnehmen** to raise money on the security of the assets; **~ auftreiben** to raise (scare up, *US coll.*) money, to raise cash, to finance, to work the oracle *(sl.)*; **~ für ein Unternehmen auftreiben** to find the money for an undertaking, to finance an institution; **~ für j. aufwenden** to spend money on s. o.; **~ aufzählen** to count up money; **~ ausgeben** to lay out (spend) money; **wenig ~ für sein Auto ausgeben** to run a car at small cost; **viel ~ für Bücher ausgeben** to spend a small fortune on books; **~ falsch ausgeben** to misspend money; **sein ganzes ~ ausgeben** to go through all one's money; **~ mit vollen Händen ausgeben** to go the paces, to be on a big spending binge, to be off on a spending spree, to make the money fly, to spend money with both hands (without stint, like water); **~ hemmungslos ausgeben** to spend money without stint (like water); **~ leicht ausgeben** to spend money with a free hand; **eine Menge ~ ausgeben** to spend lots of money; **sein ~ für nichts und wieder nichts ausgeben** to throw away one's money for nothing; **~ scheffelweise ausgeben** to squander money; **~ spekulativ ausgeben** to venture money in speculation; **sein ~ umsonst ausgeben** to spend one's money to no purpose; **verschwenderisch ~ ausgeben** to spend lavishly; **jem. mit ~ aushelfen** to aid s. o. with money; **mit seinem ~ auskommen** to live within one's means; **mit wenig ~ auskommen** to live on little money; **~ ausleihen** to lend money; **~ auf Bodmerei ausleihen** to lend money on bottomry; **~ gegen Sicherheiten ausleihen** to lend money on security; **~ auf Zinsen ausleihen** to put out money (lend) at interest, to place (lend) money on interest; **~ mit vollen Händen ausschütten** to be off (go) on a spending spree; **~ ausspucken** *(fam.)* to spill money; **sich mit genügend ~ ausstatten** to line one's purse well; **jem. gegen Vorlage seines Personalausweises ~ auszahlen** to pay s. o. a sum upon submission of proof of identity; **sich um ~ balgen** to scramble for money; **restliches ~ behalten** to keep the odd money; **Teil des ~es behalten** to retain part of the money; **~ beiseiteschaffen** to finance money away; **für sein ~ etw. [Gleichwertiges] bekommen** to get one's money's-worth; **etw. für sein ~ geboten bekommen** to have a run for one's money; **von jem. keinen Pfennig ~ bekommen** not to see the colo(u)r of s. one's money; **Verfügungsgewalt über sein ~ bekommen** to come into one's own money; **~ abgezählt bereithalten** no change given; **~ bereitstellen** to finance; **~ beschaffen** to find [the] (furnish) money, to provide funds; **jem. ~ besorgen** to provide s. o. with money; **aus lauter ~ bestehen** to be made of money; **j. um sein ~**

betrügen to do s. o. out of his money; **j. um sein ganzes ~ betrügen** to fleece s. o. of (jockey, do s. o. out of) all his money; **~ bewilligen** to grant money; **jem. für sein ~ etw. bieten** to give s. o. a run for his money; **j. eilig um ~ bitten** to rush s. o. for money; **Ehemann dringend um mehr ~ bitten** to importune a husband for more money; **j. um sein ~ bringen** to relieve s. o. of his money; **jem. um sein ganzes ~ bringen** to fleece s. o. of all his money; **das große ~ bringen** to bring in big money; **~ unter die Leute bringen** to put money into circulation; **~ in Verkehr bringen** to pass the coin; **j. in betrügerischer Weise um sein ~ bringen** to get the money from s. o. by trick; **~ bei einer Bank deponieren** to deposit money with a bank; **mit dem ~ der Kasse durchbrennen** to make off with the money (cash), to shoot the moon *(Br., sl.)*; **~ durchbringen** to waste money; **~ einfordern** to demand payment; **~ einkassieren** to pocket cash; **~ einnehmen** to receive money; **~ einschießen** to give in, to put into, to contribute capital; **~ in den Wirtschaftskreislauf einschleusen** to pump money into the economic system; **mit ~ einspringen** to chip in *(US)*; **~ einstecken (einstreichen)** to pocket money; **jds. ~ einstreichen** to finger s. one's money; **sich sein ~ sehr genau einteilen** to make a penny go a long way; **~ eintragen** to bring in, to yield; **~ eintreiben** to enforce payment, to recover a debt; **~ bei einer Bank einzahlen** to put money in[to] (deposit money with) a bank; **~ auf ein Konto einzahlen** to pay money into an account; **schlechtes ~ einziehen** to call in coins; **~ entnehmen** to draw money; **viel ~ erfordern** to call for a lot of money; **~ ergattern** to dig up *(US sl.)*; **~ durch Zahlkarte überwiesen erhalten** to be paid out in cash by the postman; **~ erheben** to raise money; **~ auf betrügerische Weise erlangen** to get money by fraud; **jem. um sein ~ erleichtern** to part s. o. from his money; **~ erpressen** to press for money, to ramp *(Br., sl.)*; **gestohlenes ~ ersetzen** to replace stolen money; **im ~ ersticken** to be rolling in money; **~ flüssigmachen** to ease money free; **aus öffentlichen ~ern fördern** to subsidize; **~ auf Bodmerei geben** to advance money on bottomry; **ins ~ gehen** to run into money *(coll.)* (up into large amounts); **mit seinem ~ geizen** to be very near with one's money; **~ bei jem. gewinnen** to cash in on s. o.; **~ haben** to be worth money (in stock, in cash); **~ ausstehen haben** to have money owing; **~ auf der Bank haben** to have funds with (money in) a bank; **~ bei einer Bank stehen haben** to keep money at a bank; **genügend ~ zum Bauen haben** to have ample means for building; **~ bei sich haben** to have money on one, to carry money about one; **etw. ~ beiseite gelegt haben** to have a little money in reserve; **eigenes ~ haben** to have money of one's own; **für sein ~ etw. haben** to have a run for one's money; **genügend ~ haben** to have money in sufficiency; **nicht genügend ~ haben** to feel the need of money, to be in want of money; **bei einem Geschäft ~ zugesetzt haben** to be a few dollars out-of-pocket as a result of a transaction; **sein ~ gut angelegt haben** to get good value for one's money; **haufenweise ~ (~ wie Heu, Mist) haben** to have scads (lots, piles) of money, to be simply coining money, to have money to burn (blow), to have money galore; **~ in der Kasse haben** to have cash in hand; **kaum ~ haben** to be hard up [for money]; **kein (Mangel an) ~ haben** to get aground, to be short of stuff (pressed for funds); **kein ~ bei sich haben** not to have any money on one, to have no cash on o. s.; **kein ~ mehr haben** to have empty pockets; **scheffelweise ~ haben** *(fam.)* to have lots of money; **sein ~ in englischer Staatsanleihe angelegt haben** to be interested in British funds; **~ in Staatspapieren angelegt haben** to have money in the funds *(Br.)*; **~ bei jem. stehen haben** to have money lodged with s. o.; **schönes Stück ~ gespart haben** to have saved a nice bit of money; **Taschen voller ~ haben** to have one's pockets full of money; **~ im Überfluß haben** to have scads (lots, piles) of money, to have money to burn; **Unmenge ~ haben** to have a pot of money; **~ zur Verfügung haben** to have money at one's disposal, to have money to the fore; **viel ~ zur Verfügung haben** to have a big bankroll; **so viel ~ zur Verfügung haben** to have so much money in hand; **viel ~ haben** to have a large income; **~ zurückgelegt haben** to have money laid aside, to have money put by; **~ zu jds. Verfügung halten** to hold money to s. one's order; **am ~ hängen** to be a slave to money; **nach ~ heiraten** to marry money; **~ herausbekommen** to get change; **~ herausgeben** to give change; **~ aus jem. herausholen** to get money out of s. o.; **~ aus jem. herauskitzeln** to worm money out of s. o.; **~ aus jem. herauslocken** to elicit (entice, worm) money out of s. o.; **~ aus jem. herauspressen** to wring money out of s. o.; **~ herausrücken** to part with one's money; to fork out, to cough up *(sl.)*; **~ bei jem. herausschinden** to extract money from s. o.; **~ aus etw. herausschlagen** to make money out of s. th.; **~ zum Fenster herauswerfen** to throw money down the drain; **~ aus jem. herausziehen** to extract money from s. o.; **~ herbeischaffen** to raise money, to supply the needful; **sein ganzes ~ hergeben** to part with all one's money; **mit seinem ~ nur so herumschmeißen** to play ducks and drakes with one's money; **Satz für tägliches ~ hinaufsetzen** to mark up call money *(US)*; **sein ~ mit beiden Händen zum Fenster hinauswerfen** to throw money down the drain; **~ in ein Land hineinpumpen** to pump money into a country; **~ hineinstecken** to embark money; **~ bei jem. hinterlegen** to lodge (deposit) money with s. o.; **~ bei einer Bank hinterlegen** to place money on deposit with a bank; **~ bei Gericht hinterlegen** to bring money into the court; **~ horten** to hoard money; **~ investieren** to invest capital; **~ in Grundbesitz investieren** to put money into land; **mit ~ klimpern** to chink; **mit dem ~ knausern** to stint money; **um sein ~ kommen** to lose one's money; **zu ~ kommen** to come by money; **plötzlich zu ~ kommen** to strike a lead (it rich); **plötzlich zu viel ~ kommen** to come into the big money; **schnell zu ~ kommen** to make a quick buck *(sl.)*, to shake the pagoda *(India)*; **schwer ~ auftreiben können** to be hard set to find money; **sich von seinem ~ schwer trennen können** not to like to part with one's money; **nicht mit ~ umgehen können** not to know how to handle money, not to be able to keep money; **~ kosten** to require money; **Haufen ~ kosten** to cost a packet of money; **schweres ~ kosten** to cost a great deal of money; **j. schweres ~ kosten** to be a heavy burden on s. o.; **anständige Stange (schönes Stück) ~ kosten** *(fam.)* to run to (cost) a pretty penny, to come to a deal of money; **viel ~ kosten** to cost a good deal [of money]; **sein ~ arbeiten lassen** to put one's money out at interest; **sein ~ nicht arbeiten lassen** to let one's money lie idle; **jem. um sein ~ betteln lassen** to let s. o. whistle for his money; **~ springen lassen** to bleed well *(sl.)*; **sehr ins ~ laufen** to run into very large sums; **von seinem ~ leben** to live on one's capital; **~ auf die Bank legen** to put money in[to] a bank; **~ auf die hohe Kante legen** to put money by, to put away for a rainy day; **~ auf den Tisch legen** *(fam.)* to put down the money, to shell out one's money, to plank down the ready *(US)*; **~ leihen** *(jem.)* to loan (lend) money, *(von jem.)* to borrow; **~ auf Bodmerei leihen** to borrow (raise, take) money on bottomry; **~ von einem Freund leihen** to borrow money off a friend; **sein ~ loswerden** to get rid of one's money, to drop money *(sl.)*; **~ machen** to make money; **zu ~ machen** to convert into cash, to turn into money (cash), to coin; **~ locker machen** to spring money *(Br., coll.)*; **aus seinem ~ mehr machen** to manage one's money more effectively; **schnell ~ machen** to make money hand over fist; **~ münzen** to coin (stamp) money; **~ nachschießen** to pay an additional amount (sum); **gutes ~ schlechtem ~ nachwerfen** *(fam.)* to throw good money after bad; **herausgegebenes ~ nachzählen** to count one's change; **~ aus der Ladenkasse nehmen** to take money from the till; **~ prägen** to coin money; **bei Freunden hemmungslos ~ pumpen** to feel no qualms about borrowing money from friends; **~ reinbuttern** *(fam.)* to kick in *(US sl.)*; **~ zu einem bestimmten Zweck sammeln** to make up a purse; **~ für wohltätige Zwecke sammeln** to canvass on *(Br.)* (in, *US*) behalf of charity; **~ auf die Seite schaffen** to finance money away; **~ scheffeln** to be coining (shovelling up) money, to be coining money; **monatlich ~ nach Hause schicken** to remit money home each month; **mit dem ~ nur so um sich schmeißen** to scatter money broadcast, to fling one's money about, to blow one's money *(sl.)*; **~ aus dem Fenster schmeißen** to fling one's money out of the window, to throw money down the drain; **~ schöpfen** to create money; **~ schulden** to owe money; **viel ~ schulden** to be involved in debts; **im ~ schwimmen** to be rolling in cash (money, wealth), to be coining money, to strike it rich (oil, *US*), to bucket money, to have loads of money; **aufs ~ aus sein** to be after (out for) money, to be on the make *(sl.)*; **bei ~ sein** to be flush of money (in funds), to be in cash (the chips, *sl.*); **nicht mit ~ zu bezahlen sein** to be worth its weight in gold; **mit ~ freigebig sein** to be open-handed with money; **knapp bei ~e sein** to be hard up (in low water), to be short of money; **nicht bei ~ sein** to be short of money (out of cash, out of funds); **mit ~ reichlich (wohl) versehen sein** to have a well-lined purse, to be flush of money; **scharf aufs ~ aus sein** to be keen on money making; **völlig ohne ~ sein** to be penniless (broke); **~ sparen** to save money; **um ~ spielen** to play for money, to game; **~ in ein Geschäft stecken** to put capital into a business; **sein ~ ins Geschäft stecken** to lock up one's cash in one's trade; **sein ganzes ~ ins Geschäft stecken** to sink all one's money in the concern; **enorm viel ~ in sein Geschäft stecken** to spend a fortune over one's business; **~ in ein Unternehmen stecken** to sink money in an undertaking; **~ aus der Ladenkasse stehlen** to abstract money from a till; **~ für**

ein Unternehmen zur Verfügung stellen to put up money for an undertaking; **nach ~ stinken** to stink of money *(sl.)*; **sich ~ in die Taschen stopfen** to shove money into one's pocket; **viel ~ zu verdienen suchen** to go in for money; **sein letztes ~ mit jem. teilen** to share one's last crust (penny) with s. o.; **~ zur Sparkasse tragen** to put money into the savings bank; **~ unmittelbar übergeben** to hand over the money direct; **~ überweisen** to transmit (transfer) money; **jem. ~ überweisen** to put s. o. in cash, to send s. o. a remittance; **telegrafisch ~ überweisen** to transfer money by cable; **~ überzählen** to count out money; **mit seinem ~ sehr geizig umgehen** to be very neat (tight) with one's money; **großzügig mit fremdem ~ umgehen** to be generous with other people's property; **leichtsinnig mit Vaters ~ umgehen** to play fast and loose with father's money; **sorglos mit seinem ~ umgehen** to be very flush with one's money; **sparsam mit seinem ~ umgehen** to husband one's money; **[fremdes] ~ umrechnen** to reduce money; **in [bares] ~ umsetzen** to turn into money (cash), to realize; **sein ~ dreimal jährlich umsetzen** to turn one's money three times a year; **falsches ~ unterbringen** to fob off false coin; **~ unterschlagen** to embezzle trust funds, to convert money to one's own use; **j. mit ~ unterstützen** to assist s. o. with money; **~ verauslagen** to disburse money; **~ verdienen** to make (earn) money; **Haufen ~ verdienen** to make stacks of money; **~ wie Heu (Mist) verdienen** to be simply coining money, to make money hand over fist; **auf einen Schlag viel ~ verdienen** to earn a lot of money in one scoop; **schweres ~ verdienen** to earn big (heavy) money, to line one's pocket; **eine Stange ~ verdienen** to make a pile of money; **an einer Sache ein schönes Stück ~ verdienen** to make a pretty penny out of s. th.; **viel ~ verdienen** to earn big money, to have a large income, to do well; **enorm viel ~ verdienen** to be simply coining money; **damit kann man viel ~ verdienen** there is money in it; **sein ~ auf anständige Art und Weise (ehrlich) verdienen** to turn an honest penny; **~ vereinnahmen** to receive money; **~ vergeuden** to trifle away one's money; **schrankenlos ~ verleihen** to lend money without limits; **~ bei etw. verlieren** to lose money on s. th.; **bei etw. sehr viel ~ verlieren** to drop a lot of money; **sein ganzes ~ verlieren** to tap out *(sl.)*; **jem. sein ganzes ~ vermachen** to leave one's money to s. o.; **sein ~ verplempern** to squander money; **~ verpulvern** to blow money *(sl.)*; **sich ~ verschaffen** to procure money; **sich ~ durch Betrug verschaffen** to obtain money by fraud; **sich das nötige ~ verschaffen** to raise the wind *(fam.)*; **sein ~ verschleudern** to make pots and pans of one's property, to throw one's money about; **viel ~ verschlingen** to cost a mint of money; **j. mit ~ versehen** to keep s. o. in money, to supply s. o. with funds, to finance s. o.; **sein ~ verspekulieren** to finance one's money away *(US)*; **~ gleichmäßig verteilen** to divide money equally; **fremdes ~ für sich verwenden** to convert funds to one's own use; **sein ~ gut verwenden** to make good use of one's money; **jem. sein ~ vorenthalten** to keep s. o. out of money; **~ vorschießen (vorstrecken)** to advance money; **~ für einen Hausbau vorsehen** to destine money to build a house; **jem. ~ vorzählen** to count money before s. o.; **ausländisches ~ wechseln** to change foreign currency; **von allen Leuten (Seiten) um ~ angegangen werden** to be pressed for money from all quarters; **mit ~ nur so um sich werfen** to fling away one's money, to fling one's money about, to throw money about like dirt, to throw away handfuls of money; **sein ~ auf die Straße werfen** to throw money down the drain; **sein ~ nicht wiederbekommen** to be put out of pocket; **für sein ~ etw. haben wollen** to want one's money's-worth; **im ~e wühlen** to be wallowing (rolling) in money; **in barem ~ zahlen** to pay in cash; **in deutschem ~ zahlen** to pay in German money; **sein ~ zählen** to tell one's money *(US)*; **jem. ~ aus der Tasche ziehen** to relieve s. o. of his money, to shake s. o. down *(US sl.)*; **~ seiner Zweckbestimmung zuführen** to appropriate money; **sein ~ zurückbekommen** to recover one's money, to get one's money back; **~ zurückerstatten** to refund money; **~ an den Eigentümer zurückgeben** to restore (refund) money to the owner; **zuviel gezahltes ~ zurückgeben** to return an overpaid amount; **schönes Stück ~ zurücklegen** to put a good deal of money aside; **~ für unvorhergesehene Ereignisse zurücklegen** to reserve money for unforeseen contingencies, to put aside for a rainy day; **sein ~ zurückverlangen** to want [to get] one's money back; **sein ~ zusammenhalten** to take care of one's money; **~ zusammenkratzen** to scrape up a sum of money, to scratch together, to scramble up money; **ein bißchen ~ zusammenkratzen** to rake together a little money; **~ zusammenscharren** to scramble up money; **sein ~ zusammenwerfen** to pool one's resources; **~ zuschießen** to contribute money; **~ zuweisen** to appropriate funds;

~ öffnet alle Türen money is a passport to everything; **~ spielt keine Rolle** money is no object;

~abfindung monetary indemnity, pecuniary compensation (satisfaction), cash settlement; **~abfluß** drain of money, efflux of funds; **~abfluß zu einer Flut aufwallen lassen** to turn the outflow of money into a flood; **~abhebung** draft [of money], withdrawal of [a sum of] money, drawing, cashing; **~abhebung in Notfällen** emergency withdrawal; **~abschöpfung** absorption of purchasing power; **~abwertung** devaluation (devalorization) of the currency; **~abzug** drain of money; **~adel** moneyed aristocracy, plutocracy.

Geldanforderung requisition for money, money demand, *(Geldmarkt)* currency demands;

~en für die Ferien- und Reisezeit holiday currency demands; **~en zum Halbjahresultimo** mid-year demands; **~en zum Jahresultimo** year-end need for cash *(US)*.

Geldangebot money supply, supply of money, *(Börse)* bid.

Geldangelegenheiten money affairs (concerns, matters), pecuniary affairs;

sich mit ~ beschäftigen to deal in money; **in ~ großzügig sein** to be liberal of money; **jem. alle ~ überlassen** to leave all money matters to s. o.

Geldanhäufung treasury of money.

Geldanlage money investment, sinking;

~n cash items;

todsichere ~ perfectly safe investment of money; **vorteilhafte ~** profitable (remunerative) investment of money;

~ bei ersten Adressen money placed with first-rate borrowers.

Geld|anleger investor; **~anleihe** loan; **~anspannung** stringency *(US)*, squeeze *(Br.)*; **~ansprüche** pecuniary (money) claims, right to money; **~anweisung** remittance, draft, money (post-office) order *(Br.)*, postal [money] order *(US)*; **telegrafische ~anweisung** telegraphic money order, cable transfer, express money order *(US)*; **~aristokratie** moneyed aristocracy, plutocracy; **~aufbringung** raising money; **~auflage** impost, imposition, tax.

Geldaufnahme raising of money, taking up of capital, borrowing;

befristete ~ temporary borrowing; **kurzfristige ~** short-term borrowing;

~ zu niedrigeren Zinssätzen als der Handelsgewinn equity trading.

Geld|aufwand expenditure; **~aufwendungen für den persönlichen Schutz** protection money; **~aufwertung** revalorization (revaluation) of the currency; **~ausfuhr** exportation of money; **~ausfuhrverbot** money embargo.

Geldausgabe expenditure, cash disbursement;

vorübergehende ~ laying out of money;

zur ~ bereit sein to put one's hand into one's pocket.

Geld|ausgänge withdrawals, cash drawings; **~ausgleich** settlement of payment, *(zwischen Banken)* clearing, evening up; **~aushungerung** money starvation; **~auslagen** outlays; **~ausleiher** moneylender, money broker; **~ausleihung** moneylending; **~ausweitung** increase of money in circulation, expansion of the money supply, monetary expansion; **durch Devisenabflüsse bedingte ~ausweitung** inflows swelling the money supply; **~auszahler** cashier, *(Bank)* paying teller.

Geldbedarf need (want) of money, borrowing demand, requisite money, monetary needs, sum required, pecuniary (financial) requirements, *(Bank)* cash requirements, *(Geldmarkt)* currency demands, demands for money, *(Gesamtwirtschaft)* money (monetary) supply;

wachsender ~ money supply growth;

~ der öffentlich-rechtlichen Kreditnehmer public debtor cash requirements;

seinen ~ decken to find accommodation for one's needs; **zunehmenden ~ hundertprozentig decken** to provide fully for the increasing monetary needs.

Geldbedarfs|entwicklung money-supply trend; **~sollziffer** money supply target; **~zunahme** run-up in the money supply; **~zuwachs** money supply growth.

Geld|beihilfe monetary grant, subsidy; **~beitrag** contribution, grant; **~beiträge einsammeln** to collect contributions; **~beitreibung** recovery of money; **~belohnung** pecuniary (monetary) reward, remuneration; **~bereitstellung** appropriation of funds, *(Parlament)* ways and means; **~ beschaffer** fund raiser; **~beschaffung** raising money, procurement of funds, finding of capital, *(Parlament)* ways and means; **~beschaffungskosten** cost of money, money cost; **~beschaffungsverkäufe** money-raising transactions; **gesamter ~bestand** cash on hand, stock of money, money (monetary) stock; **~bestände** monetary (money) holdings.

Geldbetrag money [amount], amount of money, monetary contribution, purse;
von der Bank abgehobener ~ sum withdrawn from the bank; **beigetriebener** ~ money made; **bestimmter** ~ certain sum; **gleichwertiger** ~ equality money; **kleiner** ~ small sum of money; **ungeheurer** ~ prodigious sum of money; **ungenügender** ~ small bread *(sl.)*; **für Vergnügungszwecke vorgesehener** ~ happy money;
~ **ohne Sicherheiten** nonsecured money;
~ **abheben** to withdraw a sum of money; **enormen** ~ **fest anlegen** to nail down an enormous amount of money; **jem. einen** ~ **anvertrauen** to entrust s. o. with a sum of money; ~ **beisteuern** to contribute a sum of money; ~ **bewilligen** to vote a sum of money; ~ **bei einer Bank einzahlen** to pay money into a bank, to bank an amount; **enormen** ~ **festlegen** to nail down an enormous amount of money; **jem. einen** ~ **gutschreiben** to place an amount to s. one's credit; **bestimmten** ~ **für Forschungszwecke zur Verfügung stellen** to earmark a sum of money for research; ~ **stiften** to contribute a sum of money; **jem. einen** ~ **überweisen** to remit a sum of money to s. o.; ~ **verwenden** to use a sum of money; **geliehenen** ~ **zurückgeben** to repay a sum of money borrowed.
Geldbeträge sums, funds;
nicht abgeholte ~ unclaimed funds; **unterwegs befindliche** ~ money in the post *(Br.)* (mail, *US*); **beschlagnahmte** ~ attached funds; **eingehende** ~ takings, money coming in, *(Zahlungsbilanz)* money receivable; **festliegende** ~ tied-up funds, lockup *(Br.)*; **nicht zur Ausschüttung gelangende** ~ nondistributable funds; **ohne Auflagen zur Verfügung gestellte** ~ string-free money; **investierte** ~ invested capital; **zusätzliche** ~ additional finance;
unwahrscheinliche ~ **ausgeben** to spend incredible sums of money; ~ **aus einem Fonds entnehmen** to take money out of a fund; **im Streit befangene** ~ **auf neutrale Konten führen** to hold the money in dispute independently; **unberechtigte** ~ **über eine Privatfirma schleusen** to route an unauthorized payment through a private company; **für die Bereitstellung der erforderlichen** ~ **verantwortlich sein** to be responsible for cash forecasting; **große** ~ **verwalten** to handle large sums of money.
Geldbeutel moneybag, purse, pocket, wallet, bag *(Br.)*;
aus dem eigenen ~ out of one's own stock (pocket); **für jeden** ~ **erschwinglich** within the reach of a small purse;
dicker ~ fat purse; **magerer** ~ a light purse;
jem. um seinen ~ **erleichtern** to pick (drain) s. one's purse; **Daumen auf den** ~ **halten** to tighten the purse strings; **jds.** ~ **leeren** to drain s. one's purse; **über den** ~ **verfügen** to hold (command) the purse strings; **seinen** ~ **zücken** to unstring one's purse; ~ **noch fester zuhalten** to zip one's pockets tighter.
Geldbewegungen fluctuations of money, currency movements.
Geldbewilligung grant of money, *(parl.)* appropriation of funds, vote of supplies;
~ **in Etappen** fragmentary appropriation.
Geldbewilligungsklausel *(parl.)* money clause *(Br.)*.
Geld|bezüge remuneration; ~**börse** moneybag, purse; **seine** ~**börse zücken** to dip into (unstring) one's purse; ~**brief** money *(US)* (insured, *Br.*, cash) letter; ~**briefträger** money postman; **großer** ~**brocken** large chunk of money; ~**buße** amends, fine, penalty; **jem. eine** ~**buße auferlegen** to amerce s. o.; ~**charakter** monetary nature; ~**darlehn** loan; ~**deckung** cover; ~**depot** money on deposit, deposit money, money lodged; ~**disponent** liquidity manager; ~**disponent eines Konzerns** group cash manager; ~**disponibilitäten** available funds; ~**disposition** monetary arrangements, cash (liquidity) management; **langfristige** ~**dispositionen** cash forecast; **für die** ~**disposition verantwortlich sein** to be responsible for cash forecasting; ~**dispositionsmaßnahmen im ganzen Konzernbereich straffen** to tighten up the cash-management procedures throughout the world; ~**eingang** money received, moneys paid in, receipt of money; ~**eingänge** takings, receipt of money, receipts; ~**einheit** monetary unit; ~**einkommen** money income; ~**einlage** deposit, money paid in; ~**einnahmen** money income, [cash] receipts, takings; ~**einnehmer** money taker, collector, *(Bank)* receiving teller *(US)*; ~**einschuß** money paid in, injection of new capital; ~**einsendung** remittance in cash; ~**einstandskosten** cost of money; ~**einwurf** *(Automat)* slot; ~**einziehung** collection, recovery of money; ~**einziehung durch die Post** postal collection; ~**empfang** receipt of money; ~**empfänger** recipient of a payment, payee.
Geldentschädigung money relief, pecuniary compensation (satisfaction), indemnity;
gerichtlich festgesetzte ~ money condemnation.
Geldentwertung fall (depreciation) of the currency, currency depreciation, depreciation of coin, decline in the value of money, devaluation of money, inflation.
Geldentwertungs|ausgleich equalization for currency depreciation; ~**rate** inflation rate.
Geldentzug drain of money.
Gelder means, sums of money, funds, purse;
langfristig angelegte ~ long-term (funded) capital; **nicht angelegte** ~ unemployed money; **aufgenommene** ~ borrowed funds, borrowings; **aufgewandte** ~ money employed; **an Kunden ausgeliehene** ~ *(Bilanz)* advances against customers; **ausgezahlte** ~ cash disbursements; **ausstehende** ~ outstanding debts, outs, accounts receivable *(US)*; **unterwegs befindliche** ~ money in the post *(Br.)* (mail, *US*); **befristete** ~ tied-up funds, lockup *(Br.)* time deposits *(US)*; **benötigte** ~ necessary funds; **vom Parlament bewilligte** ~ money provided by Parliament *(Br.)*; **durchlaufende** ~ cash in transit; **eingefrorene** ~ blocked funds, frozen money; **eingegangene** ~ cash receipts; **eingehende** ~ money pouring in, receipt of money, receipts; **täglich fällige** ~ sight (demand, *US*) deposits; **festgelegte, festliegende** ~ tied-up funds, lockup *(Br.)*, time deposits *(US)*; **flüssige** ~ ready money, available capital, disposable funds, liquid assets; **fremde** ~ *(Bankbilanz)* funds from outside sources, third-party funds, deposit by customers; **kurzfristige** ~ money at short notice *(Br.)*, demand deposits *(US)*, short-term loans *(US)*; **langfristige** ~ time money, long-term loans *(US)*, deposit accounts *(US)*; **mündelsichere** ~ trustee investment *(Br.)*, trust fund *(US)*; **öffentliche** ~ public moneys (purse, funds, *Br.*); **stillgelegte** ~ nonearning reserve; **tägliche** ~ sight (demand, *US*) deposits; **unverzinsliche** ~ dormant funds; **jederzeit verfügbare** ~ money on hand, floating money, disposable funds; **von einer Bank verwaltete** ~ banker's (bank) funds; **treuhänderisch verwaltete** ~ trustee investment *(Br.)*, trust fund *(US)*; **zweckgebundene** ~ earmarked funds;
~ **auf Abruf** money at call; ~ **mit Laufzeit** time deposits;
~ **abziehen** to withdraw funds (deposits); **öffentliche** ~ **bestimmungsgemäß ausgeben** to use public money only for legitimate purposes; ~ **ausleihen** to put money out to loan; **öffentliche** ~ **bereitstellen** to make the necessary public funds available; ~ **beschaffen** to furnish (procure) money; ~ **bewilligen** *(Parlament)* to vote supplies (funds); **seine** ~ **einziehen** to call in one's money; **gesperrte** ~ **freigeben** to release funds; **dicke** ~ **haben** to have a fat income; **unermeßliche** ~ **haben** to have lots of money; **öffentliche** ~ **unterschlagen (veruntreuen)** to misappropriate public funds, to misapply public money; ~ **anderen als den vorhergesehenen Zwecken zuführen** to alienate funds from their proper destination; ~ **zweckbestimmen** to earmark funds; ~ **zweckentfremden** to alienate funds from their proper destination.
Geld|erlös money earnings; ~**ersatz** token money, auxiliary currency, representative money *(US)*; ~**ersparnis** economy, savings; ~**erwerb** moneymaking; **auf** ~**erwerb ausgehen** to seek a livelihood.
Geldeswert money's worth, value in money.
geldeswerte Gegenleistung pecuniary consideration.
Geld|fachmann professional money manager; ~**fälscher** counterfeiter, smasher *(Br.)*; ~**fälschung** counter-feasance, counterfeiting of money, forgery of bank notes; ~**flüssigkeit** liquidity, *(Geldmarkt)* glut (ease) of money (in money rates), easy (easiness of the) money market, easy money *(US)*; ~**forderung** claim for money, money claim (demand), monetary claim, pecuniary claim (demand), *(ausstehender Gelder)* money due, outstanding money; ~**forderungen des Kapitalverkehrs** financial debts; ~**frage** financial question, question (matter) of money; ~**fülle** abundance (glut) of money; ~**funktion** function of money; ~**geber** moneylender, financial backer, advancer, financier, investor, *(Förderer)* sponsor, *(Hypotheken)* mortgagee; ~**gefüge** monetary structure; ~**gesamtbestand** monetary aggregate; ~**geschäft** money (financial, cash) transaction; ~**geschäfte** money dealings, financial affairs, monetary transactions; ~**geschäfte machen** to finance; ~**geschenk** gift of money (cash), cash gift (donation), pecuniary present, purse, gratuity, pouch *(Br., sl.)*, *(Trinkgeld)* tip; ~**gier** thirst for money, cupidity, avarice, itch for money.
geldgierig moneygrubbing, covetous, avaricious.
Geld|gründe, etw. aus ~**gründen tun** to do s. th. for money; ~**hahn aufdrehen** to turn on the money tap; ~**hahn wieder aufdrehen** to loosen its stranglehold on the money supply; ~**hahn zudrehen** to turn off the money supply tap; ~**hamsterer** hoarder of money; ~**handel** money dealing, *(Firma)* cash management; ~**händler** money dealer, liquidity (cash) manager, money-

lender, money jobber *(Br.)* (broker), moneymonger; ~**händler von Kapitalsammelstellen** institutional money manager; ~**händler sein** to deal in money; ~**heirat** money match, mercenary marriage, marriage of interest; ~**heirat eingehen** to marry money; ~**herrschaft** plutocracy; ~**hilfe** pecuniary aid (assistance); ~**hinterlegung** deposit of money, cash deposit; ~**horter** money hoarder; ~**hortung** hoarding of money, currency hoarding; ~**hortungsfaktor** piggy-bank factor; ~**inflation** money inflation, inflation of the currency; ~**institut** financial (lending) institution, finance *(US)* (moneylending) company; **öffentliches** ~**institut** public financial institution, depository [institution] *(US)*, depository bank *(US)*; ~**jäger** money getter; ~**kapitalanlage** pecuniary investment, investment of funds; ~**kasse** strongbox, chest, *(Laden)* till, *(Registrierkasse)* cash register; ~**kassette** till, money chest, strongbox, cashbox; ~**kaufkraft** purchasing power; ~**kiste** money chest, strongbox; ~**klemme** financial straits, pecuniary difficulty (embarrassment); **zeitweilige** ~**klemme** money squeeze; **in einer** ~**klemme sein** to be in a jam.

geldknapp pressed for money.

Geld|knappheit dear money, money (scarcity, stringency, *US*, tightness), monetary pressure, pressure for money, shortness (shortage, tightness, lack, scarcity) of money, tight money; **zeitweilige** ~**knappheit** money pinch; ~**kosten** cost of money; ~**kreditsystem** money credit system; ~**kreislauf** circular flow of money, circulation of money.

Geldkurs demand (money) rate, demand price, bid quotations (price), *(Devisen)* [bankers'] buying rate;
~ **und Briefkurs** bid and asked quotations, closing bid and asked prices;
~**wert** standard; ~**zettel** market report.

Geld|lade till; ~**legat** pecuniary legacy; ~**leistung** payment in cash, *(Krankenkasse)* cash benefit; ~**leitsätze** key-money rates; ~**leute** moneyed people, plutocrats.

geldlich monetary, pecuniary, financial;
~**e Einbuße** money damage; ~**e Gesamtnachfrage** overall currency demands; **in** ~**er Hinsicht** financially; ~**e Unterstützung** pecuniary aid (assistance); ~**er Vorteil** pecuniary benefit.

Geld|lohn money wage; ~**lotterie** lottery; ~**macht** financial power (strength), money power; ~**makler** money (bill) broker; ~**mangel** impecuniosity, paucity of money, lack of funds (money), monetary pressure, pressure for money, low water, squeeze *(Br.)*, money stringency *(US)*; ~**mann** financier, moneyed man.

Geldmarkt money (cash, financial) market;
amerikanischer ~ **und Kapitalmarkt** Wall Street; **angespannter** ~ tight money market, tightness of the money market; **empfindlicher** ~ sensitive market; **flüssiger** ~ easy market, ease in money rates; **gespaltener** ~ two-tier money market; **lebhafter** ~ active money market; **Londoner** ~ Lombard Street; **schwankender** ~ tottering state of the money market;
Druck auf den ~ **ausüben** to place pressure on the money market; ~ **beanspruchen** to be a debtor in the money market; ~ **stark in Anspruch nehmen** to tap the money market heavily; **auf dem** ~ **aktiv sein** to be a creditor in the money market; **sich dem** ~ **gegenüber strikt neutral verhalten** to take an apparently neutral line towards the money market;
~**anlage** financial investment; ~**anleger zum Rentenkauf verführen** to tempt investors out of the money market into bonds; ~**anspannung** tightening of the money market, monetary strain; ~**ausleihungen** short-term borrowings.

geldmarktbedingt, seine ~**en Balancierungskünste wieder aufnehmen** to begin its new money-minded balancing act.

Geldmarkt|bedingungen money-market conditions; **sich auf erleichterte** ~**bedingungen einstellen** to reflect easier money circumstances; ~**bericht** money market report, money article; ~**beschränkungen über Bord werfen** to kick over the monetary traces.

geldmarktempfindlich sensitive to money-market influences.

Geldmarkt|enge stringency on the money market, jam in the money market *(US)*; ~**entwicklung** tendency of the money market; ~**erleichterungen** monetary ease; **sich für** ~**erleichterungen einsetzen** to commit o. s. to easing money; **Tendenz in der Politik der** ~**erleichterungen fortsetzen** to continue their turn toward ease in money rates; ~**experte** financial market professionalist; ~**flüssigkeit** easiness of the (easy, *US*) money market; ~**geschäft** money-market business (transaction); ~**geschäfte** money market operations; ~**instrumentarium** instruments (tools) of monetary policy, money-market instruments, monetary policy instruments, monetary and fiscal techniques; ~**investition** financial investment; ~**klemme** difficulty in the money market, pecuniary embarrassment, jam in the money market *(US)*; **kurzfristige** ~**kredite** money at call and short notice; ~**krise** crisis in the money market, monetary (financial) crisis; ~**lage** money-market situation; ~**papiere** money-market securities; ~**politik der Bundesnotenbank** Federal Reserve monetary policy *(US)*; **harte** ~**politik betreiben** to hold to restrictive monetary policies.

geldmarktpolitisch|e Änderungen shift in monetary policies; ~**e Änderungen vornehmen** to shift monetary policy; ~**e Erleichterungen in Erwägung ziehen (zulassen)** to be about to relax money; ~**e Erleichterungen zulassen** to relax monetary policy; ~**es Instrumentarium** tools of monetary policy; ~**e Konsequenzen auslösen** to produce a ripple effect on the money market.

Geldmarkt|regulativ tools of monetary policy; ~**regulierung** money-market regulations; **im Rahmen der** ~**regulierung** under its money market regulating arrangements; ~**sätze** market rates of interest; **leichte** ~**sätze** easy money rates; ~**sätze des Eurodollarmarktes** Eurocurrency money market rates; ~**schwankungen** fluctuations in the money market.

geldmarkttechnisch|e Erleichterungen easing of monetary policy; **verschärfte** ~**e Maßnahmen** clampdown on money; ~**e Möglichkeiten der Regierung** monetary techniques at the government's disposal.

Geldmarkt|verkehr, sich für Erleichterungen des ~**verkehrs einsetzen** to favo(u)r easier money; ~**verknappung** money scarcity, stringency of the money market; ~**verknappung beseitigen** to loosen the lid on tight money; ~**verschuldung** money-market indebtedness; **erschwerte** ~**versorgung** pressure on money supply; ~**versteifung** stiffening of prices, tightening of money conditions; ~**vorschriften** money-market regulations; ~**zins** money rate; ~**zinsen** short-term interest rates.

Geldmenge quantity of money, money supply;
verfügbare ~ stock of money.

Geldmengenpolitik money stock policy, policy of money supply.

Geldmittel funds on hand, [money] means, pecuniary (financial) resources, sums, purse, finances, exchequer;
beschränkte ~ limited resources; **fehlende** ~ lack of funds; **öffentliche** ~ public means (funds); **unzureichende** ~ scanty means; **verfügbare** ~ available funds;
~ **anderweitig anlegen** to convert funds to another purpose; ~ **aufbringen (beschaffen)** to put up (raise) funds; ~ **für ein Unternehmen auftreiben** to finance an institution; ~ **bereitstellen** to appropriate funds, to find cash, to bankroll *(US)*; ~ **für den Zinsendienst bereitstellen** to provide funds for payment of interest; ~ **beschaffen** to raise funds; ~ **bewilligen** to vote funds, *(parl.)* to vote the supplies; **mit kurzfristigen** ~**n finanzieren** to finance with short-term money; **gesperrte** ~ **freigeben** to release funds; **geringe** ~ **haben** to be short of money (pressed for funds); **keine** ~ **zur Verfügung haben** to have no funds available; **über die zur Verfügung stehenden** ~ **hinaus kaufen** to overtrade; ~ **zur Verfügung stellen** to ladle out funds; ~ **für ein Unternehmen zur Verfügung stellen** to finance the costs of an undertaking; **über** ~ **verfügen** to have money at one's disposal; **nur über beschränkte** ~ **verfügen** to have only limited resources; **mit** ~**n versehen** to furnish with funds, to put in funds; **j. mit** ~**n versehen** to set (put) s. o. up in (furnish, supply s. o. with) funds; ~ **anderen als den vorgesehenen Zwecken zuführen** to alienate funds from their proper destination;
~**umlauf** total money in circulation.

Geld|motiv money motive; ~**münze** coin; ~**nachfrage** money demand, demand for money; ~**nachfrage aus Vorsorgegründen** precautionary demand; ~**nehmer** borrower, *(Hypothekarkredit)* mortgagor; ~**neuordnung** currency (monetary) reform; ~**not** shortness of money, financial straights, tightness, money difficulties, squeeze *(Br.)* money stringency *(US)*; **in** ~**nöten** on the rocks; **aus seinen** ~**nöten herauskommen** to get out of one's financial difficulties; ~**notiz** demand quotation; ~**onkel** sugar daddy; ~**opfer** offertory; **unter schweren** ~**opfern** at a heavy cost of money; ~**paket** money parcel, packet of money; ~**pfändung** attachment of funds; ~**politik** monetary (financial) policy; **expansive** ~**politik** expansive monetary policy; **restriktive** ~**politik** money restrictiveness.

geldpolitisch|neutral sein to have no effect on the money market; **sich um die** ~**e Aufgabe kümmern** to handle the monetary side; ~**er Kurs** monetary policy; ~**e Maßnahmen** monetary policy devices; ~**e Maßnahmen des Finanzministeriums** treasury directives *(Br.)*.

Geld|posten sum of money, item; ~**prägung** coining of money; ~**prämie** bonus; ~**preis** interest, *(Preis)* cash price; ~**preis**

gewinnen to win the purse; ~**protz** moneybag, money bug *(US sl.)*; ~**quelle** source of money (income), pecuniary resources; ~**quelle entdecken** to strike a lead (it rich, oil, *US*); ~**quittung** accountable receipt; ~**reform** currency (monetary) reform; ~**regulierung** money-market control (regulation); ~**reichtum** glut of money; **tatsächliche nach Steuerzahlungen erzielte ~rendite** real post-tax rate of return on money; ~**rente** periodic payment, money payments, penny mail (rent, *Br.*), *(Unfall)* compensation *(US)*; ~**reserve** store of money, reserve fund, *(Bank)* cash (money) reserve; **kleine ~reserve haben** to have a little money in reserve; **ohne ~reserven** poor; ~**restriktion** monetary restrictiveness; ~**rolle** rouleau; ~**rückgabezusicherung** money-back guarantee; ~**rückzahlung** repayment, reimbursement, refund; ~**sache** money matter; ~**sack** moneybag, bank bag, pouch for money.

Geldsammlung collection, gathering, purse, drive to raise funds, whip-round *(Br.)*, *(für bestimmte Zwecke)* fundraising campaign;
zweckbestimmte ~ collection in aid of an undertaking;
~ ins Werk setzen to start a fund, to put up a purse, to put on a drive; **~ veranstalten** to raise funds, to collect contributions; **~ für j. veranstalten** to pass the hat round for s. o.; **~ für Wohltätigkeitszwecke veranstalten** to organize the raising of funds for charitable purposes.

Geldsätze money (loan) rates, rates for money on loan, market rates;
billige ~ cheap money; **kurzfristige ~** short-term market rates; **~ am offenen Markt** open-market rates, open rates *(US)*;
~ abschwächen to ease money rates; **~ herabsetzen** to mark down money rates; **~ heraufsetzen** to mark up money rates.

Geld|schatulle cashbox; ~**schatz** hoard of money.

Geldschein bank note *(Br.)*, bank bill *(US)*;
beschädigter ~ mutilated [bank] note; **falscher ~** counterfeit note;
~ wechseln to break a note;
zusammengerolltes ~bündel roll *(US sl.)*; ~**entwertung** defacement of a bank note; ~**tasche** notecase *(Br.)*, wallet, billfold *(US)*.

Geld|schiff *(fig.)* ship; ~**schleier** money veil; ~**schlitz** slot; ~**schneiderei** usury, extortionate charge, extortion, ramp *(Br., sl.)*, sharp practices; ~**schöpfung** creation of money (currency), expansion of the money supply; ~**schöpfung vornehmen** to create money (currency).

Geldschrank money chest, strongbox, safe [deposit];
diebessicherer ~ burglarproof safe; **eiserner ~** cash safe; **feuerfester ~** fireproof safe (strong box); **feuer- und diebessicherer ~** fire and burglar-resisting safe;
~ aufbrechen (knacken) to crack (break open) a safe;
~**fabrikant** safeman, safe builder, safemaker; ~**fabrikation** safemaking; ~**knacker** safe lifter, safeblower, safebreaker, safecracker, safe buster, cracksman, mob, pete-man *(sl.)*; ~**knackerei** safebreaking, safecracking.

Geld|schraube fester anziehen to tighten the monetary screw; ~**schublade** money (cash) drawer; ~**schuld** money (financial) debt; ~**schwemme** glut of money; ~**schwierigkeiten** pecuniary difficulties, money troubles; ~**schwierigkeiten haben, in ~schwierigkeiten sein** to be in embarrassed circumstances (pushed for money, in Queer Street), to be hard up (in low waters); ~**schwierigkeiten noch nicht überwunden haben** to be still under the weather; ~**sender** remitter; ~**sendung** remittance [in cash]; ~**sog** drain of money; ~**sorgen** money troubles (worries), pecuniary embarrassment, economic pressure, financial straits; **von ~sorgen bedrängt** troubled about money matters; ~**sorgen haben** to be hard up (in low water); ~**sorte** denomination; ~**sorten** foreign cash; **ausländische ~sorten** foreign coins and notes; ~**sortenzettel** specie list; ~**spende** distribution of money in charity, cash donation, money gift; ~**spritze** infusion of funds; ~**stabilität** monetary stability; ~**stillegung** sterilization of money; ~**stolz** purse pride.

Geldstrafe fine, pecuniary penalty (punishment), money bote (penalty), amercement, amende, mulct, forfeit;
einer ~ unterliegend finable; **mit einer ~ verbunden** liable to a fine;
hohe ~ heavy fine; **kollektive ~** joint fine; **dem richterlichen Ermessen überlassene ~** fine left to the discretion of the judge; **unbedeutende ~** nominal fine;
~ für unerlaubte Abwesenheit *(mil.)* straggling money; **~ für ungebührliches Benehmen** fine for disorderly conduct; **~ in bestimmter Höhe** determinate fine; **~ wegen Überschreitung der Ausgangszeit** *(mil.)* gate bill *(Br.)*;
~ auferlegen, mit einer ~ belegen to fine, to impose (levy) a fine, to surcharge; **~ beitreiben** to recover (entreat, exact) a fine; **~ bezahlen** to pay (return) a fine; **~ wegen falschen Parkens bezahlen** to pay a fine for illegal parking; **mit einer ~ davonkommen** to get (be let) off with a fine; **~ erlassen** to grant release from (remit) a fine; **~ für j. festsetzen** to assess a fine on s. o.; **~ gegen j. verhängen** to inflict a fine on s. o.; **zu einer ~ verurteilen** to fine; **~ verwirken** to incur a fine (mulct); **mit einer ~ wegkommen** to be let off with a fine; **mit einer hohen ~ belegt werden** to be heavily fined.

Geldstrafenklausel penalty clause.

Geldströme rivers of money, monetary flows;
~ in die Sozialausgabenetats einschleusen to channel money into social expenditure;
gegenläufige Güter- und ~ bilateral flow.

Geldstruktur monetary structure.

Geldstück coin, piece of money, bean *(sl.)*;
beschädigtes ~ battered coin; **einzelne ~e** loose change; **gefälschtes ~** counterfeit [coin];
jem. ein falsches ~ andrehen to palm off (foist) a bad coin on s. o.; **einem Bettler ein ~ in die Tasche stecken** to thrust a coin into a beggar's pocket; **~ grabschen und in seine Tasche stecken** to whip a coin into one's pocket.

geldsüchtig money-mad, mercenary.

Geldsumme [sum of] money, amount of money, fund, purse;
bestimmte ~ certain sum of money; **enorme ~** vast amount of money; **kleine ~** trifle;
~ aussetzen to offer (hold out) an amount; **j. eine gewaltige ~ kosten** to cost s. o. no end of money; **größere ~n verwalten** to handle a lot of money.

Geld|summenvermächtnis general bequest (legacy); ~**surrogat** auxiliary currency, token money, money substitute, representative money *(US)*; ~**system** monetary system; ~**täschchen** pocket book, purse; ~**tasche** purse, *(Anzug)* charge pocket; ~**technokraten** monetary technocrats; ~**theoretiker** monetarist, money-supply economist, money theorist; ~**theorie** theory of money, currency theory; ~**transaktion** monetary transaction; ~**transport** transport of money; ~**transportwagen** armo(u)red car; ~**überfluß** glut (abundance) of money; ~**überhang, ~überschuß** surplus (excess) money, excessive supply of money, abundance (backlog, superfluity) of money.

Geldüberweisung remission (transmission) of money, money transmission, remittance, resource transfer, [money] transfer;
telegrafische ~ express (telegraphic) money order, money order telegram, telegraph remittance, wire transfer *(US)*;
~ durch die Post money order *(Br.)*, post-office *(Br.)* (postal money, *US*) order; **~ in jeder frei konvertierbaren Währungseinheit** remittance in any convertible currency.

Geldüberweisungsverkehr, postalischer post-office financial service *(US)*.

Geldumlauf currency of money, circulation (flux, flow) of money, money (monetary) circulation;
gesamter ~ total money in circulation;
~ pro Kopf der Bevölkerung per capita circulation;
~ künstlich steigern to inflate the currency.

Geld|umsatz money turnover, returns; ~**umstellung** currency, conversion; ~**umtausch** exchange of currency; ~**unterschlagung** embezzlement of trust money, wrongful abstraction, abstraction of funds; ~**unterstützung** money relief, pecuniary aid (assistance), financial aid (assistance); ~**unterstützung erhalten** to receive financial support; ~**verbilligung** cheapening of money; ~**verbindlichkeit** pecuniary obligation.

Geldverdienen moneymaking, earning;
nur ans ~ denken to set one's heart on making money; **einfach nicht zum ~ kommen** to be in too great a hurry to make money; **aufs ~ aus sein** to be keen on moneymaking, to be all for making money; **immer aufs ~ scharf sein** to always have an eye to the main chance.

Geld|verdiener moneymaker, *(Ernährer)* breadearner, breadwinner; ~**verfassung** monetary structure; ~**verflüssigung** watering down of money; ~**vergütung** pecuniary (monetary) reward; ~**verkehr** money transfer, currency, circulation of money; **seinen täglichen ~verkehr abwickeln** to handle one's day-to-day money matters; ~**verkehrsteuer** circulation tax *(US)*; ~**verknappung** scarcity of money, money shortage, monetary restraint (tightness), squeeze *(Br.)*, stringency on the money market *(US)*, fiscal stringency *(US)*.

Geldverlegenheit pecuniary difficulty (embarrassment), involvement;
in ~ in narrow straits, pressed for money, embarrassed, tight; **sich in ~ befinden, in ~ sein** to be hard up [for money], to be in embarrassed circumstances, to be in a jam, to be at a loss

(pushed, embarrassed, pressed) for money (in pecuniary embarrassment), to be embarrassed by lack of money; **in äußerster ~ sein** to be on the rocks (one's beam-ends), to be down on one's uppers *(Br.)*; **in großer ~ sein** to be hard set to find money.

Geldverleih, gewerbsmäßiger moneylending, borrowing; **wucherischer ~** loan sharking *(US)*;
~ und Kapitalverleih money and capital transactions.

Geldverleiher, generöser ~ soft touch *(sl.)*; **gewerbsmäßiger ~** money dealer (broker), moneylender, moneymonger, lender of money; **wucherischer ~** loan shark; **zweifelhafter ~** shady financier;
sich mit ~n einlassen to entangle o. s. with money-lenders; **~n ausgeliefert sein** to be in the hands of moneylenders.

Geld|verleihvertrag moneylending agreement; **~verlust** pecuniary loss, loss of money; **~vermächtnis** disposal of money by will, general bequest, pecuniary legacy; **~vermehrung** increase of the currency; **~vermittler** money (bill) broker; **~vermögen** monetary wealth, financial assets; **~vermögensbildung** monetary wealth formation; **~vermögenswerte** cash (liquid) assets; **~vernichtung** destruction of money; **~verpflichtungen** commitments, *(Bilanz)* debts *(Br.)*, accounts receivable *(US)*; **~verschlechterung** deterioration of currency; **~verschwendung** waste of money, dissipation of funds.

Geldversorgung money supply;
verbesserte ~ money-supply growth;
inländische ~ gefährlich aufblähen to leak damaging into a country's internal money supply; **~ im eisernen Griff (Würgegriff) halten** to keep an iron grip (a stranglehold) on the money supply; **~ der Wirtschaft auf der Steuerseite unterstützen** to copy the management of the money supply on the fiscal side.

Geld|versorgungspolitik betreiben, zurückhaltende to curb the money supply; **~verteilung** division of money; **~verteuerung** currency revaluation, up in the cost of money; **~verwalter** treasurer; **~verwaltung übertragen** to hand over the purse strings; **~verzinsung** money interest; **~volumen** volume of money, money supply; **~vorrat** *(Geldmarkt)* money supply, *(Bank)* supply of money, cash reserve (in vaults), funds available, pocket, wad *(US sl.)*; **~vorrat einer Bank** cash in vaults *(US)*; **~vorschuß** advance of money, cash advance; **~waage** coin balance; **gepanzerter ~wagen** turtle *(sl.)*; **~währung** monetary standard; **~wechselgeschäft** exchange business; **~wechseln** money changing; **j. beim ~wechseln übers Ohr hauen** to ring the changes *(sl.)*; **~wechsler** money dealer (agent, changer), bill (money) broker.

Geldwert value of money, monetary (money) value, *(Hypothek)* intangible value, *(Wert in Geld)* cash value;
dem ~ nach in terms of money;
abnehmender ~ monetary erosion;
~ haben to be worth money.

geldwert, von ~er Art of pecuniary condition.

Geldwert|änderungen changes in the value of money; **~beständigkeit** currency stability; **~korrektur** monetary correction; **~minderung** depreciation of money; **~rückgang** fall in the value of money; **~schuld** pecuniary obligation; **~schwankungen** fluctuations in the value of money, monetary fluctuation; **~stabilität** stability of money, currency stability; **~theorie** commodity theory of money; **~verlust** fall (loss) in the value of money; **~verschlechterung** deterioration of the value of money.

Geld|wesen monetary matters, money system, finance; **~wirtschaft** money economy, monetary economics, finance.

geldwirtschaftlich, in ~er Hinsicht in the monetary sphere.

Geld|zähler receiving (money) teller; **~zahlung** cash payment; **~zählung** counting money, tale; **~zeichen** token; **~zentrum** money center *(US)* (centre, *Br.*); **~zins** interest on money, rate of interest; **~zirkulation** circulation of money (bank notes), currency of bank notes (money), capital flow; **~zufluß, ~zugang** influx (infusion) of money (cash) inflow; **~zunahme** money growth; **~zuschuß** money allowance, additional (extra) pay; **~zuwachs** money growth; **~zuwachsrate** rate of money growth; **~zuweisung, ~zuwendung** appropriation of funds, allowance of money.

gelegen situated, sided, located *(US)*, *(günstig)* opportune, convenient, fit, proper, suitable;
außerhalb ~ outlying, out-of-town; **am Berghang ~** on the mountain side; **günstig ~** fairly situated; **hoch ~** high up; **am höchsten ~** uppermost; **an der See ~** seaside; **an der Straße ~** near the road; **weit ~** far;
jem. sehr ~ kommen to suit s. o. perfectly; **~ sein** to be situated (located, *US*); **schön ~ sein** to be in a pleasant situation; **jem. viel am Verkauf ~ sein** to be anxious to sell;
einsam ~er Bauernhof lonely farmstead; **ruhig ~e Wohnung** flat in a quiet neighbo(u)rhood; **zu ~er Zeit** in due time.

Gelegenheit chance, opportunity, occasion, opening, turn, bargain, crack *(coll.)*, convenience *(coll.)*, room;
bei ~ as occasion arises; **bei anderen ~en** at other times; **bei besonderen ~en** occasional; **bei erster ~** at the first opportunity, at your earliest convenience; **bei jeder ~** on all occasions; **bei passender ~** when occasion serves; **bei jeder passenden und unpassenden ~** at the drop of a hat *(US coll.)*;
außergewöhnliche ~ exceptional opportunity; **besondere ~** special occasion, bargain; **einmalige ~** once-in-a-lifetime opportunity; **ergriffene ~** catch; **feierliche ~** state occasion; **günstige (gute) ~** good opportunity, advantage, vantage, chance, clear swing *(US)*, break *(US)*, innings *(Br.)*;
~ zu laufenden Kontaktmöglichkeiten opportunity for roll-over contacts;
günstige ~ abwarten to wait (bide) one's time; **~ benutzen** to profit by an opportunity; **günstige ~ benutzen** to take advantage of (improve the) occasion, to avail o. s. of an opportunity; **günstige ~ beim Schopf ergreifen** to jump at a bargain, to leap at an opportunity, to take time by the forelock, to avail o. s. of an opportunity; **~ zur Rückfahrt finden** to have a lift home; **jem. die ~ geben** to afford s. o. the opportunity; **jem. laufend ~ zur Verbesserung seiner Französischkenntnisse gewähren** to allow s. o. every facility for improving his French; **sich eine ~ entgehen lassen** to let an opportunity slip, to miss one's mark; **~ ungenutzt lassen** to pass up the chance; **von einer sich bietenden ~ bereitwillig Gebrauch machen** to embrace an opportunity; **von einer ~ profitieren** to improve the shining hour *(fam.)*; **günstige ~ verpassen (vorübergehen lassen)** to miss one's chance (the bus, *sl.*); **jem. eine ~ verschaffen** to provide an opportunity for s. o.; **günstige ~ wahrnehmen** to seize an opportunity, to take one's chance; **auf eine ~ warten** to wait for an opening.

Gelegenheits|agent casual agent; **~arbeit** odd job, casual (occasional) labo(u)r (employment), temporary work, jobbing, char *(Br.)*, chore *(US)*; **~arbeiten verrichten** to do odd jobs, to job; **~arbeiter** casual, casual worker (labo(u)rer, employee), occasional hand, handyman, jobber, jobbing man, knockabout *(Australia)*; **~auftrag** odd job, hack, jack, floater *(US)*; **~bekanntschaft** chance acquaintance, pickup; **~bekanntschaften** ships that pass in the night; **~beschäftigung** casual employment (occupation), irregular employment, odd job, char *(Br.)*, chore *(US)*; **~besuch** occasional (accidental) visit; **~dichter** part-time poet; **~dieb** sneak thief; **~einnahmen** casual emoluments; **~expedition** special (private) carrier; **~frachtführer** special (private) carrier; **~gedicht** occasional poem; **~geschäft** bargain, good deal, joint adventure *(US)*; **~geschenk** occasional gift; **~gesellschaft** single adventure *(Br.)*, particular (occasional, special) partnership, joint (casual) adventure *(US)*, joint enterprise; **~gewinn** casual profit; **günstiger ~kauf** [good] bargain, chance (bargain, casual) sale, chance purchase, pickup; **~kauf auf einer Auktion machen** to pick up a bargain at an auction; **Reste und ~käufe** remnants and oddments; **~käufer** shoppers on the lookout for a bargain; **~kunde** casual (stray, street) customer; **~politiker** political Jack; **~schauspieler** utility man; **~schiffahrt** occasional navigation; **~schriftsteller** occasional writer; **~spediteur** special (private) carrier; **~täter** infrequent offender; **~trinker** social drinker; **~verbrecher** casual criminal; **~verkauf** casual sale.

gelegentlich from time to time, at one's convenience, casual, occasional, incidental, at one's leisure;
~e Anfälle occasional fits; **~e Ausgaben** casual expenses, incidentals; **~e Bemerkung** occasional remark; **~e Beschäftigung** casual employment; **~er Kunde** stray (street) customer; **~er Leser** casual (occasional) reader; **~es Wetten** casual betting.

gelehrt erudite, learned;
~e Abhandlung scholarly essay (treatise); **~e Gesellschaft** learned society.

Gelehrten|dünkel donnish conceit; **~familie** family of scholars; **in ~kreisen** among scholars; **~welt** commonwealth of learning.

Gelehrter scholar, man of letters, learned (professional) man, erudite;
ausdauernder ~ hard student; **gebildeter ~** accomplished scholar; **großer ~** fine scholar;
bedeutender ~ sein to be no mean scholar.

Geleier, das endlose ~ des Pfarrers the parson's endless drone.

Geleise track, line, road, permanent way *(Br.)*, *(fig.)* groove; **ausgefahrene** ~ beaten track; **gewohntes** ~ rut;
im gewohnten ~ bleiben to travel in the same groove; **j. aus seinem ~ bringen** to lift s. o. out of the rut; **alles wieder ins ~ bringen** to put right, to fix everything *(US)*.

Geleit escort, escorting party, convoy;
zum ~ *(Buch)* prefatory note, foreword;
freies (sicheres) ~ safe conduct; **letztes** ~ funeral procession; **j. das ~ geben** to escort (accompany) s. o.; **jem. das ~ zum Bahnhof geben** to see s. o. off at the station; **jem. das letzte ~ geben** to pay the last hono(u)rs to s. o.; **einer Nachschubkolonne ~ geben** to convoy a supply column; **einem Schiff ~ geben** to escort a ship; **jem. freies ~ gewähren** to grant s. o. safe conduct; **Handelsfahrzeug im ~ eines Zerstörers fahren lassen** to convoy a merchant ship by a destroyer; **unter ~ reisen** to travel under escort;
~boot escort vessel, convoy ship; **~brief** safeguard, protection, pass, [letter of] safe conduct; **~dienst** convoy service.

geleiten to accompany;
Gäste in den Speisesaal ~ to usher guests into the dining room; **nach Hause** ~ to escort (see s. o.) home; **Passagiere zum Flugplatz** ~ to shepherd passengers to an airline; **j. an seinen Platz** ~ to show s. o. to his place; **schützend** ~ to convoy.

geleitet headed, directed;
wirkungsvoll ~ efficiently run.

Geleit|fahrzeug escort vessel, convoy ship; **~flugzeug** escort plane; **~flugzeugträger** escort carrier; **~mannschaft** escorting party; **~schein** pass, passport, navicert, transire; **~schiff** escort vessel, convoy ship; **~schutz** escort, convoy, screen; **~schutzaufgabe** escort duty; **~wort** preface, foreword; **~zettel** navicert, transire, certificate; **~zerstörer** destroyer escort.

Geleitzug convoy, escort, fleet train;
~ mit Unterseebooten angreifen to attack a convoy by submarines; **Truppentransport im ~ über den Atlantik eskortieren** to convoy troop ships across the Atlantic; **im ~ fahren** to sail under convoy; **~ festhalten** to block a convoy; **~ zusammenstellen** to assemble a convoy;
~schiff convoy ship, escort vessel.

Gelenk joint, knuckle, hinge;
kardanisches ~ Cardan joint;
~fahrzeug articulated vehicle.

gelenkige Finger nimble fingers.

Gelenkkupplung flexible coupling.

gelenkt *(Preise)* controlled, administered;
~e Wirtschaft controlled (directed) economy.

gelernt skilled, trained.

gelesen|und genehmigt read and approved; **nie** ~ *(Anzeige)* chunk;
viel ~ haben to have turned many books in one's life.

Gelichter riff-raff, rabble.

geliefert delivered;
verzollt ~ delivered customs cleared;
~ sein *(erledigt)* to have had it, to be dished *(sl.)*;
~e Waren goods sold and delivered; **noch nicht ~e Waren** undelivered goods.

geliehen on loan, borrowed.

gelinde gentle, mild, soft;
um es ~ auszudrücken to put it mild[ly];
mit ~m Grausen with a touch of horror; **~re Saiten aufziehen** to come down a peg or two; **~ Strafe** mild (slight) punishment; **von ~r Wut gepackt** thoroughly angry.

Gelingen, gutes best of luck;
einem Unternehmen gutes ~ wünschen to wish an enterprise every success.

gelingen, schlecht to turn out badly; **vortrefflich** ~ to be a notable success.

gellen to shrill, to pierce;
in den Ohren ~ to make one's ears ring.

gellend piercing, shrill;
~ lachen to shriek with laughter;
~es Gelächter screeching laughter; **~er Schrei** piercing scream.

geloben to vow, to pledge;
feierlich ~ to swear a solemn oath; **~, Stillschweigen zu bewahren** to make a solemn promise to observe secrecy; **ewige Treue** ~ to swear eternal fidelity.

Gelöbnis vow, solemn promise.

gelöscht *(Waren)* landed.

gelten to be regarded as, *(gültig sein)* to be in force (effective, valid, operative, in operation), to rule, to run, to hold true, *(Münze)* to pass, to be current, *(Text)* to prevail, *(wert sein)* to be worth (valid), to sell at a price, to hold good;
vom ersten April an ~ to operate as from (of, *US*) the first of April; **als ausgemacht** ~ to be taken for granted; **als eingebildet** ~ to be regarded as conceited; **als nicht eingereicht** ~ to be regarded as never being submitted; **als Geizkragen** ~ to have the reputation of being a miser; **bis H** ~ *(Fahrkarte)* to read to H; **jeweils** ~ to be applicable for the time being; **nicht mehr** ~ *(Gesetz)* to be no longer operative, *(Paß)* to be no longer valid; **heute nicht mehr** ~ to be no longer applicable; **noch** ~ to hold good; **nur für Normalfälle** ~ to apply only to normal cases; **als reich** ~ to pass for a rich man; **als richtig** ~ to be deemed to be true; **sinngemäß** ~ to apply analogously; **als Sonderfall** ~ to be treated as an exceptional case; **als Sonderling** ~ to be looked upon as eccentric; **überall** ~ to hold in all cases; **viel bei jem.** ~ to carry weight with s. o.; **bis auf weiteres** ~ to hold good until further notice; **bei jem. wenig** ~ to count for little with s. o.; **~ lassen** to let pass; **seinen Fehler ~ lassen** to acknowledge the corn *(coll.)*.

geltend acknowledged, *(Gesetz)* effective, in force (operation), operative, valid, *(Münze)* current, *(Sitte)* prevailing;
nicht ~ gemacht unclaimed;
~e Bestimmungen current regulations; **~er Lohntarif** prevailing rate; **~e Meinung** prevailing opinion; **~e Preise** ruling (current) prices; **~es Recht** law in force; **~er Vertrag** valid contract; **~es Völkerrecht** accepted international law; **~e Währung** legal tender, lawful money *(US)*.

geltend machen to enforce, to put forward, to assert, to file, *(Forderung im Konkursverfahren)* to prove;
Anspruch ~ to lodge (assert) a claim; **seinen Einfluß** ~ to use (exercise) one's influence, to make one's influence felt; **Einrede** ~ to enter a plea; **Einwand** ~ to raise an objection; **als Entschuldigung** ~ to plead as excuse; **Forderung** ~ to enforce a claim; **gerichtlich** ~ to go to law; **seine Gründe** ~ to defend one's case; **seine Rechte** ~ to vindicate (insist on) one's rights; **Verjährung** ~ to plead the statute of limitations.

Geltendmachung enforcement, assertion, insistence;
gerichtliche ~ enforcement through a court; **nachträgliche** ~ subsequent claim; **rechtzeitge** ~ vigilance; **verspätete** ~ laches; **~ eines Anspruchs** raising (assertion) of a claim; **~ von Einfluß** exercise of influence; **~ einer Einrede** entering a plea; **~ einer Forderung** enforcement (lodging) of a claim; **~ seines Rechts** vindication of one's rights; **~ eines Unterhaltsanspruchs** recovery of maintenance; **~ eines Vermieterpfandrechts** distress for nonpayment of rent; **~ eines Vorrechts** exercise of a privilege; **~ des Zeugnisverweigerungsrechts** plea of the privilege *(US)*;
gerichtliche ~ des Schadens ausschließen to preclude recovery by suit.

Geltung *(Ansehen)* repute, authority, standing, credit, value, account, operation, *(Bedeutung)* consequence, weight, importance, *(Gültigkeit)* effect, force, validity, *(Münze)* currency; **allgemeine** ~ currency, general acceptance; **subsidiäre** ~ subsidiary force;
~ eines Landes in der Welt prestige of a country;
~ behalten to remain valid; **zur ~ bringen** to assert, to put forward, to enforce; **sich zur ~ bringen** to assert o. s., to throw one's weight; **seine Worte zur ~ bringen** to emphasize one's words; **~ erlangen** to become effective; **~ haben** to be in force (valid, operative), to run, to take effect; **allgemeine ~ haben** to be generally accepted; **keine ~ mehr haben** to be inoperative (no longer in operation); **noch ~ haben** to be still in effect; **zur ~ kommen** to become effective, *(Theorie)* to win recognition, to gain acceptance; **in der Masse kaum zur ~ kommen** to be hardly noticed in the crowd; **vorteilhaft zur ~ kommen** to show to advantage; **in ~ sein** to be valid; **seine ~ verlieren** *(Land)* to suffer loss of prestige; **sich ~ verschaffen** to make one's personality felt, to establish a reputation for o. s.; **einem Gesetz ~ verschaffen** to enforce a law; **sich zur ~ zu bringen wissen** to know how to put o. s. in a good light.

Geltungsbedürfnis egotism, egoism, self-assertion;
~ haben to assert o. s., to hanker after appreciation, to have a craving for praise.

Geltungsbereich *(Abkommen)* area, coverage, scope, territory covered, sphere of operation, *(Anwendungsgebiet)* range (field) of application, *(Banknoten)* currency, *(Gericht)* competence, jurisdiction, *(Gesetz)* purview, scope, range;
räumlicher ~ territorial application, area of applicability; **sich überschneidender** ~ overlapping coverage;
~ eines Abkommens scope of a convention; **~ eines Vertrages** operation of a treaty;
in den ~ eines Gesetzes fallen to come within the purview of a law, to be located in the area in which a law is valid.

Geltungsdauer [duration of] validity, force, *(Patent)* life;
~ **eines Nutzungsrechts** running of a benefit;
~ **von einem Monat haben** to be valid for a month.
Geltungs|frage *(pol.)* matter of prestige; ~**gebiet** area, territory covered, coverage, scope; ~**konsum** conspicuous consumption.
Gelübde *(Religion)* vow;
~ **ablegen** to take a vow; **durch ein ~ gebunden sein** to be under a vow.
gelüftet, nicht unventilated.
gelungen successful, *(erheiternd)* amusing, capital, funny;
~ **aussehen** to look too funny for words;
~**e Arbeit** successful piece of work; ~**e Geschichte** capital story.
Gelüst itch, craving, desire, appetite.
GEMA [etwa] Performing Rights Society *(Br.)*.
Gemächer, sich in seine ~ zurückziehen to retire to one's private quarters.
gemächlich easy-going;
~ **leben** to take things easy;
~**es Leben führen** to lead an easy life; ~**er Spaziergang** gentle stroll; **in ~em Tempo** leisurely.
Gemahl consort, spouse, husband.
Gemälde painting, picture;
~ **erstellen** to execute a painting (portrait); ~ **für echt halten** to take a painting for genuine;
~**ausstellung** exhibition of paintings; ~**galerie** art (portrait) gallery; ~**sammlung** collection of paintings.
Gemarkung boundary, bounds.
gemäß pursuant, accordant (in accordance) with, according to, subject to, in compliance with;
~ **Ihren Anordnungen** in compliance with your instructions; ~ **den nachfolgenden Bestimmungen** as hereinafter provided; **seinen Mitteln ~ beitragen** to contribute according to one's means; **einem Vertrag ~ handeln** to act in conformity with a contract.
gemäßigt moderate, temperate;
~**e politische Anschauungen** moderate political views; ~**es Klima** temperate climate; ~**e Linke** left centre *(Br.)* (center, *US*); ~**e Partei** moderate party.
Gemäßigter *(Politik)* moderate, centrist.
gemein *(allgemein)* universal, general, public, common, *(einfach)* ordinary, common, *(ordinär)* vulgar, plebeian, indecent, low, filthy, dirty, *(unfair)* dirty, low, ugly, little, menial;
j. ~ behandeln to treat s. o. shabbily, to play the dirty on s. o. *(Br.)*; **viel ~ haben** to have much in common; **sich ~ machen** to make o. s. cheap; **sich mit jem. ~ machen** to be sociable with s. o.;
~**er Ausdruck** vulgar expression; ~**es Benehmen** unrefined manners; ~**er Bruch** vulgar fraction; ~**er Handelswert** common market value; ~**e Handlung** mean action; ~**er Kerl** nasty fellow (specimen), heel *(US)*; **der ~e Mann** the man in the street; ~**er Soldat** private; ~**e Sprache** coarse language; ~**er Streich** dirty trick; **jem. einen ~en Streich spielen** to play a shabby trick on s. o.; **das ~e Volk** the lower classes; ~**er Wert** principal value, market value; ~**er Witz** indecent (blue, *Br.*) joke; **für das ~e Wohl** for the common good (weal).
Gemein|benutzungsrecht common right; ~**besitz** joint ownership; ~**betrieb** public utility [undertaking].
Gemeinde community, [civil] parish, borough *(Br.)*, local government unit *(US)*, municipality, *(Kirche)* parish, body of worshippers;
zur Stadt erhobene ~ township *(Br.)*, incorporated town *(US)*; **grenznahe ~** frontier district; **hebeberechtigte ~** rating authority; **kreisangehörige ~** noncountry borough, urban district *(Br.)*; **kreisfreie ~** county borough; **ländliche ~** rural community, village *(US)*; **städtische ~** municipality, township *(Br.)*, incorporated town *(US)*;
einer ~ Requisitionen auferlegen to make requisitions upon a community; **~ besichtigen** to perambulate the parish; **der ~ zur Last fallen** to become chargeable to (a charge upon, to go on) the parish *(Br.)*, to come upon the town (parish) *(US)*; **von der ~ unterhalten werden** to be (go) on the parish.
Gemeindeabgaben local (borough, municipal, county) rates *(Br.)*, municipal (local) taxes *(US)*, town dues, parochial rates;
vorteilhafte ~ remunerative duties;
Vergünstigungen bei den ~ beantragen to claim rating relief *(Br.)*.
gemeindeabgabenbegünstigt rate-aided *(Br.)*.
Gemeindeabgaben|pflichtiger ratepayer *(Br.)*; ~**system** rating system.
Gemeinde|abwässerverband sewage disposal district; ~**acker**, ~**anger** common, village green; ~**amt** municipal (local government) office; ~**angelegenheiten** parochial business, business of the community, community (municipal, county) affairs; ~**angestellter** local government officer *(Br.)*, municipal employee *(US)*; ~**anleihe** municipal *(US)* (local-authority, *Br.*) loan; ~**arbeiter** municipal worker; ~**aufgabe** corporate purpose *(Br.)*, local government function; ~**aufsichtsbehörde** local government supervisory board; ~**ausgaben** municipal expenses; ~**aushang** community bulletin board; ~**ausschuß** local board *(Br.)*, board of supervisors *(US)*; ~**autonomie** local self-government; ~**bank** municipal bank; ~**beamter** municipal officer *(US)*, parish officer (clerk) *(Br.)*, parochial officer, local government officer *(Br.)*; ~**behörde** municipal corporation (authority, *US*), corporate (parish) authority *(Br.)*, local government *(Br.)*; ~**beschluß** council's resolution; ~**bestimmungsrecht** local option; ~**betrieb** communal undertaking, communal (municipal, civil) enterprise, municipal undertaking; ~**bezirk** community (county, *Br.*) district, parish, borough *(Br.)*; ~**blättchen** parish magazine; ~**bürger** freeman; ~**bürgerrecht** freedom of the borough *(Br.)*; ~**diener** beadle; ~**dienste** municipal services.
gemeindeeigen municipal, owned by the parish.
Gemeinde|eigentum common [property], municipal property; ~**eigentum privatisieren** to enclose common land; ~**einheit** local unit; ~**einnahmen** revenue of the city council, local revenue; ~**einrichtung** communal organization (institution); ~**einwohner** local resident; ~**entwicklung** community development; ~**finanzen** local government (municipal) finance; ~**fürsorge** parochial relief, community care; ~**gebiet** rating area *(Br.)*; ~**gefängnis** county jail *(US)*; ~**grenzen** parochial boundaries, boundaries of a municipality, corporate limits; ~**grundstück** community land; ~**gruppe** community group; ~**gut** common; ~**haus** town house (hall), meeting hall, *(Kirche)* parish house; ~**haushalt** local government (municipal) budget; ~**haushaltungen belasten** to burden the finances of the communities; ~**haushaltswesen** local *(Br.)* (municipal, *US*) budgeting; ~**helfer** *(Kirche)* lay worker; ~**hoheit** local self-government; ~**kasse** borough fund; ~**kirchenrat** parochial council *(Br.)*; ~**land** common, common land (field, ground), public (communal) land, townland; ~**lasten** municipal charges; ~**leben** communal life; **am ~leben regen Anteil nehmen** to move into the center of common affairs; ~**lehrling** parish apprentice *(Br.)*; ~**liste** *(Wahl)* local list; ~**mitglied** corporate member, parishioner; ~**obligationen** local improvement *(Br.)* (municipal, *US*) bonds; ~**ordnung** local byelaw *(Br.)*, municipal ordinance (charter) *(US)*, Local Government Act *(Br.)*; ~**organisation** communal organization; ~**pfarrer** parish priest; ~**pflege** parish welfare; ~**politik** local politics; **engstirnige ~politik** vestrydom; ~**polizei** country constabulary, city police; ~**polizist** parish (county) constable (officer); ~**prüfungsamt** internal audit office *(Br.)*.
Gemeinderat parish (local) council *(Br.)*, local (municipal) board, *(Kirche)* court of assistance, *(Stadtrat)* borough council *(Br.)*, city *(US)* (municipal, town) council, urban council *(Br.)*; **vom ~ gebilligt werden** to go through the town council.
Gemeinderats|beschluß council resolution; ~**mitglied** member of a local council *(Br.)*, [common] councilman *(US)*, parish councillor *(Br.)*, capital inhabitant *(Br.)*, municipal councillor; ~**sitz** municipal seat; ~**sitzung** parish *(Br.)*, (town, *US*) meeting; ~**wahlen** municipal *(US)* (local, *Br.*) elections.
Gemeinde|rechnungsprüfer internal auditor *(Br.)*; ~**recht** local government *(Br.)* (municipal) law, local law *(US)*; ~**saal** parish (common) hall; ~**satzung** city (municipal) ordinance *(US)*, charter of a borough, local byelaw *(Br.)*, municipal charter *(US)*; ~**schreiber** parish clerk *(Br.)*; ~**schulden** municipal (local) debts; ~**schule** parish (public, *Br.*, parochial, council) school, proprietary establishment; ~**schwester** parish (district, visiting) nurse; ~**sekretär** parish clerk *(Br.)*; ~**sitzung** parish *(Br.)* (town, *US*) meeting; ~**statut** municipal ordinance (charter) *(US)*, local statute (byelaw) *(Br.)*.
Gemeindesteuer|n local (municipal) taxes *(US)*, municipal (local, borough) rates *(Br.)*;
landwirtschaftliche Grundstücke von der ~ befreien to derate agricultural land *(Br.)*;
~**betrag** rating *(Br.)*; ~**einnehmer** rate collector *(Br.)*; ~**pflichtiger** common (general) vestry *(Br.)*; ~**system** rating *(Br.)* (local tax, municipal tax, *US*) system; ~**zahler** ratepayer *(Br.)*.
Gemeinde|straße country (local) road; ~**tafel** community bulletin board; ~**tag** [etwa] National Association of Parish Councils *(Br.)*; ~**umlage** municipal (borough) rates *(Br.)*, local assessment; ~**umlagengesetz** Rating Act *(Br.)*; ~**unterstützung**

parish (poor) relief *(Br.)*; **auf ~unterstützung angewiesen sein** to be thrown upon the parish (town, *US*); **~veranlagung** local assessment; **~veranstaltung** municipal function; **~verband** municipal corporation *(US)*, [etwa] National Association of Parish Councils *(Br.)*; **~verbindungsweg** third-class road; **~verfassung** local constitution (ordinance) *(US)*, local byelaw *(Br.)*, municipal charter (ordinance) *(US)*; **~vermögen** municipal (corporate, *Br.*) property; **~versammlung** parish (town, *US*) meeting; **~vertretung** parish (local) council *(Br.)*, municipal council *(US)*; **~verwaltung** municipal *(US)* (county) government, municipal administration, local authorities (government) *(Br.)*, town management *(US)*, municipality, civic authorities; **~verwaltungsbeamter** parish officer (clerk) *(Br.)*, town clerk *(US)*; **~vorstand** community council; **~vorsteher** mayor, reeve *(Br.)*, town council (clerk, *Br.*); **~wahlberechtigter** parochial (local) elector; **~wahlen** local *(Br.)* (municipal, *US*) elections; **~wähler** local (parochial) elector; **~wahlliste** parish (burgess) list; **~wald** communal forest; **~weg** common way; **~weide, ~wiese** common [land], dole meadow; **zur ~weide zugelassen** commonable; **~wirtschaft** municipal trading; **~zentrum** community center *(US)* (centre, *Br.*), community house *(US)*; **~zoll** town toll; **~zugehörigkeit** *(rel.)* church membership; **~zuschuß** municipal aid; **~zweckverband** union of local administrations.

gemeindlich local, municipal, communal;
~e Gewerbetätigkeit municipal trading; **mit ~er Unterstützung** rate-aided *(Br.)*, on the parish *(Br.)* (town, *US*); **~e Zwecke** municipal purposes.

Gemeineigentum collective goods, public ownership, common property;
ins ~ überführen to communize, to municipalize, to nationalize.

Gemeiner *(mil.)* man.

gemeinfrei in the public domain.

Gemein|freierklärung des Schutzrechtes dedication to the public; **~gebrauch** common (public) use; **~gefahr** danger to life and limb.

gemeingefährlich constituting a public danger;
~ sein to constitute a public danger, to be dangerous to the public;
~es Verbrechen felony; **~er Verbrecher** dangerous criminal, public enemy *(US)*.

Gemein|gefährlichkeit public danger; **~gläubiger** *(Konkurs)* creditor at large, general creditor.

gemeingültig generally accepted.

Gemeingut common property (good).

Gemeinheit dirty (nasty) trick, nastiness, rottenness;
~en sagen to make nasty remarks; **sich die größten ~en an den Kopf werfen** to hurl the crudest abuses at one another.

Gemeininteresse public interest.

Gemeinkosten fixed (general, apportionable, indirect) costs, dead charges, overhead[s] [expenses], general (indirect) expenses, oncost *(Br.)*, burden;
abschreibungsfähige ~ overheads liable to depreciation; **steuerlich anerkannte ~** relief for overheads, tax overheads *(US)*; **zu hoch angesetzte ~** overabsorbed charges; **zu niedrig angesetzte ~** underabsorbed charges; **anteilige ~** pro rata overheads; **auf die Abteilungen aufgeschlüsselte ~** departmental burden; **verrechnete ~** applied cost, absorbed expenses (burden);
~ umlegen to allocate general expenses;
~abweichung overhead variance; **~ansatz** assessment of overheads; **~anteil** overhead rate, share of overheads; **~aufteilung** overhead allocation, burden adjustment; **~konto** overhead charges account; **~löhne** indirect labo(u)r cost; **~material** indirect (nonproductive) material; **~satz** overhead rate; **~überdeckung** overabsorbed overheads (burden); **~umlage** overhead distribution, apportionment of indirect costs; **~unterdeckung** underabsorbed burden (overheads); **~verrechnungsbasis** burden base; **~verrechnungssatz** burden absorption rate; **~zuschlag** plant-wide burden rate.

Gemein|last *(Versicherung)* common burden; **~nutz** commonweal, public weal, common (general) welfare.

gemeinnützig nonprofit-making, public-minded, for the public weal;
nicht ~ noncharitable;
~er Betrieb nonprofit (public-service) enterprise *(US)*; **~e Einrichtung** public utility, charitable institution, welfare organization (institution); **gebührenfreie ~e Einrichtung** pure charity; **~er Fonds** charity fund; **~e Gesellschaft** nonprofit corporation *(US)*; **~es Krankenhaus** nonprofit hospital; **~es Unternehmen** nonprofit-making (public-utility) undertaking, public institution; **~e Vereinigung** charitable corporation; **in ~er Weise** on a nonprofit basis; **~er Zweck** public purpose.

Gemeinnützigkeit public-mindedness, charity, *(Kommunalvermögen)* public capacity;
~ einer Zuwendung charitable nature of a gift;
~ zuerkennen to hold to be charitable.

Gemein|nützigkeitsverordnung Charities Act *(Br.)*; **~platz** truism, commonplace, platitude, stereotype, cliché, copybook maxim, bromide *(US)*.

gemeinsam joint, joint and several, jointly, conjoint, [in] common, conjunct *(Scot.)*, general, combined, collective, mutual;
~ besitzen to be joint owners, to hold in common; **Haus ~ besitzen** to own a house jointly; **~ erben** to inherit jointly; **vieles ~ haben** to have a lot of things in common; **~ haften** to be jointly and severally liable; **etw. ~ tun** to do s. th. as a body; **~ vorgehen** to take joint action;
~er Agrarfonds *(EG)* Joint Agricultural Funds; **~e Anmelder** joint applicants; **~e Anschaffungen** jointly acquired property; **~e Anstrengungen** united efforts; **~es Arbeitsverhältnis** common service; **~er Ausschuß** joint committee; **~e Bemühungen** combined efforts; **~es Benutzungsrecht** right of common; **~e Beschwerde** joint complaint; **~er Betrieb** joint operation (working); **~er Botschafter** joint ambassador; **~er Eigentümer** joint owner; **~es Einkommen** *(Eheleute)* combined income; **~e Entschließung** *(parl.)* joint resolution; **~e Erbschaft** joint heritage *(US)*; **~e Erfindung** joint invention; **~e Erklärung** joint statement; **~er Fonds** joint stock, community fund; **~es Forschungsunternehmen** joint research; **unser ~er Freund** our mutual friend; **~e Gefahr** *(Havarie)* common danger (peril); **~es Gesundheitsprogramm verschiedener Unternehmen** cooperative health plan; **~er Gläubiger** joint creditor; **~e Grundlage** common ground; **~e Haftung** joint [and several] liability, joint responsibility; **~e Haushaltsführung** joint household; **~e Interessen** mutual (common) interests; **~e Interessen haben** to have interests in common; **~e Kasse** common purse; **~e Kasse machen** to put one's funds in common; **~es Konto** joint (participation) account; **~ anfallende Kosten** common expenses; **~e Leitung** joint management; **~e Mahlzeit** communal meal; **~er Markt** Common Market; **dem ~en Markt beitreten** to joint the Common Market; **~e Maßnahmen** concerted action; **~er Nenner** common denominator; **auf ~e Rechnung** on joint account; **~e Sache mit jem. machen** to join hands (make common cause, act in common) with s. o.; **~er Schlichter** joint arbitrator; **~e Schritte unternehmen** to take joint action; **~e Schuld** joint debt; **~er Schuldner** joint debtor; **~e Sitzung** joint meeting, *(parl.)* joint session; **~es Stellenvermittlungsbüro** joint hiring hall *(US)*; **~ begangene Straftat** joint offence; **~es Testament** joint will; **~es Unternehmen** joint venture; **~er Verhandlungsausschuß** joint negotiating panel; **~es Vermögen** joint property; **~e Versammlung** *(ECU)* Common Assembly; **~er Vertreter** joint agent; **~e Visitenkarte** collective card; **~es Vorgehen** joint (concerted, combined) action, joint operation; **~er Warenbezug** cooperative buying; **~es Ziel** common goal.

Gemeinschaft community, fraternal group, collective, fellowship, *(EG)* Community, *(Handel)* cooperative, partnership, *(Verband)* association;
in ~ mit in cooperation, jointly; **in ungeteilter ~** in common; **Atlantische ~** Atlantic Community; **eheliche ~** conjugal community; **Europäische ~** European Community; **häusliche ~** joint household, domestic life;
~ nach Bruchteilen community by undivided shares; **~ zur gesamten Hand** joint ownership; **Europäische ~ für Kohle und Stahl** European Coal and Steel Community;
einer ~ Requisitionen auferlegen to make requisitions upon a community; **in eine ~ aufnehmen** to fellowship *(US)*; **mit jem. in ~ leben** to live in close companionship with s. o.

gemeinschaftlich in common, joint[ly], conjointly, general, combined, collective, concerted, cooperative;
~ handeln to take joint action; **Kosten ~ tragen** to share the expenses; **~ verklagt werden** to be sued jointly;
~er Abschluß joint bargain; **~er Anspruch** joint right; **~ Bedachte** joint beneficiaries; **in ~em Besitz** in common; **~es Depot** joint deposit; **~e Eigentümer** joint owners; **~ begangene unerlaubte Handlung** joint tort; **~es Konto** joint account; **~e Nutznießung** joint use, common user; **~es Nutznießungsrecht am Grundbesitz** right of common; **~e Versorgungsgüter** common supplies; **~er Vertrag** joint contract; **~er Vertrieb** cooperative distribution; **~es Vorgehen** concerted (joint, combined) action; **~er Zustellungsdienst** cooperative delivery.

Gemeinschafts|abkommen joint venture agreement; ~**anlage** collectively owned installation; ~**anschluß** *(Telefon)* party line; ~**antenne** shared (combined) aerial, community antenna; ~**arbeit** combined (coop) work, teamwork, bandwork, *(Autoren)* composite work, joint authorship; ~**aufgabe** joint task; ~**ausgaben** *(EG)* Community expenses; ~**besitz** joint ownership; ~**besteller** *(Zeitung)* joint subscribers; ~**beteiligung** joint venture; ~**betrieb** joint operation (working), common enterprise.

gemeinschaftsbewußt community-conscious.

Gemeinschafts|bewußtsein community consciousness; ~**beziehungen** *(EG)* Community relations; ~**bilanz** consolidated balance sheet; ~**depot** joint deposit, alternative safe-custody *(Br.)* (custodianship, *US*) account; ~**dienst** community service; ~**ebene** *(EG)* at Community level; ~**eigentum** community of goods, collective ownership, ownership in common, community estate, *(Grundstück)* tenancy in common; ~**einkauf** group (combine) buying, joint purchase, cooperative purchasing, collective shopping, *(unabhängiger Einzelhändler)* voluntary chain; ~**einkäufer** group buyer; ~**einrichtungen** community institutions; ~**erfindung** joint invention; ~**erholung** collective recreation; ~**erziehung** co-education; ~**etat** *(EG)* Community budget; ~**farm** collective farm; ~**felder** open fields.

gemeinschaftsfeindlich antisocial.

Gemeinschafts|finanzierung group financing; ~**fonds** joint stock, pool, mutual trust *(US)*; ~**forschung** joint research; ~**foto** *(Journalismus)* pool photo; ~**gefühl** communal sense, community consciousness; ~**geist** team spirit; ~**geschäfte** business on joint account, syndicate transactions; ~**gründung** joint establishment; ~**güter** collective goods; ~**haus** community (neighbo(u)rhood) house; ~**hilfe** mutual assistance, *(EG)* Community aid; ~**kandidat** joint nominee; ~**kapital** pooled fund; ~**kasse** common fund; ~**kauf** combine (group) buying, cooperative purchasing, collective shopping; ~**käufer** *(pl.)* group buyers; ~**klage** class action; ~**kontenrahmen** uniform system of accounts; ~**kontingent** *(EG)* Community quota; ~**konto** joint (community) account; **eheliches** ~**konto** husband-and-wife joint account; ~**konto mit Verfügungsrecht der Überlebenden** survivorship account; ~**kredit** joint and several (syndicate) credit; ~**küche** communal canteen (kitchen); ~**leben** community life; ~**maßnahmen** *(EG)* Community action; ~**organ** *(EG)* Community organ (institution); ~**patent** joint patent; ~**planung** *(Betrieb)* group policy; ~**police** joint policy, *(Betrieb)* group policy; ~**politik** *(EG)* Community policy; ~**präferenzen** *(EG)* Community preferences; ~**preise** *(EG)* Community prices; ~**produktion** coproduction; ~**projekt** community project; ~**raum** common room, *(Hotel)* lounge, *(Universität)* combination room *(Br.)*; ~**recht** *(EG)* Community law; ~**reise** group trip, organized (packaged, *US*) tour; ~**rente** group (joint) annuity; ~**schaltung** *(Fernsehstation)* linkup, *(Rundfunkstationen)* hookup; ~**schuld** *(Ehepaar)* community debt; ~**schule** nondenominational (desegregation) school, mixed school *(Br.)*; ~**sekretariat** typing (secretarial, typists') pool; ~**sendung** *(Rundfunk)* full net, hookup, *(Fernsehen)* linkup; ~**sinn** public spirit; ~**steuer** *(EG)* Community tax; ~**strafe** joint fine; ~**täter** joint tortfeasors; ~**unternehmen** joint undertaking (enterprise, venture), joint adventure *(US)*, cooperative venture; ~**unternehmungen** community works; ~**unterricht** group instruction; ~**verfahren** *(EG)* Community procedure; ~**verhalten** communication behavio(u)r; ~**verkauf** cooperative selling (sales), consolidation sales; ~**vermögen** social wealth; ~**versicherung** group (collective) insurance, *(Kraftfahrzeuge)* fleet insurance; ~**vertrag** joint compact (contract); ~**vertrieb** cooperative marketing; ~**vorhaben** community project, *(ENEA)* joint services; ~**weide** open meadow; ~**werbesendungen** cooperative programme *(Br.)*; ~**werbung** association (group, joint, cooperative, *Br.*, coop) advertising; ~**werbung in Funk und Fernsehen** participating program(me); ~**werbung von Händlern und Herstellern** vertical cooperative advertising; ~**zentrum** community center *(US)* (centre, *Br.*); ~**zollkontingente** *(EG)* Community tariff quotas.

Gemeinschuldner *(Konkurs)* bankrupt merchant, [adjudicated] bankrupt, common debtor *(Scot.)*;
entlasteter ~ discharged (certificated, *Br.*) bankrupt; **nicht entlasteter** ~ undischarged (uncertified, *Br.*) bankrupt; **rehabilitierter** ~ certificated bankrupt *(Br.)*;
Einspruch gegen die Entlassung eines ~**s einlegen** to file an objection to a bankrupt's discharge; ~ **entlasten** to discharge (whitewash, *Br.*) a bankrupt.

Gemein|schuldnerin insolvent company; ~**sinn** public spirit; ~**unkosten** indirect cost, overheads, oncost *(Br.)*, burden.

gemeinverständlich easy to understand, popular;
~ **darstellen** to popularize;
klare und ~**e Anweisungen** plain and popular instructions; ~**es Buch** popular book; ~**er Zeitungsartikel** article written in a popular style.

Gemein|wert common market value; ~**wesen** community; ~**wirtschaft** social economy.

gemeinwirtschaftlich socialized.

Gemeinwirtschaftsbank trade-union bank.

Gemeinwohl common weal, public policy (good);
auf das ~ **bedacht** public-minded (-spirited).

gemessen measured;
~ **an** in terms of; **im Lichten** ~ measured in the clear;
~ **sprechen** to weigh one's words;
~**en Schrittes** with measured steps; **in** ~**en Worten** in well-considered words.

Gemetzel slaughter, butchery, massacre.

gemietet hired.

Gemisch *(Benzin)* mixture, *(Bevölkerung)* motley crowd, *(fig.)* mash;
gasarmes ~ weak mixture.

gemischt mixed, miscellaneous, *(mil.)* combined;
~**er Ausschuß** mixed committee, combined board, joint committee *(Br.)*; ~**er Fonds** *(Kapitalanlagegesellschaft)* mixed fund; ~**e Gesellschaft** mixed company, medley; ~**es Konto** mixed account; **in** ~**en Kreisen verkehren** to associate o. s. with dubious characters; ~**e Ladung** mixed cargo (carload, *US*); ~**e Lebensversicherung auf den Erlebens- und Todesfall** combined endowment and life insurance; ~**e Schiffsversicherung** mixed policy; ~**e Sendung** mixed shipment (carload, *US*); ~**es Sortiment** mixed assortment; ~**e Stichprobe** mixed sample; ~**er Vertrag** mixed contract; ~**e Warensendungen** miscellaneous collections of goods, mixed goods; ~**e Wirtschaftsform** mixed economy; ~**er Zug** mixed train.

Gemischt|bauweise composite construction; ~**unternehmen** all-purpose corporation.

Gemischtwaren groceries, general merchandise *(US)*;
~**geschäft**, ~**handlung**, ~**laden** grocery [business], general shop *(Br.)* (store, *US*), universal provider *(Br.)*, variety store *(US)*; ~**händler** grocer, general dealer *(Br.)*, universal provider *(Br.)*.

gemischtwirtschaftliches Unternehmen semi-public (mixed) enterprise, quasi-public company, mixed ownership property *(US)*.

Gemunkel whispering, *(Gerücht)* gossip.

Gemurmel murmuring.

Gemüse vegetables;
frisches ~ fresh vegetables; **junges** ~ *(fig.)* young folk, small fry; ~**anbau** vegetable growing, truck farming *(US)*; ~**ecke** *(im Garten)* vegetable plot; ~**eintopf** hotpot; ~**garten** kitchen garden; ~**gärtner** trucker, truckster *(US)*; ~**gärtnerei** market garden, grocery store; ~**geschäft** vegetable shop (store), grocery store *(US)*; ~**händler** greengrocer; ~**kost** green food; ~**laden** vegetable shop, grocery store *(US)*; ~**markt** vegetable market; **dünne** ~**suppe** slumgullion *(US sl.)*.

gemustert patterned, *(bedruckt)* printed.

Gemüt mind, disposition, feeling;
ängstliche ~**er** nervous people; **sonniges** ~ cheerful disposition; **aufgeregte** ~**er beruhigen** to pour oil on troubled waters; ~**er der Leser erregen** to arouse the feelings of the readers; **sich etw. zu** ~**e führen** to treat o. s. to s. th.; **sich gelegentlich ein Gläschen zu** ~**e führen** to take a drop now and then; **sich einen Krimi zu** ~**e führen** to afford o. s. the luxury of reading a detective story; **freundliches** ~ **haben** to have a cheerful disposition, to be easy in one's mind; **goldenes** ~ **haben** to have a heart of gold; **harmloses** ~ **haben** to be without malice; **kindliches** ~ **haben** to have the soul of child; **sich bei jem. aufs** ~ **schlagen** to weigh heavily on s. one's mind.

gemütlich cozy, snug, homely, *(Charakter)* good-natured, easy-going;
alles antik ~ all chintz and warming pans;
~ **frühstücken** to have a leisurely breakfast; **es sich** ~ **machen** to make o. s. comfortable; ~ **bei einem Glas Wein zusammensitzen** to relax over a glass of wine;
~**er Abend** pleasant evening; ~**e Ecke** cosy corner; ~**es Leben führen** to live a life of ease; ~**er Spaziergang** stroll; ~**es Stübchen** snuggery; ~**e Tasse Kaffee** quiet cup of coffee.

Gemütlichkeit coziness, snugness, *(Beschaulichkeit)* leisure, *(Mensch)* easygoing disposition;
da hört die ~ **auf** that's the limit (the last straw).

Gemüts|art temperament; ~**bewegung** emotion, affection, chord; **heftige ~bewegung** passion; ~**erschütterung** emotion, trauma.

gemütskrank mentally disordered.

Gemüts|krankheit mental disturbance; ~**mensch** warm-hearted person; ~**ruhe** composure; **in aller ~ruhe zusehen** to watch calmly; ~**verfassung** frame of mind.

Gen gene.

genannt named, called, aforesaid, *(Preis)* nominal;
namentlich nicht ~ unnamed; **oben** ~ above mentioned;
~**er Kurs** nominal price.

genau accurate, exact, exacting, just, precise, nice, by the square, *(im einzelnen)* full, in detail, detailed, minute, *(Kurs)* due, *(pedantisch)* meticulous, scrupulous, painstaking, *(pünktlich)* punctual, punctilious, to the minute, *(sorgfältig)* careful, thorough, close, *(streng)* strict;
ganz ~ by rule and line; ~ **genommen** strictly speaking;
~ **vor seiner Nase** right under s. one's nose; ~ **an dieser Stelle** just at that spot; ~ **um 12 Uhr** at twelve o'clock sharp; ~ **zur richtigen Zeit** in the nick of time;
auf die Sekunde ~ **ankommen** to arrive on the dot; ~ **aufpassen** to pay close attention; ~ **berechnen** to make a close calculation; **auf fünf Stellen** ~ **berechnen** to calculate correct to five decimal places; ~ **in den Berufsverkehr geraten** to end up right in the middle of the rush hours; **sich** ~ **an eine Vorschrift halten** to comply strictly with a rule; ~ **kennen** to know inside out; **j.** ~ **beobachten lassen** to keep s. o. under close observation; **j.** ~ **nachahmen** to give a perfect imitation of s. o.; ~ **nachprüfen** to check carefully; **es ganz** ~ **nehmen** to draw it fine *(coll.)*; **es nicht so** ~ **nehmen** not to stand upon niceties, to take it easy; **es mit der Wahrheit nicht so** ~ **nehmen** to stretch the truth; **es mit seinen Worten sehr** ~ **nehmen** to be meticulous in the choice of words; **in Geldsachen** ~ **sein** to be scrupulous in money matters; **peinlich** ~ **sein** to dot the i's and cross the t's; **in Ehrensachen peinlich** ~ **sein** to be punctilious on the point of hono(u)r; **sehr** ~ **sein** to be very particular; **nicht** ~ **stimmen** *(techn.)* to be out of true; **auf den Pfennig** ~ **stimmen** to be correct to the last halfpenny (cent, *US*); ~ **wiedergeben** to reproduce in facsimile, to make a facsimile of;
~**er Abfahrtstermin** precise moment of departure; ~**e Abschrift** true copy; ~**e Adresse** full address; ~**e Angaben** full details; ~**e Anweisung** precise order, exact direction; ~**e Auskunft** detailed information; ~**e Befolgung** strict adherence; ~**e Beobachtungen anstellen** to make close observations; ~**er Bericht** detailed account; ~**e Beschreibung** faithful description; ~**er Betrag** exact (precise) amount; ~**e Darstellung des Sachverhalts** full statement of facts; ~**e Definition** precise definition; ~**e Details geben** to give exact details; ~**e Einhaltung** strict observance; ~**e Einzelheiten** full particulars; ~**e Erklärung** correct statement; ~**es Gegenteil** the very opposite; ~**es Gewicht** true weight; ~**er Kostenvoranschlag** detailed estimate; ~**e Nachbildung** faithful imitation; ~**e Prüfung** careful examination, close (careful) inspection; ~**e Sachkenntnis** intimate knowledge; ~**er Tachometer** accurate speedometer; ~**e Überprüfung** close check; ~**e Übersetzung** accurate (close, exact) translation; ~**e wissenschaftliche Untersuchung** painstaking scientific research; ~**e Vermessung** detailed survey; ~**e Waage** true scales; ~**er Wert** exact value; ~**e Wiedergabe** faithful reproduction; ~**er Wortlaut** exact wording; ~**e Zeit** right (exact, correct) time; ~**e Zinsberechnung** accurate interest.

genaugenommen strictly speaking.

Genauigkeit accuracy, exactness, closeness, fidelity, justness, truth;
mit großer ~ by the card;
pedantische ~ punctiliousness;
~ **bei der Erledigung seiner Aufgaben** punctuality in carrying out one's duties; ~ **einer Übersetzung** closeness (fidelity) of a translation.

Genauigkeits|krämer purist; ~**quote** accuracy rate.

Gendarm rural policeman, county constable.

Gendarmerie county constabulary, rural police.

genehm agreeable.

genehmigen to approve, to agree to, to adopt, *(bevollmächtigen)* to authorize, *(bewilligen)* to grant leave, *(einwilligen)* to affirm, to consent, to [give one's] assent, to okay *(US)*, *(erlauben)* to permit, to give permission, *(Vertrag)* to ratify, to confirm, to approbate, to sanction;
amtlich ~ to license; **Antrag** ~ to carry a motion; **sich eine halbstündige Arbeitspause** ~ to enjoy a break from work for half an hour; **Bilanzabschluß** ~ to approve [of] a balance sheet; **Darlehen** ~ to grant a loan; **freizügig** ~ *(parl.)* to vote on a liberal scale; **sich gern einen** ~ to take a drop now and then; **Gesetzesantrag** ~ to pass a request (bill); **Gesuch anstandslos** ~ to grant an application without objection; **Gewinn- und Verlustrechnung** ~ to approve profit-and-loss account; **Haushaltsplan** ~ to vote the estimates, to pass the budget; **nicht** ~ to disapprove; **Plan** ~ to approve (okay, *US*) a plan; **Tagesordnung** ~ to adopt the agenda; **Woche Urlaub** ~ to allow a week's holiday; **Vorschlag** ~ to accept a proposal;
noch Zeit haben, sich einen zu ~ to just have time for a quick one.

genehmigt approved, permitted, sanctioned, authorized, confirmed, assented, okay *(US)*, *(Radiotelefonie)* affirmative;
nicht ~ unsanctioned;
gelesen und ~ read and approved;
stillschweigend ~ **werden** to get a quiet go-ahead;
~**es Anleihekapital** authorized bonds; ~**es Grundkapital** authorized capital (capital stock, *US*); ~**e Lebenshaltungskostenklausel** permissive wage-adjustment clause; ~**er Preis** approved price; ~**er Urlaub** leave of absence.

Genehmigung *(Behörde)* licence, license *(US)*, permit, *(Bestätigung)* affirmation, consent, approbation, endorsement, *(Bevollmächtigung)* authorization, *(Bewilligung)* grant, allowance, *(Billigung)* approval, acceptance, assent, *(Erlaubnis)* leave, permit, permission, *(Staatsvertrag)* ratification, confirmation, establishment, sanction, *(Zugeständnisse)* concession;
mit ~ ... under licence ...; **mit behördlicher** ~ with the approval of the authorities; **mit besonderer** ~ by special permission; **mit freundlicher** ~ **von** by favo(u)r (courtesy, *US*) of; **mit Ihrer** ~ by your leave; **mit richterlicher** ~ by leave of court; **nach vorheriger** ~ after permission; **ohne unsere** ~ without our consent; **vorbehaltlich nachträglicher** ~ subject to ratification; **mit** ~ **des Autors** under licence (with the sanction) of the author; **mit** ~ **der Behörde** with the approval of the authorities; **mit** ~ **des Gerichts** by leave of court;
allgemeine ~ general licence; **amtliche** ~ official approval (authorization), licensing; **ausdrückliche** ~ express permission (authority); **baupolizeiliche** ~ permission for building, building permit *(US)*; **behördliche** ~ permission by the authorities, licence; **besondere** ~ special permit; **devisenrechtliche** ~ foreign-exchange permit; **ehemännliche** ~ husband's authorization; **als Volljähriger erteilte** ~ ratification made after full age; **finanzamtliche** ~ approval of the fiscal authorities; **gebührenpflichtige** ~ *(Konzession)* local taxation licence; **gerichtliche** ~ sanction (approval) of the court; **königliche** ~ Royal assent *(Br.)*; **ministerielle** ~ approval by the ministry; **nachträgliche** ~ sanction, ratification, adoption *(US)*; **schriftliche** ~ written approval; **staatliche** ~ government clearance (permit); **stillschweigende** ~ connivance, implied consent; **vorherige** ~ prior approval; **widerrufliche** ~ revocable licence;
~ **zum Abschluß von Versicherungsgeschäften** authorization to transact insurance; ~ **durch die Anteilseigner** shareholders' (stockholders', *US*) approval; ~ **zur Ausübung eines Berufes** professional licence; ~ **zur Ausübung eines Gewerbes** trade (business) licence, commercial privilege, concession *(US)*, letters of business *(Br.)*; ~ **einer Bilanz** approval of a balance sheet; ~ **eines Darlehens** granting of a loan; ~ **des Finanzministeriums** treasury consent; ~ **durch das Gericht** leave of the court, court approval; ~ **durch die Geschäftsleitung** management permission; ~ **eines Gesuches** consent to a request; ~ **der Gewinn- und Verlustrechnung** approval of profit and loss account; ~ **zum Halten eines Hundes** dog licence; ~ **des Jahresberichts** adoption of the annual report; ~ **des Liquidators** sanction of the liquidator; ~ **des Protokolls** approval of the minutes; ~ **der Regierung** government go-ahead; ~ **der Tagesordnung** adoption of the agenda;
von jds. ~ **abhängen** to be subject to s. one's approval; ~ **einholen** to seek s. one's approval, to apply for consent (permission); ~ **erhalten** to obtain permission, to receive s. one's approval; ~ **erteilen** to grant permission, to give approval, *(Behörde)* to license *(Br.)*, to authorize, to empower, *(Ratifikation)* to [give] sanction, to ratify; **etw. nach eingeholter** ~ **tun** to do s. th. under licence; **der** ~ **unterliegen** to be subject to approval; ~ **verweigern** to disaffirm; **jem. zur** ~ **vorlegen** to submit for s. one's approval; ~ **widerrufen (zurückziehen)** to withdraw a permit, to withdraw (revoke) one's consent.

Genehmigungs|antrag application for a permit, *(Konzession)* licence application; ~**bedingungen** conditions of approval.

genehmigungsbedürftig in need of (subject to) [s. one's] approval, subject to permission.

Genehmigungs|befugnis authority to approve; ~**behörde** approving authority, authorizing body; ~**bescheid** notice of approval; ~**bescheid für die Errichtung neuer Bürohäuser** office development permit *(Br.)*; ~**bescheinigung** certificate of approval; ~**beschluß** *(AG)* confirming vote; ~**erfordernisse** licensing requirements.

genehmigungs|fähig approvable; ~**frei** not subject to approval.

Genehmigungs|gebühr licence fee (tax); **einmalige** ~**gebühr** basic concession, acquisition fee; ~**grenze** *(Bank)* sanctioning limit; ~**klausel** ratification clause.

genehmigungspflichtig in need of (subject to) approval (authorization), subject to s. one's consent (approval);
~ **sein** to depend on a permission;
~**er Etat** authorization budget; ~**es Gewerbe** licence case *(US)*.

Genehmigungs|schreiben letter of approbation; ~**stempel** approved stamp; **zusätzlicher** ~**stempel** counterstamp; ~**system** permit system; ~**urkunde** written permit, instrument of approval; ~**verfahren** licensing procedure; ~**vermerk** signature of approval, approved stamp, *(Paß)* visa; ~**voraussetzungen** permit requirements; ~**vorbehalt** obligatory approval; ~**vorschriften** licensing provisions; ~**widerruf** revocation of a license.

geneigt prone, inclined, willing, *(abschüssig)* sloping, *(Dach)* inclined;
~ **machen** to dispose; ~ **sein** to feel disposed, to feel inclined; ~ **sein, j. zu bevorzugen** to be predisposed in s. one's favo(u)r; **durchaus** ~ **sein, jem. zu glauben** to be quite willing to believe s. o.;
~**er Leser** gentle reader; **jem. ein** ~**es Ohr leihen** to lend an ear to s. o.

Geneigtheit inclination, favo(u)rable disposition.

General, kommandierender commanding general;
~**abkommen** general agreement; ~**abrechnung** full settlement of a claim; ~**agent** general agent; ~**agentur** general agency business; ~**amnestie** general pardon; ~**anwalt** *(EG)* advocate general; ~**auftrag** standing order; ~**bebauungsplan** general building scheme, zoning code *(US)*.

General|bevollmächtigter general (managing, universal) agent; ~**direktion** management, executive board *(US)*, general executives *(US)*; ~**direktor** director general, general manager, president; **stellvertretender** ~**direktor** executive vice-president *(US)*; ~**direktor einer Aktiengesellschaft** president of a limited liability company *(US)*; ~**gouvernement** government general, governor generalship; ~**gouverneur** governor general; ~**index** *(Statistik)* composite index number; ~**inspekteur** inspector *(US)* (surveyor, *Br.*) general.

generalisieren to generalize.

General|klausel blanket, omnibus (general, basket, *US*) clause, *(Tarif)* dragnet clause; ~**konsul** consul general; ~**konsulat** consulate general; ~**konto** *(Weltwährungsfonds)* General Account; ~**kosten** overheads, burden, undistributed cost, establishment charges, oncost *(Br.)*; ~**linie** general line; ~**linie einhalten** to work along a general line; ~**lizenz** general license; ~**lizenznehmer** general licensee; ~**nenner** common denominator; ~**police** comprehensive insurance, blanket (compound, general, floating, block) policy, *(Seeschadensversicherung)* declared policy; **für etw. eine** ~**police nehmen** to insure s. th. against all risks; ~**policenbestimmungen** open policy terms; ~**probe** *(Theater)* dress rehearsal; ~**quartiermeister** quartermaster general; ~**quittung** receipt in full; ~**quittung ausstellen** to receipt in full; ~**rückversicherungsvertrag** automatic reinsurance contract; ~**schlüssel** skeleton key; ~**schuldverschreibung** general bond; ~**sekretär** secretary general; ~**sekretär einer Gewerkschaft** president of a trade union; ~**staatsanwalt** director of Public Prosecutions *(US)*, attorney general *(Br.)*, Lord Advocate *(Scot.)*, prosecutor of the pleas *(New Jersey)*; ~**stab** *(mil.)* general staff, Horse Guards *(Br.)*.

Generalstabs|chef *(mil.)* chief of staff; ~**karte** military (ordnance, *US*) map; ~**offizier** general staff officer; ~**schule** [etwa] general service school *(US)*.

General|streik general (mass) strike; ~**synode** General Assembly.

generalüberholen to recondition;
Motor ~ to overhaul the engine of a car.

generalüberholtes Auto reconditioned automobile.

Generalüberholung complete overhauling, overall examination, *(Auto)* reconditioning, overhaul, turnaround.

Generalunkosten [general] overheads, indirect (undistributed) cost, establishment (fixed) charges, fixed (general, nonproductive) expenses, burden, oncost *(Br.)*;
zu den Gestehungsunkosten hinzutretende ~ loading;
~**posten** overhead item; ~**verteilung** overhead allocation.

General|unternehmer main (general) contractor; ~**unternehmervertrag** prime contract; ~**untersuchung** checkover; ~**verpfändung** floating mortgage (charge).

Generalversammlung *(AG)* general (corporate) meeting, *(Senat und Abgeordnetenhaus, UNO)* general assembly;
außerordentliche ~ called (extraordinary, general, special, *US*) meeting of shareholders (stockholders, *US*); **halbjährliche** ~ *(Bank von England)* general court; **konstituierende** ~ founders' meeting; **ordentliche** ~ regular (annual, stated, ordinary, *US*) general meeting; **gesetzlich vorgeschriebene** ~ statutory meeting *(Br.)*;
~ **der Vereinten Nationen** general assembly of the United Nations;
~ **abhalten** to hold a general meeting; ~ **einberufen** to summon a general meeting *(Br.)*, to call a meeting of the shareholders (stockholders, *US*); ~ **vertagen** to adjourn a general meeting.

General|versammlungsprotokoll minutes of a corporate meeting, corporate minutes; ~**versicherung** comprehensive (all-in, all-loss) insurance; ~**versicherungspolice** blanket (compound, block, floating) policy.

Generalvertreter head (general, chief) agent, universal (principal, general-commission) agent, sole representative, franchised distributor *(US)*;
~**seminar** franchise seminar *(US)*.

Generalvertretung general (head, chief) agency, general agency business;
~ **für ein Auto haben** to have the exclusive rights for a car; **Dienste einer** ~ **zur Verfügung stellen** to supply franchise services.

Generalvertretungsabkommen general agency agreement.

Generalvollmacht general power (authority, proxy), letter of attorney in fact, full power of attorney;
jem. ~ **erteilen** to invest s. o. with full powers.

Generalzahlmeister Paymaster General.

Generation generation, age;
die gegenwärtige ~ the present age; **heranwachsende** ~ rising generation; **kommende** ~ oncoming generation; **vergangene** ~**en** past generations.

Generations|dauer average lifetime of man, generation; ~**konflikt** generation clash; ~**probleme** demographic problems; ~**wechsel** alternation of generations.

Generator motor generator, gas producer;
~**gas** producer gas.

generell general, universal, overall, blanket *(US)*;
~**e Ausnahme** general exception; ~**e Erlaubnis** general licence, blanket permission *(US)*; ~**e Maßnahmen** blanket measures *(US)*; ~**e Preiserhöhung** overall increase of prices; ~**e Tendenz** overall tendency.

genesen to recover, to convalesce;
von einer schweren Krankheit ~ to recover from a serious illness.

Genesender convalescent.

Genesung healing, recovery, convalescence.

Genesungs|heim convalescent hospital; ~**urlaub** sick leave.

Genfer|Konvention Geneva Convention; ~ **Welturheberrechtsabkommen** World Copyright Convention.

genial|veranlagt sein to be gifted with genius;
~**e Erfindung** brilliant invention; ~**er Mensch** genius.

Genick, steifes stiff neck;
sich das ~ **brechen** to break one's neck; **jem. das** ~ **brechen** to cook s. one's goose *(coll.)*; **den kleinen Geschäftsinhabern das** ~ **brechen** to ruin small business; **j. beim** ~ **packen** to take s. o. by the scruff of the neck; **jem. im** ~ **sitzen** to breathe down s. one's neck.

Genie genius;
verkommenes ~ genius gone to seed;
ein ~ **erfordern** to take a genius; **mathematisches** ~ **sein** to have a genius for mathematics.

genieren, sich to feel embarrassed (awkward).

genießbar eatable, edible, *(Getränk)* drinkable, potable;
heute nicht ~ **sein** *(fig.)* to be in a bad humo(u)r today.

genießen to have the benefit of, *(Recht)* to enjoy;
große Achtung ~ to be held in high esteem; **gute Erziehung** ~ to receive a good education; **Feinheiten eines Stils** ~ to appreciate the subleties of a style; **seine Ferien** ~ to enjoy one's holidays; **seine Freizeit in vollen Zügen** ~ to get the most out of one's leisure; **Geldausgeben** ~ to revel away money; **Kredit** ~ to enjoy credit; **sein Leben im Kreis der Familie** ~ to relish one's simple family life; **sein Leben in vollen Zügen** ~ to enjoy o. s. to the full, to live on the fat of the land; **4% Rabatt** ~ to be subject to 4% discount; **Recht** ~ to enjoy a right; **guten Ruf** ~ to have a good

reputation; **jds. Vertrauen** ~ to be in the confidence of s. o.; **Vorrang vor jem.** ~ to take priority over s. o.; **Wein** ~ to savo(u)r a wine;
nicht mehr zu ~ **sein** to be no longer edible.
Genießer connoisseur, gourmet, free liver, sport *(US coll.)*;
stiller ~ **sein** to maintain a discreet silence.
genormt standardized;
~**e Produktion** standardized production; ~**e Waren** standardized commodities.
Genosse associate, companion, [political] comrade, fellow, affiliate, confrere, consociate, partner;
~**n** privies.
Genossenschaft cooperative association *(US)*, cooperative [society], *(Br.)*, body corporate, *(Gilde)* guild, trade, fellowship;
eingetragene ~ registered society; **gewerbliche** ~ industrial cooperative society *(Br.)*; **landwirtschaftliche** ~ agricultural cooperative society, farm (rural) cooperative *(US)*;
in eine ~ **umwandeln** to change a firm to cooperative ownership.
genossenschaftlich cooperative, corporative;
~ **organisiert** cooperative[ly];
~**es Denken** cooperative spirit; ~**er Ein- und Verkauf der Landwirte** cooperative farming; ~**e Großhändlervereinigung** cooperative wholesale society; ~**e Grundlage** cooperative basis; ~**es Kreditinstitut** cooperative bank, mutual savings bank *(US)*; ~**es Kreditwesen** cooperative banking; ~**e Organisation** cooperative organization; ~**es Versicherungswesen** cooperative insurance; ~**er Vertrieb** cooperative marketing; ~**e Wohnungen** cooperation apartments; ~**er Wohnungsbau** cooperative housing; ~**er Zusammenschluß** cooperation.
Genossenschafts|anteil share; ~**bank** cooperative bank (banking society), bank for cooperatives *(US)*, mutual savings bank *(US)*; **landwirtschaftliche** ~**bank** farm loan bank *(US)*; ~**bewegung** cooperation movement; ~**gesetz** Industrial and Provident Societies Act *(Br.)*, Cooperative Law *(US)*; ~**kapital** cooperative stock; ~**kasse** cooperative bank, mutual savings bank *(US)*; ~**laden** cooperative store; ~**mitglied** cooperative member, cooperationist; ~**register** register general, register of cooperative societies *(Br.)* (of cooperatives, *US*); ~**unternehmen** cooperative enterprise; ~**verband** Cooperative Union *(Br.)*; **internationaler** ~**verband** International Cooperative Alliance; ~**verkauf** cooperative sales (selling); ~**vertrag** deed of association; ~**vertrieb** cooperative marketing; ~**wesen** cooperative system, *(Banken)* cooperative banking, *(Verbraucher)* consumer cooperative.
Genrebild conversation piece.
Gentleman, perfekter perfect gentleman;
~**vereinbarung** gentleman's (gentlemen's) agreement.
genug enough, sufficient, galore;
mehr als ~ **haben** to have enough and to spare.
Genüge sufficiency;
allen Anforderungen ~ **tun** to satisfy (meet) all requirements.
genügen to suffice, to be sufficient (adequate);
den Anforderungen ~ to meet the requirements; **im Augenblick** ~ to be enough for the present; **den Vorschriften** ~ to comply with the rules.
genügend ample, sufficient, enough, satisfactory, well, *(Examen)* passing;
nicht ~ **frankiert** insufficiently paid;
nicht ~ **Arbeitskräfte haben** to be short of labo(u)r, to be short-handed; ~**e Menge** sufficient amount; ~**e Vorräte** adequate supplies; ~ **Zeit haben** to have plenty of time.
genügsam modest [in one's demands].
Genugtuung satisfaction, gratification;
~ **über etw. empfinden** to get a kick out of s. th.; ~ **über die Anerkennung seiner Arbeit empfinden** to feel satisfaction at having one's ability recognized; ~ **leisten** to make satisfaction.
Genuß enjoyment, pleasure, delight, *(Nutznießung)* beneficial use, profit;
übermäßiger ~ excessive consumption;
~ **von rohem Obst** eating of raw fruit; ~ **von Rauschgift** taking of drugs; ~ **eines Rechtes** exercise (enjoyment) of a right, *(ungestört)* quiet enjoyment; ~ **von Wein** drinking of wine;
Geschichte mit ~ **erzählen** to tell a story with great relish; **in den** ~ **einer Erbschaft gelangen** to come into an inheritance; **in den** ~ **eines Stipendiums gelangen** to be on a foundation; **in den vollen** ~ **kommen** to get the full flavo(u)r of; **j. in den** ~ **einer Sache kommen lassen** to give s. o. the benefit of s. th.; **Buch mit** ~ **lesen** to enjoy reading a book; **für den menschlichen** ~ **ungeeignet sein** to be unfit for human consumption; **wirklich ein** ~ **sein** to be a treat, to be really delicious; **jem. mit** ~ **zuhören** to have pleasure in listening to s. o.;
~**aktie** bonus share (stock, *US*), dividend share.
Genüsse des Lebens sweets of life.
Genuß|mensch man of pleasure, pleasure lover; **hochbesteuerte** ~**mittel** heavily taxed semiluxuries; ~**mittelindustrie** luxury food industry; ~- **und Nahrungsmittelmesse** food and drink fair; ~**rechte** participating rights; ~**schein** participating certificate; ~**schein für den Vorstand** management share *(US)*.
genußsüchtig pleasure-seeking.
genutzt, gewerblich used for business purposes; **rein industriell** ~ *(Bezirk)* devoted to industry.
geöffnet *(Ausstellung)* open;
ganzjährig ~ open throughout the year; **ganztägig** ~ open round the clock; **die ganze Nacht** ~ open all night; **weit** ~ wide open *(US sl.)*.
Geographie, physikalische physical geography; **politische** ~ political geography.
geographisch in ... gelegen sein to be physically located in ...
Geologie, praktische economic geology.
geölt, wie like clockwork; **wie ein** ~**er Blitz** like a streak of lightning.
Geopolitik geopolitics.
geordnet orderly, assorted, tidy, *(Konto)* straight;
nach Nummern ~ in numerical order; **zeitlich** ~ chronological;
~**e Lebensweise** regular habits; ~**er Rückzug** orderly retreat; **in** ~**en Verhältnissen leben** to live in comparative comfort.
gepachtet haben to hold under a lease.
Gepäck luggage *(Br.)*, baggage *(US)*, stuff *(coll.)*, *(mil.)* impediments;
fast ohne ~ light-handed;
aufgegebenes ~ registered luggage *(Br.)*, checked baggage *(US)*; **nicht aufgegebenes** ~ unchecked baggage *(US)*; **unterwegs befindliches** ~ baggage en route *(US)*; **zur Aufbewahrung gegebenes** ~ left luggage *(Br.)*; **großes** ~ heavy luggage (baggage, *US*); **persönliches** ~ effects, dunnage, personal luggage *(Br.)*; **zuschlagpflichtiges** ~ extra luggage *(Br.)*, excess baggage *(US)*;
~ **mit Übergewicht** overweight luggage *(Br.)* (baggage, *US*);
~ **[in der Wohnung] abholen** to check out the baggage *(US)* (luggage, *Br.*), to collect one's luggage *(Br.)* (baggage, *US*); ~ **vom Bahnhof abholen** to transfer luggage *(Br.)* (baggage, *US*) from the station; **sein** ~ **aufgeben** to check one's luggage *(Br.)*, to send one's luggage in advance *(Br.)*, to have one's luggage registered *(Br.)*, to check one's baggage *(US)*; ~ **ausfolgen** to deliver baggage *(US)* (luggage, *Br.*); ~ **befördern** to transmit luggage *(Br.)* (baggage, *US*); ~ **zum Bahnhof befördern** to run the luggage *(Br.)* (baggage, *US*) to the station; **jds. persönliches** ~ **beschlagnahmen** to seize s. one's personal effects; ~ **[zollamtlich] durchsuchen** to examine the baggage *(US)* (luggage, *Br.*), to search s. one's trunks; ~ **mit sich führen** to carry luggage *(Br.)* (baggage, *US*) with one; **sein** ~ **abgegeben haben** to have one's things at the luggage office *(Br.)*; **drei Stück** ~ **haben** to have three pieces of luggage *(Br.)* (baggage, *US*); **sich um das** ~ **kümmern** to take care of the luggage *(Br.)* (baggage, *US*); **sein** ~ **am Bahnhof lassen** to park one's bag at the station; **sein** ~ **zollamtlich abfertigen lassen** to get one's luggage *(Br.)* (baggage, *US*) through the customs; **sein** ~ **bekleben lassen** to have one's luggage labelled *(Br.)*; **überflüssiges** ~ **mitnehmen** to encumber o. s. with unnecessary luggage *(Br.)* (baggage, *US*); **mit nur wenig** ~ **reisen** to travel lightly; **für das** ~ **sorgen** to see to the luggage *(Br.)* (baggage, *US*); ~ **untersuchen** to examine the luggage *(Br.)* (baggage, *US*); **sein** ~ **verstauen** to bestow one's luggage *(Br.)* (baggage, *US*); ~ **auf dem Rücksitz des Autos verstauen** to pack the luggage in the dickey of the car; ~ **zustellen** to deliver luggage *(Br.)* (baggage, *US*);
~**abfertiger** luggage *(Br.)* (baggage, *US*) clerk; ~**abfertigung** dispatch of luggage *(Br.)*, baggage dispatch *(US)*, parcels office *(US)*; **durchgehende** ~**abfertigung** all-cargo service; ~**abfertigungsstelle** left-luggage office *(Br.)*, baggage office *(US)*; ~**abgabe** cloakroom, checkroom *(US)*, *(Abgeben des Gepäcks)* depositing of luggage *(Br.)* (baggage, *US*); ~**abholung** collection of luggage *(Br.)* (baggage, *US*); ~**ablage** *(Bahn)* luggage *(Br.)* (baggage, *US*) rack; ~**abschnitt** luggage *(Br.)* (baggage, *US*) check; ~**adresse** baggage (luggage, *Br.*) label; ~**anhänger** luggage tag *(Br.)*, baggage *(US)* (luggage, *Br.*) label, baggage label holder *(US)*; ~**anhänger festmachen** to attach a label to the luggage *(Br.)* (baggage, *US*); ~**annahmestelle** left-luggage *(Br.)* (baggage, booking, *US*) office, baggage room *(US)*, parcels office *(US)*.

Gepäckaufbewahrung registration of luggage *(Br.)*, checking of baggage *(US)*, parcels office *(US)*, *(Raum)* left-luggage (parcel) office *(Br.)*, [baggage] checkroom *(US)*, baggage deposit *(US)*, cloakroom;
sein Gepäck bei der ~ abholen to claim one's things from the left-luggage office *(Br.)*.

Gepäckaufbewahrungs|beamter cloakroom attendant, baggage clerk *(US)*; ~**gebühr** cloakroom fee; ~**raum** cloakroom, [baggage] checkroom *(US)*, luggage *(Br.)* (baggage, *US*) room, *(Bus)* rumble; ~**schein** left-luggage ticket *(Br.)*, luggage receipt *(Br.)*, baggage *(US)* (cloakroom) check, cloakroom check (ticket); ~**stelle** left-luggage office *(Br.)*.

Gepäck|aufgabe registration of luggage *(Br.)*, checking of baggage *(US)*, *(Aufgabestelle)* left-luggage office *(Br.)*, baggage counter *(US)*; ~**aufzug** luggage lift *(Br.)*, service elevator *(US)*; ~**ausgabe[stelle]** baggage pickup (room) *(US)*, delivery office; ~**auslieferung** baggage service *(US)*; ~**bahnsteig** baggage *(US)* (luggage, *Br.*) platform; **automatische ~beförderungsanlage** automated cargo-handing facility; ~**buch** parcel book; ~**durchsuchung** search of trunks; ~**empfangsschein** delivery (baggage, *US*) check; ~**ermittlung** baggage tracing *(US)*; ~**halle** baggage hall *(US)*; ~**halter** *(Auto)* baggage *(US)* (luggage, *Br.*) carrier; ~**hinterlegungsschein** left-luggage ticket *(Br.)*, cloakroom check (ticket); ~**karren** luggage trolley *(Br.)*, baggage cart *(US)*; **kleiner ~karren** depot wagon *(US)*; ~**netz** *(Bahn)* baggage *(US)* (luggage, *Br.*) rack; ~**nummer** baggage tag *(US)*; ~**raum** checkroom *(US)*, baggage room *(US)*, *(Auto)* luggage area (space, compartment), well; **betretbarer ~raum** walk-in baggage room *(US)*; **zollamtliche ~revision** luggage *(Br.)* (baggage, *US*) examination; ~**schalter** luggage registration window *(Br.)*, luggage *(Br.)* (baggage, *US*) counter (office); ~**schein** luggage check (receipt, ticket, voucher, chit) *(Br.)*, cloakroom ticket, baggage check (claim, ticket) *(US)*, counterfoil; ~**schließfach** luggage locker *(Br.)*; ~**selbstbedienung** self-claim baggage system *(US)*; ~**ständer** luggage stand *(Br.)*; ~**stück** [piece of] luggage *(Br.)*, parcel, bag, case, baggage *(US)*.

Gepäck|träger ticket (luggage) porter *(Br.)*, baggage porter *(US)*, baggageman *(US)*, *(Fahrrad)* luggage carrier *(Br.)*; ~**trägergebühr** porter's fee, porterage; ~**troß** *(mil.)* baggage train; ~**übergewicht** overweight luggage *(Br.)*, excess baggage *(US)*; ~**verlust** loss of baggage *(US)* (luggage, *Br.*), baggage loss *(US)*; ~**versicherung** luggage *(Br.)* (baggage, *US*) insurance; ~**wagen** carriage for goods (luggage, *Br.*), baggage van (wagon, car) *(US)*; **kleiner ~wagen** luggage trolley *(Br.)*, baggage truck *(US)*; ~**zettel** baggage *(US)* (luggage, *Br.*) label, label-direction card, counterfoil; **ohne ~zettel** unlabelled; ~**zustellung** parcel (baggage, *US*) delivery.

geparkt, schräg angle-parked.

gepfändet distressed, distrained, attached, seized;
fruchtlos ~ not satisfied, nulla bona; **nicht ~** unseized;
~ sein to be under seizure.

Gepfändeter distrainee.

gepfefferte Rechnung salted account, swinging bill.

gepflastert paved;
mit Kopfsteinen ~ cobbled; **mit guten Vorsätzen ~** paved with good intentions.

gepflegt neat, nice, *(Manieren)* cultivated, cared-for, polished, refined;
~**es Äußeres** sleek appearance; ~**er Rasen** well-groomed lawn;
~**e Weine** selected wines.

Gepflogenheit convention, custom, usage, habit, existing practice, praxis;
den parlamentarischen ~en entsprechend parliamentary;
diplomatische ~en diplomatic customs; **gesellschaftliche ~en** social customs; **kaufmännische ~en** business usage; **örtliche ~** local custom; **uralte ~** in memorial usage;
alle ~en im Armenhaus workhouse ins and outs;
von jds. ~ abhängig sein to depend on the attitudes of s. o.

geplagt tormented, vexed, harassed, plagued, worried.

Geplänkel skirmish;
~ mit jem. haben to have a tiff with s. o.

geplant planned, projected;
gemeinsam ~ concerted;
~**e Produktion** budgeted production.

Geplapper patter, chatter, jabber, babbling.

Geplauder small talk, chat, chatter.

Gepräge pattern, type;
~ geben to hallmark; **einer Sache sein ~ geben** to leave one's mark upon s. th.; **sehr individuelles ~ haben** to be of a highly individual character.

geprägt embossed;
neu ~ newly coined.

Geprellter sucker, dupe, mug.

geprüft, mit Erfolg passed; **~ von** checked by;
~ werden to be under consideration;
~**er Bücherrevisor** chartered *(Br.)* (incorporated, *US*) accountant.

Gequassel yak, twaddle, piffle.

Gequatsche gossip, chattering, yak.

gerade direct, straight, *(aufrecht)* upright, erect, *(ehrlich)* straightforward, honest;
~ erschienen *(Buch)* just out;
j. ~ und offen ansehen to look at s. o. frankly; **sich ~ mit einer Frage beschäftigen** to be dealing with a question right now, to be presently engaged with a problem; **~ genug zum Leben haben** to make both ends meet; **~ wieder kein Geld haben** to have run out of cash again; **fünf ~ sein lassen** to stretch a point;
~ dabei sein to be just about it;
geht ~ noch so hin would pass in a crowd;
das ~ Gegenteil the very opposite; **~ Linie** straight line; **in ~r Linie von jem. abstammen** to be a direct descendant of s. o.; **~r Mensch** upright (honest) person; **~ Nummer** even number; **~n Weg gehen** to walk the straight and narrow.

geradeaus straight ahead.

geradeheraus open, frank, straightforward;
sehr ~ sein to be blunt (outspoken).

gerädert, sich wie ~ fühlen to be dead beat (whacked, *Br.*, bushed, *US*).

geradestehen, für etw. to take the responsibility (stand up) for s. th.; **für j. ~** to stand surety for s. o.

geradezu point-blank;
~ verrückt sheer nonsense;
jem. ~ auf den Leib geschnitten sein to have been written for s. o.

geradlinig *(Abstammung)* lineal;
~ verlaufen to run in a straight line;
~**er Verlauf** *(Grenze)* straight line.

gerammelt voll packed, crowded to capacity, crammed, jammed, packed.

Gerät tool, gear, appliance, device, implement, instrument, furniture, utensil, apparatus, equipment;
~e paraphernalia, fittings, fixings *(US)*;
elektrische ~e electrical appliances; **landwirtschaftliche ~e** farm utensils, farming (agricultural) implements; **sparsames ~** saver;
~ zur Messung des Alkoholspiegels drunkometer *(sl.)*;
Werkzeuge, Instrumente und ~e *(Bilanz)* tooling and implements.

Geräte|ausstattung equipment; ~**bau** toolbuilding, toolmaking; ~**fahrzeug** tool car; ~**hersteller** appliance producer, toolbuilder, toolmaker; ~**herstellung** toolbuilding, toolmaking; ~**kammer** toolroom; ~**konto** equipment account; ~**miete** equipment rent.

geraten to get into;
in Abhängigkeit ~ to lose one's independence; **an die falsche Adresse ~** to be barking up the wrong tree; **aneinander ~** to come to blows; **unter ein Auto ~** to be run over by a car; **auf die schiefe Bahn ~** to go to the bad, to backslide; **in Brand ~** to catch fire; **auf den Gedanken ~** to hit upon the idea; **in große Gefahr ~** to run into danger; **in schlechte Gesellschaft ~** to fall into bad company; **gut ~** to turn out well; **sich in die Haare ~** to fall foul of each other; **in die Hauptverkehrszeit ~** to get caught in the rush hour; **aus dem Häuschen ~** to fly off the handle *(US)*; **ins Hintertreffen ~** to be outmanoeuvred; **in Not ~** to become destitute; **in Rückstand ~** to fall into arrears; **in eine Sackgasse ~** *(Verhandlungen)* to reach a deadlock; **ins Schleudern ~** to get into a skid; **hinter jds. Schliche ~** to be up to s. one's tricks; **in Schulden ~** to run into debt; **in Schwung ~** to get into one's stride; **ins Stocken ~** *(Verhandlungen)* to make no progress, *(Verkehr)* to be blocked (held up), to become congested; **aus der Übung ~** to get out of practice; **an den Unrechten ~** to catch a Tartar; **nach seinem Vater ~** to take after one's father; **in Vergessenheit ~** to sink into oblivion; **in Versuchung ~** to feel tempted; **jem. zum Vorteil ~** to redound to s. one's advantage.

Geräte|park depot; ~**raum** toolroom; ~**schild** instrument name plate, name plate; ~**schuppen** tool house (shed); ~**steckdose** plug box, tool socket; ~**stecker** coupler plug; ~**störung** instrumental disturbance; ~**vermietung** equipment leasing; ~**verlust** loss of equipment; ~**wagen** tool car (truck, waggon), *(Feuerwehr)* equipment tender.

Geratewohl, aufs haphazard, hit or miss, at random;
sich aufs ~ bewerben to apply on the off-chance of a job; **aufs ~ eine Auswahl treffen** to select a specimen at random.
Gerätschaften implements, equipment, appurtenances, utensils, plant.
geraumer Zeit, seit for a fairly long time.
geräumig spacious, roomy.
Geräusch noise, sound;
dumpfes ~ thud.
geräuscharm silent, noiseless.
Geräusch|auflagen noise restrictions; **~bekämpfung** suppression of noise; **~boje** sonobuoy.
geräuschdämpfend sound-absorbing.
Geräusch|dämpfer silencer, muffler *(US)*; **~kulisse** background music, sound effects.
geräuschlos silent, noiseless;
~e Schreibmaschine noiseless typewriter.
Geräusch|losigkeit silence, noiselessness; **~messer** psophometer; **für die Gerichte annehmbare ~normen entwickeln** to develop effective noise standards acceptable to the courts; **~pegel** noise level; **~unterdrückung** noise suppression; **~verringerung um zehn Phon** 10-decible reduction.
Geräusper, verlegenes hums and haws.
gerechnet, in bar reckoned in cash; **im ganzen ~** reckoned in the aggregate.
gerecht *(berechtigt)* just, justified, rightful, legitimate, *(billig)* fair, equitable;
~ und angemessen just and proper; **~ und zumutbar** just and reasonable;
j. ~ behandeln to treat s. o. fairly; **in allen Sätteln ~ sein** to be able to cope with anything; **~ urteilen** to hold the scales even; **~ verteilen** to distribute fairly; **allen Anforderungen ~ werden** to meet all requirements; **einer Aufgabe ~ werden** to come up to a task; **einer Rolle ~ werden** to do justice to a part; **seinem Ruf ~ werden** to live up to one's reputation;
seinen ~en Lohn bekommen to get one's deserts (what is coming to one; **~er Preis** fair price; **~e Sache** righteous cause; **sich für eine ~e Sache einsetzen** to speak for a just cause; **der ~en Strafe für seine Verbrechen entgegensehen** to be brought to justice for one's crimes; **~es Urteil** just and lawful decision.
gerechtfertigt justifiable, justified, reasonable, warrantable;
völlig ~ sein to have good cause for doing s. th.;
~er Anspruch legitimate claim.
Gerechtigkeit justice, justness;
ausgleichende ~ poetic[al] (retributive, commutative, distributive, corrective) justice; **soziale ~** social justice; **unparteiliche ~** even-handed justice;
~ in der Sache selbst substantial justice;
sich der ~ anheimgeben to surrender o. s. to justice; **Lauf der ~ aufhalten** to interfere with the course of justice; **für die ~ eintreten** to stand with justice; **j. der ~ entziehen** to hide s. o. from justice; **~ erfahren** to obtain justice; **der ~ in den Arm fallen** to stand in the way of justice; **~ handhaben** to distribute justice; **der ~ ihren Lauf lassen** to let justice take (have) its course (way); **jem. ~ widerfahren lassen** to do s. o. justice; **~ den Todesstoß versetzen** to defeat the ends of justice; **~ wiederherstellen** to revive justice.
Gerechtigkeitsgefühl sense of justice.
Gerechtsame privilege, franchise, prerogative;
~ einer Stadt city freedom.
Gerede talk, rumo(u)r, gossip;
albernes ~ silly talk; **großspuriges ~** bragging, big talk; **gute ~** elocution; **hochtrabendes ~** grandstand stuff *(sl.)*; **leeres ~** empty talk, wash, whishy-washy; **scheinheiliges ~** hypocritical talk; **schwülstiges ~** bombastic (swollen, pompous, high-flown) talk; **sinnloses ~** nonsense, bunkum *(sl.)*; **unzusammenhängendes ~** desultory conversation;
kein ~ ohne Hintergrund no smoke without fire;
ziemliches ~ auslösen to cause a good deal of comment; **j. ins ~ bringen** to tell tales about s. o., to gossip about s. o.; **auf das ~ der Leute wenig geben** to take not much count of what people say; **ins ~ kommen** to get o. s. talked about; **dem ~ Glauben schenken** to give credence to gossip; **alles nur ~ sein** to be all talk.
geregelt *(Schaden, Schuld)* liquidated, regular;
gütlich ~ werden to be disposed of by agreement;
~es Leben führen to lead a steady life.
gereichen, jem. zur Ehre to do s. o. credit; **jem. nicht zur Ehre ~** to reflect discredit upon s. o.; **der Universität zur Ehre ~** to redound to the fame of the university; **jem. zum Verderben ~** to bring about s. one's ruin.
gereizt irritable, touchy, itchy, *(angriffslustig)* with one's hackles up;
~ antworten to answer irritably; **~ sein** to be in a temper, to get one's monkey up.
gerettetes Vermögen salvaged property.
gereuen, j. to cause s. one's regret.
Gericht [law] court, court of justice, *(Gang)* course, dish, *(Gebäude)* law court, court house, *(Richter)* judge, bench, *(Sitzungsperiode)* session, *(Verhandlung)* hearing, trial;
bei ~ anhängig pending before the court; **dem ~ vorgeführt** brought to trial; **nach dem Ermessen des ~s** left to the discretion of the court; **von ~s wegen** by order of the court; **vor ~** in open court; **vor ein ~ gehörig** cognizable; **vor einem ordnungsgemäß besetzten ~** coram judice; **vor einem unzuständigen ~** coram non judice; **vor versammeltem ~** before a full court; **zu ~ sitzend** sitting;
angerufenes ~ court invoked; **ausgegangenes ~** *(Restaurant)* dish that is off; **ordnungsgemäß besetztes ~** regularly constituted court; **voll besetztes ~** full court; **erkennendes ~** trial court *(US)*; **erstinstanzliches ~** court of first instance (exercising original jurisdiction), circuit (local) court *(US)*, *(Hauptverhandlung)* trial court, inferior (small claims) court; **ersuchtes ~** court applied to; **fliegendes ~** ambulatory court, eyre; **gleichgeordnetes ~** coordinate court; **höheres ~** court above, superior court; **„Hohes ~"** your hono(u)r; **innerstaatliches ~** domestic court; **internationales ~** international court; **Jüngstes ~** The Last Judgement, doomsday; **kaltes ~** *(Restaurant)* cold dish; **das letzte ~** *(fig.)* the last assize; **letztinstanzliches ~** court of last resort; **nachgeordnetes ~** lower court; **niederes ~** interior (base) court; **oberstes ~** supreme court; **ordentliches ~** court of justice, court of ordinary jurisdiction (of record); **nicht ortsgebundenes ~** ambulatory court; **tagendes ~** open court; **in Permanenz tagendes ~** court available at all times; **übergeordnetes ~** superior court, court above; **untergeordnetes ~** inferior (lower) court, court below, court of requests *(Br.)*; **zuständiges ~** court of competent jurisdiction; **für Ehescheidungen zuständiges ~** divorce court; **für Hoch- und Landesverratsfälle zuständiges ~** Court of Oyer and terminer *(Br.)*; **für den Lieferanten zuständiges ~** competent court of the vendor; **ausschließlich örtlich zuständiges ~** local venue; **zur Auslegung eines Testaments zuständiges ~** court of construction; **zweitinstanzliches ~** appellate court, court of appeal;
~ für Berufungen in Zollsachen Court of Customs Appeal; **~ erster Instanz** inferior court, court of first instance, common law bench *(Br.)*, county court *(Br.)*, Circuit Court *(US)*, King's (Queen's) Bench [Division] *(Br.)*; **~ letzter Instanz** court of last resort; **~ zweiter Instanz** appellate court; **~ für bürgerliche Rechtsstreitigkeiten** civil court *(US)*; **~ der belegenen Sache** forum rei sitae; **~ mit sachlich beschränkter Zuständigkeit** court of limited jurisdiction, limited (inferior) court;
~ abhalten to hold court; **~ anrufen** to invoke the aid of the court; **~ auftragen** to put on a dish; **vor ~ auftreten** to appear at the bar; **für jem. vor ~ auftreten** to appear for s. o.; **vor ~ für j. aussagen** to give evidence on s. one's behalf in a law court; **beim ~ Kreditaufnahme beantragen** *(Konkursverwalter)* to apply to the court for permission to borrow; **~ mit einer Sache befassen** to lay a matter (bring a dispute) before the court; **~ parteiisch besetzen** to pack a court; **vor ~ beweisen** to prove to the satisfaction of the court; **~ um Weisungen bitten** *(Konkursverwalter)* to make application to the court for directions; **j. vor ~ bringen** to bring s. o. up before the (haul s. o. into) court; **Mitgliedsstaat wegen Verletzung der Gemeinschaftsrichtlinien vor ~ bringen** to take a country to court for breaking community rules; **Sache (Streitigkeit) vor ~ bringen** to take a case to (bring a dispute before the) court, to institute an action at law; **bei ~ einreichen** to put in court, to file a claim in court, to box *(Scot.)*; **~ einsetzen** to set up court; **bei ~ einzahlen** to pay into the court; **vor ~ erscheinen** to appear in court, to attend at a trial, to make one's appearance; **nicht vor ~ erscheinen** to [make] default; **persönlich vor ~ erscheinen** to attend personally in court; **~ um Richtlinien ersuchen** to apply to the court for directions; **unter die Zuständigkeit eines ~s fallen** to come within the jurisdiction of a court; **vor ~ gehen** to go before the court, to go to law, to law, to take legal action; **dem ~ Rechnung zu legen haben** to be responsible to the court; **Geld bei ~ hinterlegen** to pay into the court; **~ irreführen** to perpetrate a fraud on the court; **vor ~ kommen** to become before the judge, *(Person)* to go on trial; **j. vor ~ laden** to summon s. o., to cite (convene) s. o. before a court; **vor ~ geltend machen** to plead at the bar; **dem ~ glaubhaft machen** to

prove to the satisfaction of the court; **den ~en obliegen** to vest in the courts; **über j. zu ~ sitzen** to sit in judgment upon s. o.; **vor ~ stehen** to be up for (stand upon one's, be on) trial, *(Täter)* to underlie the law *(Scot.)*; **sich dem ~ stellen** to surrender o. s. to the court; **vor ~ stellen** to put on trial, to arraign; **Aufmerksamkeit des ~s zu erregen suchen** to seek court attention; **sich vor ~ verantworten** to answer a charge; **vor ~ verhandeln** to hold pleas, to try a case; **j. bei ~ verklagen** to bring an action against s. o.; **sich vor ~ schriftlich verpflichten** to recognize; **sich selbst vor ~ verteidigen** *(Strafrecht)* to address the jury in one's own defence; **j. vor ~ vertreten** to appear for s. o.; **Fall vor ~ vertreten** to present a case, to hold a brief, to plead a cause; **sich selbst vor ~ vertreten** to represent o. s. in court; **für das ~ verwahren** to hold for the court; **Fall an ein anderes ~ verweisen** to remand a case to another court; **bei ~ vorbringen** to allege; **Frage dem ~ zur Entscheidung vorlegen** to submit a question to the court for decision; **dem ~ einen Fall als Berichterstatter vortragen** to report to the court; **sich beschwerdeführend an das höhere ~ wenden** to appeal to the court above; **vom ~ entlassen werden** to go hence; **vor ~ gestellt werden** to go on trial; **dem ~ zur Entscheidung vorgelegt werden** to come up before a court; **sich vor ~ wiederfinden** to land in court; **Fall vor ein anderes ~ ziehen** to evoke a case; **Fall durch Berufung an ein anderes ~ ziehen** to remove a cause by appeal; **vor ~ zitieren** to cite before the court; **j. vor ~ zitieren** to cite s. o. before the court; **Fall an ein unteres ~ zurückverweisen** to relegate a case, to remit to a lower court; **den ~en zustehen** to vest in the courts; **den Anordnungen des ~s zuwiderhandeln** to fail to comply with a court order.

gerichtlich judicial, juridical, jurisdictional, by legal process, judicatory, forensic, justiciary, at law;
~ **und außergerichtlich** in legal and nonlegal matters, judicial and extrajudicial; ~ **bestätigt** *(Testament)* admitted to probate; **sich mit jem. ~ auseinandersetzen** to have a lawsuit with s. o.; **Sache mit jem. ~ austragen** to fight s. o. through the courts; **wirtschaftliche Streitigkeiten ~ austragen** to litigate a commercial dispute; **Zahlungen ~ beitreiben** to enforce payments; ~ **belangen** to process; **j. ~ belangen** to have the law against s. o., to bring s. o. to justice; ~ **beschlagnahmen** to levy an attachment; ~ **feststellen** to establish in court; ~ **eintragen lassen** to file; **Anspruch ~ geltend machen** to enforce a claim; ~ **vorgehen** to take action at law; **gegen j. ~ vorgehen** to take s. o. to court, to have the law of (institute proceedings against) s. o.; **j. ~ vorladen** to serve notice (process) on s. o.;
~**e Abhilfe erzielen** to obtain judicial redress; ~**e Anforderung** invocation; ~**e Ankündigung** legal notice; ~**e Anordnung** order of the court, judicial order, injunction; **vorläufige ~e Anordnung** rule nisi *(Br.)*; ~**e Auflage** court ban; ~**e Auseinandersetzung** lawsuit, court litigation; ~**e Auseinandersetzung gewinnen** to win a court fight; ~**e Auslegung** court interpretation; ~**e Beglaubigung** legalization; ~**e Beschlagnahme** attachment, judicial sequestration; ~**e Besitzeinweisung** vesting order; ~**e Bestallung** appointment by the court; ~**e Beurkundung** legalization; ~**e Entscheidung** judicial decision (determination, act), decision of a court; ~**e Entscheidung beantragen** to sue for a court order, to go before the court; ~**e Feststellung** court declaration; ~**es Geständnis** judicial confession; ~**e Hilfe in Anspruch nehmen** to seek redress in court; ~**e Hinterlegung** bail; ~**e Inanspruchnahme** resort to court; ~**e Kenntnis** judicial notice; ~**e Klage** action in law; ~**e Liquidation** winding up by the court; ~**er Liquidationsbeschluß** winding-up order, liquidation subject to the supervision of the court; ~**e Maßnahmen** court action; ~ **festgesetzte Miete** judicial rent; **ohne ~e Mitwirkung** out of court; ~**es Nachspiel haben** to have a sequel in court; ~ **bestellter Pfleger** judicial factor; ~**er Sachverständiger** expert appointed by the court; ~**e Schritte einleiten** to institute legal proceedings; ~**e Tätigkeit** judicial business; ~**e Trennung** judicial separation; ~ **bestellter Treuhänder** judicial trustee; ~**e Untersuchung** judicial inquiry; ~**e Urkunde** judicial document; ~**es Urteil** judgment, *(Strafakt)* verdict; ~**es Veräußerungsverbot** restraint of alienation *(Br.)*; ~**es Verbot** court injunction; ~**es Verfahren** judicial proceedings; ~**es Verfahren beschleunigen** to speed up judicial business; ~**e Verfolgung** prosecution; **sich der ~en Verfolgung entziehen** to evade justice; ~**e Verfügung** court injunction, writ; **aufgrund ~er Verfügung** by order of the court; ~**er Vergleich** court settlement; ~**e Verhandlung** hearing, trial; ~**e Versteigerung** judicial sale, sale by order of the court; ~**er Vertrag** judicial convention; ~**e Verurteilung** sentence; ~**es Vorgehen** court action; ~**e Vorladung** summons; ~ **bestellter Vormund** guardian by appointment of the court.

Gerichts|akten case (court, judicial) records, court rolls (papers), records of nisi prius *(Br.)*; **zu den ~akten einreichen** to file with the court; **vorläufige ~anordnung** rule nisi; ~**archiv** court archives; ~**assessor** [etwa] assistant judge; ~**auflage zur Unterlassung (Vornahme) einer Handlung** writ of mandamus *(US)*; ~**ausdruck** forensic term.

Gerichtsbarkeit jurisdiction, judicial authority;
ausländische ~ foreign jurisdiction; **ausschließliche ~** exclusive jurisdiction; **erstinstanzliche ~** original jurisdiction; **freiwillige ~** voluntary jurisdiction, noncontentious business; **inländische ~** national jurisdiction *(Br.)*; **konkurrierende ~** coordinate jurisdiction; **nichtausschließliche ~** concurrent jurisdiction; **örtliche ~** territorial jurisdiction; **im gleichen Rang stehende ~** coordinate jurisdiction; **streitige ~** contentious jurisdiction; **übertragene ~** delegated jurisdiction; **zusätzliche ~** cumulative jurisdiction;
~ **in Nachlaßsachen** jurisdiction in probate matters;
ordentliche ~ ausschließen to oust the jurisdiction of a court; ~ **ausüben** to exercise jurisdiction; **einer ~ unterstehen (unterworfen sein)** to be subject (amenable) to (under a) jurisdiction.

Gerichts|beamter court official, judicial (legal) officer, clerk of assize *(Br.)*; **protokollführender ~beamter** master; ~**beauftragter im Entmündigungsverfahren** master in lunacy *(Br.)*; ~**befehl** injunction, court order, writ, precept; ~**behörde** judicial authority, court of justice; ~**beisitzer** associate (puisne, *US*) judge; ~**berichterstattung** court reports.

Gerichtsbeschluß court decree (decision), interlocutor *(Scot.)*, court (judicial) ruling, judicial order, bench warrant, order of the court;
beschwerdefähiger ~ remedial mandatory writ; **formeller ~** formal decree of a court; **vorläufiger ~** order (rule, *Br.*) nisi;
~ **über die Aufhebung der ehelichen Gemeinschaft** separation order;
~ **aufheben** to discharge a writ (an order of the court); ~ **erlassen** to enter a decree, to rule; ~ **erwirken** to obtain an order; ~ **verkünden** to pass judgment, to rule; **sich einem ~ widersetzen** to refuse compliance with a court order.

Gerichts|bezirk judicial circuit *(US)* (district), jurisdiction, area of a district, division, judicial township *(US)*, Justice Ayres *(Scot.)*; **zuständiger ~bezirk** venue; **zu einem ~bezirk gehören** to lie within the jurisdiction; ~**bibliothek** county library; ~**bote** usher, messenger, marshall *(US)*; ~**buchhalter** accountant of a court; ~**chemiker** public analyst; ~**diener** usher, beadle, messenger, tipstaff, marshall *(US)*, paritor; ~**dolmetscher** court interpreter; **vereidigter ~dolmetscher** official translation expert for the courts; ~**eingangsstelle** seal office *(Br.)*.

Gerichtsentscheidung court decision (order), judicial decision (determination, ruling), determination of a court, legal decision, *(Urteil)* judgment, adjudication;
~**en** law reports;
inzident getroffene ~ collateral estoppel; **maßgebliche ~** authority; **vorläufige ~** order nisi, rule nisi *(Br.)*; **wirtschaftsfreundliche ~** court ruling favo(u)rable to industry;
~ **beantragen** to sue for a court order; ~ **fällen** to give a ruling; ~ **zu jds. Gunsten fällen** to give a ruling in favo(u)r of s. o.; **sich über eine gegenteilige ~ hinwegsetzen** to defy an adverse court ruling.

Gerichtserfahrung trial experience.

Gerichts|fälle, anstehende ~fälle erledigen to clear the docket (forum, *US*); ~**ferien** nonterm, recess *(US)*, long vacations *(Br.)*; **in den ~ferien** out of term; ~**gebäude** law court, courthouse *(US)*, pretorium *(Scot.)*; ~**gebrauch** judicial custom; ~**herr** magistrate, judge, court-baron *(Br.)*.

Gerichtshof [law] court, court of justice, bar, [judicatory] tribunal, judicature, judicial assembly;
vor versammeltem ~ in open court;
Internationaler ~ World Court; **Ständiger Internationaler ~** International Court of Justice; **niedriger ~** inferior court; **oberster ~** Supreme Court of Judicature, High Court of Justice *(Br.)*, Supreme Court *(US)*; **vollzähliger ~** sitting in banc;
~ **der Europäischen Gemeinschaft** European Community Court of Justice;
~ **einsetzen** to constitute a tribunal; **dem ~ einen Fall als Berichterstatter vortragen** to report to the court.

Gerichts|hoheit jurisdiction, judicial authority; ~**hoheit in Arbeitsrechtsfragen** industrial jurisdiction; ~**instanz** instance; ~**kanzlei** court registry, record office *(Br.)*; ~**kasse** taxing master's office; ~**kenntnis** judicial notice; ~**klausel** *(Völkerrecht)* jurisdictional clause.

Gerichtskosten court costs (fees, *Br.*), legal costs *(Br.)*, [taxable] costs, law (legal) expenses, litigation expenses *(US)*, law charges;
~ **auferlegen** to order to pay the costs; ~ **festsetzen** to tax the costs; ~ **anteilig auf die Parteien verteilen** to apportion the costs to the sides;
~**entscheidung** judgment (certificate, *Br.*) for costs, bill of taxed costs; ~**festsetzung** bill of costs; ~**rechnung** bill of costs *(US)*; ~**vorschuß** security for costs.
Gerichts|kundigkeit judicial cognizanee; ~**medizin** forensic (legal) medicine, medical jurisprudence.
gerichts|medizinisch medicolegal; ~**notorisch** of judicial notice; ~**notorische Tatsachen** jurisdiction notice.
Gerichtsordnung court practice, standing rules of a court.
Gerichtsort forum;
zuständiger ~ venue;
~ **bestimmen** to fix a venue; ~ **verlegen** to change the venue.
Gerichts|periode session, law term; ~**person** court officer; ~**personal** court personnel; ~**polizei** bailiff; ~**präsident** presiding (president) judge, chief judge *(US)*; ~**praxis** law practice; ~**protokoll** record of a court, court rolls, entry of judgment; ~**reporter** police reporter; ~**saal** court [room], judgment hall; ~**saal räumen lassen** to have the court cleared, to order the court to be cleared; ~**sache** judicial business, matter, case; ~**sachverständiger** expert appointed by the court; ~**schranke** bar; ~**schreiber** keeper of the records, clerk [of the court], registrar, recorder, marshal, actuary; ~**siegel** seal of the court.
Gerichtssitzung [sitting of a] court, court hearing, session, banc, diet;
in öffentlicher ~ in open court; **zwischen einzelnen** ~**en** out of term;
~ **abhalten** to sit in court; ~ **eröffnen** to declare a court in session.
Gerichts|spalte judgment column; ~**sprache** legal terminology; ~**sprengel** circuit, perambulation; ~**spruch** judgment, ruling of a court; ~**stadium** court stage.
Gerichtsstand venue, [place of] jurisdiction, legal domicile;
allgemeiner ~ general jurisdiction; **ausschließlicher** ~ exclusive jurisdiction; **dinglicher** ~ court where the subject matter is situated; **konkurrierender** ~ concurrent jurisdiction; **vereinbarter** ~ special jurisdiction; **zuständiger** ~ proper venue, jurisdiction of subject matter;
~ **der Erbschaft** probate jurisdiction; ~ **des Erfüllungsortes** forum contractus, place of contracting; ~ **der unerlaubten Handlung** forum actus; ~ **in Nachlaßsachen** probate jurisdiction; ~ **des Tatorts** criminal jurisdiction; ~ **des Wohnsitzes** territorial jurisdiction, court of domicile;
~ **ablehnen** to refuse to acknowledge a jurisdiction; ~ **vereinbaren** to stipulate a jurisdiction.
Gerichts|standsvereinbarung, ~**standsklausel** clause stipulating jurisdiction, jurisdictional clause, venue; ~**statistik** judicial statistics; ~**stil** style of court; ~**system** judiciary; ~**tag** judicial (legal, court) day, day of hearing, *(fig.)* doom; **allgemeiner** ~**tag** general return day; ~**tagebuch** appearance docket; ~**tagung** assize; ~**tätigkeit** judicial function.
Gerichtstermin day of hearing, appearance day, term, sitting of the court, *(Friedensrichter)* session of the peace;
anstehender ~ issuable term;
~ **anberaumen (ansetzen)** to fix (assign) a day for a hearing in court; ~ **versäumen** to default.
Gerichts|urkunde judicial document, court record; ~**urteil** judicial decision (determination), court order, judgment, sentence of a court, *(Strafprozeß)* verdict; ~**urteil in zweiter Instanz bestätigen** to uphold a decision; ~**usance** practice of the courts, court practice.
Gerichtsverfahren legal (judicial, judiciary) proceedings, proceedings at law, court (legal) procedure, procedure of a court, style of a court of justice, *(einzelnes Verfahren)* lawsuit, process, court suit (procedure), trial process;
durch ein ordentliches ~ by due process of law;
abgekürztes ~ summary proceedings; **fehlerhaftes** ~ mistrial; **gerechtes und objektives** ~ fair and impartial trial; **schriftliches** ~ trial by certificate; **schwebendes** ~ pending proceedings; **unzuständiges** ~ improper legal proceeding;
~ **unkonventionell abwickeln** to cut corners in legal procedure *(coll.)*; ~ **gegen j. anstrengen** to institute (take) legal proceedings against s. o.; **neues** ~ **in Gang bringen** to bring a fresh court suit; ~ **einleiten** to take action; ~ **einstellen** to drop court proceedings; ~ **für ungültig erklären** to annul judicial proceedings; ~ **protokollieren** to record proceedings of a court.
Gerichts|verfassung judiciary, system of justice; ~**verfassungsgesetz** Judicature Act *(Br.)*, Judiciary Act *(US)*; ~**verfügung** judicial order (writ), order of the court, bench warrant; **zwingende** ~**verfügung** peremptory mandamus.
Gerichtsverhandlung hearing in court, judicial (court) proceedings, court hearing, *(Strafverfahren)* trial of an action;
in öffentlicher ~ at bar, in open court;
~ **vor dem Einzelrichter** trial before a single judge (at nisi prius);
~ **abhalten** to hold (sit in) court; ~ **eröffnen** to open court; **ungestörte** ~ **sicherstellen** to fence *(Scot.)*; **sich einer** ~ **unterziehen** to stand one's trial.
Gerichts|vollzieher sheriff's officer, minister, [bound] bailiff *(Br.)*, marshal *(US)*; **beauftragter** ~**vollzieher** special bailiff; ~**vollzieherkosten** sheriff's fees; ~**vorsitzender** presiding judge; ~**wachtmeister** court guard, tipster, court marshal *(US)*, usher; ~**weg beschreiten** to go to law (before the court); ~**wesen** judiciary.
Gerichts|zeit, allgemeine general term; ~**zeitung** law review; ~**zuständigkeit** venue, jurisdiction.
gerieren, sich vornehm to play the gentleman.
gering small, little, slight, scanty, petty, *(billig)* cheap, *(gewöhnlich)* low, coarse, *(minderwertig)* inferior, low, *(unbedeutend)* paltry, insignificant, trifling;
~ **gerechnet** at least;
~**er** *(Wert)* inferior;
~**e Abschwächung** *(Börse)* slight decline; ~**e Anforderungen an j. stellen** to make no great demands on s. o.; ~**es Angebot** poor supply; ~**es Ansehen genießen** to be held in low esteem; ~**e Ansprüche stellen** to be moderate in one's demands; **mit** ~**en Ausnahmen** with few exceptions; ~**e Aussichten** bad lookout; ~**es Einkommen** slender (low) income; ~**e Entfernung** short distance; ~**e Erfolgsaussichten** slim chances of success; ~**e Fahrlässigkeit** slight negligence; ~**e Fortschritte machen** to make little progress; ~**er Gewinn** small profit; ~**e Gewinnchance** slim chance of profit; **von** ~**er Herkunft sein** to be of humble origin; ~**e Kenntnisse** scanty knowledge; ~**er Lohn** low wages; **keine** ~**e Meinung von sich haben** to think no small beer of o. s.; ~**e Menge** small quantity; ~**e Miete** low lease; **mit** ~**en Mitteln** with limited means; **über** ~**e Mittel verfügen** to be scarce of money; ~**er Ölverbrauch** low oil consumption; **zu einem** ~**en Preis verkaufen** to sell at a low price; ~**e Qualität** inferior (cheap, poor) quality; ~**e Schwierigkeiten** minor difficulties; ~**e Tiefe** *(Gewässer)* shallowness; ~**er Tiefgang** shallow draught; ~**er Verbrauch** low consumption; ~**es Vergehen** petty offence; ~**er Verlust** trivial loss; ~**e Vertrautheit mit einem Thema** slender acquaintance with a subject; ~**er Vorrat** scant supply; **von** ~**em Wert** of trifling value; ~**eren Wert angeben** to understate the value; ~**e Zunahme** slight increase.
geringachten to set little store by;
j. ~ to have a low opinion of s. o.; **Gefahr** ~ to make light of a danger; **jds. Rat** ~ to take little heed of s. one's advice.
geringer werden to decline, to decrease, to fall off, to diminish, to abate.
geringfügig trifling, trivial, petty, slight, fiddling, inappreciable, little, minor, *(Betrag)* paltry, insignificant, inconsiderable, *(wertlos)* frivolous, vile, worthless;
~ **nachgeben** to decline slightly;
~**e Abänderungen** minor changes; ~**e Angelegenheiten** trivial matters; **aus** ~**em Anlaß** from a trifle; **mit** ~**en Ausnahmen** with but few exceptions; ~**er Betrag** petty amount, paltry sum; ~**er Fehler** slight (trifling) error; ~**er Geldbetrag** small sum of money; ~**e Mängel** minor defects; ~**e Menge** negligible quantity; ~**er Preis** low (cheap) price; ~**e Reparaturen** minor repairs; ~**er Schaden** negligible damage; ~**e Schwierigkeiten** petty difficulties; ~**e Summe** insignificant (paltry) sum; ~**er Tiefgang** shallow draft; ~**er Umsatz** little business; ~**e Unbequemlichkeiten** little discomforts; ~**er Unterschied** negligible difference; ~**e Verletzung** minor injury; ~**er Verlust** insignificant (trivial) loss; ~**er Verweis** small one *(sl.)*.
Geringfügigkeit smallness, slightness, negligibility, triviality, paltriness, pinhead, *(Verbrechen)* petty nature, bagatelle;
~ **einer Summe** paltriness of an amount;
Verfahren wegen ~ **einstellen** to dismiss a case for want of sufficient ground.
geringhaltig low-grade, base, poor, below standard, *(Münze)* of base alloy.
geringschätzen to set little store by, to depreciate, to derogate, to disdain;
etw. ~ to think lightly of s. th., to hold s. th. cheap.

geringschätzig derogatory, disparaging, disdainful, contemptuous, depreciatory;
j. ~ ansehen to give s. o. a look of contempt; **~ behandeln** to pooh-pooh; **~ lächeln** to smile scornfully; **~ sprechen** to speak degradingly.
Geringschätzung contempt, disregard, disdain, scorn;
j. mit ~ behandeln to treat s. o. with contempt.
geringst slightest, least;
nicht die ~e Ahnung haben not to have the foggiest idea; **nicht die ~en Aussichten** not a dog's chance; **~es Gebot** *(Auktion)* lowest bid; **~e Kleinigkeit** merest trifle, at the drop of a hat; **~e meiner Sorgen** the least of my worries; **nicht den ~en Unterschied machen** not to make two straws' difference *(coll.)*; **nicht den ~en Zweifel haben** not to have the slightest doubt.
Geringste minimum, slightest detail, single thing;
nicht im ~n not in the least; **nicht das ~ davon** not a little of it; **nicht das ~ ausmachen** not to make two straws' of difference *(coll.)*; **nicht das ~ erreichen** not to get to first base *(sl.)*; **sich nicht im ~n verantwortlich fühlen** to feel in no way responsible; **sich nicht das ~ daraus machen** not to care a fig (straw) about it; **nicht das ~ übersehen** not to miss a thing no matter how small; **nicht das ~ verstehen** not to understand a single thing.
geringstmöglich least possible.
geringverzinslich at low interest rates.
geringwertig base, coarse, poor, of small value, rejected, inferior, of low quality;
~ sein to be of little value;
~e Anlagegüter *(Einkommensteuer)* inadmitted assets; **~es Erz** low-grade ore; **~e Waren** inferior (low-quality) goods.
gerinnen lassen, das Blut in den Adern to make one's blood curdle.
Gerippe skeleton, *(Arbeit)* outline, *(Gebäude)* carcass, *(Mensch)* bag of bones, *(Schiff)* frame;
wie ein wandelndes ~ aussehen to be a living skeleton.
gerissen cunning, clever, crafty, slick, wily, wide *(Br., sl.)*;
~ ausgedacht cleverly thought out;
ganz schön ~ sein to be up to a thing or two; **~er als der Spion sein** to outsmart a spy *(US coll.)*.
gern|gegeben willing, voluntary; **~ geschehen** don't mention it, you are welcome *(US)*; **am wenigsten ~ gesehen** least favo(u)rite; **liebend ~** with great pleasure;
j. schrecklich ~ haben to like s. o. a hell of a lot; **~ und gut 500 DM kosten** to cost DM 500 easily; **~ hier sein** to like it here; **etw. ~ tun** to be pleased (love) to do s. th.;
das hört man ~ that's good news; **der kann mich mal ~ haben** he can go to hell;
~ gesehener Gast very welcome guest.
Gernegroß would-be, show-off, whippersnapper, heavy swell *(Br.)*.
Geröll pebbles, boulders, detritus;
~halde scree, talus *(US)*.
Geruch odo(u)r, *(Wohlgeruch)* scent, fragance;
durchdringender ~ penetrating odo(u)r;
in schlechtem ~ stehen to be in bad repute; **im ~ eines Geizhalses stehen** to have the name of a miser.
Geruchs|belästigung malodo(u)r; **~film** acromarama *(Br.)*; **~sinn** olfactory sense; **~verschluß** trap.
Gerücht rumo(u)r, report, grapevine, scuttlebutt *(US sl.)*;
begründetes ~ well-grounded rumo(u)r; **grundloses ~** idle rumo(u)r; **hartnäckiges ~** persistent rumo(u)r; **rufschädigende ~e** hurtful rumo(u)rs; **umlaufendes ~** floating rumo(u)r; **unbestätigtes ~** vague rumo(u)r; **unverbürgtes ~** unconfirmed rumo(u)r; **allgemein verbreitetes ~** common report;
böse ~e über j. im Umlauf evil reports afloat about s. o.;
~e ausstreuen to spread a rumo(u)r; **~ bestätigen** to confirm a rumo(u)r; **sich heimlich ein ~ erzählen** to whisper a tale; **allerlei ~e über die Liquiditätsschwierigkeiten einer Firma hören** to hear much talk about a company's solvency; **~ lancieren** to float a rumo(u)r; **einem ~ nachgehen** to trace back a rumo(u)r; **einem ~ keinen Glauben schenken** to give no credence to a rumo(u)r; **~ in Umlauf setzen** to start a rumo(u)r, to put about a rumo(u)r, to set a town agog; **~ verbreiten** to spread a report [rumo(u)r], to rumo(u)r, to vent a tale; **~ vertuschen** to blanket a rumo(u)r; **~ bis zu seinem Ursprung zurückverfolgen** to trace a rumo(u)r back to its source.
Gerüchtemacher rumo(u)rer, panicmonger.
gerüchteweise, nur it's mere hearsay;
~ verlautet it is rumo(u)red.
gerufen, wie well met;
jem. wie ~ kommen to come in the nick of time.
gerührt touched, moved.
geruhsam quiet, peaceful.
Gerümpel garbage, stuff, junk, deadwood, lumber;
~verkauf garbage sale.
Gerüst scaffold, stage, *(Bohrgerät)* derrick, *(Plan)* skeleton, outline, framework;
das gesamte ~ der vorgebrachten Argumente the whole fabric of argument;
~ abschlagen to take down a scaffold; **~ aufstellen** to [furnish a] scaffold; **Haus mit einem ~ umgeben** to scaffold a house;
~bau scaffolding.
gerüstet prepared, ready.
Gerüstkran gantry crane.
gerüttelt Maß full measure.
gesagt, kurz in a nutshell; **oben ~** above-mentioned; **ganz offen ~** straight from the shoulder *(sl.)*; **unter uns ~** between you and me and the gatepost (lamppost);
es sich ~ sein lassen to take a hint.
gesalzene Rechnung salt account, swing(e)ing bill.
gesammelt *(Werke)* collected.
gesamt all, whole, aggregate, entire, collective, general, overall, overhead, blanket *(US)*, total, all-in-all, allout, en bloc, *(Haftung)* joint and several;
~e Bevölkerung whole country, entire (total) population; **~e Familie** whole family; **zur ~en Hand** jointly, in common; **~e Handelsbilanz** overall trade balance; **~er Industriequerschnitt** all-industry average; **~e Kosten** total (overall) costs, total outlay (expenses); **~en Markt erfassen** to blanket the entire market; **~es Nettoeinkommen** total net income; **~es Vermögen** entire fortune; **~e Vermögensverwaltung** general administration of an estate.
Gesamt|ablehnung der Geschworenen challenge to the panel *(Br.)*; **~abmessungen** overall measurements; **~absatz** total marketing (sales); **~abschluß** *(Rundfunkwerbung)* blanket contract; **~abschreibung** total allowance; **~abtretung** general assignment; **~abweichung** *(der Istkosten von den Standardkosten)* gross variance; **~aktiva** total assets; **~angebot** total supply; **~angebotskurve** aggregate supply curve; **~annuität** complete annuity; **~anordnung** general plan; **~ansicht** general view; **~anstieg** overall increase.
Gesamtarbeits|kräftereserve total possible labo(u)r force; **~losigkeit** overall unemployment; **~vertrag** collective agreement; **~zeit** total hours of work.
Gesamt|aufkommen total yield (revenue); **~auflage** *(Zeitung)* general circulation, net press (total print) run; **~aufnahme** establishing shot; **~aufstellung** general statement; **~auftrag** *(Werbung)* block booking; **~auftragswert** total value of goods ordered, *(Baufirma)* total work on hand; **~auftrieb der Weltwirtschaft** international (world-wide) boom; **~aufwand** aggregate expenditure, total outlay; **~aufwand im Inland** gross domestic expenditure; **~aufwand der Wirtschaft** business spending; **~ausbeute** total recovery (take, haul); **~ausfuhr** national export, total exports; **~ausgabe** complete edition; **~ausgaben** outright expenses, outgoings, total expenditure; **tatsächliche ~ausgaben** expenses incurred; **~ausgleich** settlement in full; **~auslagen** total (outright) expenses; **~ausschuß** general (joint) committee; **~außenhandel** aggregate foreign trade; **~ausstoß** total output, aggregate output; **~ausweis** consolidated financial statement; **~bearbeitungszeit** operating time; **~bedarf** total demand (requirements), entire need; **~bedingungen** overall conditions; **~belastung** connected (total) load; **offene ~belastung** *(Grundstück)* floating charge *(Br.)*; **~belegschaft** total workforce, force of men employed; **~bereich** total field; **~bericht** overall report; **~besitz** entirety of estate, general property; **~bestand** total stock on hand; **~beteiligung** joint interest; **~betrachtung** general survey.
Gesamtbetrag aggregate (total, entire) amount, sum total;
~ der täglichen Debet- und Kreditsalden einer Verrechnungsstelle clearinghouse balance; **~ der Einkünfte** aggregate income; **~ der von einer Girozentrale bei der Bank eingehenden Schecks** in-clearing; **~ der Verbindlichkeiten** total liabilities; **~ der Wechsel- und Scheckforderungen einer Bank an die Girozentrale** out-clearing;
~ von 100 Pfund erreichen to reach a total of £ 100.
Gesamt|betrieb whole concern; **~betriebswert** going-concern value; **~bevölkerung** entire (total) population, whole country; **auf die ~bevölkerung umrechnen** to project to the entire population; **~bewertung** total evaluation; **~bezüge** compensation (remuneration) package; **~bilanz** consolidated balance sheet; **volkswirtschaftliche ~bilanz** national accounts, national [income] accounting, blue book *(Br.)*; **~bild** overall picture; **~bürgen** joint guarantors; **~bürgschaft** collateral (joint) guaranty, joint surety; **~demission nehmen** to resign in a body;

~dimensionen eines Zimmers overall measurements of a room; **~dividende** total dividend; **~dotierung** remuneration package; **~durchschnitt** total average; **~eigenkapital** total proprietorship; **~eigentum** aggregate property, *(gemeinschaftliches Eigentum)* joint title, *(Kollektiv)* collectivity; **~eigentümer** joint owners; **~eindruck** general effect (impression); **~einfuhr** total imports; **~einfuhrkontingent** overall import quota; **~eingänge** total receipts; **~einkommen** entire (gross, aggregate, total) income, total revenue; **gemeinsames ~einkommen** total joint income; **progressive ~einkommensteuer** surtax *(Br.)*; **~einlage** total subscription; **~einnahme** total receipts, business; **~eintrag** compound entry; **~einzahlungen** total deposits; **~entschädigung** total indemnity (compensation); **~entwicklung** overall trend; **~entwicklung der Gewinne negativ beeinflussen** to drag down the overall profit picture; **~erbe** universal (sole) heir, sole legatee *(US)*; **~erfindung** joint invention; **~ergebnis** global (total, overall) result; **~ergebnisrechnung** statement of income and accumulated earnings; **~erhebung** universal census; **~erlös** total (entire) proceeds, overall profit; **~ersparnis** total saving; **~ertrag** entire (total) proceeds, total revenue, aggregate profit, *(Erzeugung)* aggregate (total) output; **~erzwingung** total output (production, turnout), *(Industrie)* net output; **~etat** summary (overhead, master, overall) budget, *(Werbeagentur)* billing; **~etat ablehnen** to throw out the whole budget; **~etat mit allem Drum und Dran ablehnen** to reject the whole budget lock, stock and barrel; **~familie** joint family; **~fassungsvermögen** total capacity; **flexibel in die ~finanzierung mit einbeziehen** to incorporate flexibly in the overall financing; **~fläche** total area; **~fluggewicht** full load, all-up [weight]; **~forderung** total claim; **~frachtsatz** joint rate; **~gebiet** entire territory; **~gebühr** inclusive charge; **~gehalt** salary package; **~geldstrafe** collective fine; **~genehmigung** block licence; **~geschäftsführung** general management; **~gewicht** total load (weight); **höchstzulässiges ~gewicht** maximum permissible weight; **~gewinn** overall profit; **~gläubiger** joint and several creditors; **~gut** *(Gütergemeinschaft)* common property, goods in communion *(Scot.)*, community property *(US)*; **~haftung** joint liability, joint guaranty; **~hand** co-ownership; **~handel** total (aggregate) trade; **~handelsbilanz** total balance of trade; **~handlungsvollmacht** joint procuration.

Gesamthands|besitz estate of joint tenancy; **~besitzer** tenant in common; **~eigentum** tenancy (estate) in common, joint tenancy (title), estate by the entirety, joint ownership, *(Ehegatten)* tenancy by the entirety, *(Erbengemeinschaft)* parcenary, coparcenary; **~eigentum besitzen** to hold joint property, to have joint ownership; **~eigentum in Bruchteilseigentum umwandeln** to sever a joint tenancy; **~eigentümer** joint tenant, *(Erbe)* parcener; **~eigentümer sein** to participate in an estate, to hold joint property; **~eigentumsrecht** joint property interest; **~gemeinschaft** joint ownership; **~gläubiger** joint creditors; **~schuldner** joint debtors; **~vermögen** jointly owned assets; **~verpflichtung** joint promise.

Gesamthaushalt[splan] master (summarized, overall) budget.

Gesamtheit complex, entirety, body, gross, mass, aggregate, aggregation, whole;
als ~ collectively;
~ der Beschäftigten overall employment; **~ der Fürsorgeempfänger** relief population; **~ der Gläubiger** general body of creditors; **~ der Haushaltsbewilligungen** obligations incurred; **~ der Maßnahmen** group of actions; **~ der betrieblichen Sozialaufwendungen** penalties *(US)*; **~ der Steuerfreibeträge** total allowances due *(Br.)*.

Gesamt|hersteller joint producer; **~herstellungskosten** total cost price; **~hochschule** comprehensive university *(Br.)*; **erfaßte ~hörerzahl** cumulative audience; **~hypothek** blanket (general, collective, joint, aggregate, consolidated, *US*) mortgage; **~hypothek bilden** to consolidate mortgages *(US)*; **~index** overall index; **~inhalt einer Urkunde** body of a document; **~inlandsinvestitionen** gross domestic investment; **~investitionen** total investments; **~jahreseinkommen** total annual revenue; **~kapazität** global (total) capacity; **~kapitalausstattung** total capitalization; **~kassenumsatz** total turnover; **~katalog** *(Bibliothek)* union catalog(ue); **~kaufbetrag** aggregate amount of purchase; **~konkursliste** Central Register of the Department of Official Receivers; **~kontingent** overall quota; **~konzeption** master plan; **~kosten** total cost (expense, outlay), overall costs; **~kosten einer Pensionsregelung übernehmen** to pick up the entire cost of a pension plan; **~kurswert** total market value; **~lage** general situation; **wirtschaftliche ~lage** general level of business, overall economic outlook; **~länge** overall length; **~lebensdauer** *(Lebensversicherung)* joint lives; **~leistung** overall efficiency, total output, *(Energie)* total power; **volkswirtschaftliche ~leistung** gross national product; **~leistungsvermögen** total capacity; **~leserzahl** *(Zeitung)* reader circulation; **~liquidation** joint liquidation, complete winding-up; **~liquidität** total liquidity ratio; **~masse** total (general) estate; **deflationistische ~maßnahmen** reflationary package; **~menge** total balance; **~mieteinnahmen** total rentroll; **~mitgliederversammlung** general meeting; **~nachfolge** universal succession; **~nachfolger** universal successor; **~nachfrage** all-out demand; **wirksame ~nachfrage** effective demand; **~nachfragekurve** total demand curve; **~nachlaß** aggregate (total, aggregate) estate; **dem ~nachlaß zufallen** to fall back into residue; **~nachweis** overall index; **~nettoeinkommen** total net income; **~niveau** overall level; **~nutzen** total utility; **~nutzung** joint use; **~nutzungsdauer** *(Maschine)* physical life; **~obligo** overall engagement; **~organisation** overall organization; **~pachteinnahmen** total rentroll; **~plan** general (overall) plan, master schedule; **~planung** overall planning, master scheduling; **unternehmerische ~planung** corporate planning *(US)*; **~police** joint policy; **~position** overall position; **~prämie** total premium; **~preis** allround (overhead, lump-sum) price; **~preisindex** *(Sozialprodukt)* average price level.

Gesamtproduktion total output (production), total turnout, *(Industriezweig)* net output;
volkswirtschaftliche ~ national output;
~ der Landwirtschaft agricultural output;
zu etw. 40% an der ~ beteiligt sein to account for about 40 per cent of the net output.

Gesamt|produktionskosten total production costs; **~prokura** joint signature; **~prüfung** general examination; **~quittung** receipt in full; **volkswirtschaftliche ~rechnung** national [income] accounting, national accounts, blue book *(Br.)*; **~rechte erwerben** to buy rights outright; **~rechtsnachfolge** universal succession; **~rechtsnachfolger** universal successor; **~regelung** overall settlement; **~reservenbedarf** *(Währung)* overall reserve needs; **~revision** overall examination; **~risiko** overall risk; **~rücklage** accumulated reserves; **~schaden** necessary (general) damages, *(Feuerversicherung)* total loss; **fingierter ~schaden** constructive total loss; **~schadenshaftung** unlimited liability; **~schätzung** overall estimate; **~schau** survey; **~schema** overall plan; **~schulausbildung** comprehensive secondary education *(Br.)*; **~schuld** entire (total, whole, gross, *US*) debt, *(gemeinsame Schuld)* joint and several debt, *(Ehepaar)* community debt; **~schuldner** joint and several debtors; **als ~schuldner haften** to be liable jointly and severally.

gesamtschuldnerisch joint and several, solidary;
~ haftbar liable jointly and severally;
~ haften to be liable jointly and severally;
~e Haftung joint and several responsibility, joint liability; **~es Zahlungsversprechen** joint and several bond (note, *US*).

Gesamtschuldnerschaft solidarity, joint liability.

Gesamt|schuldschein joint promissory note; **~schuldschein ohne Einrede der Vorausklage** joint and several bond (note, *US*); **~schuldverpflichtung** joint and several obligation, joint obligation; **~schuldversprechen** joint and several bond (note, *US*); **~schule** comprehensive school *(Br.)*; **~schülerzahl** total school population; **internationale ~situation** world situation.

gesamtstaatlich national.

Gesamt|stärke *(mil.)* overall strength; **~status** consolidated statement; **~statut** general statute (law); **~steigerung** overall increase; **~steueraufkommen** tax levy, total sum raised by treasury receipts; **~stimmenzahl** total votes cast; **~stimmenzahl eines Landes** national vote; **~strafe** cumulative sentence; **~streitkräfte** joint forces.

Gesamtsumme [sum] total, grand total, total amount, footing, global (gross) sum, aggregate [amount];
~ der Abschreibungen *(Bilanz)* accumulated depreciation; **~ der Abzahlungskredite** instal(l)ment credits outstanding.

Gesamt|tarifvertrag area-wide bargaining; **~tonnage** total tonnage; **~tonnagesatz** cargo rate; **~überblick über ein Projekt** general outline of a scheme; **~überholung** collective overhaul; **~überschuß** total surplus; **~übersicht** overall survey, overhead statement; **~übertragung des Schuldnervermögens zwecks Gläubigerbenachteiligung** fraudulent transfer of property; **~umfang** total volume; **~umlaufvermögen** total current assets; **~umsatz** aggregate (overall) sales, total sales (turnover), global turnover, total volume of sales, *(Bergbau)* vend *(Br.)*; **~umsatz der in den konsolidierten Jahresabschluß einbezogenen Gesellschaften** total sales of the consolidated companies; **~umsatz der im Stadtzentrum gelegenen Geschäfte** downtown sales *(US)*; ~**unternehmen** whole concern; ~**veranlagung** overall assessment; ~**verantwortung** corporate responsibility; ~**verantwortung im Vorstandsbereich übernehmen** to assume responsibility in the overall operating management; ~**verband** head organization.

gesamtverbindlich haften to be liable jointly and severally.

Gesamt|verbindlichkeit joint and several obligation, joint (gross, *US*) liability; ~**verbindlichkeiten** *(Bilanz)* total liabilities; ~**verbrauch** overal consumption; ~**verdienst** full-time (total) earnings; ~**verdienst bei Anwendung des Prämienlohnsystems** piecework earnings; ~**vereinbarung** package deal, *(Tarifabkommen)* collective agreement; ~**vergleich** joint composition; ~**vergleich mit den Gläubigern** compounding with one's creditors; ~**vergütung** compensation (remuneration) package; **übliche fünfstellige ~vergütung für leitende Angestellte** normal senior remuneration package into five figures; ~**verhalten** collective behavio(u)r; ~**verkäufe** aggregate sales, bulk sale *(US)*; ~**verkaufseinnahmen** sales revenue; ~**verkaufswert** aggregate sales value.

Gesamtverlust overall (total) loss;
nur bei ~ total loss only;
~**e** *(mil.)* total casualties;
geschätzter ~ total estimated deficiency; **tatsächlicher** ~ actual total loss.

Gesamt|vermächtnisnehmer universal (general) legatee; ~**vermögen** estate and effects, assets, aggregate estate; **steuerpflichtiges ~vermögen** aggregate taxable property; ~**verpflichtung** total (gross, *US*) liability, *(gemeinsame Verpflichtung)* joint obligation; **seine ~verschuldung abschätzen** to reckon the size of one's total indebtedness; ~**versicherung** comprehensive (all-in, all-risks, all-loss, *US*) insurance; ~**vertrag** joint contract; ~**vollmacht** joint power of attorney, collective power; ~**volumen** total volume; ~**vorgang des Erteilungsverfahrens** *(Patentwesen)* file wrapper history; ~**vorsatz** general intent; ~**vorstand** general management; ~**werk** *(Autor)* collected works; ~**wert** total (aggregate) value, *(fundierte öffentliche Anleihe)* omnium; ~**wert der Aktiva** total assets; ~**wert des Wechselobligos** total value of discounts outstanding; ~**wirkung** overall effect, ensemble; ~**wirtschaft** overall economy, total trade, national economy.

gesamtwirtschaftliche|Leistungsfähigkeit overall economic potential; ~ **Nachfrage** overall economic demand.

Gesamt|wohl common weal (welfare); ~**zahl** total number, [grand] total, *(Bevölkerung)* population; **mögliche ~zahl der eingeschalteten Funk- und Fernsehgeräte** available audience; **erfaßte ~zahl der Hörer (Zuschauer)** cumulative (accumulative) audience; **monatliche ~zahlung** all-in-one monthly payment; ~**zahlungsbilanz** overall balance of payments; ~**zeichnung**, ~**zeichnungsberechtigung** joint signature; ~**zeit von fünf Jahren** aggregate period of five years; ~**zufuhr** aggregate (total) arrivals; ~**zuladungsgewicht** dead-weight tonnage; ~**zuschauerzahl** all-over attendance.

Gesandter minister resident, foreign minister, envoy;
außerordentlicher ~ extraordinary envoy; **außerordentlicher und bevollmächtigter** ~ minister plenipotentiary and envoy extraordinary; **päpstlicher** ~ legate; **ständiger** ~ resident.

Gesandtschaft legation, embassy, *(ständige)* mission *(US)*.

Gesandtschafts|attaché attaché; ~**bericht** dispatch; ~**gebäude** legation, embassy; ~**kanzlei** chancellery; ~**personal** legation, mission; ~**rat** counsel(l)or.

Gesang|der Vögel music of the birds;
falsches ~buch haben to belong to the wrong party.

Gesangseinlage, j. um eine ~ bitten to knock s. o. down for a song *(fam.)*.

Gesangverein glee club.

gesättigter Markt saturated market.

geschädigt injuriously affected, *(Gehirn)* touched.

Geschädigter injured (wronged) party, aggrieved person, *(Unfall)* sufferer, victim, *(Versicherung)* claimant.

geschaffen sein, für etw. wie to be the right man for s. th.

geschafft haben, es to be in smooth waters.

Geschäft business, *(Arbeit)* work, *(Börse)* trading, *(Beruf)* shop, vocation, occupation, business, *(Branche)* trade, business, line, *(Büro)* office, *(Firma)* enterprise, commercial house, firm, concern, establishment, undertaking, company, *(Geschäftsabschluß)* bargain, deal, dealing, transaction, operation, *(Geschäftslokal)* [business] premises, shop, *(Gewerbe)* occupation, trade, job, business, calling, employment, *(Handel)* commerce, trade, market *(US)*, *(Laden)* shop *(Br.)*, store *(US)*, *(Sache)* affair, matter, *(Spekulationen)* venture, *(Vorschlag, coll.)* proposition;
ans ~ gefesselt hog-tied to business; **in ~en** on (engaged in) business; **in ein anrüchiges ~ verwickelt** entangled in a shady business; **voller ~e** shoppy;
~**e** dealings, transactions, interests, operations;
die ~e gehen sehr schlecht there is very little doing;
abgeschlossenes ~ business transacted, deal, completed (executed) transaction; **hohe Gewinne abwerfendes** ~ [business] bonanza; **altrenommiertes** ~ well-established firm; **angesehenes** ~ respectable firm; **anrüchiges** ~ hole-and-corner (shady) business; **anziehendes** ~ improvement in business; **von Anfang an schlecht aufgezogenes** ~ business muddled at the start; **ausgedehntes** ~ extensive trade; **bankähnliche ~e** supplementary banking functions; **bankfremde ~e** nonbanking business (activity); **in Betrieb befindliches** ~ going concern; **in Liquidation befindliches** ~ firm in liquidation; **betreffendes** ~ business in question; **im großen betriebenes** ~ business transacted at large; **auf gemeinschaftlicher Basis betriebenes** ~ joint-purse arrangement; **betriebseigenes** ~ captive shop *(US)*, company store *(US)*; **blühendes** ~ flourishing trade, thriving business; **dickes** ~ big deal; **dringende ~e** pressing business; **dunkles** ~ shady deal (business), funny business, racket *(sl.)*; **effektives** ~ actual business; **gut eingeführtes** ~ well-established business; **einschlägiges** ~ stockist *(Br.)*, one-line shop (store), limited-line retailer *(US)*; **einträgliches** ~ remunerative (lucrative, profitable) business, paying concern; **erstklassiges** ~ first-rate (-class) firm; **faires** ~ square deal; **unter Konkursanfechtung fallende ~e** protected transactions; **faules** ~ shady (hole-and-corner) business, queer transaction; **fingiertes** ~ bogus transaction; **flottes (flottgehendes)** ~ rattling trade, land-office business *(US coll.)*; **fragwürdige ~e** equivocal transactions *(US)*; **führendes** ~ leading firm; **gut fundiertes** ~ sound business [firm]; **gebührenfreie ~e** transactions free of charge; **dem Betrieb gehöriges** ~ captive shop *(US)*, company store *(US)*; **in der Hauptgeschäftsgegend (im Stadtzentrum) gelegenes** ~ central area shop, downtown (inner-city) store *(US)*; **gewagtes** ~ risky undertaking, speculation, speculative enterprise; **gewinnbringendes** ~ profitable enterprise (business); **glänzendgehendes (glänzendes)** ~ booming (roaring) business, gold mine, [business] bonanza; **glattes** ~ *(Börse)* swimming market; **große ~e** *(Börse)* large trade; **gutes** ~ pennyworth, [good] bargain, good stroke of business, big (good) deal; **leidlich gute ~e** fair business; **gutgehendes** ~ flourishing trade, going concern (firm); **stark konjunkturbedingtes** ~ highly cyclical business; **laufende ~e** regular business, day-to-day business, current transactions, current (daily) business, pending business; **lebhaftes** ~ *(Börse)* brisk trading (business); **zugrunde liegendes** ~ underlying transaction; **lohnendes** ~ paying (remunerative) business; **lukratives** ~ lucrative transaction; **mattes** ~ dull business; **mittelgroßes** ~ medium-sized store *(US)*; **nachbörsliches** ~ interoffice deal, afterhours dealing *(Br.)*, business in the street *(Br.)*; **nutzbringendes** ~ profitable business; **persönliches** ~ *(Börsenmakler)* insider trading; **preisdrückendes** ~ cut-price store *(US)*; **preisgünstiges** ~ economy-priced shop, cheap-Jack (-John) *(coll.)*; **reelles** ~ fair dealing firm; **renommiertes** ~ well-reputed firm; **rentables** ~ paying concern, paying business, *(Einzelgeschäft)* profitable business, paying transaction; **ruhiges** ~ slack business; **schlechtes** ~ bad (losing) bargain, poor business, no catch; **schmutziges** ~ dirty business; **schrumpfendes** ~ contracting business; **sicheres** ~ safe business; **sittenwidriges** ~ constructive (equitable, legal) fraud, transaction contrary to the policy of the law; **solides** ~ solid enterprise (firm), substantial house, *(Einzelgeschäft)* sound business; **steuerpflichtiges** ~ taxable transaction; **überseeisches** ~ overseas business; **unbedeutendes** ~ picayune business; **undurchsichtige ~e** hole-and-corner dealings; **unreelles** ~ dishonest business; **unrentables** ~ business that does not pay, not a paying business, white elephant; **unsittliches** ~ unconscionable bargain (transaction); **unvollständiges** ~ uncompleted transaction; **väterliches** ~ father's business; **verbandseigene ~e** interassociation transactions *(US)*; **verbotene ~e** illegal sales; **verdächtiges** ~ queer transaction; **verlustbringendes** ~ losing business; **vermitteltes** ~ transaction arranged; **vorteilhaftes** ~ bargain, deal; **wenig ~e** *(Börse)* little trade (doing); **wichtiges** ~ serious business; **zunehmendes** ~ improvement in trade; **zweideutige ~e** funny business; **zweifelhafte ~e** shady transactions;
~**e mit dem Ausland** foreign trade; ~ **mit erstklassiger Bedienung** high-class service store *(US)*; ~ **in dem nur mit Devisen eingekauft werden kann** hard-currency shop; ~ **in kleinen Effektenabschnitten** odd business *(US)*; ~ **auf Geben**

und Nehmen put and call; ~ **im großen** business transacted at large; ~ **mit Industriekundschaft** industrial outlet; ~**e auf Kommissionsbasis** commission dealings, transactions for third account; ~ **mit erstklassigem Kundenkreis** business with first-rate connections; ~ **unter dem Ladentisch** under-the-counter trading; ~ **in guter Lage** well situated business; ~ **auf feste Lieferung** time bargain; ~ **mit kleiner Marge** tight bargain; ~ **um jeden Preis** hard-nosed business; ~ **für Produkte des täglichen Bedarfs** neighbo(u)rhood shop; ~ **für eigene Rechnung** transaction for own account; ~**e für fremde Rechnung** transaction on third account; ~**e auf laufende Rechnung** dealings for the account; ~ **im Stadtzentrum** central area shop, downtown store *(US)*; ~**e im großen Stil** business transacted at large;

~**e nach etw. abklappern** to go round the shops looking for s. th.; ~ **um jeden Preis abnehmen** to steal business at any price; ~ **absagen** to call off a deal; ~ **abschließen** to drive (strike, close, conclude, enter into) a bargain, to conclude (settle, transact) a business, to enter into a transaction; ~ **erfolgreich abschließen** to wrap up a business deal; ~ **mit Gewinn abschließen** to make a profit out of a transaction; ~ **abtreten** to give up one's business; ~ **abwickeln** to settle a business, *(liquidieren)* to wind up (straighten) one's affairs, to regulate disordered finances; **umfangreiche** ~**e abwickeln** to trade in a large way; ~ **des Gemeinschuldners abwickeln** to wind up the debtor's business; ~ **ankurbeln** to drum up business; **in einem** ~ **anlegen** to invest in a business; **wieder im** ~ **anlegen** to plough (plow, *US*) back in business; **j. für das** ~ **anlernen** to train s. o. to business; ~ **annullieren** to vitiate a transaction; ~ **anregen** to enliven a business; ~ **aufgeben** to go out of (give up, discontinue [one's], dissolve, cut) business, to get out, to give up (leave off) trade, to shut up shop *(US)*, to wind (fold) up *(US)*, *(sich zur Ruhe setzen)* to retire from business; **sein** ~ **auflösen** to liquidate a business, to give up one's business, to wind (shut) up *(US)*; ~ **aufmachen** to set up shop (a business); ~ **großzügig aufziehen** to open a business on a large scale; **sein** ~ **ausdehnen** to expand one's business; **sich im** ~ **nicht mehr auskennen** to be out of the whole business; **aus dem** ~ **ausscheiden** to retire from business; **aus einem** ~ **aussteigen** to go out of business, to fold up *(US)*; ~ **beeinträchtigen** to affect business; ~ **begründen** to settle down in business, to establish o. s.; **sein** ~ **besorgen** to ply one's trade; **jds.** ~**e besorgen** to look after s. one's affairs; **bankmäßige** ~**e besorgen** to supply banking facilities; **j. an einem** ~ **beteiligen** to give s. o. a financial interest in a business; **sich an einem** ~ **beteiligen** to have a share in a venture; ~ **betreiben** to conduct (operate) a business, to run a shop, to carry on (ply) a trade; ~**e betreiben** to play a trade, to do business; **eigenes** ~ **betreiben** to operate one's own business, to be one's own master; **seine** ~**e freizügig betreiben** to deal at arm's length; ~**e mit geliehenem Kapital betreiben** to trade on the equity *(US)*; ~**e in großem Maßstab betreiben** to carry on business on a large scale; ~ **zu Kreditauskunftszwecken beurteilen** to rate a business; **im** ~ **bleiben** to stay in business; **im** ~ **tätig bleiben** to remain active (stay) in business; ~ **zu einem erfolgreichen Abschluß bringen** to put through a business deal, to bring a business to a successful conclusion; **vorteilhaftes** ~ **zum Abschluß bringen** to drive a good bargain; ~ **auf die Beine bringen** to set a business on feet; ~ **wieder in die Höhe bringen** to put a business back on its feet again; ~ **zustande bringen** to secure a business; **immer (ganze Zeit) nur ans** ~ **denken** to always have an eye to business, to be businessman all the time; **j. aus dem** ~ **drängen** to squeeze (force) s. o. out of business; ~**e weiterführen dürfen** to remain in possession of the business; **in ein** ~ **einbrechen** to crack a crib; **ins** ~ **einbringen** to bring into business; **sich [erneut] auf ein** ~ **einlassen** to embark [again] upon a business; **sich auf gewagte** ~**e einlassen** to dabble in speculative concerns; ~ **einleiten** to initiate a deal; ~ **einrichten** to fit out a shop; **seinem Sohn ein** ~ **einrichten** to set up a son in trade; **in ein** ~ **einsteigen** to start a business; **in ein gutgehendes** ~ **einsteigen** to get on the bandwaggon; **j. in sein** ~ **einstellen** to give s. o. a job; ~ **erledigen** to dispatch a business; ~**e aller Art erledigen** to handle any sort of business; **laufende** ~**e erledigen** to deal with current business; ~ **eröffnen** to open a trade (business), to set up shop, to start in business; ~ **errichten** to settle down (set up) in business, to establish o. s., to establish a (set up, start in) business; **sein** ~ **erweitern** to expand one's business; ~ **mit der gesamten Ausstattung erwerben** to buy a shop with all fixtures; **j. im** ~ **etablieren** to set s. o. up in business; ~ **finanzieren** to finance a business; ~ **fortführen** to continue a business; ~ **des Gemeinschuldners fortführen** to carry on the bankrupt's business; ~ **im eigenen Interesse fortführen** to continue a business for one's own ends; ~ **bis zur Liquidierung fortführen** to continue the business for the purpose of winding up; ~ **eines Verstorbenen fortführen** to continue a deceased's business; ~ **führen** to carry on (conduct) a business, to carry on a trade, to manage the concern, to run (manage) a shop; ~ **unter seinem Namen führen** to carry on the business under one's name; **ins (in sein)** ~ **gehen** to go to the office; ~ **rentabel gestalten** to put business on a payable basis; ~ **gründen** to set up shop [for o. s.]; **neues** ~ **gründen** to launch a new business enterprise; ~**e mit jem. haben** to have business with s. o.; **bedeutendes** ~ **haben** to be in a large way of business; **sein eigenes** ~ **haben** to be in business on one's own account; **gutgehendes** ~ **haben** to drive a good trade; **kleines** ~ **haben** to be in a small way of business; **Nase für [gute]** ~**e haben** to have a keen eye for a bargain; **aus dem** ~ **herausdrängen** to squeeze out of business; ~ **hochbringen** to work up a business; **jem. für ein** ~ **interessieren** to enlist s. o. in an enterprise; **sich nur für sein** ~ **interessieren** to be intent on one's business, to be businessman all the time, to be all business; ~ **in Bausch und Bogen kaufen** to buy the whole stock [of a business]; ~ **von der Pike auf kennen** to know the business inside out; **sich nur um sein** ~ **kümmern** to be intent on one's (attend strictly to) business; **sich nicht um sein** ~ **kümmern** to neglect one's business; **sich bei einem** ~ **registrieren lassen** *(für Marken)* to register with a tradesman; ~ **leiten** to be at the head of the business; ~ **liquidieren** to wind up one's affairs (a business company); ~**e machen** to transact business, to merchandise, to deal, to monger; ~ **mit der Dummheit der Leute machen** to trade upon the people's ignorance; **gewagte** ~**e machen** to speculate; **glänzende** ~**e machen** to drive a roaring trade; **große** ~**e machen** to do a large business; **gutes** ~ **machen** to strike a bargain (it rich, *US*), to get in on a good deal, to find s. th. a good pennyworth, to get (secure) a purchase; **gute** ~**e machen** to have a good run (be in a good way) of business; ~ **rückgängig machen** to set aside a transaction, to break off an engagement; **schlechtes** ~ **machen** to bring one's eggs (hogs) to the wrong market, to do badly, to be in a bad way of business; **unerlaubte** ~**e machen** to indulge in illicit transactions; **unsaubere** ~**e machen** to racketeer; **einem** ~ **nachgehen** to follow a business, to pursue an occupation; **seinen** ~**en nachgehen** to attend to (go about) one's business, to ply a trade; **fleißig seinen** ~**en nachgehen** to be diligent in one's business; **ungesetzlichen** ~**en nachgehen** to carry on an illegal transaction; ~ **offenhalten** to keep a shop open; **seine** ~**e ordnen** to compose one's affairs; **bei einem** ~ **profitieren** to profit by a bargain; **mit einem guten** ~ **rechnen** to calculate on a good trade; **von** ~**en reden** to talk shop (about business); **in** ~**en reisen** to travel on business; **sein** ~ **schließen** to close down a shop, to put up the shutters, to shut up shop *(US)*; **an einem** ~ **beteiligt sein** to have an interest (a share) in a business; **nach dem Krieg groß ins** ~ **gekommen sein** to boom after the war; **in** ~**en großzügig sein** to be liberal in business; **hinter seinen** ~**en her sein** to be a keen businessman; **in seinen** ~**en pünktlich sein** to be punctual in one's dealings; **einen Tag nicht im** ~ **sein** to get away from the office for a day; **in** ~**en unterwegs sein** to be on one's tour (away, out), to travel on business; **in** ~**en zuverlässig sein** to be exact in business, to pass for as good as one's word; **im** ~ **stecken** to be invested in a business; **Geld in ein** ~ **stecken** to invest money in a business, to put money into an undertaking, to embark capital in a trade; ~**e tätigen** to do business; **gutes** ~ **tätigen** to make a good deal by, to get a purchase; **im laufenden Monat keine** ~**e mehr tätigen** *(Versicherung)* to write no new business for the month; ~ **übernehmen** to take over (succeed to) a business; ~ **voll übernehmen** to purchase the sole interest in a business; **jem. ein** ~ **übertragen** to turn a business over to s. o.; ~ **auf seinen Sohn übertragen** to make over the business to one's son; **j. bei einem** ~ **übervorteilen** to jockey s. o. in a transaction; **kleines** ~ **unterhalten** to carry on business in a small way; ~**e einer Gesellschaft der Revision unterziehen** to investigate the affairs of a company; **bei seinen** ~**en verdienen** to gain by one's business; **an einem** ~ **groß verdienen** to be a great gainer by a bargain; **sein** ~ **vergrößern** to expand one's business; **sein** ~ **verkaufen** to sell out one's business; ~ **um die Hälfte verkleinern** to reduce a business one half; **seine** ~**e vernachlässigen** to neglect (shirk) one's business; **sein** ~ **verstehen** to know one's business, to know one's trade (how to turn a penny); **sein** ~ **aus dem Effeff verstehen** to have the whole business at one's fingertips; ~ **auf der Grundlage der Gegenseitigkeit vorbereiten** to arrange a transaction on mutual principles; ~**e wegnehmen** to grab business; **laufende** ~**e weiterführen** to deal with current business; ~ **nicht weiterführen** to cease to carry on business; **im**

~ **benötigt werden** to be required at the business; **sich seinen ~en widmen** to attend to (go about) one's business; **sich erneut ganz dem ~ widmen** to devote o. s. anew to business; ~ **wiedereröffnen** to resume business; **gute ~e machen wollen** to carry pigs to market; ~ **rückgängig machen wollen** to rue a bargain; **von einem ~ zurücktreten** to rescind a bargain; **sich vom (aus dem) ~ zurückziehen** to give up one's (withdraw from, quit) business; **sich von einem ~ zurückziehen** to declare a bargain off, *(fam.)* to back out; **sein Geld aus einem ~ zurückziehen** to withdraw one's money from a business; **sich wieder seinen ~en zuwenden** to turn one's thoughts to business again; **sich einem neuen ~ zuwenden** to take up another business;
das ~ geht weiter business as usual.
geschäftehalber on business.
Geschäfte|macher profiteer, jobber, racketeer, carpetbagger, hustler *(US sl.)*; ~**macherei** profiteering, jobbery.
geschäftig bustling, expeditious, busy, busybodyish, fussy, throng;
~**es Treiben** hustle and bustle.
Geschäftigkeit bustle, stirabout;
übertriebene ~ fuss, busybodyness;
~ **unserer Tage** hurry of modern life;
~ **entfalten** to manifest great activity **von hektischer ~ sein** to be positively jumping with activity.
G[e]schaftlhuber busybody, bustler, nosy Parker *(fam.)*.
geschäftlich commercial, mercantile, businesslike, business-wise, on business, trade;
~ **betrachtet** from a business point of view; **rein ~** at arm's length; ~ **unerfahren** inexperienced in business; ~ **verhindert** prevented (held up) by business;
sich ~ auszahlen to make business sense; **sich ~ betätigen** to be engaged in business; **j. ~ etablieren** to set up s. o. in trade; ~ **nach A fahren** to be going to A on business; ~ **mit jem. zu tun haben** to do business with s. o., to have dealings with s. o.; **sich ~ niederlassen** to set up in business; ~ **beteiligt sein** to hold shares in business enterprises; ~ **tätig sein** to be [engaged] in (do, transact) business; ~ **unterwegs (verreist) sein** to be away on business (out on one's tour), to travel on business; **j. ~ sprechen** to see s. o. on business; **j. ~ voranbringen** to give s. o. a boost in business; ~ **aufgehalten werden** to be detained [in the office] by business; **nur ~ benutzt werden** *(Auto)* to be used entirely for business; **mit jem. ~ zusammenarbeiten** to do business with s. o.;
~**e Angaben** business data; ~**e Angelegenheit** business matter (pursuit, affair); **in einer ~en Angelegenheit** on business; **seine ~en Angelegenheiten selbst besorgen** to conduct one's business affairs; **in einer ~en Angelegenheit unterwegs sein** to be away on business; ~**es Ansehen** credit, [business] reputation, standing; ~**e Anstrengungen** business tensions; ~**e Antwortsendungen** business reply items; ~**e Auswirkungen** business effects; **mit jem. nur auf rein ~er Basis verhandeln** to deal with s. o. at arm's length; ~**e Bekanntmachung** trade publication; ~**e Besprechung** business conference (conversation, negotiations); ~**e Beziehungen** business relations; **in ~en Dingen zuverlässig sein** to be exact in business; ~**e Dispositionen** business measures; **jem. ~en Einblick gewähren** to give s. o. sight into the business; ~**e Einkäufe** business buying; ~**e Einstellung** business attitude; ~**e Empfehlung** business reference; ~**e Entscheidung** business decision; ~**e Entwicklungsmöglichkeiten** business development possibilities; ~**e Erfahrungen als Führungskraft** business experience at management level; ~**er Erfolg** business winner; **nach ~en Gesichtspunkten** along commercial lines; ~**e Grundlage erweitern** to spread one's business base; ~**e Interessen** business (commercial) interest; ~**e Konkurrenz** trade rivalry; ~**er Kredit** commercial credit; ~**er Mißerfolg** business fiasco; ~**e Mitteilungen** business publications, *(Rundfunk)* commercial announcements; ~**e Möglichkeiten** business ways (opportunities); ~**e Nachrichten** business news; ~**e Niederlassung** business location; ~**e Nötigung** business compulsion; ~**es Risiko** business risk; **kurz vor dem ~en Ruin stehen** to be on the verge of bankruptcy; **vom ~en Standpunkt aus gesehen** from a business point of view; **früh vielversprechendes ~es Talent zeigen** to show early business promise; ~**e Tätigkeit** business (economic) activity; ~**er Teil** business end *(coll.)*; **zum ~en Teil kommen** to get down to brass tacks; **in ~em Ton** in a businesslike tone; ~**e Umgangsformen** business manners; ~**es Unternehmen** business venture, *(Firma)* commercial enterprise, business corporation; ~**e Unternehmung** commercial operation; ~**e Verabredung** business appointment; ~**e Veränderungen** business changes; ~**e Verbindungen** business links; ~**e Vereinigung** business league; ~**e Verhandlungen** business conference (negotiations); ~**e Verpflichtungen** business commitments; ~**er Vertreter** business agent; ~**er Vorschlag** business proposition; ~**er Zusammenbruch** business failure; **vor dem ~en Zusammenbruch stehen** to face the collapse of one's business, to steer near receivership;
ich komme ~ my call is a business one.
Geschäftsablauf course of business;
normaler (regelmäßiger, üblicher) ~ regular course of business, usual (normal) course of [employer's] trade;
~ **verzögern** to hamper the progress of business.
Geschäftsabschluß business transaction, making a deal (bargain), completion of a transaction, consummation of a deal, wheel *(sl.)*, *(abgeschlossenes Geschäft)* commercial transaction (operation), *(fürs laufende Jahr)* annual report;
einzelner ~ *(Börse)* bargain *(Br.)*;
~ **ohne Gewinn und Verlust** break-even transaction;
~ **tätigen** to make a deal; ~ **vorlegen** to submit the annual accounts, to disclose a balance sheet; **einem ~ zustimmen** to adopt a transaction;
~**bericht** annual report.
Geschäftsabschlüsse transactions, business, dealings, *(erhaltene Aufträge)* orders secured;
~ **betreffend** transactional;
einige ~ a few contracts; **nachbörsliche ~** business in the street; **im Haushaltsplan vorgesehene ~** budgeted transactions;
~ **mit Kreditgewährung** credit dealings;
vertrauliche ~ offenlegen to disclose secret transactions; ~ **tätigen** to effect transactions; **große ~ tätigen** to deal in a big volume.
Geschäfts|abschlußvollmacht general power to transact business; ~**abteilung** sales department (division); ~**abwicklung** conduct of business, windup of a business; ~**adresse** business address; ~**agentur** general agency; ~**akten** business documents; ~**aktiva** [firm] assets; ~**anbahnung** introduction of business, invitation to treat; ~**andrang** rush, run, pressure of business.
Geschäftsangelegenheiten business affairs, pieces of business;
in ~ on business;
laufende ~ routine business affairs;
wichtige ~ ungeeigneten Leuten übertragen to entrust serious business to irresponsibles.
Geschäfts|ankündigung trade publication; ~**anreiz** business inducement; ~**anschluß** *(tel.)* office extension; ~**anschrift** business address; ~**anspannung** rush, pressure of business.
Geschäftsanteil interest in a firm (business), business interest, [partnership] share, capital share, interest, *(Rückversicherung)* quota;
~**e** holdings in a business company;
maßgeblicher ~ controlling interest;
seinen ~ abgeben to sell out one's share of a business; ~**[e] besitzen (haben)** to have a concern (hold shares, have a share) in a business; ~ **an einer OHG erwerben** to purchase an interest in a trading partnership; **jem. einen ~ überlassen** to give s. o. a partnership in one's business; ~ **übernehmen** to buy an interest in a firm; **seinen ~ verkaufen (veräußern)** to sell out (dispose of) one's share of a business.
Geschäfts|antwortsendungen business reply items; ~**anzeige** [business] advertisement, *(im Laden)* show card, shop bill; ~**anzeigen** *(Zeitung)* business columns; ~**anzug** lounge *(Br.)* (business, *US*) suit; ~**arithmetik** business arithmetic; ~**art** line (type) of business; ~**aufgabe** retiring (retirement) from (giving up, abandonment of, termination of a) business; **wegen ~aufgabe** owing to the closing of business; **wegen ~aufgabe zu verkaufen** for sale, owner retiring from business; ~**auflösung** liquidation of a business, winding up of a business; ~**aufschwung** boom, upturn, brisk trade.
Geschäftsaufsicht *(Konkursverfahren)* temporary receivership *(Br.)*, *(im Laden)* shop walker, store superintendent *(US)*, floorwalker *(US)*;
alleinige ~ anvertraut bekommen to be left in sole charge of a business; **Antrag auf ~ stellen** to make application for receivership; **unter ~ gestellt werden** to be put under receivership.
Geschäfts|auftrag commission, order; ~**ausdehnung** expansion (extension) of business; ~**ausfallversicherung** loss-of-profit insurance; ~**ausgaben** expenditure of a business, business expenses; ~**ausrüstung** [store] equipment *(US)*; ~**aussichten** commercial (sales) prospects, business outlook (prospects); ~**ausstattung** store equipment *(US)*, *(Bilanz)* furniture and equipment, *(OHG)* partnership personalty *(US)*; **energie-**

sparende ~ausstattung energy-saving equipment; **~ausweitung** expansion (extension) of business, expansion of the trade, accretion of business *(Br.)*; **~ausweitung durch monopolartige Rohstofflieferungen** backward integration; **~auto** commercial car (automobile, *US*); **~bank** businessman's (business, commercial) bank, merchant bank *(Br.)*; **~bankwesen** commercial banking; **~-, Fabrik- und andere Bauten** *(Bilanz)* office, factory and other buildings; **~bedarf** office stationery; **~bedingungen** terms of trade (business), trading (trade, business) conditions; **allgemeine ~bedingungen** standard-form contract conditions; **günstige ~bedingungen** easy terms; **~beendigung** completion of a transaction; **~beginn** starting of an enterprise, commencement of business; **vor ~beginn** before commencing business; **~begründung** establishment; **~belebung** enlivening of (recovery in) business, trade (business) revival; **allmähliche ~belebung** gradual pickup in industrial activity; **~beleg** transaction record, voucher.

Geschäftsbereich business line, scope (sphere) of activity (business), area of operations, function, *(Ausschuß)* terms of reference, *(Minister)* portfolio, *(Zugehörigkeit)* jurisdiction;
außerhalb des ordnungsgemäßen ~s *(Gesellschaft)* outside the powers; **ohne ~** *(Minister)* without portfolio;
ministerieller ~ [minister's] portfolio; **unternehmerische Fähigkeiten voraussetzende ~e** business systems allied with entrepreneurial skill;
örtlichen ~ ausweiten to enlarge the local area of operations.

Geschäftsbericht business record (report), operating (financial, year-end, annual, *Br.*) report, working statement, *(Gesellschaft)* report and accounts, director's (annual) report, *(Konzern)* report of the group, *(Marktbericht)* market report;
~ einer Bank bank statement (return);
~ nach Steuerbilanzgründen abfassen to report one's operations one way for tax purposes; **~ fälschen** to fake a business report.

Geschäfts|besitzer shop *(Br.)* (store, *US*) owner; **~besorgung** business errand, *(für Dritten)* commission, proxy, *(Erledigung)* discharge of business; **~besorgung erledigen** to carry out a commission; **~besorgung übernehmen** to undertake a business; **~besorgungsvertrag** contract for personal services, mandate, agency agreement; **~besprechung** business conference; **~besuch** business call; **~besucher** business visitor; **~beteiligung** interest in a firm (business), business interest, share; **~beteiligung besitzen** to hold shares in business enterprises.

Geschäftsbetrieb commercial pursuit, transacting (transaction of) business, operation of a business, *(Firma)* business [establishment], business operation, business enterprise (outfit, concern), unit, commercial concern (enterprise, pursuits), *(Geschäftsgang)* office routine;
in ~ in the course of business;
ähnlicher ~ business of similar nature; **dezentralisierter ~** departmentalized business *(US)*; **eingerichteter ~** established business; **eingestellter ~** discontinued business; **familieneigener ~** family-owned business; **gleichartiger ~** business of same nature; **kaufmännischer ~** commercial undertaking; **üblicher ~** usual course of business; **unbefugter ~** unauthorized business; **wirtschaftlicher ~** economic enterprise;
~ mit besonders hohem Risiko high-risk business;
~ aufbauen to build up a business; **~ ausweiten** to expand company business; **~ beginnen** to commence business (trading); **~ einstellen** to cease to do business, to cease trading (business); **~ eröffnen** to commence business; **~ unterhalten** to do business.

Geschäfts|beurteilung business judgment; **~bevollmächtigter** agent, representative, partner, trustee, *(Gewerkschaft)* walking delegate; **~bewertung** survey of an enterprise; **~bezeichnung** trade name; **~beziehung** commercial (business) relation.

Geschäftsbeziehungen business relations (relationship), business connections, transactions, *(Staat)* trade relations;
enge ~ close relations; **lebhafte ~** very good business connections; **wechselseitige ~** mutual trading;
~ anbahnen (anknüpfen) to initiate business relations, to establish business connections; **~ mit einer Firma aufnehmen** to open up a business connection (to get in) with a firm; **in ~ mit jem. stehen** to transact business (have business relations) with s. o., to trade (deal, correspond) with s. o.; **~ unterhalten** to entertain business connections, to do business with s. o.

Geschäfts|bezirk *(Gerichtsvollzieher)* bailiwick; **~bilanz** balance sheet (statement, *US*) of a business enterprise; **~block** business block *(US)*; **~bogen** letterhead; **~branche** line of business, business line; **gleichartige ~branche** *(Konkurrenzklausel)* similarity of business; **~branche generell für gewinnträchtig halten** to reckon a business generally as prosperous; **~brauch** business usage.

Geschäftsbrief business letter;
persönlich gehaltener ~ personal letter in business; **kühler ~** business-like letter; **üblicher ~** routine business letter;
fast nur in ~en üblich sein to be little used outside a business letter;
~muster model business letter.

Geschäftsbücher books, shopbooks *(US)*, ledgers, business records, account (commercial, office) books, trading accounts;
ausweislich der ~ as shown by the books;
kaufmännische ~ commercial books of account;
~ einer Aktiengesellschaft corporate books; **~ einer Offenen Handelsgesellschaft** partnership books;
~ frisieren to salt the books; **~ übertragen** to post the books.

Geschäfts|buchführung financial accounting, company bookkeeping; **bessere ~chancen** better business bet; **~dispositionen** business measures; **~drang** rush of business; **~dreirad** delivery tricycle; **~drucksachen** commercial items; **~eigentümer** principal, business owner, shop (store, *US*) owner; **~einkäufe** business buying; **~einkommen** business income; **~einlage** contribution to (share in) capital, money invested, partnership share, share (capital) in a business, investment in the business; **~einnahmen** business income (proceeds); **~einrichtungen** office equipment, *(Laden)* shop (store, *US*) equipment; **feste ~einrichtung** fixed place of business; **~einstellung** discontinuance of business; **~eintritt** joining a firm; **~empfehlung** business (trade) reference, *(vom Inhaber aus)* offer of services; **grundsätzliche ~entscheidungen** policymaking; **~entwicklung** development of business, business development.

geschäftserfahren versed in trade, experienced in business, smart;
sehr ~ sein to be well versed in business.

Geschäftserfahrung experience in business (trade), business experience, business knowledge;
~en im Bereich der leitenden Angestellten senior level business experience;
ohne ~en sein to be new to business; **über erhebliche ~en verfügen** to be well versed in business.

Geschäfts|erfolg commercial (business) success, sell; **~ergebnis** trading (operating) result, *(Gesellschaft)* company result, *(Handelsfirma)* trading result, *(Versicherungsgesellschaft)* underwriting (insurance) result; **~erlaubnis** permisssion to transact business, business (trading) licence; **~erlaubnis für Treuhandgeschäfte** *(Bankwesen)* trust powers; **~erlaubnis erteilen** to accord permission to transact business, to issue a licence; **~erledigung** dispatch of business; **~eröffnung** establishment, starting in (opening of a) business, setting up shop *(US)*, commencement of business, *(Ladenöffnung)* taking down the shutters; **vor ~eröffnung** before commencing business; **~eröffnung Anfang November** shop will open at the beginning of November; **~errichtung** establishment, setting up shop *(US)*; **~ersparnisse** business savings; **~ertrag** proceeds, trading (operating) income; **~erweiterung** expansion (extension) of business; **~erwerb** purchase of a business; **~etat** business budget.

geschäftsfähig of sane (sound) mind, legally competent (responsible), capable to act in law (of contracting), [legally] competent to contract;
beschränkt ~ responsible to a limited extent; **nicht ~** incompetent; **voll ~** of full legal capacity;
beschränkt ~ sein *(Minderjähriger)* to be under a special disability; **nicht ~ sein** to have no capacity to act; **~ werden** to cease to be under disability.

Geschäftsfähiger, beschränkt person under disability; **voll ~** person of full age and capacity.

Geschäftsfähigkeit legal (contractual) capacity, capacity to act (contract), competence;
bedingte (beschränkte) ~ limited capacity, special disability, legal incapacity, limited (restricted) competence; **mangelnde ~** incompetency, [legal] incapacity; **unbeschränkte ~** unlimited capacity.

Geschäfts|fähigkeitsalter age of capacity; **~fahrt** business trip; **~finanzen** business finance; **~finanzierung** business (trade) financing; **~flaute** slump, stagnation of business, stagnant trade; **~flug** business flight; **~flugzeug** business aircraft; **~förderung** business promotion; **~fortführung** carrying on (continuation of) a business; **~fragen** management problems; **~frau** woman dealer (trader), tradeswoman, business woman; **selbständige ~frau** feme-sole trader (merchant) *(Br.)*, free dealer (trader).

geschäftsfrei nonbusiness;
~**er Nachmittag** early-closing day; ~**er Sonnabend** Saturday closing.

Geschäfts|freund [business] correspondent, business associate, business friend (guest, client); **Angelegenheit seinem** ~**freund übertragen** to entrust a matter to one's correspondent; ~**freundschaft** business friendship.

geschäftsführend acting, managing, executive, *(stellvertretend)* in charge of affairs;
~**er Ausschuß** managing (management, executive) committee, board of management; ~**er Direktor** acting manager; ~**er Gesellschafter** managing partner; ~**es Organ** executive body; ~**e Regierung** caretaker government; ~**er Vorstand,** ~**es Vorstandsmitglied** general manager, managing director *(Br.)*, member of the executive board.

Geschäftsführer [business] manager, director, administrator, factor, managing agent (clerk, director), *(AG)* vice principal, *(Bevollmächtigter)* attorney [in fact], *(im Sinn des BGB)* agent, executive *(US)*, runner *(US)*, *(Gesellschaft)* managing partner, *(Hotel)* hotel manager, *(Laden)* director, manager, store manager *(US)*, *(Verein)* executive secretary *(US)*;
alleiniger ~ sole manager; **gerichtlich bestellter** ~ special manager; **eigentlicher** ~ virtual manager; **äußerst erfolgreicher** ~ top-performing manager; **parlamentarischer** ~ whip *(Br.)*; **stellvertretender** ~ deputy manager, stand-in-charge;
~ **ohne Auftrag** agent of necessity, gestor, volunteer; ~ **einer Kapitalanlagegesellschaft** investment trust manager; ~ **eines Mittelstandsbetriebes** small business manager;
~ **abberufen** to remove a manager; ~ **bestellen** to appoint a manager; **um den** ~ **bitten** to inquire for the manager; **j. vorübergehend als** ~ **einsetzen** to put s. o. in temporary charge; ~ **sein** to manage the business; ~ **einer GMBH sein** to act as a director of a limited company; ~ **verlangen** to ask for the manager;
~**anteil** management share; ~**honorar** management fee; ~**in** manageress; ~**tätigkeit** managership.

Geschäftsführung conduct of business, [business] management, managership, *(fremder Geschäfte)* agency, *(Laden)* store management;
nach Ansicht der ~ in the judgment of the management;
alleinige ~ sole management; **von mehreren ausgeübte** ~ multiple management; **betrügerische** ~ fraudulent trading; **energische** ~ strong management; **fahrlässige** ~ miscarriage; **kaufmännische** ~ business management; **oberste** ~ top management; **ordnungsgemäße** ~ proper conduct of business; **schlechte** ~ mismanagement, poor (bad) management; **tatsächliche** ~ *(Doppelbesteuerungsabkommen)* effective management; **strafbare unsaubere** ~ criminal mismanagement;
~ **ohne Auftrag** agency of necessity, negotiorium gestio *(Latin)*, intromission *(Scot)*;
~ **abgeben** to turn over the management; ~ **ausüben** to manage a business; **neue** ~ **einsetzen** to draft in a new management; **neue** ~ **haben** to be under new management; **mit der** ~ **beauftragt sein** to be in charge of the management; **an der** ~ **entscheidend beteiligt sein** to take a large-scale share in the management; **ziffernmäßig zu 50% an der** ~ **beteiligt sein** to have a technical 50 - 50 voice in management; **voll in die** ~ **eingeschaltet sein** to be given full swing in the conduct of business; **auf schlechte** ~ **zurückzuführen sein** to be due to bad management; **an der** ~ **teilnehmen** to share (take part) in the management; ~ **von Grund auf umstrukturieren** to structure one's management from scratch; **von der** ~ **zurücktreten** to resign from management.

Geschäftsführungs|ausschuß management committee; ~**befugnis** manager's authority; ~**kosten** management (executive) expenses; ~**vereinbarung** management agreement.

Geschäftsgang [run (course) of] business, course of trade, *(Bote)* errand, commission, *(Tendenz)* business trend, trend of affairs;
allgemeiner ~ general office procedure; **flotter** ~ brisk state (briskness) of trade; **normaler (regelmäßiger)** ~ ordinary [course of] business; **täglicher** ~ daily routine [of business]; **schleppenden** ~ **aufweisen** to have a hard sledding; ~ **heben** to increase business.

Geschäftsgebaren dealing, business policy (manners), *(Anlagegesellschaft)* performance;
anständiges ~ fair practices, fair (square) dealings; **betrügerisches** ~ business fraud, fraudulent manipulation (trading); **korrektes (lauteres, reelles)** ~ straight (fair, plain) dealings; **ordnungsgemäßes** ~ proper conduct of business; **standeswidriges** ~ unethical business practices; **unlauteres** ~ unfair [trade] practices.

Geschäftsgebäude office building, commercial property, business premises;
mehrstöckiges ~ multiple-stor(e)y business building;
~- **und Wohngebäude** *(Bilanz)* buildings.

Geschäfts|gebrauch business (trade) usage, shop practice; ~**gebühr** *(Anwalt)* consultation fee.

Geschäftsgegend business district (quarter, section), the City *(Br.)*, downtown district (area) *(US)*, trading center *(US)*, location *(US)*, *(Einzelhandel)* shopping area (district), shoppy neighbo(u)rhood;
gut eingeführte ~ established location *(US)*; **teure** ~ high-rent location *(US)*.

Geschäfts|geheimnis trade (business) secret; ~**geheimnis preisgeben** to divulge a trade secret; ~**geist** business acumen, commercial spirit; ~**gelegenheit** business opportunities; ~**gespräch** business conversation, pipe *(sl.)*; ~**gestaltung** trend of affairs.

geschäftsgewandt smart, quick, skilled (versed) in business.

Geschäftsgewandtheit smartness, business skill (acumen, capacity).

Geschäftsgewinn business gain, commercial (business, operating) profit, profits of the business, trading profit *(Br.)*;
~ **für das Jahr 1981** trading profit for 1981; ~ **ab Sanierung** dated earned surplus *(US)*;
~ **mittels Abschreibungen auf das Anlagevermögen steuerlich als Verlust ausweisen** to convert a trading profit into a loss for tax purposes by means of capital allowance *(Br.)*; ~ **mit einem höheren Steuersatz veranlagen** to assess a business profit at a higher rate.

Geschäfts|gläubiger firm's (trade) creditors; **abteilungsweise** ~**gliederung** line organization; ~**grundlage** underlying basis of a contract; ~**grundlage erweitern** to spread one's business base; ~**grundlage wegfallen lassen** to cause the frustration; ~**grundsätze** business policy, operating principles; ~**grundstück** business property (premises), office premises, commercial land (property), establishment, place of business, commercial (store, *US*) property, shop property; ~**grundstück vermieten** to lease business property; ~**grundstückstaxe** business property appraisal; ~**gründung** setting up in business, business organization, business creation, *(Gesellschaft)* formation of partnership; **fundierte** ~**gründung vornehmen** to build up a business on a sound basis; ~**guthaben** credit balance; ~**guthaben bei einer Genossenschaftsbank** paid-up shares in a cooperative society; ~**haus** business enterprise (house), commercial establishment, place of call, firm, [mercantile] house, *(Bürogebäude)* business (office) premises, *(Ladengeschäft)* store building *(US)*; ~**herr** master, proprietor, *(Auftraggeber)* principal; **ungenannter** ~**herr** undisclosed principal; ~**herrn sofort verständigen** to inform the principal immediately; ~**inhaber** proprietor, business owner, head (owner) of a firm, shopkeeper *(Br.)*, storekeeper *(US)*; **alleiniger** ~**inhaber** individual proprietor; ~**insolvenz** commercial insolvency.

Geschäftsinteresse interest in a business, business interest (concerns);
~**n** business concerns;
im ~ **fahren** to drive on one's master's business; ~**n einer Firma im Ausland wahrnehmen** to travel abroad in the interests of a business firm.

Geschäfts|inventar business inventory, *(Bilanz)* office furniture and equipment, *(OHG)* partnership personalty *(US)*; ~**investition** business investment; ~**irrtum** *(jur.)* mistake as to the existence of the subject matter.

Geschäftsjahr business (commercial, trading, official) year, *(Regierung)* financial year *(Br.)*, fiscal year (period) *(US)*;
abgelaufenes ~ last (past) business year; **vom Kalenderjahr abweichendes** ~ natural business year *(US)*; **sehr erfolgreiches** ~ banner sales year; **gutes** ~ profitable year, year of good trading; **laufendes** ~ current business year; **schlechtes** ~ poor year;
~ **ohne Dividendenausschüttung abschließen** to pass a dividend *(US)*; **im nächsten** ~ **nur mit Mühe gewinnträchtig werden können** to run into more earning troubles next year.

Geschäfts|kapital [firm's] capital, trading (share, *Br.*) capital, stock in trade, stock *(Br.)*, capital (joint) stock *(US)*; ~**karte** business (trade, calling, *US*) card; ~**katalog** trade list, catalog(ue); ~**kenntnisse** knowledge of business, business experience (knowledge); ~**klugheit** business sense (acumen); ~**kniffe** tricks of the trade; ~**kodex** business code; ~**konkurrenz** industrial competition; ~**konto** business (overhead-charges) account; ~**korrespondenz** business correspondence (writing), routine correspondence; ~**korrespondenz erledigen** to deal with business correspondence; ~**kosten** business (office, overhead) expenses; **laufende ~kosten** recurring cost *(US)*; **auf ~kosten laufen** *(Auto)* to run on expenses; ~**kredit** commercial credit, business borrowing, business credit, credit of a firm, *(Anleihe)* business loan; ~**kredite** commercial (business) lendings, commercial (business) borrowing.

Geschäftskreis walk, province, sphere of action, field of activity, scope of operation (business), department;
in ~en in commercial (business) circles;
ausgedehnter ~ extensive business.

Geschäftskunde [business] customer, client.

geschäftskundig experienced, skilled in business, versed in trade.

Geschäftslage state of business, business standing, status, stand *(US)*, *(Belegenheit)* situation, [store] location *(US)*, *(Geschäftsaussichten)* business outlook (prospects, situation), *(Wirtschaft)* state of affairs (the market), market trend;
teure ~ high-rent location; **unsichere** ~ uncertain state of business;
günstige ~ haben to be in a desirable location.

Geschäftsleben business [life], business movement (world), mercantile affairs;
im ~ in business;
Privatdinge das ~ beeinflussen lassen to let pleasure interfere with business; **im ~ großzügig sein** to be liberal in business; **im ~ zuverlässig sein** to be exact in business; **im ~ stehen** to be in business; **ins ~ treten** to go out to (enter into) business; **sich aus dem ~ zurückziehen** to quit (bail out of public) business.

geschäftsleitend managing, managerial, executive.

Geschäftsleiter managing clerk (director, *Br.*), [general-office] manager, director, *(Laden)* store manager *(US)*.

Geschäftsleitung conduct of business, *(Geschäftsführer)* [store, *US*] management, managerial staff, *(AG)* board of directors, directorate, corporate (executive) management, store management *(US)*;
nach Ansicht der ~ in the judgment of the management;
tatsächliche ~ *(Doppelbesteuerungsabkommen)* effective management;
neue ~ einsetzen to draft in a new management; **~ haben** to manage the concern; **~ übernehmen** to assume the direction of a business.

Geschäftsleitungskosten executive expenses, costs of management.

Geschäftsleute tradespeople, tradesmen, tradesfolk, trading class, dealers, businessmen, business people;
nur für ~ no admittance except on business;
führende ~ business executives (leaders), key businessmen, big businessmen; **kleine** ~ small businessmen;
~ auf einer Dienstreise itinera[n]cy;
kleine ~ vom Markt verdrängen to cut out the small traders.

Geschäfts|lizenz business licence; ~**lokal** [business] office, [business] premises, [place of] business, shop *(Br.)*.

geschäftslos *(Börse)* dull, dead, slack, inactive, lifeless, featureless.

Geschäftslosigkeit dullness, slackness, dead, deadness, inactivity;
allgemeine ~ general stagnation of business.

geschäftslustig enterprising, brisk.

Geschäftsmann businessman, man of business, commercial (city, *Br.*) man, merchant, trader, tradesman;
einflußreicher ~ big businessman; **unternehmerisch eingestellter** ~ go-ahead businessman; **gerissener** ~ smart businessman, wheeler-dealer *(US)*; **gewiefter** ~ shrewd businessman; **hochqualifizierter** ~ high-level businessman; **kleiner** ~ small businessman, petty trader; **pfiffiger** ~ smart bargainer; **tüchtiger** ~ good businessman, active man of business; **wohldotierter** ~ high-placed businessman;
sich als guter ~ erweisen to prove o. s. a good businessman; **~ sein** to be in trade (in the city); **ausgezeichneter ~ sein** to have excellent business capacity; **geborener ~ sein** to be cut out for business; **geschickter ~ sein** to be well-versed in trade; **guter ~ sein** to have a good head for business; **nur ~ sein** to be all business; **versierter ~ sein** to be well versed in business; **~ werden** to engage (settle down) in business, to set up shop *(US)*.

geschäftsmäßig businesslike, commercial, merchantlike, *(rein mechanisch)* routine, mechanical;
nicht ~ unbusinesslike;
~ aussehend business looking;
~ erledigen to do in a businesslike way.

Geschäfts|mäßigkeit businesslikeness; ~**merkmale** features of business.

Geschäftsmethoden business practice (policy), business methods;
einheitliche ~ standard of business forms; **unlautere** ~ unfair [methods of] competition, unfair [business] practices, improper practices; **unsaubere** ~ sharp practices;
~ und Absatzmethode *(Agenturgeschäft)* market-survey method;
über unerlaubte ~ hinwegsehen to blink at sharp practices.

Geschäfts|miete shop rent; **bezahlte ~miete** rent paid for business premises; ~**mitteilung** trade publications, business communication (notice); ~**möglichkeit** opening for business, trade opportunity; ~**moral** business ethics, commercial morality; **strenge Maßstäbe an die ~moral anlegen** to set a high standard of business morality; ~**motiv** transaction motive; ~**nachfolger** successor; ~**nachlässigkeit** neglect of one's business; ~**nachteil** trading handicap; ~**name** business (trade) name, style; ~**neugründung** new establishment; ~**nummer** *(Brief)* reference number.

Geschäftsordnung routine orders, standing (business, *US*) rules, bylaws *(US)*, *(Gericht)* rules, *(parl.)* standing order (rules), rules of order, *(Tagesordnung)* agenda;
in Übereinstimmung mit der ~ in order; **im Widerspruch zur** ~ out of order; **zur ~!** a point of order!;
für eine Tagung geltende ~ sessional orders *(Br.)*; **gemeinsame** ~ joint rule *(US)*;
~ des Bundestages parliamentary law;
~ aufstellen to draw up the rules of procedure; **~ einhalten** to observe the rules of procedure; **sich eine ~ geben** to fix the rules of procedure; **zur ~ sprechen** to rise to order; **das Wort zur ~ verlangen** to raise a point of order.

Geschäftsordnungs|antrag procedural motion; ~**ausschuß** standing orders (organizing, House Rules, *US*) committee.

Geschäfts|organisation business (office) organization; ~**papiere** commercial documents (papers), business records; ~**partner** [business] associate, partner; **j. als ~partner aufnehmen** to admit s. o. as partner; ~**periode** fiscal period; ~**personal** staff, personnel, employees; ~**planung** budgeting; ~**politik** policies of a business, business policy (economics, *Br.*), *(Anlagefonds)* policy, *(Gesellschaft)* corporate policy *(US)*, general policy of the business; **schriftlich niedergelegte ~politik** *(Gesellschaft)* policy document.

geschäftspolitische|Aussage policy formulation; **~ Probleme** business policy issues; **~ Tagung** policy meeting.

Geschäfts|position bargaining position; **wettbewerbsbeschränkende ~praktiken** *(Kartellrecht)* business practices, restrictive trade practices *(Br.)*; ~**praxis** office routine, trade (commercial) practice; ~**prinzip** business principle; ~**prognose** business outlook, forecasting; ~**projekt** business project; ~**protokoll** *(AG)* corporate minutes; ~**prüfung** internal audit, auditing; ~**rahmen** sphere (scope) of business.

Geschäftsraum parlor *(US)*, *(Laden)* store space;
Benutzung als ~ office use.

Geschäftsräume office, business (shop) premises, chambers *(Br.)*, store space *(US)*;
ausgedehnte ~ extensive premises; **dringend reparaturbedürftige** ~ premises badly in need of repair;
in neue ~ verlegen to transfer to new premises.

Geschäfts|raummiete, bezahlte paid rent for business premises; ~**referenz** trade reference; ~**reingewinn** net trading profit (avails, *US*).

Geschäftsreise business tour (travel), business mission (trip, round), journey on business, itineration, industrial tour *(US)*;
~ ins Ausland foreign business trip;
~ mit zwingenden Gründen belegen to justify a trip with good business reasons; **~ unternehmen (sich auf einer ~ befinden)** to travel for the (on) business.

Geschäfts|reisender business traveller, commercial (travel(l)ing) salesman, sales clerk (agent, *US*), commercial man *(US)*, drummer *(US)*; ~**reklame** business advertising, goodwill propaganda, trade publicity (advertising), *(Laden)* store advertising *(US)*; ~**reserven** business reserves; ~**risiko** commercial (mercantile, trade, trading, business) risk, risk of business; ~**routine** office routine, trade practice, experience in business (trade); ~**rückgang** decline in (falling off of) business, business contraction, *(Konjunktur)* [business] recession, trade recession, dip, downturn; **saisonbedingter ~rückgang** seasonal slump; ~**sache** matter of business, business matter; **in ~sachen gut beschlagen sein** to be well versed in business; ~**sanierung** recapitalization (reorganization) of business, financial reorganization.

geschäftsschädigendes Verhalten discreditable conduct of business.

Geschäfts|schädigung trade libel; **~schließung** shutdown, closing of business; **~schluß** closing time (hours); **nach ~schluß** after [business] hours; **früher ~schluß** early closing; **~schulden** business debts (liabilities), trade debts, *(Gesellschaft)* company liabilities, debts of a business enterprise; **~schwankungen** business fluctuations; **~schwerpunkt** bulk of one's business; **~sinn** business acumen, business (commercial) spirit, commercialism.

Geschäftssitz establishment, office, place (location, *US*) of business, business location *(US)*, commercial domicile, situs *(lat.)*;
eingetragener ~ principal establishment (place of business), registered office *(Br.)*; **steuerlicher ~** location for tax purposes *(US)*, business situs;
seinen ~ begründen to fix one's residence in a city; **~ verlegen** to vacate one's place of business, to transfer an office.

Geschäfts|sitzung business meeting (conference); **~sorgen** business troubles; **~sparte** branch (class, line) of business; **~sparte aufgeben** to diversify away from a business; **in einer ~sparte tätig sein** to deal in a line, to engage in a line of business; **~spesen** travelling (business) expenses; **~sprache** business language (slang); **~stadt** commercial (trading) town; **~statistik** business statistics.

Geschäftsstelle agency, branch, [secretary's] office, secretariat[e], department, bureau, *(Bank)* branch office, *(Gericht)* registrar's office *(Br.)*, registry *(Br.)*, court's office;
eingetragene ~ principal establishment, registered office *(Br.)*;
nachgeordnete ~ subsidiary corporation;
~ eines Konkursgerichtes registrar of a bankruptcy court; **~ des Nachlaßgerichtes** Probate Office, probate court registry, district probate registry *(Br.)*;
~ unterhalten to maintain an office; **25 ~n unterhalten** to have 25 branch offices in operation.

Geschäfts|stellenleiter *(Gericht)* country (district) clerk *(US)*, justice's clerk, clerk of the court *(US)*; **~stellennetz** network of branches; **~stil** business (commercial) style; **geschraubter ~stil** commercial jargon; **~stille** dullness, lull in business, dull time [of business], stagnation, slackness in trade, depression, dead; **~stillstand** stoppage of business; **~stockung** business stagnation, stagnation of (lull in) business, slackness (slump) in trade (of business), stagnant state of business, economic slowdown, depression; **~straße** business (commercial, shopping, shoppy) street; **~struktur** business structure, pattern of trade.

Geschäftsstunden business (office) hours, *(Bank)* banking hours;
außerhalb der ~ out of business hours;
bestimmte ~ stated hours of business.

Geschäftstag business day;
glänzender ~ red one *(sl.)*; **kein ~** nonbusiness day.

geschäftstätig|in ... engaged in trade, business within ...;
~ bleiben to stay in business; **~ sein** to be doing one's business.

Geschäftstätiger practical tradesman.

Geschäftstätigkeit business activity (operations), continuous operation, doing business, economic function;
lustlose ~ sluggish business pace; **normale ~** ordinary course of business, *(Sonntagsruhe)* common labo(u)r; **übliche ~** secular business; **unerlaubte ~** *(Sonntagsschutzgesetze)* worldly employment or business; **weitgestreute ~** spread of business; **hauptsächliche ~ der Gesellschaft** principal activities of the company;
~ aufnehmen to begin operations; **im Rahmen der üblichen ~ handeln** to act in the ordinary course of one's business; **~ Tag für Tag genauestens überwachen** to keep a finger on the pulse of business activity day by day.

Geschäftsteilhaber associate, partner, *(in Schottland)* confident person;
abwickelnder ~ liquidating partner; **stiller ~** sleeping *(Br.)* (silent, *US*) partner.

Geschäfts|telefonate business telephone calls; **~träger** proxy, representative, *(dipl.)* chargé d'affaires, deputy *(Australia)*.

Geschäftstransaktion trading transaction;
außerhalb der satzungsmäßigen Befugnisse vorgenommene ~ ultra-vires transaction;
~ mit Gegendeckung *(Börse)* hedging transaction;
~ verbuchen to make an entry of a transaction.

Geschäftstrick business trick.

geschäftstüchtig efficient, skilled in trade, well versed in business, hard-headed, smart;
nicht ~ dilatory in undertaking business;
~ sein to be a good businessman.

Geschäfts|tüchtigkeit business capacity (acumen), smartness; **~typ** line of business; **~übergabe**, **~übergang** transfer of a business; **~übernahme** taking over a business, takeover; **nach ~übernahme** under new management; **~übersicht** business report, daily state of affairs; **~übertragung** transfer of a business, business transfer.

geschäftsüblicher Ausdruck business cliché.

Geschäfts|übung shop (trade) practice; **~umfang** volume of business, *(Geschäftskreis)* scope of business; **üblicher ~umfang** ordinary amount of business; **~umkreis** trading radius; **~umsatz** turnover, total sales; **abnehmender ~umsatz** slower business; **~umsätze** transactions, dealings, sales; **nicht zur Flugzeugindustrie gehörige ~umsätze** nonaviation turnover; **~umschlag** *(Brief)* commercial envelope.

geschäftsunfähig incompetent to make a contract, not responsible, disabled, declared incapable of managing one's own affairs, incapacitated, incapable of acting in law, entirely without understanding;
dauernd ~ permanently incapable;
für ~ erklären to adjudge incompetent; **jem. für ~ erklären lassen** to have s. o. declared incapable of managing his own affairs; **~ sein** to lie (be) under disability.

Geschäftsunfähiger mentally incompetent, incapacitated person, person under disability.

Geschäftsunfähigkeit mental incapacity (incompetency, *US*), legal incapacity, general disability, incapacity to act in law, incapacity to contract;
~ wegen Geisteskrankheit disability of an insane person (a lunatic), mental incapacity, legal insanity; **~ wegen Volltrunkenheit** incapacity through drunkenness.

Geschäftsunkosten business (office, operating) expenses, expenditure of a business, *(Gemeinkosten)* burden, overhead [expenses], oncost *(Br.)*, *(Reisespesen)* travelling expenses;
absetzbare ~ *(Einkommensteuer)* expense account *(Br.)*; **allgemeine ~** indirect expense, office-operating costs, overheads; **steuerlich anerkannte ~** legitimate business expenses; **laufende ~** expense in carrying on business, recovering costs, office-operating costs;
~aufteilung overhead allocation.

geschäftsunkundig unexperienced in business, unfit for business, nonbusiness.

Geschäfts|unlust sluggish market, sluggishness; **~unterbrechung** interruption of business; **~unterbringung** office accommodation; **~unterhaltungskosten** office-operating costs; **~unterlagen** business records, office files, *(Gesellschaft)* papers of a business concern, books of a corporation (company); **~unternehmen** [commercial] enterprise, business enterprise (entity, undertaking, *Br.*), commercial establishment (undertaking); **~usancen** business usage (custom); **~veräußerung** sale of a business; **~verbindlichkeiten** [business] commitments, business obligations.

Geschäftsverbindung business connection (connexion, *Br.*), business association (relations, relationship), commercial relations, *(Bank)* correspondence;
langjährige ~ connection of long standing; **laufende ~** *(Bank)* continuous dealings;
[neue] ~ anbahnen (anknüpfen) to make business contacts, to enter (open) new (establish) business connections (relations);
~ mit jem. aufrechterhalten to transact business with s. o.; **neue ~ herstellen** to build up a new connection; **in ~ stehen** to be engaged (have) business relations; **mit jem. in ~ stehen** to transact business with s. o., to have dealings (business connections, trade) with s. o., to be connected in business (business connections); **in ~ treten** to open up business relations, to enter into business connections; **~en unterhalten** to keep up business dealings.

Geschäfts|vereinbarung business concert, trading arrangement; **~vereinigung** business league; **~verfahren** trade practice, trade process, business policy; **~verhalten** business attitude (style); **bewußt gleichlaufendes ~verhalten** *(Kartellrecht)* conscious parallel business behavio(u)r (parallelism, *US*); **~verhältnis eingehen** to enter into a partnership; **~verkauf** sale of a business.

Geschäftsverkehr dealings, commercial intercourse, course of business, business transactions, business writing;
im gewöhnlichen ~ in the ordinary course of business;
lebhafter ~ lively dealings; **wechselseitiger ~** mutual dealings; **~ vor Konkurseröffnung** dealings prior to the date of a receiving order; **~ zwischen Konzerngesellschaften** intercompany operations;
~ über ein Konto abwickeln to use an account for trade (business) purposes; **~ haben** to have business connections, to deal with.

Geschäfts|verlagerung drift of trade; ~**verlauf** business trend; **im normalen** ~**verlauf** within the ordinary course of business; ~**verlegung** removal *(Br.)* (relocation) of business.

Geschäftsverlust business (trading, operating) loss, loss of profits (earnings);
von der Versicherung nicht gedeckter ~ loss not covered by the insurance company;
~ **infolge leerstehender Räume** vacancy loss;
~**e erleiden** to lose business; ~**e zu gleichen Teilen tragen** to contribute equally towards the losses sustained by a firm; **steuerlich nicht verbrauchte** ~**e gegen Gesamteinkünfte des vorangehenden Veranlagungszeitraums verrechnen** to relate back unrelieved trading losses against the total profits of the preceding accounting period.

Geschäfts|vermittler intermediary; ~**vermögen** business (firm) property, ordinary (business) assets, stock in trade, *(Betriebskapital)* working (trading) capital; ~**vernachlässigung** neglect of one's business; ~**verpflichtungen** business commitments; ~**verstand** business acumen (savvy, *sl.*); ~**verteilung** allocation of duties, *(Kammer)* assignment (distribution) of business; ~**verteilung vornehmen** *(Kammer)* to assign business; ~**verteilungsplan** chart of the organization, organization (organizational) chart, *(Gericht)* seal-paper *(Br.)*; ~**vertrag** trading (business) contract; ~**vertrag abschließen** to contract; **einheitliche** ~**verträge** standards of business contracts; ~**verzeichnis** *(Gericht)* cause list.

Geschäftsviertel business quarter (section, zone), commercial section, downtown *(US)*, *(Läden)* shopping area (district), city *(Br.)*, center *(US)*;
nach dem ~ **zu** into the city *(Br.)*, down *(US)*;
im ~ **gelegen** downtown *(US)*;
zentrumnahes ~ retail trading zone.

Geschäfts|visum business visa; ~**vollmacht** power of attorney.

Geschäftsvolumen volume of business, business volume;
~ **verdoppeln** to double business; ~ **verringern** to slim down operations; **mit abnehmendem** ~ **fertig werden** to ride out a contraction of business.

Geschäfts|voraussetzungen schaffen to lay the foundations of a business; ~**vorfall,** ~**vorgang** accountable event, business case (transaction), piece of business, transaction; **besondere** ~**vorfälle** special business; ~**vorfälle aufzeichnen** to record business transactions; ~**vorgänger[in]** predecessor [company]; ~**vorhaben** business project (plan, scheme); ~**vorschau** forecasting, budgeting; ~**vorschlag** business proposition; ~**vorstand** management; ~**vorteil** trading advantage; ~**wagen** commercial (business, company, fleet) car, *(Lieferwagen)* delivery van; **auf dem üblichen** ~**weg** in the ordinary way of business.

Geschäftswelt business community (front, interests), financial (commercial) men, world of business, commercial (business) world;
in der ~ **verankert** anchored in business;
internationale ~ businessmen engaged in international trade; **schwer auf der** ~ **lasten** *(Steuern)* to press heavily on the tradesmen; **für die** ~ **sehr verlockend sein** to have commercial glamo(u)r.

Geschäfts|werbung treibende Firma business advertiser; ~**wert** goodwill, enterprise (firm's) value, value of business; ~**zeichen** reference (file) number, file reference, *(Warenzeichen)* trademark.

Geschäftszeit business (office, official) hours, *(Laden)* shop hours;
außerhalb der ~ outside [of] business hours;
stille ~ quiet hours; **umsatzschwache** ~ dead hours.

Geschäfts|zeitraum trading period; ~**zentrum** chief seat of commerce, business center *(US)* (part of a [trading] town), business community, trading center *(US)*, *(Läden)* shopping center *(US)* (centre, *Br.*, district), shoppy part of a city, downtown *(US)*; ~**zimmer** office, bureau, *(mil.)* orderly room; ~**zone** business area; ~**zunahme** growth (increase, accretion) of business *(Br.)*; ~**zusammenbruch** business (trading) failure; ~**zusammenschluß** business combination, merger; ~**zuwachs** growth of business.

Geschäftszweck business purpose (edge);
nur zu ~**en** strictly for business;
allgemeiner ~ general nature of business;
~ **einer Gesellschaft** corporate object;
~ **ändern** to change one's line of business.

Geschäftszweig line (branch, way) of business, business line (branch), walk, department, trade [section];
~**e** commercial lines;
alle ~**e** all lines of business; **besonderer** ~ particular branch; **in einem** ~ **arbeiten** to engage in a line of business; ~ **aufgeben** to drop out of a business; **einem** ~ **nachgehen** to pursue a line of business.

geschaltet, parallel *(el.)* connected in parallel, in multiple;
schnell ~ **haben** to have been quick on the uptake.

geschätzt valued, *(angesehen)* esteemed, respected;
nicht ~ unprized;
sehr ~ **sein** *(Börse)* to be at a premium;
~**er Kostenbeitrag** estimated cost.

Geschehen event, happening, occurrence;
dramatisches (erregendes) ~ drama; **konjunkturelles** ~ cyclical trend.

geschehen to chance, to come to pass, to happen, to occur;
in jds. Interesse ~ to be for the sake of s. o.;
sehr bald war es um seine Ruhe ~ his peace was soon scattered;
~ *(a.)* done;
kürzlich ~ recent.

Geschehnis event, occurrence, happening, incidence.

gescheit clever, bright, intelligent, wise;
j. für außergewöhnlich ~ **halten** to describe s. o. as really clever; **aus etw. nicht** ~ **werden können** not to be able to make head or tail of it; **nicht ganz** ~ **sein** to be crazy (gone off one's head); **hinterher genauso** ~ **sein** to be none the wiser;
~**er Einfall** bright idea.

gescheitert wrecked;
~ **sein** to prove a bad egg.

Geschenk gift, present, *(lit.)* gift horse, *(Geldgeschenk)* gratuity, *(Schenkung)* gift, donation;
gern gegebenes ~ willing gift; **großzügiges** ~ generous gift; **königliches** ~ princely gift; **kostbares** ~ rich (top-of-the-line) gift; **mitgeführte** ~**e** gifts accompanying s. o.; **unerwartetes** ~ spontaneous gift; **üppiges** ~ bumper present;
~**e herkömmlicher Art** gifts of a habitual nature; ~ **an Geschäftsfreunde** business gifts;
~ **nicht annehmen** to repudiate a gift; **jem. ein** ~ **aufdrängen** to press a gift [up]on s. o.; **an einem** ~ **etw. auszusetzen haben** to look a gift horse in the mouth; **j. etw. zum** ~ **machen** to make a gift (donation, present) of s. th. to s. o.; ~ **zu schätzen wissen** to appreciate a gift;
~**abonnement** gift subscription; ~**annahme** acceptance of a gift.

Geschenkartikel giftware, gift articles, fancy goods;
~**abteilung** gift department; ~**geschäft** gift (souvenir) shop; ~**katalog** gift selection catalog(ue); ~**verkauf** gift selling.

Geschenk|ausgabe gift book; ~**buch** gift book; ~**einkäufe** gift purchases; ~**korb** hamper.

geschenkmäßig verpacken to giftwrap.

Geschenk|packung gift wrapping, presentation pack; ~**paket** gift parcel (package); **in** ~**papier eingepackt** gift-wrapped; ~**segen** shower *(US)*; ~**sendung** gift parcel (package).

geschenkt! spare your breath!;
es nicht einmal ~ **nehmen** wouldn't take it as a gift, not to give it houseroom.

geschenkweise as a free gift (giveaway piece).

Geschichte history, *(Erzählung)* narration, story, tale, *(Sache)* proposition, *(coll.)* business, affair;
in die ~ **eingegangen** storied;
abgeschmackte ~ insipid tale; **immer die alte** ~ the same old story; **aufgewärmte alte** ~ warmed-over cabbage; **dunkle** ~ funny business; **erfundene** ~ made-up story; **faule** ~ fishy account; **die ganze** ~ the whole caboodle *(fam.)*; **gruselige** ~ creepy story; **heikle** ~ tricky business; **nette** ~ pretty concern; **rührselige** ~ sob story *(US)*; **schöne** ~ pretty mess; **seltsame** ~ queer story; **skandalöse** ~ carryings-on; **übertriebene** ~ highly colo(u)red tale; **unangenehme** ~ nasty business, go; **unglaubwürdige** ~ lame story, unlikely tale; **unwahrscheinliche** ~ steep story; **nicht unwahrscheinliche** ~ plausible story; **verwirrte** ~ jumbled story; **wunderliche** ~ quaint tale;
~ **ohne Fortsetzung** one-shot;
der ~ **angehören** to be past and done with *(coll.)*; ~ **groß aufmachen** to run a big story; ~ **gierig in sich aufnehmen** to drink in a story; **alte** ~**n aufwärmen** to rake up old stories; **sich hemmend auf den Fortgang der** ~ **auswirken** to get in the way of a story line; ~ **mit allen Mitteln ins Gespräch bringen** to lug in a story; ~ **erfinden** to fabricate (cook) a story; ~**n erzählen** to pitch a yarn; ~**n über j. erzählen** to tell stories about s. o., to get s. o. into trouble; ~ **immer wieder zum Besten geben** to dine out on a story; **ganze** ~ **satt haben** to be fed up with it; **mit einer außergewöhnlichen** ~ **herausrücken** to come out with an extraordinary story; ~ **in allen Einzelheiten kennen** to know the long and the short of a matter; ~ **kürzen** to cut a long story

short, to boil down a story; **alte ~n begraben sein lassen** to let sleeping dogs lie; **ganze ~ fallen lassen** to drop the whole thing (matter); **~ glaubwürdig erscheinen lassen** to lend colo(u)r to a story; **~n machen** to play all sorts of pranks; **~ interessanter machen** to pep up a story; **in die ~ eingegangen sein** to have found a place in history; **schöne ~ sein** to be a pretty kettle of fish; **~ vollständig wiedergeben** to relate a story in its entirely; **auf eine bewegte ~ zurückblicken** to look back on a colo(u)rful past; **Rad der ~ zurückdrehen** to put the clock back; **~ zusammenfassen** to gather up the threads of a story;
mach keine ~n don't be a fool.
Geschichtenerzähler spinner, story teller.
geschichtlich historic;
~es Ereignis historic event; **~ bedeutsamer Ort** historic spot.
Geschichts|fälschung falsification of history; **~klitterung** deformation (twisting) of history; **~quellen** historical sources; **~schreibung** historiography; **~stunde** history lesson; **~unterricht** history lessons; **~unterricht in einer Klasse erteilen** to instruct a class in history.
Geschick fate, destiny, *(Geschicklichkeit)* hand, skill, knack;
widriges ~ adverse fate;
viel ~ für Handarbeiten haben to be skilled at handicraft; **~ haben, mit Kindern gut umzugehen** to have a knack with children; **~e eines Volkes lenken** to rule over a nation; **sich mit ~ aus einer Affäre ziehen** to get out of it very neatly.
Geschicklichkeit skill, faculty, workmanship, handiness, craft, expertness;
handelsübliche ~ ordinary skill in an art; **praktische ~** executive ability.
Geschicklichkeitsspiel game of skill.
geschickt skil(l)ful, dexterous, skilled, facile, nimble, versed, diplomatic, well;
etw. ~ anfangen to go about it gingerly *(fam.)*; **~ sein** to be neat with one's hands; **sehr ~ in etw. sein** to be a good hand at s. th.; **~ mit Kunden umzugehen wissen** to handle customers with practised skill;
~e Arbeit facile work; **Zeugen durch ~e Fragen aufs Glatteis führen** to trip a witness by skilful practices; **sehr ~e Hände haben** to be clever with one's hands; **~er Lügner sein** to be a clever liar, to be facile in inventing lies; **~er Schachzug** clever move; **~er Verhandler sein** to have negotiating skill.
geschieden divorced;
nicht ~ undivorced;
~ werden to obtain a divorce;
~e Leute sein to be through with one another.
Geschiedene[r] divorcee;
zweimal ~ two-time loser *(sl.)*.
Geschiedenenrente maintenance alimony.
Geschirr crockery, crocks *(fam.)*, ware, the dishes, pots and pans, *(Ausrüstung)* tackle, equipment, *(Pferd)* harness;
feuerfestes ~ ovenware; **goldenes ~** plate *(Br.)*;
~ abwaschen to wash up the dishes; **einem Pferd das ~ anlegen** to harness a horse; **sich tüchtig ins ~ legen** to put one's shoulder to the wheel, to buckle down to it;
~ablage plate rack; **~schrank** cupboard, dresser *(Br.)*; **~spüler** dishwasher; **~trockner** plate rack.
geschlagen defeated, beaten;
sich ~ geben to recognize defeat, to own o. s. beaten, to throw in the towel, to yield the palm to s. o., to acknowledge the corn *(US)*.
geschlängelt *(Fluß)* meandering, tortuous.
Geschlecht sex, *(Familie)* family, house, blood, name, *(Gattung)* genus, species, kind;
nach ~ern getrennt coordinate;
das andere ~ the opposite sex; **kommende ~er** unborn generations; **das menschliche ~** the human race, mankind; **das schwache ~** the gentle sex.
Geschlechterfolge genealogy.
Geschlechtsverkehr sexual intercourse.
geschliffen *(Edelstein, Glas)* cut, *(Stil)* polished, refined, smooth.
geschlossen closed, defunct, shut, *(einmütig)* solid, in a body, *(Handlung)* closely knit, *(Kurszettel)* sales transacted, paid, *(Tagung)* closed, private, *(Wahl)* en bloc;
wegen Auftragsmangels ~ closed down because of lack of orders; **am Nachmittag ~** early closing day, closed for a half holiday; **im Sommer ~** closed in the summer; **vorübergehend ~** temporarily closed;
~ ankommen to arrive in a body; **~ antreten** to turn in full force; **einen Monat lang ~ bleiben** *(Theater)* to be dark for a month; **~ demissionieren** to resign in a body; **~ Ferien machen** *(Betrieb)* to be closing down for the holidays; **~ sein** *(el.)* to be at make; **~ für etw. sein** to be all in favo(u)r of (solid for) s. th.; **im Sommer ~ sein** to have closed for the summer; **~ hinter jem. stehen** to go solid for s. o.; **~ für einen Vorschlag stimmen** to vote unanimously for a proposal; **~ von einem Konzern übernommen werden** to be completely taken over by a concern;
~er Angriff concerted attack; **~e Baueinheit** self-contained unit; **~er Bestand** *(Abschreibungsmethode)* closed-end account; **~er Deich** continuous embankment; **~es Depot** trust deposit; **~e Gesellschaft** private company; **~er Güterwagen** closed freight car, boxcar *(US)*; **~es Konto** closed account; **~e Ladung** *(Schiff)* bulk commodity; **~e Ortschaft** built-up area; **in ~er Sitzung** in closed session, in camera *(Br.)*; **Untersuchung hinter ~en Türen führen** to hold an inquiry behind closed doors; **hinter ~en Türen tagen** to sit behind closed doors; **~er Verband** *(Fahrzeuge)* convoy, escort, *(Flugzeuge)* close (tight) formation; **~e Versammlung** indoor meeting; **~e Vorstellung** private performance; **~er Wagen** *(Auto)* sedan, saloon *(US)*; **in sich ~e Wohnung** self-contained flat.
geschluckt werden, von jem. to go down with s. o.; **von einem Großkonzern ~** to be completely taken over by a big concern.
Geschmack palate, taste, zest;
nicht nach meinem ~ not my cup of tea, not my mark;
angenehmer ~ relish; **ausgefallener ~** extravagant taste; **fader ~** insipid taste; **schlechter ~** low taste; **verwöhnter ~** sophisticated taste; **nicht verwöhnter ~** budget taste;
einer Sache keinen ~ abgewinnen not to relish the prospect; **~ an einem Plan bekommen** to enter a plan with zest; **~ an etw. finden** to take a fancy to s. th., to come to like s. th.; **etw. nach seinem ~ finden** to find s. th. to one's taste; **langsam an einer Sache ~ finden** to come round to (grow upon) an idea; **~ haben** to be a man of taste; **angenehmen ~ haben** to have a delicious flavo(u)r; **ganz besonderen ~ haben** to have a flavo(u)r all of its own; **auf den ~ kommen** to get to like s. th., to taste blood; **dem öffentlichen ~ schmeicheln** to cater for public taste; **nach jds. ~ sein** to be after s. one's heart; **nicht nach jedermanns ~ sein** not to be everyone's taste; **jds. ~ treffen** to hit s. one's fancy; **gegen den guten ~ verstoßen** to perpetrate a breach of good taste, to commit an offence against good taste, to overstep the lines of good taste.
geschmackbildende Wirkung haben to develop one's taste.
Geschmäcker, völlig verschiedene ~ haben to differ widely in their tastes;
~ sind verschieden there is no accounting for taste.
geschmacklos dry, plain, atrocious *(coll.)*;
~e Bemerkung remark in doubtful (bad) taste.
Geschmacklosigkeit bad taste, crudity, atrocity *(coll.)*.
Geschmacks|änderung change in style; **~frage** matter of taste.
Geschmacksmuster design patent;
eingetragenes ~ registered design;
~eintragung registration of designs *(Br.)*; **~gesetz** Designs Act *(Br.)*; **~rolle** Register of Designs *(Br.)* (Inventions, *US*); **~schutz** protection of registered designs *(Br.)*.
Geschmacks|richtungen, verschiedene dissimilar tastes; **~sache** matter of taste; **~sinn** gustatory sense; **~test** flavo(u)r preference test; **feine literarische ~unterschiede** discriminating taste in literature; **~verirrung** lapse of taste; **~wandlung** change in taste.
geschmackvoll tasteful, neat, chic *(coll.)*;
~ mit Blumen dekoriert tastefully decorated with flowers; **~ gekleidet** dressed in perfect taste;
nicht sehr ~ sein not to be in good taste;
~ eingerichtetes Zimmer stylishly furnished room.
geschmeidig supple, soft, pliant, flexible, glossy, *(geistig)* pliable, supple, elastic;
sich der neuen Lage ~ anpassen to adapt o. s. easily to the new situation;
~er Charakter pliable character.
Geschmeidigkeit pliancy, suppleness, *(fig.)* flexibility, adaptability.
Geschmeiß vermin, scum, dregs, riff-raff, rabble.
Geschmiere smearing, *(Schrift)* scribble.
geschmiert, wie on wheels.
geschmuggelt smuggled, hot, moonshine *(sl.)*.
Geschmunzel smirk, good-natured smile.
geschnappt, von der Polizei nabbed by the police.
Geschnatter *(fig.)* chattering, babbling.
geschniegelt spruced up, dapper, keen *(US sl.)*;
~ und gebügelt spick and span.
Geschöpf creature, thing;
albernes ~ silly thing; **klägliches ~** poor creature;
~ seiner Phantasie figment of one's imagination.

Geschoß stor(e)y, floor, *(mil.)* bullet, projectile, missile;
ballistisches ~ ballistic missile; **ferngelenktes** ~ guided missile; **im obersten** ~ **wohnen** to live on the top floor;
~**aufschlag** impact of a missile; ~**bahn** trajectory; ~**garbe** cone of fire; ~**höhe** height; ~**kopf** head, nose.
geschraubt unnatural, *(Stil)* stilled, mannered, artificial.
Geschrei shouting, whoop, yelling, exclamation;
anfeuerndes ~ cheers, acclamation;
viel ~ **und wenig dahinter** much ado about nothing, much cry for little wool;
viel ~ **um Kleinigkeiten machen** to make a big fuss over trifles.
geschrieben written;
eigenhändig ~ holograph; **mit der Hand** ~ handwritten; **mit der Maschine** ~ typewritten, typed; **ungleich** ~ *(Buch)* patchy;
~**es Recht** statute (written) law.
geschuldet due, owing.
geschult trained.
Geschütz gun, cannon;
schweres ~ **auffahren** *(fig.)* to bring heavy artillery into play; ~**e in Stellung bringen** to emplace the guns;
~**bedienung** gunners' crew; **entfernter** ~**donner** distant rumbling of guns; ~**feuer** gunfire; ~**führer** *(mar.)* quarter gunner; ~**mannschaft** gunners' crew.
geschützt secure, privileged, immune;
gesetzlich ~ protected by law, proprietary; **nicht** ~ *(Urheberrecht)* uncopyrighted; **patentamtlich** ~ protected by letters patent, patented; **urheberrechtlich** ~ protected by copyright;
nicht mehr ~ **sein** *(Patent)* to be in the public domain *(US)*; **während der nächsten 21 Jahre** ~ **sein** to be protected for a period of 21 years;
durch Zollschranken ~**e Industrie** protected industries.
geschwächt in a reduced state, *(Börse)* weak, low, depressed;
weiterhin gesundheitlich ~ **sein** to still continue in weak health;
~**e Gesundheit** broken health.
Geschwader *(Flugzeug)* wing, group *(US)*, *(Schiffe)* squadron;
gemeinsam operierendes ~ flying circus;
~**flug** wing-formation flying; ~**kommodore** wing commander *(US)*.
Geschwafel twaddle, drivel, waffle *(sl.)*.
geschwängert pregnant, impregnated.
Geschwätz idle (shallow) talk, rigmarole, palaver, gab, twaddle, drivel, eyewash *(sl.)*, wind, trumpery, spiel *(US sl.)*;
ewiges ~ eternal chatter *(coll.)*; **hochtrabendes** ~ high-falutin language; **leeres** ~ idle gossip, rattle *(sl.)*, windbaggery *(sl.)*; **nichts als** ~ all talk and no do; **sentimentales** ~ mush *(sl.)*; **unentwegtes** ~ perpetual chatter.
geschwätzig loquacious, verbose, windy.
geschweige denn let alone, to say nothing of.
geschwellt, vor Stolz puffed up with pride.
geschwind swift, fast, quick, in a jiffy.
Geschwindigkeit speed, rate, velocity, *(Eile)* expedition, haste;
mit einer ~ **von** at a velocity of; **mit erlaubter** ~ on the peg *(US sl.)*; **mit größter (höchster)** ~ at the top of one's speed, against time, full out, at full lick *(Br., sl.)*; **mit einer** ~ **von 50 km in der Stunde** at a speed of 30 miles an hour;
vertraglich ausbedungene ~ designed speed; **durchschnittliche** ~ average speed; **enorme** ~ tremendous speed; **tagsüber durchschnittlich erzielte** ~ average day-time speed; **fahrplanmäßige** ~ *(Zug)* scheduled speed *(US)*; **geringe** ~ low speed; **geringere** ~ less speed; **gestoppte** ~ timed speed; **gleichmäßige** ~ uniform speed; **gute** ~ good going; **halsbrecherische** ~ breakneck speed; **hohe** ~ express speed; **kritische** ~ *(Flugzeug)* stalling speed; **überhöhte** ~ excessive speed; **unverminderte** ~ unrelenting speed; **zulässige** ~ permissible speed;
~ **über Grund** ground speed; ~ **des Lichtes** velocity of light;
~ **beibehalten** to maintain the speed; ~ **drosseln** to cut back speed; ~ **erhöhen** to increase speed, to speed up, to accelerate; **mit höchster** ~ **fahren** to drive at top (put on full) speed; **mit überhöhter** ~ **fahren** to drive at an excessive speed; ~ **auf einer kontrollierten Strecke feststellen** to test the speed over a measured mile; ~ **herabsetzen** to cut speed; **nur noch mit einer** ~ **von fünfzig Stundenkilometern reisen** to ease a car down to 30 miles; **mit einer** ~ **von 100 Stundenkilometern reisen** to travel at a rate of 60 miles an hour; **zulässige** ~ **überschreiten** to exceed the speed limit; ~ **verlangsamen** to decelerate, to ease down, to lessen (lower) speed, *(Zug)* to slacken up; **seine** ~ **vermindern** to decrease one's speed; ~ **wiederaufnehmen** to resume speed; **an** ~ **zunehmen** to gather pace.
Geschwindigkeits|abfall *(Flugzeug)* loss of flying speed; ~**abnahme** loss in speed, deceleration; ~**anzeiger** speed indicator (recorder), speedometer; ~**begrenzung** speed limit (restriction, regulation); **ohne** ~**begrenzung** unrestricted; ~**begrenzungsschild** speed-limit sign; ~**bereich** speed range; ~**beschränkung** speed restriction (limit); ~**beschränkung für eine Straße aufheben** to remove the restrictions on a street, to derestrict a road; ~**beschränkung für eine Straße festsetzen** to restrict a road; ~**beschränkungsaufhebungsschild** derestriction sign; ~**grenze** speed limit; **j. wegen Überschreitung der** ~**grenze anzeigen** to have s. o. up for exceeding the speed limit; ~**grenze überschreiten** to exceed the speed limit; ~**kontrolle** speed control (check); ~**kontrolleur** speed cop; ~**messer** speed indicator, speedometer; ~**prüfung** *(Schiff)* speed trial; ~**regler** overspeed gear; ~**schild** speed-limit signpost, *(Aufhebungsschild)* derestriction sign; ~**skala** speed spectrum; ~**stufen** gradation of speeds; ~**überschreitung** exceeding the speed limit, speeding violation *(US)*; **wegen** ~**überschreitung bestraft werden** to be fined for speeding; ~**verlust** *(Flugzeug)* pancaking, stalling; ~**vorschriften** speed regulations; ~**zähler** tachometer; **unbegrenzte** ~**zone** derestricted area; ~**zunahme** gathering of speed.
Geschwindschritt *(mil.)* quick time.
Geschwister brothers and sisters;
halbblütige ~ half blood.
geschwollen inflated, bombastic, pretentious, mouth-filling.
Geschworene jurors, jury, recognitors *(Br.)*, lay people, good country *(Scot.)*, pais;
unanfechtbare ~ good jury; **unvoreingenommene** ~ unpartial jury;
~ **in der Hauptverhandlung** traverse jury;
~ **abberufen** to withdraw jurors; ~ **ablehnen** to challenge a jury, to challenge the array; ~ **über die wesentlichen Rechtsgrundsätze aufklären** to instruct jurors; ~ **auslosen** to draw (call) the jury; ~ **auswählen** to strike a jury; ~ **nach Befragung auswählen** to poll jurors; ~ **beeinflussen** to labo(u)r a jury; ~ **einzeln befragen** to poll the jurors *(US)*; **die** ~**n belehren** to instruct the jury; ~ **bestechen** to embrace jurors, to charge (fix, *US*) a jury; ~ **für sich einnehmen** to win the jury; ~ **einschließen** to inclose a jury; ~ **einsetzen** to impanel a jury; ~ **entlassen** to discharge the members of the jury; ~ **zwecks Urteilsfindung entlassen** to leave the jury to find their verdict; ~ **ernennen** to array a panel; ~ **für sich freundlich stimmen** to win over the jury.
Geschworenen|ablehnung challenge to the array (panel); **grundsätzliche** ~**ablehnung** general challenge; ~**anklageschrift** bill of indictment; ~**ausschuß** jury; ~**bank** common jury, jury box, petit jury; **auf der** ~**bank sitzen** to be (serve) on the jury; ~**bank aus parteiischen Geschworenen zusammenstellen** to pack a jury; ~**beeinflussung**, ~**bestechung** embracery of jurors, jury fixing, bracery; ~**entscheid in öffentlicher Sitzung** public verdict.
Geschworenengericht jury [trial], coroner's (crown, *Br.*) court;
besonders ausgeprägtes ~ struck jury; **blockiertes** ~ hung jury; **großes** ~ grand jury *(US)*; **mehrsprachiges** ~ mixed jury; **beruflich qualifiziertes** ~ special jury; **unparteiisches** ~ fair jury.
Geschworenenliste jury panel, panel of jurors, array;
in die ~ **eintragen** to [im]panel; ~ **veröffentlichen** to return a list of jurors; ~ **zusammenstellen** to strike a jury *(US)*.
Geschworenenspruch jury award;
einstimmiger ~ unanimous voice of a jury; **rechtsgültiger** ~ true verdict; **rechtswidriger** ~ verdict contrary to law;
~ **durch das Los** chance verdict; ~ **im versiegelten Umschlag** sealed verdict.
Geschworenentätigkeit jury service.
Geschworenenurteil general verdict;
öffentlich verkündetes ~ public verdict;
~ **in Einzelfragen** special finding; ~ **durch das Los** verdict by lot;
~ **fällen** to return a verdict.
Geschworenen|verzeichnis juror's book; ~**vorladung** venire *(US)*.
Geschworener juryman, jurator, talesman;
nicht mehr als ~ **einberufen werden können** to be exempt from jury service; **als** ~ **tätig sein, als** ~ **fungieren** to serve as a juror, to sit (serve) on a jury; **als** ~ **einberufen werden** to be called to jury service.
geschworener Gegner sworn enemy.
Gesegneten, die wenig vom Glück the least fortunate (underdogs).
gesehen und genehmigt seen and approved.
Geselle journeyman, little master *(Br.)*;
voll ausgebildeter ~ full-fledged journeyman; **fahrender** ~ travelling journeyman, wayfarer; **sturer** ~ *(fig.)* insular mind; **als** ~**n einstellen** to indenture.
gesell|en, sich zu jem. to join s. o.;
gleich und gleich ~**t sich gern** birds of a feather flock together.

Gesellen|arbeit journeywork; ~**brief** certificate of apprenticeship; ~**lohn** journeyman wage, approved journeyman's rate; ~**prüfung** journeyman's examination, test of apprenticeship; ~**stück** diploma piece; ~**zeit** terms of apprenticeship.

gesellig sociable, social, conversable;
~ **beisammensitzen** to spend a social evening; ~ **sein** to be fond of company;
~**es Beisammensein** social gathering, setout; ~**e Veranstaltung** social occasion; ~**es Wesen** social animal.

Geselligkeit social life, company, entertaining, good fellowship;
~ **lieben** to be fond of company; ~ **pflegen** to entertain a great deal.

Geselligkeitsverein social organization.

Gesellschaft society, social order, *(Akademie)* institute, *(Einladung)* party, setout, *(Gruppe)* crowd *(US sl.)*, *(Handelsgesellschaft)* company, corporation *(US)*, body, *(Teilhaberschaft)* partnership firm, [co]partnership, *(Vereinigung)* society, association, union, fellowship;
abgebende ~ vendor company; **abgewickelte** ~ dissolved company; **abhängige** ~ controlled company, subsidiary company (corporation, *US*); **angegliederte** ~ associated company *(Br.)*, affiliated corporation *(US)*, affiliate; **geographisch aufgegliederte** ~ multidivision corporation *(US)*; **aufgelöste** ~ dissolved company (corporation, *US*), company wound up, defunct company; **aufnehmende** ~ *(Fusion)* absorbing company; **nicht auf den Betrieb eines Handelsunternehmens ausgerichtete** ~ nontrading company; **mit zu geringem Eigenkapital ausgestattete** ~ equity-starved company; **mit allen Rechten ausgestattete** ~ complete corporation; **ausgewählte** ~ select company; **ausländische (auswärtige)** ~ foreign (alien, *US*) corporation, alien company, overseas company *(Br.)*; **ausschüttende** ~ dividend-paying company; **Verlustausgleich beantragende** ~ claimant company; **befreundete** ~ corresponding company, correspondent; **beherrschende** ~ controlling company; **bergrechtliche** ~ mining company; **auf mündlicher Vereinbarung beruhende** ~ oral partnership; **bestehende** ~ actual society; **aus mehreren Personen bestehende** ~ corporation aggregate *(US)*; **beteiligte** ~ participating company; **privatwirtschaftlich betriebene** ~ privately held company; **bürgerliche** ~ middle-class society; **nur in Schablonen denkende** ~ punch-card society; **dividendenlose** ~ company paying no dividends; **einbringende** ~ *(Fusion)* vendor company; **eingegliederte** ~ integrated company; **fortschrittlich eingestellte** ~ forward-looking company; **handelsgerichtlich eingetragene** ~ incorporated company *(Br.)*, registered (chartered) corporation *(US)*; **nicht eingetragene** ~ unincorporated *(Br.)* (unregistered, *US*) corporation; **emittierende** ~ issuing company; **enteignete** ~ dispossessed company; **Gewinnabführungsbeträge entgegennehmende** ~ claimant company; **neu entstandene** ~ resultant (newly formed) company; **durch Simultangründung entstandene** ~ nonprospectus company *(Br.)*; **im Handelsregister erloschene** ~ defunct company; **fehlerhaft errichtete** ~ defective company; **exklusive** ~ select party; **federführende** ~ pilot company; **feine** ~ polite society, the great world; **formierte** ~ aligned society; **fortbestehende** ~ standing company; **äußerst freizügige** ~ permissive society; **fusionierende** ~ merger company; **fusionierte** ~ merged company; **die ganze** ~ the whole lot; **ordnungsgemäß gegründete** ~ de jure corporation *(US)*; **aus Steuergründen vorübergehend gegründete** ~ collapsible corporation *(US)*; **für einen besonderen Zweck gegründete** ~ special partnership; **gelehrte** ~ learned society; **gut geleitete** ~ well-managed company; **im Handelsregister gelöschte** ~ defunct company; **gemeinnützige** ~ friendly society, nonprofit-making company, benevolent (public-service, eleemosynary, public utility, membership, *US*) corporation; **gemischte** ~ diverse lot, medley; **gemischtwirtschaftliche** ~ quasi-public company **geschlossene** ~ private party, club; **gesittete** ~ polite society; **gewinnabführende** ~ surrendering company; **gute** ~ the great world, polite society; **die sogenannte gute** ~ the so-called high society; **halbstaatliche** ~ semigovernmental corporation *(US)*; **handeltreibende** ~ commercial partnership; **herrschende** ~ controlling company; **klassenlose** ~ classless society; **konsolidierte** ~ consolidated company; **nicht konsolidierte** ~ nonconsolidated company; **kontrollierende** ~ proprietary (controlling) company; **staatlich kontrollierte** ~ publicly-owned corporation *(US)*; **konventionelle** ~ set party; **konzessionierte** ~ licensed company, chartered corporation; **jederzeit kündbare** ~ partnership at will; **leoninische** ~ leonine partnership; **an der Grenze der Rentabilität liegende** ~ marginal company; **liquidierte** ~ dissolved company; **literarische** ~ literary society; **lustige** ~ jolly crowd; **marktbeherrschende** ~ company dominating the market; **nahestehende** ~ associated company *(Br.)*, affiliated corporation *(US)*; **öffentlichrechtliche** ~ public company (corporation, *US*); **privatrechtliche** ~ private corporation *(US)*; **privilegierte** ~ chartered company *(Br.)*; **rechtsfähige** ~ incorporated (registered) company *(Br.)*, corporation de jure; **nicht rechtsfähige** ~ corporation de facto *(US)*, unincorporated (unregistered) company *(Br.)*; **reformierte** ~ reform society; **sich rückversichernde** ~ *(Versicherungswesen)* reinsured carrier; **rückversicherte** ~ reinsured carrier; **sanierte** ~ reorganized company (corporation) *(US)*; **schuldende** ~ debtor company (corporation, *US*); **selbständige** ~ independent company; **staatliche** ~ government company, publicly owned corporation *(US)*; **stille** ~ dormant (secret, silent, *US*) partnership, partnership in commendam; **stillgelegte** ~ defunct company *(Br.)*; **effektiv tätige** ~ operating company; **treuhänderisch tätige** ~ corporation acting as trustee *(US)*; **tolerante** ~ permissive society; **übernehmende** ~ *(Fusion)* surviving (transferee) company; **übertragende** ~ *(Fusion)* transferor company; **unseriöse** ~ dubious (wildcat) company; **veräußernde** ~ vendor company; **geschäftlich verbundene** ~ associated company *(Br.)*; **verpachtende** ~ lessor company; **verpachtete** ~ nonoperating company; **verschachtelte** ~**en** interrelated companies; **verstaatlichte** ~ nationalized company; **vertrauenswürdige** ~ reliable firm; **vorgeschobene** ~ dummy corporation *(US)*; **vornehme** ~ rank and fashion, polite society, the great world; **zugelassene** ~ chartered corporation;
~ **zur Absatzfinanzierung** sales finance company; ~, **deren Aktien an der Börse gehandelt werden** quoted company; ~ **zur Aufbewahrung von Wertgegenständen** safe company *(US)*; ~ **mit öffentlich-rechtlichen Befugnissen** quasi-public company (corporation, *US*); ~ **zur Bekämpfung des Wettbewerbes** Council of Better Business Bureaus; ~ **mit Börsenprospekt** prospectus company; ~ **mit Dividendenbeschränkung** limited-dividend corporation *(US)*; ~ **mit gesetzlich vorgeschriebener Devisenbeschränkung** limited-dividend corporation *(US)*; ~ **vor Eintragung** quasi corporation *(US)*; ~ **zur Errettung Ertrinkender** Royal Humane Society; ~ **zur Erschließung von Baugelände** industrial development company, development concern *(US)*; ~ **ohne Erwerbszweck** nonprofit-making company; ~ **mit überproportionalem Fertigungsprogramm** overdiversified company; ~ **zur Finanzierung der Viehzucht** cattle-loan company; ~ **zur Finanzierung von Warenkrediten** commercial company; ~ **auf Gegenseitigkeit** mutual society; ~ **ohne Geschäftsbetrieb** inactive company; ~ **mit Geschäftssitz im Ausland** nonresident company; ~ **mit begrenztem Gesellschafterkreis** close corporation; ~ **an der Grenze der Rentabilität** marginal company; ~ **mit beschränkter Haftung** [etwa] exempt private (limited) company *(Br.)*, limited liability company *(Br.)* (corporation, *US*), a type of close corporation *(US)* under German law; ~**en des Handelsrechtes** commercial corporations (partnerships), trading companies; **fidele** ~ **in geschlossenem Kreis** pink tea *(sl.)*; ~ **zur Leitung eines öffentlichen Versorgungsbetriebes** public service corporation *(US)*; ~ **mit beschränktem Mitgliederkreis** close company *(Br.)* (corporation, *US*); ~ **mit beschränkter Nachschußpflicht** company limited by guarantee *(Br.)*; **ausländische** ~ **mit Niederlassung in England** overseas company *(Br.)*; ~ **mit breitgestreutem Produktionsprogramm** diversified company (corporation, *US*); ~ **des bürgerlichen Rechts** [etwa] partnership at will, nontrading partnership, civil (unlimited) corporation *(US)*; ~ **kraft Rechtsscheins** partnership by estoppel *(Br.)*; ~ **in ausschließlichem Schachtelbesitz** wholly owned corporation *(US)*; ~ **zum Schutz der Bürgerrechte** Civil Liberties Union *(US)*; ~ **mit Vorstandswahl in der Hauptversammlung** open corporation;
sich einer ~ **anschließen** to make one of a party; ~ **auflösen** to liquidate a company, to dissolve a business company, to wind up a company (partnership); **aus einer** ~ **ausscheiden** to retire (withdraw) from a partnership; **sich seine** ~ **sorgfältig aussuchen** to pick one's company; **aus einer** ~ **austreten** to take one's name off the books, to withdraw from a society; **sich in schlechter** ~ **befinden** to be in bad company; ~ **beherrschen** to control a company; **einer** ~ **beitreten** to enter (join) a company; **einer** ~ **als Mitglied beitreten** to affiliate o. s. to (with) a society, to enter a society; **schlechte** ~ **darstellen** to make strange bedfellows; **Gefahr für die menschliche** ~ **darstellen** to be a danger to society; **seine Arbeitskraft in eine** ~ **einbringen** to contribute one's services to a company; **in die** ~ **einführen** to bring out; ~ **handelsgerichtlich eintragen** to register (incorpo-

rate) a company (corporation); **in eine ~ eintreten** to join a company, to enter a society; **in eine ~ als Teilhaber eintreten** to enter a company as partner; ~ **errichten** to establish a company, to create (organize) a corporation *(US)*; **Rendite bei einer ~ erwirtschaften** to put a company in the black *(US coll.)*; **zwei ~en fusionieren** to unite two companies; ~ **geben** to give (toss, *sl.*) a party; **einmal im Jahr eine ~ geben** to give a racket once a year; **in ~ gehen** to go out; **zur besten ~ gehören** to move in the leading circles; **zu den Stützen der ~ gehören** to belong to the pillars of society; **in schlechte ~ geraten** to get in bad company, to get in law habits, to be thrown with bad companions; ~ **gründen** to establish a partnership, to incorporate (float, *Br.*, found, form, promote, set up, start) a company, to create a corporation *(US)*; **mit jem. eine ~ gründen** to join company (start a company jointly) with s. o.; **neue ~ gründen** to float a new business company; ~ **aus den roten Zahlen herausführen** to administer a company from red to black *(US coll.)*; ~ **nicht verpflichten können** to have no power to bind a company; ~ **lancieren** to promote a company; ~ **im Handelsregister löschen lassen** to withdraw partnership registration, to take a company off the books; **jem. ~ leisten** to provide companionship, to keep s. o. company; ~ **leiten** to manage a firm; ~ **liquidieren** to dissolve a business company (partnership), to liquidate (wind-up) a company; **als ~ prozessieren** to sue in its corporate name; ~ **ins Leben rufen** to institute a society; **Finanzen einer ~ sanieren** to rehabilitate a company financially, to reconstruct a company, to reorganize a company; **an verschiedenen ~en beteiligt sein** to have holdings in several companies; **mit 100.000 Dollar an einer ~ beteiligt sein** to have an interest of $ 100.000 in a company; ~ **übernehmen** to take over a company; ~ **nur nominell übertragen** to transfer a company on paper; **in eine ~ umwandeln** to form (convert) into a company; **Abend in ~ verbringen** to spend a social evening; ~ **verklagen** to prosecute a company; **in eine ~ aufgenommen werden** to be admitted into a company (partnership, introduced as partner); **in die ~ eingeführt werden** to come out, to make one's debut.

Gesellschafter member of a company *(Br.)*, member of a corporation *(US)*, partner, associate, corporate member, *(Aktiengesellschaft)* shareholder, stockholder *(US)*, *(Gefährte)* companion, attendant;
abwickelnder ~ liquidating partner; **ausgeschiedener ~** retired (past) partner; **ausscheidender ~** retiring (outgoing, withdrawing) partner; **vom Konkurs nicht betroffener ~** solvent partner; **neu eintretender ~** incoming partner; **Gesellschaftsverhältnis fortsetzender ~** surviving partner; **geschäftsführender ~** active (managing, working) partner, active owner; **guter ~** *(Geselligkeit)* good mixer, conversationalist; **beschränkt haftender ~** special (limited) partner; **persönlich haftender ~** general (ordinary, *Br.*, unlimited, associated, responsible) partner; **nicht persönlich haftender ~** subordinate partner *(Br.)*; **unbeschränkt haftender ~** general (unlimited) partner; **konzernfremder ~** outside shareholder; **liquidierender ~** liquidating partner; **minderjähriger ~** infant partner, infant member of a partnership; **nomineller ~** nominal (quasi, holding-out) partner; **scheinbarer ~** ostensible partner; **stiller ~** dormant (silent, secret, *Br.*, sleeping) partner; **tätiger ~** active partner; **nicht tätiger ~** inactive partner; **verbleibender ~** continuing (surviving) partner; **verstorbener ~** deceased partner; **vorgeschobener ~** ostensible partner; **zahlungsunfähiger ~** partner in default;
~ **mit gleichen Geschäftsanteilen** equal partners; ~ **einer Handelsgesellschaft** proprietor in a trading company; ~ **einer Offenen Handelsgesellschaft** general partner;
als ~ aufnehmen to introduce as partner; **j. als ~ ausgeben** to hold s. o. out as a partner; **als ~ ausscheiden** to withdraw (retire) from a partnership; **als ~ persönlich haften** to be personally liable as a partner; **guter ~ sein** to be a good mixer; ~ **werden** to become partner of a firm, to join a company, to enter into a partnership;
~**abfindung** buying out of a partner; ~**anteil** share, partnership (business) interest; ~**aufnahme** admission in a partnership; ~**beschluß** corporate resolution; ~**darlehen** loan made by a partner; ~**entnahmen** drawing by partners, proprietor's drawing; ~**gewinn** partnership profit; ~**haftung** liability of partners, partnership liability; ~**kapital** members' capital, partnership funds; ~**konkurs** bankruptcy of partners, bankruptcy of a partnership, partnership bankruptcy; ~**konto** partnership account; ~**pflichten** partner's duties; ~**rechte** partner's rights; ~**register** stock register *(US)*; ~**verhältnis begründen** to create a partnership; ~**verlust** partnership loss; ~**versammlung** company (corporate, corporation, *US*) meeting; ~**versicherung** partnership life insurance; ~**vertrag** articles of partnership, partnership agreement; ~**verzeichnis** stock register *(US)*; ~**vollmacht** authority of a partner, partner's authority; ~**wechsel** change of partner.

gesellschaftlich social, *(jur.)* corporate;
~ **nicht voll akzeptiert** marginal; ~ **gewandt** easy-mannered; ~ **organisiert** cooperative;
sich ~ unmöglich gemacht haben to have fallen into disgrace with one's companions; ~ **nicht erfolgreich sein** to be a social failure; ~ **nicht integriert sein** to feel no state in society;
~**e Assimilation** social adaption; ~**er Aufstieg** social advancement; ~**en Funktionen dienen** to serve a social function; ~**es Gefüge** social fabric, fabric of society; ~**e Gepflogenheiten beeinflussen** to influence social usage; ~**e Isolierung** social isolation; ~**es Leben** company; **sich vom ~en Leben zurückziehen** to retire into obscurity; ~**e Schichtung** stratum; ~**e Stellung** social position (standing, status); **Einbußen in seiner ~en Stellung hinnehmen müssen** to sink in the social scale; **keinerlei ~en Umgang haben** to be cut off from all society; ~**e Umgangsformen** social habits; ~**er Untergang** social distance; ~**e Veranstaltung** social gathering (event); ~**es Verhalten** social interaction; ~**e Verhaltensweise** social code of good manners; ~**er Verkehr** social life (intercourse); ~**e Verpflichtungen** social commitments (engagements); ~**en Verpflichtungen nachkommen** to fulfil(l) social obligations; ~**er Vorgang** social process.

Gesellschafts|abend evening party, soirée; ~**akten** company files; ~**angelegenheiten** partnership concerns (affairs), corporate business *(US)*; ~**angestellter** *(AG)* corporate official *(US)*; ~**anspruch** partnership claim.

Gesellschaftsanteil partnership share, share in a partnership, partnership interest, holding in a business company, *(AG)* share, stock *(US)*;
bei Umwandlung in eine Kapitalgesellschaft als Kaufpreis übernommene ~e vendor's shares;
~**e übernehmen** to subscribe for shares in a company.

Gesellschafts|anzug formal (regulation, party, full) dress, *(Frack)* tails, dinner jacket, tuxedo *(US)*; **im ~anzug** in full dress; ~**auflösung** dissolution of partnership; ~**bedürfnis** affiliation want; ~**befugnisse** *(AG)* corporate powers; ~**berechtigung** corporate existence *(US)*; ~**bericht** company report, corporation report *(US)*, *(Verein)* secretary's report; ~**beschluß** company resolution, *(AG)* corporate resolution *(US)*; ~**bestimmungen** *(Ergänzungsstatut)* corporate byelaws *(US)*; ~**beteiligung** share, interest; ~**bilanz** company statement, *(AG)* corporate balance sheet (statement, *US*); ~**bücher** company books, *(AG)* corporate books; ~**buchhaltung** company bookkeeping, corporation accounting *(US)*; ~**depot** custody held for a partnership; ~**eigentum** company ownership, partnership property, *(AG)* corporate ownership (property) *(US)*; ~**einkommen** corporate *(US)* (partnership) income; ~**einkünfte** company (corporation, corporate, *US*) earnings; ~**einlage** contribution to capital, investment in a company; ~**entwicklung** corporate development *(US)*.

gesellschaftsfähig out;
nicht ~ not fit for good society, unpresentable, out to lunch *(sl.)*; **noch nicht ~** not yet out;
nicht ~e Person outsider.

Gesellschaftsfahrt organized (packaged, *US*) tour.

gesellschaftsfeindlich antisocial, unsocial, asocial.

Gesellschafts|finanzwesen *(AG)* corporation finance *(US)*; ~**fonds** joint stock; ~**forderung** partnership claim.

Gesellschaftsform corporate form (structure), *(Soziologie)* social system;
~**en** forms of business organization;
in eine öffentlich-rechtliche ~ umwandeln to go public.

gesellschaftsfremd outside the ordinary course of business.

Gesellschafts|führung corporate management *(US)*; ~**fusion** corporate merger (amalgamation) *(US)*; ~**garantie** company's guarantee; ~**geschäft** corporate business; ~**gewinn** partnership (company) profit (earnings), *(AG)* corporation earnings *(US)*, corporate (corporative) profit *(US)*; ~**gewinne vor Konzerneingliederung** preacquisition profits; ~**gläubiger** creditor of a firm (partnership), partnership (corporate, *US*) creditor; ~**gründer** organizer, incorporator *(US)*, promoter of a company; ~**gründung** company promotion, establishment (flotation, formation) of a company (corporation, *US*); ~**haftung** corporate liability *(US)*; ~**handlung** *(AG)* corporate act *(US)*; ~**hierarchie** pecking order; ~**jahr** company's financial year *(Br.)*; ~**journalist** gossip columnist.

Gesellschaftskapital capital of a partnership, a company's resources (capital), partnership funds (stock), funds of a company, company's funds, ownership interest, *(Eigenkapital einer AG)* capitalization, net worth *(US)*, stockholders' equity *(US)*, *(Grundkapital einer AG)* joint capital *(Br.)*, capital (joint) stock *(US)*, corporate (corporation) capital *(US)*; **ausgewiesenes (genehmigtes, satzungsmäßiges)** ~ stated (nominal, *Br.*, authorized, *Br.*) capital, authorized capital stock *(US)*; **unverwässertes** ~ dry capital; **verwässertes** ~ watered stock.

Gesellschafts|klasse [social] class; **die niedrigen ~klassen** the under classes; **~konkurs** partnership bankruptcy; **~konkurs einleiten** to force a company into a chapter 10 proceeding *(US)*; **~konto** partnership account, company (corporate, *US*) account; **~konzession** corporation licence; **~kreis** walk, circle; **höchste ~kreise** highest walks of life; **sich in den besten ~kreisen bewegen, in den besten ~kreisen verkehren** to move in the best society (exclusive circles); **~kritiker** social commentator, gossip columnist (writer); **~leben** social organization; **in das ~leben Eingang finden** to insinuate o. s. into society; **~leitung** company (corporate, *US*) management; **~löwe** social lion, socialite *(US)*, party boy; **~mehrheit** majority of a company; **~mensch** social lion, cookie-pusher; **~mittel** partnership funds, corporate funds *(US)*; **~nachrichten** society news; **~name** partnership name, corporate name *(US)*; **~ordnung** social scale (code); **durch Titelsucht bestimmte ~ordnung** pecking order; **freiheitliche ~ordnung** free social order; **~organe** executive bodies of a company (corporation); **langfristige ~politik** company strategy.

gesellschaftspolitisch sociopolitical.

Gesellschafts|privilegien *(AG)* corporate franchise *(US)*, charter; **~prospekt** company prospectus; **~protokoll** corporate minutes *(US)*; **~räume** reception (public) rooms, recreational space, *(Hotel)* hotel lounge; **~rechnung** rule of partnership, corporate statement; **~recht** law of partnership, partnership law, company law *(Br.)*; **~rechte** corporate rights; **~reformer** society reformer; **~register** stock register, register of companies *(Br.)* (corporations, *US*); **~reingewinn** corporate surplus *(US)*; **~reise** organized (conducted, guided, packaged, *US*) tour; **~reise in der Touristenklasse** economy excursion; **~sanierung** rehabilitation of the finances of a company, corporate reorganization *(US)*; **~satzung** *(AG)* articles of association *(Br.)* (incorporation, *US*), *(OHG)* articles of partnership, *(Verein)* society's rules.

Gesellschaftsschicht social order, social bracket, stratum;
zu einer ~ gehörig class;
höhere ~en first classes, higher brackets; **niedrige ~en** lower orders; **die oberen ~en** the fashionable world (upper ten); **tonangebende** ~ establishment.

Gesellschafts|schulden *(AG)* corporation debts *(US)*, *(OHG)* partnership liabilities, partnership (company's) debts; **vor [nach] dem Ausscheiden entstandene ~schulden** debts incurred before [after] retirement; **~siegel** common *(Br.)* (corporate, *US*) seal; **~sitz** head office, location of the registered office, registered office *(Br.)*, residence of a company (corporation, *US*); **~spalte** society (gossip) column; **~spiele** indoor diversions; **~spitzen** leading lights; **~statuten** memorandum and articles of association *(Br.)*, partnership articles, articles of partnership, *(AG)* articles of incorporation *(US)*, corporate byelaws *(US)*, regulations of a corporation *(US)*; **~statuten einhalten** to observe the articles of association; **~steuer** incorporation (corporate, *US*) tax; **~struktur** corporate structure *(US)*, *(Soziologie)* setup; **~stück** *(Theater)* drawing-room play; **~stufe** social scale; **~system** framework of society; **zustimmungspflichtige ~tätigkeit** corporate action *(US)*; **sich im Rahmen der üblichen ~tätigkeit halten** to act in the ordinary course of a partnership; **~transaktion** partnership transaction; **~unternehmen** business (commercial) enterprise; **~urkunde** charter of incorporation; **~verbindlichkeiten** company debts (liabilities), corporate liabilities.

Gesellschaftsverhältnis partnership;
~ **beenden** to dissolve a partnership; **mit jem. ein ~ eingehen** to enter into partnership with s. o.; ~ **fortsetzen** to carry on in a partnership.

Gesellschafts|verlust partnership loss, *(AG)* corporate loss; **~verluste vor Konzerneingliederung** preacquisition losses; **~vermögen** *(AG)* corporate assets (estate) *(US)*, corporation money *(US)*, company (corporate, corporation, *US*) property, *(OHG)* assets of a company (partnership), partnership assets (property, stock, estate, goods); **in das ~vermögen vollstrecken** to levy execution into the company's property; **~versammlung** company *(Br.)* (corporate, corporation, *US*) meeting; **~vertrag** *(AG)* articles and memorandum of association *(Br.)*, articles of incorporation *(US)*, *(OHG)* contract (articles, deed) of partnership, company agreement, partnership agreement (articles, contract, deed), *(Soziologie)* social contract (compact); **~vertrag verletzen** to commit a breach of the partnership agreement; **~zimmer** *(Hotel)* parlo(u)r, reception room; **~zweck** partnership purpose, objects of a company, company's object, *(AG)* corporate purpose (object) *(US)*; **~zweckbestimmung** objects clause.

gesendet werden to be on the air.

Gesenk drain pit.

gesenkt depressed.

Gesetz law, parliamentary act, *(Erlaß)* act, enactment, decree, *(Gesetzesvorlage)* bill;
aufgrund eines ~es by virtue of (under the) law; **bei Inkrafttreten des ~es** when the law comes into effect; **im Sinne dieses ~es** within the meaning of this law; **kraft ~es** by operation of law; **mit den ~en vereinbar** consistent with law; **nach dem** ~ under the law; **nach Recht und** ~ according to law; **unmittelbar kraft ~es** ipso jure; **vom ~ vorgeschrieben** prescribed by law, mandatory; **wie es das ~ vorsieht** as by law enacted; **wird folgendes ~ beschlossen** be it further enacted that;
allgemeines ~ public statute; **ungenau angewandtes** ~ loosely administrated law; **nicht mehr angewendetes [formal noch nicht aufgehobenes]** ~ obsolete law; **anwendbares** ~ law applicable; **aufgehobenes** ~ extinct law; **befristetes** ~ temporary statute; **bestehendes** ~ existing law; **von der Regierung eingebrachtes** ~ administration bill *(US)*; **einheitliches** ~ uniform law; **einschlägiges** ~ relevant law; **aus besonderem Anlaß erlassenes** ~ law made for the occasion; **formgerecht erlassenes** ~ enrolled bill; **im Verordnungswege erlassenes** ~ decree law; **erläuterndes** ~ expository statute, declaratory law; **geltendes** ~ established law, law in force; **geschriebenes** ~ statutory (written) law, statute; **gewerbepolizeiliche ~e** factory acts *(Br.)*; **unanwendbar gewordenes** ~ dormant law; **gültiges** ~ operative (established) law; **unerläßlich notwendige ~e** must legislation *(US)*; **oberstes** ~ cardinal law; **ökonomisches** ~ economic law; **rückwirkendes** ~ ex-post-facto (retroactive) law; **nicht rückwirkendes** ~ nonretroactive law; **strenges** ~ strict (exact) law; **umfassendes** ~ comprehensive law; **zeitlich unbeschränktes** ~ perpetual statute; **ungeschriebenes** ~ unwritten law; **ungültiges** ~ dead law; **verabschiedetes** ~ law on the books; **allgemein verbindliches** ~ public (general) statute; **verbrauchsbeschränkendes** ~ sumptuary law; **verfassungswidriges** ~ unconstitutional law; **verschärftes** ~ reinforced law; **hastig zusammengestoppeltes** ~ improvised law; **zwingendes** ~ binding (peremptory) law, mandatory statute;
~ **von Angebot und Nachfrage** general law of demand, law of supply and demand; ~ **über die Anwendung anderer Gesetzesvorschriften** reference statute; ~ **zur Aufrechterhaltung von Ruhe und Ordnung** Public Order Act *(Br.)*; ~ **zur Aufrechterhaltung der Vollbeschäftigung** Employment Act *(US)*; ~ **über Bausparkassen** Building Societies Act *(Br.)*; ~ **zur Beschränkung der Gastwirtshaftung** Hotel Proprietors Act *(Br.)*; ~ **vom abnehmenden Bodenertrag** law of diminishing returns; ~ **über die Bodeninanspruchnahme durch die öffentliche Hand** Lands Clauses Act *(Br.)*; ~ **über das Bundesaufsichtsamt für das Versicherungswesen** Federal Credit Union Act *(US)*; ~ **über die Direktwahlen zum Europaparlament** European Direct Elections Bill *(Br.)*; ~ **zur Einführung der Sommerzeit** Daylight Saving Act *(Br.)*; ~ **der seltenen Ereignisse** *(Statistik)* poisson distribution; ~ **über die Errichtung gemeinnütziger Stiftungen** Charities Act *(Br.)*; ~ **vom abnehmenden Ertragszuwachs** law of returns to scale; ~ **der Europäischen Gemeinschaften** European Communities Bill; ~ **in der Fassung vom ...** law as amended on ...; ~ **zur Finanzierung des sozialen Wohnungsbaues** Housing Finance Act *(Br.)*; ~ **über Formerfordernisse** Statute of Frauds *(Br.)*; **ungeschriebene ~ der Gastfreundschaft** code of hospitality; ~ **über die Gemeinschaftsaufgabe zur Verbesserung der regionalen Wirtschaftsstruktur** Town and Country Planning Act *(Br.)*; ~ **des abnehmenden Grenznutzens** law of diminishing utility; ~ **der abnehmenden Grenzproduktivität** law of diminishing marginal productivity; ~ **zur Heilung fehlerhafter Verwaltungsakte** validating statute; ~ **der komparativen Kosten** law of comparative costs; ~ **mit rückwirkender Kraft** law with retroactive effect, retrospective law; ~ **gegen Landstreicherei** Vagrancy Act *(Br.)*; ~ **über Lebensversicherungsanstalten** Assurance Companies Act *(Br.)*; ~ **über die Neufestsetzung von Einheitswerten** Rating and

Valuation Act *(Br.)*; ~ **über die Preisbindung von Markenartikeln** Fair Trading Act *(Br.)*, Fair Trade Act *(US)*; **~e und [Rechts]verordnungen** laws and regulations; ~ **zur Regelung von Entlassungsabfindungen** Redundancy Payments Act *(Br.)*; ~ **über amtlich zu führende Register** Recording Act *(US)*; ~ **zum Schutz der ehelichen Wohnung** Matrimonial Home Act *(Br.)*; ~ **von Ursache und Wirkung** law of cause and effect; ~ **zur Verbesserung der betrieblichen Altersrente** Act of the Improvement of Works Pension Scheme *(Br.)* (of Corporate Pension Plans, *US*); ~ **zur Verhütung von Kapitalanlagenbetrug** Prevention of Fraud Act *(Br.)*; ~ **über Versicherungsgesellschaften** Insurance Companies Act *(Br.)*; ~ **mit dispositiven Vorschriften** enabling statute; ~ **zur Wahrung des Bankgeheimnisses** banking secrecy law; **~e gegen den unlauteren Wettbewerb** Unfair Trade Practices Acts *(US)*; ~ **der großen Zahlen** law of large numbers;

~ **abändern** to amend a bill, to revise a law; **gültige ~e abändern** to alter the legislation in force; **vom ~ abgehen** to vary from a law; ~ **ablehnen** *(Parlament)* to kill a bill; ~ **abschaffen** to extinguish a law; ~ **mit Inhalt anfüllen** to back a law with action; ~ **annehmen** to carry a law; **dem ~ Gewalt antun** to strain a law; ~ **anwenden** to apply (administer, dispense) a law, to put a law into force (operation); ~ **mit aller Strenge anwenden** to put a law in force with all its rigo(u)r; ~ **aufheben** to repeal (abolish, abrogate) a law; ~ **ausarbeiten** to draft a bill; ~ **auslegen** to construe (expound) a law; ~ **in unberechtigter Weise auslegen** to stretch a law; ~ **[als Interessent] beeinflussen** to lobby a bill; ~ **befolgen** to comply with a law, to obey (abide by, observe) a law; ~ **nicht befolgen** to disobey the law, to be disobedient to the law; ~ **beobachten** to keep the law; **über ein ~ beraten** to debate a bill; **sich auf ein ~ berufen** to refer to an act; ~ **beschließen** to carry (pass) a bill; ~ **zur Anwendung bringen** to bring a law into action, to carry out a law, to put a law into operation; ~ **mit aller Strenge zur Anwendung bringen** to put a law into operation in all its rigo(u)r; ~ **wieder zur Anwendung bringen** to bring a law into force again; ~ **durchführen** to execute (implement) a law; ~ **durchpeitschen** to jam a bill through Congress *(US)*, to rattle (rush) a bill through the House *(Br.)*; ~ **einbringen** to initiate legislation, to introduce (table, *Br.*) a bill; ~ **einführen** to institute a law; ~ **einhalten** to abide by (adhere to) a law; **für das ~ eintreten** to maintain the law; **Gewohnheitsrecht zum ~ erheben** to erect a custom into law; ~ **erklären** to expound a law; **Vorzüge eines ~es erlangen** to secure the immunities of a statute; ~ **erlassen** to enact a law (legislation), to legislate, to promulgate; ~ **gegen Glücksspiele erlassen** to legislate against gambling; **unter ein ~ fallen** to come under (be governed by) a law; **in den Anwendungsbereich eines ~es fallen** to come under the provisions of a law; ~ **neu fassen** to revise a statute; **Lücke im ~ finden** to find a loophole in the law; **dem ~ genügen** to satisfy a statute; **mit dem ~ in Konflikt geraten** to run (fall) foul of the law; **sich an ein ~ halten** to keep within a law; **~e handhaben** to execute (dispense) justice, to implement a law; ~ **ergehen lassen** to pass a law; **dem ~ Folge leisten** to abide by the law; ~ **machen** to make a law; ~ **wirkungslos machen** to make a law of no effect; ~ **mißachten** to set a law at naught; **im ~ nachlesen** to read up in a law; **im ~ nachschlagen** to consult the law; **Schutz eines ~es in Anspruch nehmen** to claim the benefit of a law; **über ein ~ referieren** to report a bill; **sich nach ungeschriebenen ~en richten** to live up to the code; **in einem ~ enthalten sein** to be embodied in a law; **fest durch ~e gebunden sein** to be locked firmly into law; **mit dem ~ in Konflikt geraten sein** to be against the law; **durch ~ geregelt sein** to be regulated by law; **zum ~ geworden sein** to have become law, to have been entered into the statute books; **vor dem ~ gleich sein** to be equal before the law; **dem Zwang des ~es unterworfen sein** to be bound by law; **vor dem ~ verantwortlich sein** to be amenable to law; **in die Schlingen eines ~es verstrickt sein** to be caught in the meshes of a law; ~ **außer Kraft setzen** to invalidate (rescind) an act; ~ **vorübergehend außer Kraft setzen** to suspend the operation of a law; ~ **in Kraft setzen** to give effect to a law, to put a law into force (operation); **über dem ~ stehen** to be above the law; **unter dem Schutz der ~e stehen** to be under the guardianship of the law; ~ **übertreten** to transgress (trespass against) a law; ~ **umgehen** to get around (dodge, circumvent) a law; ~ **umstoßen** to subvert a law; **dem ~ unterliegen** to be amenable to law; **sich dem ~ unterwerfen** to conform (submit) o. s. to law; ~ **verabschieden** to carry (pass) a bill, to pass an act; **~e verfassen** to write legislation; **einem ~ zur Annahme verhelfen** to get through a bill; ~ **verkünden** to promulgate a law; **dem ~ Nachdruck verleihen** to enforce the law; ~ **verletzen** to break (infringe, violate) a law; **einem ~ Geltung verschaffen** to enforce a law; **dem ~ Respekt verschaffen** to enforce obedience to the law; **gegen das ~ verstoßen** to violate (offend against, contravene) a law; **gegen den Geist eines ~es verstoßen** to circumvent the spirit of a law; **gegen die ~e der Höflichkeit verstoßen** to offend against the law of courtesy; ~ **verwässern** to water down a bill; **zu ~ werden** to pass into law; **dem ~ Achtung zollen** to respect the law; **zwei ~e zusammenfassen** to consolidate two bills; **dem ~ zuwiderhandeln** to run counter to a law;

~abänderungsvorschlag einbringen to give notice of an amendment [to a bill]; **~änderung** amendment [to a bill]; **~änderung vornehmen** to dispose of an amendment; **~annahme** carrying (passage) of a bill.

Gesetzantrag [draft for a parliamentary] bill;
von den Wählern ausgehender ~ indirect initiative *(US)*;
sich gegen einen ~ aussprechen to deliver o. s. against a bill; ~ **zu Fall bringen** to kill a bill in Parliament; ~ **nicht durchbringen** to lose a bill; ~ **einbringen** to lay a bill before the House; ~ **erläutern** to exhibit a bill; ~ **durch Vertagung zunichte machen** to count out *(Br.)*, to table a law *(US)*.

Gesetz|anwendung application of a law, law enforcement; **entsprechende ~anwendung** equity of a statute; **~artikel** chapter; **~aufhebung** revocation (repeal, abrogation) of a law; **~auslegung** interpretation of a law, statutory interpretation; **~beratung** reading of a bill; **~blatt** Official Register *(US)*, Official Gazette *(Br.)*, statutes at large *(US)*; **~brecher** lawbreaker; **~buch** statute book, code; **Bürgerliches ~buch** Civil Code.

Gesetzentwurf draft law (statute), model act *(US)*;
aussichtsloser ~ lame duck bill *(sl.)*; **von allen Parteien eingebrachter ~** nonparty bill; **noch nicht erledigter ~** remanet *(Br.)*; **umfassender ~** all-embracing bill;
~ **abändern** to amend a law; ~ **ablehnen** to throw out (drop) a bill; ~ **annehmen** to carry (pass) a bill; **Verabschiedung eines ~es aufhalten** to obstruct (block) a bill; **in einen ~ aufnehmen** to write into a bill; ~ **ausarbeiten** to draw up a [parliamentary] bill; ~ **beeinflussen** to lobby a bill; ~ **befürworten** to look favourably on a bill; ~ **in einem Ausschuß begraben** to bottle a bill in a committee; ~ **abschließend behandeln** to round off a bill; ~ **im Plenum bekämpfen** to oppose a bill on the floor; ~ **in zweiter Lesung beraten** to give a second reading to a bill; ~ **beschließen** to carry (pass) a bill; ~ **bei den Ausschußberatungen blockieren** to block a bill in a committee; ~ **zu Fall bringen** to kill (table, *US*) a bill; ~ **durch das Parlament bringen** to engineer a bill through the House (Congress, *US*); ~ **bis zur Vertagung diskutieren** to talk out a bill *(Br.)*; ~ **durchs Parlament durchpeitschen** to rattle (railroad) a bill through Congress *(US)*, to rush a bill through the House *(Br.)*; ~ **einbringen** to introduce (bring in, present, table, *Br.*) a bill; ~ **einschränken** to write restrictions in a bill; ~ **erläutern** to exhibit a bill; ~ **stückweise erledigen** to closure a bill by compartments; ~ **fallenlassen** to jettison (table, *US*) a bill; ~ **initiieren** to promote a bill in Parliament; ~ **liegenlassen** to allow a bill to lie on the table, to table a bill *(US)*; ~ **vor einer gesetzgebenden Körperschaft zur Debatte stellen** to call up a bill before a legislative body; ~ **einem Ausschuß überweisen** to commit a bill, to refer a bill to a committee; ~ **verabschieden** to carry (pass) a bill; ~ **ohne besondere Abstimmung verabschieden** to pass a bill without a division; **Beratung eines ~es verhindern** to block (obstruct) a bill; ~ **verschleppen** to filibuster a bill *(US)*; ~ **mit dem Stempel der Demokratischen Partei versehen** to put a democratic stamp on a bill; ~ **verwässern** to water down a bill; ~ **dem Oberhaus vorlegen** to send up a bill to the Upper House *(Br.)*; ~ **wieder vorlegen** to report a bill *(Br.)*; ~ **zurückstellen** to shelve *(Br.)* (table, *US*) a bill, to allow a bill to lie on the table, to lay a bill on the table *(US)*; ~ **an den Ausschuß zurückverweisen** to recommit a bill.

Gesetzes|absicht intention of a law; **rechtsgestaltender ~akt** act of law; **~begriff** legal term; **~bereinigung** revision of a statute; **~beschluß** legislative act; **~beschreibung** nomography.

Gesetzesbestimmungen legal provisions, provisions of a law, dispositions of a statute;
~ **befolgen** to observe the provisions of an act; **sich auf ~ berufen** to invoke the provisions of a statute; ~ **bewußt mißachten** to act in defiance of a law.

Gesetzes|einheit unity of the law; **~erbe** statutory heir; **~form** statutory form; **~formel** enacting clause, legal formula; **~gleichheit** isonomy; **~initiative** legislative initiative *(US)*; **~kenntnis** familiarity with the law; **~kollision, ~konflikt** conflict of laws; **~kommentar** legal commentary; **~komplex** body of laws; **~konkurrenz** *(Strafrecht)* merger *(US)*.

Gesetzeskraft force (strength) of a law, legal force;
~ **erlangen** to pass into law; ~ **haben** to have legal force; ~ **verleihen** to enact.
gesetzeskundig versed in law.
Gesetzes | lücke gap (loophole) in a law; ~**lücke entdecken** to find a loophole in a law; ~**maschinerie in Bewegung setzen** to put the law into motion; **strittige** ~**materie** contentious matter of legislation; ~**mißachtung** outlawry, defiance of the law; ~**novelle** amended version of a law; ~**paket** legislative package; ~**paragraph** paragraph; ~**recht** statute (statutory, enacted, written) law; ~**rolle** statute roll; ~**sammlung** statute book, code, compendium of laws, statutes at large *(US)*; ~**text** wording (text) of a law; ~**titel** rubric of a statute, title of an act, rubric.
gesetzestreu law-abiding.
Gesetzes | treue law-abidingness, obedience to the law; ~**übertreter** offender, lawbreaker, scofflaw; ~**übertretung** malfeasance, contravention (violation) of a law, lawbreaking; ~**übertretung begehen, sich einer** ~**übertretung schuldig machen** to act contrary to (commit an offence against the) law; ~**umgehung** evasion (circumvention, evasion) of the law; ~**unkenntnis** ignorance of the law; ~**verabschiedung** enactment of a law, passing of a bill; ~**verächter** despiser of the law; ~**verbot** statutory prohibition; ~**verkündung** promulgation of a law; ~**verletzer** wrongdoer, lawbreaker; ~**verletzung** breach (infringement, infraction, violation) of law, lawbreaking; **fahrlässige** ~**verletzung** negligent violation of a statute; **allgemeine** ~**vermutung** general presumption of the law; ~**veröffentlichung** promulgation of a law; ~**verordnung** ordinance, decree law; ~**verstoß** lawbreaking, violation of a law; ~**vollziehung** execution of a law; ~**vorbehalt** reservation.
Gesetzesvorlage bill, draft of a parliamentary bill, legislative proposal, stage legislation;
gemischte ~ hybrid bill *(Br.)*;
~ **ohne Gegenstimmen** unopposed bill; ~ **der Regierung** public bill;
~ **abändern** to amend a bill; ~ **ablehnen** to negate a bill; ~ **abwürgen** to strangle a bill; ~ **in dritter Lesung behandeln** to read a bill for the third time; ~ **bekämpfen** to oppose a bill; ~ **durchpeitschen** to rattle a bill through the House *(Br.)*, to jam (railroad) a bill through Congress *(US)*; ~ **einbringen** to initiate (introduce) legislation (a bill), to bring in (file, table, *Br.*) a bill; ~ **aufs tote Gleis schieben** to pigeonhole (shelve, *Br.*, table, *US*) a bill; ~ **an einen Ausschuß überweisen** to commit a bill; ~ **nicht unterzeichnen** to retain a bill unsigned, to pocket a bill *(US)*; ~ **verwerfen** to reject a bill; ~ **dem Plenum mit Abänderungsvorschlägen vorlegen** to report a bill with amendments; ~ **zurückstellen** to shelve *(Br.)* (table, *US*) a bill.
Gesetzes | vorschriften requirements of the law, statute; **materielle** ~**vorschriften** declaratory part of a law; ~**widerspruch** antinomy; ~**wortlaut** text of a law; ~**zweck** intention of a law, policy of the law *(US)*.
gesetzgebend legislative, lawgiving, lawmaking, constitutive;
~**e Gewalt** legislative power, legislature; ~**e Körperschaft** legislative body; ~**es Organ** legislative branch; ~**e Tätigkeit** legislative action *(US)*; ~**e Versammlung** legislative assembly.
Gesetzgeber lawgiver, lawmaker, legislator, institutor of law, enactor;
sich zum ~ **aufspielen** to be a law unto o. s.
gesetzgeberisch legislative, legislatorial;
~**e Absicht** intention of a law, policy of the law *(US)*; ~**e Funktion** legislative function; ~**er Rat** legislative council.
Gesetzgeberstil legislative style.
Gesetzgebung legislation, legislature, lawmaking, lawgiving;
durch einen Akt der ~ by legislative act;
arbeitsrechtliche ~ labor legislation *(US)*; **Kostenlawine auslösende** ~ cost-increasing legislation; **ausschließliche** ~ exclusive legislation; **delegierte** ~ subordinate legislation; **ergänzende** ~ amendatory legislation; **geltende** ~ legislation in force; **gewerkschaftsfeindliche** ~ anti-labo(u)r legislation; **gewerkschaftsfreundliche** ~ pro-labo(u)r legislation; **inländische** ~ internal (national, municipal) legislation; **innerstaatliche** ~ domestic legislation; **konkurrierende** ~ concurrent legislation; **soziale** ~ social legislation; **staatliche** ~ government legislation; **verwässerte** ~ watered-down legislation; **vorgesehene** ~ draft legislation; **zukünftige** ~ prospective legislation;
~ **des Bundes** Federal legislation; ~ **mit rückwirkender Kraft** retroactive (retrospective, ex-post-facto) legislation; **landwirtschaftliche** ~ **für Nebenbetriebe** [etwa] homestead exemption laws *(US)*; ~ **zur Regelung von Sozialabfindungen** redundancy legislation *(Br.)*; ~ **zum Schutz des Verbrauchers** consumer protection legislation; ~ **für den Wohnungsbau** housing legislation;
~ **auf den neuesten Stand bringen** to update legislation; ~ **initiieren** to initiate legislation; **Körperschaft durch** ~ **ins Leben rufen** to legislate a corporation into existence.
gesetzgebungsähnlich quasi-legislative.
Gesetzgebungs | akt enactment, legislative act; ~**ausschuß** legislative (assembly) committee; ~**befugnis** lawmaking power; ~**funktion** legislative function; ~**gewalt** legislative power; ~**kompetenz** legislative power, prerogative; ~**maßnahmen** legislative act; ~**notstand** emergency legislation; ~**organ** lawmaker, legislator; ~**paket** legislative package; ~**periode** legislative period; ~**politik** legislative policy; ~**programm** legislative program(me); ~**recht** legislative power; ~**verfahren** legislative process (procedure); ~**vorbehalt** reserve of bills *(Br.)*; **auf dem** ~**wege** by legislative action; ~**werk** body of law.
gesetzlich legal, lawful, legitimate, statutory, legislative;
~ **bestimmt** prescribed by law; ~ **geschützt** patent[ed], proprietary *(US)*, *(Warenzeichen)* registered; ~ **strafbar** punishable by law; ~ **verboten** forbidden by law; ~ **verpflichtet** legally bound, responsible, liable; ~ **vorgeschrieben** prescribed by law, statutory; ~ **zulässig** legal, lawful;
~ **verpflichtet sein** to be statutorily obliged (bound by law);
~**e Abgaben** statutory levies; ~**e Abhilfe** legal remedy; ~ **vorgeschriebenes Alter** legal age; ~**er Anspruch** legal claim; ~**e Anweisung** legal order; ~**e Bestimmungen** statutory (legal) provisions; **unter die** ~**en Bestimmungen fallen** to come within the scope of the law; ~ **vorgeschriebenes Deckungsverhältnis** *(Bank)* legal requirement; ~**es Eigentumsrecht** legal estate (title); ~**er Erbe** lawful (statutory, *US*) heir, heir apparent *(Br.)*, intestate successor, heir-at-law *(US)*; ~**e Erben** legal distributees, lawful issue; **als** ~**e Erben erben** to succeed to an intestate estate; ~**e Erbfolgeordnung** legal (intestate) succession; ~**er Feiertag** legal holiday *(US)*, bank holiday *(Br.)*; ~**e Fiktion** legal fiction; ~**e Forderungsrechte** lawful things in action; ~**e Form** statutory form; ~**e Formalitäten** legal formalities; ~**e Frist** statutory period; ~**e Gebühren** legal fees; ~ **vorgeschriebene Generalversammlung** statutory meeting; ~ **vorgeschriebene Geschäftsbücher** statutory books *(Br.)*; ~**e Grundlage** legal base; **auf** ~**er Grundlage** on a statutory footing; ~**e Gültigkeit** validity; ~**er Güterstand** legal community, statutory regime *(US)*; ~**e Haftpflicht** legal (statutory) liability; ~**e Haftungsbestimmungen** statutory provisions, regarding liability; ~**e Kündigungsfrist** legal notice to quit, statutory notice; ~**e Maßnahmen** statutory action; ~**e Meile** statute mile; ~**es Mindestalter** legal age; ~**es Minimum** statutory minimum; ~**es Pfandrecht** lien by operation of the law, statutory lien; ~**er Rahmen** legal framework; ~ **vorgeschriebene Reserven** *(Bank)* legal (lawful, *US*) reserve; ~**e Rücklage** legal reserve; ~ **begründeter Schadensersatzanspruch** lawful damages; ~**er Straftatbestand** statutory offence; ~ **anerkannter Streik** legal strike; ~ **anerkannter Tarif** *(Bahn)* legal rate; ~ **vorgeschriebenes Treuhandeigentum** statutory trust *(Br.)*; ~**es Treuhandverhältnis** involuntary trust; ~**es Veräußerungsverbot** restraining order; ~**e Verjährungsfrist** statutory period of limitation; ~**e Verjährungsvorschriften** statute of limitations; ~**e Vermutung** artificial presumption; ~**e Verpflichtung** statutory liability, legal obligation; ~**er Vertreter** legal representative, statutory agent; ~**e Vertretungsmacht** statutory agency; ~ **vorgeschriebene Voraussetzungen** statutory requirements; ~**er Vormund** guardian by nature, statutory guardian; ~**e Vorschrift** public act; ~ **vorgeschriebener Wohnsitz** legal residence, necessary domicile; ~**es Zahlungsmittel** lawful (legal, *Br.*) tender, legal *(Br.)* lawful currency (money, *US*); ~**er Zinssatz** legal rate of interest; ~**es Zurückbehaltungsrecht** lien by operation of law.
Gesetzlichkeit legalism, lawfulness, legitimacy.
gesetzlos lawless, illegal, anarchic, anarchistic.
Gesetzloser outcast.
Gesetzlosigkeit anarchy, anarchism.
gesetzmäßig legal, legitimate, lawful, in conformity with the (according to) law, constitutional;
~**er Erbe** lawful (statutory, *US*) heir, heir apparent *(Br.)*.
Gesetzmäßigkeit lawfulness, legitimacy, legality;
historische ~**en** historical patterns.
gesetzt steady, settled, *(Buch)* composed;
fortlaufend ~ run-on;
~ **den Fall** supposing, assuming;
~ **werden** to be set in type; ~**er werden** to sober down;
in ~**em Alter** in advanced years.

gesetzwidrig contrary to law, illegal, illicit, unlawful, malfeasant, lawless, disorderly;
~**e Entlassung** wrongful dismissal.
Gesetzwidrigkeit illegality, unlawfulness.
gesichert secure[d], covered, *(garantiert)* guaranteed, warranted *(US)*;
hypothekarisch ~ secured by mortgage; **nicht** ~ unsecured, unwarranted *(US)*; **durch Schuldverschreibungen** ~ bonded; **Zukunft seiner Kinder** ~ **haben** to have settled the future of one's children; ~ **sein** to be covered, *(Gläubiger)* to hold security;
~**e Anleihe** collateral (secured) loan; ~**e Forderung** privileged (preferential, preferred) debt; **dinglich** ~**e Forderung** debt covered by a security; ~**er Gläubiger** secured (catholic) creditor; ~**er Kredit** secured loan; ~**e Obligationen** secured bonds *(US)*; ~**e Stellung** permanent position.
Gesicht face, countenance, vision;
mit steinernem ~ stone-faced; **von** ~**ern verfolgt** haunted by visions;
abgehärmtes ~ pinched face; **ausdrucksloses** ~ blank face; **aus Fernsehsendungen bekanntes** ~ telly-familiar face *(Br.)*; **katzenfreundliches** ~ smooth face; **strahlendes** ~ radiant face; **verblüfftes** ~ blank face; **vor Schmerz verzerrtes** ~ face contorted with pain; **zweites** ~ second sight;
wahres ~ **eines Menschen** true character of a person; ~ **einer Zeitung** face of a paper;
entschlossenes ~ **aufsetzen** to put on a firm countenance; **offizielles** ~ **aufsetzen** to put on one's Whitehall face *(coll.)*; **der Wahrheit ins** ~ **blicken** to face the truth; **Sache ein anderes** ~ **geben** to put a new complexion on a matter; **der Stadt ein freundliches** ~ **geben** to make the town look cheerful; **über das ganze** ~ **grinsen** to grin like a cheshire cat (a street-door knocker); ~ **eines Verbrechers haben** to have the physiognomy of a criminal; **jem. ins** ~ **lügen** to lie to s. one's face; **böses** ~ **machen** to look cross; ~ **wie drei Tage Regenwetter machen** to pull a face as long as a fiddle, to look like a dying duck in a thunderstorm; **jem. etw. gerade ins** ~ **sagen** to tell s. o. s. th. straight from the shoulder; **den Tatsachen ins** ~ **schauen** to face the facts (music); **jem. etw. ins** ~ **schleudern** to fling s. th. in s. one's teeth; ~**er schneiden** to pull faces; **jem. wie aus dem** ~ **geschnitten sein** to be the very image of s. o.; **jem. ins** ~ **springen** to murder s. o. *(coll.)*; **jem. gut zu** ~ **stehen** to suit s. o. well, to benefit s. o.; **sein** ~ **verlieren** to lose one's face; **sein** ~ **wahren** to save one's face; **sein wahres** ~ **zeigen** to show one's true colo(u)rs; **schiefes** ~ **ziehen** to make a wry face.
Gesichtsausdruck face, countenance;
undurchdringlicher ~ deadpan expression.
Gesichtsfarbe, gesunde healthy complexion.
Gesichtsfeld view, visual view, range of sight;
weites ~ wide field of vision;
~ **des Fahrers behindern** to obscure the vision of the driver.
Gesichtskreis [mental] horizon, purview, eye, beat;
außerhalb unseres ~**es** beyond our vision;
begrenzter ~ constricted outlook, limited view; **enger** ~ parochial point of view;
seinen ~ **erweitern** to enlarge one's view (the mind), to broaden one's outlook; **j. ganz aus seinem** ~ **verloren haben** to have lost sight of s. o.; **in jds.** ~ **treten** to come into s. one's world.
Gesichts|maske face mask; ~**puder** face powder.
Gesichtspunkt point of view, viewpoint, criterion, facet, aspect;
unter bankgeschäftlichen ~**en** for banking reasons; **nach kommerziellen** ~**en** along commercial lines; **vom sozialen** ~ **aus** under its social aspect;
wirtschaftlicher ~ economic angle;
etw. von allen ~**en aus betrachten** to consider s. th. from all points of view (all angles of a question); ~ **vortragen** to submit a proposition.
Gesichts|sinn visual sense, vision; ~**straffung** face lifting; **jem. einen** ~**verlust in der Öffentlichkeit beibringen** to take away from s. one's public image; ~**winkel** visual angle; **harte** ~**züge** hard features.
Gesinde domestic servants;
in der ~**stube** belowstairs.
Gesindel vermin, riffraff, rabble, trash;
lichtscheues ~ underworld mob, shady characters.
gesinnt minded, disposed, oriented;
günstig ~ favo(u)rable;
jem. freundlich ~ **sein** to be well disposed towards s. o.; **sozial** ~ **sein** to be socially minded;
liberal ~**er Politiker** liberal-minded politician; **fortschrittlich** ~**es Unternehmen** forward-looking company.

Gesinnung mind, character, attitude, colo(u)r;
aufrührerische ~ insurrectionism; **edle (noble)** ~ noble sentiment, high mind; **politische** ~ political conviction (opinion); **vornehme** ~ nobility of mind;
seine ~ **ändern** to change one's attitude, *(Politiker)* to cross the floor; **von anständiger** ~ **sein** to be of good moral character; **seine wahre** ~ **zeigen** to show one's true colo(u)r; **an jds. freundlicher** ~ **nicht zweifeln** to have no doubt about s. one's friendly attitude.
Gesinnungsgenosse fellow traveller.
gesinnungslos sein to be a man without character.
Gesinnungs|lump timeserver; ~**lumperei** opportunism, timeserving; ~**wandel,** ~**wechsel** about-face, turnabout *(US)*, voltface.
gesittet well-bred;
~**es Betragen** good manners.
Gesöff, dünnes muck, dishwater, slops *(Br., coll.)*, wish-wash, whipbelly *(sl.)*.
gesondert separate, several, parcelled, on its merits, *(Postversand)* under separate cover;
~ **berechnet werden** to be charged for extra.
Gesottenes und Gebratenes boiled meat and roast meat.
Gespann team, couple;
komisches ~ odd couple;
gutes ~ **abgeben** to hunt (run) in couples.
gespannt tense, strained, tiptoe, *(neugierig)* curious, anxious;
aufs höchste ~ **sein** to be on tenterhooks; ~ **auf j. warten** to be very anxious that s. o. should come; ~ **auf das Wahlergebnis warten** to wait eagerly for the result of the elections; **jem.** ~ **zuhören** to hang on s. one's lips;
~**e Beziehungen** strained relations; ~**e Lage** tense situation; **bis zum Zerreißen** ~**e Nerven** nerves stretched to the breaking point.
Gespanntheit|der Lage tense situation, tension; ~ **unseres gegenwärtigen Verhältnisses** our present strained relations.
Gespenst ghost, spectre, phantom;
~ **der Vergangenheit** skeleton at the feast;
~ **der Arbeitslosigkeit heraufbeschwören** to raise the spectre of redundancies; ~**er sehen** to see ghosts (things).
Gespenstergeschichte ghost story.
gespensterhaft ghostlike, spooky, ghostly.
Gespenster|schiff phantom ship; ~**stunde** witching hour.
gespenstische Atmosphäre ghostly atmosphere.
gesperrt stopped, blocked, closed, earmarked;
~ **gedruckt** spaced;
für Fahrzeuge ~ closed for vehicles; **halbseitig** ~ closed on one side; **für Lastwagen** ~ closed for heavy motor traffic; **für Militär** ~ off limits *(US)*, out of bounds *(Br.)*; **Straße für Durchgangsverkehr** ~ *(Straßenschild)* road closed ahead; **für Werbesendungen** ~ blocked-out;
~**e Berufszweige** closed professions; ~**es Guthaben** frozen assets; ~**es Konto** blocked account; ~**er Scheck** earmarked (stopped) check *(US)* (cheque, *Br.*); ~**e Vermögenswerte** blocked property.
gespickt, mit Zitaten interlarded with quotations;
~**e Brieftasche** stuffed wallet.
gespielt werden *(Theaterstück, Film)* to be on show.
Gespinst, seidenes silken tissue;
~ **von Hoffnungen** edifice of one's hope; ~ **von Lügen** web of lies.
Gespött derision, ridicule, mockery;
~ **der Stadt** joke of the village;
j. zum ~ **machen** to make a mock of s. o.; **sich zum** ~ **machen, zum** ~ **der Leute werden** to become an object of derision, to make a laughingstock (exhibition) of o. s.; **sein** ~ **mit jem. treiben** to ridicule (mock) s. o.
Gespräch conversation, talk, interview, discourse, *(Diskussion)* discussion, *(Telefon)* call;
ins ~ **eingeflochten** interlocutory;
abgehendes ~ outgoing call *(tel.)*; **angeregtes** ~ snappy conversation; **im Gang befindliche** ~**e** talks under way; **dienstliches** ~ *(Telefon)* business (official) call; **dringendes** ~ *(Telefon)* urgent (priority) call; **gebührenpflichtiges** ~ *(Telefon)* call charged for; **zu Hause geführte** ~**e** at-home discussions; **gelehrtes** ~ learned discussions; **handvermitteltes** ~ *(Telefon)* manually operated call; **harmloses** ~ harmless talk; **informelles** ~ informal conversation; **klärendes** ~ illuminating talk; **R-**~ *(Telefon)* reverse-charge call *(US)*, transferred charge call *(Br.)*; **vertrauliches** ~ private talk; **vorbereitetes** ~ organized talk; **wissenschaftliches** ~ colloquium, learned discussion; **zwangloses** ~ informal talk, converse;

~ **unter vier Augen** face-to-face talk (discussion); ~**e über die Begrenzung der strategischen Kernwaffen** Strategic Arms Limitation Talks, SALT; ~**e auf Botschafterebene** discussion at ambassador level; ~**e auf höchster Ebene** summit talks; ~ **mit Gebührenansage** *(Telefon)* advise duration and charge call; ~**e im engsten Kreis auf höchster Ebene** high-level talk-in; ~ **der ganzen Stadt** talk of the town; ~ **im Stehen** stand-up talk; ~**e am runden Tisch** round-table talks; ~ **mit Voranmeldung** *(Telefon)* person-to-person (personal) call;
~ **abbrechen** to break off a conversation; ~ **abmelden** *(Telefon)* to cancel a call; ~ **anknüpfen** to broach a conversation; ~ **mit jem. anknüpfen** to enter into a conversation with s. o.; ~ **anmelden** *(Telefon)* to book (place, *US*) a call; ~ **annehmen** *(Telefon)* to accept a call; **in einem ~ ganz nebenbei anschneiden** to cover leisurely in an interview; **sich an einem ~ beteiligen** to participate in the conversation; **ins ~ bringen** to talk up *(US)*; ~ **auf die politische Lage bringen** to lead the conversation round to the political situation; ~**e auf Botschafterebene durchführen** to hold talks at the level of ambassadors; **sich in ein ~ einmischen** to chip (butt) into a conversation; ~ **eröffnen** to start a conversation; ~ **fortsetzen** to carry on a conversation; ~ **führen** to conduct a conversation; **ausgedehntes ~ führen** to linger in conversation; ~ **in englischer Sprache führen** to carry on a conversation in English; **R-~ führen** *(Telefon)* to make a call-collect *(US)*; **stundenlanges ~ führen** to sustain a conversation for hours; **vertrauliches ~ führen** to converse; **dem ~ eine andere Richtung geben** to divert the conversation; ~ **mit jem. unter vier Augen haben** to have a confidential conversation; ~ **in Gang halten** to keep the ball up (rolling); **R-~ herstellen** *(Telefon)* to reverse the charge; **mit jem. ins ~ kommen** to engage in a conversation (make contact with) s. o.; ~ **auf etw. lenken** to work the conversation round to s. th.; **sich ins ~ mischen** to chime in; ~ **auf einen anderen Anschluß umstellen** *(Telefon)* to forward a call; ~ **vermitteln** *(Telefon)* to put a call through; **jem. in ein ~ verwickeln** to engage s. o. in a conversation; ~ **wiederaufnehmen** to carry on a conversation; **sich bei politischen ~en richtig wohlfühlen** to be in one's element when taking part in a political debate.

gesprächig talkative, loquacious, conversational, conversable.

Gesprächs | abwicklung *(Telefon)* handling of calls; ~**anmeldung** *(Telefon)* booking (placing, *US*) a call; ~**aufzeichner** conversation (tape) recorder; ~**beendigung** discontinuance of conversation; ~**beherrscher** meeting monopolizer; ~**belegzettel** *(Hotel)* traffic sheet; **zur ~belustigung beitragen** to be the life of the conversation; ~**dauer** length of conversation, *(Telefon)* duration of a call; ~**dichte** *(Telefon)* frequency of calls; ~**form** interlocutory form; ~**führer** interviewer; **vertrauliche ~führung** intimate nature of a conversation; ~**führung an sich reißen** to take the conversational lead, to monopolize (engross) a meeting; **mit jem. nicht auf ~fuß stehen** not to be on speaking terms with s. o.; ~**gebühr** *(Telefon)* tariff, charge [for calls]; **R-~gebühr** reverse charge; ~**gebühreneinheit** *(Telefon)* unit charge; ~**gegenstand** topic of a conversation, talking point; **seinen ~knochen wieder aufnehmen** to return to one's muttons; ~**notiz** notes, memo; ~**partner** auditor, partner, interlocutor, collocutor; **gewandter ~partner** conversationalist; ~**pause** lull in the conversation; ~**rahmen** scope of talks; ~**runde beherrschen** to take the conversational lead, to engross (monopolize) the conversation; ~**stadium** talking stage; ~**stil** conversational style; **plötzliche ~stille** gap in a conversation; ~**stoff** talking point, food for conversation, subjects, topics; **allgemeinen ~stoff abgeben** to make a noise in the world; ~**teilnehmer** interlocutor.

Gesprächsthema talking point, topic of discussion;
~ **an den Haaren herbeiziehen** to drag in a subject by the head and ears; **wieder zu seinem ~ zurückkehren** to return to one's muttons.

Gesprächsthemen, verbotene forbidden subjects of conversation; **vorgeschlagene ~** suggested topical outline;
~ **ununterbrochen wechseln** to jump from one subject to another.

Gesprächs | überwachung *(Telefon)* supervision of calls; ~**uhr** *(Telefon)* speaking clock, time check, chargeable time indicator.

gesprächsweise in the course (by way) of conversation, interlocutory, colloquial.

Gesprächs | zähler, ~**zeitmesser** *(Telefon)* chargeable time indicator.

gespreizt wide apart, astraddle *(fig.)*, pompous, affected, pretty, finical;
sich ~ ausdrücken to use a pompous style.

gesprochen spoken;
~**er Kurs** nominal price.

Gestade foreshore.

gestaffelt graduated, graded, differential, *(Arbeitszeit)* staggered, *(mil.)* echeloned, *(Steuern)* progressive, graduated;
~**e Arbeitszeit** staggering of hours; ~**es Besteuerungssystem** graduated taxation; ~**e Preise** graduated prices; ~**er Rabatt** adjusted discount; ~**e Steuer** graduated tax; **nach oben ~e Steuer** progressive tax; **nach unten ~e Steuer** degressive tax; ~**er Tarif** flexible (graduated) tariff, sliding scale, *(Anzeigen)* rate scale *(US)*, *(Einkommensteuer)* tapering rates; ~**e Zinsen** graduated interest; ~**er Zinssatz** progressive rate; ~**er Zoll** differential duty.

Gestalt shape, form, fashion, *(Aussehen)* appearance, presence, *(Figur)* figure, character, *(Theater)* person;
in ~ von Geld in terms of money;
dunkle ~ obscure character; **schwankende ~en** wavering shapes;
~ **annehmen** *(Pläne)* to fall into (take) shape, to take form, to materialize *(US)*; **allmählich ~ annehmen** to be gradually taking shape, to develop gradually; **endgültige ~ annehmen** to shape up *(coll.)*; **im Kopf eines Autors ~ annehmen** to develop in an author's mind; **sich in seiner wahren ~ zeigen** to show one's true colo(u)r.

gestalten to form, to shape, to [put into] fashion, to work up, *(arrangieren)* to arrange, to organize, *(Buchausstattung)* to make (get) up, *(künstlerisch)* to lay out, to create, to design; **sich ~** to take shape, to shape up *(US)*;
Abend sehr nett ~ to make it a very pleasant evening; **Bericht lebendig ~** to give colo(u)r to a report; **Charakter ~** to mo(u)ld a character; **sich zu einem Erfolg ~** to turn out a success; **seine Freizeit ~** to organize one's leisure time; **seine Freizeit abwechslungsreich ~** to vary one's spare-time activities; **neu ~** to reorganize; **baulich neu ~** to redevelop; **jds. Persönlichkeit ~** to mo(u)ld s. one's character; **Programm ~** to arrange a program(me); **Schaufenster ~** to dress a window; **sich schwierig ~** to run up against difficulties; **unterschiedlich ~** to vary.

gestaltend creative.

Gestalter creator, creative artist, designer, fashioner, *(Werbeagentur)* art director.

gestalterisch creative, designing.

gestaltet shaped, turned;
bei so ~en Verhältnissen such being the case.

Gestaltung formation, *(Druck)* presentation, development, shape, *(Formgebung)* forming, designing, *(Freizeit, Programm)* arrangement, organization, *(Künstler)* laying out, creation, *(Organisation)* arrangement, organization;
grafische ~ design; **individuelle ~** *(Urheberrecht)* literary composition; **künstlerische ~** artistic planning, design, *(Agenturkosten)* talent; **redaktionelle ~** editorial preparation; **typografische ~** typographic design; **übersichtliche ~** well-ordered arrangement;
~ **einer Ausstellung** arrangement of an exhibition; ~ **eines Buches** make-up (getup) of a book; ~ **des Firmengesichts** mo(u)lding of the corporate image.

Gestaltungs | arbeit creative work; ~**chef** *(Werbeagentur)* art (creative) director; ~**grundlage** *(Werbung)* copy platform; ~**klage** action in rem; ~**mangel** defect of design; ~**urteil** judgment in rem.

Gestammel stammer, stutter.

gestandenes Mannsbild fine figure of a man.

geständig sein to plead (confess o. s.) guilty, to confess a crime.

Geständnis confession, admission, admitted statement;
auf Grund seines eigenen ~ses on his own confession (admission);
ausdrückliches ~ direct admission; **außergerichtliches ~** extrajudicial confession; **bloßes ~** naked confession; **erpreßtes ~** extortion, squeeze; **erzwungenes ~** forced confession; **formelles ~** simple confession; **freiwilliges ~** voluntary confession; **gerichtliches ~** judicial confession; **mittelbares ~** implied confession; **umfassendes ~** full (plenary) confession, plenary admission; **unfreiwilliges ~** involuntary confession;
~ **vor Gericht** judicial admission; ~ **auf dem Totenbett** deathbed confession;
~ **ablegen** to confess o. s. guilty, to confess a crime; **freiwilliges ~ ablegen** to volunteer a confession; **kein ~ ablegen** to refuse to confess; **umfassendes ~ ablegen** to make a full confession, to confess fully; **jem. ein ~ abpressen** to wring (wrench, force) a confession [of guilt] from s. o., to make s. o. squeal; ~ **verweigern** to refuse to confess; ~ **widerrufen** to retract a confession.

Gestank nasty smell, stench, reek.
gestatten to permit, to allow, to admit;
jem. Einblick in die Bücher ~ to give s. o. access to the books;
nicht ~ to disallow.
gestattet, Eintritt nicht no entry (admittance); **Rauchen nicht** ~ no smoking, please.
Gestattung, ausdrückliche express grant; **widerrufliche** ~ precarious right.
Gestattungsvertrag licence agreement.
gestaut trimmed;
schlecht ~ out of trim.
Geste gesture, motion, *(dipl.)* handsome gesture;
als höfliche ~ as an act of courtesy;
~ **der Freundschaft** gesture of friendship;
j. mit einer herablassenden ~ **entlassen** to dismiss s. o. with a condescending wave of one's hand; **freundliche** ~ **machen** to make a friendly gesture.
gestehen to confess, to admit, to own up;
seine Schuld ~ to confess o. s. guilty; **die Wahrheit** ~ to tell the truth.
Gestehungs|kosten first (prime, original, producing, actual, production) cost, *(Wiederbeschaffungskosten)* replacement costs; ~**kosten plus Gewinnspanne** cost-plus *(US)*; ~**preis** cost price, flat (production) cost; **durchschnittlicher** ~**preis** average cost price; **unter dem** ~**preis verkaufen** to sell below cost price; ~**wert** cost price.
gesteigerter Absatz increased sales.
Gestein [living] rock;
abbauwürdiges ~ *(Goldabbau)* pay dirt; **erzhaltiges** ~ ore-bearing rock; **loses** ~ loose rock; **taubes** ~ attle, waste.
Gestell skeleton, [storage] rack, framework, support, *(für Bücher)* shelf;
~ **für Broschüren** rack of pamplets;
dürres ~ bag of bones;
schrecklich dürres ~ **sein** to look like a bean-pole;
~**brett** shelf.
gestellt, schlecht badly situated; **schlechter** ~ worse off;
auf sich selbst ~ **sein** to be left to one's own devices.
Gestellung *(Verkehrsmittel)* provision;
~ **eines Akkreditivs** opening of a letter of credit; ~ **eines Bürgen** putting in of bail; ~ **von Geiseln** delivery of hostages; ~ **von Planen** hiring of tarpaulins; ~ **zusätzlicher Sicherheiten** replenishment of a loan.
Gestellungsbefehl calling up, induction order *(US)*;
~ **erhalten** to be called to the colo(u)rs.
Gestellungskosten original cost.
gestempelt stamped.
gestern yesterday;
nicht von ~ **sein** not to have been born yesterday, to be no fool.
gesteuert controlled.
gestiefelt und gespornt ready for the journey.
gestiegen sein *(Preise)* to run high;
im Kurs ~ to be quoted higher.
Gestik gestures.
gestimmt disposed.
gestohlen stolen, purloined;
es kann mir ~ **bleiben** and welcome to it; **sein Geld kann mir** ~ **bleiben** to hell with his money.
gestoppt|er Preis stop price;
~ **werden** to be brought to a stand.
gestorben departed, dead;
weder ~ **noch für tot erklärt** full life.
gestört disturbed;
~ **sein** *(tel.)* to be down (out of order); **geistig** ~ **sein** to be deranged [in one's mental faculities].
Gestotter stammer, stutter.
gestrandet stranded, aground, [ship]wrecked, *(fig.)* high and dry, castaway.
Gestrandeter social outcast, castaway.
gestrenger Vater strict father.
gestreut, risikomäßig *(Kapital, Produktion)* diversified.
gestrichen painted, *(drucktechn.)* deleted, *(Kurs)* no quotation;
frisch ~! wet paint!; **aus dem Protokoll** ~ struck out (stricken, *US*) from the record; ~ **voll** brimful, full to the brim;
~**es Papier** coated paper, *(Börse)* nonquoted stock; **die im Text** ~**en Stellen** sentences deleted from the text; ~**es Wort** deleted word.
gestriegelt spick-and-span.
Gestrüpp brushwood, undergrowth, underbush;
~ **von Verordnungen** jungle (maze) of regulations.
gestundet deferred.
Gestürzten attackieren to kick a man when he's down *(fam.)*.
gestützt supported, propped, upborne, underlaid;
auf Tatsachen ~ founded on facts;
~**er Kurs** pegged exchange rate.
Gesuch request, petition, plea, application, suit;
in Erledigung eines ~**es** in answer to a request;
dringendes ~ earnest request; **gemeinsam eingebrachtes** ~ collective petition; **erneuertes** ~ reapplication; **schriftliches** ~ written request;
~ **um ein Stipendium** application for a scholarship;
~ **schriftlich abfassen** to couch a request in writing; ~ **ablehnen (abschlägig bescheiden)** to deny (reject) a request, to dismiss (refuse) a petition; ~ **aufsetzen** to draw up a request (petition); ~ **bearbeiten** to take charge of (handle) a request; ~ **befürworten** to second a petition; ~ **anstandslos bewilligen** to grant an application without objection; ~ **einreichen** to make a request, to prefer (present, file, put up) a petition, to file (send in) an application; **schriftliches** ~ **einreichen** to apply in writing, to apply by letter; ~ **beim Gericht einreichen** to enter a petition; ~ **entgegennehmen** to receive (hear) a petition; ~ **genehmigen** to fall in with a request, to grant a petition; **einem** ~ **stattgeben** to comply with (accede to, grant) a request, to accord a petition; **jem. ein** ~ **vorlegen** to refer a request to s. o.;
~ **in Betracht ziehen** to attend to a request;
~**formular** application form; ~**steller** petitioner, applicant.
gesucht wanted, *(Börse)* asked, sought after, in demand, *(Redeweise)* stilted, affected, *(Ware)* wanted, in vogue;
für sofort ~ wanted immediately; **nicht** ~ *(Börse)* without inquiry; **steckbrieflich** ~ wanted by the police; **Stelle** ~ situation wanted; **ziemlich** ~ in tolerable demand; **zu kaufen** ~ required;
~ **sein** to come into demand, to be sought; **sehr** ~ **sein** to be in great (brisk) demand, *(Börse)* to be at a premium; **wenig** ~ **sein** to be in little demand;
~**er Ausdruck** strained (labo(u)red) expression; **mit** ~**er Höflichkeit** with studied politeness; ~**er Vergleich** far-fetched comparison.
Gesuchter, steckbrieflich person wanted.
gesund healthy, healthful, wholesome, fit, well, *(Lebensversicherter)* of sound health;
~ **wie ein Fisch im Wasser** as sound as a bell, as fit as a fiddle;
geistig ~ of sound mind; **nicht** ~ weak; **wirtschaftlich** ~ financially sound;
~ **und munter** alive and kicking; ~ **und wohlbehalten** safe and sound;
~ **aussehen** to have a healthy look; ~ **bleiben** to keep body and soul together; **branchenmäßig erfolgreich und finanziell** ~ **sein** to have established successful and financially sound records in its industry; **nicht ganz** ~ **sein** to be a bit touched; **sehr** ~ **für j. sein** to do s. o. a world of good; ~ **werden** to convalesce, to recuperate;
~**e Ertragslage** health of earnings; ~**e Farbe** healthy complexion; ~**e Finanzgebarung** sound finance; ~**e Firma** sound business house; ~**e Glieder haben** to be sound in wind and limb; ~**es Klima** salubrious climate; ~**e Lebensweise** healthy way of living; ~**er Menschenverstand** common sense, horse sense; ~**es Unternehmen** sound business; ~**es Urteil haben** to have a sound (clear) judgment; ~**es Verhältnis** healthy relationship; ~**e Währung** hard (sound) currency.
Gesund|beter faith-healer; ~**brunnen** mineral waters.
Gesundheit [physical] health, *(Geschäft)* soundness, solvency;
bei bester ~ in the pink (best of health); **bei blühender** ~ in glowing health; **von eiserner** ~ as hard as nails;
ernsthaft gefährdete ~ seriously impaired health; **geschwächte** ~ impaired health; **gestärkte** ~ improved health; **öffentliche** ~ public health; **schwächliche** ~ fragile (tender) health; **zarte** ~ delicacy;
zum Nachteil seiner ~ **zu lange arbeiten** to work long hours to the detriment of one's health; **Toast auf jds.** ~ **ausbringen** to drink to the health of s. o.; **jds.** ~ **beeinträchtigen** to impair (derange, affect) s. one's health; **sich bester** ~ **erfreuen** to be alive and well; **seine** ~ **festigen** to conserve (improve) one's health; **labile** ~ **haben** to be of delicate health; **zerrüttete** ~ **haben** to be broken in health; **seine** ~ **ruinieren** to play the devil with one's health; **seine** ~ **schädigen** to injure one's health; **bei bester** ~ **sein** to be in the best of health; **von strotzender** ~ **sein** to be in the full flush of health; **von zarter** ~ **sein** to be of delicate health; **seine** ~ **aufs Spiel setzen** to risk (gamble with, play with) one's health; **vor** ~ **strotzen** to be in rude (the very picture of, look the picture of) health, to be glowing with health; **seine** ~ **wiederherstellen** to recoup one's health.

gesundheitlich | schlecht dran sein to be in a poor state of health, to be in bad health;
~**e Einrichtungen** sanitary installations; **j. aus ~en Gründen freilassen** to free s. o. for health reasons; ~**e Risiken** health hazards; ~**er Schaden** injury to health; ~**e Vorkehrungen treffen** to sanitate.
Gesundheits | amt Board of Health, health authorities, sanitary (health) board, public health center *(US)*; ~**apostel** sanitarian.
Gesundheitsattest health certificate, certificate of health, *(Schiff)* bill of health;
negatives ~ touched (foul) bill of health; **positives** ~ clean bill of health;
~ **überprüfen** to examine a bill of health.
Gesundheits | auflagen health provisions; ~**beamter** health officer, sanitary inspector; ~**behörde** sanitary authorities, Sanitary Board, health administration, health authorities, board of health; ~**beschädigung** injury to health; ~**bestimmungen** health provisions, sanitary regulations; ~**bonus der Firma** health check on the firm.
Gesundheitsdienst medical (sanitary) services, health and sanitation, medical department;
staatlich gelenkter ~ socialized medicine; **öffentlicher** ~ public *(US)* (national, *Br.*) health service;
~ **für Bedürftige** Medicaid *(Br.)*.
Gesundheits | einrichtungen public health facilities *(US)*, health services *(Br.)*; ~**fanatiker** sanitarian.
gesundheitsfördernd healthful, beneficial to the health, wholesome;
~**e Umgebung** wholesome surroundings.
Gesundheits | förderung, gewerbliche industrial sanitation; ~**fürsorge** health care, *(für über 65jährige)* Medicare *(US)*; ~**fürsorger** health visitor.
gesundheitsgefährdend health-endangering, unhealthy, harmful;
~**e Bestandteile** deleterious ingredients.
Gesundheitsgesetz bill on health care *(US)*;
~**gebung** health laws.
gesundheitshalber for reasons of health.
Gesundheits | maßnahme public health (sanitary) measures, health activity; ~**minister** Minister of Health; ~**ministerium** Ministry of Health *(Br.)*, Department of Health *(US)*; ~-, **Erziehungs- und Wohlfahrtsministerium** Department of Health, Education and Welfare *(Br.)*; ~- **und Sozialministerium** Department of Health and Social Security *(Br.)*; ~**nachweis** health certificate.
Gesundheitspaß health certificate;
einwandfreier ~ *(Schiff)* clean bill of health;
~ **mit Einschränkungen** *(Schiff)* foul bill of health; ~ **mit Vermerk** touched bill of health.
Gesundheitspflege hygiene;
betriebliche ~ employee health welfare, industrial sanitation; **öffentliche** ~ public *(US)* (national, *Br.*) health service; **vorbeugende** ~ preventive medicine.
Gesundheits | pfleger health visitor; ~**polizei** sanitary police; **gemeinsames** ~**programm verschiedener Unternehmen** co-operation health plan; ~**risiko** health risk; **aus** ~**rücksichten** for reasons of health; ~**schaden** injury to health.
gesundheitsschädlich dangerous to (destructive of) health, unhealthy, adverse (inimical) to health, insanitary, obnoxious.
Gesundheits | schädlichkeit insanitariness; ~**statistik** health statistics; ~**überwachung** sanitary control; ~**verordnungen,** ~**vorschriften** sanitary regulations (provisions); **internationale** ~**vorschriften** International Sanitary Regulations; ~**vorsorge** health care (protection), preventive medicine; ~**vorsorgewesen** health care system.
Gesundheitswesen sanitary affairs, sanitation;
betriebliches ~ industrial health; **öffentliches** ~ public health, health administration, health and sanitation, National Health Service *(Br.)*.
gesundheitswidrig unhealthy, insanitary, unwholesome.
Gesundheits | zentrum health center *(US)* (centre, *Br.*); ~**zeugnis** quarantine certificate.
Gesundheitszustand [state of] health, physicial condition, condition of one's health;
einwandfreier ~ sound health; **schlechter** ~ ill-health, low state of health; **unstabiler** ~ precarious state of health;
sich um jds. ~ **Sorgen machen** to be concerned about s. one's health.
Gesundmarktwert *(Transportversicherung)* sound market value.
gesund | schreiben, j. *(Arzt)* to certify that s. o. is cured; **sich** ~**schrumpfen** to shrink to profitable size; **sich** ~**stoßen** *(fam.)* to make a packet *(Br., sl.)*.
Gesundung recovery, healing, recuperation of health, restoration from sickness, *(Wirtschaft)* rehabilitation, restoration;
finanzielle ~ reorganization.
gesunken foundered, sunken;
~**er Meeresspiegel** lowered level; ~**e Preise** diminished (dropped, sagged) prices; ~**es Riff** submerged reef.
getäfelte Wände panelled walls.
getan, nach ~**er Arbeit ist gut ruhn** rest is sweet after a hard day's work; **gesagt,** ~ no sooner said than done.
getarnte | Diktatur masked dictatorship; ~ **Geschütze** masked guns.
getätigt done;
im Ausland ~ offshore.
geteilt divided, separated, *(Börse)* split;
mit ~**en Gefühlen** with mixed feelings; ~**es Land** divided nation; **in einer Frage** ~**er Meinung sein** to differ on a question;
~**e Freude ist doppelte Freude** joy shared is joy doubled.
getilgt liquidated, redeemed, paid, settled.
getönt tinted;
rosa ~ touched with rose.
Getöse din, clamo(u)r, deafening noise;
~ **der Schlacht** clash of arms, din of a battle;
~ **um etw. machen** to make a fuss about s. th.
Getöteter dead (killed) person.
getragen *(Kleider)* used;
~ **sprechen** to speak in a solemn and dignified manner.
getrampelt, zu Tode crushed to death.
Getränk beverage, tap, drink;
~**e nicht einbegriffen** drinks extra;
alkoholfreie ~**e** nonalcoholic beverages; **alkoholisches** ~ drink, spirits, alcoholic drinks; **berauschendes** ~ intoxicating liquor, intoxicant; **eisgekühltes** ~ ice drink; **erfrischendes** ~ refreshment; **scharfe** ~**e** hard liquors, hard drinks; **steuerpflichtige** ~**e** excisable drinks;
sich an ~**en schadlos halten** to take it out in drinks; ~**e servieren** to serve refreshments; **j. mit alkoholischen** ~**en traktieren** to liquor s. o. up.
Getränke | ausschank drinking outlet (kiosk), counter, bar, refreshment kiosk (counter); **alkoholfreier** ~**ausschank** soft-drink parlo(u)r; ~**automat** drink dispenser; ~**bude** refreshment kiosk, stall; ~**herstellung** manufacture of beverages; ~**industrie** beverage (drinks) industry; ~**karte** *(Restaurant)* wine card; ~**kellner** wine waiter; ~**marke** tavern token; ~**sorte** tap; **hervorragende** ~**sorte** excellent tap; ~**stand** refreshment counter (kiosk); ~**steuer** tax on alcohol, excise on liquors *(US)*, beverage tax.
Getratsch gossip, twaddle;
leeres ~ empty talk.
getrauen, sich to dare to, to have the courage; **sich technische Übersetzungen nicht** ~ not to feel able to do technical translations; **sich nicht** ~**, jem. zu widersprechen** not to dare to contradict s. o.
getraut, standesamtlich married at a registry.
Getreide grain, corn *(Br.)*, cereals;
~ **auf dem Halm** standing grain, crop; ~ **in Säcken** bagged grain;
~ **anpflanzen** to plant a field with corn; ~ **aufkaufen** to make a corner in wheat; **mit** ~ **handeln** to trade in grain;
~**anbau** grain (crop, corn, *Br.*) growing, cultivation of cereals; ~**aufkäufer** kidder *(Br.)*; ~**aufzug** grain elevator; ~**ausfuhr** grain export; ~**ausfuhrland** grain-exporting country; ~**börse** corn *(Br.)* (grain) exchange, grain pit; ~**einfuhr** grain imports, imported cereals; ~**einkäufer** grain purchaser; ~**ernte** grain crop (harvest) *(US)*; ~**erzeugung** grain (corn, *Br.*) production; ~**feld** cornfield; ~**handel** grain trade; ~**händler** grain merchant (dealer), corn factor *(Br.)*; ~**käufe** grain purchases; ~**ladung** grain cargo; ~**lager** grain depot; ~**land** cornland; ~**lieferungen** grain deliveries; ~**makler** grain (corn, *Br.*) broker; ~**markt** grain (corn, *Br.*) market; ~**preise** grain (cereal) prices; ~**produktion** grain (corn) production; ~**reserven** grain reserves; ~**sack** grain sack; ~**silo** grain storage, [grain] harvester; ~**speicher** cornloft, granary *(US)*; ~**termingeschäfte** grain futures trade *(US)*; ~**überschuß** grain surplus (carryover), surplus wheat; ~**waage** grain weigher; ~**wechsel** grain bill; ~**wirtschaftsjahr** *(EG)* marketing year; ~**zoll** corn tax.
getrennt separate, severable, several, apart, discrete, distinct;
~ **lebend** *(Ehepartner)* living separately and apart;
etw. ~ **aufbewahren** to keep s. th. separate; **verschiedene Aspekte** ~ **betrachten** to distinguish between the various aspects; ~ **halten** to keep asunder; ~ **veranlagen** to assess separately;

~e **Anlagen** *(Pensionskasse)* separate accounts; ~e **Besteuerung** separate taxation; ~e **Kasse machen** to go Dutch; ~e **Planungsrechnung** separable programming; **mit ~er Post** under separate cover; ~e **Rechnung** separate bill, Dutch treat; ~es **Schuldanerkenntnis** *(Ehefrau)* separate acknowledgement; ~e **Steuererklärung** separate return; ~en **Urlaub machen** to take separate holidays; ~e **Veranlagung** separate assessment; ~e **Zimmer** separate rooms.

Getrenntleben separation;
gerichtlich angeordnetes ~ limited divorce, judicial separation, separation by order of the court; **unberechtigtes** ~ obstinate desertion.

Getriebe wheelwork, *(Auto)* [driving] gear, gearbox, gearing, *(fig.)* bustle, hustle, *(Uhr)* clockwork;
automatisches ~ automatic gearbox (transmission); **synchronisiertes** ~ synchromesh gearbox;
~ **mit Druckknopfschaltung** selective transmission; ~ **des Verwaltungsapparates** the wheels of government;
Sand ins ~ **streuen** to throw a spanner (monkey wrench) into the works; **mit einem** ~ **versehen** to gear, to provide with gearing;
~**bremse** transmission brake; ~**gehäuse** gearbox, gear (transmission) case; ~**kasten** pinion box; ~**öl** transmission (gear) oil; ~**pumpe** gear pump; ~**rad** gear wheel; ~**schaden** gearbox trouble; ~**übersetzung** gear ratio; ~**welle** gear (transmission) shaft.

getroffen stricken, hit, struck;
empfindlich ~ touched to the quick; **tief** ~ heart-stricken;
sich ~ **fühlen** to take s. th. personally; **schwer** ~ **sein** to be hard hit.

getrost confident, hopeful, *(ohne Bedenken)* without hesitation;
~ **in die Zukunft blicken** to face the future confidently; **sich bei seinen Freunden** ~ **Geld pumpen** to feel no qualms about borrowing from one's friends.

Getue fuss, ado, fanfare, dog, time *(US coll.)*;
affektiertes ~ airs and graces;
großes ~ **machen** to make a lot of fuss, to take on *(coll.)*, to put on airs.

Getümmel turmoil, tumult, hurly-burly;
unbeschreibliches ~ tremendous turmoil, fearful tumult, chaos;
sich ins ~ **stürzen** to hurl o. s. into the fray.

Getuschel whisper, whispering.

Getute tooting.

geübt practised, experienced, versed;
sehr ~ **in etw. sein** to be a good hand at; **im Übersetzen technischer Texte sehr** ~ **sein** to have considerable experience in translating technical texts;
~e **Schneiderin** skilled dressmaker.

Gewächs plant;
bösartiges ~ malignant tumo(u)r; **edles** ~ good wine; **unser eigenes** ~ our own vintage.

gewachsen, übermäßig overgrown;
jem. ~ **sein** to be a match for s. o., to measure up to s. o. *(US)*;
den geschäftlichen Anstrengungen nicht mehr ~ **sein** to be no longer equal to the strain of business; **sich einer Lage** ~ **zeigen** to cope with (be equal to) a situation, to rise to the occasion.

Gewächshaus greenhouse, hothouse, glasshouse, conservatory *(Br.)*.

gewagt risky, hazardous, bold;
~er **Film** daring film; ~e **Konstruktion** bold piece of construction; ~e **Sache** touch-and-go affair; ~es **Spiel spielen** to be skating on thin ice; ~es **Unternehmen** speculative venture, risky undertaking; ~er **Witz** blue (off-colo(u)r) joke.

gewählt elected, elect, *(Stil)* polite, refined;
einstimmig ~ elected unanimously; **nicht** ~ unsuccessful; **nicht wieder** ~ unreturned;
sich ~ **ausdrücken** to express o. s. elegantly; ~ **sein** to be in;
einstimmig ~ **werden** to be chosen by general consent; **für die Dauer von sieben Jahren** ~ **werden** to be elected for a term of seven years; **ins Parlament** ~ **werden** to be elected (returned) into Parliament; **zum Vorsitzenden** ~ **werden** to be voted into the chair.

gewahr aware;
eines Fehlers ~ **werden** to realize a mistake.

Gewähr guarantee, guaranty, security, warranty, warrant, undertaking;
ohne ~ without engagement, subject to correction, no guarantee, *(Fahrplan)* subject to change; **unter** ~ warranted, guaranteed;
stillschweigende ~ implied warranty;
keine ~ **für Bruch** no guarantee against breakage; ~ **für zugesicherte Eigenschaften** warranty of fitness;
~ **leisten (übernehmen)** to guarantee, to undertake a guarantee, to guaranty, to warrant; **volle** ~ **leisten** to fully guarantee; **keine** ~ **übernehmen** to accept no responsibility.

gewähren to grant, to allow, to concede, to accord, to afford, to confer;
Anleihe ~ to grant a loan; **Asyl** ~ to grant asylum; **Aufschub** ~ to grant (allow) a respite; **herrliche Aussicht** ~ to command a superb view; **jem. eine Belohnung** ~ to confer a reward on s. o.; **Bitte** ~ to grant a request; **Büchereinsicht** ~ to give access to the books; **Darlehen** ~ to grant a loan; **Diskont** ~ to allow a discount; **jem. Einlaß** ~ to admit s. o.; **Entschädigung** ~ to pay compensation, to indemnify; **jem. Erleichterungen** ~ to grant s. o. facilities; **Frist** ~ to accord (grant) a respite; **Fristverlängerung** ~ to grant extension (respite) of time; **jem. ein Interview** ~ to favo(u)r s. o. with an interview; **jem. eine Konzession** ~ to license s. o.; **Kredit** ~ to grant a credit; **Nachlaß** ~ to grant a reduction, to allow a discount; **jem. Obdach** ~ to give s. o. shelter; **keinen Pardon** ~ to give no quarter; **Provision** ~ to accord a commission; **Rabatt** ~ to allow an abatement; **Steuerfreibetrag** ~ to grant an exemption; **Strafaufschub** ~ to reprieve; **Unterhaltszuschuß** ~ to grant an allowance; **Vorrecht** ~ to grant a privilege; **Vorteil** ~ to offer an advantage; **Zahlungsfrist** ~ to allow a debtor time to pay;
~ **lassen** to indulge; **jem.** ~ **lassen** to give s. o. line enough, to give s. o. full play.

Gewährenlassen, wissentliches connivance.

gewährleisten to guarantee, to guaranty, to warrant, *(sichern)* to ensure, to secure;
Frieden ~ to ensure peace; **pünktliche Lieferung** ~ to warrant punctual delivery; **Sicherheit des Staates** ~ to ensure the safety of the state.

Gewährleistung guarantee *(Br.)*, guaranty *(US)*, warrant of merchantability, warranty;
unter Ausschluß der ~ without guarantee, with all faults, caveat emptor;
gesetzliche ~ implied warranty *(US)*; **vertragliche** ~ warranty in the contract, express warranty *(US)*;
~ **von Durchschnittsqualität** average quality protection, warranty of merchantability *(US)*; ~ **für zugesicherte Eigenschaften** express warranty; ~ **wegen Rechtsmangels** warranty of title, title warranty; ~ **für Sachmängel** warranty of fitness (goods); ~ **des Verkäufers** caveat venditor; ~ **der Vollmacht** warranty of authority;
~ **übernehmen** to give a warranty.

Gewährleistungs|anspruch warranty claim; ~**ansprüche erfüllen** to stand back (behind) *(Br.)* a guarantee, to fill the warranty; ~**ausschuß** caveat emptor; ~**bruch** breach of warranty; ~**erklärung** express warranty; ~**fehler** defect covered by a warranty, redhibitory defect (vice) *(US)*; ~**frist** period of warranty; ~**garantie** performance guarantee *(Br.)*; ~**klage** redhibitory action *(US)*; ~**klausel** clause of warranty, warranty clause; ~**kosten** warranty costs.

Gewährleistungspflicht guarantee *(Br.)*, guaranty *(US)*, warranty responsibility;
nicht eingehaltene ~ breach of warranty; **gesetzliche** ~ implied warranty *(US)*; **vereinbarte** ~ warranty of fitness *(US)*;
seiner ~ **nachkommen** to pay under a guarantee *(Br.)* (guaranty, *US*).

Gewährleistungs|versicherung des Produzenten (Warenherstellers) producer's liability insurance *(US)*; ~**vertrag** warranty deed.

Gewahrsam safekeeping, custody, occupancy, charge, hold, keeping, *(Bank)* deposit, safe custody, *(Haft)* detention, lockup, confinement;
in polizeilichem ~ in police custody; **in sicherem** ~ in safe custody; **unter** ~ under restraint;
amtlicher ~ official custody; **tatsächlicher** ~ actual occupation;
j. in polizeilichen ~ **geben** to give s. o. in charge (in custody); **in** ~ **nehmen** to take into custody, *(festsetzen)* to arrest; **in jds.** ~ **sein** to be in s. one's custody; **in sicherem** ~ **sein** to be in safekeeping.

Gewahrsams|bruch malfeasance in office; ~**inhaber** bailee; **geduldeter** ~**inhaber** quasi tenant at sufferance; ~**inhaber eines Kindes** guardian by nature; ~**klausel** *(Versicherung)* bailee clause; ~**macht** *(pol.)* detaining power, captor.

Gewährsmangel defect covered by (under) a warranty, redhibitory vice (defect) *(US)*.

Gewährsmann reference, referee, source, informant, authority, *(Bürge)* guarantee *(Br.)*, guaranty *(US)*, warrantor, voucher;

sicherer ~ reliable authority;
j. als ~ angeben to quote s. o. as one's authority; **seinen ~ nicht preisgeben** to refuse to disclose the name of one's informant; **j. als ~ vorladen** to vouch s. o. to warranty.
Gewährs|schein *(Kommissionsgeschäft)* del credere bond *(Br.)*; **~träger** guarantor.
Gewährung allowance, grant, granting, accordance, concession;
~ **einer Ausbildungsbeihilfe** training grant, educational allowance; ~ **von Auslandshilfe** pumping in foreign aid; ~ **eines Darlehns** granting a loan; ~ **von Entschädigung ohne Untersuchung der Unfallursache** no-fault insurance plan; ~ **einer Frist** granting (allowance) of time; ~ **eines Kredits** allowance (granting) of a credit; ~ **verbilligter Landesdarlehen mit Grundbuchsicherung** option mortgage system; ~ **einer Lizenz** concession of a licence; ~ **eines Lombardkredites** lending on collateral; ~ **einer Prämie** allowance of a bonus; ~ **mildernder Umstände** allowance of extenuating circumstances; ~ **einer Umzugsbeihilfe** allowance for removal *(Br.)*; ~ **von Unterschlupf** harbo(u)ring; **erneute ~ einer Unterstützung** resumption of a grant; ~ **eines Vorschusses** grant of an advance; ~ **preislicher Vorteile** price concessions; ~ **von Zahlungsaufschub** extension (prolongation) of time; ~ **betrieblicher Zusatzrenten zur staatlichen Altersversorgung** providing occupational benefits in addition to those provided by the state.
Gewalt power, authority, force, violence, arm, gripe, grip;
in ehemännlicher ~ under coverture; **in der ~ eines Tyrannen** in the grip of a tyrant; **mit** ~ at the point of the sword; **mit aller** ~ with might and main; **mit nackter** ~ by sheer force; **mit sanfter** ~ by gentle force;
absolute ~ absolute power; **ausübende** ~ administrative power, executive [power]; **brutale** ~ brute force (strength); **elterliche** ~ custody of the children; **gesetzgebende** ~ legislative [power]; **höchste** ~ supreme power, supremacy; **höhere** ~ *(Recht der unerlaubten Handlungen)* superior force, Act of God, main act, vis major, force majeure, unforeseen circumstances; **konkurrierende ~en** concurrent powers; **konsularische** ~ consular power; **nackte** ~ open force; **öffentliche** ~ public authority; **physische** ~ physical force; **richterliche** ~ authority of the court, judicial power (authority); **rohe** ~ brute violence; **unumschränkte** ~ sovereign power (prerogative); **unwiderstehliche** ~ *(Fahrlässigkeitshaftung)* superior force; **väterliche** ~ paternal power, authority of father; **vollziehende** ~ executive [power], executive (administrative) authority;
~ **oder Bedrohung** force and fear; ~ **der Empfindung** strength of s. one's feelings; ~ **einer Rede** force of a speech;
jem. ~ androhen to offer violence to s. o.; **jem. ~ antun** to lay violent hands on s. o.; **einem Mädchen ~ antun** to ravish (rape) a girl; **einem Text ~ antun** to do violence to a text; ~ **anwenden** to use force, to practise violence; ~ **in Notwehr anwenden** to use force in self-protection *(US)*; **magische ~ über j. ausüben** to cast a spell over s. o.; **Stadt in seine ~ bringen** to bring a town under one's power; **Eintritt mit ~ erzwingen** to force one's way; **sich mit aller ~ an einer Hoffnung festhalten** to cling desperately to a hope; **jem. unumschränkte ~ geben** to make s. o. sovereign; **in jds. ~ geraten** to fall into s.one's hands; ~ **über etw. haben** to have s. th. within one's grasp; **j. in seiner ~ haben** to have s. o. in one's power (in the hip), to have s. o. in one's pocket; **höchste ~ haben** to be supreme; **j. völlig in seiner ~ haben** to have s. o. by the short hairs *(sl.)*; **sich vollkommen in der ~ haben** to have complete control of o. s.; **seine Zunge unter ~ haben** to curb (bridle) one's tongue; ~ **in Händen haben** to be in authority; **j. mit sanfter ~ hinausbefördern** to show s. o. gently but firmly to the door; ~ **an sich reißen** to seize power; **unter jds. ~ sein** to be at the mercy of s. o.; **den ~en des Sturmes ausgesetzt sein** to be exposed to the fury of the elements; **unter väterlicher ~ stehen** to be under paternal authority; ~ **über sein Auto verlieren** to lose control of one's car; **sich mit aller ~ gegen etw. wehren** to fight tooth and nail; **der ~ weichen** to yield to force; **mit richterlicher ~ ausgestattet werden** to be invested with judicial powers; **mit ~ reich werden wollen** to stop at nothing to get rich;
~akt act of violence; **öffentliche ~akte** street violence; **~androhung** threat of violence, mailed fist; **~anmaßung** usurpation of power; **~anwendung** force, actual violence, stronghand, mailed fist, assault; **unzulässige ~anwendung** *(Verhör)* third degree; **~anwendung im Notwehrfall** use of force in self-protection *(US)*.
Gewaltenteilung division of powers, power sharing.
Gewalt|haber ruler, tyrant, dictator; **~herrschaft** rule of force, high hand, despotism, tyranny; **~herrschaft ausüben** to tyrannize; **~herrscher** tyrant, despot.
gewaltig powerful, mighty;
sich ~ anstrengen to make tremendous efforts; **sich ~ irren** to be very much mistaken;
~e Anzahl huge number; **von ~en Ausmaßen** of huge dimensions; **~e Gemeinheit** dirty trick; **~e Hitze** tremendous heat; **~en Hunger haben** to be terribly hungry; **~e Truppenansammlung** enormous force of troops; **~er Unterschied** vast difference.
Gewaltige bosses, leaders, top brass;
die ~n der Autoindustrie the big noises in the motor-car industry.
Gewalt|inhaber holder of power; **~kur gegen die Inflation** drastic measures to cure inflation.
gewaltlos nonviolent;
~er Widerstand passive resistance.
Gewalt|losigkeit nonviolence; **~lösung** drastic solution; **~marsch** forced march, five-mile hike *(coll.)*; **~maßnahmen** violent measures; **~maßnahmen ergreifen** to have resort to force; **~methode** shotgun approach; **~politik** policy of force.
gewaltsam by force, forcibly, with a strong hand, by violent means, by the head and ears;
~ **in ein Haus eindringen** to force one's way into a house; **j. ~ aus dem Schlaf reißen** to waken s. o. suddenly;
~e Besitzergreifung forcible entry and detainer; **~er Tod** violent death; **eines ~en Todes sterben** to die by violence.
Gewalt|streich tour de force, coup; **~tat** outrage, [act of] violence.
gewalttätig violent, brutal;
~ **werden** to lay violent hands on.
Gewalttätigkeit, zu ~en geneigt easily provoked to violence;
studentische ~ student violence;
~ **mit Vaterlandsgefühlen bemänteln** to use patriotism as a cloak for violence.
Gewalt|verbrechen act (crime) of violence, violent crime; **~verbrecher** desperate criminal, cutthroat, brutal gangster; **~verzicht** renunciation of force; **~verzichtsabkommen** nonaggression treaty.
Gewand garment, costume, clothes;
im ~ eines Menschenfreundes under the guise of a philanthropist;
in neuem ~ erscheinen *(Zeitschrift)* to appear with a new look.
gewandt efficient, versed, proficient, competent, nimble, agile, experienced, versed;
sich ~ aus der Affäre ziehen to extricate o. s. from a difficulty;
~es Auftreten elegant manners; **~er Diplomat** skilled diplomat; **~er Geschäftsmann** shrewd businessman; **~er Geschäftsmann sein** to be well versed in business [matters]; **~e Sekretärin** competent (efficient) secretary; **~er Stil** easy-flowing style; **~e Umgangsformen** easy manners.
Gewandtheit dexterity, facility, skill, knack;
diplomatische ~ diplomatic skill.
gewappnet proof.
gewartet *(Maschine)* maintained;
nicht ~ werden to suffer from neglect.
gewärtig, eines Winkes on the watch.
gewärtigen, zu ~ haben to be in for s. th.; **schwere Strafen zu ~ haben** to be liable for severe punishment.
Gewäsch idle talk, trumpery, jabber, wash, eyewash *(sl.)*;
leeres ~ wish-wash, trash, rabble, windbaggery *(sl.)*; **sentimentales** ~ milk and water; **sinnloses** ~ twaddle.
Gewässer waters;
in chinesischen ~n in Chinese waters;
fließende ~ bodies of running water; **zum Hoheitsgebiet gehörige** ~ closed sea; **größeres** ~ public pond; **inländisches (innerstaatliche)** ~ internal (inland) waters; **neutrale** ~ neutral waters; **öffentliche** ~ public waters; **schiffbare** ~ navigable (public) waters; **stehendes** ~ dead water, stagnant waters; **stilles** ~ quiet waters; **unterirdische** ~ subterranean waters; **verschmutztes** ~ polluted pond;
~güte water quality; **~schutz** pollution control; **~verunreinigung** water pollution.
Gewebe web, fabric, tissue, textile, texture;
dichtes ~ dense texture;
~ **von Lügen** web of lies;
~muster pattern (design) of a fabric.
Gewehr rifle, gun;
mit dem ~ auf j. anlegen to point a rifle at s. o.; **sein ~ entsichern** to release the safety catch of one's rifle; ~ **sichern** to put a rifle on safe *(US)*; **jem. das ~ wegnehmen** to disarm s. o. of his rifle;
~exerzieren rifle exercise; **~fabrik** rifle factory; **~pyramide** pile of arms; **~reiniger** pull-through; **~schuß** gunshot.

geweiht devoted, dedicated;
dem Untergang ~ doomed to destruction.

Gewerbe business, trade, *(Beruf)* calling, profession, occupation, vocation, shop, job *(US)*, *(Handwerk)* craft, *(Industrie)* industry, *(Industriezweig)* line of business, branch of industry;
in Ausübung eines ~s in pursuance of a trade;
ambulantes ~ itinerant trade (trading), runaway shop, travelling vendors, peddlery, peddling; **anmeldepflichtiges** ~ trade subject to a licence; **aufblühendes** ~ boom industry; **noch in der Entstehung begriffenes** ~ embryo industry; **besonderes** ~ particular branch; **dienstleistendes** ~ service industries; **dunkles** ~ shady business; **ehrbares** ~ honest trade, gentle calling; **einträgliches** ~ profitable trade; **gefährliches** ~ dangerous trade (industry); **genehmigungspflichtiges** ~ trade subject to a licence; **gesundheitsschädliches** ~ offensive trade; **grafisches** ~ printing trade; **handwerkliches** ~ handicraft [business], craftman's establishment; **horizontales** ~ streetwalking; **kaufmännisches** ~ merchanthood, merchantry, business (commercial) occupation; **konzessioniertes** ~ licensed traffic (trade); **landwirtschaftliches** ~ noncommercial trade; **im öffentlichen Interesse liegendes** ~ business affected with a public interest; **modeabhängiges** ~ fashionable trade; **nützliches** ~ useful trade; **ortsansässiges** ~ local trade; **nicht registriertes** ~ unincorporated enterprise; **schimpfliches** ~ discreditable profession; **schmutziges** ~ dirty business; **sittenwidriges** ~ immoral trade; **stehendes** ~ nonitinerant trading; **durch Industrialisierung überholtes** ~ industry bypassed by industrialization; **unterentlohntes** ~ sweatshop industry; **verbotenes** ~ no lawful trade; **zünftiges** ~ incorporated trade;
~ **belästigender Art** noxious trade; **Handel und** ~ commerce and industry; ~ **der Steuerumgehung** tax avoidance industry; ~ **im Umherziehen** runaway shop, itinerant trade (trading), peddlery, pedlary;
sein Kapital in einem ~ **anlegen** to buy o. s. into an industry; ~ **anmelden** to register a trade (business); ~ **ansiedeln** to locate industry; ~ **ausüben (betreiben)** to carry on (drive, exercise, ply, pursue, follow) a trade, to run a business; ~ **beginnen** to open a trade; ~ **nach kaufmännischen Gesichtspunkten betreiben** to carry on a trade on a commercial basis; **auf Gewinn gerichtetes** ~ **betreiben** to carry on business in common with a view to profit; ~ **erlernen** to learn a trade; **sein** ~ **bei erkannter Insolvenz fortsetzen** to continue trading after knowledge of insolvency; **etw. zum** ~ **machen** to professionalize s. th.; **einem** ~ **nachgehen** to prosecute (ply) a trade, to pursue a line of business; **im gleichen** ~ **tätig sein** to be on the same game;
~**abfall** industrial refuse; ~**anmeldung** registration of business; ~**antrag** business application; ~**antragsteller** commercial applicant; ~**aufseher** factory inspector industrial executive *(US)*, umpire; ~**aufsicht** factory (labo(u)r, trade) inspection; ~**aufsichtsamt** factory inspectorate division, industrial executive *(US)*; ~**aufsichtswesen** factoryship; ~**ausbildung** industrial training; ~**ausbildungsgesetz** Industrial Training Act *(Br.)*; ~**ausschuß** trade committee; ~**ausschuß für das Hotel- und Gaststättenwesen** Hotel and Catering Industry Board *(Br.)*; ~**ausstellung** industrial (trade) exhibition, trade show (fair) *(Br.)*; ~**ausübung** exercise (pursuit) of a trade; ~**bank** industrial bank; **Handels- und** ~**bank** trade bank; ~**befugnis**, ~**berechtigung** [business (trade)] licence, commercial privilege, letters of business *(Br.)*, concession *(US)*; **ausschließliche** ~**berechtigung** monopoly; ~**besteuerung** business taxation.

Gewerbebetrieb business, business entity (establishment), factory, trade, industrial (business) enterprise, workshop, manufacturing establishment;
belästigender ~ offensive (noxious) trade; **schon bestehender** ~ existing business;
~ **im Umherziehen** itinerant trade (trading), peddling, peddlery, pedlary, runaway shop;
~ **ausüben** to carry on a trade; ~ **beeinträchtigen** to affect the trade; ~ **beginnen** to commence trading (business).

Gwerbe|einkünfte profits from trade, trading revenues (receipts); ~**erlaubnis** trade licence, concession *(US)*; ~**ertrag** income from a business, business (trading) profit, operating profit, trading income, returns; ~**ertragssteuer** earned-income tax *(US)*, business profits (trade) tax; ~**erzeugnis** industrial product, manufacture; ~**fläche** floor space; ~**flächensteuerung** floor-space policy *(Br.)*; ~**freiheit** economic freedom, freedom (liberty) of trade; ~**gebiet** industrial area, manufacturing district, works area *(Br.)*; ~**genehmigung** trade licence, commercial privilege, letters of business *(Br.)*, concession *(US)*; ~**gericht** court of trade, industrial tribunal (arbitration board) *(Br.)*; ~**gerichtsbarkeit** industrial arbitration; ~**gesetzgebung** inspection laws, Factory Acts *(Br.)*; ~**grafik** industrial art; ~**gruppe** category of industry; ~**hygiene** industrial hygiene; ~**inspektor** factory inspector; ~**kapital** trade (trading, industrial) capital; ~**kontrolle** factory inspection; ~**konzession** [business (trade)] licence, letters of business *(Br.)*, commercial privilege, concession *(US)*; ~**krankheit** occupational (industrial) disease *(Br.)*; ~**kunde** technology.

gewerbekundig technological.

Gewerbe|kundiger technologist; ~**lehrer** commercial teacher, trade master, technical instructor; ~**lizenz** [business] licence, trade licence, letters of business *(Br.)*; ~**lizenz erteilen** to accord permission to transact business; ~**lizenzantrag** business application; ~**müll** trade refuse; ~**museum** industrial museum; ~**ordnung** statute of labo(u)rers *(Br.)*; ~**polizei** factory inspection.

gewerbepolizeiliche|Anordnung factory regulations; ~ **Bestimmungen** factory acts; ~ **Gesetzgebung** inspection laws, statute of labour *(Br.)*; ~ **Überprüfung** factory inspection.

Gewerbe|räume trade premises; ~**recht** factory (industrial, *Br.*) law.

Gewerbeschein [business] licence, licence to carry on a trade, trading certificate *(Br.)*, letters of business *(Br.)*;
~ **für den Einzelhandel** retail licence;
ohne ~ **tätig sein** to peddle without a licence;
~**gebühr** regulation charge.

Gewerbe|schiedsgericht Industrial Arbitration Board *(Br.)*; ~**schule** industrial *(Br.)* (vocational, technical, trade, *US*) school, technical high school *(US)*; ~**schulunterricht in den verschiedensten Fächern erteilen** to teach many useful trades; ~**schutzgesetz** Safeguarding of Industry Act *(Br.)*; ~**schutzgesetzgebung** Factories Acts *(Br.)*; ~**stand** trading class; ~**statistik** industrial statistics.

Gewerbesteuer occupation (professional, trade, business) tax, *(Konzessionsabgabe)* license tax *(US)*;
~ **jeglicher Art** tax in respect of any trade *(Br.)*.

Gewerbesteuer|befreiung exemption from business tax; ~**bescheid** business tax notice; ~**erklärung** occupation tax return; ~**meßbescheid** occupation tax assessment; **der** ~**pflicht unterliegen** to be subject to license tax *(US)*.

gewerbesteuerpflichtig subject to licence.

Gewerbesteuer|pflichtiger recognized merchant; ~**satz** business scale rate; ~**wesen** business taxation.

gewerbetätig industrial, commercial.

Gewerbetätigkeit industrial employment (activity, work), trading activity, trade activities, industrialism;
gemeindliche ~ municipal trading;
~ **ausüben** to carry on a trade or business.

gewerbetreibend manufacturing, trading, *(Handwerker)* handicraft.

Gewerbetreibende tradesfolk, tradespeople.

Gewerbetreibender industrialist, manufacturer, tradesman, trader, businessman, *(Handwerker)* [handi]craftsman;
kleiner ~ small (petty) trader; **selbständiger** ~ independent businessman;
~ **sein** to exercise a trade.

Gewerbe|unfallversicherung industrial accident insurance; ~**unfallversicherungsgesetz** workmen's compensation law *(Br.)*; **steuerlich als** ~**unkosten behandeln** to charge as trade expense for tax purposes; ~**usancen** professional customs; ~**verband** trade association; ~**verlust** trading loss; ~**verzeichnis** trade directory; ~**zeichen** brand, mark, trademark; ~**zentrum** occupational center *(US)* (centre, *Br.*); ~**zulassung** trade (business) licence; ~**zweck** business purpose, industrial use, objects of a company; **zu** ~**zwecken** for the purpose of the trade, for commercial purposes; ~**zweckklausel** *(Satzung)* objects clause.

Gewerbezweig trading line, [line of] industry, branch of trade, trade branch;
von der Krise betroffene ~**e** depressed industries; **dienstleistungsorientierte** ~**e** service-orientated industries; **umweltfreundliche** ~**e** nonpolluting industries; **unterbesetzter** ~ short-staffed industry;
~**e wirtschaftlich zusammenfassen** to amalgamate industries.

gewerblich industrial, commercial, business;
nicht ~ noncommercial, nonbusiness;
~ **beschäftigt** gainfully employed;
~ **tätig sein** to follow (carry on, ply) a trade, to carry on a trade or business; **Erfindung** ~ **verwerten** to put an invention to commercial use; **nicht** ~ **genutzt werden** to have nonindustrial use;

~e **Abwässer** trade effluent; ~e **Bauten** commercial and industrial buildings; ~e **Betätigung** commercial activities; ~er **Betrieb** manufacturing (industrial, business) enterprise; ~es **Eigentum** industrial property; ~es **Einkommen** business income, operating (trading) profit, trading income, income from a business; ~e **Einnahmen** trading receipts; ~es **Erzeugnis** manufactured (industrial) product; ~es **Fahrzeug** commercial vehicle; ~e **Genossenschaft** industrial cooperative society; ~er **Güterverkehr** goods *(Br.)* (freight, *US*) traffic; ~er **Kraftwagenverkehr** road contractors (haulage); ~e **Kreditgenossenschaft** industrial finance company, cooperative bank; ~e **Niederlassung** commercial establishment; ~e **Nutzung** commercial use; ~e **Produktion** factory production; ~e **Räume** business (trade) premises; ~er **Rechtsschutz** protection of inventions (industrial property); ~e **Schiedsgerichtsbarkeit** industrial (trade) arbitration; ~e **Schutzmarke** industry (industrial) label; ~e **Schutzrechte** industrial property rights; ~e **Tätigkeit** industrial activity (employment, work), trade; ~es **Unternehmen** commercial enterprise; ~er **Verbrauch** industrial consumption; ~er **Verbraucher** industrial user, manufacturing consumer; ~es **Vermögen** industrial property; ~e **Verwertung** industrial use; ~e **Wirtschaft** manufacturing trade, trade and industry; ~er **Zweck** business purpose, industrial use; **zu ~en Zwecken** for commercial purposes.

gewerbsmäßig business, professional, on a commercial scale;
nicht ~ nonprofit;
etw. ~ betreiben to do s. th. for profit, to make a business out of s. th.;
~e **Hehlerei** receiving stolen goods; ~e **Unzucht** prostitution; ~er **Verkäufer** common seller.

Gewerkschaft trade (labor, *US*) union, *(Bergbau)* mining company;
keiner ~ angehörend nonunion;
staatlich anerkannte ~ registered trade union *(Br.)*; **für Tarifverhandlungen (als Tarifpartner) anerkannte** ~ certified union *(US)*; **Streikposten aufstellende** ~ picketing union; **bergrechtliche** ~ cost-book company *(Br.)*; **betriebsfremde** ~ outside union; **freie** ~ free trade union; **gelbe** ~ peaceful (yellow, *US*, company, *US*) union; **gesamtstaatliche** ~ national union; **konfessionelle** ~ denominational union; **ortsansässige** ~ resident union; **mehrere Berufsgruppen umfassende** ~ multicraft union; **unabhängige** ~ independent [union]; **wirtschaftliche** ~ peaceful (yellow, *US*) union;
~, **die jeden Arbeiter als Mitglied aufnimmt** open union *(US)*; ~ **Bau, Steine und Erden** [etwa] building union; ~ **öffentlicher Dienste** public service (servants' trade) union; ~ **Druck und Papier** [etwa] National Graphical Union *(Br.)*, print union; ~ **für Fach- und Führungskräfte, Büro- und Computerangestellte** Association of Professional, Executive, Clerical and Computer Staff *(Br.)*; ~ **der Filmangestellten** film workers' union; ~ **mit Mitgliedersperre** closed union *(US)*; ~, **die Mitgliedszwang für neu eintretende Betriebsangehörige durchgesetzt hat** modified-shop union;
einer ~ angehören to belong to a trade union; **aus der ~ ausschließen** to black up *(sl.)*; **aus der ~ austreten** to quit the union; **einer ~ als Mitglied beitreten** to join a union; ~ **gründen** to establish a union, to unionize; **sich zu einer ~ vereinigen** to unionize.

Gewerkschaftler [trade] unionist, union agent.

gewerkschaftlich [trade-]unionist;
~ **organisiert** unionized; **nicht ~ organisiert** nonunion;
sich ~ betätigen to be an active unionist; ~ **organisieren, sich ~ vereinigen** to unionize, to organize;
~er **Abstimmungsblock** trade-union block vote; ~ **organisierter Arbeiter** unionist worker; ~es **Ausbildungszentrum** trade-union training centre; ~es **Einverständnis** trade-union's agreement; ~e **Forderungen** union demands; ~e **Kampfmaßnahmen** union combative measures; ~e **Solidarität** union solidarity; ~e **Tätigkeit** union business; ~e **Vertretung** union representation; ~es **Vertretungsrecht** union jurisdiction; ~e **Zustimmung** trade-union approval; ~e **Zwangsveranstaltung** mandatory union meeting.

Gewerkschafts|abkommen union contract; ~**anerkennung** union recognition; ~**angehöriger** [trade] unionist, union man; ~**angestellter** union official (officer, *US*); ~**aufgaben** union duties; ~**ausschuß** [trade-]union (labor, *US*) committee, panel of trade unions, joint council; ~**austritt** union resignation; ~**ausweis** [union] card, pie card *(sl.)*; ~**bank** union (labour, *Br.*) bank; ~**beauftragter** shop steward; ~**beitrag** union contribution, union dues, subscription to a trade union, trade-union subscription, labo(u)r-union due; ~**bewegung** trade-union movement, unionism; ~**bezirk** union section; ~**bund** trade-unions congress *(Br.)*, Federation of Labor *(US)*; ~**büro** union office; ~**druck** union pressure; ~**einrichtung** union organization.

gewerkschaftsfeindlich antiunion, antilabo(u)r, unfair to union labo(u)r;
~e **Einstellung**, ~es **Verhalten** antiunion attitude, blackleggery *(Br.)*.

Gewerkschafts|feldzug union crusade; ~**finanzen** union finances; ~**forderungen** demands of labo(u)r, union demands (claims).

gewerkschaftsfreundlich pro-union, pro-labor *(US)*.

Gewerkschafts|führer [trade] union (labo(u)r) leader; ~**führung** union leadership; ~**funktionär** labo(u)r (trade) union official, union officer (organizer) *(US)*, walking delegate; ~**gefüge** trade-union structure; ~**gegner** antiunionist, nonunionist, nobill *(sl.)*; ~**gegnerschaft** nonunionism; ~**gelder** union funds; ~**geschichte** trade-union history; ~**gesetze** Trade-Union Acts; ~**gründer** union organizer; ~**gründung** trade-union formation; ~**haus** union building (headquarters); ~**institut** labo(u)r research association; ~**interessen** union interests; ~**kasse** union funds (treasury); ~**kongreß** union meeting (conference); ~**konkurrenz** union rivalry; ~**kreise** labo(u)r circles; ~**marke** *(an Waren)* union label.

Gewerkschaftsmitglied union member (man), unionist;
einfaches ~ rank-and-file member (unionist); **streikendes** ~ striking member;
Stimmen der ~er verlieren to lose the trade-union voice.

Gewerkschafts|mitgliedschaft union membership; **aufrechterhaltene ~mitgliedschaft als Beteiligungsvoraussetzung** maintenance of membership; ~**mittel** union funds; ~**monopol** union shop system *(US)*; ~**monopolabkommen** closed shop agreement *(US)*; ~**nachrichtendienst** union news service *(US)*; ~**organ** union publication; ~**organisation** labo(u)r organization *(US)*; ~**ortsverband** local trade council *(Br.)*, local *(US)*.

gewerkschaftspflichtiger Betrieb closed (union) shop.

Gewerkschafts|politik [trade-]union policy; **betriebliche ~politik** company labo(u)r policy; ~**presse** trade-union (labor, *US*) press; ~**rechte** union rights; ~**reform** labo(u)r reform; ~**reformgesetz** labo(u)r reform bill; ~**richtlinien** trade-union rules; **gegen die ~satzungen verstoßen** to blackleg *(Br.)*; ~**sekretär** trade-union secretary; ~**sieg** union victory; ~**solidarität** union solidarity; ~**sonderbeitrag** union assessment; ~**sprecher** union spokesman; **anerkanntes ~statut** approved trade-union rule book *(Br.)*; ~**stimmen verlieren** to lose the trade-union voice; ~**struktur** structure of trade unionism; ~**tätigkeit** trade-union activity; ~**tätigkeit in seinem Betrieb nicht zulassen** to keep a union out of one's plant; ~**umlagen** union assessments; ~**unterhändler** union negotiator; ~**verband** alliance *(Br.)*, national union *(US)*, federation of trade unions; **Amerikanischer ~verband** American Federation of Labor (AFL); **örtlicher ~verband** local *(US)*; ~**vereinbarung** union agreement.

Gewerkschaftsvereinigung [trade] unionism;
fachliche ~ industrial unionism; **Internationale** ~ International Federation of Trade Unions.

Gewerkschafts|vermittlung, ohne ~vermittlung handeln to go nonunion *(US)*; ~**vermögen** trade-union funds; ~**versammlung** union meeting; ~**vertreter** trade-union delegate, union representative (agent), walking (business) delegate, business manager (agent) *(US)*, local *(US)*; ~**vertreterwahl** union representative election; ~**vertretung** labo(u)r representation; ~**vorschriften** union regulations; **sich ~vorschriften unterwerfen** to unionize; ~**wesen** trade unionism, unionism *(US)*; **betriebliches ~wesen** industrial unionism; ~**zeitung** trade-union paper; ~**zugehörigkeit** trade- (labor, *US*) union affiliation, union membership, unionship; **zwangsweise ~zugehörigkeit** compulsory union membership.

Gewicht weight, *(Belastung)* load, *(Edelmetall)* troy weight, *(Einfluß)* authority, heaviness, *(fig.)* stress, *(Handelsgewicht)* avoirdupois;
nach ~ by weight (the ounce); **ohne** ~ weightless; **von geringem spezifischen** ~ light;
ausgeladenes (ausgeliefertes) ~ weight delivered weight; **äußerstes** ~ ultimate weight; **eingehendes** ~ inward weight; **nochmals ermitteltes** ~ reweigh; **falsche** ~e false weights; **fehlendes** ~ short weight; **einverständlich festgelegtes** ~ agreed weight; **frachtpflichtiges** ~ chargeable weight; **geeichtes** ~ stamped weight; **genaues** ~ true weight; **zu geringes** ~ weight under; **geschätztes** ~ estimated weight; **gesetzliches** ~ standard weight; **gleiches** ~ stamped weight; **handelsübliches** ~

commercial weight, avoirdupois; **höchstzulässiges ~** maximum permissible weight; **zu hohes ~** overweight, overload; **knappes ~** underweight; **lebendes ~** live weight; **zu leichtes ~** short weight; **ordentliches ~** regular weight; **reelles ~** full weight; **spezifisches ~** specific weight (gravity); **totes ~** dead weight; **volles ~** honest (full) weight; **zollpflichtiges ~** dutiable weight; **zulässiges ~** permissible weight;
~ der Ladung freight (shipping) weight; **Maße und ~e** weights and measures; **~ der Verpackung** weight of packing; **~ einer Zeugenaussage** gravity of a testimony;
einer Sache ~ beimessen to lay emphasis on s. th.; **kein ~ beimessen** to attach no importance to; **mit einem ~ belasten** to [load with] weight; **Papiere mit einem ~ beschweren** to keep papers down with a weight; **~ eichen** to gauge the weight; **ins ~ fallen** to count, to be of importance, to tip the scales; **nicht ins ~ fallen** to be of no importance; **gutes ~ geben** to give full weight; **großes ~ haben** to carry weight; **nicht das nötige (kein volles) ~ haben** to fall short of (be deficient in) weight; **wenig ~ haben** not to count for much; **nach dem ~ kaufen** to purchase by weight; **auf etw. ~ legen** to lay stress on s. th.; **Maße und ~e stempeln** to seal weights and measures; **~ überschreiten** to exceed the weight; **nach ~ verkaufen** to [sell by] weight; **sein ~ in die Waagschale werfen** to make one's authority felt.

gewichtig important, weighty, momentous, formidable, *(Münze)* of full (standard) weight;
~e Entscheidung momentous decision; **~e Miene aufsetzen** to assume an air of importance; **~e Persönlichkeit** influential person, person of weight, big shot *(coll.)*; **~e Rede** significant speech.

Gewichtigkeit ponderosity, importance, weightiness.

Gewichts|abgang loss in weight, underweight, shortage; **gewöhnlicher ~abgang und Schwund** trade losses; **~abnahme** decrease in weight; **zulässige ~abweichung** tolerance, remedy of weight, discrepancy in weight; **den ~anforderungen entsprechen** to make one's weight; **~angabe** declaration [of weight]; **falsche ~angabe** false report of weight, *(Spediteur)* false billing; **~aufschlag** additional weight, overweight; **~ausfall** underweight; **~bescheinigung** certificate of weight, weight certificate; **~beschränkungen** weight limitations; **~eichung** adjustment of weights; **~einheit** unit of weight, standard weight; **erste ~erhöhung** *(Post)* first weight step; **~fracht** dead weight; **~grenzen** weight limits; **~kontrolle** checking of (testing for) weight, *(Zoll)* test weighing; **~kontrolleur** check weigher *(Br.)*; **~losigkeit** weightlessness; **~manko** deficiency (shortage) in weight, weight deficiency, weight shortage; **~nota** weight note; **~porto** postage by weight; **~prüfung** testing for (checking of) weight; **~schwund** loss of weight, shrinkage; **~tabelle** table of weights; **~tonne** ton weight, freight ton; **englische ~tonne** long (gross, shipper's, shipping) ton; **~überschuß** excess (surplus) weight; **~unterschied** difference in weight; **~vergütung** tret; **~verlust** loss of weight, shortage, *(Flüssigkeit)* ullage, *(Münze)* shortness of weight; **~verlust auf dem Transport** loss in transit; **~verminderung** diminution in weight; **~zeugnis** certificate of weight; **~zoll** specific duty; **~zugabe, ~zuschlag** makeweight, additional weight, *(Gepäck)* excess luggage charge *(Br.)*; **~zunahme** increase in weight.

gewieft cunning, artful, clever, smart, sly;
~er Geschäftsmann shrewd (smart) businessman.

gewiegter Anwalt astute (Philadelphia, *US*) lawyer.

gewillkürt|e Erbfolge testamentary succession; **~es Treuhandverhältnis** express trust.

gewillt willing, prepared.

Gewinn profit, gain, gainings, getting, increment, *(Einkünfte)* emolument, spoil, *(Erfolg)* benefit, *(Ertrag)* receipts, proceeds, return, yield, produce, avails *(US)*, *(Ertrag aus Grund und Boden)* issue, *(gute Gelegenheit)* catch, bargain, market, *(aus Gewerbebetrieb)* profit, earnings, gain, *(Gewinnspanne)* [profit] margin, *(Kursgewinn)* increase, advance, gains, *(Lotterie)* prize, *(Nutzen)* advantage, account, fruit, *(Spekulation)* gain, *(Spiel)* winnings, *(Überschuß)* surplus;
auf ~ gerichtet with a view to profit, for pecuniary benefit, profitmaking, commercial; **auf gemeinschaftlichen ~ und Verlust gerichtet** on joint profit and loss; **mit ~** at a profit, profitably; **nicht auf ~ gerichtet** noncommercial, nonprofit[-making];
~ abwerfend paying, remunerative;
abgeführter ~ amount surrendered; **an konzernfremde Gesellschaften abgeführter ~** *(Bilanz)* mandatory profit distributions under agreement; **abgezweigter ~** profit set aside; **abrechnungspflichtiger ~** profit subject to accounting; **im Rechnungsabschnitt angefallener ~** accounting profit; **im Geschäft angelegter ~** retained earnings *(US)*, earnings ploughed *(Br.)* (plowed, *US*) back; **angemessener ~** fair return (profit), reasonable return; **angesammelte ~e** accumulated profits; **rapid ansteigende ~e** soaring profits; **auffallende ~e** striking gains; **auf die Abteilungen aufgeschlüsselter ~** departmental profit; **ausgeschüttete ~e** distributed profits; **nicht ausgeschütteter ~** undivided (undistributed, unappropriated) profit, retained earnings; **noch nicht ausgeschütteter ~** accumulated profits; **ausgewiesene ~e** reported profits; **ausgezahlter ~** *(Versicherung)* bonus in cash; **ausschüttungsfähiger ~** distributable earnings, profit available for appropriation, unappropriated earned surplus *(US)*; **außerordentlicher ~** nonrecurring profits; **beachtlicher ~** substantial gain; **steuerlich bereinigter (berichtigter) ~** adjusted profit; **auf Neubewertung beruhender ~** appreciated surplus; **besteuerungsfähiger ~** taxable gain; **betriebsbedingter ~** operating profit; **betriebsfremder ~** nonoperating profit; **betrügerische ~e** fraudulent gains; **buchmäßiger ~** book (accounting) profit; **dicker ~** fat profit; **echter ~** actual profit; **ehrliche ~e** honest profits; **einbehaltene ~e** undistributed profits, retained earnings *(US)*; **einmaliger ~** nonrecurring (banner) profit; **entfallender ~** attributable profit; **entgangener ~** ceasing (lost, prospective) profit, ceasing gain, lucrum cessans *(Latin)*; **nicht entnommener ~** retained income (earnings, profit) *(US)*, unwithdrawn (nondrawn) profit, profit ploughed (plowed, *US*) back; **aus Kapitalherabsetzungen entstandener ~** recapitalization surplus *(US)*; **im Liquidationszeitraum entstandene ~e** profits arising during a winding up; **ergaunerter ~** plunder *(sl.)*; **erheblicher ~** substantial gain; **erhoffter ~** anticipated profit; **zu erwartender (erwarteter) ~** prospective (anticipated) profit, lucrative interest; **aus Arbeit zu erwirtschaftender ~** profit derivable from work; **erzielter ~** realized (secured) profit, profit made; **beim Autoverkauf erzielter ~** profit on sale of a motor car; **an der Börse erzielte ~e** profits on exchange; **leicht erzielter ~** *(Börse)* velvet *(US)*; **tatsächlich erzielter ~** actual profit; **in Übersee erzielte ~e** overseas gains; **eventueller ~** contingent profit; **früherer ~** past earnings; **gelegentliche ~e** casual profits; **geringer ~** small profit; **gewerblicher ~** operating (industrial, commercial) profit; **glänzende ~e** booming profits; **glatter ~** clear profit; **unerwartet hoher ~** bonanza *(US)*; **imaginärer ~** expected profit; **inflationsbedingter ~** inflation-generated profit; **zur Ausschüttung kommender ~** distributable profit; **körperschaftssteuerpflichtige ~e** profits chargeable to corporation tax; **laufender ~** current earnings; **mäßiger ~** light (slight) profit; **mitgenommener ~** realized profit; **müheloser ~** easy profit; **optimaler ~** optimum profit; **realisierter ~** realized profit (revenue); **nicht realisierter ~** unrealized profit; **noch nicht realisierter ~** contingent profit; **unrealisierter rechnerischer ~** paper (calculated) profit; **reiner ~** net profit (avails, *US*); **rückständige ~e** back profits; **schwindende ~e** shrivel(l)ing profits; **sicherer ~** certain percentage; **stattlicher ~** handsome profit; **für die Aktionäre zur Verfügung stehender ~** profit attributable to shareholders *(Br.)* (stockholders, *US*); **zur Ausschüttung zur Verfügung stehender ~** distributable earnings, profit available for appropriation, unappropriated earned surplus *(US)*; **stehengelassener (stehengebliebener) ~** retained *(US)* (unrealized, left) profit, retained income *(US)*, profit ploughed *(Br.)* (plowed, *US*) back; **steigender ~** growing profit; **steuerpflichtiger ~** attributable profit before taxation, taxable (chargeable, assessable) profit, chargeable gain; **tatsächlicher (tatsächlich erzielter) ~** actual profit; **thesaurierter ~** accumulated (unappropriated) profit, profit retained *(US)*, retained earnings (profit, surplus), retained income, accumulated earnings; **überschießender (überschüssiger) ~** excess (surplus) profit, surplus income (profit); **unausgeschütteter ~** undistributed (undivided) profits, retained earnings; **unerlaubte ~e** illicit profits; **unerwarteter ~** windfall profit; **unlautere ~e** sordid gains; **unrealisierte ~e** paper profits; **unrechtmäßiger ~** illegal profit; **der Steuerpflicht unterliegende ~e** profits brought within the charge of tax, chargeable gains; **der Körperschaftssteuer unterworfene ~e** profits chargeable to corporation tax; **unverteilter ~** unappropriated [earned, *US*] surplus, undistributed (nondistributed) net profit *(Br.)*, undivided profit; **veranlagungspflichtiger ~** chargeable gain, profit brought within the charge of tax; **verfügbarer ~** available profit; **für die Dividendenausschüttung verfügbarer ~** unappropriated profit, unappropriated earned surplus *(US)*; **nach Rückstellung auf Rücklagekonto verfügbarer ~** net surplus *(US)*; **verkürzter ~** shave-off profit; **versteckter ~** hidden

(secret) profit; **zu versteuernder** ~ taxable profit (earnings); **versteuerter** ~ taxed profit; **zu verteilender** ~ distributable earnings; **verteilter** ~ distributed profit, appropriated surplus; **nicht verteilter (verwertbarer)** ~ accumulated profit, unappropriated [earned, *US*] surplus, surplus earnings *(US)*; **nicht verwendete** ~**e** unapplied profits; **vorgetragener** ~ accumulated profit, profit carried forward; **vorweggenommener** ~ anticipated bonus, deferred profit; **wesentliche** ~**e** material gains; **zugeflossene** ~**e** accrued profits; **den Rücklagen zugeführte (zugewiesene)** ~**e** *(Bilanz)* appropriated earnings *(US)*, earned surplus *(US)*, profit retained and added to reserve; **gesetzlich zugerechneter** ~ profit appendant; **vertraglich zugerechneter** ~ profit appurtenant; **nicht zugewiesener** ~ unappropriated profit; **zurechenbarer** ~ attributable profit; **zusätzlicher** ~ extra profit; **nicht zweckgebundener** ~ available (disposable) surplus; **einbehaltene** ~**e und Abschreibungen** retained cashflow; ~ **nach Abzug von Steuern** after-tax earnings (profit); ~ **vor Abzug von Steuern** pretax profit (earnings), earnings (profit) before tax; ~ **je Aktie** earnings per share (stock, *US*); ~ **vor Berücksichtigung der Steuern** pretax profit; ~ **aus Beteiligungen** investment profit, profit due from participation; ~ **aus Buchwerterhöhungen** appreciated surplus, surplus of appreciation; ~ **vor Fusionierung** profit prior to consolidation; ~**e im Geschäftsjahr** *(Versicherung)* underwriting (insurance) profits; ~**e aus einem nicht genehmigten Gewerbe** unlawful profits; ~ **aus Gewerbebetrieb** business profit; ~ **aus der Hauptbetriebstätigkeit** operating profit; ~ **bei Kalkulation zu Marktpreisen nach Abzug fälliger Steuern** current cost profit after deducting taxation payable; ~ **aus Kapitalanlagen** income from capital investment; ~ **je Kapitaleinheit** profitability ratio *(US)*; ~**e aus Monopolen** *(Bilanz)* profits from patents and secret processes *(Br.)*, monopoly profits *(US)*; ~ **aus Neubewertung** reappraisal surplus; ~ **aus Prägung von Scheidemünzen** minor coinage profit fund *(US)*; ~ **nach Steuern** profit after taxes; ~ **vor Steuern** pretax profit (earnings); ~ **aus Veräußerungen** sales profit; ~**e aus dem Verkauf von Anlagegütern** profits on the sale of fixed assets; ~ **und Verlust** profit and loss account, losings and winnings; ~ **vor Vornahme von Abschreibungen** profit before depreciation; ~ **nach Vortrag** *(Bilanz)* profit balance; ~**e aus Wertpapieranlagen** income from securities, investment income;

~ **abführen** to surrender a profit; **seinen** ~ **vom Wettbüro abholen** to collect one's winnings from the betting shop; **mit** ~ **abschließen** to show a profit; **Transaktion mit** ~ **abschließen** to make a profit out of a transaction; ~**e abschöpfen** to siphon (skim) off (cream away) profits; ~ **abwerfen** to leave (bring in, render, yield, return) profit, to leave a margin, to be profitable, to pay; **angemessenen** ~ **abwerfen** to yield a fair profit, to bring an adequate return; ~**e aktivieren** to capitalize profits; **mit** ~ **arbeiten** to operate (run) at a profit (in the black, *US coll.*), to be on a profitable basis, to work with good result; **wieder mit** ~ **arbeiten** to be back in the black *(US coll.)*; ~ **anteilsmäßig aufteilen** to prorate profits; ~ **untereinander aufteilen** to split the profit; ~ **aufweisen** to show profit; **seine** ~**e aufzehren** to eat up (improve away) one's profits; ~ **und Verlust durchschnittlich ausgleichen** to give and take, to average; ~ **ausschütten** to distribute a surplus, to divide profits; ~**e nachteilig beeinflussen** to hurt profits; ~ **beschneiden** to trim profits; **j. am** ~ **beteiligen** to give s. o. a share in the profits; **mit** ~ **betreiben** to be on a profitable basis, to operate profitably, to be in the black *(US coll.)*; **Bergwerk mit** ~ **betreiben** to work a mine at a profit; ~ **bringen (einbringen)** to be profitable, to show profit, to pay, to bring in, to yield a handsome profit; ~**e einkalkulieren** to compute profits; **unberechtigten** ~ **einstecken** to pocket a profit *(sl.)*; ~ **einstreichen** to reap a profit, to sweep the board; **gewaltige** ~**e einstreichen** to make huge profits; **unerlaubte** ~**e einstreichen** to make illicit profits, to pocket a profit *(sl.)*; ~ **entnehmen** to draw the profits; ~ **nicht entnehmen** to plough (plow, *US*) back earnings; ~ **ermitteln** to determine profit; ~ **erzielen** to realize (operate at, make) a profit, to come out of the red *(US coll.)*, to secure (draw) profits, to fetch a price; **angemessenen** ~ **erzielen** to turn a healthy profit; **anständige** ~**e erzielen** to make fair profits; **gute** ~**e erzielen** to realize large profits; **hohe** ~**e erzielen** to make huge profits; **10 Pfund** ~ **erzielen** to be ten pounds to the good; ~ **feststellen** to ascertain (determine) the profit; **Anteil am** ~ **haben** to have a share in the profit; **reinen** ~ **ergeben haben** to have netted; **bisher noch keinen** ~ **gemacht haben** to have produced zero profit to date; **nur geringen** ~ **von etw. haben** to get little out of it; **seine** ~**e niedrig halten** to hold down profits; **mit einem** ~ **herauskommen** *(Lotterie)* to win a prize; ~**e hochschrauben** to kick up earnings; ~ **kassieren** to lock in the profit; **dicke** ~**e kassieren** to mop profits; **unverhofft zu einem** ~ **kommen** to come into a windfall; **lukrative** ~**e buchungstechnisch in Steueroasen anfallen lassen** to book most of one's lucrative business through tax havens; **große** ~**e bei der letzten Wahl machen** to make large gains in the last election; ~ **mitnehmen** to take profits, to pick up bargains; ~**e realisieren** *(Börse)* to reap (realize, take) profits, to cash in; **mit** ~ **rechnen** to look to profit; ~**e scheffeln** to rake in profits; **am** ~ **beteiligt sein** to have an interest (share) in profits, to share in the profits; **geistiger** ~ **sein** to enrich one's mind; **ganzen** ~ **aufs Spiel setzen** to play on the velvet *(US)*; ~ **teilen** to share gains, to pool profits, to cut *(US sl.)*; **am** ~ **teilnehmen** to partake of the profits; ~ **thesaurieren** to retain the profit; ~ **und Verlust zu gleichen Teilen tragen** to go shares; ~**e transferieren** to repatriate (remit) profits; **sich von jem. ohne** ~ **und Verlust trennen** to break even with s. o.; **mit** ~ **verkaufen** to sell to advantage (at a profit), *(Wertpapiere)* to sell at a premium; ~ **verrechnen** to appropriate profits; **mit späteren** ~**en verrechnen** to carry forward long-term losses *(US)*; ~ **mit einem Verlust verrechnen** to set off a gain against a loss; ~**e verschleiern** to conceal profits; ~ **verteilen** to divide (distribute) the profits (proceeds); ~ **unter die Angestellten verteilen** to allocate the profit among the employees; **thesaurierte** ~**e für Investitionen verwenden** to retain profits for expansion; ~ **verzeichnen** *(Börse)* to post (record) gains; **kleine** ~**e verzeichnen** to register (show) small gains; **große** ~**e vorweisen** to exhibit large profits; **mit einem** ~ **winken** to hold forth hopes of profit; ~ **mit etw. erzielen wollen** to do s. th. for profit; **schnell** ~ **machen wollen** to be out for quick killing *(fam.)*; **großen** ~ **zeitigen** to result in a large profit; ~ **ziehen aus** to take advantage of, to benefit from, *(Lotterie)* to draw a prize; ~ **aus einem Geschäft ziehen** to make a profit on a transaction; **keinen bedeutenden** ~ **aus etw. ziehen** to extract no unusual profit from s. th.; ~**e steuerlich zurechnen** to allocate (attribute) profits;

~**abfall** profit drop, skid in profits; ~**abführung** surrender of profits, profit transfer; ~**abführungssteuer** excess profits tax; ~**abführungsvertrag** surrender-of-profits agreement; ~**abnahme** fall in profits.

Gewinnabrechnungsgemeinschaft *(Schiffahrt)* tonnage pool; ~ **im Passagierverkehr** passenger pool; ~ **für Verkehrseinnahmen** joint-purpose agreement *(Br.)*.

Gewinn|abschluß profit balance; ~**abschöpfung** taxing away (skimming off) excess profits; ~**abschöpfung vornehmen** to siphon (skim) off (cream away) profits; **in** ~**absicht** with a view (eye) to profit, for pecuniary benefit; ~**absichten** profit goals; ~**aktivierung** capitalization of profits; ~**analyse** surplus analysis, analysis of surplus; ~**anlagegeschäft** *(Börse)* pyramiding transaction; ~**ansammlung** accumulation of profits, *(Lebensversicherung)* surplus accumulation; ~**anspruch** profit claim, *(Aktionär)* dividend right; ~**anstieg** rise in (buildup of) profits; ~**anstieg nicht fortsetzen** to swerve off the road of profitable growth.

Gewinnanteil [profit] share, share of profit, percentage (share, quota, portion, slice) of profits, portion of the gain, royalty, *(AG)* dividend [share], *(Rückversicherung)* profit commission, *(Versicherung)* bonus, profit;
aufgeschobener ~ accumulation (deferred) dividend; **ausgezahlter** ~ bonus in cash; **betrügerischer** ~ rake-off *(US sl.)*; **rückständiger** ~ reversionary dividend; **vorweggenommener** ~ *(Lebensversicherung)* anticipated bonus;
~ **jedes Teilhabers** interest of each partner in a transaction;
~**e steuerlich auf ein bestimmtes Jahr aufteilen** to apportion part of the profits to a particular tax year; ~ **von 8% ausschütten** to make a distribution of 8%; **gleichen** ~ **haben** to participate equally in a transaction.

Gewinnanteils|festsetzung *(Versicherung)* bonus declaration; ~**plan** profit sharing plan; ~**schein** dividend warrant (coupon).

Gewinnaufschlag markup, markon *(US)*;
~ **auf die Herstellungskosten** cost-plus pricing; ~ **auf das Warenlager** inventory markup.

Gewinn|- und Verlustaufstellung earnings statement (report, *US*); ~**aufteilungsgenehmigung** *(Finanzamt)* apportionment clearance; ~**ausfall** lost profit, loss of earnings (profits); ~**ausfallversicherung** profit insurance; ~**ausgleich** *(Spediteur)* cross subsidization; ~**ausschließungsvereinbarung** nonprofit agreement.

Gewinnausschüttung division (distribution) of profit;
verdeckte ~ undisclosed channeling of profits, hidden profit distribution;
~ **in Form von Gratisaktien** property dividend.

Gewinnaussichten profit prospects (outlook, expectations);
gute ~ nap hand;
große ~ **haben** to be (play) on velvet *(US)*.
Gewinn|ausweis earnings (income, *US*) statement, trading report, corporate earnings report *(US)*; ~**basis** profitable (profit) basis; ~**begrenzung** limitation (ceiling) of profits; ~**belastung** surplus charge; ~**berechnung** calculation (computation, determination) of profit.
gewinnberechtigt participating, profit-sharing;
~ **sein** to partake the profits;
~**e Aktien** participating shares (stocks, *US*); **zusätzlich** ~**e Vorzugsaktien** participating preferred ordinaries.
Gewinn|bereich black *(US coll.)*; ~**berechtigung** participating rights.
Gewinnberichtigung reconciliation of surplus, surplus adjustment;
vorjährige ~**en** adjustment of prior year's profits.
Gewinnbeschränkung limitation (control, ceiling) of profits.
gewinnbeteiligt participating, profit-sharing;
nicht ~ *(Versicherungsnehmer)* nonparticipating;
~ **sein** to participate, to share in (partake of) profits;
~**e Versicherung** participating insurance; ~**e Versicherungspolice** participating policy.
Gewinnbeteiligung sharing of profit, profit (gain) sharing, share (interest) of profit, participation in profits, percentage, rake, *(Lebensversicherung)* investment income, special settlement dividend, stock premium, *(Vorstandsmitglied)* fringe benefit;
mit ~ *(Lebensversicherung)* with profits [endowment basis scheme]; **ohne** ~ *(Lebensversicherung)* nonparticipating;
aufgeschobene ~ deferred profit sharing; **unmittelbare** ~ immediate participation; **zusätzliche** ~ *(Lebensversicherung)* dividend addition;
~ **der Arbeitnehmer** employee profit sharing, employee participation in industry, co-partnership of labo(u)r, labo(u)r copartnership, industrial partnership, worker participation;
~ **einführen** to initiate (start) a profit scheme; **jds.** ~ **vermindern** to cut down s. one's profits.
Gewinnbeteiligungs|fonds profit-sharing fund (trust); ~**kartell** gross-money pool; ~**konto** profit-sharing account; ~**kosten** *(Lebensversicherung)* cost of dividends; ~**obligationen** profit-sharing bonds.
Gewinnbeteiligungsplan profit-sharing plan;
~ **für die Angestellten** staff bonus system;
steuerlich begünstigter ~ qualified stock plan; **steuerlich begünstigter** ~ **oder Pensionsplan** qualified plan (trust, stock, *US*);
~ **ins Leben rufen** to initiate a profit-sharing system.
Gewinnbeteiligungs|rechte participating rights; ~**system** *(Arbeitnehmer)* profit-sharing plan, bonus system, share acquisition scheme *(Br.)*, *(Lebensversicherung)* contribution plan, with profits scheme; ~**vereinbarung** profit agreement (arrangement), participation agreement; ~**vertrag** profit agreement (arrangement), gross-money pool, *(Versicherung)* participating contract; ~**vertrag abschließen** to set up a profit-sharing plan; ~**ziele** profit-sharing goals; ~**zulage** profit-sharing bonus.
Gewinn|betrag profit amount; ~**betrieb** profitable operation.
gewinnbezogen profit-orientated.
Gewinn|bilanz earnings (income, *US*) statement; ~**bonus** profit-sharing incentive.
gewinnbringend profitable, gainful, lucrative, profit-producing (-making), remunerative, revenue-earning, profit-earning, moneymaking, pay, paying, payable, advantageous;
~ **anlegen** to invest advantageously (one's money to good account);
~**e Anfangskurse** bargain basement prices; ~**e Anlage** paying (profitable) investment; ~**e Beschäftigung** gainful occupation; ~**es Geschäft** paying business; ~**e Kapitalanlage** remunerative investment, *(Landeszentralbank)* earning assets; ~**e Spekulation** profitable speculation; ~**es Unternehmen** profitable enterprise; **in** ~**er Weise** productive.
Gewinnchance chance (show) of winning, chance of success, fighting chance, *(Erträgnisse)* profit opportunity (chance), chance of profit, opportunity for gain;
mit guten ~**n** odds-on; **ohne** ~ unlikely to win;
jem. eine ~ **geben** to give s. o. the edge; ~**n verbessern** to shove up profits.
Gewinn|eigenschaft profit-making ability; ~**einbehaltung** retention of profits; ~**einbruch** profit slump; **erneuter** ~**einsatz** parlay.
gewinnen to win, to gain, to get, *(aus Altmaterial)* to salvage, to recover, *(Bergbau)* to mine, to acquire, to win, to extract, to obtain, *(verdienen)* to earn, to make, to net;
bei etw. ~ to make gains of; **j. für etw.** ~ to land s. o.; **j. für sich** ~ to bring s. o. into one's (obtain s. one's) interest, to make a conquest of s. o.; **j. zu etw.** ~ to get s. o. round;
Ansehen ~ to win a reputation; **j. zu seiner Ansicht** ~ to bring s. o. round to one's opinion; **jds. Aufmerksamkeit** ~ to attract s. one's attention; **Ausschuß für sich** ~ to be solid with a committee; **ganz anderes Aussehen** ~ to put a new complexion on a matter; **neue Bedeutung** ~ to take on a new meaning; **bei näherer Bekanntschaft** ~ to improve on closer acquaintance; **an Boden** ~ to gain ground; **j. zum Bundesgenossen** ~ to win s. o. over as an ally; **Einfluß** ~ to gain influence; **Einfluß auf j.** ~ to win upon s. o.; **Fahrt (Geschwindigkeit)** ~ *(Schiff)* to pick up (gather) speed; **allmählich Gestalt** ~ to be gradually taking shape; **haushoch** ~ to win hands down; **rasch die Herzen der Zuhörer** ~ to win one's audience over; **Krieg** ~ to win a war; **Kunden** ~ to acquire customers; **am Kurs** ~ to benefit by the exchange; **mit Leichtigkeit** ~ to win hands down; **in der Lotterie** ~ to draw a prize in a lottery; **öffentliche Meinung für sich** ~ to get the public on one's side; **jds. Mitarbeit** ~ to enlist s. o.; **Neuland** ~ to reclaim land, to break new ground; **Oberhand** ~ to gain the upper hand, to wax *(US)*; **Preis** ~ to win a prize; **Preisausschreiben** ~ to win a competition; **seinen Prozeß** ~ to gain one's cause, to recover in one's lawsuit; **10 Punkte** ~ *(Kurs)* to gain 10 points; **offene See** ~ *(Schiff)* to gain the open sea; **es über sich** ~ to find it in one's heart; **spielend** ~ to win hands down; **Stipendium** ~ to win a scholarship; **Ufer** ~ to reach the shore; **jds. Unterstützung** ~ to gain s. one's support; **am Verkauf eines Grundstücks** ~ to make a profit on the sale of a property; **Vorteil über j.** ~ to gain an advantage over s. o.; **Wahlen** ~ to win the elections;
Zeit zu ~ **suchen** to play for time.
gewinnend captivating, charming, attractive, engaging;
~**e Art haben** to have an engaging manner; **mit** ~**em Lächeln** with a charming smile.
Gewinnentnahme withdrawal of profits.
Gewinnentwicklung profit development, profit trend, performance of earnings;
bessere ~ pickup in profits;
~ **je Aktie** earnings per share.
Gewinner winner, gainer;
~ **einer Wahl** vote winner;
~ **sein** to be in the money (profits); **schließlich der** ~ **sein** to have the right end of the stick *(fam.)*; **sicherer** ~ **sein** to have the gain in one's hands; **auf den** ~ **setzen** to tip the winner.
Gewinn|ergebnis result; **sich in** ~**erhöhungen niederschlagen** to pay off in increased profits; ~**ermittlung** calculation (computation, determination) of profits; ~**ermittlung durch Betriebsvermögensvergleich** accrual method; ~**erosion** erosion of profits, profit erosion; ~**ertrag** increment[al] return, proceeds, profits; ~**erwartungen** profit expectations; **berechtigte** ~**erwartung** reasonable expectation of profit; **spekulative** ~**erwartungen** paper profits; ~**erzielung** making a profit, profit making, realization of profits; **zur** ~**erzielung** for the purpose of gain; ~**explosion** profit explosion; ~**faktor** profitable earner, profit maker, plus factor; **veränderliche** ~**faktoren** profit variables *(US)*; ~**feststellung** ascertainment of profits; ~**feststellungsbescheid** *(Firma)* notice of assessment, assessment notice; ~**fonds aus der Prägung von Scheidemünzen** minor coinage profit fund *(US)*.
gewinnförderndes Element profit builder.
Gewinn|formel winning formula; ~**garantie** profit guarantee; ~**garantievertrag** profit-guaranteeing contract; ~**gemeinschaft** profit-pooling agreement, pooling of profits, pool; ~**größen** profit variables *(US)*; ~**gutschriftssystem** *(Lebensversicherung)* reversionary bonus plan; **schwaches** ~**jahr** year of small profits; ~**kalkulation** calculation (computation) of profits; ~**klassifizierung** classification of profits; ~**konjunktur** boom, prosperity; ~**konto** profit account, *(Betriebsgewinn)* earned-surplus account *(US)*, *(Kapitalgewinn)* capital surplus account; **auf** ~- **und Verlustkonto buchen** to pass to profit and loss account; ~**kontrolle** profit control; ~**kürzung** curtailment of profits; ~**lage** earnings base, profit situation; ~**liste** list of awards, prize list; ~**los** winning (drawing) number; ~**los ziehen** to draw the winner.
Gewinn|marge profit margin, margin of profit; ~**marge beschneiden** to cut into profits; ~**margen auf ein Minimum reduzieren** to pare margins to the bone; ~**maximierung** maximization of profit, profit planning.
gewinnmindernd rent- (profit-) reducing.

Gewinn | minimum marginal profit; ~**mitnahme** revenue realization, *(Börse)* profit taking; **große** ~**mitnahme** scoop; ~**möglichkeit** profit opportunity (potentiality), opportunity for gain; ~**motiv** profit-seeking motive; ~**nummer** *(Lotterie)* winning number; ~**obligationen** participating (income, *US*, reorganization, *US*) bonds, participating debentures, profit bonds *(US)*; ~**optimismus** optimism on profits.

gewinnorientiert profit-centered, profit-motivated.

Gewinn | orientierung profit orientation; ~- **und Verlustperiodenrechnung** income statement *(US)*; ~**plan** *(Lebensversicherung)* flat bonus system; ~**planung** profit planning, projection of profit; ~**planziel** profit target; ~**pooling** pooling of profits *(US)*, profit pooling; ~**position beibehalten** to stay profitable; ~**posten** surplus item; ~**potential** profit potential.

Gewinnprämie, aufgeschobene deferred bonus; **vorweggenommene** ~ anticipated bonus.

Gewinn | prognose profit forecast; ~**projektion** projection of profits, profit projection; ~**prozentsatz** current yield; ~**quote** profit share, *(Toto)* dividend; **volkswirtschaftliche** ~**quote** capital's share; ~**rate** rate of profit (gain); **umfangreichen** ~**realisationen unterworfen sein** to come in for heavy liquidations; ~**realisierung** realization of profit, income (revenue) realization, *(Börse)* profit taking; **sich steuerlich kräftig auswirkende** ~**realisierungen** bunched gains.

Gewinnrechnung profit (surplus, *US*) account;
Kapital- und ~ capital and surplus *(US)*.

Gewinn- und Verlustrechnung profit and loss account, operating statement *(US)*, statement of revenue and expenditure (of profit and loss, *US*), statement of income *(US)*, income (earnings) statement *(US)*;
konsolidierte ~ consolidated profit and loss (income, *US*, earnings) statement, consolidated profit and loss account, consolidated statement of earnings *(US)*; **vergleichende** ~ comparative income statement *(US)*; **mit Prüfungsvermerk versehene** ~ audited statement; **zusammengesetzte** ~ cumulative profit and loss *(US)*;
~ **in Kontoform** single-step income statement; ~ **in Staffelform** reducing-balance (statement) form; ~ **mit Vergleichszahlen aus dem Vorjahr** comparative income statement *(US)*;
~ **genehmigen** to approve profit and loss accounts.

Gewinn | rezession recession in profits; ~**rückgang** drop-off (drop, fall) in profits (earnings), profit decline (dip, drop), profit squeeze; **rasanter** ~**rückgang** profit slide; ~**rücklage** retained income, appropriated (earned) surplus *(US)*, surplus reserve; ~**rücklage für Erweiterungsinvestitionen bilden** to retain profit for expansion; ~**rücklagen für Forschungszwecke einsetzen** to plough *(Br.)* (plow, *US*) back profits into research; ~**rückstellung** surplus reserve, ploughing *(Br.)* (plowing, *US*) back of earnings, appropriated (earned, *US*) surplus *(US)*; ~**saldo** profit balance; ~- **und Verlustsammelkonto** profit and loss summary account; ~**satz** rate of gain (profit); ~**schätzung** estimate of profits; ~**schrumpfung** profit shrinkage, diminution of profits; ~**schuldverschreibungen** participating (income) bonds *(US)*, participating (income) debentures *(Br.)*, parliamentary debentures, reorganization bonds *(US)*.

Gewinnschwelle pay-off stage, break-even point, profitability level, profitable basis;
~ **erreichen** to be on a profitable basis, to come out of the red *(US coll.)*; ~ **beinahe erreichen** to break even; ~ **noch nicht erreicht haben** to be still in the red *(US coll.)*; ~ **wieder erreicht haben** to get back into profit, to be back in the black *(US coll.)*; ~ **überschritten haben** to be on a profitable basis (in the black, out of the red, *US coll.*); ~ **überschreiten** to turn the profit corner.

Gewinn | schwellendiagramm break-even chart; ~**sicherung** profit taking; **disproportionale** ~**situation** leveraged position; **verbesserte** ~**situation** improvement in profits; ~**situation der Unternehmer** corporate earnings *(US)*.

Gewinnspanne margin of profit, profit margin;
enge (geringe) ~ narrow margin line; **geringste** ~ small spread; ~ **nach Begleichung der Steuern** post-tax margin of profit; ~ **vor Steuerabzug** pretax margin of profit;
zu niedrige ~ **haben** to cut one's profit too fine.

Gewinn | spitze maximum profit; ~**steigerung** profits rise, earnings growth; ~**steuer** profits tax *(Br.)*; ~**streben**, ~**sucht** profit motive, private advantage, profit-seeking, pursuit of profit, greed for profits (of gain), acquisitiveness; **aus** ~**sucht** with an eye to profit, for pecuniary benefit, mercenarily.

gewinnsüchtig acquisitive, profit-seeking, greedy of gain;
in ~**er Absicht** with an eye to profit, for pecuniary benefit, mercenarily.

Gewinn | teile steuerlich auf ein bestimmtes Jahr aufteilen to apportion part of profits to a particular tax year; ~**teil zurücklegen** to reserve a part of the profit; ~**teilung** pooling of profits, profit pooling (sharing); ~**thesaurierung** accumulation (retention) of profits.

gewinnträchtig profit-bearing, big-time.

Gewinn | träger profit[able) earner; ~**transfer** repatriation (remittance) of profits; ~**trend** profitability (profit) trend; ~**überschuß** surplus, surplus profit *(US)*; **den allgemeinen Rücklagen zugewiesener** ~**überschuß** surplus transferred to general reserves, appropriated (earned) surplus *(US)*; ~**überschußkonto** surplus account; ~**übersicht** earnings *(US)* (surplus) statement, statement of earned surplus *(US)*; ~-**Umsatzverhältnis** *(Aktienbewertung)* profit margin *(US)*.

Gewinnung *(Bodenschätze)* winning, production, extraction, *(Förderung)* output, *(Neuland)* reclamation;
~ **von Bodenschätzen** mineral extraction; ~ **von Nebenprodukten** recovery of by-products.

Gewinnungs | anlage extracting plant; ~**kosten** production cost.

Gewinn | verband *(Pensionsplan)* experience rating; ~**verbesserung** profit improvement; ~**verdeckung** profit squeeze; ~**vergleich** earnings comparison; **zeitlich verlagerte** ~**vergütungen** deferred compensation plan *(US)*; ~**verhältnis** profit ratio; ~**verheimlichung** concealment of profits; ~**verknappung** profit pinch; ~**verlegung** shift of earnings; ~**verlust** loss [of profit], sacrifice, loss of earnings; ~**verlustversicherung** loss of profits insurance; ~**verschleierung** concealment of profits; ~**verteilung** division (distribution) of profits, repartition, dispersion of profits; ~**verteilung vornehmen** to divide profits.

Gewinnverteilungs | kartell gross-money pool; ~- **und Verlustverteilungskonto** profit and loss appropriation account; ~**schlüssel ändern** to change the allocation of profit; ~- **und Verlustverteilungsschlüssel** profit and loss sharing ratio; ~**vorschlag** proposed appropriation of profits.

Gewinnverwendung appropriation of funds (profits).

Gewinnverwendungs | aufstellung, ~**rechnung** earnings (earned surplus) statement *(US)*, statement of retained earnings *(US)*; ~**rücklage** retained income, unappropriated [earned, *US*] surplus.

Gewinn | voraussage machen to spot the winner in a race; ~**vorschau** earnings estimate, profits projection (forecast); ~**vortrag** unappropriated balance, undistributed (undivided) profits, reserved surplus, accumulated income (earnings, profit, surplus) *(US)*, profit carryforward, surplus brought forward *(US)*; ~**vortrag aus dem Vorjahr** profit brought forward from the previous year; ~**vortragskonto** retained earnings account *(US)*; ~**vortragsrechnung** statement of earned surplus (retained earnings) *(US)*; ~**vorwegnahme** *(Börse)* discounting of earnings; ~**zahlen** profit figures, *(Lotterie)* winning numbers; ~**ziehung** drawing of prizes; ~**ziffern** profit figures.

Gewinnzone *(Bilanz)* profitable basis, break-even point, black *(US coll.)*;
in der ~ in the black *(US coll.)*;
wieder in die ~ **bringen** to bring back into the black *(US coll.)*; **Unternehmen in die** ~ **führen** to boost a company into the black *(US coll.)*; **in der** ~ **sein** to be in the black *(US coll.)*, to break even.

Gewinn | zunahme advance in profits, earnings growth; ~**zurechnung** *(Körperschafts-, Einkommensteuer)* allocation (attribution) of profits; ~**zuschlag** markup; ~**zuteilung** bonus distribution; ~**zuwachs** earnings (profit) growth, advance in profits; ~**zuwachssteuer** increment income tax; **zu** ~**zwecken** for purpose of gain.

Gewinnst winnings;
schönen ~ **machen** to get a fine haul.

Gewirr enger Gassen maze of narrow streets.

Gewissen conscience;
nach bestem ~ to the best of one's belief; **vom** ~ **gepeinigt** pursued by remorse;
elastisches ~ wide (lax) conscience; **gutes** ~ clear conscience; **schlechtes** ~ guilty conscience; **soziales** ~ social conscience; **weites** ~ elastic conscience;
~ **beeinflussen** to work upon the conscience; **sein** ~ **befragen** to examine one's conscience; ~ **erheblich belasten** to lie heavy on one's conscience; **sein** ~ **beruhigen (entlasten)** to clear (ease) one's conscience; **sein** ~ **erforschen** to ransack one's conscience; **sein** ~ **erleichtern** to unburden one's conscience, to relieve one's mind; **seinem** ~ **folgen** to obey the dictates of one's conscience, to make it a matter of conscience; **sich von seinem** ~ **beunruhigt fühlen** to feel the pricks of conscience; **schlechtes**

~ **haben** to have a guilty conscience; **schlechtes ~ wegen seiner geringen Hilfeleistung haben** to feel rather mean for not helping more; **schwer auf jds. ~ lasten** to lie heavy on s. one's conscience; **jem. ernst ins ~ reden** to make a heart-felt appeal.
gewissenhaft conscentious, earnest, nice, *(übergenau)* painstaking, scrupulous;
~ sein to be conscientious, to have a tender conscience;
~er Gelehrter exact scholar; **~er Mensch** painstaker; **~e Untersuchung** thorough examination.
gewissenlos unscrupulous, ruthless, unprincipled;
an jem. ~ handeln to treat s. o. unscrupulously.
Gewissens|belastung load on one's conscience; **~bisse** remorse, worm (pangs, qualms, twinge) of conscience; **von ~bissen geplagt** conscience-smitten; **~frage aus etw. machen** to make s. th. a matter of conscience; **aus ~gründen** on grounds of conscience, for conscience sake; **Wehrdienst aus ~gründen ablehnen** to be a conscientious objector; **~klausel** conscience clause; **~konflikt** conflict of conscience; **~not** moral dilemma; **~pflicht** moral duty; **~prüfung** self-examination; **~qual** agony of remorse; **unter ~zwang handeln** to act under moral constraint.
gewissermaßen in a way, to a certain extent, so to speak.
Gewißheit, absolute dead certainty.
Gewitter thunderstorm, thunder and lightning, lightning storm; **häusliches ~** domestic storm;
wie ein reinigendes ~ wirken to clear the air, to reduce the tension;
~bildung formation of a thunderstorm; **~bö** squall, thundergust *(US)*; **~front** thundery front; **~herd** storm center; **~neigung** thundery tendency; **~schauer** thundershower; **~schwüle** sultriness; **~stimmung** thundery atmosphere, *(fig.)* explosive atmosphere; **in ~stimmung sein** to be in a black mood; **~störung** perturbation, atmospheric disturbances, atmospherics; **~sturm** thunderstorm; **~- und Sturmschadensversicherung** storm and tempest insurance; **~wolken** thunderclouds, *(fig.)* storm clouds.
gewittrig thundery.
gewitzter Bursche smart (bright) fellow.
gewogen weighted, *(fig.)* fond, attached to, favo(u)rably inclined towards;
jem. nicht ~ sein to have no liking for s. o.; **~ und zu leicht befunden werden** to be weighed and found wanting;
~er Mittelwert mean average; **~er Preisindex** weighted price index.
Gewogenheit favo(u)rable attitude, favo(u)r.
gewöhnen, sich an Disziplin to accustom o. s. to discipline; **sich an eine Fremdsprache ~** to familiarize o. s. with a foreign language; **Kinder an Pünktlichkeit ~** to get children used to punctuality; **sich an ein Klima ~** to acclimatize o. s.
Gewohnheit habit, custom, use, usage, consuetude, practice;
aus ~ from habit; **ganz gegen seine ~** contrary to one's usual habit; **nach ~ und Vermutung** habit and repute *(Scot. law)*; **althergebrachte ~en** old customs; **eingefleischte ~** institution *(coll.)*; **eingewurzelte ~** confirmed habits; **feste ~** fast (regular) habit; **müßige ~** inactive habits; **üble ~en** evil courses;
von einer festen ~ abgehen to depart from a custom, to discontinue a habit; **~ ablegen** to get out of (outgrow) a habit; **schlechte ~en annehmen** to fall (lapse, get, glide) into bad habits; **~ aufgeben** to grow out of a habit; **~ zum Gesetz erheben** to erect a custom into law; **außer ~ kommen** to fall into decay; **es zur ~ werden lassen** to make a habit of it; **~ daraus machen** to make a practice of it, to make it one's practice; **etw. aus reiner ~ tun** to do s. th. by sheer force of habit.
Gewohnheitsdieb common thief.
gewohnheitsmäßig usual, customary, habitual, routine, mechanical, consuetudinary;
etw. rein ~ tun to do s. th. by sheer force of habit.
Gewohnheits|mensch creature of habit, routinist; **~mißbrauch** habitual effects of an abuse.
Gewohnheitsrecht legal custom *(US)*, unwritten (tacit, consuetudinary, *US*, customary) law, *(ersessenes Recht)* prescriptive right;
durch ~ begründet authorized by usage;
internationales ~ customary international law; **kaufmännisches ~** commercial (mercantile) custom, custom of the trade (of merchants);
~ zum Gesetz erheben to erect a custom into law.
gewohnheitsrechtlich conventional, customary.
Gewohnheits|sache matter of habit, matter of knack; **~tier** creature of habit; **~trinker** confirmed (habitual, common) drunkard, habitual drinker; **~unrecht** *(fig.)* sanction of custom; **~verbrecher** habitual (common) criminal, habitual persistent offender *(US)*, outlaw, rounder *(US sl.)*; **~verbrechergesetz** Prevention of Crimes Act; **~wetter** betting man.
gewöhnlich habitual, customary, ordinary, usual, medium, *(vulgär)* common, vulgar, trivial;
ausgesprochen ~ downright common;
~er Akzent common accent; **~er Aufenthaltsort** habitual residence; **~e Ausdrücke gebrauchen** to be vulgar of speech; **~e Beschäftigung** usual occupation; **~er Bruch** vulgar fraction; **in ~er Fracht** paying freight as customary; **~e Korrespondenzschrift** small hand; **im ~en Leben** in everyday life; **~er Soldat** private; **unter ~en Umständen** in the ordinary course of events.
gewohnt usual, customary, habitual, *(vertraut)* familiar;
in ~er Weise in the usual way; **zur ~en Zeit** at the usual time.
gewöhnt accustomed;
sich an etw. ~ haben to have grown used to s. th.
Gewöhnung habituation.
Gewölbe, feuerfestes fireproof vault; **unterirdisches ~** undercroft.
gewonnen|es Spiel haben to be almost home and dry; **bei jem. ~es Spiel haben** to have s. o. eating out of one's hand; **jds. Vertrauen ~ haben** to be in s. one's confidence;
wie ~ so zerronnen that lightly come, lightly go.
Gewühl cram, crowd, throng;
im ~ der Menge in the milling crowd;
dichtes ~ crush.
gewunden winding, twisting, tortuous;
sich ~ ausdrücken to express o. s. in a roundabout way.
gewünscht, wie as required, in accordance with your wishes.
gezähmt tame.
gezeichnet drawn, *(Anleihe)* subscribed, *(unterschrieben)* signed;
nicht ~ undrawn; **richtig ~** in drawing; **voll ~** fully subscribed;
~ und unterschrieben marked and numbered.
Gezeichneter marked man.
Gezeiten tides;
~hafen tidal harbo(u)r; **~kraftwerk** tidal power station; **~marke** tidemark; **~messer** tidal gauge; **~rechner** tide predictor; **~tafel** tide table, time table; **~verspätung** retardation of the tide; **~wasser** tide waters; **~wechsel** change of the tide.
Gezeter clamo(u)r, scolding, nagging.
gezielt well-aimed, selective;
~e Absatzpolitik selective selling; **~e Investitionspolitik** ad-hoc investment policy; **~e Steuersenkungen** selective tax reductions; **~e Werbung** direct (selective) advertisement (advertising).
geziemen, sich für j. to befit s. o.
geziemend due, appropriate, beseeming, befitting, decorous;
~ von der Verlobung seiner Tochter Nachricht geben to be happy to announce the engagement of one's daughter; **j. ~ von etw. in Kenntnis setzen** to inform s. o. respectfully of s. th.
geziert prim, namby-pamby, pretty;
~ sprechen to be mealy-mouthed; **~ tun** to prim o. s. up.
Geziertheit primness, niminy-piminess.
gezogen *(Los)* drawn;
~er Wechsel draft, drawn bill.
Gezogener *(mil.)* enlistee, inductee *(US)*.
gezwungen under constraint (compulsion) constrained, forced;
sich ~ benehmen to behave stiffly; **zu etw. ~ sein** to be under the necessity of doing s. th.;
~e Höflichkeit forced politeness.
gezwungenermaßen willy-nilly, under duress.
Ghetto ghetto;
~bewohner ghetto resident; **~bezirk** ghetto area.
Ghostwriter ghostwriter, ghost.
Gicht|eines Hochofens throat of a furnace;
~bühne top gallery.
Giebel gable;
~haus gabled house.
gieren *(mar.)* to yaw.
gierig greedy, voracious, gluttonous;
Angebot ~ annehmen to accept an offer with alacrity, to jump at an offer; **neue Ideen ~ in sich aufnehmen** to absorb new ideas eagerly; **~ essen** to eat greedily, to gulp down; **nach Neuigkeiten ~ sein** to be eager for news; **neuen Kriminalroman ~ verschlingen** to devo(u)r a new detective novel;
mit ~en Augen with covetous eyes.
Gierung *(fig.)* yaw.
Gießbett pig bed.
gießen to pour, *(in Form)* to mold, to mould, to cast;
sich einen hinter die Binde ~ to wet one's whistle; **Öl auf die Wogen ~** to pour oil on troubled waters; **in Strömen ~** to be raining cats and dogs.

Gießer mo(u)lder.
Gießerei foundry;
~**industrie** foundry industry.
Gießkanne watering can.
Gießkannenprinzip, Subventionen nach dem ~ verteilen to give everyone a slice of the budget.
Gift poison;
schleichendes ~ slow poison;
~ beibringen to administer poison; **~ nehmen** to take poison; **~ und Galle spucken** to fume and rage; **jem. ~ verabreichen** to give s. o. a dose of poison; **sein ~ verspritzen** to spit venom; **darauf kannst du ~ nehmen** you can bet your life on it;
~**becher** death cup; ~**beibringung** administering poison.
giften, sich über etw. to make one's blood boil.
Giftgas [poison] gas;
~ verwenden to apply poison gas.
giftig poisonous, *(fig.)* venomous, malicious, vicious;
j. ~ anfahren to spit in s. one's face; **j. ~ ansehen** to look at s. o. daggers drawn; **~ auf j. sein** to be cross with s. o., to have a spite against s. o.; **plötzlich ~ werden** to suddenly turn nasty;
~**e Bemerkung** spiteful remark; ~**e Kritik** vicious (venomous) criticism; ~**e Kröte** *(fig.)* spiteful creature; ~**e Wirkung** toxic effect.
Gift|mischer preparer of poison, *(fig.)* scandalmonger; **sich als ~mischer gegen j. betätigen** to make a scurrilous attack on s. o.; ~**mord** poisoning; ~**mörder** poisoner; ~**schlange** *(fig.)* viper; ~**schrank** *(Apotheke)* poison cabinet, *(Bibliothek)* collection of immoral books; ~**stoff** toxicant; ~**trank** poison; ~**zwerg** spiteful creature, wasp.
gigantisch colossal, giant, gigantic, enormous.
Gigolo gigolo, poodle-faker *(sl.)*, mover.
Gilde guild, corporation, fellowship (guild) trade, company;
~**n und Zünfte** city companies *(City of London)*.
Gimpel ninny, easy mark (victim) *(sl.)*, fool, simpleton, deadhead *(sl.)*, pigeon *(sl.)*.
Gipfel peak, pitch, top, summit, climax, apex, pinnacle, height, altitude, high tide, pink, tiptop;
auf dem ~ seiner Laufbahn at the height of one's career; **auf dem ~ seiner beruflichen Möglichkeiten** at the top of the tree (ladder);
~ des Ehrgeizes height of ambition; **~ der Höflichkeit** pink of politeness; **~ des Ruhms** pitch of greatness; **~ der Vollendung** prime of perfection;
~ erreichen to top the hill, to win the summit; **~ des Ruhms erreicht haben** to be at the height of one's glory;
das ist der ~ that is the limit!, that beats everything (tops the lot);
~**abkommen** summit agreement; **wirtschaftliche ~diplomatie** economic summitry; ~**ebene** summit level; **absolute ~höhe** absolute ceiling; ~**konferenz** top-level (-notch, -flight, summit) conference; ~**konferenz für Wirtschaftsfragen** economic summit; ~**konferenzteilnehmer** summiteer; ~**leistung** peak performance; ~**politik** summitry; ~**punkt** peak, point, *(Karriere)* culminating point; **auf dem ~punkt** culminant; ~**punkt des Ruhms** highest point of glory; ~**stürmer** pyramid climber; ~**treffen** summit meeting; ~**verhandlungen** summit talks.
Gips plaster, gypsum;
gebrochenes Bein in ~ legen to put a broken leg in plaster;
~**abguß** plaster cast; ~**decke** stucco ceiling; ~**verband** plaster bandage.
Giralgeld credit currency (money), bank money *(US)*, fiduciary (fiat, current account) money *(US)*, money in account *(Br.)*, deposit money *(Br.)* (currency, *US*);
sekundäres ~ derivative deposit;
~**schöpfung** creation of means of payment, creation of bank credit (deposits) *(Br.)*; ~**schöpfungsmultiplikator** credit multiplier.
Girant indorser, endorser;
späterer ~ subsequent endorser (indorser);
~ aus Gefälligkeit accommodation endorser (indorser); **~ ohne Verbindlichkeit** qualified endorser (indorser);
sich beim ~en erholen to have recourse to the endorser (indorser) of a note.
Girat endorsee, indorsee.
girierbar endorsable, indorsable, negotiable, transferable by endorsement.
girieren to endorse, to indorse, to place an endorsement (indorsement);
blanko ~ to endorse (indorse) in blank; **voll ~** to endorse (indorse) in full.
Girierfähigkeit capacity to endorse (indorse).
giriert endorsed, indorsed;
blanko ~ endorsed (indorsed) in blank; **ordnungsgemäß ~** duly endorsed (indorsed);
~**er Wechsel** indorsed bill.
Girierung endorsement, indorsement;
~ eines Schecks indorsement of a cheque *(Br.)* (check, *US*).
Girlande garland, festoon, wreath;
mit ~n bekränzen (schmücken) to string with festoons, to festoon.
Giro endorsement, indorsement, *(Übertragung)* assignment, transfer;
mit ~ versehen endorsed, indorsed; **ohne ~** unendorsed, unindorsed;
~ bestätigt endorsement (indorsement) confirmed; **~ fehlt** endorsement (indorsement) required; **~ ungenau** endorsement (indorsement) irregular;
bedingtes ~ *(Br.)* conditional endorsement (indorsement); **beschränktes ~** restrictive (qualified) endorsement (indorsement), conditional indorsement; **fehlendes ~** lack of endorsement (indorsement); **gewöhnliches ~** regular endorsement (indorsement); **offenes ~** blank endorsement (indorsement); **unbeschränktes ~** absolute endorsement (indorsement); **volles ~** direct indorsement;
~ einer Bank bank indorsement; **~ ohne Verbindlichkeit** endorsement (indorsement) without recourse, qualified indorsement;
durch ~ übertragen to transfer by endorsement (indorsement); **mit ~ versehen** to endorse, to indorse; **~ verweigern** to refuse to back a bill; **durch ~ zurückgeben** to endorse (indorse) back;
~**abschnitt** bank slip; ~**abteilung** check (cheque, giro, *Br.*) (clearing) department; ~**anweisung** transfer order *(Br.)*; ~**ausgleichsstelle** clearinghouse; ~**bank** deposit clearing (transfer) bank, bank of circulation, clearing (cheque) bank *(Br.)*; ~**bestätigung** confirmation of indorsement; ~**buch** passbook; ~**einlagen** [clearing-bank] deposits; ~**fälschung** forged endorsement (indorsement); ~**geschäft** [business of] clearing; ~**gläubiger** bill creditor; ~**guthaben** credit (current account) balance *(US)*; ~**guthaben der Wirtschaft** private sector current bank accounts; ~**kasse** clearinghouse; ~**konto** drawing *(US)* (checking, cheque, *Br.*, giro) account, account current *(US)*, clearing (running, transfer) account; ~**konto bei der Landeszentralbank** Federal Reserve Bank account *(US)*; ~**konto besitzen** to hold a Giro (drawing, checking) account; ~**kontor** clearinghouse; ~**kunde** checking account depositor, current account customer *(US)*; ~**kundschaft** clearing bank customers; ~**obligo** contingent liability of bills discounted; ~**provision** transfer commission; ~**rechnung** drawing (checking) account; ~**sammeldepot**, ~**sammelverwahrung** collective (omnibus) deposit; ~**scheck** clearinghouse check *(US)* (cheque, *Br.*); ~**stelle** clearinghouse; ~**stempel** transfer (indorsement) stamp; ~**system** clearinghouse (check, *US*) system; ~**überweisung** bank (credit) transfer, bank giro *(Br.)*; ~**verband** clearinghouse association; ~**verbindlichkeit** indorser's liability; ~**verbindlichkeiten** *(Bilanz)* liabilities on account of endorsements, contingent liabilities on bills discounted *(Br.)*; **aus ~verbindlichkeiten schulden** to be contingently indebted; ~**verkehr** transfer business, [business of] clearing, clearinghouse business, clearing (clearinghouse) system; **allgemeiner ~verkehr** general clearing; ~**verkehr durch die Post** National Girobank services available at post offices; ~**vertrag** clearing agreement; ~**wesen** cheque system *(Br.)*, clearinghouse business; ~**zahlung** bank transfer; ~**zentrale** clearinghouse *(Br.)*; ~**zettel** bank slip; ~**zusätze** additions to indorsement.
Gitter lattice, trellis, grating, *(el.)* grid, *(vor Kamin)* fender, guard, *(Landkarte)* grid, *(Zaun)* fence, railings;
hinter ~n sitzen to be behind bars;
~**fenster** lattice; ~**netz** *(Landkarte)* grid; ~**netzkarte** gridded map; ~**tür** lattice; ~**vorspannung** *(el.)* bias; ~**werk** grating.
Glacehandschuhe kid gloves;
j. mit ~n anfassen to handle s. o. with kid gloves, to give s. o. kid-glove treatment; **j. nicht gerade mit ~n anfassen** to handle s. o. without gloves.
Glanz shine, gloss, lustre, shine, dazzle, varnish, *(Edelstein)* brilliance;
im vollen ~ ihrer Schönheit in the full radiance of her beauty; **äußerer ~** outward splendo(u)r; **falscher ~** veneer; **metallischer ~** metallic lustre (luster); **verschwundener ~** vanished glory;
~ des Goldes shine of gold; **~ des Hofes** splendo(u)r of the court;

Prüfung mit ~ bestehen to do brilliantly in an examination; **mit ~ und Gloria durchfallen** to come a cropper, to flunk; **j. mit ~ und Gloria hinausschmeißen** to chuck s. o. out on his ears *(coll.)*; **einer Sache den ~ nehmen** to take the gilt off the gingerbread; **sich im ~ seines Ruhmes sonnen** to bask in one's fame; **einem Jahrhundert ~ verleihen** to be the glory of the age; **einer Sache ~ verleihen** to lend glamo(u)r to; **seinen ~ verlieren** to lose its polish; **sich mit ~ aus der Affäre ziehen** to find a brilliant solution;
~abzug glossy print.

glänzen to shine, to glitter;
durch Abwesenheit ~ to be conspicuous by one's absence; **vor Freude ~** *(Gesicht)* to beam with joy; **in Mathematik ~** to be brilliant in mathematics.

glänzend fine, superior, shining, shiny, glossy, *(fig.)* brilliant, excellent, nailing *(sl.)*, *(Fotoabzug)* glossy, *(glitzernd)* flashy, *(Papier)* glossy, *(Perle)* lustrous, bright, glossy, *(Schuhe)* polished;
nicht gerade ~ less-than-highly polished;
~ mit jem. auskommen to be hand in glove with s. o.; **~ aussehen** to look splendid; **sich ~ bewähren** to give a first-rate account of o. s.; **~ klappen** to work out beautifully; **Papier ~ machen** to glaze paper; **jem. ~ passen** to fit s. o. to a nicety; **etw. ~ verstehen** to have the knack of it;
~e Aussichten bright prospects; **~e Gelegenheit** golden opportunity; **~e Geschäfte machen** to drive a roaring trade; **~en Gesprächspartner abgeben** to shine in conversation; **~e Idee** brilliant (bright) idea; **~e Konjunktur** booming economy; **in ~er Laune sein** to be in sunny mood; **~er Redner** brilliant speaker; **~er Reinfall** fiasco comedown, washout *(sl.)*, complete flop; **~er Stoff** lustrous fabric; **in ~en Verhältnissen** in flourishing circumstances; **~es Zeugnis** excellent report; **~e Zukunft** bright future.

Glanz|leder patent leather; **~leistung** bright (brilliant) performance; **~licht** *(Foto)* highlight.

glanzlos *(Papier)* mat.

Glanz|mittel polish; **~nummer** star performance (turn, *Br.*); **~papier** calendered paper; **auf ~papier gedruckt** glossy; **~periode** heyday, palmy days; **seine ~periode überschritten haben** to be past one's prime; **~punkt** highlight; **~rolle** star turn; **~stelle** purple passage, fat; **~stück** master stroke, brilliant performance, stunt, feat, *(Sammlung)* gem, showpiece, piece de resistance, *(Theater)* star turn, draw; **~zeit** golden age, heyday, boom; **in seiner ~zeit** at the peak of one's career.

Glas glass;
bewehrtes ~ armo(u)r-proof glass; **feuerfestes ~** fireproof (Jena) glass; **graviertes ~** engraved glass; **kugelsicheres ~** armo(u)r-proof (bullet-proof) glass; **splittersicheres ~** shatterproof (safety) glass;
bei einem ~ Wein besprechen to discuss s. th. over a glass of wine; **sein ~ bis zum Rand füllen** to fill one's glass to the pretty; **ein ~ zuviel getrunken haben, zu tief ins ~ geschaut haben** to have had a glass too much, to have had one over the eight *(fam.)*;
~auge glass (artificial) eye.

Gläschen, sich gelegentlich ein ~ zu Gemüte führen to drink a drop now and then.

Glasdach, mit einem ~ versehen glass-roofed.

Glaser glazier;
~diamant diamond pencil.

Glaser|ei glassworks; **~meister** master glazier.

Glas|fabrik glasswork, glass factory; **~haus** greenhouse, glasshouse *(Br.)*; **wer im ~haus sitzt soll nicht mit Steinen schmeißen** people who live in glass-houses should not throw stones; **~hauswirkung** (Atmosphäre) greenhouse effect.

glasieren to glaze, *(Metall)* to enamel.

Glasindustrie glass industry.

glasklar clear-cut.

Glas|- und Porzellanladen glass and china shop; **~palast** crystal palace; **~papier** glass paper; **~perle** glass bead, Venetian pearl; **~sachen** glassware; **~schaden** glass claim; **~scheibe** glazing; **farbige ~scheibe** tinter; **~schild** glass sign; **~tür** French door; **~versicherung** plate-glass insurance; **~waren** glassware, crystal; **~wolle** glass wool.

glatt even, plain, level, smooth, *(Bruch)* clean, *(Mensch)* sleek, suave, well-oiled;
so ~ wie ein Aal as slippery as an eel;
~ abstreiten to deny flatly; **~ aufgehen** to work out exactly; **~ vonstatten gehen** to go off without a hitch; **~ gewinnen** to win hands down; **Effekten ~ hereinnehmen** to take in stock without charging contango; **~ landen** to land safely; **sich ~ lesen lassen** to read smoothly; **~ erfunden sein** to be pure fabrication; **j. ~ umwerfen** *(Nachricht)* to bowl s. o. over; **sich ~ weigern** to flatly refuse;
~e Ablehnung flat refusal; **~er Betrugsfall** clear case of fraud; **für die ~e Erledigung einer Angelegenheit sorgen** to ensure the smooth settlement of a business; **~es Geschäft** clear profit; **~es Gesicht** unwrinkled (smooth) face; **~er Höfling** smooth-tongued courtier; **~e Landung** *(Flugzeug)* safe landing; **~e Lüge** outright (downright) lie; **~e tausend Mark** a cool thousand; **~e 1000 DM kosten** to cost easily a thousand marks; **~er Mord sein** to be tantamount to murder; **~es Nein** flat no; **~e Niederlage** complete defeat; **~es Papier** smooth (shiny) paper; **~es Parkett der Politik** slippery ground of politics; **~e Prolongation** *(Börse)* carrying over; **~e Rechnung machen** to round off a bill; **keine ~e Sache** not at all plain sailing; **~er Satz** *(drucktechn.)* straight (solid) matter; **~e See** smooth (unruffled) sea; **~er Stoff** smooth fabric; **~e Straße** slippery road; **~e Summe** round sum; **~er Unsinn** sheer nonsense; **~e Verdrehung der Tatsachen** complete distortion of facts; **~er Verlauf einer Operation** uncomplicated course of an operation; **~es Versagen** complete failure, fiasco; **~er Wahnsinn** utter madness; **~e Wahrheit** plain truth; **in ~em Widerspruch zu einander stehen** to be in complete contradiction to one another; **~e Zahl** round figure; **~er Zufall** pure chance; **~e Zunge** glib tongue.

Glattdeck flush deck.

Glätte *(Stil)* smoothness;
~ auf den Straßen slipperiness of the roads.

Glatteis glazed frost *(Br.)*, glaze *(US)*, black ice;
sich aufs ~ begeben to skate over thin ice; **j. aufs ~ führen** to lead s. o. up the garden path; **Zeugen aufs ~ führen** to trip a witness.

glatthobeln to plane smooth.

glattstellen to settle, to liquidate, to clear, *(Börse)* to realize, to liquidate, to even up *(US)*, to clear, to close a speculative position;
Konto ~ to settle an account.

Glattstellung *(Börse)* realization, liquidation, evening up *(US)*, closing of a speculative position, position closing;
~ von Hausseengagements liquidation of longs (long positions); **~ eines Kontos** settlement (liquidation) of an account; **übliche ~en am Wochenende** usual weekend realizations (evening-up process, *US*);
umfangreichen ~en unterworfen sein to come in for heavy liquidations.

Glattstellungs|auftrag realizing (realization) order; **~geschäft** evening-up transaction *(US)*; **~konto** realization (liquidation) account; **~verkauf** realization (realizing) sale, sell-off.

glattwalzen, Straße mit der Dampfwalze to iron out a road with a steam roller, to steamroller.

glattweg flatly, point-blank, outright;
~ ablehnen to refuse flatly (point-blank); **~ belügen** to tell a downright lie; **etw. ~ vergessen** to forget s. th. completely.

Glättzahn *(Buchbinderei)* polisher.

glattzüngig reden to oil the tongue.

Glaube faith, belief, *(Religion)* religious belief;
auf Treu und ~n in good faith; **im guten ~n** bona fide, in good faith; **in bösem ~n** mala fide; **in gutem ~n darauf** in reliance thereon; **in schlechtem ~n** in bad faith;
guter ~ good faith, bona fides; **öffentlicher ~** prima facie evidence; **schlechter ~** bad faith;
Treu und ~n im Geschäftsverkehr full faith in business policy; **unerschütterlicher ~ an die Zukunft** unshakeable faith in the future;
sich auf seinen guten ~n berufen to plead one's good faith; **an seinem ~n festhalten** to hold firm to one's belief; **öffentlichen ~n genießen** to be prima facie evidence; **in gutem ~n handeln** to act in good faith; **seinen guten ~n geltend machen** to assert one's good faith; **jem. ~n schenken** to take s. one's word for it; **einem Bericht ~n schenken** to give credit to a report; **jedem Gerücht ~n schenken** to believe any rumo(u)r; **einer Geschichte überhaupt keinen ~n schenken** not to believe a word of a story; **einer Sache ~n schenken** to put faith in s. th.

glauben to believe, to deem, to think;
jem. aufs Wort ~ to take (believe in) s. one's word;
dran ~ müssen to kick the bucket, to kick off *(sl.)*.

Glaubens|bekenntnis creed, confession (profession) of faith, *(Politik)* platform; **~bewegung** religious movement; **~formen** creeds; **~freiheit** religious freedom, freedom of religion; **~gemeinschaft** confession, fellowship, communion, religious community; **~richtung** persuasion; **~wechsel** conversion.

glaubhaft plausible, authentic, creditable, colo(u)rable; **eidesstattlich ~ gemacht** founded on an affidavit; **sehr ~ klingen** to sound very convincing; **~ machen** to substantiate, to show to the satisfaction, to establish credibly (a prima facie case); **Aussage ~ machen** to substantiate a statement; **dem Gericht ~ machen** to prove to the satisfaction of the court; **in der vorgeschriebenen Weise ~ machen** to furnish satisfactory evidence;
~e Geschichte plausible story; **~er Zeuge** credible witness.

Glaubhaftigkeit eines Zeugen credibility of a witness.

Glaubhaftmachung plausibility, authentication, substantiation, prima facie evidence;
nach erfolgter ~ after being proved;
hinreichende ~ satisfactory proof, prima facie evidence;
~ von Ansprüchen authentication of claims; **~ durch Unterlagen** documentation.

Gläubiger creditor, demander, debtee, obligee;
von seinen ~n bedrängt pressed by one's creditors;
zur Befriedigung der ~ for the purpose of paying the creditors; **abgefundene ~** paid-off creditors; **absonderungsberechtigter ~** preferential (secured, *US*) creditor; **alle ~** general body of creditors; **antragstellender ~** petitioning creditor; **aussonderungsberechtigter ~** creditor with a colo(u)rable claim; **Vollstreckung betreibender ~** executing (attaching) creditor; **bevorrechtigter ~** prior (secured, *US*, privileged, preferential, *Br.*, preferred, *US*) creditor; **nicht bevorrechtigter ~** unprotected (unsecured, *US*, simple contract) creditor, creditor at large; **diverse ~** sundry creditors; **drängender ~** urgent creditor; **einfacher ~** general creditor; **buchmäßig festgestellter ~** book creditor; **gerichtlich festgestellter ~** judgment creditor; **unbefriedigt gebliebener ~** dissatisfied creditor; **gemeinsamer ~** joint obligee; **dinglich gesicherter ~** existing (catholic, lien, *US*) creditor; **doppelt gesicherter ~** double creditor; **einfach gesicherter ~** single creditor; **erstklassig gesicherter ~** catholic creditor; **hypothekarisch gesicherter ~** mortgagee, mortgage creditor; **teilweise gesicherter ~** partly secured creditor; **voll gesicherter ~** fully secured creditor *(US)*; **gewöhnlicher ~** simple contract creditor; **gleichrangige ~** equally ranking creditors, creditors ranking equally, creditors who rank equally (with equality of rights); **inländischer ~** domestic creditor; **nachrangiger (nachstehender) ~** subsequent (junior, deferred) creditor; **persönlicher ~ [eines Gesellschafters]** individual creditor; **pfändender ~** attaching (execution) creditor; **privilegierter ~** prior (privileged) creditor; **ranggleiche ~** creditors who rank equally; **sichergestellter ~** secured (general) creditor; **Konkursantrag stellender ~** petitioning creditor; **unredlicher ~** fraudulent creditor; **verschiedene ~** sundry creditors; **voraussichtliche ~** creditors expected to rank; **bereits vorhandene ~** antecedent creditors; **vorrangiger ~** senior creditor; **zustimmender ~** assenting creditor; **einem Vergleich nicht zustimmender ~** dissenting (nonassenting) creditor; **zwangsvollstreckender ~** attaching (executing) creditor; **zweitrangiger ~** secondary creditor;
~ einer Aktiengesellschaft corporate creditor; **~ einer vor [verschleiernder] Vermögensübertragung entstandenen Forderung** antecedent creditor; **~ aus Kontokorrentgeschäften** trade creditor; **~ einer verbrieften Schuld** specialty creditor; **~ von Sicherheiten** holder of s. one's securities; **~ nach durchgeführtem Vollstreckungsverfahren** executive creditor;
seine ~ abfinden to settle with (pay off) one's creditors; **mit seinen ~n akkordieren** to make a composition (to compound) with one's creditors; **sich mit seinen ~n auseinandersetzen** to arrange with one's creditors; **seine ~ voll auszahlen** to pay one's creditors in full; **seine ~ befriedigen** to discharge creditors, to compound with (satisfy, meet the claims of) one's creditors; **~ begünstigen** to favo(u)r (prefer) a creditor; **seine ~ benachteiligen** to defeat one's creditors; **~ mit einer Ratenzahlung beruhigen** to put off a creditor with an instal(l)ment; **~ betrügen** to defraud a creditor; **einzelne ~ bevorzugen** to prefer one creditor over others (a creditor over one's other creditors); **seinem ~ entkommen, sich seinen ~n [durch die Flucht] entziehen** to evade (run away from) one's creditors, to skate *(sl.)*; **sich mit seinen ~n verglichen haben** to have got whitewashed *(Br.)*; **seine ~ hinhalten** to delay (put off) one's creditors; **seine ~ mit leeren Versprechungen hinhalten** to feed one's creditors with empty promises; **~ hintergehen** to defeat one's creditors; **von seinen ~n verklagt werden können** to be liable to be proceeded against by one's creditors; **Vergleich mit seinen ~n schließen** to come to terms (compound) with one's creditors; **von seinen ~n bedrängt sein** to be dunned by one's creditors; **~ sicherstellen** to secure a creditor; **sich mit seinen ~n vergleichen** to settle (compound, compose) with one's creditors, to get a whitewash *(Br.)*; **sich mit seinen ~n wegen eines Zahlungsaufschubs verständigen** to arrange with one's creditors for an extension of time; **sich vor seinen ~n verstecken** to keep house *(Br.)*; **~ vertrösten** to put off creditors; **~n den Zugriff verwehren** to hinder creditors;
~abfindung settlement with (paying off) one's creditors; **~anfechtung** contestation of a voidable preference; **~anspruch** creditor claim; **gerichtlich festgestellter ~anteil** creditor's bill; **~antrag** creditor's petition, application of creditors; **auf ~antrag** upon the application of a creditor; **~aufsicht** creditor control; **~ausgleich** arrangement with creditors; **~ausschuß** body of creditors, committee in a winding up *(Br.)*, *(zur Untersuchung)* committee of inspection *(Br.)*, creditors' committee *(US)*; **~auswechslung** subrogation of a creditor; **~auszahlung** payment of creditors; **~bank** creditor bank; **~befriedigung** satisfaction of (paying off) creditors; **bevorrechtigte ~befriedigung** preferential (preferred, *US*) payment; **~begünstigung** fraudulent (undue, *Br.*) preference; **beabsichtigte ~begünstigung** voluntary preference; **sich der ~begünstigung schuldig machen** to prefer one creditor over others; **~behinderung** defrauding creditors; **~behinderung betreiben** to delay creditors; **~beirat** committee of inspection *(Br.)* (creditors, *US*), creditors' committee *(US)*; **~benachteiligung** fraudulent trading (conveyance), defeating of (fraud on) a creditor; **vorsätzliche ~benachteiligung** intent to delay or defraud creditors; **~beschluß** resolution of creditors; **~beschränkung** marshalling of remedies; **~bestechung** bribery of a creditor; **~bevorzugung** fraudulent preference; **~buch** creditors' ledger; **~forderung** creditor claim; **~gefährdung** jeopardizing a creditor's interest; **~gemeinschaft** body of creditors.

Gläubigerin woman creditor.

Gläubiger|interesse creditor claim, creditor interest; **~interessen wahrnehmen** to represent the interests of creditors; **~klassen** classes of creditors; **~konten** accounts with creditors; **~kontrolle** creditor control; **~land** creditor nation (country), lending country; **~liste** list of creditors, schedule of a bankrupt's creditors *(US)*; **~mehrheit** majority of creditors; **zahlen- und wertmäßige ~mehrheit** majority in number and value of creditors; **~mehrheit nach der Höhe der angemeldeten Forderungen** majority in value of the creditors; **~nation** creditor nation; **~position** creditor position; **~prozentsatz** proportionate share of a creditor, dividend; **~rang** ranking of a creditor; **~rangordnung feststellen** to marshall creditors; **~recht** creditor interest, right of a creditor; **~rechte erhalten** to enter into the rights of a creditor; **~schädigung** defeating of (fraud on) creditors; **~schutz** protection of creditors; **gerichtlich anerkannten ~schutz genießen** to be protected from one's creditors by court decree; **~schutzverband** trade protection society; **~staat** creditor state; **~stellung** creditor position; **~stellung erhalten** to enter into the rights of a creditor; **~streit** interpleader issue; **~vereinigung** association of creditors.

Gläubigervergleich legal settlement, settlement (agreement, composition, arrangement) with one's creditors, composition in bankruptcy, reorganization *(US)*;
außergerichtlicher ~ composition by deed of arrangement *(Br.)*;
~ beantragen to file a petition for an arrangement; **~ schließen** to settle (arrange, compound) with one's creditors.

Gläubiger|-Schuldnerverhältnis creditor-debtor relation; **~verluste** losses of creditors; **~versammlung** creditors' meeting, meeting of creditors; **~versammlung einberufen** to call (give notice of) a meeting of the creditors; **~vertreter** creditor's representative; **~verwaltung [eines bankrotten Geschäfts]** creditor management; **~verzeichnis** list of creditors, schedule of a bankrupt's estate *(US)*; **~verzug** creditor's delay; **~vollstreckung** execution by creditors; **~vorrang** priority of creditors; **~wechsel** subrogation; **~zustimmung** consent of creditors, creditor's assent.

glaubwürdig colo(u)rable, creditable, on good authority, credible, plausible, presumable *(verbürgt)* authentic, reliable, *(zuverlässig)* trustworthy, worthy of credit;
unbedingt ~ of unquestioned authority;
aus ~er Quelle, von ~er Seite on good authority, from a reliable source; **~er Zeuge** credible witness.

Glaubwürdigkeit credit, credence, plausibility, credibility, authenticity, trustworthiness;
mangelnde ~ untrustworthiness;
~ einer Geschichte plausibility of a story;

einer Geschichte ~ beimessen to credit a story; **~ erringen** to establish one's credibility; **j. seine öffentliche ~ verlieren lassen** to discredit s. o. with the public; **einem Bericht ~ verleihen** to lend countenance to a report; **öffentliche ~ verlieren** to lose one's credit with the public; **~ eines Zeugen in Zweifel ziehen (erschüttern)** to impugn the character of (impeach) a witness.

Glaubwürdigkeitsgrad degree of credibility.

gleich same, [a]like, identical, *(auf gleicher Höhe)* even, level, *(gleichwertig)* equal, equivalent, *(sofort)* immediately, right;
~ zum Anfang at the very beginning; **~ daneben** right beside; **~ um die Ecke** just round the corner; **~ nach dem Frühstück** straight after breakfast; **~ gegenüber** directly opposite;
j. ~ behandeln to put s. o. on the same footing; **j. ~ erkennen** to recognize s. o. immediately; **~ sein** to be on a par with; **~ mit einer Ausrede bei der Hand sein** to be never at a loss for an excuse; **~ wieder zurück sein** to be back in a moment; **~ Null setzen** to equate to zero;
~ und ~ gesellt sich gern birds of a feather flock together;
~en Anteil haben to go equal shares; **zu ~en Bedingungen** on equal terms; **~e Bezahlung** equal pay; **~e Chancen** even odds; **unter ~en Chancen kämpfen** to meet on even ground; **~en Datums** of the same date; **~e Entlohnung** equality of pay; **~e Erfindung** same invention; **~es Ergebnis haben** to amount (come) to the same thing; **~en Fehler wiederholen** to make the very same mistake again; **~er Gewinn** even break; **von ~er Größe** equal in size; **vom ~en Kaliber** cast in the same mould; **in der ~en Lage** in the same boat; **~er Lohn für ~e Leistung** equal pay for equal work; **~er Meinung sein** to endorse an opinion; **jem. etw. mit ~er Münze heimzahlen** to pay s. o. back in his own coin; **Preise auf dem ~en Niveau halten** to maintain the same level of prices; **mit ~er Post** by the same post (mail); **~er Preis** same price; **bei ~er Punktzahl** in case of equality in points; **~er Rang** equal (equality of) rank; **mit jem. im ~en Rang stehen** to be even with s. o., to be on an equal footing with s. o.; **~e Rechte** equal rights; **~es Schicksal erleiden** to suffer the same fate; **mit ~em Schreiben** under the same cover; **von ~er Stärke** of equal strength; **~e Stufe** same level; **mit jem. auf der ~en Stufe stehen** to be on the same level (on an equality) with s. o.; **zu ~en Teilen** in equal parts, equally; **zu ~en Teilen an den Kosten beteiligt sein** to contribute equal shares to the expenses; **unter sonst ~en Umständen** all other things being equal; **unter ~en Voraussetzungen arbeiten** to work under the same conditions; **vom ~en Wert** equivalent; **zur ~en Zeit** simultaneously; **~e Ziele verfolgen** to pursue a common goal.

gleichaltrig contemporary, of the same age, even-aged;
~ sein to be the same age.

Gleichaltrigengruppe peer group.

gleichartig similar, homogeneous, analogous, congenial;
~e Produktionseinheiten equivalent units; **~es Thema** like subject.

gleichbedeutend equivalent, equal in value, synonymous.

Gleichbehandlung equality of (equal) treatment, nondiscrimination.

gleichberechtigt having equal rights, on equal terms, concurrent, equal, on an equal footing, *(mit neuen Aktien)* pari-passu, *(Gläubiger)* equally ranking;
jem. ~ gegenübertreten to meet s. o. on equal terms; **~ sein** to have equal rights, *(Gläubiger)* to rank equally, *(mit neuen Aktien)* to rank pari-passu with; **nicht ~ sein** to suffer inequality of status;
~es Mitglied equal member.

Gleichberechtigte, j. als ~n behandeln to treat s. o. as an equal.

Gleichberechtigung equality of rights, equal status, *(Frau)* emancipation;
auf der Grundlage der ~ on a footing of equality;
politische ~ equality of status, political equality;
~ von Mann und Frau equal rights of men and women;
für die ~ kämpfen to fight for equal rights.

Gleichberechtigungsinteresse erwecken to bring out sexist instincts.

gleichbleiben, fast to be about static.

gleichbleibend constant, unchanging, *(einheitlich)* uniform, *(Markt)* invariable, steady;
~e Belegschaft stable force; **~e Dividendenpolitik** conformity in dividend politics; **~e Kosten** constant costs; **~er Lohn** same pay; **~e Nachfrage** steady demand; **~e Politik** unwavering policy; **~e Prämie** level premium; **~e Preise** unchanged prices; **~e Qualität** unvarying quality; **~e Rente** level annuity; **~e Temperatur** constant temperature; **~er Text** same text.

Gleiche|s same thing;
auf das ~ herauskommen to amount to the same; **genau das ~ sagen** to say exactly the same thing; **~s mit ~m vergelten** to give tit for tat, to pay s. o. back in his own coin; **~s mit ~m vergüten** to give s. o. a dose of his own medicine *(fam.)*.

gleichen resemble, to be like;
wie ein Ei dem anderen ~ to be as like as two peas.

gleichförmig *(Arbeit)* monotonous, *(Beschleunigung)* uniform, equal, constant;
~ buchen to enter in conformity;
~e Buchung entry in conformity.

Gleichförmigkeit uniformity, conformity.

gleich|gelagert mit einem früheren Rechtsstreit sein to be on all fours; **~geordnet** ranking equally, coordinate, coequal; **~gerichtet** parallel; **~geschaltet** coordinated.

gleichgestellt on an equal footing, coordinate, treated as equal;
~ behandeln to treat equally; **jem. ~ sein** to be on a par with s. o.

Gleichgestellter equal, coordinate.

Gleichgewicht equilibrium, balance, poise;
aus dem ~ gebracht unbalanced; **im ~** well-balanced;
binnenwirtschaftliches ~ domestic equilibrium; **fehlendes konjunkturelles ~** economic imbalance; **nukleares ~** nuclear parity; **partielles ~** particular equilibrium; **politisches ~** balance of power; **seelisches ~** evenness of disposition, poise of mind; **soziales ~** social stability; **totales ~** general equilibrium; **wirtschaftliches ~** economic equilibrium;
~ von Angebot und Nachfrage equation of demand and supply; **~ der Kräfte** balance of power; **~ auf allen Märkten** general equilibrium; **~ zwischen privater Produktion und öffentlichem Leistungsangebot** social balance; **~ des atomaren Schreckens** nuclear terror balance; **~ bei Unterbeschäftigung** underemployment equilibrium; **~ der Zahlungsbilanz** equilibrium of the balance of payments;
Etat ins ~ bringen to balance the budget; **das ~ in Europa stören** to disturb the balance of power in Europe; **seelisches ~ wiederherstellen** to restore the poise of mind.

Gleichgewichts|preis equilibrium price, normal price; **~störung** unbalance, *(Währungsparität)* disequilibrium; **~theorie** equilibrium theory; **~zins** neutral rate of interest; **~zustand** equilibrium level.

gleichgültig dry, without feeling, neglectful, indifferent, *(unwichtig)* trivial;
jem. ~ sein to be immaterial to s. o.; **jem. ziemlich ~ sein** to matter little to s. o.;
über ~e Dinge sprechen to talk about trivial matters; **in ~em Ton** in an indifferent tone.

Gleichgültigkeit indifference;
~ der USA in Fragen der europäischen Politik detachment of the United States from European affairs;
seine ~ bekunden to disinterest o. s.; **in ~ versinken** to sink into apathy.

Gleichheit equality, *(Ähnlichkeit)* likeness, identity, evenness;
~ der politischen Ansichten identity of political opinion; **~ der Beteiligung** unity of interests; **~ vor dem Gesetz** equal protection of the law *(US)*; **~ der Preise** parity of prices;
für die ~ eintreten to preach up equality.

Gleichheitsgrundsatz principle of equality;
von der Verfassung geforderter ~ constitutional requirement of uniformity.

gleichkommen, jem. to be equal to s. o.; **einer Absage ~** to be nothing short of a refusal; **einem Verrat ~** to be tantamount to treason.

Gleichlauf synchronism.

gleichlaufend parallel.

gleichlautend conformable, in conformity with, identical, parallel, of the same tenor;
~ buchen to enter (pass) in conformity;
~e Abschrift duplicate, true (exact, identical) copy; **~e Buchung** entry in conformity; **~e Erklärungen** identical statements; **~e Note** identical note; **~e Stelle** parallel passage.

gleichmachen to level, to even;
dem Erdboden ~ to raze to the ground.

Gleichmacher egalitarian, leveller.

Gleichmacherei egalitarianism.

gleichmacherisch egalitarian.

gleichmäßig equal, coequal, regular, flat, even, running, uniform, *(Qualität)* straight *(US)*;
~ zu den Kosten beitragen to contribute equal shares (equally) to the expenses;
~e Begünstigung equal benefit; **~e Belastung** evenly distributed load; **~e Beschleunigung** uniform acceleration; **~e Besteuerung** uniformity in taxation; **~e Gesichtszüge** regular features; **~e Wärme** constant temperature.

Gleichmäßigkeit equality.
Gleichmäßigkeitsklausel uniformity clause.
Gleichmut equal mind;
mit ~ ertragen to bear with equanimity.
gleichmütig even-tempered, equal, with unconcern.
gleichnamiger Ort place of the same name.
Gleichnis parable, simile;
in ~sen reden to speak in parables.
gleichordnen to coordinate.
Gleichordnung coordination.
Gleichrang equal rank, equality of rank;
~ haben to have equal rank, to rank equally, *(mit neuen Aktien)* to rank pari-passu.
gleichrangig equally ranking, of equal rank, on an equal footing, coordinate, *(mit neuen Aktien)* pari-passu;
~ sein to be on an equal footing, to take rank with s. o., to rank equally, to be of the same standing (equal footing), *(neue Aktien)* to rank as pari-passu;
~er Gläubiger equal-ranking creditor; **~es Zurückbehaltungsrecht** concurrent lien.
gleichschalten to bring into line, to coordinate, to homogenize;
sich ~ lassen to toe the line.
Gleich|schaltung coordination, homogenizing; **~schrift** duplicate, second copy.
gleich|setzen, einen Begriff mit einem anderen to equate one term with another; **~stehen mit** *(pol.)* to tie; **~stehend** of equal standing; **~stellen** to coordinate, to put on the same footing, to put on a par with, to equalize.
Gleichstellung equal treatment, equalization, coordination;
bürgerliche ~ emancipation; **staatsrechtliche ~** equality before the law.
Gleichstrom direct (continuous) current;
~generator direct current generator.
gleichtun, es jem. to emulate s. o.
Gleichung equation;
~ aufstellen to form an equation.
gleichwertig of the same value, equivalent, on a par, adequate;
~ machen to par; **~ sein** to countervail, to be of the same class (of the same standard); **jem. ~ sein** to be a match for s. o.;
~er Geldbetrag equality money.
Gleichwertigkeit equal value, equality, equivalence, *(Leistung)* equal standard;
~ mehrerer patentierter Erfindungen substantial equivalent of patented devices; **~ der Währungen** equivalence of currencies.
gleichzeitig contemporaneous, concurrent, at the same time, simultaneous, of the same date;
sich ~ abspielen to happen at the same time; **~ über Rundfunk und Fernsehen senden** to simulcast;
~e Anwesenheit simultaneous presence; **~es Anziehen der Preise** overall increase of prices; **~er Tod** simultaneous death *(US)*; **~e Versicherung** *(Feuerversicherung des gleichen Objekts bei mehreren Anstalten)* concurrent fire insurance.
Gleichzeitigkeit simultaneousness, concomitance, concomitancy.
gleichziehen, mit jem. to draw level (catch up) with s. o.; **mit der Konkurrenz ~** to catch up with one's competitors.
Gleis track, line;
auf dem toten ~ *(fig.)* high and dry, sidetracked;
ausgefahrenes ~ *(fig.)* rut; **belegtes ~** occupied track; **totes ~** dead track, unused line, sidetrack *(US)*;
im gewohnten ~e bleiben to travel in the same groove; **aus dem gewohnten ~ bringen** to unsettle; **~ freimachen** to clear a track; **auf ein totes ~ geraten** to get bogged down, to reach a deadlock, to run into a brick wall, *(beruflich)* to get into a blind-alley job; **aus dem ~ springen** to fly off the track, to jump (run off) the rails, to run off the metals, to be derailed; **ausgefahrene ~e verlassen** to leave the beaten track;
~abnutzung track wear; **~abschnitt** track section; **~abzweigung** branch line; **~anlage** railroad tracks *(US)*, rail facilities; **~anlagen erneuern** to rebuild tracks; **~anlagenausbau** track improvement; **~anordnung** group of sidings; **~anschluß** junction, siding; **privater ~anschluß** private siding, *(Industrieunternehmen)* industrial track; **~arbeiten** track maintenance; **~arbeiter** tracklayer; **~bau** tracklaying; **~begeher** permanent-wayman; **~dreieck** triangular junction; **~kette** caterpillar track, crawler track; **~kettenantrieb** caterpillar (crawler) drive; **~kettenfahrzeug** tracklaying vehicle (tractor), caterpillar; **~körper** permanent way; **schienengleiche ~kreuzung** level crossing, frog *(US)*; **~lagergebühr** track storage; **~miete** side rent; **~netz** network of lines.
gleißen to gleam, to shine.
gleißend|es Licht dazzling light; **~e Versprechungen** glittering promises.
Gleis|sperre line-blocking device; **~strang** line, track; **~system** roadbed; **schienengleicher ~übergang** level crossing *(Br.)*, grade crossing *(US)*, frog *(US)*; **~unterhaltung** track maintenance; **~unterhaltungskosten** track costs; **~waage** weighbridge, railroad scales *(US)*.
Gleit|bahn glide path, *(Stapellauf)* launching ways; **~bombe** *(mil.)* glider bomb; **radargelenkte ~bombe** bat; **~boot** hydroplane, glider.
Gleiten slide, glide.
gleiten to glide, to slide, *(Preise)* to skid;
Münze in seine Tasche ~ lassen to slip a coin into one's pocket; **unbemerkt aus dem Zimmer ~** to slip unnoticed from a room.
gleitend|e Arbeitszeit flexible working (staggering of) hours, flextime *(Br.)*; **~er Lohn** sliding wage; **~e Lohnskala** sliding wage scale; **~e Neuwertversicherung** reinstatement insurance; **~e Prämie** sliding-scale premium; **~er Preis** escalation price; **~e Preisskala** escalator formula (provision, clause); **~e Skala** sliding scale; **~er Zoll** sliding-scale tariff.
Gleitfläche tread.
Gleitflug to glide, gliding flight;
im ~ in a glide;
~ machen to glide; **zum ~ übergehen** to go into a glide;
~landung glide landing; **~zeug** sailplane, glider.
Gleit|klausel escalator (rise and fall) clause, escalator provision; **~klauselsystem** escalator plan; **~komma** *(Datenverarbeitung)* floating point; **~kufe** *(Flugzeug)* skid; **~lohntarif** sliding wage scale; **~mittel** lubricant; **~preis** escalation price, price subject to adjustment.
Gleitschutz *(Auto)* antiskid (nonskid) device;
mit ~profilen versehen nonskidding; **~reifen** nonskid tire (tyre, *Br.*); **~vorrichtung** antiskid device.
Gleit|strahl [radio-landing] beam; **~zoll** sliding-scale tariff.
Gletscher glacier;
~eis inland ice; **~spalte** ice pinnacle; **~zunge** snout.
Glied limb, member, *(mil.)* rank, file, *(Unfallversicherung)* bodily member;
in Reih und ~ in rank and file;
fehlendes ~ missing link; **hinteres ~** *(mil.)* rear rank; **künstliches ~** artificial limb;
~ in der Beweiskette missing link in the chain of evidence;
seine Vorfahren bis ins fünfte ~ kennen to trace back one's ancestors for five generations; **aus dem ~ treten** to break rank, to fall out.
Glieder|bus articulated (trolley) bus; **~kette** *(Tank)* track.
gliedern *(anordnen)* to arrange, to order, to organize, *(aufgliedern)* to divide, to subdivide, to apportion, to break down, *(Gläubiger)* to marshal, *(gruppieren)* to classify, to group, *(mil.)* to organize, to distribute;
sich in drei Absätze ~ to be composed of three parts; **in drei Abschnitte ~** to divide in three parts; **seine Gedanken ~** to marshal one's thoughts; **neu ~** *(mil.)* to reorganize a unit; **nach Stoffgebieten ~** to classify by subjects; **in sechs Teile ~** *(Buch)* to break down into six parts.
Glieder|puppe *(Schaufenster)* display model, lay figure; **~taxe** *(Versicherung)* dismemberment schedule; **~triebwagen** *(Bahn)* gasoline rail car.
Gliederung *(Anordnung)* organization, arrangement, *(Aufgliederung)* subdivision, breakdown, apportionment, *(Aufsatz)* outline, *(Gläubigeransprüche)* marshalling, *(Gruppierung)* classification, grouping, *(mil.)* distribution, organization, *(Verband)* affiliation;
berufliche ~ breakdown of occupations; **dramatische ~** dramatic construction; **fachliche ~** professional division; **geographische ~** geographical division; **naturräumliche ~** physical regionalization; **regionale ~** regional division;
~ der Bilanz balance-sheet structure; **~ nach Einkommensgruppen** breakdown according to income brackets; **~ von Konten** classification of accounts; **~ der Kosten** cost structure, breakdown of costs; **~ nach Sachgebieten** functional classification; **~ der Sicherheiten** marshalling of securities; **~ von Truppen** organization of troops; **~ der Waren nach Zolltarifen** classification in customs tariffs.
Gliederungsmerkmale constituent elements.
Glieder|verlust loss of limbs, dismemberment; **~wagen** articulated streetcar *(US)*.
Gliedstaat member (constituent) state.
glimmen to glimmer, to gleam, *(Asche)* to smoulder.
glimmende|Asche embers; **schwach ~ Hoffnung** a flicker of hope; **~ Zigarre** glowing cigar.

Glimmstengel gasper, weed, fag *(coll.)*.
glimpflich lenient, mild;
~ **davonkommen** to get off lightly;
~**e Strafe** mild punishment.
glitschig *(Straße)* slippery.
glitzern to glitter, to glisten.
glitzernd sparkling, flashy.
global global, world-wide, overall, aggregate, across-the-board, through the line, blanket *(US)*;
~ **bewilligen** to vote as a lump sum;
~**e Auswirkungen** world-wide consequences; ~**er Lohnanstieg** all-round (across-the-board) wage increase; ~**es Patent** complete (blanket, *US*) patent; ~**e Preiserhöhung** general (overall) price increase; ~**e Wirtschaftsprobleme** global economic problems; ~**es Wissen** allround knowledge; ~**e Zahlungsbilanz** overall balance of payments.
Global|abdeckung global settlement; ~**abrechnung** *(Banken)* clearing; ~**abschluß** *(Rundfunk)* blanket contract; ~**aktie** stock certificate, multiple certificate *(Br.)*; ~**angebot** global (comprehensive) offer; ~**anstieg** across-the-board boost; ~**anstieg der Preise** overall (general) increase of prices; ~**auftrag** aggregate amount of purchase; ~**belastung** omnibus charge; ~**berechnung** aggregate calculation; ~**betrag** aggregate amount, inclusive (round, global) sum; ~**bewilligung** block (token) vote; ~**darlehen** loans en bloc; ~**darstellung** overall picture; ~**deckung** *(Versicherung)* umbrella coverage; ~**einsparung** overall cut; ~**finanzierung** block financing; ~**geschäft** package deal; ~**hypothek** unlimited mortgage, blanket (general) mortgage; ~**information** comprehensive information; ~**klausel** *(Grundstücksübertragung)* all the estate; ~**kontingent** overall (global) quota; ~**kredit** block credit; ~**kürzung** allround cut; ~**pfandbestellung** *(Bausparkasse)* omnibus charge; ~**police** all-risks insurance policy; ~**preis** allround (lump-sum) price; ~**regelung** global (overall) settlement; ~**steuer** single tax; ~**streik** all-out strike; ~**summe** global amount (sum); ~**tarif** blanket rate; ~**überschuß anreichern** to shore up the overall surplus; ~**untersuchung** overall study; ~**verbot** blanket prohibition; ~**verpfändung** floating charge *(Br.)*; ~**verpflichtung** blanket bond; ~**versicherung** comprehensive (global, blanket, all-loss, *US*) insurance; ~**versicherung der Büroeinrichtung** office floater *(US)*.
Globetrotter globocrat, globe-trotter.
Globus globe.
Glocke bell;
etw. an die große ~ hängen to proclaim from the housetops; **jem. sagen, was die ~ geschlagen hat** to tell s. o. where to get off; **wissen, was die ~ geschlagen hat** to know what's in store for one.
Glocken|anker *(el.)* bell-type armature; ~**boje** bell buoy; ~**geläut** bell ringing; ~**isolator** petticoat insulator; ~**spiel** carillon, chime.
glorios|es Durcheinander glorious mess; ~**er Reinfall** flop, fiasco.
Glossa[rium] glossary.
Glosse gloss, personnel paragraph, squib, annotation, marginal note, *(Zeitung)* leaderette;
über alles seine ~n machen to scoff at everything; ~**n schreiben** to gloss, to paragraph.
Glossenschreiber paragraphist *(Br.)*, paragraph writer *(US)*, paragrapher.
glossieren to gloss, to paragraph, to comment, to explain by notes.
Glotz|kasten *(fam.)* goggle box; ~**röhre** the tube *(US sl.)*.
Glück luck, chance, fortune, sun, ship;
auf gut ~ at a venture, on the off-chance, at random, on spec, hobnob; **von seinem ~ überwältigt** stunned with one's good fortune;
junges ~ new-found happiness; **launisches ~** fickle fortune; **unerhofftes ~** windfall; **ungetrübtes ~** unclouded happiness; **ungewöhnliches ~** bread buttered on both sides; **viel ~** good luck;
~ **bei der Auslosung** luck of the draw; ~ **im Spiel** lucky at cards; ~ **im Unglück** a blessing in disguise;
sein ~ im Spielsaal ausprobieren to try one's luck at the gaming tables; **jds. ~ oder Unglück bedeuten** to make or mar s. o. *(fam.)*; **jem. kein ~ bringen** to bring s. o. bad luck; **auf gut ~ zu jem. gehen** to go to s. o. on the off-chance; ~ **haben** to have fortune on one's side, to make a strike, to strike oil, to lick out *(US)*; **kein ~ mehr haben** to be through with one's stars; **unverschämtes ~ haben** to have had the devil's own luck, to be bloody lucky; **sein ~ machen** to make one's fortune (pile), to make one's way in life; **jds. ~ machen** to make s. o.; **von ~ sagen** to thank one's lucky stars; **vom ~ verlassen sein** to be down on one's luck; **sein ~ aufs Spiel setzen** to push one's luck; **sein ~ in der Fremde suchen** to seek one's fortune in a new country; ~ **und Unglück mit jem. teilen** to share the good times and the bad times with s. o.; **sein ~ versuchen** to try (run) one's fortune (luck), to mortgage one's happiness *(fam.)*; **etw. auf gut ~ versuchen** to have a fling at s. th., to run for luck *(US)*; **sein ~ machen wollen** to push (crowd, *US*) one's fortune; **jem. ~ wünschen** to wish s. o. well;
~ **und Glas wie leicht bricht das** glass and luck brittle muck; **jeder ist seines ~es Schmied** everyone carves his own destiny.
glucken, ganzen Tag zu Hause to be a stay-at-home.
glücken to succeed, to be successful.
glücklich lucky, fortunate, happy, pleased;
sehr ~ aussehen to look blissfully happy; **es ~ hinter sich haben** to be well out of it; **in ~er Ehe leben** to be happily married; **sich ~ schätzen** to count o. s. fortunate;
~**e Ankunft** safe arrival; ~**er Einfall** happy thought; **zu einem ~en Ende führen** to bring a business to a successful conclusion; ~**en Griff tun** to strike it lucky *(US)*; **unter einem ~en Stern geboren sein** to be born under a lucky star; ~**e Umstände** fortunate circumstances; ~**es Vorzeichen** happy portent; ~**e Wortwahl** felicity in the choice of words.
glücklos unfortunate, up the creek *(sl.)*.
Glücks|automat fruit machine *(Br.)*, one-armed bandit *(US)*; ~**beutel** lucky dip *(Br.)*, grab bag *(US)*; ~**bringer** mascot, talisman; **als ~bringer aufbewahren** to keep for luck.
glückselig happy, beatific, blissful.
Glücks|fall stroke of luck, lucky hit, chance, piece of good luck, lucky incident, godsend, fluke; ~**geld** *(Effektenhandel)* luck money; ~**göttin** goddess fortune; ~**güter** earthly goods; **j. mit ~gütern überschütten** to pour down blessings on s. o.; ~**hafen** raffle stall; ~**jäger** fortune hunter; ~**kind** spoiled child of fortune, lucky bargee, fortunate; **ein ~kind sein** to be born with a silver spoon in one's mouth; ~**lotto** bingo; ~**pfennig** lucky penny, pocket piece; ~**pilz** lucky dog (beggar), up [start]; ~**rad** the wheel of fortune, Fortune's wheel, lottery wheel; ~**ritter** adventurer, fortune seeker, gentleman of fortune; ~**sache** matter of luck, lottery.
Glücksspiel hazard, game of chance, confidence game, gambling;
gewerbliches ~ commercialized gambling; **verbotenes ~** unlawful game;
Gesetze gegen das ~ erlassen to legislate against gambling; **j. zum ~ verleiten** to inveigle s. o. into gambling;
~**automat** one-armed bandit *(US)*, fruit-machine *(Br.)*; ~**gerät** gambling device; ~**ring** gambling ring.
Glücks|spieler gambler; ~**stern** lucky star; **seinem ~stern vertrauen** to follow one's star.
Glückssträhne good fortune, run of luck;
~ **haben** to be in luck's way, to be in luck; **auf eine ~ stoßen** to run into a lucky streak.
Glückstag red-letter (lucky) day;
als ~ bezeichnen to mark with a white stone.
glückstrahlende Braut radiant bride.
Glücks|treffer bonanza, lucky hit (shot), lucky strike *(US)*; ~**treffer landen** to draw (score) a hit, to strike it lucky *(US)*; ~**umstand** fortunate circumstance; ~**vertrag** aleatory contract; ~**zeichen** good omen.
Glückwunsch|adresse congratulatory address; ~**ansprache** congratulatory speech.
Glückwünsche congratulations, felicitations;
jem. seine ~ aussprechen to congratulate s. o.; **jem. seine ~ zum neuen Jahr aussprechen** to wish s. o. a happy New Year; ~ **überbringen** to carry congratulations.
Glückwunsch|karte greeting (congratulation) card; ~**schreiben** letter of congratulation, congratulatory letter; ~**telegramm** congratulatory telegram, greetings telegram, message of greetings *(US)*; **sich ein paar ~worte abringen** to force out a few words of congratulation.
Glühbirne [electric] bulb.
glühen to glow, to be red-hot;
vor Begeisterung für eine Idee ~ to be fired with enthusiasm for an idea.
glühend glowing, live, warm;
j. ~ beneiden to be green with envy at s. o.; **j. ~ lieben** to be passionately in love with s. o.; **sich etw. ~ wünschen** to desire s. th. ardently;
in ~en Farben von jem. sprechen to speak in glowing terms of s. o.; ~ **roter Himmel** fiery red sky; ~**e Hitze** scorching heat; ~**e Kohlen** live coals; ~**e Kohlen auf jds. Haupt sammeln** to heap

coals of fire on s. one's head; **wie auf ~en Kohlen sitzen** to be on tenterhooks (like a cat on hot bricks), to be on pins and needles *(US)*; ~**er Ofen** fiery furnace; ~ **heißer Tag** scorcher, blazer *(coll.)*; ~**es Verlangen** fervent desire; ~**e Wangen** burning cheeks.

Glüh|faden filament; ~**lampe** incandescent lamp.

Glut glow, embers, live coals;
~ **des Sommers** scorching heat of the summer;
~ **anfachen** to fan the fire.

Gnade grace, clemency, mercy, quarter;
von jds. ~ abhängen to lie at s. one's mercy; **j. um ~ anflehen** to entreat (pray) s. o. to show mercy; **Richter um ~ anflehen** to implore a judge for mercy; **sich der ~ des Gerichts anheimgeben** to cast o. s. upon the mercy of the court; **sich jem. auf ~ und Ungnade ausliefern** to throw o. s. on s. one's mercy; **um ~ bitten** to appeal for mercy, to quarter; **in ~n entlassen** to dismiss graciously; **sich auf ~ und Ungnade ergeben** to surrender unconditionally, to place o. s. under s. one's power; ~ **vor jds. Augen finden** to find favo(u)r in s. one's sight; **bei seinen Richtern keine ~ finden** to receive no clemency at the hand of one's judges; **um ~ flehen** to cry for quarter, to crave for mercy; ~ **für Recht ergehen lassen** to temper justice with mercy; **keine ~ walten lassen** to show no mercy; **zu viel ~ walten lassen** to err on the side of mercy.

Gnaden|akt act of grace; ~**ausschuß** clemency board; ~**beweis** favo(u)r; **eines ~beweises unwürdig** undeserving of mercy; **für einen ~beweis plädieren** to lean towards mercy; **bei jem. das ~brot essen** to live on s. one's charity; **einem alten Dienstboten das ~brot geben** to keep an old servant on; **einem Pferd das ~brot geben** to put a horse out to grass; ~**empfehlung** recommendation for mercy; ~**empfehlung geben** to lean towards mercy; ~**erlaß** act of grace; ~**erweis** executive pardon, oblivion; **jem. einen ~erweis gewähren** to give s. o. a grant of clemency; ~**frist** period of grace; **ohne ~frist** unreprievable; ~**gesuch** petition of mercy (clemency); ~**gesuch ablehnen** to refuse a clemency plea; ~**gesuch einreichen** to petition for a reprieve (mercy); ~**instanz** clemency board.

gnadenlos merciless, ruthless, *(Kampf)* without quarter;
geringste Verfehlungen ~ verfolgen to have no mercy on the slightest mistakes;
~**e Verfolgungsjagd** relentless chase.

Gnaden|recht mercy, prerogative of pardon *(Br.)*; ~**sache** clemency case; ~**stoß** coup de grâce; ~**stoß geben** to give the finishing stroke; ~**tage** days of grace; ~**tod** mercy killing; **auf dem ~wege** by special (way of) grace.

gnädig merciful, *(Strafe)* lenient, mild;
~ **lächeln** to smile condescendingly; ~ **davongekommen sein** to have got away rather lightly; ~ **mit jem. verfahren** to treat s. o. leniently.

Gold gold, international money *(coll.)*;
aus reinem ~ made of gold; **in ~ rückzahlbar** redeemable in gold; **mit ~ überzogen** overlaid with gold; **treu wie ~** true as steel;
auf dem Transport befindliches ~ bullion at transit; **echtes ~** sterling gold; **freies ~** *(Schatzamt)* free gold; **gediegenes ~** native (solid, virgin) gold; **gemünztes ~** coined gold, effective; **18karätiges ~** common gold, gold 18 carats fine; **24karätiges ~** twenty-four carat gold; **legiertes ~** alloyed gold; **pures ~** pure gold; **reines ~** real (clean, true, pure) gold; **schlechtes ~** base gold; **ungemünztes ~** bullion, bar gold; **im Sonderdepot verwahrtes ~** earmarked gold;
~ **in Barren** ingot gold, gold bullion; ~ **von geringem Feingehalt** base gold; ~ **von gesetzlicher Feinheit** standard gold; ~ **in Klumpen** gold in nuggets; ~ **und sofort fällige Staatsbankguthaben** treasury cash;
~ **als Währungsgrundlage aufgeben** to demonetize gold; **mit ~ aufwiegen** to pay a heavy price; ~ **auswaschen** to wash gravel for gold, to pan out gold; **in (mit) ~ bezahlen** to pay in gold; ~ **in der Kehle haben** to have a beautiful voice; ~ **für ausländische Rechnung im Depot halten** to hold gold earmarked for foreign accounts; **im ~ schwimmen** to be wallowing in money; **nicht mit ~ zu bezahlen sein** to be worth one's weight in gold; **mit ~ überziehen** to gold-plate; ~ **waschen** to wash for gold;
durch ~ gedeckte Währung currency backed by gold;
es ist nicht alles ~ was glänzt all that glisters is not gold; **Reden ist Silber, Schweigen ist ~** speech is silver, silence is gold;
~**abbau** gold mining; ~**abfluß** gold outflow, efflux (outflow) of gold (bullion), drain in bullion *(Br.)*; ~**abflüsse nach dem Inland zurückbringen** to repatriate gold; ~**abwanderung** efflux (drain) of gold; ~**abzüge** gold drain, gold withdrawals, withdrawals of gold; ~**ader** vein of gold; **auf eine ~ader stoßen** to strike it rich *(US)*; ~**agio** gold premium, premium on gold; ~**aktien** gold shares *(Br.)* (stocks, *US*); ~**angebot** gold supply; **ankauf** gold buying (purchase); ~**ankäufer** gold purchaser; ~**ankaufspreis** gold-buying price; ~**anleihe** loan on a gold basis, gold loan; ~**arbitrage** arbitrage in gold (bullion); ~**auflage** overlay of gold.

Goldausfuhr gold export;
~**barren** export bar; ~**punkt** gold (export specie, bullion, gold-exchange) point; ~**verbot** embargo on gold, gold embargo.

Goldausgleichsfonds gold settlement fund.

Goldbarren gold bar (ingot), bullion, ingot of gold;
amtlich auf Feingehalt geprüfter ~ assay office bar;
~ **im Wert von ca. 8000 $** export bar *(US)*; ~**- oder Silberbarren** commercial bar *(US)*;
~**preis** gold-bullion price; ~**währung** gold-bullion standard.

Gold|basis gold basis; **auf ~basis** on gold; ~**bergwerk** gold mine.

Goldbestand gold holdings (reserves, reserve stock);
auswärtiger ~ *(Bilanz)* bullion abroad; **die gesetzlich vorgeschriebenen Reserven übersteigender ~** free gold *(US)*;
~ **und Silberbestand** bullion [reserve].

Gold|bestände gold holdings, gold coin and bullion; ~**- und Devisenbestände** gold and foreign exchange holdings; ~**bewegung** gold movement; ~**block** gold bloc; ~**blockländer** gold-bloc countries; ~**bonds** gold bonds *(US)*; ~**brosche** gold brooch; ~**deckung** gold backing (cover, coverage); **zwanzigprozentige ~deckung** twenty per cent gold coverage; ~**deckung aufgeben** to abolish (lift) the gold cover; ~**deckungsprinzip** currency principle (doctrine) *(US)*; ~**depotschein** gold depositary certificate; ~**devisenwährung** gold (indirect, irredeemable, foreign) exchange standard; ~**dollar** gold (standard) dollar; ~**einfuhr** gold import; ~**einfuhrpunkt** import specie point; ~**einheiten** terms of gold; ~**einzahlung** gold subscription; ~**embargo** embargo on gold, gold embargo.

goldene|Berge versprechen, jem. to promise s. o. the moon and stars; ~ **Brücke** golden bridge; ~ **Hochzeit** golden wedding; ~**r Mittelweg** happy mean.

Gold|ersatzrolle des Dollars dollar's reserve role; ~**export** gold export; ~**feld** gold field; ~**fieber** gold rush; ~**fonds** gold fund, gold pool; ~**franken** gold franc; ~**fund** gold strike; ~**fundgebiet** gold diggings; ~**garantie** gold backing; ~**gebiet** gold field; ~**gehalt** percentage of gold, gold content.

goldgerändert gilt-edged.

Gold|gewicht troy weight; ~**gewinnung** production of gold, gold production; ~**gräber** gold digger; ~**gräberkolonie** camp *(US)*; ~**grube** gold mine, bonanza, golcanda; **wahre ~grube** a regular gold mine, bonanza; ~**gulden** gold florin.

goldhaltige Erde pay gravel (ground).

Gold|handel gold trade; **konzessionierter ~händler** authorized dealer in gold *(Br.)*; ~**hortung** gold hoarding.

goldig aussehen to look sweet.

Gold|import gold import; ~**index** gold index; ~**kernwährung** gold bullion standard; ~**klauseln** gold clauses, gold bugs; ~**klumpen** nugget; ~**kurs** rate of gold, gold rate; ~**kurswährung** gold exchange standard; ~**lager** deposit of gold; ~**land** gold-producing country; ~**legierung** allegation (alloy) of gold, gold alloy; ~**mangel** scarceness (scarcity) of gold; **gespaltener ~markt** two-tier gold market; ~**markt in einen freien und einen offiziellen Markt aufspalten** to split the gold market into a free and an official market; ~**medaille** gold medal; ~**mine** gold mine; ~**minenaktien** goldmining shares, gold shares *(Br.)*; ~**minenbezirk** gold field; ~**münze** gold coin, gold; ~**münze zu 5 Dollars** half-eagle *(US)*; ~**münze zu 10 Shilling** half sovereign *(Br.)*; ~**münzprägung** gold coinage; ~**münzwährung** gold coin standard; ~**obligationen** gold bonds *(US)*; ~**parität** gold parity; ~**pfandbriefe** gold bonds *(US)*; ~**prägung** gold printing; ~**preis** gold price, price of gold; **gespaltener ~preis** two-tier gold price (price of gold), dual gold price; ~**produktion** production of gold, gold production.

Goldpunkt gold (specie, bullion) point;
oberer ~ export specie point; **unterer ~** import specie point.

Gold|rausch gold rush, yellow fever; ~**rente** gold annuity; ~**reserve** gold (bullion) reserve; ~**reserve bei ausländischen Noteninstituten** earmarked (earmarking of) gold; ~**reservenaufwertung** revaluing of gold reserves.

goldrichtig dead right.

Gold|sand wash dirt; ~**schatz** treasure of gold; ~**schmied** goldsmith; ~**schmiedearbeit** goldsmithery; **mit ~schnitt** *(Buch)* gilt-edged; ~**schulden** debts owed in bullion; ~**sendung** gold shipment; ~**spekulation** speculation in gold.

Goldstandard gold standard (currency);
~ **abschaffen** to go off the gold standard; ~ **aufgeben** to

abandon the gold standard; ~ **vorübergehend aufheben** to suspend the gold standard; **für Aufrechterhaltung des ~s eintreten** to support the gold standard; ~ **verlassen** to go off the gold standard.

Gold|stück gold coin (piece), goldfinch *(Br.)*, yellow boy *(Br., sl.)*, shiner *(sl.)*; ~**suche** prospecting for gold; ~**sucher** gold prospector; ~**termingeschäft** gold future contract; ~**tranche** *(Weltwährungsfonds)* gold tranche; ~**tranchenziehungsrechte** gold tranche rights; ~**transport** gold consignment (transportation); ~**überschuß** surplus of gold; ~**umlauf** gold circulation; ~**umlaufwährung** gold specie standard; ~**umsätze** turnover in gold; ~**valuten** gold exchanges; ~**verbrauch** gold consumption; ~**verkäufe an die private Kundschaft einstellen** to bring the closing of the gold window to private people; ~**verluste** gold loss; ~**versendung** shipment of gold; ~**versorgung** supply of gold, gold supply; ~**vorkommen** occurrence (deposit) of gold, incidence of gold; ~**vorrat** stock of gold, gold supply; **auswärtige ~vorräte** bullion abroad; ~**waage** assay (bullion) balance; **jedes Wort auf die ~waage legen** to weigh up every word, to be meticulous in the choice of words.

Goldwährung gold standard (currency);
in ~ der USA in gold coin of the USA;
reine ~ gold specie standard;
~ **und Silberwährung** gold and silver currency;
~ **aufgeben** to come off the gold standard.

Goldwährungs|block gold bloc; ~**land** gold-standard country.

Goldwäscherei gold washing.

Goldwert value in gold, gold value;
~ **und Silberwert einer geprägten Münze** bullion value;
~**basis** gold value basis; ~**garantie** *(Weltwährungsfonds)* gold value guarantee; **volle ~garantie** outright gold-value guarantee.

goldwertgesichert sein to carry a gold-value guarantee.

Goldwert|klausel gold clause; ~**schwund** reduction in the gold value.

Gold|zahlung gold payment; ~**zertifikat** gold certificate *(US)*; ~**zufluß** gold inflow, influx of gold.

Golf gulf, *(Sport)* golf;
~**platz** golf links; ~**strom** gulf stream.

Gondel gondola, *(Luftschiff)* cabin, nacelle;
~**bahn** cable railway.

Gong gong.

gönnen, jem. etw. not to begrudge s. o. s. th.; **sich etw. ~** to indulge one's taste, to treat o. s. to s. th.; **jem. einen Blick ~** to glance at s. o.; **jem. das liebe Brot nicht ~** to grudge s. o. the food he eats; **jem. etw. von Herzen ~** to be so glad for s. o.; **jem. nicht das kleinste Vergnügen ~** to grudge s. o. his pleasures; **sich ein arbeitsfreies Wochenende ~** to treat o. s. to a good weekend holiday; **jem. kein freundliches Wort ~** never to have a kind word for s. o.; **jem. nur eine kurze Zeit des Glückes ~** to grant s. o. only a short period of happiness.

Gönner well-wisher, friend, sponsor, promoter, protector, furtherer, patronizer, countenancer;
hilfreicher ~ der Armen a good friend of the poor.

gönnerhaft patronizing, condescending.

Gönner|miene patronizing air; ~**schaft** patronage, sponsorship; **einem jungen Autor seine ~schaft zuwenden** to extend one's protection to a young author.

Goodwill goodwill;
~**werbung** institutional campaign (advertising).

gordischer Knoten Gordian knot.

Gösch union jack.

Gosse gutter, kennel, runnel;
Kind aus der ~ auflesen to take a child out of the gutter; **jds. Namen durch die ~ ziehen** to drag s. one's name through the mire.

Gott god, lord;
wie ~ einen geschaffen hat dastehen to stand in one's birthday suit; **den lieben ~ einen guten Mann sein lassen** to live for the day, to let things go happy; **wie ~ in Frankreich leben** to live in clover (in the lap of luxury); **über ~ und die Welt reden** to talk of this and that; **von ~ und der Welt abgeschieden sein** to be cut off from the rest of the world; **dem lieben ~ den Tag stehlen** to laze away one's time; **etw. um ~es Lohn tun** to do s. th. for nothing; ~**es Mühlen mahlen langsam** the mills of God grind slowly but exceeding small.

Götter, von allen ~n verlassen sein to be out of one's mind, to be crazy.

Götterdämmerung twilight of the gods.

Gottesdienst divine service, religious service, worship;
öffentlicher ~ public worship; ~**ordnung** liturgy; ~**störung** disturbance of public or religious worship.

gottesfürchtig devout.

Gottes|geschenk godsend; ~**haus** place of worship, house of worship, house of God; ~**haus entweihen (schänden)** to violate a church.

gotteslästerliche Sprache blasphemous words.

Gotteslästerung blasphemy, profanity.

gottverlassenes Nest godforsaken hole, dead-and-alive place, one-horse town *(US coll.)*.

Götze idol;
Geld zu seinem ~n machen to make an idol of wealth.

Götzen|bild graven image; ~**diener** worshipper of idols; ~**dienst** image worship.

Gouaschetechnik gouache.

Gourmet gourmet, epicure;
~ **sein** to be food-minded.

Gouvernante governess.

Gouvernement government territory.

Gouverneur state governor, executive;
dem ~ zustehend vested in the governor;
designierter ~ governor select *(US)*; **stellvertretender ~** deputy (lieutenant, *US*) governor;
j. als ~ einsetzen (ernennen) to appoint (establish) s. o. governor.

Gouverneurs|amt governorship *(US)*; ~**gebäude** government house; ~**reise** gubernatorial trip; ~**stelle** governorship *(US)*; ~**wahl** gubernatorial election; ~**wohnung** Executive Mansion *(US)*.

Grab grave, tomb;
offenes ~ open grave;
~ **ausheben** to dig a grave; **j. ins ~ betten** to lay s. o. to rest; **frühes ~ finden** to die before one's time, to be brought to an early grave; **sein ~ in den Wellen finden** to find a watery grave; **jem. ins ~ folgen** to die after s. o.; **j. zum ~ geleiten** to follow s. o. to the grave-side; **sich sein eigenes ~ schaufeln** to dig one's own grave; **verschwiegen wie ein ~ sein** to be as tight as wax; **mit einem Fuß im ~e stehen** to have one foot in the grave; **etw. zu ~e tragen** to ring the knell of s. th.; **Hoffnung zu ~e tragen** to bury a hope; **sich im ~ umdrehen** to turn in one's grave.

Graben ditch, trench, *(Tätigkeit)* digging;
~ **ausheben** to excavate a trench; **im ~ landen** to land in the ditch;
~**krieg** trench, mine warfare; ~**system** trenches.

graben, nach Gold to dig for gold; **Schacht ~** to sink a shaft; **Tunnel ~** to drive a tunnel.

Grab|geleit the last hono(u)rs; ~**gewand** grave clothes; ~**inschrift** monumental inscription; ~**platte** brass *(Br.)*; ~**rede** funeral oration; ~**schändung** desecration of a grave; ~**stätte** burying ground, sepulchre, burial spot (place); ~**stättenpflege** maintenance of tombs; ~**stein** headstone, monument; ~**steinkosten** cost of tombstone; ~**stelle auf Dauer kaufen** to purchase a cemetery plot in fast.

Grad degree, grade, order, extent, measure, rate, *(Qualität)* class, quality, *(Rang)* step, rank, *(Skala)* point, *(Strafrecht)* degree; **bis zu einem gewissen ~** to a certain extent, up to a point, in some measure; **im Besitz eines akademischen ~es** graduate; **im ersten ~e verwandt** in the first remove; **im höchsten ~e zuwider** distasteful in the extreme; **im ~ eines Obersten** of the rank of a colonel; **in hohem ~e** to a large extent, highly; **in hohem ~e verdächtig** highly suspicious;
akademischer ~ academic degree (rank), university degree; **unterster akademischer ~** pass degree *(Br.)*; **ehrenhalber verliehener akademischer ~** honorary degree; **geringer ~** *(Kurse)* shade; **höchster ~** extreme;
~ **der Arbeitslosigkeit** level of unemployment; **höchster ~ der Dummheit** height of stupidity; **höchster ~ der Erregung** highest pitch of excitement; ~ **des Folgeschadens** remoteness of damages; **acht ~ Kälte** eight degrees of frost; ~ **der Neuheit** *(Patent)* novel feature; **7 ~ unter Null** seven points below zero; **höchster ~ an Reinheit** *(Diamant)* first water; ~ **des Verschuldens** extent of liability;
15 ~ Celsius anzeigen to register 15 degrees centigrade; **akademischen ~ besitzen** to hold a degree; **in ~e einteilen** to graduate, to grade; **akademischen ~ erlangen** to take a degree; **seinen akademischen ~ in Oxford erlangen** to graduate at (from, *US*) Oxford, to have received one's degree from Oxford; **jds. Interesse in höchstem ~e erregen** to excite s. one's interest to the highest pitch; **bei Null ~ frieren** to freeze at 32 degrees Fahrenheit; **akademischen ~ verleihen** to confer a degree;

~**einteilung** scale division, scaling, graduation; ~**messer** indicator, *(fig.)* criterion; ~**messer für den Wohlstand eines Landes sein** to be an index of a country's prosperity.
graduell gradual, by degrees;
~**e Lebenskostenerhöhung** gradual increase in the cost of living.
graduieren to graduate, to receive a degree.
Graduiertenkursus graduate course.
Graduierter graduate, magister.
Grafik graph, engraving, graphic arts;
gewerbliche ~ industrial (commercial) art.
Grafiker commercial artist;
freier ~ free-lance (freelance) artist.
Grafik|händler print seller; ~**handlung** print shop.
grafisch graphic;
~ **darstellen** to graph, to diagram;
~**er Beruf** printing craft; ~**er Betrieb** printing establishment;
~**e Darstellung** graphical representation, graph, diagram.
Gram grief, sorrow, ruefulness;
vom ~ **gebeugt** grief-stricken, prostrated with grief;
vor ~ **sterben** to die of a broken heart; **sich vor** ~ **verzehren** to pine away with grief.
gram sein, jem. to harbo(u)r a grudge against s. o.
grämen, sich to grieve (sadden) o. s.; **sich zu Tode** ~ to pine away with grief.
gramgebeugt grief-stricken.
Grammatik grammar, *(Buch)* grammar book;
französische ~ **pauken** to drill French grammar;
~**fehler machen** to offend against grammar.
grammatisch nicht korrekt ungrammatical.
Grammophon gramophone, phonograph *(US)*;
~ **anstellen** to put on the gramophone;
~**nadel** phonograph needle, stylus; ~**platte** record, gramophone disk; ~**vorführung** gramophone recital.
Gran *(Perle)* grain.
Granate shell, egg *(sl.)*, *(Gewehr)* rifle grenade;
krepierte ~ exploded shell; **nicht krepierte** ~ dud.
Granat|feuer shell-fire; ~**werfer** *(mil.)* trench mortar.
Grandezza grandeur, grandeeship, grand air.
grandios grandiose, grand, magnificent;
~**e Aussicht** magnificent view; ~**e Idee** splendid idea.
Granit granite;
auf ~ **beißen** to knock one's head against a brick wall.
Graphologe graphologist, graphological expert.
Graphologie graphology.
Gras grass;
ins ~ **beißen** to bite (kiss, *coll.*) the dust, to kick the bucket *(sl.)*;
~ **wachsen hören** to hear the grass grow, to see far into a millstone (a brick wall); ~ **darüber wachsen lassen** to let bygones be bygones; ~ **zertrampeln** to trample down the grass.
grasen to graze, to pasture;
in fremden Gärten (auf einer anderen Wiese) ~ to poach on s. one's preserves.
Gras|gerechtigkeit profit à prendre; ~**land** grass; ~**narbe** turf.
grassieren to be rife (rampant, prevalent), to rage;
es ~ **Gerüchte** rumo(u)r has it.
grassierend widespread, epidemic, raging.
gräßlich ghastly, hideous, atrocious;
~ **langweilig** terribly dull;
~**er Mensch** horrible person; ~**es Verbrechen** hideous (abominable) crime; ~**es Wetter** awful (beastly) weather.
Grat ridge, edge;
~**anfall** *(Dach)* hip; ~**balken** hip rafter.
Grätenmuster herringbone pattern.
Gratifikation bonus, gratuity, bounty, money present;
nicht produktionsbezogene ~ nonproduction bonus;
~ **in bar** cash bonus; ~ **für die Belegschaft** staff bonus.
Gratifikations- und Vergünstigungswesen fringe benefit program(me).
gratis gratis, without payment (cost), gratuitous, for nothing, as a free gift, free of charge (costs), uncharged for, into the bargain;
etw. ~ **bekommen** to get it for nothing;
~ **und franko** free of charge and postage paid.
Gratisaktie free share, bonus share (stock, *US*), bonus on shares, capital (scrip) bonus *(Br.)*, stock dividend *(US)*, melon *(US)*, plum *(US)*;
ohne Anspruch auf ~**n** ex capitalization;
~**n anderer Gesellschaften** property dividends; ~ **mit Wahlrecht der Barabfindung** optional dividend;
~**n gewähren** to declare a dividend in stock of the corporation *(US)*; ~ **verteilen** to make distribution in stock.
Gratis|aktienausgabe bonus (scrip, *Br.*) issue; ~**angebot** *(Werbung)* [free] deal, premium; ~**anteil** bonus; ~**beilage** free supplement; ~**exemplar** presentation (specimen, personal, desk) copy; ~**kostprobe** sampling by taste; ~**kupon** incentive premium; ~**muster** free sample; ~**nummer** specimen number (presentation), specimen (desk) copy; ~**obligationen** *(an Stelle von Barverzinsung)* interest bonds; **variable** ~**obligationen** variable interest bonds; ~**plakat** free posting; ~**probe** free trial (sample); ~**reise** free trip; ~**vorführung** free demonstration (performance); ~**zeitschrift** free publication; ~**zuteilung** bonus distribution.
Gratulant congratulant.
Gratulation congratulation, felicitation.
Gratulations|besuch congratulatory visit; ~**karte** congratulation card; ~**kur** reception; ~**schreiben** letter of congratulation, congratulatory letter.
gratulieren to congratulate, to felicitate.
grau grey, gray;
alt und ~ **werden** to live to a grey age;
~**er Alltag** drab of life; **das** ~**e Elend bekommen** to be down in the mouth, to be in the dumps, to have the blues *(coll.)*; ~ **verhangener Himmel** grey and overcast sky; ~**er Markt** *(Pfandbriefe)* grey market; ~**en Rock anziehen** to join the army; **in** ~**er Vorzeit** in the dim and distant past; ~**e Wolken** wolly clouds.
Graubuch *(pol.)* grey book.
Grauen dread, fear;
j. mit ~ **erfüllen** to fill s. o. with horror.
grauen to be dawning;
jem. vor der Prüfung ~ to shudder to think of the examination.
grauenhaft dreadful, horrible;
~**er Fraß** muck *(sl.)*.
graumelierte Schläfen haben to be greying at the temples.
grausam cruel, atrocious, awful;
~**e Enttäuschung erleben** to experience a bitter disappointment.
Grausamkeit cruelty, atrocious act;
seelische ~ *(Scheidungsverfahren)* law (mental, *US*) cruelty, indignity; **unerträgliche** ~ *(Scheidungsrecht)* intolerable cruelty.
Grausen horror;
da kann man das große ~ **bekommen** it gives you the creeps.
grausig ghastly, dreadful, horrible;
~**er Anblick** horrible sight.
Grauzone green area, *(Arbeitslosigkeit)* intermediate area.
Gravier|anstalt engraving establishment; ~**arbeit** engraving.
gravieren to engrave, to cut.
gravierend aggravating, serious;
~**e Umstände** aggravating circumstances.
Gravitationskraft gravitational force.
gravitätisch einherschreiten to move with dignity.
Gravur intaglio, engraving.
grazil slender, delicate.
graziös graceful, with grace.
greifbar tangible, ready, on hand, handy, corporeal, concrete;
Buch ~ **haben** to have a book at hand;
~**e Ergebnisse** tangible results; ~**e Gestalt annehmen** to materialize; ~**e Mittel** available funds; **in** ~**e Nähe rücken** to come within reach; ~**e Vermögenswerte** tangible assets, corporeal property; ~**er Wert** tangible value.
Greifen grasp;
zum ~ **nahe** within one's reach;
~ **der Räder** grip of the wheels;
dem Erfolg zum ~ **nahe sein** to have success within one's grasp.
greifen to grip, to grasp, to seize, *(Anker, Rad)* to bite, *(Bremsen)* to grip, *(Zahnrad)* to engage;
Anschuldigungen aus der Luft ~ to fabricate allegations; **jem. unter die Arme** ~ to back s. o. with money, to help s. o. financially; **in den Beutel** ~ to dig deep into one's pocket; **im Dunkeln um sich** ~ to grope in the dark; **an jds. Ehre** ~ to attack s. one's hono(u)r; **zur Flasche** ~ to take to drinking; **mit beiden Händen nach einem Angebot** ~ to jump at an offer; **in die Kasse** ~ to rob the till; **zu einer List** ~ to resort to a ruse; **nach der Macht** ~ to seize power; **zu drastischen Maßnahmen** ~ to have recourse to drastic measures; **Personen eines Schauspiels aus dem Leben** ~ to draw the characters of a play from life; **Preis zu hoch** ~ to put the price too high; **mit seiner Schätzung zu hoch** ~ to make too high an estimate; **zur Selbsthilfe** ~ to resort to self-help; **um sich** ~ to be rampant, to spread; **schnell um sich** ~ to make rapid progress; **nach den Sternen** ~ to reach for the stars; **nach einem Strohhalm** ~ to clutch (grasp) at a straw; **zu den**

Waffen ~ to take up arms; **in ein Wespennest** ~ to stir up a nest of hornets;
tief in die Tasche ~ **müssen** to pay the devil; **mit den Händen zu** ~ **sein** to be obvious.
Greifer *(Filmkamera)* claw, *(Kran)* grab, *(Polizist)* sleuth, *(Zeilensetzmaschine)* elevator.
Greis graybeard, greybeard;
ehrwürdiger ~ venerable old man; **seniler** ~ dotard, doter.
Greisenalter old age, secondary childhood;
rüstig ins ~ **gehen** to live to a virile old age.
Greisenherrschaft gerontocracy.
grell glaring, dazzling;
~**er Blitz** brilliant flash of lightning; ~**er Schrei** piercing cry; ~**es Sonnenlicht** dazzling sunlight; **mit** ~**er Stimme** in a shrill voice.
Gremium body, group, committee, panel, board;
beratendes ~ advisory body (panel); **entscheidendes** ~ decision team; **internationales** ~ international organization; **besonders zusammengestelltes** ~ blue-ribbon panel;
~ **von Sachverständigen** committee (body, panel) of experts; ~ **von Wirtschaftsprüfern** accountancy body;
einem ~ **angehören** to be on a panel; **beschlußfähiges** ~ **bilden** to constitute a quorum; **als kollegiales** ~ **handeln** to act as a body; **j. aus einem** ~ **wählen** to elect s. o. from among the members present.
Grenz|abfertigung customs clearance; ~**abkommen** boundary convention, border treaty; ~**abschnitt** border district; ~**anbieter** marginal seller; ~**arbeiter** frontier worker; ~**arbeitgeber** nonprofit employer; ~**aufseher** customhouse officer; ~**ausweis** transit pass; ~**bahnhof** border (frontier) station; ~**beamter** border official; ~**befestigung** fortification; ~**befeuerung** boundary beacons; ~**begeher** perambulator; ~**begehung** perambulation, processioning; ~**bereich** suburb, frontier, confines; ~**bereich des Wissens** frontier of knowledge; ~**bereinigung,** ~**berichtigung** rectification of boundaries, frontier revision; ~**bescheinigung** frontier certificate, permit; ~**bestimmung** location *(US)*; ~**betrag** marginal income; ~**betrieb** marginal company (firm, producer, undertaking); ~**bevölkerung** frontier (border) population; ~**bewohner** borderer, frontiersman *(US)*; ~**bezirk** frontier (border, marginal) district, suburb; ~**dorf** border village.
Grenze frontier, border[line], boundary, bound, *(Grenzgebiet)* confines, *(Leistungsfähigkeit)* margin, *(Limit)* limit, *(Linie)* demarcation line, *(Rand)* edge;
an der ~ near the boundary; **bis an die** ~ **des Anständigen** near the knuckle; **in** ~**n** within limits; **in engen** ~**n** within narrow bounds; **innerhalb der** ~**n** within the precincts of; **innerhalb bestimmter** ~**n** within the marks; **ohne feste** ~ open-end;
angemessene ~**n** manageable limits; **äußerste** ~ extremity, utmost limit, extreme point, range, outboundary *(US)*; **stark befestigte** ~ strongly fortified border; **genau bestimmte** ~**n** well defined limits; **enge** ~**n** narrow limits; **nicht genau festgelegte** ~ no definite frontier; **nicht festliegende** ~**n** ambulant boundaries; **künstliche** ~ private boundary, artificial frontier (boundary); **natürliche** ~ public boundary; **obere** ~ upper limit; **regionale** ~**n** parochial boundaries; **strittige** ~ disputed (controversial) frontier; **untere** ~ lower limit; **verteidigungsfähige** ~ security border;
~ **der Arbeitswilligkeit** marginal disutility of labor *(US)*; ~**n des Geschäftslebens** business confines; ~ **der menschlichen Leistungsfähigkeit** limit of human performance; ~ **zwischen Recht und Unrecht** line between right and wrong; ~ **der Rentabilität** margin of profitability, break-even point; ~ **des Verbrauchs** margin of consumption; ~**n des Wachstums** limits to growth; **äußerste** ~**n des Weltraums** utmost confines of space;
~ **abstecken** to draw a boundary, to demarcate, to delimit; **genaue** ~**n angeben** to define; **an der** ~ **seiner Mittel ankommen** to reach the limits of one's resources; ~ **begehen** to perambulate; **sich hart an der** ~ **des Erlaubten bewegen** to sail near (close) to the wind; ~ **bilden** to form a boundary; **in seinen** ~**n bleiben** to keep within one's purlieus; **über die** ~ **entkommen** to escape over the border; ~**n festlegen** to determine (fix, mark out, designate, define) boundaries, to delimit, to demarcate; ~**n neu festlegen** to relocate *(US)*; ~**n einer Bergbaukonzession festlegen** to locate a mining claim; **über die** ~ **gehen** to cross the border; **bis zur** ~ **seiner Leistungsfähigkeit gehen** to work to capacity; **gemeinsame** ~ **haben** to touch each other, to march; **sich in engen** ~**n halten** to continue in a narrow range; **über die** ~**n des guten Geschmacks hinausgehen** to exceed the bounds of good taste; **sich über alle** ~**n hinwegsetzen** to pass all bounds; **seine** ~**n kennen** to know one's metes and bounds (one's limitations); **jds.** ~**n kennen** to know the length of s. one's foot; **über die** ~ **locken** to decoy across the frontier; ~**n revidieren** to revise boundaries; **an die** ~ **des Lächerlichen rühren** to verge on the ridiculous; ~ **des Erlaubten überschreiten** to overstep the line, to break the bonds, to offend against proprieties; ~ **seiner Vollmacht überschreiten** to exceed (overstep) one's authority; ~ **verletzen** to violate the frontier; ~ **hermetisch verschließen** to seal off the border; **Feind aus den** ~**n vertreiben** to drive the enemy out of the country; ~**n gegenüber jem. wahren** to observe the proprieties; **nahe der** ~ **wohnen** to live on the frontier; ~ **ziehen** to fix a boundary; **irgendwo eine** ~ **ziehen** to draw a line somewhere; **scharfe** ~ **ziehen** to make a clear distinction, to draw hard and fast lines.
Grenzeinkommen marginal revenue (income).
grenzen an to border, to verge, *(Grundstück)* to be adjacent (contiguous), to adjoin;
an Wahnsinn ~ to be little short of madness.
grenzenlos boundless, unlimited;
~ **dumm** utterly stupid;
~ **sein** to know no bounds; ~ **glücklich sein** to be happy beyond measure; **j.** ~ **verachten** to despise s. o. immeasurably;
~**er Weltraum** unbounded space.
Grenz|ertrag marginal revenue, marginal return (profit, yield); ~**ertragskurve** marginal product curve; ~**erzeugnis** end product, marginal product; ~**fall** borderline (marginal) case; ~**festsetzung** demarcation, determination; ~**festung** barrier, frontier fort; ~**flughöhe** service ceiling; ~**fluß** frontier river; ~**forderung** territorial claim; ~**formalitäten** frontier formalities; ~**frage** boundary question; ~**gänger** frontier worker (crosser); ~**gebiet** frontier area (land, zone), border area (district), borderland, confines, march, *(Studium)* borderline; **strittiges** ~**gebiet** debatable ground (land); ~**gebiet des Wissens** borderland of science; ~**graben** boundary ditch; ~**haus** house on the border; ~**kapazität** maximum capacity; ~**kapital** marginal capital; ~**kapitalkoeffizient** marginal capital-output ratio; ~**kommission** border commission; ~**konflikt** frontier (border) incident, boundary dispute; ~**konto** marginal account; ~**kontrolle** frontier (border) control, *(Zoll)* customs inspection; ~**kontrollstelle** checkpoint; ~**korrektur** frontier revision, rectification of boundaries.
Grenzkosten marginal (incremental, extra, terminal) costs;
~ **für die letzte Produkteinheit** marginal unit costs;
~**ergebnis** economic profit; ~**kalkulation** direct costing *(US)*, marginal costing *(Br.)*; ~**lehre** differential costing.
Grenz|kreditnehmer marginal borrower; ~**krieg** border war; ~**kurs** marginal rate; ~**land** outland, borderland, frontier land *(US)*; ~**landgebiet** frontier region; ~**last** maximum load; ~**leistungsfähigkeit des Kapitals** marginal efficiency of capital; ~**linie** boundary line, borderline, line of demarcation; ~**linien** *(Grundstück)* metes and bounds; ~**mal** landmark, boundary mark; ~**marke** boundary mark; ~**markierungsbake** boundary beacon; ~**mauer** party wall; ~**nachbar** adjacent owner.
grenznahe Gemeinde frontier district.
Grenznähe der Arbeit marginal disutility of labo(u)r.
Grenznutzen marginal profit (utility), degree of utility, final (diminishing) utility, margin of profitableness;
~ **der Arbeit** marginal utility of labo(u)r;
~**lehre** marginal utility theory; ~**schule** marginal utility school; ~**theorie** marginal utility (marginalist) theory, marginal theory of value.
Grenz|opfer marginal disutility; ~**passierschein** transit pass; ~**pfahl** boundary post; ~**pfähle verrücken** to move one's stakes; ~**pfosten** boundary pole; ~**plankostenrechnung** direct *(US)* (marginal, *Br.*) costing; ~**polizei** border police; ~**polizeistation** border police post; ~**posten** *(Grenzschutz)* boundary post, frontier station; ~**prinzip** marginal principle; ~**problem** frontier problem; ~**produkt** marginal product, end product; ~**produktivität** marginal productivity (productiveness, utility, disutility); ~**produktivität der Arbeit** zero productivity of labo(u)r, marginal disutility; ~**produktivitätstheorie** marginal productivity theory [of wages]; ~**produzent** marginal producer; ~**provinz** frontier province; ~**punkt** checkpoint, border point; ~**punkte** *(Grundstück)* bounders *(US)*; ~**rate der Substitution** marginal rate of substitution; ~**regelung** demarcation, delimitation; ~**region** frontier district; ~**revision** border revision; ~**schein** frontier pass; ~**schicht** marginal increment; ~**schließung** closing of the frontier; ~**schutz** border service, frontier service *(Br.)*; ~**schutzleiter** border patrol official; ~**schwierigkeiten** border troubles; ~**sicherungsbetrag** terminal subscription; ~**sperre** embargo on frontier trade, prohibition

of frontier traffic, *(Hindernis)* closed frontier; ~**staat** bordering state; ~**stadt** border (frontier, front) town, town on the frontier; ~**stamm** marginal tribe; ~**station** frontier (border) station, border point, checkpoint; **ab ~station** delivered at frontier; ~**stein** border (boundary) stone, landmark, terminus, monument; ~**steine setzen** to set boundary stones; ~**steinentfernung** removal of a landmark; ~**stempel** frontier stamp; ~**streife** border patrol; ~**streifen** *(Bauerngrundstück)* balk, *(Staaten)* frontier zone; ~**streitigkeit** boundary dispute (suit); ~**überbau** encroachment, superstructure; ~**übergang** border (boundary) crossing, crossing of the frontier; ~**übergangspunkt**, ~**übergangsstelle** frontier (border) point, frontier station, crossing point, checkpoint.
grenzüberschreitend frontier-crossing;
~**er Verkehr** border-crossing traffic.
Grenz|überschreitung frontier (border) crossing; ~**überschreitungskosten** *(EG)* frontier crossing costs; ~**übertritt** border (frontier) crossing; **zollfreier ~übertritt** free entry; ~**überwachung** border (frontier) control; ~**veränderung** alteration of borders; ~**vereinbarung** border treaty; **[kleiner] ~verkehr** [local] frontier traffic, cross-border traffic; ~**verlängerung** extension of a boundary; ~**verlauf** running of the border line; ~**verletzung** violation of the frontier, border violation; ~**verletzung begehen** to violate a frontier; ~**vermessung** surveying a boundary; ~**verrückung** removal of a landmark; ~**vertrag** treaty of limits; ~**verwirrung** confusion of boundaries; ~**wache** border warden; ~**wert** marginal value, *(fig.)* critical value; ~**zaun** boundary fence; ~**zeichen** natural boundary, landmark, boundary mark, terminus; ~**ziehung** demarcation, delimitation, *(Schürfrecht)* marking out of a claim; ~**zoll** customs; ~**zollamt** customs office, frontier customhouse; ~**zollbehörde** customs authorities; ~**zone** border zone; ~**zwischenfall** border (frontier) incident (clash).
Gretchenfrage 64thousand dollar (begging the) question.
Greuel abhorrence, horror;
~ **des Krieges** horrors of war;
~ **vor etw. empfinden** to abominate (have a horror of) s. th.; ~**nachrichten** atrocity stories; ~**propaganda** atrocity propaganda; ~**tat** atrocious crime, atrocity; ~**taten begehen** to commit outrages (atrocities).
Griesgram grumbler, grouser, sourpuss, *(alt)* sour old man.
griesgrämig sour, morose, sullen.
Griff hold, grip, grasp, butt, *(Stiel)* helve;
mit eisernem ~ with a grip of iron;
~ **nach der Macht** attempt to seize power; ~ **zu schärferen Maßnahmen** recourse to sterner measures; ~ **nach den Sternen** reaching for the stars, crying for the moon;
j. weiterhin im ~ behalten to hang on s. o.; **Konjunktur in den ~ bekommen** to have a grip on the economy; **seine Partei in den ~ bekommen** to establish a grip on one's party; **Problem in den ~ bekommen** to get to grips with a problem; **sich an einem ~ festhalten** to hang on to the handrail; **etw. im ~ haben** to have the knack of s. th.; **etw. fest im ~ haben** to keep a tight hold of s. th., to have s. th. by the tail *(sl.)*; **j. im ~ haben** to hold s. o. down, to have a considerable lead over s. o.; **Problem fest im ~ haben** to have a thorough grasp of a problem; ~**e kloppen** *(mil.)* to do rifle drill; **sich mit ein paar ~en erledigen lassen** to fix easily; **seinen ~ lockern** to loosen one's hold; **falschen ~ tun** to make the wrong choice; **glücklichen ~ tun** to strike a bonanza (it rich, *US*); **mit einem neuen Angestellten einen glücklichen ~ tun** to strike it lucky with a new employee; **tiefen ~ in seinen Beutel tun** to dip deep in one's pocket; **einen ~ in die Kasse tun** to dip (break) into the till.
griffbereit handy, ready to hand, at one's fingertips.
Griffel slate pencil, stylus.
Grill grill, gridiron, broiler *(US)*.
Grille *(fig.)* whim, whimsy, fancy;
jem. die ~n schon austreiben to knock stupid ideas out of s. o.; ~**n fangen** to be in low spirits, to mope; ~**n im Kopf haben** to have a head full of whims; **jem. ~n in den Kopf setzen** to put ideas into s. one's head.
grillen to grill.
Grillenfänger morose person.
Grillraum grillroom.
Grimassen schneiden to pull a face.
grimmig furious, fierce;
~ **kalt sein** to be bitterly cold;
~**er Hunger** severe hunger.
Grinsen grin, sneer;
höhnisches ~ derisive grin; **schadenfrohes** ~ smirk.
grinsen, über das ganze Gesicht to grin all over one's face; **wie ein Honigkuchenpferd** ~ to grin like a Cheshire cat (a street-door knocker); **spöttisch** ~ to smirk.
Grippe influenza, flu;
häßlichen ~anfall haben to have a bad go of flu; ~**epidemie** influenza (flu) epidemic; **fünf ~fälle** five cases of influenza; ~**virus** flu bug *(fam.)*.
Grips savvy, brains.
grob coarse, *(Arbeit)* rough, uneven;
~ **fahrlässig** grossly negligent; ~ **gerechnet** at a rough estimate; ~ **gesagt** roughly speaking;
j. ~ anfahren to snap at s. o.; ~ **bearbeiten** to roughwork, to rough-machine; **j. ~ behandeln** to treat s. o. in a rude way; ~ **überschlagen** to make a rough estimate; ~ **mit jem. umgehen** to treat s. o. roughly; ~ **umreißen** to give a rough outline; ~ **werden** to become rude (offensive);
~**e Antwort geben** to give a rude answer; ~**e Arbeit** rough work; ~**e Beleidigung** gross insult; ~**e Fahrlässigkeit** gross (crash) negligence; ~**er Fehler (Schnitzer)** gross mistake, howler, serious blunder; ~**en Fehler machen** to make a serious blunder; ~**e Gesichtszüge** coarse features; **aus ~em Holz geschnitzt** tough stuff; ~**er Kerl** rude fellow; ~**e Kost** plain fare; ~**er Raster** coarse screen; ~**e Schätzung** rough estimate; ~**e Schrift** grotesque type; ~**e See** rough sea; ~**e Umrisse** rough outline; ~**er Undank** gross ingratitude; ~**er Unfug** public nuisance; ~**e Unterteilung** rude classification; ~**e Worte gebrauchen** to say rude things.
Grob|abstimmung flat tuning; ~**bearbeitung** roughworking, rough-machining; ~**blech** heavy plate; ~**blechwalzwerk** plate rolling-mill ~**einstellung** rough adjustment; ~**gewicht** gross weight.
Grobheiten rude remarks, rudeness;
jem. ~ an den Kopf werfen to say rude things to s. o.
Grobian boor, churl, ruffian.
gröblich gross;
j. ~ beleidigen to offend s. o. seriously; **sich ~ irren** to be grossly mistaken; ~ **gegen eine Bestimmung verstoßen** to commit a gross violation of a rule.
Grob|passung *(Maschine)* loose fit; ~**raster** coarse screen; ~**schmied** ironsmith, blacksmith.
Gröbste, aus dem ~n heraus sein to be out of the wood.
Grobwalzwerk plate-rolling mill.
Grog rum, grog;
sich einen steifen ~ machen to mix o. s. a stiff peg.
grölen to bawl, to howl;
Beifall ~ to howl approval.
grölendes Gelächter raucous laughter.
Groll ranco(u)r, grudge, resentment;
heimlichen ~ gegen j. hegen to harbo(u)r a grudge against s. o.; **seinen ~ verbergen** to harbo(u)r quiet resentment.
grollen to harbo(u)r resentment, *(Gewitter)* to rumble, to mutter; **jem.** ~ to have a grudge against s. o., to harbo(u)r a resentment against s. o.
grollend zurückziehen, sich to withdraw resentfully.
Gros gross, twelve dozen, *(mil.)* main body;
~ **der Arbeiter** majority of the workers; ~ **des Heeres** bulk of the army; ~ **der abgegebenen Stimmen** bulk of the votes cast; ~ **der Tagesordnungspunkte** majority of the agenda; ~ **der Wähler** majority of the voters.
gros, en wholesale.
Groschen penny, cent;
meine paar ~ my few pennies;
keinen ~ Geld bei sich haben not to have a halfpenny on one; **nicht für einen ~ Verstand haben** to be a blockhead; **keine zwei ~ wert sein** not to be worth a brass farthing *(Br.)* (plugged nickel, *US*); **jeden nur möglichen ~ sparen** to save every penny one can; **ein paar ~ nebenbei verdienen** to earn a few extras; **seine paar ~ zusammenhalten** to look after one's money;
bei ihm fällt der ~ pfennigweise he is slow in the uptake;
~**automat** penny-in-the-slot (coin) machine; ~**blatt** penny magazine *(Br.)*, tabloid (yellow) paper; ~**heft**, ~**roman** penny horrible (dreadful) *(Br.)*, novelette *(Br.)*, dime novel *(US)*; ~**presse** yellow paper, penny press; ~**schreiber** penny-a-liner; ~**sparkasse** penny bank.
groß great, large, tall, big, wide, high, *(ausgewachsen)* grown up; **außerordentlich** ~ imperial, of superior size; **gleich** ~ equal in size; **normal** ~ full size; **riesig** ~ gigantic; **überdurchschnittlich** ~ king-size; **ungeheuer** ~ enormous, huge, immense; **ungewöhnlich** ~ bumper; ~ **vertreten** well represented;
beim Provinzpublikum ~ ankommen to go down very well with a provincial audience; **sich ~ aufspielen** to give o. s. airs, to act up

(US); ~ **auftreten** to make a big show; ~ **im Geschäft bleiben** to stay very big; ~ **dastehen** to cut a fine figure; ~ **und edel denken** to have lofty ideas; ~ **herausbringen** to launch, to star; ~ **hergehen** to go with a swing; ~ **schreiben** *(Rechtschreibung)* to write a word with a capital letter, to capitalize; **bei jem.** ~ **angeschrieben sein** to be in s. one's good books; ~ **in Form sein** to be in capital (crashing, *US*) form; ~ **im Geldausgeben sein** to be a great one for spending money; **ein wenig zu** ~ **geraten sein** to be on the large side;

~ **angelegter Angriff** large-scale attack; **~e Anzahl** great number of people; **~e Auflage** *(Zeitung)* wide circulation; **~er Auftrag** heavy order; **~er Aufwand** large expenditure; **j. mit ~en Augen ansehen** to look at s. o. wide-eyed; **~e Ausgaben** heavy expenses; **~e Auswahl** wide variety of products (choice); **~en Bahnhof für j. veranstalten** to give s. o. a red-carpet reception; **in ~er Besetzung erscheinen** *(Delegation)* to appear in full force; **~er Betrag** large sum; **~er Buchstabe** capital letter; **jem. ~en Dank schulden** to be greatly indebted to s. o.; **jem. einen ~en Dienst erweisen** to do s. o. a good turn; **~er Dummkopf** terrible fool; **in ~er Eile sein** to be in a hurry; **~er Einfluß** great deal of influence, pull; **~es Einkommen** large income; **~e Fahrt** deep-sea navigation; **~e Ferien** long vacation; **~es Feuerwerk** grand display of fireworks; **~e Fortschritte machen** to make great progress (strides); **zu meiner ~en Freude** much to my delight; **auf ~em Fuße leben** to live in great style; **~es Gefolge** large retinue; **~es Geld** bank notes; **~e Geschäftsabschlüsse tätigen** to deal in big volume; **~e Havarie** general average; **~en Herrn spielen** to lord it *(coll.)*, to give o. s. airs; **~e Hitze** intense heat; **~es Hotel** large hotel; **~e Kinder** grown-up children; **~e Koalition** great coalition; **~er Krieg** major war; **~e Kursspanne** wide quotation; **~e Linie** underlying principle; **~es Los** first prize; **~e Menge Arbeit** pile of work; **~e Mode sein** to be all the vogue (go now); **sich ~e Mühe geben** to go to great trouble; **sich in ~er Not befinden** to be in dire want (sore need); **~e Pause** long interval; **~e Politik** high-level politics; **~e Politikerfamilie** family of great politicians; ~ **angelegtes Projekt** large-scale project; **das ~e Publikum** the general public; **2000 Quadratmeter** ~ **sein** to be 2000 square meters; **kein ~er Redner sein** not to be much of a speaker; **~e Reise** long journey; **~e Rolle spielen** *(Theater)* to figure large; **~e Rosinen im Kopf haben** to fly high; **~er Schaden** severe loss; **~e Schnauze haben** to talk big, to brag; **~er Spielraum** wide margin; **~e Stücke von jem. halten** to think well of s. o.; **~e Stücke von sich halten** to think no small beer of o. s.; **~en Teil seines Einkommens im Provisionswege verdienen** to get the bulk of one's income by way of commission; **~es Tier** *(pol.)* bigwig, big shot; **in ~er Toilette** in evening dress; **~e Töne spucken** to make a boast of s. th.; **in ~em Umfang** on a large scale; **~e Verallgemeinerung** wide generalization; **~er Verlust** severe (heavy) loss; **~es Vermögen** great (large) fortune; **die ~e Welt** the fashionable world, top drawer, the four-hundred *(US)*; **von ~em Wert sein** to be of high value; **~es Wörterbuch** bulky dictionary; **~e Ziele haben** to fly high; **in ~en Zügen schildern** to give a broad outline.

Groß|abnahme industrial consumption, quantity (heavy) buying; **~abnehmer** bulk (heavy, quantity) buyer, large user (customer), outlet; **~abschluß** large contract; **~aktionär** principal (controlling) shareholder (stockholder, *US*).

groß angelegt large-scale.

Groß|angriff large-scale attack; **industrielle ~anlagen** large-scale industrial units; **~anleger** big investor; **~antiquariat** wholesale antiquarian (secondhand) booksellers; **~anzeige** display advertising.

großartig grand, unique, imperial, magnificent, swell;

~ **geschrieben** brilliantly written;

~ **mit jem. auskommen** to be hand in glove with s. o.; ~ **klappen** to work beautifully; ~ **tun** to put on airs;

~e Sache fine piece of business.

Groß|artigkeit einer Landschaft grandeur of a landscape; **~aufkauf** engrossing; **~aufnahme** *(Film)* close-up, bust, full screen, *(Foto)* big shot; **in ~aufnahme heranrücken** to zoom; **~auftrag** large (tall, volume) order, *(Börse)* big ticket order; **~band** large volume; **~bank** big banking house, big bank; **~bankwesen** large-scale banking, group banking *(US)*; **~bauer** large farmer; **~baustelle** large building site; **~bauten** capital works; **~behälter verladen** to handle containers.

Großbetrieb large establishment, large-scale enterprise (industry), big concern, big business *(US)*;

dezentralisierter ~ deconcentrated industry; **landwirtschaftlicher** ~ farming on a large scale, extensive farming;

~ **der chemischen Industrie** large chemical concern;

~ **haben** to trade in a large-scale way.

großbetriebliche Produktion wholesale production.

Groß|brandbereich *(Feuerversicherung)* conflagration area; **~buchhändler** wholesale bookseller; **~buchstabe** capital letter, majuscule, *(drucktechn.)* upper-case letter; **in ~buchstaben schreiben** to use block capitals; **~bürgertum** substantial (upper) middle class.

Größe size, extent, *(Bedeutung)* greatness, *(Berühmtheit)* celebrity, lion, star, *(Fassungsvermögen)* capacity, *(Größenordnung)* order, *(Größenverhältnis)* dimensions, *(Körpergröße)* height, *(Menge)* quantity, *(Rauminhalt)* bulk, volume, *(Stern)* magnitude, *(Summe)* amount;

in allen ~n und Ausführungen in all sizes and styles; **in gangbaren ~n** fair-sized; **nach ~n geordnet** in order of size, sized; **von mittlerer** ~ middle-sized;

nicht gängige ~ odd size; **genormte** ~ standardized (basic) size; **handelbare** ~ *(Börse)* regular lot; **kolossale** ~ jumbo size; **lagergängige** ~ stock size; **marktfähige** ~ commercial size; **mittlere** ~ middling size; **nächsthöhere** ~ next larger size; **natürliche** ~ *(techn.)* full scale; **preisbereinigte** ~ real term; **seelische** ~ nobility of soul; **übersehbare** ~ negligible quantity; **unbekannte** ~ dark horse; **vorschriftsmäßige** ~ regulation size;

~ **auf medizinischem Gebiet** great name in the field of medicine; ~ **der auf dem Spiel stehenden Interessen** magnitude of the interests at stake; ~ **in der Literatur** literary lion; ~ **eines Verbrechens** enormity of a crime;

der ~ **nach ordnen** to arrange according to size; **Ereignis von wirtschaftlicher** ~ **sein** to be an event of great significance.

Großeinkauf bulk buying (purchase, purchasing), lump sum (quantity, bulk, volume, *US*) purchase, purchase in bulk *(US)*, volume order;

im ~ bulk-purchased;

~ **tätigen** to buy in quantity.

Groß|einkäufer wholesale purchaser, wholesale (quantity, heavy) buyer; **~einkaufsgelegenheit** service center *(US)* (centre, *Br.*); **~einkaufsgenossenschaft** cooperative wholesale society *(Br.)*, wholesale cooperative *(US)*, wholesale purchasing company; **~einlage** large denomination deposit; **~einsatz** large-scale operations; **~eltern** grandparents.

großen, im in *(US)* (by the, *Br.*) bulk;

im ~ und ganzen on the whole, by and large, in the mass;

im ~ einkaufen to buy goods wholesale; **im ~ und ganzen unverändert sein** *(Kurse)* to be steady on the whole; **der Regierungspolitik im ~ und ganzen zustimmen** to approve at large of the government's policy.

Größen|angaben statement of size; **besondere ~ausmaße anlegen** to do things on a noble scale; **~beschränkungen** size restrictions; **~einteilung** sizing, size group; **~gleichheit** equality in size; **~klasse** size, size group; **nach ~klassen** according to size.

Größenordnung order of magnitude;

in der ~ **von** in the order (neighbo(u)rhood) of, on the scale of, *(Preise)* in the range of; **in jeder** ~ on every scale;

Kredite nach ihrer ~ **aufteilen** to scale credits.

Größenverhältnis *(math.)* proportion, ratio;

im ~ **3 : 4 gezeichnet** drawn on a scale of three to four.

Größenverhältnisse scale, dimensions;

wirtschaftliche ~ economies of scale;

~ **verändern** to scale up (down).

Größenwahn delusion of grandeur, megalomania;

an ~ **leiden** to suffer from a swelled head.

größenwahnsinnig werden to get too big for one's boots *(sl.)*.

Groß|erzeuger mass (large, quantity, big) producer; **~erzeugung** volume production; **~exporte** large-scale exports; **~fabrikation** mass (quantity) production, wholesale manufacture; **~fahndung** manhunt; **~fahrzeuge** heavy equipment; **~familie** extended family; **~feuer** large fire, conflagration; **~film** superproduction; **~finanz** high finance, moneyed interests.

großflächige Anzeigen large-scale space ads *(US)*.

Groß|flughafen air terminal, international airport; **~flugzeug** aerobus, jumbo jet; **~format** large size, *(Briefumschlag)* commercial size; **im ~format** large-sized.

großformatig large-sized.

Großfrachtflugzeug supercargo plane, flying boxcar *(US)*, sky truck *(US)*.

großgemustert large-patterned.

Groß|gepäck registered luggage *(Br.)*, checked baggage *(US)*; **~gerät** *(mil.)* major equipment; **~grundbesitz** landed interests, landed aristocracy, large- (many-) acred landlords; **~grundbesitz parzellieren** to parcel out land into small holdings; **~grundbesitzer** holder (owner) of a large estate, [many-acred] landlord, great landowner.

Großhandel wholesale [trade], wholesale dealing, merchant trading, jobbing *(US)*;
im ~ by the gross, by wholesale; **im ~ und Einzelhandel** wholesale and retail;
nur den ~ beliefern to supply wholesalers only; **~ betreiben** to buy and sell on a large-scale, to do big business, to carry on (do) a wholesale business, to wholesale, to job *(US)*; **~ umgehen** to eliminate wholesalers; **im ~ verkaufen** to [sell by] wholesale.

Großhandels|artikel wholesale goods; **nur ~artikel führen** to be wholesale only; **~aufgaben** wholesale (wholesaling) functions; **~betrieb** wholesale house; **~bezirk** wholesale district; **~einkauf** quantity buying (purchase), wholesaling; **~einkäufer** quantity buyer; **~erzeugnisse** wholesale goods; **~filiale** wholesale branch; **~firma** wholesale house (firm); **~funktionen** wholesale (wholesaling) functions.

Großhandelsgeschäft wholesale business (shop, store, *US*), *(einzelnes)* wholesale operation;
~ an Einzelkäufer wholesale dealing in small quantities;
~ betreiben to do a wholesale business, to wholesale.

Großhandels|gewerbe wholesale business, jobber's trade *(US)*; **~haus** wholesale warehouse, jobbing house; **~höchstpreis** maximum wholesale price; **~index** wholesale price index; **~kaufmann** wholesale merchant, wholesaler; **~kaufmann mit eigenem Lager** full service wholesaler; **~kredit** wholesale credit; **~lager** wholesale stock; **~markt** wholesale [produce] market; **~netz** wholesaling network; **~notierungen** wholesale quotations; **~partie** wholesale lot.

Großhandelspreis wholesale (trade) price, wholesale cost;
zum ~ by wholesale;
~e wholesale quotation;
zu ~en einkaufen to buy [at] wholesale, to buy goods wholesale;
~index index number of wholesale prices, wholesale price index; **~niveau** wholesale price level.

Großhandels|rabatt quantity (wholesale) discount, trade allowance; **~spanne** wholesale margin; **~unternehmen** wholesale enterprise (establishment), cash-and-carry concern; **~verband** wholesale association, federation of wholesale organizations *(Br.)*; **~verdienstspanne** wholesale margin; **~verkauf, ~verkäufe** wholesale selling, selling by wholesale; **~verkäufer** wholesale salesman; **~verteiler[stelle]** distributor; **~verteilung** distribution; **~vertreter** wholesale representative, distributing agent, distributor; **~zentrum** wholesale center *(US)* (centre, *Br.*).

Großhändler wholesale merchant (dealer), distributor, wholesaler, jobber *(US)*, large merchant, salesman *(US)*, tycoon *(US)*;
auftragsvermittelnder ~ drop shipper, drop shipment wholesaler, desk jobber *(US)*; **beschränkt zugelassener ~** limited-function wholesaler *(US)*;
~ für Industriebetriebe industrial distributor; **~ ohne eigenes Lager** waggon jobber *(US)*, truck wholesaler *(US)*; **~ mit breitem Sortiment (für alle Warengattungen)** general-line jobber;
genossenschaftliche ~vereinigung cooperative wholesale society.

Groß|handlung wholesale business (firm); **~havarie** gross average; **~hersteller** large-scale (mass) producer; **~herstellung** large-scale (mass) production; **~industrie** large-scale (big) industry, large industrial concerns *(Br.)*, large corporations *(US)*, big business *(US)*; **~industrieller** magnate of industry, industrial captain (magnate), big industrialist, business magnate, captain of industry, business tycoon.

großindustrielles Unternehmen large-scale industrial concern.

Grossist wholesale (quantity) buyer, wholesale dealer (trader), wholesaler;
~ ohne eigenes Lager (für Partiewaren) desk jobber *(US)*, drop shipper.

Grossisten|preis wholesale cost (price); **~tarif** quantity rate.

großjährig of age, major;
~ werden to come of age, to reach one's majority.

Groß|jähriger major; **~jährigkeit** full age, majority; **~kampfschiff** capital ship; **~kapital** haute (high) finance; **~kapitalist** capitalist, tycoon *(US)*; **~kaufmann** wholesale dealer (merchant, trader), wholesaler, warehouseman; **~klima** macroclimate; **~konfektion** wholesale fashion trade; **~konzern** group, big concern, trust, conglomerate *(US)*; **~kopfeter** big bug *(sl.)*.

großkotzig puffed up, big bully *(US coll.)*.

Groß|kraftwerk high-power station; **~kunde** big customer; **~lager** bulk storage; **~lagerhaus** wholesale warehouse; **~lautsprecher** high-power loudspeaker; **~lebensversicherung** ordinary life insurance *(US)* (assurance, *Br.*); **~lieferant** bulk supplier; **~lieferant eines Kaufhofes** rack jobber *(US)*; **~lieferung** bulk supplies; **~loge** *(Freimaurer)* grand lodge; **~macht** great (first-rate) power; **einer ~macht ein Mandat über ein Land übertragen** to mandate a country to one of the powers; **seine ~machtstellung verlieren** to lose one's position as a great power; **~markt** supermarket; **~markteinkauf** supermarket shopping; **~mutter** grandmother; **das kannst Du Deiner ~mutter erzählen** tell that to the horse marines.

Grossobuchhandel wholesale bookseller.

Groß|offensive *(mil.)* major offensive, push; **~oktav** large octavo; **~packung** family size, giant package; **in ~packung** economy-sized.

Großraum large area;
im ~ von N. in the environs (area) of N.;
~ einer Stadt environs of a town;
~büro open-plan office; **~fahrzeug** large-capacity train; **~flugzeug** jumbo jet.

großräumig roomy, spacious.

Großräumpflug bulldozer.

Großraum|tanker giant tanker; **~transporter** bulk carrier; **~wirtschaft** large-area economy; **~zeug** large-capacity car.

Groß|reinemachen heavy cleaning; **~rohr** big-diameter tube; **~rohrproduktion** big-diameter production; **~rundfunksender** high-power (clear-channel, regional, *Br.*) station; **~schaden** heavy (severe) loss; **~schlächterei** meat house *(coll.)*, packing house *(US)*; **~schreibung** capitalization.

Großserien|fertigung, ~herstellung, ~produktion large-scale (mass, quantity) production.

groß|sprecherisch boasting, bragging, tall; **~spurig** pretentious, overbearing, arrogant, haughty.

Großstadt large town, city, *(Weltstadt)* metropolis;
außerhalb der ~ extra-metropolitan;
sich als ~ entpuppen to turn out to be a big city;
~ausgabe *(Zeitung)* metropolitan paper; **~bezirk** metropolitan district (territory); **~entwicklung** metropolitan development; **kreisfreie ~** incorporated city, county borough, municipal corporation *(US)*.

Großstädter city dweller.

Großstadt|gebiet metropolitan (big-city) area (region), urban center *(US)* (centre, *Br.*); **~geräusche** busy hum of a large city; **abgeschwächtes ~geräusch hören** to hear the noise of a city subdued to a drone; **~getriebe hassen** to hate the racket of a city.

großstädtisch metropolitan.

Großstadt|konzept metro concept; **~lunge** lung of a city; **eleganter ~mensch** city slicker *(sl.)*; **~presse** big-city press; **~randgebiet** subtopia; **~verbrauch** metropolitan consumption; **~verbraucher** metropolitan consumer; **~verkehr** big-city traffic; **~verlockungen** inducements of a large town, attractions (allurements) of a big city; **~verwaltung** metro-[politan] government (authority); **~vorort** metropolitan suburb.

Groß|tat great achievement; **~teil** major part; **~teil der Anhänger** mainstream of adherents; **~teil der Bevölkerung** large proportion of the population; **~tuerei (~tun)** bragging, boasting.

großtun to brag, to boast, to put on the dog;
sich mit seinem Wissen ~ to make a display of one's knowledge.

Großunternehmen large-scale (big) enterprise, big business *(US)*; **städtische ~ zugunsten von Kleinbetrieben und ländlichen Fertigungseinheiten aufgeben** to diversify out of large-scale urban industries into small-scale units and village industries; **~ haben** to buy and sell on a large scale.

Groß|unternehmer large-scale (big) enterprise, big business; **~veranstaltung** mass rally; **~verbraucher** bulk (heavy, large-scale) consumer, large (heavy) user; **~verdiener** big-income earner; **~verdiener sein** to make a lot (stacks) of money; **~verkauf** wholesale [selling]; **~verkäufer** wholesale dealer; **~versandgeschäft** mail-order house *(US)*; **~versuch** large-scale test; **~verteiler** distributor, wholesaler; **~vertrieb** large-scale distribution; **~vieh** great cattle; **~wetterkarte** synoptic chart; **~wetterlage** general weather situation; **~wild** big game; **~wildjagd** big-game shooting.

großzügig liberal, generous, handsome, profuse, open-handed;
Geschäft ~ aufziehen to open a business on a large scale;
~ Geld ausgeben to launch out, to go the pace; **sich ~ erweisen** to do the handsome thing, to come down handsomely; **als ~ gelten** to earn a reputation for generosity; **~ sein** to take wide views; **fast zu ~ sein** to be generous to excess, to be generous to a fault; **~ bei Geschäften sein** to be free in business;

~es **Angebot** liberal offer; ~e **Bewilligungen vornehmen** to vote on a liberal scale; ~ **eingerichtetes Büro** handsomely equipped office; ~es **Gehalt** generous salary; ~e **Straßenführung** system of spacious and well-planned roads.

Großzügigkeit generosity, liberality;
grandiose ~ imperial generosity;
jds. ~ **ausnutzen** to draw on s. one's generosity; **j. an** ~ **übertreffen** to outbid s. o. in generosity.

Grotesk|film slapstick film; ~**schriften** grotesque.

Grotte grotto.

Grube excavation, cavity, *(Bergbau)* mine, pit, *(für Autoreparatur)* repair pit, *(Zeche)* coal mine, pit, works, colliery;
aufgelassene ~ abandoned (shutdown) mine; **im Tagebau betriebene** ~ opencast mine *(Br.)*, strip mine *(US)*; **enteignete** ~ expropriated mine;
~ **abbauen** to work a mine; ~ **auflassen** to shut down a mine; ~ **ausbeuten** to mine coal; ~ **befahren** to inspect a mine; ~ **mit Arbeitern belegen** to man a mine; ~ **mit Gewinn betreiben** to work a mine at a profit; **in eine** ~ **einfahren** to descend into (go down) a mine; **jem. eine** ~ **graben** to set a trap for s. o.

grübeln to muse, to meditate, to ponder;
über sein Mißgeschick ~ to brood over a misfortune; **stundenlang** ~ to be brooding for hours.

Gruben|abbau mining, working of mines, *(im Tagebau)* opencast working *(Br.)*, stripping *(US)*; ~**anteil** mining share, royalty; ~**arbeiter** [coal]miner, pitman, pithand, underground man, collier; ~**arbeiter sein** to work in the mines; ~**aufseher** inspector of mines; ~**aufsicht** inspection of mines; ~**aufsichtsbeamter** inspector of mines; ~**bahn** tramway; **senkrechter** ~**bau** well; ~**beauftragter** deputy *(Br.)*; ~**betrieb** mining, working of a mine; ~**bewetterung** mine ventilation; ~**brand** fire in a coal mine, mine fire; ~**distrikt** mining (coal) area; ~**erz fördern** to wind up ore from a mine; ~**explosion** mine (colliery) explosion; ~**feld** ground of a mine, coal field; ~**förderung** output of a mine; ~**gas** mine (marsh) firedamp, methane; ~**gasexplosion** gas explosion; ~**gelände** pitsite; ~**halde** mine dump; ~**holz** mining timber, pitwood; ~**industrie** mining industry; ~**kohle** pit coal; ~**lampe** safety (miner's) lamp; ~**pächter** contractor, charter master *(Br.)*; ~**preis** pithead price; ~**riß** plan of a mine; ~**schacht** shaft; ~**schließung**, ~**stillegung** mine shutdown (closing); ~**senkung** subsidence; ~**sicherheit** mine safety; ~**stempel** pit prop; ~**ventilator** mine fan, ventilator, ventilation shaft; ~**verschalung** mine tubbing; ~**vorstand** mining board; ~**wagen** mine car, tub; ~**wetter** damp.

Gruft [family] vault, sepulchre, tomb.

Grün *(Verkehrsampel)* green;
bei ~ **durchfahren** to cross on the green; **ins** ~**e fahren** to make a sally into the country, to go for a trip in the country; **bei Mutter** ~ **schlafen** to sleep in the open; **dasselbe in** ~ **sein** to be six of one and half a dozen of the other.

grün green, *(fig.)* green, inexperienced, unripe;
sich ~ **und blau ärgern** to kick o. s. for *(coll.)*; **j.** ~ **und blau schlagen** to beat s. o. black and blue; **jem. nicht** ~ **sein** to have no time for s. o.; ~ **und gelb vor Neid werden** to be green with envy;
sie waren einander nicht ~ there was no love lost between them; **über die** ~**e Grenze gehen** to cross the border illegally; ~**es Holz** green (unseasoned) wood; ~**er Junge** greenhorn; ~**es Licht** *(Verkehr)* green light; ~**es Licht für ein Vorhaben erhalten** to receive green light for a project; **jem.** ~**es Licht geben** to give the green light to s. o.; ~**e Minna** Black Maria *(Br., coll.)*, patrol waggon *(US)*, paddy wagon *(sl.)*, pie wagon *(US sl.)*; ~**es Pfund** *(EG)* green pound; ~**er Plan** farm program(me); ~**er Salat** dressed lettuce; ~**e Weihnachten** green Christmas; ~**e Welle** *(Verkehrsampel)* linked (synchronized) traffic light (pacer), 50 signals set a 50 km p.h.; ~**e Witwe** grass widow; ~**e Woche** Agricultural Show; **auf einen** ~**en Zweig kommen** to make progress, to rise in the world, *(Firma)* to break even.

Grün|anlagen green [belt], public land, parks, terrace *(US)*; **Freiflächen und** ~**anlagen** open-space area; **regionaler** ~**bereich** green wedge; ~**buch** *(pol.)* green book.

Grund ground, land, *(Baugrund)* building lot *(US)* (plot), *(Begründung)* cause, *(Fundament)* foundation, *(See)* bottom, floor, *(Ursache)* cause, occasion, rise, *(Vernunftsgrund)* reason;
auf ~ **von** by reason (virtue) of; **auf eigenem** ~ **und Boden** on one's own property; **auf** ~ **Gesetzes** under the law; **auf** ~ **eines Irrtums** due to an error; **auf dem** ~ **des Meeres** on the bottom of the sea; **auf** ~ **dieser Nachricht** as a result of this news; **auf** ~ **der Tatsache** on the strength that; **aus gleichem** ~**e** by the same token; **aus wichtigem** ~**e** *(Vertragsrecht)* for cause; **dem** ~**e und der Höhe nach** on the merits or in terms of amount; **im** ~**e genommen** at bottom, as a matter of fact, actually, strictly speaking; **im tiefsten** ~**e seines Herzens** in one's heart of hearts; **in** ~ **und Boden** out and out, completely, thoroughly; **mit gutem** ~ with good reason, well, with propriety; **ohne besonderen** ~ for the hell of it *(sl.)*; **ohne hinreichenden** ~ without just cause; **vom** ~ **auf** up from the ground; **von** ~ **aus verschieden** entirely different;
genau angegebener ~ specific cause; **ausreichender** ~ probable cause; **ausschlaggebender** ~ overriding reason; **kein erdenkbarer** ~ no earthly reason; **ernsthafter** ~ solid consideration; **gesetzlicher** ~ lawful cause; **hinreichender** ~ sufficient reason, probable cause; **stichhaltiger** ~ sound reason, reasonable ground; **nicht stichhaltiger** ~ unsound reason; **triftiger** ~ reasonable and probable cause, valid reason; **verfahrensrechtlicher** ~ procedural ground; **wichtiger** ~ just cause, cogent ground;
kein ~ **zur Besorgnis** no cause for alarm; ~ **und Boden** land, ground, real estate; **billiger** ~ **und Boden** low value lands *(US)*; **dazugehöriger** ~ **und Boden** premises; **unergiebiger** ~ **und Boden** deficient estate; **kein** ~ **zur Eile** no need for hurry; **kein** ~ **zum Eingreifen** no occasion to intervene; ~ **für hinreichenden Verdacht** justifiable cause for suspicion;
von ~ **auf ändern** to renew from top to bottom; **seine Meinung von** ~ **auf ändern** to change one's ground; ~ **angeben** to assign a (tell the) reason; **triftigen** ~ **angeben** to show cause; **zur fristlosen Kündigung aus wichtigem** ~**e berechtigen** to justify summary dismissal; ~ **und Boden besitzen** to own land; **Sache dem** ~ **nach entscheiden** to decide a case on its merits; **hinreichenden** ~ **geben** to account for; **der Sache auf den** ~ **gehen** to get down to bedrock (rock-bottom), to probe deep into a matter; **auf** ~ **geraten** to run aground; ~ **haben** to be within one's depth; **keinen** ~ **zur Beschwerde haben** to have no ground for complaint; ~ **zur Klage haben** to have reason (cause) to complain; ~ **zur Kündigung haben** to have grounds for giving notice; **etw. von** ~ **auf kennen** to know a subject inside out; **einem Gerücht auf den** ~ **kommen** to trace a rumo(u)r; **einer Sache auf den** ~ **kommen** to get to the bottom of the matter; **auf** ~ **laufen** to run aground; **Krug bis zum** ~ **leeren** drink the cup to the dregs; ~ **für ein Gebäude legen** to lay the foundations; ~ **zu einer völlig neuen Wissenschaft legen** to lay the foundation for an entirely new science; ~ **und Boden landwirtschaftlich nutzen** to use land for agricultural purposes; **j. in** ~ **und Boden reden** to talk s. o. down (one's head off); **sich in** ~ **und Boden schämen** to be thoroughly ashamed; **auf festem** ~ **sein** to stand on firm ground; **ohne jeden** ~ **sein** *(Beschwerde)* to be quite unfounded; **wahrer** ~ **für etw. sein** to be at the bottom of s. th.; **j. in** ~ **und Boden verdammen** to condemn s. o. outright; **etw. von** ~ **auf verstehen** to have the knack of (be a good hand at) it, to be death on s. th.; **ohne jeden** ~ **verhaftet werden** to be arrested without any reason given; **in** ~ **und Boden wirtschaften** to bring to total ruin;
~**abgabe** ground rent *(Br.)*, tax on land *(US)*, land tax *(US)*; ~**anliegen** basic concern; ~**anstrich** ground (priming) coat; ~**arbeitsbewertungspunkte** basic job factor points; **augenblickliche** ~**auflage** *(Zeitung)* current circulation; ~**ausbildung** initial training, primary education *(Br.)*, basic course; **fliegerische** ~**ausbildung** basic flying training; **nur eine** ~**ausbildung genossen haben** to be only half educated; ~**aussage** *(Anzeige)* creative copy; ~**ausstattung** basic facilities, initial equipment; **soziale** ~**ausstattung** basic amenities; ~**bedarf** basic requirements; ~**bedeutung** primary meaning of a word; ~**bedingung** prerequisite, fundamental (basic, main) condition, standard clause.

Grundbegriff fundamental conception (idea), fundamental clause, basic condition, basic idea;
~**e der Absatzwirtschaft** basic grounding in marketing; ~**e der Buchführung** principles (fundaments) of bookkeeping; **nicht einmal die** ~**e des Finanzwesens begreifen** not to know the ABC of finance; **einem Schüler die** ~**e im Französischen beibringen** to ground a pupil in French.

Grund|beitrag basic fee, flat-rate contribution; ~**belastung** land charge.

Grundbesitz ground, land, [landed] property (estate), ownership of land, holding of land, landholding, tenement, legal estate in land, real estate (property), realty, estate, corporeal hereditaments *(Br.)*, interest in land, interests in real estate, tenure, freehold property, hereditable property *(Scot.)*, heritage *(Scot.)*, subjects *(Scot.)*, *(Hausbesitz)* house property;
ohne ~ landless;
abgeschlossener ~ close, plot of land *(US)*; **ausgedehnter** ~ vast estate; **bäuerlicher** ~ peasant holding; **[hypothekarisch]**

belasteter ~ encumbered estate; **eingetragener** ~ registered land *(Br.)*; **nicht im Grundbuch eingetragener** ~ unregistered land *(Br.)*; **der Verfügungsfreiheit entzogener** ~ settled land; **ererbter** ~ ancestral estate; **freier** ~ free tenement, freehold [property] *(Br.)*, freehold tenure *(Br.)*; **gemeinsam geerbter** ~ coparcenary; **gewerblich genutzter** ~ commercial property; **industriell genutzter** ~ industrial property; **landwirtschaftlich genutzter** ~ agricultural holding; **zu Wohnzwecken genutzter** ~ residential property; **gepachteter** ~ leasehold property; **unterhalb der Ertragsgrenze liegender** ~ rentless land; **öffentlicher** ~ public land (domain, *US*); **bis zum Meer reichender** ~ estate extending to the sea; **staatlicher** ~ public land (domain, *US*), state lands *(US)*; **städtischer** ~ city real estate (property), town property *(Br.)*; **steuerpflichtiger** ~ ratable property *(Br.)*; **teilbarer** ~ partible land; **unveräußerlicher** ~ entailed property; **beschränkt vererblicher** ~ fee tail; ~ **mit gebundener Erbfolge** estate in tail; ~ **einer Gesellschaft** partnership realty; ~ **auf Lebenszeit** estate for life; ~ **und bewegliches Vermögen** land and chattels;
~ **in Bauerngüter aufteilen** to slice an estate into farms; **seinen** ~ **belasten** to charge one's land; ~ **besteuern** to levy taxes on land; ~ **entschulden** to free an estate of encumbrances, to disencumber an estate; ~ **erben** to succeed (be heir) to an estate, to take land by descent (devise); ~ **erwerben** to buy some land; ~ **haben** to own land; **etw.** ~ **haben** to have a small property in the country; **erheblichen (umfangreichen)** ~ **haben** to own acres of land (large estates); **gemeinsamen** ~ **haben** to own land by the entireties; **gemeinsam** ~ **geerbt haben** to hold an estate in parcenary; **seinen** ~ **schuldenfrei machen** to rid one's estate of debt; ~ **parzellieren** to parcel (divide) an estate, to lay out one's estate for sale in lots; ~ **steuerlich veranlagen** to value an estate; ~ **veräußern** to convey land, dispone *(Scot.)*; ~ **als Fideikommiß vererben** to entail; ~ **vermachen** to devise, to demise; ~ **testamentarisch vermachen** to devise by will;
~**abgabe** real-estate levy; **parzellierter** ~**anteil** freehold land *(Br.)*.

grundbesitzend landowning, landed.

Grundbesitzentwertungsfonds real-estate depreciation fund.

Grundbesitzer landholder, landowner, landed proprietor (proprietary), possessory lord;
kleinbäuerlicher ~ peasant proprietor; **kleine** ~ the small holders; **unmittelbarer** ~ terre-tenant;
~ **mit Fideikommißbindung** tenant in tail;
~ **sein** to have landed property; ~ **werden** to get an estate.

Grundbesitzertum land ownership.

Grund|besitzwerttabelle valuation list *(Br.)*; ~**bestandteil** element, primary component (ingredient); **wichtige** ~**bestandteile erfolgreicher Staatskunst** important elements in a good government; ~**betrag** basic (original) amount, *(Steuer)* basic allowance; ~**betrag des Urlaubsgeldes** basic holiday allowance.

Grundbuch land register *(Br.)*, real-estate register *(US)*, registry of deeds *(US)*, register of Sasines (deed) *(Scot.)*, deed registry *(Irland)*;
~ **berichtigen** to rectify the register; ~ **einsehen** to examine the public records, to search the land register *(Br.)*, [etwa] to clear a title; ~ **einsehen lassen** to have the title searched; **ins** ~ **eintragen lassen** to make an entry in the land register *(Br.)*, to enter at the Register of Deeds Office *(US)*; **Hypothek ins** ~ **eintragen lassen** to register a mortgage, to have a mortgage recorded in the office of the register of deeds *(US)*; **Hypothek im** ~ **löschen lassen** to enter satisfaction; **jem. im** ~ **[im Range] vorgehen** to have priority over s. o. in claim on mortgaged property;
beglaubigte ~**abschrift** certified copy from the land register *(Br.)*; ~**amt** Office of the Land Registry *(Br.)*, land registry *(Br.)*, registry of deeds *(US)*, register of title, title registration office *(US)*, register of deeds (titles) *(Scot.)*, real-estate recording office *(US)*, local deeds registry *(Ireland)*; ~**auszug** abstract of title *(Br.)*, land certificate *(Br.)*, office copy of the Land Register *(Br.)*, certificate of title *(US)*; **einwandfreier** ~**auszug** good merchantable abstract of title *(Br.)*; ~**auszug anfertigen** [etwa] to make an abstract from the documents of title; ~**beamter** registrar of deeds *(US)*, recording officer *(US)*, recorder; ~**berichtigung** rectification of register; ~**bescheinigung** certified copy from the land register; ~**bestimmungen** land registration rules; ~**bezirk** land district *(US)*; ~**blatt** [etwa] land registry general map *(Br.)*, real-estate map *(US)*; ~**einsicht** search of the [land] register, inspection of the register *(Br.)*, [etwa] examination of title, title search *(US)*; **befriedigende** ~**einsicht** good record title; ~**eintragung** [etwa] title of record, land (deed) registration *(Br.)*, registration with the land registry (of land) *(Br.)*, registration of land (title, deeds), entry made in the register *(Br.)*, real-estate recording *(US)*, title registration *(US)*; **falsche** ~**eintragung** error in the register; ~**eintragung beantragen** to apply for a registration as proprietor; ~**gebühren** land registry fees *(Br.)*, registry fees *(US)*.

grundbuchlich|vorbelastet sein to be subject to prior encumbrances;
~**e Sicherheiten** freehold securities.

Grundbuch|ordnung Land Registration Act *(Br.)*, [etwa] Land Transfer Act *(Br.)*; ~**papiere** real-estate records; ~**richter** Registrar at the Land Charges Department *(Br.)* (of the land office, *US*); ~**system** registry system; ~**unterlagen prüfen** to inspect the documents of title; ~**vermerk** notice in the land register *(Br.)*; ~**vermutung** conclusive evidence of title; ~**zwang** compulsory registration of title *(US)*.

Grunddienstbarkeit rent charge, landed (real) servitude *(Scot., US)*, [right of] easement;
ununterbrochen ausgeübte ~ continuous easement; **subjektiv dingliche** ~ easement appurtenant; **negative** ~ negative easement; **öffentlich-rechtliche** ~ public easement; **beschränkt persönliche** ~ easement in gross *(US)*; **positive (unbeschränkte)** ~ positive (affirmative) easement;
~ **einräumen** to grant an easement; ~ **löschen** to extinguish an easement.

Gründe grounds, reasons;
aus diesen ~**n** on these grounds; **aus formellen** ~**n** as a matter of form, for the sake of formality, for form's sake; **aus persönlichen** ~**n** on personal grounds; **aus politischen** ~**n** for reasons of policy, on political grounds; **aus rechtlichen (juristischen)** ~**n** on legal grounds; **aus religiösen** ~**n** on religious grounds; **aus steuerlichen** ~**n** for taxation purposes; **aus verschiedenen** ~**n** on a number of counts; **aus verschiedensten** ~**n** for a variety of reasons; **aus wirtschaftlichen** ~**n** for economic reasons; **aus** ~**n der Klugheit** for reasons of policy; **aus** ~**n der Sicherheit** for safety reasons; **aus** ~**n der Staatsräson** for reasons of state; **mit** ~**n versehen** substantiated; **ohne Angabe von** ~**n** without stating reasons;
die früher aufgeführten ~ the above reasons; **berechtigte** ~ legitimate reasons; **erhebliche** ~ substantial reasons; **flache** ~ *(Fischerei)* shallow; **geschäftliche** ~ business reasons; **plausible** ~ ostensible reasons; **private** ~ private reasons; **schwerwiegende** ~ serious reasons, deep-lying causes; **steuerliche** ~ tax reasons; **stichhaltige** ~ valid reasons; **zwingende** ~ compelling (cogent) reasons;
~ **die stark gegen die Wahrheit von Nachrichten sprechen** strong presumption against the truth of the news; **die tiefsten** ~ **eines Waldes** the innermost depth of a forest; ~ **für und wider** pros and cons;
~ **anführen** to produce reasons; **zwingende** ~ **anführen** to clinch an argument; **seine** ~ **angeben** to show cause (reasons); **seine** ~ **darlegen** to state one's reasons; **Fall nach materiellen** ~**n entscheiden** to decide a case on its merits; **stichhaltige** ~ **ins Feld führen** to advance sound arguments; **seine ganz besonderen** ~ **haben** to have one's own peculiar reasons; **gute** ~ **haben** to have good grounds; **aus wohlüberlegten** ~**n handeln** to act upon good grounds; **seine** ~ **geltend machen** to defend one's case; **wahre** ~ **für etw. sein** to be at the bottom of it; ~ **für die Arbeitslosigkeit untersuchen** to investigate the causes of unemployment; ~ **verschleiern** to obscure the issue; ~ **vorbringen** to show reasons (cause), to establish grounds, to motivate; **seine** ~ **zusammenstellen** to marshal one's arguments.

grundehrlich as straight as a die.

Grundeigentum landed property (estate), freehold property, land (real) estate, realty, real property, demesne, ownership of (title to) land, *(OHG)* partnership realty;
belastetes ~ imperfect ownership, mortgaged property (estate); **freies** ~ fee simple absolute, domain, frank tenement, freehold; **im Wert gestiegenes** ~ improved real estate; **lastenfreies** ~ perfect ownership *(US)*; **nachlaßfähiges** ~ estate of inheritance *(US)*; **unbelastetes** ~ perfect ownership *(US)*; **unbeschränktes** ~ fee simple; **verbrieftes** ~ record title; **unbeschränkt vererbliches** ~ property held in fee simple; **gesetzlich vererbtes** ~ freehold in law;
~ **und bewegliche Sachen** land and chattels;
~ **besitzen** to hold land (in demesne); **unbelastetes** ~ **erwerben** to obtain title free of a mortgage; **über sein** ~ **frei verfügen können** to own the freehold.

Grundeigentümer landowner, owner of land, landed proprietor, land (property) owner, ground landlord, owner of real estate, (property) tenant in fee simple, superficiary;

freier ~ freeholder, freehold owner; **unbeschränkter** ~ tenant in fee simple;
~ **sein** to own (hold) land.

Grund | einführung basic introduction; ~**einheit** *(mil.)* basic unit; ~**einkommen** basic income; **jds.** ~**einstellung teilen** to share s. one's basic position; ~**eis** ground (anchor) ice.

gründen to ground, *(einrichten)* to establish, to create, *(einsetzen)* to set up, to institute, to endow, *(Fabrik)* to plant, *(Geschäft)* to open, to establish, to set up, *(Gesellschaft)* to found, to float, to form, to start, to promote, to create, to organize, *(schaffen)* to create;
Aktiengesellschaft ~ to organize (promote) a corporation; **sich auf bloße Annahmen** ~ to be based on mere supposition; **Familie** ~ to found a family; **Filiale** ~ to establish a branch office; **sich auf Fleiß und Sparsamkeit** ~ to flow from industry and economy; **eigenes Geschäft** ~ to set o. s. up in business; **neue Gesellschaft** ~ to float a new business company; **Handelsfirma** ~ to establish a business; **seinen eigenen Hausstand** ~ to set up house (for o. s.); **seine Meinung auf Tatsachen** ~ to found one's opinions on facts; **Reich** ~ to build up an empire; **Stadt** ~ to found a new city; **sein Urteil auf einen Verdacht** ~ to base one's judgment on a suspicion.

Gründer promoter, floater, organizer, founder, originator, institutor, projector, incorporator *(US)*;
berufsmäßiger ~ **von Gesellschaften** professional (companies) promoter;
~**aktien** promoter's shares (stocks, *US*), original issue (founder's) stock *(US)*; **zurückgegebene** ~**aktien** donated stock *(US)*; ~**anteile** initial shares, founders' shares (stock, *US*), original issue stock *(US)*; ~**anteil besitzen** to be in on the ground floor; ~**anteil erhalten** to be let in on the ground floor; ~**bank** parent bank; **sich zu den** ~**bedingungen beteiligen** to get in on the ground floor; ~**bericht** statutory report; ~**familie** founder's (proprietary, *Br.*) family.

Grunderfordernisse principal (prime) requisites.

Gründer | gesellschaft original (constituent) company, parent company (concern, corporation, establishment); ~**gewinn** founder's profit; ~**konsortium** promoting syndicate *(Br.)*; ~**lohn** founder's profit; ~**parteitag** inaugural convention.

Grundertragssteuer farmer's tax *(Br.)*.

Gründerversammlung founder's (organization) meeting, meeting of incorporators (to organize).

Grunderwerb purchase (acquisition) of land;
freihändiger ~ offhand buying of ground *(US)*;
j. vom ~ **im Erbschaftswege ausschließen** to disable s. o. from inheriting real estate.

Grunderwerbs | bescheinigung *(Zwangsversteigerung)* certificate of purchase; ~**kosten** cost of site, purchase cost of real estate; **steigende** ~**kosten** rising costs of land; ~**steuer** tax on the conveyance of real estate, realty transfer tax *(US)*.

Gründerzeit period of promotion.

Grund | erzeugnis primary product; ~**faktoren** primary factors.

grundfalsch utterly (absolutely) wrong.

Grund | farbe ground colo(u)r; **in den** ~**festen erschüttern** to rock the foundations; ~**fischerei** sedentary fishery; ~**fläche** acreage, *(Erde)* surface, *(Haus)* floor space (area); ~**form** type; ~**formel** basic formula; ~**freibetrag** *(Einkommensteuerformular)* basic abatement, basic relief *(US)*; ~**freiheiten** *(Verfassung)* fundamental freedoms; ~**gebühr** base fee, basic charge, *(Bank)* basis of charge, *(el.)* flat rate *(US)*, *(Telefon)* telephone subscription (rate), telephone rental, subscription rental *(Br.)*, line charge; ~**gebühr nebst Verbrauchstarif** *(Gas, Elektrizität)* two-charge rate, two-part tariff; ~**gedanke** leading idea, keynote; ~**gedanke einer Ausstellung** keynote of an exhibition; **als** ~**gedanken enthalten** to keynote; ~**gehalt** base (regular) pay, basic (base) salary, class rate, basic content; **garantiertes** ~**gehalt** guaranteed rate; ~**gesamtheit** *(Statistik)* population; ~**geschäft** underlying transaction; ~**gesetz** fundamental law, *(pol.)* constitutional law, constitution, institution, organic law *(US)*; ~**haltung der Börse** prevailing tone of the market; ~**haltung beibehalten** *(Börse)* to maintain the tone.

grundhäßlich ugly as sin.

Grund | herr possessory lord, seignior; ~**herrschaft** *(hist.)* manor; ~**idee** *(Werbung)* keynote (root) idea.

grundieren to ground, to prime.

Grundierfarbe priming colo(u)r.

Grundindustrie basic industries.

Grundkapital *(AG)* capital stock *(US)* (fund), nominal capital *(Br.)*, stock capital *(US)*, share (registered) capital *(Br.)*, original stock *(US)*, *(Bank)* fund *(Br.)*, capital stock *(US)*, *(Nominalkapital)* nominal capital *(US)*;
zur Zeichnung aufgelegtes ~ issued capital *(Br.)*, issued capital stock *(US)*; **eingetragenes** ~ registered capital; **zusätzlich eingezahltes** ~ additionally contributed capital; **genehmigtes** ~ authorized capital *(Br.)*, authorized capital stock *(US)*; **satzungsgemäßes** ~ statutory capital; **stimmberechtigtes** ~ relevant share capital *(Br.)*; **geringst zulässiges** ~ minimum capital;
zur Zahlung auf das ~ **auffordern** to levy assessment *(US)*; ~ **um ... erhöhen** to increase the original capital *(Br.)* (stock capital, *US*) by ...; ~ **herabsetzen** to reduce the capital stock *(US)* (share capital, *Br.*);
~**verwendung** use of funds.

Grund | karte master card; ~**kenntnisse** basic skills; **volkswirtschaftliche** ~**kenntnisse** grounding in economics; ~**kenntnisse im Lesen, Schreiben und Rechnen** standards of literacy and numeracy; ~**kontingent** basic quota; **skizzierte** ~**konzeption** *(Anzeige)* outline; ~**konzeption für den Mediaeinsatz** basic media conception; ~**kosten** real (bulk-line, basic) costs; **erforderlicher** ~**kurs** *(Schule)* prerequisite.

Grundlage base, basis, foundation, fundament, bedrock, substratum, *(fig.)* pedestal, *(Gebäude)* fundamental, groundwork, *(Unterlagen)* datum, data;
auf der ~ **der Gegenseitigkeit** on a basis of reciprocity; **auf gesetzlicher** ~ on a statutory footing; **auf internationaler** ~ on an international basis; **auf sicherer** ~ on a steady foundation; **auf unparteiischer** ~ on a nonpartisan basis; **jeder** ~ **entbehrend** devoid of any foundation;
~**n** *(Wissenschaft)* elements, rudiments;
genossenschaftliche ~ cooperative basis; **gesetzliche** ~ statutory basis, legal basis; **regionale** ~ regional basis; **solide** ~ solid foundation; **gesunde wirtschaftliche** ~ sound economic basis; **rein wirtschaftliche** ~ profit-and-loss basis;
~ **späterer Entwicklung** basis for future development; ~ **des Erfolgs** corner stone of success; **sittliche** ~ **für die Erziehung** ethical basis for education; ~**n der modernen Gesellschaft** foundations of modern society; ~ **der Preisberechnung** basis of prices; ~ **großer sozialer Umwälzungen** underlying cause of great social upheavals; ~ **einer Wissenschaft** rudiments of a science;
als ~ **dienen** to serve as a basis; **jeder** ~ **entbehren** to be without any foundation, to be off base, *(Klage)* to be destitute of merits; **Geschäft auf einer soliden** ~ **errichten** to build up a business on a sound basis; ~**n der Gesellschaft erschüttern** to shake the foundations of society; **gemeinsame** ~ **für Verhandlungen finden** to find common ground for negotiations; ~ **für ein Vermögen legen** to found a fortune; **Einkünfte zur** ~ **der Besteuerung nehmen** to base taxation on the revenue; ~**n für den Anlagenpark schaffen** to build up the asset base; ~ **für seine späteren Erfolge schaffen** to lay the foundation for one's future success; **auf eine gesündere finanzielle** ~ **stellen** to put on a better financial footing; ~ **eines Unternehmens verbreitern** to spread its business base.

Grundlagen | ausarbeitung *(Anzeige)* conception; ~**forschung** basic research; ~**last** land charge.

grundlegend basic, primary, fundamental, elementary, radical;
~**e Abhandlung** treatise of fundamental importance; ~**e Änderungen vornehmen** to make fundamental changes; ~**er Beitrag** fundamental contribution; ~**e Bücher** basic reading; ~**e Lektüre** basic reading; ~**es Material** basic data; ~**e Planung** basic planning; ~**e Tatsachen** basic facts.

Grund | legung foundation; ~**lehrgang** basic course; ~**leistung** *(Krankenkasse)* basic benefit; ~**lektüre** basic reading.

gründlich solid, thorough, well thought out, deep, ingoing, detailed, hot and strong, six ways to Sunday *(sl.)*, *(Kenntnisse)* profound, well-grounded;
seine Meinung ~ **ändern** to alter one's opinion radically; ~ **arbeiten** to be thorough in one's work; **etw.** ~ **ausnutzen** to take full advantage of s. th.; **jem. etw.** ~ **austreiben** to knock s. th. out of s. o.; ~ **in etw. einsteigen** to go deeply into s. th.; **Zimmer** ~ **reinigen** to give a room a thorough cleaning; **jem.** ~ **die Meinung sagen** to give s. o. a few home truths, to give s. o. a piece of one's mind; **sich** ~ **täuschen** to be sadly mistaken; ~ **überholen** *(Auto)* to overhaul thoroughly; ~ **Bescheid wissen** to know all about it;
~**er Arbeiter** thorough worker; ~**e Ausbildung** thorough training; ~**e Enttäuschung** quite a disappointment; ~**e Kenntnisse haben** to be thoroughly versed, to know one's trade; ~**e Reform** radical (sweeping) reform; ~**er Reinfall** flop, washout, blue, ruin *(sl.)*; ~**es Studium** detailed study.

Grundlinie *(Statistik)* base line, *(Theorie)* outline;
~**n der Außenpolitik** main features of foreign policy.

Grundlohn basic wage (pay), base wage rate;
~ **einschließlich von Normalzuschlägen** standard labo(u)r rate; ~**satz** base rate of pay (earnings); ~**satz und Prämie** standard labo(u)r rate; ~**tarif** base wage rate.
grundlos bottomless, unfathomable *(fig.)*, idle, groundless, gratuitous;
~**e Beschuldigungen** unfounded accusations; ~**es Gerücht** unfounded rumo(u)r; ~**e Lüge** gratuitous lie; ~**er Verdacht** gratuitous suspicion.
Grund|maß *(Statistik)* basic dimensions; ~**maßstab** *(Physik)* unit; ~**mauer** base, building foundation; ~**modell** initial form; ~**nahrungsmittel** essential (basic) foodstuffs, basic items (provisions); ~**pacht** ground rent; **lebenslängliche** ~**pacht** lifehold; ~**pächter** land tenant, landholder; ~**patent** basic patent; ~**pfandbrief** mortgage bond, real-estate bond *(US)*; ~**pfandgläubiger** mortgagee.
Grundpfandrecht encumbrance, landed security, charge by way of legal mortgage *(Br.)*, mortgage of land, mortgage lien, hypothecary right;
durch ~**e gesichert** secured by mortgages;
formloses ~ general equitable charge; **vertragliches** ~ conventional (common-law) mortgage;
~**e und sonstige Grundstückslasten** *(Bilanz)* charges and mortgages;
~ **auf seinem Grundbesitz bestellen** to encumber one's real property.
grundpfandrechtlich besichern to secure by mortgage on real estate.
Grund|pfandrechtsbescheinigung charge certificate; ~**pfandverzeichnis** register of charges *(Br.)*, land charges register *(Br.)*; ~**pfeiler** pillar, main support, keystone.
Grundplan *(Architekt)* ground plan, plot;
in einen ~ **aufnehmen** to plot;
~**aufteilung** plotting of subdivision.
Grund|prämie *(Versicherung)* basic key rate; ~**preis** standard [purchase] (basic) price, net cost, *(pro Einheit)* unit price; **abänderungsfähiger** ~**preis** target price; ~**prinzip** fundamental (cardinal, guiding, first) principle; ~**problem** fundamental problem; ~**produkte** primary (basic) products.
Grundrecht *(Naturrecht)* natural right;
~**e** *(pol.)* constitutional (substantial, civil) rights;
verfassungsmäßig geschützte ~**e** personal rights, privileges and immunities *(US)*; **wirtschaftliche** ~**e** economic rights;
~ **der Konsumfreiheit** basic principle of freedom for the consumer.
Grund|regel principal, fundament, ground, rule; ~**rente** annual (economic, net, pure, true) rent, census, *(Pensionsplan)* primary insurance amount *(US)*, basic pension, *(Sozialversicherung)* primary benefit; **pauschale** ~**rente** basic flat-rate pension; ~**rentenformel** primary benefit formula; ~**richtung** general tendency.
Grundriß ground (floor) plan, *(Anlageplan)* layout, *(Festung)* trace, *(Lehrbuch, Leitfaden)* compendium, sketch, outline;
~ **der Wirtschaftsgeschichte** outlines of economic history;
~ **abstecken** to peg out the ground plan; ~ **aufnehmen** to table a plan; ~ **eines Hauses aufnehmen** to trace out the plan of a house.
Grundsatz principle, axiom, gospel, postulate, rule;
beherrschender ~ overriding principle; **entscheidender** ~ precedent; **oberster** ~ leading principle;
~ **der Gefährdungshaftung** doctrine of strict liability; ~ **der Gegenseitigkeit** rule of comity, reciprocity principle; ~ **der Haftbeschränkung** principle of limited liability; ~ **der Mehrheitsentscheidung** majority rule; ~ **der Nichthaftung bei Verschulden der Gegenseite** sudden peril rule; ~ **der Notwendigkeit der Erschöpfung innerstaatlicher Rechtsmittel** local remedies rule; ~ **der Produzentenhaftung** manufacturer's liability doctrine; ~ **wirtschaftlich vernünftiger Regelung** *(Kartellrecht)* rule of reason *(US)*; ~ **von Treu und Glauben** expectation of good faith in business dealings; ~ **der gemeinwirtschaftlichen Verkehrsbedienung** common carrier principle; ~ **des freien Wettbewerbs** let-alone principle; ~ **der liberalen Wirtschaftspolitik** Fair Deal *(US)*;
von einem ~ **abgehen** to deviate from a principle; ~ **aufstellen** to lay down a principle; **es sich zum** ~ **machen** to make it a rule;
~**besprechung** policy discussion; ~**debatte** principle debate; ~**denken** hard-core thinking.
Grundsätze lines, policy;
nach diesen ~**n** along these lines; **nach den festgesetzten** ~**n** on the lines laid down; **nach gleichen** ~**n** on an equal footing; **nach kaufmännischen** ~**n** according to business principles;
allgemein anerkannte ~ generally recognized principles; **berufsethische** ~ professional standards; **besteuerungspolitische** ~ cannons of taxation; **feste** ~ fixed principles; **hohe moralische** ~ high moral code; **parteipolitische** ~ party platform; **politische** ~ politics; **sittliche** ~ ethical principles; **standesrechtliche** ~ cannons of professional ethics; **strenge** ~ rigid principles; **völkerrechtliche** ~ principles of international law, Comity of Nations; **widerstreitende** ~ warring principles;
~ **ordnungsgemäßer Buchführung und Bilanzierung** good accounting principles *(US)*; **personalpolitische** ~ **eines Unternehmens** manpower policy; ~ **der Wirtschaftsordnung** basic principles of the economy;
jem. ~ **einprägen** to transfuse principles into s. o.; **an seinen** ~**n festhalten** to stick (live up) to one's principles; **zu den** ~**n guter Verwaltung gehören** to be the principle of good government; **eiserne** ~ **haben** to have cast-iron principles; **in äußerst noblen** ~**n fundiert sein** to proceed from the most noble principles; **gegen die** ~ **der Demokratie verstoßen** to be contrary to the tenets of democracy.
Grundsatz|entscheidung leading decision; ~**erklärung** declaration of policy, policy statement, statement on policy, manifesto *(US)*; **präzise** ~**erklärung** definite statement of policy.
Grundsatzfrage fundamental question;
~**n** major policies;
politische ~**n** basic policy issues;
in den ~**n zu einer Einigung gelangen** to reach a general agreement on fundamentals.
Grundsatzgesetzgebung legislative framework.
grundsätzlich fundamental, cardinal, basic, principal, on principle, principally;
sich ~ **einigen** to agree in principle; ~ **dagegen sein** to refuse on principle;
~**e Aufgaben** basic functions; **von** ~**er Bedeutung** of cardinal importance; ~**e Entscheidung** leading decision; ~**er Gegner** opponent on principle; ~**e Meinungsverschiedenheiten** basic differences of opinion; ~**e Rede** platform speech.
Grundsätzliches fundamentals;
über ~ **verhandeln** to talk turkey *(sl.)*.
Grundsatz|programm policy statement, *(Partei)* party platform; ~**referat** fundamental paper; ~**urteil** test case *(US)*; ~**urteil beantragen** to sue for damages at large; ~**vereinbarung** open contract.
Grundschul[aus]bildung elementary education (instruction), primary education *(Br.)*;
seine ~ **erfolgreich abschließen** to obtain basic school-leaving qualification.
Grundschuld [etwa] dry mortgage, land charge *(Br.)*;
~ **bestellen** to register (create) a charge on land *(Br.)*;
~**brief** certificate of charge *(Br.)*; ~**verschreibung** mortgage debenture *(Br.)*.
Grund|schule elementary (primary, grade, *US*) school, junior school *(Br.)*, grades *(US)*; ~**schulbildung** primary (elementary) education; ~**schüler** primary scholar, elementary student *(US)*.
Grundschulklassen junior forms *(Br.)*, grades *(US)*;
erste vier ~ junior forms *(Br.)*; **letzte** ~ senior school *(Br.)*;
~ **und Oberschulklassen** elementary and secondary grades *(US)*.
Grundschul|lehrer grade teacher *(US)*; ~**stufen** primary grades *(US)*; ~**unterricht** primary instruction, grades *(US)*; ~**unterricht erteilen** to teach in the grades *(US)*; ~**wesen** elementary school system, grades *(US)*.
Grund|standardkosten basic standard costs; ~**statut** primary franchise *(US)*.
Grundstein foundation (memorial) stone, headstone;
~ **legen** to lay the foundation, *(fig.)* to lay the corner stone.
Grundsteinlegung foundation of a house;
~ **vornehmen** to lay the foundation stone, to perform groundbreaking ceremonies.
Grundstellung *(mil.)* attention.
Grundsteuer land (property, *US*) tax, local rate *(Br.)*, tax on land *(US)*, residential levy;
~ **und Gebäudesteuer** land and building tax *(US)*; **fällige** ~ **und Gebäudesteuer** property tax payable *(Br.)*;
von der ~ **befreien** to exempt from land tax *(US)*, to derate of local taxes *(Br.)*; ~ **erheben** to levy a rate *(Br.)*; ~ **ermäßigen** to reduce the taxes on a house; **zur** ~ **veranlagen** to assess landed property;
~**ablösung** redemption of land tax *(US)*; ~**ausschuß** Commissioners of Supply, local valuation court *(Br.)*; ~**befreiung**

exemption from land tax *(US)*, derating of local taxes *(Br.)*; ~**befürworter** land taxer *(US)*; ~**erleichterung** derating of local taxes *(Br.)*; ~**kapitalisierung** capitalization of land taxes *(US)*; ~**neufestsetzung** new valuation for rating purposes; ~**pflichtiger** rate-payer.

grundsteuerpflichtiges Grundstück ratable estate (property).

Grundsteuer|rolle register of taxes; ~**satz** realty (local) rate; ~**schätzung** rating valuation; ~**veranlagung** assessment on landed property *(US)*, property tax assessment *(Br.)*; ~**veranlagungsstelle** land-tax parish *(US)*, rating authority *(Br.)*; ~**vergünstigung** land tax relief *(US)*, rating relief *(Br.)*.

Grundstimmung *(Börse)* undertone, prevailing tone.

Grundstock basis stock, foundation, *(Stammkapital)* original funds;
~ **einer Büchersammlung** main body of a book collection, nucleus of a library.

Grundstoff basic (raw) material, primary product;
~**e** primary commodities (products);
gewerbliche ~**e** industrial basic materials;
~**bereich** basic industry sector; ~**industrie** primary (basic, commodity) industries; ~**markt** primary commodities market; ~**preis** basic-material price; **im** ~**sektor** in the basic sector.

Grund|strecke *(Bergbau)* wall *(Br.)*; ~**strich** *(drucktechn.)* stem.

Grundstück plot [of land], land, property, piece (parcel) of land, close, lot *(US)*, *(Bauplatz)* building site (plot), building lot *(US)*, location *(US)*, yard, *(mit Gebäuden)* premises;
auf dem ~ on these premises; **mit einem** ~ **verbunden** incident to a piece of land; **mit einem** ~ **fest verbunden** running with the land;
~**e** things real (immovables), *(Bilanz)* land, real estate; **abgeholztes** ~ cut-over land; **abgeräumtes** ~ cleared site; **in sich abgeschlossenes** ~ enclosure, land enclosed; **von einer Vermögensverwaltung zum Verkauf angebotenes** ~ land held on trust for sale; **angrenzendes** ~ adjoining property, adjacent parts of land; **aufgegebenes** ~ relinquished (abandoned) land; **zu Spekulationszwecken aufgekaufte** ~**e** accommodation lands; **bahneigenes** ~ railway *(Br.)* (railroad, *US*) property; **baureifes** ~ developed land, building estate; **bebaute** ~**e** built-up area, developed real estate, improved (built-on) property; **nicht bebautes** ~ idle (undeveloped) land, new land *(US)*, empty lot *(US)*; **bebaute und unbebaute** ~**e** *(Bilanz)* land, real estate and buildings, freehold land and buildings *(Br.)*; **beherrschendes** ~ dominant tenement; **[hypothekarisch] belastetes** ~ land conveyed by way of mortgage, affected (mortgaged, burdened, charged) estate, encumbered (mortgaged, onerous) property (estate); **belastungsfähiges** ~ land that may be mortgaged; **benachbartes** ~ adjacent (adjoining) land, neighbo(u)ring premises; **billigeres** ~ back land; **dienendes** ~ servant land; **als Kreditsicherheit dienendes** ~ property charged as security for a debt; **eigengenutztes** ~ owner-occupied land; **eingefriedetes** ~ land enclosed, enclosure; **nicht eingefriedetes** ~ overt pound; **grundbuchlich eingetragenes** ~ registered property, recorded land; **einmaliges** ~ property rarity; **nicht eintragungspflichtige** ~**e** overriding interests *(Br.)*; **enteignetes** ~ condemned property; **grundbuchlich erfaßtes** ~ recorded (registered, *Br.*) land; **erschlossenes** ~ improved property, developed real estate; **frei erworbenes** ~ nonancestral estate; **freies** ~ vacant property; **ähnlich gelegenes** ~ similarly located property; **im Sanierungsgebiet gelegenes** ~ slum property; **am Wasser gelegenes** ~ waterfront property; **zentral gelegenes** ~ downtown property *(US)*; **gemeindeeigenes** ~ municipal (parish) property; **gemeinschaftliches** ~ joint estate; **in Besitz genommenes** ~ executed estate; **genutztes** ~ seated (used) land; **forstwirtschaftlich genutztes** ~ timber estate; **gewerblich genutztes** ~ industrial property, commercial land, business premises; **landwirtschaftlich genutztes** ~ agricultural *(Br.)* (farm) land; **nicht genutztes** ~ vacant property; **zum Verkauf gestelltes** ~ property listed for sale *(US)*; **im Wert gestiegenes** ~ improved real estate; **herrenloses** ~ disclaimed property; **herrschendes** ~ dominant land (estate, tenement); **hypothekisiertes** ~ mortgaged premises; **lastenfreies** ~ unencumbered estate; **staatliche** ~**e** government land; **städtisches** ~ city property (real estate), town lot *(US)*; **steuerpflichtiges** ~ rat(e)able property (estate) *(Br.)*; **treuhänderisch übereignetes** ~ land conveyed on trust; **einem Treuhänder zum Verkauf übertragenes** ~ trust for sale *(Br.)*; **umfriedetes** ~ enclosed land; **nicht umfriedetes** ~ unenclosed land; **unbebautes** ~ idle (undeveloped) land, new land *(US)*, plot of unbuilt ground, empty lot *(US)*; **unbelastetes** ~ clear estate, estate free from encumbrances; **ungenutztes** ~ unseated (unused) land; **einer eintragungsfähigen Belastung unterliegendes** ~ property subject to a registrable charge; **nicht frei vererbliches** ~ entail; **verlassenes** ~ disclaimed property; **verpachtetes** ~ land out at rent, leased (let) property, demised premises; **gewerbsmäßig verpachtetes** ~ property let commercially;
~ **des Berechtigten** *(Dienstbarkeit)* dominant tenement; ~ **im Besitz von Kapitalsammelstellen** institutionally owned real estate; ~**e des jeweiligen Eigentümers** shifting severalties; ~**e und Gebäude** *(Bilanz)* land *(Br.)* (real estate, *US*) and buildings; ~ **und Gebäude, Maschinen und maschinelle Anlagen** *(Bilanz)* land, buildings, plant and machinery *(Br.)*, property, plant and equipment *(US)*; ~ **in gleicher Lage** similarly located property; ~ **in lebenslänglicher Nutznießung** estate for life; ~**e und grundstücksgleiche Rechte** *(Bilanz)* real estate and equivalent rights; ~ **mit Straßenfront** frontage; **kleines** ~ **zu verkaufen** *(Anzeige)* small property for sale; ~, **in das Zwangsvollstreckung betrieben wird** extended land;
~ **abschätzen** to estimate an estate; ~ **abschreiben** to write down property; ~ **abstecken** to mark out (stake off) a claim; **an ein** ~ **angrenzen** to neighbo(u)r with an estate; **belastetes** ~ **aufgeben** to abandon a mortgaged estate; ~ **auflassen** to transfer (convey, assure, surrender) land; ~ **ausmessen** to survey a property; **landwirtschaftlich genutzte** ~**e von den Gemeindesteuern befreien** to derate property of local taxes *(Br.)*; ~ **belasten** to encumber real property; ~ **hypothekarisch belasten** to mortgage a piece of real estate, to charge land; ~**e zu Besicherungszwecken belasten** to charge land as security; ~ **beleihen** to lend on mortgage; ~ **mit Vorkaufsberechtigung besitzen** to settle upon land subject to preemption *(US)*; ~ **betreten** to enter premises; **widerrechtlich jds.** ~ **betreten** to trespass upon s. one's property; ~ **im Grundbuch eintragen** to make an entry in the land register *(Br.)*, to enter an estate at the Register of Deeds Office *(US)*; ~ **enteignen** to amerce an estate to the Crown *(Br.)*, to take private property for public use; ~ **entschulden** to free an estate of encumbrances, to disencumber an estate; ~**e erschließen** to lay land out in a community, to develop building lots *(US)*; ~ **lastenfrei erwerben** to get a property free from all encumbrances; ~**e zur Bebauung mit Geschäftshäusern freigeben** to zone for *(US)* (throw a property into) business use; ~ **einem Makler an die Hand geben** to list property with a broker *(US)*; **an ein** ~ **grenzen** to neighbo(u)r with an estate; ~ **gepachtet haben** to hold under land lease; ~ **kaufen** to buy some land; **auf einem** ~ **lasten** to run with the land; ~ **lastenfrei machen** to free a property from mortgage (encumbrances), to disencumber an estate; ~ **in Pacht nehmen (pachten)** to take land on lease, to take a lease of a piece of land; ~ **parzellieren** to parcel (divide) an estate, to divide an estate into lots *(US)*; ~ **räumen und herausgeben** to quit and yield up; ~ **realisieren** to bank an estate; **in** ~**en angelegt sein** to be locked up in land; **mit einem** ~ **verbunden sein** to be incident to a piece of land; ~ **umschreiben** to alienate an estate; ~ **umzäunen** to hedge in a piece of ground; ~ **steuerlich veranlagen** to appraise property for taxation, to value an estate, to rate property; ~ **veräußern** to dispose of land; ~ **an die tote Hand veräußern** to alienate in mortmain, to amortize land; ~ **verpachten** to lease property; ~ **pauschal verpachten** to let off (lease) a property as a whole; ~**e zusammenschreiben** to assemble parcels of land.

Grundstücks|abgrenzung limitation (lines) of an estate; ~**abschätzung** valuation of an estate, real-estate appraisal; ~**abschreibung** depreciation on land (of premises, of property owned), property (real-estate) depreciation, allowance on premises; ~**absteckung** marking out of a claim; ~**abtretung** conveyance of real estate, transfer of title to land; ~**agent** real-estate salesman; ~**angebot** real-estate offering, supply of land; ~**angelegenheit** real-estate subject; ~**angelegenheiten** conveyancing (real-estate) matters; ~**anlage** real-estate investment; **gewerbsmäßige** ~**anlagen** commercial investment in property; **seinen** ~**anspruch aussitzen** to hold down a claim *(Br.)*; **auf** ~**ansprüche verzichten** to sign away one's interest in an estate; ~**anteil** portion of an estate; ~**anzeigen** *(Zeitung)* real-estate columns; ~**areal aufkaufen** to buy land on a large scale; ~**auflassung** conveyance of real estate, transfer of title to land, grant to uses; ~**auflassungsurkunde** transfer deed, deed in fee (of conveyance), record by way of conveyance; ~**aufsplitterung** property carve-up; ~**auswahl** selection of site.

Grundstücksbelastung mortgage of (charge on) land, land charge, encumbrance on land, registered (land) charge *(Br.)*, real burden *(Scot.)*;
nachrangige ~ subsequent charge *(Br.)*;
~ **löschen** to discharge an encumbrance; ~ **vornehmen** to create a charge.

Grundstücks|belastungsurkunde memorandum of charge; ~**belegenheit** location of land (property), lie of the ground; ~**benutzung** licence, use of land; ~**benutzungsrecht** license *(US)*; ~**beschreibung** real-estate picture, description of property (land), parcels; ~**besichtigung** viewing of land, inspection of property *(Br.)*; ~**besichtigung durchführen** to make a survey of an estate; ~**besitz** landed property; **echter** ~**besitz** actual seisin, seizing; ~**besitzer** real-estate owner, owner of land, *(pl.)* landed men; **ortsansässiger** ~**besitzer** resident landowner; **wirklicher** ~**besitzer** terretenant; **entfernbarer** ~**bestandteil** movable fixture; **wesentliche** ~**bestandteile** immovable fixtures; **zum beweglichen Vermögen gehörende** ~**bestandteile** quasi personalty; ~**beteiligungen** real-estate holdings; **zusätzliche** ~**beurkundung** derivative conveyance; ~**bewertung** assessment, survey, land valuation, valuation of an estate, valuing real estate, real-estate appraisal; ~**bewertung für Kommunalsteuerzwecke** valuation for rating purposes; ~**büro** real-estate office; ~**darlehn** real-estate loan; ~**darlehn aufnehmen** to raise a loan on an estate; **schmale** ~**ecke** pick of land.

Grundstückseigentum proprietorship, landed (real) estate, landed property, freehold, title to land, property, tenancy; **nur auf dem Papier bestehendes** ~ paper title; **zum Verkauf gestelltes** ~ property listed for sale *(US)*; **unbeschränkt vererbares** ~ fee simple, freehold estate *(Br.)*;
~ **einem Makler in die Hand geben** to list property with a broker *(US)*.

Grundstückseigentümer [real] estate owner, property owner, owner of land, occupier of premises, freehold owner, freeholder, landholder, landed proprietor;
unbeschränkter ~ owner in fee simple;
~ **zu Bruchteilen** tenants in common;
~ **sein** to hold land;
~**haftpflicht** owner's public liability.

Grundstücks|eigentumsurkunde title deed; ~**eignung** fitness of property; ~**einkünfte** land revenue, property (real-estate) income, rents and profits from land; ~**enteignung** compulsory land purchase *(Br.)*, eminent domain *(US)*; ~**entschädigung** indemnity for expropriation, special benefit land damages *(Br.)*, compensation money *(US)*; ~**entschuldung** disencumberment of an estate; ~**entwicklungskosten** property development costs; **widerrechtliche** ~**entziehung** real wrong; ~**erschließung** land (property) development.

Grundstückserschließungs|abgabe development land tax *(Br.)*; ~**gesellschaft** development agency, land (real-estate) developer, site planner; ~**kosten** property development costs; ~**plan** land-development project.

Grundstücks|erträge *(Bilanz)* income from rents and profits of land, issue of an estate; ~**erwerb** purchase of property (land), land acquisition; ~**erwerb mittels eines Bankkredits finanzieren** to purchase property with money to be advanced by a bank; ~**erwerber** purchaser of property; **lastenfreier** ~**erwerber** third possessor *(US)*; **sich als** ~**erwerber eintragen lassen** to enter land *(US)*; ~**finanzen** real-estate finance; ~**finanzierung** real-estate financing; ~**fläche** plot of land, lot *(US)*, land area; **große** ~**flächen parzellieren** to slice up large parcels of land; ~**fonds** proprietary fund; **[im Ausland vertriebener]** ~**fonds** [offshore] real-estate fund *(US)*; **unrechtmäßig gezogene** ~**früchte** mesne profits *(Br.)*; ~**genossenschaft** land trust; ~**geschäft** real-estate industry, *(einzelnes)* real-estate transaction, land *(US)* (property) deal; ~**gesellschaft** proprietary (land-leasing, property, real-estate) company, real-estate corporation (trust) *(US)*, land (realty, *US*) company; ~**gesetz** Vendor and Purchaser Act; ~**grenzen** boundary lines of an estate, butts and bounds, commarchio; ~**grenzen festlegen** to mark the bounds of an estate, to locate the lines of a property *(US)*; ~**haftung** occupier's liability; ~**handel** real-estate business; ~**hauptbuch** property ledger; ~**höchstpreise** land ceilings; ~**hypothek** mortgage on real estate *(US)*; ~**inanspruchnahme** forced use of land; ~**interessen** real-estate interests, interests in real estate; ~**investition** real property investment; ~**kauf** land (property) purchase, purchase of real estate; ~**kauf finanzieren** to finance purchase of property; ~**käufer** purchaser of land; ~**kaufvertrag** real covenant, real-estate closing, land (estate) contract, agreement of sale and purchase *(Br.)*, contract for the sale of land *(Br.)*, purchase and sale agreement *(Br.)*, *(mit Rechtsgarantie)* warranty deed *(US)*; **rechtsverbindlicher** ~**kaufvertrag** binding contract for land; **schuldrechtlicher** ~**kaufvertrag** bond for title; ~**kaufvertragsformular** blank deed; ~**klage** land action; ~**komplex aufteilen** to slice a piece of property; ~**konjunktur** boom in real estate; ~**konsortium** real-estate syndicate; ~**konto** premises (real-estate) account; ~**konzern** property conglomerate; ~**kredit** land credit, real-estate loan (credit); ~**last** charge on land, estate (land) charge, encumbrance; **vertragliche** ~**lasten** onerous provisions.

Grundstücksmakler real-estate agent (broker, dealer, operator) *(US)*, estate (house) agent *(Br.)*, land agency (agent, *US*, jobber, broker, *Br.*), realtor *(US)*;
~ **für gewerbliche Grundstücke** industrial broker;
einem ~ **an die Hand geben** to list with (place in the hands of) a real-estate broker *(US)*; ~ **sein** to trade in real estate;
~**büro** estate office (agency), land agency *(Br.)*; ~**gebühr** estate agent's fees *(Br.)*, real-estate brokerage *(US)*.

Grundstücks|markt real-estate (property, *Br.*) market, *(Zeitungsspalte)* real-estate column (section); ~**meliorationen** land improvements, improvements of real estate; ~**miteigentümer** joint estate; ~**nachbar** adjoining landowner, neighbo(u)r; ~**nachlaß** estate of inheritance; ~**nachrichten** newspaper real-estate pages; ~**nießbrauch** estate in usufruct; **lebenslanger** ~**nießbrauch** estate for life, life estate; ~**nutzung** enjoyment of land, land use; **befristetes** ~**nutzungsrecht** base fee; ~**obligationen** real-estate bonds *(US)*; ~**pacht** land tenure, ground lease (rent), lease of land, *(mit fester Pachtdauer)* estate for years; **billige** ~**pacht** bargain-basement lease of property; ~**pachtvermittlung** lease brokerage; ~**pachtvertrag** ground lease; ~**papiere** brief of title.

Grundstücksparzelle lot *(US)*, plot (portion) of land, parcel, allotment *(Br.)*;
~**n vereinigen (zusammenschreiben)** to link up one's land, to incorporate a field in an estate, to assemble parcels of land.

Grundstücks|parzellierung breaking up an estate, parcelling of land into small holdings; ~**parzellierung vornehmen** to parcel land into small holdings; ~**pfandrecht** hypothecary right; ~**portefeuille** property portfolio; ~**preis** real-estate price *(US)*, land cost (price), property price *(Br.)*; ~**preis nachträglich erhöhen** to gazump *(Br.)*; ~**projekt** real-estate project; ~**prozeß** land action; ~**räumungsklage** action to recover land, dispossess proceedings *(Br.)*.

Grundstücksrecht interest in land, legal estate (interest), real-estate interest, *(Immobilienrecht)* land law, law of real property *(US)*, real property law *(US)*, heritable right *(Scot. law)*;
älteres ~ paramount title; **anerkanntes** ~ vested estate; **aufschiebend bedingtes** ~ executory estate;
jem. ~**e übertragen** to vest an estate in s. o., to vest s. o. with rights in an estate; ~**e in Geldansprüche umwandeln** to convert from rights in land to rights in money.

Grundstücks|register property register, land records *(US)*; ~**reklame** real-estate advertising; ~**rendite** income from rents and profits from land; ~**rente** rent charge; ~**schätzer** real-estate appraiser; ~**schätzung** valuation of an estate, land (real-estate) appraisal; ~**schätzung vornehmen** to value a property; ~**sicherheit** land as security; ~**spekulant** land jobber, property (land) speculator; ~**spekulation** realty (property, land) speculation, land jobbing, speculation in real estate, real-estate venture *(US)*; ~**spezialist** property lawyer; ~**tausch** real-estate exchange; ~**taxe** valuation of an estate, real-estate appraisal; ~**teilfläche** plot of land, lot *(US)*; ~**teilung** division of land, partition; ~**transaktion** real-estate transaction; ~**übereignung** alienation (conveyance) of real estate, transfer of title to land; ~**überlassung** assurance of property, surrender, closing of title *(US)*; ~**überlassung an die tote Hand** mortmain; ~**übernahmevertrag** purchase and sale agreement *(US)*; ~**übernehmer** surrenderee.

Grundstücksübertragung conveyance of land, alienation (conveyance, conveyancing) of real estate, transfer of real estate *(US)*, assignment of property, real estate transfer *(US)*, demise, transfer of title for land;
lastenfreie ~ overreaching conveyance *(Br.)*; **unentgeltliche** ~ voluntary disposition of land, voluntary transfer of property;
~ **mit (ohne) gleichzeitige Grundbucheintragung** conveyance with (without) registration; **treuhänderische** ~ **zur Obligationensicherung** trust deed; ~ **gegen Stundung des Kaufpreises** living pledge; ~ **in der Zwangsversteigerung** foreclosure conveyance;
~ **vornehmen** to transfer (convey, assure, surrender) land, to demise.

Grundstücks|umschreibung alienation (conveyance) of an estate; ~ **umschreibung vornehmen** to alienate an estate; ~**unterhaltungskosten** cost of carrying real estate *(US)*; ~**unterlagen** title deed, real-estate records *(US)*; ~**urkunde** muniments of title, title (quitclaim) deed, warranty (real covenant) deed *(US)*; ~**veräußerung** alienation of land, conveyance of real property;

~**verkauf** sale of land, property (land) sale, real-estate dealing (selling, marketing, *US*); ~**verkäufe auf Abzahlungsbasis** instalment land sales; ~**verkäufer** vendor of a piece of land (an estate), real-estate salesman *(US)*; ~**verkaufsangebot** offer to sell property; ~**verkaufsvertrag** estate contract, real covenant, warranty deed *(US)*; ~**verkaufsvertrag unter gleichzeitigem Abschluß eines langjährigen Pachtvertrages** sell-and-lease agreement; ~**verkehr** property dealing, real estate transactions; ~**vermächtnis** specific devise; ~**vermessung** survey of land, land surveying; ~**vermittler** real-estate consultant; ~**vermittlung** real-estate agency (office) *(US)*, land (estate, *Br.*) agency; ~**vermögen** realty, real estate, landed property; ~**verpfändung** mortgage of land; ~**verpfändung bis zur Schuldtilgung durch den laufenden Ertrag** living pledge; ~**versicherung** property insurance; ~**vertrag** contract for sale of land, deed of real estate, real covenant, warranty deed *(US)*; ~**vertragsunterzeichnung** real-estate closing; ~**verwalter** estate (property) manager, steward, bailiff; ~**verwaltung** estate (property) management, management of property; ~**verwaltung en bloc übernehmen** to swallow up property portfolios; ~**verwertungsgesellschaft** development company; ~**verzeichnis** register of properties, list of real estate *(US)*; ~**vorkaufsrecht haben** to have an option on a piece of land, to settle upon land subject to preemption; ~**vorvertrag** preliminary agreement.

Grundstückswert land (plottage, real-estate, property, *Br.*) value, value of land (property, *Br.*), *(Einheitswert)* basic value;

~**e** real-estate securities;

durch Baulanderschließung gestiegener ~ development value inherent in the land; **steuerlicher** ~ site value; **hypothekarische Belastung übersteigender** ~ equity; **zufälliger** ~ adventitious value of land;

~ **nach Abschreibung** net real estate; **erhöhter** ~ **durch Ortserschließung** development value of land;

~ **fortschreiben** to adjust the real-estate value; ~**e steigen lassen** to enhance the value of land; ~ **schätzen** to estimate the value of land (property, *Br.*);

~**schätzung** site-value rating.

Grundstücks|wesen real-estate field; ~**zubehör** part and pertinent, quasi realty; ~**zusammenschreibung** assembling parcels of land.

Grund|studium basic study; ~**stufe** *(Schule)* elementary education, grade *(US)*; ~**tabelle** basic table; ~**tarif** base rate, class basis (rate), *(Feuerversicherung)* basis rate, *(Spediteur)* basic rate, *(Werbung)* standard rate; **einheitlicher** ~**tarif** *(Körperschaftssteuer)* basic rate *(Br.)*; ~**tarifvertrag** basic national contract; ~**tatsachen** bottom facts *(US)*; ~**taxe** standard (base, basis) rate; ~**tendenz** *(Börse)* primary trend; ~**tendenz einer Rede** tenor of a speech; ~**ton** *(Börse)* prevailing tone, undertone, *(pol.)* keynote.

Gründung foundation, creation, *(Aktiengesellschaft)* formation, promotion, organization *(US)*, *(Errichtung)* erection, setting up, establishment, *(Einrichtung)* institution, plantation;

schwindelhafte ~ bogus concern, bubble company *(Br.)*, bucket shop *(US)*; **vorläufige** ~ tentative organization;

~ **von Filialen** establishment of branches; ~ **einer Firma** organization of business, business organization, establishment of a corporation; ~ **eines Geschäfts** setting up in (organization of a) business, opening of a business; ~ **einer Gesellschaft** floating (formation, incorporation, establishment) of a company (partnership, corporation); ~ **eines Kartells** establishment (formation) of a cartel; ~ **von Krankenhäusern** organization of hospitals; ~ **des Gemeinsamen Marktes** Common Market formation; ~ **von Tochterunternehmen** founding of subsidiaries; ~ **eines Unternehmens** inception of an enterprise; ~ **eines Vereins** organization of a club;

fehlerhafte ~ **heilen** to cure the fatally defective organization.

Gründungs|akt foundation, establishment; ~**akten** organization files *(US)*; ~**arbeiten** development work; ~**aufwand** organization expenses (cost) *(US)*, promotion money (expense) *(Br.)*, promoter's expenses, original cost, expenses of formation, preliminary (formation) expenses *(Br.)*, *(Versorgungsbetrieb)* original cost; ~**ausschuß** organizing *(US)* (promotion, *Br.*) committee; ~**bank** investment bank; ~**bedingungen** articles of association (incorporation, *US*); ~**bericht** statutory report; ~**bescheinigung** certificate of incorporation; ~**bilanz** registration statement; ~**einlage** original (beginning) investment; ~**feier** inaugural ceremonies; ~**fieber** promoterism; ~**fonds** original fund; ~**geschäft** promotion of companies, organization of corporations *(US)*; ~**gesetz** organic act *(US)*; ~**gremium** founding body; ~**jahr** year of foundation (organization, *US*); ~**kapital** original (initial, nominal, *Br.*) capital, share capital *(Br.)*, original investment, capital stock *(US)*; ~**konjunktur** company-floating boom; ~**konsortium** underlying syndicate *(US)*; ~**kosten** promotion expense (money) *(Br.)*, promoter's (organization) expenses (costs) *(US)*, costs of promotion *(Br.)*, setup costs, expenses of formation, formation expenses, preliminary expenses *(Br.)*; ~- **und Unterparikosten** preliminary and issue expenses *(Br.)*; ~**mitglied** charter (founder) member, corporator, incorporator *(US)*, *(Verein)* original (founder) member; ~**protokoll** memorandum of association; ~**schwindel** bubble *(Br., sl.)*, promoterism; ~**stadium** *(AG)* development stage; ~**statut** organic act *(US)*; ~**steuer** organization tax *(US)*; ~**stock** original stock; ~**tag** foundation day; ~**urkunde** [corporate] charter, settlement deed, *(Bank)* organization certificate *(US)*, *(AG)* articles (memorandum, *Br.*) of association, articles of organization *(US)*, corporate articles *(US)*, corporation charter *(US)*; ~**urkunde und Satzung** memorandum and articles of association *(Br.)*; ~**versammlung** founders' (organization, *US*) meeting, meeting of incorporators *(US)* (to found); ~**vertrag** memorandum of association, articles of association (organization) *(US)*; ~**vorgang** establishment, setup, foundation; ~**zeitpunkt** time of incorporation; ~**zeugnis** certificate of organization *(US)*, organization certificate *(US)*; ~**ziele** original aims of an association.

Grund|unterricht grounding; ~**unterschied** fundamental difference; ~**unterstützung** basic benefit; ~**ursache** primary (bottom) cause; ~**vergütung** basic compensation (pay); ~**vergütung eines Jahresvertrages erhöhen** to raise the ante on s. one's annual contract; ~**verkehrssteuer** tax on the conveyance of real estate.

grundverkehrt utterly wrong;

~ **sein** to be a fundamental mistake.

Grundvermögen [landed (fixed)] property, property in land, real (landed) estate, fast estate;

gebundenes ~ entailed estate; **gemeindeabgabenpflichtiges** ~ ratable property;

~ **und bewegliche Sachen** land and chattels;

sein ~ **flüssigmachen (realisieren)** to turn one's land (real estate) into money (personal property), to convert realty into personalty; **der öffentlichen Hand** ~ **zu wohltätigen Zwecken überlassen** to mortify land for a charitable purpose *(Scot.)*.

Grundverpflichtung basic obligation.

grundverschieden entirely different;

von seinem Bruder ~ **sein** to be a great contrast to one's brother.

Grund|versorgungssystem basic scheme; ~**vertrag** principal contract, *(pol.)* basic treaty; ~**vollmacht** primary powers; ~**voraussetzungen** basic requirements; ~**vorrat** base stock; ~**wasser** underground (ground) water; ~**wasserschicht** water bed; ~**wasserspiegel** water table (level); ~**wehrdienst** basic military service; ~**welle** ground swell, *(el.)* fundamental; ~**werbeaussage** basic message; ~**wert** land value, *(Statistik)* base, *(Zinsrechnung)* original number; **moralische** ~**werte** the simple verities; ~**wertsteigerung** appreciation of real estate; ~**widerspruch** immanent contradiction; ~**zahl** cardinal number; ~**zahlungsbilanz** basic balance of payments; ~**zehnter** royalty; ~**zeitraum** basic period (time); ~**ziffer** basic rate; ~**zins** annual rent; ~**zug** distinctive mark, main feature, characteristic.

Grundzüge|der Physik fundamentals of physics; ~ **eines Planes** main outlines of a scheme; ~ **einer Vereinbarung** memorandum outlines; ~ **eines Vertrages** features of a contract;

Thema in seinen ~**n bearbeiten** to outline the characteristics of a subject.

Grundzuteilung basic ration.

Grüner *(Polizist)* copper, cop.

Grün|filter *(Foto)* green filter; ~**fläche** *(Städteplanung)* open space, green belt; ~**flächenplanung** open-space planning; ~**futter** green forage, ensilage; ~**gürtel** green (thermal) belt; ~**horn** greenhorn *(coll.)*; ~**kramhändler** greengrocer; ~**kramladen** greengrocery; ~**land** meadow land, grassland; ~**schnabel** greenhorn, John Raw, young shaver, whipper-snapper, fledgeling *(Br.)*, jackaro *(Australia)*, kid *(sl.)*; ~**span** verdigris; ~**streifen** verge, strip of turf, parkway, parking; ~**zone** green (thermal) belt.

Gruppe body, group, panel, crowd *(US sl.)*, *(Arbeiter)* team, crew, gang, section, band, *(Flieger)* squadron, wing, *(Haufe)* troop, cluster, flock, batch, herd, *(Klasse)* class, category, *(Kollektiv)* collective, *(Luftwaffe)* group *(US)*, wing *(Br.)*, *(Maschinenaggregate)* set, *(mil.)* squad, section, *(Serie)* series, *(Steuer)* bracket, *(Tourismus)* outfit *(US)*;

abgespaltene ~ breakaway group, splinter party, split; **vom Großhandel begünstigte** ~ wholesale-sponsored group; **berufsgleiche** ~**n** job families; **bewaffnete** ~ band; **noch nicht eingearbeitete** ~ awkward squad; **nicht konkurrierende** ~**n** noncompeting groups; **politische** ~ political group; **ständige** ~ *(UNO)* standing group; **zusammenhängende** ~ *(Werbeagentur)* chain;

~ **von Banken** group of banks, banking syndicate; ~ **von Bergsteigern** party of mountaineers; ~ **von Börsenspekulanten** clique of brokers; ~ **ähnlicher Erzeugnisse** product family; ~ **von Geldgebern** sponsoring group; ~ **von Gläubigern** association (class) of creditors; ~ **von Häusern** set of houses; ~ **landwirtschaftlicher Interessenvertreter im Parlament** farm bloc *(US)*; ~ **von Maklern** *(Geldausleihungen)* loan crowd *(US)*; ~ **von Personen** class of persons; ~ **von Rebellen** rebel group; ~ **von Reportern** panel of reporters; ~ **von Sachverständigen** panel of experts; ~ **von Schulkindern** troop of school children; ~ **von Spaziergängern** parade, assembly of promenaders; ~ **von Zuschauern** cluster of spectators;

~ **bilden** to form groups; ~**n in den Straßen bilden** to gather in knots in the streets; **in** ~**n einordnen** to classify; **zu einer** ~ **gehören** to belong to a class; **in** ~**n herumstehen** to cluster around; **sich zu einer** ~ **zusammenschließen** to team up; **in** ~**n zusammenstehen** to stand about in knots; **einer** ~ **zuteilen** to squad.

Gruppen|abend *(Jugendliche)* youth evening; ~**abschreibung** composite life method of depreciation, group depreciation; ~**abschreibungsverfahren** *(Speditionsbuchführung)* group plan; ~**akkord** group incentive; ~**akkord[arbeit]** group piecework [plan]; ~**akkordlohn** group piece rate; **gewinnbeteiligte** ~**altersversorgung** with-profits group pension scheme; ~**analyse** clustering analysis; ~**anpassung** group accommodation; ~**arbeit** teamwork, bandwork; ~**aufnahme** group picture; ~**ausbildung** group training; ~**beitrag** group contribution; ~**bezahlung** group payment (piece rate); ~**bild** group picture; ~**bildung** formation of groups, groupage, grouping; ~**boycott** concerted refusal to deal; ~**denken** team thinking; ~**disziplin** *(Kartellwesen)* restricted (concerted) practices, quasi agreement *(US)*; ~**dynamik** group dynamics; ~**egoismus** sectional self-interest; ~**ehe** group (communal) marriage; ~**einteilung** classification; ~**entscheidung** group decision; ~**fahrkarte** party ticket; ~**faktor** *(Statistik)* group factor; ~**fehlschluß** ecological fallacy; ~**flug** charter flight; ~**führer** *(mil.)* section (squad, *US*) leader; ~**gemeinschaft** community group; ~**gespräch** group (panel, *US*) discussion; ~**großstadt** conurbation; ~**index** group index; ~**interessen** sectional interests, pressure groups; ~**interview** group interview; ~**kohäsion** group cohesiveness; ~**kommandeur** *(mil.)* group commander; ~**lebensversicherung** group-term life insurance; ~**leistung** group output (production); ~**leistungslohnsystem** group piecework system; ~**leiter** group manager (executive); ~**lohn** group compensation, group payment (piece rate); ~**police** master policy, *(Fahrzeuge)* fleet policy; ~**prämie** group bonus; **kollektives** ~**prämiensystem** group (non-piecework) bonus plan; ~**praxis** group practice; ~**prüfung** group test; ~**reise** organized (packaged, *US*) tour, group trip; **verbilligte** ~**reise** group-rate travel; ~**rentenversicherung** group annuity insurance; ~**rentenversicherungssystem** deposit administration (group-annuity) pension plan; ~**risikoversicherung für vorzeitige Todesfälle** group life insurance; ~**schalter** *(el.)* gang switch, group breaker, multiple switch; ~**schaltung** *(el.)* multiple connection; ~**schule** platoon school; ~**solidarität** group solidarity; ~**spannung** group tension; ~**tarif** group (groupage) rate, *(Spediteur)* class rate; **pauschalierter** ~**tarif** *(Versicherung)* wholesale group rate; ~**überlegenheit** *(Soziologie)* group ascendancy; ~**umsatz** *(Konzern)* consolidated sales; ~**unterricht** group tuition (instruction); ~**veränderung** *(Gehälter)* classification change; ~**vergleich** *(Statistik)* group comparison; ~**verkauf** *(Kraftfahrzeuge)* fleet sale.

Gruppenversicherung group (collective) insurance;

~ **für leitende Angestellte** executives' company group insurance; ~ **mit Beitragsleistung der Beteiligten** contributory group insurance; ~ **für Kraftfahrzeuge** fleet insurance; ~ **für vorzeitige Todesfälle** group life insurance.

Gruppen|versicherungsschutz für leitende Angestellte executives' company group protection; ~**versicherungssystem** group scheme, *(Kraftfahrzeuge)* fleet plan; ~**wähler** *(tel.)* group selector; ~**wechselwirkung** group interaction.

gruppenweise zusammenfassen to [bracket together in a] group.

Gruppen|zelt bell tent; ~**zusammenfassung** *(Statistik)* sample make-up.

gruppieren to arrange in groups, to group, to assort.

Gruppierung grouping, arrangement in groups, assortment, alignment.

Grusel|film horror film, thriller, grusical; ~**geschichte** creepy, spine-chilling story, tale of horror, horror novel.

Gruseln creeps, creepy feeling.

grusel|n, sich to shiver, to have the creeps; **j.** ~**n machen** to make s. o. shiver, to give s. o. the creeps;

mich ~**t es** I have got the willies.

Gruß greeting, salutation;

jem. seinen ~ **entbieten** to present one's compliments to s. o.;

~**bekanntschaft** nodding acquaintance; ~**botschaft** complimentary message.

Grüße greetings, respects, regards, compliments;

mit freundlichen ~**n** with kind regards, yours sincerely, sincerely yours *(Br.)*;

herzliche ~ warm (kind) regards;

~ **zum Fest** season's greetings;

~ **übermitteln** to present one's regards; ~ **schriftlich übermitteln** to convey greetings by letter.

Grüßen greeting, *(mil.)* salutation;

jem. vom ~ **kennen** to be on nodding terms with s. o.

grüßen to greet, to salute;

j. mit einem Kopfnicken ~ to give s. o. a nod; **respektvoll** ~ to pull one's forelock; **j. mit einer Verbeugung** ~ to bow to s. o.;

j. ~ **lassen** to remember o. s. to s. o.

Gruß|formel salutation; **mit jem. auf** ~**fuß stehen** to have a nodding acquaintance with s. o.; ~**wort** message of greetings.

Grütze gumption *(coll.)*, grey matter *(Br.)*;

ein bißchen ~ **im Kopf haben** to have a bit of gumption.

gucken to peep, to look;

sich die Augen aus dem Kopf ~ to look all over the place; **um die Ecke** ~ to poke one's head round the corner; **neugierig aus dem Fenster** ~ to peer out of the windows; **zu tief ins Glas** ~ to have had a drop too much (one too many); **in die Röhre** ~ to be left in the cold; **durchs Schlüsselloch** ~ to peep through a keyhole; **in alle Töpfe** ~ to poke one's nose in everything.

Guckloch eyehole, spyhole, inspection hole, peep[-hole], peeper *(coll.)*.

Guerilla|kämpfe guerilla; ~**kämpfer** guerilla, bushfighter; ~**krieg** guerilla warfare.

gültig *(Fahrkarte)* available, valid, good, *(Münze)* current, good, passable, *(rechtsgültig)* legal, valid, good in law, lawful, in force, binding, effective, operative, *(unverfälscht)* authentic, genuine, *(zulässig)* admissible;

allgemein ~ blanket *(US)*; **formell und materiell** ~ valid in form and fact; **drei Monate** ~ valid for three months; **nicht mehr** ~ no longer operative, ineffective, obsolete; **noch** ~ still in force;

~ **bis Ultimo** good this month; ~ **erst bei Vertragsabschluß** subject to contract; ~ **bis auf Widerruf** *(Börsenauftrag)* good until recalled (cancelled), valid until recalled;

~ **bleiben** to hold true (good); **für** ~ **erklären** to make valid, to validate; ~ **machen** to render (make) valid, to validate; ~ **sein** to be valid (in force), to run, *(Kurs haben)* to pass, to be in circulation (current, *Br.*); **allgemein** ~ **sein** to pass current; **nicht in allen Fällen** ~ **sein** not to hold in all cases; **einen Monat** ~ **sein** to be available for one month; **nicht mehr** ~ **sein** to be no longer current (in force, out of circulation), *(Paß)* to have expired; **noch** ~ **sein** to survive intact, to be still on the books, *(Gesetz)* to be still in vigo(u)r; **als** ~ **angenommen werden** to pass for current;

unwiderruflich ~**es und bestätigtes Akkreditiv** irrevocable and confirmed letter of credit; ~**e Auslegung** authentic interpretation; ~**er Beweis** valid proof; ~**e Eheschließung** valid marriage; ~**e Entschuldigung** valid excuse; ~**er Fahrschein** valid ticket; **in** ~**er Form** in due form; ~**es Gesetz** operative (established) law; ~**e Prosa** contemporary prose; ~**e Quittung** good receipt; ~**er Rechtsanspruch** valid title; ~**es Testament** genuine (valid) will; ~**e Unterschrift** authentic signature; ~**e Urkunde** effective (valid) instrument; ~**er Vertrag** valid (legally binding) contract; ~**es Zahlungsmittel** legal tender, lawful money *(US)*.

Gültigkeit validity, force, effect, *(Fahrkarte)* availability, *(Gesetzlichkeit)* legality, vigo(u)r, *(Münze)* currency, *(Zulässigkeit)* admissibility;

allgemeine ~ currency, general acceptance; **teilweise** ~ particular validity; **volle** ~ *(ausländisches Urteil)* full faith and credit;

~ **einer Offerte** duration of an offer; ~ **eines Passes** validity of a passport; ~ **eines Patents** duration of patent; ~ **eines Testaments** genuineness (validity) of a will; ~ **eines Vertrages** force of an agreement, validity of a contract; ~ **einer Wahl** validity of an election;

~ **eines Testaments anfechten** to contest (dispute) the validity of a will; ~ **aufheben** to invalidate; ~ **seiner Forderung begründen** to make good one's claim; ~ **bestreiten** to challenge the validity; ~ **eines Testaments bestreiten** to contest (dispute) a will; ~ **eines angefochtenen Testaments beweisen** to establish the validity of a disputed will; ~ **erlangen** to become effective (operative); **allgemeine** ~ **haben** to be universally accepted; **rechtliche** ~ **haben** to be valid in law, to run, *(Zahlungsmittel)* to be legal tender (lawful money, *US*); **einen Monat** ~ **haben** to be available for a month; **rechtliche** ~ **haben** to be valid in law; ~ **eines Testaments bestätigen lassen** to prove a bill; ~ **verbürgen** to authenticate; ~ **verlängern** to extend the validity; ~ **verleihen** to authenticate; ~ **verlieren** to expire, to become invalid, to be deprived of validity.

Gültigkeitsbereich range of validity, *(Gesetz)* scope.

Gültigkeitsdauer validity, run, running, limit, life, validation period, *(Fahrschein)* period for which a ticket is available, *(Vertrag)* life, *(Wettervorhersage)* valid time;
~ **einer Offerte** duration of offer; ~ **einer Police** validity of a policy;
~ **verlängern** to extend the validity; ~ **einer Fahrkarte verlängern** to extend a ticket.

Gültigkeits|erfordernisse prerequisites of validity; ~**erklärung** validation, legalization; ~**klausel** testing clause; ~**verlängerung** extension of validity; ~**vermerk** *(Scheck)* certification; ~**vermutung** presumption of validity.

Gummi gum, *(Radiergummi)* rubber, eraser;
künstliche ~ synthetic rubber;
~**abdichtung** rubber seal; ~**absatz** rubber heel; ~**aktien** rubber shares *(Br.)* (stock, *US*), rubbers; ~**band** rubber band; ~**bereifung** rubber tyres *(Br.)* (tires, *US*).

gummieren to gum.

Gummierstift glue dispenser.

gummierter Briefumschlag adhesive envelope.

Gummierung gum;
mit unbeschädigter ~ with original gum;
mit einer ~ **versehen** to gum.

Gummi|industrie rubber industry; ~**knüppel** police baton *(Br.)*, rubber truncheon *(Br.)*, billy club *(US)*; ~**knüppel benutzen** to truncheon; **mit dem** ~**knüppel vorgehen** to make a baton charge; ~**linse** *(Foto)* zoom lens; ~**paragraph** elastic clause; ~**reifen** rubber tyre *(Br.)* (tire, *US*); ~**ringe** rubber bands; ~**schlauch** rubber tube (hose); ~**schuhe** overshoes; ~**stempel** rubber stamp; ~**stiefel** Wellington boots, Wellingtons; ~**stoßstange** rubber bumper; ~**waren- und Reifenindustrie** tyre and rubber industry *(Br.)*; ~**wärmflasche** hot-water bottle; ~**werte** rubber shares *(Br.)* (stocks, *US*), rubbers.

Gunst favo(u)r, goodwill, grace, *(Begünstigung)* patronage, partiality;
in besonderer ~ in high favo(u)r;
~ **der Stunde ausnutzen** to go while the going is good, to make hay while the sun shines; **sich in jds.** ~ **einschmeicheln** to work o. s. into s. one's favo(u)r; **seine** ~ **entziehen** to withdraw one's favo(u)r; **sich jds.** ~ **erschleichen** to wind into s. one's favo(u)r; **jem. eine** ~ **erweisen** to confer a favo(u)r on s. o.; **jem. eine** ~ **gewähren** to do (grant) s. o. a favo(u)r; **jem. seine** ~ **gewähren** to extend one's patronage to s. o.; **jds.** ~ **verloren haben** to be in s. one's black books; **seine** ~ **verschenken** to shed favo(u)rs; **sich jds.** ~ **verscherzen** to get in wrong with s. o. *(US)*;
~**beweis,** ~**bezeigung** mark of favo(u)r, favo(u)r, countenance; ~**bezeigung dankbar anerkennen** to acknowledge a favo(u)r; **mit** ~**bezeigungen überschütten** to heap favo(u)rs on s. o.

Gunsten, zu ~ **von** *(Buchhaltung)* to s. one's credit, to the benefit of, in favo(u)r of; **zu meinen** ~ to the credit of my account; **zu** ~ **eines Dritten** for the benefit of a third party;
Saldo zu Ihren ~ **aufweisen** to show a balance to your credit; **zu jds.** ~ **aussagen** to give evidence in s. one's favo(u)r, to witness for s. o.; **sich zu jds.** ~ **aussprechen** to find for s. o.; **zu jds.** ~ **einen Scheck ausstellen** to write out a check *(US)* (cheque, *Br.*) in s. one's favo(u)r; **zu jds.** ~ **entscheiden** to decide in s. one's favo(u)r; **im Zweifelsfall zu jds.** ~ **entscheiden** to give s. o. the benefit of the doubt; **zu jds.** ~ **intervenieren** to make intercession for s. o.; **sich zu jds.** ~ **neigen** to preponderate in favo(u)r of s. o.; **zu jds.** ~ **sprechen** to say a good word for s. o.; **bei jem. in** ~ **stehen** to be in s. one's good graces; **sich zu jds.** ~ **wenden** to sway to s. one's side; **zu jds.** ~ **gewürdigt werden** to be weighted in favo(u)r of s. o.

günstig advantageous, favo(u)rable, promising, fair, convenient, opportune, well;
ununterbrochen ~ **aufgenommen** *(Werbung)* favo(u)rably continued;
~ **abschneiden** to come off well; **etw.** ~ **aufnehmen** to give s. th. a favo(u)rable reception; **j.** ~ **beurteilen** to pass a favo(u)rable judgment on s. o.; **es für** ~ **halten** to see fit; ~ **für j. sein** to stand in s. one's favo(u)r; **jem.** ~ **gesinnt sein** to be well-disposed towards s. o.;
~**es Angebot** favo(u)rable offer; ~**e Anzeichen** favo(u)rable auspices; ~**en Augenblick abpassen** to watch one's time; ~**en Ausgang erwarten lassen** to be in a promising state; **zu** ~**en Bedingungen** on easy terms; ~**e Bedingungen erzielen** to reach favo(u)rable terms; ~**er Bescheid** favo(u)rable answer; ~**en Eindruck machen** to make a favo(u)rable impression; **im** ~**sten Fall** at best; ~**e Gelegenheit** opportunity, chance; ~**e Gelegenheit abwarten** to wait one's opportunity, to bid one's time; ~**e Gelegenheit finden** to find a convenient opportunity; **zu besonders** ~**em Kurs** at a favo(u)rable rate of exchange; **sich im** ~**en Licht zeigen** to show o. s. in a favo(u)rable light; ~**er Preis** favo(u)rable price; ~**e Stellung** advantageous position; **unter einem** ~**en Stern geboren sein** to be born under a lucky star; ~**e Stunde** auspicious hour; ~**er Umrechnungskurs** favo(u)rable exchange rate; ~**en Verlauf nehmen** to make good progress, to go off well; ~**e Vorzeichen** favo(u)rable auspices; ~**e Wendung nehmen** to take a turn for the better; **bei** ~**em Wetter** weather permitting; ~**er Wind** fair wind; ~**er Zeitpunkt** opportune moment; ~**er Zufall** stroke of good luck.

günstigenfalls at best.

Günstling favo(u)rite, minion, creature.

Günstlingswirtschaft acceptance of persons, favo(u)ritism, spoils system *(US)*.

Gurgel throat;
jem. die ~ **abschnüren** to strangle s. o., *(fig.)* to cut s. one's throat; **jem. die** ~ **durchschneiden** to cut s. one's throat; **sein ganzes Vermögen durch die** ~ **jagen** to spend an estate in drinking; **seine** ~ **schmieren** to wet one's whistle; **jem. das Messer an die** ~ **setzen** to hold a knife at s. one's throat.

Gurkenzeit, saure silly season.

Gürtel waist belt, *(geogr.)* zone;
~ **von Festungsanlagen** cordon of forts; ~ **von Grünanlagen** green belt;
seinen ~ **enger schnallen** to tighten one's belt, to pull one's belt together;
~**bahn** circular railway, belt line *(US)*; ~**linie** waistline; **unterhalb der** ~**linie** below the belt; ~**reifen** *(Auto)* radial-ply tyre *(Br.)* (tire, *US*).

Guß gush, stream, jet, *(drucktechn.)* casting, founding;
aus einem ~ all of one piece (founding);
in einen heftigen ~ **geraten** to get caught in a heavy shower;
~**form** mould *(Br.)*, mold *(US)*.

Gut *(Besitz)* property, possessions, *(Gutshof)* estate, farm, landed estate (property), *(Rittergut)* manor, demesne, country seat (site), *(Vermögen)* property, assets, effects, *(Ware)* goods, merchandise, wares;
angeschwemmtes ~ driftage; **anvertrautes** ~ trust charge; **bewegliches** ~ movables, personalty, personals, personal property; **eingebrachtes** ~ separate estate, dotal property; **unrechtmäßig erworbenes** ~ ill-gotten gains; **gerettetes** ~ salvage; **gestohlenes** ~ stolen property; **heimgefallenes** ~ property escheated, escheat; **herrenloses** ~ abandoned property, waif, stray, derelict, goods unclaimed; **irdenes** ~ earthenware; **kostbares** ~ precious asset; **quasi öffentliches** ~ merit good; **spezifisch öffentliches** ~ purely public good; **schwimmendes** ~ *(Ware)* cargo (goods) afloat, venture; **seetriftiges** ~ flotsam; **sperriges** ~ bulky goods; **unbewegliches** ~ immovables; **veränderliches** ~ *(Versicherung)* shifting property; **verderbliches** ~ perishables;
eingebrachtes ~ **der Ehefrau** separate (dotal) property; **Hab und** ~ goods and chattels, belongings;
~ **bewirtschaften** to work a farm; **jds.** ~ **erben** to succeed to s. o.; ~ **auf j. als Fideikommiß vererben** to entail an estate on s. o.; **sein** ~ **um zehn Morgen vergrößern** to annex ten acres to one's farm; ~ **verwalten** to factor an estate; ~ **in Grund und Boden wirtschaften** to bring a farm to total ruin;
unrecht ~ **gedeiht nicht gut** ill-gotten goods never prosper.

gut good, okay, *(günstig)* favo(u)rable, well, *(vorteilhaft)* advantageous, profitable;
~ **bezahlt** well paid; ~ **erhalten** well-preserved, in good condition, *(Haus)* in good repair; ~ **geführt** well-run; **keineswegs so** ~ not near so good; **kurz und** ~ in short; **nicht im Entferntesten so** ~ not a patch on; **nicht mehr** ~ no longer wearable; ~ **situiert** well-off, well-to-do, well-fixed *(US)*, on one's legs; **so** ~ **wie erledigt** as good as settled; **so** ~ **wie sicher** practically certain, a sure thing; **überraschend** ~ to a miracle; ~

und wohlbehalten in good order and well conditioned; **ziemlich** ~ passably good; **ziemlich ~ bis mittelmäßig** fair to middling; ~ **ankommen** to arrive safely; **für ~ befinden** to think fit; **j. ~ behandeln** to be kind to s. o.; **etw. ~ beherrschen** to have the knack of it; **~en dritten Platz belegen** to come in a good third; ~ **davonkommen** to get off cheaply, to have a narrow squeak; ~ **gehen** *(Absatz)* to meet with ready sale (a ready market), to sell (start) well; **es ~ haben** to be well off (lucky), to come off well; **es sehr ~ haben** to live at rack and manger; **etw. ~ hinter sich gebracht haben** to be well out of it; **sich ~ halten** *(Person)* to be well preserved, *(Speisen)* to keep well; **jem. ~ zustatten kommen** to stand s. o . in good stead; ~ **rechnen können** to be quick at figures; **es sich ~ gehen lassen** to do o. s. proud; ~ **machen** to make amends, to compensate, to shape up very well; ~ **sein für** *(Kredit genießen)* to be good for; **bei jem. ~ angeschrieben sein** to be in s. one's good books; ~ **gehalten sein** *(Kurse)* to maintain a good tone; ~ **gestellt sein** to be well off, to be in easy circumstances; **nicht halb so ~ sein wie es sollte** not to be a quarter as good as it should be; ~ **bei Kasse sein** to be flush (in funds); ~ **in Schuß sein** to be in good shape; **stellenweise ~ sein** *(Buch)* to be good in patches; **jem. für eine bestimmte Summe ~ sein** to be s. o. good for a sum, to enjoy credit to the extent of a certain amount with s. o.; **sich wieder ~ sein** to be friends again; **sich mit seinem Vorgesetzten ~ stehen** to stand well with one's chief; **sehr ~ werden** *(Wetter)* to come off very fine; **jem. ~ zureden** to coax s. o. into doing s. th.;

~en Absatz finden to find a ready market, to meet with a ready sale, to sell readily; **~e Allgemeinbildung** good general education; **sein ~es Auskommen haben** to enjoy a competence, to be in easy circumstances; **~er Einfall** brainwave; **~e Fahrt** pleasant journey; **aus ~er Familie stammen** to stem from a good line (stock); **auf ~em Fuß mit jem. stehen** to be on good terms with s. o.; **~es Gehalt verdienen** to earn a good salary; **~es Geschäft** lucrative (profitable) business; **gegen den ~en Geschmack verstoßen** to overstep the lines of good taste; **~er Glaube** good faith, bona fides; **kein ~es Haar an jem. lassen** to run s. o. down; **~er Hoffnung sein** to be in the family way; **~es Jahr** profitable year; **~e Kameradschaft** good fellowship; **in ~ unterrichteten Kreisen** in well-informed quarters; **~e Mittelsorte** good middling quality; **~e Nachrichten** glad tidings; **~e Nummer bei jem. haben** to be in s. one's good books; **~e Partie** good match; **~e Qualität** high quality; **aus ~er Quelle** from a reliable source; **~er Rechner sein** to be quick at figures; **seine ~en Sachen anziehen** to put on one's best bib and tucker; **~en Schluck nehmen** to take a swig at the bottle; **alles von der ~en Seite sehen** to look on the bright side of things; **gegen die ~en Sitten verstoßen** to act contrary to good morals; **~e Stellung** good place (billet); **~e Stellung haben** to have a snug berth; **~es Stück vorankommen** to make headway (good progress); **~e Stunde** full (solid) hour; **~e halbe Stunde** a full half hour; **~e Verhältnisse** favo(u)rable circumstances; **kein ~er Verlierer sein** to be a bad loser; **~e Ware für sein Geld bekommen** to get good value for one's money; **~e Weile Zeit haben** to have plenty of time; **~es Wetter** fine weather; **nicht für Geld und ~e Worte** not for love or money; **die ~e alte Zeit** the good old times, the piping times of yore; **in ~em Zustand** in good order, good-conditioned.

Gutachten [expert] opinion, expertise, testimonial, survey, advice, report, *(Schätzung)* appraisal, *(Schiedsgutachten)* award; **anwaltliches ~** attorney's (lawyer's) opinion; **ärztliches ~** medical certificate (opinion); **demoskopisches ~** public opinion poll; **gerichtsmedizinisches ~** forensic opinion;

~ **eines Anwalts** attorney's (counsel's, *Br.*, lawyer's) opinion; ~ **der Minderheit** dissenting (dissentient, separate) opinion *(US)*; ~ **eines medizinischen Sachverständigen** opinion of a medical expert;

~ **abgeben (erstatten)** to deliver (render) an opinion, to give an expert opinion; ~ **einholen** to take counsel's opinion, to obtain an opinion;

~entwurf draft opinion; **~gebühr** expert's fees, *(Versicherung)* survey fee.

Gutachter expert, advisor, *(Schätzer)* appraiser, valuer, assessor, *(Schiedsrichter)* arbitrator, *(Versicherungsgesellschaft)* surveyor, adjuster;

ständiger ~ consultant; **vereidigter ~** sworn appraiser;

~ **in Buchführungsfragen** auditing expert;

~ **ernennen** to appoint an expert; ~ **hinzuziehen** to consult an expert, to take expert advice;

~ausschuß advisory committee, panel (committee) of experts; **~bericht** expert's report, *(Versicherung)* surveyor's report, survey; **~gruppe** expert group; **~kommission** advisory committee, committee of experts; **in ~kreisen** among experts; **~tätigkeit** advisory service; **~verfahren** *(Völkerrecht)* advisory procedure.

gutachtlich advisory, expert, consultatory, authoritative;

sich ~ äußern to give an expert opinion;

~e Aussage eines Sachverständigen expert testimony; **~e Äußerung** expert opinion; **~e Bewertung** official appraisement; **~e Tätigkeit** advisory service; **~e Zeugenaussage** expert evidence.

gutartiger Verlauf einer Krankheit harmless course of an illness.

Gut | befund approval; **~bereich** *(Statistik)* acceptance region.

gutbringen to credit;

jem. etw. ~ to place to the credit account of s. o.

gutbürgerliche Küche plain cooking.

Gutdünken discretion, pleasure, judgment;

dem ~ überlassen discretionary; **nach ~** at (upon) discretion, at pleasure;

nach ~ handeln to act without restraint (as one thinks fit), to use one's discretion; **etw. jds. ~ überlassen** to leave to s. one's discretion.

Gut | es good;

alles ~e zum Geburtstag happy returns of the day; **das ~e an der Sache** the good thing about it;

nichts ~es im Schilde führen to be up to no good; **Sache zum ~en lenken** to give a matter a favo(u)rable turn; **des ~en zuviel tun** to overdo it; **Böses mit ~em vergelten** to return evil for good; **sich zum ~en wenden** to change for the better, to come to the good.

Güte goodness, kindness, good nature, amicableness, *(Beschaffenheit)* quality, grade, class, sort, excellence, *(Entgegenkommen)* courtesy, kindness;

der ~ nach qualitative; **von erster ~** first-rate (-class), *(Diamant)* of the first water; **von gleichmäßiger Art und ~** of uniform kind and quality; **von marktfähiger ~** marketable; **von mittlerer Art und ~** of medium kind and of merchantable quality; **von ungleicher ~** varying in quality;

durchschnittliche ~ standard quality; **erste (erstklassige) ~** first rate, top (first-rate) quality; **handelsübliche ~ und Beschaffenheit** good merchantable quality and condition; **minderwertige ~** inferior (poor) quality; **übergroße ~** overflowing kindness; **in ~ abmachen** to settle amicably; **jds. ~ mißbrauchen** to encroach (impose) upon s. one's kindness; **vollendete ~ sein** to be the perfection of kindness;

~anforderungen quality requirements; **hohe ~anforderungen** exacting standards of quality; **~antrag** request for a conciliatory procedure; **~aufpreis** quality markup; **~bestimmung** quality designation (description); **~eigenschaften** quality characteristics; **~einteilung** grade labelling, grading; **den ~erfordernissen entsprechen** to be up to standard; **~faktor** factor of merit, *(Telefonleitung)* quality factor; **~grad** efficiency factor, quality, grade, standard.

Güteklasse grade, class, quality category;

nach ~n eingeteilt graded;

in ~n einstufen to grade.

Güteklassen | bezeichnung grade labelling; **~einteilung** grading.

gütemäßig in quality.

Güteprüfung quality control.

Güter merchandise, commodities, goods, articles, property, possessions;

aufgeopferte ~ *(Havarie)* sacrificed goods; **aufgestaute ~** stowage; **bahnlagernde ~** goods at the railway depot *(Br.)*; **unterwegs befindliche ~** goods in transit (en route); **bewegliche ~** personal assets; **bewirtschaftete ~** rationed goods; **der Bedürfnisbefriedigung dienende ~** convenience goods; **eingelagerte ~** merchandise in storage, stored goods; **analog einzustufende ~** *(Spediteur)* analogous articles; **feuergefährliche ~** inflammable cargo, combustibles; **flüssige ~** wet goods; **gefahrbringende ~** hazardous (dangerous) goods; **gefährliche ~** dangerous cargo; **genormte ~** standardized commodity (commodities); **geringwertige ~** goods of inferior quality; **gewerbliche ~** manufactured goods; **haltbare ~** durable goods; **über den Eigenbedarf hinaus hergestellte ~** surplus commodities; **im Inland hergestellte ~** home-produced goods; **hochwertige ~** high-grade goods; **immaterielle ~** things in action, *(Bilanz)* intangible assets; **irdische ~** earthly possessions, wordly goods; **kurzlebige ~** nondurable goods, nondurables; **lagerfähige ~** inventoriable goods; **langlebige ~** durable goods; **lebenswichtige ~** essential goods, essentials; **nicht lebenswichtige ~** nonessentials, nonessential goods, nonessential elements; **mangelhafte ~** defective goods; **materielle ~** tangible goods; **öffentliche ~** social goods;

schwimmende ~ goods afloat; **seetriftige** ~ flotsam, shipwrecked goods; **sperrige** ~ measured (bulky) goods, goods shipped in bulk, bulk commodities; **unverkäufliche** ~ unsalable goods; **unverzollte** ~ bonded goods; **unwirtschaftliche** ~ onerous goods; **verderbliche** ~ perishable goods (commodities); **lose verladene** ~ measured (unpacked, bulk) goods; **aus Raummangel nicht verladene** ~ goods not loaded due to lack of space; **vermischte (vermengte)** ~ commingled goods; **versicherte** ~ insured goods; **verstaute** ~ stowdown; **vertretbare** ~ fungible things, fungibles, representative commodities; **verzollte** ~ duty-paid goods; **niedrig verzollte** ~ low-duty goods; **weltliche** ~ worldly goods; **wertbeständige** ~ goods of stable value; **zollpflichtige** ~ dutiable goods;
~ **aller Art** goods, wares and merchandise; ~ **des gehobenen Bedarfs** luxury and semi-luxury goods, high-quality goods, conventional necessities; ~ **des täglichen Bedarfs** necessities, convenience goods *(US)*; ~ **und Dienstleistungen** goods and services; ~ **mit unbeschränkter Erbfolge** estate with inheritance absolute; **hochwertige** ~ **des Massenkonsums** high-volume and highly acceptable branded consumer goods; ~ **für Messen und Ausstellungen** exhibits at trade fairs; ~ **höherer Ordnung** higher goods; ~ **mit sozialem Preis** utility goods *(Br.)*; ~ **mit längerer Umschlagsdauer** slow-moving goods; ~ **mit hoher Umschlagsgeschwindigkeit** articles of quick sale; ~ **der gewerblichen Wirtschaft** industrial goods (commodities); ~ **unter Zollverschluß** bonded (warehouse) goods;
immaterielle ~ **abtreten** to assign choses in action; ~ **befördern** to dispatch goods, to haul freight; ~ **[aus einem verunglückten Schiff] bergen** to make salvage of goods, to recover shipwrecked goods; **auf seinen ~n leben** to live on one's estates; ~ **löschen** to unload (discharge) goods, to wharf; ~ **transportieren** to wag(g)on goods; ~ **verfrachten** to transport goods by truck; ~ **verladen** to dispatch (load) goods; ~ **über Bord werfen** to [make] jettison;
~**abfertigung** dispatch (forwarding, consignment) of goods, *(Abteilung)* goods office (department) *(Br.)*, freight service (agency) *(US)*, forwarding (freight, *US*) office; ~**abladeplatz** goods platform *(Br.)*; ~**agent** estate agent; **volkswirtschaftliches** ~**angebot** total supply of goods; ~**angebot steigern** to increase the amount of goods; ~**annahme** receiving of goods, *(Stelle)* receiving (goods, *Br.*) office, goods department *(Br.)*; ~**aufzug** hoist, freight elevator *(US)*, goods lift *(Br.)*; ~**ausgabe** delivery of goods, *(Stelle)* goods *(Br.)* (freight, *US*) office; ~**ausstoß** output of goods; ~**austausch** exchange of goods (commodities); ~**bahnhof** goods yard (station) *(Br.)*, freight depot (yard) *(US)*; ~**bahnsteig** goods platform *(Br.)*; ~**ballen** bale; ~**bedarf** demand of goods; ~**beförderung** forwarding of goods, shipping of goods *(US)*, shipment *(US)*, freight service *(US)*; ~**begleitschein** bill of lading, freight bill *(US)*, waybill *(US)*, freight note *(Br.)*; ~**beschlagnahme** seizure (confiscation) of goods; ~**besichtiger** surveyor; ~**bewegungen** goods traffic *(Br.)*, freight traffic *(US)*; ~**boden** warehouse floor; ~**einteilung** classification of goods; ~**erwerb** acquisition, conquest *(Scot.)*; ~**erzeugung** production of goods; ~**expedition** dispatch, dispatching office, forwarding agency; ~**fernverkehr** long-distance goods traffic *(Br.)*, long-distance freight traffic, long-haul freight traffic *(US)*, long haulage, long hauls on the railroad *(US)*, long-distance haulage (hauling, transport) *(US)*, highway transportation *(US)*.

Güterfernverkehrs|genehmigung, allgemeine A licence *(Br.)*; ~**genehmigung für Werksverkehr** C licence *(Br.)*; ~**unternehmen** truck carrier, general haulier.

Güter|flugverkehr commercial air transportation; ~**flugzeug** freight-carrying aircraft, freight plane (carrier), airfreighter, cargo aeroplane; ~**fluß** flow of goods.

Güterfracht|tarif rail tariff; ~**verkehr** rail freight traffic ~**versicherung** cargo (freight, *US*) insurance.

Güterfreigabe freight release.

Gütergemeinschaft joint property, *(Ehepaar)* communal estate (tenure), community property *(US)*, *(pol.)* community of goods;
allgemeine ~ universal partnership, community property; **vertraglich vereinbarte eheliche** ~ conventional community; **gesetzliche** ~ legal communion, community property *(US)*;
sein Eigentum in die ~ **einbringen** to bring one's property into the communal estate.

Güter|gleis goods line *(Br.)*; ~**halle** goods depot *(Br.)*, freight shed *(US)*; ~**hof** goods *(Br.)* (freight, *US*) yard; ~**industrien** production goods industry; ~- **und Dienstleistungskäufe** purchase of goods and services; ~**kopfstation** freight terminal; ~**kraftverkehr** truckage *(Br.)*, road haulage (transport, *Br.*), haulers (hauliers, *Br.*) and carterers; ~**kraftverkehrsunternehmen** road haulage company; ~**kreislauf** circular flow of goods; ~**ladeplatz** platform, landing stage; ~**laderaum** loading space; ~**lagerung** freight storage; ~- **und Dienstleistungen** real resources; ~**magazin** store, warehouse; ~**makler** estate *(Br.)* (land, *US*) agent, land jobber, realtor *(US)*; **beförderte** ~**menge** density of freight; ~**nahverkehr** short-distance (haul) freight traffic, short hauls *(US)*, shorthaul *(US)*; ~**niederlage** freight *(US)* (goods, *Br.*) depot; ~**produktion** production of goods; **eheliches** ~**recht** matrimonial regime *(US)*; **immaterielle** ~**rechte** incorporeal rights; **vertragsmäßiges** ~**recht** contractual regime *(US)*; ~**rechtsvertrag** marriage settlement, settlement in trust, system of marital property *(US)*; **vorehelicher** ~**rechtsvertrag** antenuptial marriage agreement; ~**schlächter** land jobber; ~**schnellzug** rattler *(sl.)*; ~**schuppen** goods depot (loft, *Br.*), freight house (shed, station) *(US)*, warehouse *(US)*; ~**sendung** consignment; ~**spediteur** freight forwarder *(US)*, common carrier *(US)*, haulage contractor; ~**spedition** common carrier, trucking agency (company) *(US)*, haulage-contracting business; ~**speicher** goods loft (shed) *(Br.)*, freight (goods, *Br.*) depot, warehouse *(US)*, freight shed *(US)*; ~**spekulant** land jobber; ~**spekulation** land jobbing; **gesetzlicher** ~**stand** *(Ehe)* statutory regime *(US)*; **vertraglich vereinbarter** ~**stand** contractual regime *(US)*; ~**strom** stream (flow) of goods, real flow; ~**tarif** goods tariff *(Br.)*, railroad freight *(US)* (goods, *Br.*) rates, railroad charges *(US)*, railway *(Br.)* (freight, *US*) tariff, *(bevorzugter Luftfrachttarif)* commodity rates *(US)*; ~**tonnage** freight tonnage; ~**transport** transport of merchandise (freight, *US*), carriage of goods *(Br.)*, freight transportation *(US)*, conveyance of goods; ~**transport per Bahn** carriage of goods by rail; ~**transport zu öffentlich festgelegten Tarifsätzen durchführen** to carry goods at published fare on set schedules *(US)*; ~**transportversicherung** insurance of goods in transit, freight (transit) insurance; ~**trennung** *(Eheleute)* split, separation of property (estate); **notarielle** ~**trennung** notarial separation; ~**umlauf** circulation of goods; ~**umschlag** goods turnover, transhipment; ~**umschlagstelle** rail and water terminal, freight distributor; ~**verbrauch** consumption of goods; ~**vereinigung** *(zwecks Erbausgleichs)* hotchpot; ~**verkauf** sale of goods.

Güterverkehr merchandise (freight, *US*, goods, *Br.*) traffic, movement of freight *(US)* (goods, *Br.*), goods carried *(Br.)*, freight system *(US)*, *(per Bahn)* rail transport *(Br.)*;
freier ~ free flow of goods; **zwischenstaatlicher** ~ interstate transport, intrastate shipment *(US)*;
~ **und Kapitalverkehr** goods and capital movement; ~ **mit Lastwagen** road transport *(Br.)* (haulage), transport of goods by road *(Br.)*, highway transportation *(US)*.

Güter|verkehrslinie railroad freight line *(US)*; ~**verkehrssteuer** mileage tax *(US)*; ~**verlader** loader, shipper *(US)*, shipping agent *(US)*; ~**verlustversicherung** common carriers' insurance; ~**vermengung** confusion of goods; ~**versand** dispatch, shipping (shipment) of goods *(US)*; ~**versicherungspolice** cargo policy; ~**versorgung** supply of goods; ~**verteilung** distribution of goods; **mengenmäßige** ~**verteilung** proportional distribution of goods; ~**verwalter** land steward.

Güterwagen goods vehicle *(Br.)*, waggon *(Br.)*, freight car (waggon) *(US)*, truck *(Br.)* (tonnage, *US*, merchandise) car;
gedeckter ~ goods van *(Br.)*, house car, boxcar *(US)*; **geschlossener** ~ closed freight car *(US)*, covered waggon *(Br.)*, closed wagon *(US)*, box waggon *(Br.)*, boxcar *(US)*, gondola car *(US)*; **offener** ~ flat [car] *(US)*, open waggon, platform carriage *(Br.)* (car, *US*), goods truck *(Br.)*, general service car;
~ **zur Entladestelle dirigieren** to spot a freight car *(US)*;
in ~ **befördern (verladen)** to put aboard a train, to entrain, to load goods, to [ship by] freight *(US)*, to truck *(US)*; **im** ~ **verschicken** to van, to [ship by] freight *(US)*;
~**ladung** waggonload *(Br.)*, carlot *(US)*, carload *(US)*; ~**transport** trucking *(Br.)*, truckage *(Br.)*, shipment *(US)*, freight service *(US)*.

Güter|waggon [box] waggon *(Br.)*, boxcar *(US)*, freight car (waggon) *(US)*; **zwanzig** ~**waggons stellen** to make twenty waggons available; ~**wert** goods value; ~**wirtschaft** merchandising.

güterwirtschaftliche Analyse real analysis.

Güterzug goods train *(Br.)*, freight train *(US)*;
~ **auflösen** to break up a train; **umsonst in einem** ~ **mitfahren** to fit the rods *(sl.)*;
~**lokomotive** goods locomotive (engine) *(Br.)*, freight locomotive (engine) *(US)*, *(schwere)* consolidated engine, consolidation locomotive *(US)*; ~**verkehr** freight-train service *(US)*.

Güterzustellung freight delivery.
Güte|schutz quality protection; **~stelle** *(jur.)* conciliation court; **statistische ~überwachung** quality control; **~verfahren** *(jur.)* conciliation; **~vorschlag** *(jur.)* conciliatory proposal; **~vorschrift** quality specification; **~zeichen** quality label, brand, certification mark *(US)*, trademark; **~zeichen für mehrere Produkte** collective mark.
gutgehendes Geschäft flourishing business, going concern, roaring rade, business bonanza *(US)*.
gutgeschrieben, jds. Konto credited to s. one's account;
jem. ~ werden to appear in s. one's credit.
Gutgewicht tret, tare.
gutgläubig bona fide, in good faith;
~er Besitzer bona-fide holder; **~er Dritter** innocent [third] party; **~er Eigentümer** bona fide holder for value; **~er Erwerb** innocent purchase, bona fide acquisition; **~er Erwerber** bona fide purchaser, good faith taker *(US)*; **~er Inhaber** bona fide holder, innocent holder for value.
Gutgläubigkeit eines Kunden ausnutzen to trade on the credulity of a client.
Guthaben *(Anlagevermögen)* assets, *(Bilanz)* money owing to us, accounts receivable *(US)*, receivables *(US)*, *(Konto)* credit [balance], money on account, balance in s. one's favo(u)r, deposit account (balance) *(US)*;
im ~ *(Bankbilanz)* to the good; **ohne ~** without funds in hand; **täglich abhebbares ~** call money, daily balance; **antizipative ~** deferred credits [to income]; **ausreichendes ~** *(Scheck)* sufficient funds, sufficiency of funds; **nicht ausreichendes ~** insufficient funds; **ausstehende ~** outstanding accounts, receivable assets *(US)*; **dubiose ~** doubtful accounts; **eingefrorene ~** frozen assets; **sofort einlösbare ~** liquid (quick, *US*) assets; **nicht voll einbringlich erscheinende ~** nonredeemable assets; **täglich fälliges ~** current (demand, *US*, sight) deposit; **flüssige ~** cash assets; **nicht flüssige ~** frozen assets; **Ihr gegenwärtiges ~** amount (balance) standing to your credit; **gesperrtes ~** blocked credit balance; **kein ~** no assets (effects, funds); **kompensationsfähiges ~** clearing item; **längerfristige ~** time and saving deposits; **laufendes ~** cash on current account; **öffentliche ~** public deposits; **privates ~** private deposit; **transitorische ~** deposits in transit; **umsatzloses ~** dormant balance; **ungenügendes ~** insufficient funds; **unterhaltenes ~** credit balance maintained; **nicht von Banken unterhaltene ~** *(Bilanz)* individual deposits; **bei der Zentralnotenbank unterhaltene ~** legal (minimum, *US*) reserve, safety fund *(US)*, *(Bilanz)* deposits with the central bank; **unzureichendes ~** insufficient balance; **verbleibendes ~** remaining balance; **verfügbares ~** amount standing to the credit, available balance (funds); **frei verfügbare ~** free assets; **jederzeit verfügbares ~** money at call, call money, sight deposits; **zinsloses ~** free balance; **nicht zurückgefordertes ~** unclaimed balance;
~ des Auslands foreign-held balances; **~ im Ausland** foreign deposits; **~ bei einer Bank** bank balance, deposit in a bank; **~ bei [anderen] Banken** *(Bilanz)* due from banks; **~ bei Bausparkassen** deposits with building societies; **~ der Bundesnotenbank** public funds *(Br.)*; **~ bei anderen Etatstiteln** due from other funds; **~ bei Finanzinstituten** *(Bankbilanz)* balances with financial institutions; **~ der öffentlichen Hände** government deposits, public deposits *(Br.)*; **~ auf Inkassokonto** bills for collection; **~ auf Kontokorrentkonto** *(Bankbilanz)* deposits by customers; **~ bei Kreditinstituten** *(Bankbilanz)* cash in banks (at bankers); **~ privater Kundschaft** *(Bankbilanz)* deposits by customers, individual deposits; **freie ~ bei der Landeszentralbank** free reserves *(US)*; **~ auf Postscheckkonten** giro account *(Br.)*, postal cheque *(Br.)* (check, *US*) account; **~ staatlicher Stellen** government (public, *Br.*) deposits; **~ in konvertierbarer Währung** Eurocurrency;
~ auf einen Monat fest anlegen to fix a deposit for 30 days' notice; **~ aufweisen** to show a credit balance; **~ auf zwei Monate festlegen** to fix a deposit for two months; **eingefrorene ~ freigeben** to deblock frozen accounts, to unfreeze funds; **~ pfänden** to garnish an account; **als jds. ~ ausgewiesen sein** to stand to s. one's credit; **~ sperren** to block an account; **in jds. ~ stehen** to figure to s. one's credit; **bei der Notenbank zinslos ~ unterhalten** to maintain balances interest-free with the central bank (Bank of England, *Br.*, Federal Reserve Bank, *US*); **sein ~ zusammenrechnen** to sum [up] one's cash account;
~abzug withdrawal of deposits, outflow of funds; **~gutschein** gift token; **~inhaber** account holder, holder of a banking account; **~klausel** *(Bankwesen)* sufficient-funds clause; **~konto** credit [balance], [bank] deposit account (balance); **~posten** credit item; **~saldo** credit bank balance, account showing a credit balance, balance due to us (receivable, *US*), deposit balance; **~scheck ausschreiben** to issue a check *(US)* (cheque, *Br.*) against an account; **~übertragung** assignment of funds.
gutheißen to consent, to sanction, to approve, to o. k. *(US)*, to okay *(US)*.
gütig, mit Ihrer ~en Erlaubnis with your kind permission.
gütlich voluntary, amicable, friendly, *(außergerichtlich)* out of court;
sich ~ einigen to settle amicably;
~e Einigung friendly arrangement, amicable (out-of-court) settlement; **sich auf ~em Wege einigen** to come to an amicable arrangement.
gut|machen to make amends, to make up for; **~mütig** good-natured, kind-hearted.
Gutmütigkeit, jds. ~ mißbrauchen to presume s. one's kindness.
gutnachbarlich neighbo(u)rly;
~ handeln to act in a neighbo(u)rly fashion;
~es Verhältnis good-neighbo(u)rliness.
gutsagen to stand bail, to warrant.
Guts|arbeiter cottager; **~besitzer** gentleman farmer, big landowner, landed proprietor, squire *(Br.)*, farmer *(US)*, farmholder *(US)*; **~bewirtschaftung** cultivation, husbanding, farm management *(US)*.
Gutschein *(Bezugsschein)* coupon, ticket, *(Bon)* chit, *(Einzahlungsbeleg)* credit slip, *(Garantieschein)* quality warrant, warrant letter *(US)*, *(Prämie)* free-gift coupon, premium, token, gift voucher, giveaway *(US)*, courtesy card, trading stamp, *(Schuldschein)* promissory note, bond, *(Wertpapier)* voucher check;
auf den Inhaber lautender ~ bond payable to bearer; **portofreier ~** free-post coupon;
~ in Form eines um die Ware gewickelten Streifens package-band premium; **~ zu Geschenkzwecken** gift certificate;
~einlösung redemption of a coupon, coupon redemption; **~heft** coupon book; **~system** credit-coupon plan.
gutschreiben to credit;
jem. ~ to pass to s. one's credit, to enter to the credit of s. o.; **einem Angestelltenkonto Unternehmensaktien ~** to credit an employee in the company books with shares of stock; **jem. (jds. Konto) einen Betrag ~** to credit an account, to credit s. o. with a sum, to place (enter) an amount (a sum) to s. one's credit; **Gegenwert einem Konto ~** to place the proceeds to the credit of an account, to credit the proceeds to an account; **jem. einen Saldo ~** to balance in favo(u)r of s. o.; **zuviel ~** to overcredit; **zuwenig ~** to undercredit.
Gutschrift crediting, credit entry, *(Posten)* credit item;
nur zur ~ auf Konto des genannten Zahlungsempfängers a/c payee only *(Br.)*; **~ Eingang vorbehalten** entering short; **gegenseitige ~en** mutual credits; **irrige ~en** erroneous credits; **vorläufige ~** short entry;
~ für ausländische Steuern und bezahlte Kapitalertragssteuern tax credit *(US)*;
~ erteilen to pass to the credit; **~ stornieren** to reverse a credit entry; **zur ~ überreichen** to transfer for value.
Gutschrifts|anzeige, ~aufgabe advice of credit, credit advice (memorandum, note, *US*); **~aufgabe erteilen** to send a credit advice; **~beleg** *(im internen Bankverkehr)* credit slip *(Br.)* (ticket, *US*); **~kladde** *(Börse)* credit blotter; **~mitteilung** credit note; **~posten** credit item; **~stornierung** credit returns account; **~zettel** credit memorandum *(US)*, credit advice.
Guts|gebäude agricultural building, farmhouse *(Br.)*; **~grenze** lines of an estate; **~haus** farmhouse *(Br.)*, manor house; **geräumiges ~haus** rambling mansion; **~haus und dazugehörende Ländereien** mansion and lands pertaining thereto; **~herr** landlord, lord of the manor, squire *(Br.)*, farmer *(US)*, farmholder *(US)*; **~herrschaft** lords of the manor; **~hof** farm, manor, estate, farmyard; **~inspektor** land agent (steward) *(Br.)*, managing man, farm bailiff *(Br.)*, estate (farm, *US*) manager.
gutsituierte Geschäftsleute well-to-do businessmen.
Guts|pacht farm tenancy; **~pächter** tenant farmer.
gutstehen für to answer for, to guarantee, to stand bail.
Guts|verkauf disposal of an estate by sale; **~verwalter** managing man, land steward *(Br.)*, bailiff *(Br.)*, estate agent *(Br.)*, estate (farm, *US*) manager, land agent *(US)*, commissioner; **~verwaltung** estate (farm) management.
Gymnasialausbildung general grammar-school education.
Gymnasiast grammar-school student.
Gymnasium grammar school *(Br.)*, senior high school *(US)*; **humanistisches ~** secondary grammar school.
Gymnastik physical exercises, *(tägliche)* daily dozen *(fam.)*.

H

Haager Abkommen Hague Convention.

Haar, aufs ~ genau to a nicety, to a tittle; **mit Haut und ~** bones and all, completely, altogether; **um ein ~** by a hairsbreadth, within (by a fraction of) an inch; **um kein ~ besser** not a bit better;
~ **in der Suppe** fly in the ointment;
an den ~en herbeigezogen erscheinen to seem far-fetched; **~ in der Suppe finden** to find a hair in the soup; **jem. die ~e vom Kopf fressen** to eat s. o. out of house and home; **sich in die ~e geraten** to go for one another, to fall foul of each other; **sich aufs ~ gleichen** to be like two peas in a pod; **mehr Schulden als ~e auf dem Kopf haben** to be up to one's ears in debt; **~e auf den Zähnen haben** to be a tough customer; **an einem ~ hängen** to hang by a thread (on by the eyelids); **an den ~en herbeiziehen** to drag by head and shoulders; **jem. kein ~ krümmen** not to do any harm to s. o.; **kein gutes ~ an jem. lassen** to pick s. o. to pieces; **kein gutes ~ an einem Vorschlag lassen** to pull s. one's proposal to pieces; **einem die ~e zu Berge stehen lassen** to make one's hair stand on end; **sich keine grauen ~e wachsen lassen** not to lose sleep over it; **sich in den ~en liegen** to be at loggerheads, to be by the ears; **~e lassen müssen** to have to fork up *(US sl.)*, to come across with *(sl.)*, to have to pay through the nose; **sich vor Verzweiflung die ~e raufen** to tear one's hair; **um kein ~ besser sein** to be not a whit the better for it; **an den ~en herbeigezogen sein** to be far-fetched; **um ein ~ überfahren worden sein** to have been within an ace of being run over; **j. um ein ~ treffen** to miss s. o. by a fraction of an inch;
ich könnte mir die ~e raufen I would kick myself.

haarbreit, nicht ein not an inch.

Haardraht gold wire.

Haaresbreite, um by a hair's breadth (hairsbreadth, shave);
um ~ entkommen to escape by a hair's breadth (hairsbreadth); **nicht um ~ nachgeben** not to yield (budge) an inch; **um ~ verlieren** to lose by a neck.

haar|feiner Unterschied hairline (subtle) distinction; **~feinen Unterschied machen** to make a hairline distinction.

haargenau to a hair, to a toucher;
~ **getroffen** dead on the mark; ~ **passen** to suit to a T.

haarig hairy, *(fig.)* stiff, tough;
~es Examen stiff examination; **~e Geschichte** fishy business.

haarklein to the last detail;
~ **erklären** to explain to the minutest details.

Haar|nadelkurve hairpin bend; **~riß** *(Glasur)* craze, *(techn.)* microflaw.

haarscharf by a hair's breadth (hairsbreadth);
~ **daneben** a near miss; ~ **das Richtige** the cat's whiskers *(sl.)*; ~ **davonkommen** to have a narrow escape; **sich ~ an seine Weisungen halten** not to depart by a hair's breadth (hairsbreadth) from one's instructions; **~en Unterschied machen** to make a hairline distinction.

Haar|schnitt haircut; **militärischer ~schnitt** crew cut; **~spalter** hairsplitter, refiner; **~spalterei betreiben** to split hairs, to quibble.

haarsträubend hair-raising.
~e Geschichte hair-raising story; **~er Unsinn** frightful nonsense.

Haarstrich hairstroke, hairline.

Hab und Gut chattels, chose in possession, goods, wares and merchandise, fortune, goods and chattels.

Habe having, effects, belongings, possessions, goods [and chattels], movable estate, property;
bewegliche ~ movable property; **persönliche ~** personal things (belongings), personal estate, personal effects, personals; **keine pfändbare ~** *(Gerichtsvollziehervermerk)* nulla bona; **meine restliche ~** what remains; **unbewegliche ~** chattels real, immovables;
j. um seine ~ beneiden to envy s. one's possessions; **seine ganze ~ auf etw. setzen** to put one's shirt upon s. th. *(sl.)*; **seine ganze ~ verlieren** to lose all one's belongings.

Haben credit [side], assets, *(Bilanz)* creditors, credit items;
Soll und ~ credit and debit, assets and liabilities;
im ~ buchen to [place to the] credit, to enter on the credit side; **ins ~ kommen** to go into credit; **im ~ stehen** to be entered on the credit side.

haben to have, *(besitzen)* to possess, to be in possession of, *(im Laden führen)* to sell;
sich ~ to carry on, to make a fuss about; **j. zum Besten ~** to pull s. one's leg; **es eilig ~** to be in a hurry; **es gut ~** to sit pretty *(US sl.)*, to be well off; **j. völlig in der Hand ~** to hold s. o. in the palm of one's hand; **es in sich ~** *(Getränk)* to be pretty strong; **keinen Pfennig ~** to have not a penny to bless o. s. with, not to have a penny to one's name; **etw. unter sich ~** to be in control (charge) of s. th.; **viel für sich ~** to have everything in one's favo(u)r; **zu ~ sein** *(Börse)* to be on the market, *(Ware)* to be obtainable (for sale).

Haben|bestände assets, credit items; **~buchung** credit entry.

Habenichts have-not, lack-all.

Haben|posten credit entry (balance, item); **~saldo** credit (active) balance; **ausreichenden ~saldo aufweisen** to be sufficiently in credit; **~seite** credit [side]; **auf der ~seite zu verbuchen sein** to go among the credits; **~zinsabkommen** agreement on creditor interest rates; **~zinsen** interest due, credit interest [rates], creditor interest rates, interest on deposits (credit balances).

Habenzins|nummer credit (black) number *(Br.)*; **~satz** credit (deposit) rate.

Habgier greed, greediness, avarice, cupidity, exorbitance.

habgierig greedy, covetous, avaricious.

Habgieriger grasper.

habhaft werden, jds. to get hold of s. o.; **einer Sache ~** to lay one's hands on s. th.; **eines Verbrechers ~** to catch a criminal.

Habilitation habilitation, inception.

Habilitationsschrift inaugural dissertation.

habilitieren, sich to habilitate, to incept, to qualify as a university tutor.

Habilitierung habilitation.

Habitus deportment, carriage, behavio(u)r.

Habseligkeiten belongings, effects, goods, traps;
seine ~ in eine kleine Tasche stopfen to stuff one's belongings into a small bag.

Habsucht greed.

Hackbeil chopper, cleaver.

Hacke hoe, *(Absatz)* heel;
sich die ~n ablaufen to run one's legs off; **jem. auf die ~n treten** to tread on s. one's heels; **seine ~n zusammenschlagen** to click one's heels.

hacken to hack, to chop, to peck;
Loch ins Eis ~ to cut a hole in the ice.

Hackfleisch mincemeat, ground meat *(US)*;
~ **aus jem. machen** to make mincemeat of s. o., to make cold meat of s. o. *(sl.)*.

Hackfrucht root crop.

Hader paper rags, discord, quarrel, wrangle.

hadern to wrangle;
mit seinem Schicksal ~ to quarrel with one's lot.

Haderpapier rag paper.

Hafen harbo(u)r, port, haven;
im ~ in; **ohne ~** harbo(u)rless;
anzulaufender ~ port of call; **vom Land eingeschlossener ~** landlocked harbo(u)r; **eisfreier ~** ice-free port (harbo(u)r); **gesperrter ~** unequipped port; **innerer ~** inner harbo(u)r, close port *(Br.)*; **kleiner ~** creek *(Br.)*; **künstlicher ~** artificial harbo(u)r, artificial port; **natürlicher ~** natural harbo(u)r, natural port; **offener ~** open harbo(u)r; **sicherer ~** anchorage, haven of refuge; **sturmsicherer ~** safe harbo(u)r; **vereister ~** icebound harbo(u)r; **vorbestimmter ~** direct port; **zugelassener ~** approved port;
~ **der Europäischen Gemeinschaft** Community port; **~ mit Zollager** bonded port;
im ~ ankern to harbo(u)r; **~ anlaufen** to put into (stop at, touch, call at, make a call at) a port; **~ anlaufen und dort bleiben** to touch and stay; **~ ausbaggern** to clean out a harbo(u)r; **aus einem ~ auslaufen** to clear (run out of) a port, to leave harbo(u)r, to undock; **in den ~ bringen** to carry into port; **in den ~ einlaufen** to drop in (come, make, fetch, put) into port, to enter a harbo(u)r, to put into harbo(u)r, to cross the bar, to enter a port, to arrive in harbo(u)r; **sicher in den ~ einlaufen** to reach port safely; **~ erreichen** to reach a port; **mit Maschinenschaden im ~ festliegen** to be held up in port with engine trouble; **~ schließen** to close a port; **aus dem ~ heraus sein** to be free of the harbo(u)r; **~ sperren** to shut up (blockade) a port; **~ verlassen** to steam out of the harbo(u)r; **auf einen ~ zuhalten** to make for a port;
~abgaben harbo(u)r (dock, port) dues; **~abgrenzung** harbo(u)r line; **~amt** harbo(u)r board, port authority, Docks Board

(Br.), surveyor of the port *(US)*; **sich beim ~amt melden** to report to the port authority; **~anlagen** port construction site, harbo(u)r (port) installations (facilities, equipment), docks; **~anlauferlaubnis** liberty of a port.
Hafenarbeiter docker *(Br.)*, dock labo(u)rer (worker), wharf worker (man, porter), quay-side (cargo) worker, lumper, stevedore, long-shoreman *(US)*;
~streik waterfront strike.
Hafenauf|enthalt stay in a port; **~seher** harbo(u)r master, port warden *(US)*; **~sichtsamt** port authorities, surveyor of the port *(US)*, Docks Board *(Br.)*.
Hafen|ausbau port development, port improvement; **~bahn** harbo(u)r railway; **~bahnfracht** port carriage; **~bahnhof** harbo(u)r (marine) station; **~beamter** boarding officer (clerk, *Br.)*, landing waiter, naval officer *(US)*; **~becken** basin, dock; **~behörde** port (dock) authority, harbo(u)r board (authority); **staatliche ~behörde** National Port Council *(Br.)*; **~bereich** limits of port; **~besuch** port call; **~betrieb** port operation; **~betriebsgesellschaft** port-operators' association; **~blockade** naval blockade; **~brauch** custom at the port; **~damm** jetty, mole, pier, breakwater; **~dienstleistungen** harbo(u)r duties; **~dockgelder** pierage; **~einfahrt** entrance to a harbo(u)r, port entrance, harbo(u)r mouth, inlet; **~einnehmer** collector of a port; **~einrichtungen** harbo(u)r installations, harbo(u)r facilities; **~fahrzeug** harbo(u)r craft; **~feuer** harbo(u)r lights, dock light; **~gebiet** port area; **~gebühren** [port] toll, port charges (dues), anchorage, groundage *(Br.)*, pierage, harbo(u)r dues (rates), keelage; **~gefahr** port risk; **~geld** groundage, dock dues, berthage, keelage, duty of anchorage; **~gesundheitsamt** port sanitary authorities; **negative (positive) ~gesundheitsbescheinigung** foul (clean) bill of health; **~instandhaltungsabgaben** pierage; **~interessen** port interests; **~kapitän** port captain; **~kommandant** port master, port admiral *(Br.)*; **~kommandantur** port-admiral's office *(Br.)*; **~kommissar** harbo(u)r master, dockmaster; **~konnossement** port bill of lading; **~kosten** [port] toll, port dues, pierage; **~leistungen** harbo(u)r service; **~meister** harbo(u)r master, dockmaster, overseer (warden) of a port, port reeve, warden *(US)*; **~meisteramt** port authority, harbo(u)r board; **~ordnung** harbo(u)r (port) regulations; **~pilot** dock pilot, loadsman; **~platz** [sea] port, harbo(u)r; **einem Schiff einen ~platz zuweisen** to give place to a ship; **~polizei** harbo(u)r guard, harbo(u)r (dock) police, police of port; **~risiko** *(Versicherung)* port risk; **~schlepper** tugboat, harbo(u)r tug; **~schleppergebühr** loadmanage; **~schleuse** dock gate; **~schließung** closing a port; **~sperre** closing of a port, embargo, blockade, harbo(u)r barrage; **~sperre vornehmen** to block up a harbo(u)r; **~stadt** maritime city, port, seaport; **~usancen** custom at the port, particular trade of port; **~verwaltung** port authority (administration, management), dock authorities, harbo(u)r board (authority); **~viertel** dockland, dock area, the docks, waterfront; **~wache** harbo(u)r police, harbo(u)r guard, harbo(u)r watch, water guard; **~zoll** harbo(u)r dues (charges), [port] toll; **~zollamt** comptroller of the customs; **~zugang verwehren** to exclude from a port.
Hafer oats.
Haft detention, hold, ward, confinement, imprisonment, lock-up, custody;
in ~ under arrest, in prison (custody), detained;
strenge ~ close confinement; **ungesetzliche ~** unlawful detention; **vorbeugende ~** detention on remand;
~ ohne Sprecherlaubnis incommunication;
~ für j. anordnen to commit s. o. to prison; **vorübergehende ~ anordnen** to remand, to recommit temporarily; **~ antreten** to begin one's sentence; **in ~ behalten** to detain; **in ~ bleiben** to be remanded; **aus der ~ entlassen** to disincarcerate, to release from custody (prison), *(gegen Kautionsgestellung)* to remand on bail; **in ~ halten** to keep (have, hold) in custody, to detain, to hold prisoner; **j. in strenger ~ halten** to keep s. o. in close confinement; **j. unter Mordverdacht in ~ halten** to hold s. o. for murder; **in ~ nehmen** to place under confinement, to lay (put)in hold, to arrest; **aus der ~ vorgeführt werden** to be brought up on remand, to come out *(Br.)*;
~anordnung remand in custody, committitur; **verlängerte ~anordnung** detainer; **~anstalt** prison, prison house, jail *(US)*, gaol, lockup, *(für Jugendliche)* detention home; **~aufhebung** release from custody.
haftbar responsible, answerable, accountable, [legally] liable; **einzeln ~** severally liable; **gesamtschuldnerisch ~** jointly and severally responsible (liable); **insgesamt und einzeln ~** jointly and severally liable; **nicht ~** unanswerable, not liable, unaccountable; **noch ~** undischarged of an obligation; **persönlich ~** personally (individually) liable; **selbstschuldnerisch ~** liable at once, primarily liable *(US)*; **strafrechtlich ~** responsible; **subsidiär ~** secondarily liable;
j. ~ machen to render (hold) s. o. liable; **gesamtschuldnerisch ~ machen** to make jointly and severally liable; **j. für den Schaden ~ machen** to hold s. o. responsible for a damage; **j. für die ganze Schuld ~ machen** to hold s. o. liable for the whole debt; **Spediteur voll ~ machen** to hold the carrier responsible for the full value; **als Streitgenossen ~ machen** to render jointly liable; **~ sein** to be obliged (liable); **nur beschränkt ~ sein** to have limited liability; **für den Erfüllungsgehilfen ~ sein** to be vicariously liable; **für die Folgen seiner Fahrlässigkeit gesetzlich ~ sein** to be liable in law for the results of one's own negligence; **als Hauptschuldner ~ sein** to be liable for the debt of the principal; **nur bis zur Höhe seines verhältnismäßigen Verlustanteils ~ sein** not to be liable for more than one's rat(e)able share of a loss; **seinem Kunden bis zur Höhe des entstandenen Schadens ~ sein** to be liable to a customer to the extent of a loss; **persönlich ~ sein** to be personally answerable (individually liable), to incur personal liability.
Haftbefehl warrant of commitment (to arrest), detention order, writ of attachment, [writ of] detainer, mittimus, tag *(sl.)*;
aufgrund eines ~s inhaftiert legally committed;
mündlicher ~ parol arrest; **richterlicher ~** bench warrant;
~ für entsprungenen Sträfling escape warrant; **~ zur Vorführung des Beklagten** writ of capias *(US)*;
~ ausfertigen to execute a warrant of arrest; **~ gegen den Beschuldigten aufrecht erhalten** to recommit a prisoner, to remand the accused in custody *(US)*; **~ gegen einen Verdächtigen erlassen** to warrant the arrest of a suspected criminal; **~ gegen j. erwirken** to take out a warrant against s. o.; **ohne ~ festnehmen** to arrest without a warrant; **~ mit Protokoll wieder zustellen** to return a warrant.
Haft|beschwerde einlegen to appeal against an order of arrest; **~dauer** term of imprisonment; **~einweisung** mittimus.
haften to be liable (answer, be answerable) for, to respond *(US)*, *(garantieren)* to guarantee, to be guarantee for, to warrant, to vouch, *(Kleber)* to stick, to adhere;
für j. ~ to be responsible for s. one's actions; **bedingt ~** to be contingently liable; **für vorsätzliche Beschädigung ~** to be liable for voluntary waste; **beschränkt ~** to have a limited liability; **als Bürge für j. ~** to stand guarantee (surety) for s. o.; **für den Erfüllungsgehilfen ~** to be vicariously liable; **für die Folgen seiner Fahrlässigkeit rechtlich ~** to be liable in law for the results of one's negligence; **aus Gefährdung ~** to be strictly and absolutely liable; **gemeinsam (gesamtschuldnerisch) ~** to be jointly and severally liable; **als Gesellschafter ~** to be liable for partnership debts; **für fahrlässige Handlungen seiner Angestellten als Erfüllungsgehilfe ~** to be vicariously liable for acts of negligence by one's employees; **aus unerlaubter Handlung ~** to attract liability in tort; **für unerlaubte Handlungen seines Vertreters ~** to be liable for the torts of one's agent; **für den Hauptschuldner ~** to be liable for the principal; **nur bis zur Höhe seines verhältnismäßigen Verlustanteils ~** not to be liable for more than one's rat(e)able share of a loss; **wie eine Klette an j. ~** to stick like a burr to s. o.; **für einen Mangel ~** to warrant for a defect; **persönlich ~** to be personally liable (liable individually); **für einen Schaden ~** to be liable (responsible, held liable) for a charge; **auf Schadensersatz ~** to be responsible for a loss; **für eine Schuld ~** to be answerable for a debt; **für jds. Schulden ~** to be liable for s. one's debts; **selbstschuldnerisch ~** to be liable as principal debtor (at once, primarily liable, *US*); **solidarisch ~** to be severally liable; **unbeschränkt ~** to be liable without limitation; **unmittelbar ~** to be primarily responsible; **mit seinem ganzen Vermögen ~** to be liable to the extent of one's property; **wechselrechtlich ~** to become liable on a bill;
im Gedächtnis ~ bleiben to stick in the memory, to leave an impression on one's mind; **im Unterbewußtsein ~ bleiben** to cling to the side of the mind.
haftend, beschränkt ~er Gesellschafter limited partner; **persönlich ~er Gesellschafter** general partner.
Haftender obligor;
selbstschuldnerisch ~ primary debtor.
Haftentlassung release from prison, discharge [from custody];
bedingte ~ parole;
~ gegen Sicherheitsleistung bailment, release (remand) on bail; **jds. ~ anordnen** to order s. one's release from prison, *(gegen Kautionsgestellung)* to remand a prisoner on bail; **~ eines Untersuchungshäftlings erwirken** to bail out a prisoner.

Haft|entlassungsanordnung order for release from prison; ~**entschädigung** compensation for false imprisonment; ~**ersuchen** charge sheet; ~**etikett** adhesive label; ~**folie** adhesive foil; ~**fortdauer anordnen** to recommit a prisoner, to remand the accused in custody *(US)*; ~**geld** prison fee; ~**grund** reason of arrest; ~**kaution** bail bond; ~**ladung** limpet bomb.

Häftling remanded (remand) prisoner, detainee, *(KZ)* concentration-camp prisoner;
auf Bewährung vorzeitig entlassener ~ ticket-of-leave man *(Br.)*, probationer; **entsprungener** ~ prison breaker; **jugendlicher** ~ young prisoner; **mittelloser** ~ poor prisoner; **politischer** ~ state (political) prisoner.

Haft|liste charge sheet *(Br.)*; ~**lokal** house of detention, *(mil.)* guardhouse, military lockup, detention barracks.

Haftpflicht liability, responsibility, accountability, obligation;
mit beschränkter ~ with limited liability;
anteilmäßige ~ pro-rata liability; **beschränkte** ~ limited liability; **gesetzliche** ~ legal liability, third-party personal injury liability *(Br.)*, liability created by statute, statutory liability; **mittelbare** ~ secondary liability; **persönliche** ~ personal liability; **solidarische** ~ solidarity; **unbeschränkte** ~ absolute (unlimited) liability; **unmittelbare** ~ primary liability; ~ **gegenüber Dritten** third-party indemnity (liability) *(Br.)*; ~ **für das Reisegepäck** liability for baggage *(US)*;
~ **ablehnen** *(Versicherung)* to decline responsibility; ~ **ausschließen** to negative a liability; **von einer** ~ **befreien** to discharge (release, free) from a liability; **sich gegen** ~ **versichern** to insure against one's legal liability for injury or damage to others, to insure against third-party risk *(Br.)*;
~**anerkenntnis** liability bond; ~**anspruch** liability claim; ~**anteil** proportion of liability; ~**ausschluß** nonliability; ~**beschränkung** limitation of liability; ~**gesetz** [employers'] liability insurance law; ~**höchstgrenze** maximum liability.

haftpflichtig [legally] liable [for damages], answerable for a debt, bound, responsible, accountable;
selbstschuldnerisch ~ liable at once, primarily liable *(US)*; **subsidiär** ~ secondarily liable *(US)*;
j. ~ **machen** to hold s. o. liable; ~ **sein** to be liable (answerable) [for damages].

Haftpflichtiger party liable.

Haftpflicht|mindestgrenze minimum liability; ~**police** liability policy, third-party risk policy *(Br.)*; **allgemeine** ~**police** general liability policy; ~**prozeß** liability suit; ~**risiko** third-party risk *(Br.)*; **berufliches** ~**risiko** risk incident to employment; **gesamtes** ~**risiko** *(Unfallversicherung)* general accident portfolio; ~**umfang** liability coverage; ~**verbindlichkeiten** liabilities from third-party risks; ~**versicherer** public liability insurance company.

Haftpflichtversicherung public liability insurance, *(privat)* third-party indemnity insurance, *(Unfall)* accident (third-party accident, *Br.*) insurance;
berufliche ~ professional [risks indemnity] insurance; **kombinierte** ~ **und Diebstahlsversicherung** *(Auto)* comprehensive liability and property damage insurance *(US)*; **kombinierte** ~ **und Kaskoversicherung** *(Auto)* automobile personal liability and property damage insurance, comprehensive insurance *(Br.)*; **öffentlich-[rechtlich]e (staatliche)** ~ public [bodily] liability insurance; **private** ~ third-party indemnity (accident, *Br.*) insurance; **reine** ~ *(Kraftfahrzeug)* third-party only policy *(Br.)*;
~ **für Geschäftsfahrzeuge** commercial auto insurance; ~ **im Grundstücksverkehr** conveyance insurance; ~ **bis zur Höhe der gesetzlichen Haftung** legal liability insurance; ~ **für Privatfahrzeuge** personal auto insurance; ~ **für ein unbekannt abgebliebenes Schiff** retroactive insurance; ~ **gegen Veruntreuung** fidelity insurance;
der Aufsichtsbehörde gegenüber den Nachweis einer ~ **erbringen** to file an indemnity policy from an insurance company with the department; **gesetzliche** ~ **unterhalten** to carry insurance against legal liability *(US)* (third-party liability, *Br.*).

Haftpflichtversicherungspolice general liability (indemnity, third-party risk, *Br.*) policy;
reine ~ *(Autoversicherung)* third-party only policy.

Haftpflichtvoraussetzungen conditions precedent to liability.

Haftprüfung reviews of remand cases, Habeas Corpus;
Untersuchungshäftling zur ~ **sofort vorführen** to bring a prisoner before the court immediately.

Haftprüfungskammer remand court.

Haftprüfungstermin writ of Habeas Corpus;
~ **anordnen** to assign a writ of Habeas Corpus; ~ **suspendieren** to suspend the habeas corpus Act.

Haftprüfungsverfahren personal replevin, review of remand cases;
über die Rechtmäßigkeit einer Inhaftierung im ~ **entscheiden** to judge the legality of the imprisonment; **im** ~ **freilassen** to set a prisoner at large on habeas corpus; ~ **verzögern** to delay habeas corpus; **im** ~ **vorgeführt werden** to appear on remand *(Br.)*.

Haft|psychose prison psychosis; ~**richter** committing magistrate; ~**schale** contact lens.

Haftstrafe custodial sentence, detention on remand;
ausgesetzte ~ split sentence; **zur Bewährung ausgesetzte** ~ probationary custody; **lebenslängliche** ~ life sentence, lifer *(sl.)*;
Mörder zu lebenslanger ~ **verurteilen** to condemn a murderer to life imprisonment.

Haftsumme amount guaranteed.

Haftung liability, responsibility, accountability, obligation;
durch eine ~ **gedeckt** covered by a guarantee; **mit Ausschluß der** ~ nonliable; **mit beschränkter** ~ with limited liability, limited; **unter Ausschluß jeder** ~ no liability whatever, nonliable;
anteilsmäßige ~ pro-rata liability; **außervertragliche** ~ noncontractual liability; **beschränkte** ~ limited liability; **deliktsähnliche** ~ quasi tort; **doppelte** ~ *(Bankaktionäre)* double liability *(US)*; **erhöhte** ~ additional responsibility *(US)*; **finanzielle** ~ financial responsibility *(US)*; **gegenseitige** ~ *(Schiff)* cross liability; **gesamtschuldnerische** ~ joint and several liability; **gesetzliche** ~ liability created by statute, statutory liability, third-party personal injury liability *(Br.)*, *(Betriebsprüfer)* legal liability; **individuelle** ~ personal liability; **primäre** ~ *(Wechsel)* primary obligation; **sekundäre** ~ secondary liability *(US)*; **selbstschuldnerische** ~ primary liability; **solidarische** ~ joint and several liability; **strafrechtliche** ~ criminal liability; **unbeschränkte** ~ unlimited (absolute, full, strict) liability; **unmittelbare** ~ primary liability; **vertragliche** ~ contractual obligation (liability); **völkerrechtliche** ~ international responsibility; **wechselrechtliche** ~ liability for endorsement; **zivilrechtliche** ~ civil responsibility (liability);
~ **einer Aktiengesellschaft** corporate liability; ~ **des Arbeitgebers** liability of employer; ~ **nach konkursrechtlichen Bestimmungen** liability of bankruptcy jurisdiction; ~ **für Dritte** vicarious liability; ~ **des Ehegatten für im Rahmen der Schlüsselgewalt getätigte Ausgaben** husband's responsibility for wife's expenditure; ~ **bei Einsturz von Gebäuden** liability for the collapse of a building; ~ **des Erben** liability of an heir; ~ **des Erfüllungsgehilfen** accountability of a vicarious agent; ~ **für den Erfüllungsgehilfen** vicarious liability, rule of agency; ~ **für Fahrlässigkeit des Erfüllungsgehilfen** liability for negligence of servants, sole-actor doctrine; ~ **des Gastwirts** liability towards guests (of innkeeper); ~ **ausscheidender Gesellschafter** liability of retiring partners; ~ **eines nachschußpflichtigen Gesellschafters** liability of a contributory *(Br.)*; ~ **für Gesellschaftsschulden** liability for partnership debts; ~ **des Grundstückseigentümers** occupier's liability; ~ **aus unerlaubter Handlung** tortuous liability, liability for damage, liability [for negligence] in tort; ~ **des Herstellers** manufacturer's liability (warranty); ~ **für Liefermängel** liability for defects of the goods delivered; ~ **eines Liquidators** liability of liquidator; ~ **auf Schadensersatz** liability for damages (losses); ~ **für eingegangene Schulden** liability for debts contracted; ~ **des überlebenden Schuldners** survival of joint liability; ~ **des Spediteurs** liability of a common carrier; ~ **für Substanzschäden** *(Pächter)* impeachment of waste; ~ **des Tierhalters** liability for animals; ~ **im Todesfall oder für Körperverletzungen** liability for death or bodily injury to third parties; ~ **für Unfallschäden** responsibility for an accident; ~ **wegen Untätigkeit** liability for noncompliance; ~ **für Verkehrssicherheit** occupier's liability; ~ **des Vermieters** landlord's liability; ~ **für fremdes Verschulden** vicarious liability; ~ **ohne Verschulden** absolute (strict) liability; ~ **infolge arglistigen Verschweigens** liability for fraudulent misrepresentation; ~ **aus Vertrag** contractual liability; ~ **für Weglassung wichtiger Angaben** *(Prospekterstellung)* liability for omissions;
~ **ablehnen** to decline (deny) responsibility (liability); ~ **aufgrund der Versicherungsbedingungen ablehnen** to deny liability under a policy; **j. von der** ~ **ausnehmen (befreien)** to exempt s. o. from liability; **aus der** ~ **ausscheiden** to be released from liability; ~ **ausschließen** to exclude (negative) liability; **von der** ~ **befreien** to absolve (relieve, free) from liability; **von jeglicher** ~ **befreien** to discharge from all liability; ~ **begründen** to create liability; ~ **beschränken** to limit liability; ~ **eingehen** to

contract a liability; **sich der ~ entziehen** to avoid liability; **persönliche ~ der Einzelgesellschafter herbeiführen** to pierce the corporate veil *(US)*; ~ **übernehmen** to assume (undertake, contract a) liability, to underwrite; ~ **für j. übernehmen** to assume the responsibility for s. one's debts; ~ **für den unbezahlten Rechnungssaldo übernehmen** to hold the sack for the whole of the balance unpaid *(US)*; **von der ~ befreit werden** to be exonerated from an obligation.

Haftungs|ansprüche Dritter third-party liability claims; **~anteil** proportion of liability.

Haftungsausschluß nonliability, nonwarranty, exemption (exclusion, disclaimer, waiver) of liability;
völliger ~ no recourse;
~ **bei Beschlagnahme** warranted free from capture; ~ **bei der Haftpflichtversicherung** *(Kraftfahrzeug)* collision damage waiver; ~ **bei Seeuntüchtigkeit** rotten clause; ~ **bei Tod infolge Teilnahme an rechtswidrigen Unternehmungen** violating law clause; ~ **für leicht verderbliche Waren** memorandum clause.

Haftungs|befreiung relief (exemption) from liability; **~befreiung zu erreichen suchen** to seek relief from one's responsibilities; **~beschränkung** limitation of liability, *(Bürge)* right of division *(Scot.)*; **~beschränkungen** limits of liability; **~beschränkung des Transportunternehmers auf eigenes Verschulden der Angestellten** risk note; **~beschränkungsgrundsatz** principle of limited liability; **~beschränkungsklausel** *(Seeversicherung)* memorandum clause; **gesetzliche ~bestimmungen** statutory provisions regarding liability; **~buchung** liability entry; **~durchgriff** piercing the corporate veil *(US)*; **~entstehung** creation of liability; **~erklärung** liability bond, contract of suretyship; **~erweiterung** extended liability.

haftungsfähig, beschränkt of limited capacity.

Haftungs|fonds guarantee fund; **~freiheit für Schäden berufsüblicher Werkzeuge** simple tools doctrine; **~freistellung** exemption (release) from liability, indemnity against liability; **~freistellungsklausel** indemnity clause; **~freistellungsvertrag** contract of indemnity, indemnity contract; **~grenze** *(Versicherung)* limit (limitation) of indemnity; **~grund** responsible cause; **~kapital** share capital, capital stock *(US)*; **~klausel** liability clause; **~obligo** liability reserve; **~prinzip für kindergefährdende Spieleinrichtungen** turntable doctrine; **~prozeß** liability suit; **~quote** proportion of liability; **~risiko** risk of liability, third-party risk; **~schaden** liability loss; **~schuldner** indemnitor *(US)*; **~summe** liability coverage, amount covered; **~träger** party liable; **~übernahme** assumption of liability, undertaking; **~übernahmevertrag** hold-harmless agreement; **~umfang** accountability, accounting unit, measure of liability, liability coverage; **seinen ~umfang beschränken** to reduce one's liability; **~verbindlichkeiten** commitments, liabilites; **~versprechen** bond; **~verzichtsklausel** waiver of exemption; **~vorschriften** liability provisions; **explosionsartige ~zunahme** liability explosion.

haftuntauglich unfit to undergo detention.

Haft|unterbringung, offene liberty of the rules; **~verlängerung für eine Woche anordnen** to remand for a week; **~verlängerungsbefehl** detainer; **gestaffelte ~verschärfungsstufen** the first, second, third division; **~verschonung gegen Kautionsgestellung gewähren** to let to bail; **~vollzug** execution of punishment; **~vorführung** committal for trial; **~zeit** term of imprisonment.

Hagel hail, graupel *(US)*;
~ **von Flüchen** volley (hail, stream) of oaths; ~ **von Schimpfworten** torrent of abuse; ~ **von Schlägen** hail of blows; ~ **von Vorwürfen** volley of reproaches.

hageldicht auf j. fallen *(Schläge)* to hail down on s. o.

Hagelkorn hailstone.

hageln to be hailing, to hail.

Hagel|schaden damage caused by hail; **~schauer** hailstorm; **durch ~schlag zerstört** destroyed by hail; **~versicherung** hail insurance; **~wetter** hailstorm.

hager lean, thin, raw-boned, lanky.

Hahn cock, rooster, *(Gas, Wasser)* tap *(Br.)*, faucet *(US)*;
~ **im Korbe** cock of the walk;
~ **aufdrehen** to turn a tap; **jem. den roten ~ aufs Dach setzen** to set s. one's house on fire;
kein ~ kräht danach nobody cares a fig about it.

Hain hurst, grove, bosk.

Häkchen, was ein ~ werden will krümmt sich beizeiten just as the twig is bent, the tree's inclined.

Haken *(fig.)* rub, snag, catch, hitch, trouble, *(auf Liste)* tick, mark, check *(US)*, *(Öse)* hook;
kurzer ~ *(Boxhieb)* short blow;
~ **und Öse** hook and eye; ~ **an einer Sache** fly in the ointment; **mit einem ~ befestigen** to hook up; ~ **haben** *(fig.)* to have a string to (catch, snag in) it; ~ **schlagen** *(fig.)* to make a quick turn;
~umschalter *(tel.)* switch hook.

halb half;
~ **geschenkt sein** to be a giveaway price; **nur ~ so schlimm sein** not to be as bad as all that; **etw. nur ~ tun** to do s. th. by halves; **~er Arbeitstag** half holiday; **~er Dollar** half dollar *(US)*; **~er Fahrpreis** half fare (rate); **mit ~er Fahrt** at half speed; **~es Gehalt** half pay; **nur mit ~em Herzen dabei sein** to do s. th. in a half-hearted manner; **~e Maßnahmen** half-way measures; **nur mit ~em Ohr zuhören** to listen with one ear, to be a half-listener; **~e Portion** *(fam.)* shrimp; **~er Preis** half price; **~er Punkt** *(drucktechn.)* hair space; **alle ~en Stunden** every half hour; **auf ~em Wege entgegenkommen** to meet half way.

Halbabteil *(Bahn)* half compartment, coupé *(Br.)*.

halb|amtlich semiofficial, demi- (quasi-) official, officious; **~automatisch** semiautomatic.

Halb|blut half-blood, half-caste; **~bruder** half brother, uterine brother.

halbdienstlich semiofficial.

Halbdunkel der Geschichte twilight of history.

halbe-halbe fifty-fifty;
mit jem. ~ machen to go halves (fifty-fifty) with s. o.

Halb|edelstein semiprecious stone; **~erzeugnisse** unfinished goods.

Halbes, nichts ~ und nichts Ganzes neither fish, flesh nor good red herring.

Halbfabrikate semimanufacture, semifinished articles (products, manufactures), business goods, work in process *(US)* (progress, *Br.*), unfinished goods, half-finished (semifinished, intermediate) products;
~ **der Produktionsindustrie** semimanufactured production goods;
~bestand work-in-process inventory *(US)*; **~löhne** work-in-process labor *(US)*; **~material** work in process *(US)* (progress, *Br.*) material; **~ziffern** work-in-progress figures *(Br.)*.

halbfertig half-finished, semifinished;
~e und fertige Erzeugnisse work-in-process and finished goods *(US)*.

Halbfertig|fabrikate, ~waren intermediate goods (products), primary products, business (semimanufactured, semifinished) goods;
~ **der Produktionsindustrie** semimanufactured production goods.

halbfett gedruckt boldfaced, medium-faced.

Halb|finale semifinal; **~format** *(Foto)* half-frame; **in ~franz** half-bound; **~franzband** quarter binding, half-calf.

halbgebildet semiliterate.

Halbgebildeter smatterer.

halbgeschäftlich semibusiness.

Halb|geschoßfenster flemish window; **~gewebeband** half-fabric binding; **~heiten** halfway measures.

halbherzig|e Maßnahmen halfway measures; **~er Versuch** half-hearted attempt.

halbieren to halve;
Differenz ~ to split the difference.

Halbierungsmethode *(Statistik)* split-half method.

Halb|insel peninsula; **~invalide** semi-invalid; **~invalide sein** to be partially disabled; **~jahr** half year, semester, *(Schule)* half.

Halbjahres|abschluß midyear settlement, half-yearly rest; **~ausweis** midyear (semiannual) statement, half-year (midyear) return *(Br.)*; **~dividende** midyear (semiannual) dividend; **~geld** six-month loan; **~prämie** semiannual premium; **~rate** semiannual (half-yearly) instal(l)ment; **~rechnung** midyear settlement, semiannual (six-month) account; **~schrift** semiannual magazine; **~ultimo** midyear settlement; **~urlaub** a six-months' leave; **~zahlung** half-yearly payment; **~zeitschrift** biannual; **~zins** semiannual interest.

halbjährlich half-yearly, semiannual[ly], six-monthly;
~ **bezahlen** to pay every six months;
~er Vertrag six-month contract.

halblaut sprechen to speak in a subdued voice.

Halb|lederband half-leather binding; **~leinen** half cloth; **~leiter** semiconductor; **~luftreifen** cushion tyre.

halbmast half-mast;
~ **flaggen** to [fly at] half-mast; **auf ~ setzen** to half-mast.

halb|militärisch paramilitary; **~monatlich** twice a month, fortnightly *(Br.)*.

Halbmonats|lohn fortnightly wage *(Br.)*; **~schrift** biweekly, fortnightly review *(Br.)*; **~zahlung** fortnightly payment *(Br.)*.

halböffentlich semipublic.
Halb|pacht sharecrop *(US)* (metayer, *Br.*) system, **~pächter** produce-sharing farmer, metayer *(Br.)*, sharecropper *(US)*, farmer working on shares *(US)*.
Halbpart half share, fifty-fifty;
~ mit jem. machen to go half and half (halves) with s. o.; **~ verlangen** to cry halves.
Halb|pension partial board, European plan *(US)*; **~pensionär** half[-day] boarder.
halbseitig|gesperrt *(Straße)* closed on one side;
~e Anzeige half-page advertisement; **~er Bericht** report covering half a page.
Halbsold retainer pay.
halbstaatlich semigovernmental;
~e Einrichtung quasi-governmental corporation.
Halbstarker teddy boy *(Br.)*, skinhead *(sl.)*.
halbstarr *(Luftschiff)* semirigid.
halbstündlich half-hourly;
~er Abstand interval of half an hour.
halbtägig, halbtags half-time, part-time;
[nur] ~ arbeiten to work half time; **~ beschäftigt sein** to be on (employed) part-time.
Halbtags|arbeit part-time employment (work); **~arbeiter** half-timer, half-time (part-time) worker; **~beschäftigung** half-day (-time) job, part-time employment (job); **~beurlaubung** part-time day release; **~bezahlung** part-time worker rate; **~kraft** part-time worker, half-timer, part-timer; **~lohn** half-day wage; **~stelle** part-time job; **~verdienst durch Fabrikarbeit** part-time factory earnings.
Halb|teil *(jur.)* moiety; **~ton** *(Foto)* halftone; **~tonätzung** half-tone photoengraving; **~totale** *(Film)* medium shot; **~wahrheiten** half-truths.
halbwegs halfway.
Halb|welt demimonde, outskirts of society; **~wert** *(Statistik)* median; **~wissen** smatter, smattering, half knowledge.
halb|wöchentlich half-weekly; **~wüchsig** adolescent, half-grown, teenage *(US)*.
Halb|wüchsiger adolescent, teenager, youth; **als ~wüchsiger** in one's early teens; **~zeit** half time; **~zeitbeschäftigung** working half-time; **~zeug** semimanufacture (semifinished, business) goods, intermediate products.
halbzivilisiert semicivilized.
Halde waste heap, tip, *(Bergbau)* dump;
Kohle auf ~ schütten to dump (stockpile) coal.
Halden|abfälle tailings; **~bestände** dump (pithead) stocks; **~bevorratung** stockpiling; **~gelände** dumping ground.
Hälfte half [share], *(jur.)* moiety;
bessere ~ split level; **jds. bessere ~** s. one's better half *(coll.)*; **die größere ~** the lion's share (taking);
~ des Gewinns half the profits;
auf die ~ herabsetzen (reduzieren) to halve, to cut by half; **an der ~ des Unternehmens beteiligt sein** to go half share; **um die ~ gestiegen sein** to have increased by half; **Kosten zur ~ tragen** to pay half the cost;
Kinder zahlen die ~ children half-price;
~anteil half share.
hälftig|an einer Firma beteiligt sein to have a half interest in a firm; **Kosten ~ tragen** to contribute equal shares to the expense.
Halle hall, vestibule, saloon, aula, *(Bahnhof)* station hall, concourse *(US)*, *(Flugplatz)* hangar, *(Hotel)* lobby, lounge, hall.
Hallen|aufseher market watchman; **~schwimmbad** indoor swimming pool; **~vorplatz** *(Flugplatz)* apron.
Hallo hallo, hello, hullo *(Br.)*;
großes ~ hullabaloo.
Halluzinationen phantasm, hallucinations, visions;
~ haben to be seeing things.
Halm, Ernte auf dem ~ pfänden to seize the crop; **Ernte auf dem ~ verkaufen** to sell the crop standing.
Hals, aus vollem at the top of one's voice; **bis zum ~** over head and heels, up to hub *(US)*; **~ über Kopf** head over heels, helterskelter, headlong;
jem. den ~ abschneiden to cut s. one's throat; **Sache in den falschen ~ bekommen** to get hold of the wrong end of the stick; **den ~ nicht voll genug bekommen** to have an itch for money; **im ~e stecken bleiben** *(Worte)* to stick in one's throat; **sich den ~ brechen** to break one's neck; **jem. den ~ brechen** to ruin s. o., to do s. o. in *(sl.)*; **einer Flasche den ~ brechen** to crack a bottle; **~ über Kopf davonlaufen** to take to one's heels; **jem. um den ~ fallen** to fling one's arms around s. one's neck; **um ~ und Kragen gehen** to be a matter of life and death; **in den falschen ~ geraten** to go down the wrong way (s. one's Sunday throat, *US*); **j. auf dem ~ haben** to be saddled with s. o., to have s. o. on one's back; **etw. auf dem ~e haben** to be hard put to it; **Kloß im ~ haben** to have a lump in one's throat; **unverkäufliches Lager am ~ haben** to have a lot of unsalable stock; **das Wasser bis zum ~ stehen haben** to be head over heels in debt; **die ganze Welt auf dem ~ haben** to have everyone about one's ears; **jem. einen Prozeß an den ~ hängen** to land s. o. with (get s. o. into, *US*) a lawsuit; **jem. immer am ~e hängen** to be always in s. one's pocket; **jem. sein ganzes Leben lang wie ein Mühlstein am ~ hängen** to be a millstone round s. one's neck all his life; **sich auf den ~ laden** to let o. s. in for; **sich erhebliche Verbindlichkeiten auf den ~ laden** to saddle o. s. with a heavy task, to heavily commit o. s.; **seinen ~ retten** to save one's neck; **seinen ~ riskieren** to risk one's neck; **sich vom ~ schaffen** to doff, to dispose of, to get rid of, to make a bonfire of; **sich jem. vom ~e schaffen** to job s. o. off; **sich etw. vom ~e schaffen** to get rid of s. th.; **jem. die Polizei auf den ~ schicken** to set the police on s. o.; **aus vollem ~e singen** to sing at the top of one's voice; **bis zum ~ in etw. stecken** to be up to one's neck in s. th.; **bis zum ~ in den Schulden stecken** to be over head and heels in debt; **sich den ~ verrenken** to crane one's neck, to rubberneck;
die Sache hängt mir zum ~ heraus I am fed up with it;
~abschneider hawk, cutthroat, loan shark *(US)*.
halsabschneiderisch cutthroat.
Halsband *(Hund)* collar.
halsbrecherisches Tempo breakneck pace.
Hals|kette necklace; **~-Nasen-Ohren-Arzt** ear-nose-and-throat specialist, otorhinolaryngologist.
halsstarrig stubborn, obstinate, wilful, headstrong.
Halsweh haben to have a sore throat.
Halt halt, foothold, stop, *(Griff)* hold, grip, *(Stütze)* support, stay, prop;
sittlicher ~ moral support, ballast, mainstay;
~ der Familie mainstay of the family;
seinen inneren ~ in der Religion finden to find a sure support in religion; **keinen inneren ~ haben** to have no backbone, to be a man of no stability; **~ verlieren** to lose one's hold.
haltbar durable, lasting, stable, firm, *(Anzug)* sustainable, *(Argument)* tenable, perishable, *(Farbe)* faste) fast;
begrenzt (beschränkt) ~ semidurable; **nicht ~** *(Theorie)* untenable;
Nahrungsmittel ~ machen to preserve (process) food; **äußerst ~ sein** to stand any amount of hard wear; **~ verpacken** to pack for a long shelf-life;
begrenzt ~e Lebensmittel perishables.
Haltbarkeit *(Lebensmittel)* durability, solidity, fastness, stability, wear, shelf-life, *(Farbe)* fastness;
größere ~ longer shelf-life.
Haltbar|keitsprüfung endurance test; **~machung** preparation, treatment for preservation.
Halte|gurt safety belt; **~linie** stop line.
Halten|eines Kraftfahrzeugs keeping a car (motor vehicle);
Fahrzeug zum ~ bringen to bring a vehicle to a stop; **Fahrzeug rechtzeitig zum ~ bringen** to stop a car just in time; **Vormarsch des Feindes zum ~ bringen** to hold the enemy's advance.
halten to keep, *(glauben)* to deem, to believe, to think, *(Zug)* to stop;
sich ~ to hold one's own, *(Festung)* to hold out, *(fortleben)* to linger, *(Kurse, Preise)* to remain firm, to be maintained, to keep their ground, to rule steady, to support, to hold, *(Lebensmittel)* to keep, *(Theaterstück)* to hold the stage; **sich an eine Abmachung ~** to abide by an agreement; **sich abseits ~** to hold aloof; **sich vor Lachen den Bauch ~** to split one's sides with laughter; **nichts davon ~** to think nothing of; **j. in hohen Ehren ~** to hold s. o. in great esteem; **j. für einen Engländer ~** to put s. o. down as an Englishman; **sich für etw. für zu fein ~** to think s. th. beneath o. s.; **nicht viel auf Formen ~** to be no stickler for formality; **in Gang ~** to keep going; **für gastfreundlich ~** to rate as hospitable; **getrennt ~** to keep separate; **j. in Gewahrsam ~** to keep s. o. in custody; **es mit zwei Parteien gleichzeitig ~** to run with the hare and hunt with the hounds; **sich gut ~** *(Anzug)* to wear well, *(Börse)* to maintain a good tone; **sich dauernd hoch ~** *(Kurse)* to continue high; **Hochzeit ~** to celebrate one's marriage; **j. knapp ~** to keep s. o. on short commons; **Kraftfahrzeug ~** to keep a car (motor vehicle); **j. für 10.000 DM für kreditwürdig ~** to consider s. o. trustworthy to the extent of DM 10.000; **Kurs ~** to hold one's course; **j. auf dem laufenden ~** to keep s. o. posted; **sich auf seinem Spezialgebiet auf dem laufenden ~** to keep abreast of one's field; **jem. den Mantel ~** to help s. o. into (on with) his coat; **Marktanteil ~** to hold on the

market; **j. für den nächsten Ministerpräsidenten** ~ to tip s. o. for the next Prime Minister *(coll.)*; **seinen Mund** ~ to hold one's tongue; **sich nicht** ~ *(Theorie)* to be untenable; **etw. in Ordnung** ~ to keep s. th. going; **es für seine Pflicht** ~ to deem it one's duty; **Preise auf dem gleichen Niveau** ~ to maintain the same level of prices; **sich rechts** ~ *(Verkehr)* to keep to the right; **es für richtig** ~ to deem it right to do so; **schadlos** ~ to indemnify; **sich schadlos** ~ to recover one's losses, to have one's redress, to have recourse against; **Schläfchen** ~ to take (have) a nap; **mit seiner Meinung an sich** ~ to help one's own counsel; **es stets mit dem Sieger** ~ to side with the stronger party; **sich an die Spielregeln** ~ to play the game; **jem. die Stange** ~ to back s. o.; **seine Stellung** ~ to hold one's job, to hold the pass (down a job, *US*); **Stellung offen** ~ to keep a job open; **jem. eine Strafpredigt** ~ to read s. o. a lecture; **seine Kinder sehr streng** ~ to be very strict with one's children; **große Stücke von jem.** ~ to have a high opinion of s. o., to think well of s. o.; **sich tapfer** ~ to behave bravely; **sich eng an den Text** ~ to stick closely to the text; **Tier** ~ to keep an animal; **seinen Titel** ~ *(Rekord)* to retain one's title; **Plan für undurchführbar** ~ to hold that a plan is impracticable; **sich an eine Vereinbarung** ~ to abide by an agreement; **unter Verschluß** ~ to keep under lock and key; **Vertrag** ~ to adhere to an agreement; **viel von jem.** ~ to think quite a lot of s. o.; **nicht viel von jem.** ~ to have a poor opinion of s. o., to think little of s. o.; **nicht viel von etw.** ~ to think poorly of s. th.; **Vorlesung** ~ to deliver a lecture; **sich an seinen Vormann** ~ to have recourse against the preceding party; **vorrätig** ~ to keep in store, to have in (on, *US*) stock; **einen Vorschlag gegen den anderen** ~ to compare one proposal with another; **sich an die bestehenden Vorschriften** ~ to abide by the existing regulations; **Wache** ~ to keep watch; **sich wacker** ~ *(Kranker)* to hold one's own; **sich weitgehend** ~ *(Nebel)* to persist in most areas; **wenig von etw.** ~ to set little store by s. th.; **sein Wort nicht** ~ to go back on one's word; **Zeitung** ~ to subscribe for *(US)* (take in, *Br.*) a newspaper; **sein Zimmer ordentlich** ~ to keep one's room tidy; **zu jem.** ~ to range o. s. with s. o.;

sich nicht ~ **lassen** *(Theorie)* to be untenable; ~, **was man verspricht** to live up to one's reputation.

Halte|platz stopping place, stop, pull up *(Br.)*, *(Taxi)* taxi rank *(Br.)* (stand); ~**punkt** stop, *(Bahn)* wayside station, *(Flugzeug)* taxi holding position.

Halter keeper, holder;
~ **eines Kraftfahrzeuges** automobile (motor-vehicle, car) owner.

Halte|seil, ~**strick** tether line, tether.

Haltesignal halt (danger) signal, *(Bahn)* stop sign;
automatisches ~ *(Bahn)* automatic block signal;
~ **überfahren** to run past a [stop] signal.

Haltestelle station, stop, stopping place, stopover, *(Omnibus)* bus stop, *(Straßenbahn)* tram stop;
vereinbarte ~ set-down point;
~ **auf Verlangen** request stop.

Halte|stellensäule bus-stop pillar; ~**straße** stop street; ~**verbot** *(Schild)* no waiting.

Halteverbots|bestimmungen waiting restrictions; ~**grenze** no-waiting area; ~**straße** no-waiting street, clearway *(Br.)*; ~**zone** no-waiting area, no-stopping zone.

Haltezeichen stop (halt) signal, *(Bahn)* block signal.

haltlos *(labil)* weak, unstable, unsteady, *(Theorie)* without foundation;
~**es Gerücht** unfounded rumour.

haltmachen to stop, to halt.

Haltung attitude, posture, deportment, stance, carriage, mien, post, *(Ansicht)* ground, *(Börse)* tone, tendency, *(mil.)* attention;
abwartende ~ look (wait-and-see) position, attitude of expectancy; **distanzierte** ~ hands-off attitude; **drohende** ~ threatening attitude; **wenig entgegenkommende** ~ unreceptive attitude; **entschlossene** ~ firm stand; **feste** ~ *(Börse)* firmness, strength, *(pol.)* firm attitude; **auf Spezialwerte beschränkte feste** ~ *(Börse)* selective strength; **sehr feste** ~ *(Börse)* buoyant performance; **matte** ~ *(Börse)* flatness, dullness; **politische** ~ political attitude, stand; **unentschlossene** ~ straddle; **ungezwungene** ~ easy carriage; **unnachgiebige** ~ intransigent (unbending) attitude;
~ **einer Nation** tone of a nation; ~ **zum Schluß** *(Börse)* final tone;
~ **annehmen** to pull o. s. together, *(mil.)* to stand to attention; **legere** ~ **annehmen** to assume an easy posture; **stramme** ~ **annehmen** to stand to attention; **oppositionelle** ~ **im Kongreß aufgeben** to recede from one's opposition *(US)*; ~ **beibehalten** to maintain an attitude; ~ **bewahren** to preserve one's dignity (composure), to keep one's countenance; **bei seiner ablehnenden** ~ **bleiben** to maintain a negative attitude; ~ **einnehmen** to take a stand; **feste** ~ **einnehmen** to preserve a firm attitude; **gleiche** ~ **einnehmen** to take the same side; **neutrale** ~ **einnehmen** to maintain a neutral attitude; **strenge** ~ **einnehmen** to take a rigid line; **theatralische** ~ **einnehmen** to strike an attitude; **in schwankender** ~ **verkehren** *(Börse)* to fluctuate; **feste** ~ **zeigen** *(Börse)* to show a bold front;
selbst in der Armut ~ **zu wahren wissen** to live in genteel poverty.

Halunke rascal, scoundrel, rogue, blackguard.

hämisch malicious, malignant, spiteful;
sich ~ **über etw. freuen** to gloat over s. th.;
~**e Bemerkung** malicious remark.

Hammel, um auf besagten ~ **zurückzukommen** to return to our muttons;
jem. die ~**beine langziehen** to give s. o. a telling-off, to make s. o. toe the line.

Hammelsprung *(parl.)* division;
im ~ **abstimmen** to divide the house *(Br.)*.

Hammer, unter dem under the hammer;
unter den ~ **bringen** to bring under the hammer; **zwischen** ~ **und Amboß geraten** to get between the devil and the deep blue sea; **unter den** ~ **kommen** to come under the hammer.

hämmern to hammer, to pound;
auf ein Klavier ~ to hammer at the keys; **auf der Schreibmaschine** ~ to pound the typewriter; **an eine Tür** ~ to pound on a door.

Hampelmann jumping jack.

Hamsterer hoarder, shyster *(US)*;
~ **von Lebensmitteln** food hoarder.

Hamsterlager eines Geizkragens a miser's hoard.

Hamstern hoarding;
~ **von Lebensmitteln** food hoarding.

hamstern to hoard;
~ **gehen** to go shopcrawling *(Br.)*.

Hand, an ~ **von** based on; **an** ~ **von Beispielen** with the aid of examples; **aus erster** ~ immediate, first-hand; **aus zweiter** ~ secondhand, at second hand, unoriginal; **aus dritter** ~ at third hand; **im Bereich der öffentlichen** ~ in the public sector; **im Besitz der öffentlichen** ~ public-owned, under government control; **in privater** ~ in private hands; **mit der** ~ manually; **mit der** ~ **gemacht** manual; **mit der** ~ **zu greifen** within hand-reach; **mit eigener** ~ in own writing; **mit geschickter** ~ skilfully, deftly; **mit harter** ~ with a heavy hand; **mit sicherer** ~ with sure touch; **unter der** ~ by private contract, privately, under the counter, sub rosa, on the side *(Br.)*, on the Q. T.; **von** ~ **zu** ~ hand to hand; **von hoher** ~ on high authority; **von langer** ~ **vorbereitet** planned well in advance; **zur** ~ **gehend** to hand; **zur gesamten** ~ jointly; **zur ungeteilten** ~ jointly;
glückliche ~ green fingers *(coll.)*; **hilfreiche** ~ helping hand; **letzte** ~ ultimate owner (user); **öffentliche** ~ state sector; **rechte** ~ *(fig.)* righthandman, right arm; **tote** ~ dead hand, mortmain;
rechte ~ **des Chefs** right-hand man of the boss; ~ **aufs Herz** hand on heart; ~ **des Meisters** touch of the master;
um die ~ **eines Mädchens anhalten** to ask for a girl's hand in marriage; ~ **anlegen** to lend a hand; **letzte** ~ **anlegen** to add the finishing touches, to finalize, to put the last hand to; ~ **in** ~ **mit jem. arbeiten** to work hand-in-glove (in close cooperation) with s. o.; **seine** ~ **ausstrecken** to offer one's hand; **100 DM auf die** ~ **bekommen** to receive DM 100 clear; **unter der** ~ **erfahren** to get to know on the quiet; ~ **gegen j. erheben** to offer to strike s. o.; **sich unter der** ~ **erkundigen** to make unofficial inquiries; **an die** ~ **geben** to give an option, *(Grundstück einem Makler)* to list *(US)*; **fest an die** ~ **geben** to make a firm offer; **etw. aus der** ~ **geben** to part with s. th.; **jem. ein Vorzugsrecht an die** ~ **geben** to give s. o. the first refusal; **Wechsel aus der** ~ **geben** to give a bill from hand; ~ **in** ~ **gehen** to be accompanied by; **jem. zur** ~ **gehen** to wait on s. o., to lend s. o. a helping hand; **einem flott von der** ~ **gehen** to do s. th. with great ease; **jem. aus der** ~ **gleiten** to slip out of s. one's hand; **immer eine Antwort bei der** ~ **haben** to have one's answer pat; **immer eine Ausrede an der** ~ **haben** to be always ready with an excuse; **freie** ~ **haben** to have free scope; ~ **und Fuß haben** to hold water; **weder** ~ **noch Fuß haben** *(Anklage)* to be without any foundation; **kein Geld bei der** ~ **haben** to have no money on one; **glückliche** ~ **haben** to be able to turn one's hand to most jobs; **glückliche** ~ **mit Blumen haben** to have green fingers; **glückliche** ~ **im Umgang mit**

Kindern haben to have a way with children; **eine hohle ~ haben** to be open to bribery; **Inlandsmarkt fest in der ~ haben** to keep a tight grip of the home market; **lockere ~ haben** to be quick with a slap; **Nachricht aus der ersten ~ haben** to have a piece of news straight from the horse's mouth; **offene ~ haben** to have an itching palm; **sich in der ~ haben** to have control of o. s.; **Situation voll in der ~ haben** to have a good grip of the situation; **seine ~ im Spiel haben** to have a finger in the pie; **immer einen Verbandskasten zur ~ haben** to always keep a first-aid kit ready; **j. völlig in der ~ haben** to have s. o. in the palm of one's hand (a pull over s. o.), to have s. o. on toast *(Br., sl.)*; **die ~ auf den Beutel halten** to tighten the purse-strings; **~ auf der Tasche halten** to be close fisted, to hold the purse-strings tightly; **aus erster ~ kaufen** to purchase (buy) first hand; **freie ~ lassen** to give free rein, to allow s. o. a free hand (run, a blank check), to leave s. th. to s. one's discretion; **jem. völlig freie ~ lassen** to give full scope to s. o.; **von der ~ in den Mund leben** to live from hand to mouth, to lead a hand-to-mouth existence; **~ an sich legen** to attempt suicide; **~ an j. legen** to lay violent hands on s. o.; **~ an etw. legen** to turn one's hand to s. th.; **~ an die Arbeit legen** to take a piece of work in hand; **Arbeit aus der ~ legen** to lay work aside; **die ~ für etw. ins Feuer legen** to take one's oath on s. th., to stake one's life on s. th.; **letzte ~ an etw. legen** to give the finishing touch[es]; **~ ans Werk legen** to put one's hand to the plough; **jem. aus der ~ lesen** to read in s. one's hand; **auf der ~ liegen** to be obvious; **in jds. ~ liegen** to be up to s. o., to be within s. one's power; **Sache in die ~ nehmen** to take a matter in hand, to take the direction of affairs *(coll.)*; **mit eiserner ~ regieren** to rule with a rod of iron, to rule with a heavy hand; **keine ~ rühren** not to lift a finger; **nicht von der ~ zu weisen sein** not to be brushed aside; **etw. mit der linken ~ tun** to throw one's bread upon the waters; **an die tote ~ veräußern** to mortmain; **unter der ~ verkaufen** to sell privately (by private bargain, under the counter); **in die ~ versprechen** to promise solemnly; **mit der ~ bedient werden** to be hand-operated; **von der öffentlichen ~ unterstützt werden** to live upon the parish; **eine ~ wäscht die andere** one good turn deserves another; **~abzug** *(drucktechn.)* hand print; **~akten** reference files, *(Anwalt)* brief, pleadings; **~apparat** *(Scot.)* handset.

Handarbeit manual (unskilled, hand, common) labo(u)r (work), hand's turn, handiwork, handwork;
in ~ hergestellt craftsman-made;
feine ~ fancywork;
~en machen to needle.

Handarbeiter manual worker (labo(u)rer), handworkman, blue-collar worker *(US)*;
ohne ~ auskommen to dispense with hand labo(u)r.

Handaufheben *(Abstimmung)* show of hands;
durch ~ abstimmen to vote by show of hands.

Hand|ausgabe pocket edition; **~bearbeitung** hand tooling; **~bedienung** manual control (operation); **~betrieb** manufacture by hand.

handbetrieben hand-operated.

Hand|bibliothek reference library; **~breit** hand, a hand's breadth; **~bremse** parking brake.

Handbuch handbook, desk book, compendium, companion, manual, vademecum, *(Nachschlagebuch)* reference book;
~ für Ausbildungsfragen instruction manual; **~ für Betriebsprüfer** accounting manual; **~ der Finanzen** financial handbook; **~ für die Geschäftsführung** management guide; **~ für den Interviewer** field writer's manual; **~ für Verkäufer** sales manual.

Händchen für Blumen haben to have green fingers.

Hand- und Spanndienste arriage and carriage.

Handdruck block print.

Hände, durch Heben der *(parl.)* by show of hands; **zu ~n von** care of (c/o) *(Br.)*, attention of *(US)*; **zu treuen ~n** care of *(Br.)*, attention of *(US)*;
gierige ~ der Geldverleiher clutches of the moneylenders;
die öffentlichen ~ public sector (authorities);
jem. in die ~ arbeiten to play into s. one's hands; **Geld mit vollen ~n ausgeben** to spend money like water (with both hands); **~ im Spiel behalten** to keep one's hand in; **etw. in die ~ bekommen** to obtain possession of s. th.; **jem. in die ~ fallen** to fall into s. one's clutches; **einem Erpresser in die ~ fallen** to fall into the hands of a blackmailer; **mit offenen ~n geben** to give open-handedly; **durch viele ~ gehen** to pass through many hands; **in jds. ~ gelangen** to come to hand; **zwei linke ~ haben** his fingers are all thumbs; **seine ~ im Spiel haben** to have one's finger in the pie; **alle ~ voll zu tun haben** to be up to the elbows in work, to have a good deal (heaps of things) to do, to have one's work cut out *(coll.)*, to have much work on hand; **mit leeren ~n kommen** to come empty-handed; **sich die ~ reichen können** to be birds of a feather; **von seiner ~ Arbeit leben** to live by the sweat of one's brow; **in jds. ~ legen** to resign (put) into s. one's hands; **~ in den Schoß legen** to twiddle one's thumbs, to sit back; **in jds. ~n liegen** to be vested in s. o.; **Zügel behutsam aber fest in die ~ nehmen** to bring a gentle but firm hand into the management; **sich die ~ reiben** to rub one's hands; **jem. auf die ~ sehen** to watch s. o. closely; **in festen ~n sein** to be unlikely to change hands, *(Mädchen)* to be permanently attached; **an ~n und Füßen gebunden sein** to have one's hands tied; **mit den ~n zu greifen sein** to be as plain as pikesstaff; **jem. in die ~ spielen** to play into s. one's hands; **jem. Geheimakten in die ~ spielen** to pass secret documents on to s. o.; **seine ~ in die Tasche stecken** to plunge one's hands into one's pocket; **j. auf ~n tragen** to wait on s. o. hand and foot; **jem. etw. zu getreuen ~n übergeben** to leave s. th. in charge of s. o., to commit in trust of s. o.; **in andere (fremde) ~ übergehen** to pass into other (change) hands; **jem. etwas zu treuen ~n überlassen** to entrust the care of s. th. to s. o.; **seine ~ in Unschuld waschen** to wash one's hands of it; **sich mit ~n und Füßen wehren** to fight tooth and nail; **unter den ~n zerrinnen** to run through one's fingers; **mit beiden ~n zugreifen** to grasp an opportunity, to take time by the forelock; **~ über dem Kopf zusammenschlagen** to throw up one's hands;
viele ~ machen rasch ein Ende many hands make light work;
~druck handgrip; **~klatschen** handclap.

Handel commerce, trade, *(Abmachung)* agreement, *(Einzelgeschäft)* business, deal, dealing, transaction, *(Handelsstand)* the traders, *(Markt)* market, *(Tausch)* barter, exchange, truck, *(Vorfall)* affair, business, *(Warenaustausch)* traffic, trading;
für den ~ bestimmt commercial; **im ~** by way of trade, on the market; **nicht mehr im ~ erhältlich** off the market; **vom ~ abgeschnitten** debarred from commerce; **zum amtlichen ~ zugelassen** admitted (listed, *US*) on the stock exchange;
ambulanter ~ nonestablished retail trade, peddlery, pedlary *(Br.)*, peddling; **ausgedehnter ~** extensive trade; **ausgeglichener ~** balanced trade; **bilateraler ~** bilateral trade; **binnenstaatlicher ~** intrastate trade *(US)*; **blühender ~** roaring trade, commercial prosperity; **darniederliegender ~** languishing trade; **ehrlicher ~** square deal, bone-fide bargain; **erlaubter ~** lawful trade; **inländischer ~** domestic trade; **innereuropäischer ~** intra-European trade; **inoffizieller ~** *(Börse)* unofficial trading; **intervalutarischer ~** cross exchange *(Br.)*; **konzessionierter ~** licensed traffic, lawful trade; **lebhafter ~** brisk trade; **mittelständischer ~** small traders (business men); **schwunghafter ~** roaring trade; **sichtbarer ~** visible trade; **stockender ~** stagnant trade; **überseeischer ~** oversea trade, overseas (transmarine) commerce; **unerlaubter ~** illicit (clandestine) trade; **unvorteilhafter ~** bad bargain; **verbotener ~** illegal dealing; **völkerrechtlich verbotener ~** illegal trade; **zwischenstaatlicher ~** interstate commerce, interstate (intrastate, *US*) trade;
~ mit dem Ausland commerce with foreign nations, export trade, foreign commerce; **~ in Bezugsrechten** rights dealing *(US)*; **~ mit Billigerzeugnissen zwecks Umsatzsteigerung** trading down *(US)*; **~ in Edelmetallen** bullion trade; **~ in kleineren Effektenabschnitten** odd-lot trading *(US)*; **~ innerhalb der EG-Länder** intracommunity trade; **~ zwischen den Einzelstaaten** interstate (intrastate) commerce *(US)*; **~ mit landwirtschaftlichen Erzeugnissen** agricultural commerce; **~ mit Erzeugnissen der Landwirtschaft** agricultural trade; **~ mit dem Feinde** trading with the enemy; **~ und Gewerbe** trade and industry; **~ zwischen den Kolonien** intercolonial trade; **~ mit Luxusgütern** luxury trade; **~ in kleinen Mengen** retail trade; **geduldeter ~ neutraler Staaten** precarious trade; **~ im Umherziehen** hawking, itinerant trade, peddling, peddlery, pedlary *(Br.)*; **~ und Verkehr** trade and transport; **~ mit leicht verderblichen Waren** perishable traffic; **~ mit Waren höherer Preislage und größerer Gewinnspanne** trading up *(US)*; **~ auf dem Wasserwege** water-borne commerce; **~ in nicht notierten Werten** off-board (-floor) trading *(US)*; **~ mit gestohlenen Wertpapieren** stolen-securities traffic; **~ mit nicht notierten Wertpapieren** over-the-counter trading *(US)*; **~ mit nicht zum offiziellen Börsenverkehr zugelassenen Wertpapieren** over-the-counter market *(US)*; **~ und Wirtschaft** trade and industry;
~ abbrechen to break a bargain; **~ ableiten** to divert trade from a country; **~ abschließen** to conclude a sale, to strike (bind) a bargain, to consummate a deal; **~ aufgeben** to quit business; **~ aufkündigen** to break a bargain; **~ aufmachen** to open a trade, to set up shop *(US)*; **~ behindern** to intercept trade; **~ wieder beleben** to reanimate (revive) trade; **in den ~ bringen** to

commercialize; ~ **einhalten** to stick to a bargain; **in den ~ kommen** to be marketed; **guten ~ machen** to do a good stroke of business; ~ **rückgängig machen** to undo a bargain, to rescind a contract; **im ~ sein** to be sold (on the market); **im freien ~ erhältlich sein** to be sold commercially; **nicht mehr im ~ sein** to be no longer on the market; **zum ~ an der Börse zugelassen sein** to be accepted for trading (listed, *US*) at the stock exchange; ~ **treiben** to [carry on (follow) a] trade, to traffic, to market, to handle, to carry on commerce with, to buy and sell, to deal; **bedeutenden ~ treiben** to do a lot of trade; **unter der Firma ... ~ treiben** to trade under the name (style) of ...; **wilden ~ treiben** to interlope; **über einen ~ einig werden** to strike hands upon a bargain; ~ **wiederbeleben** to revive trade.

Händel suchen to pick a quarrel.

handelbar salable, marketable, *(Wertpapier)* negotiable; **börsenmäßig ~** admitted to (listed at, *US*) the stock exchange; **jederzeit ~ sein** *(Wertpapier)* to constitute a good delivery.

Handeln *(Tätigwerden)* doing, action, activity, *(Handeltreiben)* trading, bargaining;

eigenmächtiges ~ unauthorized act; **fahrlässiges ~** active negligence; **gemeinschaftliches ~** concerted action; **gewaltloses ~** nonviolent action; **rechtswidriges ~** malfeasance; **schlüssiges ~** acceptance inferred from conduct; **selbständiges ~** *(Arbeitgeber-Arbeitnehmer)* deviation; **verspätetes ~** delayed action;

~ **für andere** agency; **fehlerhaftes ~ an Bord** unproper navigation; ~ **auf eigene Gefahr** voluntary assumption of risk; ~ **im guten Glauben** bona-fide operation.

handeln to act, to take action, to proceed, to operate, *(feilschen)* to haggle, to chaffer, to bargain, *(Geschäft betreiben)* to be in business, to carry on a trade, to negotiate, *(Handel treiben)* to trade, to deal, to traffic, to buy and sell, to handle, to monger, *(auf den Markt bringen)* to market, to sell, *(tauschen)* to merchandise, to barter;

mit etw. ~ to carry on the trade of s. th.; **in gewinnsüchtiger Absicht ~** to act with an eye to profit; **mit Aktien ~** to job; **von Amts wegen (kraft seines Amtes) ~** to act in an official capacity; **auftragsgemäß ~** to act in compliance with one's orders; **ganz nach eigenem Belieben ~** to suit one's own convenience; **gemäß den Bestimmungen ~** to act in accordance with the rules; **von den deutsch-englischen Beziehungen ~** to deal about (treat of) the Anglo-German relations; **an der Börse ~** to quote (list, *US*) on the stock exchange; **bösgläubig ~** to act mala fide; **fahrlässig ~** to act carelessly; **gemeinsam ~** to act conjointly, to make corporate action; **gegen das Gesetz ~** to act contrary to law; **seinen Grundsätzen gemäß ~** to live up to one's principles; **nach Gutdünken ~** to act as one thinks fit; **gutgläubig ~** to act bona fide, to act in good faith; **auf eigene Initiative ~** to act in one's individual capacity; **gegen jds. Interessen ~** to act adversely to s. one's interests; **gegen die Interessen seines Mandanten ~** to operate against one's client; **nach seinem eigenen Kopf ~** to abound in one's own sense; **aus eigener Machtvollkommenheit ~** to act independently; **im eigenen Namen ~** to act on one's own behalf; **in fremdem Namen ~** to act as agent; **ganz offen ~** to act aboveboard; **rechtswidrig ~** to offend the law; **sich um eine wichtige Sache ~** to be a matter of importance; **sofort ~** to take immediate action; **in Überschreitung seiner Befugnisse ~** to act ultra vires; **mit Übersee ~** to do business with overseas countries; **überstürzt ~** to go off half cock; **aus innerster Überzeugung ~** to act from conviction; **umsichtig ~** to act with caution; **unredlich ~** to play foul; **außerhalb seiner Vertretungsbefugnisse ~** to act beyond the scope of one's authority; **innerhalb seiner Vertretungsmacht ~** to act within the scope of one's authority; **vorsätzlich ~** to act deliberately; **vorschriftsmäßig ~** to act in accordance with the regulations (rules); **unter Zwang ~** to act under duress;

mit sich ~ lassen to be accommodating, to abate.

handelnd acting, active.

Handelnder doer, actor.

Handelsabkommen commercial treaty (accord, convention), treaty of commerce, commercial agreement, trade agreement (pact), economic trading agreement;

allgemeines Zoll- und ~ General Agreement on Tariffs and Trade (GATT); **zweiseitiges ~** bilateral trade agreement;

~ **mit Meistbegünstigungsklausel** reciprocal trade agreement.

Handels|abmachung trading arrangement; ~**abordnung** trade delegation; ~**abschlag** markdown [on selling price] *(US)*; ~**abteilung** *(Konsulat)* commercial section; ~- **und Wirtschaftsabteilung** *(Auswärtiges Amt)* trade service; ~**adreßbuch** trade (business) directory; ~**agent** commercial *(US)* (mercantile) agent, commission merchant; ~**agentur** mercantile (commercial) agency; ~**akademie** mercantile academy, commercial (business, *US*) school; ~**akzept** trade acceptance; **ausstehende ~akzepte** *(Bilanz)* trade acceptances receivable *(US)*; ~**angebot** trade offering; ~**angelegenheit** commercial concern; ~**artikel** articles of merchandise, commercial articles, commodities, wares; **gesetzlich geschützte ~artikel** patented articles; ~**attaché** commercial attaché (counsellor, secretary), trade-service diplomat; ~**aufschlag** markup; ~**ausdruck** commercial (mercantile) term; ~**auskunft** trade enquiry; ~**auskunftei** credit-reporting agency; ~**ausschuß** committee of commercial men, trade commission, trade committee *(US)*; ~**aussichten** trade prospects; ~**ausstellung** trade show (exhibition) *(Br.)*; ~**austausch** trade exchange; ~**ausweitung** expansion of trade, expansion of commerce; ~**bank** commercial bank (credit company), acceptance house, merchant bank[er] *(Br.)*, trading bank *(Australia)*; ~- **und Gewerbebank** trade (commercial) bank; **seine ~bankfunktionen ausdehnen** to expand its merchant banking arm; ~**bedingungen** trading (trade) conditions, *(Austauschrelation)* terms of trade; ~**bedürfnisse** trade demand; ~**befugnis** licence; ~**beilage** *(Zeitung)* commercial supplement; ~**berechtigung** trade licence; ~**bericht** commercial (mercantile) advice, market report, city article *(Br.)*.

Handelsbeschränkungen impediment to (restraint of) trade, trade restrictions;

~ **aufheben** to lift the discriminations; ~ **unterwerfen** to place restrictions on foreign trade.

Handels|besprechungen commercial negotiations, industrial conference, trade talks; ~**bestimmungen** economic clauses; ~**beteiligung** trade sharing; ~**betrieb** business, commercial establishment (business, enterprise), firm; ~**bevollmächtigter** commercial agent; ~**bewilligung** licence; ~**bezeichnung** trade (commercial) name, commercial term, brand.

Handelsbeziehungen mercantile (trade) connections, trade relations, commercial relations (relationship);

dreiseitige ~ three-cornered trade relations; **gespannte ~** trade tension;

multilaterale ~ wieder in Gang bringen to relaunch the multinational trade negotiations; ~ **zwischen zwei Ländern zum Stillstand bringen** to interrupt the flow of commerce between two countries; ~ **einstellen** to cease dealings; ~ **erwägen** to contemplate trade; ~ **unterhalten** to maintain trade relations; ~ **verstärken** to build up trade.

Handelsbilanz trade (visible) balance, balance of trade, merchandise balance *(US)*, *(Firma)* commercial balance sheet;

aktive ~ active trade balance, favo(u)rable (active) balance of trade; **defizitäre (passive) ~** passive (adverse) trade balance, unfavo(u)rable (adverse) balance of trade; **negative ~** debit trade balance; **passive ~** passive trade balance, unfavo(u)rable balance of trade; **positive ~** positive trade balance;

~ **der Steuerbilanz weitgehendst angleichen** to report pretty much on the same basis as one's tax form; **bei der ~ längere Abschreibungsfristen anwenden** to report on a longer depreciable life basis; **aktive ~ aufweisen** to run (show) a favo(u)rable trade balance; ~ **ausgleichen** to redress the balance of trade; ~ **verschlechtern** to deteriorate the trade balance;

~**defizit** trade balance deficit; ~**erträge** gains of trade; ~**lücke** trade gap; ~**überschüsse** surpluses of balance of trade, trade balance surpluses; **für ~zwecke** for financial reporting.

Handels|blatt trade journal, financial paper; ~**blockade** economic blockade; ~**brauch** trade usage, custom of merchants (the trade), usage of trade, commercial practice; **strenger ~brauch** hard and fast rule; ~**bräuche des Buchhandels** commercial practices of the bookselling trade; ~**brief** business letter; ~**bücher** account (trade) books; ~**bücher aufbewahren** to retain [trade] books; ~**chance** opening for trade; ~**dampfer** merchant ship, merchantman, trading vessel; ~**defizit** trade deficit; **gewaltiges ~defizit ausgleichen** to slim its enormous trade gap; ~**delegation** trade mission (delegation); ~**dienstorganisation** Trade Commissioner Service *(Br.)*; ~**dünger** commercial fertilizer; ~**einheit** *(Börse)* unit of trade, trading unit, lot.

handelseinig werden to strike a bargain, to make (come to) terms.

Handels|einschränkungen restraints of trade; ~**englisch** business English; ~**erfahrungen** experience in trade; ~**ergebnis** trading performance; ~**erlaubnis** trade (trading) licence, license *(US)*; ~**erlaubnis für Ausländer** staple; ~**erleichterungen** trade [promotive] facilities; ~**erschwerung** restraint of trade; ~**erzeugnis** trading item; ~**fach** branch of industry, line of business.

handelsfähig negotiable, merchantable.

Handels|faktura invoice; ~**firma** business firm, commercial [house], commercial establishment (concern), mercantile house, merchandising concern (establishment); **gelöschte ~firma** extinct firm; ~**firma ruinieren** to wreck a commercial house; ~**flagge** merchant flag, Red ensign *(Br.)*; **billige ~flaggen** flags of convenience; ~**flotte** merchant marine; **durch den Krieg stark mitgenommene ~flotte** war-riddled merchant fleet (marine); ~**flottenkapazität** fleet capacity; ~**frau** femesole trader, free dealer (trader); ~**freiheit** free trade, freedom of trade; ~**fürst** merchant prince; ~**gebiet** commercial field, trade area; ~**gebräuche** custom, trade practices, practice of merchants; ~**gehilfe** office clerk, *(Verkäufer)* shop assistant, *(Voluntär)* volunteer; ~**gemeinschaft** trading community; ~**genossenschaft** copartnership, company; ~**geographie** commercial geography; ~**gepflogenheit** trade practices, custom; ~**gericht** [etwa] commercial court *(Br.)*, tribunal of commerce *(US)*.

handelsgerichtlich|eingetragen registered, incorporated *(US)*; ~ **eintragen** to register *(Br.)*, to incorporate *(US)*; ~**e Eintragung** registration, incorporation *(US)*; ~**e Eintragungsurkunde** certificate of registration *(Br.)* (incorporation, *US*); **unter seiner ~en Firma verklagt werden** to be sued in its corporate name; ~**er Firmenname** trade name.

Handelsgeschäft commercial establishment (house), business (mercantile) concern, mercantile business, *(einzelnes)* commercial transaction, trading (commercial) operation, deal; ~e commercial dealings (operations); ~ **betreiben** to be engaged in a commercial business, to [carry on a] trade.

Handelsgesellschaft [trading (registered), *Br.*] company, trading corporation (partnership), commercial partnership, mercantile partnership *(US)*, business corporation; **eingetragene** ~ registered *(Br.)* (incorporated, *US*) company; **gutgläubige** ~ bona-fide business corporation; **inländische** ~ resident company; **konzessionierte** ~ chartered company *(Br.)*; **Offene** ~ general partnership, ordinary partnership *(US)*; **privilegierte** ~ chartered company *(Br.)*; **rechtsfähige** ~ incorporated company *(Br.)*; **staatliche** ~ state trading company; ~ **zur Durchführung einer einmaligen Transaktion** single adventure *(Br.)*, special (particular) partnership *(US)*; ~ **auflösen** to wind up a business company; ~ **als fortgeführt behandeln** to treat a partnership as a continuing business; **Offene** ~ **in eine GmbH umwandeln** to turn a partnership into a limited company.

Handelsgesetz commercial law; ~**buch** [etwa] Uniform Commercial Code; ~**gebung** commercial (trade) legislation.

Handels|gespräche trade talks; ~**gewerbe** business, trade; ~**gewerbe betreiben** to carry on (run) a business, to exercise (follow, ply) a trade; ~**gewicht** avoirdupois [weight]; ~**gewinn** trading (business) profit; **unerlaubter ~gewinn** trade windfall; ~**gewohnheiten** trade practices, custom.

handelsgünstig good for trade.

Handels|gut merchandise; ~**gut mittlerer Art und Güte** fair average quality; ~**güter** commodities, wares, merchandise, trade goods; ~**hafen** commercial port (harbo(u)r), trading port; ~**haus** commercial establishment (house), mercantile (business) house, business enterprise, [trading] firm, trading house; **solides ~haus** house of standing; ~**herr** proprietor of a commercial establishment, merchant principle; **nicht tarifgebundene ~hindernisse** nontariff barriers; ~**hochschule** commercial college, business school, mercantile academy; ~**index** trade (business) index; ~**innung** guild; ~**interessen** commercial interests.

Handelskammer chamber of commerce, board of trade *(US)*; **Industrie- und** ~ Chamber of Industry and Commerce, *(in USA)* United States Chamber of Commerce *(US)*; **Internationale** ~ International Chamber of Commerce; ~**verband** association of chambers of commerce.

Handels|kapitän master of a trading vessel; ~**kette** chain trade; ~**klasse** grade, class, quality; ~**klausel** trade stipulation; ~**kniffe** trade dodges; ~**kommissionär** commission merchant; ~**kompanie** trading corporation; ~**konferenz** trade conference; **Genfer ~konferenz** Geneva Trade Conference; ~**konkurrenz** trade rivalry; ~**konzern** trading combine; ~**konzession** licence; ~**korrespondent** business (economic) correspondent; ~**korrespondenz** commercial (business) correspondence, commercial papers (post); ~**korrespondenzkursus** commercial correspondence course; ~**kredit** commercial credit, business loan; ~**kreditbrief** commercial letter of credit; **durchschnittlicher ~kreditsatz** average business loan rate; ~**kreise** merchants, business circles; **bewaffneter ~kreuzer** armed merchant cruiser; ~**krieg** commerce destroying, tariff (trade) war, economic warfare; ~**krise** commercial (economic) crisis; ~**kunde** commercial science; ~**kursus** business (commercial) course; ~**lager** dealer stock; ~**lehrer** commercial teacher; ~**lehrling** merchant apprentice; ~**luftfahrt** commercial aviation; ~**macht** trading nation; ~**makler** mercantile (commercial) broker, mercantile agent; ~**mann** merchant, trader, tradesman; ~**marine** mercantile (merchant) marine, merchant service; **durch den Krieg stark mitgenommene ~marine** war-riddled merchant marine; ~**marke** brand name, trademark, mark, ideograph *(US)*.

handelsmäßig according to usance.

Handels|menge number of transactions; ~**messe** trade fair *(Br.)*; ~**metropole** commercial metropolis; ~**minister** President of the Board of Commerce, President of the Board of Trade *(Br.)*, Secretary of State for Trade *(Br.)*, Secretary of Commerce *(US)*; ~**ministerium** Board of Trade *(Br.)*, Department of Commerce *(US)*, Commerce Department *(US)*; ~ **und Industrieministerium** Department of Trade and Industry *(Br.)*; ~**mißbrauch** trade abuse; **Mitwirkung bei einer Vereinbarung über Abstellung von ~mißbräuchen** trade practice submittal *(US)*; ~**mission** trade mission (delegation); ~**mittelpunkt** commercial (business) center *(US)* (centre, *Br.*); ~**möglichkeiten** trading possibilities; ~**monopol** trade monopoly; ~**moral** business morals (morality); ~**münze** current coin; ~**muster** sample [of merchandise], pattern of trade; ~**nachbar** trading neighbo(u)r; ~**nachrichten** financial columns, city article *(Br.)*; ~**name** trade (business) name, style of a business firm; **unter dem ~namen firmieren** to trade under the style; ~**nation** trading nation; ~**niederlage errichten** to staple; ~**niederlassung** trading post (station), trade settlement, staple, commercial factory, commercial location; ~**objekte** trade-offs; ~**offensive** trade offensive; ~**organisation** business (trade) organization; **internationale ~organisation** international trade organization; ~**papier** commercial instrument, negotiable paper; **kurzfristiges ~papier** commercial paper; ~**parität** commercial parity *(US)*; ~**partner** [business] partner, trading partner; ~**platz** trading post (town), staple place, marketing center *(US)* (centre, *Br.*), market; ~**platz ersten Ranges** emporium, commercial center *(US)* (centre, *Br.*).

Handelspolitik commercial (trading, trade) policy; **protektionistische** ~ protectionist trading policies; ~ **der offenen Tür** open-door policy.

handelspolitisch|e Abmachungen trade agreements; ~**e Anregungen** trade-policy initiative; ~**e Auswirkungen** trade-policy effects; ~**e Beziehungen** trade relations; ~**er Graben** trade-policy moat; ~**e Initiative** trade-policy initiative; ~**e Instruktionen** trade-policy instructions; ~**e Kursänderung** trade-policy shift; ~**e Lösung** trade-policy solution; ~**e Maßnahmen** trade measures; ~**e Praktiken** commercial policy devices; ~**er Querkopf** biassed trade freak; ~**e Spaltung** trade split; ~**e Vorteile** trade benefits.

Handels|position commercial position; ~**praktiken** trade practices; ~**preis** market price; **üblicher (laufender, jetziger, gegenwärtiger) ~preis** current price; **unter dem normalen ~preis verkaufen** to sell below dealer costs; ~**privileg** trade privilege, right of staple; ~**produkt** trading item; ~**qualität** commercial quality; ~**rabatt** trade discount; ~**raum** trade area; ~**recht** law merchant, custom of merchants, mercantile (commercial) law.

handelsrechtliche Auseinandersetzungen schiedsgerichtlich beilegen to settle trade disputes by arbitration.

Handelsreferent *(Konsulardienst)* commercial agent *(US)*.

Handelsregister [etwa] Register of Companies (Corporations, *US*), Registrar of business names *(Br.)*, Companies Registry (Registration Office, *Br.*); **ins ~ eintragen** to register *(Br.)*, to incorporate *(US)*; **beim ~ hinterlegen** to file with the Register of Companies *(Br.)*; **sich beim ~ eintragen lassen** to file accounts with the Register of Companies *(Br.)*; **Firma im ~ löschen** to remove a firm from the register, to deregister *(Br.)* (disincorporate, *US*) a firm; **einer Firma die Eintragung ins ~ versagen** to refuse to register a firm; ~**auszug** extract from a registered statement; ~**eintragung** certificate of registration *(Br.)* (incorporation, *US*).

Handels|reisender commercial travel(l)er, commercial *(Br.)* (travel(l)ing) salesman, sales representative, bagman *(Br.)*, runner *(US)*, drummer *(US)*; ~**risiko** trading (trade) hazard, business risk; ~**rückgang** loss of trade; ~**sache** *(Gericht)* commercial case (cause); ~**schiedsgerichtsbarkeit** commercial arbitration; **Internationaler ~schiedsgerichtshof** Court of International Commercial Arbitration.

Handelsschiff merchant (mercantile) vessel (ship), merchantman, regular trader, cargo steamer;
im Krieg gebautes ~ war-built merchant ship;
~ **entladen** to discharge a merchant vessel; ~ **im Schutzgeleit eines Zerstörers fahren lassen** to convoy a merchant ship by a destroyer;
~**fahrt** merchant shipping *(Br.)* (service), maritime commerce; **die ~fahrt** *(Börse)* the shipping interests.
Handelsschiffahrts|gesetz Merchant Shipping Act *(Br.)*; ~**verordnung** Merchant Shipping Regulations *(Br.)*.
Handelsschiffer merchant seaman.
Handelsschiffs|auftrag merchant ship order; ~**kapitän** master mariner.
Handelsschranken impediment to (barriers of) trade, trade walls (barriers);
nicht tarifgebundene ~ nontariff barriers; **zwischenstaatliche** ~ interstate trade barriers;
~ **abbauen** to reduce the barriers of trade, to dismantle trade barriers; **auf Zolldisparitäten beruhende** ~ **abbauen** to ease nontariff barriers of trade.
Handels|schulausbildung commercial (business) education, education for commerce; ~**schulden** business (commercial) debts; ~**schule** commercial school (college), school of commerce, trade school *(US)*, secretarial college; ~**sitte** usage of trade; ~**sitz** registered office, commercial domicile; ~**sorte** merchantable qualitiy, commercial variety; ~**spanne** trade margin, [profit] margin, margin of profit, markup [on selling prices]; **allen Artikeln einheitlich dieselbe ~spanne berechnen** to put a flat markup on all items; ~**sparte** line of commerce; ~**spekulation** venture; ~**sperre** stoppage of trade, embargo; ~**sperre aufheben** to lift an embargo; ~**sprache** business language; ~**staat** trading state; ~**stadt** mercantile (business) town, trading port, emporium; ~**stand** commercial occupation, mercantile (trading) classes, merchants, tradespeople, trade; ~**statistik** trade statistics, Board of Trade returns (figures); ~**stockung** stoppage of trade; ~**straße** highway of commerce, trade route; ~**streitigkeit** trade dispute; ~**ströme** currents of trade, trade currents; ~**ströme eines Landes umleiten** to divert trade from a country; ~**stützpunkt** trading post; ~**system** mercantile system; ~**tätigkeit** commercial occupation (services), business (commercial) activity; ~**teil** *(Zeitung)* commercial supplement, financial columns (part), city article *(Br.)*; ~**töchter** trading subsidiaries; ~**tonnage** freight tonnage; ~**überschüsse** trade surplus[es].
handelsüblich commercial, customary in trade, in accordance with usage;
~**e Abkürzungen** commercial signs; ~**e Bezeichnung** trade name, brand, description; ~**es Gewicht** commercial weight, avoirdupois weight; ~**er Preis** market price; ~**e Qualität** merchantable quality; ~**er Rabatt** trade (commercial) discount; ~**e Verpackung** standard packaging; ~**e Vertragsformeln** trade terms.
Handels|unkosten trade expenses; ~**unternehmen** commercial establishment (business, enterprise), mercantile (business) enterprise, merchandising (trading) concern; **öffentlich-rechtliches ~unternehmen** public trading body; **staatliches ~unternehmen** state trading enterprise; ~**usance** usage of trade, trade practices, custom of merchants, merchant's rule; ~**verbindungen** business (trade) connections, trade relations, economic intercourse; ~**verbot** stoppage of trade, embargo; ~**verdienst** perquisites of trade; ~**vereinigung** commercial combination, trading association; ~**verhältnisse kennen** to understand the market.
Handelsverkehr commerce, traffic, trafficking, trade, trade flows, market, mercantile operations, economic intercourse;
ausgeglichener ~ balanced trade; **erhöhter** ~ stepped-up trade; **innergemeinschaftlicher** ~ trade within the community; **innerstaatlicher** ~ internal commerce; **lebhafter** ~ active commerce; **zwischenstaatlicher** ~ international commerce;
~ **neutraler Staaten** neutral commerce;
~ **sperren** to embargo; ~ **unterbrechen** to intercept the trade; ~ **mit dem Ausland untersagen** to interdict trade with foreign nations (countries).
Handels|verkehrslinien trade routes; ~**verlagerung** *(EG)* trade diversion.
Handelsvertrag commercial treaty (contract, alliance, agreement), trade agreement (treaty, pact), trading contract;
gegenseitiger ~ reciprocal trade agreement;
~ **abschließen** to enter into a treaty of commerce, to sign a trade agreement; ~ **mit dreimonatiger Frist kündigen** to denounce a trade pact with three months notice.
Handelsvertrags|partner trade (trading) partner; ~**verhandlungen** negotiations for a commercial treaty; ~**vollmacht** commerce clause *(US)*.
Handels|vertreter commercial *(US)* (mercantile, *Br.*, sales, business, trade) agent, commercial travel(l)er, commercial canvasser *(Br.)*, drummer *(US)*, sales representative, factor; ~**vertretervereinbarung,** ~**vertretervertrag** agency agreement; ~**vertretung** commercial (mercantile) agency, sales agency; **unabhängige ~vertretung** general agency business; ~**vertretung für eine Firma haben** to be agents for a company; ~**volk** mercantile (trading) nation; ~**volumen** trading (trade) volume, volume of trade; ~**vorrat** stock-in-trade; ~**vorrechte** preferences, economic priorities; ~**vorschriften** business regulations; ~**vorteil** commercial advantage, preference; ~**ware** article of merchandise, wares, merchant's (trade) goods; ~**wechsel** commercial paper (note, bill), mercantile (trade, business) paper, trade bill (acceptance), bill down on goods sold; **erstklassiger ~wechsel** fine bill (trade paper); ~**weg** channels of commerce (trade), trade channels; ~**welt** trading community, business world; ~**wert** commercial (market, trading, trade, economic) value, trade-in value, *(einer Ware)* commercial (merchantable) quality; **gemeiner ~wert** common market value; ~**wesen** trade matters; ~**wissenschaft** commercial science; ~**wörterbuch** business dictionary; ~**zeichen** trademark, brand, description; ~**zeitschrift** trade magazine (journal); ~**zensus** census of distribution; ~**zentrum** center *(US)* (centre, *Br.*) of commerce, hub of commerce, trading (commercial) center *(US)* (centre, *Br.*), staple, entrepôt, mart, emporium; ~**zerstörer** commerce destroyer; ~**ziffern** trade data; ~**zone** trading (trade) area, business zone; ~**zweig** branch of industry, line of business.
handeltreibend trading, commercial, mercantile.
Handeltreibender trader, tradesman, merchant, dealer.
Hände|ringen wringing one's hands; ~**schütteln** handshake.
Hand|exemplar copy for private use, author's copy; ~**feger und Schaufel** dustpan and brush; ~**fertigkeit** dexterity, manual skill; ~**fertigkeitsunterricht** craft classes; ~**fesseln** manacles.
handfest tangible, substantial, solid;
~**e Argumente** solid arguments; ~**er Beweis** cast-iron proof; ~**e Klausel** ironclad clause; ~**e Lüge** downright (brazen, thumping, *fam.*) lie; ~**er Verdacht** well-founded suspicion.
Hand|feuerwaffen small arms, handguns; ~**feuerwaffen führen** to carry fire arms; ~**fläche** palm.
handgearbeitet handmade, handworked, hand-wrought, self-made.
Handgebrauch, zum for daily use.
Handgeld imprest (earnest, bargain) money, handsel, advance, *(Pächter)* key money, *(Schiff)* prest money;
bei Nichtabschluß des Kaufvertrages zurückzahlbares ~ deposit subject;
als ~ **geben** to give in prest.
Handgelenk, aus dem offhand, off the cuff;
aus dem ~ **schütteln** to do it just like that.
handgemacht handmade.
handgemein werden to fight hand to hand, to come to blows, to come to handgrips, to come to grips, to exchange blows.
Handgemenge scuffle, hand-to-hand fight, scrimmage, mêlée, dogfight, affray, mix-up, grapple;
wirres ~ rough and tumble *(fam.)*;
in ein ~ **geraten** to come to close quarters.
Handgepäck personal luggage *(Br.)* (baggage, *US*), luggage travel(l)ing with the passenger *(Br.)*, hand baggage *(US)*, grip *(US)*, *(Flugpassagier)* cabin (carry-on) luggage *(Br.)*;
abgegebenes ~ left luggage *(Br.)*; **mit ins Flugzeug genommenes** ~ carry-on (cabin) luggage *(Br.)*;
sein ~ **aufbewahren lassen** to leave one's luggage *(Br.)* (baggage, *US*) in the cloakroom;
~**aufbewahrung** left-luggage office *(Br.)*, parcel room *(Br.)*, cloakroom, baggage room *(US)*; ~**schließfach** baggage locker *(US)*; ~**wagen** baggage truck *(US)*.
handgerecht handy.
Handgeschenk manual gift.
hand|geschöpft *(Papier)* handmade; ~**geschrieben** handwritten.
Handgranate hand grenade, bomb.
handgreiflich violent;
~ **gegen j. werden** to lift one's hand against s. o.
Handgreiflichkeiten violence, blows, wigs on the green *(coll.)*;
Ausweg in ~ **suchen** to resort to fisticuffs.
Handgriff handgrip, handle, *(Kunstgriff)* manoeuvre, manipulation;
mit einem einzigen ~ with a flick of the wrist;

notwendige ~e kennen to know the tricks of the trade; **den ganzen Tag keinen ~ tun** not to lift a finger all day long; **Maschine mit wenigen ~en zusammenbauen** to assemble a machine very quickly.

Handhabe handle, pretext, ways, means, handsel, instrument; **gesetzliche ~** legal grounds;
seinen Feinden eine ~ gegen sich bieten to give one's enemies a handle against one; **der Verleumdung eine ~ bieten** to give a handle for calumny; **als ~ dienen** to serve as a pretext; **~ gegen j. finden** to have a leverage to bring to bear on s. o.; **jem. eine ~ geben** to give s. o. an occasion, to give s. o. a handle against o. s.; **keine ~ gegen j. haben** to have nothing on s. o. *(fam.)*.

handhaben to administer, to manage, to handle, to manipulate, to play, *(Maschine)* to operate, to work;
betrügerisch ~ to rig; **Gerechtigkeit ~** to administer justice; **Gesetz ~** to administer the law; **seine Werkzeuge ~** to handle one's tools;
sich leicht ~ lassen to handle easily, to be easy to manipulate.

Handhabung handling, management, manipulation, operations, application, use, execution, administration;
betrügerische ~ rigging; **elastische ~** *(Vorschrift)* flexible use; **leichte ~** easy handling;
~ gleicher Arbeitsbedingungen für alle fair employment practices *(US)*; **~ von Beschränkungen** administration of restrictions; **~ der Einkommensteuerbestimmung** income-tax practice; **~ der Gerechtigkeit** distribution of justice.

Hand|karren handcart, trolley *(Br.)*, pushcart; **~katalog** ready reference catalog(ue); **~kauf** handsale, purchase in lump; **~koffer** suitcase, overnight case, portmanteau *(Br.)*, valise *(US)*, grip *(US)*; **~köfferchen** handbag; **~kuß** kiss on the hand; **mit ~kuß nehmen** to take gladly.

Handlanger day labo(u)rer, jack, journeyman, underling, handyman *(US)*, jobber, jockey *(Br.)*, *(auf dem Bau)* hod carrier, hodman *(Br.)*, *(politisch)* puppet, stooge, instrument, mate, subworker, jobber;
immer nur den ~ machen to do always the donkey work; **~ sein** to fetch and carry;
~dienste donkey work; **~dienste leisten** to jack-all, to be s. one's dog's-body.

Händler trader, tradesman, merchant, [market] dealer, monger, marketeer, barterer, *(Börse)* stockjobber, *(Kleingewerbe)* chandler, *(Ladenbesitzer)* shopkeeper, storekeeper *(US)*;
ambulanter (fliegender, umherziehender) ~ itinerant (door-to-door) trader, costermonger, hawker, barrowman *(Br.)*, pedlar *(Br.)*; **fliegender ~** peddler *(US)*; **unbedeutender ~** petty dealer; **zugelassener ~** franchised (authorized) dealer;
~ in kleinen Effektenabschnitten odd-lot dealer *(US)*; **~ mit eigenem Lager** stockist *(Br.)*, rack jobber *(US)*; **~ mit alten Möbeln** furniture broker; **~ mit großen (bedeutenden) Umsätzen** heavy dealer; **~ in festverzinslichen Werten** bond trading officer;
~ nicht mehr beliefern to withhold supplies of goods from a dealer; **~ erstmalig einschalten** to handsel a dealer; **Vormachtstellung als ~ wiedergewinnen** to refill its dealer forecourts;
~analyse dealer research; **eingedruckte ~anschrift, ~aufdruck** dealer imprint; **~befragung** dealer survey (research), shop audit; **~gefolgschaft** dealer force; **~gruppe bei einer Versteigerung** ring of dealers at an auction; **~interview** dealer interview; **eingebaute ~kodierung** built-in dealers' coding; **~kontrolle** dealer control; **~lager** dealer inventory; **~marge** trade discount; **~marke** private (dealer) brand; **~nachlaß** dealer's rebate; **~netz** dealer network; **~organisation** dealer organization (outlet); **~preis** trade price; **~rabatt** distributor's (trade) discount, dealer's rebate (allowance, abatement, discount), functional discount, discount allowed to dealers, discount earned; **~stand** pitch; **~überwachung** dealer control; **~verband** retail association *(US)*; **~verdienstspanne** dealer markup; **~vereinbarung** distributor agreement; **~vereinbarung mit Ausschließlichkeitsklausel** exclusive dealer arrangement *(US)*; **~vereinigung** dealer organization, retail association *(US)*; **~werbung** trade advertising, dealer merchandising plan; **~wettbewerb** dealer incentive contest; **~zeitschrift** trade paper; **~zettel** *(Börse)* slip.

Handleuchte portable lamp.

handlich convenient-sized, handy, manageable;
~es Format handy size; **in ~er Nähe** within easy reach.

Handlichkeit handiness.

Handlung act, action, deed, proceeding, *(Drama)* plot, *(Laden)* business, shop *(Br.)*, store *(US)*, *(Roman)* plot;
aus unerlaubter ~ founded on tort;
betrügerische ~ fraudulent activity (act), deceit; **fahrlässige ~** negligent act; **fehlerbeseitigende ~** curative act; **feindselige ~** *(Völkerrecht)* act of hostility, hostile act; **zur Last gelegte ~** offence charged with; **genehmigungsfähige ~** act capable of ratification; **hoheitsrechtliche ~** act of state; **komplizierte ~** *(Roman)* intricate plot; **kriegerische ~** act of war; **nachträgliche ~** postfactum; **offenkundige ~** overt act; **pflichtwidrige ~** *(Beamter)* misfeasance, malfeasance; **rechtswidrige ~** private wrong, act of illegality, malfeasance, unlawful (illegal) act; **vorsätzliche rechtswidrige ~** malicious act; **richterliche ~** judical act; **schuldhafte ~** wrongful act; **staatsfeindliche ~en** subversive activities; **strafbare ~** penal act, tort subject of penalty, punishable offence (act), criminal (public) offence; **unerlaubte ~** actionable tort (nuisance), tortious act, delict, civil (private) wrong, *(auf hoher See)* maritime tort; **einklagbare (schadensersatzpflichtige) unerlaubte ~** actionable wrong; **fahrlässig begangene unerlaubte ~** negligence in tort; **gemeinsam begangene unerlaubte ~** joint trespass, joint tort; **vorsätzlich begangene unerlaubte ~** wilful tort; **unfreundliche ~** *(pol.)* unfriendly act; **unsittliche ~** immoral offence; **unüberlegte ~** thoughtless action, rush (sudden) impulse; **unzüchtige ~** indecent liberties, indecency; **verräterische ~** foul play; **vorbereitende ~** *(Strafrecht)* preparation; **vorsätzliche ~** wilful act; **widerrechtliche ~** illegal act; **willenlose ~** involuntary act; **willkührliche ~** moral action;
~ des Erfüllungsgehilfen vicarious performance (act); **strafbare ~ eines Ersttäters** first offence; **unerlaubte ~en Jugendlicher** juvenile wrongdoing; **~ auf eigene Rechnung** separate trade; **~en und Unterlassungen** acts and omissions;
unerlaubte ~ begehen to commit a tort; **Schadensersatz wegen unerlaubter ~ erlangen** to obtain damages in tort; **aus unerlaubter ~ haften** to be liable in tort; **für die unerlaubten ~en seines Vertreters haften** to be liable for the tort of one's agent; **durch ~en bewußt irreführen** to act a lie; **aus unerlaubter ~ klagen** to sue for tort; **auf unerlaubte ~ lauten** to sound in tort; **ohne ~ sein** to lack movement; **für seine ~en verantwortlich sein** to be responsible for one's actions; **an einer strafbaren ~ teilnehmen** to participate in committing an offence; **j. zu überstürzten ~en verleiten** to stampede s. o. into doing s. th.

Handlungsablauf *(Film, Roman)* plot, denouement.

handlungsarm *(Drama)* plotless.

Handlungs|beauftragter agent; **keine ~befugnis haben** to have no capacity to act.

handlungsbereit und verfügungsberechtigt ready and willing.

Handlungsbevollmächtigter proxy, attorney in fact, managing agent, signing clerk *(Br.)*, *(Handelsagent)* commercial (mercantile, general) agent.

handlungsfähig capable, competent, *(bevollmächtigt)* authorized (entitled) to act;
~ sein to have capacity (be capacitated) to act; **nicht ~ sein** not to be free to act.

Handlungsfähigkeit capacity to act, mental capacity (competence).

Handlungsfreiheit free scope (rein), freedom of action, elbow room, rope;
volle ~ full discretion to act;
in der auswärtigen Politik absolute ~ besitzen to be free to act in foreign affairs; **jds. ~ einschränken** to tie s. one's hands; **jem. volle ~ gewähren** to give s. o. plenty of rope; **volle ~ haben** to have full discretion.

Handlungs|gehilfe [merchant's (office)] clerk, *(Verkäufer)* shop assistant, *(Volontär)* volunteer; **als ~gehilfe arbeiten** to clerk; **~lehrling** clerk, commercial apprentice (trainee), learner; **~reisender** commercial travel(l)er, sales representative, travel(l)ing sales agent (salesman) *(US)*, merchant, agent, canvasser, commercial traveller *(Br.)*, bagman *(Br.)*, runner *(US)*, drummer *(US)*, knight of the road; **~spielraum** behavio(u)r (action) space.

handlungsunfähig incompetent to act, incapable of acting, immobilized;
~ sein not to be of responsible age, to have no capacity to act; **~ werden** to become paralysed.

Handlungsunfähigkeit incompetency to act;
~ der Regierung government paralysis.

Handlungsunkosten [general] overhead, overhead charges (cost, expenses), charges of merchandise *(Br.)*, commercial (undistributed) cost, burden, profit and loss expenses, oncost *(Br.)*;
auf die Abteilungen aufgeschlüsselte ~ departmental overhead (burden);
~konto overhead charges account; **auf ~konto buchen** to charge to expense.

Handlungsvollmacht power [of attorney], authority to act, proxy, *(Prokura)* procuration;
beschränkte ~ limited authority.

Handlungsweise course (line) of action, *(Methoden)* methods, practices, deal, *(Verfahren)* proceedings, procedure, dealing; **diskriminierende** ~ discriminatory action; **gesetzwidrige** ~ malpractice; **unverantwortliche** ~ reckless conduct;
jds. ~ **falsch auslegen** to put a wrong interpretation on s. one's actions; **jds.** ~ **nicht billigen können, jds.** ~ **mißbilligen** to disapprove of s. one's action (conduct); **jds.** ~ **zustimmen** to endorse s. one's action.

Hand|muster dummy; ~**presse** manual press; ~**pumpe** hand pump; **jem.** ~**reichungen leisten** to catch and ferry for s. o.; ~**satz** *(drucktechn.)* hand composition, casework; ~**schaltung** *(Auto)* manual shifting *(US)*; ~**schein** note of hand, promissory note; ~**schellen** manacles, handcuffs, darbies, nippers *(coll.)*; **jem.** ~**schellen anlegen** to clap handcuffs on s. o., to handcuff s. o.; ~**schenkung** absolute (manual) gift; ~**schlag** handshake; ~**schreiben** autograph (handwritten) letter.

Handschrift handwriting, [writing] hand, writing, [original] script;
ausgeschriebene ~ running (current) hand; **deutliche** ~ clear hand; **gespreizte** ~ sprawling handwriting; **gewöhnliche** ~ *(im Gegensatz zur Kurzschrift)* longhand; **kaufmännische** ~ commercial (business) hand; **gut lesbare** ~ readable handwriting; **schwer lesbare** ~ writing difficult to read; **miserable** ~ shocking handwriting; **passable** ~ fair handwriting; **schlechte** ~ paw *(coll.)*; **schöne** ~ good handwriting;
~ **entziffern** to make out a handwriting; **jds.** ~ **erkennen** to know s. one's character, to recognize s. one's writing; **schöne** ~ **haben** to write a good hand; **ungelenke** ~ **haben** to write in in a rude hand; **zierliche** ~ **haben** to write in a small hand; **jds.** ~ **kennen** to know s. one's character; **gute** ~ **schreiben** to write a good hand; **seine** ~ **verstellen** to disguise one's handwriting.

Handschriften|abteilung *(Bibliothek)* manuscript department; ~**deuter** graphologist; ~**deutung** handwriting analysis; ~**probe** specimen of one's handwriting; ~**untersuchung** handwriting analysis.

handschriftlich handwritten, in writing, manuscript;
sich ~ **verpflichten** to bind s. o. in writing;
~**e Bewerbung** handwritten application.

Handschuh, seine ~**e ausziehen** *(fig.)* to take the gloves off; **jem. den** ~ **hinwerfen** to fling down the gauntlet to s. o.;
~**fach** *(Auto)* glove compartment; **verschließbares** ~**fach** lockable glove compartment; ~**nummer** glove size.

Hand|setzer *(drucktechn.)* hand compositor; ~**siegel** manual seal; **königliches** ~**siegel** privy signet.

handsigniert hand-signed.

Hand|stempel green hand stamp *(US)*; ~**streich** *(mil.)* raid, surprise, attack, coup de main, *(v.)* surprise, attack, *(pol.)* stroke; **im** ~**streich nehmen** to take by surprise; ~**täschchen** vanity bag, purse *(US)*; ~**tasche** handbag, gripsack, purse *(US)*; ~**taschenraub** handbag snatching; ~**teller** palm; ~**tuch** towel, *(schmales Stück Land)* strip of land; **das** ~**tuch werfen** to throw in the towel, to throw in the sponge; **im** ~**umdrehen** in no time (a jiffy, a trice), in the turning of a hand, in less than no time, in the twinkling of an eye, before you could say Jack Robinson, in two shakes of a duck's tail, like smoke *(sl.)*; ~**verkauf** private (over-the-counter) sale, handsale.

handvermittelt *(Telefon)* manually operated.

Hand|vermittlung *(Telefon)* manual remote-control switchboard; ~**voll Münzen** handful of coins; ~**wagen** handcart, truck, gocart, *(Postbote)* mail cart *(Br.)*.

Handwerk [handi]craft, skilled crafts, small trade;
zu Hause ausgeübtes ~ homecraft; **dienstleistendes** ~ service trade; **erlernbares** ~ apprenticeable trade;
~ **ausüben** to pursue a trade; **sein** ~ **restlos beherrschen** to be a consummate master of one's craft; ~ **betreiben** to ply (follow, pursue) a trade; ~ **erlernen** to learn a craft; **j. ein** ~ **erlernen lassen** to put s. o. to a trade; **jem. das** ~ **legen** to put a spoke in s. one's wheel; **jem. ins** ~ **pfuschen** to meddle in s. one's affairs; **sein** ~ **verstehen** to know one's onions (oil, oats).

Handwerker craftsman, handicraftsman, artisan, artificer, tradesman, mechanic, operative, workman;
geschickter ~ artist;
~ **im Hause haben** to have the workmen in; ~ **sein** to exercise a handicraft;
bevorrechtigte ~**forderung** mechanic's lien; ~**innung** trade (craft) guild; ~**messe** mechanic's fair; ~**prüfung** trade test, journeyman's examination; ~**stand** craftsmanship; ~**tum** handicraftsmanship; ~**zunft** trade (craft) guild.

handwerklich|hervorragende Arbeit piece of excellent craftsmanship; ~**er Beruf** handicraft (skilled) trade; ~**er Berufsstand** handicraft pursuits, skilled trade; ~**er Betrieb** handicraft, craftman's establishment; ~**er Einmannbetrieb** one-man handicraft; ~**e Geschicklichkeit** ordinary skill in an art; ~**es Können** trade proficiency.

Handwerks|arbeit handicraft; ~**ausbildung** artisan training; ~**beruf** skilled trade, handicraft pursuits (trade); ~**betrieb** handicraft, handicraft business, craftsman's establishment; ~**brauch** trade rule; ~**bursche** journeyman; ~**geräte** tools (implements) of trade; ~**gilde**, ~**innung** trade (craft) guild, livery company *(Br.)*; ~**kasten** do-it-yourself kit; ~**kniff** mechanical dodge *(coll.)*; ~**lehrling** apprentice.

handwerksmäßig handicraft, mechanical.

Handwerks|meister craftmaster, master [craftsman], artificer; ~**ordnung** mechanic's institute; ~**prüfung** trade test; ~**register** trade register; ~**schule** school of arts and crafts, art school; ~**tasche** kit bag; ~**zeug** kit, set of tools, implements of trade, findings *(US)*.

Handwörterbuch concise dictionary.

Handzeichen sign manual, initials, mark, *(Abstimmungsverfahren)* show of hands, *(drucktechn.)* hand, index, fist;
Auto durch ~ **anhalten** to motion a car to stop; **sein** ~ **setzen** to make one's mark.

Handzettel handbill, throw-away leaflet, dodger *(US)*.

Hang inclination, propensity, tendency, lurch, ply, *(Abhang)* slope, declivity, proclivity;
krimineller ~ criminal disposition;
~ **zur Grausamkeit** cruel disposition;
zu starken ~ **zum Alkohol haben** to be too partial to the bottle; ~ **zur Faulheit haben** to have a lazy fit; **unverbesserlichen** ~ **zum Lügen haben** to have a great propensity for lying; ~ **zur Schwermut haben** to have a tendency to melancholy; **an einem** ~ **gebaut sein** to stand on a hillside.

Hänge|ablage suspended filing; ~**ablagesystem** flat-top suspended system; ~**antenne** trailing antenna; ~**bahn** aerial cableway, suspension railway; ~**brücke** suspension (chain) bridge; ~**decke** suspended ceiling; ~**kommission** *(Ausstellung)* hanging committee; ~**kran** travelling crab; ~**matte** hammock.

Hangen und Bangen anxious suspense.

Hängen suspension;
mit ~ **und Würgen durchkommen** just to scrape through one's examination.

hängen to hang, to be suspended, *(Schachpartie)* to be adjourned;
an etw. ~ to care for (be very attached to) s. th.; **an jem.** ~ to be very devoted to s. o.; **voller Äpfel** ~ to be laden with apples; **seinen Beruf an den Nagel** ~ to pack up one's job; **an seinem Besitz** ~ to cling to one's possessions; **an alten Bräuchen** ~ to be attached to old customs; **in Englisch** ~ *(Schüler)* to have trouble in English; **an einem seidenen Faden** ~ to hang by a hair (one's eyelids, a single thread); **sehr an seiner Familie** ~ to be very fond of his family; **an seinem Geld** ~ to be a slave to money; **etw. an die große Glocke** ~ to shout s. th. from the rooftops; **an jds. Hals** ~ to hang onto s. one's neck; **sein Herz an etw.** ~ to set one's heart on s. th.; **beim Kaufmann** ~ to be in the red with the grocer *(US coll.)*; **voller Kleider** ~ to be full of clothes; **sich wie eine Klette an j.** ~ to cling to s. o. like ivy; **an jds. Lippen** ~ to hang on s. one's lips; **in der Luft** ~ *(Person)* to be at a loose end; **noch völlig in der Luft** ~ to be still up in the air; **Mantel nach dem Wind** ~ to blow hot and cold, to temporize; **niedriger** ~ to soft-pedal; **schief** ~ *(Bild)* to be hanging crooked; **sich an die Strippe** ~ to get on the phone *(coll.)*; **stundenlang am Telefon** ~ to be stuck to the telephone; **über einer Wiese** ~ *(Hubschrauber)* to hover over a lawn; **ewig im Wirtshaus** ~ to be always in the pub.

Hangendschichten *(Bergbau)* upper beds.

Hänge|plakat hanger card; ~**registratur** suspended pocket filing; ~**schild** hanging sign.

Hang|schutzbepflanzung strip cropping; ~**täter** habitual offender.

Hansdampf in allen Gassen jack of all trades, Johnny on-the-spot *(US)*.

Hänselei teasing, ragging *(fam.)*.

hänseln to tease, to josh, to chip, to rag.

Hanswurst funny man, harlequin, buffoon, clown.

hantieren to be busy.

hapern, am Geld to be short of (stuck for, *fam.*) money; **an den Vokabeln** ~ to be weak in vocabulary.

Happen bite, bit, nibble, morsel;
fetter ~ good catch, golden opportunity;

nicht ein ~ Brot not a morsel of bread;
~ essen to pick a bit, to have a snack (quick meal); **sich einen fetten ~ entgehen lassen** to let an opportunity slip.
happig greedy;
ein bißchen ~ a bit steep;
~er Preis stiff price.
Happy-End happy end;
mit ~ upbeat.
Harakiri harakiri, happy dispatch.
Härchen, jem. kein ~ krümmen not to touch s. one's hair.
Harlekin Harlequin.
harmlos harmless;
Sache als ~ darstellen to whitewash an affair;
~er Irrer village innocent; **~e Lüge** white lie; **mit ~er Miene** with an air of innocence; **~e Vergnügungen** innocent pleasures.
Harmonie harmony, union.
harmonieren to go with, to harmonize, to cotton;
mit jem. ~ to sort well with s. one's character; **gut miteinander ~** to make fine music together; **nicht ~** *(Farben)* to clash; **mit dem Teppich ~** *(Vorhang)* to tone in with the carpet; **mit seiner Umgebung ~** to be in tune with one's surroundings.
Harmonika|akte bellows (accordion, concertina) file; **~falz** concertina fold; **~gang** *(Schnellzug)* vestibule; **~tür** accordion (concertina) door.
harmonisch harmonic, musical;
~ verlaufen to go off very well (with a swing);
~es Dasein führen to live in perfect harmony.
harmonisieren *(Steuern, Tarif)* to harmonize.
Harmonisierung *(Steuern)* harmonization;
~ der Mehrwertsteuer vat harmonization; **~ von Steuern** fiscal harmonization.
Harnisch armo(u)r;
j. in ~ bringen to get a rise out of s. o. (s. one's monkey up), to provoke (enrage) s. o.; **in ~ geraten** to get in a furious temper.
Harpune harpoon.
harpunieren to harpoon.
hart hard, difficult, rough, tough, firm, *(Krimi)* violent, *(mühevoll)* troublesome, laborious, *(streng)* severe, vigorous, oppressive;
~ am Feind at close quarters with the enemy; **~ an der Grenze des Anständigen** near the knuckle; **~ wie Stahl** as hard as adamant; **~ wie Stein** hard as a rock (brick);
~ aneinandergeraten to have a set-to *(coll.)*; **jem. ~ ankommen** to be tough on s. o.; **~ arbeiten** to work hard, to be hard on it; **~ bestrafen** to punish with severity; **~ auf ~ gehen** to be going to be a fight to the finish; **j. ~ mitnehmen** to take it out of s. o. *(coll.)*; **jem. ~ auf den Fersen sein** to tread on s. one's heels; **~ im Nehmen sein** to have enough muscle; **~ an der Grenze stehen** *(Haus)* to be close to the frontier; **~ an der Grenze des Krieges stehen** to be on the brink of war; **j. ~ treffen** to be a hard blow for s. o.; **jem. ~ zusetzen** to do hardship to s. o., to keep after s. o.;
~e Arbeit hard work; **~e Bedingungen** onerous terms; **~er Brocken** tough job; **~er Bursche** tough guy; **~es Geld** coin[ed] money, hard *(US)* (solid) cash, specie; **~es Klima** rigorous climate; **~e Ladung** heavy lading; **~e Landung machen** to land heavily; **~es Leben fern von aller Zivilisation führen** to lead a rough life away from civilization; **~e Nuß zu knacken haben** to have a hard nut to crack; **~en Schädel haben** to be stubborn; **~er Schlag für j. sein** to be tough on s. o.; **jem. einen ~en Schlag versetzen** to deal s. o. a heavy blow; **durch eine ~e Schule gegangen sein** to have gone through the mill; **~en Stand haben** to have no easy time of it; **~en Stand bei jem. haben** to have a great deal of trouble with s. o.; **~e Stimme** harsh voice; **~e Strafe** severe punishment; **~es Urteil** harsh judgment; **~er Verlust** heavy (severe) loss; **~e Währung** hard currency; **~ erarbeitetes Wissen** hard-acquired knowledge; **~e Worte** harsh (hard) words; **~e Zeiten durchmachen** to have a hard time of it.
Härte hardship, hardiness, granite, *(Strenge)* severity;
unbillige ~ undue hardship;
Gesetz mit aller ~ anwenden to put the law into operation in all its rigo(u)r; **zu unbilliger ~ führen** to lead to undue hardship; **~ lindern** to relieve hardship; **~n vermeiden** to avoid anomalies;
~ausgleich hardship allowance, *(Dienstentlassung)* severance pay (allowance) *(US)*, dismissal compensation, redundancy payment *(Br.)*; **jem. einen ~ausgleich gewähren** to indemnify s. o. for a hardship; **~fall** case of hardship, hardship (extreme) case; **~fälle mildern** to relieve hardship; **~fonds** relief (severance) fund, *(für Entlassungen)* redundancy payment fund *(Br.)*; **~grad** *(Metall)* temper; **~klausel** hardship clause; **~paragraph** *(Steuer)* small-income relief clause *(Br.)*; **~regelung** settlement of hardship cases; **~zulage** allowance for hardship conditions, hardship allowance; **besondere ~zulage bei Berufsunfähigkeit** special hardship allowance *(Br.)*.
Hartfaserplatte hardboard.
Hartgeld specie, coin, coined money, coinage, hard cash (money) *(US)*, solid cash, metallic currency (money);
nicht in ~ einlösbar nonspecie.
hartgesotten hard-boiled;
~er Verbrecher tough (hardened) criminal.
Hartgummi hard rubber, vulcanite.
hart|herzig hard-hearted; **~köpfig** stubborn.
Hartmetall hard metal.
hartnäckig insistent, unbending, tough, stubborn, *(Krankheit)* inveterate;
~ bleiben to square one's shoulders; **~ bei seiner Meinung bleiben** to stick to one's guns; **sein Recht ~ verfechten** to be tenacious of one's rights;
~e Forderung persistent demand; **~er Kampf** obstinate contest; **nach ~em Leugnen** after persistent denial; **~er Widerstand** obstinate resistance; **~en Widerstand leisten** to offer stubborn resistance.
Hartnäckigkeit eines Bittstellers urgency of a petitioner.
Hart|papier laminated (manila, *US*, kraft) paper; **~spiritus** solid alcohol.
Hartwährungs|konto hard-currency account; **~länder** hard- (strong-) currency countries.
Hasardeur gambler, adventurer.
Hasard|spiel hazard, gambling; **~spieler** gambler.
haschen, nach Komplimenten to fish for compliments.
Häscher myrmidon, tracker.
Hase hare;
alter ~ old hand (stager), old soldier, old-timer; **furchtsamer ~** coward;
wissen, wie der ~ läuft to know which way the wind lies (blows); **furchtsam wie ein ~ sein** to be as timid as a rabbit; **kein heuriger ~ sein** to be no greenhorn; **den alten ~n gegenüber jem. spielen** to come the old soldier over s. o. *(sl.)*;
da liegt der ~ im Pfeffer there's the rub, that's the nigger in the woodpile *(coll.)*.
Hasen|fuß funk, coward; **~panier ergreifen** to take to one's heels.
hasenrein, nicht ganz something fishy about it.
Hass|erwecken to excite hatred; **tödlichen ~ hegen** to have a mortal hatred.
hassen, wie die Pest to hate like the plague (poison).
häßlich|wie die Sünde as ugly as sin;
~e Geschichte nasty business.
Haßliebe empfinden to love to hate.
Hast hurry, haste, press, precipitance, precipitation;
in größter ~ in great (hot) haste, post-haste; **in wilder ~** in a tearing hurry;
blinde ~ panic haste;
~ des modernen Großstadtlebens whirl of modern life in a big city.
hasten to hurry, to haste, to rush.
hastig hasty, hurried;
mit einem ~en Blick zur Tür with a swift glance to the door; **~e Mahlzeit** hurried meal; **~er Rückzug** precipitate retreat; **~ geschriebene Zeilen** a few lines written in haste.
Haube *(Auto)* bonnet, *(Haartrockner)* drier, *(Krankenschwester)* cap;
unter die ~ bringen to marry off.
Hauch whiff, touch, tinge, trace, breath, suggestion;
~ von Abenteuer adventure touch; **~ von Ironie** touch of irony; **~ eines Lächelns** ghost of a smile; **~ von Parfüm** waft of perfume; **~ von Romantik** touch of romance; **~ von Schwermut um sich verbreiten** to spread an aura of melancholy.
hauchen, eine Antwort to whisper an answer.
Haudegen, alter old war horse.
hauen to strike, to hit, *(Bergbau)* to break down;
Bargeld auf den Tisch ~ to plank down the ready; **sich in die Falle ~** to go between the sheets; **mit der Faust auf den Tisch ~** to bang one's fist on the table; **alles Geld auf den Kopf ~** to blow (blue, *Br.*) one's money; **alles kurz und klein ~** to make a matchwood of s. th.; **Öffnung in die Wand ~** to cut an opening in the wall; **j. übers Ohr ~** to pull a fast one on s. o., to fleece s. o.; **j. in die Pfanne ~** to settle s. one's hash, to haul s. o. over the coals, to make mincemeat of s. o.; **über die Stränge ~** to get out of hand; **Stufen in die Felsen ~** to hew steps in the rock;
~, daß die Fetzen fliegen to make the feathers fly.
Häufchen|Leute handful of people;
wie ein ~ Elend aussehen to be a picture of misery.

Haufen heap, pile, peck, mass, assemblage, flock, cluster, pack, *(mil.)* troop, *(Pöbel)* mob, crew, crowd *(US sl.)*;
in dichten ~ in flocks;
bewaffneter ~ armed crowd; **großer** ~ herd; **verlorener** ~ forlorn hope;
~ **Arbeit** lots (loads, stacks) of work; ~ **Bücher** heaps (pile, crowd) of books; ~ **Dummheiten** pack of nonsense *(sl.)*; **zügelloser** ~ **eines ehemaligen Eliteregiments** disorderly rabble of a former crack regiment; ~ **Fehler** crop of mistakes; ~ **Geld** pots (lots, loads, pile, sight) of money, loot, big money, package *(sl.)*, packet *(Br., sl.)*; **ganzer** ~ **von Kindern** a whole host of children; ~ **Leute** crowds of people; ~ **von Lügen** pack of lies; ~ **Menschen** crowds (power) of people; ~ **Rechnungen** swarm of bills; ~ **von Schwierigkeiten** mountain of difficulties, deuce to pay; ~ **Sorgen** peck of trouble; ~ **Spielmarken** stack; ~ **Zeitungen** pile of newspapers; ~ **von Zeugen** crowd of witnesses;
~ **Fragen aufwerfen** to need a lot of asking; **jem. einen** ~ **von Schwierigkeiten bereiten** to put s. o. to a lot of trouble; **j. über den** ~ **fahren** to knock (run) s. o. down; ~ **Dummheiten von sich geben** to talk a lot of punk; ~ **Geld gewinnen** to win a parcel *(sl.)*, to make a packet *(Br., sl.)*; ~ **Geld haben** to have loads (lots) of money; ~ **Kinder haben** to have lots of children; ~ **Schulden haben** to have loads of debts; ~ **Geld kosten** to cost a great deal (a packet, *Br., sl.*) of money; **auf einen** ~ **schichten** to stack (pile) up; **j. über den** ~ **schießen** to shoot s. o. down; **bei seinem** ~ **sein** *(Br., sl.)* to be in the Forces; ~ **von Fragen stellen** to ask a lot of questions; ~ **Geld verdienen** to earn a packet, to make a pile of money; **sich in hellen** ~ **versammeln** to throng; **alles auf einen** ~ **werfen** to throw everything into a heap; **alle guten Manieren über den** ~ **werfen** to throw propriety to the winds; **alle Pläne über den** ~ **werfen** to upset the applecart.
häufen to heap [together], to pile;
sich ~ *(Rechnungen)* to pile up, to amass, *(Verbrechen)* to become frequent.
Haufendorf bunched village.
haufenweise in crowds (flocks, herds);
~ **hereinkommen** to pour in.
Haufenwolke woolpack cloud, cumulus.
häufig frequent, numerous;
~ **auftreten** to occur frequently; ~ **sein** to abound, to be frequent; ~**er werden** to increase, to become more frequent; ~**er Besucher** frequent visitor.
Häufigkeit frequency, incidence;
proportionale ~ *(Statistik)* proportional frequency; **relative** ~ relative frequency;
~ **des Erscheinens** *(Anzeigen)* frequency of publication; ~ **von Verbrechen** crime rate, frequency of crimes.
Häufigkeits|funktion frequency function; ~**kurve** frequency curve; ~**moment** frequency moment; ~**studie** frequency study; ~**stufen** quantiles; ~**tabelle** frequency table (chart); ~**theorie der Wahrscheinlichkeit** frequency theory of probability; ~**verhältnis** frequency rate; ~**verteilung** *(Statistik)* frequency (binomial) distribution; ~**wert** frequency value.
Haupt head;
bemoostes ~ veteran; **entblößten** ~**es** bareheaded;
~ **der Verschwörung** chief engineer of the plot;
sein ~ **erheben** to lift up one's head; **Gegner aufs** ~ **schlagen** to vanquish one's opponent; **Reform an** ~ **und Gliedern verlangen** to demand sweeping reforms;
~**abkommen** principal agreement; ~**abrechnung** annual (general) balance sheet; ~**absatzgebiet,** ~**absatzmarkt** main (major, chief) market, prime market area; ~**abschluß** annual statement *(US)*; ~**abschlußbilanz** annual balance sheet; ~**abschlußübersicht** work sheet *(US)*; ~**abschnitt** *(Gesetz)* title; ~**abteilung** central department; ~**ader** original vein; ~**agent** head agent; ~**agentur** general (head, principal) agency; ~**akte** basic fact file; ~**aktionär** leading (principal, main) shareholder *(Br.)* (stockholder, *US*); ~**akzent** *(ling.)* primary stress.
hauptamtlich full-time;
~ **arbeiten** to work on a full-time basis;
~**e Beschäftigung** full-time job.
Haupt|angeklagter principal defendant; ~**angelegenheit** primary business; ~**angriffsziel** principal target; ~**anklagepunkt** main charge; ~**anliegen** major concern, key objective; ~**anschluß** *(el.)* service box, *(Installation)* mains connection, *(Telefon)* direct [exchange] line; ~**anschluß stillegen** to disconnect the supply; ~**anspruch** *(Patent)* primary (main) claim; ~**anteil** major portion; ~**anwärter** prime candidate; ~**anziehungspunkt** focus of attention; ~**apparat** *(Telefon)* master telephone; ~**arbeit** chief labo(u)r; ~**argument** principal argument; ~**artikel** chief product, *(Firma)* major selling line, *(Waren)* staple articles (commodities, goods), staples, *(Zeitung)* leader, leading article; ~**attraktion** chief attraction, star turn *(Br.)*; ~**aufenthaltsort** headquarters; ~**aufgabe** basic job, key task; ~**aufseher** chief warden; **sein** ~**augenmerk darauf richten** to pay particular attention to it; ~**ausfuhr** bulk of export; ~**ausfuhrgüter** chief exports; ~**ausgabe** main edition; ~**ausgang** main exit; ~**aussage einer Rede** main features of a speech; ~**ausschuß** general (main) committee, *(Kommunalverwaltung)* management committee; ~**bahnhof** main (railroad, *US*) station, depot *(US)*, central [railway] station *(Br.)*; ~**balken** principal rafter; ~**bankplatz** banking center *(US)* (centre, *Br.*); ~**bausaison** peak construction season; ~**bedenken** key concern; ~**bedeutung** primary meaning; ~**bedeutung einer Ansprache** substance of a speech; ~**bedingungen** main (essential) conditions, prerequisites; ~**begründung einer Klage** declaration in chief, primary allegation; ~**begünstigter** principal beneficiary; ~**belastung** mainstream charge, *(el., Verkehr)* peak [load]; ~**belastungszeuge** star prosecution witness; ~**berichterstatter** general correspondent; ~**beruf** chief (principal) occupation, main profession, leading business.
hauptberuflich as a regular (permanent) occupation, professional, full-time;
~ **als Gewerkschaftsvertreter arbeiten** to work full-time as a trade-union official.
Haupt|beschaffungsstelle central equipment bureau; ~**beschäftigung** leading business, chief occupation, full-time job, major (principal) occupation; ~**bestandteil** chief ingredient, primary component, essential part, *(Anzeige)* body matter, *(Mahlzeit)* substantials; ~**bestandteil von etw. bilden** to be part and parcel of s. th.; ~**betrag** total amount; ~**betreiber** prime mover; ~**betrieb** headquarters, principal place of business; ~**betriebszeit** main (peak) season, rush hours; ~**bett** *(Fluß)* natural channel; ~**beweggrund** leading motive; ~**beweisgrund** principal argument; ~**bilanz** general balance sheet; ~**blickfang** *(Anzeige)* primary appeal, eye appeal (catcher); ~**börse** high change.
Hauptbuch ledger [book], shopbook *(US)*, book of final entry, public ledger;
in Tabellenform geführtes ~ ledger journal;
~ **der Aktionäre** shareholders' *(Br.)* (stockholders', *US*) ledger, stock book *(US)*; ~ **einer Filiale** branch ledger; ~ **mit sämtlichen Hauptbuchkonten** general ledger (journal); ~ **in Loseblattbuchführung** loose-leaf ledger;
~ **abschließen** to balance the ledger; **in das** ~ **eintragen** to enter into the ledger, to post an item in the ledger; **das** ~ **führen** to keep the ledger; ~ **vollständig nachtragen** to post up the ledger; ~ **saldieren** to balance the ledger;
~**auszug** ledger abstract (report); ~**eintragungen** ledger postings; ~**folio** ledger folio; ~**führer** ledger clerk (keeper); ~**führung** ledger work; ~**halter** senior clerk (cashier), head bookkeeper, accountant general *(Br.)*, chief accountant *(Br.)*; ~**haltung** general bookkeeping department; ~**konto** general (ledger) account, primary account; ~**kontrolle** ledger control; ~**posten** ledger item; ~**sammelkonto** control account.
Haupt|bürge principal surety; ~**büro** chief (head, home, main, *US*) office, headquarters; ~**büro eröffnen** to headquarter *(US)*; ~**darsteller** *(Theater)* leading man, principal [actor], headliner; **als** ~**darsteller auftreten** to star; ~**darstellerin** leading lady; ~**daten noch einmal durchnehmen** to go over the main facts again; ~**depot** *(mil.)* base depot; ~**diskussionsredner** principal in a debate; ~**durchgangsstraße** main thoroughfare; ~**effekt** *(Statistik)* main effect; ~**eigenschaft** primary quality; ~**eigentümer** general owner; ~**einfahrt** main entrance, driveway *(US)*; ~**einfuhr** bulk of import[s]; ~**einfuhrwaren** principal imports; ~**eingang** main (grand) entrance, front door, *(Zirkus)* marquee; ~**eingangstor** main gate; ~**einkäufer** head buyer of a firm, chief purchaser; ~**einkommen,** ~**einkünfte** principal income, basic compensation; ~**einnahmequelle** major part of revenue, major means of income, staple earner; ~**einwand gegen j.** chief objection to s. o.; ~**eisenbahnlinie** main (trunk, *US*) line; ~**entschädigung** basic compensation; ~**erbe** sole heir, *(Grundbesitz)* residuary devisee; ~**erfindung** basic invention; ~**erfordernisse** principal (prime) requisites; ~**ernährer** breadwinner; ~**erwerbszweig** main profession; ~**erzader** discovery vein; ~**erzeugnisse** staple products, staple merchandise, staples; ~**fach** *(Schule)* main (special) subject, major *(US)*; ~**fach studieren** to major in a subject *(US)*; ~**fahrrinne** trunk; ~**faktoren** primary factors; ~**feind** enemy number one; ~**feldwebel** sergeant major, sergeant 1st class *(US)*, top sergeant *(US coll.)*; ~**fernsehzeit** prime time; ~**feststellung** main assessment; ~**feststellungszeitraum** main assessment

period; ~**figur** protagonist; ~**figuren eines Romans** central figures in a novel; ~**filiale** main branch; ~**film** [star] feature, feature picture, full-length film; ~**flöz** mother lode; ~**flügel** main wing; ~**fluglinie** main line; **inländische** ~**fluglinie** domestic trunk route; ~**folio** ledger folio; ~**förderstrecke** entry, mother gate; ~**forderung** key demand, *(Schuld)* principal [claim]; ~**frachtvertrag** head charter; ~**frage** main issue, cardinal question, sixty-four thousand dollar question; ~**gasleitung** gas main; ~**gebäude** main building, body; ~**gedanke** *(Anzeige)* key note; ~**gedingenehmer** *(Bergbau)* contractor; ~**gegenstand** main subject, staple; ~**gericht** main dish, piece de resistance, entrée *(US)*; ~**geschäft** head office, parent store, headquarters, *(Schwerpunkt)* bulk of one's business, bread-and-butter business.

Hauptgeschäfts|führer general (head) manager, principal; ~**gegend** central shopping (business) district; ~**sitz** principle (capital, main) place of business; ~**stelle** head (main, principal) office, headquarters, *(Gericht)* Central Office; ~**straße** high street; ~**stunden** peak hours, busy period; **sich im** ~**viertel niederlassen** to fix one's residence in the city; ~**weg** main channel; ~**zeit** rush (peak) hours, peak sales period.

Haupt|geschmacksrichtung staple flavo(u)r; ~**gesellschafter** chief partner; ~**gesellschaftsraum** *(Hotel)* main lounge; ~**gesprächsstoff** leading topics of the hour; ~**gesprächsthema abgeben** to form the staple of a conversation; ~**gewerbezweck** *(Unternehmen)* main object; ~**gewicht in seiner Rede auf ... legen** to emphasize ... in one's speech; ~**gewinn** capital (first, grand, great, highest) prize, *(Einkommensteuer)* bulk of profit, major part of the revenue, *(Tombola)* jack pot, *(Lotterie)* capital (first, grand) prize; ~**gläubiger** principal (chief) creditor; ~**gleis** main track; ~**grund** main (prime) reason; ~**grundsatz** leading principle; ~**gruppe** chief group; ~**hahn** master valve; ~**hahn abstellen (abdrehen)** to cut off the water at the main; ~**handelsartikel** staple goods, staples; ~**handelsplatz** staple town; ~**handelsware** staple [goods]; ~**herausgeber** editor-in-chief; ~**industriezweige** staple industries; ~**inhaber** principal owner.

Hauptinhalt substance, essence;
~ **einer Klage** gist of an action; ~ **einer Rede** tenor (substance) of a speech; ~ **eines Vertrages** essence of a contract.

Haupt|interessensgebiet field of major professional interest; ~**intervenient** *(jur.)* intervening party; ~**intervention** *(jur.)* claim of cognizance or conusance, interpleader; ~**kabel** main cable; ~**kampflinie** *(mil.)* line of defence, main line of resistance; ~**kanal** public (trunk) sewer, mother ditch *(US)*; ~**kartei** master file; ~**kasse** chief cashier, teller's department; ~**kassierer** chief (head) cashier, cashier in charge of operations, paying teller *(US)*; ~**katalog** main catalog(ue); ~**knotenpunkt** main junction; ~**konkurrent** chief rival; ~**konto** ledger account; ~**kontor** headquarters; ~**kontrollkonto** master control account; ~**kostenstelle** cost center *(US)* (centre, *Br.*); ~**kredit** primary credit; ~**kunde** main (primary) customer; ~**lager** *(mil.)* base camp; ~**lagerstätte** major deposit; ~**lebenszweck** chief purpose in life; ~**leidenschaft** master passion; ~**leidtragender** principal sufferer; ~**leistung** main accomplishment, primary obligation; ~**leiter** *(el.)* prime conductor; ~**leitung** headquarters, general management, *(el.)* mains, primary *(US)*, *(Telefon)* main (trunk) line; ~**lieferant** major supplier, original (prime, general, main) contractor; ~**linie** main line (track), central line of railway *(Br.)*, principal railroad *(US)*, main (trunk) line *(US)*, trunk route *(US)*, *(Flugverkehr)* trunk airline *(US)*; ~**linien** outlines; ~**mahlzeit** chief meal; ~**mangel** principal defect; ~**markt** principal (main) market; ~**masse** bulk; ~**masse seines Vermögens** bulk of one's property, general estate; ~**material** chief material; ~**melodie** theme song; ~**merkmal** main (key) features; ~**miete** chief rent; ~**mieter** master tenant (lessee), head lessee; ~**mietvertrag** proprietary (master) lease; ~**mitarbeiter** chief assistant; ~**motiv** *(Werbung)* keynote idea; ~**nachfrage** chief demand; ~**nachricht** *(Rundfunk)* lead story; ~**nahrungsmittel** staple (principal) food; ~**niederlage** staple *(US)*; ~**niederlassung** main office *(US)*, main establishment, principal establishment (place of business), main seat of activity, major subsidiary, registered office *(Br.)*, *(Bank)* head office, headquarters; ~**nummer** chief attraction, star turn *(Br.)*; ~**nutznießer** primary beneficiary; ~**organ** *(UNO)* principal organ; ~**pacht** chief rent; ~**pachtvertrag** proprietary (head) lease; ~**patent** original (basic, pioneer, main) patent; ~**person** key man, feature, principal, headliner *(US)*, kingpin *(coll.)*; ~**pfeiler** centerpiece; ~**pflicht** principal covenant; ~**plan** *(Etat)* master budget; ~**planet** primary planet; ~**platz** *(Bankwesen)* banking center *(US)* (centre, *Br.*); ~**police** original policy; ~**postamt** head (main, general, *Br.*) post office; ~**probe** *(Theater)* dress rehearsal; ~**problem** main (top) issue, biggest headache; ~**produkte** staple articles (commodities, goods), staples; ~**produktion** principal product line; ~**prozeß** main case; ~**prozeß nach Pfändung** forthcoming *(Scot. law)*; ~**prozeßbevollmächtigter** senior counsel; ~**prüfer** senior accountant, *(Patentamt)* examiner in chief.

Hauptpunkt chief point;
~**e** *(Klage)* merits, gist;
~**e einer Kontroverse** burden of argument; ~**e einer Rede** heads of a speech; ~**e einer Vereinbarung** heads of an agreement.

Haupt|quartier headquarters; ~**quelle** key resource, main source; ~**quittung** general receipt; ~**rechenschaftsbericht** audit; ~**rechnung** general account (bill); ~**redner** principal speaker; ~**reeder** principal owner; ~**register** general table of contents, *(Warenzeichen)* principal register; ~**reisezeit** tourist season; ~**repräsentant einer Firma** leading agent of a firm; ~**revisor** senior accountant; ~**richtung** mainstream; ~**rohr** street main; ~**rolle** central role, *(Theater)* lead, leading (principal) part; ~**rolle spielen** to be the principal performer, to have a major (leading) role, *(fig.)* to play the first fiddle; **in der** ~**rolle zeigen** *(Film)* to feature; ~**rücklage** primary reserve.

Hauptsache main point, main thing, primary, essential, brass tacks, merits, principal, principal matter, high spot *(US)*, substance, *(jur.)* main issue;
in der ~ on the whole, *(jur.)* on the merits;
~ **im Leben** main line *(sl.)*; ~ **nebst Zinsen** principal and interest;
sich auf die Klage zur ~ **einlassen** to join issue; **in der** ~ **entscheiden** to give judgment on the (deal with a case on its) merits; **zur** ~ **kommen** to get down to brass tacks, to come to the main point; **in der** ~ **für den Export produzieren** to produce mainly for export; **zur** ~ **verhandeln** to plead to the merits.

hauptsächlich primary, principal, main, master, cardinal.

Haupt|saison busy (peak, main) season; ~**satz** *(gr.)* principal clause, simple sentence; ~**satzung** general statute, *(Kommunalverwaltung)* [etwa] standing orders; ~**schalter** *(Bahn, Post)* main booking office, *(el.)* master switch; ~**schema** staple; ~**schlager** theme song; ~**schlüssel** master key, passkey; ~**schöffe** foreman of the jury; ~**schriftleiter** chief (general, managing) editor, editor-in-chief; ~**schriftleitung** editorial board; ~**schuld** principal debt; ~**schuldiger** chief culprit, major offender.

Hauptschuldner principal [debtor], primary party;
~ **ausklagen** to discuss a principal debtor; ~ **freistellen** to release the principal debtor; **für den** ~ **haften** to be liable for the debt of the principal.

Haupt|schwierigkeiten main difficulties; ~**seite** *(Zeitung)* front (feature) page; ~**sender** main transmitter, key (basic) station *(US)*, basic network, main transmitter; ~**sendezeit** prime time; ~**sendezeit einer Fernsehgruppe** network prime time; ~**sicherung** *(el.)* main fuse; ~**sitz** headquarters, principal establishment (place of business); ~**sitz einer Behörde** headquarters of an agency; **seinen** ~**sitz haben** to headquarter; ~**sorge** primary concern, main worry; ~**spalte** main column; ~**spediteur** destination (issuing, transportation) carrier; ~**speicher** *(Datenverarbeitung)* general storage; ~**spielfilm** feature film; ~**stadt** capital, principal town.

hauptstädtisch capital, metropolitan.

Haupt|standesamt General Register Office *(Br.)*; ~**standesbeamter** Superintendent Registrar *(Br.)*; ~**stelle** main branch (office); ~**steuereinnehmer** receiver general of the public revenue *(Br.)*; ~**steuertermin** main tax-filing date; ~**stollen** *(Bergwerk)* headway; ~**straße** principal street, main street (road, *US*), artery, high street *(Br.)*, broadway *(US)*, highway, *(Ausstellung)* midway *(US)*; **in die** ~**straße einmünden** to open into the main road; ~**strecke** artery, arterial highway, main route (road), *(Eisenbahn)* arterial (trunk) railway *(Br.)*, main (trunk, *US*) line; ~**streitpunkt** main issue; ~**strom** body of a river; ~**stromkabel** main cable; ~**stromleitung** mains; **mit den** ~**strömungen der Partei nicht mehr ganz übereinstimmen** to be out of step with the mainstream of the party; ~**stütze** main support, mainstay, right arm, keystone, pillar; ~**stütze seiner Familie** chief support of one's family; ~**stütze einer Partei** pillar of a party; ~**summe** *(Kapital)* principal; ~**täter** principal, offender, chief (major) offender, chief culprit; ~**tätigkeit** principal activity, key performance; ~**tätigkeitsgebiet** key performance area; ~**tatsache** leading fact.

Hauptteil principal part, trunk, body, bulk, gross, *(Anzeige)* running body (text);

~ **eines Gesetzes** body of a law; ~ **einer Rede** body of a speech; ~ **einer Schuld** bulk of a debt; ~ **einer Urkunde** body of an instrument;
~ **einer Arbeit hinter sich bringen** to break the neck of a task; ~ **seines Einkommens im Provisionswege verdienen** to get the bulk of one's income by way of commission.
Haupt|telegrafenlinie main (trunk, *US*) line; ~**tendenz** mainstream; ~**text** *(Anzeige)* body [copy].
Hauptthema main topic;
~ **einer Rede** keynote of a speech;
vom ~ **abkommen** to digress from the main subject; **auf das** ~ **kommen** to get to the point.
Haupt|titel full title; ~**träger** principal member, mainstay; ~**träger der städtischen Finanzen** mainstay of the city's finances; ~**träger einer Politik** keystone of a policy; ~**treffer** first prize; ~**treppe** grand staircase; ~**tribüne** grandstand; ~**triebfeder eines Unternehmens sein** to be the prime mover of an enterprise; ~**umschlagplatz** staple place, *(landwirtschaftliche Erzeugnisse)* primary point *(US)*; ~**unkosten** key costs; ~**untergebener** major subordinate; ~**unterhändler** chief negotiator; ~**unternehmer** main contractor; ~**unterstützungsempfänger** recipient of unemployment relief, dole drawer *(Br.)*; ~**veranlagung** *(Einkommensteuer)* basic assessment; ~**verantwortung** *(Kartellrecht)* primary responsibility *(US)*; ~**verbandsplatz** main dressing (clearing, *US*) station; ~**verbindlichkeit** principal (primary) obligation; ~**verbindung** key link; ~**verbindungsstraße** main communication road; ~**verbraucher** principal consumer; ~**verbrauchsgebiet** principal area of consumption; ~**verdächtiger** prime suspect; ~**verdienst** principal income; ~**verfahren** criminal procedure, trial; ~**verfahren eröffnen** to arraign.
Hauptverhandlung trial of an action, hearing;
ergebnislose ~ abortive trial; **gemeinsame** ~ joint trial; **sofortige** ~ trial instanter;
Angeklagten (Zeugen) zur ~ **laden** to summon a defendant (witness) to stand.
Hauptverhandlungs|gegenstand principal subject matter; ~**punkte** heads of negotiations; ~**termin** final trial.
Hauptverkaufs|raum main floor; ~**tag** major selling day; ~**zeit** peak season, rush (peak) hours.
Hauptverkehr arterial traffic, rush hours, peak of traffic.
Hauptverkehrs|ader artery; ~**linie** heavy traffic (trunk, *US*) line, main stem *(US)*; ~**straße** thoroughfare, major highway, high (main) road, trunk route *(Br.)*, trunk line *(US)*, classified road *(Br.)*, arterial highway *(US)*, main drag *(sl.)*; ~**straßen** arteries of traffic; ~**strom** main current of traffic; ~**weg** key road, main artery; ~**zeit** rush (busy, crowded) hours, peak hours of traffic, peak time, rush-hour peak; ~**zeit umgehen** to beat the rush hours.
Haupt|vermieter master lessor; ~**verpflichtung** principal covenant, primary obligation.
Hauptversammlung general (company, *Br.*, stockholders', *US*) meeting, annual general meeting *(Br.)*, regular (corporate) meeting *(US)*, meeting of shareholders *(Br.)* (stockholders, *US*);
außerordentliche ~ extraordinary general meeting *(Br.)*; **von den Aktionären beantragte** ~ requisitioned meeting; **besonders einberufene** ~ called meeting; **ordentliche** ~ stated (ordinary, *Br.*, general, regular, *US*) meeting;
alle Formalitäten bei einer ~ **beachten** to hold a meeting on a formal basis; **über eine** ~ **berichten** to cover a meeting of shareholders *(Br.)* (stockholders, *US*); ~ **einberufen** to call a meeting of shareholders *(Br.)* (stockholders, *US*), to summon shareholders *(Br.)* (stockholders, *US*), to summon a general meeting *(Br.)*; **Satzungserfordernisse für eine** ~ **erfüllen** to constitute a valid meeting; ~ **eröffnen** to call a general meeting to order *(US)*; ~ **vertagen** to adjourn a meeting.
Hauptversammlungs|bericht statutory report; ~**berichte** *(Zeitung)* company comments *(Br.)*; ~**beschluß** resolution at general meeting, company resolution, corporate resolution *(US)*; ~**erfahrungen** meetings practice; ~**richtlinien** regulations governing meetings; ~**spalte** *(Zeitung)* company meeting's column *(Br.)*; ~**termin** annual meeting day; ~**verlauf** proceedings at a general meeting.
Haupt|versicherer direct-writing company (carrier); ~**versicherter** *(Rückversicherung)* original insured; ~**versorgungsbasis** key supply; ~**verteidiger** leader for the defense (defence, *Br.*); ~**vertrag** primary (principal, original) contract; ~**vertreter** general (head, principal) agent; ~**verwaltung** central administration (management), head office management, *(Sitz)* headquarters, main office *(US)*; ~**verwaltungsbeamter** [etwa] chief executive officer; ~**verwaltungsorgan** central governing body; ~**vollmacht** primary powers; ~**vorbringen** material allegation; ~- **und Hilfsvorbringen** disjunctive allegation; ~**vorkommnisse in jds. Leben** principal events in s. one's life; ~**vorstand** executive board; ~**wache** police headquarters; ~**wachtmeister** master (police) sergeant; ~**währung** metropolitan currency; ~**wasserrohr** water main; ~**wasserstraße** artery; ~**werk** *(Autor)* standard work; ~**wirtschaftsdaten für die Konjunkturbeurteilung** key business indicators; ~**wirtschaftsgebiete** primary fields of business; ~**wohnsitz** main residence; ~**wohnung** principal dwelling; ~**wort** noun, substantive; ~**zeuge** material (principal, key) witness; ~**ziel** prime target, major (key) objective, principal object; ~**zielscheibe** principal target; ~**zollamt** Excise Office *(Br.)*, Bureau of the Customs *(US)*; ~**züge** outlines; ~**zweck** primary aim (purpose); ~**zweig** main branch.
Haus house, building, premises, dwelling, home, hearth, *(Firma)* firm, *(parl.)* chamber, House *(Br.)*, *(Mieter)* tenement, *(Wohnsitz)* residence, abode, domicile;
ans ~ **gefesselt** housebound; **auf Ersuchen des** ~**es** at the desire of the manager; **aus gutem** ~ of a good family, patrician; **außer** ~ outdoors; **bei mir zu** ~**e** at my [private] house, in my home; **frei** ~ free of charge, no charges for delivery, carriage free (paid); **hinter dem** ~ at the rear of the house; **im** ~**e** within the house, indoors, indoor, on the premises; **im Fall des Unbewohntseins eines** ~**es** in case of vacancy of a property; **im nächsten** ~ next door; **nach** ~**e zu** homewards; **nicht zu** ~ out; **von** ~ **zu** ~ from door to door, warehouse to warehouse; **vor versammeltem** ~ before a full house; **zu** ~**e** at home, homelike; **zu** ~**e ein Tyrann und draußen ein Feigling** a lion at home, a mouse abroad;
achtbares ~ respectable firm; **alleinstehendes** ~ detached house; **sehr altes** ~ ancient house; **verfallenes altes** ~ dilapidated old house; **zum Verkauf angebotenes** ~ house advertised for sale; **fertig angeliefertes** ~ prefabricated house; **angesehenes** ~ respectable firm; **angrenzendes** ~ contiguous house; **verwahrlost aussehendes** ~ poor-looking house; **ausverkauftes** ~ *(Theater)* capacity (full) house; **im Bau befindliches** ~ house under construction (in course of erection); **beschlußfähiges** ~ *(Parlament)* quorum; **beschlußunfähiges** ~ no house; **schlecht besetztes** ~ *(Theater)* small house; **billig zu bewirtschaftendes** ~ house inexpensive to run; **bewohntes** ~ occupied house; **vom Eigentümer bewohntes** ~ owner-occupied property; **bezugsfertiges** ~ vacant possession; **sofort bezugsfertiges** ~ *(Anzeige)* house for sale with immediate possession; **dreistöckiges (vierstöckiges,** *US*) three-story house; **einzelstehendes** ~ detached house (residence); **erdbebensicheres** ~ quakeproof house; **fideles** ~ jolly dog; **mit Mitteln des sozialen Wohnungsbaus finanziertes** ~ social house *(Br.)*, council dwelling *(Br.)*; **freistehendes** ~ detached house (residence); **führendes** ~ leading firm; **massiv gebautes** ~ solid building; **gegenüberliegendes** ~ house opposite; **am Stadtrand gelegenes** ~ ribbon building; **gelehrtes** ~ pundit; **gemietetes** ~ tenement; **geräumiges** ~ ample house; **im Montagebau hergestelltes** ~ prefabricated house; **leerstehendes** ~ vacant house; **mehrstöckiges** ~ multistorey building; **mietfreies** ~ rent-free house; **möbliertes** ~ furnished house; **modernes** ~ modern (up-to-date) house; **öffentliches** ~ house of ill repute, brothel; **transportables** ~ mobile house; **übelbeleumdetes** ~ sporting house; **überbelegtes** ~ overcrowded house; **der Mieterschutzgesetzgebung unterliegendes** ~ controlled house *(Br.)*; **volles** ~ good house; **zum Bersten volles** ~ *(Theater)* packed house; **zahlungsfähiges** ~ solvent merchant;
~ **für gehobene Ansprüche** executive-level house; ~ **mit angebauter Garage** house with a garage attached; ~ **in vernünftigen Größenabmessungen** decent-sized house; ~ **und Hof** house and home, toft and croft; ~ **auf dem Lande** country house; ~ **und Nebengebäude** premises; ~ **mit zweierlei Niveau** split-level house; **erstes** ~ **am Platz** leading fashion house; ~ **mit drei Schlafzimmern** three-bedroom model; **letztes** ~ **einer Straße** end house of a street;
~ **abdecken** to dismantle a roof; ~ **abreißen** to dismantle (knock down) a house; **jem. ein** ~ **zum Preis von 45.000 Dollar anbieten** to offer s. o. a house for $ 45.000; **sein** ~ **als Sicherheit anbieten** to offer one's house as a guarantee; ~ **an die Gasversorgung anschließen** to lay on gas to a house; ~ **an das Kabelfernsehnetz anschließen** to serve a home with cable television service; **j. zu** ~ **antreffen** to find s. o. at home; **Mieterschutzbestimmungen für ein** ~ **aufheben** to free a house from the provisions of the Rent Restriction Act *(Br.)*; **j. in sein** ~ **aufnehmen** to give s. o. houseroom; **in einem** ~ **aus- und eingehen** to have the run of a

house; **aus einem ~ ausziehen** to move out of (vacate) a house; **~ bauen** to build a house; **j. nach ~e begleiten** to see s. o. home, to guide s. o. to his house; **j. zu ~e behalten** to keep s. o. at home; **~ besichtigen** to go over a house; **kleines ~ auf dem Lande besitzen** to have a small property in the country; **sein ~ bestellen** to arrange one's business affairs, to set one's house in order; **jds. ~ nicht mehr betreten** not to darken s. one's door; **~ bewohnen** to occupy a house; **auf ein ~ bieten** to bid for a house; **zu ~e bleiben** to stay at home, to keep in, to keep within doors, to keep (stay) indoors; **in ein ~ einbrechen** to break into a house, to crack a crib; **in ein ~ einlassen** to admit into a house; **jem. das ~ einrennen** to live on s. one's doorstep; **sich in einem ~ einrichten** to establish o. s. in a house; **jem. ein ~ einrichten** to furnish a house for s. o.; **in ein ~ einziehen** to move into a house; **ganz auf Zweckmäßigkeit abgestelltes ~ entwerfen** to plan a house for convenience; **~ erben** to inherit a house; **~ lastenfrei erwerben** to buy a house free from all debt; **außer ~ essen** to dine out; **mit der Tür ins ~ fallen** to come straight to the point; **~ feuerversichern** to insure one's house against fire; **keinen Mieter für sein ~ finden** not to get a tenant for one's house; **von zu ~e fortgehen** to leave home; **gastfreies ~ führen** to keep open doors, to keep open house, to entertain; **großes ~ führen** to keep an establishment, to entertain a great deal, to live in great style; **von ~ zu ~ gehen** to go from door to door; **eigenes ~ haben** to have a house of one's own; **stets ein volles ~ haben** *(Theater)* to play to capacity audience; **~ ganzjährig voll vermietet haben** to have a property 100 per cent rented at all times; **Einfälle wie ein altes ~ haben** to have crazy ideas; **sehr an zu ~e hängen** to be deeply attached to one's family; **j. aus dem ~ herauswerfen** to bootleg (pitch) s. o. out of the house; **nicht in ein ~ hineinkönnen** to have got the key of the street; **~ auf Abbruch kaufen** to buy a house for its material; **aus gutem ~e kommen** to be a man of good family; **auf den Tisch des ~es legen** to pay on the dot; **~ mieten** to rent a house; **sofort bezugsfähiges ~ mieten** to rent a house with immediate possession; **~ auf ein Jahr mieten** to take a house (home) for a year; **~ mit Vorkaufsrecht mieten** to rent a building with the option of purchase; **~ hüten müssen** to be confined to the house; **~ hypothekisieren müssen** to plaster a house *(sl.)*; **~ plündern** to ravage a house; **~ räumen** to vacate (empty) a house; **zu ~e sein** to be at home; **nie zu ~e sein** to live in the street; **fideles ~ sein** to be as merry as a cricket (lark); **für j. nicht zu ~ sein** not to be at home to s. o.; **nirgendwo zu ~e sein** to have neither house nor home; **von ~e aus reich sein** to be born rich, to be born with a silver spoon in one's mouth; **auf einem Gebiet völlig zu ~e sein** to feel perfectly at home on a subject (up one'bs alley, *sl.*), to know one's trade; **wieder zu ~e sein** to be back home; **vor einem leeren ~ spielen** to play to empty benches; **von ~ aus wenig sprechen** to never talk much; **aus gutem ~e stammen** to be of a good line; **aus königlichem ~e stammen** to be of royal descent; **das ganze ~ auf den Kopf stellen** to turn the whole house upside down; **~ zur Verfügung stellen** to allot a house to live in; **~ für Etagenwohnungen umbauen** to make a house over into several apartments; **~ in Wohnungen umbauen** to turn a house into flats; **~ unterspülen** to mine the foundation of a house; **~ gegen jds. Willen verkaufen** to sell a house over s. one's head; **~ in Einzelwohnungen vermieten** to let off (rent) a house into flats; **j. aus seinem ~ weisen** to order s. o. out of one's house; **außerhalb des ~es eingenommen werden** to be eaten out; **~ wiederaufbauen** to rebuild a house; **~ an ~ mit jem. wohnen** to live next door with s. o.; **nach ~e zurückkehren** to home; **~ zuschließen** to shut up a house;
~abzahlungssystem contract system *(US)*; **~agentur** house agency, *(Versicherungsgeschäft)* own case agent (agency); **~anbau** extension to a house; **~andacht** private devotion.

Hausangestellte [domestic] servant, menial [servant], maidservant *(US)*, servant (hired) girl, domestic [worker], lady help *(US)*;
als ~ beschäftigt out;
langjährige ~ servant of old standing; **im Haus wohnende ~** resident housekeeper;
einer ~n ein Zeugnis ausstellen to give a servant a good character; **~ einstellen (engagieren)** to take s. o. into one's service, to hire a servant; **~ wieder einstellen** to engage a servant again; **~ entlassen** to turn out a servant; **~n wegen Unredlichkeit entlassen** to discharge a servant for being dishonest; **Stelle als ~ haben** to be in a place; **~ kündigen** to serve notice upon a servant, to give a servant the sack *(sl.)*; **sich eine ~ leisten** to keep a servant; **zugleich ~r und Gärtner sein** to perform the functions of servant and gardener combined; **~ werden** to go into service.

Haus|angestelltenvermittlung domestic agency; **~ankauf** home purchase; **über einen ~ankauf verhandeln** to negotiate for the purchase of a house; **~anlage** *(Telefon)* interoffice telephone; **~anschluß** *(Gas)* gas main, *(Telefon)* telephone connection (connexion, *Br.*); **~anschlußkasten** *(el.)* house connection box; **~anzug** house dress; **~apotheke** medicine chest; **~arbeit** housework, house (indoor) work, chore *(US)*, *(Schule)* homework, prep *(coll.)*, assignment *(US)*; **~arbeit verrichten** to do family work, to chore *(US)*; **~arbeiten** housekeeping chores; **~arrest** house arrest; **~arrest haben** *(Kind)* to have to stay indoors; **~arzt** general practitioner, family doctor, family physician, *(Hotel)* house physician, *(Kurhaus)* resident doctor; **~aufgaben** homework, prep *(coll.)*, assignment *(US)*; **~aufgaben machen** to do one's prep[arations]; **~aufseher** *(Internat)* house master *(Br.)*.

hausbacken homely.

Haus|bank borrower's bank, company's bank; **~bar** liquor (cocktail) cabinet; **~bau** house construction, housebuilding; **billiger ~bau** low-cost home construction; **~bau mit Nachbarschaftshilfe** house raising *(US)*; **~bedarf** household requirements, truck; **nur für den ~bedarf** for home use only; **~beschlagnahme** requisition of a house; **~besetzer** squatter *(Br.)*; **unberechtigte ~besetzung durchführen** to squat *(Br.)*; **~besichtigung** tour of the house; **~besitz** house-ownership, house property; **~- und Grundbesitz** home ownership.

Hausbesitzer householder, house-owner, owner of a house, property owner, *(Eigenheim)* home owner *(US)*, *(pl.)* occupants of a house, *(Vermieter)* landlord;
unabhängiger ~ freeholder;
~ sein to be in occupation of a house; **~ werden** to invest in home property;
~verband, ~vereinigung property owners' association.

Haus|besuch *(Arzt)* house (doctor's) call, home visitation; **~bewertung** valuation on a house; **~bewohner** inhabitant of a house, occupant, householder *(Mieter)* tenant, lodger; **ständiger ~bewohner** housekeeper, occupier; **~bibel mit Familieneintragungen** family bible; **~bibliothek** private library; **~boot** houseboat, house barge *(Br.)*; **auf einem ~boot wohnen** to houseboat; **~brand** domestic fuel, house coal; **~bursche** *(Hotel)* boots *(sl.)*.

Häuschen small house, cottage;
ganz aus dem ~ in a great taking, worked up, off one's onion; **leicht aus dem ~** easily upset;
j. aus dem ~ bringen to get s. one's shirt out *(sl.)*, to blow s. one's tops *(sl.)*; **aus dem ~ geraten** to fly off the handle *(sl.)*; **aus dem ~ sein** to be off balance, to cut up *(US sl.)*; **völlig aus dem ~ sein** to be in a flutter of excitement.

Haus|dame *(Hotel)* matron; **~detektiv** *(Warenhaus)* house detective; **~diebstahl** domestic theft; **~diener** manservant, valet, houseman, *(Hotel)* porter, houseboy, boots *(sl.)*; **~druckerei** in-plant printing plant *(US)*; **~durchsuchung** house search; **rechtswidrige ~durchsuchung** unreasonable search; **~durchsuchungsbefehl** search warrant; **~durchsuchungsbefehl für die Polizei ausstellen** to authorize a constable to enter and search the premises; **~eigentümer** owner of a house, house owner, householder; **~eigentümer sein** to have a house of one's own; **~eigentümer-Haftpflichtversicherung** property owner's liability insurance; **~eingang** threshold; **~einladung** home entertaining; **~einrichtung** furniture, appointments; **~einweihung** housewarming party.

hausen to dwell, to live, to reside;
furchtbar ~ *(Flut)* to cause havoc; **gemeinsam ~** to hive; **in einer Kellerwohnung ~** to live in a cellar; **in den Vorräten ~** to be heavy on supplies.

Häuser, verstreut liegende scattered (straggling) houses;
volle ~ haben to play to full houses;
~block block [of houses] *(US)*, square *(US)*; **~block weiter oben** squares up; **~front** row of houses; **~halde** housing stock; **fabrikmäßige ~herstellung** prefabrication of houses; **~komplex** set (group) of houses, block of buildings *(US)*; **~makler** realtor *(US)*, house farmer *(Br.)*, real-estate agent (broker) *(US)*; **~markt** houses offered for sale; **~meer** ocean of houses; **~reihe** line of buildings.

Hauserrichtung house construction.

Häuserteilanfertigung, fabrikmäßige prefabrication of houses.

Haus- und Grundstückserträge income from buildings and landed property (real estate, *US*).

Häuser|verwalter [real-]estate agent, realtor *(US)*; **~viertel** quarter, block *(US)*.

Haus|erwerb house purchase; **~erwerb im Abzahlungswege** house purchase by instalment payment; **~erwerber** house property purchaser; ~**flagge** *(Reeder)* burgee; ~**flur** [entrance] hall, landing passage *(Br.)*, corridor, *(Diele)* entrance hall, hallway *(US)*; ~**frau** housewife, mistress, hostess; **methodisch arbeitende** ~**frau** orderly housewife; ~**frauenzeitschrift** women's (service) magazine; ~**freund** gallant; ~**friedensbruch** breach of close, forcible entry into a building, domestic violence, homesecken *(Scot.)*; ~**garten** back garden, backyard *(US)*; ~**gebrauch** domestic use; **nur für den** ~**gebrauch** for domestic use only; ~**gehilfin** domestic servant; ~**gemeinschaft** housemating, household; ~**genosse** inmate, housemate, fellow lodger; ~**geräte** household goods; ~**gewalt** power of the keys; ~**gewerbe** cottage industry; ~**grundstück** freehold house; **hypothekarisch belastetes** ~**grundstück** mortgaged building.

Haushalt household, family ménage, establishment, *(Budget)* budget, estimates, *(Haushaltung)* housekeeping;
im ~ **vorgesehen** budgeted; **im** ~ **nicht vorgesehen** extra-budgetary; **nicht zum ordentlichen** ~ **gehörig** below-the line *(Br.)*; **zum ordentlichen** ~ **gehörig** above-the-line *(Br.)*; **ausgeglichener** ~ balanced budget, balance of budget; **nicht ausgeglichener** ~ adverse (unbalanced) budget; **außerordentlicher** ~ double (extraordinary) budget; **mit Wahlgeschenken belasteter** ~ giveaway budget; **defizitärer** ~ adverse budget; **gemeinsamer** ~ common household; **gemischter** ~ composite household; **genehmigter** ~ approved budget; **getrennter** ~ separate establishment; **individueller** ~ private household; **kommunaler** ~ local *(Br.)* (municipal, *US*) budget; **ordentlicher** ~ ordinary budget; **private** ~**e** private households; **städtischer** ~ city economy; **unausgeglichener** ~ unbalanced (adverse) budget;
~ **mit Steuergeschenken** give-away budget; ~ **als Verbrauchereinheit** household consumer; ~ **des Verteidigungsministeriums** defence budget;
~ **annehmen** to pass the budget; **im** ~ **arbeiten** to do housework; ~ **auffüllen** to fatten a budget; **seinen** ~ **auflösen** to break up one's household, to give up housekeeping; ~ **aufstellen** to prepare (make up) the estimates *(Br.)*; ~ **ausgleichen (ins Gleichgewicht bringen)** to balance the budget, to set the budget on its feet again; ~ **der Gemeinden belasten** to burden the finances of the communities; ~ **durcheinanderbringen** to throw a budget out of gear; ~ **einbringen** to bring in (introduce) the estimates *(Br.)*; **angespannten** ~ **entlasten** to ease the stress on the budget; **jem. den** ~ **führen** to manage (run) s. one's house, to keep house (housekeep) for s. o., to do for s. o.; ~ **genehmigen** to vote the estimates *(Br.)* (budget); **seinen eigenen** ~ **haben** to keep house; **großen** ~ **haben** to keep a large establishment; ~ **das ganze Jahr über kontrollieren** to work around the year on the budget; **übersetzten** ~ **kürzen** to trim fat from one's budget; **im** ~ **der Eltern leben** to live with one's parents; **in jds.** ~ **leben** to live in s. one's family; ~ **leiten** to take hold of the housework; ~ **auf Streichungsmöglichkeiten hin überprüfen** to scan the budget for possible cutbacks; ~ **überschreiten** to exceed the budget; **festgelegten** ~ **nicht überschreiten** to hold the budget line; ~ **verwalten** to have charge of the budget; ~ **vorlegen** to present (open, introduce) the budget, to bring in the estimates *(Br.)*; ~ **zusammenstreichen** to slash a budget.

haushalten to be economical, to economize, to husband;
~ **für j.** to keep house for s. o.

Haushälterin lady housekeeper.

haushälterisch housekeeperly, *(sparsam)* housewifely, economical, thrifty, sparing;
~ **sein** to husband, to economize;
~**er Mensch** economizer.

Haushalts|abfälle household refuse; ~**abnehmer** household consumer; ~**abstriche** budget cuts; ~**abteilung** budget-making (budgetary) agency, budget department, *(Kaufhaus)* hardware department; ~**abteilung des Finanzministeriums** Bureau of the Budget *(US)*; ~**abteilungsleiter** budget director, director of the budget; ~**abweichungen** budget variance; ~**änderungen** budget changes; ~**anforderungen beschneiden** to prune budget requests; ~**angehörige** family group; ~**ansatz** draft budget, estimates *(Br.)*; ~**ansatz zurückführen** to rein back a budget; ~**ansätze nicht erreichen** to fall below budget figures; ~**arbeiten** household duties; **leichte** ~**arbeit** light housekeeping; ~**artikel** household gear, domestic articles; ~**aufstellung** budgeting, making up of a budget, income engineering *(US)*; ~**ausgaben** budgetary (budget) expenditure; ~**ausgleich** budget equilibrium *(Br.)* (balancing); **antizyklischer** ~**ausgleich** cyclical budgeting; ~**ausschuß** budget (appropriation, *US*) committee, budgetary commission (board), Committee of Supply *(Br.)*, House Ways and Means Committee *(US)*; ~**ausweis** budget statement; **wöchentlicher** ~**ausweis** week's budget statement; ~**ausweitung** budget busting; ~**bedarf** household requirements; ~**bedürfnisse** *(Etat)* budget (budgetary) needs; ~**befragung** sample of householders; ~**befugnisse** budgetary powers; ~**behörde** budgetary authority, budget agency *(US)*; ~**beratungen** budget debate (session, trading, *US*), budgetary negotiations; ~**bericht** budget report; ~**beschränkungen** budgetary restraints; ~**besteuerung** splitting system; ~**bewilligung** budget grant, budgetary appropriations, voting the estimates *(Br.)*; ~**bewilligungsausschuß** budgetary committee (board), appropriation (budget) committee, Committee of Supply (Ways and Means, *Br.*), House Ways and Means Committee *(US)*; ~**buch** housekeeping book; ~**buchführung** family accounting; ~**debatte** budget issue (debate); ~**debatte durchführen** to debate on the budget.

Haushaltsdefizit budget[ary] deficit, deficit in the budget, fiscal deficit, adverse budget;
aus der Vollbeschäftigungspolitik entstandene ~**e** full employment budget deficits;
~ **ausgleichen** to balance an adverse budget; ~ **herbeiführen** to put the budget in the red *(US coll.)*; **sich ein großes** ~ **leisten** to run a large budget deficit.

Haushalts|disziplin budgetary discipline; ~**einkommen** family income; ~**einnahmen** budgetary receipts; ~**einrichtung** household furniture; ~**einsparungen** budgetary economies, budget savings, retrenchment of budgetary expenditure; ~**entwurf** proposed budget; **ausweitende** ~**ergänzungen** budget-busting additions; ~**experte,** ~**fachmann** budget specialist (analyst, man), budgeteer; ~**fehlbetrag** fiscal (budgetary) deficit, adverse budget; ~**formular** budget form; ~**frage** budgetary question.

haushaltsfremd extra-budgetary.

Haushalts|führung housekeeping, homemaking, management of a house; **gemeinsame** ~**führung** joint household, common domestic life; ~**gebarung** budgetary framework; ~**gegenstände** household commodities (utensils, assets), household effects (stuff), housewares.

Haushaltsgeld housekeeping allowance (money), household income;
mit dem ~ **auskommen** to make the housekeeping money stretch, to budget; **etw. vom** ~ **bezahlen** to pay s. th. out of the housekeeping money; **mit dem** ~ **geizen** to scrimp one's household.

Haushalts|geräte domestic (household) appliances, household goods (equipment); **elektrische** ~**geräte** electric-powered household gadgets; ~**geschäft** hardware shop; ~**gesetz** Appropriation Act *(Br.)*, Consolidated Act *(Br.)*, Budget and Accounting Act *(US)*, Finance Act *(Br.)*; ~**gleichung** budget equation; **lebenswichtige** ~**güter** household essentials; ~**hilfe** household help (home, domestic) help; **vom Betrieb gestellte stundenweise** ~**hilfen** home helper system; **im Haushalt lebende** ~**hilfe** resident housekeeper; ~**höchstgrenze festsetzen** to fix an extreme limit for the budget; ~**jahr** budgetary (budget, financial, *Br.*, fiscal, *US*) year; ~**kleidung** housewear; ~**kommissar** *(EG)* budget commissioner; ~**kontrolle** budgetary control; ~**kosten** household operating costs; ~**kredit** budget credit; ~**kunde** domestic economy; ~**kunst** domestic economy; ~**kürzungen** budget cuts (slash), budget cutting; ~**kürzungen vornehmen** to prune a budget; ~**lage** budgetary position; ~**lehrgang** household arts; ~**liste** census paper.

haushaltsmäßig budgetary, in accordance with the estimates *(Br.)*.

Haushalts|messe exhibition of household appliances; ~**mißbrauch** budget dissavings.

Haushaltsmittel budgetary appropriation (funds, means), budget funds (means);
ausgegebene, jedoch noch nicht angewiesene ~ obligated balance; **bereitgestellte (bewilligte)** ~ budgetary appropriations; **bewilligte** ~ budget grant; **bewilligte, jedoch noch nicht ausgegebene** ~ obligations outstanding; **kommunale** ~ county general fund; **noch zur Verfügung stehende** ~ unallotted appropriation; **frei verfügbare** ~ unapplied cash;
~ **nicht voll ausschöpfen** to underspend on the budget; ~ **bewilligen** to vote supplies (the estimates, *Br.*); ~ **zuteilen** to apportion budget funds;
~**bereitstellung** budgetary appropriation.

Haushalts|nachtrag supplementary budget (estimate, *Br.*); ~**packung** family size, giant package; ~**panel** family research panel; ~**periode** budget period.

Haushaltsplan budget, the estimates *(Br.)*;
den ~ **betreffend** budgetary; **im** ~ **vorgesehen** budgeted; **im** ~ **nicht vorgesehen** extra-budgetary;

gesamter ~ master budget; **normaler** ~ business-as-usual budget; **städtischer** ~ city budget;
~ **aufstellen** to draw up the estimates *(Br.)*, to prepare (draw up) the budget, to [make a] budget *(US)*; ~ **bewilligen** to vote the estimates *(Br.)*; ~ **einbringen** to introduce the budget; ~ **einhalten** to keep to the budget; **in den** ~ **einstellen** to budget for; ~ **genehmigen** to vote the budget (estimates, *Br.*); ~ **überschreiten** to exceed the budget (estimates, *Br.*); **im** ~ **unterbringen** to budget *(US)*; ~ **verabschieden** to pass the budget; **in einem** ~ **verstecken** to bury in a budget; ~ **vorlegen** to present the budget, to bring in the estimates *(Br.)*.

Haushaltsplanung budgeting.

Haushaltspolitik budgetary practices (policy);
antizyklisch (konjunkturell) ausgerichtete ~ cyclical budgeting; **langfristige** ~ long-range budgeting; **restriktive** ~ restrictive budget policy; **jeden Einzelposten grundsätzlich zur Diskussion stellende** ~ zero-base budgeting approach.

Haushalts|posten budgetary item, item included in the budget; **~postenausgleich** interfund settlement; **~programm** budget program(me); **Ausgaben im ~rahmen halten** to keep spending within the budgetary plan; **~rechnung** household bill (budget), *(Etat)* budgetary (proprietary) account; **~rechnungsführung** budgetary accounting; **~recht** budget law *(US)*.

haushaltsrechtlich budgetary;
~ **genehmigt sein** to fall within the budget;
~e Bestimmungen budgetary regulations; ~ **genehmigte Kredite** credits falling into the budget; **~e Kreditgenehmigung** interfund borrowing.

Haushalts|rede budget message (speech, statement); **~rede halten** to open the budget; **~referent** budgetary officer *(US)*; **~reform** budgetary reform; **~reinigungsmittel** detergents; **~rest** unspent appropriations; **~satzung** budget ordinance; **~schlußtermin** budget deadline *(US)*; **~schwierigkeiten** budget difficulties; **~sektor** personal sector; **~spezialist** budget man (specialist, analyst), budgeteer; **~stichprobe** sample of households; **~streichungen** budget slashing; **~system** budgetary (budget) system; **mittelfristiges ~system** medium-term budgetary framework; **~tarif** *(el.)* flat rate; **vom Handel übernommene ~tätigkeit** built-in maid service.

haushaltstechnischer Fehler budgetary error.

Haushalts|titel budget item (heading); **~titel auflösen** to deobligate; **~titelauflösung** deobligation; **~transaktionen** budgetary operations; **~trennung** maintaining separate households; **~überschreitung** exceeding the budget; **~überschreitung vermeiden** to hold the budget line; **~überschuß** [unappropriated] budget surplus, unspent appropriation *(US)*; **~umfang endgültig festlegen** to wrench a budget into final shape; **~utensilien** housefurnishings; **~verabschiedung** budget resolution; **~verbrauch** domestic (household) consumption; **~verbraucher** household consumer; **~vereinbarung** budgetary arrangements; **~verfahren** budgetary procedure; **~verordnung** appropriation ordinance *(US)*; **~versicherung** householder's insurance; **~volumen** total budget.

Haushaltsvoranschlag estimate of expenditure, budgetary (annual) estimate *(Br.)*, budget proposal, *(parl.)* the Estimates *(Br.)*, budget work sheets *(US)*;
ausgelasteter ~ balanced budget;
~ **abändern** to amend an appropriation bill; ~ **annehmen** to approve the budget; ~ **bewilligen** to vote the appropriation (estimates, *Br.*, supplies, funds); ~ **kürzen** to shave the budget (estimates, *Br.*); ~ **überschreiten** to exceed the estimates *(Br.)* (budget); ~ **vorlegen** to open the budget.

Haushalts|vorbereitung budgetary preparation; **~vorgriff** advances on the succeeding budget, credit *(Br.)*; **~vorlage** appropriation *(Br.)* (budget, *US*) bill, budget document; **~vorschlag** proposed budget; **~vorschriften** budgetary regulations; **~vorstand** householder; **~waren** household wares (commodities); **~zuweisung** budgetary appropriation.

Haushaltung housekeeping, household;
~en residential customers.

Haushaltungs|bedarf household requirements; **~buch** housekeeping book; **~einkommen** household income; **~fragebogen** census paper; **~gegenstände** household stuff (goods, articles, utensils), household wares; **~geld** household income, housekeeping allowance; **~kosten** family expenses, household operating costs; **~möbel** household furniture; **~rechnung** budgetary account, budget report *(US)*; **~schule** domestic science college; **~vorstand** housefather, household head, head of a family, householder, housemaster.

Hausherr head of the family, master of the house, *(Hauswirt)* landlord, *(Gastgeber)* host.

Hausherrin lady of the house.

haushoch vast, enormous, huge, smashing;
~ **gewinnen** to win hands down; **j.** ~ **schlagen** to trounce s. o.; **allen anderen** ~ **überlegen sein** to be head and shoulders above the rest; ~ **verlieren** to lose by a large margin.

haushoh|e Mehrheit vast majority; **~e Schulden** vast debts; **~er Sieg** out-and-out victory; **~e Verluste** huge losses; **~e Wellen** mountaineous seas.

Haushund house dog.

Hausieren hawking, trafficking, [itinerant] peddling, peddlery, pedlary *(Br.)*;
~ **verboten!** No canvassing allowed!; **Betteln und** ~ **verboten!** No canvassers! No hawkers! No circulars!

hausieren to peddle, to hawk, to vend, to huckster;
~ **gehen** to canvass from door to door, to higgle; **mit einer Geschichte** ~ **gehen** to spread a story, to hawk news about.

Hausierer peddler *(US)*, pedlar *(Br.)*, hawker, canvasser, itinerant vendor (salesman, dealer, trader), home-service (door-to-door, doorstep) salesman, trucker, huckster, higgler, roadsman, cadger, chapman *(Br.)*, boomer *(US)*;
~gewerbe, ~tum hawking business, itinerant trade, peddling, peddlery, pedlary *(Br.)*, door-to-door canvassing.

Hausier|geschäft peddlery *(US)*, pedlary *(Br.)*; **~gewerbeschein** peddler's (pedlar's, *Br.*)licence; **~handel** house-to-house selling, itinerant peddling (trade), peddling, peddlery, pedlary *(Br.)*, doorstep trading; **~handel treiben** to peddle, to canvass from door to door; **~schein** peddler's (pedlar's, *Br.*) licence.

Haus|industrie domestic industry (system), home (cottage) industry, homework, outwork; **~inhaber** houseowner; **~installation** indoor installation; **~instandhaltungskosten** occupancy expenses; **~instandsetzung** building repair; **~kauf** purchase of a building, house deal; **auf dem Hypothekenmarkt finanzierte ~käufe** new homes purchased with conventional mortgages; **~käufer** house (home, *US*) buyer, house purchaser; **übliche ~-zu-~klausel** standard warehouse-to-warehouse clause; **~kleid** overall; **~kleidung** indoor dress, household wear; **~klingel** doorbell; **~konzert** musicale; **~korrektor** *(Verlag)* indoor reader, proofreader; **~korrektur** printer's proof; **~lehrer** visiting (private) teacher, family tutor, coach, governor; **~lehrerin** governess.

Häusler cottager.

häuslich domestic, homely, housekeeping;
sich ~ **einrichten** to settle down; **sich** ~ **niederlassen** to make o. s. at home; ~ **eingestellt sein** to be domesticated;
~e Angelegenheiten family affairs; **~e Arbeiten** housework; **~er Ärger** domestic trouble; **~e Atmosphäre** homely atmosphere; **~e Aufgabe** homework; **~e Gemeinschaft** joint household; **~en Herd verlassen** to leave home; **im ~en Kreis** in the family circle; **in seinem ~en Leben** in his home life; **~er Mensch** homebody *(US coll.)*; **~e Zwecke** domestic purposes.

Häuslichkeit family life.

Haus|lieferant von Menüs take-away restaurant; **~macht eines Kandidaten** strength of a candidate; **~mädchen** housemaid, house chambermaid *(Br.)*; **~mannskost** plain (homely, ordinary) fare, home cooking; **nur ~mannskost** merely ordinary *(US)*; **~marke** private (own) brand, *(Händler)* dealer's brand; **~meister** doorkeeper, custodian, concierge, caretaker, hall (house) porter, janitor *(US)*; **ständig anwesender ~meister** resident porter; **als ~meister tätig sein** to janitor *(US)*; **~meisterin** woman caretaker, concierge, janitress *(US)*; **~miete** leasing of a house, rent; **~müll** residential domestic) refuse *(US)*; **~mutter** housemother; **~nummer** street (house) number; **~ordnung** rules of the house, *(Hotel)* hotel regulations; **beim ~personal** below stairs; **~plakette** house plate; **~putz** spring (house) cleaning; **~rat** gear, household equipment (goods, furniture, stuff, effects), housefurnishings, personal chattels; **~ratsersatzbeschaffung** replacement of household goods (effects); **~ratsversicherung** household (house and contents) insurance; **kombinierte ~- und ~ratsversicherung** householder's comprehensive insurance, domestic policy; **~ratsverteilung** division of household effects; **~recht** power of the keys, domiciliary right; **~reinigung** house cleaning; **~revision** internal audit; **~sammlung** round collection; **~schätzung** valuation on a house; **~schlüssel** latch (front-door, check, *Br.*) key; **~schwamm** dry rot.

Hausse rise, bull movement (market), bullish demonstration, price rally, boom market;
konjunkturbedingte ~ cyclical boom; **plötzliche** ~ fireworks;
~ **auf dem Immobilienmarkt** property boom; ~ **auf dem Markt für mündelsichere Anlagewerte** boom in the giltedged market *(Br.)*; ~ **im Museumsbau** museum boom;

auf ~ kaufen to bull the market, to bull; **à la ~ liegen** to be all bulls; **auf lange Sicht auf eine ~ setzen** to be bullish in the long run; **auf ~ spekulieren** to speculate on a rise, to go in (buy, operate) for a rise, to buy long, to gamble on a rise in prices, to [go a] bull; **erwartete ~ am Markt überschätzen** to overdiscount the market *(US)*.
hausseartige Kurssteigerung bullish price rise.
Haussebedingungen boom conditions.
Haussebewegung bull movement, bullish demonstration (performance), upward tendency;
abnehmende ~ subsiding boom; **künstliche ~** ballooning;
~ fortsetzen to continue bullish.
Hausse | börse bullish (boom) market; **~engagement** bull account *(Br.)*, the long interest (account, *US*); **~einfluß** bullish influence; **~geschäft** bull transaction; **~- und Baissegeschäfte** longs and shorts; **~gruppe** bull pool; **~kauf** purchase for a rise, bull purchase; **~kauf tätigen** to buy long; **~kurs** boom price; **~markt** bullish (bull [stock], boom, rising) market; **~marktabschwächung** bull market's dotage; **~moment** bull point; **~nachricht** bullish report; **~neigung** up tendency, tendency towards high prices; **~partei** bull clique, long side *(US)*, operators for a rise, constructive side of the market *(US)*; **~periode** period of buoyancy (upward tendency), bull phase; **seine Verkäufe über eine ~periode verteilen** to sell on a slice; **~phase** boom period; **~position** bull account *(Br.)* (position), long account *(Br.)*, long interest *(Br.)* (account, *US*), long position; **~position hereingeben** to give on a bull; **~spekulant** bull, inflater, operator (speculator) for a rise; **~spekulation** bull transaction (speculation, operation), bullish operation, speculation (dealing, operating) for a rise; **kurze ~spekulation** free ride; **~stimmung** bullish tendency (tone, mood, market); **in ~stimmung sein** to be all bull, to feel bullish; **~tendenz** bullishness, bullish tendency; **starke ~tendenz** strong upward tendency.
haussetendenziös bullish, bull;
sich kaum ~ auf einen Aktienkurs auswirken to be hardly bullish news for a share price.
Hausseverkauf long sale.
Haussier bull, long, inflator;
geschlagener ~ stale bear;
~ werden to run bull.
haussieren to feel bullish, to be all bulls (in a bullish mood), to whirl upward, to move upward rapidly.
haussierend bullish;
~e Kurse booming prices.
Haus | sprechanlage house phone, subscriber's set, interphone, intercom *(coll.)*; **~stand** household; **seinen ~stand gründen** to set up house[keeping]; **~steuer** house duty; **~suchung** domiciliary visit *(Br.)*, search of a house, house check *(US)*; **~suchung vornehmen** to search a house; **~suchungsbefehl** search warrant; **genormte ~teile vorfertigen** to prefabricate; **~telefon** interoffice communication, intercom *(coll.)*, house phone, interphone; **~tier** domestic animal, animal that has been domesticated, creature; **zu ~tieren machen** to domesticate; **~tochter** mother's help, lady help *(Br.)*; **~tor** main entrance; **~tür** front (entry, street, outer) door; **~türschlüssel** latchkey; **~tyrann** lion at home, cock on his own dunghill *(coll.)*; **~umbau** house conversion; **~verkauf** house deal, *(Hausierer)* door-to-door selling (market); **~vermietung** lease of a house, house-letting; **~versicherung** home insurance; **~verwalter** property manager, real-estate agent, realtor *(US)*, *(Portier)* house steward, caretaker, porter, concierge, janitor *(US)*; **~verwaltung** property management, householding, housekeeping *(US)*; **neues ~viertel** new housing estate; **kostenlose ~vorführung** free demonstration in the home; **~wart** caretaker, porter, concierge, janitor *(US)*; **Viertel des ~wertes anzahlen** to deposit a quarter of the price of the house; **~wert mit 140.000 Dollar festsetzen** to value a house at $ 140.000; **~wirt** landlord; **~wirtin** landlady; **~wirtschaft** domestic economy, family industry.
hauswirtschaftlich domestic, economic;
~e Geräte household appliances.
Hauswirtschafts | kunde domestic economy; **~lehre** household (home, *US*) economics; **~leiterin** homemaker; **~schule** domestic science college; **~unterricht** home-economic class *(US)*.
Haus | zeitschrift company magazine, house organ; **~zentrale** extension board, private branch exchange, subscriber's set.
Hauszins rent;
~steuer tax on inhabitant houses, inhabitated house duty *(Br.)*; **~steuer erheben** [etwa] to assess a building.
Hauszustellung[sdienst] store-door service *(US)*.
Haut, mit ~ und Haar bones and all, neck and crop *(fam.)*; **naß bis auf die ~** soaked to the skin;
ehrliche ~ soul of hono(u)r;
nur aus ~ und Knochen bestehen to be nothing but skin and bone; **mit heiler ~ davonkommen** to come off with a whole skin, to save one's skin (bacon), to get out from under *(US)*; **aus der ~ fahren** to jump out of one's skin, to go off the handle; **dicke ~ haben** to be thick-skinned, to have a thick skin; **nicht aus seiner ~ herauskönnen** not to be able to change one's skin (to get outside one's pudding, *sl.*); **auf der faulen ~ liegen** to lie down on the job, to take it easy; **seine ~ retten** to save one's bacon; **grundehrliche ~ sein** to be honest up to the hub; **in jds. ~ stecken** to stand in s. one's shoes; **seine ~ zu Markte tragen** to risk one's own skin, to stick one's neck out; **sich mit ~ und Haaren seiner Arbeit verschreiben** to put one's heart and soul into one's work; **sich in seiner ~ nicht wohlfühlen** to feel uneasy; **nicht in jds. ~ stecken wollen** not to like to be in s. one's shoes;
keiner kann aus seiner ~ heraus no leopard can change his spots;
zum Aus-der-~-Fahren for crying out loud.
Hautevolee the upper ten [thousand], the four hundred *(US)*.
Hautverpflanzung skin grafting.
Havarie average, ship damage, damage by sea;
nicht gegen ~ versichert free of average; **nicht gegen besondere ~ versichert** free of particular average; **nicht gegen große und besondere ~ versichert** free of all average;
große ausländische ~ foreign general average; **besondere ~** particular (simple) average; **einfache ~** partial (simple, common) average; **große ~** general (gross) average; **kleine ~** particular average; **schwere ~** serious damage;
~ nach Seegebrauch average accustomed;
~ aufmachen to assess the damage, to settle the average; **Ersatz für ~ erhalten** to recover average; **~ erleiden (machen)** to make (suffer) average, to suffer damages, to meet with a casualty, to go bad; **~ ertragen** to bear average;
~agent average agent; **~attest** captain's (ship's) protest; **~aufmachung** assessment (statement) of damage, settlement of average; **~aufopferung** average sacrifice; **~beitrag** average contribution; **gemeinsamer ~beitrag** general average contribution; **~berechnung** adjustment of average, average adjustment (statement); **~bericht** damage report; **~dispacheur** average adjuster; **~einschuß zur großen Havarie** general average cash deposit; **~erklärung** average statement, ship's (captain's) protest; **~experte** average stater.
havariefrei free of average.
Havarie | gelder average charges (expenses, expenditure, money); **~gutachten** damage survey; **~klausel** average clause; **große ~klausel** general average clause; **~kommissar** claims (average) agent, average adjuster, surveyor; **~kommissar mit Schadensregulierungsvollmacht** claims settling agent; **~kosten aufmachen** to settle the average; **~rechnung** average account (bill, adjustment); **~regelung** average adjustment; **~revers** average bond.
havariert sea-damaged.
Havarie | sachverständiger average adjuster, dispacheur; **~schaden** average loss, damage by sea water; **~schadensaufstellung** statement of average; **~schein** average bond, certificate of average; **~umlage** general average contribution; **~verpflichtung** average bond; **große ~versicherung** general average bond; **~verteilung** average adjustment; **~vertrag** average agreement; **~vertreter** average adjuster (stater, agent); **~waren** average (damaged) goods; **~zertifikat** certificate of average, survey report.
Hebamme midwife.
Hebammendienst midwifery service.
Hebe | bühne lifting platform, rising floor; **~gebühr** [collection] rate; **~gewicht** working load; **~kran** lifting (hoisting) crane.
Hebel lever;
~ ansetzen to operate a lever, *(fig.)* to apply pressure; **alle ~ in Bewegung setzen** to move heaven and earth, to leave no stone unturned; **am längeren ~ sitzen** to have more pull; **~ umlegen** to turn a switch.
Hebeliste assessment (tax, *US*) roll, tax book *(US)*, tax-payers' (income-tax) list, register of taxes.
Hebelwirkung leverage effect;
~ der Fixkosten operating leverage, operational gearing.
Heben heave.
heben to raise, to lift, *(Bruch)* to reduce;
sich ~ *(Kurse)* to advance, to rise, to go up, *(Lebensstandard, Umsatz)* to rise, to improve; **sich ~ und senken** to rise and fall;

Anker ~ to weigh anchor; **Auto** ~ to lift (jack up) a car; **einen** ~ to wet one's whistle *(coll.)*; **gern einen** ~ to be fond of the bottle; **Fremdenverkehr** ~ to promote tourism; **Glas aufs Wohl des Hausherrn** ~ to raise one's glass to the health of the host; **j. in den Himmel** ~ to extol (laud) s. o. to the skies; **Kind aus der Taufe** ~ to sponsor a child; **Lebensstandard** ~ to raise (improve) the standard of living; **Preisniveau** ~ to raise the level of prices; **Schatz** ~ to dig up a treasure; **gesunkenes Schiff** ~ to refloat a sunken ship; **Tür aus den Angeln** ~ to unhinge a door; **Welt aus den Angeln** ~ to set the world on fire; **Zug aus den Schienen** ~ to derail a train;
einen ~ **gehen** to go and have one.

Hebe|recht rating authority *(Br.)*, local tax power *(US)*; ~**rolle** tax (taxpayers') list, assessment roll, tax book *(US)*; ~**satz** rate of assessment, collection rate; ~**schiff** salvage ship; ~**schleuse** canal lock; ~**stelle** receiver's office; ~**vorrichtung** lifting jack; ~**werk** hoisting engine, *(Kanal)* lift.

Hebung increase, *(Förderung)* promotion, improvement;
~ **des Fremdenverkehrs** promotion of tourist traffic; ~ **des Lebensstandards** improvement of the standard of living.

Hecht, toller dashing fellow;
~ **im Karpfenteich** pike in a fish-pond, wolf among the lambs.

Heck stern, poop, *(Auto)* rear, tail;
~**anker** stern anchor; ~**antrieb** rear drive.

Hecke hedge;
dichte ~ thickset hedge; **lebende** ~ quick hedge;
Grundstück durch eine ~ **abgrenzen** to hedge off a piece of ground.

Hecken|springer *(Flieger)* hedgehopper *(sl.)*; ~**schütze** sniper.

Heck|fenster *(Auto)* rear window, *(Schiff)* poop port; ~**flosse** *(Auto)* tail fin; ~**gepäckträger** luggage (baggage, *US*) grid.

hecklastig *(Flugzeug)* tail-heavy.

Heck|laterne stern lantern; ~**leuchte** *(Auto)* rear light; ~**licht** *(Flugzeug)* taillight; **mit** ~**motor** rear-engined; ~**pfennig** pocket piece, luck penny; ~**raddampfer** stern-wheeler; **beheizte** ~**scheibe** heated rear window; ~**schütze** rear gunner; ~**streifen** rear waistband; **aufklappbare** ~**tür** *(Kfz.)* tailgate.

Heer army, armed force, *(Schwarm)* host, swarm;
im ~ **dienend** with the colo(u)rs;
nur aus Freiwilligen bestehendes ~ all-volunteer armed force;
stehendes ~ regular (standing) army, military establishment;
~ **von Arbeitern** army (rank) of workmen; ~ **der Arbeitslosen** army of the jobless; ~ **von Beamten** host of officials;
ins ~ **eintreten** to join the ranks; **im** ~ **dienen** to serve with the colo(u)rs; ~ **unterhalten** to subsidize an army.

Heeres|auftrag army contract; ~**bedarf** army requirements; ~**bericht** daily war bulletin; ~**beschaffung** army procurement; ~**bestände** stores; ~**betreuung** army welfare center *(US)* (centre, *Br.*); ~**dienstvorschriften** army manual; ~**etat** army vote; ~**fachschule** army industrial college *(US)*; ~**gruppe** army group; ~**gut** military property; **oberste** ~**leitung** supreme command; ~**lieferant** army contractor (agent, broker); ~**lieferant sein** to purvey to the army; ~**lieferungen** army supplies; ~**ministerium** Department of the Army *(US)*; ~**streife** army patrol; ~**verpflegungsamt** army commissary; ~**verwaltung** army organization; ~**waffenamt** Ordnance Department *(US)*.

Heer|führer military leader, commander of an army; ~**lager** camp.

Hefe des Volkes scum (dregs) of mankind.

Heft *(Broschüre)* booklet, pamphlet, brochure, *(Schule)* notebook, exercise book, *(Zeitschrift)* number, issue;
~ **mit Kontrollabschnitten** counterfoil book;
in monatlichen ~**en erscheinen** to appear in monthly issues; ~ **in der Hand haben** to hold the reins, to be on top (in the saddle), to be at the helm; **jem. das** ~ **aus der Hand nehmen** to take the reins out of s. one's hands;
~**apparat** stapler.

heften to fasten, to tack, *(mit Klammer)* to staple, *(drucktechn.)* to whipstitch, to stitch;
Blick auf etw. ~ to rivet one's eyes on s. th.; **Buch mit Draht** ~ to wire-stitch a book; **sich an jds. Fersen** ~ to follow upon s. one's heels; **jem. einen Orden an die Brust** ~ to pin a medal on s. o.; **Zettel an die Tür** ~ to stick up a note on the door.

Hefter stitcher, *(Akte)* file.

Heftfaden *(Buchbinder)* sewing thread.

heftig violent, fierce, vehement;
leicht ~ **werden** to lose one's temper (flare up) quickly;
~**e Abneigung** strong dislike; ~**e Attacke** violent attack; ~**e Auseinandersetzung** violent controversy, fierce encounter; ~**es Fieber** high fever; ~**e Konkurrenz** severe (keen) competition; ~**e Kopfschmerzen** splitting headache; ~**e Leidenschaft** burning passion; ~**es Verlangen** ardent (fierce) desire; **jem.** ~**e Vorwürfe machen** to reproach s. o. violently; ~**er Wind** fierce wind.

Heftigkeit violence, intensity;
~ **einer Attacke** violence of an attack; ~ **eines Unwetters** violence of a storm.

Heft|klammer [paper] clip, staple; ~**lage** *(Buchbinden)* signature; ~**mappe** file; ~**maschine** stapler, stapling machine, *(drucktechn.)* stitcher; ~**öse** staple; ~**pflaster** adhesive (sticking) plaster, adhesive *(US)*; ~**pistole** gun stapler; ~**preis** single-copy price; ~**rand** margin; ~**schnur** band, bandstring; ~**verschlüsse** fasteners; ~**zange** stapling tongs; ~**zwecke** drawing pin *(Br.)*, thumbtack *(US)*.

Hegemonie hegemony, supremacy.

hegen to nurse, to tend;
Groll gegen j. ~ to hold a grudge against s. o.; **Haß gegen j.** ~ to feel hatred towards s. o.; **Hoffnungen** ~ to entertain hopes; **Verdacht** ~ to harbo(u)r suspicion.

Heger gamekeeper, preserver *(Br.)*.

Hehl, kein ~ **daraus machen** to be quite frank about it, to make no secret of it.

Hehler receiver [of stolen goods], resetter *(Br.)*, accessory after the fact, fence *(sl.)*, lock *(sl.)*, stop *(sl.)*;
als ~ **fungieren** to receive stolen goods.

Hehlerei receiving stolen goods, reset theft *(Scot.)*;
~ **begehen** to receive stolen goods.

Hehlerware stuff, stolen goods, cache, swag *(sl.)*, plant *(sl.)*;
~ **verkloppen** to stuff *(sl.)*; ~ **zurückgeben** to kick back *(US sl.)*.

Heide heath *(Br.)*.

Heiden|angst blue funk; ~**angst haben** to have the jitters, to be scared stiff (to death), to have a holy fear *(fam.)*; ~**arbeit** devil of a job; ~**arbeit sein** to be no end of a benefit; ~**geld** pot of money; ~**geld kosten** to cost like all creation (the earth); ~**lärm** fearful row, terrific din, racket; ~**lärm veranstalten** to kick up a row, to raise hell.

heidenmäßig viel Geld verdienen to be simply coining money.

Heiden|spaß high time *(sl.)*; ~**spektakel** heck of a row; ~**spektakel veranstalten** to raise the roof.

heikel delicate, prickly, ticklish, slippery, sensitive, *(wählerisch)* hard to please, fussy, particular;
äußerst ~ **sein** to be pretty near the knuckle, to be of great delicacy; **mit seinem Essen sehr** ~ **sein** to be very fussy (particular) about one's food.
sich im ~**sten Stadium befinden** to be at their most delicate.

heikle|r Auftrag delicate mission, tricky job; ~ **Frage** delicate (kittle) question; ~ **Lage** trouble, ticklish situation; ~**s Problem** knotty problem; ~ **Situation** hot seat; ~**s Thema** delicate subject.

Heil welfare, *(Nutzen)* benefit;
sein ~ **in der Flucht suchen** to seek refuge in flight, to take to one's heels.

heil safe, unscathed, *(Geschirr)* unbroken;
~ **machen** to mend.

Heil|- und Pflegeanstalt mental home hospital, insane asylum *(US)*, mental institution *(US)*, hospital for mental diseases *(US)*, sanitorium *(US)*; **in eine** ~**anstalt einweisen** to detain compulsorily; ~**bad** medicated bath, spa.

heilbarer Mangel curable defect.

Heil|behandlung therapeutic treatment, cure; ~**berufe** medical professions; ~**brunnen** mineral spring.

heilen to heal, to cure;
j. von einer Krankheit ~ to cure s. o. of an illness; **Rechtsmangel** ~ to cure (remedy) a defect.

heilend curative.

Heil|fürsorge medical care, sanitation; ~**gewerbe** therapeutics; ~**gymnastik** remedial gymnastics.

heilighalten, Sonntag to keep the Sabbath.

Heilig|keit der Ehe sanctity of marriage; ~**keit der Verträge** sanctity of treaties; ~**tum** sanctum, sanctuary, temple, shrine; ~**tum schänden** to defile a sacred place.

heilkräftig medicinal.

Heil|kräuter medicinal herbs; ~**kunde** medicine; ~**kurort aufsuchen** to take the waters.

heillos utter, terrific;
~ **durcheinander sein** to be knocked all of a heap; ~ **verfahren sein** to be in a muddle;
~**e Angst** blue funk, panic; ~**es Durcheinander** topsy-turvy, hopeless mess; ~**es Durcheinander anrichten** to make a muddle of it; ~**es Geld kosten** to cost an unholy amount of money.

Heil|methode therapy, cure; **psychologische** ~**methode** mental healing; ~**mittel** remedy; ~**mittel gegen die Arbeitslosigkeit**

cure for unemployment; ~**mittelverabfolgung** medicamentation; ~**praktiker** healer, physiotherapist; ~**quelle** well, mineral spring, waters; ~**quellen** the waters *(dial.)*.
heilsam wholesome, healthy;
~**e Tracht Prügel** sound thrashing.
Heilstätte sanatorium.
Heilung cure, *(Vertrag)* ratification *(US)*.
Heil|verfahren cure, medical treatment, therapy; ~**wirkung** curative effect.
Heim home, house, hearth, *(Erziehungsanstalt)* borstal institution, reform school *(US)*, *(Studenten)* hostel *(Br.)*;
~ **für sittlich Gefährdete** house of refuge; ~ **für Geisteskranke** mental (insane, *US*) asylum; ~ **für gefallene Mädchen** preservatory *(US)*;
in einem ~ **aufwachsen** to grow up in an orphanage; **eigenes** ~ **haben** to have a home of one's own; **seinen Großvater in einem** ~ **unterbringen** to home one's grandfather; **Kind in einem** ~ **unterbringen** to place a child in a foster home;
~**arbeit** indoor work; **industrielle** ~**arbeit** homework, cottage industry, outwork, putting-out system; ~**arbeiter** taker-in, outside worker, outworker, homeworker.
Heimat native country, homeland, home;
in der ~ at home; **nach der** ~ **bestimmt** *(Schiff)* homeward (inward) bound;
sich nach der ~ **sehnen** to long for home; **jem. zur zweiten** ~ **werden** to become s. one's second home; **in die** ~ **zurückkehren** to return home;
~**anschrift** home address; ~**bahnhof** *(Waggon)* home station, station of attachment; ~**basis** home base; ~**berechtigung** settlement; ~**boden** one's native soil; ~**flotte** home fleet *(Br.)*; **zum** ~**flughafen zurückkehren** to home; ~**front** home front; ~**gebiet** home territory *(US)*; ~**gemeinde** native town; ~**hafen** home (registered) port, port of registry (commission); ~**kriegsgebiet** zone of interior.
Heimatland homeland, home country *(Br.)*, home state, native country (land), country of one's birth, *(Immigrant)* old country;
mein ~ my native shore;
in sein ~ **zurückkehren** to return to one's own country.
heimatlich native;
j. ~ **anmuten** to remind s. o. of home;
~**e Gefühle** nostalgic feelings; ~**e Küste** one's native shore; ~**e Mahlzeit** homely meal; ~**e Sitten** local customs.
heimatlos without hearth or home, *(staatenlos)* stateless;
~**e und verwahrloste Kinder** waifs and strays.
Heimat|loser refugee, displaced person; ~**museum** local history museum; ~**ort** native place, *(Schiff)* port of registry; ~**recht** domiciliary law, domestic law, [right of] settlement; ~**schuß** blighty wound *(Br., sl.)*; ~**staat** country of nationality (origin), native country, home state; ~**stadt** native (one's home, *US*) town; **bezahlter** ~**urlaub** paid home leave; ~**urlaub antreten** to go home on furlough; ~**urlaub erhalten** to get leave to go home; ~**vertriebene** exiles from home; ~**vertriebener** displaced person, war refugee, expellee; ~**zeitung** local paper.
Heimaufsicht institutional care.
heimbringen, j. to see s. o. home.
Heimerziehung approved school education.
Heimfahrt homeward voyage;
auf der ~ **befindlich** inward bound, inbound.
Heimfall lapse, devolvement, confusion;
~ **durch Erbschaft** devolution, reversion; ~ **an den Fiskus** escheat *(US)*; ~ **an den Grundstückseigentümer** freehold reversion;
~**anspruch** revisionary interest, interest in expectancy.
heimfallen to revert, to lapse;
an den Staat ~ to revert by escheat (to the crown) *(Br.)*.
heimfällig revertible, reversionable.
Heimfalls|klausel defeasance clause; ~**möglichkeit** reversionary potential.
Heimfallsrecht [estate in] reversion, default of heirs, caduciary right, escheatage, reverter, *(Völkerrecht)* right of aubine;
mögliches ~ possibility of reverter; **subsidiäres** ~ contingency with double aspect; **unmittelbares** ~ immediate reversion.
Heimfalls|rechtsfolge escheated succession; ~**rente** reversionary annuity; ~**steuer** reversion value duty.
Heimgang death, passing away;
auf dem ~ on the way home.
Heimgegangener departed.
heimgesucht, von einem Erdbeben struck by an earthquake;
von schweren Bombenangriffen ~ **werden** to suffer heavy airraids;
von Heuschrecken ~**e Gebiete** locust-infested fields; **von Streiks** ~**e Gebiete** strike-ridden areas; **von Überschwemmungen** ~**e Gebiete** flood-stricken areas.
Heim|industrie cottage (home, domestic) industry, domestic system; ~**insasse** inmate.
heimisch domestic, native, home, internal, local;
sich in einer Wissenschaft ~ **fühlen** to feel at home in a branch of knowledge; ~ **werden** to acclimatize; **in einer Stadt** ~ **werden** to be based in a city;
~**e Atmosphäre** homely atmosphere; ~**e Fabrikate** home manufactures (-produced goods); ~**e Gewässer** inland waters; **am** ~**en Herd** round the fireside; ~**e Industrie** native (home, domestic) industry; ~**e Industrie fördern** to foster home industries.
Heim|kehr homecoming; ~**kehrer** repatriate, homecomer, returnee; ~**kino** home cinema (television); ~**leiter** warden, housemaster *(Br.)*, headmaster; ~**leiterin** house-mother, matron.
heimleuchten, jem. to send s. o. away with a flea in his ear.
heimlich secret, clandestine, concealed, underhand, hidden, furtive;
~ **und anrüchig** hole-and-corner;
jem. ~ **anblicken** to steal a glance at s. o.; **sich** ~ **davonmachen** to bolt, to take French leave; **jem.** ~ **entwischen** to give s. o. the slip; ~ **gehen** to leave unnoticed, to disappear quietly; ~ **horchen** to eavesdrop; **sich** ~ **treffen** to meet secretly; **etw.** ~ **wegschaffen** to spirit s. th. away; **jem.** ~ **ein paar Geldstücke zustecken** to slip a few coins into s. one's pocket;
~**e Blicke** stealthy glances; ~**e Eheschließung** clandestine marriage; ~**e Machenschaften** underhand dealings; ~**er Mangel** hidden defect; ~**er Nachdruck** surreptitious edition, piracy; ~**es Plätzchen** silent place; ~**e Schätze** concealed treasures; ~**er Verdacht** secret suspicion; ~**e Zusammenkunft** clandestine (secret) meeting.
Heimlichkeit secrecy, clandestineness, furtiveness, stealth.
Heimlichtuerei mystery.
Heimreise homeward voyage, home journey;
auf der ~ **begriffen** *(Schiff)* homeward (inward) bound, homebound; **auf seiner** ~ on his passage home.
Heim|schaffung repatriation; ~**schule** residential school; ~**sparbüchse** home safe *(Br.)*; ~**stätte** national home, homecroft *(Br.)*, homestead *(US)*; **vollstreckungsgeschützte** ~**stätte** urban homestead *(US)*.
Heimstätten|besitzer homecrofter *(Br.)*, homesteader *(US)*; ~**grundstück** homecroft *(Br.)* (homestead) lot (estate) *(US)*; ~**siedler** homesteader *(US)*, homecrofter *(Br.)*; ~**vollstreckungsfreibetrag** homestead exemption *(US)*; ~**vollstreckungsschutz** homestead law *(US)*; ~**werk** Homecroft Scheme *(Br.)*, Homestead Act *(US)*.
heimsuchen to strike, to infest, to visit;
Land mit der Pest ~ to smite a country with the plague.
Heimsuchung plague, calamity, misfortune, tragedy, *(Seuche)* visitation, *(Ungeziefer)* infestation;
schwere ~**en erleiden** to suffer great ills.
Heimtücke perfidy, maliciousness.
heimtückisch perfidious, treacherous, malicious, underhand;
~**e Krankheit** insidious illness; ~**er Mord** treacherous murder.
Heimunterbringung part III accommodation *(Br.)*.
heimwärts homeward;
seine Schritte ~ **lenken** to set out for home.
Heim|weg homeward way, way home; **sich auf den** ~**weg machen** to make for home; ~**weh** homesickness.
heimwehkrank homesick, pining for home.
Heimwirtschaft domestic system.
heimzahlen, es jem. to pay s. o. out for s. th. *(Br.)*, to serve s. o. out, to quit scores with s. o., to get one's own back, to get even with s. o. *(US coll.)*; **jem. mit gleicher Münze** ~ to pay s. o. back in his own coin.
Heinzelmännchen good people.
Heirat, formlose consensual marriage; **gültige** ~ lawful marriage; **vorteilhafte** ~ good marriage;
~ **unter nahen Verwandten** intermarriage;
~ **zustande bringen** to make a match of it; **einer** ~ **seine Zustimmung versagen** to oppose a marriage; **einer** ~ **zustimmen** to approve of a marriage.
heiraten to marry, to go off *(coll.)*, to step off the carpet *(sl.)*;
ohne das Einverständnis seiner Eltern ~ to marry without the knowledge of one's parents; **reich** ~ to marry a fortune; **j. schließlich (letzten Endes) doch** ~ to end up by marrying s. o.; **nicht standesgemäß** ~ to marry below one's station; **Frau wegen ihres Vermögens** ~ to marry s. o. with eye on her fortune.

Heirats|absichten serious (hono(u)rable) intentions; **~alter** marriageable age, age of marriage; **durchschnittliches ~alter** average marrying age; **~antrag** offer (proposal) of marriage, proposal, popping the question; **~antrag ablehnen** to refuse an offer of an marriage; **~antrag machen** to make known one's intentions, to propose, to pop the question, to speak one's piece *(sl.)*; **~anzeige** announcement of marriage, wedding announcement; **~beihilfe** marriage grant; **~beschränkungen** conditions in restraint of marriage; **~buch** marriage notice book, register of marriages; **~einwilligung versagen** to refuse consent to the marriage; **~erlaubnis** marriage licence (lines, *Br.*), consent of marriage; **besondere ~erlaubnis** special licence *(Br.)*; **standesamtliche ~erlaubnis** registrar's licence.

heiratsfähig marriageable, nubile;
nicht ~ unmarriageable;
~ sein to be of age to marry (of an age to be married);
in ~em Alter of a marrying age.

Heirats|fähigkeit marriageable age, capacity of marry, marriageableness; **~genehmigung** marriage licence; **~gut** dowry, marriage portion; **~kandidat** aspirant for s. one's hand, suitor; **~register** register of marriages, marriage notice book; **~schein** marriage certificate (lines, *Br.*); **~schwindler** impostor; **~statistik** marriage statistics; **~urkunde** marriage certificate (document); **~vermittler[in]** marriage broker, matchmaker, shotgun *(sl.)*; **~vermittlung** marriage brokerage, matrimonial agent, matchmaking; **~vermittlungsbüro** matrimonial agency, marriage brokerage; **~versprechen** marriage promise, promise of marriage; **~vertrag** marriage settlement, articles (contract) of marriage; **~ziffer** marriage rate; **~zulage, ~zuschuß** needs of a woman.

heiß *(gestohlen)* hot;
drückend ~ sulty, oppressive; **erstickend ~** suffocatingly hot; **glühend ~** red hot; **kochend ~** boiling hot;
wie die Katze um den ~en Brei herumlaufen to beat about the bush; **einem kalt und ~ den Rücken herunterlaufen** to go hot and cold all over; **sich ~ laufen** *(Motor)* to run hot; **~ machen** to heat up; **jem. die Hölle ~ machen** to make things warm (it hot) for s. o.; **jem. den Platz zu ~ machen** to make the place too hot for s. o.; **sich die Köpfe ~ reden** to have a heated debate; **~ umstritten sein** to arouse great controversy;
~er Draht *(pol.)* hot line; **~es Eisen** hot potato; **~es Eisen anfassen** to bring up a controversial subject; **~es Geld** hot money; **~er Krieg** hot war; **~ umkämpfter Platz sein** to be an object of bitter fighting; **~e Spur verfolgen** to be hot on the trail; **~es Thema** sore subject, delicate matter; **~er Tropfen auf dem Stein** a drop in the ocean; **~er Wunsch** fervent desire; **~e Würstchen** hot dogs;
was ich nicht weiß, macht mich nicht ~ what the eye does not see the heart does not grieve.

heißblütig sein to have a quick temper.

Heißblütigkeit quickness of temper;
~ der Jugend hot blood of youth.

heißen to be named (called);
j. einen Lügner ~ to call s. o. a liar; **j. willkommen ~** to bid s. o. welcome;
das will nichts ~ that means nothing.

Heißhunger keen appetite.

heißhungrig ravenous, voracious;
sein Essen ~ herunterschlingen to wolf down one's food.

Heißluft hot air;
~ballon fire balloon, hot-air balloon, montgolfier; **~heizung** hot-air heating; **~motor** hot-air engine.

Heißmangel hot press.

heißumstritten highly controversial.

Heißwasser|anlage hot-water connections; **~bereiter** geyser *(Br.)*; **~speicher** boiler.

heiter gay, merry, cheerful, smiling, *(Wetter)* bright, clear, fine, unclouded;
das Leben von seiner ~en Seite betrachten to look on the sunny side of things; **j. ~ stimmen** to cheer s. o. up.

Heiterkeit glee, mirth, *(Wetter)* brightness.

Heiterkeitserfolg bei jem. erzielen to make s. o. cry with laughter.

heiterst, in ~er Laune in high spirits.

Heiz|anlage heating system; **elektrischer ~apparat** electric heater.

heizbar heatable;
~er Waggon heater car.

Heiz|batterie filament battery; **~decke** electric blanket.

heizen to heat, to turn on the heating, *(Ofen)* to fire, to light;
Zimmer mit Gas ~ to heat a room with gas; **mit Kohle ~** to fire (burn) coal; **mit Öl ~** to have oil heating.

Heizer heater, fireboy, boilerman, stoker, fireteaser *(Br.)*.

Heiz|faden filament; **~fläche** heating surface; **~gas** fuel gas; **~gerät** heating apparatus, heater; **~kessel** boiler; **~kissen** heating cushion (pad); **~körper** heater, radiator; **~kosten** heating expenses; **~kostenbeihilfe** heating allowance; **~kraft** heating quality; **~material** fuel; **elektrischer ~ofen** electric heater; **~öl** fuel (heating) oil; **~ölsteuer** tax on fuel oil; **~platte** hot plate; **~raum** fireroom, furnace room, *(Schiff)* stokehold; **~schlange** heating coil; **~strahler** convector heater.

Heizung heating, firing, *(Heizkörper)* radiator, heater;
elektrische ~ electric heating;
~ abstellen to turn off the heating; **~ anstellen** to turn on the heating; **~ installieren** to install a heating system.

Heizungs|anlage heating plant (installation); **~keller** fireplace, fireroom, furnace room; **~kosten** fuel (heating) costs; **~periode** heating period; **~technik** heat-power engineering.

Heizwert heating power, thermal value, calorie intensity.

Hektik hectic state;
~ des modernen Großstadtlebens whirl of modern life in a big city; **~ des modernen Lebens** the press of modern life.

hektisch hectic;
~ arbeiten to work at white heat;
~es Leben führen to lead a hectic life; **~e Nachfrage** keen demand; **~e Zeit durchmachen** to have a hectic time.

Hektograph hectograph.

hektographieren to hectograph, to manifold.

hektographierter Abzug manifold.

hektographisch hectographic, autographic, self-recording.

Held hero, *(Theater)* protagonist;
~ des Tages lion of the day;
~en im letzten Kapitel sterben lassen to kill off the hero in the last chapter; **kein ~ in Englisch sein** to be no great shakes in English; **den ~en spielen** to play the hero's part; **als ~ sterben** to die like a hero, to die game; **zum ~ des Tages werden** to become the hero of the hour.

Helden|epos heroic tales; **~friedhof** military cemetery; **~gedenktag** Memorial Day *(US)*; **~keller** funkhole *(sl.)*; **~rolle in einem Stück spielen** to play the hero's part; **jugendliche ~rollen spielen** to play juvenile leads; **~tat** heroic deed; **nicht gerade eine ~tat** nothing to be proud of; **~tod sterben** to die like a hero, to die game; **~verehrung** hero-worship.

Helfen helping.

helfen to help, to aid, to assist, to lend a helping hand, to relieve;
j. ~ to roll a log for s. o. *(US)*; **bei einer Arbeit ~** to assist in doing a job; **jem. auf die Beine ~** to give s. o. a leg up; **finanziell ~** to extend financial aid; **jem. finanziell auf die Beine ~** to help s. o. to pick up the pieces, to set s. o. up again; **sich gegenseitig ~** to take in one another's washing; **j. mit Geld ~** to aid s. o. with money; **j. aus einer verwickelten Lage ~** to disembroil s. o.; **j. aus der Patsche ~** to get s. o. out of a scrape; **sich selbst ~** to shift for o. s.; **jem. auf die Sprünge ~** to jog s. one's memory; **jem. auf die Spur ~** to put s. o. on the track; **jem. unabsichtlich ~** to play s. one's game; **jem. beim Wiederaufbau ~** to aid s. one's recovery;
sich nicht mehr zu ~ wissen to be at one's wit's end, to be at a loss; **nur zu gern ~ wollen** to be proud to be of assistance.

helfend helping, helpful, auxiliary.

Helfer helper, aider, aid, backer, second, *(Ordner)* steward;
freiwilliger ~ voluntary worker;
~ in Steuersachen tax counsel[(l)or] (preparer).

Helfershelfer stooge, accomplice, bottleholder *(coll.)*, *(Strafrecht)* accessory during the fact.

hell light, clear, *(Foto)* intense, *(klug)* clever, wide *(Br., sl.)*;
~ brennen to burn brightly; **über etw. ~ begeistert sein** to wax enthusiastic over s. th.;
~e Begeisterung unbounded enthusiasm; **~es Bier** light (pale) beer *(US)*, lager *(Br.)*; **in ~en Flammen stehen** to be ablaze (in flames); **seine ~e Freude an etw. haben** to be delighted with s. th.; **~es Köpfchen haben** to be a bright chap, to have a good head on one's shoulders; **in ~en Scharen kommen** to flock; **am ~en Tage** in broad daylight; **~er Unsinn** utter nonsense; **in ~er Verzweiflung** in complete despair; **~er Wahnsinn** sheer madness; **in ~er Wut** in a blazing temper; **~es Zimmer** light room.

hellauf von etw. begeistert sein to wax enthusiastic about s. th.

Heller penny, stiver, mite, farthing *(Br.)*, dump *(sl.)*;
keinen roten ~ wert not worth a rap (picayune, cent, whoop, brass farthing), not worth a thin dime *(US sl.)*;
jem. sein Geld bis zum letzten ~ abnehmen to fleece s. o. of every halfpenny; **auf ~ und Pfennig bezahlen** to pay to the last penny (scot and lot); **seine Schulden auf ~ und Pfennig bezahlen** to pay

twenty shillings in the pound; **j. bis auf den letzten ~ enterben** to cut s. o. off with a shilling; **keinen roten ~ dafür geben** not to care a copper *(US)*; **keinen roten ~ haben** not to have a bean; **sich keinen roten ~ darum scheren** not to care a brass farthing.
hellhörig *(Wohnung)* poorly soundproofed;
~ **werden** to prick up one's ears.
hellicht, am ~en Tage in broad daylight.
Helling assembly hangar, slipway, way, stocks, *(Flugzeug)* building cradle;
~**gerüst** staging.
Hell|sehen second sight, clairvoyance; ~**seher** visionary, clairvoyant; ~**seherin** wisewoman.
hellseherisch visionary.
hellwach sein to be wide awake.
Helm helmet.
Hemd shirt;
j. bis aufs ~ ausziehen to fleece s. o. of his money; **bis aufs ~ ausgezogen sein** not to have a shirt to one's back;
das ~ ist näher als der Rock charity begins at home.
Hemdenfabrikant shirt manufacturer.
hemdsärmelig shirt-sleeve.
Hemisphäre hemisphere;
außerhalb der westlichen ~ extra-continental *(US)*.
hemmen to handicap, to impede, to hinder, to obstruct, to restrain, to estop from, to block, to check, *(jur.)* to estop, *(verzögern)* to delay;
Entwicklung ~ to retard (arrest) development; **wirtschaftliche Entwicklung** ~ to hamper the progress of business; **Fortschritt** ~ to impede progress; **Gang einer Maschine** ~ to stop the working of a machine; **Lauf einer Frist** ~ to suspend the running of a time; **Machtzuwachs eines Staates** ~ to stunt the growth of a nation; **Verjährungsfrist** ~ to interrupt the statute of limitations; **Vormarsch der Truppen** ~ to hold up the advance of troops.
hemmend handicapping, stunting;
sich ~ auf jds. ganze Entwicklung auswirken to be a drag on s. one all his life;
~**e Wirkung** restraining action.
Hemmnis hindrance, obstruction, obstacle, impediment, handicap, hamper, clog;
finanzbedingte ~se financial handicaps; **konventionelle ~se** shackles of convention; **wirtschaftliches** ~ economic handicap; ~**se für den internationalen Handel** impediments to international trade;
~ **für den Außenhandel darstellen** to be an impediment to foreign trade; **etw. als schweres ~ empfinden** to feel s. th. as a severe handicap.
Hemmschuh drag, stumbling block (stone), skid pan *(Br.)*;
konjunktureller drag on recovery;
~ **der Etikette** trammels of etiquette.
Hemmung restraint, suspension, estoppage, check, arrest, *(psychologisch)* inhibition, *(Verjährung)* interruption;
assoziative ~ association interference; **psychologische** ~ inhibition;
~ **der Verjährungsfrist** interruption (suspense) of the statute of limitations;
keine ~en haben to feel no inhibitions; **alle ~en fallen lassen** to let down the bars, to cut loose; **jds. natürliche ~en lockern** to weaken s. one's inhibitions.
hemmungslos unrestrained, unbridled;
sich ~ betrinken to get beastly drunk (drunk to the light); ~ **weinen** to weep without restraint; **völlig ~ werden** to cut loose.
Hemmungslosigkeit unrestraint;
krankhafte ~ moral insanity.
henken to hang [on the gallows].
Henker deathman, public executioner, hangman, Jack Ketch *(Br.)*;
zum ~ hang it all;
auf den ~ warten to be for the high jump.
Henkers|knecht henchman; ~**mahlzeit** last meal; ~**tod** halter.
Henkerstrick halter, rope for hanging.
herabdrücken to depress, to lower, to abate, to beat down;
Kurse ~ to bear the market; **Preise** ~ to force down the prices.
herabgesetzt reduced, cut, depressed, at a reduced price;
im Werte ~ depreciated; **nicht** ~ unreduced; **und** ~ *(Aktienkapitalzusatzbezeichnung)* and reduced;
~**es Kapital** reduced capital; ~**er Preis** reduced price; **etw. zu ~en Preisen kaufen** to buy s. th. at a bargain.
herablassen, sich to vouchsafe, to condescend, to deign; **sich zu keiner Antwort** ~ not to deign s. o. an answer; **Boot** ~ to lower a boat; **j. an einem Seil** ~ to lower s. o. on a rope.
herablassend, in einem ~en Ton in patronizing tone.
Herablassung condescension, vouchsafement;
j. mit ~ behandeln to treat s. o. patronizingly, to patronize s. o.
herabmindern to reduce, to lower, to diminish;
Geschwindigkeit ~ to reduce (cut) speed.
herabsehen, auf j. to look down one's nose.
herabsetzbar reducible.
herabsetzen to lower, to reduce, to make a reduction, to depress, to bring down, to decrease, to abate, to diminish, to put down, *(Konkurrenzerzeugnisse)* to disparage, to slander, *(kürzen)* to cut, to curtail, *(Löhne)* to nibble, to cut, to lower, to curtail, *(im Rang)* to degrade, *(verächtlich machen)* to belittle, to disparage, to decry;
j. ~ to cry s. o. down, to say black is one's eye; **seine Ausgaben** ~ to cut down one's expenses; **beruflich** ~ to disparage in a profession; **Diskont[satz]** ~ to lower (reduce, cut) the discount (bank, *Br.*, rediscount, *US*) rate; **Geheimhaltungsstufe** ~ to downgrade security classifications; **Geschwindigkeit** ~ to slow down, to decrease (cut) speed; **Kapital** ~ to reduce (write down) capital; **Kaufpreis** ~ to abate the purchase price; **j. in der öffentlichen Meinung** ~ to lower s. o. in the eyes of public opinion; **Mieten** ~ to lower the rents; **Mindestdiskontsatz** ~ to cut the prime *(US)* (minimum lending rate, *Br.*); **Preis** ~ to lower the price; **Preise stark** ~ to chop prices; **Produktion** ~ to curtail (curb) production; **scharf** ~ to scale down; **jds. Spesensatz** ~ to cut down s. one's expenses; **Steuerfreibetrag** ~ to reduce the tax credit rate *(US)*; **Steuern** ~ to reduce taxes; **Tarif** ~ to cut the rates; **im Wert** ~ to lessen, to depress, to depreciate; **Zinssatz** ~ to lower the rate of interest.
herabsetzend *(Reklame)* disparaging;
sich ~ äußern to speak disparagingly;
~**e Werbung** knocking *(Br.)* (competitive, *US*) copy.
Herabsetzung lowering, reduction, cut, cutting [down], bringing (levelling) down, *(Kapital)* cut, reduction, *(Konkurrenzerzeugnis)* disparagement, *(Kürzung)* curtailment, *(Löhne, Steuern, Tarif)* abatement, *(Ruf)* detraction, belittlement, *(Wertminderung)* depreciation;
proportionale ~ abatement in proportion;
~ **des Aktienkapitals** stock depreciation *(US)*, reduction of share capital *(Br.)*; ~ **des Diskontsatzes** reduction in (lowering of) the discount (bank, *Br.*, rediscount, *US*) rate; ~ **der Ergänzungsabgabe** surtax reduction; ~ **des Fremdkapitalanteils** low gearing; ~ **der Geheimhaltungsstufe** downgrading of securitiy classifications; ~ **der Geschwindigkeit** decrease in speed; ~ **des Grundkapitals** reduction of share capital *(Br.)* (capital stock, *US*); ~ **des Kapitals** decrease in capital; ~ **des Kaufpreises** abatement of purchase money; ~ **des Kleinhandelspreises** retail reduction; ~ **der Löhne** wage cut; ~ **der Miete** abatement of rent; ~ **des Mindestdiskontsatzes** cut in the minimum lending rate *(Br.)* (prime rate, *US*); ~ **des Münzwertes** debasement of coinage; ~ **der Preise** price slashing (cut, reduction); ~ **der Punktzahl** *(Rationierung)* downpoint; ~ **der Qualität von Waren** slander of goods; ~ **des Schadensersatzes** reduction of damages; ~ **der Steuerfreibetragssätze** reduction in the tax credit rate *(US)*; ~ **der Truppenstärke** cut in strength; ~ **des Wertes** diminution in value; ~ **der Zinssätze** interest rate cut.
Herabsetzungsklausel abatement clause.
herabsteigen, von seinem hohen Roß to come off of the high horse.
herabstoßen, auf j. wie ein Geier to drop upon s. o. like a ton of bricks.
herabwürdigen to belittle, to degrade;
sich zu etw. ~ to abase (lower) o. s.; **j. zur reinsten Maschine** ~ to reduce s. o. to a mere machine.
Herabwürdigung abasement, degradation, vulgarization, *(Konkurrenzerzeugnisse)* disparagement.
heran|arbeiten, sich an eine Lösung to work one's way towards a solution; **zum Facharbeiter ~bilden** to train to become a skilled worker.
Heranbildung *(Stab)* training, building;
~ **von Nachwuchskräften** executive training.
heranfahren, an die Straßenseite to pull over to the side of the road;
so nahe als möglich ~ to sail up as near as possible.
heranführen, Truppen to assemble troops.
Herangehen approach.
herangehen to approach;
an eine Arbeit ~ to tackle a piece of work (job); **an jds. Bankkonto** ~ to touch s. one's bank account; **an eine Sache** ~ to put one's hand to a task; **ungern an etw.** ~ to go to it like a bear to the stake; **vorsichtig an etw.** ~ to take it slow.

herankommen to draw near;
an j. ~ to get to (reach) s. o.; **an seine früheren Arbeiten nicht** ~ not to reach the standard of s. one's earlier works; **dicht an j.** ~ to come right up to s. o.;
etw. an sich ~ **lassen** to wait and see what happens.

herankommendes Auto oncoming car.

heranmachen, sich an j. to approach s. o.; **sich an ein Problem** ~ to tackle a problem.

heranreichen, an j. to measure up to s. o.; **an j. nicht** ~ not to be in the same class with s. o.; **bis an den Wald** ~ to stretch as far as the wood.

heranreifen, zu einer Schönheit to grow into a beauty.

heranrücken to draw near, to approach;
dicht an j. ~ to move up very close to s. o.; **in Großaufnahme** ~ to zoom.

heranschaffen to supply;
Material ~ to transport material.

heran|schlängeln, sich an j. to sidle up to s. o.; **sich an den Feind ~schleichen** to stalk the enemy; **sich an ein Problem ~tasten** to grapple with (get down to) a problem; **etw. an j. ~tragen** to approach s. o. with s. th.

herantreten, an j. to contact (accost, approach) s. o.; **an seinen Arbeitgeber mit einer Gehaltserhöhung** ~ to approach one's employer about an increase in salary (a raise, *US*); **mit einer Bitte an j.** ~ to ask a favo(u)r of s. o.; **an einen Kunden** ~ to approach (contact) a customer; **an j. mit einem Vorschlag** ~ to make a suggestion to s. o.

heranwachsen, im Wege des Zukaufs zu einem Konzern to take the conglomerate route.

heranwachsend adolescent, adult;
~e Generation rising generation.

Heranwachsender juvenile adult *(Br.)*, minor *(Scot.)*, kid *(US)*.

heranwagen, sich an etw. to dare to do s. th., to make bold, to venture; **sich an die Herausgabe der Betriebszeitung** ~ to try one's hand at editing the staff magazine; **sich an eine Übersetzung** ~ to attempt a translation.

heranziehen *(Fachkraft)* to consult, to call in, to enlist, *(zu einer Umlage)* to assess, to rate;
j. zur Beitragsleistung ~ to collect dues from s. o.; **zur Besteuerung** ~ to levy a tax on; **j. zur Hilfe** ~ to call upon s. o. to help; **einschlägige Literatur** ~ to consult the relevant literature; **Nachfolger** ~ to train a successor; **seine Notizen** ~ to consult one's notes; **Sachverständigen** ~ to call in an expert; **j. zur Unterstützung** ~ to enlist s. one's services; **zum Wehrdienst** ~ to call to the colo(u)rs, to conscript, to draft *(US)*, to induct *(US)*; **zu zusätzlichen Zahlungen** ~ to assess for additional payment.

Heranziehung enlistment;
~ **eines zweiten Arztes in einem Krankheitsfall** association of a second doctor in a case; ~ **von Kapital** mobilization of capital; ~ **zur Kommunalabgabe** rating *(Br.)*; ~ **von Quellen** reference to authorities; ~ **eines Sachverständigen** consultation of an expert; ~ **zu Steuern** imposition of taxes, taxation; ~ **zu zusätzlichen Zahlungen** assessment for additional payments.

herauf|arbeiten, sich to work one's way (o. s.) up (o. s. into a good position); **sich vom Zugabfertiger zum Abteilungspräsidenten ~arbeiten** to work up from a train dispatcher to division superintendent; **öffentlich bekannte Persönlichkeit die Treppe ~befördern** to kick a public man upstairs; **j. ~bemühen** to trouble s. o. to come upwards.

heraufbeschwören to conjure up, to precipitate;
etw. ~ to ask for trouble; **Diskussion** ~ to provoke a discussion; **alte Erinnerungen** ~ to call up old memories; **Gefahren** ~ to court dangers, to pose hazards.

herauf|schalten *(el.)* to step up; **auf 100 km ~schnellen** to creep up to 60 miles an hour.

heraufsetzen to increase, to raise, *(Preise)* to mark (put) up;
Aktienkapital ~ to increase the share *(Br.)* (stock, *US*) capital; **Diskontsatz** ~ to increase the discount (bank, *Br.*, rediscount, *US*) rate; **Geldsätze** ~ to mark up call money; **Herstellungskosten** ~ to increase the cost of goods; **Höchstkurs** ~ to lift the top; **Preise** ~ to raise prices; **Schulentlassungsalter** ~ to raise the school-leaving age; **Steuer** ~ to put up a tax; **Warenpreise** ~ to increase the cost of goods; **Zinsfuß** ~ to increase the rate of interest.

Heraufsetzung increase, *(Preise)* markup;
~ **des Diskontsatzes** raising the discount (bank, *Br.*, rediscount, *US*) rate; ~ **des Kapitals** capital increase; ~ **des Schulentlassungsalters** raising of the school-leaving age.

heraufziehen *(Gewitter)* to draw on (near).

heraus, aus der Stadt outside the town;
~ **mit der Sprache!** speak out!

heraus sein *(Buch)* to be out (published);
aus diesem Alter ~ to have passed this age; **aus dem Ärgsten** ~ to be out of the wood; **fein** ~ to sit pretty; **aus seinen Schwierigkeiten** ~ to have got over one's difficulties.

heraus tun, etw. aus sich to do s. th. on one's own initiative.

herausarbeiten, sich ~ **aus** to climb out of; **sich aus dem Schnee** ~ to work one's way out of the snow; **Tatsachen scharf** ~ to bring out the facts in full relief.

herausbeißen, neuen Angestellten to elbow out a newcomer.

herausbekommen to make (find, nose) out, to get the hang of s. th., *(rechnen)* to figure out *(US coll.)*;
Antwort aus j. ~ to elicit a reply from s. o.; **sein Geld wieder** ~ to get one's money back; **Geständnis aus jem.** ~ to get a confession out of s. o.; **Wechselgeld** ~ to get change;
~, **was los ist** to get wise to what's happening.

herausbringen *(Buch)* to bring (get) out, to publish, to edit, *(Fabrikat)* to turn (get) out, to come out with, to put (launch) on the market;
Antwort aus j. ~ to elicit a reply from s. o.; **Buch rechtzeitig** ~ to get out a book on time; **neues Erzeugnis** ~ to launch a new product; **Nachricht groß** ~ to splash (feature) a piece of news; **Schauspielerin groß** ~ to launch an actress.

herausfahren to move out, *(Bergbau)* to come up;
jem. ~ *(Bemerkung)* to escape from s. o.; **Auto aus der Garage** ~ to drive the car out of the garage; **aus der Station** ~ to pull out of the station; **Vorsprung** ~ to build up a lead.

herausfinden, Fehler ~ to discover mistakes; **genau** ~ to pin down; **sich aus Schwierigkeiten** ~ to extricate o. s. from a difficulty; **etw. sofort** ~ to see s. th. with half an eye;
~, **wie der Hase läuft** to find out how the wind lies.

heraus|fischen, Münze aus der Tasche to fish out a coin from one's pocket; **~fliegen** *(Angestellter)* to be fired (sacked) *(sl.)*.

Herausforderer challenger.

herausfordern to challenge, to throw down the gauntlet, to provoke, to ask for trouble;
etw. ~ to ask for it, to stick one's neck out *(sl.)*; **zur Kritik** ~ to invite (ask for) criticism; **Schicksal** ~ to challenge fate; **Widerspruch** ~ to provoke contradiction; **zum Zweikampf** ~ to call s. o. out.

herausfordernd challenging, defiant, provoking, provocative;
j. ~ **ansehen** to look defiantly at s. o.;
~e Haltung einnehmen to bid defiance to s. o.

Herausforderung challenge, provocation;
wirtschaftliche ~ economic challenge;
~ **annehmen** to accept a challenge; **wie eine** ~ **klingen** to sound like a challenge; **auf eine** ~ **reagieren** to act under provocation.

Herausgabe surrender, *(Briefmarken)* issue, *(Bücher, Zeitungen)* publishing, publication, issue, editing, bringing out, *(Frachtgut)* handing out, delivery, *(Rückerstattung)* restoration, restitution, *(Übergabe)* delivery, handing over;
der ~ **unterliegend** repleviable;
~ **eines Berichts** publication of a report; ~ **von Gefangenen** surrender of prisoners; ~ **gestohlener Gegenstände** restitution of stolen goods;
auf ~ **klagen** to bring an action of detinue; ~ **verlangen** to demand restitution; ~ **eines Kindes verlangen** to demand the surrender of a child; ~ **verweigern** to refuse delivery; **sich an die** ~ **der Betriebszeitung wagen** to try one's hand at editing the staff magazine;
~anspruch claim and delivery, claim for conversion, revindication, claiming back; **~anspruch wegen nichteingehaltenen Heiratsversprechens** entry for marriage in speech; **~beschluß bei zweiter unberechtigter Mietpfändung** writ of recaption; **~klage** revindication (petitory, *Scot.*) action, writ of replevin *(US)*; **~verfügung** *(Pfandsache)* replevy; **~verpflichteter** party to surrender; **~verweigerung** forcible detainer.

herausgeben to hand over, to surrender, *(Briefmarken)* to issue, *(Bücher, Zeitung)* to publish, to edit, to issue, *(übergeben)* to hand over, to deliver, *(zurückgeben)* to restore, to restitute;
Gefangenen ~ to surrender a prisoner; **einem Kunden falsch** ~ to give wrong change to a customer, to short-change *(US)*; **neu** ~ to reedit; **Wechselgeld** ~ to give change for.

Herausgeber [executive] publisher, executive editor;
als ~ **fungieren** to edit;
~gremium joint editors; **~in** woman editor; **~tätigkeit** editorial (editing) work.

herausgegeben von edited (published) by.

herausgehen, aus sich to unbend, to come out of one's shell *(fam.)*, to liven up; **aus Aktien** ~ to switch out of stocks; **auf die Straße** ~ to overlook the street;
jederzeit ~ **können** to have free exit at all times.

heraus|gehende Post outgoing mail; **bunt ~geputzt** dressed up to the nines (fit to kill), spiffed up *(sl.)*; **~geschmissen werden** to get the gate *(US)*, *(Angestellter)* to be fired (sacked) *(sl.)*; **groß ~gestellt** widely heralded; **in der Presse ~gestellt werden** to be given a great buildup in the press; **über die anderen ~gewachsen sein** to have risen above one's equals; **~geworfen werden** to get the boot (sack) *(sl.)*, to be fired (sacked) *(sl.)*; **j. ~greifen** to single s. o. out; **wahllos ~greifen** to pick out at random; **den Bogen ~haben** to have the knack (hang) of it; **sich aus einer Sache ~halten** to keep out of a business.

Heraushaltung keeping out.

heraus|hängen *(Fahne)* to hang out; **zum Halse ~hängen** *(fig.)* to be fed up with it; **j. ~hauen** to get s. o. out of a hole; **jem. aus einem Auto ~helfen** to help s. o. out of a car; **j. aus einer Schwierigkeit ~helfen** to pull s. o. through, to see s. o. through difficulties.

herausholen to get (take) out, to extract;
Auto aus dem Schlamm ~ to extricate a carriage from the mud; **Erfolg ~** to score a success; **Geld aus jem. ~** to get (worm) money out of s. o.; **hohe Gewinne aus einer Firma ~** to derive great profits from a company; **Informationen aus jem. ~** to extract information from s. o.; **Kind aus einem Waisenhaus ~** to take a child away from an orphanage; **das Letzte aus sich ~** to give one's utmost; **Zugeständnis aus jem. ~** to elicit an admission from s. o.

heraus|kehren, seine Überlegenheit to show off one's superiority; **Vorgesetzten ~kehren** to act the boss; **Geld aus jem. ~kitzeln** to worm money out of s. o.; **~klagen** to sue out; **~klamüsern** to puzzle out.

Herauskommen turnout, outcome, result.

herauskommen *(mit einem Artikel)* to come out with, to put (launch) on the market, *(Buch)* to be published, *(Lotterielos)* to come up;
auf dasselbe ~ to be all the same, to make no difference; **aus seinen Geldnöten ~** to get out of one's financial difficulties; **mit einem Gewinn ~** to win a prize; **groß ~** to make a hit, to be a box-office success *(US)*; **nichts Gutes ~** to come a cropper; **aus einer schwierigen Lage ~** to extricate o. s. from a difficulty; **in Lieferungen ~** to be issued in instal(l)ments; **mit einem Lotteriegewinn ~** to draw a prize; **mit seiner Meinung ~** to splash it out; **mit einem neuen Modell ~** to launch a new model on the market; **nicht ~** *(Los)* not to be drawn; **mit der Sprache ~** to own up, to pop *(US)*.

heraus|komplimentieren, j. to bow s. o. out; **sich ~kristallisieren** to crystallize, to take shape; **Buchstelle ~lassen** to strike a passage out of a book; **j. aus einer Geschichte ~lassen** to leave s. one's name out of a story; **auf die Straße ~laufen** to run into the street; **aus einem Brief ~lesen** to read into a letter; **aus einer Erklärung ~lesen** to gather from a statement.

herauslocken, etw. aus jem. to extricate s. th. from s. o., to coax s. th. out of s. o.; **Geheimnis aus jem. ~** to coax a secret out of s. o.; **Geld aus jem. ~** to wheedle money out of s. o.; **ins Freie ~** *(Wetter)* to draw out into the open; **j. aus seiner Reserve ~** to draw s. o. out.

heraus|machen, sich *(Firma)* to make good progress, to turn out well; **Flecken ~machen** to remove a stain; **j. aus etw. ~manövrieren** to manoeuvre s. o. out of s. th.; **sich aus einer schwierigen Lage ~manövrieren** to extricate o. s. from a difficulty.

Herausnahme bestimmter Gebiete *(Völkerrecht)* removal of specified territories.

herausnehmbar removable.

herausnehmen to take out, to remove;
sich gegenüber jem. zu viel ~ to make free (take liberties) with s. o.; **sich Frechheiten ~** to be impertinent; **sich Freiheiten ~** to take liberties; **Schüler aus der Schule ~** to take a pupil from school.

heraus|picken, sich die schönsten Rosinen to take the pick of the bunch; **mit etw. unbedacht ~platzen** to blunder out; **mit der Wahrheit ~platzen** to blurt out the truth; **Geld aus jem. ~pressen** to squeeze money out of s. o.; **Geständnis aus jem. ~pressen** to wrest a confession from s. o.; **einige Tränen ~pressen** to squeeze out a few tears; **~putzen** to trim up, to trick out (up); **aus einem Sportstadium ~quellen** to surge out of a sports stadium; **über alle anderen ~ragen** to tower above everyone; **aus den Ereignissen ~ragen** to rise above events; **sich aus einer schwierigen Situation ~reden** to talk one's way out of a difficulty; **Buchseite ~reißen** to tear a page out of a book; **j. aus dem Schlaf ~reißen** to startle s. o. from his sleep; **Kind aus seiner vertrauten Umgebung ~reißen** to remove a child from familiar surroundings.

herausrücken, Geld to cough up *(US sl.)*, to fork out *(sl.)*; **mit einer außergewöhnlichen Geschichte ~** to come out with an extraordinary story; **mit der Sprache ~** to own up, to pop *(US)*; **mit der Wahrheit ~** to come clean *(sl.)*.

heraus|rufen to call out; **~rutschen** *(Bemerkung)* to slip out; **Möbel ~schaffen** to remove furniture.

herausschälen, sich *(Begabung)* to become apparent, *(Problem)* to crystallize, to take shape; **sich aus einer Diskussion ~** to emerge from a discussion; **besondere Idee ~** to single out an idea; **sich aus seinen Kleidern ~** to peel off one's clothes; **wesentliche Punkte einer Rede ~** to extract important passages from a speech.

Herausschieben von Zahlungen postponement of payment.

heraus|schieben, etw. bis zur letzten Minute to drive s. th. to the last minute; **Zahlungen ~schieben** to postpone payment; **aus einer Seitenstraße ~schießen** *(Auto)* to swing out of a side street; **~schinden** to eke out; **Geld aus jem. ~schinden** to extract money from s. o.; **zusätzliche Urlaubswoche ~schinden** to wangle an extra week's holiday.

herausschlagen, aus dem Fenster *(Flammen)* to leap out of the window; **Geld aus einer Sache ~** to get one's money's worth; **Orden für sich ~** to wangle a decoration for o. s.; **allerlei Vorteile ~** to gain all kinds of advantages.

heraus|schmeißen to kick downstairs, to turf out *(Br., sl.)*, *(Angestellte)* to fire, to sack *(sl.)*, *(aus dem Auto)* to shell out *(sl.)*; **Betrunkenen aus dem Lokal ~schmeißen** to chuck a drunken man out of a pub; **Unfähige ~schmeißen** to weed out the incompetents; **~schneiden** to cut out; **sich ~schwindeln** to talk one's way out; **~setzen** *(Mieter)* to evict, to eject, to turn out.

Herausspringen einer Sicherung blow of a fuse.

heraus|springen *(Sicherung)* to blow out; **aus dem Fenster ~springen** to jump out of the window; **wieviel wird für mich dabei ~springen?** how much do I get out of it?; **~sprudeln** to well up, to bubble out; **seine Unglücksgeschichte ~sprudeln** to pour out one's tale of misfortune; **sich mächtig ~staffiert haben** to be dressed to kill.

herausstellen to point out;
besonders ~ to emphasize, *(Presse)* to feature, to highlight *(US)*; **sich ~** to turn out, to emerge, to come to light; **sich als falsch ~** to prove false; **sich als Fälschung ~** to prove to be a forgery; **groß ~** to give a build-up; **lobend ~** to write up; **sich als mißglückt ~** *(Anlage)* to turn sour; **Nachricht besonders ~** to splash up a piece of news; **in einer Rede klar ~** to present clearly in a speech; **sich als richtig ~** to prove correct; **Schauspielerin ~** to launch an actress; **Schwierigkeiten klar ~** to lay stress on difficulties; **sich als unbegründet ~** to turn out (be proved) unfounded; **jds. Verdienst ~** to notice s. one's services; **sich als wahr ~** to turn out to be true.

heraus|streichen to delete, to cross out; **sich ~streichen** to blow one's own trumpet; **Absatz ~streichen** to delete (strike out) a paragraph; **aus dem Theater ~strömen** to trickle out of the theatre; **sich die besten Sachen ~suchen** to take the pick of the bunch; **aus seiner Reserve ~treten** to come out of one's shell *(fam.)*; **~verlangen** to reclaim, to replevin *(US)*; **aus seinen Kleidern ~wachsen** to outgrow one's clothes; **~werfen** to put out, *(Beamten)* to boot out of office, *(kündigen)* to fire, to sack *(sl.)*; **j. ~werfen** to turn s. o. out of the house; **sich irgendwie ~winden** to wangle through somehow, to wriggle out of s. th.; **sich aus einer schwierigen Situation ~winden** to extricate o. s. from a difficult situation; **~wirtschaften** to earn, to obtain, to work at a profit; **durch Einsparungen ~wirtschaften** to economize; **Geld für eine Reise ~wirtschaften** to save up money for a holiday.

Herauswurf firing *(coll.)*, sack *(sl.)*.

herauszahlen to pay out;
jem. seinen Anteil ~ to pay s. o. out.

herausziehen *(Geld)* to withdraw;
j. aus dem Bett ~ to drag s. o. out of bed; **Geld aus jem. ~** to get money out of s. o.; **aufs Land ~** to move into the country; **sich leidlich aus einer Sache ~** to shuffle out of an awkward situation; **jedes Wort aus jem. ~** to wrest every word from s. o.

herbeieilen to rush to the scene.

herbeiführen to cause, to effect, to precipitate, to bring about;
Besserung ~ to bring about an improvement; **Einigung ~** to reach an agreement; **Mißverständnisse ~** to give rise to misunderstandings; **Unfall ~** to cause an accident; **Zahlungsunfähigkeit vorsätzlich ~** to contemplate insolvency.

Herbeiführung causation, initiation;
vorsätzliche ~ der Zahlungsunfähigkeit contemplation of insolvency.

herbei | holen to fetch; **Polizei ~rufen** to call the police; **~schaffen** to procure, to provide; **Geld ~schaffen** to raise funds (the wind, *sl.*); **jds. Rückkehr ~sehnen** to long for s. one's return; **in Scharen ~strömen** to come in crowds, to flock in; **Taxi ~winken** to signal a taxi; **Wochenende ~wünschen** to be longing for the weekend; **an den Haaren ~ziehen** to drag by head and shoulders.
herbemühen, sich to trouble to come.
Herberge inn, road house, house of accommodation, housing, harbo(u)r, *(Jugendherberge)* hostel;
~ bei jem. finden to find lodgings in s. one's house; **einem Flüchtling ~ geben** to give shelter to a fugitive.
Herbergsvater host, dossman *(Br., sl.)*.
Herbst | des Lebens fall of life;
~artikel fall merchandise *(US)*; **~belebung** autumn upswing; **~ferien** autumn holiday; **~mode** autumn *(Br.)* (fall, *US*) fashion.
Herd hearth, *(fig.)* focus, center *(US)* (centre, *Br.*);
am heimischen ~ by the fireside;
elektrischer ~ electric stove; **häuslicher ~** fireside;
~ des Aufruhrs center *(US)* (centre, *Br.*) of a rebellion; **~ eines Erdbebens** centre of an earthquake; **~ mit vier Kochstellen** cooker with four hot plates; **~ der Unruhen** focus of unrest; **seinen eigenen ~ gründen** to set up for o. s.; **zum heimischen ~ zurückkehren** to return home;
eigner ~ ist Goldes wert there's no place like home, nothing like leather;
~buch herdbook.
Herde herd, flock, *(fig.)* drove;
~ hüten to tend a flock; **mit der ~ laufen** to follow the crowd.
Herden | instinkt herd instinct; **wie ~vieh ins Wartezimmer treiben** to herd into the waiting room.
Herdplatte hot plate.
herein come in;
~ in die gute Stube pile in *(coll.)*, roll up, step in *(US)*.
Hereinbekommen einer Schuld getting in of debt.
hereinbekommen *(Außenstände)* to recover debts, *(Ware)* to get in;
seine Außenstände nicht ~ not to clear one's expenses; **seine Verluste durch Börsentransaktionen wieder ~** to recoup one's losses in gaining on the stock exchange.
hereinbitten, j. to bid s. o. to come in, to ask (invite) s. o. in.
hereinbrechen *(Dämmerung)* to fall, *(Winter)* to set in;
über ein Land ~ to befall a country.
Hereinbringen | der Ernte harvesting, gathering in of the crop, harvest collection; **~ eines Geschäftes** business getting.
herein | bringen to bring in, *(Ernte)* to gather, *(Geschäft)* to get; **~drängen** to crowd (push) in; **~fahren** to drive in.
Hereinfall disappointment, let-down, *(Theaterstück)* flop.
hereinfallen to fall into a trap;
mit etw. ~ to make a mistake (boo-boo, *US fam.*) with s. th.; **auf diese Art von Reklame leicht ~** to be a pushover for that sort of advertising; **auf Schmeicheleien ~** to succumb to flattery; **auf einen Schwindler ~** to be taken in (tricked) by a swindler; **mit dem Wetter ~** to be unlucky with the weather;
j. ~ lassen to trap s. o., to do s. o. in the eye.
hereinführen to show (usher) in.
hereingeben *(Wertpapiere)* to deposit, to give on.
Hereingeber *(Börse)* depositor, giver-on *(Br.)*.
hereingelegt, ganz schön ~ worden sein to have been badly let down; **ganz schön ~ werden** to get nicely left *(coll.)*.
Hereingelegter victim, dupe.
herein | geleiten to usher in; **~genommen** *(Wertpapiere)* taken in; **zufällig ~geschneit kommen** to happen *(US coll.)*; **Aufträge ~holen** to canvass (solicit) orders.
Hereinholung von Aufträgen solicitation (canvassing) of orders.
herein | kommen *(Aufträge)* to come in, to perk up, *(Geld)* to roll in; **gut ~kommen** *(Geld)* to come in well, to pour in; **~komplimentieren** to usher in.
hereinlegen, j. to fool s. o., to do s. o. in the eye, to let (take) s. o. in *(Br., sl.)*, to hoodwink s. o., to do s. o. down *(Br., coll.)*, to brown s. o. *(Br., sl.)*, to pull a fast one on s. o. *(sl.)*; **j. richtig (ganz schön) ~** to sell s. o. a pup, to pull s. th. on s. o. *(coll.)*, to do s. o. nicely *(sl.)*, to play a pretty trick upon s. o.; **j. in gemeiner Weise ~** to do s. o. dirt *(US sl.)*.
Hereinnahme purchase, *(Reportgeschäft)* taking in *(Br.)*, carrying over, *(Wechsel)* discounting of bills.
hereinnehmen to take in stock, *(Börse)* to carry over, to take in *(Br.)*;
zum Diskont ~ to discount; **Ware ~** to take in stock; **Wechsel zum Inkasso ~** to accept bills for collection.
Hereinnehmer *(Reportgeschäft)* receiver, taker [in] *(Br.)*.
herein | nötigen, j. to urge s. o. to come in; **Menschen in einen schon überfüllten Bus ~pferchen** to pack people into an already overcrowded bus; **in ein Zimmer ~platzen** to burst into a room; **~rasseln** *(Prüfling)* to run into deep water; **j. ~reiten, ~reißen** to get s. o. into a mess; **sich selbst ~reiten** to get o. s. into a bad fix; **nächsten Patienten ins Behandlungszimmer ~rufen** to call the next patient into the office (surgery, *Br.*); **für einen Augenblick ~schauen** to drop in for a moment; **Geschenke ins Haus ~schmuggeln** to sneak presents into one's house; **~schneien** *(fam.)* to drop in; **~spaziert kommen** to trot in; **~strömen** *(Aufträge)* to flow (pour) in; **ins Zimmer ~stürmen** to dash into the room; **j. in etw. ~ziehen** to drag s. o. into s. th.; **leicht ~zulegen sein** to be an easy mark.
Herfahrt journey (way) back.
herfallen, über j. to be down on s. o., to walk into s. o.; **über ein Buch ~** to attack a book;
Her | fracht inward cargo, home freight; **~gabe** delivery, handing over, surrender; **~gang** course of events.
hergeben, für eine Diskussion nichts not to offer enough for a discussion; **sein ganzes Geld ~** to part with all one's money; **seinen Namen zu etw. ~** to lend one's name to s. th.; **seine letzten Reserven ~** to go all out; **sich zu einer Sache ~** to lend o. s. to a transaction.
her | gebracht customary, usual; **weit ~geholte Gründe** farfetched reasons; **~gelaufener Kerl** vagabond, tramp, bum *(US)*; **~gelaufenes Gesindel** riff-raff.
hergestellt made, produced, manufactured;
in Deutschland ~ made in Germany; **fabrikmäßig ~** factory-made, fabricated, manufactured; **teilweise maschinell ~** part-machined; **maschinenmäßig ~** machine-made; **ordnungsgemäß ~** properly manufactured;
genügend ~ werden to be in good production; **nicht mehr ~ werden** to be no longer in production.
herhalten müssen to have to pay;
als Gesprächsstoff ~ to have to serve as a topic.
Hering, eingelegter pickled herring;
richtiger ~ sein to be as thin as a rake; **wie die ~e sitzen** to be packed like sardines.
herjagen, hinter etw. to chase off after s. th. *(coll.)*; **hinter dem Geld ~** to be keen on moneymaking, to worship mammon.
Herkommen custom, observance, tradition, ancestry, use, usage, *(Herkunft)* descent, family, lineage, extraction;
durch ~ sanktioniert sanctioned by usage.
herkommen to issue, to proceed, *(Schiff)* to sail from;
von überall ~ to arrive from all quarters.
herkömmlich conventional, customary, usual, ordinary.
Herkulesarbeit labo(u)r of Hercules.
Herkunft descent, descendance, nativity, spring, origin, birth, blood, family background, *(Waren)* provenance;
ausländischer ~ of foreign origin; **von edler ~** of noble stem; **von einfacher ~** of simple birth; **von unbekannter ~** of unknown origin; **von vornehmer ~** of gentle extraction;
gesellschaftliche ~ social background; **örtliche ~** regional origin;
englischer ~ sein to be British by birth; **von unbekannter ~ sein** to be of obscure origin.
Herkunfts | bescheinigung certificate of origin, origin brand; **~bezeichnung, ~kennzeichen** mark of origin, informative labelling; **~land** country of origin, producing (shipping) country; **~nachweis** proof of origin; **~ort** point of origin *(US)*; **~ortsschau** point-of-purchase display; **~zeugnis** certificate of origin.
herlaufen, hinter jem. to run after s. o.
herleiten, seine Abkunft to trace one's descent; **sein Eigentumsrecht von jem. ~** to derive one's title from s. o.
Herleitung derivation;
~ eines Anspruchs deduction of a claim.
hermachen, etw. to be effective, to look impressive; **sich über j. ~** to go for s. o. *(fam.)*, to pull s. o. to pieces; **sich über die Arbeit ~** to pitch into the work, to get down to a job; **sich über das Essen ~** to pitch into the pie; **von etw. viel ~** to make a great fuss about s. th.
Hermes | bürgschaft [etwa] Export Credit Guarantee; **~gesellschaft** [etwa] Export Credits Guarantee Department *(Br.)*, Foreign Credit Insurance Association *(US)*.
hermetisch | abgeschlossen hermetically sealed; **~ abriegeln** to shut down like a clam; **Gegend ~ abriegeln** to seal off an area.
hernehmen to get, to take;
j. richtig ~ to put s. o. through the mill; **j. scharf ~** to give s. o. a good talking to.

Herr gentleman, *(Gebieter)* master, lord;
mein alter ~ my old man, my governor; **besserer ~** distinguished gentleman;
sich als feinen ~n aufspielen to be highty and mighty; **sich jem. gegenüber als ~n aufspielen** to lord it over s. o.; **zweierlei ~en dienen** to serve two masters; **seinen ~n und Meister finden** to meet one's match; **sein eigener ~ sein** to be one's own master, to be independent; **nicht ~ freier Entschlüsse sein** to have one's hands tied; **~ im Hause sein** to be master in one's own house; **~ der Lage sein** to master (be the master of) a situation, to have a situation under control (the ball on one's feet, *Br.*); **nicht mehr ~ seiner Sinne sein** to have lost control of o. s.; **den großen ~n spielen** to act like the boss, to come the fine gentleman *(Br.)*; **einer Epidemie ~ werden** to bring an epidemic under control; **einer Lage ~ werden** to outface a situation; **seiner Schwierigkeiten ~ werden** to tide over one's difficulties; **wie der ~ so's Geschirr** like master, like man.
Herren|abend stag party, bull session *(US)*; **~artikelgeschäft** hosiers, haberdashery *(US)*, clothing store *(US)*; **~ausstatter** gentlemen's outfitter, haberdasher *(US)*, hosier; **~essen** stag dinner; **an einem ~essen teilnehmen** to sling the bull *(sl.)*; **~fahrer** owner-driver; **~gesellschaft** stag party, bull session *(US)*; **~haus** mansion (manor) house, manor, residence; **großes ~haus** handsome residence, stately home; **~leben führen** to live like a lord.
herrenlos vacant, unappropriated, unowned, ownerless, abandoned, in abeyance, derelict, unpossessed;
~ sein *(Grundstück)* to lie in franchise;
~e Aktie unclaimed share (stock, *US*); **~es Auto** abandoned car; **~es Gut** derelicts; **~e Sachen** res derelicta, derelicts; **~es Tier** stray.
Herren|mode men's fashion; **~modeartikel** hosiery, haberdashery *(US)*; **~modenhändler** hosier, haberdasher *(US)*; **~reiter** gentleman-jockey; **~sitz** gentleman's residence, mansion house, manor residence; **~toilette** men's room; **~zimmer** smoking room, study.
Herrgott God, the Lord;
dem lieben ~ den Tag stehlen to eat the bread of idleness.
Herrgottsfrühe, in aller at an unearthly hour.
herrichten to arrange, to furbish [up], *(Zimmer)* to do up, to tidy, to clear;
Auslage ~ to dress a shop window; **behelfsmäßig ~** to rig up; **Bett für die Nacht ~** to make up a bed for the night; **für einen Empfang ~** to arrange for a reception; **altes Haus ~** to renovate (refurbish) a house; **Zimmer als Büro ~** to adapt a room to office use; **Zimmer neu ~** to redecorate a room.
Herrichtung| eines Zimmers als Büro adaptation of a room to office use; **handelsübliche ~ der Ware** customary preparation of goods.
Herrin mistress, lady.
herrisch imperious, domineering, *(hochfahrend)* high-handed, overbearing;
~es Auftreten overbearingness; **in einem ~en Ton reden** to speak in a sharp key.
herrlich magnificent, grand, great, marvel(l)ous, splendid;
~ und in Freuden leben to live on the fat of the land;
~e Aussicht magnificent view; **~es Feuerwerk** grand display of fireworks; **~er Sonnenuntergang** marvel(l)ous sunset; **~es Wetter** glorious (splendid) weather.
Herrschaft reign, sovereignty, rule, rulership, dominion, sway, throne, mastery, helm, *(größerer Landbesitz)* seigniority, demesne, domain, *(Kontrolle)* grasp, power, control, grip;
bei der ~ abovestairs; **unter französischer ~** under French dominion;
territoriale ~ territorial power; **unumschränkte ~** rule absolute *(Br.)*;
~ über ein Fahrzeug control of a motor car; **~ des Gesetzes** reign of law; **~ über die Meere** control of the seas, maritime reign; **~ der Mehrheit** majority rule; **~ des Pöbels** mob rule, ochlocracy; **~ der Verbraucherherrschaft** consumers' sovereignty;
~ antreten to assume the reins of government; **~ ausüben** to wield power; **~ über ein Land ausüben** to dominate over a people, to rule over a country; **Volk unter seine ~ bringen** to bring a people under one's sway; **~ an sich reißen** to seize power; **unter jds. ~ stehen** to be ruled by s. o., to be under the sway of s. o.; **~ über sein Auto verlieren** to lose control of one's car.
herrschaftlich manorial, *(elegant)* grand, elegant, imposing;
~er Diener gentleman's servant.
Herrschafts|antritt accession to power; **~ausübung** jurisdiction.
Herrschaftsbereich domain, sovereignty;
seinen ~ ausdehnen to extend one's power; **~ eines Staates ausdehnen** to aggrandize a state; **in jds. ~ leben** to be under s. one's dominion.
Herrschafts|gebiet dominion, sovereign territory; **britisches ~gebiet** foreign dominion *(Br.)*; **~gewalt** jurisdiction.
Herrschaftsrecht vested estate;
aufschiebend bedingtes ~ executory remainder; **vertragliches ~** conventional estate;
~ an einem Grundstück legal estate in land.
Herrschaftssystem begründen, neues to set up a new order.
herrschen to govern, to rule, to sway, to be supreme, to be at the helm, *(Mode)* to be en vogue, *(Krankheit)* to become rife, *(Monarch)* to rule, to reign;
despotisch ~ to domineer; **über ein Königreich ~** to reign over a kingdom; **unumschränkt ~** to have absolute power, to wield omnipotent control; **über ein Volk ~** to rule over a country, to dominate over a people.
herrschend ruling, dominant, governing;
~e Gesellschaftsschichten ruling classes, establishment; **~es Grundstück** dominant estate (tenement), superior estate; **~e Lehre** prevailing doctrine; **~e Meinung** received opinion (doctrine); **~e Mode** leading (prevailing, current) fashion; **~e Partei** party in power; **~es Unternehmen** controlling company; **hierzulande ~e Vorurteile** prejudices prevailing in this country.
Herrscher sovereign, prince, ruler, dynast, throne, dominator, governor;
vom Parlament kontrollierter ~ constitutional ruler; **rechtmäßiger ~** lawful ruler;
nur dem Namen nach ~ sein to rule nominally;
~familie royal family; **~geschlecht** dynasty; **~gewalt** sovereign power (prerogative); **~haus** dynasty, ruling family.
her|rühren to emanate from, to originate with, to stem from; **aus dem Krieg ~rühren** to date from the war; **wie am Schnürchen ~sagen** to have s. th. at one's finger-tips; **Entscheidung vor sich ~schieben** to keep putting off a decision; **hinter jem. ~spionieren** to spy upon s. o.; **~stammen** to derive, to come (stem) from.
herstellbar producible;
maschinell ~ machinable.
Herstellbarkeit producibility.
herstellen to make, to fabricate, to manufacture, to produce, to turn out, *(verarbeiten)* to process;
Beziehungen ~ to establish relations; **Erfindungsgegenstand ~** to produce an invention; **fabrikmäßig ~** to manufacture, *(Hausteile)* to prefabricate; **Film ~** to produce a film; **Gebäude wieder ~** to restore a ruined building; **Geschäftsverbindung zu jem. ~** to establish business relations with s. o.; **wirtschaftliches Gleichgewicht ~** to establish an economic balance; **in der Hauptsache für den Export ~** to produce mainly for export; **künstlich ~** to synthesize; **lagermäßig ~** to make for stock; **maschinell ~** to machine; **als Massenartikel ~** to mass-produce; **in der Minute 100 Stück ~** to turn out a hundred a minute; **Produkte maschinenmäßig ~** to produce goods by machinery; **Produktionsaufträge in einem fremden Werk herstellen lassen** to hive off production; **serienmäßig ~** to serialize; **für j. eine Telefonverbindung ~** to put s. o. through; **Verbindung mit jem. ~** to make contact with s. o.; **Verbindung vom Haus zur Garage ~** to connect the house with the garage; **Waren verschiedenster Beschaffenheit (Qualität) ~** to manufacture goods in various qualities; **Waren ohne fremde Kräfte ~** to manufacture articles without exterior help; **zusammen ~** to coproduce.
herstellend producing.
Hersteller maker, fabricator, fabricant, producer, operator, manufacturing man, manufacturer, *(Film)* producer, *(Verlag)* production assistant;
direkt absetzender ~ direct-marketing (-selling) manufacturer; **mit geringen Selbstkosten arbeitender ~** low-cost operator; **teurer ~** high-cost producer;
~ mit breitem Produktionsprogramm diversified producer (manufacturer);
~auslage producer's display; **~firma** manufacturer, manufacturing firm, *(Film)* producer; **~gewinn** producer's surplus; **~gruppe** manufacturing group; **~marke** producer's (manufacturer's, maker's) mark; **~preis** producer's cost (factory) price; **~typenbezeichnung** production certificate; **~umsatzsteuer** manufacturer's excise tax; **~verband** producer association; **~vermerk** *(drucktechn.)* impress, imprint; **~werbung** producer advertising; **gemeinsame Händler- und ~werbung** vertical cooperative society; **~werk** manufacturing enterprise (establishment); **~zeichen** trademark.

Herstellung making, make, fabrication, manufacture, manufacturing, producing, production;
in der ~ in process;
fabrikmäßige ~ wholesale (mass-production) manufacture; **großtechnische** ~ large-scale manufacture; **maschinelle** ~ machining, machine production; **serienmäßige** ~ serialization, mass (serial, volume) production, production in bulk;
~ **von Abzügen** developing of prints; ~ **einer vollstreckbaren Ausfertigung** preparation of a document for execution; ~ **einer Ausgabe** issue production; ~ **von Automobilen** fabrication of automobiles; ~ **am laufenden Band** standardized mass (line) production; ~ **falschen Beweismaterials** fabrication of evidence; ~ **freundschaftlicher Beziehungen** *(Völkerrecht)* rapprochement, establishment of cordial relations; ~ **der Druckunterlagen** production; ~ **von Eisen-, Blech- und Metallwaren** production of hardware; ~ **der ehelichen Gemeinschaft** restitution of conjugal rights; ~ **schnell verbrauchbarer Güter** soft-goods production; ~ **transportabler Häuser** mobile-home manufacturing; ~ **von Konfektionsware** apparel manufacture *(US)*; ~ **von Massengütern** quantity manufacturing, production in bulk (of manufactured goods); ~ **von Produktionsaufträgen in einem fremden Werk** hive-off of products; ~ **eines Telefonanschlusses** connection of a new telephone; ~ **einer Verbindung** establishment of a connection, contracting; ~ **von Zeichentrickfilmen** animation of cartoons; ~ **eines Zeitschriftenheftes** issue production; ~ **des früheren Zustandes** restitution of the former state; ~ **des ursprünglichen Zustands** restoration of the original position;
sofort mit der ~ **beginnen** to rush off into production; **mit der serienmäßigen** ~ **beginnen** to start full production; ~ **einschränken** to curtail production; ~ **einstellen** to discontinue the manufacture; **in der** ~ **begriffen sein** to be in process of production; ~ **steigern** to step up production; **Vorbereitungen für die** ~ **treffen** to arrange for the manufacture; **sich zusätzlich auf die** ~ **verlegen** to expand into manufacturing.

Herstellungs|abteilung manufacturing division, *(Verlag)* production department (division); ~**anlagen** manufacturing facilities; ~**art** production method; ~**aufwand** production cost, *(Versorgungsbetrieb)* original cost; ~**beginn eines Erzeugnisses** inception of a product; ~**berechnung** costing, cost accounting; ~**bereitschaft** readiness to go into production; ~**beschränkungen** production restrictions; ~**betrieb** manufacturing enterprise (establishment, company, firm, place, corporation, *US*), manufactory, *(Vorgang)* manufacturing operations; **billigster** ~**betrieb** lowest-cost manufacturer; ~**betrieb mit breitgestreutem Produktionsprogramm** diversified producer; ~**dauer** production time; ~**firma** manufacturing company; ~**gang** manufacturing process; ~**gebiet** production area; ~**gesellschaft** manufacturing company (corporation, *US*); ~**jahr** year of manufacture, *(Münze)* date; ~**konto** manufacturing (production) account.

Herstellungskosten cost of manufacturing (manufacture, goods manufactured), manufacturing cost (expenses), manufacturer's price, expenses of production, factory (production, processing) cost, indirect expenses, *(Selbstkosten)* cost price, prime cost, actual costs, *(Verleger)* cost of production;
effektive ~ actual costs; **reine** ~ mere cost of production;
~ **zuzüglich Normalgewinnzuschlag** price of production;
~ **verbilligen** to cheapen (reduce) the cost of manufacture;
~**berechnung** cost accounting, costing.

Herstellungs|land producing (manufacturing) country; ~**leiter** production manager, *(Verlag)* production manager; ~**lizenz** licence (license, *US*) to manufacture, manufacturing licence; ~**lizenz ausnutzen** to manufacture under licence; ~**methode** manufacturing process; ~**monopol** manufacturing monopoly; ~**muster** preproduction model; ~**nummer** manufacturer's number; ~**ort** place of production (manufacture), manufacturing place; ~**politik** product policy; ~**posten** manufactured item, lot; ~**prämie** bounty.

Herstellungspreis cost of manufacture, manufacturing (manufacturer's, production) price, producer's cost price, *(Selbstkosten)* cost price, prime cost, actual costs;
scharf kalkulierte ~**e** strict cost prices;
mit einem ~ **von ... zu Buch stehen** to stand at cost at ...; **unter dem** ~ **verkaufen** to sell below cost.

Herstellungs|programm manufacturing (production) program(me), production schedule; **rationalisiertes** ~**programm** production rationalization; **sein** ~**programm abrunden** to round off one's production; ~**projekt** manufacturing project; ~**prozeß** manufacturing (industrial, production) process, productive technique; ~**prozeß durch bessere Fabrikationsmethoden steigern** to increase production by better methods; ~**rechte** manufacturing (production) rights; **alleiniges** ~**recht haben** to have the exclusive rights in a production; ~**stätte** producing center *(US)* (centre, *Br.*); ~**system** production system; ~**unternehmen** manufacturing enterprise (establishment); ~**verbot** production prohibition.

Herstellungsverfahren manufacturing (production) process, production (manufacturing) technique, manufacturing service (method), operating procedure;
geheimes ~ secret [manufacturing] process; **industrielles** ~ industrial techniques (process of manufacture), know-how; **patentiertes** ~ proprietary industrial process; **rationelles** ~ efficient manufacturing process.

Herstellungs|vertrag manufacturing agreement; ~**vorschriften** production prescriptions; ~**werk** manufacturing enterprise (establishment, plant).

Herstellungswert production value, *(Selbstkosten)* value at cost, cost value, prime cost;
mit einem ~ **von ... zu Buch stehen** to stand at cost at ...

Herstellungs|zeichen [maker's] brand, trademark; ~**zeit** period of production, production time.

hertrödeln, hinter den anderen to linger behind the others.

herüber|schaffen to carry (get) over; **j. zu sich** ~**ziehen** to win s. o. over, to get s. o. on one's side *(fam.)*.

herum about, around *(US)*, in the neighbo(u)rhood of;
~**albern** to horse around *(fam.)*; **sich mit jem.** ~**ärgern** to keep getting annoyed with s. o.; **stundenlang an seinem Radiogerät** ~**basteln** to have an hour's tinker at the radio set; ~**bekommen** to win over; **Tag irgendwie** ~**bekommen** to spend the day somehow; **in einem Buch** ~**blättern** to leaf (page, *US*) through a book; ~**bummeln** to stroll, to saunter along; **bei den Schularbeiten** ~**bummeln** to dawdle over one's homework; **an einer Sache** ~**doktern** to fiddle over a job; ~**drehen** to turn about; **sich im Kreis** ~**drehen** to rotate on its own axis, *(Gedanken)* to get round in circles; **jem. das Wort im Munde** ~**drehen** to twist s. one's words.

herumdrücken, sich to shirk, to dodge, to evade, to stall *(US)*; **sich um etw.** ~ to weasel out of s. th. *(coll.)*; **sich um die Beantwortung einer Frage** ~ to dodge a question; **sich um die Bezahlung seiner Schulden** ~ to evade payment of one's debts; **sich um eine Entscheidung** ~ to shirk a decision; **sich um den Militärdienst** ~ to dodge military service.

herumdrucksen to squirm;
an einer Antwort ~ to hum and haw over an answer.

herumerzählen, etw. to tell s. th. abroad; **Geschichte** ~ to spread a story; **etw. überall** ~ to bruit it (bandy a story) about.

herumexperimentieren to try various methods.

Herumfahren auf Fahrgastsuche *(Taxi)* plying for hire *(Br.)*, cruising.

herumfahren to travel about;
um ein Hindernis ~ to drive round an obstacle; **um die ganze Insel mit dem Motorboot** ~ to go right round the island in a motorboat; **auf Kundensuche** ~ *(Taxi)* to cruise, to ply for hire *(Br.)*; **im Nebel im Kreis** ~ to go round in a circle in the fog; **stundenlang in der Stadt** ~ to drive (ride, *US*) around town for hours; **um die Stadt** ~ to bypass the town; **in der ganzen Welt** ~ to roam about the world.

herum|faseln to tell a long rigmarole; ~**flanieren** to ooze, to fool along, to scrounge around; **auf den Straßen** ~**flanieren** to idle about the street; **in ganz Europa zu seinem Vergnügen** ~**fliegen** to wing around the Continent on pleasure; **überall** ~**fragen** to ask everywhere.

herumführen, jem. to show s. o. round; **jem. an der Nase** ~ to lead s. o. by the nose, to lead s. o. up the garden path; **jem. in der Stadt** ~ to take (show) s. o. all over the town.

herumfuhrwerken, in der Küche to muck about in the kitchen *(Br., sl.)*.

herumfummeln to fumble (fiddle, mess) around, to monkey about with s. th.;
stundenlang an seinem Radio ~ to have an hour's tinker at the radio.

herumgehen *(Zeit)* to pass;
in großem Bogen um j. ~ to give s. o. a wide berth; **um etw. in weitem Bogen** ~ to keep clear of s. th.; **bei allen Familienangehörigen** ~ to pass round to all the members of the family; **um das ganze Grundstück** ~ *(Zaun)* to encircle the entire estate; **wie die Katze um den heißen Brei** ~ to beat around the bush; **um den Kern der Sache** ~ to evade (dodge, shirk) the issue; **jem. im Kopf** ~ to pass through s. one's head; **im Kreis** ~ to go round in a circle; **jem. wie ein Mühlrad im Kopf** ~ to make s. one's head swim; **schnell** ~ *(Ferienzeit)* to have passed

quickly, *(Gerücht)* to be spread abroad quickly; **in der Stadt ~** to wander through the town; **im Zimmer ~** to pace the floor; **Melodie im Kopf ~ haben** to have a tune on the brain *(fam.)*.

herumgeistern, unruhig im Haus to wander restlessly about the house; **in jds. Kopf ~** to be in s. one's mind.

herumgekommen sein, in der Welt to have seen the world.

herumhacken, auf etw. to cross the T's; **auf jem. ~** to find fault with s. o., to peck at s. o., to pull to s. o. to pieces; **auf einem Kind dauernd ~** to be always on at a child.

herumhantieren, an Geräten to monkey about with tools; **in der Küche ~** to be busy in the kitchen; **an seinem Radiogerät ~** to fool about with one's wireless set; **an einem Schlüsselloch ~** to fumble at a lock; **in seinen Unterlagen ~** to meddle in one's papers, to shuffle one's notes.

herum|horchen to keep one's ears open; **im Nebel ~irren** to have lost one's way in the fog; **ziellos in den Straßen ~irren** to wander aimlessly in the streets; **an einem Problem ~kauen** to ponder (chew) over a problem; **auf dem Klavier ~klimpern** to strum on the piano; **an einem Problem ~knobeln** to puzzle over a problem, to rack one's brains about s. th.; **~kommandieren** to hector, to huff, to boss (order) about; **Leute gern ~kommandieren** to be fond of ordering people about.

herumkommen, um eine Bestimmung to get round a clause; **um staatliche Regulierungsfesseln ~** to escape from the shackles of state regulations; **um eine Schwierigkeit ~** to get round a difficulty; **in der Welt ~** to see life, to get round in the world.

herum|kramen, in alten Akten to rummage among old papers; **in einer Schublade ~kramen** to rummage in a drawer; **in seinen Taschen ~kramen** to fumble in one's pockets; **j. ~kriegen** to win s. o. round *(sl.)*, to cajole s. o. into doing s. th.; **j. durch Betrug ~kriegen** to shanghai s. o.; **Tag schon irgendwie ~kriegen** to kill the day somehow; **an jem. ~kritisieren** to find fault with s. o.; **an einem Angebot ~kritteln** to nibble at an offer; **j. in der Stadt ~kutschieren** to drive s. o. around town; **den ganzen Tag in der Stadt ~latschen** to trapse the streets; **frei ~laufen** *(Verbrecher)* to be at large; **planlos in der Gegend ~laufen** to kick about; **in Lumpen ~laufen** to go in rags; **im ganzen Haus ~liegen** to lie kicking about the house; **den ganzen Tag am Strand ~liegen** to laze about on the beach all day; **nichts ~liegen lassen** to keep things picked-up; **seine Unterlagen ~liegen lassen** to leave one's papers lying about.

Herumlungerer layabout, loafer.

Herumlungern prowling.

herumlungern to traipse, to trapes, to trapse, to slouch, to stick around, to hang about, to prowl, to maroon *(Br., sl.)*, to hang round *(US)*, to hang out *(sl.)*, to suck around *(sl.)*;
in den Straßen ~ to loaf (prowl) about the streets; **an den Straßenecken ~** to loaf at street corners.

herumlungernd auf das Öffnen der Kneipen warten to hang about at street corners for the pubs to open.

herum|mäkeln, an etw. to grumble (moan) about s. th., to pick holes in s. th.; **an jem. ~mäkeln** to carp at s. o.; **am Essen ~mäkeln** to be fastidious (particular) about one's food; **mit seinem Essen ~manschen** to trifle away with one's food; **~meckern** to grumble, to gripe about *(US sl.)*, to quetch *(sl.)*.

herummurksen to tinker, to mess about;
an einem Brief ~ to sit over a letter; **an seinem Radioapparat schon eine Stunde ~** to have an hour's tinker at the radio; **an einem Schloß ~** to fiddle with a lock.

herum|nörgeln to grumble, to grouse, to gripe about *(US sl.)*, to quetch *(sl.)*; **an j. ~nörgeln** to find fault with s. o., to nag (pick) at s. o.; **~pfuschen** to tinker, to fiddle, to potter, to mess about; **an einer Urkunde ~pfuschen** to tamper with a document; **an seinem Essen ~picken** to pick at one's food.

herumplagen, sich mit etw. to bother o. s. about s. th.; **sich den ganzen Tag mit dem Haushalt ~** to slave away all day in the house; **sich stundenlang mit einer Übersetzung ~** to spend hours sweating over a translation; **sich mit widrigen Umständen ~** to be struggling with adversity;
sich damit ~ ein Haus zu finden to have much bother in finding a house.

herumposaunen to bandy (bruit it) about.

Herumprobieren trial and error.

herum|probieren to have a try at s. th.; **sich mit einem Problem ~quälen** to plod on a problem; **~raten** to make a random guess; **~rätseln** to figure out; **~reden** to quibble; **um ein Thema ~reden** to argue round and round a subject; **~reichen** to hand (pass) round; **j. ~reichen** to lionize s. o.; **j. in der Gesellschaft ~reichen** to introduce s. o. into society; **ziemlich viel ~reisen** to travel a great deal; **um die ganze Welt ~reisen** to travel round the world, to travel all over the world; **ziellos ~reisen** to knock around; **Steuer ~reißen** to swing the wheel, *(fig.)* to alter one's course radically.

herumreiten, auf jem. dauernd to carp (keep on) at s. o.; **auf Kleinigkeiten ~** to pettifog[ulize]; **auf einer Nebenfrage ~** to ride on a side issue; **dauernd auf ein Thema ~** to harp on the same thing, to rub it in.

herum|rühren, in alten Geschichten to rake up old stories; **um jem. ~scharwenzeln** to dance attendance on s. o.; **j. ~schicken** to give s. o. the roundabout *(US)*.

herumschlagen, sich mit etw. to fight one's way with s. th.; **sich mit einer Behörde ~** to battle with an authority; **sich mit dem Finanzamt ~** to tussle with the tax and revenue office; **sich mit schwierigen Kunden ~** to meet with considerable sales resistance; **sich mit einem Problem ~** to wrestle (grapple) with a problem.

herum|schleichen, um ein Haus to creep around a house; **~schlendern** to stooge around, to saunter along.

herumschleppen to drag about, to schlep along *(US sl.)*;
zwei schwere Koffer ~ to lug two heavy suitcases about with one; **sich mit einem Problem ~** to have a load on one's mind; **Schuldkomplex mit sich ~** to have a feeling of guilt; **Sorgen mit sich ~** to saddle o. s. with troubles.

herum|schmeißen, mit seinem Geld nur so to play ducks and drakes with one's money; **~schnüffeln** to poke and pry, to sneak about, to snook, to smell about; **in anderer Leute Sachen ~schnüffeln** to poke one's nose into other people's business; **um j. ~schwänzeln** to dance attendance on (bow and scrape to) s. o.; **in der Welt ~schweifen** to roam about the world; **~schwenken** *(Kamera)* to pan; **zu Hause ~sitzen** to sit at home; **untätig ~sitzen** to loll (idle, laze) about; **~spazieren** to stroll around; **an etw. ~spielen** to fiddle (tinker) with s. th.; **auf dem Klavier ~spielen** to strum the piano; **~spionieren** to poke and pry, to nose (snoop) around; **sich ~sprechen** to get about, to spread; **in jds. Kopf ~spuken** to be on (lurk in) s. one's mind; **dauernd ~stänkern** to be always grumbling.

Herumstehen loitering.

herumstehen to be standing about, *(flanieren)* to loiter;
in Gruppen ~ to cluster around.

herumstöbern to rummage around;
in alten Akten ~ to rummage among old papers; **in allen Ecken und Enden ~** to poke about in every corner; **im ganzen Haus ~** to hunt high and low.

herumstochern, in seinem Essen to peck (pick) at one's dinner (food); **im Feuer ~** to poke the fire.

herumstolzieren to strut around;
im Dorf ~ to nose about the village; **mit der ganzen Familie im Park ~** to parade one's whole family in the park; **in neuen Kleidern ~** to flaunt one's new clothes.

herumstreichen, ums Lager to prowl round the camp.

Herumstreifen gad.

herumstreifen to roam, to ramble.

herumstreiten, sich mit jem. to wrangle (squabble) with s. o., to cross swords with s. o.; **sich mit einer Behörde ~** to battle with an authority; **sich mit dem Finanzamt ~** to tussle with the tax and revenue office.

Herumstreunen loitering;
wegen ~s angezeigt werden to be accused of loitering with felonious intent.

herum|streunen to stray, to loaf, to slouch, to prowl, to maroon *(Br., sl.)*, *(Hund)* to roam about; **~strolchen** *(Kinder)* to roam about; **in der Stadt ~stromern** to knock about downtown *(US)*; **~stümpern** to fiddle about.

herumsuchen, in allen Ecken to hunt high and low, to poke about in every corner; **nach jem. im ganzen Ort ~** to search s. o. all over the place; **in alten Papieren ~** to rummage among old papers; **in seinen Taschen ~** to forage (grope) in one's pockets; **vergeblich in einem Wörterbuch ~** to search through a dictionary for a word not included.

herum|sumpfen to be on the tiles *(sl.)*; **um jem. ~tanzen** to dangle round s. o., to dance attendance on s. o.; **jem. auf der Nase ~tanzen** to play s. o. up no end; **im Dunkel ~tappen** to grope in the dark; **im Dunkeln ~tasten** to fumble in the dark; **~tollen** to rollick, to romp, to frolic.

herumtragen to carry about (around);
Geheimnis mit sich ~ to carry a secret around with one; **Kummer mit sich ~** to nurse one's grief *(fam.)*; **Neuigkeit ~** to spread a piece of news; **Problem mit sich ~** to have s. th. on one's brain.

herum|trampeln, auf jds. Gefühlen to trample on s. one's feelings; **jem. auf dem Kopf ~trampeln** to play s. o. up no end; **~tratschen** to noise abroad, to gossip.

Herumtreiben loitering;
~ **in gesetzwidriger Absicht** loitering with intent to commit an offence.
herumtreiben, sich to roam (knock, hang, muck, *Br., sl.*) about; **sich in den Kneipen** ~ to hang about in the pubs; **sich müßig** ~ to gad about (abroad); **sich die halbe Nacht** ~ to be out half the night; **sich auf der Straße** ~ to knock (loaf) about the streets.
Herumtreiber runabout, loafer, rover, layabout, streetraker.
herum|trödeln to idle [poke] about, to dillydally *(coll.)*; **~tüfteln** to niggle, to potter, to fidget; **~vagabundieren** to tramp the country, to bum around *(US)*; **Problem im Kopf ~wälzen** to roll a problem round in one's mind; **sich schlaflos in seinem Bett ~wälzen** to toss and turn sleeplessly in one's bed; **in einer Ausstellung ~wandern** to stroll around an exhibition; **im Land ~wandern** to hike about the country.
herumwerfen, mit Fachausdrücken to talk shop; **mit seinem Geld** ~ to chuck one's money around; **Kurs (Steuer)** ~ *(fig.)* to change one's policy radically; **sich im Schlaf** ~ to toss and turn in one's sleep.
herum|werkeln, im Garten to potter about in the garden; **~wirtschaften** to potter about, to be always on the hop.
herumwühlen, im Dreck to burrow in the mud; **in alten Geschichten** ~ to rake up old stories; **in seinem Koffer** ~ to rummage in one's suitcase; **im Schmutz** ~ *(Schriftsteller)* to wallow in filth; **in alten Unterlagen** ~ to root among old papers; **in alten Wunden** ~ to probe a wound with one's finger.
herum|wursteln to fiddle (mess, tinker, fumble) about; **dauernd ~zanken** to be constantly quarrel(l)ing (squabbling); **~zeigen** to show around; **im Land ~ziehen** to move about in the country, to roam about the world; **~ziehender Händler** itinerant vendor; **~zigeunern** to rove, to roam about; **an einer Sache ~zukauen haben** to get one's teeth into s. th.
herunter, fünf Punkte ~ **sein** *(Kurs)* to be off five points; **~brennen** to burn down.
herunterbringen *(Preise)* to reduce, to lower;
keinen Bissen mehr ~ not to be able to swallow another mouthful; **j. finanziell** ~ to smash (wreck)s. o.; **Koffer** ~ to bring down the luggage.
herunterdrücken, Aktienkurse to pull down the prices of stocks; **Kurse** ~ to bear the market; **Preise** ~ to beat (cut, force) down the prices.
herunter|fahren to descend; **mit dem Fahrstuhl ~fahren** to ride down in a lift; **~fallen** *(Flugzeug)* to crash, to pile up, to abort *(sl.)*; **Treppe ~fallen** to fall downstairs; **~gegangen** *(Kurs)* down; **[im Preise] ~gegangen sein** to be down.
Heruntergehen sinking, decline, fall.
heruntergehen to go down, to decline, to fall, to drop, to ease off, *(Flugzeug)* to plane down;
etw. ~ *(Kurse)* to ease a fraction; **in den ersten Gang** ~ to change (shift, *US*) down into first [gear]; **mit der Geschwindigkeit** ~ to reduce speed, to slow down; **mit dem Preis** ~ to reduce (lower) the price; **in der Qualität** ~ to drop in quality; **Treppe** ~ to go downstairs; **im Wert** ~ to recede in value.
heruntergekommen deteriorated, in reduced circumstances, behindhand, badly off, decayed, ruined, broken down, *(äußerlich)* down-at-heel, dowdy, seedy, *(Hof)* run-down, mismanaged;
~ **sein** to be at a low ebb, to be on the downgrade (down and out, on the beach, *sl.*); **sittlich** ~ **sein** to become depraved; **völlig** ~ **sein** *(Wirtschaft)* to have gone to rack and ruin (to pot, *fam.*);
~es Individuum a down-and-out; **in ~em Zustand** *(Geschäft)* in a run-down condition, *(Haus)* in a dilapidated condition.
herunter|geputzt werden to be put on the carpet *(Br.)*; **~gesetzt** cut-price; **~handeln** to beat down, to get a price reduced, to knock off; **~haspeln** to reel off; **jem. eine ~hauen** to give s. o. a box on the ear, to slap s. one's face; **Brief auf der Schreibmaschine ~hauen** to pound out a letter on the typewriter; **jem. die Treppe ~helfen** to help s. o. downstairs; **Flugzeug ~holen** to shoot down an airplane; **Sitz ~klappen** to turn down a seat; **~kommen** *(Flugzeug)* to come down, *(Geschäft)* to deteriorate, to go to pot, *(gesundheitlich)* to go downhill, *(Person)* to come down in the world, to go to the dogs; **Fluß ~kommen** to come down the river; **völlig ~kommen** to go to rack and ruin (to pot, *fam.*), to go to the dogs; **keinen Bissen mehr ~kriegen** not to be able to swallow another mouthful; **~lassen** to let down; **Jalousie (Rolläden) ~lassen** to lower the Venetian blinds; **Straße ~laufen** to pound along a road; **jem. kalt und heiß den Rücken ~laufen** to have the shivers; **an der Wand ~laufen** *(Wasser)* to run down the wall; **~leiern** to drone out; **Gedicht ~leiern** to rattle off a poem; **j. ~machen** to pull s. o. to pieces, to haul s. o. over the coals; **Bild ~nehmen** to unhang a picture; **Buch vom Regal ~nehmen** to take a book down from the shelf; **schweren Sack ~plumpsen lassen** to flop down a heavy bag; **~purzeln** *(Kurse)* to tumble; **~putzen** to rebuke, to rag, to pick to pieces, to carpet *(Br.)*, to trim *(sl.)*, to slam *(US sl.)*; **j. gehörig ~putzen** to come down on s. o. like a ton of bricks, to rake s. o. over the coals; **Gedicht ~rasseln** to rake off a poem; **~reißen** to pull down, *(kritisieren)* to pick apart, to slash, to pull down, to slate, to pan *(US)*; **Theaterstück ~reißen** to slate (pan, *US*) a play.
Herunterschalten downshift *(US)*.
herunter|schalten *(Gang)* to change (shift, *US*) down, to downshift *(US)*; **~schießen** to shoot down; **sein Essen ~schlingen** to wolf down one's food; **~schlucken** to swallow, to gulp down; **etw. ~schlucken** *(fig.)* to pocket one's pride; **Beleidigung ~schlucken** to swallow an insult; **~schrauben** to scale down; **Ausgaben ~schrauben** to cut down expenses; **seine Ansprüche ~schrauben** to moderate one's claims; **auf j. ~sehen** to look down on s. o.; **~sein** to be in poor health; **mit den Nerven völlig ~sein** to be all nerves, to have one's nerves frayed at both ends.
heruntersetzen to reduce, to lower, to mark (scale) down, to abate, to depreciate;
j. in jds. Achtung ~ to lower s. o. in s. one's estimation; **Gehalt stark** ~ to slash a salary; **Warenpreise** ~ to lower the price of goods.
Heruntersetzung lowering, reduction.
herunterspielen *(fam.)* to play it down (low), to soft-pedal;
Gerüchte ~ to play down rumo(u)rs; **Nachricht** ~ to play down (downplay, *US*) a piece of news.
herunter|steigen to descend, to climb down; **j. von seinem hohen Roß ~steigen lassen** to knock s. o. off his perch; **j. von einer Mauer ~stoßen** to push s. o. off a wall; **j. von seinem hohen Piedestal ~stoßen** to knock s. o. off his perch; **sich vom Balkon ~stürzen** to fling o. s. down from the balcony; **vom Dach ~stürzen** to fall off the roof; **Treppe ~stürzen** to come rushing down the stairs; **~wirtschaften** to run down, to bring low, to mismanage; **Beleidigung ~würgen** to swallow an insult; **Schmuckstücke vom Ladentisch ~zerren** to whip jewels from the counter; **j. auf sein niedriges Niveau ~zerren** to drag s. o. down to one's own level; **~ziehen** to pull down.
hervorbrechen, aus dem Hinterhalt to burst out of ambush; **aus den Wolken** ~ *(Sonne)* to break through the clouds.
hervorbringen to produce, to turn out, to generate, to give birth to;
vor Überraschung keinen Ton ~ **können** to be speechless with surprise.
Hervorbringung production, turnout, generation.
hervorgehen to spring from, to result;
aus einer Ehe ~ to issue from a marriage; **siegreich aus einem Kampf mit jem.** ~ to be victorious over s. o.; **aus einer Sache siegreich** ~ to come out of s. th. with flying colo(u)rs; **aus einem Schreiben nicht** ~ not to be clear from a letter; **aus einer Universität** ~ to have been trained in a university; **gestärkt aus den Wahlen** ~ to emerge in a strong position from the elections.
hervorheben to emphasize, to accentuate, to lay stress on, to highlight *(US)*, *(drucktechn.)* to display, to throw up;
jds. gutes Benehmen lobend ~ to commend s. o. upon his good manners; **durch fetten Druck** ~ to print in bold type; **Idee** ~ to give prominence to an idea; **Punkt besonders** ~ to insist upon a point; **in seiner Rede** ~ to emphasize in one's speech; **Textstelle** ~ to make a passage stand out through print; **Unterschiede** ~ to bring out differences; **jds. Verdienste** ~ to extol s. one's merits; **jds. Verdienste in einer Rede** ~ to notice s. one's services in a speech.
Hervorhebung accentuation, emphasizing, *(drucktechn.)* display;
unter besonderer ~ stressing particularly.
hervor|holen, Buch to produce a book; **Sträfling aus seinem Versteck ~holen** to drag a prisoner out of his hiding place; **aus seinem Versteck ~kommen** to come out of one's hiding; **aus den Wolken ~kommen** *(Sonne)* to break through the clouds; **~kramen** to rummage out; **keinen Hund hinter dem Ofen ~locken** not to tempt anybody; **~ragen** *(Berg)* to rise; **aus den anderen ~ragen** to tower above the others.
hervorragend fine, superior, first-class (-rate), outstanding, eminent, preeminent, topping, stellar, distinguished, banner *(US)*;
Rolle ~ **spielen** to act one's part well;
~er Balken projecting beam; **~es Essen** excellent food; **in ~em Maße an einem Erfolg beteiligt sein** to be largely due to s. one's efforts; **~e Persönlichkeiten des Landes** outstanding figures of a country; **von ~er Qualität** of first-class quality; **~e Sekretärin**

first-rate secretary; ~**er Staatsmann** eminent statesman; ~**e Stellung einnehmen** to hold a high-level position; ~**er Unterhändler** top negotiator; **sich in ~er Weise verdient gemacht haben** to have rendered excellent services.
Hervorruf *(Theater)* curtain call.
hervorrufen to give rise, to cause, to excite, to evoke, to call forth;
Ärgernis ~ to give rise to (create) a scandal; **Bedarf** ~ to create a demand; **künstliche Hausse** ~ to balloon *(US)*; **Lächeln** ~ to evoke a smile; **Mitleid** ~ to provoke pity; **Neid** ~ to excite envy; **Panik** ~ to give rise to panic; **soziale Unruhen** ~ to create social unrest; **Verbraucherinteresse** ~ to excite customers' interest.
Hervorrufung sozialer Unruhen creation of social unrest.
hervorschießen, wie Pilze *(Häuser)* to shoot (spring up) like mushrooms.
hervorstechend outstanding, striking, conspicuous, salient;
~**e Landschaftsmerkmale** outstanding features of a landscape; ~**e Merkmale** salient characteristics.
hervortreten to emerge, to appear;
als Bühnenschriftsteller ~ to make one's name as a playwright; **literarisch** ~ to distinguish o. s. in the field of literature; **nicht** ~ to keep in the background; **plastisch** ~ to stand out in relief; **plötzlich** ~ to pop up; **als Produzent hervorragender Geräte** ~ to make a name for themselves as producers of quality instruments; **aus der Reihe** ~ to step out of line, *(fig.)* to make a name for o. s.; **mit einem Roman** ~ to come to the fore with a novel;
Einzelheiten deutlicher ~ **lassen** to show up the details more clearly.
hervortun, sich to distinguish o. s., to make o. s. conspicuous, to win distinction, *(sich wichtig machen)* to give o. s. airs, to show off; **sich durch Frechheit** ~ to be known for one's impudence.
hervor|wagen, sich mit etw. an die Öffentlichkeit ~**wagen** to dare to appear in public with s. th.; **Flasche Wein** ~**zaubern** to produce a bottle of wine from nowhere; **Kaninchen aus einem Hut** ~**zaubern** to conjure a rabbit out of a hat.
Herz heart, *(Herzstück)* center, core, heart;
im tiefsten Grunde seines ~**ens** in his heart of hearts; **im Innersten meines** ~**ens** in my heart's core; **in tiefstem** ~**en** in the depth of one's heart; **mit allen Fasern seines** ~**ens** with every fibre of one's being; **von ganzem** ~**en** with heart and soul, from the bottom of one's heart;
mitfühlendes ~ tender heart;
weiches ~ **in rauher Schale** rough diamond;
sein ~ **ausschütten** to disburden one's mind, to talk it out; **jem. sein** ~ **ausschütten** to open one's heart to s. o.; **jem. das** ~ **brechen** to break s. one's heart; **es übers** ~ **bringen** to find the heart to do, to prevail upon o. s.; **es nicht übers** ~ **bringen** not to find it in one's heart; **das** ~ **erfreuen** to rejoice one's heart; **jds.** ~ **erobern** to win s. one's heart; **sich ein** ~ **fassen** to pluck up (take) heart, to take courage; **dem Zuge seines** ~**ens folgen** to follow the dictates of one's conscience; **etw. auf dem** ~**en haben** to have s. th. on one's mind; ~ **für die Armen haben** to feel for the poor; ~ **auf dem rechten Fleck haben** to have one's heart in the right place; ~ **in der Hose haben** to have one's heart in one's boots, to quake in one's shoes *(fam.)*; **schwaches** ~ **haben** to have a weak heart; ~ **aus Stein haben** to have a heart of stone, to be as hard as a flint *(fam.)*; **Stein vom** ~**en haben** to have a load off one's mind; **zu viel** ~ **haben** to be too tender-hearted; **weites** ~ **haben** to be big-hearted; **jds. Wohl und Weh am** ~**en liegen haben** to have s. one's welfare at heart; **sein** ~ **an etw. hängen** to set one's heart on s. th.; **jds.** ~ **höher schlagen lassen** to bring a flutter to s. one's heart; **etw. ans** ~ **legen** to set (lay) s. th. to heart; **j. von ganzem** ~**en lieben** to love s. o. with all one's heart; **jem. am** ~**en liegen** to lie at s. one's heart; **seinem** ~**en Luft machen** to find a vent for one's feelings, to give vent to one's feelings; **aus seinem** ~**en keine Mördergrube machen** to reveal one's naked heart; **an jds.** ~**en nagen** to prey on s. one's mind; **sich etw. zu** ~**en nehmen** to take s. th. to heart; **sein** ~ **in die Hand nehmen** to pluck up courage; **j. auf** ~ **und Nieren prüfen** to put s. o. to the acid test; **sich das** ~ **aus dem Leibe reden** to talk one's head off; **j. ans** ~ **rühren** to touch s. o. to the heart; **j. ins** ~ **schließen** to become fond of s. o.; **mit ganzem** ~**en bei der Arbeit sein** to have one's heart in one's work; **nur mit halbem** ~**en dabei sein** to do s. th. in a half-hearted manner; **jem. ans** ~ **gewachsen sein** to be dear to s. o.; **im Innersten seines** ~**ens glücklich sein** to feel a great gladness at heart; **ein Mann nach meinem** ~**en sein** to be a man after my heart; **ein** ~ **und eine Seele sein** to be hand in glove; **traurigen** ~**ens sein** to be sad at heart; **unauslöschlich in jds.** ~ **eingegraben sein** to be engraved on s. one's heart; **an gebrochenem** ~**en sterben** to die of a broken heart; **Groll gegen j. im** ~**en tragen** to bear s. o. ill will; **Kind unter dem** ~**en tragen** to be with child (in the family way); **sein** ~ **auf der Zunge tragen** to wear one's heart upon one's sleeve; **j. bis ins Innerste seines** ~**ens treffen** to cut (stab) s. o. to the heart; **etw. leichten (schweren)** ~**ens tun** to do s. th. with a light (heavy) heart; **dem** ~**en weh tun** to make one's heart bleed; **jds.** ~ **verhärten** to harden s. one's heart; **sein** ~ **an j. verlieren** to give (lose) one's heart to s. o.; **sich einer Sache mit allen Fasern seines** ~**ens verschreiben** to put one's heart and soul into a business; **den Weg zu den** ~**en der Menschen zu finden wissen** to know how to find one's way into people's hearts; **etw. von ganzem** ~**en wünschen** to desire s. th. with all one's (have s. th. at) heart; **jem. das** ~ **zerreißen** to play upon s. one's heartstrings; **einem Plan von ganzem** ~**en zustimmen** to give one's hearty approval to a plan;
sagen, was man auf dem ~**en hat** to speak one's mind.
herzählen, Namen an den Fingern to count off the names on one's fingers.
Herz|anfall heart attack; ~**beanspruchung** heart strain; ~**beschwerden** heart complaint (trouble); **sein** ~**blut an etw. gesetzt haben** to have set one's heart on doing s. th.
Herzeleid heartbreak, grief.
herzen to cuddle, to caress, to fondle, to hug.
Herzens|anliegen haben, besonderes to have a cause particularly at heart; ~**brecher** heartbreaker; **aus tiefstem** ~**grund** from the bottom of one's heart.
herzensgut|sein to be of good heart;
~**e Seele sein** to have a heart of gold.
Herzenslust, nach to one's heart's content;
es sich nach ~ **wohl sein lassen** to indulge o. s. to one's heart's content.
Herzenswunsch dearest wish.
herzerfrischende Neuigkeiten heartening news.
Herzfehler heart complaint (failure).
herzhaft|er Appetit hearty appetite; ~**es Lachen** hearty laugh.
herziehen to move here;
etw. hinter sich ~ to trail s. th. behind one; **über j.** ~ to go on at s. o., to run s. o. down, to pull s. o. to pieces, to rail against s. o.; **über die Briten** ~ to twist the lion's tail.
Herz|infarkt heart failure, cardiac infarction; ~**klopfen haben** to have one's heart in one's mouth; ~**leiden** heart trouble.
herzlich hearty, cordial;
~ **gern** with the greatest of pleasure; ~ **willkommen** nice to see you;
jem. ~ **schlecht gehen** not to feel very well at all; ~ **wenig damit anfangen können** not to help s. o. at all; ~ **wenig davon verstehen** to understand precious little of s. th.; **von jem.** ~ **aufgenommen werden** to be received cordially by s. o.;
jem. sein ~**es Beileid aussprechen** to offer s. o. one's condolences; **j. seinen** ~**sten Dank aussprechen** to express one's heart-felt thanks to s. o.; ~ **wenig Einfluß** fat lot of influence; ~**er Empfang** warm reception; ~**ste Glückwünsche** heartiest congratulations; ~**e Glückwünsche zum Geburtstag** many happy returns of the day; ~**e Grüße** kind regards; **mit** ~**en Grüßen** yours sincerely; ~**e Worte** sincere words.
Herzlichkeit cordiality, sincerity;
demonstrative ~ demonstrative cordiality.
Herz|schrittmacher heart pacemaker; ~**stück** central point, core, *(Weiche)* frog; ~**versagen** heart failure.
Hetz|artikel inflammatory article; ~**blatt** yellow paper, gutter press, smearsheet.
Hetze agitation, instigation, [smearing] campaign, mischief-making, *(Eile)* hurry, rush;
~ **des Großstadtlebens** rush of city life; ~ **des modernen Lebens** whirl of modern life;
in einer dauernden ~ **sein** to be always on the run; **massive** ~ **gegen j. veranstalten** to conduct a virulent campaign against s. o.
hetzen to agitate, to stir up, *(Jagd)* to hunt, to bait, to course, *(verfolgen)* to hunt, to hound, to chase;
sich ~ to hurry, to rush; **gegeneinander** ~ to set at odds (loggerheads); **nach Gewinn** ~ to chase for profit; **Hund auf j.** ~ to set the dog on s. o.; **zum Krieg** ~ to be a warmonger; **durch die Straßen** ~ to hurry through the streets; **j. zu Tode** ~ to hunt s. o. to death.
Hetzer agitator, demagogue, rabble-rouser;
staatsgefährliche ~ seditionary.
Hetz|feldzug gutter-press campaign; ~**flugblätter** subversive literature; ~**jagd** *(pol.)* witchhunt; ~**jagd auf j. veranstalten** to conduct a virulent campaign against s. o.; ~**rede** virulent (inflammatory, incendiary) speech; ~**schrift** slanderous pamphlet.

Heu, frei gestapeltes hay in stack;
~ **aufstaken** to pitch hay; **Geld wie ~ haben** to be rolling in (have pots of) money; **sein ~ im Trockenen haben** to be set for life; **zum zweiten Mal ~ machen** to make one's second cut; **wie ~ und Stroh durcheinander sein** to be all at sixes and sevens; ~ **wenden** to toss hay;
~**boden** hay loft; ~**bündel** wisp of hay.
Heuchelei hypocrisy, insincerity.
heucheln to feign, to play the hypocrite;
voll ausgelastet zu sein ~ to pretend to be very busy.
Heuchler hypocrite, feigner, make-believe, dissembler.
heuchlerisch hypocritical, two-faced;
~ **reden** to cant.
Heuer hire, pay, wages;
~**abtretungsschein** allotment note; ~**baas** shipping master *(Br.)*, crimp *(sl.)*; ~**buch** [seaman's] pay-book; ~**büro** shipping office *(Br.)*, seamen's employment agency.
heuern to engage, to enlist, to hire *(US)*, to recruit *(US)*;
Schiff ~ to charter a ship.
Heuernote advance note.
Heuernte hay harvest;
zweite ~ latter grass.
Heuervertrag ship's articles, company service contract *(Br.)*, *(Schiff)* charterparty.
Heugabel pitchfork.
Heulboje whistling buoy.
Heulen *(Radio)* howler;
~ **und Zähneklappern** weeping, wailing and gnashing of teeth;
~ **des Sturms** howling of the storm.
heulen to cry, to bawl, to weep, *(Sirene)* to wail, *(Sturm)* to howl, to rage, to rave, to blow great guns;
vor Schmerzen ~ to cry with pain; **mit den Wölfen** ~ to follow the crowd, to howl with the pack *(fam.)*.
heulend, das ~e Elend bekommen to get the blues (maudlin), to have the dismals.
Heul|suse crybaby; ~**tonne** whistling buoy.
Heu|schober haycock, rick; **als ~wiese benutzen** to meadow.
Hexe witch, sorceress.
hexen to work miracles.
Hexen|jagd *(pol.)* witch hunt; **wie ein ~kessel sein** to be agitated like boiling water; ~**sabbat** devil among the tailors; ~**schuß** lumbago; ~**verfolgung** witch hunt.
Hexerei witchcraft.
Hieb blow, stroke, thrust;
auf den ersten ~ at the first attempt;
~**e bekommen** to get a thrashing; **auf ~ und Stich fechten** to fight cut-and-thrust; ~ **parieren** to ward off a blow; **jem. einen ~ versetzen** to have a dig at s. o.; **seiner Konkurrenz manchen ~ versetzen** to play a number of tricks on one's competitors; **auf einen ~ fällt kein Baum** Rome was not built in a day; **der ~ galt dir** that was aimed at you; **dieser ~ hat gesessen** that struck home.
hieb- und stichfest watertight;
~ **beweisen** to give cast-iron proof; **nicht ~ sein** not to hold water.
hier local, spot;
alle ~ entstehenden Verbindlichkeiten any liabilities arising hereunder.
Hierarchie der leitenden Angestellten managerial hierarchy.
hierarchische Ordnung hierarchical order.
hier|durch by the presents, hereby; ~**durch wird bestätigt** this is to certify; ~**mit** herewith, by the presents; ~**mit sei kundgetan** know all men; ~**nach** hereafter; ~**zulande** in this country.
hiesige Industrie local industry.
Hilfe help, helping, assistance, hand, backing, lift, standby, auxiliary, favo(u)r, *(Haushalt)* domestic help, *(Hilfsaktion)* relief, rescue, *(Unterstützung)* aid, assistance, favo(u)r, crutch; **auf die ~ von Freunden angewiesen** dependent upon friends; **mit staatlicher** ~ with government support; **ohne** ~ unaided; **ohne fremde** ~ off one's own bat;
ärztliche ~ medical assistance; **ausländische** ~ foreign aid; **erste** ~ first aid; **finanzielle** ~ grant, financial aid (assistance); **gegenseitige** ~ mutual aid; **gern gewährte** ~ willing help; **großzügige** ~ unstinting help; **praktische** ~ positive help; **technische** ~ technical assistance; **treue** ~ yeoman's service; **wenig oder gar keine** ~ little or no help; **projektfreie wirtschaftliche** ~ untied aid; **projektgebundene wirtschaftliche** ~ tied aid;
~ **bei der Erstellung der Rechnungsunterlagen** accountancy service; **kleine ~ für das Gedächtnis** aids to memory;
Armen ~ anbieten to extend help to the poor; ~ **des Gerichts anrufen** to appeal to the law; **j. um ~ ansprechen** to appeal to s. o. for help; **ohne ~ auskommen** to manage without help; **sofortiger ~ bedürfen** to be in instant need of help; **jds. ~ nicht benötigen** to have no occasion for s. one's help; **j. um ~ bitten** to seek s. one's aid, to appeal to s. o. for help; **jem. zu ~ eilen** to spring to s. one's assistance; **einem in Seenot geratenen Schiff zu ~ eilen** to go out to a ship in distress; ~ **einstellen (entziehen)** to withdraw aid; **um ~ ersuchen** to ask for help; ~ **finden** to get assistance; ~ **gewähren** to afford assistance; **massive finanzielle ~ gewähren** to step in with massive aid; **jem. zu ~ kommen** to come to s. one's help, to come to the rescue of s. o., to run to s. one's aid; ~ **angedeihen lassen** to render assistance; ~ **zuteil werden lassen** to render assistance; ~ **leisten** to help, to assist, to aid; **jem. erste ~ leisten** to apply first aid to s. o.; ~ **des Gerichts (richterliche ~) in Anspruch nehmen** to seek redress in (enlist the aid of the) court; **mit jds. ~ rechnen** to bank upon s. one's help; **Feuerwehr zu ~ rufen** to call in the fire brigade to help; **bei jeder Kleinigkeit um ~ rufen** to cry wolf too often; **auf fremde ~ angewiesen sein** to be dependent on the help of others; **der Geschäftsleitung eine große ~ sein** to aid management; ~ **in der Not sein** to arrive in the nick of time; **wirkliche ~ für j. sein** to lend effective help to s. o.; **unserer ~ würdig sein** to deserve our help; **Rat und ~ bei jem. suchen** to seek s. one's advice and support; **jem. ~ verweigern** to refuse help to s. o.; **weder Rat noch ~ wissen** to be at one's wit's end.
hilfeflehender Blick imploring glance.
Hilfeleistung assistance [effort], help, aid [efforts], relief, rescue; **finanzielle** ~ financial service; **gegenseitige** ~ mutual assistance; **staatliche ~en** government subsidies; **technische** ~ technical aid; **unterlassene** ~ *(jur.)* [etwa] culpable neglect;
~**en auf finanziellem Gebiet** subsidiary payments; ~ **für in Seenot geratene Schiffe** assistance to ships in distress, rescue, salvage;
Flüchtlingen ~en gewähren to provide relief for refugees.
Hilfe|ruf, ~signal cry for help, *(Schiff)* distress call (signal), SOS;
einziger ~ desperate cry for help;
~ **des Roten Kreuzes** appeal by the Red Cross;
~ **auffangen** to pick up a distress call; ~ **ausstrahlen** to radio an urgent appeal.
Hilfestellung support, backing up;
jem. in einer Diskussion ~ geben to back s. o. up throughout a discussion.
hilfesuchend|ansehen, j. to look imploringly at s. o.; **sich ~ an j. wenden** to turn to s. o. for help.
hilflos helpless;
~ **allein gelassen sein** to turn adrift in the world;
~**er alter Mann** feeble old man.
Hilfloser destitute.
Hilflosigkeit, gänzliche utter helplessness;
jds. ~ ausnutzen to exploit s. one's helpless situation.
hilfreich helping, helpful, forthcoming;
sich ~ bei der Beschaffung einer gut bezahlten Stellung für einen Freund erweisen to be instrumental in finding well paid work for a friend; ~ **sein** to lend a hand; **nicht sehr ~ sein** to count for little; **seinen Freunden stets ~ zur Seite stehen** to be always ready to help one's friends.
Hilfs|abkommen auf Gegenseitigkeit mutual-aid plan; ~**abteilung** auxiliary department; ~**adresse** *(Wechsel)* accommodation address, address in case of need; ~**akkreditiv** ancillary letter of credit.
Hilfsaktion provident scheme, relief work, rescue operation;
finanzielle ~ campaign to raise funds; **staatliche** ~ state rescue;
~ **einleiten** to organize relief measures.
Hilfsangebot, spontanes spontaneous offer of help;
~ **machen** to offer assistance.
Hilfs|angestellter emergency man; ~**anlage** *(Betrieb)* emergency set; ~**antenne** dummy antenna; ~**antrag** alternative relief, alternative pleading; ~**antrieb** booster; **jem. einige ~anweisungen hinterlassen** to jot down a few hints for s. o.; ~**arbeit** unskilled work.
Hilfsarbeiter unskilled (subsidiary, auxiliary) worker, supernumerary, *(Assistent)* assistant, *(Aushilfe)* help[er];
kümmerlich bezahlter ~ savage *(sl.)*; **eingewanderter** ~ hunky *(US sl.)*; **wissenschaftlicher** ~ unestablished assistant.
Hilfs|arzt house officer, intern *(US)*; ~**aufruf** aid appeal; ~**aufwand** aid expenditure; ~**aufzeichnungen** subsidiary records; ~**ausschuß** relief (emergency, distress, auxiliary) committee; ~**beamter** supernumerary.
hilfsbedürftig in need of assistance, needy, indigent;
~**e Familie** needy family;
sehr ~ sein to be in sore need.

Hilfs|bedürftiger needy person; ~**bedürftigkeit** indigence, distress, need; ~**bemühungen** assistance effort.
hilfsbereit ready to help, friendly, favo(u)rable, cooperative;
wenig ~ tardy in offering help;
~ **anderen helfen** to be forward in helping others.
Hilfs|bereitschaft readiness to help others, cooperation, accommodation; ~**betrieb** ancillary undertaking, service department *(US)*; **industrielle** ~**betriebe** subsidiary industries (undertakings); ~**betriebskonto** service department account *(US)*; ~**bogen** *(Bilanz)* work sheet; ~**briefträger** temporary postman.
Hilfsbuch handbook, auxiliary book, *(Buchführung)* subsidiary ledger, *(für Erstellung der Konzernbilanz)* elimination ledger; ~**halter** assistant bookkeeper.
Hilfsdienst help, aid, assistance, *(Autofahrer)* service station, *(Industrie)* ancillary service, *(Notdienst)* help (aid) scheme, emergency department, *(Rotes Kreuz)* first-aid service;
freiwilliger ~ voluntary service;
~ **für Autofahrer anrufen** to ring up the scout car (automobile association patrol); **besonderen** ~ **einrichten** *(Rotes Kreuz)* to organize a first-aid service; ~ **leisten** to render assistance.
Hilfs|einkäufer assistant buyer; ~**einrichtungen** support facilities; ~**einwendung** supplemental plea; ~**ersuchen** appeal for help, invocation of aid; ~**expedition** relief expedition; ~**fahrzeug** emergency (light-duty) vehicle, *(Marine)* naval auxiliary *(US)*; ~**fallschirm** pilot parachute; ~**flugplatz** auxiliary airfield, feeder airport; ~**fonds** relief (aid, emergency) fund; ~**funktion** auxiliary (ancillary)function; ~**gelder** subsidiary coins, aid moneys (funds), subsidies, grant-in-aid *(Br.)*; ~**gelder zahlen** to subsidize; ~**gemeinschaft** relief organization; ~**gerät** labo(u)r-saving appliance; ~**geschworener** talesman; ~**gesuch** request for help; ~**industrie** ancillary industry; ~**ingenieur** *(mar.)* assistant engineer; ~**kasse** relief (provident) fund, *(Verein)* friendly (benefit, *Br.*) society, slate club *(Br.)*; ~**kassenbuch** subsidiary cashbook; ~**kassierer** assistant cashier, assistant paying teller *(US)*; ~**kessel** donkey boiler; ~**kolonne** breakdown gang; ~**komitee** emergency (distress, relief) committee; ~**konsortium** aid consortium; ~**kontenbuch** subsidiary journal.
Hilfskonto subsidiary (auxiliary, adjunct) account;
~ **für Kostenberechnungen** cost ledger;
~**buch** subsidiary journal.
Hilfskostenstelle nonproductive department.
Hilfskraft help, helper, subsidiary worker, aid, assistant, auxiliary, *(Behörde)* supernumerary;
wissenschaftliche ~ research assistant;
~ **eines Gutsverwalters** land reeve.
Hilfskräfte emergency hands;
~ **gesucht** *(Inserat)* hands wanted;
~ **im Büro** secretarial help;
unbedeutende ~ small fry *(sl.)*.
Hilfs|kreuzer converted (armed merchant) cruiser, boarding ship, auxiliary [cruiser]; ~**landeplatz** emergency landing field; ~**lazarett** field hospital; ~**lehrer** deputy lecturer, substitute teacher; **wissenschaftlicher** ~**lehrer** unestablished teacher; ~**lehrkraft** assistant *(US)*; ~**lehrmittel** teaching aid; ~**leistungen** assistance effort; ~**löhne** indirect labo(u)r; ~**lokomotive** second engine; ~**mannschaft** rescue party.
Hilfsmaßnahmen emergency measures, relief operations;
nicht funktionierende staatliche ~ **aufheben** to ban self-defeating state aids; ~ **einstellen** to close down aid operation.
Hilfs|material nonproductive material, supplies; ~**mitglied** deputy member.
Hilfsmittel resources, purse, auxiliary means, *(Notbehelf)* expedient, makeshift, shift, resort, organ, stopgap, remedy;
alle ~ **anwendend** total;
finanzielle ~ financial aid; **letztes** ~ last resort; **technische** ~ mechanical aids; **alle verfügbaren** ~ all available resources;
~ **zum Be- und Entladen** devices for loading and unloading; ~ **für den Schulunterricht** teaching aids; **audiovisuelle** ~ **für den Unterricht** audiovisual aids;
~ **für Entwicklungsländer bereitstellen** to make aid available for developing countries; **seine** ~ **einsetzen** to make a draft on one's means; **zur Durchführung eines Auftrags alle** ~ **mobilisieren** to throw all resources into a job; **jds.** ~ **in Anspruch nehmen** to draw on s. o.
Hilfs|motor servo (auxiliary) motor, *(Schiff)* auxiliary engine, kicker *(sl.)*; **mit** ~**motor ausgestattet** motor-assisted; ~**organ** auxiliary (subsidiary) body.
Hilfsorganisation relief organization (agency), welfare association;
freiwillige ~ voluntary agency;
~**en der Vereinten Nationen** specialized agencies of the United Nations.
Hilfs|person helper, aid, assistant; ~**personal** ancillary (auxiliary) workers, helpers; ~**polizei** special police; ~**polizist** special constable, special deputy, vigilante *(US)*; ~**postamt** suboffice; ~**produkt** substitute [commodity].
Hilfsprogramm emergency-aid (subsidy, relief) program(me);
technisches ~ **der UNO** Expanded Programme for Technical Assistance (EPTA); **nicht verklausuliertes** ~ no-strings aid program(me);
~ **zur Kinderernährung in Entwicklungsländern** food for peace program *(US)*.
Hilfs|projekt aid project; ~**prüfer** assistant (junior) accountant, *(Patentrecht)* assistant examiner; ~**pumpe** *(Schiff)* donkey pump; ~**quelle** [re]source, expedient, *(wissenschaftliche Arbeit)* material.
Hilfsquellen resources, potential, purse;
ohne ~ resourceless;
industrielle ~ industrial resources; **latente** ~ potential resources; **örtliche** ~ local resources; **noch nicht probierte** ~ untapped resources; **steuerliche** ~ tax resources; **unerschöpfliche** ~ inexhaustible resources; **ungenutzte** ~ untapped resources;
Land nach und nach seiner ~ **berauben** to drain upon a country's resources; **neue** ~ **erschließen** to open up new resources; **seine** ~ **mobilisieren** to mobilize one's resources; **seine** ~ **in Anspruch nehmen** to draw upon (on) one's resources.
Hilfs|rakete booster; ~**redakteur** assistant editor, subeditor, copyman *(US)*; ~**revisor** junior (assistant) accountant, assistant auditor (controller); ~**richter** judge pro tempore, deputy judge, assistant [judge], master *(US)*; ~**schicht** relief (swing, *US*) shift; ~**schiene** dead rail; ~**schiff** relief ship; ~**schöffe** reserve juror, talesman; ~**schule** special school for educationally subnormal children, approved school *(Br.)*; ~**schulunterricht** remedial education; ~**schwester** assistant nurse; ~**signal** distress signal; ~**spalte** *(Buchhaltung)* auxiliary column; ~**spende** relief aid; ~**stab** support team; ~**station** outstation; ~**stelle** aid center *(US)* (centre, *Br.*); ~**stoffe** auxiliary material; ~- **und Betriebsstoffe** operating supplies; **Roh-,** ~- **und Betriebsstoffe** *(Bilanz)* raw materials and supplies; ~**testamentsvollstrecker** assumed executor; ~**testamentsvollstreckerzeugnis** ancillary letters testamentary *(US)*; ~**trupp** rescue party, *(Instandsetzung)* breakdown gang; ~**truppen** auxiliary (subsidiary) troops, auxiliaries; ~**verein** benefit club, provident (benevolent) society *(Br.)*; ~**verein auf Gegenseitigkeit** mutual aid society; ~**versprechen abgeben** to promise one's help; ~**volumen** aid volume; ~**vorbringen** alternative submission (pleading); ~**wagen** emergency car.
hilfsweise alternatively.
Hilfs|werk relief organization (agency), charitable organization; **soziales** ~**werk** welfare association (institution), charitable organization; ~**zahl für Prämienreserveberechnung** valuation constant; ~**zettel** reminder; ~**zug** relief (emergency, supply, breakdown, wrecking) train; ~**zusage** aid grant; **feste** ~**zusage** pledge of aid; **der Stahlindustrie mit generellen** ~**zusagen, Anleihen und Staatsgarantien Mittel zuführen** to pump aid, loans and guarantees into the steel industry.
Himmel sky, heaven, *(Paradies)* promised land, paradise;
aus heiterem ~ out of a clear (the blue) sky; **im** ~ **und auf Erden** in heaven and earth; **um** ~**s willen** for pity's sake, good gracious, good heavens; **unter freiem** ~ under the open sky; **wie im siebenten** ~ in the seventh heaven, high up in the skies;
bedeckter ~ overcast sky; **düsterer** ~ heavy sky; **freier** ~ open; **politischer** ~ political horizon; **siebenter** ~ paradise;
~ **auf Erden** heaven on earth;
aus allen ~**n fallen** to be stunned (flabberghasted); **vom** ~ **fallen** to appear (come) out of the blue; **sich wie im siebenten** ~ **fühlen** to tread (walk) on air, to be floating on the clouds; ~ **auf Erden haben** to lead the life of Riley *(US coll.)*; **in den** ~ **heben** to talk up, to crack up; **j. in den** ~ **heben** to extol s. o. to the skies; **das Blaue vom** ~ **herunterlügen** to lie like a trooper, to lie in one's throat; **das Blaue vom** ~ **herunterreden** to talk the hind leg off a donkey, to talk nineteen to the dozen; **wie ein Blitz aus heiterem** ~ **kommen** to come like a bolt from the blue; **j. in den** ~ **loben** to elevate (extol, laud) s. o. to the skies; **unter freiem** ~ **schlafen** to sleep in the open; **wie im siebenten** ~ **sein** to swing from the chandeliers; **neuer Stern am literarischen** ~ **sein** to shine as a new star in the literary firmament; ~ **und Hölle in Bewegung setzen** to move heaven and earth; **jem.** ~ **und Erde versprechen** to promise s. o. the moon.

himmelangst werden, jem. to be in a blue funk *(coll.)*.
Himmelfahrts|kommando forlorn hope; ~**nase** pug-nose.
himmelhochjauchzend - zu Tode betrübt the thrill of victory, heartbreak of defeat;
~ **sein** to laugh on the wrong side of the mouth.
himmelschreiendes Unrecht outrageous injustice.
Himmels|laboratorium skylab; ~**reklame** aerial (sky) advertising; ~**richtung** cardinal point, direction; **die vier** ~**richtungen** the four quarters of the globe, the four winds; **in alle** ~**richtungen verstreut sein** to be scattered to the four corners of the earth, *(im Zimmer)* to be all over the shop; ~**schreiber** skywriter; ~**schrift** aerial advertisement, skywriting; ~**stürmer** highflier.
himmelweit immense, enormous;
~ **auseinander sein** to be poles apart;
~**er Unterschied** a world of difference.
himmlisch wonderful, marvel(l)ous, heavenly, delicious, out of this world *(coll.)*;
~**es Essen** marvel(l)ous food; ~**e Fügung** providence; ~**e Geduld** patience of Job; **die** ~**en Heerscharen** the host of heaven.
Hin und Her, ewiges chopping and changing.
hin und wieder on and off.
hin und zurück there and back, out and home, going and coming, outward and inward.
hin- und herfahren to shuttle, to commute *(US)*.
Hin- und Herfracht freight out and home.
hin- und herschwanken, in seiner Meinung to wobble (waver) between two opinions.
Hin- und Herwechsel exchange and reexchange.
Hin- und Rück|fahrkarte return, return (round trip, *US*) ticket; ~**fahrt** voyage out and home, journey there and back, round trip *(US)*; ~**reise** out and home voyage; ~**reiseversicherung** insurance out and home.
hinab|schleusen *(Schiff)* to lock down; ~**steigen** to descend, to climb down.
hinarbeiten, auf etw. to work one's way up; **jahrelang auf etw.** ~ to work for s. th. for years.
hinauf|arbeiten, sich vom Zugabfertiger zum Abteilungspräsidenten to work up from the dispatcher to division superintendent; **sich** ~**bemühen** to take the trouble to go upwards; **mit dem Aufzug zum 10. Stock** ~**fahren** to go up to the tenth floor in a lift; **Treppe** ~**fallen** to be kicked upstairs.
hinaufgehen to go up;
auf das Podium ~ to mount the platform; **stark** ~ *(Preise)* to go up sharply.
hinauf|geleiten to show s. o. upstairs; **Koffer ins Gepäcknetz** ~**heben** to lift a suitcase onto the luggage rack; ~**schnellen** *(Kurs)* to soar, to splurge *(US)*; ~**schrauben** *(Preise)* to push (screw, level, drive) up, to boost prices, to push to a level; **Produktion** ~**schrauben** to step up production; **Steuern um 20%** ~**schrauben** to raise taxes by 20 per cent; **sich hoch** ~**schwingen** to fly a high pitch; ~**setzen** *(Preise)* to increase, to raise, to mark up; **auf der Erfolgsleiter weiter** ~**steigen** to advance further on the ladder of success; **bis auf 50 Grad** ~**steigen** *(Temperaturen)* to reach the fifties; ~**treiben** *(Preise)* to run (push, send, force) up; **Aktienkurs** ~**treiben** to boom (bull) a stock; **Rolläden** ~**ziehen** to pull up the venetian blinds.
hinaus, auf Jahre for many years; **aufs Meer** ~ out to sea; **nach hinten** ~ *(Zimmer)* at the back; **nach Süden** ~ *(Zimmer)* facing the South; **über sein Gehalt** ~ over and above s. one's salary; **über das Grab** ~ beyond the grave; **über das Normalmaß** ~ more than usual; **über die Zeit** ~ beyond the time limit;
über dieses Alter ~ **sein** to have passed this age; **darüber** ~ **sein** to be past it; **auf Jahre** ~ **versorgt sein** to have enough to live on for years; **hoch** ~ **wollen** to be a highflyer;
j. mit einem Fußtritt ~**befördern** to kick s. o. outside; ~**begleiten** to show (see) out; **j. aus seiner Stellung** ~**beißen** to elbow s. o. out of his position; **über die beabsichtigte Zeit** ~**bleiben** to stay beyond one's time; **j. aus einer Stellung** ~**drängen** to oust s. o. from his position; **j.** ~**ekeln** to worry (freeze, *US*) s. o. out; **ins Land** ~**fahren** to drive out into the country; **j. aufs Meer** ~**fahren** to take s. o. out to sea; **über ein Signal** ~**fahren** to go beyond a signal; ~**finden** to find one's way out; ~**fliegen** to be fired (sacked) *(sl.)*, to get the sack (push) *(sl.)*; **in hohem Bogen** ~**fliegen** to be thrown out on one's ear; **aus der Schule** ~**fliegen** to be expelled from school.
hinausgehen, über den Antrag des Staatsanwaltes *(Urteil)* to be more severe than the public prosecutor's recommendation; **über jds. Befugnisse** ~ to exceed s. one's authority; **auf Betrug** ~ to be tantamount to fraud; **über jds. Erwartungen** ~ to surpass s. one's expectations; **auf den Garten** ~ *(Tür)* to lead into the garden; **über jds. Möglichkeiten** ~ to be beyond s. one's means; **nicht über fünfzig Pfund** ~ not go higher than £ 50; **über einen Spaß** ~ to be going beyond a joke; **auf die Straße** ~ *(Fenster)* to face the street; **über seine Versprechungen** ~ to be better than one's word.
hinaus|gekommen sein, den ganzen Tag nicht aus dem Haus not to have been out of the house all day; ~**geschmissen werden** to get thrown out, to get the gate *(US)* (sack, push, *sl.*); ~**geschoben** deferred; ~**geworfen** *(mil.)* cashiered; **Fahnen aus dem Fenster** ~**hängen** to hang flags out of the window; **j. aus dem Haus** ~**jagen** to drive s. o. out of the house; **auf das Gleiche** ~**kommen** to come to the same thing; **j.** ~**komplimentieren** to bow s. o. out; ~**lassen** to leave out; **darauf** ~**laufen** to end up that way; **auf eine Sauferei** ~**laufen** to definitely end in a drinking bout; **Schiff aus dem Hafen** ~**lotsen** to pilot a ship out of the harbo(u)r; **Neuigkeiten** ~**posaunen** to broadcast (spread) the news; **über seine Zeitgenossen** ~**ragen** to tower above one's contemporaries; **sich auf j.** ~**reden** to lay the blame at s. one's door; **sich auf Krankheit** ~**reden** to plead ill health; **aus dem Fenster** ~**reichen** to hand out of the window; **Einladungen** ~**schicken** to send out invitations.
Hinausschieben der Zahlungen postponement of payments.
hinausschieben to postpone, to delay, to defer, to put off, to retard;
Abfahrt um zwei Stunden ~ to postpone one's departure for two hours; **Fälligkeit eines Wechsels** ~ to prolong (renew) a bill of exchange; **Hausputz immer wieder** ~ to put off the spring cleaning again and again; **Protest** ~ to delay protest.
hinaus|schießen, über die Landemarke to overshoot the mark; **über das Ziel** ~**schießen** to overstep the mark *(fam.)*; **mit seiner Kritik über das Ziel** ~**schießen** to go too far with one's criticism; **j.** ~**schmeißen** to give s. o. the sack *(sl.)*, to chuck s. o. out *(Br., sl.)*, to fire s. o.; **Angestellten kurzerhand** ~**setzen** to chuck an employee out without more ado; **Mieter** ~**setzen** to evict a tenant; **Unruhestifter kurzerhand** ~**setzen** to turn out the troublemaker on the spot.
hinaus|spähen, durch den Vorhang to peer through the curtain; **aus dem Fenster** ~**springen** to leap (jump) out of the window; **Blumen auf den Balkon** ~**stellen** to put flowers out on the balcony; **aus dem Stadion auf die Straße** ~**strömen** to pour out of the stadium into the street; **aus dem Fenster** ~**stürzen** to fall out of the window; **auf die Straße** ~**stürzen** to rush out of the house; **j. auf den Friedhof** ~**tragen** to bear s. o. out to the grave; **jds. Namen in die ganze Welt** ~**tragen** to spread s. one's name all over the world; **auf das Meer** ~**treiben** to drift out to sea; ~**trompeten** to broadcast; **über etw.** ~**wachsen** to outgrow s. th.; **über sich selbst** ~**wachsen** to surpass (rise above) o. s.; **sich auf das Eis** ~**wagen** to venture out onto the ice; **sich mit einer Erkältung nicht** ~**wagen** to dare not go out with a cold.
hinauswerfen to throw (kick, chuck) out, to put s. o. out of the room, *(kündigen)* to sack *(sl.)*, to fire *(sl.)*, to swap *(sl.)*;
j. in hohem Bogen ~ to knock s. o. into the middle of next week; **Geld zum Fenster** ~ to throw money down the drain; **j. aus der Wohnung** ~ to turn s. o. out of his lodgings, to evict a tenant.
hinauswollen, auf etw. to drive at s. th.; **hoch** ~ to be ambitious, to fly high.
Hinauswurf instant dismissal, sacking *(sl.)*, sack *(sl.)*, gate *(US)*, chuck *(Br., sl.)*;
jem. mit dem ~ **drohen** to threaten to dismiss s. o., to threaten s. o. with the sack *(sl.)*.
hinausziehen to delay, to put on the shelf (long run, *US*);
sich ~ *(Abreise)* to be delayed, *(Arbeit)* to take longer than expected, *(Diskussion)* to go on longer than expected, *(Verhandlungen)* to drag on; **aufs Land** ~ to move into the country.
hinauszögern to retard, to delay, to protract;
sich ~ *(Aufbruch)* to be delayed; **Angelegenheit** ~ to drag one's feet; **Aufbruch zum Büro** ~ to shirk going to the office.
hin|begeben, sich to proceed to; **j.** ~**begleiten** to accompany s. o.; **sich** ~**bemühen** to take the trouble to go there; **Taxi** ~**bestellen** to order a taxi; ~**bestellt werden** to be called up to; **irgendwie** ~**biegen** to manage somehow.
Hinblick, im ~ **auf** with a view (regard) to;
nur im ~ **auf Lebensmittel zutreffen** to be true only of food prices.
hinbringen *(Zeit)* to spend, to pass, to kill;
Kinder zur Schule ~ to take the children to school; **sein Leben kümmerlich** ~ to lead a miserable existence; **sein Leichtsinn wird ihn ins Gefängnis** ~ his carelessness will land him in prison.

hindämmern, vor sich to be half-awake.
hinderlich in the way, impeding, hindering, *(lästig)* burdensome, cumbersome;
jem. ~ **sein** to be in s. one's way, to hamper s. o., to be a nuisance to s. o.; **dem konjunkturellen Fortschritt** ~ **sein** to hamper the progress of business.
hindern to estop, to hinder, to obstruct, to prevent, to hamper, to restrain, to block;
j. ~ to be in s. one's way, to prevent s. o. from doing s. th.; **j. an der Arbeit** ~ to hinder s. o. in his work, to keep s. o. from working; **j. an der Ausübung seiner Pflichten** ~ to obstruct s. o. in the execution of his duty; **j. an der Beantwortung eines Briefes** ~ to hinder s. o. in answering a letter; **Fortschritt** ~ to impede progress; **j. in seiner Karriere** ~ to stop s. o. in mid-career; **j. am Schlafen** ~ to prevent s. o. from sleeping; **Verkehr** ~ to block (obstruct) the traffic; **Vollstreckung** ~ to hinder and delay.
Hindernis hindrance, hamper, clog, countercheck, fetter, bar, obstacle, obstruction, block, check, hitch, drawback, *(Hemmnis)* handicap, drag, impediment;
eingetretene ~**se** intervening circumstances; **gesetzliches** ~ legal bar, statutory foreclosure; **künstliche** ~**se** artificial obstacles; **steuerliches** ~ fiscal drag; **unvorhergesehene** ~**se** unforeseen circumstances;
~ **für die Europäische Einigung** stumbling block in the unification of Europe; ~ **für den Weltfrieden** obstacle to world peace;
~**sen begegnen** to meet with obstacles; ~ **beseitigen** to remove (smooth away) an obstacle; ~ **für die Eintragung darstellen** to be an obstacle to registration; ~ **errichten** to impose a block on; **sich als** ~ **für jds. Beförderung herausstellen** to prove an obstacle to s. one's promotion; **sich über alle** ~**se hinwegsetzen** to brush aside all obstacles; ~ **überwinden** to clear an obstacle; **gesetzlicher** ~**grund** impediment, legal bar; ~**rennen** obstacle race; **zur Erlangung einer behördlichen Genehmigung das reinste** ~**rennen zurücklegen** to have to fight tooth and nail to get a permission.
Hinderungsgrund objection, impediment, *(jur.)* estoppel;
~ **für jds. Beförderung sein** to be an impediment to s. one's promotion.
hindeuten to point to, to indicate;
auf eine konjunkturelle Besserung ~ to show signs of improvement; **auf jds. Schuld** ~ to point to s. one's guilt; **auf einen frühen Winter** ~ to suggest the possibility of an early winter.
hindurch | arbeiten, sich durch ein Buch to work one's way through a book; **sich nicht mehr** ~**finden können** to be all at sea *(coll.)*; **sich durch die Menge** ~**kämpfen** to wriggle one's way through the crowd; **sich durch Schwierigkeiten** ~**kämpfen** to battle one's way through difficulties; **sich durch die tägliche Arbeit** ~**quälen** to worry through the work of the day; **sich** ~**schlängeln** to needle one's way through; **sich durch die Fahrzeuge** ~**schlängeln** to thread one's way between the carriages; **sich wie ein roter Faden durch das ganze Buch** ~**ziehen** to run through the whole book; **sich zwischen den Fahrzeugen** ~**zwängen** to nip in and out of the traffic; **sich durch eine Menschenmenge** ~**zwängen** to thread one's way through a crowd.
hinein | arbeiten, sich in etw. to get the hang of s. th.; **Haus in einen Hang** ~**bauen** to build a house into a hillside; **Schwierigkeiten in einen Prüfungstext** ~**bauen** to incorporate a great many difficulties into an examination paper; **Schlüssel nicht** ~**bekommen** not to be able to get the key into the keyhole.
hineinbringen, Disziplin in eine Klasse to enforce discipline into a class; **keinen Sinn in einem Text** ~ not to be able to make any sense of a sentence; **scharfen Ton in eine Diskussion** ~ to introduce a harsh tone into a discussion; **Vorfall nicht in die Zeitungen** ~ to keep an incident out of the papers; **Zwiespalt in eine Familie** ~ to cause discord and quarrels in a family.
hinein | bugsieren, in eine gute Stellung to manoeuvre into a good job; **Gäste ins Wohnzimmer** ~**bugsieren** to steer guests into the living-room; **sich in jds. Lage** ~**denken** to imagine o. s. in s. one's position; **sich in eine Stellung** ~**drängeln** to edge one's way into a job; **sich in eine volle Straßenbahn** ~**drängen** to wedge (squeeze) o. s. into a crowded tram; **seine Sachen in einen Koffer** ~**drücken** to ram one's clothes into a suitcase; **Wagen in die Garage** ~**fahren** to drive the car into the garage; **j. in die Stadt** ~**fahren** to take s. o. into town; **in einen parkenden Wagen** ~**fahren** to run into (hit) a parked car.
hineinfinden, sich in etw. to get into the knack of s. th.; **sich langsam** ~ to be beginning to find one's feet; **sich in sein Schicksal** ~ to resign o. s. to one's fate; **sich in seine Umgebung** ~ to adjust o. s. to one's environments.
hinein | fressen, seinen Ärger in sich to swallow (gulp down) one's anger; ~**führen** to usher; **in den Wald** ~**führen** to lead into the wood; ~**geben** *(Börse)* to give on *(Br.)*; ~**geboren** to the manner born; **etw.** ~**geheimnissen** to try to find a hidden meaning, to read mysteries in s. th.
hinein | gehen *(in einen Saal)* to go in, to accommodate, to seat, to hold; **in ein Gebäude** ~**gelangen** to get into a building; ~**geleiten** to usher in.
hineingeraten, in den Berufsverkehr to get caught in the rush-hour traffic; **in schlechte Gesellschaft** ~ to get into bad company; **in ein Gewitter** ~ to get caught in a storm; **in eine Sackgasse** ~ *(fig.)* to come up against a blank wall; **in eine unangenehme Situation** ~ to involve o. s in trouble.
hinein | gerissen werden, in jds. Zusammenbruch to be involved in s. one's ruin; **in einen Streit mit jem.** ~**gezogen sein** to be embroiled with s. o.; **sich in fremde Angelegenheiten** ~**hängen** to poke one's nose into other people's business; **in eine Familie** ~**heiraten** to marry into a family; **jem. ins Auto** ~**helfen** to help s. o. into the car; **jem. in den Mantel** ~**helfen** to help s. o. on with his coat; **in einen Text zu viel** ~**interpretieren** to read too much into a text; **falschen Sinn** ~**interpretieren** to read into a sentence what is not there.
hineinknien, sich in etw. to get right down to s. th.; **sich in eine Aufgabe** ~ to buckle down to a task; **sich in ein Problem** ~ to get to grips with a problem; **sich in sein Studium** ~ to buckle down to one's studies.
hineinkommen, in einen Schneesturm to be caught in a snowstorm; **schnell in eine Sprache** ~ to find a language to present little difficulties; **in ein Zimmer** ~ to enter a room.
Hineinkopieren printing-in.
hinein | kriechen, jem. hinten to kiss s. one's arse; **j. ins Haus** ~**lassen** to let s. o. in; **direkt in ein Auto** ~**laufen** to walk right (run) into a car; **in den Tag** ~**leben** to live in a happy-go-lucky way; **anderen Sinn in einen Text** ~**legen** to alter the meaning of a text; **in eine Klausel** ~**lesen** to read into a clause; **sich in eine Sprache** ~**lesen** to read o. s. into a language; **zuviel in einen Text** ~**lesen** to read too much into a text; **in eine dunkle Affäre** ~**leuchten** to throw light on a shady affair; **ins Fenster** ~**leuchten** *(Sterne)* to shine through the window; **in einen bewaffneten Konflikt** ~**manövrieren** to manoeuvre a state into an armed conflict; **in den Schulunterricht** ~**nehmen** to include in the school syllabus; **in ein Schloß** ~**passen** to fit a lock; **in einen Waggon** ~**pferchen** to cram into a rail car; **in jds. Angelegenheiten** ~**pfuschen** to meddle in s. one's affairs; **in ein Zimmer** ~**platzen** to burst into a room; **neue Bestimmung in einen Text** ~**praktizieren** to smuggle a new clause into a text; **erste 240 Mio Pfundtranche in den Bankenapparat im Januar** ~**pressen** to squeeze the first 240 m tranch of the tap in January banking month; **sich in einen Bus** ~**quetschen** to wedge o. s. in a bus; **seine Sachen in den Koffer** ~**quetschen** to cram one's things into a suitcase.
hineinreden to chip in *(coll.)*;
jem. ~ to interrupt s. o.; **jem. in alles** ~ to interfere with everything s. o. is doing; **jem. in seine Angelegenheiten** ~ to interfere in s. one's affairs; **ins Leere** ~ to talk at random.
hinein | regnen, ins Zimmer to be raining into the room; **weit ins Meer** ~**reichen** to stretch far out to sea; **j. in eine unangenehme Sache** ~**reißen** to involve s. o. in a sorry business; **sich selbst** ~**reiten** to get o. s. into a bad fix; **j. schön** ~**reiten** to get s. o. in a pickle; **direkt in ein Auto** ~**rennen** to run straight into a car; **nur kurz in eine Sache** ~**riechen** to have a look-see *(Br.)*; **zu tief ins Glas** ~**schauen** to have a drop too much; **bei jem. kurz** ~**schauen** to look s. o. up; **kurz in die Zeitung** ~**schauen** to have a dip into the newspaper; **in die Menge** ~**schießen** to shoot into the crowd; **sich ins Haus** ~**schleichen** to sneak into the house; ~**schlittern** to slip into; **in eine Affäre** ~**schlittern** to get mixed up in an affair; **in einen Krieg** ~**schlittern** to drift into a war; **sich** ~**schmuggeln** to gate-crash; **in eine Gesellschaft** ~**schneien** to drop into a party; **sich in die Lage eines anderen** ~**setzen** to imagine o. s. in s. one's situation; ~**stecken** *(investieren)* to invest, to make investments, to tie (lock, *Br.*) up; **seine Nase überall** ~**stecken** to poke one's nose in everything; **sich in eine panische Angst** ~**steigern** to work o. s. up into a panic; **Essen in sich** ~**stopfen** to eat one's fill, to cram o. s. with food; **Papiere in eine Schublade** ~**stopfen** to cram papers into a drawer; **seine Sachen in einen Koffer** ~**stopfen** to jam (ram) one's things into a suitcase; **in eine Stadt** ~**strömen** to pour into a town; **in ein Zimmer** ~**stürmen** to rush into a room; **sich in die Arbeit** ~**stürzen** to plunge into business; **sich blindlings in den Kampf**

~stürzen to hurl o. s. into the fray; **ins Zimmer ~stürzen** to dash into the room; **Möbel ins Haus ~tragen** to carry furniture into a house; **Stollen in einen Berg ~treiben** to drive a tunnel into a mountain; **ins Haus ~treten** to enter a building; **sich in j. ~versetzen** to identify o. s. with s. o.; **in etw. ~wachsen** to get the hang of s. th.; **Blick in ein Buch ~werfen** to have a dip into a book.

hineinziehen, j. in etw. to drag s. o. into s. th.; **j. in eine Affäre ~** to involve s. o. in a sorry business; **in eine Auseinandersetzung ~** to embroil in a quarrel; **Volk in einen Krieg ~** to embroil a nation in a war.

hineinzwängen, sich in einen Bus to wedge o. s. into a bus.

hinfahren, j. zum Flugplatz to drive (take) s. o. to the airport.

hin- und herfahren to shuttle, to commute *(US)*.

Hin | fahrkarte one-way ticket *(US)*; **~- und Rückfahrkarte** return, return (round trip, *US*) ticket; **~fahrt** journey there, *(Seereise)* voyage (passage) there; **nur für die ~fahrt** one-way *(US)*; **~- und Rückfahrt** voyage out and home, journey there and back, round trip *(US)*.

hinfallen, der Länge nach to fall full length.

hinfällig frail, feeble, decrepit, prostrate, *(Gesetz)* superseded, no longer applicable, *(Klausel)* void, invalid;
~ machen to invaliditate, to render invalid, to supersede; **~ werden** *(Vermächtnis)* to lapse, *(Vertragsbestimmung)* to be cancelled (invalidated), to become void;
~er alter Mann frail old man.

Hinfälligkeit frailty, decrepitude, debility, weakness;
~ eines Vermächtnisses lapse of a legacy.

hinflegeln, sich to loll, to sprawl; **sich auf einen Stuhl ~** to flop down on a seat.

hinfliegen to fly there, to take a plane;
mit der nächsten Maschine ~ to take the next plane.

Hin | flug outgoing (outward) flight; **~fracht** freight out, outward cargo (freight); **~- und Herfracht** freight out and home.

hinführen, zum Bahnhof to lead to the station.

Hingabe devotion;
durch ~ eines Pfandstücks by way of a pledge; **unter ~ seines Lebens** at the cost of one's own life;
~ erfüllungshalber accord and satisfaction;
restlose ~ an seinen Beruf utter devotion to one's profession; **mit leidenschaftlicher ~ lieben** to love passionately; **sich mit beharrlicher ~ seinen wissenschaftlichen Aufgaben widmen** to be constant in one's devotion to scientific studies.

hingeben, sich seiner Arbeit völlig to dedicate o. s. completely to one's work; **sein ganzes Geld ~** to part with all one's money; **sich der Hoffnung ~** to cherish a hope; **sich falschen Hoffnungen ~** to have illusions; **sein Leben ~** to sacrifice one's life; **sein Leben für sein Vaterland ~** to give one's life as a sacrifice for one's country; **sich einer Sache ~** to give o. s. up to s. th.; **sich seinen Träumen ~** to cherish a dream; **sich der Verzweiflung ~** to abandon o. s. to despair.

Hingebung devotion;
j. mit großer ~ pflegen to care for s. o. with devotion.

hingebungsvoll devoted.

hingegeben, völlig devotedly attached.

hingehen *(vergehen)* to pass, to slip by;
etw. ~ lassen to shut one's eyes to s. th., to overlook s. th.; **jem. etw. ungestraft ~ lassen** to let s. o. get away with it.

hin | gehören, nicht *(Bemerkung)* to be out of place; **~gerissen sein** to be carried away (in raptures, entranced with); **sich zu jem. ~gezogen fühlen** to feel drawn towards s. o.

Hinhaltemanöver delaying tactics, stall *(US sl.)*.

hinhalten to delay, to put off, to keep in suspense, to stall off *(US sl.)*;
j. ~ to make s. o. wait, to put (fob, *US*) s. o. off; **j. mit der Bezahlung ~** to keep s. o. out of money; **Feind ~** to keep the enemy at bay; **j. mit der Gehaltserhöhung ~** to keep s. o. waiting a long time for a raise *(US)* (rise, *Br.*); **Gläubiger ~** to delay creditors; **seine Gläubiger mit leeren Versprechungen ~** to feed one's creditors with empty promises; **jem. die Hand ~** to extend (hold out) one's hand to s. o.; **seinen Kopf für etw. ~** to hold the baby *(Br., sl.)* (the bag, *US*), to carry the can; **j. pausenlos ~** to give s. o. the runaround *(US)*.

hinhaltend dilatory, delaying;
~e Politik stalling tactics; **~er Widerstand** delaying action.

Hinhaltungstaktik delaying tactics, stall *(US sl.)*.

hinhauen to hit, *(funktionieren)* to work alright;
seine Arbeit nur ~ to scurry through one's work; **Artikel für eine Zeitschrift ~** to knock off an article for a magazine; **Brief ~** to scribble a letter; **Buch ~** to slam a book on the table; **den ganzen Kram ~** to chuck up the whole thing; **lang ~** to fall flat on the ground; **sich für eine halbe Stunde ~** to kip down for half an hour *(coll.)*;
das wird ~ that will do.

hinhören, nur halb to be only half listening; **nicht richtig ~** not to listen properly.

Hinkebein dot-and-carry-one.

hinken to [walk with a] limp, *(Vergleich)* to be lame.

hinkend lame;
~e Währung limping standard.

hin | knallen, Buch to slam the book on the table; **mit seinem Geld ~kommen** to live within one's means; **mit der Zeit gerade ~kommen** to have enough time; **es gut ~kriegen** to make a neat job of it, to rustle up *(US sl.)*; **etw. ~kritzeln** to jot down, to scratch a note; **ein paar Worte ~kritzeln** to scrawl a few words; **nicht ~langen** not to be enough (sufficient).

hinlänglich sufficient, adequate;
~ unterrichtet worden sein to have been sufficiently informed; **kein ~er Beweggrund** an inadequate motive; **~er Gegenwert** sufficient consideration; **~es Kapital** sufficient funds.

hinleben, auf ein Ziel to direct one's life towards a goal.

hinlegen, sich to lie down; **seine Karten offen ~** to put one's cards on the table; **Rolle nur so ~** to perform a part brilliantly.

hinlenken, jds. Aufmerksamkeit auf etw. to draw s. one's attention to s. th.; **Unterhaltung auf die politische Lage ~** to lead the conversation round to the political situation.

hinmetzeln to slaughter, to butcher;
wahllos ~ to slaughter without discrimination.

Hinnahme, stillschweigende acquiescence.

hinnehmen, Beleidigung to put up with an affront; **jds. Entscheidung ~** to submit to s. one's judgment; **gelassen (ruhig) ~** to put up with, to take calmly; **unpassende Heirat niemals ~** to never acquiesce in an unsuitable marriage; **sein Schicksal ~** to resign o. s. to one's fate; **als selbstverständlich ~** to take for granted; **stillschweigend ~** to take it lying down; **Trennung von seiner Familie ~** to submit to the separation of one's family; **auf Treu und Glauben ~** to take on trust; **jds. Unverschämtheiten ~** to submit to s. one's insolences.

hinneigen, mehr zu der Auffassung to be more inclined to believe.

Hinneigung inclination, leaning;
pazifistische ~en haben to have leanings towards pacifism.

hin- und herpendeln, zwischen zwei Ländern to shuttle back and forth between two countries.

hinpfuschen, Arbeit to muddle through a piece of work.

Hin- und Herpolitik stop-go policy.

hinquälen, sich to drag on, to wear out.

hinreichend ample, adequate, sufficient;
~e Erklärung satisfactory explanation; **~er Gegenwert** sufficient consideration; **~er Grund** sufficient cause; **über ~e Mittel verfügen** to have sufficient funds (means) at one's disposal; **~e Reserven** adequate reserves; **~e Sicherheit** sufficient security; **~er Verdacht** reasonable suspicion; **~e Vorräte** adequate supply of provisions.

Hinreise *(Schiff)* voyage out, outward journey *(Br.)*;
auf der ~ begriffen outward bound.

Hin- und Rückreise out and home voyage;
~versicherung insurance out and home.

hinreißen *(begeistern)* to carry away, to ravish, to enchant;
zu Beifallsstürmen ~ to raise the house; **j. zur Bewunderung ~** to send s. o. into raptures, to enrapture s. o.;
sich zu keinen Äußerungen ~ lassen to refuse to be drawn; **sich zu einer Bemerkung ~ lassen** to be foolish enough to make a remark; **sich zum Mitleid ~ lassen** to let o. s. be stirred to pity; **sich vom Zorn ~ lassen** to give way to one's anger.

hinreißend enchanting, entrancing, ravishing;
~ aussehen to look breath-taking;
~e Beredsamkeit rousing eloquence; **~es Lächeln** captivating smile; **~e Stimme** fascinating voice.

hinrichten to execute, to carry out an execution;
j. in der Gaskammer ~ to gas s. o.; **j. durch den Strang ~** to execute s. o. by hanging; **auf dem elektrischen Stuhl ~** to electrocute.

Hinrichtung execution;
öffentliche ~ public execution;
~ durch den Strang execution [by hanging]; **~ auf dem elektrischen Stuhl** electrocution, electric chair.

Hinrichtungs | befehl death warrant, executionary order; **~kommando** firing party (squad); **~stätte** place of execution; **~termin** execution deadline.

hin- und herrollen to tumble and toss.

hin | schaffen to carry, to transport; **etw. ~schaukeln** to swing it *(fam.)*.

Hinscheiden departure, decease, demise.
hin | schicken, Vertreter to send a delegate; ~**schielen** to cast a glance, to steal a furtive glance; ~**schlachten** to slaughter, to butcher; **der Länge nach ~schlagen** to measure one's length on the ground; ~**schleichen** *(Zeit)* to drag; **j. zum Arzt ~schleifen** to drag s. o. to the doctor; ~**schlendern** to saunter, to stroll; **sich ~schleppen** *(Unterhaltung)* to drag, *(Zeit)* to wear out; **sich über Jahre ~schleppen** *(Prozeß)* to drag on for years; **Buch ~schleudern** to fling down a book; **Artikel ~schludern** to knock off an article; ~**schmachten** to pine away, to languish; **alles ~schmeißen** to chuck up one's job (the whole thing, the sponge); **Geld ~schmeißen** to plank down the ready; ~**schreiben** to write there; **Wort mühselig ~schreiben** to trace a word laboriously; ~- **und herschütteln** *(Bus)* to jog up and down; ~- **und herschwanken** to oscillate; ~**schwinden** *(Vorräte)* to dwindle (melt) away, *(Zeit)* to wear out.
Hinsehen, bei näherem on closer examination.
hinsehen, nicht zu genau not to look too closely.
hinsein to be broken, *(Auto)* to be a write-off, *(Ruf)* to be ruined; **völlig** ~ to be carried away.
hinsetzen, sich to sit down, to take a seat; **sich zum Lesen** ~ to sit down to read.
Hinsicht respect, view, consideration;
in finanzieller ~ financially; **in jeder** ~ in all respects, in every way, for all the world, perfect in all things; **in kultureller** ~ cultural; **in mancherlei** ~ in several ways; **in politischer** ~ from a political point of view; **in tatsächlicher und rechtlicher** ~ in fact and law.
hinsichtlich concerning, with regard to, referring, in point of.
hinsiechen to pine away, to languish.
hinstellen, j. als Beispiel to hold s. o. up, as an example; **jem. das Essen** ~ to serve s. o. his dinner; **es so** ~ to make it appear; **sich als Tugendbold** ~ to represent o. s. as a model of virtue; **als unbedeutend** ~ to play down *(Br.)*, to downplay *(US)*, to softpedal.
hinsteuern, auf etw. to be driving (aiming) at; **auf den Konkurs** ~ to steer near receivership; **nach Norden** ~ to head north; **Unterhaltung auf die Politik** ~ to lead the conversation round to the political situation.
hinstreben, zur Kneipe to head for the pub.
hinstrecken, nach Norden to stretch (range) to the north; **j. mit einem einzigen Schlag** ~ to knock s. o. flat.
hinströmen to flock in there.
hintansetzen to disregard, to ignore;
Gläubigerinteressen ~ to prejudice the rights of creditors; **persönliche Wünsche immer** ~ to always put personal wishes last.
hintanstehen to take second place.
hinten at the back, in the rear;
ganz ~ **im Wald** deep in the forest; **weit** ~ **im Buch** towards the end of the book;
von ~ **anfangen** to start at the wrong end; **sich** ~ **anstellen** to join the end of the queue; **j. von** ~ **und vorn bedienen** to wait on s. o. hand and foot; **mit seiner Arbeit** ~ **bleiben** to lag with one's work; ~ **einsteigen** to enter at the rear; **nach** ~ **hinausliegen** *(Wohnung)* to face the back; **j.** ~ **hineinkriechen** to lick s. one's boots *(coll.)*; **j. am liebsten von** ~ **sehen** to be glad to see the back of s. o.; ~ **im Auto sitzen** to sit in the back of the car; **von** ~ **überfallen** to attack from the rear; **nicht wissen wo** ~ **und vorn ist** not to know which end is up.
hintenherum in a roundabout way, on the crook *(sl.)*;
~ **ergattern** to wangle, to get under the counter; **es** ~ **gehört haben** to have heard it in a roundabout way (on the grapevine); **jem. etw.** ~ **sagen** to tell s. o. s. th. on the quiet; ~ **verkaufen** to sell on the quiet.
Hinter | achsantrieb rear drive; ~**achse** rear axle; ~**ansicht** back view; ~**bänkler** *(Parlament)* backbencher *(Br.)*; **sich auf die ~beine setzen (stellen)** to dig one's heels in, to offer a stiff resistance, to get on one's hind legs; ~**bliebene** surviving dependants, survivors, relicts, bereaved.
Hinterbliebenen | bezüge surviving dependant's allowance *(US)*, *(Witwe)* widow's benefit *(Br.)*; ~**fürsorge** maintenance of survivors; ~**pension** [war] pension, *(Eheleute)* survivor's pension; ~**rente** death (survivor's, *US*, dependant's, *Br.*) benefit, *(Kriegsrente)* parent's insurance benefit *(US)*, [war] pension; ~**rente der Witwe** *(Sozialversicherung)* widow's insurance benefits *(US)*; ~**versicherung** survivor's *(US)* (survivorship) insurance; ~- **und Invalidenversicherung** Old-Age (Survivor's and Disability) Insurance *(US)*; ~**versorgung** provision for dependants.
Hinterbliebener survivor.
hinterbringen, jem. etw. to pass on to s. o., to inform s. o. of s. th.
Hinterbringer informant, telltale.
Hinterbühne backstage;
auf der ~ upstage.
hintereinander right of the reel, *(ohne Pause)* without interruption (a break), *(zeitlich)* in succession, consecutively;
dicht ~ one close after the other; **für drei Tage** ~ for three days running;
acht Stunden ~ **arbeiten** to work for eight hours at a stretch; **seine Arbeit** ~ **fertigmachen** to finish one's work in one go; **wochenlang** ~ **geregnet haben** to have been raining for weeks on end;
~**fahren** to drive in a column; ~**gehen** to walk in single (Indian) file; **Batterien ~schalten** to connect batteries in tandem.
Hintereinander | fliegen rat race; ~**schaltung** tandem connection.
Hintereingang rear (back) entrance;
~ **benutzen** to use the back entrance.
Hinter | füße, sich auf die ~füße stellen to get on one's hind legs, to offer a stiff resistance; ~**galerie** *(Schiff)* balcony; ~**gebäude** rear building.
Hintergedanke ulterior motive;
in ihren ~n in the back of their minds;
etw. ohne ~n sagen to say s. th. quite innocently.
hintergehen to defraud, to double-cross, to deceive, to delude, to hoodwink, to beguile, to trick;
j. ~ to double-cross s. o., to play s. o. foul; **bevorrechtigte Gläubiger** ~ to defraud secured creditors; **Zoll** ~ to defraud the revenue, to evade customs duty.
Hintergehung | bevorrechtigter Gläubiger defrauding secured creditors; ~ **des Zolls** defraudation of the revenue, evasion of customs duty.
Hintergrund background;
im ~ **der Bühne** upstage;
politischer ~ political background;
sich scharf vom ~ **abheben** to define itself against the background; **etw. ganz in den** ~ **drängen** to push into the background, to push s. th. into the shade; ~ **erläutern** to fill in the background; **sich im** ~ **halten** to efface o. s., to take a back seat *(coll.)*; **aus dem** ~ **operieren** to drive from the back-seat; **in den** ~ **rücken** to play down; **in den** ~ **treten** to take a back seat; **vorläufig in den** ~ **treten** to go into temporary eclipse;
~**bericht** inside story.
Hintergründe | eines Skandals aufdecken to probe into a scandal; ~ **einer Entscheidung ausleuchten** to go behind a decision; ~ **eines Falles kennen** to speak with inside knowledge, to be inside on a matter *(US)*, to know the inner history of an affair.
Hintergrundgeräusche *(Radio)* background.
hintergründig enigmatical, inscrutable, *(verborgen)* secret, obscure, cryptic;
~ **antworten** to answer in a subtle way;
~**e Absichten** secret intention; ~**es Lächeln** cryptic smile.
Hintergründiges der politischen Intrige arcana of political intrigue.
Hintergrund | informationen background briefings; ~**material** background material (stuff); **historisches ~material zur Verfügung stellen** to historiate; ~**musik** background music.
Hinterhalt ambush;
j. aus dem ~ **angreifen** to ambush s. o.; **in einen** ~ **geraten** to walk (fall) into an ambush; **etw. im** ~ **haben** to have s. th. in reserve (up one's sleeve); ~ **legen** to lay (to prepare) an ambush; **im** ~ **liegen** to lie in ambush; **j. aus dem** ~ **überfallen** to ambush (waylay) s. o.
hinterhältig sneaky, artful, insidious, furtive;
~**e Methoden** underhand methods.
Hinterhaus back building;
~**verschwörer** backstreet conspirator; ~**wohnung** rear flat.
hinterherhinken to lag behind;
mit seinen Zahlungen ~ to be behindhand with one's payments.
hinterher | laufen, jem. to run after s. o.; ~**sein** to be keen on it; ~**trollen** to trail along.
Hinter | hof back yard, inner court, courtyard; **asoziale ~hofeinflüsse auf die Erziehung** slum (back-street) education; ~**land** hinterland, back country *(US)*, upstate *(US)*; **ins ~land reisen** to travel up-country.
hinterlassen *(Erbschaft)* to leave, *(Grundbesitz)* to devise, *(Vermächtnis)* to give and to bequeath;
jem. etw. ~ to escheat an estate to s. o.; **keine Erben** ~ to leave no issue; **sein Geld einem Krankenhaus** ~ to will one's money to a hospital; **jem. ein Haus** ~ to leave s. o. a house; **Nachricht** ~ to leave word (a message); **nichts als Schulden** ~ to leave nothing but debts; **keine Spuren** ~ to leave no traces; **kein Testament** ~

to die intestate; **sein ganzes Vermögen seiner Frau** ~ to leave all one's property to one's wife;
jem. etw. auszurichten ~ to leave a message with s. o.

Hinterlassenschaft property left, estate, assets, inheritance *(US)*;
jds. ~ antreten to step into a dead man's shoes.

Hinterlassung devisal, estate, heritage;
unter ~ von Schulden leaving unsettled debts;
ohne ~ eines Testaments sterben to die intestate.

hinterlassungsfähig bequeathable.

hinterlegen to lodge, to deliver in trust, *(bei einer Bank)* to deposit, to bank, *(Waren)* to consign, to bail;
Betrag ~ to deposit an amount; **bis zur Erfüllung einer Vertragsbedingung** ~ to place in escrow; **in der Garderobe** ~ to leave in the cloakroam; **Geld bei jem.** ~ to deposit money with s. o.; **bei Gericht** ~ to pay into the court, to deposit in court; **Kaution für j.** ~ to put up bail for s. o.; **Schlüssel beim Nachbarn** ~ to leave the key with the neighbo(u)r; **seinen Schmuck** ~ to leave one's jewel(le)ry in safe custody; **als Sicherheit** ~ to deposit (lodge) as underlying security *(US)*; **Summe** ~ to deposit a sum in the hands of a third party; **Testament** ~ to deposit a will; **unwiderruflich** ~ to deposit irrevocably; **Urkunde** ~ to place an instrument in escrow; **Wertpapiere** ~ to deposit securities, to place securities in a deposit *(US)* (safe custody, *Br.*).

Hinterleger depositor, bailor, bailer, consignor *(Scot. law)*.

hinterlegt, nicht undeposited;
~**e Aktie** deposited share (stock, *US*); ~**er Betrag** deposit; ~**es Geld** money deposited, trust money.

Hinterlegung deposit, deposition, depositation, bailment, *(Hinterlegungsvertrag)* contract of bailment, delivery in escrow, escrow agreement, *(Waren)* consignment, consignation *(Scot.)*;
gegen ~ von on depositing of; **gegen ~ erstklassiger Aktien** subject to the deposit of collateral security consisting of first-rate stocks *(US)*;
gerichtliche ~ lodgment, bringing money (payment) into court; **öffentliche** ~ custody of the law; **vereinbarte** ~ voluntary deposit; **vertraglich vereinbarte** ~ conventional deposit; **vorläufige** ~ delivery in escrow;
~ **in bar** cash deposit; ~ **von Besitzurkunden** deposit of title deeds; ~ **von Geld** lodging of money; ~ **bei Gericht** lodgment, bringing money (payment) into court; ~ **des Grundschuldbriefes** deposit of the land certificate *(Br.)*; ~ **der Ratifizierungsurkunden** deposit of the instruments of ratification; ~ **von Stimmrechtsermächtigungen** deposit of proxies; ~ **von Urkunden** depositing of documents; ~ **von Wertpapieren** deposit of securities;
durch ~ einer Sicherheitssumme decken to margin; **gegen ~ einer Kaution freigelassen werden** to be released on bail.

Hinterlegungs|abteilung *(Bank)* escrow department; ~**befugnis** authority to deposit; ~**beleg** depositary certificate; ~**benachrichtigung,** ~**bescheid** notice of payment in, notice of deposit *(Br.)*; ~**bescheinigung** certificate of funds (deposit), depository (trust) receipt; ~**betrag** money deposited, *(bei Aktienzeichnung)* application money *(Br.)*, *(Börse)* margin; ~**erklärung** trust declaration.

hinterlegungsfähig eligible to serve as collateral *(US)*.

Hinterlegungs|gebühr fee for custodianship; ~**gelder** money deposited, trust money; ~**geschäft** deposit business; **einseitiges** ~**geschäft** bailment for the sole benefit of one party; ~**kasse** lodgment office; ~**konto** escrow account, margin account *(US)*; ~**konto für Sicherheitsleistungen** suitor's deposit account; ~**kosten** costs of deposit; ~**ordnung** Public Trustee Act *(Br.)*, Trustee Reliefs Act *(US)*; ~**ort** place of deposit; ~**quittung** deposit receipt, depositary certificate; ~**schein** depository (trust) receipt, certificate of deposit (funds), trustee's certificate, deposit warrant (certificate).

Hinterlegungsstelle bailee at law, escrow holder, lodgment office, *(Bank)* depositary, depository, deposit company *(Br.)*;
amtliche ~ legal custodian, bailee at law; **staatlich anerkannte** ~ authorized depository *(Br.)*; **einfache** ~ bare (simple) trust *(US)*; **gesetzliche** ~ legal custodian; **öffentliche** ~ Public Trustee Office *(Br.)*;
~ **für Devisenwerte** authorized depository *(Br.)*; ~ **mit besonderen Vollmachten** special trust *(US)*.

Hinterlegungs|summe money deposited, *(Börse)* margin; ~**urkunde** depository (trust) receipt, memorandum of deposit *(Br.)*.

Hinterlegungsvertrag deposit, deposition, escrow agreement, agreement of deposit, contract of bailment, bailment agreement (contract);
entgeltlicher ~ lucrative hire, bailment for hire; **normaler** ~ regular deposit; **unentgeltlicher** ~ gratuitous bailment; **zweiseitiger** ~ bailment for hire.

Hinterlist deceit, cunning, craftiness, *(Tücke)* treachery, insidiousness;
durch ~ by deceitful means.

hinterlistig deceitful, insidious, crafty, cunning;
~ **in eine Falle gelockt werden** to be lured into a trap;
~**es Angebot** insidious offer; ~**es Spiel betreiben** to play an underhand game.

Hintermann backer, ringleader, wirepuller, bottleholder *(coll.)*, *(Wechsel)* subsequent indorser (endorser);
einflußreicher ~ agent of influence, fat cat *(sl.)*; **finanzieller** ~ financial backer;
Informationen an seinen ~ weiterleiten to pass on one's information to s. o. behind the scenes.

Hintermänner, dunkle shady characters.

Hintern backside, bottom;
Hummeln im ~ haben to have ants in one's pants; **j. in den ~ treten** *(fam.)* to kick s. one's bottom.

Hinterrad back wheel;
~**aufhängung** rear suspension; ~**dampfer** stern-wheeler.

hinterrücks behind s. one's back;
j. ~ angreifen to attack s. o. from behind; **j. ~ verleumden** to stab s. o. in the back.

Hinter|seite back, *(Haus)* rear; ~**sinn** deeper meaning; ~**sitz** back seat; **ins ~treffen geraten** to drop behind the rear *(fig.)*, to fall behind, to get outmanoeuvred; ~**treiben** counteraction.

hintertreiben to frustrate, to thwart, to prevent, to wreck;
Annahme eines Gesetzesantrags ~ to block the passage of (ca-canny) a bill; **jds. Beförderung** ~ to prevent s. o. from being promoted; **Gesetzgebung** ~ to obstruct legislation; **jds. Pläne** ~ to thwart (frustrate) s. one's plans; **Verhandlungen** ~ to prevent negotiations taking place.

Hintertreibung frustration, circumvention, prevention, *(Gesetztreibung)* obstruction, ca-cannyism.

Hintertreppe private staircase, backstairs;
auf der ~ reich werden to get rich by devious ways.

Hintertreppen|eingang backstair entrance; ~**politik** backstairs politics; ~**roman** penny dreadful *(Br.)*, dime novel *(US)*, washy novel.

Hintertür back (rear) door;
durch die ~ *(fig.)* by indirect channels, by a side door;
durch die ~ eindringen to slip in by the back door; **durch die ~ wiederkommen** to come in again by the back door.

Hintertürchen *(fig.)* loophole, bolthole;
~ **zur Inanspruchname der Börse im Notfall** back-door route into the market;
sich ein ~ offenhalten to leave o. s. a way out.

Hinter|türklausel *(pol.)* joker *(US sl.)*; ~**wäldler** country bumpkin, clodhopper, yokel, hillbilly *(US)*, hick *(US)*.

hinterwäldlerisch countrified, hillbilly, rustic, *(Idee)* backyard, homespun.

hinterziehen to misappropriate, to embezzle, *(Steuern)* to defraud, to evade;
Einkommensteuer ~ to defraud the revenue, to evade paying taxes (a tax); **Zoll** ~ to evade customs duty.

Hinterziehung defraudation, defraud, embezzlement, evasion;
~ **der Einkommensteuer** evasion of income tax; ~ **öffentlicher Mittel** misappropriation of public funds; ~ **von Steuern** defraudation of the revenue; ~ **des Zolls** defraudation of the customs.

Hinterzimmer backroom.

hinterzogene Einkommensteuer evaded income tax.

hinüber|fahren, über die Grenze to cross the frontier; **zum Nachbarn ~gehen** to walk over to the neighbo(u)r's house; **auf die andere Straßenseite ~gehen** to cross the road; ~**sein** to have given up one's ghost, to have popped off, *(betrunken)* to be well away *(coll.)*.

Hinüberwechseln vom Staatsdienst in die Wirtschaft shuttling between government and business.

hinüberwechseln, ins Lager des Feindes to go over to the enemy camp; **zu einer anderen Partei** ~ to change sides, to rat; **vom Staatsdient in die Wirtschaft** ~ to shuttle between government and business.

hin- und zurückversichern to insure out and home.

Hinweg way there (out).

hinweggehen, über Details to skid over details; **flüchtig darüber** ~ to touch on it only lightly; **über gewisse Punkte** ~ to skip over certain points; **mit Stillschweigen darüber** ~ to pass over it in silence.

hinweg|gekommen sein, nie über einen Verlust to have never got (gotten, *US*) over a loss; **~geschwemmt werden** to be carried off one's legs; **über schwierige Stellen ~gleiten** to glide over the difficult passages; **jem. über eine bestimmte Zeit ~helfen** to tide s. o. over; **darüber ~kommen** to get over it; **über etw. ~lesen** to skim over s. th.; **j. ~lotsen** to jockey s. o. away; **über seine Zuhörer ~reden** to be past (talk over the heads of) one's audience.

hinwegsehen to overlook, to shut one's eyes to;
über eine Beleidigung ~ to ignore an insult; **darüber ~** to let it pass; **auf der Straße über j. völlig ~** to cut s. o. dead in the street.

hinwegsetzen, sich to disregard, to ignore; **sich über alles ~** to cut across all the lines; **sich mit seinen Anordnungen über j. ~** to give orders over s. one's head; **sich über alle Bedenken ~** to set aside all scruples; **sich über einen Einwand ~** to ignore an objection; **sich rücksichtslos über eine frühere Entscheidung ~** to override a former decision; **sich über ein Gesetz ~** to disregard a law; **sich über eine Sitte ~** to reject a custom.

hinweg|täuschen, j. über etw. to mislead (blind) s. o.; **über eine Tatsache ~täuschen** to obscure a fact; **sich mit dem Gedanken darüber ~trösten, daß** to console o. s. with the thought that.

Hinweis indication, reference, hint, tipoff, lead, clue, allusion, point, pointer *(US)*, shady *(sl.)*, *(Zeitung)* announcement;
unter ~ auf Absatz with reference to section;
dringender ~ injunction; **geschäftsmäßiger ~** business notice; **gesetzlicher ~** statutory reference; **versteckter ~** allusion;
einige ~e für das Abendprogramm a few details of the evening program(me); **~e für das Anlagegeschäft** leads for investors; **~e für die Benutzung des Lexikons** notes for the user of this dictionary; **~ auf Fortsetzung des Versicherungsverhältnisses** renewal papers; **~e für Touristen** hints for tourists;
~ am Schwarzen Brett anbringen to post an announcement on the notice board; **verschiedene ~ enthalten** to contain various references; **~ geben** to drop a hint; **einem ~ nachgehen** to follow up a clue.

hinweisen to indicate, to point out;
j. auf etw. ~ to point out (indicate) to s. o.; **nachdrücklich darauf ~** to make it quite clear, to emphasize; **j. auf seine Pflicht ~** to point out to s. o. his duty.

hinweisend indicative;
~es Fürwort demonstrative pronoun.

Hinweis|preis *(EG)* indicated price; **~schild** roadside (direction) sign; **~signal** *(Telefon)* beep; **~tafel** signboard; **~zeichen** *(Verkehr)* directional sign, signpost.

hinwelken to wither away, *(Mensch)* to fade away.

hinwerfen, auf den Boden to throw (fling) s. th. down; **jem. den Fehdehandschuh ~** to throw down the gauntlet to s. o.; **den ganzen Krempel ~** to chuck up the whole thing; **ein paar Zeilen ~** to jot down a few lines.

hinwirken to work towards, to use one's influence, to bring s. th. about.

Hinz und Kunz Tom, Dick and Harry, the populace, hoi polloi, plebs, every man Jack, every mother's son *(coll.)*.

hinziehen to delay, to protract;
sich ~ to drag on, *(Straße)* to extend; **Angelegenheit ~** to drag out an affair; **sich am Fluß ~** *(Grenze)* to run along the river; **sich bis zum Fluß ~** to extend as far as the river; **sich über mehrere Monate ~** *(Verhandlungen)* to spread over several months; **Prozeß ~** to drag on (protract) a lawsuit, to delay proceedings; **sich zum Semesterschluß endlos ~** to drag on towards the end of a term; **Verhandlungsablauf ~** to drag out the negotiating process; **sich noch einige Zeit ~** to progress for some time.

hinzielen auf to aim at, to drive at *(coll.)*.

hinzögern to put off, to delay, to retard.

hinzufügen to add, to append, *(beifügen)* to enclose, to subjoin, *(Gebäude)* to annex.

Hinzufügung [super]addition;
unter ~ adding.

hinzu|gefügt adscript, appendant, appended, additional; **~gewählt** co-optative; **Aktien ~kaufen** to buy more shares (stocks, *US*); **~kommen** to be added, *(Krankheit)* to supervene; **~kommend** additional, further; **~rechnen** to add, to include; **Mehrwertsteuer ~rechnen** to include the value-added tax.

Hinzurechnung addition, inclusion;
unter ~ adding.

Hinzuschlagen addition;
~ der Zinsen zum Kapital capitalization of interest.

hinzu|schlagen, Zinsen zum Kapital to capitalize interest; **~setzen** to add; **seinen Namen ~setzen** to append one's name.

Hinzuwahl cooption, cooptation.

hinzuwählen to coopt.

hinzuziehen to call in, to consult;
Anwalt ~ to consult a barrister; **Sachverständigen ~** to call in an expert.

Hinzuziehung consultation, calling in;
unter ~ von with the assistance of.

Hiobsbotschaft Job's (bad) news.

Hirn, sein ~ zermartern to rack one's brains.

Hirngespinst product(ion) (coinage) of the brain, chimera, vapo(u)r, wild fancy, phantasy, pipe dream;
~e figments of the imagination;
~en nachjagen to run a wild-goose chase.

Hirnschaden mental injury.

hirnverbrannte Idee crazy idea.

Hirtenbrief pastoral letter, charge.

Hissen einer Flagge hoisting of a flag.

hissen, Flagge to hoist a flag.

Histörchen anecdote;
pikante ~ erzählen to tell spicy stories.

Historiker historian;
aus der Sicht des ~s from the historian's point of view.

historisch historical;
~ ungeschehen machen to expunge from the history books;
~belegt sein to have a historical record;
~er Film historical film; **~es Gemälde** historical painting; **~er Roman** historical novel; **~e Schule** *(Volkswirtschaft)* historical school.

Hit hit;
~parade top of the pops.

Hitze, in der ~ des Gefechts in the press of the fight, in the heat of the moment;
fliegende ~ *(med.)* hot flushes; **gräßliche ~** outrageous heat; **große ~** violent heat; **schwüle ~** melting heat; **sengende ~** torrid heat; **verlorene ~** waste heat;
sich bei ~ schlecht halten not to keep in hot weather;
~auswirkungen spüren to suffer from the effects of the hot weather; **~barriere** heat (thermal) barrier.

hitzebeständig heat-proof (-resisting).

Hitze|blitz *(Atombombe)* heat flash; **~grad** degree of heat; **~mauer** heat barrier; **~periode** spell of hot weather, heat, hot spell, sizzle spell of weather; **~welle** heat wave, sizzle spell of weather.

hitzig hot-headed, hot-tempered, *(jähzornig)* choleric, irascible, peppery;
~ werden to fly into a passion, to work o. s. up;
~e Auseinandersetzung heated debate.

Hitz|kopf hothead, tartar, wildcat; **~schlag** heatstroke.

Hobby|fahrzeug recreational vehicle; **~fotograf** amateur photographer; **~raum** rumpus room *(US)*.

Hobel plane;
~bank planing bench; **~eisen** plane bit; **~messer** planer, planing tool.

Hobeln planing.

Hoch *(Wetter)* high-pressure area, anticyclone, high *(coll.)*.

hoch high, tall, lofty, great, *(im Kurs)* up, stiff, *(im Preis)* high, hard;
~ bezahlt highly paid; **effektiv zu ~** definitely too high; **unbestimmt ~** open-end; **zu ~** excessive, exorbitant; **[nicht] zu ~ gegriffen** [not] overstated; **zu ~ versichert** overinsured;
wenn es ~ kommt at the utmost;
Hände ~! hands up! stick 'em up! *(coll.)*; **~ oben im Norden** away up in the north; **~ im Preis** dear, high, high-priced, hard, steep, expensive;
jem. etw. ~ anrechnen to give s. o. credit for s. th.; **zu ~ bemessen** to overassess, to overrate; **etw. zu ~ einschätzen** to set too high a value on s. th.; **~ fliegen** to fly at a high altitude; **~ hergehen** to go with a swing; **~ hinauswollen** to hitch one's waggon to a star, to fly high; **~ zu stehen kommen** to cost dear; **einen Meter ~ liegen** *(Schnee)* to be one meter *(US)* (metre, *Br.)* deep; **~ sein** to amount to, *(Preis)* to be expensive (dear); **für j. zu ~ sein** to be too deep for (above) s. o.; **ziemlich ~ sein** *(Preise, Kurse)* to be on the high side; **~ begabt sein** to be highly gifted; **~ besteuert sein** to be highly rated (heavily taxed); **~ im Kurse stehen** to rule high; **Nase ~ tragen** to walk with one's head high, to be stuck up, to put on airs, to be high-hat *(US)*; **~ verlieren** to suffer a crushing defeat; **~ und heilig versprechen** to swear by all that is holy; **~ gewertet werden** to take a high rank; **~ wohnen** to live high up; **zwei Treppen ~ wohnen** to live on the second (third, *US*) floor;
wer ~ steigt, fällt tief the higher you climb the farther you fall.

hochachtbar respectable.

hochachten, j. to have a high regard for s. o., to esteem s. o. highly.

Hochachtung esteem, respect, hono(u)r;
bei aller ~ with all due deference; **mit vorzüglicher** ~ yours faithfully, very respectfully yours, yours very truly *(US)*;
größte ~ profound respect;
~ **abnötigen** to impose respect; **jem. mit aller** ~ **begegnen** to show great respect to s. o.; **jem.** ~ **bezeigen** to pay tribute to s. o.; **jem. seine** ~ **für eine Entdeckung bezeugen** to render homage to s. o. for a discovery; **große** ~ **vor jem. haben** to hold s. o. in great hono(u)r.

hochachtungsvoll [most] respectfully [yours], faithfully yours, my respectful compliments, yours very truly *(US)*.

Hochadel peerage.

hoch|aktuell topical; ~**aktuelle Nachrichten** front-page news; ~**angesehen** of high repute (standing), highly respected; ~**angesehen sein** to rise high in public esteem.

Hochantenne overhead (elevated) aerial (antenna, *US*).

hocharbeiten, sich aus eigener Kraft to make good under one's own steam; **sich mühsam** ~ to hew a career for o. s., to emerge from poverty, to work one's way up (o. s. up to a post); **sich vom Zugabfertiger zum Abteilungspräsidenten** ~ to work up from a dispatcher to division superindendent.

hochaufgeschossen lanky.

Hochbahn overhead (elevated) railway *(Br.)* (railroad, *US*), L *(US)*, el *(US coll.)*.

Hochbau building above ground, multi-stor(e)y (high-rise) building, *(Errichtung)* surface (architectural) engineering;
~**arbeiter sein** to ride the air *(sl.)*; ~**ingenieur** structural engineer; ~**saison** peak construction season.

Hoch|bauten multi-story buildings; ~**bauunternehmen** building (construction) firm, contractors.

hoch|begabt highly gifted; ~**beladen** heavily laden; ~**besteuert** heavily taxed, high-duty; ~**besteuerte Artikel** high-duty goods; ~**betagt** advanced in years.

Hochbetrieb rush [period], bustle, hustle, bustling activity;
vorweihnachtlicher ~ Christmas rush;
~ **auf den Bahnhöfen** rush at the stations;
~ **haben** to be humming with activity, to be full of stir.

Hoch|bildkarte relief map; ~**blüte** full bloom, *(fig.)* heyday.

hochbocken, ein Auto to jack up a car.

hochbringen, j. to get a rise out of s. o.; **Geschäft** ~ to make a concern going, to pit a business on its feet again, to bring a company back into the black *(US coll.)*; **Industrie künstlich** ~ to spoon-feed industry; **etw. mühsam** ~ to grind it out *(fam.)*.

Hoch|brücke viaduct; ~**bunker** surface airraid shelter; ~**burg** stronghold, repository; ~**decker** high-wing aircraft; ~**deutsch** high German.

hoch|dienen, sich im Büro to work one's way up by the clerical route; ~**dotierte Stellung** highly paid job.

Hochdruck high pressure, drive, *(drucktechn.)* relief printing;
mit ~ with full blast;
mit ~ **arbeiten** to go ahead at full speed;
~**ausläufer** ridge of a high-pressure area, ridge; ~**betrieb** drive, rush; ~**gebiet** high-pressure area, high *(coll.)*; ~**keil** wedge; **automatisch gesteuerte** ~**klimaanlage** automatically controlled high-pressure air-conditioning system; ~**reifen** high-pressure tyre *(Br.)* (tire, *US*).

Hoch|ebene tableland, plateau; ~**elastikreifen** cushion tyre *(Br.)* (tire, *US*).

hoch|elegant stylish, slick *(sl.)*; ~**empfindlich** highly sensitive, *(Film)* rapid; ~**entwickelt** highly developed, advanced, sophisticated; ~**erfreut sein** to be well-pleased; ~**explosiv** highly explosive.

hochfahren, immer gleich to flare up immediately, to fly off the handle; **aus dem Schlaf** ~ to wake up with a start.

hochfahrend highhanded, overbearing;
~**es Wesen** arrogant manner, highhandedness, overbearingness.

hochfein choice, superfine, de luxe, classy;
~**e Familie** genteel family; ~**es Hotel** posh (plush, *Br.*) hotel, plushery *(sl.)*; ~**es Mädchenpensionat** high-toned finishing school for girls.

Hochfinanz haute (high, big, *US*) finance, world of high finance;
New Yorker ~ Wall Street.

hochfliegen *(Ballon)* to ascend, *(Brücke)* to blow up.

hochfliegend high-flown, ambitious, *(Stil)* lofty.

Hoch|flut floodtide; ~**flut von Verbrechen** deluge of crimes; **in** ~**form sein** to be on top of one's form (in the pink of condition); ~**format** *(Inserat)* high size, upright side and across, *(Foto)* panel.

hochfrequent high-frequent.

Hochfrequenz high frequency;
~**drossel** *(el.)* low-pass filter; ~**strom** high-frequency current; ~**verstärker** high-frequency amplifier.

Hochgarage multistorey car park.

hochgeachtet of high standing (repute);
~ **sein** to be held in high esteem, to rate *(sl.)*.

Hoch|gebirge high mountainous region; ~**gebirgsalm** high Alpine pastureland; ~**gehen** *(Preise)* upward tendency.

hochgehen to go upwards, *(fig.)* to blow up, to hit the ceiling, *(Mine)* to explode, *(Preise, Kurse)* to advance, to go up, to rise, *(Vorhang)* to go up;
sprunghaft ~ to jump, *(Kurse)* to skyrocket;
Mine ~ **lassen** to explode a mine; **Verbrecherbande** ~ **lassen** to round up a gang of criminals.

hoch|gehende See heavy sea, swell; ~**geistig** intellectual, highbrow *(coll.)*, sophisticated; ~**gelegen** high-level; ~**gelehrter Mann** great scholar.

Hochgenuß für j. sein to be a treat for s. o.

hochgeschraubte Forderungen exaggerated demands.

Hochgeschwindigkeits|windkanal high-speed wind tunnel; ~**zug** high-speed train.

hoch|gesinnt noble-minded, high-toned; ~**gespannt** wound up to a high pitch; **in** ~**gespannter Erwartung sein** to be on tenterhooks; ~**gesteckte Ziele** high-pitched aims.

hochgestellt of high rank;
~**er Beamter** highly-placed official; ~**e Persönlichkeit** high-up *(coll.)*, very important person (V.I.P.).

Hochgestellter, sozial socialite.

hochgestochen overbearing, stuck up *(coll.)*;
~ **schreiben** to write in a high-flown style;
~**er Kerl** high-brow; ~**er Stil** inflated (high-flown) style; ~**e Unterhaltung** high-faluting conversation.

hoch|gewachsen tall; ~**gezüchteter Motor** beefed-up engine.

Hochglanz high polish, mirror finish;
auf ~ **bringen** to slick up; **sein Französisch auf** ~ **bringen** to polish up one's French; **auf** ~ **polieren** to give a shine to the brass-works;
~**abzug** glossy photographic print; ~**folie** glazing sheet, ferrotype tin *(US)*; ~**magazin** slick *(US sl.)*; ~**papier** box enamel paper.

hochgradig high-grade, highly concentrated;
~**e Nervosität** extreme nervousness; ~**er Unsinn** utter nonsense.

hochhalten to upbear, to uphold, *(Preise)* to keep up, to peg;
sich dauernd ~ *(Kurse)* to continue high; **jds. Andenken** ~ to treasure s. one's memory.

Hochhaus multi-stor(e)y (high-rise) building, skyscraper *(US)*;
~**garage** parking garage, autosilo; ~**hotel** high-rise hotel; ~**sucht** skyscraperitis.

Hochheben, durch ~ **der Hände abstimmen** to vote by show of hands.

hoch|heben to lift, to raise; ~**herrschaftliches Haus** lordly mansion; ~**herziges Geschenk** generous present; ~**industrialisiert** highly industrial; ~**industrialisierte Länder** fully industrialized countries; ~**intelligent** sophisticated; ~**kant** on edge, upright; ~**kant stellen** to upend; ~**kantig herauswerfen** to chuck out; ~**kantig hinausfliegen** to be fired (given the sack) *(coll.)*.

Hochkapitalismus mature capitalism.

hochkomfortabel luxurious, with all modern conveniences.

hochkommen to rise in the world, to make one's way, *(Frage)* to bob up;
wieder ~ to find one's feet again;
jem. die Galle ~ **lassen** to make s. o. fly off the handle; **j. nicht** ~ **lassen** to stand in s. one's way.

Hoch|kommissar High Commissioner; ~**kommission** High Commission.

Hochkonjunktur cyclical boom, boom times, peak season (time), booming economy, high-level business, [wave of] prosperity;
~ **des Waffengeschäfts** arms boom;
~ **bremsen** to curb the boom; ~ **erleben (haben)** to live in the full swing of prosperity, to be booming, to be on the upswing;
~**niveau** boomtime level; ~**periode** prolonged boom, period of general prosperity; ~**phase** phase of the boom.

hoch|konzentriert highly concentrated; **seine Ärmel** ~**krempeln** to roll up one's sleeves.

hochkultivierter Mann highly cultured man.

Hochkultur advanced civilization.

Hoch|land highland, tableland, upland; ~**leistung** *(Maschine)* heavy duty, high performance, *(Sport)* first-class performance, *(Wissenschaft)* great achievement.

hochleistungsfähig high-powered.
Hochleistungs|motor heavy-duty (high-efficiency, high-pressure) engine; ~**öl** heavy-duty oil; ~**stahl** high-quality tool steel; ~**wagen** competition car.
Hochlichtautotypie highlight half-tone.
hochliquide highly liquid, cash-rich.
hochmodern latest style, highly up-to-date, newfangled, ultramodern, streamlined, spiffy *(sl.)*;
~**es Kleid** very stylish dress; ~**e Kontrollmethode** streamlined control; ~**e Möbel** ultramodern furniture; ~**e Wohnung** high-bracket flat.
Hochmut arrogance, haughtiness, pride;
~ **kommt vor dem Fall** pride must have a fall (goeth before destruction).
hoch|mütig arrogant, haughty, inflated, overbearing, with a high hand; ~**näsig** standoffish, toplofty, snobby, ripstage; ~**näsig sein** to be stuck-up.
Hoch|näsigkeit toploftiness; ~**nebel** high stratus.
hoch|nehmen j. to pull s. one's legs, to josh s. o., *(preislich)* to soak s. o. *(US sl.)*, to fleece s. o.; ~**notpeinliche Lage** highly embarrassing situation.
Hochofen blast furnace;
~**schlacke** iron dross.
hochpäppeln, Industrie to spoon-feed industry.
Hochparterre raised ground floor, first floor *(US)*.
hochprozentig of a high percentage.
hochqualifiziert highly qualified, high-calibre *(Br.)* (-level, -potential);
~**e Erzeugnisse** high-class goods; ~**e Verkaufstechnik** high-pressure salesmanship.
hoch|ragen to tower; **sich** ~**rappeln** *(Kranker)* to struggle to one's feet, to pick up.
Hoch|rechnung computer forecast; ~**reißen** *(Flugzeug)* zoom.
hoch|reißen *(Flugzeug)* to zoom; **j. aus dem Schlaf** ~**reißen** to startle s. o. out of his sleep; ~**rentierlich** high-coupon.
Hochruf cheer;
brausende ~**e** ringing cheers;
mit ~**en begrüßen** to cheer.
Hochsaison peak (high, height of the) season.
hoch|satiniert super-calendered; ~**schalten** to uplift; ~**schätzen** to esteem highly, to hold in high esteem.
Hoch|schätzung esteem, high regard; ~**schaukeln** *(pol.)* escalation.
hoch|schaukeln to escalate; ~**schießen** *(Flammen)* to leap, to shoot up; **Rakete** ~**schießen** to launch a rocket; **an der Kaimauer** ~**schlagen** to lash up against the quay; ~**schnellen** *(Kurse)* to skyrocket *(US)*, *(Preise)* to leap, to jump, to soar; **Forderungen** ~**schrauben** to exaggerate claims.
Hochschul|absolvent [university] graduate; ~**abschluß** university examination; ~**anstellung** university appointment; ~**ausbildung** university training (education), higher education; **gleichzeitige** ~**ausbildung und Berufsausübung** part-time schooling alternating with part-time employment.
Hochschulbildung university (college, higher) education;
~ **haben** to have been to college.
Hochschule college, university, academy;
landwirtschaftliche ~ agricultural college; **Technische** ~ engineering (technical) college; **tierärztliche** ~ veterinary college;
~ **der bildenden Künste** academy of fine arts; ~ **für Lehrerbildung** training college *(Br.)*, teachers' college *(US)*; ~ **für Musik** academy for music.
Hochschüler student, undergraduate.
Hochschul|führer calendar *(Br.)*, catalog *(US)*; ~**gebäude** campus building; ~**kursus,** ~**lehrgang** college course, university extension; ~**kursus für Gasthörer** extramural course *(Br.)*; ~**lehrer** university lecturer (professor, don); ~**ordnung** [university] calendar *(Br.)* (catalog, *US*); ~**politik** campus politics; ~**qualifikation** university level; ~**reife** [etwa] general certificate of education *(Br.)*, advanced (A) level; **mit anerkannter** ~**reife** matriculated; **kostenloses** ~**studium** free university education.
hochschwanger sein to be near one's time.
Hochsee the open sea, deep sea, outsea;
~**dampfer** ocean-going ship; ~**fischer** trawler; ~**fischerei** deep-sea fishing, sea fishery; ~**fischereiboot** trawler; ~**flotte** ocean-going fleet; ~**hafen** deep-water port; ~**schiff** seagoing vessel, deep waterman; **für** ~**schiffe befahrbar** navigable by seagoing vessels; ~**schiffahrt** high-seas navigation, ocean-shipping (-carrying) trade; ~**schiffsmakler** ocean freight broker; ~**schlepper** ocean-going tug.
hochseetüchtig ocean-going, seagoing.
Hochseeverkehr ocean transportation (traffic).
Hochsommer midsummer, high summer.
hochsommerlich midsummery.
Hochspannung, politische political high tension.
Hochspannungs|isolator high-tension insulator; ~**leitung** high-voltage transmission line, high-tension transmission cable; ~**mast** pylon; ~**transformator** high-voltage transformer.
hochspielen to play up.
höchst highest, topmost, uppermost, precious *(coll.)*;
~ **amüsant** most amusing;
aufs ~**e** to the highest degree;
aufs ~**e erschrocken sein** to be alarmed; **aufs** ~**e gestiegen sein** to have reached a climax; **aufs** ~**e überrascht sein** to be greatly surprised;
in ~**er Aufregung sein** to be in a flurry (in wild excitement); ~**e Auszeichnung** highest award (decoration); **auf** ~**en Befehl** by order of the supreme command; ~**er Beleihungswert** maximum loan value (advance); ~**er Betrag** maximum [amount]; ~**e Bewertung erzielen** to hit top ratings; **auf** ~**er Ebene** at the highest (top) level; ~**e Einkommensteuerstufen** top brackets; ~**er Gang** top gear; ~**es Gebot** closing (highest) bid; ~**e Gefahr** extreme danger; ~**e Geheimhaltung** utmost secrecy, cosmic; **mit** ~**er Geheimhaltung behandelt werden** to get top-secret treatment; ~**es Gericht** supreme court; **in** ~**em Grade** in the highest degree; ~**e Instanz** last instance; ~**e Kreditsätze** ceilings on loans (lending); ~ **wichtige Position** key position; ~**er Preis** maximum price; ~**en Preis bei einem Wettbewerb gewinnen** to win the top hono(u)rs in a competition; **in** ~**er Sorge sein** to be extremely worried; ~**e Sorgfalt** utmost care; ~**en Stand erreichen** to reach the highest level; **an** ~**er Stelle** in first place; ~**er Steuersatz** maximum tax rate; **j. in den** ~**en Tönen loben** to sing s. one's praise, to extol s. o. to the skies; ~**er Verkaufspreis** maximum selling price; ~**e Zeit** high time; ~ **ärgerlicher Zwischenfall** most annoying incident.
Höchst|alter maximum age; ~**altersgrenze bei der Einstellung** maximum hiring age limit *(US)*.
Hochstand der Preise high level of prices.
Höchstangebot highest offer.
Hoch|stapelei imposture, high-class robbery, confidence trick, imposture, swindling; **geistige** ~**stapelei** intellectual dishonesty; ~**stapler** impostor, swindler, confidence (con) man, highflyer, counterfeit, mobsman.
Höchst|auflagen erzielend best-selling; ~**ausschlag** *(el.)* maximum deflection; ~**bedarf** peak of the demand; ~**beitrag** maximum contribution; **zulässige** ~**belastung** peak (maximum) load, *(Stromverbrauch)* peak load; ~**beschäftigungszeit** maximum hours of work; ~**besitz** maximum holding.
höchstbesteuert subject to the highest tax rate.
Höchstbetrag highest amount, maximum [amount], *(Preisgrenze)* limit, *(Versicherung)* office limit;
bis zum ~ **von** up to the amount of;
~ **eines eingeräumten Akzeptkredits** acceptance line; ~ **eines Banksaldos** maximum bank advance.
Höchstbetrags|hypothek running-account mortgage *(Br.)*; ~**klausel** open-mortgage clause.
Höchst|bewertung optimum rating; ~**bietender** best (highest) bidder, highest offerer; **erforderliches** ~**darlehn** maximum advance required; ~**dauer** maximum time limit; ~**dividende** maximum dividend.
hochstecken, seine Ziele to aim (fly) high.
hochstehend distinguished, high-ranking, grand, *(drucktechn.)* superior, *(Papiere)* high-priced, *(Preis)* high;
gesellschaftlich ~ of high social standing, great;
~**er Beamter** high official; ~**e Persönlichkeit** high-up *(coll.)*; ~**e Persönlichkeiten** high-ranking persons, upper ten, top drawer *(sl.)*.
hochsteigen to escalate, *(Ballon, Rauch)* to rise, to ascend.
höchsteigen, in ~**er Person** in person.
Höchst|einkommen, für die Körperschaftssteuerberechnung in Frage kommendes maximum relevant income; **anhaltende** ~**einnahmen** maximum long-time returns; ~**einstellungsalter** maximum hiring age limit *(US)*.
höchstens at the best, at the outside, not exceeding;
~ **eine Woche bleiben** to stay for a week at the outside.
Höchst|entschädigung limit of compensation; ~**entwertung** maximum depreciation; ~**ertrag** maximum yield; **im** ~**fall** at the utmost; **in** ~**form sein** to be on the top of one's form (up to the mark, with it, *sl.*); ~**gebot** closing (highest, last) bid, best offer, maximum [bid]; ~**gebühr** maximum tax; ~**gehalt** maximum salary, ceiling; ~**geldstrafe** maximum fine.

Höchstgeschwindigkeit maximum (top, permissible) speed;
mit ~ all out, on top;
gesetzlich vorgeschriebene ~ regulation speed; **zugelassene (zulässige)** ~ speed limit;
~ **für Kraftfahrzeuge** motor-vehicle speed limit;
an ~ **erreichen** *(Auto)* to do in top; **mit** ~ **fahren** to travel at full (top) speed, to floor *(sl.)*; ~ **überschreiten** to exceed the speed limit.
Höchstgewicht maximum weight, working load, *(im Postverkehr)* rate limit *(US)*.
Höchstgrenze ceiling, maximum [limit], *(Versicherung)* gross line, *(Anzeige)* maximum linage;
gesetzliche ~ *(Preise)* price ceiling;
praktische ~ **von 50% des Bruttosozialprodukts** de facto 50% ceiling of gross domestic product; ~ **für Lohn- und Gehaltssteigerungen** limit on wage rises *(Br.)*; ~ **für ungedeckte Notenausgabe** fiduciary limit; ~ **des Selbstbehalts** net line; ~ **der Versicherungspflicht** maximum liability;
~ **für Ausgaben festsetzen** to put a ceiling on spending; ~ **für Kommunalausgaben festsetzen** to set cash limits on local authority spending.
Höchstgrößen *(im Postverkehr)* size limits.
Hochstimmung, in ~ **sein** to be in high glee (spirits).
Höchst | kapazität maximum capacity (quota), optimum capacity; ~**kontingent** maximum quota; ~**kredit** line of credit *(US)*, credit line *(US)* (limit, *Br.*).
Höchstkurs top (maximum, peak, highest) price, maximum rate, high record, market top;
neuer ~ new high;
~**e erreichen** to reach peak levels; **neue** ~**e erreichen (erzielen)** to establish new high records, to move (rise, break) into new high ground *(US)*; **in rascher Steigerung neue** ~**e erzielen** to shoot into new high ground *(US)*; **sprunghaft steigen und einen neuen** ~ **erzielen** to jump into new high ground *(US)*; ~ **heraufsetzen** to raise (lift, *US*) the top; **zu** ~**en kaufen** to buy at the top of the market; **neue** ~**e verbuchen** to register a new top; **zu** ~**en verkaufen** to sell at best.
Höchst | ladegewicht maximum load; ~**last** maximum (peak) load; ~**laufzeit** remaining life.
Höchstleistung top (maximum, peak) output, record, peak (maximum, best) performance, *(Maschine)* maximum efficiency (power), *(Sport)* record [performance], *(Versicherung)* maximum benefit;
produktive ~ *(Mensch)* productive efficiency;
~ **der modernen Technik** greatest achievement of modern technology;
mit ~ **laufen** *(Maschine)* to be running flat out.
Höchstleistungs | einrichtung high-production equipment; ~**fähigkeit** optimum capacity; ~**grenze** peak capacity.
Höchst | lohn peak (maximum) wage; **festgesetzte** ~**löhne** wage ceilings; ~**maß** maximum; ~**maß an Takt** maximum amount of tact; **gesetzliche** ~**miete** rent ceiling.
höchstmöglich at the highest possible;
~**er Einkommensausgleichseffekt** maximum social advantage;
~**e statistische Meßzahl** optimum statistic.
Höchst | niveau optimum level; ~**pension** maximum pension.
höchstpersönlich purely personal, in the flesh;
~ **kommen** to come in person;
~**es Recht** personal servitude.
Höchstpreis highest (outside, peak, maximum, top) price, peak maximum [rate];
festgesetzter (gesetzlicher) ~ ceiling [price]; **unüberschreitbarer** ~ not-to-exceed ceiling price;
möglicher ~ **für Konsumartikel** consumers' surplus;
~ **erzielen** to secure the best value; ~**e festsetzen** to clamp ceilings on prices; **zum** ~ **verkaufen** to sell at the highest price, *(Börse)* to sell at best; ~**e zahlen** to pay top prices;
~**bestimmungen** maximum price regulations; ~**grenze** upper price limit.
Höchst | produktion top (maximum, peak) output; ~**punkt** peak; ~**rabatt** maximum rebate.
Hochstraße elevated highway, flyover, overpass *(US)*.
höchstrichterliche Entscheidung decision of the supreme court.
Höchstsatz highest (maximum, top, ceiling) rate, upper limit, maximum [charge];
bis zum ~ **von** up to the amount of;
steuerlicher ~ top tax rate.
Höchstsätze, nahezu ~ **erreichen** to enter at close to record rates; ~ **im ersten Vierteljahr erreichen** to peak in the first quarter; ~ **erzielen** to pour in at record rates.
Höchst | schuld debt limit; ~**spanne** maximum margin.
Höchststand high, highest (peak) level, top, maximum, *(Kurse)* top price;
absoluter (einmaliger) ~ all-time high; **neuer** ~ new high; **vorläufiger** ~ temporary peak;
~ **der Flut** top of the tide; ~ **der Produktion** peak of production; **auf seinen wirtschaftlichen** ~ **bringen** to upgrade economically; ~ **erreichen** to reach the peak; **neuen** ~ **erreichen** to move into (reach a) new high *(US)*; **erstmals den** ~ **vom März wieder überschreiten** to break through its previous March peak.
Höchststärke *(mil.)* maximum strength.
höchststehend uppermost.
Höchst | strafe maximum punishment (term); **j. zu einer** ~**strafe verdonnern** to throw the book at s. o. *(sl.)*; ~**stundenklausel für 26 Arbeitswochen** *(Teilzeitbeschäftigung)* one thousand hour clause; ~**tarif** *(Spediteur)* maximum rate, *(Versicherung)* maximum tariff; ~**temperatur** maximum temperature; **Maßnahmen gegen den** ~**verbrauch treffen** to cope with peak consumption; ~**verbrauchertarif** *(el.)* demand rate; ~**vergünstigung** maximum benefit; ~**verkaufspreis** maximum selling price.
höchstwahrscheinlich in all probability.
Höchst | wert maximum (top, peak) value; ~**werte von 102 bis 108 Phon für Flugzeuge zulassen** to establish maximum noise level for airlines of between 102 and 108 decibels; ~**wertung** optimum rating; ~**zahl** maximum number; ~**ziffer** ceiling (maximum) figure; ~**zinsen** interest ceilings; ~**zinssatz** maximum rate of interest, top interest rate; **gesetzlich nicht erlaubter** ~**zinssatz** usurious rate of interest; ~**zoll** maximum tariff, *(Einfuhr)* maximum import duty; ~**zuladung** maximum useful load.
höchstzulässige Geschwindigkeit maximum speed, limit speed.
hochtönende Phrasen high-sounding phrases.
Hochtonlautsprecher high-power loudspeaker, tweeter.
Hochtouren, auf at full blast *(coll.)*;
auf ~ **bringen** to bring to full capacity; **auf** ~ **kommen** *(fig.)* to hit one's stride; **auf** ~ **laufen** to get into full swing, to run at full speed (flat-out), to be in high gear.
hochtourig high-compression (-powered).
Hoch | tourist mountaineer; ~**touristik** mountaineering.
hochtrabend toplofty, windy;
~**es Geschwätz** high-falutin language; ~**er Titel** high-sounding title.
Hochtreiben durch Scheingebote by-bidding.
hochtreiben to force up, to boost *(US)*;
Kurse ~ to bull the market; **Preise** ~ to push up prices.
hochverdient of high merit.
Hochverrat high treason;
~ **begehen** to commit treason, to levy war against the King *(Br.)*.
Hochverräter traitor to one's country.
hochverräterisch seditious, treasonable;
in ~**er Absicht** traitorously; ~**e Reden** seditious words; ~**e Verhandlungen** treasonable negotiations.
Hochverrats | anklage exhibiting a charge of treason; ~**handlung** treasonable act; ~**verfahren** suit of the king's peace.
hochverzinslich yielding high interest;
~ **sein** to yield high interest.
Hochwald timber forest, high forest.
Hochwasser flood, waters, spate *(Br.)*, *(Gezeitenwechsel)* high tide;
mittleres ~ mean high water;
~ **führen** to be in spate *(Br.)*; **dem** ~ **weichen müssen** to flood out; **vom** ~ **fortgerissen werden** to be swept away by the flood; **vom** ~ **aus dem Haus getrieben werden** to be flooded out of the house;
~**damm** flood dam; ~**gebiet** flood plain; ~**geschädigter** flood victim; ~**katastrophe** flood disaster; ~**kontrolle** flood control; ~**risiko** flood risk; ~**schaden** flood damage; ~**schutz** flood prevention; ~**stand** high-water level; ~**standsmarke,** ~**standszeichen** flood-mark, high-water mark; ~**versicherung** flood (wave damage) insurance; ~**zeit** floodtime.
hochwertig high-cost (-grade, -class, -quality), of high quality, top grade *(US)*, *(Nahrungsmittel)* concentrated;
technisch ~ of high technical standard;
~**e Abzahlungsverkäufe** high-ticket instalment sales; ~**e Anlagewerte** high-grade investments, blue chips *(US)*; ~**es Benzin** high-grade fuel (petrol); ~**es Gas** rich gas; ~**e Papiere** high-grade issues; ~**e Qualitätsarbeit** superior (first-class) workmanship, work of high quality; ~**es Spezialgeschäft** high-class specialty store *(US)*.
Hochwinter midwinter.

Hochzeit wedding, marriage, *(historisch)* high time;
eiserne ~ diamond wedding; **goldene** ~ golden wedding; **silberne** ~ silver wedding;
j. zur ~ **einladen** to bid s. o. to a wedding; **kurz vor der** ~ **stehen** to be on the point of getting married; **auf zwei** ~**en tanzen wollen** to want the penny and the bun (the cake and the halfpenny).
Hochzeits|datum date of marriage; ~**empfang** wedding reception, shower party *(US)*; ~**essen** wedding breakfast; ~**feier-[lichkeiten]** wedding [ceremony]; **intime** ~**feier** quiet wedding; ~**geschenk** wedding present, *(Bräutigam)* handsel; ~**gesellschaft** wedding party; ~**kuchen** wedding cake; ~**paar** newly married couple; ~**reise** wedding tour (trip), honeymoon [trip]; ~**tag** wedding aniversary (day), nuptial day; **erster** ~**tag** paper wedding; ~**tag festlegen** to name the day (a day for the wedding), to set the wedding date; ~**zeremoniell** marriage rites.
Hochziehen heave, *(Flugzeug)* pull-out, zooming.
hochziehen *(Flugzeug)* to nose (pull) up, to zoom, *(mit Winde)* to winch;
Flagge ~ to hoist a flag; **Haß künstlich** ~ to build up hatred; **Mauer** ~ to erect a wall; **Nase** ~ to snuffle; **Rolläden** ~ to pull up the blinds; **Vorhang** ~ *(Theater)* to draw (ring up) the curtain.
Hochzinspolitik policy of high interest rates.
hochzüchten to breed selectively.
hocken, über seinen Büchern to pore over one's books; **immer zu Hause** ~ to be a stay-at-home; **in seinem Zimmer** ~ to be sitting in one's room.
Höcker hump;
~**hindernis** *(mil.)* dragon's teeth.
Hof yard, court, *(Bauernhof)* farm, farmstead, farmyard, homestead, *(Gefängnis)* yard, *(Hofraum)* court[yard], *(Schule)* playground, schoolyard;
frei ~ free farmyard;
großer ~ large estate, manor; **verpachteter** ~ leased farm;
~ **bewirtschaften** to farm land; ~ **halten** to hold a court; **auf den** ~ **hinausgehen** to overlook the yard; **einem Mädchen den** ~ **machen** to court a girl; ~ **verpachten** to let a farm to a tenant; **bei** ~**e vorstellen** to introduce at court; **bei** ~**e empfangen werden** to be received at court; **bei** ~**e vorgestellt werden** to be represented at court, to come out;
~**almanach** court calendar (guide); ~**amt** appointment at court; ~**ball** court ball; **einflußreiche** ~**beamte** the palace; ~**dame** waiting gentlewoman; ~**erbe** [etwa] special heir; ~**erbfolgeordnung** entail; ~**erwerbsdarlehn** tenant purchase loan *(US)*.
Hoffnung, von ~ **beflügelt** inspired with hope; **zwischen** ~ **und Angst hin- und hergerissen** distracted between hope and fear; **fast gar keine** ~ **mehr** precious little hope; **nicht die geringste** ~ not a grain of hope; **unbegründete** ~**en** unfounded hopes; **keine** ~ **auf eine Vereinbarung** no prospect of agreement; **zu den besten** ~**en berechtigen** to promise well; **jds.** ~**en ein jähes Ende bereiten** to dash s. one's hopes *(fam.)*; **sich trügerischen** ~**en hingeben** to deceive o. s. with a fond hope; **jds.** ~**en zunichte machen** to undo (dash, shatter) s. one's hopes, to defeat s. o. of his hopes; **seine** ~**en zu hoch schrauben** to pitch one's hopes too high; **jds. einzige** ~ **sein** to be s. one's sole trust; **seine** ~**en auf j. setzen** to lay (pin) one's hopes on s. o., to bank on s. o.; **auf etw. große** ~**en setzen** to have high hopes for s. th.; **sich in seinen** ~**en täuschen** to fail in one's hopes.
Hoffnungskauf speculative purchase.
hoffnungslos without resource, hopeless;
~ **betrunken** dead drunk; ~ **krank** incurably ill;
~ **krank sein** to be at a desperate pass; ~ **verloren sein** *(Kranker)* to be past all hope, *(Schiff)* to be lost without hope;
~**er Fall** hopeless case; ~**er Versuch** attempt doomed to failure; **in einem** ~**en Zustand sein** to be in a hopeless state.
Hoffnungslosigkeit desperation.
Hoffnungsschimmer glimmer (gleam, ray) of hope;
schwacher ~ weak flicker of hope;
~ **ausfindig machen** to detect a ray of hope; **endlich einen** ~ **sehen** to see daylight at last.
Hoffnungsstrahl flash (ray) of hope.
hoffnungsvoll|er junger Mann promising youth; ~**es Zukunftsbild** optimistic view of the future.
Hofgut domain.
hofieren, j. to fawn upon s. o., to pay one's attention to s. o., to flatter s. o., *(Mädchen)* to court a girl.
Hofknicks curts(e)y, genuflection *(US)*.
höflich polite, civilized, complimentary, courteous, urbane;
~, **aber bestimmt** with a certain cheerful firmness; **erstaunlich** ~ markedly polite;
~ **bleiben** to keep a civil tongue in one's head; **sich von seiner** ~**sten Seite zeigen** to do the polite *(fam.)*.
höflicherweise in civility.
Höflichkeit civility, courtesy;
aus Gründen der ~ on principles of comity; **mit angeborener** ~ with a homebred courtesy;
angeborene ~ innate courtesy; **äußerste** ~ pink of courtesy; **kriecherische** ~ cringe, cringingness; **liebenswürdige** ~ sweet politeness;
~**en austauschen** to exchange civilities; **j. mit kühler** ~ **empfangen** to receive s. o. with frozen formality; **es an** ~ **fehlen lassen** to be wanting in courtesy; **jem.** ~**en sagen** to pay compliments to s. o.; **die** ~ **in Person sein** to be the pink of politeness; **sich in** ~ **üben** to practise politeness; **sich von der äußersten** ~ **zeigen** to be exquisitively polite.
Höflichkeitsbesuch courtesy visit (call), duty (formal morning) call;
~ **abstatten (machen)** to pay a duty (courtesy) call (one's compliments).
Höflichkeits|bezeigung duty, reverence, compliment, devoir, attention; ~**floskeln** forms of address, phrases of civility.
Höflichkeitsform form;
~**en** etiquette, decorum, proprieties;
internationale ~**en** international courtesies;
~**en wahren** to observe the proprieties.
Höflichkeits|geste duty, reverence; **einige** ~**phrasen erlernen** to learn some polite phrases; ~**schlußformel** complimentary prefixes (suffixes).
Hof|lieferant, königlicher purveyor by appointment to the Royal Family *(Br.)*; ~**lieferantendiplom** royal warrant *(Br.)*; ~**marschall** Lord Chamberlain *(Br.)*; ~**nachrichten** court circular *(Br.)*; ~**[raum]** courtyard, yard; **umschlossener** ~**raum** curtilage; ~**staat** retinue, court, The Household *(Br.)*; ~**tracht** court fashion; ~**trauer** court mourning; ~**veräußerung** conveyance of a farm; ~**wirtschaft** farming; ~**zeremoniell** court etiquette.
hoh|es Alter erreichen to live to a great age; ~**es Amt bekleiden** to be high-placed; ~**e Anforderungen stellen** to make great demands; ~**es Ansehen genießen** to be held in high repute; ~**er Beamter** high official.
Hohe Behörde *(EG)* High Authority.
hoh|er Blutdruck high blood-pressure; **um** ~**e Einsätze spielen** to play for high stakes; **in** ~**er Fahrt** at full speed; ~**es Fieber haben** to be running a high temperature; ~**es Fremdkapital** high-geared capital; ~**es Gehalt** high salary; ~**e Geldstrafe** heavy fine.
Hohes Gericht *(Anrede)* Your Lordship *(Br.)* (Honor, *US*).
hohe| Geschwindigkeit high speed; ~ **Ideale** high ideals; **auf die** ~ **Kante legen** to put away for a rainy day.
Hohe|r Kommissar High Commissioner; ~ **Kommission** High Commission.
hoh|e Luftfeuchtigkeit high moisture content; ~**e Meinung von jem. haben** to think highly of s. o.; ~**e Meinung von sich haben** to think no small beer of o. s.; ~**e Obrigkeit** the powers that be; ~**es Pflichtgefühl** high sense of duty; ~**e Politik** high politics; **sehr** ~**er Preis** exorbitant (steep) price; ~**en Preis erzielen** to fetch a high price; **zu einem** ~**en Preis verkaufen** to sell at a high price; **maßlos** ~**e Preise verlangen** to stick it on; **von** ~**em Rang** high-ranking; ~**e Rechnung** long bill; **auf einem** ~**en Roß sitzen** to perk it, to be on one's high horse; ~**e See** open sea; ~**er Seegang** rough sea; ~**e Staatsstellung innehaben** to be high-up in the civil service; ~**er Stand** high level; ~**e Stellung bekleiden** to be high in office; ~**e Sterblichkeitsrate** high mortality; ~**e Steuerstufe** high bracket; **bei** ~**er Strafe** under a heavy penalty; ~**e vertragsschließende Teile** high contracting parties; ~**e Temperatur** high temperature; ~**es Tier** bigwig, big shot *(sl.)*, high-up *(coll.)*; ~**e Verschleißquote** high mortality; ~**er Wellengang** high waves; ~**er Würdenträger** bigwig, cordon bleu; ~**er Zinsfuß** high rate of interest.
Höhe height, highness, altitude, *(Ausmaß)* extent, measure, *(Bedeutung)* importance, *(Breitengrad)* latitude, *(Höhepunkt)* height, peak, pinnacle, *(Preise)* level, *(Strafe)* degree, *(Summe)* amount, *(Tunnel)* headroom;
auf der ~ *(fig.)* abreast, up to par; **auf gleicher** ~ *(Bahnübergang)* at grade *(US)*, *(Fahrzeuge)* level, abreast; **auf der** ~ **seiner Laufbahn** at the height of one's career; **auf der** ~ **seines Ruhms** at the pinnacle of one's fame; **bis zur** ~ **von up to** the limit, not exceeding, at most; **bis zur** ~ **der geleisteten Anzahlung** to the extent of such payment; **der** ~ **nach** in terms of amount; **in der** ~ **von** to the amount of, amounting to; **in beliebiger** ~ to any extent; **in gleicher** ~ *(drucktechn.)* flush; **in**

schwindelnder ~ at a giddy height; **nicht auf der** ~ not up to the mark, off one's swing; **nicht ganz auf der** ~ below average; **von bewaldeten ~n umgeben** surrounded by wooded hills;
absolute ~ height above sea level; **astronomische** ~ astronomical level; **beherrschende** ~ commanding height; **gleiche** ~ level; **kritische** ~ *(Flugzeug)* critical altitude; **lichte** ~ headroom, *(Brücke)* clearance; **vorgeschriebene** ~ prescribed level;
~ **des Bevölkerungszuwachses** rate of increase of the population; **durchschnittliche** ~ **des Diskontkredits** line of discount; ~ **des Einkommens** size of income; ~ **einer Gefängnisstrafe** term of imprisonment; ~ **einer Grundstücksbelastung** extent of a charge; ~ **der Kosten** amount of costs; ~ **eines Kredits** credit limit *(Br.)* (line, *US*); ~ **unter dreihundert Metern** zero; ~ **der Preise** level of prices, price level; ~ **des Schadens** measure (extent) of damage; ~ **des zugesprochenen Schadensersatzes** quantum of damages; ~ **der gestellten Sicherheiten** value of securities; ~ **des Streitwertes** amount in controversy, jurisdictional amount; **~n und Tiefen des Lebens** ups and downs of life; ~ **des Unterstützungssatzes** level of relief; ~ **der Verschuldung** amount of indebtedness; ~ **des Versicherungsanspruches** amount of claim; ~ **des Zinsfußes** rate of interest;
Schaden in ~ **von 1000 DM anrichten** to cause damage amounting to DM 1000; **sich in die** ~ **arbeiten** to work one's way up; **sich auf der gleichen** ~ **behaupten** *(Kurse)* to continue high; **Kapital in** ~ **von 100.000 £ benötigen** to need funds to the amount of £ 100.000; **in die** ~ **bringen** to work up; **Geschäft wieder in die** ~ **bringen** to put a business back on its feet again; **auf gleiche** ~ **bringen** to level; ~ **eines Beitrages festsetzen** to assess the contribution; **sich nicht ganz auf der** ~ **fühlen** not to feel up to scratch (a bit out of sorts), to be off colo(u)r; **in die** ~ **gehen** *(Kurse)* to rise, to go upwards (up), to look up; **plötzlich in die** ~ **gehen** to [go up with a] jump, *(Kurse)* to skyrocket *(US)*; **mit den Preisen in die** ~ **gehen** to rise prices; **Preise auf der gleichen** ~ **halten** to maintain the same level of prices; **j. bis zur** ~ **von ... für kreditwürdig halten** to consider s. o. trustworthy to the extent of ...; **gegenwärtige** ~ **nicht halten können** not to be able to maintain its present level; ~ **einer Miete schiedsgerichtlich festlegen lassen** to refer the amount of rent to arbitration; **Geschenk in der** ~ **von 100 £ machen** to make a present to the value of £ 100; **auf halber** ~ **eine Rast machen** to rest halfway; ~ **messen** to take sight; **in die** ~ **schießen (schnellen)** *(Kind)* to shoot up, *(Kurse)* to blaze, to soar, to whirl upwards, to leap ahead, to skyrocket *(US)*; **Preise in die** ~ **schrauben** to force (send) up prices; **auf der** ~ **sein** to be up to the mark (on top of one's form, to be in tip-top form, to be with it *(sl.)*; **geistig nicht ganz auf der** ~ **sein** to be a little wrong in the upper storey; **gesundheitlich auf der** ~ **sein** to be up to par; **wissenschaftlich auf der** ~ **sein** to keep abreast of the latest developments in science; **auf der** ~ **seiner Leistungsfähigkeit angelangt sein** to have reached one's peak; **bis zur** ~ **von ... überzogen sein** to be overdrawn to the extent of ...; **auf gleicher** ~ **mit jem. stehen** to be on a level with s. o.; **senkrecht in die** ~ **steigen** *(Preise)* to zoom; **in die** ~ **treiben** to inflate, *(Kurse)* to enhance, to raise, to push (force, rush, *US*) up, to boom *(US)*, to boost *(US)*, to skyrocket *(US)*; **Aktie um 44 Punkte auf 640 in die** ~ **treiben** to bid up a stock 44 points to 640; **~n und Tiefen des Lebens des Lebens zu ertragen wissen** to take the rough with the smooth; **das ist doch die** ~ that beats everything, that's the limit (it, *US*).

Hoheit sovereignty, supreme power;
Königliche ~ *(Anrede)* Your Royal Highness.

hoheitlich sovereign;
~er Akt act of state; **~e Befugnisse ausüben** to exercise sovereign powers, to sovereignize.

Hoheits|abzeichen national ensign (emblem), *(Flugzeug)* national marking; **staatlicher ~akt** act of state; **~flagge** national flag.

Hoheitsgebiet territorial jurisdiction, sovereign (national) territory;
neutrales ~ neutral territory; **überseeische ~e** oversea (overseas) territories;
~ **der Vereinigten Staaten von Nordamerika** United States territory;
~ **betreten** to enter the territory.

Hoheitsgewalt sovereign power (prerogative), sovereignty.

Hoheitsgewässer territorial sea (waters), jurisdictional (home) waters, marine belt;
ausländische ~ foreign waters; **auf Gewohnheitsrecht beruhende** ~ historial waters;
~ **der Vereinigten Staaten** waters of the United States.

Hoheits|grenze three-mile limit, limit of territorial waters, territorial limits; **~handlung** act of state.

Hoheitsrecht sovereign power, dominion;
~e sovereign (rights, powers), royal privileges (prerogatives), regality;
~e über eine natürliche Person jurisdiction in personam;
~e ausüben to sovereignize, to exercise sovereign power (jurisdiction).

hoheitsrechtliche|Eingriffe restraint of princes and rulers; ~ **Funktionen** sovereign powers; ~ **Funktionen ausüben** to sovereignize.

Hoheits|verletzung violation of the border; **~verwaltung** public administration; **~zeichen** national emblem, *(Flugzeug)* nationality marking.

Höhen|abstand *(Flugzeug)* clearance, *(Verbandsflug)* vertical spacing; **~angabe** altitude reading; **~anzug** pressure suit; **~ballon** sky-hook *(US sl.)*; **~barometer** mountain barometer, altimeter, orometer; **~bomber** stratofortress; **~flosse** stabilizer, tail plane *(US)*; **~flug** high-altitude flying; **geistiger ~flug** flight of fancy; **~flugrekord** altitude record; **~flugzeug** high-altitude aircraft; **~forschungsrakete** sounding rocket.

höhengleiche Kreuzung level (grade, *US*) crossing.

Höhen|kabine pressurized cabin; **~karte** contour map (relief); **~klima** mountain climate; **~krankheit** mountain (height) sickness; **~kurort** high-altitude health resort; **in größeren ~lagen** higher up; **~leitwerk** horizontal tail surface; **~linie** contour line; **~linienkarte** contour map; **~messer** height measure, altitude recorder; **~rücken** ridge; **~ruder** *(Flugzeug)* elevator; **~schreiber** altigraph; **~sonne** *(med.)* sunray lamp; **~sonnenbehandlung** ultra-violet ray heatment; **~steuer** elevator, airfoil; **~umlaufbahn** *(Satellit)* altitude range; **~wind** upper wind.

Höhepunkt height, pitch, peak, peak level, point, pinnacle, high tide, culmination, culminating point, climax, tiptop, highlight, head, summit, *(Theater)* crisis;
auf dem ~ at the full; **auf dem** ~ **der Debatte** in the heat of the debate;
dramatischer ~ strong situation; **jahreszeitlicher** ~ peak of the year;
~ **des Abends** high spot of the evening; ~ **einer Geschichte** highlight of a story; ~ **seiner Laufbahn** top of s. one's career; ~ **der Macht** zenith of power; ~ **eines Programms** principal features of a program(me);
sich dem ~ **zu bewegen** to near the climax; ~ **einer festlichen Veranstaltung darstellen** to crown a feast; ~ **erreichen** to culminate, to climax; **neuen** ~ **erreichen** to hit a new level; **seinen** ~ **erreichen** to reach one's climax; ~ **seiner Laufbahn erreichen** to round off (reach) the culmination of one's career; **zum dramatischen** ~ **führen** to lead up to the final event of a drama; ~ **seiner Laufbahn überschritten haben** to be past one's peak; **auf dem** ~ **sein** *(Krankheit)* to be at its worst;
das ist doch der ~ that beats everything (tops all).

Höher, nicht nach ~em streben to have no higher pretensions.

höher higher, superior;
nicht ~ **als** not exceeding;
~ **bewertet** of higher value, *(Effekten)* high-priced;
~ **bewerten** to rate higher; ~ **bieten** to make a higher bid, to overbid; **Mieten** ~ **festsetzen** to screw up rents; ~ **als die Stadt liegen** to be on a higher level than the town; ~ **notieren** to mark up; ~ **sein** *(Kurs)* to exceed; ~ **denn je stehen** *(Kurse)* to be at an all-time high;
~es Angebot higher offer; **~e Ansprüche stellen** to make great demands; **~er Beamter** higher-grade (senior) official; **~e Berufsstände** professional classes; **~e Bildung** higher education; **~es Dienstalter** seniority; **~en Gang einschalten** to shift into high gear; **~es Gebot** higher bid; **~e Gesellschaftsschichten** first classes; **~e Gewalt** Act of God, fortuitous event; **~e Instanz** higher echelon, higher court; **in ~en Lagen** on higher grounds; **~e Lehranstalt** senior high school; **~en Orts** by higher authorities; **in ~en Regionen schweben** to live in the clouds; **~e Schulbildung** secondary education; **~e Schule** senior high school; **~e Schulklassen** upper (higher) forms; **~er Staatsdienst** higher grades of the civil service.

höherbewertet of higher value.

Höherbewertung write-up, writing up;
~ **von Anlagegütern** appreciation of fixed assets *(US)*; ~ **der Lagervorräte** appreciation of stocks; ~ **einer Währung gegenüber dem Dollar** currency appreciation against the dollar.

Höher|einstufung upgrading; **~entwicklung** refining; **~gebot** higher bid.

höher|gelegen upper; **~gestellt sein** to be superior in rank.
Höhergruppierung upgrading, reclassification.
höher|schrauben, Preise to screw up the prices; **~stehend** higher ranking, upper.
Höherstehender, gesellschaftlich social superior.
Höherversicherung increased insurance.
hohl *(Buchrücken)* hollow, *(Hand)* cupped, *(nichtssagend)* vain, empty;
~e Hand haben to be greased; **~e Hand machen** to brace, to panhandle; **aus der ~en Hand trinken** to drink from one's cupped hand; **etw. aus der ~en Hand zahlen** to be the merest chickenfeed to s. o.; **~en Kopf haben** to be empty-headed; **keine ~e Nuß dafür geben** not to give twopence (a red cent, *US*) for it; **~e Redensarten** a few nothings, empty phrases; **damit kaum einen ~en Zahn füllen können** not to be enough to keep a sparrow alive.
Hohlblockstein hollow block.
Höhle cave, cavern, hollow, *(Versteck)* den;
~ **des Löwen** the lion's den;
~n erforschen to pothole *(Br., coll.)*; **in ~n leben** to live in caves; **sich in die ~ des Löwen wagen** to put one's head into the lion's mouth, to beard the lion in his den.
Höhlen|forscher speleologist, spelunker *(US)*, potholer *(Br., coll.)*; **~forschung** speleology; **~wohnung** cave dwelling.
Hohl|heit *(fig.)* vanity, emptiness; **~leiter** *(el.)* wave guide; **~raum** hollow; **~spiegel** concave mirror.
Hohn mockery, scorn, derision;
der reinste ~ a mere mockery;
überall ~ und Spott ernten to become the derision of the wohle nation; **Gesetz zum ~ machen** to make a mockery of the law; **j. mit ~ und Spott überschütten** to heap scorn on s. o.;
~gelächter derisive laughter.
höhnisch scoffing, mocking, scornful, derisive, *(verächtlich)* disdainful;
~e Bemerkung scoffing remark; **jds. Ruf durch ~e Bemerkungen verunglimpfen** to sneer away s. one's reputation; **~es Lächeln** scornful smile.
Hohnlächeln scornful smile.
hohn|lächelnd with a scornful smile; **Vorschlag ~lachend zurückweisen** to scorn a proposal, to dismiss a proposal with scorn; **dem Gesetz ~sprechen** to make a mockery of the law, to act in defiance of the law.
Höker hawker, barrowman *(Br.)*, chapman *(Br.)*, costermonger, huckster, street pedlar;
~handel hawking, costermonger's trade; **~laden** huckstery.
hökern to hawk, to huckster, to higgle.
Höker|waren hawker's goods; **~weib** market woman.
Hokuspokus hocuspocus, hanky-panky, juggle, jiggery-pokery *(Br., coll.)*.
Holdinggesellschaft holding (controlling, proprietary) company, parent company (establishment);
staatliche ~ National Enterprise Board *(Br.)*; **tätige ~** operating holding company; **übergeordnete ~** top holding company;
~ **im Eigentum einer Bank** bank holding company.
Holdingsystem holding-company system.
holen to fetch, to go for;
j. aus dem Bett ~ to get s. o. out of bed; **sich einen Korb ~** to get the gate; **Polizei ~** to call the police; **j. ans Telefon ~** to call s. o. to the telephone;
Buch ~ kommen to come after a book.
Holländern dutch stitching.
Hölle|auf Erden hell on earth;
jem. die ~ auf Erden bereiten to lead s. o. a dog's life; **die ~ auf Erden haben** to suffer hell on earth; **jem. die ~ heiß machen** to play hell and tommy with (make it hot for) s. o., to give s. o. hell, to lead s. o. a dog's life, to worry the life out of s. o., to call s. o. over the coals;
der Weg zur ~ ist mit guten Vorsätzen gepflastert the way to hell is paved with good intentions.
Höllen|angst haben to be scared stiff (in a blue funk); **~feuer** hell-fire.
Höllenlärm hell-fire, racket;
ein ~ a deuce of a row;
~ **schlagen** to raise the devil about it; ~ **veranstalten** to make a hell of a noise *(coll.)*.
Höllen|maschine infernal machine, time bomb; **~qualen** torment of Tantalus.
Hollerith|karte punched card; **~maschine** punched-card machine; **~verfahren** card-index system.
höllisch infernal, devilish, fiendish;
~ **aufpassen** to watch out like the dickens *(coll.)*;
~e Angst haben to be scared stiff (in a blue funk); **~e Arbeit** tremendous lot of work; **~en Durst haben** to be parched with thirst; **~en Lärm veranstalten** to make a hell of a noise *(coll.)*; **~en Respekt vor jem. haben** to respect s. o. tremendously; **jem. einen ~en Schrecken einjagen** to scare s. o. to death.
holographisches Testament abfassen to write one's will in holograph.
holperig *(Stil)* jerky, clumsy, *(Straße)* bumpy;
~ **lesen** to read jerkily.
Holperigkeit bumpiness.
holpern *(Wagen)* to bump, to jolt;
über das Pflaster ~ to jolt over the cobbles.
Holschuld *(Vermieter)* rent lying in render *(Br.)*.
holterdiepolter helter-skelter, hurry-skurry, pell-mell.
Holz wood, timber, lumber *(US)*;
aus dem selben (gleichen) ~ geschnitzt cast in the same mold (mould), of the same stamp; **mit ~ bewachsen** wooded; **abgelagertes ~** well-seasoned wood; **abgestorbenes ~** dead wood; **astreines ~** wood free from knots; **bearbeitetes ~** sided (squared) timber; **drittklassiges ~** cull; **dürres ~** dry wood; **gesundes ~** hearty timber; **grünes ~** unseasoned timber; **unbearbeitetes ~** rough (undressed) timber;
~ **auf dem Stamm** growing timber;
~ **fällen** to cut timber, to fell trees; ~ **flößen** to float wood; **morsches ~ herausschneiden** to clean out the deadwood; ~ **auf dem Stamm kaufen** to buy timber on the stump; **aufs ~ klopfen** to touch wood; ~ **sägen** to lumber, to saw timber; **trockenes ~ sammeln** to gather dry sticks; **aus dem ~ sein, aus dem Helden geschnitzt werden** to be of the stuff that heroes are made of; **aus völlig anderem ~ geschnitzt sein** to be quite a different cut; **aus dem gleichen ~ geschnitzt sein** to be a chip of the same block; **aus härterem ~ geschnitzt sein** to be made of sterner stuff; ~ **stapeln** to stack wood; ~ **in den Busch tragen** to carry coals to Newcastle;
~abfall waste wood; **~abhieb** cutting, lumbering *(US)*; **~anstrich** wood finishing; **~anteil** estover; **~arbeiten** woodwork; **~arbeiter** woodworker, woodcutter, logger, lumberjack *(US)*; **~auktion** wood (timber) auction; **~auskleidung** wainscotting, panelling; **~baracke** shanty, shack; **~bearbeitungsindustrie** woodworking industry; **~bestand** stand; **~block** wood block, saw horse, wooden horse; **~brücke** wooden bridge; **~bündel** faggot; **~diele** board, wood (boarded) floor; **~druck** woodcut; **~druckwalze** printing roller; **~dübel** dowel; **~einschlag** rate of felling.
Holzentnahmegerechtigkeit common of estovers, plough-bote;
~ **zum Ausbessern von Hecken und Zäunen** hay-bote; ~ **für Hausreparaturen** house-bote.
hölzern woody, *(fig.)* clumsy, awkward, stiff, gauche.
Holz|erzeugung timber production; **~fachwerk** timber framing; **~fällen** woodcutting, logging, felling of trees; **~fäller** woodcutter, timberman, lumberman *(Canada, US)*, lumberjack *(US)*; **~fällerweg** skid road; **~faserplatte** fibreboard; **~faß** wooden barrel; **~feuer anzünden** to light a wood fire; **~feuerung** heating with wood; **~floß** log, raft, float.
holzfreies Papier wood-free paper.
Holz|fußboden wooden floor; **~gasgenerator** wood-gas producer; **~gerüst** scaffolding; **~hacker** woodchopper.
holzhaltiges Papier wood-containing paper.
Holzhammer mallet, beetle;
j. etw. mit dem ~ beibringen to drum s. th. into s. one's head; **j. mit dem ~ traktieren** to use sledge-hammer arguments *(coll.)*;
~methode hard sell, sledge-hammer arguments *(fam.)*.
Holz|handel timber (lumber, *US*) trade; **~händler** timber merchant, lumberman *(US)*; **~industrie** wood-based industry, woodwork and timber industry; **~kiste** wooden box; **~klotz** log; **~knüppel** cudgel; **~kohle** charcoal.
Holzkohlen|brikett charcoal briquette; **~[brenn]ofen** charcoal kiln; **~vergaser** charcoal-gas producer.
Holz|konstruktion timber construction; **~lager** timber depot; **~lagerplatz** woodyard, timberyard; **~lieferant** timber contractor; **~maserung** grain; **~nagel** treenail; **~nutzungsrecht** common of estovers; **~pflaster** wood pavement; **~platte** slat of wood; **~schneidekunst** woodcutting; **~schnitzer** wood carver; **~schnitzerei** wood carving; **~spanplatte** chipboard; **~stamm** timber; **~stempel** *(Bergbau)* prop; **~stoß** pile of wood, woodpile; **~tonne** wood.
holzverarbeitende Industrie wood-working (lumbering, *US*) industry.

Holz|verarbeitung wood processing; ~**verband** timberwork; ~**verkleidung** wainscot, panelling, timbering; ~**verschalung** planking, boarding; ~**verschlag** wooden crate; **auf dem ~weg** on the wrong track; ~**wirtschaft** lumber industry, ~**wolle** wood wool; ~**zwischenlagerplatz** dropping ground.

Homer, selbst ~ schläft gelegentlich Homer sometimes nods.

homogener Markt perfect market.

Honig honey;
türkischer ~ turkish delight;
~ schleudern to drain the honeycomb; **wie ~ schmecken** *(Lob)* to be honey for one's soul; **jem. ~ um den Mund (ums Maul) schmieren** to butter s. o. up, to soft-soap s. o.;
keine reine ~lecke not to be all beer and skittles.

honigsüß as sweet as honey, honeyed;
~e Worte honeyed words.

Honorant *(Wechsel)* payer of hono(u)r.

Honorar professional fee, honorarium, terms, six, six and eightpence, *(Anwalt)* counsel's (solicitor's, *Br.*) fee, [retaining] fee, retainer, *(Autor)* royalty, *(Belohnung)* gratification, *(Entlohnung)* remuneration, reward;
für ein mäßiges ~ at a reduced (modest) fee;
ärztliches ~ medical fee; **festes ~** salary compensation, general retainer; **fettes ~** plump (stiff) fee; **gewaltiges ~** stiff fee; **besonders vereinbartes ~** special retainer; **vorläufiges ~** retainer;
sein ~ beziehen to draw one's salary; **große ~e einstreichen** to pocket large fees; **~ liquidieren** to charge a fee; **~ teilen** to split a fee; **jem. ein ~ zahlen** to pay s. o. a fee; **~ an einen Anwalt zahlen** to fee a lawyer;
~**abrede** fee arrangement; ~**abrede treffen** to operate on a fee basis; ~**abteilung** royalty department; ~**anspruch** claim to remuneration; ~**aufstellung** royalty statement; ~**aufteilung** fee splitting; ~**aufwand für die Wirtschaftsprüfer** *(Bilanz)* remuneration of auditors; **hohe ~einnahmen haben** to pocket large fees; ~**festsetzung** bill of costs *(Br.)*; ~**forderung** fee payable.

honorarfrei free of charge.

Honorar|klausel *(Treuhänder)* charging clause; ~**konsul** honorary consul; ~**konsulat** honorary consulate; ~**professor** ordinary (full) professor, associate [professor] *(US)*; ~**rechnung** bill of costs *(Br.)*; **übliche ~regelung** *(Anwalt)* usual agency terms; ~**teilung** fee splitting; ~**vereinbarung treffen** to operate on a fee basis; ~**vertrag** special retainer; ~**vertrag mit einem Anwalt schließen** to retain an attorney; ~**vorschuß** retaining fee.

Honoratioren notabilities, notables, dignitaries, persons of standing, civic headliners *(US)*.

honorieren to fee, *(Wechsel)* to hono(u)r;
j. ~ to [pay a] fee [to] s. o.; **nicht ~** to refuse payment, *(Wechsel)* to dishono(u)r a bill of exchange, to leave in sufferance; **Scheck ~** to cash a check *(US)* (cheque, *Br.*); **Wechsel ~** to protect (hono(u)r, answer, redeem, cash, meet) a bill of exchange.

honoriert stipendiary, paid.

Honorierung payment of a fee, remuneration, *(Wechsel)* hono(u)ring, protection, discharge, taking up.

Hopfen|ernten to pick hops;
bei ihm ist ~ und Malz verloren he is a hopeless case (dead loss);
~**anbau** hop growing; ~**anbaugebiet** hop district; ~**händler** hop-merchant; ~**pflücker** hop picker.

hops|gehen to go to pot (west), *(Flieger)* to write o. s. off *(sl.)*, *(Person)* to pop off, to write o. s. off *(sl.)*; **Dieb ~ nehmen** to nab a thief; **~ sein** to be done for, to have pegged out.

Hör|apparat hearing aid; ~**bericht** wireless report, commentary.

horchen to listen;
angespannt ~ to strain one's ears; **an der Wand ~** to listen at the door, to eavesdrop.

Horcher eavesdropper;
der ~ an der Wand hört seine eigne Schand listeners never hear good of themselves.

Horch|funk interception; ~**gerät** sound locator; ~**posten** listening station.

Horde horde.

Hörempfang audio reception.

Hören *(Radio)* listening in;
jem. eine herunterhauen, daß ihm ~ und Sehen vergeht to knock s. o. into the middle of next week;
ihm verging ~ und Sehen he was absolutely stupefied by what was happening.

hören to hear;
auf j. ~ to pay attention to s. o.; **zu seinem Bedauern ~** to be sorry to learn; **nicht auf jds. Bitten ~** to turn a deaf ear to s. one's entreaties; **auf die Klingel ~** to answer the bell; **auf den Namen ~** to answer to the name; **auf diesem Ohr schlecht ~** to turn a deaf ear to s. th.; **Radio ~** to listen to the radio; **sich gern reden ~** to like to hear o. s. talk; **Sachverständigen ~** to call in (consult) an expert; **überall ~** to hear it from all quarters; **Vorlesung ~** to attend a course of lectures; **das Gras wachsen ~** to hear the grass grow, to see far into a mill stone (through a brick wall);
etw. zu ~ bekommen to listen to a few home truths; **sich ~ lassen** to sound all right; **nichts ~ wollen** to turn a deaf ear, to stop one's ears; **nichts von einem Hilfsersuchen ~ wollen** to shut one's ears to all appeals for help; **nie ~ wollen** to never listen to reason.

Hörensagen hearsay;
vom ~ by hearsay, from mere report;
vom ~ wissen to have it only from hearsay, to have secondhand knowledge.

Hörer *(Radio)* listener-in, *(pl.)* audience, *(Telefon)* receiver, earpiece, *(Universität)* student, auditor;
~ abnehmen to lift the receiver; **~ auflegen** to replace (restore) the receiver;
~**analyse** listener (audience, *Br.*) research; ~**befragung** listener (audience, *Br.*) research; ~**bericht** diary method; ~**brief** listener's letter; ~**forschung** listener research; ~**gesamtheit bei Programmende** audience flow; ~**korrespondenz** listener's correspondence; ~**kreis** audience; ~**post** listeners' correspondence; ~**publikum** [listening] audience; ~**schaft** listenership, audience, *(Universität)* students; ~**statistik** audience rating; ~**umfrage** listener (audience) research; ~**umfrage zu einer bestimmten Sendung** listenership research *(US)*; ~**wunsch** listener's request.

Hör|fehler auditory defect; ~**folge** radio serial.

Hörfunk sound broadcasting, blind radio *(US)*;
~**buchungsbüro** radio booking office; ~**kabine** broadcasting cabin; **rührselige ~serie** soap opera; ~**werbung** radio advertising.

Hörgerät deaf- (hearing) aid.

hörgeschädigt hearing impaired.

hörig compliant, enslaved;
einer Partei ~ sein to be dependent on a party; **jem. sexuell ~ sein** to be sexually enslaved to s. o.; **jem. völlig ~ sein** to feed out of s. one's hand, to be s. one's slave.

Hörigkeit subjection, compliance.

Horizont horizon, purview, *(Stadt)* skyline;
mit engem ~ untravel(l)ed;
enger ~ parochial point of view; **geistiger ~** beat; **natürlicher ~** visible horizon; **politischer ~** political horizon; **sichtbarer ~** local horizon;
sich am ~ abheben to stand out on the horizon; **am ~ aufsteigen** to top the horizon; **~ erweitern** to broaden the mind (the outlook); **über jds. ~ gehen** to pass s. one's comprehension, to be beyond s. one's comprehension (compass); **beschränkten ~ haben** to have a limited horizon; **hinter dem ~ versinken** to dip below the horizon.

horizontal horizontal, level;
~e Ausdehnung horizontal expansion; **~es Gewerbe** street walking, prostitution; **~es Kartell** horizontal combine; **sich in ~er Lage befinden** to be level; **~e Verschmelzung von Konkurrenzfirmen** horizontal integration; **~er Zusammenschluß** horizontal amalgamation.

Horizontal|ablage horizontal files; ~**ablenkung** *(Fernsehen)* line (horizontal) deflection; ~**konzern** horizontal combine; ~**verschiebung** continental drift.

Hör|kopf *(Tonband)* playback head; ~**muschel** earpiece.

Horn *(Auto)* hooter, horn, *(Material)* horn, keratin;
ins gleiche ~ blasen to sing the same song; **ins ~ stoßen** to sound the horn.

Hornberger Schießen, wie das ~ ausgehen to be a flash in the pan, to come to nothing, to be a flop.

Hörnchen cornet, *(für Eis)* ice-cream cone.

Hörner, sich die ~ abstoßen to sow one's wild oats; **einem Ehemann ~ aufsetzen** to cuckold a husband; **j. auf die ~ nehmen** to go for s. o.; **Stier bei den ~n nehmen** to take the bull by the horns; **jem. die ~ zeigen** to show one's teeth to s. o.

Hornissennest, in ein ~ stechen to stir up a nest of hornets, to bring a hornet's nest about one's ears.

Hornsignal preparative *(mil.)*.

Hörorgan auditory organ.

Horoskop horoscope, ascendant;
jem. das ~ stellen to cast s. one's horoscope (nativity).

Hörprobe trial hearing, *(Sänger)* audition.

horrend exorbitant, shocking, stupendous;
~ **teuer sein** to be frightfully expensive;
~**er Preis** terrific (exorbitant) price; ~**e Summe** colossal amount.

Hörrohr ear trumpet.

Horror horror;
~ **vor jem. haben** to be scared of s. o.; ~ **vor der Öffentlichkeit haben** to have a horror of publicity; ~ **vor einer Prüfung haben** to be terribly afraid of an examination; ~ **vor einer Reise haben** not to be able to bear the thought of a journey;
~**film** horror film.

Hör|rundfunk sound broadcasting; ~**saal** lecture room, auditorium; ~**spiel** radio play (drama).

Horst nest, eyrie, *(Flieger)* air base.

Hort *(Bollwerk)* stronghold, bulwark, place of refuge, sanctuary, *(Kinderhort)* day nursery;
~ **des Freihandels** stronghold of free trade; ~ **der Freiheit** bulwark of liberty; ~ **der Nibelungen** hoard of the Nibelungs.

horten to accumulate, to hoard, to stockpile, to treasure up *(Br.)*;
Vorräte ~ to hoard supplies.

Hortung hoarding, stockpiling, accumulation;
~ **von Arbeitskräften** labo(u)r hoarding.

Hortungs|käufe stockpiling purchases, *(Kundschaft)* panic buying (purchase); ~**politik** stockpiling policy; ~**tempo beschleunigen** to step up one's stockpiling pace.

Hör|verlust loss of hearing; ~**weite des Testierenden** presence of testator; **auf** ~**weite herankommen** to come within hearing distance.

Hose trousers, pants *(coll.)*;
~**n runter!** show your hand!;
~**n gestrichen voll haben** to be scared stiff (in a blue funk); **einem Kind die** ~**n strammziehen** to give a child a spanking.

Hosen|boden, sich auf den ~**boden setzen** to pull one's socks up; **einem Kind den** ~**boden versohlen** to give a child a spanking; ~**boje** *(mar.)* breeches buoy; **Hände an die** ~**naht** hands to sides; **etw. wie seine** ~**tasche kennen** to know s. th. inside out (all to pieces, *US*); **Stadt wie seine** ~**tasche kennen** to know a town like the back of one's hand.

hospitieren to attend lessons as an auditor, to audit *(US)*;
bei einer Partei ~ to be an associate of a party.

Hotel, Ia high-class hotel; **altrenommiertes** ~ old-line hotel; **erst[klassig]es** ~ first (high) -class hotel, tiptop hotel; **feudales** ~ swell hotel; ~ **garni** residential hotel, lodging house, apartment hotel *(US)*; **im Stadtzentrum gelegenes** ~ downtown hotel *(US)*; **schwimmendes** ~ floating hotel; **zweitklassiges** ~ second-class hotel;
~ **für Anspruchsvolle (gehobene Ansprüche)** quality hotel; ~ **für Autoreisende** motel *(US)*; ~ **für Geschäftsreisende** commercial hotel; ~ **der Mittelklasse** medium-priced hotel; ~ **der gehobenen Mittelklasse** upper-bracket hotel; ~**s am Platze** local hotels; ~ **der mittleren Preisklasse** medium-priced hotel; ~ **der Spitzenklasse** exclusive (luxury) hotel;
in einem ~ **absteigen** to put up at a hotel; **sich in einem** ~ **anmelden** to sign the hotel register, to sign a registration form, to check in with a hotel *(US)*; **sich in einem** ~ **einlogieren** to put up at a hotel; **seine Mittagsmahlzeiten in einem** ~ **einnehmen** to board at a hotel; ~ **auf das Modernste einrichten** to fit up a hotel with modern comforts and conveniences; **im** ~ **speisen** to take one's meals in the hotel; ~ **nach Rechnungsbegleichung verlassen** to check out of a hotel *(US)*; **in ein** ~ **verwandeln** to hotelize; **in einem** ~ **wohnen** to lodge (stay) at a hotel;
~**anbau** annex to a hotel; ~**angestellte** hotel staff; ~**angestellter** hotel clerk (employee, worker); ~**anmeldung** registration with a hotel; ~**anzeiger** hotel directory; ~**aufbewahrung** hotel safe deposit; ~**aufnahmevertrag** hotel accommodation agreement; ~**bar** hotel bar; ~**besitzer** hotelkeeper, proprietor of a hotel, hotel proprietor, hotelier, maître d'hôtel; ~**betrieb** hotel operation, *(Unternehmen)* hotel company; ~**bett** hotel bed; **überschüssige** ~**betten** hotel bedrooms surplus; ~**bus** station bus; ~**detektiv** house detective, dick *(sl.)*; ~**diele** [hotel] lounge, lobby, foyer; ~**diener** boots *(Br.)*; ~**direktion** hotel management; ~**direktor** manager of a hotel, hotel manager; ~**eigenschaft** hotelhood; ~**einheit** hotel unit; ~**eröffnung** opening of a hotel; ~**fach** hotel business; ~**fachschule** catering and hotel management school; ~**filiale** hotel subsidiary; ~**führer** hotel manager; ~**führung** hotel management (directory); ~**gast** visitor, guest; ~**gebäude** hotel building; ~**gelände** hotel site; ~**gewerbe** hotel business (trade); ~**- und Gaststättengewerbe** hotel and catering industry; ~**größe** hotel size; ~**grundstück** hotel site; ~**gutschein** hotel voucher; ~**halle** entrance hall, lobby, foyer, lounge.

Hotelier hotelkeeper, proprietor of a hotel, hotelier;
~ **sein** to keep an inn;
~**gewerbe** hotel business (trade).

Hotel|kapazität hotel capacity; ~**kette** hotel chain; ~**möglichkeiten** hotel accommodations; ~**nachweis** hotel broker (guide); ~**omnibus** station bus; ~**ordnung** hotel (guest) regulations; ~**page** page, callboy, button boy, bellboy *(US)*, bellhop *(US sl.)*; ~**pension** residential hotel, boardinghouse, private hotel *(Br.)*; ~**personal** hotel servants (staff); ~**portier** lodge (hotel) porter, hotel concierge, desk clerk *(US)*; ~**quartier** hotel accommodation; ~**quartier besorgen** to reserve hotel accommodation.

Hotelrechnung bill for hotel, [hotel] bill;
seine ~ **bezahlen** to check out of a hotel *(US)*; ~ **nicht bezahlen** to skip a hotel *(sl.)*; **große** ~ **haben** to run up a bill in a hotel.

Hotel|reservierung hotel booking; ~**reservierung vornehmen** to book hotel accommodation in advance; ~**restaurant** hotel dining room; ~**spesen** hotel expenses; **betriebseigene** ~**suite** company hotel suite; ~**unterbringung**, ~**unterkunft** hotel (sleeping) accommodation; ~**verzeichnis** hotel guide; ~**wesen** hotel field (trade); ~**wirtschaft** hotel industry.

Hotelzimmer hotel room (bedroom);
~ **zu einem annehmbaren Preis** moderate-price room;
~ **abbestellen** to cancel a room at a hotel; ~ **bestellen** to secure a room in a hotel, to book a hotel room *(Br.)*; ~ **telegrafisch bestellen** to telegraph to a hotel for a reservation; ~ **modernisieren** to update a hotel room; **vom** ~ **aus seiner Arbeit nachgehen** to work from a hotel room; ~ **telegrafisch vorbestellen** to telegraph to a hotel for reservation.

Hottentotten, wie die ~ **leben** to live like savages.

Hubraum piston displacement, *(Kubikinhalt)* cubic capacity;
~**leistung** power per unit of displacement, power output.

hübsch pretty, handsome, nice *(coll.)*, *(Gegend)* attractive, lovely;
~ **gelegen** nicely situated; **ganz** ~ **teuer** rather expensive;
sich ganz ~ **geirrt haben** to have made a big mistake; **sich** ~ **machen** to spruce o. s. up;
~**er Abend** pleasant evening; ~**e Bescherung** pretty kettle of fish; ~**es Durcheinander** devil among the tailors; ~**e Entfernung** quite a distance; ~**es Sümmchen** tidy sum of money, nice little sum, pretty penny; ~**es Vermögen** handsome fortune.

Hubschrauber helicopter, aerocab, windmill *(sl.)*, eggbeater *(sl.)*;
~**bus** helicopter bus, helibus; ~**landeplatz** heliport, helidrome, helicopter terminal, airstop; ~**miete** helicopter hire; ~**pilot** helipilot.

Hubstapler lift truck.

Hucke|voll Heu load of hay;
jem. die ~ **vollhauen** to give s. o. a good thrashing; **jem. die** ~ **vollügen** to tell s. o. a pack of lies.

Huckepack piggy-back;
j. ~ **tragen** to carry s. o. pick-a-back;
~**anhänger** piggyback trailer; ~**ausfuhrsystem** piggyback export scheme; ~**auto** trailer on flat car *(US)*; ~**flugzeug** pick-a-back plane, piggyback *(sl.)*; ~**schiff** roll-on (roll-off) vessel; ~**verkehr** roll-on (roll-off) service, rail piggyback, piggyback [rail] service.

Hudelei skimping, scamping.

hudelig|arbeiten to skimp;
~**e Arbeit** slopwork, slovenly (slipshod) work.

hudeln to scamp;
bei seiner Arbeit ~ to be sloppy with one's work.

Hufeisentafel horseshoe table.

Hügel hill, hillock;
am Abhang eines ~**s** on the hillside; **zwischen** ~**n liegend** embedded between hills;
~ **ohne zu schalten herauffahren** to climb a hill in top gear.

hügelartig erheben, sich to hill.

hügelig hilly, undulating.

Hügeligkeit lay of the land.

Hügellandschaft hilly country, hills.

Huhn, dummes silly goose; **verdrehtes** ~ queer bird, crazy person, screwball *(US fam.)*;
auch ein blindes ~ **findet mal ein Korn** every dog has its day.

Hühnchen chicken;
mit jem. ein ~ **zu rupfen haben** to have a bone to pick (a nut to crack, crow to pluck) with s. o.

Hühneraugen, jem. auf die ~ **treten** to tread on s. one's corns, to tread on s. one's toes.

Hühner|brühe chicken broth; ~**futter** chickenfood; ~**hof** poultry yard.

Hühnern, mit den ~ **aufstehen** to rise with the lark; **mit den** ~ **zu Bett gehen** to go to bed early.

Huld favo(u)r;
jem. seine ~ schenken to bestow one's favo(u)r on s. o.
huldigen, jem. to do (pay) homage to s. o.; **dem Alkohol ~** to be addicted to the bottle; **dem Grundsatz ~, daß** to embrace the principle that; **dem Laster ~** to indulge in vice; **dem Mammon ~** to worship the golden calf.
Huldigung homage, ovation, tribute;
jem. seine ~ darbringen to pay homage to s. o.; **jds. ~en entgegennehmen** to accept s. one's tribute, to receive s. one's ovation.
Huldigungseid oath of allegiance.
Hülle cover, covering, wrapper, jacket, blanket, *(Brief)* envelope, *(Ballon)* envelope, *(für Dokumente)* folder, jacket, case, *(Luftschiff)* hull;
in ~ und Fülle in abundance (showers);
durchsichtige ~ transparent cover; **sterbliche ~** mortal frame; **wertlose ~** husk;
~ und Fülle cut and come again; **~ der Nacht** cloak of the night; **~ des Schweigens** veil of silence;
seine ~n abstreifen to take off one's clothes; **seine alten ~n abwerfen** to put off the old man *(sl.)*; **Geld in ~ und Fülle haben** to have plenty of money; **in ~ und Fülle leben** to live in grand style (abundance); **durch äußere ~n zum Kern einer Sache vordringen** to penetrate through the outer coverings to the heart of a matter.
hüllen, Leiche in ein Leichentuch to shroud a corpse; **sich fester in seinen Mantel ~** to wrap one's coat closer around one; **j. in Samt und Seide ~** to clothe s. o. in silk and satin; **sich in tiefes Schweigen ~** to wrap o. s. in profound silence.
human humane;
seine Angestellten sehr ~ behandeln to treat one's employees with humanity;
aus ~en Gründen for humanitarian reasons.
humanisieren to humanize.
Humanisierung humanization.
humanistisch humane;
~ gebildet with a classical education;
~e Abteilung classical side *(Br.)*; **~e Bildung** classical education; **~e Denkweise** classic turn of mind; **~es Gymnasium** grammar (high, *US*) school.
humanitär humanitarian, compassionate;
~e Belange humanitarian concerns; **~e Bestrebungen** humanitarian endeavo(u)rs.
Humanität humanity.
Humanitäts | duselei sentimental humanitarianism; **~verbrechen** crime against humanity.
Humanvermögensrechnung human resource accounting.
Humbug humbug, gammon *(Br.)*, spoof *(Br., sl.)*;
~ reden to talk nonsense.
Hummeln im Hintern haben to have ants in one's pants.
Humor humo(u)r;
kein bißchen (keinen Funken) ~ no trace of humo(u)r;
schwarzer ~ blue devils; **trockener ~** dry humo(u)r, dry sense of humo(u)r;
Sinn für ~ besitzen to be of a humorous turn; **etw. mit ~ ertragen** to take s. th. good-humo(u)redly.
humorig humorous.
humoristische | Ader vein of humo(u)r; **~ Erzählung** humorous (funny) story; **~ Zeichnung** cartoon.
humorvoll sein to be of a humorous turn.
humpeln to hobble, to limp;
leicht ~ to walk with a slight limp.
Humpen tankard.
Humus humus, mould, mold *(US)*.
Hund dog, hound, *(Bergbau)* truck, mine car, tram, cub, lorry, hound, *(fig.)* despisable person;
auf den ~ gekommen down and out, out at elbows;
unter allem ~ beneath contempt; **wie ein geprügelter ~** with his tail between his legs;
armer ~ poor fellow; **blöder ~** stupid ass; **falscher ~** yellow dog; **fauler ~** lazy dog; **feiger ~** cur, pudding heart; **gemeiner ~** dirty skunk *(sl.)*; **öffentlich geprügelter ~** poor pussy on the public pavement; **herrenloser ~** ownerless dog; **scharfer ~** vicious dog; **tollwütiger ~** mad dog; **weiße ~e** *(Wellen)* white crests; **wildernder ~** unlawful dog;
~ anmelden to take out a dog licence; **j. wie einen ~ behandeln** to lead s. o. a dog's life, to treat s. o. like dirt; **j. auf den ~ bringen** to reduce s. o. to beggary; **wie ein junger ~ frieren** to be as cold as charity; **~ an der Leine führen** to keep one's dog on the lead; **vor die ~e gehen** to go to the dogs (devil, pot, *sl.*); **~ halten** to harbo(u)r a dog; **~ auf j. hetzen** to set a dog at s. o.; **mit ~en hetzen** to dog; **auf den ~ kommen** to go to the dogs (to wrack and ruin), to go down in the world; **wie ~ und Katze leben** to lead a cat-and-dog life; **~ an die Kette legen** to chain up a dog; **ganz auf dem ~ sein** to have reached rock bottom; **müde wie ein ~ sein** to be dog-tired; **wie ein bunter ~ bekannt sein** to be known all over the place; **mit allen ~en gehetzt sein** to know the tricks of the trade, to be an artful dodger (up to snuff, *sl.*); **vor die ~e werfen** to throw to the dogs;
das Mitbringen von ~en ist nicht gestattet! no dogs!; **Vorsicht, bissiger ~!** beware of the dog!;
da liegt der ~ begraben there is a nigger in the woodpile; **den letzten beißen die ~e** the devil takes the hindmost; **das ist ein dicker ~** that's a clanger, it's a piece of damned cheek; **kommt man über den ~, kommt man auch über den Schwanz** once you've broken the back of it, the rest is easy; **man soll schlafende ~e nicht wecken** to let sleeping dogs lie.
Hündchen, jem. wie ein ~ folgen to follow s. o. like a dog.
Hunde | abteil dog box *(Br.)*, doghouse; **~arbeit** grind, drudgery; **~ausstellung** dog show; **~besitzer, ~halter** keeper of a dog, dogowner; **~decke** dog blanket.
hundeelend dog-sick;
~ aussehen to look wretched; **sich ~ fühlen** to feel as sick as a dog.
Hunde | fänger dog catcher; **~führer** *(Polizei)* handler; **~halteerlaubnis** dog licence; **~hütte** doghouse, kennel; **in einer ~hütte leben** to live in a dunghill.
hundekalt beastly cold.
Hunde | koppel brace of hounds; **~kuchen** dog cake (biscuits); **~leben führen** to lead a dog's life; **~leine** dog lead; **~liebhaber** dog fancier; **~loch** doghole; **das reinste ~loch sein** not to be better than a dunghill; **~marke** dog licence (license, *US*), *(Erkennungsmarke)* identity disk *(Br.)*, dog tag *(US sl.)*; **~meute** pack of hounds.
hundemüde dog-tired, dead tired.
Hundepension boarding home for dogs.
Hundert, vom per cent;
in die ~e gehen to run into three figures.
hundert, einmal in ~ Jahren vorkommen to happen once in a blue moon;
~e von Ausreden haben to have dozens of excuses.
Hundertdollar | aktie full stock *(US)*; **~schein** hundred dollar note *(US)*, C *(US sl.)*.
Hunderter hundred dollar note *(US)*.
hunderterlei Weise, auf in a hundred different ways.
hundertfünfzigprozentig fanatic, ardent, ultra, dyed in the wool;
~er Ire dyed-in-the-wool Irishman; **~er Nationalist** ultranationalist, out-and-out nationalist.
Hundert | fünfzigprozentiger lunatic fringe; **~jahrfeier** centenary.
hundertjähriges Jubiläum centenary.
hundertprozentig out-and-out, perfect, thoroughgoing, downright;
~ garantiert sure fire *(fam.)*;
sich ~ engagieren to turn on the heat *(sl.)*; **mit jem. ~ einverstanden sein** to be in perfect agreement with s. o.; **~ übereinstimmen** to agree wholly; **sich ~ auf etw. verlassen** to rely on it absolutely; **etw. ~ wissen** to know s. th. for sure;
~er Alkohol pure alcohol; **~er Amerikaner** super (a hundred per cent) American; **~e Beteiligung** a hundred percent participation; **~er Egoist** thoroughpaced egoist; **~e Preiserhöhung** price increase of one hundred percent; **~er Unsinn** utter nonsense; **in ~er Vergrößerung** enlarged a hundred times.
Hundertprozentiger out-and-outer *(sl.)*, hundred-percenter.
Hundertsatz percentage.
Hundertstelstelle percentile.
hundertstückweise kaufen to buy by the hundred pieces.
Hunde | schnauze, kalt wie eine as cool as a cucumber; **treue ~seele besitzen** to have a dog-like devotion; **~steuer** dog tax (licence, *Br.)*; **~steuer zahlen** to take out a dog licence *(Br.)*; **~wache** *(mar.)* dogwatch, midwatch, middle watch *(US)*; **~wetter** beastly weather; **~zwinger** dog kennels.
hündisch servile, cringing, fawning, toadyish;
jem. ~ ergeben sein to have an abject devotion to s. o.;
~e Ergebenheit dog-like devotion; **~er Gehorsam** slavish obedience; **~e Unterwürfigkeit** abject obsequiousness.
Hundsfott dastard, scoundrel, blackguard.
hundsföttisch low-down, base, dastardly.
hundsgemein mean, low;
sich ~ benommen haben to have behaved beastly;
~es Wetter beastly weather.
hundsmiserabel wretched, rotten, lousy *(sl.)*;
sich ~ fühlen to feel absolutely rotten (lousy, *sl.*).

hundsmiserable | Handschrift atrocious handwriting; **~s Wetter** awful (wretched) weather.
Hundstage dog-days.
Hunger hunger, *(Appetit)* stomach, *(Sehnen)* craving, longing; **vom ~ getrieben** under the stimulus of hunger;
nagender ~ pangs of hunger; **quälender ~** pinch of hunger;
~ nach Lob hunger for praise;
keinen richtigen ~ haben to have no real appetite; **an ~ sterben** to die of hunger; **seinen ~ stillen** to satisfy one's hunger;
~ ist der beste Koch hunger is the best sauce;
Worte stillen den ~ nicht hungry bellies have no ears;
~blockade hunger blockade; **~gebiet** famine-affected area; **~kur** starvation (reducing) diet, slimming course; **~kur durchführen** to be on a starvation diet; **~leider** starveling, pauper.
Hungerlohn destitution (starvation) wages, sweated money, pittance, penny fee *(Br.)*;
für ~ hergestellt sweated;
für ~ arbeiten to sweat; **ganzen Tag für einen ~ arbeiten** to work all day for a mere pittance.
Hunger | marsch hunger march; **~marschierer** hunger marcher.
hungern to feel hungry, to tighten one's belt, *(sich sehnen)* to crave, to long, to hanker;
freiwillig ~ to starve o. s.; **nach Liebe ~** to crave for affection;
nach Lob ~ to hunger for praise;
~, um schlank zu werden to be on a starvation diet;
sich zu Tode ~ to starve o. s. to death; **nach Wissen ~** to be hungry for knowledge.
hungernde Bevölkerung starving population.
Hunger | ration short-commons; **~revolte** food riot.
Hungersnot famine.
Hungerstreik hunger (bread) strike;
in einen ~ eintreten to go on a hunger strike, to hunger-strike;
~ Durchführender hunger striker.
Hunger | tod starvation; **~tod sterben** to die of starvation; **am ~tuche nagen** to dine with Duke Humphrey.
hungrig hungry;
~ wie ein Wolf dog-hungry, as hungry as a hunter;
~es Gesicht machen to have a hungry look;
einem ~en Magen ist schlecht predigen hungry bellies have no ears.
hunzen, bei seiner Arbeit to slobber away with one's work.
Hupe horn, hooter, toot *(Br.)*;
~ betätigen to honk the horn; **nicht mehr von der ~ heruntersteigen** to drive on the horn.
hupen to toot, to honk the horn.
Hupen | signal, ~zeichen hooter signal, honk.
hüpfen, vor Freude to leap with joy.
Hup | konzert chorus of hooters; **~verbot** no hooting.
Hürde obstacle, barrier, hurdle;
handelspolitische ~n barriers to trade;
alle ~n nehmen to clear all the hurdles; **alle ~n mühelos nehmen** to take everything in one's stride.
Hure strumpet, whore, tart, prostitute.
Huren | bock whoremaster, lecher; **~gegend, ~viertel** red-light district; **~haus** brothel; **~kind** *(drucktechn.)* widow; **~wirtin** brothel-keeper.
Hurra hurrah, hurray;
~patriot hundred-percenter, flagwaver, spread-eagle *(US)*; **~patriotismus** hundred-percentism, flagwaving, spread-eagleism *(US)*; **mit ~rufen begrüßen** to cheer.
Hurrikan hurricane, wind storm.
hurtig nimble, swift.
Husarenstück coup de main.
Husch, jem. auf einen ~ besuchen to pay s. o. a flying visit, to pop in on s. o.
Husch-Husch, im in a hurry;
im ~ arbeiten to work slovenly, to do slopwork.
husten, auf etw. not to care a fig (straw); **er kann mir etw. ~** he can whistle for it, he can wait for me till doomsday.
Hut hat, *(Obacht)* watch, *(Schutz)* protection, keeping;
in Gottes ~ in God's keeping;
alter ~ in neuer Verpackung an old parcel in new string;
gegensätzliche Meinungen unter einen ~ bekommen to reconcile conflicting opinions; **etw. in jds. ~ geben** to commit s. th. to s. one's care; **jem. etw. auf den ~ geben** to give s. o. a good dressing down; **eins auf den ~ kriegen** to get a crack on the nut; **~ herumgehen lassen** to pass the hat round; **jem. den ~ hochgehen lassen** to make s. o. see red (s. one's blood boil); **seinen ~ nehmen** *(fig.)* to resign, to step down; **j. in seine ~ nehmen** to take care of s. o.; **auf der ~ sein** to be on watch, to keep one's weather eye open, to be wary of, to keep one's powder dry, to be careful enough, to watch out *(US coll.)*; **ein alter ~ sein** to be old hat *(fam.)*; **~ vor jem. ziehen** to take off one's hat to s. o.;
das kannst du dir an den ~ stecken! you can keep it!;
schließlich ging ihm der ~ hoch finally he blew his top;
~ablage hatrack.
hüten to guard, to protect;
sich vor Erkältungen ~ to guard against colds; **Geheimnis ~** to keep a secret; **Schatz ~** to guard a treasure; **sich schwer ~** to take jolly good care not to do it; **Zimmer ~** to stay indoors;
seine Zunge ~ to mind one's tongue;
Bett ~ müssen to be confined to one's bed.
Hüter keeper, guardian, upholder;
~ des Gesetzes arm of the law.
Hut | laden hat shop; **~macher** hatmaker, hatter; **das geht mir über die ~schnur** that puts the lid on it; **~ständer** hatstand, hat peg, hat tree *(US)*.
Hütte hut, cottage, shed, shack, cabin, crib, cot, barrack, tabernacle *(US)*, *(Berghütte)* lodge, *(Hundehütte)* kennel, *(Jagdhütte)* hunting lodge, *(Industrie)* smelting works, foundry, steelworks, ironworks, *(Schutzhütte)* refuge;
in meiner bescheidenen ~ under my humble roof;
verlassene ~ deserted hut;
aus einigen kümmerlichen ~n bestehen to consist of a few miserable cottages.
Hütten | arbeiter ironworker, foundry worker, steel worker; **~bewohner** cottager; **~fachmann** metallurgist; **~industrie** iron and steel industry; **~kunde** metallurgy; **~techniker** metallurgical engineer; **~werk** smelting plant (works), steelworks.
Hydrant hydrant, fireplug.
Hydraulikanlage hydraulic system.
hydraulisch betätigt hydraulically operated.
Hygienekonferenz health conference.
Hygieniker public health specialist.
hygienisch hygienic, sanitary.
hypermodern ultramodern, newfangled, up to the minute.
Hypnose | schlaf hypnotic sleep; **~zustand** hypnotic state.
hypochondrisch hypochondriac, valetudinarian.
Hypothek mortgage, hypothec, charge *(Br.)*;
frei von ~en unencumbered, unmortgaged; **mit einer ~ belastet** covered by a mortgage, encumbered, mortgaged;
abgelöste ~ paid-off mortgage; **sicherungsweise abgetretene ~** blanket bond (mortgage); **wieder aufgefüllte (beliehene) ~** remortgage; **von einer Aktiengesellschaft aufgenommene ~** corporate mortgage; **aufgewertete ~** revalorized mortgage; **nicht aufstockungsfähige ~** closed mortgage *(coll., US)*; **vertraglich ausbedungene ~** conventional mortgage; **mit Indexklauseln ausgestattete ~** index-linked mortgage; **formgerecht bestellte ~** completed (technical) mortgage; **für mehrere Gläubiger bestellte ~** contributory mortgage; **bevorrechtigte ~** senior mortgage; **drittrangige ~** third mortgage; **eingetragene ~** recorded *(US)* (registered, *Br.*) mortgage; **kraft Gesetzes entstandene ~** legal mortgage (hypothec), tacit mortgage; **durch Gerichtsurteil entstandene ~** judicial hypothec; **erst[stellig]e ~** legal mortgage *(Br.)*, first *(Br.)* (senior, *US*) mortgage; **formgerechte ~** technical mortgage; **mit einer Lebensversicherung gekoppelte ~** insured mortgage; **gelöschte ~** discharged mortgage; **gewöhnliche ~** common-law mortgage; **nachrangige (im Rang nachstehende, nachstellige) ~** overlying (subsequent, junior, *US*, puisne, *Br.*) mortgage, submortgage, surcharge; **notleidende ~** defaulted mortgage; **in Anrechnung auf den Kaufpreis übernommene ~** purchase-money mortgage; **unablösliche ~** irredeemable mortgage; **unkündbare ~** irredeemable mortgage; **dem Betrag nach unveränderliche ~** closed mortgage; **voll valutierte ~** limited open-end mortgage; **nicht voll valutierte ~** open-end mortgage; **verbilligte ~** option mortgage; **verfallene ~** default (foreclosed) mortgage; **treuhänderisch verwaltete ~** trust mortgage; **im Rang vorgehende (vorrangige) ~** senior *(US)* (prior [recorded, *US*], underlying) mortgage; **mehreren Gläubigern zustehende ~** participating mortgage; **zweitrangige ~** second mortgage;
~ zu mörderischen Bedingungen cutthroat mortgage; **~ über einen festen Betrag** fixed mortgage; **~ zur Erschließung von Baugelände** development mortgage; **~ auf landwirtschaftlich genutzten Grundbesitz** farm mortgage; **~ zur Sicherung von Inhaberschuldverschreibungen** adjustment mortgage; **~ mit Tilgungsstreckung** low-start mortgage;
~ ablösen to redeem (pay off) a mortgage, to dismortgage; **~ amortisieren** to pay off (extinguish) a mortgage; **~ aufnehmen**

to take a mortgage; ~ **bei einer Bausparkasse aufnehmen** to effect a mortgage with a building society; ~ **auf ein Grundstück aufnehmen** to take a mortgage on real estate, to borrow (raise) money on [the security of] an estate; ~ **auf ein Haus aufnehmen** to raise a mortgage on a house; **mit einer** ~ **belasten** to [encumber with a] mortgage; ~ **bestellen** to mortgage, to deliver (create, register, complete) a mortgage, to create a charge *(Br.)*; **nachrangige** ~ **bestellen** to submortgage; **aus einer** ~ **die Zwangsvollstreckung betreiben** to execute a mortgage, to foreclose on a mortgage [deed, *US*], to levy an execution; ~ **[ins Grundbuch] eintragen** to register *(Br.)* (record, *US*) a mortgage; ~ **für verfallen erklären** to foreclose (close, *US coll.*) a mortgage; **mit der Verzinsung und Amortisation seiner** ~ **in Verzug geraten** to default on one's mortgage payment; ~ **(Darlehn gegen eine** ~**) gewähren** to lend on mortgage; ~ **kündigen** *(Gläubiger)* to call in a mortgage, to foreclose a mortgage, *(Schuldner)* to give notice of redemption; ~ **ins Grundbuch eintragen lassen** to have a mortgage recorded in the office of the registrar of deeds *(US)*; ~ **auf einem Grundstück eintragen lassen** to place a mortgage on a property; **auf eine** ~ **leihen** to lend (borrow) on mortgage; ~ **im Grundbuch löschen** to release (discharge, cancel) a mortgage, to enter satisfaction; ~ **beim Heimathafen registrieren** to register a mortgage at the port of registry; **mit der** ~ **des verlorenen Krieges belastet sein** to be encumbered with the burden of a lost war; ~ **tilgen** to extinguish (pay off, clear [off], repay, satisfy, cancel, redeem, wipe off) a mortgage; ~ **übernehmen** to take over a mortgage; ~ **[unter Anrechnung auf den Kaufpreis] übernehmen** to assume a mortgage; ~**en vereinigen** to pool mortgages; ~ **zurückzahlen** to pay off (redeem, clear off, wipe off, satisfy, repay) a mortgage; ~**en verschiedenen Ranges zusammenschreiben** to tack mortgages; **aus einer** ~ **zwangsvollstrecken** to execute a mortgage, to levy an execution on s. one's estate, to foreclose a mortgage *(US)*.

Hypothekar|darlehn loan on mortgage, mortgage loan; ~**darlehn aufnehmen** to issue a mortgage; ~**geschäft** mortgage transaction; ~**gläubiger** mortgage creditor.

Hypothekarisierung hypothecation.

hypothekarisch hypothecary, on (by way of a) mortgage;
~ **belastbar** mortgageable; ~ **belastet** mortgaged, encumbered, under and subject; ~ **nicht belastet** unencumbered, unmortgaged; ~ **gesichert** secured by mortgage;
~ **belasten** to borrow money on the security of an estate, to [encumber with a] mortgage, to hypothecate; **Grundstück** ~ **belasten** to mortgage a piece of real estate; **sein Haus** ~ **belasten** to mortgage one's house; ~ **belastet sein** to be encumbered with a mortgage; ~ **sicherstellen** to secure (cover) by mortgage;
~**e Belastung** mortgage debt (charge, *Br.*); ~**e Beleihung eines Grundstücks** raising of a mortgage on an estate; ~ **gesichertes Darlehn** mortgage loan; ~ **belastetes Eigentum** mortgaged property; ~**e Forderung** mortgage claim; ~ **belasteter Grundbesitz** mortgaged property; ~**e Klage** foreclosure suit *(US)*; ~ **gesicherter Kredit** credit on mortgage; ~ **gesicherte Pfandbriefe** first mortgage bonds; ~**e Schuld** mortgage debt; ~ **gesicherte Schuldurkunde** mortgage note *(US)*; ~ **gesicherte Schuldverschreibung** mortgage debenture; ~**e Sicherheit** mortgage, mortgage security; **Geld gegen** ~**e Sicherheit aufnehmen** to borrow on mortgage by deposit of a titled deed *(Br.)*; ~**e Verpflichtungen** mortgage obligations, mortgages outstanding (payable, *US*); **zu** ~**en Zwecken** for mortgage purposes.

Hypothekar|kredit mortgage (real-estate) loan, mortgage advance; ~**kredit aufnehmen** to borrow money on the security of an estate; ~**pfandbriefe** mortgage debentures; ~**schuld** mortgage debt; ~**schuldverschreibungen** [corporate] mortgage bonds *(US)* (debentures, *Br.*); ~**verschuldung** mortgage borrowing; ~**versicherung** mortgage guarantee insurance.

Hypotheken|ablösung redemption of a mortgage; ~**ablösungsrecht** equity of redemption; ~**abschlüsse** mortgage sales; ~**abteilung** *(Bank)* mortgage department; ~**abtretung** assignment (release) of a mortgage, mortgage assignment; ~**amortisation** extinguishment of a mortgage; ~**angebot** mortgage facility; **knappes** ~**angebot** shortage of mortgage money, reduced availability of mortgage funds; ~**anlage** investment in mortgages; ~**anlagenkäufe** mortgage buying; ~**anleihe** mortgage loan; ~**anstalt** mortgage bank; ~**aufwertung** revalorization of mortgages; ~**ausfall** mortgage loss; ~**ausleihungen** mortgage lending; ~**auszahlung** payment of a mortgage loan; ~**bank** mortgage (land) bank, mortgage loan and investment company *(US)*; ~**bankgeschäft** mortgage bank business; ~**bankinstitut** mortgage lending institution; ~**bedarf** demand for new mortgages; ~**belastung** mortgage charge *(Br.)*, charge by way of legal mortgage *(Br.)*, encumbrance, incumbrance; ~**beleihung** borrowing on mortgages; ~**bereitstellung** mortgage service; ~**beschaffung** mortgage assistance; ~**besitzer** mortgagee; ~**bestellung** delivery (creation) of a mortgage, mortgage contract; ~**bewilligungsurkunde** instrument of charge *(Br.)*, deed of trust *(US)*; ~**brief** mortgage deed (instrument, certificate, note, *US*); **treuhänderisch hinterlegter** ~**brief von Gesamthandsgläubigern** party mortgage; ~**buch** registrar of mortgages, mortgage registry.

Hypothekendarlehn loan on mortgage, mortgage loan;
erststelliges ~ first mortgage loan; **auf dem Eigenheim gesichertes** ~ home mortgage loan;
~ **durch Tilgungsleistungen abtragen** to reduce the principal amount on a mortgage; ~ **aufnehmen** to raise money on an estate; **langfristiges** ~ **bei einer Kapitalsammelstelle aufnehmen** to borrow on mortgage from a long-term institutional lender; ~ **geben (gewähren)** to lend (borrow) money on mortgage.

Hypotheken|darlehnsvertrag mortgage agreement; ~**eigentümer** mortgagee; ~**eintragung** registration *(Br.)* (recording, *US*) of a mortgage; ~**finanzierung** mortgage financing; ~**finanzierung durch Bausparverträge** building society mortgage financing; ~**finanzierung mit Tilgungsstreckung vermitteln** to introduce a low-start mortgage scheme; ~**fonds** mortgage pool, equity funding.

Hypothekenforderung claim on mortgage, mortgage debt (claim), hypothecary claim;
~**en** *(Bilanz)* mortgages receivable *(US)*;
gepfändete ~ defaulted (distressed) mortgage; **nachstehende** ~ junior *(US)* (puisne, *Br.*) mortgage claim;
~ **abtreten** to assign a mortgage.

Hypothekenformular mortgage form.

hypothekenfrei free and unencumbered, unmortgaged.

Hypothekengarantie|kasse mortgage underwriting agency *(US)*; ~**versicherung** mortgage guaranty insurance; ~**versicherungsprämie** mortgage guarantee premium.

Hypotheken|gelder, verknappte reduced availability of mortgage funds, shortage of mortgage money; ~**geldgeber** mortgage lender; ~**geschäft** mortgage business (investments); ~**gesellschaft** mortgage loan and investment company *(US)*; ~**gesuch** application for a mortgage, mortgage loan application; ~**gewährung gegen Abtretung einer Versicherung für den Erlebensfall** mortgage endowment scheme.

Hypothekengläubiger mortgage creditor, holder of a mortgage, mortgagee of land, encumbrancer;
erstrangiger ~ legal mortgagee; **in guten Glauben handelnder** ~ bona fide mortgagor; **im Range nachstehender (nachrangiger)** ~ subordinate (subsequent) mortgagee, junior encumbrancer; **im Rang vorgehender** ~ prior mortgagee;
~ **sein** to hold a mortgage; **vorgehenden** ~ **von einer nachrangigen Eintragung unterrichten** to serve notice of mortgage.

Hypotheken|höchstsatz maximum mortgage interest rate; ~**inhaber** mortgage creditor; ~**institut** mortgage (land) bank; ~**klage** foreclosure action *(US)*; ~**klausel** *(Feuerversicherung)* mortgage clause; ~**knappheit** shortage of mortgage money; ~**konto** mortgage account, mortgage payable account *(US)*.

Hypothekenkredit mortgage loan;
erststelliger ~ first mortgage loan;
~ **aufnehmen** to borrow on mortgage.

Hypotheken|kündigung notice of redeemption; ~**laufzeit** mortgage period; ~**löschung** discharge (extinguishment) of a mortgage, cancellation of a mortgage *(US)*; ~**makler** mortgage broker; ~**markt** market for mortgages, mortgage market; ~**märkte verstärkt mit Etatsüberschüssen anreichern** to force-feed mortgage markets with big budget surpluses; ~**moratorium** mortgage moratorium; ~**pfandbrief** bond and mortgage, mortgage note (debenture, *Br.*); ~**pfandbriefinhaber** mortgage debenture stockholder; ~**pfandrecht** hypothecary right; ~**rang** rank[ing] of mortgages; **nicht eingehaltene** ~**raten** mortgage payment delinquency; **mit einer** ~**rate auf sein Eigenheim in Verzug kommen** to miss a payment on one's home; ~**recht** law of mortgages; ~**register** [etwa] register of land charges *(Br.)*, registrar of mortgages, charges register *(Br.)*, mortgage registry (recording, *US*) office; ~**rückzahlungen** mortgage payment; ~**schein** mortgage note (certificate, *US*, deed).

Hypothekenschuld hypothecary (mortgage) debt, debt on mortgage, mortgage liability, encumbrance;
frei von ~**en** unencumbranced, unmortgaged;
~**en** *(Bilanz)* mortgages payable *(US)*;

noch bestehende ~ face of a mortgage;

~ **bezahlen** to disencumber an estate, to satisfy (pay off, cancel, wipe off) a mortgage.

Hypothekenschuldner mortgager, mortgagor, reverser *(Scot.)*, debtor on mortgage, mortgage debtor, hypothecator;

ursprünglicher ~ original mortgagor.

Hypotheken|schuldverschreibung mortgage bond *(US)* (debenture, *Br.*); ~**stelle** rank of a mortgage; ~**stock** portfolio of mortgages; ~**subventionierungssystem** mortgage subsidy system; ~**tilgung** extinguishment (redemption, discharge, paying off) of a mortgage, repayment of a mortgage debt, mortgage amortization, mortgage payment; ~**übernahme** assuming (assumption) of a mortgage; ~**urkunde** mortgage deed (certificate); ~**valuta** mortgage money; **restliche ~valuta** balance outstanding on a mortgage; ~**vereinigung** pooling of mortgages, tacking; ~**vereinigungsanspruch** right to tack *(Br.)*; ~**verkehr** mortgage business; ~**vermittler** mortgage broker; ~**vermittlung** mortgage broking; ~**verschuldung** mortgage indebtedness; ~**versicherungsanstalt** mortgage insurance company; ~**vertrag** mortgage transaction; ~**verzeichnis** statutory register of mortgages; ~**verzinsung** interest on mortgage; ~**vormerkung** mortgage caution; ~**vorrang** priority of a mortgage; ~**wert** value of a mortgage; ~**werte** mortgage papers; ~**zinsen** mortgage interest (rates); ~**zinssatz** rate of interest on mortgage loan, mortgage [interest] rate; ~**zinszahlungen** mortgage interest payments; ~**zusage** mortgage guarantee; **feste (verbindliche) ~zusage** firm commitment *(US)*; ~**zusage mit Staatsgarantie** government-backed mortgage; ~**zusammenschreibung** pooling of mortgages, tacking *(Br.)*; ~**zuschußwesen** mortgage subsidy scheme; ~**zwangsvollstreckung** execution levied upon the property, foreclosure *(US)*.

hypothekisierbar mortgageable.

hypothekisieren to hypothecate, to bond, to mortgage, to encumber.

Hypothekisierung hypothecation, charge by way of legal mortgage *(Br.)*.

Hypothese hypothesis.

hypothetisch hypothetical, *(Gesetz)* constructive;

~**er Fall** moot case; ~**e Frage** hypothetical question; ~**e Jahrespacht** hypothetical yearly tenancy.

Hysterie dämpfen to quiet hysteria.

I

I-Tüpfelchen, bis aufs to a T (dot, toucher, crumb);
jds. Anweisungen bis zum ~ ausführen not to depart an inch from s. one's orders; **Vertrag bis aufs ~ erfüllen** to live up to the letter of a contract.
Ich self, ego;
das eigene (liebe) ~ number one, one's own interests; **mein anderes ~** my alter ego (other self);
nur noch ein Schatten seines früheren ~s sein to be worn to a shadow;
ich | bewußt self-aware; **~bezogen** self-centered, egocentric, egoistic; **weniger ~bezogen** less personalized;
Ich | form, in der in the first person; **~sucht** egoism, egotism, selfishness.
Ideal ideal, hearththrob perfection;
schwer zu erreichendes ~ a counsel of perfection *(coll.)*; **hohe ~e** high ideals;
~auto ideal car; **~bewerber** ideal applicant.
ideales Ferienwetter ideal weather for a holiday.
Idealfall, im in ideal circumstances.
idealisieren to idealize.
Idealismus idealism.
Idealist idealist.
idealistisch idealistic.
Ideal | konkurrenz *(Strafrecht)* [etwa] concurrence of offences; **~verein** voluntary association *(US)*; **~vorstellung** ideal; **~wechsel** accommodation bill.
Idee idea, conception, conceit, image, imagination, flash, brilliant burst, *(Nuance)* shade, trace, fraction, drop, suggestion, *(Werbung)* idea, notion;
ohne jede ~n innocent of ideas; **voller ~n** pregnant with ideas; **voller neuer ~n** full of new ideas; **von einer ~ besessen** obsessed with an idea;
drollige ~ quaint idea; **famose ~** first-rate idea; **fixe ~** craze, bee in one's bonnet, mad point, crank, obsession; **großartige ~** rich idea; **gute ~** good plan; **kluge ~** brainwave; **konfuse ~n** muddy ideas; **nicht ausgegorene politische ~n** half-baked policies; **nicht realisierbare ~** impracticable idea; **tolle ~** insane idea; **unausgegorene ~n** half-baked (crude) ideas; **unentwickelte ~n** germinal ideas; **unklare ~n** indeterminate ideas; **vage ~** foggy idea, lax (vague) idea; **verkaufsfördernde ~** promotional idea *(US)*;
eine ~ zu klein a trifle too small;
j. von einer ~ abbringen to cure s. o. of an idea; **sich jds. ~n aneignen** to appropriate s. one's ideas; **seine ~n der neuen Lage anpassen** to orient one's ideas to new conditions; **~n assoziieren** to connect (associate) ideas; **~ aufgreifen** to seize on a notion; **~n in sich aufnehmen** to imbibe ideas; **~ ausnutzen** to cash in on an idea; **jem. törichte ~n austreiben** to knock stupid ideas out of s. o.; **j. mit einer ~ behelligen** to possess s. o. with an idea; **~ mit Beschlag belegen** to pre-empt an idea; **~ praktisch und wirksam zur Anwendung bringen** to put an idea into effective organizational action; **jem. eine ~ einbläuen** to hammer an idea into s. one's head; **jem. neue ~n einimpfen** to inoculate s. o. with new ideas; **je. eine ~ einpflanzen** to plant an idea in s. one's mind; **jem. eine ~ eintrichtern** to indoctrinate s. o. with an idea; **an einer ~ festhalten** to cherish an idea; **seinen ~n in einer Ansprache konkrete Form geben** to embody one's ideas in a speech; **fixe ~ haben** to have s. th. on one's brain; **nicht die geringste ~ haben** not to have the faintest idea; **~ fallen lassen** to relinquish an idea; **skeptisch auf jds. ~n reagieren** to pour cold water on s. one's ideas; **aus einer ~ Kapital schlagen** to cash in on an idea; **von einer ~ besessen sein** to be possessed with an idea; **von einer fixen ~ besessen sein** to be dominated by one idea; **jem. eine ~ in den Kopf setzen** to infatuate s. o. with an idea; **mit der ~ spielen** to toy with an idea; **mit der ~ spielen auszuwandern** to play with the idea of emigrating; **voller ~n stecken** to bubble with ideas; **voller hervorragender ~n stecken** to be teeming with bright ideas; **neuen ~n aufgeschlossen gegenüber stehen** to be hospitable to new ideas; **einem Autor eine ~ stehlen** to derive an idea from an author; **~n verbreiten** to disseminate ideas; **seine ~n vortragen** to present one's ideas; **für eine ~ werben** to start an idea on its way; **durch jds. ~n gefördert werden** to improve on s. one's ideas.
ideell, rein ~er Wert purely sentimental value; **~er Wert einer Firma** goodwill of a firm.
Ideen | anreger, ~gestalter *(Werbung)* visualizer *(US)*, ideas man *(Br.)*.
ideenarm bankrupt of ideas;
~ werden to become poorer in ideas.
Ideen | armut penury of ideas; **~assoziation** association of ideas; **~findung** brainstorming; **~gemeinschaft** community of ideas; **grafischer ~gestalter** ideas man *(Br.)*, visualizer *(US)*; **~gestaltung** visualizing *(US)*; **~kreis** range of ideas.
ideenlos bankrupt of ideas.
Ideen | losigkeit penury of ideas; **~mann** *(Werbung)* ideas man *(Br.)*, visualizer *(US)*; **~programm** *(Werbefeldzug)* copy platform.
ideenreich | er Mensch man of ideas; **~e Persönlichkeit sein** to be a man full of new ideas.
Ideenreichtum productivity;
über großen ~ verfügen to bubble with ideas; **sich auf ~ verlassen** to feed on ideas.
Ideen | sitzung brainstorming; **~skizze** scribble, rough, *(Anzeige)* layout; **~spezialist** *(Werbung)* ideas man *(Br.)*, visualizer *(US)*; **~verbreiter** idea-monger; **~vorrat** bank of ideas; **~wirbel** brainstorming.
Identifikation identification.
identifizierbar identifiable;
leicht ~ *(Hehlergut)* hot.
identifizieren to identify;
sich mit jem. ~ to identify o. s. with s. o.
Identifizierung identification;
~ eines Verbrechers identification of a criminal; **~ von Verkehrsopfern** identification of persons killed in a road accident.
Identifizierungszeichen identification mark, tally.
identisch identical, same;
~e Erklärungen identical statements.
Identität identity;
~ bestätigen to identify; **jds. ~ feststellen** to establish the identity of s. o.; **seine ~ nachweisen** to prove one's identity; **seine ~ verheimlichen** to conceal one's identity.
Identitäts | ausweis identification (identity) card, identity certificate; **~feststellung** identification; **~glied** *(Datenverarbeitung)* identity element (unit); **~irrtum** mistaken identity; **~karte** identification (identity) card, identity certificate; **~marke** *(mil.)* identification disk *(US)* (tag); **~nachweis** submission of proof of identity, identity certificate, certificate of identity, *(Zoll)* certificate of origin; **~nachweis führen** to submit proof of identity; **~täuschung** impersonation, imposture; **~urkunde** certification of a man's name; **~verwechselung** mistaken identity; **aufgrund einer ~verwechslung festgenommen werden** to be arrested because of mistaken identity; **~zeichen** identification mark.
Ideologe ideologist.
Ideologie, totalitäre totalitarian ideology.
ideologische | Neigungen ideological leanings; **~ Risse überbrücken** to bridge the ideological rift.
Idiom idiom;
fremdes ~ foreignism.
Idiomatik idiom.
idiomatisch idiomatic;
~e Redewendung idiom; **~e Redewendungen gebrauchen** to express o. s. idiomatically.
Idiosynkrasie idiosyncrasy, allergy;
~ gegen j. haben to have a strong aversion towards s. o.
Idiot idiot, insane person, fool, natural.
Idiotenhügel nursery slope.
idiotensicher foolproof.
Idiotie idiocy, *(große Dummheit)* folly, stupidity.
idiotisch idiotic, stupid, foolish, daft *(coll.)*.
Idol idol, image.
idyllisch idyllic, pastoral.
IG | Druck und Papier National Graphical Union *(Br.)*; **~ Metall** [etwa] Metal Workers Union.
Igelstellung *(mil.)* hedgehog.
Ignorantentum ignorantism.
ignorieren, to ignore, to take no notice, to disregard;
j. ~ to give s. o. the cold shoulder; **jds. schlechtes Benehmen ~** to overlook s. one's bad behavio(u)r; **j. völlig ~** to ignore s. one's existence, to cut s. o. dead *(coll.)*.
Ignorierung deliberate disregard.
illegal illegal, unlawful, hot;
~ gepumpt und verschifft *(Öl)* hot;

sich ~ betätigen, ~ sein to belong to an underground (a resistance) movement;
~**e Geschäfte** illegal transactions; ~**e Tätigkeit** illegal activities.
Illegalität illegality, illegal status, unlawfulness.
illegitim illegitimate, born out of wedlock, nameless;
~**es Kind** illegitimate (natural) child, child born out of wedlock, love child.
Illegitimität illegitimate birth, illegitimacy.
illiquide nonliquid, illiquid, insolvent, short of liquid assets (funds);
~**e Guthaben** frozen assets.
Illiquidität illiquidity, nonliquid position, insolvency, shortage of liquid assets (funds).
Illumination illumination.
illuminieren, festlich to illuminate.
illoyal disloyal.
Illoyalität disloyalty, perfidy.
Illusion illusion;
keinerlei ~en haben to be free of illusion; **sich einer ~ hingeben** to cherish an (labo(u)r under an) illusion, to delude o. s. with false hopes; **in ~en leben** to build castles in the air; **j. zu einer ~ verleiten** to work off an illusion on s. o.; **sich in ~en wiegen** to lend o. s. to illusions, to live in a fool's paradise.
Illusionist illusionist, dreamer;
hoffnungsloser ~ sein to be in the clouds.
illusorisch illusory, hypothetical.
Illustration illustration, figure;
~**en in einen Text einbauen** to tie in illustrations in a text.
Illustrations|druck illustration (cutwork) printing; **satiniertes oder kalandriertes ~druckpapier** calendered or glazed illustration-printing paper; ~**skizze** thumbnail sketch; ~**wert** illustrative value; **zu ~zwecken** for illustration purposes.
Illustrator illustrator.
illustrieren to illustrate;
Text ~ to illustrate, to tie in illustrations in a text.
illustriert illustrated;
reichhaltig (üppig) ~ profusely illustrated;
~**er Katalog** trade catalog(ue); ~**e Zeitung** illustrated paper (magazine), pictorial.
Illustrierte illustrated paper.
Illustrierten|foto pinup; ~**schönheit** pinup [girl].
Illustrierung illustration.
Image image;
berufliches ~ career image;
~ **pflegen** to cultivate an image;
~**pflege** image polishing, cultivation of one's image; ~**werbung** prestige (goodwill, indirect-action) advertising.
imaginär imaginary, notional, visionary;
~**e Abstandssumme** notional premium; ~**er Gewinn** imaginary profit.
Imaginationswert imaginary value.
Imbiß snack, refreshment, refection, luncheon, bait *(Br.)*;
im Stehen eingenommener ~ stand-up lunch;
kleiner ~ in Notfällen emergency snack; ~ **im Selbstbedienungsspeisewagen** buffet snack;
~ **einnehmen** to snack, to bait *(Br.)*;
~**halle** snack bar (counter); ~**stand im Freien** open-air bar; ~**stube** lunch counter, snack (quick-lunch) bar *(US)*, bistro, luncheonette, tea shop *(Br.)*, nookery; ~**stubenkonzession** snack-bar concession.
Imitation imitation, copy, *(Fälschung)* fake, forgery, counterfeit.
Imitations|leder imitation leather; ~**schmuck** imitation jewellery, flash (flashy) jewellery (jewelry, *US*).
Imitator imitator.
imitieren to fake;
j. ~ to imitate (impersonate) s. o.
Immaterial|güter intangible property, intangibles, incorporeal chattels; ~**rechte** choses in action, incorporeal chattels; ~**schaden** nominal damage.
immateriell immaterial, incorporeal, intangible;
~**e Anlagewerte** *(Patente, Firmenwert)* fixed (intangible) assets, incorporeal chattels; ~**er Firmenwert (Geschäftswert)** goodwill of a business; ~**er Schaden** nominal damage; ~**es Vermögen** intangible property; ~**e Vermögensrechte** immaterial property; ~**e Vermögenswerte** intangible assets; ~**er Wert** *(Firma)* goodwill; ~**e Werte von Bedeutung** intangibles of value.
Immatrikulation matriculation, enrol(l)ment, registration *(US)*, entering one's name for the term.
Immatrikulations|bescheinigung certificate of enrolment; ~**bestimmungen** enrol(l)ment regulations; ~**erfordernisse** registrable qualifications; ~**gebühr** registration *(US)* (enro(l)lment, *Br.)* fee, cost of enrolment; ~**rückgang** dropoff in enrolments; ~**unterlagen** enrol(l)ment records.
immatrikulieren, sich [~ lassen] to matriculate to university entrance, to be admitted to *(Br.)* (enrol, register at, *US*) a university, to enter one's name for the term; **Studenten ~** to matriculate a student.
immatrikuliert matriculated, on the boards *(Cambridge, Br.)*;
~ **sein** to have one's name on the book *(Br.)*.
Immatrikulierter matriculate.
Immatrikulierung matriculation, enrol(l)ment.
immer und ewig without end.
immerfort from first to last.
immerwährend perpetual, perennial, perdurable.
Immigrant immigrant.
Immigration immigration.
Immission *(Gas)* intromission;
~**en** *(Grundstück)* noxious air, nuisance.
Immissions|auflagen emission standards; ~**schutz** pollution protection; ~**schutzgebiet** air pollution control area.
Immobiliar|arrest attachment of real property; ~**erbe** real representative; ~**investmentfonds** real-estate investment trust; ~**klage** real action; ~**kredit** credit on landed property, real-estate credit; ~**kreditbank** land bank; ~**nachlaß** real-estate assets; ~**pfandrecht** mortgage; ~**pfändung** seizure of real estate (property); ~**sicherheit** real security *(US)*; ~**vermögen** real estate (property, assets), realty, landed property (estate), properties; **sein ~vermögen flüssig machen** to turn one's land into money; ~**versicherung** residence insurance.
Immobilien real things (estate), realty, immovables, things immovable, landed property, immovable property *(US)*;
sein Geld in ~ anlegen to put one's money into land; ~ **besitzen** to have landed property, to own acres of land;
~**anlageberater** real-estate investment counsel(l)or; ~**anlagegesellschaft** real-estate trust, property investment company; ~**anlagemarkt** property investment market; ~**besitz** real-estate holdings; ~**besitz verwalten** to manage real estate; ~**beteiligungsgeschäft** syndicating business; ~**beteiligungsgesellschaft** syndicating company; ~**büro** real-estate office (agency), land agency *(US)*, estate agency *(Br.)*; ~**erträge** rents of a property; ~**erwerb** real property purchases; ~**fachmann** specialist in the property field; ~**firma** property outfit, real-estate company (corporation), estate agency *(Br.)*.
Immobilienfonds property and share-dealing company, real-estate investment trust, real-estate fund;
geschlossener ~ closed-end property fund; **offener ~** open-end real property investment fund; **im Ausland vertriebener ~** offshore real-estate fund *(US)*.
Immobilien|geschäft real-estate (property) business; ~**geschäfte machen (~geschäft haben)** to trade in real estate; ~**gesellschaft** real-estate company (corporation), property-dealing company, property corporation; ~**handel** dealing in real estate, real-estate transactions; **im ~handel einen guten Ruf genießen** to be widely respected in the property world; ~**händler** house agent *(Br.)*, land agent (broker, *Br.*), real-estate dealer (broker), location factor *(US)*, realtor *(US)*; ~**hausse** boom in the property market; ~**konto** property (premises) account; ~**lizenz** real-estate licence; ~**makler** real-estate dealer (broker) *(US)*, house agent, real-estate agent *(US)*, estate agent *(Br.)*, land agency *(US)*, trade dealer in land, land agent (jobber, broker, *Br.*), location factor *(US)*, property developer, realtor *(US)*; **dem Verband nicht angeschlossener ~makler** unattached real-estate agent *(US)*; **vereinigte ~maklerkammern** association of real-estate boards; ~**markt** real-estate market (section), property market, *(Zeitungsteil)* real-estate column (pages); ~**markt für Stadtkerngrundstücke** inner-city market; ~**recht** real property (real-estate) law; ~**rendite verkürzen** to bring property yields down; ~**spekulant** property speculator; ~**tätigkeit** real-estate activities; ~**teil einer Zeitung** real-estate pages (column); ~**trust** real-estate trust; ~**verkauf** sale of property; ~**vermögen** real (landed) property, immovable property *(US)*; ~**versicherung** residence insurance; ~**verwalter** property manager, *(Versicherungsgesellschaft)* estates manager; ~**wirtschaft** land economy.
immobilisieren to immobilize;
Kapitalien ~ to tie (lock, *Br.*) up capital [in landed property].
Immobilisierung immobilization, annexation.
Immobilität immobility.
immun immune;
gegen beruflichen Ärger ~ geworden sein to have become immune from (impervious of) the drawbacks of one's job.
immunisieren to immunize.

Immunität immunity, [privilege of] freedom from arrest, inviolability, *(Abgeordneter)* privilege of Parliament, parliamentary privilege;
unter die ~ fallend privileged;
absolute ~ absolute privilege; **bedingte ~** conditional privilege; **gesetzlich begründete ~** statutory privilege; **diplomatische ~** diplomatic privilege (immunity); **eingeschränkte ~** qualified immunity; **parlamentarische ~** parliamentary immunity; **persönliche ~** privilege from arrest; **richterliche ~** judicial privilege; **strafrechtliche ~** immunity from prosecution;
~ gegen eine Krankheit immunity from a disease;
~ eines Abgeordneten aufheben to revoke the liberty of freedom from arrest, to waive immunity, to suspend a member of parliament; **aufgrund seiner ~ sich jedem Gerichtsverfahren entziehen** to have immunity against any legal proceedings; **~ genießen** to be free from arrest; **diplomatische ~ genießen** to enjoy diplomatic immunity; **~ gewähren** to grant immunity, to privilege from arrest; **Mitgliedern gesetzgebender Versammlungen ~ gewähren** to privilege legislators from arrest.

Immunitäts|aufhebung *(Abgeordneter)* suspension of a member of Parliament; **~klausel** words of exemption; **~recht** personal law; **auf ~rechte verzichten** to waive one's right to immunity; **~verletzung** breach of privilege.

Imperialismus imperialism.

Imperialist imperialist.

imperialistisch imperialistic.

Imperium empire;
in einem ~ aufgehen to merge in an empire.

Impf|anstalt vaccine institute; **~arzt** vaccinator, vaccinist, inoculator.

impfen to inoculate, to vaccinate;
sich ~ lassen to get vaccinated.

Impf|gegner objector to vaccination; **~ling** vaccinee; **~pflicht** compulsory vaccination; **~schein** vaccination certificate, certificate of vaccination; **~stoff** vaccine.

Impfung vaccination, inoculation;
erneute (wiederholte) ~ revaccination.

Impf|zeugnis vaccination certificate, certification of vaccination; **~zwang** compulsory vaccination.

impliziert implicit.

Imponderabilien imponderables.

imponieren, jem. to impress s. o., to command s. one's respect;
jem. nicht ~ to cut no ice with s. o.

imponierend imposing, impressive;
~e Wissensdarbietung imposing display of knowledge.

Import import [trade], importation;
billige ~e cut-price (low-price) imports; **kontingentierte ~e** rationed imports; **symbolische ~e** token imports; **übermäßige ~e** overimportation; **unsichtbare ~e** invisible imports; **zollfreie ~e** [duty-]free imports; **zeitweilig zollfreie ~e** temporary admissions;
~e unter Zollvormerkschein entry under bond;
~e beschränken to reduce imports; **~e drosseln** to curb imports; **~e kontingentieren** to fix import quotas; **~e liberalisieren** to decontrol imports; **sich ~e sichern** to book imports;
~abgabe import surcharge (levy); **~abgaben endgültig abschaffen** to liquidate import duty; **~abteilung** import department; **~agent** import agent; **~akkreditiv** import letter of credit; **~anstieg** increase of (jump in) imports; **~anreiz** import incentive; **~antrag** import application; **~artikel** articles of importation, imported articles (stocks), imports; **nicht kontingentierte ~artikel** nonquoted imports; **~aufnahmefähigkeit** import capacity; **~aufschlag** import markup; **~ausgleichsabgabe** import equlization fee (tax, *US*); **~bedarf** import requirements; **~begrenzungsabkommen** import limitation agreement; **~beihilfen** import subsidies; **~bescheinigung** import certificate (clearance), clearance inwards; **~beschränkungen** import restrictions; **~beschränkungen einführen** to put on import restrictions; **verschärfte ~beschränkungen erlassen** to tighten import restrictions; **~bestimmungen** import regulations; **~bestimmungen vereinfachen** to simplify import inspection requirements; **~bewilligung** import authorization (licence); **~bewilligungsantrag** import application; **~buchhändler** import trade bookseller; **~deklaration** import declaration, entry inwards, bill of entry *(Br.)*; **~depot** import deposit *(Br.)*; **~drosselung** restriction (curb) of imports; **~einschränkungen** limitation of imports; **~embargo** import ban, embargo on imports; **~erklärung** entry (declaration) inwards, bill of entry *(Br.)*; **~erleichterungspolitik** policy of easing imports.

Importeur importer, import merchant;
~ von Agrarerzeugnissen farm importer.

Import|finanzierung financing of imports; **~firma** importing firm (house), import house, importer; **selbständige ~firma** freelance importers; **~flut** import tide; **~förderung** promotion of imports; **~garantie** import guarantee; **~genehmigung** import licence; **~genehmigungsverfahren** import licensing; **~geschäft** import business (trade), *(einzelnes)* import transaction; **~gesellschaft** import firm (house), importer; **~gewinn** import gain; **~güter** imported goods, imports; **~hafen** port of import (entry), import (inward) port; **~handel** import (passive, inward) trade; **~handelsfirma** importing firm; **~händler** import merchant; **~haus** importing firm, importer; **~hemmnis** import handicap (bar); **~hinterlegungssumme** import deposit *(Br.)*.

importierbar importable.

importieren to import;
Arbeitskräfte ~ to import labo(u)r from another country.

Import|industrie importing industry; **~kaufmann** import merchant, importer; **~kommissionär** import commission agent; **~konnossement** inward bill of lading; **~kontingent** import quota; **~kontingente festsetzen** to apportion quotas on import; **~kontingentierung** fixing of import quotas; **~kontrolle** control of imports, import control; **~kredit** credit for imports, import (domestic, *US*) credit; **~kreditbrief** import letter of credit; **~kürzungen** import cuts; **~land** importing country; **~liberalisierung** decontrol of imports; **~liste** import list; **~lizenz** import licence (permit); **~monopol** import monopoly; **~prämie** bounty on importation; **~preis** import price; **~quote** import quota (rate); **~regelung** import arrangement; **~restriktionen** import restrictions; **~rohstoffe** imported raw materials; **~rückgang** decline (fall-off, turn-down) in imports, import reduction; **~schleuse** import sluice-gate; **~schonfrist gewähren** to switch off the import tap; **~schutzzölle** protective tariff on imports; **~sicherungsprogramm** program(me) of anticipating imports; **inflationsbedingter ~sog** inflation-induced pull of imports; **~sonderzoll** surcharge on imports; **~sperre** embargo on imports; **~steigerung** increased (increase in) imports; **~steuer** import excise tax *(US)*; **~stopp** cessation of (embargo on) imports; **~subvention** import subsidy; **~überschuß** import surplus; **~verbot** import prohibition (ban), embargo; **~verfahren** import procedure; **~verlagerung** shift of imports; **~vertreter** import agent; **~volumen** volume of imports; **~ware** articles of import, importation, imported stocks (goods), imports; **~waren einführen** to handle imported goods; **~ware zwecks Zollfestsetzung klassifizieren** to impost imports *(US)*; **~wert** import value; **~wirtschaft** import trade; **~zahlen** import figures; **~zoll** duty on importation, import duty; **~zwischenhändler** merchant shipper.

imposant imposing, impressive, grand;
~er Anblick awe-inspiring sight; **~e Erscheinung sein** to be a man of impressive build; **~es Schauspiel** striking spectacle.

imprägnieren to impregnate, to process, to waterproof.

Imprägnierung impregnation, waterproofing, preparation, textile processing.

Impresario impresario, projector, manager.

Impressum printer's imprint, *(Zeitung)* masthead.

Imprimatur good for printing, O.K. *(US)*, okay *(US)*;
~ erteilen to sign for press.

Improvisation improvisation, impromptu event, *(Musik)* extemporization, impromptu.

Improvisationsspiel jam session.

Improvisator extemporary speaker.

improvisieren to improvize, to hit off, to knock together (up);
politische Persönlichkeit ~ to hit off a political personnage.

improvisiert extemporary, extemporaneous, on the spur of the moment, impromptu;
~es Essen improvised meal.

Improvisiertes impromptu, pickup *(US sl.)*.

Impuls impulse, impulsion, impetus, *(Radar)* blip;
konjunkturelle ~e economic impetus; **plötzlicher ~** rash (sudden) impulse;
unter einem ~ handeln to do s. th. on a sudden impulse, to act on the spur of the moment; **einer Sache neuen ~ verleihen** to give fresh impetus to s. th.;
~geber *(Computer)* digit emitter; **~gegenstände** impulse items.

impulsiv impulsive, vivid;
~ handeln to be impulsive in one's actions, to act on impulse (the spur of the moment);
~e Geste impulsive gesture; **~er Mensch** man of impulse.

Impuls|käufe impulse buying; **~kaufgegenstände** impulse goods (items, *US*); **~peilung** direction finding.

imstande sein to be able to do (capable of doing);
zu allem ~ to stop at nothing.

in Frage | kommen, für j. nicht to lie outside the sphere of s. one's activities; ~ **kommend** possible *(coll.)*.
in Frage stellen to call into question, *(gefährden)* to endanger, to jeopardize;
alles wieder ~ to put everything back into the melting pot.
inaktiv inactive, *(mil.)* retired;
~**es Mitglied** inactive (nonactive) member; ~**er Teilhaber** sleeping partner.
inaktivieren to retire, to superannuate.
Inaktivierung retiring, superannuation.
Inaktivität inactivity, *(mil.)* retired state.
inaktuell not topical, *(Theorie)* out of date.
In | angriffnahme start, tackling, attack; ~**ansatzbringen von Sterbefällen** *(Pensionsfonds)* discounting for mortality.
Inanspruchnahme use, utilization, availment, employment, in road, *(geistige)* engrossment, absorption;
im Fall der ~ in case of implementation; **ohne** ~ **öffentlicher Mittel** without recourse to public funds; **wegen starker** ~ owing to pressure of business;
finanzielle ~ financial drain; **starke** ~ drain; **zeitliche** ~ claim on (demand upon) one's time;
~ **von Abschreibungen** claim to capital allowance; ~ **eines Anwalts** employment of a solicitor *(Br.)*, retaining a lawyer; ~ **eines Autos für Geschäftszwecke** use of a car for business; ~ **einer Bank am Platze** employment of a local bank; **erhöhte** ~ **der Banken** increased borrowings from the banks; ~ **zweier Fahrbahnen** lane straddling; ~ **von Firmenmitteln für die Bedürfnisse leitender Angestellter** use of company resources for the private gain of senior officials; ~ **eines Fonds** use of a fund; ~ **einer Garantie** service under a guarantee; ~ **ungebetener Gastlichkeit** intrusion upon a company; **starke** ~ **des Geldmarktes** pressure on the money market; **übermäßige** ~ **von Geldmitteln** drain on financial resources; ~ **des Gerichts** resort to court; ~ **von Hilfsmitteln** drain on the resources; ~ **des Kapitalmarktes** recourse to the capital market; ~ **eines Kredits** availment of a credit line, recourse to a credit, borrowing, using (utilization of a) credit; ~ **der Landeszentralbankfazilitäten** [etwa] member-bank borrowings *(US)*; **starke** ~ **der Mitarbeiter (des Personals)** heavy demands on the staff; ~ **des Mitbürgen** benefit of division; ~ **öffentlicher Mittel** recourse to public money; ~ **der Priorität** claiming priority; ~ **von Raum** occupancy of space; ~ **des Rentenmarktes** tap of the gilt-edged market *(Br.)*; ~ **von Sachleistungen** requisitioning; ~ **von Vergünstigungen des Doppelbesteuerungsabkommens** claiming double-tax relief *(Br.)*; ~ **von jds. Zeit** demand upon s. one's time.
Inaugenscheinnahme inspection;
~ **durch das Gericht** judicial survey; ~ **des Tatorts** viewing the scene of crime.
Inauguraldissertation inaugural dissertation, thesis.
Inauguration inauguration.
inaugurieren to inaugurate.
Inbegriff essence, entirety, aggregate, complex, *(Verkörperung)* embodiment;
mit ~ **sämtlicher Spesen** all charges included;
~ **des Bösen** a devil incarnate; ~ **der Güte** embodiment of kindness; ~ **der Selbstsucht** personification of selfishness; ~ **der Weisheit** incarnation of wisdom.
inbegriffen inclusive, included, including;
alles ~ terms inclusive, all-in *(Br.)*; **mit** ~ implied, implicit; **nicht** ~ implicit.
Inbesitznahme appropriation, occupation, taking possession, seizure;
körperliche ~ seizin in fact; **tatsächliche** ~ actual entry; **unerlaubte (unrechtmäßige)** ~ unlawful (wrongful) entry; **vorherige** ~ preoccupation;
~ **eines Grundstückes** appropriation of a piece of land, seizin; ~ **vor Zeugen** open entry;
~**recht** right of entry.
Inbetriebnahme opening, putting into operation (in motion);
~ **eines Hotels** opening of a hotel.
Inbetriebsetzung start, starting, opening, putting into operation, initial operations.
Inbrunst fervo(u)r, ardo(u)r.
inbrünstig ardent, fervent, passionate;
~**es Gebet** fervent prayer.
Indemnität indemnity, exemption from responsibility.
Indemnitätsbeschluß act of indemnity.
Indent | kaufmann indent merchant; ~**vertrag** indent contract.
Index index, *(Inhaltsverzeichnis)* register, table of contents;
mit einem ~ **gekoppelt** index-linked;
gekreuzter ~ crossed-weight index [number]; **gewogener** ~ weighted index [number]; **saisonbedingter** ~ seasonally adjusted index; **unbewerteter** ~ unweighted index; **verketteter** ~ chain index;
~ **der Aktienkurse** index of share prices *(Br.)*, (stocks, *US*), stock price index *(US)*, all-share index *(Br.)*, Dow Jones index *(US)*; ~ **der Arbeitslosenzahl** unemployment index; ~ **der Baukosten** index of building (construction) costs; ~ **der Bruttostundenlöhne** index of gross hourly wages; ~, **dem der Durchschnitt von 1914 mit 100 zugrunde liegt** index based on 1914 averages as 100; ~ **der Einzelhandelspreise** retail-price index; ~ **der Erzeugerpreise** index of manufacturing prices; ~ **der Großhandelspreise** wholesale-price index; ~ **des gesamten Handelsgewinns** index of total gain from trade; ~ **der Industrieaktien** index of industrial shares; ~ **der katholischen Kirche** expurgatory index; ~ **der Lebenshaltungskosten** cost-of-living index; ~ **der industriellen Nettoproduktion** index of industrial production, national production index; ~ **als typisch erachteter Stammaktien** industrial ordinary index; ~ **der Verbraucherpreise** consumer price index;
~**anleihe** loan tied to an index; ~**automatik des Zinses** automatic interest adjustment; ~**berechnung** computation of an index; ~**familie** typical average family; ~**fonds** index fund.
indexgebunden tied to an index, index-linked.
Indexierung indexation;
~ **der Steueranfangsbeträge (des unteren Proportionalbereichs)** indexation of tax thresholds; ~ **von Steuerfreibeträgen** indexation of personal tax allowances; **gesamte** ~ **der Steuern** indexation package.
Index | karte index card; ~**klausel** escalator (index) clause; ~**kopplung** index linking; ~**kurve** index curve; ~**lohn** index wage; ~**lohnerhöhung** index wage rise; ~**preis** index-linked price; ~**rente** earnings-related pension; ~**stanzung** *(drucktechn.)* tab; ~**system** indexation system; ~**verbindung** index linking; ~**vergleich der Familienlebensunterhaltskosten** family expenditure survey *(Br.)*; ~**verknüpfung** index linking; ~**versicherung** floating policy; ~**währung** multiple (tabulator) standard, commodity (neutral) money; ~**zahl**, ~**ziffer** index number (figure); ~**ziffern der Börsenkurse** Standard and Poor's indices *(US)*.
Indianerreservate tribal lands.
Indienststellung putting into service, *(Schiff)* commission.
Indifferenzkurve expenditure curve;
volkswirtschaftliche ~ social (community) indifference curve.
indignieren, j. to rouse s. one's indignation.
indigniert indignant, angry.
Indikator indicator;
bedeutsame konjunkturindexempfindliche ~**en** sensitive leading business indicators.
indirekt indirect, intermediate;
etw. ~ **erreichen** to achieve s. th. by oblique ways;
~**e Arbitrage** indirect (triangular, *US*) arbitration; ~**e Befragungsmethode** indirect opinion method; ~**e Beleuchtung** indirect lighting; ~**e Devisenarbitrage** indirect exchange; ~**es Mittel** indirect means, side wind; ~**e Rede** indirect speech; ~**e Steuern** indirect taxes; ~**es Vorgehen** indirection.
Indiskretion indiscretion, leakage;
gezielte ~ news (inspired) leak, calculated indiscretion;
~ **begehen** to commit an indiscretion; **gezielte** ~ **begehen** to leak s. th. into (to the) press; **sich einer** ~ **schuldig machen** to be guilty of an indiscretion; **gezielte** ~**en über Ergebnisse von Kabinettssitzungen vornehmen** to leak cabinet proceedings.
indiskutabel out of court (the question).
indiskutable | s Benehmen impossible behavio(u)r; ~**r Plan** plan not worth discussing.
indisponibel *(Kapital)* not available.
indisponiert indisposed, not well, off colo(u)r;
sich ~ **fühlen** to be off one's oats; ~ **sein** to have a slight illness.
Individual | anspruch personal claim; **steuerliche** ~**belastung** individual tax burden; ~**haftung** several liability.
Individualisierung individualization.
Individualismus, krasser rugged individualism.
Individualist individualist.
Individualität individualism, individuality, individual character.
Individual | rechte personal rights; ~**versicherung** personal (individual) insurance.
individuell individual, particular;
~ **beurteilt** judged on one's own merit; ~ **verschieden sein** to vary from case to case;
sehr ~**e Ansichten vertreten** to be individual in one's views; ~**er Geschmack** personal taste.

Individuum individual person;
schäbiges ~ mean individual; **zweifelhaftes** ~ doubtful character.
Indiz indication, pointer.
Indizien, durch ~ **beweisen** to circumstantiate;
~**beweis** presumptive (circumstantial, indirect, resumptive) evidence, inferential proof; **j. aufgrund geringen** ~**materials verurteilen** to condemn s. o. on slight evidence.
indossabel indorsable, endorsable, transferable by indorsement;
nicht ~ nonnegotiable, unendorsable, not negotiable.
Indossament indorsement, endorsement;
durch ~ **übertragbar** negotiable, indorsable, endorsable, transferable by indorsement; **mit** ~ **versehen** indorsed, endorsed;
in der Form abweichendes ~ irregular indorsement (endorsement); **beschränktes** ~ conditional (qualified, restrictive) indorsement (endorsement); **fiduziarisches** ~ fiduciary indorsement (endorsement); **gefälschtes** ~ forged indorsement (endorsement) **teilweises** ~ partial indorsement; **unbefugtes** ~ unauthorized indorsement; **unbeschränktes** ~ absolute indorsement; **unvollständiges** ~ incorrect indorsement (endorsement); **vollständiges** ~ full indorsement;
~ **aus Gefälligkeit** accommodation indorsement; ~ **ohne Obligo (Rückkehr)** indorsement (endorsement) without recourse; ~ **nicht in Ordnung** irregular indorsement; ~ **nach Protest** indorsement (endorsement) under (supra) protest; **durch** ~ **begeben** to endorse, to indorse; **durch** ~ **übertragen** to indorse, to endorse; **Wechsel durch** ~ **übertragen** to indorse (endorse) a bill of exchange; ~ **verbürgen** to guarantee an indorsement (endorsement); **mit einem** ~ **versehen** to provide with an indorsement.
Indossaments|fälschung forgery of an endorsement; ~**haftung** endorser's liability; ~**provision** indorsement commission; ~**verbindlichkeiten** endorsement liabilities; ~**vollmacht** power to indorse.
Indossant indorser, endorser;
nachfolgender ~ subsequent indorser; **vorgehender** ~ previous indorser (endorser).
Indossantenhaftung liability of indorser.
Indossat[ar] indorsee, endorsee, *(Wertpapiere)* transferee.
indossierbar indorsable, endorsable, negotiable.
Indossierbarkeit negotiability.
indossieren to indorse, to endorse, to place an indorsement (endorsement), to negotiate, *(fremde Wechsel)* to back;
blanko ~ to indorse (endorse) in blank; **an eine bestimmte Person** ~ to endorse specially.
Indossierer *(fremder Wechsel)* backer.
indossierfähig negotiable, indorsable, endorsable.
indossiert indorsed, endorsed;
nicht ~ unindorsed, unendorsed.
Induktionsstrom induced current *(el.)*.
induktive Methode objective method.
industrialisieren to industrialize.
industrialisiert industrial[ized].
Industrialisierung industrialization.
Industrialisierungs|programm industrialization program(me); ~**prozeß** process of industrialization; **für** ~**zwecke** for use of industrialization.
Industrie [manufacturing] industry;
in der ~ **beschäftigt** industrial, engaged in industry; **in der ganzen** ~ **geltend** industry-wide; **mit starker** ~ industrial;
mit voller Ausnutzung der Kapazität arbeitende (voll ausgelastete) ~ industry producing at its maximum output; **mit geringen Unkosten (niedrigen Selbstkosten) arbeitende** ~ low-cost industry; **bearbeitende** ~ manufacturing industry; **durch Saisonschwankungen beeinflußte** ~ seasonally unstable industry; **Nachbarschaft beeinträchtigende** ~ nuisance industry; **von den Banken beherrschte** ~ banker-controlled industry; **auf einen Staat beschränkte** ~ intra-state industry *(US)*; **von der Krise betroffene** ~ depressed industry; **bodenständige** ~**n** stable industries; **chemische** ~ chemical industry; **in die Arbeitslosenfürsorge einbezogene** ~ covered industry; **einheimische** ~ home (domestic, native) industry; **eisenschaffende** ~ iron and steel industry; **eisenverarbeitende** ~ iron-working industry; **elektronische (elektrotechnische)** ~ electronics engineering industry; **über das ganze Land sich erstreckende** ~ nation-wide industry *(US)*; **exportintensive** ~ export-oriented industry; **feinmechanische** ~ precision engineering industry; **führende** ~ leading industry; **gefährliche** ~ dangerous industry; **staatlich gelenkte** ~ state-controlled industry; **zollpolitisch geschützte** ~ sheltered *(Br.)* (protected, *US*) industry; **holzverarbeitende** ~ wood-working industry; **junge** ~ infant industry; **kapitalintensive** ~ highly geared industry; **keramische** ~ ceramics industry; **von den Banken kontrollierte** ~ banker-controlled industry; **kunststoffverarbeitende** ~ plastics-processing industry; **lebenswichtige** ~ vital industry; **metallverarbeitende** ~ metal-working industry; **in die Arbeitslosenfürsorge miteinbezogene** ~ covered industry; **mittlere** ~ medium-sized industry; **nachgelagerte** ~**n** downstream industries; **ortsansässige** ~ local industry; **pharmazeutische** ~ pharmaceutical industry; **produktionswichtige** ~ essential industry; **saisonbedingte** ~ seasonal industry; **schutzzollbedürftige (noch in den Kinderschuhen steckende)** ~ infant industry, industry still in its infancy; **stahlverarbeitende** ~ steel-using industry; **standortunabhängige** ~ foot-loose industry; **störende** ~**n** nuisance industries; **staatlich subventionierte** ~ subsidized (bounty-fed, *Br.*) industry; **traditionelle** ~ traditional industry; **überregionale** ~ nation-wide industry *(US)*; **übersetzte** ~ overcrowded industry; **unterbesetzte** ~ undermanned (short-staffed) industry; **durch Staatsaufträge unterstützte** ~ sheltered (bounty-fed) industry *(Br.)*; **nicht durch Staatsaufträge unterstützte** ~ unsheltered industry *(Br.)*; **verarbeitende** ~ manufacturing (finishing, processing, process) industry; **an Bedeutung verlierende** ~ industry that is falling off; **verstaatlichte** ~ public ownership of industry; **vollausgelastete** ~ industry producing at its maximum output; **zweitrangige** ~**n** second-tier industries;
~ **mit Arbeitermangel** undermanned industry; ~ **für landwirtschaftliche Betriebsmittel** agriculture (farming) industry; ~ **für Güter des gehobenen Bedarfs** sophisticated industry; ~ **in den Kinderschuhen** infant industry, industry still in its infancy; ~ **in Staatseigentum** state-owned industry; ~ **der Steine und Erden** extractive industry;
~ **neu ausrüsten** to retool industry; **einheimische** ~ **steuerlich begünstigen** to benefit local industry; **einheimische** ~**n fördern** to foster (beef up) home industries; ~**n integrieren** to form industries into a vertical trust; ~ **paralysieren** to cripple industry; ~ **ins Leben rufen** to create an industry; **Wachstum der** ~ **verlangsamen** to slow down industrial expansion; ~ **verstaatlichen** to nationalize industry; **zur** ~ **werden** to become industrialized;
~**abbau** running down of an industry; ~**abbauprogramm** dismantling program(me); ~**abgase** waste gas; ~**abnehmer** industrial customer; ~**absatz** industry sales, sales to industry; ~**abwässer** trade effluent; ~**aktien** industrial equities (shares, *Br.*, stocks, *US*); ~**aktiengesellschaft** industrial company (corporation, *US*); ~**aktienindex** index of industrial shares (stocks, *US*), Dow Jones Index; ~**akzept** industrial bill; ~**anlage** industrial unit (plant), manufacturing plant (establishment); ~**anlagen** industrial installations, *(Investitionen)* industrial investments; **hochwertige** ~**anlagen** high-type industries; ~**anlagenvermietung** plant leasing; ~**anleihe** industrial loan (bond, issue); ~**ansiedlung** industrial colony; **gelenkte** ~**ansiedlung** planned location of industry.
Industriearbeiter industrial labo(u)rer (worker), factory (production) worker, workman;
~**gewerkschaft** industrial union; ~**löhne** industrial wages; ~**schaft** industrial classes.
Industrie|areal industrial site (estate, *Br.*); ~**artikel** manufactured goods; ~**ausdehnung** industrial expansion; ~**ausfuhr** exports of manufacture; ~**ausschuß** industry panel; ~**ausstattung** [industrial] equipment; ~**ausstellung** industrial exhibition (exposition), industries fair; ~**ausstoß** industrial output; ~**ausweitung** industrial expansion; ~**bahn** industrial railway *(Br.)* (railroad, *US*), tap line (feeder); ~**bank** industrial bank (banker); ~**bauten** industrial construction; ~**beobachter** industry observer; ~**berater** industrial counsel(l)or (engineering consultant), consultant to industry, management (executive search) consultant; ~**beratung** consulting engineering firm; ~**beratungsdienst** industrial service; **in einem anderen** ~**bereich Fuß fassen** to gain a foothold in another industry; ~**bericht** industrial report; ~**besatz** industrial job ratio; ~**beschäftigte** industrial employees; ~**beteiligung** industrial participation (interests), *(Arbeitnehmer)* industrial partnership.
Industriebetrieb manufacturing establishment (plant), industrial concern (plant), industrial enterprise;
sämtliche Phasen durchführender ~ continuous industry; **störende** ~**e** nuisance industries;
~ **auf der grünen Wiese** exurbia;
~ **auf der grünen Wiese ansiedeln** to create industry from the ground up; **in einem anderen** ~ **Fuß fassen** to gain a foothold in another industry.

Industrie|betriebslehre industrial science, industrial organization *(Br.)*; **~bezirk** industrial area (district), manufacturing (industrial) district; **~chemie** chemical engineering; **~demontage** industrial dismantling, dismantling of industries; **~diamant** industrial diamond; **~dunst** smog; **~durchschnitt** industrial average; **gesamter ~durchschnitt** all-industrial average; **~emissionen** industrial issues, *(Verunreinigung)* nuisance; **~entwicklungsprogramm** industrial development program(me); **~erfahrung** industrial experience; **~erfahrung mit dem Universitätsleben verbinden** to blend industrial experience with academic life; **~erwartungsland** industrial estate *(Br.)*; **~erzeugerpreise** industrial producer prices; **~erzeugnis** industrial product, manufactured article (product, goods), manufacture; **~erzeugnisse** manufactured goods; **~erzeugung** industrial output (production), factory production; **~finanzierung** financing of industry; **mittel- und langfristiges ~finanzierungsgeschäft** medium and long-term industrial financing; **~finanzierungsgesellschaft** industrial finance (loan) company; **~firma** industrial firm (undertaking, enterprise); **~förderung** encouragement (promotion) of industry; **~förderungsgesellschaft** industrial development company; **~forschung** industry (industrial) research; **~führer** captain of industry; **~gas** producer gas; **~gebiet** industrial area (community), economic territory, manufacturing district; **für ~gebiete vorgesehen sein** to be zoned for manufacturing enterprises *(US)*; **~gegend** industrial section (area), manufacturing district, economic district (quarter); **~gelände** industrial site (land, estate, *Br.*); **~gesetzgebung** factory acts (legislation); **~gewerkschaft** industrial union, blue-collar union *(US)*; **~gewerkschaft Bau, Steine, Erden** [etwa] builders' and construction workers' union; **~gewerkschaftsbewegung** industrial unionism; **~gewerkschaftsverband** Congress of Industrial Organizations; **~gigant** titan of industry, industry giant; **~gleis** industrial track; **~grundstück** industrial property (land), factory site; **~grundstoffe** basic industrial materials; **~gruppe** industrial group; **~güter** industrial goods; **~güterpreise** prices of industrial goods; **~index** industrial index; **~ingenieur** industrial engineer; **~investitionen** industrial investments; **~- und Handelskammer [der USA]** [United States] Chamber of Commerce *(US)*; **~kanal** flume; **~kapazität** industrial capacity; **~kapital** industrial capital; **~kapitalismus** industrial capitalism; **~kapitän** captain of industry, tycoon *(US)*; **~kartell** industrial cartel; **~klassifikation** industrial classification; **~klub** economic club *(US)*; **~koeffizient** industry ratio; **~komplex** industry (industrial) complex; **~könig** captain of industry, tycoon *(US)*; **~konsortium** industrial consortium; **~kontenrahmen** industrial accounting system; **~konzentration** localization of an industry, territorial (regional) division of labo(u)r; **~konzern** industrial concern (combination), conglomeration; **~kredit** industrial credit; **~kreditbank** industrial bank, [etwa] Industrial and Commercial Finance Corporation Ltd. *(Br.)*; **~kreditsatz** corporation bank rate *(Br.)*; **~kreise** industrial circles; **aus ~kreisen** according to industry sources; **~kundschaft** *(Werbeagentur)* industrial accounts; **~land** industrial state (nation), industrialized country; **hochentwickeltes ~land** advanced industrial country; **~länder** advanced countries; **~lieferant** industry contractor; **~lieferungen** industrial supplies.

industriell industrial;
~ hergestellt made in a factory, tailor-made *(sl.)*;
~er Abnehmer industrial customer; **~er Absatzmarkt** industrial sales; **~e Anlagen** industrial installations; **~e Bauinvestitionen** plant investment; **~er Bereich** industrial sector; **~e Beteiligung** industrial participation; **~e Betriebseinheit** industrial unit; **~e Daten** industry figures; **~e Entwicklung** industrial (industry) development; **~e Erschließung** industrial development; **~e Erschließungsgenehmigung** industrial development certificate; **~es Erzeugnis** industrial (manufactured) product; **~e Expansion** industrial expansion; **~e Fachausbildung** industrial training; **~e Fachzeitschrift** industrial magazine; **~e Formgebung** industrial design; **~e Großanlagen** large-scale industrial units; **~e Kapazität** industrial capacity; **~e Leistungen** industrial achievements; **~ gefertigtes Produkt** industrial product; **~es Rechnungswesen** industrial accounting; **~e Reservekapazität** industrial reserve capacity; **~e Revolution** industrial revolution; **~e Rezession** industry slump; **~e Tätigkeit** industrial work (employment); **~e Umwälzung** industrial revolution; **~e Verwertung** industrial exploitation; **~er Vorreiter** industrial leader; **~es Wachstum** industrial growth; **~er Wettbewerb** industry competition; **~es Zentrum** hub of industry; **~er Zusammenschluß** industrial combination.

Industrieller industrialist, industrial [producer], manufacturer, millowner *(Br.)*;
führender ~ top industrialist.

Industrie|macht industrial power; **~magnat** captain of industry, tycoon *(US)*; **~markt** *(Börse)* industrial market (list), *(Börsenbericht)* „industrials"; **~messe** industries fair, industrial exhibition (fair); **~minister** Secretary of State for Industry *(Br.)*; **~ministerium** Department of Trade and Industry; **~monopol** industrial monopoly; **~müll** trade refuse; **~nation** industrial nation (power), advanced country; **~normen** industry standards; **~normung** standardization of industry; **~obligationen** industrial bonds (securities), private bonds, business corporation (corporate) bonds *(US)*; **~ödland** derelict land; **~organisation** industrial machine *(US)*; **~papiere** industrial bonds (issues, securities, stocks), industrials; **~park** industrial establishment *(Br.)*, trading estate *(Br.)*; **~pension** industry pension; **~plan** industrial plan; **~planung** planning of industry; **~politik** industrial policy; **~potential** industrial potential; **von der Königin verliehene ~preis** Queen's award of industry; **~produkte** industrial (manufactured) goods, manufactures, industrial products; **~produktion** industrial output (production), factory production; **~produktion erhöhen** to step up industrial production; **~produktivität** industrial productivity; **~programm** industrial plan; **zum Skelett abgemagertes ~reservoir** skeletal industrial base; **~schau** industrial display; **~schuldverschreibungen** private (industrial) bonds, corporate (corporation) bonds *(US)*; **~schutzbeauftragter** safety representative.

industrieschwach less industrialized.

Industrie|sektor sector of industry, industrial sector; **~siedlung** industrial (trading, *Br.*) estate; **mit öffentlichen Mitteln unterhaltene ~siedlung** industrial colony; **~sparte** line of industry; **von der Rezession besonders betroffene ~sparten** recession-hit industries; **~spionage** industrial espionage; **~staat** industrial state (nation, country), industrialized country (nation); **starker ~staat mit passiver Handelsbilanz** mature creditor nation; **zu einem ~staat machen** to industrialize; **~stadt** industrial city, manufacturing town; **~standard** industrial standard; **~standort** location of industry, industrial location; **~stellung** position in industry; **~struktur** industrial structure; **~strukturpolitik** industrial location policy; **~subventionen** industrial subsidies; **~syndikat** trust, conglomerate; **~syndikate bilden** to trustify; **~system** industrial system; **~tarif** *(el.)* industrial tariff; **~tätigkeit** industrial employment (work); **~überalterung** industry obsolescence; **~umsätze** industrial sales; **~umsetzung** industrial transference; **~unternehmen** industrial concern (establishment, corporation, undertaking, organization), manufacturing enterprise (establishment, concern); **~verband** industrial organization (association, *US*), industry association, federation of industries; **~verbindungen** industrial affiliations; **~verlagerung** translocation (relocation) of industry; **~vermögen** industrial wealth (properties); **~vertreter** manufacturer's agent *(US)*; **~vertriebskosten** manufacturer's cost price; **~viertel** industrial area (district, estate), manufacturing quarter; **~waren** manufactured goods (items); **~warenzoll** duty on manufactures; **~werbung** industrial advertising; **~werk** factory, plant, works, manufacturing establishment; **~werte** *(Börse)* industrial equities (securities, issues, features), industrials; **~wirtschaft** industrial economy; **neues ~zeitalter heraufführen** to establish a new industrial regime; **~zensus** industrial census, census of production; **~zentrum** industrial (manufacturing) center *(US)* (centre, *Br.*), hub of industry; **~zusammenballung** hive of industry, conglomerate, conglomeration; **~zusammenschluß** industrial combination; **~zwecke** industrial purposes.

Industriezweig manufacturing branch, manufacture, industry, line (group, branch, section) of industry, industrial division; **autarker ~** self-contained industry; **höher besteuerte ~e** higher-taxed industries; **von der Krise betroffene ~e** depressed (crisis-ridden) industries; **devisenschwache ~e** soft-goods industries; **devisenstarke ~e** hardgoods industries; **dienstleistungsorientierte ~e** service-oriented industries; **engverzahnter ~** close-knit industry; **exportintensive ~e** export-intensive branches of industry; **gebundene ~e** regulated industries *(US)*; **durch Einfuhrzölle (Zollschranken) geschützte ~e** sheltered *(Br.)* (protected, *US*) industries; **zollpolitisch nicht geschützte ~** unsheltered *(Br.)* (unprotected, *US*) industries (trades); **unter staatliche Aufsicht gestellte ~e** regimed industry; **saisonabhängige ~e** seasonally unstable industries; **übersetzter ~** overcrowded industry; **unterbezahlte ~e** sweated industries; **verstaatlichte ~e** nationalized industries;

~e **mit geringer Arbeitsintensitätsquote im Verhältnis zur Gesamtproduktion** industries with low employment output ratio;
~ **begründen** to originate an industry; ~ **beherrschen** to control an industry; ~ **beleben** to revive an industry; **neugegründeten ~ fördern** to nurse an infant industry; ~ **ins Leben rufen** to create an industry; ~ **unter Staatsaufsicht stellen** to bring an industry under state control; **ganze ~e stillegen** to shut down whole industries; ~e **in der gesamten europäischen Gemeinschaft völlig umstrukturieren** to restructure industry throughout the community; ~ **verlagern** to relocate industry.

ineinander | arbeiten to play into one another; **~geschachtelte Sätze** incapsulated sentences; **~greifen** to interlink, to be interconnected; **~greifend** interlocking; **~passen** to fit into one another, to nest, to dovetail; **~schalten** to interlock; **sich bei einem Unfall ~schieben** *(Waggons)* to telescope at an accident; ~ **übergehen** to merge into one another.

Inelastizität des Angebots rigidity of supply.

Inempfangnahme reception, receipt.

infam infamous, disgraceful, shameful;
sich ~ benehmen to behave disgracefully.

Infamie infamy, infamous act, foul deed.

Infanterie infantry;
~ausbildung infantry training; **~geschütz** close support gun.

Infanterist infantryman, infantry soldier, footslogger *(sl.)*.

infantil infantile, childish.

Infektion infection;
auf eine ~ zurückzuführen attributed to an infection.

Infektions | abteilung *(Krankenhaus)* isolation ward; **~herd** center of infection; **~kranke isolieren** to segregate people with infectious diseases; **~krankenhaus** isolation hospital, quarantine; **~krankheit** infectious disease; **~zeit** infection period.

Infiltration *(pol.)* infiltration.

infiltrieren to infiltrate.

infizieren to contaminate, to infect;
sich ~ to catch infection; **sich die Hand ~** to poison one's hand.

Infizierung infection, contamination.

Inflation inflation;
durch Lohnsteigerungen angeheizte ~ wage-fuelled inflation; **durch Staatsausgaben angeheizte ~** government-spending-boosted inflation; **durch Lohnerhöhungen ausgelöste ~** wageled inflation; **durch Nachfrageüberhang ausgelöste ~** demand-pull inflation; **durch Nachfrageverschiebungen ausgelöste ~** demand-shift inflation; **durch Produktionskostensteigerung ausgelöste ~** cost-push inflation; **durch Lohnsteigerungen bedingte ~** wage-push inflation; **dosierte ~** pent-up inflation; **galoppierende ~** runaway (galloping) inflation; **mit langsamem Wachstum des Sozialprodukts gekoppelte ~** stagflation; **gesteuerte ~** pent-up inflation; **hausgemachte ~** home-grown inflation; **importierte ~** imported inflation; **sektoral induzierte ~** sectoral inflation; **kostenbedingte ~** cost-induced inflation; **kostentreibende ~** cost-push inflation; **kriegsbedingte ~** war-caused inflation; **lohninduzierte ~** wagepush inflation; **nachfrageüberhangsbedingte (nachfrageinduzierte) ~** demand-pull inflation; **nachlassende ~** let-up in inflation; **preisgestoppte ~** price-frozen inflation; **schleichende ~** creeping (persistent) inflation; **sektorale ~** bottleneck inflation; **übermäßige ~** hyperinflation; **unaufhaltsame ~** runaround inflation; **vorübergehend unterdrückte ~** suppressed inflation; **verheerende ~** wildfire inflation; **verlangsamte ~** slowdown in inflation; **versteckte ~** hidden (masked) inflation; **wiederbelebte ~** inflation revival; **zügellose ~** runaway inflation; **zurückgestaute ~** suppressed (repressed) inflation;
~ **der Nahrungsmittelpreise** food-price inflation; ~ **bei gleichzeitigem Produktivitätsrückgang** slumpflation;
~ **abbremsen** to put a brake on inflation; ~ **anheizen** to kindle (prime, fuel) inflation; ~ **als letztes Hilfsmittel anwenden** to resort to inflation; ~ **bekämpfen** to combat (battle) inflation; ~ **stärker bekämpfen** to take a stronger stand against inflation; ~ **in den Griff bekommen** to bring inflation under control, to cure inflation; ~ **neu beleben** to rekindle inflation; ~ **bremsen (dämpfen)** to curb inflation; ~ **durchführen** to inflate [the volume of money]; ~ **durchmachen** to undergo inflation; **der ~ den Nährboden entziehen** to squeeze inflation out of their system; ~ **fördern** to encourage inflation; **der ~ Einhalt gebieten** to halt inflation; ~ **herbeiführen** to inflate the currency; ~ **stabilisieren** to level-peg inflation; **mit der ~ fertig werden** to lick inflation; ~ **zügeln** to curb inflation; ~ **zurückdrängen** to hold the line on inflation.

inflationär inflationary, inflated;
~e **Auswirkungen lediglich vorübergehend konterkarieren** to bottle up inflationary forces; ~e **Entwicklungen vorantreiben** to make inflation worse; ~ **bedingte Konjunktur** inflation boom; ~e **Kräfte in den Griff bekommen** to grapple with inflationary forces; ~er **Preisanstieg** inflationary hike; ~e **Preise** inflated prices; ~e **Verhältnisse** inflationary conditions; ~e **Verzerrung** inflation bias.

Inflationist inflationist.

inflationistisch inflationary, inflationist;
~er **Druck** inflationary pressure; ~es **Gegenmittel** inflation antidote; ~e **Konjunktur** inflation boom; ~e **Kräfte in den Griff bekommen** to grapple with inflationary forces; ~e **Kreditausdehnung** credit inflation; ~e **Politk** inflationary policy; ~e **Tendenz** inflationary tendency (trend); ~e **Wirkung** inflatory effect.

Inflations | abbau durch gezielte Maßnahmen disinflation; **~abkühlung** cooling of inflation; **~angst** inflation phobia (panic); **~anhänger** inflationist; **~anpassung von Kapitaleinkünften** capital-income adjustment; **~anzeichen** signals for inflation; **~ausgleich** inflationary adjustment; **~auswirkungen** effect (impact) of inflation.

inflationsbedingt inflation-induced, inflationary;
nach Abrechnung der ~en Erhöhung after inflation retention; ~ **steigen** to rise with inflation.

Inflations | bedingungen inflationary conditions; **~bekämpfung** fight against inflation, inflation fighting, antiinflationary strategy; **~bekämpfungsprogramm** anti-inflation program(me); **~belastung** bite of inflation.

inflationsbereinigt adjusted to inflation, inflation-adjusted, after adjustment of inflation.

Inflations | beschleunigung acceleration of inflation; **~chaos** inflationary chaos; **~damm** hedge against inflation; **~dämpfung** curbing of inflation; **~drohung** inflationary threat; **~drosselung, ~eindämmung** dampening down (curbing) of inflation; **~druck** impact of inflation, inflationary pressure (impact, squeeze).

inflationsempfindlich vulnerable to inflation;
~e **Ware** inflation-prone goods.

Inflationsentwicklung, der ~ laufend angepaßt periodically rebased.

inflationserfahren experienced in inflation.

Inflations | erfahrung inflationary experiences; **~erosion** erosion from inflation; **~erscheinung** inflationary phenomenon, symptom of inflation; **~erwartung** expectation of inflation, inflationary expectations; **~faktor** inflationary factor.

inflationsfeindlich anti-inflationary.

Inflations | fieber inflationary fever; **~gefahr** inflation danger, danger (risk) of inflation.

inflationsgeschützt inflation-hedged.

Inflations | gewinn inflationary profit (gain), inflation gain; **~hinweise** inflationary signposts; **~hysterie** inflation phobia (panic); **~index** index of inflation; **~indikator** indicator to inflation; **~klima** inflationary climate; **~kräfte** inflationary forces; **~lücke** inflationary gap; **~maßnahmen** protection against inflation; **~mentalität** inflationary psychology; **~moment** inflation factor; **~niveau** level of inflation; **~opfer** victim of inflation.

inflationsorientiert sein to tend to inflation.

Inflations | periode period of inflation; **~politik** inflationary policy; **~prognose** inflation forecast; **~prozeß** process of inflation; **~psychologie** inflationary psychology.

Inflationsrate rate of inflation, inflation rate;
anormale ~ hyperinflation; **einstellige ~** single-figure inflation; **zweistellige ~** double-digit inflation;
~ **verlangsamen** to slow down inflation.

Inflations | rückgang let-up (reduction) in inflation; **~rückkehr** resumption of inflation; **sich den ~sätzen anpassen** to keep up with inflation; **~schraube** inflationary spiral; **~schutz** protection against inflation, inflation shelters.

inflationsicher inflation-proof;
Abschlüsse durch Umstellung von Dollar- auf Goldbasis ~ machen to hedge against inflation by gearing the dollar value of contracts to gold;
~e **Kapitalanlage** inflation-proof investment.

Inflationssicherung hedge against inflation;
automatische ~ built-in inflation proofing; **zusätzliche ~** top-up cover against inflation;
~ **der Löhne** inflation proofing of wages.

Inflations | spirale inflationary spiral; **zeitweilige ~stabilität** inflation plateau; **explosive ~steigerung** inflation explosion; **~steigerung auf dem gleichen Niveau wie die internationale Konkurrenz halten** to hold inflation down to the level of international competition; ~**symptome** symptoms of inflation; ~**tempo** inflation pace; **verlangsamtes ~tempo** slowdown of inflation; ~**tendenzen** inflationary tendencies; ~**ursache** causation of inflation; ~**verlangsamung** slowing (slowdown) of inflation; ~**vorteile** benefits of inflation; ~**währung** inflated currency; ~**warnung** inflation alert; ~**welle** wave of inflation; ~**wert** inflated value; ~**wirkungen** effects of inflation; ~**zeit** inflationist (inflationary) period, inflationary times, period of inflation; ~**zeit durchmachen** to undergo inflation.

Inflationszunahme acceleration of inflation, up in inflation, inflation potential;
rasante ~ inflationary upsurge;
~ **beschleunigen** to accelerate inflation.

inflatorisch inflationary;
nicht ~ uninflated;
~ **bedingt** inflation-induced;
~**e Kräfte** inflationary forces; ~**e Lücke** *(Staatsausgaben)* inflationary gap; ~**e Tendenzen eindämmen** to curb the inflationary tendencies.

Informant informer, informant, finger *(sl.)*.

Informatik computer science.

Information [piece of] information, news, communication;
nach den neuesten ~en according to the latest information; **zur** ~ for reference (information);
angebliche ~ alleged piece of information; **auswärtige ~en** advices from abroad; **nur für den Anwalt bestimmte ~en** privileged communication; **eingehende ~en** inside information; **an Ort und Stelle eingeholte ~en** local information; **geheime** ~ secret information, dope; **geschäftliche ~en** business information; **durch Aussageverweigerung geschützte ~en** privileged information; **spärliche ~en** a few crumbs of information; **mir zur Verfügung stehende ~en** information in my possession; **technische ~en** mechanical information; **ungenügende (unzureichende) ~en** inadequate information; **vertrauliche** ~ confidential (restricted, private) information; **zusammenhanglose ~en** loose pieces of information; **zuverlässige** ~ authentic information;
~ **für den internen Dienstgebrauch** restricted information circular; ~ **der Führungskräfte** management information; ~**en aus erster Hand (Quelle)** immediate information, information straight from the horse's mouth, inside *(US sl.)*, poop *(sl.)*; **mangelnde ~ über wesentliche Tatsachen** failure to supply material information; ~ **über betriebsinterne Vorgänge** inside information;
~**en über Steuersünder austauschen** to swap information on tax evaders; **neue ~en zu einem Thema beitragen** to throw fresh light on a subject; ~**en beschaffen** to secure information, to furnish data; **üblicherweise ~en über jem. einholen** to rely for information on s. o.; ~**en über etw. erhalten** to gain (obtain) information, to get a line on s. th.; **zusätzliche ~en erhalten** to receive news from another quarter; **Computer mit ~en füllen** to feed a computer with information; ~**en aus Büchern gewinnen** to quarry information from books; **geheime ~en über die feindlichen Absichten vorliegen haben** to have secret intelligence of the enemy's plan; ~**en aus jem. herausholen** to extract information from s. o.; ~**en herauskitzeln** to fish for information; ~**en zukommen lassen** to convey information; **unerlaubte ~en zukommen lassen** to disclose confidential information; ~**en löschen** *(Computer)* to cancel information; **sich bei der ~ melden** to contact the information desk; ~**en nachprüfen** to check up on information; ~ **preisgeben** to divulge information; **als vertrauliche ~ für j. bestimmt sein** to be for s. one's private ear; ~**en zu erlangen suchen** to dig for information; ~**en verarbeiten** *(Computer)* to process data; **jem. ~en verdanken** to be indebted to s. o. for information; **über erstklassige ~en verfügen** to be well primed with information; **sich ~en verschaffen** to gather information; **j. stets mit den neuesten ~en versehen** to keep s. o. posted.

Informations|abteilung credit department; ~**amt** information office; ~**artikel** educational piece; ~**austausch** information sharing; ~**austauschvereinbarung** *(Auftragswesen)* information-sharing agreement; ~**bank** information bank; ~**bedürfnisse** information needs; ~**bereich** area of information, *(Zeitung)* news coverage; ~**bericht** informational record, *(Parlament)* green paper *(Br.)*; **wirtschafts- und sozialpolitischer ~bericht** white paper *(Br.)*; ~**beschaffung** provision of information; ~**besprechung** briefing conference; ~**blatt,** ~**brief** newsletter, newspaper press, newssheet; ~**büro** inquiry (intelligence) office, information agency (bureau, *US*); **staatliches ~büro** government information office; ~**darstellung** display; ~**dichte** *(Computer)* packing density; **wirtschaftlicher ~dienst** trade information, information service; **sein Gedächtnis mit unnötigen ~einzelheiten belasten** to lumber one's mind with useless bits of information; ~**fluß** communication; ~**fluß pro Zeiteinheit** flow rate; ~**freiheit** freedom of information; **unauflösliche ~grundeinheit** *(Computer)* bit.

informationshalber for information.

Informations|kanal public medium; ~**kartell** open price system; ~**lücke** communication gap, newslag.

Informationsmaterial information (research, handout) material, *(Abwehr)* intelligence;
auf Wunsch Übersendung von ~ literature on request;
gesperrtes ~ classified information; **kostenloses** ~ free literature; **unterschwelliges** ~ soft-sell material; **veröffentlichtes** ~ information disclosure;
~ **für Abgeordnete** parliamentary papers;
~ **ausgraben** to ferret out information; **umfangreiches ~ zutage fördern** to yield a rich harvest of information; ~ **preisgeben** to disclose (divulge) confidential information; **von sich aus ~ zur Verfügung stellen** to volunteer some information; ~ **zurückhalten** to hold back information.

Informations|ministerium Ministry of Information; ~**mittel** information media; ~**möglichkeiten** facilities for the supply of information; ~**netz** network of information; ~**pflicht** obligation to disclose; ~**programm** information program(me); ~**prospekt** information kit; ~**quelle** source (repository) of information, information service, *(geheime)* pipeline; ~**recht** right to make inquiries; ~**reise** field trip, fact-finding (briefing) tour; ~**schriften** specialized literature; ~**sitzung** briefing meeting; ~**speicherung** *(Computer)* information (data) storage; ~**speicherverfahren** data storage process; ~**stand** information desk (stand); ~**stelle** information bureau (office), inquiry (intelligence) office, communication agency *(US)*; ~**system** information system; ~**tätigkeit** information[al] activity; ~**träger** *(Computer)* data set; ~**übermittlungsverfahren mittels Elektronik** electronic data transmission process; ~**verarbeitung** data (information) processing; ~**weg** lines of communication; ~**werbung** informative advertising; **regierungsamtliches ~wesen** government information service; ~**wiedergewinnung** *(Datenverarbeitung)* information retrieval; ~**wirtschaft** controlling *(US)*; **Verantwortlicher für die betriebliche ~wirtschaft** controller; ~**zentrale** information center *(US)* (centre, *Br.*), central office of information.

informatives Gespräch informative talk.

informatorisch informative, informatory;
~**e Aufgaben erfüllen** to handle information.

informell, sich völlig ~ geben to be no stickler for formalities;
~**e Gruppen** informal groups.

informieren to inform, to instruct, to acquaint, to prime;
sich ~ to inform o. s., to secure information, to make inquiries, to inquire about, to acquaint o. s.; **sich über j.** ~ to gather information about s. o.; **j. falsch** ~ to give s. o. false information, to misinform s. o.; **j. über einen Sachverhalt** ~ to instruct s. o. of a fact; **vorweg** ~ to tell off *(sl.)*.

informiert informed, advised, in the picture, next *(US sl.)*;
falsch ~ misinformed;
als ~ gelten to be deemed to have notice; **sehr gut ~ sein** to have a great stock of information; **über etw. nicht ~ sein** to have no knowledge about s. th.;
~**e Stellen** informed quarters.

Infragestellung calling into question, *(Gefährdung)* endangering, jeopardizing;
~ **einer Zeugenaussage** impeachment of a witness.

Infrarot|fotografie infra-red photography; ~**gerät** infra-red equipment, *(mit Bildwandler)* snooper scope; ~**grill** infra-red grill; ~**heizung** infra-red heating; ~**visier** sniperscope.

Infrastruktur infrastructure;
~**bedarf** deficiency in infrastructure; ~**kapital** public overhead capital; ~**kredite** infrastructural credits; ~**raum** infrastructural region; ~**vorhaben** infrastructural project.

Ingangbringen bringing into action;
~ **von Verhandlungen** setting on foot of negotiations.

Ingangsetzung starting, launching, putting into operation.

Ingenieur engineer, technical officer;
ausführender ~ project engineer; **beratender** ~ consultant engineer; **leitender** ~ chief engineer;
~ **für Sanitäranlagen** sanitary engineer;
~**arbeit** civil engineering work; ~**bau** constructural engineering; ~**beruf** engineering; ~**büro** consulting engineering firm; ~**laufbahn einschlagen** to take up the vocation of engineering; ~**nachwuchs** recruits to engineering; ~**schule** school of engineering; ~**wesen,** ~**wissenschaft** [science of] engineering.

Inhaber holder, bearer, *(Besitzer)* possessor, *(Eigentümer)* proprietor, owner, *(Gasthof)* innkeeper, *(Geschäft)* principal, proprietor, head, *(Grundstück)* occupant, occupier, *(Wechsel)* bearer, holder *(US)*;
auf den ~ lautend in bearer form, made out to bearer; **zahlbar an den ~** payable to bearer;
alleiniger ~ sole owner; **augenblicklicher (gegenwärtiger) ~** actual holder; **wechselmäßig berechtigter ~** bona-fide holder for value; **früherer ~** former owner, prior holder; **gutgläubiger ~** bona-fide holder, innocent holder for value, holder in due course (good faith) **jeweiliger ~** holder for the time being; **nachfolgender ~** subsequent holder; **rechtmäßiger ~** lawful (legitimate) owner, true holder, *(Thron)* pretender; **schlechtgläubiger ~** mala-fide holder; **ursprünglicher ~** former holder; **~ eines Abzahlungsgeschäftes** tallyman *(Br.)*; **~ von Aktien** shareholder *(Br.)*, stockholder *(US)*; **~ eines verbotenen Alkoholausschanks** jointist; **~ eines Bankkontos** owner (holder) of a banking account; **~ eines Berechtigungsscheins** permit holder; **~ eines Besserungsscheines** income bondholder; **~ von Eisenbahnaktien** railway shareholder *(Br.)*, railroad stockholder *(US)*; **~ eines Gasthauses** innkeeper; **~ eines Gemeinschaftskontos** joint-account holder; **~ eines akademischen Grades** graduate; **~ einer Grunddienstbarkeit** rent charger; **~ eines Hotels** proprietor of a hotel, hotel owner; **~ von Namensaktien** registered shareholder *(Br.)*, stockholder of record *(US)*; **~ eines Passes** bearer of a passport; **~ eines Patentes** proprietor (holder) of a patent, patent owner, patentee; **~ einer Planstelle** established civil servant *(Br.)*, career civil servant *(US)*; **~ eines Postscheckkontos** giro account holder *(Br.)*; **~ einer Preismedaille** [prize] medallist; **~ eines Schuldscheins** noteholder; **~ einer Schuldverschreibung** debenture holder *(Br.)*; **~ eines Spezialgeschäfts** limited-line retailer, stockist *(Br.)*; **~ von Staatspapieren** fundholder; **~ von Stammaktien** ordinary shareholder *(Br.)* (stockholder, *US*); **~ der entscheidenden Stimme** odd man; **~ eines Urheberrechts** owner of a copyright; **~ einer Vollmacht** holder of a power of attorney; **~ einer Vorzugsberechtigung** priority permit holder; **~ eines Warenzeichens** trademark owner, registered user *(Br.)*; **entgeltlicher ~ einer Wechselgutschrift** holder for value of a bill; **~ eines Zurückbehaltungsrechts** lienor; **~ eines Zwischenscheins** scrip holder;
den ~n der alten Aktien neue Aktien zu ... anbieten to offer new shares (stock, *US*) to the holders of old ones at ...; **auf den ~ ausstellen** to issue (make out) to bearer; **auf den ~ lauten** to be made out in the name of the holder; **wirkliche ~ von Stimmrechtsaktien ausfindig machen** to flush out the beneficial holders of voting shares; **~ einer Dauerfahrkarte sein** to have a season ticket, to commute *(US)*; **~ wechseln** to change hands; **~aktie** bearer share, share payable to bearer, transferable share, bearer stock *(US)*; **~aktienzertifikat** share warrant [to bearer], stock certificate to bearer *(US)*; **~anleihe** bearer loan; **~indossament** endorsement made out to bearer; **~klausel** bearer clause; **~konnossement** bearer bill of lading; **~kreditbrief** open letter of credit; **~lagerschein** negotiable warehouse receipt *(US)*; **~obligation** bearer bond (debenture), bond (debenture) payable to bearer, *(ohne Giro)* clean bond *(US)*, *(mit Zinsschein)* coupon bond *(US)*.

Inhaberpapier bearer instrument (security), instrument payable to bearer;
begebbares ~ negotiable instrument; **erstklassige ~e** floaters *(Br.)*.

Inhaber|police policy to bearer, bearer policy; **~scheck** bearer cheque *(Br.)* (check, *US*), cheque *(Br.)* (check, *US*) to bearer, open cheque *(Br.)* (check, *US*); **in einen ~scheck umwandeln** to turn into a bearer cheque *(Br.)* (check, *US*).

Inhaberschuldverschreibung bearer (registered) debenture (bond, *Br.*), debenture payable to bearer, *(mit Zinsschein)* coupon bond *(US)*;
~en bearer bonds, investment securities *(US)*;
~en ohne Giro (Einschränkung) clean bonds *(US)*.

Inhaber|wechsel promissory note made out to bearer, bill payable to bearer; **~zertifikat** bearer certificate, depositary receipt; **~zinsschein** interest coupon payable to bearer; **~zwischenschein** scrip payable to bearer.

inhaftieren to arrest, to imprison, to put in jail, to detent, to detain, to take into custody, to incarcerate.

Inhaftierter person imprisoned, detained person.

Inhaftierung confinement, detention in jail, body execution, detainment, imprisonment, incarceration, prison;
~ eines Vollstreckungsschuldners committal of a judgment debtor.

Inhaftierungsvollmacht power of committal *(Br.)*.

Inhalt contents, amount, matter, *(Dokument)* purport, *(Körper)* volume, content, *(Rauminhalt)* capacity, *(Schrift)* tenor, subject matter, docket, *(Überblick)* summary, *(Urteil)* tenor; **des ~s** purporting, to the effect that; **gleichen ~s** of the same tenor;
~ unbekannt contents unknown;
wesentlicher ~ essence, substance, *(Brief)* tenor;
wesentlicher ~ einer Ansprache the head and front of a speech; **~ eines Briefes** contents of a letter; **~ eines Dreiecks** area of a triangle; **~ eines Gesprächs** substance of a conversation; **~ eines Schiedsspruches** term of an award; **~ eines Würfels** volume of a cube;
wesentlichen ~ eines Vertrages berühren to go to the root of a contract; **Brief folgenden ~s erhalten** to receive a letter to the following effect; **Leben ohne ~ führen** to lead an empty life; **einem abstrakten Rahmenwerk konkreten ~ geben** to put meaningful flesh on a bony structure; **~ seines Lebens sein** to be s. one's whole life; **~ eines Gesprächs wiedergeben** to recount the substance of a conversation.

inhaltlich textual;
~ abweichen to read differently.

Inhalts|analyse *(Rede, Zeitung)* contents analysis; **~angabe** specification of contents, statement of contents, argument, *(Buch)* summary, *(Zoll)* declaration of contents; **~anzeige** table of contents.

inhaltsarm of little substance.

Inhalts|aufstellung schedule of contents; **~berechnung, ~bestimmung** *(Fläche)* calculation of an area, *(Körper)* determination of volume; **~beschreibung** nature (description) of contents.

inhalts|gleich of equal area; **~leeres Dasein** empty existence; **~los** empty, devoid of substance; **~reich** full of matter; **~schwer** profound.

Inhalts|übersicht synopsis; **~vermerk** docket, bordereau; **mit ~vermerk versehen** to docket.

Inhaltsverzeichnis table (statement) of contents, catalog(ue), index, register, contents, docket;
alphabetisches ~ alphabetical table;
mit einem ~ versehen to index;
~wert declared value.

Initiale initial, paragraph, *(drucktechn.)* cockup;
mit seinen ~n abzeichnen to initial[ize].

Initial|preiselastizität impact price elasticity; **~werbung** pioneering advertising; **~zünder** trigger, primer, exploder; **~zündung** primer, *(fig.)* booster, *(Konjunkturmaßnahmen)* priming the pump *(US)*.

initiativ on one's own initiative, enterprising, aggressive, go-getting *(US)*;
selbst ~ werden to do s. th. on one's own initiative;
~ veranlagter Mensch go-getter *(US)*.

Initiativantrag eines Abgeordneten private member's bill.

Initiative initiative, enterprise, getup *(US)*, pep, gumption, drive, go;
auf seine ~ at his instigation (initiative); **aus eigener ~** on one's own initiative;
gesetzgeberische ~ legislative initiative; **handelspolitische ~** trade-policy initiative; **persönliche ~** private initiative; **politische ~n** policy initiatives; **privatwirtschaftliche ~** private enterprise; **unternehmerische ~** industrial initiative;
~ beflügeln to stimulate action; **~ besitzen** to be enterprising, to have pep; **keine ~ besitzen** to be lacking (lack) initiative; **~ ergreifen** to take the initiative, to initiate, to make a move *(coll.)*, to take the ball; **~ in einer Angelegenheit ergreifen** to move in a matter; **aus eigener ~ handeln (auf eigene ~ tun)** to act in one's individual capacity, to do on one's own initiative; **~ vermissen lassen** to be lacking in drive, to lack gumption (initiative); **staatliche ~ unterstützen** to participate in a government drive.

Initiativrecht *(Volksbegehren)* initiative, power of initiative.

Initiator initiator.

Injektion injection.

Injektionsspritze injection syringe.

Inkarnation embodiment, incarnation;
~ des Bösen devil incarnate.

Inkassi collections;
ausländische ~ foreign collections; **auswärtige ~** out-of-town collections *(US)*, out collections *(US)*; **spesenfreie ~** free items *(US)*;
~ auf Banken in der Provinz country collections; **~ auf nicht der Stadtabrechnung angeschlossene Banken** walks *(Br.)*; **~ durch**

Boten collections by hand; ~ **von Ratenzahlungen** instal(l)ment collections; ~ **auf Regionalbanken** country collections; ~ **besorgen** to effect collections; ~ **eines Unternehmens übernehmen** to undertake the collections for a firm.

Inkasso encashment, debt collecting, collection;
zum ~ for collection;
direktes ~ direct collection;
~ **von Lieferantenschulden** trading-debts collection; ~ **zum Pariwert** par collection; ~ **von Schecks zum Pariwert ohne Abzug der Spesen** par collection of checks *(US)*;
~ **besorgen** to procure payment, to cash, to effect encashment;
~ **eines Wechsels besorgen** to attend to the collection of a bill;
Wechsel zum ~ **einsenden** to send bills to be cashed (for collection); **zum** ~ **von Kundenzahlungen berechtigt sein** to effect the collection of a firm; **zum** ~ **übernehmen** to receive for collection; **zum** ~ **vorlegen (vorzeigen)** to present for collection;
~**abschnitt** collection item; ~**abteilung** collection (debt-collecting) department; ~**abteilung für Zinsscheine** coupon collection department; ~**agent** agent of collection, collecting agent; ~**anstrengungen** collection efforts; ~**anweisung** remittance letter; ~**anzeige** advice of collection; ~**arbeit** collection work; ~**auftrag** encashment (collection) order; ~**auftrag für Dividendenzahlungen** dividend mandate; **einer Bank** ~**auftrag erteilen** to entrust a bank with the collection; ~**aufwand** collection expenses; ~**auskunft** tracer information *(US)*; ~**auskunftsabteilung** tracer department *(US)*; ~**auskunftsformular** tracer blank *(US)*; ~**aviso** collection advice; ~**bank** collecting bank (banker); ~**beamter** collection clerk, collector, person cashing, *(Bank)* note teller *(US)*; ~**bearbeiter** collection manager, collector; ~**beauftragter** collecting agent; ~**bedingungen** conditions for collection; ~**befugnis** power to collect; ~**bericht** clearinghouse report, tracer *(US)*; **schleppend eingehende** ~**beträge** slow collections; ~**bevollmächtigter** collection agent; ~**bote** *(Bank)* walk clerk *(Br.)*; ~**brief** collection letter; ~**büro** collection (debt-collecting) agency, claim agent; ~**dienst** collection service; ~**dienst für eine Firma besorgen** to effect the collection for a firm; ~**einrichtungen** collection devices; ~**einzugsauftrag** collection order; ~**einzugsgebiet** *(Kleinlebensversicherung)* debit; ~**ermächtigung** letter of delegation; ~**erträge** collection proceeds; ~**forderungen** uncollected items *(US)*; ~**forderungen an Banken** *(Bilanz)* collections due from banks; ~**formular** collection form; ~**gebühr** collection fee (commission); ~**gegenwert** collection proceeds; ~**geschäft** collection work, collecting (collection) business; ~**gesellschaft** collection (collecting) agency; **eigene** ~**gesellschaft** house collection agency; ~**giro,** ~**indossament** indorsement for collection only, restrictive indorsement; ~**karteikarte** collection card; ~**kommis** collection clerk; ~**kommission** collection commission; ~**konto** collection account; ~**korrespondenz** collection correspondence; ~**kosten** collection expense; ~**mandat** encashment order; ~**mandatar** debt collector, collecting (claims) agent, collection agency (agent); ~**methoden** collection methods; ~**nummer** collection number; ~**ort** place of collection; ~**papier** collection item; ~**politik** collection policy; ~**posten** collection item, walks items *(Br.)*; ~**provision** commission for collecting, collection commission (fee), *(Versicherung)* renewal commission; ~**reisender** collector, collecting agent; ~**rückstand** lag in collections; ~**scheck** collection check *(US)* (cheque, *Br.*); ~**schreiben** collection letter; ~**spesen** cost of collection, collection charges (expense), collecting (recovering) charges (expenses), walk charges *(Br.)*; ~**stelle** collection (claims) agent, collecting (collection) agency, outside collector; ~**system** collection system; ~**tarif** collecting rates; ~**tarif der dem Abrechnungsverkehr angeschlossenen Banken** clearinghouse exchange rates; ~**tätigkeit** collection activities; ~**tratte** agency draft; ~**unternehmen** collection agency; ~**verfahren** collection technique (proceedings); ~**vertreter** agent of collection, collection (claims) agent, collecting agent, collector; ~**vollmacht** letter of delegation, power to collect, collecting power; ~**wechsel** short (country) bill, bill for collection, collection item; ~**wechselkonto** collection (float, *US*) ledger; ~**zeit** time of collection.

Inkaufnahme acquiescence;
trotz ~ **einiger Nachteile** although we had to put up with certain disadvantages.

inklusive inclusive;
~ **Dividende** cum dividend *(Br.)*, dividend on *(US)*; ~ **aller Transportkosten** inclusive of all transport costs; ~ **Ziehung** including drawing.

Inklusivpreis inclusive terms.

Inkognito incognito;
~ **lüften** to reveal one's identity; **sein** ~ **nicht lüften** to preserve one's incognito.

inkognito incognito.

inkommodieren to trouble;
j. ~ to trouble (incommode, inconvenience) s. o.; **sich für j.** ~ to put o. s. out on s. one's account.

Inkompatibilität incompatibility.

inkompetent incompetent.

Inkompetenz *(Richter)* incompetence.

inkonventionell, völlig uninhibited.

inkonvertibel inconvertible.

Inkonvertibilität inconvertibility.

Inkorporation incorporation.

inkorporieren to incorporate.

inkorporiert corporate, incorporated.

inkorrekt incorrect, inaccurate;
~ **gekleidet** improperly dressed;
sich ~ **benehmen** to commit improprieties.

Inkorrektheit incorrect act, impropriety.

Inkraft|bleiben remaining in force; ~**setzung** putting into force, enactment, validation; **erneute** ~**setzung** revalidation; ~**treten** taking effect, effective date; **bei** ~**treten des Gesetzes** when the law comes into effect.

inkriminieren to incriminate.

Inkriminierung incrimination.

Inkubationszeit period of incubation, incubation period, latent period.

Inland inland, interior, home country *(Br.)*, homeland;
im ~ within the country (realm), inward; **im** ~ **und Ausland** at home and abroad;
für das ~ **bestimmt** for home consumption (use); **im** ~ **erzeugt** home-produced; **im** ~ **geboren** native-born; **im** ~ **hergestellt** home-made, domestic;
im ~ **aufgenommen werden** *(Produktion)* to be absorbed by the internal market.

Inländer native, subject, citizen, inhabitant, inlander, *(Devisengesetze)* national resident, resident inside the sterling area *(Br.)*;
devisenrechtlich ~ **sein** to be resident for exchange-control purpose inside the Scheduled Territories *(Br.)*;
~**begünstigung** nativism *(US)*; ~**behandlung** treatment of nationals, national treatment; ~**behandlungsklausel** national treatment clause; ~**konvertierbarkeit** resident convertibility.

inländisch inland, domestic, native, internal, home, inward, home-made;
~**e Abgaben** internal charges; ~**e Aktien** home shares *(Br.)* (stocks, *US*); ~**er Bedarf** domestic (internal, home) demand; ~**es Erzeugnis** native product, domestic article, home manufacture (product); ~**e Gesetzgebung** internal legislation; ~**er Handel** domestic (internal) trade; ~**e Industrie** domestic (home) industry; ~**e Kapitalgesellschaft** domestic corporation *(US)*; ~**e Steuern und Abgaben** internal revenue taxes *(US)*; ~**er Steuerpflichtiger** resident taxpayer; ~**er Verbrauch** home consumption; ~**e Waren** home-made goods; ~**e Wasserstraßen** inland waterways; ~**e Wertpapiere** home stocks *(Br.)*.

Inlands|abgabe inland duty; ~**absatz** domestic (home) sales; ~**anlagen** domestic investments; ~**anleihe** home (domestic, internal) loan, internal bonds; ~**aufenthalt** stay in one's home country; ~**auflage** *(Zeitung)* national print run; ~**aufträge** domestic ordering (orders), orders from domestic customers, home-market orders; ~**ausgaben im Etatsrahmen halten** to hold domestic spending within the budgetary plan; ~**bedarf,** ~**bedürfnisse** domestic needs, internal (domestic, home) consumption (demand), home requirements; ~**belieferung** supplies to domestic customers; ~**besitz** property held by residents; ~**bestellung** domestic order; ~**brief** inland letter; ~**bruttosozialprodukt** gross domestic product; ~**dienst** *(mil.)* service at home, home service, *(Post)* domestic *(US)* (inland, *Br.*) service; ~**einkommen,** ~**einkünfte** domestic income; ~**eis** ice sheet; ~**emission** internal (domestic) issue; ~**erzeuger** domestic (inland, home) producer; ~**erzeugnis** domestic article; ~**erzeugnisse** home-produced (home-made) goods; ~**erzeugnisse durch Zollschranken vor der Auslandskonkurrenz schützen** to protect domestic products from foreign competition by trade barriers; ~**erzeugung** domestic output; ~**finanzierung** domestic financing.

Inlandsflug|linie internal air route; ~**lizenz** cabotage; ~**preis** domestic air fare; ~**verkehr** inland air traffic.

Inlands|forderungen claims against internal debtors; ~**gebühren** internal charges; ~**geschäft** domestic business, home trading (business, sales); ~**geschäfte** home sales; ~**gesellschaft** domestic operation; ~**hafen** domestic port; ~**handel** domestic (internal, home) trade; ~**inkassi** inward collections; **gesamte** ~**investitionen** gross domestic investment; ~**kapazität** domestic capacity; ~**kapital** domestic capital; ~**kartell** domestic cartel; ~**konjunktur** internal boom; ~**konto** internal account; ~**korrespondent** home (domestic) correspondent; ~**kunde** domestic customer; ~**liquidität** domestic liquidity; ~**luftfahrt** inland air traffic; ~**markt** domestic (home, inland) market; ~**mitteilungen** internal communications; ~**nachfrage** domestic (home) demand; ~**nachfrage dämpfen** to curb domestic demand; ~**nachrichten** home news; ~**organisation** home organization; ~**paket** inland (domestic) parcel; ~**porto** inland (domestic) postage, inland rate of postage *(Br.)*.

Inlandspost inland mail *(Br.)*, domestic mail *(US)*;
~**anweisung** inland *(US)* (domestic postal, *Br.*) money order; ~**gebühren** domestic rates *(Br.)*; ~**tarif** inland postage rates *(Br.)*; ~**verkehr** internal mail *(US)* (domestic postal, *Br.*) service.

Inlands|preis domestic (home-market, inland selling) price, home rate; ~**produkte** domestic products, home-made goods; ~**produktion** home manufacture, domestic production; ~**reisekreditbrief** domestic travel(l)ers' letter of credit; ~**rezession** domestic recession; ~**satellit** domestic satellite; ~**schuld** internal debt; ~**schuldverschreibungen** internal bonds; ~**spediteur**, ~**speditionsgeschäft** inland carrier, country shipper *(US)*; ~**strecke** domestic route; ~**tarif** inland tariff, domestic (home) rates, home tariff; ~**telegramm** domestic (inland, *Br.*) telegram; ~**umsatz** domestic (home) turnover (sales); ~**unternehmen** home enterprise; ~**verbindlichkeiten** internal (domestic) liabilities; ~**verbrauch** internal (domestic) consumption, home use (consumption); **ziviler** ~**verbrauch** home civilian use; ~**verbraucher** domestic consumer; ~**verkaufsleiter** home sales manager; ~**verkehr** inland traffic; ~**vermögen** assets held within the country; ~**verschuldung** internal (interior) debt; ~**vertreter** domestic (resident, home) factor; ~**vertretung** home agency; ~**währung** internal (home, national) currency; ~**wechsel** domestic bill of exchange *(US)*, inland bill of exchange *(Br.)*; ~**wert** domestic valuation, home consumption value; **amerikanischer** ~**wert** American value; ~**wohnsitz** municipal (national) domicile; ~**zahlung** domestic (inland) payment; ~**zahlungen** inland payments.

inliegend inclosed, enclosed, attached, subjoined.

Innehaben occupancy, tenure, possession;
tatsächliches ~ actual occupation;
~ **eines Amtes** tenure of office; ~ **eines Lehrstuhles** tenure of a chair.

innehaben to occupy, to have and hold, to own, to possess, to fill; **Amt** ~ to fill a post, to hold an office; **Lehrstuhl** ~ to hold a professorship; **Vorsitz** ~ to occupy the chair; **Wohnung** ~ to occupy an apartment.

innehalten to make a pause, to cease;
mitten in der Arbeit ~ to stop in the middle of one's work.

innen befindlich inner.

Innen|abmessungen interior dimensions; ~**abschnitt** *(Anzeige)* gutter bleed; ~**adresse** inside address; ~**ansicht** interior view; ~**antenne** indoor aerial, built-in antenna; ~**architektur** indoor decoration; ~**aufnahme** indoor photo, interior, *(Film)* indoor (studio) shot; ~**ausbau** indoor installation; ~**auslage** interior display; ~**ausstatter** interior decorator; ~**ausstattung** interior decoration, *(Auto)* interior appointments, *(Schiff)* inboard accommodation; ~**beleuchtung** interior lighting; **türabhängige** ~**beleuchtung** *(Auto)* interior courtesy light; ~**betrieb** indoor work; ~**bezirke einer Stadt** central parts of a town; ~**bild eines Erzeugnisses** *(Werbung)* ghost view; ~**bordmotor** inboard motor; ~**dekorateur** interior decorator; ~**dekoration** interior decoration; ~**dienst** office work, indoor service; **im** ~**dienst tätig sein** to work indoors; ~**durchmesser** internal diameter; ~**einlage** *(Zeitung)* inserts *(US)*; ~**einrichtung** interior equipment; ~**geld** inside money; ~**hafen** inner harbo(u)r; ~- **und Außenhandelsamt** Bureau of Foreign and Domestic Commerce *(US)*; ~**hof** quadrangle, patio; ~**ladung** inboard cargo; ~**leben** inner life; **sich auf sein** ~**leben einstellen** to introvert one's mind; ~**leitung** *(el.)* internal wiring; ~**lenker** *(Auto)* inside-drive car, limousine (saloon, *Br.*) car, sedan *(US)*; ~**maße** inside dimensions; ~**mauer** inside wall; ~**minister** Home Secretary *(Br.)*, Secretary of State for Home Affairs *(Br.)*, Secretary of the Interior *(US)*, home minister *(India)*; ~**ministerium** Ministry of the Interior (Internal Affairs), Home Department, Home Office *(Br.)*, Department of the Interior *(US)*, Interior Department *(US)*; **dem** ~**ministerium unterstehen** to be under the authority of the Home Office *(Br.)*; ~**plakat** *(Verkehrsmittel)* car card; ~**platz in einem Bus** inside seat in a bus; ~**politik** home affairs *(Br.)*, internal politics, domestic policy.

innenpolitisch internal, domestic, in the domestics;
~**e Angelegenheiten** internal (home, *Br.*) affairs; ~**e Auseinandersetzungen** domestic quarrels; ~**e Debatte** debate on home affairs; ~**e Fragen** home affairs *(Br.)*, domestic issues; **auf** ~**em Gebiet** on the home front; ~**e Probleme** domestic problems; ~**e Schwierigkeiten** domestic difficulties; ~**e Spannungen** internal strain.

Innen|rand, weißer inner margin; ~**raum** interior; ~**revision** internal audit [department]; ~**revisor** internal auditor; ~**seite** interior, inner page, inside; ~**spalte** *(Inserat)* gutter; ~**spiegel** *(Auto)* inside mirror, *(Buchbinderei)* end paper.

Innenstadt center *(US)* (centre, *Br.*) of a town, city center *(US)* (centre, *Br.*), downtown *(US)*, the City *(Br.)*;
in der ~ downtown *(US)*;
tote ~ dead city;
in die ~ **hineinfahren** to go up town *(Br.)* (downtown, *US*).

Innen|temperatur indoor temperature; ~**titel** title page; ~**tür** inner door; ~**umsatz** *(Konzern)* intercompany sales; ~**umsatzerlöse** intercompany profits; ~**verhältnis** inner relationship *(US)*; ~**verpackung** internal packing; ~**welt** mental world; ~**wirtschaft** domestic business.

innenwirtschaftliches Gleichgewicht domestic equilibrium.

inner interior, internal, inside, inward;
~**e Abhängigkeit** interdependence; ~**e Angelegenheiten** interior (internal, home, *Br.*) affairs; ~**e Anleihe** internal loan; ~**e Beschaffenheit und Inhalt unbekannt** inside and contents unknown; ~**e Beziehung** interrelation; ~**er Halt eines Staates** backbone of a country; ~**e Mission** Home Mission; ~**e Staatsschuld** interior debt, internal national debt; ~**e Unruhen** civil commotion; ~**er Verderb** inherent deterioration; ~**e Verletzung** internal injury; ~**er Wert** intrinsic value; ~**er Widerspruch** inconsistency.

innerbetrieblich intercompany, intradepartmental, works-internal, inplant *(US)*, in-plant *(US)*;
~**e Altersversorgung** company-financed pension plan; ~**e Aufsicht** internal control; ~**e Ausbildung** employee (in-plant, *US*) training; ~**e Berufsförderung** in-service training *(US)*; ~**e Beziehungen** employee relations; ~**e Kontaktpflege** human relations; ~**e Leistungsverrechnung** intercompany elimination; ~**er Markenwettbewerb** intrabrand competition; ~**er Posten** intercompany item; ~**e Revision** internal audit; ~**er Revisionsbeamter** internal auditor; ~**e Überwachung** in-house control; ~**er Vergleich** intern (interfactory) comparison studies.

Inner|es interior;
im ~**en des Waldes** in the heart of the forest;
~**es eines Kontinents** continental interior;
j. einen Blick in sein ~**es tun lassen** to reveal one's soul to s. o.

inner|europäischer Handel intra-European trade; ~**gebietlich** intraregional; ~**gemeinschaftlicher Handel** *(EG)* intra-Community trade.

innerlich inner, inward, inside, *(med.)* internal;
~ **anzuwenden** for internal use; ~ **gefestigt** morally firm;
~ **überzeugt sein** to be convinced in one's heart of hearts.

inner|organisatorisch operational; ~**parteilich** intraparty.

innerst|e Gefühle inmost feelings; **jem. seine** ~**en Gefühle offenbaren** to reveal one's heart to s. o.; ~**es Wesen ausmachen** to be at the heart of s. th.

innerstaatlich national, municipal, internal, intrastate *(US)*;
~**es Gericht** domestic court; ~**e Probleme** internal (home, *Br.*) affairs; ~**es Recht** municipal (internal, domestic) law; ~**e Steuern** internal taxes.

innerstädtisch municipal, within a town.

Innerste, bis ins to the core;
im ~**n seines Herzens glücklich sein** to feel a great gladness at heart; **j. bis ins** ~ **seines Herzens treffen** to cut s. o. to the heart.

inne|werden to become conscious (aware); ~**wohnen** to inhere; ~**wohnend** inherent, intrinsic.

innig close, intimate;
jem. ~ **zugetan sein** to be affectionately devoted to s. o.

innigster Wunsch most heart-felt desire.

Innovation innovation;
~**en in der Industrie einführen** to make technical innovations in industry.

Innung [trade] guild, craft guild, corporation;
ganze ~ **blamieren** to let the side down *(coll.)*.

Innungs|brief charter of incorporation; ~**haus** trade hall; ~**wesen** guild system.

inoffiziell inofficial, unofficial, off the record *(US)*, in an unofficial capacity, straw *(US)*;
~e Probeabstimmung unofficial (straw, *US*) vote.
inopportun inopportune, out-of-place;
~e Bemerkung ill-timed remark.
Input-Output-Analyse input-output-analysis.
Inrechnungstellung invoicing, billing.
Insasse inmate, occupant, dweller, *(Fahrgast)* passenger, *(Gefängnis)* inmate, *(Invalidenhaus)* inpensioner *(Br.)*;
~ eines versicherten Fahrzeugs occupant of an insured car;
~ eines Gefängnisses sein to lie in prison.
Insassenunfallversicherung motor-vehicle passenger insurance *(US)*, auto bodily injury insurance, passenger accident insurance, medical payments coverage insurance.
Inschrift inscription, writing, *(Münze)* legend;
nicht mehr lesbare ~ obsolete inscription;
~ entziffern to make out an inscription; **mit einer ~ versehen** to inscribe.
Insektenvertilgungsmittel insecticide, vermin killer.
Insel island;
schwimmende ~ floating island;
~ der Ruhe und des Friedens oasis of rest and peace;
auf einer einsamen ~ aussetzen to maroon; **j. zu einer ~ hinüberfahren** to take s. o. over to an island; **wie auf einer ~ leben** to live on an island; **~ mit dem Festland verbinden** to join an island with the mainland;
~bahnhof loop station; **~bahnsteig** island platform; **~bewohner** islander; **~gelände** island site; **~gruppe** cluster of islands; **~kette** string of islands; **~klima** insular climate; **~kontinent** island continent; **~lage** insularity; **~plazierung** *(Inserat)* island position; **~welt** archipelago.
Inserat insertion, insert, advertisement, ad *(US)*;
ohne ~e without inserts, adless *(US)*;
an mehreren Seiten textangeschlossenes ~ cut-in advertisement;
~ aufgeben to put in (insert, issue) an advertisement; **~e sammeln** to canvass; **durch ~ suchen** to advertise for.
Inseraten|annahme advertisement department, advertising office; **~blatt** advertising paper; **~büro** advertising agency; **~preisliste** advertising rates, rate card *(US)*; **~reklame** newspaper advertising; **~sammler** canvasser; **~tarif** advertising rates; **~teil** advertising columns, advertising space; **~werber** advertising (advertisement) canvasser.
Inserent advertiser, space buyer.
Inserieren insertion, advertising.
inserieren to insert, to advertise for;
unter Umgehung einer Agentur ~ to place the advertising direct; **in einer Zeitung ~** to put an advertisement in a newspaper, to advertise in a paper.
Insertion insert, insertion, advertising, putting in;
mit der Bitte um ~ in Ihrer Zeitung for favo(u)r of publication in your columns;
kostenlose ~ free insertion.
Insertions|auftrag space order; **~gebühren, ~kosten** advertising fees (charges); **~jahr** contractual year; **~vertrag** advertising contract.
insgeheim secretly, in one's heart.
insgesamt in the aggregate, all told, as a body, neck and crop;
~ betragen to total.
Insichgeschäft *(jur.)* agent and patient;
~ abschließen to transact on one's own account.
Inskriptionsgebühren registration fees.
Insolvent insolvent, bankrupt.
insolvent insolvent, bankrupt, in failing circumstances;
für ~ erklärt werden to be adjudicated insolvent, *(Börsenmakler)* to be hammered on the stock exchange *(Br.)*.
Insolventen|fonds insolvency fund; **~liste** black list.
Insolvenz insolvency, default, bankruptcy;
geschäftliche ~ commercial insolvency.
Insolvenzen|fonds insolvency guarantee fund; **~risiko** insolvency risk; **~statistik** insolvency statistics.
Insolvenz|erklärung declaration of insolvency, debtor's declaration; **~feststellung** *(Börsenmakler)* hammering on the stock exchange *(Br.)*; **~verluste** winding-up losses.
Inspekteur supervisor, visitor.
Inspektion inspection, visit, survey, examination, *(Auto)* servicing;
~ durch das Gesundheitsamt sanitary inspection;
sein Auto regelmäßig zur ~ bringen to have one's car serviced regularly; **~ eines Autos durchführen** to inspect a car; **~ haben** to have the auditors in.
Inspektions|ausschuß review committee; **~bericht** survey; **~bezirk** inspectorate; **~dienst durch Versicherungsexperten** inspection service; **~fahrt** tour of inspection, visiting round; **~hafen** port of survey; **~personal** inspection personnel.
inspektionspflichtig visitable.
Inspektions|recht visitorial right; **dem Verpächter ein ~recht über den Reparaturzustand auszuüben gestatten** to allow the lessor to view the state of repair of the premises; **~reise** tour of inspection, visiting round; **~stab** inspectoral staff; **~verfahren** inspection process.
Inspektor inspector, superintendent, overseer, *(auf Gut)* estate manager, farm bailiff *(Br.)*, farm manager *(US)*, *(Polizei)* police officer;
~ des Gesundheitsamtes sanitary inspector.
Inspiration inspiration.
inspirieren to inspire, to spirit, to prompt, to fire, to inflame.
inspiriert inspired.
Inspizient superintendent, *(mil.)* chief *(US)*, *(Theater)* stage manager.
inspizieren to inspect, to visit, to examine, to tour, *(Bergbau)* to survey, *(Bücher)* to audit;
Truppen ~ to visit troops.
Installateur sanitary engineer, fitter, *(el.)* electrician, *(Gasanschluß)* gas fitter, *(Klempner)* plumber;
~werkstatt plumber's shop, plumbery.
Installation fitting, finishing, installation, *(el.)* wiring, *(Schlosser)* plumbing;
ohne ~ unplumbed;
~ einer Heizungsanlage heating installation; **~ einer Maschine** setting up of a machine; **~ eines Telefonapparates** connection of a new telephone;
mit ~en versehen to wire.
Installations|anlagen indoor plumbing; **~arbeiten** plumbing, plumbery; **~kosten** cost of equipment (erection), installation cost; **bauseitig anfallende ~kosten** on-site installation costs; **~werkstatt** plumber's shop, plumbery.
Installieren fitting, installation.
installieren to install, to equip, *(el., Gas)* to finish, *(Schlosser)* to plumb;
sich ~ to fix o. s. up, to settle down in business; **in einem Amt ~** to install [in an office]; **Betrieb ~** to equip a shop with tools, to fit a workshop; **in einer Fabrik neue Maschinen ~** to equip a works with new plant, to retool a factory; **Heizung ~** to install a heating system; **Maschine ~** to install (set up) a machine; **neu ~** to fit with new plumbing; **Telefonapparat ~** to connect a new telephone; **sich in einer hübschen kleinen Wohnung ~** to settle in a nice little flat.
installiert, elektrisch wired for electricity.
Installierung installation, instalment.
instand halten to maintain, to keep in repair (order), to service.
instand setzen to repair, to restore, to put in order, to refit, to maintain, to do up;
Straße ~ to fit a road for traffic; **wieder ~** to re-instate; **selbst wieder ~ und sich behelfen** to make do and mend;
etw. ~ lassen to put s. th. in repair.
Instandhaltung maintenance [and repair], upkeep, preservation;
laufende ~ current maintenance (upkeep); **unterlassene ~** postponed maintenance work; **vorbeugende ~** preventive maintenance;
Aufwendungen und ~ upkeep and improvements; **Unterhalt und ~** maintenance and repair;
~ des Mobiliars upkeep of furniture; **~ von Straßen und öffentlichen Wegen** maintenance of public roads and highways;
für die ~ eines Flugplatzes Sorge tragen to maintain an airport.
Instandhaltungs|abkommen maintenance contract; **~abteilung** maintenance department (section); **laufende ~arbeiten** general maintenance work; **~aufwand** cost of repair, maintenance charges (expenses); **~konto** maintenance-expense account; **~kosten** cost[s] of maintenance, maintenance charges (expenses), expenses of upkeep, upkeep expenses, cost of repair; **laufende ~kosten** carrying charges; **~mannschaft** maintenance personnel, housekeeping crew; **~- und Pflegemaßnahmen** maintenance engineering; **~personal** maintenance employees (personnel); **allgemein übliche ~richtwerte** universal maintenance standards; **~umlage** maintenance assessment; **~verpflichtung** *(Pächter)* impeachment of waste; **~vertrag** maintenance contract; **~vorschriften** maintenance instructions; **~zeitfolge** period of maintenance.
inständig earnest, urgent, *(beharrlich)* insistent;
j. ~ bitten to beseech (implore) s. o.

Instandsetzung repair, reparation, putting in order;
außergewöhnliche ~en extraordinary repairs;
~ **einer Wohnung** housing rehabilitation.
Instandsetzungs|abteilung maintenance department; **~arbeiten** repair work, repairs; **laufende ~arbeiten** general maintenance work; **während der ~arbeiten geschlossen sein** to be closed during repair; **~auftrag** repair order.
instandsetzungsbedürftig in need of repair.
Instandsetzungs|darlehn home-improvement loan; **~dienst** repair service; **~halle** maintenance hall; **~konto** maintenance-expense account; **~kosten** maintenance expenses (costs), cost of repair, repair costs, repairing charges, repairs, reparation costs, *(Haus)* rehabilitation costs, expenditure on repair; **~kredit** home-improvement loan; **~rücklage** maintenance reserve; **~werkstatt** repair shop; **~zuschüsse** improvement grants.
Instanz instance, authority, *(Gericht)* instance;
in der ersten ~ in the first instance; **in der letzten ~** in the last resort (instance);
beaufsichtigende ~ supervising (superior) authority; **erste ~** first instance; **fiskalpolitische ~en** fiscal authorities; **höhere ~** superior (supervising) authority, appellate court, court above, higher echelon (instance); **letzte ~** last instance (resort); **untere ~** lower instance; **zuständige ~** competent authority;
höhere ~ anrufen to appeal to a higher court; **Angelegenheit mit einer höheren ~ besprechen** to take a matter up with a higher authority; **Prozeß bis zur letzten ~ durchfechten** to fight a case to final judgment; **in erster ~ entscheiden** to deliver a judgment in the first instance; **in letzter ~ entscheiden** to make a final decision; **gegen j. durch alle ~en prozessieren** to fight s. o. through the courts; **in der letzten ~ sein** to be in the last stage of appeal; **in der ersten ~ zuständig sein** to have original jurisdiction; **~en überspringen** to jump channels, *(bei Gericht)* to leapfrog; **sich an die nächsthöhere ~ wenden** to appeal to the court above; **in der ersten ~ abgewiesen werden** to lose a case in court in the first instance.
Instanzenweg normal [official] channels, stages of appeal;
~ **einhalten** to go through channels; ~ **nicht einhalten** to ignore (jump) channels.
Instanzenzug stages of appeal;
administrativer ~ administrative channels.
Instinkt instinct;
auf natürlichen ~en beruhend natural; **aus ~** by instinct, instinctively, by the seat of one's pants *(sl.)*;
seinem ~ folgen to follow one's nose; **feinen ~ für etw. haben** to have a flair for s. th.; **niedere ~e wachrufen** to arouse the baser feelings.
instinktiv by instinct, instinctively;
~ **handeln** to act on instinct, to fly by the seat of one's pants *(sl.)*.
instinktmäßig by instinct, instinctively.
Institut institute, institution, establishment, home, hall *(US)*, *(Erziehung)* boarding school, *(Heim)* asylum, home;
demoskopisches ~ institute for population research; **Naturwissenschaftliches ~** Science Hall *(US)*; **wissenschaftliches ~** scientific institution;
~ **zur Auflagen- und Hörerschaftskontrolle** single audit system of circulations *(US)*; ~ **für Fragen der Konjunkturpolitik** institute for business-cycle research; ~ **für Städteplanung** town-planning institute *(US)*; ~ **zum Studium von Verkehrsfragen** Institute of Transport *(Br.)*.
Institution institution;
gemeinnützige ~ nonprofitmaking (philanthropic) institution; **neue ~** young institution; **öffentliche ~en** public institutions; **staatliche ~en** governmental institutions; **wirtschaftliche ~en** economic institutions.
institutionalisieren to institutionalize.
Institutionalisierung institutionalization.
institutionell institutional;
~er Anleger institutional investor; **~e Werbung** institutional (goodwill) advertising.
Instituts|gebäude institution; **~leiter** institute leader.
instruieren to instruct, to direct, to brief;
Anwalt ~ to brief a barrister; **genau ~** to give detailed instructions; **jem. über einen Sachverhalt ~** to instruct s. o. of the facts of a case.
instruiert, genauestens von seinem Anwalt primed by one's lawyer.
Instruktion instruction, direction, order, *(an Anwalt)* brief;
gemäß Ihren ~en pursuant to your instructions; **ohne ~en** briefless;
handelspolitische ~en trade-policy instructions; **schriftliche ~en** written instructions;
~ **eines Anwalts** briefing (instructions to) a barrister, brief to counsel *(Br.)*;
~ **nicht befolgen** to contravene an instruction; **~en einholen** to ask for instructions; **detaillierte ~en erhalten** to receive full and particular instructions; **jem. ~en erteilen** to give s. o. instructions; **einem Anwalt ~en erteilen** to brief a barrister, to give instructions to a solicitor *(Br.)*; **jem. genaueste ~en geben** to give s. o. full directions; **seine ~en überschreiten** to exceed one's instructions; **~en zuwiderhandeln** to disregard (contravene) instructions.
Instruktions|buch instruction book, manual; **~gebung** briefing.
instruktionsgemäß according to instructions.
Instruktions|konferenz briefing conference; **~stunde** *(mil.)* lecture.
Instrument *(Urkunde)* legal instrument, deed, copy, transcript, *(Werkzeug)* instrument, tool, device, implement, appliance;
kreditpolitisches ~ credit instrument; **präzises ~** exact instrument; **wirtschaftspolitisches ~** instrument by economic policy;
~e und Geräte tools and implements;
~e ablesen to read off instruments; ~ **nach Richtwerten einstellen** to adjust an instrument by guide marks; **nach ~en fliegen** to fly by instruments.
Instrumentalmusik instrumental music.
Instrumentarium, gesamtes absatzpolitisches marketing mix; **geldmarktpolitisches ~** instruments of monetary policy; **konjunkturpolitisches ~** economic policy tools; **kreditpolitisches ~** credit instrument.
Instrumenten|ausrüstung instrumentation; **~bau** instrument making; **~beleuchtung** panel light; **~brett** panel, *(Auto)* dashboard, *(Flugzeug)* instrument board; **~fehler** instrumental error; **~flug** instrument (blind) flying; **~flugregeln** instrument flight; **~landung** instrument landing; **~macher** toolmaker; **~skala** instrument (instrumental) scale, *(Auto)* instrument panel; **~tafel** instrument board.
inszenieren *(Theater)* to stage-manage, to enact, *(Film)* to produce a film;
Besprechnung ~ to bring about a conference; **neu ~** to re-enact; **sich schlecht ~ lassen** not to stage well.
inszeniert werden to reach the stage.
Inszenierung *(Theater)* enactment, staging, getup, production.
intakt intact, *(Vertrag)* unbroken.
Intarsie inlay.
Integration, horizontale horizontal integration; **politische ~** political integration; **schrittweise ~** progressive integration; **vertikale ~** vertical integration; **wirtschaftliche ~** economic integration.
Integrations|basis basis of integration; **~bewegung** integration movement; **~prozeß** integration process; **~zeitraum** integration period.
integrieren to integrate, to incorporate, to absorb;
Industrien ~ to form industries into a vertical trust; **neue Kräfte in den Arbeitsprozeß ~** to absorb new workers in the labo(u)r force.
integrierend interlocking;
~er Bestandteil integral part.
integriert integrated, integral;
voll ~ fully integrated;
~es Informationssystem für die Unternehmensführung integrated management information system; **~e Versorgungsbetriebe** integrated public utility system; **~e Wirtschaft** integrated economy.
Integrierung integration, absorption;
politische ~ political integration; **wirtschaftliche ~** economic integration;
~ **neuer Kräfte in den Arbeitsprozeß** absorption of new workers in the labo(u)r force.
Integrität integrity.
Intellekt intellect;
hervorragener ~ first-class brain.
Intellektualismus intellectualism, sophistication.
intellektuell intellectual, high-brow *(coll.)*, sophisticated, egg-headish *(US sl.)*;
betont ~ third-programme *(Br.)*;
~er Hochmut high-browism.
Intellektueller intellectual[ist], professional man, sophisticated person, high-brow, long-hair *(sl.)*, egghead *(US sl.)*, wig *(sl.)*.
intelligent intelligent, understanding, knowledgeable;
~ **sein** to be quik of understanding.

Intelligenz intelligence, brain, brain capacity, intellectual understanding;
was die ~ anlangt in point of intelligence;
große ~ great intellectual power; **vorhandene ~** mental furniture, furniture of one's mind;
seine ~ beweisen to prove one's cleverness; **geringe ~ erkennen lassen** to show little intelligence; **kein Anzeichen besonderer ~ sein** not to pretend to intelligence;
~bestie powerful brain, intellectual heavyweight, whiz, wizard *(sl.)*; **~blatt** advertiser; **~grad** standard of intelligence; **altersbezogener ~grad** mental age; **großes ~niveau** high plane of intelligence; **~prüfung** mental (intelligence) test, comprehensive examination, omnibus; **~quotient** intelligence quotient, I.Q.; **gutes Ergebnis bei der Prüfung des ~quotienten erzielen** to score high on an intelligence quotient test; **~schicht des Landes** intellect of the country *(coll.)*; **~test** intelligence [-quotient] test, comprehensive examination.
Intendant director, *(mil.)* commissary, intendant, *(Theater)* stage manager.
Intendantenamt intendency.
Intendanz directorship, managership.
Intensität intensity, depth.
intensiv intensive, thorough, *(Foto)* intense;
~ nachdenken to ponder, to rack one's brains; **Thema sehr ~ studieren** to make an intensive study of a subject;
~e Anbaumethoden high farming; **~e Bewirtschaftungsmethoden** intensive methods of agriculture; **~e Wirtschaft** intensive agriculture.
intensivieren to intensify;
Konjunktur ~ to stimulate business.
Intensivierung intensification, stimulation.
Intensiv|kultur intensive cultivation of land, high farming; **~kursus** total course; **~methode** direct method; **~sprachkursus** crash language course; **~station** intensive care unit; **~werbung** intensive advertising.
interalliiert interallied.
Interdependenz interdependence.
interessant interesting, of interest, juicy *(coll.)*, *(auffallend)* remarkable, striking, conspicuous;
höchst ~ hot *(sl.)*;
Sache ungeheuer ~ finden to be exhilarated to the point of intoxication about s. th.; **sich ~ machen** to do s. th. for effect, to put on the highty and mighty, to act up *(US)*;
~e Frau attractive woman; **~e Stelle** interesting place; **~e Vergangenheit** dubious past.
Interessantes, nichts nothing to write home about; **nichts ~ in der Zeitung** nothing interesting in the newspaper.
Interesse interest, concern, stake, share, fancy, care, regard, *(Akkordarbeit)* inducement, incentive;
das öffentliche ~ berührend affected with a public interest; **durch gemeinsame ~n verbunden** knit together by common interests; **für das eigene ~** for one's own hand; **gegen das öffentliche ~ [verstoßend]** contrary to public policy; **im öffentlichen ~** for the public benefit, in the public interest, *(Beamtenentlassung)* good for service; **im ~ der Allgemeinheit** for the common good; **im ~ der Kürze** for the sake of brevity; **ohne jedes ~** void of interest; **ohne ~ für die Öffentlichkeit** not of public concern; **unseren ~n abträglich** detrimental to our interests; **von aktuellem ~** of present interest; **von allgemeinem ~** of general interest; **von unmittelbarem ~** on the nail; **von untergeordnetem ~** of minor interest;
allgemeines ~ general interest; **rechtlich anerkanntes ~** legal interest; **berechtigtes ~** legitimate interest; **berufliches ~** interest in the job; **beschränkte ~n** provincial interest; **beteiligte ~n** the interest at issue; **divergierende ~n** divergent interests, **eigenes ~** private interest; **entgegenstehende ~n** conflicting (jarring) interests; **erhöhtes ~ an** upsurge of interest in; **erlahmendes ~** languishing interest; **fehlendes ~** lack of interest; **finanzielles ~** moneyed (pecuniary) interest; **gegenseitiges ~** mutual interest; **geldwertes ~** pecuniary interest; **gemeinsame ~n** common interests; **geschäftliches ~** liking for (interest in) business, *(Geschäftsanteil)* stake in a business; **kaufmännische ~n** business (commercial, mercantile) concerns; **kollidierende ~n** conflicting interests; **lebenswichtige ~n** vital interests; **außerhalb des eigentlichen Studiums liegendes ~** outside interest; **literarische ~n** literary pursuits; **lokale ~n** sectional interests; **maßgebendes ~** controlling interest; **nachlassendes ~** flagging interest; **nationales ~** national interest; **öffentliches ~** public interest (policy); **reges ~** warm interest; **sachliches ~** impersonal interest; **steuerliches ~** fiscal concern; **unantastbare ~n** sacred interest; **unmittelbares ~** direct interest; **untergeordnetes ~** subordinate interest; **unternehmerähnliches ~** partner-like stake; **unvermindertes ~** unabated interest; **vermögensrechtliches ~** pecuniary interest; **versicherbares ~** insurable interest; **nicht versicherungsfähiges ~** prohibited risk; **vielseitige ~n** multiple interests; **vorübergehendes ~** transient interest; **weitgespannte und liberale ~n** catholic tastes and interests; **weltliche ~n** terrestrial interests; **wesentliches ~** substantial interest; **widerstreitende ~n** incompatible (clashing, conflicting) interests; **wirtschaftliche ~n** economic interests;
~n der Allgemeinheit common interests; **~ des Ausschusses** committee attention; **unersättliches ~ an Skandalgeschichten** voracious appetite for scandals; **aufrichtiges ~ an jds. Wohlergehen** true interest in s. one's welfare;
widerstreitende ~n ausgleichen to accommodate conflicting interests; **sich nachteilig auf jds. ~n auswirken** to be prejudicial (prove injurious) to s. one's interests; **jds. ~n beeinträchtigen** to injure (impair, hurt, be hurtful to, interfere with) s. one's interests; **jds. ~n nicht berücksichtigen** to set back s. one's interests; **sich auf Wahrnehmungen berechtigter ~n berufen** to plead justification; **~n berühren** to affect interests; **immer nur an seine eigenen ~n denken** to be always thinking of number one; **eigenen ~n dienen** to serve one's own interests; **jds. ~n dienen** to suit s. one's interests; **dem öffentlichen ~ dienen** to serve (perform in) the public interest; **sich für jds. ~n einsetzen** to safeguard s. one's interests; **seiner Arbeit ~ entgegenbringen** to show interest in one's work; **eigenen ~n entgegenstehen** to interfere with one's private interests; **~ erwecken** to interest, to catch s. one's fancy; **kein ~ finden** to be void of interest; **jds. ~ fördern** to further s. one's interests; **jds. ~n gefährden** to jeopardize s. one's interests; **j. für seine ~n gewinnen** to gain s. o. over; **~ haben für** to take an interest in, to have a concern in, to be in the market for; **an Büchern kein ~ haben** to show disinclination towards books; **gemeinsame ~n haben** to have interests in common; **keinerlei gemeinsame ~n haben** to have nothing in common with s. o.; **an etw. überhaupt kein ~ haben** to care naught for s. th.; **materielles ~ an etw. haben** to have a stake in s. th.; **sein eigenes ~ im Auge haben** to consult (study) one's own interests; **gegen jds. ~n handeln** to act adversely to s. one's interests; **gegen die ~n seines Kunden handeln** to operate against one's client; **besonderes ~ hervorrufen** to be of peculiar interest; **kein besonderes ~ hervorrufen** to receive no particular notice; **mit jds. ~n kollidieren** to collide (come into collision) with s. one's interests; **sich um seine eigenen ~n kümmern** to have the eye to the main chance; **seine ~n in eine andere Richtung lenken** to rechannel one's interests; **in jds. ~ liegen** to be in s. one's interest; **in festverwurzeltem ~ liegen** to reside in entrenched interests; **im öffentlichen ~ liegen** to benefit public welfare, to benefit the public interest, to be in the public interest; **sein geschäftliches ~ nicht sichtbar machen** to retain one's business privacy; **~ an etw. nehmen** to take an interest in s. th.; **seine persönlichen ~n offenlegen** *(Vorstandsmitglied)* to declare one's interests; **sich gegen das öffentliche ~ richten** to operate against the public interest; **seinen ~n schaden** to quarrel with one's bread and butter; **jds. ~n schädigen** to be harmful (prejudicial) to s. one's interests; **jds. ~n ernstlich schädigen** to prejudice seriously s. one's interests; **jds. ~n abträglich sein** to be of prejudice (prejudicial) to s. one's interests; **im öffentlichen ~ tätig sein** to act for the common good; **im Mittelpunkt des öffentlichen ~s stehen** to be in the limelight, to be large in the public eye; **jds. ~n verletzen** to run counter to s. one's interests; **das ~ verlieren** to lose interest; **seine ~n verteidigen** to build defences for one's interests; **~n vertreten** to safeguard interests; **jds. ~n vertreten** to look after (see to) s. one's interests; **seine eigenen ~n vertreten** to fight for one's own hand; **jds. ~n als Beobachter [vor Gericht] vertreten** to hold a watching brief for s. o. *(Br.)*; **gewissen früheren ~n vorgehen** to overreach certain prior interests; **~n wahren** to safeguard interests, *(Börsenmakler)* to protect (guard) interests; **seine ~n wahren** to fight for one's own hand; **jds. ~n ordnungsgemäß wahren** to be loyal to s. one's interests; **seine politischen ~n wahren** to mend one's fences *(US sl.)*; **jds. ~n wahrnehmen** to uphold (safeguard) s. one's interests, to be loyal to the interests of s. o.; **seine eigenen ~n wahrnehmen** to attend to (look after, act in) one's interests, to mend one's fences *(US sl.)*; **seine ~n nicht wahrnehmen** to be neglectful of one's interests; **jds. ~ an einer Angelegenheit wecken** to interest s. o. in a cause (plan); **beträchtliches ~ für etw. zeigen** *(Börse)* to give a fair amount of support to; **plötzlich ~ zeigen** to sit up and take notice *(US coll.)*; **mit jds. ~n zusammenstoßen** to come into collision (collide) with s. one's interests.

interesselos uninterested, indifferent, incurious, languishing, languid, listness, keycold *(dial.)*.
Interesselosigkeit languidness, indifference, incuriosity, disinterest.
Interessen|abstimmung agreement of interests; ~**abwägung** weighing of interests; ~**bereich** sphere of influence (interest); ~**förderung von jem.** furtherance of s. one's interests; ~**gebiet** sphere of influence (interests), zone of influence (operations); **besondere** ~**gebiete haben** to have outside interests; ~**gegensatz** interference of interests, contrariety (conflict) of (clashing) interests; ~**gegensätze** jarring interests.
Interessengemeinschaft community of interest, solidarity, privity, fraternity, *(Arbeitsgemeinschaft)* working agreement, *(Bank)* combination, *(Kartell)* syndicate, combine, trust, *(Poolvertrag)* pool, pooling of interest, pooling agreement (contract);
politische ~ combine, pressure group;
~ **mit unbeschränkter Geschäftsführungsvollmacht** blind pool; ~ **mit jem. eingehen** to enter into combination with s. o.; **einer** ~ **unterwerfen** to pool; **sich in einer** ~ **zusammenfinden** to strike hands.
Interessen|gruppe pressure group, junto, lobby, interests; ~**käufe** *(Börse)* support buying; ~**kollision** collision of interests, divergent (conflict of) interests, conflicting interests; ~**kollision mit jem. haben** to collide with s. one's interests; ~**kollision hervorrufen** to bring interests into conflict; ~**konflikt** conflicting interests, lappage; **seinen** ~**kreis begrenzen** to circumscribe one's interests; **seine** ~**lage herausfinden** to know where one's interests lie; ~**politik** pressure-group policy; ~**sphäre** zone of influence (operations), sphere of influence (interests).
Interessent party interested (concerned), *(potentieller Käufer)* prospective purchaser (buyer), prospect *(US)*, *(Lobbyist)* lobbyist;
~**en** interested parties, interests, *(politisch)* pressure group; **möglicher** ~ prospect *(US)*; **tatsächlicher** ~ real party concerned.
Interessenten|gruppe, ~**verband** interest (pressure) group, faction; **englische** ~**gruppe** British interests; ~**kreis** interested parties, *(potentielle Käufer)* prospective buyers, prospects *(US)*; ~**papiere** manipulated shares *(Br.)* (stocks, *US*).
Interessen|übereinstimmung harmony of interests; ~**verband** syndicate, pressure (interest) group, combine, pool.
interessenverbunden united in interest.
Interessen|vereinigung pooling of interests; ~**verflechtung** interlocking interests; ~**verknüpfung** pooling of interests; ~**vertreter** representative of [special] interests; **bezahlter** ~**vertreter** bendable lobbyist; ~**vertretung** representation of interest; ~**vorlage** hybrid bill *(Br.)*; ~**wahrung** protection (safeguarding) of interests; ~**widerstreit** conflict (collision) of interests; ~**zusammenschluß zwecks einheitlicher Verkaufspolitik** organized market.
interessieren to interest, to intrigue;
sich für etw. ~ to interest (concern) o. s., to take an interest in s. th., *(Unternehmen)* to be interested in (in the market for) s. th.; **sich nur für technische Dinge** ~ to have a mechanical turn; **sich kaum für Politik** ~ to take no great interest in politics; **sich politisch** ~ to mix (dabble) in politics; **j. für eine Sache** ~ to interest s. o. for a cause (a plan), to win s. o. over to a cause.
interessiert concerned, interested;
~ **sein** to be full of life; **einseitig** ~ **sein** to have a single-track mind (single eye); **ernsthaft** ~ **sein** to mean business *(coll.)*; **an etw.** ~ **sein** to feel an interest in s. th.; **finanziell** ~ **sein** to be financially interested; **an einem Unternehmen finanziell** ~ **sein** to have a financial interest in an undertaking; **nicht daran** ~ **sein** not to be very keen on it; **an einem Problem nicht** ~ **sein** to dissociate o. s. from (disinterest o. s. in) a question; **politisch übermäßig** ~ **sein** to have politics on the brain *(coll.)*; **an etw. unmittelbar** ~ **sein** to have a direct interest in s. th.; **weder** ~ **noch beteiligt sein** to have neither part nor lot in it.
Interessierte|r interested person;
literarisch ~ the literary kind.
interfraktionell interparty.
interimistisch provisional, temporary, transitory.
Interims|abkommen temporary agreement; ~**aktie** interim share, provisional share certificate *(Br.)*, interim stock certificate *(US)*, *(Teilaktie)* stock scrip *(US)*; ~**anleiheschein** temporary receipt, scrip; ~**ausschuß** interim commitee; ~**band** provisional volume; ~**bestimmungen** provisional regulations; ~**bilanz** interim balance sheet (earnings statement, *US*); ~**broschur** provisional brochure; ~**buchung** suspense entry.
Interimschein *(Aktie)* bearer scrip, provisional bond, scrip certificate *(Br.)*, interim (temporary) [stock] certificate *(US)*, *(Inhaberschuldverschreibung)* bond certificate *(US)*;
auf den Namen lautender ~ registered scrip;
~ **über die erfolgte Anlieferung von Gütern zur Verschiffung** dock receipt *(US)*; ~ **einer Eisenbahnaktie** railway scrip *(Br.)*; ~**inhaber** scrip holder; ~**wechsel** provisional (interim) bill, bill at interim; ~**zettel** counter check; ~**zollschein** sight entry.
Interims|dividende interim dividend, dividend on account; ~**kabinett** caretaker government, interim administration (cabinet); ~**kommission** interim committee; ~**konto** suspense (interim) account; ~**quittung** interim (provisional) receipt; ~**regierung** provisional (caretaker) government.
inter|konfessionell *(Schule)* interconfessional, interdenominational, undenominational; ~**kontinental** intercontinental.
Interkontinental|bomber intercontinental bomber; ~**geschoß** intercontinental ballistic missile, ICBM; ~**rakete** intercontinental rocket; ~**verkehr** intercontinental travel.
Interlinearmanuskript interlined manuscript.
Intermezzo intermezzo.
interministeriell interministerial;
~**er Ausschuß** departmental committee.
intern internal, interior, private;
Angelegenheit ~ **regeln** to settle an affair among oneselves (privately); **sich** ~ **verständigen** to come to a private arrangement;
~**e Abmachung** private (internal) agreement (arrangement); ~**e Angelegenheiten** internal affairs; ~**e Kosten** degression internal economies of scale; ~**e Preissteigerungen** price increases on the home market; ~**e und externe Schüler** boarders and day pupils; ~**e Streitigkeiten** internal quarrels.
Interna einer Sache kennen to know the inside of an affair.
Internat boarding home (school), public school *(Br.)*, house, hall, pension;
~ **und Internatsgebäude** existing public school.
international|ausgerichtet internationally orientated; ~ **eingestellt** international minded;
~**es Abkommen** international convention.
International|e Absatzwirtschaftliche Vereinigung International Marketing Association (IMA); ~**e Anwaltsvereinigung** International Bar Association; ~**e Arbeitervereinigung** International Working Men's Association; ~**e Arbeitgeber-Organisation** International Organization of Employers; ~**es Arbeitsamt** International Labo(u)r Office; ~**e Arbeitsorganisation** International Labo(u)r Organization (IAO); ~**e Atomenergiekommission** International Atomic Energy Agency (IAEA); ~**er Ausschuß für Frequenzregistrierung** International Frequency Registration Board; ~**er Beratender Ausschuß für den Funkdienst** International Radio Consultative Committee; ~**er Ausschuß für den** ~**en Suchdienst** International Commission for the International Tracing Service; ~**er Beratender Ausschuß für den Telegrafen- und Fernsprechdienst** International Telegraph and Telephone Consultative Committee; ~**es Ausstellungsamt** International Exhibitions Office; ~**e Bank für Wiederaufbau** International Bank for Reconstruction and Development; ~**e Berufssystematik** International Standard Classification of Occupation; ~**er Bund freier Gewerkschaften** International Confederation of Free Trade Unions; ~**es Büro für Geistiges Eigentum** International Bureau of Intellectuell Property; ~**es Büro für Maße und Gewichte** International Bureau of Weights and Measures.
internationaler Devisenmarkt international exchange market.
International|er Eiswachdienst im Nordatlantik International Sea Patrol Service in the North Atlantic; ~**e Energie-Agentur** International Energy Agency; ~**es Energieprogramm** International Energy Programme; ~**er Entschädigungsfonds bei Ölverschmutzungsschäden** International Oil Pollution Compensation Fund; ~**e Entwicklungsorganisation** International Development Association (IDA); ~**e Entwicklungsstelle** International Development Agency; ~**er Fernmeldeverein** International Telecommunications Union (I.T.U.); ~**e Finanzierungsgesellschaft** International Finance Corporation (IFC); ~**e Flüchtlings-Organisation** International Refugee Organization (IRO); ~**e Flußanliegergemeinschaft** International River Community.
international|er Frachtbrief international consignment note; ~**er Geld- und Kapitalverkehr** international money and capital transactions.
International|er Gemeindeverband International Union of Local Authorities; ~**er Genossenschaftsverband** International Co-operative Alliance.

internationale Gepflogenheiten international usage.
International|er Gerichtshof International Court of Justice; ~**e Gesundheitsvorschriften** International Sanitary Regulations.
internationale Gewässer international waters.
Internationale Gewerkschaftsvereinigung International Federation of Trade Unions.
internationales Gewerkschaftswesen international trade unionism.
International|e Handelskammer International Chamber of Commerce; ~**e Handelsorganisation** International Trade Organization (ITO); ~**er Hotelverband** International Hotel Association; ~**e Hydrographische Konferenz** International Hydrographic Conference; ~**es Institut für Führungsaufgaben in der Technik** International Institute for the Management of Technology; ~**es Institut für die Vereinheitlichung des Privatrechts** International Institute for the Unification of Private Law; ~**er Jugendherbergsverband** International Youth Hostel Federation; ~**es Komitee vom Roten Kreuz** International Committee of the Red Cross; ~**e Kommission für Be- und Entwässerung** International Commission on Irrigation and Draining; ~**e Kommission für die Nordwestatlantische Fischerei** International Commission for the Northwest Atlantic Fisheries; ~**e Kommission für Landwirtschaftliche Industrien** International Commission for Agricultural Industries; ~**e Kommission zum Schutz des Rheins gegen Verunreinigung** International Commission for the Protection of the Rhine against Pollution.
internationaler Kreditverkehr international lending.
Internationale Kriminalpolizei-Organisation International Criminal Police Organization (Interpol).
internationales Luftrecht international air law.
Internationaler Luftverkehrsverband International Air Transport Association (IATA).
international gebräuchliche Maßeinheit *(Statistik)* international unit.
International|er Normenausschuß International Standardization Organization (ISO); ~**e Organisation der Arbeitgeber** International Organization of Employers; ~**e Organisation für Fernmeldewesen** International Telecommunication Union; ~**e Organisation für Normung** International Standards Organization; ~**e Pilotenvereinigung** International Federation of Airline Pilots' Association.
international|e Postanweisung international money order; ~**es Privatrecht** international private law.
International|er Rat für Meeresforschung International Council for the Exploration of the Sea; ~**e Recherchenbehörde** *(Patentwesen)* International Searching Authority.
internationales Recht international law.
Iinternational|er Reederverein International Shipping Federation; ~**es Rohstoffabkommen** International Commodity Agreement; ~**es Rotes Kreuz** International Red Cross.
international|er Rückantwortschein international reply coupon; ~**e Schiedsgerichtsbarkeit** international arbitration.
Internationale Schiffahrtskammer International Chamber of Shipping.
international|e Seemeile international nautical mile; ~**er Seeverkehr** international maritime traffic.
International|es Signalbuch International Code of Signals; ~**e Standardklassifikation der Berufe** International Standard Classification of Occupation; ~**es Statistisches Institut** International Statistical Institute.
internationaler Straßenverkehr international road traffic.
International|e Studienzentrale für die Erhaltung und Restaurierung von Kulturgut International Centre for the Study of Preservation and Restoration of Cultural Property; ~**es Suchtstoffkontrollamt** International Narcotics Control Board; ~**e Systematik der Wirtschaftszweige der Vereinten Nationen** International Standard Industrial Classification of all Economic Activities; ~**es Tierseuchenamt** International Office of Epizootics.
internationaler Transitverkehr international transit.
International|e Übereinkunft über den Eisenbahnfrachtverkehr International Agreement on Railway Freight Traffic; ~**e Union für die Erhaltung der Natur und der natürlichen Hilfsquellen** International Union for Conservation of Nature and Natural Resources; ~**er Verband für Berufsberatung** International Association for Vocational Guidance; ~**er Verband für die Veröffentlichung der Zolltarife** International Union for the Publication of Customs Tariffs; ~**er Verband für Wohnungswesen, Städtebau und Raumplanung** International Federation for Housing and Planning.
internationale Vereinigung international confederation.
Internationale|Vereinigung zum Schutz gewerblichen Eigentums International Association for the Protection of Industrial Property; ~ **Verkehrsluftfahrtorganisation** International Civil Aviation Organization.
international|e Verkehrszeichen international road signs; ~**es Verlagsrecht** international copyright; ~**e Verpflichtung** international obligations.
Internationaler Währungsfonds International Monetary Fund (IMF).
internationales Währungssystem international monetary system.
Internationales Warenverzeichnis für den Außenhandel Standard International Trade Classification.
international geschütztes Warenzeichen international trademark.
International|er Weizenrat International Wheat Council; ~**er Werbeverband** International Advertising Association (IAA).
international gehandelte Wertpapiere international securities (stocks, *US*).
International|e Wirtschaftskonferenz International Trade Conference; ~**e Wirtschaftszweigssystematik** International Standard Industrial Classification of all Economic Activities.
internationaler Zahlungsverkehr international payments.
International|es Zentrum für die Beilegung von Investitionsstreitigkeiten International Centre for the Settlement of Investment Disputes; ~**e Zivilluftfahrt Organisation** International Civil Air Organization (ICAO).
internationalisieren to internationalize.
Internationalisierung internationalization.
Internats|angehöriger internal (boarding) student, boarder *(Br.)*; ~**gast**, ~**schüler** pensioner, boarder; ~**kosten** boarding school costs (fee); ~**platz** boarding place; ~**schüler** boarding (internal) student, boarder *(Br.)*; **bevorrechtigter** ~**schüler** parlour boarder *(Br.)*.
Interner resident pupil.
internieren to intern, to detain.
Internierter internee, detainee.
Internierung internment, internation *(US)*.
Internierungs|befehl internment order; ~**haft** internment detention by the police; ~**lager** internment camp, compound; ~**macht** detaining power.
Internist internist, internal specialist.
Internspeicher *(Datenverarbeitung)* internal memory.
interparlamentarischer Ausschuß interparliamentary committee.
Interpellant interpellant, interpellator, interrogator.
Interpellation *(parl.)* interpellation, question;
~ **einbringen** to give notice of a question, to interpellate.
interpellieren *(parl.)* to interpellate, to ask a formal question.
Interpol International Criminal Police Organization.
Interpretation interpretation, construction;
ausdehnende ~ extensive interpretation; **einschränkende** ~ restrictive interpretation; **falsche** ~ misinterpretation; **auf Schallplatte (Tonband) festgehaltene** ~ record performance; **richterliche** ~ judicial interpretation; **weitgehende** ~ liberal construction.
Interpretations|klausel interpretation clause; **zwei** ~**möglichkeiten zulassen** to admit two interpretations.
interpretieren to interpret, to construct;
ausdehnend ~ to put a wide interpretation on; **Buchpassage** ~ to interpret a difficult passage in a book; **falsch** ~ to misinterpret; **jds. Schweigen als Ablehnung** ~ to interpret s. one's silence as refusal; **Vertrag** ~ to interpret a contract; **weitgehend** ~ to put a wide interpretation on.
interpunktieren to punctuate.
Interpunktion punctuation;
ohne ~ unpointed.
Interpunktionszeichen punctuation mark, stop;
mit ~ **versehen** to point;
moderne ~**verwendung** open style of punctuation.
Interregnum interregnum.
interstellar interstellar.
Intervall interval;
in ~**en** off and on;
lichte ~**e** *(Irrer)* period of lucidity;
~**prognose** quantitative forecasting.
intervalutarischer Kurs foreign exchange rate.
Intervenient intervening party, intervenient, intervenant, intervener, intervenor, *(Prozeß)* interpleader, *(Wechsel)* acceptor for hono(u)r;
als ~ **zahlen** to pay for hono(u)r.
intervenieren to intervene, to intermediate, to intercede, to interfere, *(Prozeß)* to interplead;

am Effektenmarkt ~ to give supporting orders; **zu jds. Gunsten** ~ to make intercessions for s. o.; **als Notadressat** ~ to accept for hono(u)r, to intervene in case of need; **in einem Streit** ~ to interpose in a dispute.
intervenierend interventional.
Intervention intervention, interference, intercession, *(Kursstützung)* supporting order, banking support, *(Prozeß)* joinder of parties, third-party notice, interpleader, *(Wechsel)* acceptance (payment) for hono(u)r, act of honor *(US)*;
per ~ by supra protest;
bewaffnete ~ armed intervention; **staatliche** ~ government (state) intervention, state interference, *(in der Wirtschaft)* direct intervention in the economy, interference with private business; **wirtschaftliche** ~ industrial (economic) intervention; ~ **des wahren Eigentümers** compulsory demand [against vendor]; ~ **der Währungsbehörde** exchange intervention;
für staatliche ~en eintreten to favo(u)r statutory policy; **mit seiner ~ fast nichts erreichen** to intervene to little purpose.
Interventionismus state intervention, interventionism.
Interventionist interventionist.
interventionistisch interventionistic.
Interventions|akzept acceptance for (upon) hono(u)r (supra protest), supraprotest (collateral, *US*) acceptance; **~annahme** acceptance for (upon) hono(u)r (supra protest); **~anspruch** adverse claim; **~auftrag** *(Bank)* supporting order; **~ausgaben** *(EG)* intervention expenditure; **~berechtigter** party entitled to intervene; **~bestände** intervention holdings; **~fonds** *(Finanzministerium)* equalization account *(Br.)*; **~grenze** *(Börse)* stop limit; **~handlung** intervening act; **~käufe** *(Börse)* supporting orders (purchases), *(Währungsfonds)* intervention buying; **in mäßigem Umfang Dollar-~käufe durchführen** *(Bundesnotenbank)* to intervene on a reasonable scale to buy dollars; **sämtliche DM für ~käufe verwenden** to use all its D-marks in interventions; **~klage** interpleader; **~klage erheben** to interplead; **~konsortium** supporting syndicate; **~kosten** *(EG)* intervention expenditure; **~krieg** war of intervention; **~kurs** *(Währungsfonds)* intervention price; **~maßnahmen** *(EG)* intervention measures; **~plan** intervention scheme; **~politik** intervention policy; **~preis** *(EG)* intervention price; **~preissystem** *(EG)* price support scheme; **~protest** protest of intervention; **~provision** commission for intervention; **~punkt** *(Bundesnotenbank)* intervention point; **~recht** right to intervene, right of intervention; **~stelle** *(EG)* intervention agency; **~syndikat** supporting syndicate; **~verfahren** interpleader proceedings; **~zahlung** payment by intervention (supra protest, for hono(u)r).
Interview interview;
erlistetes ~ stolen interview; **im einzelnen festgelegtes** ~ checklist interview, quantitative interview; **gezieltes** ~ focus interview; **informelles** ~ qualitative (open-ended) interview; **mündliches** ~ personal interview; **telefonisches** ~ telephone interview; **zentriertes** ~ focused interview;
~ **zustande bringen** to arrange an interview; **jem. ein** ~ **gewähren** to grant s. o. an interview, to favo(u)r s. o. with an interview, to give out an interview to s. o. *(US)*; **bei einem** ~ **Quatsch reden** to fudge an interview; **der Presse jedes** ~ **verweigern** to refuse to give any interview to journalists;
~anweisung interviews guide, assignment sheet.
interviewen to interview.
Interviewer [field] interviewer, pollster, field investigator.
Interviewleit|anweisung interview guide; **~faden** assignment sheet.
Interzonen|abkommen interzonal agreement; **~handel** interzonal trade; **~handelsabkommen** interzonal trade agreement; **~paß** interzonal travel permit; **~verkehr** interzonal traffic.
Intestat|erbe legal (lawful) heir, heir at law *(US)*; **als ~erbe erben** to succeed to an intestate estate; **~erbfolge** intestate succession, distribution; **~erblasser** intestate; **~nachlaß** intestate estate.
Inthronisation enthronement.
inthronisieren to enthrone.
intim intimate, familiar, *(Atmosphäre)* intimate, cosy;
mit jem. ~ befreundet sein to be close friends (be very intimate) with s. o.;
~e Beziehungen close (intimate) relations; **~e Beziehungen zu einer Frau unterhalten** to be on intimate terms with a woman; **~er Charakter eines Gesprächs** intimate nature of a conversation; **~e Erfahrungen** sexual experience; **~e Freunde** bosom friends; **Abend im ~en Kreis verbringen** to dine with a few intimate friends; **~e Mitteilung** confidential message; **~e Musik** soft music.
Intimität intimacy, familiarity, closeness;
sich ~en jem. gegenüber erlauben to take liberties with s. o.
Intimsphäre privacy, private-life sphere, sanctum, penetralia;
in der ~ in the privacy of the home;
jds. ~ verletzten to invade (intrude upon) s. one's privacy.
intolerant intolerant.
Intoleranz intolerance.
Intrigant intriguer, manoeuvrer, schemer.
intrigant intriguing, scheming.
Intrige scheme, intrigue, cobweb, frame-up *(US sl.)*;
~n intrigue, underhand manoeuvres, practice;
kleine ~n little schemes; **politische ~n** political machinations; **unbedeutende** ~ subordinate plot; **widerwärtige** ~ devilish plot; **jem. durch ~n zu einer Anstellung verhelfen** to intrigue to get s. o. an appointment.
Intrigen|nest hotbed of intrigue; **~netz** web of intrigues; **~spiel** engineering.
Intrigieren mischief-making.
intrigieren to intrigue, to contrive, to scheme, to frame *(sl.)*.
introvertiert withdrawn, unsociable.
Introvertiertheit introversion.
Intuition intuition;
sich weitgehend auf seine ~ verlassen to be a purely intuitive operator.
intuitiv intuitive.
Inumlaufsetzen von Falschgeld passing counterfeit money.
invalid invalid, disabled.
Invalide physically disabled, disabled (incapacitated) person (worker), permanent invalid, civil pensioner, *(mil.)* invalid;
Soldaten als ~n entlassen to invalid a man out of the army; **zum ~n machen** to invalid; **~n schieben** to trundle a disabled person.
Invaliden|fürsorge disablement relief; **~haus** hospital.
Invalidenrente *(Altersrente)* old-age annuity (pension), retirement pension, primary benefit *(US)*, *(Arbeitsunfähigkeit)* disablement annuity, disablement benefit (pension) *(Br.)*, industrial injuries benefit *(Br.)*, disability pension (insurance benefit, *US*), *(Unfallrente)* invalidity pension, accident indemnity;
beitragsfreie ~ noncontributory invalidity pension;
~ **für Angehörige** industrial death benefit for widows and other dependants *(Br.)*; ~ **bei Beschädigungen unter 20%** disablement gratuity *(Br.)*; ~ **an Blinde** blindness disability payment.
Invaliden|rentner old-age pensioner, annuity holder; **~unterstützung** disability (disablement) benefit; **steuerfrei erhaltene ~unterstützung** tax-free disability payment; **~versicherung** *(Altersversicherung)* social security tax, *(Arbeitsunfähigkeit)* disablement (disability, *US*) insurance.
Invalidenversicherungs|beitrag *(Altersversicherung)* social security contribution, *(Arbeitsunfähigkeit)* health insurance contribution *(Br.)*; **~leistung** disablement (disability, *US*) benefit.
Invalidität disablement, permanent incapacity, disability *(US)*, invalidism, invalidity;
dauernde ~ permanent disability (disablement); **partielle** ~ partial disability (disablement); **vollständige** ~ total disability; **vorübergehende (zeitweilige)** ~ temporary disability (disablement).
Invaliditäts|anspruch disablement claim; **~fonds** disability fund *(Br.)*; **~grad** degree of disablement, disability rate *(Br.)*; **~klausel** disability clause; **~rente** *(Altersversicherung)* old-age pension, *(Arbeitsunfähigkeit)* disablement annuity; **~versicherung** disablement (disability, *US*) insurance.
Invasion invasion, descent upon the enemy;
~ **bei jem. veranstalten** to invade s. one's house *(fam.)*.
Invasionsarmee invading army (force);
unter einer ~ schmachten to be under the heel of the invader.
Invasions|beschuldigung charge of invasion; **~krieg** war of invasion; **den ~truppen Feuerschutz gewähren** to cover the landing of the invading army; **~versuch** invasion attempt; **~zeit** invasion period.
Inventar inventory, stock on hand, accountable (expendable, *US*) stores, schedule, *(Büroeinrichtungen)* office furniture and equipment, *(Fabrik)* implements and machinery, *(Landwirt)* furnishings and fixtures;
anfängliches ~ beginning (opening) inventory; **tatsächlich aufgenommenes** ~ physical inventory (stocktaking, *Br.*); **buchmäßiges** ~ book inventory; **festes** ~ fixtures; **laufend geführtes** ~ continuous (going, running, perpetual) inventory; **landwirtschaftliches** ~ farm stock; **lebendes** ~ livestock; **totes** ~ dead stock, *(Bilanz)* implements and machinery; **unbewegliches** ~ installed property;

~ **zum Anschaffungspreis** inventory at cost; ~ **zu Beginn des Geschäftsjahres** beginning inventory; ~ **zum Schluß des Geschäftsjahres** closing inventory;
~ **aufnehmen (errichten)** to [make up the] inventory, to take inventory (stock), to list; **zum** ~ **gehören** to be part of the inventory;
~**abschreibung** inventory writedown; ~**aufnahme** inventory [taking], stocktaking, taking stock; **tatsächliche** ~**aufnahme** physical inventory (stocktaking); ~**aufstellung** making up an inventory, inventory schedule (sheet), listing of property; ~**bewertung** valuation of inventory, inventory valuation, inventory pricing; ~**blatt** inventory sheet; ~**buch** inventory (balance-sheet) book, inventory register, stock ledger; ~**erbe** beneficiary heir; ~**errichtung** [making up an] inventory, stocktaking *(Br.)*; ~**errichtungsliste** inventory list; ~**fehlbetrag** inventory shortage; ~**frist** inventory period; ~**gegenstand** inventory item; ~**herabsetzung** inventory reduction.

inventarisieren to [make] inventory, to take inventory (stock), to catalog(ue);
Bücher ~ to enter in the accession book.

Inventarisierung stocktaking, [making up an] inventory, listing.

Inventarisierungsnummer *(Bibliothek)* inventory number.

Inventar|karte, ~**karteiblatt** inventory (stock) card; ~**konto** inventory (furniture and fixture) account; ~**kontrolle** inventory checking; ~**liste** inventory; ~**nummer** inventory number; ~**posten** inventory item; ~**preis** inventory price; ~**prüfung** inventory audit (checking); ~**prüfungsbescheinigung** inventory certificate; ~**stücke** surplus stock; **kleine** ~**stücke** small fixtures; ~**veränderung** change in inventory, inventory changes; ~**verlust** inventory loss; ~**versicherung mit der Auflage von Veränderungsmeldungen** reporting insurance; ~**verzeichnis** plant ledger, inventory, inventory record (schedule, sheet), contents of inventory, stock register, *(Konkurs)* statement of affairs.

Inventarwert inventory value, value of inventory, *(Investmentfonds)* net asset value;
~ **von 5000 Dollar haben** to inventory at $ 5000;
~**berichtigung** inventory valuation adjustment; ~**schwankungen** inventory fluctuations.

Inventur stocktaking *(Br.)*, inventory [taking] *(US)*, inventory audit, list of assets and liabilities;
laufende (permanente) ~ book (continuous, perpetual) inventory *(US)*; **tatsächliche** ~ physical inventory *(US)* (stocktaking, *Br.*);
~ **durch körperliche Bestandaufnahme** physical inventory *(US)* (stocktaking, *Br.*);
~ **machen** to take stock *(Br.)*, to [take] inventory *(US)*, to make up an inventory *(US)*; **im Januar** ~ **machen** to take inventory (stock) in January; ~ **überwachen** to observe an inventory;
~**arbeiten** inventory proceedings *(US)*; ~**aufnahme** stocktaking *(Br.)*, inventory [taking] *(US)*; **tatsächliche** ~**aufnahme** physical stocktaking (inventory); ~**ausverkauf** clearance (inventory, *US*) sale, stocktaking sale *(Br.)*; ~**bestandsaufnahme** physical inventory; ~**bewertung** inventory valuation; ~**blatt** inventory *(US)* (stock, *Br.*) sheet; ~**buch** inventory book *(US)*; ~**erstellung** stocktaking, inventory taking; ~**fehlbetrag** inventory shortage; ~**frist** stocktaking *(Br.)* (inventory, *US*) period; ~**kosten** cost of stocktaking *(Br.)*, inventory costs; ~**lohn** inventory labor *(US)*; ~**menge** inventory quantity *(US)*; ~**preis** inventory price; ~**prüfung** inventory verification (audit) *(US)*, stocktaking *(Br.)*; ~**tag,** ~**termin** inventory cut-off date *(US)*; ~**überwachung** inventory observation *(US)*; ~**verkauf** clearance (stocktaking, *Br.*) sale; ~**verzeichnis** inventory record (sheet, schedule); ~**wert pro Einheit** inventory value per unit.

Inverkehrbringen putting in circulation, issue;
~ **von Falschgeld** uttering false notes; ~ **von Falschnachrichten** spreading false news.

Invertergerät *(tel.)* inverter.

Inverzugsetzung notice of default.

investieren to invest [capital], to place (make, effect) investments;
5% des Anlagevermögens in Beleihungen beweglichen Vermögens ~ to invest 5% of their assets in chattel paper; **in Anlagewerten** ~ to place in investments; **für die Einführungskampagne** ~ to invest in initial publicity; **erneut** ~ to restart investing; **seine Ersparnisse in einem Geschäft** ~ to invest one's savings in a business enterprise; **in Grundstücken** ~ to make investments in real estate, to invest one's money in real estate; **günstig** ~ to invest advantageously; **Kapital** ~ to invest capital; **kurzfristig** ~ to invest on a short-term basis; **langfristig** ~ to make long-term investments; **mehr** ~ to make greater investments; **in Rüstungswerten** ~ to touch shares of armament firms; **tausend Pfund in Staatspapieren** ~ to invest £ 1000 in government stock; **vorteilhaft** ~ to make a good investment; **hauptsächlich in Wertpapieren** ~ to invest primarily in securities; **in Wohngrundstücken** ~ to invest in house property.

investiertes Kapital capital invested.

Investierung investment, placement;
~ **von Kapital** investment of funds.

Investition investment, investing, placement, capital spending; **für Arbeitskräfte aufgewandte** ~**en** investment in men (human capital); **außerbetriebliche** ~**en** outside investments; **bauliche** ~**en** expenditure on building; **betriebliche** ~**en** plant investment; **durchgeführte** ~**en** capital expenditure; **echte** ~ real investment; **erstklassige** ~ choice investment; **erwartete** ~**en** investment anticipation; **bitter fehlende** ~**en** investment famine; **festverzinsliche** ~**en** fixed-interest-bearing investments; **mit eigener Betätigung gekoppelte** ~**en** direct investments; **geschäftliche** ~**en** trade investments *(Br.)*; **gewinnbringende** ~**en** earning investments (assets); **indirekte** ~**en** portfolio investment; **infrastrukturelle** ~**en** infrastructure investments; **kapitalsparende** ~ capital-saving investment; **kurzfristige** ~**en** temporary investments; **langfristige** ~**en** long-term capital investments, permanent investments; **laufende** ~**en** current investments; **lohnende** ~**en** profitable (remunerative) investments; **maschinelle** ~**en** capital expenditure on machinery; **mißglückte** ~ mistaken investment; **mittelfristige** ~**en** intermediate-term investments; **mündelsichere** ~**en** gilt-edged *(Br.)* (high-grade, *US*, trustee, *Br.*) investments; **risikoärmere** ~**en** *(Investmentfonds)* defensive portion; **risikoreichere** ~**en** *(Investmentfonds)* aggressive portion; **schlechte** ~ poor investment; **soziale** ~**en** social investments; **spekulative** ~**en** aggressive (special-situation) investments; **dirigistisch gelenkte staatliche** ~**en** centrally planned government investments; **übermäßige** ~**en** excessive investments; **von wirtschaftlichen Überlegungen unabhängige** ~**en** autonomous investments; **unvorteilhafte** ~ unprofitable investment; **verzinsliche** ~**en** interest-bearing investments; **auf lange Sicht vorgenommene** ~**en** long-lived investments; **werterhöhende** ~**en** internal improvements *(US)*;
~**en für menschliche Arbeitskräfte** investment in men (human capital); ~**en im Ausland** investments abroad, foreign investments; ~**en für den Automatisierungsprozeß** spending to automate (for automation); ~**en auf dem Bausektor** construction spending; ~**en im kommunalen Bereich** local authorities' investment; ~**en in die Betriebseinrichtungen** equipment investment; ~**en in Ersthypotheken** first-mortgage investments; ~**en zur Erzielung kurzfristiger Kapitalerträge** revenue (income) expenditure; ~**en im Filialbereich** branch investments; ~**en in Geschäftsgrundstücken** commercial real-estate investments; ~**en der öffentlichen Hand** public sector investment, public-capital expenditure; ~**en im Immobiliensektor** real-estate investments; ~**en im Inland** domestic investments; ~**en für den Maschinenpark** equipment investments; ~**en in nachgelagerte Produktionen** downstream investments; ~**en zu Rationalisierungszwecken** investments undertaken for rationalization purposes; ~**en mit fester Rendite** fixed-yield investments; ~**en mit verteiltem Risiko** diversification of one's investment; ~**en in Wertpapieren** portfolio investments; ~**en auf dem Wohnungsbausektor** residential investments; ~**en bei Zweigunternehmen** branch investments;
Umfang der vorgesehenen ~**en leicht anheben** to raise (trim) slightly the current rate of spending; ~**en der Unternehmen auslösen** to trigger off entrepreneurial investments; **für** ~**en im Ausland auswerfen** to dole out in overseas investments; ~**en bremsen** to check investment; **für** ~**en empfehlen** to single out for investment; **als langfristige** ~ **empfehlen** to advise retention of longer commitments; **als** ~ **für lange Sicht gelten** to have long-term appeal; **nur sofort rentierliche** ~**en machen** to invest only in short-hand gain; **zusätzliche Ertragschancen durch** ~**en auf bisher vernachlässigten Gebieten verbessern** to generate additional earnings through investments in special undervalued situations; ~ **vornehmen** to place (effect) investments, to invest; **bevorzugt weiterhin langfristige** ~**en vornehmen** to keep up the booming pace of capital investment; **überstürzte** ~**en vornehmen** to rush into new investment; ~**en im Ausland vornehmen** to plough in foreign investments; ~**en in Grundbesitz vornehmen** to make investments in real estate; **mit immer weiteren** ~**en winken** to hold out the carrot of yet more investments.

Investitions|abschreibungen investment allowance *(Br.)*; ~**absichten** investment intentions; ~**absprache** planning agreement; ~**abzahlungsberechnung** pay-back method.

investitionsähnlicher Charakter investment-like feature.

Investitions|anleihe investment loan; ~**anreiz** incentive to invest, investment incentive; **spekulativer** ~**anreiz** speculative investment attraction; ~**anstrengung** investment spurt; ~**antrag** investment proposal; ~**aufgabe** capital project; ~**aufschwung** investment upturn; ~**aufträge der öffentlichen Hand** public-sector investment orders; ~**aufwand** capital expenditure (spending, investment), fixed capital (investment) expenditure, investment outlays; **reiner** ~**aufwand nach Abschreibungen** net investment; ~**aufwand im Fertigungssektor** manufacturing investment; ~**ausgaben** investment spending, capital expenditure; ~**ausschuß** investment committee; ~**ausweitung** expansion of investment; ~**bank** investment bank; **Europäische** ~**bank** European Investment Bank; ~**bedarf** investment demand; **attraktive** ~**bedingungen für industriell weniger erschlossene Gebiete schaffen** to attract investment to poorer regions; ~**befugnis** power of investment; ~**beihilfe** investment aid; ~**bemühungen** investment efforts; ~**beratung** investment banking job; ~**bereich** investment area; **gesamter** ~**bereich** all aspects of capital expenditure; ~**bereitschaft** propensity (inclination, readiness) to invest; **Alibi für die mangelnde** ~**bereitschaft beseitigen** to remove the no-investment alibi; ~**beschlüsse** investment decisions; ~**beschränkungen** investment restrictions; ~- **und Produktionsbeschränkungen** restriction of investments and production; ~**beschränkung in Richtung auf bestimmte Sparten** restriction of investment of special classes; ~**bestand** investment total; ~**bestimmungen** investment clauses; ~**betrag** amount invested, investment sum; **fehlgeleitete** ~**beträge** misappropriated capital funds; ~**beurteilung** investment (capital expenditure) appraisal; ~**boom** investment boom; **gute** ~**chancen im Immobiliensektor** property investment opportunities; ~**darlehen** investment loan; ~**dispositionen** investment disposition; ~**drosselung** capital expenditure cutback, checking of investment activities; **rollender** ~**einsatz** leapfrogging investments; ~**empfänger** investee; ~**entschluß** decision to spend, investment decision, capital investment decision-making; ~**erfahrung** investment experience; **gute** ~**ergebnisse** good investment records; ~**fähigkeit** ability to invest; ~**finanzierung** investment financing; **Bereitschaft zu** ~**finanzierungen** financing propensity to invest; ~**flut** investment surge; ~**fonds** investment fund, capital pool; **für Zeiten wirtschaftlichen Niederganges zur Verfügung stehender** ~**fonds** investment reserve fund; ~**förderung** promotion of investments, investment promotion; ~**fragen** investment matters; ~**freibetrag** investment allowance; ~**freigabe** release of investment funds; ~**freudigkeit** propensity (inclination, readiness) to invest; ~**funktion** investment function; ~**gefälle einseitig auf kurzfristige Projekte verschieben** to skew the investment pattern towards shorter-lived projects; ~**geschäft** investment banking (business); **im** ~**geschäft erfolgreich sein** to prosper in institutional business; ~**gesichtspunkte** investment angles; ~**grad** rate of investment; ~**grundsatz** investment standard; ~**grundstück** investment property.

Investitionsgüter capital (investment) goods (assets), fixed-capital goods;
hochwertige ~ high-quality investment goods; **kurzfristige** ~ limited-life (short-lived) assets; **langlebige** ~ long-lived assets; **verbrauchsnahe** ~ consumer capital-type goods;
~ **mit einer zehnjährigen Nutzungsdauer** investments with a useful life of ten years;
~ **ersetzen** to replace capital goods; **Abschreibungen auf** ~ **steuerlich vortragen** to carry forward capital allowance *(Br.)*;
~**aufwand** capital-goods outlay; ~**bereich** capital-goods sector; ~**industrie** capital-goods (investment) industry; ~**konjunktur** boom in the capital-goods industry, capital-spending boom; ~**markt** industrial market; ~**produzent** capital-goods manufacturer; ~**werbung** industrial advertising.

Investitionshaushalt capital expenditure budget.

investitionshemmend disincentive to investment.

Investitions|hilfe investment assistance (aid); ~**hilfeabgabe** capital levy; **erwartete** ~**höhe** investment anticipation; ~**impuls** incentive to invest; ~**kapital** capital investment (invested), investment capital; ~**kapital für Erweiterungsprojekte** development capital; **privates** ~**kapital in Entwicklungsländern zum Einsatz bringen** to steer private investment into less developed countries; ~**klima** investment climate; ~**konjunktur** boom in capital investment, investment boom; ~**konjunktur anheizen** to fuel the fires of inflationary boom in business investments; ~**kontrolle** control of investment, investment control; **staatliche** ~**kontrolle** public investment control; ~**kontrolle weniger scharf handhaben** to scrap investment controls; ~**kosten** capital expense (charge), investment charges (expense); **nicht abschreibungsfähige** ~**kosten** uncoverable cost; ~**kredit** loan for the purpose of investment, investment credit (loan); ~**kriterium** investment criterion; ~**kürzungen vornehmen** to impair investments; ~**leistungen** investments effected, investment performance; ~**lenkung** direction of capital investments, control of investment, investment control; **bereitgestellte** ~**mittel** capital appropriation, investment funds; ~**mittelbedarf einschränken** to reduce the requirements for capital; ~**möglichkeit** ability to invest, investment outlet (opportunities, media, *US*); ~**müdigkeit** reluctance to invest; ~**multiplikator** investment multiplier; ~**nachfrage** investment demand; ~**nachholbedarf** pent-up investment demand; ~**neigung** propensity to invest, capital intention; ~**niveau** level of investment; ~**objekt** investment object; ~**pessimismus** investor pessimism; ~**plan** capital investment plan, capital (spending) budget; ~**planung** planned investment, capital budgeting; ~**politik** capital planning, investment policy; **bewegliche** ~**politik** investment approach; **zielbewußte** ~**politik** selective investing.

investitionspolitische Maßnahmen measures in the fields of capital investment.

Investitions|prämie, steuerliche investment tax credit; ~**prognose** capital forecasting; ~**programm** capital [expenditure] program(me), investment plan, program(me) of investment; **rasch ein breitgestreutes** ~**programm anstreben** to grow rapidly through diversification; **Streichungen bei dem** ~**programm der öffentlichen Hand vornehmen** to slash the public sector's program(me); ~**projekt** investment (capital) project, capital expenditure subject; ~**prozeß** investment process; ~**quote** level of investment, investment quota (ratio); **optimale** ~**quote** golden rule of accumulation; ~**rate** rate of investment; ~**rechnung** capital expenditure account; ~**rendite** investment return (yield); **höchste** ~**rendite** highest rate of return on investment; ~**rentabilitätsschätzung** investment appraisal; ~**richtlinien** investment rules; ~**risiko** investment risk, risk of investment, business risk; **hohes** ~**risiko** *(EEC)* primary risk; ~**rückgang** decline of (in) investment, fall in investment; ~**rücknahme** disinvestment; ~**schema** pattern of investment; ~**schutzabkommen** investment guaranty treaty; ~**schwerpunkt** priority of capital expenditure; ~**schwund** drop in investments; ~**sektor** capital-goods sector; ~**sparkurve** investment-saving curve; ~**spritze** shot in the arm *(coll.)*; ~**steigerung** induced investment; ~**steuer** investment tax; ~**streuung vornehmen** to diversify; ~**strom** flow of investment; ~**tabelle** investment schedule.

Investitionstätigkeit capital expenditure activity, investment activities;
nachlassende ~ decline of (in) investment; **rege** ~ brisk investment activity;
~ **bremsen** to check investment; ~ **hofieren** to court investment; ~ **verringern** to cut back on investment.

Investitions|tempo pace of investment, investment activity; ~**tempo drosseln** to slow down investment; ~**tendenz** investment trend; ~**termin** vesting day; ~**träger** investor; ~**überhang** investment backlogs; ~**übersicht** capital spending survey; ~**überwachung** investment supervision; ~**unlust** unwillingness to invest.

investitionsunlustig bleiben to remain gun-shy on capital investment.

Investitions|verbot investment ban; ~**vergünstigung** investment allowance; ~**verlangsamung** slowdown in investments; ~**verlust** loss on investment, investment loss; ~**verzinsung** investment yield; ~**volumen** volume of investment; ~**vorgang** investment activity.

Investitionsvorhaben investment plan (project), capital budget (project);
auswärtige ~ investment abroad; **bitter fehlende** ~ investment famine; **langfristiges** ~ long-term capital project; **zurückgestellte** ~ deferral of investment program(me)s;
~ **mit durchschnittlichem Risiko** *(EEC)* secondary risk; ~ **mit geringem Risiko** *(EEG)* tertiary risk;
~ **fördern** to encourage capital investment.

Investitions|vorteil investment merit; ~**weg** investment route; ~**wert** investment value; ~**williger** prospective investor; ~**zeitraum** period of investment; ~**ziel** investment goal (target); ~**zulage** investment premium (bonus), investment tax incentive, investment grant; ~**zunahme zustande bringen** to bring forward more investment; ~**zuschuß** investment (capital) grant; ~**zuschuß [in Fördergebieten]** regional development grant *(Br.)*; ~**zuwachs** increase of investment; ~**zweck** investment purpose; **für ~zwecke bestimmen** to earmark for investment; ~**zyklus** investment cycle.

Investivlohn participation wage.

Investment | anleger investor, unit holder *(Br.)*; ~**anteil** certificate of participation (interest, *US*), investment fund unit *(Br.)*, investment certificate, collateral trust certificate *(US)*, unit in unit trusts *(Br.)*, share *(US)*; ~**anteile ausgeben** to put units in issue *(Br.)*; ~**anteile ohne Provisionsaufschlag erwerben** to buy certificates on a no-load basis; ~**anteilseigner** unitholder *(Br.)*, shareholder *(US)*; ~**bank** investment company.

Investmentfonds investment fund (trust), unit trust *(Br.)*, profit-sharing trust;
aus Aktien und Obligationen bestehender ~ balanced fund *(US)*; **zur Konjunktursteuerung gebildeter ~** countercyclical investment fund; **an den Aktienindex gekoppelter ~** index fund; **von Treuhändern geleiteter ~** uniform trust; **geschlossener ~** closed-end fund *(US)*; **offener ~** open-end fund *(US)*; **thesaurierender ~** cumulative fund; **versicherungseigener ~** in-house fund; **im Ausland vertriebener ~** offshore mutual fund *(US)*; **von einer Versicherungsgesellschaft verwalteter ~** insurance-run mutual fund;
~ mit sofortiger Anlage der zufließenden Mittel cash-fund trust; **~ mit strengen Anlagevorschriften (festgelegten Anlagewerten)** nondiscretionary trust *(Br.)*; **~ mit unbeschränkter Anteilsausgabe** open-end investment fund *(US)*; **~ auf Basis eines Trusts** trust fund; **~ mit begrenzter Emissionshöhe (mit festem Grundkapital)** closed-end fund *(US)*; **~ mit beliebiger Emissionshöhe** open-end fund *(US)* **~ mit Leihkapital** leverage fund *(US)*; **~ mit auswechselbarem (veränderlichem) Portefeuille** flexible fund; **~ mit begrenzt auswechselbarem Portefeuille** semi-fixed fund; **~ mit feststehendem Portefeuille** fixed fund; **~ mit auswechselbarem Wertpapierbestand** flexible fund, managed fund;
~**vermittlung** mutual fund brokerage *(US)*.

Investmentgesellschaft investment company (trust), unit [investment] trust *(Br.)*, mutual fund *(US)*;
abhängige ~ investment affiliate; **staatlich anerkannte ~** registered unit trust *(Br.)*; **nach eigenem Ermessen anlegende ~** management trust (investment company); **steuerlich privilegierte ~** regulated investment company *(US)*; **von einer Versicherungsgesellschaft verwaltete ~** insurance-run mutual fund *(US)*;
~ mit breitgestreutem Aktienportefeuille general management trust, discretionary trust *(Br.)*; **~ mit konstantem Anlagefonds** close investment company *(US)*, closed-end investment *(US)* (unit, *Br.*) trust; **~ ohne Anlagestreuung** nondiversified company *(US)*; **~ mit eigenverantwortlicher (freizügiger) Anlagenverwaltung** managed list trust, general management trust, management investment company; **~ mit steuerfreiem Auslandssitz** offshore fund *(US)*; **~ mit Austauschrecht der Investitionseffekten** managed-list (flexible) trust *(US)*, flexible unit trust *(Br.)*; **~ mit festgelegtem Effektenbestand** fixed investment trust *(US)*; **~ mit beschränkter Emissionsmöglichkeit** closed-end investment company *(US)*; **~ mit auswechselndem Portefeuille** flexible unit trust *(Br.)*, flexible (managed) trust *(US)*.

Investment | käufer certificate buyer *(US)*, unit buyer *(Br.)*; ~**sparen** investment saving; ~**trust** investment trust; ~**vertragssystem** mutual fund contractual plan *(US)*; ~**wesen** mutual fund industry *(US)*.

Investmentzertifikat certificate of participation (interest, *US*), unit *(Br.)*, sub-unit certificate *(Br.)*, unit in unit trusts *(Br.)*, collateral trust certificate *(US)*, [mutual investment] share *(US)*;
an der Börse gehandeltes ~ investment certificate; **mit einer Lebensversicherung gekoppeltes ~** mutual fund-insurance package *(US)*;
bis zu 150 ~e einer Serie besitzen to hold up to 150 units of an issue; **~ stückeln** to split a certificate; **~e zurücknehmen** to repurchase units *(Br.)*.

Investmentzertifikatsbesitz unit trust holdings *(US)*.

Investor investor, unit holder *(Br.)*.

Inzahlunggeben giving in payment.

Inzahlungnahme trade-in.

Inzidentfeststellungsverfahren interpleader, interlocutory proceedings.

Inzucht in[-and-in] breeding.

Ionosphäre ionosphere.

irdisch earthy, earthly, mundane, terrestrial;
~e Güter wordly goods.

irgend | wann at some time; ~**wie** one way or another.

Ironie, beißende biting irony;
~ des Schicksals irony of fate.

ironisch | sprechen to speak with one's tongue in one's cheek;
~**er Unterton** tinge of irony.

ironisieren to speak ironically.

irre idiotic, insane, mad, crazy, *(verirrt)* astray;
wie ~ arbeiten to work at white-hot speed; **wie ~ schreien** to cry blue murder; **~ sein** to suffer from mental disorder; **ganz ~ vor Freude sein** to be beside o. s.; **~ werden** to get mixed-up (muddled, confused); **an jem. ~ werden** to lose faith in s. o.; **vor Schmerzen ~ werden** to go out of one's mind with pain;
~ Angst mad fear; **mit einem ~n Blick** with a wild look in one's eyes; **~ Reden führen** to talk in a demented way; **in einem ~n Tempo fahren** to drive with breakneck speed.

Irredenta irredentist movement.

irreführen to mislead, to misguide, to delude, to mystify;
j. über seine Absichten ~ to mislead s. o. as to one's intentions; **Behörden ~** to mislead the authorities; **durch Handlungen bewußt ~** to act in lie; **öffentliche Meinung bewußt ~** to practise deception on the public; **Polizei ~** to put the police on a wrong track;
sich ~ lassen to be taken in *(coll.)*; **sich leicht ~ lassen** to be easily deceived.

irreführend delusive, deceptive, fallacious, misleading;
~e Angaben misleading statement; **~e Auskunft** misleading information; **~e Bezeichnung** misleading indication; **~es Warenzeichen** deceptive mark; **~e Werbung** deceptive (misleading) advertising.

Irreführung disguise, misguidance, deception, misleading, mystification, bluff, fraud, delusion, camouflage;
bewußte ~ der öffentlichen Meinung wilful deception of the public; **~ der Post** mail fraud.

irregehen to lose one's way, to go astray;
in der Annahme ~ to be wrong assuming.

irregeleitete Jugend misguided young people.

irregulär *(mil.)* irregular;
~e Truppen irregulars, partisan troops.

irreleiten to lead astray, to misguide.

irrelevant irrelevant, immaterial, off the mark.

Irrelevanz irrelevance, *(Unschlüssigkeit)* impertinence.

irremachen, j. to confuse (disconcert, bewilder) s. o.

Irren ist menschlich to err is human.

irren, sich to err, to be mistaken (wrong); **sich gründlich in jem. ~** to completely misjudge s. o.; **sich in der Hausnummer ~** to go to the wrong number; **von Ort zu Ort ~** to wander from place to place; **sich in jds. Person ~** to mistake s. o. for somebody else; **sich in der Straße ~** to take the wrong road, to mistake one's way; **sich in der Zeit ~** to mistake the time.

Irren | anstalt lunatic asylum, mental institution *(US)*, mental hospital *(Br.)*, insane asylum *(US)*, madhouse, reception institute, retreat; ~**arzt** mental specialist, alienist, mad-doctor; ~**fürsorgegesetz** Mental Health Act *(Br.)*; ~**haus** mental home, asylum, madhouse; **im ~haus** confined in an asylum; ~**heilanstalt** mental hospital *(Br.)* (institution, *US*), insane asylum *(US)*; ~**wärter** asylum attendant.

Irrer idiot, fool, insane person, mentally disordered person;
mordlustiger ~ homicidal lunatic.

Irresein insanity;
manisch-depressives ~ maniacal-depressive (circular) insanity.

Irrgarten maze;
~ von Durchführungsbestimmungen regulatory maze.

irrig devious;
~e Meinung mistaken opinion.

irritieren to irritate, to annoy;
j. ~ to rub s. o. the wrong way.

Irr | läufer misrouted document, misplaced letter, miscarriage; ~**licht** will-of-the-wisp, lantern jack.

Irrsinn lunacy, insanity;
reiner ~ sheer madness, plumb crazy *(US)*.

irrsinnig insane, mad, lunatic, mentally deranged;
~ teuer outrageously (shockingly) expensive;
sich ~ freuen to be as pleased as Punch; **~ aufgeregt sein** to be in a state of excitement; **~ viel Geld verdienen** to make pots of money;
~e Angst blue funk; **~e Hitze** tremendous (terrific) heat; **in ~em Tempo** at a breakneck speed.

Irrsinniger madman, lunatic.

Irrtum error, mistake, *(Fehler)* wrong, trip, *(Mißverständnis)* misapprehension;
im ~ in the wrong; **völlig im ~** off one's base *(US sl.)*; **~ vorbehalten** subject to correction, barring error; **beachtlicher ~** operative mistake; **beiderseitiger ~** mutual mistake, mistake common to both parties; **einseitiger ~** unilateral error; **entschuldbarer ~** honest mistake; **fundamentaler ~** fundamental error; **grober ~** bad mistake; **grundlegender ~** fundamental (capital) error; **rechtlicher ~** mistake of law; **tatsächlicher ~** mistake of fact; **allgemein verbreiteter ~** common mistake; **weit verbreiteter ~** popular fallacy (error); **verhängnisvoller ~** fatal mistake;
~ von fundamentaler Bedeutung für den Vertragsabschluß common mistake as to a fact fundamental to the agreement; **~ über die rechtliche Bedeutung einer abgegebenen Willenserklärung** mistake in expression of true agreement; **~ im Beweggrund** mistake as to the nature of the subject matter; **~ über wesentliche Eigenschaften** mistake as to the quality of the subject matter; **~ über eine wesentliche Eigenschaft einer Person** mistake as to the character of a person; **~ bei der Formulierung der Vertragsofferte** mistake by the offerer in expressing his intentions; **~ über die Geschäftsgrundlage** mistake as to the existence of the subject matter; **~ über die Identität des Vertragspartners** mistake as to the identity of the person contracted with; **~ im Motiv** mistake as to the nature of the subject matter, mistake in the inducement *(US)*; **~ über die Person** mistaken identity; **~ über die Rechtsnatur der unterschriebenen Urkunde** mistake as to the nature of the document signed; **~ über eine Tatsache** mistake of fact; **~ über eine für den ganzen Vertrag wesentliche Tatsache** mistake as to a fact fundamental to the entire agreement; **~, der die Vertragsentstehung verhindert** operative mistake; **~ über den Vertragsgegenstand** mistake as to the quality of the subject matter, error as to the subject matter; **beiderseitiger ~ über den Vertragsgegenstand** mutual mistake as to the identity of the subject matter of the contract; **~ über die Vertragsgrundlage** fundamental error, fundamental mistake as to the tenor of words; **~ beider Vertragsparteien** mistake common to both parties; **einseitiger ~ über den Vertragspartner** unilateral mistake as to the identity of the person contracted with; **~ infolge fehlender Willenseinigung** discordant error; **~ über den Wortlaut einer Erklärung** fundamental mistake as to the tenor of words;
sich im ~ befinden to stand in error, to labo(u)r under a mistake (misapprehension); **~ berichtigen** to rectify an error; **auf einem ~ beruhen** to be due to a mistake; **~ bei jem. erregen (erzeugen)** to lead s. o. into error; **~ klarstellen** to clear up a misunderstanding; **~ korrigieren** to rectify an error; **seinen ~ teuer bezahlen müssen** to pay dearly for one's mistake; **jem. einen ~ nachweisen** to prove s. o. wrong, to convict s. o. of an error; **im ~ sein** to be in error;
ein ~ ist ausgeschlossen there can be no mistake.

Irrtümer und Auslassungen vorbehalten errors and omissions excepted.

irrtümlich erroneous, by mistake, mistaken, by error;
~ einen fremden Schirm mitnehmen to take s. one's umbrella in mistake for one's own; **~ zustellen** to deliver by mistake; **~e Anschuldigung** false accusation; **~e Erklärung** mistaken statement.

Irrtums|anfechtung recission for innocent misrepresentation; **~anzeige** communication of an error; **schriftliche ~erklärung** memorandum in error; **~erregung** deception; **~vorbehalt** clause reserving errors; **~vorbehalt machen** to speak under correction; **~wahrscheinlichkeit** *(Statistik)* error probability, level of significance.

Irrwahn delusion.

Irrweg wrong track;
sich auf einem ~ befinden to be on the wrong track (tack); **auf ~e geraten** to go astray.

Iso|gewinnkurve iso profit curve; **~kostenlinie** iso cost line; **~kurve** conto(u)r line.

Isolationismus isolationism;
sich dem ~ zuwenden to turn isolationist.

Isolationist isolationist.

isolationistisch isolationistic;
~e Politik isolationistic policy.

Isolations|fehler eines Kabels fault in the insulation of a cable; **~folter** sensory deprivation; **~material** insulating material.

Isolator insulator.

Isolierband insulating (electrician's) tape.

isolieren to quarantine, to segregate, *(el.)* to insulate, *(pol.)* to isolate;
Gefangenen ~ to seclude a prisoner; **Land politisch und wirtschaftlich völlig ~** to quarantine a country; **j. vollständig ~** to cut s. o. dead.

Isolier|glocke *(el.)* petticoat; **~haft** solitary confinement, incommunication; **~krankenhaus** detention hospital; **~station** *(Krankenhaus)* casual ward.

isoliert isolated, insular, withdrawn;
etw. ~ betrachten to keep s. th. in a watertight compartment.

Isolierung *(el.)* insulation, *(Kranke)* quarantine, *(Rassen)* segregation, *(pol.)* isolation;
mangelnde ~ defect in insulation;
~ von Gefangenen seclusion of prisoners.

Isolierzelle solitary confinement.

Ist|aufkommen *(Steuer)* tax yield; **~ausgabe** actual expenditure; **~ausstoß** actual rate of output; **~bestand** real amount, actual stock, balance actually in hand; **~betrag** actual amount; **~bilanz** actual balance sheet; **~einnahmen** actual proceeds (receipts); **~etat** performance (program[me]) budget.

Istkosten actual costs;
angefallene ~ historic costs;
~abweichung deviation of actual costs; **~buchführung** historical accounting.

Ist|prämie premium paid; **~reserve** reserve maintained, actual reserve; **~stärke** *(Betrieb)* manpower, total (effective, actual) strength, *(mil.)* effective force, total strength, effective, quantum of forces; **~stärke herabsetzen** to cut down military manpower; **~stärkemeldung** *(mil.)* actual report; **~stunden** actual manhours; **~stundenverdienst** actual hourly earnings; **~wert** true value, *(Versicherung)* actual cash value; **~zeit** time taken, *(Zeitstudie)* clock (actual) hours, actual time.

J

Ja *(Funker)* affirmative;
mit einem ~ antworten to answer in the affirmative; **mit ~ stimmen** to vote in the affirmative.

Jacke jacket;
~ wie Hose six of one and half a dozen of the other;
jem. die ~ vollhauen to trim (dust) s. one's jacket.

Jackett jacket.

Jagd [game] hunting, hunt, shooting, *(fig.)* hunt, *(Radar)* hunting, *(Verfolgung)* chase;
~ nach Arbeitskräften pirating (raiding) of manpower; **~ nach dem Geld** chase for money; **~ nach Gelegenheitskäufen** *(Börse)* bargain-hunting; **~ nach dem Glück** pursuit of happiness; **~ nach dem Mörder** murder hunt; **~ nach dem Reichtum** scramble for wealth; **~ nach einem Verbrecher** hunt for a criminal;
~ ausüben to pursue game; **auf die ~ gehen** to go a-hunting, to gun; **auf politisch verdächtige Personen ~ machen** to witch-hunt persons said to be disloyal politically *(coll.)*; **~ pachten** to rent a shoot, to lease shooting rights *(US)*; **auf der ~ nach Antiquitäten sein** to be out for curios; **~ auf seinem Gelände verpachten** to sell the shooting on an estate;
~aufseher gamekeeper, game warden *(US)*; **~ausflug** hunting expedition; **~ausübung** pursuit of game; **~ausübungsberechtigter** holder of a hunting licence.

jagdbares Wild fair game.

Jagd|berechtigung shooting licence *(Br.)*, hunting permit *(US)*; **~beute** kill, killing; **~bezirk** hunting district; **~bomber** fighter-bomber; **~bomber zur Panzerbekämpfung** tank buster; **~dieb** poacher; **~duldung** frank-chase; **~erlaubnis** gaming licence; **~flieger** pursuit (fighter) pilot; **~fliegerschutz** fighter cover; **~flugzeug** fighter [aircraft], pursuit plane, chaser; **~frevel** poaching; **~frevler** poacher, game hog *(US)*; **~gebiet** hunt, hunting ground; **~gehege** game reserve; **~gelände** hunting ground; **~geschwader** fighter group *(Br.)* (wing, *US*); **~gesellschaft** shoot; **~gesellschaft zusammenstellen** to get up a shooting party; **~gesetze** game laws; **~gewehr** sporting gun; **~gründe** stalking grounds, *(fig.)* purlieu; **in die ewigen ~gründe eingehen** to be gathered to one's fathers; **in seine alten ~gründe zurückkehren** to return to one's old home; **~horn** hunting horn; **~hund** game dog, hunting dog, hound, hunter; **unabgeführter ~hund** *(fig.)* unlicked cub; **sich wie unabgeführte ~hunde aufführen** to come in like young Turks; **~hütte** hunting lodge (box), shooting box; **~pächter** game tenant, game farmer; **~recht** game laws, forest shooting rights, chase *(Br.)*; **~revier** shooting (hunting) ground, chase *(Br.)*, coverside, shoot; **~schein** shooting (game, gaming) licence, hunting permit *(US)*; **~schein lösen** to take out a certificate (shooting licence); **~schlößchen** hunting seat; **~schutz** *(mil.)* fighter umbrella; **~sperre** *(mil.)* fighter screen; **~staffel** *(mil.)* pursuit squadron; **~tasche** gamebag; **~wild** beast of the chase; **~zeit** game (open) season.

jagen to hunt, to chase;
j. ins Bockshorn ~ to bully s. o.; **Brücke in die Luft ~** to blow up a bridge; **aus dem Dorf ~** to hunt from the village; **Feind aus dem Lande ~** to drive the enemy out of the country; **j. in die Flucht ~** to put s. o. to flight; **nach dem Glück ~** to hunt after fortune; **j. aus dem Hause ~** to turn s. o. out of the house; **sich eine Kugel durch den Kopf ~** to blow one's brains out; **nach dem Reichtum ~** to scramble for wealth; **j. zum Teufel ~** to send s. o. packing; **Vermögen durch die Gurgel ~** to squander a fortune on drink.

Jäger game hunter;
~latein cock-and-bull story.

jäh sudden, unexpected, abrupt;
~er Abbruch diplomatischer Beziehungen abrupt rupture of diplomatic relations; **~es Erwachen** *(fig.)* rude awakening; **~ abfallende Schlucht** precipitous gorge; **~er Tod** sudden death.

jählings precipitate.

Jahr year;
auf ~ und Tag for a year and a day; **auf ~e hinaus** for years to come; **bei ~en** advanced; **das ganze ~ hindurch** all the year round, throughout the year; **für ein akademisches ~** sessional *(Br.)*; **im ~ der Eheschließung** in the year of marriage; **im laufenden ~** this year; **im Laufe der ~e** in the course of years; **in den besten ~en** in the prime of life; **in nicht so guten ~en** in off years; **pro ~** per annum; **vom nächsten ~ ab** as from next year; **abgelaufenes ~** last (past) year; **akademisches ~** college year, session *(Br.)*; **anrechnungsfähiges ~** *(Sozialversicherung)* year of coverage; **aufeinanderfolgende ~e** successive years; **beginnendes ~** incoming year; **bewegte ~e** wild (turbulent) years; **bürgerliches ~** civil year; **dahinschwindende ~e** passing years; **jedes darauffolgende ~** each succeeding year; **entscheidende ~e** key years; **finanziell erfolgreichstes ~** most financially rewarding year, banner year; **zu Ende gehendes ~** dying year; **gewinnschwaches ~** year of small profits; **kommende ~e** years ahead; **laufendes ~** current (present) year; **letztes ~** closing year; **normales ~** common year; **steuerpflichtiges ~** taxable (financial, fiscal, *US*) year; **turbulente ~e** wild years; **vorrangegangenes ~** past (old) year, previous (preceding) year; **die goldenen zwanziger ~e** the roaring twenties;
~e wirtschaftlichen Aufschwungs upswing years; **~ wirtschaftlicher Blüte** booming year; **entscheidende ~e der Entwicklung** formative years; **~e zwischen den Kriegen** the inter-war years; **~ in dem der Präsident gewählt wird** presidential year *(US)*; **~ wirtschaftlichen (konjunkturellen) Rückgangs** recession (economically depressing) year; **~ der Thronbesteigung** regent year *(Br.)*; **~ des Versicherungsbeginns** year of issue;
Mietvertrag über ein ~ abschließen to hire s. th. by the year; **seine ~e absitzen** *(Verurteilter)* to serve one's time; **zwanzig ~e Gefängnis bekommen** to get twenty years; **ein ~ brummen** to do a stretch *(Br., sl.)*; **innerhalb eines ~es fertigstellen** to complete within a year; **die besten ~e hinter sich haben** to be past one's prime; **viele ~e halten** to wear for years; **auf fünf ~e gewählt sein** to be elected for a term of five years; **1000 Pfund im ~ verdienen** to have a thousand a year *(Br.)*; **auf ein ~ vermietet werden** to be let by the year; **auf ~e zurückgeworfen werden** to be set back for a number of years; **hinter dem letzten ~ zurückbleiben** to be off from last year; **seit ~en zusammenarbeiten** to have been working together for years.

Jahrbuch yearbook, almanac, annual register *(Br.)*;
nautisches ~ nautical almanac; **statistisches ~** statistical abstract;
an einem ~ mitarbeiten to annualize.

jahrelang lasting for years;
~ daran gearbeitet haben to have worked on it for years on end *(fam.)*;
~e Erfahrung years of practice, many years of experience; **~e Freundschaft** friendship of long standing.

jähren, sich to have occurred (be) a year ago.

Jahresabonnement annual ticket, annual (yearly) subscription;
~ nehmen to take out a year's subscription.

Jahresabrechnung annual (yearly) settlement (account).

Jahresabschluß [annual] accounts, annual balance [sheet] *(Br.)*, annual financial statement, year-end closing *(US)*, annual settlement (statement, report, *Br.*);
festgestellter ~ established statement of accounts; **konsolidierter ~** consolidated balance sheet;
~ feststellen to establish statement of accounts; **~ machen** to make up one's accounts; **~ manipulieren** to mishandle the financial statement; **mit dem ~ beschäftigt sein** to be balancing the books of the year, to make up one's accounts; **~ vorlegen** to present the balance sheet;
~arbeiten balancing of the books; **mit den ~arbeiten beschäftigt sein** to be balancing the books for the year; **~bilanz** annual balance sheet, year-end closing *(US)*; **~buchung** year-end closing entry *(US)*; **~prüfung** public accounting, annual (general) audit; **~zahlungen** end-of-the-year payments; **~ziffern** year-end figures *(US)*.

Jahres|abschreibung annual depreciation; **~absetzungsbetrag** annual rate of depreciation; **~anfang** beginning (commencement) of a year; **ohne ~angabe** *(Bibliothekskatalog)* no date; **~anleihe** annuity; **~arbeitsverdienst** annual average earnings; **~ausgaben** annual expenses; **~ausgleich** year-end adjustment *(US)*, *(Steuerausgleich)* end-of-the-year equalization payments; **~ausweis** annual report (return, statement, *US*); **~auszug** [annual] accounts; **~bedarf** annual (yearly) requirements, annual (yearly) consumption; **~beitrag** yearly (annual) subscription; **~beitrag zum Pensionsfonds** yearly pension levy.

Jahresbericht financial (annual, *Br.*) report (return), annual statement *(US)*, statement of accounts *(US)*;
für die Angestellten zusammengestellter ~ employees' annual report;
~ nebst Bilanz sowie Gewinn- und Verlustrechnung statement of income and surplus *(US)*; **~ mit Vergleichsziffern aus dem Vorjahr** comparative statement.

Jahres|beschäftigung, durchgängige year-round (year-long) employment; ~**bestandsaufnahme** annual stocktaking (inventory); ~**betrag** annual amount; ~**bilanz** annual balance [sheet] *(Br.)*; ~**budget** annual budget; ~**defizit** annual deficit; ~**dividende** annual dividend; ~**durchschnitt** annual average; ~**durchschnittsverdienst** annual average earnings.

Jahreseinkommen annual income, yearly income (revenue), returns during the year, annuity, total net income;
garantiertes ~ guaranteed annual income;
~ **von 60.000 DM haben** to be in receipt of DM 60.000 a year.

Jahres|einkünfte yearly income, returns during the year; ~**einnahme** annual receipts (revenue, pension), yearly revenue, *(Bilanz)* net income for the year; ~**endbeanspruchung** year-end need for cash; ~**ende** end of the year, year end; ~**entschädigung** annual compensation; ~**erfolg** annual review; ~**ergebnis** results for the year; **bilanzgeprüftes** ~**ergebnis** audited result; ~**erhebung** annual survey, *(UNO)* annual review; ~**ertrag** annual compensation (receipts, income, proceeds, profit), yield for the year, *(Haus)* annual value *(Br.)*, purchase, *(Landwirtschaft)* yearly output; **voller** ~**ertrag** full annual value; ~**ertragswert** yearly value of land; **zehnfacher** ~**ertragswert** ten years' purchase; ~**erzeugung** annual output; ~**etat** annual budget; ~**fahrkarte** annual season ticket; ~**fehlbetrag** annual deficit; ~**feier** anniversary; ~**förderung** annual output; ~**frist** period of a year, one-year period; **binnen (innerhalb)** ~**frist** in the course (space) of (within) a year; **nach** ~**frist** after a year; ~**garantie** 12-month guarantee; **von der gefahrenen Kilometerzahl unabhängige** ~**garantie** *(Autoverkauf)* 12 months unlimited mileage warranty; ~**gebühr** annual fee, *(Patent)* renewal fee, annuity; **pauschale** ~**gebühr** combined annual fee; ~**gebühr erlassen** to remit an annuity; ~**gehalt** annual salary (pay); **ein** ~**gehalt** one year's pay; ~**gehalt beziehen** to be hired on a yearly basis; ~**geld** *(Bankwesen)* one-year money; ~**gewinn** yearly earnings, annual (yearly) profit, income (profit) for the year; ~**gratifikation** bonus; ~**hauptversammlung** annual general meeting *(Br.)*; ~**haushalt[splan]** annual budget; ~**höchststand** annual peak; ~**honorar** annual fee; ~**inventur** annual stocktaking *(Br.)* (inventory, *US*); ~**kapazität** annual capacity; ~**karte** annual ticket; ~**klasse** class; ~**kontingent** yearly quota, annual contingent; ~**kursus für Erwachsene** sessional course *(Br.)*; ~**lauf** course of the year; ~**lohn** annual wage; **garantierter** ~**lohn** annual wage guarantee *(Br.)*; ~**lohnsteuerausgleich** end-of-the-year equalization payments; ~**meldung über bezahlte Löhne und Gehälter** wages declaration.

Jahresmiete annual (a year's) rent, year's rental, yearly leasing;
übliche ~ rackrent *(Br.)*;
~ **im voraus bezahlen** to pay the rent annually in advance.

Jahres|mitgliedskarte annual membership card; ~**mitte** midyear; ~**modell** *(Auto)* year model; ~**nettoertrag** total net income; ~**niederschlag** annual precipitation; ~**pacht** yearly letting; **hypothetische** ~**pacht** hypothetical yearly tenancy; **auf** ~**pacht vergeben** to farm out for a year; ~**pensum** annual syllabus; ~**police** annual policy; ~**prämie** annual premium, *(Angestellter)* end-of-tax-year bonus, *(Versicherung)* annual rate; ~**produktion** annual production (output), yearly production (output); ~**prüfung** general (annual) audit; ~**rate** annual instal(l)ment, annuity; ~**rechnung** [annual] accounts, annual settlement; ~**reingewinn** clear annual value, net income for the year; ~**rendite** annual return.

Jahresrente annuity, appanage;
fällige ~ annuity due;
jem. eine ~ **aussetzen** to settle an annuity on s. o.; **jem. eine** ~ **von 4000 Pfund gewähren** to allow s. o. £ 4000 a year; ~ **von 400 £ haben** to have £ 400 in one's own right.

Jahresrevision annual (complete, general) audit.

Jahresschluß close of the year, year end;
~**bericht** year-end report *(US)*; ~**bilanz** postclosing balance sheet; ~**bilanz verschönern** to dress up the year-end books *(US)*; ~**buchung** year-end closing entry *(US)*; ~**dividende** year-end dividend *(US)*; ~**examen** end-of-year examination; ~**feier** *(Schule)* speech day *(Br.)*; **unverteilte** ~**gewinne** undivided profits at end of year; ~**vergütung** year-end compensation *(US)*; ~**ziffern** year-end figures *(US)*.

Jahres|soll budget provisions; ~**steigerungsrate** annual rate of increase; ~**stempel** datemark; ~**tag** anniversary; ~**tagung** annual convention (conference); **immer noch auf dem** ~**tiefstpunkt verharren** to be still bumping along near its low for the year; ~**überschuß** year's net earnings, net income for the year; ~**übersicht** annual review, *(Bilanz)* annual report (return, statement, *US*); ~**ultimo** end of the year, year end; ~**ultimobeanspruchung** end-of-year pressure; ~**umsatz** annual turnover (sales, volume), turnover per annum; ~**umsatz haben** to turn over per annum; ~**urlaub** annual leave; ~**urlaub von sechs Wochen beinhalten** to carry with it the right to six weeks' annual leave; ~**verbrauch** annual (yearly) consumption; ~**verdienst** annual average earnings; ~**verlust** annual loss; ~**versammlung** annual meeting (assembly); ~**versicherung** annual policy; ~**vertrag** contract good for one year; ~**verzeichnis** annual list; ~**voranschlag** annual estimates *(Br.)*; ~**wechsel** turn of the year; **mit den besten Wünschen zum** ~**wechsel** with the compliments of the season; ~**wende** turn of the year; ~**zahl** year; **ohne** ~**zahl** with no indication of the year; ~**zahlung** yearly (annual) payment, annuity.

Jahreszeit season;
von den ~**en abhängig** seasonal; **der** ~ **angemessen** *(Wetter)* seasonable;
beste ~ pride of the season; **tote** ~ off (dull, dead) season.

jahreszeitlich seasonal;
~ **bedingt sein** to be due to seasonal factors;
~**e Belebung** seasonal increase; ~**er Rückgang** seasonal recession; ~ **bedingte Schwankungen** seasonal variations (fluctuations).

Jahres|zeitraum period of one year; ~**zinsen** annual interest, annuity; ~**zinssatz** annual rate of interest; ~**zuschuß** yearly allowance, *(Staat)* annual grant; **regelmäßiger** ~**zuwachs** current annual increment.

Jahrgang *(Dienstalter)* age group (grade), *(mil.)* class, *(Schule)* class, *(Veröffentlichung)* annual set (publication), *(Wein)* vintage;
kostbarer alter ~ rare old vintage; **geburtenstarker** ~ age (population) bulge; **geburtenstarker** ~ **Jugendlicher** teenage population bulge;
~ **1981** class of 1981;
~ **aufrufen** to call up an age group; **fehlenden** ~ **einer Zeitschrift nachbestellen** to order the missing volume of a periodical.

Jahr|gänge, die jüngeren preteen; ~**geld** pension, allowance; **am Anfang des** ~**hunderts** in the early part of the century; **einmal im** ~**hundert** once in a blue moon; ~**hundertwende** turn of the century.

jährlich annual, by the year, yearly, per annum;
~ **wiederkehrend** annual; ~ **zahlbar** annually payable;
~ **400 Pfund einbringen** to rent £ 400 a year; **viermal** ~ **erscheinen** to be issued four times a year; ~ **zahlen** to pay by the year;
~**e Abrechnung** annual balance; ~ **fälliger Betrag** sum due annually; ~**e Dividende** annual dividend; ~**e Generalversammlung** annual general (yearly) meeting; ~**e Rente** annuity; ~ **erhobene Steuer** annual tax; ~**es Stipendium** annual stipend; ~ **erscheinende Veröffentlichung** annual; ~**e Wachstumsrate** year-to-year growth ratio; ~**e Zahlungen** yearly payments; ~ **erscheinende Zeitschrift** annual magazine.

Jahrmarkt country fair, mart, market;
~ **der Eitelkeiten** Vanity Fair.

Jahrmarkts|bude booth; ~**geschenk** fairing; ~**leute** fairground entertainers; ~**tag** fair day; ~**verkäufer** itinerant vendor.

Jahr|tausend millenium; ~**zehnt** decade.

Jähzorn violent fit of temper.

jähzornig hot-tempered;
leicht ~ **werden** to fly off the handle.

Jakob, billiger cheap Jack.

Jalousie window shade, [venetian] blind;
~ **herunterlassen** to lower the blinds.

Jammer wretchedness, misery, *(Wehklagen)* lamentation, wailing;
Bild des ~**s bieten** to be a picture of misery;
~**gestalt** wretched (poor) figure; ~**lappen** spineless creature, wet.

jämmerlich miserable, wretched;
~ **unterbezahlt** miserably underpaid;
sich ~ **aufführen** to behave abominably;
~**er Anblick** sorry sight; ~**e Arbeit** slipshod work, slopwork; ~**e Behausung** wretched house; ~**es Dasein führen** to eke out a scanty living; ~**e Figur abgeben** to cut a poor figure; ~**er Kerl** spineless creature; ~**e Unterkunft** miserable dwelling; **in** ~**en Verhältnissen leben** to live in misery and want (wretched poverty).

Jammern wail, lamentation, moaning and groaning;
ständiges ~ everlasting moaning.

jammern to wail, to lament, to sing sorrow, to laugh on the wrong side of one's mouth;
nach seiner Mutter ~ *(Kind)* to whimper for its mother.

jammernd wailing, moaning.
jammerschade great pity, deplorable, great shame.
Ja-Neinfrage dichotomous question.
Januarposition *(Bank)* January position.
Ja|sager stooge, yes man; ~**stimmen** yea, affirmative votes, *(Politik)* aye, pro; ~**stimme abgeben** to vote in the affirmative.
jäten to weed.
Jauche|faß manure tank; ~**grube** cesspool, cesspit; ~**wagen** manure cart.
jauchzende Menge exultant crowd.
Jawort approval, consent.
jeder für sich individually, every man for himself.
jedermann every person, old and young.
jenseitiges Ufer opposite bank.
Jenseits other (next) world;
im ~ gone to kingdom come;
das ~ the world beyond;
j. ins ~ **befördern** to expedite s. o. into kingdom come, to launch s. o. into eternity *(fam.)*.
jenseits von 40 sein to be on the wrong side of forty.
Jeton counter.
jetzige Preise current prices.
jetzt, gleich first off *(US sl.)*.
Jeunesse dorée gilded youth.
jeweilig in each (the individual) case, from time to time.
Jobber *(Börse)* [stock]jobber.
Joch, sein ~ **abschütteln** to throw (cast off) the yoke; **sich unter das** ~ **beugen** to come under the yoke.
Jokus fun, joke.
Jolle jolly.
Jongleur juggler.
Jonglieren jugglery.
jonglieren to juggle, *(arrangieren)* to fiddle it;
ungeschickt ~ to fumble; **mit Zahlen** ~ to juggle with figures.
Jota, kein not a jot (iota, whit);
kein ~ **nachgeben** not to swerve a jot, not to yield an iota of one's privileges.
Jour at-home day;
~ **abhalten** to give weekly receptions.
Journaille gutter (yellow) press.
Journal journal [book], daybook, shopbook *(US)*, diary, register, *(Zeitung)* newspaper;
amerikanisches (in Tabellenform geführtes) ~ ledger-type journal; **anerkanntes** ~ ledger journal; **mehrspaltiges** ~ multicolumn journal;
Hauptbuch und ~ ledger journal;
~ **für einfache Buchführung** simple journal; ~ **zur chronologischen Verbuchung gewährter Darlehn** loan register *(US)*;
~ **durchlaufen** to run through the journal; **ins** ~ **eintragen** to journalize, to enter in the daybook; ~ **führen** to maintain a journal, to journal, to journalize; **ins** ~ **übertragen** to post into the journal;
~**beleg** journal voucher; ~**blatt** journal form; ~**buchung** journal entry; ~**eintragung** journalization; **zusammengesetzte** ~**eintragung** compound journal entry.
journalisieren to journalize;
Kasse ~ to bring the cash through the journal.
Journalismus journalism, presswork.
Journalist journalist, newspaper man, news (gazette, space) writer, space bandit *(sl.)*, writer for the press, publicist, pressman *(sl.)*, *(eines Amtsblattes)* gazetteer;
akkreditierte ~**en** news corps; **bestinformierter** ~ best-posted journalist; **nach der Zeile bezahlter** ~ penny-a-liner, staff writer; **freier** ~ independent journalist, freelancer; **auf politischem Gebiet recherchierender** ~ investigative political journalist; **reißerisch schreibender** ~ sensational journalist; **unabhängiger** ~ freelance writer;
Beruf eines ~**en ausüben** to write for the press (papers); **als freier** ~ **tätig sein** to free-lance.
Journalisten|ausweis press credentials; ~**beruf** profession of journalism; ~**frühstück** press luncheon; **ausgewählte** ~**gruppe** press contingent; ~**kontingent** press pool; ~**liste** press list; ~**mappe** press kit; ~**reise** press junket; ~**stand** journalism, the press; ~**stil** journalese; ~**verband** National Union of Journalists *(Br.)*; ~**vereinigung** fraternity of the press, press association.
journalistisch journalistic;
sich ~ **betätigen,** ~ **tätig sein** to practise journalism, to write for the press (in the papers), to be a journalist;
~**e Betreuung** press coverage; ~**e Erfahrungen** journalistic experience; ~**e Fähigkeiten** journalistic skills.
Journal|nummer reference number; ~**posten** journal item.
jovial jovial, genial, jolly.
Jubel jubilation, exultation, rejoicing;
~ **und Trubel** merrymaking;
~**fest** jubilee; ~**geschrei** cheers, cheering; **alle** ~**jahre einmal** once in a blue moon *(fam.)*.
jubeln to jubilate, to rejoice, to be exultant, to exult;
vor Freude ~ to shout with joy; **zu früh** ~ to count one's chickens before they are hatched.
Jubilar jubilarian.
Jubiläum jubilee, anniversary;
fünfundzwanzigjähriges ~ silver jubilee;
~ **begehen** to observe (celebrate) an anniversary.
Jubiläums|ausgabe, ~**briefmarke** anniversary (jubilee) stamp; ~**geld** anniversary bonus; ~**marke** jubilee stamp; ~**schrift** anniversary publication.
juckt, es ~ **mir in den Fingern** I am itching to ...; **das** ~ **mich nicht** I don't care a fig; **das Geld** ~ **mir in der Tasche** the money is burning a hole in my pocket.
Judikatur judicature, case law.
Jugend youth, juveniles, young people;
in der frühesten ~ in the first blush of youth; **seit der frühesten** ~ since childhood; **seit meiner** ~ up from my youth; **von** ~ **an** from the cradle;
meine ~ my early life; **militärmüde** ~ draft-weary youth; **studentische** ~ university students; **stürmische** ~ wild youth; **vertane** ~ misspent youth;
sich in der ~ **austoben** to have one's fling; **in der** ~ **Dummheiten machen** to go wrong in early life; **in der Blüte der** ~ **sein** to be in the prime of one's youth; **über die erste** ~ **hinaus sein** to be past one's prime; **der** ~ **Weisheit lehren wollen** to put an old head on young shoulders;
~ **kennt keine Tugend** boys will be boys;
~**alkoholismus** under-age drinking; ~**alter** adolescence, teenage; ~**amt** youth welfare service; ~**amtsleiter** Children's officer *(Br.)*; ~**arbeit** juvenile labo(u)r, youth employment; ~**arbeitslosigkeit** youth unemployment; ~**arbeitsschutzgesetz** Young Persons Employment Act *(Br.)*; ~**arrest** *(Schule)* detention; ~**bewahranstalt** remand centre *(Br.)*, *(für Kinder unter 15 Jahren)* reception centre *(Br.)*; ~**buch** juvenile book; ~**bücherei** children's library; ~**erinnerungen** childhood memories.
jugendfrei suitable for children, *(Film)* carrying a U certificate; **nicht** ~ carrying an X certificate.
Jugendfreizeitheim youth club.
Jugendfürsorge welfare of children, child welfare;
~**gesetzgebung** child welfare legislation.
jugendgefährdende Schriften harmful publication.
Jugend|gefängnis remand home, reform school *(US)*, little school *(sl.)*; ~**gericht** juvenile *(US)* (children's) court; ~**gesundheitsdienst** child guidance center *(US)* (centre, *Br.*); ~**gruppe** youth group; ~**heim** youth center *(US)* (centre, *Br.*); **durch Spenden unterhaltenes** ~**heim** voluntary home; ~**helfer** youth worker; ~**herberge** youth hostel; ~**herbergsbenutzer** hosteler; ~**herbergsverband** youth-hostel association *(Br.)*; ~**irresein** precocious dementia; ~**jahre** puppyhood; ~**klub** youth center *(US)* (centre, *Br.*); ~**kriminalität** juvenile (youth) delinquency, teenage crime; ~**lager** youth camp.
jugendlich youthful, adolescent, fresh, blooming;
sich einen ~**en Kraftakt leisten** to be doing one's youth thing; ~**er Strafgefangener** juvenile prisoner; **als** ~**er Straftäter eingestuft werden** to be tabelled as juvenile delinquent; ~**er Täter** *(Verbrecher)* juvenile delinquent (offender), young offender; ~**e Unreife** juvenility.
Jugendlicher juvenile, juvenile adult *(Br.)*, youth, teenager, young person, adolescent, kid *(US)*.
Jugend|literatur juvenile literature; ~**meisterschaft** junior championship; ~**organisation** youth organization, junior branch; ~**pflege** youth welfare service, youth activities; ~**pfleger** child welfare worker, youth officer; ~**psychologe** guidance counsellor; ~**roman** juvenile fiction; ~**schutz** child welfare; ~**schutzgesetz** Children and Young Persons Act *(Br.)*; ~**strafanstalt** remand centre (house, *Br.*), training institute *(US)*, technical school *(US)*, vocational institution *(US)*, junior detention center *(Br.)*; ~**strafgericht** young offender court; ~**straftat** juvenile offence; ~**täterschaft** juvenile delinquency; ~**torheiten** youthful indiscretions; ~**treffen** youth meeting; ~**verbot** adults only; ~**verfehlung** juvenile offence; ~**wahnsinn** adolescent insanity; ~**wohlfahrt** child welfare; ~**wohnheim** hostel; ~**zeit** young (youthful) days; **in seiner** ~**zeit** in the first blush of one's youth; ~**zeitung** youth paper; ~**zentrum** youth center *(US)* (centre, *Br.*).

jung young, fresh, inexperienced, juvenile;
für seine Jahre ~ aussehen to wear one's years well; **nicht mehr ganz ~ sein** to be no chicken;
~e Aktie new share (stock, *US*); **~es Gemüse** *(fig.)* small fry; **~es Glück** new-found happiness; **vielversprechender ~er Mann** youth of great promise, promising youth; **~es Unternehmen** infant company; **~er Wein** new wine.
Jung|akademiker postgraduate; **~arbeiter** junior employee, young worker; **~brunnen** fountain of youth.
Junge boy, lad, youngster, *(eines Tieres)* newly born animal, puppy, young;
dummer ~ stupid fellow; **grüner ~** greenhorn; **schlauer ~** sly fox; **schwerer ~** thug, tough guy *(US)*.
Jungenstreich prank.
Jünger disciple, adherent, follower.
jünger junior, *(Recht)* puisne;
~er Teilhaber junior partner.
Jungfer, alte old-womanish maid, old spinster, tabby.
Jungfern|fahrt maiden trip (voyage), virgin cruise, inaugural voyage (run); **~flug** inaugural flight; **~rede** maiden speech; **~schrift** *(drucktechn.)* brevier.
Jungfrau virgin;
unberührte ~ *(jur.)* innocent woman, virgo intacta.
jungfräulich virginal, maidenlike;
~er Boden virgin soil.
Jungfräulichkeit maidenhood, maidenhead.
Junggeselle bachelor, single man;
eingefleischter ~ old (confirmed) bachelor.
Junggesellen|bude bachelor flat, digs *(coll.)*; **~stand** bachelorhood, bachelordom; **~steuer** bachelor's tax; **~wirtschaft** bachelor's ménage; **~wohnung** bachelor apartment (flat), digs *(coll.)*.
Jung|gesellin unmarried woman, spinster, maid; **~lehrer** assistant teacher.
Jüngling, eingebildeter conceited pup.
Jünglingsalter boyhood, adolescence.
jüngste Vergangenheit recent past.
Jung|tier young animal; **~türke** *(pol.)* young Turk; **~volk** small fry.
Junior junior;
~chef, ~partner junior director (partner), *(Anwaltskanzlei)* junior barrister.
Juniorengruppe junior group.
Junker squire.
Junkertum landed aristocracy, squirarchy.
Junktim package deal.
Junta junta;
militärische ~ military junta;
~mitglied junta member.
Jura|studieren to follow (smatter, read, study, go in for) the law, to read for the bar, to eat one's dinner (terms) *(Br.)*;
~student law student, lexer *(sl.)*; **~studium** law studies; **~studium beenden** to keep term *(Br.)*.
jure, de by right.
Juris|diktion jurisdiction; **~prudenz** jurisprudence.
Jurist legal practitioner (expert), jurist, legist, *(Anwalt)* lawyer;
in der Sprache des ~en in legal parlance;
~ im Angestelltenverhältnis employed lawyer;
j. zum ~en ausersehen to design s. o. for the bar; **sich als guter ~ erweisen** to approve o. s. as a good lawyer; **~ sein** to be in the law, to profess (follow the) law; **~ werden** to follow the law, to enter (go into) the legal profession; **zum ~en erzogen werden** to be brought up for the bar.
Juristen|ausbildung legal training; **~ausdruck** legal (forensic) term; **~beruf** legal profession, long robe; **~deutsch** lawyer's jargon, legalism; **im ~deutsch aufgesetzt** artificially drawn; **~jargon** legalese, legalism; **~laufbahn einschlagen** to go into the legal profession, to follow the law; **~sprache** legal language, legalism; **~stand** legal profession; **~vereinigung** law association.
juristisch legal, juridical, for legal purports, jural;
~ ausgebildet learned in the law; **~ ausgedrückt** in legal parlance; **~ einwandfrei** watertight;
sich ~ beraten lassen to take legal advice; **~ vorgebildet sein** to have had legal training;
~e Abteilung legal department; **~e Angelegenheit** judicial business; **~e Aufgabe** legal function; **~e Ausbildung** legal (law) training (qualification); **~er Ausdruck** law (legal) term (expression); **~er Beistand** *(Berater)* legal adviser; **~e Beziehungen** jural relations; **~er Fachausdruck** forensic (legal) term; **~e Fakultät** faculty of law, school of law *(US)*, law school *(US)*; **~e Formalität** legal formality; **~e Kenntnisse** knowledge of the law; **~e Laufbahn** legal career; **~e Laufbahn einschlagen** to go in for law, to enter the legal profession; **~er Mitarbeiter** legal assistant; **~e Person** artificial (legal, juristic, *US*) person, legal personality, *(Körperschaft)* body corporate, corporation; **~e Person gründen** to incorporate; **~es Problem** moot question; **~er Redakteur** legal editor; **~er Sachverständiger** legal expert; **~e Streitfrage** issue of a dispute; **~es Studium** law studies; **~er Verstand** legal mind; **~e Zeitschrift** law review.
Jury selection committee, *(Strafrecht)* jury, country.
justieren *(drucktechn.)* to adjust, to justify, to gauge.
Justierung justification, adjustment.
justifizieren to justify, to check.
Justitiar legal adviser, corporation counsel *(US)*, *(Aktienbank)* public officer *(Br.)*;
~ des Finanzministeriums Treasury Solicitor *(Br.)*.
Justiz judicature, justice;
käufliche ~ venal justice;
der ~ überstellen to commit for trial;
~amtmann certifying officer, keeper of the records *(US)*, registrar, clerk; **~apparat** judicial authorities; **~beamter** officer of the law (justice), legal (law) officer, judicial officer, court official; **~behörde** judicial authorities; **~beitreibung** collection of legal notes; **~fehler** clerical misprision; **~gebäude** courthouse, law court; **~hoheit** judicial power; **~inspektor** clerk of the court; **~irrtum** lapse (miscarriage) of justice, judicial error; **~minister** Minister of Justice, Attorney General *(US)*; **stellvertretender ~minister** Solicitor General *(US)*; **~ministerium** Justice Department *(US)*, Department *(US)* (Ministry) of Justice; **~mord** judicial murder; **~palast** palace of justice, Hall of Justice, The Law Courts *(Br.)*; **~rat** [etwa] inner barrister *(Br.)*, King's (Queen's) counsel *(Br.)*; **~reform** judicial reform; **~sekretär** clerk of court; **~verwaltung** judicial department, administration of justice; **~verwaltungsgesetz** Administration of Justice Act *(Br.)*; **~wachtmeister** court guard, tipstaff; **~wesen** judicial affairs (branch), judiciary.
Juwel *(fig.)* gem, jewel.
Juwelen jewelry, jewels, jewellery, pennyweight *(sl.)*;
mit ~ dicht besetzt thickset with jewels;
unechte ~ imitation jewellery;
~ in Gold fassen to mount jewels in gold.
juwelenbesetzt studded with jewels.
Juwelen|transportpolice jewel(l)er's block policy; **~versicherung** jewelry insurance.
Juwelier jeweller;
~arbeit jewellery; **~geschäft, ~laden** jeweller, jewelry store *(US)*, jewel(le)ry shop.
Jux lark, prank.
Juxtebuch voucher book.

K

Kabarett[vorführung] cabaret (floor, *US*) show, satirical revue, vaudeville performance (show) *(US)*;
~besitzer cabaretier; **~nummer** revue number.

Kabel cable, line, wire *(el.)* lead, *(Telegramm)* cable[gram];
armiertes ~ armo(u)red cable; **mehradriges ~** multicore cable; **transatlantisches ~** transatlantic (submarine) cable; **unterirdisches ~** underground cable; **unterseeisches ~** submarine cable;
~ auslegen to lay a cable; **~ losmachen** to detach a cable; **~ in Betrieb nehmen** to open a cable; **~ schicken** to [send a] cable; **~ verlegen** to lay out a cable; **~ verwickeln** to foul a cable;
~adresse cable address; **~angebot** cabled offer; **~anschluß** cable connection (connexion); **~antwort** cable reply; **~anweisung** cable money order; **~auftrag** cable order; **~auszahlung** telegraphic (cable) transfer; **~auszahlungssätze** cable rates; **~bericht** cable report; **~brief** cabled letter; **~dampfer** cable steamer; **~depesche** cable[gram]; **~diskontsatz** cable rate; **~endverschluß** pothead; **~fernsehbetrieb** cable television operations; **~fernsehen** cable television; **~fernsehteilnehmer** cable subscriber; **~kurs** cable rate; **~legung** laying a cable, cable-laying.

kabeln to [send a] cable.

Kabel|nachricht cable information, cable message; **~netz** cable network; **~notierung, ~preis** cabled quotation; **~satz** cable rate; **~satz für Termingeschäfte** futures cable rate *(US)*; **~schacht** manhole; **~spesen** cable expenses; **~trommel** drum wheel; **~überweisung** cable (telegraphic) transfer, cable order; **~verbindung** cable connection; **auf dem ~wege** by cable.

Kabine cabin, *(Abteil)* compartment, stateroom, *(Aufzug)* cage, *(Seilbahn)* car cabin, *(tel.)* booth, call box *(Br.)*;
schalldichte ~ blimp;
~ erster Klasse first-class cabin;
in ~n einteilen to cabin off.

Kabinen|dampfer cabin cruiser; **~dienst** *(Flugzeug)* catering service; **~gepäck** cabin baggage; **~klasse** cabin class; **~koffer** cabin (steamer) trunk; **~passagier** cabin passenger; **~reservierung** reservation of berths; **~roller** cycle (bubble) car, scooter.

Kabinett cabinet, closet, *(pol.)* cabinet, government;
nur aus Zivilisten bestehendes ~ all-civilian cabinet; **Geheimes ~** Privy Chamber;
aus dem ~ ausscheiden to resign from the cabinet; **~ bilden** to form a cabinet (government); **Sitz im ~ haben** to have a seat in the cabinet; **ins ~ nehmen** to take into Downing Street *(Br.)*; **~ stürzen** to overthrow the government; **~ umbilden** to reshuffle (to make changes, revamp) the cabinet (government);
~format *(Foto)* cabinet size; **~schrank** cabinet.

Kabinetts|amt cabinet office; **~ausschuß** cabinet committee; **~beschluß** cabinet decision, command paper *(Br.)*; **~bildung** cabinetmaking, forming a government; **~eintritt** entrance upon a ministerial office; **~empfehlung** cabinet advice; **~frage** cabinet issue; **~justiz** arbitrary government; **~kollege** cabinet colleague; **~krise** cabinet (government) crisis; **~liste** list of cabinet members; **~liste zusammenstellen** to pick a cabinet; **~maßnahmen** cabinet action; **~mehrheit** majority of the cabinet; **~minister, ~mitglied** minister, Secretary of State *(Br.)*, Cabinet Minister *(Br.)*, cabinet officer *(US)*, member of the cabinet (government), cabinet member (minister, *Br.*), officer *(US)*, counsellor *(Br.)*, public man; **als ~mitglied vorgesehen sein** to be slated for the cabinet; **~order** order in council *(Br.)*; **~regierung** cabinet government (rule); **~siegel** privy seal; **~sitz** seat (post, position) in the cabinet, cabinet job; **~sitzung** cabinet meeting (council), meeting of the cabinet, ministerial meeting; **gezielte Indiskretionen über ~sitzungen veranlassen** to leak cabinet proceedings; **~stück** *(fig.)* clever move; **~system** cabinet system of government; **~umbildung** shakeup of the cabinet, cabinet reshuffle, change in the cabinet, general posting in the cabinet; **~verfügung** order in council *(Br.)*; **~zustimmung** cabinet approval.

Kabriolet cabriolet, convertible *(US)*, drophead coupé.

Kachel tile;
~n legen to tile.

Kacheln tiling.

Kachelverkleidung tile wainscot.

Kadaver corps, dead body, cadaver, carcass;
~gehorsam servile obedience.

Kader cadre, *(Betrieb)* key personnel, skeleton staff;
~ einer Partei nucleus of a party;
~truppen einer Partei stalwarts of a party.

Kadett cadet.

Kadetten|anstalt cadet school, military school *(US)*; **~messe** gun room *(Br.)*; **~schiff** cadet ship.

Kadi, zum ~ gehen to go to law.

kaduzieren *(Aktien)* to declare forfeited, to forfeit.

Kaduzierung von Aktien cancellation (forfeiture) of unissued shares (stocks, *US*).

Kaffee, dünner washy coffee; **sehr starker ~** varnish remover *(sl.)*;
~ verkehrt milk coffee;
das ist ja kalter ~ that's old hat;
~anbau coffee growing; **~automat** coffee vending machine; **~börse** coffee exchange; **in der ~branche sein** to be in the coffee trade; **~bude** coffee-stall; **~budenbesitzer** coffee vendor; **~filter** coffee filter; **~kanne** coffee pot; **~kränzchen** hen party *(coll.)*; **~maschine** coffee machine; **~mühle** coffee mill; **~pause** tea (coffee, *US*) break.

Kaffer *(fig.)* blockhead, country bumpkin.

kahl bald, *(Landschaft)* bare, barren, bleak;
~pfänden to levy on the entire property.

Kahl|rasur close shave; **~schlag** deforestation; **~schlag vornehmen** to deforest.

Kahn boat, barge, lighter;
mit jem. ~ fahren *(fig.)* to lead s. o. up the garden path; **in den ~ gehen** to turn in, to go between the sheets; **im ~ sitzen** to be in clink (jug, *US*);
~fahrer boatman; **~fahrt** boat trip.

Kai dock, pier, quay, wharf;
ab ~ ex wharf (quay), ex dock *(US)*; **ab ~ unverzollt** ex quay duties unpaid; **ab ~ verzollt** ex quay duty paid; **frei ~** free on quay; **längsseits ~** alongside the quay, berthed;
auf dem ~ abstellen to wharf; **am ~ festmachen** to berth, to wharf, to dock; **Schiff am ~ festmachen** to lay a ship alongside the quay; **am ~ löschen** to discharge at the quay; **mit einem ~ versehen** to [furnish with a] wharf;
~ablieferungsbescheinigung dock receipt, wharfinger's certificate *(Br.)*; **~anlagen für den Warenumschlag** waterfront facilities; **~anlieferung** delivery at quay; **~annahmeschein** dock (wharfinger's) receipt (certificate, *Br.*); **~anschluß** dock siding; **~arbeiter** stevedore, longshoreman *(US)*; **~aufseher** wharfmaster, wharfinger; **~benutzung** *(Ladegelegenheit)* wharfage; **~besitzer** wharfinger; **~empfangsbestätigung, ~empfangsschein** dock (quay) receipt, wharfinger's receipt (certificate, *Br.*); **~gebühren** wharfage, wharf duty (dues), berthage, pierage, quayage, quay dues; **~geld** pierage, quayage; **~konnossement** wharf bill of lading; **~lagergeld** quay rent; **~lagerschein** wharfinger's warrant *(Br.)*; **an der ~mauer festmachen** to make fast at the quay side; **~meister** wharfmaster, wharfinger; **~quittung** dock receipt, wharfinger's certificate *(Br.)*.

Kaiser emperor;
~reich empire; **~wetter** queen's weather.

Kai|umschlag quay transhipment; **~versicherung** quay insurance.

Kajüte cabin, berth;
erste ~ saloon; **große ~** state room; **vordere ~** fore cabin *(Br.)*;
~ erster Klasse first-class cabin.

Kajüten|bett berth; **~passagier** cabin (saloon) passenger.

Kajüts|fahrgast cabin-class passenger; **~junge** cabin (mess) boy; **~klasse** cabin class; **~treppe** companion way.

Kalamitäten woes;
in ~ geraten to get into trouble (a mess, a fix).

kalandern to roll, to calender.

Kalauer pun, corney joke *(US)*, Joe Miller.

Kalender calendar, almanac;
hundertjähriger (immerwährender) ~ perpetual calendar;
~ abreißen to tear off the calendar; **~ angleichen** to adjust the calendar; **rot im ~ anstreichen** to chalk up, to mark as a red-letter day; **in einem ~ eintragen** to calendar;
~angleichung adjustment of the calendar; **~block** date (calendar, *US*) block; **~jahr** calendar (civil, legal) year; **~monat** calendar month; **~tag** calendar day (date), civil day, natural (entire) day; **~vierteljahr** calendar quarter.

Kalfaktor *(Gefängnis)* trustee.

Kali potash.

Kaliber calibre *(Br.)*, caliber *(US)*, gauge *(mil.)*;
vom gleichen ~ cast in the same mo(u)ld, tarred with the same brush;
schweres ~ **auffahren** to bring up one's heavy artillery; **alle vom gleichen** ~ **sein** to be all of a piece, to be all tarred with the same brush.
Kalibergwerk potassium mine.
Kalk lime;
~**anstrich** whitewash; ~**steinbruch** limestone quarry.
Kalkül calculus;
ins ~ **ziehen** to include in one's calculations.
Kalkulation [preliminary] calculation, computation, *(Kostenrechnung)* cost accounting (keeping), costing;
falsche ~ miscalculation, wrong calculation; **knappe** ~ close (exact) calculation; **marktwirtschaftliche** ~ calculation in conformity with the market; **pauschale** ~ blanket costing; **überschlägliche** ~**en** back-of-envelope calculations; **übliche** ~ standard calculation; **vorherige** ~ previous (preliminary) calculation; **vorsichtige** ~ conservative calculation;
~ **zu Marktpreisen** current cost accounting;
~ **aufstellen (vornehmen)** to make a calculation, to work out the figures; **jds.** ~**en durcheinanderbringen** to throw out s. o. in his calculations; **j. in seine** ~**en entsprechend einbeziehen** to take s. o. sufficiently into account.
Kalkulationsabteilung costing (cost accounting) department, cost-finding division.
Kalkulationsaufschlag markup, markon *(US)*;
~ **auf den Einstandspreis** markup on cost; ~ **auf das Inventar** inventory markup; ~ **auf den Verkaufspreis** markup on retail.
Kalkulations|aufschlagssatz markup percentage; ~**basis** calculation basis; ~**buch** cost ledger, cost book; ~**büro** estimating office, costing (cost accounting) department; ~**faktor** calculation item; ~**fehler** calculating error, miscalculation, mistake in (wrong) calculation; ~**grundlage** calculation basis; **jds.** ~**grundlage über den Haufen werfen** to throw out (upset) s. one's calculation; ~**methode** method of calculation, pricing practices; ~**norm** cost standard; ~**preis** calculated price; ~**prüfung** budgetary service; ~**quote** markup percentage; ~**stundensatz** calculated hourly rate; ~**system** pricing (delivered price, *US*) system, cost accounting system; ~**tabelle** pricing schedule; ~**unterlagen** cost-accounting records; ~**verfahren** pricing practices; ~**zuschlag** markup, markon *(US)*; **endgültiger** ~**zuschlag** maintained markup.
Kalkulator controller, calculator, *(Kostenrechnung)* cost keeper, cost accountant.
kalkulatorisch calculatory, calculable;
~**e Kosten** imputations.
kalkulieren to calculate, to compute, to reckon, to estimate;
über den Daumen ~ to operate a crude rule of thumb; **falsch** ~ to miscalculate, to miscount; **genaustens** ~ to cut it fine; **knapp** ~ to calculate closely; **Kosten** ~ to cost-account; **Kostenaufwand eines Unternehmens** ~ to reckon the cost of an undertaking; **Neubaukosten eines Hauses** ~ to estimate the costs of a new house; **Preis sehr vorsichtig** ~ to establish a price at a low level;
gut ~ **können** to be quick at accounts.
kalkuliert, aufs äußerste cut-rate; **richtig** ~ budget-priced; **schärfstens** ~ completely priced;
falsch ~ **haben** to be out in one's calculation; **scharf** ~ **sein** to be cut very fine;
~**e Kosten** imputed costs; **scharf** ~**er Preis** close price.
Kalorien|gehalt caloric content; ~**menge** caloric intake.
kalorienreich calorie-rich.
Kalorienwert calorific value.
kalt cold, *(fig.)* iron, frozen *(US)*, frigid;
~ **wie eine Hundeschnauze** cool as a cucumber;
j. ganz ~ **lassen** to be nothing to s. o.; **jem.** ~ **über den Rücken laufen** to give s. o. the shivers; ~ **gegen j. sein** to treat s. o. distantly, to be cold with s. o.; **weder** ~ **noch warm sein** not to care a rap; **Heizung auf** ~ **stellen** to turn the heating off;
~**e Angst** blue funk; ~**es Büfett** stand-up buffet; ~**e Dusche** *(fig.)* wet blanket; ~**e Dusche verabfolgen** to bring down to earth, to pour cold water on s. one's enthusiasm, to cold-pick *(sl.)*; ~**er Empfang** chilly (cold) reception; ~**e Füße bekommen** *(fig.)* to have cold feet; ~**er Krieg** cold war; ~**er Krieger** *(pol.)* cold warrior; ~**e Miete** rent exclusive of heating; **jem. die** ~**e Schulter zeigen** to give s. o. the cold shoulder; ~**e Verachtung** cold disdain.
kaltblütig cold-blooded, in cold blood;
in der Gefahr ~ **bleiben** to remain calm in the face of danger; **auf** ~**e Weise** in a cold-blooded way.
Kaltblütigkeit coldbloodedness;
seine ~ **wiedergewinnen** to smooth one's crumpled feathers.
Kälte coldness, *(fig.)* coolness, chilliness;
vor ~ **erstarrt** numb with cold;
beißende ~ hard (sharp) frost; **plötzlich eintretende** ~ sudden onset of cold weather; **schneidende** ~ piercing (pinching) cold;
j. mit ~ **behandeln** to be cool with s. o., to treat s. o. distantly;
vor ~ **zittern** to shiver with cold;
~**anlage** cold storage (refrigeration) plant.
kältebeständig nonfreezing, cold-proof.
Kälte|einbruch invasion of cold air, *(plötzlicher)* cold snap; ~**erzeugung** refrigeration; ~**gefühl** chill; ~**grad** degree of frost; ~**industrie** refrigeration industry; ~**ingenieur** refrigeration engineer; ~**maschine** refrigerator; ~**periode** cold snap, spell of cold weather; ~**rückfall** return of the cold weather; ~**schutz** protection against the cold; ~**schutzmittel** antifreeze; ~**technik** refrigeration engineering; ~**techniker** refrigeration engineer; ~**welle** cold wave.
kaltgestellt high and dry, sidetracked, on the shelf;
~ **werden** to be left out in the cold.
kaltherzig sein to have a cold heart.
kaltlächeld without scruple, unscrupulously;
~ **tun** to be as cold as marble.
Kaltlagerung cold storage.
kaltlassen, j. to leave s. o. cold.
Kaltluft, polare polar air;
~**front** cold front; ~**keil** wedge of cold air.
kalt|machen to do s. o. in, to put out of the way, to liquidate, to bump off *(sl.)*; ~**rechnend** hard-nosed; ~**schnäuzig** cheeky *(coll.)*.
Kaltstart cold start.
kaltstellen, j. to freeze s. o. out, to shunt (sidetrack) s. o., to dish (shelve, *sl.*); **j.durch Beförderung** ~ to kick s. o. upstairs.
Kamel camel, *(Dummkopf)* clot, fool;
~**karawane** camel train.
Kamellen, olle *(fam.)* past history, chestnut *(coll.)*.
Kamera camera;
kümmerliche ~ pop bottle *(sl.)*; **versteckte** ~ hidden camera;
~ **laden** to thread a film;
~**assistent** camera assistant; ~**auszug** extension.
Kamerad comrade, pal, chum, peer, mate, companion, fellow.
Kameradenschinder bully.
Kameradschaft good fellowship, *(Bergbau)* pair.
kameradschaftlich companionable, comradely.
Kameradschafts|abend companionship; ~**ehe** companionate marriage; ~**geist** team spirit.
Kamera|einstellung camera shot; ~**führung** camera work; **unerfahrener** ~**gehilfe** punk *(sl.)*; ~**mann** cameraman, movie man, cinematographer; **fahrbarer** ~**tisch,** ~**wagen** camera truck, dolly *(sl.)*.
Kamin chimney, flue;
offener ~ fireplace;
etw. in den ~ **schreiben** to write off as a total loss;
~**aufsatz** chimney pot; ~**brett** fireboard; ~**geschichten** fireside tales; ~**gitter** fireguard; ~**kehrer** chimney sweep; ~**vorsatz** fender.
Kamm, über einen ~ **scheren** to lump with; **alles über einen** ~ **scheren** to measure everything with the same yardstick; **jem. den** ~ **stutzen** to trim s. one's wings;
bei ihnen liegt der ~ **neben der Butter** their room is a regular pigsty; **ihm schwillt der** ~ he has got a swollen head.
Kammer closet, room, *(Behörde)* chamber, board, *(Gericht)* court of law, *(mar.)* cabin, cupboard, closet, *(parl.)* house, *(Senat)* division;
erste ~ lower house; **zweite** ~ upper house, revisionary (second) chamber;
~ **für Handelssachen** [etwa] commercial court *(Br.)*;
vor die ~ **kommen** to come up before the court;
~**auflösung** dissolution of Parliament; ~**diener** valet, manservant.
Kämmerei budget office.
Kämmerer treasurer, chief financial officer *(Br.)*.
Kammer|gericht final court of appeal *(US)*; ~**herr** chamberlain, gentleman in waiting; ~**jäger** vermin destroyer, exterminator; ~**konzert** chamber concert.
Kämmerlein closet;
im stillen ~ **trauern** to suffer one's grief in private.
Kammer|mitglied member of chambers; ~**orchester** chamber orchestra; ~**schleuse** *(mar.)* tidelock; ~**sitzung** full court (session), bank; ~**spiele** little theatre *(Br.)*; ~**steward** cabin boy; ~**vorsitzender** presiding judge; ~**zofe** lady's maid.

Kammgarnanzug worsted suit.
Kampagne campaign;
~ **zur Mitgliederwerbung** membership drive.
Kampf struggle, warfare, *(mil.)* fight, battle, action;
erbitterter ~ mortal struggle; **mit allen Mitteln geführter** ~ tooth-and-nail battle; **harter** ~ uphill struggle; **politischer** ~ political struggle; **regelrechter** ~ stand-up fight; **ständiger** ~ running battle; **wechselvoller** ~ dingdong struggle;
~ **um den Absatz** fight for the market; ~ **gegen die Armut** struggle with poverty; ~ **ums Dasein** struggle for existence; ~ **bis zur Entscheidung** fight to the finish; ~ **um den Geldbeutel** pocketbook battle; ~ **zwischen zwei Kandidaten** straight fight; ~ **auf Leben und Tod** life-and-death struggle; ~ **um die Macht** struggle for power; ~ **Mann gegen Mann** hand-to-hand fight; ~ **mit geistigen Waffen** battle of brains;
jem. den ~ **ansagen** to declare war on s. o.; **zum** ~ **antreten** to climb down into the arena; ~ **aufnehmen** to join battle, to enter the contest; **in den** ~ **eingreifen** to take up the cudgels; **im** ~ **fallen** to be killed in action; **hoffnungslosen** ~ **führen** to fight a loosing battle; ~ **gegen Windmühlen führen** to tilt at windmills; **sich einen erbarmungslosen** ~ **liefern** to fight with the gloves off; **mit dem Feind im** ~ **stehen** to be at grips with the enemy; **sich zum** ~ **stellen** *(mil.)* to accept combat; **im** ~ **umkommen** to fall; **sich für einen langen** ~ **vorbereiten** to bunker down for a long battle; **Regiment in den** ~ **werfen** to throw a regiment into action;
~**abbruch** ceasefire; ~**abstimmung** crucial vote; ~**aktion** militant action; ~**ansage** challenge; ~**auftrag** *(mil.)* task, mission; ~**bahn** arena; **in die** ~**bahn treten** to enter the arena.
kampf|begierig eager to fight; ~**bereit** ready to fight, combatant.
Kampfbomber fighter-bomber.
Kämpfe fighting.
Kampf|einheit combat branch, tactical unit; ~**einheiten** combat job.
kämpfen to fight, to struggle, to contend;
wie Aasgeier um die Nachfolge ~ to fight like vultures over the succession; **bis zum letzten Blutstropfen** ~ to die in the last ditch; **bis zum bitteren Ende** ~ to fight out the battle to the end, to fight to the finish; **für eine Sache** ~ to fight for one's cause; **mit unvorhergesehenen Schwierigkeiten** ~ to wrestle with unforeseen difficulties; **mit den Tränen** ~ to fight one's emotion; **gegen Wind und Wellen** ~ to battle against wind and wave.
kämpfende Truppen front-line troops.
Kampferfahrung combat practice.
kampferprobte Truppen veteran troops.
Kampfesmut martial spirit.
kampffähig *(Panzer)* serviceable, effective.
Kampf|fahrzeug fighting vehicle, combat car *(US)*; ~**feld** battlefield, combat zone, *(pol.)* ring; ~**flieger** bomber (fighter) pilot; ~**flugzeug** fighter-bomber, strike aircraft, dive bomber, warplane, pea-shooter *(sl.)*; ~**fonds** *(Gewerkschaft)* strike fund; ~**fondszuschuß** fund contribution; ~**front** firing line, front line; ~**führung** conduct of operations, warfare; **psychologische** ~**führung** psychological warfare; ~**gas** poison gas; ~**gebiet** combat area (zone).
Kampfgeist, nachlassender ~ **des Feindes** failing morale of the enemy;
j. seines ganzen ~**es berauben** to take all the fight out of s. o.; **noch über genügend** ~ **verfügen** to have plenty of fight left; **wenig** ~ **zeigen** to put up little fight.
Kampf|geschwader tactical wing (group, *US*); **mitten im** ~**getümmel** in the thick of the fight; ~**gliederung** order of battle; ~**gruppe** combat group (team), task force; ~**gruppenstab** combat command; **sich stets wie ein** ~**hahn aufführen** to live like a fighting cock.
Kampfhandlung action, combat, commitment, battle, operation, engagement, show *(sl.)*;
~**en** active hostilities;
betriebliche ~ industrial action; **streikähnliche rechtswidrige** ~**en** irregular industrial action short of a strike *(Br.)*;
~**en einstellen** to break off action, to cease fire.
Kampf|hubschrauber combat (attack) helicopter; ~**kraft** fighting strength, *(Schiff)* fighting efficiency (qualities); ~**kraft einer Flotte** fighting efficiency of a fleet; **keinerlei** ~**kraft mehr haben** to shrink to a nullity; ~**linie** line of battle, fighting line; **vorderste** ~**linie** front.
kampf|los ergeben, sich to surrender without a shot being fired; ~**lüstern sein** to show fight.
Kampf|marke fighting brand; **gewerkschaftliche** ~**maßnahmen** union combative measures; ~**mittel** weapon; ~**moral eines Heeres** moral of an army; ~**müdigkeit** operational fatigue; ~**offerte** competitive offer; ~**panzer** battle tank; ~**pause** lull in fighting; ~**platz** arena, cockpit; ~**platz betreten** to enter the arena; ~**preis** competitive (cut-rate, cutthroat, price-war) price; **gezielte** ~**preise** predatory price differentials *(US)*; ~**richter** umpire; ~**schauplatz verlegen** to shift one's ground; ~**schule** *(mil.)* special service school; ~**staffel** fighter squadron; **aufgelockerter** ~**stil** sparse manner of fighting; ~**stoff** [chemical] agent; ~**streik** offensive strike; ~**tarif** fighting tariff; **lebhafte** ~**tätigkeit** violent fighting; ~**teilnehmer** *(Sport)* combatant, contestant; ~**truppe** fighting forces, line; **zur** ~**truppe gehörig** regular; ~**übung** tactical exercise.
kampfunfähig disabled, *(Panzer)* unserviceable, crippled;
~ **machen** to put out of action, to disable; **Schiff** ~ **machen** to put a ship out of action.
Kampf|unfähigkeit disablement *(mil.)*, disability; ~**verband** combat unit; ~**wagen** armo(u)red vehicle, combat car *(US)*; ~**wert** combat efficiency; ~**zoll** retaliatory duty (tariff), penal rate; ~**zone** battle (combat, *US*) zone.
kampieren to camp, to hang out *(sl.)*;
im Freien ~ to camp out; **auf dem Sofa** ~ to bed down (kip down) on the sofa *(sl.)*.
Kanal channel, canal, passage, water gang, *(Abwässer)* drain, sewer, *(Frequenzverband)* program(me) channel, *(für Kabel)* duct, tunnel;
geschlossener ~ locked canal; **künstlicher** ~ canal;
~ **anlegen** to build a canal; ~ **mit Schleusen ausstatten** to lock a canal; **über den** ~ **fahren** to cross the channel; ~ **voll haben** *(fam.)* to be fed up with it; ~ **räumen** to clear a canal from obstruction; **durch einen** ~ **verbunden sein** to be linked with (joined by) a canal;
~**abgaben** canal tolls; ~**abkommen** canal treaty; ~**abschnitt** reach; ~**arbeiter** canal (sanitation) worker, ditcher, waterworker, navvy *(Br.)*; ~**bagger** canal dredger; ~**bau** *(Abwässer)* sewers; ~**-, Landstraßen- und Eisenbahnbauten** internal improvements *(US)*; ~**boot** canal boat; ~**dampfer** cross-channel steamer; ~**deckel** manhole cover; ~**durchfahrschein** passing ticket; ~**durchfahrt** passage through a channel.
Kanäle, auf mehreren ~**n gleichzeitig** *(Fernseher)* in syndication; **offizielle** ~ regular machinery.
Kanal|fährenunternehmen cross-channel transport operator; ~**fracht** carriage by channel, channel freight; ~**gase** sewer gases; ~**gebiet** canal zone; ~**gebühr** canal toll (dues); ~**gesellschaft** canal company; ~**hafen** channel port.
Kanalisation main supply, mains, *(Häuser, Straßen)* drainage, drains, sewerage, sewers;
städtische ~ town mains;
an die ~ **anschließen** to connect to the mains; **an die** ~ **angeschlossen sein** to be on the drain, to have sewerage service; **mit** ~ **versehen** to drain, to sewage.
Kanalisations|anlage sewage plant; ~**anschluß** sewerage connection; ~**arbeiter** sewerman, drainer; ~**kosten** cost of drainage; ~**netz** sewerage, system of sewers; **Gebäude ans** ~**netz anschließen** to drain a building; **am** ~**netz angeschlossen sein** to have sewerage service; ~**öffnung** manhole; ~**rohr** sewer pipe; ~**schleuse** canal lock; ~**system** drainage [system], sewer system, sewerage.
kanalisieren to canal, to canalize, to channelize, *(Abwässer)* to drain, to sewer, to sewage;
sein Wissen ~ to funnel know-how.
Kanalisierung drainage, sewerage, canalization.
Kanal|netz sewage system; ~**reiniger** flusher; ~**schacht** manhole; ~**schiffahrt** canal navigation; ~**schleuse** canal lock; ~**sohle** bottom of a sewer; ~**system** *(Bewässerung)* irrigation system, *(Entwässerung)* drainage; ~**tunnel** channel tunnel; ~**verbindung** connection between rivers; ~**verkehr** canal (cross-channel) traffic; ~**wähler** *(Fernsehen)* channel selector; ~**zone** canal zone.
Kandare, an jds. under s. one's thumb;
~ **anziehen** to apply the curb; **j. an der** ~ **haben** to keep s. o. in check; **j. fest an der** ~ **haben** to keep a tight rein on s. o.; **Ehemann fest an der** ~ **haben** to be tied to a wife's apron strings; **j. an die** ~ **nehmen** to put a curb on s. one's passions.
Kandidat candidate, aspirant, *(Bewerber)* applicant, appointee *(US)*, competitor, *(parl.)* contestant, *(Prüfling)* examinee;
akzeptierter ~ recipiendary; **aufgestellter** ~ nominee; **sorgfältig ausgesuchter** ~ hand-picked candidate; **aussichtsreichster** ~ front runner, strong candidate; **wenig bekannter** ~ dark horse; **durchgefallender** ~ sorehead; **einziger** ~ unopposed candidate; **empfohlener** ~ coupon candidate; **geeigneter** ~ eligible candidate; **gemeinsamer** ~ fusion candidate; **gewählter** ~

successful candidate; **möglicher** ~ prospect; **offizieller** ~ ticket *(US)*; **seriöser** ~ strong candidate; **umstrittener** ~ contestee *(US)*; **wahrscheinlicher** ~ probable;
~ **der Arbeiterpartei** Labour candidate *(Br.)*; ~ **mit Erfolgsaussichten** available candidate *(US)*;
~**en ablehnen** to turn down (refuse) a candidate; **sich als** ~ **anbieten** to offer o. s. as candidate; ~**en aufstellen** to nominate (run, present, set up, put up, propose) a candidate, to slate for for nomination *(US)*; **als** ~ **auftreten** to put in for election, to put up, to stand for; **ungeeignetsten** ~**en auswählen** to pick the least deserving candidate; ~**en in Vorschlag bringen** to propose (recommend) a candidate for a post; **sich als** ~ **in Vorschlag bringen** to offer o. s. as a candidate; **einem** ~**en die Zustimmung erteilen** to rubberstamp a candidate; **völlig unbekannten** ~**en fördern** to promote s. o. from the shadows; **alle Stimmen einem** ~**en geben** to plump for a candidate *(coll.)*; ~ **lancieren** to groom a candidate for office *(US)*; **sich als** ~ **aufstellen lassen** to put one's name down, to offer o. s. (stand, *Br.*) as candidate, to stand for a constituency *(Br.)*, to run in an election; ~**en ministrabel machen** to license a candidate for a ministry; ~**en prüfen** to examine (question) a candidate; ~**en mit großer Mehrheit schlagen** to snow under a candidate *(US)*; **letzter unter den** ~**en sein** to be at the bottom of the list; **ziemlich sicherer** ~ **sein** to be a fairly safe bet; **als** ~ **aufgestellt sein** to be in nomination; **als** ~**en in der engeren Wahl stehen** to be on the short list of candidates; **als** ~ **für das Amt des Sekretärs zur Verfügung stellen** to put up for the secretaryship; **für einen** ~**en stimmen** to ballot for a candidate *(US)*; ~**en unterstützen** to back up (boost, endorse) a candidate; ~**en vorschlagen** to propose (recommend) a candidate; ~**en im Plenum vorschlagen** to make nominations from the floor *(US)*; **sich als** ~ **vorstellen** to come forward as a candidate; ~ **wählen** to poll a candidate; **vorgeschlagenen** ~**en wählen** to vote the straight ticket *(US)*; **als** ~ **zurücktreten** to withdraw one's candidature; **der Aufstellung eines** ~**en zustimmen** to adopt a candidate *(Br.)*.

Kandidatenaufstellung nomination of (putting up, adoption of, *Br.*) a candidate;
erstmalige ~ fresh nomination.

Kandidatenliste list of candidates (nominates, nominees), party list, leet *(Scot.)*, ticket *(US)*;
provisorische ~ slate *(US)*;
~ **der Partei** party ticket *(US)*;
~ **aufstellen** to put forward a list of candidates; **j. von der** ~ **streichen** to remove s. o. from the ticket *(US)*; **vorgeschriebene** ~ **wählen** to vote the straight ticket *(US)*.

Kandidaten|nominierung nominating (nomination, putting up of) candidates; ~**wahl** return *(Br.)*; **offener** ~**wettbewerb** political free-for-all.

Kandidatur candidateship, candidature *(Br.)*, candidacy *(US)*;
~ **annehmen** to agree to be a candidate; ~ **unterstützen** to support a candidate; **jds.** ~ **unterstützen** to canvass for s. o.; **seine** ~ **zurückziehen** to withdraw one's candidature *(Br.)*, to stand down.

kandidieren to [stand as] candidate, *(Politiker)* to stand *(Br.)* (run, *US*) for an office, to put up, to campaign *(US)*, to be in the run *(US)*;
für etw. ~ to offer o. s. (stand) as candidate; **aus verfassungsrechtlichen Gründen nicht ein drittes Mal für den Gouverneursposten** ~ **können** to be constitutionally barred from seeking a third term as governor; **für das Parlament** ~ to contest a seat in (put up for) Parliament; **für eine Stellung** ~ to apply (run) for an office (a position); **für eine Wahl** ~ to run in an election; **für einen Wahlkreis** ~ to contest a borough *(Br.)*.

Kanister canister, jerrican *(Br.)*, container.

Kannbestimmungen permissive legislation.

Kanne jar, jug, mug;
wie mit ~**n gießen** to rain cats and dogs; **in die** ~ **steigen müssen** to be sconced *(Br.)*.

Kannegießer, politischer dabbler in politics.

kannibalisch cannibalistic;
~ **hungrig** as hungry as a wolf;
sich ~ **wohl fühlen** to feel on top of the world.

Kannibalismus, in den ~ **zurückfallen** to revert to cannibalism.

Kann|leistungen voluntary contribution; ~**vorschrift** discretionary clause, optional rule, permissive provision.

Kanone gun, cannon, crackjack, *(fig.)* big shot, ace, wizard *(sl.)*, oner *(sl.)*, mastermind *(US)*, shark *(US sl.)*;
voll wie eine ~ drunk as a lord;
mit ~**n auf Spatzen schießen** to break a butterfly on the wheel; ~ **auf einem Gebiet sein** to be a whale at; **unter aller** ~ **sein** to be abominable (lousy, *coll.*).

Kanonen|boot gunboat; ~**bootdiplomatie** gunboat diplomacy; ~**donner** rumble (thunder) of cannons; ~**futter** cannon fodder; ~**kugel** cannon ball, round shot; ~**rohr** gun barrel; **heiliges** ~**rohr!** good heavens!; ~**schlag** *(Feuerwerk)* petard; ~**schuß** gunshot; ~**schußweite** gun-shot range.

Kanonier gunner, cannoneer.

kanonisches Recht canon[ical] law.

Kanossa, nach ~ **gehen** to eat humble pie.

Kante edge;
an allen Ecken und ~**n** here, there and everywhere;
es an allen Ecken und ~**n fehlen haben** to be terribly short of everything; **Geld auf die hohe** ~ **legen** to put money by for a rainy day; **viel Geld auf die hohe** ~ **legen** to salt away a lot of money.

Kantine canteen, company *(US)* (industrial retail) store, factory snack shop, cafeteria, lunchroom *(US)*, *(mil.)* mess hall, commissary mess, post exchange *(US)*, PX;
~ **betreiben** to run a canteen.

Kantinen|arbeit canteen work; ~**belieferung** industrial catering; ~**einrichtungen** canteen facilities; ~**fahrzeug** clubmobile; ~**leiter**, ~**pächter** canteen manager; ~**lieferant** industrial caterer; ~**tätigkeit** canteen work; ~**verwaltung** catering department; ~**wirt** canteen keeper.

Kanton canton.

Kantonalwahlen cantonal elections.

Kantonist, unsicherer bad customer, phony, dead beat *(US)*.

Kanzel pulpit, *(Flugzeug)* nose, cockpit, turret, *(Jäger)* shooting stand *(US)*, blind hide *(Br.)*;
~**predigt** pulpit oratory; ~**redner** pulpit orator.

Kanzlei chancery, chancellery, *(Anwalt)* law office, bureau, chambers *(Br.)*, chancellery, *(Gericht)* chancery, *(Rechnungsabteilung)* accounts department;
große ~ **haben** to have a large practice;
~**abteilung** secretarial department; ~**arbeit** clerical profession, desk; ~**beamter** office clerk; ~**bogen** legal cap, foolscap; ~**bote** office (official) messenger; ~**deutsch** officialese; ~**diener** messenger; ~**gericht** court of chancery; ~**kraft** solicitor's clerk *(Br.)*, usher.

kanzleimäßig clerical.

Kanzleipapier foolscap, briefpaper; ~**personal** office staff; ~**schrift** engrossing (court) hand, secretary type; ~**sprache**, ~**stil** gobbleygook *(US)*, officialese; ~**tätigkeit** chamber work; ~**vorstand** *(Diplomatie)* chancellor; ~**vorsteher** chief clerk, *(Anwaltsbüro)* senior clerk.

Kanzler chancellor;
~**amt** chancellery, chancellorship; **sich um das** ~**amt bewerben** to campaign for the chancellorship.

Kanzleramtsausschuß [etwa] cabinet-office committee.

Kanzlist clerk, copying clerk, writer.

Kap cape, foreland, point, head, headland;
~ **passieren** to weather a cape.

Kapazität capacity, potentiality, *(Fachmann)* authority, expert, mastermind *(US)*, *(Maschine)* efficiency;
nicht ausgelastete ~ below-capacity working; **voll ausgenutzte** ~ full operating capacity; **brachliegende** ~ unused capacity; **freie** ~ spare (surplus) capacity; **industrielle** ~ industrial capacity; **überschüssige** ~ excess capacity; **ungenutzte** ~ idle *(US)* (spare, *Br.*) capacity; **unzureichende** ~ undercapacity; **verfügbare** ~ capacity available;
~ **eines Betriebes** plant capacity; ~ **der Wirtschaft** industrial capacity;
seine ~**en in stärkerem Maße ausfahren** to roll along at a pace closer to its capacity; **seine** ~ **voll ausfahren** to be working (work) to capacity; ~ **voll ausnutzen** to work to capacity; ~ **fast voll ausnutzen** to operate close (at near to) capacity; ~ **kaum zu 75% ausnutzen** to work to 75% or less of capacity; ~ **ausweiten** to extend (expand) capacity; ~ **einschränken** to curtail capacity; ~ **erhöhen** to raise capacity; ~**en der einzelnen Länder reduzieren** to reduce national capacity; ~ **auf seinem Gebiet sein** to have a great name in one's field; ~**en um 50% verkleinern** to cut back capacity by 50%.

Kapazitäts|angleichung adjustment of capacity; ~**auslastung**, ~**ausnutzung** use of (employment to) [plant] capacity, capacity utilization (working); ~**ausnutzungsgrad**, ~**auslastungsquotient** capacity load factor; ~**ausnutzungslücke** capacity utilization gap; ~**ausweitung** growth (extension) in (expansion of) capacity, capacity extension; ~**effekt** capacity effect; ~**erfordernisse** capacity requirements; ~**grenze** limit of capacity; **volkswirtschaftliche** ~**grenze** ceiling of the economy; **7% unterhalb der** ~**grenze laufen** to operate 7% below its potentiality; ~**nutzungsgrad** load factor; ~**problem** capacity problem; ~**reduzierung** reduction of capacity, capacity cutback; ~**reserve** reserve capacity; ~**schwund** loss of capacity; ~**steuerung** capacity control; ~**überhang**, ~**überschuß** surplus capacity; ~**überwachung** capacity control; ~**verringerung** capacity cutback; **rasante** ~**zunahme** surge of capacity.

Kapelle chapel, *(Musik)* band, orchestra;
mit Spitzenmusikern besetzte ~ all-star band.

Kapellmeister conductor, *(für Tanzmusik)* bandleader.

Kaperbrief letter of marque.

Kaperei betreiben to go privateering.

kapern to privateer, to go privateering, to capture, *(Flugzeug)* to hi[gh]jack;
Schiff ~ to make prize of a ship.

Kaper|schiff privateer, pirate, marque, corsair; ~**schiff ausstatten** to fit out a ship for privateering; ~**wesen** privateer practice, privateering.

kapieren to grasp, to catch on, to cut a tooth, to see the light *(fam.)*, to cotton on *(fam.)*, to tumble *(US sl.)*;
schnell ~ to be quick on the uptake; **schwer** ~ to be slow to catch on.

Kapital capital *(Eigenkapital von Kapital- und Personalgesellschaft)* equity [capital], proprietary capital, proprietorship *(US)*, net worth *(US)*, capital ownership *(US)*, *(Geldmittel)* funds, means, resources, *(Kapitalmacht)* moneyed interest, capitalists, *(Stammkapital einer AG)* authorizied capital stock *(US)* (share capital, *Br.*), [joint] stock *(Br.)*, stock (corporate) capital *(US)*, *(zum Unterschied von Zinsen)* principal;
aus dem ~ **gezahlt** paid out of capital; **mit herabgesetztem** ~ *(Aktiengesellschaft)* and reduced;
amortisiertes ~ sunk (redeemed) capital; **angegebenes** ~ declared capital; **angelegtes** ~ funded (invested, investment) capital; **im Ausland angelegtes** ~ capital invested abroad; **in Grundstücken angelegtes** ~ capital invested in real property, real capital *(US)*; **langfristig angelegtes** ~ long-term funded capital, capital investment, investment spending; **nicht angelegtes** ~ idle money; **risikotragend angelegtes** ~ risk (venture) capital; **in Wertpapieren angelegtes** ~ property capital; **anlagesuchendes** ~ capital-seeking investment; **arbeitendes** ~ productive (employed, active, net working) capital; **aufgebrachtes** ~ capital produced; **aufgenommenes** ~ borrowed money (capital); **zur Einzahlung aufgerufenes** ~ called-up capital; **noch nicht aufgerufenes** ~ uncalled capital; **effektiv ausgegebenes** ~ issued capital *(Br.)* [stock, *US*]; **noch nicht ausgegebenes** ~ unissued capital *(Br.)* [stock, *US*], granted capital; **ausgewiesenes** ~ declared (stated) capital; **buchmäßig ausgewiesenes** ~ book equity; **ausländisches** ~ foreign capital (equity); **autorisiertes** ~ authorized capital *(Br.)* [stock, *US*]; **bares** ~ cash capital; **zu niedrig bemessenes** ~ low-geared capital; **effektiv benötigtes** ~ real capital; **aus Vorzugsaktien bestehendes** ~ preferred capital stock *(US)*; **aus kumulativen Vorzugsaktien bestehendes** ~ cumulative preferred stock *(US)*; **aus verkäuflichen Waren bestehendes** ~ bona-fide capital; **betriebsnotwendiges** ~ fixed (permanent) working capital; **bewilligtes** ~ authorized capital *(Br.)*, authorized capital stock *(US)*; **blockiertes** ~ blocked funds, frozen capital; **brachliegendes** ~ capital lying idle, unemployed funds, dead (idle, unproductive capital, loose) capital, idle money; **deklariertes** ~ declared capital; **dividendenberechtigtes** ~ capital entitled to a dividend; **einbezahltes** ~ paid-up capital; **eingebrachtes** ~ brought-in (contribution to) capital, capital brought in; **eingefordertes** ~ called-up capital; **eingefrorenes** ~ frozen capital, blocked funds; **eingeschossenes** ~ deposit[ed] capital; **eingesetztes** ~ invested capital, capital employed; **eingezahltes** ~ paid-in (paid-up) capital; **noch nicht eingezahltes** ~ uncalled capital; **tatsächlich eingezahltes** ~ present capital; **teilweise eingezahltes** ~ partly paid-up capital; **voll eingezahltes** ~ capital fully paid, paid-up capital; **nicht voll eingezahltes** ~ partly paid-up capital; **eisernes** ~ money sunk *(US)*; **engagiertes** ~ tied- (locked-, *Br.*) up capital; **fälliges** ~ matured capital; **fehlgeleitetes** ~ misappropriated capital; **festgelegtes** ~ tied- (locked-, *Br.*) up capital, lockup *(Br.)*; **festgesetztes** ~ declared capital; **festliegendes** ~ frozen (fixed) capital; **fiktives** ~ fictitious capital; **flüssiges** ~ liquid (circulation) capital, funds in hand, liquid resources, available funds; **freies** ~ disengaged (unemployed, unused, uninvested) capital; **fremdes** ~ borrowed capital; **geistiges** ~ immaterial capital, intangible assets; **gemeinsames** ~ pooled fund; **genehmigtes [und noch nicht ausgegebenes]** ~ granted (registered, authorized, *Br.*) capital, authorized capital stock *(US)*, unissued capital stock *(US)*; **geringes** ~ small capital; **geringfügiges** ~ nominal capital *(US)*; **gezeichnetes** ~ capital subscribed; **haftendes** ~ authorized capital; **herabgesetztes** ~ reduced capital; **hinlängliches** ~ ample means; **investiertes** ~ invested capital; **konstantes** ~ constant capital; **kündbares** ~ withdrawable (redeemable) capital; **langfristiges** ~ long-term capital; **menschliches** ~ human capital; **neues** ~ fresh (additional) capital; **nominelles** ~ nominal capital *(US)*; **persönliches** ~ immaterial capital; **privates** ~ private capital (means); **produktives** ~ employed (engaged) capital; **reales** ~ tangible property; **nicht realisierbares** ~ fixed (locked-up, *Br.*) capital; **registriertes** ~ registered (authorized, *Br.*) capital, authorized capital stock *(US)*; **satzungsmäßiges** ~ statutory capital; **schrumpfendes** ~ shrinking capital; **stehendes** ~ fixed capital; **zur Verfügung stehendes** ~ disposable capital; **stimmberechtigtes** ~ voting stock; **totes** ~ unemployed (unused, unapplied) funds, dead (barren, dormant) money, dead assets, dead stock, capital (money) lying idle, unproductive (unapplied) capital; **umlaufendes** ~ floating (circulating) capital; **unangelegtes** ~ capital lying idle; **unaufgerufenes** ~ uncalled capital; **unbeschäftigtes** ~ idle capital, capital lying idle; **ungenutztes** ~ unemployed capital; **unkündbares** ~ irredeemable capital; **unproduktives** ~ dead capital; **völlig unzureichendes** ~ capital inadequate to the needs of a transaction, shoestring *(US sl.)*; **ursprüngliches** ~ natural capital; **verantwortliches** ~ registered (authorized) capital; **verfügbares** ~ capital that can be made available, available capital, expendable (available) funds; **[um Zinsen] vermehrtes** ~ compound discount; **[durch Verlust] vermindertes** ~ impaired capital; **vom Staat verwaltetes** ~ state-operated funds *(US)*; **verwässertes** ~ watered stock; **verzinsliches** ~ interest-bearing capital; **volleingezahltes** ~ capital fully paid; **gesetzlich vorgeschriebenes** ~ legal capital; **wechselndes** ~ variable capital; **werbendes** ~ interest-bearing (working, quick) capital; **zinsfreies** ~ free capital; **zinstragendes** ~ interest-bearing capital; **zurückgezahltes** ~ redeemed capital;
~ **einer Aktiengesellschaft** share capital *(Br.)*, [joint] stock *(Br.)*, corporate (stock) capital *(US)*; ~ **einer Bank** bank's capital, bank assets, capital resources; ~ **einer Firma** funds of a firm; ~ **einer Gesellschaft** capital of a partnership, a company's resources; **anderes** ~ **als Grund und Boden** artificial capital; ~ **eines Investmentfonds** certificate capital; ~ **und Spesen** principal and charges; ~ **einer Vermögensverwaltung** settlement capital; ~ **einer Versicherungsgesellschaft** insurance stock; ~ **nebst Zinsen** principal and interest, amount; ~ **samt aufgelaufenen Zinsen** principal with interest accrued;
~ **abschöpfen** to absorb capital; ~ **abschreiben** to write off capital; ~ **abziehen** to alienate capital; **sein** ~ **anbrechen (angreifen)** to make incursions into (holes in, inroads upon) one's principal, to touch the (break into one's) capital, to invade the principal *(US)*; ~ **anlegen** to embark money, to embark capital, to invest capital; ~ **fest anlegen** to tie (lock, *Br.*) up capital; **sein** ~ **in verschiedenen Gewerbesparten anlegen** to diversify one's capital; ~ **anlocken** to attract capital; **mit fremdem** ~ **arbeiten** to trade with borrowed money (on the equity); **mit großem** ~ **arbeiten** to dispose of a large capital; **gesamtes** ~ **aufbrauchen** to draw out all the principal; ~ **aufbringen** to start a fund, to raise money; **neues** ~ **zur Finanzierung von Entwicklungsaufträgen aufbringen** to raise growth capital; ~ **aufnehmen** to raise capital (funds); **neues** ~ **aufnehmen** to take up new capital; **neues** ~ **zur Durchführung von Betriebserweiterungen aufnehmen** to raise additional capital for new plant facilities; ~ **zur Einzahlung aufrufen** to make a call for (call up) capital; ~ **aufstocken** to reequip capital, *(AG)* to increase the capital stock *(US)* (share capital, *Br.*); **sein** ~ **aufzehren** to eat up one's capital; ~ **wieder ausführen** to repatriate capital; ~ **zinsfrei ausleihen** to lend out money free of interest; **mit** ~ **ausstatten** to furnish (endow, provide) with capital; **Industriezweig mit** ~ **ausstatten** to raise money for an industry; ~ **berichtigen** to adjust the capital; ~ **beschaffen** to finance, to procure (furnish) capital (funds), to raise the money; ~ **durch Aktienausgabe beschaffen** to raise equity finance; **neues** ~ **auf dem bewährten Weg der Aktienausgabe beschaffen** to get new capital through the equity security route; **Geschäft mit geliehenem** ~ **betreiben** to trade on the equity; ~ **bilden** to accumulate capital; **im Ausland aus unversteuertem Einkommen** ~ **bilden** to build up capital abroad from untaxed income; ~ **blockieren** to tie (lock, *Br.*) up capital; ~ **einbringen (einschießen)** to contribute capital; **sein** ~ **schwerpunktartig einsetzen** to make the most of one's resources; ~ **einzahlen** to pay capital; ~ **einziehen** to call in capital; ~ **erhöhen** to increase the capital, *(AG)* to raise the capital stock *(US)* (share capital, *Br.*); ~ **festlegen** to

immobilize (tie up, *US*, lock up, *Br.*) capital; ~ **flüssigmachen (freisetzen)** to liberate (mobilize) capital, to realize assets; **kein eigenes ~ haben** to have no resources of one's own, to trade on the equity; **sein ~ nicht angegriffen haben** to have kept one's capital intact; ~ **herabsetzen** to write down capital, to reduce the share capital *(Br.)* (capital stock, *US*); ~ **heranziehen** to attract capital; ~ **hineinstecken (investieren)** to invest capital; ~ **investieren** to invest capital; ~ **nicht zurückzahlen können** to default in the repayment of principal; ~ **kündigen** to call in capital (money), to recall capital; **vom ~ leben** to live on *(Br.)* (off) the capital; ~ **aus etw. schlagen** to make propaganda capital out of s. th., to cash in on s. th., to capitalize on s. th. politically, to parlay *(US)*; **als Partei aus einer Sache ~ schlagen** to make party capital; **Zinsen zum ~ schlagen** to capitalize interest; ~ **zur Verfügung stellen** to provide (furnish) with capital; ~ **umgruppieren** to regroup capital; **in ~ umwandeln** to convert into capital; ~ **der staatlichen Zwangswirtschaft unterwerfen** to conscript capital; **über das erforderliche ~ verfügen** to have the money required; ~ **verringern** to reduce the share capital *(Br.)* (capital stock, *US*); ~ **verstärken** to extend the financial basis, *(erhöhen)* to increase capital; ~ **verwalten** to administer funds; ~ **verwässern** to water stocks; **Dividende vom ~ zahlen** to pay a dividend out of capital; ~ **zeichnen** to subscribe capital, *(Übernahmekonsortium)* to underwrite capital; ~ **zuführen** to introduce capital; **neues ~ zuführen** to infuse fresh capital; ~ **aus dem Ausland zurückführen** to repatriate capital; ~ **zurückziehen** to recall capital, to withdraw funds; ~ **zusammenlegen** to write off capital, to reduce the capital stock *(US)*; **sein ~ zusammenschießen** to club together, to pool funds; **dem ~ zuschlagen** to add to the capital; **dem ~ zuzurechnen sein** to be of a capital nature;

~**abfindung** capital indemnification, lump-sum settlement, settlement in cash; ~**abfluß** outflow (efflux) of capital, capital drain; ~**abfluß drosseln** to limit capital outflow; ~**abflußrechnung** cashflow statement; ~**abgabe** capital levy; ~**ablösung** capital redemption; ~**abschöpfung** depletion of capital; ~**abschreibung** writing down of capital, capital depreciation; **einkommensteuerlich nicht anerkannte ~abschreibung** capital items disallowed for income-tax purposes; ~**abschreibung vornehmen** to write down capital; ~**abtragung** repayment (redemption) of capital; ~**abwanderung** exodus (migration, emigration) of capital, capital drain, drain of specie; ~**abzug** alienation of capital, withdrawal of funds, capital drain; ~**akkumulation** capital accumulation; ~**änderung** alteration of capital; ~**angabe** statement of capital; ~**angebot** capital supply; ~**anhäufung** accumulation, accumulated surplus.

Kapitalanlage [capital] investment, capital assets, *(Anlage von Kapital)* employment (investment, placement) of capital, capital spending;

als ~ for investment purposes; **zur ~ geeignet** suitable for investment;

nicht ablösbare ~n noncommutable investment; **attraktive ~** attractive investment; **ausgesuchte ~** choice investment; **ausländische ~n** investment from abroad; **außerbetriebliche ~** outside investment; **bestimmungswidrige ~** *(Investmentsfonds)* improper investment; **erstklassige ~** high-grade (high-class, choice) investment, prime (gilt-edged, *Br.*) investment; **ertragreiche ~** profitable investment; **feste (fixe) ~** fixed capital, lockup *(Br.)*; **gesetzwidrige ~** improper investment; **gewinnbringende ~n** income-earning assets (investment); **inflationssichere ~** inflation-proof investment; **kurzfristige ~n** temporary (short-term) investments; **langfristige ~n** long-dated (long-term, long-time) capital investments (spending), fixed (permanent) investment; **lohnende ~** profitable (remunerative) investment; **mittelfristige ~** medium-term investment; **mündelsichere ~** gilt-edged *(Br.)* (high-grade, safe, trustee, *Br.*, trust fund, *US*, legal, *US*) investments, prime investment; **notleidende ~** defaulted investment; **planmäßige ~** capital planning; **private ~** private investment; **produktive ~** productive investment (assets); **leicht realisierbare ~n** liquid investments; **risikoreiche ~n** *(Kapitalanlagegesellschaft)* aggressive investments, special-situation investments; **schlechte ~** poor investments; **sichere ~n** secure (safe) investments, safety of capital; **spekulative ~** speculative (special-situation) investment, *(Kapitalanlagegesellschaft)* aggressive investment; **ungünstige ~** poor investment; **unproduktive ~** unproductive investment, dead assets; **unvorteilhafte ~** unprofitable investment; **verzinsliche (zinsbringende) ~** interest-bearing investment; **ordnungsgemäß vorgenommene ~** prudent investment; **vorsichtige ~** conservative investment; **vorteilhafte ~** good investment; **zulässige ~** *(Investmentgesellschaft)* qualified investment *(US)*;

~ **im Ausland** foreign investment; ~ **einer Bausparkasse** society investments; ~**n in Ersthypotheken** first-mortgage investments; ~ **mit fester Rendite** fixed-yield investment; ~ **zu Renditezwecken** nonspeculative investment; ~ **zu Spekulationszwecken** speculative (special-situation) investment; ~ **von Tilgungsfondsmitteln** sinking-fund investment; ~ **in immateriellen Werten** intangible investment; ~ **in Wertpapieren** portfolio investment; ~**n in Wohngrundstücken** residential holdings;

brachliegende ~n anderweitig einsetzen to redeploy a wasting capital asset; ~ **erhöhen** to increase the amount of capital contributed; **in eine steuerfreie ~ umwandeln** to convert investment into a nontaxable form; **bevorzugt weiterhin langfristige ~n vornehmen** to keep up the booming pace of capital investment;

~**fonds** unit trust fund *(Br.)*; **kurzfristige ~gebiete** short-term capital areas; **im ~geschäft erfolgreich tätig sein** to prosper on institutional business.

Kapitalanlagegesellschaft investment trust company, investment company, mutual fund *(US)*, unit [investment] trust *(Br.)*;

abhängige ~ investment affiliate; **staatlich anerkannte (zugelassene) ~** registered unit trust *(Br.)*; **nach eigenem Ermessen anlegende ~** management trust (investment company); **steuerlich privilegierte ~** regulated investment company *(US)*; **zugelassene ~** registered investment company;

~ **mit breit gestreutem Aktienportefeuille** discretionary trust *(Br.)*; ~ **mit geschlossenem Anlagefonds** closed-end investment company *(US)*; ~ **mit umfassendem Anlagefonds** general management trust; ~ **mit konstantem Anlagekapital** closed-end investment trust; ~ **ohne Anlagenstreuung** nondiversified company *(US)*; ~ **mit eigenverantwortlicher Anlagenverwaltung** managed list trust, general management trust; ~ **mit freizügiger Anlageverwaltung (mit Freizügigkeit in der Anlagepolitik)** management trust (investment company); ~ **mit steuerfreiem Auslandsitz** offshore fund; ~ **mit festgelegtem Effektenbestand** fixed [investment] trust, fixed unit trust *(Br.)*; ~ **mit auswechselbarem Portefeuille** flexible unit trust *(Br.)*, flexible (managed) trust *(US)*; ~ **mit vorgeschriebener Risikosteuerung** diversified investment company;

Gesetz über ~en Investment Company Act.

Kapitalanlagegüter capital assets (goods);

veraltete ~ out-of-date capital;

~ **mit beschränkter Lebensdauer** limited-life assets;

Abschreibungen auf ~ steuerlich vortragen to carry forward capital allowance *(Br.)*.

Kapitalanlage|institut investment institution; ~**konto** capital asset account; ~**politik** capital planning; ~**programm** capital improvement program(me); ~**stelle** professional investor; **staatliche ~stelle** institutional unit of government; **von einer ~stelle abgestoßen werden** to come under institutional liquidation; ~**vermögen** capital assets; ~**vertrag** investment contract, unit trust plan *(Br.)*; ~**verwaltungsgesellschaft** closed-end investment company; ~**vorhaben** investment intentions; **festverzinsliche ~werte** investment bonds; ~**wesen** mutual fund industry; ~**zertifikate** unit trust holdings.

Kapitalanlagen|abschreibung capital allowance *(Br.)*; ~**berater** investment adviser, security analyst *(US)*; ~**beratung** investment advice, security analysis *(US)*; ~**beratungsgesetz** Investment Adviser Act; ~**bewertung** appreciation of assets, security analysis *(US)*; ~**gesetz** Prevention of Fraud Act *(Br.)*.

Kapitalanleger investor, institutional client;

berufsmäßiger ~ professional investor; **einzelner ~** individual investor; **erfahrener ~** seasoned investor; **vertrauensvoller ~** trusting investor;

~ **in Grundstücken** real-estate investor.

Kapitalansammlung [capital] accumulation, amassing (accumulation) of capital.

Kapitalansammlungs|plan plan of accumulation, accumulation schedule (plan); ~**schein** accumulation unit; ~**vertrag** accumulation agreement.

Kapitalanteil share in capital, [capital] share, capital interest, ownership interest, percentage of capital, share of stock, stock share, *(Beteiligung)* interest in a firm, [economic] interest, *(Bilanz)* capital, *(Leibrente)* capital element;

ausschlaggebender ~ control in ownership interest, controlling [stock] interest; **beschränkt stimmberechtigter ~** voting pool stock;

festverzinslicher ~ am Gesamtkapital capital gearing;

gleiche ~e haben to share equally in the capital; ~ **kaufen** to purchase interest.

Kapitalanteils | recht, voll eingezahlte ~rechte in Aktien umwandeln to convert fully paid shares into stock; **~schein** share, certificate of stock, stock certificate.

kapitalarm short of funds, lacking capital, capital-starved.

Kapital | aufbringer contributor of capital, investor; **~aufbringung** raising (contribution) of capital, capital contribution, capital raising, putting up of funds; **~aufbringung mittels Börsenprospektes** prospectus method; **~aufnahme** taking up (raising of) capital, capital borrowing; **erster ~aufruf** first call; **~aufstellung** capital account; **~aufstockung** capital reequipment (increase), increase in capital, increase of capital stock *(US)* (share capital, *Br.*).

Kapitalaufwand capital expenditure (outlay, spending, cost), revenue expenditure, financial expense;
über Unkosten abzubuchender ~ revenue charges; **aktivierungspflichtiger ~** charges to capital, capital charges; **volkswirtschaftlicher ~** national capital spending;
~ für weitere Ausbauten capital improvement; **großer ~ für Forschungsarbeiten** large outlay on scientific research; **~ für das Sachanlagevermögen** fixed capital expenditure; **~ für technische Verbesserungen** capital improvement; **~ der Wirtschaft** industry spending.

Kapitalaufwands | berechnung capital expenditure evaluation; **~vorschau** capital expenditure budget.

Kapitalaufwendungen capital spending (disbursements, expenditure);
als Betriebsausgaben abgebuchte ~ charges to revenue, revenue charges.

Kapital | aufzehrung capital consumption; **~ausfuhr** capital export, remittances abroad; **~ausfuhrland** capital-exporting country; **~ausgleich** capital hotchpot; **~ausrüstung** capital equipment, capitalization; **~ausschüttung** capital distribution, stock dividend *(US)*.

Kapitalausstattung capitalization, *(Bilanz)* capital equipment (endowment), endowment with capital, capital resources;
knappe ~ low gearing; **multinationale ~** multinational funding; **ungenügende ~** insufficient capitalization; **vollständige ~** total capitalization;
~ einer Gesellschaft capitalization of a company;
gute ~ haben to be well provided with capital; **~ vornehmen** to capitalize, to endow with capital.

Kapital | ausstattungsergebnis capitalization result; **~ausstattungskosten** capital equipment costs; **~auswanderung** exodus (migration) of capital; **~ausweitung** capital expansion; **~auszahlung** capital payment (distribution); **~barwert berechnen** to capitalize; **~basis** capital (financial) base, capital (financial) requirements, demand for (supply of) capital (funds), capital demand (needs), want of money; **~basis verstärken** to increase the capital; **~bedarf** need for capital, capital needs, capital requirements, capital demand; **langfristiger ~bedarf** demand for long-term investment capital; **~bedürfnisse** capital requirements; **langfristiges ~bedürfnis sichtbar machen** to put out its own demand for long-term capital; **~beitrag** contribution to capital; **~belastungen** charges on capital, capital charges; **~bereitstellung** provision (supply) of capital.

Kapitalbereitstellungs | gemeinschaft money pool; **~konto** capital appropriation account; **~kosten** commitment charges; **~provision** commitment commission.

Kapital | berichtigung adjustment of capital, capital adjustment; **~berichtigungsaktie** scrip issue *(Br.)*, stock dividend *(US)*; **~beschaffung** provision (procurement) of capital (funds), finding of means, capital raising, financing; **~beschaffung durch Aktienausgabe** equity financing; **~beschaffungsstelle** capital raiser; **~besitz** holding of capital; **~besitzer** capital owner.

Kapitalbeteiligung [financial] interest, ownership share, [equity] participation, equity interests, *(Aktienanteil)* share, stock *(US)*, *(Aktienzeichnung)* stock subscription;
amerikanische ~en in Deutschland American interests in Germany;
amerikanische ~en ausweisen to have some degree of ownership by U.S. capital; **~ verkaufen** to sell an interest.

Kapitalbetrag amount of capital, capital [amount], capital sum, *(im Gegensatz zu Zinsen)* principal amount (sum), principal;
nur dem ~ nach eintragungsfähig registrable as to principal only;
pauschaler ~ lump sum of capital;
~ zurückzahlen to return a capital sum.

Kapitalbeträge, über Gewinn- und Verlustkonto abgebuchte capital items charged against profits;
überschüssige ~ abziehen to drain off capital funds; **große ~ zur Verfügung haben** to have large capital at one's disposal, to dispose of a large capital.

Kapitalbewegung capital movement, flow of capital, flotation; **~en** capital transactions;
kompensatorische (kurzfristige) ~en short-term movements of capital; **langfristige ~en** long-term movements of capital;
~ zum Halbjahresultimo mid-year movement of funds; **~en zwischen Industrieländern** cross investment; **~en zum Monatsultimo** monthly movements of funds.

Kapital | bewertung capital valuation (rating, *US*); **~bewertungsergebnisse** capital-rating result *(US)*; **~bewertungsziffern** capital-rating figures *(US)*; **~bewilligung** allocation (appropriation) of funds; **~bilanz** balance of capital transactions, balance on capital account; **~bildung** capital accumulation (formation), amassing of capital; **rasche ~bildung ermöglichen** to enable capital to build up at a faster rate; **~bonus** capital bonus *(Br.)*, stock dividend *(US)*.

Kapitälchen *(drucktechn.)* small capitals.

Kapital | decke, knappe low gearing; **unzureichende (knappe) ~decke haben** to lack the requisite (be strapped for) capital; **~deckung** recovery of capital, capital [investment] recovery.

Kapitaldeckungs | fonds *(Lebensversicherung)* unearned premium reserve; **~stock** *(Bausparkasse)* guarantee stock, *(Versicherung)* unearned premium reserve; **~verfahren** *(Versicherung)* level premium system.

Kapital | dienst service of capital; **~dienst sicherstellen** to service its capital investment; **~dienst und ~transfer** interest payments and transfer of capital; **~disposition** provision (supply) of capital; **~dividende** capital dividend, dividend on capital; **~eigner** equity (capital) owner; **~einbringung, ~einzahlung** contribution of capital, capital contribution; **~einbuße** capital loss, leakage; **~einfuhr** import of capital, capital import; **ausländische ~einfuhr abbremsen** to stem the inflow of foreign funds; **~einfuhrland** capital-importing country; **~einkommen, ~einkünfte** unearned income (revenue), capital gain, investment income *(US)*, equity earnings, capital receipts, capital revenue, income from interest; **500 £ an ~einkünften haben** to receive £ 500 from investments.

Kapitaleinlage contribution to capital, capital contribution (paid up), stake, invested capital, principal, money sunk *(US)*;
nicht rückzahlbare ~ guarantee stock;
~ eines Gesellschafters contribution to capital by a partner;
~ erhöhen to increase the amount of capital contributed.

Kapitaleinleger contributor of capital, investor.

Kapitaleinsatz capital appropriation, use (employment) of capital;
vorsichtiger ~ husbanding of capital;
seinen ~ verringern to reduce one's equity stake;
~übersicht capital appropriation survey.

Kapital | einschuß contribution to capital, capital paid [up], partly paid-up capital; **~einzahlung** put-in capital; **~einziehung** retirement of stock; **~emission** capital issue, capital flotation; **~emissionskosten** underwriting costs; **~empfehlungsliste** list of recommended capital projects; **~entblößung** depletion of capital; **~entnahme** withdrawal of capital; **~entschädigung** capital indemnification, lump-sum settlement; **~entstehung** funds generation; **~entwertung** depreciation of capital, capital depreciation; **~entwertungskonto** capital depreciation account; **~entwertungsrücklage** provision for depreciation of investments (capital); **~entwicklung** capital changes; **~erhaltung** maintenance of capital, capital conservation.

Kapitalerhöhung capital increase, further issue of capital, increase of [share] capital (in capital stock, *US*);
~ genehmigen to approve an increase of capital; **~ vornehmen** to increase the capital (share capital, *Br.*, capital stock, *US*), to make a call for funds, to make a new issue of stock.

Kapital | erhöhungsangebot equity offerings; **~erhöhungskosten** capitalization expenditure; **~erlös** profit on investment.

Kapitalertrag unearned income, profits of capital, return on capital stock employed *(US)* (investment), investment return (revenue, *Br.*), capital yield, income return *(US)*;
~ von 15% bringen to yield 15 per cent.

Kapital | erträge, ~erträgnisse unearned (investment) income, capital gains, capital receipts, proceeds from capital, gains derived from capital, equity earnings, return on income *(US)*;
in neuen Investmentzertifikaten angelegte ~ income reinvested in units; **zur Erstellung von Fernstraßen aufgewandte ~** trunk-road investment; **körperschaftssteuerfreie ~** franked investment income *(Br.)*; **der Körperschaftssteuer unterliegende (steuerabzugspflichtige) ~** unfranked investment income *(Br.)*;

~ **nach Steuerabzügen** franked investment income; ~ **vor Steuerabzug** nonfranked income *(Br.)*;
~ **lediglich der Körperschaftssteuer unterwerfen** to charge unfranked income to corporation tax only *(Br.)*.
Kapitalertragsbilanz net investment income.
Kapitalertragssteuer [etwa] capital-gains tax, capital-yields tax *(Br.)*, *(im Abzugswege)* federal transfer (withholding) tax *(US)*, tax withheld on dividends *(US)*;
~ **erheben** to withhold capital-gains tax;
~**satz** withholding rate *(US)*.
Kapital|ertragswert capitalized (earning-capacity) value; ~**etat** capital budget; ~**export** capital export; ~**exporteur** exporter of capital; ~**fehlbetrag** stock shortage; ~**fehlleitung** misappropriated (misappropriation of) capital funds; ~**festlegung** immobilization (tying-up, locking up) of capital *(Br.)*, lock-up *(Br.)*; ~**flucht** exodus (flight) of capital, capital flight; ~**fluß** flow of capital, capital flow, *(aus Umsatz)* cashflow; ~**flußrechnung** cashflow statement; ~**fonds** capital pool, working fund; ~**forderung** capital due; **keine ~forderung gegen den Schuldner durchsetzen können** to have no equity in the debtor; ~**freisetzung** liberation of capital.
Kapitalgeber capital-giver, furnisher of capital, moneylender, investor, financier;
ausländischer ~ foreign investor;
~ **mit hoher Einkommensteuerprogression** high-bracket investor; ~ **für den Pfandbriefmarkt** bond-market investor.
Kapitalgefüge capital construction.
Kapitalgesellschaft commercial (business) corporation *(US)*, joint-stock company, company limited by shares *(Br.)*, corporate enterprise;
ausländische ~ alien corporation *(US)*; **inländische** ~ domestic corporation *(US)*; **investierende** ~ corporative investor; **staatliche** ~ government corporation;
~ **mit [un]begrenzter Haftung** [un]limited company *(Br.)*;
seine Firma in eine ~ umwandeln to incorporate one's business.
Kapitalgewinn capital profit, capital gain, capital benefit, *(Anlagegewinn)* investment profit;
steuerpflichtiger ~ chargeable capital gain; **nicht steuerpflichtiger** ~ reserve of capital, capital reserve;
der Behandlung als ~ unterworfen sein to qualify for capital-gains treatment;
~**abgabe** capital-gains levy; ~**ausschüttungen** capital-gains distribution; ~**berechnung** capital-gains computation; ~**konto** capital-gains (surplus, *US*) account.
kapitalgewinnsteuerpflichtig sein to be liable to capital-gains tax.
Kapitalgüter [fixed] capital goods;
teure ~ big-ticket durables;
~ **für mehrere Zwecke** free capital goods;
~ **schaffen** to create capital goods;
~**bereich** capital-goods area, capital investment goods sector;
~**industrie** capital-goods [investmen] industries; ~**investitionen** investment in capital goods, capital spending (investment);
~**konjunktur** capital-goods boom; ~**strom** flow of capital investment; ~**verringerung** diminution of capital goods.
Kapitalherabsetzung reduction of share capital *(Br.)* (capital stock, *US*), capital reduction *(US)*;
~ **vornehmen** to write down the capital, to reduce the share capital *(Br.)* (capital stock, *US*); **einer ~ nicht zustimmen** to object to the reduction of share capital *(Br.)*.
Kapital|herabsetzungsvorschlag capital reduction plan; ~**hilfe** capital aid, capital assistance; ~**höhe** capital [amount], amount of capital.
Kapitalien capital [assets], funds, means, resources;
ohne ~ fundless;
brachliegende ~ unapplied funds; **für Betriebsumstellung erforderliche** ~ reconversion investment; **reichliche** ~ ample means;
~ **anlegen** to embark capital; ~ **aufbringen** to raise capital; ~ **flüssigmachen** to liquidate capital; **seine ~ zusammenwerfen** to pool one's resources.
Kapital|import import of capital, capital import; ~**intensität** high gearing; **gesteigerte ~intensität** capital deepening.
kapitalintensiv capital-intensive;
~**e Unternehmen** high-cost enterprise.
Kapitalintensivierung extension of the financial basis.
Kapitalinteresse financial (moneyed) interest;
maßgebendes ~ controlling stock interest.
Kapitalinteressenten beschaffen to procure funds.
Kapital|investierung, ~investition investment in capital goods, capital (equity) investment, investment of funds, capital (investment) spending;
auswärtige ~ investment from abroad; **produktivitätsfördernde** ~ productivity-improving investment; **steuerbegünstigte** ~ tax investment; **ordnungsgemäß vorgenommene** ~ prudent investment;
übermäßige ~en in Debitoren overinvestments in receivables *(US)*; ~**en der öffentlichen Hand** public investments; **übermäßige ~en in Warenständen** overinvestment in inventories; **fehlende ~en der privaten Wirtschaft** lack of private investment;
vor ~en zurückschrecken to fight shy of capital.
kapitalisierbar capitalizable, fundable, convertible.
kapitalisieren to capitalize, to finance, to fund, *(in Geld umwandeln)* to convert into capital, to realize;
nochmals ~ to recapitalize; **Rente** ~ to capitalize an annuity.
kapitalisiert capitalized, funded;
nicht genügend ~ undercapitalized;
~ **werden** to be capitalized;
~**er Aufwand** capitalized expenses; ~**e Kosten** capitalized expenses; ~**er Wert** capitalized value.
Kapitalisierung realization, *(Rente)* capitalization;
~ **einer Gesellschaft** capitalization of a company (corporation, *US*); ~ **von Gewinnen** capitalization of profits; ~ **einer Rente** capitalization of an annuity.
Kapitalisierungs|anleihe funding loan; ~**aufwand** capitalization unit; ~**faktor** capitalization of earnings; ~**marktwert** market capitalization value; ~**methode** capitalization method; ~**satz** rate of capitalization, capitalization rate.
Kapitalismus capitalism.
Kapitalist capitalist, moneyed man, financier, plutocrat, stockholder;
~**en** moneyed interest (people), high finance;
~ **werden** to become a rich man, to capitalize.
kapitalistisch capitalistic;
~**es System** capitalistic system; ~**es Unternehmen** capital venture; ~**es Wirtschaftssystem** capitalistic economics.
kapitalknapp capital-short, low-geared;
~ **sein** to be strapped for capital.
Kapital|knappheit shortage of capital, capital shortage; ~**koeffizient** *(volkswirtschaftliche Erfolgsrechnung)* capital output ratio, capital coefficient; **marginaler ~koeffizient** incremental capital-output ratio; ~**konsolidierung** consolidation of funds.
Kapitalkonto share account, capital [stock], proprietorship account, equity account;
liberalisiertes ~ liberalized capital account;
auf ~ übernehmen to capitalize, to charge to capital account.
Kapital|kontrolle capital accounting, *(AG)* stock control *(US)*;
~**konzentration** concentration of ownership (capital); ~**kosten** capital expenditure (cost), *(Emission)* underwriting costs; **aktivierte ~kosten** capital charges, charges to capital; **durchschnittliche ~kosten** cost of capital; ~**kraft** sound financial position, financial strength (standing).
kapitalkräftig financially sound, financially strong, in good financial standing, substantial;
~ **sein** to be well provided with capital, to have ample means, to be in funds.
Kapital|krise stringency in the [money] market; ~**leistung** capital transaction; ~**lenkung** direction of capital, investment control; ~**lücke** capital gap; ~**macht** financial strength; ~**mangel** shortage (lack, deficiency) of capital, want of funds (capital).
Kapitalmarkt capital (equity) market;
freier ~ open market; **privater** ~ private placement market;
~ **für Fremdwährungsinvestitionen** investment currency market *(Br.)*;
~ **nur geringfügig beanspruchen** to have little recourse to the capital market; ~ **pfleglich behandeln** to nurse the capital market; ~ **fördern** to encourage the capital market; **auf den ~ gehen** to go to the captial market; ~ **in Anspruch nehmen** to resort (have recourse, access) to the capital market, to obtain capital from the general public; ~ **überbeanspruchen** to crowd out the capital market; **Papiere auf dem ~ unterbringen** to market securities to the public;
zentraler ~ausschuß city capital market committee; ~**dirigismus** planned capital market; ~**entspannung** easing of the capital market; ~**förderung** encouragement of the capital market; ~**klima** capital market conditions; ~**konjunktur** boom in the equity market; ~**lenkungsausschuß** capital issue committee; ~**lücke für Mittelbetriebe schließen** to plug the equity gap for medium-sized companies; ~**papiere** equities, gilts *(Br.)*; ~**pflege** nursing the capital market; ~**politik** capital market policy; ~**publikum** investing public, investors;

~publikum in Anspruch nehmen to turn to private sources of capital; **~sätze** capital market rates; **~situation** conditions in the capital market; **~verflechtung** interpenetration of capital markets; **~verhältnisse** conditions in the capital market; **~zins** price of money; **freier ~zins** open market rates.

kapitalmäßig, sich ~ beteiligen to take up a financial interest, to participate on an equity basis;
~e Aktionärsmehrheit majority of stockholders *(US)* (shareholders, *Br.*); **~e Bindung** financial relationship; **auf ~er Grundlage** on the basis of share capital.

Kapital|mehrheit controlling interest, *(AG)* majority shareholding (stockholding, *US*); **~mehrheit eines Unternehmens erwerben** to acquire a controlling interest in a concern; **~menge** [amount of] capital.

Kapitalmittel capital [equipment], funds, means, financial resources;
nicht ausgegebene ~ unspent appropriations; **unzulängliche ~** inadequate resources;
~ vorsichtig einsetzen to husband capital; **nur über begrenzte ~ verfügen** to have only limited capital available.

Kapital|nachfrage demand for capital, capital demand; **~nachfragender** capital-seeking investor, borrower; **~nettoertrag** net capital gain; **reale ~nettorendite** net real return on equity; **~nettoverlust** net capital loss; **~not** scarcity of capital; **~nutzungsertrag** return on capital employed, [capital] yield; **~prämie** capital bonus *(Br.)*, stock dividend; **~produktivität** investment productivity; **~prognose** capital forecasting; **~quellen** supplies of money, [capital] resources, financial resources, funds; **~rechnung** capital (stock, *Br.*) account; **~- und Gewinnrechnung** capital and surplus *(US)*; **~reichtum der Wirtschaft** surplus of capital; **~reingewinn** net capital gain; **~relation** current ratio; **~rendite** yield on investment, return on capital employed (investment), investment income (revenue, *Br.*), *(in bar)* cash refund annuity; **höhere ~rendite** higher return on capital employed, greater return on equity; **~rentabilität** earning power of capital employed; **~rente** capitalized annuity; **~reserve** reserve capital, reserve fund; **~reserve im Falle der Liquidation** reserve capital, rest capital *(Br.)*; **~rückfluß** reflux of capital, capital recapture (recovery) rate; **~rückflußberechnung** payback method; **~rückflußdauer** payback (payoff, payout) period *(US)*; **~rückführung** repatriation of capital; **~rückwanderung** reflux of capital; **~rückzahlung** repayment of principal (capital), return of capital; **~sammelbecken** capital reservoir; **~sammelstelle** investing institution, institutional investor (buyer, lender) *(US)*, accumulation trust; **staatliche ~sammelstelle** government depository *(US)*; **~sammelstellenkonto** institutional account; **~sanierung** capital reconstruction; **~sättigungspunkt** capital saturation; **~schmälerung** encroachment upon one's (impairment of) capital, negative earned surplus, [capital] impairment; **~schöpfung** creation of capital, capital accumulation (creation); **~schrumpfung** shrinking capital, dwindling assets; **~schuld** principal.

kapitalschwach capital-poor, lacking capital, financially weak.

Kapital|schwund dwindling assets, shrinking capital; **~seite** equity section; **~sektor** capital field; **~sicherheit** capital safety (security); **langfristige ~sicherheit mit großen Erträgen kombinieren** to combine a high income with capital security in the long term; **~sicherung** preservation of capital; **~spritze** injection of new capital, capital injection, shot in the arm *(coll.)*.

kapitalstark financially sound, financially strong, substantial.

Kapital|stärke financial strength, sound financial position; **~stau** piling up of capital; **~steuer** capital levy, tax on capital, loan-capital duty *(Br.)*; **vom Finanzamt zurückzuerstattender ~steueranteil** net rate of tax *(Br.)*; **~steuerung** investment control; **~stock** capital fund; **~strom** capital flow; **~ströme umlenken** to redirect capital; **~struktur** capital (financial) structure, capital position, capital construction; **~strukturschema** setup; **~strukturverhältnis** capital structure ratio; **~substanz** net worth *(US)*; **~suche** search for capital; **auf ~suche sein** to scratch around for funds; **~summe** capital [sum], principal, *(Versicherung)* insurance principal; **~tilgung** redemption of principal, capital redemption; **~transaktion** capital transaction; **~transfer[ierung]** transfer of capital, capital transfer; **~übernahmeplan für Arbeitnehmer** employee stock ownership plan *(US)*; **~überschuß** redundant capital, capital surplus *(US)*; **~überschußposten** capital surplus item *(US)*; **~übertragung, ~überweisung** transfer of capital [stock], remittance of capital, capital transfer; **~umdispositionen** reinvestments, capital movements; **~umdispositionen vornehmen** to reinvest; **~umgruppierung** regrouping of capital; **~umlauf** circulation of capital, capitalization; **~umlenkung** redirection of capital; **~umschichtung** regrouping of capital; **~umschlag** capital sales, capital turnover; **~umschlagshäufigkeit** sales volume rate, total assets turnover; **~umschlagsplatz** financial centre *(Br.)* (center, *US*); **~umschlagsverhältnis** capital turnover rate; **~umstellung** *(AG)* reorganization; **~umstrukturierung** capital reconstruction; **~veränderung** capital change; **~verbindlichkeit** capital liability; **~verbindungen** capital connections; **~verbrauch** capital consumption; **~verbrechen** capital crime (offence, felony); **~verbrechen begehen** to compound a felony; **~verflechtungen** capital (financial) interrelation, capital link, interlacing of capital, capital connections; **wechselseitige ~verflechtung** cross ownership; **~verflüssigung** liberation of capital; **~verhältnis** capital ratio; **~verkehr** movement of capital, capital movement, capital transactions; **freier ~verkehr** free movement of capital; **~verkehr beschränken** to restrict the free movement of capital; **~verkehrssteuer** [etwa] transfer tax *(US)*, transfer stamp tax *(Br.)*; **~verknappung** tightness of money, lack of capital; **~verlagerung** capital flow, shifting of capital; **~verlust** capital loss, leakage; **~verlustkonto** capital loss account; **~verlustreserve** investment reserve fund; **~vermehrung** increase of share capital *(Br.)* (capital stock, *US*); **~verminderung** writing off, cut (impairment) of capital, capital reduction; **~vermögen** moneyed capital, property of a capital nature, funded property, capital assets, capital sum, wealth fund, *(Einkommensteuerformular)* shares and securities, *(Kapitalanlagegesellschaft)* investment estate; **~verpfändungen** charges on capital; **~verpflichtungen** capital liabilities, deficiency to owners; **~verschlechterung** capital impairment; **~verschleiß** capital depreciation; **~verschuldung** capital liability.

Kapitalversicherung endowment insurance (assurance, *Br.*);
~ auf den Erlebensfall pure endowment insurance (assurance, *Br.*); **~ mit bestimmter Verfallzeit** insurance for a fixed term.

Kapital|versicherungsgesellschaft stock insurance corporation *(US)*; **~versorgung** provision (supply) of capital, capital supply; **~verteilung** distribution of capital, *(Anlagen zu Kapital)* current ratio; **~verwaltung** fund administration; **~verwaltungsgesellschaft** investment trust; **~verwässerung** watering of stock, stock watering; **~verwendung** capital appropriation, employment of capital, application (employment, placement) of funds; **anderweitige ~verwendung** displacement of funds; **~verwendungsnachweis** statement of application of funds, capital reconciliation statement *(Br.)*; **~verwertung** capital investment; **~verzehr** depreciation of capital, capital depreciation (consumption).

Kapitalverzinsung interest on capital accounts (principal), rate of return *(US)*, return on capital employed (investment), investment return (revenue, *Br.*);
gute ~ fair return on investment; **landesübliche ~** normal returns; **reale ~** real return on investment.

Kapital|verzinsungsfunktion rate of return function; **~volumen** total capital; **~wachstumsrate** capital growth rate; **~wanderung** capital movement, capital flow.

Kapitalwert capital value, *(Police)* cash value, *(Rente)* present value;
~ berechnen to capitalize; **~ in eine Rente umwandeln** to transfer the cash into an annuity;
~methode net present-value method; **~tabelle** *(Versicherung)* cash-value table; **~zuwachs** unearned increment.

Kapitalzahlung commutation, capital payment;
~ oder Rentenzahlung insurance option;
durch ~ abfinden to commute;
~tabelle cash-value table.

Kapital|zeichnung [stock] subscription; **~zeichnungsliste** stock subscription record *(US)*; **~zins[en]** rate of interest, interest on capital; **~zufluß** flow (inflow) of capital, capital flow (inflow), influx of capital; **~zufuhr** import of capital; **~zurückzahlung** repayment of principal.

Kapitalzusammen|ballung concentration of ownership; **~legung** capital reduction, reduction of capital stock *(US)*, *(Fusion)* merger; **~legung vornehmen** to write off capital; **~setzung** capital structure.

Kapitalzuschuß capital subsidy, grant.

Kapitalzuwachs capital gain (accretion, appreciation, *Br.*), appreciation of principal, addition during the year to capital account, *(Investmentfonds)* capital growth, capital increase; **~bilanz** statement of earned surplus *(US)*; **~konto** capital surplus account *(US)*; **~steuer** tax on capital gains, capital-gains tax, capital gains levy.

Kapitän captain, master;
~ **auf großer Fahrt** master mariner; ~ **auf kleiner Fahrt** master of a coasting vessel, skipper; ~ **auf mittlerer Fahrt** home-trade master; ~ **bei der Handelsmarine** merchant captain, master of a trading vessel; ~ **der Landstraße** long-haul driver, trucker; **einem ~ vorübergehend die Ausübung seines Berufs untersagen** to suspend a skipper's certificate.
Kapitäns | heuer master's wages; ~**kajüte** captain's cabin; ~**patent** master's certificate; **sein ~patent bekommen** to obtain one's master's certificate; ~**patent besitzen** to qualify as a captain.
Kapitel chapter, heading, category, head;
am Schluß des ~s sub finem; **über dieses ~** on this head; **ausgewähltes ~** select chapter; **einführendes ~** introductory chapter; **eingeschobenes ~** inter-chapter;
trauriges ~ unserer Geschichte dark period of our history;
~ **abschließen** to close a chapter; **in ~ einteilen** to chapter; **um auf ein anderes ~ zu kommen** to change the subject; **jem. ein ~ lesen** to give (read) s. o. a lecture;
das ist ein ganz anderes ~ that is another story; **dieses ~ wäre erledigt** that's that;
~**überschrift** heading, title.
Kapitulation surrender, capitulation;
bedingungslose ~ unconditional surrender.
Kapitulations | bedingungen *(mil.)* terms of surrender, surrender terms; ~**urkunde** capitulation.
kapitulieren to surrender, to capitulate, to haul down one's flag;
unter gewissen Bedingungen ~ to surrender upon terms; **bedingungslos ~** to surrender unconditionally; **vor jds. Beredsamkeit ~** to yield s. one's eloquence; **nicht ~** to nail one's colo(u)rs to the mast.
Kapo *(Gefängnis)* trustee.
Kappe cap, beret;
auf jds. ~ gehen to pay the bill, to pick up the tap *(US)*; **etw. auf seine ~ nehmen** to take the blame for it;
gleiche Brüder gleiche ~n birds of a feather flock together.
Kappen von Wrackteilen cutting away wreckage.
kappen *(Ankertau)* to cut, *(Baum)* to top.
Kapriolen machen to play pranks.
kaprizieren, sich auf etw. to be dead set on s. th.
Kapsel module.
kaputt out of order (fix, whack, *coll.*), in pieces, packed up, broken, conked, ramshackle *(sl.)*, haywire *(US)*, gone on the blink *(US)*, *(total ermüdet)* fagged out *(US)*, dead beat, done up *(coll.)*, bushed *(US)*;
sich ~arbeiten to work o. s. to death, to wear (fag) o. s. out; ~**fahren** to smash up, to ruin; ~**gehen** to break in (fall to) pieces, to get out of order, to get smashed, to bust, to pack up *(fam.)*, *(Röhre)* to phut, *(sterben)* to kick the bucket *(sl.)*, *(Unternehmen)* to go bust, to fold up *(Br.)*, *(zusammenbrechen)* to crack up; **bei unsachgemäßer Behandlung schnell ~gehen** to wear out under rough usage; **sich ~lachen** to split one's sides with laughter, to be laughing fit to kill o. s.
kaputtmachen to break, to smash, to ruin, to bust, to drive to the dogs;
j. ~ to knock s. o. down; **sich ~** to fag o. s. out; **sich durch harte Arbeit völlig ~** to exhaust o. s. by hard work; **seines Vorgängers Leistungen ~** to undo the good work of one's predecessor; **Telefon ~** to put a telephone out of action.
kaputtschlagen to smash to pieces;
jem. alle Knochen ~ to crush s. o. to a pulp, to make matchwood of s. o.
kaputtwerfen, Fenster to smash a window.
kaputtzukriegen, er ist nicht you can't get the edge on him.
Karacho, mit with gusto;
mit ~ fahren to ride hell for leather.
Karambolage crash, collision;
~ **mit jem. haben** to run into (collide with) s. one's car, *(fig.)* to pick a quarrel with s. o.
karambolieren *(Auto)* to crash, to collide, to cannon into.
Karat carat;
Gold von vierundzwanzig ~ twenty-four carat gold;
~**gewicht** troy weight; ~**gold** alloyed gold.
Karawane caravan.
Karawanen | führer caravaneer, caravan leader; ~**handel** caravan trade; ~**straße** caravan route; ~**zug** caravan train.
Karawanserei caravansary.
Kardan | aufhängung cardanic suspension; ~**gelenk** gimbal (universal) joint, universal coupling; ~**welle** cardan (propeller) shaft.
Kardinal cardinal;
~**bischof** cardinal bishop.
kardinale Bedeutung cardinal importance.
Kardinal | punkt cardinal point; ~**tugenden** cardinal virtues; ~**würde** cardinalship, hat.
Karenz *(Wettbewerb)* restraint of trade;
~**entschädigung** waiting allowance; ~**klausel** *(Wettbewerb)* restraint clause; ~**vereinbarung** restraint agreement; ~**zeit** *(Anleihe)* redemption-free period, *(Emissionen)* close season, *(Versicherung)* waiting (qualifying) period, period of waiting, *(Wettbewerbsverbot)* competitive restriction.
karg scant, scanty, meager, meagre *(Br.)*, frugal, *(Boden)* barren, poor;
~ **bemessen** to give scant measure;
~ **bemessen sein** *(Zeit)* to be strictly limited;
~**e Kost** slender diet; ~**es Lob** faint praise; ~**er Lohn** scanty wages.
kargen, mit seinem Lob nicht to be unstinting in one's praise; **mit Trinkgeldern ~en** to be tight-fisted.
kärglich poor, meagre, sparse;
sein ~es Auskommen haben to eke a scanty living; ~**es Mahl** frugal meal; ~**e Reste** scanty remains.
Karikatur caricature, cartoon, travesty *(US)*, takeoff *(coll.)*;
als ~ darstellen to cartoon; ~ **zeichnen** to caricature.
karikaturenartig caricatural.
Karikaturen | reihe in Fortsetzungen cartoon; ~**seite** comic strips, funnies *(US sl.)*.
Karikaturist caricaturist, cartoonist *(US)*.
karikaturistische Zeichnung caricature, cartoon *(US)*.
Karikaturzeichner caricaturist, cartoonist *(US)*.
karikieren to caricature, to [make] a cartoon.
karitativ charitable, eleemosynary;
~ **oder förderungswürdig** charitable or deserving; ~ **und menschenfreundlich** charitable and philanthropic; ~ **oder wohltätig** charitable or benevolent;
sich ~ betätigen to do works of charity;
~**er Beitrag** *(Einkommensteuer)* charitable contribution; ~**e Einrichtung** charitable institution; ~**es Unternehmen** charitable enterprise; ~**er Verband** charitable organization; ~**e Vereinigung** charitable corporation; ~**e Zwecke** charitable purposes; **sein Vermögen für ~e Zwecke bestimmen** to leave one's money to charity.
Karneval carnival.
karnevalistisch carnivalesque.
Karnevals | maske carnival mask; ~**schlager** carnival song; ~**veranstaltung** carnival show.
Karo | muster checker; ~**papier** design paper.
Karosserie car (carriage) body, bodywork, coach;
gepanzerte ~ armo(u)red car body; **stromlinienförmige ~** streamlined (torpedo) body;
~**arbeit** bodywork, coachwork; ~**ausführung** coach (body) style; ~**bau** coachbuilding, styling; ~**bauer** bodymaker, coachbuilder, coachmaker; ~**blech** plate; ~**firma** car-body firm, bodymaking plant; ~**zeichner** stylist.
Karre cart, *(Schubkarre)* wheelbarrow;
alte ~ old crock, rattletrap, jaloppy;
jem. an die ~ fahren to upset s. one's applecart.
Karree | bilden to form a square; **ums ~ gehen** to go round the block.
Karren cart, truck, flivver *(sl.)*;
~ **in den Dreck fahren** to make a mess of it (muddle of an affair); ~ **laufen lassen** to let things slide; **sich vor jds. ~ spannen lassen** to be roped in to do s. one's donkey work; ~ **schmieren** to oil the wheels; ~ **aus dem Dreck ziehen** to clear up a mess.
karren to cart;
Abfall auf den Misthaufen ~ to wheel the rubbish to the dump.
Karrenladung cartload.
Karriere career, course, *(Galopp)* full galopp (tilt), run;
erstaunliche ~ career of resounding progress;
jds. ~ stark beeinträchtigen to take toll of s. one's career; **jds. ~ beenden** to be the end of s. o.; ~ **einschlagen** to enter upon a career; ~ **machen** to make (carve out) a career for o. s., to work one's way up, to get ahead *(US)*; **seiner ~ schaden** to injure one's prospects; **von ausschlaggebender Bedeutung für jds. ~ sein** to determine s. one's career; **seine ~ aufs Spiel setzen** to lay one's career on the line;
~**diplomat** professional (career) diplomatist; ~**macher** careerist, climber.
karrieremäßig günstig auswirken, sich to be a good step careerwise.
Karrieremuster career pattern.
karriere | süchtig eager about one's progress; ~**verdächtiger Bursche** whiz-kid *(US sl.)*.

Karte card, *(Bewirtschaftung)* ration card, coupon, *(Eintrittskarte)* admission ticket, *(Fahrkarte)* ticket, *(Landkarte)* map, *(Postkarte)* postcard, *(Restaurant)* bill of fare, menu [card], *(Schiff)* chart, *(Visitenkarte)* business card;
auf ~n on (with, *US*) coupons; **statt ~n** *(Todesanzeige)* no cards;
flächengetreue ~ equal-area chart; **grüne ~** *(Versicherung)* green card; **perforierte ~** stub card; **politische ~** political card; **randgelochte ~** margin-punched card; **ungültige ~** ticket no longer available; **winkeltreue ~** equal-angle map;
~ im Maßstab 1 : 100.000 map on a scale of 1/100.000; **~ im großen Maßstab** large-scale map;
seine ~ bei jem. abgeben to leave one's card on s. o.; **~ abstempeln** *(nach Arbeitsschluß)* to check (clock) out *(Br.)*, *(bei Arbeitsbeginn)* to check (clock) in *(Br.)*; **von einem Gebiet eine ~ anlegen** to make a map of a district; **seine ~n aufdecken** to show one's hand, to come out into the open; **zusammenklappbare ~ aufschlagen** to open out a folding map; **~ auf dem Boden ausbreiten** to spread a map on the floor; **seine beste ~ ausspielen** to play one's trump card; **seine letzte ~ ausspielen** to make one's last bid; **Kurs auf der ~ einzeichnen** to chart a course; **nach der ~ essen** to eat à la carte; **nach der ~ fahren** to drive by the map; **schlechte ~n haben** to have a bad hand; **alle ~n in seiner Hand halten** to turn up trumps; **auf ~n kaufen** to buy on (with, *US*) coupons; **Stelle auf der ~ mit einem Kreuz kennzeichnen** to mark a place on a map with a cross; **~ lesen können** to be able to read maps; **sich nicht in die ~n schauen lassen** not to show one's hand; **jem. die ~n legen** to tell s. one's fortune; **seine ~n auf den Tisch legen** to put one's cards on the table; **~ lochen** to punch (clip) a ticket; **auf ~n erhältlich sein** to go (be) on points; **alles auf eine ~ setzen** to run the risk of losing everything, to put one's shirt on s. th., to put all one's eggs in one basket, to go nap, to go for broke *(fam.)*, to play double or quits *(fam.)*, to shoot one's wad; **auf die falsche ~ setzen** to back the wrong horse; **~n spielen** to play cards; **mit offenen ~n spielen** to show one's hand; **mit verdeckten ~n spielen** to conceal (cover) one's hand; **~ stechen** *(Betrieb)* to clock in (out), to punch one's card; **~ stempeln** *(bei Arbeitsbeginn)* to check in; **~ studieren** to consult a map; **auf der ~ suchen** to look up on a map; **seine ~ vorzeigen** to show one's ticket.

Kartei card-index [file], file, card catalog(ue), filing cabinet;
leicht handhabbare ~ card-index of easy reference;
~ der laufenden Bestellungen current-order card-index;
~ anlegen to card-index; **~ für einen neuen Kunden anlegen** to enter a new client in the card index; **Karten in eine ~ einordnen** to file cards in the card index; **~ führen** to keep files; **~ auf dem laufenden halten** to keep a card index up to date;
in ~form card-indexed; **in ~form erfassen** to card-index; **~karte** index (record, file) card, data sheet; **~karte eines Abzahlungskunden** hire-purchase card *(Br.)*; **~kartenpapier** index board, cardboard *(US)*; **~kartensystem** card-index system; **~kasten** filing box, *(Bibliothek)* card catalog(ue); **~reiter** tab, signal, index clip; **~schrank** filing (card-index) cabinet; **~schublade** filing drawer; **~system** card (filing) system; **~trog** card-index tray; **~unterlagen über den einzelnen Arbeiter** work report; **~zettel** index slip.

Kartell cartel, pool, industrial combine (monopoly), monopoly agreement *(Br.)*, ring *(Br.)*, trust *(US)*, combination [in restraint of trade] *(US)*;
ausländisches ~ foreign cartel; **horizontales ~** horizontal combine; **internationales ~** international cartel;
~ der Linienfluggesellschaften scheduled carriers' cartel;
sich einem ~ anschließen to join a cartel; **~ auflösen** to break up a cartel, to split the structure of a cartel; **einem ~ beitreten** to join a cartel; **~ bilden** to pool, to cartelize; **~e entflechten** to decartelize; **den Zwangsbestimmungen eines ~s unterwerfen** to cartelize; **zu einem ~ vereinigen** to cartelize; **~ vergrößern** to expand a cartel;
~abkommen restrictive trading agreement *(Br.)*, pooling agreement (contract) in restraint of trade *(US)*; **~abmachung, ~absprache** cartel agreement (negotiations), restrictive agreement; **~abteilung** cartel office, antitrust division *(US)*.

kartellähnliche Absprachen loose (contract) combinations *(US)*.

Kartellamt cartel office, Registrar of Restrictive Trade Practices *(Br.)*, Registrar of Restrictive Trading Agreements *(Br.)*, Office for Fair Trading *(Br.)*, Antitrust Division *(US)*.

Kartellamts|bestimmungen verletzen to violate the antitrust statutes *(US)*; **~leiter** director-general of fair trading *(Br.)*; **~verfahren** monopoly charge, antitrust suit *(US)*.

Kartell|angelegenheit cartel matter; **~anhänger** cartelist, *(pl.)* pro-cartel people; **~anteile** cartel (pool) interests; **~antrag** application for a cartel; **~anwalt** antitrust lawyer *(US)*; **~auffassungen** ideas in respect of monopolies; **~auflösung** cartel relinquishment; **~aufsicht** supervision of cartels; **~aufsichtsbehörde** monopolies and mergers commission, monopoly commissioner *(Br.)*; **~ausschuß** cartel bureau, Antitrust Committee *(US)*; **~behörde** Antitrust Division *(US)*, Registrar of Restrictive Trade Practices *(Br.)*, Office for Fair Trading *(Br.)*, cartel office *(Br.)*; **Mißtrauen der ~behörde zerstreuen** to get through antitrust suspicions *(US)*; **~beseitigung** cartel relinquishment; **~bestimmungen** cartel regulations, antitrust provisions *(US)*; **~bestimmungen verletzen** to violate the antitrust statutes *(US)*; **~beteiligung** cartel participation; **~beziehungen** cartel relationship (participation); **~bildung** formation of cartels; **~brecher** trust buster *(US sl.)*; **~bürokratie** cartel bureaucracy; **~duldung** tolerance of cartels; **~entflechter** trust buster *(sl.)*; **~entflechtung** cartel dispersal, decartelization, trust busting *(sl.)*; **~entflechtungsbehörde** decartelization agency; **~erzeugnis** cartelized product; **~experte, ~fachmann** antitrust specialist (expert) *(US)*.

kartellfähig able to form a cartel.

Kartellfähigkeit ability to form cartels.

kartellfeindlich antitrust, anticartel.

Kartell|firmen cartel companies; **~fragen** cartel problems; **~führer** leader of a cartel; **~gebiet** antitrust field; **~gegner** anticartel people; **~gericht** cartel court, Restrictive Practice Court *(Br.)*; **~gesetz** Restrictive Trade Practices Act *(Br.)*, Monopolies and Restrictive Practices Act *(Br.)*, Statute of Monopolies *(Br.)*, Monopolies and Merger Act, Sherman Act *(US)*; **Verstöße gegen die ~gesetze vor Gericht bringen** to chase up antitrust injuries *(US)*; **~gesetzgebung** legislation on cartels, antimonopoly legislation, antitrust laws (legislation) *(US)*; **~gründung** establishment of a cartel; **~idee** idea of cartels; **~interessen** cartel interests.

kartellisieren to cartel, to cartelize, to pool.

kartellisierende Industrie cartelized industry.

Kartellisierung cartelization, pooling.

Kartellisierungs|methoden cartel practices; **~system** cartel ramifications.

Kartell|klage antitrust suit (action, charge) *(US)*, monopoly charge; **~kontrolle** cartel control; **~konvention** *(Völkerrecht)* cartel; **~kündigung** cartel termination; **~leistung** cartel output; **~manipulationen** cartel manipulations; **~maßnahme** restrictive trade practices *(Br.)*; **~mitglied** member of a cartel; **~organisation** trading combine, cartel combination in restraint of trade *(US)*; **~politik** cartelizing (antitrust, *US*) policy; **gebundene ~preise** fixed cartel prices; **~probleme** cartel (monopoly), problems; **~recht** right of combination, cartel law, antitrust law *(US)*.

kartellrechtliche Verbindungen cartel connections.

Kartell|spezialist antitrust specialist *(US)*, expert on antitrust law *(US)*, cartelographer; **~stabilität** stability of cartels; **~tätigkeit** cartel activities; **~teilnehmer** cartel participant.

kartellunschädlicher Tatbestand gateway *(Br.)*.

Kartell|usancen cartel habits; **~verbindungen** cartel connections; **~verbot** ban on cartelization, cartel ban.

Kartellvereinbarung cartel (restrictive trade, restrictive trading, *Br.*) agreement (arrangement), contract in restraint of trade;
~en cartel negotiations;
registrierte ~ registered agreement *(Br.)*; **wettbewerbsbeschränkende ~** cartel (restrictive trade, *Br.*) agreement (arrangement), cartel regulations (negotiations), contract (agreement) in restraint of trade *(Br.)*, restrictive trading agreement *(Br.)*;
~ zur Durchsetzung von gebundenen Wiederverkaufspreisen agreement for collective enforcement of conditions as to resale prices;
gegen eine ~ verstoßen to break the rules of a cartel.

Kartell|vereinigung producers' association, trading combine; **~verfahren** antitrust suit *(US)*, monopoly charge; **~verhandlungen** cartel negotiations; **~verkauf** pool selling; **~verordnung** cartel decree; **~vertrag** cartel agreement (arrangement), pooling contract (agreement), restrictive trade (practices) agreement *(Br.)*; **~vorschriften** cartel regulations, rules of a cartel, antitrust provisions *(US)*; **~wesen** antitrust field *(US)*, cartelism.

kartellwillig willing to form a cartel.

Karten|aufnahme mapping; **~ausgabe** booking office *(Br.)*, ticket window *(US)*; **~automat** ticket slot machine; **~behälter** map case; **~bild** cartographic representation; **~blatt** map sheet; **~brett** map board; **~brief** letter card; **~entfernung** distance on the map, cartographical distance; **~futteral** map cover; ~**gitter** map grid; **jem. einen ~gruß schicken** to send s. o. a postcard; ~**halter** map holder; ~**haus** *(fig.)* house of cards, *(Schiff)* charthouse; **wie ein ~haus zusammenfallen** to collapse like a house of cards, to come to nought, to end in smoke; ~**hersteller** map maker; ~**inhaber** card holder; ~**kunde** cartography, map reading; ~**kunststück** trick with cards, card trick; ~**kunststücke beherrschen** to be clever at card tricks; ~**legen** fortune telling; ~**legerin** fortune teller; ~**lesen** map reading; ~**locher** *(Computer)* card punch; ~**maßstab** map scale; ~**material** maps; ~**netz** skeleton map, grid; ~**papier** fine cardboard; ~**periode** ration period.

kartenpflichtig rationed, couponed;
~ **sein** to go on points, to be rationed.

Karten|projektion map projection; ~**reiter** tab; ~**sammlung** collection of maps; ~**schalter** booking office *(Br.)*, ticket window (office) *(US)*; ~**schrank** map and plan file; ~**skizze** skeleton map; ~**spiel** card game, game of cards, *(Glücksspiel)* game of chance; ~**spieler** card player; ~**ständer** card rack; ~**stelle** local food office *(Br.)*, ration-card agency *(US)*, ration board *(US)*; ~**tasche** map case; ~**tisch** card table, *(Leitstelle)* filter board; ~**umsatz** ticket sales; ~**verkauf** ticket booking, booking *(Br.)* (ticket, *US*) office, *(Theater)* box office; ~**vorverkauf** advance booking *(Br.)*, advance ticket sale; ~**wirtschaft** rationing system; ~**zeichnen** map making; ~**zeichner** cartographer, mapper; ~**zimmer** chartroom.

Kartoffel, heiße hot potato;
~**n von unten ansehen** to push up the daisies; **etw. wie eine heiße ~ fallen lassen** to drop s. th. like a hot potato (chestnut);
die dümmsten Bauern haben die dicksten ~n fortune favo(u)rs fools;
~**anbaugebiet** potato-growing district; ~**miete** potato pit; ~**nase** turnip.

Karto|gramm cartogram; ~**graph** cartographer, map maker, mapper; ~**graphie** cartography, map-making, mapping.

kartographisch cartographical, map-making;
noch nicht ~ erfaßt unmapped;
~ **aufnehmen (darstellen)** to map.

Karton cardboard, board, pasteboard, paper box, quire, *(Schachtel)* carton, cardboard box;
glatter ~ Bristol board;
~ **für Briefumschläge** envelope file.

Kartonage cartonage, cardboard;
~**arbeit** pasteboard work.

Kartonagenhersteller carton factory.

Kartoneinlagen cardboard fillers.

kartonieren *(Buch)* to bind in boards.

kartoniert *(Buch)* [bound] in boards, paperback.

Kartonpapier box card, cardboard.

Kartothek card-index [file], card catalog(ue), filing cabinet;
~ **anlegen** to card-index;
~**ausgabe** loose-leaf edition; ~**karte** file (index) card.

Karussell roundabout, ride, turnabout, merry-go-round;
~ **der Zeit** whirligig of time.

Kaschemme dive, joint *(US)*, doss house *(sl.)*.

kaschieren to hide, to conceal, to camouflage, *(Papierherstellung)* to laminate, to line.

kaschiertes Papier laminated paper.

Käse cheese;
das ist doch alles großer ~ that's rubbish.

Kaserne barracks;
in die ~ einrücken to return to barracks.

Kasernen|arrest confinement to barracks; **4 Tage ~arrest erhalten** to be confined to barracks for four days; ~**dienst** barracks duty; ~**gebäude** barrack; ~**hof** barrack square; ~**hofton** barrack-room language; ~**leben** life in barracks; ~**stube** barrack room.

kasernieren to barrack.

Kasino casino, *(Betrieb)* catering department, *(mar.)* mess, *(Verein)* clubhouse;
~ **für leitende Angestellte** executive dining room, canteen used exclusively for executives;
~**abteilung** catering department; ~**besitzer** casino owner; ~**offizier** catering officer; ~**ordonnanz** mess attendant, mess (dining room, *US*) orderly; ~**raum** mess room, *(mar.)* mess hall; ~**vorstand** mess council.

Kaskade cascade, waterfall.

Kaskaden|bombenwurf cascade bombing; ~**schaltung** tandem (cascade) connection; ~**verstärker** cascade amplifier.

Kasko|und Maschinen hull and machinery;
~**interesse** hull interest; ~**police** hull policy, comprehensive insurance policy; **teilweise gedecktes ~risiko** comprehensive coverage *(US)*; ~**schutz** collision coverage; ~**versicherer** *(Schiff)* hull underwriter; ~**versicherung** collision insurance, automobile personal liability and property damage insurance *(US)*, vehicle insurance *(US)*, *(Schiff)* hull insurance, *(Teilkasko)* comprehensive automobile and property damage insurance *(US)*, comprehensive motorcar insurance *(Br.)*; **hundertprozentige (vollgedeckte) ~versicherung** full-coverage collision insurance; ~**versicherungspolice** comprehensive insurance policy.

Kasperl harlequin, Punch.

Kassa cash;
gegen ~ for [ready] cash;
per ~ bezahlen to pay in cash;
~**abzug** cash discount; ~**anweisung** cash order.

Kassabuch cashbook;
kleines ~ petty cashbook;
~ **für tägliche Kassenumsätze** cash balance book *(Br.)*.

Kassa|devisen spot foreign currency; ~**diskont** cash discount; ~**fluß** cashflow, cash value; ~**gegenbuch** counter cashbook; ~**geschäft** cash (ready money) business, cash-on-invoice basis, *(Börse)* cash operation (sale, transaction), dealing for cash, *(Devisen)* spot deal [exchange], spot exchange transaction; ~**kauf** cash buying (purchase), buying outright *(US)*; ~**käufer** cash buyer (purchaser); ~**konto** petty cash account; ~**kurs** price for cash, cash price, cash quotation (rates), *(Devisen)* spot quotation (price, rate); ~**lieferung** *(Devisen)* spot delivery; ~**makler** *(Devisen)* spot broker; ~**markt** cash market, *(Devisen)* spot market (outlet, *US*); ~**order** *(Börse)* cash order; ~**papiere** securities dealt in for cash, *(Devisen)* securities quoted on the spot market; ~**posten** cash entry; ~**preis** cash price, price for cash, cash market value, *(Devisen)* spot price; ~**regulierung** cash payment (settlement); ~**schaden** cash claim; ~**skonto** cash discount, discount for cash; **2% ~skonto geben** to allow 2 per cent cash discount.

Kassation *(jur.)* cassation, annulment.

Kassationsgerichtshof Trial Court of Appeal *(US)*, Supreme Court of Errors *(Connecticut)*.

Kassa|umsatz *(Devisen)* spot sales; ~**verkauf** *(Börse)* cash sale; ~**ware** *(Devisen)* spot commodities; ~**werte** *(Devisen)* securities dealt with (quoted) on the spot market.

Kasse cash, *(Bahnhof)* booking office *(Br.)*, ticket window *(US)*, *(Bank)* cashier's (teller's, *US*) department, cashier's office, *(Barangebot)* cash offer, *(Bargeld)* cash [on hand], ready money, the ready, jack *(sl.)*, hardtack *(sl.)*, *(Börse)* spot cash, *(Finanzen einer Firma)* finances, Exchequer *(fam.)*, *(Fonds)* means, resources, *(Geldschrank)* safe, strongbox, box, *(Kassenschalter)* cash (paying) office, pay desk, *(Kino)* paybox, box (ticket) office, *(Krankenkasse)* health insurance, sick (sickness) fund, *(Ladenkasse)* cashbox, shop till, money chest, *(Quästur)* bursary, *(Registrierkasse)* cash register, *(Staatskasse)* Exchequer *(Br.)*, Treasury Department *(US)*, *(Theater)* box (booking, *Br.*) office, ticket window *(US)*, *(Unterstützungskasse)* relief fund, *(Verwaltung)* finance, cash (finance) department, *(Zahltisch)* counter;
an der ~ *(Bank)* over the counter (window), *(Theater)* at the booking *(Br.)* (ticket, *US*) office; **bei ~** in funds, financial, in the money *(sl.)*; **gegen ~** in ready cash, for cash, cash on delivery, *(Wertpapiere)* for delivery, spot; **gegen ~ gekauft** bought for cash; **gegen sofortige ~** spot (for prompt) cash, payable cash down; **gut bei ~** flush of money, well-heeled *(US sl.)*; **knapp bei ~** short of cash; **netto ~** net (spot) cash, *(Börse)* for money; **nicht bei ~** short of means (money), out of cash, out of funds; **nur gegen ~** for cash only; **per ~** *(Devisen)* on spot terms, *(Wertpapiere)* for cash *(US)*, cash *(US)*, payable cash down; **rein netto ~** net cash without discount; **schlecht bei ~** short of money, money-starved, hard up;
auszahlende ~ paying office; **gemeinsame (gemeinschaftliche) ~** joint account, common purse (fund), kitty; **getrennte ~** separate account, Dutch treat; **kleine ~** petty cash; **leere ~** bare (depleted) treasury; **öffentliche ~** county (public) funds, public treasury; **sofortige ~** cash down, ready, ready money, ready (spot, *US*) cash; **tägliche ~** *(Bank)* counter cash;
~ **bei Bestellung** cash with order; ~ **gegen Dokumente** cash against documents; ~ **bei Lieferung** cash on delivery; ~ **mit 2% Skonto** less 2 per cent cash discount; **netto ~ im voraus** net cash in advance;
~ **abnehmen** to balance the cash; ~ **abstimmen** to tally (count, *US*, make up) the cash, to count the daily receipts; ~ **wieder auffüllen** *(Partei)* to replenish its funds; **volle ~ bringen** to be a box-office success *(US)*; **mit der ~ durchbrennen (durchgehen)** to make (run) off (bolt) with the money (cash), to shoot the

moon *(sl.)*; ~ **führen** to keep cash, to act as a cashier, to hold the purse, to bear the bag; **getrennte** ~ **führen** to go Dutch; **in die** ~ **greifen** to rob (dip into) the till; **Geld in der** ~ **haben** to have cash in hand; **~n halten** *(öffentlicher Haushalt)* to maintain cash funds; **jem. knapp bei** ~ **halten** to keep s. o. short of money; ~ **journalisieren** to enter the cash into the journal; **per (gegen bare)** ~ **kaufen** to buy for cash (outright, *US*), *(Devisen)* to buy on a spot basis (for spot cash); ~ **machen** to tally (count) up *(US)* the cash, to count the daily receipts, to make (reckon, *Br.*) up the cash; **gemeinsame** ~ **machen** to put one's funds in common, to have a common purse, to pool expenses; **getrennte** ~ **machen** to go Dutch; **Griff in die** ~ **machen** to dip into (rob) the till; **volle** ~ **machen** *(Film)* to be a box-office success *(US)*; ~ **pfänden** to seize the till; ~ **schließen** to count the receipts; **bei** ~ **sein** to be in funds (cash, stock, flush of money), to have plenty of (be up for) cash; **gut bei** ~ **sein** to be pretty flush with funds, to be in the chips (in pocket); **knapp bei** ~ **sein** to be short of cash; **nicht bei** ~ **sein** to be out of cash; **nicht gut (schlecht) bei** ~ **sein** to be in low funds (water); ~ **stürzen** to count the cash; **~n unterhalten** *(öffentliches Rechnungswesen)* to maintain cash funds; **über die** ~ **verfügen** to have one's hand in the till, to hold the purse strings tightly; **sich an der** ~ **vergreifen** to tamper with the cash; **gegen** ~ **verkaufen** to sell for cash (outright, *US*); **an der** ~ **zahlen** to pay at the desk.

Kassen | abgänge outflow of cash; **~abhebung** cash drawing; **~abschluß** cash settlement, cash statement, cash results, making up the cash; **bei ~abschluß** when balancing the cash; **~abstimmung** proving cash, cash reconciliation; **~abteilung** cashier's office; **~abteilung für Auszahlungen** paying departmentt; **~abzüge** cashflow; **~amtsystem** panel system *(Br.)*; **~anspannung** cash drain; **~anweisung** cash note, pay *(Br.)* (cash) voucher, pay bill *(Br.)*, *(Bank)* payment voucher, bank bill *(US)*, treasury bond *(Br.)* (treasury note, certificate, *US*), cash order.

Kassenarzt panel doctor *(Br.)*;
als ~ **zugelassen** on the panel *(Br.)*;
einem ~ **überweisen** to place on a doctor's panel.

kassenärztliche Behandlung panel patient treatment *(Br.)*.

Kassen | arztpraxis panel practice *(Br.)*; **zur ~arztpraxis zugelassen sein** to be working under the panel system *(Br.)*; **~aufnahme** cash audit (auditing); **~aufsichtsbeamter** chief cashier, cashier in charge of operations; **~ausfall** cash deficit, adverse balance *(Br.)*; **~ausgabebeleg** cash disbursement record; **~ausgänge** cash disbursement (payments); **~ausgangsbuch** cash disbursements book; **~ausweis** cash statement; **~auszahlungen** cash disbursements; **~beleg** journal (cash) voucher, cash record, *(Barverkauf)* sales record (slip, ticket, warrant, check, *US*), *(Portokasse)* petty cash voucher; **abgezeichneter ~beleg** slip initialled by the cashier; **~bericht** cash report, treasurer's (financial) report, balance sheet; **periodischer ~- und Bankbericht** cash statement; **~bestand** balance in cash (on hand), cash on hand, cash balance (assets), amount in cash, *(Bank)* real reserve, stock in the till, till money *(US)*, cash in vaults *(US)*, *(Bilanz)* cash, cash holdings, effects; **~bestand der Filialen** *(Bankfilialen)* cash at branches; **~bestand und Bankguthaben** *(Bilanz)* cash assets; **schwache ~bestände haben** to run short of cash; **~bilanz** cash balance; **~bilanz ziehen** to balance the cash; **~block** cash pad; **~bon** sales voucher, receipt; **~bote** bank messenger, collecting clerk, *(Ladengeschäft)* cashboy.

Kassenbuch [cash]book, till book;
~eintragung cash (cashbook) entry; **~führung** cash accounting; **~halter** cash accountant; **~haltung** cash accounting; **~saldo** cash (cashbook) balance.

Kassen | buchung cash entry; **~budget** cash budget; **~büro** pay (cashier's) office, *(Auszahlung)* cash department; **~darlehn** cash (money) loan; **~defizit** deficit in an expense fund, adverse cash balance *(Br.)*, cash deficit, *(Irrtum)* short of cash, cash short *(US)*; **~diebstahl** embezzlement (misappropriation) of funds; **~diener** bank messenger; **~differenzkonto** over and short account *(US)*; **~disponent** cashier, teller *(US)*; **~disposition** cash arrangements; **~eingang** cash receipts; **~eingangsbuch** cash receipts journal.

Kasseneinnahme takings, cash (box office, *US*, gate) receipts, box-office takings *(US)*;
~ **ansteigen lassen** to send up gate receipts;
~buch cash receipts book; **~journal** cash receipts journal.

Kassen | einnehmer cashier, receiving teller *(US)*, *(Einkassierer)* collector; **~eintrag[ung]** cash entry (item); **~entwicklung** cash position; **~erfolg** office bomb, box-office success *(US)*; **~fehlbetrag** shortage in the cash, cash deficit, adverse cash balance *(Br.)*; **~führer** cashier, treasurer, teller *(US)*; **~führung** cashkeeping; **~führung haben** to be in charge of the cash; **~fülle** glut of money; **~gebarung** cash management; **~gehilfe** assistant cashier; **~geschäfte** cash transactions; **~gewinn** cash earnings; **~guthaben** cash assets, cash in hand (vault, *US*); **~gutschein** trading cheque *(Br.)*; **~halle** cash office; **~haltung** cash management, holding of money; **~haltungstheorie** cash balance theory; **~journal** cash journal, cash blotter; **~kladde** rough cashbook, cash diary, waste book *(Br.)*; **~knüller** office bomb, box-office success *(US)*; **~konto** cash (cashier's) account; **~kontrolle** cash audit.

Kassenkredit *(Notenbank)* cash advance;
~ **bei der Landeszentralbank** reserve bank credit *(US)*; **~e der Notenbank an die öffentlichen Haushalte** ways and means advances *(Br.)*;
~zusage cash advance facilities.

Kassen | lage *(Flüssigkeit)* cash position, cash situation; **~leistung** *(Krankenkasse)* medical benefits; **~liquidität** liquidity; **~mädchen** cash girl; **~magnet** *(Film)* box-office draw *(US)*; **~manko** cash deficit, adverse cash balance *(Br.)*, short *(US)*; **~mankogeld** cash indemnity; **~markt** cash (spot) market.

kassenmäßig cash;
~ **durchleiten** *(Bank)* to pass through one's books;
~e Ausgaben cash expenditure; **~e Entwicklung** cash position; **~es Minimum** minimum cash reserves; **~er Spielraum** cash margin.

Kassen | mitglied *(Krankenkasse)* health-service (panel, *Br.*) patient; **~mittel** cash money, cash resources; **~obligationen** treasury bonds *(Br.)*, deposit certificates; **~patient** health-service (panel, *Br.*) patient; **~pfändung vornehmen** to seize the till; **~position** *(Flüssigkeit)* cash position; **~posten** cash item; **~praxis** panel practice *(Br.)*; **zur ~praxis zugelassen sein** to be working under the panel system *(Br.)*; **~prüfer** cash auditor.

Kassenprüfung cash check, proving cash, *(Revision)* cash audit[ing];
~ **durchführen (vornehmen)** to prove (check) the cash, *(Revision)* to audit the cash.

Kassen | quittung cash (cashier's) receipt, sales check *(US)*; **~rabatt** cash discount.

Kassenraub payroll robbery;
~ **durchführen** to rob s. o. of the payroll;
~versicherung paymaster's robbery insurance.

Kassen | raum cash office, *(Kino)* paybox; **~rekord** box-office record *(US)*; **~reserve** reserve in cash, cash resources, *(Bank)* real (primary) reserve, petty money *(US)*; **~revision** cash audit[ing], checkup (verification) of the cash; **~revisor** cash auditor; **~saldo** balance in cash, balance on hand, cash balance.

Kassenschalter paybox, pay (cash, cashier's) desk, *(Bahnhof)* booking office *(Br.)*, ticket office (window, *US*), *(Bank)* [teller's, *US*] counter, bank counter, window *(US)*, *(Theater)* box office;
~ **für Auszahlungen** paying teller's counter (window, *US*); ~ **für Einzahlungen** receiving teller's counter (window, *US*);
am ~ **auszahlen** to pay out money across the counter, to pay over the counter (window, *US*).

Kassen | scheck bank cheque *(Br.)*, cashier's (counter) check *(US)*, *(Barscheck)* open (uncrossed) check *(US)* (cheque, *Br.*); **~schein** *(Anweisung)* cash order, slip, check *(US)*, *(Banknote)* bank note (bill, *US*), *(Kassenzettel)* sales slip (ticket, warrant), *(Krankenkasse)* sickness certificate, *(Schatzanweisung)* treasury bill (note) *(US)*, currency note; **entwertete ~scheine** cancelled notes; **schlechte ~scheine** wild-cat currency *(US)*; **~schlager** jack-pot winner, great draw, box-office success (draw) *(US)*, blockbuster *(US)*, office bomb, *(Film)* film hit, smash *(sl.)*; **echter ~schlager** bona-fide smash hit *(sl.)*; **späte ~schließung** late cutoff of the admission; **nach ~schluß** after banking hours; **~schrank** safe, money vault *(US)*; **~schublade** cash drawer; **~sieger** box-office champion *(US)*; **~skonto** cash discount; **~stand** balance on hand, cash position (situation); **~standkoeffizient** cash-position ratio; **~status** cash position; **~strazze** cashbook; **~stunden** banking (business) hours.

Kassensturz proving cash;
~ **machen** to cash up, to tally (count, *US*) up, to make up (balance) the cash, to check the day's takings, to count the daily receipts.

Kassensystem national health insurance plan *(Br.)*.

Kassenüberschuß surplus [in cash], cash surplus, *(irrtümlich)* cash overs, excess cash, overage of cash *(US)*;
~ **der öffentlichen Hand** budget surplus.

Kassen | überschüsse und Fehlbeträge cash shorts and overs *(US)*; **~umsatz** cash turnover (transactions); **~verein** [etwa] clearinghouse association; **~verkehr** cash transactions, over-the-counter business (trading) *(US)*; **~verlust** cash deficit *(US)*, adverse cash balance; **~verwalter** treasurer, [chief] cashier, cash clerk; **~verwaltung** cash department; **~voranschlag, ~vorschau** cash budget *(US)*; **~vorschuß** cash advance; **~vorschüsse** *(Bundesnotenbank)* deficiency advances *(Br.)*; **~vorstand, ~vorsteher** chief cashier *(US)*; **~wart** cashier, cash clerk, *(Verein)* treasurer; **~wart abgeben** to keep the cash, to hold the purse; **~wesen** cash accounting; **~zahnarzt** panel dentist *(Br.)*; **~zettel** sales check *(US)* (slip), check slip, sales ticket *(US)*, coupon check *(US)*; **~zettelkontrolle** sales check control; **~zufluß, ~zugänge** cashflow, inflow of cash; **~zwang** *(Krankenkasse)* compulsory (national) health insurance *(Br.)*.

Kassette strongbox, cashbox, coffer, *(Buch)* box, clipcase, *(für Dokumente)* deedbox, *(Fernsehen)* cartridge, *(Film)* magazine, plateholder, cassette, dark slide, *(für Geschenkpackungen)* gift carton, *(Kassettendecke)* coffer, woffle, panel, *(für Schmuck)* jewel box, casket, chest, *(Tonband)* cassette;
in ~ *(Buch)* boxed;
bespielte ~ pre-recorded (program(me)) cartridge; **verschließbare ~** lockbox;
unbespielte ~ mit einstündiger Laufzeit blank one-hour cassette.

Kassetten | decke coffered ceiling; **~fernsehen** electronic video recording, cartridge television, cartrivision.

Kassettenfernseh | film cartridge movie for television program(me); **~gerät** video cassette machine; **~rechte** cartridge television rights.

Kassetten | gerät cassette (tape) recorder; **~größe** size of cassettes; **~spieler, ~spielgerät** cartridge (cassette) player.

Kassiber stiffy *(sl.)*, kite *(US sl.)*.

kassieren to cash, to collect, to do the receiving, to bag *(fam.)*, *(Beamten)* to supersede, *(beschlagnahmen)* to confiscate, *(Offizier)* to cashier, to break, *(Urteil)* to quash, to reserve, to set aside, *(verdienen)* to earn, to make, to pocket;
Bombengehalt ~ to earn a packet; **täglich sechzig Dollar ~** to earn sixty dollars a day; **Geld ~** to take [in, *US*] money; **Hälfte des Gewinns ~** to pocket half of the takings (profit); **hohe Honorare ~** to pocket large fees; **Provision ~** to make (charge) a commission; **Rädelsführer ~** to collar the ringleader; **Rechnungsbetrag ~** to collect a bill; **Schmuggelware ~** to confiscate contraband goods; **seine Tantiemen ~** to draw one's fees; **Urkunde ~** to invalidate a document; **Wechsel ~** to collect a check *(US)* (cheque, *Br.*); **Zeitungsgeld monatlich ~** to collect the money for the newspaper once a month;
~ gehen to cash in; **darf ich jetzt ~?** would you mind paying now?

Kassierer cashier, cash (counter) clerk, cashkeeper, receiver, bank teller *(US)*, *(Geldeinnehmer)* money taker, collector, *(Geldzähler)* money teller, *(Kassenwart)* treasurer, paymaster, *(Kino)* box-office clerk;
erster ~ chief cashier, first (paying) teller *(US)*; **stellvertretender ~** assistant paymaster (cashier); **zweiter ~** assistant cashier, second (receiving, *US*) teller, disbursing officer *(US)*;
~ für Auszahlungen first (paying, *US*) teller, disbursing officer *(US)*; **~ für Einzahlungen** second (receiving, *US*) teller; **~ für postalisch eingehende Überweisungen** mail teller *(US)*;
~ sein to keep the cash, to do the receiving.

Kassierer | in lady cashier; **~posten** tellership *(US)*.

Kastanien aus dem Feuer holen to pull the chestnuts out of the fire.

Kästchen cassette, casket, *(Kreuzworträtsel)* square.

Kaste caste, class;
~ der Politiker race of politicians;
aus einer ~ ausstoßen to outcast.

Kastellan caretaker, castellan, constable of a castle.

Kasten box, case, coffer, *(Aushang)* showcase, *(Fahrzeug)* crate, *(Kittchen)* jug, clink, booby hatch *(sl.)*, stir *(sl.)*, glasshouse, big house *(US sl.)*;
alter ~ *(Auto)* flivver *(sl.)*, *(Bus)* ramshackle old bus, *(Schiff)* crate, tub;
schwarz umrandeter ~ *(Zeitung)* black-edged box;
~ für Kleinbuchstaben lower case; **~ für ausgehende Post** out-tray;
etw. auf dem ~ haben *(fam.)* to have brains (s. th. on the ball, *US sl.*); **nicht viel auf dem ~ haben** to be slightly cracked (without much grey matter); **nicht alles im ~ haben** to have bats in the belfrey, to be wrong in the upper storey; **im ~ sitzen** to be in jug (clink);
~aufbau *(Auto)* panel body; **~bier** bottled beer; **~förderungsanlage** box-type conveyer system; **~geist** class-consciousness; **~herrschaft** caste system; **~kipper** car dump; **~lieferwagen** box truck; **~loser** outcast; **~möbel** unit furniture; **~satz** *(Zeitungskopf)* ear pieces (spaces); **~schloß** rim lock; **~wagen** *(Eisenbahn)* boxcar, box waggon *(Br.)*; **~wesen** caste system.

Katafalk catafalque;
an einem ~ vorbeidefilieren to file past a catafalque.

Katalog catalog(ue), list;
alphabetischer ~ alphabetical (dictionary) catalog(ue); **ausführlicher ~** descriptive catalog(ue); **bebilderter ~** illustrated price list; **beschreibender ~** descriptive catalog(ue); **nach Sachgebieten geordneter ~** classified catalog(ue); **systematischer ~** subject catalog(ue);
~ für Einkäufer buyer's guide; **~ der Grundrechte** declaration of rights; **ganzer ~ geldmarktpolitischer Maßnahmen** package of monetary relief; **~ mit Preisangaben** price list; **~ mit losen Seiten** loose-leaf catalog(ue);
im ~ aufführen to [carry in a] catalog(ue), to cataloguize; **in einen ~ aufnehmen** to insert (list) in a catalog(ue); **~ aufstellen** to catalog(ue); **~ durchblättern** to skim through a catalog(ue); **im ~ streichen** to delete from a catalog(ue); **nur nach ~ verkaufen** to sell from one's catalog(ue); **neuen ~ versenden** to forward a new catalog(ue); **~ zusammenstellen** to compile (work on) a catalog(ue);
~aufnahme entry in a catalog(ue); **~bearbeiter** catalog(u)er.

katalogisieren to catalog(ue), to card-index, to list.

katalogisiert catalog(u)ed;
nicht ~ uncatalog(u)ed.

Katalogisierung catalog(u)ing.

Katalogisierungsstelle catalog(u)ing agency.

katalogmäßig angeordnet in catalog(ue) form.

Katalog | möbel ready-made furniture; **~nummer** catalog(ue) (index) number; **~posten numerieren** to number the items in a catalog(ue); **~preis** catalog(ue) (list[ing]) price; **~zettel** catalog(ue) card; **auf Wunsch kostenlose ~zusendung** catalog(ue) sent free on request.

Katapult launcher;
mit ~ starten to launch;
~flugzeug catapult airplane; **~sitz** ejection (ejector) seat; **~start** launch, catapult take-off.

Kataster cadaster, cadastre *(Br.)*, lot book, cadastral survey (map, plan), valuation list *(Br.)*, (roll, *Scot.*);
~amt land registry *(Br.)*; **~anlage** cadastration; **~aufnahme** cadastral survey; **~auszug** cadastral extract; **~beamter** land surveyor and valuer; **~bewertung** cadastral valuation; **~buch** cadastral survey, lot book *(Br.)*; **~karte** cadastral map.

katastermäßig cadastral.

Kataster | nummer tract (cadastral) number; **~plan** cadastral map (plan, survey, plat); **~planeinheit** cadastral unit, plot *(US)*, plat *(US)*; **~wert** land value.

katastrophale Überschwemmung disastrous flood.

Katastrophe catastrophe, disaster, calamity;
einmalige ~ unparalleled disaster; **finanzielle ~** financial disaster; **nationale ~** public disaster;
vor einer ~ bewahren to snatch out of the fire; **am Rande einer wirtschaftlichen ~ stehen** to be on the brink of an economic disaster.

Katastrophen | alarm emergency alert; **~anzeichen** disaster signal; **~ausrüstung** emergency equipment; **~ausschuß** disaster committee; **~bekämpfung** disaster control; **~betroffene** victims of a catastrophe; **~deckung** *(Rückversicherung)* calamity coverage; **~dienst** emergency relief service; **~einsatz** emergency assignment; **~einsatzverband** disaster unit; **~fall** unforeseen calamity, disaster situation.

Katastrophengebiet disaster (distressed) area;
vom Erdbeben betroffenes ~ earthquake area;
zum ~ erklären to design a major disaster area.

katastrophen | gefährdetes Gebiet disaster-prone area; **~geschädigt** disaster-struck (-stricken).

Katastrophen | geschädigte, 100.000 Dollar für die ~geschädigten bewilligen to vote $ 100.000 for the sufferers; **~hilfe** disaster relief; **~hilfsprogramm** disaster relief program(me); **~jahr** disastrous year; **~politik** disastrous policy; **~risiko** fundamental (catastrophe) risk; **~rücklage** *(Versicherung)* castrophe reserve (surplus); **~rückversicherung** catastrophe reinsurance; **~schaden** catastrophic loss; **~schock** shock loss *(US)*; **~schutz** disaster prevention council; **~serie** string (run) of disaster; **~theorie** catastrophism; **~vorschau** disaster forecasting; **~wagnis** catastrophe hazard (risk); **~warnung** emergency action notification.

Kategorie category, class, order, line, head, rating, *(Statistik)* category, bracket, *(Wertpapiere)* denomination;
unter eine ~ bringen to categorize, to classify, to label, to blanket *(US)*; **unter eine andere ~ fallen** to fall under another category; **zu einer ~ gehören** to come under (fall within) a category.
kategorisch categorical;
~ ablehnen to refuse flatly;
~e Behauptung categorical statement; **~es Dementi** categorical denial; **~es Nein** flat refusal.
kategorisieren to categorize, to classify, to label, to blanket *(US)*.
Kategorisierung categorization, classification, label(l)ing.
Kategorisierungsbestimmungen label(l)ing requirements.
Kater male cat, tomcat *(fig.)*, hangover, the morning after [the night before], holdover *(sl.)*;
wie ein verliebter ~ doting;
kastrierter ~ doctored tomcat; **moralischer ~** pangs of conscience;
seinen ~ im Alkohol ersäufen to take a hair of the dog that bit you;
~frühstück hangover breakfast *(sl.)*; **~idee** crazy idea, harebrained scheme; **~stimmung** the morning after the night before *(coll.)*.
Katheder|blüte boner *(sl.)*; **~sozialismus** socialism of the chair; **~sozialist** professorial socialist.
Kätner cottager, crofter.
Kattun calico, cotton cloth (fabric);
~ kriegen to get it in the neck *(coll.)*;
~drucker cotton printer.
Katzbuckelei cringing, servility, bootlicking *(coll.)*.
katzbuckeln to sneak, to cringe, to lick s. one's boots, to heel, to kotow *(fam.)*;
vor einem reichen Verwandten ~ to fawn on a rich relative.
Kätzchen kitten, catkin.
Katze|im Sack *(fam.)* blind bargain;
~ im Sack kaufen to buy a pig in a poke; **~ aus dem Sack lassen** to let the cat out of the bag; **wie ~ und Hund leben** to live a cat-and-dog life; **naß wie eine ~ sein** to be like a drowned rat; **alles für die ~ gewesen sein** to have been wasted effort; **mit jem. ~ und Maus spielen** to play cat and mouse with s. o.; **der ~ die Schelle umhängen** to bell the cat;
bei Nacht sind alle ~n grau when candles are away all cats are grey; **die ~ läßt das Mausen nicht** the leopard cannot change his spots; **wenn die ~ aus dem Haus ist, tanzen die Mäuse auf dem Tisch** when the cat's away, the mice will play.
Katzenauge *(Fahrrad)* reflector, *(Verkehrsbahn)* cat's eye.
katzenfreundlich velvet, oversweet;
~es Lächeln saccharine smile; **~er Ton** honeyed tones.
Katzen|jammer black dog *(coll.)*, the morning after, heebie-jeebie *(US sl.)*, hangover *(sl.)*; **~jammer haben** to be hung-over *(US)*; **~musik** Dutch concert, charivari; **~sprung** hop, skip and jump, a stone's throw *(Br.)*, spell *(US coll.)*; **~tisch** separate table; **~wäsche machen** to give s. th. a lick and a promise.
Kauderwelsch lingo, peddler's French, double-Dutch, gibberish, jargon, down the road;
~ der Funkamateure jargon of radio technicians;
~ reden to talk double-Dutch (gibberish).
kauen to chew, to masticate;
an den Nägeln ~ to bite one's nails; **Worte zwischen den Zähnen ~** to drawl one's words;
an einem Problem zu ~ haben to have s. th. on one's brain.
Kauf buying, purchase, purchasing, *(Erwerbung)* bargain, acquisition;
beim ~ when buying; **durch ~** by purchase; **zum ~ angeboten** on offer;
fester ~ outright purchase; **fingierter ~** sham (mock) purchase; **freier ~** sale by private treaty, voluntary sale; **günstiger ~** good bargain (buy), find; **teurer ~** overpurchase; **wohlfeiler ~** pennyworth bargain, good cheap (bargain), steal;
~ auf Abzahlung instal(l)ment buying, hire purchase *(Br.)*, purchase on deferred terms *(US)*; **~ gegen Akzept** purchase for acceptance; **~ zur Ansicht** purchase on approval (subject to inspection); **~ von Anzeigenraum** space buying; **~ unter Ausschluß von Gewährleistungsansprüchen** sale with all faults; **~ auf Baisse** short purchase *(US)*, bear purchase *(Br.)*; **~ gegen bar** purchase for cash, cash (ready money) purchase; **~ in Bausch und Bogen** lumpsum purchase, purchase in the lump; **~ nach Beschreibung** sale by description; **~ auf Besicht (wie besehen)** as seen, sale on inspection; **~ sofort lieferbarer Devisen** spot purchase; **~ für einen Dritten** fiduciary coemption; **~ mit Eigentumsübergang** executed sale; **~ unter Eigentumsvorbehalt** conditional sale; **~ aufgrund von Erinnerungswerbung** repeat sale *(US)*; **~ nach Erprobung** sale by test; **~ aus zweiter Hand** secondhand sale; **~ eines Hauses** purchase of a house, home purchase; **~ à la Hausse** bull (speculative) purchase; **~ gegen Kassa** cash purchase; **~ aufgrund übersandten Katalogs** catalog(ue) sale; **~ auf Kreditbasis** basis purchase on account, credit sale; **~ auf Lieferung** purchase on term, forward purchase, purchase for future delivery *(US)*; **~ gegen sofortige Lieferung** purchase for daily delivery; **~ nach Muster** sale to pattern; **~ auf Probe** sale (purchase) on approval (trial), approval (memorandum) sale on approval; **~ nach Probe** purchase according to (by) sample (pattern); **~ auf eigene Rechnung** purchase for own account; **~ auf feste Rechnung** firm purchase, purchase on account; **~ auf fremde Rechnung** buying on third account; **~ mit Rückgaberecht** memorandum buying, sale and return; **~ zu Spekulationszwecken** purchase on speculation; **~ auf Teilzahlung** hire purchase *(Br.)*, deferred-payment purchase *(US)*; **~ mit Umtauschrecht** sale with exchange privilege; **~ und Verkauf** buying and selling, trade *(US)*; **~ mit Vorbehalt** conditional purchase; **~ wie die Ware steht und liegt** sale with all faults; **~ nach Warenbeschreibung** sale by description; **~ von Wertpapieren** purchase of investment securities; **sukzessiver ~ von Wertpapieren zu verschiedenen Kursen** buying on a scale, scaling *(US)*; **~ auf Zeit** time bargain, forward (future, *US*) purchase; **~ zu verschiedenen Zeiten und zu verschiedenen Preisen** *(Börse)* split purchase; **~ auf Ziel** purchase on term (credit);
~ abschließen to effect a sale, to make a purchase, to close (make) a bargain; **zum ~ anbieten** to offer for sale; **zum ~ aufgeben** to give a buying order; **wohlfeilen ~es davonkommen** to get off cheaply; **zum ~ einladen** *(Schaufenster)* to be an invitation to buy; **durch ~ erwerben** to acquire by purchase; **~ rückgängig machen** to rescind a sale; **~ tätigen** to make (conclude) a purchase; **zum ~ von etw. verführen (verleiten)** to entrap into buying s. th., to trick s. o. into purchasing; **vom ~ zurücktreten** to repudiate (retire from, cancel) a purchase;
~abneigung sales resistance; **~abrechnung** *(Börse)* bought note.
kaufabschließender Appell *(Anzeige)* rider, close.
Kaufabschluß purchase, conclusion of a bargain;
beim ~ at the time of purchase, in making the contract;
~ durch Handschlag hand sale;
~ tätigen to make a bargain (purchase).
Kauf|abschlüsse *(Börse)* buying orders; **~absicht** purchase (buying) decision; **aus den Umständen zu entnehmende ~absicht** quasi purchase; **~andrang** pressure to buy, buying pressure; **~angebot** offer to buy, offer of purchase, purchase offer, bid; **~anlaß** buying motive; **~anreiz** inducement to buy, sales inducement, buying incentive, merchandise (selling) appeal, buy signal, pull, come-on *(US sl.)*; **~antrag** offer to buy; **~anwärter** prospective buyer, prospect *(US)*; **~anweisung** *(Betriebsabteilung)* purchase requisition; **~appell** sales (selling) appeal.
Kaufauftrag purchase (buying, buyer's, buy) order, *(aus dem Ausland)* indent, *(Börse)* sales (purchase) form;
limitierter ~ *(Börse)* stop order;
~ für Abschnitte zu verschiedenen Kursen split order *(US)*;
~ erteilen to give a purchase (buying) order; **plötzlich ~ erteilen** to jump into the market.
Kauf|auftragsformular purchase order form; **~ausweis** certificate of purchase.
kaufbar purchasable.
Kauf|bedingung buying conditions, purchase terms; **~beeinflussung** purchasing influence; **~belebung** increase in sales; **~bereitschaft** disposition to buy, animation among buyers, consumer acceptance; **~bestimmungen** purchase terms; **~bewilligung** docket *(Br.)*; **~bindungspolitik** buy-American policy; **~brief** bill of emption (sale), *(Grundstück)* title deed.
Käufe *(Börse)* buying orders;
durch ~ gehalten supported;
bedeutende ~ heavy purchases; **aufgrund von Warenproben getätigte ~** sales made on the basis of samples; **lebhafte ~** active buyers; **spekulative ~** speculation (speculative) purchases;
~ am offenen Markt open-market purchases, purchases on the open market; **~ und Verkäufe** *(Börse)* bids and offers;
auf ~ hin festliegen to be firm (steady) on account of buying orders; **auf eine Hausse hin ~ tätigen** to buy for a rise.
Kauf|eigenheim freehold property; **~einflüsse** buying influences.
Kaufen buying, purchase;
plötzliches und unmotiviertes ~ impulse buying.

kaufen to buy, to [make a (acquire by)] purchase, *(bestechen)* to bribe, to subsidize, to corrupt, to suborn;
bei jem. ~ to deal at s. one's shop; **auf Abzahlung** ~ to buy on the instal(l)ment (hire-purchase, *Br.*) (deferred-payment, *US*) system; **antiquarisch** ~ to buy secondhand; **auf der Auktion** ~ to buy at *(US)* (by, *Br.*) auction; **sich ein Auto** ~ to buy o. s. a car; **auf Baisse** ~ to buy on a fall; **gegen bar** ~ to buy (purchase) for cash; **in Bausch und Bogen** ~ to purchase wholesale; **Beamten** ~ to bribe an official; **auf Besicht** ~ to purchase subject to inspection; **nach Besicht** ~ to buy after inspection; **billig** ~ to make a bargain, to buy (pick up) cheap; **billig ~ und teuer verkaufen** *(Börse)* to reload; **auf Borg** ~ to buy on the sleeve *(US)* (on tick, *Br.*); **für ein Butterbrot** ~ to pick up for a song; **aufgrund plötzlicher Eingebung** ~ to buy on impulse; **ab Fabrik** ~ to buy on ex works terms; **fertig** ~ to buy ready-made; **fest** ~ to buy firm (on contract); **en gros** ~ to buy wholesale; **Grundstück** ~ to buy some land; **gutgläubig** ~ to buy in good faith; **aus erster Hand** ~ to purchase at first hand; **aus zweiter Hand** ~ to buy secondhand; **auf Hausse** ~ to buy for a rise; **Holz auf dem Stamm** ~ to buy timber on the stump; **direkt beim Hersteller** ~ to buy off the shelf; **hundertstückweise** ~ to buy by the 100 [pieces]; **nach Katalog** ~ to purchase from a catalog(ue); **auf Kreditbasis** ~ to buy on credit (trust); **auf Lieferung** ~ *(Börse)* to buy forward (for settlement, *Br.*, future delivery, *US*); **am offenen Markt** ~ to buy (purchase) in the open market; **nach Maß** ~ to buy to measure; **für einen Pappenstiel** ~ to buy for a mere song; **pauschal** ~ to buy on a lump-sum basis; **zu festen Preisen** ~ to buy on a scale; **auf Probe** ~ to buy on trial; **auf Pump** ~ to buy on the sleeve *(US)* (on tick, *Br.*); **mit Rabatt** ~ to buy at a market discount; **auf Raten** ~ to buy on the instalment (hire-purchase system, *Br.*, deferred-payment system, *US*); **auf Rechnung** ~ to purchase on account, to buy firm (on contract); **für feste Rechnung** ~ to buy outright; **für fremde Rechnung** ~ to buy for third account; **auf zukünftige Rechnung** ~ to take on futures account; **regelmäßig bei X** ~ to shop regularly at X's; **Rentenwerte** ~ to buy funds; **Rückprämie** ~ to take for the put *(Br.)*; **zum Selbstkostenpreis** ~ to buy at cost price; **zu Spekulationszwecken** ~ to buy for speculative account; **spottbillig** ~ to buy for a mere song; **von der Stange** ~ to buy ready-made (off the peg); **stark** ~ *(Börse)* to load; **Stimmen** ~ to buy votes; **auf Stottern** ~ to buy on the never-never (instal(l)ment, hire-purchase, *Br.*, deferred-payment, *US*) system; **auf Termin** ~ to purchase forward (for future delivery, *US*), to buy for the account *(Br.)* (for settlement, *Br.*); **teuer** ~ to give a long price; **zu teuer** ~ to overbuy, to overpurchase; **fast umsonst** ~ to buy for a mere song; **etw. unbesehen** ~ to buy s. th. unsight; **über die zur Verfügung stehenden Geldmittel hinaus** ~ to buy beyond one's means, to overtrade; **unter Verzicht auf entgegenkommende Finanzierungszusagen** ~ to buy without soft finance; **jds. ganzen Vorrat** ~ to buy up s. one's stock; **Ware lose oder verpackt** ~ to buy bulk or packed goods; **wohlfeil** ~ to buy at a low rate; **auf Zeit** ~ to buy forward (on credit, *US*);
sich anheischig machen zu ~ to profess to purchase;
~ **gehen** to go shopping; **zu ~ gesucht** *(Anzeigen)* required; **zu ~ sein** to be obtainable.

Kauf|entgelt purchase consideration; ~**entscheid** buying (purchasing) decision.

Kaufentschluß buying impulse;
~**analyse** *(Werbung)* activation research.

Käufer purchaser, purchasing party, buyer, vendee *(US)*, emptor, salegoer, prospect *(US)*, bargainee, *(Abnehmer)* taker, *(Auktion)* bidder, *(Kunde)* customer, store buyer, *(Kurszettel)* buyers, bid money, *(im Laden)* shopper, store buyer *(US)*;
in Ermangelung eines ~s failing a purchaser; **nach ~s Wahl** option to put, optional with the buyer; **ohne** ~ no buyers; **Risiko beim** ~ let the buyer beware, caveat emptor;
im Ausland ansässiger ~ nonresident buyer; **betrogener** ~ defrauded purchaser; **bösgläubiger** ~ mala-fide purchaser; **schnell entschlossener** ~ ready buyer, wrap-up *(US sl.)*; **gutgläubiger** ~ purchaser in good faith, bona fide purchaser; **scharf kalkulierender** ~ economic buyer; **letztinteressierter** ~ marginal buyer; **mittelbarer** ~ subpurchaser; **möglicher** ~ potential customer (buyer), prospect *(US)*; **normaler** ~ full-price purchaser; **ortsansässiger** ~ resident buyer; **potentieller** ~ prospective buyer (consumer), would-be buyer, potential buyer, prospect *(US)*; **preisempfindlicher** ~ price-finicky customer; **rechnender** ~ economic buyer; **späterer** ~ subsequent buyer; **überseeischer** ~ indentor; **umsichtiger** ~ discriminating purchaser; **ungenannter** ~ undisclosed buyer; **unschlüssiger** ~ marginal purchaser;
~ **eines Grundstücks** purchaser of land (property); ~ **aus zweiter Hand** secondhand buyer, subpurchaser; ~ **beim Räumungsverkauf** buyer of clearance lines; ~ **in Übersee** indentor, buyer overseas; ~ **einer Vorprämie** giver for a call *(Br.)*; ~ **eines Wechsels** purchaser of a bill (note);
potentielle ~ abschrecken to deter potential buyers; **als ~ auftreten** to be in the market; ~ **für verkaufte Waren belasten** to debit a purchaser (customer) with (for the amount of) goods sold; ~ **finden** to meet with a ready market; **zu Lasten des ~s gehen** to be paid by the buyer; **zur Verfügung des ~s halten** to hold subject to the seller's order;
~**andrang**, ~**ansturm** rush on a shop, buying wave; ~**gruppe** buyer category, market grouping, customer group; ~**hausse** purchasing high; ~**in** *(Firma)* purchasing company (party); ~**konsortium** group of buyers; ~**land** purchasing (buying) country; ~**liste** buyer's list.

Kauferlös purchase proceeds.

Käufer|markt buyer's market; ~**monopol** buyer's monopoly; ~**pflichten** buyer's obligations (duties); ~**ring** sales ring; ~**ring bilden** *(Auktion)* to knock out *(Br.)*; ~**schicht** spending group; **übliche ~schicht** ordinary run of buyers; ~**seite** world of buyers; ~**streik** buyer's (consumer's) strike; ~**unlust** consumer's resistance; ~**verhalten** purchase pattern; ~**verzeichnis** buyer's list; ~**widerstände**, ~**zurückhaltung** buyer's (consumer's) resistance, resistance to high prices.

kauffähig purchasable.

Kauffahrer merchantman, merchant ship.

Kauffahrtei|flotte merchant fleet (marine); ~**schiff** trading vessel, merchantman, merchant ship (vessel), mercantile vessel; ~**schiffahrt** commercial navigation.

Kauf|formular purchase form; ~**frau** feme-sole trader, free dealer (trader); **festes ~gebot** firm bid; ~**gegenstand** object of purchase.

Kaufgeld purchase money (price);
~**finanzierung** purchase-money financing; ~**hypothek** purchase-money mortgage; ~**kredit** purchase-money loan; ~**minderung**, ~**nachlaß** purchase-money allowance; ~**obligationen** purchase-money bonds; ~**verpflichtung** purchase-money obligation.

Kauf|gelegenheit opportunity to buy; ~**genehmigung** permission to purchase; ~**gesuch** offer to buy, bid, *(Anzeige)* [articles] wanted, required; ~**gewohnheiten** *(Kundschaft)* custom, buying (consumer) habits; ~**gewohnheit annehmen** to acquire a habit of buying; ~**gut** goods bought; ~**halle** bazaar.

Kaufhaus departmental *(Br.)* (department, *US*) store, [variety chain] store, stores *(US)* universal providers *(Br.)*, warehouse *(Br.)*;
billiges ~ limited-price variety store, five-and-ten *(US)*;
~ **mit gemischtem Warenkreis** variety chain store;
~ **mit Waren versehen** to stock a warehouse with goods *(Br.)*;
~**detektiv** store detective, dick *(US)*; ~**werte** stores.

Kauf|hemmung buyer's (consumer, buying) resistance; ~**herr** city merchant, trader; ~**interesse** buying interest, inclination (desire) to buy.

Kaufinteressent intending purchaser, intending buyer, prospective (would-be, potential) buyer, prospect *(US)*, up *(sl.)*, *(Auktion)* bidder;
ernsthafter ~ seriously disposed buyer; **keine ~en** no bidders.

kaufinteressiert prepared to buy.

Kauf|kontingent purchase quota; ~**kontrakt** bill of sale (emption), sales contract.

Kaufkraft purchasing (buying) power, spending power, value;
in reeller ~ in real terms;
effektive ~ real purchasing power; **überschüssige** ~ surplus of spending power, excessive buying power; **frei verfügbare** ~ discretionary buying power;
~ **des Geldes** purchasing power of money; ~ **einer Verbraucherschicht** consumption capacity;
überschüssige ~ abschöpfen to absorb buying (skim off surplus purchasing) power; **an ~ verlieren** to decline in purchasing power;
~**abschöpfung** absorption of excess buying power; ~**entzug** drain on purchasing power.

kaufkräftig able to purchase;
~**es Publikum** crowd of eager shoppers.

Kaufkraft|index purchasing power index; ~**lenkung** control of purchasing power; ~**minderung** reduction of purchasing power; ~**parität** purchasing power parity; ~**paritätstheorie** purchasing power parity theory; ~**schwund** dwindling purchasing power; ~**stabilität** stability of purchasing power; ~**steigerung** increase in purchasing power; ~**theorie des Geldes**

banking theory *(Br.)*; ~**überhang** excessive (backlog of) purchasing power; ~**verschlechterung** deterioration of the purchasing value of money; ~**wert** purchasing value of money.

Kauf|kredit vendor credit; ~**kurs** buying rate; ~**laden** [merchant's] shop *(Br.)*, store *(US)*; ~**leute** mercantile men, merchants, tradesmen.

käuflich for (on) sale, purchasable, by purchase, buyable, *(bestechlich)* bribable, venal, hireling, mercenary, corrupt, corruptible;
nicht ~ not for sale, unpurchasable, *(nicht bestechlich)* incorruptible, not to be bribed;
~ **erwerben** to acquire by purchase; **nicht** ~ **sein** to be above taking a bribe; **weder für Geld noch für gute Worte** ~ **sein** not to be had for love nor money;
~**e Beamte** corruptible government officilas; ~**e Justiz** venal justice; ~**es Mädchen** prostitute, harlot; ~**e Presse** corrupt press.

Käuflichkeit *(Bestechlichkeit)* corruptibility, venality.

Kauf|liebhaber prospective (would-be) buyer, prospect *(US)*; ~**limit** buying limit, *(Börse)* stop-loss order.

Kauflust inclination (disposition, eagerness, propensity) to buy, animation among buyers, buying desire;
erneute ~ fresh demand; **geringe** ~ little animation among buyers; **gesteigerte** ~ buying spree;
abnehmende ~ **der Verbraucher** consumer spending slowdown.

kauflustig eager (inclined) to buy;
~**e Menge** crowd of eager shoppers.

Kauflustiger intending (prospective, would-be) purchaser, willing buyer, prospect *(US)*.

Kaufmann merchant, *(Gemischtwarenhändler)* grocer, *(Geschäftsinhaber)* shopkeeper, storekeeper *(US)*, businessman, man of business, *(Großhändler)* wholesaler, merchant, *(Händler)* dealer, trader, tradesman, *(kaufmännischer Angestellter)* clerk, employee, *(Kleinhändler)* retail dealer, retailer, *(Verkäufer)* salesman, shop assistant;
als ~ **tätig** engaged in commerce;
alteingesessener ~ resident dealer; **gerissener** ~ smart businessman; **geschäftstüchtiger** ~ sharp dealer; **gewerbesteuerpflichtiger** ~ recognized merchant; **gewiegter** ~ shrewd businessman; **hochqualifizierter** ~ high-level businessman; **kleiner** ~ petty trader, retailer; **ordentlicher** ~ serious businessman; **selbständiger** ~ established merchant, independent dealer, single (sole) proprietor *(US)*; **umsichtiger** ~ prudent businessman; **wagemutiger** ~ speculative merchant; ~ **mit offenem Ladengeschäft** tradesman;
erfolgreichen ~ **abgeben** to make a successful businessman; **sich bei einem** ~ **als Kunden eintragen lassen** to register with a tradesman; **seinen Sohn** ~ **werden lassen** to set up one's son in trade; **sich als** ~ **niederlassen** to set up shop, to open a trade; ~ **sein** to be in business; **als** ~ **ausgebildet sein** to have had business training; **sehr guter** ~ **sein** to know the tricks of the trade; ~ **werden** to go into business, to turn merchant, to set up shop.

kaufmännisch commercial, mercantile, trading, businesslike;
~ **geschult** brought up in business; **nicht** ~ nonmercantile; **nicht** ~ **beschäftigt** nontrading;
~ **ausgebildet sein** to be skilled in business; ~ **gewandt sein** to have a head for business, to be a shrewd businessman; ~ **tätig sein** to be in business (the trade), to be engaged in business;
~**es Akzepthaus** merchant banker; ~**er Angestellter** clerk, employee; ~**e Ausbildung** commercial education, business training (education), business study; ~**er Beruf** commercial profession, business occupation; ~**en Beruf ergreifen** to go into business, to turn merchant; **einer** ~**en Betätigung nachgehen** to be engaged in commercial activities; ~**er Betrieb** business enterprise, commercial establishment; ~**e Beziehungen** business connections; ~**e Buchführung** merchant's accounts; ~**e Denkweise** business thinking; ~**e Erfahrungen sammeln** to get wise to the ways of businessmen; ~**es Fach** commercial line; ~**e Fähigkeiten** business acumen, business ability, business accomplishments; ~**e Gepflogenheiten** customs of merchants; **nach** ~**en Gesichtspunkten** from a commercial point of view, businesslike; ~**e Grundsätze** business principles; ~**e Handschrift** business hand; ~**e Interessen** commercial interests; ~**e Korrespondenz** business correspondence; ~**er Kredit** commercial loan; **im ordentlichen** ~**en Leben üblich sein** to be consistent with sound commercial practice; ~**e Lehre** apprenticeship; ~**er Lehrgang** commercial course; ~**er Lehrling** business trainee, apprentice; ~**er Leiter** business (commercial) manager, *(Warenhaus)* merchandise manager, front desk *(US)*; ~**es Personal** office employees, staff, personnel; ~**es Rechnen** commercial arithmetic; ~**es Thema** commercial subject; ~**es Unternehmen** trading corporation; ~**es Urteilsvermögen** business judgment; ~**es Zurückbehaltungsrecht** right of stoppage in transit.

Kaufmanns|beruf commercial profession, business occupation; ~**brauch** custom (law) of merchants, usage of trade; ~**fach** mercantile line; ~**familie** business family; ~**frau** merchant's wife, *(selbständig)* feme-sole trader; ~**gehilfe** shop assistant; ~**gehilfenprüfung** business college (school) examination; ~**gericht** commercial arbitration; ~**gilde** merchant guild, body of merchants; ~**gut** merchandise; ~**innung** merchant guild; ~**kreise** commercial circles, businessmen; ~**prüfung bestehen** to graduate from a business college *(US)*; ~**schaft** [body of] merchants, commercial world (men), trade, mercantile community, factory; ~**stand** the trade, commercial (business) profession, business community; ~**vereinigung** trade club *(Br.)*.

Kauf|möglichkeit buy; ~**motiv** buying motive; ~**neigung** inclination to buy; **der Verbraucherschaft Einblick in die** ~**neigungen geben** to let consumers in on the shopping tips; ~**note** *(Makler)* sales (bought, *Br.*) note; ~**objekt** proposition; ~**option** option of (to) purchase, buying (buyer's, *Br.*) option, call option; ~**option ausüben** to take up an option; ~**order** buying (purchasing) order; ~- **und Verkaufsorder zu verschiedenen Zeiten** *(Börse)* buying on a scale, scaling *(US)*; ~**orgie** buying binge; ~**potential** purchasing power.

Kaufpreis purchase money (price), [sales] price;
~ **bezahlt** price paid;
~ **erlegen** to pay the sales price; ~ **für ein Haus in bar erlegen** to buy a house outright; ~ **herabsetzen (mindern)** to reduce (abate) the purchase price; ~ **überweisen** to render the price of a purchase; ~ **zurückerstatten** to refund the purchase price;
~**finanzierung** purchase money financing; ~**genehmigung** approval of the purchase price; ~**minderung**, ~**nachlaß** abatement of purchase money, purchase money allowance; ~**rate** instal(l)ment; ~**rückerstattung**, ~**vergütung** restitution of the purchase money; ~**schuld** purchase money obligation.

Kauf|reflektant prospective (would-be, potential) buyer, intending buyer (purchaser), prospect *(US)*; ~**stimmung** buying mood; ~**summe** purchase (contract) price, purchase money; ~**überlegungen** buying considerations; ~**unlust** sales (consumer) resistance, disclination to buy.

kaufunlustig disinclined to buy.

Kauf|urkunde purchase deed, *(Grundstück)* deed of bargain and sale, *(Eigentumstitel)* title deed; ~**vereinbarung** sales agreement; ~**verhalten** buying behavio(u)r; ~**verpflichtung** obligation to buy, *(Börse)* commitment *(US)*.

Kaufvertrag sales agreement, contract to sell *(US)*, [contract for] sale, act (deed) of sale, sales (purchase) contract, purchase deed, bargain and sale, bill of emption, bargain, *(Grundstück)* title deed, *(Schiff)* bill of sale;
noch zu erfüllender ~ executory sale; **erfüllter** ~ executed sale; **notarieller** ~ special contract under seal; **obligatorischer** ~ executory (executorial) contract, agreement to sell;
~ **ohne Eigentumsvorbehalt** absolute sale; ~ **unter Eigentumsvorbehalt** conditional sales contract; ~ **über künftige Lieferungen** contract to sell for future delivery; ~ **über bewegliche Sachen** contract for the sale of goods;
~ **gegen Zahlung einer Geldbuße annullieren** to annul a sale by paying a fine; ~ **unterzeichnen** to sign a sales contract; **vom** ~ **zurücktreten** to rescind (repudiate) a sales contract (purchase).

Kauf|vertragsvordruck purchase agreement form; ~**vorrecht** purchase privilege; ~**vorurteil** buying prejudice.

kaufweise by way of purchase.

Kauf|welle buying wave; ~**wert** purchasing (market) value, purchase consideration.

kaufwillig inclined to buy.

Kauf|williger willing buyer; ~**wut** urge to buy, buying craze; ~**zeit** time of purchase; ~**zentrum** shopping center *(US)* (centre, *Br.*); ~**zettel** contract (bought, *Br.*) note; ~**zurückhaltung** buying resistance; ~**zwang** obligation (pressure) to buy; **kein** ~**zwang** free inspection invited.

kausales Rechtsgeschäft valuable consideration.

Kausal|bedingung causal condition; ~**geschäft** valuable consideration.

Kausalitätsprinzip principle of causality.

Kausalkette chain of causation.

Kausalzusammenhang causal connection, causality, chain of causation, relation (correspondence) between cause and effect, natural sequence of events;
nicht im ~ **stehend** remote;

unmittelbarer ~ proximate connection; **unterbrochener** ~ efficient-intervening cause; **[nicht] unterbrochener** ~ *(Versicherungsrecht)* [un]broken sequence;
Ergebnis mit einer Ursache in ~ **bringen** to relate a result with a cause; ~ **unterbrechen** to break the chain of causation.

Kautelen safeguards.

Kaution bail [bond], bailment, deposit, caution, risk money, financial bond, guarantee *(Br.)*, security *(US)*, recognizance, safe pledge, surety *(US)*, *(Zwangsvollstreckung)* replevin bond; **gegen** ~ under bond; **gegen** ~ **freigelassen** [released] on bail; **ohne** ~ on one's own recognizance;
hinterlegte ~ caution money; **hohe** ~ ample bail; **vom Liquidator zu stellende** ~ liquidator's security; **wertlose** ~ straw bail; **zugelassene** ~ special bail;
~ **eines öffentlichen Amtsträgers** official (cumulative, *US*) bond; ~ **eines Bauunternehmers** construction bond; ~ **bei der Einreichung einer Berufung** appeal bond; ~ **für die Freigabe beschlagnahmter Waren** delivery bond; ~ **für die Gerichtskosten** security for costs; ~ **des Konkursverwalters** receiver's bond; ~ **des Lagerinhabers** warehouse bond; ~ **des Nachlaßverwalters** administrator's bond; ~ **im Pfändungsverfahren** replevin bond; ~ **eines Staatstreuhänders** public bond; ~ **des Testamentsvollstreckers** executor's bond; ~ **gegen Veruntreuung** fidelity bond; ~ **für zukünftiges Wohlverhalten** surety for the peace, security for good behavio(u)r; ~ **für Zollspeicherbenutzung** warehouse bond;
~ **anbieten** to offer surety; ~ **zur Haftverschonung anbieten** to tender bail; **sich gegen** ~ **auf freiem Fuß befinden** to be out on bail; ~ **für verfallen erklären** to forfeit a security; **j. gegen** ~ **freilassen** to admit (remand, *Br.*) s. o. to (let s. o. out on) bail; **als** ~ **hinterlegen** to deposit as underlying security; ~ **schießen (verfallen) lassen** to jump (skip) bail, to forfeit one's bail; ~ **leisten** to stand bail, to pay a deposit (guaranty); ~ **stellen** to bail, to give (furnish, stand) bail, to put in bail, to bail, to furnish security, to provide (stand) security, to [post a] bond, to enter in recognizance; ~ **für j. stellen** to become bail for s. o.; ~ **verlangen** to ask for a guarantee; ~ **verwirken** to forfeit one's bail; **gegen** ~ **freigelassen werden** to be let out on bail.

Kautions | angebot zwecks Haftverschonung tender of bail; **~bestellung** bailment; **~betrag** amount of security; **~depot** guarantee deposit; **~effekten** guarantee securities; **~effektenkonto** guarantee security account; **~erklärung** surety bond; **durch ~erlegung auf freien Fuß bringen** to bail out.

kautionsfähig bailable, able to put up bail, mainpernable, able to deposit securities.

Kautionsgesellschaft guarantor corporation.

Kautionsgestellung bailment, *(für Erscheinen vor Gericht)* safe pledge, recognizance, *(Zwangsvollstreckung)* redelivery bond; ~ **unter Eid** caution juratory *(Scot. law)*;
~ **ablehnen** to refuse [to grant] bail; **sich nach** ~ **auf freiem Fuß befinden** to be out on bail; **bis zur** ~ **in Haft behalten** to hold for bail; **ohne** ~ **von der Untersuchungshaft verschont bleiben** to be released on one's own recognizance; **durch** ~ **auf freien Fuß bringen** to bail out; **j. gegen** ~ **frei lassen** to release (remand, *Br.*) s. o. out on bail.

Kautions | gewährung admission to bail; **~hinterlegung** guarantee deposit; **~höhe** caution money, security; **~hypothek** general (blanket) mortgage; **~kredit** collateral loan; **~leistung** suretyship, bailment; **~mißbrauch** abuse of bail; **~nachschuß** supplementary bond; **~nehmer** guarantor.

kautionspflichtig liable to give security.

Kautions | regreß recourse of guarantee *(Br.)*; **~schuld** debt due to recognizance; **~stellung** depositing of security; **~summe** amount of guarantee, caution money, surety, security; **~summe einbüßen** to run off one's cover; **~urkunde** security (surety) bond; **~verfall** bail jumping *(US)*.

Kautionsverpflichtung fiduciary (surety) bond;
ohne ~ nonbailable;
~en zwecks Verlagerung zollpflichtiger Waren request note;
~ **eingehen** to enter into a surety bond.

Kautionsversicherung surety insurance *(US)*, fidelity guarantee insurance *(Br.)*, [bond of] fidelity insurance *(US)*.

Kautionsversicherungs | geschäft surety business; **~gesellschaft** bonding (guarantee, *Br.*) company, guarantee society *(Br.)*, surety company *(US)*; **~police** three-d-policy; **~risiko** fidelity guarantee risk; **~schein zwecks Versicherung aller in einem Werk beschäftigten Angestellten** position bond *(US)*.

Kautions | vertrag surety bond; **~wechsel** security bill; **~zweck** exigency of a bond.

Kautschukplantage rubber estate.

Kauz, komischer queer bird (customer), queer fellow, card *(coll.)*.

Kavalier gallant, gentleman, knight, *(Verehrer)* admirer, beau;
~ **der alten Schule** old-fashioned gentleman; ~ **der Straße** knight of the road;
~ **vom Scheitel bis zur Sohle sein** to be every inch a gentleman.

kavaliermäßig gentlemanlike, chivalrous.

Kavaliersverbrechen slight offence, peccadillo.

Kavalkade cavalcade.

Kavallerie, leichte light horse;
~ **und Infanterie** horse and foot;
~angriff cavalry charge.

Kavallerist cavalryman, trooper.

keck daring, bold, cheeky, nervy *(sl.)*;
~ **an j. schreiben** to have the cheek to write to s. o.; ~ **sein** to have a sauce;
~e Antwort cheeky (fresh, *US*) answer; **~es Hütchen** pert little hat.

Kegel skittle, pin, *(drucktechn.)* body size;
mit Kind und ~ with kith and kin (bag and baggage);
wie die ~ **fallen** to go down like ninepins;
~bahn skittle alley (ground); **~junge** pinboy, skittle boy; **~partie** skittling (bowling, *US*) session; **~schieben** skittles, ninepins bowling *(US)*.

Kehle throat, gorge;
heisere ~ hoarse voice;
sich die ~ **anfeuchten** to wet one's whistle; **jem. finanziell an die** ~ **gehen** to have a stranglehold on s. o.; **in die falsche** ~ **geraten** to go the wrong way *(coll.)*; **wie zugeschnürte** ~ **haben** to have a lump in one's throat; **aus voller** ~ **lachen** to roar with laughter; **jem. die** ~ **zuschnüren** to choke (strangle, throttle) s. o.

Kehl | kopfmikrophon throat microphone; **~ziegel** gutter tile.

Kehraus | machen to make a clean sweep; **zum** ~ **spielen** to play the last dance.

Kehre turn, bend, corner, loop, U-turn;
in spitzen ~n zum Gipfel ansteigen *(Straße)* to climb to the summit in a series of hairpin bends.

kehren, sich nicht an jds. Anweisungen to take no heed of s. one's orders; **sich zum Besten** ~ to come right in the end; **der Heimat den Rücken** ~ to leave one's home; **sein Mäntelchen nach dem Winde** ~ to sail with every shift of wind, to turn one's coat; **das Oberste zu unterst** ~ to turn everything topsy-turvy; **jem. den Rücken** ~ to turn one's back on s. o.; **Straße** ~ to sweep the street.

Kehrmaschine [road] sweeper.

Kehrricht rubbish, dirt, refuse, dust *(Br.)*, outsweepings;
das geht dich einen feuchten ~ **an** mind your own business;
~haufen rubbish heap; **~schaufel** dust pan *(Br.)*.

Kehr | schleife hairpin bend; **~seite** *(Münze)* reverse, tail; **die ~seite der Medaille** the reverse of the medal, the other side of the shield.

Kehrtkurve *(Flugzeug)* turn;
hochgezogene ~ Immelmann turn.

kehrtmachen to turn on one's heels, to turn tail;
schleunigst ~ to beat a hasty retreat.

Kehrtwendung about-face;
hundertprozentige ~ U-turn;
volle ~ **machen** to turn 180° right round; **hundertprozentige** ~ **vollziehen** to make an about-face.

keifen to yell, to squabble, to scold, to bicker.

keifende Stimme nagging voice.

Keil wedge, *(Zwickel)* gusset, gore;
~ **hineintreiben** to drive in a wedge; ~ **zwischen zwei Freunde treiben** to estrange two friends;
~bahnhof stub station.

Keile thrashing, hiding;
tüchtige ~ **bekommen** to get a sound thrashing.

keilen *(Studenten)* to canvass;
Studenten für eine Verbindung ~ to pledge (pheeze, *US sl.*) a student for a fraternity.

Keilerei scrap, dust-up, scuffle, strong-arm work *(US)*, mix *(sl.)*, roughhouse *(sl.)*.

Keil | form, in in arrowhead formation; **~formation** *(mil.)* wedge, formation; **~inschrift** wedge inscription, cuneiform; **~rahmen** *(drucktechn.)* quoin chase; **~riemen** vee belt, V belt.

Keim germ, bud;
~ **einer Idee** germ of an idea; **zarte ~e einer jungen Liebe** first tender awakenings of young love; ~ **der Zwietracht** seeds of discord;
Aufruhr im ~ **ersticken** to nip the rebellion in the bud; **im** ~ **vorhanden sein** to be in an embryonic state; **~e treiben** to sprout, to shoot, to bud.

keimfreie Milch sterilized milk.

Keimzelle *(fig.)* basic unit.
kein|e Deckung no funds; ~ **Konto** no account; ~**e der Parteien** neither party.
keines|falls on no account, in no way, in no case, not by any possibility; ~**wegs** in no circumstances.
Keks biscuit, cookie *(US).*
Kelch goblet, chalice;
~ **bis zur Neige leeren** to drink the cup to the dregs; ~ **des Leidens bis zur Neige leeren** to drain the cup of sorrow to the dregs;
der ~ ist noch einmal an mir vorbeigegangen I had a narrow squeak *(coll.).*
Kelle ladle, scoop, *(Signalstab)* disk;
nehmen, was die ~ gibt to take pot-luck.
Keller *(Schutzraum)* shelter, *(Wohnung)* cellar, basement;
splittersicherer ~ splinterproof shelter;
~ **einer Bank** bank vault; ~ **einer Burg** dungeon of a castle;
im ~ unterbringen to store in the cellar;
~**decke** basement ceiling.
Kellerei wine cellar.
Keller|geschäft basement shop; ~**geschoß** cellarage, [English] basement *(US)*, underground story, understairs; **hohes ~geschoß** stor(e)y in the basement; ~**geschoßabteilung** *(Warenhaus)* basement shop (store, *US*); ~**lokal** underground bistro, beer (night) cellar *(Br.)*, dive bar, dive *(Br.)*; ~**meister** cellarman; ~**miete** cellarage; ~**raum** cellarage, cellar; ~**restaurant** underground bistro, dive bar; ~**wechsel** accommodation (fictitious, *Br.*, bogus, pro-forma) bill, spurious note, kite *(Br.)*; ~**wechsel ausstellen** to fly a kite *(Br.)*; ~**wohnung** underground dwelling, basement flat.
Kellner waiter, *(auf Schiff)* steward;
~**gehilfe** waiter's assistant, omnibus *(coll.).*
Kellnerin barmaid, waitress.
Kellnerlehrling busboy *(US).*
keltern, Weintrauben to press (tread) the grapes.
Kennbuchstabe code letter.
kennen to know, to be acquainted;
j. genauestens ~ to know s. o. in and out; **gründlich ~** to have a thorough knowledge; **j. nur vom Grüßen ~** to be on nodding terms with s. o.; **j. gut ~** to know s. o. well, to be on visiting terms with s. o.; **j. oberflächlich ~** to have a nodding acquaintance with s. o.; **Sache in- und auswendig ~** to know s. th. inside out (the rights of a case); **Stadt wie seine eigene Westentasche ~** to know a town like the back of one's hand; **j. zu ~ behaupten** to claim acquaintance with s. o.; ~ **müssen** *(jur.)* to know or to be chargeable with knowledge, to be deemed to have notice.
kennenlernen to become acquainted with;
j. ~ to make s. one's acquaintance, to meet s. o., to get to know s. o.; **j. näher ~** to dig under s. one's skin; **auf der Straße ~** to pick up on the street.
Kennenmüssen constructive notice, imputed knowledge.
Kenner authority, connoisseur, expert, adept, specialist, professional;
mit ~auge (~blick) with the eye of an expert; ~**miene aufsetzen** to assume the air of a connoisseur.
Kenn|karte identity (identification) card; ~**marke** identifying badge, *(mil.)* tag, identification mark; ~**melodie** *(Rundfunk)* signature tune; ~**nummer** index (reference) number.
kenntlich identifiable, recognizable, discernible, *(bezeichnet)* label(l)ed, marked;
~ **machen** to identify, to mark, *(Waren)* to label, to ticket; **in den Büchern ~ machen** to mark in the books; **abgetretene Konten ~ machen** to bookmark assigned accounts; **durch Schilder ~ machen** to signpost; ~ **gemacht sein** to be marked.
Kenntlichmachung identification, *(Etikett)* label(l)ing, marking, *(Beschilderung)* signposting;
~ **abgetretener Konten** bookmarking of assigned accounts.
Kenntnis knowledge, privity of knowledge, notice, note, information;
aus eigener ~ from first-hand knowledge; **bei voller ~ der Tatsachen** in full possession of the facts; **zur ~ gebracht** made known, brought to the attention; **zur ~ und weiteren Veranlassung** for information and further action;
genaue ~ full (intimate) knowledge; **oberflächliche ~** slight knowledge, smattering; **tatsächliche ~** actual notice (knowledge); **unmittelbare ~** intuitive knowledge; **unterstellte ~** imputed knowledge, constructive notice; **vermutete ~** implied notice; **vertrauliche ~** confidential information; **verwertbare ~** working knowledge; **vorherige ~** preacquaintance; **zurechenbare ~** *(jur.)* constructive (actual, *Br.*, imputed) notice;
~ **des menschlichen Charakters** insight into human character; **eigene ~ des Gerichts** judicial cognizance, judicial (jurisdiction) notice; ~ **aufgrund einer Mitteilung** express notice; ~ **aus eigener Wahrnehmung** personal knowledge;
jegliche ~ von einem Plan abstreiten to deny any knowledge of a plan; ~ **von einem Vorfall bekommen** to hear of an incident; ~ **von der Gefährdung eines anderen besitzen** to have knowledge of another's peril; **jem. etw. zur ~ bringen** to bring (call) s. th. to s. one's notice; **der Polizei einen Unfall zur ~ bringen** to notify the police of an accident; ~ **erlangen** to be given notice of, to become aware of; **jem. ~ geben** to bring to s. one's attention; **zur ~ geben** to notify; **zur ~ gelangen** to come to the attention; ~ **haben** to be aware, to be on notice *(US)*; ~ **von etw. nehmen** to take notice of (note) s. th., to take cognizance of s. th.; **amtlich von etw. ~ nehmen** to take notice of s. th.; **einverständlich von etw. ~ nehmen** to understand and agree; **von einer Erklärung ~ nehmen** to note a statement; **in ~ setzen** to acquaint, to notify, to warn, to apprise; **j. in ~ setzen** to inform s. o.; **j. von seinen Absichten in ~ setzen** to give s. o. notice of one's intentions; **in ~ aller Tatsachen sprechen** to speak with full knowledge of the facts; **sich ~ über etw. verschaffen** to inform o. s. about s. th.; **nicht offiziell zur ~ genommen werden** to lie on the table.
Kenntnisgabe publication.
Kenntnisnahme notice, note, [taking] notice, cognizance;
mit der Bitte um ~ kindly note; **zur ~** for the attention of;
zur ~ vorlegen to deliver in.
Kenntnisse accomplishments, attainments, experience, *(Fähigkeiten)* attainments, *(technisch)* know-how;
allerneueste ~ up-to-the-minute knowledge; **ärztliche ~** medical knowledge; **auf Erfahrung beruhende ~** practical knowledge; **erworbene ~** acquired knowledge; **geringe ~** small stock of knowledge; **gründliche ~** in-depth knowledge, thorough knowledge; **juristische ~** knowledge of the law; **kaufmännische ~** commercial knowledge; **technische ~** technical knowledge; **umfassende ~** extensive (exact, complete, allround) knowledge; **vertrauliche ~** confidential information; **während der Ehe übermittelte vertrauliche ~** confidences communicated during marriage;
umfassende ~ des Absatzwesens competence in marketing; **profunde ~ auf dem Gebiet des Einzelhandels** understanding in depth of retail marketing; **solide ~ auf dem volkswirtschaftlichen Gebiet** sound background as a general economist; ~ **der europäischen Marktsituation** knowledge of markets in Europe; **besondere ~ nicht erforderlich** *(Annonce)* special knowledge not required;
sich mit seinen ~n brüsten to take pride in one's knowledge; **seine ~ erweitern** to improve one's stock of learning; **gute ~ auf der Universität erwerben** to receive a good education at the university; **einige ~ im Französischen haben** to have a working knowledge of French; **gründliche ~ in seinem Fach haben** to know one's trade; **hinlängliche ~ haben** to have a competence of learning; **rudimentäre ~ des Polizeiapparates haben** to have a background in law enforcement; **umfassende ~ auf einem Gebiet haben** to know s. th. perfectly; **wohlfundierte ~ von etw. haben** to be well-grounded in s. th.; **über solide ~ der englischen Sprache verfügen** to have a good grounding in English; **seine ~ verwerten** to apply one's knowledge.
Kennwort watchword, code word, password, cipher (code) word, *(Zeitungsinserat)* box number, key, *(mil.)* parole;
~**anzeige** box-number advertisement.
Kennzahl code number, indicative figure, indicator, *(Fernschreiber)* dialling code, exchange number, *(Telefon)* area code prefix;
wirtschaftliche ~en economic statistics;
~ **des Absatzes** standard of distribution.
Kennzeichen sign, [distinctive, distinguishing] mark, symbol, distinctive feature, distinction, *(Abzeichen)* badge, *(Auto)* registration number, *(Eigentumszeichen)* earmark, brand, *(Güteabzeichen)* hallmark, label, brand, *(Unterscheidungsmerkmal)* criterion, characteristic, earmark, difference, character;
amtliches ~ *(Auto)* registration number, licence plate; **besondere ~** characteristic signs, *(Paß)* special peculiarity *(Br.)*; **irreführende ~** misleading marks; **polizeiliches ~** *(Auto)* registered (licence, *US*) number, identification (number) plate, number of a car, licence plate *(US)*, registration plate *(Br.)*, *(Flugzeug)* aircraft marking;
mit ~ versehen to put a mark on;
~**beleuchtung** *(Auto)* number (licence, *US*) plate lights; ~**mißbrauch** *(Markenartikel)* passing off one's goods as those of another make *(US)*; ~**schild** *(Auto)* number (licence, *US*) plate.

kennzeichnen to identify, to mark, to hallmark, to designate, to describe, to feature, *(charakterisieren)* to distinguish, *(Waren)* to label, to ticket, *(zweckbestimmen)* to earmark;
Flasche mit einem Etikett ~ to label a bottle; **genau** ~ to mark clearly; **Kiste** ~ to mark a case; **seine Kleidung namentlich** ~ to mark one's clothes with one's name; **Konsignationsware genau** ~ to mark clearly consigned goods; **durch eine punktierte Linie** ~ to mark by a dotted line; **gewisse Posten mit einem Kreuz** ~ to put a cross against certain items; **Urkunde** ~ to earmark a document; **Waren** ~ to identify goods by marks; **Weg durch Schilder** ~ to mark out a path.
kennzeichnend distinctive, characteristic, typical;
~ **sein** to be characteristic.
Kennzeichnung identification, labelling, ticketing, marking, *(Zweckbestimmung)* earmarking;
~ **von Markenerzeugnissen** marking of articles patented.
Kennzeichnungs|bestimmungen, ~**vorschriften** labelling provisions, marketing instructions, marketing (labelling) requirements; ~**leuchtfeuer** beacon.
Kennziffer index, code (index, key) number, key, *(Aktenzeichen)* reference number, *(Bank)* rating, *(Fernschreiber)* dialling code, exchange number, *(Insertion)* box number, key;
mit ~ **versehen** to key, to code;
~**anschrift** keyed address; ~**anzeige** box-number advertising; ~**ausstattung** keying; ~**kupon** keyed coupon; ~**werbung** keyed advertising, keying of advertisements.
Kentern upset;
Boot zum ~ **bringen** to overturn a boat.
kentern to capsize, to overturn, to turn turtle *(coll.)*.
Keramik ceramics, pottery, ware.
keramische|Erzeugnisse pottery; ~ **Industrie** ceramics industry.
Kerbe notch, nick;
in die gleiche ~ **hauen** to back s. o. up.
Kerbholz criminal record;
allerlei auf dem ~ **haben** to have a smoky past *(US sl.)*.
Kerker dungeon, pound, hell, cage, *(Strafmaß)* imprisonment;
~ **bei Wasser und Brot** imprisonment on a bread and water diet; ~**meister** warden of a prison; ~**zelle** dungeon.
Kerl chap, fellow, duck, dog *(coll.)*, guy *(US sl.)*;
anständiger ~ square shooter *(US coll.)*; **kleiner dicker** ~ humpty dumpty; **dummer** ~ tame cat; **famoser** ~ brick *(fam.)*; **großartiger** ~ nailer *(sl.)*; **gutmütiger** ~ easy-going chap; **langweiliger** ~ meal *(sl.)*; **netter** ~ decent fellow *(coll.)*; **ein patenter** ~ a man and a brother *(Br.)*; **schlauer** ~ knowing card; **toller** ~ pip *(sl.)*; **unangenehmer** ~ nasty fellow; **wilder** ~ wild fellow;
j. für einen anständigen ~ **halten** to vote s. o. a fine fellow; **famoser** ~ **sein** to be a regular brick *(fam.)*.
Kern marrow, pivotal point, heart, main issue, quick, substance, *(Atomphysik)* nucleus, *(Hauptsache)* gist, core, essence, heart, root, *(Klage)* gist of an action;
im innersten ~ **getroffen** deeply hurt, cut to the marrow, stung to the quick; **im** ~ **verdorben** rotten to the core;
~ **einer Angelegenheit** root of a matter, nucleus (crux, nub, *US*) of a matter; ~ **der Arbeitslosen** hard core; ~ **der Beweisführung** burden of an argument; ~ **einer Partei** nucleus (hard core) of a party; **des Pudels** ~ the very heart (essence) of a matter; ~ **der Sache** crux of the matter, nucleus of an affair; **guter** ~ **in einer rauhen Schale** rough diamond; ~ **einer Stadt** heart (center) of a city, city core; ~ **eines Vertrages** essence (root) of a contract; ~ **einer Sache bilden** to be at the heart of s. th.; **um den** ~ **einer Sache herumreden** to beat about the bush; **zum** ~ **einer Sache kommen (vorstoßen)** to come to the heart of the matter, to pierce beneath the show of a thing, to come to the crucial point; ~ **einer Sache treffen** to hit the nail on the head; **am** ~ **einer Sache vorbeigehen** to be beside the point;
wer den ~ **essen will, muß die Nuß knacken** he that will eat the kernel must crack the nut;
~**bestandteil** *(Anzeige)* body; ~**brennstoffe** nuclear fuels; ~**energie** nuclear energy; ~**energieanlage** nuclear site; ~**energienutzung** use of nuclear energy; ~**explosion** nuclear explosion; ~**forschung** nuclear research; ~**frage** crucial problem, sticking point; ~**fusion** nuclear fusion; ~**gebiet** core area; ~**gedanke** central idea.
kerngesund as fit as a fiddle, sound as a bell (dollar).
Kern|industrie nuclear industry; ~**kraftanlage,** ~**werk** nuclear power plant (station); ~**problem** crucial question (issue), central issue; ~**punkt** main issue, marrow, *(Klage)* gist; ~**reaktor** atomic (chain) reactor, chain-reacting pile; ~**reaktoranlage** nuclear power station (plant); ~**reaktorgelände** reactor site; ~**seife** curd soap; ~**spaltung** nuclear fission; ~**spaltungsauslöser** atomic-fission trigger; ~**stück** basic item, *(Anzeige)* bold type, *(Ausstellung)* centerpiece; ~**technik** nuclear engineering; ~**teilung** nuclear division; ~**truppe** crack unit; **unsere** ~**truppen** choice of our troops; ~**umwandlung** nuclear transmutation; ~**verschmelzung** nuclear fusion.
Kernwaffen nuclear weapons;
~**mitbesitz** nuclear sharing; ~**verbot** denuclearization; ~**versuch** nuclear test; ~**verteidigung** nuclear defence.
Kernzerfall disintegration of the nucleus, nuclear disintegration.
Kerze candle.
Kerzen|dinner candlelight dinner; ~**halter** candleholder; ~**licht** candlelight; **bei** ~**licht** by candle-light; ~**stummel** candle ends.
keß jaunty, saucy, pert.
Kessel kettle, pot, pan, *(Industrie)* boiler, tank, *(mil.)* pocket;
mit Öl geheizter ~ oil-fired furnace;
~ **flicken** to tinker; ~ **überwachen** to inspect a boiler;
~**anlage** boiler plant; ~**bau** boilermaking; ~**dampf** live steam; ~**druck** boiler pressure; ~**flicker** tinker; ~**treiben** dragnet, battue shoot, witch hunting; ~**treiben gegen j. veranstalten** to close in on s. o.; ~**wagen** tank waggon (car, *US*), tanker.
Kette chain, train, *(Gefangener)* bond, fetter, *(mil.)* flight;
~ **von Angebot und Gegengebot** bargaining path; ~ **von Fahrzeugen** string of vehicles; ~**n der Konvention** shackles of convention; ~ **von Nachwahlmißerfolgen** string of by-election failures; ~ **von Unglücksfällen** an Iliad of woes; ~ **von Widersprüchen** set of contradictions;
sich in eine ~ **einreihen** to get into line, to queue up; **j. in** ~**n legen** to put s. o. in irons (fetters); **Hund an die** ~ **legen** to chain up a dog; **Schiff an die** ~ **legen** to arrest a ship; ~ **vorlegen** to put the chain across.
Ketten|antrieb chain drive; ~**bankwesen** chain banking; ~**blitz** chain[ed] lightning; ~**brief** chain letter; ~**fahrzeug** tracked vehicle; ~**geschäft** chain (multiple, *Br.*, integrated, *US*) store; ~**handel** chain trade; ~**hund** watch dog; ~**laden** chain store *(US)*, multiple shop (firm) *(Br.)*, multiple-store enterprise *(US)*, integrated store *(US)*; ~**läden** multiples *(Br.)*; ~**ladensteuer** chain-store tax *(US)*; ~**ladenunternehmen** chain-store business *(US)*, multiple shop *(Br.)*, integrated store *(US)*; ~**raucher** chain smoker; **nukleare** ~**reaktion** nuclear chain reaction; ~**reaktion auslösen** to trigger a chain reaction; ~**stich** *(Buchbinderei)* kettle stitch; ~**unternehmen** chain, multiple-store enterprise *(US)*.
keuchen to gasp, to puff, to wheeze, to pant.
Keule club, cudgel.
keusch chaste, pure.
kichern to giggle, to snigger, to titter, to snicker.
Kickstarter kick starter.
Kieker, j. auf dem ~ **haben** to be out for s. one's blood, to have the knock in on s. o. *(sl.)*.
Kiel, Schiff auf ~ **legen** to lay down a ship (a ship on keel);
~**geld** keelage, careenage; ~**linie** line ahead; **in** ~**linie** fore-and-after.
kieloben treiben to float keel up.
Kielschwert centre-board, centerboard *(US)*.
Kielwasser wake, wash;
im ~ **eines Schiffes** in the wake of a ship;
in jds. ~ **segeln** to be dragged in the heels of s. o., to be in the wake of s. o.
Kien, auf dem ~ **sein** to be on one's toes (on the ball, *US*).
Kies pebble, gravel, *(Geld, coll.)* gingerbread, lolly *(Br., sl.)*, dough *(US sl.)*, chink *(sl.)*, tin, dibs *(sl.)*, sponduliks, rhino *(Br.)*, sugar *(sl.)*, the needful *(sl.)*, shiners *(sl.)*;
~**gewinnung** sand and gravel working; ~**grube** gravel pit; ~**weg** gravel path.
Killer-Satellit anti-satellite.
Kilo|gebühr *(Buchhandel)* kilo charge; ~**kalorie** therm.
Kilometer kilometer, kilometre *(Br.)*;
gefahrene ~ mil(e)age;
~ **fressen (verschlingen)** to eat up a distance (miles);
geringer ~**anteil einzelner Frachtstücke** lower interdrop mil(e)age; ~**anzeiger** mil(e)age recorder, odometer; ~**berechnungsgrundlage** mil(e)age basis; ~**fresser** mile-eater, speed merchant, road monster; ~**geld** mil(e)age allowance, mil(e)age charge, allowance for travel(l)ing expense, *(Eisenbahn)* car mil(e)age, truck rates; ~**pauschale** flat mil(e)age rate; ~**preis** standard rate per mile; ~**satz** rate per car-mile, distance rate, standard rate per mile; ~**schild** distance marker; **nach einem** ~**schlüssel bezahlen** to pay on a mil(e)age basis; ~**stand** *(Auto)* mil(e)age; ~**stein** milestone; ~**tarif** mil(e)age rate, distance tariff; ~**zähler** mileometer, distance indicator, mil(e)age recorder, odometer, *(Fahrrad)* cyclometer.

Kilowattstunde kilowatt, lamp hour, unit of electricity *(Br.)*, Board of Trade unit.

Kimm *(mar.)* visible horizon.

Kind child, issue, kid *(sl.)*;
~**er nicht mitgerechnet** not counting the children; **mit ~ und Kegel** with bag and baggage;
nicht adoptierte ~er unadopted children; **angenommenes ~** adopted child; **anormales ~** defective child; **unterdurchschnittlich ausgebildetes ~** educationally subnormal child; **ausgesetztes ~** exposed child; **behindertes ~** handicapped child; **von der Fürsorge betreutes ~** charity child; **eheliches ~** legitimate child, child born in wedlock; **elternlose ~er** unadopted children; **empfangenes, noch nicht geborenes ~** existing person; **für ehelich erklärtes ~** special bastard; **schwer erziehbares ~** maladjusted (intractable) child; **evakuiertes ~** evacuee child; **frühreifes ~** precocious child; **außerehelich geborenes ~** bastard *(US)*, child born out of wedlock; **moralisch gefährdetes ~** wayward child *(US)*; **geistiges ~** brain child *(coll.)*; **heranwachsendes ~** growing child; **kindergeldberechtigtes ~** qualifying child; **nachträglich legitimiertes ~** special bastard, mantle child; **minderjähriges ~** infant, minor; **nachgeborenes ~** posthumous child; **natürliches ~** natural child; **neugeborenes ~** new-born child; **noch nicht schulpflichtige ~er** preschool[-age] children, preschoolers; **schwieriges ~** unmanageable child; **unter Vormundschaft stehendes ~** child in tutelage; **uneheliches ~** bastard [child] *(US)*, natural (chance, love, *Br.*) child, child born out of wedlock; **ungeborenes ~** unborn child; **unmündiges ~** incapable child; **unschuldiges ~** babe in the woods; **untergeschobenes ~** changeling; **unterhaltsberechtigtes ~** child entitled to maintenance; **unversorgtes ~** dependent child; **verhaltensgestörte ~er** autistic children; **verwahrlostes ~** neglected (derelict) child; **heimatlose und verwahrloste ~er** waifs and strays; **verzogenes ~** spoilt child;
~**er zahlen die Hälfte** children half price; ~**er und Jugendliche** children and young persons; **~ auf der Universität (in Universitätsausbildung)** college-age child, child receiving full-time education at a university; ~**er und Unzurechnungsfähige** wards of court;
~ annehmen (adoptieren), an ~es Statt annehmen to mother (adopt) a child; **~ einer Amme anvertrauen** to put a child to a nurse; **in der Betreuung der ~er aufgehen** to be devoted to one's children; ~**er aufziehen** to raise a family; **~ recht und schlecht aufziehen** to drag up a child *(coll.)*; **~ mit dem Bade ausschütten** *(fig.)* to empty the baby with the bathwater; **neugeborenes ~ aussetzen** to abandon (expose) a new-born child; **ungezogene ~er disziplinieren** to discipline badly behaved children; **~ enterben** to abdicate a child; **~ entführen** to kidnap a child; ~**er zu guten Staatsbürgern erziehen** to train [up] children to be good citizens; **~ in Pflege geben** to put a child out to a nurse, to farm out a child; **~ zu beaufsichtigen haben** to have charge of a child; ~**er am Rockzipfel hängen haben** to have children underfoot; **Frau und ~er zu unterhalten haben** to have a wife and children to keep (support); **~ ruhig halten** to keep a child quiet; **die ~er mit den Sünden der Väter heimsuchen** to visit the sins of the fathers upon the children; **~ von der Schule nehmen** to withdraw a child from school; **~ beim Namen nennen** to call a spade a spade; **wie das ~ im Hause sein** to be one of the family; **seine ~er sicherstellen (versorgen)** to settle [the future of] one's children; **sich gut auf ~er verstehen** to have a knack with children; **mit ~ern umzugehen wissen** to know how to treat children; **seine ~er völlig unversorgt zurücklassen** to leave one's children in utter neglect.

Kinder|abteilung *(Warenhaus)* children's department; ~**arbeit** employment of children, children's labo(u)r *(Br.)*, child labor *(US)*.

kinderarmes Land country with a low birth rate.

Kinder|aufzucht child rearing; ~**beaufsichtigung** child minding; ~**beihilfe** dependency allowance, child allowance *(Br.)*, allowance for dependants; ~**beratungsstelle** child guidance clinic; ~**betreuung** care of children; ~**bewahranstalt** day nursery; ~**buch** children's storybook (book), juvenile; ~**ermäßigung** reduction for children, *(Einkommensteuer)* tax allowance for dependants, children's allowance, child relief *(Br.)*; ~**erziehung** upbringing of children; ~**fahrkarte** half ticket; ~**fernsehen** kidvid *(fam.)*; ~**fest** children's party; ~**fest veranstalten** to give the children a treat; ~**fräulein** nursery governess; ~**freibetrag** allowance for dependants, child tax allowance *(Br.)*, child relief *(Br.)* (exemption, *US*); **zusätzlicher ~freibetrag** additional personal allowance for children *(Br.)*; ~**früherziehung** early childhood education; ~**funk** children's hour; ~**garten** nursery [school], kindergarten.

Kindergeld family allowance *(Br.)*, child allowance *(US)* (benefit, *Br.*), children's allowance;
bar ausgezahltes ~ cash child benefit *(Br.)*; **steuerfreies ~** tax-free child benefit *(Br.)*;
~**abzug** family allowance deduction *(Br.)*; ~**bestimmungen** children's allowance regulations; ~**erhöhung** increase in child benefit *(Br.)*; ~**gesetz** Family Allowance Act *(Br.)*; **erhöhte ~sätze** increased rates of child benefits; ~**schema** family allowance scheme *(Br.)*, child benefit system.

Kinder|heim children's home; ~**hilfswerk der Vereinten Nationen** United Nations Children's Fund; ~**hort** day nursery, crèche *(Br.)*; ~**hüten** babysitting; ~**jahre** infancy, childhood; **sich auf ~kleidung spezialisieren** to specialize in children's wear; ~**krankheiten** infantile diseases, children's troubles, *(fig.)* teething troubles; ~**krippe** day nursery, crèche *(Br.)*; ~**landverschickung** child evacuation scheme; ~**lehrer** infant teacher.

kinderleicht as easy as shelling peas (winking, *Br.*, *sl.*, kiss my thumb, *sl.*, rolling off a log, *US*, potty, *sl.*);
~ sein to be simplicity itself (as easy as pie, *sl.*);
~**e Sache** child's play.

Kinderlied nursery rhyme.

kinderlos childless, without issue, issueless;
~ sein to have no children.

Kinder|mädchen mother's help, baby minder; ~**märchen** fairy tale; ~**prozentsatzzunahme** increase in child population.

kinderreiche Familie large family.

Kinderschlafsaal night nursery.

Kinderschuhe, in den ~n in leading strings, in its infancy;
seine ~ austreten to cut one's eye teeth; **den ~n entwachsen** to emerge from childhood; **aus den ~n heraus sein** to be past a boy; **noch in den ~n stecken** *(Industrie)* to be still in its pupilage.

Kinder|schutz protection of children; ~**schutzgesetzgebung** Child Labor Laws *(US)*; **geprüfte ~schwester** trained (dry) nurse; ~**sendung** *(Fernsehen)* kidvid *(fam.)*.

Kinderspiel easy job, pushover, child's play, white meat *(sl.)*;
nur ein ~ a mere trifle;
ein ~ sein to be as easy as shelling peas (kiss my thumb, *sl.*, as pie);
~**platz** playground; ~**zeug** *(fig.)* plaything, toy.

Kinder|station *(Krankenhaus)* children's ward; ~**sterblichkeitsrate** infant-death rate.

Kinderstube, gute mannerliness;
gute ~ gehabt haben to be well-bred; **im Galopp durch die ~ geritten sein** to have been badly brought up.

Kinder|stunde *(Radio)* children's hour; ~**tagesstätte** day nursery, day-care center, crèche *(Br.)*; ~**vernachlässigung** child neglect; ~**vers** nursery rhyme; ~**wagen** baby carriage *(US)*, perambulator *(Br.)*, push pram *(Br., coll.)*; ~**wärter** babysitter; ~**wärterin** baby farmer; ~**zahl** number of children; ~**zeitschrift** children's magazine; **als ~zimmer entworfen** designed as a children's playroom; ~**zulage**, ~**zuschlag**, ~**zuschuß** child bounty *(US)*, dependency bonus (allowance), child's special allowance, child benefit.

Kindes|alter infancy, childhood; **im ~alter** of tender age, young; ~**annahme** adoption of children; ~**aussetzung** exposition (exposure, abandonment) of a child; **j. von ~beinen an kennen** to have known s. o. since he was in petticoats; **erste ~bewegungen im Mutterleib** quickening; ~**entführer** kidnapper; ~**entführung** kidnapping; ~**erziehung** child development; ~**mißhandlung** cruelty to children; ~**pflicht** filial duty; ~**raub** child stealing; ~**tötung** child destruction, infanticide; ~**unterschiebung** substitution of a child; ~**unterschiebung begehen** to substitute a child; **mutmaßlicher ~vater** reputed father; ~**verhältnis** parental relationship; ~**vermögen** child's property; ~**vernachlässigung** neglect of children.

Kindheit childhood;
von ~ an from being a child.

Kindheits|alter childhood, pupilarity *(Scot.)*; ~**erinnerungen** childhood memories, recollections of childhood; **unbeschwerte ~tage** gay youth; **j. in die ~tage zurückversetzen** to take s. o. back to his childhood days.

kindisch childish, childlike, bread-and-butter *(coll.)*;
sich ~ über etw. freuen to be as pleased as Punch;
~**e Fragen stellen** to ask silly questions; ~**er Greis** dotard; ~**es Wesen** infantilism, puerility.

Kindischwerden second childhood, dotage.

kindliches Gesicht baby face.

Kinkerlitzchen knicknacks, trivialities, gimcrackery, toy.

Kino cinema *(Br.)*, picture [theater], film, the screen, motion picture *(US)*, movies *(sl.)*;

j. zum ~ **einladen** to pay for s. o. at the cinema; ~ **frequentieren** to patronize a cinema; **ins** ~ **gehen** to go to the movies *(sl.)* (films, pictures, cinema, flicks, *Br., sl.*);
~**besitzer** exhibitor; ~**besitzer sein** to own a cinema; ~**besuch** cinema attendance; ~**besucher** cinema (movie, *US*) goer; ~**eintrittspreis** movie admission price *(US)*; ~**gänger** filmgoer; ~**kasse** box office, paybox; ~**leinwand** cinema screen; ~**narr** cinema addict, movie hound *(US)*; ~**narr sein** to be nuts about films; ~**orgel** theater (cinema) organ; ~**programm** cinema (film, movie, *US*) program(me); ~**publikum** film people, filmgoers, movie audience *(US)*; ~**reklame** cinema advertising, film advertisment *(Br.)*, screen (movie, *US*) advertisement (advertising); ~**vorstellung** cinema (film, movie, *US*) performance; ~**werbung** film *(Br.)* (screen, program(me)) advertising; ~**wesen** cinematography.

Kintopp *(fam.)* flicks *(Br., sl.)*, pictures, movies *(US)*;
in den ~ **gehen** to go to the movies.

Kiosk [concession] stand, kiosk, outlet, *(Zeitungen)* bookstall *(Br.)*, newsstand *(US)*;
~ **besitzen** to run a stand; **am** ~ **nicht zu haben sein** to be off newsstands;
~**absatz**, ~**verkauf** *(Zeitungen)* newsstand distribution (sale) *(US)*.

Kippbrücke *(Lastwagen)* dump body.

Kippe *(Müllhalde)* dump, junk yard (heap) *(US)*, *(Zigarette)* cigarette end, fag (dog, *US*) end, snipe *(sl.)*;
auf der ~ *(fig.)* touch and go;
~ **machen** to go fifty-fifty (halves); **auf der** ~ **stehen** to be touch and go, *(Firma)* to hang in the balance, *(Regierung)* to be wavering on the edge of collapse, *(Schüler bei der Versetzung)* to be a borderline case;
auf der ~ **stehende Firma** shaky firm.

Kipp|einrichtung, ~**vorrichtung** tip, tipping device, tilter, tipper *(US)*, dump body, device for dumping.

Kippen tilt;
durch ~ **entleeren** to tip out.

kippen, gern einen to like to crook (lift) one's elbow; **Kiste** ~ to tip (tilt) up a case; **Kohlen in den Laderaum** ~ to dump (shoot) coal into the ship's hold; **aus den Latschen** ~ to be flabbergasted (dumbfounded).

Kipp|fenster bottom-hung window; ~**hebel** tilting device.

kipplig shaky;
~ **sein** to be touch and go.

Kipp|schalter *(el.)* tumbler switch, flip switch *(el.)*; ~**schaltung** *(Radar)* sweep circuit; ~**stromgenerator** saw-tooth generator; ~**wagen** tip truck (waggon), tipper, tipcart, tilt cart, dumper, dumpcart, dumping truck (waggon).

Kirche, im Schoße der within the pale of the church;
aus der ~ **austreten** to sever o. s. from (leave) the church; ~ **im Dorf lassen** to draw the line somewhere; ~ **ums Dorf tragen** to do s. th. in a roundabout way; ~ **vom Staat trennen** to divorce Church from State; **von der** ~ **betrieben werden** to be church-run.

Kirchen|archiv parish record (register); ~**ausschuß** church committee; ~**austritt** leaving one's church; ~**behörde** parish (church) authority; **im** ~**bereich** within the sacred precincts; ~**besuch** church attendance; ~**buch** church (parish) register; ~**buchauszug** extract from the church register; **säkularisiertes** ~**eigentum** secularized church property; **bewegliche** ~**feste** movable church feasts; ~**freigut** frank-almoigne; ~**gemeinde** parish; **örtliche** ~**gemeinde** parish church; **alle** ~**glocken läuten lassen** to fire the church bells; ~**gut**, ~**ländereien** church lands, alms lands *(Br.)*; **so arm wie eine** ~**maus** poor as a church mouse (Job's cat, *US*); ~**rat** court of assistance, consistory; ~**register** church register, parish register (record); ~**schändung** profanation of a church, sacrilege; ~**staat** Pontifical State; ~**steuer** church rate *(Br.)* (tax, *US*); ~**vermögen** church property; ~**versammlung** church assembly *(Br.)*; ~**vorstand**, ~**vorsteher** church warden *(Br.)*, parochial (church) council *(Br.)*, parish office *(Br.)*, vestry *(Br.)*, vestryman; ~**zugehörigkeit** church membership.

Kirch|geld contribution to the Church; ~**hof** churchyard.

kirchliche|Feier church ceremony; ~ **Körperschaft** spiritual corporation; ~ **Trauung** church wedding.

Kirch|spiel parish; ~**turmspolitik** parish-pump policy, parochial (peanut, *US fam.*) politics, provincialism; ~**weih** dedication day.

Kirmes church fair, feast.

kirre kriegen, j. to get the better of s. o.

Kirschen, mit jem. nicht gut ~ **essen sein** to be an awkward customer.

Kissen pillow, cushion, pad;
~**bezug** pillow slip (case).

Kiste chest, coffer, box, case, crate;
alte (klapprige) ~ jaloppy, rattletrap, *(Fahrrad)* jigger *(sl.)*, *(Flugzeug)* kite *(sl.)*, crate *(sl.)*; **mit Blech ausgeschlagene** ~ tin-lined case; **faule** ~ *(fig.)* shady (fishy) business; **die ganze** ~ kit and caboodle *(US sl.)*; **gebrauchte** ~ secondhand case; **schwierige** ~ tricky job; **tolle** ~ big spree; **verstärkte** ~ extra strong box;
~ **Tee** *(Teehandel)* quarter chest of tea, whole chest;
~ **aufbrechen** to prize a box open; ~**n und Kasten füllen** to line one's pockets; ~**n und Kasten voll haben** to be well-heeled *(US sl.)*; ~ **Zigarren kaufen** to buy a box of cigars; ~ **mit der Bahn schicken** to forward a box by passenger train; ~ **schon schmeißen** to manage it somehow; **in** ~**n verpacken** to case, to crate.

Kisten|ausschlagpapier casing paper; ~**brett** boxboard; ~**deckel zunageln** to hammer down the lid of a box; ~**maß** boxed volume; ~**öffner** nail wrench; ~**verschlag** crating.

kistenweise kaufen to buy by the case.

Kitsch trash, tawdry, trite, slush, sentimental, corn *(sl.)*;
~ **in Reinkultur** unadulterated trash;
~**film** slushy (oversentimental, mawkish) film.

kitschig trashy, sloppy, junky, corny *(US sl.)*;
~**er Schmuck** tawdry, cheap finery.

Kitsch|roman pop, tearjerker *(US)*, sob stuff *(US)*, penny dreadful, dime novel *(US)*; ~**serie** *(Rundfunk, Fernsehen)* soap opera *(US sl.)*.

Kitt putty, filler, *(fig.)* cement, solder.

Kittchen booby hatch *(sl.)*, coop *(sl.)*, cooler *(sl.)*, mill *(sl.)*, calaboose *(US sl.)*, jug *(sl.)*, quod *(sl.)*, stir *(sl.)*, clink *(sl.)*, [bull] pen *(US sl.)*, big house *(US sl.)*;
im ~ in hock, up the river *(coll.)*, out of town *(sl.)*;
aus dem ~ **entweichen** to go over the wall *(sl.)*; **im** ~ **sitzen** to be in jug, to do a stretch *(Br.)*; **ins** ~ **stecken** to send s. o. up, to jug *(sl.)*, to slough *(sl.)*.

Kittel *(Arbeiter)* overall, frock, smock *(US)*.

kitten to cement, to putty;
zerbrochene Freundschaft ~ to mend a broken friendship.

Kitzel tickle, tickling sensation;
dem Publikum einen ~ **verschaffen** to titillate the audience; ~ **nach etw. verspüren** to have an itch for s. th.

Kitzeln tickle, titillation *(coll.)*.

kitzeln, j. ~ **etw. zu tun** to itch s. o. to do s. th.; **jds. Eitelkeit** ~ to tickle s. one's vanity.

kitzlig ticklish, tricky, delicate;
~**e Lage** razor's edge; ~**es Problem** tricky problem.

Klacks trivial matter;
sich über jeden ~ **aufregen** to fly off the handle at everything *(US sl.)*; **nur ein** ~ **für j. sein** to be able to easily afford it.

Kladde notebook, rough (auxiliary) book, scribble (scribbling, *Br.*) block, petty journal, memorandum book, daybook, rough copy, blotter *(US)*, wastebook *(Br.)*;
~ **für Sollbuchungen** debit blotter *(US)*.

Kladderadatsch mess, muddle, shambles, cracker *(sl.)*;
ganzen ~ **aufräumen** to tidy up the whole mess.

klaffen to gape, to yawn.

kläffen to bark, to yap, to yelp.

klaffend|er Abgrund wide gulf; ~**e Lücke** yawning gap; ~**er Unterschied** world of difference; ~**er Widerspruch** patent contradiction; ~**e Wunde** gaping wound.

Kläffer yelping dog, *(fig.)* grumbler.

Klafter fathom, *(Holzmaß)* cord;
~**holz** cordwood.

klafterweise by fathoms.

klagbar actionable, suable, enforceable;
nicht ~ unenforceable;
~ **vorgehen** to go to law, to take legal action;
~**er Anspruch** enforceable claim.

Klagbarkeit suability, actionability, enforceability.

Klage complaint, moan, *(Beschwerde)* complaint, grievance, *(vor Gericht)* action [at law], legal action, lawsuit *(US)*, suit at law *(US)*, *(Jammer)* lamentation, wail, *(in Scheidungssachen)* petition;
im Wege der ~ by bringing an action; **mit der** ~ **abgewiesen** dismissed for want of equity;
unter den Parteien abgestimmte ~ friendly suit; **neu angestrengte** ~ fresh suit; **anhängige** ~ pending action; **dingliche** ~ real action, action in rem; **zuerst eingegangene** ~ junior writ; **erfolglose** ~ abortive trial; **an keinen besonderen Gerichtsstand gebundene** ~ transitory action; **gemeinsame** ~ joint action;

getrennte ~n several actions; **gegenstandslos gewordene ~** abortive action; **leichtfertige oder schikanöse ~** frivolous or vexatious action; **negatorische ~** injunction proceedings (suit); **obligatorische (schuldrechtliche) ~** personal action, action in personam; **öffentliche ~** popular action; **petitorische ~** petitory action *(Scot.)*; **possessorische ~** possessory action; **privatrechtliche ~** private action; **schuldrechtliche und dingliche ~** mixed action; **selbständige ~** separate action; **substantiierte ~** particular statement; **unzulässige ~** action that does not lie; **verspätete ~** action barred by lapse of time; **vorliegende ~** claim under consideration; **wechselrechtliche ~** action on a bill of exchange, summary procedure on a bill of exchange *(Br.)*; **zivilrechtliche ~** civil action; **überall zulässige ~** transitory action;

~ **einer Aktiengesellschaft** corporate action; ~ **eines Aktionärs gegen seine Gesellschaft** shareholder's bill; ~ **wegen Amtsanmaßung** quo warranto; ~ **auf Anerkennung einer Forderung** declaratory action; ~ **auf Anerkennung der Vaterschaft** paternity suit, bastardy case (proceedings) *(US)*; ~ **auf Anfechtung von Hauptversammlungsbeschlüssen** shareholders' (stockholders', *US*) representative action; ~ **auf Anfechtung eines Vertrages** action for avoidance of contract; ~ **auf Anordnung der Vermögensverwaltung** administration action (order, *Br.*); ~ **auf Aufhebung der Ehe** suit of nullity of marriage; ~ **auf Aufhebung eines Patentes** action for forfeiture of a patent; ~ **auf Aufhebung eines Vertrages** action for avoidance of contract, revocatory action; ~ **auf abgesonderte Befriedigung** *(Konkursverfahren)* creditor's bill; ~ **aus ungerechtfertigter Bereicherung** trover, action for money had and received *(Br.)*; ~ **aus Besitz** possessory action; ~ **auf Besitzeinräumung** action for possession *(Br.)*; ~ **wegen Besitzstörung** action of trespass; ~ **auf Bezahlung des Kaufpreises** action for payment; ~ **in Ehesachen** matrimonial suit; ~ **auf Eigentumsverschaffung** adjudication in implement; ~ **auf Einleitung (Eröffnung) des Zwangsvollstreckungsverfahrens** hypothecary action, foreclosure action (suit) *(US)*; ~ **wegen Entlassung aus unsozialen Gründen** action for unfair dismissal; ~ **auf Erfüllung des Vertrages** action to claim specific performance of contract; ~ **auf Erlaß einer einstweiligen Verfügung** civil suit for injunction; ~ **auf Erstattung von Zinsrückständen** action for the recovery of arrears of interest; ~ **auf Feststellung des Bestehens eines Rechtes** declaratory action; ~ **auf Feststellung des Eigentums** action to quiet title; ~ **auf Feststellung der Unwirksamkeit einer Kündigung** action for wrongful dismissal; ~ **mit vorgeschriebener Formulierung** formed action; ~ **am Gerichtsstand der belegenen Sache** local action; ~ **wegen Gewährleistungsbruches** action for breach of warranty, redhibitory action *(US)*; ~ **aus unerlaubter Handlung** action in tort (for conspiracy); ~ **auf Herausgabe** action for conversion; ~ **auf Herausgabe des Eigentums** revindication action, action of detinue (for recovery), petitory action *(Scot.)*; ~ **auf Herausgabe eines Grundstücks** action in expropriation of real property, trespass to try title; ~ **auf Herausgabe des Witwenteils** writ of dower; ~ **wegen Kürzung des Pflichtteils** action in abatement; ~ **nebst Ladung** original process; ~ **auf Leistungserfüllung** action for specific performance; ~ **auf Löschung eines Patents** action for forfeiture of a patent; ~ **wegen Mietrückständen** action for recovery of arrears; ~ **auf ordnungsgemäße Nachlaßabwicklung** administration action *(Br.)*; ~ **auf Naturalerfüllung** action for specific performance; ~ **auf Nichtigkeitserklärung** nullity suit; ~ **auf Räumung** action of ejectment (for possession, *Br.*, for removing, *Scot.*); ~ **auf Rechnungslegung** account render, action of account, creditor's bill; ~ **in bürgerlichen Rechtsstreitigkeiten** civil (common-law) action; ~ **auf Rückgabe gepfändeter Sachen (Gegenstände)** action in replevin, action for redemption, redemption action; ~ **auf Rücknahme einer fehlerhaften Sache** redhibitory action *(US)*; ~ **auf Rückzahlung eines Darlehens** action of debt; ~ **auf Schadensersatz** action for damages, damages suit; ~ **auf Schadensersatz wegen Nichtabnahme** action at law for damages caused by nonacceptance; ~ **auf Schadensersatz wegen Nichterfüllung** action at law for damages caused by nondelivery, action for assumpsit; ~ **auf Schadensersatz wegen Rufschädigung** action for tort of libel; ~ **auf Schadensersatz wegen arglistiger Täuschung** action for damages for deceit; ~ **auf Schadensersatz wegen fahrlässigen Verhaltens** action of negligence; ~ **auf Schadensersatz wegen Verletzung der Gewährleistungspflicht** action for damages for breach of warranty; ~ **auf Scheidung** petition for divorce; ~ **aufgrund gewährter Sicherheiten** action on the security; ~ **gegen den Staat** suit against the state; ~ **wegen nicht erfüllter Übergabe von Sachen** action for failing to deliver goods; ~ **auf Unterhalt** maintenance suit, action for support *(US)*; ~ **auf Unterlassung** injunction suit, *(Wettbewerb)* cease and desist order *(US)*; ~ **im ordentlichen Verfahren** plenary action *(US)*; ~ **auf angemessene Vergütung** action on a quantum meruit; ~ **wegen Verletzung des Urheberrechtes** action for infringement of copyright; ~ **aus Vertrag** action on contract; ~ **auf Vertragsannullierung** relief in chancery; ~ **auf Vertragserfüllung** action to claim specific performance of a contract; ~ **wegen (aus) Vertragsverletzung** action for breach of contract, writ of covenant; ~ **auf Wandlung** action for cancellation of a contract, redhibitory action *(US)*; ~ **wegen unlauteren Wettbewerbs** passing-off action; ~ **auf Wiederherstellung der ehelichen Lebensgemeinschaft** action for restitution of conjugal rights, adherence *(Scot.)*; ~ **auf Zahlung des Kaufpreises** action at law for the purchase price, action for payment;

~ **abändern** to amend a statement of claim; ~ **abweisen** to dismiss (close) an action (a case), to set a claim aside, to find for the defendant, to put (rule) out of court; **Kläger mit seiner ~ abweisen** to nonsuit the plaintiff; ~ **kostenpflichtig abweisen** to dismiss a case with costs; ~ **wegen Prozeßverschleppung abweisen** to dismiss a case for want of prosecution; ~ **als unbegründet abweisen** to ignore a bill, to dismiss a complaint on its merits; ~ **androhen** to threaten to sue (with a suit); ~ **anstrengen** to sue, to intend (maintain, bring, file, institute, enter) an action, to bring a case before the court; ~ **gegen j. anstrengen** to enter (institute) an action (bring a suit) against s. o.; ~ **wegen Verleumdung gegen j. anstrengen** to sue s. o. for libel; **in laute ~n ausbrechen** to break into loud lamentations; **sich zu einer ~ äußern** to refer to the merits of a case; ~ **beantworten** to answer to a charge; ~ **begründen** to substantiate a claim, to make an action; **sich an einer ~ beteiligen** to be a party to a writ; **mit einer ~ durchdringen** to succeed in an action; ~ **einbringen** to declare; **sich auf eine ~ einlassen** to join an issue, to enter an appearance, to appear in an action, to defend; ~ **einreichen** to put in suit, to prefer (file, *US*) a suit, to file (lodge) a complaint; ~ **gegen j. einreichen** to institute a suit (lay s. th.) against s. o.; ~ **gegen eine Gesellschaft einreichen** to prosecute a company; ~ **mit Hilfe eines Prozeßvormundes entgegennehmen** to defend by their guardians appointed for that purpose; **sich einer ~ enthalten** to refrain from taking legal action; **sich in ~n über etw. ergehen** to indulge in complaints about s. th.; ~ **erheben** to bring (institute, enter, maintain) an action, to exhibit a bill, to commence a lawsuit *(US)*, to file a suit *(US)*, *(Staatsanwalt)* to lay an indictment; ~ **gegen j. erheben** to take action (lodge information) against s. o., to sue s. o. at law; **bei Gericht ~ erheben** to sue in court; ~ **im eigenen Namen erheben** to maintain an action in one's own name; ~ **wegen Verletzung eines Patents erheben** to bring an action for infringement of a patent; ~ **auf Vertragsanfechtung erheben** to bring an action for rescission of contract; ~ **für zulässig erklären** to declare an action admissible; ~ **für zuständig erklären** to entertain an action; **Schmerzen ohne ~n ertragen** to suffer pains without complaining; ~ **fallenlassen** to drop a court case, to drop (abandon, discontinue) an action; **Zulässigkeit einer ~ feststellen** to declare an action dismissible; **Grund für eine ~ geben** to give rise to an action; **Grund zur ~ haben** to have reason to complain; **keinen Grund zur ~ haben** to have no cause (ground) for complaint; ~ **wegen Widerstands gegen die Staatsgewalt zu erwarten haben** to face a charge of resisting arrest; **seine ~ nicht begründen können** to fail to make out one's case; **es auf eine ~ ankommen lassen** to venture a lawsuit; ~ **leugnen** to disclaim; ~ **anhängig machen** to bring an action, to institute legal proceedings; **seine Ansprüche in einer ~ geltend machen** to join two causes of action; **einer ~ stattgeben** to sustain (allow) an action; ~ **auf Vertragsverletzung stützen** to sue for breach of contractual obligations; ~ **substantiieren** to substantiate an action; ~ **unterlassen** to forbear a suit; **verschiedene ~n miteinander verbinden (vereinigen)** to cumulate several causes of action; ~ **als unzulässig verwerfen** to dismiss an action; ~**n vorbringen** to article; **seine ~ vortragen** to state one's case; **mit einer ~ abgewiesen werden** to lose a case, to be nonsuited, to be put (ruled) out of court; ~ **nicht zulassen** to nonsuit; ~ **zurücknehmen** to abandon (drop, relinquish, withdraw) an action (a suit), to drop one's ligitation; ~ **als unbegründet zurückweisen** to ignore a bill of indictment; ~ **zustellen** to serve a writ;

~**abänderung** amendments of a statement of claim; ~**abweichung** departure; ~**abweichung vornehmen** to make a departure in pleading, to depart.

Klageabweisung involuntary nonsuit, judgment against the plaintiff, dismissal of action;
zwingende ~ peremptory nonsuit;
~ **wegen Unschlüssigkeit** compulsory nonsuit; ~ **durch Versäumnisurteil** judgment by default; ~ **mit Zustimmung der Parteien** dismissal agreed.
Klage|abweisungsantrag motion for dismissal, plea in bar; ~**abweisungsantrag stellen** to direct a nonsuit; ~**änderung** amendments to a pleading (complaint), amendment of an action, abatement of civil proceedings, departure, mutation of libel; ~**androhung** *(Patentwesen)* threats action *(Br.)*; ~**ankündigung** notice of action.
Klageanspruch claim, cause of action;
begründeter ~ clear (good) title;
~ **auf Kaufpreiszahlung** action for the price of goods; ~ **aus einem gültigen Vertrag** cause of a valid contract;
~ **begründen** to give rise to an action; ~ **bestreiten** to defend a claim (suit, *US*); **seinen** ~ **beweisen** to prove one's case; ~ **spezifizieren** to file particulars of a case; ~ **auf mehrere Klagen verteilen** to split a cause of action.
Klageanstrengung bringing (filing) an action, suing, institution of legal proceedings.
Klageantrag motion in court (for judgment, *Br.*), prayer of process, bill of particulars, pleading, counsel's brief *(Br.)*;
~ **abändern** to amend a pleading (statement of claim); ~ **einreichen** to draw pleadings; **gemeinsamen** ~ **einreichen** to file a class action motion; **einem** ~ **stattgeben** to find for the plaintiff [as claimed], to grant the relief sought in the petition;
~ **stellen** to plead; ~ **zurückziehen** to withdraw a pleading;
~ **auf prozeßleitende Anordnungen** summons for directions *(Br.)*.
Klageausschlußfrist limitation of action.
Klagebeantwortung defendant's answer (plea), answer [to a charge], [statement of] defence, points of defence *(Br.)*, defences *(Scot.)*, record *(Scot.)*, cross bill, *(UNO)* counter memorial;
formelle ~ memorandum of appearance *(Br.)*; **vollständige** ~ full answer;
~ **einreichen** to deliver a defence; **bei der** ~ **Gegenansprüche geltend machen** to deliver a counterclaim with the defence.
Klage|befugnis right of (to bring) action; ~**begehren** prayer of process, relief sought; **dem** ~**begehren stattgeben** to find for the plaintiff.
Klagebegründung substantiation (statement) of claim, stating part of a bill, condescence *(Scot. law)*, record *(Scot.)*, count *(US)*;
abgekürzte ~ endorsement of a writ, special indorsement of writ *(Br.)*, general count *(US)*; **substantiierte** ~ particular statement *(Br.)*, special count *(US)*; **umfassende** ~ full answer, omnibus count *(US)*; **zusammengefaßte** ~ inducement, general count *(US)*; **zusätzliche** ~ novel assignment *(US)*.
Klagebegründungsformeln, übliche common counts *(US)*;
~ **bei Zahlungsklagen** money counts *(US)*.
Klage|behauptung allegation of fact; ~**behauptungen bestreiten** to defend an action, to enter an appearance, to make a plea against the general issue; ~**benachrichtigung** notice of action, *(Kartellverfahren)* notice of reference.
klageberechtigt entitled to sue.
Klage|berechtigung right to sue, standing *(US)*; ~**beschleunigung** speed of action; ~**betrag** amount in controversy, jurisdictional amount *(US)*.
Klageeinlassung [entry of] appearance, appearing, defence in action, joinder of issue;
seit ~ since the commencement of the suit;
bedingte ~ conditional appearance; **beschränkte** ~ special appearance; **vorbehaltlose** ~ general appearance.
Klage|einreichung filing of (entering) an action; ~**entgegnung** answer, defendant's plea; ~**ergänzung** supplemental bill, supplemental complaint *(US)*.
Klageerhebung bringing (filing, raising, *Scot.*) an action, application to the court, suing, institution of legal proceedings, commencement of an action, *(Ladung)* originating summons;
vor ~ before suit was brought; **zum Zeitpunkt der** ~ at the time the action was brought.
Klage|erhebungsfrist time limitation; ~**erneuerung** revival of an action; ~**erweiterung** amendment to a pleading.
Klageerwiderung defendant's plea (answer), articles approbatory *(Scot. law)*, [statement of] defence, certification;
unschlüssige ~ irrelevant answer; **zusätzliche** ~ supplemental answer;
~ **einreichen** to respond.
Klage|formel formula, production of suit; ~**frist** period of limitation, time limitation, period for initiating legal action; ~**gegenstand** substance of an action, object (cause) of an action; **vom** ~**gegenstand abweichen** to depart.
Klagegrund gist (cause, object, ground) of an action, count *(US)*, action;
berechtigter ~ clear (good) title; **geeigneter** ~ proper subject for an action; **voraussichtlich vorhandener** ~ probable ground;
selbständigen ~ **abgeben** to be actionable per se; ~ **leugnen** to plead a demurrer.
Klageleugnung general demurrer, peremptory exception, traverse, negative assertion;
qualifizierte ~ special pleading; **vollständige** ~ disclaimer.
Klage|lied anstimmen, nicht enden wollendes to be everlastingly moaning and groaning; ~**mauer** Wailing Wall; ~**mitteilung** notice of action, *(Strafverfahren)* judicial process; ~**möglichkeit** judicial remedy; **ausreichende** ~**möglichkeit** adequate remedy.
Klagen wail, lamentation, complaining.
klagen to wail, to laugh on the wrong side of one's mouth, *(vor Gericht)* to institute an (take legal) action, to go to law, to take action at law, to sue in court, to declare, to commence a suit *(US)*;
im Armenrecht ~ to sue in forma pauperis; **auf Erfüllung** ~ to sue for specific performance; **auf Erlaß einer einstweiligen Verfügung** ~ to bring an action for injunction; **aufgrund eines Gesetzes** ~ to sue under a law; **aus unerlaubter Handlung** ~ to bring an action for tort; **über Kopfschmerzen** ~ to complain of a headache; **jem. sein Leid** ~ to pour out one's troubles to s. o.; **im Namen einer AG** ~ to sue in the right of a corporation *(US)*; **aus eigenem Namen** ~ to maintain an action in one's own name; **unter seinem handelsgerichtlichen Namen** ~ to sue in its corporate name; **wegen Nichterfüllung eines Vertrages** ~ to sue for breach of contractual obligation; **aus Patentverletzung** ~ to bring an action for infringement of a patent; **auf Räumung** ~ to sue for eviction; **auf Schadensersatz** ~ to sue (bring an action) for damages; **auf Schadensersatz wegen unerlaubter Handlung** ~ to sue for torts; **auf Schadensersatz wegen Unterschlagung** ~ to sue in tort for conversion; **auf Scheidung** ~ to seek a (sue for, file a petition for) divorce; **gegen j. wegen Verleumdung** ~ to sue s. o. for libel; **aus einem Vertrag** ~ to sue on (claim under) a contract; **auf Vertragsaufhebung** ~ to bring an action for rescission; **aus Vertragsbruch (Vertragsverletzung)** ~ to sue for breach of contractual obligations; **aus einem Wechsel** ~ to sue for a claim on a bill of exchange; **über das schlechte Wetter** ~ to grumble about the bad weather; **auf Zahlung des vertraglich vereinbarten Gehalts** ~ to sue for one's salary under a contract.
klagend lamenting, moaning, complaining, wailing;
~**e Partei** plaintiff, prosecuting party.
Klagenhäufung consolidation (cumulation) of actions, *(unzulässige)* misjoinder of action, multifariousness;
objektive ~ joinder of causes of action; **subjektive** ~ joinder of parties.
Klagepunkt count, ground (cause) of action;
~e heads of a charge, particulars;
allgemeine ~e general issue.
Kläger plaintiff, claimant, party suing, suitor, prosecuting party, pleader, complainant, demandant, institutor, actor, pulsator, orator *(US)*, *(Beleidigungsklage)* libellant, *(Scheidungssache)* petitioner, complaining spouse;
fingierter ~ John Doe; **minderjähriger** ~ infant plaintiff;
~, **dem das Armenrecht bewilligt ist** pauper; ~ **in Prozeßstandschaft** nominal plaintiff, guardian ad litem, *(für Minderjährigen)* near friend; ~ **im Räumungsprozeß** ejector;
~ **mit der Klage abweisen** to nonsuit the plaintiff; ~ **aufrufen** to call the plaintiff; **als** ~ **auftreten** to appear as plaintiff, to complain in a court of law, to prosecute; **als Prozeßbevollmächtigter für den** ~ **auftreten** to appear for the plaintiff; **zugunsten des** ~**s entscheiden** to find for the plaintiff; **Forderung des** ~**s erfüllen** to satisfy a claimant; **dem** ~ **obliegen** *(Beweislast)* to reside with the plaintiff; **als** ~ **nicht prozeßfähig sein** to be under a disability to sue; **mit dem** ~ **ein Abkommen treffen** to stipulate with the plaintiff.
Klagerecht right to bring action, right of action (to sue);
verwirktes ~ nonclaim;
~ **gegen jem. haben** to have a cause of action against s. o.
Klägerin complaining party, plaintiff company, demandress, *(Scheidungsverfahren)* complaining spouse.
klägerisch|er Anwalt counsel for the plaintiff; ~**e Partei** the plaintiff; ~**es Vorbringen** allegation of facts.
klägerischerseits for the plaintiff.

Klagerubrum rubrum, title of an action, title of declaration, commencement of a declaration.
Klagerücknahme abandonment (discontinuance, withdrawal) of action, withdrawal of one's suit *(US)*, nolle prosequi;
freiwillige ~ voluntary nonsuit (discontinuance);
~ **aus Rechtshängigkeitsgründen** confession of defense (defence, *Br.*);
~ **dem Beklagten anzeigen** to serve on the defendant a notice of discontinuance.
Klage|sachantrag motion in judgment; ~**sache** action (suit) at law, cause, litigation, lawsuit.
Klageschrift plaint, writ, statement of claim, complaint, declaration, libel *(US)*;
detaillierte ~ bill of particulars;
~ **anfertigen** to frame a writ, to draw a pleading; **seine** ~ **einreichen** to make one's declaration, to file (lodge) a complaint;
~ **zustellen** to issue (serve) a writ;
~**satz** writ; ~**satz mit Ladung zustellen** to issue a writ; ~**zustellung ins Ausland** notice of writ of summons.
Klage|substantiierung substantiation (statement, *Br.*) of claim, statement of particulars; ~**summe** sum claimed, jurisdictional amount *(US)*; ~**tatsachen** allegation of facts; ~**unterlassung** forbearance, refraining from action; ~**veranlassung** occasion prompting an action; ~**verbindung,** ~**vereinigung** joinder (consolidation, cumulation) of actions; **unzulässige** ~**verbindung** misjoinder of actions; ~**verfahren** action of (suit at) law; ~**verjährung** limitation of (barring of an) action; ~**verwirkung** laches in bringing suit; ~**verzichtsvereinbarung** covenant of nonclaim (not to sue); ~**voraussetzungen** admissibility of an action.
Klagevorbringen particulars of a claim, allegation;
beeidigtes ~ affidavit of merits; **ersatzweises** ~ ancillary relief;
bewußt falsches ~ false answer;
~ **abändern** to amend a pleading, to depart; **gesamtes** ~ **bestreiten** to make a plea against the general issue; **sein** ~ **unter Beweis stellen** to prove one's case.
Klageweg, auf dem by bringing suit, by way of action;
~ **beschreiten** to take legal action, to go to law, to institute legal proceedings; **Rückzahlung einer Anzahlung im** ~ **fordern** to sue for the return of a deposit.
Klagezurück|nahme withdrawal of action; ~**weisung** nonsuit, dismissal of an action (proceedings).
Klagezustellung service of process, original writ;
ersatzweise ~ substituted service, constructive service of process; **öffentliche** ~ service by publication.
kläglich pitiable, pitiful;
~**en Anblick bieten** to cut a sorry figure, to be the picture of misery; ~**e Behausung** wretched house; ~**es Ende finden** to perish miserably; ~**e Leistung** poor performance; **der** ~**e Rest** all that is left; **mit** ~**er Stimme** in a pitiful voice; **in einer** ~**en Verfassung sein** to be in a sorry plight; **sich in einem** ~**en Zustand befinden** to be in a deplorable state.
Klamauk din, shindy, fuss;
~ **um einen Film** ballyhoo about a film;
~ **machen** to kick up a row, to skylark, to make a din.
Klammer bracket, parenthesis, *(Bindeglied)* binding force, *(Büroklammer)* paper clip, *(drucktechn.)* parenthesis, *(Heftklammer)* staple, cramp, clip, *(techn.)* dog iron, *(Wäscheklammer)* peg, clothespin;
in ~**n** in brackets;
eckige ~**n** square brackets; **runde** ~**n** round (curved) brackets, curves;
wie eine eiserne ~ **ums Herz** like an iron grip round one's heart;
Bemerkung in ~**n hinzufügen** to add a remark in parenthesis; **in** ~**n setzen** to insert (enclose) in brackets, to bracket a word, to parenthesize;
~**affe** *(fig.)* pillion rider; ~**eisen** cramp, dog; ~**heftmaschine** stapler, stapling machine.
klammern to fasten, to join;
sich an j. ~ to cling close to s. o.; **sich an die Hoffnung** ~**, gerettet zu werden** to cling to the hope of being rescued; **sich an Illusionen** ~ to lend o. s. to illusions; **sich an eine Planke** ~ to clutch to a plank; **sich an jeden Strohhalm** ~ to clutch at every straw; **Wäschestücke an eine Leine** ~ to peg (pin, *US*) clothes on a line.
Klammer|satz bracketed sentence; ~**zahl** circled (bracketed) figure.
klammheimlich furtively, stealthily;
etw. ~ **erledigen** to do s. th. on the quiet *(coll.)*.
Klamotte *(sl.)* toy;
alte ~ oldie, oldy, *(Auto)* jaloppy *(US)*, rattletrap.
Klamotten slop;
alte ~ rags, duds, stuff, old clothes, togs;
aus der ~**kiste kommen** to be an oldy one.
Klang sound, tone;
ohne Sang und ~ unceremoniously;
dreidimensionaler ~ stereophonic sound; **gedämpfter** ~ dull sound;
guten ~ **haben** *(fig.)* to be regarded highly, to figure; **guten** ~ **in der Wirtschaft haben** to have a good reputation among business people; **ohne Sang und** ~ **verschwinden** to sneak off (away), to skip town; **ohne Sang und** ~ **entlassen werden** to be fired (sacked) *(sl.)*;
~**blende** tone control; ~**charakter** tone quality.
Klänge, unter den ~**n der Nationalhymne** to the strains of the national anthem.
Klang|effekt sound effect; ~**farbe** tone colo(u)r (quality); ~**fülle** sonority.
klanggetreue Wiedergabe high-fidelity reproduction.
Klang|güte tone quality; ~**höhe** pitch; ~**körper** orchestra.
klanglich|ausgezeichnet sein to have a very good tone;
~**e Wiedergabe** sound reproduction.
klanglos, sang- und ~ **entlassen** fired *(sl.)*, sacked *(sl.)*.
Klang|reflektor *(Film)* cheese cutter, barn; ~**regelung** tone control; ~**regler** tone correction device; ~**treue** high fidelity.
klangvoller Name illustrious name.
Klangwiedergabe sound reproduction.
klappbar collapsible, folding.
Klapp|bett folding (disappearing) bed; ~**boje** nun buoy; ~**brücke** bascule bridge; ~**deckel** hinged lid.
Klappe valve, *(Bett)* bunk, kip *(Br.)*, sack *(US)*, *(Briefumschlag)* flap, *(Falltür)* trapdoor, *(Film)* slate, *(Landungsboot)* ramp, *(Lastwagen)* folding tail gate, *(Telefonzentrale)* drop indicator, *(freche Schnauze)* mouth, trap *(sl.)*, gob *(sl.)*;
~ **eines Tisches** leaf of a table;
jem. eins auf die ~ **geben** to give s. o. a sock in the face; **in die** ~ **gehen** to go between the sheets; **seine** ~ **halten** to shut one's trap *(sl.)*; **große** ~ **schwingen, große** ~ **haben** *(fam.)* to have a big mouth, to brag.
Klappen, zum ~ **bringen** to bring to a head.
klappen to go off well, to go according to plan, to fold;
Autositz nach vorn ~ to tip the car-seat forward; **nicht** ~ to fall through, not to come off, to be no success; **wie am Schnürchen** ~ to go off without a hitch (like clockwork); **Sitz** ~ to fold (turn up) a seat; **gegen die Wand** ~ *(Tür)* to bang against the wall.
Klappen|schrank manual remote-control switchboard; ~**text** clip-sheet; ~**ventil** butterfly valve.
Klapper|gestell bag of bones, rattlebones; ~**kasten,** ~**kiste** lizzy *(sl.)*, *(Schiff)* old tub, *(altes Auto)* puddle jumper *(sl.)*, rattletrap, rattler, jaloppy *(US)*, *(Flugzeug)* kite *(sl.)*, crate *(sl.)*.
Klappern rattle, clatter, chatter.
klappern to rattle, to clatter, *(mit den Zähnen)* to chatter;
vor Kälte ~ to be shivering; **mit der Sammelbüchse** ~ to rattle the begging bowl; **durch die Straßen** ~ *(Fahrzeug)* to rattle through the streets.
Klapp|fenster transom window, *(Auto)* quarter-light (vent, *US*), wing; ~**flügel** folding wing; ~**kamera** folding camera; ~**luke** *(Dach)* skylight; **illustrierter** ~**prospekt** sales folder.
klapprig ramshackle, *(Mensch)* on one's last legs;
sich ~ **auf den Beinen fühlen** to feel a bit shaky.
Klapp|schnitte sandwich; ~**sitz** drop (rumble) seat, *(Auto)* jump seat *(US)*, tilting bucket seat; ~**stuhl** folding (camp, deck) chair, folding stool; ~**tisch** collapsible (folding, drop) table, gate-legged table; ~**verdeck** *(Auto)* folding hood, convertible top; **mit** ~**verdeck** *(Auto)* convertible.
Klaps slap, pat, clap;
~ **auf den Hosenboden** spank on the bottom;
einen ~ **haben** to be a bit dotty, to have a screw loose; **einen** ~ **kriegen** *(fig.)* to go off one's rocker (nutty, *US sl.*);
~**mühle** *(coll.)* booby hatch *(sl.)*, loony bin *(Br.)*, nut house (factory, college) *(sl.)*.
klar clear, bare, manifest, distinct, *(Luft, Wasser)* fair, *(leuchtend)* vivid, *(offensichtlich)* plain, explicit, obvious, *(Schiff)* clear, ready, *(Stil)* crisp, *(unzweideutig)* unambiguous, clear;
klipp und ~ clear-cut; ~ **ausgedrückt** expressed in clear terms; ~ **zum Start** ready to take off;
so ~ **wie Kloßbrühe** as plain as the nose on one's face, as plain as pikestaff *(fam.)*; **so** ~ **wie dicke Tinte** as plain as print (clear as daylight);
sich ~ **abzeichnen** to become apparent; ~ **und deutlich sagen** to

make one's meaning perfectly plain; ~ **sein** to be obvious; **sich noch nicht** ~ **sein** not to be quite sure; **sich über etw.** ~ **sein** to be clear about s. th.; **völlig** ~ **sein** to stand to reason;
~**e Absage erhalten** to receive a definite no; ~**e Antwort** plain answer; ~**e Aussprache** distinct pronunciation; **bei** ~**em Bewußtsein** fully conscious; ~**er Fall von denkste** clear case of wishful thinking; ~**e Handschrift haben** to have a clear hand; ~**er Kopf** lucid mind, clear head; ~**e Momente** *(Geisteskranker)* lucid intervals; ~ **erkennbares Risiko** obvious risk; ~**e Sache** plain (plane) sailing; ~**e Sicht** high visibility; ~**er Stil** transparent style; **in** ~**en Verhältnissen leben** to lead a steady life; ~**e Verhältnisse schaffen** to clear the air; ~**e Vertragsbestimmungen** clear-cut provisions of a contract; ~**e Vorstellung über etw. haben** to form a true notion of s. th.; ~**e Vorstellung über seine Verwendungsmöglichkeiten haben** to be vocal about one's assignments.

Kläranlage sewage farm (plant), clarification plant.

klaren, im aware of; **völlig im** ~ to fully realize;
sich über die möglichen Folgen völlig im ~ **sein** to be well aware of the possible consequences.

klären to clarify, *(Abwässer)* to purify sewage;
Angelegenheit ~ to clear up a matter; **die Dinge** ~ to explain matters; **Mißverständnis** ~ to clear up a misunderstanding; **Schuldfrage endgültig** ~ to find out who was at fault in an accident; **Unfallschuldfrage** ~ to find out the blame for an accident.

klärendes Wort sprechen to say a few words in explanation.

Klärgrube catch pit, cesspit.

Klarheit clearness, clarity;
~ **seiner Gedanken** lucidity of one's thoughts; ~ **der Linienführung** clear lines; ~ **der Rede** coherence of speech;
~ **in eine Sache bringen** to throw light on a matter; ~ **über jds. Schicksal gewinnen** to get to know what has become of s. o.

klarieren to clear the customs.

Klarierung clearance.

Klarierungs | brief clearing bill, jerque note *(Br.)*; ~**gelder** clearance; ~**schein** bill of clearance, clearance certificate.

klarkommen to get clear;
mit etw. ~ to manage all right; **mit jem.** ~ to get along with s. o.; **vom Lande** ~ to clear the land; **mit einem Problem** ~ to get to grips with a problem.

klarlegen to explain, to lay open.

Klarmachen zum Gefecht general quarters.

klarmachen to point out, to make clear, to explain;
jem. etw. ~ to make s. th. plain to s. o., to drive s. th. home to s. o., to put s. th. across to s. o., to clear s. one's mind; **Flugzeug** ~ to handle a flight; **jem. die ihm bevorstehenden Gefahren deutlich** ~ to lay before s. o. the dangers he is running; **jem. etw. mit Gewalt** ~ to drum s. th. into s. one's head; **Schiff zum Gefecht** ~ to clear the ship for action; **jem. seinen Standpunkt gehörig** ~ to give s. o. a good dressing down; **jem. das Törichte seines Verhaltens** ~ to point out to s. o. the folly of his conduct.

Klar | scheibe *(Gasmaske)* antimist disk; ~**schiff** readiness for action.

Klärschlamm sludge.

Klarschreiber printer.

klarsehen to understand, to realize, to keep a clear head, to see one's way clear;
in einer Sache ~ to see clear in a matter; **endlich in einer Sache** ~ to see daylight at last.

Klarsicht | folie transparent foil; ~**hülle** window envelope; ~**mittel** screenwash additive; ~**packung** transparent pack; ~**scheibe** demister.

klarstellen to clear up, to clarify, to make evident, to settle, to eludicate;
undeutliche Stelle ~ to remedy an ambiguous passage.

Klarstellung explanation, clarification.

Klärteich settling pond.

Klartext text in clear, uncoded text, hard copy;
im ~in clear, decoded;
im ~ **senden** to transmit in plain language, to transmit in clear.

Klärung clearing up, clarification;
~ **von Fragen** resolution of questions;
noch der ~ **bedürfen** to be still up in the air.

klarwerden, jem. to be borne upon (become clear to) s. o.; **jem. blitzartig** ~ to recognize in a flash; **sich über seine Lage** ~ to take stock of one's situation.

Klasse class, category, rate, *(erstklassig)* classy *(sl.)*, *(Qualität)* class, quality, sort, brand, *(Schicht)* order, estate, *(Schiff)* class, rating, *(Schule)* form, standard *(Br.)*, class, grade *(US)*, *(Steuerklasse)* bracket, *(Wertpapiere)* denomination;
in der zweiten ~ *(Krankenhaus)* semiprivate; **nach** ~**n eingeteilt** classified;
die arbeitenden ~**n** the working-class population; **begüterte** ~**n** leisured classes; **besitzende** ~**n** proprietary (moneyed) classes; **erste** ~ *(Grundschule)* first form *(Br.)* (grade, *US*); **erster** ~ grade A *(US)*, *(Abteil)* first-class, *(Krankenhaus)* private, *(Ware)* first-rate; **ganz große** ~! smashing! terrific!; **herrschende** ~**n** governing (ruling) classes; **oberste** ~ *(Schule)* sixth form; **überfüllte** ~**n** overcrowded classes; **untere** ~**n** lower classes, low orders; **unterste** ~**n** lowest range, *(Schiffsregister)* E *(Br.)*; **zweiter** ~ *(Eisenbahn)* second (tourist, *US*) class;
1. ~ **und Touristenklasse kombiniert** mixed;
~ **für sich darstellen** to hold a position all its own; **in** ~**n einteilen** to classify; **erster** ~ **fahren** to go first; **zu einer** ~ **gehören** to belong to a class; **zur A-**~ **gehören** *(Schiff)* to be classed A; **zu den Hotels der ersten** ~ **gehören** to be a first-class hotel; **erster** ~ **liegen** *(Krankenhaus)* to have a private room; **zweiter** ~ **reisen** to travel (go) second (tourist, *US*) class; ~ **für sich sein** to top everything; **große** ~ **sein** to be smashing; **alle** ~**n der Bevölkerung treffen** *(Preisanstieg)* to affect all classes; ~ **überspringen** to skip a class; **in die nächste** ~ **versetzen** to move up; **in die nächsthöhere** ~ **versetzt werden** to go up a form; ~ **wiederholen** *(Schule)* to stay down [in a class]; **zu einer** ~ **zählen** to rate; ~ **für englischen Erstunterricht zusammenstellen** to form a class for beginners in English;
~**fahrer** top-notch driver; ~**frau** smasher, dish.

Klassen | ältester top boy; ~**arbeit** paper, schoolwork, classwork *(US)*; ~**arbeit,** ~**aufsatz schreiben** to do a form test, to write a paper; ~**aufsicht** observation; ~**aufsicht führen** *(bei Examen)* to proctor, to invigilate a class; ~**ausflug** school treat, class outing; ~**bester sein** to be at the top of one's class.

klassenbewußt class-conscious.

Klassenbewußtsein class consciousness (feeling).

klassenbildend classificatory.

Klassen | bildung formation of classes; ~**breite** class interval; ~**buch** classbook *(US)*, class (masters') register, mark book; **Schüler ins** ~**buch eintragen** to give a pupil a black mark.

klassendiskriminierend class-distinctive.

Klassen | dünkel pride of rank; ~**durchschnitt** average of a class; ~**einteilung** classification, rating, ranging; ~**erster** head of the class, top of the form, dux *(Br.)*; ~**erster sein** to head one's class; ~**feind** class enemy; ~**gegensätze** class antagonism; ~**geist** team spirit; ~**gesetzgebung** class legislation; ~**größe** class size, *(Statistik)* class interval; ~**haß** class hatred; ~**interesse** class interest; ~**kamerad** schoolmate, classmate, form mate, class fellow; ~**kampf** class struggle (war, warfare); ~**kampfdoktrin** doctrine of class struggle; ~**kampfempfinden** class-warfare ideas; ~**lehrer,** ~**leiter** class teacher, form master.

klassenlos classless.

Klassen | losigkeit classlessness; ~**lotterie** class (serial, Dutch) lottery; ~**ordner** monitor; ~**platz** *(Schule)* position in class; ~**primus** head of the class, top of the class (form); ~**raum** classroom; ~**register** *(Schiffe)* classification register; ~**schranken** class barriers; ~**solidarität** class solidarity; ~**spiegel** seating plan of a class; ~**sprecher** class captain (prefect); ~**stärke** *(Schule)* class load; ~**steuer** classified (graduated) tax; ~**tarif** classified advertisement; ~**treffen** class meeting; ~**übungen** class exercises; ~**unterricht** classroom instruction; ~**unterschied** class distinction (difference); ~**vorrechte** class privileges; ~**vorurteil** rank (class) prejudice, class bias; ~**ziel erreichen** to go up into a higher class; ~**ziel nicht erreichen** to stay down, to be retained *(US)*; ~**zimmer** form room, classroom; ~**zugehörigkeit** class affiliation.

Klassewagen smashing car;
zweiter ~ second-class carriage *(Br.)*.

Klassifikation classification, qualification.

Klassifikations | attest *(Schiff)* classification certificate; ~**system** system of classification, classification system; ~**vermerk** *(Bibliothek)* class number; ~**zahlen** classification statistics.

klassifizierbar classable;
nicht ~ nondescript.

klassifizieren to classify, to class, to arrange in classes, to categorize, to rank, to range, to sort, to label, to digest, *(aufschlüsseln)* to break down, *(finanziell)* to rate.

klassifiziert classified;
nicht ~ innominate;
~**e Schuldverschreibungen** classified bonds.

Klassifizierung classification, arrangement in classes, qualification, grading, *(Aufschlüsselung)* breakdown, *(finanziell)* rating, *(Tarif)* express classification;

vergleichende ~ cross tabulation, cue sheet;
~ des Verhaltens attitude rating.
Klassifizierungs|ausschuß *(Seeschadensversicherung)* classification society; **~gesellschaft** *(Schiffe)* classification society; **~system** classification system.
Klassiker standard writer, classic author.
klassisch classic[al];
~es Beispiel classic example; **~er Baustil** classical architecture; **~er Fall versuchten Betruges** clear case of fraud; **~e Philologie studieren** to study the classics; **~e Sprachen** classical languages; **~e Waffen** conventional weapons; **~er Zeuge** credible witness.
Klatsch smack, clap, *(Gerücht)* gossip, tittle-tattle, talk;
~ **verbreiten** to spread gossip;
~base scandalmonger, gossipmonger, blab, talebearer, tattle, tabby, telltale; **~blatt** gutter paper, yellow paper *(US)*.
Klatsche *(Schule)* trot *(sl.)*, crib *(Br.)*, pony *(US)*, mule;
als ~ benutzen to [ride a] pony *(US)*, to crib *(Br.)*, to skin *(sl.)*.
Klatschen applause, clapping.
klatschen *(Beifall)* to clap, to applaud, *(Klatschgeschichten erzählen)* to spread gossip, to tittle-tattle, *(in der Schule)* to sneak *(Br., sl.)*, to tattle *(US)*;
stürmischen Beifall ~ to applaud wildly; **Buch auf den Tisch ~** to fling a book onto the table; **gegen die Fensterscheiben ~** *(Regen)* to patter against the window panes; **mit seinem Nachbarn ~** to have a gossip with one's neighbo(u)r; **gegen die Uferpromenade ~** *(Wellen)* to slap against the promenade.
Klatschgeschichten piece of gossip;
mit seinen ~ hausieren gehen to peddle one's gossip wares; **in ~ schwelgen** to revel in gossip; **~ verbreiten** to spread scandal.
klatschhaft gossipy.
Klatsch|kolumnist gossip writer; **~maul** scandalmonger.
klatschnaß soaking wet.
Klatsch|nest hotbed of gossip; **~spalte** *(Zeitung)* gossip (society) column; **in den ~spalten auftauchen** to make the society columns; **~spalten füllen** to provide matter for gossip; **~spaltenjournalist** gossip columnist (writer); **~stadt** yak-yak city *(US)*.
klatschsüchtig gossip-mongering.
Klatschtante old gossip, gossipmonger;
Stoff für die ~n abgeben to make good gossip.
klauben to gather, to collect;
an jedem Wort etw. zu ~ wissen to quibble at every word.
Klaue *(Handschrift)* paw *(coll.)*, fist, scrawl, scribble;
in den ~n des Lasters in the grip of vice;
in jds. ~n fallen to get into s. one's clutches;
er hat eine fürchterliche ~ his writing is a scrawl.
Klauen pinching, pilfering.
klauen to pilfer, to pick and steal, to dip, to lurch, to touch, to lift, to bag *(sl.)*, to find, to snoop, to snaffle *(sl.)*, to snitch *(sl.)*, to pinch, to whip, to palm *(US sl.)*;
Buch aus einer Bibliothek ~ to filch a book out of a library; **jem. die Uhr ~** to abstract a watch from s. o. *(coll.)*.
Klause hermitage, *(Studierzimmer)* retreat, den.
Klausel [contract] clause, article, reserved power, *(Bedingung)* condition, stipulation, *(Vorbehalt)* provision, proviso;
durch besondere ~n geschützt hedged in by clauses; **ohne ~n** no strings attached;
aufhebende ~ *(Testament)* derogatory clause; **bedingte ~** conditional clause; **eingefügte ~** inserted clause; **in arglistiger Absicht eingefügte ~** fraudulent clause; **handschriftlich eingefügte ~** hand-written clause; **einschränkende ~** restrictive clause, restrictive provision; **entgegenstehende ~** stipulation to the contrary; **handelsübliche ~** customary clause; **hinterlistige ~** joker *(US sl.)*, bug; **[orts]übliche ~** customary clause; **salvatorische ~** escape clause; **übliche Haus-zu-Haus ~** standard warehouse-to-warehouse coverage; **unumgehbare ~** ironclad clause; **vertragsauflösende ~** resolutory condition; **vorgedruckte ~** printed clause; **zusätzliche ~** additional (added) clause; **zwingende ~** mandatory clause (provision) *(US)*;
~ über die sofortige Fälligkeit acceleration clause; **~n für die Festsetzung neuer Preise** repricing provisions; **~ hinsichtlich des Gerichtsstandes** jurisdictional clause; **~ zugunsten des Grundpfandgläubigers** *(Feuerversicherung)* union mortgage clause; **~ über Haftung für versteckte Mängel** latent-defect clause; **~ frei von besonderer Havarie** free-of-particular average clause; **~ frei von großer Havarie** general average clause; **~ über Schadensabwendung und Schadensminderung** *(Seeversicherung)* sue and labour clause *(Br.)*; **~ hinsichtlich der Schiedsgerichtsbarkeit** arbitration clause; **~ gegen mißbräuchliche Schiffsbenutzung** trade warranty; **~n für Seeschadensversicherung** institute-cargo clauses *(Br.)*; **~ über den Selbstbehalt** co-insurance clause; **~ zur Sicherstellung der Zahlung angemessener Löhne** fair-wage clause; **~ für die Verschiffung lebender Tiere** livestock clause *(Br.)*; **~ für beiderseitiges Verschulden** both-to-blame collision clause; **~ eines Vertrages** article of an agreement, contract clause; **~ Wert anerkannt** admitted-value clause; **~ für Zusatzleistungen im Unfalltod** accidental death benefit clause;
mit ~n absichern to guard by clauses; **~ anfechten** to dispute a clause; **~ eng auslegen** to construe a clause narrowly; **einem Vertrag ~n beifügen** to add clauses to a contract; **~ aufnehmen lassen** to have a clause inserted; **durch vertragliche ~n schützen** to guard by clauses; **an eine ~ gebunden sein** to have a string to it.
Klausur enclosure, *(Arbeit)* paper, test;
~ für Fortgeschrittene progress test;
in strenger ~ leben to live in strict seclusion; **~ schreiben** to sit for (do) a paper;
~arbeit test paper; **~tagung** private session, closed-door meeting.
Klaviatur, die ganze ~ des Geschäfts souverän beherrschen to have the whole gamut of a business at one's fingerends (fingertips).
Klavier, ausgedientes tuneless piano;
~ spielen to play the piano; **auf zwei ~en spielen** to do two things at once, to have a foot in both camps; **~ üben** to practise on the piano;
~abend piano recital; **~konzert** piano concerto.
Klebe|apparat gummed-tape sealer; **~band** Scotch tape, *(Film)* splicing tape; **~bindung** *(Buchbinderei)* adhesive binding; **~falz** hinge; **~folie** adhesive film; **~heftung** adhesive binding; **~marke** adhesive stamp; **~mittel** glue, adhesive.
kleben to glue, to stick;
jem. eine ~ to give s. o. a box on the ear; **hinter einem langsamen Auto ~** to tail a slow car *(coll.)*; **Briefmarke auf ein Kuvert ~** to stick a stamp on an envelope; **am Buchstaben ~** to stick on the letter; **gut ~** to stick well; **wie eine Klette an jem. ~** to stick like a bur on to s. o.; **Plakate ~** to stick (post) placards; **an seinem Posten ~** to hang on to one's job, to stick to one's post; **zu sehr am Text ~** to adhere too closely to a text; **Tüten ~** to be doing time, to be in jug; **Versicherungsmarken ~** to buy insurance stamps.
klebenbleiben to stick fast, *(Schüler)* to stay down, to repeat a year;
drei Tage in einer kleinen Stadt ~ to strand for three days in a little town.
Klebe|presse *(Film)* splicer; **~stelle** *(Film)* splice, joining; **~stift** adhesive stick; **~stoff** glue, gum, paste, pasting, adhesive; **~streifen** adhesive (gummed) tape, sticker *(US)*, *(Reproduktion)* masking type; **durchsichtiger ~streifen** Scotch tape; **~streifen für Einschreibesendungen** registration label; **~vignette, ~zettel** adhesive (gummed) label, sticker.
klebrig sticky;
~e Hände haben to have sticky hands, *(fig.)* to be light-fingered.
Kleckerfritze mucky pup.
kleckern to make spots (a mess);
Farbe auf den Tisch ~ to spill paint on the table.
kleckerweise in dribs and drabs;
~ eingehen to come in in dribs and drabs; **~ vorankommen** to proceed by fits and starts.
Klecks stain, mark, blot, blur, *(drucktechn.)* monk *(Br.)*;
nur ein ~ von M entfernt sein to be only a stone's throw from M.
klecksen to blot, to make a stain.
Kleeblatt[konstruktion] *(Autobahn)* cloverleaf.
Kleid garment, dress, costume, apparel, attire, clothes;
~ ändern to make alterations to a suit of clothes; **festliches ~ anlegen** *(Stadt)* to put on a festive air; **~ entwerfen** to design a dress.
kleiden, j. to dress (clothe) s. o.; **seine Drohung in höfliche Worte ~** to couch one's threat in polite words; **sich geschmackvoll ~** to dress with fine taste; **j. gut ~** to become (suit) s. o.; **sich nach der neuesten Mode ~** to dress in the latest fashion; **j. in Samt und Seide ~** to lay s. o. out in lavender *(sl.)*.
Kleider, abgelegte left-off clothing; **abgetragene ~** old clothes; **fertige ~** store (ready-made, off-the-peg) clothes, reach-(hand-) me-downs;
kostspielige ~ bevorzugen to have expensive tastes in clothes; **in seine ~ fahren** to hurry into one's clothes; **~ von der Stange kaufen** to buy ready-made clothes; **zwei Tage nicht aus den ~n gekommen sein** not to have been to bed for two days;
~ machen Leute fine feathers make fine birds;

~ablage cloakroom, checkroom *(US)*, garment rack *(US)*; ~**fabrikant** clothing manufacturer; ~**geld** clothing (dress) allowance, *(mil.)* outfit allowance; ~**geschäft** clothing shop *(Br.)* (store, *US*), outfitter; ~**haken** clothes hook; ~**händler** wardrobe dealer; ~**kabine** fitting room; ~**kammer** *(mil.)* clothing stores, *(mar.)* slop room; ~**karte** clothing ration book; ~**kartenabschnitt** clothing coupon; ~**kiste** *(mar.)* slop chest; ~**kupon vom Tuchballen abschneiden** to cut off a yard of cloth from the roll; ~**ordnung** dress regulation; ~**puppe** dummy, lay figure; ~**reste zusammenstückeln** to piece together odds and ends of cloth; ~**sack** duffel bag, *(mar.)* kit bag; ~**schrank** wardrobe, clothes press; ~**ständer** clothing rack (tree), coat tree *(US)*; **dürr wie ein** ~**ständer** as thin as a rake (rail, *US*); ~**stoff** dress material; ~**zulage**, ~**zuschuß** clothing (dress) allowance.

Kleidung clothing, clothes, dress, apparel, garment, attire;
in gewöhnlicher ~ out of livery;
ärmliche ~ poor dress; **auffallende** ~ loud dress; **extravagante** ~ way-out clothes; **fertige** ~ off-the-peg (ready-made) clothes; **geschmackvolle** ~ neat dress; **konventionelle** ~ classic clothes; **korrekte** ~ proper clothes (dress); **für ein derartiges Ereignis korrekte** ~ clothes proper to such an occasion; **saloppe** ~ casual attire; **schlampige** ~ disarray; **schwarze** ~ black; **warme** ~ warm clothes;
seine ~ **namentlich kennzeichnen** to mark one's clothes with one's name; **auf seine** ~ **größten Wert legen** to be particular about one's dress; **für jds. Nahrung und** ~ **sorgen** to feed and clothe s. o.

Kleidungsstücke garments, clothing, personal chattels *(Br.)*;
abgelegte (ausrangierte) ~ castoff clothes; **pfändungsfreie** ~ wearing apparel;
notwendige ~ **und Bettücher** necessary wearing apparel and bedding.

Klein | er little boy, lad, youngster;
~**en in der Krone haben** to be tipsy; **Ware im** ~**en verkaufen** to retail goods, to sell goods retail.

klein small, little, minor, short, petty, *(geringfügig)* fractional, *(jung)* young;
sehr ~ tiny, teeny, minute *(coll.)*; **ein** ~ **wenig** smidgeon *(US fam.)*, a tiny (wee) bit;
~ **anfangen** *(Unternehmen)* to start from scratch; ~ **beigeben** to draw in one's horns, to sing small, to climb down, to knuckle under; ~ **von jem. denken** to have a low opinion of s. o.; **sich ganz** ~ **und häßlich machen** to lay low *(sl.)*; **bis ins** ~**ste ausgearbeitet sein** to be worked down to the last detail; **aus** ~**en Verhältnissen stammen** to have a humble background, to spring from humble stock; **im** ~**en verkaufen** to sell by (at, *US*) retail; **ganz** ~ **und häßlich werden** to come down a peg or two (off the high horse), to stick (tuck) one's tail between one's legs, to deflate;
~**e Aktienbeteiligung** smallholdings; ~**e Aktionäre** smallholders; ~**e Alltagssorgen** small worries of life; ~**er Anfang** humble (small) beginning; ~**e Anfrage** *(parl.)* interpellation, question; ~**e Anzeigen** classified advertisements, smalls; ~**e Auflage** short number; ~**er Ausflug** short trip; ~**e Ausgaben** petty (minor) expenses, petty cash; **dubiose** ~**e Bank** shoestring bank; ~**er Bauernhof** subsistence farm, cottage farming, small holding *(Br.)*; ~**er Beamter** petty official; ~**er Betrag** small sum, petty cash; **mein** ~**er Bruder** my little brother (kid, *US*); ~**er Dieb** smalltime thief; ~**e Einlagen** small deposits; ~**e Fahrt** *(Schiff)* dead slow; ~**er Fehler** slight mistake, trifling error; ~**e Fische** *(fig.)* small potatoes *(US)*; ~**en Gang einschalten** to shift to low gear; ~**er Geist** narrow-minded person, small pot *(sl.)*; ~**es Geld** small change; ~**er Geldbetrag** small sum of money; **auch für einen** ~**en Geldbeutel erschwinglich sein** to be within the reach of a small purse; ~**e Geldscheine** low-value notes; ~**e Geldsumme** small sum of money; ~**es Geschäft unterhalten** to carry on business in a small way; ~**e Geschäftsleute** small businessmen; ~**er Geschäftsmann** petty trader (shopkeeper); ~**er Gewerbetreibender** small tradesman; ~**es Glas Bier** half-pint of beer; **der** ~**e Grundbesitz** the smallholders; **in einem bescheidenen** ~**en Haus wohnen** to live in a modest little house; ~**e Intrigen** little schemes; ~**e Kasse** petty cash, imprest fund; ~**es Kassenbuch** petty cash book; ~**e Kiste** box; ~**e Kosten** petty charges; ~**er Krieg** minor war; ~**er Ladenbesitzer** small shopkeeper; ~**e Leute** simple people; ~**es Lexikon** pocket dictionary; ~**ere Mängel** minor defects; **der** ~**e Mann [auf der Straße]** the ordinary man in the street; ~**e Pause** short break; ~**e Portokasse** petty cash; ~**e Preise** short rates; **in** ~**em Rahmen** small-scale; ~**e Rationen** short rations; **auf** ~**stem Raum** in a confined space; ~**ere Reparaturen** minor repairs; **jem. einen** ~**en Schrecken einjagen** to give s. o. quite a scare; ~**e Sendungen** small consignments; ~**er Sparer** small investor; ~**e Spesen** small (petty) charges; **mit** ~**em Stammkapital** in a small way; ~**e Steuerreform** minor tax reform; ~**e Stücke** *(Wertpapiere)* small denominations; ~**er Umweg** slight detour; ~**e Unterbrechung** short interruption; **in** ~**en Verhältnissen leben** to live in quite a small way; **aus** ~**en Verhältnissen stammen** to have a humble background, to spring from humble stock; ~**es Vermögen** small fortune; ~**e Verzögerung** slight delay; ~**e Wohnung** small flat; ~**e Zurechtweisung** dressing down.

Klein | abnehmertarif *(el.)* flat rate [tariff]; ~**addiermaschine** pocket adding machine, electronic computer; ~**aggregat** farm lighting generator; ~**aktie** baby share, penny stock *(US)*; ~**aktionäre** small shareholders *(Br.)*, smallholders; ~**anleger betreuen** to cater for the small investors.

Kleinanzeigen classified advertisements (announcements), smalls, want (small) ads *(US)*;
~**abteilung** classified ad department *(US)*; ~**spalte** classified columns; ~**wesen** small-size advertising; ~**zuschlag** short notice charge.

Kleinarbeit spadework;
mühevolle ~ painstaking work; **tägliche** ~ routine work;
sich um die ~ **kümmern** to take care of the details; ~ **leisten** to grind small.

Klein | auto runabout, baby (compact, *US*) car, pony; ~**bahn** light (narrow-gauge, branch) railway (railroad, *US*); ~**bahnhof** light railway (way, *US*) station; ~**bauer** smallholder, cotter, crofter, dirt (little, small) farmer; ~**bauernbetrieb** cottage farming; ~**bauernhof** subsistence farm; ~**behälter** small container; ~**besitz an Aktien** smallholding.

Kleinbetrieb splinter operation, small establishment, small firm (enterprise), small-scale operator, small merchandising unit *(US)*;
~**e** small industries;
landwirtschaftlicher ~ subsistence farm cottage farming, small holding *(Br.)*;
~ **und Mittelbetriebe** medium and small-scale enterprises, small business *(US)*.

Kleinbild | film miniature film; ~**kamera** pocket (miniature-sized) camera; ~**projektor** slide projector.

Klein | buchstabe small letter, lower case; ~**bühne** little theatre *(Br.)*; ~**bürger** petty bourgeois, babbit *(US)*; ~**bürgertum** lower middle class; ~**bus** minibus, microbus; ~**diebstahl** pilferage, pickery, petty larceny *(US)*; ~**druck** small type, minuscules; ~**eisenwarenbranche** hardware trade; ~**empfänger** portable radio receiver (set), transistor radio; ~**familie** *(Soziologie)* elementary family; ~**flughafen** air-park; ~**flugzeug** grass-hopper; ~**format** note size, *(Buch)* smaller version; ~**funkgerät** walkie-talkie; ~**garten** allotment *(Br.)*; ~**gartensystem** allotment system *(Br.)*; ~**gärtner** allotment holder *(Br.)*.

kleingedruckt in small type (print).

Kleingedrucktes small print.

Kleingeld small change, small (fractional, broken) money, loose cash, loose change, fractional currency *(US sl.)*, fractional coins *(US)*;
das nötige ~ the wherewithal (needful, *sl.*);
jem. mit ~ **aushelfen** to accommodate s. o. with change.

kleingestückelt of low denomination;
~**e Aktie** fractional share; ~**e Schuldverschreibungen** fractional debentures, small bonds *(US)*; ~**e Wertpapiere** small denominations.

Kleingewerbe small-scale trade (service business);
~**betrieb** small-scale operator, small merchandising unit *(US)*; ~**händler** small businessman, petty dealer, small (retail) tradesman; ~**steuer** retail trade (business), shopkeeping; ~**treibender** small businessman (tradesman).

Kleingrundstück, von Hecken umschlossenes pickle.

kleinhalten, Kosten to keep down the expenses.

Kleinhandel retail trade (business), shopkeeping;
im ~ by (at, *US*) retail.

Kleinhandels | betrieb small-scale operator, small merchandising unit *(US)*; ~**funktion** retail function; ~**geschäft** retail shop (store, *US*); ~**industrie** retail industry.

Kleinhandelspreis retail [selling] price, resale price;
herabgesetzter ~ markdown price *(US)*;
~ **bereits bei der Bestellung festsetzen** to preretail an order.

Kleinhandels | rabatt retail discount, *(bei frühzeitiger Warenlieferung)* anticipation; ~**umsatzsteuer** retail sales tax; ~**verkauf** retail issue, sale by (at, *US*) retail; ~**verkaufspreis** retail [selling] price, retail value, resale price; ~**volumen** volume of retail sales.

Kleinhändler retail dealer (trader), retailer, petty dealer, small tradesman, shopkeeper *(Br.)*, *(in Schnittwaren)* mercer *(Br.)*.
Kleinhandwerker small master, garretmaster *(Br.)*.
Kleinholz matchwood, kindling;
~ **aus jem. machen** to make matchwood (mincemeat) of s. o.; **in ~ verwandeln** to smash to pieces.
Kleinigkeit bagatelle, trifle, shade, drop, farthing, fig, picayune, chickenfeed *(US sl.)*, hair, bit, penny, easy proposition, pinpoint, whit, pin, nothing, inch, pushover, molehill, shadow, little, small change *(US)*, pinhead, iota, fillip;
~**en** small things;
allerlei ~en odds and ends; **bloße ~** mere trifle; **eine ~** a thumb's breadth; **keine ~** no light (small) matter, no joke ; **unerledigte ~en** loose ends;
sich mit ~en abgeben to piddle, to peddle, to be busy about trifles; **sich nicht mit ~en abgeben** to do things on the big, to go the whole figure *(US)*, not to stick on (at) trifles; **auf jede ~ achten** to draw it fine *(coll.)*; **bei jeder ~ aufbrausen** to fire up at the least thing; **sich über ~en aufregen** to fret (fume, get into a fuss) over (worry about) trifles; **auf die kleinsten ~en eingehen** to enter into the smallest details; **~ essen** to have a snack (bite); **für eine ~ kaufen** to buy for a mere song; **keine ~ kosten** to cost a pretty penny; **nur eine ~ kosten** to cost only a trifle; **bei ~en Umstände machen** to strain at a gnat; **~ für j. sein** to easily afford it; **sich in ~en verlieren** to get lost (bogged down) in details; **seine Zeit mit ~en verschwenden** to waste one's time with trifles.
Kleinigkeits|krämer fussbudget, stickler, pettifogger, newsmonger; ~**krämerei** pettifoggery, pettifogging.
Klein|industrie light industry; ~**kaliberwaffe** small-bore weapon.
kleinkariert *(fig.)* hidebound.
Kleinkaufleute small traders.
Kleinkind infant.
Kleinkinder small children (fry);
~**bewahranstalt** crèche *(Br.)*; ~**schule** petty school; ~**spielgruppe** play group.
Klein|kleckersdorf godforsaken hole, back of beyond, one-horse town *(US coll.)*, hick town *(US sl.)*; ~**konjunktur** boomlet; ~**konjunktur in Warenpreisen** commodity price boomlet; ~**kraftrad** moped, autocycle; ~**kram** bits and pieces, odds and ends, truck; ~**krankenhaus** cottage hospital.
Kleinkredit small loan, small advance, loan for consumption;
persönlicher ~ small personal loan;
~**bank** Morris Plan bank *(US)*; ~**geschäft** small loan lending.
Kleinkrieg guerilla warfare.
kleinkriegen to break, to ruin;
j. ~ to cut s. o. down to size, to take s. o. down a peg or two, to break s. o.; **sein Vermögen bald ~** to make short work of (get through) one's fortune;
sich ~ lassen to allow o. s. to be ordered about; **sich nicht ~ lassen** to keep up one's pecker, to stand the gaffs *(US sl.)*.
Klein|küche kitchenette; ~**kunstbühne** cabaret, little theatre *(Br.)*, vaudeville show *(US)*.
Kleinland|besitz small holding *(Br.)*; ~**besitzer** small holder *(Br.)*; ~**besitzer sein** to have several smallholdings in the country *(Br.)*; ~**gesetz** Small Holdings and Allotments Act *(Br.)*; ~**wirt** peasant proprietor, petty farmer.
kleinlaut subdued;
~ **antworten** to answer in a subdued manner; ~ **werden** to sing small, to shut up.
Kleinlebensversicherung industrial *(US)* (low-rate) insurance, industrial home service assurance *(Br.)*.
Kleinlebensversicherungs|geschäft industrial business; ~**police** industrial life policy.
kleinlich mean, paltry, petty-minded, hidebound, ungenerous, *(Politik)* grandmotherly;
in finanziellen Dingen äußerst ~ sein to be rather mean in money matters; **in Geldsachen ~ sein** mean in money matters; ~**e Auslegung** narrow interpretation.
Kleinlichkeit paltryness, meanness, petty-mindedness, littleness.
Klein|lieferwagen delivery car *(Br.)*, delivery van, pickup *(US)*; ~**luftschiff** blimp *(US)*; ~**malerei** *(Literatur)* minute description; ~**möbel** occasional furniture.
kleinmütig weak-spirited.
Klein|obligationen baby bonds *(US)*; ~**od** jewel; ~**oktav** crown octavo; ~**omnibus** minibus; **auf freiwilliger Basis betriebener ~omnibusdienst** volunteer-run minibus service; ~**pächter** smallholder; ~**pachtvertrag** cottier tenancy *(Ireland)*; ~**preisgeschäft** five-and-ten (dime) shop *(US)*, penny shop *(Br.)*; ~**rentner** pensioner, small fundholder; ~**schaden** *(Versicherung)* minor loss.
kleinschreiben, Wort to write a word with a small initial letter.
Klein|schreibmaschine portable typewriter; ~**schreibmaschinentype** elite; ~**sendungen** small consignments; ~**serie** job lot.
Kleinserien|anfertigung job-lot (jobbing) production; ~**hersteller** small-lot (job-lot) producer; ~**herstellung** small-lot (job-lot) production.
Klein|siedler smallholder *(Br.)*; ~**siedlerstelle** smallholding; ~**siedlung** smallholding; ~**sparer** small investor (saver); ~**sparerkonto** small savings account; ~**sparkasse** penny bank; ~**staat** small state; ~**staaterei** particularism; ~**stadt** small town, whistle stop; ~**städter** provincial, suburbanite, small towner *(US)*.
kleinstädtisch small-townish;
~**es Wesen** suburbanity, provincialism.
Kleinst|betrag trifle; ~**betrieb** small (infant) business, hole in the wall *(sl.)*; **im ~format** miniaturized; ~**kind** baby; ~**kinderschule** infant school *(Br.)*; ~**laden** bantam shop *(US)*; ~**lastwagen** pickup *(US)*; ~**motor** pilot motor; ~**rennwagen** go-cart; ~**taxi** minicab; ~**U-Boot** midget submarine; ~**verdiener** small wage earner; ~**wagen** sub-compact car, minicar, bubblecar, runabout, cyclecar, bubble *(US)*; ~**wohnung** small flat, flatlet.
Kleinverbrauchertarif *(el.)* flat rate *(US)*.
Kleinverkauf retail, small issue;
im ~ absetzen to sell by *(Br.)* (at, *US*) retail.
Kleinverkäufer retailer.
Kleinverkaufs|preis retail price; ~**spanne** retail margin; ~**wert** retail value.
Kleinvieh small cattle;
~ **macht auch Mist** many a mickle makes a muckle.
Kleinwagen baby (small, compact, *US*) car, subcompact;
~**fabrik** small-car plant; ~**markt** small-car market; ~**umsatz** smallcar sales.
Klein|wohnung flatlet *(Br.)*, small dwelling, maisonette; ~**zeug** small deer, oddments, trifle.
Kleister paste;
dünner ~ *(Buchbinderei)* paste water.
kleistern, jem. eine to give s. o. a box on the ear, to clout s. o.; **Plakat an die Wand ~** to paste a poster on the wall.
Klemme hole, awkward situation, shortage, scarcity, pinch, corner, fix, jam, nonplus, quagmire, scrape, mire, bay, dilemma, chancery, box, tight, fobble *(coll.)*, *(finanziell)* squeeze, straits, tightness [of money];
in der ~ up the tree *(sl.)*, in the soup (a scrape, a cleft stick), between the devil and the deep blue sea, under hatches, up a stump *(US)*, in a (on the) spot *(sl.)*;
j. ganz schön in die ~ bringen to land s. o. in a nice fix; **in eine ~ geraten** to get into a scrape (mess), to be thrown into a dilemma; **jem. aus der ~ helfen** to get (pull) s. o. out of a hole (fix) *(fam.)*; **in der ~ sein (sitzen)** to be in a tight corner (a jam, chancery, a dilemma, in the cart, *Br.*, a pickle, the wrong box, a plight, up the pole, *sl.*), to have not a leg to stand on; **tüchtig in der ~ sitzen** to hold the wolf by the ears, to be in a tight squeeze; **sich aus der ~ ziehen** to get o. s. out of a fix.
klemmen to wedge, to jam, *(Fenster, Tür)* to be stuck;
sich hinter j. ~ to get on to (work on) s. o.; **sich hinter seine Arbeit ~** to keep one's nose to the grindstone, to get down to work; **sich etw. unter den Arm ~** to tuck s. th. under one's arm; **sich den Finger in der Tür ~** to pinch (nip) one's finger in the door.
Klemm|schraube thumbscrew; ~**vorrichtung** clamp, clamping (gripping) device.
Klempner tinsmith, whitesmith, plumber;
~**arbeit** tinsmithing, plumbery, plumbing; ~**handwerk** tinwork, tinworking, plumbing; ~**waren** tinware; ~**werkstatt** tinsmith's works (shop), plumber's shop, plumbery.
Kleptomanie kleptomania.
Klerus body of clergy, clergy.
Klette, wie ~n aneinanderhängen to stick together like glue; **sich wie eine ~ an j. hängen** to stick like a bur (leech) to s. o., to cling to s. o. like ivy.
Kletter|eisen crampon, climbing iron; ~**maxe** cat burglar, porch climber *(sl.)*.
klettern *(Barometer, Preis, Temperatur)* to rise, to go up, to climb, *(Flugzeug)* to climb;
ins Bett ~ to turn in, to go between the sheets; **nach oben ~** to hop upwards; **bis auf 150 Stundenkilometer ~** to climb to 150 kilometres an hour.
Kletterpartie climb.
Klicke clique, coterie, set;
~ **bilden** to form a little clique; **zur ~ gehören** to be one out of the box (one of the crowd); **sich in einer ~ vereinigen** to clique.

Klient client, customer, patron;
ohne ~en *(Anwalt)* briefless;
~en cliency;
gut verdienender ~ high-income client;
jem. ~en abjagen to alienate s. one's clients; **~en beraten** to advise a client; **~en betreuen** to serve a customer; **gegen die Interessen seines ~en verstoßen** to operate against one's client.
Klientele clientele, cliency, goodwill, patronage, custom, customers, connection, connexion *(Br.)*.
Klientenkonto verwalten to hold a client's money.
Klientin client company.
Klima climate, sky, *(fig.)* atmosphere, climate;
abscheuliches ~ rank climate; **gemäßigtes ~** temperate climate; **gesundes ~** salubrious climate; **konjunkturelles ~** economic temperature, business climate; **mildes ~** soft (warm, genial) climate; **trockenes ~** dry climate; **ungünstiges ~** uncongenial climate;
angenehmes ~ in einem Betrieb pleasant office atmosphere; **sich an das ~ gewöhnen** to acclimatize (acclimate, *US*) o. s.; **~ für die Entwicklung revolutionärer Verhältnisse schaffen** to create a revolutionary climate; **jedem ~ gewachsen sein** *(Konstitution)* to defy every climate; **an ein ~ gewöhnt sein** to be seasoned to a climate;
~änderung change in climate.
Klimaanlage air conditoner, air-conditioning unit (system);
automatische ~ automatic climate control;
mit einer ~ ausstatten to air-condition.
Klima|bedingungen climatological conditions; **~bereinigung** improvement in climate; **entscheidender ~einfluß** essential influence of climate; **~gerät** air conditioner; **~ingenieur** air-conditioning engineer; **~kammer** environment chamber.
Klimakterium change of life.
Klima|steuerung, automatische automatic climate control; **~technik** air-conditioning engineering; **~therapie** climatotherapy.
klimatisch|er Kurort health resort; **~e Veränderungen** changes in the climate.
klimatisieren to air-condition.
klimatisiert air-conditioned.
Klimatisierung air-conditioning, *(Zimmer)* room conditioning.
Klima|tologe climatologist; **~veränderung** climate change; **~verhältnisse** climate condition; **~wechsel** change in climate, climate change; **~zone** heaven.
Klimbim fuss, rubbish, junk, trashery;
schrecklicher ~ noisy goings-on;
großen ~ machen to make a racket, to kick up a row; **ganzen ~ wegwerfen** to junk the whole lot.
klimpern, mit dem Geld in der Tasche to jingle the money in one's pocket; **auf dem Klavier ~** to strum on the piano; **mit den Wimpern ~** to flutter one's eyelashes.
Klinge, scharfe ~ führen to be a hard-hitting opponent; **mit jem. die ~n kreuzen** to cross swords with s. o.; **j. über die ~ springen lassen** to put s. o. to the sword, to scuttle s. one's career; **gute ~ schlagen** to play a good knife and fork.
Klingel bell;
elektrische ~ gong;
auf die ~ drücken to press the bell.
Klingelbeutel collection (alms) bag;
mit dem ~ herumgehen to take up a collection *(US)*.
Klingel|draht bell wire; **~knopf** [call] button; **~knopf drücken** to touch the bell; **~leitung** bell wire.
Klingeln *(tel.)* ring, ringing, *(Theater)* bell.
klingeln to ring, to pull the bell;
j. aus dem Bett ~ to knock s. o. up; **zwei Minuten ~** *(Wecker)* to be ringing for two minutes.
Klingel|schnur bell pull; **~transformator** bell transformer; **~zeichen** bell [signal].
Klingen, bei jem. eine Saite zum ~ bringen to touch s. one's heartstrings.
klingen to sound, to resound, to ring;
aufgeregt ~ to have an excited ring; **beunruhigend ~** to have a sinister sound; **faul (verdächtig) ~** to sound fishy; **glaubhaft (plausibel) ~** to sound feasible; **jem. in den Ohren ~** to ring in s. one's ears; **wie eine Übersetzung ~** to read like a translation; **überzeugend ~** to look the winning argument; **nicht sehr überzeugend ~** not to carry much conviction; **wahr ~** to have the ring of truth in it;
mir ~ die Ohren my ears are burning.
klingend, etw. in ~e Münze umsetzen to make money out of it; **in ~er Münze zahlen** to pay in specie (hard coin); **mit ~em Spiel** with the band playing.

Klinik clinic, hospital;
ambulante ~ outpatient clinic; **fahrbare ~** mobile clinic, clinicar;
in die ~ eingeliefert werden to be brought to hospital;
~aufenthalt stay in a hospital; **~behandlung** hospital treatment.
klinisch|e Behandlung hospital treatment; **~er Fall** hospital patient; **~er Tod** clinical death.
Klinke latch, *(tel.)* jack;
jem. die ~ in die Hand drücken to show s. o. the door; **die ~ putzen** to go (canvass) from door to door.
Klinken|putzen doot-to-door selling, canvassing; **~putzer** hawker, peddler, pedlar.
Klinkerbau clinker-work.
klipp und klar perfectly clear, clear-cut, straight out, point-blank;
~ beweisen to prove beyond doubt; **jem. ~ seine Meinung sagen** to give s. o. a piece of one's mind.
Klippe cliff, rock, reef, skerry, *(Schwierigkeit)* obstacle, hurdle, difficulty;
auf eine ~ auflaufen to run on the rocks; **an einer ~ scheitern** to founder on a rock, *(Verhandlungen)* to break down because of a stumbling block; **alle ~n überwinden** to clear all the hurdles; **~ umschiffen** to turn the corner.
klippenreich|e Küste rocky coast; **~es Unternehmen** hazardous undertaking.
Klirren *(Gläser)* clink, chink.
klirren *(Gläser)* to clink, to chink, *(Ketten)* to rattle, to jangle, to clank, *(Schlüssel)* to jingle.
klirrender Frost severe (crisp) cold.
Klischee printing block, cast, cut, engraving, cliché *(Br.)*, *(fig.)* stereotype, cliché, *(Galvano)* galvano, electrotype, *(Negativklischee)* negative plate, *(Rasterklischee)* half-tone block, *(Stereoplatte)* stereotype plate, *(Strichklischee)* line block;
ausgeklinktes ~ mortise; **nicht mehr benutztes ~** dead plate; **fotomechanisches ~** process block; **kombiniertes ~** combination plate; **unmontiertes ~** unmounted block; **zusammengesetztes ~** composite plate;
~ herstellen to plate; **fotografische ~s herstellen** to photograve; **nur in ~s denken können** to be compartmentalized; **~ nachschneiden** to tool a block;
~abzug block pull, engraved plate, engraving; **~anstalt** engraving establishment, cliché manufacturer *(Br.)*, blockmaker; **~anzeige** advertising block; **~begriff** stereotyped idea; **~fuß** block base.
klischeehaft cliché-ridden, stereotyped.
Klischee|hersteller blockmaker, process engraver, photoengraver; **~herstellung** engraving; **fotomechanische ~herstellung** blockmaking, [photo]engraving (process-engraving) process; **~herstellungskosten** blockmaking charges; **~montage** composition; **~platte** engraving plate; **~vorlage** copy; **~vorstellung** stereotyped idea; **den ~vorstellungen in einigen Romanen Glauben schenken** to go by some kinds of fiction; **~wort** cliché.
klischieren to dab, to plate, to electrotype, to stereotype;
galvanisch ~ to electrotype; **Seite ~** to cast a page.
klitschnaß soaking (dripping) wet.
klitzeklein teeny-weeny.
Klo lavatory, toilet, loo *(coll.)*.
Kloake sewer, cesspool.
Kloakenwasser sewage.
klobig cumbersome, clumsy-looking, *(Benehmen)* loutish;
~e Handschrift clumsy handwriting; **~e Schuhe** heavy shoes; **~e Umgangssprache** uncouth manners.
klönen to chat, to have a chinwag.
Klopfbrett *(drucktechn.)* planer.
Klopfen *(Motor)* knock.
klopfen to knock (rap) at, *(Herz)* to pound, to throb, *(Motor)* to knock, to pink;
an das Barometer ~ to tap the barometer; **auf den Busch ~** to beat about the bush; **jem. auf die Finger ~** to give s. o. a rap over the knuckles; **an sein Glas ~** to tap one's glass; **Nagel in die Wand ~** to knock a nail into the wall; **jem. anerkennend auf die Schulter ~** to pat s. o. on the back; **an die Tür ~** to tap at the door; **sich vor Vergnügen auf den Schenkel ~** to slap one's thighs.
klopffest antiknock, nonpinking.
Klopf|festigkeit antiknock quality; **~zeichen** trap, knock.
Klosett toilet, lavatory, water closet, loo *(fam.)*;
~papier toilet paper.
Kloß clod, clump, lump, *(gastron.)* dumpling;
~ im Hals haben to have a lump in one's throat.

Kloster monastery, nunnery, convent;
~**bruder** monk; ~**einband** monastic binding.
klösterlich monastic, secluded.
klöterig, sich ganz ~ **fühlen** to feel rotten (lousy, *sl.*).
Klotz block, lump, log;
~ **am Bein** drag, millstone round s. one's neck;
sich einen ~ **ans Bein binden** to tie a millstone round one's neck;
wie ein ~ **schlafen** to sleep like a top;
auf einen groben ~ **gehört ein grober Keil** it takes a bully to know a bully.
klotzig clumsy, *(sehr)* awfully, terribly;
~ **viel Geld haben** to have piles of money, to be stinking rich.
Klub club, association;
exklusiver ~ exclusive (select) club;
~**abend** club night; ~**beitrag** club fee (money, subscription); ~**ecke** lounge corner; ~**einrichtung** club facilities; ~**garnitur** three-piece suite; ~**haus** club house (buildings), *(Studentenverbindung)* chapter house *(US)*; ~**hauskomitee** house committee; ~**jacke** blazer; ~**kamerad** clubmate, stable companion *(coll., Br.)*; ~**lokal** club premises; ~**mitglied** clubmate, clubfellow; ~**mitgliedschaft** club membership; ~**personal** club employees (staff); ~**sekretär** club manager; ~**sessel** lounge chair; ~**statuten** club law; ~**viertel** *(London)* clubland; ~**zeremoniell** club etiquette; ~**zimmer** clubroom, *(Hotel)* parlo(u)r.
klucken, bei jem. to park o. s. on s. o.
Kluft gap, crevice, cleft, fissure, chasm, *(fig.)* gap, gulf, *(Kleider)* togs, *(Lücke)* hiatus;
unüberbrückbare ~ unbridgeable gulf;
~ **zwischen Arm und Reich** the gulf between the rich and the poor; ~ **zwischen den Generationen** generation gap;
sich in seine beste ~ **schmeißen** to put on one's best bib and tucker; ~ **überbrücken** to bridge the gap; ~ **vertiefen** to widen a gap.
klug intelligent, clever, bright, shrewd, diplomatic, knowledgeable;
etw. ~ **anstellen** to go about it cleverly; **sich besonders** ~ **dünken** to think no small beer of o. s.; **sein Geld** ~ **einteilen** to make a penny go a long way; **aus etw. überhaupt nicht** ~ **werden können** not to be able to make head or tail of it; **so** ~ **sein** to be clever enough; **genauso** ~ **wie vorher sein** to be not any (none) the wiser; **viel zu** ~ **sein** to be too clever by half; **aus jem. nicht** ~ **werden** not to know what to make of s. o.; **aus einem Brief nicht** ~ **werden** not to be able to make sense of a letter; ~ **wählen** to choose sensibly; **sich mit Bemerkungen** ~ **zurückhalten** to wisely refrain from making any comment;
~**e Einkäufe** judicious purchases; **mit** ~**er Einsicht** with wise insight; **politisch** ~**e Entscheidung** politically sound decision; ~**e Fragenbeantwortung** intelligent answers to questions; **alles nur** ~**es Gerede sein** to be a lot of hot air; ~**er Geschäftsmann** shrewd (prudent) businessman; ~ **durchdachtes Projekt** cleverly thought-out project; ~**er Schachzug** clever move; ~**e Wahl** sensible choice.
Klugheit intelligence, cleverness, wisdom, discretion, prudence;
staatsmännische ~ statesmanlike prudence;
~ **außer acht lassen** to throw prudence to the wind; **aus** ~ **schweigen** to wisely remain silent; **sich in seiner** ~ **sonnen** to flatter o. s. on one's cleverness.
Klugscheißer *(coll.)* wiseacre, wisehead, wise guy, knowall, clever dick.
Klump, Auto in ~ **fahren** to smash a car; **in** ~ **gehen** to be smashed to pieces; **j. in** ~ **schlagen** to reduce s. o. to pulp, to make matchwood of s. o.
Klumpen lump, dump *(Br.)*;
~ **Gold** gold in nuggets;
~**auswahlverfahren** *(Statistik)* cluster sampling.
Klüngel clique, cabal, coterie, set, junto;
zum ~ **gehören** to be one of the crowd;
~**wirtschaft** cliquishness, boss rule *(US)*, cronyism *(US)*.
Knabe boy, lad;
alter ~ old chap (top, *sl.*), old fruit *(Br., sl.)*.
Knabenalter boyhood.
knacken *(Eis)* to crack, *(Feuer)* to crackle;
Geldschrank ~ to blow (bust, break, crack) a safe;
jem. eine harte Nuß zu ~ **geben** to give s. o. a hard nut to crack.
Knacker miser, skinflint;
alter ~ old fogey *(sl.)*.
Knacks crack, snap, click;
schweren ~ **bekommen** *(Freundschaft)* to suffer a severe blow; **leichen** ~ **haben** to be crackbrained; **sich einen** ~ **holen** to catch it.
Knall bang, crack, pop, explosion, *(Schallmauer)* sonic boom, *(Streit)* row, quarrel;
~ **und Fall** all of a sudden, on the spot, slapdash;
~ **und Fall abberufen** to recall abruptly; ~ **und Fall entlassen** to fire *(sl.)*, to sack *(sl.)*; **mit einem lauten** ~ **explodieren** to explode with a loud bang; **einen** ~ **haben** to be crackbrained; **sich** ~ **und Fall verlieben** to fall in love at first sight; **Tür mit einem** ~ **zuwerfen** to slam a door;
~**bonbon** snapper; ~**effekt** punch line, coup de theatre.
knallen to crack, *(explodieren)* to detonate, to fulminate, *(Feuerwerk)* to bang, to go pop, *(Zündung)* to misfire;
mit den Absätzen ~ to click one's heels; **Buch auf den Tisch** ~ to slam a book on the table; **auf die Dächer** ~ *(Sonne)* to beat down on the rooftops; **j. über den Haufen** ~ to shoot s. o. down; **Hörer auf die Gabel** ~ to slam down the receiver; **Korken** ~ **lassen** to pop a cork; **jem. ein paar Kugeln auf den Pelz** ~ to fire a few shots at s. o.; **jem. eins vor den Latz** ~ to clout s. o.; **gegen eine Mauer** ~ to crash into a wall; **mit der Peitsche** ~ to crack the whip; **ins Schloß** ~ *(Tür)* to close with a bang.
knallende Farben loud colo(u)rs.
Knall|erbse squib *(Br.)*; ~**frosch** jumping jack *(Br.)*, grasshopper *(US)*; ~**gas** oxyhydrogen gas.
knallhart hard-core *(fam.)*.
Knall|kapsel *(Bahnsignal)* detonator; ~**kopf** ninny, blockhead, dunderhead, flat *(sl.)*.
knapp short, narrow, *(Gehalt, Lohn)* scanty, meagre, *(Geldmarkt)* tight, close, stringent, *(Stil)* concise, terse, tight, succinct, *(Ware)* scarce, scant, scanty, *(vor Zahlen)* just under, a little less than;
kurz und ~ short and to the point; **sehr** ~ by a short head;
~ **an Arbeitskräften** short of hands, short-handed; ~ **bemessen** *(Zeit)* limited; ~ **dran** on a budget; ~ **gerechnet** at the lowest estimate; ~ **bei Kasse** short of cash, low in cash, in low water, shy of money *(US sl.)*; ~**e zwei Monate** just under two months;
~ **unter der Rentabilitätsgrenze** marginal;
~ **abwiegen** to cut it fine; ~ **auskommen** to make both ends meet, to rub along; ~ **über ein Ereignis berichten** to report briefly on an event, to cover with a few lines; ~ **disponieren** to show caution in the placing of orders; ~ **dem Konkurs entgehen** to bring back from the brink of bankrupty; **Wahl** ~ **gewinnen** to win an election with a narrow margin; **j.** ~ **bei Kasse halten** to keep s. o. short of money; ~ **vor dem Abgrund zum Halten kommen** to stop within inches of the ravine; ~ **rechnen** to cut it fine; ~ **sein** to be in short supply, to be short of, to lack, to be lacking; **finanziell sehr** ~ **sein** to be hard pushed (up); ~ **bei Kasse sein** to be short of (pinched for) money, to be in narrow straits (low funds); ~ **mit der Zeit dran sein** to be pressed for time; ~ **werden** *(Vorräte)* to run low, to run (fall) short, to be running low; ~**er werden** to narrow; ~ **zusammenfassen** to summarize, to give a concise summary;
~**es Angebot** scanty supply; ~**e Antworten** answers short and to the point; **sein** ~**es Auskommen haben** to earn a bare living; ~**e Berechnung** conservative estimate; ~**e Beschreibung** thumbnail description; ~**e Darstellung** terse (concise) account; ~**e Finanzdecke** shortage of finance; ~**es Geld** tight money; ~**es Gewicht** short weight; ~**es Hypothekenangebot** shortage of mortgage money; ~**e Kost** meagre fare; ~**e Kreditmittel** credit stringency; ~**e Mahlzeit** small meal, meagre fare; ~**e Mehrheit** narrow (bare) majority; ~**e Mittel** narrow means; **mit** ~**er Mühe** with difficulty; ~**e Nahrungsmittelzuteilung** short commons; **mit** ~**er Not davonkommen** to have a narrow escape (shave, squeak, *coll.*); ~**e Rationen** short rations (allowances); ~**e Reserven** low reserves; ~**e Stunde** short hour; ~**er Tatsachenbericht** condensed statement of facts; **sich mit einer** ~**en Verbeugung verabschieden** to leave with a curt bow; ~**er Vorsprung** narrow margin; ~**e Waren** critical items, scarce articles (goods, commodities); **für eine** ~**e Woche nach Paris kommen** to come to Paris for the inside of a week; ~**er Wohnungsraum** housing shortage; **etw. mit** ~**en Worten sagen** to be brief and to the point; ~**e Zeiten** hard times; ~ **verfehltes Ziel** near miss; ~**e Zuteilung** scant allowance.
Knappe *(Bergbau)* miner, mineworker, coalminer, pitman.
knapphalten, j. to keep s. o. short of money; **seinen Sohn** ~ to scrimp one's son for money.
Knappheit shortage, scantiness, deficiency, lack, penury, *(Geldmarkt)* scarcity, squeeze, tightness, stringency;
infolge der zeitweiligen ~ owing to the temporary scarcity;
~ **an Arbeitskräften** shortage of manpower, manpower shortage, labo(u)r scarcity; ~ **an Lebensmitteln** food shortage.
Knappheits|erscheinung tightness, shortage, scarceness, scarcity; ~**kurs** scarcity price.

Knappschafts|kasse miners' provident (benefit) fund, miners' insurance; ~**rente** miners' pension; ~**verband** miners' union.
Knast jug, booby, big house, bull pen *(US sl.)*, clink, cooler *(sl.)*;
~ **schieben** to be in jug, to do a stretch *(Br.)*;
~**bruder** fellow convict, gaol bird, jailbird *(sl.)*.
knattern to crackle, *(Motorrad)* to put-put.
Knäuel ball, clew, *(Menge)* crowd, cluster, bunch;
~ **von Menschen** throng of people; ~ **aufgeregter Reporter** bunch of excited reporters; ~ **neugieriger Zuschauer** crowd of inquisitive onlookers;
~ **bilden** *(Menschen)* to cluster, to throng; ~ **der Ereignisse entwirren** to unravel the tangle of events.
Knauser scraper, niggard, curmudgeon, pinchfist.
Knauserei pinching, parsimony, nearness, cheese paring.
knauserig parsimonious, mean, stingy, niggardly, penny-pinching *(sl.)*, skimpy, ungenerous, illiberal.
knausern to scant, to pinch, to scrimp, to be a niggard;
mit dem Geld ~ to be tight-fisted, to skimp with money; **mit den Vorräten** ~ to scant with provisions; **mit seiner Zeit** ~ to be stinting with one's time.
Knautschkommode accordion, squeeze-box.
Knebel gag;
jem. einen ~ **in den Mund stecken** to gag s. o.
knebeln to gag, *(Presse)* to muzzle, to gag, to suppress, *(durch Schutzzölle)* to fetter.
Knebelung der Presse muzzling of the press.
Knecht farmhand, ploughman;
~ **der öffentlichen Meinung** slave of public opinion;
Volk zu ~**en machen** to reduce a people to slavery.
knechten to enslave, to subjugate;
Volk ~ to tyrannize (oppress) a people.
knechtisch servile, slavish;
j. ~ **behandeln** to treat s. o. like a slave;
~**e Gesinnung** servile disposition, servility.
Knechtschaft slavery, bondage, yoke.
kneifen to pinch *(fig.)*, to back out, to funk, to turn tail, to shirk, to hedge, to crawfish *(US)*, to take water *(US sl.)*;
vor einer unangenehmen Diskussion ~ to dodge an unpleasant discussion; **vor jeder Endscheidung** ~ to avoid taking decisions.
Kneifzange pliers, pair of pincers (nippers).
Kneipe tavern *(US)*, public house *(Br.)*, pub *(Br.)*, saloon *(US)*, rum hole *(sl.)*, jerry *(Br., sl.)*, barrel house *(US sl.)*, pot house, boozer *(Br., sl.)*, tavern, dive *(Br.)*, joint *(sl.)*;
anrüchige ~ disreputable bar; **billige** ~ sawdust saloon (parlor) *(US sl.)*; **bis nach Mitternacht offene** ~ finish *(Br.)*; **ominöse** ~ bucket shop;
sich schnell einen in der ~ **genehmigen** to call at a pub for a quick one *(Br.)*.
kneipen to carouse, to booze, to tipple.
Kneipenbesitzer publican, barkeeper, saloonkeeper *(US)*.
Kneip|ier saloonkeeper *(US)*, publican; ~**tour** drinking spree, binge, booze, bat *(US sl.)*; ~**tour machen** to go on a bat (spree).
kneten, Charakter to mould (mold, *US*) a character.
Knick *(Papier)* fold, crease, dog's-ear, *(Straße)* bend, curve;
~ **in einer Kurve** dip in a curve.
knicken to [make a] bend, *(Papier)* to crease;
Bäume wie Strohhalme ~ *(Tornado)* to break (snap) the trees like matchwood; **jds. Hoffnungen** ~ to dash (crush) s. one's hopes; **jds. Stolz** ~ to hurt s. one's pride.
Knicker scraper, close hand, curdmudgeon, muckworm, cheap skate *(US sl.)*.
Knickerei nearness, stinginess, niggardliness, parsimony, cheese-paring.
knickerig skimpy, stingy, niggardly;
~ **bei Kleinigkeiten und verschwenderisch im Großen** penny-wise and pound foolish.
Knickerigkeit closeness, niggardliness, parsimony, tightness.
knickern to palter, to stint, to scrimp.
Knicks genuflection, curtsy.
Knie knee, *(Rohrstück)* knee, elbow;
j. auf ~**n anflehen** to ask for s. th. on one's bended knees; **in die** ~ **brechen** to sink to one's knees; **etw. übers** ~ **brechen** to rush into an affair; **auf die** ~ **fallen** to drop on one's knees; **vor jem. auf die** ~ **fallen** to go down on one's knees to s. o.; **vor dem Geld auf den** ~**n liegen** to worship money; **bis an die** ~ **im Wasser stehen** to be standing knee-deep in water; **j. auf die** ~ **zwingen** to bring s. o. to his knees; **Unternehmen aus finanziellen Gründen auf die** ~ **zwingen** to force a company to its financial knees.
Kniefall prostration;
~ **vor jem. machen** to prostrate o. s. before s. o.
kniefällig bitten, j. to ask s. o. on one's bended knees.
kniehoch knee-deep.
knien to be on one's knees, to kneel;
sich in die Arbeit ~ to knuckle (buckle) down to work; **sich in ein Problem** ~ to knuckle down to a problem *(US)*.
Knie|raum *(Auto, Flugzeug)* legroom; ~**stiefel** overknee boots; ~**stück** knee, elbow.
knietief im Wasser mid-leg (knee-) deep in water.
Kniff dodge, knack, catch, fetch, fixup, trick, stratagem, pinch, lurk *(Br., sl.)*, *(im Papier)* crease, wrinkle;
~**e** craft, trickery, ropes, doubling;
allerlei ~ **und Schliche anwenden** to use all sorts of tricks and dodges; ~ **herausbekommen** to get the knack of it; ~ **heraushaben** to have got the knack of it; **alle** ~ **kennen** to know the tricks of the trade, to be up to all the dodges (snuff, *sl.*); **hinter jds.** ~ **kommen** to see through s. one's tricks; **durch geschickte** ~ **etw. seinem Ziel näherbringen** to manipulate s. th. towards objectives.
kniffen *(Papier)* to double up.
knifflig finicky, prickly, tricky, niggling, intricate;
~**e Frage** tricky question.
Knigge kennen, seinen to be well posted on one's etiquette, to know one's Emily Post *(US)*.
knipsen *(Fahrkarte)* to punch, to clip, *(fotografieren)* to photo;
Bild ~ to take a snapshot; **Fahrkarte** ~ to punch (clip) a ticket;
mit den Fingern ~ to snap one's fingers.
Knips|schalter snap switch; ~**zange** ticket punch.
Knirps whippersnapper, urchin, shrimp;
frecher kleiner ~ naughty little beggar.
knirschen *(Bremse)* to grind, *(Schnee)* to crunch;
mit den Zähnen ~ to grind one's teeth.
knirschendes Geräusch crunching (grinding) noise.
knistern to crackle;
mit Papier ~ to rustle paper.
knistert, es ~ **im Gebälk** the rafters are creaking, *(fig.)* there is trouble ahead; **es** ~ **vor Spannung** the air is electric.
Knittelreim doggerel.
knitter|fest, ~**frei** creaseless, noncreasing, creaseproof, wrinkle-resistant, uncreasable.
Knobelbecher dicebox.
Knochen bone;
bis auf die ~ **durchnäßt** soaked to the skin;
seine müden ~ **ausruhen** to rest one's weary limbs; **nur aus Haut und** ~ **bestehen** to be nothing but a bag of bones; **sich bis auf die** ~ **blamieren** to make a terrible fool of o. s.; **jem. durch alle** ~ **fahren** to shake s. o. to the core; **keinen Mumm in den** ~ **haben** to have no guts; **Grippe noch in den** ~ **sitzen haben** not to have shaken off the flu; **seine** ~ **hinhalten** to take the rap; **seine** ~ **riskieren** to risk one's neck; **konservativ bis auf die** ~ **sein** to be an out-and-out conservative; **reaktionär bis in die** ~ **sein** to be a prototypical reactionary; **jem. alle** ~ **im Leibe zusammenschlagen** to make matchwood (mincemeat) of s. o.;
nimm deine ~ **weg** get your paws out of the way.
knochendürr all skin and bones, skinny, spindly.
Knochengerippe sein, wahres to be as thin as a rake.
Knochenmühle boneshaker, grindstone;
wieder in die ~ **zurückkehren müssen** to have to go back to the old grind.
Knödel im Hals haben to have a lump in one's throat.
Knöllchen traffic violation fine, motoring fine *(Br.)*.
Knopf button;
reicher ~ wealthy devil;
auf den ~ **drücken** to press (push) the button; ~ **und Kragen verlieren** to lose one's shirt;
ihm ist ein ~ **aufgegangen** at last the penny has dropped.
Knopfdruck pressure on the button;
durch einen ~ **auslösen** to push-button;
~**radio** push-button radio.
Knopfloch buttonhole.
Knopflöcher, aus allen ~**n grinsen** to grin like a Cheshire cat.
Knospe bud, eye, gemma.
Knoten knot, *(Bahn)* junction, *(Schiffsgeschwindigkeit)* knot;
fester ~ hard knot;
mit einem ~ **befestigen** to knot; ~ **durchhauen** to cut the Gordian knot; **einen** ~ **haben** to have snag in it; ~ **lösen** to unravel a plot; ~ **ins Taschentuch machen** to tie a knot in one's handkerchief *(fam.)*;
bei ihm ist endlich der ~ **geplatzt** the penny (nickel, *US*) has dropped;
~**amt** *(Telefon)* tandem office; ~**bahnhof** junction; ~**punkt** nodal point, hub, *(Eisenbahn)* junction, *(Fernverkehr)* basing point, *(Verkehr)* center *(US)*, centre *(Br.)*.

Knülch, langweiliger dull bloke.
knüllen to crumple, to crease.
Knüller smash hit, scoop, bumper, whopper *(coll.)*, *(Buch)* best-seller, *(Film)* thriller, *(Journalismus)* scoop;
absoluter ~ the clincher;
zum ~ werden to be getting its kicks *(sl.)*.
knüpfen to [make a] knot, to attach;
zarte Bande ~ to form a sentimental attachment; **Bedingungen an etw. ~** to attach conditions to s. th.; **Freundschaft ~** to strike up a friendship; **Freundschaftsbande enger ~** to strengthen friendly relations; **große Hoffnungen an etw. ~** to have high hopes for s. th.; **bestimmte Vorstellungen an eine Melodie ~** to have a definite association with a tune.
Knüppel cudgel, *(Polizei)* mace, truncheon;
~ am Bein haben to be hampered by an obligation; **jem. einen ~ zwischen die Beine werfen** to put a spoke in s. one's wheel, to throw a spanner in the works;
da liegt der ~ beim Hund it is Hobson's choice;
~damm ground bridge, boardwalk, corduroy road *(US)*.
knüppeldick haben, es to be fed up with it.
Knüppel|holz logs; **~schaltung** *(Auto)* floor-mounted gear change.
knurren to growl, to snarl, *(Magen)* to rumble;
immer etw. zu ~ haben to be always grumbling about s. th.
knurrender Magen rumbling stomach.
Knusperhäuschen gingerbread house.
knusprig crunchy, crisp, *(fig.)* attractive, bonny.
Knute whip, knout;
jem. unter seiner ~ haben to have s. o. under one's thumb; **unter jds. ~ stehen** to be in s. one's clutches.
Knüttel bat, cudgel.
koalieren *(pol.)* to enter into a coalition, to coalize.
Koalition coalition, fusion;
~ politischer Parteien fusion of political parties;
~ eingehen to form (enter into) a coalition, to coalize; **~ sprengen** to disrupt a coalition; **~ umbilden** to reshuffle a coalition.
Koalitions|anhänger coalitioner, coalitionist; **~ausschuß** coalition committee; **~bildung** formation of a coalition, coalition formation; **Gespräche auf ~ebene führen** to carry on talks on a coalition level; **~freiheit** freedom of association; **~gespräche** coalition talks; **~kabinett** coalition government; **~kämpfe** coalition infighting; **~minister** coalition minister; **~partei** coalition party; **~partner** coalition partner; **~problem** coalition problem; **~recht** freedom of association.
Koalitionsregierung coalition government (cabinet), coalition rule;
~ auseinanderbrechen to prize (prise) open a coalition; **~ im Amt bestätigen** to keep a coalition in office; **~ umbilden** to reshuffle a coalition; **~ zusammenschustern** to patchwork a coalition; **~ zustande bringen** to work out a coalition.
Koalitions|wahlliste mixed ticket; **~ziel** coalition goal.
Kochbuch cookery-book *(Br.)*, cookbook *(US)*.
Köche, viele ~ verderben den Brei too many cooks spoil the broth.
Kochen|mit Sonnenenergie solar cooking;
j. zum ~ bringen to make s. one's blood boil; **Volksseele zum ~ bringen** to stir up a people to rebellion.
kochen to cook, *(fig.)* to simmer, *(Motor)* to boil, to percolate; **Wäsche ~** to boil the washing; **vor Wut ~** to be boiling with rage.
kochend heiß boiling hot.
Köcher, etw. auf dem ~ haben to have a clever head.
kochfertig *(Speisen)* ready-to-cook.
kochfest boil-proof.
Koch|gerät cooking appliance (apparatus); **~geschirr** *(mil.)* mess-tin.
Köchin cook.
Koch|kiste fireless cooker *(US)*; **~kunst** cookery; **~kursus** cookery course; **~möglichkeit** kitchen facilities; **~nische** kitchenette; **~rezept** recipe.
Kode [cipher] code;
~ benutzen to write a dispatch in code; **~ entschlüsseln** to break a code;
~adresse code address; **~benutzung** use of code; **~brief** code letter; **~buch** code book; **~nachricht** code message; **in einen Apparat seine ~nummer eingeben** to key into a machine a personal code number.
Köder bait, decoy, stool pigeon, allurement, come on *(US sl.)*;
~ für die Wähler vote catcher;
~ nach jem. auswerfen to throw out a bait for s. o.;
~brief decoy letter.
ködern to entice, to allure, to lure, to bait, to decoy;
jem. mit großen Versprechungen ~ to lure s. o. with bright prospects;
sich ~ lassen to swallow the bait; **sich nicht ~ lassen** not to rise to the bait.
Kode|schlüssel key to a code; **~wort** codeword.
Kodex code, codex, rule-book;
~ von Vorschriften discipline, body of law.
Kodierung codesheet.
kodifizieren to codify, to code, to digest.
Kodifizierung codification, code.
Kodizill codicil, rider.
Koeffizient ratio.
Koexistenz coexistence;
friedliche ~ peaceful coexistence.
koexistieren to coexist.
Koffer case, suitcase, portmanteau *(Br.)*, travelling bag *(US)*, grip *(US)*, *(blaue Bohne)* pill *(mil., sl.)*;
großer ~ trunk; **kleiner ~** valise *(Br.)*;
~ absetzen to plump down a suitcase; **~ aufgeben** to check a trunk *(US)*; **~ auspacken** to unpack a trunk (one's things); **~ zur Bahn bringen** to take the luggage *(Br.)* (baggage, *US*) to the station; **seinen ~ zur Gepäckaufbewahrung geben** to leave one's bag in the cloakroom; **seinen ~ beim Bahnhof lassen** to park one's bag at the station; **seine ~ packen** to pack one's trunks (bags); **seine Kleidung in den ~ stopfen** to ram one's clothes into a suitcase; **ein paar Sachen in seinen ~ stopfen** to put a few things together in a handbag;
~anhänger luggage *(Br.)* (baggage, *US*) bag, label holder; **~apparat** portable set; **~brücke** *(Auto)* luggage grid *(Br.)*; **~damm** cofferdam *(mar.)*; **~deck** *(Schiff)* trunk deck; **~einsatz** trunk tray; **~fernsehgerät** portable television set; **~radio** table radio, portable radio set; **~raum** *(Auto)* luggage (baggage, trunk, *US*) compartment, car boot *(Br.)*, luggage boot *(Br.)*, trunk *(US)*; **~raumleuchte** boot *(Br.)* (trunk, *US*) light; **~schreibmaschine** portable typewriter; **~träger** porter.
Kohl, alter hash, rehash;
alten ~ aufwärmen to drag up an old story, to rake up old quarrels (the past); **~ reden** to talk through one's hat *(sl.)*.
Kohle coal, *(Moneten)* dough *(US sl.)*, chink *(sl.)*, dibs *(sl.)*, sponduliks *(US sl.)*, beans *(sl.)*;
anstehende ~ unworked coal; **bituminöse ~** fat coal; **im Tagebau gewonnene ~** opencast coal; **glühende ~n** live coals; **magere ~** lean coal; **minderwertige ~** low-quality coal;
~n abbauen to mine (extract) coal; **~ bunkern** to bunker, to recoal; **sich mit ~ eindecken** to lay in coal; **~n einkellern** to store coal; **~ einnehmen** to coal; **~n hauen** to cut coal; **~ laden** to bunker; **~ nachlegen** to pile more coal on; **glühende ~n auf jds. Haupt sammeln** to heap coals of fire on s. one's head; **~n schaufeln** to move dirt *(sl.)*; **~ auf Halde schütten** to dump coal *(US)*; **wie auf [glühenden] ~n sitzen** to be on tenterhooks, to sit (be) on pins and needles, to sit on thorns; **~n trimmen** to hew coal; **viel ~ verbrauchen** *(Maschine)* to be very heavy on coal; **~hydrierung** hydrogenation of coal; **~mikrofon** carbon microphone.
Kohlen|abbau coal mining; **~abbaugerechtigkeit** royalty; **~abgabe** coal levy; **nicht mit größeren ~anforderungen von den Versorgungsbetrieben rechnen** not to expect a large coal demand from the utilities; **~ausfuhr** coal export; **~becken** coal bed.
kohlenbeheizt coal-fired.
Kohlen|bergarbeiterstreik coal strike; **~bergbau** coal-mining industry; **~bergbauleitung** Combined Coal Control Group; **~bergwerk** coal mine, pit, colliery; **~bewirtschaftung** coal control; **~bunker** coal bunker; **~deputat** allowance of free coal; **~distrikt** coal field; **~eimer** coal scuttle; **~einsatz** input of coal; **~feld ausbeuten** to work a coal field; **~feuerung** coal firing; **~flöz** coal bed, (bank, *US*), seam; **~förderung** coal output; **tägliche ~förderung pro Kopf** coal output per man per day; **~gas** coal gas; **~gebiet** coal-mining district, coal area; **~grube** coalpit; **~grube ausbeuten** to mine coal; **~hafen** coaling port (station); **~halde** coal bank, coal stockpile, pithead stocks; **~händler** dealer in coal, coal merchant, coal factor *(Br.)*, coal hawker; **~heizung haben** to heat with coal; **~industrie** coal industry; **~knappheit** coal shortage; **~krise** coal crisis; **~ladung** load of coal; **~lager** coal field (depot, yard, bank, *US*); **~lieferant** coal contractor (supplier); **~lieferungen** coal supply; **~lieferungsvertrag abschließen** to make a contract for supply of coal; **~mangel** coal famine; **~nebenprodukte gewinnen** to recover byproducts from coal; **abbauwürdige ~reserven** workable reserves of coal; **~revier** coal area, coal field, coal-

mining district; ~**schätze eines Gebiets erschließen** to develop a coal area; ~**schaufel** coal shovel; ~**schiff** coal ship, collier; ~**schiffe** keels; ~**schuppen** coal shed (house); ~**schütte** coal shuttle; **kritische** ~**situation** coal pinch; ~**station** coaling station; ~**staub** coal dust; ~**träger** coal heaver; ~**transport** coal transport; ~**transportband** coal conveyer; ~**trimmer** trimmer, coal heaver; ~**überhang** coal glut; ~**übernahme** coaling; ~**verbrauch** coal consumption; ~**vergeudung** wastage of coal; ~**verkaufsbüro** coal sales office; ~**versand** coal transport; ~**versorgung** coal supplies; ~**vorkommen** coal deposit; ~**vorrat** coal reserves; ~**vorrat ergänzen** to recoal; **ausreichenden** ~**vorrat eingelagert haben** to have enough coal in; ~**waggon** coal wag(g)on (truck, car, *US*), tender; ~**waggon fahren** to hurry a coal waggon *(Br.)*; ~**zeche** coal mine, colliery; ~**zug** coal train, coaler, black snake *(sl.)*.

Kohle|papier carbon paper; ~**zeichnung** charcoal drawing.

Koje berth, cabin, bunk, *(Ausstellungsstand)* booth, *(Schiff)* cot.

Kokain cocaine, coke, snow, white stuff *(sl.)*;
~**süchtiger** snowbird *(sl.)*.

kokett coquettish.

kokettieren, mit jem. to [play the] coquette (flirt) with s. o.; **mit seinem Alter** ~ to play up one's age; **mit einer Idee** ~ to toy with an idea; **mit dem Kommunismus** ~ to be a fellow-traveller.

Koks coke;
~**eisen** coke iron; ~**feuerung** coke-firing; ~**kohle** coking coal; ~**ofen** coke oven.

Kolben *(Motor)* piston;
jem. eins auf den ~ **geben** to give s. o. a crack on the nut; ~**antrieb** piston drive; ~**blitz** *(Foto)* flashgun; ~**hub** upstroke (travel) of a piston; ~**motor** piston (reciprocating) engine; ~**pumpe** piston pump; ~**ventil** piston valve; ~**verdrängung** piston displacement.

Kolchose collective farm.

Kolik gripes *(coll.)*.

Kollaborateur collaborator, quisling.

kollaborieren to collaborate.

Kollaps collapse *(med.)*.

Kollation *(Buchführung)* collation, *(Erbausgleich)* putting in hotchpot.

kollationieren to compare, to collate, *(abhaken)* to check [off], *(ablesen)* to call over, *(Konten)* to reconcile;
Telegramm ~ to repeat back a telegram.

Kollationierung comparison, collation, *(Erbausgleich)* hotchpot, *(Konten)* reconcilement.

kollationspflichtig liable to be put in hotchpot.

Kolleg course of lectures;
dreistündiges ~ **über Steuerprobleme** three-hour lecture on tax problems;
~ **abhalten** to [give a] lecture; ~ **belegen** to enter one's name (enrol) for a course of lectures; ~ **besuchen** to go to (attend) a lecture.

Kollege colleague, workfellow, fellow worker, adjunct, peer, friend, assessor, confrère, associate, *(auf Regierungsebene)* opposite number, counterpart;
mein geehrter ~ my learned friend; **mein geschätzter** ~ my respected colleague, my hono(u)rable friend *(Br.)*.

Kollegenrabatt *(Buchhändler)* trade discount.

Kolleg|gelder college tuition, lecture fees; ~**heft** notebook.

kollegial collegial, helpful, friendly, cooperative;
sich ~ **verhalten** to act as a good friend;
~**es Verhalten** loyal (helpful) attitude.

Kollegial|behörde board, governmental department; ~**gericht** panel of judges.

Kollegialität colleagueship, fellowship.

Kollegial|system collegial system; ~**verhältnis** congenial relationship.

Kollegium board, panel, body, council, committee, *(Schule)* teaching staff, faculty *(US)*, hall *(US)*.

Kollekte collection, whip round, *(Kirche)* offertory;
~ **veranstalten** to make a collection, to pass the hat round.

Kollektion collection [of patterns], assortment, selection, set, parcel, range;
komplette ~ full set (range) [of samples]; **unvollständige** ~ broken assortment;
~ **aller einschlägigen Artikel** the whole range of articles; ~ **neuer Hüte** new lot of hats;
~ **zusammenstellen** to assort samples.

Kollektiv community, common ownership, collective body, *(pol.)* collective.

kollektiv collective, congregate, joint;
~**e Bewirtschaftung** collective farming; ~**e Geldstrafe** joint fine; ~**es Gütezeichen** collective mark; ~**e Selbstverteidigung** *(UNO)* collective self-defence; ~**e Sicherheit** *(pol.)* collective security; ~**es Sparen** social savings.

Kollektiv|abkommen *(Industrie)* collective labo(u)r agreement; ~**anzeige** composite advertisement; ~**arbeit** teamwork, collaboration; ~**arbeitsvertrag** collective labo(u)r agreement; ~**bedürfnisse** merit wants, social wants proper; ~**begriff** collective; ~**besitz** collective ownership; **landwirtschaftlicher** ~**betrieb** collective farm; ~**bewußtsein** collective consciousness; ~**eigentum** collective ownership, collective goods; ~**einbürgerung** collective naturalization; ~**einrichtung** collective organization; ~**formel** collective formula; ~**frachtbrief** blanket waybill; ~**frieden** collective peace; ~**garantie** collective guarantee; ~**geldstrafe** combined fine; ~**haftung** joint liability, *(Völkerrecht)* collective liability.

kollektivieren to collectivize.

Kollektivierung collectivization.

Kollektivismus collectivism.

kollektivistisch collectivistic.

Kollektivklausel joint clause.

Kollektivlebensversicherung group life insurance;
~ **für Darlehnsnehmer ungedeckter Kleinkredite** group insurance.

Kollektiv|marke collective mark; ~**maßnahmen ergreifen** to take collective measures; ~**note** *(dipl.)* collective note; ~**prokura** joint power of attorney, joint signature; ~**sparen** group saving; ~**strafe** collective punishment; ~**unternehmen** concerted under-taking; ~**verantwortung** collective responsibility; ~**vereinbarung** collective [bargaining] agreement; ~**verhandlung** collective bargaining; ~**verpflichtung** joint bond; ~**versicherung** blanket (group, blanket-clause) insurance; ~**vertrag** [collective] labo(u)r agreement, collective wage (bargaining) agreement, *(Völkerrecht)* collective treaty, convention; **obligatorische** ~**verträge einführen** to make collective contracts mandatory; ~**vertragsverhandlungen** collective bargaining; ~**vollmacht** joint power of attorny; ~**wirtschaft** collective economy; ~**zeichen** collective trademark; ~**zeichnung** joint signature.

Koller outburst of rage;
~ **kriegen** to fly into a tantrum.

kollerig quick-tempered, in a tantrum.

Kolli packages.

kollidieren to come into collision, to clash;
mit einem Anspruch ~ *(Patentgesetz)* to conflict with a claim; **mit dem Gesetz** ~ to come into conflict with the law; **mit jds. Interessen** ~ to clash (come into collision) with s. one's interests.

kollidierend concurrent, clashing;
~**e Interessen** clashing (conflicting) interests.

Kollier collier, collar, necklace, neckband.

Kollision collision, conflict, clash, *(Patent)* interference, *(Recht)* concurrence;
in ~ *(Schiff)* foul;
~ **von Interessen** clash of interests; **heftige** ~ **mit der Polizei** violent collision with the police;
~ **vermeiden** to fend off a collision.

Kollisions|gefahr risk of collision; ~**klausel** *(Schiff)* collision clause, *(Auto)* running-down clause; ~**klausel für beiderseitiges Verschulden** both-to-blame collision clause; ~**kurs** *(Schiff)* collision course; ~**normen** conflicting rules; ~**patent** interfering patent; ~**recht** conflict of laws; ~**risiko** collision risk; ~**schaden** collision (impact) damage; ~**sicherung** prevention of collisions; ~**urkunde** preliminary act.

Kollo pareel.

Kolloquium colloquium, conference.

Kollusion collusion.

kolonialähnlich quasi-colonial.

Kolonial|anleihe colonial (insular) bonds; ~**bank** colonial bank *(Br.)*; ~**beamter** colonial civil servant; ~**besitz** colonial possessions; ~**gebiet** colonial power; ~**handel** colonial trade; ~**herrschaft** colonial rule.

kolonialistisch colonialist.

Kolonial|krieg colonial war; ~**macht** colonial power, colonizer; ~**mandat** mandated colony; ~**ministerium** colonial department; ~**papiere** colonial securities (stocks), colonials; ~**politik** colonial policy, colonialism; ~**produkte** colonial produce; ~**regierung** colonial government; ~**reich** colonial empire; ~**status** dominion status; ~**system** colonialism; ~**verwaltung** colonial administration; ~**volk** colonial people.

Kolonialwaren colonial produce (products), colonial goods (wares), groceries, grocer's wares;

~geschäft grocer's shop (store, *US*), grocery, grocery outlet (store) *(US)*; **~handel** grocery business (trade); **~händler** provision dealer (merchant), colonial merchant, grocer, *(en gros)* engros (wholesale) grocer; **~handlung** grocer's shop (store, *US*), grocery.

Kolonial | werte *(Börse)* colonials; **~zeit** colonial era.

Kolonie colony, colonial possession, settlement;
junge ~ infant colony;
nach den ~n ausführen to export colonially; **einer ~ die Unabhängigkeit gewähren** to raise a colony to the status of a substantive nation; **~ gründen** to establish a colony; **in den ~n leben** to live in the colonies.

Kolonisation colonization.

Kolonisator colonizer, settler.

kolonisieren to colonize, to plant.

Kolonisierung colonization.

Kolonist colonist, colonial, settler.

Kolonnade addition footing.

Kolonne column, convoy, *(Arbeiter)* gang, group, crew;
fliegende ~ flying column; **Fünfte ~** *(pol.)* fifth column;
~ von Kraftfahrzeugen queue (string) of cars, column of motor vehicles;
~ addieren to add up columns; **aus einer ~ ausscheren** to pull out of a column; **sich in eine ~ einreihen** to join a column; **in ~ fahren** to drive in a column; **in geschlossener ~ marschieren** to march in close column; **~ überholen** to overtake a string of cars.

Kolonnen | anfang head of a column; **~arbeit** gang work; **~bogen** columnar sheet; **~brücke** *(mil.)* pontoon (trestle) bridge; **~fahrt** driving in a column (convoy); **~flug** javelin formation; **~führer** group leader, gang boss *(US)*; **~schiff** leading ship; **an der ~spitze** at the head of the column; **~springer** *(Autofahrer)* queue jumper; **~steller** *(Schreibmaschine)* tabulator; **~werbung** group canvassing.

kolorieren to colo(u)r, to tone.

koloriert colo(u)red.

Kolorit colo(u)ring;
lokaler ~ local colo(u)r;
~ einer Stadt atmosphere of a town.

Koloss colossus, gigantic statue.

kolossal colossal, gigantic;
jem. ~ imponieren to impress s. o. tremendously; **~ viel Geld verdienen** to be simply coining money;
~e Anstrengungen stupendous efforts; **~e Dummheit begehen** to make a colossal blunder; **~e Entfernung** vast distance; **~es Gebäude** huge building; **~e Reklame** gigantic publicity; **~er Schrecken** tremendous fright.

Kolossalfilm spectacular.

Kolportage trashy literature;
~roman trashy novel, penny dreadful *(Br.)*, dime novel *(US)*.

Kolporteur newsmonger, rumo(u)rer.

kolportieren, Gerücht to spread a rumo(u)r; **Skandale ~** to peddle scandals *(fam.)*.

Kolumne column, page.

Kolumnen | breite *(Druck)* measure, column width; **~leiste** running head; **~maß** printer's gauge, rule, scale; **~schreiber** syndicated (newspaper) columnist; **~titel** catchword, running title (head), headline; **lebender ~titel** live headline.

kolumnenweise page by page.

Kolumnen | zeilenmaß printer's gauge, rule; **~ziffer** folio (page) number.

Kombinat combine.

Kombination combination, guesswork, *(Flieger)* flying suit;
messerscharfe ~en razor-sharp deductions;
~ für einen Safe combination used to open a safe.

Kombinations | ausgabe combined edition; **~druck** colo(u)r printing; **~effekt** combined effect; **~gabe** reasoning power; **mit ~gabe und Risikoinkaufnahme vorgehen** to cut and dry; **~möbel** unit furniture; **~patent** combination; **bequem zu begleichender ~preis** easy-to-pay package price; **~rabatt** *(Anzeige)* combined edition discount; **~schloß** combination (letter-keyed) lock; **~schrank** multipurpose cabinet; **~tarif** combined rate, *(Anzeigen)* combination rate.

kombinieren to combine, *(Logik)* to deduct, to guess;
hohe Leistung mit geringem Benzinverbrauch ~ to combine high performance with fuel economy; **richtig ~** to guess right; **sich beliebig ~ lassen** to be arranged in any desired combination.

kombiniert | e Abschreibungs- und Erhaltungsmethode combined depreciation and upkeep method; **~e militärische Aktionen** combined actions; **~er Anzeigenpreis** combined rate; **~e Ätzung** combination plate; **~er Frachttarif** combination mil(e)age and rate prorate *(US)*, combination rate; **~er Verband** combined force; **~es Wert- und Ursprungszeugnis** combined certificate of value and origin *(Br.)*.

Kombi | wagen carryall *(US)*, beach wagon *(US)*, estate car *(Br.)*, station wagon *(US)*; **~zange** combination pliers.

Kombüse caboose, galley.

Komet comet.

kometenartiger gesellschaftlicher Aufstieg meteoric rise in the social scale.

Kometenbahn orbit of a comet.

kometenhafte Laufbahn meteoric career.

Kometenschweif tail of a comet.

Komfort comfort, convenience, accommodation, ease;
mit dem allerneuesten ~ with all modern conveniences;
aller ~ every modern comfort; **bester ~** main comfort;
nur kümmerlichen ~ erhalten to receive a few grains of comfort;
mit allem ~ ausgestattet sein, über den allerneuesten ~ verfügen to be fitted with all modern comfort, to have all modern conveniences; **auf den üblichen ~ verzichten** to do without the convenience one is used to.

komfortabel comfortable, cosy, snug;
~ leben to live in comfort (in comfortable circumstances, at ease); **sehr ~ wirken** *(Haus)* to have an air of comfort; **~ wohnen** to be comfortably housed.

Komfort | bedürfnis, modernste ~bedürfnisse befriedigen to be the last word in comfort and convenience; **~wohnung** luxury flat.

Komik comic, humo(u)r;
unfreiwillige ~ unintentional humo(u)r;
nicht einer gewissen ~ entbehren not to be without its funny side; **~ einer Sache sehen** to see the comic side of a situation; **von unwiderstehlicher ~ sein** to be irresistibly comical.

komisch peculiar *(coll.)*, comic, humo(u)rous, curious *(coll.)*;
jem. ~ kommen to behave oddly towards s. o.; **selten ~ sein** to be too funny for words; **in Gelddingen ziemlich ~ sein** to be very peculiar in money matters; **jem. ~ zumute sein** to feel queer all over; **einem ~ vorkommen** to find s. th. strange;
~e Figur abgeben to cut a funny figure; **~es Gefühl haben** to feel in one's bones; **~es Individuum** caution; **~er Kauz** odd stick, queer type (bloke); **~e Oper** comic opera; **~e Rolle** comic part; **~er Verein** rum lot.

Komische, das ~ daran ist the funny part about it.

komischerweise funnily enough.

Komitee committee;
zwischenstaatliches ~ für europäische Auswanderung Intergovernmental Committee for European Migration;
~ einsetzen to set up a committee.

Komma, auf zwei Stellen hinter dem ~ abrunden to correct to two decimal places; **~ setzen** to insert a comma.

Kommandant commander, commandant, commanding officer, *(Festung)* governor, *(Schiff)* captain;
stellvertretender ~ second-in-command.

Kommandantur headquarters.

Kommandeur commanding officer, commander.

kommandieren to command, to be in command, to order;
gern ~ to like to order people about; **zu einem Lehrgang ~** to detach for a course;
sich nicht gern ~ lassen not to like it being ordered about.

kommandierend commanding;
~er General commanding general.

Kommandit | anteil limited partnership interest; **~beteiligung** participation in a limited parnership.

Kommandite partly-owned subsidiary.

Kommanditeinlagen, in Höhe ihrer ~ haften to be liable up to their contributions.

Kommanditgesellschaft limited partnership, partnership limited by shares;
~ auf Aktien scrip (joint stock) company *(US)*.

Kommanditist special (limited) partner, commanditaire.

Kommanditisten | anteil limited partnership interest; **~haftung** limited partner's liability.

kommanditistisch beteiligt sein to carry limited liability in a partnership.

Kommandit | kapital special (partner's) capital; **~vertrag** articles of partnership.

Kommando command, order, *(Abteilung)* party;
~ abstellen to detail off a squad; **~ führen** to be in command; **unter jds. ~ stehen** to be under s. one's command; **~ übergeben** to hand over the command to; **~ übernehmen** to hoist one's flag; **einem Offizier ein ~ übertragen** to designate an officer for a command;

~**behörde** headquarters; ~**bereich** command; ~**brücke** pilot bridge, *(fig.)* commanding height; ~**flagge** distinguishing pennant; ~**gerät** *(Flugabwehr)* fire director; ~**gewalt über ein Schiff ausüben** to have charge or conduct of a ship; ~**raum** control room; **geheime** ~**sache** top secret; ~**stand** central station, *(Kriegsschiff)* communication room; ~**stelle** head, staff; ~**system** system of control; **im** ~**ton** in a tone of command; ~**turm** *(U-Boot)* conning tower; ~**unternehmen** landing party *(Br.)*, commando raid; ~**werte** *(Flugabwehrgeschütz)* fire-director data; ~**wirtschaft** command economy; ~**zentrale** control center *(US)* (centre, *Br.*).

Kommastelle decimal figure.

Kommata, ein paar ~ einsetzen to stick in a few commas; **~ falsch setzen** *(math.)* to misplace the decimal point.

Kommen coming, arrival;
freies ~ und Gehen free issue and entry, run of the house; **sein ~ ankündigen** *(Auto)* to give notice of approach; **im ~ sein** to be on the way up; **wieder stark im ~ sein** to make a strong comeback.

kommen *(Post)* to come, to arrive;
~ und gehen *(Mode)* to pass;
jederzeit ~ und gehen dürfen to have the run of the house; **zu etw. ~** *(Erbe)* to come by; **völlig anders ~** to turn out very differently; **nicht zum Briefschreiben ~** not to find time for one's correspondence; **an den Falschen ~** to bark up the wrong tree; **oft im Fernsehen ~** to be often on television; **nicht vom Fleck ~** to get nowhere, not to make any progress; **in einen besonderen Fonds ~** to go to a special fund; **ins Gefängnis ~** to be sent to prison; **hinter jds. Geheimnis ~** to discover s. one's secret; **zu Geld ~** to come into money; **jem. grob ~** to treat s. o. rudely; **unter den Hammer ~** to be on the auction block; **in den Handel ~** to come on the market; **zu einem Handgemenge ~** to come to blows; **auf den Hund ~** to go to the dogs; **auf eine Idee ~** to hit upon an idea; **in die Jahre ~** to be getting on in years; **jem. zur Kenntnis ~** to be brought to s. one's notice; **für Tage nicht aus den Kleidern ~** not to see one's bed for days; **sofort aufs Konto ~** to go straight into the bank account; **wieder zu Kräften ~** to regain one's strength; **ins Krankenhaus ~** to be taken to hospital; **in eine mißliche Lage ~** to get into a bad fix; **kaum unter Menschen ~** to seldom meet other people; **wegen der Miete ~** to come to collect the rent; **nicht auf jds. Namen ~** not to remember s. one's name; **gleich nach dem Präsidenten ~** to rank next to the president; **an die Reihe ~** to be s. one's turn; **in die Reinigung ~** to be taken to the cleaners; **vor den Richter ~** to be brought before a judge; **ins Schleudern ~** to get into a skid; **hinter jds. Schliche ~** to find out about s. one's tricks; **jem. mit Schmeicheleien ~** to try to flatter s. o.; **Ostern aus der Schule ~** to be leaving school at Easter; **an den ältesten Sohn ~** to fall to the eldest son; **kurz auf Politik zu sprechen ~** to touch politics; **auf einen Sprung ~** to pay a flying visit; **jem. teuer zu stehen ~** to cost s. o. dearly; **zum Stillstand ~** to come to a standstill; **ans Tageslicht ~** to come to light; **richtig auf Touren ~** to hit one's stride; **zu der Überzeugung ~** to realize; **aus der Übung ~** to get out of practice; **nicht von ungefähr ~** to be no accident; **nach seinem Vater ~** to take after one's father; **vor die Vereinten Nationen ~** to be placed before the United Nations; **nächste Woche zur Verhandlung ~** to come up for hearing next week; **um sein ganzes Vermögen ~** to lose all one's fortune; **mit 100 DM nicht weit ~** DM 100 doesn't go very far; **auf die Welt ~** to be borne; **durch den Zoll ~** to pass through the customs.

kommen lassen, Arzt to send for a doctor; **nichts auf j. ~** not to have anything said against s. o.; **nicht näher ~** to keep off.

kommend | e Generation rising generation; ~**e Jahre** future years; ~**er Mann sein** to be the up-and-coming man (a comer, *US sl.*); ~**er Politiker** rising politician; ~**e Woche** next week.

Kommentar commentary, comment, annotation, descant, *(Textbuch)* textbook;
beigefügter ~ pendant note; **entstellter ~** garbled comment; **juristischer ~** legal commentary; **redaktioneller ~** editorial comment; **überholter ~** obsolete textbook;
~ ablehnen to decline to comment; **sich jeden ~s enthalten** to refrain from comments; **~ geben** to comment; **~ verfassen** to write a commentary; **mit einem ~ versehen** to annotate;
~**frage** open-ended question.

Kommentator commentator, annotator, *(für Textbücher)* textbookwriter, text writer, glossarist, expositor, *(juristische Bücher)* law writer;
politischer ~ commentator on politics.

kommentieren *(Buch)* to comment, to annotate;
etw. ~ to make one's comments upon s. th., to pass remarks on s. th.

kommentierend commentatory, commentarial.

Kommentierung annotation.

kommerzialisieren to commercialize.

Kommerzialisierung commercialization.

kommerziell commercial;
in ~er Weise commercially; **nicht ~** noncommercial, nonprofit; **~ gesehen vernünftig sein** to make good business sense.

Kommilitone fellow student.

Kommis clerk, employee, *(Verkäufer)* salesman, salesclerk *(US)*.

Kommiß army, armed forces, uniform, service.

Kommissar commissioner, *(pol.)* commissary, commissioner, *(Polizei)* inspector, superintendent, police commissioner *(US)*;
~ für Entwicklungsländer *(EG)* development commissioner; **~ für Wettbewerbsfragen** *(EG)* competition commissioner.

Kommissariat superintendent's office *(Br.)*, commissariat, commissionership, *(Polizei)* police station;
jem. ein ~ übertragen to commission s. o.

kommissarisch commissarial, temporary, vicarious, provisional;
Amt ~ ausüben to hold an office in commission;
~**e Funktionen** provisional duties; **unter ~e Verwaltung stellen** to put under provisional administration.

Kommission commission, committee, board, *(Auftrag)* commission, order, *(Entgelt)* commission [fee], charge, brokerage;
in ~ *(Waren)* in commission (consignment), on sale and return, on commission, on condition;
beratende ~ advisory committee; **gemischte (paritätische) ~** joint commission; **ständige ~** standing committee, permanent commission;
~ aus Beteiligungen underwriting commission; **~ von Fachleuten** committee (panel) of experts, blue-ribbon panel *(US)*; **~ der Europäischen Gemeinschaft** Commission of the European Communities;
~ bilden (einsetzen) to set up (appoint) a committee, to establish a commission; **~ erledigen** to execute a commission; **in ~ geben** to consign, to send on consignment, to send [goods] on return; **Waren in ~ geben** to deliver goods on sale and return; **~ kassieren** to make a commission; **Waren in ~ nehmen** to take goods on sale and return, to take goods on a commission basis (on consignment); **Wertpapiere in ~ nehmen** to take securities on a commission basis; **auf ~ schicken** to send on commission, *(Juwelen)* to send on memorandum; **Mitglied in einer ~ sein** to sit on a committee; **in ~ übernehmen** to take on a commission basis; **einer ~ unterliegen** to be subject to a commission; **gegen ~ verkaufen** to sell on commission.

Kommissionär commission agent (merchant), middleman, consignment agent, mercantile agent *(Br.)*, *(Buchhandel)* wholesaler, *(Empfänger einer Warensendung)* consignee, *(Makler)* broker, *(Verkaufsagent)* factor;
unselbständiger ~ agent middleman, half-commission man *(Br.)*.

Kommissionärs | gesetz Factor's Act *(Br.)*; ~**pfandrecht** factor's lien.

Kommissions | agent commission agent; **beigefügte ~anzeige** covering advice, memorandum; ~**artikel** goods on commission (in trust), consignment, memorandum goods (package) *(US)*; ~**auftrag** consignment.

Kommissionsbasis commission basis;
auf ~ [verkauft] on sale and return, factored, sold on commission;
auf ~ arbeiten to operate on a commission basis; **auf ~ übernehmen** to take on a commission basis; **auf ~ verkaufen** to factor, to sell [goods] on commission.

Kommissions | bericht committee report; ~**bezug** purchase on commission, *(Buchhändler)* outright purchase with right to return; ~**buch** order book; ~**buchhandel** wholesale bookselling; ~**buchhändler** wholesale bookseller; ~**einkauf** purchase on commission; ~**firma** commission merchant; ~**gebühr** commission, factorage; ~**geschäft** agency (agent's) business, factorage, commission agency (merchant), *(einzelnes)* commission dealing, commission business, sale and return, transaction for third account; ~**geschäfte machen** to trade (buy and sell) on commission; ~**gut** goods on commission (in trust), articles on commission, consignment, memorandum goods (package) *(US)*; ~**handel** agency (agent's) business, factorage, commission marketing, transaction for third account; ~**haus** commission merchant; ~**kauf** purchase on commission; ~**konto** consignment (memorandum, *US*) account; ~**lager** stock on consignment (commission); ~**lieferung vornehmen** to supply on a consignment (commission) basis; ~**makler** commission broker; ~**mitglied** committee member, commissioner; ~**mitglieder** *(EG)* members of the commission;

~**mitglied sein** to be (sit) on a commission (committee); ~**note** broker's note (confirmation, *US*), memorandum *(US)*; ~**nummer** order number; ~**provision** commission on sale effected, factorage; ~**rechnung** consignment invoice; ~**reisender** commercial travel(l)er, travel(l)ing salesman; ~**rimesse** remittance on third account; ~**satz** commission; ~**schein** consignment note, memorandum [bill] *(US)*; ~**sendung** consignment; ~**sitzung** committee meeting; ~**verkauf** consignment sale (marketing), sale on consignment (and return), memorandum sale *(US)*; ~**verkauf mit Selbsteintritt** bailment sale; ~**verlag** commission publishers; ~**vertrag** consignment, consignment contract; ~**vertreter** consignment agent.

Kommissionsware goods on commission (consignment), goods on sale and return (in trust), consigner's merchandise, consignment [goods], memorandum goods (package) *(US)*;
angekündigte ~ billed order; **erstmalige** ~ initial consignment.

Kommissionswarenbuch order consignment book.

kommissionsweise on consignment, on (by way of) commission (memorandum, *US*), on an agency (commission) basis;
~ **überlassen** to send on commission; **Waren** ~ **verkaufen** to sell goods on commission, to factor; ~ **versandt werden** to be shipped on memorandum *(US)*;
~**r Verkauf** consignment sale (marketing).

Kommißstiefel army boots;
~ **anziehen müssen** to be drafted.

Kommode chest of drawers, bureau *(US)*.

kommunal communal, local *(Br.)*, municipal;
~ **verbürgt** guaranteed by local authorities *(Br.)*;
~**e Auszahlungsanweisung** county warrant; ~**e Befugnisse** county powers; ~**e Behörden** local government, municipal authorities; ~**er Betriebsmittelfonds** county general fund; ~**e Ebene** local scale; ~**e Einflüsse** local influences; ~**e Einrichtungen** municipal services, communal organization (facilities); ~**e Finanzen** local government finance *(Br.)*; ~**e Finanzzuweisung** grants-in-aid *(US)*; ~**e Gebietskörperschaften** local authorities; ~**e Gesetzgebung** local legislation; ~**e Gewaltenausübung** municipal action; ~**e Gewerbetätigkeit** municipal trading; ~**e Grundstückslast** local land charge; ~**e Mittel** county funds; ~**es Rechnungswesen** municipal accounting; ~**es Schuldscheindarlehen** county warrant; ~**e Schuldverschreibungen** municipal bonds *(US)*; ~**er Sektor** municipal segment; ~**e Selbstverwaltung** local self-government *(Br.)*, municipal government; ~**e Selbstverwaltungsfunktionen** local government functions; ~**e Steuern** municipal rates (taxes), local rates *(Br.)*; ~**e Unterstützung** municipal support (aid); ~**er Versorgungsbetrieb** municipal (municipally owned) utility; ~**e Vertretungskörperschaft** local government council; ~**e Verwaltungsstelle** local unit of government; ~**e Wirtschaftstätigkeit** municipal trading; ~**e Zahlungsunfähigkeit** municipal default; **für** ~**e Zwecke** for county (municipal) purposes.

Kommunalabgaben local *(Br.)* (municipal) taxes, town (parish, local, municipal) rates *(Br.)*;
allgemeine ~ general rates *(Br.)*;
~ **und Steuern** rates and taxes *(Br.)*;
~ **erheben** to levy a rate *(Br.)*; **als Grundstücksbesitzer für** ~ **haftbar sein** to become liable for rates as occupier *(Br.)*;
~**ablösung** compounding of rates *(Br.)*; ~**anforderung** rate demand *(Br.)*.

kommunalabgaben|frei wohnen to live a rate-free life *(Br.)*; ~**pflichtig** ratable *(Br.)*.

Kommunalabgaben|quittung rates receipt *(Br.)*; ~**wesen** municipal taxation.

Kommunal|angelegenheiten county business, county affairs, local affairs *(Br.)*, municipal affairs *(US)*; ~**angestellte** employees of municipal governments *(US)*; ~**anlagen** municipal facilities, communal organizations.

Kommunalanleihe municipal bonds *(US)*, municipal securities *(US)*, local authority loan (bonds) *(Br.)*, municipal stocks *(Br.)*, corporation loan *(Br.)*;
~**n** municipals, municipal (local, *Br.*) bonds, municipal loans; **ausländische** ~ foreign municipal bonds *(US)*; **der Verbesserung öffentlicher Anlagen dienende** ~ improvement bonds *(US)*; **nicht vollwertige** ~ quasi- (semi-) municipal bonds *(US)*;
~**n zur Kanalisationsfinanzierung** sewer bonds.

Kommunal|arbeiter municipal worker; ~**aufgaben** county affairs; ~**aufwendungen**, ~**ausgaben** municipal expenses *(US)*, local expenditure *(Br.)*, environmental services *(Br.)*; ~**bank** municipal (city) bank; ~**beamter** local government officer *(Br.)*, local public official *(Br.)*, county (municipal) officer *(US)*; ~**bedarf** local wants; ~**bediensteter** paid officer of a council; ~**behörden** local authorities (government) *(Br.)*, municipal authorities *(US)*; ~**betrieb** communal enterprise, civil (municipal) enterprise, municipal undertaking (corporation, *US*); ~**bezirk** municipal district *(US)*, township *(Br.)*, county; ~**bürgschaft** local government guarantee *(Br.)*; ~**darlehn** local authority loan *(Br.)*, municipal loan *(US)*; **in** ~**eigentum** municipally owned; ~**einnahmen**, ~**einkünfte** revenues of the city council, local revenue *(Br.)*; ~**einrichtung** communal organization, community facility; ~**emission** municipal issue; ~**etat**, ~**haushalt** local budget *(Br.)*, municipal budget *(US)*, county general fund; ~**finanzen** municipal finances *(US)*, local government finance *(Br.)*; ~**gebäude** municipal building.

kommunalgebührenpflichtige Konzession local taxation licence.

Kommunal|grundstück community land; ~**haushalt** local budget *(Br.)*, municipal budget; ~**hilfe** community support.

kommunalisieren to communalize, to municipalize.

Kommunalisierung communalization, municipalization.

Kommunalkrankenhaus community hospital.

Kommunalkredit advances to local authorities *(Br.)*, municipal loan (credit) *(US)*;
~**anstalt** municipal bank; ~**aufnahme** local authority borrowing *(Br.)*; ~**institut** municipal savings bank; ~**ordnung** Control of Borrowing Order *(Br.)*.

Kommunal|leistungen local (municipal) services; ~**nachrichten** local news; ~**obligationen** corporation stock *(Br.)*, county bonds, municipal papers (bonds, *US*), local *(Br.)* (general obligation) bonds; **nicht vollwertige** ~**obligationen** quasi- (semi-) municipal bonds *(US)*; ~**obligationen für den Ausbau der Gemeindeanlagen** local improvement bonds *(Br.)*; ~**papiere** municipal securities (papers) *(US)*, local authority stock *(Br.)*; ~**planung** local planning *(Br.)*; ~**politik** local politics *(Br.)*; ~**politiker** local politician *(Br.)*.

kommunalpolitisch|e Aufgaben local government jobs *(Br.)*;
sich ~ **betätigen** to be active in local politics *(Br.)*.

Kommunal|recht local government law, local law, municipal (territorial) law *(US)*; ~**reform** municipal reform; ~**schuldanleihe** municipal bonds (stocks); ~**schulden** local debts *(Br.)*, municipal debts *(US)*; ~**schuldschein** municipal instrument of indebtedness *(US)*, municipal (county) warrant *(US)*, local authority bond *(Br.)*; ~**schuldverschreibungen** municipals, local bonds *(Br.)*, communal securities, county debentures, municipal bonds *(US)* (stocks, *Br.*).

Kommunalsteuer|für aus Verbesserung öffentlicher Einrichtungen entstandene Werterhöhung local tax *(US)*;
~**aufkommen** local revenue *(Br.)*; ~**gesetz** Local Taxation Act *(Br.)*.

Kommunalsteuern municipal (local) taxes *(US)*, [local] rates *(Br.)*.

Kommunalsteuerpflicht rat(e)ability.

kommunalsteuerpflichtig ratable *(Br.)*, ratepaying *(Br.)*.

Kommunalsteuer|pflichtiger, ~**zahler** ratepayer *(Br.)*; ~**satz** municipal tax rate, ratal *(Br.)*; ~**senkung** reduction of rates *(Br.)*; ~**wesen** local tax system *(US)*, local taxation *(Br.)*, municipal taxation.

Kommunal|straße adopted road (street); ~**struktur** municipal structure; ~**umlage** county rate *(Br.)*; ~**veranstaltungen** municipal functions; ~**verband** municipal corporation *(US)*, communal organization, National Association of Parish Councils *(Br.)*; ~**verbindlichkeiten** municipal debts *(US)*; ~**verfassung** local constitution; ~**vermögen** county treasury (fund, property), general revenue fund, municipal property *(US)*; ~**verschuldung** indebtedness of local authorities *(Br.)*, municipal indebtedness *(US)*; ~**verwaltung** local government *(Br.)*, county (municipal) government *(US)*, municipalism; **in** ~**verwaltung überführen** to municipalize, to communalize; ~**verwaltungsgesetz** Local Government Act *(Br.)*; ~**verwaltungsstelle** local unit of government *(Br.)*; ~**wahlen** municipal elections (polling) *(US)*, local government elections *(Br.)*, local elections *(Br.)*, regional elections; ~**wähler** communal elector; ~**wahlergebnis** local election results *(Br.)*; **pauschaler** ~**zuschuß** block grant *(Br.)*; ~**zwecke** municipal purposes.

Kommune *(Gemeinde)* municipality, *(pol.)* community.

Kommunikations|forschung communication research; ~**linie** life line; ~**markt** communication market; ~**mittel** means of communication, communication media; ~**schwierigkeiten** lack of communications.

Kommuniqué communiqué, bulletin, official statement, briefing;
offizielles ~ formal communiqué;
~ **herausgeben** to [issue a] bulletin, to issue a communiqué.

Kommunismus communism;
mit dem ~ **sympathisieren** to fellow-travel *(US)*.

Kommunist communist, Red;
getarnter ~ cryptocommunist;
als ~en schikanieren to red-bait *(US)*.
kommunistenfreundlich sein to fellow-travel *(US)*.
Kommunisten|sympathisant fellow traveller; **~verfolgung** red baiting *(US sl.)*.
kommunistisch communist, red;
~e Partei Communist Party.
Kommutationswertspalte commutation column.
Komödiant actor, comedian, *(fig.)* hypocrite, play-actor;
aufgeplusterter ~ stand-up comedian.
Komödie comedy, *(fig.)* farce;
leichte ~ light comedy; **reinste** ~ complete farce;
jds. ~ durchschauen to see through s. one's little game; **~ spielen** to play-act, *(fig.)* to put on an act.
komödienhafte Elemente comic elements.
Komödienschreiber comic playright.
Kompagnon partner.
Kompakt|siedlungen industrial estates; **~wagen** compact car.
Kompanie *(historisch, mil.)* company;
~chef company commander; **~geschäft** joint venture; **~stärke** company strength; **~trottel** sad sack *(US sl.)*.
komparative Kosten comparative costs.
Komparse *(Film)* extra, supernumerary, super, bit-player.
Komparserie extras, supers.
Kompaß compass;
~abweichung deviation of the magnetic needle; **~fehler** compass error; **~haus** binnacle; **~karte** compass card; **~kreisel** gyroscope; **~kurs** [compass] heading; **~nadel** magnetic needle; **~peilung** compass bearing; **~regulierer** pilot; **in allen ~richtungen suchen** to play around the compass; **~rose** compass rose (card); **~strich** point.
Kompendium handbook, field guide, compendium, manual, abstract, summary.
Kompensation compensation, setoff, offset *(US)*, *(Schecks)* clearing.
Kompensations|abkommen offset (barter) agreement; **~anspruch** compensation claim; **~betrag** amount of compensation.
kompensationsfähige Guthaben clearing items.
Kompensations|fonds compensation (equalization) fund; **~geschäft** barter (offsetting) transaction, compensation deal, *(Switchgeschäft)* switch; **~grundlage** basis of compensation; **~kasse** clearinghouse; **~klausel** *(Feuerversicherung)* schedule form; **~konto** compensation account, *(Scheckausgleich)* clearing account; **~kredit** compensating credit; **~kurs** rate of compensation (settlement); **~order** cross order *(US)*; **~regelung** compensatory adjustment; **~schema** compensation plan (scheme); **~verkehr** barter trade, *(Schecks)* clearing; **~zoll** countervailing duty.
kompensieren to compensate, to set off, to offset *(US)*, to counterbalance, to counterweigh, to counterpoise, *(Scheck)* to clear;
Forderung durch eine andere ~ to set off one claim against another; **sein bescheidenes Gehalt durch sparsame Lebensweise** ~ to offset a small salary by living economically; **frühere Verluste** ~ to offset earlier losses *(US)*.
Kompensierung compensation, setoff, offset *(US)*, *(Scheck)* clearing;
~ **von Verkauf und Kauf** *(Börse)* crossing trade *(US)*.
kompetent competent, authorized, authoritative, responsible, answerable, cognizant;
~ **sein** *(Fachmann)* to be an expert (authority) on a subject; **nicht** ~ **sein** *(Gericht)* to have no jurisdiction;
von ~er Seite from an authoritative source; **~e Stellen** competent authorities.
Kompetenz competence, authority, authoritativeness, responsibility, *(Gericht)* cognizance, jurisdiction;
jds. ~ **anzweifeln** to question s. one's authority; **in die** ~ **eines Gerichtes fallen** to come under the cognizance of a court; **nicht in jds.** ~ **fallen** to go beyond s. one's cognizance; **in die** ~ **der Verwaltungsgerichte fallen** to come within the jurisdiction of the administrative courts; **in kulturellen Fragen keine** ~ **haben** *(Bundesregierung)* to have no legislative authority in cultural matters; **seine** ~ **überschreiten** to exceed one's authority;
~abgrenzung jurisdictional limits; **~artikel** *(Satzung)* objects clause; **~bereich** [sphere of] jurisdiction; **seinen ~bereich überschreiten** to exceed one's competence; **~frage** matter of competence; **~konflikt** concurrence of jurisdiction, conflict of laws; **~streit** clash of power, *(Gericht)* concurrence of jurisdiction, jurisdictional dispute; **~überschreitung** excess of authority.
Kompilation compilation;
~ **eines Buches** bookmaking.
Kompilator compiler.
kompilieren to compile.
Komplementär general (unlimited, responsible) partner, ordinary partner *(Br.)*.
komplementär complementary;
~e Güter *(Volkswirtschaft)* complementary (joint demand, *US*) goods; **~e Güternachfrage** complementary demand.
Komplementär|anteil general partner's interest; **~bedarf** joint demand; **~bedürfnisse** complementary needs; **~güter** complementary (joint demand, *US*) goods.
Komplementarität complementarity.
Komplet two-piece.
komplett complete, entire, whole, positive *(coll.)*, plumb *(US coll.)*;
~ **verrückt sein** to be as mad as a March hare (hatter);
~e Ausrüstung complete outfit; **~e Belegnummer** complete voucher copy; **~er Idiot** utter fool; **~er Reinfall** blue ruin *(sl.)*; **~es Schlafzimmer** fully furnished bedroom; **~er Unsinn** utter (downright) nonsense.
komplettieren to complete, to complement, to raise to the full number;
sein Lager ~ to replenish one's stock.
Komplettierungs|ansage *(Rundfunk)* time holder; **~anzeige** rate holder.
Komplex complex, body, nexus, mass, aggregation, *(Grundstück)* plot of land, *(fixe Idee)* fixed idea;
~ **industrieller Anlagen** industry complex; ~ **von 10 Millionen Pfund** total amount of 10 million pounds; ~ **von Tatsachen** body of facts;
~ **abreagieren** to work off a complex.
Komplikation complication;
[politische] ~en imbroglios;
sofern nicht weitere ~en eintreten if no complications set in.
Kompliment compliment;
fade ~e insipid compliments; **überschwengliche ~e** gushing (effusive) compliments; **übliche ~e** necessary compliments; **zweischneidiges** ~ back-handed compliment;
mit einem ~ **beginnen** to open with a compliment; **nach ~en fischen** to be out (fish) for compliments; **jem. ein** ~ **machen** to pay s. o. a compliment, to flatter s. o.; **auf ~e aus sein** to be fishing for compliments.
Komplize accomplice, accessory, partner in crime, sidekicker *(US fam.)*;
j. zum ~n eines Verbrechens machen to involve s. o. in a crime; **seine ~n preisgeben** to turn informers; ~ **eines Verbrechens werden** to become a party to a crime.
Komplizenschaft partnership in crime.
komplizieren to complicate;
unnötig ~ to make work.
kompliziert complicated, complex, embarrassed, involved, dark;
sich ~ **ausdrücken** to express o. s. in a complicated way;
~e Berechnungen complex calculations; **~e Handlung** *(Roman)* intricate plot; **~es Regierungssystem** complex system of government; **~es Satzgefüge** involved period; **~e Zusammenhänge eines Falles** intricacies of a case.
Kompliziertheit complicacy, complexity, intricacy.
Komplott plot, conspiracy, intrigue, confederacy, common plan and scheme *(US)*;
in ein ~ **verstrickt** ensnarled in a plot;
~ **anzetteln** to devise a plot; ~ **gegen die Regierung anzetteln** to conspire against the government; ~ **aufdecken** to spring a plot; ~ **aushecken** to knit up a plot *(fam.)*; ~ **entdecken** to discover (smell out) a plot; ~ **schmieden** to lay (weave) a plot (complot), to conspire, to put up a job *(sl.)*; ~ **vereiteln** to foil a plot;
~teilnehmer conspirator.
Komponente constituent, component.
komponieren to compose.
Komposition *(einer Anzeige)* make-up, layout *(US)*, *(Musik)* musical composition, music;
eigene ~ own composition; **wunderbare** ~ *(Kleid)* wonderful creation;
~ **erlesener Duftstoffe** blend of choice aromatic essences.
Kompositionselemente, gebrauchsgrafische art work.
Kompositum compound word.
Kompost|erde compost; **~haufen** compost heap.
Kompott stewed fruit, compote [dish].
kompreß solid;
~ **gesetzt** tightly (close) set.
Kompression *(Motor)* compression.

Kompressionsdruck compression pressure.
Kompressor compressor, supercharger.
komprimieren to compress;
Gewinnspanne ~ to narrow the profit margin.
komprimiert compressed, tight.
Kompromiß compromise, composition, half measure, halfway house;
zu keinem ~ **bereit** uncompromising;
eine Art ~ a compromise of sorts; **von den Parteien erzielter** ~ compromise arrived at by the parties;
zu einem ~ **gelangen** to come to an arrangement; ~ **schließen** to compromise;
~**angebot** compromise package; ~**bereitschaft** readiness to reach a compromise; **Spielraum für** ~**bereitschaft lassen** to allow a compromise; ~**entscheidung der Geschworenen** compromise verdict; ~**formel** compromise formula; **sich auf eine** ~**formel einigen** to agree to a compromise; ~**gesetz** compromise bill; ~**haltung** compromise position; ~**kandidat** compromise candidate.
kompromißlos thoroughgoing, intransigent, uncompromising, hard-shell *(US coll.)*.
Kompromiß|losigkeit intransigence; ~**lösung** compromise agreement, settlement; **einer** ~**lösung zustimmen** to agree to a compromise; ~**plan** compromise plan; ~**politik** policy of compromise, middle-of-the-road policy; **in einer** ~**situation** over a barrel; ~**vereinbarung** compromise agreement; ~**vorschlag** suggested compromise; ~**wahlliste** mixed ticket *(US)*.
kompromittieren to compromise;
sich ~ to commit (compromise) o. s.
Kompromittierendes über j. erfahren, etw. to get s. th. on s. o. *(US)*.
kompromittiert werden, durch Fotoveröffentlichungen to be compromised by the publication of photos.
Kondensator *(el.)* capacitator, condenser;
~**lautsprecher** electrostatic loudspeaker.
kondensieren to condense, to boil down.
Kondensstreifen *(Flugzeug)* vapo(u)r trail(s), contrail(s).
Kondition *(Sport)* condition, fitness;
nicht in ~ out of condition;
keine ~ **haben** to lack stamina; **in erstklassiger** ~ **sein** to be in the pink of condition; **seine frühere** ~ **zurückgewinnen** to come back.
Konditionen conditions, terms, *(Zahlungsbedingungen)* terms of payment;
kostengünstige ~ accommodating terms; **übliche** ~ usual conditions;
~ **erfüllen** to comply with the conditions; ~ **festsetzen** to stipulate the conditions (terms);
~**kartell** conditions cartel; ~**vereinbarung** agreement on sales conditions.
konditionieren to condition.
Konditions|kauf qualified sale; ~**schwäche** lack of stamina.
Konditor cake baker, confectioner, pastry cook.
Konditorei confectionery *(US)*, candy store *(US)*, tea room, cakehouse, coffee house *(US)*, coffeeroom, café.
Konditorware confectionery, pastry.
Kondolenz|liste caller's register, book (register) of condolence; **sich in die** ~**liste eintragen** to sign the register of condolence; ~**papier** mourning paper; ~**schreiben** letter of condolence, consolatory letter.
kondolieren, jem. to offer one's sympathy to s. o.
Konfekt conserve, confection.
Konfektion ready-made things (clothing), off-the-peg clothing, reach- (hand-, *US*) me-downs.
Konfektionär ready-made clothier, slop dealer, slopseller.
konfektionieren to confection.
konfektioniert ready-made (-make), ready for wear, reach-me-down, off the peg.
Konfektions|abteilung *(Warenhaus)* ready-made department; ~**anzug** ready-made suit, reach-me-down, hand-me-down *(US)*; ~**arbeiter** slopworker; ~**artikel** ready-made clothes, confection, slopwork, slops; ~**betrieb** clothing factory; ~**geschäft** ready-made dress shop; ~**größe** standard size; ~**händler** slopseller; ~**industrie** apparel manufacture; ~**kleidung** ready-made (made-up) clothes, *(fam.)* reach- (hand-, *US*) me-downs, slopwork; **billiger** ~**laden** slopshop; ~**ware** ready-to-wear (made-up) clothes, slopwork, slops; ~**warenabteilung** ready-to-wear department.
Konferenz conference, meeting, session, symposium, parley;
außerhalb der (am Rande einer) ~ outside a conference;
bevorstehende ~ forthcoming conference; **sofort einberufene** ~ on-the-spot meeting, meeting called at short notice; **formelle** ~ formal conference; **lange** ~ long session;
~ **auf höchster Ebene** top-level (-notch) conference; ~ **am runden Tisch** round-table conference; ~ **hinter verschlossenen Türen** closed-door conference (meeting);
~ **abhalten** to hold a conference (meeting); ~ **beenden** to close a meeting; ~ **einberufen** to call (convoke, convene) a meeting; ~ **erneut einberufen** to reconvene a conference; **zu einer** ~ **zu viele Teilnehmer einladen** to overstaff a meeting; **in einer** ~ **das Wort ergreifen** to address a meeting; ~ **leiten** to preside over a conference; **bei einer** ~ **mitmachen, an einer** ~ **teilnehmen** to take part (sit, *US*) in a conference; ~ **vertagen** to adjourn a meeting;
~**ablauf** conference proceedings; ~**anlagen** conference facilities; ~**anzug** morning dress; ~**auftakt** prelude to a conference; ~**bedingungen** *(Schiffseigner)* conference terms; ~**beginn auf 10 Uhr festsetzen** to schedule a meeting for ten o'clock; ~**bericht** conference report, report of a conference; ~**beschluß** decision reached at a conference, resolution of a meeting; ~**diplomatie** diplomacy in conference, conference diplomacy; ~**dolmetscher** conference interpreter; ~**ebene** conference platform; ~**empfehlungen** conference recommendations; ~**fracht** conference rate; ~**gespräch** *(Telefon)* conference call (phone); ~**leiter** conference leader; ~**mitglied** conference member, conferencee *(US)*, *(wichtiges)* conferencier; ~**ort** meeting place; ~**plattform** conference platform; ~**programm** conference program(me); ~**saal** conference chamber (hall); ~**schaltung** intraorganizational conference, *(Rundfunk)* hookup; ~**stadium** stage of a conference; ~**teilnehmer** conference delegate (member), conferee *(US)*; ~**teilnehmer sein** to take part (sit, *US*) in a conference; ~**tisch** conference (round) table; ~**verhandlungen** conference negotiations; ~**zentrum** conference center *(US)* (centre, *Br.*); ~**zimmer** conference room, *(Hotel)* commercial room.
konferieren to deliberate, to confer, to hold a conference (meeting);
mit jem. ~ to have a talk with s. o.; **mehrere Stunden über die finanzielle Lage** ~ to confer for hours on the financial situation.
Konfession religious belief, confession, denomination, persuasion;
allen ~**en zugänglich** open to all sects.
konfessionalisieren to denominatialize.
Konfessionalisierung, Konfessionspolitik denominalization.
konfessional confessional, denominalizational.
konfessionell|e Schule denominational (parochial) school; ~**er Streit** sectarian feud.
konfessions|gebunden denominational; ~**los** undenominational.
Konfessions|proporz confessional (sectarian) arithmetic, *(pol.)* power sharing; ~**schule** denominational (confessional) school, *(durch Spenden unterhaltene)* voluntary school *(Br.)*.
Konfetti confetti;
~**parade** ticker-tape reception.
Konfirmand confirmee.
Konfirmation confirmation.
konfirmieren to confirm.
Konfiskation condemnation, seizure, forfeiture, confiscation;
~ **des Führerscheins** forfeiture of a driving licence; ~ **von Schmuggelware** seizure of contraband; ~ **des Vermögens** distraint of property.
Konfiskations|verfahren condemnation proceedings; ~**verfügung** confiscation order.
konfiskatorisch confiscatory.
konfiszierbar forfeitable, sequestrable, confiscable.
konfiszieren to condemn, to confiscate, to forfeit, to make seizure, to seize, to escheat, *(Völkerrecht)* to sequester;
jds. Führerschein ~ to forfeit s. one's driving licence; **Schmuggelware** ~ to confiscate contraband goods.
konfisziert confiscated, condemned, forfeited, seized;
vom Zoll ~ confiscated by the customs authorities;
vom Staat ~ **werden** to be forfeited by the state;
~**es Grundstück** condemned property.
Konfiszierung condemnation, confiscation, seizure, forfeiture, *(Völkerrecht)* sequestration.
Konfitüre jam, preserve, confiture *(US)*.
Konflikt conflict, clash, concurrence, controversy, dispute;
bewaffneter ~ clash of arms, armed conflict; **offener** ~ open conflict; **ökonomischer** ~ economic conflict;
langanhaltender ~ **zwischen Arbeitgebern und Arbeitnehmern** long drawn-out conflict between employers and workers;

~ **auf dem Verhandlungswege beilegen** to settle a dispute by negotiation; **in ~ geraten** to clash; **mit dem Gesetz in ~ geraten sein** to run foul of (be in trouble with) the law;
~**herd** focus of conflict; ~**situation** conflict situation; **weiteren ~stoff schaffen** to leave a further hostage to fortune.

konform conform[able], in conformity;
Ihrer Aufgabe ~ conformable to your advice;
~ **buchen** to enter (book) in conformity; **mit jem. ~ gehen** to be agreed (in agreement, in accordance) with s. o., to run with s. o., to fall into s. one's line; **in der Außenpolitik ~ gehen** to concur on questions of foreign policy; **mit jds. Büchern ~ gehen** to correspond with the books of s. o.

Konformist conformist.

konformistisch conformist;
~**e Einstellung** conformist belief.

Konfrontation crunch, clash, *(Zeuge)* confrontation;
~ **mit Dritten** collision of persons.

Konfrontationslage confrontation situation.

konfrontieren to front, to confront;
Angeklagten mit Zeugen ~ to bring the accused face to face with the witnesses; **zwei Meinungen ~** to contrast two opinions; **j. mit einem Problem ~** to leave s. o. with a problem; **zwei Zeugen ~** to confront two witnesses.

konfrontiert, mit etw. ~ sein to be beset by (faced with) s. th.; **mit etw. ~ werden** to have to face s. th.

Konfrontierung *(Zeugen)* identification parade, confrontation.

konfus confused, muddled, mixed-up;
ganz ~ all at sea;
völlig ~ sein to be in a muddle, to be getting all mixed-up, to be utterly confused;
~**e Ideen** scatterbrained ideas; ~**e Rede** confused speech; ~**es Zeug reden** to talk through one's hat.

Konfusion *(jur.)* confusion of debts, merger;
gesetzliche ~ merger by operation of law;
~ **von Grundstückslasten und -rechten** merger of charges on property.

Konfusionsrat muddled person.

kongenial congenial;
~ **sein** to be of the same high standard;
~**er Partner** ideal partner.

Konglomerat conglomerate, conglomeration, mixed bag *(fam.)*.

Kongreß congress, assembly, meeting, conference, convention *(US)*;
protektionistisch eingestellter ~ protectionist congress;
~ **auf Bundesebene** state-wide convention;
~ **abhalten** to hold a congress; **an einem ~ teilnehmen** to attend a congress;
~**abgeordneter** member of the House of Representatives, congressman; ~**abgeordneter sein** to sit in Congress *(US)*; ~**abstimmung** congressional vote; ~**ausschuß** congressional committee *(US)*; ~**bibliothek** Library of Congress *(US)*; ~**debatten** congressional debates *(US)*; ~**halle** congress hall; ~**mitglied** congressman *(US)*, member of congress *(US)*; **rangältestes ~mitglied** ranking member *(US)*; ~**partei** *(Indien)* congress party; **seinen ~sitz aufgeben und sich zurückziehen** to vacate one's seat in Congress by resignation *(US)*; ~**sitzung**, ~**tagung** meeting (sitting) of a congress; **vollständige ~sitzung** general term *(US)*; ~**stadt** convention city; ~**teilnehmer** congress member; ~**untersuchung** congressional inquiry *(US)*; ~**wahlen** congressional elections *(US)*; ~**wesen** convention business; ~**zentrum** convention center *(US)* (centre, *Br.*).

König king;
j. zum ~ krönen to crown s. o. king; ~ **sein** to wear the crown.

Königin queen;
~**witwe** queen dowager.

königlich royal, *(fig.)* fit for a king;
sich ~ amüsieren to have a whale of a time; **j. ~ belohnen** to reward s. o. richly; **j. ~ bewirten** to treat s. o. in a princely manner;
~**e Familie** royal family; ~**es Geschenk** princely gift; ~**es Privileg** royal prerogative; ~**e Zustimmung** royal assent.

Königreich kingdom, realm.

Königs|format *(Werbung)* king size; ~**hof** royal court (household); ~**mord** regicide; ~**titel** regal (royal) title; ~**tum** kingship, royalty; ~**würde** royalty.

Konjunktur market conditions (prospects), state of the economy, economic conditions, economic (upward) trend, [business] boom, business outlook (activity), *(Kreislauf der Wirtschaft)* business (trade) cycle, market swing *(US)*;
abklingende ~ faltering economy; **abschwächende ~** slowing economy; **absinkende ~** downward trend; **von Lohnerhöhungen angetriebene ~** wage-led boom; **anhaltende ~** continuing boom; **ansteigende ~** increasing economic activity; **expansive ~** boom; **glänzende ~** booming economy; **günstige ~** favo(u)rable market conditions; **inflationistische ~** inflation boom; **kleine ~** boomlet; **nachlassende ~** economic slowdown, economic slackening, slackening (declining) market; **politische ~** favo(u)rable political climate; **rezessive ~** declining economy; **rückläufige ~** business (economic) slump, slowing economy, economic dip, subsiding boom; **scheinbare ~** specious boom; **sinkende ~** recession; **steigende ~** upward trend, revival, boom; **überhitzte ~** overheated (excessive, excess) boom; **überschäumende ~** over-exuberant economy; **ungünstige ~** unfavo(u)rable business situation; **verlangsamte ~** slowdown in economic activity; **vorübergehende ~** boomlet; **schwächer werdende ~** slowing economy, economic dip; **zukünftige ~** business future;
~ **der Bauwirtschaft** building boom; ~ **auf dem Exportgebiet** export boom; ~ **in Farbfernsehgeräten** colo(u)r-set boom; ~ **im Immobiliengeschäft** boom in real estate; ~ **in der Investitionsgüterindustrie** boom in capital investment; ~ **im Konsumgüterbereich** consumer boom; ~ **in der Schiffsbauindustrie** business condition in the shipbuilding industry, shipbuilding boom; **rückläufige ~ der Schiffsbauindustrie** shipping slump; ~ **auf dem Wohnungsbausektor** upsurge in housing;
[überhitzte] ~ abkühlen to cool off an [overheated] economy; ~ **anheizen** to heat up the economy; ~ **ankurbeln** to turn the economy around, to enliven business; ~ **wieder ankurbeln** to turn the economy back up again; ~ **anregen** to stimulate business activity; ~ **ausnutzen** to take advantage of the economic situation; ~ **beeinflussen** to affect the economy; ~ **in zunehmendem Maße negativ beeinflussen** to take a bigger bite out of the economy; ~ **in den Griff bekommen** to have a grip on (come to grips with) the economy; ~ **beleben** to improve the economic conditions, to revive economic activity; **hinreichend ~ bremsen** to take enough of the pep out of the economy; ~ **wieder zum Anlauf bringen** to get the economy back on the tracks; ~ **auf größeres Tempo bringen** to ride the economy at full gallop; ~ **dämpfen** to place a check on (restrain, curb) the boom; ~ **eindämmen** to slow down the economy; ~ **entspannen** to ease the economic situation; ~ **mit einem weiteren kleinen Trick am Leben erhalten** to keep the economy jogging along by another little fix; ~ **fördern** to stimulate (pep up) economic activity; ~ **im Griff haben** to handle the economy; ~ **in Grenzen halten** to keep the economy on the straight and narrow; ~ **gerade noch im Schwung halten** to keep the economy ticking over; ~ **im Zaum halten** to keep the economy on the straight and narrow; ~ **intensivieren** to stimulate business (economic) activity; **mit Hilfe der Gewerkschaften die ~ zugrunde richten können** to have the union muscle to wreck the economy; ~ **auf Hochtouren laufen lassen** to keep the economy in high gear; ~ **steuern** to handle (manage) the economy; ~ **stützen** to underpin the economy; **einer erwarteten ~ im voraus Rechnung tragen** to discount the market; ~ **überhitzen** to overtake (overheat) the boom, to overheat the economic activity; ~ **verlangsamen** to slow economy; **der ~ eine Spritze verpassen** to give the economy a shot in the arm; ~ **zügeln** to curb the boom, to hold the economy back.

konjunkturabhängig cyclical;
~**e Industrie** cyclical industry.

Konjunktur|abkühlung slackening of the economic trend, cooling of the economy, cyclical slowdown; ~**abkühlung herbeiführen** to cool the economy; ~**ablauf** business (economic) cycle; ~**abschwächung** downward business trend, slackening of the economic trend, economic slowdown, weakness of economic activity, softening in business conditions, falloff in the economy; ~**abschwung** downward swing, [cyclical] downturn, cyclical downswing, recession; ~**analyse** trend (business-cycle, business, cyclical, economic) analysis; ~**analytiker** business analyst; ~**änderung** cyclical trend, change in the economic activities, turn in the market.

konjunkturanfällig sensitive to business movements.

Konjunktur|ankurbelung enlivening of business, economic stimulation; ~**ankurbelungspaket** economic package; **erster ~anlauf** first flutter of an upturn; ~**anlauf herbeiführen** to get the economy on the tracks; ~**anpassung** business-cycle adjustment; **allmähliche ~anpassung** rolling adjustment; ~**anregung** stimulation of business activity, cyclical stimulation; ~**anreiz** economic stimulus, economic stimulation; ~**anspannung** economic strain.

Konjunkturanstieg upward business trend, cyclical recovery, economic upswing, business progress, upturn in business

[cycle], economic recovery (upswing), upward business trend, upswing, uplift, trend increase, economic upturn, growth in the economy, up in business activity;
leichter ~ gradual pickup in industrial activity; **maßvoller** ~ modest advance in business; **verlangsamter** ~ slowdown in the recovery.

Konjunktur|anstoß geben to give the economy a push; ~**anzeichen** economic indicator; ~**atmosphäre** economic atmosphere.

Konjunkturaufschwung business revival, business upturn, economic rebound, upward business trend, upswing, upturn in the business cycle, cyclical upswing, trade revival, economic boom (recovery);
ausfuhrbestimmter ~ export-led recovery; **saisonbedingter** ~ seasonal upward trend; **selbstbewirkter** ~ homemade upswing; ~ **feststellen** to report a marked improvement in business; ~ **intensivieren** to strengthen the cyclical upswing.

Konjunktur|auftrieb business prosperity, upward phase, trade revival; ~**auftriebe und** ~**rückgänge** cyclical ups and downs; **im** ~**auftrieb sein** to be on the upgrade; ~**ausgleich** levelling out of business fluctuations, seasonal adjustment; ~**ausgleichsrücklage** countercyclical reserve; ~**aussichten** business outlook (prospects), cyclical prospects, prospects of the market (of the economy), economic aspects (prospects), market outlook (conditions); **gute** ~**aussichten** bright economic outlook; ~**ausweitung** business expansion; ~**barometer** trade (business) barometer, business (economic) indicator, indicator of business.

konjunkturbedingt cycle-induced, cyclically induced, for cyclical reasons;
~**e Arbeitslosigkeit** cyclical unemployment; ~**er Nachfragerückgang in Stahl** cyclical fall in steel demand; ~**er Preisanstieg** cyclical price increase; ~**e Produktionssteigerung** cyclical improvement in production.

Konjunktur|bedingungen boom (business) conditions; **verzerrte** ~**bedingungen** competitive distortions; ~**beeinflussung** economic influences; ~**befragung** anticipation survey; ~**beherrschung** grip on the economy; ~**belebung** increase in business activity, economic recovery (revival, upturn), business (cyclical) recovery; ~**beobachter**, ~**berater** economic forecaster, economic pundit, business analyst; ~**beobachtung** economic forecasting; ~**beratungsgremium** economic policy team; ~**bericht** business forecast, market (economic) report, report on business; ~**beruhigung** easing of cyclical strains; ~**besserung** business upturn, economic recovery, trade revival.

konjunkturbestimmend cyclical.

Konjunkturbeurteilung business (economic) forecasting.

Konjunkturbewegung cyclical movement;
rückläufige ~ business downturn, decline in economic activity; **verlangsamte** ~ business slowdown;
zyklische ~ **abschaffen** to buck the stop-go business cycle.

Konjunktur|bild economic (business) picture; ~**bremse zurückhaltend anwenden** to ease the economic brakes.

konjunkturdämpfende Maßnahmen countercyclical measures.

Konjunktur|dämpfung curbing the boom; ~**dämpfung auf einzelnen Gebieten** rolling adjustment; ~**dämpfungsmaßnahmen** countercyclical measures; ~**daten** economic data, economic information; ~**debatte** economic [policy] debate, discussion of cyclical questions; ~**diagnose** market (trend, business-cycle, cyclical) analysis; ~**diagnostiker** market analyst; ~**drosselung** economic throttle; ~**dynamik** business-cycle dynamics; ~**einbruch** economic dip; **scharfer** ~**einbruch** sharp decline in economic activity; **mit dem** ~**einbruch fertig werden** to buck the business cycle *(US)*; ~**einflüsse** cyclical influences; **negative** ~**einwirkung** disincentive to business.

konjunkturell cyclical, economic;
sich ~ **auswirken** to tell on the economy; **sich** ~ **erweitern** to show an upward tendency; **sich** ~ **kaum mehr erweitern** to show hardly any further upward trend;
~**e Abschwächungen erfahren** to show a downward trend of economic activity; ~**e Aktivität** economic activity; ~**er Anstieg** upward trend; ~**e Anstrengungen** cyclical strains; ~**e Arbeitslosigkeit** cyclical unemployment; ~**er Aufschwung** cyclical upswing; ~**er Auftrieb** cyclical uptrend, business prosperity, trade revival, upswing; ~**en Auftrieb haben** to boom; ~**e Auftriebskräfte** business prosperity; ~**e Auftriebstendenz** upward (boom) trend; ~**e Aufwärtsbewegung** cyclical upward movement, up-cycle; ~**e Aufwärtstendenz** boom trend; ~**e Ausweitung** expansive trend; ~**e Auswirkungen** economic implications; ~**e Belebung** economic recovery (revival, activity), business recovery; ~**e Besserung** cyclical improvement; ~**e Bremse** drag on the recovery; **ausreichende** ~**e Bremsen betätigen** to take enough of the pep out of the economy; ~**e Entwicklung** economic (cyclical) trend, business tendencies; ~**e Entwicklungstendenzen** trends in the economy; ~**e Erholung** booming recovery; ~**e Faktoren** cyclical factors; ~**e Fehlanpassung** cyclical maladjustment; ~**e Festigkeit** strength of the economy; ~**e Flautenbewegung** sluggish pace of business; ~**e Fortschritte machen** to move further along the recovery track; ~**e Initialzündung** pump priming *(US)*; ~**es Klima** economic temperature (climate); ~**en Niedergang erleben** to be on the downgrade; ~**e Preissteigerung** cyclical rise in prices; ~ **unbeeinflußbarer Rest an Arbeitslosen** hard core of unemployment; ~**er Rückgang** cyclical decline; ~**e Schwankungen** market (cyclical) fluctuations, cyclical irregularity; ~**e Situation** business situation; ~**e Stagnation** economic stagnation; ~**e Strömungen** trends in the economy; ~**e Talfahrt** downtrend in economic activity; ~**e Talfahrt auffangen** to cushion the downswing; ~**e Tatsachen ans Tageslicht bringen** to nose out economic truths; ~**e Tendenz** economic trend, cyclical (business) tendency; ~**e Tendenzänderung** changes in the underlying trend; ~**e Ungewißheit** economic uncertainty; ~**e Veränderung** economic change; ~**e Verschlechterung** economic downturn; **auf** ~**e Verschlechterungen empfindlich reagieren** to be sensitive to downturns; ~**er Wandel** change in the economic activities; ~**e Wechselphasen** alternating phases of the cyclical trend; ~**er Wellenberg** peak time; ~**er Wendepunkt** business cycle turning, business turning point.

konjunkturempfindlich sensitive to business movements (economic fluctuations);
~**e Industrie** cyclical industry.

Konjunktur|empfindlichkeit sensitivity to economic (business) fluctuations; ~**entspannung** easing of cyclical conditions; ~**entspannung herbeiführen** to ease the economic situation; ~**entwicklung** economic development (trend), business formation, cyclical trend, market trend, trend of business; **sich in kumulierender Weise negativ auf die** ~**entwicklung auswirken** to exert cumulative downward pressure on economic activity; **der** ~**entwicklung entgehen** to buck the trend.

Konjunkturerholung pickup in economic activity, cyclical recovery;
höchstmögliche ~ maxirecovery; **konsumbedingte** ~ consumerled recovery; **rückläufige** ~ shortfall in the recovery.

Konjunktur|ermattungstendenzen shakeout tendency; ~**erwartung** expected trend of the market, business outlook (prospects); ~**fachmann** expert on business cycles; ~**faktoren** cyclical factors; ~**flaute** slack in the economy, economic slackening, flat economy, recession of business activity; ~**förderung** stimulation of business activity, cyclical stimulation; ~**förderungsprogramm** government program(me) to stimulate economic activity; ~**forscher** economic researcher, market research worker; ~**forschung** market (business, economic) research; ~**forschungsabteilung** economic research division; ~**forschungsinstitut** economic (business) research institute; ~**gebiet** cyclical field.

konjunkturgerecht, als ~ **anzusehen sein** to be in line with cyclical policy.

Konjunktur|geschwindigkeit business tempo; **sein gebrechliches Staatsschiff in ruhige** ~**gewässer steuern** to see one's frail craft through to calmer economic waters; ~**gewinn** boom (competitive, *US*) profit; ~**horizont** economic horizon; ~**horizont aufhellen** to lighten the economic horizon; ~**impuls** stimulation of business activity; ~**indikator** economic indicator, business cycle indicator; **nachhinkender** ~**indikator** lagging indicator; ~**institut** institute for business-cycle research, business research institute, economic research organization, market researcher, National Institute of Economic and Social Research *(Br.)*; ~**jahr** boom year; ~**jahre** years of prosperity.

Konjunkturklima business (economic) climate;
verschlechtertes ~ worsening of the economic climate;
~ **stören** to stir up the economic waters.

Konjunktur|krankheiten economic ills; ~**krise** trade depression, economic crisis; ~**kurve** cyclical (economic) trend; ~**kurve einbeulen** to put a big dent in the economy; ~**lage** market conditions, economic (cyclical) situation, state (trend) of the market (economy), economic situation; **in die ausgedörrte** ~**landschaft hineinpumpen** to pump into the arid economic landscape; ~**leistung** economic performance; ~**lenkung** handling of the economy, economic management, cycle riding; ~**maßnahmen** economic policy measures; ~**maßnahmen auf dem Gebiet der Einkommenspolitik** national incomes policy; ~**modell** typical boom; ~**mulde** depression low, dip in business, recession trough; **sich von der ~mulde im Versicherungsgeschäft erholen** to recover from the trough in the underwriting cycle; ~**nachrichten** economic news.

konjunkturneutral sein to have no effect on the cyclical trend.

Konjunktur|niveau level of economic activity; **hohes ~niveau aufrechterhalten** to keep the economy running at a high level; ~**optimismus** optimistic business outlook, business confidence; ~**periode** trade-cycle period, period of prosperity, business boom, boom (trend, economic) period, market swing, swing in the business cycle *(US)*; **rückläufige ~periode** slowdown period.

Konjunkturphase business cycle, boom period;
abgeschwächte ~ period of decline in economic activity; **rückläufige ~** economic downswing, downward phase (swing), slump period;
sich in einer ~ befinden to experience a boom.

Konjunkturplanung cyclical budgeting.

Konjunkturpolitik cyclical (economic) policy, stabilization policy;
antizyklische ~ compensatory fiscal policy; **langfristige ~** economic strategy; **monetäre ~** countercyclical monetary policy; **sektorale ~** economics of industrial organization; **antizyklische ~ mittels steuerpolitischer Maßnahmen** functional finance;
~ in den Griff bekommen to keep tabs on the state of the economy; **stabile ~ betreiben** to stabilize the economy; **antiinflationistische Maßnahmen in der ~ ergreifen** to build antiinflationary forces into the economy; **ausgeglichene ~ treiben** to remain on an even keel.

Konjunkturpolitiker economic policymaker, forecaster, market researcher, National Bureau economist *(US)*.

konjunkturpolitisch cyclical, economic;
~ unerwünscht cyclically undesirable;
~er Aktivismus economic policy activism; **~e Entschlüsse** anticyclical (cyclical) policy resolutions; **~e Erwägungen** cyclical considerations; **aus ~en Gründen** for anticyclical (cyclical) reasons; **~e Lage** cyclical situation; **~e Maßnahmen** economic policy measures; **~er Mitarbeiter** economic policy official; **~e Überlegungen** cyclical considerations; **~e Verhandlungspunkte** economic-policy agenda; **~es Ziel** economic policy goal.

Konjunktur|problem economic (cyclical) problem; ~**prognose** business forecast (prediction, outlook), economic forecasting, outlook for the economy; **~prognose vornehmen** to forecast the course of business; ~**prognostiker** business forecaster, prognosticator, market researcher; ~**programm** business-boosting program(me), [anti]cyclical program(me); ~**rate** trend rate.

konjunkturreagibel sensitive to economic fluctuation (business movements).

Konjunkturregulativ regulator of the economy, economic regulator.

konjunkturrhythmisch cyclical.

Konjunktur|rhythmus business cycle; ~**risiko** market (economic) risk; ~**ritter** timeserver, *(pol.)* opportunist, henchman, carpetbagger.

Konjunkturrückgang slump in trade, regressive business trend, business slump, downtrend, decline in prosperity, recession, [market] depression, economic (business) down-turn, down cycle, cyclical fall, cyclical decline, economic decline, economic setback;
kopfsprungartiger ~ headlong dive into a slump;
anhaltender ~ in der Bauindustrie continuing slump in construction;
~ erfahren to show a depression.

Konjunktur|rückschlag recession, economic dip, business (economic) setback, slowdown in economic activity; ~**sachverständiger** economic expert, market researcher, National Bureau economist *(US)*; ~**schatten** seamy side of business activities, economic drawback; ~**schema** cyclical pattern; **zyklische ~schrumpfung** cyclical contraction of general business activity; ~**schwäche** cyclical decline; ~**schwankungen** cyclical fluctuations [in business]; ~**sensibilität** sensivity to economic fluctuations; ~**spritze** pump priming *(US)*, shot in the arm *(coll.)*; ~**stabilisierung** stabilization of the economy; ~**stabilität** economic stability; ~**statistik** economic statistics; ~**steuerer** economic manager, cycle rider.

Konjunktursteuerung handling of the economy, economic management, cycle riding;
~ unter Inkaufnahme von Risiken economic brinkmanship;
~ beherrschen to handle the economy; **~ mit dem Ziel steigender Nachfrage nach Arbeitsplätzen vornehmen** to run the economy at a high level of job-creating demand.

Konjunktur|stimulus stimulation of business activity, cyclical stimulation; ~**stockung** economic slowdown; ~**studie** business-cycle study; ~**sturz** business slump, cyclical fall, economic tailspin; ~**stützung** under-pinning of the economy; ~**stützungsmaßnahmen** support for economic activity; ~**tal** recession trough, economic dip; ~**tempo** pace of business activity, business tempo; **~tempo verlangsamen** to slow down the pace of business; ~**tendenz** cyclical trend; **allgemeine ~tendenz** general trend of business conditions; **steigende ~tendenz** upward trend; ~**terminologie** business-cycle terminology; ~**test** market research; ~**theoretiker** market research worker, forecaster, National Bureau economist *(US)*; ~**theorie** theory of economic trends; ~**therapie** compensatory fiscal policy, countercyclical compensatory government policy; ~**tief** depression low (level), economic trough; ~**trend** economic trend; ~**überhitzung** economic overheating, overtaxing (overtaking, overheating) of the boom; ~**umbruch** turn in the market; **~umbruch auf der ganzen Linie** world-wide slump; ~**umschwung** break in the economic trend, market (cyclical) swing *(US)*.

konjunkturunempfindlich resistant to the slowdown.

Konjunktur|unempfindlichkeit resistance to the slowdown; ~**unsicherheit** economic uncertainty.

konjunkturunwirksame Maßnahmen cyclical maladjustment.

Konjunktur|veränderung business change; ~**verbesserung** progress of business; ~**verhältnisziffern** boom proportions; ~**verkauf** seasonal sale; ~**verlangsamung** economic (business) slowdown, slowing of the economy; **~verlangsamung bis zum Stillstand voraussagen** to predict a marginal slowdown; ~**verlauf** path of the economy, economic trend (course), cyclical trend, cyclical course, business (economic) cycle; **zyklischer ~verlauf** cyclical movement; **~verlauf im Versicherungsgeschäft** underwriting cycle; ~**verschlechterung** worsening in business, worsening of the economy; ~**vorhersage**, ~**vorschau** forecast budget, economic forecasting (forecast); ~**welle** strength of the economy; ~**wende** economic turnaround, cyclical swing *(US)*, market swing *(US)*; ~**ziffern** economic indices; ~**zügelung** curbing of the boom; ~**zusammenbruch** complete slump; **sich weiter dem ~zusammenbruch nähern** to push the economy further towards a slump; ~**zuschlag** cyclical surtax.

Konjunkturzyklus trade (economic, business) cycle, cycle of economy;
rückläufiger ~ down cycle;
~ mit den Augen eines Arbeitszeitkontrolleurs beobachten to have a timekeeping attitude towards economic cycles.

Konklave conclave.

konkludent|es Eingeständnis implied admission; **~ geschlossener Vertrag** implied contract.

Konkordat concordat.

konkret concrete, tangible, real, *(Idee)* precise, definite, exact;
ganz ~ gesprochen in terms of facts;
sich ~ ausdrücken to be explicit;
~e Angaben definite data; **~er Anlaß** exact cause; **~e Anweisungen** exact directions; **~er Beweis** tangible proof; **~e Ergebnisse** tangible results; **~er Fall** concrete (individual) case; **~e Formen annehmen** to crystallize, to materialize; **~e Form geben** to embody, to give shape to; **~er Schaden** special damage, actual loss; **im ~en Sinn** in the literal sense.

konkretisieren to appropriate, to concretize, to concrete;
Eigentum ~ to appropriate goods to the contract; **sich ~** *(Forderung)* to crystallize.

konkretisiert appropriated.

Konkretisierung concretization, application, appropriation, *(Forderung)* crystallization;
~ des Eigentums appropriation to the contract; **~ von Gattungsschulden** appropriation of unascertained goods.

Konkubinat illicit cohabitation, cohabination in state of adultery, concubinage.

Konkurrent competitor, rival [trader], rival in business, *(Wettbewerb)* contestant;
preisdrückender ~ cut-price competitor;
als ~ auftreten to set up in competion; **~en ausstechen** to flog a competitor; **~en ausschalten** to eliminate a competitor; **als ~en gegenüberstehen** to pit against each other; **~en schlagen** to make up a competitor; **seinen ~en noch immer gewachsen sein** to be still up to one's competitors; **seine ~en überflügeln** to gain an advantage over (get the start of) one's competitors, to

transcend one's competitors; **~en unterbieten** to undercut a competitor; **~en aus der Firma verdrängen** to oust a rival from office.

Konkurrenz competition, [trade] rivalry, emulation, *(Konkurrenten)* competitors, rivals in business, competing producers; **außer ~** out of competition, not competing, unrival(l)ed; **ausländische ~** foreign competition; **die ~** the other shop; **halsabschneiderische ~** cutthroat competition; **inländische ~** domestic competition; **lebhafte ~** active competition; **meine ~** my competitors in trade; **mögliche ~** potential competition; **monopolistische ~** monopolistic competition; **mörderische ~** cutthroat competition; **offene ~** active competition; **preisdrückende (preisunterbietende) ~** cut-price competitor (competition); **ruinöse ~** destructive (ruinous, cutthroat) competition; **scharfe ~** keen (severe) competition; **schwache ~** weak competition; **starke ~** strong competition; **unlautere ~** fraudulent (mean) competition, unfair competition in trade; **wirksame ~** workable competition *(US)*;

~ der Markenartikel brand competition; **~ mittels niedriger Preise** low-price competition;

zur ~ abwandern to switch to a rival firm; **gegen eine ~ ankämpfen (aufkommen)** to contend with competition; **~ anschwärzen** to disparage a competitor; **es mit der ~ aufnehmen** to sustain (cope with) competition; **~ ausschalten** to eliminate competition; **der ~ die Spitze bieten** to defy competition; **der ~ die Stirn bieten** to meet competition; **sich gegen die ~ im Markt durchsetzen** to hold one's own in competitive markets; **ausländische ~ eindämmen** to curb foreign competition; **~ fürchten** to be afraid of competition; **der ~ das Nachsehen geben** to leave the competitors behind; **der ~ Einhalt gebieten** to check competition; **zur ~ gehen** to go over to the other side; **mit der ~ gleichziehen** to catch up with the competitors; **es mit der ~ zu tun haben** to meet with competition; **es mit der ~ aufnehmen können** to be able to cope with (match) competition; **keine ~ aufkommen lassen** to defy competition; **sich [gegenseitig] ~ machen** to set up a competition, to compete with each other; **~ schlagen** to make up on a competitor; **einheimische Erzeugnisse durch Zollschranken vor ausländischer ~ schützen** to protect domestic products from foreign competition by trade barriers; **scharfer ~ ausgesetzt sein** to be exposed to severe competition, to be up against stiff competition; **seiner ~ noch immer gewachsen sein** to be still up with one's competitors; **der ~ immer um eine Nasenlänge voraus sein** to be one jump ahead of one's competitors; **mit jem. in ~ stehen** to be in competition with s. o.; **mit jem. in ~ treten** to enter into rivalry (competition) with s. o.; **über eine erfolglose ~ triumphieren** to crow over an unsuccessful rival; **der ~ Einhalt tun** to check competition; **gesamte ~ überflügeln (übertreffen)** to lead all competitors, to excel all one's rivals; **seine ~ überflügeln** to get the jump on one's competitors; **~ unterbieten** to undersell (undercut) competitors; **vor der ~ verbergen** to palm *(sl.)*; **~ aus dem Markt verdrängen** to put competitors out of business; **jem. gebührende ~ verschaffen** to give s. o. a good run for his money; **der ~ zuvorkommen** to forestall a competitor;

~angebot competitive bid (quotation), competing offer,rival supply, rival bid; **~angriff** competitive assault; **~anschwärzung** trade disparagement, slander of title; **~artikel** competitive product; **~auslese** [competitive] selection; **~ausschaltung** elimination of competitors; **~ausschluß** competition clause; **~ausschreibung** invitation to tender (of tenders); **~ausschreibung veranstalten** to put up for competition; **~banken** banking rivals, rival banks; **~bedingungen** competitive conditions; **~bekämpfung** interference with competitors; **~beschränkungen** restraint of trade (competition); **~betrieb** rival plant (manufacturer), rival business concern, competitor, competitive enterprise, competing producer (outfit); **~betrieb eröffnen** to set up a business in competition; **~drohung** competitive threat; **~druck** pressure (stress) of competition, competitive pressure; **~einstellung** competitive spirit; **~erzeugnisse** competing (competitive) products, competitive articles (line, brand, products), competitor's goods, rival products, rival commodities; **~erzeugnisse madig machen** to start a whispering campaign against s. one's products; **~fabrikat** rival product, competitive material.

konkurrenzfähig able to compete (to meet competition), competitive, *(Ware)* marketable;

preislich ~ price-competitive;

auf dem Exportmarkt ~ bleiben to face world competition for export markets; **~ sein** to meet competition; **im Preis ~ sein** to be competitively priced.

Konkurrenzfähigkeit competitive power (ability, capacity, position), competitiveness.

Konkurrenzfirma competitor, competing (competitive) firm, rival company (firm), business rival, *(Fabrikation)* competing producer, competing outfit, competing corporation *(US)*;

~ mit unanständigen Geschäftsmethoden cutthroat competitor; **~ gründen** to set up a business in competition; **~ vom Markt verdrängen** to drive a competitor out of business.

Konkurrenz|geschäft rival business (firm, shop), competing business; **~geschäft eröffnen** to start in opposition to s. o.; **~gesellschaft** competing corporation, rival company (plant); **~gesinnung** competitive spirit; **~gewerbe** competitive industries; **~gründe** competitive reasons; **Unterbieten aus ~gründen** squeeze pricing *(US)*; **~industrien** competitive industries; **~kampf** competitive thrust, business struggle, interference with competitors, economic struggle, trade rivalry; **erbarmungsloser ~kampf** rat race; **weltoffener wirtschaftlicher ~kampf** economic cutthroat competition; **~klausel** competition (restraint) clause, restrictive covenant, stipulation in restraint of trade; **~lage** competitive situation; **ungleiche ~lage** competitive imbalance; **~land** competing country; **~lohn** competitive wage.

konkurrenzlos unrivalled, without competition, matchless, unmatched, inapproachable;

~ dastehen to defy all competition, to be far ahead of one's competitors.

Konkurrenz|losigkeit inapproachability, matchlessness; **~marken** competing brands; **~maßnahmen** competitive moves; **~möglichkeiten** potential competition; **~neid** professional jealousy; **~preis** competitor's (competitive) price; **~problem** competitive problem; **~programm** *(Rundfunk)* opposite program(me); **~punkt** *(Spediteur)* competition point; **~stärke** power to compete; **~streit zweier Gewerkschaften** rival union dispute; **~tarif** competitive rate; **~tätigkeit** competitive activity; **eifrige ~tätigkeit** competitive zeal.

konkurrenzunfähig unable cutting, to compete.

Konkurrenz|unterbietung cutting, price squeezing *(US)*; **~unternehmen** business rival, rival [in] business, competitor; **gegen ~unternehmen aufkommen müssen** to contend with competition.

Konkurrenzverbot restraint of trade (competition), exclusivity stipulation *(Br.)*;

auf bestimmte Berufe beschränktes (beruflich oder geographisch abgegrenztes) ~ special restraint of trade; **überall gültiges ~** general restraint of trade; **zeitweiliges ~** bargain or contract in restraint of trade.

Konkurrenz|vereinbarung restrictive covenant, restraint agreement; **~verhältnisse** competitive conditions; **ungleiches ~verhältnis** competitive imbalance; **~verkehr** competitive traffic; **~vertrag** *(Eisenbahn)* competitive tariff; **~vorteil** competitive advantage; **~ware** competing merchandise, competitor's goods; **~ware anschwärzen** to run down (disparage) the goods of a competitor; **~werbung** competitive advertising; **~wirtschaft** competitive economy.

konkurrieren to compete, to rival;

mit jem. ~ to stand (be) in competition with s. o.; **mit anderen Ländern ~** to compete with other countries; **mit einem Preis ~** to compete with a price; **mit einem Produkt ~** to rival a product; **mit den Besten ~ können** to hold one's own with the best.

konkurrierend competing, competitive, concurrent;

nicht ~ noncompeting;

~e Ansprüche concurrent claims; **~es Gesetz** conflicting law; **~e Interessen** clashing interests; **~es Verschulden** contributory negligence.

Konkurs bankruptcy, [business] failure, wall, *(Br.)*, *(Konkursmasse)* bankrupt estate;

in ~ bankrupt, under receivership; **kurz vor dem ~** faced with (verging on) bankruptcy;

~e *(Zeitung)* black list;

von den Gläubigern beantragter ~ involuntary bankruptcy *(US)*; **betrügerischer ~** fraudulent bankruptcy; **durch Gläubigerantrag herbeigeführter ~** involuntary bankruptcy; **leichtsinniger ~** wilful bankruptcy; **unverschuldeter ~** simple bankruptcy;

~ auf Antrag des Konkursschuldners voluntary bankruptcy *(US)*; **~ mit Inanspruchnahme des Bürgen** open insolvency;

~ abwenden to avoid bankruptcy proceedings; **~ abwickeln** to administer a bankrupt's estate, to liquidate a bankrupt's affairs; **seinen ~ anmelden** to file one's petition (a declaration of bankruptcy), to file a petition in voluntary bankruptcy *(US)*, to declare o. s. a bankrupt, to strike a docket, to go through the hoops, to pay ten shillings in the pound; **seine Forderung zum ~ anmelden** to prove one's claim in bankruptcy; **~ aufheben** to terminate (stop) bankruptcy proceedings; **~ gegen j. beantragen** to bring bankruptcy proceedings against s. o.; **Rechtswirkungen eines ~es beilegen** to attach the incidents of a bankrupt; **~ einstellen** to terminate (close) bankruptcy proceedings; **über jds. Vermögen den ~ erklären** to declare (adjudicate) s. o. judicially to be a bankrupt; **~ eröffnen** to institute bankruptcy proceedings; **schließlich zum ~ führen** to culminate in bankruptcy; **in ~ gehen (geraten)** to go (become) bankrupt, to fail, to wind up *(US)*, to become insolvent, to go to the wall *(Br.)*; **~ machen** to be in Queer Street *(Br.)*, to go to the wall *(Br.)*, to go in bankruptcy (receivership), to wind up *(US)*; **im ~ sein** to be bankrupt; **vor einem ~ stehen** to be faced with bankruptcy; **kurz vor dem ~ stehen** to totter on the verge of bankruptcy; **in der Liste der ~e stehen** to have one's name (appear) in the gazette; **j. zum ~ treiben** to force (throw) s. o. into bankruptcy, to drive s. o. to the wall *(Br.)*; **seinen Schuldner in den ~ treiben** to throw a debtor into bankruptcy; **über j. den ~ verhängen** to declare s. o. judicially to be bankrupt, to adjudicate (adjudge) s. o. [to be] bankrupt; **~ vermeiden** to stave off bankruptcy; **gerade noch am ~ vorbeisteuern** to bring back from the brink of bankruptcy; **auf den ~ zusteuern** to drift towards bankruptcy, to head for bankruptcy, to steer near receivership; **j. zum ~ zwingen** to force s. o. into bankruptcy;

~ablauf procedure in bankruptcy; **~abwendung** avoidance of bankruptcy proceedings; **~abwicklung** administration of a bankrupt's estate; **~abwicklungsbilanz** realization and liquidation statement, statutory statement of affairs *(Br.)*, schedule of a bankrupt's debts *(US)*; **~androhung** bankruptcy notice; **~androhung mit Zahlungsaufforderung** judgment (debtor) summons *(Br.)*; **Schuldner zur Zahlung unter ~androhung auffordern** to serve a bankruptcy notice on a debtor; **~anmeldegebühr** filing costs; **~anmeldung** declaration of (petition in) bankruptcy, *(durch Gemeinschuldner)* voluntary petition *(US)*; **~anmeldung vornehmen** to file one's schedule *(US)* (a declaration of bankruptcy); **auf alle ~ansprüche verzichten** to give up all claims upon a bankrupt.

Konkursantrag bankruptcy petition, [filing of a] petition in bankruptcy;

von den Gläubigern gestellter ~ creditors' petition, petition for adjudication; **selbst gestellter ~** voluntary petition *(US)*;

~ mangels Masse abweisen to dismiss a petition on cause that the assets will be exhausted by costs; **über einen ~ noch nicht entscheiden** to adjourn a petition in bankrupty; **~ des Schuldners genehmigen** to adjudicate (adjudge) to be a bankrupt; **~ stellen** to file one's petition (a declaration of bankruptcy), to file a bankruptcy (Bankruptcy Act) petition (a petition in voluntary bankruptcy, *US*); **~ gegen j. stellen** to bring bankruptcy proceedings against s. o.

Konkurs|anzeige bankruptcy notice; **~aufhebung** discharge of a bankrupt.

Konkursaufhebungs|antrag petition for discharge of a bankrupt *(US)*; **~bescheid** bankrupt's certificate, order of discharge *(Br.)*; **~beschluß** order of *(Br.)* (for, *US*) discharge; **~beschluß annullieren** to revoke an order of *(Br.)* (for, *US*) discharge.

Konkurs|ausschüttung division of a bankrupt's estate; **~beendigung** closing of bankruptcy proceedings; **~begehren** bankruptcy petition; **~beginn** commencement of a bankruptcy; **~beschlag** bankruptcy inhibition; **~beschluß** receiving (winding up, *US*) order; **~bestimmungen** bankruptcy rules; **~beteiligter** party in interest; **~bilanz** realization and liquidation statement, statutory statement of affairs *(Br.)*, schedule of a bankrupt's debts *(US)*; **~bilanz erstellen** to file a declaration of bankruptcy, to file one's schedule *(US)*; **~delikt** criminal offence under bankruptcy law, bankruptcy offence, act of bankruptcy, fraudulent alienation (conveyance, preference); **~dividende** quota, dividend of a bankrupt's estate; **~einstellung** closing of bankruptcy proceedings; **~einstellungsbeschluß** order of *(Br.)* (for, *US*) discharge.

Konkurserklärung [filing of a] petition in (declaration of) bankruptcy, *(durch das Gericht)* adjudication in bankruptcy; **selbst beantragte ~** voluntary bankruptcy *(US)*;

jem. eine ~ zustellen to serve s. o. with a bankruptcy notice.

Konkurseröffnung adjudication in bankruptcy, receiving order *(Br.)*;

~ aufheben to annul an adjudication; **~ beantragen** *(Schuldner)* to file a petition; **~ gegen j. beantragen** bring bankruptcy proceedings (present a petition) against s. o.; **Antrag auf ~ stellen** to file one's petition (a declaration of bankruptcy).

Konkurseröffnungsantrag [filing of a] petition in bankruptcy, bankruptcy petition, *(Gläubigerantrag)* petition for adjudication;

~ stellen to file one's petition (a declaration in bankruptcy), to strike a docket *(Br.)*.

Konkurseröffnungsbeschluß adjudication order, winding-up order *(US)*, adjudication of (decree in) bankruptcy, decree of adjudication;

~ gegen Gesamtschuldner joint fiat; **vorläufiger ~** receiving order *(Br.)*, winding-up order;

~ mit Erfolg anfechten to comply with a bankruptcy notice; **~ zugestellt erhalten** to be served with a bankruptcy notice; **~ erlassen** to sign a decree in adjudication, to make an order for the winding up *(Br.)*; **~ zustellen** to serve with a bankruptcy notice.

Konkurseröffnungs|termin date of adjudication; **~verfahren** [involuntary] bankruptcy proceedings.

konkursfähig, für ~ erklären to adjudicate s. o. judicially to be a bankrupt.

Konkursfall bankruptcy case;

~ amtlich bekanntgeben to gazette a case of bankruptcy; **als ~ veröffentlicht werden** to appear in the gazette, *(Makler)* to be hammered *(Br.)*.

Konkursforderung claim provable in bankruptcy;

anerkannte ~ proved debt (claim); **anmeldefähige ~** provable claim (debt); **bevorrechtigte ~** preferential (preferred, *US*, privileged) debt, privileged claim; **nicht bevorrechtigte ~** unsecured debt; **nicht beweisfähige ~** nonprovable claim; **festgestellte ~** debt proved in proceedings of bankruptcy, proved debt; **gesicherte ~** secured claim *(US)*; **gewöhnliche ~** simple debts; **im Range nachgehende (nachrangige) ~** deferred debt; **nicht nachweisbare ~** nonprovable claim;

~ anerkennen to allow a bankruptcy claim; **~ anmelden** to file a bankruptcy claim, to prove a claim in bankruptcy (against the estate), to turn in a proof of debt; **nach Verwertung der Sicherheit seine restliche ~ anmelden** *(aussonderungsberechtigter Gläubiger)* to prove for the balance of one's debt; **als ~ anerkannt sein** to have been admitted provable in bankruptcy; **als bevorrechtigte ~ behandelt werden** to rank as preferred debt.

konkursfreies Vermögen property exempt from distribution in bankruptcy, unattachable property.

Konkurs|gefahr danger of bankruptcy; **~gegenstände** assets of a bankrupt's estate, bankruptcy subjects; **~gericht** court of bankruptcy, bankruptcy court; **~gesetzgebung** bankruptcy laws.

Konkursgläubiger bankruptcy creditor, petitioning creditor, *(pl.)* parties in interest;

Konkursverfahren betreibender ~ petitioning creditor; **bevorrechtigter ~** preferential (preferred, *US*) creditor; **einfacher ~** general creditor; **teilweise gesicherter ~** partly secured creditor *(US)*; **voll gesicherter ~** fully secured *(US)* (catholic) creditor; **nachrangige ~** deferred creditors; **privilegierter ~** secured creditor;

~ benachteiligen to make a fraudulent conveyance.

Konkurs|grund, ~handlung act of bankruptcy, act of insolvency; **~kosten** bankruptcy costs; **~lager** bankrupt stock; **in der ~liste erscheinen** to appear in the gazette, to be gazetted.

Konkursmasse assets of a bankrupt, bankrupt's estate, bankruptcy assets, debtor's property, property of a debtor, mass; **verteilte ~** distributed assets;

seine Ansprüche an die ~ anmelden to sue for admittance; **~ ausschütten** to divide a bankrupt's estate, to liquidate the assets of a bankrupt; **~ liquidieren** to liquidate the assets of a bankrupt, to sell up; **~ zugunsten der Gläubiger verwalten** to administer an estate for the benefit of the creditors; **aus der ~ zahlen** to pay out of the trust estate.

Konkurs|nachteile disadvantage of bankruptcy; **~ordnung** *(US)*, Bankruptcy Act *(Br.)*, National Bankruptcy Act *(US)*, Chandler Act *(US)*; **~pfleger** trustee in bankruptcy; **~quote** dividend of a bankrupt's estate, liquidation dividend, quota, status schedule; **übermäßige ~quote** surplus dividend; **~quote von 40% ausschütten** to pay 40 per cent out of the estate; **~recht** law of bankruptcy, bankrupt law.

konkursrechtlich|belangt werden können to be liable to be proceeded against under the bankruptcy law;

~en Bestimmungen unterliegen to be amenable to the bankruptcy laws (subject to bankruptcy jurisdiction); **von den ~en Schutzbestimmungen profitieren** to take the benefit of the bankruptcy laws; **~es Veräußerungsverbot** bankruptcy inhibition; **~e Zuständigkeit** bankruptcy jurisdiction.

konkursreifer Nachlaß insolvent estate.

Konkurs|richter bankruptcy commissioner, referee *(US)* (registrar, *Br.*) in bankruptcy, magistrate in bankruptcy (of a bankruptcy court); **beauftragter ~richter** commissioner of bankrupts; **~richtlinien** bankruptcy rules; **~sache** bankruptcy case, case (matter) of bankruptcy; **~sache abwickeln** to liquidate a bankrupt's affairs; **~schulden** bankrupt's debts; **bevorzugt zu befriedigende ~schulden** preferential (preferred, *US*) debts.

Konkursschuldner bankrupt [merchant], insolvent debtor, bankrupt debtor, adjudicated bankrupt;
betrügerischer ~ fraudulent bankrupt; **entlasteter (rehabilitierter)** ~ discharged (certificated, *Br.*) bankrupt; **fahrlässiger** ~ negligent bankrupt; **freiwilliger** ~ voluntary bankrupt; **rehabilitierter** ~ discharged (certificated, *Br.*) bankrupt; **nicht rehabilitierter (entlasteter)** ~ undischarged (uncertificated, *Br.*) bankrupt;
~ **aufgrund eigenen Antrags** voluntary bankrupt;
Waren aus dem Vermögen des ~s aussondern to take the goods out of the order and disposition of the bankrupt; **Entlastung als ~ erhalten** to get one's discharge, to be whitewashed *(Br.)*; **Geschäfte des ~s fortführen** to carry on the bankrupt's business; ~ **rehabilitieren** to discharge (whitewash, *Br.*) a bankrupt.

Konkurs|status statement of affairs *(Br.)*, schedule *(US)*; **~tabelle** realization and liquidation statement, statutory statement of affairs *(Br.)*, schedule of a bankrupt's debts *(US)*; **Forderung zur ~tabelle anmelden** to lodge a proof in bankruptcy; **~tabelle aufstellen** to marshal securities; **~verbrechen** act of bankruptcy, *(Gläubigerbegünstigung)* fraudulent preference; **~verbrechen begehen** to commit a bankruptcy offence; **wegen ~verdachts verhaftet werden** to be arrested on suspicion of fraudulent bankruptcy.

Konkursverfahren bankruptcy proceedings (procedure), proceedings in (process of) bankruptcy, bankruptcy action;
normales ~ ordinary bankruptcy;
~ **aufheben** to discharge a bankrupt, to grant the bankrupt's discharge; ~ **noch einmal aufrollen** to reopen a case of bankruptcy; **Aufhebung des ~s beantragen** to apply to the court for an order of (for one's) discharge; ~ **einleiten** to initiate (open) bankruptcy proceedings; ~ **einstellen** to stop bankruptcy proceedings; **über jds. Vermögen das ~ eröffnen** to institute bankruptcy proceedings against s. o., to adjudicate (declare s. o.) judicially a bankrupt; ~ **erwirken** to sue out a commission of bankruptcy; ~ **über das Schuldnervermögen fortsetzen** to proceed with the bankruptcy of a debtor; **infolge eines ~s seine Geschäfte nicht wahrnehmen können** to suffer from bankruptcy disabilities; **in ein ~ verwickelt sein** to be thrown into a bankruptcy action.

Konkurs|vergehen commission of an act of bankruptcy, bankruptcy offence, fraudulent preference; **~vergehen begehen** to commit an act of bankruptcy; **~vergleich** composition in bankruptcy; **~vergleich vorschlagen** to present a petition for compositon; **~vergleichsverfahren** compositon proceedings; **~verhängung** adjudication in bankruptcy (of a bankrupt); **~verlust** loss due to bankruptcy; **~vermögen** property of a bankrupt, bankrupt's property; **~verschleppung** obstructing proceedings of bankruptcy; **~verschleppung begehen** to obstruct proceedings of bankruptcy; **~versicherungsgesellschaft** indemnity company.

Konkursverwalter liquidator of an estate, administrator (trustee) of a bankrupt's estate, trustee (curator) in bankruptcy *(Br.)*; **behördlich bestellter (amtlicher)** ~ official receiver *(Br.)*, liquidator in winding up by the court *(US)*; **vom Gemeinschuldner vorgeschlagener** ~ assignee for the benefit of creditors; **vorläufiger** ~ official receiver *(Br.)*;
~ **im Zwangskonkurs** receiver in bankruptcy;
~ **bestellen** to appoint a receiver for the bankrupt's estate; **auf den ~ übertragen** to vest in the official receiver (trustee in bankruptcy) *(Br.)*;
~bericht official receiver's report; **~bestellung** appointment of a receiver (trustee in bankruptcy, *Br.*); **~einsetzung** fiat in bankruptcy; **~gebühren** receiver's expenses; **~kaution** bankruptcy bond; **~zeugnis** receiver's certificate.

Konkurs|verwaltung administration of a bankrupt's estate, bankruptcy administration, receivership *(Br.)*, trusteeship in bankruptcy *(US)*; **vorläufige ~verwaltung** official receivership; **~verwaltungskosten** administration (official receiver's) expenses; **~voraussetzung** act of bankruptcy; **~vorrecht** privilege; **~vorschriften** rules of bankruptcy; **~weg einschlagen** to take the bankruptcy route; **~zustand** bankrupt condition, bankruptcy.

Können ability, faculty, efficiency, skill, aptitude;
durchschnittliches ~ reasonable skill; **fachliches** ~ technical competence; **handwerkliches** ~ manual skill; **technisches** ~ know-how;
sein ganzes ~ ausspielen to have a heyday; **sein wahres ~ zeigen** to do justice to o. s.

können, praktisch alles to turn one's hand to most jobs; **kein Deutsch** ~ to speak no German; **sich nicht einigen** ~ to be unable to agree; **sich selbst erhalten** ~ to shift for o. s.; **viel auf seinem Gebiet** ~ to be an authority in one's subject; **es mit jem. gut** ~ to get on with s. o.; **nicht mehr** ~ to be exhausted (at the end of one's tether); **gut rechnen** ~ to be smart (good) at figures; **Sache in- und auswendig** ~ to know the rights of a case; **etw. im Schlaf** ~ to know s. th. backwards; **für einen Unfall nichts** ~ not to be to blame for an accident.

Könner expert, authority, specialist, artist, schemer, dab *(Br.)*, dabster *(Br.)*, oner *(US)*.

Konnexionen haben to have influential friends.

Konnossement bill of lading, *(Original)* original bill of lading (B/L), *(1. Kopie)* shipping bill (order), *(2. Kopie)* skippers' memorandum;
auf den Inhaber ausgestelltes ~ bill of lading to bearer; **auf den Namen ausgestelltes** ~ straight bill of lading *(US)*; **an Order ausgestelltes** ~ order bill of lading; **durchgehendes** ~ through bill of lading; **echtes** ~ clean bill of lading; **eingeschränktes (faules)** ~ foul bill of lading; **reines** ~ clean bill of lading; **staatliches** ~ government bill of lading; **unreines** ~ unclean (foul) bill of lading;
~ **in dreifacher Ausfertigung** bill of lading drawn in three copies; ~ **mit Kopien** set of bills; ~ **ohne Vorbehalt** clean bill of lading;
~ **ausstellen** to make out a bill of lading.

Konnossements|bestimmungen provisions (stipulations) of bill of lading; **~datum** date of bill of lading; **~garantie** letter of indemnity; **~klausel** bill-of-lading clause; **ungezeichnete ~kopie** memorandum copy of a bill of lading; **~teilschein** split bill of lading; **~vermerk** remark endorsed on a bill of lading; **~vertrag** bill-of-lading contract.

Konsekutivübersetzung consecutive interpretation.

Konsens *(jur.)* consent, assent, meeting of minds *(US)*.

konsenspflichtig subject to approval.

konsequent consequent, consistent;
~ **bleiben** to remain (stand) firm; ~ **denken** to think logically; ~ **nein sagen** to say no every time; **sein Ziel ~ verfolgen** to pursue one's goal resolutely;
~e Bemühungen unremitting efforts; **~er Freund der arbeitenden Bevölkerung** consistent friend of the working classes; **äußerst ~er Mensch** whole-hogger.

Konsequenz consequence, consistency, sequel, effect;
schwerwiegende ~en serious consequences;
Plan mit ~ durchführen to carry out a plan with determination; **seine Bemühungen mit großer ~ fortsetzen** to leave no stone unturned; **bis zur letzten ~ kämpfen** to fight to the bitter end; **~en auf sich nehmen (tragen)** to bear (abide by) the consequences, to face the music; **~en ziehen** to do the obvious thing; **juristische ~en gegen j. ziehen** to take legal steps against s. o.

konservativ conservative, rightist, old-time, tory;
übertrieben ~ overconservative, reactionary;
~ **regieren** to govern on conservative lines; ~ **eingestellt sein** to be conservative;
~er Flügel conservative wing; **~e Grundsätze** conservatism; **~e Partei** conservative party.

Konservativer Conservative, blue *(Br.)*;
engstirniger ~ diehard, High Tory *(Br.)*; **verkrusteter** ~ standpat *(US)*.

Konservativismus conservatism.

Konservator conservator, curator, *(Museum)* keeper.

Konserven tinned *(Br.)* (canned, *US*) foods (goods, provisions), preserved goods, preserves, conserves;
ausschließlich von ~ leben to live out of tins (cans, *US*);
~arbeiter can worker *(US)*; **~büchse** tin *(Br.)*, can *(US)*; **~dose** tin *(Br.)*, can *(US)*; **~fabrik** tinning factory *(Br.)*, packing company (house, plant) *(US)*, packhouse *(US)*, cannery *(US)*; **~fabrikant** packer *(US)*, canner *(US)*, tinner *(Br.)*; **~fabrikation** tinning *(Br.)*, canning *(US)*; **~fleisch** tinned (canned, *US*, potted, bully) meat; **~glas** preserving (fruit, *US*) jar; **~industrie** tin (can, *US*) industry, packing trade *(US)*; **~öffner** tin (can, *US*) opener; **~produktion** tin *(Br.)* (can, *US*) production, pack *(US)*; **~vergiftung** food (can, *US*) poisoning.

konservierbar conservable, preservable.

konservieren to conserve, to preserve;
in Büchsen ~ to tin *(Br.)*, to can *(US)*, to pack *(US)*.
konservierend conservatory.
konserviert canned *(US)*, tinned *(Br.)*;
sich gut ~ **haben** not to look one's age, to carry one's age well.
Konservierung conservation, preservation, tinning *(Br.)*, canning *(US)*, packing *(US)*;
~ **von Lebensmitteln** food conservation.
Konservierungs|methode pack; ~**mittel** preservative, conservative.
Konsignatar consignee;
~**mächte** consignatory power.
Konsignation consignment;
Waren in ~ **nehmen** to take goods on consignment.
Konsignations|ausfuhr export of consignment goods; ~**buch** order book; ~**faktura** proforma (consignment) invoice; ~**geschäft** consignment marketing (sale), memorandum sale *(US)*; ~**güter** consignment [goods, stock]; ~**konto** commission (consignment) account; ~**lager** storehouse, warehouse, consignment stock, custodian warehouse *(US)*; ~**lager unterhalten** to carry stocks; ~**lagerei** commission agency (business), custodian warehouse *(US)*; ~**rechnung** consignment invoice; ~**sendung** consignment; ~**verkauf** consignment sale (marketing), memorandum sale *(US)*; ~**vertrag** contract of consignment; ~**ware** merchandise lying in a warehouse, consigned goods, consignment [stock, goods], memorandum goods (package) *(US)*; ~**wechsel** value bill.
konsignationsweise on consignment (commission, memorandum, *US*), on a commission basis.
konsignieren to consign, to send on consignment (memorandum, *US*).
konsignierte Waren consignment (memorandum, *US*) goods.
Konsilium consultation.
Konskription *(mil.)* enlistment, enrolment.
Konsole [supporting] bracket, console.
konsolidieren to consolidate, to fund;
neu ~ to refund; **sich** ~ to be in the general bottoming area.
konsolidiert funded, *(Bilanz)* consolidated;
nicht ~ *(Bilanz)* unconsolidated, *(Schuld)* unfunded;
~**e Anleihe** consolidated (funded) loan; ~**e Bilanz** consolidated balance sheet (statement); ~**e Gesellschaft** consolidated company; ~**e Gewinn- und Verlustrechnung** consolidated profit and loss statement; ~**er Konzernabschluß** consolidated [annual statement of] accounts; ~**e Schuld** funded (consolidated) debt; ~**e Staatsanleihe** consolidated annuities; ~**e Staatspapiere** consols *(Br.)*, consolidated funds (stocks) *(Br.)*, consolidated bonds *(US)* (annuities); ~**e Verbindlichkeit** funded liability.
Konsolidierung consolidation, funding, conversion into permanent debt, merging;
politische ~ political consolidation;
~ **von Bankkrediten** funding of bank advances; ~ **der schwebenden Schuld** funding of the floating debt; ~ **von Schulden** debt consolidation; ~ **der Staatsschuld** consolidation of the national debt.
Konsolidierungs|anleihe funding (consolidated) loan, funding stock, funded loan; ~**ausgleichsposten** excess arising in consolidation; ~**bogen** consolidating financial statement; ~**gewinn** surplus from consolidation; ~**kredit** consolidated loan; ~**maßnahmen** consolidated (consolidation) measures; ~**programm** funding program(me); ~**prozeß** consolidation process; ~**rücklage** consolidation reserve; ~**schuldverschreibungen** funding bonds; ~**wesen** funding system.
Konsols consols *(Br.)*, consolidated funds (stocks) *(Br.)*, bank (consolidated) annuities *(Br.)*, consolidated (unified) bonds *(US)*.
Konsorte associate, syndicate member, underwriter, participant *(US)*.
konsortial consortial, syndical.
Konsortial|anleihe syndicate loan; ~**anteil** underwriting share, share in a syndicate, syndicate quota; ~**anteil übernehmen** to purchase a portion of a new issue; ~**aufwendungen** underwriting expense; ~**bank** underwriting bank, syndicate (member) bank; ~**beteiligung** underwriting share, underwriting participation, syndicate participation *(US)*, partnership in a syndicate; ~**beteiligungen** *(Bilanz)* syndicate holdings; ~**bildung** syndication; ~**führer[in]** leading underwriter, *(Bank)* originating banker (house), leading bank; ~**führung** syndicate management; ~**führung haben** to lead a syndicate; ~**geldbeträge** joint account money; ~**geschäft** business on joint account, underwriting (syndicate) business, *(einzelnes)* syndicate operation (transaction); ~**geschäfte** *(Bank)* syndicate banking; **multinationale** ~**geschäfte** international multibank syndications; ~**gewinn** underwriting (syndicate) profit; ~**gründung** organization of a syndicate; ~**gruppe** underwriting (syndicate) group; ~**hilfe** consortium aid.
konsortialiter by way of a syndicate.
Konsortial|konto syndicating account, joint (syndicate, underwriting, participation, *US*) account; ~**kredit** joint credit, syndicate (participation, *US*) loan, syndicate credit; ~**kreditgeber** joint creditors; ~**kreditnehmer** joint borrowers; ~**kurs** syndicate price; ~**marge** underwriter's commission; ~**mitglied** syndicate member, syndicator, underwriter, underwriting house, purchaser, consortium partner; **führendes** ~**mitglied** syndicatee, leading underwriter; ~**provision** spread, underwriter's commission, purchase commitment; ~**quote** underwriting share, syndicate quota; ~**sitzung** underwriter's meeting; ~**spesen** underwriting fee; ~**verpflichtungen** *(Bilanz)* underwriting (purchase) commitments; **seine** ~**verpflichtungen voll erfüllen** to take up the remainder of one's underwriting obligations; ~**vertrag** underwriting contract (agreement), syndicate agreement.
Konsortium consortium, syndicate, underwriting group, *(Emissionen)* purchase (selling) syndicate;
ausgebendes ~ distributing syndicate *(US)*; **übernehmendes** ~ original syndicate *(US)*;
~ **von Banken** bank consortium, banking syndicate;
~ **anführen** to head a consortium; ~ **bilden** to [form a] syndicate; **Anleihe an ein** ~ **geben** to put a loan into the hands of a syndicate.
Konsortiumsmitglied syndicate member, purchaser, underwriter.
Konspiration conspiracy, plot.
Konspirator conspirator, plotter.
konspirieren to [hatch a] plot, to conspire.
konstant constant, steady, *(fest)* standing, basic;
~ **bleiben** *(Wetter)* to last; ~ **an seinen Prinzipien festhalten** to remain constant to one's principles;
jds. Namen mit ~**er Bosheit falsch schreiben** to insist on spelling s. one's name wrong; ~**e Dividendenpolitik** conformity in dividend politics; ~**e Geschwindigkeit** maintained speed; ~**e Größe** constant; ~**es Kapital** constant capital; ~**e Kosten** constant costs; ~**e Nachfrage** steady demand; ~**e Preise** constant (steady) prices; ~**e Skalenerträge** constant returns to scale; ~**e Wachstumsrate** steady-rate growth; ~ **schlechtes Wetter** consistently bad weather.
Konstanttaste *(Computer)* constant key.
konstatieren to state, to establish, *(Gericht)* to find;
überall zu ~ **sein** to be perceived everywhere.
Konstatierung statement.
Konstellation, politische political situation, political subdivision *(US)*.
Konsternation consternation, dismay.
konsternieren to consternate, to fill with consternation, to strike with dismay.
konsterniert filled with dismay, taken aback;
völlig ~ **sein** to be wholly at a loss.
konstituieren to constitute, to form, to set up, to organize;
sich ~ *(Parlament)* to assemble; **Ausschuß** ~ to appoint a committee; **sich als Ausschuß** ~ *(parl.)* to resolve themselves into a committee; **sich als Körperschaft** ~ to incorporate.
konstituierend constituent;
~**e Versammlung** constituent assembly.
konstituiert, ordnungsgemäß duly constituted by law.
Konstituierung constitution, organization.
Konstitution *(körperliche Verfassung)* constitution;
robuste ~ tough physique; **schwache** ~ weak constitution;
eiserne ~ **haben** to have an iron constitution; **schwache** ~ **haben** to have poor health.
Konstitutionalismus constitutionalism.
konstitutionell constitutional, organic, limited;
~ **machen** to constitutionalize;
~**e Monarchie** constitutional monarchy; ~**e Regierung** constitutional government; ~**e Schwäche** constitutional weakness.
Konstitutions|schwäche *(med.)* weakness of constitution; ~**urkunde** written constitution.
konstitutiv constitutive;
~**e Wirkung** constitutive effect.
konstruieren to design, to imagine, *(bauen)* to construct, to build, to draw, to erect;
Flugzeug ~ to design an aircraft; **Gegensätze** ~ to create differences; **stromlinienförmig** ~ to streamline.
konstruiert designed, built, *(Stil)* forced, artificial;
~**es Alibi** fabricated (invented) alibi.

Konstrukteur constructor, design engineer, designer, machinist, craftsman *(US)*, *(Bauten)* erecting engineer, *(Schiffsbau)* draughtman, draftsman.

Konstruktion construction, design, model, *(Bau)* structure, building, *(fig.)* setup, scheme, device;
fehlerhafte ~ defective construction; **moderne ~** modern structure;
gewaltige ~ aus Beton und Glas a huge construction of reinforced concrete and glass; **~ einer Eisenbahn** planning of a railway line; **~ von Maschinen** mechanics.

Konstruktions|abteilung design department; **~änderung** change in design.

konstruktionsbedingt structural.

Konstruktions|büro drawing *(Br.)* (drafting) office, drafting room *(US)*, technical bureau, engineering (designing) department; **ins ~büro zurück** back to the drawing board; **zehn Jahre für den Weg vom ~büro über die Ausführung zur Inbetriebnahme benötigen** to take ten years from the drawing board to construction and into operation; **neue ~elemente beinhalten** to embody new features; **~entwurf** engineering design; **~fehler** faulty design, fault of construction, structural defect (error), *(Maschine)* constructional defect (error), defect in machinery, fault in the construction of a machine, flaw; **grundlegender ~fehler** basic design flaw; **~firma** engineering firm, engineering shop; **~formel** graphic formula; **~ingenieur** construction (design) engineer; **~kosten** cost of construction, engineering charges, *(Bau)* building cost (expenses); **~merkmale** constructive features; **~plan** erection scheme.

konstruktionstechnisch constructional.

Konstruktions|teil structural component; **~verbesserungen** structural improvements; **~vereinfachung** simplification of design; **~verfahren** method of construction; **~zeichnung** mechanical (working) drawing (plan).

konstruktiv constructive;
sich bei einer Sitzung ~ verhalten to be constructive at a meeting;
~er Geist constructive mind; **~er Vorschlag** constructive suggestion.

Konsul consul;
~ formell anerkennen to recognize a consul.

Konsular|abkommen consular convention (treaty, deal); **~abteilung** *(Botschaft)* consular section; **~agent** consular agent; **~beamter** consular officer; **~behörde** consular authority; **~bezirk** consular district; **~dienst** consular service; **~einnahmen** consular receipts; **~gebühren** consular fees; **~gericht** consular court; **~gerichtsbarkeit** consular jurisdiction.

konsularisch consular;
~e Amtshandlungen consular transactions; **~er Aufgabenbereich** functions of a consul; **~es Aufgabengebiet** consular assignment; **~e Beziehungen** consular relations; **~er Dienst** consular service; **~e Ernennung** consular appointment; **~e Funktionen** consular functions; **~es Korps** consular corps; **~e Privilegien** privileges of a consul; **~er Rang** consular rank; **~er Schutz** consular protection; **~e Tätigkeit** activities of a consul; **~er Titel** consular title; **~er Vertreter** consular agent (representative); **~e Vertretung** consular agency.

Konsular|korps consular corps; **~matrikel** consular register; **~papiere** consular documents; **~status** consular status; **~vertrag** consular convention; **~vertreter** consular agent (representative); **~vertretung** consular representation.

Konsulat consulate, consulship, consular office.

Konsulats|abteilung consular section (department); **~akten** consular archives; **~angehöriger** consular employee; **~angelegenheit** consular affair; **~beamter** consular officer, *(mit der Berechtigung, Eheschließungen vorzunehmen)* marriage officer; **~befugnisse** jurisdiction of a consulate; **~bericht** consular report; **~bescheinigung** consular certificate; **~bezirk** consular district; **~dienst** consular service; **~einnahmen** consular revenues; **~faktura** consular invoice (document); **~faktura ausstellen** to prepare a consular invoice; **~fakturen beglaubigen lassen** to get the consular invoices legalized; **~flagge** consular flag; **~funktionen** consular functions; **~gebühren** consular charge (fees), consulage; **~gericht** consular court; **~kanzlei** chancellery; **~papiere** consular documents; **~posten** consular post; **~programm** consular program(me); **~rechnung** consular invoice; **~sichtvermerk** consular visa; **~siegel** consular seal; **~system** consular system; **~vertrag** consular treaty (convention); **~vorschriften** consular regulations; **~zeit** consulship.

Konsultation consultation, deliberation, discussion;
~ in der Praxis *(Arzt)* office call; **~en auf Regierungsebene** consultations on cabinet level;
in ~en eintreten to enter into deliberations (consultations); **Experten zur ~ hinzuziehen** to take expert advice.

Konsultations|gebühren consultation fees; **~mechanismus** machinery for consultation; **~pflicht** compulsory consultation; **~verfahren** *(EG)* consultation procedure; **laufendes ~verfahren** continuing system of consultation.

konsultative Funktionen ausüben to act in an advisory capacity.

Konsultativ|pakt *(Politik)* consultative pact; **~verfahren** advisory procedure.

konsultieren to consult, to deliberate, to seek s. one's advice;
seinen Anwalt ~ to consult one's lawyer, to confer with one's counsel *(Br.)*; **Arzt ~** to see (consult) a doctor; **Experten ~** to seek the opinion of an expert.

Konsum consumption, *(Konsumladen)* cooperative store (shop, *Br.*), coop *(coll.)*;
demonstrativer ~ conspicuous consumption; **inländischer ~** home (domestic) consumption; **privater ~** private consumption;
für den ~ ausgeben to spend on consumption goods; **sich jeden ~ leisten können** to be able to afford anything;
~artikel consumer goods (items), articles of consumption; **~aufwand** consumption expenditures; **gesamtwirtschaftliche ~ausgaben** consumer expenditures; **~ausweitung** increased consumption; **täglicher ~bedarf** daily consumer needs; **sich den ~bedürfnissen anpassen** to gear to consumer needs; **~bereitschaft** consumer acceptance; **an der Grenze liegende ~bereitschaft** marginal propensity to consume; **~beschränkungen** restrictions set on consumption; **~beschränkungen auf dem Kraftfahrzeugsektor** automotive austerity; **erste Maßnahmen zur Erleichterung in der ~beschränkung treffen** to lift the austerity lid a bit; **~betrieb** consumer enterprise.

konsumbewußt consumer-oriented.

Konsumbewußtsein consumer orientation.

konsumbezogen consumption-oriented.

Konsum|darlehn consumer credit; **~drosselung** curbs on consumption; **externer ~effekt** bandwaggon (snob) effect; **frei verfügbares ~einkommen** discretionary income; **~einschränkung** cut in consumption.

Konsument consumer, user;
wiederholt angesprochene ~en *(Werbung)* repeat audience; **~en und Produzenten** consumers and producers.

Konsumenten|aggressivität militancy of consumers; **~bedarf** consumer demand; **~bedürfnisse** consumer needs; **~bedürfnisse befriedigen** to cater for the needs of one's customers; **~befragung** consumer research (inquiry, survey); **postalische ~befragung** contact mail panel; **vollkommene ~befriedigung** total utility; **~beschwerden** consumer complaints; **~einkommen** consumer income; **~finanzierung** consumer financing.

konsumentenfreundlich consumer-conscious (-minded).

Konsumenten|funktion consumption function; **repräsentative ~gruppe** consumer group (panel); **~irreführung** misleading of consumers; **~kaufkraft** consumer purchasing power; **~kreditwerbung** consumer credit advertising; **~nachfrage** consumer demand; **~preis** consumer price; **~preisindex** consumer price index; **~rente** consumer's surplus; **~souveränität** consumer sovereignty; **~verband** consumers' union; **~vereinigung** consumer organization; **~verhalten** consumer behavio(u)r; **~werbung** direct (consumer) advertising; **~zeitalter** age of consumerism.

Konsum|erhöhung increased consumption; **~explosion** burst of consumption; **~finanzierung** consumer financing; **~forschung** consumer research.

konsumfreudiges Zeitalter consumer-orient[at]ed age.

Konsum|freudigkeit propensity to consume; **marginale ~freudigkeit** marginal propensity to consume; **~funktion** consumption function; **~gebiet** consumption area; **~genossenschaft** consumer cooperative, retail cooperative (industrial and provident, *Br.*) society; **~genossenschaft des Einzelhandels** cooperative retail society, retail co-operative society *(Br.)*; **~geschäft** cooperative shop (store, *US*), coop *(coll.)*; **~gewohnheiten** habits of consumption, consumer buying habits; **~gut** article of consumption, consumer product.

Konsumgüter consumer (consumption, convenience, *US*) goods, consumer products, goods for consumption, semidurable (first-order shopping) goods *(US)*, consumption capital;
dauerhafte ~ consumer durables; **kurzlebige ~** perishable (semidurable) consumer goods *(US)*, perishables, soft goods; **langlebige ~** long-life consumer goods, consumer hardgoods, durable goods, consumer durables;
~bereich consumer goods sector; **~betrieb** consumer subsidiary; **~industrie** consumer-goods industry; **~konjunktur** con-

sumer-goods boom; ~**leasing** consumer-goods leasing; ~**markt** consumer market; ~**messe** trade fair for consumer goods; ~**nachfrage** demand for consumer goods; ~**vermietung** consumer-goods leasing.
konsumierbar consumable.
konsumieren to consume.
Konsumierung consumption.
Konsum|knappheit consumer shortage; ~**kontrolle** consumer clampdown; ~**kraft** consumptive power, consumption capacity, power to consume; ~**kredit** consumer (consumption, instalment) credit, consumption loan; ~**kredite gewähren** to lend for consumption; ~**kreditbeschränkungen** restrictions of consumer credits; ~**kreditgenossenschaft** industrial finance company; ~**laden** cooperative shop *(Br.)* (store, *US*), coop *(coll.)*; ~**neigung** propensity to consume; ~**niederlage** cooperative store.
konsumorientiert consumer-orient[at]ed.
Konsum|orientierung consumer orientation; ~**quote** consumption ratio; ~**rückgang** drop in consumption; ~**schatten** neglected consumer markets; ~**sphäre** consumer goods sector; ~**steigerung** increased (growth in) consumption, expansion of consumption; ~**steuer** consumption tax, excise tax *(US)*; ~**stoß** surge of consumption; ~**theorie** theory of demand.
Konsumtionsgüter consumer (consumption) goods; ~**industrie** consumption-goods industry.
Konsumtivkredit consumption (consumer, retail, *US*) credit; ~**beschränkungen** consumer credit restrictions; ~**lenkung** consumer credit control; ~**wirtschaft** consumer credit industry.
Konsum|trend consumption trend, flood of demand; ~**verein** cooperative purchasing (industrial and provident, *Br.*) society, cooperative store *(US)*, cooperative society *(Br.)*, the stores *(Br.)*; ~**vereinsgesetz** Industrial and Provident Societies Act *(Br.)*; ~**vereinsmitglied** cooperator; ~**verhalten** consumer habits (behavio(u)r); ~**vermögen** consumers' (consumption) capital; ~**verzicht** abstention, deferred demand; ~**verzicht treiben** to refrain from consumption; ~**vorschau** consumption prospect; ~**waren** consumer (consumption, current, first order, *US*) goods; ~**welle** flood of demand; ~**werbung** consumer advertising; ~**ziffern** consumption figures; ~**zuwachs** consumption gain.
Kontakt contact, liaison, *(el.)* contact;
berufliche ~**e** professional contacts; **enger** ~ close contact; **geschäftliche** ~**e** business contacts; **hergestellter** ~ contact established; **persönlicher** ~ face-to-face contact;
~**e anknüpfen** to establish contacts; ~ **mit jem. aufnehmen** to get into touch with s. o.; **in ständigem** ~ **miteinander bleiben** to hear regularly from one another; ~ **haben** to be in touch; **unmittelbaren** ~ **mit jem. haben** to be in direct contact with s. o.; ~ **schließen** *(el.)* to make the circuit; **in engem** ~ **sein** to touch shoulders (elbows); **mit jem. in** ~ **stehen** to be in contact (touch) with s. o.; **mit jem. brieflich in** ~ **treten** to contact s. o. by mail;
~**aufnahme** establishment of a contact; **erste** ~**aufnahme** initial contact; **persönliche** ~**aufnahme** personal contact; ~**büro** lobbying office, liaison mission.
Kontakter contact man, liaison consultant (man) *(US)*, *(Werbeagentur)* account executive;
leitender ~ account supervisor.
kontaktfähig sociable.
Kontakt|fähigkeit sociability; ~**herstellung** making contacts.
Kontaktieren contacting.
Kontakt|interview contact interview; ~**kosten** calling cost; ~**mann** contact man, liaison consultant (man) *(US)*, *(Kriminalpolizei)* informer, informant, source, *(Werbeagentur)* account executive; ~**mann zur Presse** press-relations counsellor (officer), press officer; ~**mine** *(mil.)* contact mine; **laufende** ~**möglichkeiten** opportunity for roll-over contacts; **gute** ~**möglichkeiten mit allen nur möglichen Leuten haben** to have good opportunity to come into contact with all sorts of people; ~**person** contact man, *(medizinisch)* contact; ~**pflege** human (public) relations; ~**schale** contact lens; ~**station** *(Raumschiff)* tracking station; ~**stelle** contact point, liaison office; ~**streifen** *(Foto)* contact print; ~**umfrage** contactual survey.
Konten, debitorische accounts having a debit balance, accounts receivable *(US)*; **ungenügend gedeckte** ~ overextended accounts *(US)*; **sorgfältig geführte** ~ straight accounts; **interne** ~ intercompany accounts; **kreditorische** ~ accounts having a credit balance, accounts payable *(US)*; **laufende** ~ current accounts, demand deposits *(US)*; **tote (unbewegte)** ~ dead accounts; **zedierte** ~ assigned accounts; **zweifelhafte** ~ doubtful accounts;
~ **zwecks späterer Gutschrift** deferred accounts; ~ **von Kapitalssammelstellen** institutional accounts; ~ **von Organgesellschaften** intercompany accounts;
~ **ablesen** to call over accounts; ~ **abrechnen** to square accounts; ~ **abstimmen** to reconcile accounts; ~ **nach ihrer Fälligkeit aufgliedern** to age accounts; ~ **ausgleichen** to equalize (square) accounts; ~ **in Ordnung bringen** to adjust accounts; **seine** ~ **in Ordnung bringen** to get one's accounts square; ~ **wieder in Ordnung (Übereinstimmung) bringen** to readjust accounts; ~ **auf den neuesten Stand bringen** to bring accounts up to date, to post accounts; ~ **durchgehen** to go through accounts; **gesperrte** ~ **freigeben** to release blocked accounts; ~ **frisieren** to juggle the accounts; ~ **glattstellen** to settle (adjust) accounts; ~ **prüfen** to audit accounts; ~ **sperren** to block accounts; ~ **überprüfen (überwachen)** to audit (control) accounts; ~ **zusammenlegen** to merge (pool) accounts;
~**abgleichung** balancing of accounts; ~**abrechnung** settlement of accounts; ~**abschluß** making up (balancing of, reconciliation of) the accounts; ~**abstimmung** squaring (adjustment, agreement, reconciliation) of accounts, accounting equation; **monatliche** ~**abstimmung** monthly reconciliation; ~**abweichung** discrepancy between two accounts; ~**analyse** account analysis; ~**aufgliederung** account classification (dissection, analysis), breakdown of accounts *(US)*; ~**ausgleich** squaring of accounts, fan-out; ~**bearbeiter** accounts supervisor; ~**berechnung** computation of accounts; ~**bewegung** changes in accounts; ~**blatt** accounting form; ~**dotierung** allocation of accounts; ~**einteilung** classification of accounts; ~**fälschung** manipulation (falsification) of accounts; ~**freigabe** release of blocked accounts; ~**führer** keeper of an account; ~**führung** accounting, accountancy, bookkeeping; **bei der** ~**führung Unregelmäßigkeiten begehen** to tamper with (cook) the accounts; ~**glattstellung** adjustment (squaring) of accounts; ~**gliederung** classification of accounts; ~**gruppe** group of accounts; ~**inhaber** holder of a [banking] account, account holder, depositor, customer of a bank; ~**plan** chart (schedule) of accounts; ~**rahmen** standard chart of accounts; **funktionale** ~**rechnung** activity (functional) accounting; ~**regulierung** adjustment (squaring) of accounts.
Kontensaldo balance;
der Höhe nach feststehender ~ liquidated account; **täglicher Zinsberechnung zugrunde liegender** ~ interest balance *(US)*;
~ **abtreten** to assign an account.
Konten|sparen account savings; ~**sperre** blocking of accounts; ~**sperre aufheben** to release blocked accounts, to unfreeze funds; ~**sperre vornehmen** to stop accounts; ~**übertragung** transfer to another account; ~**überwacher** account supervisor; ~**unstimmigkeiten** discrepancy between two accounts; **treuhänderische** ~**verwaltung** fiduciary accounting; ~**verzeichnis** accounts opened and closed book *(Br.)*; ~**zergliederung** account classification, dissection (analysis) of accounts, account analysis; ~**zettel** cargo (freight) list; ~**zusammenlegung** pooling (merger) of accounts.
Konterbande contraband [articles], contraband goods, prohibited goods (articles);
absolute ~ absolute contraband; **bedingte (gelegentliche)** ~ conditional (relative, occasional) contraband; **keine** ~ innocent goods, lawful goods *(US)*;
als ~ **beschlagnahmt werden** to be seized as contraband.
Kontermarke countermark, *(Theater)* pass-out check *(Br.)*, pass check *(US)*, passing-out list.
Kontermine *(Börse)* bear speculation, the bears, short interest *(US)*.
konterminieren *(Börse)* to sell a bear, to speculate for a fall, to be short of the market *(US)*, to countermine.
kontern, erfolgreich to launch a successful counterattack.
Konter|presse proof press; ~**revolution** conterrevolution; ~**revolutionär** counterrevolutionary; ~**zettel** counter check.
Kontext context;
Text und ~ **stimmen nicht überein** words and figures differ.
kontieren to allocate an account.
Kontierung allocation of an account.
Kontiguitätsgrenze contiguous zone.
Kontinent continent, mainland;
aufstrebender ~ emerging continent; **autarker** ~ self-contained continent.
kontinental continental.
Kontinental|hafen continental port *(Br.)*; ~**klima** continental climate; ~**mächte** Continental (European) Powers; ~**plateau** continental shelf.

Kontingent quota, share, allocation, allotment, contingent, *(Truppen)* contingent;
nicht am ~ **beteiligt** nonquota;
nicht ausgenutztes ~ unused quota; **erschöpftes** ~ exhausted quota; **gesetzlich festgelegtes** ~ legislated quota; **freies** ~ free quota; **globales** ~ overall quota; **jährliches** ~ annual contingent, yearly quota; **in Frage kommendes** ~ applicable quota;
~**e aufstocken** to increase quotas; ~ **aufteilen** to [allocate the shares in a] quota; ~**e aushandeln** to bargain for quotas; ~ **bewilligen** to grant a quota; ~ **erhöhen** to increase (raise) a quota; ~ **erschöpfen** to exhaust (use up) a quota; ~ **festlegen (festsetzen)** to fix by quotas, to quota, to allocate; ~**e für Einfuhren festsetzen** to apportion quotas for imports; ~ **kürzen** to reduce a quota; **unausgenutzte** ~**e ins nächste Jahr übertragen lassen** to allow unfilled quotas to carry into next year; **sein** ~ **übernehmen** to contribute one's quota; ~ **überziehen** to exceed a quota; **über ein** ~ **verfügen** to dispose of a quota;
~**erhöhung** quota increase.
kontingentfreie Einfuhren nonquota imports.
kontingentieren to fix a contingent, to fix by quotas, to quota, to allocate, *(Devisen)* to ration;
Banknoten ~ to limit the fiduciary issue; **Export** ~ to allocate export quotas.
kontingentiert quota, subject to a quota system, *(Devisen)* rationed;
nicht ~ nonquota, *(Devisen)* nonrationed;
~**e Ware** quota goods; **nicht** ~**e Waren** nonquota goods.
Kontingentierung fixing (allocation) of quotas, quota system (restriction), limitation;
~ **von Devisen** rationing of foreign exchange; ~ **der Einfuhr** limitation of imports; ~ **der Notenausgabe** limitation of the fiduciary issue.
Kontingentierungs|bescheinigung quota certificate; ~**gesetz** quota bill; ~**grundlage** quota basis; ~**satz** quota; ~**system** quota system, *(Devisen)* rationing system; ~**vertrag** quota agreement; ~**vorschriften** rationing regulations; ~**zuweisung** allocation of quotas.
Kontingents|abrechnung quota accounting; ~**anteil** quota share; ~**antrag** application for a quota; ~**aufhebung** suspension of a quota; ~**aufstockung** quota increase; ~**aufteilung** allocation of shares in a quota; ~**aushandlung** quota bargaining; ~**beschränkungen** quota restrictions; ~**erhöhung** quota increase; ~**festsetzung** fixing of quotas; ~**kürzungen** quota cuts; ~**land** *(Einwanderungsbestimmungen)* quota country; ~**träger** quota agent; ~**vereinbarung** quota agreement; ~**zuweisung** quota allotment.
Kontingenztafel contingency table.
kontinuierlich continual, continued, continuous;
~**e Walzenstraße** continuous (tandem) mill.
Kontinuität continuity.
Konto account, *(Guthaben)* balance;
à ~ [received] on account, a vista; **zum Ausgleich eines** ~**s** to settle (in settlement of) an account;
abgerechnetes ~ settled account; **abgeschlossenes** ~ closed account, account ruled off; **abgesichertes** ~ secured account; **abgetretenes** ~ assigned account; **allgemeines** ~ general account; **als sicher angesehenes** ~ well-regarded account; **ausgeglichenes** ~ balanced account; **belastetes** ~ account debited; **beschlagnahmtes** ~ account attached; **lange bestehendes** ~ long-standing account; **debitorisches** ~ debit (debtor) account; **doppeltes** ~ duplicate account; **eingefrorenes** ~ frozen account; **erkanntes** ~ account credited; **fingiertes** ~ pro-forma (fictitious) account; **gebundenes** ~ time deposit; **gedecktes** ~ secured account; **ungenügend gedecktes** ~ overextended account *(US)*; **debitorisch geführtes** ~ debit (debtor) account; **hilfsweise geführtes** ~ adjunct account; **im Inland geführtes** ~ inland account; **gemeinsames** ~ participation account; **gemeinschaftliches** ~ joint account; **gemischtes** ~ mixed account; **beim Drittschuldner gepfändetes** ~ garnishee account; **gesperrtes** ~ blocked account (deposit); **internes** ~ internal (intercompany) account; **kein** ~ no account (no ac); **kreditorisches** ~ account showing a credit balance, creditor account; **laufendes** ~ current account, working (personal, running, continuing, checking, *US*, drawing, *US*, open, *US*) account, demand deposit *(US)*; **laufendes** ~ **mit ständigem Kreditsaldo** credit account; **lebendes** ~ personal (customer's) account; **normales** ~ ordinary account; **offenes** ~ open (current, checking, *US*, drawing) account; **offenstehendes** ~ open (unsettled) account; **persönliches** ~ private account; **reguliertes** ~ settled account; **revolvierendes** ~ revolving account; **rückständiges** ~ delinquent account; **ruhendes** ~ broken (inactive, dead, *Br.*) account; **steuerbegünstigtes** ~ tax-favo(u)red account; **tägliches** ~ account current, checking account *(US)*; **totes** ~ *(Sachkonto)* nominal (impersonal, *Br.*) account, *(umsatzloses)* sleeping (inactive, dead, *Br.*) account; **transitorisches** ~ suspense (suspended) account; **überzogenes** ~ overdrawn account, overdraft; **umsatzloses (unbewegtes)** ~ dormant (broken, inactive, inaccurate, dead, *Br.*, inoperative, *Br.*) account; **umsatzträchtiges** ~ active account; **ungedecktes** ~ unsecured account; **unpersönliches** ~ impersonal *(Br.)* (nominal) account; **unverzinsliches** ~ account bearing no interest, noninterest-bearing account; **verfallenes** ~ aging account; **versichertes** ~ insured account *(US)*; **verzinsliches** ~ interest-bearing account; **vorjähriges** ~ last year's account; **vorläufiges** ~ suspense (provisional) account; **zediertes** ~ assigned account; **zinstragendes** ~ interest-bearing account; **zweckgebundenes** ~ earmarked account;
~ **Abschreibungen** depreciation account; ~ **für Abschreibungsrücklagen** depreciation reserve account; ~ **der Anlagewerte** fixed-asset (capital) account; ~ **des Ausstellers** drawer's account; ~ **Beteiligungen** investment (syndicate) account; ~ **für Diverse** sundries (sundry persons', *Br.*) account; ~ **für nachträglich eingegangene Dubiosen** bad-debts collected account *(US)*; ~ **für Gelder der öffentlichen Hand** public account; ~ **eines nicht entlasteten Gemeinschuldners** account with an undischarged bankrupt; ~ **der Hauptniederlassung** head-office account; ~ **Investierungen** investment account; **laufendes** ~ **mit ständigem Kreditsaldo** credit account; ~ **mit Kündigungsfrist** fixed (time, *US*) deposit; ~ **einer Organgesellschaft** intercompany account; ~ **für Privatentnahmen** drawing account; ~ **in laufender Rechnung** balance on current account; ~ **für Sonderziehungen** *(Weltwährungsfonds)* special drawing account; ~ **beim Stammhaus** head-office account; ~ **mit häufigen (hohen) Umsätzen** active account; ~ **für kurzfristige Verbindlichkeiten** liability account; ~ **zur vorläufigen Verbuchung unklarer Posten** over and short account; ~, **aus dem die Verwendung des Reingewinns ersichtlich ist** appropriation account; ~ **überfälliger Wechsel** bills overdue account; ~ **für laufende Zahlungen** budget account; ~ **zweifelhafter Zinseingänge** reserve (suspense, *Br.*) interest account;
vom ~ **abheben** to draw (make a draft) on an account; ~ **abrechnen** to settle (balance) an account; ~ **abschließen** to balance (close and rule, run off, post) an account; ~ **alimentieren** to place an account in funds; ~ **anlegen** to open an account; **Betrag auf jds.** ~ **anweisen** to have an account credited to s. one's account; ~ **aufgliedern** to analyse (break down, *US*) an account; ~ **aufheben (auflösen)** to eliminate (close) an account; **sein** ~ **auflösen** to withdraw one's account; ~ **aufstellen** to make up an account; ~ **ausgleichen** to balance (settle) an account, *(begleichen)* to discharge an account, to quit scores, to settle (discharge) an account; ~ **zugeteilt bekommen** to be assigned an account; ~ **belasten** to debit an account, to pass to the debit of (charge against) an account; ~ **mit einem Betrag belasten** to pass an account (place a sum) to the debit of an account; **jds.** ~ **mit einem Betrag belasten** to charge an amount to s. one's account, to place a sum to s. one's debit; ~ **mit sämtlichen Unkosten belasten** to charge an account with all the expenses; ~ **bereinigen** to clear up an account; **Richtigkeit eines** ~**s bestätigen** to verify an account; ~ **debitieren** to pass (place) to the debit of (debit) an account; ~ **dotieren** to place an account in funds; ~ **durchsehen** to go over an account; ~ **einrichten** to open an account; **auf ein** ~ **einzahlen** to pay into an account; **Betrag auf jds.** ~ **einzahlen** to pay in a sum to s. one's credit; ~ **entlasten** to approve an account; ~ **zugeteilt erhalten** to be assigned an account; ~ **erkennen** to credit an account; ~ **mit dem Gegenwert erkennen** to credit the proceeds to an account; ~ **eröffnen** to open an account; ~ **bei einer Bank zugunsten von ... eröffnen** to open an account with a bank to the favo(u)r of ...; ~ **für j. errichten** to open an account in s. one's name; **auf einem** ~ **erscheinen (figurieren)** to appear in an account; ~ **führen** to keep an account; **auf das** ~ **der Regierungspartei gehen** to be to the credit of the party in power; ~ **glattstellen** to discharge (settle) an account; **einem** ~ **gutschreiben** to credit (pass, place to the credit of) an account; ~ **haben** to keep an account; ~ **bei einer Bank haben** to have a bank account (an account with a bank); **sein** ~ **überzogen haben** to have an overdraft; **über ein** ~ **mittels Scheckkarte verfügen können** to hold an account under current check-card arrangements; ~ **kreditieren** to pass (place) to the credit of an account; ~ **kündigen** to call up an account; ~

anwachsen lassen to run up an account; ~ **sperren lassen** to order an account to be blocked; ~ **unausgeglichen lassen** to let an account stand over; ~ **löschen** to close and rule an account; **um Errichtung eines ~s nachsuchen** to solicit for an account; **auf ~ nehmen** to take on credit; ~ **pfänden** to garnish (attach, *US*) the balance of an account; ~ **prüfen** to analyse (check, examine) an account; ~ **regulieren** to regulate an account, to even up an account in funds; ~ **saldieren** to balance an account; **faules ~ versuchsweise sanieren** to nurse an account *(Br.)*; ~ **schließen** to close an account; ~ **sperren** to block (freeze) an account; **auf jds. ~ setzen** to pass (put down) to s. one's account; ~ **überprüfen** to go over an account; **Geld auf ein anderes ~ überschreiben** to transfer money to another account; **sein ~ überschreiten (überziehen)** to overdraw (overcheck, *US*) one's account, to make an overdraft *(US)*, *(fam.)* to overdraw the badger *(Br.)*; **sein ~ nur begrenzt überziehen** to keep one's overdraft within reasonable limits; ~ **laufend überziehen** to run up overdrafts *(US)*; ~ **unterhalten** to maintain (keep, operate) an account; ~ **bei einer Bank unterhalten** to have (hold) an account with a bank; **kreditorisches ~ unterhalten** to keep an account on a nonborrowing basis; ~ **bei der Landeszentralbank unterhalten** to have a deposit account with the Federal Reserve Bank *(US)*; **auf ein ~ verbuchen** to enter into an account; **über jds. ~ verfügen** to sign on s. one's account; **Saldo eines ~s ziehen** to balance an account; **einem ~ zuschlagen** to add to an account;
~**abhebung** drawing on an account; ~**abhebung vornehmen** to make a draft on (withdraw from) one's account, to draw on an account; ~**abrechnung** computation of account, *(Bankauszug)* bank reconciliation statement; ~**abrechnung nicht anerkennen** to question the computation of an account; ~**abschluß** closing, balancing (making up) an account, rest *(Br.)*; **halbjähriger ~abschluß** accounts to be settled every six months; ~**abstimmung** bank reconciliation; ~**abtretung** assignment of an account; ~**abwicklung** running of an account; ~**änderung** change of account; ~**anerkennung** approval of account; ~**anreicherung** feeding of an account; ~**auflösung** closing (elimination, *US*) of an account; ~**aufstockung** buildup of an account; ~**auftrag** account mandate; ~**ausgleich** account balance.

Kontoauszug statement (abstract, extract) of account, account statement, accounts receivable statement *(US)*, customer's (bank) statement, pass sheet *(Br.)*;
bestätigter ~ verification statement, account stated *(US)*; **nebenstehender ~** affixed statement of account;
~ **per 31. Dezember** statement of account closed per December 31st;
~ **anfertigen** to make an abstract from (draw up a statement of) an account; ~ **zur Prüfung beifügen** to subjoin a statement of account for audit; **Richtigkeit eines ~s bestätigen** to verify an account (an abstract, *Br.*); ~ **vergleichen** to audit an abstract of account.

Konto|auszugsbestätigung verification of an account, account stated *(US)*, reconcilement (statement) blank *(US)*; ~**belastung** debit; ~**bereinigung,** ~**berichtigung** correction (adjustment) of an account; ~**besitzer** account holder; ~**bestand** balance; ~**bestätigung** verification statement *(Br.)*, reconcilement (statement) blank *(US)*; ~**bestätigungsformular** verification form *(Br.)*; ~**bewegung** account transactions; ~**bezeichnung** name (title) of an account, account title, account heading; ~**blatt** account form; ~**blätter** ledger sheets; ~**buch** account book, account passbook, tally, book of accounts, record, *(Kunde)* bankbook, passbook, deposit book *(US)*; **die ~bücher stimmen nicht** the account books won't (don't) add up; ~**buchersparnisse** passbook savings; ~**buchseite** folio; ~**einlagen** account deposits; ~**eröffnung** opening an account; ~**eröffnungsantrag** application for an account; ~**fälschung** cooking of an account; ~**freigabe** unblocking of an account; ~**führer** account manager, account supervisor; ~**führung** keeping (working) an account, *(Abteilung)* accounts department; ~**führungsgebühren** account-carrying charges; ~**führungssystem** accounting system; **besondere ~führungsvereinbarung** special account agreement; ~**gegenbuch** tally, *(Kunde)* passbook, bankbook, deposit book *(US)*; ~**guthaben** credit balance, *(pl.)* account deposits; ~**guthaben pfänden** to garnish (attach, *US*) a bank account; ~**gutschrift** credit advice (memorandum, note, *US*); ~**inhaber** holder of an account, account holder, depositor, *(Bank)* customer of a bank; ~**karte** account card; ~**kopf** title of an account, account title.

Kontokorrent current (open, *US*, running) account, account current;
schriftlich anerkanntes ~ settled account;
Posten auf dem ~ verbuchen to pass an item to the current account;
~**abhebungen** drawings on current accounts; ~**ausleihungen** lending on current account; ~**auszug** statement of account, accounts receivable statement *(US)*; ~**bedingungen gewähren** to grant open-account facilities *(US)*; ~**bestätigung** account stated *(US)*, verification form *(Br.)*, reconcilement (statement) blank *(US)*; ~**buch** current account ledger, *(Kreditoren)* accounts payable ledger *(US)*, *(Debitoren)* accounts receivable ledger *(US)*; ~**buch einer Bank** bank ledger, money lent and lodged book *(Br.)*; ~**debitor** debtor in account current; ~**einlagen** call money *(Br.)*, deposits on current account, demand (current account) deposits; ~**forderungen** current account receivables *(US)*; ~**geschäft** deposit banking, current account business; ~**gläubiger** current account customer, trade creditor; **vereinbarte ~grenze** overdraft limit; ~**guthaben** balance at bank on current account, bank (current account) balance.

Kontokorrentkonto book (current, *Br.*, running, continuing, open, *US*, checking, *US*) account, account current, demand deposit *(US)*;
debitorisch geführtes ~ borrowing account *(Br.)*; **kreditorisch geführtes ~** nonborrowing account *(Br.)*, credit current account; **überzogenes ~** overdraft on current account; **unbesichertes ~** unsecured account;
~ **einer Bank mit Konten bei anderen Banken** bank ledger, money lent and lodged book *(Br.)*;
laufendes ~ mit den Zinsen des Kreditkontos belasten to debit interest on a loan account to an active current account; ~ **führen** to conduct a current account; ~ **haben** to have a running account.

Kontokorrentkredit current account advance, credit (overdraft) in current account, personal (cash) credit, loan on overdraft, deposit (open) credit *(US)*;
nicht gedeckter (unbesicherter) ~ uncovered advance (overdraft);
~ **gewähren** to grant overdraft facilities; **um Einräumung eines ~s nachsuchen** to ask the banker for an overdraft.

Kontokorrent|kreditor creditor in account current; ~**kunde** current account customer, current account user; ~**mindestguthaben** compensating balance; ~**provision** overdraft commission (fee); **unwidersprochener ~saldo** fitted accounts; ~**schuldner** trade debtor, debtor in account current; ~**transaktionen** current account operations; ~**verbindlichkeiten** current account liabilities, deposit liabilities *(US)*; ~**verhältnis** mutual accounts; ~**verkehr** current account business, deposit banking *(US)*; **im ~verkehr stehen** to have an open (a running, current) account; ~**vertrag mit gleichbleibend gestellten Sicherheiten** continuing agreement; ~**zinsen** interest on current account, overdraft interest, demand deposit rates *(US)*; **gesetzliche ~zinsen** legal interest [rate].

Konto|kosten bank (account-carrying) charges; ~**name** title of an account, account title, account name; ~**nummer** account number; ~**pfändung** garnishment of a banking account.

Kontor [merchant's] office, counter, countinghouse *(Br.)*.

Kontoregulierung settlement of an account.

Kontorflagge burgee.

Kontorist clerk.

Kontoristin lady clerk.

Konto|saldo account balance; **versuchte ~sanierung** nursing of an account *(Br.)*; ~**schiebung** wangling (manipulation) of an account; **rechte ~seite** right-hand side; ~**sperre** blocking (stopping) of an account; ~**spesen** *(Bank)* account-carrying charges.

Kontostand bank balance, state (position) of an account;
täglicher ~ day-to-day position;
~ **preisgeben** to divulge the state of an account; **täglichen ~ überwachen** to supervise the day-to-day running of an account; ~ **laufend überwachen** to keep an account under constant observation.

Konto|tagesauszug daily statement; ~**überschrift** account title; ~**übertrag** transfer of an account; ~**übertragungszeitraum** posting period; ~**überzieher** overdrawer; ~**überziehung,** ~**überzug** [bank] overdraft, overdrawn account; **laufende ~überziehung** hard-core overdraft; ~**überziehungsprovision** overdraft commission; ~**umbuchung** transfer to another account; **bankinterne ~umbuchung** bancogiro; ~**umsatz** account turnover, ratio of sales to receivables *(US)*; ~**unterhaltung** maintenance of an account; ~**unterlagen** account files; ~**veränderung** change in account; **gesamten**

~**verkehr untersagen** to stop all operations on an account; ~**verwendung** account operation; ~**vollmacht** authority to sign an account, mandate; **jem. ~vollmacht erteilen** to empower s. o. to operate on an account; ~**vortrag** balance carried forward; ~**zahlung** payment on account.

Kontrabuch tally, account book.

kontradiktorisch *(Recht)* contradictory, contentious;
~ **verhandeln** to hear a case;
~**e Sache** contentious matter; ~**es Urteil** contradictory judgment; ~**es Verfahren** adversary proceedings.

Kontrahent contractor, contracting party, party to a contract, contrahent, stipulator, contractant, covenantor;
~**en** contracting parties.

kontrahieren to contract;
mit sich selbst ~ to act as principal and agent;
Anleihe ~ to negotiate a loan; **Schulden** ~ to incur debts.

Kontrahierung von Schulden contraction (incurrence) of debts.

Kontrahierungs|freiheit liberty to contract; ~**zwang** contractual obligation.

Kontrakt contract, covenant, article, agreement;
laut ~ as per contract;
~ **abschließen** to enter into an agreement;
~**abschlüsse** contracts placed; ~**arbeit** bargain work; ~**bruch** breach of covenant.

kontraktbrüchig contract-breaking;
~**e Partei** defaulting party.

kontraktlich contractual, stipulated;
~ **gebunden** under (bound by) contract, articled.

Kontraposition contra item.

konträr contrary;
~**e Meinungen** opposing opinions.

Kontrast contrast;
als ~ für jds. Klugkeit dienen to serve as a foil for s. one's cleverness.

kontrastarm *(Foto)* flat.

Kontrast|bild contrast picture; ~**farben** colo(u)rs in contrast; ~**filter** contrast film; ~**foto** hard-contrast picture; ~**fotometer** contrast photometer.

kontrastieren to contrast.

kontrastlos *(Foto)* flat.

Kontrastprogramm *(Rundfund)* opposite programm(me).

Kontribution contribution;
~**en auferlegen** to put under (levy a) contribution; **einem Land ~en auferlegen** to lay a country under contribution.

Kontributionsplan *(Lebensversicherung)* contribution method.

Kontroll|abschnitt checking form, coupon, counterfoil *(Br.)*, stub *(US)*; ~**abschnitt und Abreißblatt** counterfoil and leaf; ~**abteilung** auditing department; ~**angestellter** checkout clerk; ~**apparat** checking instrument; **periodische ~aufstellungen** *(Makler und Banken)* comparisons; ~**ausschuß** governing commission, supervisory (control) committee; ~**beamter** controller, examiner, control officer, *(Straßenbahn)* floating inspector, supervisor; ~**befugnis** supervisory power, authority to control, *(Forstbehörde)* conservancy *(Br.)*; ~**behörde** supervisory authority (board, *Br.*), board of control; ~**beleg** voucher, counterfoil, *(Makler)* comparison slip *(US)*; ~**bestimmungen für die Stadtausdehnungen festlegen** to control urban growth; ~**bild** *(Fernsehen)* monitoring picture; ~**blatt** counterfoil *(Br.)*, stub *(US)*; ~**buch** controlling account *(US)*, *(Arbeiter)* time sheet *(US)*, *(Kunde)* cheque book *(Br.)*, passbook, bankbook, deposit book *(US)*; ~**buch für ein Kontokorrentkonto** current register *(Br.)*.

Kontrolle control, supervision, surveillance, examination, tab, grasp, *(Prüfung)* supervision, verification, *(Revision)* auditing, *(persönliche Überprüfung)* screening, *(Untersuchung)* examination, inspection, check[ing], checkup;
außer ~ geraten out of control; **unter** ~ in hand, under control; **absolute** ~ entire control; **ärztliche** ~ medical inspection; **parlamentarische** ~ parliamentary control; **strenge** ~ strict control; **zentrale** ~ overhead control;
betriebsinterne ~ der Arbeitsabläufe operational audit; ~ **der öffentlichen Ausgabenwirtschaft** public spending control; ~ **des Außendienstes** field control; **betriebsinterne ~ der Buchführung** accounting control; ~ **nach Erscheinen** post check; **automatisch justierte ~ der Farbeinstellung** *(Fernseher)* keyed automatic colo(u)r gain control; ~ **der Fertigung** supervision of manufacture; ~ **an der Grenze** formalities at the frontier; ~ **der Lagervorräte** inventory control; ~ **des Marktes** control of the market, market supervision, *(durch zwei Firmen)* duopoly; ~ **durch das Parlament** parliamentary control; ~ **des Verkaufspersonals** field control; ~ **der Wirtschaft** industrial control;
scharfe ~n anwenden to put a leash on s. th.; ~ **ausüben** to exercise (wield) control, to keep a firm hand on; **praktisch die ~ ausüben** to have practical control of; ~ **über sich behalten** to keep a check on one's temper; **unter ~ bekommen** to get under control; **schleudernden Wagen wieder unter ~ bekommen** to pull a car out of a skid; **sich der ~ entziehen** to get out of control; **sich jeder ~ entziehen** to take the bit between one's teeth; **außer ~ geraten** to get out of hand; **etw. unter ~ haben** to have s. th. securely packaged, to keep tabs on s. th. *(Br.)*; **Situation vollkommen unter ~ haben** to have s. th. (an affair) well in hand, to master a situation; **unter jds. voller ~ sein** to be under s. one's thumb; **unter ~ stehen** to be under control, *(Bewährungssystem)* to be under police supervision; **unter ~ stellen** to place under supervision; **regelmäßiger ~ unterliegen** to be subject to regular inspection; **einer gründlichen ~ unterziehen** to check thoroughly; **leicht die ~ über sich verlieren** to easily fly off the handle *(US)*; ~ **verschärfen** to increase the control.

Kontrollempfänger *(Fernsehen)* monitoring receiver.

Kontrolleur controller, supervisor, *(Fracht)* tally clerk (keeper), check taker, checker, tallyman, *(Eisenbahn)* ticket inspector, guard, *(Schaffner)* checkman *(US)*;
~**stelle** controlship.

Kontroll|flüge durchführen to fly air patrols; ~**funktionen** regulatory (supervisory) powers; ~**funktionen ausüben** to exercise supervisory control; ~**gang** *(Polizei)* beat, *(Wächter)* round; ~**gerät** checking device; ~**grenze** *(Statistik)* control limit; ~**gruppe** *(Untersuchung)* control group.

kontrollierbar controllable, checkable.

kontrollieren to control, *(abstreichen)* to tick off, *(Bücher)* to audit, to inspect, *(nachprüfen)* to verify, *(prüfen)* to check, to supervise, to control, to tally, to inspect, to check up;
etw. ~ to ride hard on s. th.; **Bücher** ~ to audit (inspect) the books; **genauestens** ~ to cross-check; **Güte eines Erzeugnisses** ~ to inspect the quality of a product; **Hälfte der Aktien** ~ to hold over half of the shares; **Instrumente** ~ to keep a check on the instruments; **Markt** ~ to command (regulate) the market; **Preise** ~ to administer prices; **Rechnungsposten** ~ to verify the items of a bill; **Reisende an der Grenze** ~ to check the papers of travellers at the frontier; **Tagesumsätze genau** ~ to keep close tabs on daily sales *(Br.)*; **Unternehmen durch Aktienmehrheit** ~ to control a company by holding a majority of the shares.

kontrollierende Gesellschaft controlling company.

kontrolliert controlled;
~**e Abrüstung** controlled disarmament.

Kontroll|karte control card, *(Arbeitszeitkontrolle)* time card; ~**kasse** cash register; ~**knopfregelung auf dem Armaturenbrett** dashboard control knob; ~**kommission** control commission; ~**konto** controlling account, checkbook; ~**lampe** pilot lamp; ~**leiter** controller; ~**leuchte** *(Auto)* indicator light, *(Flugzeug)* pilot light, *(Warnlampe)* warning lamp; ~**liste** check list, tally sheet, checkroll, *(mil.)* muster roll; ~**marke** check [mark] *(US)*, inspection stamp, *(Zeitkontrolle)* time card, time ticket; ~**markenabnehmer** *(Theater)* check taker; ~**maßnahmen** measures of control; ~**methoden** control methods; ~**muster** counter sample; ~**nummer** test (reference, check) number, *(Kennziffer)* code number; ~**organ** controlling (supervisory) body, *(Staat)* state regulator; ~**organisation** control organization.

kontrollpflichtig subject to control.

Kontroll|platz *(tel.)* monitor position; ~**prüfung** test, check; ~**pult** *(Radio, Fernsehen)* monitoring board; ~**punkt** point of control, checkpoint; ~**rat** Control Council; ~**rechnung** checking account; ~**recht** *(Bücher)* audit privilege; ~**register** counter account; ~**relais** control (pilot) relay; ~**satellit** spy satellite; ~**schalter** control switch; ~**schein** control ticket, check *(US)*, counterfoil *(Br.)*, *(Arbeitszeitkontrolle)* time ticket (card), *(Theater)* pass-out check *(Br.)*; ~**schirm** *(Fernsehen)* monitoring screen; ~**stelle** control office, *(Betrieb)* auditing agency, *(Kapitalanlagegesellschaft)* auditors; ~**stempel** time stamp, countermark; ~**stichprobe** reference sample; ~**streifen** *(Fluglotsen)* strip; ~**system** system of controls; ~**tätigkeit ausüben** to exercise supervisory control; ~**telegramm** repeated message; ~**turm** *(Flugplatz)* control tower; ~**uhr** time clock, time recorder, journeyman (master) clock, control clock, telltale, watchman's clock; ~**uhr stechen** to check in (out); ~**untersuchung** check inspection; ~**vermerk** stamp, check mark; ~**versuch** control experiment; ~**verzeichnis** counter account; ~**vorrichtung** checking device; ~**zeichen** tick, tally, countermark, check mark; ~**zettel** checking form, inspection ticket, counterfoil, tally; ~**ziffer** key (desk) number; ~**zweck** control purpose.

kontrovers controversial;
~**e Ansichten** controversial opinions.
Kontroverse controversy, dispute, conflict, contestation, antagonism;
scharfe ~ tussle; **wortreiche** ~ wordy conflict;
allerlei ~**n auslösen** to give rise to much controversy; ~ **mit jem. austragen** to have it out with s. o.; ~ **im Verhandlungswege beilegen** to settle a dispute by negotiation; **sich zu einer größeren politischen** ~ **entwickeln** to swell into a major political controversy; ~ **mit jem. haben** to carry on a controversy with s. o.
Kontur outline, line;
verschwommene ~**en** soft outlines;
elegante ~**en eines Wagens** elegant outline of a car;
~**en aufzeichnen** to line in a contour;
~**karte** contour map; ~**schrift** open type, outline; **in** ~**zeichnung** in outline.
Konus cone, neck.
konvenieren, jem. to suit (be suitable for) s. o.
Konvention convention, treaty, agreement;
~**en** conventional proprieties, customs;
gesellschaftliche ~**en** social conventions;
einer ~ **beitreten** to accede to a convention; **sich den gesellschaftlichen** ~**en fügen** to conform to the usages of society; **sich über alle** ~**en hinwegsetzen** to throw one's cap over a windmill, to be a law unto o. s.; ~**en wahren** to observe the respectabilities.
Konventional | heirat marriage of convenience; ~**strafe** presumptive (liquidated, stipulated) damages, penal sum, penalty for nonfulfil(l)ment of contract; ~**strafe einklagen** to sue for liquidated damages; ~**strafbestimmung** liquidated damages clause; ~**tarif** conventional tariff; ~**zinsen** stipulated interest.
konventionell conventional, formal, ready-made, customary, usual;
übertrieben ~ ossified;
~**e Kräfte** *(mil.)* conventional forces; ~**en Krieg in einen Atomkrieg eskalieren** to escalate conventional war into nuclear warfare.
Konversation conversation;
belanglose ~ small talk, racket jawing *(sl.)*;
~ **mit jem. beginnen** to enter into a conversation with s. o.;
lebhafte ~ **führen** to carry on a lively conversation.
Konversationslexikon encyclop(a)edia, holdall *(coll.)*;
wandelndes ~ **sein** to be a walking library *(fam.)*.
Konversationston conversational tone.
Konversion, echte effective conversion; **zwangsweise** ~ compulsory conversion;
~ **einer Anleihe** loan conversion.
Konversions | abkommen convertibility agreement; ~**angebot** conversion offer; ~**anleihe** conversion loan; ~**ausgabe** conversion issue; ~**bestimmungen** conversion provisions; ~**betrag** conversion amount; ~**guthaben** conversion balance; ~**kasse** conversion office, clearinghouse; ~**klausel** conversion feature, convertibility clause; ~**konto** conversion account; ~**kurs** conversion price; ~**prämie** conversion premium; ~**recht** right of conversion, conversion privilege; ~**satz** rate of conversion, conversion rate; ~**schuldverschreibungen** convertible bonds; ~**tabelle** conversion table (chart); ~**vorrecht** right of conversion.
Konvertibilität | der Währung convertibility of currency;
~ **in Etappen wieder herstellen** to restore convertibility by easy stages.
konvertierbar convertible;
beschränkt ~ partly convertible; **nicht** ~ inconvertible, unconvertible; **voll** ~ fully convertible;
~**e Papiere** convertible securities; ~**es Papiergeld** convertible paper currency; ~**e Vermögenswerte** convertible assets.
Konvertierbarkeit convertibility [of currency];
beschränkte ~ restricted convertibility; **freie** ~ external convertibility.
Konvertierbarkeitsklausel convertibility clause.
konvertieren *(Religion)* to be converted, to get religion *(fam.)*.
konvertiert converted;
nicht ~ unconverted.
Konvertierung conversion.
Konvertierungsangebot conversion offer.
Konvoi convoy;
~ **mit Unterseebooten angreifen** to attack a convoy by submarines; **Schiffe im** ~ **begleiten** to convoy ships; ~ **auf den Weg bringen** to dispatch a convoy; **im** ~ **fahren** to sail under (drive in) convoy; ~ **festhalten** to block a convoy.
konzedieren to concede, to accord, to grant.
Konzentration concentration, integration, merger;
horizontale ~ horizontal integration; **industrielle** ~ territorial (regional) division of labo(u)r, industrial concentration; **mangelnde** ~ lack of concentration; **vertikale** ~ vertical integration; **wirtschaftliche** ~ industrial concentration;
~ **einer Industrie** industrial concentration, localization of an industry; ~ **wirtschaftlicher Macht** concentration of economic power; ~ **des statistischen Materials** reduction of data; **vertikale** ~ **in vorgelagerten Produktionsstufen** backward integration; ~ **von Truppen** concentration of troops; ~ **der Wirtschaft** economic concentration (integration);
hohes Maß an ~ **verlangen** to require great (a great degree of) concentration.
Konzentrations | bewegungen integration movements; ~**genehmigung** merger clearance *(US)*; **große** ~**kraft verlangen** to require great concentration; ~**lager** detention (concentration) camp; ~**maßnahmen** concentration measures; ~**minderung** disvestiture; **staatliches** ~**prinzip** cut-off principle; ~**problem** concentration issue; ~**prozeß** process of concentration; ~**prozeß der Wirtschaft** economic concentration, process of integration; ~**tendenz** trend of concentration; ~**theorie** theory of concentration; ~**vermögen** power of concentration; ~**vorgang** process of concentration, industrial merger; **beschleunigter** ~**vorgang** speedup in concentration.
konzentrieren to concentrate, to major on, to center, to integrate;
sich ~ to put one's thoughts together; **sich auf etw.** ~ to focus (capitalize) on s. th.; **sich auf eine Arbeit** ~ to settle down to work; **seine Bemühungen auf ein Problem** ~ to focus one's efforts on a problem; **all seine Energie auf etw.** ~ to channel all one's energies into s. th.; **sich um ein Gebiet** ~ to be localized (centered) in an area; **sich ganz aufs Geschäft** ~ to attend strictly to business, to wipe it off *(sl.)*; **polizeiliche Nachforschungen** ~ to concentrate police investigations; **sich auf zwei Punkte** ~ to concentrate on two points; **sich auf Staatsaufträge** ~ to focus on the government market; **sich um eine Stadt** ~ to center on a town; **sich in den Städten** ~ to concentrate in the cities; **Truppen** ~ to concentrate troops; **sich völlig** ~ to pour it on *(sl.)*; **wieder** ~ to reconcentrate; **sich auf die kostengünstig arbeitenden Zechen** ~ to concentrate on the mines operating most economically.
konzentriert concentrated, focussed, *(knapp)* in tabloid form;
ganz auf seine Arbeit ~ centered on one's work;
~**e Angriffe** concentrated attacks; ~**e Nahrungsmittel** concentrated food.
Konzept concept, *(Entwurf)* foul paper (copy), rough copy, first draft, minute, pattern;
~ **einer Rede** draft of a speech;
vom ~ **ablesen** to read from one's notes; **Redner durch Zwischenrufe aus dem** ~ **bringen** to heckle (confuse, throw out) a speaker with interruptions; **sein** ~ **durchsetzen** to have one's way; **aus dem** ~ **kommen** to lose the thread; **ohne** ~ **sprechen** to speak off the cuff *(US)*; **jem. das** ~ **verderben** to spoil s. one's plans, to upset s. one's applecart;
~**buch** sketch book; ~**halter** *(Schreibmaschine)* copyholder.
Konzeption conception, idea, *(Anzeige)* layout;
entwicklungspolitische ~ development policy conception.
Konzeptpapier scribbling paper, common foolscap;
mittelfeines ~ draft paper.
Konzern combination, combine, conglomerate, multicorporate enterprise *(US)*, group of companies, affiliated group of corporations *(US)*, multi-corporate enterprise *(US)*, business trust *(US)*;
kurzfristig gebildeter ~ limited trust *(US)*; **horizontaler** ~ horizontal combine (combination); **vertikaler** ~ lateral combination, integrated (vertical) trust *(US)*;
~ **der holzverarbeitenden Industrie** timber group; ~ **mit breitgestreutem Produktionsprogramm** multiproduct group; **wohl ausgewogener** ~ **mit einem breiten Sortiment integrierter Gesellschaften** well-balanced integrated group of complementary companies;
im Wege des Zukaufs zu einem ~ **heranwachsen** to take the conglomerate route to growth; **in einem** ~ **zusammenfassen** to bracket together in a group;
~**absatz** intercompany sale, group's sales; ~**abschluß** group accounts; **konsolidierter** ~**abschluß** consolidated [annual statement of] accounts, group accounts.
konzernähnlicher Charakter quasi-trust character *(US)*.
Konzern | aktien conglomerate shares (stocks, *US*); ~**angebot** conglomerate bid, group-wide offer; ~**angestellter** big-company executive; **leitender** ~**angestellter** group executive;

~**anreiz** impetus to combination; ~**ausgleich** *(konsolidierte Bilanz)* intercompany elimination (squaring); ~**ausweis** group statement; ~**bedarf** group demand; ~**beteiligungen** shares (stocks, *US*) in subsidiary companies; ~**betrieb** affiliated company (organization), division of a conglomerate; ~**bewegung** combination movement; ~**beziehungen** group relationship, intercompany (intercorporate) relations; ~**bilanz** consolidated (group) balance sheet, combined (group, consolidated) financial statement *(US)*; ~**bilanzsumme** group's balance-sheet total; ~**bildung** consolidation, merger; **ungesetzliche** ~**bildung** *(Kartellgesetz)* unlawful combination; ~**buchführung**, ~**buchhaltung** group accounts, entity accounting; ~**buchgewinn** intercompany profit; ~**buchhalter** group accountant; ~**chef** group chairman; ~**darlehn** lending to a group, *(Darlehn innerhalb des Konzerns)* intercompany loan.

konzerneigene Revision group internal audit.

Konzern|eigenmittel group's own funds; ~**einkauf** syndicate buying; ~**einnahmen** consolidated returns (income); ~**entflechtung** deconcentration *(US)*, decartelization; ~**entwicklung** combination (trust, *US*) movement; ~**erträge vor Steuern** group revenue before taxation; ~**etat** overall company budget; ~**fahrzeug** group vehicle; ~**finanzchef** group financial director, group treasurer; ~**firma** affiliated (associated) company; ~**forderungen** intercompany claims (equities); ~**fremder** outsider; ~**fusion** conglomerate merger; ~**geschäfte** group activities, intercompany operations; ~**geschäftsbericht** consolidated report; ~**gesellschaft** affiliated (associated, allied) company, subsidiary [company], related (constituent) company, consolidated company *(Br.)*, affiliated (consolidated) corporation *(US)*, group member.

Konzerngewinn profit of the group, intercompany (group) profit;
~ **vor Steuern** group profit before taxation;
~**anteil** group share of profits; ~ **und Verlustrechnung** statement of consolidated income, consolidated profit and loss statement.

Konzern|gruppe [consolidated] group, affiliate group of a corporation, link-up; ~**guthaben** intercompany assets; ~**handel** group trading.

konzernintern intercorporate, within the group;
~**e Ertragsbelastungen** intercompany charge on income; ~**e Umsätze** intercompany *(Br.)* (intercorporate) transactions; ~**e Verrechnungen** intergroup eliminations.

Konzern|jahresergebnis group result for the year; ~**jurist** corporation counsel *(US)*; ~**konto** consolidated (group) account; ~**kredit** intercompany loan, group borrowing; ~**leitung** group management, central management of a combine; ~**rücklagen** consolidated earned surplus *(US)*; ~**schulden** intercompany debts; ~**spitze** group management; ~**syndikus** corporation counsel *(US)*; ~**tagung** company-wide meeting; ~**tätigkeit** group's activities; ~**tochter** affiliate group of a corporation; ~**transaktionen** group dealings; ~**umsatz** external (group) turnover (sales), intercompany (consolidated) sales, group dealings; ~**unternehmen** associated company *(Br.)*, affiliated company (corporation, *US*), consolidated (related) corporation *(US)*, trading group; ~**verbindlichkeiten** intercompany liabilities; ~**verflechtung** interlocking combine; ~**verhältnis** intercorporate relations, group relationship; ~**verlust** group's (intercompany) loss; ~**vermögen** group assets; ~**versicherung** captive insurance; ~**vertrag** trust agreement *(US)*; ~**verwaltung** group management; ~**vorstand** group board; ~**ziel** conglomerate target; ~**zusammenhänge** interlocking (holdings) of firms; ~**zusammenschluß von Gesellschaften** corporate combination; **einen Ausweg in weiteren** ~**zusammenschlüssen sehen** to see a way out in the conglomerate route.

Konzert concert;
~ **der Großmächte** *(Historie)* Concert of Europe;
~ **geben** to give a concert;
~**abend** recital; ~**aufführung** concert presentation; ~**besucher** concert goer; ~**flügel** concert grand; ~**halle** music (concert) hall; ~**halle mieten** to hire a concert hall.

konzertieren to give a concert, to concertize *(US)*;
im Freien ~ to perform alfresco.

konzertierte Aktion concerted action.

Konzert|meister concertmaster; ~**raum** concert room; ~**saal** concert hall; ~**zeichner** *(Börse)* stag *(Br.)*; ~**zeichnung von neu aufgelegten Wertpapieren** stagging of new issues *(Br.)*; **Markt durch** ~**zeichnungen beeinflussen** to stag the market *(Br.)*.

Konzession concession, *(Bank)* charter, federal (state) charter *(US)*, *(Erlaubnis)* permit *(Br.)*, *(Privileg)* grant, patent, privilege, *(Verkaufsrecht)* licence, franchise *(US)*;
ohne ~ unlicensed;
ausgehandelte ~ bargaining give; **besondere** ~ special (personal) franchise *(US)*; **erloschene** ~ expired licence; **noch nicht genehmigte** ~ *(Bank)* open charter; **grundstücksgekoppelte** ~ real privilege *(Br.)*; **internationale** ~ international settlement; **öffentlich rechtliche** ~ licence under public law, franchise; **übertragene** ~ holdover; **vorläufige** ~ interim licence, preliminary concession *(US)*;
~ **zum Ausschank alkoholischer Getränke** excise licence *(Br.)*, liquor license *(US)*, license for the sale of alcoholic drinks; ~ **zur Ausübung eines Gewerbes** trading (business) licence; ~ **zum Betrieb einer Druckerei** printer's licence; ~ **zum Betrieb eines Taxiunternehmens** hack license *(US)*; ~ **zur Gründung einer Gesellschaft** franchise of a corporation, corporation license; ~ **für eine Omnibuslinie** franchise for a bus service *(US)*; ~ **für eine Schnellgaststätte** fast-food franchise *(US)*; ~ **für später** executory licence;
~ **ändern** *(Bank)* to amend a charter; ~ **beantragen** to apply for a licence (concession); **sich eine** ~ **beschaffen** to take out a licence; ~ **besitzen** to be licensed, to hold a licence, to be franchised *(US)*; **um eine** ~ **einkommen** to apply for a licence; ~ **entziehen** to withdraw a concession, to withdraw a licence, to revoke a licence, to disenfranchise; ~ **erteilen** to grant a concession (privilege), to issue (grant) a licence, *(Bank)* to grant a charter; ~ **haben** to be licensed, to hold a licence; ~**en machen** to make concessions; ~ **suspendieren** to suspend a license *(US)*; ~ **verleihen** to grant a license, to franchise *(US)*; **sich eine** ~ **verschaffen** to take out a licence; ~ **zurücknehmen** to revoke a licence, to withdraw a concession, to revoke a grant.

Konzessionär concession(n)aire, concessionary, grantor, licensee, licence holder, franchisee *(US)*;
städtischer ~ city concession(n)aire.

konzessionieren to [grant a] license, to franchise *(US)*, *(Bank)* to charter.

konzessioniert licensed, concessionary, franchised *(US)*, *(Bank)* chartered;
nicht ~ unlicensed;
~**es Gewerbe** licensed (licenced, *US*) trade, licensed traffic; ~**er Spirituosenhandel** licensed victuallers *(Br.)*; ~**er Verkaufsvertreter** licensed dealer; ~**es Wirtshaus** licensed house (premises) *(Br.)*.

Konzessionierung licensing, franchising *(US)*.

Konzessions|abgabe licence fee *(Br.)* (tax, *US*), franchise (privilege) tax *(US)*, municipal compensation *(US)*; ~**abteilung** department of licensing affairs; ~**änderung** *(Bank)* amendment of a charter; ~**antrag** licence application; ~**ausschuß** licensing committee; ~**aussteller** licenser *(Br.)*, franchiser *(US)*; ~**bedingungen** terms of concession; ~**behörde** licensing agency; ~**belassung** retention of a licence; ~**bereich** permit-issuing locality.

konzessionsbereit willing to make concessions.

Konzessions|bestimmungen licensing regulations; ~**einkünfte** concession revenue; ~**entziehung**, ~**entzug** revocation of a licence, licence revocation; ~**erfordernisse erfüllen** to prove up on a concession *(US)*; ~**erneuerung** renewal of a concession; ~**erteilung** licensing, public grant, franchise *(US)*, franchising *(US)*, *(an Bank)* grant[ing] of a charter; ~**erwerb** licence buying; ~**gebiet** franchise field; ~**gebühr** charter (licence, concession) fee, franchise (privilege) tax *(US)*, bonus, mise money, *(Bank)* charter fee; **einmalige** ~**gebühr** basic concession acquisition fee; ~**gelände** franchise site *(US)*; ~**gewährung** licensing, franchising *(US)*, secondary (special) franchise *(US)*; ~**grenzen** *(Bank)* limits of charter powers; ~**grundlage** concession basis; ~**inhaber**, ~**nehmer** concession(n)aire, person duly licensed, licensed person, grantee, holder of a licence, licence holder, claim holder, franchisee *(US)*, franchise owner *(US)*, concessionary *(US)*, *(Bank)* grantee of charter; ~**klausel** *(Zollbehörde)* escape clause *(US)*; ~**periode** period of a licence.

konzessionspflichtig subject to a licence (franchise, *US*).

Konzessions|rechte concessionary rights, dealership rights; ~**rücknahme** revocation of a grant; ~**rücknahmeklausel** escape clause *(US)*; ~**steuer** licence tax, franchise (privilege) tax *(US)*; ~**system** licence (franchise) system; ~**träger** grantee, licensee, claim holder; ~**umfang** *(Bank)* charter powers; ~**urkunde** *(Bank)* charter, organization certificate; ~**verfahren** licence proceedings; ~**vergabe**, ~**verleihung** licensing, franchising *(US)*, *(Bank)* grant of a charter; ~**vergeber** licenser, franchiser *(US)*; ~**verlust** forfeiture, loss of corporate franchise *(US)*; ~**vertrag** licensing (franchise, *US*) agreement; ~**verzicht** *(Bank)* surrender of a charter; **im** ~**wege** concessionary; **im** ~**wege vergeben** to let out on a concession basis; ~**wesen** licence

(franchise, *US*) system, licensing system, franchise field *(US)*, franchising industry *(US)*; ~**zeit** chartered time, permitted hours *(Br.)*.
Konzil synod, council.
konziliant conciliatory, conciliative.
konzipieren to draw up, to draft, to outline.
Kooperation, in ~ mit der Betriebsleitung in cooperation with the management;
betriebliche ~ employee cooperation *(Br.)*;
~ auf dem Währungsgebiet monetary cooperation.
Kooperations|ausschuß der gewerblichen Wirtschaft business co-operation committee; ~**vereinbarung** cooperation agreement.
kooperativ coöperative.
kooperieren to coöperate, to play ball *(US coll.)*.
Kooptation coöptation, coöption.
Kooptationsrecht right to coöpt.
kooptieren to coöpt, to coöptate.
Kooptierter coöptee.
Kooptierung coöption, coöptation.
Koordinaten|kreuz crosshairs; ~**netz** map grid, *(math.)* net; ~**system** coördinate system.
Koordination coördination.
Koordinationsaufgaben coördination functions, function of co-ördination.
Koordinator coördinator, *(Pressekorrespondenz)* news desk;
~ des Investitionsbereichs controller of investments.
koordinieren to coördinate, to pool.
koordiniert coördinate[d];
nicht ~ incoördinate;
nicht genügend ~ sein to lack coördination;
~**e Dienststelle** coördinate authority; ~**e Politik** coördinated policy.
Koordinierung coördination, *(zeitlich)* timing;
unter ~ durch das Kanzleramt with cabinet-office coördination;
mangelnde ~ incoördination;
~ des Transportwesens coördination of transport (transportation, *US*); **~ auf dem Verwaltungsgebiet** administrative coördination.
Koordinierungs|aufgabe function of coördinating, coördination function; ~**ausschuß** coördinating committee (body); ~**befugnis** coördination decision; ~**büro** coördinating office; ~**maßnahme** trade-off; ~**stelle** coördinating office; ~**verfahren** coördination procedure.
Kopf head, *(Titel)* title, heading, caption *(US)*, *(Verstand)* brains;
auf dem ~ stehend *(Druck)* turned; **aus dem ~** from memory; **pro ~ der Bevölkerung** per head (capita, poll); **über jds. ~ hinweg** over s. one's head; **von ~ bis Fuß** from top to toe; **wie vor den ~ geschlagen** dumbfounded, nowhere *(US)*;
bedeutender ~ great thinker; **heller ~** clear head, whizz-kid *(US sl.)*; **kluger ~** strong mind, brains, headpiece *(coll.)*;
~ oder Adler *(Münze)* heads or tails; **~ eines Briefes** letterhead; **~ an ~** neck and neck; **~ einer Münze** face side of a coin; **~ einer Rechnung** billhead; **~ einer Seite** top of a page; **~ eines Unternehmens** soul (real head) of an enterprise (a business); **~ oder Wappen** pitch and toss;
jem. den ~ abreißen to knock s. o. into a cocked hat *(sl.)*, to have s. o. on the ropes; **jem. den ~ abschlagen** to strike off a man's head; **jem. das Haus über dem ~ anzünden** to set fire to s. one's house; **im ~ ausrechnen** to reckon (work out) in one's head; **auf jds. ~ eine Belohnung aussetzen** to set a price on s. one's head; **im Gegensatz zu allen anderen einen kühlen ~ behalten** to keep calm amid the excitements; **~ über dem Wasser behalten** *(fig.)* to keep one's head above water; **roten ~ bekommen** to get red in the face; **kühlen ~ bewahren** to keep a cool head; **10 DM pro ~ bezahlen** to pay DM 10 each; **~ einziehen** to make o. s. small; **seinen ~ mit Tatsachenmaterial füllen** to store one's mind with facts; **jem. etw. auf den ~ geben** to take s. o. down a peg or two; **einem durch den ~ gehen** to pass through one's head, to cross one's mind; **um ~ und Kragen gehen** to be a matter of life and death; **~ an ~ durchs Ziel gehen** to finish neck and neck; **seinen ~ für sich haben** to have a will of one's own; **nur Autos im ~ haben** to talk and think cars; **benommenen ~ haben** to feel dizzy; **Brett vor dem ~ haben** to be slow in the uptake; **kein Dach über dem ~ haben** to be made homeless; **nichts als Dummheiten im ~ haben** to be always up to some mischief; **Grütze im ~ haben** to have plenty of brains; **harten ~ haben** to be stubborn as a mule; **große Rosinen im ~ haben** to fly high; **schweren ~ haben** to have a bad (thick, *fam.*) head; **seinen ~ voll haben** to have a lot on one's mind; **~ hoch halten** to keep one's pecker up; **Geld auf den ~ hauen** to go the pace, to be on a big spending spree; **jem. im ~ herumgehen** to run in s. one's head, to revolve in s. one's mind; **j. auf dem ~ herumtanzen** to tyrannize s. o.; **~ zum Fenster hinausstecken** to pop (poke) one's head out of the window; **auf 5 Pfund pro ~ zu stehen kommen** to work out at £ 5 a head; **den ~ kosten** to cost one's life; **sich ein Angebot durch den ~ gehen lassen** to consider an offer; **sich einen Vorschlag durch den ~ gehen lassen** to think a proposal over, to turn over a project; **~ hängen lassen** to droop; **sich von jem. den ~ verdrehen lassen** to be swept off one's feet by s. o.; **bei einer Wahl ~ an ~ liegen** to be neck and neck in an election; **j. um einen ~ kürzer machen** to behead s. o.; **~ hinhalten müssen** to hold the baby *(Br., sl.)* (can, bag, *US*), to take the blame for it; **um seinen ~ zu retten** to save one's skin; **~ und Kragen riskieren** to stick one's neck out; **sich eine Kugel durch den ~ schießen** to blow one's brains out; **sich aus dem ~ schlagen** to put s. th. out of one's mind; **seinen ~ mißbilligend schütteln** to shake one's head disapprovingly; **~ eines Aufstands sein** to head a riot; **fähiger ~ sein** to have brains, to be a man of parts; **nicht ganz richtig im ~ sein** to have lost a button; **maßgebender ~ eines Unternehmens sein** to be the ruling spirit in a firm; **~ einer Verschwörung sein** to engineer a plot; **nicht auf den ~ gefallen sein** not to be born yesterday, to be no fool; **wie vor den ~ geschlagen sein** to be quite stunned; **über jds. ~ gewachsen sein** *(Schwierigkeiten)* to have got on top of s. o.; **sich etw. in den ~ setzen** to get an idea (take it) into one's head; **bis über den ~ in Schulden stecken** to be head over heels (up to the ears) in debt *(fam.)*; **~ in den Sand stecken** to bury one's head in the sand; **~ an ~ stehen** to stand shoulder to shoulder, to stand packed together; **völlig auf dem ~ stehen** to be topsy-turvy (upside down); **jem. in den ~ steigen** to go to the head; **etw. auf den ~ stellen** to play mischief with s. th., to turn everything topsy-turvy; **alles auf den ~ stellen, um ein verlorengegangenes Testament zu finden** to hunt high and low for a missing will; **das ganze Haus auf den ~ stellen** to turn a house upside down; **Stadt auf den ~ stellen** to paint the town red, to make whoopee *(US sl.)*; **jem. vor den ~ stoßen** to put s. o. off; **alle Leute mit seiner Aufgeblasenheit vor den ~ stoßen** to put everybody off by one's lordly airs; **~ hoch tragen** to be proud of o. s.; **Nagel auf den ~ treffen** to hit the nail on the head; **etw. im ~ umrechnen** to convert (reckon, work out) s. th. in one's head; **jem. den ~ verdrehen** to turn s. one's head; **seinen ~ verlieren** to lose one's head; **~ und Kragen beim Spiel verlieren** to gamble away one's fortune; **jem. über den ~ wachsen** to get beyond s. one's control, to get on top of s. o.; **jem. gehörig (tüchtig) den ~ waschen** to give s. o. a dressing down, to wash s. one's hair, to send s. o. away with a flea in his ear; **jem. das Dach über dem ~ wegnehmen** to pull up s. one's root; **auf den ~ gestellt werden** *(Auto)* to be turned right over; **sich gegenseitig Beleidigungen an den ~ werfen** to hurl insults at each other; **mit dem ~ durch die Wand wollen** to ram one's head against the wall, to go full tilt at everything; **jem. soundso viel pro ~ zahlen** to pay s. o. so much a head; **sich über etw. den ~ zerbrechen** to cudgel one's brains about s. th.; **seinen ~ aus der Schlinge ziehen** to wriggle out of it, to save one's hide; **jem. den ~ zurechtrücken** to bring s. o. to his senses (bearing), to tell s. o. what is what; **jem. auf den ~ zusagen** to tell s. o. outright; **seine Hände über dem ~ zusammenschlagen** to throw up one's hands in surprise;
mir schwirrt der ~ my head is swimming; **nicht wissen wo einem der ~ steht** not to know whether one is coming or going;
~**ansage** *(Fernsehstück)* opening announcement; ~**arbeit** brainwork, headwork, mental (white-collar, *US*) work; ~**arbeiter** brainworker, headworker, black-coated worker *(Br.)*, white-collar man (worker) *(US)*; ~**bahnhof** loop station, terminus *(Br.)*, terminal *(US)*; **vereinigter ~- und Durchgangsbahnhof** combination station; ~**bahnsteig** end platform; ~**bedeckung** head dress, headwear; ~**betrag** amount per head, capitation fee, per-capita quota; ~**blatt** *(Zeitung)* local edition; **standardisierter ~bogen** *(Patentwesen)* standardized front page; ~**briefbogen** letterhead.
Köpfchen savvy, mastermind *(US)*;
~ haben to have brains; **kluges ~ haben** to have one's head screwed on the right way.
Köpfe, nach ~n per capita;
führende ~ eines Landes leading figures of a country;
über die ~ seiner Zuhörer hinwegreden to be over the heads of one's audience; **sich bei einem Angriff blutige ~ holen** to return with severe losses from an attack; **sich bei den ~n kriegen** to be at loggerheads with one another, to go for another; **~ zusammenstecken** to put heads together, to get into a huddle;

Dritte brauchen sich hierüber nicht die ~ zu zerbrechen it is not for others to wonder; **viele ~, viele Sinne** so many heads, so many minds; **zwei ~ wissen mehr als einer** two heads are better than one.

köpfen to behead, to decapitate, *(Baum)* to top, to pollard.

Kopfende head, top, upper end.

Kopfeslänge, um ~ gewinnen to win by a head.

Kopf|filiale main branch; **~gebühr** capitation fee; **~geld** allowance per head, *(Sträfling)* blood money, head money *(US)*, bounty offered.

kopfgesteuerter Motor overhead engine.

Kopf|höhe headroom; **in ~höhe** on a level with the head; **~hörer** headset, headphone, earphone; **~hörer für den Unterrichtszweck** educational headphone; **~jäger** *(Arbeitskräfte)* headhunter; **~kissen** pillow; **~lampe** headlight.

kopflastig top-heavy, top-hampered, nose-heavy;
~es Programm head-start program(me); **~e Verwaltung** top-heavy organization.

Kopf|lastigkeit top (nose) -heaviness; **~leiste** *(Buch)* headband *(US)*, *(Zeitung)* head, headpiece.

kopflos headless, *(überstürzt)* panicky, panic-stricken, precipitate;
vor Angst ~ sein to be panic-stricken; **völlig ~ werden** to hit the panic-button;
~e Entscheidung headlong decision; **~e Flucht** headlong flight.

Kopf|mehrheit majority in numbers; **~nicken** nod; **mit einem ~nicken** with a wag of one's head; **~note** headnote; **~nuß** cuff on the head; **~preis** price, award offered for apprehension; **~quote** per-capita quota; **~rampe** end-loading platform; **~rechnen** mental arithmetic; **~-an-~-Rennen bei einer Wahl** desperately close-run election.

kopfscheu confused, intimidated, alarmed;
Redner ~ machen to throw out an orator, to disconcert a speaker; **~ werden** to become confused.

Kopfschmerzen headache;
wahnsinnige ~ haben to have a splitting headache; **sich über die politische Entwicklung ~ machen** to be worried by the political situation.

Kopf|schuß shot in the head; **~schütteln** shake of the head; **~seite** *(Zeitung)* front page.

kopfsprungartigen Konjunkturrückgang erfahren to drive headlong into a slump.

Kopf|stand *(Flugzeug)* nose-over; **~stärke** strength; **~station** railhead, loop station, terminus *(Br.)*, terminal *(US)*; **~steg** *(drucktechn.)* top reglet, headstick, head margin.

kopfstehen, vor Aufregung to be besides o. s. with joy.

Kopf|steinpflaster cobblestone pavement; **~steuer** capitation (personal, poll) tax, capitation fee, head money; **~stück** heading, headpiece, *(Klaps)* rap on the head *(coll.)*; **~stütze** headrest, *(Auto)* roll bar; **verstellbare ~stütze** adjustable head restraint; **~teil** individual quota, *(Rakete)* head; **nach ~teilen** per capita.

kopfüber head foremost, topsy-turvy;
sich ~ in ein Abenteuer stürzen to fling o. s. head-first into an adventure; **sich ~ in eine eingehende Beschreibung stürzen** to plunge headlong into a description.

Kopf|überschrift account title; **~verletzung** head injury; **~wäsche** *(fig.)* dressing down; **~weh** headache.

Kopfzahl number of persons;
~ der Besatzung crew size; **~ der Bevölkerung** number of the population;
nach der ~ abstimmen to vote by head.

Kopf|zählung head count; **~zeile** top line; **~zerbrechen** puzzling one's brains; **sich über die Schuldenbezahlung ~zerbrechen machen** to rack one's brains to think of a way of paying one's debts.

Kopie copy, counterpart, *(Durchschlag)* carbon [copy], flimsy *(Br.)*, transcript, *(Film)* print, *(Kopieren)* copying, *(Nachbildung)* imitation, facsimile, reproduction, replica, *(Pause)* tracing, *(Zweitschrift)* duplicate, duplication, manifold, print, counterpart, double;
beglaubigte ~ exemplified (examined) copy, certified true copy; **notariell beglaubigte ~** notarized copy; **gleichlautende ~** conformed copy *(US)*; **vierfach vorhandene ~n** quadruplicate copies; **wortgetreue ~** close copy; **zusätzliche ~** blind carbon copy, *(Werbematerial)* dupe;
~ einer Rechnung copy of an invoice;
~ anfertigen to [make a carbon] copy, to duplicate; **~ beglaubigen** to certify a copy; **~ beifügen** to attach a copy;
~anfertigung copying; **~apparat** copying apparatus (machine), copier, printer, duplicator; **~apparateindustrie** copier business; **~buch** copybook, copying (duplicating) book; **~buch für eingehende und ausgehende Avise** advice book; **~einrichtung** copying equipment; **~herstellung** ingrossing.

Kopieranstalt printing establishment (office, shop).

kopieren to [make a] copy, to write out, to pattern, to print off, to trace over, *(nachahmen)* to imitate, *(nachbilden)* to reproduce, to replicate, *(vervielfältigen)* to duplicate;
Filmschauspieler ~ to imitate a film actor; **jds. Stil ~** to imitate s. one's style.

kopierfähig copiable, copyable.

Kopier|farbband copying ribbon; **~gerät** photostat, copying equipment, copying machine (apparatus), copier, *(Foto)* printing equipment; **~leinwand** tracing cloth; **~licht** printing light; **~maschine** copying machine, copier; **~original** original copy; **~papier** printing-out paper, flimsy, *(Foto)* printing paper; **~presse** copying press, letter press; **~stift** stylus, copying pencil.

kopiert *(Foto)* printed.

Kopier|tinte copying (indelible) ink; **~unkosten** copying costs; **~verfahren** copying process, *(Foto)* printing process.

Kopiewechsel ziehen to draw bills in sets.

Kopilot copilot, second pilot, *(Luftwaffe, sl.)* meter reader.

Kopist copying clerk, copier, copyist, scribe, writer.

Koppel pasture, enclosure, pen, *(mil.)* waist belt;
auf der ~ weiden *(Pferde)* to be grazing in the paddock.

koppeln to join, to connect, to couple, to tie in;
Urlaubsfahrt mit einer Geschäftsreise ~ to combine business with pleasure; **zwei Waggons aneinander ~** to couple two railway coaches.

Koppeltarif coupled rate.

Kopplungs|geschäft package (tying-in, *US*) deal, tie-in, tying agreement (arrangement); **~klausel** tying (tie-in, *US*) clause; **~manöver** *(Raumschiffe)* docking, linkup; **~programm** *(Raumschiff)* docking program(me); **~verkauf** tie-in (combination, bundle, tied, *US*) sales, tying-in sale *(US)*; **~vertrag** *(Kartellrecht)* tying contract *(US)*.

Koproduktion coproduction.

Koproduktionsvertrag coproduction agreement.

Korb basket;
~ Wäsche basketful of washing;
einen ~ bekommen to get the mitten *(coll.)*; **jem. einen ~ geben** to turn s. o. down, to give s. o. the gate, to jilt at s. o.;
~flasche carboy, demijohn, wicker flask; **~macher** basket maker; **~möbel** wicker furniture; **~sessel** wicker (basket) chair; **~wagen** wicker perambulator; **~waren** basketry.

Kordel string, twine, cord;
Päckchen mit ~ verschnüren to tie up a parcel with string.

Kordon cordon;
~ bilden to ring; **~ um ein Gebiet ziehen** to cordon off an area.

Korken cork;
~ knallen lassen to pop a cork; **nach dem ~ schmecken** to taste of the cork;
~geld corkage; **~knall** pop of a cork; **~zieher** corkscrew, *(Flugzeug)* spin; **~zieherhose** baggy trousers.

Korn corn, grain, cereals, *(Visiereinstellung)* front sight, foresight;
~ anbauen to grow corn; **jem. aufs ~ nehmen** to seek s. o. out, to put s. o. on the spot *(US)*, to draw a bead on s. o. *(US)*; **Mann von echtem Schrot und ~ sein** to be a man of great caliber (calibre, *Br.*);
~anbau growing corn; **~boden** granary, loft; **~speicher** granary.

Körnchen grain, ounce;
~ Wahrheit grain (element, modicum) of truth; **auch nicht ein ~ Wahrheit** no particle of truth.

Korn|feld cornfield; **~kammer** garner.

Körper body, corpus;
am ganzen ~ through every pore;
am ganzen ~ zittern to tremble all over;
von kräftigem ~bau powerfully built.

körperbehindert disabled, physically handicapped.

Körper|behinderte handicapped (disabled) persons, disabled people; **~berechnung** solid geometry, cubature.

Körperbeschädigung physical disability;
lebenslängliche ~ permanent injury; **unfallbedingte ~** injury by accident.

Körper|ertüchtigung physical training; **~fülle** embonpoint, corpulence; **~glied** bodily member; **~kraft** physical strength, vigo(u)r.

körperlich bodily, physical, corporal, corporeal, material;
alle ~en Anstrengungen vermeiden to avoid any form of

physical exertion; ~e **Arbeit** manual (bodily) labo(u)r; ~e **Bestandsaufnahme** physical inventory; ~e **Frische** physical fitness; ~es **Gebrechen** physical defect; ~e **Gegenstände** things corporeal; ~e **Leistungsfähigkeit** physical capacity; ~e **Untersuchung** bodily search; ~e **Verfassung** physical shape; ~er **Zwang** physical compulsion.

Körper|pflegemittel toilet articles; **berufsbedingte ~schäden** occupational wear and tear.

Körperschaft body corporate, corporation, incorporation, incorporated body, corpus, *(jur. Person)* artificial person;
als ~ corporately; **nicht als ~ eingetragen** incorporate; **beratende ~** deliberative body, general assembly *(US)*; **aus mehreren Gesellschaften bestehende ~** aggregate corporation; **bundesunmittelbare ~** federal corporation *(US)*; **gemeinnützige ~** benevolent corporation, public-service (nonprofit-making, nontrading) corporation (organization); **gesetzgebende ~** legislative body (assembly), General Court *(US)*, House of Assembly; **inländische ~** domestic corporation *(US)*; **keine ~** not incorporated; **kommunale ~** municipal corporation; **öffentlich-rechtliche ~** statutory company (corporation), public body, public corporation *(US)*; **unabhängige politische ~** independent body politic; **selbstverwaltungsähnliche ~** quasi-municipal corporation *(US)*; **steuerpflichtige ~** taxpayer corporation;
~ des Privatrechtes corporate enterprise, private corporation *(US)*; **~ des öffentlichen Rechts** public body, public corporation, statutory company (corporation, *US*);
j. in eine ~ aufnehmen to aggregate s. o. to a society; **sich in einer ~ zusammenschließen** to become incorporated.

körperschaftlich corporate, corporative;
~ organisiert incorporated.

Körperschafts|besteuerung corporate taxation *(Br.)*; **~bildung** incorporation; **~eigentum** corporate property.

Körperschaftssteuer [general] corporation income *(US)* (corporation, corporate, *Br.*) tax, income tax on corporations *(US)*;
zuviel gezahlte ~ corporation tax overprovided in previous years; **gegen Vorschüsse verrechnete ~** mainstream corporation tax; **vorausgezahlte ~** advance corporation tax;
~ auf Dividenden aus Schachtelbeteiligungen intercorporate tax on dividends; **~ für nicht ausgeschüttete Erträge** accumulated earnings tax *(US)*;
~ ausrechnen to impute corporation tax; **~ erheben** to charge corporation tax; **von der ~ befreit sein** to be exempt from corporation tax; **der ~ unterliegen** to be within the charge of corporation tax;
~anrechnung imputation of corporation tax *(Br.)*; **~anrechnungssystem** imputation system *(Br.)*; **~befreiung** exemption from corporation tax; **~berechnung** corporation tax computation; **fälliger ~betrag** corporation tax due; **~erklärung** corporation (corporate, *Br.*) income-tax return; **für die ~festsetzung nicht anwendbar sein** to have no application under corporation tax; **~freibetrag** corporate income-tax exemption *(US)*; **~gesetz** income and corporation taxes act; **~gesetzgebung** corporation tax legislation; **~gesetzgebung vereinfachen** to simplify the tax laws applicable to companies *(Br.)*; **~herabsetzung** corporate tax cut *(Br.)*; **~pflicht** corporation tax liability.

körperschaftssteuerpflichtig sein to be liable to pay corporation (corporation income, *US*, corporate, *Br.*) tax.

Körperschaftssteuerrestzahlung mainstream corporation tax.

Körperschaftssteuersatz corporate *(Br.)* (corporation) tax rate, rate of corporation tax;
ermäßigter ~ für Kleinbetriebe small companies rate *(Br.)*; **einem einheitlichen ~ vor der Ausschüttung unterworfen sein** *(Dividende)* to suffer income tax at the basic rate at source.

Körperschaftssteuer|schuld corporation tax liability; **~system** scheme of corporation tax, corporation tax scheme (system); **~vergünstigung** corporate tax privilege *(Br.)*; **~vorauszahlungen** advance payments of corporation tax.

Körperverletzung bodily (personal, physical) injury, damage to person, *(Strafrecht)* battery, assault *(US)*;
fahrlässige ~ negligent bodily harm; **gefährliche ~** atrocious assault and battery; **gewaltsame ~** criminal assault and battery; **leichte ~** simple battery; **schwere ~** wounding, great (grievous) bodily harm (injury), serious injury, mutilation, *(Strafrecht)* aggravated assault *(US)*, assault and battery of a high and aggravated nature; **zufällige unbeabsichtigte ~** excusable assault; **unfallbedingte ~** injury caused by an accident; **versuchte ~** simple assault; **vorsätzliche ~** malicious injury;
~ mit tödlichem Ausgang felony murder *(US)*; **vorsätzliche ~ mit tödlichem Ausgang** manslaughter;
j. wegen ~ zivilrechtlich belangen to sue s. o. for civil injury.

Korporation corporation, incorporation, *(Studentenschaft)* fraternity *(US)*.

Korporations|rechte, ohne incorporate; **~siegel** common seal; **~urkunde** certificate (articles) of incorporation; **~urkunde einer Bank** bank charter, organization certificate *(US)*.

korporativ corporate, corporative;
~ handeln to act as (in) a body;
~e Vereinigung body corporate.

Korps, diplomatisches diplomatic body (corps);
~bereich *(mil.)* corps area; **~geist** party spirit.

Korpus *(drucktechn.)* long primer.

Korreferat supplementary paper.

korrekt correct, accurate, proper, to the book;
~ gekleidet properly dressed; **nicht ~** *(Stil)* faulty;
äußerst ~ sein to be letter-perfect; **nicht ganz ~ sein** not to be quite honest; **sich immer äußerst ~ verhalten** to be perfectly straight in all one's dealings;
~es Geschäftsgebaren straight dealings.

Korrektheit correctness, rectitude, correctitude, propriety, honesty, accuracy;
~ in finanziellen Dingen financial probity;
sich äußerster ~ befleißigen to behave with utmost correctitude.

Korrektiv corrective.

Korrektor corrector [of the press], proofreader, press (printer's) reader;
wissenschaftlicher ~ editorial reader;
~gehilfe copyholder; **~stelle** readership.

Korrektur correction, rectification, *(Abänderung)* alteration, *(Börsenkurs)* adjustment, *(Druck)* correction of the press, *(Korrekturbogen)* proof sheet;
bei der ~ under correction; **mit ~en zwischen den Zeilen** interlined with corrections;
druckfertige ~ press proof; **erste ~** first proof; **letzte ~** final (second) revise, second revisal, press proof; **schlechte ~** badly corrected proof; **verbesserte ~** revised proof; **zweite ~** revisal;
~ einer Buchung rectification of an entry; **~ einer Examensarbeit** correction of an examination paper; **~en der Extremwerte** *(Statistik)* end corrections; **~ einer Grenze** rectification of a boundary; **~ von Schularbeiten** correction of school children's work;
~en abziehen to pull proofs; **~en auf einem Manuskript anbringen** to mark a copy; **~en besorgen** to proof-correct, to read the proofs; **~en zum Druck geben** to pass a proof for press; **~en lesen** to hold copy, to read proofs, to proofread, to proof-correct, *(Hauskorrektur)* to make the first (rough) correction;
~ überprüfen to revise; **~ vornehmen** to make a correction;
~abzug copy (first) proof, impress copy, proof sheet; **letzter ~abzug** final proof; **~abzug anfertigen** to work off (pull) a proof; **~angaben** corrections for type; **~bogen** proof [sheet], revised proof; **druckfertige ~bogen** press revise, revised (press) proof; **fehlerloser ~bogen** clean printer's proof; **~eintragungen in roter Tinte** corrections in red ink.

Korrekturen|besorgung, ~lesen proof correction, correction of a proofsheet, proofreading, copyholding; **~leser** proofreader, press (printer's) corrector, corrector [of the press], copyreader, copyholder.

Korrektur|fahne [galley] proof; **~fahnen lesen** to read (correct) galley proofs; **~lack** correction fluid; **~posten** correcting and adjusting item; **~terminal** editing terminal; **~vorschrift** directions for correctors, proofreading instructions; **~zeichen** proofreader's corrections (mark), proof correction marks, mark (sign) of correction.

Korrespondent *(Berichterstatter)* [newspaper] correspondent, press agent (correspondent), contributing editor, stringer, *(Bank)* out-of-town correspondent, correspondent bank *(US)*, *(Geschäftsfreund)* business friend, *(Handelshaus)* correspondence clerk, *(Sekretär)* corresponding secretary, *(Verkaufsabteilung)* sales correspondent;
ständiger ~ staff correspondent; **überseeischer ~** overseas correspondent; **für Berlin vorgesehener ~** correspondence-elect for Berlin;
~ für mehrere Zeitungen syndicated correspondent;
seinen ~en mit etw. beauftragen to entrust a matter to one's correspondent.

Korrespondenten|berichte, zusammengefaßte points from letters; **~liste** list of correspondents, *(für Reisekreditbriefinhaber)* letter of indication; **~netz** network of correspondents.

Korrespondentreeder ship's husband, managing owner of a ship.
Korrespondenz correspondence, *(Papiere)* papers, *(Post)* letters, post *(Br.)*, mail *(US)*;
frühere ~ letters exchanged; **miteinander geführte (unsere)** ~ correspondence that has passed between us; **geschäftliche** ~ business correspondence; **mit Eingangsstempel versehene** ~ time-stamped correspondence;
~ **mit jem. abbrechen** to cut off one's correspondence with s. o.; ~ **ablegen** to place the correspondence in one's files; **seine** ~ **verschlossen aufbewahren** to keep one's letters under lock and key; **seine** ~ **durchsehen** to go through one's mail; ~ **einstellen** to discontinue (drop) a correspondence; ~ **erledigen** to attend to the correspondence; ~ **führen** to conduct a correspondence, to act as correspondent; **in** ~ **stehen** to be in correspondence (communication); **in** ~ **treten** to enter into correspondence; ~ **unterhalten** to carry on a correspondence; ~ **wiederaufnehmen** to resume correspondence with;
~**bank** banker's correspondence, advising bank, out-of-town correspondent, banker's correspondence, correspondent bank *(US)*; ~**bankverbindungen** links with corresponding banks; ~**büro** news (press) agency, clipping bureau *(US)*; ~**faktor** corresponding factor; ~**karte** correspondence card; ~**kursus** correspondence course; **gewöhnliche** ~**schrift** small hand; ~**spediteur** connecting carrier, correspondent forwarder; ~**versicherung** home-foreign insurance *(Br.)*.
korrespondieren, miteinander to correspond, to exchange letters.
korrespondierendes Mitglied corresponding member.
Korridor corridor *(Br.)*, passage, passageway, hall, vestibule, *(Entenschnabel)* panhandle *(US)*;
breiter ~ lobby.
korrigieren to correct, to rectify, to red-pencil;
Aufsatz ~ to correct an essay; **mit Blaustift** ~ to blue-pencil; **Börsenkurs** ~ to mark up (down, adjust) the rate of exchange; **Druckfahnen** ~ to proofread, to read for press (proofs); **seine Einstellung** ~ to alter one's attitude; **Eintragungen** ~ to rectify entries; **Maschineneinstellung** ~ to readjust a machine; **Rechnungsbetrag** ~ to correct an amount; **mit Rotstift** ~ to red-pencil.
korrigiert rectified.
Korrosionsschutz corrosion preventive;
doppelter ~ **der Gesamtkarosserie** double protection of body-shell against corrosion.
korrumpieren to corrupt, to debauch.
korrupt corrupt, bribable, depraved, rotten *(Br.)*;
durch und durch ~ rotten to the core;
~**e Methoden** venal practices; ~**er Politiker** venal politician; ~**e Staatsbeamte** corruptible government officials; ~**e Verwaltung** bribable administration.
Korruption corruption, corrupt practices, maladministration, jobbery, bribery, venality, graft *(US)*;
schamlose ~ unblushing corruption;
~ **der Öffentlichkeit** corruption in public life;
mit der ~ **in einer Stadt aufräumen** to clean up a city; **j. der** ~ **beschuldigen** to accuse s. o. of bribery.
Korruptions|anklage charge of corruption; **einer** ~**anklage entgegensehen** to face a charge of corruption; ~**fälle aufspüren (politisch ausnutzen)** to muck-rake *(US)*; ~**seuche** pest of corruption; ~**skandal** bribery scandal; ~**sumpf** hotbed of corruption; ~**unwesen** bribery and corruption; ~**vorbringen** corruption allegation.
Korso parade, procession.
Korvette corvette.
koscher kosher, straight, on the level, o.k.;
nicht ganz ~ phony *(US sl.)*, fishy, shady, hedge.
Kosmetik|er cosmetician, beautician *(US)*; ~**koffer** vanity bag (case, box); ~**salon** beauty shop (parlo(u)r).
kosmetische Mittel cosmetics, make-up.
Kosmopolit cosmopolite, cosmopolitan.
kosmopolitischer Weitblick cosmopolitan outlook.
Kosmos cosmos;
expandierender ~ expanding universe.
Kost food, fare, diet, *(Beköstigung)* board[ing], *(Wechsel)* pension, carrying over;
auf schmale ~ **gesetzt** kept on short commons;
einfache ~ simple diet, plain food; **fettarme** ~ low-fat diet; **freie** ~ free meals, run of one's teeth; **karge** ~ slender diet; **magere (knappe)** ~ poor fare, low diet; **substanzlose** ~ low diet; **unverdauliche** ~ indigestible diet; **vegetarische** ~ vegetarian diet;
~ **und Logis** room and board, board and lodging; **freie** ~ **und Wohnung** free board and lodging;
abwechslungsreiche ~ **bieten** to offer a rich variety of dishes; **in** ~ **geben** to board out, *(Börse)* to give on *(Br.)*; **freie** ~ **haben** to have one's board free; **in** ~ **nehmen** to take as a boarder, to board, *(Börse)* to take in; **in** ~ **sein** to board in (at); **auf schmale** ~ **setzen** to pinch s. o. for food, to put on a low diet (s. o. on short commons); **nur leichte** ~ **vertragen** to take only light food.
kostbar precious, valuable, *(teuer)* expensive, costly.
Kostbarkeit costly thing, preciousness;
~**en** valuables, treasures;
literarische ~**en** literary gems.
Kosten cost, costs, *(Auslagen)* expense[s], outlay, *(Gebühren)* charges, fees, *(Preis)* price, cost, *(Spesen)* charge[s];
abzüglich der ~ charges deducted, after deduction of charges (costs), less expenses (charges); **alle** ~ **eingeschlossen** including all charges; **auf** ~ **von** at the expense of; **auf eigene** ~ at one's own expense; **auf gemeinsame** ~ at joint expense, dividing [the] expenses; **auf jds.** ~ at the cost of s. o.; **auf meine** ~ to my cost, at my expense; **auf seine eigenen** ~ at his own charge; **auf** ~ **der Allgemeinheit** at public expense; **auf** ~ **und Gefahr** at the cost and risk of; **auf** ~ **der Qualität** at the expense of quality; **auf** ~ **der Reederei** at ship's expenses; **auf** ~ **des Staates** at public expense; **aufgrund der** ~ owing to the expenses; **ausschließlich der** ~ exclusive of costs; **einschließlich der** ~ including costs; **frei von den** ~ free of charges, cost-free; **gegen Erstattung der baren** ~ with out-of-pocket expense; **mit Einschluß aller** ~ all expenses included; **mit großen (hohen)** ~ **verbunden** at great cost, cost-effective; **mit** ~ **verknüpft** involving expense; **mit Rücksicht auf die** ~ in deference to cost; **nach Abzug aller** ~ all expenses deducted; **ohne** ~ no charge, *(Wechselaufdruck)* no expense [to be incurred], without expenses, *(Protest)* no protest; **ohne Rücksicht auf die** ~ without regard to cost; **ohne zusätzliche** ~ for no extra fare; **unter Auferlegung der** ~ awarding the costs; **unter Einschluß sämtlicher** ~ all costs included; **unter Nachnahme der** ~ charges forwarded, expenses charged forward; **unter Tragung der** ~ on payment of the costs; **zur Deckung der** ~ to cover the cost; **zuzüglich der** ~ expenses not included (to be added);
~ **gedeckt** expenses covered;
abnehmende ~ decreasing costs; **abschreibungsfähige** ~ service cost; **abzugsfähige** ~ deductible charges; **abzurechnende** ~ off charges; **aktivierte** ~ capitalized expenses; **allgemeine** ~ overhead expenses; **alternative** ~ opportunity costs; **nicht in bar anfallende** ~ noncash costs; **gemeinsame anfallende** ~ *(Fracht- und Passagierdienst)* common expense; **zukünftig anfallende** future costs; **angefallene** ~ expenses incurred; **vor der Gründung angefallene** ~ preliminary expenses *(Br.)*; **bei der Versilberung tatsächlich angefallene** ~ actual expenses of realization of the assets; **steil ansteigende** ~ skyrocketing (soaring) costs; **anteilsmäßige** ~ proportional (proratable, *US*) costs; **auferlegte** ~ taxable costs; **aufgelaufene** ~ accrued charges, costs incurred (accrued), accumulated charges; **auflaufende** ~ accruing costs; **außergerichtliche** ~ out-of-court expenses; **außerplanmäßige** ~ expenditure not budgeted for; **von der Kostenstelle nicht beeinflußbare** ~ uncontrollable expenses; **beitreibbare** ~ recoverable costs; **nicht beitreibbare** ~ irrecoverable expense; **besondere** ~ special charges; **beträchtliche** ~ considerable costs, heavy expense; **degressive** ~ regressive costs; **direkte** ~ direct cost (expenses), traceable cost; **diverse** ~ promiscuous charges; **durchlaufende** ~ transit costs; **eingegangene** ~ expenses involved; **einmalige** ~ nonrecurrent costs (expenses); **eintreibbare** ~ recoverable costs; **entscheidungsrelevante** ~ relevant costs; **entstandene** ~ costs incurred, accrued charges (cost); **bei der Konkursabwehr entstandene** ~ costs of resisting the bankruptcy proceedings; **entstehende** ~ accruing costs; **daraus entstehende** ~ costs arising from it; **bei der Geschäftsführung notwendigerweise entstehende** ~ costs necessarily incurred in the conduct of business; **nicht erfaßte** ~ imputed cost; **genehmigte erhöhte** ~ *(Prozeß)* treble costs *(US)*; **erstattete** ~ reimbursed expenses; **nicht anderseitig erstattete** ~ expenses not otherwise received; **erstattungsfähige** ~ *(Prozeß)* party and party (taxable) costs; **nicht erstattungsfähige** ~ untaxable costs; **daraus erwachsende** ~ costs attendant on; **nicht faktorbezogene** ~ nonfactor costs; **fallende** ~ decreasing (declining) costs; **fällige** ~ outstanding costs; **feste (fixe)** ~ fixed charges (costs), constant (unavoidable) cost, standby costs; **[noch] nicht festgesetzte** ~ *(Gericht)* untaxable cost; **festliegende** ~ assured costs; **festsetzbare** ~ taxable costs; **feststehende (fixe)** ~ fixed (standby) cost; **festzusetzende** ~ costs to be taxed; **fortlaufende** ~ overheads; **geschätzte** ~ estimated cost; **gesetzliche** ~ legal costs *(Br.)*; **in**

Rechnung gestellte ~ billed costs; **gewöhnliche** ~ ordinary expenses; **gleichbleibende** ~ constant costs; **indirekte** ~ indirect costs; **individuelle** ~ private costs; **kalkulatorische (kalkulierte)** ~ imputed cost; **kapitalisierte** ~ capitalized costs; **komparative** ~ comparative costs; **konstante** ~ constant (standing, standard) costs, general charges; **kumulierende** ~ accruing costs; **kurzfristige** ~ short-run costs; **laufende** ~ running (standing) charges, running (current) expenses; **leistungsabhängige** ~ variable costs; **an der Grenze der Wirtschaftlichkeit (Rentabilität) liegende** ~ marginal (incremental) costs; **mittelbare** ~ indirect costs; **nachkalkulierte** ~ post-mortem cost; **notwendige** ~ related cost; **pauschalierte** ~ bunched cost; **private** ~ internal effects; **progressive** ~ progressive costs; **proportionale** ~ proportional costs; **relative** ~ relative costs; **nicht relevante** ~ sunk cost; **rückläufige** ~ decreasing (declining) costs; **sämtliche** ~ full costs; **steil in die Höhe schießende** ~ skyrocketing costs; **spezifische (spezifizierte)** ~ special (direct) costs; **nahe der Rentabilitätsgrenze stehende** ~ marginal (incremental) costs; **steigende** ~ rising (increasing) costs; **stellvertretende** ~ *(Havarie)* substituted expenses; **tatsächliche** ~ actual costs; **übermäßige** ~ excessive (charges) costs; **auf Kapitalkonto übernommene** ~ capitalized costs; **auf den Tageswert umgerechnete** ~ adjusted costs; **unerhebliche** ~ insignificant expenses; **unerschwingliche** ~ enormous costs; **ungewisse** ~ variable cost; **unproduktive** ~ incidental expenses of production; **untragbare** ~ prohibitive cost; **variable (veränderliche)** ~ variable cost, out-of-pocket costs; **proportionale variable** ~ average variable costs; **veranschlagte** ~ estimated costs; **verbundene** ~ composite costs; **damit verbundene** ~ expense involved; **mit der Anschaffung verbundene** ~ purchase-related costs; **vereinbarte** ~ agreed costs; **vermeidbare** ~ escapable cost; **verschiedene** ~ sundry (miscellaneous) expenses; **verzerrte** ~ distorted costs; **voraussichtliche** ~ prospective costs; **vorkalkulierte** ~ standard costs, predetermined (scheduled, target) cost; **wachsende** ~ growing expenditure; **wechselnde** ~ controllable cost, variable cost (expenses); **wirkliche** ~ actual cost (expense); **rechtlich zulässige** ~ legitimate costs; **zunehmende** ~ increasing (rising) cost; **zurechenbare** ~ apportionable costs; **zusätzliche** ~ additional charges (expense, costs), added costs, extra charges;

~ **der Abschreibung** depreciation charges; ~ **nach Abschreibungen** amortized cost; ~ **des Abtransportes** transportation inland costs; ~ **vor Abzug des Bardiskonts** billed cost; ~ **des Anlagevermögens** asset costs; ~ **vor Anlauf der Fertigung** starting-load cost; ~ **der Anschlußeinrichtung** *(tel.)* installation charges; ~ **der weiteren Ausbildung** advancement costs *(US)*; ~ **und Auslagen** charges, costs and expenses; ~ **des Beklagten** defendant's costs; ~ **der Bergung** salvage cost (charges); ~ **bei voller Betriebsausnutzung** capacity costs; ~ **für Betriebsbauten** plant construction costs; ~ **der Betriebseinstellung (Betriebsstillegung)** shutdown costs; ~ **der Betriebsführung** operating costs; ~ **der Buchführung (Buchhaltung)** accounting (bookkeeping) costs; ~ **zum Buchwert** amortized cost; ~ **der Ernteeinbringung** harvesting expenses; ~ **der Erstellung des Jahresberichts** annual report costs; **immaterielle** ~ **und Erträge** nonpecuniary costs and benefits; ~ **pro Exemplar** per-copy costs; ~ **für Fahrten zwischen Wohnung und Betrieb** cost of travel between home and work; ~ **der Gebäudeerrichtung** cost of a structure; ~ **der Geldbeschaffung** cost of money; ~ **eines Gerichtsverfahrens** costs of going to court; ~ **der Geschäftsführung** executive (management) expenses; ~ **der Geschäftsstelle** agency cost; ~ **der Gesundheitsvorsorge** health care costs; ~ **der Haushaltsführung (Haushaltung)** household operating costs, household expenditure; ~ **der Instandhaltung** cost of maintenance; ~ **der Kapitalausstattung** capital equipment cost; ~ **des Konkursverfahrens** cost of preserving and administering the bankrupt's estate, bankruptcy costs, costs of adjudication; ~ **der Konkursverwaltung** administration (official receiver's) expenses; ~ **pro Kopf der Bevölkerung** per capita costs; ~ **der Lagerhaltung** holding costs, outlays for inventories, house charges *(US)*; ~ **der Lebenshaltung** cost of living; ~ **für Leichterung** lighterage charges; ~ **für die Leichterung und Verbringung an Land** lighterage and wharfage charges; ~ **des Liquidators** liquidator's expenses; ~ **des Löschens** charges for unloading; ~ **der Luftfrachtbeförderung** airfreight expenses; ~ **der Montage** cost of erection, assembly costs; ~ **der Nachlaßverwaltung** expenses of administration; ~ **der Pflichtverteidigung** costs of poor prisoner's defence; ~ **einer Projektdurchführung** running costs of a project; ~ **für das Rangieren** switching charges; ~ **eines Rechtsstreits** costs of issue; **erstattungsfähige** ~ **eines Rechtsstreites** costs as between party and party; ~ **der Rechtsverfolgung** law costs; ~ **für Rettungsmaßnahmen** salvage costs; ~ **zum anderthalbfachen Satz** double costs, double cash; ~ **zum zweieinhalbfachen Satz** treble costs; ~ **eines Schiedsgerichtsverfahrens** costs of umpirage; ~ **der Testamentserrichtung** testamentary expenses; ~ **des Unterhalts eines Lastkraftwagens** motor-van expenses *(Br.)*; ~ **der Unterhaltung eines Kraftfahrzeuges** automobile-operating (maintenance) costs; ~ **zuzüglich Verdienstspanne** cost-plus *(US)*; ~ **der Vermögensverwaltung** *(Treuhänder)* administration expenses; ~ **der Verpackung** packaging costs; ~, **Versicherung und Fracht** cost, insurance and freight, c.i.f.; ~ **des Vertriebs** marketing cost; ~ **der gesamten Warenlieferung** costs of goods sold; ~ **der notariellen Wechselvorlage** expense of noting; ~ **für immaterielle Werte** intangible costs; ~ **der Wiederbeschaffung** replacement cost; ~ **einer Wohnung** housing price; ~ **der Zollabfertigung** cost of customs clearance; ~ **im Zwischenverfahren** interlocutory costs;

~ **gehen zu Lasten von** costs to be borne by; ~ **spielen keine Rolle** expense is no object;

~ **steuerlich absetzen** to deduct costs; ~ **der Büromiete steuerlich absetzen** to claim the cost of rent of premises as a deduction; **für** ~ **und Logis arbeiten** to work for one's board; **jem. die** ~ **aufbrummen** to land s. o. with the costs; ~ **der Staatskasse aufbürden** to award the costs against the state; ~ **auferlegen** to allocate (order to bear) the costs, to award the costs; ~ **aufgliedern** to itemize costs; ~ **gegeneinander aufheben** to divide the costs between the parties; **für die** ~ **aufkommen** to bear (meet, pay) the expenses; ~ **aufschlüsseln** to break down expenses; ~ **aufteilen** to apportion (assign) costs; ~ **eines gemeinsamen Abendessens aufteilen** to split the cost of a dinner party; **sich die voraussichtlich entstehenden** ~ **ausrechnen** to reckon the probable costs; ~ **im Griff behalten** to keep track of costs; ~ **auferlegt bekommen** to be condemned in (ordered to pay) the costs; ~ **in den Griff bekommen** to control costs; **Konto mit sämtlichen** ~ **belasten** to charge an account with all the expenses; ~ **berechnen** to count (figure up, calculate, compute) the costs; **sich auf jds.** ~ **bereichern** to get rich at s. one's expense; ~ **berücksichtigen** to consider the expense; ~ **bestreiten** to bear the costs (expenses), to cover (meet) the expenses; **sich an den** ~ **gleichmäßig beteiligen** to contribute equally to the expense; **sich an den** ~ **schlüsselmäßig beteiligen** to pool expenses; **entstandene** ~ **bezahlen** to pay the costs incurred; ~ **decken** to cover (reimburse) the expenses, to defray the costs; **seine** ~ **decken** to get back one's expenses; ~ **einrechnen** to include expenses; ~ **einsparen** to cut back on costs; **über die** ~ **entscheiden** *(Urteil)* to carry costs; ~ **ermitteln** to ascertain the costs; ~ **ersetzen** to refund the costs; **entstandene** ~ **erstatten** to reimburse the expenses incurred; **dem Zeugen seine** ~ **erstatten** to reimburse the witness for his expenses; ~ **festsetzen** to fix (determine) the costs; **beträchtliche** ~ **aufgewandt haben** to have gone to considerable expense; ~ **für Subventionen zu tragen haben** to foot the subsidy bill; ~ **niedrig halten** to hold (keep) down costs, to keep costs in line, to keep a lid on costs; ~ **kalkulieren** to cost-account; **auf seine** ~ **kommen** to cover one's expenses, to pay one's way, to have a run for one's money; **geistig und materiell auf seine** ~ **kommen** to make the best of both worlds; ~ **nicht mehr verkraften können** to run one's costs through the roof; **auf jds.** ~ **leben** to live at s. one's expense, to sponge on s. o. *(coll.)*; ~ **machen** to be an (go to) expense; ~ **nachgehen** to keep track of costs; ~ **nachprüfen** to tax costs; ~ **niederschlagen** to cancel the costs; ~ **niedrighalten** to keep a lid on costs; ~ **reduzieren** to cut costs; ~ **scheuen** *(fam.)* to balk at an expense; **keine** ~ **scheuen** to spare no expenses (costs); **weder Mühe noch** ~ **scheuen** to spare neither effort nor expense; **mit großen** ~ **verbunden sein** to involve much expense; **mit weiteren (zusätzlichen)** ~ **verbunden sein** to involve additional charges; **zu den** ~ **verurteilt sein** to be cast (ordered) to pay the costs; ~ **sparen** to save expenses; ~ **steigern** to run up the costs; **sich in große** ~ **stürzen** to go to great expense; **sich mit jem. die** ~ **teilen** to go halves (share the expenses) with s. o.; ~ **tragen** to defray the expense (charges), to pay for [the shot], to meet the expenses; **alle** ~ **für jem. tragen** to carry all expenses for s. o.; ~ **mit jem. zu gleichen Teilen (gemeinsam) tragen** to go halves (share the expenses) with s. o.; ~ **übernehmen** to pay expenses; **entstandene** ~ **übernehmen** to pay the costs incurred; **Hälfte der** ~ **übernehmen** to go halves with s. o.; **gesamte** ~ **einer Pensionsregelung übernehmen** to pick up the entire cost of a pension plan; ~ **einer Reise übernehmen** to defray the expenses of a trip; ~ **auf die Staatskasse übernehmen** to charge an expense to the public debt; ~ **eines Unternehmens übernehmen** to bear the cost of an undertaking; ~ **umlegen** to apportion the costs; ~ **veranschlagen** to evaluate (estimate) expenses, to figure up the costs; ~ **vergüten** to reimburse expenses; **überflüssige ~ vermeiden** to economize; ~ **unmittelbar auf die Abteilung verrechnen** to charge cost directly to the department; ~ **verteilen** to spread the cost; **jem. große ~ verursachen** to put s. o. to great expense; **phantastische ~ verursachen** to lash out into expenditure; **zu den ~ verurteilen** to order (cast) to pay the costs; **Beklagten zu den ~ des Prozesses verurteilen** to condemn the defendant in cost; **gestiegene ~ ohne Verschlechterung der Wettbewerbssituation weitergeben** to pass on rising cost without becoming uncompetitive; **auf ~ der Allgemeinheit unterhalten werden** to be maintained at public expense; **auf gemeinsame ~ von Verleger und Autor veröffentlicht werden** to be published at joint expense of publisher and author; ~ **nach sich ziehen** to carry costs; **hohe ~ nach sich ziehen** to involve great expense; ~ **zurückerstatten** to refund (reimburse) expenses.

kosten to cost, *(erfordern)* to require, *(Speisen)* to taste, *(wert sein)* to be worth;
etw. 100 $ ~ to cost a matter of $ 100; **Geld ~** to require money; **jem. Geld ~** to cost s. o. money; **Haufen Geld ~** to cost a packet of money; **heilloses Stück Geld ~** to cost an unholy amount of money; **jede Menge Geld ~** to cost no end of money; **viel Geld ~** to cost a good deal; **mindestens ~** to cost at least; **nur Pfifferlinge ~** to cost peanuts; **glatte tausend Pfund ~** to cost easily a thousand pounds; **ungefähr ~** to cost roughly; **kleines Vermögen ~** to cost the earth (a small fortune); **viel ~** to cost dearly;
sich sein Hobby etw. ~ lassen to pay dearly for one's whistle.

Kosten|abbau cost reduction, retrenchment, cost cut, cost cutting; **~abbauzeichen erkennen lassen** to show signs of retrenchment; **~ablehnung** disallowance of costs; **~abrechnung** cost sheet; **~abschreibung** cost recovery; **~abteilung** cost center *(US)* (centre, *Br.*), cost department; **~abwälzung** cost passalongs; **~abweichung** cost variance; **~abzug** deduction of costs; **~analyse** analysis of expenses, cost (account) analysis, systems analysis; **~analytiker** cost analyst; **~anerkenntnis** allowance of costs; **~anfall** accrual of cost; **~anfechtung** appeal against costs; **~angaben** cost data; **pauschale ~angaben** blanket; **~angleichung** cost adjustment; **~anpassung** cost adjustment; **~ansatz** assessment of cost.

Kostenanschlag cost account, estimate of costs, computation of costs, calculation, statement of costs;
zu niedriger ~ underestimate; **niedrigster ~** lowest computation; **ungefährer ~** rough estimate of expenses;
~ **machen** to give an estimate, to cost a job.

Kostenanstieg increase in cost;
plötzlicher ~ jump in costs, cost boost; **rasanter ~** surge in costs.

Kostenanteil cost fraction (rate), share of the expense, portion of the cost, partial cost;
abgeschriebener ~ expired cost, cost written off; **zunehmender ~** increasing costs;
~ **pro Anfrage** cost per reply (enquiry);
jem. seinen ~ in Rechnung stellen to bill s. o. for his share of cost; **seinen ~ tragen** to pay one's way.

Kosten|art type of costs, expense category *(Br.)*; **~auferlegung** awarding the costs; **~aufgliederung, ~aufschlüsselung** classification of expenses (accounts), expense classification, breakdown (itemization) of costs, cost breakdown; **funktionelle ~aufgliederung** functional division of expenses *(US)*; **~aufhebung** no costs; **mit ~aufschlag von** costed at; **~aufstellung** statement of costs (charges, expenses), schedule (sheet) of expenses, cost distribution (assignment), cost statement (sheet), *(Kalkulation)* cost allocation; **~aufteilung** assignment of costs, cost allocation (assignment); **~aufteilung vornehmen** to apportion the expenses; **~aufteilungsverfahren** absorption costing; **~auftrieb** upward push on costs, uptrend in cost.

Kostenaufwand expenditure, expense incurred, cost, outlay;
ohne großen ~ with no considerable outlay;
augenblicklicher ~ current outlay (cost); **bargeldloser ~** noncash expenses; **geschätzter ~** estimated cost; **hoher ~** high cost run-up; **mittelbarer ~** indirect expense; **unmittelbarer ~** direct expense; **unnützer ~** expired cost; **für Abschreibungen zugelassener ~** qualifying expenditure;
~ **für Betriebserweiterungen** expenditure on additional plant; ~ **für ungenutzte Kapazität** idle capacity cost; ~ **zu Marktpreisen** current cost; ~ **nach Steuerbegleichung** after-tax cost;
~ **aktivieren** to capitalize cost; ~ **berechnen** to cost a job; **geringen ~ haben** to hold down costs; ~ **eines Unternehmens kalkulieren** to reckon the cost of an undertaking; **sich nur nach bedeutendem ~ anderweitig gewerblich nutzen lassen** not to be adaptable without considerable outlay for other trade.

Kosten|ausgleich *(Börse)* cost averaging; **~ausgleichsbetrag** money compensatory amount; **automatischer ~ausgleichsfaktor** built-in cost-of-living adjuster; **~auslagen** outlay [cost], recoverable cost; **~auswirkungen auf den Haushalt** budgetary costs; **~beamter** *(Gericht)* taxing master.

kostenbedingt governed by cost.

Kosten|befreiung exemption from costs; **~begleichung** defrayal; **~begrenzung** cost limit; **~beitrag** contribution to the expenses; **~beitreibung** collection of charges; **~belastung** burden of costs, expense loading (charge); **~beleg** cost card (record, voucher); **~berechnung** computation of costs, calculation of expenses, *(Anwalt)* bill of costs, *(Aufstellung)* statement of expenses, *(Kalkulation)* cost accounting, costing; **~berechnung vornehmen** to cost a job; **~berechnungsmethode** cost method; **~berichtigungskonto** cost ledger; **~bescheinigung** *(Gericht)* allocatur, judge's certificate; **~beschluß** judgment (certificate, *Br.*) for costs; **~bestandteile** elements of costs, cost elements; **~bestimmung** cost finding; **~beteiligung** sharing of costs, cost sharing; **~betrag** amount of expenses; **~bewegung** fluctuation of costs.

kostenbewußt cost-conscious.

Kosten|bewußtsein cost-consciousness; **~bild** cost picture; **~blatt** *(Produktionsauftrag)* cost sheet; **~bruchteil** cost fraction; **~buch** cost book; **~buchhaltung** cost [book]keeping (accountancy, accounting).

kostendeckend marginal;
nicht ~ sein not to earn one's keep.

Kostendeckung cost recovery;
zur ~ to cover the cost;
~ **sicherstellen** to cover production costs.

Kostendeckungsprinzip cost-of-service principle.

Kostendegression decreasing trend in costs;
interne ~ internal economies of scale;
~ **durch optimale Betriebsvergrößerung** economies of scale; ~ **der Massenproduktion** scale effect.

Kosten|denken cost-consciousness; **~diagramm** break-even chart; **~druck** pressure of costs, cost pressure (squeeze); **~druckinflation** cost-push inflation; **~einheit** cost (costing) unit; **~einschätzung** estimating, cost estimate; **~einsparer** cost cutter; **~einsparung** economy, cost cutting (saving), reduction of expenses; **~einsparung vornehmen** to cut back on costs, to pare down expenditure; **~eintreibung** collection (recovering) of charges; **~elemente** elements of cost, cost elements.

Kostenentscheidung judgment for costs, certificate for costs *(Br.)*;
~ **vorbehalten** costs reserved;
~ **beinhalten** *(Urteil)* to carry costs; ~ **überprüfen** to review taxation.

Kosten|entwicklung cost trend; **~erfassung** ascertainment of costs, cost finding; **~erfordernisse** expense requirements; **~erhebung** levy of costs; **~erhöhung** rising (increasing) increase in cost; **~erhöhungen auffangen** to absorb increases in costs; **~erhöhungen teilweise selbst tragen** to absorb part of the cost increase; **~erlaß** waiver of fees; **~ermittlung** cost accounting, costing; **~ersatz** reimbursement of expenses incurred; **~ersatzanspruch** claim for the expenses incurred.

Kostenersparnis cost saving;
~se durch optimale Betriebsvergrößerung economies of scale; **bedingte ~se eines gesamten Industriezweiges** external economies;
~ **von 30% gegenüber den Konkurrenzfirmen erzielen** to save 30% on costs versus competitors.

Kosten|erstattung compensation for outlay incurred, reimbursement of expenses incurred; expense reimbursement; **~eskalation** escalation of costs; **~fachmann** cost accountant (analyst); **~faktor** cost factor, factor cost.

kostenfällig verurteilt werden to be sentenced to bear (be ordered to pay) the costs.

Kostenfestsetzung assessment (determination) of costs, *(Gericht)* taxing (taxation) of costs *(Br.)*, taxed bill of costs *(US)*;
bei der ~ gekürzt taxed off *(US)*;
~ **gegen den Prozeßgegner** taxation between party and party.

Kostenfestsetzungs|beamter taxing master, taxing officer; **~bescheid, ~beschluß** taxed bill of costs *(US)*, taxation of costs *(Br.)*, allocatur.

Kosten|feststellung cost finding, determination of cost; **~fluß** flow of costs; **~folgen** consequential costs; **~folgen haben** to carry costs; ~**forderungen** costs receivable *(US)*; ~**frage** question of costs, cost issue (problem); **die ~frage spielt keine Rolle** expense is no object.

kostenfrei free of charge, free off all (clear of) charges, all charges paid, cost-free, expenses covered, free of expense (cost).

Kosten|freiheit exemption from charges; ~**funktion** cost function; ~**gefüge** cost structure; ~**gegenkonto** cost control account; ~**gliederung** classification of expenses, breakdown of costs; ~**grundlage** cost basis [of accounting]; ~**gruppe** cost bracket; ~**güter** factors of production; ~**güterpreis** input price; ~**haftung** liability for costs; ~**haftungserklärung** undertaking to pay the costs; ~**hinterlegung** *(bei Gericht)* security for cost; ~**höchstbeträge** maximus charges; ~**höhe** amount of costs; ~**index** standard cost system; ~**inflation** inflation costs, costpush inflation.

kostenintensiv cost-intensive (-effective).

Kosten|kalkulation cost estimate (keeping, finding), estimation of cost; **verantwortlich aufgeteilte ~kalkulation** responsibility costing, cost accounting; **funktionale ~kalkulation** functional statement; ~**konto** cost account, account of charges; ~**kontrolle** cost control, control of costs; ~**kurve** cost line (curve); ~**last** burden of costs, expense loading; ~**lawine** avalanche of costs; ~**legung** cost allocation; ~**leiter** cost ladder; ~**lenkung** cost guidance (control); ~**liquidation** *(Anwalt)* bill of costs.

kostenlos gratuitous, gratis, cost-free, costless, free [of cost], free of charge;
etw. ~ abgeben to give s. th. away free; **etw. ~ bekommen** to get s. th. for nothing; **~ sein** to go free of charge; **sonnabends ~ zugänglich sein** to be open free on Saturdays;
~**es Abonnement** complimentary subscription; ~**e Insertion** free insertion; ~**er Kursus** noncredit course; ~**e Lieferung** delivered free of charge; ~**e redaktionelle Werbung** free puff *(Br.)*.

kostenmäßig, sich ~ auswirken to make a showing on cost; **ganzen Betrieb ~ durchforsten** to cut costs throughout a company.

Kosten|methode cost approach; ~**miete** minimum rent, cost rent *(Br.)*; ~**minderung** reduction in costs; **schlechte ~moral haben** to be slow in payment of costs ~**nachkalkulationsprinzip** cost-plus system; ~**nachnahme** charges to be collected; ~**nachteil** cost disadvantage; ~**nachweis** documentation of cost; ~**nachweis für hergestellte und verkaufte Waren** cost of goods sold *(US)*; ~**nachzahlung** subsequent payment of costs; ~**niederschlagung** cancellation of charges, *(Gericht)* waiving court costs; ~**niveau halten** to hold the line on costs; ~**nummer für einzelne Arbeiten** job number; ~**nutzenanalyse** cost-benefit analysis; ~**ordnung** schedule of fees *(US)*.

kostenorientiert cost-oriented.

Kostenorientierung cost orientation.

kostenpflichtig liable to pay the costs;
~ abweisen to dismiss with costs; **j. ~ verurteilen** to award costs against s. o.

Kosten|plan cost budget; ~**planziel** cost target.

Kostenpreis cost price, prime cost;
zum ~ at cost;
~**e in Durchschnittspreisen des Vergleichjahres ausdrücken** to express cost prices in average prices for the year which is the best; **unter dem ~ verkaufen** to sell below cost price (at a loss); ~**schere** cost-price squeeze.

Kosten|problem cost problem; ~**progression** increasing trend of costs, diseconomies of sale; ~**prozentsatz** percentage of cost; ~**punkt** factor cost, cost issue (point); ~**rechner** cost clerk (keeper, accountant).

Kostenrechnung account of charges, bill (statement) of costs, *(Gericht)* taxed bill of costs *(US)*, taxation of costs *(Br.)*, *(Kalkulation)* cost system (accounting), costing, *(System)* cost accountancy method;
gerichtlich anerkannte erhöhte ~ extra (special) allowance;
~ für Einzelfertigung job cost system; **~ für Serienfertigung** process costing (cost system);
~ anerkennen to allow costs; **~ des Anwalts feststellen** to tax the bill of costs; **anwaltliche ~ überprüfen** to review costs (taxation, *Br.*).

Kostenrechnungs|art cost method; ~**blatt** job-order cost sheet; ~**karte** job-order cost card; ~**methode,** ~**prinzip** job cost method.

Kostenrechnungssystem [job] costing, cost [accounting] system;
~ für auftragsweise Fertigung job-order costing *(US)*, specificorder cost method; **~ mit vorausgeschätzten Kosten** estimating cost system;
~ einführen to install a cost system.

Kostenrechnungsverfahren costing, cost accounting (system);
~ für auftragsweise Forderung job-order costing *(US)*, specificorder cost system; **~ mit vorausgeschätzten Kosten** estimating cost system.

Kosten|regulierung settlement of costs; **höchste ~rentabilität** cost effectiveness; ~**rest** residue of expenditure; ~**rückgang** decrease in costs; **ohne ~rücksicht** without regard to cost; ~**rückstand** recoverable (residual) costs; ~**rückstand nach Abzug der Substanzverringerung** depleted cost; ~**satz** *(Klinik)* tariff; **niedrigster ~satz** lowest cost range; ~**schätzung** cost estimate; ~**schuldner** party liable for costs; ~**schwelle** *(Verlagerung)* cost transfer; ~**seite** cost side; ~**senkung** cost reduction (cutting); **zur ~senkung beitragen** to cut down on costs; ~**senkungsplan,** ~**senkungsprogramm** cost-reduction (-cutting) program(me); ~**sicherheit** idemnity for costs.

kostensparend cost-saving (-cutting).

Kosten|spezifikationsverfahren direct (marginal, *Br.*) costing; ~**spirale** spiral(l)ing of costs; ~**sprung** cost speedup, jump in costs; ~**stand** level of costs; ~**stand niedrig halten** to hold the line on costs; **vom ~standpunkt aus** from the standpoint of cost; ~**steigerung** price rise, increase in costs, cost increase (push), rise in expenditure (costs); **sprunghafte ~steigerung** cost booze; ~**steigerung auf die Preise abwälzen** to pass on cost increases to prices; ~**steigerungsfaktor** cost increase factor; ~**stelle** burden center *(US)* (centre, *Br.*); **nach betrieblichen Fabrikationszweigen aufgeteiltes ~stellenkonto** departmental expense account; ~**stellenrechnung** cost centre accounting *(Br.)*, cost location accounting *(US)*; ~**streuung** spreading of costs; ~**struktur** cost structure; ~**sturm** cost hurricane; ~**tabelle** cost chart (schedule); **aus einem ~tal heraussteuern** to coast one's way out of a loss; ~**teilung** cost sharing; ~**tendenz** cost trend; **vollsteckbarer ~titel** enforceable certificate for costs *(Br.)*; ~**träger** unit of cost, cost (costing) unit; ~**trägerrechnung** cost unit accounting; ~**überhöhung** excessive costs; ~**übernahme** assumption of costs, cost absorption; ~**überprüfer** comptroller; ~**überschlag** approximate estimate; ~**überschreitung** cost overrun; ~**übersicht** cost survey; ~**überwachung** cost control; ~**überwachungsprogramm** cost control program(me); ~**umlage,** ~**umlegung** apportionment (distribution) of cost (expenses), cost allocation (distribution, assignment); ~**unterdeckung** cost deficit; ~**unterlagen** cost data; ~**unterschied** cost difference; ~**untersuchung** cost studies; ~**urteil** order to tax (pay) costs, judgment (certificate, *Br.*) for costs; ~**veränderungen** cost changes; ~**verantwortung** cost consciousness; ~**vergleich** comparison of costs, cost comparison; ~**vergleich zwischen Straße und Schiene** comparison of road and rail costs; ~**vergleichsmiete** economic rent; ~**verlauf** cost trend, pattern of expenditure; ~**verrechnung** allocation of cost; ~**verringerung** reduction (diminution) of expenses, cost reduction, retrenchment, cut; ~**verteilung** cost (expense) distribution, distribution of costs (expenses), *(Gericht)* allocatur, *(Werbeausgaben)* allocation of costs; **steuerbedingte ~verteilung** cost recovery for tax purposes; ~**verteilungsschema** lapsing schedule; ~**verteuerung** cost overrun; ~**verzehr** consumption of costs; ~**verzeichnis** bill of costs, statement of charges; ~**voranschlag,** ~**vorschau** estimate of costs, cost prediction (estimate), bid, pre-estimate, preliminary estimate, estimated charges, budget; ~**voranschlag für einen Garagenanbau** specification for building a garage; ~**voranschlag machen** to draw up an estimate; ~**vorauszahlung** expense prepayment; ~**vorschuß** [charges paid in] advance, advanced expense, advance on costs, payment on account of cost, *(für den Anwalt)* retainer, retaining fee, dives costs *(sl.)*, *(Eisenbahn)* advanced charge, *(Gericht)* security for costs; ~**vorschuß in Rechnung stellen** *(Anwalt)* to charge a retainer.

Kostenvorteil cost advantage (benefit), wind to profit;
~**e bei der Verwendung von Kohle** coal's cost advantage;
~ methodisch untersuchen to use a cost-benefit approach.

Kosten|vorurteil *(jur.)* allocatur, certificate for costs *(Br.)*; ~**wert** cost value; ~**wertberichtigung** cost absorption.

kostenwirksam cost-effective.

Kosten|wirkung cost effect; ~**zahl** expense figure; ~**zahlung** payment of costs; ~**ziffern** expense figures; ~**zunahme** increase in costs, increasing costs; ~**zurechnung** cost distribution; ~**zuschlag** oncost *(Br.)*, excess charge.

Kost|gänger boarder, lodger; ~**geber** *(Börse)* giver on *(Br.)*.

Kostgeld free board, boarding money, pension, allowance, board [wages], *(Börse)* carrying-over (continuation) rate *(Br.)*, contango rate *(Br.)*;
~ zahlen to put on board wages;
~**empfänger** recipient of an allowance.

Kostgeschäft *(Börse)* contango *(Br.)*, backwardation (carrying-over, continuation) business *(Br.)*.

köstlich delicious, tasty, savo(u)ry, dainty;
sich ~ amüsieren to have a whale of a (a wonderful) time; **~e Zeit** killing time.

Köstliches pearl.

Köstlichkeit deliciousness, tastiness, savo(u)r;
exotische ~en exotic delicacies; **literarische ~** literary gem.

Kost | nehmer *(Börse)* receiver, taker-in *(Br.)*; **~probe** sample, sampling demonstration, *(Kosten)* taste; **~probe seiner Fähigkeiten geben** to give an earnest of one's talent; **~probenverteilung** sampling.

kostspielig costly, pricy, expensive, high-priced, *(übermäßig)* extravagant, sumptuous;
~es Freizeitvergnügen expensive hobby; **~e Lebensführung** sumptuous living; **~es Verfahren** wasteful process; **~e Werbung** expensive advertising.

Kostspieligkeit costliness, expensiveness, dearness.

Kostüm costume, *(Maskenfest)* fancy dress;
maßgeschneidertes ~ tailor-made suit;
~ball fancy-dress ball; **~berater** *(Film)* costume adviser, stylist; **~bildner** costume designer.

kostümieren, sich to dress up; **sich als Seeräuber ~** to disguise o. s. as a pirate.

kostümiert in costume, disguised.

Kostüm | probe dress rehearsal; **~stück** costume piece; **~verleih** dress hire, costumer *(US)*, costumier.

Kost | verächter, kein ~verächter sein to be fond of good fare; **~wechsel** bill on deposit (in pension).

Kot, etw. in den ~ ziehen to drag s. th. in the mud (mire).

Kotau kotow;
~ machen to kotow.

Kotelett chop, cutlet;
~en side whiskers, sideburns *(US)*, sideboards *(sl.)*.

Köter tyke, cur, pooch *(US sl.)*.

Kotflügel mudguard, splasher, fender *(US)*.

Kotze kriegen können to make s. o. sick.

kotzen, man hat schon Pferde ~ sehen pigs might fly.

kotzübel as sick as a dog.

Krach crash, crack, bang, noise, racket, din, *(Ärger)* row, kickup *(US sl.)*, *(Börse)* smash, collapse, debacle, panic;
~ mit ihrem Freund tiff with her boy-friend; **~ in der Vorstandsetage** board-room row;
mit seinen Nachbarn ~ bekommen to have a row with one's neighbo(u)rs; **oft ~ miteinander bekommen** to quarrel often; **mit einem ~ einstürzen** to collapse with a deafening noise; **mit einem ~ zu Boden fallen** to fall with a thud; **zu einem ~ an der Börse führen** to bring about a crash at the stock exchange; **~ mit jem. haben** to have a rumpus with s. o.; **~ nicht aushalten können** not to be able to stand the racket; **~ machen** to make a noise, to kick up a breeze; **derartigen ~ machen** to make so much din; **unwahrscheinlichen ~ machen** to kick up no end of a racket; **~ schlagen** to kick up a row, to kick up a fuss, to raise hell.

Kraft power, strength, energy, sap, *(Arbeitskraft)* worker, employee, *(Kapazität)* capacity, *(Widerstandskraft)* resistance, *(Wirksamkeit)* force, effect, power;
aus eigener ~ on one's own account; **außer ~** repealed; **in ~** in force, *(Vertrag)* valid; **mit aller ~** with might and main; **mit bindender ~** binding; **mit letzter ~** with a final effort; **mit rückwirkender ~** retroactively; **noch in ~** unrepealed, *(Vertrag)* unrescinded; **zeitweilig außer ~** temporarily suspended;
bindende ~ binding force; **von einem Motor gelieferte ~** power supplied by a motor; **rückwirkende ~** *(Gesetz)* retroactive (retrospective) effect; **treibende ~** moving power, driving force, spirit, soul; **treibende ~ hinter dem Aufruhr** animating spirit of the rebellion; **treibende ~ für bestimmte Gesetzgebungstätigkeit** sponsor for certain legislation; **zuverlässige ~** reliable worker; **zwingende ~** *(Argument)* stringency;
dritte ~ im Parlament third force in parliament;
mit reduzierter ~ arbeiten to operate on a shorter wave-length; **in ~ bleiben** to hold good, to remain in force, to run on; **sich mit ganzer ~ dahintersetzen** to spend all one's energies, to turn on the heat *(US)*; **sich aus eigener ~ emporarbeiten** to work one's way up; **rückwirkende ~ haben** to have retrospective effect; **verbindliche ~ haben** to oblige, to be of binding authority; **in ~ treten lassen** to put into force; **mit voller ~ laufen** *(Maschine)* to be running at full capacity; **mit aller ~ darauf losgehen** to go at it hammer and tongs; **neue ~ schöpfen** to rally; **ausgezeichnete ~ sein** to be a first-class worker; **außer ~ sein** to be invalid, *(Gesetz)* to be repealed, to become inoperative; **in ~ sein** to be in force (effective, in operation), to rule; **noch in ~ sein** to be still in vigo(u)r; **am Ende seiner ~ sein** to be completely exhausted; **Mensch ohne ~ und Saft sein** to lack pep, to have no go; **treibende ~ des Ganzen sein** to be the driving force behind the scene; **außer ~ setzen** *(Gesetz)* to repeal, to abrogate, to overrule, to deprive of effect, *(Vertrag)* to make invalid, to invalidate, to cancel, to annul, to set aside, to rescind, to override; **vorübergehend außer ~ setzen** to suspend; **in ~ setzen** to put into force (operation), to give effect to; **erneut in ~ setzen** to revalidate, to reenact; **vor ~ strotzen** to be bursting with health; **außer ~ treten** to lapse, to expire, to become invalid (inoperative, void), to cease to have force, (to be effective); **zeitweilig außer ~ treten** to fall into abeyance, **in ~ treten** to become effective (operative, law), to come into effect (force, operation), to take effect, to enure, to be of force; **am 1. Januar in ~ treten** to take effect on January 1st; **rückwirkend in ~ treten** to become retroactive; **mit dem Tag der Veröffentlichung in ~ treten** to come into force on the date of publication; **wieder in ~ treten** to revive, *(Patent)* to reinstate; **einer Sache seine ganze ~ widmen** to employ all one's energies in s. th.

kraft | seines Amtes by (in) virtue of his office; **~ Gesetzes** by operation of law.

Kraft | abgabe power transmission; **~akt** strong-arm act; **sich einen jugendlichen ~akt leisten** to be doing one's youth thing; **~anlage** power station (plant); **~anschluß** power supply connection; **~anstrengung** effort, strain; **in einer einmaligen ~anstrengung** at one heat; **~anstrengung unternehmen** to wind o. s. up for an effort; **~antrieb** power drive; **~aufwand** energy, strain, link *(US)*; **~ausdrücke** strong language; **~bedarf** power requirements; **~betrieb** power installation; **~brühe** beef tea; **~dreirad** motor tricycle; **~droschke** taxi [cab].

Kräfte forces;
im Vollbesitz seiner geistigen ~ in full possession of one's faculties, of sound mind and memory *(US)*; **mit all meinen ~n** to the utmost of my power, with all my might; **nach besten ~n** to the best of one's ability, for all one is worth;
antiinflationistische ~ antiinflationary forces; **neu in den Arbeitsmarkt eintretende ~** new entrants onto the labo(u)r market; **fortgeschrittene ~** progressive forces; **freie ~** available manpower (labo(u)r); **geistige ~** mental powers; **herkulische ~** Herculean strength; **konventionelle ~** *(mil.)* conventional forces; **marktbestimmende ~** market determinants; **linkslastige militante ~** left-wing militants; **reaktionäre ~** forces of reaction; **rechtsextremistische ~** right-wing extremist forces; **rechtsoppositionelle ~** antileft forces; **tüchtige ~** qualified personnel; **ungelernte ~** unskilled workers; **weibliche ~** female workers; **wirtschaftliche ~** economic forces;
~ innerhalb und außerhalb des Marktes market and nonmarket forces;
mit überlegenen ~n angreifen to attack with superior forces; **alle ~ anspannen** to strain every nerve, to summon up one's energy; **sich nach besten ~n bemühen** to use one's best endeavo(u)rs; **~ gemeinsam einsetzen** to pool one's forces; **mit seinen ~n haushalten** to husband one's strength; **allmählich wieder zu ~n kommen** to recover one's (gather) strength; **Problem mit vereinten ~n lösen** to solve a problem with united effort; **seine ~ gegen j. messen** to match one's strength against s. o.; **gut bei ~n sein** to be fit; **im vollen Besitz seiner geistigen ~ sein** to be of sound mind and memory *(US)*; **seine ~ vergeuden** to prostitute one's energies; **seine ~ verlieren** to decline; **die im Außendienst tätigen ~ verstärken** to back up the local field forces; **nach seinen besten ~n versuchen** to try to the best of one's ability; **seine ~ verzetteln** to waste one's energy;
~beanspruchung drain on the strength; **~bedarf** manpower (labo(u)r) requirements; **~einheit** unit of force; **gemeinsamer ~einsatz** pooling of efforts; **~mangel** manpower (labo(u)r shortage, shortage of manpower; **~rückgang** decline of strength; **wechselseitiges ~spiel** interplay of forces; **~verfall** loss of strength; **militärisches ~verhältnis** military ratio of strength; **~verteilung** order of battle; **~zersplitterung** *(mil.)* dispersal of troops.

Kraftfahr | abteilung transport unit, motor pool; **~betrieb** operating of a motor vehicle; **~dienst** motor transport service.

Kraftfahrer [car] driver, motorist, automobilist, carman;
~hotel auto court, motel *(US)*; **~reiseversicherung** autotravel insurance; **~verband** automobile association *(Br.)*.

Kraftfahr | linie bus route (line, *US*); **~park** motor pool; **~sport** motoring; **~straße** major (motor) road; **~technik** automative engineering; **~wesen** motoring, automobilism.

Kraftfahrzeug motor (power-propelled) vehicle, [motor]car, auto, automobile *(US)*;

bei einem Zusammenstoß schwer beschädigtes ~ motor car badly dented in a collision; **im Linienverkehr eingesetztes** ~ auto stage; **teils geschäftlich teils privat genutztes** ~ car used partly during employment and partly privately; **privates** ~ private car; **zugelassenes** ~ legally operating automobile *(US)*; **neu zugelassene** ~**e** new car registrations;
~ **der Mittelklasse** economy car;
~ **abmelden** to cancel a motor-vehicle registration; ~ **anmelden** to register a motor vehicle; **jds.** ~ **benutzen** to operate s. one's automobile *(US)*; **in einem** ~ **fahren** to motor, to drive a car; ~ **im Zustand der Trunkenheit fahren** to drive a car while intoxicated; ~ **führen** to drive a car, to operate a motor vehicle *(US)*; **unfallsicheres** ~ **mit niedrigen Reparatureigenschaften kreieren** to design a car with lower accident and repair-cost potential; ~ **zukünftig nur noch privat nutzen** to transfer a car from business to private use; ~**e für den Transport zum Flugplatz stellen** to provide door-to-airport limousine service; ~ **zur Verfügung stellen** to provide a car; ~ **steuern** to drive a car, to operate a motor vehicle *(US)*; **auf** ~**e verladen** *(mil.)* to embus;
für ~**e nicht zu benutzen** unfit for motor vehicles;
~**abgase** car exhaust; ~**abnahme** auto trial; ~**anhänger** trailer; ~**anmeldung** motor-vehicle registration; ~**ausstellung** motor (auto) show; ~**bau** automobile (automotive, *US*) engineering, car manufacturing; ~**beförderung** automobile transportation *(US)*; ~**besitzer** automobile *(US)* (car) owner; ~**bestand** car park, motor-vehicle ownership, number of vehicles registered; ~**betrieb** automobile operation, *(Firma)* motor-car manufacturer; ~**branche** automobile business; ~**brief** car licence, motor-vehicle registration certificate *(US)*; ~**dichte** traffic density; ~**erwerb** motor-vehicle acquisition; ~**führer** driver of a motor vehicle, motor-vehicle driver, operator of a motor vehicle *(US)*; ~**gewerbe** motor trade.

Kraftfahrzeughaftpflicht motor-vehicle third-party liability;
~**unkosten** motorcar (auto) liability costs; **allgemeine** ~**versicherung** motorcar liability insurance, motor-vehicle liability (public liability motor, *Br.*) insurance; ~**versicherungspolice** standard automobile public liability policy *(US)*.

Kraftfahrzeug|haftung motor-vehicle third-party liability, automobile public liability *(US)*; ~**halter** owner of an automobile *(US)*, automobile *(US)* (car) owner, owner of a car, motor-vehicle owner; ~**halter sein** to use (own) a motor vehicle; ~**halterhaftung für Familienangehörige** family service (car) rule, family automobile (purpose) doctrine *(US)*; ~**haltung** car maintenance, maintenance of an automobile *(US)*; ~**handel** motor trade; ~**händler** dealer in motor vehicles, motorcar dealer (trader); ~**industrie** motorcar (automobile, *US*, automotive) industry; ~**ingenieur** motor engineer; ~**insassenversicherung** motor-vehicle passenger insurance *(Br.)*, medical payment coverage *(US)*; ~**kennzeichen** registration plate *(Br.)*, licence number *(US)*; ~**klasse** class of a vehicle; ~**kolonne** string of cars, motorcade *(US)*; ~**kosten** motorcar (automobile, *US*) expenses; ~**kredit** motorcar (auto) loan; ~**markt** car market; ~**mechaniker** auto mechanic; ~**motor** motor-vehicle engine; ~**papiere** automobile ownership documents, car (driving, motor-vehicle) licence; ~**park** *(mil.)* park, *(Unternehmen)* fleet, motor pool; ~**pauschalsteuer** flat-rate car-licence fee; ~**police** motor (automobile, *US*) policy; ~**produktion** auto production; ~**programm** auto schedule; ~**reparaturwerkstätte** motor-vehicle (automobile, *US*) repair shop, motor repairs, service station; ~**sammelversicherung** fleet insurance; ~**schein** motor-vehicle registration certificate *(US)*, car licence; ~**schlosser** motor fitter, auto[mobile] mechanic *(US)*; ~**sektor** motor-car industry; ~**steuer** automobile (motor-vehicle, *US*) tax, motor-vehicle duty, motor tax *(Br.)*; ~**steuereinkünfte** motor-tax receipts; ~**technik** automobile engineering; ~**unfall** automobile *(US)* (motor[-vehicle]) accident; ~**unterhaltung** auto maintenance; ~**unterhaltungskosten** cost of motoring, car expenses, automobile operating (motorcar) costs *(US)*; ~**verband** motoring organization, car association; ~**verkehr** vehicular (motor[-vehicle]) traffic, motor transportation; **gewerbsmäßiger** ~**verkehr** commercial motoring and road transport; ~**vermietung** renting of cars, car hire service, car rental service *(US)*; ~**vermietung für Selbstfahrer** self-drive cars for hire; ~**versicherer** auto insurer; ~**versicherung** motor-vehicle *(US)* (motor transportation, auto, automobile [collision], *US*, motor, motorcar, car) insurance, motor-vehicle duty *(Br.)*; **kombinierte** ~- **und Kaskoversicherung** comprehensive motorcar insurance *(Br.)*; ~**versicherung unterhalten** to carry a public liability motor insurance.

Kraftfahrzeugversicherungs|geschäft automobile *(US)* (auto) underwriting; ~**gesellschaft** auto insurance underwriter, auto insurer, motor insurers; **tariffreie** ~**gesellschaft** nontariff insurer *(Br.)*; **tarifgebundene** ~**gesellschaft** tariff company *(Br.)*; ~**nehmer** auto insurance customer; ~**police** motor policy; ~**prämie** auto premium, motor insurance premium *(Br.)*; ~**sätze** motor tariff, motor (auto) insurance rates; ~**schadensersatzanspruch** auto insurance claim; ~**schutz** auto coverage; ~**stelle für den Schadensausgleich ungedeckter Haftungsfälle** motor insurers' bureau *(Br.)*; ~**system mit Prämien für unfallfreies Fahren** merit pricing (no-claim bonus, *Br.*) system *(US)*; ~**tarif** *(Haftpflichtversicherung)* motor tariff, motor (auto) insurance (auto liability) rates; ~**vertrag** automobile insurance contract *(US)*; ~**wesen** motor-vehicle insurance business; ~**zubehör** automobile accessories *(US)*; ~**zulassung** licensing of a motor vehicle, motor-vehicle (car) licence, road licence *(Br.)*; ~**zulassung erhalten** to take out a licence for a car; ~**zulassungsgebühr** vehicle licence duty; ~**zulieferungsbetrieb** auto industry supplier, car components manufacturer, automotive supplier *(US)*; ~**zulieferungsindustrie** auto supplier (components, parts) industries; ~**zuschuß** car allowance.

kräftig strong, vigorous, virile;
~ **mit anpacken** to make no bones about getting down to it; ~ **anziehen** *(Kurse)* to recover sharply; ~ **für j. eintreten** to stand up for s. o.; **Kurse** ~ **herunterdrücken** to squeeze down prices; **jem.** ~ **die Meinung sagen** to give s. o. a piece of one's mind; ~ **gestiegen sein** to have gone up considerably; ~ **sinken** to drop heavily; **dem Wein** ~ **zusprechen** to do justice to the wine;
~**er Arbeiter** hefty worker; ~**e Ausdrücke** strong language; ~**e Gewinne erzielen** to be good gainers; ~**es Hoch** strong high; ~**er Kursanstieg** sharp advance, abrupt rise, buoyant market; ~**e Mahlzeit** substantial meal; ~**e Prügel** a good thrashing; ~**er Regen** heavy rain; ~**en Schluck aus der Flasche nehmen** to take a swig at the bottle; ~**e Suppe** nutritious soup; ~**er Umsatzrückgang** heavy drop in sales; ~**e Unterstützung** strong-arm treatment.

kräftigen, sich *(Kurs)* to improve, to recover, *(nach Krankheit)* to go stronger, to recuperate, to recover from an illness; **Dollarkurs** ~ to strengthen the dollar price; **seine Gesundheit** ~ to improve one's health.

kräftigend *(Luft)* bracing, invigorating;
~**e Mahlzeit** fortifying meal; ~**es Mittel** restorative, tonic.

Kräftigung invigoration, strengthening, *(Kurse)* recuperation;
~ **des Dollarkurses** strengthening of the dollar price.

Kräftigungsmittel tonic, restorative.

kraftlos inefficient, feeble, prostrate, exhausted, *(Markt)* languid, *(Vertrag)* [null and] void, invalid;
für ~ **erklären** to invalidate, to declare null and void, *(Wechsel)* to cancel; **Testament für** ~ **erklären** to invalidate a will; **Wertpapiere für** ~ **erklären** to retire (annul) securities; ~ **sein** to lack energy; ~ **werden** to cease to have force, to be invalid;
~**er Mensch** feebling; ~**e Stimme** thin voice.

Kraftloserklärung annulment, invalidation, *(Wechsel)* cancellation;
~ **von Aktien** forfeiture of shares; ~ **verlorengegangener Wertpapiere** annulment of bonds, retirement (invalidation) of securities.

Kraft|losigkeit weakness, feebleness, debility, *(jur.)* invalidity; ~**meier** strong-arm man, tough guy *(US)*; ~**meierei** strong-arm methods, swagging; ~**mensch sein** to be as strong as an ox; ~**nahrung** nutriment; ~**omnibus** motor coach; ~**papier** kraft paper; ~**postlinie** motorbus line; ~**probe** endurance test, workout; **entscheidende** ~**probe** showdown; ~**quelle** power source; ~**rad** motorcycle; **große** ~**reserven haben** to have a great reserve of energy; ~**sinn** kinetic sense; ~**station** power station.

Kraftstoff [driving] fuel, petrol *(Br.)*, motor spirit, gas *(coll.)*, gasoline *(US)*;
wenig ~ **verbrauchen** to be good on fuel economy;
~**anlage** fuel system; ~**anzeiger** gasoline *(US)* (fuel) gauge; ~**behälter** fuel tank, petrol tank *(Br.)*, gasoline container *(US)*; ~**düse** fuel jet; ~**einspritzung** fuel injection; ~**filter** fuel filter; ~**gemisch** fuel mixture; ~**industrie** fuel industry; ~**lager** fuel oil depot; ~**leitung** fuel (petrol, *Br.*) pipe; ~**preis** fuel price; ~**pumpe** fuel pump; ~**verbrauch** fuel (petrol, *Br.*) consumption; ~**verbrauch auf 100 km** mil(e)age per gallon; ~**vorräte** fuel reserves; ~**warnlicht** low-fuel quantity warning light; ~**zufuhr** fuel supply; ~**zuleitung** fuel feed; ~**zuteilung** fuel allocation, petrol ration (allowance) *(Br.)*, gasoline allowance *(US)*.

Kraftstrom power;
~**verbrauch** power consumption.

kraftstrotzend bursting with health.
Kraftverkehr motor traffic, road transport *(Br.)*.
Kraftverkehrs | abgaben motor-vehicle duties; **~industrie** road haulage industry *(Br.)*; **~ordnung** Road Traffic Act *(Br.)*; **~unternehmen** motor-transport agency; **~versicherung** motor-vehicle (transportation, automobile, *US*) insurance.
Kraftwagen [motor]car, motor van *(Br.)*, automobile *(US)*, auto, motor vehicle;
geländegängiger ~ cross-country car;
~beförderung motor transport *(Br.)*, motor traffic; **~benutzung für Geschäftszwecke** use of a car for business; **~bestand** car park, car (truck) fleet; **~führer** motorist, driver; **~kolonne** convoy, column of motor vehicles; **~park** motor pool, fleet of cars; **~spedition** commercial (common) trucking company; **~sport** motor sport; **~verdeck** automobile deck; **~verkehr** motor traffic, road haulage.
Kraft | werk power plant (station); **~wörter** strong language; **geistiges ~zentrum** spiritual powerhouse.
Kragen collar;
einem an den ~ gehen to get it in the neck; **j. am ~ haben** to have one's thumb in s. one's eye; **j. am ~ kriegen** to pinch s. o.; **j. den ~ platzen lassen** to fly off the handle, to go off the deep end; **Dieb beim ~ nehmen** to collar a thief; **Kopf und ~ riskieren** to risk one's neck, to stick one's neck out; **einem Huhn den ~ umdrehen** to wring a chicken's neck; **Kopf und ~ verlieren** to dissipate one's fortune;
~nummer collar size; **meine ~weite** my cup of tea; **jds. ~weite sein** to be up s. one's street, to suit s. o. to a T.
Krähe crow;
eine ~ hackt der anderen kein Auge aus dog does not eat dog.
Krähen | nest *(mar.)* crow's nest; **~winkel** godforsaken hole, one-horse (hick, *US sl.*) town; **aus ~winkel stammen** to come from the back of beyond.
krakeelen to kick up a row (shindy), to roister.
Krakeeler squabbler, rowdy, brawler.
Krakelfüße, Krakelei scribble, scrawl, spidery handwriting.
krakelige Schrift spidery handwriting.
Kralle claw;
die ~n zeigen to show fight, to turn nasty.
krallen, sich an etw. to clutch on to s. th.; **seine Finger in etw. ~** to dig one's fingers into s. th.
Kram kit, caboodle, *(Plunder)* plunder *(US coll.)*, junk, stuff, rubbish, show *(sl.)*;
der ganze ~ the whole outfit *(coll.)*; **unnützer ~** trash;
den ganzen ~ satt haben to be sick of the whole business; **jem. in seinen ~ hineinreden** to poke one's nose into s. one's affairs; **den ganzen ~ hinschmeißen** to chuck up the whole thing; **jem. genau in den ~ passen** to suit s. o. to the ground (s. one's purpose); **den ganzen ~ schmeißen** to run (boss, *US*) the show; **mit nutzlosem ~ vollgestopft sein** to be stuffed with rubbish; **seinen ~ zusammenhalten** to keep track of one's things.
kramen to rummage about;
in alten Akten ~ to rummage among old papers; **in seinen Erinnerungen ~** to walk down memory lane.
Krämer small dealer, monger, grocer, shopkeeper *(Br.)*, cheap Jack, chandler, merchant, shopkeeper;
~geist mercantilism, miserliness, petty mind.
krämerhaft shoppy, miserly, petty-minded.
Kramladen chandlery, cheap-Jack shop, swagshop, grocery store *(US)*;
~ führen to deal in goods of all kinds.
Krampe dog iron, staple.
Krampf cramp, *(Anfall)* spasm, convulsion;
~ im Fuß bekommen to have cramp in one's foot;
was für ein ~! what a bind!
krampfartiger Hustenanfall spasmodic attack of coughing.
krampfhaft *(Lachen)* forced;
sich ~ bemühen, eine Unterhaltung in Gang zu bringen to make frantic efforts to get a conversation going; **~ über etw. nachdenken** to rack one's brains about it;
~e Anstrengungen machen to make desperate efforts.
Kran crane, derrick;
~ausleger crane jib; **~führer** crane operator (driver), derrickman; **~gebühren, ~geld** cranage, crane dues.
krängen *(Schiff)* to [give a] heel, to tilt, to lie along.
Krängung heel, list.
krank ill, sick, diseased, afflicted, unsound, unhealthy;
gefährlich ~ critical; **hoffnungslos ~** incurably ill;
~ an Körper und Seele diseased in body and mind;
sich ~ ärgern to get furious with o. s.; **~ aussehen** to look ill (poorly); **sich ~ fühlen** to have a sensation of discomfort; **sich ~ lachen** to double up (split one's sides) with laughter; **j. ~ machen** to drive s. o. mad; **j. ~ melden** to report s. o. sick; **j. ~ schreiben** to put s. o. on the sick list, to give s. o. a medical certificate; **ganz ~ vor Aufregung sein** to be all worked up; **~ geschrieben sein** to be on the sick list; **~ vor Heimweh sein** to be homesick; **immerfort ~ sein** to be a confirmed invalid; **lebensgefährlich ~ sein** to be dangerously ill (on the danger list); **unheilbar ~ sein** to be past cure; **oft ~ gewesen sein** to have a bad health record; **~ spielen, sich ~ stellen** to feign illness, to malinger, to sham illness, to play the old soldier; **~ werden** to be taken (fall) ill, to sicken, to catch a disease;
~es Gemüt haben to be mentally sick; **~es Herz** weak (ailing) heart; **~en Magen haben** to have stomach trouble; **~e Phantasie** diseased imagination; **~es Unternehmen** failing company; **~e Wirtschaft** ailing economy; **~er Zahn** bad tooth.
Kranke | r sick person, patient, invalid, case;
ambulant behandelter ~r outpatient; **unheilbar ~r** incurable; **jedem ~n im Hospital einen Besuch abstatten** to get round every patient in a ward; **~n behandeln** to doctor a sick man.
kränkeln to be in poor health;
am Vielparteiensystem ~ to suffer because of the multiparty system; **längere Zeit ~** to be ailing for a long time.
kränkelnd valetudinarian;
~es Kind sickly child.
kranken to be afflicted with;
an Kapitalmangel ~ to be strapped for capital; **an schlechter Organisation ~** to have a faulty organization.
kränken to hurt, to disoblige, to aggrieve, to mortify;
sich über etw. ~ to feel hurt (offended, grieved); **j. ~** to cause offence to s. o., to hurt s. one's feelings; **j. empfindlich ~** to cut (pare) s. o. to the quick; **jds. Stolz ~** to wound s. one's pride.
Kranken | abteilung infirmary, ward; **~anstalt** hospital, clinic; **gemeinnützige ~anstalt** nonprofit hospital; **~attest** certificate of illness; **~ausfallquote** illness frequency rate; **~auto** motor ambulance; **~behandlung** medical treatment; **~behandlung ablehnen** to refuse treatment; **~behandlungsraum** ambulance room; **~beihilfe** sickness allowance (compensation, relief); **~bericht** sick report, bulletin; **~besuch** visit, sick call; **~besuche machen** to visit one's patients, to go the round; **~betreuung von Sozialfällen** district visiting *(Br.)*; **~bett** sickbed, cot; **auf dem ~bett dahinsiechen** to linger out one's days on a sickbed; **ans ~bett gefesselt sein** to be confined to bed; **~blatt** case (medical) record.
kränkend wounding, hurtful, offending;
seine Kritik auf ~e Art äußern to be very offensive in one's criticism; **~e Bemerkungen** offending remarks.
Kranken | diät sick diet; **~fahrstuhl** wheel (bath, invalid) chair; **~fürsorge** medical assistance (care); **~geld** sickness (sick) pay, sick benefit, sickness benefit *(US)* (allowance, *Br.*), sickness compensation (allowance), *(bar ausgezahltes)* sickness cash benefit *(Br.)*; **staatliches ~geld** state sickness benefit *(Br.)*; **~geld beziehen** to draw sickness benefits *(Br.)*; **~geldansprüche** sick-pay rights; **~geschichte** case (medical) history.
Krankenhaus hospital, clinic;
im ~ in hospital (dock, *sl.*);
allgemeines ~ general hospital; **privat finanzierte (durch Subventionen unterhaltenes) ~** hospital financed by voluntary efforts, voluntary hospital; **gemeinnütziges (öffentliches, mit öffentlichen Mitteln unterhaltenes) ~** public (nonprofit) hospital; **städtisches ~** city hospital; **subventioniertes ~** voluntary hospital, hospital financed by voluntary efforts;
~ des staatlichen Gesundheitsdienstes health-service hospital *(Br.)*; **~ für ansteckende Krankheiten** fever hospital; **~ für Matrosen** marine hospital *(US)*;
j. in ein ~ aufnehmen to admit s. o. into hospital; **~ aufsuchen** to enter a hospital; **~ ausbauen** to build an extension to a hospital; **j. auf dem schnellsten Wege zum ~ bringen** to rush s. o. to [the] hospital; **in ein ~ einweisen** to send s. o. to hospital, to hospitalize *(US)*; **ins ~ kommen** to sell out to the yankees *(sl.)*; **im ~ liegen** to lie (be) in [the] hospital; **im ~ behandelt werden** to be under treatment in hospital;
~abteilung für ambulante Patienten outpatient department; **~arzt** resident physician, hospital doctor, physician to a hospital, intern; **~aufenthalt** hospital stay, hospitalization *(US)*; **zwangsweiser ~aufenthalt** detention in hospital; **~aufnahme** adoption into (admission to) hospital, hospitalization; **~aufnahmevertrag** hospitalization agreement *(US)*; **~ausfallquote** illness frequency rate; **~bau** hospital building; **~behandlung** hospital treatment (care); **stationäre ~behandlung** in-patient treatment; **sich einer ~behandlung unterziehen** to go into dock *(sl.)*; **~beihilfe** in-hospital benefit; **~besuch**

hospital visit; ~**besuch machen** to make a call at the hospital; ~**bett stiften** to endow a bed in hospital; ~**decke** hospital blanket; ~**einfahrt** hospital entrance; ~**einlieferung,** ~**einweisung** referral to hospital, hospitalization *(US)*; ~**entlassung** discharge from hospital; ~**errichtung** building of a hospital; ~**facharzt** hospital consultant (specialist); ~**finanzen** hospital finance; **neuer** ~**flügel** new wing to a hospital; **neuen** ~**flügel anbauen** to add a new wing to a hospital; ~**gebäude** hospital premises; ~**geld** hospital fee; ~**helfer** hospital aid (worker); ~**insasse** patient in hospital, hospital patient, hospitaler; **kostenlos behandelter** ~**insasse** ward patient; ~**inspektion** hospital review; ~**kosten** hospital costs (expenses, charges); ~**kostenversicherung** hospital cost insurance; ~**küche** hospital kitchen; ~**leistungen** hospital services; ~**mäzen** hospital's patron; ~**pflege** hospital (nursing) care; ~**pflegekosten** hospital ward costs; ~**pflegesatz** hospital allowance; ~**rechnung** hospital bill; ~**schwester** hospital nurse; ~**system** hospitalism; ~**tagegeld** hospital fee; ~**tagegeldversicherung** hospital fee insurance; ~**unterbringung** hospital room and board, hospitalization *(US)*; ~**unterlagen** hospitalization records *(US)*; ~**versicherung** insurance for private medical treatment; ~**versicherungsbeitrag** health contribution; ~**versorgung** hospital provision (accommodation); ~**vertrag** hospitalization contract *(US)*; ~**verwaltung** management of a hospital, hospital administration (board, management); ~**verwaltungsausschuß** hospital management committee; ~**zusatzversicherung** hospital benefit insurance; ~**zuschuß** in-hospital benefits; ~**zuschußversicherung** hospital benefit insurance; ~**zustände** hospitalism.

Krankenhilfe sick benefit *(Br.)*;
ärztliche ~ medical benefit.

Krankenkasse sick-benefit (sickness) fund;
private ~ provident association (fund) *(Br.)*; **staatliche** ~ health insurance fund *(Br.)*;
einer ~ **angehören** to be insured against sickness.

Krankenkassen|arzt panel doctor *(Br.)*; ~**beitrag** National Health Service contribution *(Br.)*; ~**bestimmungen** health service provisions *(Br.)*; ~**gebühren** health service charges *(Br.)*; ~**leistung** health service benefit *(Br.)*; ~**mitglied sein** to subscribe to a health insurance; ~**system** health-insurance plan *(US)*, panel system *(Br.)*.

Kranken|kost [sick] diet, invalid diet; **auf** ~**kost gesetzt sein** to be put upon a diet; ~**kosten** health costs; ~**lager** sickbed; ~**leistungen** health services; ~**liste** *(mil.)* sick list; ~**pflege** care of the sick, nursing care; ~**pflegeanstalt** nursing home *(Br.)*; ~**pflegeberuf** nursing; ~**pfleger** orderly, watcher; ~**pflegerin** sicknurse; **als** ~**pflegerin tätig sein** to sicknurse; ~**pflichtversicherung** compulsory health insurance; ~**revier** *(mil.)* infirmary, dispensary, *(Schiff)* sick bay; ~**saal** ward; ~**satz** illness frequency rate; ~**schein** sickness (sick) certificate.

Krankenschwester sicknurse;
praktisch ausgebildete ~ practical nurse; **diensthabende** ~ nurse on duty; **erfahrene** ~ experienced nurse; **staatlich geprüfte** ~ registered nurse *(US)*, state-registered *(Br.)* (practical, *US*) nurse;
~**ausbildung** training of nurses; ~**beruf ergreifen** to take up nursing as a career.

Kranken|stand sickness figure; ~**station** *(Schiff)* sick bay (berth); ~**stube** sickroom; ~**stuhl** bath (wheel) chair; ~**tagegeld** daily sickness benefit; ~**trage** stretcher, litter; ~**transportdienst** ambulance service; ~**unterstützung** sick benefit; ~**unterstützungsverein** sick club; ~**urlaub** sick leave; **bezahlter** ~**urlaub** paid sick leave.

krankenversichert sick-insured.

Krankenversicherung health *(Br.)* (medical, sickness, *US*) insurance;
staatliche ~ national health insurance *(Br.)*;
~ **zur Abdeckung besonders hoher Risiken** catastrophe insurance;
~ **abschließen** to insure against illness.

Krankenversicherungs|beitrag national health contribution *(Br.)*; ~**bezüge** sickness benefit (allowance, *US*); **staatliche** ~**einrichtungen** governmental health insurance plan *(US)*; ~**police** sickness indemnity policy; ~**schutz** medical plan.

Kranken|versorgung älterer Menschen medical care for the aged; ~**wagen** motor ambulance, hospital carriage; **im** ~**wagen befördern** to ambulance; ~**wärter** hospital (medical) attendant, watcher, ward orderly; ~**zimmer** sickroom; ~**zulage** health welfare benefit; ~**zusatzversicherung** supplementary sickness insurance; ~**zustandsmeldung** sick report.

kränker worse.

Krankfeiern malingering.

krankfeiern to malinger, to swing the lead *(Br., sl.)*.

krankhaft morbid;
~**e Verschwendungssucht** obsessive extravagance.

Krankheit illness, disease, complaint;
durch ~ **gehindert** laid low by sickness; **wegen** ~ **abwesend** absent because of sickness;
angeborene ~ hereditary (congenital) disease; **ansteckende** ~ contagious (infectious) disease; **noch nicht ausgebrochene** ~ dormant disease; **beruflich bedingte** ~ occupational disease; **bösartige** ~ virulent (pernicious) disease; **chronische** ~ chronic illness; **ekelerregende** ~ repulsive disease; **gefährliche** ~ serious illness; **hartnäckige** ~ stubborn illness, obstinate disease; **heimtückische** ~ insidious disease; **meldepflichtige** ~**en** notifiable diseases; **organische** ~ structural disease; **quarantänepflichtige** ~ disease subject to quarantine regulations; **schleichende** ~ lingering disease, creeping sickness, languishing illness; **schwere** ~ *(Lebensversicherung)* severe illness; **simulierte** ~**en** feigned diseases; **tödliche** ~ mortal disease; **übertragbare** ~ contagious disease; **unerwartete** ~ precipitate illness; **wiederkehrende** ~ recurring disease; **zunehmende** ~ progressive disease;
~ **als Grund angeben** to allege ill health as a reason; ~ **unsachgemäß behandeln** to tamper with a disease; ~ **einschleppen** to introduce an illness; **sich mit** ~ **entschuldigen** to excuse o. s. on the grounds of illness; **sich nach einer schweren** ~ **erholen** to get over a serious illness; **wegen** ~ **fehlen** to be absent through illness; **von einer** ~ **genesen** to rise from a sickbed; **j. von einer** ~ **heilen** to heal s. o. of a disease, to cure s. o. of an illness; **wegen** ~ **nicht ausgehen können** to be confined to the house by illness; ~ **lokalisieren** to locate the seat of a disease; **vor** ~ **schützen** to guard against disease; **wegen** ~ **beurlaubt sein** to be on sick leave; ~ **simulieren** to feign illness, to put on the invalid; **schwere** ~ **überstehen** to come through a serious illness; ~ **übertragen** to transmit (communicate) a disease; ~ **auf j. übertragen** to give s. o. a disease; **Nachwirkungen einer** ~ **verspüren** to feel the effects of an illness; ~ **vorschützen** to pretend to be ill, to pretext sickness, to malinger; **einer** ~ **widerstehen** to fight back a disease; ~ **auf Verschmutzung zurückführen** to attribute a disease to filth; **sich eine** ~ **zuziehen** to contract a disease (an illness), to develop an illness, to fall ill.

krankheitsanfällig prone to a disease, predisposed to illness.

Krankheits|beginn onset; ~**bereitschaft** diathesis; ~**bericht** medical report, bulletin; ~**bild** clinical picture; ~**erscheinung** symptom; ~**erscheinungen eines Betriebes** business ailments.

Krankheitsfall case;
im ~ in the event of sickness;
sich um einen ~ **unablässig kümmern** *(Arzt)* to be unremitting in one's attention to a case; **sich für den** ~ **versichern** to insure against illness.

Krankheits|folgen after-effects of a disease; **aus** ~**gründen aufgeben müssen** to be compelled by illness to resign.

krankheitshalber on account of illness.

Krankheits|herd seat of a disease; ~**kosten** illness costs; **außerhalb der Klinik anfallende** ~**kosten** out-of-hospital expenses; ~**phasen** periods of a disease; ~**prozentsatz** sickness rate; **größere Personenzahl ernsthaftem** ~**risiko aussetzen** to expose a substantial number of persons to serious risk of illness; ~**rücklage** allowance for possible illness; ~**rücklagen bilden** to allow for possible illness; ~**satz** sickness rate; ~**schadenspolice** sickness indemnity policy; ~**schutz** sickness cover; ~**stoff** contagious matter; ~**tag** day of sickness; ~**urlaub** sick leave; ~**ursache entdecken** to discover (trace) the cause for an illness (a disease); ~**verbreitung** communication of disease; ~**verhütung** prevention of [a] disease; ~**verlauf** course of a disease; ~**zeichen** symptom; ~**ziffer** sick rate; ~**zustand** case, condition of a patient; **sich im** ~**zustand verschlimmert haben** to be a change for the worse of a patient.

kränklich weak, poorly *(coll.)*;
~ **aussehen** to want some colo(u)r.

Kränklichkeit morbidity.

Krankmelder sick caller.

Krankspielen simulation, malingering.

Kränkung mortification, abuse, wound;
~ **von jds. Stolz** hurt to s. one's pride;
unter ~**en leiden** to writhe under insults; **jem.** ~**en zufügen** to cause offence to s. o.

Kranwagen crane (breakdown, *US*) truck, derrick car *(US)*.

Kranz wreath;
~ **niederlegen** to lay a wreath.

Kränzchen circle.
Kranzniederlegung wreath-laying ceremony.
Kranzspende floral tribute;
~n verbeten no flowers, please.
krasser | Außenseiter rank outsider; ~ **Egoist** blatant egoist.
Kratzer scrap, scratch.
Kratzfuß machen to make a leg.
Kräuselung ripple.
Kraut, wie ~ und Rüben higgledy-piggledy;
wie ~ und Rüben durcheinanderliegen to be in a pretty mess; **ins ~ schießen** to go to weed, to run wild.
Krauter, junger sprout; **kleiner ~** smallholder.
Krautjunker squireling.
Krawall disorder, uproar, rumpus, row, riot;
politische ~e political riots;
wegen etw. ~ schlagen to kick up a row, to make a rumpus; **auf ~ aus sein** to be looking out for trouble.
Krawattennadel scarf pin.
Kreation creation.
kreativ *(Werbung)* creative;
~es Denken creative thought.
Kreatur creature, thing;
elende ~ vile creature; **minderwertige ~** worm.
Krebs | bekämpfung cancer control; **~untersuchung** cancer check-up.
Kredit credit, loan, advance, *(Anschreibenlassen)* tick *(Br.)*, score credit *(US)*, *(Ansehen)* public (general) credit, business reputation, *(Kreditlinie)* credit line *(US)* (limit, *Br.*), line *(US)* (limit, *Br.*) of credit, *(Kreditwürdigkeit)* credit rating (standing), *(Vorschuß)* advance;
auf ~ on (upon) credit, on trust *(US)*, on tick *(Br.)*; **auf ~ verkauft** sold on credit; **ohne ~** uncredited;
abgelehnter ~ declined credit; **sich selbst abwickelnder ~** self-liquidating loan; **neu aufgenommener ~** fresh credit; **wieder auflebender ~** revolving credit; **auftragsgebundener ~** tied loan; **beanspruchter ~** used credit, credit in use; **nicht beanspruchter (benötigter) ~** unused (unemployed) credit; **begrenzter ~** limited credit; **besicherter ~** covered (secured, collateral, *US*) loan, loan against security (upon collateral security, *US*); **hypothekarisch besicherter ~** real-estate loan, credit on mortgage; **bestätigter ~** guaranteed (confirmed, *Br.*) credit; **billiger ~** easier (low-interest) credit, soft loan; **durchgeleiteter ~** transmitted credit; **durchlaufender ~** transitory credit; **eingefrorener ~** frozen credit (loan), blocked credit, nonliquid loan; **eingeräumter ~** credit limit *(Br.)*, credit line *(US)*, line of credit *(US)*; **blanko eingeräumter ~** blank (open, *US*) credit; **monatlich eingeräumter ~** a month's credit; **der Regierung eingeräumter ~** loan made to the government; **sich automatisch erneuernder ~** revolving [letter of] credit, revolving fund loan *(US)*; **erstrangiger ~** first-rate credit; **bei Sicht fälliger ~** sight credit; **sofort fälliger ~** call (demand) loan; **festbegründeter ~** established credit; **kurzfristig finanzierter ~** short-term credit; **gebündelte ~e** loan package; **gebundener ~** tight credit; **gedeckter ~** secured loan, collateral credit *(US)*; **durch verschiedenartige Sicherheiten gedeckter ~** mixed loan; **genehmigter ~** authorized loan; **in Anspruch genommene ~e** credits in use, used credits, *(Bilanz)* borrowings; **noch nicht bis zum Höchststand in Anspruch genommener ~** unused portion of a credit; **noch nicht bis zum Höchststand in Anspruch genommener ~ auf hypothekarischer Basis** open mortgage; **geschäftlicher ~** commercial loan; **geschwächter ~** impaired credit; **gesicherter ~** secured loan (advance), collateral credit *(US)*; **hypothekarisch gesicherter ~** real-estate loan; **durch erststellige Hypothek gesicherter ~** first-mortgage loan; **durch Lombardierung verschiedenartiger Wertpapiere gesicherter ~** mixed loan; **von einem Konsortium (konsortialiter) gewährter ~** syndicated credit; **von Lieferanten gewährter ~** credit granted by suppliers; **einem Minderjährigen gewährter ~** loan to an infant; **zinslos gewährter ~** credit given flat; **gewerblicher ~** industrial loan; **herausgelegte ~e** loans granted; **hypothekarischer ~** real-estate (mortgage) loan; **interne ~e** *(an Zweigniederlassungen einer Bank)* house debits; **kaufmännischer ~** commercial loan; **knapper ~** tight credit; **kündbarer ~** credit on call, loan on notice; **kurzfristiger ~** short credit, short-term credit, fixture; **landwirtschaftlicher ~** agricultural loan; **längerfristiger ~** medium-term loan; **langfristiger ~** long (long-term, long-time) loan; **kurzfristig finanzierter langfristiger ~** roll-over credit; **laufender ~** open (standing) credit; **lieferungsgebundener ~** tied credit; **mittelfristiger ~** *(Eurodollarmarkt)* medium-term credit; **mittelständischer ~** small-business investment credit (administration loan, *US*); **offener ~** open (blank) credit *(US)*, uncovered (unsecured) loan, *(laufendes Konto)* account current, drawing account; **projektfreier ~** untied credit; **projektgebundener ~** tied credit; **prolongierter ~** extended credit; **refinanzierbarer ~** refinanceable credit; **revolvierender ~** revolving credit; **rückzahlbarer ~** repayable credit; **innerhalb 24 Stunden rückzahlbarer ~** overnight loan *(US)*; **schöpferischer ~** creative credit; **staatsverbürgter ~** government-backed credit; **zur Verfügung stehender ~** supply of credit [available]; **transitorischer ~** temporary credit; **überzogener ~** overdraft, overdrawn credit; **unbeeinträchtigter ~** *(Kreditwürdigkeit)* unimpaired credit; **unbegrenzter (unbeschränkter) ~** unlimited credit; **unbestätigter ~** unconfirmed (uncovered) letter of credit *(Br.)*; **ungedeckter (ungesicherter) ~** open *(US)* (unsecured, uncovered) credit, blank advance, loan without security (collateral, *US*); **unkündbarer ~** irrevocable credit; **unsicherer ~** unsafe loan, shaky credit; **unverzinslicher ~** credit given flat; **unwiderruflicher ~** irrevocable letter of credit; **widerruflicher ~** revocable (unconfirmed, *Br.*) letter of credit; **wiederauflebender ~** revolving credit; **zinsloser ~** interest-free loan, credit given flat; **zinsverbilligter ~** low-interest credit, credit given at a reduced rate, soft loan; **verbindlich zugesagter ~** advance commitment, standby credit; **zusätzlicher ~** additional credit; **zweckgebundener ~** tied loan (credit); **nicht zweckgebundener ~** no-purpose (untied) loan; **zweiseitiger ~** bilateral loan;
~ gegen Bürgschaft loan against surety; **~ für Gebäudewerterhöhungen** loan for improvement of property; **öffentlicher ~ an einen Gewerbebetrieb** industrial advance; **~ bis zur Höhe von** credit within the limit of; **~ in begrenzter Höhe** limited credit; **~ in festgesetzter Höhe** line-of-credit loan *(US)*; **~e an Kreditinstitute** lending to bank customers; **~ mit begrenzter Laufzeit** time loan, fixture; **~ in laufender Rechnung** credit in current account; **~ gegen Sicherheit** credit against security (collateral, *US*); **~ gegen Sicherungsübereignung** field warehouse loan; **~ für einen Spitzenbetrag** gap loan; **~ gegen Verpfändung der Schiffsfracht** respondentia loan; **~ in fremder Währung** foreign currency credit; **~ auf eingelagerte Waren** storage credit; **~ gegen Wertpapierlombard** lending on security, collateral loan *(US)*; **~ zu niedrigem Zinssatz** low-interest credit, soft loan;
~ abdecken to repay a credit; **~ abwickeln** to liquidate (repay) a loan; **~ dem Wert der gestellten Sicherheit anpassen** to mark a loan to the market *(US)*; **~ aufbrauchen** to eat up (use) a credit; **~e nach ihrer Größenordnung aufführen** to scale credits; **~ aufnehmen** to borrow money, to raise a loan (credit); **erforderlichen ~ aufnehmen** to raise any money requisite; **~ für den Ankauf eines Grundstücks aufnehmen** to borrow for the purchase of land; **~ für den gesamten Kaufpreis aufnehmen** to borrow the whole of the purchase price; **~ ausschöpfen** to exhaust a loan; **~ etappenweise entsprechend den nachgewiesenen Bauleistungen auszahlen** to make an advance in stages against production of architect's certificate; **~ beantragen** to request a loan, to apply for a credit; **~ bekommen** to obtain (get) a credit; **~ zurückgezahlt bekommen** to receive a loan back; **~ für j. bereitstellen** to place a loan at s. one's disposal; **sich durch Wechselreiterei ~ beschaffen** to fly a kite *(Br.)*; **~ bewilligen** to grant a loan, to pass a credit vote; **~ nur ratenweise bewilligen** to vote a credit in instal(l)ments; **auf ~ des Ehemannes einkaufen** to pledge one's husband's credit; **~ einräumen** to grant a loan, to allow a credit; **einem Kunden einen ~ einräumen** to allow a customer an advance; **~ einrichten** to establish a credit; **~ einschränken** to reduce (restrict) a credit; **für einen ~ einstehen** to respond for a credit *(US)*; **~ entziehen** to draw in a loan, to withdraw a credit; **auf ~ erhalten** to receive on tick *(Br.)* (trust, *US*); **auf Antrag einen persönlichen ~ erhalten** to obtain a personal loan upon application; **zinslosen ~ erhalten** to borrow money flat; **~ erhöhen** to increase a credit line *(US)* (limit, *Br.*); **~ eröffnen** to open a loan (credit, credit line, *US*, credit limit, *Br.*); **~ bei jem. eröffnen** to establish a credit with s. o.; **~ zu jds. Gunsten eröffnen** to open a credit account in s. one's favo(u)r; **sich ~ erschleichen** to obtain credit by fraud; **~ erschüttern** to affect the credit; **~ geben** to loan (out), to grant a credit; **auf ~ geben** to [give on] credit, to chalk up, to [give upon] trust *(US)*; **jem. ~ in Höhe von 100 Dollar geben** to give s. o. credit for $ 100; **jds. ~ gefährden** to undermine s. one's credit; **nur begrenzten ~ genießen** to enjoy very restricted credit; **unbegrenzten ~ genießen** to enjoy unlimited credit; **~ gewähren** to grant (make) a loan, to grant a credit, *(anschreiben)* to [give upon] trust *(US)*, to tick *(Br.)*; **abgesicherten ~ gewähren** to lend on security, to loan on collateral *(US)*; **keinen ~ gewähren** to

withhold a credit; **nur sehr kurzfristigen ~ gewähren** to give very short credit; **~ nur in einem bestimmten Rahmen gewähren** to allow a credit not beyond a certain figure; **gegen Sicherheit (Lombardierung von Wertpapieren) ~ gewähren** to lend on security, to loan on collateral *(US)*; **zinslosen ~ gewähren** to give a flat credit; **~ bei jem. haben** to be in credit (have interest) with s. o.; **keinen ~ haben** to be without credit; **j. für einen ~ von 4000 $ für gut (sicher) halten** to consider s. o. safe for a credit of $ 4000; **auf ~ kaufen** to buy on credit (time, trust, *US*), to purchase on account, to buy on (go upon) tick *(Br.)*; **~ kündigen** to draw in a loan, to withdraw (call in) a credit; **~ kürzen** to curtail a credit; **~e einfrieren lassen** to lay up credits; **Waren auf ~ liefern** to supply goods on account (credit); **mehr als üblich faule ~e abschreiben müssen** to have more bad loans to write off than usual; **um größere ~e nachsuchen** to ask for larger credits; **um zusätzlichen ~ nachsuchen** to ask for further credit; **~ in Anspruch nehmen** to utilize (use) a credit, to run a line *(US)* (limit, *Br.*) of credit, to take up (use) a credit; **seinen ~ bei jem. in Anspruch nehmen** to make interest with s. o.; **höhere ~e in Anspruch nehmen** to ask for larger credits; **bei der Bank in erhöhtem Maße ~e in Anspruch nehmen** to increase the borrowings at the bank; **~ prolongieren** to renew a credit; **~ prüfen** to check a credit; **~ refinanzieren** to refinance a loan; **~ schöpfen** to create credit; **~ schwächen** to discredit; **~ sperren** to block a credit; **im ~ stehen** to be on the credit side; **seinen ~ überschreiten (überziehen)** to stretch (strain, outrun, surpass) one's credit, to overdraw one's account, to make an overdraft; **eingeräumten ~ überziehen** to run over the credit limit *(Br.)* (line, *US*); **~ untergraben** to undermine credit; **~e vergeben** to deal in credits; **auf ~ verkaufen** to sell on credit (tick, *Br.*, trust, *US*); **~ verkürzen** to curtail a credit; **~ verlängern** to extend [the term of] a credit; **eingeräumten ~ verlängern** to extend the validity of a credit; **~ verschaffen** to furnish (provide) with credit; **~ mit 12% verzinsen** to pay 12 per cent interest on a loan; **~ eines Unternehmens wiederherstellen** to re-establish a firm's credit; **~ zurückzahlen** to repay a loan (credit); **fälligen ~ zurückzahlen** to meet a loan when due;
~abkommen credit arrangement (agreement), loan agreement; **~abteilung** credit (loan) department; **~abteilung einer Bank** bank loan department; **~akte** credit folder; **~andrang** credit strain; **~anfrage ablehnen** to turn thumbs down on a loan.

Kreditangebot credit offer, supply of credit, tender of a loan;
gebündeltes ~ credit (loan) package; **unzureichendes ~** credit poverty;
umfassendes ~ sicherstellen to arrange for a credit package.

Kredit|anspannung strain on credit, credit strain; **~ansprüche** credit needs; **~anstalt** credit institution (association, bank, *Br.*); **~anstalt für Wiederaufbau** Reconstruction Loan Corporation; **~anteil** portion of a loan.

Kreditantrag application for a credit (an advance), loan (credit) application, loan demand;
~ stellen to apply for a credit line *(US)* (limit, *Br.*).

Kreditantrags|formular credit-application form; **~steller** credit (loan) applicant.

Kreditapparat machinery of credit, credit facilities;
~ auf Schwung bringen to pump up credit.

kreditäre Geldabschöpfung creation of currency (money).

Kredit|armut credit poverty; **~art** class of credit.

Kreditaufnahme borrowing, raising of credit (loan);
befristete ~ temporary borrowing; **nicht genehmigte ~** unauthorized borrowing; **kurzfristige ~** short-term borrowing; **langfristige ~** long-term borrowing; **satzungswidrige ~** ultra vires borrowing; **staatliche ~** government borrowing;
~ durch Abtretung von Debitoren borrowing on accounts receivable *(US)*; **hohe ~ der öffentlichen Hand** high level of public borrowing; **~ durch Kommunalbehörden** borrowing by local authorities; **~ durch einen gerichtlich bestellten Liquidator** borrowing by a liquidator appointed by the court; **~ durch einen Nachlaßverwalter** borrowing by a representative; **~ zu gleichbleibenden Zinssätzen** fixed-interest borrowing; **~ unter Zuwiderhandlung gegen die Satzungen** ultra vires borrowing; **beim Gericht ~ beantragen** *(Konkursverwalter)* to apply to the court for permission to borrow; **~ erleichtern** to shade credit standards; **~ durch einen Hauptversammlungsbeschluß genehmigen lassen** to ratify the borrowing by resolution in general meeting;
~befugnis *(Vorstand)* power to borrow [money], borrowing capacity (power), capacity to borrow, borrowing authorization; **satzungsgemäß gestattete ~befugnis** statutory power to borrow; **~grenze** borrowing limit; **~koeffizient** borrowing ratio; **~möglichkeiten** borrowing facilities.

Kredit|auftrag credit order; **~aufwand** credit expense; **~ausdehnung** credit expansion, expansion of a loan; **inflationistische ~ausdehnung** credit inflation; **~ausfall** credit loss; **~auskunft** commercial credit information, credit statement, credit enquiry *(Br.)*, *(Report)* credit agency report, trade reference, special rating *(US)*; **gegenseitige ~auskunft** credit interchange; **~auskunftei** credit bureau, credit reporting agency, credit enquiry *(Br.)*, mercantile agency *(US)*; **~auskunftsbeurteilung** credit rating; **~auskunftsbogen** loan ticket; **~auskunftsorganisation, ~auskunftsverband** credit service organization; **~auslese** selective credit control; **~ausschuß** credit (loan) committee; **~ausweitung** credit expansion (extension); **übermäßige ~ausweitung** credit inflation; **~auszahlungen** total credits extended; **~bank** credit (loan) bank; **landwirtschaftliche ~bank** land bank, Agricultural Credit Corporation *(US)*; **~basis** credit basis; **jem. etw. auf ~basis anbieten** to offer s. o. a loan of s. th.; **~beanspruchung** use of credit, credit usage, recourse to credit, borrowing; **~bearbeiter** credit man *(US)*, loan officer; **~bearbeitung** credit work, loan processing *(US)*; **~bearbeitungsgebühr** loan fee.

Kreditbedarf borrowing needs (requirements), credit requirements, demand for loans (advances), loan (credit) demand;
unabgebauter laufender ~ hard core in borrowing;
~ der Banken bank-loan demand; **~ der öffentlichen Hand** public-sector borrowing requirements;
erheblichen ~ auslösen to build up a lot of loan demand.

Kreditbedarfsspitze maximum borrowing requirements.

Kreditbedingungen terms of credit, credit terms (conditions);
günstige ~ easy terms;
~ erleichtern to liberalize credit; **seine ~ verschärfen** to tighten up on one's credit terms.

Kredit|bedürfnis loan demand, credit requirements, borrowing (credit) needs; **~begrenzung** cash limit *(Br.)*, credit limit *(Br.)* (line, *US*), line (limit, *Br.*) of credit.

kreditbereit ready to lend (borrow).

Kredit|bereitschaft readiness to borrow; **~bereitstellung** granting of a credit, allocation of funds; **~bericht** credit report; **~beschaffung** procurement of a loan, credit supply; **~beschaffungskosten** cost of borrowing; **~beschränkung** contraction of credit issues, clampdown of credit, credit contraction (restriction, squeeze, rationing); **~beschränkungen verfügen** to impose curbs on credit; **~beschränkungsbestimmungen** *(Börse)* margin rules *(US)*; **~besicherung** safeguarding of a credit; **~besonderheiten** particulars of a loan; **~bestätigung** confirmed credit; **~bestimmungen** terms of a loan; **~betrag** amount of a loan (credit), amount credited; **offener ~betrag** unused portion of credit; **~betrug** credit robbery, obtaining money by false pretences; **~betrug begehen** to obtain money by false pretences (by fraud); **~beurteilung** checking credit, audit for credit purposes, credit rating *(US)*; **~bewilligung** credit vote (authorization), granting a credit (loan); **verzögerte ~bewilligungen** votes of credit subject to delay; **~bewilligungsvorlage** appropriation bill; **~beziehung** debtor-creditor relation; **~blatt** valuation sheet; **~bremse** credit brake (restraint); **~bremse zur Anwendung bringen** to clamp down on credits.

Kreditbrief letter (bill) of credit, credit [letter];
bestätigter ~ confirmed letter of credit; **dokumentarischer ~** documentary letter of credit; **noch nicht in Anspruch genommener ~** letter of credit not yet utilized; **an eine bestimmte Bank gerichteter ~** direct letter of credit; **auf englische Pfund lautender ~** sterling [letter of] credit; **ungültiger ~** invalid letter of credit; **unwiderruflicher ~** irrevocable letter of credit; **widerruflicher ~** revocable letter of credit;
~ mit Dokumenten document[ed] credit; **~, dessen Gültigkeit sofort nach Finanzierung der Waren erlischt** straight letter of credit; **~, bei dem die dagegen gezogenen Wechsel bei Sicht fällig sind** sight letter of credit;
~ ausstellen to issue a letter of credit, to emit a bill of credit; **~ausstellung** emission of bills of credit; **~inhaber** holder (beneficiary) of a letter of credit.

Kredit|buchung credit entry; **~bürge** guarantor of credit; **~bürgschaft** credit guarantee *(Br.)*, continuing (special) guaranty *(US)*; **~dauer** length of credit; **~deckungsklausel** security clause; **~dirigismus** regulation of credits; **~disagio** debt discount; **~drosselung, ~einengung** credit restrictions (squeeze); **~drosselungspolitik** restrictive credit policy; **~einräumung** granting (allowance) of credit, establishment of a credit, credit vote (granting); **~einräumung im Ausland** foreign lending; **~einrichtungen** credit facilities (devices); **~einschätzung** audit for credit purposes, credit rating *(US)*; **~einzelheiten** particulars of a credit; **~empfänger** beneficiary, debtor; ~**engagements** credit commitments; ~**entscheidung** credit decision; ~**entwicklung** borrowing trend; ~**entziehung** withdrawal of credit; ~**erhöhung** credit expansion, increase of credit, further advance; ~**erhöhung infolge Kontoüberziehung** forced loan; **sein gutes Aussehen zur ~erlangung ausnützen** to run one's face *(US sl.)*; ~**erleichterungen** easing of credit (ease in, relaxion in) credit; ~**erleichterungen einführen** to make credit easier; ~**ermächtigung** credit authorization; ~**eröffnung** opening a credit; ~**ersuchen** loan application, application for a credit; ~**expansion** credit expansion (extension), expansion of a loan; ~**fachmann** manager of a credit, credit manager (analyst man).

kreditfähig good, [financially] sound, creditable, responsible, solvent, solid, worthy of credit, *(vertrauenswürdig)* trustworthy, reliable;
jem. bis zu einer Höhe von 4000 $ für ~ halten to consider s. o. trustworthy to the extent of $ 4000.

Kreditfähigkeit credit standing (status, capacity), creditability, borrowing power, solidity, soundness, strength, *(Vertrauenswürdigkeit)* trustworthiness, reliability, reliableness;
geschätzte ~ financial (credit) standing, credit rating *(US)*;
zweifelhafte ~ doubtful standing;
~ eines Darlehnsnehmers responsibility of one seeking a loan; **jds. ~ schädigen** to impair s. one's credit; **jds. ~ in Frage stellen (in Zweifel ziehen)** to question the responsibility of s. o. seeking a loan.

Kredit | faktor credit element; ~**fall** loan granted.

Kreditfazilitäten credit (borrowing, overdraft) facilities, credit accommodation;
nicht in Anspruch genommene ~ unused loan commitments;
seine ~ äußerst behutsam in Anspruch nehmen to lock in one's loan commitments; **einer Firma ~ zur Verfügung stellen** to grant a firm credit (overdraft) facilities; **über ~ bei einer Bank verfügen** to have credit with a bank.

Kredit | finanzierung borrowing, lending; ~**förderung** trade facilities; ~**form** type of credit; ~**garantiegemeinschaft** credit union.

Kreditgeber lender, borrower, loan creditor, credit grantor;
letztbereiter ~ marginal lender;
~ hypothekarisch sicherstellen to secure a loan by mortgage.

Kredit | gebiet credit field; ~**gebühr** credit service (loan) charge; ~**gebung** granting (making) a loan; ~**gefährdung** injury to reputation; ~**gefüge** credit structure; ~**geld** deposit currency, bank money; **[sofort erteilte] ~genehmigung** [spot] credit approval (authorization).

Kreditgenossenschaft credit cooperative (association, union, *US*), mutual loan society *(Br.)*, cooperative saving organization *(US)*;
gewerbliche ~ industrial loan (finance) company; **landwirtschaftliche ~** agricultural credit corporation, production credit association *(US)*.

Kredit | geschäft *(einzelnes)* credit transaction (operation), *(Gewerbe)* lending (credit) business, credit field; ~**gesellschaft** industrial finance (trust, *US*) company.

Kreditgesuch application for credit, loan (credit) application, credit request;
~ ablehnen (abschlägig bescheiden) to refuse a request for credit, to withhold a credit; **~ bewilligen** to pass a credit vote; **~ einreichen** to apply for credit.

Kreditgewährung lending or loaning money on credit, support of credit, credit accommodation, award of a loan, borrowing;
haushaltsrechtliche ~ interfund borrowing; **kurzfristige ~** granting of short-term credits; **langfristige ~** credit stretching; **objektgebundene ~ an Entwicklungsländer** tied aid; **verbotene ~** prohibited loan;
~ mit offengelegter Forderungsabtretung notification type of a loan;
geringe Ansprüche bei der ~ stellen to shade credit standards.

Kredit | gewerbe moneylending, credit field (lending, business), banking [business]; ~**gewerbe anmelden** to register under the Moneylenders Act *(Br.)*; ~**gewinnabgabe** debts profit levy; ~**grenze** limit of credit *(Br.)*, credit limit *(Br.)* (margin), line of credit *(US)*, credit line *(US)*, *(Verrechnungsabkommen)* swing; ~**grundsätze** credit principles; ~**hahn öffnen** to open the credit tap; ~**hai** loan shark *(US)*; ~**hergabe** borrowing, lending, granting credit; ~**hilfe** financial aid; **staatliche ~hilfe** government financial credit; ~**höchstgrenze** limit of credit *(Br.)*, credit line *(US)*; ~**höchstsätze** ceilings on loans; ~**höhe** amount (extent) of a loan (credit).

kreditieren *(gutschreiben)* to [pass (place) to the] credit, *(Kredit gewähren)* to sell (give) on credit, to [give on] trust *(US)*, *(fam.)* to give on tick *(Br.)*.

kreditiert | sein to be credited;
~**e Beträge** credited amounts; ~**e Importe** imports on credit.

Kreditierung crediting, *(Gutschriftsanzeige)* credit advice (note).

Kredit | inanspruchnahme recourse to credit, use of credit, credit use (usage); **erhöhte ~inanspruchnahme** increased borrowings; ~**inflation** credit inflation; ~**information** credit information (report); ~**informationsabteilung** credit information department; ~**informationsaustausch** watch and warning service.

Kreditinstitut credit (financial) institution, financial establishment, financial house *(Br.)* (institution), credit bank *(Br.)*, moneyed corporation *(US)*;
mit einer Nachlaßverwaltung beauftragtes ~ corporate trustee; **landwirtschaftliches ~** farm credit agency *(US)*, farm mortgage company *(US)*; **öffentlich-rechtliches ~** publicly owned credit institution, public financial institution.

Kredit | instrumentarium credit instrument; ~**jahr** credit year; ~**kapazität** credit capacity; ~**kapital** borrowed capital; ~**karte** credit card, master charge *(US)*.

Kreditkarten | ausgabestelle credit-card organizer; ~**besitzer** credit-card holder; ~**gebühr** credit-card charge; ~**inhaber** credit-card holder; ~**system** credit-card service.

Kredit | kasse loan (credit, *Br.*) bank; ~**kassenschein** bill of credit; ~**kauf** purchasing (buying) on credit, credit (charge, *US*) purchase, credit shopping, *(Abzahlungskauf)* instalment purchase, deferred payment system *(US)*, hire purchase *(Br.)*; **übermäßiger ~kauf** overtrading; ~**knappheit** shortage of credits, credit squeeze (stringency); ~**komponente** credit factor; ~**konditionen** credit terms (conditions); ~**konsortium** financial syndicate, syndicate of bankers; ~**kontingent** portion of a credit; ~**kontingentierung** rationing of credit, credit allocation.

Kreditkonto credit (loan, personal) account;
privates ~ credit private account;
~ für j. einrichten (eröffnen) to open a loan (tick, *Br., fam.*) account for s. o., to arrange account terms for s. o.

Kredit | kontrolle, staatliche checking of bank credits, credit control; ~**kosten** borrowing costs (expenses), credit cost (expense, charges), cost of credit; ~**krise** financial crisis; ~**kunde** credit (charge-account) customer, borrower; ~**kunde der öffentlichen Hand** public sector borrower; ~**kunden mit einer Gebühr belasten** to charge customers for holding cash in their tills; ~**kundenwerbung** soliciting loans; ~**kündigung** notice of withdrawal of credit; ~**lage** financial situation, credit rating *(US)*; ~**laufzeit** period of credit, credit period, term of a loan; ~**lenkung** selective credit control, regulation of credit, credit management; ~**lieferungen** supplies on a deferred payment basis *(US)*; ~**limit** credit limit *(Br.)* (line, *US*); ~**limit aufheben** to cancel a credit limit *(Br.)* (line, *US*).

Kreditlinie credit limit *(Br.)*, limit of credit *(Br.)*, line of credit *(US)*, credit (cash) line *(US)*;
nicht in Anspruch genommene (ausgenutzte) ~ unused (unavailed) credit line *(US)* (limit, *Br.*);
gleichzeitige ~n bei mehreren Kreditinstituten multiple lines *(US)* (limits, *Br.*) of credit;
bei seiner Bank eine ~ beantragen to ask one's bank for a line of credit *(US)* (credit limit, *Br.*); **einjährige ~ eingeräumt erhalten** to obtain a line of credit to run for one year *(US)*; **~ erhöhen** to increase a credit line *(US)* (limit, *Br.*); **~ eröffnen** to open a credit (credit line, *US*, credit limit, *Br.*); **~ für ein Konto festsetzen** to place a credit limit on an account *(Br.)*, to establish a credit line for an account *(US)*; **~ offenhalten** to run a line of credit *(US)* (credit line, *US*, credit limit, *Br.*); **~ überschreiten** to exceed a credit, to run over the credit limit *(Br.)* (line, *US*).

Kredit | liste *(Banken)* black list; ~**lockerung** easing of credits; ~**makler** loan agent, money broker; ~**marge** limit of credit *(Br.)*, credit limit *(Br.)*, credit line (margin) *(US)*, *(Handelsvertrag)* swing; ~**markt** money (credit) market, money and capital market; ~**märkte heftig in Anspruch nehmen** to draw heavily on the credit market; ~**marktmittel** credit resources.

kreditmäßiger Einsatz borrowing, lending.

Kredit | maßnahmen credit policy measures; ~**maßnahmen lockern** to ease credit controls; ~**mechanismus** credit machinery; ~**mißbrauch** credit abuse.

Kreditmittel credit instrument (resources), loan funds;
etatisierte ~ budgeted loans; **objektgebundene ~** earmarked funds; **staatliche ~** state loans;
~ bereitstellen to make credit available; **~ einschränken** to contract credit.

Kreditmöglichkeiten credit resources, borrowing facilities;
~ einschränken to contract credit; **~ erweitern** to expand credit.

Kredit|monopol fiscal (financial) monopoly; ~**nachfrage** demand for credit, credit demand (requirements), loan demand; ~**nachfrage der Wirtschaft** business demand for credit; ~**nachsuchender** credit applicant (candidate); ~**nahme** borrowing, lending.

kreditnehmendes Land borrowing country.

Kreditnehmer borrower, debtor, beneficiary;
letzter ~ final borrower; **öffentlich-rechtlicher** ~ public debtor; ~ **aus der Industrie** industrial borrowers; ~ **zu Schuldtilgungszwecken** debit raiser;
größere Schar von ~**n aufscheuchen** to flush out a string of borrowers.

Kreditnehmerin borrowing company (corporation, concern).

kreditneutral sein to have no effect on the credit standing.

Kredit|normen credit standards; ~**not** credit shortage; ~**offerte machen** to offer a loan.

Kreditor creditor, *(Bank)* depositor.

Kreditoren creditors, *(Bilanz)* accounts due (payable, *US*);
fiktive ~ fictitious liabilities; **verschiedene** ~ sundry creditors; ~ **und Debitoren** assets and liabilities, accounts payable and accounts receivable *(US)*; ~ **aus Hypotheken** mortgage due (payable, *US*); ~ **in laufender Rechnung** account current creditors; ~ **aus Schuldverschreibungen** bonds payable *(US)*; ~ **aus Wechseln** bills (notes) payable *(US)*;
~**buch** creditors' (purchase) ledger; ~**buchhalter** voucher (accounts payable, *US*) clerk; ~**buchhaltung** accounts payable department *(US)*; ~**journal** purchase register; ~**konto** creditor account; ~**verzeichnis** list of creditors, schedule of accounts payable *(US)*.

Kreditorganisation credit organization *(US)*.

kreditorisch, mit seiner Bank nur ~ **arbeiten** to maintain cash balances at a bank on a nonborrowing account; ~ **werden** to go into credit;
~ **geführtes Konto** nonborrowing account.

Kredit|papier credit instrument; ~**plafond** *(Betrieb)* borrowing limit, *(Bankdirektor)* loan (portfolio) ceiling; ~**politik** credit (loan, lending) policy; **restriktive** ~**politik** tight (restrictive) credit policy, tight money; **staatliche** ~**politik** government's credit policy, stop-go *(Br.)*.

kreditpolitisch|es Instrumentarium credit instrument, measures of credit policy; ~**e Lage** credit situation; ~**e Maßnahmen** credit policy measures; ~**e Restriktionsmaßnahmen** measures of credit restriction; ~**e Situation** credit situation.

Kredit|portefeuille credit portfolio; ~**posten** credit entry (item), entry on the credit side; ~**potential** lending (borrowing) power; ~**preis** lending rate; ~**preisverhältnis** loan-to-price ratio; ~**programm** lending program(me); ~**prolongation** extension (renewal) of a credit; ~**provision** procuration fee (money), bonus; ~**prüfer** credit analyst (investigator); ~**prüfung** credit analysis (checking), audit for credit purposes, checking credit, means test *(Br.)*, loan appraisal, credit rating *(US)*; ~**prüfungsdienst** credit-checking service; ~**quellen** credit resources; **verschiedene** ~**quellen erschließen** to tap alternative sources of credit; **nicht in Anspruch genommene** ~**quote** unused portion of a credit; ~**rahmen** credit limit *(Br.)* (line, *US*); **durchschnittliche** ~**rate für Geschäftskredite** average business loan rate; ~**rationierung** credit rationing; ~**registratur** credit files; **staatliche** ~**regulierung** regulation of credits, credit control; ~**reserve** borrowing reserve; ~**restriktion** credit restriction (restraint, deflation, brake, stringency, squeeze), loan restrictions; **generelle** ~**restriktionen** *(Bundesnotenbank)* quantitative credit restrictions *(Br.)*; **einzelne gezielte** ~**restriktionen** qualitative credit restrictions *(Br.)*; ~**richtlinien** rules of credit, credit rules (standards); ~**richtsätze** regulations in regard to credits; **augenscheinliche** ~**risiken beseitigen** to remove the apparent risk barriers.

Kreditrisiko credit risk;
~ **berechnen** to appraise a credit risk; ~ **übernehmen** to assume the credit risk;
~**versicherung** credit risk insurance.

Kredit|rückflüsse amortization of loans; ~**rückführung** reduction in the volume of a credit; **unmöglich gewordene** ~**rückführung** loan default; ~**rückzahlung** repayment of an advance (a credit); ~**sachbearbeiter** credit man, loan officer; **erfahrener** ~**sachbearbeiter** qualified lending officer; ~**sachverständiger** credit expert (man).

Kreditsaldo credit (loan) balance;
durchschnittlicher ~ deposit line *(US)*; **mein gegenwärtiger** ~ the balance standing to my credit; **auf Gewinn- und Verlustkonto vorzutragender** ~ credit to be carried forward to profit and loss account; **durchschnittlicher** ~ **eines Depositenkontos** deposit line *(US)*, line of deposit *(US)*;
~ **zu meinen Gunsten ausweisen** to present (show) a balance to my favo(u)r.

Kredit|schädigung damage to credit (reputation), injurious falsehood *(Br.)*, discredit; ~**schädigung nachweisen** to prove the damage to one's credit; **am** ~**schalter Schlange stehen** to be waiting at the loan window; ~**schöpfung** creation of bank credit; ~**schöpfungsmultiplikator** money supply expansion multiplier; ~**schraube** credit squeeze; ~**schraube anziehen** to tighten credits; ~**schrumpfung** contraction of credits; ~**schutzverein** trade protection society *(Br.)*; ~**schwindel** obtaining money by false pretences; **auf der** ~**seite** to the good; ~**sektor** credit field; ~**selektion** selective credit control.

Kreditsicherheit security, collateral *(US)*;
auswechselbare ~ floating security; **persönlich gestellte** ~ direct security;
Aktien als ~ **verwenden** to apply shares as collateral security *(US)*.

Kredit|situation credit situation; ~**sonderkonto** special loan account; ~**spanne** credit margin; ~**sperre** lending stop, stoppage of credit, freezing of credit, loan embargo; ~**spielraum** credit limit *(Br.)* (line, *US*), credit margin; ~**spitzenbetrag** residual amount of a credit; ~**spritze** credit injection; ~**status** credit standing (rating, *US*); ~**stopp** stoppage of credit, lending stop; ~**strom** flow of credit; ~**suchender** applicant for credit, credit applicant (candidate).

kreditsuchendes Unternehmen would-be borrower.

Kredit|sucher credit applicant; ~**summe** amount (extent) of a loan (credit); ~**system** credit system, *(Ratenzahlung)* instal(l)ment (hire-purchase, *Br.*, deferred-payment, *US*) system; **landwirtschaftliches** ~**system** farm credit system *(US)*; ~**täuschung** obtaining money by false pretences; **nicht in Anspruch genommener** ~**teil** unused portion of a credit, credit reserves, unused credit; ~**tilgung** repayment of a credit; **noch nicht in Anspruch genommene** ~**tranche** undrawn portion of a loan; ~**übereinkommen** credit agreement (arrangement); ~**überschreitung** overdrawing of an account, overdraft; ~**überspannung** overexpansion of credit, *(generell)* credit inflation; **staatliche** ~**überwachung** control of an advance, credit control; ~**überwachungsstelle** credit-control authority; ~**überziehung** overdrawing of an account, overdraft; ~**überziehungsprovision** overdraft commission; ~**umfang** extent of a credit; ~**unkosten** borrowing costs, credit expense (charges, cost); ~**unterlagen** credit files; ~**unterlagen mit gefälschten Angaben** false papers; ~**unterlagenprüfung** checking credit, audit for credit purposes, credit rating *(US)*; ~**unternehmen** credit institution.

kreditunwürdig unworthy of credit.

Kredit|valuta loan money; ~**verein[igung]** guarantee society, credit union *(US)*, loan society *(Br.)*; **gemeinnütziger** ~**verein** remedial loan society; **gewerblicher** ~**verein** industrial loan society; ~**vereinbarung** credit (borrowing) arrangement (agreement); **allgemeine** ~**vereinbarungen** *(GATT)* general arrangements to borrow; ~**verflechtung** interlocking credit relationship; ~**verhältnis** creditor debtor relationship; ~**verhandlungen** loan talks; ~**verkauf** credit sale, sale of merchandise on credit; ~**verkäufe in offener Rechnung** credit sales on open accounts; ~**verkehr** lending, borrowing, credit transactions; **internationaler** ~**verkehr** international lending (borrowing); ~**verkehr mit dem Ausland** external credit transactions; ~**verknappung** credit restriction (tightness, squeeze, crunch), restriction (stringency) of credit; ~**verlängerung** extension of a loan, credit extension; ~**verlängerung gewähren** to extend a credit; ~**verlust** credit (loan) loss; ~**vermittler** financial agent, loan broker; ~**vermittlungsbüro** credit agency; ~**versicherung** loan insurance, credit (bad debts, guarantee, *Br.*, guaranty, *US*) insurance; ~**versicherungsgesellschaft** credit insurer; ~**versicherungspolice** credit insurance policy; ~**versorgung** credit supply; ~**verteuerung** increase in the cost of credit.

Kreditvertrag credit agreement (arrangement), loan agreement;
für Investitionszwecke im voraus vereinbarter langfristiger ~ standby credit agreement.

Kreditverwaltung credit management.

Kreditvolumen volume of credits, credit volume, total borrowings;
~ **insgesamt** total credits extended; **kurzfristiges** ~ volume of short-term credits;
~ **der öffentlichen Hand** total borrowings of public authorities;
~ **erhöhen** to create further bank money *(US)*.

Kredit|vordruck credit form *(US)*; ~**vorschlag** credit suggestion; ~**vorteile** credit facilities; ~**wechsel** credit bill; **auf dem ~wege** by raising a credit; **im ~wege erwerben** to buy on credit terms.

Kreditwesen credit system (field), financing;
genossenschaftliches ~ cooperative banking; **landwirtschaftliches ~** farm credit system *(US)*;
~**gesetz** Moneylenders' Act *(Br.)*.

Kredit|wirtschaft credit economy, lending business; **restriktive ~wirtschaft** quantitative credit restrictions *(Br.)*; ~**wucher** loan sharking *(US)*; ~**wucher treiben** to practise usury; ~**wucherer** loan shark *(US)*; ~**wünsche** borrowing demands; **weitere ~wünsche abschlägig bescheiden** to refuse further credit.

kreditwürdig good, [financially] sound, solvent, solid, creditable, worthy of credit, credit-worthy, *(vertrauenswürdig)* reliable, trustworthy;
jem. zu einer Höhe von 10.000 $ für ~ halten to consider s. o. trustworthy to the extent of $ 10.000;
~**e Firma** sound business house.

Kreditwürdigkeit creditabilitiy, borrowing power, credit position (worthiness), credit, standing, soundness, solidity, strength, *(Vertrauenswürdigkeit)* reliability, trustworthiness;
geschäftliche ~ bis zu ... trustworthiness in the way of business to the extent of ...;
für die ~ einstehen to pledge the credit.

Kreditwürdigkeits|liste credit rating book *(US)*; ~**prüfung** credit standing (investigation, rating, *US*); ~ **und Verwendungsprüfung** means and purpose test.

Kredit|zinsen interest on borrowed money (loans), interest due (receivable, *US*); ~ **und Debetzinsen** interest pro and contra; ~**zinssatz** interest rate, lending rate *(US)*; ~**zügel** credit restrictions (crunches); ~**zurückziehung** withdrawal of credit; ~**zusage** credit approval, advance commitment, standby credit, promise of a loan; **für Investitionszwecke im voraus vereinbarte langfristige ~zusage** standby credit agreement; ~**zusammenfassung** contraction of credit issues; ~**zustimmung** loan sanction; **zu ~zwecken überprüfen** to audit for credit purposes.

Kreide chalk;
hoch bei jem. in der ~ stehen to be up to one's ears in debt to s. o.

kreidebleich white as a sheet.

Kreidezeichnung chalk (crayon) drawing.

kreieren to create;
Mode ~ to set the fashion.

Kreierung creation.

Kreis circle, quarter, *(Bezirk)* borough *(Br.)*, parish *(Br.)*, county *(US)*, district *(US)*, minor civil division *(US)*, civil county *(Scot.)*, *(el.)* circuit, *(Gesellschaft)* set, *(Gruppe)* group, walk of life, *(Wirkungskreis)* sphere, section;
aus allen ~en der Bevölkerung from all walks of life; **aus ~en der Industrie verlautet** according to industry sources; **im ~e seiner Familie** among his own people; **in ~en außerhalb der Firma** in outside quarters; **in ~en des Auswärtigen Amtes** in Foreign Office circles; **in diplomatischen ~en** in diplomatic quarters; **in finanziellen ~en** in financial circles; **in kaufmännischen ~en** in commercial circles; **in unterrichteten ~en** in informed quarters; **in weiten ~en** widely; **in weiten ~en geteilt** broadly shared;
ausgewählter ~ elite circle; **begüterte ~e** propertied classes, well-to-do people; **einflußreiche ~e** influential circles; **eingeweihte ~e** well-informed quarters, insiders; **erlesener ~** coterie; **geselliger ~** social gathering; **literarischer ~** literary set (group); **maßgebende ~e** influential circles; **politische ~e** political circles; **führende politische ~e** high places; **gut unterrichtete ~e** well-placed sources;
~ **der Begünstigten** class of benificiaries; **weite ~e der Bevölkerung** large groups (wide sections) of the population; **ganzer ~ von Fragen** whole range of questions; ~ **von Geldgebern** sponsoring group; ~ **der Interessen** sphere of interests; **kleiner ~ von Lesern** small readership; ~**e der Wirtschaft** business quarters, commercial circles;
~ **der Fürsorgeberechtigten ausweiten** to expand the welfare rolls; **weite ~e der Bevölkerung betreffen** to affect wide sections of the population; **sich im ~ bewegen** *(Überlegungen)* to reason in a circle; ~ **bilden** to form a circle; **im ~ der Familie feiern** to celebrate at a family gathering; **sich nur im ~ der Familie wohl fühlen** to feel happy only among one's own people; **zum ~ der Vertrauten gehören** to belong to the inner circle; **aus dem engen ~ seiner Interessen nicht herauskommen** to be unable to go beyond the narrow sphere of one's interests; **im ~ herumlaufen** to go round (in a circle); **jds. ~e stören** to bother s. o.; **in den führenden ~en verkehren** to move in the leading circles; **in bestimmten ~en gerüchtweise verlauten** to be rumo(u)red in certain quarters; **weite ~e ziehen** to have repercussions; **immer weitere ~e ziehen** *(Gerücht)* to spread further and further, *(Skandal)* to involve more and more people; ~**e über dem Flugplatz ziehen** to circle above the airport;
mir dreht sich alles im ~e my head is spinning; **die Beerdigung findet im kleinsten ~e statt** funeral private;
~**abschnitt** segment, sector; ~**amt** county (district) office.

kreisangehörige Stadt [etwa] noncounty borough *(Br.)*, urban district *(Br.)*.

Kreis|angelegenheiten county business (affairs); ~**arzt** medical officer of health; ~**aufgaben** functions of a county; ~**ausschnitt** sector; ~**ausschuß** county council *(Br.)*, district committee; ~**ausschußmitglied** county council(l)or *(US)*.

Kreisbahn orbit;
in eine niedrige ~ bringen to park in a low orbit; **Satelliten in eine ~ um die Erde bringen** to blast a satellite into an orbit; **in eine ~ um den Mond einschwenken** to enter an orbit around the moon;
~**geschwindigkeit** orbital velocity; ~**raketensystem** fractional orbital bombing.

Kreis|beamter county officer *(US)*; ~**beauftragter** county *(US)* (district) commissioner; ~**behörde** county office, district (local) authority *(Br.)*; ~**branddirektor** fire chief.

kreischen jar, to shriek, *(Zugbremse)* to grate, to screak *(US)*, *(Bremse)* to screech;
vor Vergnügen ~ to be screaming with pleasure.

kreischend, mit ~en Bremsen zum Halten kommen to screech to a halt; ~**e Stimme** shrill voice.

Kreis|diagramm circular (pie) chart; ~**direktor** [etwa] county manager *(US)*; **auf ~ebene** at county level; ~**einteilung** division of a circle.

Kreisel top, whirligig, *(physikalisch)* gyroscope;
~**aufhängung** gyro mounting; ~**gerät** gyroscope, gyropilot.

kreiselgesteuert gyro-operated.

Kreisel|kompaß gyrocompass, gyroscope sextant; ~**stabilisierung** gyro stabilization; ~**steuerung** gyroscope control.

kreisen to revolve, to rotate, *(Runde machen)* to circle;
über dem Flugplatz ~ to circle (circuit) above the airport; **immer um einen Punkt ~** *(Gedanken)* to reason in a circle; **um die Sonne ~** *(Planet)* to revolve around the sun; **über der Stadt ~** to circle over the town; **um ein bestimmtes Thema ~** to revolve about one single subject; **im Warteraum ~** *(Flugzeug)* to orbit.

kreis|förmige Bahn circular orbit; ~**freie Stadt** incorporated city, county borough, municipality *(US)*, municipal corporation *(US)*.

Kreis|gebiet county; ~**gefängnis** county jail; ~**gericht** district (county, *Br.*) court, quarter session division *(Br.)*; ~**gesundheitsamt** local health authority; ~**hauptstadt** county seat *(Br.)*; ~**haushalt** budget of a borough (county, *US*); ~**kämmerer** county treasurer *(US)*; ~**krankenhaus** district general hospital, county hospital.

Kreislauf blood circulation, *(fig.)* cycle;
~ **der Spekulation** speculative cycle; ~ **der Wirtschaft** trade *(Br.)* (business, *US*) cycle;
~ **anregen** to stimulate circulation; **in den ~ zurückführen** *(Geld)* to recycle;
gesamtwirtschaftliches ~modell macroeconomic model of income determination; ~**störung** circulatory disorder, disturbance of circulation.

Kreis|planungsbehörde local planning authority; ~**rat** county council(l)or *(Br.)*, district committy; ~**ratsmitglied** county counci(l)lor; ~**richter** district judge; ~**schaubild** circle chart; ~**schule** council school; ~**stadt** municipal (county) town (borough) *(Br.)*, county seat *(US)*; ~**steuern** county rates; ~**straße** county road *(US)*, local road; ~**tag** county (district) council *(Br.)*.

Kreistags|abgeordneter, ~mitglied county councillor; ~**sitzung** county session *(Br.)*; ~**wahlen** local elections *(Br.)*, municipal elections *(US)*.

Kreis|umlage county (district) rate *(Br.)*; ~**verband** county corporate; ~**verkehr** circular (rotary) traffic, roundabout [system of traffic], merry-go-round; **im ~verkehr** gyratory *(Br.)*; ~**verkehrsregelung** roundabout traffic system; ~**vermögen** county property (treasury); ~**verwaltung** county government; ~**wahlausschuß** election board.

Krematorium crematorium, crematory *(US)*.

Krempel duds, stuff, lumber, things;
der ganze ~ the whole concern (outfit);
seinen ~ aufräumen to tidy up one's things; **ganzen ~ satt haben** to be fed up with the whole business; **den ganzen ~ hinschmeißen** to chuck up the whole thing.

krepieren to kick the bucket, to snuff it, *(Granate)* to explode.
Krepp | papier crêpe paper, crinkled paper; ~**sohle** rubber (crape) sole.
Krethi und Plethi ragtag and bobtail, hoi polloi, common herd.
Kretin cretin, dim-witted person.
Kreuz cross, *(Handzeichen)* mark;
Rotes ~ Red Cross;
zu ~e kriechen to truckle, to eat humble pie, to eat one's words; **ein bißchen zu ~e kriechen** to eat a small helping of humble pie; **j. aufs ~ legen** to euchre s. o. *(US sl.)*, to take s. o. in, to pull a fast one on s. o., to thwart s. one's plans; **jem. Geld aus dem ~ leiern** to wheedle money out of s. o.; **zu ~e kriechen müssen** to return by the weeping cross; **sein ~ auf sich nehmen** to bear one's cross; **mit einem ~ unterschreiben** to make one's cross.
kreuz und quer zig-zag, criss-cross;
~ **durch die Stadt laufen** to go all over the town.
Kreuzauswertung *(Umfrage)* cross tabulation, cross sectional analysis.
Kreuzband [newspaper] cover, wrapper;
unter ~ under wrapper (cover);
unter ~ **schicken** to send by bookpost, to post in wrappers.
Kreuzelastizität der Nachfrage cross elasticity of demand.
kreuzen *(Scheck)* to cross, crossing;
sich ~ *(Briefe)* to cross in the post, *(Interessen)* to clash, to run counter, *(Straße)* to cross, to intersect;
Klinge mit jem. ~ to cross swords with s. o.
Kreuzer, leichter protected cruiser; **schwerer** ~ armo(u)red cruiser.
Kreuzfahrt holiday (training) cruise;
~ **machen** to cruise; ~ **unternehmen** to [go on a] cruise.
Kreuzfeuer running fire;
~ **von Fragen** barrage (running fire) of questions, cross fire; ~ **der Kritik** battery of criticism;
ins ~ **nehmen** to cross-question; **im** ~ **der öffentlichen Meinung stehen** to be under the cross-fire of public opinion.
kreuzfidel fit as a fiddle, merry as a lark (cricket).
Kreuz | hacke pick; ~**kurs** cross rate.
kreuzlahm stiff as a poker;
j. ~ **schlagen** to beat s. o. to a pulp.
Kreuztabellierung cross tabulation.
Kreuzung crossing, crossover, crossroads, cross, crosspoint, *(Bahn)* junction, *(Scheck)* crossing;
beschrankte ~ crossing with gates; **besondere** ~ *(Scheck)* special crossing *(Br.)*; **gefährliche** ~ *(Straßenschild)* dangerous crossing; **geregelte** ~ controlled crossing; **höhengleiche (schienengleiche)** ~ level *(Br.)* (grade, *US*) crossing; **planfreie** ~ grade-separated crossing; **rechtwinklige** ~ T-junction; **ungeregelte** ~ uncontrolled crossing;
~ **mit polizeilicher Verkehrsregelung** police-controlled junction; ~ **nur zur Verrechnung** nonnegotiable crossing;
bei Gelb über die ~ **fahren** to shoot (crash) the amber *(US sl.)*; **bei Rot über die** ~ **fahren** to shoot the traffic lights, to run a red light.
Kreuzungsbahnhof junction.
kreuzungsfrei free of crossroads, intersection-free *(US)*.
Kreuzungs | punkt intersection; ~**verkehr** crossroads.
Kreuzverhör cross-examination (-question);
ins ~ **nehmen** to cross-examine, to cross-question, *(in Versammlung)* to heckle; **Verbrecher einem strengen** ~ **unterwerfen** to grill a criminal *(US sl.)*.
Kreuz | verweis cross reference; ~**weg** cross section; **am ~weg seines Lebens** at the crossroads; ~**worträtsel** crossword puzzle; ~**worträtselzeitung** crossword paper; ~**zeichen** *(drucktechn.)* dagger, *(Handzeichen)* cross; ~**zug** crusade, campaign; ~**zug durchführen** to crusade.
Kribbelgefühl tingling sensation.
kribbelig edgy, on edge, fidgety, jittery, jumpy, *(gereizt)* fretful;
j. ~ **machen** to set s. one's teeth on edge, to give s. o. the jitters, to get on s. one's nerves; **ganz** ~ **sein** to be on pins and needles; ~ **werden** to get fidgety.
Kribbeln pin, pins and needles, jimjams *(fig.)*.
kriechen to sneak, to worm, to kotow *(fam.)*, *(Verkehr)* to crawl;
vor jem. ~ to fall over s. o.; **ins Bett** ~ to get between the sheets; **jem. in den Hintern** ~ to lick s. one's boots; **jem. auf den Leim** ~ to let o. s. be taken in; **auf allen vieren** ~ to crawl on all fours, to go on one's hands and knees; **vor seinem Vorgesetzten** ~ to crawl to one's boss, to toady to the boss.
Kriecher creeper, sneak, toady, crawler, reptile, bootlick, underling, understrapper, truckler, lackey;
gemeiner ~ lion's provider.
Kriecherei toadyism, flunkeyism, servility.
kriecherisch toadyish, crawling, servile;
einem Polizisten ~ **begegnen** to cringe before a policeman; **jem.** ~ **schmeicheln** to flatter s. o. servilely.
Kriech | öffnung, ~**durchlaß** creep, close opening; ~**spur** *(Autobahn)* creeper lane; ~**strom** creeping current *(sl.)*.
Krieg war, warfare;
am Rande eines ~es on the verge of a war; **für den** ~ **gerüstet** prepared for war; **im** ~ **befindlich** at war; **in einen** ~ **verwickelt** embroiled in a war; **vom** ~ **stark mitgenommen** war-battered; **während des ~es** for the duration of war;
allgemeiner ~ perfect war; **ohne Kriegserklärung begonnener** ~ unsolemn war; **begrenzter** ~ limited war; **völkerrechtlich erklärter** ~ solemn war; **heißer** ~ hot war; **kalter** ~ cold war, war of nerves; **kleinerer** ~ minor war; **konventioneller** ~ conventional war; **mörderischer** ~ murderous war; **subversiver** ~ insurgency war; **totaler** ~ total war[fare]; **unbarmherziger** ~ cruel war; **unblutiger** ~ dry war;
~ **auf allen Fronten** war on a large scale; ~ **ohne Kriegserklärung** undeclared war; ~ **und Kriegsgeschrei** war and rumo(u)rs of war; ~ **bis aufs Messer** war to the knife (death); ~ **mit konventionellen Waffen** conventional war;
~ **ächten** to outlaw war; **einem Land einen** ~ **aufzwingen** to force war upon a country; ~ **beenden** to bring war to an end; ~ **beginnen** to go to war; **in den** ~ **eintreten** to enter into the war; ~ **von neuem entfachen** to rekindle a war; **sich vom** ~ **erholen** to rebound from the war; **einem Land den** ~ **erklären** to declare war upon a country; ~ **eröffnen** to go to war; **konventionellen** ~ **in einen Atomkrieg eskalieren** to escalate a conventional war into nuclear warfare; ~ **führen** to maintain a (levy, wage) war, to bear arms against, to be at war with; **zum** ~ **hetzen** to warmonger; **in einen** ~ **hineinschlittern** to drift into a war; **es auf einen** ~ **ankommen lassen** to resort to war; ~ **lokalisieren** to quarantine a war; **zum** ~ **rüsten** to prepare for war; **zum** ~ **schreiten** to resort to war, to war; **in einen** ~ **verwickelt sein** to be [engaged] in a war; **auf den** ~ **zurückzuführen sein** to date from the war; **vom** ~ **sprechen** to sound the note of war; **am Rande eines ~es stehen** to be on the brink of war; **sich in einen** ~ **stürzen** to plunge into war; ~ **ins Feindesland tragen** to carry war into the enemy's land; **im** ~ **umkommen** to be killed in the war; ~ **verhindern** to prevent (avoid) a war; ~ **durch Abschreckung verhindern** to deter war; ~ **verlieren** to lose a war; ~ **vermeiden** to avoid a war; ~ **vorbereiten** to plan for a war; ~ **in die Länge ziehen** to protract a war.
kriegen to get, to receive, to pan out *(US coll.)*, *(verdienen)* to earn;
es mit der Angst zu tun ~ to get scared; **Heimweh** ~ to grow homesick; **etw. zu hören** ~ to get a good talking to; **Kopfschmerzen** ~ to get a headache; **seinen verdienten Lohn** ~ to get a fair reward for one's labo(u)r; **Mörder** ~ to catch a murderer; **schwer zu** ~ difficult to obtain; **die Wut** ~ to fly off the handle.
Krieger military man, warrior;
~**denkmal** war memorial.
kriegerisch belligerent, bellicose, martial;
~**e Besetzung** belligerent occupation; ~**e Handlung** act of war, warlike operation; ~**er Konflikt** armed conflict.
Kriegerwitwe war widow.
Kriegerwitwenpension war widow's pension.
kriegführend, nicht nonbelligerent;
~**e Mächte** belligerent powers.
Kriegs | abgabe war levy; ~**ächtung** outlawry of war.
kriegsähnlich | e Handlung measures short of war; ~**er Zustand** warlike state.
Kriegs | akademie Imperial Defence College *(Br.)*, Staff (War, *US*) College; ~**anleihe** war loan, national war (defence) bonds, war saving certificates *(Br.)*, victory loan *(Br.)*, liberty bonds *(US)*; ~**anstrengungen** war efforts; ~**arsenal** war arsenal; ~**artikel herstellen** to turn out instruments of war; ~**auflage** contribution; ~**ausbruch** outbreak (erruption) of a war; ~**ausführung** war grade of product; ~**ausgaben** wartime expenditure; ~**ausrüstung** war equipment; ~**ausschlußklausel** free-of-capture-and-seizure clause; ~**ausweitung** extension of war, widening of war; **sich von den ~auswirkungen erholen** to recover from the effects of a war; ~**auszeichnungen** war medals, hono(u)rs of war; ~**bedarf** war material.
kriegsbedingt due to the war, war-conditioned;
~**e Einstellung** war hirings; ~**e Notwendigkeit** wartime emergency; ~**e Rationierung** wartime rationing.
Kriegs | beginn commencement of war; ~**beil ausgraben** to take up the hatchet, to dig up the tomahawk; **volle ~bemalung** war paint *(fam.)*.

kriegsbereit prepared for war.

Kriegs|bereitschaft preparedness (readiness) for war; **Armee in ~bereitschaft halten** to keep the army on a war footing; **~bericht** war report, dispatch *(Br.)*; **im ~bericht lobend erwähnt werden** to be mentioned in dispatches *(Br.)*; **~berichterstatter** war correspondent (reporter).

kriegsbeschädigt disabled in the war, [war-]disabled.

Kriegs|beschädigtenrente war pension; **~beschädigter** war-disabled, ex-service man; **~beschädigung** war disablement; **~besteuerung** wartime (war) taxation; **~bestimmungen** wartime regulations; **~beteiligung** cobelligerency; **~betrieb** war plant; **~beute** spoils of war, loot; **~bewirtschaftung** wartime control; **~brauch** custom and usages of war; **~buch** war book; **auf ~dauer** for the duration (during the continuance) of the war.

Kriegsdienst service in the field;
sich freiwillig zum ~ melden to enlist for the army in a war; **~ tun** to see service;
~verweigerer conscientious objector, war resister; **~verweigerung** conscientious objection.

Kriegs|drohung threat of war; **~drohungen ausstoßen** to menace with war; **~einkommen** wartime earnings; **~einsatz** action; **~einstellungen** war hirings; **~eintritt** entry (entering) into the war; **~einwirkungen** effects of the war; **durch ~einwirkungen** as a result of the war; **~ende** end of the war; **~entschädigung** war indemnity (damage compensation), reparation; **~entschädigung für bewegliches Vermögen** private chattel scheme *(Br.)*; **~ereignis** event of the war; **~erfahrung** smell of powder; **~erklärung** declaration of war; **überstürzte ~erklärung abgeben** to be too precipitate in declaring war; **zur Abgabe von ~erklärungen berechtigt sein** to be vested with the power to declare war; **~erlebnisse** wartime experiences; **~eröffnung** opening of bostilities.

kriegserprobt war-proof.

Kriegs|erscheinung wartime phenomenon; **~ersparnisse** war savings; **im ~fall** in case of war; **für den ~fall vorgesehen sein** to contemplate a state of war; **~finanzierung** war financing; **~flagge** white ensign *(Br.)*; **~flotte** fleet, naval forces; **~flüchtling** war refugee; **~flugzeug** warplane.

Kriegsfolgen sequel (progeny, repercussions, results) of the war;
zu den ~ gehören to follow on the heels of war;
~rente war pension.

Kriegs|folgeschäden war-induced damage; **~freiwilliger** volunteer.

Kriegsführung conduct of war, belligerence, warfare;
bakteriologische (biologische) ~ bacteriological (germ, biological) warfare; **energische ~** vigorous prosecution of a war; **ideologische ~** ideological warfare; **psychologische ~** psychological warfare; **radioaktive ~** radioactive warfare;
~ großen Ausmaßes large-scale warfare.

Kriegs|funktionen ausüben, entscheidende to figure in the war; **~furcht** war scare; **auf ~fuß mit jem. stehen** to be at daggers drawn with s. o.; **~gebiet** region of war, military area, war (operational) zone; **~gefahr** war risk, hazards of war; **~gefahrklausel** war-risk clause.

Kriegsgefangenen|entschädigung compensation for prisoners of war; **~freigabe** redemption of prisoners of war; **~lager** prisoner-of-war camp; **~status** prisoner-of-war status.

Kriegs|gefangener prisoner of war; **befreiter ~gefangener** liberee; **~gefangenschaft** captivity, prisoner-of-war status; **~gegner** antiwar protester; **~geisel** scourge of war; **~gerät** war material (tools, equipment); **~gerede hören** to hear talk of war; **~gericht** provost court, court-martial; **vor ein ~gericht stellen** to court-martial; **~gerichtsverfahren** procedure of court-martial; **~gerüchte** rumo(u)rs of war; **~geschehen** events of the war; **~geschrei** war cry, whoops; **~gesetz** emergency law; **~gesetzgebung** wartime legislation; **~gewinn** war profit; **~gewinnler** war profiteer; **~gewinnsteuer** express profits duty *(Br.)*, war profits tax *(US)*; **~gewohnheitsrecht** custom and usages of war; **~glück** fortunes of war; **~glück entscheiden lassen** to appeal to the sword; **~gräberfürsorge** war-graves commission; **~greuel** horrors of war; **~gründe** war circumstances; **~hafen** man-of-war harbo(u)r, naval port; **~handlung** act of war; **~handwerk** trade of war; **~hausse** war boom; **~heimkehrer** repatriate, home-coming prisoner; **~held** war hero; **~hetze** warmongering, war agitation; **~hetzer** warmonger, war agitator.

kriegshetzerisch bellicose, jingoistic.

Kriegs|hinterbliebene war victims; **~hysterie** war [time] hysteria; **~industrie** wartime (war) industry; **zurückgeführter ~internierter** repatriate; **~invalide** war-disabled, war pensioner; **~jahre** years of the war; **geburtenschwache ~jahrgänge** low birth-rate of the war years; **~kabinett** war cabinet; **~kamerad** fellow soldier, brother-in-arms; **~kasse** war (military) chest; **~kind** war baby; **~klauseln** institute-war *(Br.)* (war-risk) clauses; **~konjunktur** war boom; **~konterbande** contraband of war; **~kontribution** contribution; **einer Stadt ~kontributionen auferlegen** to punish a town; **~kontrollkommission** war control commission; **~kosten** war expenses, cost (expense) of war; **~kunst** war; **~lasten** war burden; **~lazarett** base hospital; **~lieferungen** war deliveries (supplies); **~list** ploy, stratagem, ruse of war, trick; **~lohn** wartime wage.

kriegslüstern trigger-happy.

Kriegs|macht military establishment; **~marine** navy, the senior service *(Br.)*; **~maschinerie** war machine.

Kriegs|maßnahmen war efforts; **~material** war material, munition of war, military stores; **überschüssiges ~material** surplus war property; **~minister** army minister, Secretary of State for War *(Br.)*; **~ministerium** War Office *(Br.)*, War Department *(US)*, Department of War *(US)*, Target A *(sl.)*; **~moloch** juggernaut of war.

kriegsmüde war-weary.

Kriegs|müdigkeit war weariness; **~nachwirkungen** aftermath of war; **~neurose** combat fatigue, battle (operational) fatigue; **~notstandsgesetz** Defence of the Realm Act *(Br.)*; **~opfer** war victim; **~opferfürsorge** care for war victims; **~opferversorgung** pension scheme for war victims; **~partei** war party; **auf dem ~pfad** to be on the warpath; **nachnukleare ~phase** broken-back war; **~potential** war-making potential, military resources, armament; **~prise** prize of war; **~produktion** wartime (war, defense, *US*, defence, *Br.*) production; **~propaganda** war (wartime, belligerent) propaganda; **~psychose** war scare; **~recht** martial (military) law, law of arms; **~recht verhängen** to impose martial law; **~rechtsverhängung** imposition of martial law; **~rechtsverhängung wieder aufheben** to lift martial law; **~reparationen** war reparations; **~richter** provost.

Kriegsrisiko hazards (risks, perils) of war, war risk;
~klausel war-risk clause; **~police** war-risk policy; **~versicherung** war-risk insurance.

Kriegs|rücklage *(Versicherung)* war reserve; **~rüstung** implements of war, war planning; **~schäden** war damage; **~schädenamt** compensation office; **~schadensgesetz** war damages bill; **~schadenshilfe** war-damage assistance; **~schadensvergütung** war indemnity; **~schatz** war chest; **~schauplatz** theatre (zone) of war, scene of operations; **europäischer ~schauplatz** European theatre; **auf einem anderen ~schauplatz einsetzen** to redeploy; **~schiff** man-of-war, warship, battleship, naval ship; **~schiffsbau** naval architecture; **~schuld** war guilt.

Kriegsschulden war debts;
zwischenstaatliche ~ interstate war debts *(US)*;
~ erlassen (streichen) to cancel war debts;
~streichung cancellation of war debts.

Kriegs|schuldner war debtor; **~schuldverschreibungen** war bonds; **~schule** officers training corps; **~spiel** war game.

kriegsstark on a war footing.

Kriegs|stärke war footing (establishment), armament; **~steuer** contribution, excess profits duty *(Br.)*, war (excess profits) tax *(US)*; **~tagebuch** historic record.

kriegstauglich fit for active service.

Kriegs|taumel martial rage; **~teilnehmer** combatant, campaigner; **ehemaliger ~teilnehmer** war veteran *(US)*; **~teilnehmerabfindung** war veterans' bonus; **~treiber** warmonger; **~tribun** military tribune; **~ursache** cause of the war; **~ursache sein** to lead up to the war; **~verbrechen** war crime; **~verbrecher** war criminal; **~verdienstorden** Distinguished Service Cross *(US)* (Order, *Br.*); **~verherrlichung** glamo(u)r of war; **~verhütung** prevention of war; **~verletzung** war injury; **~verlust** war loss; **~verluste** war casualties; **~verrat** relieving the enemy; **~verrat begehen** to relieve the enemy; **~verräter** war traitor; **~verschollenheit** presumption of death due to war; **~versehrtenrente** disability pension; **~versehrter** war-disabled, war cripple, disabled veteran *(US)*; **~versicherung** war-risk insurance; **~verteuerung** wartime price increase.

kriegsverwendungsfähig fit for active service.

Kriegsverwüstungen desolation caused by war.

Kriegsvorbereitungen preparations for war, warlike preparations;
umfassende ~ getroffen haben to be in good preparation for war; **~ treffen** to prepare for war.

Kriegs|vorräte war stocks (stores), munition; **~waffen** military weapons; **~waise** war orphan; **~werkzeuge** instruments of war.

kriegswichtig | en Beruf ausüben to be in a reserved occupation; **~e Güter** strategic goods.
Kriegs | wirtschaft wartime economy; **~wirtschaftskontrolle** wartime business control; **~wolken** clouds of war; **während der ganzen ~zeit** throughout the war; **~zeiten ausgenommen** except in time of war.
kriegszerstörtes Land war-worn country.
Kriegs | ziel war aims; **~zone** war zone; **~zug** military expedition; **~zulage** field allowance, war bonus; **~zuschlag** war increase.
Kriegszustand belligerency, militancy, war footing, state of war;
im ~ at war;
bestehender ~ existence of a state of war;
~ erklären to declare a state of war; **mit einem Land im ~ sein** to be at war with a country.
Kriminal | abteilung criminal investigation department; **~beamter** police detective, plain-clothes policeman, C.I.D. (F.B.I., *US*) officer, trap, hard hole *(sl.)*, bull *(US sl.)*, stool *(sl.)*; **~fall** criminal case; **~film** detective film, thriller, **~inspektor** detective (police) inspector.
Kriminalist detective [officer].
Kriminalistik criminalistics.
kriminalistische Untersuchungen criminal investigation.
Kriminalität criminalism, criminality, delinquency.
Kriminalitätsziffer crime rate.
Kriminalkommissar superintendent.
kriminalkundlich penological.
Kriminal | polizei detective police (force), detective bureau of the police force, Scotland Yard *(Br.)*, Criminal Investigation Department (C.I.D.) *(Br.)*, Federal Bureau of Investigation (F.B.I.) *(US)*; **~roman** detective story (novel), crime fiction, thriller, murder mystery, mistery novel, whodunit *(sl.)*; **~schriftsteller** crime writer, detective novelist; **~statistik** criminal statistics; **~strafkunde** penology; **~stück** crime play; **~stück ohne Fortsetzung** *(Rundfunk)* one-shot whodunit *(sl.)*; **~wissenschaft** criminology.
kriminell malfeasant, criminal;
~e Preise cutthroat prices; **~e Veranlagung** criminal disposition (leanings).
Krimineller criminal;
geisteskranker ~ Broadmoor patient *(Br.)*.
Krimskrams candle end, rubbish, trash, junk, odds and ends, trashery, pretties *(US)*, *(wertloses Zeug)* knickknack, trinket.
Krippe crib, feeding trough, *(bequeme Stellung)* cushy job, *(Tagesheim für Kleinkinder)* day nursery, crèche *(Br.)*;
an die ~ drängen *(fig.)* to climb onto the bandwaggon; **an der ~ sitzen** *(fig.)* to live in clover.
Krise crisis, conjuncture, crunch, hump, *(Börse)* shake-out;
andauernde ~ continuing crisis; **finanzielle ~** financial crisis; **politische ~** political crisis; **wirtschaftliche ~** business (economic) depression, slump in trade, cyclical downswing; **~ des Berufsverkehrs** commuter crisis *(US)*; **~ auf dem Kapitalmarkt** crisis in the money market; **~ auf dem Wohnungsmarkt** housing crisis;
~ beseitigen to ease the crisis; **~ durchlaufen** to pass through a crisis; **~ durchstehen (überstehen)** to walk to the brink, to meet the (get over, weather) a crisis; **~ gerade noch vermeiden** to come very close to the brink; **einer ~ vorausgehen** to preface a crisis.
kriseln to be on the brink of a crisis, *(Ehe)* to run upon the rocks.
Krisenabgaben für Einfuhren emergency import duties.
krisenanfällig crisis-prone, prone to crisis.
Krisen | anfälligkeit proneness to crisis; **~bestände** emergency stocks.
krisenbetroffene Industriezweige crisis industries.
krisenbewußt crisis-conscious.
krisenfest panic- (crisis-) proof, *(Konjunktur)* depression- (slump-) proof;
nicht ~ sein to be of low economic strength.
Krisen | fonds crisis (emergency) fund; **~gebiet** trouble area, danger zone.
krisenhaft critical.
Krisen | händler slump merchant; **~herd** trouble spot, storm center *(US)* (centre, *Br.*); **potentielle ~herde** potential crisis-breeding elements; **~jahr** depression year; **~kontrolle** crisis management; **~kürzung** crisis cut; **~lösung** crisis solution; **~plan** contingency plan; **~politik unter Eingehung außerordentlich hoher Risiken** brinkmanship; **~politiker** brinkman; **~punkt erreichen** to draw to a crisis (head).
krisensicher crisis- (depression-, panic-) proof.
Krisen | situation crisis situation; **~situation im Börsenaufschwung** rally juncture; **in eine ~situation geraten** to come to the crunch; **~stab** emergency (crisis) staff; **~stadium** crisis stage; **~steuer** emergency tax; **~steuerung** crisis management; **~stimmung** crisis feeling; **~welle** wave of depression; **~zeit** times of depression, crisis days, time of pressure (crisis), juncture, depression era *(US)*; **in einer ~zeit zusammenbrechen** to fail in a depression; **~zentrum** crisis center *(US)* (centre, *Br.*).
Krisis crisis, juncture.
Kristall | anhänger lustre, chandelier; **~glas** crystal.
Kristallisation crystallization.
kristallisieren, sich to crystallize.
kristallklar as clear as crystal.
Kriterium criterion.
Kritik criticism, nicety, *(Buchbesprechung)* review, reviewal, critique;
unter aller ~ hopelessly below standard;
abfällige ~ adverse criticism; **beißende ~** incisive criticism, mock *(US sl.)*; **heftige ~** loud criticism; **konstruktive ~** constructive criticism; **lobhudelnde ~** puff; **negative (scharfe) ~** pan *(US sl.)*; **nützliche ~** healthy criticism; **sachliche ~** fair comment; **scharfe ~** discriminating (severe) criticism, slam *(US)*; **tödliche ~** venomous criticism; **vernichtende ~** slashing (destructive) criticism; **vernünftige ~** sane criticism;
sich der ~ aussetzen to lay o. s. open to criticism; **sich der öffentlichen ~ aussetzen** to lay o. s. open to public censure; **gute ~en bekommen** to have a good press; **schlechte ~en bekommen** to receive unfavo(u)rable criticism; **~ herausfordern** to challenge criticism; **jds. ~ in den Wind schlagen** to take little heed of s. one's criticism; **~ schreiben** to review, to write a critical examination; **beißender ~ ausgesetzt sein** to be under the lash of criticism; **über alle ~ erhaben sein** to be beyond criticism; **~ üben** to make a criticism; **an allem nur ~ üben** to look on everything with a critical eye; **j. einer ~ unterziehen** to launch censures against s. o.; **etw. seiner ~ unterziehen** to pass criticism on s. th.
kritikempfindlich vulnerable (sensitive) to criticism.
Kritiker critic, literator, *(Bücher)* reviewer;
scharfer ~ slasher;
bei den ~n durchfallen to fail with the critics; **Beifall der ~ finden** to win critical acclaim.
kritiklos indiscriminating;
~ hinnehmen to eat up.
Kritiklosigkeit indiscrimination.
kritisch critical, crucial, trying, judicial;
j. ~ mustern to cast disapproving glances at s. o.;
~e Abhandlung criticism; **~es Alter** change of life; **~e Bemerkung** critical remark; **~e Meinungsäußerungen zu Kunst- und literarischen Fragen** critical opinions on art and literature; **~e Situation meistern** to turn the corner; **~es Stadium** crisis stage; **~e Umstände** critical circumstances.
kritisieren to critizise, to reprehend, to trounce, to call down;
etw. ~ to pass a criticism on s. th., to pick holes in s. th.; **jem. ~** to find fault with s. o.; **jds. Arbeit ~** to critizise s. one's work; **heftig ~** to scorch; **Roman abfällig ~** to give a novel an unfavo(u)rable review; **scharf ~** to pick apart, to be severe on, to pan *(US sl.)*; **j. scharf ~** to give s. o. a sound slating; **stets nur ~** to be always finding fault.
Krittelei fault finding.
kritzlige Handschrift scrawling (spidery) handwriting.
Kroki sketch map.
Krokodilstränen crocodile (false) tears, Job's-tears.
Krondomäne demesne of the crown.
Krone crown, diadem, *(fig.)* pearl;
halbe ~ half a crown *(Br.)*;
~ aller Frauen paragon of womanhood; **~ des Märtyrertums** palm of martyrdom; **~ der Schöpfung** the top of all creation; **der ~ anheimfallen** to be annexed to the Crown *(Br.)*; **~ aufsetzen** to crown; **um dem Ganzen die ~ aufzusetzen** to put the lid on a thing *(Br.)*, to top it all; **der ~ entsagen** to abdicate a throne; **einen in der ~ haben** to be slightly tipsy (under the weather); **im Besitz der ~ sein** to be owned by the crown; **jem. in die ~ gestiegen sein** to have gone into s. one's head; **~ tragen** to wear the crown;
was ist denn dem in die ~ gefahren? what's bitten him?
krönen, mit Erfolg to crown with success; **festliche Veranstaltung ~** to crown a feast.
Kron | gut demesne of the crown, crown estate, domain, royal demesne, fiscal lands; **~juwelen** jewels of the crown, crown jewels; **~kolonie** crown colony *(Br.)*; **~land** crown estates (lands) *(Br.)*; **~lehen** fief, custodian [lease]; **~leuchter** chandelier, lustre; **~prinz** crown prince; **~rat** Privy Council *(Br.)*.

Krönung coronation, crowning, *(fig.)* crowner, crown, splendo(u)r;
~ **des Abends** crowning event of the evening; ~ **seiner Arbeit** crown of one's labo(u)rs; ~ **eines Festes** highlights of a celebration; ~ **einer Laufbahn** culmination of a career;
~ **des Abends darstellen** to crown a feast.
Krönungs | eid coronation oath; ~**feierlichkeiten** coronation ceremony; ~**insignien** regalia; ~**zug** coronation procession.
Kronzeuge chief witness, Queen's *(Br.)* (State's, *US*) evidence, approver *(Br.)*;
zum ~n werden to turn King's (Queen's, *Br.*, State's, *US*) evidence.
Kroppzeug small deer (fry), riff-raff.
Krösus nabob, croesus;
wie ein ~ leben to live like a king; ~ **sein** to have pots of money.
Kröte toad;
giftige ~ poisonous creature; **nette kleine** ~ cute little thing; **nur noch ein paar ~n haben** to have only a few coppers left; **eine ~ schlucken** to eat crow; **giftig werden wie eine ~ sein** to swell like a toad.
Krücke crutch;
an ~n gehen to go on crutches.
Krückstock crooked (walking) stick.
Krug jar, jug, mug.
Krümchen wee bite, crumb, bit;
kein ~ übrig lassen to eat every bit of one's dinner; **nicht ein ~ Interesse zeigen** not to show the slightest interest.
Krume, Krümel crumb, *(Acker)* mould, mold *(US)*.
krumm crooked, bent, wry, stooping;
sich ~ und schief lachen to double with laughter; **keinen Finger ~ machen** not to lift a finger; **etw. ~ nehmen** to take s. th. amiss, to take umbrage at; **j. ~ und lahm schlagen** to beat s. o. to a pulp; **vor Alter ~ werden** to bend down with age;
~**e Beine** crooked legs; **ein ~es Ding drehen** to be involved in some crooked business; ~**e Finger machen** to pilfer, to be light-fingered; **j. einen ~en Hund nennen** to call s. o. a dirty dog; ~**en Mund ziehen** to pull a wry face; ~**er Rücken** round shoulders; ~**en Rücken machen** to bow and scrape; ~**e Sache** bad job *(sl.)*; ~**e Tour** tortuous policy; **etw. auf die ~e Tour bekommen** to get s. th. on the crook; ~**e Wege** crooked ways.
krümmen to bend, to crook;
keinen Finger dafür ~ not to lift a finger; **Finger am Abzug ~** to have one's finger on the trigger; **seinen Rücken ~** to bow and scrape; **sich vor Schmerzen ~** to double with pain; **sich durch das Tal ~** *(Fluß)* to meander through the valley; **sich vor Verlegenheit ~** to squirm with embarrassment.
Krümmung turn[ing], bend, twist, wriggle, *(Fluß)* meander, wind;
scharfe ~ hook;
scharfe ~ machen to elbow; **sich in vielen ~en bergan winden** to wind its way up the mountain in twists and turns.
Krüppel cripple;
hilfloser ~ helpless invalid;
zum ~ machen to cripple.
Kruste crust.
Kübel tub, pail;
~ **von Schmutz über j. ausgießen** to sling mud at s. o.; **wie mit ~n gießen** to be raining cats and dogs; **Blumen in einen ~ pflanzen** to tub (box) flowers;
~**sitz** *(Auto)* bucket seat; ~**wagen** command car, jeep.
kübelweise by the bucket.
Küche kitchen, *(mil.)* cookhouse, *(Schiff)* galley, pantry;
frisch aus der ~ freshly made;
bürgerliche ~ simple (plain) cooking, homely cuisine; **kalte und warme ~ zu jeder Tageszeit** hot and cold meals all day long; **sich eine ~ anschaffen** to buy one's kitchen furniture; **gute ~ führen** to keep a good table; **in des Teufels ~ geraten** to get into a mess (trouble).
Kuchen, Stück ~ versuchen to have a taste of a cake.
Küchen | abfälle kitchen stuff, household refuse; ~**abfluß** kitchen drain.
Kuchenanteil *(Beteiligung)* piece *(sl.)*.
Küchen | bulle *(mil.)* mungy wallah; ~**dienst** *(mil.)* kitchen police; ~**garten** kitchen garden; ~**gerät** kitchen gadget (utensil), cooking outfit; ~**geschirr** kitchen ware; ~**herd** kitchen stove, kitchener *(Br.)*; ~**latein** dog-Latin; ~**mädchen** kitchen (scullery) maid; ~**maschine** mixer; **bei ihnen ist Schmalhans ~meister** they are so poor that they have to skimp; ~**personal** kitchen staff; ~**schrank** kitchen cabinet.
Kuchenstück wedge of a cake.
Küchen | verwaltung *(Betrieb)* catering department (system); ~**waage** kitchen scales; ~**wagen** mobile kitchen.
Kuckuck cuckoo;
~ **ankleben** to affix the bailiff's seal; **j. zum ~ jagen** to sack (fire) s. o. *(sl.)*;
das ganze Geld ist zum ~ all the money is gone; **geh zum ~** go to blazes (hell); **zum ~!** confound it!
Kuckucksei cuckoo in the nest.
Kuddelmuddel topsy-turvydom, razzle-dazzle *(sl.)*.
Kufe *(Flugzeug)* skid, *(Holzfaß)* vat, tub, *(Schlitten)* runner.
Kufenflugzeug sled plane.
Küfer cooper, cellarman;
~**arbeit** cooperage.
Kugel *(Erde)* sphere, ball, *(Geschoß)* bullet, *(Glücksspiel)* roulette wheel, *(Thermometer)* bulb;
verirrte ~ stray bullet;
die ~ ins Rollen bringen to start the ball rolling; **als Beamter eine ruhige ~ schieben** to get a cushy job in the civil service; **sich eine ~ durch den Kopf schießen** to blow one's brains out; ~**n wechseln** to exchange shots;
~**blitz** ball lightning; ~**fang** butt, backstop *(US)*.
kugelfest bulletproof.
Kugel | gelenk ball-and-socket joint; ~**hagel** hail of bullets; ~**lager** ball bearings; **heißgelaufenes ~lager** hot box *(US)*.
kugeln, sich vor Lachen to curl up (double) with laughter; **sich im Schnee ~** to roll in the snow.
Kugel | regen shower of lead; ~**schreiber** ball-point pen.
kugelsichere Weste bulletproof jacket.
Kugelwechsel exchange of shots.
Kuh, dumme silly goose; **trockenstehende ~** dry cow;
die ~ vom Eis bringen to make a neat job of it, to rustle up *(US sl.)*; **wie die ~ vorm Scheunentor stehen** to be completely flabbergasted;
~**dorf** one-horse *(Br.)* (hick, *US*) town, godforsaken hole; ~**handel** trading off, logrolling *(US)*, spoils-system *(US)*; **parteipolitischer ~handel** deal between parties, political huckstering; ~**handel betreiben** to logroll *(US)*; **auf keine ~haut gehen** to be past belief.
kühl cool, *(fig.)* distant, dry, without feeling, cool;
~ **aufzubewahren** to be kept in a cool place; **j. ~ behandeln** to be distant to s. o.;
mit ~er Berechnung vorgehen to act in a calculating manner; ~**e Brise** cool breeze; ~**er Empfang** chilly welcome; **jem. einen sehr ~en Empfang bereiten** to give s. o. a very cool reception; ~**en Kopf bewahren** to keep a cool head, to keep one's temper; ~**e Zurückhaltung** standoffiness, distance, ice.
Kühlanlage cold-storage (refrigerating) plant.
Kühle coolness, chilliness.
kühlen to cool, *(Industrie)* to refrigerate, *(Wein)* to chill;
seinen Durst ~ to quench one's thirst; **Motor mit Luft ~** to air-cool the engine; **seine Rache an jem. ~** to wreak one's vengeance upon s. o.; **seine Wut ~** to vent one's anger.
Kühler *(Auto)* radiator, bonnet *(Br.)*, hood *(US)*;
~ **auftauen** to thaw out the radiator;
~**abdeckung** radiator blind; ~**figur** mascot; ~**haube** radiator shell, bonnet *(Br.)*, hood *(US)*; ~**lamellen** radiator fins; ~**schutz** radiator shell; ~**schutzgitter** radiator grill *(US)* (grille, *Br.*); **selbstabschaltender ~ventilator** self-disengaging fan; ~**verkleidung** radiator grille (grill, *US*); ~**verzierung** radiator ornament.
Kühl | fleisch frozen meat; ~**gut** chilled cargo; ~**haus** cold store, coolhouse, cold-storage depot; **im ~haus lagern** to coldstore; ~**hauslagerung** cold storage; ~**kette** refrigerated (cold) chain; ~**maschine** refrigerator; ~**mittel** cooling agent; ~**raum** holding (cold-storage) room, refrigerator, cooler, freezing chamber *(Australia)*, refrigerating chamber, cool store; ~**raumladung** refrigerated cargo; ~**schiff** refrigerated (cold-storage) vessel, cold storage ship, refrigerator ship (vessel); ~**schlange** cooling (refrigerating) coil, worm; ~**schlitz** *(Auto)* air slot; ~**schrank** refrigerator, fridge, icebox *(US)*; ~**schrank zur Getränkeaufbewahrung** refrigerated bar; ~**tank** cooling tank; ~**truhe** deep freeze, freezer; ~**verfahren** refrigerating process; ~**wagen** refrigerated truck, refrigerator [car, van] *(US)*; ~**wagentransport** refrigerated traffic; ~**waggon** refrigerator car *(US)*, refrigerated van *(Br.)*, reefer *(sl.)*; ~**wasser** *(Auto)* cooling water.
kühn audacious, bold, intrepid, daring, dauntless;
nicht so ~ sein zu behaupten to dare not to say so; **so ~ sein zu fragen** to take the liberty to ask;
~**e Behauptung** daring assertion; ~**er Entschluß** brave decision; ~**ste Erwartungen** wildest expectations; ~**e Konstruktion** bold feat of engineering; **nicht in meinen ~sten Träumen** I shouldn't dream of doing it; ~**es Unternehmen** bold enterprise.
Kühnheit audacity, boldness, impudence.

Kuhstall cow-stable, cowhouse, neat house, byre *(Scot.)*.
kulant accommodating, obliging, fair, easy;
~**e Bedingungen** accommodating (generous) terms.
Kulanz obligingness, fairness, fair dealing;
Reparatur im Wege der ~ ausführen to carry out a repair at the firm's expense.
Kuli coolie, drudge, donkey, dogsbody *(sl.)*;
~**arbeit** coolie labo(u)r, donkeywork.
Kulisse *(Börse)* coulisse, professional traders *(US)*, curb (kerb, *Br.*) market, *(Theater)* side scene, scenery, flat;
hinter den ~n behind the curtain (scenes), in a back room, backstage;
sich hinter den ~n abspielen to go on (take place) behind the scenes; **hinter den ~n agieren** to work the oracle, to be behind the scenes, to pull the strings; ~**n malen** to paint the scenery; **hinter die ~n schauen** to know what is going on behind the scenes; **hinter den ~n verschwinden** to drop into the background, to fade out; ~**n wechseln** *(Theater)* to strike; **einen Blick hinter die ~n werfen** to [take a] look behind the scenes; **hinter den ~n wirken** to mastermind, to be behind the scenes; **einer Vorführung hinter den ~n zuschauen** to watch a performance from the wings (slips).
Kulissen | makler *(Kulissier)* unofficial (street, curb, kerb, *Br.*) broker, stone broker *(US)*; ~**maler** scene painter; ~**schaltung** *(Auto)* gatetype gear shift; ~**schieber** *(Theater)* sceneshifter, shifter.
Kulmination culmination, climax, apex, *(Laufbahn)* culmination.
Kulminations | höchstand closing high; ~**punkt** apex, culminating point; **auf dem ~punkt seiner Laufbahn** reaching the culmination of one's career, at the height of one's career.
kulminieren to culminate, to reach its climax.
kulminierend culminant.
Kult cult, worship.
kultivierbar cultivable, improvable, arable, growable;
nicht ~ uncultivable.
Kultivierbarkeit improvability.
kultivieren to cultivate, to till, to farm, to reclaim, to improve *(US)*, to subdue, *(fig.)* to cultivate, to refine.
kultiviert cultivated, refined, in tillage, tame *(US)*, *(fig.)* civilized, true-bred, thoroughbred, cultured;
~ sein *(Land)* to be under crop;
~**e Aussprache** refined speech.
Kultiviertheit refinement, culture.
Kultivierung cultivation, tillage, crop, improvement *(US)*, *(fig.)* refining, breaking in.
kultivierungsfähig cultivable, arable, growable, open to improvement *(US)*.
Kultivierungs | grenze margin of cultivation; ~**methode** cultivation method; ~**methode verbessern** to improve on the mode of tillage *(US)*.
Kultstätte place of worship.
Kultur cultivation, culture, civilization, *(Anbau)* cultivation, *(Anpflanzen)* growing;
noch nicht von der ~ beleckt untouched by civilization; **abendländische ~** Western civilization; **überlieferte ~** established culture; **wesenfremde ~** alien culture;
~**en eines Waldes** woodland nurseries;
~ haben to be cultured;
~**abkommen** cultural convention; ~**abteilung** cultural affairs division; ~**attaché** cultural attaché; ~**austausch** cultural exchange; ~**autonomie** independence in cultural matters; ~**banause** philistine, lowbrow; ~**bau** land improvements; ~**beflissener** culturist; ~**beilage** *(Zeitung)* arts supplement; ~**beutel** overnight bag, toilet case; ~**bezirk** reclamation district.
kulturell cultural;
~**e Einrichtungen** cultural facilities; ~**e Ereignisse** cultural activities; ~**e Folgewirkungen** culture sequences; ~**e Gebäude** historical buildings; ~**es Leben** cultural life; ~**e Mobilität** cultural mobility.
Kulturepoche period of civilization, culture epoch, culture period.
kulturfähig reclaimable, arable, tillable, cultivable;
~ machen to reclaim.
Kultur | faktor culture factor; ~**film** instructional film, documentary; ~**fläche** cultivated area; ~**form** culture pattern; ~**fragen** cultural matters; ~**gebiet** culture area; ~**geschichte** history of civilization, social history; **archäologisches ~gut** archaeological heritage; ~**güter** cultural property; **gefährdete ~güter** heritage in danger; ~**güterschutz** protection of cultural property; ~**imperialismus** cultural imperialism; ~**institut** cultural institute; ~**kritiker** culture critic; ~**land** arable land; ~**landschaft** culture area (landscape); ~**leben** cultural life; ~**leistung** cultural achievement.
kulturlos uncivilized, uncultured.
Kulturlosigkeit unculture, lack of refinement.
Kultur | mensch civilized man; ~**merkmal** culture trait; ~**politik im Ausland** cultural diplomacy; ~**programm** cultural program(me); ~**rasse** cultural variety; ~**raum** culture area; ~**redakteur** cultural editor; ~**revolution** cultural revolution; ~**schande** crime against civilization; ~**sprache** literary language; ~**staat** civilized country (nation); ~**stufe** stage of civilization, culture stage; **auf niedriger ~stufe stehend** primitive, not civilized; ~**träger** upholder of civilization, civilizer; ~**volk** civilized nation; ~**wandel** culture change; ~**welt** culture world; ~**zentrum** cultural capital, culture center *(US)* (centre, *Br.*), arts center *(US)*.
Kultus | gemeinde congregation, religious community; ~**minister** Minister of Education *(Br.)*, Education Minister, culture minister, minister of culture; ~**ministerium** Ministry of Education (Art and Culture).
Kümmeltürke, wie ein ~ arbeiten *(fam.)* to drive away at one's work, to work like a navvy (nigger, slave, dog, beaver, *US*).
Kummer sorrow, trouble, worry, grief, heartache, pain, distress, fret;
zu meinem großen ~ much to my regret;
sich seinem ~ anheimgeben to give way to grief; **jem. ~ bereiten** to grieve s. o.; **sich ~ ersparen** to spare o. s. grief; **~ mit jem. haben** to have trouble with s. o., to be concerned about s. o.; **viel ~ mit seinem Auto haben** to have a lot of trouble with one's car; **an jds. ~ Anteil nehmen** to feel with s. o. in his sorrow; **vom ~ gebeugt sein** to be weighted down with grief; **vor ~ vergehen, sich in ~ verzehren** to die of grief, to pine away, to eat one's heart out;
tiefe ~falten deep lines of care.
kümmerlich miserable, wretched, pitiable, scanty, tin-pot;
jds. ~e Ausdrucksweise penury of s. one's language; ~**e Behausung** miserable dwelling, wretched house; ~**es Einkommen** scanty income; ~**e Flüchtlingsexistenzen** miserable lives of refugees; ~**es Gehalt** miserable salary; ~**es Leben fristen** to eke out a scanty living; ~**e Vegetation** sparse vegetation; ~**e Verhältnisse** wretched circumstances; **in ~en Verhältnissen leben** to live in misery and want; ~**e Vorräte** scanty supplies.
kümmern, sich to worry (bother) o. s.; **sich um j. ~** to take care of (tend, wait on) s. o.; **sich um etw. ~** to see to it, to look after s. th.; **sich um seine eigenen Angelegenheiten ~** to have an eye to the main chance, to mind one's own business; **sich um jds. Anweisungen ~** to pay attention to s. one's instructions; **sich ganz besonders um etw. ~** to take precious good care of s. th.; **sich einen Dreck (Pfifferling) darum ~** not to care a fig (dam, straw) about it; **sich um Geldangelegenheiten ~** to take care of all money matters; **sich ums Geschäft ~** to mind the shop; **sich um ein Geschäft besonders ~** to nurse a business; **sich nicht um sein Geschäft ~** to neglect one's business; **sich um den Haushalt ~** to do the housework; **sich nach der Pensionierung um den Garten ~** to take to gardening when one retires; **sich nicht um Politik ~** not to be interested in politics; **sich den Teufel um etw. ~** to let things go hang, not to care a hang (twopence); **sich höchst wenig darum ~** to take precious little care (trouble).
Kümmernisse | des Alltagslebens worries of everyday life; **zahllose ~ des Lebens** the thousand and one worries of life.
Kumpan crony, cully, mate, pal, buddy, sidekicker *(US fam.)*;
sein Diebesgut mit seinen ~en teilen to share one's loot with one's associates.
Kumpel pitman, miner, collier, *(Kumpan)* crony, pal *(sl.)*, buddy *(US)*;
jds. ~ sein to make a pal of s. o.
Kumulation cumulation, accumulation.
Kumulations | prinzip *(Strafrecht)* cumulate penalties; ~**werte** cumulative figures.
kumulativ accumulative, cumulative;
nicht ~ noncumulative;
~**e Aktien** cumulative stocks; ~**e Dividende** cumulative dividend; ~**e Stimmabgabe** cumulative voting; ~**e Vorzugsaktien** cumulative preference shares *(Br.)*, accumulative stocks *(US)*.
kumulieren to accumulate, *(Stimmen)* to plump, to cumulate.
kumulierende Wirkung cumulative effect.
kumulierte | Stimmen cumulative votes; **~ Strafen** cumulate penalties.
Kumulierung accumulation, cumulation, combined effect.
Kumulierungssystem cumulative voting.

kündbar callable, at notice, *(Anleihe)* redeemable, redemandable, subject to redemption (denunciation), *(Kapital)* subject to call (notice), *(Rentenbrief)* terminable;
beiderseitig ~ subject to notice on either side; **jederzeit** ~ at (on) call, terminable at pleasure, at will, *(Angestellter)* at a moment's (minute's) notice; **kurzfristig** ~ at short notice; **täglich** ~ *(Kontoeinlage)* subject to call; **vierteljährlich** ~ subject to three months' notice; **nicht vorzeitig** ~ not subject to call;
halbjährlich ~ **sein** to be under six months' notice; **jederzeit** ~ **sein** *(Hofbeamter)* to hold office during Her Majesty's pleasure *(Br.)*;
~**e Anleihe** redeemable loan; ~**es Darlehn** loan at notice; **täglich** ~**es Geld** call (day-to-day) money *(Br.)*, demand deposits *(US)*; ~**er Kredit** credit on call; **jederzeit** ~**er Mieter** tenant at will; ~**e Obligationen** redeemable (optional, *US*) bonds; ~**er Vertrag** terminable contract.

Kündbarkeit terminability, *(Anleihe)* redeemableness;
mit gegenseitiger ~ subject to notice on either side.

Kunde customer, purchaser, consumer, demander, store buyer *(US)*, *(Anwalt)* client, *(Kenntnis)* note, knowledge, *(Nachricht)* information, news, *(Werbeagentur)* account;
~**n** customers, custom, patronage;
ohne ~**n** unpatronized;
in die [Kunden]kartei aufgenommener ~ registered customer; **auswärtige** ~**n** customers who have come from abroad; **bevorzugter** ~ preferential client; **bar bezahlender** ~ cash customer; **eingetragener** ~ registered customer; **fauler** ~ bad customer (egg, *US sl.*), phony *(sl.)*; **fester** ~ regular customer, patron, *(Werbeagentur)* established account; **gefährlicher** ~ rum customer; **in Konkurs gegangener** ~ bankrupt customer; **gelegentlicher** ~ stray (chance, street, casual) customer; **ganz geriebener** ~ cool customer, deep file; **hartgesottener** ~ sharp customer; **langjähriger** ~ customer of long standing, standing customer; **möglicher (potentieller)** ~ prospective customer, potential client, sales prospect *(US)*; **privater** ~ home buyer; **regelmäßiger** ~ steady customer, patronizer; **säumiger** ~ delinquent customer; **sicherer** ~ good man; **sparsamer** ~ economy-minded customer; **täglicher** ~ local customer; **treuer** ~ faithful customer; **übler** ~ ugly customer, tough, bad egg *(sl.)*, bad lot *(sl.)*; **unsicherer** ~ dead beat *(US)*; **sehr gut verdienender** ~ high-income client; **voraussichtlicher** ~ potential (prospective) customer, sales prospect *(US)*; **wichtigster** ~ key customer; **bar zahlender** ~ cash customer; **nicht zahlender** ~ defaulting customer; **zahlungsfähiger** ~ solvent client, wealthy customer; **zuverlässiger** ~ loyal customer;
~ **aus der Industrie** industrial client; ~ **in laufender Rechnung** checking-account depositor; ~ **im Stadtgebiet** home-town (city) customer; ~ **mit Zahlungsrückständen** delinquent customer;
~**n abfangen (abwerben, abziehen)** to take (entice) away (drum up, *US*) customers; **letzten** ~**n abfertigen** to serve the last customer; ~**n als verloren abschreiben** to regard a customer as lost; **Steuer auf den** ~**n abwälzen** to pass a tax on to the customer; ~**n abwerben (abziehen)** to tout customers, to take (entice) away (drum up, *US*) customers; ~**n anlocken** to bring customers, to draw customers into the store; ~**n anziehen** to appeal to customers, to attract customers, to draw customers into the store; ~**n akquirieren** to acquire (drum up, *US*) customers; **möglichen** ~**n aufsuchen** to pay a visit to a prospective customer; ~**n ausspannen** to alienate customers; ~**n bearbeiten** to high-pressure customers; ~**n bedienen** to attend to (serve) a customer; ~**n bevorzugt behandeln** to grant special favo(u)rs to a customer; **Porto dem** ~**n belasten** to charge the postage to the customer; ~**n beliefern** to forward goods to a customer; **fremden** ~**n beliefern** to shortstop *(sl.)*; ~**n mit Ware beliefern** to serve a customer with goods; ~**n besuchen** to call on a client, to canvass customers; **als** ~**n bevorzugt besuchen** to patronize; ~**n in ihren eigenen vier Wänden besuchen** to visit customers on their home ground; ~**n bevorschussen** to make advances to customers; ~**n bewirten** to entertain customers; **einem** ~**n einen Dienst erweisen** to accommodate a client; ~**n gewinnen** to acquire customers; **nur sechs** ~**n am Tag gehabt haben** *(Taxifahrer)* to have had only six fares this day; **es mit einem schwierigen** ~**n zu tun haben** to meet with considerable sales resistance; **an einen** ~**n herantreten** to approach a purchaser; ~**n anschreiben lassen** to carry a customer; ~**n abspenstig machen** to draw away customers, to knock down a customer *(sl.)*; ~**n pflegen** *(fam.)* to keep in with a customer; ~**n schleppen** to canvass for customers, to tour *(coll.)*; **regelmäßiger** ~ **sein** to patronize; ~**n überweisen** to recommend customers; ~**n zum Kauf verleiten** to allure customers to buy goods; ~**n werben** to acquire (canvass, solicit for, drum up, *US*) customers, to bring business, *(marktschreierisch)* to bark *(US sl.)*; **jem. zu seinen** ~**n zählen** to have s. one's custom; ~**n zuführen** to bring (attract, introduce) customers, to tout customers *(coll.)*.

Kunden|abwanderung drift of trade; ~**abwanderung auf andere Märkte** customers defecting to other markets; ~**abwerbung** alienation (enticement) of customers; ~**akte** *(Werbeagentur)* account folder; ~**akzept** trade acceptance, acceptance on behalf of a customer; ~**akzepte** *(Bilanz)* customers' liabilities on acceptance; ~**anlockung** enticement of customers; ~**ansehen** customer's reputation; ~**ansturm** run of customers; ~**arbeit** custom work; ~**auftrag** customer's order (mandate); ~**ausfälle** loss from bad debts; ~**auskunftsbuch** opinion list *(Br.)*; ~**außenstände** *(Bilanz)* trade accounts receivable *(US)*, trade debts; ~**auswahl** selection of customers; **gezielte** ~**auswahl** more selectivity in accepting clients; ~**bedienung** servicing of customers; ~**bedürfnisse** customer needs (requirements); ~**bedürfnisse befriedigen** to cater for the needs of one's customers; ~**beeinflussung** suggestion selling *(US)*; ~**benachrichtigung** communication to the customer; ~**berater** customer counse(l)lor, *(Werbeagentur)* account executive; ~**beratung** consumer counse(l)ling; ~**beratungsdienst** advisory service for customers; ~**beratungsgruppe** customer advisory group; ~**beratungszimmer** customers' room; ~**beschränkung** *(Kartellwesen)* customer restriction *(US)*; ~**beschreibung** *(Werbeagentur)* description of an account; ~**beschwerden** complaint from a customer, customer's complaint (grievance); ~**besuch** call on a customer, business (sales) call, calling on customers, travel to clients; ~**betreuer** *(Werbeagentur)* account executive, account manager; ~**betreuung** aftersales service; ~**betrieb** customer's trade (company); ~**beurteilung durch die Bank** customer's position at the bank; ~**bewirtung** entertainment of customers.

kundenbewußt customer-directed.

Kunden|beziehungen client relations; ~**bonus** sales discount; ~**buch** customers' (individual) ledger; ~**buchhalter** accounts receivable accountant *(US)*; ~**darlehen** loan to customer; ~**depot** safe custody *(Br.)* (custodianship, *US*) account.

Kundendienst service [to the customer], customer service, servicing of consumers, repair (after-sales) service;
kostenloser ~ gratuitous service; **zusätzlicher** ~ subsidiary services;
~ **für Autofahrer** auto servicing; ~ **an Ort und Stelle** on-the-spot service; **telephonischer** ~ **für Touristen** teletourist scheme; **im** ~ **betreuen** to service; **sein Auto alle 5000 km zum** ~ **bringen** to send the car in for service every 3000 miles; **sein Auto laufend zum** ~ **bringen** to have one's car regularly serviced; **guten** ~ **haben** to provide with intelligent service;
~**abteilung** service department; ~**konzept** service concept; **vertraglich festgelegte** ~**leistungen** contract services; ~**regelung** servicing arrangement; ~**stelle** service depot; ~**werkstatt** service station; ~**zentrum** *(Kraftfahrzeug)* service garage.

Kunden|diskont sales discount; ~**effekten** customer's investment; ~**einkaufsbetrag** customers' purchase; ~**einlagen** customer deposits, *(Bankbilanz)* liabilities of a bank; **täglich fällige** ~**einlagen** *(Bankbilanz)* customers' sight deposits; ~**empfehlung** customer recommendation; ~**etat** *(Werbeagentur)* account; ~**fang** canvassing, touting *(coll.)*; **für den** ~**fang berechnet** catchpenny; ~**fänger** tout, drummer, clicker *(Br., sl.)*, puller-in *(US)*.

kundenfeindlich against the interests of customers.

Kunden|finanzierung financing of customers; ~**finanzierungsbank** discount company (corporation, *US*); ~**firma** client company.

Kundenforderungen *(Bilanz)* uncollected debts, receivables from customers *(US)*, account receivables *(US)*;
abgetretene ~ pledged accounts receivable *(US)*; **überfällige** ~ extended receivables *(US)*;
buchmäßig weiterhin als ~ **behandeln** to keep on the books as receivables *(US)*.

Kunden|gelder customers' (client) money; ~**geschäft** transaction for third account; ~**geschenke** gifts to customers; ~**geschmack** consumers' taste; ~**gruppe** customer (consumer) group; ~**guthaben** customer's [credit] balance, consumer deposit; ~**informationsdienst** customer relations; ~**interesse** customer interest; ~**kartei** list of customers, customer list; **alphabetisch angeordnete** ~**kartei** alphabetic arrangement of customers; ~**karteikarte** customers' card; ~**kontakt** client contact.

Kundenkonto trade account, customer's ledger (account), personal (charge, *US*) account, monthly (depositor's) *(Br.)* account;
mit bestimmter Kreditlinie ausgestattetes ~ budget charge account *(US)*;
~ **für kurz- und langfristige Dispositionen** mixed account;
~**blatt** customer's ledger sheet.

Kundenkredit consumer credit, accounts receivable credit (loan) *(US)*, customer's loan, retail credit *(US)*;
~**e** *(Bankbilanz)* bank advances;
kurzfristiger ~ store credit *(US)*;
~ **des Kaufmannes** retail book credit;
~ **beantragen** to seek retail credit *(US)*;
~**auskunftei**, ~**austauschstelle** trade group interchange *(US)*, retail credit [exchange] bureau *(US)*; ~**bank** hire-purchase finance house *(Br.)*, consumer credit agency, instalment house *(US)*, personal loan company *(US)*; ~**geschäft** retail creditor *(US)*; ~**karte** charge card; ~**konto** customer's credit account, retail charge account *(US)*; ~**konto eröffnen** to arrange account terms; **jem. ein ~konto zugestehen** to grant open account terms to s. o.; ~**linie** customers' limit.

Kundenkreis circle of customers, custom, [range of] customers, clientele, constituency, consumer group, *(Firmenwert)* goodwill;
erstklassiger ~ first-rate connections; **fester** ~ regular customers; **sein gesamter** ~ all his customers; **großer** ~ large patronage (custom).

Kunden|kritik consumer criticism; ~**liste** list of customers, client list, customer register, *(Bank)* abstract; **sich in eine ~liste eintragen lassen** to register with a tradesman; ~**loyalität** customers' loyalty; ~**name** customer's name; ~**nummer** customer number; ~**portefeuille** customer's portfolio; ~**rabatt** discount for customers, customer allowance, sales (consumer) discount, patronage refund *(US)*; ~**raum** customers' room; ~**reklamation** customer's complaint; ~**sachbearbeiter** customer's man, *(Werbeagentur)* account executive; ~**scheck** customer's check *(US)* (cheque, *Br.*); ~**skonti** discounts granted; ~**stamm** regular customers, custom, connection; **sich einen ~stamm schaffen** to work up a connection; **auf ~suche herumfahren** *(Taxi)* to ply for hire, to cruise; ~**termineinlagen** customers' term (time, *US*) deposits; ~**treue** customer loyalty; ~**umsätze** customer (consumer) sales; ~**unterlagen** *(Werbeagentur)* account records; ~**unterschrift** customer's signature; ~**verbindlichkeiten** customer's obligations; ~**verhalten** consumer behavio(u)r; ~**verhältnis** customer relationship; **direkter ~verkauf** direct-to-customer selling; ~**verkäufe** consumer (customer) sales; ~**verkehr** customer (consumer) traffic; ~**verlust** loss of custom; ~**verpflichtung** customer's undertaking (obligation); ~**verzeichnis** customer register; ~**vorliebe** consumers' taste; ~**vorurteil** customer prejudice; ~**wechsel** trade bill (paper), customer's acceptance (bill), bill on customers, private bill of exchange, *(Bilanz)* customer's notes, trade notes receivables *(US)*, bills receivable *(US)*; ~**wechselbuch** notes receivable register *(US)*; ~**werbeabteilung** canvassing department.

kundenwerbend business-getting.

Kunden|werber canvassser, drummer *(US)*, runner *(Br.)*, tout; **marktschreierischer ~werber** barker *(US sl.)*; ~**werbung** solicitation of customers, canvassing of orders, acquiring (getting) business, touting [for customers], *(Reklame)* consumer advertising (advertisement, *Br.*); **telefonische ~werbung** telephone solicitation; ~**werbung auf eine völlig neue Basis stellen** to restructure one's whole approach to customers; ~**wettbewerb** customer (consumer) contest; ~**widerstand** customer (consumer) resistance.

Kundenwünsche customer (consumer) wants;
auf die ~ abstellen to aim at the needs of customers; ~**n Vorrang einräumen** to put customer demands first; ~ **erfüllen** to attend to the wants of customers; ~ **unverzüglich erledigen** to meet one's customers' wishes without delay.

Kunden|zahl number of customers; ~**zeitschrift** external house organ, sales bulletin, shopping news; ~**zuführung** introduction of customers.

Kundgabe [public] announcement, promulgation, publication;
feierliche ~ proclamation.

kundgeben to notify, to give notice, to manifest;
feierlich ~ to proclaim; **öffentlich** ~ to announce to the public.

Kundgebung demonstration, rally, *(Meinungsäußerung)* manifestation, manifest, declaration;
auf einer ~ at a demonstration;
~ **auflösen** to disperse a demonstration; ~ **durchführen** to demonstrate; **auf einer ~ sprechen** to speak at a meeting; **an einer ~ teilnehmen** to take part in a demonstration; ~**en veranstalten** to manifest, to demonstrate.

Kundgebungsteilnehmer manifestant, demonstrator;
~ **festnehmen** to take demonstrators into custody; ~ **durch polizeiliche Maßnahmen zerstreuen** to disperse demonstrators by the police.

kundgetan, hiermit wird allen know all men by these presents.

kündigen to give notice, to cancel, *(Anleihe)* to give notice of withdrawal (redemption), *(Arbeitgeber)* to give notice [to quit] (warning), to dismiss, *(Arbeitnehmer)* to sign off *(US)*, to quit one's job *(US)*, *(Kapital)* to call in, to recall, to demand repayment, *(Mieter)* to give notice to quit, to vacate, *(Obligationen)* to call in, *(Vertrag)* to denounce, to terminate;
jem. ~ to terminate s. one's employment; **seinem Arbeitgeber** ~ to give one's employer notice that one intends to leave, to give one's master warning; **dem Arbeitnehmer** ~ to terminate s. one's employment, to give an employee warning *(Br.)*; **sein Arbeitsverhältnis** ~ to give warning; **sein Arbeitsverhältnis fristlos** ~ to terminate employment without notice; **zum nächsten Ersten** ~ to give a month's notice; **Handelsabkommen mit dreimonatiger Frist** ~ to denounce a trade pact with three months' notice; **mit wöchentlicher Frist** ~ to give one week's notice; **jem. fristgemäß** ~ to give s. o. due warning; **jem. fristlos** ~ *(Arbeitgeber)* to dismiss s. o. at a moment's notice (summarily), to dismiss s. o. without notice (summarily, immediately), to terminate s. one's employment without notice, to sack (fire) s. o. on the spot *(sl.)*, *(Arbeitnehmer)* to quit an employment (one's job, *US*) without notice; **aus wichtigem Grund** ~ to give notice for cause; **Hausangestellten fristlos** ~ to dismiss a servant without notice; **Hypothek** ~ to call in (foreclose) a mortgage; **Konto** ~ to call up an account; **Kredit** ~ to call (draw) in a loan, to withdraw a credit, to demand repayment of a loan; **jem. kurzfristig** ~ to give s. o. short notice; **Mietvertrag** ~ to terminate a lease; **mit Monatsfrist** ~ to give a month's warning (notice); **Obligationen** ~ to call in bonds; **ordnungsgemäß** ~ to give due notice; **jem. rechtzeitig** ~ to give s. o. fair warning; **schriftlich** ~ to give written notice; **von sich aus** ~ to resign voluntarily, to leave of one's own volition; **Staatsvertrag** ~ to denounce a treaty; **termingerecht** ~ to give due notice; **sozial ungerechtfertigt** ~ to dismiss an employee unfairly *(Br.)*; **Vereinbarung jederzeit fristlos** ~ to terminate an agreement at any time without notice; **seinem Vermieter** ~ to give one's landlord notice [of leave]; **Versicherung** ~ to give notice of cancellation of the insurance policy; **Vertrag** ~ to cancel (revoke) a contract; **vertragsgemäß** ~ to give notice in accordance with the contract; **acht Werktage vorher** ~ to give eight clear working days notice; **seine Wohnung** ~ to give notice of one's intention to leave.

Kündigung notice [to quit (to leave)], warning, *(Abkommen)* denunciation, *(Anleihe)* notice of redemption, *(Arbeitgeber)* dismissal, discharge, *(Arbeitnehmer)* termination, resignation, *(Beamter)* removal from office, *(Kapital)* calling in, recalling, *(Mieter)* warning, notice to quit, *(Vermieter)* notice to leave, *(Vertrag)* revocation, cancellation, termination, denouncement;
auf jederzeitige ~ at a minute's warning; **auf tägliche** ~ at (on) call; **mit einstündiger** ~ at an hour's notice; **mit monatlicher (vierteljährlicher)** ~ subject to a month's (three months') notice; **ohne ~ rückzahlbar** at call;
außerordentliche ~ dimissal for exceptional reasons, *(Versicherung)* short rate cancellation; **befristete** ~ dismissal with notice; **berechtigte** ~ discharge for just cause; **dreimonatige** ~ three months' notice; **einseitige** ~ arbitrary (one-sided) notice; **frühzeitig erfolgte** ~ long notice; **vom Angestellten erzwungene** ~ constructive discharge; **fristgemäße** ~ dismissal with notice, termination by notice; **nicht fristgemäße** ~ *(Mieter)* dismissal without notice; **fristlose** ~ summary termination, termination without notice; **gesetzliche** ~ legal notice to quit; **grundlose** ~ discharge without cause; **halbjährige** ~ six months' notice; **kurzfristige** ~ short-term cancellation; **monatliche** ~ monthly (a month's) notice, a month's warning; **nahegelegte** ~ *(Beamter)* involuntary resignation; **ordnungsgemäße** ~ due and proper (lawful) notice; **rechtzeitige** ~ due notice; **schriftliche** ~ written notice, notice in writing; **termingerechte** ~ due notice; **unberechtigte** ~ unjust discharge; **sozial ungerechtfertigte** ~ unfair dismissal *(Br.)*; **vorzeitige** ~ premature notice; **willkürliche** ~ arbitrary notice; **wöchentliche** ~ seven days' (week's) notice; **ordnungsgemäß zugestellte** ~ due and proper notice; **zweiwöchentliche** ~ two weeks notice;

~ **eines völkerrechtlichen Abkommens** notice of denunciation of a convention; ~ **eines Angestelltenverhältnisses** loss of service; ~ **einer Anleihe** call for redemption of a loan; ~ **eines Arbeitsverhältnisses (Dienstverhältnisses)** notice of termination of employment; ~ **von Einlagen** notice of withdrawal of funds; ~ **aus wichtigem Grund** notice for cause; ~ **einer Hypothek** foreclosure; ~ **eines Kredits** notice of withdrawal of credit; ~ **des Miet-, Pachtverhältnisses** notice to quit (vacate); ~ **zum Quartalsende** three months' notice to the end of a calendar quarter; ~ **zur Rückzahlung** notice of withdrawal, withdrawal notice; ~ **eines Staatsvertrages** notice of termination of a treaty; ~ **des Vermieters** notice by a landlord; ~ **eines Versicherungsvertrages** notice of cancellation of an insurance policy; ~ **eines Vertrages** contract cancellation, termination (cancellation, annulment) of a contract; ~ **des Waffenstillstandes** denunciation of an armistice; ~ **von Wertpapieren** notice of withdrawal; ~ **einer Wohnung** notice to quit;
zur ~ aufrufen *(Obligationen)* to call for redemption; **jem. die ~ aussprechen** to give s. o. notice; **einem Angestellten mit der ~ drohen** to threaten an employee with dismissal; **sechswöchige ~ einhalten** to give six weeks' notice; **gesetzlich begründeten Widerspruch gegen eine ~ einlegen** *(Mieter)* to establish a statutory ground of opposition; **seine ~ einreichen** to give in one's notice; **einmonatliche ~ erhalten** to receive an immediate month's warning; **Einwand sozial ungerechtfertigter ~ erheben** to claim unfair dismissal; ~ **erhalten haben** to have received a dismissal notice, *(Mieter)* to be under (have) notice to leave (quit); ~ **hinausschieben** to postpone a notice; **zu seiner ~ als Mieter ordnungsgemäß Stellung nehmen** to serve an appropriate counternotice; **einem Mieter die ~ zustellen** to give a tenant notice to quit, to serve notice upon a tenant.

Kündigungs|abfindung redundancy payment *(Br.)*, severance benefit *(US)*; **~absicht** notice of withdrawal; **seinem Arbeitgeber von seiner ~absicht Kenntnis geben** to give one's employer notice that one intends to leave; **~bedingungen** terms of termination; **~benachrichtigung** notice of cancellation (dismissal), *(Mieter)* notice to quit, *(Vertrag)* notice of cancellation, *(Wertpapiere)* notice of withdrawal; **~benachrichtigung zustellen** to issue a dismissal notice; **~bestimmungen** *(Vertrag)* cancellation clause (conditions), *(Mietvertrag)* tenure provisions; **~brief** letter terminating employment; **~entschädigung** dismissal compensation (pay), severance benefit (pay) *(US)*, redundancy payment *(Br.)*.

Kündigungsfrist term (period, length) of notice, notice period, warning, *(Bankwelt)* withdrawal period;
mit dreimonatiger ~ subject to three months' notice; **mit einjähriger ~ abhebbar** withdrawable at one year's notice; **ohne ~** without notice [given]; **ohne Einhaltung der erforderlichen ~** without giving the requisite notice; **unter Einhaltung einer ~** observing a term of notice;
angemessene (ausreichende) ~ reasonable (correct) notice; **monatliche ~** one month's notice; **unzureichende ~** insufficient notice; **gesetzlich vorgeschriebene (gesetzliche) ~** legal (statutory) notice to quit; **wöchentliche ~** one week's (seven days') notice;
~ **für beide Seiten** notice to be given on both sides;
bis zum Ende der ~ arbeiten to work out a written notice; ~ **einhalten** to observe a term (the period) of notice; ~ **nicht einhalten** to leave without notice; **mit halbjährlicher ~ angestellt sein** to work under a written six-months contract; **monatliche ~ vereinbaren** to agree upon a period of one month's notice; **auf Einhaltung der ~ verzichten** to waive notice.

Kündigungs|gelder restricted cash, fixed (time, *US*) deposits, deposits at short notice *(US)*; **~grund** ground for giving notice, reason for a dismissal; **ausreichender ~grund** sufficient notice; **~hypothek** mortgage repayable in a lump sum; **~klausel** cancellation clause, *(Abkommen)* clause of denunciation, *(Angestellter)* termination clause; **~mitteilung** notice to quit (leave), *(an Angestellten)* notice of dismissal, dismissal notice; **~nachricht** *(Wertpapiere)* notice of withdrawal; **~prozentsatz** resignation ratio, *(Mieter)* quit ratio (rate); **~recht** right to give notice (of termination), *(Anleihe)* redeemable feature, *(Vertrag)* cancellation privilege; **freie ~rechte des Vermieters weitgehend einschränken** to affect in considerable measure the rights of landlords; **~schreiben** written notice, notice in writing, *(Angestellter)* letter of resignation, *(Arbeitgeber)* dismissal notice, *(Bank)* letter of withdrawal, *(Wertpapiere)* written notice of withdrawal; **offizielles ~schreiben** formal notice to terminate one's engagement; **sein ~schreiben abgeben** to send (hand) in one's resignation.

Kündigungsschutz call protection, *(Mieter)* rent control *(Br.)*; **dem Mieter ~ gewähren** to protect the tenant; ~ **in Anspruch nehmen** to claim the protection of the Rent Acts *(Br.)*;
~bestimmungen rent restrictions *(Br.)*; **einem Angestellten gegenüber die ~frist einhalten** to give an employee the amount of notice to which he is entitled.

Kündigungs|termin term of notice, *(Vertrag)* cancellation date; **bis zum Schluß des ~termins bleiben** to serve out one's notice with s. o.; **~wirkung** effect of [giving] notice; **~zeitraum** amount of notice.

Kundin woman customer, *(Firma)* customer company, client, client company.

kundmachen to make known, to announce;
feierlich ~ to proclaim; **öffentlich ~** to make a public announcement.

Kundmachung manifestation, announcement;
amtliche ~ official announcement; **öffentliche ~** public notice.

Kundschaft custom, patronage *(coll.)*, clientele, business, buyers, connection, connexion *(Br.)*, constituency, *(Einzelkunden)* customers, *(Firmenwert)* goodwill;
auf die Wünsche der ~ eingestellt customer-directed; **mit guter ~** with a good clientele; **ohne ~** uncustomed; **zur Unterrichtung der ~** for customer orientation;
anspruchsvolle ~ demanding customers; **ausgedehnte ~** wide connection; **feste ~** steady customers; **meine ~** my class of business; **unzufriedene ~** consumer dissatisfaction; **gut verdienende ~** upper-income customers;
~ **mit niedrigerem Einkommen** lower-income customers;
jem. die ~ abjagen to alienate s. one's clients; ~ **anlocken** to draw customers into the store; ~ **anziehen** *(Anzeige)* to pull custom *(US)*; **seine ~ wegen schlechter Bedienung aufgeben** to take away one's patronage because of poor service; ~ **bedienen** to serve customers; **neue ~ bekommen** to get new customers; ~ **besuchen** to canvass customers; ~ **erhalten** to retain customers; **sich ~ erwerben** to build up custom, to get business, to work up a connection; ~ **gewinnen** to acquire customers; **vornehme ~ haben** to have a select patronage; **wenig ~ haben** to have little custom; **über mangelnde ~ nicht zu klagen haben** to lack no clients; ~ **abspenstig machen** to draw (entice) away customers; **sich die Aufmerksamkeit seiner ~ sichern** to key one's publicity; ~ **übernehmen** to acquire the goodwill; **seine ~ verlieren** to lose business (one's customers); **mit ~ versorgen** to custom; **auf ~ warten** *(Taxifahrer)* to ply for hire *(Br.)*, to cruise; **jem. die ~ wegnehmen** to entice away the custom of s. o.; **um ~ werben** to solicit for customers.

Kundschafter scout, secret agent, intelligencer, spy.

Kundschafts|beziehungen customer relations; **~verpflichtungen aus dokumentarischen Krediten und Akzeptverbindlichkeiten** *(Bilanz)* customers' liabilities.

kundtun to make known, to announce, *(öffentlich)* to manifest, to proclain.

künftig|erscheinende Bücher forthcoming books; **~e politische Entwicklung** political development to come; **~e Generationen** rising generations; **~es Programm** coming program(me).

Kunst art, *(Kunstfertigkeit)* skill, dextery;
abstrakte ~ abstract art; **angewandte ~** applied art; **brotlose ~** unremunerative occupation; **schwarze ~** black art;
~ **des Gefallens** knack of pleasing; ~ **des Verkaufens** salesmanship;
j. nach allen Regeln der ~ betrügen to swindle s. o. right and center *(US)* (centre, *Br.*) left; **mit seiner ~ am Ende sein** to be at one's wit's end, to come to the end of one's tether; **seine ~ versuchen** to try one's hand;
~ **geht nach Brot** art goes a-begging; **das ist keine besondere ~** that's as easy as shelling peas;
~akademie academy of arts; **~auktion** art sale; **~ausdruck** art expression, technical term; **~ausstellung** art exhibition (show); **~banause** philistine, lowbrow; **~bauten** constructive work; **~beilage** *(Zeitung)* art supplement; **~besitz** art possessions; **~blatt** art print; **~denkmal** monument of art; **~diebstahl** art theft; **~druck** art printing; **~druckabzug** art pull *(Br.)*, glossy print (proof) *(US)*; **~druckkarton** art cardboard; **~druckpapier** coated (art, enamelled) paper; **mattes ~druckpapier** art matt paper *(Br.)*, art matt *(US)*; **~dünger** artificial fertilizer (manure).

Künste, bildende imitative arts; **darstellende ~** performing arts; **schöne ~** fine (polite) arts;
alle ~ der Überredung anwenden to use all tricks of persuasion; **alle ~ der Verführung spielen lassen** to use all one's wiles; **j. nach allen Regeln der ~ verprügeln** to give s. o. a good thrashing; **seine ~ vorführen** to show off (one's mettle).

Kunst|epoche art period; ~**erzeugnis** work of art, *(künstlich)* plastic (synthetic) product; ~**etat** budget for acquiring art; ~**faser** artificial (synthetic) fibre; ~**faserproduktion** synthetic fibre production; ~**faserproduzent** synthetic fibre producer; ~**fehler** maltreatment, professional malpractice; ~**fertigkeit** workmanship, deftnes, dexterity, technique, skillfulness, skill; ~**flieger** stunt pilot, stunter; ~**flug** stunts, aerobatics, stunt (trick) flying; ~**flugstaffel** aerobatic team; ~**förderung** promotion of arts; ~**galerie** art (picture) gallery; ~**gärtner** nurseryman, horticulturist; ~**gegenstand** art work; ~**gegenstände** articles of virtue, objects of art; ~**genuß** aesthetic, delight.

kunstgerecht|erledigen, etw. to be skilful in doing s. th.;
~**e Übersetzung** expert translation.

Kunstgewerbe applied art, arts and crafts, *(angewandte Kunst)* industrial art;
~**laden** arts-and-crafts shop; ~**schau** craft show; ~**schule** polytechnic school.

Kunst|gewerbler industrial artist, artificer; ~**glas** ornamental glas; ~**glied** artificial limb.

Kunstgriff manoeuvre *(Br.)*, device, trick, dodge, artifice;
allerlei ~e anwenden to use all sorts of tricks; **alle ~e kennen** to know all the tricks of the trade.

Kunst|gummi synthetic rubber; ~**halle** art gallery; ~**handel** art trade; ~**händler** art dealer; ~**handlung** art (craft[s]) shop; ~**handwerk** arts and crafts; ~**handwerker** industrial artist, artificer, artisan.

kunsthandwerkliche Gegenstände art-and-craft items.

Kunst|harz synthetic resin; ~**harzklischee** plastic block; ~**historiker** art historian; ~**hochschule** academy of arts; ~**kalender** art calendar; ~**kenner** art connoisseur, virtuoso; ~**kritik** art criticism; ~**kritiker** art critic; ~**leder** imitation leather; ~**lederband** leatherette binding; ~**lehrer** art teacher.

Künstler craftsman, artisan, artist, artificer, virtuoso, *(Unterhaltungskünstler)* entertainer;
ausübender ~ performer; **bedeutender ~** no mean artist; **hervorragender ~** notable artist;
~**agentur** art representation; ~**arbeit** art [work]; ~**fest** artists' party; ~**garderobe** dressing room; ~**gilde** art guild; **von ~hand entworfen** designed by an artist.

künstlerisch|e Anerkennung innerhalb der maßgebenden Kreise finden to receive top professional recognition; ~**e Ausstattung** artistic getup; ~**e Darstellung** artistic performance; ~**er Entwurf** art design; ~**e Fähigkeiten** artistry; **von ~en Gesichtspunkten** artistically; ~**er Leiter** artistic director; ~**er Leiter einer Sendung** art director of a program(me); ~**er Leiter einer Werbeagentur** creative director; ~**es Urheberrecht** artistic copyright; ~**er Wert** art value, artistic merit.

Künstler|kolonie colony of artists; ~**launen** artistic temperament; ~**lokal** artists' haunt; ~**mähne** mop; ~**name** stage (professional) name, pen name, nom de plume; **das ist ~pech** that's really bad luck; ~**schrift** fancy type; ~**sprache** artistic slang; ~**verein** art league; ~**viertel** artist's quarter; ~**volk** show folk; ~**werkstatt** studio.

künstlich artificial, man-made, imitated, *(falsch)* false, faked, spurious;
~ **hergestellt** synthetic;
sich ~ aufregen to get excited about nothing; ~ **herstellen** to synthetize; **Kurse ~ hochhalten** to peg the market; ~ **ernährt werden** to be artificially fed; **Verhandlungen ~ in die Länge ziehen** to intentionally prolong negotiations;
~**e Antenne** phantom (dummy) antenna; ~**e Atmung** artificial respiration; ~ **gehaltene Devisenkurse** pegged exchange; ~**es Lachen** forced laugh; ~**e Lunge** iron lung; ~**er Nebel** smoke screen; ~ **gehaltene Preise** pegged prices.

Kunst|licht artificial light; ~**liebhaber** virtuoso; ~**literatur** art literature.

kunstlos amateurish, unsophisticated, simple.

Kunst|maler painter; ~**markt** art market; ~**museum** art museum; ~**narr** art bug; ~**pause** *(Redner)* telling pause; ~**pause einlegen** to pause for effect; ~**sachverständiger** art expert, adept, connoisseur; ~**sammler** art collector; ~**sammlung** art collection; ~**schätze** art treasures; ~**schmiedearbeit** wrought ironwork; ~**schule** school of arts, art school; ~**schütze** marksman; ~**seide** artificial silk, rayon; ~**sprache** artificial language, cant.

Kunststoff plastics, artificial resin, synthetic (plastic) material, man-made fibre;
~**erzeugnis** plastic products; ~**folie** plastic film; ~**industrie** plastics industry; ~**klischee** plastic block (stereo); ~**überzug** plastic coating.

kunststoffverarbeitende Industrie plastics-processing industry.

Kunststopfen invisible mending.

kunststopfen to mend invisibly.

Kunst|straße made-up road; ~**stück** trick, feat, sleight-of-hand trick, conjuration; ~**stück zuwege bringen** to pull off the trick *(US)*; **verschiedene ~stücke können** to know a trick or two; ~**student** art student; ~**tischler** cabinetmaker; ~**tischlerarbeit** cabinet work; ~**tischlerei** cabinetmaking; ~**unterricht** art lessons; ~**urheberrecht** copyright for works of art; ~**verein** art league.

kunstverständiges Urteil expert opinion on art.

Kunstverständnis art appreciation.

Kunstwerk work of art, art work, artistic work;
~**e** articles of virtue;
dem Staat hinterlassene ~e works of art bequeathed to the nation;
~ **vernichten (zerstören)** to destroy a work of art.

Kunst|wert, abstrakter abstract; ~**wolle** recovered wool, shoddy; ~**wort** coined (invented) word; ~**zeitschrift** art journal; ~**zentrum** art center *(US)* (centre, *Br.*).

kunterbunt *(Farbe)* multicolo(u)red, particolo(u)red, *(Programm)* varied, diversified;
~ **durcheinander** higgledy-piggledy;
alles ~ durcheinander erzählen to relate everything pell-mell;
~**es Durcheinander** complete muddle.

Kupfer, feuervergoldetes vermeil;
~**aktien** coppers, copper issues; ~**ätzung** copper etching; ~**ausfuhrland** copper exporter; ~**bergwerk** copper mine; ~**draht** copper wire; ~**druck** plate printing; ~**druckpapier** plate paper; ~**geld,** ~**münze** copper [coin]; ~**haut** galvanic shell; ~**klischee** electrotype, copper block *(Br.)*; ~**legierung** copper alloy; ~**münzen** coppers; ~**platte** copper plate; ~**stecher** etcher, engraver; ~**stich** print, copper engraving; ~**tiefdruck** copperplate printing, photogravure, rotogravure *(US)*; ~**tiefdruckpapier** printing paper for copper engravings; ~**tiefdruckmaschine** copper-plate printing machine; ~**werk** copperworks; ~**werte** *(Börse)* copper issues, coppers.

Kupon [dividend] coupon, dividend warrant, *(Scheck)* block slip, counterfeit *(Br.)*, stub *(US)*, *(Zinsschein)* dividend warrant, coupon;
ohne ~ coupon off, ex coupon; **samt ~** cum dividend;
abgetrennter ~ detached coupon; **ausstehende ~s** outstanding coupons; **noch nicht zur Zahlung eingereichter ~** matured coupon; **laufender ~** current coupon; **notleidende ~s** outstanding coupons; **rückständiger ~** coupon in arrears; **zum Einzug übersandter ~** coupon sent for collection; **verfallener ~** lapsed coupon; **fällig werdender ~** maturing coupon;
~ **in Form einer Bestellkarte** return coupon;
~**s abschneiden (abtrennen)** to detach coupons; ~**s einreichen** to present (deposit) coupons;
~**abschlag einbringen** to recover the coupon; ~**abtrennung** detaching of coupon; ~**besitzer** coupon holder; ~**bogen** coupon sheet, sheet of coupons; ~**einlösung** coupon service; ~**inhaber** coupon holder; ~**kasse** coupon-paying department; ~**kassierer** coupon teller, coupon collection teller *(US)*; ~**konto** coupon book (ledger), coupon payments account *(US)*; ~**scheck** coupon check *(US)* (cheque, *Br.*); ~**schneiden** detaching (clipping) of coupons; ~**schneider** coupon clipper *(US)*, scissorbill *(sl.)*; ~**skonto** coupon payments account *(US)*; ~**steuer** tax on coupons (dividend), coupon tax; ~**termin** coupon date; ~**zahlstelle** paying agent; ~**zinsen** interest on coupons.

Kuppel dome, cupola.

Kuppelei procuration, pandering;
gewerbsmäßige ~ professional pandering;
~ **treiben** to pander.

kuppeln to couple, to join, *(Auto)* to clutch;
zweimal ~ to double-declutch.

Kuppel|pelz verdienen, sich einen to arrange a match; ~**produkte** linked products; ~**stange** coupling rod.

Kuppler procurer, pimp, pander.

Kupplerin bawd, panderess.

Kupplung *(Auto)* clutch, coupling, *(techn.)* gripe, *(Waggon)* connector;
automatische ~ automatic coupling; **hydraulische ~** fluid coupling;
~ **langsam kommen lassen** to engage the clutch slowly; ~ **schleifen lassen** to slip the clutch.

Kupplungs|angebot combination offer, joint supply; ~**belag** clutch facing (lining); ~**einrichtung für Raumschiffe** space docking arrangement; ~**gehäuse** clutch case; ~**kette** coupling chain; ~**lager** clutch bearing; ~**manöver** *(Raumschiff)* docking; ~**pedal** clutch pedal; ~**scheibe** clutch disk (plate), coupling disk; ~**stecker** connection plug; ~**welle** clutch shaft.

Kur cure, course, treatment;
~ **erfolgreich abschließen** to effect a cure; **Erfolg einer** ~ **garantieren** to guarantee a cure; ~ **in Bath machen** to take the waters at Bath; **j. in die** ~ **nehmen** to bring s. o. to book, to haul s. o. over the coals; **sich einer** ~ **unterziehen** to go through (undergo) a cure, to cure; ~ **verschreiben** to prescribe a cure; **zur** ~ **geschickt werden** to be sent to a health resort.

Kür *(Sport)* voluntary.

Kur|anlagen resort facilities; ~**anstalt** sanatorium.

Kurant|geld currency, current money; ~**münze** standard coin.

Kuratel guardianship, tutelage;
unter ~ **stehen** to be in ward (the custody of a guardian); **j. unter** ~ **stellen** to appoint a guardian for s. o.

Kurator curator, trustee [in charitable uses], administrator, warden, guardian, committee *(Br.)*, regent *(US)*;
~**amt** wardenship.

Kuratorium body of curators, board of trustees (regents, *US*), trusteeship, governing body (panel), curatorium, curatory *(Scot.)*.

Kur|aufenthalt stay at a health resort; ~**bad** watering place, spa, health resort; ~**behandlung** hydropathic treatment.

Kurbel handle, crank, *(Auto)* starting handle;
~**dach** crank-operated sliding roof; ~**fenster** wind-down window; ~**welle** crankshaft.

Kurdirektion administrative committee of a health resort.

küren, zur Schönheitskönigin to elect a beauty queen.

Kur|gast cure guest, visitor; ~**haus** hydropathic *(Br.)*; ~**hotel** resort hotel.

Kurie curia.

Kurier courier, dispatch carrier, express messenger *(Br.)*, poster;
~ **abfertigen** to dispatch a messenger; **als** ~ **unterwegs sein** to courier;
~**abteilung** Foreign Messengers Service; ~**dienst** courier service.

kurieren to cure, to heal;
j. von seinen Vorurteilen ~ to cure s. o. of his prejudices.

Kurier|flugzeug courier airplane; ~**gepäck**, ~**post** diplomatic pouch (bag); ~**tasche** dispatch bag *(US)*; ~**wagen** courier; ~**weg** courier route; ~**wesen** courier service.

kurios odd, queer, strange;
~**e Geschichte** strange story; ~**er Kauz** queer fellow, rum fellow *(Br.)*.

Kuriosität oddness, queerness;
der ~ **halber erzählen** to tell for kicks.

Kuriositäten curiosities, curios;
~**händler** curiosities (curio) dealer; ~**kabinett** curio gallery; ~**museum** dime museum *(US)*.

Kuriosum in der Familie darstellen to represent s. th. unique in a family.

Kurort health (spring) resort, spa, the waters;
mondäner ~ luxury resort;
~ **aufsuchen** to resort to the springs, to [visit] a spa.

Kur|park park; ~**pfuscher** quack, charlatan; ~**pfuscherei** quackery, charlatanry.

Kurrent|geld current money; ~**schrift** running hand.

Kurs price, market rate (price), market, *(Kursus)* course, *(Lehrgang)* course, *(politische Linie)* line, *(Notierung)* quotation, value, *(Schiff)* course, *(Termingeschäft)* forward (future, *US*) rate, *(Umlauf)* circulation, *(Unterrichtsstunde)* session, *(Wechselkurs)* rate of exchange, exchange rate;
außer ~ **[gesetzt]** out of circulation; **bei sinkenden** ~**en** at reduced prices; **bei steigenden** ~**en** in a rising market; **bei weichenden** ~**en** at prices dropping off; **hoch im** ~ *(fig.)* at a premium; **ohne** ~ without official quotation, not quoted, unlisted *(US)*, *(Börsenbericht)* no transactions; **unter dem** ~ below parity rate; **zu dem im Indossament angegebenen** ~ at the exchange as per indorsement; **zu verschiedenen** ~**en limitiert** on a scale; **zum** ~ **von** at the rate of exchange (parity) of; **zum angeführten** ~ at the quoted exchange; **zum ersten** ~ at the opening [price]; **zum gegenwärtigen** ~ at the current rate of exchange (present quotation); **zum günstigsten** ~ *(Wechselkurs)* at the most favo(u)rable rate; **zum höchsten** ~ at the highest rate of exchange; **zum mittleren** ~ at the parity rate; **zum verzeichneten** ~ at the rate [of exchange] quoted;
keinen ~ **habend** not quoted, unlisted *(US)*;
abbröckelnde ~**e** slackening prices; **abflauende** ~**e** dropping (receding, sagging) prices; **abwartender** ~ waiting course; **amtlicher** ~ market (official) rate, official quotation, *(Wechselkurs)* currency [rate of exchange]; **annähender** ~ approximate rate; **ansteigender** ~ rising price; **anziehender** ~ rising market rate; **knapp aufrechterhaltener** ~ barely supported price; **außerbörslicher** ~ curb [market] price, inofficial quotation, outside market; **äußerster** ~ bottom price; **bestehender** ~ ruling rate; **bezahlter** ~ real exchange; **davonlaufende** ~**e** soaring prices; **um Bruchteile differierender** ~ close price; **doppelter** ~ two-way price *(Br.)*; **durchschnittlicher** ~ middle price; **echter** ~ true rate; **effektiver** ~ actual quotation; **entsprechender** ~ reasonable price; **erster** ~ opening price (rate); **heute erzielte** ~**e** rates obtained at today's market; **fallender** ~ declining (receding, dropping, sagging) price, *(Wechselkurs)* falling rate; **fester** ~ fixed (established) rate, fixed (firm) price; **nicht fester** ~ fluctuating rate; **festgelegter** ~ *(Schiff)* lane; **fiktive** ~**e** forced quotations; **fortlaufender** ~ currently adjusted rate; **fortschnellende** ~**e** buoyant prices; **freier** ~ inofficial price; **garantierter** ~ guaranteed rate of exchange; **gedrückte** ~**e** depressed (slackening, low level of) prices; **gegenwärtiger** ~ current rate (price); **künstlich gehaltene** ~**e** pegged prices, *(Wechselkurs)* pegged exchange [rate]; **tatsächlich gehandelte** ~**e** bargains made, actual quotations; **gemachter** ~ real exchange; **gesamteuropäischer** ~ all-European course; **gesetzlicher** ~ legal rate; **gestiegener** ~ advanced (increased) price; **gestützter** ~ pegged (supported) price; **gleichbleibender** ~ steady course; **grauer** ~ grey rate; **günstiger** ~ *(Wechselkurs)* favo(u)rable exchange rate; **haussierende** ~**e** booming (soaring) prices; **höchster** ~ highest quotation (price), peak (top) price; **hoher** ~ high rate; **laufender** ~ current quotation, *(Wechselkurs)* running course of exchange; **leichter** ~ snap course; **letzte** ~**e** last prices (quotation), closing prices; **limitierter** ~ limited price; **manipulierter** ~ manipulated price; **mittlerer** ~ mean course; **nachbörslicher** ~ kerb [stone] *(Br.)* (curb) [market] price, price after hours, street price *(Br.)*; **nachgebende** ~**e** sagging (receding, declining, crumbling, slackening) prices; **nachgeholter** ~ *(Examen)* make-up *(US)*; **neuer** ~ new tack; **niedriger (niedrigst kalkulierter)** ~ low rate (price); **niedrigster** ~ lowest quotation (possible price), bargain level, bottom price; **nomineller** ~ nominal price (exchange); **fortlaufend notierte** ~**e** consecutively quoted prices; **notierter** ~ quoted (listed, *US*) price; **zuletzt notierter** ~ last quotation; **offizieller** ~ official quotation; **östlicher** ~ eastern route; **politischer** ~ orientation of policy; **rückläufige** ~**e** drooping rates, retrograde prices, down market, bears *(US)*; **schwankende** ~**e** fluctuating prices, fluctuating quotation (rates), *(Wechselkurs)* flexible rate; **sinkende** ~**e** sagging (falling, declining) prices; **spekulativer** ~ speculative price; **niedrigst stehende** ~**e** hardpan prices *(US coll.)*; **steigende** ~**e** rising market, up, bulls *(US)*; **rasch steigende** ~**e** soaring prices; **telegrafische** ~**e** tape prices; **übersteigerter** ~ exaggerated (outbid) quotation; **uneinheitliche** ~**e** mixed market; **ungünstiger** ~ *(Wechselkurs)* unfavo(u)rable exchange rate; ~ **unverändert** *(Devisen)* exchange the same; **variabler** ~ variable exchange; **veränderlicher** ~ fluctuating market rate *(US)*; **bei fast keinem Umsatz verzeichnete** ~**e** untested prices; **weichende** ~**e** receding prices; **weicher** ~ *(Politik)* soft line;
~ **bei telegrafischer Auszahlung** cable rate; ~**e von Dividendenwerten** equity prices; ~ **über Grund** *(Flugzeug)* track; ~ **in Prozenten** rate per cent; **agrarpolitischer** ~ **der Regierung** government's agricultural policy; ~ **für Sichtpapiere** sight rate; ~**e für Sorten und Devisen auf europäischen Plätzen** continental rates *(Br.)*; ~**e mit großer Spanne zwischen Geld- und Briefkurs** wide prices; ~ **für Termindevisen** forward exchange rate; ~ **für Termingeschäfte** forward (futures, *US*) rate, futures price *(US)*; ~ **nach vorn** onward course; ~**e für mündelsichere Wertpapiere** gilts prices *(Br.)*;
vom ~ **abkommen** to get (to be blown) off course; ~ **absetzen** *(Schiff)* to prick off (chart, plot) the course; **vom** ~ **abweichen** to go off course; **vom offiziellen** ~ **abweichen** to deviate from the official line; ~ **ändern** *(fig.)* to haul, *(Schiff)* to alter the course; ~ **angeben** to state a price, *(Wechselkurs)* to quote a rate; ~ **des Pfundes an den Dollar anhängen** to peg the value of the pound to the dollar; **sich zu** ~**en für die Erwachsenenbildung anmelden** to sign up for evening classes; **besondere** ~**e für Aktienpakete aushandeln** to negotiate prices on block trades; ~**e beeinflussen** to have an effect on the market, *(Wechselkurs)* to affect the rate of exchange; ~**e unzulässig beeinflussen** to rig the market; **sich auf dem gestrigen** ~ **behaupten** to remain stationary at yesterday's prices; **weiterhin hohe** ~**e behaupten** to continue to rule high; ~ **belegen** to take a course; ~ **bestimmen** to fix a price; ~**e zu neuem Höchststand bringen** to push the

market into new high ground; **~e auf einen neuen Tiefstand bringen** to carry the price to a new low level; **~ decken** to cover the rate; **auf die ~e drücken** to depress the market (prices), to bear the stocks *(Br.)*, to force down the prices, to cause a fall in prices; **~e durch Verkäufe drücken** to raid the market; **~ einhalten** to stay on the course; **~ einschlagen** to course; **entgegengesetzten ~ einschlagen** to go on (take) an opposite course; **neuen ~ einschlagen** to adopt a new course, *(Regierung)* to adopt a new line (policy); **realistischen ~ einschlagen** to pursue a realistic course; **~ erhöhen** to advance the price; **~ erzielen** to reach a price; **~ fahren** to chart a course; **im ~ fallen** to [experience a] fall, to fall (go down) in price, to recede, to sag in price, to go down; **plötzlich im ~ fallen** to break; **~ festlegen** to lay the course; **seinen ~ festlegen** to chart one's course; **~ festsetzen** to fix (mark) a price, *(Wechselkurs)* to fix the rate; **seinen ~ festsetzen** to keep one's way; **~ feststellen** to fix a price; **~e börsenmäßig feststellen** to quote (list, *US*) prices; **~ freigeben** *(Wechselkurs)* to float the exchange rate; **am ~ gewinnen** to benefit by the exchange; **~ haben auf** to make (head) for; **gesetzlichen ~ haben** to be legal tender (lawful money, *US*); **seinen ~ halten** *(Schiff)* to hold (keep) one's course; **sich auf dem gestrigen ~ halten** to remain stationary at yesterday's price; **~ des britischen Pfundes niedrig halten** to keep down the sterling exchange rate; **~ herabdrücken** to depress (force down) the price; **~ herabsetzen** to lower the rate; **~ heraufsetzen** to advance (improve) the price (rate); **~ hinauftreiben** to force (push up, send up) the price; **~e hochtreiben** to boom (rig) the market; **aus dem ~ laufen** to yaw; **auf ~ liegen** to head for; **~ auf das offene Meer nehmen** to set course for the open sea; **~ notieren** to quote (list, *US*) a price; **~e ausschließlich Dividende notieren** to quote prices exdividend; **vom ~ abgekommen sein** *(Schiff)* to be off her course; **außer ~ setzen** to withdraw (recall) from circulation, to call in, to demonetize *(Br.)*; **schlechtes Geld außer ~ setzen** to call in clipped money; **Geldmünzen außer ~ setzen** to withdraw coins from circulation; **in ~ setzen** to circulate; **wieder in ~ setzen** to remonetize *(Br.)*; **~ sichern** *(Wechselkurs)* to fix (cover, hedge) a rate; **im ~ sinken** to lower in value; **~e stabilisieren** to stabilize prices; **im ~ stehen** to be quoted (listed, *US*) at; **hoch im ~ stehen** to be in great demand, to be all the rage (in full vogue), *(Börse)* to rule (be) high, to be up; **hoch bei jem. im ~ stehen** to be in s. one's good books; **sehr hoch im ~ stehen** *(Schauspieler)* to be a great box-office attraction; **wieder hoch im ~e stehen** to be back in favo(u)r; **im ~ steigen** to [experience a] rise, to improve, to advance (increase) in price, to be a rising market, to go up; **bei jem. im ~ steigen** to go up in s. one's opinion; **plötzlich im ~ steigen** to have a sudden rise, to skyrocket *(US)*; **~e steigern** to boom (rig) the market; **~ steuern** to steer a course; **~ stützen** to support a price, *(Wechselkurs)* to peg the exchange, to support a currency; **Abschlüsse auf New York zum ~ von ... tätigen** to effect exchange deals on New York at ...; **~e in die Höhe treiben** to make a market, to push (force, send) up prices, to boom the market, to skyrocket *(US)*; **~e künstlich in die Höhe treiben** to rig the market; **~ von 480 überschreiten** to cross 480; **~ verfolgen** to course, to pursue one's steady course; **vom ~ abgetrieben werden** *(Schiff)* to blow out of its course; **zum ~ von ... notiert werden** to be quoted (listed, *US*) at the rate of ...;

~e bessern sich prices are improving; **~e bleiben fest** prices are running high; **~e bleiben stabil** prices continue stable; **~ bröckeln ab** prices are easing off (crumbling [off]); **~ erholen sich** prices are improving; **~e erreichen ihr altes Niveau** prices recover their old level; **~e fallen** prices are declining (dropping), prices are on the decline; **~e flauen ab** prices are sagging; **~e geben nach** prices are softening; **~e gehen zurück** prices are crumbling (receding); **~e gingen sprunghaft höher** prices jumped; **~e halten sich** prices remain steady; **~e haussieren** prices are booming (skyrocketing, *US*); **~e liegen gebessert** prices have improved; **~e liegen höher** the market is high; **~ liegen eine Kleinigkeit niedriger** prices are a shade lower; **~e liegen unverändert** prices remain unchanged; **~ mangels Nachfrage gestrichen** no quotation, only sellers; **~e schwächten ab** the quotations weakened; **~e schwanken** prices are fluctuating; **~e sind abgebröckelt** prices have eased [off]; **~e sind abgeschwächt** prices have eased [off], market off *(US)*; **~e sind fest** prices are firm; **~e sind gefallen** prices have dropped (gone down); **~e sind gestiegen** prices have advanced (gone up); **~e sind rückläufig** prices are easing off; **~e sind unverändert** prices have remained unchanged; **~e sind zurückgegangen** prices have receded; **~e sinken** prices are declining (dropping); **~e steigen** prices are going up (advancing); **~e verfallen** prices are collapsing; **~e werden fester** prices become firmer; **~e zeigen eine rückläufige Bewegung** prices show a downward tendency; **~e ziehen an** prices are advancing (hardening, going up); **~e ziehen heftig an** prices rise sharply; **~e zogen an** prices have hardened;

~abbröckelung crumbling of prices; **~abfall** price decline; **~abschlag** drop (fall, reduction, decline) in prices, *(Devisen)* backwardation, deport, *(Disagio)* discount quotation, reduction in prices, *(Terminhandel)* discount quotation; **~abschwächung** weaker tendency in prices, weakness of prices, weak market, price weakness, concession, market softening, lowering of prices; **~abschwächung um einen Bruchteil** a fractional ease; **~abweichung** difference in the rates, *(Schiff)* deviation from the course; **~änderung** changes in prices, price changes, *(Politik)* shift, reorientation, *(Schiff)* alteration of course, *(Wechselkurs)* change in the exchange rate; **~änderungen** price changes; **~angabe** stock-exchange quotation; **~angleichung** *(Wechselkurs)* adjustment of rates; **~anomalie** unwarranted price level.

Kursanstieg improvement in prices (rates), run-up of prices, uptrend in prices, price advance, upturn, upward movement, up, rise, rising market;
erneuter ~ recovery of prices; **leichter ~** moderate rise; **scharfer ~** sharp advance, abrupt rise;
~ auf breiter Front widely spread improvement (rise).

Kurs|anweisung diversion order; **~anzeiger** *(Börse)* stock price indicator, *(Flugzeug)* direction indicator; **~anzeigetafel** exchange board.

kursanziehend rising, improving.

Kursaufbesserung improvement in prices, turn of exchange, [price] improvement;
mit kleinen ~en schließen to close with small advances.

Kurs|aufschlag price increase, improvement, *(Devisen)* contango, *(Termingeschäft)* premium; **~aufschwung nehmen** to show a rising tendency; **~auftrieb** upward movement, upturn in quotations; **~auftrieb hervorrufen** to give a fillip to the market; **~auftriebsmöglichkeiten** upside potential; **~ausschläge** range of price movements; **~barometer für Anlagewerte** investment barometer *(US)*; **~basis** price basis; **~beeinflusser** manipulator, stockjobber *(US)*; **~beeinflussung** manipulation, stockjobbing *(US)*, stockjobbery *(US)*, stock juggling *(US)*; **~beeinflussung vornehmen** to manipulate the market; **~befestigung** stronger tendency in prices; **~begrenzung** price limit; **~berechnung** *(Devisen)* calculation of exchange, *(Börse)* exchange (price) calculation; **~bereich** range of prices; **~bericht** market (stock exchange) report, list of quotations, daily quotations, *(Devisen)* exchange list (advice), statement of exchanges; **amtlicher ~bericht** official quotation, stock exchange list; **~beruhigung** *(Wechselkurs)* stabilization of the exchange rate; **~besserung** price advance, improvement; **~beständigkeit** steadiness in value.

kursbestimmend price-ruling, *(Wechselkurs)* rate-fixing.

Kurs|bestimmung *(Schiff)* fixing of a course; **~betrug** share pushing.

Kursbewegung price range (movement), movement of prices, stock trend, *(Devisen)* range of rates;
~en price (share) movements;
heftige ~en pyrotechnics *(US)*; **rückläufige ~** retrograde movement of prices, declining price trend;
abwärts gerichtete ~ haben to be in a downward price movement.

Kurs|bildung *(Börse)* price range (determination); **~bindung** pegging the exchanges; **~blatt** daily quotations, note of exchange, stock-market report *(US)*, list of stock-exchange quotations *(Br.)*, list of (market) quotations *(Br.)*, stock-exchange list *(Br.)*; **amtliches ~blatt** stock-exchange daily official list *(Br.)*; **~blatt für Freiverkehrswerte (unnotierte Werte)** over-the-counter report *(US)*; **~buch** *(Eisenbahn)* railway (railroad, *US*) guide, timetable, schedule *(US)*, Appleton *(US)*; **alphabetisches ~buch** ABC *(Br.)*.

Kürschner furrier, skinner;
~arbeit furs and skins.

Kürschnerei furrier's trade.

Kurs|depesche telegraphic exchange quotation, exchange telegram; **tägliche ~depesche** daily telegraphic quotation; **~depression** break in prices stock-market slump; **~deroute** price collapse; **~differenz** *(Devisen)* difference of exchange, *(Börse)* [price] difference, price spread *(US)*; **~druck** pressure of prices, raid; **~durchschnitt** average price; **~einbruch** break [in prices], sudden fall; **starker ~einbruch** sharp break in prices, stock-market slump, sharp break on the stock market;

~**einbuße** loss (decline) in price; ~**einbuße bis zu 10% erleiden** to suffer a loss in exchange up to 10 per cent; ~**entwicklung** trend (movements) of prices, stock trend, *(Rentenwerte)* trend of quotations, *(Spielraum)* price range; **durchschnittliche** ~**entwicklung** market average; **rückläufige** ~**entwicklung** downward movement of prices, declining price trend; ~**erhöhung** rise in price, price advance (increase); **vereinzelte** ~**erhöhungen** scattered advances; ~**erholung** recovery of prices (the market), rally (comeback) in prices, price rally, recuperation of prices; ~**ertragsmultiplikator** price earnings multiple; ~**ertragsverhältnis** price-earnings ratio.

kursfähig current, *(Aktie)* quotable, listable *(US)*;
nicht ~ out of circulation;
~ **sein** to be quoted (listed, *US*).

Kursfall decline in prices;
plötzlicher ~ break, stock-market slump, sudden decline;
starker ~ brisk decline.

Kurs|favorit stock-market favo(u)rite; ~**festigung** hardening (stiffening, strengthening, recover) of the market; ~**festsetzer** market maker.

Kursfestsetzung [price] quotation, price determination, mark *(Br.)*, market making, *(Devisen)* rate-fixing *(US)*;
~ **im Wege des Zurufs** public call *(US)*;
gegen eine ~ **protestieren** to lodge an objection to the mark *(Br.)*.

Kurs|feuer *(Schiff)* leading light, *(Flugzeug)* airways beacon; ~**freigabe** *(Wechselkurs)* floating of the exchange rate; ~**garantie** exchange-rate (decline) guarantee; ~**gefälle** price differential; ~**gefüge** price structure, *(Wechselkurs)* rate structure; ~**geschäft** trading on rates; ~**geschäft ohne Verlust abschließen** to average out; ~**gestaltung** trend in prices.

Kursgewinn *(Börsengewinn)* turn of the market *(Br.)*, market profit, stock price gain, *(Devisengeschäft)* exchange profit, profit by (gain of) exchange;
realisierter ~ realized capital gain; **wesentliche** ~**e** substantional gains;
~ **des Effektenhändlers** jobber's turn *(Br.)*;
~ **von 41 Punkten verzeichnen** to score an advance of 41 points; ~**rendite** earnings (price) yield basis; ~**steuerbestimmungen** capital-gains tax provisions; ~**verhältnis** price-earnings ratio; ~**zuwachs** gain in stock-market prices.

Kurs|handel trading on rates; ~**hausse** price rally; ~**herabsetzung** lowering of rates; ~**höhe** price strength.

kursieren to circulate, to be in circulation, to be current (in circulation), *(Gerücht)* to go [round], to have it, to circulate;
~ **lassen** to bandy about.

kursierend current, in circulation, *(fig.)* flying;
~**es Geld** currency.

Kurs|index price (stock-exchange) index; ~**intervention** price (exchange) intervention, pegging operation.

kursiv *(Druck)* italic, cursive, in italics;
~ **drucken** to italicize, to print in italics;
~ **gedruckt** in italics; ~ **gesetzte Wörter** words in italics.

Kursivdruck cursive type;
durch ~ **hervorheben** to italicize.

Kursivschrift italic type;
in ~ in itlic type (italics);
in ~ **setzen** to italicize.

Kurs|klausel *(Wechselkurs)* exchange clause; ~**korrektur** price adjustment; ~**korrektur vornehmen** *(Schiff)* to correct the course; ~**limit** limited price, limit; ~**limit festlegen** to limit a price.

Kursmakler stockbroker, exchange broker, specialist *(US)*;
vereidigter ~ sworn broker;
~ **sein** to job shares.

Kurs|manipulation manipulation of the market; ~**marge** rate margin; **vorher festgelegte** ~**marke unterschreiten** to slide below a trading range anchored in a special plateau; ~**marktzins** money rate; ~**meldung** quotation; ~ **und Ertragsmultiplikator** price-earnings multiple.

Kursniveau price (stock market) level;
durchschnittliches ~ average volume of transactions; **stabiles** ~ stability of price levels;
~ **aufblähen** to bolster the quotation level; ~ **künstlich beeinflussen** to boom (rig) the market; **hohes** ~ **haben** to rule high; ~ **vertiefen** to sink the level of prices.

Kursnotierung *(Devisen)* quotation of foreign-exchange rates, exchange quotation, direct exchange, exchange list (advice), *(Börse)* prices quoted, price quotation, marking;
amtliche ~ official quotation; **erste** ~ first board; **laufende** ~**en** consecutively quoted prices; **letzte** ~**en** latest (going-to-press) prices, latest quotations from the stock exchange; **offizielle** ~ official quotation; **uneinheitliche** ~ split quotation; **verbindliche** ~ firm quotation;
~ **von Freiverkehrswerten** over-the-counter *(US)* (unofficial, *Br.*) quotation; ~**en für Industriewerte** industrial share prices;
~ **ohne Zinsberücksichtigung** flat quotation *(US)*;
~ **aussetzen** to suspend (stop) the quotation.

Kursnotiz market quotation.

kursorischer Überblick cursory survey.

Kurs|parität equivalence of exchange, parity of exchange, exchange parity; ~**peilung vornehmen** *(Schiff)* to take one's bearing; ~**pflege** supporting purchases; ~**regulierung** price regulation, *(für Anleihen)* price support; ~**risiko** price risk, *(Devisen)* risk of exchange, foreign-exchange risk.

Kursrückgang decline [in prices], receding (sagging, dropping) prices, reaction (drop, fall) in prices, drop in the price of the stock, price drop (recession, setback, fall) stock-market setback, price decline, fall in stocks, market decline, drop in share prices, *(Devisen)* reduction in the exchange rate, depreciation;
allgemeiner ~ decline on the stock market (in stock prices), retreat; **beträchtlicher** ~ considerable decline in prices, material recession; **geringer** ~ shading;
~ **der Aktienkurse** decrease in share prices, *(heftig)* heavy fall in stocks; ~ **der Staatspapiere** fall of rents;
~ **erfahren (erleiden)** to experience a decline (fall) in prices, to crumble; **leichten** ~ **erleiden** to suffer a slight reaction.

Kurs|rückschlag decline in prices, price setback, price drop, sagging prices; ~**schnitt** unfair profit; ~**schreiber** *(Schiff)* course protactor.

Kursschwankungen movement in exchange rates, fluctuations in the exchange, exchange fluctuations, *(Börse)* price oscilliations (fluctuations), fluctuation in prices (of the market), ups and downs of the market;
starke ~ wide prices, sharp swings;
geringe ~ **aufweisen** to move in a narrow range; ~ **unterliegen (unterworfen sein)** to be subject to price fluctuations.

Kurssicherung forward guarantee (cover), *(Wechselkurs)* foreign-exchange (rate) guarantee (guaranty), foreign-exchange cover.

Kurssicherungs|geschäft hedging transaction; ~**klausel** hedge clause; ~**kosten** cost of exchange-rate guarantee.

Kurs|spanne exchange difference, *(Börse)* turn of the market; **große** ~**spanne** wide quotations; ~**spekulant** premium hunter, market manipulator (operator); ~**spekulation** manipulation, speculation on the stock exchange, market making; ~**spielraum** *(Wechselkurs)* rate margin; ~**sprünge** jump in prices, price jumps, spurts, bull movements; ~**stabilisierung** price stabilization; ~**stabilität** stability of prices, price stability, *(Wechselkurse)* exchange stability.

Kursstand price level, level of prices, *(Wechselkurs)* rate of exchange;
bei dem gegenwärtigen ~ at present prices;
abgeschlossener ~ resistance point *(US)*; **hoher** ~ high rate; **stabilisierter** ~**stand** level-pegging;
niedrigsten ~ **erreichen** to touch the bottom; **alten** ~ **wieder erreichen** to recover the old level; ~ **halten** to hold the level.

Kurssteigerung price advance, advance in prices, improvement, rise [in prises], appreciation in (run-up of, *US*) prices, going up, *(Wechselkurs)* appreciation in value;
auf ~**en wartend** long;
beträchtliche ~**en** substantial rises; **plötzliche** ~ boom, pinch, sudden advance in prices; **starke** ~ upward surge of prices; **überproportionale** ~ price rise out of proportion;
~**en in Spezialwerten** advances in special shares (stocks, *US*); **erhebliche** ~ **aufweisen** to show great improvement; ~ **erfahren** to be a rising market, to experience an advance; **zu neuen** ~**en führen** to carry to higher price levels; **plötzliche** ~**en hervorrufen** to rig the market.

Kurs|steigerungsprognose rise forecast; ~**steigerungstendenz** tendency for prices to increase; ~**steuergerät**, ~**steuerung** *(Flugzeug)* gyropilot, autopilot, automatic pilot; ~**streichung** nonquotation; ~**struktur** exchange-rate structure.

Kurzsturz sudden fall, fall in (collapse of) prices, nose dive, price slump *(sl.)*, panic, deroute, back-off, break *(US)*;
~ **auffangen** to cushion the decline; **heftigen** ~ **erfahren** to slump heavily.

Kursstützung support of prices, price support, peg, pegging the prices, *(Wechselkurs)* rate supporting, pegging the exchange; **ermessensmäßig vorgenommene vorsichtige** ~ discretionary crawling peg;

~**en durchführen (unternehmen)** to peg (hold) the market, *(Wechselkurs)* to peg the exchange rate.

Kursstützungs|aktion price-support scheme; ~**aktion unternehmen** to rescue (hold, peg) the market; ~**faktoren** stabilizing factors of the market; ~**käufe** supporting purchases; ~**maßnahmen** price-support activities; ~**periode** price-support period; ~**programm** price-supporting program(me).

Kurs|tabelle, ~**tafel** quotation (big) board; ~**tag** settling day; ~**telegramm** telegraphic exchange quotation; ~**tendenz** tendency of prices, trend in prices, price (market) trend; **steigende** ~**tendenz** upward tendency; ~**treiber** market rigger; ~**treiberei** market making, forcing up the prices, market rigging, rigging the market, stockjobbing *(US)*, stockjobbery *(US)*, stock juggling *(US)*, bull campaign *(US)*; ~**übersteigerung** excessive prices; **elektronisches** ~**umrechnungsgerät** electronic currency converter; ~**umschwung** price swing, sudden change; ~**unsicherheit** insecurity in share prices; ~**unterschied** price difference (spread), margin, *(Devisen)* margin of the exchange rate; **große** ~**unterschiede** wide prices; **reiner** ~**unterschied** net change.

Kursus course [of lectures], class, school, lecture, session;
kostenloser ~ noncredit course; **vollständiger** ~ full-credit course;
~ **für freies Sprechen** speaking course in public; ~ **an der Volkshochschule** extension course;
~ **abhalten** to give a course of lectures; **zu einem** ~ **abkommandieren** to detach for a course; **sich zu einem** ~ **anmelden** to sign up for a course; ~ **belegen** to enrol(l) for a course; ~ **besuchen** to attend the classes at; ~ **zur fachlichen Fortbildung besuchen** to attend evening classes; ~ **durchlaufen** to go through a course; **an einem** ~ **teilnehmen** to take (attend, join) a course; **an einem** ~ **für Fortgeschrittene teilnehmen** to take part in a course for advanced students;
~**leiter** instructor; ~**material** course material; ~**tätigkeit** course work; ~**teilnehmer** enrollee, trainee, student.

Kurs|veränderung *(Politik)* reorientation, *(Schiff)* alteration of course; **keine** ~**veränderungen** *(Börse)* exchanges without variation; ~**verbesserung** [price] improvement; **durch** ~**vergleich feststellen** to arbitrate; ~**verhalten** price action; ~**verhältnis** *(Wechselkurs)* rate of exchange; ~**-Ertragsverhältnis** earnings-to-sales (price-earnings) ratio.

Kursverlust shrinkage in the price of stocks, loss of price, loss on securities, price (market) loss, *(Devisen)* depreciation, loss on exchange;
durchschnittlicher ~ **gewichtet nach dem Handelsvolumen** *(Währungsabkommen)* trade-weighted average depreciation;
~**e hinnehmen müssen** to meet with losses on the stock exchange;
~**reserve** investment reserve fund; ~**versicherung** insurance against redemption at par.

Kurs|verschiebung shift of prices; ~**versetzung** *(Schiff)* drift; ~**wagen** through carriage (coach, *Br.*), through car *(US)*; ~**wechsel** *(Schiff)* alteration of course; **außenpolitischer** ~**wechsel** reorientation of foreign policy; **hundertprozentiger** ~**wechsel** *(pol.)* turnabout.

Kurswert market price (value), quoted value, value at issue, *(Devisen)* market rate;
oberhalb des ~**es notiert** quoted (listed, *US*) above the market price; **unter** ~ below quotation; **zu verschiedenen** ~**en** on a scale;
veränderlicher ~ fluctuating market value;
~ **haben** to be quoted (listed, *US*) on the stock exchange; ~**e notieren** to mark stock.

Kurswiedergabegerät, automatisches automatic quotation system.

Kurszettel exchange (price) list, printed exchange, note of exchange, list of [market] quotations, list of stock-exchange quotations *(Br.)*, stock-exchange list *(Br.)*, stock list (record, *US*), *(Devisen)* exchange-rate quotation, bill of course of exchange;
amtlicher ~ official (quoted, *Br.*) list, official price list;
~ **der Industriewerte** industrial list.

Kurs|zusammenbruch price collapse, collapse of the market; ~**zuschlag** *(Reportgeschäft)* contango (continuation, carrying-over) rate *(Br.)*.

Kurtage brokerage.

Kurtaxe visitors tax.

Kurve curve, bend, turn, *(Seismograph)* trace, *(Statistik)* curve, graph, trend;
fallende ~ sloping curve; **flache** ~ flat curve; **gefährliche** ~ dangerous corner; **scharfe** ~ sharp corner; **überhöhte** ~ banked curve; **unübersichtliche** ~ blind bend (turning);
~ **ausfahren** to round a curve; **sich in einer ansteigenden** ~ **befinden** to be on a rising curve; ~ **grafisch darstellen** to plot a curve; **um eine** ~ **fahren** to swing round a corner; **zu schnell in den** ~**n fahren** to take curves at high speed; ~ **fliegen** *(Flugzeug)* to do a banking turn; **zu stark in die** ~ **gehen** to overbank; **die** ~ **weg haben** to have the knack (hang) of it; **die** ~ **kratzen** to make tracks *(coll.)*; **sich in die** ~ **legen** *(Flugzeug)* to bank; ~ **nehmen** to take (turn, negotiate) a corner; ~ **zu scharf nehmen** to cut a close corner; ~ **schneiden** to cut a corner; **Wagen aus der** ~ **tragen** to force a car out of the bend.

kurven, zu schnell um die Ecke to take a curve at a high speed; **über dem Flugplatz** ~ to circle over the airfield; **um einen Platz** ~ to drive round and round a square.

Kurven|anstieg aufweisen to trace a flat line; ~**ausbau** banking of a road at a bend; ~**darstellung** graph; ~**fahrt** cornering; ~**lage** cornering characteristics, *(Flugzeug)* bank; **gute** ~**lage haben** to hold the road well on corners; ~**lineal** pliancy rule.

kurvenreich winding, twisting, twisty;
~**e Straße** tortuous road; ~**e Strecke 5 km!** *(Straßenschild)* bends for 5 km!

Kurven|schneiden cutting corners; ~**schreiber** *(Computer)* curve plotter; **schlechte** ~**sicht** blind corner; ~**überhöhung** banking of a road at a bend.

kurz short, *(Art der Abfassung)* short, brief;
~ **ausgedrückt** briefly put; **zu** ~ **gekommen** underdog, underprivileged; ~ **gesagt** in a phrase (a nutshell, *sl.*); ~ **und gut** in short; ~ **und knapp** short and to the point; ~ **und schmerzlos** quick and easy;
seit ~**em** for the last few days; **über** ~ **oder lang** sooner or later; **vor** ~**em** a short while ago; ~ **vor einer Katastrophe** tettering on the edge of disaster; ~ **vor Toresschluß** at the last moment;
~ **abbrechen** to break off abruptly; **j.** ~ **abfertigen** to be short (brief) with s. o., to treat s. o. in an off-hand manner; **j.** ~ **abweisen** to cut s. o. short; ~ **angebunden antworten** to answer curtly; **j.** ~ **vorher benachrichtigen** to give s. o. short notice; **sich** ~ **besinnen** to reflect for a moment; **Lage** ~ **besprechen** to discuss a situation briefly; **jem.** ~ **und bündig erklären** to tell s. o. straight out; **sich** ~ **fassen** to be brief, to make it short; **j.** ~ **halten** to put s. o. on small allowances (short-commons, short rations); **seinen Sohn** ~ **halten** to scrimp one's son for money; ~ **hereinschauen** to pop in for a short visit; **zu** ~ **kommen** to get less than one's share; **j.** ~ **abfahren lassen** to send s. o. packing; **um es** ~ **zu sagen** the long and the short of it; **alles** ~ **und klein schlagen** to make matchwood of; ~ **vor dem Bankrott stehen** to be on the verge (brink) of bankruptcy; ~ **treten** to reef one's sails, to take in a reef; ~ **zusammenfassen** to summarize, to recapitulate briefly;
~**er Abriß** brief outline; ~**e Ansprache** short address; ~**e Antwort** curt answer; ~**er Artikel** paragraph; ~**en Atem haben** to have no staying power; ~**er Aufenthalt** brief sojourn; ~**er Aufschub** short delay; ~**er Bericht** brief report; **von** ~**em Bestand** short-lived; ~**er Besuch** flying visit; ~**er Brief** short letter; ~**e Darstellung** summary; ~**e Entfernung** short way off; ~**en Entschluß fassen** to come to a quick decision; ~**e Erklärung** brief explanation; **auf eine** ~**e Formel bringen** to reduce to simple terms; ~**e Freiheitsstrafe** short-term prison sentence; ~**e Frist** short notice; ~**er Galopp** hand-gallop, canter; ~**es Gedächtnis haben** to have a bad memory; **sich** ~**e Notizen machen** to jot down; ~**en Prozeß mit jem. machen** to give s. o. short shrift; ~**en Prozeß mit etw. machen** to make short work of it; ~**e Sachdarstellung** brief account; ~**e See** choppy sea; ~**e Sicht** short sight; **auf** ~**en Strecken eingesetzt** *(Bus)* used on short runs; ~**er Urlaub** short holiday; ~**er Wechsel** short-dated (-sighted) bill; **mit** ~**en Worten** in a few words; **vor** ~**er Zeit** a short time ago; **auf** ~**e Zeit verreisen** to go away for a short time; ~**er Zeitraum** short period; **nach** ~**em Zögern** after hesitating for a moment; **am** ~**en Zügel** on a short rein.

Kurz|abschreibung accelerated allowance; ~**anschrift** cable (telegraphic) address.

Kurzarbeit part time [work], short hours (time), short-time work (working);
Beschäftigung in ~ *(zwecks Bekämpfung der Arbeitslosigkeit)* staggering short (of shifts), *(zwecks Vermeidung von Entlassungen)* work-sharing;
~ **einführen** to put on short time.

kurzarbeiten to be on part (short) time, to work short time.

Kurzarbeiter short- (part-) time worker, short-term employee, part timer;
als ~ **beschäftigt** placed on short time;
j. als ~ **beschäftigen** to short-time s. o.; ~ **sein** to be on part (short) time;

~**geld** short-time benefit, temporary employment subsidy *(Br.)*; **lohnabhängiges ~geld** earnings-related supplement *(Br.)*; ~**unterstützung** shortened work-week allowance; ~**zuschüsse** temporary employment subsidy *(Br.)*.

Kurzarbeits|bestimmungen short-time provisions; ~**programm zur Vermeidung von Entlassungen,** ~**vereinbarung** share-the-work plan *(US)*, share-the-work agreement; ~**wochen in der Industrie auslösen** to put industry on short weeks.

Kurz|artikelschreiber paragraphist, par writer, paragrapher *(US)*; ~**ausbildung** intensive training; ~**ausgabe** abridged (abbreviated) edition; ~**bericht** summary; **als ~beschreibung für** as shorthand for; ~**bezeichnung** abbreviation; ~**biographie** short biography, biographical sketch, profile; ~**biographie schreiben** to profile.

Kürze shortness, brevity;
der ~ halber for brevity's sake; **in aller ~** in a nutshell *(coll.)*; **lakonische ~** laconic reply;
~ der Zeit lack of time;
in ~ erscheinen to be published shortly;
in der ~ liegt die Würze brevity is the soul of wit.

Kürzel abbreviation, *(Kurzschrift)* grammalog(ue).

kürzen to reduce, to abate, *(Ausgaben, Gehälter)* to cut down, to curtail, *(Buch)* to abridge, to condense, *(Rationen)* to cut, to slash;
einem Arbeiter den Lohn ~ to dock a worker's wage; **Arbeitszeit ~** to reduce working time; **Artikel um die Hälfte ~** to cut an article by half; **Bruch ~** to reduce a fraction; **drastisch ~** to slash; **jem. das Gehalt ~** to cut down (reduce) s. one's salary; **übersetzten Haushalt ~** to trim fat from one's budget; **Legate anteilsmäßig zur Schuldentilgung ~** to abate legacies pro rata to pay debts; **Löhne ~** to scale down wages; **bereitgestellte Mittel um 4% ~** to trim one's appropriations by 4 per cent; **jds. Pension (Ruhegehalt) ~** to retrench s. one's pension; **Rationen ~** to slash rations; **Spesenetat ~** to cut down expenditure; **Unterhaltszuschuß ~** to curtail an allowance [of money]; **nach dem Verhältnis der Beträge ~** to reduce pro rata.

Kurzengagement *(Theater)* snap.

kürzer werden *(Manuskript)* to run in, *(Tage)* to draw in.

kürzeren, den ~ ziehen to come off second best (out of the little end of the horn), to get the dirty end of the stick, to get the worst of it, to be topped; **den ~ bei einem Geschäft ziehen** to be the loser in a business.

kurzerhand without further ado, without delay;
~ ablehnen to turn down without hesitation; **~ entlassen** to dismiss on the spot.

Kürzezeichen *(drucktechn.)* breve.

Kurzfassung abridged edition (version), *(Nachrichten)* rundown, wrap-up of the news *(US)*;
~ eines Patents title of a patent; **~ eines Urteils** head-note; **~ eines Vertrags** short-form agreement.

Kurz|film short subject, filmlet, short *(Br.)*, quickie *(US)*, minute movie *(US)*; ~**form** abbreviated form; **Notizen in ~form zusammenfassen** to sum up in note form.

kurzfristig short, at short date (duration), short-dated, short-timed, short-sighted, short-run;
~ kündbar at short notice; **~ lieferbar** for short delivery;
~ anlegen to invest at short notice; **j. ~ beschäftigen** to employ s. o. temporarily;
~**e Anlage** temporary investment; **als ganz ~e Anlage** for a turn; ~**e Anlagewerte** short-maturing securities; ~**e Anleihe** short-term loan; ~**er Anschlag** temporary posting; ~**e Aussichten** short-term prospects; ~**e Bankvorschüsse** day-to-day advances; ~**e Darlehn** short[-term] money; ~**er Devisenwechsel** short exchange *(Br.)*; ~**e Dispositionen der Kundschaft** hand-to-mouth orders by customers; ~**e Einlagen** deposits at short notice, short (demand, *US*) deposits, sight deposits; ~**e Finanzierung** short-term financing; ~**es Geld** money at short notice, short loan *(US)*; ~**e Geldaufnahmen** short-term borrowings; **~ entstehende Kosten** short-run costs; ~**er Kredit** short-term loan (credit, advance), *(innerhalb 24 Stunden rückzahlbar)* overnight loan *(US)*; ~**e Kündigung** *(Vertrag)* short-term cancellation; ~**e Maßnahmen** short-term measures; ~**er Pachtvertrag** short lease; ~**er Plan** short-range plan; ~**er Schatzwechsel** treasury bill; ~**e Schuldscheine** short-term notes, short notes *(US)*; ~**e Verbindlichkeit** short-term liability; ~**e Verpflichtung** quick liability, short-term obligation; ~**er Wechsel** short (-sighted, -dated) paper.

Kurzfristigkeit short date.

kurzgefaßt brief, concise, condensed.

Kurz|geschichte short story; ~**interview** contact interview; ~**katalog** *(Bibliothek)* finding list; ~**kommentar** short commentary; ~**lebensversicherung mit abnehmendem Auszahlungsbetrag** decreasing term assurance *(Br.)*; ~**lebensversicherung mit möglicher Prämienfortzahlung durch das Kind** child's deferred assurance *(Br.)*.

kurzlebig short-lived, expendable, wasting, fugitive;
~ sein to be a flash in the pan;
~**e Anlagegüter** short-life (lived) assets; ~**e Berühmtheit** a nine-days wonder; ~**e Konsumgüter (Verbrauchsgüter)** perishable consumer goods, nondurable consumer goods, perishables; ~**e Wirtschaftsgüter** short-lived (wasting) assets.

Kurzlebigkeit *(Waren)* perishability.

kürzlich recently, a short time ago.

Kurz|meldung brief report, news-flash *(US)*; ~**nachrichten** news summary, news item (in brief), wrapup of the news *(US)*, newsflash *(US)*; **spritzige ~notiz** squib *(sl.)*; ~**operette** musical tabloid; ~**parker** short-term parker; ~**parkzone** limited parking zone; ~**protokoll** summary record, *(Parlament)* votes and proceedings; ~**prüfung** *(Schule, coll.)* quiz; ~**referat** lecturette.

kurzschließen *(el.)* to short-circuit.

Kurzschluß *(el.)* short circuit, cutout;
seelischer ~ mental blackout;
~ haben *(fig.)* to have a blank; **~ verursachen** to short-circuit;
~**appell** *(Werbung)* short-circuit appeal; ~**handlung** mental blackout.

Kurzschrift stenography, shorthand;
in ~ stenographic[al];
in ~ aufnehmen to take down in shorthand; **englische ~ beherrschen** to take English shorthand; **in ~ schreiben** to write shorthand;
~ ist erwünscht, aber nicht Bedingung *(Anzeige)* shorthand is an advantage but not essential.

kurzschriftliche Notizen shorthand notes.

Kurzsemester session *(US)*.

kurzsichtig near-sighted;
~**e Politik** short-sighted policy.

Kurz|spielfilm quickie *(US)*, short *(Br.)*; ~**strecke** short distance; **auf ~strecken eingesetzt** *(Bus)* used on short runs.

Kurzstrecken|flug hop; ~**flugzeug** short-range aircraft (airbus); ~**fracht** short haul; ~**frachtgeschäft** short-haul business *(US)*; ~**rakete** short-range missile; ~**senkrechtstarter** short-take-off vertical-landing aeroplane; ~**verbindung** low-traffic short hop.

Kurz|streik quickie strike *(US)*; ~**stunde** short lecture; ~**szene** *(Film)* spot; ~**titel** short title.

kurztreten to ease up, to go easy with one's money.

Kürzung deduction, diminution, decrease, *(Ausgaben, Gehälter)* cut, cutting down, curtailment, retrenchment, reduction, cutback *(US)*, *(Bruch)* reduction, *(Buch)* abridgement, condensation, cut, *(Kurzschrift)* contraction, *(Rationen)* cut, slashing;
verhältnismäßige ~ der Entschädigung im Fall einer Unterversicherung average in fire insurance; **~ des Gehalts** salary cut (reduction), retrenchment of salary; **~ des Haushalts** cut in the budget; **~ ausländischer Hilfsprogramme** foreign-aid cut; **~ von Investitionsvorhaben** cutback in capital spending; **~ der Löhne** cut (reduction) of wages, wage-rate cutting, dockage *(US)*; **~ der Rationen** cut in rations; **~ des Raumfahrtprogramms** aerospace cutback; **~ des Ruhegehalts** retrenchment of a pension; **~ der Staatsausgaben** cuts in government expenditure; **~ eines Vermächtnisses** abatement of a legacy;
~ des Gehalts erfahren to have one's salary docked; **für eine scharfe ~ vorgesehen sein** to be in for a sharp reduction; ~**en vornehmen** to cut, to make cuts in, to take in a reef; ~**en in einem Artikel vornehmen** to make cuts in an article; ~**en im Haushalt vornehmen** to slash the budget; **erhebliche ~en bei den Sozialleistungen vornehmen** to make painful cuts in welfare.

Kürzungs|betrag amount of reduction; **etatsmäßig vorgesehene ~sätze verhindern** to prevent cost-cutting of the budget rate; **eigenständige ~ und Kompilierungstätigkeit** *(Urheberrecht)* fair abridgement; ~**vorschläge eines Ausschusses** committee cut; ~**ziel** cutback target.

Kurz|urlaub short leave (holiday), out *(Br., coll.)*; **auf ~urlaub sein** *(mil.)* to be on pass *(US)*; ~**versicherung** term insurance, term assurance *(Br.)*; **prolongierte ~versicherungspolice** extended-term policy.

Kurzwaren petty wares (goods), narrow goods, small wares *(Br.)*, haberdashery *(Br.)*, dry goods *(US)*, notions *(US)*, *(Metallwaren)* hardware;
~**händler** haberdasher *(Br.)*, dry-goodsman *(US)*, *(Metallwaren)* dealer in hardware; ~**handlung** haberdashery *(Br.)*, dry goods store *(US)*, *(Metallwaren)* hardware store.

kurzweg flatly, bluntly;
Angebot ~ ablehnen to flatly decline an offer; **~ ableugnen** to deny flatly; **sich ~ entscheiden** to decide on the spur of the moment; **Vertrag ~ unterschreiben** to sign a contract without further ado.

Kurzweil amusement, entertainment, diversion.

kurzweilig entertaining, amusing.

Kurzwelle short wave;
auf ~ senden to broadcast on the short-wave band.

Kurzwellen | amateur ham; **~band** short-wave band; **~behandlung** short-wave treatment; **~bereich** short-wave range; **~empfänger** short-wave radio (receiver); **~lupe** short-wave bandspread tuning; **~sender** short-wave transmitter; **~sendung** short-wave transmission; **~telefonie** short-wave telephony.

Kurz | werbefilm filmlet, short *(Br.)*, quickie *(US)*; **~wort** contraction, curtailed word; **~zug** short train.

kuscheln, sich an j. to cuddle (snuggle) up to s. o.; **sich in sein Bett ~** to snuggle up in one's bed.

kuschen to lie down, to crouch, to knuckle under;
vor einem Lehrer ~ to cringe before a teacher.

Kußhand, mit ~ loswerden to get rid of s. th. easily; **jem. eine ~ zuwerfen** to blow a kiss to s. o.

Küste coast[line], shore; waterside;
gefährliche ~ foul coast;
an der ~ inshore; **an der ~ stationiert** *(mil.)* shore-based; **längs der ~** alongshore; **vor der ~ gelegen** offshore;
eingeschnittene ~ indented inshore; **von Piraten heimgesuchte ~** coast preyed upon by pirates; **stürmische ~** wild coast;
~ entlangfahren to range (run down) the coast; **langsam an der ~ entlangfahren** to coast along slowly; **sich von der ~ fernhalten** to clear the coast; **von der ~ nicht freikommen** *(Schiff)* to cling to the coast; **an der ~ liegen** to front the sea; **~ verlassen** to put off from the shore; **an die ~ getrieben werden** to be driven ashore.

Küsten | befestigung reinforcement of the coast; **~bewohner** borderer on the sea, coastman; **~bezirk** coastal district; **~blockade** coast blockade; **~dampfer** coasting steamer (trader).

küsteneinwärts inshore.

Küsten | eis, loses panic ice; **~fahrer** coasting trader, coaster, trader; **~fahrt** coasting (coastwise) trade; **~fahrzeug** coaster, coasting vessel, hovel(l)er; **~fischerei** inshore (coastal) fishery; **~flugzeug** coastal aircraft; **~fracht** coasting cargo; **~frachtfahrt** coasting trade; **~front** beachfront; **~gebiet** coastal district (area), littoral zone; **~gewässer** coast (offshore, adjacent) waters, tidewater, territorial sea; **~handel** intercoastal (coast) trade; **~handelsplatz** seaboard market; **~land** maritime country, foreside *(US)*; **~linie** coastline, shoreline; **~linie anfressen** *(See)* to eat away the coastline; **~lotse** coast (inshore) pilot.

küstennahe | Fischerei offshore fisheries; **~ Ölfelder** offshore fields.

Küsten | nähe offshore; **sich in ~nähe halten** to keep inshore; **~nebel** sea fog; **~patrouille** shore patrol; **~pilot** coasting pilot; **~provinz** maritime province; **~radar** shore-based radar; **~schiff** home-trade ship; **~schiffahrt** coastal navigation (shipping), coasting (coastwise) trade, cabotage; **~schiffahrt treiben** to be in the coasting trade, to coast; **~schiffer** master of a coasting vessel, skipper; **~sockel** maritime shelf; **~staat** coastal state; **~stadt** coastal city, maritime town; **~station** *(Funkstelle)* coast station; **~streife** shore patrol; **~streifen** seashore; **~strich** coastline; **~verkehr** coastal traffic, home-trade navigation, coasting (intercoastal) trade; **~vermessung** coast survey; **~versetzung** change in the coast-line, beach drifting; **~verteidigung** coastal defence; **~vorland** foreshore; **~wachboot** coastguard cutter, patrolman vessel; **~wachdienst** coast guard; **~wache** coast patrol; **~wachschiff** coast-guard cutter, coasting vessel; **~wachstation** coastguard station; **~zolldienst** customs waterguard service *(Br.)*.

Küster lay (parish) clerk *(Br.)*, verger, sacristan, sexton.

Kustos custodian, warden, keeper, guardian.

Kutsche coach, carriage;
alte ~ crock.

Kutscher coach driver, coachman, whip;
~brief bread-and-butter letter; **~sitz** coach box.

kutschieren to [drive a] coach;
mit dem neuen Auto in der Gegend ~ to drive around with the new car; **zum Bahnhof ~** to drive to the station.

Kutsch | pferd coach horse; **~weg** carriage road.

Kutter cutter.

Kuvert envelope, *(Restaurant)* cover;
passende ~s envelopes to match;
weiteres ~ auflegen to lay another place; **~ verschließen (zukleben)** to stick down an envelope.

kuvertieren to [put into an] envelope.

Kuvertiermaschine enveloping machine.

Kux share in a mine, mining share (stock, *US*);
~e *(Börsenbericht)* mines;
~buch cost book *(Br.)*; **~inhaber** shareholder in a mine.

Kybernetik cybernetics.

L

L-Dock offshore dock.
Laban, langer bean-pole.
labberig *(Hand)* limp, *(Speise)* wishy-washy, insipid.
laben, sich to refresh o. s., *(fig.)* to feast.
labender Trunk refreshing (quickening) draught.
labern to prattle, to tattle.
labil unstable, instable, weak;
~**er Charakter** unstable character; ~**er Gesundheitszustand** weak (fragile) health; ~**e Nachfrage** instability of demand.
Labilität *(Wirtschaftslage)* instability.
Labor laboratory, lab.
Laborant laboratory worker, assistant chemist.
Laboratorium laboratory;
fliegendes ~ flying laboratory, skylab;
~ **zur Bestimmung des Feingehalts von Metallen** assay office.
Labor|ausstattung laboratory equipment; ~**experiment** laboratory experiment; ~**gebäude** lab block *(US)*; ~**gerät** laboratory apparatus.
laborieren to be afflicted with;
an einer Grippe ~ to have been suffering from the flu.
Labor|tätigkeit laboratory work; ~**untersuchung,** ~**versuch** laboratory test.
Labourregierung labo(u)r rule.
Labsal feast;
~ **für die Augen** a sight for sore eyes.
Labyrinth labyrinth, maze;
~ **der Paragraphen** maze of laws; ~ **von Straßen** maze of streets; **sich in einem** ~ **verlieren** to lose o. s. in a labyrinth.
labyrinthartig labyrinthine.
Lache puddle, *(fam.)* laugh;
fettige ~ dirty laugh;
~ **von Blut** pool of blood.
Lächeln, gewinnendes winning smile;
~ **für die Öffentlichkeit** public grin.
lächeln, dankbar to smile happily; **einfältig** ~ to simper; **über das ganze Gesicht** ~ to be all smiles; **verlegen** ~ to give an embarrassed smile; **vielsagend** ~ to smile significantly.
lächelnde Gesichter smiling faces.
Lachen laugh, laughter;
befreiendes ~ laughter of relief; **leises** ~ chuckle; **zwerchfellerschütterndes** ~ side-splitting laughter;
sich das ~ **nicht verkneifen können** to be seized with uncontrollable laughter; **von krampfartigem** ~ **geschüttelt werden** to be convulsed (rock) with laughter;
ihm wird das ~ **schon vergehen** I soon will make him laugh on the wrong side of his face.
lachen, sich einen Ast to roll up with laughter; **sich ins Fäustchen** ~ to laugh up one's sleeve (in one's beard); **jem. ins Gesicht** ~ to laugh in s. one's face; **sich kringelig (krumm und schief)** ~ to split one's sides with laughter; **sich kugelig** ~ to double up with laughter; **leise vor sich hin** ~ to chuckle under one's breath; **schallend** ~ to roar (shout, scream) with laughter; **Tränen** ~ to cry with laughter, to laugh till one cries;
nichts zu ~ **haben** not to be on a bed of roses; **bei jem. nichts zu** ~ **haben** to be no laughing matter with s. o.;
da ~ **ja die Hühner** it's enough to make a cat laugh *(fam.)*.
lachend laughing;
Vorschlag ~ **ablehnen** to laugh down a proposal; **jds. Drohungen** ~ **abtun** to laugh at s. one's threats; ~ **sein Einverständnis geben** to laugh one's approval;
mit einem ~**en und einem weinenden Auge** laughing and crying at the same time, with mixed feelings; ~**er Dritter** tertius gaudens; ~**e Erben** joyful heirs.
Lacher auf seiner Seite haben to have the laugh on one's side.
lächerlich ridiculous, absurd, jesting, derisory, ludicrous;
j. ~ **machen** to make fun of (poke fun at) s. o., to make s. o. look ridiculous, to hold s. o. up to ridicule; **sich** ~ **machen** to lay o. s. open (expose o. s.) to ridicule, to make a fool (an exhibition) of o. s.; **sich nur** ~ **machen** to gain nothing but ridicule; **beinahe** ~ **sein** to verge on the ridiculous;
~**es Angebot** derisory offer; ~**e Ausrede** ridiculous excuse; **für einen** ~**en Betrag arbeiten** to work all day for a mere pittance; ~**e Figur abgeben** to make a laughing-stock of o. s.; ~**e Forderung** preposterous claim; ~**e Frage** absurd question; ~**e Kleinigkeit** mere trifle.
Lächerliche|s, das ~ **an der ganzen Sache** the ridiculous side of the situation.
Lächerlichkeit ridiculousness, absurdity;
j. der ~ **preisgeben** to hold s. o. up to ridicule; **sich über** ~**en streiten** to argue about trivialities.
Lachgas laughing gas.
lachhafte Ausrede ridiculous excuse.
Lachkabinett hall of mirrors.
lacht, wer zuletzt ~, ~ **am besten** he laughs longest who laughs last.
Lack lacquer, varnish, paint;
schnelltrocknender ~ quick-drying lacquer;
~ **der westlichen Zivilisation** veneer of Western civilization;
Kratzer im ~ **haben** *(Auto)* to have a scratch in the paintwork;
der erste ~ **ist schon ab** she is no chicken;
~**arbeit** lacquering, paint work.
lackieren to varnish, to lacquer, to enamel, to paint, to japan;
Kotflügel neu ~ to repaint a fender (mudguard, *Br.*).
lackiert sein *(fig.)* to be in a fix;
~**er Affe** dude, conceited ass; ~**e Möbel** lacquered (japaned) furniture; ~**es Papier** varnished paper.
Lackierung lacquering, coating, *(Auto)* cellulose varnish, paintwork;
~ **mit Schutzschicht** coated finish.
Lackierwerkstatt *(Auto)* paint shop.
Lackleder patent leather.
Lade|anlage loading facility (plant); ~**baum** derrick; ~**begleitschein** shipping note *(Br.)*.
ladebereit ready for loading (to take cargo).
Lade|bereitschaft zugesichert guaranteed for cargo; ~**bestimmungen** loading regulations; ~**block** cargo block; ~**brief** bill of lading; ~**brücke** loading bridge; ~**buch** cargo book; ~**bühne** ledge, [loading] platform, loading jack *(US)*; ~**dock** loading dock; ~**einrichtungen** loading plant; ~**erlaubnis** loading permit; ~**fähigkeit** cargo (carrying) capacity, *(Schiff)* [cargo] tonnage, load [displacement], *(gewichtsmäßig)* deadweight; ~**fähigkeitsangaben** *(LKW)* factory rating.
ladefertig ready for loading (to take cargo).
Lade|fläche loading space (area), *(Waggon)* load platform; ~**frist** time for loading, loading time, loading days; ~**gebühren** loading charges; ~**gerät** loading equipment, *(Batterie)* battery charger; ~**gerüst** cargo stage; ~**geschäft** loading and unloading; ~**geschwindigkeit** speed of loading; ~**gestell** loading (handling) platform; ~**gewicht** load, shipping weight, gross delivery weight, *(Schiff)* load [displacement]; ~**gewicht während einer Reise** actual displacement; ~**gleis** loading track (side); ~**gut** freightage, cargo, freight; ~**hafen** port of lading, shipping (loading) port; ~**hemmung** *(Schußwaffe)* stoppage, jam; ~**hemmung haben** to be jammed, *(fig.)* not to be able, to find one's words; ~**höhe** *(Lastwagen)* loading platform; ~**kai** loading wharf (quay); ~**kapazität** carrying capacity; ~**klappe** *(Lastwagen)* tailboard, tail (end) gate *(US)*; ~**kosten** loading (handling) charges; ~**kran** loading crane, hoisting engine; ~**linie** load line, plimsoll line, waterline; ~**liste** loading list, shipper's manifest, freight list; ~**luke** cargo hatch (port), tonnage opening; ~**mannschaft** loading hands; ~**marke** load line, high watermark; ~**maschine** charging generator ~**meister** chief loader, *(Bahn)* railway goods manager; ~**menge** load.
Laden shop *(Br.)*, store *(US)*, outfit, repository, market *(US)*, *(Fenster)* shutter, blind, *(Kram)* show *(sl.)*, *(ganze Sippschaft)* caboodle shebang, business, *(Verladen)* loading, *(Vorladen)* summons, citation;
im ~ **gekauft** store *(US)*; **im** ~ **vorrätig** kept in store *(US)*;
wohl assortierter ~ well-assorted shop; **betriebseigener** ~ industrial (company) store *(US)*; **billiger** ~ cheap *(US)*; **gut eingerichteter** ~ well-furnished shop; **der ganze** ~ the whole outfit *(coll.)*; **gut geführter** ~ well-managed shop; **im Stadtzentrum gelegener** ~ downtown (inner-city) store *(US)*; **offener** ~ open shop; **schicker** ~ posh place; **vermieteter** ~ store for rent *(US)*; **zollfreier** ~ duty-free shop; **nur von der Straße aus zugänglicher** ~ lockup shop;
~ **mit erstklassiger Bedienung** high-class service store *(US)*; ~ **um die Ecke** corner store *(US)*; ~ **und Löschen** loading and unloading; ~ **und Löschen zu Lasten des Schiffs** gross terms; ~ **in der Nachbarschaft** neighbo(u)rhood store *(US)*; ~ **im Parterre** basement store; **betriebseigener** ~ **eines Versorgungsbetriebes** utility-operated store *(US)*;
seinen ~ **aufmachen** to open one's shop; **auf den** ~ **aufpassen** to mind the store *(US)*; ~ **ausplündern** to knock over a store *(sl.)*;

~ **besorgen** to take the counter; **Schwung in den ~ bringen** to put life into an enterprise, to make things hum; ~ **dichtmachen** to put (run) up the shutters, to shut up shop; **regelmäßig in einem ~ einkaufen** to patronize a shop; ~ **einrichten** to fit out a shop; ~ **eröffnen** to open (set up, start) a shop, *(frühmorgens)* to take down the shutters; ~ **mit der ganzen Ausstattung erwerben** to buy a shop with all fixtures; **j. an den ~ fahren** to bite s. one's head off; ~ **führen (haben)** to keep [a] shop, to storekeep *(US)*; **ganzen ~ satt haben** to be sick of the whole shebang, to be fed up with it *(coll.)*; ~ **wieder voll haben** to have got a good skinful again *(sl.)*; **seinen ~ dicht halten** to keep one's mouth shut; **ganzen ~ hinschmeißen** to chuck up one's job *(coll.)*, to pull the pin *(sl.)*; ~ **offenhalten** to keep a shop open; ~ **schließen** to shut (close) up shop, to put up the shutters; **ganzen ~ schmeißen** to run (boss, *US coll.*) the show; **müder ~ sein** *(fig.)* to be as dull as ditchwater; **in einem ~ ausgestellt sein** to be on view in a shop; ~ **übernehmen** to take over a shop; **im ~ verkaufen** to sell across (over) the counter; ~ **vermieten** to rent (lease) a shop; **j. im ~ kurzfristig vertreten** to keep shop for s. o.; ~ **zumachen (zuschließen)** to shut up shop, to put up the shutters.

laden to load, to lade, *(einladen)* to invite, *(Fracht)* to [take in] freight, to embark cargo, *(Schiff)* to ship, to take shippings, *(vorladen)* to summon, to cite;
Aktionäre zur Hauptversammlung ~ to summon shareholders to *(Br.)* (give notice to stockholders of, *US*) a general meeting; **Batterie ~** to charge a battery; **Batterie kurzzeitig stark ~** to boost a battery; **Beteiligte ~** to summon the parties; **blind ~** *(Geschütz)* to load with blank cartridges; **in Boote ~** to load into boats; **erneut ~** *(Gericht)* to resummon; **j. zum Essen ~** to invite s. o. to dinner; **Fracht aufs Schiff ~** to ship the cargo; **j. vor Gericht ~** to cite s. o. before the court, to summon (serve a summons on) s. o.; **allgemeinen Haß auf sich ~** to incur universal hatred; **Kohlen ~** to bunker; **schwere Schuld auf sich ~** to incur great guilt upon o. s.; **Schuldner vor Gericht ~** to summon a debtor; ~ **und sichern** *(Gewehr)* to load and to stock; **j. unter Strafandrohung ~** to subpoena s. o.; **Stückgüter ~** to freight (ship, *US*) by parcel; **schwere Verantwortung auf j. ~** to saddle s. o. with a great responsibility; **zu viel ~** to overload; **aus dem Wagen ~** to unload a cart; **auf einen Waggon ~** to load onto a waggon; **j. als Zeugen ~** to summon s. o. to appear as a witness;
j. ~ lassen to take out a summons against s. o.;
~**angestellter** shop (store, *US*) employee, shopman *(Br.)*, shop assistant *(Br.)*, salesman *(US)*; ~**arbeiter** shopworker, store worker *(US)*; ~**aufseher** shopwalker *(Br.)*, floorwalker *(US)*; ~**aufsicht innehaben** to tend store *(US)*; ~**auslage** store display (layout) *(US)*; ~**ausstatter** shop fitter; ~**ausstattung** shop fittings, store equipment (decoration) *(US)*; ~**ausstellung** store show *(US)*; ~**beschäftigung** situation in a store.

Ladenbesitzer merchant, shopkeeper *(Br.)*, storekeeper *(US)*, store owner *(US)*, proprietor of a shop;
kleiner ~ small shopkeeper *(Br.)*;
~ **sein** to keep shop *(Br.)*, to storekeep *(US)*.

Laden|besitzerin tradeswoman; ~**bestände** stocks; ~**besuch** shopping [expedition], store visit *(US)*; ~**besucher** shopper, visitor; ~**betrieb** shopkeeping, storekeeping *(US)*; ~**buch** shopbook; **j. zu einem ~bummel mitnehmen** to trot s. o. round; ~**dekoration** store decoration *(US)*; ~**detektiv** shop (store, *US*) detective; ~**dieb** shoplifter, shopbreaker, grabman, snatch *(sl.)*; ~**diebstahl** shoplifting, shopbreaking; ~**diebstahlsrisiko** risk of shoplifting; ~**diener** shopman, counterjumper *(fam.)*; ~**einbrecher** smash-and-grab raider; ~**einbruch** shopbreaking; ~**einbruch begehen** to break and enter a shop; ~**einrichtung** shop fittings *(Br.)*, store fittings *(US)*; ~**fenster** shopwindow; ~**fläche** shopfloor space; ~**front** shop front, storefront *(US)*; ~**gehilfe** shop (sales) assistant.

Ladengeschäft shop *(Br.)*, store *(US)*, business;
betriebseigenes ~ company (retail) store *(US)*; **offenes ~** open shop;
~ **mit besonderem Bedienungsfenster** drive-in store *(US)*;
~ **betreiben** to run (keep) a shop (store, *US*); ~ **eröffnen** to set up shop.

Laden|gestelle, geschlossene blind fixtures; ~**glocke** shop bell; ~**grundstück** shop property, store property (premises) *(US)*; ~**handel** retail trade, store business *(US)*; ~**hüter** shelf warmer, old stock, back number, drug on the market, sticker *(US)*, dormant stock, dead (unsalable, stale) article, deadwood, sleeper *(US)*, shop-worn merchandise *(US)*, shopkeeper *(Br., sl.)*, *(Buch)* plug *(sl.)*; ~**hüter sein** to be a drug on the market; ~**inhaber** occupier of a shop, shopkeeper *(Br.)*, shopman *(Br.)*, storekeeper *(US)*, store owner *(US)*.

Ladenkasse cash drawer, stand, [shop] till, cash register;
~ **pfänden** to seize the till; **sich an der ~ vergreifen** to knock down the till *(sl.)*.

Laden|kette chain of shops (stores, *US*); ~**kittel** shopkeeper's smock; ~**klingel** shop bell; ~**mädchen** shopgirl *(Br.)*, shopmaid *(Br.)*, salesgirl, countergirl; ~**miete** shop rent (lease), store lease (rental) *(US)*; ~**öffnungszeit** opening hours.

Ladenpreis retail (selling) price, *(Buchhandel)* publication (publishing, public, published) price;
empfohlener ~ recommended retail price; **gebundener ~** *(Buchhandel)* controlled retail price;
~**schutz** resale (retail) price maintenance *(Br.)* fair-trade pricing *(US)*.

Laden|raum store space *(US)*, shop (store, *US*) premises; ~**reklame** store advertising *(US)*; ~**schild** [shop] sign, facia.

Ladenschluß shop closing time, closing time, shutting up shop;
nach ~ after hours, afterhours;
früher ~ early (half-day, *Br.*) closing;
~**gesetz** Shops Early Closing Act *(Br.)*; **gesetzliche ~zeit** compulsory closing time; ~**zeiten** closing hours.

Laden|schwengel counterjumper *(coll.)*; ~**stadt** shoppy part of a town, storefront center *(US)*; ~**straße** shopping (shoppy) street, shopping promenade, promenade street.

Ladentisch counter, desk, shopboard;
unter dem ~ under the counter;
hinter dem ~ stehen to be behind the counter; **über den ~ verkaufen** to sell across the counter;
~**auslage** counter display.

Laden|tür shop door; ~**überfall** store robbery *(US)*.

Ladenverkauf retail (store, counter, *US*) sales;
ungesetzlicher ~ under-the-counter sales;
~ **und Marktverkauf** sale in market overt;
~ **am Sonntag** Sunday store opening *(US)*.

Ladenverkäufer shop assistant *(Br.)*, clerk *(US)*, sales clerk *(US)*, salesman *(US)*.

Ladenverkaufspreis selling (retail, resale) price;
10% vom ~ *(Autorenhonorar)* royalty of 10 per cent on the published price;
gebundener ~ fixed retail price.

Ladenverkaufs|zeiten shop (shopping) hours; ~**zentrum** shop commercial complex, storefront center *(US)*.

Ladenwerbung shop (store, *US*) advertising.

Lade|papiere shipping documents (papers); ~**pforte** [car] port, load cargo; ~**plan** storage plan, *(Flugzeug)* loading diagram; ~**platz** wharf, loading place (berth, dock, bay), goods platform.

Lader loader, lader, packer, cargo worker.

Laderampe [loading] ramp, loading platform, dock *(US)*.

Laderaum stowage, freight (cargo, loading) space, *(Eisenbahnwaggon)* accommodation, *(Flugzeug)* freight (cargo) compartment, *(Schiff)* ship's hold;
mit großem ~ full-bottomed;
freier ~ surplus cargo space;
~ **eines Waggons** accommodation of a railway carriage;
~**vorausbestellungen** freight bookings.

Laderisiko loading risk.

Ladeschein bill of lading, carrier's receipt, receiving note, consignment, certificate of shipment, shipping bill (note) *(US)*, *(Schlußkonossement)* domestic bill of lading;
laut ~ vom ... as per consignment of ...;
abgestempelter ~ backed note; **nicht übertragbarer ~** straight bill of lading;
~ **an Order ausstellen** to prepare an order bill of lading.

Lade|schluß closing for cargo; ~**sektor** cargo compartment; ~**spesen** loading charges; ~**stelle** loading place (point), berth, place of shipment *(US)*, *(Batterie)* battery charging station; ~**tage** running days; ~**tätigkeit** loading and unloading; ~**tiefgang** load draft; ~**tonnage,** ~**verdrängung** load displacement, displacement loaded; ~**vermögen** loading capacity, *(Schiff)* deadweight capacity, load displacement, displacement loaded; ~**vermögen für Ballast** dead-weight capacity; ~**verzeichnis** freight (cargo) list, *(Zoll)* shipper's (ship's) manifest; ~**verzögerung** delay in loading; ~**vorgang** loading and unloading; ~**vorrichtung** loading equipment (tackle, facilities); ~**vorschrift** loading pamphlet; ~**wasserlinie** load waterline; ~**zeit** laying days, period of shipment, time for loading, loading time; **gebührenfreie ~zeit** free time; ~**zettel** receiving note, post bill (note) *(US)*.

lädiert|aussehen to look the worse for wear;
~**e Briefmarke** damaged stamp; ~**es Image** tarnished image; ~**er Ruf** tarnished (clouded) reputation.

Ladung load, loading, lading, burden, portage, lug *(coll.)*, *(Aktionäre)* calling, notice, *(Eisenbahn)* freight, goods, freightage, cargo, portage, *(Laden)* loading, lading, *(Schiff)* cargo, freight, shipload, shipment, bulk, stowdown, *(Vorladung)* [writ of] summons, citation, *(Vorladung unter Strafandrohung)* subpoena, *(voller Waggon)* truckload, wag(g)onload, *(Warensendung)* consignment, freight, freightage, shipment *(US)*;
ohne ~ empty, clear, freightless, *(Schiff)* in ballast; **trotz ~ nicht erschienen** contumacious;
abgehende ~ outward cargo (freight); **nicht befestigte** ~ insecure load; **unterwegs befindliche** ~ floating cargo; **zu weit beförderte** ~ overcarriage; **falsch deklarierte** ~ wrongly declared cargo; **nicht deklarierte** ~ undeclared cargo; **durchgehende** ~ through shipment *(US)*; **erneute** ~ *(Gericht)* resummons; **feuergefährliche** ~ inflammable cargo; **flüssige** ~ liquid cargo; **geballte** ~ pole charge, *(mil.)* concentrated charge, demolition charge *(mil.)*; **geborgene** ~ cargo saved; **gefährliche** ~ dangerous cargo; **in Säcke gefüllte** ~ bag cargo; **gemischte** ~ general (mixed, *Br.*) cargo; **geschlossene** ~ *(Schiff)* bulk cargo; **über Bord geworfene** ~ jettison; **lose** ~ shifting cargo; **zu weit mitgenommene** ~ overcarriage; **öffentliche** ~ *(Gericht)* service by publication, edital citation *(Scot. law)*; **schriftliche** ~ letters citatory; **schwimmende** ~ floating cargo; **sperrige** ~ measurement (bulky) cargo; **trockene** ~ dry goods; **unbeanstandete** ~ *(internationales Recht)* lawful goods; **unverpackte** ~ *(Schiff)* bulk [cargo], bulky cargo; **verderbliche** ~ perishable cargo; **verzögerte** ~ delay in loading; **volle** ~ full cargo (load); **wertvolle** ~ valuable cargo; **zahlende** ~ revenue freight;
~ **mit Aufforderung zur Klagebegründung** rule to show cause; ~ **mit abgekürzter Frist** short summons; ~ **zur Hauptverhandlung** notice of a meeting, originating summons; **ordnungsgemäße** ~ **zu einer Hauptversammlung** due calling of a general meeting; ~ **Kohlen** haul of coals; ~ **unter Strafandrohung** subpoena; ~ **Stückgüter** general (mixed) cargo, mixed (less-than) carload *(US)*; ~ **zum Termin vor dem Einzelrichter** summons for directions; ~ **aller am Verfahren beteiligten Personen** general monition; ~ **zur mündlichen Verhandlung** notice of trial; ~ **zur mündlichen Verhandlung und zur Klageerwiderung** summons ad respondensus; ~ **eines Zeugen** subpoena of a witness; ~ **durch öffentliche Zustellung** service by publication; ~ **bei der Zwangsvollstreckungsintervention** interpleader summons;
~ **zu löschen anfangen** to break bulk; **sich für eine rechtzeitige** ~ **zu weit entfernt aufhalten** to be beyond summoning distance; ~ **brechen** to break bulk; ~ **einnehmen** to load [up], *(Schiff)* to take in freight (cargo), to embark (take in, load a) cargo; **volle** ~ **einnehmen** to take in the full complement of cargo; **gerichtliche** ~ **erhalten** to be served with a summons; **trotz** ~ **nicht vor Gericht erscheinen** to be contumacious; **ohne** ~ **fahren** *(Schiff)* to sail in ballast; ~ **ergehen lassen** to issue a summons; **jem. einen Schriftsatz mit** ~ **zustellen lassen** to have a writ issued against s. o.; **einer** ~ **Folge leisten** to answer a summons (upon a writ), to put in an appearance; ~ **löschen** to discharge (land) a cargo, to unload [cargo], to unlade, to discharge, *(Schiff)* to clear a ship of her cargo; ~ **nehmen** to be loading; ~ **nach A übernehmen** to load for A; ~ **überprüfen** to examine the cargo; ~ **verfügen** *(Gericht)* to issue a summons; ~ **verringern** to lighten; ~ **versichern** to take a risk on a cargo; ~ **verstauen** to stow freight; ~ **vervollständigen** to get full cargo; ~ **mit Durchführungsbericht vorlegen** *(Gerichtsvollzieher)* to return a writ of summons; ~ **über Bord werfen** to jettison the cargo; **ohne** ~ **zurückkehren** to return light; ~ **zusammenstellen** to assort a cargo; **jem. eine** ~ **zustellen** *(Gericht)* to serve s. o. with a summons (a writ, citation).
Ladungs|aufkommen tonnage loaded; ~**aufseher** supercargo; ~**beamter** summoner; ~**buch** cause book; ~**einheit** manifest ton; ~**empfänger** consignee, receiver; ~**fähigkeit** carrying capacity (capability), *(Schiff)* tonnage, load displacement; ~**frist** notice of appearance; **abgekürzte** ~**frist** shorter notice; **qualifizierte** ~**frist** *(Hauptversammlung)* special notice; ~**gewicht** load, shipping weight *(US)*, *(Schiff)* tonnage, load displacement; ~**hafen** port of loading; ~**kontrolleur** tally clerk; ~**kosten** lading (shipping, *US*) charges; ~**manifest** captain's (shipper's, ocean, *US*) manifest; ~**manko** short tonnage; ~**pfandrecht** cargo lien; ~**police** cargo policy; ~**prüfer** cargo checker; ~**schaden** damage caused by unloading; ~**schreiben** *(Gericht)* [writ of] summons, notification, citation; ~**steg** pier; ~**tonne** manifest ton; ~**träger** charge carrier; ~**tüchtigkeit** *(Schiff)* fitness; ~**überschuß** surplus tonnage; ~**verlust** loss of cargo; ~**verzeichnis** freight list, carrier's (loading) manifest, waybill, *(Schiff)* shipper's (captain's, ocean, *US*) manifest; ~**verzeichnis anmelden** to manifest; ~**vorgang beenden** to finish loading up; ~**wert** value of cargo; ~**wurf** jettison of cargo; ~**zustellung** service of a writ of summons, *(Hauptversammlung)* service of notice.
Lafette *(mil.)* mounting.
Laffe dandy, jackanapes;
eingebildeter ~ conceited (puppy) ass.
Lage state, position, situation, condition, footing, circumstances, lines, *(Belegenheit)* site, aspect, locality, situs, exposure, location *(US)*, *(Buchbinderei)* quire, gathering, *(Flugzeug)* altitude, *(Garnitur, Satz)* set, *(Schicht)* layer, tier, *(Schicksal)* fate, lot, *(Straßenlage)* road-holding facilities, roadability, *(Wein)* site;
in einer gefährlichen ~ out on a limb *(coll.)*; **in günstiger** ~ fairly situated, on a good wicket; **in höherer** ~ on higher ground; **in mißlicher** ~ in a trying condition (bad way); **in einer schönen** ~ *(Grundstück)* in a desirable location *(US)*; **in einer schwierigen** ~ far gone; **in einer unvorteilhaften** ~ in a disadvantageous position; **in einer verteufelten** ~ in a dilemma; **in verzweifelter** ~ with one's back to the wall, between the devil and the deep blue sea; **in einer verzwickten** ~ up a stump *(US)*; **je nach** ~ **des Falles** as the case may be; **nach** ~ **der Dinge** under these (according to) circumstances, as matters stand; **nur der augenblicklichen** ~ **Rechnung tragend** short-term;
allgemeine ~ general situation; **allgemeine** ~ **in Europa** outlook in Europe; **angespannte** ~ *(Betrieb)* overextension; **außenpolitische** ~ foreign situation; **bedrängte** ~ embarrassment; **erhöhte** ~ *(Haus)* hill side; **ernste** ~ grave situation; **exponierte** ~ exposed position; **fatale** ~ delicate situation, a predicament; **finanzielle** ~ financial showing (position, condition), pecuniary circumstances; **gesunde finanzielle** ~ sound financial position; **gute finanzielle** ~ strong finances; **meine finanzielle** ~ my worldly circumstances; **gefährliche** ~ distress, state of danger, tight spot; **gegenwärtige** ~ present state of affairs; **geschäftliche** ~ status; **gespannte** ~ tense atmosphere, strained condition; **gesunde** ~ healthy position; **heikle** ~ trouble; **hilflose** ~ chancery; **hoffnungslose** ~ hopeless plight; **innenpolitische** ~ local political situation; **isolierte** ~ insularity; **kitzlige** ~ ticklish situation; **komplizierte** ~ wheels within wheels; **kreditpolitische** ~ credit situation; **kritische** ~ strange pass, critical position (situation), precipice, razor's edge; **liquiditätspolitische** ~ liquidity status; **mißliche** ~ precarious situation, hole, awkward situation, jam *(coll.)*, predicament; **örtliche** ~ local situation, location *(US)*; **peinliche** ~ embarrassing situation; **politische** ~ political situation; **rechtliche** ~ legal position; **schwierige** ~ exigency, exigence, awkward position, predicament; **steuerliche** ~ tax status, taxation position; **strategische** ~ strategic position; **unangenehme** ~ plight; **ungünstige** ~ disadvantage; **unhaltbare** ~ pocket *(sl.)*; **verzweifelte** ~ desperate situation; **wirtschaftliche** ~ economic outlook; **allgemeine wirtschaftliche** ~e general economic outlook;
~ **der Arbeiter** conditions of the workers; ~ **auf dem Arbeitsmarkt** manpower situation; **angespannte** ~ **am Arbeitsmarkt** strained situation on the labo(u)r market; **finanzielle** ~ **eines laufenden Betriebes** going-concern position; ~ **der Dinge** state of affairs; ~ **am Effektenmarkt** stock-market situation; **finanzielle** ~ **[des Ehemanns im Scheidungsfall]** faculties; **finanzielle** ~ **einer Firma** financial standing of a firm; ~ **eines Grundstücks** site, situs, locality, location *(US)*; **sonnige** ~ **eines Hauses** sunny situation of a house; ~ **der öffentlichen Haushalte** public finance situation; ~ **des Marktes** state of the market; ~, **in der alles möglich ist** situation full of potentialities; **zwei** ~**n Seide** two thicknesses of silk; **gute** ~ **für den Standort neuer Industriezweige** suitable location for new factories *(US)*; **eine** ~ **Steine** a course of bricks;
jem. seine ~ **auseinandersetzen** to explain one's position to s. o.; ~ **ausgeben** *(Wirtshaus)* to stand a round (treat all round); **jds. ungünstige** ~ **ausnutzen** to hit a man below the belt (when he is down); **sich in einer kritischen** ~ **befinden** to be in an insecure position; **sich in einer scheußlichen** ~ **befinden** to be in an awkward predicament; **sich finanziell in einer schlimmen** ~ **befinden** to be at one's beam-ends; **aus einer schwierigen** ~ **befreien** to untangle; **j. aus einer schwierigen** ~ **befreien** to get s. o. out of a fix; ~ **in allen Auswirkungen begreifen** to take in a situation; **jem. in einer schweren** ~ **beistehen** to help s. o. at a dead lift; ~ **besprechen** to discuss the situation; ~ **bestimmen** to locate; **in die richtige** ~ **bringen** to right; **j. in eine schiefe** ~ **bringen** to land s. o. in an awkward position; ~ **richtig einschätzen** to form a true estimate of the situation; **nach** ~ **der**

Akten entscheiden to decide on its merits; ~ entspannen to relieve the tension; Ernst der ~ erkennen to realize the seriousness of a situation; seine ~ klar erkennen to find one's bearings; sich in der ~ fühlen to feel up to; Überblick über die internationale ~ geben to survey the international situation; in eine mißliche ~ geraten to get into a scrape; schöne ~ haben to be in a pleasant location (US); unvergleichliche ~ haben to be unrivalled for its position; aus einer schwierigen ~ herauskommen to extricate o. s. from a difficulty; schwierige ~ mit Würde meistern to bear o. s. with dignity in difficult circumstances; ~ peilen to size up a situation, to find out how the land lies; neue ~ schaffen to put a new face on things; in der ~ sein to be able (prepared, in a position) to; in jds. ~ sein to be in s. one's shoes; in bedrängter ~ sein to be hard up, to be down on one's uppers (fam.), to have one's back to the wall; in gleicher ~ sein to be in the same boat; in der glücklichen ~ sein ... to be fortunate enough to ...; Herr der ~ sein to master a situation; in einer hilflosen ~ sein to be on the ropes; in einer mißlichen ~ sein to stand in an awkward position, to be behind the eight; in einer mißlichen finanziellen ~ sein to be in financial difficulties; momentan in einer mißlichen ~ sein to be awkwardly situated just now; nicht in der ~ sein, etw. zu tun to be unfit to do s. th.; höchst riskante ~ sein to be a touch-and-go situation; in einer schlimmen ~ sein to be in a fix (up a tree, coll.); in einer üblen ~ sein to be down on one's luck; in gleich übler ~ sein to be in the same box (boat); in einer unangenehmen ~ sein to be awkwardly placed; in einer verflixten ~ sein to be between the devil and the deep blue sea; in einer verzwickten ~ sein to find o. s. in a hole; auf eine besondere ~ abgestellt sein to be tailor-made to meet a special situation; der ~ nicht gewachsen sein not to be equal to the occasion; in ~n setzen (drucktechn.) to gather; eine ~ stiften (spendieren) to serve a round of drinks, to stand (treat) all round; ~ überblicken to assess (review) a situation; ~ laufend einer Überprüfung unterziehen to keep a situation under review; ~ vollständig verändern to turn the tables; sich in jds. ~ versetzen to put o. s. in s. one's position (place), to imagine o. s. in another's position; in eine hilflose ~ versetzen to turn turtle (sl.); in die ~ versetzen, nicht mehr arbeiten zu müssen to relieve s. o. of the necessity of working; j. in die ~ versetzen, in Pension zu gehen to enable s. o. to retire; sich in einer schwierigen ~ wiederfinden to be placed in difficult circumstances; finanzielle ~ einer Firma richtig wiedergeben to represent fairly the financial position of a company; nicht in jds. ~ sein wollen not to like to be in s. one's shoes; sich einer ~ gewachsen zeigen to rise to the occasion; ~änderung business trend; kontraktive ~änderung regressive business trend; ~bericht background (situation) report, fact-finding survey, summary (estimate) of the situation, situation report; ~besprechung briefing; ~besprechung abhalten to discuss the situation, to brief; ~bestimmung orientation; ~betrachtungen views on the situation; ~beurteilung assessment of the situation.

Lagenabbau excavation in layers.

lagenweise in layers (tiers).

Lage|ort situs (lat.); ~plan layout, groundplan, site plan, plan of site, sketch map, survey.

Lager (Anhaltelager) detention (internment) camp, (Flüchtlinge) camp, encampment, (Gebäude) storehouse, warehouse (US), depot, (mil.) training center (US) (centre, Br.), (Parteipolitik) camp, (Stapelplatz) dump, (Vorrat) store, stock, stockpile, inventory, assortment, supply, holding;

ab ~ [lieferbar] ex store (warehouse, US); auf ~ in (on) stock, in (on) hand, stocked, in store, (Wein) on tap; auf ~ geblieben left on hand; im ~ vorrätig carried on stock; nicht auf ~ out of stock, unstored, unstocked; vom unversteuerten (unverzollten) ~ out of bond;

bedeutendes ~ considerable stock; bescheidenes ~ shakedown; gering bestücktes ~ low stock; erschöpftes ~ depleted (exhausted) stocks; festes ~ (mil.) permanent camp; beweglich geführtes ~ buffer stock; gegnerisches ~ (pol.) opposition camp; geheimes ~ stash, (Lebensmittel) cache; stark gelichtetes ~ heavily depleted stocks; zu großes ~ overstock; sofort realisierbares ~ readily marketable staples; reich sortiertes ~ well-assorted (-selected) stock; sozialistisches ~ socialist camp; überhöhtes ~ inflated stocks; übervolles ~ top-heavy inventory; unabsetzbares ~ frozen inventory; unvollständiges ~ incomplete stock; wohlassortiertes ~ well-selected (-assorted) stock;

~ und ~bestand stock and inventory; ~ von Fertigwaren finished stock, stock of finished goods; ~ in allen Sorten stock of all kinds; ~ aus Stroh bed of straw;

~ abbauen to reduce (cut, liquidate) inventory (US), to run down stocks; ~ abbrechen (mil.) to strike a camp; sein ~ abstoßen to liquidate one's stock of goods, to sell out; ~ angreifen to draw on stocks; feindliches ~ angreifen to attempt an enemy's camp; ~ anlegen to lay in stock; auf ~ arbeiten to work on stock; im ~ aufbewahren to store goods; sein ~ auffrischen to renew one's stock; ~ wieder auffüllen to stock up, to restock (US), to replace (refill, replenish) the stock, to recruit supplies; ~ auflösen (pol.) to close down a camp; ~ aufnehmen to [take an] inventory; ~ aufschlagen to pitch a (establish) one's camp, to encamp; ~ aufstocken to build up an inventory; sein ~ aufsuchen to repair to one's bed; ~ ausrichten to true off a bearing; mit einem ~ ausstatten to stock; ~ ausverkaufen to clear out; jem. sein ~ bereiten to make the bed for s. o.; ~ beschlagnahmen to condemn stores; auf ~ bleiben to remain on the shelf; auf ~ bringen to store, to lodge (deposit) in a warehouse (US); j. in ein ~ einweisen to send s. o. to a camp; dem ~ entnehmen to take out of store; sein ~ ergänzen to replenish one's inventory (stock), to refill (replace) the stock; ~ nicht mehr ergänzen to withdraw from stock; im ~ festsitzen to sit in stockpile; in einem ~ Aufnahme finden to be taken into a camp; zu großes ~ führen to be overstocked; auf ~ haben to [hold in] store, to keep (carry) in (have on, US) stock, to stock an article, to have on the shelf, to keep on ice (US); immer eine Ausrede auf ~ haben to always have one's excuse pat; nicht [mehr] auf ~ haben to be out of stock (an article); reichhaltiges (umfangreiches) ~ haben to be heavily stocked, to carry heavy stock, to have a wide range of goods; nur gängige Sorten auf ~ haben to have only conventional designs in stock; zu viel auf ~ haben to overstock; stets volles ~ haben to prevent short delivery; immer ein paar Witze auf ~ haben to always have a few jokes up one's sleeve; unverkäufliches ~ auf dem Halse haben to have a lot of unsalable stock; auf ~ halten to stock [an article], to keep [in stock], to keep in store; ~ knapp halten to keep down an inventory; zu beiden ~n Verbindung halten to have a foot in both camps; Waren auf ~ halten to carry goods in stock; auf ~ legen to lodge in a warehouse (US), to stock goods, to lay in; im ~ liegen to be in stock, to lie in a warehouse (US); ~ liquidieren to sell out, to liquidate one's stock of goods; auf ~ nehmen to stock, to warehouse, to lay in goods (stock), to put goods into stock, to store away (up); neue Sendung von Büchern aufs ~ nehmen to receive new supplies of books; wieder auf ~ nehmen to restock (US); ~ räumen to unstock a store, to clear off old stock, to sell out; j. an sein ~ rufen to call s. o. to one's bedside; ~ säubern (pol.) to police a camp (US); auf ~ sein to be in stock; sich in mehrere ~ spalten (pol.) to split up into several parties; im gleichen ~ stehen (fig.) to be on the same side; seine Möbel aufs ~ stellen to warehouse one's furniture; ins feindliche ~ überlaufen to change sides, to flop over (coll.), to rat (sl.); in einem ~ unterbringen to camp; zu kleines ~ unterhalten to understock; umfangreiches ~ unterhalten to have a wide range of goods; ganzes ~ verbrauchen to work up all the stock; ~ drastisch vermindern to cut back drastically on stockpiles; sein ~ vervollständigen to replenish one's stock; j. wochenlang aufs ~ werfen to keep s. o. in bed for weeks;

~abbau inventory cutting (reduction), cutting of inventory, negative investment, disinvestment (US), reduction of stocks, stock reduction (cut), stockshedding, drop in stocks, inventory liquidation (US), depletion of inventories, inventory decumulation, (durch Auftragskürzung) destocking; drastischen ~abbau durchführen to cut back drastically on the stockpiles; ~abbaurate, ~abbausatz rate of stockshedding; ~abgang inventory decrease; ~abnahme stock shrinkage; ~abschreibung inventory writedown; ~abstoßung liquidation of inventories (US), inventory liquidation; ~anfertigung production (producing) for stock; ~anforderung stores (stock, purchase) requisition; ~angleichung inventory adjustment; erhebliche ~ankäufe tätigen to lay in stock pretty heavily; ~anlieferungen store supplies; ~anreicherung inventory accumulation; Tempo der ~anreicherung beschleunigen to step up one's stockpiling pace; ~anstieg growth of inventory, inventory growth; ~apfel apple that is a good keeper; ~arbeiter storeman, stock boy, warehouse laborer (hand, boy) (US); ~arbeiterin stock girl; ~artikel articles in stock, stock articles; ~aufbau buildup of stocks, stock (store) building; ~auffüllung inventory buildup (accumulation, increase), stock accumulation (replacement), replenishment of stocks, restocking (US); ~auffüllungsprozentsatz rate of stock building; erhebliche ~aufkäufe tätigen to lay in stocks pretty heavily; ~auflösung liquidation of an inventory; ~aufnahme stocktaking, inventory taking (US); ~aufnahmefähigkeit storage capacity; ~**aufseher** storeman, storer, storekeeper *(Br.)*, warehouseman *(US)*, warehouse keeper *(US)*, *(Anhaltelager)* overseer of a camp; ~**aufstellung** inventory sheet; ~**aufstockung** inventory buildup, stock (store) building, stockbuilding, stockpiling; ~**aufstockungsvereinbarung** walking possession agreement; ~**auftrag** stock (stocking-up, store) order; **probeweiser erteilter** ~**auftrag** stock trial order; ~**aufwand** outlay for inventories; ~**aufwertung** write-up of stock value.

Lageraum *(mil.)* briefing room.

Lager|ausdehnung inventory size; ~**ausgabenanordnung** withdrawal (delivery) order, *(Rohstoffe)* materials requisition slip; ~**ausrüstung** camping equipment; ~**ausschuß** campship; ~**auswahl** stock selection; ~**bedarf** stock requirements; ~**bedingungen** storing conditions; ~**befundbuch** inventory [book] *(US)*; ~**begrenzung** stock limit; ~**behälter** storage container, ~**bereicherung** addition to [our] stores.

Lagerbestand stock [in (on) hand], stocks inventory, unsold inventory, stockpile, inventory holdings, leftover (trading) stocks, statement of goods, goods on hand;

ohne ~ unstocked;

durchschnittlicher ~ average stock; **geringer** ~ low inventory; **geschätzter** ~ estimated inventory; **höchster** ~ stock peak; **zu hoher** ~ inflated stocks;

~ **auffüllen** to replace (refill, replenish) the stock, to restock *(US)*; ~ **aufnehmen** to [make up an] inventory, to take stock.

Lagerbestands|auffüllung replacement of inventories, inventory building (buildup, accumulation), restocking *(US)*; ~**durchschnitt** average stock; **fortlaufende** ~**feststellung** continuous inventory; ~**karte** stock record (ledger) card; ~**prüfung** inventory verification; ~**veränderungen** inventory changes; ~**verzeichnis** inventory; ~**verzeichnis aufnehmen** to [make up an] inventory, to take stock; ~**wert** inventory value.

Lager|bestellung store order, fill-in reorder; **bedarfsgerechte** ~**bestellung** requirement-related ordering of stock; ~**betrieb** storage operation, *(Unternehmen)* field warehouse; ~**bewertung** inventory (stock, merchandise) valuation; **erhöhte** ~**bewertung** stock appreciation; ~**bewertung zu Einkaufspreisen** base-stock method; ~**bewertungsausgleich** inventory valuation adjustment; ~**bewertungsmethode** inventory valuation method; ~**bewirtschaftung** inventory control.

lagerbewußt inventory-conscious.

Lager|bezugsschein stores (stock, purchase) requisition; ~**bier** stock beer; ~**bild** inventory picture; ~**bildung** stock (store) building, stockpiling.

Lagerbuch warehouse (store, inventory, stock) book, *(Teil des Hauptbuches)* stock ledger;

~**führung** stock record division, store accounting; ~**halter** stores ledger clerk; ~**haltung** store accounting, stock record division; ~**haltung in Form offener Posten** stock bookkeeping as unpaid items; ~**konto** stock (stores) ledger account.

Lager|bühne warehouse floor *(US)*; ~**büro** camp office; ~**bursche** stock (warehouse, *US*) boy; ~**butter** cold-storage butter; ~**dauer** warehouse (storage) period, operating cycle; ~**defizit** inventory shortage; ~**disponibilität** stock availability; ~**dispositionen** stockpile dispositions, stockpiling behavio(u)r.

Lagerei storage service, warehousing.

Lager|einkäufe inventory buying; ~**einrichtungen** storing (warehouse, *US*) facilities, storage accommodation (devices); ~**empfangsbescheinigung** warehouse receipt *(US)*; ~**ergänzung** replenishment of stock; ~**ergänzung vornehmen** to replenish one's inventory (stock); **periodische** ~**erneuerung** revolvement of stocks; ~**erzeugnisse** warehouse goods.

lagerfähig storable;

nur begrenzt ~ **sein** to be stored for a limited period only.

Lager|fähigkeit storage capacity; ~**fahrzeug** warehouse truck; ~**fertigung** production for stock; ~**feuer** camp fire; ~**finanzierung** stocking finance; ~**finanzierung durch mittel- oder langfristigen Kredit** inventory loan; ~**fläche** storage area, floor space; ~**freisetzung** stockshedding; ~**frist** time for free storing; ~**funktion** storage function; ~**gebäude** storage building, storehouse, warehouse *(US)*; ~**gebühren** storing (warehouse, *US*) charges, *(für nicht abgeholte Ware)* yardage; **übermäßige** ~**gebühren** excessive rates of storage; ~**geld** storage (storing) charges, demurrage *(coll.)*, warehousing charges (expenses) *(US)*; ~**geschäft** storage (storing) business, warehousing *(US)*; ~**gewinn** inventory profit; ~**gleisanschluß** warehouse track; ~**größe** stock (inventory) size; ~**gruppe** inventory group; ~**gut** stock, stored (bonded, warehouse, *US*) goods, goods in storage; ~**hafen** warehousing port; ~**halle** warehouse, storehouse.

Lagerhalter storekeeper *(Br.)*, store clerk *(Br.)*, stock keeper, stockman *(US)*, *(selbständig)* warehouseman *(US)*, warehouse clerk *(US)*;

~**konossement** custody bill of lading; ~**pfandrecht** warehouseman's lien *(US)*.

lagerhaltig stocked.

Lagerhaltung stockkeeping, storing, storekeeping, warehousing *(US)*;

überhöhte ~ inflated stocks; **vermehrte (verstärkte)** ~ increase in stocks, increased stocking.

Lagerhaltungs|dienst storage service; ~**kontrolle** inventory control; ~**kosten** storage charges (costs), stockholding costs, warehousing costs *(US)*; ~**kredit** storage credit; ~**spezialist** inventory controller.

Lagerhauptbuch stores ledger, stock record.

Lagerhaus staple house, storehouse, storage, depot, store, packhouse, depository of goods, warehouse *(US)*, *(für Getreide)* granary, silo, *(aus abgeteilten Stockwerken)* loft, *(für Waffen)* magazine;

ab ~ ex store (warehouse, *US*);

öffentliches ~ public warehouse;

~ **für zollpflichtige Güter** licensed warehouse *(US)*; ~ **für nicht zollpflichtige Güter** wharf; ~ **für unverzollte Waren** bonded store (warehouse, *US)*;

in einem ~ **einlagern** to store in a warehouse;

~**aufstockung** store building; ~**besitzer** dock (warehouse, *US*) owner; ~**gebühr** storage (warehouse) charges; ~**genossenschaft** cooperative warehouse society *(US)*; ~**gesellschaft** storage (warehousing, *US*) company, dock company; ~**gewerbe** storage business, warehousing *(US)*; ~**kosten** storage charges (costs), warehouse charges *(US)*; ~**verwalter** warrant clerk.

Lager|herstellung production for stock; ~**höchststand** stock peak; ~**hof** storage, yard, dock [warehouse]; ~**hofbesitzer** wharfinger; ~**hortung** inventory hoarding; ~**hüter** shelf warmer; ~**insasse** camp inmate; ~**investition** investment in stock, inventory investment, capital investment on inventories; **hohe** ~**investitionen** heavy stock; ~**ist** store *(Br.)* (warehouse, *US*) clerk, warehouse boy *(US)*, warehouseman *(US)*, stockman *(US)*; ~**kapazität** warehouse *(US)* (storage) capacity; ~**karte** stores ledger (perpetual inventory) card; ~**kartei** inventory record; ~**katalog** stock catalog(ue); ~**keller** cellar, vault; ~**klischee** stock cut; ~**knappheit** stock shortage; ~**kommandant** *(mil.)* camp commander; ~**konto** store (stock, warehouse, *US*) account, *(Lagerbuchkonto)* stock (stores) ledger account.

Lagerkontrolle stock (stores, inventory) control, inventory checking;

laufende ~ perpetual inventory control system;

~ **nach Wareneinheiten** unit control *(US)*.

Lagerkontroll|führer stock (store, *Br.*, warehouse, *US*) clerk; ~**haltung** inventory control; ~**system** inventory control system; ~**verzeichnis** stock register, inventory [register].

Lager|kosten cost of storage, storage (storing) charges, yardage, carrying (warehousing, *US*, warehouse, *US*) charges, warehousing costs *(US)*; **übermäßige** ~**kosten** excessive rates of storage; ~**leben** life in a camp; ~**leben führen** to be in camp; ~**leitung** camp authorities; ~**liste** inventory, stock register (sheet); ~**manko** inventory shortage; ~**marke** store mark.

lagermäßig herstellen to make for (work on) stock.

Lager|mathematik arithmetic of inventory; ~**miete** storage, store *(Br.)* (warehouse, *US*) rent, store hire, *(Kosten)* cost of storage, storage charges (costs), warehouse charges *(US)*; ~**mietenkonto** warehouse rent account; ~**minderung** decrease of stocks; ~**möglichkeiten haben** to share storage (warehouse, *US*) facilities.

Lagern storing, lodging, stockpiling, warehousing *(US)*.

lagern to store, to stockpile, to deposit, to [put in] warehouse *(US)*, *(abstützen)* to support, *(mil.)* to park, to dump, *(im Freien stapeln)* to dump, *(v./i.)* to be stored (warehoused, *US*), *(im Schiff)* to stow away;

sich ~ to lie down, to settle o. s.; **j. bequem** ~ to lay s. o. in a comfortable position;

auf Betonpfeilern ~ *(Brücke)* to rest on concrete piers; **sich um das Feuer** ~ to sit down around the fire; **im Freien** ~ to camp out; **kühl** ~ to cold-store; **sich im Schatten eines Baumes** ~ to rest in the shade of a tree; **vor den Toren der Stadt** ~ *(mil.)* to camp outside the gates of the town; **Waren in einem Lagerhaus** ~ to store (warehouse, *US*) goods; **Wein** ~ to cellar wine; **unter Zollverschluß** ~ to bond;

bei jem. etw. ~ **haben** to have s. th. in custody with s. o.; ~ **lassen** to keep in store (warehouse, *US*).

Lager|nummer store (storing) number; ~**ordnung** stock arrangement.

Lagerpfandschein deposit warrant, warrant for goods *(Br.)*, warehouse receipt *(US)*, warehouse keeper's receipt *(Br.)*, *(für per Schiff importierte Waren)* dock warrant;
begebbarer ~ warehouse keeper's warrant; **nicht begebbarer** ~ warehouse keeper's certificate *(Br.)*;
~ **als Kreditsicherheit verwenden** to use a warehouse receipt as security for a loan *(US)*.

Lager|planung stock planning, stockpiling; ~**planziel** stockpiling (inventory) target; ~**platz** depot, entrepôt, storing place, yard, *(im Freien)* camp, *(Holz)* lumberyard, *(Kohle)* coal yard, *(Rastplatz)* resting place, *(Stapelplatz im Freien)* dump, *(Zeltplatz)* camping ground; ~**politik** stockpiling policy, policy of stocking; **vorsichtige** ~**politik betreiben** to keep down an inventory; ~**politik völlig durcheinanderbringen** to knock the inventory picture out of focus.

lagerpolitisches Ziel inventory (stockpiling) target.

Lager|preiszettel stock tag; ~**probeauftrag** stock trial order; ~**produktion** inventory building; ~**prüfung** inventory control, stocktaking; ~**prüfungsbescheinigung** inventory certificate; ~**rabatt** stock rebate; ~**raum** storage, stowage, storeroom, storage closet (place, space), stock room, warehouse [room] *(US)*, warehouse space *(US)*; ~**räume** storage area; ~**räumung** removal of stores, clearance; ~**rechnung** store (warehouse, *US*) account; ~**reserve** inventory reserve; **über** ~**reserven von sechs Wochen verfügen** to have an average of six weeks' stocks in hand; ~**restbestand** leftover, residue of stocks; ~**rezession** inventory recession; ~**risiko** storage risk; ~**rückgabemeldung** returned stores report; ~**rückgang** drop in stocks.

Lagerschein warrant for goods *(Br.)*, storage check, warehouse receipt (certificate, bond, warrant) *(US)*, *(Getreidespeicher)* elevator receipt *(US)*, *(Kailagerhaus)* wharfinger's receipt, dock warrant *(Br.)* (receipt, *US*), *(Speicher)* delivery order;
begebbarer ~ transferable warrant, warehouse keeper's warrant *(Br.)*; **nicht begebbarer** ~ warehouse keeper's certificate *(Br.)*;
~ **über eingelagerte Waren** produce warrant; ~ **für sicherungsübereignete, beim Eigentümer verbliebene Waren** field warehouse receipt *(US)*;
für eingelagerte Waren einen ~ **ausstellen** to issue a warehouse warrant for goods *(US)*; **durch** ~ **sichern** to secure by warrant *(US)*;
~**ausstellung** issuing of a warehouse warrant *(US)*; ~**inhaber** warehouse receipt holder *(US)*; ~**register** *(Kailager)* dock warrant register; ~**vorschüsse** advances on warrant.

Lager|schloß builder's lock; ~**schriften** *(Druckerei)* type on store; ~**schrumpfung** dwindling of stocks, stock shakeout; ~**schuppen** shed; ~**schwierigkeiten** inventory woes; ~**spesen** storage charges (costs), storing expenses, warehouse charges *(US)*; ~**stätte** resting place, *(geologisch)* deposit; **abbauwürdige** ~**stätte** productive bed; ~**teilnehmer** camper; ~**treffen** camp meeting; ~**überschuß** warehouse surplus *(US)*, surplus stockpiles; ~**überwachung** stock (inventory) control; ~**umfang** inventory size; ~**umschlag** inventory (stock, merchandise) turnover; ~**umschlagsgeschwindigkeit** rate of stock turnover; ~**umschlagsverhältnis** inventory (stock-) sales ratio.

Lagerung storing, storage, stowage, housing, warehousing *(US)*;
während der ~ while storing;
unsachgemäße ~ careless storage;
~ **sicherungsübereigneter Waren** field warehousing *(US)*, custodian warehouse *(US)*; ~ **unter Zollverschluß** storing in a bonded warehouse *(US)*, warehousing under bond *(US)*.

Lagerungs|fähigkeit storage capacity; ~**gebühren** cost of storage, storage (storing) charges, stowage, warehousing expenses *(US)*; **übermäßige** ~**gebühren** excessive rates of storage; ~**geschäft** storage business, warehousing [business] *(US)*, warehouse line *(US)*; ~**kosten** storage charges, cost of storage, warehousing expenses *(US)*; ~**möglichkeit** storage accommodation (facilities); ~**möglichkeiten haben** to share storage (warehouse, *US*) facilities; ~**zinsen** storage interest.

Lager|veralterung obsolescence of stock; ~**verlust** shrinkage of stocks; ~**versicherung** warehouseman's liability insurance; ~**versicherung mit [vierteljährlicher] Bestandsmeldung** stock declaration policy; ~**versicherungspolice** stock policy; ~**vertretung** storage agency; ~**verwalter** storeroom (stock) clerk, stock manager, store keeper *(Br.)*, stockman *(US)*, warehouse keeper (manager) *(US)*, warehouseman *(US)*; ~**verzeichnis** inventory record (register); ~**vorarbeiter** storehouseman, warehouse foreman *(US)*; ~**vorrat** stock, supply; ~**vorrat in der Verkaufsabteilung** forward stock.

Lagervorräte stocks, stores;
geringe ~ low inventory;
~ **abbauen** to liquidate an inventory; **in** ~**n anlegen** to put into the inventory, to stockpile; ~ **ansammeln** to build up inventories; ~ **knapp bemessen** to keep down an inventory; **auf** ~**n festsitzen** to sit on stockpiles; **umfangreiche** ~ **haben** to carry heavy stock.

lagervorrätig carried in stock.

Lager|vorratssteuer floor tax; ~**vorrichtungen** storage (warehousing, *US*) accommodation (facilities); ~**vorschüsse** advance on warrants; ~**wache** *(mil.)* quarter guard *(Br.)*; ~**wachstum** stock growth; ~**waren** storage (warehouse, *US*) goods, stock [articles]; ~**wert** inventory value, stock figure; ~**wertveränderung** variation in inventory prices; ~**wirtschaft** trade of storing, updating of inventory, stockpiling; ~**zeit** time of storing, storing time; ~**zins** storage, warehouse rent *(US)*; ~**zugänge** incoming stocks, addition to stock; ~**zunahme** growth of inventory, inventory growth.

lagerzyklischer Aufschwung stepup in inventory growth.

Lagerzyklus inventory investment cycle, stock-building cycle;
~ **positiv beeinflussen** to step up the pace of stockbuilding (one's stockpiling pace).

Lage|skizze *(mil.)* sketch, map; ~**tisch** *(mil.)* operations board; ~**verbesserung** improvement in the situation; ~**zimmer** situation room *(US)*.

Lagune lagoon.

lahm lame, *(gelähmt)* paralyzed, crippled, *(Geschäfte)* slack, slackening, flagging, *(Hand)* numb;
j. krumm und ~ **schlagen** to give s. o. a brutal thrashing;
ziemlich ~**e Angelegenheit** pretty dull affair; ~**e Ente** lame (lazy) dog, lame duck, slow coach, slowpoke *(US coll.)*; ~**e Entschuldigung** lame (paltry, thin) excuse; ~**er Verein** moribund organization *(US)*.

lähmen to cripple, to petrify, to paralyse;
jds. Energie ~ to sap s. one's energy; **Industrie** ~ to paralise industry; **jds. Konzentration** ~ to numb s. one's concentration; **Sinne** ~ to deaden one's senses; **durch einen Streik** ~ to cripple by a strike; **Wirtschaft des Landes** ~ to cripple the nation's economy.

Lahmheit stiffness, *(Entschuldigung)* feebleness, weakness.

lahmlegen to black, to boycott, to petrify, to stymie, *(Handel)* to paralyse, to cripple, *(mil.)* to neutralize;
gegnerische Offensive ~ to neutralize the enemy offensive; **Verkehr** ~ to obstruct the traffic; **vollständig** ~ to bring to an absolute standstill; **Wirtschaft des Landes** ~ to cripple the nation's economy.

Lahmlegung blacking, boycott, paralysation, petrification, *(mil.)* neutralization.

Lähmung paralysation, crippling, *(Verkehr)* stoppage, obstruction, block;
~ **der Arbeitsbereitschaft durch Fürsorgeleistungen** poverty trap;
gegen die ~ **des Gesamtverkehrs angehen** to stave off traffic paralysis; ~ **der gesamten Stahlindustrie zur Folge haben** to paralise the whole steel industry.

Laie lay person, layman, outsider, nonexpert, dilettante;
auf diesem Gebiet ein absoluter ~ **sein** to be a greenhorn in this field.

Laien|bruder lay brother; ~**gesellschaft** lay corporation.

laienhaft lay, amateurish, dilettante;
~ **ausgedrückt** in layman's terms;
~ **ausgeführte Arbeit** amateurishly executed piece of work.

Laien|publikum general public; ~**richter** lay justice (judge, *US*); ~**spiel** amateur theatrical; ~**spielgruppe** drama group, amateur dramatics; ~**sprache** unprofessional language.

Lakai lackey, waiting man, flunkey *(US)*.

Lakaiennatur pampered menial.

Laken, frische clean sheets.

lakonische Kürze laconic brevity.

lallen *(Baby)* to babble, *(Betrunkener)* to mumble, to speak thickly, *(Kranker)* to mutter.

Lamelle *(Kühler)* fin, rib, *(Kupplung)* disk.

lamentieren to moan, to lament, to wail;
immerzu ~ to be everlastingly moaning; **über Kleinigkeiten** ~ to wail over trifles; **über seine Mißhelligkeiten** ~ to lament over one's misfortune.

Lametta silver tinsel, *(Orden)* old iron *(Br., sl.)*, fruit salad *(US sl.)*.

laminieren *(Buchbinderei)* to laminate.

Lamm lamb, kid;
so geduldig wie ein ~ **sein** to have the patience of Job (a saint).

Lämmerwolke cirrocumulus.

lammfromm as meek (mild) as a lamb.

Lampe lamp, *(Licht)* light;
im Verbrauch billige ~ low-consumption lamp;
~ **an der Decke aufhängen** to hang a lamp from the ceiling; ~ **ausmachen** to switch out the light; **neue** ~ **einschrauben** to screw in a new bulb; **sich einen auf die** ~ **gießen** to wet one's whistle; **mit** ~**n versehen** to lamp.

Lampen|docht lamp-wick; ~**fassung** lamp holder; ~**fieber** stage fright; ~**fieber haben** to have the go-fever; ~**halter** lamp bracket; ~**licht** lamplight; ~**schirm** lamp shade.

Lampion Chinese lantern.

lancieren to launch, to float;
j. ~ to start s. o. on a career, to carve out a career for (launch) s. o.; **Anleihe** ~ to float a loan; **Artikel in die Zeitung** ~ to get an article in the newspaper; **neues Ereignis** ~ to launch a new product; **Gerücht** ~ to float a rumo(u)r, to set a rumo(u)r afloat; **Gesellschaft** ~ to promote (organize) a company, to float a new business company; **Sache** ~ to push the boat out *(coll.)*; **j. in eine Stellung** ~ to pitchfork s. o. into a position.

lanciert werden to get a start in business.

Lancierung einer Anleihe floating (flotation) of a loan; ~ **eines Gerüchtes** floating a rumo(u)r; ~ **einer Gesellschaft** company promotion.

Land country, land, *(Ackerboden)* ground, soil, *(Gebiet)* territory, region, *(Grund und Boden)* [piece of] land, landed property, plot, lot *(US)*, *(Nation)* country, state, power, *(Staatsgebiet)* state;
an ~ **angeschwemmt** washed ashore; **auf dem** ~**e** down in the country, out of town *(Br.)*; **auf dem** ~**e aufgewachsen** grown up in the country; **aus dem ganzen** ~ from all over the country; **außer** ~**es** abroad; **bekannt in Stadt und** ~ known far and wide; **dicht am** ~**e** close inshore; **im** ~**e** at home; **im eigenen** ~**e** at home, native, inland; **im ganzen** ~ throughout the country (nation); **sich über das ganze** ~ **erstreckend** nation-wide; **über** ~ **und Meer** by land and sea; **vom** ~ **umschlossen** landlocked;
abgetretenes ~ ceded territory; **nicht akkreditiertes** ~ nonaccredited state; **anbaufähiges** ~ plowland *(US)*, ploughland *(Br.)*, arable land; **nicht anbaufähiges** ~ barren land; **angebautes** ~ cropland, farmland; **nicht dem Weltpostverein angehörendes** ~ nonunion country *(Br.)*; **angeschwemmtes** ~ alluvial soil, alluvion; **assoziiertes** ~ *(EG)* associated country; **aufgegebenes** ~ abandoned land; **baureifes** ~ building site (lot, *US*), developed land; **bebautes** ~ build-up area; **kommunistisch beherrschtes** ~ communist-ruled country; **bergbaufähiges** ~ mineral land; **bergiges** ~ mountainous country; **besetztes** ~ country under occupation; **besiedeltes** ~ settled country; **dicht besiedeltes** ~ densely populated region; **bestelltes** ~ cultivated (cleared) land, tillage; **am Verrechnungsabkommen [nicht] beteiligtes** ~ [non]clearing country; **bewaldetes** ~ forest, timber; **selbst bewirtschaftetes** ~ own (home) farm, demesne land; **nach wissenschaftlichen Erkenntnissen bewirtschaftetes** ~ land farmed on scientific principles; **brachliegendes** ~ fallow, waste building site; **nicht devisenbewirtschaftetes** ~ free (hard)-currency country; **devisenschwaches** ~ short-of-exchange country; **eigengenutztes** ~ demesne land; **grundbuchlich eingetragenes** ~ registered land; **einladendes** ~ inviting country; **enteignetes** ~ land taken; **privat erschlossenes** ~ privately-developed land; **wenig ertragreiches** ~ red-clay country; **festes** ~ dry land, continent; **fettes** ~ rich land; **finanzschwaches** ~ financially weak country; **finanzstarkes** ~ key financial nation; **flaches** ~ flat (level) country; **fruchtbares** ~ fertile soil; **zum Sterlingblock gehörendes** ~ scheduled territory *(Br.)*; **höher gelegenes** ~ upland; **urbar gemachtes** ~ cultivated (cleared) land; **forstwirtschaftlich genutztes** ~ forested land; **landwirtschaftlich genutztes** ~ agricultural land; **zugrunde gerichtetes** ~ prostrate country; **gerodetes** ~ cleared forest land; **hochentwickeltes** ~ advanced industrial country; **industrialisiertes** ~ industrialized country (nation); **hoch industrialisiertes** ~ highly developed country; **industrieschwaches** ~ less industrialized country; **keilförmiges Stück** ~ wedge; **für Zwangsenteignung in Frage kommendes** ~ land subject to compulsory acquisition; **kreditnehmendes** ~ borrowing country; **kriegführendes** ~ nation at war; **kriegszerstörtes** ~ war-worn country; **lieferndes** ~ country of delivery; **an der Grenze der Rentabilität liegendes** ~ marginal land; **melioriertes** ~ improved land; **rückständiges** ~ backward country; **schmales Stück** ~ strip of land; **Stück** ~ property, tract of land *(US)*; **Stückchen** ~ patch; **Ackerbau treibendes** ~ agrarian country; **überlassenes Stück** ~ concession; **unbebautes** ~ wild (new, *US*) land; **unfruchtbares** ~ barren (waste) land, infertile soil; **unterentwickeltes** ~ underdeveloped country; **urbares** ~ arable land; **valutaschwaches** ~ country with a low monetary standard, soft-currency country; **valutastarkes** ~ country with a high monetary standard, hard-currency country; **verpachtetes** ~ leased land; **währungsschwaches** ~ soft-currency country; **währungsstarkes** ~ strong (hard) -currency country; **das weite** ~ the open country; **wüstes** ~ waste land; **zugewiesenes** ~ grant *(US)*;
~ **mit Devisenbewirtschaftung** exchange-controlling country; ~ **mit Handelsbilanzüberschüssen** payments-surplus country; ~ **und Leute** a country and its inhabitants; ~, **wo Milch und Honig fließt** land flowing with milk and honey; ~ **mit Papierwährung** soft-currency country; ~ **der Verheißung** promised land; ~ **ohne Verrechnungsabkommen** nonclearing country; ~ **mit harter (stabiler) Währung** hard-currency country; ~ **des Wohnsitzes** country of established residence; ~ **mit einem Zahlungsbilanzüberschuß** creditor nation; ~ **ohne Zugang zum Meer** landlocked country;
der See ~ **abgewinnen** to reclaim land from the sea; **vom** ~**e abhalten** to lie off; **jem.** ~ **abnehmen** to conquer territories from s. o.; ~ **abstecken** to peg out; ~ **zu Vorratszwecken ankaufen** to acquire land in advance of development; ~ **anlaufen (ansteuern)** to make [the] land, to make for the shore; **Stellung an** ~ **annehmen** *(Seemann)* to swallow the anchor; ~ **ansteuern** to sight (lay) the land; **sich außerhalb des** ~**es aufhalten** to stay abroad; **auf dem** ~**e aufwachsen** to be brought up on a farm; ~ **ausmachen** to make land; ~ **bebauen (bestellen)** to cultivate the country, to till the land; **sich an** ~ **begeben** to put to land; ~ **nach und nach seiner Hilfsquellen berauben** to drain upon a country's resources; ~ **bereisen** to travel (pass) over a country, to tour a nation; **kleines Stück** ~ **besitzen** to have a small property in the country; ~ **bewilligen** to grant land; **400 Morgen** ~ **bewirtschaften** to farm 400 acres of land; **sich im** ~**e breitmachen** to overrun a country; **an** ~ **bringen** to put ashore, to disembark; ~ **wirtschaftlich wieder auf die Beine bringen** to put a country economically on its feet again; ~ **durchstreifen** to roam the country; **das ganze** ~ **erfassen** to be of a nation-wide scope; ~ **erforschen** to explore a country; ~ **oder Schiffsziele erkunden** *(mil.)* to spot positions of the enemy; ~ **für den Handel erschließen** to open a country to trade; ~ **erwerben** to buy some land, to homestead *(US)*; **an** ~ **gehen** to go ashore, to land, to disembark; **aufs** ~ **gehen** to go into the country; **außer** ~**es gehen** to leave the country for good, to go abroad, to abjure the state; **ins** ~ **gehen** *(Jahre)* to pass; ~ **gewinnen** to gain land from the sea, to reclaim land; **im** ~**e um sich greifen** to overrun the country; ~ **zu eigen haben** to hold land in fee; **sich dicht am** ~ **halten** to hug the land; **aufs** ~ **hinausfahren** to drive down into the country; ~ **politisch und wirtschaftlich völlig isolieren** to quarantine a country; ~ **auf Vorrat kaufen** to acquire land in advance of development; ~ **und Leute kennen** to see the world; ~ **ausbluten lassen** to bleed a country white; ~ **verarmen lassen** to impoverish a people; ~ **verfallen lassen** to allow land to go out of cultivation; ~ **brach liegen lassen** to allow land to lie fallow; **auf dem** ~**e leben** to live in the country; ~ **urbar machen** to cultivate the soil; **sich dem** ~**e nähern** to close with the land; ~ **in Kultur nehmen** to bring land under cultivation; **sich auf dem** ~**e niederlassen** to take up one's abode (establish o. s.) in the country; ~ **parzellieren** to divide (parcel out) land into smallholdings; ~ **pflügen** to plough (plow, *US*) the land; **über** ~ **reisen** to travel across country; **zu** ~**e reisen** to travel by land; **etw. außer** ~**es schmuggeln** to smuggle s. th. out of the country; **langsam** ~ **sehen** *(fig.)* to see daylight at last; **außer** ~**es sein** to be abroad (in foreign parts); **dem festen** ~ **vorgelagert sein** to be off the mainland; **Lotsen an** ~ **setzen** to land the pilot; ~ **sichten** to make (come in sight of) land; **für Ruhe und Ordnung im** ~ **sorgen** to maintain law and order; **vom** ~ **stammen** to originate from the country; **ins** ~ **übergehen** *(Vorort)* to fringe into the country; **aufs** ~ **umziehen** to move into the country; ~ **veräußern** to dispose of land; ~ **vergewaltigen** to throttle the freedom in a country; ~ **in einem Stück verkaufen** to sell land as a whole; ~ **verlassen** to get out of a country; ~ **für immer verlassen** to leave the country for good; ~ **aus der Sicht verlieren** to lose sight of the land; ~ **vermessen** to survey a district; **Belange eines** ~**es vertreten** to represent a country; **des** ~**es verweisen** to exile; **Ausländer des** ~**es verweisen** to expel an alien; ~ **für öffentliche Zwecke verwenden** to reduce land to public use; **aufs** ~ **vordringen** *(Meer)* to encroach upon the land; **vom** ~**e wegziehen** to abandon the countryside; **an** ~ **getrieben (geschwemmt) werden** to be washed ashore; **aus dem** ~**e gewiesen werden** to be banished from the country; **auf dem** ~**e wohnen** to dwell in the country; **ungestört auf dem** ~**e**

wohnen to be deeply buried in the countryside; **aufs ~ ziehen** to move into the country; **Boot an ~ ziehen** to beach a boat; **sich eine reiche Frau an ~ ziehen** to hook a rich wife; **Millionär an ~ ziehen** to catch a millionaire; **aufs ~ zuhalten** to bear with the land; **sich wieder auf dem ~e zurechtfinden** to get on one's land legs; **sich aufs ~ zurückziehen** to go to grass, to bury o. s. in the country, to rusticate, to ruralize; **~ zuweisen** to assign (grant) land;
~abfindung land damages, compensation money *(US)*; **~abgabe** surrender of land; **~abschnitt** section of land *(US)*; **~adel** landed aristocracy (gentry, *Br.*); **~ankauf** land purchase; **~anker** shore anchor; **~anschlag** *(Werbung)* rural areas posting; **~anwachs** alluvion; **~arbeit** agricultural (farm) labo(u)r, farm work; **~arbeit verrichten** to be at the ploughtail.
Landarbeiter agricultural (rural, farm, country) worker, farm labo(u)rer (boy), farmhand *(US)*, hired (field) hand, village farmer, labo(u)rer in husbandry, cottager *(Br.)*;
~ auf Naturallohnbasis tasker, sharecropper *(US)*;
~ sein to work on the land;
~knappheit shortage of agricultural workers; **~lohn** agricultural (farm) wage; **~schaft** farm force; **~tarif** wage scale for farm workers; **~wohnung** farm labo(u)rer's cottage.
Landarzt country doctor.
landauf, landab all over the country.
Land|aufenthalt stay in the country, rustification; **~aufkauf** *(spekulativ)* land-grabbing; **spekulativer ~aufkäufer** land-grabber; **~aufnahme** survey of land, surveying, ordnance survey *(Br.)*; **~aufteilung** land subdivision, division of land.
landaus, landein far and wide.
Land|ausnutzung land use; **~bau** agriculture, husbandry; **~bauschule** agricultural college; **~beschaffung** private land grant; **~besitz** landholding, landed property (estate), realty, estate; **gemeinsamer ~besitz** multiple tenure; **großer ~besitz** extensive grounds; **~besitzer** landowner, landed proprietor; **~bestellbezirk** rural delivery (country, *Br.*) district; **~bevölkerung** rural population, country people; **~bewilligung** grant of land; **~bewohner** countryman, country dweller, landman, hind *(Br.)*; **~bezirk** rural (country) district *(Br.)*; **~briefträger** rural postman (carrier, *US*); **~brot** coarse brown bread; **~brücke** landbridge; **~butter** farm butter.
Lande|anflug landing approach, approach flight; **~anfluggerät** homing device; **~anweisung** landing instructions; **~automatik** automatic landing system.
Landebahn *(Flugzeug)* airstrip, landing strip, runway *(Br.)*, apron;
behelfsmäßige ~ und Startbahn flight strip;
über die ~ hinausschießen to overshoot the runway;
~leuchte landing floodlight, runway light; **~sicht** runway visual range.
Lande|bake airport (approach) beacon; **~bedingungen** landing conditions; **~bremsschirm** brake (air-brake) parachute; **~brücke** landing stage, jetty, pier; **schwimmende ~brücke** float; **~deck** *(Flugzeug)* flight (landing) deck *(US)*.
Landedelmann gentleman farmer, squire *(Br.)*.
Lande|einrichtungen landing facilities; **~einschränkungen** restrictions on landing; **~erlaubnis** permission to land, landing permit (clearance); **~erlaubnis erteilen** to clear up for full-stop landing; **auf ~erlaubnis warten** *(Flugzeug)* to stooge around; **~fackel** wing-tip flare; **~fähre** ferry rocket; **~fallschirm** air-brake (brake) parachute; **~feld** landing ground; **~feuer** landing light, airport beacon; **~fläche** landing area; **~flughafen** airport of arrival; **~funkfeuer** airport (approach) beacon; **~gebiet** *(mil.)* landing area; **~gebühr** landing fee (charge); **~- und Wartegebühren** landing and service charges; **~genehmigung** *(Flugzeug)* permission to land, landing permit (clearance); **~geschwindigkeit** landing speed; **~gestell** landing chassis (gear).
Land|eigentümer landed proprietor, landowner; **~einfriedung** enclosure.
landeingeschlossen landlocked.
landeinwärts inland, towards the interior, upward, up country; **~ gehen** to go inland; **~ gelegen** landward; **~ marschieren** to march up-country.
Landeinweisung extension of title.
Lande|karte landing ticket; **~klappe** flap; **~knüppel** *(Flugzeug)* landing gear; **~kopf** beachhead; **~kosten** landing charges; **~kreuz** air tree; **~kufe** skid; **~kurs** approach path; **~kurssender** localizer; **~licht** aerodrome beacon, approach (landing) light; **~manöver** landing, alighting, touchdown; **~möglichkeit** *(Flugzeug)* landing strip.
Landen landing, *(Flugzeug)* landfall, landing, alighting.
landen to land, to touch land, to debark, to disembark, to dock, *(Ballon)* to drop to earth, *(Flugzeug)* to alight, to make (effect) a landing, to land, to roll out, to descend, to come (touch, put) down *(US)*;
schließlich im Ehehafen ~ to end up by marrying; **fahrplanmäßig ~** to put down on the airport in time, *(Schiff)* to land according to schedule *(US)*; **glatt ~** to touch down (land) smoothly, to make a good landing; **glücklich ~** to make a safe landing; **in einem Hafen ~** to fetch up at a port; **weich auf dem Mond ~** to make a soft landing on the moon; **bei jem. damit nicht ~** to cut no ice with s. o.; **im Papierkorb ~** to end up in the wastepaper basket; **bei der Polizei ~** to end up in a police court; **nach mehrfachem Berufswechsel bei der Polizei ~** to land after changing one's occupation several times finally in the police force; **großen Schlag ~** to score a big success, to strike twelve; **schlecht ~** to make a bad landing; **sicher ~** to make a safe landing, to land an airliner safely; **im Straßengraben ~** to be ditched; **Truppen ~** to disembark troops; **auf dem Wasser ~** to alight on the water, to land on the sea, *(Raumkapsel)* to splash down on the water.
Landenge neck, isthmus.
Lande|pfad *(Flugzeug)* approach path; **~piste** landing strip, runway; **~plan** *(mil.)* landing schedule; **~platz** landing place (platform, site), quay, wharf, pier, *(Flugzeug)* landing field (ground), *(mil.)* landing area; **~punkt** touchdown point.
Länder, aus aller Herren from all quarters of the globe;
lange besiedelte ~ old countries; **devisenschwache ~** soft-currency countries; **englischsprechende ~** English-speaking countries; **Erdöl exportierende ~** oil exporters; **hoch industrialisierte ~** highly developed countries; **kriegszerstörte ~** war-worn countries; **unter kommunistischer Herrschaft stehende ~** countries of Communist obedience;
~ mit Devisenkontrolle exchange-controlling countries; **~ mit mittlerer Finanzierungskraft** middle-income countries; **~ des Sterlingblocks** scheduled territories *(Br.)*; **~ ohne Verrechnungsabkommen** nonclearing countries; **~ der dritten Welt** third-world countries;
mit anderen ~n konkurrieren to compete with other countries; **zwei ~ miteinander verbinden** to bind two countries together.
Lande|rad undercarriage wheel; **~rakete** ferry rocket.
Länder|anteil *(Weltwährungsfonds)* country share; **~bank** state bank.
länderbesteuert state-taxed.
Länderbesteuerung [etwa] state taxation *(US)*.
Landerecht landing rights.
Ländereien land, landed property (estate), grounds;
angrenzende ~ dependencies of an estate; **ausgedehnte ~** broad lands; **staatliche ~** government land; **umfangreiche ~** extensive grounds; **vom Grundstücksbesitzer selbst verwaltete ~** demesne, manor house;
~ aufteilen to make purparty; **von großen ~ umgeben sein** to have extensive grounds.
Länder|grenze national border; **~gruppe** country group; **~haushalt** state budget *(US)*; **~komplex** group of countries comprised; **~kunde** regional geography; **~mittel** government grants; **~risiko** country risks.
Landerschließung exploitation of a country, development.
Landerschließungsvorhaben real-estate development project.
Länder|spiel *(Sport)* international; **~staatsangehörigkeit** state citizenship *(US)*.
Landerwerb land acquisition, *(spekulativ)* land-grabbing.
Landerziehungsheim boarding school.
Landes|abgaben internal (state, *US*) taxes; **statistisches ~amt** statistical office; **~angehöriger** subject, citizen, national; **~angehörigkeit** citizenship; **~anleihe** domestic loan; **~arbeitsamt** regional labo(u)r office (exchange) *(Br.)*; **~aufnahme** Ordnance Survey *(Br.)*; **~aufsichtsamt für das Kreditwesen** bank commissioner *(US)*; **~aufsichtsamt für das Versicherungswesen** Insurance Commissioner; **~bank** regional (state) *(US)* bank; **~bedarf** home consumption; **~bedarf decken** to supply the needs of the country; **~behörden** [etwa] regional authorities; **~beschreibung** topography; **~besteuerung** state taxation *(US)*; **~brauch** general custom, custom of the country, custom of the Realm *(Br.)*.
Landeschein landing account (certificate, ticket);
~werfer landing lights.
Landesdarlehn, grundbuchlich gesichertes option mortgage *(Br.)*.
landeseigen state-owned, government-owned.
Landes|erzeugnisse home produce, native products, products of a country; **~fabrikate** domestic manufactures; **~farben, ~flagge** national colo(u)rs; **~flagge** national flag.

landesflüchtig fugitive;
~ **werden** to flee from a country.

Landes|gebiet territory; ~**geschäftsstelle einer Vereinigung** provincial branch of an association; ~**gesetzgebung** internal legislation; ~**gesundheitsamt** executive council; ~**grenze** land border, national boundary *(US)*; ~**gruppe** national committee; ~**hauptkasse** paymaster's office; **hauptstadt** capital, chief town of a country; ~**haushalt** state budget; ~**herr** sovereign, ruler; ~**hoheit** sovereignty; ~**industrie** home industry.

Landesinnere depth of a country, hinterland;
ins ~ inland, upward, towards the interior;
sich ins ~ **begeben** to get up country;
~ **erforschen** to explore the inland.

Landes|interesse national interest; ~**kind** native; ~**kirche** Established Church *(Br.)*; ~**kultur** land improvements; ~**kulturkredit** improvement loan; ~**kulturplan** reclamation project; ~**liste** [etwa] regional list; ~**listensystem** [etwa] regional list system; ~**meister** national champion; ~**minister** state minister; ~**mittel** regional aid funds *(Br.)*; ~**münze** inland coin; ~**planung** regional planning (development).

Landesplanungs|amt regional economic planning board *(Br.)*; ~**rat** regional economic planning council *(Br.)*; ~**stelle** regional planning agency.

Landes|produkte home (inland) commodities, inland produce, domestics, produce of the country; ~**prüfungsausschuß** regional examining body; ~**rechnungshof** board of audit; ~**recht** national (domestic) law; ~**regierung** national (state, *US*) government; ~**schlichter** [etwa] National Wage Board *(Br.)*; ~**schuld** national debt; ~**sitte** general (national) custom; ~**sitten und Gebräuche** custom of the country (realm, *Br.*); ~**sozialgericht** [etwa] Local Appeal Tribunal *(Br.)*; ~**sprache** national (vernacular) language, vernacular; ~**steuerausschuß** state tax commission *(US)*; ~**steuern** state taxes.

Landesteg landing platform (ramp).

Landes|teil quarter, region; ~**tracht** national dress.

Landestrahl landing beam.

Landestrauer national mourning.

Lande|strecke alighting run; ~**streifen** air (flight) strip.

landesüblich customary, usual, vulgar;
~**er Zinsfuß** usual rate of interest.

Landes|universität regional college, provincial (state, *US*) university; **in der** ~**valuta** in the legal currency of a country; ~**verband einer Gewerkschaft** central labor union *(US)*; ~**vermessung** ordnance survey *(Br.)*; **amtliche** ~**vermessung** Ordnance Survey *(Br.)*; ~**verrat** high treason, parricide; ~**verrat begehen** to commit treason; ~**verräter** traitor to his country, war traitor, parricider.

landesverräterisch treasonable, parricidal;
~**e Konspiration** treasonable negotiation; **in** ~**er Weise reden** to talk treason.

Landes|verratsprozeß treason trial; ~**versicherungsamt** regional insurance office; ~**verteidigung** national defence; ~**verweisung** exile, ban, deportation, banishment; ~**währung** home (legal, local, national, domestic) currency, current (lawful, *US*) money, money of account; **in der** ~**währung** in the legal currency of the country; **gängige** ~**währung** current coin of the realm *(Br.)*; ~**zeit** zone time.

Landeszentralbank [etwa] Federal Reserve Bank *(US)*;
fast alle Einrichtungen der ~ **in Anspruch nehmen** to get most of the Federal Reserve services *(US)*; **Konto bei der** ~ **unterhalten** to have a special deposit with the Bank of England *(Br.)*, to have a deposit account with the Federal Reserve Bank *(US)*.

landeszentralbankfähige Verbindlichkeiten auf Einlagekonten eligible deposit liabilities.

Landeszentralbank|gesetz [etwa] Federal Reserve Act *(US)*; ~**guthaben** [etwa] balance with the Bank of England *(Br.)*, deposit account with the Federal Reserve Bank *(US)*; ~**guthaben in Höhe von 1/8 für besondere Barguthaben unterhalten** to back every £ 100 of extra cash which one holds with an extra of £ 12.50 of reserve assets; ~**kredit** Federal Reserve credit *(US)*; ~**präsident** Federal Reserve Agent *(US)*; ~**zahlen** Federal Reserve figures *(US)*.

Landeszugehörigkeit nationality.

Lande|triebwerk *(Mondfähre)* lunar module engine; ~**trupp** landing party; ~**überwachungsradar** approach surveyance radar; ~**verbot** landing restriction; ~**verfahren** approach (landing) system; ~**vorhersage** landing forecast; ~**zeichen** landing mark; ~**zone** landing area, *(Fallschirm)* dropping zone.

land|fein machen, sich to spruce o. s. up; ~**fest gewordene Insel** tied island.

Land|flucht drift from the land, rural exodus, migration from the countryside; **von der Industrialisierung ausgelöste** ~**flucht** industry-induced exodus from farm to factory; ~**flugzeug** landplane; ~**fracht** land carriage, conveyance by land; ~**frachtvertrag** contract of carriage; ~**frau** country woman, farmwife.

landfremd alien, foreign.

Land|frieden King's peace; ~**friedensbruch** affray, violation of law and order, unlawful assembly, mobbing and rioting *(Scot.)*; ~**friedensbruch begehen** to break the peace; ~**funk** agricultural program(me); **feste** ~**funkstelle** ground station; ~**gang** gangway, shore leave; ~**gangsausweis** liberty ticket; ~**gangsgelder** seaman's shore allowance; **weite** ~**gebiete** extensive territories; ~**gendarm** rural policeman; ~**gemeinde** rural community (township, *US*), county borough *(Br.)*; ~**gericht** [etwa] district (county) court, Court of Common Pleas *(US)*; ~**gerichtsrat** [etwa] district judge.

landgestützt *(mil.)* land based.

Land|gewinnung land reclamation, reclamation of land; ~**gewinnungsprojekt** reclamation project; ~**gut** country seat, estate; **ganz hübsches** ~**gut** tidy farm; ~**handel** land-borne trade; ~**haus** country house, country seat, chalet, *(klein)* cottage, country box *(Br.)*; **altertümliches** ~**haus** old-world cottage; **strohgedecktes** ~**haus** thatched cottage; ~**heer** land army (forces); ~**hunger** land hunger.

landhungrig land-hungry.

Land|jugend rural youth; ~**karte** map; **kostenlose** ~**karte zur Umgehung von Verkehrsstauungen** free beat-the-jam map; **seine Reiseroute auf der** ~**karte einzeichnen** to trace [out] one's route on the map; ~**kartenzeichner** map maker, cartographer; ~**kauf** land purchase; ~**konzession** concession of land; ~**korridor** land corridor; ~**kreis** [etwa] administrative county *(Br.)*, rural borough *(Br.)*, rural district; ~**krieg** land warfare.

landläufig general, generally accepted;
~**er Ausdruck** widely-used expression; ~**e Meinung** general opinion; **im** ~**en Sinn** in popular usage.

Landleben country life;
sich auf das ~ **umstellen** to ruralize.

ländlich rural, agricultural, countrylike, rustic, pastoral, *(kleinstädtisch)* small-townish, crossroad *(US)*;
~-**sittlich** untouched by civilization;
in ~**er Abgeschiedenheit leben** to live in rural seclusion; ~**er Bezirk** country (rural) district; ~**e Einfachheit** rustic simplicity; ~**e Gebiete** rural sections, grassroots *(US)*; ~**e Gegend** rural (country) area, rural district *(Br.)*, grassroots *(US)*; ~**e Kreditgenossenschaft** agricultural credit corporation; ~**es Leben** country life, rustication; ~**es Leben führen** to rusticate; ~**e Szene** pastoral; ~**e Verbraucherschaft** agricultural clientele.

Land|luft country air; ~**macht** continental power; ~**marke** *(mar.)* landmark, mark; ~**maschinen** agricultural machinery, farm equipment (implement); ~**messer** surveyor; ~**mine** land mine; **ständige** ~**nahme durch das Meer** the ocean's steady usurpation of the land; ~**nahmeschein** float *(US)*; ~**nebel** inland fog; ~**nutzung** use of land; ~**pacht** tenure of land, agricultural (farm) tenancy, lease, homestead lease *(Australia)*; ~**partie** excursion into the country, rural excursion, junket, junketing party; ~**partie machen** to make a sally into (pop down to) the country, to go about the country, to junket; ~**parzelle** plot of land, lot *(US)*; ~**pfeiler** *(Brücke)* end abutment; ~**plage** *(fig.)* pest, plague, public nuisance; ~**polizei** rural police; ~**polizist** rural policeman; ~**pomeranze** country wench; **freie** ~**postzustellung** rural-free delivery; ~**rat** [etwa] county officer; ~**ratte** landman, landlubber, lubber; ~**recht** common law; ~**reform** land reform; ~**route** overland route; ~**rücken** ridge, swell.

Landschaft landscape, countryside, scenery, *(Bezirk)* land, province, rural borough (district), country, territory;
hügelige ~ hilly country; **gegenwärtige politische** ~ current political scenery; **zersiedelte** ~ subtopia;
sich gut der ~ **anpassen** to fit well into the landscape; ~ **charakterisieren** to feature a landscape; ~ **verschandeln** to be a blot on the landscape.

landschaftlich scenic, regional;
~ **verschieden** scenically different;
~ **verschönern** to landscape; ~ **verunstalten** to be a blot on a landscape;
~**e Beschaffenheit** topography of an area; ~**e Formen** topographical features; ~**e Schönheit** scenic beauty.

Landschafts|bild landscape, panorama; ~**bilder malen** to paint landscapes; ~**film** scenic film, scenerical; ~**gärtnerei** landscape architecture *(US)*; ~- **und Freizeitgelände** scenic and recreational property; ~**gestalter** landscape gardener; ~**gestal-**

tung landscape gardening; ~**maler** landscape painter, landscapist; **hervorstechende ~merkmale** outstanding features of a landscape; ~**schutzamt** Countryside Commission *(Br.)*; ~**schutzgebiet** Area of outstanding Natural Beauty *(Br.)*, natural reserve; ~**verband** agricultural association.

Land | schenkung land grant; ~**schule** village school; ~**senkung** subsidence.

Landser private, footslogger, Tommy Atkins *(Br.)*, dogface *(US sl.)*.

Landsitz country seat, manor, demesne, country site (house, retreat, home, estate), residence;
hübscher ~ nice place in the country.

Lands | knecht, wie ein ~knecht fluchen to swear like a trooper; ~**leute** fellow countrymen; ~**mann** fellow patriot (countryman); ~**mannschaft** compatriotism.

Landspitze headland, cape.

Landstraße country lane, country (local, parish, public, main) road, public way, common highway, highroad;
an der ~ gelegen roadside;
angrenzende ~ adjoining highway; **offene ~** open road;
~ erster Ordnung main highway, classified *(Br.)* (primary) road;
~ entlangtrotten to peg the highway; **zur ~ erster Ordnung erheben** to classify a road *(Br.)*; **~ instandhalten** to keep a highway in repair; **von der ~ verschwunden sein** to have slid off the map.

Landstreicher vagabond, vagrant, tramp, tramper, vag *(sl.)*, rogue *(Br.)*, hobo *(US)*, prowler, runabout, rover, hedge bird, bum *(US sl.)*.

Landstreicherei vagrancy, vagabondage, hoboism *(US)*.

Landstreicher | jargon hobo use *(US)*; ~**lager** jungle *(sl.)*, hobo camp *(US)*; **richtiges ~leben führen** to be for ever on the prowl; ~**roman** novel of a hobo life *(US)*; ~**tum** vagrancy, hoboism *(US)*.

Landstreifen tract [of land];
in kleine ~ aufteilen to separate into small fields.

Landstreitkräfte *(mil.)* land forces, land army.

Landstrich tract of land, region, country, province, district;
überfluteter ~ overflowed land;
~ urbar machen to clear the ground.

Land | stück tract [of land]; ~**sturm** *(mil.)* home reserves, posse comitatus; **~- und Seestützpunkt** amphibious base; ~**tag** diet, [etwa] state assembly.

Landtags | abgeordneter member of a diet; ~**sitzung** diet; ~**wahlen** state (regional) elections.

Landtechnik agricultural engineering.

Landtransport conveyance (carriage) by land, land carriage;
~**risiko** land risk; ~**versicherung** transport insurance.

Landung landing, *(Ausladung)* discharge, *(Ausschiffung)* debarkation, disembarkation, *(Flugzeug)* landing, landfall, alighting, descent, touchdown, arrival;
erzwungene ~ forced landing; **glatte ~** safe landing; **mißglückte ~** balked landing *(US)*; **weiche ~** smooth landing;
~ mit Bodensicht contact landing; **~ auf dem Mond** lunar landing; **~ mit abgestelltem Motor** dead-stick landing;
zur ~ ansetzen to come in to land, to stand by for descent; **einer feindlichen ~ Widerstand leisten** to dispute a landing by the enemy; **glatte ~ machen** to make a good landing; **harte ~ machen** to land too heavily; **Flugzeug zur ~ zwingen** to force a plane down.

Landungs | abteilung *(mil.)* landing party; ~**bake** approach beacon; ~**boot** landing craft (ship); **flaches ~boot** flat-bottomed boat, beetle boat *(Br.)*; **kleines ~boot** assault boat; ~**brücke** ferry bridge, landing stage, jetty, pier, gangplank; **schwimmende ~brücke** floating pier, float; ~**fahrzeug** ramp boat; **großes ~fahrzeug** assault ship; ~**gebiet** *(mil.)* landing area; ~**gestell** landing gear; ~**gewicht** *(Flugzeug)* landing weight; ~**hafen** port of landing, *(Flugzeug)* port of call; ~**karte** landing ticket; ~**korps** *(mil.)* landing detachment; ~**kosten** landing charges; ~**mast** *(Luftschiff)* mooring mast; ~**offizier** beachmaster; ~**rolle** *(Schiff)* landing bill; ~**trupp** *(mil.)* landing force, landing party *(Br.)*; ~**unternehmen** landing operation; ~**versuch** *(mil.)* attempted landing; ~**vorgang** *(mil.)* landing operation; ~**welle** *(mil.)* landing wave; ~**zoll** quayage.

Land | urlaub shore leave, free gangway, liberty ticket; ~**verbesserung** land improvements; ~**verbindung** land link; ~**verkehr** land transport; **~- und Binnenwasserverkehr** surface traffic; ~**vermessung** ordnance survey, surveying, land measuring; ~**verschickung** evacuation of inhabitants; ~**verteilung** distribution of land, land grant *(US)*; ~**volk** country folk, grassroots *(US)*; ~**vorsprung** headland.

landwärts onshore.

Land | wasserflugzeug sea and land aircraft, amphibian plane; ~**weg** country lane, farm road, overland route; **auf dem ~wege** by land, overland; **auf dem ~wege verschicken** to send by land; ~**wehr** militia, territorial army *(Br.)*; ~**wehrbezirk** militia district; ~**wehrmann** territorial *(Br.)*; ~**wein** wine of the country; ~**wind** offshore wind, breeze.

Landwirt peasant [proprietor], farmer, husbandman, granger, cultivator;
über den Eigenbedarf hinaus produzierender ~ commercial farmer; **selbständiger ~** owner-farmer, dirt farmer *(US coll.)*; **verschuldeter ~** farm debtor.

Land- und Forstwirte farmers and foresters.

Landwirtschaft agriculture, rural economy (economics), farming, husbandry, *(Anwesen)* farm, estate;
industriell betriebene ~ factory farm; **intensive ~** intensive cultivation; **mechanisierte ~** mechanized farming, motorized agriculture; **praktische ~** practical agriculture;
~ betreiben to farm, to be engaged in farming; **in der ~ tätig sein** to work on a farm; **~ subventionieren** to featherbed (carry, *US*) the farmers.

landwirtschaftlich agricultural, rural, agrarian, farming;
~**e Absatzorganisation** agricultural marketing association; ~**e Aktienbanken** joint-stock land banks; ~**e Anlagen** agricultural assets; ~**er Arbeiter** farm worker, farmhand, agricultural labo(u)rer; ~**e Arbeitskräfte** agricultural workforce; ~**e Ausstellung** agricultural fair (show); ~**e Bauten** farm (agricultural) buildings; ~**er Beratungsdienst** Agricultural Advisory Service *(Br.)*; ~**e Beschäftigung** agricultural employment; **~ genutzter Besitz** agricultural holding; ~**er Betrieb** farm, agricultural enterprise (estate); ~**e Betriebseinheit** agricultural unit; ~**e Betriebseinrichtung** agricultural plant; ~**e Betriebsfläche** agricultural area, farm land (real estate); ~**e Betriebsführung** farming [business], farm management *(US)*; ~**e Betriebsgenossenschaft** agricultural cooperative society; ~**e Betriebslehre** agricultural economics; ~**es Betriebsvermögen** farming stock; **~ genutzter Boden** area under cultivation, cultivated land; ~**er Eigenbetrieb** home (owner-operated, *US*) farm; ~**er Erschließungskredit** farming development loan; ~**er Erzeugerpreis** agricultural (farm) price; ~**e Erzeugnisse** farm (agricultural) produce (products), agricultural commodities; ~**e Erzeugung** agricultural production; ~**e Fachzeitschrift** farm publication, agricultural paper; ~**er Familienbetrieb** family-sized farm; ~**e Gebäude** farm buildings; **~ genutztes Gebäude** agricultural (farmyard) building, farmery *(Br.)*; ~**es Gebiet** agricultural (rural) district; **auf ~em Gebiet** in the field of agriculture; ~**e Gebiete** rural sections; ~**e Gegend** agricultural area; ~**e Genossenschaft** farmers' cooperative, agricultural cooperation, farming association; ~**e Genossenschaftsbank** farm loan bank, agricultural credit society; ~**es Genossenschaftswesen** Federal Farm Loan System *(US)*; ~**e Geräte** farm implements (utensils); ~**er Großbetrieb** farming on a large scale, large farming; ~**e Hochschule** agricultural (land) college; ~**es Hypothekendarlehen** farm mortgage; ~**es Institut** farmer's institute; ~**es Inventar** farm stock; ~**er Kleinbesitz** small holding *(Br.)*; ~**er Kredit** agricultural credit, farm loan; ~**e Kreditbank** Agricultural Credit Corporation *(US)*; ~**e Kreditgenossenschaft** agricultural credit corporation; ~**es Kreditinstitut** agricultural credit organization, farm credit agency *(US)*; ~**es Kreditwesen** farm credit system; ~**e Maschinen** farm implements (equipment), agricultural machinery; ~**er Musterbetrieb** model farm; ~**er Nebenbetrieb** part-time farm, small farming; ~**e Nebenerwerbssiedlung** homestead *(US)*, homecraft *(Br.)*; ~**e Nebengebäude** outlying farm buildings; ~**e Notlage** agricultural depression; ~**es Nutzland** area under cultivation; ~**er Pachtvertrag** farm lease; ~**e Pfandbriefe** farm loan bonds; ~**es Produkt** agricultural (farm) product; ~**e Produktion** farm output; ~**e Tarifzugeständnisse** farm concessions; ~**e Tätigkeit** farming operations; ~**e Überschußprodukte** farm surpluses; ~**er Verlustbetrieb** submarginal farm; ~**es Vermögen** agricultural property; ~**e Vermögenswerte** agricultural assets; ~**e Verschuldung** rural indebtedness; ~**e Versicherung** agricultural insurance; ~**e Zwecke** farming purposes.

Landwirtschafts | ausstellung agricultural show (fair); ~**bank** land (farmer's, agricultural, rural) bank, farm loan bank; **staatliche ~bank** Federal Land Bank *(US)*; ~**bank auf Aktien** joint-stock land bank *(US)*; ~**betrieb** agricultural enterprise, farming business; **automatisch bewässerter ~betrieb** sprinkler-irrigated farm; **vollmechanisierter und völlig durchorganisierter ~betrieb**

highly mechanized and intensively cultivated farm; ~**blatt** farm publication, agricultural paper; ~**darlehn** agricultural loan; ~**dollar** *(EG)* green money; ~**erzeugnisse** farm (agricultural) products; **preisgestützte ~erzeugnisse** basic crops *(US)*.

landwirtschaftsfreundlich proagriculture *(US)*.

Landwirtschafts|gebiet farming region; ~**hochschule** agricultural college, Aggie *(US)*; ~**institut** Farmer's Institute *(US)*; ~**kammer** Chamber of Agriculture; ~**kommissar** *(EG)* farm commissioner; ~**kredit** agricultural credit, farm loan; ~**krise** depression in agriculture; ~**lehre** agricultural economics; ~**messe** agricultural fair (show); ~**minister** Agriculture Minister *(Br.)*, Minister of Agriculture *(Br.)*, Secretary of Agriculture *(US)*, farm minister; ~**ministerium** Agricultural Department *(US)*, Department *(US)* (Board, *Br.*) of Agriculture; ~**politik** agrarian policy; ~**schule** agricultural college; ~**verband** agricultural association.

Land|zugang land corridor; ~**zukauf** addition *(US)*; ~**zunge** tongue (neck) of land, headland; ~**zustellbezirk** rural delivery district; ~**zusteller** rural postman; ~**zustellung** rural service; **freier ~zustellungsdienst** rural free delivery; ~**zuteilung** assignment of land, grant of land *(US)*, land grant *(US)*; ~**zuteilungssystem** allotment *(Br.)* (land-grant, *US*) system; ~**zuwachs** accruer (accretion) of land; ~**zuweisung** assignment of land, land grant *(US)*, grant-in-aid *(US)*.

Landzuweisungs|schein, ~urkunde land warrant (scrip, patent, *US*); ~**system** allotment *(Br.)* (land-grant, *US*) system; ~**urkunde** land patent *(US)*; ~**verfahren** allotment system *(Br.)*, land grant procedure *(US)*.

lang, über kurz oder sooner or later; **~e nach Mitternacht** well past midnight;
 sich ~ und breit über etw. auslassen to dwell at great length on a subject; **Geschichte ~ und breit erzählen** to tell a story in great detail; **nicht erst ~e um Erlaubnis fragen** not to bother to ask for permission; **sich ~e hinziehen** to linger, to drag on; **sich ~e bitten lassen** to need a lot of asking; **j. ~e warten lassen** to let s. o. cool his heels; **~e schlafen** to sleep late; **~e abwesend sein** to be away for long; **noch ~e kein Beweis sein** to be no proof at all; **noch ~e nicht fertig sein** to have not nearly finished; **noch ~e nicht gut sein** to be by no means good; **~ ziehen** *(Wechsel)* to draw a long-dated bill;
 da kannst du ~e warten you may whistle for it;
 ~e Arbeitszeit long hours; **~er Aufenthalt** extended stay; **auf die ~e Bank schieben** to put into cold storage (on the shelf); **~er Besuch** extended visit; **übermäßig ~er Besuch** long drawn-out visit; **~e Finger machen** to be light-fingered, to pilfer; **~es Gesicht machen** to pull a long face; **~en Hals machen** to crane one's neck; **von ~er Hand vorbereiten** to prepare carefully; **nach ~en Jahren** after many years; **~e bestehendes Konto** long-standing account; **~e Krankheit** protracted illness; **~e Latte** bean pole; **~e Leitung haben** to be slow on the uptake; **~e Liste** long list; **nach ~em Nachdenken** after thinking twice; **mit ~er Nase abziehen** to go away with a long face; **jem. eine ~e Nase machen** to make a long nose at s. o.; **der ~en Rede kurzer Sinn** the long and the short of it; **auf ~e Sicht** long-dated, over the long pull; **auf ~e Sicht planen** to plan well ahead; **lieben ~en Tag faulenzen** to laze away one's time; **~er Wechsel** long-dated bill; **mit ~en Zähnen essen** to pick at one's food; **in nicht allzu ~er Zeit** in the not too distant future; **vor ~er Zeit** a long time ago; **~e Zeit für eine Übersetzung benötigen** to take a long time to do a translation; **~es Ziel** long term.

lang anhaltender|Beifall prolongued applause; **~ Regen** sustained rain; **~ Schaden** protracted loss.

langatmig long-winded, lengthy;
 ~e Beschreibung lengthy description; **~e Erklärung** long-drawn explanation; **~e Reden führen** to be a long-winded talker.

Länge length, extent, *(geographisch)* longitude;
 auf die ~ gesehen from a long-range point of view;
 ~ in Meilen mil(e)age, footage;
 Interview in seiner vollen ~ abdrucken to print an interview at full length; **in die ~ schießen** to be shooting up; **in die ~ ziehen** *(Debatte)* to protract; **sich in die ~ ziehen** to linger, to drag on, *(Geschichte)* to wear on, *(Verhandlungen)* to be of a protracted nature; **Geschichte in die ~ ziehen** to spin out a story.

langen to reach;
 jem. eine ~ to fetch s. o. one; **Brief aus seiner Tasche ~** to produce a letter from one's pocket; **mit 100 DM nicht weit ~** not to go far with DM 100; **für ein paar Tage ~** to do for a couple of days;
 damit nicht ~ können not to be able to manage on it.

Längen|bestimmung determination of longitude; ~**grad** degree of longitude; ~**kreis** circle of longitude; ~**maß** linear (long) measure, measure (unit) of length; ~**toleranz** length margin.

länger longer;
 je ~ je lieber the longer the better;
 ~ als j. leben to outlive s. o.; **sich des ~en mit jem. unterhalten** to talk to s. o. for some time;
 am ~en Hebel sitzen to be in the stronger position, to carry more weight; **auf ~e Sicht gesehen** on the long pull; **~er Urlaub** longish holiday.

Längerdienender *(mil.)* long service man.

längerfristig long-range;
 ~e Einlagen time and savings deposits; **~e Kredite** medium-term loans.

langersehnt long-desired.

Langeweile boredom;
 vor ~ sterben to be bored to death; **sich die ~ vertreiben** to dispel boredom, to kill time *(coll.)*.

Lang|finger pilferer, pickpocket, sneaking thief, wire *(sl.)*, pincher *(sl.)*, lifter *(sl.)*; ~**format** oblong size.

langfristig long-term (-dated, -range), long-period, long;
 ~ gesehen in the long run;
 Kapital ~ anlegen to make capital investments; **~ investieren** to make long-term investments;
 ~e Anleihe long-term loan; **~e Anleiherechnung** long-term loan account; **~es Darlehn** long-term (-sighted, -period) loan; **~er Devisenwechsel** long exchange; **~es Durchhalten von Aktien** long-term holding of shares; **~es Geld** time money (deposit); **~e Kapitalanlage** long-dated (-term) investment; **~ angelegte Kapitalien** capital investments; **~e Kredite** long-term lendings; **~es Lieferabkommen** long-term supply arrangement; **~er Mietvertrag** long-term lease; **~es Papier** long-dated paper, long-sighted draft; **~er Pfundwechsel auf London** long Sterling; **~e Planung** long-range planning; **~e Schatzanweisung** exchequer *(Br.)* (treasury, *US*) bond; **~e Schuld** long-term debt; **~e Schuldverschreibung** long-term bond (debenture); **~e Unternehmensplanung** corporate planning *(US)*; **~e Verpflichtungen** long-term engagements (commitments); **~e Verschuldung** long-term indebtedness; **~er Vertrag** long-term contract; **~er Wechsel** long draft, long-dated bill (paper); **~ geplante Werbekampagne** preplanned advertising campaign; **~e Wettervorhersage** long-sighted weather forecast.

Langfristprognose long-range forecasting.

langgestrecktes Gebäude long building.

Langholzwagen timber cart, lumber car *(US)*.

langjährig *(Vertrag)* long-standing, of long duration;
 ~e Erfahrungen years of experience; **~e Geschäftsbeziehungen** business relations of long standing; **~e Gewohnheit** habit for many years; **~er Mietvertrag** long-term lease; **~er Wunsch** long-felt want.

langlebig durable, long-lived, lasting;
 ~e Konsumgüter long-lived consumer goods; **~e [Wirtschafts]-güter** durable goods, durables, long-lived assets.

Langlebigkeit long life, durability.

langlegen, sich to lie down, *(fig.)* to be flabbergasted.

Langmut forbearance, patience;
 ~ gegenüber jem. zeigen to be forbearing towards s. o.

längs|des Flusses alongside the river; **~ der Küste** alongshore.

Längsabweichung longitudinal aberration.

langsam slow, *(träge)* sluggish, slow-witted, dull;
 ~ im Rechnen slow at accounts;
 ~er fahren to slow down; **einem ~ besser gehen** to be gradually improving; **jem. ~ auf die Nerven gehen** to get on s. one's nerves; **nur ~ vorankommen** to make slow progress; **~er werden** to slow down;
 ~er Arbeiter slow worker; **~e Erhöhung der Geschwindigkeit** gradual acceleration; **~ steigende Preise** creeping prices **bei ~em Tempo** at a low speed; **~es Wachstum** slow growth; **~ ansteigender Weg** gradually ascending path.

Langsam|arbeiten, planmäßiges go-slow *(Br.)*, work-to-rule *(Br.)*, work according to the book *(US)*; **beim ~fahren** when driving slowly; ~**flug** low-speed flight.

Längsaufriß longitudinal view.

Lang|schläfer lie-abed, top boot; ~**schrift** *(im Gegensatz zu Kurzschrift)* longhand.

Längsformat oblong size.

Langspielplatte long-play record.

Längs|richtung longitudinal direction; ~**schnitt** longitudinal section; ~**schwelle** *(Bahn)* longitudinal sleeper (tie, *US*); **ab ~seite Schiff** from alongside ship; ~**seitslieferung** delivery alongside the vessel.

Langstrecke long distance.
Langstrecken|bomber long-range bomber, (LRB); ~**flug** long-distance flight; ~**flugbetrieb** long-distance air operation; ~**flugzeug** long-range airplane; ~**rakete** long-range rocket (missile); ~**route** long-haul route.
langweilen, sich to be bored; **j. zu Tode** ~ to bore s. o. to death.
langweilig boring, dull, tedious, humdrum;
zum Sterben ~ dull as ditchwater;
~ **sein** *(Roman)* to lack movement; ~ **werden** to pall; **zum Semesterschluß** ~ **werden** to drag up towards the end of a term; **total** ~**er Abend** thoroughly boring evening; ~**e Angelegenheit** tedious affair; **mit** ~**en Arbeiten beschäftigt sein** to be engaged in humdrum tasks; ~**e Aufgabe** weary task; ~**es Buch** dull book; ~**er Bursche** slow coach, wet sock *(sl.)*; ~**es Dasein** humdrum existence; ~**e Kleinstadt** dull little town; **äußerst** ~**er Mensch sein** to be a dreadful bore; ~**er Schluß** *(Geschichte)* tame ending; ~**e Stadt** dead-and-alive hole *(coll.)*; ~**e Vorlesung** tedious lecture.
Langwelle long wave.
Langwellen|bereich long-wave band; ~**empfang** long-wave reception; ~**sender** long-wave transmitter.
langwierig lengthy, protracted, dilatory;
~ **sein** to be long-drawn out;
~**e Aufgabe** long job; ~**e Debatte** protracted debate; ~**e Prozedur** tedious process.
langziehen, jem. die Ohren to tweak s. one's ears.
Lanze für j. brechen to take up the cudgels for s. o., to go to bat for s. o. *(US)*.
Lappalie insignificancy, bagatelle, snap, fiddle-faddle, mere trifle, piddling business, fillip, small change *(US)*;
~**n** small concerns, small potatoes *(US)*.
Lappen shred, rag, *(Geldschein)* note, bill *(US)*, skin *(US sl.)*, *(Staublappen)* duster;
jem. durch die ~ **gehen** to slip through s. one's fingers, to give s. o. the slip.
Läpperschulden *(fam.)* petty (paltry) debts;
~ **machen** to scrounge *(sl.)*.
läppisch silly, foolish;
sich ~ **benehmen** to be as silly as one can be;
~**e Summe** paltry (piffling) amount; ~**e Unterhaltung** insipid (vapid) conversation; ~**es Zeug reden** to talk nonsense.
Lapsus lapse, blunder, howler, slip;
sich einen ~ **unterlaufen lassen** to slip a cog.
Lärm noise, din, clamo(u)r, breeze, *(Motoren)* roar;
ohrenbetäubender ~ ear-splitting din; **ruhestörender** ~ disturbing noise;
~ **auf dem Marktplatz** hubbub on the market place; **viel** ~ **um Nichts** much ado about nothing, much cry for little wool;
~ **der Straße bekämpfen** to abate traffic noise; **schrecklichen** ~ **machen** to make a terrible din, to kick up a row, to whoop it (things) up *(US sl.)*; **viel** ~ **um etw. machen** to make a fuss about s. th.;
~**bekämpfung** noise control (abatement, prevention); ~**belästigung** noise pollution; ~**belastung** noise pollution; ~**einwirkung** noise level.
lärmen to kick up a row, to make a racket.
lärmend noisy, uproarious, roaring, riotous.
Lärm|höchstwerte von 102 - 108 Phon für Flugzeuge festsetzen to establish maximum noise levels for airplanes between 102 and 108 decibles; ~**intensität** noise level; ~**schlucker** noise absorber; ~**schutz** sound protection; ~**schutzbereich** noise abatement zone; ~**schutzwand** noise barrier; ~**tabelle** phonometer scale; ~**teppich** *(Flugzeug)* sound carpet; ~**verminderung** noise abatement (reduction); **den** ~**vorschriften bei Benutzung von Flugplätzen gerecht** to meet airport noise rules.
Larve mask;
einem Schwindler die ~ **vom Gesicht reißen** to unmask an imposter.
lasch lax, listless, slack, *(Händedruck)* limp;
Spesenabrechnung ~ **behandeln** to be lax in handling expenses;
~ **auf ein Angebot reagieren** to respond without much enthusiasm to an offer;
~**e Arbeitsmoral haben** to be slack at one's work; ~**er Bursche** sluggish fellow; ~**e Disziplin haben** to be lax in one's duties; ~**e Moral** lax morals; ~**es Verhalten an den Tag legen** to be lax in one's conduct.
Laschheit laxity, lack of drive, sluggishness;
~ **einreißen lassen** to be a poor disciplinarian.
Laser laser;
~**todesstrahlen** laser death rays.
Lasierfarbe transparent colo(u)r.
lassen, es bei einer Abmachung to abide by an agreement; **j. zur Ader** ~ *(fig.)* to make s. o. pay through his nose, to fleece s. o.; **einen Arzt holen** ~ to send for a doctor; **jem. etw. ausrichten** ~ to leave a message for s. o.; **j. einen Brief lesen** ~ to permit s. o. to read a letter; **400 DM für einen Abend springen** ~ to spend DM 400 for an evening out; **durchblicken** ~ to hint, to intimate; **Federn** ~ to be mauled by the critics; **Finger von etw.** ~ to let s. th. well alone; **sich fotografieren** ~ to have one's photo taken; **viel Geld auf der Rennbahn** ~ to drop a lot of money at the races; **sich etw. gesagt sein** ~ to take due note of s. th.; **alte Geschichten ruhen** ~ to let bygones be bygones; **von einer Gewohnheit** ~ to grow out of a habit; **j. grüßen** ~ to want to be remembered to s. o.; **j. nichts Gutes ahnen** ~ to give s. o. a sense of foreboding; **kein gutes Haar an jem.** ~ to pick s. o. to pieces; **jem. freie Hand** ~ to give s. o. a free hand; **j. ins Haus** ~ to let s. o. into the house; **hinter sich** ~ to outrun; **alles weit hinter sich** ~ to be far ahead of anything; **sich ein Hotelzimmer zeigen** ~ to ask to see a room in a hotel; **Katze aus dem Sack** ~ to let the cat out of the bag; **sein Leben** ~ to lose (give) one's life; **j. in einem völlig anderen Licht erscheinen** ~ to show s. o. in a completely new light; **Luft aus dem Reifen** ~ to let the air out of a tyre; **sich seine Müdigkeit nicht anmerken** ~ not to show how tired one is; **sich etw. Neues einfallen** ~ to come up with new ideas; **jem. nur das Nötigste zum Leben** ~ to leave s. o. with the bare necessities of life; **Partie zu einem herabgesetzten Preis** ~ to dispose of a lot at reduced prices; **als Pfand** ~ to leave for a pledge; **protokollieren** ~ to leave on record; **das Rauchen** ~ to give up smoking; **über etw. mit sich reden** ~ to be open to advice; **in Ruhe** ~ to let alone; **Schiff vom Stapel** ~ to launch a ship; **das Schlimmste befürchten** ~ to give rise to the greatest fears; **es sich schmecken** ~ to tuck into one's food; **in der Schwebe** ~ to leave in abeyance; **nicht mit sich spaßen** ~ not to be a man to be trifled with; **Satz stehen** ~ to keep the type standing; **stehen** ~ *(Schulden)* to leave on tick; **im Stich** ~ to let down; **sich nicht länger umgehen** ~ to be no longer avoidable; **unausgefüllt** ~ to leave blank; **j. über etw. im Unklaren** ~ to leave s. o. in the dark about s. th.; **nichts unversucht** ~ to leave no stone unturned; **Verfolger weit hinter sich** ~ to leave one's pursuers far behind; **jem. den Vortritt** ~ to yield precedence to s. o.; **freie Wahl** ~ to give the refusal; **j. wissen** ~ to inform s. o., to let s. o. know; **seine Wohnung machen** ~ to have one's flat (apartment) done over; **ein Wort mit sich reden** ~ to listen to reason; **viel zu wünschen übrig** ~ to leave much to be desired; **sich seine Zeche bezahlen** ~ to make s. o. pay one's bill; **Zeile frei** ~ to leave a line blank.
lässig nonchalant, casual, offhanded, laggard, *(mit Leichtigkeit)* hands down, easily;
~ **antworten** to give a casual answer; ~ **den dritten Platz belegen** to come in an easy third; **sich** ~ **benehmen** to be lax in one's behavio(u)r;
~**e Einstellung haben** to have a slack attitude; ~**e Eleganz** casual elegance; **seiner Arbeit gegenüber eine** ~**e Haltung einnehmen** to be lax in carrying out one's duties; **mit einer** ~**en Handbewegung** with a casual movement of one's hand.
Lässigkeit casualness, nonchalance, offhandedness.
Last load, burden, weight, lug *(coll.)*, tie *(coll.)*, *(Belastung)* encumbrance, charge, *(Fracht)* freight, cargo, *(Gewicht)* weight, charge, *(Ladefähigkeit)* tonnage, *(Steuer)* tax, duty, *(kaufmännische Verbindlichkeit)* charge, debit, *(verladenes Gut)* load, haul *(US)*;
Betrag zu Ihren ~**en** amount payable by you; **frei von** ~ *(Grundstück)* free from encumbrances; **zu jds.** ~**en** at the cost of s. o.; **zu** ~**en von** chargeable (debitable) to, for the account (to the debit, at the expense) of; **zu** ~**en des Empfängers** on receiver's account; **zu** ~**en der Gemeinde** chargeable to the parish (town, *US*); **zu** ~**en des Käufers** to be paid by the buyer; ~**en** *(Abgaben)* taxes, fiscal burden;
bedrückende ~ incubus; **dauernde** ~**en** standing charges; **finanzielle** ~**en** financial burden, charge; **jährliche** ~**en** annual charges; **kostspielige** ~ white elephant; **öffentliche** ~**en** public charges, rates and taxes; **schwere** ~ heavy lift; **soziale** ~**en** social security contributions; **steuerliche** ~**en** tax burden; **tote** ~ dead load; **gleichmäßig verteilte** ~ load evenly distributed; **zusätzliche** ~**en** additional burden;
~ **der Beweisführung** onus (burden) of proof; ~ **des Beweismaterials** weight of evidence; **erhebliche** ~**en eines Grundstücks** heavy encumbrances upon a real estate; ~ **der Jahre** onslaught of the years; **große** ~ **von der Seele** great weight off one's mind;
jem. eine ~ **abnehmen** to remove s. one's load; ~ **abschütteln** to throw off a burden; ~ **auf j. abwälzen** to shift a burden upon s.

o.; **jem. eine ~ aufbürden** to burden s. o. with s. th.; **Saldo zu Ihren ~en aufweisen** to show a balance to your debit; **j. von einer ~ befreien** to free s. o. of a burden; **sich von einer ~ befreien** to disencumber o. s. of a load; **zu jds. ~en buchen** to debit s. one's account; **jem. zur ~ fallen** to be on s. one's hands (thrown upon s. one's resources), to be (become) a burden to s. o., to burden s. o., to be an inconvenience to s. o.; **der Gemeinde (Öffentlichkeit) zur ~ fallen** to come upon the parish (town, *US*); **zu jds. ~en gehen** to fall on (be borne by) s. o.; **zu ~en des Steuerzahlers gehen** to increase the burden of the taxpayers; **jem. das ganze Leben zur ~ werden lassen** to make s. one's life a burden; **mit einer schweren ~ leben** to labo(u)r under a burden; **jem. zur ~ legen** to put the blame at s. one's door, to lay s. th. to s. one's charge, to count s. th. against s. o.; **dem Wirtschaftsminister die Finanzkrise zur ~ legen** to blame the minister for economic affairs for the financial crisis; **unter der ~ des Schnees nachgeben** to sag under the weight of the snow; **~ auf sich nehmen** to support a charge; **~ für j. sein** to be a burden to (charge on) s. o.; **von der ~ seines Amtes bedrückt sein** to be weighed down by the burden of one's office; **von der ~ der Verantwortung befreit sein** to be relieved of a responsibility; **von der ~ der Jahre gebeugt sein** to be bowed down with years; **~en tragen** to carry weights; **schwere ~ tragen** to bear a burden; **des Tages ~ und Hitze tragen** to bear the burden and heat of the day; **Betrag zu ~en eines Kontos vortragen** to charge a sum to the debit; **unter der ~ des Beweismaterials zusammenbrechen** to break down under the weight of the evidence; **unter der ~ der Unglücksfälle zusammenbrechen** to give way under the load of misfortunes;
einer trage des anderen ~ bear ye one another's burden; **Kosten gehen zu ~en von** costs to be borne by; **Portokosten gehen zu Ihren ~en** postage will be charged to your account;
~anhänger trailer; **~auto** lorry *(Br.)*, [motor] van, truck; **per ~auto** by road; **~dampfer** cargo steamer.

lasten to rest upon, *(Hypothek)* to be burdened (encumbered);
auf jds. Gewissen ~ to have a guilty conscience; **auf dem Haushalt der Gemeinden ~** to burden the finances of the communities; **auf jds. Schultern ~** to rest upon s. one's shoulders; **schwer auf jem. ~** to weigh heavy on s. one's mind.

Lasten|aufzug hoist, goods lift *(Br.)*, freight elevator *(US)*; **~ausgleich** burden sharing.

Lastenausgleichs|abgabe capital levy, equalization fee; **~amt** [etwa] board of equalization; **~fonds** equalization fund; **~plan** private chattel scheme *(Br.)*.

Lastenbeihilfe hardship allowance.

Lasten|erhöhung increase of public charges; **~fallschirm** cargo parachute; **~flugzeug** cargo plane, freight-carrying aircraft.

lastenfrei free of charges (from encumbrances), without charge of any kind;
Haus ~ kaufen to buy a home free from all debt; **~ sein** to be free from any charge;
~es Grundstück unencumbered estate.

Lasten|segler cargo-carrying glider; **~senkung** reduction of charges; **~übergang** transfer of liabilities; **gerechte ~verteilung** fair sharing of burden; **~zuschuß** hardship allowance.

Laster vice;
langes ~ lanky fellow, bean-pole;
dem ~ frönen to wallow in vice; **sich dem ~ der Völlerei hingeben** to indulge in gluttony; **~ loswerden** to kick it *(US)*.

Lästerchronik tittle-tattle of the day.

lasterhaft profligate, vicious, dissolute, wicked;
~es Leben führen to lead a dissolute life.

Lasterhaftigkeit profligacy.

Laster|höhle nest (den) of vice, sink of iniquity; **~leben führen** to lead a dissolute life.

lästerlich|es Leben riotous life; **~e Reden** profane words, profanities; **~e Reden führen** to use blasphemous language.

Lästermaul scandalmonger, slanderer, backbiter;
richtiges ~ big gossip.

Lästern profane language, blasphemy.

lästern to backbite, to gossip;
über j. ~ to talk about s. o., to make disparaging remarks about (poke fun at) s. o.; **Gott ~** to blaspheme against God.

Lästerrede abusive talk;
~n über die Regierung führen to make disparaging remarks about the government.

Lästerung slander, backbite, *(religiös)* blasphemy, profanity.

Lästerzungen wagging tongues, detractors.

Last|fuhrwerk horse-drawn cart; **~gewicht** loading weight.

lästig burdensome, onerous, cumbersome, incommodious, inconvenient, annoying, importunate business;
jem. ~ fallen to get on s. one's nerves; **jem. ~ sein** to pester s. o.; **jem. ~ werden** to be nuisance to s. o., to intrude upon s. o.;
~er Ausländer undesirable alien; **~er Besuch** tiresome visitor; **~es Kind** pestering child; **~er Mensch** insect; **~er Mensch sein** to be a nuisance; **~e Person** handful; **~er Vertrag** burdensome contract.

Lastkahn barge, lighter.

Lastkraftwagen [motor] van, lorry *(Br.)*, [motor] truck, goods vehicle *(US)*, autotruck *(US)*;
mittelschwerer ~ pickup (light) truck; **schwerer ~** heavy truck;
~ fahren to [drive a] truck, to lorry *(Br.)*;
~anhänger trailer; **~flotte, ~park** fleet of trucks (lorries, *Br.*); **~transport** motor transport; **~verkehr** motor traffic.

Last|pferd pack horse; **~schiff** vessel of charge, ship of burden, freighter, merchantman, merchant ship; **~schlepper** cargo trailer; **~schlitten** sleigh, train.

Lastschrift *(Buchung)* debit entry (item), debit [advice], debiting; **~anzeige** debit note (memorandum) *(US)*; **~beleg** debit voucher (slip), *(Bank)* bank giro debit slip; **~posten** debit item; **~verfahren** direct debiting [system], direct debiting service.

Last|tier beast of burden; **~träger** market porter.

Lastwagen [motor] van *(Br.)*, lorry *(Br.)*, [motor, automobile] truck, waggon, wagon *(US)*, autotruck *(US)*, goods vehicle *(US)*;
für ~ gesperrt closed for heavy motor traffic; **mit ~ befördert** lorry-borne *(Br.)*;
leichter ~ light van *(Br.)*; **mittelschwerer ~** light truck; **schneller ~** pickup truck *(US)*; **schwerer ~** heavy lorry *(Br.)* (truck);
~ mit Anhänger truck-trailer; **~ ohne Anhänger** straight job *(sl.)*; **~ mit Gasgenerator** gasoline truck; **~ mit Kippvorrichtung** dump truck;
~ ausrauben to hi[gh]jack a lorry *(Br.)* (truck); **mit ~ befördern** to lorry *(Br.)*, to [ship by] truck; **~ fahren** to truck, to drive a truck, to lorry *(Br.)*;
~anhänger [truck] trailer; **~beförderung** road haulage (transport), motor transport, truckage *(US)*; **~besatzung** crew of a lorry *(Br.)* (truck); **~besitzer** van (truck) owner; **~depot** trucking depot; **~fabrik** truck factory (manufacturing plant); **~fahrer** lorry *(Br.)* (truck) driver, van driver *(Br.)*, trucker *(US)*, truckman *(US)*, teamster *(US)*, driver of a truck, carman; **~fahrer sein** to lorry *(Br.)*, to truck; **sich als ~fahrer sein Geld verdienen** to truck for a living; **~fernverkehr** road haulage, road transport service *(US)*; **~firma** truck business; **~flotte** fleet of lorries *(Br.)* (trucks), truck fleet; **~gewerbe** motor carrier (road haulage, trucking) industry; **~hersteller** truck manufacturer; **~herstellung** truck manufacture, lorry production *(Br.)*; **~industrie** trucking industry; **~kolonne** convoy of trucks, trucking fleet; **~ladung** truckload *(US)*, lorry load *(Br.)*; **~markt** heavy truck market; **~miete** truck rental; **~park** fleet of lorries *(Br.)* (trucks), truck fleet; **~produktion** lorry *(Br.)* (truck) production; **~spedition** trucking; **~straße** truckway; **~tarif** truck rates; **~teilzusendung** less-than-truckload *(US)*; **~transport** motor transport *(US)*, road haulage *(Br.)*, truckage, trucking, *(mil.)* mechanical transport; **~transportunternehmen** motor [truck] carrier, truck carrier, road haulier; **~verkehr** motor traffic, truck service; **für ~verkehr gesperrt sein** to be closed for heavy motor traffic; **~verleih** truck-leasing business; **~versicherung** motor transportation insurance; **~wettbewerb** truck competition.

Lastzug trailor-tractor unit, juggernaut.

Latein Latin;
am Ende seines ~s sein to be at one's wit's end (at the end of one's tether).

lateinamerikanische Freihandelszone Latin-American Free-Trade Association (LAFTA).

latent latent, potential, dormant;
~er Fehler hidden defect; **~e Feindschaft** latent animosity; **~e Gefahr** potential danger.

Laterne lamp, lantern;
im Licht einer ~ in the light of a street lamp;
jem. einen Wink mit der ~ geben to give s. o. a broad hint; **nach einem geeigneten Kandidaten mit der ~ suchen** to hunt high and low for a possible candidate.

Laternen|anzünder lamplighter; **nur eine ~garage haben** to park under a street light; **~licht** lantern light; **~pfahl** lamp-post, electric mast.

Latifundien large estates.

Latrine latrine, earth-closet, rear *(Br., sl.)*.

Latrinenparole gossip, rumo(u)rs, scuttlebutt *(Br., sl.)*.

Latsche slipper;
in der Hitze aus den ~n kippen to pass out in the intense heat.

latschen, jem. eine to paste s. o. on the face; **auf die Bremse** ~ to slam on the brake; **über die Straße** ~ to shuffle across the street.
Latte lath, crossbar;
ganze ~ **von** a long list of; **lange** ~ lanky fellow, bean-pole; **ganze** ~ **von Nachwahlmißerfolgen** string of by-election failures; ~ **von Schulden** mountain of debts; **ganze** ~ **von Vorstrafen** long criminal record;
nicht alle auf der ~ **haben** not to be all there.
Latten|gerüst lathwork; ~**kiste** crate; ~**rost** floor grid; ~**verschlag** lattice work; ~**zaun** picket (board, *US*) fence, lattice work.
Latz bib, flab;
jem. einen vor den ~ **knallen** to clout s. o. on the head.
lau mild, balmy, gentle, *(Börsenstimmung)* dull, slack, weak, languid, sluggish, *(halbherzig)* lukewarm, half-hearted;
~**e Haltung einnehmen** to assume a lukewarm attitude; ~**er Versuch** half-hearted attempt.
Laub leaves, foliage.
Laube summerhouse, bower, bowery, arbo(u)r;
und fertig ist die ~ that's that, and Bob's your uncle.
Lauben|gang pergola, *(Mietshaus)* access balcony; ~**kolonie** allotment gardens.
Lauer, auf der on the scout, on the lurk;
auf der ~ **liegen** to lie in ambush, to be on the lurk, *(Verkehrspolizei)* to be on the prowl; **auf der** ~ **nach einer besseren Wohnung liegen** to be on the lookout for better accommodation.
lauern to lie in ambush (wait);
auf den Briefträger ~ to wait impatiently for the postman; **auf j. im Dunkeln** ~ to lurk in the dark for s. o.; **auf eine Gelegenheit** ~ to bide one's opportunity, to watch one's time; **auf Gelegenheitskäufe** ~ to be on the lookout for bargains.
lauernd lurking.
Lauerstellung, in ~ **liegen** to lie in wait (ambush).
Lauf course, process, *(Bahn)* course, track, path, *(Fluß)* course, reach[es], *(Frist)* running, *(Maschine)* movement, functioning, *(Motor)* run, running;
im ~**e von** in the course of; **im** ~ **des Gesprächs** in the course of the conversation; **im** ~ **eines Jahres** in the course of a year; **im** ~**e meines Lebens** in the course of (during) my life; **im** ~ **der Zeit** in process (progress) of time;
gezogener ~ *(Gewehr)* rifled barrel;
natürlicher ~ **der Dinge** course of nature; ~ **der Ereignisse** course of events; ~ **einer Frist** running of a period; ~ **der Gerechtigkeit** course of justice; ~ **der Geschichte** stream of history; ~ **eines Kolbens** travel of a piston; **geräuschloser** ~ **einer Maschine** quiet running of a machine; **ungleichmäßiger** ~ **einer Maschine** irregular action of a machine; ~ **von Risiken** running of risks; ~ **der Verjährungsfrist** running of the Statute of Limitations; ~ **der Welt** way of the world, goings;
~ **der Gerechtigkeit anhalten** to interfere with the course of justice; **dem** ~ **der Bahnstrecke folgen** to follow the railway line; **freien** ~ **lassen** to allow full (free) play to; **den Dingen ihren** ~ **lassen** to let things ripen; **seinen Gefühlen freien** ~ **lassen** to give rein to one's feelings, to get down on the emotional side of it; **seiner Phantasie freien** ~ **lassen** to give free rein to one's imagination; **seinen Tränen freien** ~ **lassen** to make no attempt to hold back one's tears; **seinem Zorn freien** ~ **lassen** to give vent to one's anger; **seinen** ~ **nehmen** to run its course, to have one's swing, to jog along, to go one's way; **in vollem** ~ **gegen einen Laternenpfahl rennen** to go full tilt against a lamppost; ~ **eines Flusses umleiten** to turn the channel of a stream.
Laufbahn career, course, walk, race;
auf dem Kulminationspunkt seiner ~ at the height of one's career; **seit der Geburt für eine militärische** ~ **vorgesehen** destined from birth for the army; **von entscheidendem Einfluß auf jds.** ~ determinative of s. one's career; **zu Beginn seiner** ~ at the outset of one's career;
akademische ~ academic career; **berufliche** ~ business (professional) career; **erfolgreiche** ~ fruitful career; **erstaunliche** ~ career of resounding progress; **erstrebte** ~ career objectives; **geschäftliche** ~ business career; **glänzende** ~ brilliant career; **juristische** ~ legal career; **kaufmännische** ~ business career; **makellose** ~ unblemished career; **öffentliche** ~ civil life; **parlamentarische** ~ House Career; **ruhmvolle** ~ race of glory; **wechselvolle** ~ chequered career;
sich positiv auf die ~ **auswirken** to be a good step career-wise; **jds.** ~ **entscheidend beeinflussen** to determine s. one's career; ~ **wirkungsvoll beeinflussen** to enrich a career; ~ **plötzlich beenden** to cut short a career; ~ **einschlagen** to enter a career; ~ **des Beamten einschlagen** to enter the civil service; **sich für die juristische** ~ **entscheiden** to go in for law; **sich für eine wissenschaftliche** ~ **entschließen** to engage in scientific pursuits; **Höhepunkt seiner** ~ **erreichen** to round off one's career; **j. für die** ~ **des Gelehrten erziehen** to breed s. o. for a scholar; **seine** ~ **noch nicht abgeschlossen haben** to be in mid-career; **hervorragende wissenschaftliche** ~ **aufzuweisen haben** to have strong academical credentials; **seine** ~ **krönen** to cap one's career; **für die juristische** ~ **bestimmt werden** to be bred up for the law;
~**aussichten** career prospects; ~**bestrebungen** career aspirations; ~**bewerber** civil service applicant; ~**entwicklung** career progression; ~**grundlage** career base; ~**kurve** career curve; ~**lenkung** career guidance; ~**steuerung** career management; ~**verordnung** National Civil Service Act *(US)*; ~**wechsel** change of career.
Lauf|brett planks, gangway; ~**brücke** footbridge, gangway, *(Tanker)* catwalk; ~**bühne** platform.
Laufbursche footboy, pageboy, caddie, runner, shopboy, delivery (messenger, errand, office) boy, roundsman *(Br.)*, hall boy *(US)*;
~**n machen** to office-boy, to punk *(US sl.)*.
Laufen *(Gültigkeit)* running, *(Maschine)* operating.
laufen *(gültig sein)* to be valid, to run, *(Maschine)* to go, to operate, to be in action, to run, to function, to work, *(Prozeß)* to be on the way, *(Schiff)* to make, *(Verhandlungen)* to be in progress, *(Wasserhahn)* to be dripping, *(Zeit)* to pass, to go by, to fly;
~ **von** *(Zinsen)* to be payable from; **ausgekuppelt** ~ to tick over; **in ein Auto** ~ to run into a car; **wie ein geölter Blitz** ~ to run like the wind (greased lightning, *coll.*); **durchgehend** ~ to operate day and night; **um die Erde auf einer Kreisbahn** ~ *(Satellit)* to travel round the earth in a circular orbit; **nicht fahrplanmäßig** ~ to be running behind the time (schedule, *US*); **in jeden Film** ~ to never miss a film; **im Galopp zum Bahnhof** ~ to sprint to the station; **Gefahr** ~ to run the risk; **ins Geld** ~ to run into money, to run into large amounts *(coll.)*; **wie geplant** ~ to go according to plan; **gleichzeitig** ~ to take place at the same time; **auf Grund** ~ *(Schiff)* to run aground, to strike bottom, to be stranded; **gut** ~ *(Automotor)* to hit on all four cylinders, *(Maschine)* to perform well; **in den Hafen** ~ to put into port; **schnell mal zum Kolonialwarenhändler** ~ to pop over to the grocer's; **mit dem Kopf durch die Wand** ~ **wollen** to run one's head against a brick wall; **auf eine Mine** ~ to hit a mine; **seit zehn Minuten** ~ *(Film)* to have been running for ten minutes; **j. müde** ~ to walk s. o. off his legs; **von Mund zu Mund** ~ *(Gerücht)* to go from mouth to mouth; **unter dem Namen** ~ to go under the name; **wieder normal** ~ *(Verkehr)* to go back to normal; **gegen die Parteiorganisation Sturm** ~ to run against the political machine; **von Pontius zu Pilatus** ~ to run from pillar to post; **wie am Schnürchen** ~ to go like clockwork; **Spießruten** ~ to run the gauntlet; **vom Stapel** ~ to be launched; **mit 3000 Touren** ~ to run at 3000 revolutions per minute; **mit vollen Touren** ~ *(Betrieb)* to go full blast (a humdinger, *US sl.*); **kopfüber in sein Verderben** ~ to rush headlong to one's ruin; **auf allen Vieren** ~ to go on all fours; **sich warm** ~ to warm up; **jem. über den Weg** ~ to run into s. o.; **seit vier Wochen** ~ *(Stück)* to have been on the stocks for four weeks;
sofort zu ~ **beginnen** *(Verjährungsfrist)* to run immediately; **wieder zu** ~ **beginnen** *(Verjährungsfrist)* to recommence; **Prozeß gegen j.** ~ **haben** to have taken s. o. to court; **alles** ~ **lassen** to let the world slide, to drop everything; **Schiff auf den Strand** ~ **lassen** to beach a boat.
laufend current, running, ruling, regular, constructive, *(aufeinanderfolgend)* consecutive, *(durchgehend)* continuous, *(gültig)* valid, in force, *(täglich)* present, day-to-day, routine;
~ **an der Verbesserung seiner Produkte arbeiten** to be continuously working to improve one's products; ~ **ergänzen** to keep up to date; ~ **zu tun haben** to be always kept busy; ~ **notieren** to quote consecutively; ~ **numerieren** to number consecutively;
~**en Absatz finden** to find a ready market; ~**e Akzepte** bills (notes) receivable *(US)*; ~**es Angebot** floating supply; ~**e Arbeit** daily labo(u)r; ~**er Auftrag** standing order; ~**e Ausgaben** fixed expenses; ~**es Band** conveyor belt; **am** ~**en Band** on the assembly line; **Fehler am** ~**en Band machen** to make one mistake after the other; **am** ~**en Band reden** to talk nineteen to the dozen; ~**er Bedarf** current demand; ~**er Beitrag** periodic dues (subscription); ~**e Betriebsunkosten** current operating expenses; ~**es Einkommen** regular income; ~**e Emissionen** outstanding issues; ~**e Geschäfte** regular (routine) business; ~**e Geschäftsunkosten** running expenses; ~**e Inventur** continuous

stocktaking (inventory); ~es **Jahr** current (present) year; ~es **Konto** continuing account, running account, open account *(US)*, drawing account *(US)*, account current; ~e **Kontrolle** regular inspection; ~e **Kosten** fixed (standing) charges; ~er **Kredit** open (standing) credit; ~er **Kupon** maturing coupon; **zum** ~en **Kurse** at the current price; ~er **Meter** running meter *(US)* (metre, *Br.*); ~en **Monats** instant, this month; ~e **Nachfrage** current demand; ~e **Notierung** ruling price, consecutive quotation; ~e **Nummer** serial (consecutive, running) number; ~e **Police** floating policy; ~er **Preis** market price; ~e **Produktion** current production; ~e **Rechnung** account current, current (running) account, open account *(US)*; **auf** ~e **Rechnung einkaufen** to buy on tick; **in** ~er **Rechnung stehen** to have a current account; ~e **Revisionsarbeiten** continuous audit; ~e **Risiken** pending risks; ~e **Schulden** current (running) debts; ~e **Unkosten** current expenses, cost in carrying business; ~er **Unterhaltsbetrag** permanent alimony; ~e **Verbindlichkeiten** current liabilities; ~e **Verhandlungen** negotiations carried on; ~e **Verpflichtungen** running engagements; ~er **Vertrag** running (standing) contract; ~e **Verzinsung** running yield; ~e **Wartung** routine maintenance; ~es **Wasser** running water; ~er **Wechsel** bill in circulation, unmatured bill; ~e **Wechsel** *(Bilanz)* bills (notes) receivable *(US)*; **gegenwärtig** ~e **Werbekampagne** current advertising; ~e **Zahlungen** regular payments; ~e **Zinsen** running (accruing) interest.

laufendem, auf dem up-to-date, on the ball;
auf dem ~ **bleiben** to keep o. s. posted; **j. auf dem** ~ **halten** to keep s. o. informed (advised, up to date, on the track); **sich auf dem** ~ **halten** to keep up to date; **sich auf seinem Gebiet auf dem** ~ **halten** to keep abreast of time in one's field; **auf dem** ~ **sein** to be fully informed (in the picture); **mit seiner Arbeit auf dem** ~ **sein** to be up to date with one's work; **nicht mehr auf dem** ~ **sein** to be out of date.

Läufer messenger, goer, errand boy, roundsman *(Br.)*.

Lauffeuer wildfire, head fire *(US)*;
sich wie ein ~ **verbreiten** to spread (run) like wildfire, to grapevine *(Australia)*.

Lauf|gang footwalk, *(Schiff)* gallery; ~**geschwindigkeit** *(Kamera)* film speed; ~**junge** office (bell, *US*) boy, shop boy; ~**junge sein** to office-boy; ~**karren** tram; ~**karte** routing card; ~**katze** travelling crab; ~**kran** travelling (walking) crane; ~**kunde** chance (street, stray) customer (purchaser); ~**kundschaft** irregular customers, traffic-passing trade; ~**mädchen** office (delivery) girl; ~**masche** ladder *(Br.)*, run *(US)*.

laufmaschenfest ladder-proof.

Lauf|nummer order number; ~**paß bekommen** to be sacked (fired) *(sl.)*; **jem. den** ~**paß geben** to jilt at s. o., to send s. o. packing, to sack s. o. *(sl.)*, to give s. o. his walking papers, to give s. o. the bag air *(US sl.)*; ~**planke** *(Schiff)* gangway, gangboard; ~**richtung** *(Papier)* fiber (fibre, *Br.*) direction; ~**schiene** tongue, guideway; ~**schritt** *(mil.)* double; **im** ~**schritt** at a run; **im** ~**schritt Marsch-Marsch!** double time, march!; ~**steg** gangway, runway; **neues Modell über den** ~**steg schicken** to introduce a new fashion model; ~**wagen** *(Bahn)* pony track; ~**werk** *(Lokomotive)* running gear *(Uhr)* clockwork.

Laufzeit period to run, running, run, validity, duration, life, *(Fälligkeit)* maturity, due date, *(Film)* running time, *(Lebensdauer)* useful (service, *Br.*) life, *(Maschine)* cycle, *(Telegramm)* transmission time, *(Wechsel)* term, currency, tenor;
für die volle ~ for the full term; **mit kurzer** ~ *(Wechsel)* short; **mit sechsmonatiger** ~ at six months date;
durchschnittliche ~ average (mean) due date; **einjährige** ~ maturity of one year; **mittlere** ~ mean duration; **vereinbarte** ~ *(Darlehn)* agreed life; **vertragliche** ~ contract period;
~ **eines Akkreditivs** life of a letter of credit; ~ **einer Anleihe** period of a loan; ~ **einer Belastung** running of a burden; ~ **eines Darlehens** term of a loan; ~ **eines Films** running time of a film; ~ **einer Hypothek** mortgage term *(Br.)*; ~ **einer Kommunalobligation** life of a bond; ~ **eines Kredits** term (period) of a credit, credit period; ~ **eines Mietvertrages (Pachtverhältnisses)** currency (duration) of a lease; ~ **eines Patents** life of a patent; ~ **einer Police** duration (life) of a policy, policy period; ~ **eines Vertrages** life of an agreement (a contract), term of a contract; ~ **eines Wechsels** term of a bill of exchange;
effektive ~ **feststellen** *(Wechsel)* to time; **dreißig Tage** ~ **haben** to have thirty days to run; **zwanzigjährige** ~ **haben** to have a maturity (be for a term) of twenty years;
~**ausgleich** *(Elektronik)* transit time compensation.

Laufzettel tracer, clearance chit, routing (interoffice) slip, *(Produktion)* manufacturing tag.

Lauge lye, alcaline solution;
ätzende ~ **seines Spotts** biting sarcasm.

Laune whim, whimsy, cue, fancy, fad, freak, humo(u)r;
schlechte ~ ill-humo(u)r, pet, tantrum *(coll.)*, pip *(Br., sl.)*; **sprudelnde** ~ exuberant spirits;
j. mit seiner guten ~ **anstecken** to laugh s. o. out of his bad humo(u)r; **seine schlechte** ~ **an der Ehefrau auslassen** to take it out on one's wife; **bei guter** ~ **bleiben** to keep one's tail up; **jds.** ~**n nachgeben** to indulge (give way to) s. one's whims; **einer plötzlichen** ~ **nachgeben** to do s. th. on a sudden impulse; **bester** ~ **sein** to be in a cheerful frame of mind (in strong heart); **in glänzender** ~ **sein** to be in high feather; **guter** ~ **sein** to be in a good humo(u)r; **schlechter** ~ **sein** to be out of spirits.

launenhaft moody, whimsical, full of whims (fancies), capricious;
~ **sein** to have (be a man of) moods;
~**er Filmstar** capricious film star; ~**es Wetter** changeable weather.

launig jocose, jocular, witty, clever;
~ **geschrieben** written with wit and humo(u)r;
~**e Rede** humo(u)rous speech.

launisch moody, peevish, wayward, fickle.

Laus, jem. eine ~ **in den Kopf setzen** to put ideas into s. one's head;
sich eine ~ **in den Pelz setzen** to let o. s. in for s. th.

Lauschangriff illicit wiretapping, eavesdropping.

lauschen to listen;
angestrengt ~ to strain one's ears; **an der Tür** ~ to eavesdrop at the door.

Lauscher eavesdropper;
der ~ **an der Wand hört seine eigene Schand** listeners hear no good of themselves.

lauschig|e Ecke snug corner; ~**es Plätzchen** secluded spot.

Lauschüberwachung electronic surveyance.

Lausebengel young blighter.

lausen, jem. den Beutel to clean s. o. out.

lausig lousy, rotten, miserable, wretched;
~ **kalt** beastly cold;
sich ~ **fühlen** to be down in the dumps *(coll.)*; ~ **viel Geld kosten** to cost a hell of a lot of money; ~ **weh tun** to hurt like hell;
~**es Wetter** awful (rotten) weather; ~**e Zeiten** hard times.

Laut, unartikulierte ~**e ausstoßen** to make inarticulate noises; **keinen** ~ **von sich geben** not to utter a word; **seiner Verachtung jem. gegenüber** ~ **geben** to pour out one's indignation on s. o.

laut as per, in accordance with, *(Geräusch)* loud, noisy;
seine Bewunderung ~ **äußern** to be loud in one's admiration; **sich** ~ **und deutlich äußern** to speak one's mind clearly and to the point; **Geheimnis** ~ **werden lassen** to divulge a secret; **es nicht** ~ **werden lassen** to keep mum about s. th.; **einige Wünsche** ~ **werden lassen** to voice a few wishes; ~ **loslachen** to burst out laughing; ~**er stellen** to turn up;
mit ~**em Beifall begrüßt** welcomed with loud applause; ~**es Gelächter** ringing (resounding) laughter; ~**es Geschrei erheben** to raise hue and cry; ~**e Gesellschaft** boisterous party; ~**es Lesen** reading aloud; ~**e Loblieder auf j. singen** to be loud in s. one's praise; ~**e Straße** noisy (loud) street;
~ **Aufstellung** as per statement; ~ **Auftrag** by (according to) order, as directed; ~ **Bericht** as advised; ~ **Faktura** as per invoice; ~ **Gesetz** under the law; ~ **ärztlichem Gutachten** according to expert medical opinion; ~ **Paragraph 5** as stated in paragraph 5; ~ **beifolgender Quittung** as per receipt enclosed; ~ **beiliegender Rechnung** as indicated in enclosed invoice; ~ **umstehender Rechnung** as per note behind; ~ **unserem Schreiben vom** as set forth in our letter of; ~ **Übereinkunft** by agreement; ~ **Verfügung** by decree, as directed; ~ **Vollmacht** by virtue of power of attorney; ~ **Vorschrift** according to rule, in conformity with the regulations.

lautbar, amtlicherseits wurde it leaked out from official circles that.

Lautbezeichnung phonetic transcription.

lauten to read, to run;
besorgniserregend ~ to have a sinister sound; **auf einen Betrag von 1000 Dollar** ~ to be made out to the amount of (expressed in) $ 1000; **folgendermaßen** ~ to read (to be worded) as follows; **auf 4 Monate Gefängnis** ~ to be a sentence of four months imprisonment; **auf Hochverrat** ~ *(Anklage)* to be a charge of high treason; **auf den Inhaber** ~ to be payable to bearer; **im Manuskript anders** ~ to read differently in the manuscript; **auf den Namen** ~ *(Aktie)* to be registered, *(Paß)* to be made out, in the name of; **an Order** ~ *(Wechsel)* to be payable to order; **auf Schadenersatz** ~ to sound in damages.

Läuten ring, ringing.
läuten to pull the bell;
mit der Glocke ~ to ring the bell; **j. zu Grabe** ~ to toll the bell for s. one's funeral; **zur Hochzeit** ~ to be pealing for the wedding; **Sturm** ~ to sound the alarm; **bei jem. Sturm** ~ to ring s. one's bell impatiently.
lautend | auf made out to, issued (payable) to;
auf 100 Dollar ~ for (expressed in) $ 100; **auf den Inhaber** ~ payable to bearer, in bearer form; **auf den Namen** ~ *(Aktie)* registered, *(Scheck)* payable to order; **auf den Überbringer** ~ in bearer form, payable to bearer.
lauter candid, true, honest, hono(u)rable, sincere;
~**e Absichten** honesty of purpose; **seinen** ~**en Charakter erkennen lassen** to display one's genuine character; ~ **kleine Fetzen** tiny little shreds; ~ **solche Geschichten** a whole lot of such stories; ~**e Gesinnung** sincerity; ~ **nette Leute** only nice people; ~ **Lügen** pack of lies; ~ **Unsinn** sheer nonsense; **von** ~ **Verehrern umgeben sein** to be surrounded by fans; **aus** ~ **Verzweiflung** out of sheer despair; ~**e Wahrheit** unvarnished truth.
Lauterkeit cando(u)r, integrity, sincerity;
~ **der Werbung** advertising standard; ~ **des Wettbewerbs** fair trade *(US)*.
läutern to clarify, to purify, to refine;
Charakter ~ to reform a character.
Läuterungsprozeß refining process.
Läutewerk alarm, warning bell, *(Bahn)* signal bell.
lautgehender Motor noisy engine.
lauthals at the top of one's voice;
~ **lachen** to burst out laughing.
Lautkunde phonetics.
Lautschrift phonetic writing;
in ~ **wiedergeben** to phoneticize.
Lautsprache lip language.
Lautsprecher loudspeaker, reproducer;
durch ~ **übertragen** carried by loudspeaker;
tragbarer ~ portable loudspeaker, hog-caller *(sl.)*; **zusätzlicher** ~ extensive loudspeaker;
~**anlage** loudspeaker paging device; ~**anschluß** *(Radio)* speaker socket; ~**flugzeug** polly plane; ~**übertragung im Laden** store casting *(US)*; ~**wagen** loudspeaker van, sound truck *(US)*; ~**werbung** loudspeaker advertising.
lautstark *(el.)* full, noisy;
~ **argumentieren** to argue heatedly; **sich** ~ **beschweren** to be loud in one's complaints; ~ **fordern** to scream; **sich** ~ **bemerkbar machen** to kick up a row (no end of a din);
~**er Protest** vociferous protest.
Lautstärke sound volume (level);
an ~ **verlierend** fading;
~ **regulieren** to adjust the volume;
~**regelung** volume control; ~**regelung eines Radios** control of a wireless set; ~**regler** volume increaser.
Läutstärkste the most vocal.
Lautzeichen phonogram.
lauwarm *(Heizung)* lukewarm.
Lava[strom] lava[stream].
Lavendel lavender.
lavieren to shift, to trim, to manage, to steer a middle course, to ply;
Verhandlungen ~ to manipulate negotiations.
Lawine avalanche, snowslide;
~ **von Briefen** avalanche of letters; ~ **landwirtschaftlicher Erzeugnisse** agricultural avalanche;
~ **auslösen** to trigger off an avalanche; ~ **von Protesten hervorrufen** to provoke a flood of protests.
lawinenartig | anwachsen to snowball into, to grow like mushrooms, to mushroom;
~**en Produktionsauftrag auslösen** to mushroom into a production order.
Lawinen | galerie avalanche shelter; ~**gefahr** danger of avalanches.
lawinengefährdet exposed to avalanches.
Lawinen | hang avalanche slope; ~**katastrophe** avalanche disaster; ~**rettungsdienst** avalanche rescue service; ~**warndienst** avalanche patrol; ~**warnung** avalanche warning.
lax wide, loose in character, wide open *(US sl.)*.
Laxheit laxity.
Layout, detailliertes comprehensive layout;
~ **anfertigen** to make a layout; ~ **für eine Seite fertigstellen** to lay out a printed page;
~**gestalter** layouter, layout man, artist.
Lazarett military (department) hospital;
~**einheit** hospital unit; ~**flugzeug** hospital aircraft; ~**gehilfe** hospital orderly; ~**schiff** hospital ship; ~**zug** hospital (ambulance) train.
Leasing leasing;
grenzüberschreitendes ~**geschäft** cross-frontier leasing business; ~**gesellschaft** leasing company; ~**vertrag** leasing arrangement.
Lebedame demimondaine.
Lebemann man of the world, epicurean, playboy, bon vivant, sport *(US coll.)*;
als ~ **in London großzügig Geld ausgeben** to be a man about town *(Br.)*.
Leben life, existence, *(Handel)* activity, *(Lebensführung)* living, *(Lebensunterhalt)* livelihood, subsistence, living, *(Lebhaftigkeit)* vivacity, animation, liveliness, *(geschäftiges Treiben)* bustle, to-do, activity, *(Wirklichkeit)* reality, life;
am ~ alive, above ground; **für den Rest des** ~**s** for life; **im öffentlichen** ~ in public life; **in der Blüte des** ~**s** in the prime of youth; **nach dem** ~ **gezeichnet** drawn from life; **sein ganzes** ~ **hindurch** throughout one's life; **voller** ~ full of life, *(Straße)* bustling with life;
arbeitsreiches ~ busy life; **beschauliches** ~ contemplative life; **bürgerliches** ~ civil life; **eheliches** ~ married (wedded, conjugal) life; **eintöniges** ~ monotonous life; **ewiges** ~ eternal life; **gefahrenreiches** ~ precarious life; **geregeltes** ~ level life, clean living; **geselliges (gesellschaftliches)** ~ social life, doings *(sl.)*; **kulturelles** ~ cultural life; **lockeres** ~ frivolous life; **müßiges** ~ vacuous life; **öffentliches** ~ public affairs; **ruhiges** ~ still life; **sittenstrenges** ~ moral life; **das süße** ~ life of luxury, dolce vita; **unstetes** ~ vagabond life; **üppiges** ~ fleshpots [of Egypt]; **verbundene** ~ *(Versicherung)* joint lives; **versichertes** ~ insured (assured, *Br.*) life; **wirkliches** ~ life proper; **zügelloses** ~ dissipated life; **zurückgezogenes** ~ sequestered (solitary) life; ~ **in der Familie** family life; ~ **auf dem Lande** country life; **geistiges** ~ **eines Landes** intellectual activity of a country; ~ **der unteren Schichten** lower life; ~ **in der Stadt** town life; ~ **nach dem Tode** life after death; **elendes** ~ **in der Verbannung** outcast misery; **gefährliches** ~ **eines Verschwörers** insecure life of a conspirator;
neues ~ **anfangen** to turn over a new leaf *(coll.)*; **sein** ~ **bis zur Neige auskosten** to live one's full span; ~ **auslöschen** to extinguish a life; **anständiges** ~ **beginnen** to straighten up *(US)*; **neues** ~ **beginnen** to take a new lease of life; **sein** ~ **in Frieden beschließen** to end one's life in peace; ~ **melancholisch betrachten** to have a melancholic outlook; **am** ~ **bleiben** to survive; ~ **in die Bude bringen** *(fam.)* to put [new] life into an enterprise, to make things hum *(sl.)*; ~ **in die Debatte bringen** to enliven a discussion; **mit dem** ~ **davonkommen** to escape with one's life, to overlive; **sein** ~ **so einrichten, wie man will** to find the right niche for o. s.; **sein** ~ **einsetzen** to jeopardize one's life, to pawn one's life; **sein** ~ **für die Freiheit einsetzen** to purchase freedom with one's blood; **in das öffentliche** ~ **eintreten** to enter public life; **jem. das** ~ **erleichtern** to put s. o. on easy street; **zu neuem** ~ **erwecken** to galvanize into life, to revive; **sein** ~ **fristen** to keep the pot boiling, to scrape for one's living; **kärgliches** ~ **fristen** to eke out a scanty living; **angenehmes** ~ **führen** to live (lead) a good life; **aufwendiges** ~ **führen** to live in grand style; **behagliches** ~ **führen** to live in comfort, to keep a good house; **bequemes** ~ **führen** to live in comparative comfort, to lead an easy life; **ehrliches** ~ **führen** to live honestly; **einfaches** ~ **führen** to live in a plain way; **eintöniges** ~ **führen** to live a humdrum life; **einwandfreies** ~ **führen** to live a moral life; **entbehrungsreiches** ~ **führen** to live in privation; **erfülltes** ~ **führen** to live a full (an all-round) life; **faules** ~ **führen** to eat the bread of idleness; **flottes** ~ **führen** to lead a fast life; **friedliches** ~ **führen** to live in peace and quiet; **glückliches** ~ **führen** to live happily with s. o.; **gottgefälliges** ~ **führen** to walk with God; **hektisches** ~ **führen** to lead a hectic life; **liederliches** ~ **führen** to lead a disorderly life; **luxuriöses** ~ **führen** to plush *(sl.)*; ~ **eines Millionärs führen** to live the life of a millionaire; **normales** ~ **führen** to follow standard lines; **ruhiges** ~ **führen** to lead a quiet life; **solides** ~ **führen** to lead a steady life; **sorgenloses (sorgenfreies)** ~ **führen** to live a life of ease, to lead the life of Riley *(US coll.)*; **unabhängiges** ~ **führen** to live a life of independence; **völlig ungeordnetes** ~ **führen** to live in a hugger-mugger fashion; **uninteressantes** ~ **führen** to lead a colo(u)rless existence; **unmoralisches** ~ **führen** to live an evil life; **unstetes** ~ **führen** to knock about; ~ **im Freien führen** to lead an outdoor life; ~ **in Wohlstand führen** to live in affluent (comfortable) circumtances (in easy street, *coll.*); **sein** ~ **dafür geben** to give

one's ears for it; **seinem ~ eine völlig andere Richtung geben** to strike out into a new course of life; **das ~ einer größeren Anzahl von Menschen gefährden** to endanger the life of a substantial number of persons; **gelassen durchs ~ gehen** to sail serenely through life; **auf Tod und ~ gehen** to be a matter of life and death; **zu den Persönlichkeiten des öffentlichen ~s gehören** to be a public figure; **sein ~ genießen** to enjoy life; **an häusliches ~ gewöhnen** to domesticate; **angenehmes ~ haben** to live comfortably; **gerade genug zum ~ haben** to have a bare competence, to make both ends meet; **es schwer im ~ haben** to have a hard row to hoe; **mit dem ~ abgeschlossen haben** to have finished with life; **~ in vollen Zügen genossen haben** to have drunk deep of the pleasures of life; **bewegtes ~ hinter sich haben** to have led an adventurous life; **sein ~ verpfuscht haben** to have made a mess of one's life; **jem. beim Eintritt ins ~ helfen** to give s. o. a start; **ins ~ hinausgehen** to go out into the world; **sein ~ hingeben** to sacrifice one's life; **sein ~ für j. hingeben** to lay down one's life for s. o.; **große Lücke in jds. ~ hinterlassen** to leave a big blank in s. one's life; **mit einem Räuber um sein ~ kämpfen** to contend with a robber for one's life; **das ~ kennen** to know the world; **auf tragische Weise ums ~ kommen** to come by one's death tragically; **sich ein angenehmes ~ leisten können** to have enough for one's material comforts; **sein ~ im Geist Revue passieren lassen** to pass one's life in review; **sich vom ~ nicht unterkriegen lassen** not to give in to things; **sich das ~ angenehm machen** to make one's life pleasant; **jem. das ~ zur Hölle machen** to make s. one's life a hell [upon earth], to put s. o. through the hoop, to lead s. o. a dog's life; **jem. das ~ schwer machen** to give s. o. the gaff *(US sl.)*; **sich das ~ nehmen** to take one's life, to commit suicide; **am ~ der Gemeinde regen Anteil nehmen** to move into the center *(US)* (centre, *Br.*) of common affairs; **sich in einem Schwermutsanfall das ~ nehmen** to commit suicide during a fit of depression; **sein ~ opfern** to sacrifice one's life; **jem. die Hand fürs ~ reichen** to give s. o. one's hand in marriage; **das nackte ~ retten** to escape with life and limb; **sein ~ riskieren** to carry one's life in one's hands, to expose (risk) one's life; **ins ~ rufen** to give life to, to set up, to call into being, to create, to institute, to originate; **Organisation ins ~ rufen** to call an organization into existence; **jds. ganzes ~ ruinieren** to poison s. one's whole life; **aus dem ~ scheiden** to depart from life; **beschließen, gemeinsam aus dem ~ zu scheiden** to make a suicide pact; **jem. das ~ schenken** to spare s. one's life; **einem Mörder das ~ schenken** to reprieve a murderer; **sich mehr oder weniger ehrlich durchs ~ schlagen** to live on one's wits; **aus eigener Kraft durchs ~ schlagen** to paddle one's own canoe; **sein ganzes ~ mit finanzwirtschaftlichen Fragen beschäftigt sein** to spend one's entire career on the financial side; **um sein ~ besorgt sein** to be apprehensive for one's life; **sein ~ aufs Spiel setzen** to set one's life on a chance, to risk one's life; **sein ~ mutwillig aufs Spiel setzen** to take one's life in one's hands, to play ducks and drakes with one's life; **im öffentlichen ~ stehen** to be in the limelight; **sich ins volle ~ stürzen** to launch out into the sea of life; **jem. nach dem ~ trachten** to make an attempt on s. one's life; **ins politische ~ treten** to enter politics; **für sein ~ gern tun** to give one's eye; **die Hälfte seines ~s beruflich verbringen** to live half of one's life on one's job; **sein ~ verdanken** to owe one's life; **genug zum ~ verdienen** to have a sufficiency, to get a sufficient living; **jem. das ~ vergiften** to plague s. one's life out; **sein ~ so teuer wie möglich verkaufen** to sell one's life dearly; **~ verlängern** to lengthen life; **sein ~ durch einen Unfall verlieren** to lose one's life in an accident; **sein ~ versichern** to insure one's life, to take out a life policy; **sein ~ bei einer Gesellschaft versichern** to assure one's life with a company *(Br.)*; **sein ~ verwirken** to forfeit one's life; **im ~ vorwärtskommen** to improve one's position, to make one's way; **~ bedenkenlos wegwerfen** to squander life routinely; **mit dem ~ nicht fertig werden** to be unable to cope with life; **mitten im ~ weggerafft werden** to die in one's boots; **sein ~ widmen (weihen)** to dedicate one's life; **sein ~ einer Sache widmen** to consecrate one's life to an idea; **jds. ~ zerstören** to ruin s. one's life; **j. ins ~ zurückrufen** to bring s. o. back to life; **sich vom öffentlichen ~ zurückziehen** to retire into obscurity; **sich den schönen Dingen des ~s zuwenden** to become escapist.

leben to live, to exist, to subsist, to walk, *(wohnen)* to live, to abide, to quarter;

von etw. ~ to make a living out of it; **für sich ~** to lead a retired life; **ganz für sich ~** to live in one's very house; **von seiner Hände Arbeit ~** to live on one's purchase (by the sweat of one's brow, by the work of one's hand), to earn one's living by manual labo(u)r; **am Arbeitsplatz ~** to live in; **in äußerster Armut ~** to live in straitened circumstances, to live in dire need; **au pair ~** to get food and lodging in requital of one's services; **im Ausland ~** to stay abroad; **in Baracken ~** to live in huts; **sehr bescheiden ~** to live in a small way *(Br.)*; **bescheidener ~** to draw in one's horns; **dürftig ~** to live low; **von den Einkünften seiner Frau ~** to live on one's wife; **bei seinen Eltern ~** to live with one's parents; **vom Fischfang ~** to make a living by fishing; **flott ~** to hit (go) the pace, to lead a fast life; **wie ein Fürst ~** to live like a lord; **auf gespanntem Fuß ~** to live at daggers drawn; **auf großem Fuße ~** to live on a large scale (in a lavish style), to live at rack and manger *(Br.)*, to live high on the hog *(sl.)*; **von seinem Gehalt ~** to live on one's salary; **getrennt ~** *(Eheleute)* to live apart; **nicht getrennt ~** to live together; **seinen Grundsätzen gemäß ~** to live up to one's principles; **von der Hand in den Mund ~** to live from hand to mouth; **von der öffentlichen Hand ~** to live upon the parish; **wie ein Heiliger ~** to live like a saint; **von seinem Kapital ~** to live on one's capital, to live off the income; **von Konserven ~** to live on canned food; **für die Kunst ~** to devote one's life to art; **auf dem Lande ~** to live in the country; **auf anderer Leute Kosten ~** to live at the expense of others (at rack and manger, *coll.*); **wie die Made im Speck ~** to live like a fighting cock; **wie Mann und Frau ~** to live and cohabit as husband and wife, to play at keeping house; **sehr gut miteinander ~** to be very happy together; **von seinem guten Namen ~** to trade upon one's past reputation; **von fast nichts ~** to live on air; **notgedrungen ~** to live perforce; **von seinem Privatvermögen ~** to live on one's private means; **von seiner Rente ~** to live on one's income; **in Saus und Braus ~** to live on the fat of the land, to live in grand style (at rack and manger, a riotous life); **von der Schriftstellerei ~** to live by one's pen; **ohne Sorgen (sorgenfrei) ~** to live at ease (in clover), to lead the life of Riley *(US coll.)*; **sparsam ~** to live near (close); **trotz seiner Familie völlig unabhängig ~** to cut o. s. loose from one's family; **ganz unauffällig ~** to lie low *(coll.)*; **von staatlicher Unterstützung ~** to live off government checks *(US)* (cheques, *Br.*); **üppig ~** to live well (high), to luxuriate; **im Verborgenen ~** to live in the shadow; **in der Vergangenheit ~** to live in the past; **in bedrängten Verhältnissen ~** to live in cramped conditions; **in bescheidenen (dürftigen) Verhältnissen ~** to live in modest circumstances, to live in a small way; **in guten Verhältnissen ~** to live in easy circumstances (well); **in jämmerlichen Verhältnissen ~** to live in wretched poverty (in misery and want); **über seine Verhältnisse ~** to live above one's means, to dissave, to overrun (outrun) the constable *(Br.)*; **von seinem Vermögen ~** to live on prior means; **von Wasser und Brot ~** to live on bread and water; **in Wohlstand ~** to live in affluent circumstances (clover); **von der Wohltätigkeit ~** to live on charity; **zurückgezogen ~** to live in privacy (a retired, obscure life);

zu ~ haben to have a competency; **genug zu ~ haben** to have enough to live on; **nicht mehr lange zu ~ haben** to live on borrowed time; **vom Ertrag eines Bauernhofs ~ können** to win support from a farm; **mit einer Beschuldigung ~ müssen** to be labo(u)ring under an accusation;

~ und ~ lassen to live and let live;

solange sie beide ~ *(Lebensversicherung)* during their joint lives, so long as they both shall live.

lebend geboren born alive; **getrennt ~** *(Einkommensteuerformular)* living separate and apart; **nicht getrennt ~** living with husband, living together;

~es Depotkonto securities ledger; **in guten Verhältnissen ~e Familie** family in easy circumstances; **~e Hecke** quickset hedge; **~es Inventar** livestock; **~er Kolumnentitel** live headline; **~es Konto** customer's (personal) account; **~er Registraturteil** pending correspondence; **~e Sprache** modern (living) language; **~es Wörterbuch** walking dictionary; **~er Zeuge** still living witness.

Lebende, unter den ~n inter vivos;

die ~n und die Toten the quick and the dead.

Lebender living person;

freiwillig im Ausland ~ expatriate.

Lebend|geburt live birth; **~gewicht** live weight.

lebendig live, full of life, *(Börse)* brisk, animated;

mehr tot als ~ more dead than alive;

~ bleiben to remain existent, to linger; **für j. ~ werden lassen** to bring home to s. o.; **Erinnerung ~ machen** to bring back to one's memory; **~ schreiben** to have a vivid style; **~ begraben werden** to be buried alive;

sehr ~es Kind vivacious child; **~e Phantasie haben** to have a lively imagination; **~e Schilderung eines Ereignisses** vivid description of an event; **~er Stil** crisp style.

Lebendigkeit imagination, vividness.
Lebensabend decline of life, declining years, sunset, evening of life, autumn of life *(coll.)*;
friedlichen ~ haben to end one's days in peace; **~ im Armenhaus verbringen** to end one's days in a workhouse; **~ in Italien verbringen** to spend one's remaining years in Italy.
Lebens | ablauf life cycle; **~abriß** biographical notes, vita, curriculum vitae; **kurzen ~abriß geben** to give a short personal record; **~abschnitt** period of life; **in bestimmten ~abschnitten** during certain periods of life; **neuen ~abschnitt beginnen** to begin a new chapter of life; **~ader** jugular vein, *(Verkehrslinie)* life line; **~alter** age; **mittleres ~alter** middle life; **~angst** fear of life; **~anschauung** outlook on life; **~ansprüche** basic requirements; **~arbeit** lifework.
Lebensart way of living, civility, style;
ohne ~ unrefined;
englische ~ English ways of living; **feine ~** fashion;
jem. ~ beibringen to teach s. o. manners; **feine ~ haben** to be well-bred.
Lebens | aufgabe mission in life; **es sich zur ~aufgabe machen** to make it one's lifework, to dedicate one's life to s. th.; **~aufwand** style of living; **unvertretbarer ~aufwand** extravagant living; **hohen ~aufwand haben** to live high on the hog *(sl.)*; **~äußerung** manifestation of life; **~aussichten** expectancy (prospects) of life; **~bedarf, ~bedürfnisse** livelihood, subsistence; **dringendster (notwendiger) ~bedarf** bare necessaries of life, strict necessaries; **kaum seinen ~bedarf verdienen** to earn a bare living; **~bedingungen** conditions of life, living conditions; **äußere ~bedingungen** environment; **bessere ~bedingungen für die Armen herbeiführen** to improve the conditions of the poor.
lebensbedrohende Krankheit fatal disease.
Lebensbedürfnisse necessaries (essentials, wants) of life.
lebensbejahende Einstellung positive turn of mind.
Lebens | bejahung acceptance of life; **~berechtigung** right to exist; **in jds. privaten ~bereich eindringen** to violate s. one's privacy; **~beruf** vocation; **~beschreibung** life, biography; **~bezirk** walk of life; **~bild** biographical sketch, life, vita; **~chance** chance to survive; **~daten** biographical data.
Lebensdauer age, life, length (duration, span) of life, mean time before failure, *(Anlagegut)* mortality, useful (service, *Br.*) life, *(Dauerhaftigkeit)* durability, *(Lager)* rating life, *(Nutzungsdauer)* useful life;
auf ~ for life; **auf die ~ eines Dritten** pour autre vie;
begrenzte ~ limited life; **durchschnittliche ~** *(Lebensversicherung)* standard (average duration of) life; **lange ~** longevity; **mittlere ~** average life expectancy; **mutmaßliche ~** probable (anticipation of, expectation of) life, life expectancy; **normale ~** average life span; **unterdurchschnittliche ~** substandard life; **wahrscheinliche ~**probable [duration of] life; **wirtschaftliche ~** economic (useful, service, *Br.*) life;
~ einer Batterie battery life; **~ eines Dampfers** life of a steamship; **~ einer Einrichtung** vitality of an institution; **~ eines Motors** engine life; **~ eines Schiffes** life of a ship.
lebensecht realistic, true to life.
Lebenseinstellung outlook on life;
allgemeine ~ climate of opinion; **positive ~** positive turn of mind, positivism;
positive ~ haben to hold the affirmative attitude.
Lebens | elan vital impulse; **bis ans ~ende** to the end of one's days, until death; **~energie** life blood; **~erfahrung** practical experience, knowledge of life; **~erhaltung** preservation of life; **~erinnerungen** memoirs; **~erwartung** expectancy of life, life expectancy; **unterdurchschnittliche ~erwartung** *(Versicherung)* bad life; **verkürzte ~erwartung** curtailed expectation of life; **~faden** life strings, fatal thread; **jem. den ~faden abschneiden** to deprive s. o. of his life.
lebensfähig viable, fit to live;
sich als wirtschaftlich ~ erweisen to prove viable, to be economically viable;
~es Projekt viable scheme.
Lebensfähigkeit vitality, *(Überlebensfähigkeit)* survival powers, *(Wirtschafts-unternehmen)* viability.
lebensfeindlich inimical to life;
~es Klima hostile climate.
Lebens | formen, niedere low (simple) forms of life; **hoch organisierte ~formen** highly organized forms of life; **neue ~formen hervorrufen** to create new forms of life; **~frage** vital question, matter of life and death.
lebensfremd starry-eyed.
Lebens | freude, voller full of beans, full of the joys of life; **~frist** lease of life; **seine ~frist ist abgelaufen** his life has run.
Lebensführung line of conduct;
aufwendige ~ sumptuous (high-style, extravagant) living; **mäßige ~** temperance; **unmoralische ~** vicious life;
aufwendige ~ haben to live high on the hog *(sl.)*; **bescheidene ~ haben** to lead a modest life, to live in a small way.
Lebens | führungskosten living expenses; **~gebiet** walk of life.
Lebensgefahr danger of life, mortal danger;
in ~ on the spot *(US sl.)*; **mit eigener ~** at the risk of one's own life;
keine ~ no grave danger; **unmittelbare ~** immediate danger of life;
sich in ~ befinden to be in danger (peril) of one's life, *(Kranker)* to be on the danger list; **sich in ~ begeben** to risk one's life; **j. unter eigener ~ retten** to rescue s. o. at the risk of one's own life; **in ~ schweben** to be in jeopardy [of one's life], to be in mortal danger.
lebensgefährdend perilous.
lebensgefährlich extremely dangerous, dangerous to life;
absolut ~ sein to be sheer murder; **~ erkrankt sein** to be on the danger list;
mit ~en Verletzungen dangerously (critically) injured.
Lebens | gefährte partner in life, life companion; **~geister** spirits; **die erschlafften ~geister einer Partei wieder beleben** to revive the drooping spirits of a party; **alle ~geister verloren haben** to have no kick left.
Lebensgemeinschaft partnership in life;
eheliche ~ married (conjugal) life, conjugal relations; **gewöhnliche eheliche ~ und Haushaltsgemeinschaft** ordinary domestic arrangements *(Br.)*; **häusliche ~** family life.
Lebens | genuß enjoyment of life; **~geschichte** life [hi]story, biography; **seine ~geschichte schreiben** to be writing one's life.
lebensgetreu true to life, lifelike.
Lebens | gewohnheiten way of life (living), living habits, life patterns; **vertraute ~gewohnheiten** familiar pattern of life; **seine gesamten ~gewohnheiten ändern** to change one's whole way of life; **~glück** personal happiness.
lebensgroß life-size[d];
~es Porträt full-length portrait.
Lebens | größe full (life) size; **in ~größe** as large as life; **~grundlage** basis of existence, livelihood; **j. um seine ~grundlage bringen** to deprive s. o. of his livelihood; **~grundsatz** vital principle; **~gruppe** *(Soziologie)* social group.
Lebenshaltung cost (standard, style) of living;
aufwendige ~ sumptuous (high-style, extravagant) living; **durchschnittliche ~** average standard of living;
~ einschränken to lower one's standard of living.
Lebenshaltungsfrage bread-and-butter issue.
Lebenshaltungsindex index number of cost of living, cost-of-living (consumer's price) index;
gestiegener ~ advanced cost of living.
Lebenshaltungskosten living costs (expenses), cost of living;
einfachste ~ bread-alone costs of living; **erhöhte (gestiegene) ~** advanced (increased) cost of living;
~ im Ausland foreign living costs; **~ einer Familie** family living expenses;
gestiegene ~ abbremsen to slow down the rising cost of living; **preistreibend für die ~ sein** to pace the general increase of living cost;
automatische ~angleichung cost-of-living escalator adjustment; **~anstieg** cost-of-living rise; **~ausgleichsformel** cost-of-living adjustment formula; **~behörde** Cost of Living Council *(US)*; **automatischer ~faktor** built-in cost-of-living adjuster; **~[gleit]klausel** cost-of-living [escalator] clause; **~index** cost-of-living index, index number of cost of living; **genehmigte ~klausel** permissive wage-adjustment clause; **~steigerung** cost-of-living increase.
Lebenshaltungs | preisindex cost-of-living (consumer's price) index; **~zuschuß** cost-of-living allowance.
Lebens | inhalt, sein ganzer his whole life; **~interessen** vital interests; **~jahr** year of one's life; **~kampf** battle of life, struggle for life; **~kenner** man of the world.
lebensklug wise, sophisticated.
Lebens | kostenindex cost-of-living index, index number of cost of living; **~kraft** vitality, stamina, vigo(u)r, prime; **voller ~kraft** full of life; **~kreis** personal world; **~künstler** happy-go-lucky fellow.
Lebenslage stage of life;
in jeder ~ in every condition of life;
jeder ~ gewachsen sein to prove equal to one's task, to cope with every situation; **sich in allen ~n zu helfen wissen** to know how to find a way out of every situation.

lebenslange Freundschaft lifelong friendship.
lebenslänglich for (during) life, lifelong, permanent, *(ewig)* perpetual, eternal;
~ **angestellt sein** to hold an office for life; ~ **verurteilt sein** to be sentenced for life;
~**es Amt** office for life; ~**e Anstellung** life tenure; ~**es Einkommen** life income; ~**e Mitgliedschaft** life membership; ~**er Nießbrauch** life interest, *(Grundstück)* tenancy for life, life tenancy; ~**er Nießbraucher** tenant for life, lifeholder; ~**er Nutznießer** life beneficiary; ~**e Nutznießung** life interest; ~**e Rente** life annuity; ~**e Strafe** life sentence; ~**e Treuhandverwaltung** living trust *(US)*; ~**e Unterhaltsrente** permanent alimony; ~**er Vertrag** life contract; ~**e Zuchthausstrafe** life imprisonment.
Lebenslauf course of life, career, *(schriftlich)* personal record (background), life history, curriculum vitae;
detaillierter ~ comprehensive career details;
~ **aufsetzen** to draw up a curriculum vitae; ~ **vorzulegen haben** to be required to hand in a curriculum vitae;
~**akte** *(Maschine)* service records, log-book.
Lebens|licht spark of life, vital spark; **jem. das** ~**licht ausblasen** to snuff out s. one's hopes, *(töten)* to bump s. o. off; ~**linie** life line; **voller** ~**lust** full of beans.
lebenslustig fond of life, keen to enjoy life, gay.
Lebens|maxime vital principle; ~**minimum** minimum of existence, subsistence level, bread line.
Lebensmittel provisions, victuals *(Br.)*, viands, groceries, food [supplies], foodstuffs;
abgepackte ~ packaged groceries; **dauerhafte** ~ nonperishable foodstuffs; **nicht zum Verzehr geeignete** ~ unwholesome food; **haltbare** ~ durables; **konzentrierte** ~ condensed food; **tiefgekühlte** ~ frozen food; **überflüssige** ~ spare food; **verderbliche** ~ perishables; **vitaminreiche** ~ protective food; **zollfreie** ~ free food;
~ **tierischen Ursprungs** animal products;
Vorrat an ~**n anlegen** to stock provisions; ~ **anschaffen** to market, to cater; ~ **aufkaufen** to regrate *(Br.)*; **tiefgekühlte** ~ **auftauen** to defreeze food; ~ **ausgeben** to issue provisions; ~ **beschlagnahmen** to commandeer provisions; **schlecht gewordene** ~ **beschlagnahmen** to condemn defective provisions; **sich mit** ~**n eindecken** to victual; ~ **einkaufen** to go grocery shopping; **nicht genügend** ~ **haben** to fall short of provisions; ~ **hamstern** to hoard food; ~ **konservieren** to preserve foodstuffs, to keep food on ice; ~ **liefern** to purvey; ~ **rationieren** to ration food; ~ **dem Tiefkühlverfahren unterziehen** to quick-freeze food; ~ **verfälschen** to adulterate food; **mit** ~ **versehen** to provision, to supply with provisions, to victual; ~ **verteilen** to dispense food; ~ **weiterverkaufen** to regrate *(Br.)*; ~ **zurückhalten** to hold up foodstuffs;
kostenloser ~**abschnitt** food stamp benefit; ~**abteilung** food department; ~**aktien** food shares (stocks, *US*); ~**amt** food office; ~**an- und verkauf** regrating; ~**anreicherung** food enrichment; ~**anzeigen** food ads *(US)*; ~**aufbewahrung** food conservation; ~**auswahl** choice of food; ~**auszeichnung** food labelling; ~**bedarf** food requirements; ~**behälter** food container; ~**behörde** Food and Drug Administration (FDA) *(US)*; ~**bereich** foodstuff sector; ~**betrieb** food plant; ~**bevorratung** stockpiling of foodstuffs; ~**bewirtschaftung** food rationing; ~**branche** food trade, supply branch; **in der** ~**branche** in the food line; ~**chemiker** food analyst (chemist); ~**einfuhren** food imports; ~**einkauf** grocery shopping; ~**einsparung** food conservation; ~**einzelhändler** food retailer; ~**- und Rohstofferzeugung** primary production; ~**fabrikant** food manufacturer; ~**fälschung** adulteration of food; ~**geschäft** food shop (store, *US*), grocery (grocer's) shop *(Br.)* (store, outlet, *US*), grocery *(US)*; **großes** ~**geschäft mit Selbstbedienung** supermarket *(US)*; ~**gesetz** National Food Bill *(US)*, Food and Drug Act *(Br.)*; ~**großhändler**, ~**großhandel** wholesale provision business; ~**gutschein** victualling note *(Br.)*; ~**hamsterer** food hoarder; ~**hamstern** food hoarding, hoarding of supplies; ~**handel** victual(l)ing (grocery) trade; ~**händler** victualler, provision dealer (merchant); ~**handlung** grocery shop (store, *US*), food shop; ~**industrie** food-processing (-manufacturing) industry, provisions industry; ~**inspekteur** food inspector; ~**karte** food (ration) card, ration book (ticket); ~**kartenabschnitt** food (ration) coupon *(Br.)*, point; ~**kaufhaus** supermarket; ~**kennzeichnung** label(l)ing of foodstuffs; ~**knappheit** shortage of food, food shortage, lack of food; ~**konserven** canned *(US)* (tinned, *Br.*) food; ~**konservierung** food conservation; ~**kontrolle** food control; ~**kontrolleur** food inspector (controller); ~**kürzung** food cut; ~**laden** food shop (store, *US*), grocery outlet; **fahrender** ~**laden** mobile shop; ~**laden besitzen** to keep a grocer's shop; ~**lager** supply depot, inventory of supplies, cache; ~**lagerung** food storage; ~**lieferant** purveyor, victualler, provisioner, *(fertiger Speisen)* caterer; ~**mangel** food shortage; ~**markenabschnitt** ration coupon; ~**paket** food parcel (package); ~**preisauszeichnung** food price label(l)ing; ~**preise** food prices, prices of foodstuffs; ~**produkte** food products; ~**produktion** food production; ~**ration** food ration; ~**rationierung** food rationing; ~**reserven** food reserves; ~**sendung**, ~**transport** shipment of food[stuffs], food shipment; ~**spende** food donation; ~**überschüsse** food surpluses (glut); ~**überwachung** food control; ~**verarbeitung** food processing; ~**verarbeitungsbetrieb** food-processing company; ~**verbrauch** food consumption; ~**verfälschung** adulteration of food; ~**vergiftung** food poisoning; ~**verkauf** sale of provisions; ~**verpackung** food packaging; ~**verpackungsbetrieb** food packer; ~**versand** food shipment; ~**verschwendung** food waste; ~**versorgung** food supply, supplying with provisions, victual(l)ing; ~**vorrat** food supply (stocks), provisions; ~**vorrat anlegen** to lay in a store (stock) of provisions; ~**werte** *(Börse)* food shares (stocks, *US*); ~**zufuhr abschneiden** to cut off provisions; ~**zusatz** food additive; ~**zuteilung** food ration (allowance); ~**zwangswirtschaft** food rationing.
Lebensmöglichkeit possibility to exist.
lebensmüde world-weary.
Lebensmut, neuen ~ **gewonnen haben** to take a fresh interest in life; **jem. neuen** ~ **schenken** to infuse new life into s. o.; **allen** ~ **verlieren** to lose all interest in life.
lebensnah true to life, realistic.
Lebensnähe closeness to life.
lebensnotwendig vital, essential;
~ **werden** to become vital in one's daily life;
~**er Bedarf** bare necessities of life; ~**e Dinge** necessaries; ~**e Funktionen** vital functions.
Lebens|notwendigkeit vital necessity; ~**prinzip**, ~**regel** vital principle, principle of life; ~**qualität** quality of life; ~**raum** living (vital) space; ~**recht** right to exist; ~**rente** life annuity, pension for life; ~**retter** life saver, rescuer, *(Schwimmer)* lifeguard; ~**rettung** life saving, rescue, *(Schwimmer)* lifesaving.
Lebensrettungs|gerät lifesaving apparatus; ~**gesellschaft** Royal Humane Society *(Br.)*, lifeboat association; ~**kanone** *(Schiff)* mortar; ~**medaille** lifesaving medal.
Lebens|risiko life contingency; ~**saft** sap; ~**spanne** span of life.
lebenssprühend vital, animated;
~ **sein** to be full of beans *(sl.)*.
Lebensstandard standard (level, *US*, scale, rate) of living, living standard;
jds. ~ **entsprechend** suitable to s. one's station;
angemessener ~ health and decency standard of living; **bequemer** ~ comfortable living standard; **tatsächlicher** ~ actual level of living.
Lebensstellung walk of (place in) life, position of (condition in) life, *(im Beruf)* appointment for life, permanent position (situation), establishment.
Lebensstil style of living, life style;
eleganter ~ gracious living, fashion; **persönlicher** ~ personal style;
bescheidenen ~ **haben** to live in a quiet way.
Lebensstufe, niedere low scale of existence.
lebens|treu to the life; ~**tüchtig** fit for life; ~**überdrüssig** world-weary.
Lebensumstände environment, surroundings.
lebensunfähig nonviable.
Lebensunterhalt livelihood, living [costs, expenses], sustenance, necessaries, bread, support, subsistence, maintenance;
existenznotwendiger ~ minimum subsistence level; **notwendiger** ~ minimum maintenance, bread and butter; **unsicherer** ~ precarious livelihood;
~ **von Familien** family living expenses;
sich für seinen ~ **abplacken (abrackern)** to scrape for one's living, to scrabble for one's livelihood; **dem kargen Boden seinen** ~ **abringen** to wrest a living from the soil; **für seinen** ~ **arbeiten** to work for one's living, to work in order to live; **seinen** ~ **davon bestreiten** to make a living out of it; **seinen** ~ **erwerben** to get (earn) one's living; **seinen** ~ **finden** to pick up a livelihood *(Br.)*; **seinen** ~ **mit bar entlohnter Gelegenheitsarbeit fristen** to live on cash earnings; **genug zum** ~ **haben** to pay one's way; **vertraglich nur für den notwendigen** ~ **haften** to be liable only for necessaries; **j. der Notwendigkeit entheben, sich seinen**

~ **verdienen zu müssen** to dispense s. o. from the necessity of earning his living; **jds.** ~ **sicherstellen** to supply s. one's needs, to ensure s. o. enough to live on; ~ **einer Familie sicherstellen** to support a family; **für jds.** ~ **sorgen** to provide for s. o.; **seinen** ~ **verdienen** to earn (win) one's living, to get one's bread, to earn one's bread and butter, to keep the pot boiling *(Br.)*; **nur den nackten** ~ **verdienen** to earn a bare living; **seinen** ~ **mit seiner Hände Arbeit verdienen** to earn a living by manual labo(u)r; **seinen** ~ **als Schriftsteller verdienen** to depend on one's pen for a living, to earn one's living by writing; **seinen** ~ **selbst verdienen** to support o. s.; **jem. zu einem** ~ **verhelfen** to put s. o. in the way of earning a living.

Lebensunterhalt[ung]s|kosten cost of living, living expenses; ~**zuschuß** cost-of-living allowance.

Lebens|untüchtigkeit copelessness; ~**verhältnisse** living conditions, way of life; ~**vermutung** presumption of life.

Lebensversicherer life underwriter.

lebensversichern, sich to assure one's life with a company *(Br.)*; **sich für 20.000 £** ~ to insure (assure, *Br.*) o. s. for £ 20.000; **sich gegenseitig** ~ to insure one's own life for the benefit of the other; **seine Schlüsselkräfte** ~ to take out life policies on one's key men.

Lebensversicherter life insured (assured, *Br.*).

Lebensversicherung life insurance (assurance, *Br.*), *(auf den Erlebensfall)* endowment insurance, *(auf den Todesfall)* whole-life assurance *(Br.)*, ordinary life insurance *(US)*;
abgekürzte ~ ordinary endowment (deferred annuity, limited payment) insurance, term (temporary) assurance *(Br.)*; **zur Hypothekenrückzahlung abgeschlossene** ~ mortgage redemption insurance; **vom Staat abgeschlossene** ~ governmental life insurance; **aufgeschobene** ~ deferred life assurance *(Br.)*; **erneuerungsfähige** ~ renewable term insurance; **gegenseitige** ~ assessment (mutual) life insurance; **mit einem Kapitalanlagegesellschaftsvertrag gekoppelte** ~ unit assurance *(Br.)*; **gemischte** ~ combined endowment and whole life insurance, mixed life assurance *(Br.)*; **beitragslos gestellte** ~ extended life insurance; **globale** ~ wholesale life insurance; **große** ~ ordinary life insurance; **hochwertige** ~ high-value life insurance; **prämienfreie** ~paid-up life insurance, free life assurance *(Br.)*; **staatliche** ~ government life insurance; **unkündbare** ~ noncancellable insurance;
~ **für Arbeitnehmer** industrial assurance *(Br.)*; ~ **mit laufender Beitragszahlung** life insurance in force; ~ **mit Einschluß der Kriegsgefahr** life insurance war risk included; **gemischte** ~ **auf den Erlebens- und Todesfall** combined endowment and whole-life insurance, mixed life assurance *(Br.)*; ~ **auf Gegenseitigkeit** mutual (assessment) life insurance; ~ **von Gesellschaftern** partnership (business) life insurance; ~ **mit Gewinnbeteiligung** life assurance with profits *(Br.)*, participating life insurance *(US)*; ~ **ohne Gewinnbeteiligung** life insurance without profits; ~ **über verbundene Leben** more than one life assurance *(Br.)*; ~ **mit steigender Prämie** renewable term assurance *(Br.)*; ~ **mit Prämienabbuchung vom Gehalt** salary reduction (savings) life insurance; ~ **mit abgekürzter Prämienzahlung** limited payment (pay, *US*) insurance, limited payment assurance *(Br.)*; ~ **ohne Rückkaufswert** term life insurance; ~ **für Staatsangestellte** governmental life insurance; ~ **auf den Todesfall** straight (whole) life insurance, ordinary life insurance *(US)* (assurance, *Br.*), whole-life assurance *(Br.)*; ~ **ohne ärztliche Untersuchung** nonmedical policy; **befristete** ~ **mit Verlängerungsrecht** renewable terms life insurance; ~ **gegen Zahlung einer Einmalprämie** single-premium insurance;
~ **abschließen** to insure one's life, to buy a life insurance; ~ **für j. abschließen, j. in eine** ~ **einkaufen** to write insurance upon s. one's life, to assure s. one's life *(Br.)*; ~ **auf seinen eigenen Namen umschreiben lassen** to vest an assurance on one's own name *(Br.)*; ~ **zurückkaufen** to surrender a policy.

Lebensversicherungs|abteilung life branch; ~**agent** life-insurance agent (underwriter); ~**ansprüche** life-insurance claims; ~**anstalt** life insurance office, life office; **guten** ~**aspiranten abgeben** to be a good life; ~**büro** life office; ~**charakter** life-insurance elements; **staatlicher** ~**fonds** state life-insurance fund; ~**freibetrag** *(Einkommensteuererklärung)* life insurance relief *(Br.)*; ~**gesellschaft** life[-insurance (-assurance, *Br.*)] company, life office; ~**gesellschaft auf Gegenseitigkeit** mutual life insurance company; ~- **und Sterbekassengesetz** Industrial Assurance and Friendly Societies Act *(Br.)*.

Lebensversicherungspolice life [insurance, assurance, *Br.*] policy, life, benefit certificate;
abgekürzte ~ endowment *(Br.)* (limited-payment life) policy; **zeitlich befristete** ~ term policy; **erneuerungsfähige** ~ renewable term policy; **gewinnbeteiligte** ~ life policy with profits, with profits policy, participating life policy *(US)*; **nicht gewinnbeteiligte** ~ without profits policy; **jährlich kündbare** ~ permanent life policy; **normale** ~ ordinary life policy; **steuerbegünstigte** ~ life policy qualifying for relief *(Br.)*; **umwandelbare** ~ convertible term policy;
~ **auf den Erlebnisfall** endowment policy; ~ **mit Gewinnbeteiligung** participating life policy *(US)*, life insurance with profits; ~ **ohne Gewinnbeteiligung** life insurance without profits, stock [-rate] policy; ~ **mit auf zwanzig Jahre abgekürzter Laufzeit** 20 years payment life-insurance policy; ~ **mit gleichbleibenden Prämien** ordinary life policy; ~ **mit abgekürzter Prämienzahlung** limited life policy; ~ **auf den Todesfall** straight (whole, *Br.*, ordinary, *US*) life policy; ~ **ohne ärztliche Untersuchung** nonmedical policy;
~ **abtreten** to assign a life assurance *(Br.)* (insurance) policy; **jds.** ~ **beleihen** to advance money against s. one's life policy; ~ **zur Besicherung hinterlegen** to lodge a life policy as security.

Lebensversicherungsprämie life-insurance (-assurance, *Br.*) premium, life premium;
von Jahr zu Jahr ansteigende ~ natural premium; **gesamte** ~ life rate.

Lebensversicherungs|schutz life-insurance coverage (cover, protection), life-assurance protection *(Br.)*; ~**sektor** life insurance field; ~**summe** life-insured amount, reversion; **doppelte** ~**summe bei Unfalltod** double indemnity; ~**summe in Höhe von 100.000 £ ausgezahlt bekommen** to receive 100.000 £ in life insurance; ~**treuhandfonds** life trust; ~**vertrag** life insurance (assurance, *Br.*) contract; ~**vertrag abschließen** to buy a life insurance; ~**vertreter** life underwriter (insurance agent).

lebenswahr to the life.

Lebenswahrscheinlichkeit expectation of life.

Lebenswandel way of life (living), line of conduct, walk;
mit einwandfreiem ~ clean-lived;
unmoralischer ~ profligacy, vice;
seinen bisherigen ~ **fortsetzen** to follow one's old course; **liederlichen (unsittlichen)** ~ **führen** to have a light character, to lead a disreputable (immoral) life.

Lebensweg course of life.

Lebensweise mode of living, walk;
amerikanische ~ American way of life; **billige** ~ cheap living; **bürgerliche** ~ civil ways; **eingeschränkte** ~ austerity; **geordnete** ~ regular habits; **gesunde** ~ healthy way of living; **schlichte** ~ plain living; **sitzende** ~ sedentary life; **unbekümmerte** ~ happy-go-lucky fashion; **vernünftige** ~ the correct procedure; **primitive** ~ **eines unzivilisierten Landes** crude life of an uncivilized country;
seine ~ **zum Besseren ändern** to amend one's ways.

Lebens|weisheit wisdom; ~**wende** turn of life; ~**werk** lifework.

lebenswichtig vital, essential, vitally important, pivotal;
nicht ~ nonessential;
~**e Artikel** articles of first necessity; ~**e Betriebe** key industries, *(Versorgung)* public utilities; ~**e Güter** essential goods; ~**es Interesse** vital interest; ~**er Teil** vital part.

Lebenszeichen sign of life.

Lebenszeit [term of] life, lifetime, *(Scheidungsrecht)* limited period;
auf ~ for life, permanent, lifehold, *(Rente)* during one's natural life, *(Richter)* during good behavio(u)r; **auf** ~ **angestellt** appointed for life;
durchschnittliche ~ average span of life; **natürliche** ~ **eines Menschen** natural life; **verbleibende** ~ life in being;
auf ~ **anstellen** to appoint for life; **auf** ~ **angestellt sein** to hold an office for life; **auf** ~ **Mitglied sein** to be a life member; **zum Beamten auf** ~ **bestellt werden** to become an established civil servant.

Lebensziel, jds. one's goal in life; **ohne** ~ with no object in life; **wesentliches** ~ main object in life.

Lebens|zuschnitt haben, allereinfachsten to live in the simplest possible way; **neue** ~**zuversicht** a new lease of life; ~**zyklus** life cycle.

Lebe|welt outskirts of society, fast set; **menschliches** ~**wesen** reasonable creature.

lebhaft vivid, vigorous, fresh, *(Börse)* animated, brisk, cheerful, active, lively, buoyant, *(Verkehr)* busy, frequented;
~ **und fest** *(Börse)* active and strong;
Vorschlag ~ **begrüßen** to welcome a proposal; ~ **beschreiben** to describe vividly; **sich** ~ **beteiligen** to be an active member; **sehr** ~ **sein** to be full of life, to be in good spirits; ~ **begehrt werden** to be in brisk demand; ~ **begrüßt werden** to be accorded a warm welcome;

~**er Absatz** brisk sale; ~**es Bedauern** deep regret; ~**e Börse** brisk market; ~**e Debatte** lively debate; ~**e Farben** bright colo(u)rs; ~**es Geschäft** brisk business; ~**en Handel treiben** to do a lot of trade; ~**es Interesse** keen (lively) interest; ~**es Kind** vivacious child; ~**e Konkurrenz** active competition; **zu** ~**es Muster** loud pattern; ~**e Nachfrage** strong (brisk, active) demand, cheerful market; ~**e Phantasie** lively imagination; ~**es Treiben** bustling life; ~**er Umsatz** active dealings; ~**e Unterhaltung** animated conversation (discussion); ~**er Verkehr** heavy traffic; ~**e Vorstellung** lively idea.

Lebhaftigkeit *(Börse)* animation, liveliness, briskness, buoyancy, *(Verkehr)* frequency.

leblos lifeless, *(Börse)* stagnant, dull, dead, flat.

Leblosigkeit *(Börse)* flatness, stagnation, deadness, dullness.

Lebzeiten, zu in one's lifetime, while alive (living).

Leck leak, leakage.

leck schlagen to stave, to spring a leak, *(Schiff)* to smash a hole in a ship.

Leckage, Leckwerden leakage, ullage;
frei von ~ free from leakage;
~ **und Bruch** leakage and breakage;
für ~ **in Abzug bringen** to allow a sum for leakage;
~**abzug** allowance for leakage; ~**klausel** leakage clause.

lecken, bis zum Dach *(Flammen)* to lick the roof; **sich alle zehn Finger** ~ to be very keen on s. th.

lecker delicious, savory, tasty;
~**e Happen** dainties, titbits.

Leckerbissen dainty, morsel, titbit, delicacy;
literarische ~ s. th. for literary connoisseurs;
~ **der Filmfestspiele** highlight of the film festival.

Leckereien sweets *(Br.)*, candies *(US)*, goodies;
verschiedene ~ **servieren** to serve various kinds of delicacies (dainties).

Leckermaul sein to have a sweet tooth.

Leckleitung drainage tube.

lecksicher leak-proof.

Leck|strom leakage current; ~**werden** leakage.

Leder leather;
in ~ **gebunden** leather-bound; **zäh wie** ~ *(fig.)* as hard as nails; **jem. ans** ~ **gehen** to be in for it; **einem Angestellten ans** ~ **gehen** to make it hot for an employee; **jem. das** ~ **gerben** to tan s. one's hide; **zäh wie** ~ **sein** to have an iron constitution; **jem. ans** ~ **wollen** to be out to get s. o.; **dem Redner ans** ~ **wollen** to attack the speaker sharply; **vom** ~ **ziehen** to unsheathe one's sword; **gegen jem. vom** ~ **ziehen** to let fly against s. o.;
zuschlagen, was das ~ **hält** to strike with might and main;
~**arbeit** leatherwork; ~**band** calf (leather, *US*) binding; ~**industrie** leather industry; ~**kissen** leather cushion; ~**koffer** leather suitcase; ~**mappe** leatherboard.

ledern *(Buch, Vortrag)* rapid, dry.

Leder|nacken *(mil.)* leatherneck *(US sl.)*; ~**polster** leather upholstery (car); ~**verarbeitung,** ~**zurichtung** leather dressing; ~**waren** leatherware.

ledig unmarried, single, sole, *(Frau)* discovert;
los und ~ footloose and fancy-free;
~ **bleiben** to remain a bachelor (spinster); ~ **sein** to be single; **aller Schulden** ~ **sein** to be free of all debts; **einer Sache** ~ **werden** to get rid of s. th.;
~**e Frau** feme sole, spinster; ~**es Kind** illegitimate child; ~**e Mutter** unmarried mother.

Ledigen|heim home for single persons; ~**stand** wifelessness; ~**steuer** bachelor tax.

Lediger bachelor, unmarried man.

lediglich only, simply, merely, solely;
~ **hingehen, um etw. anzusehen** to go there solely to see it; ~ **eine Frage der Zeit sein** to be simply a question of time;
~ **eine Formsache** merely a formality; ~ **durch Zufall** by a mere accident.

Lee lee side;
in ~ under the wind;
~**küste** lee-shore.

leer empty, *(eitel)* moonshine, *(Formular)* blank, *(geräumt)* evacuated, *(Geschwätz)* windy, *(Grundstück)* tenantless, *(Haus)* vacant, unoccupied, *(Land)* unmanned, *(Schiff)* light; **gähnend** ~ *(Saal)* completely empty; ~ **zurück** returned empty; ~ **ausgehen** to get nothing by it, to be left in the cold, to hold the bag *(coll.)*; **seinen Teller** ~ **essen** to clear one's plate; **etw.** ~ **kaufen** to buy s. th. unfurnished; **Zeile** ~ **lassen** to leave a line blank; ~ **laufen** to idle, to run idle; ~ **sein** *(Lager)* to be out of stock; ~ **stehen** to stand empty, to be vacant (unoccupied);
~**es Blatt** blank sheet of paper; ~**e Drohung** idle (empty) threat; ~**e Fässer** empties; **nichts als** ~**es Gerede** nothing but idle talk, gas *(coll.)*; ~**es Gerücht** unfounded (idle) rumo(u)r; ~**er Gesichtsausdruck** vacant expression; **mit** ~**en Händen kommen** to come empty-handed; **vor einem** ~**en Haus spielen** to play to empty benches; ~**er Platz** vacant seat; ~**e Pracht** pomp; ~**e Stelle** vacancy; ~**e Straßen** deserted streets; ~**es Stroh dreschen** to beat the air; ~**e Versprechungen** empty (vain, hollow) promises; ~**e Worte** empty words.

Leerabgabe *(Börse)* bearish sale *(Br.)*, short selling *(US)*;
~ **einer Position decken** to repurchase short sales *(US)*.

Leer|aktie unpaid share; ~**aufmachung** dummy; ~**band** *(Aufnahmegerät)* blank tape; ~**bus** deadhead.

Leere emptiness, vanity, vacuum;
geistige ~ vacuity;
geistige ~ **empfinden** to feel an emptiness.

leeren to empty, *(Briefkasten)* to clear, to collect;
jem. den Geldbeutel ~ to drain s. one's box, to fleece s. o. of his money; **bitteren Kelch bis zur Neige** ~ to drain the cup of sorrow to the dregs; **seinen Teller** ~ to clear one's plate.

Leer|fahrt empty run; ~**fahrtlokomotive** pilot engine; ~**fracht** dead freight; ~**fuhre haben** *(Taxi)* to deadhead; ~**gang** neutral position; ~**gewicht** dead-weight, net weight, weight when empty.

Leergut empties;
~ **zurück** returned empties;
~ **wird nicht zurückgenommen** empties are not taken back;
~**rücklauf,** ~**rücksendung** empty return running.

leerkaufen, Laden to clean out a shop.

Leerkiste empty packing case.

Leerlauf *(Gang)* neutral gear (position), idle position, idling, power off, *(Unbeschäftigtsein)* running on the spot, no-load;
im ~ out of gear;
ruhiger ~ smooth idling;
~ **in der Verwaltung** waste of energy in administration;
im ~ **fahren** *(Auto)* to coast, *(Maschine)* to run idle (with no load); **in den** ~ **schalten** to leave a car out of gear, to put the lever into neutral; **im** ~ **sein** to run in neutral gear, to tick over;
~**düse** *(Vergaser)* low-speed nozzle, idler; ~**einstellung** *(Vergaser)* idling adjustment.

leerlaufen to be running out;
Faß ~ **lassen** to run a barrel dry.

leerlaufend idle, not operating.

Leerlauf|gang neutral gear; ~**gemisch** pilot jet mixture; ~**kapazität** idle capacity *(US)*; ~**stellung** neutral position; **Gang in die** ~**stellung bringen** to slip (put) the gear into neutral; ~**strom** idling current; ~**verlust** *(Fabrik)* idle-plant expenses, *(Maschine)* no-load loss; ~**zeit** idle time, *(beim Produktionswechsel)* set-up time.

Leer|material empty, empties; ~**packung** sham package, dummy.

leerpumpen, Brunnen to exhaust the water in a well.

Leer|seite blank leaf; ~**spule** *(Tonband)* empty reel; ~**stehen** unoccupancy, vacancy *(US)*.

leerstehend unoccupied, vacant, empty;
~**es Haus** vacant house; ~**e Wohnung** unoccupied dwelling, idle tenement.

Leer|takt *(Motor)* idle stroke; ~**taste** *(Schreibmaschine)* space bar; ~**tiefgang** light draft (draught, *Br.*); ~**tonnage** dead-weight tonnage, light displacement; ~**übertragung** *(Firma)* pro-forma transfer.

Leerung *(Briefkasten)* clearance, collection.

Leerungszeit collection time.

Leerverkauf *(Börse)* bear sale *(Br.)*, *(Börse)* short sales *(US)*, *(Waren)* forward (futures) sale;
~ **tätigen** to write a call naked.

Leerverkäufe uncovered *(Br.)* (short, *US*) sales, selling stocks short *(US)*.

Leerverkäufer bear seller *(Br.)*, short seller *(US)*.

Leer|verkaufsposition *(Börse)* short position *(US)*; ~**wagen** empty [wag(g)on], deadhead; ~**wohnung** unfurnished flat (apartment); ~**zeile** space; ~**zeit** idle (nonproductive) time; ~**zimmer** vacant (empty) room, unfurnished lodging; ~**zug** deadhead.

Leeseite lee side.

leewärts leeward.

legal legal, lawful, rightful, innocent;
mit ~**en Mitteln** by lawful means; **auf** ~**em Wege** legally.

Legalisation legalization.

legalisieren to legalize, to legitimate, to validate;
Urkunde ~ to authenticate a deed.

legalisierte Erklärung duly certified declaration.

Legalisierung legalization, validation, authentication.
Legalisierungsklausel attestation clause.
Legalität legality, validity, lawfulness;
außerhalb der ~ unlawful, outside the law;
sein Handeln mit dem Mäntelchen der ~ umgeben to cover one's actions with a gloss of legality.
Legalitätskontrolle challenge of the legality of official actions.
Legat legacy, bequest, *(Grundeigentum)* devise;
bedingtes ~ conditional bequest; **vom Treuhänder verwaltetes ~** trust legacy;
~ aussetzen to admeasure a legacy; **~ einbehalten** to subtract a legacy; **~e anteilsmäßig zur Schuldentilgung kürzen** to abate legacies pro rata to pay debts.
Legatar legatee, devisee.
Legation legation, embassy.
Legations|rat, vortragender counsel(l)or of legation; **~rat erster Klasse** first secretary; **~rat zweiter Klasse** second secretary; **~sekretär** legation (third, *Br.*) secretary, secretary of a legation.
Legatsaussetzung admeasurement of a legacy.
legatsberechtigt beneficially, entitled.
Legats|entziehung revocation (ademption) of a legacy; **~verfall** lapsing of legacy; **~verkürzung** abatement.
legen, sich to lay down, *(Aufregung)* to pass off, *(Fieber)* to drop, to go down, *(Schmerz)* to ease, *(Sturm, Wind)* to die down, to abate, *(Zorn)* to calm down; **ad acta ~** to file away, to throw into the discard; **zu den Akten ~** to lay on the shelves, to pigeonhole; **sich vor Anker ~** to cast (drop) anchor; **j. auf eine Bahre ~** to lay s. o. on a stretcher; **Beschränkungen auf Einfuhren ~** to place restrictions on imports; **jem. Einquartierung ins Haus ~** to billet s. o.; **jem. die Entscheidung in die Hand ~** to leave the decision in s. one's hands; **Feuer ~** to commit arson, to set on fire; **Fundament ~** to lay the foundation; **sich über das ganze Gebiet ~** *(Nebel)* to settle over the entire area; **sich jem. aufs Gemüt ~** to prey upon s. one's mind; **Gewicht in die Waagschale ~** to put a weight on the scale; **sein Gewicht in die Waagschale ~** to make one's influence felt; **j. ins Grab ~** to rest s. o. in the grave; **Hinterhalt ~** to lay an ambush; **Hund an die Kette ~** to chain up a dog; **Kabel ~** to lay cables; **Kartoffeln ~** to plant potatoes; **jem. etw. zur Last ~** to lay the blame at s. one's door; **sich auf den Magen ~** to settle in one's stomach; **schlechte Manieren an den Tag ~** to display bad manners; **Minen ~** to mine, to lay mines; **sich ins Mittel ~** to intervene; **sich aufs Ohr ~** to take (have) a nap; **Pflaster auf die Wunde ~** to apply a plaster to a wound; **etw. an den falschen Platz ~** to misplace s. th.; **etw. wieder an den richtigen Platz ~** to restore s. th. to its proper place; **Rechnung ~** to render account; **Schienen ~** to lay a track; **sich schlafen ~** to go to bed; **Schloß vor die Tür ~** to hang a padlock on the door; **sich auf die Seite ~** *(Schiff)* to heel over; **Sitzung auf Freitag ~** to fix a meeting for Friday; **kesse Sohle aufs Parkett ~** to shake a leg; **sich auf neue Sprachen ~** to take up modern languages; **Stadt in Schutt und Asche ~** to coventrize a town; **sich nach Steuerbord ~** to list to starboard; **Steuern auf etw. ~** to levy taxes upon s. th.; **seine Stirn in Falten ~** to wrinkle (pucker up) one's forehead; **seine Stirn gegen eine Scheibe ~** to lean one's forehead against a window; **Wäsche ~** to fold the washing; **jem. nichts in den Weg ~** not to make any difficulties for s. o.; **Wein in den Keller ~** to cellar wine; **sich für eine Woche ins Bett ~** to lay o. s. off for a week; **sein Wort auf die Goldwaage ~** to weigh one's words; **sich tüchtig ins Zeug ~** to put one's shoulder to the wheel.
legendär legendary, fabulous;
~er Reichtum fabulous wealth.
Legende legend, *(Bildunterschrift)* caption, *(Zeichenerklärung)* key;
jem. ~n erzählen to pull s. one's leg.
Legendenerfinder fablemonger.
legendenhafte Darstellung legendary description.
leger shirt-sleeve, casual, informal, nonchalant;
~e Art easy manners; **~e Atmosphäre** relaxed atmosphere; **~e Handbewegung** casual gesture; **~e Kleidung** informal dress.
Lege|spiel jigsaw (picture) puzzle; **~verfahren** handsorting method.
legieren to alloy.
legierter Stahl alloy steel.
Legierung alloy, alligation, composition metal.
Legion legion.
Legionär legionary.
legislativ legislative.
Legislativbefugnisse legislative powers.
Legislative legislative [power], legislature, lawgiving.
Legislaturperiode legislative period (session), parliamentary session *(Br.)*, lifetime of a parliament;
eine ~ betreffend sessional.
legitim legitimate, lawful.
Legitimation legitimation, declaration of legitimacy, *(Indentitätsnachweis)* proof of one's identity, identification;
~ durch nachfolgende Heirat legitimation by subsequent matrimony;
Betrag gegen ~ auszahlen to pay a sum upon proof of identity.
Legitimations|aktionär proxyholder; **~brief** letter of credit; **~karte** identity card; **~papiere** identification papers, non-negotiable instruments; **~prüfung** proof of identity; **~schein** hawker's license; **~übertragung** proxy statement; **~urkunde** document of title; **~zeichen** token.
legitimieren to legitimate, to legitimatize, to authorize;
sich ~ to prove one's identity, to show one's papers; **Kind ~** to legitimize a child; **j. zur Vertragsunterschrift ~** to authorize s. o. to sign a contract.
legitimiert authorized, entitled;
aktiv ~ able (entitled) to sue, capable of suing; **passiv ~** liable to be sued;
~ sein to be authorized to act;
nachträglich ~es Kind special bastard; **~er Vertreter** authorized agent.
Legitimierung legitimation, legitimization, proof of one's identity.
Legitimität legitimacy.
Lehm clay, loam, mud;
~boden mud floor; **~grube** clay pit; **~hütte** mud hut.
Lehramt situation as teacher, teachership, preceptorate, mastership, *(Universität)* professorship;
~ antreten to enter upon a mastership; **sein ~ aufgeben** to resign one's position as teacher; **~ innehaben** to hold a teaching job.
Lehramts|anwärter trainee teacher; **~auftrag** teaching appointment; **~befähigung** teacher's diploma; **~kandidat** trainee teacher; **~prüfung** teacher's examination; **~prüfungszeugnis** teaching diploma.
Lehranstalt educational establishment (institution, endowment), academy, thinking shop *(coll.)*;
höhere ~ secondary (grammar) school, high school *(US)*; **höhere ~en** institutions of higher learning; **staatliche ~** public school.
Lehr|auftrag teaching appointment, lectureship; **~automat** automatic teaching device; **~beauftragter** lecturer, associate *(US)*; **~befähigung** teaching qualification; **~beispiel** instructive example; **~berechtigung** teacher's diploma; **~beruf** apprenticeable occupation, teaching profession, teaching job; **sich auf den ~beruf vorbereiten** to study for the teaching profession; **~betrieb** training shop, *(Hochschule)* lectures, *(Schule)* teaching; **landwirtschaftlicher ~betrieb** training farm; **~betrieb wieder aufnehmen** to recommence school; **~brief** certificate of apprenticeship, indenture.
Lehrbuch educational book, reader, reading (school) book, textbook *(US)*, manual;
reich bebildertes ~ well illustrated textbook;
~ für Anfänger primer; **~ für Stenografie** shorthand manual; **sich eng ans ~ halten** to stick close to the textbook.
Lehr|bücher, vorgeschriebene prescribed textbooks; **~bursche** apprentice.
Lehre doctrine, *(Ausbildung)* apprenticeship, *(System)* system, gospel, *(Theorie)* theory, *(Unterweisung)* instruction, tuition, teaching, training, *(Wissenschaft)* science;
in der ~ articled;
auf Erfahrung gegründete ~n lessons of experience; **herrschende ~** received opinion (doctrine), prevailing opinion;
~ von der Eigentumsvermutung doctrine of reputed ownership; **~ von der rückwirkenden Kraft** doctrine of relation back; **~ von der Überschreitung der Satzungsbefugnisse** doctrine of ultra vires; **~ der Umwandlung von Grundvermögen** doctrine of conversion; **~ von der Verjährung** doctrine of prescription; **~ von der Vertragsgrundlage** doctrine of frustration of adventure;
seine ~ absolvieren (durchmachen) to serve one's articles (time), to go through the shops; **in die ~ geben** to put out as apprentice, to put to trade, to bind s. o. apprentice, to indent s. o., to article, to indenture; **jem. einige gute ~n auf den Weg geben** to give s. o. some sound advice to take with him; **bei einem Meister in die ~ gehen** to learn from a master; **~ beendet haben** to be out of one's indenture (through one's apprenticeship); **zu jem. in die ~ kommen** to be apprenticed to s. o.; **j. in die ~**

nehmen to take s. o. as apprentice; **in der ~ sein** to be apprenticed, to serve one's articles, to be serving one's apprenticeship; **~ für j. sein** to be a lesson for s. o.; **~ aus etw. ziehen** to draw a moral from s. th.

lehren to teach, to train, to instruct, *(Universität)* to give lectures;
j. Mores ~ to teach s. o. manners;
die Zeit wird es ~ time will tell.

Lehrer teacher, schoolmaster, instructor, director, *(Privatunterricht)* tutor, coach, *(Universität)* lecturer, professor;
amtlich anerkannter ~ certificated teacher;
sich zum ~ kaum eignen to have little or no vocation for teaching; **als ~ unterrichten** to teach in a school;
~beruf teaching [job]; **~bildungsanstalt** teacher training college *(Br.)*, teachers' college *(US)*, normal school; **~buch** instruction book.

Lehrerin mistress.

Lehrer|knappheit teacher shortage; **~kollegium** teaching staff of a school, school staff; **~konferenz** teachers' council; **~mangel** shortage of teachers; **~schaft** body of teachers; **~-Schülerprozentsatz** teacher-pupil ratio; **~seminar** teachers' college (institute); **~stelle** teaching appointment, teachership, mastership; **~überschuß** teacher glut; **~zimmer** common room.

Lehr|fach teaching subject (discipline); **~film** training (educational) film.

Lehrgang [training] course, course of lectures, class school;
außerbetrieblicher ~ out-of-company course; **ganzjähriger ~** full year's course; **kostenloser ~** non-credit course; **vollständiger ~** full-credit course;
~ für Buchprüfer course of instruction in accounting; **~ im Maschinenschreiben** typing course;
zu einem ~ abstellen to detach for a course; **sich zu einem ~ anmelden** to sign up for a course; **~ in der Form gleichzeitig stattfindender Ausbildungskurse aufziehen** to structure a course on a sandwich basis; **~ mit fünf Anrechnungspunkten belegen** to take a course for five credits *(US)*; **~ durchlaufen** to go through a course; **an einem ~ als Gasthörer teilnehmen** to audit a course *(US)*.

Lehr|gangsleiter training supervisor, chief instructor; **~gangsteilnehmer** enrollee, trainee; **philosophisches ~gebäude** scheme of philosophy; **~gebiet** curriculum; **~gegenstand** subject; **~geld** premium, apprentice fee; **~geld zahlen** to learn it the hard way; **teures ~geld zahlen** to pay dearly for one's experience; **~gerüst** falsework; **~herr** master, employer; **~institut** teachers' institute.

Lehrjahr unit *(US)*;
~e apprenticeship;
erstes ~ first year of apprenticeship;
seine ~e durchmachen to serve one's apprenticeship (time), to go through the shops; **noch in den ~en sein** to be in the learning process.

Lehr|junge apprentice; **~kommando** *(mil.)* demonstration team; **~körper** school staff, *(Universität)* fellowship, faculty *(US)*; **~kraft** teaching fellow, qualified teacher; **~krankenhaus** teaching (training) hospital.

Lehrling apprentice, learner;
fauler ~ idle apprentice; **kaufmännischer ~** commercial apprentice, business trainee; **minderjähriger ~** infant apprentice; **überstellter ~** turnover *(Br.)*; **unerfahrener ~** fresh apprentice; **vertraglich verpflichteter ~** bound apprentice; **nicht bei seinem Lehrherrn wohnender ~** outdoor apprentice;
~ an einen anderen Lehrherrn abtreten to turn over an apprentice to another master; **~ annehmen** to take an apprentice; **als ~ dienen** to serve one's articles (apprenticeship); **~ einstellen** to recruit apprentices; **j. als ~ verpflichten** to indent s. o.; **als ~ eingestellt werden** to become apprenticed.

Lehrlings|anwerbung recruitment of apprentices; **~ausbilder** apprentice teacher, apprenticeship executive; **~ausbildung** apprentice (apprenticeship) training, training of apprentices; **~ausbildungsfragen** questions of apprenticeship; **~ausbildungsprogramm** apprenticeship program(me) (scheme); **~ausschuß** apprenticeship committee; **~bedingungen** conditions of apprenticeship; **~beruf** apprenticeable occupation; **~beschäftigung** employment of an apprentice; **~geld** apprentice rate (wages); **~heim** hostel for apprentices; **~jahre** apprentice age; **~liste** register of apprentices; **~lohn** apprentice rate (wages); **~programm** apprenticeship program(me); **~quote** apprenticeship ratio; **~stand** apprenticeship; **~vergütung** apprentice wages.

Lehrlingsverhältnis apprenticeship;
im ~ indented, apprenticed, articled, indentured;
in ein ~ eintreten to take up one's indenture;
~zahl apprenticeship ratio.

Lehrlings|vertrag indenture of apprenticeship, apprenticeship training agreement, apprenticeship contract (agreement); **~vertrag abschließen** to fasten an apprentice; **~werkstatt** training shop; **~wesen** apprenticeship system; **~zeit** apprenticeship [period]; **seine ~zeit beenden** to work out one's time; **mit der ~zeit beginnen** to enter into apprenticeship; **~zeugnis** certificate of apprenticeship.

Lehr|mädchen girl apprentice; **~maschine** teaching machine; **programmiertes ~material** program(m)ed instruction; **~meinung** dogma, doctrine, school of thought; **~meister** instructor, master, principal, professor; **~methode** teaching method (technique), method of instruction; **~mittel** teaching aids, educational appliances; **~mittelfreiheit** educational-material privilege; **~modell** mockup; **~personal** training staff; **~plan** teaching program(me) (plan), school curriculum, syllabus; **~plan festlegen** to lay a curriculum; **~roboter** automatic teaching device; **~saal** lecture (class) room, auditorium; **~satz** theorem, doctrine, maxim, principle, rule; **~stand** teaching profession; **~stelle** apprenticeship; **~stellenvermittlung** placement service for apprentices *(US)*; **~stoff** teaching subject.

Lehrstuhl [professional (professor's)] chair, professorship;
gestifteter ~ endowed professorship; **unbesetzter ~** vacant chair;
~ für Handelswissenschaften chair of commerce;
Berufung auf einen ~ ablehnen to refuse a chair (professorship); **auf einen ~ berufen** to chair; **~ besetzen** to fill a chair; **neuen ~ errichten** to found (establish) a new chair; **auf einen ~ berufen werden** to be offered a chair (be appointed to a professorship);
~errichtung establishment of a new chair; **~inhaber** holder of a chair.

Lehr|stunde lesson, lecture; **~system** school; **~tätigkeit** teaching; **~veranstaltungen** lectures; **~verhältnis** apprenticeship; **~verpflichtung** lectureship, lecturing duties; **~vertrag** indenture, articles of apprenticeship; **durch ~vertrag verpflichten** to indenture; **~werkstätte** shop-training department, special instruction workshop, vestibule school *(US)*.

Lehrzeit [period of] apprenticeship, term of article, probationership;
seine ~ beenden to finish one's apprenticeship; **seine ~ durchmachen** to serve one's time, to go through one's apprenticeship (the shops).

Lehrzeugnis certificate of apprenticeship.

Leib body, corpus;
drei Schritt vom ~e stay at arm's length; **mit ~ und Seele** with one's whole heart, with heart and soul;
~ Brot loaf; **~ und Leben** life and limb;
~ und Leben einsetzen to risk one's life; **jem. nicht vom ~e gehen** to dangle round s. o.; **einer Sache wirklich zu ~e gehen** to wage effective war on s. th.; **Armut am eigenen ~e zu spüren bekommen haben** to know poverty by experience; **keine Ehre im ~ haben** to have no sense of hono(u)r; **Mumm im ~ haben** to have guts; **nichts im ~e haben** to have an empty stomach; **Teufel im ~ haben** to be the devil incarnate; **unverschämten Ton am ~e haben** to be as cheeky as a cock-sparrow; **sich j. vom ~e halten** to keep aloof from s. o., to keep s. o. at distance; **sich Unannehmlichkeiten vom ~e halten** to steer clear of difficulties; **jem. mit unangenehmen Fragen auf den ~ rücken** to pester s. o. with awkward questions; **jem. immer näher auf den ~ rücken** to edge closer and closer to s. o.; **einem Problem zu ~e rücken** to tackle a problem; **sich die Lunge aus dem ~ schreien** to scream at the top of one's voice; **mit ~ und Seele bei der Arbeit sein** to put one's heart and soul into one's work; **sich mit ~ und Seele einer Sache verschreiben** to throw o. s. heart and soul into a business; **sich den ~ vollschlagen** to stuff o. s., to eat one's fill; **am ganzen ~ zittern** to tremble all over;
das Herz lacht mir im ~e my heart leaps with joy; **da tut einem ja das Herz im ~e weh** it hurts one to the quick;
auf den ~ geschriebene Rolle tailor-made part;
~arzt physician in ordinary; **~diener** body servant.

leibeigen in bondage.

Leibeigener bondsman, villein, serf.

Leibeigenschaft villeinage.

Leibeserbe heir bodily, issue, descendant, offspring, bodily heir;
ohne ~n sterben to die without issue.

Leibes|erziehung physical training; **~frucht** embryo, foetus; **~fülle** corpulence, stoutness; **~gefahr** danger to life; **mit ~kräften** with might and main; **~übungen** physical exercises, gymnastics; **~umfang** waist; **~untersuchung** bodily search; **~visitation** bodily (body, personal) search.

Leib|garde life-guard, brigade of guards, gorilla *(US)*, *(mil.)* household troops; **~gedinge** widow's dower; **~gericht** favo(u)rite dish.

leibhaftig in the flesh;
~**es Ebenbild** living image; ~**er Teufel** devil incarnate.
leiblich bodily, physical, material;
~**e Bedürfnisse** bodily wants; ~**er Bruder** full brother, brother-german; ~**er Erbe** bodily heir, heir of one's body; ~**e Hülle eines Toten** mortal remains of a dead man; ~**e Nachkommen** issue; ~**er Vetter** first cousin; ~**es Wohlbefinden** physical comfort.
Leibrente [whole] life annuity;
abgekürzte ~ temporary life annuity; **aufgeschobene** ~ deferred life annuity;
~ **für eine festgelegte Zeit** guaranteed annuity;
~ **aussetzen** to settle a life annuity.
Leibrenten|empfänger life annuitant, nominee; ~**versicherung** annuity insurance; **kollektive** ~**versicherung** group annuity assurance; ~**versicherungspolice** annuity policy; ~**vertrag** annuity insurance contract, annuity agreement; **sein Vermögen in einem** ~**vertrag anlegen** to invest one's money at life interest.
Leib|rentner life annuitant, annuity holder; ~**wache** life guard, bodyguard, gorilla *(US)*; ~**wächter** bodyguard, heavy; ~**wäsche** body clothes, underclothes, undergarment.
Leiche dead body, corpse, mortal remains, *(Druck)* out, omission;
~ **exhumieren** to resurrect (exhume) a body, to dispose of a body; **über** ~**n gehen** to be completely ruthless, to be an all-outer.
Leichen|ausgrabung exhumation; ~**begängnis** funeral, burial, obsequies, cold-meat party *(sl.)*; **an jds.** ~**begängnis teilnehmen** to pay the last hono(u)rs (final respects) to s. o.; ~**beschauer** medical examiner, coroner, crawner *(Scot. law)*; ~**bestatter** funeral director *(US)* (undertaker), mortician *(US)*; ~**bittermiene aufsetzen** to have a face as long as a fiddle; ~**dieb** body snatcher, resurrectionist; ~**fledderei** body-stripping; ~**gerüst** catafalque; ~**halle** funeral parlor *(US)*, funeral house, mortuary, deadhouse; ~**hemd** shroud; ~**kasse** burial fund; ~**öffnung** autopsy; ~**paß** corpse transport permit; ~**raub** body snatching; ~**räuber** body snatcher, resurrectionist; ~**rede** funeral sermon.
Leichenschau postmortem [examination], coroner's inquest, inquisition, crowner's quest *(Scot.)*, autopsy;
~ **abhalten** to hold a post mortem;
~**haus** morgue *(US)*, mortuary *(Br.)*, deadhouse, charnel house, morturary; ~**kommission** coroner's jury; ~**schein** post-mortem certificate; ~**verfahren** coroner's inquest.
Leichen|schmaus funeral meal, cold-meat party *(sl.)*; ~**starre** rigor mortis; ~**träger** bearer; ~**tuch** pall, winding sheet; ~**verbrennung** cremation; ~**wagen** hearse; ~**zug** funeral procession (train); **im** ~**zug mitgehen** to follow a body to the grave.
Leichnam dead body, corpse, dust, earthly remains, cadaver.
leicht light, weightless, *(geringfügig)* slight, minor, *(Markt, mühelos)* easy;
sehr ~ nice and easy; **zu** ~ under weight;
~ **angeboten** slightly on offer; ~ **beschädigt** slightly damaged; ~ **entzündlich** highly inflammable; ~ **lesbar** self-reading; ~ **möglich** quite possible; ~ **zu überreden** easy to manage, facile; ~ **verdaulich** easy of digestion, digestible; ~ **verderblich** perishable; ~ **verdient** light-earned; ~ **verständlich** easy to understand; ~ **zugänglich** easy of access;
gewogen und zu ~ **befunden** tried and found wanting;
~ **Absatz finden** to meet with a ready market; ~ **durchs Leben gehen** to go through life in a happy-go-lucky fashion; ~ **laufen** *(Maschine)* to run smoothly; **sich** ~ **lösen** to come away cleanly; **es sich** ~ **machen** to go easy; **am Schluß** ~ **sein** *(Geldmarkt)* to be an easy finish; ~ **verderblich sein** to be perishable; ~ **verrückt sein** to be a little wrong in the upper storey *(sl.)*;
~**e Abschwächung** slight decline; ~**er Anfall** slight attack; ~**e Arbeit** light work; ~**e Auffassungsgabe haben** to be quick in the uptake; **gegen** ~**e Bedingungen** on easy terms; ~ **zu pflegende Bekleidung** easy-care clothes; ~**e Beute** easy meat; ~**es Bier** light beer; ~**er Boden** light soil; ~**e Brise** gentle breeze; ~**es Erdbeben** slight earthquake; ~**e Erkältung** slight cold; ~**este Erschütterung** smallest tremor; ~**e Fahrlässigkeit** slight negligence (fault); ~**e Feldartillerie** light field artillery; ~**en Fußes** nimbly; ~ **verdientes Geld** easy money; ~**e Geldmarktsätze** easy money rates; **zu** ~**e Gewichte** light weights; **bei allem eine** ~**e Hand haben** to have the knack of it; **j. mit** ~**er Hand regieren** to go easy with s. o.; ~**e Hausarbeit** light housekeeping; ~**e Komödie** light comedy; ~**e Krankheit** light attack of illness; ~**er Kreuzer** light cruiser; ~**es Kühlmittel** low-density coolant; ~**e Lektüre** light reading, escape literature; ~**e Lokomotive** light engine; ~**es Mädchen** fast girl, hussy, loose woman, tart; ~**e Magenvergiftung** slightly upset stomach; ~**es Marschgepäck** light marching order; ~**e Sache** plain sailing; **keine** ~**e Sache** no picknick; **Einwände auf die** ~**e Schulter nehmen** to make light of s. one's objections; ~**en Schwips haben** to be tipsy; ~**es Spiel mit jem. haben** to have an easy time with s. o., to make short work of s. o.; ~**e Strafe** mild punishment; ~**er Unfall** minor accident; ~ **zerbrechliche Vase** fragile vase; ~**es Vergehen** minor offence; **mit** ~**em Vorwurf** with a touch of reproach; ~ **zu nehmender Zeitgenosse** easy person to get on with; ~**e Zunahme** slight increase.
Leicht|anlage light plant; ~**athletik** track-and-field sports; ~**bau** light-weight construction (concrete).
Leichter lighter, barge, tender, hoy, tug boat *(US)*;
in einem ~ **befördern** to lighter.
leichter *(Börse)* easier;
j. um 1000 DM ~ **machen** to fleece s. o. of DM 1000; ~ **sein** *(Geldmarkt)* to have an easier day; ~ **werden** to ease up.
leichteres Geld easier money.
Leichter|führer barge operator, bargeman, bargee *(Br.)*; ~**gebühren** lighterage; ~**kapitän** hoyman; ~**klausel** craft clause; ~**miete** lighterhire; ~**schiffer** lighterman; ~**transportgewerbe** lighterage.
Leichterung lighterage, lightening.
Leichterungskosten lighterage charges.
Leichtes light [thing];
nichts ~ no easy matter;
etw. ~ **essen** to eat s. th. light; **ein** ~ **für j. sein** to be child's play for s. o.
leichtfallen, jem. to come easily to s. o.
leichtfertig frivolous, lightly, volatile, given to trifling, wanton, reckless;
sein väterliches Erbteil ~ **ausgeben** to squander one's estate; **sich** ~ **entscheiden** to make a rash decision; ~ **handeln** to act heedlessly; ~ **über etw. reden** to speak lightly of s. th.; **sein Leben** ~ **aufs Spiel setzen** to jeopardize one's life;
~ **erhobene Forderung** frivolous claim; ~**e Gefährdung Dritter** reckless endangering of s. o. *(US)*; ~**es Gegenvorbringen** frivolous defence; ~**es Gerede** idle gossip; ~**e oder schikanöse Klage** frivolous or vexatious action; ~**er Mensch** lighthead, flyaway; ~**es Wesen** flippancy.
Leichtfertigkeit hazardous (gross) negligence, frivolity, recklessness, wantoness;
bewußt in Kauf genommene ~ constructive wilfulness.
Leicht|flugzeug light plane (aircraft), grasshopper, cub; **[Bruder]** ~**fuß** happy-go-lucky person; ~**gewicht** lightweight, featherweight.
leichtgläubig credulous, gullible, quick of belief.
Leichtgläubigkeit credulity, gullibility, easiness of belief.
Leicht|gut light cargo (goods, freight); ~**güterzug** light goods train.
Leichtheit weightlessness.
Leichtigkeit lightness, ease;
mit ~ with a wet finger, with ease, easily, well;
j. mit ~ **schlagen** to beat s. o. hollow *(coll.)*; **j. mit** ~ **überreden** to persuade s. o. easily.
Leicht|industrie light industries; ~**last** light load; ~**lastwagen** pickup truck; ~**matrose** ordinary seaman (sailor); ~**metall** light metal; ~**metallindustrie** light metals industry; ~**metallware** light metal goods.
leichtnehmen to take it easy;
das Leben ~ to have a happy-go-lucky fashion.
Leichtöl light oil.
Leichtsinn thoughtlessness, carelessness;
sträflicher ~ criminal negligence; **unbegreiflicher** ~ piece of carelessness.
leichtsinnig careless, uncareful, improvident;
alle Warnungen ~ **in den Wind schlagen** to throw all caution to the wind; **sich** ~ **in Schulden stürzen** to plunge o. s. into debts; ~ **mit fremdem Geld umgehen** to be free with other people's money (property); ~ **mit Vaters Geld umgehen** to play fast and loose with father's money;
~**er Bankrott** wil(l)ful bankruptcy; ~**e Bemerkung** frivolous remark; ~**es Fahren** reckless driving; ~**es Mädchen** giddy girl; ~**er Spieler** reckless gambler.
leichtverderbliche Waren perishable goods, perishables.
Leichtverderblichkeit perishability.
Leid pain, sorrow, grief, suffering;
vom ~ **gebeugt** grief-stricken;
seelisches ~ mental anguish; **unermeßliches** ~ boundless suffering;

sein ~ **in sich hineinfressen** to keep all one's worries to o. s., to eat one's heart out; **jem. sein ~ klagen** to hand s. o. a long tale of woe; ~ **um j. tragen** to mourn over s. one's death; **in Freud und ~ zusammenhalten** to stand by each other for better, for worse.

Leiden illness, affection, dross;
nach langem ~ after a long period of suffering;
altes ~ *(Versicherung)* previous illness; **dem Volk auferlegte ~** inflictions put upon the people; **körperliches ~** physical ailment; **nervöses ~** nervous complaints; **seelisches ~** mental disease;
~ **des Alters** afflictions of old age;
jds. ~ ein Ende bereiten to put s. o. out of his misery.

leiden to suffer;
unter Arbeiterunruhen zu ~ haben to suffer from labo(u)r troubles; **keinen Aufschub ~** to brook no delay; **entsetzlich ~** to go through an agony; **an Gedächtnisschwäche ~** to suffer from loss of memory; **bittere Not ~** to be in necessity, to undergo severe privation; **an Personalmangel ~** to be understaffed (short of staff); **an Verfolgungswahn ~** to suffer from hallucinations;
j. nicht ~ können not to be able to stand (be ill-disposed towards) s. o.; **j. absolut nicht ~ können** to have a particular dislike for s. o.

leidend suffering, ailing, afflicted;
~ **aussehen** to look ill.

Leidender patient, sick person.

Leidenschaft passion, violent emotion, ardo(u)r;
neu entdeckte ~ new-born passion; **schlummernde ~** lurking passion;
~**en entfachen** to kindle the passions, to add fuel to the flames; **jds. ~en entfachen** to raise the devil in s. o. *(coll.)*; **Sturm der ~en entfachen** to unleash a storm of controversy; ~**en entflammen** to heat the passions, to fan the flame; **einer ~ frönen** to indulge in a passion; **unselige ~en hervorrufen** to work great mischief; ~**en schüren** to work up the passions; **jds. große ~ sein** to be mad about s. th.

leidenschaftlich passionate, enthusiastic, hot-blooded, tropical;
~ **auf Ruhm bedacht** ardent in the pursuit of glory;
j. ~ lieben to be passionately in love with s. o.; **j. ~ widersprechen** to oppose (contradict) s. o. violently;
~**er Befürworter** ardent supporter; ~**e Briefe** passionate letters; ~**e Rede** passionate (impassionated) speech; ~**er Reiter sein** to adore riding.

Leidenschaftlichkeit passionateness, ardo(u)r, agitation of mind, heat.

leidenschaftslose Behandlung eines Themas dispassionate presentation of a subject.

Leidens|gefährte, ~**genosse** fellow sufferer, companion in distress; ~**geschichte** tale of woe; **jem. seine ~geschichte erzählen** to hand s. o. a long tale of woe; ~**miene aufsetzen** to put on a martyred look; ~**zeit durchmachen müssen** to go through a terrible ordeal.

leidlich tolerable, reasonable, not too bad;
~ **gehen** *(Geschäft)* to be so-so; **einem ~ gehen** to be tolerable well; ~ **Englisch sprechen** to speak English reasonably well;
~**es Essen** tolerable food; ~ **gute Geschäfte** fair business; **in ~er Gesundheit** in tolerable health; ~**es Wetter** fair-to-middling weather.

Leidtragender mourner, victim.

leidtragender Teil aggrieved party.

Leidwesen, zu meinem much to my regret.

Leier *(Geschichte)* story, tune, song;
die alte ~ the same old cant; **ewige ~** standing dish;
noch immer die alte ~ drauflhaben to be harping upon the same string.

Leierkasten street organ, hurdy-gurdy;
~**mann** organ grinder.

leiern to wind (rank) up;
auf der Drehorgel ~ to grind the street organ; **Gedicht ~** to drone out a poem; **jem. Geld aus dem Kreuz ~** to stint s. o. for (wheedle s. o. out of his) money; **an der Kurbel ~** to turn the crank.

leiernde Stimme monotonous voice.

Leih|amt pawnbroker's office, pawnshop; **aufs ~amt tragen** to pawn, to put in pawn, to hock *(US sl.)*; ~**arbeiter** employee on temporary loan; ~**bibliothek,** ~**bücherei** lending (subscription, circulating, rental, *US*) library.

Leihe loan for use, commodate loan;
unentgeltliche ~ gratuitous loan;
etw. zur ~ haben to have s. th. on loan.

Leihemballagen containers to be returned (on loan).

Leihen borrowing, lending, *(Ausleihen)* loan, lending, *(Entleihen)* borrowing.

leihen to lend, to loan, to advance, *(von jem.)* to borrow, to take on hire;
sich etw. ~ to take on hire, to borrow (rent, *US*) s. th.; **jem. seine Aufmerksamkeit ~** to lend one's ear to s. o.; **sich ein Auto ~** to take a car on hire, to rent a car; **Bücher aus der Bibliothek ~** to borrow books from a library; **Geld auf Hypotheken ~** to lend on mortgages; **Geld auf Waren ~** to advance money on goods; **Geld auf Zinsen ~** to lend [out] money at interest; **sich kurzfristig größere Geldbeträge ~** to borrow heavily on a short-term basis; **auf Lombard ~** to loan on collateral; **Tagesgeld ~** to lend day-to-day money; **jem. einen Vorwand ~** to give s. o. s. th. as a pretext; **auf Wucherzinsen ~** to practise usury.

Leiher lender, borrower.

Leih|frist lending period; **als ~gabe** as a loan; ~**gebühr** lending fee, *(Auto)* hire charges, car rental costs; ~**gelder** borrowed money, loans, loanable capital (funds), *(Tagegeld)* day-to-day loans *(Br.)*, call money *(US)*; ~**geschäft** lending business; ~- **und Pachtgesetz** *(US)* Land-and-Lease Bill.

Leihhaus pawnshop, pawnbroker's shop, (office), spout, loan office *(US)*;
etw. aus dem ~ auslösen to redeem a pawn; **ins ~ tragen** to put into pawn, to hock *(US sl.)*;
~**schein** pawn ticket.

Leih|kapital borrowed capital, borrowed (hire of) money, loan capital *(Br.)*, loanable funds; ~**kapitalien mit Kündigungsfrist** term (time, *US*) deposits; ~**kräfte** employees on temporary loan; ~**lieferungen** loaned supplies; ~**pacht** *(US)* lend-lease; **in ~pacht überlassen** to lend-lease; ~**satz** interest (lending, *US*) rate; ~**schein** pawn ticket, *(Bibliothek)* borrowing slip; ~- **und Pachtschulden** *(US)* Lend-Lease bills; **auswärtiger ~verkehr** *(Bibliotheken)* interlibrary loan; ~**vertrag** bailment, contract of loan for use.

Leihwagen rented (rent-a-) car;
selbstgefahrener ~ self-drive car;
~**gebühr** car rental costs; ~**geschäft** car rental business, rent-a-car agency (firm).

leihweise by way of (as) a loan, on loan, on hire;
von einem Museum ~ überlassen loaned by a museum;
~ **Überlassung** loan for use.

Leim glue;
auf den ~ gehen to rise to (swallow) the bait, to fall to pieces; **sich nicht auf den ~ locken lassen** not to fall into a trap.

leimen to glue;
j. ~ to take s. o. in (for a ride), to dupe s. o.; **Papier ~** to size paper.

Leim|farbe glue colo(u)r; **mit ~farbe streichen** to calcimine, to distemper *(Br.)*; ~**topf** glue pot.

Leine line, tether, *(Hund)* leash, lead;
~ **anziehen** to pull the reins; **j. an der kurzen ~ führen** to hold s. o. on a short leash; **Hund an der ~ führen** to keep a dog on the lead; **j. fest an der ~ haben** to keep a tight rein on s. o.; **Wäsche auf die ~ hängen** to hang clothes on the line; **j. an der langen ~ laufen lassen** to give s. o. his head; **j. an die ~ legen** to get s. o. under control; ~ **ziehen** to pack in *(sl.)*.

Leinen linen;
in ~ gebunden bound in cloth, clothbound;
~**band** volume bound in cloth, cloth binding; ~**decke** cloth board; ~**einband** hard-cover; ~**händler** linen dealer (draper); ~**handtuch** linen towel; ~**papier** linen paper, cloth-mounted paper; ~**prägung** linen finish; ~**umschlag** close-lined envelope.

Leinölfirnis oil varnish.

Leinwand linen, *(Buch)* cloth, *(Film)* screen, *(Segel, Zelt)* canvas;
in ~ gebunden bound in cloth, clothbound;
auf die ~ bringen to screen; **Roman auf die ~ bringen** to turn a novel into a film; **auf die ~ werfen** to project on the screen.

Leinwarenhandel linen trade.

leise quiet, soft, gentle, faint;
~ **vor sich hinmurmeln** to murmur under one's breath; ~ **sprechen** to speak in a low (faint) voice; ~**r stellen** *(Radio)* to turn down; ~ **aus dem Zimmer verschwinden** to stealthily leave the room; ~ **weinen** to weep quietly;
nicht die ~ste Ahnung haben not to have the foggiest idea; **bei der ~sten Gefahr** at the first hint of danger; **nicht der ~ste Grund** not the slightest reason; ~ **Hoffnung** faint hope; ~**s Raunen** soft murmur; **auf ~n Sohlen** on tiptoe; **sich auf ~n Sohlen davonschleichen** to steal away quietly.

Leise|treter pussyfoot; ~**treterei** mealy-mouthed behavio(u)r.

leisetreterisch pussyfooting, mealy-mouthed.

Leiste lath, ledge, *(Scheuerleiste)* skirting board, *(drucktechn.)* flourish, border.

Leisten *(Schuhmacher)* last;
alles über einen ~ schlagen to measure everything with the same yardstick;
Schuster bleib bei deinem ~ let not the cobbler go beyond his last.

leisten to perform, to do, *(ausführen)* to carry out, to execute, to effect, to realize, *(erfüllen)* to fulfil(l), to achieve, to accomplish, *(liefern)* to supply, to provide, to procure, *(Maschine)* to render service;
etw. ~ *(Auto)* to be a good performer; **sich etw. ~** to indulge one's taste, to give o. s. a treat, to blow o. s. to s. th.; **Anzahlung ~** to make *(US)* (pay, *Br.*) a deposit, to pay on account; **nützliche Arbeit ~** to perform useful work; **einem Befehl Folge ~** to carry out an order; **Beistand ~** to render assistance; **Beitrag ~** to contribute, to make a contribution; **Bürgschaft ~** to put up (stand) bail, to give security; **jem. einen Dienst ~** to render a service to s. o.; **Eid ~** to (swear) take an oath; **einer Einladung Folge ~** to accept an invitation; **Einschuß ~** to make a contribution to capital; **Ersatz ~** to pay compensation, to make restitution; **Erstaunliches ~** to do amazing things; **sich einen richtigen Fauxpas ~** to make a big blunder; **sich eine Flasche Wein ~** to treat o. s. to a bottle of wine; **Garantie ~** to guarantee, to warrant; **jem. Gesellschaft ~** to bear s. one's (keep s. o.) company; **Hilfe ~** to render (give) assistance; **Kaution ~** to go (become) bail, to stand bail, to pay a deposit, to provide security; **Nachzahlung ~** to make a subsequent payment; **Schadenersatz ~** to respond in *(US)* (pay) damages; **Sicherheit für j. ~** to stand surety for s. o.; **jem. ausreichende Sicherheit ~** to furnish s. o. with sufficient security; **Tüchtiges ~** to do a splendid job; **sich einen Urlaub ~** to afford a holiday; **Verzicht ~** to waive a claim; **einer Vorladung Folge ~** to answer a summons; **Vorschuß ~** to advance money; **Wechselbürgschaft ~** to guarantee the due payment of a bill; **Widerstand ~** to offer resistance; **Zahlung ~** to effect (make) payment;
sich eine Ausgabe ~ können to afford an expense; **sich nichts ~ können** not to be able to enjoy luxuries; **sich keinen Urlaub ~ können** not to be able to afford to go away for a holiday; **sich weder zeitlich noch geldlich ~ können** to can ill afford the time and money.

Leistung performance, effort, act, *(geleistete Arbeit)* job, piece of work, work done, flow, stroke, *(Beitrag)* contribution, *(Dienst)* service, *(Ergebnis)* result, effect, *(Erzeugung)* output, production, *(Fähigkeit)* efficiency, ability, *(Gebrauchsgüter)* serviceableness, *(Gegenleistung)* consideration, *(Haltbarkeit)* service life, *(Kraft)* power, output, *(Lieferung)* delivery, *(Maschine)* power, capacity, efficiency, performance, rating, *(Sozialversicherung)* benefit, *(Verpflichtung)* obligation, *(Verrichtung)* discharge, performance of an obligation, *(Vollendung)* accomplishment, achievement, attainment, *(Zahlung)* payment;
aufgrund gestiegener ~en due to increased output; **während des Bezuges der ~en** while drawing benefits;
abgegebene ~ output of power; **vom Versicherungsnehmer abhängige ~en** executory warranties; **ärztliche ~en** *(Versicherungsfall)* medical benefits; **ausgezeichnete ~** excellence, excellent workmanship; **außerordentliche ~** exceptional achievement, tour de force; **bankbetriebliche ~en** banking facilities; **bedeutende ~** no mean achievement; **bedingte ~** conditional obligation; **vertraglich bedungene ~** contractual obligation, obligation of a contract; **beitragsfreie ~en** noncontributory benefits; **besondere ~** comparative performance; **betriebliche ~en** personnel performance, output of the staff; **bewirkte ~** executed consideration; **eigenschöpferische ~** literary composition; **entgeltliche ~** valuable consideration; **entsprechende ~en** corresponding benefits; **fliegerische ~** aircraft performance; **freiwillige ~** voluntary; **freiwillige ~en** *(Betrieb)* fringe benefits, *(Versicherung)* ex gratia payments; **gegenseitige ~** reciprocal duty; **geldwerte ~en** performance in money; **vertraglich geschuldete ~** simple contract debt, contractual obligation; **gewerbliche ~en** commercial services; **glänzende ~** brilliant feat; **großartige (hervorragende) ~** tremendous performance, outstanding achievement, one for the book; **gute ~en** *(Ausbildung)* proficiency; **hochqualifizierte ~** high-level achievement; **höchste ~** record, peak performance; **industrielle ~en** industrial achievements; **konzerninterne ~en** intergroup services; **langfristige ~en** long-term benefits; **maximale ~** *(Maschine)* maximum output; **normale ~** normal performance; **nutzbare ~** effective power; **optimale ~** optimal performance; **produktive ~en** manufacturing efficiency; **glanzvolle schauspielerische ~** glittering debut performance; **schriftstellerische ~en** literary attainments; **soziale ~en** social welfare benefits, social contributions; **kostenlose staatliche ~en** free government services; **steuerpflichtige ~en** taxable transactions; **tadellose ~** faultless performance; **bedeutende technische ~** engineering feat; **teilbare ~** divisible performance; **überragende ~** outstanding achievement; **unentgeltliche ~en** gratuitous services, *(Überweisungsverkehr)* unilateral transfers; **unmögliche ~** impossible consideration, impossibility of performance of contract; **unteilbare ~** indivisible performance (obligation); **unvergleichbare ~** unparalleled achievement; **vereinbarte ~en** contract work *(US)*; **vermögenswirksame ~** property-creating performance; **versprochene ~** express obligation; **vertragliche ~en** contractual obligations; **gesamte volkswirtschaftliche ~** gross national product; **wiederkehrende ~en** revolving payments; **wirtschaftliche ~en** industrial achievements; **voraussichtliche zukünftige ~en** *(Sozialversicherung)* probable future payments; **zusätzliche ~** additional contribution;
~en bei der Abwicklung des Versicherungsgeschäftes claims service provided; **~ einer Anzahlung** deposit; **~ eines Dienstes** rendering a service; **~ an Erfüllungs Statt** payment in lieu of performance; **~ in den wissenschaftlichen Fächern** academic achievement; **~en zur Finanzierung des Wohnungsbaus** housing aid; **zusätzliche ~en bei einem Flug** flight additions; **~en einer Führungskraft** executive performance; **~ in Geld** pecuniary consideration; **~en für die Europäische Gemeinschaft** payments for the European Community; **~ des vertraglich Geschuldeten** specific performance; **bauwirtschaftliche ~en der öffentlichen Hand** public investment in building; **~en im Krankheitsfall** *(Versicherung)* sickness benefit *(Br.)* (allowance, *US*); **gute ~en in Latein** attainments (proficiency) in Latin; **noch nicht abgewohnte werterhöhende ~en des Mieters** unexhausted improvements; **~en in Naturalien** payments in kind, specific performance; **~en des Personals** personnel performance, output of the staff; **~ von Sacheinlagen** assets in kind brought in; **zusätzliche ~en zum Selbstkostenpreis** addition at cost; **~en der Sozialversicherung** social security benefits, public assistance benefits *(US)*; **doppelte ~ bei Unfalltod** double accident benefit *(Br.)* (indemnity, *US*); **~ an Unterhaltsberechtigte** dependency benefit *(Br.)*; **~en eines Werklieferungsvertrages** work and labo(u)r; **~en für die Wiedergutmachung** restitution payments; **~ Zug um Zug** contemporaneous performance, concurrent consideration;
~en abgelten to pay for services rendered; **~ anbieten** to offer performance; **~ andienen** to tender performance; **zur höchsten ~ anspornen** to speed up; **hervorragende ~en auf verschiedenen Gebieten aufweisen** to be distinguished in many spheres; **jds. ~ bewerten** to rate s. one's performance; **~ bewirken** to affect performance; **nach ~ bezahlen** to pay by results; **j. entsprechend dem Wert seiner ~ bezahlen** to pay for the value of s. one's service; **seine ~en sehr hoch einstufen** to rate one's services at a high value; **~en erbringen** to render services; **~en durch einen Erfüllungsgehilfen erbringen** to perform services vicariously; **gute ~ erbringen** to put up a good performance; **verjährte ~ erbringen** to perform a barred obligation; **höhere ~en von den Lieferanten fordern** to drive on contractor performance; **~en honorieren** to pay for services; **mit den ~en in Verzug kommen** to get behind with the performance of a contract, to fail to complete within contract time; **seinen vertraglichen ~en nachkommen** to fulfil one's obligations under a contract; **~ steigern** *(technisch)* to tune up; **zur ~ von Schadenersatz verurteilen** to award damages against; **~ verweigern** to refuse performance.

Leistungs|abfall decline in production, *(el.)* power drop; **~abgabe** *(el.)* power output; **kostendeckende ~abgaben** beneficial rates; **nicht kostendeckende ~abgaben** onerous rates.

leistungsabhängige|Gehaltshöchstgrenze efficiency bar; **~ Kosten** direct (variable) cost.

Leistungs|abkommen für Zechenarbeiter pit incentive deal; **~abweichung** labo(u)r efficiency variance, *(Maschine)* capacity variance; **~alter** achievement age; **~analyse** performance (merit, *US*) rating, efficiency (service) rating *(US)*, *(Rationalisierung)* value analysis; **~analyse von Vorgesetzten** rating of supervisors; **~andienung** tender of performance; **~anforderungen** performance qualifications; **~angaben** performance data, *(Personalakte)* efficiency record, *(technisch)* power rating.

Leistungsangebot tender of performance, offer;
umfassendes ~ comprehensive package of services;

~ **auf dem Bausektor** construction services;
speziell auf die Kundschaft zugeschnittenes ~ ausweiten to extend tailor-made services.

Leistungs|anreiz merit bonus, wage incentive; **~anspruch** obligatory right, *(Sozialversicherung)* right to draw benefits, *(Versicherung)* title to benefit; **~anspruch ausschließen** to disqualify from benefits; **~anspruch haben** to be entitled to benefits; **~ausgleich** compensation [for services rendered]; **~ausschluß** exclusion of benefits; **~austausch** exchange of goods and services; **~bedarf** required output, *(el.)* power demand; **~begrenzung** effort limitation; **~belastung** *(Flugzeug)* power loading; **~berechnung** rating, *(Angestellter)* calculation of benefit.

leistungsberechtigt eligible for benefit.

Leistungs|berechtigter beneficiary; **minderjähriger ~berechtigter** infant beneficiary; **~berechtigung** eligibility for benefit; **~bereich** *(Maschine)* [range of] capacity, *(Versicherung)* benefit range; **~bericht** performance (efficiency) report; **~bestimmung, ~beurteilung** performance (service, experience, efficiency) rating, performance review, appraisal performance, merit rating (review) *(US)*.

Leistungsbeurteilungs|blatt merit rating sheet *(US)*; **~prinzip** merit-rating system *(US)*; **~schema** experience rating plan; **~skala** performance (merit, *US*) rating scale; **~system** merit rating system *(US)*.

Leistungs|bewertung performance evaluation, job evaluation *(US)*, merit *(US)* (efficiency, performance) rating; **~bewertungspunkte** basic job factor points; **~bewertungsmethode** job evaluation system *(US)*.

Leistungsbilanz current account (invisible) balance, balance of current accounts;
negative ~ current account deficit, deficit on current account; **positive ~** surplus on current account, credit invisible balance; **~defizit** current account deficit; **~guthaben** credit in the invisible balance; **~überschuß** current account surplus, surplus on current account; **~überschußpolitik** beggar-my-neighbo(u)r policy.

Leistungs|buch proficiency record; **~dauer** period of benefit, indemnity period *(US)*; **~diagramm** performance chart, indicator card (diagram); **~druck** pressure to perform; **~ebene** standard; **~effekt** useful output; **~einheit** efficiency unit, unit power; **~einkommen** factor income; **~einstufung** performance (service, man) rating, merit rating (review) *(US)*; **~empfänger** recipient of services; **~entgelt** compensation, *(Gebühr)* rate *(US)*; **kostendeckende ~entgelte** remunerative rates; **~entlohnung** incentive-wage system (plan); **~entlohnung ausdehnen** to extend incentive coverage; **~entzug** withdrawal of services; **~erbringer** contractor, supplier; **~erfüllung** discharge by performance, performance, fulfil(l)ment; **~erfüllung anbieten** to tender performance; **~ermittlung** output evaluation; **~erstellung** performance.

leistungsfähig able, capable, efficient, *(ergiebig)* productive, *(Gebrauchsgüter)* serviceable, *(Motor)* powerful, *(zahlungsfähig)* able to pay, solvent;
finanziell ~ financially able, solvent, solid, sound; **körperlich ~** able-bodied; **steuerlich ~** taxpaying;
sich als sehr ~ erweisen to show up high on the efficiency list; **~ sein** to be efficient in one's work; **sehr ~ sein** *(Auto)* to have a pretty turn of speed; **auch in den nächsten Jahren noch ~ sein** to be good for several more years' service;
~es Lehrergremium efficient staff of teachers; **wenig ~er Mensch** lame duck.

Leistungsfähigkeit ability, capability, functional capacity, job efficiency, effectiveness, proficiency, form, reach, *(Brücke)* payload, *(Ergiebigkeit)* productivity, productiveness, *(Maschine)* service capacity, ability, *(Produktionsleistung)* output, *(Produktivität)* productive capacity, *(Zahlungsfähigkeit)* ability to pay, solvency;
behauptete ~ *(Unterhaltsverfahren)* allegation of faculties; **berufliche ~** job (occupational) efficiency; **betriebliche ~** productive (plant, operating) efficiency, operating competence, production capacity; **durchschnittliche ~** *(Arbeiter)* production standard; **finanzielle ~** financial capacity (ability, power), solvency, *(Staat)* viability; **gesamtwirtschaftliche ~** overall economic potential; **geschäftliche ~** business ability; **körperliche ~** physical faculty (capacity); **mangelnde ~** inefficiency; **steuerliche ~** taxable capacity; **vergleichbare ~** comparative performance; **wirtschaftliche ~** productivity, economic vitality (performance), industrial (economic) efficiency;
~ des Absatzapparates marketing efficiency; **~ eines Betriebes** *(Geschäfts)* business efficiency; **~ bei voller Kapazitätsausnutzung** full operating capacity; **~ eines Mannes** manpower; **finanzielle ~ eines Unternehmens** productiveness of an enterprise; **~ des Vorstands** management efficiency; **~ der Wirtschaft** industrial efficiency, economic vitality;
betriebliche ~ voll ausfahren to work to capacity; **seine ~ unter Beweis stellen** to prove one's potential, to show what one is made of; **finanzielle ~ einer ausgeklügelten Überprüfung unterziehen** to conduct a sophisticated examination of the financial capacity.

Leistungs|[fähigkeits]faktor performance rating (efficiency) factor, *(Produktion)* productivity factor; **mengenmäßige ~förderung** volume incentive promotion; **~garantie** performance (bid) bond *(US)*, performance guarantee *(Br.)*; **~gegenstand** subject matter.

leistungsgerechte Bezahlung payment by result, incentive wage plan.

Leistungsgesellschaft meritocracy.

Leistungsgrad level of efficiency (performance), performance (efficiency) level;
unterschiedlich hohe ~e varying degrees of excellence; **hohen ~ erreichen** to reach a high standard of efficiency; **~abweichung** physical (labo(u)r efficiency) variance; **~schätzung** performance (efficiency, merit, *US*) rating.

Leistungs|grenze marginal productivity, production limit; **~hindernis** *(bei Vertragserfüllung)* frustration; **~höchststufe** pitch of proficiency; **~höhe** *(Krankenversicherung)* rates of benefit; **~kennzahlen** standards of performance; **~klage** action to claim specific performance of contract; **aufgrund Vertrages angestrengte ~klage** action on contract; **~kontrollabteilung** efficiency department *(US)*; **~kontrolle** *(Fabrik)* efficiency survey, *(automatisch)* internal check; **~kontrollsachverständiger** efficiency expert *(US)*; **~kraft** efficiency, *(Person)* vitality; **finanzielle ~kraft** financial capacity; **wirtschaftliche ~kraft** business performance; **~kurve** *(technisch)* performance graph.

Leistungslohn payment by results, incentive pay (wage), efficiency wage *(US)*;
nicht akkordmäßiger ~ nonpiecework bonus plan; **progressiver ~** high piecework;
im ~ arbeiten to work on an incentive system;
~abkommen incentive pay agreement; **~anteil** percentage of an incentive rate; **~errechnung** incentive pay figuration; **~formel** efficiency wage plan formula *(US)*; **~satz** incentive rate; **~system** incentive wage system (plan), wage incentive payment plan, premium bonus system, efficiency bonus plan *(US)*.

Leistungs|maßstab efficiency unit; **~maximum** *(el.)* maximum output; **~minimum** *(el.)* minimum output; **~möglichkeiten** performance possibilities; **~motivation** achievement motivation; **~nachweis** proof of performance; **~niveau** level of performance, performance level; **~normen** standards of performance (efficiency); **~note** performance rating.

leistungsorientiert efficiency-orientated.

Leistungs|ort place of delivery (performance); **~pegel** level of performance; **~pflicht** obligation.

leistungspflichtig liable for service, contributory.

Leistungs|pflichtiger contributor; **~planung** budgeting results.

Leistungsprämie production (performance, merit, *US*, step) bonus, efficiency premium, *(progressiv)* accelerating premium, *(Verkäufer)* incentive, premium, bonus;
~ der Belegschaft staff productivity bonus;
besondere ~n einschließen to carry incentive arrangements.

Leistungs|prämiensystem efficiency bonus plan; **spezielles ~prämiensystem** incentive plan; **~prinzip** principle of efficiency, merit system *(US)*; **~prüfung** *(Maschine)* performance (efficiency) test, *(Mensch)* achievement test, rating *(US)*, *(Schule)* test; **~qualitäten** performance qualifications; **~querschnitt** industrial cross section; **~quotient** achievement quotient; **~reaktor** power reactor; **~reserve** *(el.)* power reserve, *(Maschine)* reserve capacity; **~rückgang** decrease in performance, *(Produktion)* decline in production; **~schätzung** efficiency rating; **~schau** trade (competitive) exhibition; **~schau der Kraftfahrzeugindustrie** motor show; **~schild** *(Motor)* name (rating) plate; **~schuldner** debtor, obligor.

leistungsschwach inefficient, *(Sender)* low-powered.

Leistungs|schwankungen fluctuations in performance; **~soll** performance level, *(Produktion)* production target, *(Vertreter)* territorial quota; **~spitze** ceiling [performance]; **~stand** standard of technology, effectiveness; **~stand erreichen** to attain a [stage of] proficiency; **~standard** performance standard.

leistungsstark powerful, *(Sender)* high-powered;
~**er Motor** high-pressure engine.
leistungssteigernd incentive.
Leistungs|steigerung increased performance (efficiency), increase in output, greater productivity; ~**störung** frustration; ~**streben** incentive; ~**stufe** level (standard) of performance, *(Kraftmaschine)* power stage; **j. in verschiedene ~stufen einteilen** to stream s. o.; ~**system** efficiency bonus plan; ~**tabelle** performance table; ~**termin** time of performance; ~**test** achievement test; ~**träger** *(Sozialversicherung)* social insurance institution; ~**überprüfung** performance review, *(verstaatlichte Industriezweige)* efficiency audit *(Br.)*; ~**überschuß** surplus on goods and services; ~**übersicht** performance chart (table); ~**unterschied** difference in performance; **regionaler ~unterschied** regional differential; ~**urteil** personal judgment, performance (efficiency, merit, *US*) rating; ~**urteil klageweise fordern** to sue for a decree of specific performance; ~**verbot an Drittschuldner** garnishee (third-party, *US*) order; ~**verbrauch** *(el.)* power consumption; ~**verlust** loss of efficiency, *(el.)* power drop; ~**vermögen** proficiency, capacity, *(Produktivität)* productive capacity, productivity; **gesamtes ~vermögen** *(Produktion)* total capacity; **wirtschaftliches ~vermögen** economic performance (efficiency); ~**verpflichtung** obligation; ~**versprechen** single (contract) obligation, *(Bietungsgarantie)* performance (bid) bond *(US)*, performance guarantee *(Br.)*; **unentgeltliches ~versprechen** gratuitous consideration; ~**verstärker** *(el.)* power amplifier; ~**versuch** duty trial; ~**verweigerung** repudiation; ~**verzeichnis** specifications, *(Baukostenvoranschlag)* bill of quantities; ~**verzug** failure to meet obligations, delay in the execution of an order; ~**volumen** volume of production; ~**voraussetzung** qualification for benefit; ~**vorgabe** standards of performance; ~**vorsprung** superior efficiency; ~**wesen** rating (merit, *US*) system; ~**wettbewerb** efficiency contest; ~**zahlen**, ~**ziffern** output figures, rates of performance; ~**zeit** time of performance; ~**zeitraum** benefit period; ~**ziele** *(Unternehmen)* basic objectives; ~**zulage** merit salary increase *(US)*, production (incentive) bonus, efficiency (merit) bonus *(US)*, proficiency pay; ~**zulagensystem für leitende Angestellte** executive incentive plan; ~**zusagen** service commitments.
Leitartikel leader, leading (editorial) article, editorial *(US)*, editorial leader (column), page-oner *(sl.)*, shirt-tail *(sl.)*;
aktueller ~ timely editorial *(US)*; **gegenüberstehender** ~ facing leader; **kurzer** ~ leaderette *(Br.)*;
~ **auf der ersten Seite** front-page editorial *(US)*;
im ~ Stellung nehmen, ~ schreiben to editorialize; ~ **veröffentlichen** to run an editorial *(US)*;
~**seite** editorial page; ~**verfasser** leader *(Br.)* (editorial, *US*) writer, paragrapher *(US)*, editor, editorialist.
Leitbild guiding principle;
~ **eines Unternehmens in der Öffentlichkeit** *(Werbung)* corporate image *(US)*;
~**erstellung** image building; ~**programm** image building program(me).
Leit|code flag; ~**devise** key currency.
leiten to lead, to guide, to master, to head, to steer, *(beaufsichtigen)* to control, to superintend, *(Betrieb)* to manage, to run, to conduct, to operate *(Br.)*, to be in charge of, to direct, *(Staat)* to govern, *(Verkehr)* to route, *(verwalten)* to administer, to administrate;
Abteilung ~ to have control (be in charge) of a department; **an die falsche Adresse** ~ to pass on to the wrong address; **Arbeit** ~ to direct a work; **Aufstand** ~ to head a rebellion; **Bank** ~ to be a bank manager; **Delegation** ~ to head a delegation; **Diskussion** ~ to be in the chair; **Expedition** ~ to lead (head) an expedition; **Fabrik** ~ to operate (run) a factory; **Flugzeug wegen Nebels nach M** ~ to divert a plane because of fog to M; **Fluß in ein anderes Bett** ~ to divert the course of a river; **Frachtsendungen** ~ to route shipments; **Gerichtsverhandlung** ~ to hold court, to try a case; **Mitarbeiterstab** ~ to run a group of people; **Produktion durch elektronische Rechenanlagen** ~ to control production by electronic computers; **Schule** ~ to be a headmaster; **Sitzung** ~ to preside at a conference, to run a meeting; **auf die richtige Spur** ~ to put on the right track; **an die zuständige Stelle** ~ to refer to the appropriate quarter; **Unternehmen nach gesunden finanzpolitischen Grundsätzen** ~ to run an organization on a sound financial basis; **Untersuchung** ~ to be in charge of an investigation; **Verhandlungen** ~ to conduct negotiations; **Versammlung** ~ to preside over a meeting, to be in the chair; **in die Wege** ~ to set on foot, to initiate;
sich von den Umständen ~ lassen to be ruled by circumstances.

leitend managing, managerial, leading, governing, executive, directorial, directory;
~**er Angestellter** executive [employee], managerial employee, managing clerk; ~**er Arzt** physician in chief; ~**er Ausschuß** steering committee; ~**er Beamter** chief officer; ~**e Berufsfunktion** managerial function; ~**er Direktor** managing director; ~**er Gedanke** governing idea, guiding thought, key note; ~**er Ingenieur** chief engineer; ~**es Personal** executive staff; ~**e Position** managerial (managing, key) position; ~**e Stellung** leading (key, senior, managerial, management, executive) position.
Leiter leader, guide, manager, head, director, chief, master, executive head, governor, *(el.)* conductor, *(Gerät)* ladder, *(Schule)* headmaster *(Br.)*, principal *(US)*;
ausziehbare ~ extension ladder; **isolierter** ~ *(el.)* insulated conductor; **kaufmännischer** ~ business (commercial) manager, *(Warenhaus)* merchandise manager, front desk *(US)*; **künstlerischer** ~ *(Werbeagentur)* art director; **stellvertretender** ~ assistant (deputy) manager; **stromführender** ~ *(el.)* hot conductor; **stromloser** ~ *(el.)* dead wire; **technischer** ~ managing engineer, technical director (manager); **verantwortlicher** ~ acting manager, responsible head; **zusammenschiebbare** ~ telescope (telescopic) ladder;
~ **einer Abteilung** head of a department, department head, departmental manager; ~ **der Abteilung Absatzförderung** marketing manager; ~ **der Auswanderungsbehörde** chief emigration officer; ~ **einer Bank** manager of a bank, bank manager; ~ **einer Behörde** commissioner, head (chief) of an agency *(US)*; ~ **des Beschaffungsamtes** procurement officer; ~ **eines Betriebes** chief manager; ~ **einer Bezirksgeschäftsstelle** district registrar; ~ **der Buchhaltung** bookkeeping (accounting) supervisor; ~ **der Datenverarbeitung** data-processing manager; ~ **einer Delegation** leader (head) of a delegation; ~ **eines Dezernats** chief of a branch; ~ **einer Dienststelle** department head, chief of an agency *(US)*; ~ **einer Diskussion** leader of a discussion; ~ **der Einkaufsabteilung** purchasing manager; ~ **der Ein- und Verkaufsabteilung** merchandise manager; ~ **zum Erfolg** ladder to success; ~ **der Exportabteilung** export manager (director); ~ **des Finanzwesens** treasurer of a corporation *(US)*, finance manager *(Br.)*, financial director *(Br.)*; ~ **des Finanz- und Rechnungswesens** finance (financial) manager *(Br.)*, treasurer of a corporation *(US)*; **alleiniger** ~ **einer Firma** sole proprietor; ~ **der Gestaltung** *(Werbeagentur)* art director; ~ **des Grundbuchamtes** chief land registrar *(Br.)*; ~ **einer Güterabfertigungsstelle** freight agent *(US)*; ~ **des Hafenamtes** surveyor of the port; ~ **der Instandhaltungsabteilung** maintenance manager; ~ **einer Konsularabteilung** head of a consular post; ~ **einer Kopffiliale** [etwa] area superintendent; ~ **der Kraftfahrzeugversicherungsabteilung** motor manager; ~ **der Kreditabteilung** credit manager; ~ **der Kulturabteilung** *(Auswärtiges Amt)* assistant secretary for educational and cultural affairs; ~ **einer Lebensversicherungsabteilung** life manager; ~ **der Marktforschung** information manager; ~ **des Münzamtes** mint-master; ~ **einer Niederlassung** branch manager; ~ **eines Orchesters** conductor of an orchestra; ~ **des Patentamtes** Commissioner of the Patent Office *(US)*; ~ **der Personalabteilung** personnel director, staff executive (manager); ~ **der Planungs- und Kontrollabteilung** controller; ~ **der Pressestelle** press officer; ~ **der Public-Relations-Abteilung** publicity manager, public-relations director; ~ **des Rechnungswesens** accounting supervisor; ~ **der Regierungsdruckerei** public printer *(US)*; ~ **einer Schule** headmaster, principal *(US)*; ~ **des Seeversicherungsgeschäftes** marine manager; ~ **des Stadtrechtsamtes** city attorney *(US)*; **kommissarischer** ~ **der Stadtverwaltung** township trustee; ~ **der Steuer- und Devisenabteilung** tax and exchange controller; ~ **des Straßenverkehrsamtes** traffic manager; ~ **der Streuungsabteilung** *(Werbeagentur)* media director; ~ **des betrieblichen Unfallschutzes** safety supervisor; ~ **einer Unfallversicherungsabteilung** accident manager; ~ **der Unterhaltungsabteilung** entertainment president; ~ **der Verkaufsabteilung** director of sales, sales manager; ~ **der Verkaufsförderung** sales-promotion manager, merchandising director; ~ **des Verkehrsamtes** traffic manager (director); ~ **einer Versammlung** chairman of a meeting; ~ **der Versandabteilung** shipping manager (clerk) *(US)*; ~ **der Versandhausabteilung** maintenance manager; ~ **der Vertriebsabteilung** marketing director, distribution manager; ~ **der Warenzeichenabteilung** trademarks officer; ~ **der Werbeabteilung** advertising manager, publicity director; **künstlerischer** ~ **einer Werbeagentur** creative director;

~ **an eine Hauswand anlegen** to pitch a ladder against a building; ~ **zum Ruhm ersteigen** to climb the ladder to success; ~ **hinaufsteigen** to climb up a ladder; ~ **einer Reisegesellschaft sein** to escort a party.

Leiterzeugnis *(EG)* pilot product.

Leitfaden guide, handbook, textbook, manual, directory, abridgement, primer, introduction, companion, compendium, vademecum, *(fig.)* clew *(US)*, clue *(Br.)*; **kraftfahrtechnischer** ~ motor manual; ~ **für Einkäufer** buyer's guide; ~ **zum Fotografieren** guide to photography; ~ **der Geschäftspolitik** policy manual; ~ **für den Interviewer** assignment sheet, guide sheet, interviewer guide; ~ **für das Rechnungswesen** accounting manual.

leitfähig *(el.)* conductive.

Leit|fall leading case; ~**feuer** leading light; ~**flächenhebel** horn; ~**frequenz** radio-directing frequency, *(Flugkörper)* homing frequency; ~**funkstelle** net control station; ~**gedanke** guiding principle (thought), governing (leading) idea, key note, motif; ~**grundsatz** leading principle, number-one guideline; ~**hammel** *(fig.)* bell-wether; ~**idee** governing idea; ~**karte** master (guide) card; ~**kreuz** *(Verkehrsregelung)* convoy cross; ~**kurs** *(Währungsschlange)* central rate; ~**linie** *(drucktechn.)* guideline, *(Verkehr)* broken line; **politisches** ~**motiv** keynote of a policy; ~**planke** crash barrier, *(Bahn)* guardrail; ~**prinzip** guiding principle; ~**punkte** *(drucktechn.)* leaders; ~**satz** governing principle; ~**sätze** terms of reference, *(Gerichtsentscheidung)* head notes; ~**schiene** *(Bahn)* conductor rail, guide-rail; ~**schiff** commodore; ~**seil** *(Flugzeug)* guideline, dragline; ~**spruch** motto; ~**stand** command post; ~**stange** *(Straßenbahn)* trolley pole; ~**station** *(Rundfunk)* control station; ~**stelle** head office; ~**stern** lodestar, *(fig.)* pole star.

Leitstrahl guide beam, [pilot] beam, ray; **auf dem** ~ **anfliegen** to come in on the beam; ~**bake** localizer, radio-range beacon; ~**empfänger** radar receiver; ~**feuer** beam rider guidance; ~**feuerung** beam rider guidance; ~**funkfeuer** radio range beacon; ~**gerät** homing device; ~**rakete** beam rider; ~**sender** radar transmitter; ~**system** beam system; ~**überwachungsradar** approach surveillance radar.

Leit|studie pilot study, exploratory (pilot) survey; ~**system** *(Rakete)* guidance system.

Leitung lead, leading, conduct, carriage, pilotage, *(AG)* board of management, *(Aufsicht)* control, *(Betrieb)* governing body, management, direction, operation *(US)*, *(el.)* circuit, conveyance, *(Führerschaft)* leadership, guidance, direction, *(Rohrleitung)* pipeline, *(Staat)* government, administration, *(Telefon)* line, wire, *(Veranstaltung)* steering committee, management, *(Versorgungsleitung)* mains, *(Vorsitz)* chairmanship, chair, presidency, *(Wasser)* line; **unter der** ~ **von A.** under the direction (guidance) of A., with A. in the chair; **unter neuer** ~ under new management (ownership); **unter wechselnder** ~ under various control; **unter** ~ **einer internationalen Kommission** under the supervision of an international committee; **besetzte** ~ *(Telefon)* line engaged (busy, *US*); **nicht besetzte** ~ free line; **fachkundige (fachmännische)** ~ professional management; **gemeinsame** ~ joint management; **oberirdische** ~ *(Telefon)* overhead line; **oberste** ~ top management, headship; **operative** ~ *(mil.)* operational control; **redaktionelle** ~ editorial management, editorship; **staatliche** ~ government control; **stromführende** ~ *(el.)* live wire; **umsichtige** ~ prudent management; **verstopfte** ~ plugged line; **verwaltungsmäßige** ~ executive management; ~ **mehrerer Abteilungen** control over several departments; ~ **einer Behörde** administrative management; ~ **der Geschäfte** conduct of affairs; ~ **einer Gesellschaft** direction (operation) of a company (an enterprise), *(AG)* corporate management; ~ **einer Hauptversammlung** conduct of a general meeting; **vorübergehende** ~ **eines Industriebetriebes** partial operation of an industry; ~ **einer Schule** running (operation, *US*) of a school; ~ **einer Vorstandssitzung** conduct of a board meeting; ~ **der Verwaltung abgeben** to pass on the administrative leadership; **in der** ~ **bleiben** *(Telefon)* to hold the line; ~ **durchprüfen** *(Telefon)* to examine (check up) on a line; **in eine** ~ **eintreten** *(el.)* to monitor a circuit; ~ **von etw. haben** to be in control of s. th.; **erhebliche Erfahrungen in der zentralen** ~ **eines Unternehmens haben** to be heavy on operational management experience; **lange** ~ **haben** to be slow on the uptake; **neue** ~ **haben** to have a new board of directors (management); **organisatorische** ~ **haben** to hold the reigns of an organization; **in der** ~ **mitzureden haben** to have a voice in the management; ~ **legen** *(el.)* to instal(l); ~ **in die Hand nehmen** undertake the management; **mit der** ~ **eines Geschäftes betraut sein** to be in charge of a business; **unter jds.** ~ **stehen** to be under conduct of s. o.; ~ **übernehmen** to assume the control, to take charge of (take over) the management; ~ **eines Unternehmens übernehmen** to assume the direction of an enterprise; **jem. die** ~ **einer Bank übertragen** to invest the management of a bank in s. o.; ~ **verlegen** to install a pipeline; **elektrische** ~**en in einem Haus verlegen** to wire a house for electricity.

Leitungs|anlage *(el.)* wiring; ~**ausfall** *(el.)* mains breakdown; ~**bau** *(Röhren)* pipelaying; ~**belastung** *(el.)* power load; ~**bruch** burst in the water main; ~**draht** lead, conducting wire; ~**entstörung** fault finding; ~**fehler** *(Telefon)* line fault; ~**führung** wiring arrangement; ~**hahn** water tap, faucet *(US)*; ~**kabel** cable; ~**kanal** cable duct, conduit, channel; ~**mast** pole, pylon; ~**netz** *(Abwässer)* sewer system, sewerage, supply network, *(el.)* wiring, mains, *(Rohrleitungen)* network of pipes, *(Überlandleitungen)* grid; **an das** ~**netz anschließen** *(el.)* to connect to the mains; ~**plan** *(el.)* wiring diagram; ~**schnur** cord, flex; ~**schutzschalter** *(el.)* cut-out; ~**störung** *(Telefon)* line fault; ~**überwacher** *(el.)* linewalker, faultfinder; ~**wähler** *(tel.)* final selector; ~**wasser** tap water; **über** ~**wasser verfügen** to have water on tap; ~**wasserversicherung** water damage insurance.

Leitvermerk *(auf Briefen)* routing, route instruction, indication of route; **mit** ~ **versehen** routed; ~ **festlegen** to route.

Leit|vermerksbestimmung routing; ~**währung** key (leading) currency; ~**weg** route; ~**wegangaben** forwarding instructions, routing order; ~**werk** *(Flugzeug)* control, tail group (fin, unit); ~**werkflosse** fixed tail surface; ~**zahl** code number, index number, *(Post)* postal code, postcode *(Br.)*, zip-code *(US)*; ~**zahlsystem** [postal] zoning system, postcode system *(Br.)*; ~**zeichen** mark, beacon; ~**zinssatz** key rate, prime rate *(US)*; **festgelegter** ~**zinssatz** formula-established prime rate *(US)*.

Lektion lesson, lection, *(Schulaufgabe)* chapter; **jem. eine** ~ **erteilen** to read s. o. a lesson, to reprimand s. o.; **wohlverdiente** ~ **für j. sein** to have been taught a lesson, to serve s. o. right.

Lektor *(Universität)* lecturer, lector *(US)*, tutor *(US)*, reader, *(Verlag)* publisher's reader, editor; **englischer** ~ reader in English.

Lektorat lectureship, readership.

Lektoren|aufgaben, ~**tätigkeit** lecturing duties; ~**erfahrung** experience as lecturer; ~**stelle** lectureship, lectorship, readership, tutorship *(US)*.

Lektorin lady reader.

Lektüre reading, reading matter, books, literature; **eilige** ~ scamper; **einschlägige** ~ pertinent literature; **schwere** ~ hard reading; ~ **zur Entspannung** escape literature (reading); ~ **für Fortgeschrittene** advanced reading; **angenehme** ~ **darstellen** to make pleasant reading; **schwer verdauliche** ~ **darstellen** to be heavy reading; **intensiv mit einer** ~ **beschäftigt sein** to be in the middle of reading.

lenkbar steerable, *(fig.)* governable, ductile, *(Luftschiff)* navigable; ~**er Ballon** dirigible balloon; **leicht** ~**es Kind** easily manageable child; ~**es Luftschiff** dirigible airship.

Lenkbarkeit navigability.

lenken to control, to govern, to guide, to direct, to lead, to rule, to head, to master, *(Fahrzeug)* to steer, to drive, *(Flugzeug)* to navigate, to fly, *(zügeln)* to pace; **jds. Aufmerksamkeit auf etw.** ~ to draw s. one's attention on s. th.; **Aufmerksamkeit des Parlamentspräsidenten auf sich** ~ to catch the speaker's eye; **jds. Aufmerksamkeit auf ein Problem** ~ to focus s. one's attention on a problem; **Gespräch auf Politik** ~ to lead the conversation round to the political situation; **privates Investitionskapital in die Entwicklungsländer** ~ to steer private investments into less developed countries; **Lichtstrahl auf etw.** ~ to flash a beam of light on s. th.; **Produktion** ~ to control production; **Rakete ins Ziel** ~ to beam a rocket to its target; **seine Schritte heimwärts** ~ to direct one's steps towards home; **erste Schritte eines Kindes** ~ to guide a child's first steps; **Verdacht auf jem.** ~ to throw suspicion on s. o.; **Verkehr** ~ to channelize traffic; **Wirtschaft** ~ to regulate the industries of a country; **sich von Gefühlen** ~ **lassen** to be governed by one's feelings; **schwer zu** ~ **sein** to be difficult to manage.

Lenker controller.

Lenk|rad steering wheel; **~säule** steering column; **~stange** *(Fahrrad)* handle bar; **~system** guidance system.

Lenkung control, direction, guidance, leading, leadership, government, *(Fahrzeug)* steering, steering gear, driving, *(Flugzeug, Schiff)* navigation, flying;
staatliche ~ government control;
~ des Außenhandels export control; **~ des Kraftfahrzeugverkehrs** motor traffic management.

Lenkungs|ausschuß governing body, steering committee; **~funktion** function of coordinating; **~maßnahmen** regulatory measures, measures of direction (control); **~organ** regulatory body; **~stelle** planning office; **~vorschriften** planned measures; **~waffe** missile.

Lenkvorrichtung guiding control.

Lenzpumpe bilge (drainage) pump.

leoninischer Vertrag leonine contract.

Leporellofalzung accordion (concertina) folding, fanfold form.

lernbar learnable;
schwer ~ difficult to learn.

Lernbegierde eagerness to learn.

lernbegierig keen (eager) to learn.

Lerndisziplin haben to have the study habits.

Lernen learning, study, *(Schulaufgabe)* homework;
programmiertes ~ program(m)ed instruction;
~ durch Beobachtung observational learning.

lernen to learn, to study, *(Lehrling)* to serve one's apprenticeship (time), *(Schulaufgaben machen)* to do one's homework;
auswendig ~ to learn by heart, to memorize; **Beruf ~** to learn a trade; **ein paar Brocken Englisch ~** to acquire a smattering of English; **aus Büchern ~** to learn from books; **aus seinen Fehlern ~** to learn from one's mistakes; **Fremdsprachen ~** to study languages; **etw. nebenbei ~** to pick up s. th. along the line; **seine Rolle auswendig ~** to study one's part; **bei einem Schneider ~** to be apprenticed to a tailor; **fleißig in der Schule ~** to work hard at school; **schwer ~** to be backward in learning.

Lernender learner, pupil.

lernfähiges System *(Computer)* memory system.

Lern|gerät teaching device; **~jahre** training time on a job; **~krankenhaus** training hospital; **~methode** teaching method; **~mittel** teaching aid; **~prozeß** learning process; **~schwester** student nurse; **~system** teaching system; **~vorgang** training process; **~zeit** apprenticeship.

Lesart version, reading, lection, interpretation;
abweichende ~ different reading; **falsche ~** misconstruction, misreading; **verschiedene ~en** contradictory versions, different reading.

lesbar readable, legible;
schwer ~ illegible, cramped;
schwer ~er Druck print difficult to read.

Lese|alter reading age; **~automat** reading machine; **~befehl** *(Computer)* read instruction; **durchschnittliche ~beteiligung** average audience rating; **~brille** reading glasses; **~buch** reader; **~fibel** primer; **~früchte** gleanings; **~genuß eines Buches durch Lesen der Besprechungen vorwegnehmen** to discount one's enjoyment of a book by reading its advance review; **~gerät** microfilm viewer, *(Datenverarbeitung)* reader, scanner; **~gewohnheiten** reading habits; **~glas** magnifying glass; **~halle** newspaper room, study hall; **ungeheuren ~hunger haben** to be a voracious reader.

lesehungrig sein to read with avidity.

Lese|kreis, ~kränzchen literary coterie, reading society; **~lampe** reading lamp; **~licht** reading lamp (light); **~lichtschalter** reading light switch; **~liste** reading list; **~liste vorschreiben** to set books to be read; **~maschine** reading machine; **~methode** reading skills.

Lesen reading, *(Vorlesung abhalten)* lecturing;
planloses ~ desultory reading;
zum ~ keine Lust haben not to be in the mood (cue) for reading; **im Zug gut zum ~ kommen** to have a good read in the train *(Br.)*; **überdimensionale Zeit auf das ~ verwenden** to give a disproportinate amount of one's time to reading.

lesen to read, *(Universität)* to lecture, to deliver lectures;
schwer zu ~ *(Handschrift)* illegible, cramped;
Ähren ~ to glean a cornfield; **Bericht über etw. ~** to read an account of it; **Buch fertig ~** to finish [reading] a book; **Buch sorgfältig ~** to peruse a book; **in jem. wie in einem offenen Buch ~** to read s. o. like a book; **alte Geschichte ~** to lecture on ancient history; **Gesetzentwurf dreimal im Parlament ~** to give a bill three readings; **jem. etw. aus der Hand ~** to read s. one's hand; **Kartoffeln ~** to pick up potatoes; **Korrekturen ~** to read proofs, to proof-read; **jem. die Leviten ~** to read s. o. a lesson, to give s. o. a good dressing down; **sich müde ~** to read o. s. asleep; **etw. mit Mühe ~** to have difficulty in deciphering s. th.; **in Ruhe ~** to read in depth; **zu viel ~** to overread; **jem. jeden Wunsch von den Lippen ~** to anticipate s. one's every wish; **zwischen den Zeilen ~** to read between the lines; **in der Zukunft ~** to read the future; **jem. die Zukunft ~** to tell s. one's fortune; **sich gut ~ lassen** to read well, to be good (pleasant) reading; **diagonal zu ~ lernen** to become a skimmer in one's reading.

lesenswert readable, worth reading;
nicht ~ unreadable;
~ sein to make good (be well worth) reading.

Lese|pause einschalten, kurze to have a short read; **~plan** reading program(me); **~probe** specimen, *(Theater)* first rehearsal; **~pult** reading desk, bookholder, bookrest.

Leser reader, *(Zeitung)* subscriber;
flüchtiger ~ skipper; **gelegentlicher ~** occasional reader; **der geneigte ~** the gentle reader; **vier Millionen ~** readership of four millions; **regelmäßiger ~** regular reader; **tatsächliche ~** reader circulation; **unersättlicher ~** voracious reader; **unkritischer ~** uncritical reader;
seine ~ mitreißen to take one's readers with one; **dem ~ das Urteil überlassen** to leave the reader to judge; **sich an seine ~ wenden** to call upon one's readers;
~analyse readership (circulation) analysis, *(Rundfunk)* audience analysis.

Leseratte voracious reader, bookish person;
~ sein to be passionately fond of reading.

Leser|briefe letters to the editor; **~briefspalte** correspondence column, letters page; **~echo** reader feedback score; **~forschung** reader (audience) interest research; **~gemeinde** reading public.

Leserin lady reader.

Leserkreis audience, readership, circle of readers, reading society;
weiten ~ haben to be widely read;
~maßstäbe audience measurements.

leserlich legible, easy to read;
~e Handschrift readable handwriting.

Leser|lichkeit legibility; **~prozentsatz** reader traffic, *(einer Anzeige)* noting advertising; **~publikum** reading public.

Leserschaft the readers, readership, audience, constituency;
große ~ general readership; **hauptsächliche ~** primary readership;
~ einer Durchschnittsauflage average issue audience; **~ der höheren Einkommensklassen** upper-income readership;
auf die Bedürfnisse der ~ Rücksicht nehmen to pay respects to the needs of the general reader; **sich an seine ~ wenden** to call upon one's readers.

Leserschafts|analyse readership analysis (survey); **~interesse** reader (audience) attention; **~kontrolle** readership test; **~qualität** quality of an audience; **~tabelle** readership chart; **~ziffern** readership figures.

Leser|stamm stock of regular readers, steady readership; **guten ~stamm haben** to have a solid core of steady readers; **~umfrage** readership (audience) analysis, readers research; **~wohlwollen** reader confidence; **~zahl** *(Zeitung)* readership, *(einer Anzeige)* noting advertising; **~zuschrift** letter to the editor.

Lese|saal newspaper (reading) room, study hall; **~signal** *(Computer)* read-back signal; **seine ~stelle wiederfinden** to find one's place; **~stoff** reading matter; **seinen ~stoff verdauen** to digest what one reads; **~stück aus einem Buch** piece out of a book; **~tag** reading day; **systematische ~tätigkeit** systematic reading; **~übung** reading practice; **~unkundiger** illiterate; **~unterricht erteilen** to give reading lessons; **~wut** mania (craze) for reading; **~zeichen** bookmark, marker; **~zeit** reading time; **schöne ~zeit in der Bahn haben** to have a good read in the train *(Br.)*; **~zimmer** reading room, newsroom; **~zirkel** reading circle (club), book club, *(Lesering)* circulating magazine, magazine subscription service; **~zirkeldienst** press mapping agency; **~zirkelwerbung** advertising in reading circles.

Lesung, dritte *(Gesetz)* final passage; **erste ~** first reading; **zweite ~** second reading;
~ eines Gesetzesentwurfes reading of a bill;
zur dritten ~ anstehen to be down for the third reading; **Gesetz in der zweiten ~ beraten** to give a second reading for a bill; **Gesetz in der dritten ~ beschließen** to give a bill its third reading; **erste ~ erfahren** to be read for the first time; **zur zweiten ~ gelangen** to reach the second reading; **Gesetzesvorlage in zweiter ~ prüfen** to consider a bill in a second reading; **auf die ~ verzichten** *(Protokoll)* to take as read; **erste ~ vornehmen** to read for the first time; **in der dritten ~ abgelehnt werden** to be rejected at the third reading.

Letzt, zu guter to crown all;
das ~e Gericht the last assize; **~er Wille** last will [and testament];
das ~e auf dem Gebiet des Komforts bringen to be the last word in comfort and convenience; **das Erste und ~e für j. sein** to be everything for s. o.; **am ~en des Monats fällig werden** to be due on the last of the month.

letzt last;
bis zum ~en to the full;
bis ins ~e ausarbeiten to work out in great detail; **bis ins ~e ausnutzen** to make the most of it; **j. bis ins ~e ausnutzen** to take every possible advantage of s. o.; **an sich als ~en denken** to put o. s. last; **sich bis zum ~en einsetzen** to do one's utmost; **als ~er eingestellt sein** to be last in; **der ~e seines Stammes sein** to be the last of one's line;
den ~en beißen die Hunde the devil take the hindmost;
j. wie den ~en Dreck behandeln to treat s. o. like dirt; **jem. die ~en Ehren erweisen** to pay one's last respects to s. o.; **seine ~e Fassung verlieren** to lose complete control of o. s.; **~er Gang** *(Hinrichtung)* the last mile; **~es Gebot** highest (last) bid; **~e Geheimnisse des Lebens** deepest mysteries of life; **sein ~es Geld mit jem. teilen** to share one's last penny with s. o.; **~e Hand an etw. legen** to give the finishing touches; **~er Heller** last penny; **~e Instanz** last resort; **~e Klasse** top class; **ein ~es Mal** one more (for the last) time; **bis zum ~en Mann kämpfen** to die in the last ditch; **nach den ~en Meldungen** according to the latest information; **~es Mittel** extreme measures; **zu den ~en Mitteln greifen** to go to extremes; **~er Modeschrei** latest craze; **~er Monat** last month; **~e Nachrichten** *(Zeitung)* latest (stop press) news; **~e Notierung** previous quotation; **seine Schulden bis auf den ~en Pfennig bezahlen** to pay scot and lot; **seinen ~en Pfennig mit jem. teilen** to share one's last crust with s. o.; **bis auf den ~en Platz gefüllt** crowded (packed) to capacity; **~er Preis** lowest price; **~e Rate** final instal(l)ment; **~e Reihen im Theater** back rows in a theatre; **jem. den ~en Rest geben** to finish s. o. off; **j. zur ~en Ruhe betten** to lay s. o. to rest; **~er Schliff** master touch; **im ~en Semester** in the last term; **meine ~e Sorge** the least of my worries; **~e Sorte** poorest quality; **~e Tankstelle vor der Autobahn** last filling station before the motorway; **~e Überlebende einer großen Familie** sole remains of a large family; **~er Versuch** final attempt; **~es Wort** *(Angeklagter)* last word; **~e Worte [auf dem Sterbebett]** dying words; **in der ~en Zeit** recently.

Letzt|angebot highest bid; **~begünstigter** ultimate beneficiary; **~bietender** last and highest bidder.

letzter hindmost.

letzt|erwähnt, ~genannt last mentioned; **~instanzlich entscheiden** to judge without appeal (in the last instance); **~instanzliches Urteil** final judgment; **~interessierter Verkäufer** marginal seller.

Letzt|kreditnehmer final borrower; **~lebender** last survivor; **~verbrauch** last (ultimate) consumption; **~verbraucher** ultimate user (consumer); **~verteiler** retailer.

letztwillig testamentary;
j. ~ bedenken to mention s. o. in one's will; **~ verfügen** to devise, to make a will, to bequeath, to wish;
~e Verfügung last will and testament.

Leucht|bake light beacon; **~boje** floating light, light buoy, beacon buoy; **~bombe** parachute flare, marker, flash bomb; **~buchstabe** illuminated letter; **~draht** filament; **~druck** fluorescent ink printing.

Leuchte torch, lantern, *(fig.)* jumbo *(sl.)*;
gerade keine ~ no great shakes *(coll.)*;
~ einer Epoche shining light of the day; **~ auf dem Gebiet der Rechtswissenschaften** legal luminary; **~ der Wissenschaft** lantern of science;
gerade keine ~ in einem Gespräch abgeben not to shine in a conversation.

Leuchteffekt illuminating effect.

leuchten to glow, to shine, *(funkeln)* to sparkle, to glitter, to twinkle, *(Schirm)* to luminesce;
jem. ~ to light the way for s. o.; **in allen Farben ~** to be ablaze with colo(u)rs; **vor Freude ~** to shine with delight, to sparkle with joy; **hell ~** *(Kerzen)* to burn brightly, *(Sterne)* to shine brightly; **schwach ~** *(Birne)* to give a dim light;
sein Licht ~ lassen to let one's light shine.

leuchtend shining, burning, glowing, glimmering, sparkling, bright, vivid, *(Punkt)* luminous, radiant;
~e Sterne twinkling stars.

Leuchter candlestick.

Leucht|fallschirm parachute light; **~feld** illuminated panel.

Leuchtfeuer [air] beacon, beacon light, *(Schiffsfeuer)* seamark, coast light;
festes ~ fixed light; **unterbrochenes ~** occulting light;
~gebühr light due, lighthouse toll.

Leucht|fleck *(Radar)* pip, luminous spot; **~gas** lighting gas; **~kraft** illuminating power, luminosity; **~kugel** flare, *(Schiff)* signal rocket; **~masse** tracer element; **~öl** illuminating oil; **~patrone** flare cartridge; **~pistole** flare (signal) pistol; **~rahmensucher** *(Fotoapparat)* brilliant-frame viewfinder; **~rakete** *(Schiff)* signal rocket.

Leuchtreklame neon sign (light advertising), translight, illuminated (electric) advertising;
bewegliche ~ spectacular;
~ auf Dächern sky signs.

Leucht|röhre luminescent lamp, fluorescent tube, vacuum discharge tube *(US)*; **~schaltbild** illuminated diagram; **~schirm** illuminated indicator, fluorescent screen, *(für Ultraschall)* oscilloscope; **~schreiber** electric newscaster; **~schrift** illuminated newsband, luminous signs; **~signal** flashing signal, flare; **~skala** luminous dial; **~spur** tracer path; **~spurgeschoß** tracer bullet; **~spurmunition** tracer ammunition; **~stoff** luminescent substance; **~stofflampe** fluorescent (luminescent) lamp; **~stoffröhre** fluorescent tube; **~turm** lighthouse, light, seamark, fire tower, watchtower, beacon; **~turmbehörde** Trinity House *(Br.)*; **~turmwärter** lighthouse keeper, lighthouseman; **~werbung** illuminated (electric) advertising, neon sign; **~zeiger** *(Uhr)* luminous hand; **~zifferblatt** luminous dial; **~ziffern** luminous figures; **~ziffernanzeige** luminous-figure representation.

Leugnen denial, disavowal, traverse;
hartnäckiges ~ persistent denial;
wiederholtes ~ eines Angeklagten repeated denials of a charge;
~ einer Forderung impugnment of a claim; **~ des Klagegrundes** traverse, plea of demurrer.

leugnen to deny, to disavow, to disown, *(bestreiten)* to contest, to traverse, to gainsay;
Beschuldigung ~ to deny a charge; **Bestehen einer Forderung** to disclaim (impugn) a debt; **Klagegrund ~** to traverse, to plead a demurrer; **jegliche Mitwissenschaft an einem Plan ~** to deny any knowledge of a plan;
das läßt sich nicht ~ there is no gainsaying it.

leugnend, nicht zu ~e Tatsachen facts that cannot be gainsaid.

Leumund reputation, repute, character, record, renown, standing;
allgemeiner ~ general credit; **einwandfreier ~** good repute (reputation); **schlechter (übler) ~** bad record (reputation), ill repute;
in bösen ~ bringen to bring into disrepute; **guten ~ haben** to be of good report; **jds. ~ zerstören** to injure s. one's reputation, to bring s. o. into disrepute, to defame s. one's character.

Leumunds|nachweis character evidence; **~zeugnis** certificate of good behavio(u)r (character), character reference, good-conduct certificate.

Leute people, persons, *(Arbeiter)* hands, staff, employees, *(Familie)* family, folk *(Br.)*, folks *(US)*, *(Hausangestellte)* [domestic] servants, establishment, *(mil.)* enlisted men;
ständig auf Achse befindliche ~ mobile people; **die ~** Mrs. Grundy; **einfache ~** simple folk, common people; **führende ~** leading lights; **junge ~** young people; **meine ~** my people; **alle möglichen ~** everyone and his uncle; **reiche ~** moneyed people; **renommierte ~** people of name; **tonangebende ~** leading features; **undurchsichtige ~** financiers of a dubious character; **unsere ~** our set; **die verantwortlichen ~** the people responsible; **vornehme ~** gentlefolk, high society;
~ vom Bau specialists, experts; **~ die nicht vom Fach sind** people outside the profession; **die ~ im Finanzministerium** the chaps in the Treasury Department *(US)*; **Land und ~** a country and its people; **~ von Rang und Namen** distinguished people, men of station;
viele ~ beschäftigen to be a large employer; **größtenteils aus alten ~n bestehen** to contain a high ratio of old people; **~ brauchen** to be short of hands (shorthanded); **Gerücht unter die ~ bringen** to spread a rumo(u)r; **zu den ~n gehören, die ...** to be one of those people who ...; **zu den ~n gehören, die sich nichts gefallen lassen** to be the kind of man who hits back; **zu den unwichtigen ~n gehören** to be in the lower echelon; **nicht genug ~ haben** to be short of hands (shorthanded); **jede Menge (eine Fülle) interessanter ~ kennenlernen** to meet no end of interesting people; **unter die ~ kommen** to become public; **schnell unter die ~ kommen** to soon get around; **wenig unter die ~ kommen** not to go out much; **sich um anderer ~**

Angelegenheiten kümmern to follow other men's business; **sich nicht um das Gerede der ~ kümmern** not to pay attention to what people say; **sich unter die ~ mischen** to mix with the crowd; **einer von unseren ~n sein** to be one of the crowd; **sich mit allen ~n gut stehen** to make friends with everybody; **hinterm Berg wohnen auch ~** you are not the only pebble on the beach;
~schinder sweater, grinder, slave driver.
leutselig amiable, gracious, welcome;
~er alter Herr affable old gentleman.
Leviten, jem. die ~ lesen to row s. o., to lecture s. o., to read the Riot Act to (drop on) s. o.
Lexikograph dictionary maker, lexicographer, vocabulist.
lexikographisch lexical.
Lexikon lexicon, dictionary, *(Konservationslexikon)* encyclop(a)edia, vocabulary, wordbook;
lebendes ~ walking dictionary;
Wort im ~ aufnehmen to include a word in a dictionary; **Wort im ~ nachschlagen** to look up a word in a dictionary; **~ zu Hilfe nehmen** to consult a dictionary;
~format lexicon format, *(Papier)* royal.
Liaison unterhalten to have an entanglement with a woman.
liberal liberal, broad-minded, open-minded, liberal-minded;
sich ~ verhalten to take a liberal turn; **für ~ gehalten werden** to pass for a liberal;
~e Ansichten vertreten to hold liberal views; **~e Bastion** liberal bastion; **~e Handelspolitik** liberal trade policy; **~es Mäntelchen** liberal cloak; **~e Partei** liberal party; **~e Partei wählen** to go liberal; **~e Stadt** open-matter town *(US sl.)*.
Liberaler liberal, whig *(Br.)*.
liberalisieren to liberalize, to free, to decontrol;
Warenliste ~ to liberalize a list of items.
liberalisiert | e Abschreibungspolitik liberalization of depreciation allowances; **~es Kapitalkonto** liberalized capital account.
Liberalisierung liberalization, *(Importe)* decontrol;
wirtschaftliche ~ trade liberalization;
~ aufheben to reimpose restrictions on imports, to deliberalize.
Liberalisierungs | abkommen liberalization agreement; **~grad** degree of liberalization; **~kodex** liberalization code; **~liste** free list; **von der ~liste streichen** to deliberalize; **~maßnahmen** liberalization measures; **~politik** policy of liberalization.
Liberalismus liberalism;
zum ~ bekehren to liberalize; **~ eindämmen** to stem back liberalism.
liberalistisch liberalistic;
~ angehaucht sein to smack of liberalism;
~e Richtung laissez-faire school.
Licht light, *(Beleuchtung)* illumination, lighting;
in günstigem ~ in favo(u)rable light; **in helles ~ getaucht** bathed in bright light;
abgeblendetes ~ *(Auto)* dimmed illumination (light), dimmed (dipped) headlight; **diffuses ~** diffuse light; **elektrisches ~** electric light; **gedämpftes ~** soft light; **gelbes ~** *(Verkehrsampel)* amber traffic light; **grelles ~** glare; **grünes ~** *(fig. und Verkehrsampel)* green light; **künstliches ~** artificial light;
~er einer Großstadt lights of a big city; **grelles ~ der Öffentlichkeit** glare of publicity; **~ und Schatten** light and shade;
~ anknipsen to turn on the light; **jem. ein ~ aufstecken** to open s. one's eyes; **~ ausschalten** to switch out the light; **bei ~ betrachtet völlig anders aussehen** to look quite different on closer examination; **ans ~ bringen** to bring to light, to disclose; **~ in eine Angelegenheit bringen** to throw light on a matter; **sich in neuem ~ darstellen** to present itself in a new light; **das ~ der Welt erblicken** to see the light [of day]; **grünes ~ für ein Vorhaben erhalten** to receive (be given) the green light (go-ahead) for a project; **jem. hinters ~ führen** to hoodwink s. o., to pull the wool over s. one's eyes; **~ brennen lassen** to keep the light on; **Sache in neuem ~ erscheinen lassen** to throw (cast) a new light upon a matter; **sich nicht leicht hinters ~ führen lassen** not to be taken in so easily; **elektrisches ~ in ein Haus legen** to wire a house for electricity; **im ~ einer Kerze lesen** to read by candlelight; **etw. ins rechte ~ rücken** to put s. th in its true light; **Sache in einem anderen ~ sehen** to see a matter in a different light; **ganze Welt in rosigem ~ sehen** to see everything through rose-colo(u)red spectacles; **wegen Fahrens ohne ~ angeklagt sein** to be charged for driving without lights; **in Finanzdingen kein großes ~ sein** to have no genius for finance; **sich ins rechte ~ setzen** to put (show) o. s. in a good light; **im ~ der Öffentlichkeit stehen** to be in the limelight; **sich selbst im ~ stehen** to quarrel with one's bread and butter; **sein ~ unter den Scheffel stellen** to hide one's light under a bushel; **sich ins rechte ~ stellen** to bring o. s. into notice; **~ auf etw. werfen** to shed light on s. th.; **falsches ~ auf etw. werfen** to cast false colo(u)rs on s. th.; **schlechtes ~ auf j. werfen** to reflect unfavo(u)rably on s. o.; **zweifelhaftes ~ auf eine Sache werfen** to cast a doubtful light on s. th.; **sich im wahren ~ zeigen** to appear in one's true light, to show one's true colo(u)rs.
licht light, bright, white, *(Schrift)* open;
~e Augenblicke haben to have one's brighter moments; **~er Durchmesser** inside diameter; **~e Höhe** headroom, headway; **~e Momente haben** *(Geisteskranker)* to have lucid intervals; **~e Schrift** light-faced type; **am ~en Tage** in broad daylight; **~e Weite einer Brücke** clear span of a bridge; **~e Weite eines Rohres** inside diameter of a pipe; **~es Zimmer** bright room.
Licht | abdeckschirm *(Fernsehen)* flag; **~anlage** lighting installation, light plant; **defekte ~anlage** *(Auto)* defective lights.
lichtarm poorly lit.
Licht | ausstrahlung radiation of light; **~band** luminous strip.
lichtbeständig light-resistant.
Licht | bild photo[graph], photographic picture, *(Diapositiv)* lantern slide; **~bildauswertung** photogrammetry; **durch ~bilder veranschaulicht** illustrated by lantern slides; **~bildervortrag** lantern (slide) lecture, lecture with slides, travelog *(US)*; **~bildwerfer** projector; **~blende** diaphram; **~blick** silver lining, clear spot in a cloudy sky; **~blitz** flash; **~bogen** arc; **~bündel** aggregation of light.
Lichtdruck phototype, heliotype, artotype, collotype *(Br.)*, photographic printing;
~platte phototype; **~presse** collotype press; **~verfahren** colotype,photogelatine process.
licht | durchlässig translucent, pervious to light; **~echt** lightfast, nonfading.
Lichteffekt light effect.
lichtempfindlich *(Film)* sensitive, photosensitive;
~ machen to excite.
Lichtempfindlichkeit film speed.
Lichtempfindlichkeitsmesser sensiometer.
Lichten *(Wald)* thinning.
lichten, sich *(Haar)* to be getting thin, *(Himmel)* to clear;
Anker ~ to weigh anchor; **Reihen der Soldaten ~** to thin the ranks of the soldiers.
Lichter | baum Christmas tree; **~glanz** illumination, *(Straßen)* blaze of lights; **~glanz der Sterne** brilliance of the stars.
lichterloh ablaze, blazing;
~ brennen to burn like a house on fire.
Lichtermeer sea of lights.
Licht | filter *(Foto)* colo(u)r (light) filter; **~flut** dazzle of light; **~geschwindigkeit** velocity of light; **~hof** *(Foto)* halo, *(Haus)* arcade, patio.
lichthoffrei free from halo, antihalo.
Licht | hofschutz antihalo base; **~hupe** headlight flasher; **~jahr** light year; **~kegel** pencil of light; **~klecks im Nebel** blur of light in the fog; **~leitung** circuit; **~leitungen in einem Haus verlegen** to wire a house for electricity; **~maschine** *(Auto)* dynamo, generator *(US)*; **~messer** photometer; **~messung** *(Foto)* exposure control; **~netz** network; **~pausanstalt** photocopying establishment; **~pausapparat** copying (blueprint) apparatus, blueprinter *(US)*; **~pause** blueprint, photocopy; **~pause machen** to blueprint; **~pausgerät** blueprint (copying) apparatus, blueprinter *(US)*; **~pauspapier** blueprint (photocopying) paper; **~pausverfahren** heliographic printing, blueprint process; **~punkt** cursor; **~quante** photon; **~recht** right to light; **~- und Fensterrecht** ancient lights *(Br.)*; **~reklame** illuminated (electric sign, neon light) advertising, sky sign, electric signs *(US)*, *(bewegliche)* spectaculars *(US)*; **~rufanlage** luminous calling system; **~satz** phototypography, photo offset, photocomposition, computerized typesetting, filmsetting; **im ~satz hergestellt** photographic; **~satzverfahren** photo-offset composing (filmsetting) system; **~schacht** well; **im Dunkeln nach dem ~schalter tasten** to feel about in the dark for the electric light switch; **~schein einer Lampe** lamp pool; **~schein verbreiten** to throw out light.
lichtscheues Gesindel shady characters.
Licht | schimmer glimmer (gleam) of light; **~schleuse** *(Foto)* light trap; **~setzmaschine** photocomposing machine; **~signal** *(Ampel)* traffic light, *(Auto)* flashlight; **~signalanlage** light-signalling system; **durch ~signale mitteilen** to blink.
Lichtspiel | haus cinema, picture house, movie theater *(US)*, movies *(US sl.)*; **~hauswerbung** picture (movie, *US*) advertisement; **~theater** picturedrome; **~wesen** cinematography.

Lichtsprechgerät blinker apparatus, heliograph, heliotrope.
lichtstark *(Objektiv)* high-speed.
Licht|stärke intensity of light, luminous intensity; **~steindruck** photolithography; **~strahl** beam (ray) of light; **~strahl auf etw. lenken** to flash a beam of light on s. th.; **~strahler** floodlight projector.
lichtunempfindlich insensitive to light.
Lichtung clearance, open felling.
Licht|verbrauch current consumption; **~verhältnisse** lighting arrangements; **~welle** light wave; **~werbung** electric sign advertising, spectaculars *(US)*; **~wert** *(Foto)* exposure value.
lieb, jem. ~ geworden sein to have grown fond of s. th.;
~er Freund dear friend; **um des ~en Friedens willen** for the safe of peace and quiet; **~es Gesicht** sweet face; **sich ~ Kind bei jem. machen** to worm o. s. into s. one's favo(u)r; **~ Kind bei jem. sein** to be in s. one's good graces; **seine ~e Not mit jem. haben** to have a lot of trouble with s. o.; **den ~en langen Tag** the livelong day, all day long; **du ~e Zeit** good heavens.
liebäugeln to ogle;
mit jem. ~ to make sheep's eyes at s. o.; **mit etw. ~** to toy with the idea; **mit der Idee ~, sich ein neues Auto zu kaufen** to flirt with the idea of buying a new car; **mit einer neuen Stellung schon lange ~** to have had one's eye on a new job for a long time.
Liebe, mit Lust und with heart and soul;
erste ~ puppy love; **leidenschaftliche ~** passionate (fervent) love; **verbotene ~** illegal love;
~ zum Beruf attachment to one's profession; **~ auf den ersten Blick** love at first sight;
mit Lust und ~ dabei sein to have one's heart in it;
~ geht durch den Magen the way to a man's heart is through his stomach; **~ macht blind** love is blind;
~diener timeserver, toady, sycophant; **~dienerei** flannel.
liebedienern to toady.
lieben to love, *(gern haben)* to like, to enjoy, to be fond of;
Musik ~ to be fond of music.
liebend gern with the greatest pleasure.
liebenswert|er alter Herr charming old gentleman; **~es Lächeln** winning smile.
liebenswürdig pretty, gentle, urbane, nice *(coll.)*, amiable, engaging, obliging, *(hilfsbereit)* kind;
~ sein to have an engaging manner.
liebenswürdigerweise kindly.
Liebenswürdigkeit amiability, charm, sweetness of temper;
angeborene ~ native charm;
jem. mit großer ~ empfangen to receive s. o. most charmingly; **jem. ~en sagen** to say nice things to s. o.; **sich ~en an den Kopf werfen** to hurl insults at one another.
Liebes|abenteuer love affair; **~brief** love letter, sugar report *(coll.)*; **~dienst** favo(u)r, good turn, kind act; **jem. einen ~dienst erweisen** to do s. o. a favo(u)r; **jem. eine ~erklärung machen** to propose to s. o., to pop the question to s. o. *(coll.)*; **~gabe** charitable gift; **~gabensendung** gift package (parcel); **~gedicht** love poem; **~geschichte** love story; **~gunst** favo(u)r; **~heirat** love match; **~heirat ohne finanzielle Grundlage** love in a cottage; **~lied** love song; **sentimentales ~lied** torch song *(US)*; **vergebliche ~mühe** lost labo(u)r; **durchgegangenes ~paar** runaway couple; **~paarbelauscher** voyeur; **~roman** love story; **~schmerz** pangs of love; **~verhältnis** love affair, liaison.
liebgewinnen to become fond of.
Liebhaber lover;
jugendlicher ~ *(Theater)* juvenile lead;
mit einem ~ durchbrennen to elope with a lover;
~aufführung amateur production; **~ausgabe** amateur edition; **~bühne** amateur theatre.
Liebhaberei hobby, fancy, fad, toy.
Liebhaber|einband amateur binding; **~preis** fancy price; **~vorstellung** private theater, amateur theatrical; **~wert** sentimental (fancy) value, personal value.
lieblich|er Duft pleasant smell; **~e Melodie** sweet melody.
Liebling favo(u)rite, idol, nursling, honey *(US)*;
~ des Direktors fair-haired boy of the manager; **~ der Familie** idol of the family; **~ der Frauen** darling of the ladies; **Mutters ~** mother's pet; **~ des Publikums** favo(u)rite with the public;
jds. ~ sein to be s. one's favo(u)rite.
Lieblings|beschäftigung favo(u)rite pursuit; **~gericht** favo(u)rite dish; **~lied** favo(u)rite tune, air; **~phrase** favo(u)rite remark; **~platz** haunt, favo(u)rite spot; **~schriftsteller** favo(u)rite writer; **~schüler** pet pupil; **Gespräch auf sein ~thema hinführen** to bring a conversation round to one's favo(u)rite subject; **auf sein ~thema zu sprechen kommen** to start on one's hobby-horse; **schon wieder über sein ~thema reden** to be on one's pet subject again; **~theorie** pet theory; **~zeitvertreib** favo(u)rite part-time.
lieblos cold, loveless.
liebst, jem. am ~en sein to suit s. o. best;
~e Beschäftigung favo(u)rite occupation.
Lied, immer das alte the same old song;
ein ~ davon singen können to know it from experience; **das Ende vom ~ sein** to be the upshot of it.
Liederabend recital.
liederlich slovenly, *(ausschweifend)* dissolute, dissipated, loose; **~e Arbeit** slipshod work, slopwork; **~ geführte Bücher** slovenly kept books; **~es Frauenzimmer** slattern, slut; **~en Lebenswandel führen** to lead a loose life, to have a light character; **~er Mensch** wastrel, rake.
Liederlichkeit sloppiness, carelessness, dissipation.
Liefer|abkommen supply contract, contract for [future] delivery; **langfristiges ~abkommen** long-term supply arrangement; **~ablehnung** refusal to supply; **~angebot** tender of delivery, supplier's offer; **~annahme** taking delivery, acceptance.
Lieferant supplier, contractor, deliverer, deliveryman, dealer, trade creditor, undertaker, vendor *(US)*, *(Kohlen)* fitter, *(Lebensmittel)* victualler, caterer, purveyor, provider, *(Möbel)* furnisher, *(Quelle)* source;
regelmäßiger ~ regular supplier; **unsere ~en** tradesmen who supply us;
~ von Ausrüstungsgegenständen outfitter; **~ für Ersatzteile** supplier of replacement parts; **~ von Fertiggerichten** industrial caterer; **~ von Raumfahrterzeugnissen** aerospace contractor; **~ von Schiffsbedarf** ship chandler;
augenblicklichen ~en beibehalten to stay with a present supplier; **~ sein** to supply; **auf ausländische ~en angewiesen sein** to depend on foreign suppliers; **höhere Leistungen von den ~en verlangen** to drive on contractor performance.
Lieferanten|angebot supplier's offer; **~anweisung** supplier's instruction; **~beziehungen** supplier relations; **~buchhalter** accounts payable accountant *(US)*; **~eingang** tradesmen's entrance; **~finanzierung** supplier's financing; **~kartei** card-index of suppliers; **~konto** *(Bilanz)* suppliers account; **~kosten** supplier's costs; **~kredit** credit granted by suppliers, supplier's (trade, short-term) credit, advance to customers; **~kreditkonto** trade account; **~liste** list of suppliers; **~nummer** supplier number; **~preis** supplier's price; **~rechnung** supplier's invoice; **offene ~rechnungen** trade accounts receivable *(US)*; **ungeprüfte ~rechnungen** unaudited invoices; **~schulden** *(Bilanz)* trade creditors (debts), suppliers, trade account payables *(US)*; **beigetriebene ~schulden** *(Bilanz)* trade debts recovered; **~skonti** trade discounts; **~tür** tradesmen's entrance; **~verbindlichkeiten** trade creditors, suppliers, trade account payables *(US)*; **~wahl** supplier choice; **~wechsel** trade acceptance; **~zahlungen** payments to suppliers.
Liefer|anweisung delivery order; **~auftrag** order of delivery, delivery (purchase) order, *(für eigene Waren an Angestellte)* store order *(US)*; **als ~auftrag vorliegen haben** to have on order; **~auto** delivery van *(Br.)*.
lieferbar deliverable, available, ready for delivery (shipment), can be supplied, *(begebbar)* negotiable, *(Börse)* good delivery, *(auf Lager)* on stock, carried in stock, available, *(marktfähig)* marketable, merchantable, salable;
auf Abruf ~ ready for delivery; **in allen Größen ~** available in all sizes; **jederzeit unbegrenzt ~** *(Wertpapiere)* on tap; **kurzfristig ~** for short delivery; **nicht ~** undeliverable, not to be had, *(Börse)* bad delivery; **nicht mehr ~** no longer on sale (available); **sofort ~** for immediate delivery, *(Börse)* spot;
~ bei Eingang der Bestellung delivery upon receipt of order; **~ nur fest** available for outright purchase only;
~ sein *(Effektengeschäft)* to constitute [a] good delivery; **beschränkt ~ sein** to be in short supply; **nicht gut ~ sein** to be bad delivery; **nicht ~ sein** not to be a delivery (available); **noch nicht ~ sein** to be not yet available for delivery; **nur ~ sein, solange der Vorrat reicht** to be supplied (available) only until stocks run out;
~es Papier good trade paper; **~er Titel** *(Buchhandel)* available title; **sofort ~e Waren** prompts *(Br.)*, *(Börse)* spot goods, spots.
Liefer|barkeit deliverability, availability, merchantableness; **~basis** basing point; **~bedingungen** terms (conditions) of delivery, delivery terms (conditions), trade terms; **~begünstigung** priority delivery; **~beleg** delivery slip.
lieferbereit ready to deliver (for delivery, for shipment);
~ sein to be prepared to supply goods.

Liefer|bereitschaft readiness for delivery (to deliver); ~**bereitschaftsgrad** service grade; ~**bewilligung** delivery order, docket *(Br.)*; ~**bezirk** cartage limit, *(Gaswerk)* service area; ~**bote** deliveryman, roundsman *(Br.)*, messenger boy; ~**buch** delivery book; ~**datum** delivery date; ~**dienst** supply service; ~**dock** delivery dock; ~**einstellung** cessation of delivery; ~**engpaß** supply bottleneck.

Lieferer deliverer, contractor, purveyor, furnisher, supplier, vendor *(US)*.

lieferfähig deliverable, able to supply, available, carried on stock, fit for acceptance;
nicht ~ unavailable, not to be had;
in drei Tagen ~ **sein** to be delivered at three days notice; **nicht** ~ **sein** to have no available stock;
~**er Zustand** deliverable condition.

Liefer|fähigkeit delivery power, ability to supply, *(Börse)* stock availability; ~**firma** supplier, supplying firm, purveyor [firm], deliverer, contractor; ~**frist** term of (fixed time for) delivery, delivery period; **10tägige** ~**frist** 10-days delivery; **länger werdende** ~**fristen** lengthening delivery periods; **zwingende** ~**frist** time is the escense of contract; ~**frist einhalten** to deliver within the specified time; ~**frist festsetzen** to stipulate a time for delivery; ~**frist überschreiten** to exceed the term of delivery; ~**fristüberschreitung** failure to keep the delivery date; ~**garantie** supply (performance) guarantee, performance bid *(US)*; ~**gebiet** *(Gaswerk)* service area; ~**gebühren** cost of delivery, delivery cost; ~**gegenstand** delivery item, object of supply, article to be supplied; ~**gemeinschaft** associative marketing; ~**genehmigung** delivery licence; ~**geschäft** *(Börse)* time bargain, futures *(US)*, *(Prämiengeschäft)* option deal, trading in puts and calls *(US)*; ~**gewicht** weight delivered, delivery weight; ~**hafen** port of delivery; ~**hindernis sofort melden** report immediately any delivery holdup; ~**kartei** term file; ~**kaution** supply guarantee, delayed delivery bond; ~**klausel** delivery clause; ~**klauseln** commercial (trade) terms; **internationale** ~**klauseln** incoterms; ~**kommando** *(Flugzeug)* ferry (specified) command; ~**konsortium** suppliers' syndicate; ~**konto** trading account; ~**kosten** cost of delivery, delivery cost; ~**kredit** supplier's credit; ~**land** supplier's country, country of delivery; ~**menge** quantity delivered, lot; ~**möglichkeit** delivery power, *(Börse)* stock availability; **begrenzte** ~**möglichkeit** limited supplies.

liefern to supply, to deliver, to furnish, to provide, to procure, to place, *(ausrüsten)* to outfit, *(Ertrag)* to yield, *(Lebensmittel)* to purvey, to cater, *(Prämiengeschäft)* to put, *(übergeben)* to surrender;
sofort zu ~ for immediate delivery, *(Börse)* spot;
für die Armee ~ to purvey for the army; **auf Bestellung** ~ to supply to order; **Beweis** ~ to furnish proof; **frei an Bord zu** ~ deliverable free on board, to be delivered on board free of charge; **gute Ernte** ~ to yield good crops; **falsch** ~ to misdeliver; **fristgerecht** ~ to deliver within the time stipulated (the specified time); **Gesprächsstoff** ~ to provide a topic of conversation; **nur an den Großhandel** ~ to supply only to wholesalers; **frei Haus** ~ to deliver to s. one's house, to deliver free door; **in Heften** ~ to issue in numbers; **Löwenanteil** ~ to supply the bulk; **Nachweis** ~ to furnish proof; **prompt** ~ to be expeditious in business; **rechtzeitig** ~ to deliver on schedule; **schnell** ~ to speed up delivery; **sofort vom Lager** ~ to deliver from stock immediately; **stockend** ~ to be slack in supplying; **Strom** ~ to supply electricity; **12 Stück pro Minute** ~ *(Maschine)* to turn out twelve pieces per minute; **Waren** ~ to deliver goods; **Waren auf Kredit** ~ to supply goods on credit; **Ware an einen Kunden** ~ to serve a customer with goods; **Ware längsseits Schiff** ~ to deliver the goods alongside the ship; **einen Zentner Ware zu wenig** ~ to short-ship a consignment by 1 cwt.; **an Wiederverkäufer** ~ to supply to the trade.

Liefer|ort point (place) of delivery; ~**pflicht** obligation to deliver; ~**pflichtsaldo** balance of commitments; ~**plan** delivery schedule; ~**posten** delivery item, lot; ~**preis** delivered (contract) price, price of delivery, delivery (purchase, contract) price; ~**quelle** source of supply; ~**rückstand** delayed delivery.

Lieferschein bill of delivery, delivery note (slip, receipt, ticket), docket *(Br.)*, supply note, shipping ticket *(US)*, tally out *(US)*, *(Kommissionsverkauf)* memorandum, bill;
frei gegen ~ free on delivery;
durch Giro übertragbarer ~ tracer.

Liefer|schwierigkeiten delivery failures (problems); ~**situation** supply situation; ~**soll** delivery quota; ~**sperre** refusal to deal *(US)*; ~**sperre für bestreikten Betrieb** hotcargo ban; ~**spesen** delivering charges, delivery cost (charges); ~**stelle** supply base; ~**stellung** supply position; ~**störung** wrongful delivery; ~**tag** delivery date (day, *Br.*), day of delivery, *(Börse)* settling day, day of settlement, payday *(Br.)*.

Liefertermin time (date, day) of delivery, fixed time for delivery, delivery date, delivery deadline *(US)*, *(Börse)* settling day, day of settlement, payday *(Br.)*;
festgesetzter ~ scheduled delivery date;
~**e unbedingt einhalten** to be very specific on delivery dates.

Lieferumfang extent (scope, *US*) of supply, supply schedule.

Lieferung delivery, deliverance, supply, supplying, furnishing, *(Buch)* instal(l)ment, part, number, issue, *(Effekten)* delivery, *(Lebensmittel)* purveyance, catering, *(Partie)* lot, parcel, shipment *(US)*, *(Schiffsladung)* cargo, *(Sendung)* consignment, invoice, *(Waggon)* carload;
auf ~ on delivery; **bei** ~ on delivery, at the time of delivery; **bei** ~ **zahlbar** payable (cash) on delivery; **bis zur** ~ pending delivery; **falls die** ~ **unterbleibt** in case of nondelivery; **im Zeitpunkt der** ~ at the time of delivery; **nach erfolgter** ~ when delivered; **was die** ~ **anbetrifft** delivery-wise; **zahlbar bei** ~ payable on delivery; **zum Nachweis der** ~ in proof of delivery; **aufgeschobene** ~ *(Börse)* deferred delivery; **vertraglich ausbedungene** ~**en** contract supplies; **bestimmungsgemäße** ~ *(Börse)* good delivery; **bevorzugte** ~ priority delivery; **nicht erfolgte** ~ lack of delivery; **fehlerhafte** ~ deficient delivery; **innerbetriebliche** ~ internal delivery; **kostenlose** ~ delivered free of charge; **künftige** ~ *(Börse)* future delivery; **kurzfristige** ~ near delivery; **mangelhafte** ~ bad delivery; **ordnungswidrige** ~ misdelivery; **prompte** ~ prompt (speedy) delivery, *(Börse)* spot delivery; **rechtzeitige** ~ good delivery; **rückständige** ~ delivery in arrears, back order; **sofortige** ~ prompt (immediate) delivery, *(Börse)* spot delivery; **spätere** ~ *(Börse)* forward (future) delivery; **steuerfreie** ~**en** tax-exempt supplies; **termingerechte** ~ delivery in due course; **umgehende** ~ immediate delivery; **unvollständige** ~ short delivery; **verrechnete** ~**en** deliveries charged on account; **versehentliche** ~ delivery by mistake; **verspätete** ~ delayed delivery; **nicht vertragsmäßige** ~ bad delivery; **nachts vorgenommene** ~ overnight delivery; **vorzeitige** ~ premature delivery; **wöchentliche** ~ weekly delivery; **zollfreie** ~ duty-free delivery; **zusätzliche** ~**en** fresh supplies;
~ **auf Abruf** delivery as required, delivery at call; ~ **am gleichen Tag des Abschlusses** *(Börse)* cash; ~**en auf Abzahlungsbasis** supplies on a deferred-payment basis *(US)*; ~ **von Aktien** delivery of stocks; ~ **und Aufstellung** supply and erection; ~ **des Auslands** import shipments; ~**en ins Ausland** deliveries overseas, export shipments; ~ **franko (frei) Bahnhof** delivered free at station; ~ **gegen Barzahlung** payment cash on delivery; ~ **frei Baustelle** delivered [on] site; ~ **frei Bestimmungsbahnhof** free station of destination; ~ **an Bord** free on board; ~ **innerhalb kürzester Frist** prompt delivery; ~ **frei Geschäft** delivered in store *(US)*; ~ **am nächsten Geschäftstag** *(Börse)* regular way *(US)*; ~**en im Großhandel** wholesale deliveries; ~ **frei Haus** delivered (delivery) free at residence; ~ **ins Haus** take-out (store-door, *US*) service; ~ **ab Kai** delivery from the quay; ~ **nach Käufers Wahl** at buyer's option; ~ **per LKW oder mit der Bahn** road or rail delivery; ~ **gegen Nachnahme** payment on delivery; ~**en auf Pacht- und Leihbasis** lease-lend deliveries *(US)*; ~ **in Raten** delivery in instal(l)ments; ~ **auf dem See- oder Binnenwasserweg** delivery by sea or by inland waterway; ~ **auf der Straße** delivery by road; ~**en am gleichen Tage** same-day deliveries; ~**en aus Übersee** sea-borne supplies; ~ **nach Wahl des Käufers oder Verkäufers** buyer's or seller's option *(US)*; ~ **nur an Wiederverkäufer** supplied to trade only;
~ **abnehmen** to take delivery; ~ **anbieten** to tender delivery; ~ **aufrechterhalten** to maintain the deliveries; ~ **bewirken** to effect delivery; **bei** ~ **bezahlen** to pay on delivery (at the door); ~**en für die Armee durchführen** to make issues to (purvey for) the army; **für prompte** ~ **einstehen** to guarantee prompt delivery of goods; ~ **einstellen** to stop delivery (supplies), to disconnect service; ~ **entgegennehmen** to accept delivery; **für eine** ~ **den Zuschlag erhalten** to secure a contract; **in** ~**en erscheinen** *(Buch)* to be published (appear) in instal(l)ments (parts), to appear in packs; **in monatlichen** ~**en erscheinen** to be issued in monthly parts; ~ **vier Wochen nach Auftragserteilung erwarten** to require delivery within four weeks of (from) order; **für pünktliche** ~ **garantieren** to warrant punctual delivery; **alle 14 Tage eine** ~ **herausbringen** *(Buch)* to issue in fortnightly parts; **auf** ~ **kaufen** *(Börse)* to buy forward (for future delivery, *US*, for settlement); **gegen sofortige** ~ **kaufen** *(Börse)* to buy

spot (outright, *US*); **auf spätere ~ kaufen** to buy ahead; **großen Wert auf regelmäßige ~ legen** to appreciate a regular delivery; **auf ausländische ~en angewiesen sein** to depend on foreign supplies; **~ sicherstellen** to assure delivery; **~ übernehmen** to tender; **auf zukünftige ~ verkaufen** to sell for future delivery (by anticipation, *US*), *(Börse)* to sell forward (ahead, for future delivery, *US*); **~ verweigern** to refuse to supply goods, to withhold supplies from a dealer; **~ vornehmen** to execute (effect) delivery; **~ gegen Barzahlung vornehmen** to make delivery on a cash basis.

Lieferungs|anforderung requisition; **~angebot** tender, bid, proposal; **~angebot machen** to tender; **~annahme** acceptance of goods, taking delivery; **~anweisung** delivery order; **~anzeige** shipping advice, *(Börse)* delivery ticket; **~aufschub** deferred delivery; **~auftrag** purchase order; **~bedingungen** conditions of sale, delivery conditions, terms of delivery; **langfristige ~bedingungen** long-term delivery conditions; **~buch** delivery book; **~datum** delivery date, day of delivery; **~frist** term of delivery; **~garantie** performance guarantee *(Br.)* (bond, *US*); **~genehmigung** delivery licence; **~genossenschaft** wholesale cooperative society; **~geschäft** *(Börse)* time bargain (purchase), negotiation of time, [business in] futures *(US)*, *(Prämiengeschäft)* option deal *(Br.)*, trading in puts and calls *(US)*; **~kauf** *(Börse)* forward purchase *(Br.)*, purchase for future delivery *(US)*; **~käufe** *(Börse)* futures *(US)*; **~kosten** delivery expenses; **~kurs** *(Börse)* delivery (making-up) price; **~markt** *(Börse)* future market *(US)*; **~ort** place (point) of delivery; **~prämie** *(Vorprämie)* premium for the cash, *(Rückprämie)* premium for the put; **~preis** making-up (contract, contracting, contracted) price, *(Börse)* quotation for futures *(US)*; **~schein** delivery order (note); **~tag** day of delivery, *(Börse)* settling day, pay day *(Br.)*; **~termin** day (date) of delivery; **~umfang** extent (scope, *US*) of supply, supply schedule; **~unfähigkeit** inability to supply goods; **~verkäufe** *(Börse)* forward sales (selling), futures *(US)*; **~verpflichtung** duty (obligation) to deliver; **~versagen** failure to meet delivery.

Lieferungsvertrag delivery contract, supply agreement (contract), *(Börse)* forward purchase *(Br.)*, contract for [future, *US*] delivery, future contract *(US)*, *(Buch)* instal(l)ment contract;
das ganze Jahr gültiger ~ contract good for a year; **unbefristeter ~** open-end contract;
~ abschließen to tender and contract for a supply; **Erfüllung eines ~es aussetzen** to defer fulfil(l)ment of a supply contract.

Lieferungs|verzögerung delay in (delayed) delivery; **~ware** *(Börse)* futures *(US)*; **~werk** *(Buch)* instalment of a publication, serial; **~wert** value delivered.

Liefer|verbot prohibition to deliver; **~verlangen** demand of delivery; **~verpflichtung** duty (obligation) to deliver; **~vertrag** supply agreement *(Börse)* forward contract, contract for [future] delivery *(US)*, futures contract *(US)*; **~vertrag mit einer Fabrik abschließen** to contract to supply a factory; **sich um einen ~vertrag bemühen** to tender for a supply of goods; **~verweigerung** withholding supply of goods from a dealer; **abgestimmte ~verweigerung** *(Kartellwesen)* concerted refusal to deal *(US)*; **~verzögerung, ~verzug** delay (default) in delivery, supply delays, deferred (delayed) delivery, delivery lag (delay); **im ~verzug sein** to be in default (late) in delivery; **~vorschriften** delivery instructions; **~wagen** delivery (motor) van *(Br.)*, delivery lorry, pickup truck, delivery car (truck, wagon, *US*); **~wagenfahrer** vanman *(Br.)*; **~wagenunkosten** motor-van expenses *(Br.)*; **~werk** supply plant; **~wert** delivery value.

Lieferzeit period for delivery, delivery time (period);
vertraglich vereinbarte ~ time of delivery as provided in the contract;
~ einhalten to deliver within the specified time; **fünf Tage ~ haben** to be delivered in five days; **~ überschreiten** to overrun the delivery time.

Liefer|zettel delivery note (slip); **~ziffer** supply index figure; **~zunahme** increase in shipments; **achttägige ~zusage nach Auftragseingang geben** to promise delivery within one week from receiving order; **~zustand** condition of the goods; **~zwang** compulsory delivery.

Liege chaise longue, couch, divan.

Liege|bett couch; **~gebühren, ~geld** *(Schiff)* quayage, quay dues, *(Waggon)* demurrage, car service; **~geldsatz** demurrage rate; **~geldvereinbarung** demurrage contract; **~halle** *(Sanatorium)* open-air wing; **~kur** rest cure.

liegen *(Getreide)* to be flattened, *(Grundstück)* to be situated (located, *US*);
bei jem. ~ to be up to s. o. to decide; **vor Anker ~** to ride at anchor; **ganzen Tag auf der Bahn ~** to spend a whole day on the train; **unter schwerem Beschuß ~** to be under heavy fire; **brach ~** to lie fallow; **schon lange unter der Erde ~** to have died a long time ago; **im richterlichen Ermessen ~** to be left to the discretion of the court; **in der Familie ~** to run in the blood; **fest ~** *(Kurs)* to hold, to be a hard spot; **festgemacht ~** to be berthed (moored); **mit der Front nach dem Fluß ~** *(Haus)* to face the river; **in einer Stadt in Garnison ~** to keep a garrison in a town; **gedrückt ~** *(Kurse)* to be under pressure; **weiterhin stark gedrückt ~** to remain under heavy pressure; **am fehlenden Geld ~** to be due to lack of money; **im Rahmen des üblichen Geschäftsverkehrs ~** to be incidental to the normal activity of a business; **günstig ~** *(Haus)* to be favo(u)rably situated; **im Hafen ~** to lie in the harbo(u)r; **auf der Hand ~** to be obvious; **jem. am Herzen ~** to lie at s. one's heart; **im Hinterhalt ~** to lie in ambush; **hoch ~** *(Kurse)* to rule high; **12 Punkte höher ~** to gain twelve points; **an der Kette ~** to be chained up; **auf Kiel ~** to be laid down on keel; **ungenutzt auf dem Konto ~** to lie idle at the bank; **wie Kraut und Rüben durcheinander ~** to be higgledy-piggledy; **wie eine schwere Last auf der Seele ~** to weigh heavy on s. one's mind, to press heavily upon s. o.; **in der Luft ~** to be in the air; **in jds. Macht ~** to lie with s. o.; **schwer im Magen ~** *(Prüfung)* to lie heavy on one's stomach; **bei 4 Millionen ~** *(Gewinn)* to amount to about four millions; **in der Mitte ~** to be half-way in between; **im Bereich der Möglichkeit ~** to be within the realms of possibility; **jem. nicht ~** not to suit s. o.; **niedrig ~** *(Kurse)* to rule low; **jem. in den Ohren ~** to pester s. o.; **preislich richtig ~** to be priced right; **mit den Nachbarn im Prozeß ~** to be engaged in a lawsuit with the neighbo(u)rs; **auf Reede ~** to ride at (lie in) the roads, to be in dock; **in Scheidung ~** to undergo divorce proceedings; **in Schutt und Asche ~** to be reduced to ashes; **schwächer ~** *(Kurse)* to be easier; **auf der Straße ~** to be in dry dock *(fam.)*, to be off the payroll; **drei Punkte tiefer ~** to be three points off; **abseits der Straße ~** to lie away from the road; **ganz dicht an der Straße ~** to be contiguous to the street; **gut auf der Straße ~** *(Auto)* to have a favo(u)rable clearance on the road; **nach Süden ~** *(Zimmer)* to have a southern aspect, to point to the south; **auf Südwestkurs ~** to be heading southwest; **jem. auf der Tasche ~** to live at s. one's expense; **der Gemeinde auf der Tasche ~** to fall upon the parish (town, *US*); **auf den Tod krank ~** to be at death's door; **in Trümmern ~** to lie in ruins; **mit seiner Vermutung goldrichtig ~** to be dead right with one's guess; **verstreut ~** *(Haus)* to straggle; **vertäut ~** to be moored; **jem. viel daran ~** to be very important to s. o.; **auf jds. Wege ~** to be on s. one's way; **hart am Winde ~** to sail close to the wind; **ganz zentral ~** to be very central (in the downtown area) *(US)*; **in den letzten Zügen ~** to be breathing one's last, to be at the point of death; **auf der Zunge ~** to have it on the tip of one's tongue;
Menge Geld auf der Bank ~ haben to have a lot of money at the bank; **Gesetzentwurf ~ lassen** to shelve a bill *(Br.)*; **~ müssen** *(Holz)* to have to season, *(Wein)* to have to stay down;
wie die Dinge zur Zeit ~ as matters stand at present.

liegenbleiben to wait, to stand over, *(Arbeit)* to pile up, to be neglected, *(Auto)* to break down, *(Briefe)* not to be sent off, *(Waren)* to remain on stock, to be left unsold, *(Zug)* to be held up.

liegend lying, *(Motor)* horizontal;
im Sterben ~ moribund; **in Trümmern ~** in ruins; **beim Volk ~** residing in the people;
~er Anschlag *(Schießen)* prone position; **~e Handschrift** sloping handwriting.

liegengeblieben uncleared, *(Brief)* not sent off.

Liegenschaften possessions, immovables, immovable (real) estate, immovable property *(US)*, landed property, lands, properties, estates, real assets *(US)*, realty *(US)*;
freie ~ charter land; **fremde ~** *(Bilanz)* third-party land;
~ aller Art lands, tenements and hereditaments *(US)*; **~ einer Handelsgesellschaft** partnership realty *(US)*; **~ und bewegliche Sachen** land and chattels.

Liegenschafts|amt real-estate (land, *US*) office; **~anteil** undivided share in land; **~konto** real-estate (premises) account, property account; **~nachlaßverwalter** real representative; **~nießbrauch** life estate; **~nutzung** use of property; **~recht** land law, law of property *(US)*, property law *(US)*; **nicht rechtsmängelfreies ~recht** nonmerchantable title; **~rechte aller Art** lands, tenements and hereditaments *(US)*; **~übertragung** conveyance; **~vertrag** contract for sale of land, real contract *(US)*; **~verwalter** estate agent, factor *(Scot.)*; **~verzeichnis** property record.

Liege | platz berth, moorage, *(Schlafwagen)* couchette, sleeping berth; **~platzgebühr** mooring dues; **~raum** rest room; **~sitz** *(Auto)* reclining seat, *(Schlafwagen)* sleeperette; **~stuhl** deck (hammock) chair; **~tage** *(Schiff)* lay (laying) days; **~wagen** couchette coach; **~wagenplatz** *(Schlafwagen)* couchette.

Liegezeit lay days, idle period;
freie ~ free time;
~ überschritten haben to be on demurrage.

Lift lift *(Br.)*, elevator *(US)*;
~boy lift (button) boy, elevator operator *(US)*.

Liga league.

liieren, sich *(Gesellschafter)* to unite, to join, to enter into an alliance, to associate, to become a partner.

liiert, eng closely connected.

Limit limit, stop order;
ausführbares ~ feasible (practicable) limit; **ausgedehntes ~** large limit; **erreichbares ~** attainable limit; **knappes ~** narrow limit; **oberes ~** upper limit; **oberstes ~** maximum limit; **unausführbares ~** limit impracticable of execution; **unteres ~** lower limit, minimum;
~ für die Gläubigerländer *(Weltwährungsfonds)* creditor limit; **~ einhalten** to keep within a limit, to stick to the price fixed; **sein ~ einschränken** to reduce one's limit; **~ erhöhen** to extend (raise) a limit; **~ festsetzen** to set (fix, give) a limit; **über das ~ hinausgehen** to go beyond the limit; **an ein ~ gebunden sein** to be bound to a limit; **~ überschreiten** to exceed a prescribed amount, to exceed (go beyond) a limit; **~ vorschreiben** to limit, to bound;
~auftrag limit order.

limitieren to limit, to fix a limit, to bound;
Ausgaben ~ to set a limit (put a stop) to expenses.

limitiert limited;
nicht ~ unlimited.

limitierter | Auftrag limited order; **~ Kurs** limited price.

Limitierung limitation.

Limit | preis limit, limited price, price ceiling; **~setzung** stop order.

Limousine limousine, saloon car *(Br.)*, coach *(US)*, sedan *(US)*;
zweitürige ~ two-door sedan *(US)*, coupé;
~ der Luxusklasse luxury-class saloon *(Br.)*; **~ ohne feste Mittelstreben** hardtop; **~ mit Trennwand zum Chauffeur** town car.

linder Regen gentle rain.

lindern to alleviate, to assuage, to palliate, to relieve, to ease, to mitigate;
jds. Ärger ~ to sooth s. o. one's anger; **Flüchtlingsnot ~** to provide relief for the refugees, to relieve the distress among the refugees; **Härten ~** to relieve hardships; **allgemeine Not ~** to relieve the common distress; **Schmerzen ~** to alleviate (ease) pain.

linderndes Mittel palliative, soothing remedy.

Linderung alleviation, palliation, relief, mitigation;
~ der Armut relief of poverty.

Lineal rule, ruler;
~ anlegen to draw a line with a ruler;
so gehen, als ob man ein ~ verschluckt hätte to walk as straight as a ramrod (stiff as a poker).

linear linear, lineal, allround, across the board;
~e Abschreibung straight-line depreciation *(US)*; **~e Abschreibungsmethode** straight-line method of depreciation *(US)*; **~er Abschreibungssatz** straight-line rate *(US)*; **~e Funktion** straight-line function; **~e Lohnerhöhung** across-the-board wage increase; **~e Planungsrechnung,** *(Datenverarbeitung)* linear programming; **~e Steuererhöhung** linear increase of taxation; **~e Steuersenkung** allround tax reduction.

Linearplanung linear programming.

Linie line, *(Abstammung)* line [of descent), descent, rank, *(Bus)* route, line, *(drucktechn.)* composing line, rule, *(Eisenbahn)* [railway, railroad, *US*] line, branch, trace, leg, *(Straßenbahn)* number, *(Tendenz)* trend, tendency, course, slant, policy;
auf breiter ~ across the board, allround, along a wide front; **auf der ganzen ~** all along the line, down the line; **in erster ~** first of all, primarily, in the first instance; **in gerader ~** direct, as the crow flies; **in der großen ~** on the whole; **in der männlichen ~** in the male line;
absteigende (aufsteigende) ~ descending (ascending) line; **stark befahrene ~** heavily travelled line; **direkte ~** direct line; **durchgehende ~** through line; **durchgezogene ~** unbroken line; **ins Stadtzentrum fahrende ~** down line *(US)*; **schwankende feindliche ~en** wavering lines of the enemy; **halbfette ~** medium rule; **aus freier Hand gezogene ~** freehand line; **harte ~** *(pol.)* hard line; **kreditpolitische ~** credit policy; **mütterliche ~** *(Erbrecht)* maternal line; **die neue ~** *(Mode)* the new look; **offene ~** *(Kredit)* unused portion; **feststehende politische ~** firm policy; **punktierte (gestrichelte) ~** dotted (broken) line; **restriktive ~** restrictive policy; **senkrechte ~** vertical [line]; **ununterbrochene ~** unbroken line; **vorderste ~** *(mil.)* line of battle; **vorgedruckte ~** blank line; **weibliche ~** *(Erbrecht)* female line;
klare ~ in einer Rede clear train of thought in a speech; **~ mit hoher Verkehrsdichte** high-density route; **~ mit Vorzugstarif** differential line; **~ einer Zeitung** editorial policy;
von jem. in direkter ~ abstammen to descend from s. o. in direct line; **auf die schlanke ~ achten** to watch one's waistline; **große ~ eines Werkes aufzeigen** to lay down the broad lines of a work; **~ über den Nordpol befliegen** to fly by the route over the North Pole; **sich in ansteigender ~ bewegen** to take an upward trend; **feindliche ~ durchbrechen** to break through the enemy's lines; **bestimmte ~ einhalten** to pursue a line of conduct; **~ der Partei einhalten** to toe the party line; **mittlere ~ einschlagen** to follow a middle course; **in die restriktive ~ einschwenken** to conform to the restrictive trend; **gleiche Abstände auf einer ~ eintragen** to mark equal distances along a line; **~ festlegen** to peg out a line; **~ halten** *(drucktechn.)* to align; **immer an der vordersten ~ kämpfen** to be always to the fore in a fight; **durch eine punktierte ~ kennzeichnen** to mark by a dotted line; **erst in zweiter ~ in Betracht kommen** to be of secondary consideration; **in der ~ der allgemeinen Wirtschaftspolitik liegen** to be in conformity with the general economic policy; **auf der ganzen ~ erfolgreich sein** to be successful all along the line, to carry all the world before one; **~ außer Betrieb setzen** *(Eisenbahn)* to close a line; **in gerade ~ stehen** *(Häuser)* to be in a straight line; **in vorderster ~ stehen** to be in the front line; **die ~ überschreiten** *(Äquator)* to cross the line; **~ verfolgen** *(pol.)* to follow a line.

Linien | abschluß *(Werbung)* package [insert], packaging; **kostensparender ~abschluß** *(Fluggesellschaft)* cost-saving package; **~bus** regular (scheduled, *US*) bus; **~diagramm** curve (line) chart; **regulärer ~dienst** commercial (regular) service, scheduled service *(US)*; **~dienst von besonderer volkswirtschaftlicher Bedeutung** essential trade routes *(US)*; **~einrahmung** *(Zeitung)* box; **~fahrt** liner transport; **~fahrtsbestimmungen** liner terms.

Linienflug scheduled *(US)* (commercial, one-line) flight;
~dienst regular service, scheduled service *(US)*; **~dienst unterhalten** to give regular service to; **~frachtschiff** cargo liner; **~frachtschiff für Sammelladungen** general cargo liner; **~frachtschiffsverkehr** cargo liner shipping; **~geschäft** *(Flugwesen)* regular service, scheduled business *(US)*; **~gesellschaft** national flag (commercial) airline, scheduled carrier *(US)*, sked *(US sl.)*; **~raten** liner rates; **~zeug** commercial (scheduled, *US*) airliner, liner; **wechselseitige Benutzung von Charter- und ~zeugen im Transatlantikverkehr ermöglichen** to split manifests on transatlantic flights.

Linien | kasten *(drucktechn.)* rule case; **~kräfte** line, staff members; **~maschine** scheduled *(US)* (commercial) airliner; **~netz** *(Omnibusse)* route network; **~organisation** scalar organization; **~papier** ruled (cartridge) paper; **~passagier** regular (scheduled, *US*) passenger; **vollen Flugpreis zahlender ~passagier** full-fare paying scheduled passenger *(US)*; **nicht gebuchte ~plätze für Teilcharter benutzen** to use spare capacity on scheduled flights *(US)*; **~schaubild** line chart; **~schiff** liner, ship of the line, *(mil.)* line-of-battle-ship, battleship; **~schiffahrt** liner voyage, regular (line) navigation; **~schiffstonnage** liner tonnage; **~sortiment** font.

linientreu *(pol.)* true to (toeing) the party line.

Linien | umrandung line border, ruled frame; **~verkehr** *(Bahn)* regular (stage) service, *(Flugzeug)* regular air service, scheduled airline service *(US)*, *(Frachtgeschäft)* line-haul movement, *(Omnibusse)* intercity traffic, *(Schiffe)* liner traffic; **~verkehrskartell** liner conference; **~zug** trace.

linieren to line, to rule.

liniertes Papier ruled paper.

Linierung ruling, *(schwach)* feint (faint) lines.

Linke, äußerste extreme left; **EG-feindliche ~** anti-market left; **gemäßigte ~** moderate left; **oppositionelle ~** opposition left; **zur äußersten ~n gehören** to belong to the extreme left.

link | er Arm left arm; **mit dem ~en Bein zuerst aufgestanden sein** to have got out of the wrong side of the bed; **~e Ecke** *(Buch)* left-hand corner; **~e Fahrbahn** left-hand lane; **unter dem Druck des ~en Flügels** under left-wing pressure; **revoltierender ~er Flügel** left-wing revolt; **Einfluß des ~en Flügels zurückdrängen**

to break the left-wing grip; **zwei ~e Hände haben** to have one's fingers all thumbs, to be more thumbs than talent; **~e Straßenseite** left-hand side of a street.

Linker left winger.

linkisch clumsy, awkward, gawky, ungainly;
sich ~ benehmen to behave awkwardly; **~ mit Kunden umgehen** to be ill at ease with customers.

links on the left, *(pol.)* left;
~ oben top left-hand corner, top left position; **~ unten** bottom left;
sich politisch ~ von der Mitte eingruppieren to place one's viewpoint left of center *(US)* (centre, *Br.*); **~ fahren** to keep to the left; **j. ~ liegen lassen** to turn one's back on s. o., to cold-shoulder s. o., to give s. o. the go-by; **sich heftig nach ~ orientieren** to swing violently to the left; **~ stehen** *(pol.)* to be a leftist; **sehr weit ~ stehen** to be very far to the left; **~ überholen** to overtake on the left.

Linksabbiegen left turn;
~ verboten no left turn.

Links|abbieger vehicle turning left; **~abbiegersignal** left-turn signal; **~abweichler** deviationist to the left; **~biegung** wind to the left.

linksbündig flush left.

Linksdrall *(pol.)* left-hand twist;
~ bei Meinungsumfragen leftward shift in opinion polls;
~ haben *(Auto)* to pull to the left.

links- oder rechtsextrem left-or right-wing extremist.

Links|extremismus left-wing extremism; **~fahrgebot** law of the road *(Br.)*.

links|gängige Schraube left-handed screw; **~gerichtet** leftist.

Links|gruppe left wing; **~händer** left-handed person; **~kartell** left-wing cartel; **~koalition** left-wing coalition; **~kurs** leftist policy.

linkslastige militante Kräfte left-wing militants.

Links|majorität, ~mehrheit left-wing majority; **~majorität herbeiführen** to install a left-wing majority; **~opposition** left-wing opposition.

linksorientiert left-wing, leftist.

Links|orientierung leftism; **~partei** left-wing party; **~politiker** left winger, leftist; **~presse** leftist party.

linksradikal of the extreme left, extreme left-wing.

Links|radikaler left-wing radical, last-ditcher, red, lefty *(sl.)*; **~regierung** left-wing government; **~ruck** swing to the left; **~schwenkung** left turn; **~sozialist** left-wing socialist.

linksstehende Organisation left-wing organization.

Links|steuerung left-hand steering (drive); **~stimmen** left-wing votes; **~unterzeichneter** signatory on the left; **~verkehr** left-hand traffic.

Linoleumdruck lino printing.

Linolschnitt lino cut.

Linotype *(Setzmaschine)* linotype;
mit ~ setzen to linotype, to keyboard;
~satz linotype composition; **~setzer** linotype operator.

Linse lens.

Linsengericht mess of pottage.

Lippe, jem. die Worte von den ~n ablesen to lip-read s. one's words; **an jds. ~n hängen** to hang on s. one's lips; **eine ~ riskieren** to speak one's mind, to give s. o. a lip *(sl.)*; **verächtlich die ~n schürzen** to purse (pout) one's lips in disdain;
kein Wort soll über meine ~n kommen not a word shall pass my lips; **riskier hier nicht so eine ~** none of your lip.

Lippenbekenntnis lip service;
nur ein ~ ablegen to give only lip service.

Lippenstift lipstick.

Liquidation liquidation, dissolution, winding up, realization, *(Anwaltshonorar)* bill of costs *(Br.)*, fee, charge, *(Arzthonorar)* doctor's bill, *(Termingeschäft)* settlement, settling;
abermalige ~ reliquidation; **freiwillige ~** voluntary winding-up (liquidation); **gerichtliche ~** liquidation (winding-up) subject to the supervision of the court; **laufende ~** current realization; **offizielle ~** formal liquidation; **stille ~** de facto dissolution;
~ unter Aufsicht des Gerichts liquidation (winding-up) subject to the supervision of the court; **~ einer Bank** suspension of a bank's charter; **~ an der Londoner Börse** stock-exchange settlement *(Br.)*; **~ der Geschäfte des Gemeinschuldners** winding up the debtor's business; **~ einer Gesellschaft** dissolution of a company (corporation), winding-up of a company; **freiwillige ~ zugunsten der Gläubiger** creditor's voluntary winding up;
~ einer Gesellschaft gerichtlich beantragen to file a petition for the winding-up of a company; **~ einer Handelsgesellschaft durchführen** to wind up a company; **~ erleichtern** to ease liquidation problems; **in ~ gehen (treten)** to wind up, to liquidate, to go (enter) into liquidation; **~ überwachen** to supervise the winding-up; **in ~ zeichnen** to sign in liquidation.

Liquidations|abrechnung account of the winding-up; **~anordnung** dissolution order; **~anteil** [liquidating] dividend; **~anteilschein** liquidation certificate; **~antrag** petition (application) for winding-up, petition in liquidation, winding-up petition; **~aufwand** liquidation expense; **~ausverkauf** clearance sale; **~bedingungen** *(Börse)* settlement terms; **~beginn** commencement of a liquidation, commencement of the winding-up; **~bericht vorlegen** to make up an account of the winding-up.

Liquidationsbeschluß winding-up resolution;
gerichtlicher ~ winding-up (dissolution) order;
~ der Hauptversammlung resolution to wind up voluntarily;
~ erlassen to make an order for the winding-up.

Liquidations|bestimmungen winding-up rules (provisions); **~bilanz** balance at liquidation, liquidating balance sheet, statement of realization and liquidation *(Br.)* (assets and liabilities), statutory statement of affairs *(Br.)*; **~bilanz aufstellen** to submit a statement of one's affairs; **~büro** *(Börse)* clearinghouse; **~datum** *(Börse)* settling day, day of settlement; **~erklärung bei Gesellschaftsauflösung** declaration of solvency; **~erlös** proceeds of a liquidation, winding-up proceeds (profit); **~firma, ~gesellschaft** winding-up corporation, company in liquidation; **~forderungen** claims in winding up; **~gewinn** winding-up profit; **~grund** ground for winding up; **~guthaben** clearing balance; **~kasse** *(Börse)* clearinghouse; **~konto** liquidation account, realization and liquidation account, *(Börse)* settlement account; **~kosten** costs of liquidation, winding-up costs, liquidation expense; **~kurs** *(Börse)* settling rate, making-up price *(Br.)*; **~masse** liquidating trust; **~plan** liquidation plan, scheme of arrangement; **~preis** realization price (figure), *(Börse)* settling (making-up, *Br.*) price; **~protokoll** winding-up minutes; **~quote** [liquidating] dividend; **~richtlinien** winding-up rules *(Br.)*; **~saldo** balance at liquidation.

Liquidations|tag, ~termin *(Börse)* ticket day, day of settlement, account *(Br.)*, pay day *(Br.)*;
zum nächsten ~ for the account *(Br.)*;
zweiter ~ making-up day *(Br.)*.

Liquidations|unterlagen winding-up records; **~verfahren** proceedings for winding up, liquidation (winding-up) proceedings; **~verfahren beantragen** to petition for the winding up; **~vergleich** winding up by arrangement, assignment for the benefit of creditors, arrangement with creditors in a voluntary liquidation, scheme of arrangement *(Br.)*; **gerichtlicher ~vergleich** settlement in court; **~verkauf** clearance (liquidation) sale; **~verlust** liquidation damages; **geschätzter ~verlust** estimated deficiency from realization of assets; **~vorrecht** preference in liquidation proceedings; **~vorschlag** liquidation plan.

Liquidationswert liquidating (breakup) value, *(Börse)* realization value, *(Investmentfonds)* net asset value;
~ einer Gesellschaft surplus assets.

Liquidator liquidator, liquidating agent, special manager *(Br.)*, *(Gesellschafter)* liquidating partner;
von der Bank bestellter ~ receiver appointed by the bank; **freiwillig bestellter ~** liquidator for the purpose of winding up; **gerichtlich bestellter ~** liquidator appointed by the court, official liquidator *(Br.)*, official receiver *(Br.)*; **vorläufig bestellter ~** provisional liquidator;
~ einsetzen to appoint a liquidator.

liquide liquid, cash-rich, ready, *(zahlungsfähig)* financial, solvent, fluid *(US)*;
äußerst ~ cash-heavy; **nicht ~** illiquid, not liquid, insolvent;
Ersparnisse ~ angelegt haben to hold savings in liquid form;
äußerst ~ sein to have cash galore;
~ Anlagewerte liquid assets; **~ Bestände** liquid holdings; **~ Firma** solvent merchant; **~ Form** liquid form; **~ Mittel** liquid capital (assets), liquid (available) funds; **~ Mittel erster Ordnung** primary liquidity; **~ Mittel zweiter Ordnung** secondary liquidity; **~ Mittel dritter Ordnung** tertiary liquidity; **im Jahresabschluß ~ Mittel von 32 Mio Pfund aufweisen** to finish the year with liquid funds of £ 32 m; **~ Mittel haben** to be liquid; **~r Nachlaß** solvent estate; **~ Reserven** *(Bank)* liquid reserves; **~ Reserven der Wirtschaft** liquid investments.

liquidierbar, innerhalb eines Jahres *(Bilanz)* payable (due) within a year.

liquidieren to liquidate, to dissolve, to wind up, *(Honorar)* to charge, to fee, *(realisieren)* to sell off, to realize, *(Termingeschäft)* to settle, *(umbringen)* to liquidate, to do in *(sl.)*; **für ärztliche Bemühungen** ~ to charge for medical care; **freiwillig** ~ to wind up voluntarily; **Gegner** ~ to liquidate opponents; **[Handels]gesellschaft** ~ to liquidate a company, to dissolve a business partnership, to wind up the affairs of a partnership (a business company); **Konkursmasse (Konkurssache)** ~ to liquidate the assets of a bankrupt (a bankrupt's affairs); **Rechnungen** ~ to settle accounts; **wieder** ~ to reliquidate; **zwangsweise** ~ to wind up compulsorily.

liquidiert wound up;
nur noch ~ werden können to end up in the hands of liquidators.

Liquidierung liquidation, dissolution, winding up, *(Honorar)* bill of costs, *(Termingeschäft)* settlement, *(Verflüssigung)* realization.

Liquidierungskosten expenses of liquidation, liquidation expense.

Liquidität liquidity, liquid position, *(Zahlungsfähigkeit)* solvency;
eingeengte ~ reduced liquidity, liquidity shortage; **internationale** ~ world liquidity; **kurzfristige** ~ short-term cash position; **mangelnde** ~ liquidity shortage, illiquidity; **uneingeschränkte** ~ *(Sonderziehungsrechte)* unconditional liquidity; **nicht vorhandene** ~ nonliquidity; **zunehmende** ~ increasing liquidity;
~ **einer Aktiengesellschaft** corporate liquidity; ~ **einer Bank** bank liquidity, liquidity of a bank, current position; ~ **der Banken (des Bankensystems)** banks' liquidity, easy money market; ~ **ersten Grades** acid test, liquid ratio; ~ **zweiten Grades** current (working-capital) ratio; ~ **eines Unternehmens** corporate liquidity;
~ **anreichern** to increase liquidity, to increase one's holdings of cash; **ausreichende ~ sicherstellen** to maintain a liquid position, to build up (maintain) liquidity; **für wirtschaftliche ~ sorgen** to put the economy on a richer monetary diet; **für ~ Sorge tragen** to build liquidity; **ausreichende ~ unterhalten** to maintain a liquid position; ~ **verbessern** to rebuild liquidity; ~ **des inländischen Bankenapparates verknappen** to cut domestic banking liquidity.

Liquiditäts|abfluß efflux of liquidity, outflow of cash; **~abnahme** decrease in liquidity; **~abschöpfung** absorption of liquidity; **~abschöpfung vornehmen** to absorb liquidity; **~absprache** liquidity arrangement; **~angebot** supply of cash; **kurzfristige ~anhäufung** *(Bankausweis)* window dressing; **~anreicherung** increasing liquidity, increase in liquidity; **~anspannung** pressure on (strain of) liquidity, monetary strain, tightness of money, tightening of the money market; **~anstieg** build-up of liquidity; **~aspekt** liquidity aspect; **~ausgleich** liquidity equalization; **~ausstattung** allocation of funds; **~ausweitung** expansion (extension) of liquidity, newly created liquidity; **~auswirkung** impact on liquidity, liquidity-creating effect; **katastrophale ~auswirkungen** disastrous effects on liquidity; **~auswirkungen abschwächen** to contain one's liquidity problems; **~bedürfnis** need for liquidity; **verstärkte ~bedürfnisse haben** to require greater liquidity.

liquiditätsbeengt short of liquid assets (funds).

Liquiditäts|beengung lack of liquidity, liquidity pinch (bind), reduced liquidity, shortage of liquid assets, *(Bank)* cash (money) squeeze; **~begrenzung** clamping down on liquidity.

liquiditätsbelastende Faktoren liquidity-reducing factors.

Liquiditäts|belastung drain on liquidity; **~beschaffung** procurement of liquidity; **~beschaffung durch Schatzwechselverkauf** front-door operation *(Br.)*; **~besserung** improvement of liquidity; **~bestimmungen** solvency rules; **~bestimmungen verschärfen** to clamp down on liquidity; **~bilanz** liquidity balance, liquid position; **~bindung** immobilization of liquid funds; **für eine ausreichende ~decke sorgen** to establish enough liquidity; **~defizit** liquidity (liquid) deficit; **~dispositionen** liquidity arrangements; **~druck** pressure (impact) on liquidity, liquidity squeeze (pressure), *(Bank)* cash squeeze; **~effekt** liquidity-creating effect; **~enge** shortage of cash, liquidity shortage; **~entzug** absorption (withdrawal) of liquidity; **~erfordernisse** liquidity requirements; **übliche ~erfordernisse** commercial standards of solvency; **~erhaltung** maintenance of liquidity; **~erwägungen** considerations of liquidity; **~falle** liquidity trap; **~fonds** pool of liquidity; **~freisetzung** release of liquid funds; **~fülle** ample liquidity; **~gefälle** liquidity differential; **um das ~gerede zu beenden** to squelch talk of a liquidity pinch; **~grad** degree (level) of liquidity, working capital (liquidity) ratio, *(Bank)* current position, cash ratio, acid-test (quick-assets, *US*) ratio; **hoher ~grad** liquid strength; **größeren ~grad als notwendig erzielen** to build up a higher liquidity ratio than the minimum; **~grundlage** liquidity basis; **~grundsätze** liquidity rules; **~guthaben** *(Bank)* liquid assets (resources); **~hemmung** clamping down (drain) on liquidity; **~hilfe** liquidity assistance; **~kennzahl, ~kennziffer** current position ratio, acid-test ratio; **~klemme** lack of liquidity, liquidity squeeze, liquidity pinch; **~knappheit** shortage of liquidity, liquidity shortage; **~koeffizient** working capital (liquidity) ratio; **~kontrolle** liquidity control; **~kredit** liquid loan; **~krise** liquidity crisis; **~lage** liquid (cash) position, *(Bank)* current position; **~mangel** shortage of liquidity; **~manipulation** *(Bilanz)* window dressing; **~marge** *(Versicherungsgesellschaft)* margin of solvency, solvency margin.

liquiditätsmäßig sichtbar werden to be based on liquidity.

Liquiditäts|maßnahmen liquidity measures, easy-money policy; **~menge** solvency margin.

liquiditätsmindernd liquidity-reducing.

Liquiditäts|mittel, sorgsam mit ~mitteln umgehen to husband meagre cash supplies; **~mulde** liquidity trough; **~neigung** liquidity preference; **~niveau** liquidity level; **allgemeines ~ und Kapitalintensitätsniveau** general level of liquidity and gearing; **~politik** policy of active ease, cheap-money policy; **angespannte ~politik betreiben** to strain liquidity.

liquiditätspolitisch|neutral sein to have no effect on liquidity; **~e Maßnahmen** policy of active ease; **~e Maßnahmen treffen** to build liquidity; **~e Möglichkeiten darstellen** to be a source of liquidity.

Liquiditäts|position liquid position; **angeschlagene ~position** illiquid position; **starke ~position** high degree of liquidity; **~priorität** order of liquidity; **~problem** liquidity (cash) problem, problem of liquidity; **~prüfung** acid (liquidity) test; **~quote** *(Banken)* cash ratio; **~reserven** monetary (liquid, liquidity) reserves, reserves of liquidity; **vorgeschriebene freie ~reserven** prescribed margins of free liquidity; **~richtlinien** liquidity rules; **~risiko** risk of liquidity; **~rückgang** decrease in liquidity, reduced liquidity; **sich auf internationalen Märkten eines ausgezeichneten ~rufes erfreuen** to establish itself firmly on the international liquidity map; **~schlacht** liquidity battle; **~schöpfung** creation of liquidity; **~schrumpfung** contraction of liquidity; **~schwierigkeiten** liquidity difficulties; **~schwierigkeiten wegen zu hoher Lagerhaltung** overtrading; **~sorgen** liquidity worries; **~spanne** liquidity (solvency) margin; **~spielraum** liquidity (solvency) margin, reserve ratio *(US)*; **~status** liquid (liquidity, current) position; **hohen ~status aufrecht erhalten** to offer a high solvency margin; **~steigerung** increased liquidity; **~steuerer** liquidity manager; **~steuerung** liquidity management; **~streben** liquidity preference; **~stützen** liquidity assistance; **~theorie** *(Keynes)* liquidity preference theory; **~überfluß** liquid surplus; **~überhang** monetary reserve, surplus (excess) liquidity; **~überhang abbauen** to reduce liquidity; **~überlegungen** considerations of liquidity; **~umschichtung** change in liquidity; **~umschwung** reversal in the money market; **~verbesserung** increase in (rebuilding of) liquidity, improvement in liquidity, liquidity improvement; **~verbesserungen für den Bankenapparat** easing of the monetary policy; **~verbesserung erzielen** to rebuild liquidity; **~verhältnis** liquidity (acid-test, quick, current) ratio; **beengte ~verhältnisse** tight money conditions; **weltbedingte ~verhältnisse** interlocking liquidity in world markets; **~verkauf** final liquidation sale; **~verknappung** reduction in liquidity, liquidity shortage; **~verlagerung** shift in liquidity; **~verlust** loss of liquidity.

liquiditätsvermindernd liquidity-reducing.

Liquiditäts|versorgung, reichliche ample supply of liquid funds; **~verstärkung** strengthening of the liquid position; **~volumen** volume of liquidity; **~vorliebe** liquidity preference; **~vorschau** cashflow budget; **~vorschriften** liquidity requirements; **~vorsorge** maintenance of liquidity.

liquiditätswirksam liquidity-creating.

Liquiditäts|wirkung liquidity-creating effect; **~zufluß** inflow (influx) of liquidity; **~zunahme** expansion of liquidity, increasing liquidity; **~zustrom** liquidity afflux.

List cunning, craft, guile, wiliness, artfulness, slyness, *(mil.)* stratagem;
durch ~ by craft; **mit ~ und Tücke** by cunning and deceit; **etw. durch ~ erreichen** to get s. th. by guile, to wangle s. th.; **jds. ~en zum Opfer fallen** to fall a victim to the wiles of s. o.; **zur ~ seine Zuflucht nehmen** to resort to tricks; **voller ~en stecken** to be full of craft; **sein Ziel durch eine ~ zu erreichen suchen** to resort to tricks to gain one's end.

Liste list, calendar, scheme, bill, account, *(Anwälte)* roll, *(detaillierte Aufstellung)* specification, *(Geschworene)* panel, *(Inventarverzeichnis)* inventory, *(Kandidatenliste)* ticket, slate *(US)*, *(Kassenärzte)* panel, *(Katalog)* catalog(ue), *(Mitglieder)* roll, list, roster, *(Register)* register, record, *(Steuer)* roll, *(Tabelle)* schedule, *(Terminliste)* agenda, docket;
am Anfang der ~ early in the list; **am Ende der** ~ at the foot of the list; **auf der** ~ on the list;
alphabetische ~ alphabetical list; **amtliche** ~ register, indenture, file; **schwarze** ~ black (stop, unfair, *US*) list;
~ **der Abgangsdaten** *(Schiffe)* sailing list, shipping card; ~ **der stimmberechtigten Aktionäre** voting list of shareholders *(Br.)* (stockholders, *US*); ~ **der zur engeren Wahl Anstehenden** short list; ~ **angemeldeter Anträge** *(Parlament)* order book *(Br.)*; ~ **der Bediensteten** checkroll; ~ **der Bewerber** list of applicants; ~ **der Bezieher** list of subscribers; ~ **empfohlener Börsenwerte** stockbroker's list of recommendations; ~ **der börsengängigen Effekten** official list; ~ **gefundener Gegenstände** found-property report; ~ **vorrangig angesetzter Gerichtstermine** preferred dockets; ~ **der Gewinner** list of awards; ~ **der Handelssachen** commercial list; ~ **der Kassenärzte** panel *(Br.)*; ~ **fauler Kunden** black book; ~ **der kreditfähigen Kunden** credit list; ~ **potentieller Kunden** sucker list *(sl.)*; ~ **der Passagiere** passenger list; ~ **der offenen Posten** statement of open items; ~ **übernommener Risiken** *(Versicherung)* risks book; ~ **der Ruhestandsbeamten** retired list; ~ **zu behandelnder Sachen** *(Gericht)* agenda, docket *(US)*; ~ **der Schulabgänger** passing-out list; ~ **der Schuldverschreibungsinhaber** register of debentures *(Br.)*; ~ **von Sonderterminen** *(Gericht)* special paper *(Br.)*; ~ **der säumigen Steuerzahler** *(Grundsteuer)* tax list; ~ **der anstehenden Strafsachen** crown paper *(Br.)*; ~ **geführter Telefongespräche** *(Hotel)* traffic sheet; ~ **der anstehenden Termine** special calendar; ~ **der Untersuchungsgefangenen** calendar of prisoners *(Br.)*; ~ **anstehender Veranstaltungen** calendar of special events; ~ **der Verbindlichkeiten** schedule of liabilities; ~, **auf die man sich verlassen kann** reliable list; ~ **eingegangener Verpflichtungen** *(Makler)* position book-keeping ~ **der Wahlberechtigten** list of voters, electoral register, poll [book]; ~ **zollfreier Waren** free list; ~ **der Wechselkurse** list of exchange; ~ **bevorzugter Werte** purchase preference list; ~ **der zum Börsenhandel zugelassenen Werte** official (the) list; ~ **börsengängiger Wertpapiere** the list; ~ **der schlechten Zahler** black book; ~ **der Zeichnungsberechtigten** signatory list, list of authorized signatures;
Namen auf einer ~ **abstreichen** to strike off names from a list; ~ **anführen** to top (head, be at the head of, stand first on) a list; ~ **anlegen** to draw up a list; **in eine** ~ **aufnehmen** to add to (include in) a list; ~ **aufstellen** to make up (compile, draw up) a list; ~ **durchsehen** to look down a list; **in eine** ~ **eintragen** to enrol(l) (enter) in a list, to catalog(ue), to impanel, to empanel, to list, to bill, to register, to put on the roll, to schedule, to post; **sich auf einer** ~ **(Namen in eine** ~**) eintragen** to give in one's name, to enter one's name on a list, to register on a list *(US)*; **j. als wohltätigen Spender für 1 Pfund in eine** ~ **eintragen** to put s. one's name down for £ 1; ~ **eröffnen** to head (top) a list; ~ **führen** to keep a list; **auf die schwarze** ~ **kommen** to be blacklisted (in the black book); ~ **schließen** to close the books; **Kandidaten auf die** ~ **setzen** to propose (slate, *US*) candidates; **auf die schwarze** ~ **setzen** to blacklist s. o., to pipe s. o. off *(sl.)*; **auf einer** ~ **stehen** to figure (appear) on a list, to be on a list (the panel); **ganz am Ende der** ~ **stehen** to come bottom of a list; **ganz oben auf der** ~ **stehen** to be right up there; **auf der schwarzen** ~ **stehen** to be in the black book (blacklisted); **an der Spitze einer** ~ **stehen** to head a list; **weit oben in einer** ~ **stehen** to be well up in a list; **weit unten auf einer** ~ **stehen** to come low in a list; **von einer** ~ **streichen** to withdraw from a list, to take s. one's name off the books; **Anwalt von der** ~ **streichen** to disbar a lawyer, to strike a lawyer off the rolls; **von der** ~ **der Mitglieder streichen** to strike off the rolls *(Br.)*; **Namen von einer** ~ **streichen** to strike a name off a list; ~ **wählen** to vote a ticket; ~ **der vorgeschlagenen Kandidaten wählen** to vote the straight ticket *(US)*; ~ **zusammenstellen** to build up a list, to schedule.

Listen|aufstellung making out of (making-up) a list; ~**auswahl** list sample; ~**führer** *(bei Wahl)* leading candidate; ~**grundpreis** catalog(ue) price.

listenmäßig erfassen to list, to register.

Listenpreis catalog(ue) (scheduled, posted, list[ing]) price, *(Werbung)* scale rate;
diskriminierender ~ rate discrimination; **empfohlener** ~ suggested list price; **festgesetzter** ~ posted price;
~**e des Herstellers einhalten** not to sell below the manufacturer's list prices; **sich beim Verkauf streng an** ~**e halten** to sell closer to list prices; **empfohlene** ~**e unterbieten** to cut prices; **unter dem** ~ **verkaufen** to sell under list price.

listenreicher Politiker crafty politician.

Listen|schluß closing of subscription; ~**system** *(Kassenärzte)* panel system, *(Politik)* party list system; **regionales** ~**system** regional list system; ~**verarbeitung** list processing; ~**wahl** list system; **von der** ~ **zur Direktwahl** from proportional representation towards single-member constituencies.

listig tricky, cunning, wily, sly;
~ **zu Werke gehen** to do s. th. on the sly; **äußerst** ~ **sein** to be a wily old bird;
~**e Bemerkungen** wily remarks; ~**er Fuchs** cunning old fox, sly dog.

Litanei, lange long song;
~ **von Beschwerden** rehearsal of grievances;
immer die gleiche ~ always the same old song;
~ **herunterleiern** to reel (drone) off a litany of grievances; **immer die gleiche** ~ **hervorbringen** to harp on the same string.

Liter litre, liter;
halber ~ pint.

literarisch literary;
~ **gebildet** lettered, literate;
sich ~ **betätigen** to take to literature;
~**er Diebstahl** plagiarism; ~**es Eigentum** literary property; ~**e Gesellschaft** literary society; ~**e Größe** literary star; ~**e Hilfsmittel** literary tools; ~**e Kontroverse** literary controversy; ~**e Kostbarkeiten** literary gems; ~**en Stil verfälschen** to vitiate the style of writing; ~**e Tagelöhner** hodmen of literature; ~**e Tätigkeit** literary activity (work); ~**e Welt** republic of letters, commonwealth of letters; ~**er Zirkel** literary group (coterie).

Literat writer, man of letters, essayist, literary man, literate;
~**en** literary people.

Literatur literature, polite learning;
benutzte ~ books consulted, books of reference; **einschlägige** ~ pertinent literature; **juristische** ~ legal literature; **unterhaltende** ~ light (escape) literature; **leicht verständliche** ~ milk for babes; **verwendete** ~ books consulted; **weltliche** ~ profane literature; **wissenschaftliche** ~ scientific writing;
~**angaben** biographical data (reference); ~**beilage** literary supplement; ~**blatt** literary review; ~**gattung** class of literature; ~**geschichte** literary history, history of literature; ~**hinweise** recommended books; ~**kritik** literary criticism; ~**kritiker** literary critic; **schöpferische** ~**periode** fecund era in literature; ~**verzeichnis** bibliography; **vergleichende** ~**wissenschaft** comparative literature; ~**zeitschrift** literary (little, *US*) magazine.

Litfaßsäule advertising (poster) pillar, hoarding, billboard *(US)*.

Lithographie lithography, print, litho.

lithographieren to lithograph.

lithographische Anstalt lithographic establishment.

Litze *(el.)* flex, cord, *(Uniform)* lace.

Litzendraht twisted (stranded) wire.

Livesendung live, camera reporting.

Livree livery.

livriert in livery;
~**er Diener** servant in livery, flunkey *(coll.)*.

Lizenz licence, license *(US)*, permit, royalty, franchise *(US)*;
ohne ~ unlicensed;
ausschließliche ~ exclusive licence; **einfache** ~ nonexclusive licence; **gebührenfreie** ~ royalty-free licence; **gebührenpflichtige** ~ licence for value; **stillschweigend gewährte** ~ implied licence; **pauschale** ~ block licence; **unbeschränkte** ~ unrestricted licence; **unentgeltliche** ~ royalty-free licence;
~ **für Alkoholverkauf** liquor licence, *(außerhalb des Ladens)* off license; ~**en auf technischem Anwendungsgebiet** defined field licenses; ~ **zum Betrieb eines Druckereibetriebes** printer's licence;
~ **beantragen** to apply for a licence; ~ **besitzen** to hold a licence; ~ **entziehen** to revoke (withdraw) a licence; ~ **als Arzt entziehen** to strike off the Medical Register; ~ **erneuern** to renew a licence; **sich eine** ~ **erschleichen** to obtain a licence by false pretences; ~ **erteilen** to [issue (grant) a] licence, *(Gewerbe)* to accord permission to transact business; **urheberrechtliche** ~ **erteilen** to grant a licence in respect of a copyright; ~ **erwerben, sich eine** ~ **geben lassen** to take out a licence; **in** ~ **herstellen** to manufacture under licence; ~ **zeitweilig außer Kraft setzen** to suspend a licence *(US)*; ~ **vergeben** to grant a licence (concession); ~ **an eine Firma vergeben** to license a firm; **seine** ~ **verlieren** to forfeit one's licence; ~ **verwerten** to exploit a

licence; **nach vom Verteidigungsministerium vergebenen ~en gebaut werden** to be build under licence from the ministry of defence; ~ **zurücknehmen** to cancel (revoke) a licence; ~**abgaben** licence fees, royalty; **frei von ~abgaben** free of royalties; ~**abkommen** licensing agreement (arrangement); ~**abkommen auf Gegenseitigkeit** cross-licensing agreement; ~**abrechnung** royalty statement; ~**anteil** royalty interest; ~**antrag** application for a licence; ~**auflagen** licensing restrictions; ~**ausgabe** licensed edition; ~**austausch** cross-licence; ~**austauschvereinbarung** cross-licensing agreement; ~**ausübung** licensing, licensing activity; ~**bau** licensed construction; ~**bedingungen,** ~**bestimmungen** terms of a licence; ~**berater** franchise consultant *(US)*.

lizenzbereit ready to grant a licence.

Lizenz|beschränkungen licensing restrictions; ~**betrieb** franchise business *(US)*; ~**bewerber** contender for a franchise *(US)*; ~**bewilligung** granting a licence, licensing; ~**bilanz** balance of licence transactions; ~**dauer** period (term) of a licence; ~**einkünfte** licensing (licence) income, royalties; ~**entziehung,** ~**entzug** revocation of a licence (grant), licence revocation, resumption of a licence; **gegenseitige ~erklärung** cross-licensing; ~**erneuerung** licence renewal; ~**erteilung** licensing, franchising *(US)*, public grant, granting (issuance of) a licence, *(an Bank)* granting a charter; ~**erträge** licence income, rights earnings; ~**fertigung** licensed construction.

lizenzfrei free of royalties, royalty-free.

Lizenzgeber licenser, grantor of a licence, grantor [of patent], *(Firma)* franchise company *(US)*.

Lizenzgebühr inventor's royalty, licence duty (fees), *(Steuer)* licence tax;
auf den Umsatz gerechnete ~ royalty on sales;
~**en beziehen** to derive royalties; ~ **festlegen** to fix a royalty.

Lizenz|gesetzgebung franchise legislation *(US)*; ~**gewährung** grant of a business, licensing ordinance.

lizenzieren to approbate, to license, to franchise *(US)*.

lizenziert licensed, concessionary;
~**e Tochtergesellschaft** franchised satellite *(US)*.

Lizenzierung|von Herstellungsverfahren licensing of process; ~ **von Patenten** licensing of patents; ~ **von Warenzeichen** trademark licensing.

Lizenz|inhaber licence (claim) holder, concessionary, licensee, franchise owner *(US)*; **alleiniger ~inhaber** exclusive licensee; ~**makler** franchise broker *(US)*.

lizenzmäßig herstellen to build under licence.

Lizenzmesse franchise show *(US)*.

Lizenznehmer holder of a licence, licence holder, licensee, franchisee *(US)*, franchise dealer *(US)*, *(Firma)* licensed (franchised, *US*) firm;
alleiniger ~ exclusive licensee; **nicht gewerbsmäßiger** ~ gratuitous licensee.

lizenzpflichtig subject to payment of royalties (to a licence).

Lizenz|registrierung franchise registration *(US)*; ~**registrierungserklärung** franchise registration statement *(US)*; ~**rücknahme** revocation (cancellation, resumption) of a licence; ~**system [für Vertreterauswahl]** *(UNO)* panel system; ~**tätigkeit** licensing business; ~**träger** licensee; ~**verfahren** licence proceedings; ~**vergabe,** ~**vergebung** licensing, franchising *(US)*, issuing a license; ~**vergabegesellschaft** franchise company *(US)*; ~**vergeber** licenser, franchiser *(US)*; ~**verkauf** sale of licences; ~**verkehr** licensing transactions; ~**verlängerung** renewal of a licence; **einer ~verlängerung zustimmen** to renew a licence; ~**verpflichtungen** licensing ties; ~**vertrag** licensing (licence, franchise, *US*) agreement, licensing contract; **gegenseitiger ~vertrag** *(Patentrecht)* cross-licensing arrangement *(US)*; ~**vertreter** franchise agent *(US)*; ~**vertretung** franchising *(US)*; ~**vertretung besitzen** to run a franchise operation *(US)*; ~**verweigerung** refusal to license; ~**verwertung** exploitation of a licence; ~**voraussetzungen,** ~**vorschriften** licensing requirements; ~**wesen** franchise business (field) *(US)*; ~**widerruf** cancellation of a licence; ~**zahlung** royalty payment; ~**zurücknahme** revocation (cancellation) of a licence; ~**zusammenfassung** package licensing.

Lob praise, commendation;
gerechtes ~ well-deserved praise;
~ **aussprechen** to express commendation; **nach ~ dürsten** to be eager for praise; **großes ~ erhalten** to win high praise; ~ **ernten** to be commended; **über alles (jedes) ~ erhaben sein** to be beyond all praise; **jds. ~ singen** to sing s. one's praises; **selten ~ spenden** to be chary of praise; **überreiches ~ spenden** to be profuse in one's praise; **j. mit ~ überschütten** to load s. o. with praise.

Lobby lobbying group, lobby;
~**honorar** lobbying fee; ~**ismus** lobbyism, lobbying; ~**ist** lobbyist; ~**tätigkeit** lobbying activities.

loben to praise, to commend;
sich selbst ~ to blow one's own trumpet; **j. wie einen Schellenkönig (über den grünen Klee)** ~ to give s. o. boundless praise; **j. überschwenglich** ~ to extol s. o. to the skies.

lobend laudatory, commendatory;
j. ~ erwähnen to speak in praise of s. o., to make hono(u)rable mention of s. o.; **im Heeresbericht ~ erwähnt werden** to be mentioned in dispatches;
jem. seine ~e Anerkennung aussprechen to express one's appreciation to s. o.

lobenswert praiseworthy, commendable.

lobeshungrig sein to be eager for praise.

Lobeshymne, überschwengliche ~n über jem. anstimmen to extol s. o. to the skies.

Lobhudelei adulation, unctuous flattery.

lobhudeln, jem. to give s. o. fullsome praise.

löblich praiseworthy, commendable;
~**e Absicht** laudable intention.

Lob|lied auf j. singen to be loud in one's praise of s. o., to sing s. one's praise, to extol s. o. to the skies; **in jds. ~preisungen ausbrechen** to break into praise for s. o.

Lobrede laudatory speech, eulogy, panegyric;
~ **auf j. halten** to pronounce a eulogy on s. o.; **j. mit ~n überschütten** to break out into praise of s. o., to plaster s. o. with praise.

Loch hole, vent, *(im Dach)* hole, leak, *(Elendsquartier)* hovel, hole, dunghill, kennel *(US sl.)*, *(Fahrweg)* pothole, chuckhole *(US)*, *(Kittchen)* jug, clink, quod *(sl.)*, glasshouse *(Br., sl.)*, calaboose *(US sl.)*, *(Öffnung)* aperture, *(im Zaun)* opening, gap;
kümmerliches ~ rotten hole of a place;
ein ~ aufreißen, um ein anderes zu stopfen to rob Peter to pay Paul; ~ **im Gesetz finden** to find a loophole in the law; **jem. ein ~ in den Bauch fragen** to pester s. o. with questions; **ein ~ haben** *(Rechnung)* not to work out; ~ **im Reifen haben** to have a puncture (flat tyre); **ins ~ kommen** to be put in clink *(coll.)*; **sich ein ~ in den Bauch lachen** to split one's sides with laughter; **aus einem anderen ~ pfeifen** *(fig.)* to blow from another quarter; **auf dem letzten ~ pfeifen** to be at one's beam-ends (at one's last gasp, on one's last legs), to be down and out; **jem. ein ~ in den Bauch reden** to talk nineteen to the dozen; **größeres ~ in den Einkaufsetat reißen** to bite deeper into the shopper's budget; ~ **in jds. Ersparnisse reißen** to make inroads upon (a large hole in) s. one's savings; **wie ein ~ saufen** to drink like a fish; **j. anderen vors ~ schieben** to let s. o. else bear the brunt of s. one's displeasure; **sich ein ~ in den Kopf schlagen** to cut one's head open; **seinen Gürtel ein ~ enger schnallen** to tighten one's belt; **im ~ sitzen** to be in jug; ~ **in die Luft starren** to stare into the distance; **j. ins ~ stecken** to put s. o. in clink *(coll.)*; ~ **stopfen** *(fig.)* to fill a gap; **in einem kümmerlichen ~ wohnen** to live in a tiny place; **jem. das ~ zeigen, das der Zimmermann gelassen hat** to show s. o. the door;
~**band** carriage tape.

lochen to punch, to perforate, to pierce;
Omnibusfahrkarte ~ to punch a bus ticket.

Locher hole puncher, paper (letter, key) punch;
~ **mit automatischer Kartenzuführung** automatic feed punch.

löcherig full of holes, holey;
~**e Beweisführung** argument full of holes.

Loch|kamera pinhole camera; ~**karte** punched (punch, tabulating) card; ~**karten ablochen** *(Computer)* to keypunch.

Lochkarten|ablage filing of punched cards; ~**abteilung** punched-card department; ~**buchhaltung** punched-card accounting; ~**erfahrung** punched-card experience; ~**index** punch-card index; ~**maschine** punched-card machine; ~**programmierung** punched-card program(m)ing; ~**schlüssel** punch-card code; ~**system** punch-card system; ~**umrechner** punched-card computer; ~**verfahren** punched-card method (system); ~**zuführung** punch feed.

Lochstreifen punched (paper) tape, magnetic papertype;
~**betrieb** tape relay; ~**code** paper tape code; ~**einheit** paper tape unit.

lochstreifengesteuert tape-controlled.

Lochstreifenkarte tape card.

Loch|verstärkerringe reinforcing rings; ~**zange** punch, punch pliers, perforator; ~**ziegel** perforated (air) brick.

Lockartikel bait, lure, [loss] leader *(US)*;
~**posten** loss-leader item *(US)*; ~**werbung** bait advertising.

locken to lure, to attract, to entice, to tempt;
mit dem Angebot besserer Bezahlung ~ to lure away with an offer of better pay; **j. auf die falsche Fährte ~** to put s. o. on the wrong track, to give s. o. a bum steer *(US)*; **jem. das Geld aus der Tasche ~** to fleece s. o. of his money; **über die Grenze ~** to decoy across the frontier; **j. in einen Hinterhalt ~** to lure s. o. into a trap; **j. mit einer glänzenden Zukunft ~** to lure s. o. with bright prospects.

löcken, gegen den Stachel to kick against the pricks.

lockend tempting, alluring, attractive;
~es Angebot tempting (attractive) offer; **in den ~sten Farben schildern** to paint in rosy colo(u)rs; **~e Versprechungen** tempting promises.

locker loose, *(liederlich)* with levity, lightly;
Schraube ~ anziehen to fasten a screw loosely; **eine Schraube ~ haben** to have a screw loose; **nicht ~ lassen** to stick to one's point, not to give in; **Geld ~ machen** to loosen one's purse strings, to fork out, to cough up, to stump up *(coll.)*, to spring money *(Br., coll.)*; **Gürtel ~ machen** to loosen one's belt; **~ in der Tasche sitzen** *(Geld)* to burn a hole in s. one's pocket; **~ werden** to become loose;
~e Bindungen loose connections; **~e Hand haben** to let fly at s. o.; **~er Kuchen** light cake; **~es Leben führen** to lead a fast life; **~es Mädchen** hussy, loose girl, lady of easy virtue; **~e Vereinbarungen** *(Kartellrecht)* loose combinations *(US)*; **~er Vogel (Zeisig)** fast liver, rake; **~e Zügelführung** slack rope.

lockern to loose, to loosen, to ease, to relax, to derestrict;
sich ~ *(Ackerkrume)* to break up, *(Dachziegel)* to become loose, *(Moral)* to grow lax, *(Schraube)* to work loose; **Bestimmungen ~** to deregulationize, to relax rules; **kreditpolitische Bestimmungen ~** to ease credit controls; **Blockade ~** to relax a blockade; **Disziplin ~** to relax (loosen) discipline; **nicht zollbedingte Einfuhrbestimmungen für auswärtige Lieferanten ~** to ease nontariff barriers to foreign suppliers; **Geldmarktbedingungen ~** to loosen the lid on tight money; **Geldmarktbestimmungen weiter ~** to continue one's run towards ease in money rates; **Kreditaufnahmebestimmungen ~** to make credit easier, to relax credit squeeze; **Zulassungsbedingungen ~** to ease admission requirements.

Lockerung loosening, *(Bestimmungen)* relaxation, easing;
~ von Beschränkungen easing of restrictions; **~ von Einschränkungsmaßnahmen** derestriction; **~ der restriktiven Geldmarktpolitik** easing of the restrictive money market policy; **~ der Geldmarktsätze** relaxation of money rates; **~ von Handelsbeschränkungen** easing of trade curbs; **~ der Kreditrestriktionen** relaxation of credit squeeze, ease in credit; **sich für eine ~ der Geldmarktbestimmungen einsetzen** to commit o. s. on easing money; **sich auf die ~ der Geldmarktbedingungen einstellen** to reflect easier money market circumstances.

Lockerungsmaßnahmen derestrictive measures.

Lock|mittel lure, bait, decoy; **~objekt** *(mil.)* decoy; **~spitzel** catch, stool, agent provocateur.

Lockungen enticements, lure, temptation.

Lock|vogel call bird, button, stool pigeon, lure, decoy [duck]; **~vogelangebot** flat catcher, bait, loss leader *(US)*; **~ware** loss leader.

lodern to blaze, to flare, to flame;
bis zum Himmel ~ to leap up to the sky; **vor Zorn ~** *(Augen)* to be ablaze with fury.

lodernd flaring, blazing, ablaze;
~er Abendhimmel blazing evening sky; **~e Flammen** leaping flames; **~e Leidenschaft** burning passion.

Löffel spoon, *(Bagger)* bucket, scoop, shovel;
~ voll Medizin spoonful of medicine;
j. über den ~ barbieren to take s. o. for a ride *(sl.)*, to suck s. o. in; **mit dem großen ~ essen** to live high on the hog *(sl.)* (at rack and manger, *Br.*); **mit dem ~ füttern** to spoon-feed; **Weisheit nicht mit ~n gefressen haben** not to be a pillar of wisdom; **eins hinter die ~ kriegen** to get a box on one's ears; **sich hinter die ~ schreiben** to have learnt one's lesson; **die ~ spitzen** to prick up one's ears;
~bagger power shovel, shovel excavator.

Logarithmentafel logarithmic (log, *fam.*) tables.

Logbuch logbook, deck book (log), ship's journal;
in das ~ eintragen to log.

Loge *(Café)* booth, *(Freimaurerei)* lodge, *(Theater)* box, lodge;
~ im ersten Rang first-tier box.

Logen|bruder freemason; **~karte** box ticket; **~platz** box seat; **~schließer** box attendant (keeper), usher; **~schließerin** usherette; **~sitz** box seat.

Logierbesuch haben to have friends to stay;
am Wochenende ~ to entertain guests over the weekend.

logieren to lodge, to room *(US)*;
bei jem. ~ to stay with s. o.; **in einem Hotel ~** to stay (lodge) at a hotel.

Logier|gast house guest; **~haus** lodging (rooming, *US*) house.

Logik, jeder ~ widersprechen to fly into the face of logic.

Logis bed, lodgings, rooms, quartering accommodation, forecastle;
Kost und ~ board and lodging;
j. in ~ nehmen to lodge (board) s. o.

logisch logical;
~ folgend consequential;
etw. ~ betrachten to look at s. th. rationally;
~er Beweis logical argument; **~e Folge** logical necessity; **~e Operation** *(Computer)* binary operation; **~er Trugschluß** non sequitur.

Logismus *(mil.)* logistics.

logistisch *(mil.)* logistic;
~er Apparat logistical apparatus; **~e Versorgung** logistical support.

Logtafel log slate.

Lohe blaze.

Lohgerber vegetable tanner.

Lohn wage, wages, hire, rate, screw *(Br., sl.)*, *(Belohnung)* reward, gratification, recompense, price, *(Bezahlung)* pay, payment, *(Entgelt)* compensation, consideration, return, *(Gehalt)* salary, *(Honorar)* fee, *(Verdienst)* earnings, *(Vergütung)* remuneration, emolument, consideration;
zum ~ für as a reward, in return for;
angemessener ~ fair wage; **netto ausbezahlter ~** nominal (take-home) wage; **von der Gewerkschaft ausgehandelter ~** union wage; **bar ausgezahlter ~** wage paid in cash; **auskömmlicher ~** living wage; **branchenüblicher ~** prevailing wage; **das Existenzminimum gerade deckender ~** maintenance (bare subsistence, *US*) wage; **durchschnittlicher ~** average wage; **effektiver ~** net wage, take-home pay, wage actually earned; **entgangener ~** lost pay, dead time; **fälliger ~** wages due; **fertigungsbezogener ~** wage based on output; **festgesetzter ~** stipulated wage; **garantierter ~** guaranteed wage; **gebührender ~** due reward; **künstlich gehaltener ~** pegged wage; **geltender ~** prevailing wage; **geringer ~** chicken-feed *(sl.)*; **Ersparnisse gestattender ~** saving wage; **außertariflich gezahlter ~** bootleg wage; **halbmonatlich gezahlter ~** fortnightly wage *(Br.)*; **einen Monat im voraus gezahlter ~** one-month advance wage; **einem Praktikanten gezahlter ~** learner wage; **stundenweise gezahlter ~** pay by the day; **tatsächlich gezahlter ~** take-home pay; **gleicher ~** equal pay; **gleitender ~** sliding wage; **gültiger ~** prevailing wage; **überdurchschnittlich hoher ~** loose (runaway) rate; **indexgebundener (indexierter) ~** index-linked wage; **über dem Existenzminimum liegender ~** living wage; **über dem amtlichen Richtlinien liegender ~** above-pay-policy wage *(Br.)*; **mittlerer ~** average (medium, *US*) wage; **ortsüblicher ~** local (standard) wage; **produktiver ~** productive wage; **progressiver ~** progressive wage; **rückständiger ~** wage in arrears, back wages (pay); **mit der Produktion steigender ~** progressive wages; **ständig steigender ~** steadily increasing wage; **übertariflicher ~** out-of-line rate; **üblicher ~** going wage; **ungenügender ~** insufficient pay; **untertariflicher ~** superannuated wage, subminimum rate; **vertraglich vereinbarter ~** contractual (stipulated) wage; **wöchentlicher ~** weekly pay;
~ nach dem letzten Abrechnungszeitraum current wage; **gleicher ~ für gleiche Arbeit** equal pay for equal work; **~ für nicht ganztägig beschäftigte Arbeitskräfte** part-time rate; **~ unter dem Existenzminimum** below-poverty wage; **wohlverdienter ~ für jds. Handlungen** just reward for s. one's actions;
vom ~ abziehen to deduct from the wage; **für zu niedrigen ~ arbeiten** to undercut (underrent) wages; **~ aufbessern** to improve (raise) wages; **~ auszahlen** to pay [out] wages; **~ ohne Steuerabzüge auszahlen** to make payment without deduction of tax; **seinen wohlverdienten ~ bekommen** to get one's desert; **auf höherem ~ bestehen** to stick out for higher pay; **j. um ~ und Brot bringen** to deprive s. o. of his livelihood; **~ einbehalten** to stop (detain) wages; **soundsoviel von jds. ~ einbehalten** to withhold (keep back) so much out of s. one's pay (wages); **5% vom ~ einbehalten** to deduct 5 per cent from the wages; **seinen wohlverdienten ~ empfangen** to get one's deserts (what is coming to one, *US*); **als ~ erhalten** to earn, to meet one's reward; **weder ~ noch gute Worte ernten** to be a fool for one's pains; **jem. ~ und Brot geben** to keep s. o. in one's pay; **~ kürzen** to cut down wages; **~ pfänden** to garnishee (attach, *US*) the

wages; **bei jem. in ~ und Brot stehen** to be in s. one's service (pay); **~ zahlen** to pay wages; **~ in Waren zahlen** to truck.

Löhne, auf die Produktivität abgestellte productivity wages; **gewerkschaftlich anerkannte ~** union wages; **in einem bestimmten Zeitabschnitt anfallende ~** current wages; **angemessene ~** fair wages; **außertarifliche ~** payments over and above the wage scale, bootleg wages; **bis zur Erstellung der Lohnliste einbehaltene ~** hold-back pay; **fällige ~** *(Bilanz)* accrued payrolls *(US)*; **an den Lebenshaltungsindex gebundene ~** index-number wages; **gestaffelte ~** progressive wages; **von der Konkurrenz gezahlte ~** competitive wages; **für Notstandsarbeiten gezahlte ~** emergency wages; **jeweils gültige ~** current rate of wages; **hohe ~** high wages; **inflationäre ~** wage inflation; **kümmerliche ~** lean wages; **produktive ~** productive wages; **unangemessene ~** unfair wages;

~ für weibliche Arbeitskräfte women's wages; **~ im Baugewerbe** building trades pay; **~ und Gehälter** cost of labo(u)r, *(Bilanz)* wages and salaries, payrolls *(US)*; **fällige ~ und Gehälter** *(Bilanz)* accrued payrolls; **~ und Materialkosten** labo(u)r and material;

~ angleichen to equalize (realign) wages; **~ auszahlen** to pay (hand) out wages; **~ drosseln** to curb wages; **~ einbehalten** to retain (detain, withhold, stop) wages; **~ erhöhen** to raise (increase) wages; **~ herabsetzen** to level (scale) down (cut, curtail, reduce) wages; **~ kürzen (senken)** to scale (level) down wages, to dock wages; **~ stoppen** to peg wages; **höhere ~ verlangen** to agitate for higher wages; **niedrige ~ zahlen** to pay bad wages; **Riesensumme an ~n zahlen** to have a huge payroll *(US)*.

Lohnabbau wage cut, cut in wages, wage reduction (deflation).

lohnabhängig earnings-related.

Lohnabhebungen withdrawal of wages.

Lohnabkommen wage (pay) agreement (settlement, pact);

auf Produktivitätszuwachs abgestelltes (produktivitätsbezogenes) ~ productivity deal;

~ mehrerer Firmen und Gesellschaften joint agreement; **~ mit garantierter Mindestbeschäftigungszeit** guaranteed wage plan.

Lohn|abrechnung[szettel] earnings statement, pay (wage) slip, *(Vorgang)* payroll work, payroll records *(US)*, wage accounting; **~- und Gehaltsabrechnung** payroll accounting *(US)*; **~abrechnungszeitraum** payroll period; **~abschlag** payment on account; **~abschlüsse** wages settlement; **~abteilung** payroll department (division, *US*); **~abtretung** assignment of wages, wage assignment; **~abweichung** payroll variance *(US)*.

Lohnabzug stoppage *(Br.)*, payroll deduction, deduction from wages (pay), cut in pay, *(bei Zuspätkommen)* dockage *(US)*, docking of pay *(US)*;

~ von Gewerkschaftsbeiträgen durch den Betrieb checkoff of labor-union dues *(US)*.

Lohnabzüge, feststehende fixed deductions *(US)*; **schwankende (variable) ~** variable deductions; **gesetzlich zugelassene ~** permitted deductions;

~ und Sozialabzüge statutory deductions; **~ für Versicherungsprämien und Pensionsbeiträge** deductions from pay for insurance and pension.

Lohn|abzugsverfahren *(Gewerkschaftsbeiträge)* checkoff system *(US)*; **~angaben** wage data; **~angebot** pay offer; **gebündeltes ~angebot** pay package; **~angleichung** wage adjustment; **automatische ~angleichung** automatic wage adjustment; **~angleichung an den Lebenshaltungsindex** cost-of-living adjustment; **automatisches ~angleichungssystem** automatic system of pay settlements; **globale ~anhebung** round-of-wage increase; **~anreiz** wage incentive; **~ansatz** wage rate; **~ansprüche** wage demands (claims); **höherer ~anspruch** wage qualification.

Lohnanstieg wage increase (rise, hike, boost, *US*), increase (upturn) in wages, pay boost, raise *(US)*;

allgemeiner (genereller, globaler, umfassender) ~ general increase, across-the-board (round-off) wage increase; **inflationärer ~** inflationary wage increase; **produktivitätsgebundener ~** productivity-related pay hike; **starker ~** pay jump;

~ mit Produktivitätszuwachs koppeln to tie wage boosts to productivity gains.

Lohnanteil portion of wage;

ruhegehaltsfähiger ~ pensionable pay; **für den wöchentlichen Lebensunterhalt zur Verfügung stehender ~** net spendable weekly average;

bestimmten ~ von jem. einbehalten to deduct (stop) so much out of s. one's wages.

Lohn|anteilsanweisung allotment note; **~arbeit** wage (paid) labo(u)r, wage-earning (job, paid, day's) work, work against payment; **~arbeiter** wage earner, paid worker, journeyman, hired man (labo(u)rer); **~aufbesserung** wage increase (increment, rise), pay boost, additional pay, wage hike, raise *(US)*; **~auftrag** subcontract, job order *(US)*; **~aufträge vergeben** to farm out, to job; **~auftragskosten** job-order cost accounting; **~auftragsvergebung** farming out; **~auftrieb** wage drift, upward tendency of wages.

Lohnaufwand cost of labo(u)r, wage costs (expenses), expenditure for wages, *(Bilanz)* labo(u)r wages;

~ plus Material und Unternehmerverdienst cost-plus.

Lohn|aufwandsprinzip cost-plus principle; **staatliche ~aufwendungen** government payrolls; **~ausbeutung** exploitation of workers, wage exploitation; **~auseinandersetzung** labo(u)r (wage) dispute; **~ausfall** dead time, loss of pay, lost pay; **~ausfallsentschädigung** dead-time compensation; **~ausgabe** cost of wages; **~ausgleich** wage adequacy (adjustment, stabilization).

Lohnausgleichs|kasse *(Gewerkschaft)* wage equalization fund; **~stelle** wage stabilization board *(US)*.

Lohnauszahlung payment of wages, payroll disbursements *(US)*, wage paying;

tägliche ~ daily payroll.

Lohnauszahlungs|anweisung allotment ticket; **~beleg** payroll voucher; **~methode, ~plan, ~system** wage payment plan.

lohnbedingt earnings-related.

Lohn|bedingungen wage conditions; **~begrenzungsabkommen** wage-control agreement; **paritätisch zusammengesetzte ~behörde** trade board *(Br.)*; **~belastung** pressure on wages; **zunehmende ~belastung** upward pressure on wages; **~berechnung** wage setting (determination), calculation of wages; **~berechnungsverfahren** wage-setting plan; **~berechnungsverfahren mit zwei Möglichkeiten** dual-pay system; **~bereich** wage sector; **~bescheinigung** wage slip; **~- und Gehaltsbeschränkung** wage control; **~bestätigung** wage statement; **auf den Lebenshaltungsindex abgestimmte ~bestimmungen** index-number wage provisions *(US)*; **bestimmte ~beträge abtreten** to assign specified amounts of earned wages; **~beutel** pay envelope; **~bewegung** wage drive (trend), trend of wages; **~bildung** wage development; **~bremse** wage (pay) curb, damp on wage increases.

Lohnbuch salary (wages) book;

~führung, ~haltung personnel (payroll) accounting, payroll journal; **~halter** paying officer, wage (pay, payroll, *US*) clerk.

Lohn|büro pay office, payroll division (department) *(US)*, wage and salary administration; **~diener** daily (hired) servant, occasional valet, sham butler; **~differenz** wage differential; **~drift** wage drift; **~druck** wage push (pressure), pressure on wages, pay squeeze; **~drückerei** rate cutting, sweating; **~durchschnitt** average wage, wage level; **~eckpfeiler** wage guidepost; **~einbehaltung** detention (stoppage of, *Br.*, withholding from, *US*) wages, wage distraint, retention of earnings (wages), deferred wages (pay); **~einbuße** dead time, lost pay; **~eingruppierung** wage classification; **~einheit** unit of wage; **~einkommen, ~einnahmen** earned (wage) income, wage earnings, income from wages; **~- und Gehaltseinnahmen** wage and salary receipts; **~einschränkung** pay curb; **~einstufung** wage classification; **niedrige ~einstufung** demotional classification change; **~empfänger** wage earner, wage-earning man, wageworker *(US)*, payroller *(US)*, *(pl.)* wage labor *(US)*; **~empfängerklasse** wage-earning group (class); **~empfehlungen** wage recommendations.

lohnen to reward, to compensate, to recompense, *(v./i.)* to be profitable;

einen Besuch ~ to be worth a visit.

löhnen to pay out wages, *(mil.)* to pay.

lohnend paying, payable, payoff, remunerative, gainful, lucrative, *(vorteilhaft)* advantageous, fat, worthwhile;

~e Beschäftigung profitable employment, remunerative occupation; **~es Buch** rewarding book; **~es Geschäft** remunerative (lucrative) business; **~e Kapitalanlage** profitable investment.

Lohn|entwicklung wage development; **~erhebung** wage statistics.

Lohnerhöhung wage increase (rise, increment, *Br.*, hike, *US*), raise *(US)*, increase of (rise in) wages, pay increase *(Br.)*;

allgemeine ~ across-the-board wage increase; **staatliche Leitlinien desavouierende ~** guideline-busting wage increase; **mit dem Inflationssatz gekoppelte ~** wage rise pegged to the rate of inflation; **indexgebundene ~** threshold payment; **rückwirkende ~** retroactive pay;

~ auf Grund besonderer Leistung merit increase;

~en **auf den Verbraucher abwälzen** to pass on wage increases to the consumer; ~ **auf 15% begrenzen** to hold wage increases to 15%; ~ **bekommen** to get an increase (a raise, *US*) in pay; ~ **fordern** to stand (stick out) for more (higher) wages; ~ **vornehmen** to increase the wages (pay), to raise wages; **globale über 10% hinausgehende** ~ **zugestehen** to dole out 10%-plus wage increases across the board.

Lohnerhöhungs|begrenzung auf 6 Pfund £ 6 pay code *(Br.)*; ~**grenze** pay target; ~**welle** spate of wage increases.

Lohn|etat wages bill *(Br.)*, payroll *(US)*; ~- **und Gehaltsetat** labo(u)r budget; ~**explosion** wage explosion; **im Bereich der öffentlichen Hände gestartete** ~**explosion** public-sector-led wage explosion; ~**faktor** coefficient of wages, wage factor in costs; ~**fertigungsvertrag** job contract; ~**festsetzung** fixing of wages, wage determination (fixing), wage (rate, *US*) setting; **automatische** ~**festsetzung** automatic wage determination; ~**festsetzung durch Betriebsrat und Betriebsführung** joint rate setting; ~**festsetzungsverfahren** wage-rate determination process, wage plan; ~**fonds** wage fund; ~**fondstheorie** wage-fund theory; ~**forderung** wage request.

Lohnforderungen wage claims (demands, challenge), pay claims; **noch nicht fällige** ~ accrued wages; **zurückgehaltene** ~ pay restraint;
sich halbwegs um Zurückhaltung bei ~ **bemühen** to pump for some form of wage restraint; ~ **durchsetzen** to push wage claims; ~ **erheben (stellen)** to stick out for higher pay (wages), to push (stand for more) wages; ~ **nachgeben** to give ground on pay; **in überhöhten** ~ **schwelgen** to go on a wage spree; **geringere** ~ **stellen** to undercut.

Lohn|formel wage formula; ~- **und Gehaltsfortzahlung im Krankheitsfall** short-term disability benefits; ~**frachtführer** common carrier of goods for hire; ~**fragen** wage matters; ~**front** wage front; ~**führerschaft** wage leadership; ~**fuhrgeschäft** carrier's business; ~**garantie** wage guarantee; ~**gärtner** jobbing gardener.

Lohngefälle wage differential;
betriebliches ~ inter-plant differential; **industrielles** ~ inter-industrial differential; **regionales** ~ regional wage and salary differentail;
vorsteuerliches ~ **einebnen** to narrow pretax differentials.

Lohn|gefüge pay (wage) structure; **sein** ~**gefüge rationalisieren** to rationalize its pay structure; ~**gelder** wage payments; **einbehaltene** ~**gelder** withheld wages, holdback pay *(US)*; ~**gerangel** wage scramble; **eisernes** ~**gesetz** iron law of wages; ~**gleichheit** wage adequacy, equality in wages (of pay); ~**gleichheitsgesetz** Equal Pay Act *(Br.)*; ~**gleitformel** escalator formula; ~**gleitklausel** escalator clause, cost-of-living escalator; ~**gleitregelung** wage escalation; ~**grundlage** time standard; ~**gruppe** wage rate group, wage scale (bracket), pay scale *(US)*; **höhere** ~**gruppen** upper pay brackets; ~**gruppierung** wage classification; ~**guthaben** unclaimed wages; ~**herabsetzung** cutting (reduction) of wages, pay reduction; ~**höhe** wage level; ~**index** wage index; ~**indexierung** wage indexation; ~**inflation** wage (wage-push) inflation, inflationary march of wages; ~**instanz** wage tribunal; ~**intensität** wage impact.

lohnintensiv wage-intensive;
~**ster Industriezweig** highest-wage industry.

Lohn|kampf wage dispute, labo(u)r conflict; ~**kampf ausfechten** to wage a dogfight; ~**kapital** wage capital; ~**karte** time card; ~**kartei** payroll file *(US)*; ~**kasse** wage fund; ~**kellner** day waiter; ~**klasse** wage group, schedule of wages, *(Bewerbung)* grade; ~**klassifizierung** wage classification; **gleitende** ~**klausel** escalator clause; ~**kode** pay code; ~**kommission** wage board; ~**konflikt** wage dispute; ~**konjunktur** wage boom; ~**konto** payroll *(US)* (wages) account, master pay record; ~- **und Gehaltskontrolle** wage and salary control; **gesetzlich vorgeschriebene** ~- **und Preiskontrollen** statutory wage-price policy; ~**korrektur** profit sharing.

Lohnkosten labo(u)r cost (rates), cost of labo(u)r, wages bill *(Br.)*, payload *(US)*;
spiralartig ansteigende ~ spiral(l)ing wage costs; **gesamte** ~ factory earnings; **steuerbedingte** ~ labo(u)r-tax matter *(Br.)*; **unmittelbare** ~ direct labo(u)r cost;
~ **je Arbeitsaufwand (Produktionseinheit)** unit wage (labo(u)r) costs;
überhöhte ~ **berechnen** to pad a payroll; **wöchentliche** ~ **erhöhen** to increase the weekly payroll;
~**anteil** payload *(US)*, labo(u)r charge; **gestiegenen** ~**anteil durch Preiserhöhungen auffangen** to recoup the increasing cost of labo(u)r by raising its prices; ~**aufteilung** payroll distribution *(US)*; ~**einsparung** wage savings; ~**erhöhung auf die Verbraucher abwälzen** to pass increased labo(u)r costs onto consumers; ~**faktor** wage factor in costs; ~**index** labo(u)r cost index; **inflationsbereinigter** ~**index** national wage index corrected to take out inflationary effects; ~**kalkulation** job pricing; ~**senkung** reduction of labo(u)r rates; ~**steigerung** increase in the cost of labo(u)r; ~**theorie** subsistence theory of wages; ~**verteilung** distribution of labo(u)r costs; **Gehalts- und** ~**vorschlag** labo(u)r [budget] estimate.

Lohn|kurve wage curve (line), earning curve; ~**kürzung** cut[ting] (reduction) of wages, pay cut, wage (rate, *US*) cut[ting], wage rate cutting, dock[age], pay cut, *(globale)* rollback *(US coll.)*; **zehnprozentige** ~**kürzung durchführen** to cut the payroll by 10 per cent; ~**kürzung vornehmen** to reduce wages; ~**kutscher** cabman, hack driver *(US)*; ~**lawine** wage avalanche; ~**leitlinien**, ~**leitsätze** pay (earnings) guidelines.

Lohnliste payroll [ledger (book, *US*)], payroll sheet *(US)*, pay bill *(US)* (sheet, *Br.*), wage sheet, payment sheet *(Br.)*;
wöchentliche ~ weekly wages return *(Br.)* (payroll, *US*);
~ **einer Fabrik** factory payroll *(US)*;
~ **aufstellen** to make out a payroll *(US)*; **j. nicht mehr auf der** ~ **führen** to throw s. o. off the payroll *(US)*; **auf der** ~ **stehen** to be on the payroll *(US)*, *(bei einer Stadt)* to be paid out of the town funds.

Lohn|listenverfahren payroll procedure *(US)*; ~**markt** wage market; ~**minimum** wage floor, living wage, wage minimum; ~**minimum für stundenweise Beschäftigung** minimum call pay *(US)*; ~**nachweis** evidence of wage paid; ~**nachzahlung** retroactive pay; ~**nebenkosten** incidental wages costs; ~**nebenleistungen** fringe benefits *(US)*.

Lohnniveau level of wages, wage (pay) level, standard of wages;
~ **und Gehaltsniveau** wage and salary level;
~ **einfrieren** to peg the wage rates;
~**anhebung** round-of- (across-the-board) wage increase;
~**unterschied** wage differential.

Lohn|ordnung wage pattern; ~**parität** wage parity; ~**pause** wage pause, pay pause *(Br.)*; ~**periode** pay period, pay[roll] period *(US)*; ~**pfändung** wage garnishment *(US)*, garnishment of wages *(US)*, *(aus Unterhaltsklage)* attachment of earnings *(Br.)*; ~**pfändungsbeschluß** attachment of earnings order *(Br.)*; ~**plafond** pay ceiling; ~**politik** wage policy; ~- **und Einkommenspolitik** incomes policy *(Br.)*; ~**politik im öffentlichen Bereich** public-sector pay policy.

lohnpolitische|Auseinandersetzungen wages disputes; ~ **Bestechungen** pay policy carrot; ~ **Führerschaft** wage leadership; ~ **Richtlinien** pay [policy] guidelines.

Lohn|posten labo(u)r item, *(Bilanz)* wages; ~**prämie** wage dividend.

Lohn-Preis|gefüge wage-price structure; ~**kontrolle** wage-price control; **gesetzlich vorgeschriebene** ~**kontrollen** statutory price policy; ~**richtzahlen** wage-price guidelines; ~**spirale** wage-price spiral, inflationary spiral.

Lohn|problem wage problem; **automatische** ~**progression** automatic [wage] progression; ~**prüfungsstelle** wage board, wage-examining bureau, pay review body *(Br.)*; ~**quote** wage share (ratio), salary ratio, ratio of wages and salaries to national product; ~**rechnung** payroll journal (sheet, record) *(US)*; ~**regelung** pay settlement, wage regulation (settlement); **auf den Lebenshaltungsindex abgestimmte** ~**regelung** index-number wage provisions; **gleitende** ~**regelung** wage escalation; ~**reglementierung** wage and salary control; **automatische** ~**regulierung** automatic wage adjustment; ~**richtlinien** pay (wage, earnings) guidelines; ~**richtung** wage drift; ~**rückstand** arrears of wages, back pay; ~**rückstände** accrued (back, arrears of) wages, back pay; **um das doppelte erhöhte** ~**rückstände** double backpay; ~**runde** across-the-board wage increase, round-of-pay policy, wage (pay) round.

Lohnsatz rate of wages (pay), wage rate, *(Satzbetrieb)* trade composition;
erhöhter ~ overtime rate; **mittlerer** ~ average rate of wages; **tariflicher** ~ standard wage rate; **übertariflicher** ~ pay in excess of standard rates; **üblicher** ~ regular rate;
unterdurchschnittlicher ~ **für behinderte Arbeiter** substandard rate; ~ **pro Tonne** *(Bergbau)* tonnage rate;
um die Hälfte erhöhten ~ **erzielen** to count time and a half; **über dem üblichen** ~ **bezahlt werden** to be in excess of standard rates.

Lohn|sätze, bestehende ~**sätze angleichen** to adjust existing wage rates; **übertarifliche** ~**sätze bezahlen** to pay in excess of the official wage rate; ~**scheck** wage check *(US)* (cheque, *Br.*); ~**schiedsgerichtsbarkeit** wage arbitration; ~**schiedsspruch** wage award; ~**schlichtung** wage mediation (arbitration); **staatliche** ~**schlichtungsstelle** National Wages Board *(Br.)*;

~schlüssel pay code *(Br.)*; **~schneider** tailor to the trade; **~schreiber** *(für Zeitung)* penny-a-liner, grub, hack[writer]; **als ~schreiber arbeiten** to penny-a-line, to devil; **~schrittmacher** pay pacesetter; **~schutzgesetzgebung** Truck Acts *(Br.)*; **~schwellenvereinbarung** threshold agreement; **~senkung** reduction of wages, wage reduction (cut[ting]); **~senkung vornehmen** to scale down wages.

Lohnskala scale of wages, wage scale;
bewegliche ~ sliding wage scale; **einheitliche ~** *(Lohntabelle)* union scale of wages; **gleitende ~** sliding wage scale, escalator clause; **zunehmende ~** incremental scale of wages.

Lohn | solidarität wage solidarity; **~sonderkonto** separate loan account; **~spanne** wage (rate) range (spread); **~spirale** wage spiral; **~stabilisierung** wage stabilization; **~stabilisierungsamt** wage stabilization board *(US)*; **~stabilizierungs- und Preissenkungspolitik** wage-freezing and price-lowering policy; **~staffelung** wage classification; **~stand** wage level; **~standardisierung** standardization of wages; **~statistik** wage statistics; **~steigerung** wage increase (raise, *US*); **verhinderte ~steigerung** wage restraint; **gesetzlich festgelegte ~steigerungsbegrenzung** formal limit on wage increase; **auf den Produktivitätszuwachs abgestellter jährlicher ~steigerungsbetrag** improvement factor.

Lohnsteuer pay-as-you-earn income tax *(Br.)*, PAYE tax *(Br.)*, withholding wage tax *(US)*;
einbehaltene ~ withheld tax from wage payment, personal withholding tax *(US)*;
~ einbehalten to withhold income tax (tax from wage payment);
~abführung deduction of wage tax, withholding income tax *(US)*; **~abrechnungen** payroll records *(US)*; **~abzug** withholding income tax *(US)*, [etwa] pay-as-you-go *(US)*, pay-as-you-earn *(Br.)*, payroll deduction *(US)*; **fällige ~abzüge** pay deductions payable *(US)*.

lohnsteuerabzugspflichtige Stelle withholding agent *(US)*.

Lohnsteuer | abzugsverfahren, ~einbehaltung payroll deduction plan *(US)*, pay-as-you-go plan *(US)*, pay-as-you-earn system (plan) *(Br.)*; **~bemessung** assessment of wage taxes; **~berechnungstabelle** tax (withholding tax, *US*) table, pay code *(Br.)*; **~bescheinigung** withholding statement *(US)*; **keine ~beträge einbehalten** to make payment without deduction of tax; **~einbehaltung** withholding income tax, pay-as-you-earn *(Br.)*, pay-as-you-go *(US)*; **~einbehaltungsverfahren** pay-as-you-earn *(Br.)* (pay-as-you-go, *US*) tax system.

lohnsteuerfrei auszahlen to make payment without deduction of tax.

Lohnsteuer | freibetrag employee's withholding exemption *(US)*, flat-rate reduction; **~freibetragsformular, ~freibetragsbescheinigung** employee's withholding exemption certificate *(US)*; **~karte** deduction card, [etwa] withholding statement *(US)*; **~kennzifferhinweis** paye coding guide *(Br.)*; **~kennziffern** pay code numbers *(Br.)*.

lohnsteuerpflichtig | sein to be liable for pay-as-you-earn income tax *(Br.)*;
~er Beruf payroll employment *(US)*.

Lohnsteuerpflichtiger pay-as-you-earn income tax payer *(Br.)*.

Lohnsteuer | richtlinien withholding regulations *(US)*; **~rückvergütung** refunding of wage tax, pay-as-you-earn income-tax refunding *(Br.)*; **~satz** withholding rate *(US)*; **~sätze auf das verbleibende Nettogehalt anwenden** to operate PAYE on the remaining net pay *(Br.)*; **~stelle** withholding agency *(US)*; **~system** withholding (pay-as-you-go) system, pay-as-you-earn income system *(Br.)*; **~tabelle** pay code *(Br.)*, withholding tax table *(US)*; **~tarif** PAYE code *(Br.)*; **~unterlagen** payroll records *(US)*; **~verfahren** pay-as-you-earn system *(Br.)*, payroll system *(US)*.

Lohnstillhalteabkommen, einjähriges one-year wage freeze.

Lohnstopp wage freeze (freezing, stop), freeze on (freezing of) wages;
~ und Preisstopp wage and price freeze (standstill), freeze of pay and prices, freeze on incomes and wages, deep freeze;
~ durchführen to freeze wages;
~politik wage-freezing policy; **~- und Preissenkungspolitik** wage-freezing and price-lowering policy.

Lohn | streifen wage (pay) slip; **~streitigkeit** dispute over pay, wage dispute (controversy), pay dispute, labor conflict *(US)*; **~struktur** wage structure; **~stückkosten** unit labo(u)r costs; **~stufe** wage (salary) bracket, wage scale; **~stunden** earned hours; **vergütete arbeitsfreie ~stunden** time paid for but not worked; **~stundennachweis** time check; **~stundensatz** labo(u)r rate; **~summe** aggregate wages, payroll total *(US)*; **tägliche ~summe** daily payroll *(US)*; **~summenaufstellung** statement of wages; **~summensteuer** selective employment tax *(Br.)*, payroll tax *(US)*; **~system** wage plan; **~tabelle** table of wages, wage table (schedule), pay scale *(US)*, scale of remunerations; **~tag** term *(Br.)*, payday, Kaiser's Geburtstag *(US sl.)*.

Lohntarif wage (compensation) rate (schedule), scale of wages, wage scale;
anderthalbfacher ~ für Überstunden overtime rate of time and a half; **erhöhter ~** overtime rate; **gewerkschaftlich festgesetzter ~** union scale *(US)*; **geltender ~** prevailing rate; **gleitender ~** sliding scale tariff, sliding wage scale; **gültiger ~** current rate of wages; **überdurchschnittlich hoher ~** loose rate; **üblicher ~** going rate;
über dem üblichen ~ bezahlt werden to be paid in excess of standard rates;
über dem ~ liegende Bezahlung payment over and above, pay in excess of standard rates;
~änderung wage-rate changes; **~forderungen** bargaining demands; **~forderungen im Bereich der öffentlichen Hand** public-sector pay claims; **neues ~system** new pay system; **~überwachung** pay control; **~veränderungen** wage-rate changes; **~vertrag** collective wage agreement; **ganzen Industriezweig umfassender ~vertrag** collective bargaining contract; **~vertragspartner** collective bargaining partners; **~wesen** wage-bargaining machinery (system); **~ziele den Steuererhöhungen anpassen** to adapt post-tax bargaining targets.

Lohn | theorie wage theory, theory of rent; **~tüte** wage packet (envelope), pay packet (envelope), pay check *(US)* (cheque, *Br.*), take-home pay (wage); **wöchentliche ~tüte** weekly take-home pay; **~tütenwerbung** pay-envelope advertising; **monatliche ~übersicht** monthly labo(u)r (payroll, *US*) summary; **~- und Gehaltsüberwachung** wage and salary control; **~- und Preisüberwachung** wage and price control; **~- und Preisüberwachungsstelle** office of wage and price stability *(US)*; **~überweisung** transfer of wages.

Löhnung payment, pay;
~ von Reservisten reserve pay.

Lohn | ungerechtigkeit, ~ungleichheit wage inequality, inequality of pay.

Löhnungs | appell *(mil.)* pay parade; **~tag** pay-off *(sl.)*, payday *(Br.)*, *(mil.)* eagle day *(sl.)*, Uncle Sam's party *(US sl.)*.

Lohnunterlagen payroll records *(US)*.

Lohnunterschied wage differential, disparity of wages;
regionaler bestimmter ~ regional wage differential; **unberechtigter ~** wage inequality.

Lohn | veränderungen wage changes; **~veredelung** processing under a job contract, job (contract, *Br.*) processing; **~vereinbarung** wage agreement; **betriebliche ~vereinbarung** labo(u)r-management contract; **an die Produktivität gekoppelte und sich selbst finanzierende ~vereinbarung** self-financing productivity deal; **~vergleich** wage comparison; **~vergütung für den Anmarschweg zum Arbeitsplatz** portal-to-portal pay; **~verhältnis** wage relationship.

Lohnverhandlungen wage talks (negotiations, bargaining), collective bargaining, pay negotiations, pay bargaining;
neue ~ wage reopening;
~ mit den Arbeitgebern führen to negotiate with employers about wage claims; **sich aus ~ völlig heraushalten** to wash its hands of pay bargaining; **größte Schwierigkeiten bei ~ machen** to be causing the most trouble on wages.

Lohn | verrechnungskonto payroll clearing account *(US)*; **~verschiedenheit** wage inequality (disparity); **~verteilung** wage distribution; **~- und Gehaltsverwaltung** wage and salary administration; **~verwirkung** forfeiture of wages; **~volumen** total payroll; **~vorauszahlung, ~vorschuß** wage advance, advance of (on) wages, advance wages; **~welle** across-the-board wage increase; **~wesen** wage costing; **~- und Gehaltswesen** wage and salary administration; **~zahltag** payday.

Lohnzahlung wage payment, payoff *(sl.)*;
vertraglich vereinbarte ~ contract wage payment; **zusätzliche ~en** wage supplements;
~ vornehmen to pay out the wages.

Lohnzahlungs | gesetz Payment of Wages Act *(Br.)*; **~methode** wage payment plan, type of wage plan; **~zeitraum** pay period, payroll period *(US)*.

Lohn | zettel payroll voucher *(US)*, pay slip; **~ziel** wage objective; **~zugeständnisse** wage concessions; **~zulage** wage increase, raise *(US)*, increased pay, supplementary wage, wage supplement.

Lohnzuschlag additional (extra) pay, wage bonus;
außertariflicher ~ payment over and above the wage scale;

~ **für außerplanmäßige Arbeiten** call-back pay; **100%iger ~ für Nacht- und Feiertagsarbeit** double time; **50%iger ~ für Nacht- und Feiertagsarbeit** time and a half; ~ **für Überstunden** overtime pay.

Lohn|zuschuß wage advance, advance wage payment, subsistence money; **~zuwachs** wage gain.

Lokal restaurant, public [eating] house *(Br.)*, place, business premises, pub *(fam.)*, property, inn, saloon *(US)*, *(Bierausschank)* beerhouse, alehouse, beer parlo(u)r;
außerhalb des ~s off the premises; **im ~ angetroffen** *(Gerichtsvollzieher)* found on premises;
billiges ~ low pub *(Br.)*; **vornehmes ~** exclusive restaurant;
~ **mit Schankkonzession** licensed premises *(Br.)*, licensed saloon (house);
~ **durchsuchen** to visit the premises; ~ **räumen** to vacate the premises; ~ **unter Protest verlassen** to leave the room under protest; **von ~ zu ~ ziehen** to go on a spree (pub crawl, *Br.*).

lokal local, regional, sectional, topical;
~er Bedarf local requirements; **~e Eifersüchteleien** sectional jealousies; **nach ~en Gesichtspunkten aufteilen** to sectionalize; **~e Interessen** sectional interests; **~e Nachrichten** local news; **~e Streitigkeiten** local quarrels.

Lokal|anästhesie local anaesthetic; **auf ~angelegenheiten in seiner Rede Bezug nehmen** to work in local references in one's speech; **~anzeiger** local advertiser; **~artikel** local item; **~augenschein** judicial survey view, viewing scene of crime; **~ausdruck** localism, local term; **~bahn** branch line, local railway *(Br.)*, suburban railway; **~bahnhof** local (way, *US*) station; **~bedarf** home consumption, local requirements; **~behörden** local authorities; **~berichterstatter** spot news reporter *(US)*; **~berühmtheiten** local notables; **~blatt** local paper; **in Dialekten gedruckte ~blätter** vernacular newspapers; **~charakter** local colo(u)r.

Lokales *(Zeitung)* local [news].

Lokal|größen local notables (talents), leaders in the community; **~handel** residential trade; **~interessen** local (sectional) interests.

lokalisierbar localizable.

lokalisieren to localize, to locate.

lokalisierte Krise localized crisis.

Lokalisierung localization, location *(US)*;
~ **eines Konflikts** localization of a conflict.

Lokalität locality, rooms, premises, *(WC)* conveniences.

Lokal|kenntnisse local knowledge; **~kenntnisse besitzen** to know a place; **~kolorit** local picture (colo(u)r); **~korrespondent** local stringer; **~markt** spot market; **~miete** shop (office) rent; **~nachrichten** local news; **~patriot** municipalist, particularist, sectionalist *(US)*, parochialist, localist; **~patriotismus** localism, parochialism, provincialism, sectionalism, sectional pride; **~politik** local politics; **~presse** local papers (press); **~redakteur** local reporter, city editor *(US)*; **~redaktion** local newsroom, city desk (office) *(US)*; **~reporter** leg man, spot news reporter *(US)*; **~seite** regional page; **~sendung** regional transmission; **~spalte** column of local news; **~stück** village farce; **~tarif** local rate; **~teil** local news; **~termin** *(Gericht)* judicial survey, viewing the scene of crime, view; **~termin abhalten** to make investigations on the spot, *(Gericht)* to view the scene of crime; **~tratsch** parish-pump gossip; **~umschreibungen** interbank clearings; **~verhältnisse** local concerns (conditions); **~verhältnisse kennen** to know the ins and outs of a place; **~werbung** local advertisement; **~werte** local stocks (securities); **~zeitung** local newspaper (paper); **~zug** local (way, *US*) train, local *(US)*.

loko on the spot;
~ **und auf Termin** spot and forward;
~ **verkaufen** to sell for spot delivery.

Loko|geschäft spot (cash) business (transaction); **~kauf** spot purchase; **~kurs** spot price; **~markt** spot market.

Lokomotiv|anhänger engine tender; **~drehscheibe** turntable.

Lokomotive locomotive [engine], iron horse *(coll.)*, *(Eisenbahn)* pot, bull *(US sl.)*;
alleinfahrende ~ light engine; **stillstehende ~** standing engine;
~ **konstruieren** to build a locomotive.

Lokomotiv|fabrik locomotive works; **~führer** engine driver, railway carman, engineer *(US)*; **~park** engine yard, fleet of locomotives; **vor dem Bahnübergang die ~pfeife betätigen** to whistle before reaching the level-crossing; **~reparatur** locomotive repairs; **~schuppen** engine (running, *Br.*) shed, enginehouse, roundhouse *(US)*.

Loko|preis loco price, spot price; **~waren** spot goods (commodities), spots.

Lokus rear *(Br., sl.)*.

Lombard lending on securities, collateral loan business *(US)*; **~anleihe** collateral loan *(US)*; **~bank** loan bank (office); **~bestände** collateral holdings (deposits, *US*); **~darlehn** loan on securities (upon collateral security, *US*), collateral loan *(US)*, lombard loan; **~debitoren** collateral loan debtors.

Lombarddeckung security, collateral security *(US)*;
erstklassige ~ darstellen to be a first-rate secured loan; **als ~ fungieren** to serve as security (collateral, *US*); ~ **verbessern** to sweeten a loan.

Lombard|depot collateral deposit *(US)*, derivative deposit; **~effekten** collateral securities.

lombardfähig suitable for loans, pawnable, eligible to serve as collateral *(US)*;
nicht ~ thrown out of loans, not eligible to serve as collateral *(US)*;
~ **sein** to be eligible as security (collateral, *US*).

Lombard|fähigkeit eligibility to serve as collateral *(US)*; **~forderung** collateral claim; **~gebühr** margin rate *(US)*; **~geschäft** lending on securities, collateral loan business *(US)*, *(einzelnes)* deposit (collateral loan, *US*) transaction; **~- und Diskontgeschäfte** loans and discounts.

lombardieren to advance (lend) money on securities, to lend (loan) on collateral *(US)*, to pawn *(Br.)*, to collaterate *(US)*, to hypothecate *(US)*;
Effekten (Wertpapiere) ~ lassen to lodge as (collaterate, *US*) securities, to have securities hypothecated *(US)*; **Waren ~** to lend money on goods; **Wechsel ~** to pledge a bill as security for a loan.

lombardiert pledged, pawned, hypothecated *(US)*;
~e Effekten pawned (collateral) securities; **~er Wechsel** bill pledged as security for an advance.

Lombardierung pawning, hypothecation *(US)*;
zweite ~ rehypothecation *(US)*;
~ **von Wertpapieren** pledging of securities, hypothecation of securities *(US)*, borrowing on collateral security *(US)*.

Lombardierungswert collateral value *(US)*.

Lombardkredit secured advance, credit against securities, lombard (collateral, *US*, Wall Street, *US*) loan, stock-market credit, loan (credit) against securities (upon collateral security, *US*);
~ **aufnehmen** to pledge securities, to borrow on collateral *(US)*; **abgesicherten ~ gewähren** to lend (loan) on collateral *(US)* (securities, *Br.*), to collaterate *(US)*.

Lombard|pfand collateral security; **~satz** lombard margin (lending, *US*) rate, rate for loans on collateral *(US)*; **~schein** qualifying agreement *(Br.)*, hypothecation certificate *(US)*; **~schuld** collateral debt.

Lombardsicherheit collateral security;
~en auswechseln to substitute different collateral; **~en erhöhen** to post additional collateral.

Lombard|sicherung durch Hinterlegung verschiedener Effekten mixed collateral; **als ~unterlage nicht gewertet werden** to be thrown out of loans, to be ineligible to serve as security (collateral, *US*); **~verkehr** collateral loan business; **~vertrag** collateral loan agreement (trust indenture, *US*); **~vorschuß** secured (collateral, *US*) advance, advance on (against) securities, stock-exchange loan; **~wechsel** loan advance (collateral, *US*) bill; **~wert** collateral (hypothecation, loan, hypothecary) value *(US)*; **~zinssatz** lombard (lending, *US*) rate.

Londoner Schuldenabkommen London Debts Agreement.

Lorbeeren, sich auf seinen ~ ausruhen to rest on one's oars (laurels); ~ **ernten** to win laurels, to carry off the bag.

Lorbeerkranz laureate wreath.

Lore lorry, tram, truck, box waggon *(US)*.

Lorokonto loro account.

Los lot, chance, *(Anleihe)* lottery bond, *(Anteil)* share, lot, portion, *(Grundstück)* plot of land, parcel, lot *(US)*, *(Lotterie)* [lottery] ticket, *(Schicksal)* fate, destiny, doom, *(Statistik)* inspection lot, *(Warenpartie)* lot, parcel, line;
durch das ~ by casting lots;
großes ~ big (first) prize;
~e ausrufen *(Auktion)* to call out the lots; ~ **auswerfen** to cast the lead; **durch das ~ entscheiden** to have a toss-up, to settle by lot; **sich in sein ~ ergeben** to submit to one's lot; **das große ~ gewinnen** to draw the first prize, to hit the jackpot *(US sl.)*; ~ **kaufen** to buy a lottery ticket; **jds. ~ teilen** to cast in one's lot with s. o.; **durch das ~ wählen** to choose by lot; **~e ziehen** to cast lots; **das große ~ ziehen** to draw the first prize, to strike it lucky *(fam.)*, to hit the jackpot *(US)*, to pick out the winners; **durch ~ zuteilen** to allot.

los loose;
etw. ~ haben to know one's stuff, to be on the ball in one's subject *(US sl.)*; **in Mathematik etw. ~ haben** to be jolly good at mathematics; **Rad ~ haben** to have got the wheel off; **nicht viel ~ haben** not to be very good; **mit etw. nicht viel ~ sein** to be nothing special; **mit jem. nicht viel ~ sein** to be a bit of a drag; **seine Pflichten ~ sein** to be free of one's commitments; **seine Schulden ~ sein** to have got rid of one's debts; **sein Geld ~ geworden sein** to never see one's money again;
bei dir ist wohl eine Schraube ~ you must have a screw loose; **dann ist der Teufel ~** there'll be the devil to pay.
Losanleihe lottery bond.
losballern to fly off the handle.
lösbar separable, removable.
losbekommen to get off;
j. aus dem Gefängnis ~ to bail s. o. out of prison.
losbrechen to break off, to prize, to pry *(US)*, *(Sturm)* to break.
Lösch|anlage fire-extinguishing apparatus; **~apparat** fire extinguisher; **~arbeiten** unloading, *(Feuerbekämpfung)* fire fighting.
lösch|bar extinguishable; **~bereit** ready to discharge.
Lösch|bescheinigung landing certificate; **~blatt** blotting paper; **~blattwerbung** blotter advertising; **~boot** fireboat; **~eimer** fire bucket.
Löschen effacement, deletion, obliteration, *(Computer)* clearance, *(Geschriebenes)* effacement, *(Hypothek)* satisfaction, *(Ladung)* discharge, unloading, unlading, unshipping, unshipment, wharfage, *(Patent)* cancellation, annulment, *(Schuld)* cancellation, liquidation, *(Tonband)* erasure;
inklusive ~ und Leichtern on landed basis;
freies ~ free discharge;
~ eines Buchungspostens extinguishment of a book account; **~ eines Feuers** extinguishing a fire; **~ einer Hypothek** discharge (extinguishment, cancellation, *US*) of a mortgage; **~ der Ladung** breaking bulk, discharge of cargo;
mit dem ~ der Ladung beginnen to break out of the hold.
löschen *(ausstreichen)* to erase, to delete, to strike out, to expunge, *(Computer)* to clear, *(Feuer)* to extinguish, to put out, *(Geschriebenes)* to efface, to blot out, *(Löschpapier)* to blot, to absorb ink, *(Schuld)* to extinguish, to redeem, to cancel, *(Tinte)* to blot, *(Tonband)* to erase, *(Waren)* to discharge, to land, to unload, to unship, to debark;
Dienstbarkeit ~ to release an easement; **seinen Durst ~** to quench one's thirst; **Eintragung ~** to cancel an entry, to vacate an entry of record; **Eintragung im Grundbuch ~** to cancel an entry in the land register *(Br.)*; **Firma im Handelsregister ~** to remove a firm from the register, to cancel a firm in the register of business names, to take a company off the books; **Güter ~** to land goods; **Hypothek ~** to extinguish (discharge, satisfy, *Br.*, cancel, *US*) a mortgage, to enter satisfaction; **Konto ~** to close an account; **Ladung ~** to discharge (land) a cargo, to unload; **Patent ~** to cancel a patent; **im Register ~** to strike off (remove from) the register, to deregister; **Satz von der Tafel ~** to wipe a sentence off the blackboard; **Schiff ~** to unload a ship; **Schiff muß schwimmend ~** discharge afloat; **teilweise ~** to lighten; **Warenzeichen im Register ~** to cancel a trademark registration;
zu ~ anfangen to break bulk; **Posten im Buch ~ lassen** to strike out (extinguish) entries.
Löscher blotter, *(Entlader)* unloader, discharger, docker, shop deliverer.
Lösch|erlaubnis discharging (landing) permit; **~fahrzeug** fire truck (-fighting vehicle); **~flugzeug** airborne fire-fighter; **~geld** unloading charges, wharfage; **~hafen** port of discharge; **~kommando** unloading party, *(Feuerwehr)* fire-brigade detachment; **~kosten** unloading charges, charges for unloading, wharfage, discharging expenses (fees), landing rates; **~mannschaft** *(Feuerwehr)* fire brigade (company, *US*); **~papier** blotting paper; **~papier zwischen Papierbögen legen** to insert blotting paper between the sheets; **~platz** port of discharge, discharging port (berth, place), *(Schiff)* unloading berth, wharf, pier, destination; **amtlich genehmigte ~plätze zollpflichtiger Waren** approved wharfs *(Br.)*; **~quantum** rate of delivery; **~risiko** unloading risk; **~schein** landing certificate; **~tage** laying days; **~taste** erasure key; **~- und Korrekturtaste** *(Computer)* clear entry key.
Löschung *(Auflösung einer Firma)* extinguishment, liquidation, *(Ausstreichung)* effacement, deletion, cancellation, *(Entladen)* discharge, unloading, landing, unshipping, debarkation, *(im Grundbuch)* cancellation, satisfaction *(Br.)*, release *(US)*;
franko ~ landed terms;
~ einer Belastung registration of satisfaction; **~ einer Buchschuld** extinguishment of a book account; **~ einer Dienstbarkeit** release of an easement; **~ eines Eintrags (einer Eintragung)** cancellation of an entry, vacation of an entry of record; **~ einer Firma im Handelsregister** cancellation (extinction) of a firm in the register of business names, removing a firm off the books; **~ einer Grundstücksbelastung** discharging an encumbrance; **~ im Handelsregister** removal from the register, deregistration; **~ einer Hypothek** satisfaction of a mortgage *(Br.)*; **~ eines Kontos** closing of an account; **~ durch Leichter** lighterage; **~ in der Warenzeichenrolle** cancellation of trademark registrations, removal of a trademark from the register;
~ beantragen *(Warenzeichen)* to apply for cancellation; **~ einer Hypothek im Grundbuch eintragen lassen** to enter satisfaction *(Br.)*.
Löschungs|anrecht cancellation privilege; **~antrag** *(Grundbuchrecht)* memorandum of satisfaction *(Br.)*, *(Patentrecht)* application for revocation; **~anzeige** notice of cancellation; **~bescheinigung** *(Waren)* landing certificate; **~bewilligung** *(Grundbuchrecht)* satisfaction (release, *US*) of mortgage; **~buch** landing book.
löschungsfähige Quittung *(Grundbuch)* deed of release, satisfaction piece *(US)*, memorandum of satisfaction *(Br.)*.
Löschungs|gebühren unloading (landing) charges, discharging fees, lastage rates, *(Leichter)* lighterage; **~geld** wharfage; **~hafen** unloading port, port of discharge (delivery), discharging port, place of transmission; **~ort, ~platz** unloading berth, port (place) of discharge, port of delivery; **~tage** lay days; **~verfahren** *(Warenzeichen)* cancellation proceedings *(US)*; **~vermerk** cancellation note, *(Grundbuch)* entry of satisfaction; **besondere ~zustimmung** *(Hypothek)* express release.
Lösch|zeit time for unloading, *(Liegezeit)* lay days; **~zug** fire brigade, engine company *(US)*.
lose loose, unpacked, in bulk, *(hemmungslos)* unbridled, *(Öl)* naked;
~ oder verpackt loose or in packages;
~ oder verpackt kaufen to buy bulk or packed goods;
~ Beilage loose insert; **~ Blätter** loose leaves; **in ~r Folge** sporadically; **~ verladene Güter** bulk goods; **~ Hand haben** to be quick with a slap; **~ Ladung** shifting cargo; **~s Mädchen** loose woman; **~es Mundwerk haben** to have a loose tongue; **~ Reden führen** to indulge in loose talk; **~r Streich** mischievous prank; **~ Verbindung** loose combination; **~r Vogel** *(fig.)* gay blade; **~ Waren** loose goods; **~ Zunge** loose tongue; **seine ~ Zunge zügeln** to bridle one's tongue; **~r Zusammenhang** slight link.
Loseblatt|ablage loose-leaf filing system; **~buch** loose-leaf book (notebook, binder); **~buchführung** loose-leaf ledger (accounts), worksheet accounts *(US)*; **~form** loose-leaf form; **~konto** loose-leaf account (notebook); **~methode** loose-leaf form; **~sammelmappe** loose-leaf binder; **~system** loose-leaf system; **~werk** loose-leaf edition.
Lösegeld ransom [money];
entsprechendes ~ equivalent ransom;
hohes ~ für j. bezahlen to pay a high ransom for s. o.; **~ von jem. erpressen** to exact a ransom from s. o.; **j. bis zur Zahlung eines ~es festhalten** to hold s. o. to ransom; **tragbares ~ fordern** to demand a moderate ransom; **gegen ein ~ freilassen** to release for a ransom; **~ verlangen** to ransom;
~forderung ransom demand; **~verpflichtung** ransom bill (bond).
loseisen to get off, *(vom Eis)* to free from the ice;
sich ~ *(Schiff)* to clear o. s. of the ice; **j. von der Bar ~** to prize s. o. away from the bar; **j. aus dem Gefängnis ~** to bail s. o. out of prison; **Geld von jem. ~** to worm money out of s. o., to extract money from s. o.
losen to cast (draw) lots, *(mit Münzen)* to toss;
mit Strohhälmchen ~ to draw straws.
Lösen|einer Fahrkarte purchase of a ticket; **~ des Fallschirms** pull-off (release) of a parachute.
lösen to loosen, to unloose;
sich ~ *(behoben werden)* to be solved (settled), *(Buchseiten)* to get loose, to start, *(Dachziegel)* to come loose, *(entwirren)* to solve, to disentangle, to unravel, *(Tapete)* to come off; **Aufgabe ~** to perform a task; **alte Bande ~** to sever old ties; **Bann ~** to break the tension; **Boot von der Boje ~** to slip the buoy; **Boot von der Vertäuung ~** to untie a boat from the mooring; **Briefmarke vom Umschlag ~** to detach (remove) a stamp from the envelope; **Ehe ~** to dissolve (annul) a marriage; **Fahrkarte**

~ to take (buy) a ticket; **Fahrkarte nach A** ~ to book for A; **Fahrkarte im voraus (Vorverkauf)** ~ to book a ticket in advance; **Fallschirm** ~ to pull off (release) a parachute; **Fesseln** ~ to free from chains; **Frage** ~ to solve a problem; **gedanklich** ~ to brainstorm *(US)*; **sich aus einem Geleitzug** ~ to detach itself from a convoy; **Handbremse** ~ to release the handbrake; **Karte im Vorverkauf** ~ to book a seat; **Knoten im Drama** ~ to unravel the plot of a play; **Kreuzworträtsel** ~ to solve a crossword puzzle; **Mathematikaufgabe** ~ to solve a mathematical problem; **Pfund vom Dollarkurs** ~ to unhook the pound from the dollar; **Platzkarte** ~ to reserve a seat; **Positionen** ~ to lighten commitments; **Schraube** ~ to loosen a screw; **sich von der gewohnten Umgebung** ~ to break away from familiar surroundings; **sich von Umwelteinflüssen** ~ to get away from one's environment; **Verbindung** ~ to discontinue a connection; **Verlobung** ~ to break off an engagement; **sich von seinen Verpflichtungen** ~ to withdraw from one's commitments, to free o. s. from obligations, to disengage o. s.; **Vertrag** ~ to terminate (rescind, set aside) a contract; **sich von Vorurteilen** ~ to outgrow a prejudice; **jem. die Zunge** ~ to loosen s. one's tongue;

sich nicht ~ **lassen** to defy solution.

losfahren to start, to depart, to leave, to drive (set) off;

direkt auf einen Baum ~ to be heading straight for a tree; **zornig auf j.** ~ to let fly at s. o.

losgehen *(Bombe)* to explode, to detonate, *(Gewehr)* to go off, *(Knopf)* to come off, *(Vorstellung)* to start, to begin;

mit Energie auf seine Arbeit ~ to tackle a piece of work; **nach hinten** ~ *(fig.)* to backfire; **auf den Kern eines Problems** ~ to go to the heart of a matter; **mit einem Messer auf j.** ~ to go for s. o. with a knife; **schnurstracks auf etw.** ~ to make a bee line for s. th.; **wieder** ~ *(Streit)* to flare up again; **unbeirrt auf sein Ziel** ~ to pursue one's goal unhesitatingly.

losgelöst isolated, separate;

Thema ~ **von einem anderen behandeln** to deal with a subject without reference to another.

Los|gemeinschaft betting society; ~**gewinner** prize winner.

losgondeln to push off.

Los|größe, wirtschaftliche standard quantity run, economic lot size; ~**kauf** buying off, redemption.

loskaufen to ransom, to buy off, to redeem;

j. ~ to pay ransom for s. o.; **sich** ~ to buy o. s. out; **sich von seinen Verpflichtungen** ~ to buy one's way out of obligations.

loskommen to get free (away);

vom Boden nicht ~ not to get off the ground; **einen Tag vom Büro** ~ to get away from the office for a day; **frühzeitig von einem Empfang** ~ to get away early from a reception; **von einer Erinnerung nicht** ~ to be imprinted on one's memory; **von seinen Schulden** ~ to get out of debt; **von einem Vorurteil** ~ to outgrow a prejudice;

von einem Gedanken nicht ~ **können** not to be able to get an idea out of one's mind.

los|koppeln, Hund to unleash a dog, to let a dog loose; ~**kriegen** to get off, to pry loose.

loslassen to let go (loose);

j. auf die Allgemeinheit ~ to let s. o. loose on the public; **wütenden Brief** ~ to dash off an angry letter; **Flut von Verwünschungen** ~ to let loose a torrent of abuse; **Hund auf einen Dieb** ~ to set the dog on a thief; **Hunde auf einen Flüchtling** ~ to turn the dogs on a fugitive; **Hund von einer Kette** ~ to unchain a dog; **jede Menge von Flüchen** ~ to let fly a volley of oaths; **Rede** ~ to run (rattle) off a speech; **Witz** ~ to crack a joke.

loslegen to wire away *(coll.)*, *(schnell fahren)* to step on the gas;

mit der Arbeit ~ to start working, to get cracking; **sofort mit seinen Beschimpfungen** ~ to blaze away with insults; **gleich mit seinen Fragen** ~ to fire off (shoot, *US*) one's questions at s. o.; **sofort** ~ to buckle down to work.

Loslösung separation, detachment;

~ **des Pfundes vom Dollar** unhooking the pound from the dollar.

Loslösungsbestrebungen separatism.

losmachen, Boot to unmoor (loose) a ship; **Hund** ~ to unchain a dog; **Kabel** ~ to detach a cable; **Schlüssel von einem Schlüsselbund** ~ to detach a key from a keyring; **sich von Verpflichtungen** ~ to free o. s. from obligations, to disengage o. s.

losmarschieren, auf die Tür to make a bee line for the door.

Losnummer ticket (lottery, lot) number.

los|platzen to be bursting with laughter; **damit** ~**platzen** to blurt it out; **sich** ~**reißen** to tear o. s. away, to break adrift.

lossagen, sich to dissociate (secede) o. s. from, to break with s. o.;

sich von seinen Freunden ~ to dissociate o. s. from one's friends; **sich von seinem Glauben** ~ to renounce one's faith; **sich von einem Kind** ~ to disown a child; **sich von der kommunistischen Partei** ~ to break with the communist party.

Lossagung dissociation, renunciation, disavowal.

losschießen *(fig.)* to plunge;

auf j. ~ to rush at s. o.

losschlagen *(angreifen)* to attack, to strike, *(Waren)* to push (make, put) off, to dispose of, to make a market of, to sell;

auf j. ~ to be hitting s. o., to let fly at s. o.; **Bücher billig** ~ to knock books; **seine alte Kollektion** ~ to sell off one's last year's range.

lossprechen, Lehrling to release an apprentice from his indenture; **j. von einer Verpflichtung** ~ to release (absolve) s. o. from an obligation.

lossteuern to head (steer) for, to make straight for;

sofort auf den Hauptpunkt ~ to come straight to the main point; **sofort auf die nächste Kneipe** ~ to make a bee line for the nearest pub; **auf den Konkurs** ~ to steer near receivership, to drift towards (head for) bankruptcy; **auf einen Krieg** ~ to be on the brink of a war; **auf den Leuchtturm** ~ to head for the lighthouse.

los|stürmen, auf j. to dart (bolt) at s. o.; **auf billige Artikel** ~**stürzen** to rush for cheap goods.

Los|trennungsbewegung separatism; ~**trommel** lottery wheel (drum).

Losung *(mil.)* pass word, watchword, *(Parteipolitik)* slogan.

Lösung solution, key, *(Entwirrung)* disentanglement;

antiinflationistische ~ noninflationary settlement; **ausgehandelte** ~ negotiated settlement; **brauchbare** ~ workable solution; **verfassungsmäßig durchführbare** ~ constitutional solution; **friedliche** ~ peaceable (peaceful) solution; **gesamteuropäische** ~ [over]all (all-out) European solution; **grafische** ~ graphical solution; **richtige** ~ *(Preisausschreiben)* winning entry;

~ **durch Differentiation** marginal approach; ~ **einer Ehe** dissolution (annulment) of a marriage; ~ **des Knotens** unravelment of the plot, denouement; ~ **eines Kreuzworträtsels** solution of a crossword puzzle; **friedliche** ~ **des Ost-West-Problems** peaceful solution to the East-West problem; ~ **eines Rätsels** answer to a mystery; ~ **eines Vertrages** termination (rescission) of a contract; ~ **des Wohnungsproblems** housing solution;

hart an der ~ **eines Problems arbeiten** to hammer away at a problem; **leichte** ~**en erreichen** to achieve the facile; ~ **finden** to hit upon a solution; ~ **eines Rätsels finden** to puzzle out; **sich an die** ~ **eines Problems machen** to set one's wits to; ~ **eines Rätsels wissen** to have the key of a riddle.

Lösungs|hilfe clue; ~**vorschlag** settlement proposal.

Losungswort *(mil.)* parole, countersign.

Losvertrieb lottery sale.

loswerden to dispose (get rid) of;

etw. ~ to get clear of s. th.; **j.** ~ to get shot of s. o. *(fam.)*; **Angestellten** ~ to get rid of an employee; **schlechte Angewohnheit** ~ to overcome a bad habit; **unerwünschten Besuch** ~ to get rid of an unwelcome visitor; **sein Geld** ~ to get rid of one's money; **in einem Geschäft sein ganzes Geld** ~ to spend all one's money in a shop; **eine Sache** ~ to get s. th. off one's hands; **j. schnell** ~ to send s. o. about his business; **seine Schulden** ~ to get out of debt; **im Spielkasino seine gesamten Ersparnisse** ~ to part with all one's savings at the casino; **Vermögen am Spieltisch** ~ to spend an estate in gaming; **Verpflichtung** ~ to get off a duty.

losziehen to set out, to start;

gegen etw. ~ to preach down s. th.; **über j.** ~ to run s. o. down, to pull s. o. to pieces.

Losziehung lottery drawing.

Lot plumb, lead;

aus dem ~ out of plumb; **nicht im** ~ out of square;

mit dem ~ **auftreffen** to strike ground; **Sache wieder ins** ~ **bringen** to set things right again, to wipe off a score; **Wassertiefe mit einem** ~ **messen** to fathom the depth of water; **wieder im** ~ **sein** to be back to normal again; **im** ~ **stehen** to be vertical.

Lötapparat soldering (brazing) outfit.

Lotblei plummet.

Lötdraht wire solder.

loten to cast (heave) the lead, to lead, to fathom, to plumb, to sound, to take the soundings.

löten to solder, to braze.

Lötlampe torch lamp.
Lotleine plumb (sounding, lead) line.
lotrecht plumb, vertical, perpendicular, normal;
nicht ~ out of plumb;
fast ~ **starten** to take off almost vertically.
Lotse pilot;
amtlich angestellter ~ branch pilot; **seeamtlich befähigter** ~ licensed pilot;
~n aussetzen (von Bord gehen lassen) to drop a pilot; **~n an Bord nehmen** to get (take) a pilot on board.
Lotsen piloting, pilotage.
lotsen to pilot, *(Auto)* to guide;
j. ins Kino ~ to drag s. o. off to a cinema; **Schiff durch den Kanal** ~ to pilot a ship through a canal (channel); **j. durch eine Stadt** ~ to guide s. o. through a town.
Lotsen|amt pilot office, pilotage; **~behörde** pilotage authority; **~bereich** pilotage district; **~boot** pilot boat (craft, cutter); **~büro** pilotage, pilot's office; **~dienst** pilot service; **~dienst an der Küste** coastal pilotage; **~fahrwasser** pilotage waters; **~fahrzeug** pilot vessel (ship); **~flagge** pilot flag (jack); **~flugzeug** *(mil.)* pathfinder; **~freiheit** free pilotage; **~gebühr** pilotage, pilotage dues; **~gebühr beim Auslaufen (Einlaufen)** pilotage outward (inward); **~geld** pilotage, lodemanage; **~gewerbe** pilot's profession; **~inspekteur** master pilot; **~kommandeur** captain of pilots, commodore; **~patent** certificate of pilot; **~prüfung abnehmen** to license a pilot; **~revier** pilotage waters; **~schein** pilot's licence; **~station** pilot station; **~strecke** pilotage waters; **~streik** pilot strike; **~zwang** compulsory pilotage.
Lotterbube debauchee, loafer, rake.
Lotterie lottery, drawing of prizes;
nicht genehmigte ~ illegal lottery;
in der ~ **gewinnen** to draw a prize in a lottery; **in der** ~ **setzen** to put in the lottery; **in der** ~ **spielen** to take lottery tickets (part in a lottery);
~anleihe lottery loan (bond); **~einnahme** lottery office; **~einnehmer** lottery agent; **~gewinn** [lottery] prize, winning ticket; **~gewinn machen (ziehen)** to draw a prize in a lottery (prize-winning ticket); **~glücksspiel** policy *(US)*; **~klasse** class; **~los** [lottery] ticket; **~losnummer** ticket number; **auf eine besondere ~losnummer setzen** to ensure a number in a lottery; **~plan** scheme of lottery; **~spiel** lottery gambling, *(Glückssache)* lottery; **~steuer** lottery tax; **~zettel** [lottery] ticket; **~ziehung** drawing lots (of prizes), lottery.
Lotter|leben dissolute (dissipated) life; **~wirtschaft** *(Betrieb)* mess, muddle, *(Haushalt)* sloppy household.
Lotto lotto, policy *(US)*, pools, number lottery, numbers game;
~ **spielen** to play at lotto (policy, *US*);
~annahmestelle policy shop *(US)*; **~gesetz** Pool Betting Act; **~schein** policy slip (ticket) *(US)*; **~spielen** policy playing *(US)*; **~spieler** lotto player; **~verkäufer** pool seller.
Lotungen vornehmen to take soundings.
Lötwerkzeug soldering tool.
Löwe, seinen Kopf in den Rachen des ~n stecken to put one's head into the lion's mouth; **sich in die Höhle des ~n wagen** to beard the lion in his den; **schlafenden ~n wecken** to rouse the sleeping lion.
Löwenanteil lion's share.
loyal loyal, allegiant.
Loyalität loyalty;
unerschütterliche ~ unswerving loyalty.
Loyalitäts|eid loyalty oath *(US)*, oath of allegiance; **~erklärung** profession of loyalty; **~erklärung vortäuschen** to profess loyalty; **~programm** loyalty program *(US)*.
Luchs, wie ein ~ **aufpassen** to have eyes like a hawk; **Ohren wie ein** ~ **haben** to have sharp ears;
~augen haben to have eyes like a hawk.
Lücke gap, break, hiatus, opening, *(Bedürfnis)* want, need, *(auf Formular)* void space, blank, *(Kassenbestand)* deficiency, deficit, *(Kreuzworträtsel)* empty space, *(Leere)* void, vacuum, *(mil.)* breach, break, *(Spalte)* fissure, crack, chink;
spürbare ~ noticeable gap; **technologische** ~ technological gap; **zu weite** ~ *(drucktechn.)* pigeonhole, rathole;
~ **in der Beweisführung** gap in an argument; **~n in Doppelbesteuerungsabkommen** double taxation loopholes; **große** ~ **zwischen zwei Gehältern** big difference between two salaries; ~ **im Gesetz** loophole in the law; ~ **in einer Hecke** opening in a hedge; **~n in einem Lattenzaun** chinks between the planks; ~ **in der Verteidigung** *(mil.)* breach in the defence;
große ~n aufweisen *(Buch)* to be mere patchwork; **~n ausfüllen** to fill a gap (the void), *(Formular)* to fill out (in) blank spaces, *(Person)* to step into the breach; ~ **im Gesetz finden** to find a loophole in the law; **fühlbare** ~ **füllen** to fill a crying need; **erhebliche ~n haben** *(Schüler)* to be remarkably ignorant; ~ **in der Kohlenversorgung hervorrufen** to give rise to a shortage in the supply of coal; **spürbare** ~ **in der Familie hinterlassen** to leap a gap in the family circle; ~ **in der Versorgung entstehen lassen** to give rise to a deficiency in the supply; **~n im Markt ausfindig machen** to find gaps in the market; ~ **schaffen** to cause a vacancy; ~ **schließen** to stop (supply, close) a gap; **fühlbare** ~ **schließen** to satisfy a long-felt want; **~n in seiner Bildung schließen** to fill in the gaps in one's education; **durch eine** ~ **im Gesetz schlüpfen** to find a loophole in the law.
Lückenbüßer stopgap, makeshift, makeweight, fill-up, stuffing, *(Anzeige)* stopgap advertisement, filler, *(Füllsel)* filler, *(Theater)* stand-in, *(Zeitung)* filler, balaam *(Br., sl.)*;
als ~ **dienen** to act as stand-in.
lückenhaft sketchy, incomplete;
~ **sein** to be patchy;
~er Bericht fragmentary report; **~er Beweis** incomplete evidence; **~e Kenntnisse** fragmentary (patchy, sketchy) knowledge.
Lückenhaftigkeit incompleteness, fragmentariness.
lückenlos without gaps (holes), complete, *(Beweis)* airtight;
sich ~ **aneinanderreihen** to form an unbroken line;
~es Alibi perfect alibi; **~er Beweis** complete evidence, airtight case; **~e Beweiskette** complete chain of evidence; **~er Lebenslauf** comprehensive career details; **~e Verkaufsanstrengungen** complete chain of sales efforts.
Luder carcass, *(Gauner)* blackguard, scoundrel, rascal, *(gemeines Weib)* hussy;
armes ~ poor devil (creature); **dummes** ~ silly ass; **feines** ~ fop; **gemeines** ~ old bitch; **kleines** ~ little so-and-so.
Luft air, *(Himmel)* sky, air, *(Spielraum)* clearance, free play, latitude, swing;
aus der ~ **gegriffen** unsubstantiated, out of the whole cloth *(US)*; **aus der** ~ **herangeführt** *(Truppen)* airlifted; **durch die** ~ airborne; **schwerer als** ~ heavier-than-air;
dicke ~ *(fig.)* tense atmosphere; **vor Hitze flimmernde** ~ air shimmering with heat; **frische** ~ crisp (fresh) air; **herrliche** ~ delicate air; **komprimierte** ~ compressed air; **milde** ~ mild air; **saubere** ~ clean air; **schlechte** ~ foul (corrupt) air, fug *(Br., coll.)*; **unsaubere** ~ impure (vitiated, vicious) air; **verbrauchte** ~ stale (puzzled) air; **verpestete** ~ tainted (vitiated, polluted) air;
~ **zwischen Achse und Lager** space between axle and bearing;
~ **aus den Reifen ablassen** to let the air out of the tyres, to deflate the tyres *(Br.)* (tires, *US*); ~ **anhalten** to hold one's breath; **sich in** ~ **auflösen** to vanish into thin air, *(Pläne)* to go down the drain, to come to nothing; **j. an die frische** ~ **befördern** to chuck s. o. out, to give s. o. the air *(US sl.)*; **j. wie** ~ **behandeln** not to give s. o. even a tumble, to ignore s. o. completely; **den festgelegten Werten für saubere** ~ **entsprechen** to meet the standards for clean air; **sich in die** ~ **erheben** *(Flugzeug)* to take off; **in die** ~ **fliegen** to blow up; **gleich in die** ~ **gehen** *(fig.)* to fly off the handle, to hit the ceiling; **frische** ~ **schöpfen gehen** to go out for some fresh air (a blow); **etw.** ~ **haben** to have a breather (a minute to spare); **in seinem Koffer noch** ~ **haben** to have still some room in one's suitcase; **völlig in der** ~ **hängen** *(Beweisführung)* to be totally unfounded; **noch völlig in der** ~ **hängen** to be still up in the air; **in der** ~ **herumfuchteln** to wave one's hands about; **in die** ~ **jagen** to dynamite; **Motor mit** ~ **kühlen** to air-cool an engine; **jem.** ~ **lassen** to give s. o. plenty of rope; ~ **nachsehen lassen** to have the air checked; **in der** ~ **liegen** *(Gerücht)* to be in the air (wind), *(Streit)* to be brewing; **seiner Entrüstung über j.** ~ **machen** to raise an outcry against s. o.; **seinen Gefühlen** ~ **machen** to find an outlet for one's emotions; **seinem Herzen** ~ **machen** to blow (let) off steam, to pour out one's trouble; **seiner Wut (seinem Zorn)** ~ **machen** to give vent to one's anger; **in die** ~ **reden** to talk to no purpose; **etw.** ~ **schaffen** to make some room; **frische** ~ **schöpfen** to take an airing (the air); **Schlag in die** ~ **sein** to be wide of the mark; **aus der** ~ **gegriffen sein** to be unfounded, to have no foundation; **völlig aus der** ~ **gegriffen sein** to be sheer invention; **an die** ~ **setzen** to sack *(coll.)*, to fire *(coll.)*, to chuck out, to bounce *(US coll.)*; **Brücke in die** ~ **sprengen** to blow up a bridge; **Löcher in die** ~ **starren** to stand there gaping; ~ **verpesten** to make the air foul, to pollute (infect, vitiate) the air; **Truppen aus der** ~ **versorgen** to airlift supplies to troops; **an die** ~ **gesetzt werden** to get the sack, to be fired; **j. in der** ~ **zerreißen** to tear s. o. limb from limb;
warte, bis die ~ **rein ist** wait until the coast is clear; **ich könnte mich in der** ~ **zerreißen** I could kick myself;

~**abkommen** air pact; ~**abwehr** antiaircraft (aerial) defence; ~**abwehrrakete** antiaircraft rocket; ~**abzug** air drain (vent); ~**akrobatik** stunt flying, aerial stunts; ~**angriff** airraid, air (aerial) attack, strike; **heftiger** ~**angriff** blitz; ~**angriff mit Brandbomben** fire blitz; ~**ansaugstutzen** *(Auto)* intake manifold; ~**ansicht** aerial view (survey); ~**aufbereitung** air conditioning; ~**aufnahme** aerial photo; ~**aufsicht** air-traffic control; ~**ballon** balloon, lighter-than-aircraft, *(lenkbar)* dirigible; ~**beförderung** carriage by air, air carriage (transport), transportation by air; **generelle** ~**beförderung nach Europa** *(Post)* all-up service *(Br.)*; ~**beförderungsvertrag** air-transport contract; ~**behälter** air vessel (tank), cylinder; ~**beobachtung** aerial observation; ~**bereifung** pneumatic tyres; ~**betankung** flight refuelling; **schwache** ~**bewegung** light wind.

Luftbild aerial (air) photo, *(Täuschung, Luftspiegelung)* mirage; ~**aufklärung** air reconnaissance; ~**aufnahmen** air photography, aerial survey; ~**gerät**, ~**kamera** aerial camera; ~**karte** aerial map, photo map; ~**vermessung** mapmaking from aerial photos, photogrammetry; ~**wesen** aerial photography.

Luft|blase air bubble, *(Metall)* blister; ~**-Boden-Flugkörper** air-to-air surface missile; ~**bombardement** aerial bombardment; ~**brücke** airlift, sky lift; **über eine** ~**brücke transportieren** to airlift [in]; ~**bus** airbus, air coach *(US)*.

Luftcharter|geschäft air chartering; ~**gesellschaft** air charter; ~**vertrag** aircraft charter agreement.

Lüftchen gentle breeze.

luftdicht airtight, airproof;
~ **verpackt** packed in an airtight container; ~ **verschlossen** hermetically sealed;
~ **abgeschlossene Tür** airtight door.

Luftdichte atmospheric density.

Luftdruck air (atmospheric) pressure, *(Reifen)* inflation pressure; ~**abnahme** decrease of pressure; ~**bremse** air brake, air pressure brake; ~**kabine** pressure cabin; ~**karte** pressure map; ~**krankheit** the bends *(fam.)*; ~**messer** barometer; ~**schreiber** barograph; ~**schwankungen** pressure variations; ~**verminderung** decompression; ~**welle** blast.

luftdurchlässig permeable to air, porous.

Luft|düse air nozzle; ~**eilfrachttarif** air express rates *(US)*; ~**eilgut** air express *(US)*.

lüften to ventilate, to clear the air, to wind, *(leicht anheben)* to raise, to lift;
vor jem. den Hut ~ to raise one's hat to s. o.; **seine Maske** ~ to reveal one's identity; **Matratzen** ~ to air the mattresses; **Schleier** ~ to lift the veil, to disclose a secret; **Vorhang** ~ to raise the curtain.

Luft|entfernung airline distance; ~**entstaubungsanlage** cyclone dust collector.

Lüfter exhaust fan, ventilator.

Luft|erhitzer air heater; ~**erscheinung** meteorological phenomenon, *(Trugbild)* phantasmagoria; ~**expressfracht** air express rate *(US)*.

Luftfahrt aviation, aerial (air) navigation, aeronautics;
zivile ~ commercial aviation;
~**abkommen** civil aviation agreement, air pact; ~**ausrüstung** aviation supply; ~**ausstellung** air show.

luftfahrtbegeistert air-minded.

Luftfahrt|behörde aviation administration, *(Bundesbehörde)* Civil Aeronautics Administration *(US)*; ~**einrichtungen** aviation facilities; ~**forschung** research in aviation, aeronautical research; ~**gesellschaft** airline (airways) company (corporation); ~**gesellschaft mit festem Fahrplan** scheduled airline *(US)*; ~**industrie** aircraft industry; ~**magazin** aviation magazine; ~**minister** Minister of Air, Minister of Aviation Supply *(Br.)*, Secretary of State for Air *(Br.)* (of the Air Force, *US*); ~**ministerium** Ministry of Aviation, Air Ministry *(Br.)*, Federal Aviation Agency *(US)*; ~**organisation** aviation [organization]; ~**politik** air policy; ~**schau** aircraft display; ~**verband** aviation organization; ~**versicherung** aviation (aircraft) insurance; ~**versicherungsgesellschaft** aviation underwriter; ~**wege** air lanes (routes).

Luftfahrzeug air vessel, aircraft;
~**führer** pilot; ~**gesetz** Civil Aviation Act *(Br.)*; ~**halter** aircraft licence holder; ~**rolle** aircraft register.

Luft|federung pneumatic cushioning; ~**feuchtigkeit** atmospheric humidity, humidity of the air; ~**feuchtigkeitsgrad** degree of humidity; **selbstregistrierender** ~**feuchtigkeitsmesser** hydrograph; ~**filter** air cleaner (filter); ~**flotte** air fleet (force), *(stark)* armada; ~**flottenmanöver** air-force manoeuvre.

Luftfracht freight by air, airfreight, air cargo;
in Leerzeiten beförderte ~ deferred airfreight;
~ **zum Vorzugstarif** commodity rate;
per ~ **transportieren** to fly out; **per** ~ **versenden** to ship by air, to forward goods by airfreight;
~**anlagen** air-cargo equipment; ~**bahnhof** air-cargo (airfreight) terminus; ~**begleitschein** air consignment note *(Br.)*; ~**benutzer** airfreight user; ~**börse** airfreight exchange; ~**brief** airbill *(US)*, airway bill, air consignment note; ~**briefnummer** airbill number *(US)*; ~**dienst** airfreight service; ~**einrichtungen** airfreight facility.

Luftfrachter airfreighter.

Luftfracht|flugzeug airfreighter; ~**führer** air carrier; ~**gebühr** airway bill fee; ~**geschäft** airfreight forwarding, air-cargo business; ~**gewerbe** air-cargo business, airfreight forwarding; ~**kosten** airfreight expenses; ~**makler** air broker; ~**markt** air-cargo market; ~**rate** air-cargo rate; **ermäßigte** ~**rate** commodity rate; ~**sendung** air shipment; ~**spediteur** air-freight (air) forwarder, common carrier by air, air-cargo carrier; ~**spedition** airfreight forwarding; ~**tarif** air-cargo rates, airfreight rates; ~**unternehmen** air-freight outfit, airfreighter; ~**verkehr** aircraft transport, air transport[ation].

Luftgebiet airspace.

luftgekühlt air-cooled.

Luft|gepäck airline bag; ~**geschwader** air squadron.

luftgestützt *(mil.)* air-based.

luftgetrocknet air-dried, *(Holz)* seasoned;
~**er Fisch** air-dried fish.

Luftgewehr air gun.

lufthaltig aeriferous.

Luft|handelsverkehr air commerce; ~**hauch** breath of air, gentle breeze; **kein** ~**hauch** no stir in the air; ~**herrschaft** air (aerial) supremacy; ~**höhe** air level; ~**hoheit** air sovereignty, sovereignty of the air; ~**hoheitsgebiet** territorial airspace; ~**hülle** *(Erde)* atmosphere.

luftig *(Kleidung, Raum)* airy, cool, light.

Luftikus happy-go-lucky fellow.

Luft|inspektion aerial inspection; **gegenseitige** ~**inspektion** open skies; ~**kabel** aerial (overhead) cable; ~**kabotage** cabotage; ~**kammer** air chamber.

Luftkampf aerial combat;
heftiger ~ dogfight;
~ **ausfechten** to wage a dogfight;
~**-Flugkörper** air-to-air missile.

Luft|kanal flue, air duct; ~**kaskoversicherung** aircraft hull insurance; ~**kissen** air cushion (pillow), cushion of air; ~**kissenfahrzeug** air-cushion vehicle, hovercraft, cushion rider; ~**klappe** air flap, *(Vergaser)* choke; ~**koffer** lightweight suitcase; ~**korridor** air lane (corridor).

luftkrank airsick.

Luft|krankheit airsickness; ~**krieg** aerial (air) war[fare]; ~**kühlung** air cooling; ~**kur** climatic treatment; ~**kurort** climatic (health) resort.

Luftlande|division airborne division; ~**kopf** airhead; ~**truppen** airborne (air, sky) troops, parachuters; ~**unternehmen** airborne (air-landed, *US*) operation.

Luftlandung airborne landing.

luftleer vacuous;
~**er Raum** *(Weltraum)* outer space; ~**en Raum schaffen** to create a vacuum; **Spaziergang im** ~**en Raum unternehmen** to walk in outer space.

Luft|linie airline, beeline, crowflight; **in der** ~**linie** as the crow flies, in a crow line; ~**linienentfernung** airline distance; ~**loch** air pocket (hole, gap), hole in the air, bump, *(Ofen)* venthole; ~**-~-Flugkörper** air-to-air missile; ~**macht** air power; ~**marschall** Air Marshal; **kalte** ~**massen** mass of cold air; ~**matratze** air mattress (bed, *Br.*); ~**meile** air mile; ~**menge** quantity of air; ~**mine** aerial (air-dropped, parachute) mine; ~**navigation** air navigation; ~**navigationskarte** aeronautical chart; ~**offensive** air offensive; ~**omnibus** airbus, air coach *(US)*; ~**omnibuspendelverkehr** air shuttle; ~**paketpost** air[mail] parcel post; ~**parade** fly past; ~**pendelbus** air shuttle; ~**perspektive** bird's-eye perspective (view); ~**pirat** aircraft hijacker, hi[gh]jacker; ~**piraterie** aerial (air) piracy, hi[gh]jacking; ~**pistole** air pistol; ~**polizei** air police; ~**polster** air bumper.

Luftpost airmail *(US)*, aerial (air) post *(Br.)*, air mail *(Br.)*;
mit (per) ~ by (per, via) airmail *(US)*, by air mail *(Br.)*, air-speeded;
per ~ **schicken** to transport mail (post) by aeroplane (airplane, *US*), to airmail *(US)*; **Brief per** ~ **schicken** to send a letter by air mail *(Br.)* (airmail, *US*);
~**aufkleber** airmail label *(US)*, air-mail label *(Br.)*; ~**auftrag** airmailing order *(US)*; ~**ausgabe** air (airmail, *US*) edition, air-

mail edition *(Br.)*; ~**beförderung** airspeeded service; ~**beförderung von Mikrofilmbriefen** airgraph; ~**bezugspreis** airmail rate *(US)*, air-mail rate *(Br.)*; ~**brief** airletter, airmail letter *(US)*, air-mail letter *(Br.)*; ~**brief aufgeben** to airmail a letter *(US)*; ~**dienst** airmail service, airmail system, air-mail service *(Br.)*; ~**drucksache** air-mail printed paper *(Br.)*, airmail printed paper *(US)*; ~**einlieferungsschein** airmail receipt *(US)*, air-mail receipt *(Br.)*; ~**empfangsbescheinigung** air consignment note; ~**format** air letter form; ~**gebühr** airmail *(US)* (air) fee, air-mail fee *(Br.)*; ~**gesellschaft** airmail *(US)* (air-mail, *Br.*) company; ~**kleber** airmail label, blue air-mail label *(Br.)*; ~**kuvert** airmail envelope *(US)*, air-mail envelope *(Br.)*; ~**leichtbrief** aerogram(me), air letter *(US)*; ~**linie** airmail line *(US)*; ~**marken** airmail stamps *(US)*, air-mail stamps *(Br.)*; ~**netz** airmail *(US)* (air-mail, *Br.*) network; ~**paket** airmail *(US)* (air-mail, *Br.*) parcel; **als ~paket verschickt werden** to be sent by the air-parcel service; ~**paketdienst** air-parcel service; ~**papier** onionskin; ~**porto** air-mail fee *(Br.)*, airmail fee *(US)*; ~**sendung** airmail *(US)* (air-mail, *Br.*) consignment; ~**streifen** airmail *(US)* (air-mail, *Br.*) label; ~**tarif** airmail rate *(US)*, air-mail rate *(Br.)*; ~**tarif für Drucksachen** air-mail printed-paper rate; ~**tarifzone** air-mail zone; ~**überweisung** airmail transfer; ~**umschlag** air-mail envelope *(Br.)*, airmail envelope *(US)*; ~**verkehr** airmail service *(US)*, air-mail service *(Br.)*; ~**zeitungsgut** newspaper sent by air, air mail newspaper, all-up newspapers; ~**zuschlag** air fee; **~- und Eilbotenzuschlag** air express; ~**zustellung** delivery by air.

Luftpumpe pneumatic (air) pump, *(Fahrrad)* bicycle pump.

Luftraum atmosphere, air space, *(Astronautik)* sky; ~**beherrschung** control of the air; ~**beobachter** *(mil.)* ground observer; ~**überwachung** air-traffic control; ~**verletzung** violation of one's airspace; ~**verteidigung** air defence; ~**verteidigungszone** air-defence identification zone.

Luft|- und Raumfahrtindustrie aerospace industry; **internationales ~recht** international air law; ~**reifen** pneumatic tyre (tire, *US*); ~**reinerhaltung** maintenance of unpolluted air; ~**reinigung** deodorization, air cleaning; ~**reinigungsanlage** air-purifying plant; ~**reise** journey by air, flight; ~**reiseverkehr** air tourism (travel); ~**reklame** skywriting, aerial (skyline) advertising; ~**rettungsdienst** air rescue service; ~**röhre** throttle; ~**rüstung** air armaments; ~**sack** wind sack, air pocket, *(Ballon)* air cell; ~**schacht** air well, ventilating (upcast, air) shaft, *(Bergbau)* air course; ~**schicht** atmospheric layer, stratum; **obere ~schichten** upper air.

Luftschiff airship, ship, vessel, dirigible, *(kleines)* blimp;
~ **in die Halle befördern** to walk an airship into the shed;
sich mit ~bau beschäftigen to do airship designs; ~**fahrt** aeronautics, aerial navigation, aerostation.

Luftschiffer aeronaut.

Luftschiff|gondel nacelle; ~**hafen** airship port; ~**halle** hangar.

Luft|schirm air umbrella; ~**schlacht** sky battle; ~**schlauch** air tube, *(Autoreifen)* inner tube; ~**schleppzug** air train; ~**schleuse** air lock; ~**schlitz** *(Motorhaube)* louvre; ~**schloß** castle in the air (Spain), daydream, air castle; ~**schlösser bauen** to build castles in the air; ~**schneise** air corridor (lane); ~**schraube** airscrew, propeller; ~**schraubenstrahl** wake; ~**schraubenturbinenwerk** turboprop (propjet) engine.

Luftschutz airraid protection (precaution), civil defense *(US)*, passive air defence;
~**alarm** airraid alarm; ~**behörde** Civil Defence Office *(US)*; ~**bund** Civil Air Guard *(Br.)*; ~**bunker** airraid shelter; **eigener ~keller** domestic shelter; ~**maßnahmen** airraid precaution measures; ~**organisation** Civil Defence Corps *(US)*; ~**sirene** airraid siren; ~**stollen** underground airraid shelter; ~**übung** airraid drill; ~**warndienst** airraid warning service; ~**wart** airraid warden, block captain, fire watcher *(Br.)*.

Luft|sicherheitsbehörde Civil Aeronautics Board *(US)*; ~**sicherung** air cover; ~**sieg** kill *(coll.)*; ~**sog** wake; ~**späher** air scout, observer; ~**spediteur** air carrier; ~**sperre** air barrage; ~**sperrgebiet** prohibited aerial space; ~**spiegelung** mirage, fata morgana; ~**sprung machen** to cut a caper, to jump for joy; ~**strahltriebwerk** jet engine; ~**straße**, ~**strecke** air route, airway; ~**streitkräfte** Air Force, combat aircraft, air arm *(Br.)*; ~**strom** airflow, wind; ~**strömung** air current; ~**strudel** wash; ~**stützpunkt** air base *(US)*; **~- und Flottenstützpunkt** air and naval facilities.

luft|tanken to refuel in the air (in flight); ~**tauglich**, ~**tüchtig** airworthy.

Luft|tauglichkeit, ~**tüchtigkeit** airworthiness; ~**tauglichkeitszeugnis** certificate of airworthiness; ~**taxi** air taxi, taxiplane; ~**torpedo** aerial torpedo (mine).

Lufttransport air transport[ation] (shipment, commerce, conveyance), movement by air, conveyance by aircraft;
~**e durchführen** to carry goods by air;
sich dem ~geschäft zuwenden to diversify into air travel; ~**gesellschaft** airline (air-cargo) carrier; ~**gesellschaft für Langstreckenflugzeuge** long-haul carrier; ~**spediteur** air carrier; ~**unternehmen** air transport undertaking; **planmäßig gewerblicher ~verkehr** commercially scheduled air transport *(US)*; ~**versicherung** air-transport insurance.

Luft|trocknung natural drying; ~**trübung** turbidity.

lufttüchtig airworthy.

Luft|turbulenz turbulence; ~**überlegenheit** air supremacy (superiority); ~**überwachung** aerial inspection; **gegenseitige ~überwachung** open skies; ~**überwachungszone** air-defence identification zone.

Lüftung ventilation, airing;
~ **eines Geheimnisses** revelation of a secret.

Lüftungs|anlage ventilator; ~**klappe** *(Auto)* ventilation flap; ~**schacht** ventilation shaft.

Luft|unterdruck air depression; ~**unterstützung für Erdkampftruppen** air support for ground troops; ~**veränderung** change of air; **jem. ~veränderung verordnen** to order s. o. a change of air; ~**verbindung** air connection (link); ~**verbindungsoffizier** air liaison officer; ~**verdrängung** air displacement.

luftverdünnt rarefied;
in ~em Raum in a partial vacuum.

Luftverkehr transport by air, air travel (service), air traffic;
flugplanmäßiger ~ scheduled *(US)* (regular, *Br.*) air service; **planmäßiger gewerblicher** ~ commercially scheduled air transport *(US)*; **nichtplanmäßiger** ~ nonscheduled air service *(US)*.

Luftverkehrs|abkommen air-transport convention (travel agreement); ~**anlagen** aviation facilities; ~**aufgabe** air-traffic job; ~**bestimmungen** air-traffic regulation, rules of the air; ~**betrieb** airline, air carrier; **[fahrplanmäßiger] ~dienst** [scheduled *(US)* (regular, *Br.*)] air service; ~**genehmigung** civil aviation permit, air carrier licence; ~**gesellschaft** airline (airways) company (corporation, *US*), aviation company, air-transport company, line; **im Inland fliegende ~gesellschaft** domestic carrier *(US)*; ~**gesellschaft der USA** US flag airline; ~**kontrolle** air-traffic control; ~**linie** airway, airline, *(Gesellschaft)* common carrier *(US)*; ~**netz** airline network; ~**ordnung** rules of the air; ~**strecke** airline; ~**tarif** airline rates; ~**unternehmen** airline company (corporation, *US*); ~**unternehmen betreiben** to operate an airline; ~**verbindungen** airline connections; ~**verhandlungen** air talks; ~**verwaltung** civil aviation board; ~**vorschriften** air-traffic rules (regulations); ~**weg** airline route, airway, skyway.

Luft|vermessung aerial survey; ~**verpestung**, ~**verschmutzung** vitiation (pollution) of the air, air pollution; ~**verschmutzer** air-pollution plant; ~**versicherung** air-risk (aviation) insurance; ~**versorgung** air feed, supply by air, airlift; ~**verteidigung** air defence; ~**verteidigungszone** air defence identification zone; ~**verunreinigung** air pollution, pollution of the air; ~**waffe** air force (arm), air corps *(US)*, Royal Air Force *(Br.)*.

Luftwaffen|amt air council *(Br.)*; ~**chef** air-force chief; ~**general** air chief marshal *(Br.)*; ~**gesetz** Air-Force Act *(Br.)*; ~**ministerium** Department of the Air Force *(US)*; ~**stützpunkt** air-force base, center base.

Luft|warndienst air-defence alert system, airraid warning service, *(Frühwarnung)* early-warning system; ~**warnung** airraid warning; ~**wechsel** change of air.

Luftweg air route, airway;
auf dem ~ by air; **auf dem ~ befördert** airshipped;
Waren auf dem ~ befördern to carry goods by air; **auf dem ~ versorgen** to airlift.

Luft|werbung skywriting, aerial advertising, publicity from the air; ~**widerstand** air resistance; ~**wirbel** air twirl (swirl, eddy), vortex, turbulence; ~**ziegel** air (ventilating) brick; ~**zirkulation** air circulation; ~**zufuhr** air supply, ventilation, passage of air; ~**zug** draught, current of air, wind; **frischer ~zug** whiff of fresh air; **kalter ~zug** cold current of air; ~**zwischenfall** air (aerial) incident.

Lug und Trug lies and deception;
sich mit ~ durchs Leben schlängeln to make a living by lying and imposture.

Lüge, faustdicke thundering lie, whacking great lie; **glatte** ~ downright lie; **grundlose** ~ gratuitous lie; **handgreifliche** ~ patent lie; **krasse** ~ whopper; **lauter ~n** parcel of lies, pack of lies; **plumpe** ~ plump lie; **unverschämte** ~ brazen lie; **vorsätzliche** ~ deliberate lie;

~ **beschönigen** to gild a lie; **j. der ~ bezichtigen** to call s. o. a liar; **j. ~n strafen** to confront s. o. with a lie, to give s. o. the lie; **~n haben kurze Beine** lies have short wings.
lügen to [tell] a lie, *(flunkern)* to tell fibs, to fabricate;
~, **daß sich die Balken biegen** to lie like a trooper, to lie like a gas-meter *(fam.)*; **wie gedruckt** ~ to lie like a book; **unverschämt** ~ to lie in one's throat; **jem. die Hucke voll** ~ to tell s. o. a pack of lies.
Lügen|bold habitual liar, fibber *(coll.)*; **~detektor** lie detector; **~geschichte** cock-and-bull story, string *(US sl.)*; **~geschichte erzählen** to spin a yarn; **~geschichte hundertprozentig glauben** to swallow it hook, line and sinker; **~gewebe** web of lies, tissue of lies, song and dance *(sl.)*; **~märchen** traveller's tale, tall story; **das reinste ~märchen** sheer invention; **~maul** bouncer.
Lügner liar, fabler, twister *(coll.)*;
bewußter ~ conscious liar; **gemeiner** ~ dirty (rotten) liar; **unverbesserlicher** ~ unmitigated liar; **vollendeter** ~ out-and-out liar;
geschickter ~ sein to be facile in inventing lies.
Luke scuttle, hatch, hatchway, port, manhole, door;
~n schließen to cover and secure the hatches.
Lukendeckel hatch cover.
lukrativ remunerative, lucrative, paying, profitable;
sehr ~ big-time *(sl.)*;
~ **sein** to be a lucrative business;
~e Anlage remunerative investment; **~es Geschäft** lucrative business (transaction); **~er Preis** remunerative price; **~es Unternehmen** paying concern.
lukullisch Lucullan, luxurious, sumptuous;
~e Genüsse mouth-watering delicacies; **~es Mahl** gourmet meal.
Lumbecken adhesive binding.
Lümmel lout, rude fellow, *(Lausbub)* rascal, ruffian.
lümmelhaft loutish, rude, ill-mannered.
lümmeln, sich to sprawl, to lounge, to slouch.
Lump rascal, rogue, backguard, scoundrel;
gemeiner ~ dirty swine;
sich wie ein ~ benehmen to behave like a swine.
Lumpen rags, rubbish;
in ~ gehüllt in rags (duds);
ständig in ~ herumlaufen to go in rags; ~ **sammeln** to pick rags, to totter *(Br.)*; **j. aus den ~ schütteln** to haul s. o. over the coals;
~ball tacky party, tramps' ball *(Br.)*; **~bündel** bundle of old rags; **~geld** paltry sum; **~gesindel** hoi polloi; **~handel** rag trade; **~händler** rag-and-bone man, dealer in rags, ragman, junkman; **~pack** rigraff, ragtag, dirty lot, blackguards; **~sack** ragbag; **~sammeln** totting; **~sammler** rubbish hunter, rag picker, rag-and-bone dealer, totter *(Br.)*, tatter *(Br., sl.)*, *(letzter Zug)* flying fornicator; **~sammlung** rag picking; **~wolf** shredding machine, shredder, devil.
lumpen lassen, sich nicht to come down handsomely, to do things in style.
Lumperei shabby (mean) trick, *(Kleinigkeit)* trifle.
lumpig shabby, tattered, ragged, *(kümmerlich)* miserable, wretched, petty, trifling;
~e fünf Minuten mere five minutes; **~e zwei Schillinge** paltry two shillings; **~es Trinkgeld** measly tip.
Lunge, eiserne iron lung;
~n der Großstadt lungs of a big city;
sich die ~ aus dem Hals schreien to shout at the top of one's voice.
Lunte fuse, slow match;
~ **ans Pulverfaß legen** to trigger off an explosion; ~ **riechen** to smell a rat, to cut one's eye *(sl.)*.
Lupe reading glass, magnifier;
unter die ~ nehmen to scrutinize closely.
lupenrein *(Diamant)* flawless;
nicht ganz ~es Geschäft somewhat fishy deal.
Lust inclination, notion, liking, desire, *(Begierde)* lust, appetite, *(Verlangen)* craving, longing;
~ **zum Kaufen** inclination to buy;
seine ~ befriedigen to gratify one's lust; **jem. große ~ bereiten** to give s. o. great pleasure; **seiner ~ frönen** to indulge one's desire; ~ **haben** to care to do, to feel in the mood; **nicht die geringste ~ haben** not to have the slightest desire; **zu nichts ~ haben** not to want to do anything; **keine besondere ~ dazu haben** not to be very keen on it; **keine ~ mehr haben** to be fed up with one's job; **keine ~ mehr zur Arbeit haben** not to feel like working any longer; **keine ~ zu einer Auseinandersetzung haben** to have no stomach for a fight; ~ **am schnellen Fahren haben** to get a kick out of driving fast; ~ **zum Leben haben** to enjoy life; ~ **auf etw. Süßes haben** to crave for a sweet; ~ **auf etw. zu trinken haben** to long for a drink; **nicht übel ~ haben, etw. zu tun** to have half a mind to do s. th.; **alle ~ an seinem Beruf verloren haben** to have lost all interest in one's profession; **jem. die ~ nehmen** to put s. o. off; **mit ~ und Liebe bei der Sache sein** to put one's heart and soul into a work.
Lustbarkeiten entertainment, amusement, diversion, gaieties;
öffentliche ~ public entertainments;
Höhepunkt der ~ sein to be the climax of the entertainment; **alle öffentlichen ~ verbieten** to put an embargo on all public rejoicings *(fam.)*.
Lustbarkeitssteuer entertainment (admission, *US*) tax;
~ **niederschlagen** to drop the admission tax *(US)*.
Lüster chandelier, lustre;
~klemme *(el.)* lustre terminal.
lüstern lascivious, lustful, lewd, *(begierig)* itching, craving;
j. ~ machen to whet s. one's appetite; **nach etw. ~ sein** to be greedy for s. th.
Lüsternheit lewdness, lustfulness, wantonness, greediness.
lustig merry, gay, jolly, jovial;
~ **und in Freuden leben** to live on the fat of the land; **sich über j. ~ machen** to poke fun at (make merry of) s. o.; **äußerst ~ sein** to be as merry as a lark (cricket);
~e Augen twinkling eyes; **~er Bursche** jolly good fellow; **~e Gesellschaft** merry party, queer lot; **in ~er Stimmung sein** to be in high spirits; ~ **gemusterte Stoffe** gaily patterned fabrics; **~er Streich** frolic, lark;
so ~ ist das auch nicht there's nothing funny about it.
Lüstling debauchee, lecher, voluptuary, sensualist.
lustlos listless, apathetic, *(Börse)* flat, dull, lifeless, sluggish, quiet, easy, slack, inactive, featureless, lackluster *(US)*, lacklustre *(Br.)*;
in erster Linie mangels Interesse ~ dull owing mainly to lack of support;
~ **essen** not to enjoy one's food; ~ **liegen** to be lifeless (laggards, *US*); ~ **schließen** *(Börse)* to leave off flat, to close on a dull note; ~ **sein** to be in a dull condition, to lack incentive, to have the blues; **völlig ~ sein** to be completely apathetic; ~ **spielen** to play half-heartedly;
~e Börse flat (inactive) market; **~en Tag hinter sich bringen** *(Börse)* to meander through a listless day; **~e Tendenz** dull tone; **~er Wochenanfang** quiet start to the week.
Lustlosigkeit flatness, dullness, inactivity, sluggishness, stagnancy, stagnation;
~ **der Börse** market inactivity;
~ **verursachen** to produce stagnancy.
Lustmord sex murder.
Lustspiel comedy;
musikalisches ~ musical comedy;
~dichter comic writer; **~film** film comedy.
Lutsch|bonbon, ~stange lollipop.
lutschen, Bonbon to suck a sweet *(Br.)* (candy).
Luv|küste weather shore; **~seite** windward, weather side.
luxuriös luxurious, extravagant, plush;
~ **eingerichtet sein** to have a luxuriously furnished house;
~es Leben führen to live (be rolling) in luxury, to have a high time, to plush *(sl.)*; **~e Lebensführung** sumptuous living.
Luxus luxury, profusion, extravagance;
durch ~ verdorben vitiated by luxury; **im ~ aufgewachsen** nursed in luxury; **vom ~ umgeben** surrounded by luxury, in the lap of luxury;
~ **seines neuen Lebens in allen Einzelheiten genießen** to luxuriate in one's new life; **sich ~ leisten können** to afford luxury; **im größten ~ leben** to wallow in luxury, to live in a lavish style; **im ~ schwelgen** to luxuriate in opulence;
~artikel luxury (fancy) goods, luxuries, fancy article(s), big-ticket items; **~ausführung** luxury (fancy) package, de-luxe model; **~ausgabe** *(Buch)* edition de luxe, extra binding; **als großformatige ~ausgabe** in coffee-table format; **~auto** luxury car; **~dampfer** luxury ocean liner; **~einband** rich binding; **~flugzeug** luxury liner; **~gegenstand** luxury; **~gesellschaft** fast society; **~gesetzgebung** sumptuary law; **~güter** luxury goods, luxuries; **~gütervertrieb** sale of luxuries; **~hotel** luxurious (luxury, exclusive) hotel, de-luxe hotel, plushery *(sl.)*; **~industrie** carriage trade, luxury industry; **~kabine** state cabin, stateroom; **~kurort** luxury resort; **~leben** life of luxury, luxury (high) life; **~leben führen** to be rolling in luxury; **~limousine** luxury saloon *(Br.)*; **~modell** de-luxe model; **~packung** fancy (luxury) packaging; **~papier** fancy paper; **~restaurant** de-luxe (carriage-trade) restaurant; **~steuer** luxury (sumptuary) tax; **~wagen** expensive (luxury) car, saloon car *(Br.)*.

Luxuswaren luxuries, fancy (luxury) goods; ~**einfuhr** luxury imports; ~**geschäft** fancy-goods business; ~**handel** luxury trade; ~**händler** dealer in fancy goods; ~**industrie** luxury industry, carriage trade.

Luxus|wohnung luxury apartment (flat), luxury housing; ~**zug** saloon *(Br.)* (Pullman, *US*) train, de-luxe train.

lynchen to lynch.

Lynchjustiz lynch law, Halifax Law, Jedbury justice, swift justice; ~ **durch Hängen** necktic party *(US sl.)*.

Lynchmord verhindern to prevent the murderer from being lynched.

lyrischer Stil lyricism.

Lyzeum girls' secondary school.

M

Maat ship's mate, qualified seaman, petty officer;
~e und Matrosen the lower deck *(Br., coll.)*.
Machart make, design, style.
machbar feasible, practicable.
Mache *(Aufmachung)* window dressing, *(Machart)* make, *(Machwerk)* put-up job, *(Täuschung)* eye-wash *(sl.)*, humbug; **etw. in der ~ haben** to have s. th. on hand; **geschickte ~ haben** *(Film, Roman)* to be cleverly constructed; **j. in die ~ nehmen** to talk to s. o. like a Dutch uncle; **in der ~ sein** to be in process.
machen to make, to manufacture, to procedure, to fabricate; **aus allem etw. ~** to turn everything to account; **Abstecher ~** to take a trip; **Abzug ~** *(Druckerei)* to pull off a proof, *(Foto)* to copy; **neuen Anfang ~** to make a fresh start, to turn over a new leaf; **Anschlag auf jds. Leben ~** to make an attempt on s. one's life; **alle nur möglichen Anstrengungen ~** to leave no stone unturned; **in Antiquitäten ~** to deal in antiquities; **sich an die Arbeit ~** to get (buck, settle down) to work, to roll up one's sleeves; **ganze Arbeit ~** to make a clean sweep of it; **j. arm ~** to impoverish s. o.; **es sich zur Aufgabe ~** to make it one's business; **Aufhebens ~** to make a fuss about it; **viel Aufhebens ~** to noise abroad; **jem. schöne Augen ~** to give s. o. the glad eye; **bankrott ~** to go bankrupt, to smash [up], to go to the wall *(Br.)*; **etw. zur Bedingung ~** to make it a condition; **jem. Beine ~** to have s. o. on the run, to keep s. o. on the trot; **jds. Bekanntschaft ~** to become aquainted with s. o.; **sich bei jem. beliebt ~** to ingratiate o. s. with s. o.; **sich bemerkbar ~** to make o. s. noticed; **bissige Bemerkungen über j. ~** to give s. o. the rough edge of one's tongue; **es sich bequem ~** to make o. s. comfortable; **Bestellung rückgängig ~** to cancel an order; **sich bezahlt ~** to pay in the long run; **sich nicht bezahlt ~** not to be worthwhile; **böses Blut ~** to make bad blood between persons; **sich ans Briefeschreiben ~** to get down to writing some letters; **jem. Dampf ~** to chivy s. o. about; **sich nichts daraus ~** not to give (care) a damn; **Doktor ~** to take a doctor's degree; **Eindruck auf jem. ~** to impress s. o.; **keinen Eindruck ~** to cut no ice, to fall flat; **seinen Einfluß bei jem. geltend ~** to exert one's influence on s. o.; **Eingabe ~** to petition; **j. zu seinem Erben ~** to appoint s. o. one's heir; **Erfindung ~** to make an invention; **sich über das Essen ~** to fall about one's food; **Examen ~** to go in (sit for) an examination; **nicht viel Federlesens ~** to make no bones about it; **fertig ~** to finish; **traurige Figur ~** to cut a poor figure; **keinen Finger krumm ~** not to lift a finger; **seinen Frieden mit jem. ~** to make one's peace with s. o.; **jem. den Garaus ~** to give s. o. the finishing stroke; **j. zum Gefangenen ~** to take s. o. prisoner; **kein Geheimnis daraus ~** to make no secret of the fact; **zu Geld ~** to run into money, to convert into cash; **Geschäfte ~** to do business, to deal with s. o.; **Gesetz wirkungslos ~** to make a law of no effect; **sich zum allgemeinen Gespött ~** to make a laughing stock of o. s.; **freundliche Geste gegenüber j. ~** to make a friendly gesture to s. o.; **Gewinne ~** to make profits; **j. glauben ~** to make s. o. belief; **glaubhaft ~** to substantiate; **sein Glück ~** to make one's pile; **sich gut ~** to be very convenient; **sich in der letzten Zeit gut ~** to make good progress recently; **j. für etw. haftbar ~** to hold s. o. liable; **sich in die Hosen ~** *(fig.)* to be in a blue funk *(coll.)*; **es schon irgendwie ~** to manage it somehow; **Kind ~** to beget a child; **j. einen Kopf kürzer ~** to behead s. o.; **um es kurz zu ~** to cut a long story short; **jem. das Leben zur Hölle ~** to make s. one's life miserable; **Licht ~** to switch on the light; **j. madig ~** to run s. o. down; **Mätzchen ~** to play one's tricks; **jem. viel Mühe ~** to put s. o. to much trouble; **jem. den Mund wässerig ~** to make s. one's mouth water; **jem. Mut ~** to encourage s. o.; **Nacht zum Tage ~** to turn night into day; **sich einen Namen ~** to make a name for o. s.; **sich nichts aus jem. ~** not to care for s. o.; **Nickerchen ~** to take a nap *(coll.)*; **gute Partie ~** to marry a fortune; **jem. plausibel ~** to make s. o. understand; **in Politik ~** *(fam.)* to dabble in politics; **aus der Politik ein Geschäft ~** to make a business of politics; **schwieriges Problem aus etw. ~** to make it tough; **Profit ~** to make one's hand; **kurzen Prozeß mit etw. ~** to make short work of it; **Prüfung ~** to undergo (go in for) an examination; **es allen recht ~** to please everybody; **seine Rechte geltend ~** to assert one's rights; **es sich zur Regel ~** to make it a rule; **Reise ~** to go on a journey, to take a trip; **gemeinsame Sache ~** to make common cause; **jem. Schande ~** to bring shame upon s. o.; **Schiedsrichter ~** to referee, to umpire; **Schluß mit jem. ~** to break off relations with s. o.; **Schulaufgaben ~** to do one's homework; **Schulden ~** to run into debt; **jem. Sorgen ~** to worry s. o., to cause s. o. trouble; **sich einen Standpunkt zu eigen ~** to adopt a mantle; **sich aus dem Staube ~** to take to one's heels, to make (clear) off; **jem. einen Strich durch die Rechnung ~** to upset s. one's plans (applecart, *coll.*); **sich einen faulen Tag ~** to have a lazy fit; **aus einem Theater ein Kino ~** to turn a theatre into a cinema; **Umstände ~** to kick up a fuss; **Umweg ~** to take a roundabout way, to make a detour; **Unfug ~** to play pranks, to be up to some mischief; **sich um etw. besonders verdient ~** to take great merit to o. s. for s. th.; **jem. Verdruß ~** to subject s. o. to annoyance; **Vermögen ~** to make a fortune; **jem. einen Vorschlag ~** to put a proposal to s. o.; **sich wegen etw. Vorwürfe ~** to blame o. s. for s. th.; **Wahlen ~** to influence elections; **seinen Weg ~** to carve out a career for o. s.; **sich auf den Weg ~** to go on one's way, to take the road; **ohne viel Wesen zu ~** without great ceremony; **sich wichtig ~** to puff o. s. up; **Witz ~** to crack a joke; **nicht viel Worte ~** not to waste words; **seiner Wut Luft ~** to give vent to one's anger; **jem. Zugeständnisse ~** to make concessions to s. o.;
sich keinen Vers darauf ~ können not to be able to make head or tail of it; **alles mit sich ~ lassen** to put up with everything; **möglichst guten Eindruck zu ~ versuchen** to put one's best foot forward.
Machenschaften practices, politics *(US)*, machinations, manipulations, intrigues, wirepulling;
betrügerische ~en fraudulent practices; **dunkle ~en** sharp practice(s), racket(s) *(sl.)*, sinister intrigues; **geheime ~** underhand manoeuvre, wire, back-door intrigues, hole-and-corner transactions; **korrupte ~** corrupt practices; **unerlaubte ~** deceptive business practices, *(Erbschaft)* vicious intromission *(Scot.)*; **unlautere ~** manipulations, sharp (deceptive business, *US*) practices;
~en im Betrieb office politics *(US)*;
jds. ~ durchschauen to see through s. one's machinations; **durch ~ erreichen** to get s. th. by a wangle; **~ vereiteln** to upset manipulations (machinations).
Macher wirepuller, prime mover, boss.
Macherlohn make, maker's wage, manufacturing price.
Machsche Zahl Mach number, critical velocity ratio.
Macht power, might, force, hold, dominion, *(Einfluß)* influence, sway, pull, leverage, *(Gewalt)* control, arm, grip, gripe, *(Heer)* military force, troops, *(Herrschaft)* command, dominion, *(Staat)* power, state;
an der ~ *(Partei)* in power (the saddle); **auf dem Höhepunkt der ~** in one's ascendancy; **aus eigener ~** on one's own responsibility; **durch die ~ der Gewohnheit** through force of habit; **mit aller ~** with might and main; **soweit es in meiner ~ liegt** as far as it lies in my power;
auswärtige ~ foreign power (government); **bedeutende ~** *(pol.)* great power; **bewaffnete ~** armed force; **feindliche ~** hostile power; **kriegführende ~** belligerent power; **neutrale ~** neutral state; **politische ~** big stick; **unumschränkte ~** absolute power; **wirtschaftliche ~** economic power;
~ der öffentlichen Meinung strength of public opinion; **~ über Tod und Leben** power of life and death;
seine ganze ~ aufbieten to exert all one's influence; **~ ausüben** to exercise power; **sich der ~ der Tatsachen beugen** to acknowledge the evidence of facts; **an der ~ bleiben** to continue (remain, survive) in power; **j. an die ~ bringen** to float s. o. into power; **Partei wieder an die ~ bringen** to sweep a party back into office; **~ zur Geltung bringen** to bring power into play; **~ in einem Lande darstellen** to be a power in the land; **~ ergreifen** to seize (assume, take) power; **zur ~ gelangen** to come (ascend) into power, to rise (attain) to power, *(Partei)* to come into office; **~ über j. gewinnen** to gain a firm hold (ascendancy) over s. o.; **große ~ über j. haben** to have a strong hold upon s. o.; **an die ~ kommen** to come into office, to gain control of the government; **wieder zur ~ kommen** to make one's comeback; **in jds. ~ liegen** to lie with s. o.; **~ an sich reißen** to seize (usurp) power; **an der ~ sein** *(Partei)* to hold (be in) office, to be in [power]; **nicht an der ~ sein** to be out; **auf dem Gipfel der ~ stehen** to have reached the zenith (be at the height) of one's power; **~ übernehmen** to come into power; **~ wieder übernehmen** to return to power; **~ übertragen** to delegate power; **zu einer ~ im Staate werden** to become a power in the state;
~ geht vor Recht might before right;

~**ablösung** change of power; ~**anhäufung** concentration of power; ~**anmaßung** usurpation of power; ~**anspruch** claim to power, fiat; ~**antritt** arrival in power; ~**apparat** machinery of power; ~**ausübung** exercise of power; **willkürliche** ~**ausübung** arbitrary action; ~**basis** power base.

Machtbefugnis authority, power, competence;
aus eigener ~ of one's own authority;
gesetzlich festgelegte ~**se** enumerated powers *(US)*;
~**se eines Vormunds** tutelary authority *(US)*;
~**se ausüben** to discharge the powers; **jds.** ~**se auf ein gewisses Ausmaß einschränken** to confine s. one's authority within certain limits; **allergrößte** ~**se innehaben** to occupy a position of highest power; **seine** ~**se deutlich machen** to make one's authority felt; **seine** ~**se mißbrauchen** to misuse one's authority; **seine** ~**se überschreiten** to exceed one's powers.

Machtbereich sphere of influence, *(jur.)* jurisdiction;
seinen ~ **ausdehnen** to extend one's power; **in seinen** ~ **mit einbeziehen** to achieve control of; ~ **seines Staates erweitern** to aggrandize a state.

Machtbeschränkung abridgement of powers.

machtbesessen power-driven.

Macht|beteiligung power-sharing; ~**block** power bloc; **neuer** ~**block afrikanischer und asiatischer Staaten** new line-up of Afro-Asian powers; ~**demonstration** show of force (muscle, sabre rattling); ~**demonstration linker Kräfte** show of left-wing strength; **mißbräuchliche** ~**demonstration durchführen** to make an excessive display of force.

Mächte, vertragsschließende contracting (signatory) powers;
~ **der Finsternis** powers of darkness;
~**gruppe** group of powers.

Macht|ergreifung assumption (usurpation, seizure) of powers; ~**faktoren der Weltpolitik** powerful forces in world affairs; ~**fülle** plenitude of power; **mit großer** ~**fülle ausstatten** to invest with great authority; ~**gefühl** sense of power; ~**gier** lust for power, letch for power *(sl.)*; ~**gleichgewicht** balance of power; ~**gruppe** pressure group, lobby.

Machthaber ruler, lord, potentate, *(pl.)* powers that be;
unrechtmäßiger ~ usurper; **unumschränkter** ~ dictator;
dem neuen ~ **huldigen** to adore the rising sun.

machthaberisch dictatorial, imperious, highhanded, autocratic;
~**e Art** domineering ways.

machthungrig insatiable of power.

mächtig powerful, potent, mighty, *(Flöz)* thick, *(riesig)* colossal, immense, huge;
sich ~ **amüsieren** to enjoy o. s. immensely; **sich** ~ **erschrecken** to be terribly frightened; **j.** ~ **gern haben** to like s. o. tremendously; **sich für** ~ **klug halten** to think no small beer of o. s.; **seiner Sinne nicht** ~ **sein** to be out of one's senses; **einer Sprache** ~ **sein** to have command of a language; ~ **gewachsen sein** to have shot up; **jem.** ~ **gut tun** to do s. o. a power of good; ~**en Bammel haben** to shake in one's shoes, to be in a blue funk; ~**e Bewegung** powerful movement; ~ **viel Geld** vast amount of money; ~**es Glück haben** to have the devil's own luck; ~**en Spaß haben** to have a lot of fun; ~**e Wellen** mighty waves.

Macht|inhaber, erfahrener connoisseur of power; ~**instrument** power instrument; ~**kampf** struggle for power, power struggle; **innenpolitische** ~**kämpfe** domestic struggles; ~**konzentration** concentration of power, power center.

machtlos powerless, helpless;
völlig ~ destitute of all power;
in einer Sache völlig ~ **sein** to be absolutely helpless in a matter.

Macht|mißbrauch abuse of power; ~**politik** power politics.

machtpolitisch by force.

Macht|probe trial of strength; **entscheidende** ~**probe** show-down; ~**sphäre** orbit; ~**spruch** fiat, peremptory order, command; **sich dem** ~**spruch seines Vaters fügen** to submit to parental authority; ~**staat** totalitarian state; ~**stellung** powerful position, purchase, ascendancy; **wirtschaftliche** ~**stellung** [dominant] market (monopolistic) power; ~**streben** thrust for power, imperialism; ~**symbole** ensigns of authority; ~**übergabe** handover of power; ~**übergang** transfer of power; ~**übernahme** assumption of (accession to, rise to) power; ~**übernahme durch die Militärs** army takeover; ~**überschreitung** excess of granted powers, ultra-vires action *(Br.)*; ~**vakuum** power vacuum; ~**verflechtung** network of influence; ~**verhältnis** balance of power; ~**verlagerung** power shift; ~**verschiebung** shift of power; ~**verteilung** distribution of power; ~**vollkommenheit** authority, power; **aus eigener** ~**vollkommenheit** of one's own authority; **richterliche** ~**vollkommenheit** discretionary power; ~**wort sprechen** to lay down the law, to put one's foot down; ~**zentrum** kernel of power, center *(US)* (centre, *Br.*) of power; ~**zunahme der Hinterbänkler** increase in the power of backbenchers; ~**zusammenballung** concentration of power; ~**zuwachs** increase in power; ~**zuwachs einer Nation hemmen** to stunt the growth of a nation's power.

Machwerk put-up job, botchwork, shoddy piece of work.

Macke haben to be nuts (off one's rocker).

Macker chap, bloke, boy friend.

Mädchen female, girl, *(Dienstmädchen)* maidservant, servant, *(Freundin)* girl friend;
sehr gefühlbetontes ~ intense young lady; **spätes** ~ old maid; ~ **für alles** maid-of-all-work, cook general *(Br.)*, general servant *(Br.)*, bottle washer; ~ **für Hausarbeit gesucht** *(Anzeige)* girl wanted for housework;
~ **aussteuern** to provide a girl with a dowry;
~**handel** white-slave trade (trading); ~**händler** white-slave trader; ~**name** maiden name; ~**namen wieder annehmen** to resume one's maiden name; **hochfeines** ~**pensionat** high-toned finishing school for girls; ~**zimmer** maid's room.

Made, wie die ~ **im Speck leben** to live like a fighting cock, to be on the gravy train *(US coll.)*.

Magazin store, storehouse, magazine, depot, depository, warehouse *(US)*, *(mil.)* depot, depository, stores, *(Zeitschrift)* periodical, review, magazine;
reichbebildertes ~ glossy magazine; **schwimmendes** ~ storeship, floating warehouse *(US)*;
~**arbeiter** stockkeeper *(Br.)*, storeman *(Br.)*, warehouseman *(US)*; ~**schiff** storeship, floating warehouse *(US)*; ~**sendung** review program(me); ~**verwalter** storekeeper *(Br.)*, warehouse keeper *(US)*, warehouseman *(US)*; ~**verwaltung** administration of stores, storekeeping, warehousing *(US)*.

Magd maidservant, *(Bauernhof)* female farm worker.

Magen stomach, tummy *(sl.)*;
auf einen leeren ~ on an empty stomach; **im** ~ under one's belt;
empfindlicher ~ weak stomach;
den Bedürfnissen seines ~**ns genügen** to satisfy the inner man *(coll.)*; **schwachen** ~ **haben** to suffer from gastric neurosis; **jem. schwer im** ~ **liegen** *(fig.)* to weigh heavy on s. one's mind; **j. auf den** ~ **schlagen** to make s. o. feel sick; **jem. den** ~ **umdrehen** to turn s. one's stomach;
~**beschwerden** stomach complaint; ~**verstimmung** stomach upset, disorder of the digestive system, indigestion.

mager meagre, thin, *(Druck)* thin, *(Kohle)* poor;
~**es Ergebnis** poor result; ~**e Ernte** lean harvest, poor crop; ~**es Gas** low-grade gas; ~**es Gemisch** lean mixture; ~**e Gewinne** light (slight) profit; ~**er Käse** skimmed-milk cheese; ~**e Kost** meagre fare; ~**es Lob** scant (faint) praise; ~**e Schrift** light-faced type; ~**es Stück Schweinefleisch** lean piece of pork.

Mager|beton lean concrete; ~**kohle** lean (poor) coal; ~**milch** skimmed milk.

magisch magical;
~**e Anziehungskraft auf seine Zuhörer ausüben** to hold one's audience spellbound; ~**es Auge** *(Rundfunkgerät)* magic (tuning) eye; ~**e Beleuchtung** magic illumination; ~**e Berührung** magical touch; ~**e Kraft eines großen Namens** the magic of a great name.

Magistrat municipal (town) council, public (municipal) corporation, municipal board (authority), municipality, magistracy.

Magistrats|amt magistrateship, municipality; ~**angelegenheit** municipal affair; ~**beamter** magistrate, municipal (county) officer; **in seiner Eigenschaft als** ~**beamter** in his function as magistrate; **zuständige** ~**behörden** magistrates entitled to adjudicate; ~**beschluß** municipal decree; ~**bezirk** magisterial district; ~**charakter** magisterial character; ~**direktor** city recorder; ~**gebäude** city hall; ~**mitglied,** ~**person** town councillor, municipal officer, selectman *(US)*, bailie *(Scot.)*; ~**sitzung** council meeting; ~**stellung** magisterial rank; ~**verordnung** magisterial decree, ordinance; ~**wahlen** municipal elections.

Magnat magnate, lord, merchant prince, mogul, baron *(US)*, tycoon *(US)*.

Magnet magnet;
~**band** magnetic tape (papertype, ribbon); **auf** ~**band aufnehmen** to [video]tape; ~**bandgerät** tape recorder, *(Fernsehen)* videotape recorder; ~**bandkassette** tape cartridge; ~**bildband** videotape; ~**bildverfahren** videotape recording system; ~**feld** magnetic field.

magnetisch|e Anziehungskraft magnetic attraction; ~**e Bildaufzeichnung** videotape recording; ~**e Mine** magnetic mine; ~**e Mißweisung** magnetic deviation; ~**er Pol** magnetic pole; ~**e Stürme** magnetic storms; ~**er Tonabnehmer** magnetic pickup.

Magnet|kassette magnetic type cassette; ~**kompaß** magnetic compass.
Magnetofon magnetophone.
Magnet|streifen data cell; ~**ton** magnetic sound; ~**tonband** magnetic ribbon, tape; ~**tonbandgerät** magnetic sound recorder; ~**tonkamera** magnetic sound camera; ~**zug** magnetic suspension train.
Mähdrescher combine harvester.
mähen to mow, *(mit Sichel)* to scythe, to sickle;
Korn ~ to cut (reap) corn; **Rasen** ~ to mow the lawn.
Mahl meal, course;
bescheidenes (karges) ~ meagre fare, bread and cheese.
mahlen *(Korn)* to grind, *(Räder)* to churn;
Kaffee ~ to grind coffee.
Mahlzeit meal, chuck *(US sl.)*;
hübsch angerichtete ~ nicely prepared meal; **kostenlos ausgegebene** ~**en** welfare meals, free lunch *(US)*; **bescheidene** ~ spare meal; **gewöhnliche** ~ ordinary meal; **hastige** ~ hurried meal; **leichte** ~ light meal; **reichliche** ~ large meal; **üppige** ~ generous meal; **während des Fluges verabreichte** ~**en** in-flight meals; **schwer verdauliche** ~ heavy meal; **volle** ~ square meal; ~ **mit vier Gängen** four-meal course; ~ **am Lagerfeuer** poke-out *(sl.)*;
~ **aufwärmen** to warm up a meal; **sich seine** ~**en selbst bereiten** to get one's own meals; ~ **in einem Restaurant ergattern** to sneak a meal in a restaurant; ~ **zu sich nehmen** to satisfy the inner man; ~ **warmhalten** to keep a dish hot; ~ **zubereiten** to prepare a meal; **bei einer** ~ **tüchtig zulangen** to do justice to a meal *(fam.)*.
Mähmaschine harvester.
Mahnbescheid summary judgment, default summons *(Br.)*.
Mahnbrief dunning (monitory, admonitory, collection, *US*) letter, [letter of] reminder, letter requesting payment, monitory, request (demand) for payment;
jem. einen ~ **schicken** to send s. o. a reminder;
~**serie** collection sequence.
mahnen to urge, to demand, *(erinnern)* to remind, *(warnen)* to warn;
j. brieflich ~ to write a monitory letter to s. o.; **Schuldner** ~ to demand payment of a debt from s. o.; **Schuldner brieflich** ~ to dun a debtor, to claim one's debts from s. o., *(dringend)* to press s. o. for payment; **j.** ~, **sein Versprechen zu halten** to urge s. o. to keep his promise; **zur Vorsicht** ~ to recommend caution.
mahnend|en Finger erheben to raise a warning finger; ~**e Stimme des Gewissens** voice of conscience.
Mahn|gebühr collection fee; ~**kartei** tickler; ~**kosten** collection expenses; ~**schreiben** dunning (monitory, collection, *US*) letter, monitory, demand note, [letter of] reminder.
Mahnung monition, admonition, demand, *(Erinnerung)* reminder, *(Warnung)* notice, warning, *(Zahlungsaufforderung)* dunning [screw], request (application) for payment;
dringende ~ urgent request; **formelle** ~ actual notice; **gerichtliche** ~ summons; **letzte** ~ pre-collection letter *(US)*; **schriftliche** ~ monitory (follow-up, dunning) letter;
letzte ~ **vor der Zwangsbeitreibung** pre-collection letter;
jds. ~**en nicht beachten** to disregard s. one's warnings; **jem. eine zweite** ~ **schicken** to send s. o. a second notice.
Mahn|verfahren summary judgment, default summons (action) *(Br.)*; **im Wege des** ~**verfahrens** by judgment note; ~**zettel** prompt note, reminder.
Mais corn *(US)*, maize *(Br.)*.
Majestät majesty.
majestätisch|er Anblick grand view; ~**es Benehmen** majestic bearing; ~**e Erscheinung** majestic appearance.
Majestäts|beleidigung lese-majesty, misprision; ~**verbrechen** high treason.
Major *(mil.)* major.
Majorat entail, entailed estate;
~ **im Mannesstamm** estate tail male;
~ **errichten (stiften)** to found an entail.
Majorats|erbe tail special; ~**gut** entail, entailed estate.
majorenn of age;
~ **werden** to come of age.
majorisieren to beat (defeat) by a majority, to outvote, to vote down.
majorisiert outvoted.
Majorisierung outvoting, defeating by a majority.
Majorität majority;
in der ~ in [the] majority;
absolute ~ absolute (clear) majority; **anteilmäßige** ~ majority in interests; **arbeitsfähige** ~ working majority; **einfache** ~ bare majority; **erdrückende** ~ overwhelming majority; **erwartete** ~ prospective majority; **geringe** ~ small majority; **große** ~ large majority; **kapitalmäßige** ~ majority in amounts; **knappe** ~ narrow majority; **qualifizierte** ~ majority in numbers; **relative** ~ relative majority; **überwältigende** ~ overwhelming (crushing) majority; **zahlenmäßige** ~ majority in numbers;
~ **der Aktionäre** majority shareholders (stockholders, *US*); ~ **von sieben Stimmen** majority (turnover) of seven votes;
sich der ~ **anschließen** to identify o. s. (come into line with, *fam.*) the majority; **in der** ~ **aufgehen** to combine with a majority; ~ **besitzen** to be in a majority over; ~ **bilden** to form the majority; ~ **der Partei an allen Klippen der Beeinflussung des Parlaments vorbei zum effektiven Einsatz bringen** to whip a party majority through the lobbies of parliament; ~ **erhalten** to gain a majority; **überwältigende** ~ **bei der Abstimmung erhalten** to carry a vote by an overwhelming majority; ~ **erzielen** to secure a majority; **nur wenige Stimmen von der** ~ **entfernt sein** to be a few votes short of a majority; **über die** ~ **verfügen** to have the majority on one's side; **mit hoher** ~ **gewählt werden** to be elected by a large majority.
Majoritäts|abstimmung majority vote; ~**aktionär** majority (controlling, *US*) shareholder (stockholder, *US*); ~**beschluß** majority vote (resolution); ~**besitzer** controlling shareholder *(Br.)* (stockholder, *US*); **einfacher** ~**besitzer** ordinary resolution; **qualifizierter** ~**besitzer** extraordinary resolution; ~**beteiligung** majority interest (ownership, stake), controlling interest (ownership); **steuerfreier** ~**kauf** *(Börse)* nontaxable exchange; ~**stellung** majority control.
Makel blemish, blot, blur, flaw, stain, brand, scar, odium;
~ **auf jds. Ruf** scar (stain) upon s. one's reputation; ~ **der Ungesetzlichkeit** infection;
jem. einen ~ **anhängen** to cast a slur on s. one's character; **mit einem** ~ **behaftet** to bear a scar; **ohne** ~ **sein** to be without blemish.
mäkelig carping, fussy, pernickety, griping *(coll.)*;
mit seinem Essen ~ **sein** to grumble about one's food.
makellos untarnished, flawless, pure, impeccable, immaculate, unexceptionable, white;
~ **sein** to be without blemish; ~ **gekleidet sein** to be immaculately dressed;
~**er Charakter** fair character; ~**e Figur** perfect figure; ~**en Lebenswandel führen** to lead an irreproachable life; ~**er Ruf** spotless (stainless) reputation; ~**er Teint** unblemished complexion.
Makellosigkeit impeccability, faultlessness.
makeln to act as a broker.
mäkeln to find fault, to gripe about *(US)*, to cavil, to be finical;
an jem. ~ to pick holes in s. o.; **an seinem Essen** ~ to be fastidious about one's food, to grumble about one's food.
Makler [merchandise] broker, go-between, middleman, agent, factor, negotiator, solicitor *(US)*, *(Börse)* [stock]broker, jobber *(Br.)*, stockjobber *(Br.)*, dealer, *(Frachtgeschäft)* freight broker, ship broker *(US)*, *(Immobilien)* real-estate broker, agent *(Br.)*, realtor *(US)*, land jobber, *(Seeversicherungsgeschäft)* marine insurance broker, *(Versicherungsgeschäft)* insurance (policy) broker;
Aufträge einsammelnder ~ drop (desk) shipper *(US)*; **freier** ~ unlicensed (outside, curbstone, street, *US*) broker, *(einer Kapitalsammelstelle)* exempted dealer; **hinzugezogener** ~ listing broker *(US)*; **selbständiger** ~ associate broker, floor broker (trader) *(US)*; **auf Provisionsbasis tätiger** ~ commission broker *(US)*; **im Rückversicherungsgeschäft tätiger** ~ surplus line broker; **vereidigter** ~ sworn broker; **amtlich zugelassener** ~ accredited (certified) broker, inside broker *(Br.)*; **nicht zur Börse zugelassener** ~ outside (curbstone, street, *US*) broker;
~ **für hochwertige Anlagepapiere** investment broker; ~ **in Auslandswechseln** foreign broker; ~ **im Befrachtungsgeschäft** chartering broker; ~ **in kleinen Effektenabschnitten** odd-lot broker (dealer, *US*); ~ **auf Großmärkten** general-line broker; ~ **für gewerbliche Grundstücke** industrial broker; ~ **für landwirtschaftlich benutzte Grundstücke** farm (land) broker; ~ **für den Handel mit ungemünztem Gold** bullion broker; ~ **für Personalkredite** personal-loan broker *(US)*; ~ **für Regierungsaufträge** five-percenter *(US)*; ~ **für den Verkauf von Schuldscheinen** note broker *(US)*;
als ~ **fungieren** to act as broker; **einem** ~ **Grundstückseigentum an die Hand geben** to list property with a broker *(US)*; **als** ~ **tätig sein** to be in the stockbroking line; ~ **werden** to take up stockbroking;
~ **verbeten!** no agents *(Br.)*!;
[ausschließlicher] ~**auftrag** [exclusive] listing *(US)*; ~**ausfüh-**

rungsspesen brokerage, carrying charges *(US)*; ~**ausschuß** brokerage board; ~**bankrott** brokerage (broker) failure; ~**beauftragung** listing *(US)*; ~**beruf** brokerage; ~**bezirk** broker's territory; ~**buchführung** stockbrokerage accounting; ~**büro** broker's office, *(Immobilien)* [real]-estate office, land agency *(US)*; ~**courtage** broker's fee (commission).

Maklerdarlehn [stock] broker's (call) loan *(Br.)*, day loan *(US)*, clearance loan;
täglich fälliges ~ day-to-day loan *(Br.)*; **kurzfristiges** ~ stock exchange (street, *US*) loan.

Maklerei jobbery, brokerage, commission business.

Makler | firma brokerage, broker's firm, firm of stockbrokers, stockbroking firm, jobbing (commission, *US*) house, *(Immobilien)* land agency, real-estate office, *(für Wechsel)* commercial paper house *(US)*; ~**forderung** broker's commission, brokerage; ~**gebühr** commission, commission rate *(US)*, broker's charge, brokerage, procuration fee, dealing costs, *(Immobilien)* real-estate brokerage *(US)*; ~**gebühren sparen** to duck broker's charges; ~**gehilfe** stockbroker's clerk; **autorisierter** ~**gehilfe** blue button *(London, Br.)*; **unberechtigter** ~**gehilfe** *(Börse)* unauthorized clerk *(Br.)*.

Maklergeschäft brokerage, broking, jobbing [business], broker's business, *(einzelnes)* brokerage (broking) operation;
freies ~ outside brokerage;
~ **betreiben** to carry on the business of broker, to job, to deal in stocks, to be a broker.

Makler | gewerbe brokerage [industry], brokerage field; ~**gruppe** board (group) of brokers; ~**gutachten** broker's award; ~**kartell** *(Immobilienhandel)* multiple (compulsory) listing *(US)*; ~**konkurs** brokerage (broker's) failure; ~**liquidation** broker's account; ~**provision** commission, brokerage, broker's commission (fee), *(Finanzmakler)* finder's fee, *(Kreditvermittlung)* procuration fee (money); ~**stand** broker's board, trading (stock, *US*) post, pitch *(Br.)*, *(Berufszweig)* brokerage industry; ~**stand für tägliches Geld an der New Yorker Börse** money post *(US)*; ~**stand für den Handel bestimmter Warengattungen** pit *(US)*; ~**syndikat** board of brokers, *(Immobilienhandel)* multiple (compulsory) listing *(US)*; ~**tätigkeit** brokerage service, broking operations; **freie** ~**tätigkeit** outside broking; ~**usancen** brokerage practices; ~**verband** *(Immobilien)* real-estate board; ~**vertrag** broker's (brokerage) contract; ~**wesen** brokerage field.

Makro | ökonomie, ~**ökonomik** macro (quantitative) economics.

Makulatur surplus sheets, spoilage, waste (setoff) paper, misprint;
~**bogen** sheet of waste paper, spoilt (waste) sheet; ~**druck** spoils; ~**papier** waste (setoff) paper, slip sheets.

Mal mark, birthmark, sign, stigma;
ein ums andere ~ by turns, alternately; **mit einem** ~ all of a sudden; **zu wiederholten** ~**en** repeatedly;
eingebranntes ~ brand; **das erste** ~ the first time; **viele** ~**e** plenty of times *(coll.)*;
Sache ein für alle ~ **erledigen** to settle a matter once and for all; **j. unzählige** ~**e fragen** to ask s. o. tons of times.

malade fühlen, sich to feel off colo(u)r.

Malariaanfälle attacks of malaria.

malen, in düsteren Farben to have a gloomy outlook; **in schwarzen Farben** ~ *(fig.)* to paint black; **aus Langeweile** ~ to doodle; **nach dem Leben** ~ to copy from life; **Teufel an die Wand** ~ to talk of the devil, to conjure up visions of dreadful possibilities; **Theaterkulissen** ~ to paint the scenery for a play; **in Wasserfarben** ~ to paint in water colo(u)rs; **Zukunft rosig** ~ to see the future through rose-colo(u)red glasses;
sich ~ **lassen** to sit for one's picture; **Küche** ~ **lassen** to have the kitchen painted.

Maler painter, *(Künstler)* painter, artist;
~ **und Anstreicher** painter and decorator;
begeisterter ~ **sein** to have a passion for painting; **einem** ~ **Modell sitzen** to sit for a painter;
~**arbeiten** painting, paintwork, paint.

Malerei, gegenstandslose nonobjective painting.

Malergeselle journeyman painter.

malerisch pictorial, picturesque, scenic.

Maler | meister master painter; ~**schule** art school.

Malheur bad luck, mishap, *(uneheliches Kind)* illegitimate baby, little bastard;
~ **mit jem. haben** to have trouble with s. o.

Mama mummy, mum, mam, mammy, mommy *(US)*, mama *(US)*.

Mammon mammon, wealth, counter *(sl.)*;
dem ~ **dienen** to worship mammon (the golden calf).

Mammut | konzern mammoth business enterprise; ~**plakat** forty-eight sheet poster; ~**unternehmen** mammoth business enterprise; ~**verluste** mammoth losses.

Management management;
hochverdienendes ~ high-income managerial people;
~**ausbildung** management training; ~**funktion ohne Eigentümerrisiko** absentee ownership; ~**institut** Institute of Management; ~**trust** flexible trust.

Manager manager;
~**ausbildung** manager education; ~**denkweise** manager thinking; ~**krankheit** managerial disease; ~**leserkreis** *(Werbung)* management audience, managerial market; ~**revolution** managerial revolution; ~**stellung** position of a manager; ~**system** managerial system; ~**technik** industrial engineering; ~**tum** managership.

Manchester | schule Manchester School; ~**tum** Cobdenism, Manchester policy.

Mandant client, customer, mandatary;
potentieller ~ potential client; **gut verdienender** ~ high-income client; **zahlungsfähiger** ~ solvent client;
~**en aus der Industrie** industrial clients;
jem. die ~**en abjagen** to alienate s. one's clients from s. o.; ~**en beraten** to advise a client.

Mandanten | gelder client money; ~**gelder verwalten** to hold a client's money; ~**liste** client list; ~**stamm** clientele.

Mandantin client company.

Mandat mandate, mandat, authority, commission, charge, *(Amtszeit)* term of office, *(Anwalt)* [counsel's] brief, warrant of attorney, retainer, *(Parlament)* seat [in Parliament], electoral mandate, *(Völkerrecht)* mandate, *(Vollmacht)* warrant, authority, proxy;
unter internationaler Aufsicht ausgeübtes ~ international mandate;
~ **annehmen** to be briefed as counsel; ~ **ausüben** *(Anwalt)* to act on behalf of a client, *(parl.)* to have a seat in parliament; **sich um ein** ~ **bewerben** *(Abgeordneter)* to canvass for a seat; ~ **erringen** to win a seat; ~ **der Wähler haben** to have the mandate of the electorate; **sein** ~ **niederlegen** *(Abgeordneter)* to resign (vacate) one's seat, *(Anwalt)* to withdraw one's counsel; ~ **für j. übernehmen** to hold a brief for s. o.; **einem Anwalt ein** ~ **übertragen** to retain a lawyer; **einer Großmacht ein** ~ **übertragen** to confer a mandate on a power, to mandate a country to one of the powers; **einem** ~ **unterstellen** to mandate; **sein** ~ **verlieren** to lose one's seat in parliament; **auf sein** ~ **verzichten** to vacate one's seat.

Mandatar proxy, procurator, mandatary;
~**mächte** Mandatory Powers.

Mandats | auftrag mandate, contract of bailment; ~**beendigung** date of completion of a mandate; ~**entzug** disengagement of a lawyer; ~**formular** mandate form; ~**gebiet** mandate, mandated territory (area); ~**herr** mandator; ~**kolonie** mandated colony; ~**macht,** ~**regierung** mandate government, mandate, mandatory [power]; ~**niederlegung** *(Abgeordneter)* vacation of one's seat, *(Anwalt)* withdrawal of counsel; ~**staat** mandatory state; ~**system** mandates system; ~**träger** mandatory representative; ~**verlust** *(Anwalt)* loss of a client, *(parl.)* loss of a seat; ~**verteilung** distribution of seats; ~**verwaltung** mandatory [power]; **gemeinsame** ~**verwaltung** condominium; ~**verzicht** vacation of one's seat.

Manege circus, circle, ring;
~**chef** ringmaster.

Mangel *(Fehlbetrag)* deficiency, deficit, *(Fehler)* defect, failure, absence, want, lack, vice, fault, *(Knappheit)* shortage, scarcity, penury, need, dearth, *(Nachteil)* drawback, disadvantage, *(Wäsche)* ironer, mangle;
aus ~ for want (lack) of; **aus** ~ **an Beweisen** for lack of sufficient evidence; **aus** ~ **an Gelegenheit** from lack of opportunity; **aus** ~ **weiterer Informationen** in the absence of further information; **aus** ~ **an Mitteln** for lack of funds, from deficiency of means; **aus** ~ **an Zeit** for want of time;
nicht abgestellter ~ unsupplied remedy; **augenscheinlicher** ~ apparent (patent) defect; **zur Wandlung berechtigender** ~ redhibitory vice (defect) *(US)*; **äußerlich erkennbarer** ~ apparent defect; **geheimer** ~ hidden (latent) defect; **heilbarer** ~ curable defect; **innerer** ~ intrinsic defect; **innewohnender** ~ inherent defect (vice); **kritischer** ~ acute shortage; **offenkundiger** ~ obvious defect; **offensichtlicher** ~ apparent (patent, obvious) defect; **schwerer** ~ serious defect; **längst spürbarer** ~ long-felt want; **unheilbarer** ~ incurable defect; **unsichtbarer** ~ invisible defect; **versteckter (verborgener)** ~ latent (hidden) defect, inherent vice; **vollständiger** ~ absence;

~ **an Arbeitskräften** manpower shortage, scarcity of workers, shortage of labo(u)r, labo(u)r scarcity (shortage), underhandedness; ~ **an selbstbewußtem Auftreten** lack of articulation; ~ **der Beweiskraft** insufficient evidence; ~ **an Devisen** foreign-exchange shortage; ~ **des Erfüllungsgeschäftes** lack (want) of delivery; ~ **an Facharbeitern** shortage of skilled workers; ~ **der gesetzlichen Form** informality; ~ **an Geld** impecuniosity, lack of funds; ~ **an Glaubwürdigkeit** creditability gap; ~ **an Kapital** lack (want, deficiency) of capital; ~ **an Lebensmitteln** shortage (shortness) of food (provisions); ~ **im Recht** defect (deficiency) of title; ~ **an Rohstoffen** scarcity of raw materials; ~ **an Schiffsraum** scarcity of tonnage; ~ **der Schlüssigkeit** inconclusiveness; ~ **an Selbstvertrauen** lack of self-confidence; ~ **der im Verkehr erforderlichen Sorgfalt** ordinary neglect (negligence); ~ **der Vertretungsbefugnis** absence of authority; ~ **an politischer Weitsicht** lack of political vision; ~ **an Wohnungen** housing shortage;
einem dringenden ~ abhelfen to supply a much-felt want; **Konkurseröffnung wegen ~ an Masse ablehnen** to dismiss a petition for return unsatisfied; ~ **beheben (beseitigen)** to remedy (cure, make good) a defect; **j. durch die ~ drehen** to put s. o. through the mill; ~ **an etw. haben** to want (be short) of s. th.; ~ **an Arbeitskräften haben** to be short of hands (shorthanded); **für einen ~ haften** to be liable for a defect; ~ **heilen** to cure a defect; **äußersten ~ leiden** to be in distress, to live in poverty; ~ **geltend machen** to raise a warranty claim; **j. in die ~ nehmen** to have s. o. on the carpet; **Prüfling in die ~ nehmen** to give a candidate a grilling; ~ **rügen** to notify a defect; **aus ~ an Aufträgen stillegen** to close down for lack of orders; ~ **verschweigen** to conceal a defect.

Mängel shortcomings;
mit allen ~n und sonstigen Fehlern with all faults and imperfections; **offenbar ohne ~** fair on its face; **von einigen stilistischen ~n abgesehen** apart from a few stylistic weaknesses;
anfängliche ~ initial shortcomings, teething troubles; **charakterliche ~** weakness of character; **kleinere ~** minor defects; **menschliche ~** human failings; **technische ~** technical deficiencies;
~ **der Ausbildung** training needs; ~ **der Betriebsanlage** shortcomings in the plant; ~ **eines Buches** faults (shortcomings) of a book;
einige ~ aufweisen to offer a few flaws; ~ **beanstanden** to find faults (defects); ~ **beseitigen (beheben)** to remove (supply, remedy) defects; ~ **im Material feststellen** to find a flaw in the material; **für ~ haften** to be liable for defects; **über kleinere ~ großzügig hinwegsetzen** to generously ignore slight imperfections; **auf ~ aufmerksam machen** to warn of defects;
~ansprüche warranty claims; **~anzeige** demonstration (notice) of defects; **~ausschluß** caveat emptor.

Mangelberuf scarce job.

Mängel|beseitigung removal (remedy) of defects; **~einrede erheben** to plead a redhibitory defect *(US)*.

Mangelerscheinungen *(med.)* deficiency symptoms;
infolge zeitweiliger ~ owing to the temporary scarcity; **kriegsbedingte ~** wartime shortages.

Mängelexemplar defective book.

mangelfrei free from defects.

Mängelgewähr warranty of fitness, express (product) warranty; **ohne ~** with all faults.

mangelhaft defective, deficient, faulty, insufficient, vicious, *(unvollständig)* incomplete, imperfect, *(Zeugnisnote)* poor, unsatisfactory;
~ **versehen** scantily provided;
~ **aufgemacht sein** to lack appeal;
~e Anpassung lack of adjustment; **~e Auskunft** inadequate information; **~e Ausrüstung** inadequate equipment; **~e Beschriftung** insufficient address; ~ **besetztes Büro** understaffed office; **~e Erfüllung** failure to perform, defective compliance; **~e Leistung** defective performance; **~e Lieferung** deficient delivery; **~e Sache** defective thing; **~e Verpackung** defective (insufficient) packing; **~e Waren** defective (faulty) goods; **~er Warenzustand** defective condition of goods; **~er Zustand** defectiveness, faultiness.

Mangelhaftigkeit defectiveness, deficiency, inadequacy, faultiness, imperfection.

Mängelhaftung warranty of fitness, express warranty;
der ~ unterliegen to be liable for defects.

Mängelklausel warranty clause.

Mangel|krankheit deficiency disease; **~lage** shortage, scarcity.

Mängelliste schedule of plights.

mangeln to be in want;
an den notwendigen Erfahrungen ~ to lack the necessary experience; **immer an Geld ~** to be always short of money; **an Kapital ~** to lack capital; **an nichts ~** to want for nothing.

mangelnd wanting, missing, lacking, absent;
~e Aktivlegitimation incapacity to sue; **~e Beschlußfähigkeit** failure to muster a quorum; **~e Beweiskraft** insufficiency of evidence; **~e Eignung** lack of ability; **~e Einsicht** lack of discernment; **~e Flüssigkeit** shortage in money accounts; **~e Gegenleistung** failure (lack) of consideration; **~e Information über wesentliche Tatsachen** failure to supply material information; **über ~e Kundschaft nicht zu klagen haben** to lack no clients; **~e Nachfrage** lack of demand; **~er Rechtsanspruch** lack of title; **~e Sorgfalt** lack of due diligence; **~e Sorgfalt des Spediteurs** carrier negligence; **~e Sorgfalt erkennen lassen** to show want of care; **~e Sparsamkeit** want of economy; **~e Unterstützung** lack of support; **~e Urteilskraft** lack of judgment; **~e Vertragserfüllung** failure to perform (of performance); **~es Vertrauen** lack of faith, want (lack) of confidence; **~e Vertretungsmacht** absence (lack) of authority; **~e Vorräte** want of provisions; **~e Zuständigkeit** want (lack) of jurisdiction.

Mängelrüge notice (demonstration) of defect, customer's complaint;
~ **berücksichtigen** to consider a complaint; ~ **erheben (geltend machen, vorbringen)** to make a complaint, to make a claim in respect of a defect, to notify a defect;
~frist einhalten to file a complaint in time.

mangels in default (for want) of, in the absence of, failing;
~ **Akzeptes protestiert** protested for nonacceptance; ~ **Akzeptes zurück** returned for want of acceptance; ~ **Annahme** for nonacceptance, for want of acceptance; ~ **Arbeitskräfte** owing to shortage of staff; ~ **Beweis** failing proof; ~ **Deckung** for want of cover (funds); ~ **Ertrag** failing yield; ~ **Masse** no funds, *(Konkursablehnung)* return unsatisfied; ~ **Nachfrage** owing to lack of demand; ~ **Nachricht** failing an answer; ~ **Übereinkunft** failing agreement; ~ **Zahlung** for want of (failing) payment.

Mangelware scarce (deficiency) goods, scarce materials (articles, commodities), goods in short supply, shortcoming goods, *(bewirtschaftet)* rationed commodities;
zur ~ werden to fall in short supply.

Mangel|warenpreis scarcity price; **~wäsche** flatwork.

Manie mania, crank, caprice.

Manier manner, form;
in der ~ von in the style of; **mit guten ~en** well-mannered;
feine ~en refined manners; **gute ~en** velvet paws; **scheinbar gute ~en** varnish of good manners; **komische ~en** funny ways; **schlechte ~en** ill manners, bad breed; **bedauerlich schlechte ~en** unfortunate lack of good manners; **tadellose ~en** polished manners; **ungeschliffene (ungehobelte) ~en** crude manners; **absolut unmögliche ~en** shocking bad manners *(fam.)*; **vollendete ~** perfect manners; **vornehme ~en** delicate manners;
sich durch bessere ~en auszeichnen to improve in manners; **sich guter ~en befleißigen** to cultivate good manners; **jem. ~en beibringen** to teach s. o. manners; **hervorragende ~en haben** to have great distinction of manners; **schlechte ~en haben** to have bad manners; **durch gute ~en verdecken** to veneer; **sich bessere ~en zulegen** to mend one's manners.

manieriert mannered, affected.

manierlich well-mannered;
sich ~ benehmen to behave well (properly); ~ **essen** to eat nicely; **seine besten ~en zur Schau stellen** to be on one's company manners;
~es Kind well-behaved child.

Manifest manifesto, *(Warenbegleitschein)* declaration, shipping bill.

Manifestation demonstration, expression.

manifestieren to manifest, to show itself.

Manipulation handling, sharp practices, engineering, *(Börse)* manoeuvre *(Br.)*, maneuver *(US)*, manipulation, *(Währung)* management, manipulation;
durch ~en beeinflußt *(Börse)* technical;
betrügerische ~en business (fraudulent) manipulations;
~ **einer Wahl** manipulation of an election;
zweifelhafte ~en durchführen to play politics.

Manipulations|bestand, ~fonds general fund; **~gebühr** handling charge; **~reserven** working reserve.

manipulierbar manoeuvrable.

Manipulieren manoeuvre, maneuver *(US)*.

manipulieren to manipulate, to manoeuvre, to plant *(sl.)*, to handle, *(Währung)* to manage, to manipulate;
Aktien ~ to manipulate stocks; **Betriebsgewinn durch allgemeine Rückstellungen** ~ to manipulate the trading profit by means of general provisions; **Bilanz** ~ to doctor (cook) a balance sheet; **an einem Briefsiegel** ~ to tamper with the seal of a letter; **geschickt** ~ to handle skillfully; **Konten** ~ to manipulate (cook, doctor) accounts; **Kurse** ~ to manipulate prices, *(hochtreiben)* to rig the market; **Posten** ~ to handle an item; **Wechselkurse** ~ to manipulate exchange rates.
manipulierend manipulatory.
Manipulierer manipulator.
manipuliert *(Börse)* manipulated, technical;
~**e Währung** managed currency.
Manipulierung | der Kurse manipulation of the market (on the stock exchange); ~ **der Währung** manipulation (management) of the currency.
Manko deficit, deficiency, defect, shortage, short, wantage, flaw, defect, *(Faß)* ullage, *(Gewicht)* short weight, underweight, *(Kasse)* deficit [of cash], deficiency, cash short;
ein ~ **sein** to be a drawback;
~**berechnung** deficiency assessment; ~**geld** cashier's allowance, cash indemnity, risk money; ~**lieferung** deficient delivery.
Mann, bis zum letzten down to the last man; **mit** ~ **und Maus** with all hands; **wie ein** ~ as one man;
angesehener ~ man of established position; **begüterter** ~ man of property; **sehr besonnener** ~ man of great discretion; **ehrenhafter** ~ man of hono(u)r; **der einfache** ~ the man in the street; **freier** ~ lawful man; **gebildeter** ~ man of education, literary (educated) man; **der geeignete** ~ s. o. to fill the post (bill); **guter** ~ set-up man; **hervorragender** ~ first; **vielversprechender junger** ~ youth of great promise; **der kleine** ~ the man in the street, common man; **der schwarze** ~ *(Kinder)* bogyman; **schweigsamer** ~ a man of few words; **tonangebender** ~ boss; **toter** ~ *(Bergbau)* goaf, gob; **verstorbener** ~ deceased husband; **vielgereister** ~ travelled man; **vielseitiger** ~ allround man, man of many parts; **wohlhabender** ~ moneyed man; **zuverlässiger** ~ reliable man; **zweiter** ~ sidekicker *(Br.)*;
~ **von Bildung** gentleman; **alle** ~ **an Bord!** all aboard!; ~ **über Bord!** man overboard!; **alle** ~ **an Deck!** all hands on deck!; ~ **der Feder** man of letters; ~ **von Format** man of high calibre; ~ **mit moralischen Grundsätzen** moral man; ~ **aus eigener Kraft** self-made man; ~ **der Mitte** centrist; ~ **der Öffentlichkeit** public man; **erfahrener** ~ **der Praxis** practised hand; ~ **hinterm Schreibtisch** desk *(coll.)*; ~ **von Stand** man of estate (prestige); ~ **von der Straße** man in the street; **der** ~ **des Tages** the man of the hour; **ein** ~ **aus dem Volke** one of the crowd (people); ~ **von Welt** a man of the world; ~ **von Wort** a man to bank on;
ein ~ **ein Wort** an honest man's word is as good as his bond; **10 DM pro** ~ **bezahlen** to pay DM 10 each; **an den** ~ **bringen** *(fam.)* to sell, to get rid of, to put off; **seine Kenntnisse an den** ~ **bringen** to show off; **Neuigkeiten an den** ~ **bringen** to pass on the news; **sich wie ein** ~ **erheben** to stand up as a body; **bis zum letzten** ~ **fallen** to be killed to the last man; **kleinen** ~ **im Ohr haben** to be nuts (crazy, a little wrong in the upper story); ~ **gegen** ~ **kämpfen** to fight hand to hand; **wie** ~ **und Frau zusammen leben** to live as man and wife; **starken** ~ **markieren** to throw one's weight around; **j. zum** ~ **nehmen** to marry s. o.; **bedeutender (einflußreicher)** ~ **sein** to be a man of consequences; **gemachter** ~ **sein** to have arrived; **auf den** ~ **dressiert sein** to be trained to attack people; ~ **für** ~ **erschienen sein** to be in full strength; ~ **vom Fach sein** to be one of the craft; ~ **von Format sein** to be of high caliber (calibre, *Br.*); ~ **in den besten Jahren sein** to be in the prime of one's life; **der starke** ~ **in einem Verband sein** to be the strong man in an organization; **den starken** ~ **spielen** to act the big cheese; **seinen** ~ **stehen** to toe the scratch, to keep one's end up, to stand one's ground; **jungen** ~ **geschäftlich unterbringen** to launch a young man into business; **mit** ~ **und Maus untergehen** to be lost with all hands, to go down with every soul on board;
wenn Not am ~ **ist** if the worst comes to the worst.
mannbar mature, marriageable, virile;
~ **werden** to reach manhood.
Männchen, kleines short little man, *(im Märchen)* manikin;
~ **malen** to doodle.
Mannequin mannequin.
Männer, für eine Geschworenentätigkeit geeignete good and lawful men; ~ **der Praxis** practical men;
~**arbeit** a man's work; **auf** ~**fang ausgehen** to go out to land s. o. for a husband.
männermordend *(hum.)* man-eating.
Männer | station *(Krankenhaus)* male ward; ~**überschuß** surplus of men; ~**wahlrecht** manhood suffrage.
Mannes | alter manhood, virility; **im besten** ~**alter** in the flower of one's strength, in the pride of manhood; ~**stamm** male line; **seinen** ~**wert beweisen** to prove a man's worth; ~**zucht** military discipline; ~**zucht verlieren** to get out of hand.
mannhaft manly, *(mutig)* brave, stout, courageous;
sich ~ **behaupten** to stand one's ground manfully;
~**en Widerstand leisten** to offer stout (manful) resistance.
mannigfach manifold;
~**e Aufgaben** manifold duties; **in** ~**en Farben** in a variety of colo(u)rs; ~**e Interessen** multifarious interests.
mannigfaltig varied, diverse, multiform, diversified, manifold; **aus** ~**en Gründen** for various (a variety of) reasons; **mit** ~**en Schwierigkeiten zu rechnen haben** to come up against all sorts of difficulties; ~**es Warenangebot** wide variety of product lines, varied assortment of goods, wide range of items.
Mannigfaltigkeit variety, diversification;
~ **der geäußerten Ansichten** diversity of opinions; ~ **an Farben** multiplicity of colo(u)rs.
männlich male, virile, *(Erscheinung)* masculine, manlike, mannish;
~**e Energie** masculine energy; ~**er Erbe** male heir; **in der** ~**en Linie** in the male line; ~**er Stil** masculine style; ~**es Wahlrecht** manhood suffrage.
Mannsbild bloke *(fam.)*, chap;
gestandenes ~ stand-up guy *(sl.)*.
Mannschaft *(Arbeiter)* team, gang, *(Belegschaft)* crew, staff, personnel, hands, *(Flugzeug)* air crew, *(mil.)* force, company, body of men, *(Schiff)* company, crew;
~**en** ranks, rank and file;
junge ~ *(Firma)* young staff; **ungezügelte** ~ wild crew; **sorgfältig zusammengestellte** ~ hand-picked team; **bunt zusammengewürfelte** ~ scratch team (crew);
Offiziere und ~**en** officers and ratings;
~ **aufstellen** to select a team; ~ **entlassen** to discharge the crew; **vor versammelter** ~ **erklären** to say in front of all men; ~ **antreten lassen** to make the men line up; ~ **retten** to take off the crew; ~ **auf ihre Posten rufen** to beat to quarters; ~ **auf dem Deck zusammenrufen** to pipe all hands on deck.
Mannschafts | aufstellung team selection; ~**bestand** establishment; ~**dienstgrad** private, enlisted grade *(US)*; **die** ~**dienstgrade** the lower deck *(Br.)*, ratings, rank and file; ~**führer** team leader, skipper; ~**geist** team spirit; ~**grade** the lower deck *(Br., coll.)*; ~**kapitän** crew's captain; ~**liste** list of the crew, crew list; ~**mitglied** member of the crew, team (crew) member, crewman; ~**quartier** crew's quarters; ~**räume** crew's accommodation, *(Schiff)* mess room; ~**stand** ranks; ~**stube** *(mil.)* privates's room; ~**transporter** personnel carrier; ~**transportwagen** armo(u)red personnel carrier; ~**unterkünfte** quarters; ~**verpflegung** maintenance of the crew; ~**wagen** troop carrier, *(Bergbau)* man-riding car.
mannshoch as tall as a man;
~ **liegen** *(Schnee)* to lie six feet deep.
mannshohe | Wellen waves six feet high; ~**r Zaun** head-high fence.
mannstoll man-mad, nymphomaniac.
Mannweib virago, termagant, amazon.
Manometer pressure (vacuum) gauge;
~**stand** pressure-gauge reading.
Manöver device, trick, manoeuvre *(Br.)*, maneuver *(US)*, *(Kunstgriff)* stroke, sham fight, stratagem, trick, device, dodge, knack;
zweifelhafte ~ sharp practices (proceedings);
~ **abhalten** to hold a manoeuvre; **an der Ostküste** ~ **durchführen** to manoeuvre off the East coast; **sein Ziel durch billige** ~ **zu erreichen suchen** to resort to cheap tricks to gain one's end; **durch geschickte** ~ **überlisten** to outmanoeuvre;
~**bombe** dummy bomb; ~**gast** manoeuvre observer; ~**gebiet**, ~**gelände** area of manoeuvres; ~**karte** ordnance survey map; ~**kritik** *(fig.)* post-mortem; ~**munition** blank ammunition; ~**schaden** manoeuvre damage.
Manövriereigenschaften eines Wagens maneuverability *(US)* (manoeuvrability, *Br.*) of a car.
manövrieren to manoeuvre, to maneuver, to handle;
sein Auto in eine schwierige Parklücke ~ to manoeuvre one's car into a difficult parking space; **jem. einen Geldschein in die Tasche** ~ to slip a note into s. one's pocket; **Gesetzesantrag durch das Parlament** ~ to railroad a bill through Congress *(US)*, to rattle a bill through the House *(Br.)*; **jem. in eine ausweglose Lage** ~ to manoeuvre s. o. into a corner *(fam.)*; **Schiff** ~ to handle a ship.

manövrierfähig manoeuvrable, maneuverable;
schwer ~ landsick.
Manövrierfähigkeit maneuverability *(US)*, manoeuvrability *(Br.)*.
manövrierunfähig disabled;
~ wegen einer undichten Stelle water-logged.
Mansarde attic [storey], garret, mansard;
mit Gerümpel angefüllte ~ attic full of junk.
Mansarden | bewohner garreteer; **~dach** curb (broken, mansard) roof, gambrel roof *(US)*; **~fenster** dormer window; **ausgebaute ~wohnung** flat in the attic, attic flat; **~zimmer** attic, garret room.
Manschette cuff;
vor jem. ~n haben to be scared of s. o.; **vor einem Examen ~n haben** to have the wind up about an exam *(sl.)*.
Mantel overcoat, coat, *(Arbeitskittel)* smock, *(Chirurg)* gown, *(Firma)* mantle, shell, cover, *(Hülle)* covering, *(Turbinenstrahltriebwerk)* shroud, *(Wertpapier)* stock certificate;
unter dem ~ der Dunkelheit under the cloak of night;
~ ablegen to take off one's coat; **etw. mit dem ~ der christlichen Nächstenliebe bedecken** to draw a curtain over s. th.; **~ des Vergessens über einen Vorgang breiten** to ring down the curtain on a scene; **seinen ~ nach dem Winde hängen** to turn one's coat, to blow hot and cold, to temporize;
~abtretungsvertrag general assignment.
Mäntelchen | des Rechts colo(u)r of law;
sein ~ nach dem Winde hängen to blow hot and cold, to sail with every shift of the wind, to turn one's coat, to come down on one side or the other of the fence.
Mantel | garantie frame guarantee; **~geschoß** jacketed projectile; **~gesetz** omnibus bill (act); **~kauf** purchase of the shell; **~note** identical note, *(Feuerversicherung)* covering note; **~police** comprehensive policy.
Manteltarif skeleton (basic) agreement;
~abkommen industry-wide (joint, master, model) agreement; **~bestimmungen** collective agreement provisions; **~struktur** national wages bargaining structure; **~vertragsverhandlungen** industry-wide bargaining.
Mantel | tasche coat pocket; **~vertrag** covering (master, basic, model, industry-wide) bargaining agreement; **~zession** general assignment.
Manual manual, note (memorandum) book.
manuell manual;
~ hergestellt made by hand.
Manufaktur manufacture;
~waren manufactured goods, *(Textilien)* textiles, dry goods *(US)*.
Manuskript manuscript, MS, matter, copy, handwriting, *(Film)* scenario, script, *(Journalist)* stuff, *(Rundfunk)* continuity;
als ~ gedruckt printed as manuscript, privately printed; **ohne ~** off the cuff;
abgesetztes ~ dead copy (matter), cast-off manuscript; **altes ~** codex; **leserliches ~** fair copy; **schlechtes ~** bad copy; **unleserliches ~** blind copy; **unübersichtliches ~** dirty copy; **unveröffentlichte ~e** unpublished manuscripts;
vom ~ ablesen to speak by the book; **~ absetzen** to cast off (set up) a manuscript, to set up type; **~ wortwörtlich absetzen** to follow copy; **~ berechnen** to cast up copy; **~ auf Schreibfehler durchsehen** to correct (go through) a manuscript for typing errors, to revise the copy; **~ in die Druckerei geben** to send a manuscript to the printers; **kein ~ mehr haben** to be out; **ohne ~ sprechen** to speak off the cuff (without notes, offhand, extemporaneously); **~ kritisch überprüfen** to review a manuscript; **~ verbessern** to correct a manuscript; **~ an die Setzer verteilen** to give out copy;
~ablehnung rejection slip; **~abschreiben** copy typing; **~abteilung** *(Rundfunk)* script (continuity) department *(US)*; **in letzter Minute vorgenommene ~änderungen** *(Rundfunk)* discrepancies; **~bearbeitung** copy styling; **~halter** copyholder; **~länge** length of a copy; **~papier** copy paper; **~teil absetzen** to cast off copy; **~umfang** calibration; **~umfangsberechnung** cast-off calibration of a copy; **~vorbereitung** copy preparation.
Mappe briefcase, briefbag, [port]folio, *(Schreibmappe)* folder.
Marathon | debatte, **~sitzung** talkathon *(US)*; **~verhandlung** marathon negotiations.
Märchen fairy tale;
reines ~ pure fiction;
~ auftischen to tell a tall tale; **wie ein ~ klingen** to sound like a fairy tale; **nur ein ~ sein** to be only a myth;
dieses ~ kannst du deiner Großmutter erzählen tell that to the marines;
~buch story (fairy-tale, fable) book; **~erzähler** taleteller, fable teller; **~erzählung** story-book account; **~figur** figure from a fairy tale.
märchenhaft | e Aussichten brightest prospects; **~e Landschaft** fairy-tale landscape; **~er Reichtum** fabulous wealth; **~e Zeit** nailing good time.
Märchen | klischee folgen, einem to follow a storybook mould; **~land** fairy-tale country, wonderland.
Margarinesteuer margarine tax.
Marge margin [of profit], markup, spread *(US)*, *(Unterschied zwischen Brief- und Geldkurs)* turn of the market;
jem. eine ~ zugestehen to allow s. o. some margin.
marginale | Ausgabenneigung marginal propensity to spend; **~ Exportquote** marginal propensity to export; **~ Konsumfreudigkeit** marginal propensity to consume.
Marginalien marginal (side) notes.
Marginalkostenpreis marginal cost pricing.
Marihuana marijuana;
~ rauchen to hit the pipe *(sl.)*;
~rauchen tea party *(sl.)*; **~zigarette** tea-stick.
Marine navy, Royal Navy *(Br.)*, marine;
bei der ~ dienen to serve in the navy; **in die ~ eintreten** to join (enter) the navy;
~akademie naval academy (college); **~amt** naval board, the Admiralty *(Br.)*, Navy Department *(US)*; **~angelegenheiten** naval affairs; **~attaché** naval attaché; **~ausdruck** nautical term; **~bedarf** marine stores; **~brigade** naval brigade; **leichte ~einheiten vor der Küste** coastal defence force; **~etat** Naval Estimates; **~fahrzeug** naval vessel; **~fliegerei**, **~flugwesen** naval aviation; **~fliegerstützpunkt** naval air station; **~flugzeug** naval airplane, seaborne aircraft, seaplane; **~haushalt** navy estimates; **~infanterie** marine infantry; **~ingenieur** naval engineer (architect); **~korps** marine corps *(US)*; **~lazarett** naval hospital; **~luftwaffe** naval air arm, Fleet Air Arm *(Br.)*; **~minister** First Lord of the Admiralty *(Br.)*, Secretary of the Navy *(US)*; **~ministerium** Admiralty *(Br.)*, Department of the Navy *(US)*, Navy Department *(US)*; **~nachrichtendienst** naval intelligence; **~offizier** naval officer; **~schule** marine college; **~station** naval base; **~stützpunkt** naval base; **~truppen** marines; **~tuch** pilot cloth; **~werft** naval docks (yard), navy yard, naval ship-repair yard.
Marionette puppet on a string, lay figure, pawn;
~ dirigieren to pull the puppet strings.
Marionetten | figur stalking horse; **~regierung**, **~staat** puppet government; **~theater** puppet show.
Mark mark, *(Grenzland)* borderland, boundary;
bis aufs ~ to the marrow; **faul bis ins ~** rotten to the core; **sich auf Tausende von ~ belaufen** to run into thousands; **bis ins ~ erschrecken** to be scared out of one's wits; **jem. durch ~ und Knochen gehen** *(Schrei)* to make s. one's blood curdle; **jem. durch ~ und Pfennig (Bein) gehen** *(Geräusch)* to pierce s. o. to the marrow; **kein ~ in den Knochen haben** to have no guts; **zwischen 5 und 10 ~ liegen** to range between 5 and 10; **mit jeder ~ rechnen müssen** to have to count every penny; **jem. das ~ aus den Knochen saugen** to suck s. one's blood; **von der Kälte bis ins ~ erstarrt sein** to be chilled to the marrow; **bis ins ~ getroffen sein** to be touched to the quick; **bis ins ~ treffen** to strike between wind and water.
markant striking, prominent, distinctive;
~er Geländepunkt prominent landmark; **~e Handschrift** bold handwriting; **~e Persönlichkeit** man of outstanding personality; **~er Stil** distinctive style; **~e Züge** well-cut features.
Marke *(Bezugsscheinwesen)* unit, coupon *(Br.)*, *(Bon)* chit, voucher, *(Briefmarke)* [postage] stamp, *(Fabrikat)* brand, make, type, *(Fahrzeug)* make, type, *(Garderobe)* check, *(Güte)* quality, sort, description, chop, *(Identitätszeichen)* identification, [identity] mark, badge, *(Kontrollmarke)* check, pass, *(Lebensmittel)* coupon, *(Markierungszeichen)* sign, mark, *(Metallmarke)* token, metal fare, *(Polizeimarke)* badge, shield, *(Rabattmarke)* trading stamp, *(Schutzmarke)* mark, trademark, brand, label, tap *(fam.)*, *(Siegel)* signet, *(Spielmarke)* counter, chip, *(Steuermarke)* revenue (fiscal, *US*) stamp, *(Wein)* vintage, growth;
auf ~n rationed, on (with, *US*) coupon, couponed; **ohne ~n** couponfree, off-ration;
abgestempelte ~ used stamp; **aufgeklebte ~** affixed stamp; **aufklebbare ~** adhesive stamp; **ausgezeichnete ~** *(Kaffee)* excellent brand; **ausländische ~** foreign brand; **bevorzugte ~** favo(u)rite brand; **unsere eigene ~** our own make; **gut eingeführte ~** popular brand (make); **eingetragene ~** registered trademark; **erstklassige ~** first-class (-rate) quality; **geschützte**

~ protected brand, registered trademark; **minderwertige ~** inferior make; **überregional verbreitete ~n** national brands; **~n in gemeinschaftlichem Eigentum** jointly owned marks; **~n abgeben** to spend (surrender) coupons; **auf ~n bekommen** to get on coupons; **~ einlösen** to cash a coupon, *(Spielmarken)* to cash in chips; **~ entwerten** to deface a stamp; **~ führen** to keep an article in stock; **komische ~ sein** to be an odd character; **Gebrauchtwagen in allen ~n verkaufen** to sell secondhand cars of all types.

Marken|abkommen trademark convention; **~album** stamp album; **~anmeldung** registration of trademark.

Markenartikel proprietary (patented, genuine, branded) articles, [name] brand, branded merchandise (staple, *US*), *(pl.)* speciality goods, trademarked commodities (goods, merchandise), patent (patented, proprietary, *US*) goods;
dominierender ~ brand leader;
~ einbauen to instal(l) branded goods; **zum ~ entwickeln** to brand; **Waren unberechtigt als ~ verkaufen** to pass off goods as those of another make *(US)*;
~preis brand price; **~wettbewerb** brand competition.

Marken|ausstellung presentation of stamps; **~barometer** brand barometer; **~benzin** high-grade petrol; **~betreuer** product (brand) manager; **~betreuung** brand management, product managing; **~bevorzugung** brand preference, brand position; **~bezeichnung** proprietary description, *(Einzelhandelsgesellschaft)* private brand; **~bild** brand image; **~bindung des Händlers** exclusive distribution (dealing); **~butter** grade A butter; **~eintragung** registration of a trademark, trademark registration; **ausgestanztes ~emblem** die-cut; **~erzeugnis** make, brand; **~erzeugnisse** trademarked commodities (goods), branded merchandise (goods), patent (patented) articles, proprietary articles; **~erzeugnis hoher Qualität** premium brand; **~etikett** brand label; **~fabrikate** trademarked goods (commodities), branded goods (commodities, merchandise), patented articles; **~fälschung** infringement of trademarks; **~firma** well-established firm.

markenfrei ration- (coupon-) free, off ration, unrationed, uncouponed.

Markengeber stamp machine.

markengebunden, nicht off-brand.

Marken|gemeinschaft brand association; **~heft** stamp booklet, book of stamps; **~identität** brand identity; **~index** brand trend survey, brand barometer; **~inhaber** trademark owner; **~lage** brand position; **~lieferant** brand supplier; **~nahrungsmittel** patent (proprietary, *US*) foods; **~name** brand (distinctive, proprietary) name, trade[mark] name.

markenpflichtig rationed, couponed;
~e Waren coupon (rationed) goods.

Marken|politik brand policy; **~preis** brand price; **~produkt** make, brand; **~recht** trademark law; **~registrierung** registration of a trademark, trademark registration; **~sammler** stamp collector; **~sammlung** stamp collection; **~schutz** protection of trademarks; **~schutzgesetz** Trademark [Registration] Act *(US)*; **~stil** brand image; **~symbol** brand image; **~tankstelle** company-owned station; **~treue** brand loyalty, consumer insistence; **~vorstellung des Verbrauchers** brand image; **~wahl** brand choice; **~ware** branded goods (commodities), patented articles, trademarked commodities, specialty goods; **~werbung** brand advertising; **innerbetrieblicher ~wettbewerb** intrabrand competition; **~wiedererkennung** brand recognition; **~wortbild** name block; **unerlaubtes ~zeichen** wildcat brand.

markerschütternder Schrei blood-curdling scream.

Marketender sutler, camp follower.

Marketender|ei sutlery, Post Exchange *(US)*, PX, Navy, Army and Air-Force Institute *(Br.)*; **~ware** small stores, Post Exchange (PX) goods *(US)*.

Marketing marketing;
~erfahrung experience in marketing; **~führungskräfte** marketing executives.

Markierboje marking buoy.

markieren to mark, to designate, *(abstecken)* to stake off, *(kennzeichnen)* to earmark, to label, *(skizzieren)* to outline, *(Tier)* to brand, *(Ware)* to brand;
Abfahrtsstrecke ~ to stake off a downhill course; **Bäume [zum Fällen] ~** to mark timber [for sawing]; **den voll Beschäftigten ~** to pretend to be very busy; **mit Bojen ~** to buoy off, to beacon; **Gegner ~** *(Manöver)* to simulate the enemy; **Grundstücksgrenzen ~** to mark the bounds of an estate; **Krankheit ~** to pretend to be ill; **den feinen Mann ~** to play the gentleman, to lord it over s. o.; **den strammen Max ~** to act big *(coll.)*; **Ort auf einer Karte ~** to mark a place on the map; **Rolle ~** *(Theater)* to walk through one's part; **Schiffswrack ~** to buoy a wreck; **mit Schildern ~** to signpost; **Strecke auf einer Karte ~** to mark a route on a map; **Weg ~** to mark out a road.

Markier|flagge guide flag; **~gerät** marker; **~stein** marker.

markiert marked, *(Weg)* signposted;
rot ~ sein to be marked in red;
~er Feind skeleton enemy; **~e Krankheit** feigned illness; **deutlich ~er Landestreifen** well marked landing strip; **~e Ware** branded goods.

Markierung mark, marking *(Br.)*, position mark, *(Filmstreifen)* cue, *(Straße)* signposting, *(Vermessung)* witness mark, *(Waren)* labelling, branding.

Markierungs|bombe parachute flare, target indicator; **~funkfeuer** radio beacon; **~pflock** peg; **~punkt** *(Inserat)* corner bullet; **~sender** fan marker; **~strich** mark, line; **~vorrichtung** *(Film)* notcher; **~wurf** cascade bombing.

Markise canvas, awning, sun blind *(Br.)*.

Markisenstoff awning cloth, duck.

Markscheide boundary;
~kunst art of surveying mines.

Markscheider underground (mine) surveyor.

Markscheidung mine survey, measurement.

Markstein landmark, boundary stone, *(fig.)* milestone, landmark;
~e in der Geschichte landmarks in history;
~ setzen to plant a landmark; **~ verrücken (versetzen)** to [re]move (shift) a landmark.

Markt market, *(Absatz)* outlet, market, *(Börse)* stock exchange, stock market, *(Geschäft)* bargain, business, sale, *(Handelsplatz)* emporium, mart, trading center *(US)* (centre, *Br.*), *(Marktplatz)* market place (square), *(Messe)* fair;
auf dem ~ in the market; **günstig auf dem ~ zu haben** in season; **nicht auf dem ~** out of season; **nicht für den ~ bestimmt** captive *(US)*;
im Freien abgehaltener ~ open-air market; **abgeschwächter ~** sagging market, market off *(US)*; **amtlicher ~** official market; **aufnahmebereiter ~** receptive market; **aufnahmefähiger ~** broad (ready) market; **beschränkt aufnahmefähiger ~** limited market; **nicht mehr aufnahmefähiger ~** long market *(US)*; **wegen spekulativer Ankäufe nicht mehr aufnahmefähiger ~** overbought market *(US)*; **bei fallenden Kursen nicht mehr aufnahmefähiger ~** oversold market *(US)*; **nicht sehr aufnahmefähiger ~** soft market; **steigende Tendenz aufweisender ~** buoyant market; **ausgeglichener ~** balanced market; **ausländischer ~** foreign market; **außerbörslicher ~** unofficial market, market in unlisted securities *(US)*; **schlecht befahrener ~** scanty market; **vom Käufer beherrschter ~** buyer's market; **nicht genügend belieferter ~** understocked (poor) market; **gut beschickter ~** market well stocked with goods; **beschränkter ~** restricted market; **von wenigen Anbietern bestimmter ~** oligopolistic market; **schlecht bestückter ~** poor market; **bewirtschafteter ~** controlled market; **effektiver ~** present market; **einheimischer ~** home (domestic) market; **einheitlicher ~** uniform market; **enger ~** narrow (limited) market; **fallender ~** declining market; **fester ~** steady market; **sehr fester ~** buoyant market; **flauer ~** flat (dull, dead, slack) market; **äußerst gedrückter ~** demoralized market; **infolge nachlassender Nachfrage gedrückter ~** heavy market; **Gemeinsamer ~** Common Market; **gesättigter ~** saturated market; **gestützter ~** pegged market; **gewerblicher ~** industrial market; **grauer ~** gray *(US)* (grey) market; **haussierender ~** bull market; **heimischer (inländischer) ~** home (domesticated) market; **heterogener ~** imperfect market; **homogener ~** perfect market; **jungfräulicher ~** virgin market; **lebhafter ~** active (brisk, cheerful, lively) market; **leerer ~** no stock available; **gedrückt liegender ~** depressed (heavy) market; **lockerer ~** easy market; **lustloser ~** inactive (featureless, flat, narrow, dull) market; **uneinheitlicher und lustloser ~** sick market *(US)*; **maßgeblicher ~** *(Kartellrecht)* relevant market *(US)*; **monopolisierter ~** captive market; **offener ~** open (competitive, free, outside, *US*) market, market overt *(Br.)*; **öffentlicher ~** public market; **potentieller ~** potential market; **reagibler ~** sensitive market; **regionaler ~** regional market; **rückläufiger ~** sagging (receding, down) market; **ruhiger ~** calm market; **schwacher ~** weak (poor) market; **auf umfangreiche Glattstellungen hin schwacher ~** liquidating market *(US)*; **schwankender ~** fluctuating market; **schwarzer ~** black market; **stagnierender ~** stagnant (languishing, trading, *US*) market; **steigender ~** rising market; **tatsächlicher ~** actual market; **teurer ~** high-priced market; **tonangebender ~** standard market; **infolge von Baisseverkäufen**

überlasteter ~ oversold account *(Br.)*; **übersättigter (mit Waren überschwemmter)** ~ glutted (overstocked) market; **überseeischer** ~ overseas market; **umfangreicher** ~ broad market; **unbearbeiteter** ~ virgin market; **unerschlossener** ~ untapped market; **vielversprechender** ~ promising market; **vollkommener** ~ perfect market; **widerstandsfähiger** ~ resistant market; **jederzeit zugänglicher** ~ freedom of entry into the market; **zurückfallender** ~ unsteady market;

~ **für Anlagewerte** investment market; ~ **der Auslandswerte** foreign market; ~ **für Automobilwerte** the motor group; ~ **für Bauerwartungsland** development land market; ~ **für Bauwerke** market for construction; ~ **für Bezugsrechte** rights market *(US)*; ~ **für Eisenbahnwerte** railway (railroad, *US*) market; ~ **für landwirtschaftliche Erzeugnisse** agricultural (farm) market; ~ **für qualifizierte Erzeugnisse** top end of the market; ~ **für Fischprodukte** fish market; ~ **für verbilligte Flüge** cheap-fare market; ~ **für Flugzeugwerte** aviation market; ~ **für Frischprodukte** fresh market; ~ **für tägliches Geld** call-money market; ~ **für langfristige Gelder** market for long-term funds; ~ **der Europäischen Gemeinschaft** Community Market; ~ **für Industrieanleihen** corporate bond market *(US)*; ~ **für Industriewerte** industrial market; ~ **für Investitionspapiere** financial market; ~ **für Kolonialwerte** colonial market; ~ **für Kommunalanleihen** local authority market *(Br.)*; ~ **für Kommunalpapiere** municipal (bond) market; ~ **für steuerfreie Kommunalwerte** tax-exempt municipal market; ~ **für wechselkursungebundene Kommunalwerte** market in floating-rate local authority securities; ~ **für Kupferwerte** copper market; ~ **mit spekulativ beeinflußten Kursen** rigged market; ~ **für Montanwerte** mining market; ~ **für Neuemissionen** new-issue market; ~ **zweiter Ordnung** secondary market; ~ **für international gehandelte Papiere** international market; ~ **für kurzfristige Papiere** short end of the market; ~ **für Pfandbriefwerte** bond market; ~ **mit steigendem Preisniveau** advancing market; ~ **für Qualitätserzeugnisse** quality market; ~ **für industrielle Schuldverschreibungen** corporate bond market *(US)*; ~ **für mündelsichere Staatsanleihen** gilt-edged market *(Br.)*; ~ **für Staatspapiere (Staatsanleihen)** consols market *(Br.)*; ~ **für Tagesgeld** overnight market, call-money market *(Br.)*; ~ **für Termingeschäfte** market for future delivery (in futures) *(US)*; ~ **für Überseewerte** overseas market; ~ **für Umweltgestaltung** environmental market; ~ **für Verbrauchsgüter** consumer market; ~ **mit großem Warenangebot** easy market; ~ **für festverzinsliche Werte (Wertpapiere)** market for fixed-interest bearing securities, bond market *(US)*; ~ **für nicht notierte Werte** off-board market *(US)*, over-the-counter market *(US)*, kerb market *(Br.)*; ~ **für international gehandelte Wertpapiere** international market; ~ **für mündelsichere Wertpapiere** gilt-edged (gilts) market *(Br.)*; ~ **für verschiedene Wertpapiere** miscellaneous market; ~ **mit starkem Wettbewerb** very competitive market;

der ~ **ist praktisch tot** there is nothing doing;

~ **abhalten** to hold a market; ~ **abtasten** to sound the market; ~ **mit kleinen Börsenumsätzen abtasten** to make a little deal in stocks as a feeler; ~ **aufkaufen** to corner the market; ~ **aufspalten** to apportion the market; ~ **aufteilen** to apportion (divide, allocate) the market; ~ **durch Spekulationsmanöver ausplündern** to milk the market; ~ **beeinflussen** to affect the market, to manipulate (rig) the market (stock exchange), to have an effect on the market; ~ **durch Konzertzeichnungen beeinflussen** to stag the market; ~ **durch Zurückhaltung beeinflussen** to wait out the market *(sl.)*; ~ **beherrschen** to hold (command, control, dominate) the market; **dem gemeinsamen** ~ **beitreten** to join the Common Market; ~ **beleben** to stimulate the market; ~ **beliefern** to supply a market; ~ **beruhigen** to calm the market; ~ **beschicken** to [send goods on the] market, to place on the market; ~ **beurteilen** to gauge the market; **auf den** ~ **bringen** to put (place, launch) on (introduce into) the market, to offer for sale, to bring out, to market *(US)*; **Aktienpaket auf den** ~ **bringen** to market one's block of shares; **Anleihe auf den** ~ **bringen** to float (issue) a loan; **neue Artikel auf den** ~ **bringen** to sell a new line in the market; **in großen Mengen auf den** ~ **bringen** *(v.)* to mass-market; **Waren im Ausland billig auf den** ~ **bringen** to dump goods on a foreign market; **aus dem** ~ **drängen** to oust from the market, to put out of business; ~ **drücken** to depress the market, to bring down prices; ~ **entlasten** to relieve the market; ~ **erdrücken** to overhang the market; **ganzen** ~ **erfassen** to blanket the entire market; ~ **erkunden** to study the market; ~ **erobern** to conquer (win) a market; ~ **spielend erobern** to romp into a market; ~ **erschließen** to tap a market, to open up; **neuen** ~ **erschließen** to open up a new market; ~ **erweitern** to extend a market; **im freien** ~ **erzielen** to earn in the open market; **aufnahmefähigen** ~ **finden** to meet with a ready (speedy) market; ~ **forcieren** to force the market; **dem** ~ **Auftrieb geben** to give a fillip to the market; **auf den** ~ **gehen** to go marketing; **aus dem** ~ **herauskommen** to come out [of the market]; **auf dem offenen** ~ **kaufen** to purchase in the open market; ~ **kennen** to understand the market; **auf den** ~ **kommen** to come out [into the market]; ~ **kontrollieren** to regulate the market; ~ **manipulieren** to manipulate the market; ~ **monopolisieren** to engross (monopolize) the market; **aus dem** ~ **nehmen** to take off (out of) the market; ~ **sättigen** to saturate the market; ~ **schaffen** to create a market; **auf dem** ~ **sein** to be at the market; **auf dem** ~ **führend sein** to be leading in its line of business; **auf dem** ~ **vertreten sein** to be found on the market; ~ **spalten** to disrupt a market; ~ **stützen** to rescue the market; **seine Haut zu ~e tragen** to do at one's own risk, to risk one's life, to go off the deep end *(sl.)*; **auf einem** ~ **in Erscheinung treten** to tap the market; ~ **überschwemmen** to flow (overstock, glut, congest, flood, swamp) the market; ~ **mit Aktien überschwemmen** to unload stocks on the market; **sein Aktienpaket auf dem** ~ **unterbringen** to market one's block of shares; **Dividendenwerte auf dem** ~ **unterbringen** to market equity securities; **vom** ~ **verdrängen** to oust from the market; **Konkurrenz aus dem** ~ **verdrängen** to drive competitors out of the market, to put competitors out of business; **auf dem** ~ **verkaufen** to market; **am offenen** ~ **verkaufen** to sell in the open market; **auf dem** ~ **verkloppen** to flog on the market; ~ **mit Waren versehen (versorgen)** to supply the market; ~ **versteifen** to glue up the market; **vom** ~ **vertreiben** to force out of the market; **auf den** ~ **werfen** to throw on the market, *(Effekten)* to unload; ~ **wiedergewinnen** to regain (win back) the market; **aus dem** ~ **ziehen** to take off (out of) the market; **verlorenen** ~ **zurückerobern** to recover a market; **auf dem** ~ **zusammenströmen** to gather in crowds on the market place;

~**abgaben** market dues; ~**abrede**, ~**absprache** marketing arrangement (agreement); ~**absatz** sale; ~**abschwächung** weakening of the market; ~**analyse** analysis of the market, marketing (market) analysis (research, inquiry, survey), commercial survey; ~**analyse vornehmen** to analyse the market; ~**angebot** market supply; ~**anlagen** investment in securities; ~**anpassungszeit** *(Börse)* time lag; ~**anspannung** tightening of the market.

Marktanteil fraction (share) of the market, market share (quota), sales quota;

größerer ~ bigger slice of the market; **notwendiger** ~ *(Kartellrecht)* appreciable part of commerce; **schrumpfender** ~ shrivelling market;

entscheidenen ~ **besitzen** to control a preponderant part of the market; **seinen** ~ **erhöhen** to up one's share of the market; **größeren** ~ **erobern** to get a bigger foot in the market; ~ **halten** to hold on the market; **sich einen noch größeren hoch rentierlichen aber konkurrenzträchtigen** ~ **sichern** to carve out an even greater share of a highly profitable yet competitive market; **sich einen großen** ~ **suchen** to carve out a large part of the market.

Markt|anteilsentwicklung market-share trend; ~**anweisung** market order *(US)*; ~**aufbau** market structure; ~**aufnahme** market acceptance; ~**aufnahmefähigkeit** receptivity of the market; ~**aufnahmetest** acceptance test; ~**aufseher** clerk of the market; ~**aufteilung** division (allocation) of markets, market sharing (segmentation); **territoriale** ~**aufteilung** territorial allocation, zoning; ~**aufteilung vornehmen** to allocate a market; ~**aufteilungsabrede** market-sharing agreement; ~**ausdehnung** expanding market; ~**ausgleich herbeiführen** to even out the market; ~**ausrufer** market crier; ~**aussichten** market prospects (outlook); **sich an der** ~**ausweitung beteiligen** to share in the expanding market.

marktbar marketable.

Markt|beanspruchung recourse to the market; ~**bedarf** market demand.

marktbedingt market-induced.

Markt|bedingungen marketing conditions; ~**bedürfnis** market demand; ~**beeinflussung** stagging the market; ~**befrager** field investigator (worker), interviewer.

marktbeherrschend market-dominating, monopolistic;

~**es Unternehmen** market-dominating enterprise, corporation dominating the market.

Markt|beherrschung control (domination) of the market, market operation (domination, dominance, control), grip on the market, monopoly; ~**belebung** trade revival, buoyancy;

~**belieferung** supplying the market, market supply; ~**beobachter** market analyst, *(Börse)* security analyst *(US)*; ~**beobachtung** market analysis (inquiry), commercial survey, *(kontinuierliche)* market observation *(US)*; ~**bereich** section of the market; ~**bereich der wechselkursfreigegebenen Euroanleihen** floating rate sector of the market; ~**bericht** market report, report (statement, review) of the market, *(Kurse)* market price list (news), quotations; **tägliche** ~**berichte** market letters *(US)*; ~**berührung** market contact; ~**beschickung** market supply.

marktbestimmender Faktor market determinant.

Markt | besuch market; ~**besucher** marketman, marketer; ~**beteiligte** market partners; ~**beteiligung** market participation; ~**beurteilung vornehmen** to gauge the market; ~**bewegungen** market fluctuations; **rückläufige** ~**bewegung** downturn in the market; ~**bewertung** market valuation (assessment); ~**bewirtschaftung** market regulation; ~**bezieher** marketman, marketer; ~**bildungsprozeß** market process; ~**bude** market stand, stall; ~**chancen** sales possibilities; ~**daten** market facts; ~**dimensionen** market size; ~**drückerei** *(Börse)* squeezing the shorts; ~**durchdringung** market penetration.

Märkte | besuchen to market; ~ **beziehen** to frequent fairs (markets); **weitere** ~ **erschließen** to carve out wider markets; **neue** ~ **für seine Erzeugnisse erschließen** to find new markets for one's manufactures; **sich spezialisierte** ~ **suchen** to move upmarket; ~ **zurückgewinnen** to win back markets.

Markt | einbruch erzielen, entscheidenden to make vast inroads into the market; ~**einfluß** staggering the market; ~**eingriff** direct intervention in the economy; **günstiger** ~**einkauf** market purchasing; ~**einkäufe** marketing; ~**elastizität** elasticity of the market, buoyancy.

marktempfindlich sensitive to business movements.

markten to market.

Markt | enge narrow market, narrowness (limitedness) of the market, limited condition; ~**entfremdung** pricing out of the market; ~**entlegenheit** remoteness of the market.

marktentscheidender Preis key price.

Markt | entwicklung market development (trend), trend of the market; ~**entwicklung über einen größeren Zeitraum** major swing *(US)*; ~**erfordernisse** market requirements; ~**erholung** recovery of the market, rally; ~**erkundung** market exploration (testing); ~**eroberung** market assumption; ~**erschließung** marketing entry, opening of (tapping) new markets; ~**erschöpfung** depletion of the market.

marktfähig marketable, salable;
nicht ~ unmarketable, unsalable;
~ **machen** to commercialize;
~**e Effekten** marketable securities.

Markt | fähigkeit marketability, salability; ~**faktoren** market factors; ~**ferne** remoteness of the market; ~**festigkeit** firmness of the market; ~**festigung** consolidation (strengthening) of the market; ~**flecken** borough, market town *(Br.)*; ~**flexibilität** flexibility of the market, market flexibility; ~**förderung** sales promotion; ~**forscher** marketing researcher, market research specialist (worker), head counter *(sl.)*.

Marktforschung market research, field survey (investigation);
stichprobenartig durchgeführte ~ purposive sampling; **kontinuierliche** ~ market observation;
~ **für ein neues Erzeugnis** product research; ~ **und Meinungsforschung** statistical sampling, *(Werbeagentur)* research; ~ **an Ort und Stelle** field (marketing) survey; ~ **in Stichproben** purposive sampling.

Marktforschungs | abteilung market research department; ~**gruppe** market research group; ~**institut** market research agency.

marktfühlig sensitive to market influences.

Markt | führer market leader, guide; ~**fülle** glut in the market.

marktgängig marketable, merchantable, current, staple, salable;
nicht ~ unmarketable, unmerchantable; **überall** ~ fungible;
~**e Preise** usual market prices; ~**e Waren** marketable products.

Markt | gängigkeit marketability, salability; ~**gebiet** market territory, marketing area; **höher entwickelte** ~**gebiete** upmarket regions; **hohe Akquisitionskosten forderndes** ~**gebiet** high-cost area; ~**gebühren** market dues; ~**gefälle** tendency of the market; ~**gefüge** market structure; ~**geld** stallage *(Br.)*, toll; ~**geltung** general standing of a business.

markt | gemäß, ~**gerecht** in conformity with the market;
Möglichkeiten im Eisenbahnfrachtverkehr der Kundschaft ~**er darstellen** to market rail freight more aggressively; ~ **verzinst werden** to carry a rate of interest in conformity with the market;
~**er Preis** fair market price.

Markt | gemeinde market town *(Br.)*; ~**gerechtigkeit** staple right (privilege), franchise, *(Konformität)* conformity with the market; ~**geschehen** market process; ~**geschehen beherrschen** to dominate trading; ~**gesundung** recovery (revitalization) of the market; ~**gleichgewicht** equilibrium of an industry; ~**größe** market volume (size); ~**halle** trade hall, covered market, market house *(Br.)*; ~**händler** marketeer, market dealer, marketman; ~**helfer** shop (warehouse, *US*) porter; ~**information** market inquiry; **umfassende** ~**informationen** market intelligence; ~**intervention** direct intervention in the economy; ~**karren** market cart; ~**kenner** *(Effekten)* stock-market observer, security analyst *(US)*; ~**kenntnis** market knowledge (analysis); ~**klima** atmosphere of the market; ~**komplex** market nexus.

marktkonform in keeping (conformity) with the market;
sich nicht ~ **entwickeln** to run against the market's favo(u)r;
~**e Mittel** [anti]cyclical measures.

Marktkonstellation state of the market, market situation.

marktkonträr sein to be incompatible with the market.

Markt | kontrolle market supervision, control of the market, *(durch zwei Firmen)* duopoly; ~**konzentration** market concentration; ~**korb** market basket.

Marktlage market position (situation), state of the market, market condition[s], course, sales situation, mood of the market;
allgemeine ~ general tone of the market; **schwache** ~ weakness of the market; **stabile** ~ stiff (stable) market;
bei der augenblicklichen ~ **keine Geschäfte machen können** to be unable to turn a penny in the present market.

Markt | leistung market performance; ~**lenkung** market regulations; ~**lücke** market hole (gap); ~**lücken finden** to find gaps in the market; ~**lücke schließen** to bridge a gap in the market; ~**macht** market forces; **gegengewichtige** ~**macht** countervailing power; **hinreichende wirtschaftliche** ~**macht** *(Kartellrecht)* sufficient economic power; ~**mechanismus** market mechanism; ~**miete** current-market (accustomed) rent; ~**modell** market pattern; **sich flexibel den** ~**möglichkeiten anpassen** to adapt o. s. flexibly to market possibilities; ~**monopol** market monopoly; ~**nachfrage** market demand, seller's market; ~**nachrichten** market news.

marktnahe close to the market.

Markt | nähe nearness (proximity) to the market; ~**notierung** market quotation; ~**öffnung** marketing entry, opening of a market; ~**ordnung** *(EG)* marketing regulation; **einzelstaatliche** ~**ordnungen** national market organizations; ~**ordnung der Europäischen Gemeinschaft** Common Market Organization; ~**ordnungsstelle** market agency; ~**organisation** *(EG)* marketing (market) organization; **gemeinsame** ~**organisation für Getreide (Obst, Gemüse)** *(EG)* common market organization of cereals (fruit, vegetables).

marktorientiert market-oriented;
~**es Verhalten** marketing behavio(u)r.

Markt | orientierung market orientation; ~**ort** market town *(Br.)*; ~**partner** market partner; ~**perspektiven** market prospects; ~**pflege** cultivation of the market; ~**pflege betreiben** to cultivate the market; ~**plan** marketing mix; ~**planung** market planning; ~**platz** market place (square), market, market stance *(Scot.)*; ~**position** market (trading) position; ~**potential** market potential.

Marktpreis market price (rate), open market price, marketable value, today's rate;
zum ~ at current market prices;
durchschnittlicher ~ certain (natural, normal) price; **im freien Kräftespiel entstandener** ~ commercial price; **freier** ~ open-market price; **gängiger** ~ going-market price; **gegenwärtiger** ~ ruling price; **herrschende** ~**e** marketable prices; **steigende** ~**e** advancing market; **üblicher** ~ fair cash market value;
~**e durch Zurückhaltung beeinflussen** to wait out the market *(sl.)*; **Ware unter dem** ~ **verkaufen** to sell goods below market price, to undercut;
~**mechanismus** price-market mechanism.

Markt | produktion production for the market; ~**prognose** market forecast (outlook).

marktreagibel sensitive to market influence.

Markt | recht [right to hold a] market, law of staple, franchise; ~**regelung,** ~**regulierung** *(EG)* regulation of the market.

marktreif ready to come into the market.

Markt | reifegestaltung product planning; ~**richtpreis** target (standard purchase) price; ~**richtwert** market standard; ~**risiko** marketing risk; ~**sachverständiger** marketing expert, *(Effekten)* security analyst *(US)*; ~**sanierung** recovery (revitalization) of the market; ~**sättigung** market saturation, saturation of consumer demands; ~**satz** market rate; ~**schaffung** marketing; ~**schreier** market crier, cheap Jack, booster, barker, puffer *(Br.)*.

marktschreierisch quackish, charlatan, blatant, showy, puffy *(Br.)*;

~**e Ankündigung** puffing advertisement (publicity) *(Br.)*, noisy advertising, ballyhoo *(US)*.

Markt|schwäche weakness in the market, market weakness; ~**schwankungen** fluctuations of the market, market swing, fluctuating market; ~**schwemme** glut in the market; ~**segment** market segment; ~**situation** market position (situation), [state of the] market; ~**spaltung** disruption of the market; ~**stand** [market] stand, stall; ~**standgebühren** market dues; ~**steigerung** rising market; ~**stelle** market agency; ~**stellung** position in the market, market position; **seine ~stellung behalten** to hold one's own; ~**steuerung** control of the market; ~**stockung** stagnation of the market; ~**strategie** marketing strategy; ~**struktur** market structure; ~**studie** market study, market-trend analysis; ~**sturz** slump in trade; ~**stützung** peg, rescue of (holding, *US*) the market; ~**stützungskosten** cost of rescue of the market; **freies ~system** free price system; ~**tag** market day; **nächster ~tag** next market; ~**tätigkeit** business; ~**tendenz** market trend; **günstige ~tendenz** promising tendency; **vollkommene ~transparenz** perfect knowledge of the market; ~**übersättigung** glutting the market, oversaturation; ~**übersicht** market review (survey); ~**umfang** market volume; ~**unbeständigkeit** unsteadiness of the market.

Marktuntersuchung market research (study, analysis, audit), [market] survey, trade research, *(Marktforschung)* marketing inquiry;

charakteristische ~ controlled sample; **methodische** ~ randomization; **regionale** ~ area sampling; **repräsentative** ~ adequate sample; **nach Schichten spezifizierte** ~ stratified sample; **stichprobenartige** ~ haphazard (random) sampling.

Markt|veränderung market change, shift in the market; ~**verband** marketing association; ~**verbot** prohibition of trade; ~**vereinbarung** marketing agreement; ~**vereinigung** marketing association; ~**verengung** tightening of the market; ~**verfassung** tone (state) of the market; ~**verflechtung** integration of markets; ~**verhalten** market behavio(u)r; ~**verhältnis** market ratio; ~**verhältnisse** market conditions; ~**verkauf** run of the market; ~**verkäufe** marketings; ~**verkehr** traffic in the market, market, marketing; **flauer ~verkehr** slack market; **offener ~verkehr** open market; ~**verlagerung** shift in the market; ~**verordnungsvorschriften** *(EG)* Common Market regulations; ~**verschiebung** shift in the market; ~**versorgung** supply of the market, market supply, marketing; ~**verstimmung** indigestion in the market; ~**vertretung** marketing agency.

marktverzerrend market-distorting.

Markt|verzerrung market distortion; ~**volumen** market volume; **vom ~volumen bestimmt werden** *(Preis)* to be determined by the amount of the market; ~**voraussagen** market forecasts; ~**vorrat** stock in the market, marketing; ~**ware** market wares, marketing products.

Marktwert market, market (marketable, commercial) value, *(Börse)* exchange value;

führende ~e *(Börse)* stalwarts of the market, leaders; **gegenwärtiger** ~ current market value; **gemeiner (üblicher)** ~ fair and reasonable market value; **veränderlicher** ~ fluctuating market value.

Markt|wesen marketing; ~**widerstand** market resistance; ~**widerstandsfähigkeit** market resistance.

Marktwirtschaft, freie free market (laissez-faire) economy, free enterprise (market) system; **gebundene** ~ controlled economy; **interventionistische** ~ economics of control; **soziale** ~ social market economy.

marktwirtschaftlich, außerhalb des ~en Bereiches outside the sphere of the market economy; ~**es Gleichgewicht** balance of market economy; ~**e Ordnung** free enterprise system.

Markt|zerrüttung market distortion, dislocation of the market; ~**zettel** market quotations; ~**zinssatz** *(Geldmarkt)* market rate of interest *(US)*; ~**zug** market train; ~**zugang** access to the market; **freier ~zugang für jeden Anbieter** freedom of entry into the market.

Marmorfußboden marble pavement.

marmorieren *(Buchbinderei)* to marble.

marodieren to maraud, to pillage.

Marotte fad, whim, fancy;

kurzfristige ~ only a passing whim; **neueste** ~ the latest fad; **einer ~ nachgehen** to indulge one's fancy.

Marsch, auf dem on the move;

~ **von 20 km** twenty kilometres walk; ~ **an die Spitze der Tabelle** progress to the top of the table; ~ **ohne Tritt** route march; **j. den ~ blasen** to give s. o. a piece of one's mind; **auf dem ~ zur Unabhängigkeit sein** to be on its way to independence; **sich in ~ setzen** to move off; **Truppen in ~ setzen** to march (dispatch, route) troops.

Marschallstab im Tornister baton in the knapsack.

Marschausrüstung marching order.

Marschbefehl marching (walking, march, *US*) orders, route [order], sailing orders;

~ **erhalten** to get the route; ~ **haben** to be under marching orders.

marschbereit ready to march.

Marschbereitschaft, in ~ sein to be ready to march.

Marsch|disziplin marching discipline; ~**fahrt** *(Schiff)* cruising speed.

marschfertig ready to march.

Marsch|gepäck *(mil.)* field pack; **leichtes ~gepäck** light marching order; ~**geschwindigkeit** *(Schiff)* marching speed, cruising speed.

marschieren to march, *(wandern)* to hike;

in geschlossener Formation ~ to march in close formation; **im Gleichschritt** ~ to be marching in step; **durch die ganze Stadt** ~ to parade through the streets; **im Zimmer auf und ab** ~ to pace up and down a room.

Marsch|kolonne marching column; **geschlossene ~kolonne** closed column; **in einer ~kolonne marschieren** *(mil.)* to troop away *(coll.)*; ~**kompaß** prismatic compass; ~**lied** marching song; ~**musik** military marches, field music; ~**ordnung** marching order; ~**richtung** *(fig.)* lines of policy; ~**route** route; ~**stiefel** walking (ammunition) boots; **schnelles ~tempo** quick time; ~**tiefe** depth of column; ~**verpflegung** marching (haversack, *Br.*) ration.

Marshallplan|gegenkonto counterpart fund; ~**konto** treasury special account *(Br.)*.

Marter torture;

seelische ~n mental torments;

~**n ertragen** to suffer (bear) torments.

martern to torture, to torment.

Marterpfahl, jem. an den ~ binden to tie s. o. to the stake.

Marterung torture.

Märtyrer, sich als ~ aufspielen to make a martyr of o. s.; **zum ~ werden** to wear the crown;

~**rolle spielen** to play the role of a martyr; ~**tod erleiden** to die a martyr, to perish at the stake.

Marxismus Marxism.

Marxist Marxist, Red.

marxistisch Marxist, red.

Masche mesh, *(fig.)* tie, trick, racket *(US sl.)*, *(Stricken)* stitch;

sehr viel bessere ~ a trick worth two of it; **neue** ~ new twist; ~ **heraushaben** to have the knack of it; **jds. ~ kennen** to be up to s. one's tricks; **immer mit derselben ~ kommen** to come along with the same old story; **durch die ~n schlüpfen** to escape the web; **durch die ~ des Gesetzes schlüpfen** to find a loophole in the law; **es mit der sanften ~ versuchen** to try it with soft soap.

Maschendrahtzaun wire screen.

Maschine machine, apparatus, *(Bahn)* locomotive, engine, *(Gerät)* implement, contrivance, appliance, apparatus, *(Flugzeug)* plane, *(Motorrad)* motorcycle, *(Schreibmaschine)* typewriter;

mit der ~ geschrieben typewritten;

~**n** machinery, equipment;

arbeitende ~ running machine; **arbeitseinsparende ~n** labo(u)r-saving machines; **automatische** ~ automatic (self-driven) machine; **in Betrieb (in Benutzung, im Gebrauch) befindliche** ~ machinery in operation (use); **betriebsbereite (einsatzbereite)** ~ machine in operating condition; **landwirtschaftliche ~n** agricultural machinery, farm equipment; **leistungsfähige** ~ efficient machinery; **stillstehende** ~ standing engine;

~**n und maschinelle Anlagen** *(Bilanz)* machinery, plant and equipment; ~**n und Ausstattung** *(Bilanz)* machines and equipment; ~**n und Einrichtungen** *(Bilanz)* plant and equipment; ~**n zur Einsparung von Arbeitskräften** labo(u)r-saving machinery; ~ **im Taschenformat** pocket-size machine; ~ **mit Tastenbedienung** key-operated machine;

~ **abstellen** to stop a machine; ~ **anhalten** to rest a machine; **weitere Versuche mit einer ~ anstellen** to put a machine to further trials; **wie eine ~ arbeiten** to do one's work mechanically; **neue ~n aufstellen** to lay down (erect, install) new machinery; **Fabrik mit den notwendigen ~n ausstatten** to tool a factory; ~ **stark beanspruchen** to impose a strain on a machine; ~ **bedienen** to operate (work) a machine; ~ **in Gang bringen** to set an engine going, to put a machine in operation; **alte** ~ **ersetzen** to replace an old machine; ~ **nur mit halber Kraft fahren** to work the engine at half power; **j. zur reinsten** ~ **herabwürdigen** to reduce s. o. to a mere machine; **mit der** ~ **herstellen** to machine; ~ **kaputtmachen** to put a machine out of order; ~ **auf Probe kaufen** to take a machine on trial; ~ **konstruieren** to design a machine; ~ **arbeiten lassen** to operate a machine; **auf der** ~ **schreiben** to type; ~ **in Betrieb setzen** to start a machine, to put a machine in operation; ~ **verfeinern** to improve a machine; ~ **kostenlos zum Ausprobieren zusenden** to send a machine for free trial.

maschine|gebucht machine-posted; ~**geschrieben** typed, typewritten.

maschinell mechanical, machinal, machined;
teilweise ~ part-machined;
~ **gebucht** machine-posted;
~ **auszeichnen** *(Preise)* to mark by machine; ~ **bearbeiten** to machine; ~ **betrieben** engine-driven;
~**e Abnutzung** machine wear; ~**e Arbeit** shopwork; ~**er Arbeitsvorgang** machine operation, mechanical process; ~**e Bearbeitung** machining; ~**e Bearbeitungsmethode** machining method; ~**er Bearbeitungszuschlag** machining allowance; ~**e Buchung** machine posting; ~**e Einrichtung** machinery; ~**e Herstellung** machinery production; ~**e Tabellierung** machine tabulation; ~**es Verfahren** mechanical process; ~**e Vorrichtungen** mechanical devices.

Maschinen|abnutzung machine wear; ~**abzug** machine proof.

Maschinenanlage machinery, power plant, set, [mechanical] equipment, *(Schiff)* engine room;
in Betrieb befindliche ~**n** operative machinery; **fest eingebaute** ~**n** trade fixtures; **Arbeitskräfte ersetzende** ~**n** labo(u)r-displacing machines.

Maschinen|anlagenkonto machinery account; **mit** ~**antrieb** power-driven; ~**arbeit** machine work; ~**arbeiter** machine (engine) fitter, machinist, shopworker *(US)*, shopman *(US)*, machine attendant (operator); ~**ausfallzeit** machine-idle time; ~**ausrüstung** *(Datenverarbeitung)* hardware; ~- **und Betriebsausrüstung** *(Bilanz)* machinery and equipment; ~**bau** constructional (mechanical) engineering, engine building, *(Industriezweig)* engineering industry; ~**bauer** mechanical engineer, machine (machinery) builder, engine builder.

Maschinenbau|erzeugnis mechanical engineering product; ~**firma** mechanical engineering company, machine shop; ~**industrie** engineering industry; ~**ingenieur** construction[al] (mechanical) engineer; ~**wesen** mechanical engineering.

Maschinen|bearbeitung mechanical treatment, machining; ~**belegungsplan** equipment analysis, job-shop sequencing *(Br.)*; **für** ~**benutzung abschreiben** to write off for depreciation of machinery; ~**betrieb** mechanical operation; **auf** ~**betrieb umstellen** to mechanize; ~**betriebsversicherung** engineering insurance; ~**brachezeit** machine downtime; ~**buchhalter** machine accountant, bookkeeping machine operator; ~**buchhaltung,** ~**buchführung** mechanical bookkeeping, machine accounting; ~**buchungssatz** machine burden unit; ~**defekt** engine trouble, machinery breakdown; ~**einsatzplan** job-shop sequencing *(Br.)*; ~**element** machine part; ~**erneuerung** machinery replacement; ~**erneuerungskonto** equipment account; ~**erzeugnisse** machine products; ~**fabrik** machine works (shop), engineering (engine) works; ~**fach** mechanical engineering; ~**führer** operator.

maschinengeschrieben manuscript, typed.

Maschinengewehr machine gun;
Feind mit ~**salven eindecken** to pepper the enemy with machine-gun fire; ~**schütze** machine gunner.

maschinenglattes Papier machine-finished paper.

Maschinen|gondel engine car; ~**gruppe** production unit; ~**haftpflichtversicherung** machinery insurance; ~**halle** machine shop; ~**haus** engine house (room); ~**hauswärter** engineman; ~**heftung** *(Buch)* machine-sewing; ~**hersteller** machinery (machine) builder; ~**industrie** engineering industry; ~**ingenieur** mechanical engineer; ~**konstruktion** machine construction; ~**kostensatz** machine burden unit; ~**kunde** mechanical engineering; ~**kurzschrift** typed shorthand; ~**lehre** practical mechanics; ~**leistung** engine output (capacity).

maschinenmäßig machinal, machined, mechanical;
nicht ~ *(fig.)* unmechanical.

Maschinen|miete machine rental; ~**öl** engine oil; ~**pacht- und Wartungsvertrag** service lease *(US)*; ~**pachtvertrag ohne Wartung** financial lease.

Maschinenpark machinery, equipment;
beweglicher ~ movable plant;
~ **einer Druckerei** printing machinery (equipment);
~**erneuerung** machinery replacement; ~**investitionen mit dem Ziel rascher Ertragssteigerung durch Verringerung der Lohnquote** investment in quick return labo(u)r-cost displacing equipment; ~**miete** equipment lease.

Maschinen|pistole submachine gun, tommy-gun; ~**produktion** machinery production; ~**raum** machine room, *(Druckerei)* pressroom, *(Schiff)* engine room; ~**reparaturwerkstätte** mechanic (machine) shop; ~**revision** press revise; ~**saal** machine shop, engine room, *(Druckerei)* pressroom; ~**satz** engine set, power unit, *(Setzen)* machine composition (setting), mechanical typesetting; ~**schaden** damage to machinery, breakdown of machinery, engine trouble (failure); ~**schlosser** mechanic, machine (engine) fitter, machinist, shopman *(US)*, shopworker *(US)*; ~**schlosserlehrling** apprentice machine fitter; ~**schreiber** typist; **in** ~**schrift** typewritten, typed; ~**schuppen** engine shed; ~**setzer** machine compositor (setter); ~**sprache** machine language; ~**stenografie** typed shorthand; ~**stunde** machine hour; ~**stundensatz** machine-hour rate; ~**teile** machine parts; ~**typisierung** specialization of machines; ~**verkauf** sale of machinery; ~**wärter** machine attendant; ~**wartung** maintenance service; ~**werkstatt** machine shop; ~**wesen** mechanical engineering; ~**zeile** slug; ~**zeitalter** age of machines, machine age; ~**zentrale** central station.

Maschinerie machinery;
komplizierte ~ **des Staates** complicated machinery of government.

Maschineschreiben typing, typewriting.

maschineschreiben to type.

Maschine|schreiber typewriter, typist; ~**schreiberin** lady typist.

Maschinist machinist, mechanic, engine operator, *(Bahn)* engine driver (runner, *US*), black gang;
erster ~ *(Schiff)* chief engineer.

Maser[ung] grain, streak, vein.

Maske guise, disguise, veil, mask, visor;
unter der ~ **der Freundschaft** under the mask of friendship;
~ **aufsetzen** to put on a mask; **seine** ~ **fallen lassen** to unmask, to throw (put) off one's mask; **jem. die** ~ **vom Gesicht reißen** to strip s. o. of his disguise; **sich hinter einer gleichgültigen** ~ **verschanzen** to put up a screen of indifference.

Masken|ball masked (fancy-dress) ball; ~**bildner** make-up artist; ~**fest** masquerade; ~**kostüm** fancy dress, masquerade; ~**verfahren** *(Foto)* masking; ~**verleih** costumier; ~**zwang** masks obligatory.

Maskerade mask, masquerade.

maskieren, sich to put on a mask.

maskiert masked;
~ **sein** to be masked; ~ **umhergehen** to masquerade;
~**e Batterie** *(mil.)* masked battery; ~**er Einbrecher** masked burglar.

Maskierung masking, mask, *(mil.)* camouflage, screen.

Maskottchen mascot.

Maß measure[ment], *(Ausdehnung)* dimension, extent, size, *(Ausmaß)* extent, degree, measure, proportion, *(Eichmaß)* gauge *(Br.)*, gage *(US)*, standard, *(Größe)* size, *(Maßstab)* scale, *(Menge)* quantity, *(Raummenge)* volume, *(Verhältnis)* rate, proportion;
in begrenztem ~ on a limited scale; **in beschränktem** ~ to a limited degree; **in hohem** ~ largely, to a large extent (degree); **in solchem** ~**e** to such an extent; **nach** ~ to order, made to measure, bespoke *(Br.)*, custom-made *(US)*; **über alle** ~**en** out of all measure;
gehäuftes (gerütteltes) ~ heaped (good) measure; **höchstes** ~ full;
~**e und Gewichte** weights and measures; **falsche** ~**e und Gewichte** false weight; ~**e eines Zimmers** dimensions (measurements) of a room;
nach ~ **anfertigen** to make to order (measure); **Zeichnung in vergrößerten** ~**en anfertigen** to draw on an enlarged scale; **in starkem** ~**e beanspruchen** to subject to great stress; **sein gerütteltes** ~ **bekommen** to get one's full share; **metrische** ~**e benutzen** to use the metric system; **jem. in hohem** ~**e Vertrauen entgegenbringen** to repose a high degree of confidence in s. o.; **menschliche Arbeitskraft in zunehmendem** ~**e durch Maschinen ersetzen** to replace human labo(u)r increasingly by machinery; **im gleichen** ~**e gelten** to apply to the same degree; **bei allem und jedem** ~ **halten** to do everything with due measure; **über das übliche** ~ **hinausgehen** to go beyond the usual limits; **nach** ~ **kaufen** to buy to measure; **sich beim Schneider** ~ **nehmen lassen**

to go to the tailor's to be measured for a suit; **mit zweierlei ~ messen** to use double standards; **~ nehmen** *(Schneider)* to measure; **jem. zu einem Anzug ~ nehmen** to take s. one's measurements for a suit; **genau ~ nehmen** *(fig.)* to take careful aim; **in weitem ~e abhängig sein** to depend largely on; **in geringerem ~ betroffen sein** to be affected to a lesser extent; **in allem ohne ~ und Ziel sein** to go beyond (pass all, know no) bounds; **in gleichem ~e steigen** to rise to the same degree; **~e und Gewichte stempeln** to seal weights and measures; **~ von jds. Kräften übersteigen** to exceed s. one's strength; **nach ~ verkaufen** to sell by measure; **nur noch in geringem ~e vorkommen** to be rarely seen nowadays; **vom modernen Leben in stärkerem ~e beansprucht werden** to suffer from the greater strains of modern life; **in vergrößertem ~ zeichnen** to draw on an enlarged scale; **j. in vollem ~e zufriedenstellen** to satisfy all requirements; **Kritik auf das rechte ~ zurückführen** to reduce criticism to proper proportions;
das ~ ist voll enough is enough;
~abteilung bespoke *(Br.)* (custom-made, *US*) department.

Massage|gerät massager; **~salon** massage parlo(u)r.

Massaker massacre, wholesale slaughter.

massakrieren to massacre, to slaughter;
ganze Bevölkerung ~ to butcher (massacre) the population.

Maß|anfertigung bespoke business *(Br.)*; **~angaben** measurements.

Maßanzug tailor-made *(Br.)* (custom-made, *US*) suit;
erstklassig sitzender ~ well-tailored suit;
~ bestellen to have a suit made to measure; **jem. Maß für einen ~ nehmen** to take s. one's measurements for a suit.

Maß|arbeit bespoke *(Br.)* (custom, *US*) work; **~band** tape measure, line; **~bestimmung** measurement.

Masse mass, bulk, body, lump, aggregate, *(Erbschaft)* estate, assets, *(Konkurs)* assets, bankrupt estate, debtor's property, *(Menge)* quantity, volume, world, *(Substanz)* matter, substance, *(Volksmenge)* crowd, loads, herd, stream, host, press, multitude;
in ~n in large quantities, wholesale, *(Menschenmenge)* in crowds (droves); **in ~n produziert** mass-produced; **in der ~ untergegangen** lost in the press; **mangels ~** *(Konkurs)* return unsatisfied;
die große ~, die breiten ~n the people at large, the masses, the common herd, the rank and file; **kritische ~** *(Atomreaktor)* critical amount; **statistische ~** population; **undefinierbare ~** *(fig.)* sausage; **ungebildete ~** rough element of the population; **~n von Arbeitslosen** large bodies of unemployed men; **~n von Besuchern** stream of visitors; **~ der Bevölkerung** bulk (mass) of the population; **~ von Briefen** shoals (volume) of letters; **~ von Büchern** loads of books; **~ von Dingen** wilderness of things; **~ von Fehlern** mass of faults (mistakes); **~n von Ferienreisenden** streams (herds, loads) of tourists; **~ von Fragen** host of questions; **~ Geld** lots (barrels, lump) of money, a lot of money; **~ der Gläubiger** general creditors; **~ von Kindern** whole host of children; **~ von Leuten** scores of people; **~ der Lohnabhängigen** wage-earning masses; **~ von Menschen** crowds of people; **~ von Schulden** loads of debts; **~ eines Vermögens** bulk of a property; **~ des Volkes** mass of the population, the people at large; **~ von Zeit** lots of time; **~ der Zuhörer** mass of the audience;
Konkursantrag mangels ~ ablehnen to dismiss a petition on cause that the assets will be exhausted by costs; **~ zum Aufruhr anstiften** to excite the people to rebellion; **in ~n auftreten** to walk about in droves, to gather in masses; **sich der Sensationslust der ~ beugen** to cater to the public demand for the sensational; **mangels ~ einstellen** *(Konkursverfahren)* to stop bankruptcy proceedings for lack of funds; **~ von Briefen erhalten** to receive shoals of letters; **~ Geld haben** to have money to burn; **die ~ hinter sich haben** to be supported by the masses; **in ~n herstellen (produzieren)** to mass-produce, to volume-produce; **sich aus der ~ hervorheben** to rise above the mediocre; **Liebling der ~n sein** to be the idol of the people; **in der großen ~ untergehen** to be lost in the crowd; **in ~n angefertigt werden** to come off the production line; **in ~n auf den Markt werfen** to throw on the market in large quantities; **Aktien in ~n auf den Markt werfen** to unload stock on the market; **aus der ~ zahlen** to pay out of the assets;
~anspruch, ~forderung *(Konkurs)* unsecured claim, nonpreferential debt; **~forderung anmelden** to prove one's claim; **~gläubiger** general (unsecured, *US*, ordinary, nonprivileged) creditor, creditor at large, *(pl.)* general body of creditors.

Maßeinheit work unit, unit of measurement, standard of measure.

Masse|konto trust fund; **~kosten** cost payable out of the estate, expenses of receivership.

Massel stroke of luck;
~eisen pig iron.

Massen|abfertigung mass treatment; **~abfütterung** mass feeding; **~abnehmer** bulk buyer; **~absatz** mass marketing (selling), volume market, wholesale [selling], selling in bulk, bulk sale, heavy sales; **~absprung** *(Fallschirmtruppe)* mass jump; **sommerferienbedingte ~abwanderung ans Meer und ins Gebirge** exodus of the people to the seaside and mountains for the summer holidays; **~andrang** crush; **~ankauf** bulk buying (purchase), quantity buying; **~anreiz** mass appeal; **~ansprache** mass approach; **~arbeitseinstellung** general strike; **~arbeitslosigkeit** mass unemployment; **~armut** pauperism; **~artikel** staple articles (commodities, goods, merchandise), staples, mass-produced articles, articles made in bulk, bulk articles (commodities); **erfolgreichste ~artikel** crowd pleasers.

Massenaufgebot *(mil.)* general levy;
~ an Anhängern large crowd of supporters; **~ von Journalisten** stream of journalists; **~ der Polizei** strong body of the police.

Massen|auflage bulk edition, *(Zeitung)* mass circulation; **~aufmarsch** political parade; **~aufnahme** group picture; **~aufträge** big orders; **~auslage** mass display; **~aussperrung** general lockout; **~beförderung** transport in bulk, conveyance in mass (in bulk); **Schiff für ~befrachtung chartern** to charter a ship by the bulk; **~belustigung** mass (universal) entertainment; **~berechnung** quantity surveying; **~besuch** mass attendance; **~betrieb auf den Universitäten** overcrowding of the universities; **auf ~betrieb eingestellt sein** *(Restaurant)* to cater for large numbers of customers; **~bewegung** mass movement; **~blatt** mass magazine (circulation newspaper); **~blätter** popular press; **~defekt** *(Atomreaktor)* packing effect; **~demonstration** mass demonstration; **~deportation** mass deportation; **~drucksachen** bulk mail, bulk printed matter; **~einbürgerung** collective naturalization; **~einfluß ausüben** to pull with the general public; **~einheit** mass unit; **~einkauf** bulk purchase, quantity buying; **~einkäufer** quantity buyer; **~einkommen** mass income; **~entlassungen** mass dismissals, massive layoffs; **~ermittlung** quantity surveying; **~erscheinung** crowd phenomenon; **~erschießung** mass execution, fusilade; **~erzeugung, ~fabrikation, ~fertigung** mass (volume, bulk, large-scale, large-lot) production, quantity manufacturing (production); **~filialbetrieb** large-scale retailing, multiple shop *(Br.)*; **~flucht** stampede, exodus; **~gesellschaft** *(Soziologie)* mass society; **~grab** common (mass) grave, the pauper's grave; **~gut** bulk commodity, carlot shipment *(US)*; **~gutabfertigung per Bahn** track delivery shipment.

Massengüter bulk articles (commodities, goods);
mit ~n beladen laden in bulk;
~ der Markenindustrie high-volume branded goods;
Schiff mit ~n beladen to load a vessel in bulk;
~industrie mass-production industry.

Massengut|frachter bulk carrier; **~ladung, ~sendung** bulk cargo, carloading *(US)*.

massenhaft in *(US)* (by the, *Br.*) bulk, wholesale, massive;
~ ankommen *(Briefe)* to cascade; **~ Bargeld haben** to have cash galore; **~ Geld haben** to have loads (scads, *US*) of money; **~ zu tun haben** *(fam.)* to have a spate of work;
~e Fehler heaps of mistakes; **~e Verkehrsunfälle** vast number of traffic accidents.

Massen|hersteller mass producer (-production enterprise); **~herstellung** mass (lot, quantity, large-scale, machine) production, quantity manufacturing (production), wholesale manufacture; **~hinrichtung** mass execution; **~hysterie** mass hysteria; **~impfung** mass vaccination; **~instinkt** herd instinct; **an den ~instinkt appellieren** to play down to the crowd; **~karambolage** pile-up, multiple crash; **~käufe** bulk purchase; **~kaufkraft** mass purchasing power; **~kommunikation** mass communication; **~kommunikationsmittel** mass media; **~konsum** high-mass (general) consumption; **~konsumgüter** mass-consumption goods; **erstklassige ~konsumgüter** high-volume and highly acceptable branded consumer goods; **~kundgebung** mass meeting (demonstration); **~kündigung** mass dismissals; **~lieferung** bulk consignment; **~markt** mass market; **~märkte** mass markets; **~media** mass[-circulation] media, means of mass communication; **~mord** mass murder, hecatomb, massacre, slaughter; **~mörder** mass murderer; **~nahrungsmittel** bulk foodstuffs; **~organisation** mass organization; **~panik** crowd panic; **~presse** popular press; **~produktion** volume (serial, large-scale, mass, lot, quantity, bulk) production, serialization, quantity manufacturing (production); ~**produktion von Wohnungseinheiten** mass-produced housing; **aufgrund von ~produktion einen einheitlichen Service leisten** to mass-produce its service; ~**produktionsgesellschaft** mass-production society; ~**psychologie** crowd psychology; ~**publikum** *(bei Werbesendungen)* admass; ~**publikum anziehen** to pull in the crowds; ~**reklame** mass advertising; ~**suggestion** mass (crowd) suggestion; **verbilligter ~tarif** bulk tariff; ~**transport** mass transportation (transit), transport in bulk, bulk transport; ~**transportproblem** mass transit problem; ~**transportsystem** mass transport system; ~**unterbringung** mass housing, collective accommodation; ~**veranstaltung** mass entertainment, monumental operation; ~**verbrauch** mass (general, bulk) consumption; ~**verbraucher** bulk (large-scale) consumer; ~**verhaftungen** mass arrests; ~**verhalten** crowd (group) behavio(u)r; ~**verkauf** mass selling, *(Effekten)* unloading; ~**verkäufe** [selling by] wholesale; ~**verkehr** mass transport (transportation), very heavy traffic *(fam.)*; ~**verkehrsmittel** public transport; ~**vernichtung** holocaust; ~**vernichtungswaffen** weapons of mass destruction; ~**versammlung** mass rally (meeting), mammoth gathering; ~**vertrieb** mass selling; ~**wahn** mass hysteria; ~**ware** articles made in bulk, staple [goods], staples, knockdown (pattern) articles; **noch unverpackte ~ware** open bulk; ~**warenhersteller** large-scale producer.

massenweise by the gross, in bulk, wholesale, skits of, in large quantities.

Massen|werbung mass advertising; ~**wirkung** mass effect; ~**wohnsiedlung** mass housing; ~**zuspruch** mass response.

Masse|schluß *(el.)* earth (ground, *US*) connection; **einfache ~schulden** ordinary (unsecured, *US*) debts; ~**schuldner** debtor of a bankrupt's estate.

Masseur masseur, massager *(US)*.

Masse|verteilung liquidating distribution, distribution of assets of a bankrupt's estate; ~**verwalter** *(auf Antrag des Gemeinschuldners)* assignee for the benefits of creditors, *(auf Antrag der Konkursgläubiger)* receiver [and manager], *(Liquidator)* liquidator, trustee in bankruptcy; ~**verzeichnis** *(Konkurs)* statement of affairs, list of assets and liabilities, inventory of property, schedule of a bankrupt's debts (creditors).

Maßfracht freighting on measurement.

Maßgabe measure, proportions;
mit der ~ subject to the proviso; **mit der folgenden ~** subject to the following conditions; **nach ~** in accordance with, according to, as provided; **nach ~ der Eingänge** in conformity with the receipts; **nach ~ des Preises** according to the price.

maßgearbeitet made to measure, bespoke *(Br.)*.

maßgebend standard, decisive, controlling, authoritative, influential, leading, proper;
jds. Laufbahn ~ bestimmen to be decisive for s. one's career; **~ sein** to govern, to prevail, to serve as a rule, to be the criterion; ~**es Buch** standard book; ~**e Fassung** authorized version; ~**e Kreise** influential circles; ~**e Leute des Wirtschaftslebens** leading figures in industry and trade; ~**e Persönlichkeiten** people of importance, leading authorities; ~**e Schicht** leading class; **von ~er Seite** from authoritative quarters; ~**er Text** authentic text.

maßgeblich authoritative, competent, decisive, leading;
~ sein *(Text)* to prevail, to govern; **für j. nicht ~ sein** to be no yardstick for s. o.; **~ beteiligt sein** to contribute considerably; **~ am Wiederaufbau des Landes beteiligt sein** to play a leading role in the reconstruction of the country;
~**e Auslegung** authentic interpretation; ~**e Behörde** competent authority; ~**e Bestimmungen** governing rules, relevant conditions; ~**e Beteiligung** controlling interest; ~**e Fassung** authorized version; ~**e Kreise** influential circles; **in ~en Kreisen** in competent quarters; ~**er Markt** relevant market *(US)*; ~**e Persönlichkeit** people who matter; ~**e Position innehaben** to hold a prominent position; **sich in den ~en Punkten geeinigt haben** to be in substantial agreement; ~**e Rolle im Leben einer Stadt spielen** to play a prominent part in civic life; **von ~er Seite** from authoritative quarters; ~**er Text** authentic text; ~**e Verhandlungen** substantial alterations.

maßgerecht true to size.

Maßgeschäft bespoke business *(Br.)*, custom tailor *(US)*.

maßgeschneidert tailor-made, bespoke *(Br.)*.

Maß|größe unit of measurement; ~**halteappell** ear bashing.

Maßhalten moderation, *(Alkohol)* temperance.

maßhalten to keep within bounds;
bei den Ausgaben ~ to show spending forbearance; **im Essen und Trinken ~** to eat and drink in moderation.

Maßhaltung self-restraint;
sich Sinn für ~ bewahren to retain a sense of measure.

massieren to massage;
sich ~ to accumulate, to accrue, *(Aufträge)* to pile up; **Truppen ~** to mass (concentrate) troops.

massiert|in Erscheinung treten to gather in masses;
~**e Aktionen** mass action; ~**es Angebot** abundant offers; ~**er Angriff** mass attack; ~**e Kürzungen** drastic cuts; ~**e Nachfrage** accumulated (pent-up) demand; ~**es Streikpostenaufgebot** mass picketing.

Massierung accumulation;
~ von Truppen massing (concentration) of troops.

massig solid, volumed, bulky, massive;
~ Schulden haben to be head over heels in debt; **~ Zeit haben** to have heaps of time;
~ Geld *(coll.)* pots of money.

mäßig moderate, reasonable, abstemious, abstinent, *(Politik)* conservative;
nur ~ beliebt sein to enjoy only a limited popularity;
~**er Alkoholgenuß** moderate consumption of alcohol; ~**e Ansprüche** moderate claims; ~**e Arbeit leisten** to do a mediocre job; ~**e Arbeitskraft** mediocre worker; ~**e Brise** moderate breeze; ~**es Einkommen** moderate income; ~**es Essen** poor food; ~**e Forderungen stellen** to be moderate (reasonable) in one's demands; ~**er Frost** mild frost; **~ begabtes Kind** child of average ability; ~**es Leben führen** to lead a steady life; ~**e Lebensführung** temperance; ~**e Leistungen** mediocre (poor) performance; ~**er Preis** reasonable price; **zu ~en Preisen** moderate-priced; ~**er Trinker** moderate drinker; **~ großes Zimmer** medium-sized room.

mäßigen, sich in seinen Ansichten to moderate one's views; **seine Ansprüche ~** to moderate one's pretensions (claims, demand); **seine Geschwindigkeit ~** to slacken one's speed; **Konjunkturtempo ~** to slow down the pace of business; **seine Ungeduld ~** to curb one's patience.

mäßigender Einfluß moderating influence.

Mäßigkeit moderateness, moderation, *(Leistung)* mediocrity, *(Lebensführung)* temperance, continence;
~ der Preise reasonableness of prices.

Mäßigkeits|apostel teetotaller, temperance preacher, blue-ribbonist; ~**verein** temperance society.

Mäßigung moderation;
sich ~ auferlegen to put a restraint upon o. s., to speak in measured tone.

massiv solid, pure;
~ kritisieren to criticize severely; **~ werden** to use strong language, to cut up rough *(coll.)*;
~**e Angriffe gegen die Regierung richten** to direct heavy attacks against the government; ~**e Deviseneinschränkungen** far-reaching currency controls; ~**er Druck** heavy pressure; ~**e Eiche** solid oak; ~**er Einsatz** large-scale operations; **~ gebautes Gebäude** solid building; **in ~em Gold** in massive gold; ~**e Lohnforderungen stellen** to go on a wage spree; ~**e Proteste** massive protests.

Massiv|bau solid building; ~**gold** solid gold.

Maß|kleidung tailor-made (bespoke, *Br.*) clothes; ~**krug** beer mug.

maßlos uncontrolled, boundless, excessive, *(ohne Maß)* immoderate;
~ dankbar immensely grateful; **~ heiß** terrifically hot;
~ sein to know no measure; **~ übertrieben sein** to be exaggerated beyond all recognition; **~ verwöhnt sein** to be terribly spoilt;
~**e Beschimpfungen** outrageous insults; **in ~e Erregung geraten** to become extremely agitated; ~**e Forderungen** excessive demands; ~**e Preise** exorbitant (terrible) prices; ~**er Schwätzer** terrible talker; **von ~em Zorn erfaßt sein** to know no bounds in one's anger.

Maßlosigkeit outrageousness, exorbitance;
~ der Worte unrestrained language.

Maßnahme measure, step, action, proceeding, provision, arrangement, provision, movement, move;
als vorübergehende ~ as a temporary measure;
einer ~ Gesetzeskraft verleihen to give a measure the force of law.

Maßnahmen, absatzwirtschaftliche marketing transactions; **angeregte ~** measures suggested; **außerordentliche ~** emergency measures; **äußerste ~** extreme measures; **behördliche ~** administrative measures; **bevölkerungspolitische ~** demographic measures; **deflationäre ~** deflationary measures; **dirigistische ~** planned measures; **diskriminierende ~** dis-

criminatory action; **disziplinäre** ~ disciplinary measures; **drastische** ~ radical (strong) measures; **einschneidende** ~ incisive measures; **einstweilige** ~ temporary measures; **feindliche** ~ hostile acts; **finanzielle** ~ financial measures; **fiskalpolitische** ~ fiscal policy; **flankierende** ~ accompanying measures; **geeignete** ~ proper measures, appropriate steps; **gefährliche** ~ edge tool; **geldpolitische** ~ monetary policy devices; **gerichtliche** ~ court action; **gesetzliche** ~ legislative act; **halbe** ~ half-measures; **handelspolitische** ~ trade measures; **hoheitliche** ~ acts of state; **konjunkturdämpfende** ~ anticyclical measures; **konjunkturfördernde** ~ stimulatory measures; **konjunkturpolitische** ~ economic policy measures; **kriegsähnliche** ~ measures short of war; **kurzfristige** ~ short-term measures; **marktkonforme** ~ [anti]cyclical measures; **marktwidrige** ~ economics of control; **marktwirtschaftliche** ~ marketing operations; **panikartige** ~ panicky measures; **politische** ~ political actions; **behelfsmäßige politische** ~ stopgap politics; **polizeiliche** ~ police action; **preisstabilisierende** ~ holding the line; **protektionistische** ~ protectionist activities; **scharfe** ~ stern steps; **staatliche** ~ government[al] action; **steueraufbringende** ~ revenue raisers; **steuerliche** ~ tax practices; **steuer- und geldmarktpolitische** ~ overexpansive fiscal and monetary policies; **übereilte** ~ rash steps; **verkaufsfördernde** ~ promotional support *(US)*; **vorbereitende** ~ preliminary measures; **vorbeugende** ~ preventive steps, preventions; **vorübergehende** ~ temporary measures; **währungspolitische** ~ monetary measures; **wettbewerbshemmende** ~ unreasonable restraint of trade *(Br.)*; **wirtschaftliche** ~ economic regulations;
~ **zur Absatzsteigerung** sales promotional efforts (practices) *(US)*; ~ **zur Bekämpfung (Beseitigung) der Arbeitslosigkeit** antiunemployment measures, unemployment relief; ~ **der Betriebsleitung** managerial decisions; ~ **gegen Bodenzerstörung** soil conservation; ~ **zur Energiesparung** energy conservation measures; ~ **zur laufenden Fertigungskontrolle** control engineering; ~ **des Gerichts** acts of court; ~ **gegen Gewohnheitsverbrecher** preventive justice; **drastische (rigorose)** ~ **zur Inflationsbekämpfung** drastic measures to cure inflation; ~ **für die Landwirtschaft** land measures; ~ **gegen die Luftverschmutzung** smoke abatement; ~ **zur Rezessionsbekämpfung** antirecession package; **durchgreifende** ~ **gegen Steuerhinterziehungen** crackdown on tax evasion; ~ **zur Verbesserung der Kampfmoral** morale raisers; ~ **zur Warenbewirtschaftung** rationing arrangements;
~ **beschließen** to pass measures; **gesetzliche** ~ **durchführen** to put through a measure of legislation; **vorgesehene** ~ **in einem Ausschuß durchsetzen** to pass measures through a committee; ~ **entschiedenen Widerstand entgegensetzen** to offer a determined opposition to a measure; ~ **ergreifen** to adopt (take) measures, to take steps (action); **äußerste** ~ **ergreifen** to proceed to extremities; **erforderliche** ~ **ergreifen** to take the requisite measures; **falsche** ~ **ergreifen** to take faulty measures; **gerichtliche** ~ **ergreifen** to institute legal proceedings; **strenge** ~ **ergreifen** to employ hard measures; **unzulängliche** ~ **ergreifen** to send a boy to mill *(coll.)*; ~ **gegen j. ergreifen** to direct measures against s. o.; **harte** ~ **gegen rücksichtslose Autofahrer ergreifen** to take strong measures against reckless drivers; ~ **rückgängig machen** to cancel measures; **unpopuläre** ~ **in Kauf nehmen** to face up to unpopularity; **zu** ~ **Zuflucht nehmen** to resort to measures; **vorbeugende** ~ **treffen** to take preventive measures; ~ **zur konjunkturellen Belebung treffen** to boost the stagnant economy; ~ **gegen den Höchstverbrauch treffen** to cope with peak consumption; ~ **gesetzlich verankern** to give a measure the force of law; **erforderliche** ~ **veranlassen** to take the necessary steps;
finanzpolitischer ~katalog financing package.

Maßrechnung measurement account.

Maßregel measure, regulation, rule;
richtige ~ step in the right direction;
sich über ~n einigen to close upon measures; **neue ~n erlassen** to make new regulations; **strenge** ~ **lockern** to relax strict rules.

maßregeln to reprimand, to proctorize;
j. ~ to crack down on s. o. *(US)*, to come down on s. o. like a ton of bricks *(coll.)*, *(disziplinarisch)* to inflict disciplinary punishment on s. o.; **Streikbeteiligte** ~ to victimize strikers.

Maßregelung disciplinary punishment, reprimand, rebuke, reprove, crackdown *(US sl.)*, *(Streikbeteiligter)* victimization;
einstweilige ~ interlocutory order.

Maß|regelungsverbot *(Streikbeteiligter)* ban on victimization; **~schneider** bespoke tailor *(Br.)*, custom tailor *(US)*; **~schneiderei** bespoke *(Br.)* (custom, *US*) tailoring.

Maßstab rule, ruler, measure, measuring rod, level, degree, *(fig.)* standard, criterion, *(auf Karten)* scale;
im ~ **1 : 5 gezeichnet** drawn to [a] scale of 1 : 5; **im lokalen** ~ within local limits; **im vergrößerten** ~ on an enlarged scale; **in großem** ~ on a large scale; **in kleinem** ~ in little;
verkleinerter ~ reduced scale; **zweierlei** ~ double standard;
~ **abgeben** to set the standard for; **Zeichnung in natürlichem** ~ **anfertigen** to make a full-scale drawing; **anderen** ~ **anlegen** to apply another standard; **strengen** ~ **an die Geschäftsmoral anlegen** to set high standards of business morality; **sich als** ~ **dienen lassen** to take s. th. as an example; **andere nach seinem eigenen** ~ **messen** to measure others by one's own yardstick; **die Dinge im großen** ~ **sehen** to see things in a large way; ~ **für den Wert eines Menschen sein** to be a criterion for s. one's worth.

Maßstäbe, nach europäischen ~n by European standards; **nach menschlichen ~n** on a human scale;
anerkannte ~ established standards; **heutige** ~ present-day standards; **strenge** ~ exacting standards;
ein Gefühl für ~ **behalten haben** to retain a sense of measure; ~ **setzen** to set measure.

maßstäblich|vergrößern (verkleinern) to scale up (down);
~e Genauigkeit extreme accuracy.

maßstabs|gerecht, ~getreu to (true to) scale;
~ **zeichnen** to protract; **Karte** ~ **zeichnen** to scale a map;
~es Modell scale model; **~e Zeichnung** scaling.

Maß|stock scale rule; **~system** system of units; **~verhältnisse** proportions, dimensions.

maßvoll within limits;
sich ~ **ausdrücken** to speak in measured terms; **sich** ~ **betätigen** to restrain one's activities;
~e Ansprüche stellen to be moderate in one's pretensions; **~e Forderungen stellen** to moderate one's demands; **~er Preis** reasonable (moderate) price.

Maßzahl physical unit;
aus Stichproben gewonnene ~ sample statistics;
~ **für Austauschrelationen** terms of trade.

Mast pole, mast.

mästen to feed up, to fatten;
sich ~ *(fig.)* to line one's pockets; **sich an anderen** ~ to batten on others.

Mast|ferkel feeding pig; **~korb** crow's nest; **~viehabgabe** growth half-penny *(Br.)*; **~werbung** sign-mast advertising.

Mater matrix, mat.

Material material, matter, *(Ausrüstung)* equipment, *(Börse)* supply, offerings, offer *(US)*, *(Handwerkszeug)* findings *(US)*, *(Stoff)* substance, stuff, body, *(Verarbeitung)* stock, *(Vorrat)* [dead] stock;
abzusetzendes ~ *(drucktechn.)* matter, manuscript; **heute angebotenes** ~ *(Börse)* offerings of stock today; **reichhaltig angebotenes** ~ *(Börse)* material offerings; **aufgearbeitetes** ~ worked material; **unterwegs befindliches** ~ supplies in transit; **in Verarbeitung befindliches** ~ stock (work) in process; **belastendes** ~ incriminating evidence; **beleidigendes** ~ defamatory matter; **unmittelbar benötigtes** ~ direct material; **bestelltes** ~ material on order; **bewährtes** ~ reliable material; **einlaufendes** ~ incoming stock; **entlastendes** ~ exonerating evidence; **für die Produktion erforderliches** ~ material required for production; **fehlerhaftes** ~ defective material; **flottantes** ~ *(Börse)* floating supply; **grundlegendes** ~ basic data; **herauskommendes** ~ *(Börse)* new issues; **kriegswichtiges** ~ strategic goods; **minderwertiges** ~ low-value material; **reichhaltiges** ~ *(Börse)* ample offerings; **rollendes** ~ *(Eisenbahn)* equipment, rolling stock; **schwimmendes** ~ *(Börse)* floating supply; **spaltbares** ~ *(Atommeiler)* fission material; **statistisches** ~ statistical (census) data; **ungeeignetes (unbrauchbares)** ~ materials unfit for the job; **urkundliches** ~ documents, documentary evidence; **verarbeitetes** ~ worked material; **verarbeitungsfähiges** ~ material fit for the job; **verwendetes (verbrauchtes)** ~ materials consumed;
~ **und Arbeitslöhne** material and labo(u)r, material and making; ~ **in Verarbeitung** stock (work) in process;
~ **einsetzen** to tool material; ~ **gemeinsam einsetzen** to pool material; **belastendes** ~ **gegen j. haben** to have s. th. on s. o. *(US sl.)*; **aus schlechtem** ~ **herstellen** to fake; ~ **sammeln** to gather evidence; **statistisches** ~ **sammeln** to collect statistical information; ~ **sichten** to sift material; **nur bestes** ~ **verarbeiten** to employ the best workmanship only; ~ **für eine wissenschaftliche Arbeit zusammenstellen** to collect material for a scientific work;
~abgang withdrawal of material; **~abnahme** quality control [of material]; **~abrechnung** material accounting; **~anforderung**

requisition of material, material requisitioned, stock requisition; ~**anlieferung** supply of material; **unmittelbarer ~aufwand** direct material costs; ~**ausgabe** giving out, issuance of material *(US)*, property issue; ~**ausgabeschein** property-issue form; ~**ausgeber** issuer of materials, storekeeper, giver-out; ~**bearbeitung** working-up of material, materials handling *(US)*; ~**bedarf** material requirements; ~**bedarfsplanung** direct materials budget; ~**behandlung** materials handling *(US)*; ~**beistellung** supply of material; ~**belege** vouchers; ~**beschaffung** material purchases; ~**bestand** materials on hand; ~**bestandskarte** perpetual inventory card; ~**bestandskonten** direct goods accounts; ~**buchführung** store accounting; ~**depot** *(mil.)* ordnance depot; ~**einheit** unit of material; ~**einkauf** material purchases; **günstiger ~einkauf** market purchasing; ~**empfangsbescheinigung** material-received report *(US)*; ~**entnahme** withdrawal of material, stock requisition; ~**entnahmeschein** material requisition slip; ~**erhaltung** *(mil.)* maintenance of equipment; ~**ermüdung** fatigue; ~**fehler** defective (faulty) material, material defect; ~**festigkeit** tensile strength; ~**gemeinkosten** indirect material costs (materials and supplies); ~**gemeinkostenzuschlag**, ~**gemeinkostensatz** material cost burden rate.

Materialien materials, material goods;
angeforderte ~ materials requisitioned; **für die Produktion erforderliche ~** materials required for production;
~**verwalter** controller of materials, storekeeper; ~**verwaltung** stationery department; ~**waggon** material car.

Materialismus materialism;
dialektischer ~ dialectic materialism; **historischer ~** historical materialism.

Materialist materialist.

materialistisch materialistic, bread-and-butter;
~ eingestellt bread-and-butter minded.

Material|knappheit shortage (scarcity) of material, material shortage; **eigenes ~konto** direct goods account; ~**kontrolle** quality control [of materials], material control.

Materialkosten material costs, costs of materials;
direkte ~ direct material costs; **indirekte ~** indirect materials; **Löhne und ~** labo(u)r and material;
~**ermittlung** material costing; ~**index** price index figure of materials; ~**plan** material budget.

Material|lager contractor's store, supplies in a factory; ~**lieferant** supplies of materials, materialman; ~**lieferung** supply of materials, stores supplies; ~**liste** bill of materials; ~**nachweis** material accounting; ~**nachweisverfahren** material accounting system; ~**preis** material costs (prices), costs of material; ~**probe** materials test, *(Muster)* specimen; ~**prüfung** material control (testing); ~**prüfungsamt** materials testing office; ~**sammelstelle** salvage dump; ~**sammlung** gathering of material; ~**schaden** defective material; ~**schlacht** war of attrition; ~**schuppen** shed; ~**schwund** wastage; ~**stelle** store department; ~**transportzeit** handling time; ~**überlegenheit** superiority in material; ~**verarbeitung** working of material, processing [of material]; ~**verbrauch** material consumption, *(Bilanz)* materials consumed; **geschätzter ~verbrauch** direct materials budget; ~**verknappung** material shortage; ~**verlust** waste, *(mil.)* loss of material; ~**versorgung** supply of materials; ~**verwalter** controller of materials, storekeeper; ~**verwaltung** materials management, stationery department, interior (internal) economy; ~**vorrat** stores, material supplies; ~**wagen** handcar, construction car, go-devil; ~**wert** value of raw material; ~**zuführung** *(Maschine)* feed; ~**zug** material train.

Materie [subject] matter;
tote ~ dead matter;
sich gründlich in einer ~ auskennen to be well versed in a subject, to know the ropes; **sich in einer ~ nicht auskennen** not to be familiar with a subject; **seine ~ völlig beherrschen** to know one's onions (oats); **mit einer ~ vertraut sein** to be familiar with a matter.

materiell material, actual, corporeal, tangible, physical, *(finanziell)* financial, pecuniary, *(rechtlich)* substantive;
~ bedeutsam of practical significance; **~ denkend** of a worldly mind; **~ und formell** in form and in fact;
Anspruch ~ prüfen to examine a claim on its merits; **~ eingestellt sein** to be keen on money making (bread-and-butter minded); **sich ~ gut stehen** to be well-off (in funds), to be well fixed *(US)*;
~**e Annehmlichkeiten** creature comforts; ~**e Bedürfnisse** material needs, necessaries of life; ~**e Grundlage** financial basis; ~**e Hilfe** pecuniary aid; **in ~er Hinsicht** financially; ~**e Interessen** financial interests; ~**e Lage** pecuniary circumstances; ~**es Recht** substantive law; **nach ~em Recht** upon the merits; ~**er Schaden** pecuniary (material) damage; ~**e Unmöglichkeit** physical impossibility; ~**e Unterstützung gewähren** to extend financial aid; ~**e Voraussetzungen** substantial requirements; ~**er Vorteil** pecuniary advantage (benefit); ~**e Vorzüge und Annehmlichkeiten** material comforts and pleasures; ~**er Wert** tangible value.

materiell-rechtlich substantial, upon the merits;
~ vortragen to plead the merits.

matern to mould, to mold *(US)*.

Matern|dienst mat (matrix) service; ~**klischee** pattern (boiler, *US*) plate; ~**pappe** flong, matrix board.

Mathematik, angewandte applied mathematics.

Mathematiker, schlechter ~ sein to be poor at mathematics.

mathematisch mathematical;
~**e Erwartung** mathematical expectation; **mit ~er Pünktlichkeit abrollen** to run off with faultless precision.

Matinee morning performance, matinee.

Matratze mattress.

Mätresse fancy woman, mistress.

Matriarchat matriarchal stage.

Matrikel register, registry books, roll;
in die ~ eintragen to enrol(l), to register.

matrikulieren to print waste.

Matrix|drucker wire printer; ~**speicher** *(Computer)* matrix memory.

Matrize matrix, mat, mould, mold *(US)*, master, die, *(Schreibmaschine)* stencil;
~ anfertigen to cut a stencil; **~ schreiben** to stencil.

Matrizen|abzug stencil; ~**karton** mat board; ~**papier** stencil paper.

Matrone dame.

Matrose seaman, sailor, shipman, jack tar, *(Marine)* blue jacket, mariner, hand, man, *(mar., Dienstgrad)* ordinary rating, seaman recruit *(US)*;
arbeitsloser ~ stranded seaman; **gewöhnlicher ~** deck hand; **unerfahrener ~** landsman;
~ der Handelsmarine swab *(mar., sl.)*; **~ auf Landurlaub** liberty man;
~**n anheuern** to hire (register) a sailor.

Matrosen|ausbeuter land shark; ~**heuer** seaman's wages; ~**kneipe** sailor's pub; ~**mißhandlungen** sea batteries.

Matsch slush, mud.

matschig muddy, sludgy, miry.

Matschwetter slushy weather.

matt weary, weak, feeble, *(Börse)* dull, stagnant, lifeless, inanimate, languid, depressed, slack, featureless, lackluster *(US)*, lacklustre *(Br.)*, *(Fotoabzug)* mat, *(Glas)* frosted, *(Papier)* mat(t), noncalendered, *(Seide)* lusterless, lustreless *(Br.)*;
~ setzen to stalemate; **seine Gegner ~ setzen** to checkmate one's opponents;
~**e Birne** pearl bulb; ~**es Geschäft** dull business; ~**er Kerzenschein** dim candlelight; ~**es Kunstdruckpapier** art mat paper *(Br.)*, art mat *(US)*; ~**es Lächeln** faint smile; ~**er Puls** weak pulse; ~**e Rede halten** to deliver a dull speech; ~**es Silber** unpolished silver; **mit ~er Stimme** in a feeble voice; ~**e Wetter** *(Bergbau)* irrespirable air.

Mattdruck mat impression.

Matte mat, *(Wiese)* meadow;
mit ~n auslegen to mat; **j. auf die ~ legen** to have s. o. on the mat.

Mattheit *(Börse)* dullness, flatness, deadness, stagnancy, lifelessness, lango(u)r.

mattiertes|Glas ground glass; **~ Papier** mat paper.

Mattigkeit exhaustion, feebleness, weariness, lassitude.

Matt|kopie mat print; ~**kunstdruckpapier** mat art paper; ~**scheibe** *(Fenster)* frosted window pane, *(Fernsehen, coll.)* screen, telly *(coll.)*, *(Foto)* focusing screen; ~**scheibe haben** to have a blank, not to be with it *(coll.)*; ~**scheibenkamera** focusing camera.

Mätzchen pranks, tricks, monkey business;
~ machen to kick up a fuss, to play pranks; **wieder ~ machen** to be up to one's silly tricks again.

mau poor, bad;
sich ~ fühlen to feel lousy (rotten), to be off colo(u)r; **~ gehen** to be dull (slack);
~**es Gefühl im Magen haben** to feel queasy.

Mauer [brick] wall, *(fig.)* curtain;
Chinesische ~ Great Wall of China; **feuerfeste ~** fire-proof partition wall; **freistehende ~** dead wall;
~ von Vorurteilen wall of prejudices;

gegen eine ~ anrennen to run one's head against a brick wall; **sich in den ~n der Stadt aufhalten** to be staging in the town; **~ bilden** to line up; **wie eine ~ stehen** to form a solid wall; **nur die nackten ~n übriglassen** to leave only the bare walls standing; **mit einer ~ umgeben** to [enclose with a] wall; **~ unterhöhlen** to undermine a wall;
~anschlag wall advertisement, poster; **~blümchen** *(fig.)* wallflower; **~konsole** wall bracket; **~krone** wall crest (crown); **~latte** roof plate.
mauern to lay bricks, *(Kartenspiel)* to stonewall, *(Sport)* to play for time.
Mauer|öffnung gap in a wall, aperture; **~schwamm** dry rot; **~stütze** land tie; **~verblendung** wall facing; **~werk** brickwork, masonry.
Maul mouth, muzzle;
sein ~ groß aufreißen to talk big, to be bragging, to boast of one's exploits; **~ und Nase aufsperren** to be flabbergasted; **mit offenem ~ dastehen** to stand with open mouth before s. th.; **jem. übers ~ fahren** to cut s. o. short, to jump down s. one's throat; **jem. eins aufs ~ geben** to give s. o. a good smack in the kisser *(sl.)*; **loses ~ haben** to have a loose tongue; **das ~ halten** to keep one's mouth shut *(sl.)*; **jem. ums ~ schmieren** to butter s. o. up; **nicht aufs ~ gefallen sein** to have a glib tongue; **jem. das ~ stopfen** to shut s. o. up; **sich über j. das ~ zerreißen** to gossip about s. o.; **schiefes ~ ziehen** to pull a wry face.
maulen to grumble, to sulk, to pout the lips;
über das Essen ~ to grumble about one's food.
Mäuler, böse scandalmongers;
sich die ~ zerreißen to wag one's tongues.
Maulesel mule.
maulfaul sein to be too lazy to speak.
Maul|held braggart, big mouth, self-professed hero; **~heldentum** braggartism; **~korb** *(fig.)* muzzle, soft pedal *(US sl.)*; **der Opposition einen ~korb umhängen** to muzzle the opposition; **~schelle** slap in the face, box on the ear; **~- und Klauenseuche** foot and mouth disease; **~tierpfad** pack road, bridle path; **~tiertreiber** mule skinner *(US)*; **~wurfsarbeiten** subversive activities.
Maurer bricklayer;
~arbeit masonry, bricklaying; **~geselle** journeyman bricklayer; **~kelle** trowel.
Maus mouse;
unscheinbare kleine ~ insignificant little creature;
so flink wie eine ~ sein to be as quick as lightning; **so naß, wie eine gebadete ~ sein** to look like a drowned rat; **mit jem. Katz und ~ spielen** to play cat and mouse with s. o.
mauscheln to talk Yiddish, *(betrügen)* to cheat.
mäuschenstill quiet as a mouse, doggo.
Mäuse *(Geld)* dough *(US)*, lolly *(Br., sl.)*, chink *(sl.)*, dibs *(sl.)*, shiners *(sl.)*;
weiße ~ *(Verkehrspolizei)* speedcops;
weiße ~ sehen to see pink elephants;
mit Speck fängt man ~ set a sprat to catch a mackerel; **wenn die Katze aus dem Haus ist, tanzen die ~ auf dem Tisch** when the cat's away the mice will play.
Mause|falle mousetrap; **~loch** mousehole.
mausen to pilfer, to snoop, to lurch, to filch, to lift, to pinch *(US sl.)*.
Mauserei pilfering, pinching *(US sl.)*.
mausern, sich to change for the better, to do very well; **sich zu einem der größten Häfen ~** to develop into one of the greatest ports; **sich vom Liberalen zum Konservativen ~** to turn from a liberal to a conservative.
mausetot as dead as a doornail, dead as mutton;
~ umfallen to drop dead.
mausig machen, sich to get on one's high horse, to make a nuisance of o. s.
Maut toll, turnpike money;
~brücke toll bridge; **~einnahmen** toll revenues; **~einnehmer** turnpike man; **~gebühr** intermediate toll.
mautpflichtige Straße turnpike road, toll highway *(US)*.
Maut|recht tollage; **~stelle** turnpike.
maximal maximum;
~ 50 Personen fassen *(Bus)* to have a maximum capacity of 50 persons;
~er Beleihungswert maximum loan value.
Maximal|belastung working (peak, maximum) load, ultimate strain; **~bestand an Vorräten** maximum inventory; **~betrag** limit, maximum amount; **~flugzeit** endurance, maximum flight time; **~forderung** maximum demand; **~geschwindigkeit** top speed, *(zugelassene)* speed limit; **~gewicht** maximum load; **~grenze** upper limit; **~kontrolle** self-retention control; **~leistung** maximum (peak) output; **~lohn** ceiling (maximum) wage; **~preis** ceiling [price], limit, top price, peak [price]; **~summe** maximum [amount]; **~tabelle** table of retentions; **~tarif** maximum tariff; **~wert** maximum value; **~zoll** maximum tariff.
Maxime dictum.
maximieren to maximize.
Maximierung der Gewinne maximization of profits.
Maximum maximum;
barometrisches ~ anticyclone, high-pressure area;
~ an Bewegungsfreiheit ultimate in freedom.
Maxirezession maxirecession.
Mäzen patron, protector, sponsor, momzer *(sl.)*.
Mäzenatentum patronage, sponsorship.
Mechaniker mechanic, operative, artisan, repairman *(US)*, grease monkey *(US sl.)*, *(Flugzeug)* flight engineer;
~ einstellen to enlist a mechanic;
~ des ADAC [etwa] patrolman of the A. A. *(Br.)*.
mechanisch mechanical, automatic, *(fig.)* routine, mechanical;
nicht ~ unmechanical; **rein ~** by rote;
völlig ~ arbeiten to do one's work mechanically; **~ herstellen** to process; **~ herunterleiern** to reel off; **~ betätigt werden** to be operated automatically; **etw. ~ wiederholen** to repeat s. th. mechanically;
~e Arbeit (Tätigkeit) routine job; **~e Kraft** power; **~es Verfahren** mechanical process; **~e Vorrichtungen** mechanical devices; **~e Werkstatt** engineering shop.
mechanisieren to mechanize, to robotize.
mechanisierte|Landwirtschaft mechanized farming; **~ Verbände** *(mil.)* mechanized forces.
Mechanisierung mechanization, robotization.
Mechanisierungsprozeß process of mechanization.
Mechanismus mechanism, apparatus, machinery, dodge;
defekter ~ faulty mechanism; **komplizierter ~** wheels within wheels;
~ von Angebot und Nachfrage mechanism of supply and demand; **~ des Verfahrens** procedural machinery.
Meckerei grumble, faultfinding, beef *(US sl.)*, gripe *(US sl.)*, squawk *(sl.)*.
Meckerer jackdaw, grumbler, stickler, kicker *(US)*.
Meckern nagging.
meckern to grumble, to complain fussily, to beef *(US sl.)*, to squawk *(sl.)*, to gripe about *(US sl.)*.
Meckerziege, chronische chronic complainer, pill *(sl.)*.
Medaille medal;
Kehrseite der ~ sein to be the reverse of the medal.
Medaillenträger prize medal(l)ist.
Media *(Werbung)* media;
~auswahl media selection; **~disponent** space buyer; **~feldzug** media campaign; **~forschung** media research; **~leiter** media manager; **~plan** media plan; **~planer** media planner; **~planung** media planning; **~reichweite** media reach; **~sachbearbeiter** media clerk.
Medien information media;
~reichweite media reach.
Medikament medicament, medicine, drug;
rezeptpflichtiges ~ prescription drug;
~ verabfolgen to medicament.
Medikamentenschrank medicine cabinet.
Medio middle of the month, mid-month;
~abrechnung, ~arrangement fortnightly (mid-month) settlement, mid-month account; **~ausweis** mid-monthly settlement; **~fälligkeiten** fortnightly commitments; **~geld** fortnightly loans; **~liquidation** fortnightly (mid-month) settlement; **~prolongation** fortnightly continuation *(Br.)*; **~thek** photographic library; **~wechsel** fortnightly bill *(Br.)*.
Meditation meditation;
zur ~ anregen to lend itself to meditation.
meditieren to meditate.
Medium medium, vehicle;
provisionspflichtiges ~ commissionable medium;
~ für Auslandsinvestitionen offshore investment vehicle;
sich der Presse als ~ für die Verbreitung seiner politischen Ansichten bedienen to use the press as a vehicle for one's political opinions.
Medizin medicine;
~ eingeben to administer a medicine; **seine ~ nehmen** to take (dose) one's medicine; **bittere ~ für j. sein** to be a bitter pill for s. o.; **~ studieren** to qualify for medicine; **~ nicht vertragen** to be intolerant of a drug.

Mediziner medical man (student).
medizinisch medical, medicinal;
~ **behandeln** to medicate;
~**e Behandlung** medication; ~**e Wissenschaft** medical science.
Medizin | mann medicine man; ~**student** medical student, medic *(US)*; ~**studium** medical course.
Meer sea, high sea, ocean;
auf dem ~ on the water;
aufrührerisches ~ insurgent sea; **freies** ~ the open sea; **geschlossenes** ~ closed sea; **das offene** ~ main sea, high (open) sea;
~ **von Blut und Tränen** a sea of blood and tears;
dem ~ **abgewinnen** to reclaim; **sich ins** ~ **ergießen** to pour itself into the sea; **übers** ~ **fahren** to cross the ocean; **ins** ~ **fließen** to flow into the sea; **Hotels wie Sand am** ~ **geben** to be no end of hotels; **auf das** ~ **hinausfahren** to put out to sea; **ins** ~ **münden** to empty itself into the sea; ~ **überqueren** to cross the waters;
~**busen** gulf; ~**enge** narrow [seas], straits, belt; ~**engenabkommen** straits convention; ~**engenkommission** straits commission.
Meeresarm sea inlet, branch of the sea.
meeresbiologisches Institut institute of marine biology.
Meeres | boden bottom of the sea, ocean bottom (floor); ~**brandung** surf, breakers; ~**bucht** bay, bight; ~**fauna** aquatic crop; ~**forscher** marine researcher; ~**früchte** seafood; ~**grund** sea-bed, ocean floor; **auf dem** ~**grund** to be stranded on the ocean floor; ~**höhe** elevation, sea level; ~**karte** ocean chart; ~**spiegel** sea level; ~**spiegelhöhe** sea-level altitude; ~**strömung** ocean current; **unergründliche** ~**tiefe** unfathomed ocean depth; ~**ufer** coast; ~**untergrund** subsoil; ~**verschmutzung** pollution of the sea; ~**wetterkunde** marine meteorology.
Meer | wasser sea water; ~**wasserbad** sea-water pool.
Mega | phon megaphone, speaking trumpet; ~**tonne** megaton; ~**volt** megavolt.
Mehr excess, surplus, *(Zuwachs)* increase, addition;
~ **an Kosten** additional expenses;
~**achsenantrieb** multiaxle drive; ~**aktienzertifikat** multiple certificate; ~**anbau** additional cultivation; ~**arbeit** extra work, surplus labo(u)r, overtime; **durch** ~**arbeit eine Lohnerhöhung erzielen** to make wages; ~**arbeitslöhne** overtime pay; ~**arbeitszuschlag,** ~**arbeitsvergütung** overtime [premium] pay, overtime compensation (bonus); ~**aufwand** additional expenditure, excess costs; ~**aufwand an Zeit** extra time spent on it; ~**ausgabe** *(Wertpapier)* overissue; ~**ausgaben** additional (increased) expenditure, excess costs (expenditure).
mehrbändig in several volumes.
Mehrbedarf additional (increased) demand, consumption excess, excess consumption.
Mehrbelastung extra charge (burden), supplementary charge, overcharge, *(Überlastung)* overload;
finanzielle ~ additional financial burden;
~ **ausgleichen** to offset an extra charge; ~ **für j. darstellen** to mean extra work for s. o.
Mehr | beschäftigung higher level of employment; ~**bestand** surplus stock; ~**betrag** surplus [amount], overplus, over, plus value, excess [amount], exceeding amount, *(aus Wertsteigerung)* appreciated surplus; ~**bewertung** excess valuation; ~**bietender** outbidder, higher bidder.
mehrdeutig ambiguous, equivocal;
~**e Frage** ambiguous question.
Mehr | deutigkeit ambiguity, equivocality; **offenkundige** ~**deutigkeit** patent ambiguity; **versteckte** ~**deutigkeit** latent ambiguity; ~**dividende** additional (extra) dividend, bonus; ~**druck** overprint; ~**einkommen** increased income, *(überschüssiges Einkommen)* surplus revenue; ~**einkommensteuer** excess-profits tax, income surtax; ~**einkommensteuerstufe** surtax bracket; ~**einnahmen,** ~**erlös** additional (surplus) receipts, surplus, additional (surplus) proceeds.
mehren, sich to increase in numbers, to grow; **seinen Besitz** ~ to increase one's possessions.
mehrere | Gebäude several buildings; ~ **Gelegenheiten** sundry occasions.
Mehr | erlösabführung surrender of additional profits; ~**ertrag** surplus [amount], increment, excess profits; ~**export** additional export.
mehrfach multiple, plural, manifold, *(wiederholt)* repeated, reiterated;
~ **lesen** to read several times; ~ **beschäftigt sein** to be engaged in several occupations;
~**er Atomsprengkopf** multiple warhead; **trotz** ~ **wiederholter Aufforderung** in spite of repeated requests; **Brief in** ~**er Ausfertigung schreiben** to make several copies of a letter; ~**e Bebauung** multiple cropping; ~**e Besteuerung** multiple taxation; **in** ~**er Hinsicht** in more than one respect; ~**es Lesen** repeated reading; ~**er Mörder** multiple murderer; ~**e Pfändung** multiple seizure; ~**e Stimmabgabe (Stimmrechtsausübung)** multiple voting; ~**es Wechselkurssystem** multiple currency system.
Mehrfach | arbitrage compound arbitrage (arbitration); ~**ausnutzung eines Kredits** multiple expansion of a credit; ~**belichtung** multiple exposure; ~**beschäftigter** moonshiner *(sl.)*; ~**besteuerung** double (multiple) taxation; ~**betrieb** *(tel.)* multiplex operation; ~**bild** *(Fernsehen)* multiple image; ~**dividende** cumulative dividend; ~**einteilung** *(Statistik)* manifold classification; ~**fallschirm** cluster; ~**formular für Eintragungen** manifold form of entry; ~**kabel** multicore cable; ~**kampfflugzeug** multiplane fighter; ~**klassifizierung** *(Statistik)* multiple classification; ~**lizenzabkommen** multiple licensee agreement; ~**lizenzen** multiple licensing; ~**schalter** *(el.)* multiple switch; ~**sprengköpfe mit voneinander unabhängiger Steuerung** *(mil.)* multiple independently targetable reentry vehicle; ~**steckdose** multiple socket; ~**stecker** *(el.)* multiple plug; ~**stimmrecht** multiple (weighted, plural) voting; ~**täter** recidivist, repeated offender; ~**telegrafie** multiplex telegraphy; **betrügerische** ~**veräußerung** stellionate; ~**vergabe an Makler** multiple listing *(US)*; ~**versicherung** double insurance, multiple-line system of insurance; ~**zoll** multiple tariff.
Mehr | fahrtenausweis go-as-you-please ticket; ~**familienhaus** community house, block of flats *(Br.)*, apartment house *(US)*, multiple-family (multifamily) dwelling; **gemeinsam erbaute** ~**familienhäuser** home club cooperative apartment houses *(US)*.
Mehrfarben | druck process (multicolo(u)r) printing; ~**klischee** process plate; ~**stift** multi-colo(u)red propelling pencil.
mehrfarbig multicolo(u)r, polychromatic.
Mehr | felderwirtschaft multicourse rotation; ~**forderung** increased demand; ~**förderung** extra output; ~**fracht** extra (additional) freight, surcharge; ~**frontenkrieg** war on several fronts; ~**ganggetriebe** multispeed transmission; ~**gebot** advance, higher (further) bid, overbid, outbidding, advance of an offer; ~**gehalt** increased salary; ~**gepäck** excess luggage *(Br.)* (baggage, *US*); ~**gewicht** overweight, surplus (excess) weight, excess of weight, overs; ~**gewinn** excess (additional) profit, excess (surplus) profit.
mehrgleisig multiple-line.
Mehrheit majority, plurality *(US)*;
in der ~ **der Fälle** in most (the majority of) cases; **in Übereinstimmung mit der schweigenden** ~ in tune with the majority in the country; **mit** ~ **beschlossen** carried by a majority of votes; **von der** ~ **überstimmt** overruled by the majority;
3/4 ~ 75 percent vote; **absolute** ~ absolute (overall) majority; **anteilmäßige** ~ majority in interest, proportionate majority; **arbeitsfähige** ~ working majority; **beschlußfähige** ~ quorum; **einfache** ~ simple (bare, clear) majority; **erdrückende** ~ crushing majority; **erforderliche** ~ requisite majority; **erwartete** ~ prospective majority; **geringe** ~ small majority; **große** ~ large majority; **hauchdünne** ~ hair's breadth majority, paper- (wafer-) thin majority; **kapitalmäßige** ~ majority in amount; **knappe** ~ narrow (shoestring, *US*) majority; **qualifizierte** ~ particular (qualified, special) majority; **regierungsfeindliche** ~ antigovernment majority; **relative** ~ relative majority, plurality *(US)*; **schwache** ~ narrow majority; **schweigende** ~ silent majority; **sichere** ~ comfortable majority; **überwältigende** ~ overwhelming, (vast, crushing, whopping) majority; **überwiegende** ~ great majority; **zahlenmäßige** ~ majority in numbers, numerical majority;
~ **parteitreuer Abgeordneter** coupon majority; ~ **der Aktionäre** majority shareholders (stockholders, *US*); ~ **gegen den Antrag** adverse majority; ~ **der stimmberechtigten Anwesenden** majority of those present and voting; ~ **von Erben** plurality of heirs; ~ **von Firmen** group of companies; ~ **der Gläubiger** majority of creditors; ~ **der Gläubiger nach der Höhe der angemeldeten Forderungen** majority in value of the creditors; ~ **der erschienenen Gläubiger und 3/4** ~ **der angemeldeten Forderungen** majority in number and three-fourths in value; **zahlen- und forderungsmäßige** ~ **der Gläubiger** majority of creditors in number and value; ~ **nach der Höhe der angemeldeten Forderungen** *(Konkursverfahren)* majority in amount of claims; ~ **von Jastimmen** affirmative vote; ~ **nach Köpfen** majority of members; ~ **einer Nation** generality of a nation; ~ **im Parlament** parliamentary majority; ~ **von**

Schuldnern und Gläubigern joint and several covenant (contract); ~ **der abgegebenen Stimmen** majority of qualified electors (voters); ~ **von sieben Stimmen** majority of seven votes; **knappe ~ von vier Stimmen** four-vote margin; ~ **von 3/4 der abgegebenen Stimmen** three-fourth majority;
sich der ~ anschließen to follow (go with) the crowd, to identify o. s. (join, side with) the majority, to come into line with the majority *(fam.)*; ~ **aufbringen (erzielen)** to secure a majority; **in der ~ aufgehen** to combine with a majority; ~ **bilden** to form the majority; **beschlußfähige ~ zustande bringen** to master a quorum; **knappe ~ zustande bringen** to drum up a new majority; ~ **erhalten** to gain a majority; **bei der Abstimmung eine überwältigende ~ erhalten** to carry a vote by an overwhelming majority; ~ **der abgegebenen Stimmen erhalten** to poll a majority of votes, to secure a majority of votes cast, to receive the majority cast; **keine regierungsfähige ~ ermöglichen** to leave no one clearly in control; **schon bei einem kleinen Wählerumschwung eine glatte ~ erreichen** to need but a small swing to win a clear majority; **erforderliche ~ erzielen** to obtain the necessary majority; **Beschluß mit einfacher ~ fassen** to take a decision by a simple majority; ~ **für sich gewinnen** to gain majority support; ~ **haben** to be in a majority over; **keine ausreichende ~ haben** to lack an outright majority; **sichere ~ haben** to command majority support; **von einer zahlen- und wertmäßigen ~ gebilligt sein** to be assented by a majority in number and value; **mit einfacher ~ verabschieden** to pass by a simple majority; **über eine ~ verfügen** to be in control of (command) a majority, to swing a majority *(US)*, to have the majority on one's side; **über eine arbeitsfähige ~ verfügen** to have a working majority; **über keine (nicht über die) ~ verfügen** to lack a majority; **mit absoluter ~ wählen** to elect by an absolute majority; **mit großer ~ gewählt werden** to be elected by a large majority of votes; **sichere ~ zusammenbringen** to muster a robust majority;
die ~ ist dafür the ayes have it.

mehrheitlich | beschlossen carried by a majority of votes;
~ **kontrollierte Tochtergesellschaft** majority-owned subsidiary.

Mehrheits | abstimmung majority vote; ~**aktionär** majority stockholder *(US)* (shareholder, *Br.*); ~**ansicht** opinion of the majority, majority opinion *(US)*; ~**bericht** majority report.

Mehrheitsbeschluß decision of the majority, majority vote (decision, resolution);
durch ~ by a majority of votes;
qualifizierter ~ extraordinary *(Br.)* (special) resolution;
einfacher ~ aller Besitzer nachgewiesener Forderungen ordinary resolution; **qualifizierter ~ aller Stimmberechtigten** special resolution.

Mehrheits | besitz, im majority-owned; ~**beteiligung** controlling (majority) interest, majority ownership, majority holding; ~**einfluß** bandwaggon effect (demand); ~**entscheidung** majority vote (decision), plurality *(US)*, *(Gericht)* divided court; ~**erfordernisse** percentage requirements; ~**führer** majority leader; ~**gesellschafter** majority partner; ~**grundsatz** majority rule; ~**herrschaft** majority (majoritarian) rule; ~**partei** majority party; ~**prinzip** majority rule; ~**rechte** majority rights; ~**regierung** majority government; **schwarze ~regierung** black majority rule (government); ~**system** majority rule; ~**vertretung** representation of the majority, majority representation; ~**votum** majority opinion *(US)*; ~**wahl** majority vote; **absolute ~wahl** election by an absolute majority, majority election.

mehrjährig of several years, lasting several years.

Mehr | kosten additional costs (expense, charges), excess costs, overruns *(US)*; ~**kreisempfänger** multicircuit receiver; ~**leistung** increased performance (efficiency), *(Dienstleistungsverkehr)* additional service, *(Produktion)* increased output (production), *(Sozialversicherungsbeitrag)* additional benefit, voluntary contribution; ~**lieferung** increased delivery.

mehr | malige Aufforderungen repeated requests; ~**monatiger Urlaub** holiday lasting several months; ~**motorig** multiengined.

Mehrparteien | haus, auf genossenschaftlicher Basis gebautes cooperative apartment house (building); ~**pluralismus** multiparty pluralism; ~**regierung** multiparty coalition; ~**system** multiple party (multiparty) system.

Mehrphasen | auswahl multiphase sampling; ~**steuer** multistage tax; ~**strom** multiphase current; ~**system** *(Besteuerung)* cumulative multistage system; ~**umsatzsteuer** multiple-stage sales tax.

mehrphasig multiphase;
~**e Auswahl** multistage sampling.

Mehr | porto additional postage, surcharge; ~**preis** higher (additional, surplus) price, price supplement, extra charge; ~**produkt** surplus produce; ~**produktion** increased output, increased production, *(Überschuß)* surplus production.

mehrprozentige Erhöhung aufweisen to rise several points.

Mehrscheibenkupplung multiple-disk clutch.

Mehrschicht | betrieb multiple-shift operation; ~**film** multilayer film; ~**kosten** multiple shift costs.

mehrseitig multilateral, multipartite;
~**es Abkommen** multilateral agreement.

mehrsitzig multiplace.

Mehrspaltenjournal multicolumn journal.

mehr | spaltig *(Anzeige)* spread; ~**sprachig** multilingual, polyglot; ~**spurig** multilane.

Mehrstaatler multiple national.

mehrstellig of several places, multidigit.

Mehr | stimmenwahl plural vote; ~**stimmenwahlrecht** multiple (plural) voting; ~**stimmrechtsaktie** multiple share, multiple stock *(US)*, multiple voting share.

mehrstöckig multistor(e)y;
~**e Verkehrsanordnung** multilevel circulation pattern.

Mehrstückpackung multiple unit item, multipack.

Mehrstufen | befragung multistage interview; ~**rakete** multistage rocket.

mehrstufig multistage;
~**e Betriebsführung** multiple management; ~**e Stichprobe** multistage sample; ~**e Untersuchung** multirange survey.

mehr | stündige Besprechungen talks lasting several hours; ~**tägiger Sitzstreik** stay-in strike; ~**teilig** *(Anbaumöbel)* multisectional, multipart.

Mehr | themenbefragung multiple survey; ~**überweisung** excess remittance; ~**umsatz** increased (surplus) turnover; ~**verbrauch** additional (excess) consumption, *(an Strom)* surcharge; ~**verbrauch an Benzin** increased petrol consumption; ~**verdienst** incentive pay; ~**völkerstaat** multinational state; ~**wegpackung** dual-use (reusable) package.

Mehrwert surplus (added, excess) value, [appreciated] surplus, *(Zuwachswert)* increment value;
~**besteuerung** value-added taxation.

Mehrwertsteuer value-added tax *(Br.)*, vat *(coll.)*;
bezahlte ~ vat borne; **ohne** ~ vat zero-rated;
~ **ausweisen** to indicate vat on an invoice;
~**erhöhung** vat increase; ~**erstattung** vat rebate; ~**erträge** value-added tax receipts.

mehrwertsteuerfrei vat-exempt.

Mehrwertsteuer | harmonisierung vat harmonization; ~**nummer** vat register number; ~**rückvergütung** value added tax rebate; ~**satz** vat rate; **höherer ~satz** higher rate of vat; ~**vorbelastung** prior vat charges; ~**vorschlag** vat proposal.

Mehrwerttheorie theory of surplus value.

mehrwöchentliche Verhandlungen several weeks of negotiations.

Mehrzahl majority, plurality, bulk, greater number, *(ling.)* plural;
in der ~ der Fälle in most (the majority of) cases;
~ **der Besucher** majority of visitors; ~ **der Bevölkerung** greater part of the inhabitants; ~ **der abgegebenen Stimmen** majority of votes; ~ **der Zuhörer** mass of the audience, cumulative audience.

Mehrzweck | bauten multiple-unit housing; ~**fahrzeug** utility van, all-purpose vehicle; ~**flugzeug** multipurpose (general-purpose) aircraft; ~**frachter** multipurpose freighter; ~**frachtflugzeug** general-purpose cargo airship; ~**möbel** multipurpose furniture; ~**verband** multipurpose joint authority; ~**waffe** multipurpose weapon; ~**waggon** general-purpose wag(g)on, combination car *(US)*; ~**wohnung** multiple-unit housing.

mehrzylindrig multicylindered.

meiden to avoid, to shun;
j. ~ to steer clear of s. o.; **Gefahr** ~ to avoid danger; **Gericht** ~ to abstain from a dish; **Gesellschaft** ~ to shun society; **Öffentlichkeit** ~ to shun publicity; **j. wie die Pest** ~ to shun s. o. like the plague; **Thema** ~ to keep off a subject; **jds. Umgang** ~ to avoid s. one's company; **was kann man nicht ~, das soll man willig leiden** what can't be cured must be endured.

Meidung, bei ~ einer Strafe on penalty of.

Meierei dairy farm, wick;
~**erzeugnisse** dairy products.

Meile, gesetzliche statute mile; **nautische** ~ nautical mile.

Meilenstein milestone, mile post, waymark;
wahre ~e in der Entwicklung bedeuten to stand out as landmarks; ~ **in jds. Leben darstellen** to be a milestone in s. one's life.

Meilentarif milage rate.
meilenweit miles away;
noch ~ auseinander sein to be still poles apart; **~ von der Wahrheit entfernt sein** to be miles from the truth *(coll.)*.
Meiler, angereicherter enriched pile.
Mein und Dein verwechseln to be light-fingered.
Meineid perjury, false oath (swearing, *Br.*);
j. zum ~ anstiften (verleiten) to suborn s. o. to commit perjury; **~ leisten (schwören)** to commit perjury, to perjure o. s.; **j. wegen ~s verurteilen** to convict s. o. of perjury.
meineidig perjured;
~ werden to break one's oath.
Meineidsverfahren prosecution of perjury.
meinen to mean, to think, to believe, to deem, *(erwägen)* to suggest;
es ernst ~ to be serious.
Meinung mind, opinion, [point of] view, ground, judgment, sight, verdict, *(Absicht)* intention, *(Bedeutung)* meaning, signification, *(Überzeugung)* conviction;
der öffentlichen ~ verantwortlich responsible for [the] public opinion; **entgegen einer weitverbreiteten ~** contrary to the widely held view; **nach meiner ~** to my way of thinking, in my eye; **nach meiner persönlichen ~** in my private opinion; **nach meiner unmaßgeblichen ~** in my humble opinion; **nach der ~ der Mehrheit** in the estimation of most people; **nach ~ der Sachverständigen** in the opinion of the experts; **ohne Rücksicht auf die öffentliche ~** heedless of public opinion; **vor den Schranken der öffentlichen ~** at the bar of public opinion;
abweichende ~ dissenting (dissentient, separate) opinion, dissent; **allererste ~** horseback opinion *(US)*; **allgemeine ~** received (common) opinion; **ehrliche ~** honest opinion; **einhellige ~** unanimous (undivided) opinion, common consent, concurrence of opinion; **entgegengesetzte ~en** conflicting views; **sich entwickelnde ~** growing opinion; **feste ~** firm opinion; **deutlich zum Ausdruck gebrachte ~** emphatic opinion; **herrschende ~** received opinion (doctrine), prevailing opinion; **irrige ~** misconception, mistaken opinion; **maßgebliche ~** opinion of official quarters; **objektive ~** candid opinion; **öffentliche ~** public (current) opinion, public sentiment, vox populi, Mrs. Grundy *(Br.)*; **schwankende öffentliche ~** pendulum of public opinion; **richterliche ~** dictum; **übereinstimmende ~** concensus of opinion; **überwiegende ~** received opinion (doctrine); **verschiedenartigste ~en** all shades of opinion; **vorgefaßte ~** bias, prejudice[d opinion], preconceived notion, prepossession; **weitverbreitete ~** current opinion; **widerstreitende ~en** clashing (jarring) opinions; **in der Begründung zustimmende ~** concurrent opinion *(US)*;
~ eines Außenstehenden outside opinion; **~ des Gerichtes** voice of the court; **~ der Schriftleitung** editorial view;
seine ~ abgeben to put forward an opinion, *(Gericht)* to render an opinion; **öffentliche ~ abschätzen** to gauge public opinion; **seine ~ ändern** to reverse one's judgment, to wheel about, to recede from one's opinion, to turn round; **seine abweichende ~ ändern** to change one's opinion (ground), to shift in one's mind; **seine ~ völlig ändern** to reverse one's opinion; **sich jds. ~ anschließen** to subscribe to (fall in with, give way to) s. one's opinion, to string along with s. o. *(sl.)*; **sich jds. ~ nicht anschließen** to take issue with s. o.; **sich im Endeffekt jds. ~ anschließen** to come round to s. one's way of thinking; **seine ~en der Öffentlichkeit aufdrängen** to protrude (obtrude) one's opinions on the public; **abweichende ~ aufgeben** *(Gericht)* to recede from an opinion; **seine ~ völlig unverständlich ausdrücken** to wrap up one's meaning in obscure language; **seine ~ äußern** to put forward (offer) an opinion, to give one's judgment, to stand up and be counted; **ungefragt seine ~ äußern** to put in two cents *(sl.)*; **seine ~ ungeniert äußern** to speak one's mind; **~en austauschen** to exchange views, to compare notes; **öffentliche ~ beeinflussen** to bias the opinion of the people, to manufacture (sway) public opinion; **seine ~ für sich behalten** to keep one's own counsel; **jem. eine ungünstige ~ beibringen** to infect s. o. with an opinion; **einer ~ beipflichten** to accede to an opinion, to agree (concur) with s. o.; **j. zu seiner ~ bekehren** to win s. o. over to one's view; **~ bestätigen** to echo a sentiment; **hartnäckig auf seiner ~ bestehen** to be tenacious of one's opinion; **sich eine ~ bilden** to form an opinion, to take a view; **sich eine wenig fundierte ~ bilden** to make up one's mind on poor grounds; **j. um seine ~ bitten** to consult s. o.; **bei seiner ~ bleiben** to persist in one's opinion; **sich in Gegensatz zur öffentlichen ~ bringen** to place o. s. in opposition to public opinion; **seine persönliche ~ zum Ausdruck bringen** to give one's own personal views; **seine ~ durchsetzen** to have one's own way; **~ der Sitzungsteilnehmer einholen** to take the census of a meeting; **~ der breiten Masse erforschen** to go down to grass-root views; **öffentliche ~ erregen** to rouse the public mind, to excite public opinion; **an seiner ~ festhalten** to cling to one's opinion, to stick to one's colo(u)rs; **seine unmaßgebliche ~ zum Besten geben** to offer one's opinion for what it may be worth; **abweichende ~ haben** to dissent from s. one's opinion; **eigene ~ haben** to know one's own mind; **noch keine feste ~ haben** to have no settled opinion; **keine vorgefaßte ~ haben** to keep an open mind; **bessere ~ von jem. haben** to think better of s. o.; **gute ~ von jem. haben** to approve of s. o.; **hohe ~ von jem. haben** to think highly of s. o.; **schlechte ~ von jem. haben** to have a poor opinion of s. o.; **gute ~ von etw. haben** to deem well of s. th.; **hohe ~ von sich haben** to think no small beer of o. s. *(coll.)*; **öffentliche ~ auf seiner Seite haben** to have public sentiment in one's pocket; **mit seiner ~ herausplatzen** to plump; **Übereinstimmung in der öffentlichen ~ herbeiführen** to line up public opinion; **seine ~ kundtun** to deliver o. s. of an opinion, to declare o. s.; **sich von seiner ~ nicht abbringen lassen** to stand to one's guns; **~en der Sitzungsteilnehmer auseinandergehen lassen** to divide the meeting; **sich von jds. ~ abhängig machen** to pin one's opinion on s. one's sleeve; **sich die öffentliche ~ dienstbar machen** to exploit public opinion; **öffentliche ~ mobilisieren** to mobilize public sentiment; **von der öffentlichen ~ keine Notiz nehmen** to sail against the wind; **zu einer ~ neigen** to incline to an opinion; **sich nach jds. ~ richten** to hang on s. one's sleeve; **seine ~ sagen** to state one's opinion, to speak one's piece, to have one's say; **jem. gehörig die ~ sagen** to give s. o. a piece of one's mind, to tell s. o. a few home truths, to cut s. o. down to size *(US)*; **offen seine ~ sagen** to give one's opinion outright; **anderer ~ sein als j.** to disagree (take issue) with s. o.; **bei einer Sache entschieden anderer ~ sein** to disagree violently with s. o.; **mit jem. einer ~ sein** to be at one with s. o.; **geteilter ~ sein** to differ in opinion, to take a different view, to be in two minds, to be mixed, to be divided on a question, to differ, to disagree, to diverge; **mit seinen Freunden geteilter ~ sein** to find o. s. in opposition to one's friends; **völlig geteilter ~ sein** to be split down the center *(US)* (centre, *Br.*); **mit jem. in allem der gleichen ~ sein** to be wholly with s. o. in thinking; **gleicher ~ sein** to endorse an opinion; **sehr unterschiedlicher ~ sein** to be differing widely in opinions; **von den ~en Dritter abhängig sein** to be governed by the opinions of others; **nicht dem Druck der öffentlichen ~ kurz vor den Wahlen ausgesetzt sein** to be free of election-eve pressure; **zu seiner ~ stehen** to have the courage of one's opinion; **mit seiner eigenen ~ in starkem Gegensatz stehen** to contrast strongly with one's own opinion; **seine ~ auf Beweise stützen** to rest one's opinion on proof; **jds. ~ teilen** to share s. one's opinion (views); **mit der öffentlichen ~ übereinstimmen** to be in harmony with public opinion; **~ übernehmen** to buy the line; **seine ~ mit Schlägen auf den Tisch unterstreichen** to punctuate one's sentences with thumps on the table; **~ verfechten** to maintain (advance, advocate) an opinion; **~ vertreten** to take the line *(coll.)*; **abweichende ~ vertreten** to dissent from s. one's opinion; **auf einmal eine völlig andere ~ vertreten** to sing on the other side of one's mouth; **~ vorbringen** to advance an opinion; **öffentliche ~ widerspiegeln** to be a reflection of (reflect) public opinion; **~ einer Menschenmenge wiedergeben** to voice the feelings of a crowd; **einer ~ zuneigen** to lean towards an opinion; **sich mit seiner ~ zurückhalten** to hold one's counsel.
Meinungsänderung reversal (shift) of opinion;
radikale (völlige) ~ *(Politik)* volte-face;
j. zu einer ~ veranlassen to induce s. o. to change his mind.
Meinungsäußerung declaration of an opinion, comment, statement (expression, deliverance) of an opinion;
bloße ~ mere opinion, simplex dictum; **redaktionelle ~** editorial view; **richterliche ~** judicial dictum;
~ eines Zeugen opinion of a witness;
freie ~ gewähren to unmuzzle; **sich um eine ~ herumdrücken** to pussyfoot *(sl.)*; **freie ~ unterdrücken** to gag.
Meinungs|austausch exchange of views (ideas), communication, symposium; **freier ~austausch** free flow of views; **Ausschlag des ~barometers verändern** to tip the balance in the swing; **~befrager** public-opinion leader, field investigator, interviewer, pollist *(US)*, pollster *(US)*; **~befragung** public-opinion poll, opinion research (poll, survey, test), census of opinion; **in der Gunst der öffentlichen ~befragung allen anderen Politikern den Rang ablaufen** to outstrip all other politicians in opinion poll ratings; **~befragung durchführen** to conduct a poll, to poll *(US sl.)*; **~bewertung** opinion rating; **~bild** public image.
meinungsbildende Persönlichkeit opinion former (leader).

Meinungs|bildner opinion former (leader); ~**bildung** making-up of one's mind, *(der Öffentlichkeit)* opinion leading; ~**forscher** public-opinion analyst, Gallup (research) man, polltaker *(US)*, pollster *(US)*.
Meinungsforschung opinion poll (survey, test), public-opinion research;
stichprobenartig durchgeführte ~ judgment sampling; **Markt- und** ~ statistical sampling;
~ **der gesamten Bevölkerung** mass observation.
Meinungs|forschungsinstitut opinion research corporation; ~**freiheit** freedom of speech (opinion); ~**gleichheit** consonance of opinions; ~**käufe** *(Börse)* speculation (speculative) purchase, speculative buying; ~**lose** don't-knows; ~**manipulation** *(Wahlen)* manipulation of an election; ~**manipulator** image merchant; **auf** ~**medien ausgerichtet** media-orientated; ~**monopol** monopoly of opinions, institutional (reputation) monopoly; ~**pflege** image polishing, public relations; ~**skala** opinion (ratings) scale; ~**test** brain-picking session; ~**übereinstimmung** agreement of views.
Meinungsumfrage opinion poll;
öffentliche ~ sounding of public opinion, [public-]opinion poll (test, research, survey); **umfassende** ~ national opinion poll;
~ **veranstalten** to take a poll; ~ **veröffentlichen** to release a poll; **ausgezeichnete Ergebnisse bei** ~**n verzeichnen** to ride high in the opinion poll;
~**institut** opinion research corporation.
Meinungsumschwung reversal of opinion, swing of public opinion, turnover, stampede *(US)*;
ziffernmäßig erfaßter ~ swing figure; **völliger** ~ somersault;
~ **der Öffentlichkeit** swing of the pendulum; ~ **zuungunsten der Regierung** antigovernment swing;
schon bei einem kleinen ~ **der Wähler eine glatte Mehrheit erreichen** to need but a small swing to win a clear majority; **auf einen** ~ **hoffen** to hope for a turn of the tide.
Meinungsverkäufe *(Börse)* sales on speculation, speculative selling (sales).
Meinungsverschiedenheit division, diversion, discord, difference (divergence, clash) of opinion, friction, dissent, dissension, upset, controversy;
ernste ~ serious disagreement; **schiedsgerichtsfähige** ~**en** differences submissible to arbitration; **unbedeutende** ~ minor difference;
~**en über die Auslegung einzelner Vertragsbestimmungen** disputes under a contract; ~**en zwischen politischen Gruppen** dissensions between rival groups in politics;
~**en ausgleichen** to accommodate differences; **seine** ~**en beilegen** to settle one's differences; **kleine** ~**en haben** to [have a] tiff; ~ **mit j. haben** to have an argument (carry on a controversy) with s. o.
Meinungs|wandel shift (reversal) of opinion; ~**wechsel** change of opinion, about-face, tergiversation.
Meise haben to have bats in the belfry *(coll.)*.
meistbegünstigt most-favo(u)red.
Meistbegünstigung *(Zoll)* preference, imperial preference *(Br.)*, most favo(u)red-nation treatment.
Meistbegünstigungs|behandlung most-favo(u)red-nation treatment; ~**klausel** most-favo(u)red nation clause; ~**prinzip** most-favo(u)red-nation principle; ~**regelung** *(GATT)* preferential arrangement; ~**satz** most-favo(u)red-nation (preferential) rate; ~**stellung** most-favo(u)red-nation status; ~**tarif** most-favo(u)red-nation (preferential) tariff, imperial preference *(Br.)*; ~**zollsatz** most-favo(u)red-nation rate of duty.
meistbietend bidding most;
~ **verkaufen** to sell by *(Br.)* (at, *US*) auction, to sell to the highest bidder.
Meistbietende|r highest (best) bidder, highest offerer;
dem ~**n zuschlagen** to allocate (knock down) to the highest bidder.
Meister master [of a trade], dabster *(Br., coll.)*, *(Handwerksmeister)* master craftsman, craftsmaster, *(Industrie)* foreman, master workman, overseer;
alter ~ *(Kunst)* old master; **gestrenger** ~ hard master;
seinen ~ **finden** to meet more than one's match; **bei einem** ~ **lernen** to learn a craft, to be apprenticed; **in seinem Fach ein** ~ **sein** to know s. th. perfectly (one's onions, what's what); **großer** ~ **im Intrigieren sein** to be a past-master in intrigue;
es ist noch kein ~ **vom Himmel gefallen** no one is born a master of his craft; **Übung macht den** ~ practice makes perfect;
~**arbeit** masterwork; ~**detektiv** ace detective; ~**dieb** crack thief *(coll.)*.
meisterhaft in a masterly manner, masterful, masterly;
etw. ~ **beherrschen** to do s. th. to perfection; **sein Fach** ~ **beherrschen** to be a master of one's art; ~ **improvisieren können** to be able to improvise to perfection;
~ **gelungene Rede** accomplished speech; ~**er politischer Schachzug** master stroke of diplomacy.
Meister|hand master touch; ~**leistung** masterly performance, master stroke; **technische** ~**leistung** brilliant feat of engineering.
meistern to master, to overcome, *(Sprache)* to command;
Schwierigkeit ~ to master a difficulty.
Meisterrecht freedom of a company *(Br.)*.
Meisterschaft championship;
~ **austragen** to compete for the championship; **es zur** ~ **bringen** to attain a mastership in; ~ **gewinnen** to gain the mastery.
Meister|stelle overseership; ~**stück** masterpiece, masterwork, feat; ~**titel gewinnen** to become a craftsmaster; ~**titel verteidigen** to defend the championship; ~**würde** mastership; ~**zug** master stroke.
Meistgebot highest (last) bid, best offer.
meistgelesene Zeitung most-read paper.
Melancholie melancholy, megrims, blues.
melancholisch melancholic;
~ **sein** to have the blues.
Melde|amt registration (registry, *US*) office; ~**bestimmungen** registration requirement; ~**bogen** registration form; ~**boot** *(mar.)* aviso; **polizeiliches** ~**buch** police blotter *(US)*; ~**fahrer** *(mil.)* dispatch rider; ~**fahrt** *(mil.)* dispatch riding; **polizeiliches** ~**formular** registration form; ~**formular ausfüllen** to enter one's name in the visitor's book; ~**frist** time to register, check-in time; ~**gänger** *(mil.)* runner; ~**hund** *(mil.)* messenger (message-carrying) dog; ~**karte** *(mil.)* message card; ~**kartei** register; ~**kopf** *(mil.)* message center *(US)* (centre, *Br.*); ~**läufer** *(mil.)* messenger; ~**liste** entry list.
melden *(amtlich)* to return, *(ankündigen)* to announce, to notify, *(mitteilen)* to advise, to notify, *(dienstlich mitteilen)* to report, *(unterrichten)* to inform, *(Zeitung)* to publish reports, *(Zug)* to signal;
sich ~ to put up one's hand, *(eintragen lassen)* to register, *(Bewerber)* to apply, *(Gläubiger)* to come forward, *(mil.)* to enrol(l); **Angestellten zur disziplinarischen Bestrafung** ~ to report an employee for misconduct; **sich für einen Arbeitsplatz** ~ to apply for a post; **den Behörden** ~ to notify the authorities; **Besucher** ~ to announce a visitor; **sich im Büro** ~ to apply (register, report) at the office; **sich zum Dienstantritt** ~ to report for service; **sich beim Empfangsschalter** ~ to come to the reception; **sich zu einem Examen** ~ to enter one's name for an examination; **sich als Freiwilliger** ~ to [enlist as a] volunteer; **sich früh** ~ *(Winter)* to set in early; **Geburt** ~ to register a birth; **sich beim Hafenamt** ~ to report to the port authorities; **sich auf ein Inserat hin** ~ to answer (reply to) an advertisement; **sich als Kandidat** ~ to come forward as candidate; **sich krank** ~ to go on sick call, to report sick; **ansteckende Krankheit den Behörden** ~ to notify the authorities of an infectious disease; **sich freiwillig zum Kriegsdienst** ~ to enlist with the army in a war; **sich zu einem Kursus** ~ to sign up for a course; **sich mit den Nachrichten wieder** ~ *(Sender)* to be on the air again with the news; **etw. der Polizei** ~ to report s. th. to the police; **sich bei der Polizei** ~ to report to the police station *(Br.)*; **sich polizeilich** ~ to register with the police; **rechtzeitig** ~ to advise in due course; **sich für eine Stelle** ~ to apply for a job; **sich zur Stelle** ~ to report o. s. present; **sich am Telefon** ~ to answer the telephone; **sich telefonisch bei jem.** ~ to get in touch with s. o. by telephone; **Unfall** ~ to report an accident to the police; **j. wegen Unpünktlichkeit** ~ to report s. one's unpunctuality; **sich vom Urlaub zurück** ~ to report back from leave; **Verlust eines Flugzeuges** ~ to post an airliner as missing; **jem. einen Vorgang** ~ to advise s. o. of an incident; **Wahlergebnisse** ~ to return election results; **sich zu Wort** ~ to ask leave (permission) to speak, to ask the floor *(US)*, to try to catch the chairman's eye;
sich ~ **lassen** to send in one's name; **sich beim Vorstand** ~ **lassen** to report to the manager.
Melde|netz *(Flugverkehr)* spotting system; ~**nummer** *(Verlagsgeschäft)* message number; ~**pflicht** compulsory registration; **von der** ~**pflicht ausnehmen** to provide an exemption from registration.
meldepflichtig subject to registration, *(mitteilungspflichtig)* notifiable, reportable, *(Zoll)* declarable;
~ **sein** to require one's registration;
~**e Krankheit** notifiable disease.

Melde|pflichtiger registrant; ~**punkt** checkpoint; ~**sammelstelle** *(mil.)* pick-up; ~**schein** registration form, *(Ausländer)* certificate of registration; ~**schluß** deadline *(US)*, closing date, *(Flugplatz)* check-in time; ~**stelle** registration office, *(Feuer)* fire-alarm point; ~**stelle für marktbeherrschende Zusammenschlüsse** Registrar of Restrictive Trading Agreements *(Br.)*; ~**tasche** *(mil.)* dispatch case; ~**vorschriften** registration requirements; ~**wesen** registration of residents; ~**zeit** *(Flugplatz)* check-in time; ~**zettel** registration form.

Meldung *(Ankündigung)* announcement, *(Anzeige)* report, *(bei Behörde)* registration, notification, *(Bericht)* report, news [item], dispatch, *(Bewerbung)* application, *(Forderungsnachweis)* proof of debt, *(mil.)* report, enlistment, *(geschäftliche Mitteilung)* advice, notice, *(telefonische Mitteilung)* message, *(Prüfung, Wettbewerb)* entry, *(Unterrichtung)* information, word, *(Wortmeldung)* leave (permission) to speak;
nach den letzten ~en according to the latest information (news); **nach bisher vorliegenden ~en** according to reports received so far;
amtliche (dienstliche) ~ official report, return; **dringende ~** priority message; **eingehende ~en** incoming dispatches; **falsche ~** false alarm; **jährliche ~** *(Gesellschaftsregister)* annual return; **kurze ~** small blurb; **letzte ~en** *(Zeitung)* stop-press (very latest) news; **nichtamtliche ~** grapevine *(coll.)*; **polizeiliche ~** police report, registration with the police; **schlagzeilenartige ~** headline, scoop; **unbestätigte ~** whispered report, unconfirmed news; **ursprüngliche ~** original dispatch; **verschlüsselte ~** coded (ciphered) message;
rechtzeitige ~ am Abfertigungsschalter *(Flugplatz)* check-in time; **~en aus dem Ausland** reports from abroad; **~ einer ansteckenden Krankheit** notification of an infectious disease; **~ der Polizei** police announcement; **~en für einen Wettbewerb** entries for a competition;
~en im Rundfunk bringen (durchgeben) to broadcast news, to make an announcement on the radio; **~ telefonisch durchgeben** to telephone a message; **~ erhalten** to receive [an item of] information; **~en aus aller Herren Länder erhalten** to receive dispatches from all parts of the world; **~ erstatten** to make one's report; **bei seinen Vorgesetzten ~ erstatten** to notify one's superiors; **~ über einen Unfall erstatten** to report an accident; **~ überbringen** to carry a message; **falsche ~en verbreiten** to circulate false news; **~ veröffentlichen** to publish a report, to break an item of news; **~ mit allem Vorbehalt veröffentlichen** to publish news with all reserve; **seine ~ zurückziehen** to withdraw from a contest, to back out; **seine ~ im letzten Augenblick zurückziehen** to scratch at the last moment.

Meliorationen amelioration [works], improvement of land, betterments, soil improvements, drainage;
wertsteigernde ~ beneficial improvements.

Meliorations|arbeiten amelioration works, ditching; ~**bezirk** drainage district; ~**darlehn** loan for the purpose of improvement, improvement loan; ~**fähigkeit** capability of being improved; ~**fonds** special-assessment (local-improvement) fund; ~**gesetze** Land Improvement Acts *(Br.)*; ~**gewinn** *(Grundstück)* general benefit; ~**kosten** cost of improvement; ~**kredit** credit granted for improvement, loan for the purpose of improvement, improvement loan; ~**obligationen,** ~**schuldverschreibungen** development (local improvement) bonds; **kommunale ~schuldverschreibungen** special assessment bonds *(US)*; ~**unternehmen** improvement company, development concern; ~**wertzuwachs** drainage benefit; ~**zuschüsse** improvement grants; ~**zweck** improvement purpose.

meliorieren to meliorate, to improve arable land *(US)*.

melken *(fig.)* to milk.

Melodie tune, air, melody;
zündende ~ catching air, catchy tune;
~ nicht aus dem Kopf verlieren to have a tune on the brain.

Membrane *(tel.)* diaphram.

Memoiren memoirs;
~**schreiber** memoirist, memorialist.

Memorandum memorandum, memo, minute *(Br.)*;
~ des Finanzministeriums treasury minute.

Memorial journal, waste (memorandum, *US*) book, daybook *(Br.)*.

Menetekel writing on the wall.

Menge quantity, amount, volume, deal, bulk, portion, lump, parcel, host, posse, pack, quantity, wag(g)on-load, grist *(US coll.)*, *(Herde)* drove, *(med.)* unit, *(Überschuß)* abundance, *(Vielzahl)* plenty, multitude, *(Volksmenge)* crowd, mass, throng, stream, press, multitude, cluster, peck, assemblage, numbers, head *(Br.)*;
der ~ nach quantitative, by volume; **in der ~ eingekeilt** in the thick of the press; **in großen ~n** in large quantity, in quantities; **in großen ~n erzeugt** large scale, commercial, bulk; **in kleinen ~n** in small amounts; **in riesigen ~n** by the shipload; **in ungenügender ~ verladen** short-shipped *(US)*;
angebotene ~ quantity supplied; **begrenzte ~** limited quantity; **bestellte ~** quantity ordered; **erhebliche ~** considerable amount; **erregte ~** excited crowd; **falsche ~** wrong quantity; **fehlende ~** missing amount; **feindselige ~** hostile crowd; **friedliche ~** orderly crowd; **garantierte ~** guaranteed quantity; **nicht zum Handel geeignete ~n** noncommercial quantities; **gelieferte ~** quantity supplied (delivered); **geringe ~** trace; **gewinnbringende ~n** paying quantities; **etwa gleiche ~n** like amounts; **große ~** lump, world; **handelsübliche ~** commercial quantity; **kauflustige ~** crowd of eager shoppers; **kleine ~** dose packet; **kritische ~** threshold dose; **ungerade ~** odd lot; **unrichtige ~** wrong quantity; **verfügbare ~** available quantity; **zollfreie ~** quantity permitted;
gewaltige ~ Arbeit great quantity of work; **große ~ von Autos** a fleet of cars; **große ~ von Briefen** a shower (mass) of letters; **große ~ von Büchern** a great many books; **große ~ Geld** loads (a lot, a mint, *coll.*, scads, *US*) of money; **jede ~ von Liebesabenteuern** ocean of affairs; **jede ~ Platz** oceans of room;
~ auseinandertreiben to break up (disperse) the crowd; **eine ~ Geld ausgeben** to spend a good deal of money; **sich einen Weg durch die ~ bahnen** to push one's way through the crowd; **sich unter die ~ begeben** to mingle with the crowd; **sich durch die ~ drängeln** to shove through a crowd, to fight one's way through the press; **sich eine ~ einbilden** to think a lot of o. s.; **in großen ~n eingehen** *(Aufträge)* to pour in; **große ~n einkaufen** to buy in large quantities, to load up; **~ durch Blicke einschüchtern** to frown defiance on a crowd; **in ~n erzeugen** to volume-produce; **Beifall der ~ finden** to earn the approbation of the public; **jede ~ Geld haben** to have lots of money; **eine ~ Zeit haben** to have plenty of time; **in der ~ untertauchen** to be swallowed up in the crowd; **jede ~ Geld verdienen** to be simply coining money; **~ Leute verhaften** to arrest a great number of people; **in großen ~n verkaufen** to sell in large numbers; **nur kleine ~n verkaufen** to deal only in small lots; **sich eine ~ Scherereien zuziehen** to come in for a lot of trouble.

mengen to mix, to blend;
sich in etw. ~ to poke one's nose into s. th.; **sich in die Angelegenheiten eines anderen ~** to meddle in s. o. else's affairs.

Mengen|abnahme quantity buying, quantitative sales; ~**abnehmer** bulk buyer; ~**absatz** quantitative sales; ~**abschlag** space (volume, quantity) discount; ~**abweichung** quantity variance (deviation), *(gegenüber Standard)* volume variance; ~**analyse** quantitative analysis; ~**änderung** changes in volume; ~**angabe** quantity mark (data); ~**anpasser** quantity adjuster; ~**auftrag** volume (quantity) order; ~**beschränkungen** quantitative (quantity) restrictions; ~**bestimmung** quantity determination; ~**bezeichnung** quantity description; ~**bonus** volume discount; ~**diskont** space (volume) discount; ~**effekt** quantity effect; ~**einheit** unit of quantity; ~**einkauf** quantity (bulk) buying, bulk purchase (purchasing); ~**einkäufe tätigen** to buy things in large quantities; ~**erlös,** ~**ertrag** quantity proceeds; ~**erzeugung** quantity (mass, volume) production; ~**index** quantum (quantity, quantitative) index; ~**kauf** quantity (bulk) buying; ~**kauf ohne Besichtigung** random purchase; ~**konjunktur** quantitative market tendencies, all-out expansion of business; ~**kontrolle** quantitative control; ~**kostenrechnung** marginal costing; ~**kurs** *(Devisen)* direct exchange; ~**leistung** production capacity, output; ~**lieferung** bulk supply.

mengenmäßig quantitative, by volume (quantities), in terms of volume, in volume terms;
~ zurückgehen to fall in volume terms;
~e Beschränkungen quantitative restrictions; **~e Staffelung** quantitative graduation; **~er Umsatz** quantity (physical) turnover.

Mengen|meßziffer *(Statistik)* quantity relative; ~**nachfrage** quantity demanded; ~**nachlaß** space (volume) discount, quantity reduction; ~**notierung** fixed exchange; ~**preis** bulk (multiple, quantity) price; ~**produkt** cross product set; ~**produktion** quantity production; ~**prüfung** verification of quantity.

Mengenrabatt quantity rate (rebate, discount, reduction), space (volume, mass, frequency, time) discount, discount for quantities, bulk rate *(Br.)*;
ohne ~ without discount, straight *(US)*;
~ bei Belegung mehrerer Zeitungen group discount;
~**preis** multiple price.

Mengen|regulierung quantity control; ~**satz** *(Setzen)* area composition; ~**staffel** quantity scale; ~**steuer** specific tax; ~**tarif** specific tariff, bulk supply rate, quantity rate; ~**tarifpreis** prices shaded for quantities; ~**toleranz** quantity variance; ~**umsatz** bulk sales *(US)*, sales volume, quantity turnover; ~**verhältnis** relative proportions, quantitative ratio; ~**verlust** loss of volume; ~**vorgabe** quantity standard; ~**vorschriften** quantitative regulations; ~**ziffer** *(Statistik)* quantity relative; ~**zoll** specific duty.

Mensch human being, man, person, individual, *(Menschheit)* human race, mankind;
alleinstehender ~ singleton; **arbeitsscheuer** ~ shirker; **aufrichtiger** ~ plain dealer; **gut aussehender** ~ good-looker; **modern eingestellter** ~ swinger; **einsichtiger** ~ prudent man; **energiegeladener** ~ live wire; **schwer zu ertragender** ~ most objectionable person; **fügsamer** ~ nose of wax; **gebildeter** ~ educated man, well-read person; **moralisch gefährdeter** ~ sick mind; **genialer** ~ genius; **intelligenter** ~ intellectual person; **introvertierter** ~ introvert; **langweiliger** ~ flat tyre *(US sl.)*; **leichtfertiger** ~ lighthead; **die meisten** ~**en** most people; **oberflächlicher** ~ butterfly; **offener and loyaler** ~ plain-dealing man; **primitiver (kulturloser)** ~ low-brow *(sl.)*; **schlichter** ~ simple person; **sparsamer** ~ saver; **sturer** ~ stubborn person, mule *(coll.)*, set person *(US)*, dour type *(Br.)*; **unerträglicher** ~ incompatible; **unsteter** ~ bird of passage; **verwahrloster** ~ tack; **verwendungsfähiger** ~ reject; **wertloser** ~ dead duck, no account *(US dial.)*; **naiv wirkender** ~ innocent-looking person; **zielloser** ~ drifter; **zugänglicher** ~ accessible person;
~ **mit modernen Anschauungen** modern; ~ **im Betrieb** human factor in business; ~ **ohne Einfluß** insignificant person; ~ **mit Energie** person of spirit; ~ **von Kultur** patrician; ~ **mit schnellem Reaktionsvermögen** nimble thinker; ~ **mit schlechtem Ruf** improper person; ~**en aus allen Schichten** people of all ranks; ~ **von ganz anderem Schlage** man of another paste; ~ **vom alten Schrot und Korn** throwback to *(fam.)*;
alten ~**en ablegen** to turn over a new leaf; **ganzen** ~**en beanspruchen** to absorb s. o.; **ungern unter** ~**en gehen** to shun society; **neue** ~**en kennen lernen** to meet fresh faces; **ganz anderen** ~**en aus jem. machen** to make a new man of s. o.; **zivilisierten** ~**en aus jem. machen** to have a civilizing effect on s. o.; **mit jem. von** ~ **zu** ~ **reden** to talk to s. o. as man to man, to have a heart-to-heart talk with s. o.; **schwer zu behandelnder** ~ **sein** to be a difficult man to get on with; **ganz gewöhnlicher** ~ **sein** to be nobody in particular; **ganz anderer** ~ **geworden sein** to feel a different man; **für** ~**en ungenießbar sein** to be unfit for human consumption.

Menschen|alter age, generation; ~**andrang** crush, throng; ~**ansammlung** gathering, aggregation (crowds) of people; ~**ansammlung in den Großstädten** overcrowding of large cities.

menschenarm impoverished in men, sparsely populated.

Menschen|art, nach after the flesh; ~**auflauf** concourse, confluence; ~**beurteilung** judgment of character; ~**feind** misantrophe, misanthropist, man-hater; ~**fluten** streams of people.

menschenfreundlich humane, philanthropic.

Menschen|führer leader (manager) of men; ~**führung im Betrieb** personnel management; **durch eine** ~**gasse gehen** to pass through a lane of people; **seit** ~**gedenken** within living memory, from time immemorial; **vor** ~**gedenken** beyond memory; ~**gedränge** throng, crush; ~**geschlecht** humankind, flesh; **Teufel in** ~**gestalt sein** to be a devil incarnate; ~**gewühl** concourse, seething, milling; **dichtes** ~**gewühl** thick of the crowd; **bei Sozialuntersuchungen zugrundegelegte** ~**gruppen** social units; **von** ~**hand geschaffen** man-made; ~**handel** slave traffic, human trade; ~**jagd** manhunt; ~**kenner** judge of character; ~**kenntnis** judgment of character; ~**kraft** mortal power.

Menschenleben lifetime;
keine ~ **zu beklagen** no loss of life; **verlorene** ~ casualties, fatalities;
rücksichtslos über ~ **hinweggehen** to bear no regard for human life.

menschenleere Straßen deserted streets.

Menschen|massen shoals (crowds, streams) of people; ~**material** manpower.

Menschenmenge gathering, hive, crowd, multitude, throng;
hereinströmende ~ in-going crowd; **zusammengequetschte** ~ squash;
übliche ~**n bei Demonstrationen** rent-a-crowd standards;
sich durch eine ~ **drängen (schieben)** to edge (push) one's way (wriggle) through the crowd.

menschenmöglich humanly possibly, earthly *(coll.)*;
alles ~**e tun** to leave no stone unturned.

Menschen|möglichkeit, das ist doch nicht die that's incredible; ~**opfer** human sacrifice; ~**potential** manpower reserve; ~**raub** abduction, kidnapping; ~**raub begehen** to kidnap; ~**räuber** kidnapper; ~**rechte** human rights; **sich für die** ~**rechte einsetzen** to speak out on human rights.

Menschenrechts|beschwerde appeal to the Human Rights Commission; ~**bestimmungen** human rights clauses; ~**bewegung** human rights movement; ~**kommission** Commission on Human Rights; ~**verletzung** human rights violation.

Menschenreservoir manpower reserve.

menschenscheu unsociable, shy.

Menschen|schicksal, erschütterndes moving story of a person's life; ~**schinder** slave driver, sweater; ~**schinderei** slave-driving, sweating.

Menschenseele human soul;
weit und breit war keine ~ **zu sehen** there wasn't a soul on the street (in sight).

Menschenskind! good Lord!, gosh!

Menschenstrom streams (crowds, shoals) of people.

menschenunwürdig|sein to be beneath human dignity;
~**e Bedingungen** inhuman conditions; ~**e Behausung darstellen** to be unfit for human habitation.

Menschen|verächter misanthropist, cynic; ~**verachtung** misanthropy, cynicism.

Menschenverstand, gesunder common (horse) sense, gumption *(coll.)*, wits; **bar jedes gesunden** ~**s** destitute of common sense; **kein bißchen gesunder** ~ not a grain of common sense; **praktischer** ~ down-to-earth common sense;
dem gesunden ~ **Hohn sprechen** to bid defiance to common sense; **gegen den gesunden** ~ **verstoßen** to outrage common sense *(fam.)*.

Menschen|welt world of men; ~**würde** dignity of man.

menschenwürdig|e Bedingungen conditions fit for human beings; ~**es Essen** food fit for human consumption.

Menschheit mankind.

menschlich human;
j. ~ **behandeln** to treat s. o. with humanity;
~**e Arbeitsstunden** man-hours; ~**e Beziehungen** human relations, *(im Betrieb)* industrial relations; **für die** ~**e Ernährung nicht geeignet** unfit for human consumption; ~**e Gebräuche** man-made customs; ~**es Kapital** human capital; **in der** ~**en Natur liegen** to be human nature; ~**e Note** human touch; ~**er Richter** merciful judge; ~**e Schwächen** human foibles; ~**e Seite** human factor; ~**es Versagen** human failure; **nach** ~**er Voraussicht** as far as we can foresee; ~**es Wesen** human being; ~**er Zug** human characteristic.

Menschliche|s, das ~**Allzumenschliche** human side.

Menschlichkeit humanity;
aus Gründen der ~ **entlassen werden** to be released on humanitarian grounds.

Menschlichkeitsverbrechen crime against humanity.

Mentalreservation mental reserve (reservation).

Menü bill of fare, menu;
fertige ~**s anliefern** to cater for.

Meriten, über besondere ~ **verfügen** to have an extra pull.

meritorisches Gut quasi-private good.

merkantil eingestellt commercialized.

Merkantilismus mercantilism, mercantile theory.

Merkantilist mercantilist.

merkantilistisch mercantilistic.

Merkblatt instruction card, leaflet, notice.

merken to become aware, to notice, to realize;
sich eine Autonummer ~ to make a note of the number of a car; **es endlich** ~ at length to be dawning on s. o.; **Fehler** ~ to detect a mistake; **an jds. Gesichtsausdruck** ~ to tell from the expression on s. one's face; **sich jds. Namen** ~ to remember s. one's name; **sofort** ~ to realize at once; **keine Spuren von einer früheren Krankheit mehr** ~ to be unable to find any traces of a former illness;
seine Absicht ~ **lassen** to reveal one's intention; **sich seine Enttäuschung nicht** ~ **lassen** not to show one's disappointment; **sich nichts** ~ **lassen** to betray one's feelings.

merklich perceptible, noticeable, appreciable;
~**e Aufwärtstendenz** distinct upward trend; ~**e Besserung** considerable improvement; ~ **spürbare Tendenz** strongly marked tendency; ~**e Umsatzzunahme** marked increase in sales; ~**e Veränderung** noticeable change.

Merkmal mark, sign, indication, hallmark, appanage, trait, *(Besonderheit)* characteristic, criterion, feature;

besonderes ~ peculiarity, special feature, speciality; **keine besonderen ~e** no distinguishing marks; **charakteristisches ~** characteristic feature, impress; **festes ~** statistical attribute; **hervorstechende ~e** salient characteristics; **qualitatives ~** *(Marketing)* attribute; **quantitatives ~** *(Marketing)* variable; **unterscheidungsfähiges ~** criterion; **wesentliches ~** attribute; **zufälliges ~** nonessential property;
geografische ~e eines Bezirks geographical features of a district; **~e einer Versuchsklasse** sample characteristics.
Merkmals|klasse *(Statistik)* category; **~vergleich** factor comparison.
Merk|posten *(Bilanz)* monitory (pro-memoria) item; **nur als ~posten bestehen** to be shown only as a record; **~wort** direction word.
meschugge off one's onion.
meßbar measurable.
Meß|betrag *(Steuer)* ratal, rate; **~brief** bill of admeasurement (tonnage), certificate of tonnage.
Messe [industries] fair, show, exhibition, market, *(Fachmesse)* dealer show, *(Kirche)* mass;
auf der ~ at the fair;
internationale ~ international trade fair; **landwirtschaftliche ~** agricultural show; **technische ~** engineering (machinery) fair; **~ im Freigelände** outdoor fair;
~ abhalten to hold a fair; **sich zu einer ~ anmelden** to register for a fair, to apply for space; **~ aufziehen** to organize a fair; **Waren auf der ~ ausstellen** to exhibit goods at a fair; **~ beschicken** to send goods to a fair; **~n besuchen** to frequent (attend) fairs; **sich an einer ~ beteiligen** to participate in a fair; **~ eröffnen** to open a fair; **~ veranstalten** to organize a fair;
~amt fair authorities; **~attraktion** fair's attraction; **~ausweis** fair pass; **~behörde** fair authorities; **~bericht** report of a fair; **~beschicker** exhibitor; **~besuch** fair attendance; **~besucher** fairgoer, fair dealer (visitor); **~beteiligung** participation in a fair; **~gebäude** fair building; **~gelände** fair site, exhibition grounds (site), fairgrounds *(US)*; **~geschenk** fairing; **~gesellschaft** exhibition corporation; **~gut** exhibition goods, goods sent to a fair; **~halle** exhibition hall; **~katalog** fair catalog[ue]; **~konzession** concession at a fair; **~leitung** management of a fair, fair authorities, exhibition board; **~lieferant** [industrial] caterer.
messen to take the measurements, to measure, *(ausloten)* to sound, *(Arbeitsvorgänge)* to time, *(Flüssigkeit, Gas)* to meter, *(mit Testlehre)* to gauge, *(mit verstellbarer Lehre)* to caliper; **sich mit jem. ~** to measure swords with s. o.; **Dritte nach seinen eigenen Fähigkeiten ~** to judge others by o. s.; **Entfernung ~** to judge a distance; **jds. Fieber ~** to take s. one's temperature; **seine Kräfte mit jem. ~** to match one's strength against (have a trial of strength with) s. o.; **sich mit einem Rivalen ~** to compete with s. o.; **Temperaturschwankungen ~** to measure changes of temperature;
sich mit jem. ~ können to be more than a match for s. o.; **sein Geld mit Scheffeln ~ können** to be rolling in money; **sich zu ~ versuchen** to try conclusions *(Br.)*.
Messeordnung exhibition regulations.
Messer knife, *(Zähler)* meter;
Kampf bis aufs ~ ausfechten to fight out the battle to the end; **etw. aufs ~ bekämpfen** to fight s. th. tooth and nail; **seinem Gegner selbst das ~ in die Hand geben** to sign one's own death warrant; **ans ~ liefern** to put on the spot *(US)*; **unters ~ müssen** to have to undergo an operation; **jem. das ~ an die Kehle setzen** to put a knife to s. one's throat; **auf des ~s Schneide stehen** to be on a razor's edge, to be a touch-and-go business.
Messerabatt trade-fair rebate.
messerscharfer Verstand razor-sharp mind.
Messe|stadt fair town; **~stand** exhibition (fair) stand; **~standgebühr** pickage *(Br.)*; **~teilnehmer** exhibitor; **~test** fair test; **internationaler ~verband** Union of International Fairs; **~versicherung** fair insurance; **~vertrag** exhibition contract; **~verzeichnis** fair directory; **~wechsel** fair bill; **~woche** fair week; **~zeit** fair period.
Meß|fähnchen surveyor's pole; **~- und Warengeld** metage; **~gerät, ~instrument** gauge, measuring instrument (apparatus), measure, meter.
Messing|beschlag brass mounting; **~schild** brass plate.
Meß|schnur, mit einer ~schnur messen to tape; **~stab** staff, dipstick; **~tabelle** measurement scale; **~tisch** plan table; **~tischblatt** survey map.
Messung measurement, gauging;
~ des Leserverhaltens audience rating;
~en vornehmen to measure.
Meß|vorrichtung measuring apparatus (tool), instrument, meter; **~zahl** index (plural) number, *(Statistik)* relative, indicative figure; **beste statistische ~zahl** *(Statistik)* optimum statistic.
Mestize quarter-breed, half-breed *(US)*.
Meta|geschäft deal (business) on joint account, *(Bankwesen)* joint venture; **~geschäfte machen** to do a joint business, to go half shares; **~konto** joint account; **~kontoinhaber** joint-account party; **~kredit** credit on joint account.
Metall, unedles base metal;
~ in Barrenform base bullion;
~e versetzen to alloy;
~abfall scrap metal; **~analyse** assay; **~arbeit** metal work; **~arbeiter** metal worker; **~arbeitergewerkschaft** metal workers union; **~band** *(Verpackung)* strap; **~bearbeitung** metal-working; **~bestand** *(Notenbank)* bullion reserve; **~börse** metal exchange, Commodity Exchange Inc. (COMEX); **~branche** metal trades; **~deckung** *(Währung)* metallic cover; **~flugzeug** all-metal airplane; **~gehalt** metal content; **~geld** specie, hard cash, real money, *(Währung)* metallic currency; **~geld und Barren** coin and bullion; **~gitter** wire fence; **~industrie** metal (metallurgic) industry.
metallische Stimme metallic voice.
Metall|klischee metal block (cut); **~marke** token, metal fare; **~probe** assay; **~schild** metal sign.
metallverarbeitend metalworking;
~e Industrie metal-processing industry.
Metall|verarbeitung metal fabricating, metalworking; **~vorrat** *(Notenbank)* bullion reserve; **~währung** metallic currency (standard).
Metallwaren metalware, metal manufactures, hardware;
~gehalt yield; **~händler** ironmonger *(Br.)*, hardwareman *(US)*; **~industrie** ironmongery *(Br.)*, hardware industry *(US)*.
Metapher metaphor;
in ~n sprechen to speak in images.
Meteorologe weatherman, weather caster *(US)*, meteorologist.
meteorologisches Institut meteorological institute.
Meter, pro laufenden per running meter *(US)* (metre, *Br.*);
~ware piece goods; **~zähler** *(Film)* film (footage) counter.
Methode method, mode, way, form, system, plan, line, means, approach, angle *(US)*, *(Verfahren)* process, technique;
analytische ~ analytical approach; **für die Berechnung von Steuerermäßigungen angewandte ~** method of granting relief; **bewährte ~** approved method; **direkte ~** *(Sprache)* direct method; **eingängige ~** handy way; **erprobte ~** proven way; **hochentwickelte ~** sophisticated method; **nützliche ~** practical method; **ökonomische ~** economic method; **räuberische ~n** *(Wettbewerb)* predatory practices; **üble (unsaubere) ~n** low-down methods; **veraltete ~n** out-of-date methods; **verwerfliche ~n** vicious practices;
~ zur Feststellung der Werbewirkung order-of-merit rating; **~ zur Überprüfung des Erinnerungswertes** aided-recall technique; **neue ~n in der Unternehmensführung** new managerial techniques;
~ anwenden to adopt a method; **andere ~n anwenden** to try another course; **falsche ~ anwenden** to go the wrong way; **nach einer ~ arbeiten** to work on a system; **sich illegaler ~n bedienen** to cross the line into illegality; **neue ~ erproben** to try out a new method; **raffinierte ~ kennen** to know a trick worth two of that *(sl.)*; **~ verbessern** to rectify a method; **nach eigener ~ vorgehen** to take one's own line, to do it one's own way.
methodisch methodical, formal, orderly;
~ arbeiten to work with method, to work systematically; **an alles äußerst ~ herangehen** to be very particular about having things done methodically; **~ geordnet sein** to be arranged in an orderly fashion;
~e Anordnung methodical scheme.
Metier trade, profession, vocation, calling;
zwielichtiges ~ ausüben to follow a dubious profession.
Metropole metropolis.
Metteur *(Druckerei)* compositor, lock-up, maker-up;
teilzeitbeschäftigte ~e und Setzer part-time composing room staff.
Metzelei butchery, slaughter, massacre.
Metzger butcher, meatman *(US)*, *(fig.)* killer;
~gang fool's errand; **~laden** butcher's shop.
Meuchelmord begehen to murder s. o. in cold blood.
Meuchelmörder cutthroat, assassin, stabber, thug *(US)*.
meuchlerisch cold-blooded;
j. ~ umbringen to murder s. o. treacherously.
meuchlings with murderous attempt.

Meute pack of hounds, *(fig.)* crowd, gang, throng;
~ **von Journalisten** swarm of journalists.
Meuterei mutiny, insubordination;
~ **anstiften (anzetteln)** to institute (plot) a mutiny; ~ **ersticken** to quell a mutiny; **der ~ schuldig sein** to be guilty of mutiny.
Meutern (Meckern) grumbling, belly-aching.
meutern to mutiny, to mutineer, to riot, *(Gefangene)* to rebel, *(meckern)* to grumble, to groan;
bei jeder Gelegenheit ~ to flare up at the least thing.
meuternde Besatzung mutinous crew.
mickrig measly, meagre;
~ **aussehen** to look peaky;
~**es Essen** skimpy meal; ~**es Gehalt** meagre salary; ~**e zwei Schillinge** paltry two shillings; ~**es kleines Zimmer** poky little room.
Mief stale air, fug *(Br., coll.)*, frowst.
miefig fuggy, frowsty, fusty, musty.
Miene countenance, face, expression, look;
mit ernster ~ with an earnest air; **mit gekränkter** ~ with an injured air; **mit unbeweglicher** ~ with an impassive expression; **ohne die geringste ~ zu verziehen** without betraying the least emotion;
allwissende ~ know-all manner; **besorgte** ~ troubled countenance; **entschlossene** ~ air of purpose; **höhnische** ~ contemptuous look;
einer der Situation entsprechende ~ aufsetzen to put on a face to suit the occasion; **ernste ~ aufsetzen** to straighten one's face; **gewichtige ~ aufsetzen** to put on a face of importance; **unschuldige ~ aufsetzen** to put on an innocent air; **ernste ~ bewahren** to keep a straight face; **finstere ~ machen** to frown, to scowl; **gute ~ zum bösen Spiel machen** to put a good countenance (face) on the matter, to do s. th. with a good grace, to grin and bear it; **keine ~ machen zu gehen** to show no signs of going; **saure ~ ziehen** to look sour.
Mienenspiel changing expressions, play of features.
mies miserable, wretched, rotten;
sich ~ fühlen to feel lousy (seedy, off colo(u)r); **einem ~ gehen** to be in a bad way; **jem. etw. ~ machen** to spoil s. one's pleasure; **j. beim Chef ~ machen** to run s. o. down with the boss; ~**es Gasthaus** wretched inn; **in ~er Laune sein** to be in a terrible mood; ~**er Ruf** odious reputation; ~**e Sache** funny business; **j. in eine ~e Situation bringen** to put s. o. to inconveniences; ~**e Unterkunft** miserable dwelling; ~**es Wetter** wretched (rotten) weather.
Miesepeter grouser, spoilsport, killjoy, gloom *(coll.)*, sourpuss *(sl.)*.
miesepetrig peevish, grumpy, morose;
~ **aussehen** to look off colo(u)r; **sich ganz ~ fühlen** to be feeling under the weather.
Miesmacher crab, defeatist, wet blanket, croak, detractor, grumbler, prophet of evil.
Miet|ablösung commutation of rent, key money; ~**ablösungswert** tenant right; ~**abteilung** renting department; ~**abtretung** assignment of lease; ~**anhebung** rent increase; ~**anlagen** rental equipment; ~**anlagengeschäft** leasing business; ~**annahme** acceptance of rent; ~**anspruch** leasehold interest; ~**anteil** rent charge; ~**anzahlung** key money, forehand rent, advance rental; ~**aufhebung** forfeiture of tenancy; ~**aufhebungsklage** action for avoidance of a lease contract; ~**aufkündigung** notice to quit; ~**aufwand** rent expense, rental expenditure; ~**ausfall** loss of rent, rent property loss, rent deficiency, renting failure, rental loss, *(Kraftfahrzeug)* loss of use; ~**ausfallpolice** rental value policy; ~**ausfallversicherung** rent and rental value insurance; ~**auto** taxicab, rented (leased, *US*) car, rented (hired) car, car for hire.
mietbar for hire, hirable, rentable, tenantable.
Miet|bedingungen *(Gegenstand)* terms of hire, *(Wohnung)* letting conditions, terms of tenancy; ~**beendigung** termination of tenancy; ~**beihilfe** rent subsidy, lodging allowance; ~**belastung** rent charge; ~**beschränkungen** rent restrictions; ~**besitz** leasehold; ~**betrag** amount of rent; ~**bringschuld** rent lying in prender *(Br.)*; ~**dauer** term of tenancy (lease); ~**droschke** hackney coach, taxicab.
Miete rent, renting, *(Entgelt für bewegliche Sachen und persönliche Dienste)* hire, hiring, charge, *(Grundstück)* lease, *(Mietverhältnis)* tenancy, lease, *(Mietzins)* rent, rental, rental instalment, *(Schober)* stock, rick, pit, stook *(Br.)*;
zur ~ on lease;
angemessene ~ fair rent; **aufgelaufene** ~ accrued rent; **wirtschaftlich berechtigte** ~ commercial rent; **bewirtschaftete** ~ controlled rent *(Br.)*; **billige** ~ low lease; **fällige** ~ rent due; **gerichtlich festgesetzte (gesetzlich festgelegte)** ~ judicial rent; **vertraglich festgesetzte** ~ rent stated in the lease; **freie** ~ uncontrolled rent *(Br.)*; **sehr geringe** ~ nominal rent; **geschuldete** ~ rent due; **gesetzliche** ~ legal (standard, *Br.*) rent; **hohe** ~ heavy (high) rent; **jahresübliche** ~ rackrent *(Br.)*; **kalte** ~ rent exclusive of heating; **mäßige** ~ moderate lease; **niedrige** ~ low rent; **nominelle** ~ peppercorn rent *(Br.)*; **ortsübliche** ~ current-market (accustomed) rent; **pauschale** ~ flat rent; **reine** ~ break-even rent; **reine ~ ohne ...** rent exclusive of ...; **rückständige** ~ rent arrear, arrears of rent, back rent, hanging gale *(Br.)*; **überhöhte** ~ overcharge of rent; **unerschwingliche** ~ rackrent *(Irland)*; **ungesetzliche** ~ black rent, rackrent; **dem Mieterschutz unterliegende** ~ controlled rent *(Br.)*; **vereinbarte** ~ rent agreed upon; **verkehrsübliche** ~ open market rent; **vorausbezahlte** ~ rent paid in advance, prepaid rent; **warme** ~ rent inclusive of heating;
~ **für eine Etagenwohnung** apartment rent; ~ **eines Geschäftslokales** lease of business premises; **reine ~ ohne Heizung** rent exclusive of heating; ~ **mit automatischer Steigerungsklausel** progressive rent; ~ **für ein Zimmer** lodging money;
~ **abwerfen** to yield a rent; **auf dem Feld eine ~ anlegen** to build a rick in the field; **mit übermäßiger ~ belasten** to rackrent *(Irland)*; **Haus zur freien ~ bewohnen** to occupy a house rent-free; ~ **schuldig bleiben** to fall behind with one's rent; **seit einem Vierteljahr die ~ schuldig bleiben** to owe for three months rent; **1000 Dollar im Jahr an ~n bringen** to rent at $ 1000 a year; ~**n einziehen** to collect (mass) rents; ~ **bar und steuerunschädlich entrichten** to pay a rent in untaxed cash; ~ **erbringen** to yield (earn) a rent; **keine ~ erbringen** to earn no rent; ~ **erhöhen** to increase the rent; **hohe ~ erzielen** to command a high rent; ~ **festsetzen** to fix a rent; **zur ~ geben** to give on lease, to let, *(Gegenstand)* to hire; **Haus zur ~ haben** to tenant a house; ~ **herabsetzen** to abate (lower) a rent; ~ **heraufsetzen** to put up the rent; ~**n kassieren** to collect (lift, *fam.*) rents; ~ **kündigen** to give a tenant notice to quit; **Kartoffeln in eine ~ legen** to store potatoes in a pit; **jds. Möbel wegen rückständiger ~ pfänden** to distrain upon s. one's furniture for rent; **drei Monate ~ schulden** to owe three months' rent; **mit der ~ im Rückstand sein** to be behindhand (in arrears) with one's rent; ~ **steigern** to raise the rent; **jem. die ~ stunden** to accord s. o. a respite for payment of the rent; **hohe (niedrige) ~ von jem. verlangen** to rent s. o. high (low); ~ **vorauszahlen** to pay the rent in advance; **zur ~ wohnen** to lodge, to live as lodger (in lodgings), to be a tenant; **sehr wenig ~ zahlen** to pay a very low rent; **seine ~ auf einmal zahlen** to pay the whole of one's rent; **seine ~ vierteljährlich postnumerando zahlen** to pay one's rent at the end of each quarter;
~**n sind gestiegen** rents have soared.
Miet|eigenschaft renting ability; ~**einigungsamt** rent tribunal *(Br.)*; ~**einigungssache** rent tribunal case; ~**einkommen**, ~**einkünfte** rental income, rent-roll, property rents; ~- **und Pachteinkünfte** rents and profits from land; ~**einkünfte abwerfen** to produce rental income; ~**einnahme** rent-roll, rent received, rental [income]; ~**einnahmenübersicht** rent schedule; ~**einzug** collection of rents.
Mieten renting, *(Flugzeug, Schiff)* chartering.
mieten to rent, to [take a (on)] lease, *(Arbeitskräfte, Sachen)* to [take on] hire, *(Flugzeug)* to charter, *(Frachtraum)* to book, *(Schiff)* to [take on] charter;
zu ~ rentable, for hire;
Auto ~ to hire (rent) a car, to take a car on hire; **Droschke** ~ to take a taxi; **Haus** ~ to take a house on lease; **monatlich** ~ to rent by the month; **vorübergehende Unterkunftsräume** ~ to rent temporary accommodation; **zu den Vertragsbedingungen des Eigentümers** ~ to lease on the landlord's terms; **Wohnung** ~ to rent a flat (an apartment, *US*); **möblierte Wohnung** ~ to rent a furnished apartment (flat, *Br.*); **Wohnung ~ und die Möbel übernehmen** to rent a flat and take over the furniture *(Br.)*; **Zimmer** ~ to engage a room; **Zimmer monatlich** ~ to rent (take) a room by the month.
Mieten|einnehmer rent collector; ~**markt** rental market.
Mietentschädigung lodging allowance.
Mieter tenant, lessee, leaseholder, renter *(US)*, *(Einzelzimmer)* lodger, roomer *(US)*, *(Gegenstände)* hirer, *(Mietzahler)* rent payer, *(Schiff)* charterer;
vom ~ zu bezahlen payable by the tenant;
alleiniger ~ sole tenant; **ausziehender** ~ waygoing (outgoing) tenant; **neu einziehender** ~ incoming (ingoing) tenant; **exmittierter** ~ evicted tenant; **gewerblicher** ~ business (commercial) tenant; **hinausgesetzter** ~ evicted tenant; **jährlich**

kündbarer ~ tenant from year to year; **jederzeit kündbarer** ~ tenant at will; **reflektierender** ~ prospective tenant; **unter Kündigungsschutz stehender** ~ statutory tenant *(Br.)*; **überforderter** ~ rackrenter; **unsicherer** ~ weak (poor) tenant; **zur Arbeiterbevölkerung zählender** ~ working-class tenant;
~ **mit erstklassiger Adresse** blue-chip tenant; ~ **im Besitz der Mietsache** tenant in possession; ~ **eines Bürogebäudes** office-building tenant; ~ **und Vermieter** landlord and tenant, *(pl.)* householders and lodgers; ~, **der seine Wassergeldgebühr in die Mietzahlung einschließt** compound householder *(Br.)*;
seinen ~n geringe Miete abverlangen to rent one's tenants low; ~ **aufnehmen** to take in lodgers; ~ **exmittieren** to turn out (eject, evict) a tenant; **keinen ~ für sein Haus finden** not to get a tenant for one's house; **einem ~ Räumungsschutz gewähren** to protect a tenant against eviction; ~ **hinaussetzen** to turn s. o. out of lodgings, to evict a tenant; **einem ~ kündigen** to give a tenant warning (notice to quit); **von vier ~n bewohnt werden** to be occupied by four tenants; **dem ~ die Kündigung zustellen** to serve notice upon a tenant;
~**belästigung** disturbance of a tenant; ~**darlehn** tenant's loan; ~**einbauten** fixtures; **der Verschönerung dienende ~einbauten** ornamental fixtures; **gewerbliche ~einbauten** trade fixtures; ~**haftpflicht** tenant's liability; ~**haftpflichtversicherung** tenant's liability insurance; ~**haftung** tenant's risk.

mieterhöhend rent-raising.

Mieterhöhung increase in rent, rent increase;
mit Instandsetzungen begründete ~ repairs increase.

Mieter|kaution security deposit [with the landlord]; ~**knappheit** tenant scarcity; **noch nicht abgewohnte ~leistungen** unexhausted improvements; ~**liste** tenant list.

Mietermäßigung remission of rent.

Mieter|pflicht tenant's obligation; ~**rechte** rights of a tenant; **gesamte ~schaft** tenantry.

Mieterschutz control of rents *(Br.)*, control of lettings *(Br.)*, relief against forfeiture, rent control *(Br.)*, Rent Act protection *(Br.)*;
gesetzlicher ~ rent restriction;
~ **gewähren** to protect the tenant; ~ **in Anspruch nehmen** to claim the protection of the Rent Acts *(Br.)*.

Mieterschutzbestimmungen rent restrictions *(Br.)*;
aufgehobene ~ decontrol provisions *(Br.)*;
~ **für ein Haus aufheben** to render a house free from the provisions of the Rent Restriction Act *(Br.)*; **den ~ unterliegen** to be subject to the Rent Restriction Act *(Br.)*.

Mieterschutzgesetz Landlord and Tenant (Rent) Act *(Br.)*, Rent Restriction Act *(Br.)*, Furnished Houses Rent Control Act *(Br.)*;
~ **und Wohngeldgesetz** Housing Rents and Subsidies Act *(Br.)*; **von der Umgehung des ~es profitieren** to exploit the Rent Act dodge *(Br.)*; **dem ~ unterliegen** to be subject to a controlled rent.

Mieterschutz|recht right of occupation; ~**vereinigung** tenant's association.

Miet|erstattungssystem, kommunales local authorities' rent rebate scheme; ~**ertrag** rental, rent-roll, rent returns, rent received, rental income; ~- **und Pachterträgnisse** rents and profits from land; ~**ertragstabelle** rent schedule; ~**ertragswert** rental (rated) value.

Mieter|verpflichtungen tenant's obligations; ~**verzug** tenant's default; ~**wahlrecht** lodger franchise.

Miet|fahrzeug rented car, for-hire vehicle; ~**festsetzung** fixing of rents; ~**fläche** renting space; ~**flugzeug** chartered plane, hired aircraft; ~**forderung** demand (claim) for the rent.

mietfrei rent-free, free of rent;
~ **wohnen** to live rent-free in a house, to have a house free of rent, to occupy a residence rent-free;
~**es Haus** rent-free house; ~**e Zweijahresperiode** 2-year rent-free period.

Miet|freigabe decontrol of rents; ~**fuhre,** ~**fuhrwerk** hired carriage, hackney coach (cab); ~**gebäude** leasehold building, multiple dwelling, tenement; ~**gebühr** rent, rental fee, *(Gegenstand)* hiring charge; ~**gegenstand** leased (rented) property, rental property, rental *(US)*; **fest installierte ~gegenstände** landlord's fixtures; ~**geld** provision of rent; ~**geldentschädigung** loss of rent compensation; **kurzfristiges ~geschäft** short leasing; ~**grundlage** rental basis; ~**grundstück** demised premises, leasehold; ~**herabsetzung** cut in (abatement of) rents; ~**herr** landlord; ~**höchstpreis** rent ceiling; ~**höhe** amount of rent; ~**höhe schiedsgerichtlich festsetzen lassen** to refer the amount of rent to arbitration; ~**holschuld** rent lying in render *(Br.)*; ~**inkasso** collection of rents; ~**interessent** prospective tenant; ~**jahr** tenancy year; ~**kauf** rent (lease) with an option to purchase; ~**kaution** key money *(Br.)*; ~**konto** rent account; ~**kontrakt** lease, tenure; ~**kosten** rental fee, housing price, rent expenses; ~**kündigung** notice to quit (vacate); **zu einer ~kündigung ordnungsgemäß Stellung nehmen** to serve an appropriate counternotice; ~**kürzung** cut in rent; ~**kutsche** hackney coach (cab); ~**ling** hireling, mercenary; ~**nachlaß** remission of rent, rent rebate; ~**nachweis für Gemeinschaftswohnungen** flatsharer's register *(Br.)*; ~**nebenkosten** ancillary costs; ~**objekt** leased (rented, rental) property; ~**pachtfläche** renting space; ~**partei über uns** the tenants of the flat above; ~**pfändung** distress for nonpayment of rent; ~**pferd** livery horse.

mietpflichtig for rent.

Mietpreis rent price, housing price, rental charge, *(Sache)* hire, hire payment;
~**e festlegen** to determine rents *(Br.)*;
~**bindung** control of rent *(Br.)*, rent control *(Br.)*; ~**entwicklung** rental development; ~**erhöhung** rent increase; ~**freigabe** decontrol of rents; ~**stopp aufgeben** to lift the rent freeze.

Miet|räume demised premises, lodgings; ~**rechnung** rent account; ~**recht** leasehold interest; ~- **und Pachtrecht** law of landlord and tenant; ~**richtsatz** reference rent; ~**rückstand** rent arrears (owing), hanging gale *(Br.)*; ~**rückstände** accrued rent; **Mieter wegen ~rückständen exmittieren** to evict a tenant for nonpayment of rent; ~**rückstände haben** to be back in (in arrears with) one's rent; ~**sache** leased property; ~**sätze** rental rates, rentals; ~**schuld** rent due; ~**schuld zu begleichen anbieten** to tender the amount of rent; **jds. Sachen wegen ~schulden pfänden** to distrain upon s. one's goods for rent; ~**schuldner** defaulting tenant; ~**senkung** reduction of (cut in) rents.

Mietshaus block of flats *(Br.)*, apartment building *(US)*, apartment *(US)* (lodging, tenement, flat, flatted) house, multiple dwelling, leasehold building, mansions *(Br.)*;
billiges ~ lower price (low-rental) dwelling unit; **heruntergewirtschaftetes** ~ run-down people's warren; **in genossenschaftlichem Besitz stehendes** ~ cooperative apartment house *(US)*; **vierstöckiges** ~ four-story apartment house *(US)*;
~ **für Einzelmieter** boarding *(Br.)* (rooming, *US*) house;
sein ~ in bewohnbarem Zustand halten to keep one's tenant house in habitable repair; **zum ~ herrichten** to tenementize;
~**bau** apartment-house construction *(US)*; ~**baustelle** apartment-house site *(US)*; ~**besitzer** apartment-house owner *(US)*; ~**bewohner** flat dweller; ~**errichtung** foundation of a block of flats *(Br.)*; ~**finanzierung** leasehold financing.

Mietskaserne barrack, mansions *(Br.)*, block, multiple dwelling, warren, tenement (apartment, *US*) house.

Miet|speicher lease store, depot, warehouse *(US)*; ~**spiegel** representative list of rents; ~**stall** livery stable, livery *(US)*; ~**steigerung** increase in rent, rent increase, raising of rents; ~**stopp** rent freeze; ~**streitigkeit** tenancy dispute; ~**summe** rental; ~**unsicherheit** insecurity of tenure; ~**verbindlichkeiten** rental commitments; ~**verbotsklausel** no-letting clause; ~**vereinbarung** tenancy agreement.

Mietverhältnis tenancy, privity of estate, lease, landlord and tenant relationship;
befristetes ~ determinable lease; **jahrweise festgesetztes** ~ tenancy from year to year; **freies** ~ uncontrolled rent; **gesetzlich geschütztes** ~ protected tenancy *(Br.)*, statutory tenancy; **gewerbliches** ~ business tenancy; **jährlich kündbares** ~ tenancy from year to year; **nach Ablauf der Pachtzeit jederzeit kündbares** ~ tenancy at will; **monatlich kündbares** ~ monthly tenancy; **bei der Schiedsstelle registriertes** ~ registered rent *(Br.)*; **dem Mieterschutz unterliegendes** ~ statutory (controlled) tenancy *(Br.)*; **vertraglich vereinbartes** ~ contractual tenancy; **sich monatlich verlängerndes** ~ month-to-month tenancy; **stillschweigend verlängertes** ~ tenancy at sufferance;
~ **unter Mieterschutzbestimmungen** controlled (statutory) tenancy *(Br.)*;
~ **abschließen** to enter into a lease; ~ **aufheben** to terminate (cancel) a lease; ~ **wegen Irrtums aufheben** to rescind a lease on the grounds of mistake; ~ **mit dem neuen Eigentümer fortsetzen** to attorn to the new owner; ~ **verlängern** to extend a lease; ~ **verletzen** to forfeit one's tenancy.

Miet|verhandlungen, in ~verhandlungen stehen to negotiate for new premises; ~**verlängerung** renewal of a lease, lease renewal; ~**verleihsystem** car-rental system; ~**verlust** loss in letting, rent deficiency, rental loss; ~**verlust erleiden** to make a loss in lettings.

Mietvertrag lease [contract], contract of premises, tenancy agreement, leasehold deed, *(Sache)* [contract of] hire, hiring agreement, *(Schiff)* charterparty;

mündlich abgeschlossener ~ parol lease; **jederzeit kündbarer** ~ tenancy at sufferance; **monatlich kündbarer** ~ tenancy from month to month; **kurzfristiger** ~ short lease; **langfristiger** ~ long-term lease; **schriftlicher** ~ written lease; **siebenjähriger** ~ lease determinable at the end of seven years; **unbefristeter** ~ general tenancy; **auf Wunsch des Mieters zu verlängernder** ~ lease renewable at the option of the tenant; **verlängerter** ~ renewed lease; **vorgedruckter** ~ printed lease form;
~ **mit Instandhaltungsklausel** repairing lease; ~ **für mehrere Jahre** estate for years; ~ **für gewerblich genutzte Räume** lease of business premises, commercial lease;
~ **abschließen** to sign (to enter into) a lease; **neuen** ~ **abschließen** to take a new lease; **mehrjährigen** ~ **über ein Haus abschließen** to take a house on lease for several years; ~ **auf ein Jahr abschließen** to hire s. th. by the year; ~ **eines Hauses erneuern** to renew the lease of a house; ~ **kündigen** to terminate a lease; ~ **aufheben lassen** to cancel (terminate) a lease; ~ **registrieren lassen** to record a lease; ~ **verlängern** to extend a lease; ~ **verletzen** to forfeit one's tenancy.

Mietvertrags|bestimmungen provisions in the lease, terms of a lease; ~**dauer** life of a lease; ~**formular** printed lease form; ~**versicherung** rent insurance.

Miet|vorauszahlung, ~**vorschuß** forehand rent, security, [payment of] rent in advance, prepayment of rent, advance rental (rent), key money *(Br.)*; ~**vorvertrag** agreement on a lease.

Mietwagen cab, cabcart, hack, hackney [carriage], *(Auto)* hired (hire-, rented) car, car for hire;
selbstgefahrener ~ self-drive car, rent-a-car;
~**fahrer** hire-car driver; ~**firma** car-rental firm, rent-a-car agency (firm, corporation); ~**flotte** rental fleet; ~**geschäft** car-hire business; ~**kosten** costs of renting a car; ~**unternehmer** car-rental (rent-a-car) company; ~**verleih,** ~**vertretung** rent-a-car (car-rental, car-hire, *Br.*) service; ~**verleihbüro** rent-a-car reservation office, rent-a-car agency (firm, corporation); ~**verleihrabatt** car-rental discount; ~**vertretung** car service, car-rental company (agency), rent-a-car agency.

mietweise on hire (lease);
Vermögensgegenstand ~ **nutzen** to employ s. th. as rental property; ~ **überlassen** to let [on lease], to put out on rental.

Mietwert letting (rental) value;
steuerlicher ~ assessed rental;
~ **eines Jahres** annual rental; ~ **der eigengenutzten Wohnung [im eigenen Haus]** imputed rent;
~ **feststellen** to ascertain the rental value;
~**versicherung** rent insurance.

Mietwohngrundstück rented property.

Mietwohnung lodgings, lodgement, tenanted dwelling, tenement, quarters, flat *(Br.)*, rental apartment *(US)*;
abgeschlossene ~ self-contained flat; **unterdurchschnittliche** ~ substandard dwelling; **den Mietschutzbestimmungen unterliegende** ~ rent-controlled flat *(Br.)*;
~ **haben** to live in lodgings; ~ **räumen** to vacate rented rooms.

Miet|zahlung payment of rent[al], rental payment; **verzögerte** ~**zahlung** delay in paying rent; ~**zeit** duration of rent, lease period, [term of] tenancy; **noch nicht abgelaufene** ~**zeit** unexpired term; **festgelegte** ~**zeit** periodical tenancy.

Mietzins rent, rental instalment, hire;
wirtschaftlich berechtigter ~ commercial rent; **vertraglich vereinbarter** ~ tenancy, interest of tenant;
~ **festlegen** to fix a rent;
~**forderung** claim (demand) for the rent.

mietzinspflichtig subject to rent.

Miet|zinsstopp rent freeze; ~**zuschlag erheben** to make an extra charge for the rent.

Mietzuschuß allowance for rent, lodging allowance, rent subsidy (supplement).

Mignon *(drucktechn.)* minion.

Mikro|aufnahme microphotograph; ~**brief** airgraph; ~**dokumentation** microcopying; ~**druck** microprint.

Mikrofilm microfilm, bibliofilm;
~**abzug** microcopy; ~**archiv** microfilm library; ~**aufnahmen machen** to microfilm; ~**lesegerät** microfilm reader.

Mikrofotografie microphotography, photomicrography, photomicroscopy.

mikrofotografisch microphotographic, photomicrographic;
~**e Darstellung** micrograph.

Mikrokopie microcopy, microprint.

mikrokopieren to microcopy.

Mikro|kopiergerät microcopying apparatus; ~**metereinstellung** micrometer adjustment; ~**miniaturtechnik** microminiaturization; ~**ökonomie** microeconomics.

Mikrophon microphone, mike *(US)*, ribbon *(sl.)*;
elektrodynamisches ~ electrodynamic microphone;
~ **mit Fernbedienung** remote-control microphone;
verstecktes ~ **anbringen** to plant a microphone;
~**hörer** handset; ~**stimme** microphone voice.

Mikro|schaltkreis microcircuit; ~**sekunde** microsecond; ~**skop** microscope; ~**welle** microwave.

Milch, entrahmte skimmed milk; **kondensierte** ~ condensed (evaporated) milk;
~ **der frommen Denkungsart** milk of human kindness;
~**ausschank,** ~**bar** milk bar, dairy lunch *(US)*; ~**bruder** foster brother; ~**diät durchführen** to be on a milk diet; ~**ertrag** milk yield; ~**geschäft** milkshop, dairy, creamery; ~**getränk** milk shake; ~**glas** frosted (porcelain) glass; ~**gutschein** milk token; ~**handelsbehörde** Milk Board *(Br.)*; ~**kaffee** white coffee; ~**kanne** milk can (churn, *Br.*); ~**laden** dairy, creamery; ~**mädchenrechnung** overoptimistic estimate; ~**mann** dairyman, milkman, milk roundsman; ~**mischgetränk** milk shake; ~**panscher** adulterator of milk; ~**produkte** dairy products; ~**produzent** dairy farmer; ~**prüfer** milk checker; ~**pulver** milk powder; ~**sammelstelle** dairy; ~**schokolade** milk chocolate; ~**straße** Milky Way, galaxy; ~**straßensystem** island universe, galaxy; ~**stützungspreis** milk support price; ~**verarbeitung** milk processing; ~**verbrauch** milk consumption; **natürliches** ~**versorgungsgebiet** natural milk shed; ~**vieh** dairy cattle; ~**wagen** milk cart (wag(g)on), milk float *(Br.)*; ~**wirtschaft** dairy farm (farming, industry, husbandry).

Milde clemency, charity, leniency;
~ **walten lassen** to show clemency.

milde mild, meek, lenient, kind, charitable, soft;
~ **gegen Straftäter** lenient towards wrongdoers;
um es ~ **auszudrücken** to put it mildly; **jds. Verhalten** ~ **beurteilen** to take a lenient view of s. one's behavio(u)r;
~ **Gaben** alms, charity; ~ **Geldstrafe** light fine; ~**s Klima** temperate climate; ~**s Lächeln** faint smile; ~ **Luft** mild air; ~**s Lüftchen** gentle breeze; ~ **Maßnahmen anwenden** to adopt lenient measures; **für eine** ~ **Strafe plädieren** to plead in mitigation; ~**s Wetter** mild weather.

mildern to alleviate, to mitigate, to extenuate, to assuage, to moderate, *(abschwächen)* to water down, to soften, to tone down, to soft-pedal;
Einfuhrbestimmungen für auswärtige Lieferanten ~ to ease barriers for foreign suppliers; **Gegensätze** ~ to reconcile differences; **Handelsbeschränkungen** ~ to ease trade curbs; **Schmerzen** ~ to alleviate (soothe) pain; **Strafe** ~ to mitigate a penalty; **jds. Zorn** ~ to tone down (soothe) s. one's anger.

mildernd mitigating, extenuating;
bei der Straffestsetzung ~ **berücksichtigen** to consider in mitigation;
~**e Umstände** extenuating circumstances, mitigating circumstances (factors); **jem.** ~**e Umstände zubilligen** *(humoristisch)* to make allowances for s. o.

Milderung mitigation;
~ **von Handelsbeschränkungen** easing of trade curbs; ~ **von Steuern** mitigation of taxes; ~ **einer Strafe** mitigation of punishment;
Armut als ~ **für eine Diebstahlstrafe anführen** to plead poverty in extenuation of a theft; **auf** ~ **der Strafe plädieren** to plead for mitigation.

Milderungsgründe extenuating circumstances.

mildtätig|e Zwecke charitable purposes; **zu** ~**en Zwecken** for charity.

Mildtätigkeit, hochherzige large charity; **private** ~ private charity.

Milieu milieu, setting, moral (social) environment (medium), social background, surroundings;
bürgerliches ~ middle-class background; **häusliches** ~ family environment; **ländliches** ~ rural environment; **soziales** ~ social medium;
sich in vertrautem ~ **befinden** to be in surroundings one knows; **aus den verschiedensten** ~**s stammen** to be drawn from every milieu.

milieubedingte Unterschiede environmental differences.

Milieu|drama milieu drama; ~**forschung** environmental research.

milieugestört maladjusted.

Milieu|schilderung background description; ~**störung** maladjustment; ~**theorie** environmentalism.

Militär military, military estate, army, force, soldiery, *(Soldat)* military man;
das ~ the sabre *(Br.)* (saber, *US*), military establishment.

militärähnlich paramilitary.

Militär|akademie military academy; ~**angehörige** military personnel; ~**anwalt** judge advocate; ~**arzt** army surgeon; ~**attaché** military (defence) attaché; ~**ausgaben** military spending (outlays); ~**ausschuß** *(Atlantikrat)* military committee *(US)*; ~**basis** military basis; **ausländische ~basis** foreign base; ~**behörden** military authorities; ~**bereich** district command *(Br.)*; ~**bündnis** military alliance.

Militärdienst active (national, *Br.*) service;
~ **ableisten** to serve with the colo(u)rs; **vom ~ befreien** to exempt from military service; **j. für den ~ untauglich machen** to disqualify s. o. for military service;
~**pflicht** compulsory military service, general (universal) conscription.

militärdiensttauglich fit for military service.

Militär|dienstzeit military service; ~**diktatur** military dictatorship; ~**fahrschein** travel(l)[ing] warrant; ~**fahrzeug** military truck; ~**flugplatz** military airfield; ~**flugzeug** military plane (aircraft), service machine; ~**gebiet** military zone (area); ~**gefängnis** military lockup, guardhouse, disciplinary barracks; ~**gericht** court martial, military tribunal (court), court of inquiry.

militärgerichtliche Fälle military causes *(Br.)*.

Militär|gerichtsbarkeit military jurisdiction; ~**gerichtshof** military tribunal; ~**gewahrsam** military custody; ~**gouverneur** military governor; ~**gutschein** travel warrant; ~**haushalt** military budget; ~**herrschaft** militarism, military rule; ~**hilfe** military assistance (aid); ~**hubschrauber** military helicopter.

militärisch military, martial;
~**er Abschirmdienst** intelligence service; ~**e Anlagen** military installations (facilities); ~**e Ausbildung** military training; ~**e Dienststelle** military office; ~**e Ehren beim Begräbnis** military hono(u)rs; **j. mit ~en Ehren bestatten** to give s. o. a military funeral; ~**e Grundausbildung** basic training; ~**e Hilfeleistung** military assistance (aid); ~**e Laufbahn einschlagen** to take up the military profession; ~**es Potential** military potential (resources); ~**e Repressalien** military reprisals; ~**er Sicherheitsdienst** military security service; ~**e Verbände** forces.

Militarismus militarism.

Militär|junta military junta, the colonels; ~**kapelle** military band; ~**konvention** convention; ~**krankenhaus** department (barracks) hospital; ~**luftfahrt** military aviation; ~**macht** military power, armament; ~**mission** military mission.

militärmüde Jugend draft-weary youth.

Militär|musik martial music; ~**person** military man, member of the armed forces; **für ~personen gesperrt** off limits *(US)*, out of bounds *(Br.)*; **seiner ~pflicht genügen** to do one's national service *(Br.)*.

militärpflichtig liable to military service;
im ~en Alter sein to be of military age.

Militär|polizei military police; ~**polizeiabteilung** provost guard; ~**polizist** military policeman, redcap *(Br., sl.)*; ~**putsch** military coup; ~**regierung** military government; ~**regime** military regime; ~**staat** garrison state; ~**staatsanwalt** judge advocate; ~**strafanstalt** military lockup, disciplinary barracks *(US)*, correctional institution *(US)*; ~**strafrecht** military law, articles of war; ~**streife** army patrol; ~**stützpunkt** military base *(US)*.

militärtechnischer Ausdruck military term.

Militär|testament, [formloses] military testament (will); ~**umsturz** military coup; ~**verdienstorden** distinguished service medal; ~**verwaltung** military government, Army Council *(Br.)*; ~**vorlage** army bill, military budget; ~**zeit** time of service; **seine ~zeit beenden** to finish one's military service; ~**zug** military train.

Miliz militia, Home Guard *(Br.)*, National Guard *(US)*.

Mille, pro per thousand.

Milliarde a thousand millions *(Br.)*, milliard *(Br.)*, billion *(US)*.

Millimeter millimetre;
nicht einen ~ von seiner Meinung abgehen not to budge the fraction of an inch from one's opinion;
~**papier** graph (cross-section, squared, *Br.*) paper; ~**preis** column millimetre; ~**zeile** millimetre line.

Million million;
~ **Tonnen** megaton;
sich auf mehrere ~en belaufen to figure out at several millions; **viele ~en haben** to be worth a million; ~**en hinterlassen** to die worth a million.

Millionär millionaire;
vielfacher ~ multimillionaire;
auf dem Weg sein, ~ zu werden to be in fair way to becoming a millionaire.

Millionenkonkurs machen to fail (go bankrupt) for a million.

millionenschwer sein to be worth a million, to have millions and millions.

Mime actor, player.

mimen to act, to play, *(nachäffen)* to imitate, to mime;
den Beleidigten ~ to act the offended party; **Kranken ~** to be pretending to be ill, to feign illness; **Unschuldigen ~** to play the innocent.

Mimik mimicry.

Mimose mimosa, sensitive plant, delicate bloom;
empfindlich wie eine ~ sein to be extremely sensitive.

mimosenhaft very touchy.

minder inferior, less;
~ **gut** of inferior quality;
in ~er Anzahl in smaller numbers; **von ~er Qualität** of inferior quality; **mit ~er Sorgfalt** less carefully.

Minder|anfertigung underrun; ~**aufkommen** deficit in taxes, revenue loss, shortfall in tax revenue; ~**ausgaben** reduced expenditure, *(Wertpapier)* underissue, reduced issue; ~**auslieferung** short delivery; ~**bedarf** reduced demand.

minder|begabt less talented, less gifted; ~**belastet** less incriminated; ~**bemittelt** of moderate (small) means; **geistig ~bemittelt sein** not to be very bright.

Minder|bemittelte underprivileged classes; ~**bestand** [cash] deficit; ~**betrag** short amount, shortage, deficit, *(Kassendefizit)* cash shortage; ~**bewertung** undervaluation, belittling, depreciation; ~**einnahme** deficiency in proceeds (receipts), smaller (shortfall in) receipts; ~**erlös** short proceeds, diminishing returns, diminished proceeds, *(Wertpapier)* discount; ~**ertrag** reduction in output, diminishing return, deficiency in proceeds; ~**gebot** underbid; ~**gewicht** short weight, underweight.

Minderheit, in der outnumbered;
nationale ~en ethnic minorities; **rassische ~en** racial minorities; **separistische ~** separatist minority; **sprachliche ~en** linguistic minorities; **widersprechende ~** dissenting minority; **sich erheblich in der ~ befinden** to be a substantial minority; **in der ~ bleiben** to find o. s. outvoted; **gewichtige ~ darstellen** to represent a substantial minority; **in der ~ sein** to be in a minority; ~ **überstimmen** to freeze out the minority; ~ **unterdrücken** to quell (oppress) a minority.

Minderheiten|frage minorities problem; ~**gruppe** minority group; ~**kabinett** minority rule; ~**rechte** minority rights; ~**schutz** protection of minorities; ~**statut** statute of minorities; ~**vertrag** minority treaty.

Minderheits|aktienbeteiligung minority stock participation *(US)*; ~**aktionär** dissentient [shareholder], minority stockholder *(US)*, minority owner (holder); ~**aktionären eine Dividende garantieren** to guarantee a dividend to minority stockholders; ~**angehöriger** minority member; ~**ansicht** minority opinion; ~**bericht** minority report; ~**beteiligung** minority interest (holding, share); ~**frage** minority problem; ~**führer** leader of a minority; ~**gruppe** minority group; ~**paket** *(Aktien)* minority holding; ~**protest** protest *(Br.)*; ~**rechte** rights of a minority group, minority rights; ~**regierung** minority government (rule); ~**votum** *(Kammer)* dissenting (dissentient) opinion *(US)*, dissent.

minderjährig under [statutory] age, minor, nonaged *(US)*;
~ **sein** to be under age;
~**e Angestellte** minor executives; ~**er Kläger** infant plaintiff.

Minderjährige minors, infant children;
~**r** minor, infant, *(Pflegling)* ward;
vernachlässigter ~ neglected minor;
~**n vertraglich binden** to be binding upon an infant; **für einen ~n ein Konto eröffnen** to open an account in the name of a minor; **einem ~n überwiegend zum Vorteil gereichen** to be substantially for a minor's benefit.

Minderjährigenstellung infancy status.

Minderjährigkeit natural infancy, legal minority, underage, tutelage, pupilage, wardship, nonage *(US)*;
sich auf ~ berufen to plead the Baby Act *(US)* (infancy);
Einwand der ~ erheben to put in a plea for infancy.

Minder|kaufmann small tradesman; ~**leistung** reduced output, shortfall in production; ~**lieferung** short shipment (delivery, supply).

mindern to diminish, to lessen, *(Preis)* to reduce, to abate, to recoup, *(Rechte)* to impair, *(Wert)* to depreciate;
sich ~ *(Erträge)* to fall off; **Geschwindigkeit ~** to slacken (reduce, lower) speed; **Kaufpreis ~** to abate the purchase price; **Not der Armen ~** to relieve the poor; **Reichtum eines Landes ~** to diminish a country's wealth.

Minder | preis reduced price, price reduction; **~umsatz** reduction in turnover, falling off in sales.

Minderung diminution, reduction, abatement, *(Wert)* depreciation, decrease in value, impairment;
~ **des Gewinns** diminution of profit; ~ **des Kaufpreises** abatement of purchase money, redhibition *(US)*; ~ **des Wertes** diminution in value;
zur ~ des Kaufpreises berechtigen to be redhibitory *(US)*, to give rise to a redhibition *(US)*; ~ **erleiden** *(Kurse)* to decline; **auf ~ des Kaufpreises klagen** to maintain a redhibitory action.

Minderungsklage redhibitory action *(US)*.

Minderwert undervalue, depreciation.

minderwertig inferior, of inferior value, base, second-rate, trashy, off, low-class, low-grade, penny-a-line, hedge, substandard;
geistig ~ subnormal;
~e Arbeit inferior workmanship; **~er Brennstoff** low-grade fuel; **~es Buch** third-rate book; **~er Charakter** base character; **~es Erzeugnis** inferior product; **~es Essen** low-quality food; **~es Fleisch** low-grade meat; **~es Material** material of inferior quality; **~e Person, ~es Subjekt** yellow dog, worthless fellow, bad egg *(sl.)*; **von ~er Qualität** of inferior quality; **~e Ware** inferior goods, trash, poor-quality goods; **~e Ware anbieten** to offer inferior goods; **~es Zeug** trash.

Minder | wertigkeit inferior quality, inferiority; **~wertigkeitsgefühl** inferiority complex, feeling of inferiority; **in der ~zahl sein** to be in the minority.

mindest least, slightest, minimal;
~ens not less than;
~ens kosten to cost at least;
nicht die ~e Ahnung von der Buchhaltung haben no to know the ABC of bookkeeping; **nicht die ~e Aussicht** not the least chance; **~en Schaden anrichten** to do only minimal damage; **jem. die ~en Sorgen machen** to be the least of s. one's worries; **nicht den ~en Zweifel haben** to have not the slightest doubt.

Mindest | abnahme minimum commercial quantity; **~abstand** minimum distance; **~akkordsatz** minimum job rate; **~alter** minimum age, age limit; **gesetzliches ~alter** legal age; **~alter zum Rentenbezug** minimum pension age; **~anforderungen** minimum requirements; **~angebot** lowest tender (bid, offer); **~anspruch** minimum claim; **~anzahl** minimum number; **~anzahlung** minimum down payment, minimum deposit; **~arbeitsbedingungen** standard conditions; **~arbeitszeit** minimum working hours; **wöchentliche ~arbeitszeit** minimum workweek; **garantierte ~auflage** *(Zeitung)* guaranteed minimum circulation; **~ausleihungssatz** minimum lending rate *(Br.)*, prime rate *(US)*, bank rate *(Br.)*; **~ausstattung** initial allocation; **~auswirkung auf die Beschäftigungslage** minimal employment; **~barzahlung** minimum cash payment; **~bedarf** minimum supply (demand); **~bedarf an Nahrungsmitteln** minimum food needs; **~beitrag** minimum contribution; **garantierte ~beschäftigung** guaranteed employment; **~beschäftigungszeit** minimum period of employment; **~bestand** minimum inventory, basic stock; **~besteuerung** minimum taxation; **~beteiligung beim Ersterwerb** *(Kapitalanlagegesellschaft)* minimum initial subscription; **~betrag** minimal amount, minimum; **garantierte ~bezahlung** guarantee pay; **~bezug** minimum purchase; **~bietender** lowest bidder; **~breite** minimum width; **~courtagesatz** minimum commission rate; **~deckung** minimum margin requirements; **~diskontsatz** minimum lending (interest) rate *(Br.)*, prime rate *(US)*; **~dividende** guaranteed dividend; **~einfuhrpreis** *(EG)* minimum import price; **~einheitskosten** unit cost standard; **~einheitssätze** minimum standard rates; **~einkommen** minimum income; **einkommensteuerpflichtiges ~einkommen** threshold income; **~einkommensgrenze unterschreiten** to be below the poverty line; **~einkommenssteuersatz** income-tax standard rate, threshold tariff; **~einkommensziffer** minimum income figure; **~einlage** minimum investment, *(Bank)* minimum deposit; **bei der Landeszentralbank unterhaltene ~einlagen** memberbank balances held as reserve *(US)*, special deposits with the Bank of England; **kalkulierte ~einnahmen** price expectancy; **~einspielergebnisse** minimum return; **~einzahlungsbetrag** *(Effektendifferenzgeschäft)* margin requirements *(US)*; **~erfordernisse** minimum requirements; **~ertrag** minimum return, lowest (minimum) yield; **~erwartung** minimum expectation; **~fordernder** lowest contractor; **~forderung** minimum claim; **~fracht** lowest (minimum) freight, minimum bill of lading; **~frachtsatz** minimum freight rate; **~freibetrag** *(Steuer)* exemption minimum, *(Wertepauschale)* standard deduction for expenses; **feststehender ~freibetrag** *(Einkommensteuer)* minimum standard deduction *(US)*; **~gebot** *(Auktion)* put-up reserved price, lowest bid; **ohne ~gebot** without reserve; **~gebühr** minimum fee, *(Post)* minimum charge; **~gehalt** minimum salary, *(in der Montanindustrie)* lowest percentage; **~geschwindigkeit** minimum speed; **~gewicht** minimum weight, *(Papier)* basic weight, *(Waggonladung)* minimum carload weight *(US)*; **~grenze** minimum (lower) limit, *(Selbstbehalt, Haftpflicht)* minimum liability, franchise *(Br.)*; **~grenze für Haftungsschäden** basic minimum limit of liability; **~größe** *(Anzeige)* minimum linage; **wirtschaftliche ~größe** minimum economic size; **~guthaben** compensating balance; **~höhe** minimum altitude; **~inventar** minimum inventory, basic stock; **~kapazität** marginal capacity; **~kapital** minimum of (minimum paid-in, *US*) capital; **~kleinverkaufspreis** minimum retail price; **~kosten** minimum cost; **gesetzliche ~kündigungsfrist** statutory minimum period of notice; **~kurs** *(Devisen)* minimum rate (price); **~leistung** *(Akkordlohn)* task, *(Produktion)* minimum capacity, *(Versicherung)* minimum terms and period of insurance; **automatisch angepaßte ~leistung** shifting minimum.

Mindestlohn minimum wage (rate), living wage;
garantierter absoluter ~ guaranteed minimum wage for all trades; **betrieblicher** ~ minimum plant rate; **garantierter** ~ guaranteed minimum wage, guaranteed base (wage) rate, *(Akkordarbeiter)* fall-back pay; **gesetzlicher** ~ legal minimum, minimum statutory wage;
garantierter ~ bei außertariflicher Arbeit call-in pay; ~ **für Arbeiter bei öffentlichen Bauvorhaben** prevailing rate *(US)*; ~ **für nur stundenweise Tätigkeit** minimum call pay *(US)*;
~normen fair labo(u)r standards; **~satz** minimum wage (union) rate; **betrieblicher ~satz** minimum plant rate; **garantierter ~satz** minimum guaranteed rate.

Mindest | maß minimum; **auf ein ~maß festsetzen** to minimize; **~menge** minimum quantity; **handelsübliche ~menge** minimum commercial quantity; **~mietzeit** minimum rental period; **~monatsgehalt** monthly minimum remuneration; **~pacht** *(Bergbau)* dead rent *(Br.)*; **~prämie** minimum rate; **~prämie zur Fortsetzung der Versicherung** natural premium.

Mindestpreis minimum (lowest possible, reserve, reserved, floor) price, *(Anzeigen)* minimum rate, lowest [possible] rate, *(Auktion)* knockdown price, *(Stahleinfuhr)* trigger price *(Br.)*;
gebundene ~e maintained minimum resale prices;
~e für den Einzelhandel festlegen to establish minimum retail prices;
~höhe floor; **~regelung** *(EG)* minimum price system.

Mindest | produktion minimum output; **~produktionspreis** opportunity costs; **~provisionssatz** minimum commission rate; **~prozentsatz** minimum percentage; **~punktwerte** minimum point values; **unter der gesetzlich festgelegten ~qualität** substandard *(US)*; **~qualitätsvorschriften** minimum quality requirements; **~rand** *(Urkunde)* minimum margin; **~rendite** lowest yield; **~rendite der Sozialversicherung** basis national insurance retirement pension; **~rentenalter** minimum pensionable age.

Mindestreserve statutory (bank, *US*) reserve, special deposits *(Br.)*, lawful (legal, minimum, bank) reserve, required reserves *(US)*, safety fund *(US)*;
erforderliche (vorgeschriebene) ~n *(Banken)* special deposits with the Bank of England *(Br.)*, minimum reserve requirements *(US)*, fractional (required) reserves *(US)*, *(Bareinlagen)* minimum cash (liquid) reserves;
~n bei der Bundesnotenbank wieder auffüllen [etwa] to restore their special deposits with the Bank of England *(Br.)* (the deposits with the reserve bank in a special account, *US*); **~n bei der Bundesnotenbank erhöhen** to increase the minimum reserve requirements *(US)* (their special depots with the Bank of England, *Br.*); **~n unterhalten** to maintain legal reserves *(US)*; **~n bei der Bundesnotenbank unterhalten** to maintain special deposits with the Bank of England *(Br.)* (deposits with the reserve bank in a special account, *US*); **zum Teil Bundesanleihe als ~n verwenden** to chip in government securities as a position of required reserves;
~bestimmungen, ~erfordernisse reserve balance requirements, special deposit requirements *(Br.)*, minimum (legal, *Br.*) reserve requirements *(US)*; **~bestimmungen bei der Bundesnotenbank erhöhen** to increase the minimum reserve *(US)* (special deposits, *Br.*) requirements; **~dispositionen treffen** to make arrangements to maintain legal reserves *(US)*; **~erhöhung** increase in minimum reserve requirements *(US)*, increase of [their] special deposits with the Bank of England *(Br.)*.

mindestreservepflichtig reserve-carrying;
~**e Einlagen** memberbank balances held as reserve *(US)*, safety fund *(US)*, special deposits with the Bank of England *(Br.)*.

Mindestreserve|politik minimum reserve policy; ~**satz** special deposits ratio *(Br.)*, minimum reserve (safety fund) ratio *(US)*; **gesetzlicher ~satz** legal reserve ratio *(US)*; **niedrige ~sätze festsetzen** to release special deposits *(Br.)*; ~**senkung** cut in the minimum reserve requirements *(US)*, release of special deposits *(Br.)*, reduction in the minimum reserves; ~**soll** required reserve, safety fund *(US)*, special deposit *(Br.)*; ~**system** safety-fund *(US)*, (special deposits, *Br.*) system; ~**verpflichtungen** minimum liabilities; ~**vorschriften** legal reserve requirements *(US)*, special deposits requirements *(Br.)*; ~**vorschriften für Bareinlagen** cash reserve requirements on deposit *(US)*; ~**vorschriften lockern** to release special deposits *(Br.)* (the deposits with the reserve bank in a special account, *US*).

Mindest|saldogebühren minimum-balance charges; ~**satz** minimum rate (price), lowest [possible] rate, *(Bankkredit)* minimum lending rate *(Br.)*, prime rate *(US)*, *(Spediteur)* minimum charge; **tariflicher ~satz** union rate; **gesetzlich zulässiger ~satz** *(Steuer)* legal minimum; ~**stärke** *(Papier)* basic size; ~**steuer** minimum tax; ~**steuersatz** marginal relief *(Br.)*, basic rate of personal tax, threshold tariff; ~**strafe** minimum-term penalty (punishment); ~**streitwert** minimum value of the matter in dispute; ~**stückgutgewicht** minimum carload weight *(US)*; ~**stücklohntarif** minimum piece rate; ~**stundenlöhne** minimum hourly rates of pay; ~**tantieme** minimum royalty; ~**tarif** minimum (line) rate, *(Löhne)* minimum wage, *(Steuer)* threshold tariff; ~**temperatur** minimum temperature; ~**umfang einer Einkommensteuererklärung** minimum income statement content; ~**umsatz** minimum turnover; ~**unternehmergewinn** normal profit; ~**unterstützungssatz** minimum benefit; **gesetzlicher ~urlaub** minimum paid holiday; ~**verdienst** minimum pay; ~**verhältnis** minimum ratio.

Mindestverkaufspreis minimum price, *(Auktion)* reserve (reservation) price;
gebundene ~e maintained minimum retail prices;
~ **für ein Bild festlegen** to place a reserve on a picture; ~ **für ein Haus festsetzen** to put a reserve price on a house; ~**e für den Einzelhandel vorschreiben** to prescribe minimum prices.

Mindest|versicherungszeit minimum terms and period of insurance; ~**versorgung** minimum supply; ~**voraussetzungen** minimum requirements; ~**vorlesungszahl belegen** *(Student)* to pass up *(sl.)*; ~**vorrat** minimum supply; ~**vorschriften über liquide Mittel** *(Bankwesen)* minimum cash reserve requirements; ~**wert** minimum (minimal) value; ~**werterhöhung** marginal increment; ~**wiederverkaufspreis** minimum resale price; ~**wohnungsbedarf** minimum housing need; ~**zahl** minimum number (figure), *(zur Beschlußfassung)* quorum; ~**zeichnungsbetrag** *(Wertpapieremission)* minimum [amount of] subscription; ~**zeit** minimum time; ~**zeitlohntarif** minimum time rate; ~**zeitraum** minimum period; ~**zinssatz** *(Diskontsatz)* base lending rate, *(Leitzins)* minimum interest (lending) rate *(Br.)*, prime rate *(US)*; ~**zoll** minimum tariff.

Mine mine, *(Bleistift)* lead, refill;
~ **auslösen** to spring (touch off) a mine; **treibende ~ aus dem Wasser holen** to fish up a mine; **auf eine ~ laufen** to strike a mine; ~**n räumen** to sweep mines; ~**n verlegen** to lay out (launch) mines; **von einer ~ getroffen werden** to be mined.

Minen|feld mine field, mined area; ~**gebiet** mine field; ~**gefahr** risk of mines; ~**gürtel** mine belt; ~**leger** mine layer; ~**radargerät** mine-watching radar; ~**räumer**, ~**räumfahrzeug** mine sweeper; ~**räumung** mine sweeping (clearance); ~**sperre** mine barrier; ~**sperrgebiet** mined area; ~**stollen** mine gallery.

Minensuch|boot mine sweeper; ~**flotte** mine-sweeping fleet; ~**flugzeug** mine-locating aircraft; ~**gerät** mine detector; ~**trupp** mine-locating detail.

Minenverleger mine-laying vessel.

minenverseucht mine-infested, mined.

Minenwerte mining shares.

Mineral mineral;
~**bad** bath, spa; ~**brunnen** well, mineral spring, waters; ~**gewinnungsrechte** mineral rights.

Mineralien minerals;
~ **abbauen** to win minerals;
~**steuer** severance tax, mineral rights duty *(Br.)*.

Mineral|industrie crude (mineral) oil industry; ~**lagerstätte** mineral deposit.

Mineraloge mineralogist.

Mineralöl mineral oil, petroleum;
~**besteuerung** petroleum taxation; ~**erzeugnis** petrochemical, mineral-oil product; ~**gesellschaft** petroleum company; ~**quelle** oil spring; ~**raffinerie** oil refinery; ~**steuer** mineral-oil tax; ~**verarbeitung** mineral-oil processing; ~**vorkommen** mineral deposit, prospect; ~**vorkommen auf dem Meeresboden** seabed minerals; ~**wirtschaft** mineral-oil industry.

Mineral|quelle mineral spring, spa; ~**vorkommen** mineral resources (deposit), placer; ~**vorkommen ausbeuten** to work mineral deposits; ~**wasser** mineral (table) water, seltzer, Vichy.

Miniatur|ausgabe miniature (scaled-down) replica, *(Buch)* miniature (vest-pocket) book, pony; ~**bauweise** *(Elektronik)* miniaturization; ~**eisenbahn** toy train, miniature railway; ~**malerei** miniature painting.

Mini|aufschwung mini-revival; ~**belebung** mini-recovery.

Minierraupe mining caterpillar.

Mini|fernseher microvision set; **erneut eine ~injektionsspritze bekommen** to receive a mini-injection of reflation; **von der Konsumseite ausgelöste ~konjunktur** consumption-led miniboom.

minimal minimum, minimal, insignificant, trifling, slightest;
~ **2000 DM damit verdienen** to earn at least DM 2000 with it; ~**e Beteiligung** little or no participation; ~**er Preis** minimum price; ~**e Unterschiede** negligible distinctions; ~**e Verluste** minimum of losses, trivial losses.

Minimal|belastung minimum load; ~**betrag** minimum [amount]; ~**dosis** curative dose; ~**fahrpreis** *(Eisenbahn)* minimum fare; ~**fracht** minimum bill-of-lading charge; ~**gehalt** minimum salary; ~**klischee** minimum block; ~**kostenkombination** least-cost combination; ~**pacht** *(Bergwerk)* dead rent *(Br.)*; ~**preis** minimum price; ~**satz** *(Post)* lowest rate of postage; ~**tarif** minimum tariff, *(Versicherungswesen)* minimum premium; ~**wert** minimum value; ~**zeichnungsbetrag** minimum subscription.

Minimum minimum;
unter dem ~ subminimum;
~ **von Geld** minimum amount of money;
Abhängigkeit von Devisenschwankungen auf ein ~ begrenzen to minimize its exposure to currency fluctuations; **auf ein ~ bringen** to minimize; **Risiko auf ein ~ reduzieren** to reduce the risk to a minimum;
~**ladung** carload.

Mini|preis mini-price; ~**rezession** mini-recession; ~**rock** miniskirt.

Minister Minister of the Crown *(Br.)*, Cabinet officer *(US)*, head of a department *(US)*, department head *(US)*, Secretary of State *(Br.)*, Secretary *(US)*, Minister;
in seiner Eigenschaft als ~ in his ministerial capacity;
amtierender ~ acting minister; **schwer ansprechbarer ~** minister difficult to get at; **außerordentlicher und bevollmächtigter ~** envoy extraordinary and minister plenipotentiary; **bevollmächtigter ~** minister plenipotentiary; **früherer ~** late (former) minister;
~ **für auswertige Angelegenheiten** Minister of Foreign Affairs, Foreign Secretary *(Br.)*, Secretary of State *(US)*; ~ **für Arbeit** Minister of Employment *(Br.)*; ~ **mit besonderen Aufgaben** [etwa] Paymaster General *(Br.)*; ~ **für Bundesbesitz** Minister of State for Industries; ~ **für Energiewirtschaft** Minister of Power *(Br.)*; ~ **für Ernährung und Landwirtschaft** Minister for Agriculture, Fisheries and Food *(Br.)*; ~ **für Finanzen** Minister of Finance; ~ **für Fragen des Umweltschutzes** Minister of Environment *(Br.)*, environmental minister; ~ **ohne Geschäftsbereich** nondepartmental minister, Minister without Portfolio; ~ **für Gesundheit, Erziehung und Sozialfragen** Secretary of Health, Education and Welfare *(Br.)*; ~ **des Inneren** Home Secretary *(Br.)*, Secretary of State for Home Affairs *(US)*; ~ **für Justiz** Lord High Chancellor *(Br.)*, Attorney General *(US)*; ~ **für Post- und Fernmeldewesen** Minister for Post and Telecommunications *(Br.)*; ~ **für Soziales** Minister of Social Security *(Br.)*; ~ **für Transport und Verkehrswesen** Secretary of State for Transportation *(US)*, Minister of Transport *(Br.)*; ~ **für Verteidigung** Defence Minister *(Br.)*; ~ **für Wirtschaft** Minister of Economic Affairs *(Br.)*; ~ **für Wohnungsbau** Minister of Housing and Local Government *(Br.)*;
~ **anklagen** to impeach a minister; ~ **in sein Amt einführen** to install a minister in a new charge; ~ **entlassen** to remove a minister from office; ~ **von der Beschuldigung der Überschreitung seiner Befugnisse freisprechen** to indemnify a minister; ~ **unter Anklage stellen** to impeach a minister; ~ **stürzen** to unseat a minister;

~**amt** portfolio, ministerial post, ministry, secretaryship; ~**amt erhalten** to attain ministerial office; **im letzten Kabinett ein ~amt innehaben** to hold an office in the last cabinet; ~**anklage** impeachment of a minister; ~**anwärter** prospective minister; ~**ausschuß** ministerial committee; ~**bank** *(Parlament)* treasury (front) bench *(Br.)*, ministerial benches; ~**bezüge** cabinet wage.

Ministerial | abkommen executive agreement; ~**abteilung** government department *(Br.)*, board; ~**abteilung für Staatsbetriebe** National Enterprise Board *(Br.)*; ~**ausschuß** interdepartmental committee; ~**beamter** ministerial officer (official), ministry official, principal *(Br.)*, department (ministry) official; **höherer ~beamter** high administrative (senior departmental, *US*) official, senior principal *(Br.)*; ~**bürokratie** executive administration (ministry, *Br.*); ~**direktor** [etwa] undersecretary, assistant secretary *(US)*; **auf ~ebene** at ministerial level; ~**erlaß**, ~**verfügung** ministerial act, ministerial *(Br.)* (departmental) order; ~**gehalt** ministerial salary; ~**rat** department head; ~**stellung** ministerial appointment; ~**tätigkeit** ministerial functions; ~**verwaltung** departmental administration; ~**zulage** extra pay for departmental officers.

ministeriell ministerial, departmental;
~**e Aufgaben** ministerial duties; ~**e Ausführungsbestimmungen** departmental regulations; **auf ~er Ebene** at ministerial level; ~**er Erlaß** ministerial order *(Br.)*, departmental order; ~**e Tätigkeit** ministerial function *(US)*; ~**e Verlautbarung** ministerial statement; ~**e Vollmachten** ministerial powers; ~**e Zustimmung** ministerial approval.

Ministerieller ministerialist.

Ministerien government officers.

Ministerium board, ministry, office *(Br.)*, government, government (governing) department *(Br.)*, government office, executive department *(US)*, *(Regierung)* government, cabinet *(Br.)*;
von ~ zu ~ intradepartmental;
fachlich zuständiges ~ government department concerned;
~ **für auswärtige Angelegenheiten (des Äußeren)** Ministry of Foreign Affairs *(Br.)*, Foreign Office *(Br.)*, State Department *(US)*; ~ **für Arbeit** Board of Works *(Br.)*, Labor Department *(US)*; ~ **für Energiewirtschaft** Ministry of Fuel and Power *(Br.)*; ~ **für die Erhaltung der natürlichen Umwelt** Department of Environmental Conservation *(US)*; ~ **der Finanzen** Department of the Treasury *(US)*, Exchequers *(Br.)*; ~ **für Forschung** Ministry of Technology; ~ **des Inneren** Home Office *(Br.)*, Department of the Interior *(US)*; ~ **für Justiz** justice department *(US)*; ~ **für Kultur** Ministry of Arts and Culture, Ministry of Education *(Br.)*; ~ **der schönen Künste** arts ministry; ~ **für Landwirtschaft** Ministry of Agriculture, Fisheries and Food *(Br.)*, Agricultural Department *(US)*; ~ **für Umweltfragen** Department of Environment *(Br.)*; ~ **für Unterricht und Wissenschaft** Department of Education *(Br.)*; ~ **für Verkehr** Department of Transportation *(US)*, Ministry of Transport *(Br.)*; ~ **für Verteidigung** Ministry of Defence *(Br.)*; ~ **für Wirtschaft** Commerce Department *(US)*, Department of Economic Affairs *(Br.)*; ~ **für Wohnungsbau** [etwa] Ministry of Public Buildings and Works *(Br.)*;
~ **ablehnen** to pass up a ministerial office; ~ **anstreben** to aim at (to be ambitious of) office; ~ **zugeteilt erhalten** to be given a ministry; ~ **übernehmen** to take an office, to enter (form) a ministry; **ins ~ berufen werden** to be called to office (the ministry).

Ministeriums | ausgaben departmental spending; ~**etat** department budget; ~**vertreter** ministry official.

Minister | kollege conjoint minister; ~**konferenz** ministerial meeting (session); ~**macher** cabinetmaker; ~**posten** ministry, cabinet office, ministerial post; ~**präsident** Prime Minister *(Br.)*; ~**präsidentschaft** Prime Ministry *(Br.)*; ~**rat** cabinet (minister) meeting, council of ministers, *(EG)* executive council, ministerial (cabinet) council; ~**resident** minister resident; ~**ressort** minister's (government) portfolio; ~**sessel** ministry, ministerial post; ~**sitz** seat in the cabinet; ~**sitzung** cabinet council *(Br.)*; ~**stelle** ministerial office; ~**treffen** ministerial meeting; ~**verantwortung** ministerial responsibility *(Br.)*; ~**wechsel** change in the ministry.

ministrabel machen, j. to license a candidate for the ministry.

Minna, grüne Black Maria, booby hatch *(sl.)*, paddy waggon *(US)*, milk waggon *(sl.)*.

Minorität, in der ~ bleiben to find o. s. outvoted; ~ **überstimmen** to freeze out the minority.

Minoritäts | aktionär minority [stock]holder *(US)* (shareholder, *Br.*); ~**beteiligung** minority interest (shareholdings, *Br.*, stockholdings, *US*, stock participation, *US*).

Minus minus [sign], *(Defizit)* deficit, deficiency, *(Nachteil)* disadvantage, drawback, shortcoming;
im ~ to the bad;
immer tiefer ins ~ geraten to plunge deeper in the red *(US coll.)*; **im vergangenen Jahr ein ~ gehabt haben** to have had a deficit in the last year; **im ~ sein** to be in the red *(US coll.)*; ~ **für j. sein** to be a point against s. o.; **als ~ gewertet werden** to be considered as a drawback.

minus minus, less, deducting;
~ **4 Grad** 4 degrees below freezing point.

Minus | bestand shortage of stock; ~**betrag** deficit, deficiency, shortage in money accounts; ~**korrektur** downward adjustment; ~**leitung** negative conductor; ~**pol** *(el.)* negative pole; ~**punkt** demerit mark, minus, drawback; ~**saldo** negative balance; ~**seite** debit side; ~**zeichen** negative sign.

Minute minute;
auf die ~ [genau] up to the minute, up to schedule *(US)*; **in letzter ~** in the heels of the hunt;
zehn ~n zu Fuß ten minutes walk; **volle zehn ~n** clear ten minutes;
auf die ~ ablaufen to go off according to schedule *(coll.)*; **in letzter ~ absagen** to decline at the last minute; **auf die ~ ankommen** to arrive on the dot (as scheduled, *US*); **jede ~ entdeckt zu werden befürchten** to live in an hourly dread of discovery; ~**n verstreichen lassen** to tick off the minutes.

Minuten | entfernung a minute's walk; ~**preis** *(Rundfunkwerbung)* rate; **Zwanzig-~verkehr** twenty-minute service; ~**zeiger** minute hand.

minutiös, minuziös scrupulously exact;
~**e Prüfung** meticulous examination; **mit ~er Sorgfalt** with scrupulous care.

Misch | batterie uni-tap contraption, water mixer; ~**bauweise** composite construction; ~**becher** shaker; ~**bestand** *(Wald)* mixed growth; ~**betrieb** mixed enterprise; ~**depot** general deposit; ~**ehe** mixed marriage; ~**eigentum** mixed property.

mischen to mix, *(Kartenspiel)* to shuffle, *(Lochkarten)* to merge;
sich in jds. Angelegenheiten ~ to meddle in s. one's affairs, to mix into s. one's business; **sich in ein Gespräch ~** to butt into a conversation; **Gift ~** to concoct poison; **sich unter die Menge ~** to mingle with the crowd.

Misch | farbe *(Anzeige)* matched colo(u)r; ~**futter** mixed feed; ~**gemüse** mixed vegetables; ~**gerät** mixer; ~**getränk** mixed drink; ~**heirat** intermarriage; ~**koks** mixed coke; ~**konten** mixed accounts; ~**konzern** conglomerate, mixed enterprise; **durch Fusion entstandener ~konzern** diversification merger; ~**ling** half-caste (-bred), [person of] mixed blood, mongrel.

Mischmasch hash, medley, mash, mishmash *(sl.)*;
~ **verschiedenster Leute** medley of all kinds of people; ~ **von Worten** jumble of words.

Misch | poke, ganze whole caboodle *(sl.)*; ~**preis** mixed price; ~**pult** control (monitoring) desk, mixing table, mixer; ~**rasse** mongrel race; ~**tatbestand** hybrid provision.

Mischung mixture, mix, compound, blend;
altbekannte ~ ancient mix.

Misch | verfahren mixing process; ~**volk** mixed race; ~**wald** mixed forest; ~**wirtschaft** mixed economy; ~**zinssatz** composite rate of interest; ~**zoll** compound duty.

Mise *(Lebensversicherung)* single premium (payment).

miserabel miserable, poor, rotten, punk *(sl.)*;
~ **aussehen** to look seedy; **sich ~ benehmen** to behave abominably; **sich ~ fühlen** to be feeling under the weather; **einem ~ gehen** to be in a bad way; ~ **kochen** to be a poor cook.

miserable | Aufführung lousy performance; ~**s Ergebnis** poor result; ~**s Essen** abominable food, lousy dinner *(coll.)*; ~**s Gasthaus** wretched inn; ~ **Laune haben** to be in a bad mood; ~ **Rede** miserable speech; ~ **Schrift** atrocious handwriting; ~**s Stück** rotten play; ~**s Wetter** beastly (dreadful) weather.

Misere plight, wretched (miserable) conditions, *(Not)* distress, misery;
wirtschaftliche ~ wretched economic state;
aus einer ~ herauskommen to get out of a mess.

mißachten to disregard, to neglect, to ignore, to pay no heed;
Anordnungen ~ to ignore an order; **Gefahr ~** to give no heed to a warning; **Gesetz ~** to pay no regard to the law; **guten Ratschlag ~** to throw prudence to the wind; **an einer Kreuzung das Vorfahrtsrecht ~** to fail to give way at a crossroads; **Vorsichtsmaßregeln ~** to neglect precautions; **jds. Widerstände gegen einen Vorschlag ~** to disregard s. one's objections to a proposal.

Mißachtung disregard, disrespect, neglect, *(Gesetze)* nonobservance;

in ~ aller Konventionen in contempt of all rules and regulations; **unter ~ jeglicher Vorsicht** with utter disregard of safety;
~ der Bürgerechte violation of the rights of citizens; **~ des Gerichts** contempt of court; **~ der Parlamentshoheit** contempt of congress *(US)*; **grobfahrlässige ~ der Rechte anderer Verkehrsteilnehmer** *(Verkehrsordnung)* reckless disregard of rights of others; **~ der Redefreiheit** violation of the right of free speech; **~ des Vorfahrtsrechtes an einer Kreuzung** failure to give way at a crossroads; **~ der erforderlichen Vorsichtsmaßregeln** neglect of proper precautions;
der ~ anheimfallen to fall by the wayside; **allgemeiner ~ ausgesetzt sein** to be exposed to public contempt; **der ~ des Gerichts schuldig sein** to be standing in contempt; **wegen ~ des Gerichts vorladen** to cite for contempt of court.
Mißbehagen uneasiness, discomposure, discomfort;
~ mit der Wohlstandsgesellschaft dissatisfaction with the affluent society;
leichtes ~ fühlen to feel slightly uneasy.
Mißbildung deformation, deformity, malformation.
mißbilligen to disapprove, to find fault with, to condemn, to deprecate;
jds. Handlungsweise ~ to disapprove of s. one's actions; **scharf ~** to reprobate.
mißbilligend | seinen Kopf schütteln to shake one's head in disapproval;
~er Blick look of disapproval.
Mißbilligung disapproval, disfavo(u)r, disallowance, reproval, deprecation, disapprobation;
öffentliche ~ public reprobation;
auf etw. mit ~ blicken to frown on s. th.
Mißbrauch abuse, improper use, misemployment, misuse, nuisance, *(Sexdelikt)* abuse;
unter ~ seiner Stellung abusing one's position;
grenzenloser ~ unmeasured abuse; **grober ~** crying (gross) abuse; **skandalöser ~** glaring abuse;
~ von Alkohol alcoholic excess; **~ im Amt** malfeasance in office, malversation; **~ der Amtsgewalt** misuse of authority, official oppression *(US)*; **~ von Ausweisverfahren** improper use of identity papers; **~ eines Automaten** misuse of a slot machine; **~ der Befugnisse über öffentliche Gelder zu verfügen** misuse of public funds; **~ von Bürgerrechten** abuse of civil rights; **~ geschützter Daten** misuse of protected private data; **~ der Ermessensfreiheit** abuse of discretionary powers (discretion, authority); **~ von jds. Güte** imposition on s. one's kindness; **~ von Haushaltsmitteln** budget dissavings; **~ vertraulicher Kenntnisse** improper use of confidential information; **~ von Kindern** exploitation of children; **~ verfahrensrechtlicher Möglichkeiten** abuse of process in court; **~ einer Monopolstellung** abuse of monopoly; **~ eines Patents** misuse of a patent; **~ politischer Positionen** misuse of official positions; **~ eines Rechtes** misuser; **~ des Vertrauens** abuse of confidence (trust); **~ eines Vertrauensverhältnisses** abuse of a fiduciary relationship; **~ der Vollstreckungsmöglichkeiten** abuse of distress;
~ abstellen to reform (remedy) an abuse, to abate a nuisance; **~ treiben** to misuse one's authority, to take an undue advantage of.
Mißbräuche, schwerer ~ beschuldigt werden to be accused of serious irregularities.
mißbrauchen to abuse, to misuse, to misapply, to make improper (bad) use of;
Ermessensfreiheit ~ to abuse discretionary powers (discretion); **jds. Gastfreundschaft ~** to trespass on s. one's hospitality; **öffentliche Gelder ~** to misapply public money, to misappropriate public funds; **jds. Güte ~** to encroach upon s. one's kindness; **Lehrling als Laufjungen ~** to use an apprentice as errand boy; **seine Position zur Bereicherung ~** to abuse one's position to line one's pockets; **jds. Vertrauen ~** to abuse s. one's confidence; **seine Vollmacht ~** to abuse one's power; **j. in sittenwidriger Weise ~** to take undue advantage of s. o.; **j. als williges Werkzeug ~** to make a mere tool of s. o.;
sich zur Spionage ~ lassen to allow o. s. to be used as a spy.
mißbräuchlich abusive, improper, wrong, wrongful;
~ benutzen to misapply, to misuse, to misappropriate;
~e Mittelverwendung misappropriation (misapplication) of funds; **~e Patentbenutzung** abuse of a patent; **~e Verwendung eines Namens** abuse of name.
mißbraucht ill-used.
mißdeuten to misconstrue, to misinterpret;
jds. Handlungen ~ to misinterpret s. one's actions.
Mißdeutung misinterpretation, misconstruction.
missen to miss, to do without;
Fernsehen nicht mehr ~ können not to be able to do without television.
Mißerfolg failure, ill success, cropper, fiasco, washout, fizzle, naught, flop, *(Examen)* plough;
finanzieller ~ financial failure; **wirtschaftlicher ~** business fiasco, flop;
mit einem ~ enden to result in failure; **~ haben** to meet with a failure, to come a cropper; **~ sein** to end in failure, *(Theaterstück)* to go flop; **als Anwalt ein ~ sein** to be a failure as a lawyer; **finanzieller ~ sein** to fail at the box office; **als ~ dargestellt werden** to be written down as a failure.
Mißernte crop failure, failure of (short) crop;
dreijährige ~n hervorbringen to fail in three running years.
Missetat misdemeano(u)r, malefaction, wrongdoing, misdoing, crime;
schreiende ~ loud offence;
~ begehen to commit a misdeed; **jds. ~en der Polizei melden** to make s. one's misdeeds known to the police; **j. wegen einer ~ ein für allemal verurteilen** to give a dog a bad name and hang him; **für seine ~en zur Rechenschaft gezogen werden** to do justice for one's crimes.
Missetäter midemeanant, wrongdoer, offender, delinquent, malefactor, criminal.
Mißfallen disapproval, disfavo(u)r, dislike;
etw. mit ~ betrachten to look upon s. th. with disfavo(u)r; **jds. ~ erregen** to incur s. one's displeasure; **sein ~ verbergen** to disguise one's distaste; **sein ~ zeigen** to show one's displeasure.
mißfallen, jem. to displease s. o., to incur s. one's displeasure.
Mißfallens | bezeigung sign of disapproval; **~kundgebung** Kentish fire, demonstration of disapproval.
mißfällig disapproving, disagreeable;
sich ~ über j. äußern to speak disparagingly about s. o.
Mißgeburt monster, monstrosity.
mißgelaunt ill-humo(u)red, bad tempered;
~ sein to be in a bad mood.
Mißgeschick ill fortune, misfortune, bad luck, mischance, trouble, disaster;
trotz dieses ~s in spite of this mishap;
vom ~ verfolgt werden to be pursued by misfortune.
mißglücken to come a cropper, to fail, to fall flat, to misfire, to end in failure.
mißglückte | Fernsehsendung videocast that did not come off; **~ Versuche** unsuccessful attempts.
mißgönnen, jem. sein Glück to begrudge s. o. his good fortune.
Mißgriff misstep, mistake, blunder, gaffe, slip of the hand, *(fig.)* break *(US)*;
~ tun to make a blunder, to make a mistake, *(falsch auswählen)* to make a bad choice.
Mißgunst envy, jealousy, malevolence;
Neid und ~ envy and resentment;
unter jds. ~ zu leiden haben to suffer under s. one's ill will; **sich jds. ~ zuziehen** to incur s. one's displeasure.
mißgünstig malevolent, begrudging, envious, jealous.
mißhandeln to maltreat, to mistreat, to manhandle, to ill-treat, to lacerate, to outrage;
j. schwer ~ to brutalize s. o.
Mißhandlung maltreatment, ill-treatment, mistreatment, misusage, abuse, *(Scheidungsrecht)* legal cruelty;
schwere ~ extreme cruelty;
~ von Gefangenen abuse of prisoners; **~ von Kindern** cruelty to children.
Miß | heirat misalliance, shotgun marriage *(US)*; **~helligkeit** discord, discordance, dissonance, unpleasantness, friction.
Mission mission, delegation, call;
in besonderer ~ on special mission; **in diplomatischer ~** on an embassy; **in geheimer ~** on a secret mission;
auswärtige ~ foreign mission; **diplomatische ~** mission; **innere ~** home (domestic) mission; **ständige ~** permanent mission;
~ des guten Willens goodwill mission;
seine ~ erfolgreich beenden to complete one's mission successfully; **j. mit einer diplomatischen ~ betrauen** to entrust s. o. with a diplomatic mission; **j. in diplomatischer ~ entsenden** to send s. o. on an embassy.
Missionar missionary.
Missions | angehörige mission staff; **~chef** head of a mission (post), mission head, chef of a mission; **~fonds** missionary box, mission fund; **~gebiet** missionary field; **~gesellschaft** missionary society; **~tätigkeit** mission, missionary work; **~wesen im Ausland** foreign missions.

Mißklang dissonance, disharmony, discord;
~ **beheben** to break the spell; ~ **in eine Familie bringen** to bring discord into a family; **mit einem ~ enden** to end on an unfortunate note.
Mißkredit discredit, disrepute, bad reputation;
in ~ bringen to [bring into] discredit; **in ~ geraten** to get in bad repute, to fall into disrepute; **in ~ stehen** to be in disrepute.
mißleiten to misdirect.
mißlich awkward, embarrassing, trying;
~ **für j. aussehen** to look pretty bad for s. o.;
~e Angelegenheit fishy business, bad egg *(coll.)*; **~e finanzielle Lage** financial embarrassment; **j. in eine ~e Lage bringen** to get s. o. into a fix; **in eine ~e Lage geraten** to get into an awkward situation; **in ~er Lage sein** to be in great trouble, to have one's back to the wall.
Mißlichkeit seiner Lage awkwardness of one's situation.
mißliebig unpopular, disagreeable;
sich bei jem. ~ machen to fall out of favo(u)r with s. o.; **sich überall ~ machen** to show o. s. in an unfavo(u)rable light.
Mißlingen failure, abortion;
jem. das ~ eines Projektes zuschreiben to blame s. o. for the failure of a project.
mißlingen to come to nought, to prove abortive, to prove an abortion, to be a flop, to fall to the ground, to founder, to backfire;
vollständig ~ to turn out a complete failure.
mißlungener Staatsstreich abortive coup.
Mißmut bad mood, sulkiness, ill humo(u)r, miff.
mißmutig sulky, moody, bad-tempered, weary, morose.
mißraten to be a failure (flop), *(Ernte)* to fail, *(Kind)* to turn out badly;
~e Arbeit failure, flop, fiasco; **~es Kind** ill-bred child.
Mißstand grievance, nuisance;
abschaffbarer ~ abatable nuisance;
~ **beseitigen** to abate a nuisance.
Mißstände | im Erziehungswesen defects in a system of education; **von sozialen ~n durch einen Krieg ablenken** to curb social discomfort by making war abroad; ~ **abschaffen (abstellen, beseitigen)** to abate a nuisance, to remedy a mischief; **schreiende ~ abschaffen** to remedy crying abuses; **auf ~ hinweisen** to draw attention to the deplorable state of affairs; **auf öffentliche ~ hinweisen** to muckrake.
Mißstimmung dissonance, discordance, strained atmosphere, ill-feeling, *(Börse)* depressed state, depression;
ohne ~ verlaufen to go off swimmingly.
Mißton | auf einer Konferenz jarring note at a conference;
in den Lobesgesang einen ~ hineintragen to sound a jarring note in the concert of praise.
Mißtrauen | erregen to arouse distrust (mistrust), to make o. s. suspicious; ~ **hervorrufen** to stir up distrust; ~ **säen** to sow the seeds of distrust.
mißtrauen to distrust, to mistrust, *(verdächtigen)* to entertain a suspicion;
jem. ~ to have no confidence in s. o.; **jds. Motiven ~** to distrust s. one's motives.
Mißtrauensantrag censure (no-confidence) motion, vote (notice) of censure;
~ **ablehnen** to reject a vote of censure; ~ **gegen die Regierung annehmen** to pass [a vote of] censure on the government; ~ **einbringen** to present (propose, put down) a motion of no-confidence; ~ **gegen die Regierung unterstützen** to vote against the government on a confidence motion.
Mißtrauensvotum censure resolution (vote), vote of no confidence, nonconfidence vote, nonplacet;
~ **annehmen** to pass a nonconfidence vote; ~ **durchbringen** to pass a vote of no confidence (nonconfidence); ~ **einbringen** to present (propose) a motion of nonconfidence, to propose a vote of censure.
mißtrauisch distrustful, mistrusting;
j. ~ mustern to look s. o. up and down suspiciously; **Ausländern gegenüber ~ sein** to have a distrust of foreigners.
Mißvergnügen annoyance, displeasure;
~ **der Aktionäre** shareholder (stockholder, *US*) discontent; **sein ~ an jem. auslassen** to subject s. o. to annoyance; **sich jds. ~ zuziehen** to incur s. one's displeasure.
mißvergnügt discontented, annoyed, cross, displeased;
über etw. ~ sein to be displeased at s. th.;
mit einem ~en Blick with a look of annoyance.
Mißvergnügter malcontent.
Mißverhältnis incongruity, disproportion, maladjustment, imbalance, *(Eigen- zu Fremdkapital)* leverage;
~ **zwischen Angebot und Nachfrage** disproportion of supply and demand; ~ **in den Größen** incongruity between the sizes; ~ **der Zahlungsbilanz** maladjustment of (imbalance in) the balance of payments;
~ **zwischen Eigen- und Fremdkapital aufweisen** to be highly leveraged; **im auffälligen ~ stehen** to be conspicuously out of proportion.
mißverständlich misleading, ambiguous;
~ **sein** to be liable to be misunderstood;
völlig ~e Antwort reply full of ambiguities; **~e Bezeichnung** misleading description.
Mißverständlichkeit eines Paragraphen beseitigen to clear up the ambiguity of a paragraph.
Mißverständnis misunderstanding, misapprehension, disaccord, mistake;
um jedes ~ auszuschließen in order to preclude any misunderstanding; **sich in einem ~ befinden** to labo(u)r under a misapprehension; ~ **beseitigen** to clear up a misunderstanding; **aus einem ~ seinen Ausgang nehmen** to originate in (ensue from) a misunderstanding.
mißverstehen to misunderstand;
sich gegenseitig ~ to be at cross purposes; **etw. völlig ~** to get hold of the wrong end of the stick.
Mißweisung *(Kompaß)* magnetic declination, *(Radar)* indicating error.
Mißwirtschaft maladministration, economic mismanagement, poor management, misgovernment, misappropriation, misrule;
finanzielle ~ unsound finance;
~ **mit öffentlichen Geldern** misappropriation of public funds.
mißwirtschaften to misgovern, to mismanage.
Mist manure, dung, muck, *(Plunder)* rubbish, junk, trash, crap *(sl.)*, bilge *(sl.)*, tripe *(sl.)*, *(Unsinn)* nonsense;
auf dem eigenen ~ gewachsen off one's own head;
absoluter ~ bullshit *(sl., vul.)*;
~ **fahren** to cart out manure; **Geld wie ~ haben** to have scads (lots, piles) of money, to have money to burn; ~ **kaufen** to buy trash; **seinen ganzen ~ loswerden** to get rid of all one's bilge; **ziemlicher ~ sein** *(Buch)* to be pretty good rot *(sl.)*; ~ **streuen** to spread manure; **großen ~ verzapfen** to talk nonsense (rubbish), to talk a lot of trash; **etw. auf den ~ werfen** to throw s. th. on the rubbish heap;
Kleinvieh macht auch ~ many a mickle makes a muckle; **red keinen ~** stop talking tripe *(sl.)*;
~beet hotbed; **~beetfenster** garden frame.
misten to manure, to dung, to muck, *(Stall)* to clean.
Mist | fink dirty fellow, dirty-minded person, pig; **~gabel** muck-rake, pitchfork; **~grube** dung hole; **~haufen** dunghill, muck heap.
mistig beastly, filthy, lousy.
Mist | karren dung cart, tumbrel; **~kerl** nasty fellow, blighter, rotter; **~stück** bad lot *(coll.)*, blighter, rotter, *(Theater)* lousy play; **~wetter** beastly weather.
Mit | aktionäre joint shareholders *(Br.)* (stockholders, *US*); **~angeklagter** codefendant; **~angestellter** fellow servant; **~anmelder** *(Patent)* joint applicants; **~antragsteller** coapplicant.
Mitarbeit cooperation, collaboration, assistance, *(an Zeitung)* contribution;
kostenlose ~ unpaid work;
jds. ~ gewinnen to enlist s. one's cooperation; **j. zur ~ heranziehen** to engage s. one's services; **j. zur wissenschaftlichen ~ heranziehen** to call in s. o. as scientific adviser; **sich zur ~ verpflichten** to pledge o. s. to cooperate.
mitarbeiten to contribute one's services, to cooperate, to collaborate, to assist, to take part;
aktiv ~ *(fig.)* to pull one's weight; **an einer Erfindung ~** to cooperate in an invention; **erfolgreich ~** to play one's part well; **besser in der Schule ~** to take a more active part in the lessons; **an einer Zeitung ~** to be on the staff of (contribute to) a newspaper.
mitarbeitende Ehefrau working wife.
Mitarbeiter colleague, cooperator, collaborator, coworker, member of the staff, staff representative *(US)*, *(Arbeitskamerad)* fellow worker, workfellow, joint labo(u)rer, associate, *(Gehilfe)* assistant, coadjutor, *(an Zeitung)* contributor, correspondent, columnist;
altgedienter (bewährter) ~ veteran hand; **fachlich ausgebildete ~** skilled (specialized, trained) staff; **ausländische ~** foreign employees; **übertariflich bezahlter ~** employee paid in excess of standard rates; **ehrenamtliche ~** voluntary staff; **für langfristige**

Planungen eingesetzter ~ long-range planner; **enge** ~ aids and assistants; **freier (freiberuflicher)** ~ *(Zeitung)* contributing editor, stringer, free lancer, freelance contributor, freelance writer; **grafischer** ~ *(Werbeagentur)* artist; **hauptamtlicher** ~ full-time member of the staff; **juristischer** ~ legal assistant; **kaufmännischer** ~ clerk; **laufender** ~ *(Zeitung)* regular contributor; **leitende** ~ executive personnel, managerial staff; **leitender** ~ senior official; **technischer** ~ technical assistant; **vertrauenswürdiger** ~ trusted aide; **wissenschaftlicher** ~ scientific adviser;
~ **im Außendienst** field worker, sales representative; ~ **in wohltätigen Einrichtungen** settlement worker; ~ **der Geschäftsleitung** managerial assistant; ~ **im Innendienst** indoor staff; ~ **in der Steuerabteilung** assistant in the taxation department, taxation assistant; ~ **einer Zeitschrift** magazinist; **ständiger** ~ **einer Zeitung** regular contributor to a newspaper;
sich mit seinen ~n beraten to consult with one's fellow workers; **seine** ~ **entlassen** to dismiss one's staff; **erfahrenen** ~ **haben** to work with an experienced colleague; **zehntausend** ~ **haben** to have a staff of 10.000 people; ~ **der Times sein** to be on the staff of the Times;
~**beziehungen im Betrieb** human relations in industry; ~**förderung** personnel development; **leistungsfähiges** ~**gremium leiten** to handle an efficient staff; ~**schulung** staff training.

Mitarbeiterstab collaboratorship, *(Zeitung)* staff;
fähiger ~ competent staff of men, efficient staff;
~ **des amerikanischen Präsidenten** White House Office *(US)*; **Unternehmensführung einem qualifizierten** ~ **anvertrauen** to entrust the working of an undertaking to a qualified staff; ~ **leiten** to run a group of people.

Mitarbeitervertrag contract of personal service.

Mit|aussteller *(Wechsel)* fellow drawer, comaker, joint maker; ~**autor** co-author; ~**autorschaft** joint authorship; ~**beauftragter** joint mandatory.

mitbegründen to be one of the founders.

Mit|begründer cofounder, charter member *(US)*; ~**begünstigter** cobeneficiary; ~**beklagter** joint defendant, codefendant, *(Scheidungsverfahren)* co-respondent.

mitbekommen to understand, to get *(coll.)*, to catch on, *(Mitgift)* to get as a dowry;
nicht alles ~ not to be able to catch everything; **belegte Brote** ~ to be given sandwiches; **jds. Erklärung** ~ to get s. one's explanation.

mit|belasten to implicate; ~**benutzen** to use jointly, to share in the use; **j. seine Bibliothek** ~**benutzen lassen** to give s. o. the use (run) of one's library.

Mit|benutzer joint (concurrent) user; ~**benutzung** joint use; ~**benutzung von jds. Bibliothek** run of s. one's library; ~**benutzungsrecht** common right, right of common; ~**berechtigter** jointly entitled person, cobeneficiary; ~**besitz** joint possession (occupation, tenancy), copartnership; ~**besitzer** joint occupant (holder, owner, tenant), concurrent user, copartner.

mitbestimmen to decide (determine) together;
paritätisch ~ to codetermine; **in einer Sache** ~ to have a say in a matter; **im Vorstand** ~ to have a voice in the management.

mitbestimmend sein to be a contributory factor.

Mitbestimmung co-management, *(Belegschaft)* joint management;
betriebliche ~ management partition, joint management, comanagement, *(paritätisch)* codetermination; **überbetriebliche** ~ external comanagement; **breit verankerte** ~ grass-roots participation;
~ **am Arbeitsplatz** shop-floor participation; ~ **im Betrieb** participation in the management, worker participation *(Br.)*; ~ **in wirtschaftlichen Fragen auf Vorstandsebene zulassen** to board-level industrial democracy.

Mitbestimmungs|beirat participation council; ~**recht** comanagement, codetermination, decision-making powers; ~**system** participation plan; ~**vereinbarung** participation agreement.

mitbeteiligen, sich an einer Sache to go in with s. o. in an undertaking.

mitbeteiligt participating, cointerested, *(Verbrechen)* privy, incriminated.

Mit|beteiligter party interested, participant, partner, associate, *(Strafrecht)* accomplice; ~**beteiligter bei Begehung einer unerlaubten Handlung** joint trespasser; ~**beteiligung** copartnership, participation, partnership.

mitbetroffen affected, conjunct.

Mitbevollmächtigter joint attorney.

mitbewerben to compete.

Mit|bewerber rival, competitor, job competitor *(US)*; ~**bewohner** cohabitant, cohabiter, flatsharer *(Br.)*.

mitbezahlen to pay one's share, to share the costs.

Mitbieten bidding.

mitbieten to bid.

Mitbringen, das ~ **von Hunden ist nicht gestattet!** no dogs!

mitbringen to bring with one;
gewaltigen Hunger ~ to have an enormous appetite; **Sachkenntnisse auf einem Gebiet** ~ to be experienced in a field; **jem. etw. aus der Stadt** ~ to get s. o. s. th. from town; **Voraussetzungen für einen Beruf** ~ to qualify for a job.

Mit|bringsel take-home (holiday) gift, *(fam.)* [travel] souvenir; ~**bürge** joint guarantor; ~**bürger** fellow citizen; **angesehener** ~**bürger** reputable citizen; ~**bürgschaft** joint security, collateral bail.

mitdecken, für jem. to lay a knife and fork for s. o.

mitdenkend cooperatively thinking.

Mitdirektor joint director (manager).

Miteigentum common ownership, coownership, joint proprietaryship, *(Erbe)* coparcenary, *(bei verschiedenem Erwerbungsgrund)* estate in common, *(Grundstück)* tenancy in common, unity of seizin;
quotenmäßiges ~ proportionate ownership;
~ **nach Bruchteilen** tenancy in common; ~ **zur gesamten Hand** joint estate (tenancy).

Miteigentümer common (joint) owner (holder, proprietor), coowner, coproprietor, parcener, *(Grundstück)* joint tenant, tenant in common, *(Schiff)* part owner;
~ **nach Bruchteilen** severalty owners; ~ **zur gesamten Hand** coparceners.

Miteinander common effort and mutual assistance.

miteinander|auskommen to get on with each other; **stundenlang** ~ **beraten** to confer for hours.

mit|einbegriffen included, inclusive; **[in Arbeitslosenfürsorge]** ~**einbezogene Industrien** covered industries; ~**einrechnen** to include in the reckoning; ~**enthalten** to imply; ~**entscheidend für einen Erfolg sein** to be partly responsible for a success.

Miterbe coparcener, coheir, joint (fellow) heir *(US)*, parcener, *(Grundstück)* coparcener.

miterben to inherit jointly (conjointly).

Mit|erbenanteil joint share in an inheritance; ~**erbschaft** joint heritage *(US)*, coparcenary, coheritage; ~**erfinder** joint (fellow) inventor, coinventor; ~**erfinderschaft** joint inventorship.

miterleben, Eisenbahnunglück to be there at the time of a railway disaster; **Vorfall** ~ to witness an incident.

Miterwerber joint purchaser.

mitfahren, umsonst to ride free, to hitchhike *(coll.)*; **j. umsonst** ~ **lassen** to give s. o. a lift.

Mit|fahrende passengers in a car; ~**fahrer** automobile guest, fellow travel(l)er, hitchhiker; ~**fahrer eines versicherten Fahrzeugs** occupant of an insured car; ~**fahrerzentrale** organized car pool; ~**fahrgelegenheit** lift.

mitfinanzieren to finance jointly.

Mitfinanzierung joint financing.

mit|freuen, sich mit jem. über etw. to rejoice with s. o. about s. th.; **mit jds. Leid** ~**fühlen** to share s. one's sorrows.

mitfühlend|es Wesen sympathetic nature; ~**e Worte** words of sympathy.

mitführen, seinen Führerschein to carry one's driving licence on one.

mitgeben *(als Mitgift)* to give as a dowry;
j. als Führer ~ to send s. o. as a guide; **seinen Kindern eine gute Ausbildung** ~ to provide one's children with a good education.

Mitgebrauch joint use.

mitgefangen, mitgehangen in for a penny, in for a pound.

Mitgefangener fellow prisoner, coprisoner.

Mitgefühl sympathy, compassion, concern;
tiefes ~ deep sympathy (concern);
jem. sein ~ **ausdrücken** to express one's sympathy with s. o.; ~ **erwecken** to arouse pity; ~ **haben** to have a sense of human sympathy; ~ **mit den Unterlegenen haben** to feel for the underdog.

mitgehen, mit jem. bis zum Bahnhof to accompany s. o. as far as the station; **begeistert** ~ *(Publikum)* to be carried away; **mit der Zeit** ~ to move with the times;
etw. ~ **lassen** to lift s. th., to help o. s. to s. th.

mitgenommen *(Fahrzeug)* ramshackle, *(Kleidung)* shabby, the worse for wear, *(Person)* run down, exhausted, under a strain;
vom Krieg stark ~ war-battered;

arg ~ **worden sein** to have been in the wars *(Br., coll.)*; ~ **werden** to get a lift.

Mitgesellschaft partner, associate.

Mitgesellschafter fellow partner.

Mitgift marriage portion, dowry, dotal property, trousseau; **nicht zur ~ gehörend** extradotal; **ohne ~** dowerless; ~ **ausschlagen** to renunciate dower; ~ **aussetzen** to dower; ~**jagd** fortune hunting; ~**jäger** fortune (dowry) hunter; ~**versicherung** marriage portion insurance.

Mitgläubiger fellow creditor.

Mitglied member, *(wissenschaftliche Gesellschaft)* fellow, member;
älteres ~ *(Gerichtshof)* bencher *(Br.)*; **anwesende und abstimmende ~er** members present and voting; **assoziiertes** ~ *(EG)* associate member; **ausscheidendes** ~ withdrawing member; **auswärtiges** ~ foreign member; **beitragspflichtige ~er** contributory members, dues payers *(US)*; **beratendes** ~ consultant member; **ehrenamtliches** ~ honorary member; **eingetragenes** ~ card-carrying (enrolled) member; **mit der offiziellen Parteipolitik nicht einverstandene ~er** members above the gangway *(Br.)*; **förderndes** ~ paying (subscribing) member; **früheres** ~ ex-member; **in Not geratenes** ~ needy member; **geschäftsführendes** ~ *(Aufsichtsrat)* managing director; **ordnungsgemäß gewähltes** ~ member duly appointed; **gründendes** ~ organizer; **hinzugewähltes** ~ coopted member, cooptee; **neues** ~ entrant, freshman member; **nichtständiges** ~ part-time (nonpermanent) member; **nominelles** ~ nominal member; **ordentliches** ~ regular (full) member; **ständiges** ~ permanent member; **stellvertretendes** ~ deputy member; **ursprüngliches** ~ charter (founder) member; **wahlberechtigtes** ~ voting member; **wichtigste ~er** key members; **zahlendes** ~ contributing (paying) member; **zahlende ~er** paid-up membership;
~ **einer Akademie** associate (corresponding member) of an academy (a society); ~ **kraft Amtes** member as of right, ex-officio member; ~ **des Aufsichtsrates** member of the board of supervisors; ~ **eines Ausschusses** committee member; ~ **eines Berufsverbandes** trade member; ~ **bei der Börse** member of the stock exchange, exchange seat; ~ **des Direktoriums** member of the board, board member; ~ **einer Fachberatergruppe** brain truster *(US)*; ~ **eines Geheimbundes** initiate member of a secret society; ~ **des Gemeinderats** member of the local council; **korrespondierendes ~ einer Gesellschaft** corresponding member of a society; ~ **der gleichen Gewerkschaft** fellow unionist *(US)*; ~ **des Kabinetts** cabinet minister *(Br.)*; ~ **eines Konsortiums** underwriter; ~ **einer gesetzgebenden Körperschaft** assembly-men, conscript fathers; ~ **auf Lebenszeit** life member; ~ **des Gemeinsamen Marktes** Common Market Country; ~ **des Oberhauses** peer; ~ **der Opposition** oppositionist; ~ **einer Partei** party member; ~ **des Parteivorstands** party official *(US)*; ~ **einer Schauspielertruppe** trouper; ~ **des Unterhauses** member of the House of Commons (M.P.); ~ **einer Untersuchungskommission** royal commissioner *(Br.)*; **~er einer Verbrauchergenossenschaft** consumer members; ~ **eines Vereins** [club] member, member of a club; ~ **des Vorstands** member of the executive board; ~ **des Wahlprüfungsausschusses** election judge; ~ **der Europäischen Währungsschlange** snake country;
~ **aufnehmen** to admit a member (to membership); **als ~ ausscheiden** to cease to be a member; ~ **ausschließen** to strike a member off the list, to expel a member; **einer Gesellschaft als ~ beitreten** to enrol(l) o. s. in a society; **viele ~er besitzen** to have a large membership; **j. als ~ eintragen** to enrol s. o. in a society; **als ~ nicht in Betracht kommen** to be ineligible for membership; ~ **sein** to belong to, to be a member; **eingetragenes ~ sein** to be upon the books; ~ **eines Ausschusses sein** to sit on a committee; **aktives ~ in einem Verein sein** to take an active part in a club; **an die ~er verschicken** to mail out to the members *(US)*; **zur Aufnahme als ~ vorschlagen** to propose for membership; **j. als ~ wählen** to elect s. o. as a member; ~ **werden** to join a club.

Mitglieder | abwerbung *(Gewerkschaft)* raiding of members *(US)*; ~**ausschluß** exclusion of a member; ~**auswahl** membership selection; ~**begrenzung** membership limitation; ~**bestand** number of members; **wechselnder ~bestand** fluctuating membership; **in ihrer ~eigenschaft** *(Satzung)* in their capacity as members; ~**haftung** liability of members; ~**liste** membership roll, membership list, club book; **auf der ~liste stehen** to be on (upon) the books; **jem. von der ~liste streichen** to drop a member from the rolls; ~**rechte** membership rights; ~**rückgang** reduction of members; ~**staat** member country; ~**überwachung** membership supervision; ~**versammlung** meeting of members, general meeting; ~**verzeichnis** membership list (register, roll), club book, *(Aktiengesellschaft)* shareholders' register *(Br.)*, stock ledger *(US)*; ~**währung** *(OECD)* member's currency; ~**werbung** membership drive, campaign for members.

Mitgliederzahl *(Partei)* enrolled strength;
beschlußfähige ~ quorum; **große** ~ large membership; **höchstzulässige** ~ maximum membership.

Mitglieder | zustimmung consent of members; ~**zuwachs** expansion of membership.

Mitglieds | abzeichen badge; **sein ~abzeichen erhalten** to get one's colo(u)rs; ~**anteil** membership interest; ~**antrag** membership application; ~**aufnahme** admission to membership, affiliation; ~**ausschluß** expulsion of a member; **vorübergehender ~ausschluß** suspension of a member; ~**ausweis** membership ticket (card); ~**beitrag** membership contribution (dues, fee), club subscription, affiliation fee; ~**beitrag von 20 Dollar zahlen** to subscribe $ 20 to a club.

Mitgliedschaft membership, fellowship, seat;
aufrechterhaltene ~ continued membership; **auswärtige** ~ associateship; **beitragsfreie** ~ free membership; **korporative** ~ association membership; **lebenslängliche** ~ life membership; ~ **von Amts wegen** ex-officio membership; ~ **in einer Gewerkschaft** union membership; ~ **bei der Landeszentralbank** federal reserve membership *(US)*;
seine ~ bei der Börse aufgeben to drop one's exchange seat; **seine ~ aufheben** to discontinue (withdraw from) membership, to take one's name off the books; **jem. von der ~ ausschließen** to exclude s. o. from membership, *(vorübergehend)* to suspend s. o. from membership; ~ **für j. beantragen** to put a name down for membership; **seine ~ beibehalten** to keep one's name on the books; **seine ~ erneuern** to renew one's membership; ~ **erwerben** to become a member, to acquire membership; ~ **verlieren** to cease to be a member, to be expelled from a society.

Mitgliedschafts | antrag application for membership, membership application; ~**ausschuß** membership committee, membership card (ticket); ~**bedingungen** membership terms; ~**begrenzung** membership limitation; ~**bewerber** applicant for admission, entrant; ~**dauer** duration of membership.

mitgliedschaftsfähig eligible for membership.

Mitgliedschafts | kosten cost of membership; ~**kreis erweitern** to expand membership; ~**liste** membership list; ~**rechte** rights in respect of membership, membership rights; **der ~rechte berauben** to dismember; ~**steuer** dues tax *(US)*; ~**verzeichnis** membership list; ~**voraussetzungen** qualifications for membership, membership requirements; ~**voraussetzungen erfüllen** to qualify for membership; ~**vorrechte** membership privileges; ~**zwang** *(Gewerkschaft)* closed shop provisions *(US)*.

Mitglieds | erklärung, beigefügte membership form provided; ~**firma** member firm (corporation); ~**gebühr** membership charge; ~**karte** membership card, ticket; ~**klasse** *(Versicherung)* occupational class; ~**klausel** new members clause; **aus ~kreisen** from among the members; ~**land** member country; ~**nummer** membership number; ~**scheck** member check (cheque); ~**staat** member state (nation); ~**währung** *(Währungsfonds)* member's currency.

mithaften to be jointly liable.

Mit | häftling fellow prisoner; ~**haftung** joint liability.

mithalten, mit der modernen Entwicklung to keep pace with modern invention; **mit der ausländischen Konkurrenz ~** to keep up with foreign competitors; **Zeitung ~** to have a joint subscription for a newspaper.

mithelfen to lend a helping hand;
bei einer Arbeit ~ to assist in doing a job.

Mit | herausgeber joint (associate) editor, coeditor, *(Buch)* subeditor; ~**hilfe** aid, assistance, cooperation; ~**hilfe bei der Wohnungsbeschaffung** housing assistance; **jem. seine ~hilfe anbieten** to offer to help s. o.; ~**hördienst** monitoring service; ~**höreinrichtung** listening (monitoring) device, monitor, *(Abhören)* wire tap (tapping).

mithören to listen in, *(abhören)* to wiretap, to monitor;
unerlaubtes ~ von Telefongesprächen wire tapping; **unberechtigt ~** to listen in, to monitor; **ganze Unterhaltung ~** to overhear the whole conversation; **letzte Vorlesung nicht ~** not to attend the last lecture.

Mit | hörer listener-in, monitor, *(unberechtigt)* wire tapper; ~**hörstelle** monitoring station; ~**hörtaste** *(Telefon)* listening (monitoring) key.

Mit | inhaber [co]partner, coowner, joint partner (holder, proprietor), associate sharer, member of a firm; ~**interessent** privy.

mitkämpfen to see action.
Mitkandidat running mate.
mitkommen, mit dem Bus to catch a bus; **bis zum Bus** ~ to accompany s. o. to the busstop; **in Englisch gut** ~ *(Schüler)* to keep up in English; **finanziell** ~ to keep abreast with, to afford it; **bei etw. nicht mehr** ~ to be beyond s. o.;
bei einer Vorlesung schwer ~ **können** to find it difficult to understand a lecture.
mitkriegführender Staat cobelligerent state.
mitlaufen to walk with s. o.;
Tonband ~ **lassen** to have the tape recorder running.
Mitläufer fellow traveller, sympathizer, follower, nominal member, hanger-on, bandwaggoner;
~ **sein** to climb (jump) on the bandwaggon;
~**effekt** bandwaggon effect; ~**typen** bandwaggon personalities.
Mitleid, von ~ **erfüllt** touched with pity;
an jds. ~ **appellieren** to appeal to s. o., to show pity; **jds. Herz mit** ~ **erfüllen** to penetrate s. one's heart with pity; **jds.** ~ **erregen** to move s. o. to pity; **öffentliches** ~ **erregen** to excite (provoke) public pity; **vom** ~ **anderer Leute leben** to live on charity; **keines** ~**s fähig sein** to be destitute of sympathy; ~ **zu erregen suchen** to tell the tale *(coll.)*; ~ **verdienen** to command sympathy.
Mitleidenschaft, in ~ **gezogen** adversely affected;
durch einen Streik in ~ **gezogen sein** to be impaired by a strike.
mitleiderregendes Aussehen pitiful appearance.
mitleidig sympathetic, compassionate;
j. ~ **ansehen** to look at s. o. with sympathy; ~ **gestimmt sein** to incline to pity.
mitleidslos unpitying, pitiless.
Mit|leiter joint manager; ~**leitung** joint directorship.
mit|lesen, mit jem. to read with s. o.; **Zeitung** ~**lesen** to have a joint subscription to a newspaper; ~**liefern** to accompany delivery.
Mitliquidator coliquidator.
mitmachen to play ball, to make one of the party, to take part, to join in;
aktiv ~ to get in on the act, to take an active part; **alles** ~ to be easy, to be a good sport; **Expedition** ~ to take part in an expedition; **bei einer Flasche Wein** to join s. o. in a bottle of wine; **kräftig** ~ to pitch in *(US)*; **zwei Kriege** ~ to live through two wars; **nicht mehr lange** ~ not to last much longer; **so eben nur mal** ~ to go along for the ride *(sl.)*; **verrückte Mode** ~ to go in for a crazy fashion; **bei etw. nicht** ~ to draw the line at s. th.; **bei einer Rettungsaktion** ~ to help in a rescue operation;
viel ~ **müssen** to have to suffer a lot.
Mitmensch fellow creature (human), fellow man, fellow, contemporary;
lästiger ~ nuisance;
~**en abstoßen** to hold off people; **über seine** ~**en zu hart urteilen** to be too harsh in one's judgment of people; **seine** ~**en zu behandeln (nehmen) wissen** to be diplomatic in dealing with people.
Mitmieter flatsharer *(Br.)*.
mitmischen to have a finger in the pie;
bei einer Schlägerei heftig ~ to join in a fight with gusto; **auf dem Weltmarkt** ~ to compete (hold one's own) in world markets.
Mitnahme|von Aktien picking up of shares; ~ **kleinster Spekulationsgewinne** scalping *(US)*.
Mitnehmen|im Auto pickup, free ride;
zum ~ take away (home), for off-consumption *(Br.)*.
mitnehmen *(ausleihen)* to borrow, *(Tourist)* to take in *(US)*;
j. ~ to make s. o. one's partner, *(überanstrengen)* to pull s. o. down, to wear s. o. out; **Aktien** ~to pick up shares; **j. arg** ~ to take toll of s. o., *(Krankheit)* to take a lot out of s. o.; **j. im Auto** ~to give s. o. a ride (lift); **Paket** ~ to take along a parcel; **Schirm** ~ to make off with an umbrella; **Schmucksachen und Bargeld** ~ *(Einbrecher)* to go off with cash and jewel(le)ry; ~**, was man kriegen kann** to pocket whatever one can get hold of;
sich im Auto ~ **lassen** to hitch a ride, to hitchhike.
Mit|pacht joint tenancy; ~**pächter** joint tenant (lessee), colessee, cotenant; ~**pachtung** joint tenancy; ~**pensionär** fellow boarder.
mitreden to put in a word or two;
aus Erfahrung ~ to base one's contribution in a conversation on experience; **bei einer Verhandlung** ~ to join in a negotiation;
Wörtchen ~ **können** to have a say in a matter.
Mit|reeder part (joint) owner, copartner in a ship; ~**reederei** coownership (joint ownership) of ships, copartnership; ~**reisender** copassenger, fellow travel(l)er (passenger).
mitreißen, Brücke to sweep away a bridge; **Publikum** ~ to carry away the audience; **Tänzer** ~ *(Band)* to infect the dancers.
mitreißende Rede rousing speech.
mit|schicken to send along, to enclose; ~**schleifen** to drag along.
mitschleppen, sein ganzes Gepäck to take the entire luggage with one; **j. zu einer Veranstaltung** ~ to take s. o. along to an event.
mitschreiben to write (take) down;
in Kurzschrift ~ to take down in shorthand; **Rede** ~ to record a speech; **Vorlesung** ~ to take lecture notes, to take notes of a lecture.
Mitschuld complicity, *(Vorschubleistung)* accessoriness;
an einem Verkehrsunfall ~ **haben** to be equally to blame for an accident; **der** ~ **stark verdächtig sein** to be strongly suspected of being an accomplice; **j. der** ~ **überführen** to prove s. one's complicity.
mitschuldig partly to blame, *(strafrechtlich)* accessory, privy;
sich ~ **machen** to be guilty in the eyes of the law; ~ **an einem Verbrechen sein** to be implicated in a crime.
Mit|schuldiger accessory, accomplice, privy; ~**schuldner** joint (fellow) debtor (obligator), codebtor; ~**schüler** fellow disciple, classmate, bookmate.
mitspielen to take part, to accompany, *(Faktoren)* to have a bearing;
jem. arg ~ to cook s. one's goose; **seinem Geschäftspartner böse** ~ to play a shabby trick on one's partner; **dem Obstgarten böse** ~ *(Sturm)* to wreak havoc among the fruit trees; **in einem Theaterstück** ~ to act in a play;
~ **müssen** to have to go along with.
Mitspieler player, participant.
Mitsprache say in a matter;
~ **bei etw. fordern** to demand a voice in s. th.
Mitspracherecht say in a matter, voice in some affairs, *(Firma)* voice in the management, codetermination;
angemessenes ~ fair say;
entscheidendes ~ **haben** to be closely involved with decisions.
mitsprechen to have one's say;
für eine Entscheidung ~ to influence a decision;
~ **können** to be able to express an opinion; **aus Erfahrung** ~ **können** to base one's contribution on experience.
mitstenografieren to take down in shorthand.
Mitstreiter comrade-in-arms.
Mittag midday, noon;
nur eine Stunde ~ **machen** to have only one hour's break for lunch; **im** ~ **seines Lebens stehen** to be in the prime of one's life.
Mittagessen, vor dem preprandial;
einfaches ~ simple lunch, piece *(US)*; **verbilligtes** ~ subsidized lunch;
~ **im Freien** alfresco lunch; ~ **in der eigenen Kantine** *(Inserat)* canteen lunch provided; ~ **zum Mitnehmen** take-out *(sl.)*; ~ **in der Tüte** nose-bag;
~ **über Spesen abrechnen** to justify a lunch as business expense; **j. zum** ~ **auffordern** to ask s. o. to stay to lunch; **etw. zum** ~ **bestellen** to order s. th. for lunch; ~ **einnehmen** to lunch;
~**bon** meal ticket; ~**zuschuß** lunch allowance.
mittägliche Ruhe noon rest, siesta.
mittags|geschlossen closed for lunch;
~ **nach Hause fahren** to be going home during lunchtime.
Mittags|ausgabe noon edition (paper); ~**gast** *(Restaurant)* lunch-time guest; ~**mahlzeit** lunch, midday snack; ~**pause** lunch (meal) break, noon (meal) interval; **einstündige** ~**pause** an hour's break for lunch; ~**ruhe** noon rest; ~**schicht** second shift; ~**spaziergang** lunch-time stroll; ~**tisch** eating place, luncheon quarter; **billiger** ~**tisch** sloppy Joe's *(sl.)*; **freier** ~**tisch** free luncheon facilities; ~**verabredung** luncheon meeting (commitment); **geschäftliche** ~**verabredung** business lunch; ~**zeit** noontime, noontime, lunch time (hour).
Mittäter fellow criminal, fellow in crime, accomplice, accessory during the fact, partner in crime, principal in the second degree, joint tortfeaser (offender);
als ~ **angeklagt** indicted for (on a charge of) complicity;
seine ~ **denunzieren** to denounce one's accomplices.
Mittäterschaft joint tortfeasers, complicity, aiding and abetting.
Mitte middle, center *(US)*, centre *(Br.)*, *(pol.)* the middle party;
ab durch die ~! off with you! scram!; **auf** ~ **gesetzt** *(drucktechn.)* centered; **in der** ~ **befindlich** mid; **in der** ~ **liegend** median; **in der** ~ **des Schiffes** amidships; **rechts von der** ~ to the right of the centre;
goldene ~ happy (golden) mean; **rechte** ~ *(pol.)* right center *(US)* (centre, *Br.*);
~ **des Hauptschiffahrtsweges** middle line of main channel; ~ **der Straße** middle of the road; ~ **der Woche** midweek;

sich politisch links von der ~ eingruppieren to place one's viewpoint left of the center *(US)* (centre, *Br.*); **goldene ~ halten** to stick to a happy medium; **sich der politischen ~ nähern** to shuffle towards the center; **Verwundeten in die ~ nehmen** to take the wounded man between them; **genau in die ~ treffen** to hit the bull's eye; **aus ihrer ~ wählen** to elect from (among[st]) themselves; **ziemlich in der ~ zwischen A und B wohnen** to live more or less halfway between A and B;
~-Linkskoalition center *(US)* (centre, *Br.*) -left coalition government.

mitteilen to let know, to inform, to advise, to transmit, to send word, *(wissen lassen)* to convey, to communicate;
jem. etw. ~ to let s. o. know, to make known to s. o., to pass s. th. on to s. o.; **sich jem. ~** to unbosom o. s. to s. o.; **amtlich ~** to notify; **seine Ansicht ~** to give one's opinion; **formgerecht ~** to give due notice; **jem. eine Nachricht schonend ~** to break the news gently to s. o.; **sich dem Publikum ~** *(Erregung)* to spread through the audience; **Resultat ~** to write the result; **jem. seinen Verdacht ~** to inform s. o. of one's suspicions; **vertraulich ~** to tell in strict confidence, to intimate.

mitteilsam conversable, communicative, talkative.

Mitteilung information, notice, communication, intelligence, *(amtliche Bekanntgabe)* notice, notification, *(Nachricht)* message, *(geschäftliche Nachricht)* advice, notice;
durch besondere ~ by special notice; **ohne vorherige ~** without prior (previous) notice;
amtliche ~en official communication (news); **ausdrückliche ~** express notice; **dienstliche ~** official communication, report; **erforderliche ~** due notice; **gegenteilige ~** notification to the contrary; **geschäftliche ~** business press; **geschäftliche ~en** commercial communications, *(Rundfunk)* commercial announcements, commercials; **durch Aussageverweigerungsrecht geschützte ~** privileged information; **gleichlautende ~** copy; **innerbetriebliche ~** interoffice memo, bucket slip; **kurze ~** card; **mündliche ~** verbal message (communication); **öffentliche ~** public announcement; **private ~** private communication; **sachdienliche ~en** pertinent information; **schriftliche ~** notice in writing, written notice (message); **telefonische ~** telephone message (communication); **telegrafische ~** telegraphic communication; **der Schweigepflicht (Ausssageverweigerung) unterliegende ~** privileged communication; **vertrauliche ~** confidential (inside) information, intimation, restricted information, private news;
~ über die Ablehnung einer Aktienzuteilung letter of regret; **~ über die Anzeigentarife** rate announcement; **~ über aufgehobene Belastungen** notice of satisfaction; **[etwa] amtliche ~ im Bundesanzeiger** gazette entries *(Br.)*; **~ über seine Eigeninteressen (Selbstbeteiligungen)** *(Vorstandsmitglied)* disclosure of interest; **~ über die Einberufung zur Hauptversammlung** special notice; **~ der Entscheidungsreife** note of issue *(US)*; **~ über die erfolgte Geschäftsausdehnung** expansion announcement; **~ über mögliche Interessenkollision** *(Vorstandsmitglied)* general notice; **~ des Justizministeriums** Justice announcement; **~ an die Öffentlichkeit** bulletin, communiqué; **~ über den Programmförderer** *(Rundfunk)* sponsorship announcement; **~ der Rechtsmittelzulassung** note of allowance; **~ der Terminfestsetzung** *(Gericht)* note of issue *(US)*; **~ über die Unzustellbarkeit** return of nihil; **~ über den Verkündungstermin** notice of judgment; **~ über die nicht erfolgte Zahlung** advice of nonpayment;
~ [am Schwarzen Brett] anschlagen to put a note on the bulletin board; **~ vertraulich behandeln** to regard a communication as confidential; **~ entgegennehmen** to take a message; **~ hinterlassen** to leave a message; **~ machen** to inform; **jem. eine ~ machen** to bring s. th. to s. one's notice; **vertrauliche ~ preisgeben** to disclose a confidence.

Mitteilungs|bedürfnis need to communicate; **~bestätigungswort** *(mil.)* message authenticator.

Mitteilungsblatt bulletin, *(Informationsblatt)* newsletter;
amtliches ~ [official] gazette (journal) *(Br.)*; **diplomatisches ~** diplomatic gazette.

Mitteilungs|pflicht duty to disclose (of disclosure); **~verzicht** waiver of notice.

Mittel instrument, vehicle, *(Durchschnitt)* average, mean, *(Geldmittel)* means, funds, resources, purse, wherewithal, capital, money, *(med.)* treatment, *(Parlament)* money, supplies *(Br.)*, appropriation, *(Vermögen)* fortune, *(Vorrat)* supply, *(Vorrichtung)* appliance, device, tool;
aller ~ beraubt destitute of all means; **aus eigenen ~n** out of one's resources; **aus Mangel an ~n** from deficiency of means, for lack of funds; **im ~** on an average; **im Besitz hinreichender ~** independent; **im Besitz verfügbarer ~** in funds; **mit reichlichen ~n ausgestattet** well-financed; **mit öffentlichen ~n finanziert** taken out of the public pocketbook; **nicht aus öffentlichen ~n unterstützt** nonprovided; **ohne ~** penniless, destitute, without resources, stranded; **unter Anwendung unerlaubter ~** by unlawful means;
angelegte ~ invested capital; **langfristig angelegte ~** long-term (funded) capital; **anregendes ~** stimulant; **arithmetisches ~** arithmetic mean; **aufgebrachte ~** funds raised; **aufgenommene ~** borrowed funds, borrowings; **aufgewandte ~** money employed; **ausländische ~** foreign capital; **ausreichende finanzielle ~** sufficiency of money; **nicht ausreichende ~** insufficient means, inadequate resources; **begrenzte ~** limited resources (means); **benötigte ~** necessary funds; **berauschende ~** intoxicants, drugs; **bereitgestellte ~** appropriated (earmarked) funds; **neu bereitgestellte ~** new appropriations; **bereitstehende ~** available funds; **beschränkte ~** limited resources; **beträchtliche ~** ample means; **bewährtes ~** proved remedy; **bewilligte ~** allocated funds; **zur Defizitdeckung bewilligte ~** deficiency appropriations; **vom Parlament bewilligte ~** budgetary appropriations, money provided by Parliament *(Br.)*; **billige ~** easy money; **brachliegende ~** idle funds, dead capital; **durchlaufende ~** transitory items; **eigene ~** own funds, resources of one's own, *(Bilanz)* capital and reserves; **eingebrachte ~** capital invested; **nicht einwandfreie ~** low-down methods; **empfängnisverhütende ~** contraceptives; **entsprechende ~** adequate means; **erforderliche ~** necessary funds; **erststellige ~** money lent on first mortgage; **festliegende ~** frozen capital, lockup *(Br.)*; **finanzielle ~** (pecuniary) financial resources; **flüssige ~** available (liquid) funds, funds on hand, near (ready) money, quick (liquid, *US*) assets (resources), current funds, liquid capital, *(Bilanz)* cash; **fremde ~** borrowed (third-party) funds, borrowed capital; **geringfügige ~** limited means; **von der Bausparkasse zur Verfügung gestellte ~** building society funds; **gewogenes ~** weighted mean; **greifbare ~** available funds; **sofort greifbare ~** quick assets; **haftende ~** amount guaranteed, guarantee fund; **hinreichende ~** sufficient funds; **investierte ~** capital invested; **kapitalmarktreife ~** funds available for the capital market; **knappe ~** narrow means; **kurzfristige ~** quick assets; **langfristige ~** long-term funds; **liquide ~** available (current) funds, liquid *(US)* (current) assets, liquid capital; **sofort verfügbare liquide ~** spot cash; **öffentliche ~** public funds (purse, money) *(Br.)*; **private ~** private means (funds); **reichliche ~** ample funds; **schmerzstillende ~** painkillers; **staatliche ~** government grant; **stärkendes ~** tonic, cordial; **die mir zur Verfügung stehenden ~** the money at my command; **alle uns zur Verfügung stehenden ~** the whole of our resources; **zur Handelsausweitung zur Verfügung stehende ~** means of extending the trade; **zusätzliche für die Masseverteilung zur Verfügung stehende ~** surplus estate funds; **terminierte ~** long-term funds; **überschüssige ~** surplus funds; **unbedeutende ~** small resources; **unerschöpfliche ~** endless resources; **unzulässige ~** undue influence; **unzureichende ~** slender means; **vagabundierende ~** hot money; **verfassungsmäßige ~** constitutional (insufficient) means; **verfügbare ~** available means (funds), funds at deposit (disposal); **alle verfügbaren ~** all available resources; **frei verfügbare ~** loose funds, quick assets; **nicht verteilte (verwendete) ~** unapplied (unappropriated) funds; **von der Bank verwaltete ~** bank funds; **treuhänderisch verwaltete ~** trustee investment *(Br.)*, trust fund *(US)*; **nicht verwendete ~** unapplied (unappropriated) funds; **im Haushaltsplan nicht vorgesehene ~** unbudgeted appropriations; **für den Wiederaufbau vorgesehene ~** funds for reconstructions; **zur Deckung vorhandene ~** coverage; **wirtschaftliche ~** economic resources; **zugesagte ~** promised funds; **zweckbestimmte (zweckgebundene) ~** earmarked (appropriated) funds; **zweckentfremdete ~** diverted (unused) funds;
~ der Direktwerbung direct-mail media; **~ für die Forschung** research funds; **~ gegen die Inflation** deflationary instrument; **liquide ~ erster Ordnung** primary liquidity; **liquide ~ dritter Ordnung** tertiary liquidity; **~ einer Pensionskasse** pension fund money; **~ einer Stiftung** endowment fund; **~ der Verkaufsförderung** sales-promotion aids; **~ für die Warenbeschaffung** merchandise budget; **~ für den Wohnungsbau** funds for housing; **~ zum Zweck** means to an end;
~ abschöpfen to siphon off funds; **~ anderweitig anlegen** to convert funds to another purpose; **~ dem Zweck anpassen** to adjust the means to an end; **äußerste ~ anwenden** to take extreme measures; **nur einwandfreie ~ anwenden** to use only proper means; **alle erdenklichen ~ anwenden** to try every

possible means; ~ **aufbringen** to raise funds; **öffentliche ~ bestimmungsgemäß ausgeben** to use public money only for legitimate purposes; **mit ~n ausstatten** to endow with capital; **sich schwer tun, mit seinen ~n auszukommen** to have a hard fight to make both ends meet; **sich jds. ~ bedienen** to use s. o. as a stepping stone; **seinen ~n gemäß beitragen** to contribute according to one's means; **sich mit allen ~n um eine Position bemühen** to jockey for a position; **notwendige ~ bereitstellen** to make the necessary funds available; ~ **beschaffen** to procure capital, to raise funds; **nur unbedeutende ~ besitzen** to have inadequate means; ~ **bewilligen** to grant the money, *(Parlament)* to vote the appropriations (supplies, *Br.*); **zusätzliche ~ in Höhe von 156 Mio Dollar bewilligen** to vote $ 156 million in extra money; **als ~ zum Zweck dienen** to serve as a means to an end; **seine ~ einsetzen** to make a draft on one's means; **alle nur möglichen ~ einsetzen** to use every possible means to do s. th.; **seine ~ gemeinsam einsetzen** to pool one's resources; **seine ~ schwerpunktartig einsetzen** to make the most of one's resources; ~ **entziehen** to strip off funds; ~ **erbitten** to appeal for funds; **das ~ errechnen** to work out the average; **etw. mit friedlichen ~n erreichen** to achieve s. th. by peaceful means; **seine ~ erschöpfen** to exhaust one's resources; ~ **festlegen** to tie (lock, *Br.*) up funds, to immobilize capital; **Projekt lediglich mit eigenen ~n finanzieren** to bet one's own resources fully on a project; ~ **und Wege finden** to contrive ways and means, to provide instruments; **Beihilfe aus öffentlichen ~n gewähren** to subsidize from public funds; **zu unredlichen ~n greifen** to have recourse to foul means; **nur beschränkte ~ haben** to have only limited resources; **nicht genügend ~ haben** to be deficient in means; **ausreichend liquide ~ haben** to be liquid; **reichliche ~ [zur Verfügung] haben** to have ample means [at one's disposal]; **alle ~ aufgebraucht haben** to be at the end of one's resources; **keine ~ mehr zur Verfügung haben** to run (be) out of funds, to be in want of money; ~ **investieren** to put out funds; **bereitgestellte ~ um 4% kürzen** to trim one's appropriations by 4 per cent; **kein ~ unversucht lassen** to leave no stone unturned; **sich ins ~ legen** to interfere, to interpose, to intercede, to intervene; **sich für j. ins ~ legen** to intervene in s. one's defence; **sich beim Vater für den Sohn ins ~ legen** to intercede with the father for the son; **zur Durchführung eines Auftrags alle ~ mobilisieren** to throw all one's resources into a job; **zu drastischen ~n Zuflucht nehmen** to resort to drastic measures; **reichlich mit ~n versehen sein** to have ample means, to be flush of money; **sich mit allen ~n zur Wehr setzen** to fight against it with every available means; ~ **zur Verfügung stellen** to ladle out funds; **seine ~ überschreiten** to live beyond one's means; **öffentliche ~ unterschlagen** to misappropriate public funds *(Br.)*, to misapply public money; **mit öffentlichen ~n unterstützen** to subsidize; **über bedeutende ~ verfügen** to have large resources; **nur über beschränkte ~ verfügen** to have only limited resources; **über geringe ~ verfügen** to be short of money; **über umfangreiche ~ verfügen** to have ample resources; **erhebliche kommunale ~ verschlingen** to run away with a lot of ratepayers' money; **mit ~n versehen** to furnish with (put in) funds; ~ **sorgfältig verwalten** to nurse resources; ~ **und Zwecke verwechseln** to confound means with ends; ~ **verweigern** *(Parlament)* to refuse supplies; **wegen fehlender ~ nicht gestartet werden** to be held up by lack of money; ~ **anderen als den vorgesehenen Zwecken zuführen** to alienate funds from their proper destination; **j. ohne ~ zurücklassen** to leave s. o. penniless; ~ **zurückstellen** to appropriate funds; ~ **zweckentfremden** to alienate funds from their proper destination; **zur Anwendung seines letzten ~s zwingen** to put to one's trumps; **ihm ist jedes ~ recht** he stops at nothing;

~**abflüsse** efflux (outflow) of funds; ~**abschnitt** *(mil.)* central sector; ~**abschöpfung** siphoning off of funds; ~**alter** *(hist.)* dark (middle) ages; **kurzfristige ~anlage** short-term investment of funds; ~**ansammlung** accumulation of funds; ~**aufbringer** fund raiser; ~**aufbringung** fund raising, mobilization (raising, procurement) of funds; ~**aufkommen** accumulation of capital, inflow; ~**aufnahme der öffentlichen Hand** public borrowing.

mittelbar indirect, intermediate, mediate;

~ **haftpflichtig** secondarily liable *(US)*;

sich ~ auf die Preise auswirken to have an indirect influence on the prices;

~**er Besitz** constructive possession; ~**e Besitzverschaffung** constructive delivery; ~**er Boykott** secondary boycott; ~**e Erbfolge** mediate descent; ~**e Patentverletzung** contributory infringement; ~**e Produktion** indirect production; ~**er Schaden** consequential (indirect) damage; ~**er Streik** secondary strike; ~**e Übergabe** constructive delivery.

Mittel|beanspruchung *(Weltwährungsfonds)* drawings; ~**behörden** regional authorities; ~**bereitstellung** appropriation of funds, supply of capital, *(Parlament)* ways and means; ~**beschaffung** raising the necessary funds, borrowing; ~**betrieb** small firm, medium enterprise, medium-sized (small, *US*) business, medium-sized store *(US)*; ~- **und Kleinbetriebe** medium and small-scale enterprises, small business *(US)*; ~**bewilligung** appropriation; ~**bewilligung verzögern** to delay its funding; ~**bindung** freezing of funds, immobilization of funds, lockup of capital *(Br.)*; ~**deck** *(Schiff)* middle deck, steerage; ~**deutschland** Central Germany; ~**ding** intermediate, cross, compromise; ~**ding zwischen Personen- und Rennwagen** cross between a passenger car and a racing car; ~**einsatz** employment of funds; **unberechtigter ~einsatz** misdirection of funds; ~**entzug** withdrawal of funds; ~**ernte** average harvest; ~**europa** Central Europe.

mitteleuropäische Zeit Central European Time.

Mittel|fahrbahn central lane; ~**farbe** intermediate colo(u)r.

mittelfein middling, good medium;

~**e Papiere** medium-grade papers.

Mittel|festlegung immobilization of funds, lockup of capital *(Br.)*; ~**frequenz** medium frequency.

mittelfristig medium-dated, medium (intermediate) -term;

~ **und langfristig** medium and long term;

~**er Kredit** medium-term loan, intermediate credit.

Mittel|fristvorhersage mean range forecast; ~**gang** *(Kino)* aisle.

mittelgroß medium-sized, middling large;

~**er Staat** medium-ranking state; ~**es Unternehmen** medium enterprise; ~**e Wohnung** medium-sized dwelling.

Mittelgröße medium (middle) size;

in ~ moderate (medium) -sized.

Mittel|grund second distance *(Br.)*; **zur guten ~klasse gehören** to be fairly average; ~**klassewagen** intermediate-sized car; ~**konservierung** resource conservation; ~**kontrolle** funds control; ~**kurs** medium (mean rate) of exchange, middle market price *(Br.)*, average rate; ~**kurs halten** *(fig., pol.)* to trim, to maintain a middle position, to keep to the middle of the road; ~**kurs zwischen Planwirtschaft und freier Wirtschaft steuern** to steer a middle course between a planned and a free economy; ~**lage** central position; ~- **und Großlandwirte** middle and large farmers; ~**linie** center *(US)* (centre, *Br.*) line, *(Strom)* middle thread, medial line.

mittellos needy, impecunious, destitute, penniless, moneyless, barehanded, fundless, out of (without) funds, without means (resources), *(Schuldner)* poor;

ersichtlich ~ obviously without means;

~ **dastehen** to be stranded; ~ **sein** to be without means (out of all); **sich auf einmal völlig ~ vorfinden** to find o. s. with nothing to the fore; ~ **zurückbleiben** to be left unprovided for (destitute); **j. ~ zurücklassen** to leave s. o. penniless.

Mittellosigkeit impecuniosity, destitution, lack of funds (means), poverty, resourcelessness;

Einwand der ~ vorbringen to plead poverty.

Mittellosigkeitszeugnis certificate of poverty *(US)*.

Mittelmaß medium (average) size;

vernünftiges ~ einhalten to strike a happy medium; **über das ~ herausragen** to rise above mediocrity; **über das ~ nicht hinausgehen** to put up but an average performance.

mittelmäßig middling, mediocre, medium, middle-rate, mean, inferior, fair, tolerable, *(begabt)* moderate, *(durchschnittlich)* average;

ziemlich ~ pretty mediocre;

~**e Begabung** medium capacity; ~**es Buch** mediocre book.

Mittel|mäßigkeit mediocrity, mediocre performance, *(Begabung)* moderateness; ~**meer** the Mediterranean; ~**nachweis** evidence of means, means test; ~**ost** Middle East; ~**partei** center *(US)*, centre *(Br.)* party; ~**pfeiler** *(Brücke)* center *(US)* (centre, *Br.*) pier.

mittelprächtig so-so, not so bad.

Mittelpreis medium (middle) price.

Mittelpunkt *(fig.)* heart, center *(US)*, centre *(Br.)*, nucleus, focus, soul, *(math.)* median point;

sprachlicher ~ speech center *(US)* (centre, *Br.*);

~ **des Interesses** focus of interest; ~ **des Lebensinteresses** center *(US)* (centre, *Br.*) of vital interest; **kultureller ~ einer Stadt** cultural center *(US)* (centre, *Br.*) of a town;

~ **eines Abends sein** to be the center of attention of an evening; **im ~ der Öffentlichkeit stehen** to be in the limelight (centre of interest), to hold the spotlights; **in den ~ stellen** to center; **sich um einen ~ versammeln** to gather round a nucleus;

~**schule** consolidated school *(US)*.

Mittel|qualität middle (middling) quality; **gute ~qualität** good middling quality; **~rückfluß** reflux of funds, *(Investmentfonds)* outflow; **~rückkaufswert** *(Versicherungsjahr)* mean reserve; **gebildete ~schicht** middle-class professional people; **gehobene ~schicht** middle upper class; **untere ~schicht** lower middle class; **~schiene** *(Bahn)* point rail; **~schrift** *(drucktechn.)* double minion; **~schulbildung** middle-school course *(Br.)*, secondary education; **~schule** middle *(Br.)* (secondary, grammar, *US*, junior high, *US*, intermediate, *US*) school; **von der ~schule ohne Abschluß abgehen** to drop out of high school *(US)*; **~schüler** secondary school pupil, high-school boy (graduate) *(US)*; **~schullehrgang** high-school course *(US)*.
mittelschwerer Lastkraftwagen light (pickup) truck.
Mittels|leute, über mehrere at third hand; **~mann** middleman, intermediary, go-between, broker; **mit jem. durch einen ~mann Verbindung aufnehmen** to get in touch with s. o. through a middleman.
Mittelsorte medium quality, average sort, seconds, middlings; **gute ~** good medium (middling) quality.
Mittelsperson intermediary, middleman.
Mittelstadt large burgh *(Scot.)*.
Mittelstand middle class[es], *(Geschäftsinhaber)* small business *(US)*;
gehobener ~ upper middle class; **gewerblicher ~** medium and small-scale enterprises, small business *(US)*.
mittelständisch middle-class;
~e Gesellschaft middle-class society; **~er Handel** small traders (business men); **~es Unternehmen** medium-sized (small, *US*) business.
Mittelstands|ausschuß small-businessmen's committee *(US)*; **~bereich** small-business sector *(US)*; **~empfehlungen** small-business recommendations *(US)*; **~kredit** small-business investment credit (administration loan) *(US)*; **~programm** middle-class program(me); **~unternehmen** medium-sized business, small-business venture *(US)*.
mittelstarker Wagen medium-powered car.
Mittel|stellung intermediate position; **~stellung zwischen Hersteller und Verbraucher einnehmen** to act as a link between producer and consumer; **~straße** *(Ausstellungshalle)* midway *(US)*.
Mittelstrecken|bomber medium-range bomber (MRB); **~flugzeug** medium-range aircraft; **~geschoß** *(mil.)* intermediate-range ballistic missile (IRBM); **~rakete** intermediate-range ballistic missile, medium-range missile; **in Europa stationierte ~raketen** theatre forces; **~verkehr** medium-range air traffic.
Mittel|streifen *(Autobahn)* center strip *(US)*, central reservation; **~stück** centerpiece *(US)*, centrepiece *(Br.)*; **~stufe** *(Schule)* shell *(Br.)*, intermediate grades; **~überhänge** surplus resources (funds); **~überlassung** borrowing, lending; **~überweisung** resource transfer; **~verteilung** resource allocation; **~verwendung** application of proceeds, disposition (use, employment) of funds, allocation of resources; **~ware** medium [goods].
Mittelweg, goldener golden (happy) mean, just medium; **~ einschlagen** to keep middle of the road, to take a middle course; **goldenen ~ einschlagen** to stick to a happy medium.
Mittelwelle *(Rundfunk)* medium wave.
Mittelwellen|bereich medium-wave range; **~empfang** medium-wave reception; **~funk** standard broadcast; **~sender** medium-wave transmitter.
Mittelwert mean [value], mean number, average value;
arithmetischer ~ arithmetic mean; **gewogener ~** weighted mean; **größter ~** extreme mean; **korrigierter ~** corrected mean; **~ errechnen** to strike a mean, to average.
Mittel|zufluß flow (influx, inflow) of funds, funds flow; **zweckentfremdete ~zuführung** alienation of funds from their natural channels.
Mittelzuweisung appropriation of funds, assignment of funds; **detaillierte ~** itemized (segregated) appropriations;
~ für das Hilfsprogramm aid appropriation; **~ an die Kommunen** general grant *(Br.)*;
seine Zuständigkeiten bei der ~ voll ausschöpfen to exercise the power of the purse.
Mitternacht, bis nach ~ arbeiten to study deep into the night, to burn the midnight oil.
mitternächtliche Stille midnight silence.
Mitternachts|ball late night ball; **~schicht** midnight (lobster, *US*) shift; **~stunden** midnight hours.
Mittestamentsvollstrecker joint executor, coexecutor.
Mittler mediator, intermediary, middleman, medium;
~ für gewerbliche Informationen publicity agent;
als ~ auftreten to act as intermediary.
mittler middle, central;
von ~em Alter middle-aged; **von ~er Art und Güte** of reasonable fitness and quality; **~e Beamtenlaufbahn** second division *(Br.)*; **~er Beamter** subordinate (minor) officer; **~e Begabung** medium talent; **~es Einkommen** middle-bracket income; **~e Einkommensschichten** middle-income classes; **~e Entfernung** middle distance; **~e Führungsschicht** middle management; **~e Gehaltsklasse** middle-earning sector; **~e Größe** middling size; **von ~er Größe** middle-sized; **~e Lebensdauer** mean life; **~e Lebenserwartung** average life expectancy; **~er Lohnsatz** average rate of wages; **~e Ortszeit** mean local time; **~er Osten** Middle East; **~e Preislage** medium range; **~e Qualität** middling, medium quality; **~e Qualitäten** medium sorts; **~e Reife** [etwa] Ordinary General Certificate of Education *(Br.)*; **~er Stadtteil** center, centre *(Br.)*, downtown *(US)*, central part of a city; **~er Tiefgang** mean draught; **~es Unternehmen** medium-sized enterprise; **~er Verfalltag** average due date; **~er Zahlungstermin** average due date.
Mittler|tätigkeit ausüben to assume the role of an intermediary; **~vergütung** agency commission.
mittragen, Verlust to share a loss.
Mittreuhänder cotrustee.
mittschiffs amidships.
Mitunternehmer cocontractor, joint contractor.
mitunterschreiben, mitunterzeichnen to countersign.
Mitunterschrift countersignature.
Mit|unterzeichner, ~unterzeichneter joint signatory, comaker; **~unterzeichnung** countersignature; **~urheberrecht** joint copyright; **~ursache** concurrent cause.
mitverantwortlich co-responsible.
Mitverantwortung joint responsibility.
mitverdienen to contribute to the family income.
mitverdienende Ehefrau working (gainfully employed) wife.
Mit|verfasser joint author; **~verfasserschaft** joint authorship; **~verkäufer** joint seller.
mitverklagen to sue jointly.
Mit|verklagter joint respondent; **~vermächtnisnehmer** joint legatee, colegatee; **~verschulden** contributory (comparative, *US*) negligence; **beiderseitiges ~verschulden** mutual contributory negligence; **~verschwörer** fellow conspirator, partner to a conspiracy; **~versicherer** coinsurer.
mit|versichern to coinsure; **~versichert** coinsured.
Mit|verursachung contributory causation; **~vormund** special (joint) guardian, coguardian; **gerichtlich ernannter ~vormund** concurator; **~vormundschaft** joint guardianship, coguardianship; **~welt** contemporaries.
mitwirken to take part, to cooperate, to assist, to contribute;
bei der Aufdeckung eines Verbrechens ~ to cooperate in solving a crime; **auf der falschen Seite ~** to play on the wrong team; **am Sturz der Regierung ~** to contribute to the government's downfall; **bei einem Verkauf ~** to attend a sale.
mitwirkend concurrent, instrumental, cooperative;
~e Ursachen contributory causes; **~es Verschulden** contributory (concurrent) negligence.
Mitwirkender participant.
Mitwirkung participation, collaboration, instrumentality, cooperation, assistance, *(Konzert)* play, performance;
notwendige ~ bei der Auswechslung des Begünstigten *(Versicherung)* substantial compliance rule; **~ an einer Patentverletzung** contributory infringement.
Mit|wissen privity; **~wisser** confidant; **~wisser sein** to be in the know; **~wisserschaft** privity of knowledge, standing by, complicity, collusion.
mitzählen to count, to be counted;
nicht ~ to be of no importance.
Mit|zeichnung countersignature; **~zessionär** coassignee.
mitziehen, nicht to stand out of line.
Mixbecher shaker.
mixen, Cocktail to mix a cocktail.
Mixer mixer, bartender;
~ in einer Eisbar soda jerker *(US sl.)*.
Mob rabble, mob, riffraff, rout, canaille.
Möbel furniture, furnishings;
einfache ~ plain furniture; **fest eingebaute ~** fixed furniture; **gebrauchte ~** secondhand furniture; **geschmacklose ~** ugly furniture, trumpery furniture; **massive ~** massive furniture; **einem Eigentumsvorbehalt unterliegende ~** furniture under distraint; **wertvolle ~** valuable furniture; **zerlegbare ~** knockdown furniture;
sich eigene ~ anschaffen to find one's own furniture; **jds. ~ ausräumen** to turn out s. one's furniture; **nur ein paar ~ besitzen**

to own only a few sticks; ~ **aus einer Wohnung entfernen** to unfurnish an apartment; **eigene ~ haben** to have one's own furniture; ~ **auf Abzahlung kaufen (abstottern)** to buy furniture on the hire-purchase *(Br.)* (deferred payment, *US*) system; **jds. ~ wegen Mietschulden pfänden** to distrain upon s. one's furniture for rent; ~ **auf den Speicher (aufs Lager) stellen (verbringen)** to store (warehouse, *US*) furniture, to put furniture in storage; **mit den ~n farblich übereinstimmen** *(Vorhänge)* to be of a piece with the furniture; **Zimmer mit ~n vollstopfen** to lumber a room with furniture; **sich neue ~ zulegen** to invest in a new suite of furniture;

~aufstellung in einem neuen Haus arrangement of furniture in a new house; **~ausstellung** furniture exhibition; **~bau** furniture making; **~beschaffung** equipment with furniture, furnishing; **~beschlag** furniture fitting; **~fabrik** furniture factory; **~fabrikant** furniture manufacturer; **~garnitur** suite of furniture; **~geschäft** house furnisher, house furnishing firm (shop), furniture shop (store, *US*); **~- und Ausstattungsgeschäft** house-furnishing firm; **~händler** furniture dealer (broker); **~hersteller** furniture builder (fitter); **~industrie** furniture industry; **~laden** furniture shop (store, *US*); **~ladung** load of furniture; **~lager** pantechnicon *(Br.)*, [furniture] warehouse *(US)*; **~messe** furniture exhibition; **~miete** rent of the furniture, hiring of furniture; **~packer** furniture packer, removal man *(Br.)*; **~politur** furniture cream (polish), cabinet varnish; **~spediteur** remover *(Br.)*, removal contractor *(Br.)*, furniture mover, house mover *(US)*, warehouseman *(US)*; **~spedition, ~speditionsfirma** moving company *(US)*, removal firm *(Br.)*; **~speicher** pantechnicon *(Br.)*, [furniture] warehouse *(US)*; **~stil** style of furniture; **~stoff** upholstery fabric; **~stück** piece of furniture; **zerlegbares ~stück** knockdown furniture; **~stück auf seinen Platz schieben** to wheel a piece of furniture into a place; **~tischler** cabinetmaker; **~tischlerei** cabinet work, cabinetmaking; **~transport** removal of one's furniture, furniture removal; **~transportbehälter** lift van; **~transportgeschäft** remover *(Br.)*, mover *(US)*, warehouseman *(US)*; **~überzug** slipcover; **~versand** furniture transport; **~wagen** furniture car, moving (removing, *Br.*) van, removal van *(Br.)*, pantechnicon [van] *(Br.)*; **unbeschrifteter ~wagen** blind waggon; **~zentrum** furniture center *(US)*.

mobil mobile, *(fig.)* active;
~ **und munter** alive and kicking;
~ **bleiben** to be free to move about; **j. ~ machen** to rope s. o. in; **äußerst ~ sein** to be always on the move; **immer noch ~ sein** to be still hale and hearty; **wieder ganz ~ sein** to be quite fit again;
~er Nachrichtentrupp field intelligence team.

Mobiliar furniture, furnishings, appointments, movables, household goods, personal effects, mobiliary;
~ **und Zubehör** furniture and fixtures;
~erbe heir to personal estate; **~hypothek** chattel mortgage; **~klage** action in replevin; **~masse eines Konkursschuldners** movable property of a bankrupt; **~miete** hiring of a thing for use; **~pfand** chattel pledge; **~pfändung** personal poinding, seizure of movables, distress, distraint; **~schuldverschreibung** bill of sale; **~sicherheit** personal security, chattel mortgage; **~vermögen** personal property (effects, estate), personalty, expediment, *(Gesellschaft)* partnership personalty; **erbschaftssteuerfreies ~vermögen** free personalty; **~vermögenssteuer** personal property tax *(US)*; **~verpfändung** chattel mortgage; **~versicherung** furniture insurance; **~verzeichnis** inventory of household furniture; **~zwangsvollstreckung** execution levied by seizure.

Mobilien movable property, movables, effects, [goods and] chattels;
~konto equipment account.

mobilisierbar mobilizable.

mobilisieren to mobilize, *(flüssigmachen)* to realize, to convert into cash;
zur Durchführung eines Auftrags alle Hilfsmittel ~ to throw all one's resources into a job; **starke politische Kräfte ~** to have political muscle.

Mobilisierung mobilization, realization;
~ **der Wirtschaft** economic (industrial) mobilization.

Mobilisierungswechsel finance bill *(US)*.

Mobilität mobility;
gesamtwirtschaftliche ~ geographical mobility;
~ **der Arbeitskräfte** mobility of manpower, free movement of labo(u)r; **regionale ~ der Betriebe** industrial mobility.

Mobilitäts|prämie mobility bonus; **~zuschuß** mobility allowance.

mobilmachen *(mil.)* to mobilize, to whip up.

Mobilmachung *(mil.)* mobilization;
~ **der [Volks]wirtschaft** economic (industrial) mobilization.

Mobilmachungs|befehl mobilization order; **~plan** plan of mobilization; **höchste ~stufe anordnen** to place on full alert; **~tag** mobilization day, M-day; **~zulage** field allowance.

möblieren to furnish, to fit up;
Büro ~ to furnish an office; **neu ~** to refurnish; **Zimmer ~** to furnish a room.

möbliert|vermieten to let furnished apartments; **~ wohnen** to live in furnished lodgings (apartments, rooms), to stay at private lodgings;
~er Herr lodger, roomer *(US)*; **~e Wohnung** furnished flat *(Br.)* (apartment, *US*); **~es Zimmer** furnished room (apartment, *US*).

Möblierung furnishing, furnishment;
~ **eines Hauses** house furnishing.

Möchtegern would-be;
~erbe would-be heir.

Modalität modality, *(Vorbehalt)* proviso;
~en modality, terms of agreement, *(Vorbehalt)* restrictive clauses, proviso;
finanzielle ~en financial arrangements;
~ **einer Emission** terms and conditions of an issue; **~en der finanziellen Hilfe** terms of the financial assistance.

Mode fashion, style, mode, vogue, go, kick;
aus der ~ gekommen out of use (fashion), outmoded, played out *(sl.)*; **in ~** in use (vogue), fashionable, in general wear, in; **mit der neuesten ~ schritthaltend** up to the minute; **nach der neuesten ~** of the latest cut, according to the latest fashion; **von der ~ beeinflußt** fashion-led;
allerneueste ~ pink of fashion, all the kick (cry, *US*); **allgemeine ~** general run; **augenblickliche ~** fashion of the moment; **gegenwärtige ~** present fashion, fashion of the period; **geltende ~** fashion look; **große ~** fad, craze, all the rage; **herrschende ~** prevailing (leading) fashion; **augenblicklich herrschende ~** current fashion; **kommende ~** rising fashion; **neueste ~** conformity to fashion, height of fashion, the new look, the latest shape, all the vogue (cry, *US*); **schlanke ~** slim look;
~ **aufbringen (einführen)** to set up (create, introduce) a fashion; **neue ~ aufbringen** to strike out a new fashion; **~ beeinflussen** to set fashion trends; **~ bestimmen** to set the fashion; **in ~ bringen** to bring into fashion; **neue ~ einführen** to bring in a new fashion; **der ~ entsprechen** to conform to a fashion; **nach der neuesten ~ entwerfen** to style; **der ~ eine andere Richtung geben** to change the fashion; **sich stets nach der neuesten ~ kleiden** to dress in the latest fashion; **aus der ~ kommen** to get (go, come) out of fashion, to get out of date, to grow out of fashion (request), to go out of vogue; **in ~ kommen** to come in (up, in use), to catch it; **~ kreieren** to create (set) a fashion, to style *(US)*; **~ machen** to lead the fashion; **~ mitmachen, sich nach der ~ richten** to follow the fashion; **bald aus der ~ sein** to have short currency; **schon lange aus der ~ sein** to have been out for a long time; **gerade ~ sein** to be currently fashionable; **als Reiseziel die große ~ sein** to be very popular as a tourist country; **in ~ sein** to be in vogue; **neueste (die große) ~ sein** to be all the vogue (go now); **wieder in ~ sein** to be back in style (fashion); **der ~ unterworfen sein** to depend upon the fashion; **nach der ~ verfertigen** to fashion; **~ werden** to come into fashion;
~änderung fashion shift, changes in style *(US)*, style trend; **~artikel** fancy article, fashion merchandise (line, wear), *(pl.)* fancy (fashion) goods, novelties; **kleine ~artikel** notions *(US)*; **schnell verkäufliche ~artikel** fast-selling style *(US)*; **~ausdruck** vogue word.

modebedingte Finanzierungsmethoden fashion in financing.

Mode|beilage fashion supplement; **~berater** fashion adviser, fashionist.

mode|bestimmend sein to lead the fashion; **~bewußt** fashion-conscious; **~bewußt sein** to dress in the latest fashion.

Mode|bild fashion plate; **~blatt** fashion magazine; **~entwicklung** fashion trend; **~farbe** fashionable colo(u)r; **neuester ~fimmel** all the kick (cry, *US*); **~fotograf** glamo(u)r photographer; **~geck** dandy, fop, dude *(US)*; **~geschäft** outfitting shop, outfitter, fancy-goods business; **~haus** fashion house; **~heft** fashion journal (magazine), ladies' paper; **wie aus dem ~heft geschnitten sein** to be the mirror of fashion; **~held** fashionmonger, nut; **~industrie** fashions trade, fashion industry; **~journal** fashion journal (magazine, book, paper), ladies' paper; **~kenntnis** fashion knowledge; **~kolumne** *(Zeitung)* fashion syndicate letter; **~kontrast** fashion contrast; **~krankheit** fashionable complaint; **~künstler** fashion artist.

Modell model, pattern, form, archetype, example, shape, *(Ausführung)* design, *(Erstkonstruktion)* working model, prototype, copy, *(Maschine)* type, design, *(Person)* [fashion] model, mannequin, *(Stanze)* print;
nach dem lebenden ~ from life;
billiges ~ economy model; **einheitliches** ~ uniform pattern; **erstes** ~ prototype; **am meisten gefragtes** ~ hard-to-have girl; **geschütztes** ~ registered design; **unsere letzten (neuesten)** ~**e** our latest designs; **maßstabgerechtes** ~ scale model; **letzte Pariser** ~**e** the latest Paris models; **platzsparendes** ~ storage model; **veraltetes** ~ model T Ford *(US coll.)*; **verbessertes** ~ **von 1981** improvement design of 1981; **verkleinertes** ~ scale model; ~ **in der Größe einer Zigarettenpackung** cigarette-pack-size model; ~**e aus einer früheren Konjunkturperiode** past cyclical time pattern; ~ **einer Stadt** model town;
einem Künstler ~ **stehen** to pose for an artist;
~**abkommen** pattern agreement; ~**bau** pattern making; ~**bauer** model (pattern) maker; ~**beispiel** textbook example; ~**eisenbahn** scenic railway; ~**fall** market model, classic case; ~**firma** sample company; ~**flugzeug** prototype (model) aircraft, mockup; ~**formen in der Wirtschaft umgestalten** to reshape business patterns; ~**haus** show (model) house; **transportables** ~**haus** model mobile home.
modellieren to model, to mould *(Br.)*, to mold *(US)*.
Modell|jahr year of manufacture; ~**klasse** demonstration class; ~**kleid** model; ~**puppe** *(Schaufenster)* dummy, display figure; ~**salon** model room; ~**schlosser** pattern maker; ~**schreiner** cabinetmaker; ~**schreinerei** pattern shop; ~**schutz** protection of registered designs; ~**skizze** artist's impression; ~**stadt** show town (city); ~**studie** pilot study; ~**tarif** pattern agreement; ~**verfahren** model experiment; ~**verpachtung** licensing; ~**vertrag** prototype (standard) contract; ~**vorhaben** pilot project; ~**werkstätte** pattern shop; ~**wohnung** housing prototype, model dwelling, show flat, modular housing; ~**zeichner** pattern designer; ~**zeichnung** pattern drawing; ~**zug** model train.
Mode|manie vogue craze; ~**messe** exhibition of fashions, fancy fair; ~**narr** fashionmonger; ~**narren** slaves to fashion; **letzte** ~**neuheit** latest fashion (invention).
Modenschau fashion display (show, parade), dress parade, mannequin parade, style show *(US)*.
Modepuppe fashion plate, *(Schaufenster)* dummy, display figure.
Moder decay, rot, putrefaction;
nach ~ **riechen** to smell rotten.
Moder|fleck *(Kleid)* mildewy patch, *(an Wand)* damp spot; ~**geruch** mouldy fust.
moderieren to moderate;
Sendung ~ to present a (act as moderator in a) broadcast program(me).
moderig rotten, decaying, putrid, decomposed.
modern fashionable, modern, new, up-to-date, of recent date, stylish, in fashion (vogue), in general wear, streamlined *(US)*, *(fortschrittlich)* progressive, advanced, go-ahead, up-to-date, *(neumodisch)* newfangled;
höchst ~ tony *(sl.)*; **sehr** ~ up-to-the minute;
~ **eingerichtet** with all appointments;
~ **sein** to be in vogue (fashion); **ganz** ~ **sein** to be all the mode (cry, *US*); **gerade** ~ **sein** to be the vogue; **lange** ~ **sein** to have a long run; ~ **werden** to grow into fashion;
~**e Ansichten** modern (advanced) views; ~**e Erziehungsmethoden** progressive education; ~ **eingestellter Geschäftsmann** go-ahead business man; ~**es Haus** modern (up-to-date) house; ~**e Kontrollmethoden** stream-lined controls (methods); ~**e Kunst** contemporary art; ~**er Mensch** progressive person; ~**e Muster** exclusive patterns; ~**e Strömungen** progressive tendencies; ~**es Unternehmen** progressive organization; ~**en Verhältnissen anpassen** to streamline; ~**e Waffen** advanced weapons; ~**e Wissenschaft** the new learning;
~ *(v.) (schimmeln)* to decay, to rot, to putrefy, to mildew.
modernisieren to modernize, to bring up to date, to streamline;
Gebäude ~ to modernize a building; **Steuereintreibungsverfahren** ~ to streamline a tax-collection system; **Verwaltungs- und Schreibarbeiten** ~ to streamline administration and paperwork.
modernisiert werden to undergo conversion.
Modernisierung modernization, streamlining.
Modernisierungs|arbeiten an einem Gebäude durchführen to modernize a building; ~**bedürfnisse** modernization requirements; ~**beihilfe** aid for modernization; ~**kredit** modernization loan; ~**programm** modernization program(me); ~**prozeß** modernization process; ~**vorhaben** modernization project.
Modernität up-to-dateness;
fortschrittliche ~ streamlined modernity.
modernste|Bauart latest type; **mit** ~**m Komfort** with all modern conveniences.
Mode|sachverständiger fashion adviser, fashionist; ~**salon** fashion bureau (house); ~**schmuck** costume jewellery; ~**schöpfer** fancymonger, fashion designer (artist), stylist *(US)*, dress designer, dressmaker; **jüngste** ~**schöpfungen** latest creations; **letzter** ~**schrei** latest craze; ~**schriftsteller** fashion writer; ~**schule** school of fashion design; ~**spionage** fashion spying; ~**torheit** fad, craze, rage; ~**variationen** variety of fashion; ~**ware** fashion (fancy) articles, fancy goods, novelties, millinery *(Br.)*; ~**warengeschäft** fancy-goods business, millinery *(Br.)*; ~**warenhändler** dealer in fancy goods, milliner *(Br.)*; ~**wechsel** style trend (change); ~**welt** fashionable people (life); ~**wort** vogue word, cant term; **mit** ~**worten um sich schmeißen** to sling it; ~**zaren sein** to be the dictators of dress and fashion; ~**zeichner** dress (fashion) designer, styler *(US)*; ~**zeichnung** fashion design (pattern); ~**zeitschrift** fashion journal (magazine), ladies' paper.
Modifikation modification, qualification.
modifizieren to modify, to qualify;
Vertrag ~ to make modifications in a contract.
modifiziert modified, qualified.
modisch fashionable, all the kick (cry, *US*), stylish *(US)*, up-to-date;
~**er Akzent** fashionable touch; ~**e Einzelheit** fashion detail; ~**e Neuheiten** novelties.
Modistin milliner *(Br.)*.
Modul module.
Modulation modulation.
modulieren to modulate.
Modus mode, modus, method, manner;
~ **der Verständigung finden** to find an area of agreement.
Mogelei cheat, sharp practices, trickery;
durch eine ~ **erreichen** to get s. th. by a wangle.
mogeln to cheat, to trick, to crib *(Br.)*, to chisel *(coll.)*, to gyp *(US sl.)*, to fudge *(US sl.)*, to pigeon *(sl.)*;
jem. etw. in die Tasche ~ to slip s. th. into s. one's pocket.
Mogelpackung deceptive packing.
Mogler cheater, tricker, cribber *(Br.)*.
Möglich|e, alles all manner of things;
im Bereich des ~**en liegen** to be in the realm of the thinkable; **im Rahmen des** ~**en liegen** to be within the bounds of possibility.
möglich possible, *(durchführbar)* practicable, feasible, *(eventuell)* potential, contingent;
durchaus ~ very well possible; **so bald als** ~ at your earliest convenience; **so früh wie** ~ as early as possible; **so weit wie** ~ as far as possible, within limits;
etw. für ~ **halten** to consider s. th. likely; ~ **machen** to manage; ~ **sein** to be in posse;
alle nur ~**en Ausflüchte gebrauchen** to make all sorts of excuses; ~**er Bedarf** potential demand; ~**en Eintritt eines Ereignisses erwägen** to consider the event of a possibility; ~**es Heimfallrecht** possibility of reverter; ~**er Kunde** potential (prospective) customer, sales prospect *(US)*; ~**e Lösung eines Problems** feasible solution of a problem; ~**er Markt** potential market; **alle nur** ~**en Mittel** every means conceivable; ~**er Plan** feasible plan; **sich gegen** ~**e Unfälle versichern** to insure against possible accidents; **für alle nur** ~**en Zwecke** for all practical purposes.
Möglichkeit possibility, potentiality, resort, posse, vista, *(Gelegenheit)* chance, opportunity, odds, *(Durchführbarkeit)* practicability, feasibility, *(Wahl)* alternative;
angesichts der ~ on the chance; **für alle** ~**en gerüstet** provided for all eventualities; **im Rahmen seiner** ~**en** within one's means; **seinen** ~**en entsprechend** according to one's means;
~**en** facilities, means;
alle ~**en** full facilities; **sehr entfernte** ~ a thousand to one [chance]; **entferntere** ~ extraordinary (remote) possibility, outside chance; **geringe** ~ off chance; **nicht die geringste** ~ not a dog's chance; **geschäftliche** ~**en** business opportunities; **mangelnde** ~**en** want of facilities; **objektive** ~**en** practical possibilities; **schwache** ~ off-chance; **unbegrenzte** ~**en** unlimited possibilities; **ungeahnte** ~**en** undreamed-of possibilities; **wirtschaftlich vertretbare** ~ economic grasp; **große wirtschaftliche** ~**en** great economic potentialities;
~ **vorzeitiger Ablösung** entitlement to commutation, redeemable right; ~ **der Nichtteilnahme** *(Weltwährungsfonds)* opting out; ~**en eines breitgestreuten Produktionsprogramms (der Produktionsauffächerung)** diversification possibilities;

~ **ausschließen** to rule out the (eliminate a) possibility; ~ **nicht berücksichtigen** to leave out a possibility; **nicht die einzige** ~ **darstellen** not to be the only avenue; **alle** ~**en einkalkulieren** to allow for (foresee) all possibilities; **alle** ~**en einschließen** to take into consideration all contingencies; **neue** ~**en eröffnen** to open up new vistas; **jem. neue** ~**en erschließen** to open new prospects to s. o.; **jem. die Wahl zwischen zwei** ~**en geben** to put s. o. on the horns of a dilemma; **die besten** ~**en haben** to be in a fair way; **sich eine** ~ **entgehen lassen** to throw away an opportunity; **seine** ~**en nutzen** to make the most of an opportunity; **sich beide** ~**en offenhalten** to have it both ways; **keine** ~ **sehen** to see no possible way; **außerhalb von jds.** ~**en sein** not to be within s. one's powers; **jede sich bietende** ~ **wahrnehmen** to take what opportunity is presented; **über jds. finanzielle** ~**en nicht Bescheid wissen** not to know the length of s. one's purse.

möglichst | es tun, sein to do one's best, to do one's utmost; **mit** ~**er Sorgfalt** as carefully as possible.

Mohren weiß waschen wollen to wash a blackamoor white.

mokieren, sich über etw. to mock at s. th., to poke fun at s. th.; **sich über jds. Anstrengungen** ~ to deride s. one's efforts.

Mole breakwater, mole, jetty, pier.

Molekül molecule.

Molekulargewicht molecular weight.

Molenkopf head of a jetty, pierhead.

Molkerei dairy, dairy farming, milkhouse, creamery;
~**betrieb** dairy [business]; ~**butter** dairy butter; ~**erzeugnisse** dairy produce; ~**fachmann** dairy expert; ~**genossenschaft** milk marketing board, dairy society; ~**produkt** dairy product; ~**wirtschaft** dairy farming.

mollig | geworden sein to have put on some weight;
~**e Decke** snug blanket; ~**e Wärme** pleasant (cozy) warmth.

Moloch juggernaut.

Moment moment, instant, factor, *(Gesichtspunkt)* aspect;
im ersten ~ under the impulse of the moment;
anregendes ~ *(Börse)* stimulant; **entscheidender** ~ crucial moment; **lichte** ~**e** lucid intervals; **retardierender** ~ delaying factor; **psychologisch richtiger** ~ psychological moment; **ungünstiger** ~ inauspicious moment; **zyklische** ~**e** cyclical factors;
richtigen ~ **abpassen** to bide one's time; **keinerlei neue** ~**e bringen** to fail to bring any new aspects; **beunruhigenden** ~ **darstellen** to cause considerable disquiet; **nur einen** ~ **dauern** to take only a minute; **j. jeden** ~ **erwarten** to expect s. o. any moment.

momentan presently, for the time being, momentary, at the moment, *(vorübergehend)* temporary, transitory;
~ **sehr viel zu tun haben** to have a lot on one's hands for the time being;
~**e politische Lage** present political situation; ~**e Laune** passing mood; ~**er Rückschlag** temporary setback; ~**e Schwierigkeiten** present difficulties.

Moment | aufnahme instantaneous photograph, snapshot; ~**schalter** quick-action (quick-make-and-break) switch; ~**verschluß** instantaneous shutter.

Monarch monarch, sovereign, king.

Monarchie monarchy, monarchial government;
absolute ~ absolute monarchy, despotic monarchy; **erbliche** ~ hereditary monarchy; **erschütterte** ~ shaken monarchy; **konstitutionelle** ~ constitutional (limited) monarchy; **parlamentarische** ~ parliamentary monarchy.

Monarchist monarchist.

monarchistische Regierungsform monarchial government, monarchy.

Monat month;
am 8. des lfd. ~s on the 8th of the month; **Ende nächsten** ~**s** by the end of next month;
alle zwei ~**e** bimonthly; **jeden** ~ monthly; **laufender** ~ current month; **letzter** ~ last month, ultimo; **nächster** ~ next month, proximo; **sechs** ~**e gültig** lasting for a period of six months; **vor anderthalb** ~**en** six weeks ago; **vorigen** ~**s** of last month (ultimo);
drei ~**e dato** at three months' date;
~**e mit 31 Tagen** odd months;
nächsten ~ **anstehen** *(Gerichtssache)* to be heard next month; **seit drei** ~**en die Miete schuldig bleiben** to owe for three months' rent; **2000 $ im** ~ **verdienen** to earn $ 2000 per month; **nächsten** ~ **fällig werden** to fall due next month.

monatlich monthly, by the month;
j. ~ **anstellen** to employ s. o. on a month-to-month basis; **seine Miete** ~ **bezahlen** to pay one's rent monthly; ~ **liefern** to send goods every month; ~ **mieten** to hire by the month;
~**er Bilanzbogen** monthly balance sheet; **sein** ~**es Gehalt bekommen** to receive one's month's pay; ~**e Kontenabstimmung** monthly reconciliation; ~**e Kündigung** a month's warning (notice); ~**e Lohnsteuertabelle** monthly wage-tax table; ~**e Lohnübersicht** monthly labo(u)r summary; ~**e Meldung über den Beschäftigungsstand** monthly report of the labo(u)r force; ~ **kündbares Mietverhältnis** monthly tenancy; ~ **erscheinende Veröffentlichung** monthly publication; ~**e Zahlung** monthly payment.

Monats | abonnement monthly ticket; **kommende** ~**abrechnung** next account; ~**abschluß** monthly settlement (statement); ~**abschnitt** period of a month; ~**abstimmung** *(Konto)* monthly reconciliation; ~**anfang** entry of the month; **zum** ~**anfang** early in the month; ~**aufstellung,** ~**ausweis** *(Bank)* monthly return *(Br.)* (statement); ~**bedarf** monthly requirements, a month's supply; ~**bericht** monthly report (review, statement); ~**bilanz** monthly balance sheet *(Br.)*; ~**durchschnitt** monthly average; ~**einkommen** monthly income; ~**endbestände** end-of-month figures; **am** ~**ende bezahlen** to settle up at the end of the month; ~**fahrkarte** monthly return (season, *Br.*, commutation, *US*) ticket; ~**frist** space (respite, period) of a month; **binnen** ~**frist** within a month; ~**gehalt** monthly pay (salary, wage), a month's pay; ~**geld** time loan, one month's time deposit *(US)*; ~**index** monthly index; ~**karte** monthly return (season, *Br.*, commutation, *US*) ticket, commuter fare *(US)*; ~**karte benutzen** to commute *(US)*; ~**karteninhaber** season-ticket holder, commuter *(US)*; ~**kompensation** monthly settlement; ~**lohn** monthly wages; ~**miete** one month's rent, monthly rental (rent, premium); ~**miete von 200 Pfund verlangen** to ask £ 200 a month as rent; ~**mittel** monthly mean; ~**prämie** monthly premium; ~**produktion** monthly production; ~**rate** monthly instal(l)ment; ~**rechnung** monthly account; ~**rhythmus** month-to-month trend; ~**schrift** monthly, monthly review (publication); ~**übersicht** monthly return; ~**ultimo** end-of-month settlement; **letzter** ~**umsatz** this month's trading; ~**urlaub bekommen** to obtain a month's leave; ~**verdienst** monthly profit; **unbedeutende** ~**verluste rot im Kalender anstreichen** to chalk up small monthly deficits; ~**verzeichnis von Neuveröffentlichungen** publisher's monthly list; ~**vorrat** a month's supply; ~**wechsel** one month's bill, *(Student)* monthly allowance; **rechnerischer** ~**wert** computed monthly value; ~**zeitkarte** monthly season (commutation, *US*) ticket; ~**zeitschrift** monthly magazine (journal, periodical); ~**zuschuß** monthly allowance.

mönchisches Leben führen to live like a monk.

Mönchsorden monastic order, community of monks.

Mond, bei abnehmendem in the wane of the moon;
abnehmender ~ old moon; **zunehmender** ~ waxing moon;
nach dem ~ **greifen** to cry for the moon; **in den** ~ **gucken können** to be left out in the cold; **weich auf dem** ~ **landen** to make a soft landing on the moon; **drei Meilen hinter dem** ~ **wohnen** to live at the back of beyond;
~**auto** moon rover (buggy); ~**fahrer** lunarnaut; ~**fenster** *(Raumfahrt)* lunar window; ~**laboratorium** lunar laboratory; ~**landefähre** lunar module; ~**landschaft** lunar landscape; ~**landung** moon (lunar) landing, touchdown on the moon; ~**oberfläche** lunar surface.

Mondschein moonlight;
du kannst mir mal im ~ **begegnen** you can go to hell (blazes);
~**spaziergang** moonlight walk; ~**tarif** off-peak telephone rates *(US)*.

Mond | sonde lunar probe, ranger *(US)*; ~**station** lunar station; ~**umkreisung** lunar orbit.

monetär monetary;
~**e Auflockerungsmaßnahmen** monetary relaxation; ~**e Basis** credit basis; ~**e Beschränkungsmaßnahmen** monetary restraint; ~**e Konjunkturpolitik** countercyclical monetary policy.

Moneten *(fam.)* chink *(sl.)*, tin *(sl.)*, dibs *(sl.)*, the ready, spondulicks *(US sl.)*, beans *(sl.)*, gingerbread *(sl.)*, dingbat *(sl.)*, rhino *(Br.)*, shiners *(sl.)*, lolly *(Br., sl.)*, hardtack *(sl.)*, stumpy *(sl.)*, jack *(US)*, dough *(US)*, sugar *(sl.)*, quiff *(sl.)*;
nötige ~ the needful *(sl.)*, wherewithal; **verfügbare** ~ scratch *(sl.)*, available cash *(sl.)*;
nicht die erforderlichen ~ **haben** not to have the wherewithal.

Monier | bauweise reinforced-concrete method of building; ~**eisen** constructional iron.

monieren to find fault with, to take exception to, to make a query, *(drängen)* to urge, to remind;
beschädigte Sendung ~ to complain that the consignment was damaged.

Monitor monitor.

Monitum reminder, query, warning.
Mono|grammpapier initial(l)ed paper; ~**grafie** monograph.
Monokel eye-glass, monocle.
Mono|kultur one-crop system; ~**metallismus** monometallism.
Monopol monopoly, sole trade, *(fig.)* preserve;
absolutes ~ absolute monopoly; **bilaterales** ~ bilateral monopoly; **gesetzliches** ~ artificial (special privilege) monopoly; **homogenes** ~ pure monopoly, isolated selling; **hundertprozentiges** ~ complete monopoly; **natürliches** ~ natural monopoly; **staatliches** ~ government (state) monopoly; **unvollständiges** ~ partial monopoly; **verbraucherfreundliches** ~ beneficial monopoly; **vollständiges** ~ outright monopoly;
~**e auflösen** to break up monopolies; ~ **ausüben** to enforce a monopoly; ~ **besitzen (haben)** to monopolize, to hold (have) a monopoly; ~ **errichten (fördern)** to foster a monopoly; ~ **mißbrauchen** to make improper use of a monopoly; ~ **verleihen** to grant a monopoly;
~**abgabe** monopoly tax; ~**abkommen,** ~**absprache** monopolistic (monopoly) agreement.
monopol|ähnlich semi-monopolistic, near-monopoly; ~**artig** monopolistic, of monopolistic character.
Monopol|artikel proprietary article; ~**ausübung** enforcement of a monopoly; ~**besitzer** monopolist; ~**betrieb** monopolistic enterprise; ~**erlöse** profits from patents and secret processes *(Br.)*; ~**erträgnisse** monopoly profits; ~**erzeugnis** proprietary article.
monopol|feindlich antimonopoly; ~**fördernd** promotive of monopoly *(US)*.
Monopol|frage monopoly issue; ~**gesellschaft** monopoly company; ~**gesetz** Monopoly Act *(Br.)*; ~**gewinn** producer's surplus, monopoly profit (rent); ~**grenze überschreiten** to pass beyond the boundaries of the monopoly; ~**industrie** monopolistic (monopolized) industry; ~**inhaber** monopolist.
monopolisieren to monopolize;
Markt ~ to engross (monopolize) the market.
Monopolisierung monopolization, engrossment.
Monopolisierungs|absicht monopoly intent; ~**tendenzen** tendencies towards monopolies; ~**versuch** attempt to monopolize.
Monopolist monopolist.
monopolistisch monopolistic;
~**e Beherrschung** monopolistic control; ~**e Geschäftsmethoden bekämpfen** to discourage monopolistic business practices.
Monopol|kapital monopolism; ~**kapitalismus** monopoly capitalism.
monopolkapitalistisch monopoly capitalist.
Monopol|kontrolle control of monopolies, monopolistic control; ~**lohn** monopolistic wage; ~**macht** monopoly power; ~**mißbrauch** abuse of monopoly, discriminating monopoly; ~**patent** patent monopoly; ~**preis** monopoly (monopolistic) price; ~**problem** monopoly problem; ~**recht** monopoly privilege; ~**rechte verletzen** to infringe monopoly rights; ~**rente** monopoly income (rent, revenue); ~**rolle** monopoly rôle.
Monopolstellung monopoly, monopoly status, exclusive control, monopolistic (monopoly) position;
finanzielle ~ pyramiding *(US)*; **verbraucherfreundliche** ~ beneficial monopoly;
~ **der Post** post office's monopoly;
Ausnutzung einer ~ **beschränken** to restrict the use of monopoly power; ~ **beseitigen** to split a monopolistic structure; ~ **haben** to monopolize a business, to hold a monopoly.
Monopol|unternehmen monopolistic (monopoly) enterprise; ~**vereinbarung** monopoly agreement; ~**verkaufswert** monopoly value; ~**vermögen** monopoly wealth; ~**versuch** attempt to monopolize; ~**wirtschaft** monopolism; ~**zwang für den Ankauf von Komplementärerzeugnissen** full-line forcing.
monoton monotonous, humdrum, tedious, drab;
~**e Arbeit** humdrum work, tedious work; ~**e Landschaft** drab landscape.
Monotonie im Arbeitsprozeß monotony of work.
Monotype *(Setzmaschine)* monotype;
~**satz** monotype composition.
Monster monster.
Monsun monsoon.
Montag, blauer St. (black, Saint) Monday *(Br.)*, blue Monday *(US)*;
blauen ~ **machen** to keep Saint Monday *(Br.)*.
Montage fitting, fixing, mounting, erection *(Aufstellen)* setting up, setup *(US)*, *(Einrichten)* installation, instal(l)ment, *(Film)* editing, montage, *(Zusammenbau)* assembly, assemblage, assembling;
~ **von Baumaterial** assemblage of building material; ~ **einer Maschine** fitting up of a machine;
~**abteilung** assembly department; ~**arbeit** assembly work; ~**arbeiten** general maintenance work; ~**arbeiter** assembly line worker; ~**band** band (belt) conveyer, conveyer belt, assembly line; ~**bandvorarbeiter** assembly-line foreman; ~**bau** prefabrication; ~**bauweise** precast construction; ~**betrieb** assembling (assembly) shop, assembly operation; ~**bild** paste-up montage; ~**bock** *(Auto)* servicing jig; **automatische** ~**einrichtungen** automated assembly facilities; ~**eisen** iron reinforcement; ~**fabrik** assembly plant, subassembly factory; ~**fehler** assembly fault.
montagefertig ready for installation.
Montage|gehalt installation salary; ~**gerüst** *(Brücke)* erecting tower, *(Hochbau)* assembling scaffold; ~**gruppe** unit assembly; ~**halle** erecting (assembly) shop, assembly hall, building shed, assembly room *(US)*; ~**kosten** cost of installation (erection), erection (setting) cost, assembly costs; **bauseitig anfallende** ~**kosten** on-site installation costs; ~**kostenberechnung** assembly cost system; ~**kran** derrick (erecting) crane; ~**leiter** erector; ~**möglichkeit** assembly capacity; ~**papier** mounting paper; ~**plan** assembly schedule; ~**rahmen** mounting frame; ~**satz** rate of erection; ~**tätigkeit** assembly operation; **fahrbarer** ~**turm** *(Rakete)* assembly tower on rails; ~**vereinbarung** assembly agreement; ~**werk** assembly plant; ~**werk errichten** to set up an assembly plant; ~**werkstatt,** ~**werkstätte** assembling (fitting) shop, assembly (assembling) shop; ~**zeichen** assembly mark, matchmark; ~**zeichnung** erection blue print; ~**zeit** setting-up (setup) time.
Montan|aktie mining share (stock, *US*), steel stock *(US)*; ~**aktien** iron and steel shares; ~**anleihe** European Coal and Steel Community loan; ~**bereich** iron and steel sector; ~**gemeinschaft** Iron and Steel Community; ~**industrie** mining (coal, iron and steel) industry; ~**markt** mining market; ~**papiere** mines; ~**umlage** Iron and Steel Community level; ~**union** European Coal and Steel Community; ~**unionsvertrag** Common Market Treaty; ~**unternehmen** mining concern; ~**werte** mines, mining securities (shares).
Monteur fitter, mechanic, *(Fließband)* assembler, *(Wartung)* maintenance man;
~**anzug** overalls, dungaree.
montierbar pick-off *(US)*.
Montieren fitting, assembling, setting up.
montieren to fit, to mount, *(aufstellen)* to set up, to erect, *(einrichten)* to install, *(am Fließband)* to assemble, *(Flugzeug)* to rig, *(zusammenbauen)* to assemble;
Büchergestell ~ to fit a bookshelf to the wall; **Film** ~ to mount a film; **Gerüst** ~ to scaffold; **Heizung** ~ to install a heating system; **Reifen** ~ to fix a tyre (tire, *US*); **Wagen** ~ to assemble a motor car.
montiert mounted.
Montierung fitting, mounting, erection, adjusting, *(Einrichtung)* installation, *(Zusammenbau)* assembly, assembling, assemblage.
Montur *(mil.)* regimentals, uniform;
in voller ~ in full rigout.
Monument monument.
Monumental|film superfilm; ~**kunst** colossal art.
Moor moor, marshland;
~ **trockenlegen** to drain marshland;
~**bad** mud bath; ~**brücke** corduroy bridge.
Moos *(Geld)* quiff *(sl.)*, brass *(fam.)*, dust *(sl.)*, wad *(US sl.)*, gilt *(sl.)*, hardtack *(sl.)*, jack *(sl.)*, lolly *(Br.)*;
~**kissen** cushion of moss.
Moped motor-assisted pedal cycle, autocycle, moped;
~**fahrer** moped rider, autocyclist.
mopsen to pinch, to swipe *(sl.)*;
sich ~ to be bored stiff.
mopsfidel as merry as a cricket (lark).
mopsig boring.
Moral ethics, tag;
brüchige ~ frail morality; **strenge** ~ strict morale;
~ **einer Geschichte** moral of a story; ~ **der Truppe** morale of the army;
zur ~ **beitragen** to build morale; ~ **der Zivilbevölkerung erschüttern** to shatter civilian morale; **Mensch ohne** ~ **sein** to be an immoralist; **öffentliche** ~ **verderben** to deteriorate the public morals; **gegen die** ~ **verstoßen** to offend against moral sentiment; **öffentliche** ~ **zersetzen** to undermine morals, to vitiate public taste; ~ **einer Geschichte ziehen** to draw the moral of an experience;

gegen die ~gesetze verstoßen to offend against morals; **gegen ungeschriebene ~gesetze verstoßen** to act against moral sentiments.

moralisch moral, ethical;
~ **einwandfrei** of good moral character; ~ **entrüstet** with moral indignation;
j. ~ aufrichten to uplift s. o. *(US)*; **sich ~ verpflichtet fühlen** to feel a moral obligation; ~ **gefährdet sein** to be in moral danger; ~ **zu etw. verpflichtet sein** to be on one's hono(u)r to do s. th.;
~**er Anreiz** moral incentive; ~**e Anwandlungen** fits of morality; ~**er Auftrieb** uplift *(US)*; ~**e Auslegung** moralization; ~**e Betrachtungen anstellen** to moralize; ~**er Defekt** moral insanity; ~**er Druck** moral duress; ~**e Empörung** moral outrage; ~**e Erbauung** moral improvement; ~**e Gewißheit** moral certainty; ~**e Grundsätze** moral principles; ~**er Imperativ** moral imperative; ~**er Katzenjammer** sting of remorse; ~ **einwandfreies Leben führen** to live a moral life; ~**e Ohrfeige bekommen** to be put to shame; ~**es Recht** moral right; ~**e Schönfärberei** moral whitewashing; ~**er Sieg** moral victory; ~**e Tugenden** moral virtues; ~**e Überzeugung** moral conviction; ~**es Urteilsvermögen** moral faculty; ~**e Verhaltensweise** moral conduct; ~**e Verpflichtung** moral consideration; ~**e Verworfenheit** moral turpitude; ~**er Wert** moral value; ~**e Wiederaufrüstung** moral rearmament.

Moralischer qualms of conscience.

Moralist moralist.

Moral|kodex ethics code; **doppelter ~kodex** double standard; ~**philosophie** moral philosophy; ~**predigt** moralization, moralism, homily; **jem. eine ~predigt halten** to preach s. o. a sermon, to give s. o. a stern lecture.

Morast quagmire, mud, slob, wash *(Br.)*;
bodenloser ~ bottomless bog;
im ~ steckenbleiben to be stuck in the mud; **Weg in einen ~ verwandeln** to turn a road into a quagmire.

Moratorium moratorium, moratory, letter of protection (respite, grace), postponement of payments;
~ **gewähren** to grant a moratory.

Moratoriumsanleihe moratory loan.

morbid morbid;
~**er Zug** taint of morbidness.

Mord murder in the first degree *(US)*, assassination, felonious homicide, killing;
wegen vierfachen ~es on four counts of murder;
bezahlter ~ hired murder; **glatter** ~ *(fig.)* sheer lunacy; **vorbedachter (vorsätzlicher)** ~ malicious killing, premeditated murder;
~ **eines Polizeibeamten** killing a policeman; ~ **und Totschlag** blood and thunder, battle royal, dirty work *(fam.)*;
j. des ~es anklagen to charge s. o. with murder; ~ **begehen** to commit murder; **fähig sein, einen ~ zu begehen** to be a potential murderer; **fast einem ~ gleichkommen** to come near to murder; **des ~es angeklagt sein** to be indicted for murder; **j. des ~es überführen** to convict s. o. of murder; **wegen ~es verurteilt werden** to be declared guilty of murder;
~**absicht** murderous intent; **j. in ~absicht anfallen** to attack s. o. murderously; ~**anklage** murder charge; **unter ~anklage** on charge of murder; ~**anschlag** attempt on s. one's life, attempted murder, murderous plot; ~**anschlag auf j. begehen** to attempt s. one's life; ~**brenner** fire-raiser, arsonist; ~**dezernat** homicide commission; ~**drohung** threat of murder.

morden to [commit] murder, to assassinate.

Mörder murderer, slayer, butcher, killer, trigger man *(sl.)*;
gedungener ~ hired assassin;
~ **dingen** to hire a murderer; **zum ~ werden** to commit murder; **aus seinem Herzen keine ~grube machen** to wear one's heart upon one's sleeve, to speak one's piece (mind); **durch ~hand fallen** to die at the hands of a murderer.

mörderisch murderous;
in ~er Absicht with murderous intent; ~**er Blick** killing glance; ~**e Hitze** terrific heat; ~**en Hunger haben** to be ravenously hungry, to be as hungry as a wolf; ~**er Kampf** mortal struggle; ~**es Klima** deadly climate; ~**e Konkurrenz** cutthroat competition; ~**es Tempo** breakneck speed, killing pace.

Mord|fall case of murder; ~**fall aufklären** to solve a murder; **mit ~gedanken umhergehen** to meditate murder; ~**gier** bloodthirstiness; ~**instrument** murderous weapon.

Mordio, Zeter und ~ schreien to cry blue murder *(coll.)*.

Mord|kommando killer squad; ~**kommission** homicide squad; **gemeinsamen ~plan ausarbeiten** to plan together to kill s. o.; ~**prozeß** murder (homicide) trial; ~**prozeß gegen j. durchführen** to try s. o. for murder.

Mords|angst blue funk; ~**angst haben** to be scared stiff; ~**aufregung** hell of a stink *(sl.)*; ~**ding** hell (devil) of a job, whopper, topper *(coll.)*, wackler *(sl.)*, oner *(sl.)*, raker *(sl.)*; ~**durcheinander** devil of a mess, devil among tailors, shambles, snafu *(US sl.)*; ~**durst** almighty thirst; ~**eile** mortal hurry; ~**erfolg sein** to go over with a bang *(US coll.)*, *(Theaterstück)* to be a box-office success *(US)*; ~**gaudi haben** to have a ripping time; ~**geschrei erheben** to scream like hell; ~**glück** incredible luck, whopping good luck; ~**kerl** topper, bouncer *(sl.)*, corker *(sl.)*, humdinger *(US sl.)*, whaler *(sl.)*; ~**krach** fearful racket, terrific noise; ~**krach schlagen** to make a fearful din, to raise hell.

mordslangweilig dull as ditchwater.

Mordslüge thumper *(coll.)*, whopper *(coll.)*.

mordsmäßig thumping, ripping *(sl.)*.

Mords|propaganda ballyhoo *(US)*; ~**sache** whopper, topper *(coll.)*, oner *(sl.)*, corker *(sl.)*; ~**spaß** real jam *(Br., sl.)*; ~**spaß haben** to have no end of fun; ~**spektakel** fearful din, pandemonium, hullabaloo, hell of a row; ~**wut haben** to be in a hell of a temper.

Mord|tat begehen to commit murder; **unter ~verdacht** under suspicion of murder; **unter ~verdacht stehen** to lie under suspicion of murder; ~**verdächtiger** murder suspect; ~**verhandlung gegen j. durchführen** to try s. o. for murder; ~**verschwörung** murderous plot; ~**versuch,** ~**anschlag** attempted murder (assassination), attempt on s. one's life, assassination attempt, felonious assault; ~**vorsatz** malice aforethought; ~**waffe** murderous (murder) weapon.

Mores lehren, j. to teach s. o. manners.

morganatische Ehe left-handed (morganatic) marriage.

Morgen morning, *(Flächenmaß)* acre;
bis zum ~ durchfeiern to feast away the night, to make a night of it;
~**ausgabe** early-morning edition; **am Vorabend gedruckte ~ausgabe** bull-day edition; **kurzer ~besuch** morning call; ~**blatt** morning paper; ~**dämmerung** prime of the day; **in der ~frühe** early in the morning; ~**gabe** morning gift, dowry; ~**grauen** daylight; **vor dem ~grauen** before daylight.

morgenländisch eastern.

Morgen|post morning post *(Br.)*, morning mail *(US)*; ~**post erledigen** to dispose of the morning post *(Br.)*; ~**rock** dressing gown, wrapper, morning gown; ~**schicht** first shift; ~**sonne** morning sunshine; **frühe ~stunden** small hours; ~**stunde hat Gold im Munde** the early bird catches the worm; ~**wache** *(mar.)* morning watch; ~**zeitung** morning paper; ~**zug** early train.

morsch decayed, rotten, worm-eaten;
~**es Gebäude** ramshackle building; ~**er Zahn** decayed tooth.

Morse|alphabet morse code (alphabet); ~**apparat** morse telegraph; ~**lampe** morse lamp.

morsen to morse.

Morse|nachricht message in morse; ~**schlüssel** morse key; ~**schreiber** inker; ~**signal** signal; ~**taste** tapper; ~**telegraph** morse telegraph; ~**zeichen** signal.

Mortalitätstafel *(Lebensversicherung)* decrement (experience) table.

Moskito|fenster screen window; ~**netz** mosquito net.

Motel motel, tourist (auto, motor) court.

Motiv motive, drive;
von geheimen ~en angetrieben impelled by secret motives;
persönliche ~e private motives; **unanständiges** ~ impure motive; **vernünftige ~e** prudential motives; **zweifelhafte ~e** impeachable motives;
~ **des Gesetzgebers** legislative motive; ~ **eines Verbrechers** criminal motive;
sich auf seine guten ~e berufen to predicate the goodness of a motive; **aus ehrenwerten ~en handeln** to act with the most hono(u)rable motives; **von niedrigen und selbstsüchtigen ~en angetrieben sein** to be actuated by low and selfish motives; **jds. ~en nicht trauen** to be distrustful of s. one's motives; **seine ~e verbergen** to veil one's motives; **seine wahren ~e verbergen** to sail under false colo(u)rs; **aus eigennützigen ~en tätig werden** to act from interested motives.

Motivation motivation.

Motivforschung motivational research.

motivieren to motivate, to explain, to give reasons;
politisch ~ to motivate politically.

Motivirrtum mistake as to the nature of the subject matter, mistake in the inducement *(US)*.

Motor engine, motor, *(Antriebskraft)* drive, power;
mit abgestelltem ~ with engine turned off; **mit voll laufendem ~** with full throttle, opened up *(US)*;

abgestellter ~ cut-off engine; **ausgefallener** ~ dead engine; **frisierter** ~ junketed engine; **laut gehender** ~ noisy engine; **kopfgesteuerter** ~ valve-in-head engine; **reibungslos laufender** ~ humdinger *(sl.)*; **luftgekühlter** ~ air-cooled engine; **starker** ~ powerful engine;
eigentlicher ~ **eines Betriebes** driving force in a firm; ~ **und Getriebe** power plant; ~ **mit Kompressor** supercharged engine; ~ **abschalten (abstellen)** to stop the engine; ~ **abwürgen** to stall (kill) an engine; ~ **anlassen** to start an engine; ~ **auseinandernehmen** to dismantle an engine; **sich nachteilig auf den** ~ **auswirken** to harm the engine; ~ **in Gang bringen** to set an engine going; ~ **drosseln** to cut down the power, to cut the gun *(sl.)*; ~ **frisieren** to soup up (junket) an engine *(US sl.)*; ~ **warmlaufen lassen** to warm up the engine; ~ **reparieren** to repair a motor; ~ **zu sehr strapazieren** to punish the engine; ~ **überholen** to overhaul an engine; ~ **zerlegen** to disassemble the engine;
~**abnutzung** motor wear; ~**anlasser** starter; ~**antrieb** motor drive; ~**aufhängung** suspension of an engine; ~**ausfall** engine breakdown; ~**barkasse** motor launch *(Br.)*; ~**bau** engine construction; ~**block** engine block; ~**boot** motorboat, powerboat, yacht; ~**defekt** engine trouble; ~**drehzahl** engine speed.
Motoren|bau engine construction, engine manufacture; ~**geräusch** roar of an engine, song of a motor; ~**öl** motor oil; ~**schlosser** motor mechanic, grease monkey *(US sl.)*; ~**werk** engine factory.
Motor|fahrzeug motor vehicle; ~**gehäuse** engine casing.
motorgetrieben power-driven.
Motorhaube hood *(US)*, bonnet *(Br.)*.
motorisieren to motorize, to mechanize;
sich ~ to buy a car.
motorisiert motorized, mobile;
~**e Truppen** mechanized forces; ~**e Verkehrsstreife** patrol car, cruiser *(US)*, traffic squad.
Motorisierung motorization, mechanization.
Motor|kühlung engine cooling; ~**leistung** engine capacity, motor power; ~**nennleistung** rated motor power; ~**nummer** engine number; ~**panne** engine breakdown (trouble); ~**pflug** tractor plough (plow, *US*).
Motorrad motorcycle, motor bicycle (bike, *fam.*);
zusammengeflicktes ~ patched-up motorcycle;
~ **mit Beiwagen** combination;
mit dem ~ **fahren** to motorcycle;
~**brille** goggles; ~**fabrik** motorcycle plant; ~**fabrikant** motorbike maker; ~**fahrer** motorcyclist, rider; ~**kleidung** riding gear; ~**piste** motorcycle track.
Motor|raum engine compartment; ~**roller** scooter; ~**säge** motor saw; ~**schaden** engine failure (trouble); ~**schiff** motor ship (vessel); ~**schlepper** traction engine; ~**schlitten** snowmobile, autosled; ~**segler** power glider; ~**spritze** fire engine; ~**störung** engine breakdown (trouble); ~**takt** cycle; ~**triebwagen** railcar; ~**wechsel** motor (engine) replacement; ~**welle** engine shaft; ~**zahl einprägen** to stamp the number of an engine.
Motte moth;
von ~**n zerfressen** moth-eaten;
du kriegst die ~**n!** what the dickens!
Mottenkiste, alte Geschichte aus der ~ **holen** to rake up an old story; **altes Stück aus der** ~ **holen** to revive an old play; **in die** ~ **verbannen** to put into mothballs.
Motten|kugel mothball; ~**pulver** moth powder; ~**schutzmittel** moth repellent.
mottensicher mothproof.
Motto motto, slogan, device, epigraph.
Mucke caprice, whim, crotchet;
jem. die ~**n austreiben** to tell s. o. where to get off; ~**n haben** to be moody (crotchety), *(Motor)* to be difficult to handle, to have got bucks, *(Plan)* to be full of snags.
Mücke mosquito, gnat, midge;
eine ~ **machen** to hop (beat) it; **aus einer** ~ **einen Elefanten machen** to make a mountain out of molehill; **von** ~**n geplagt werden** to be pestered by mosquitos.
mucken to be bolshy, to grumble;
nicht ~ not to dare to utter a word; **ohne zu** ~ without a peep; **es hinnehmen, ohne zu** ~ to take it like a lamb.
Mücken|schutzmittel mosquito repellent; ~**schwarm** host of gnats.
Mucker sanctimonious person.
Mucks feeble sound;
keinen ~ **von sich geben** to be as quiet as a mouse.
mucksch sulky, sullen.
mucksen, sich nicht not to make a peep.
mucksmäuschenstill mum;
~ **sein** to be as quiet as a mouse.
müde tired, weary, drowsy;
~ **wie ein Hund** dog-tired, dead-beat;
zum Umfallen ~ ready to drop;
~ **aussehen** to look jaded; **sich** ~ **fühlen** to feel sleepy; ~ **herumschleichen** to drag o. s. about; **nur** ~ **lächeln** to give a sickly smile; **j.** ~ **machen** to fag s. o. out; ~ **sein** to be all in (worn out); **jds.** ~ **sein** to be tired of s. o.; **einer Sache** ~ **sein** to be sick of (fed up with) it; **zum Umfallen** ~ **sein** to be too tired to stand;
~**s Gesicht** tired face; **seine** ~**n Glieder von sich strecken** to stretch one's weary bones; **mit einer** ~**n Handbewegung** with a languid gesture; ~**r Laden** moribund outfit; ~ **Stimme** languid voice.
Müdigkeit tiredness, weariness, fatigue;
unüberwindliche ~ irresistible tiredness;
vor ~ **umfallen können** to be ready to drop; ~ **vorschützen** to plead fatigue.
Muffe *(Kupplung)* sleeve *(sl.)*.
Muffel grouch, grouser, crab *(sl.)*.
muffeln to sulk, to grumble.
Mühe trouble, effort, pains, difficulty;
der ~ **wert** worth-while; **mit großer** ~ with great difficulty; **außergewöhnliche** ~ special trouble; **vergebliche** ~ lost labo(u)r; **verlorene** ~ wasted effort; **viel** ~ no little pains;
Examen mit ~ **und Not bestehen** to scrape through an examination; **sich** ~ **geben** to use diligence, to be at pains; **sich jede nur erdenkliche** ~ **geben** to spare no pains, to go out of one's way, to leave no stone unturned; **sich große** ~ **geben, um seinen Arbeitgeber zufriedenzustellen** to take great pains to please one's employer; **sich große** ~ **geben, pünktlich zu sein** to try hard to be punctual; **sich übergroße** ~ **geben** to bend over backwards; **sich nur mit** ~ **über Wasser halten können** to have difficulty in making both ends meet; **sich die** ~ **machen** to trouble, to take pains; **sich nicht die** ~ **machen** not to bother; **keine** ~ **scheuen** to spare no effort, to be unsparing in one's efforts; **weder** ~ **noch Kosten scheuen** to spare neither effort nor expense; **der** ~ **wert sein** to be worth-while; **nicht der** ~ **wert sein** not to be worth the candle; **sich die** ~ **sparen** to save o. s. the trouble.
mühelos hands down, without any effort, with ease, easy;
Examen ~ **bestehen** to walk through an examination; **Aufgabe** ~ **lösen** to have no difficulty in solving a problem; **alle Hürden** ~ **nehmen** to clear all the hurdles easily; ~ **zu haben sein** to be had for the asking; ~ **siegen** to win in a canter (hands down) *(coll.)*;
~**es Leben** life of ease; ~**er Sieg** easy victory; ~**er Weg** royal road.
mühevoll difficult, laborious, hard, troublesome;
~**es Unternehmen** arduous enterprise; ~**e Vorarbeiten** strenuous spadework.
Mühewaltung trouble, effort[s], pains;
für Ihre ~ as recompense for your trouble;
für harte Arbeit und ~ **kümmerlich entlohnt werden** to work hard and get very little for one's pains.
Mühle mill;
alte ~ *(Auto, Flugzeug)* kite *(sl.)*, jaloppy *(US)*, crate, flivver *(sl.)*;
~**n der Bürokratie** bureaucratic mill;
durch die ~ **drehen** to put through the wringer; **sich in den** ~**n des Gesetzes verfangen haben** to be caught in the toils of the law; **Wasser auf jds.** ~ **sein** to be grist to s. one's mill.
Mühlen|besitzer mill owner; ~**industrie** milling industry.
Mühlrad mill wheel;
jem. wie ein ~ **im Kopf herumgehen** to be going round and round in s. one's head.
Mühlstein millstone, ton of bricks;
jem. sein ganzes Leben lang wie ein ~ **am Halse hängen** to be a millstone round s. one's neck all his life; **wie ein** ~ **auf j. lasten** to weigh heavily upon s. o.
Mühsal great strain, drudgery, hardship, toil.
mühsam laborious, wearisome, working day, plodding, hard, difficult to bear;
sich ~ **aufrichten** to struggle to one's feet; **sich** ~ **einen Weg durch die Menge bahnen** to force one's way through the crowd; **sehr** ~ **sein** to be a laborious business; **sich** ~ **seinen Lebensunterhalt verdienen** to eke out one's livelihood; **sich** ~ **wachhalten** to make an effort to keep awake; **Beweismaterial** ~ **zusammentragen** to painstakingly piece together the evidence.
mühselig working-dog, finicky, fiddly.

Mulatte mulatto *(Br.)*, black and tan *(US)*.
Mulde *(Konjunktur)* trough;
sich vor dem Feind in einer flachen ~ verbergen to hide from the enemy in a slight depression.
Müll dust *(Br.)*, tip, soft dirt, collection, rubbish, garbage *(US)*, refuse;
abfuhrbereiter ~ dust *(Br.)*, refuse ready for collection;
~ abladen to dump (shoot) rubbish, to tip *(Br.)*; **~ aufbereiten** to recycle refuse;
~abfuhr refuse *(Br.)* (garbage, *US*) disposal (collection), rubbish collection, removal (collection, disposal) of household refuse *(Br.)*, garbage removal *(US)*, *(Gesellschaft)* cesspool clearing company, *(Wagen)* dump wagon *(US)*, dumping car, dust cart *(Br.)*; **~abfuhrmann** dustman *(Br.)*, garbage collector *(US)*; **~abfuhrunternehmer** cesspool clearing company, garbage collector *(US)*; **~abladen** dumping; **~abladeplatz** dump, dumping place, trash dump *(US)*, refuse disposal site, tipping *(Br.)*; **~ablagerung** dumping, tipping; **~aufbereitung** recycling of refuse; **~auswerter** refuse collector; **~beseitigung** refuse disposal; **~eimer** dustbin *(Br.)*, dust box *(Br.)*, ash (trash, *US*) can, garbage box (pickup, pail, can) *(US)*; **~fahrer** dustman *(Br.)*, garbage (junk) collector *(US)*, garbage man *(US)*, sanitation man; **~fahrzeug** dust cart *(Br.)*, dumping truck (waggon); **~förderungsanlage** garbage conveyer *(US)*; **~grube** dust hole, refuse pit; **~halde** refuse (rubbish) dump, garbage dump *(US)*, tip *(Br.)*; **~karren** dust cart *(Br.)*; **~kasten** dust box *(Br.)*, ash bin (can), orderly bin *(Br.)*, garbage box (can) *(US)*; **~kippe** refuse disposal site, junk heap *(US)*, trash dump *(US)*, tip *(Br.)*; **~schaufel** dust pan *(Br.)*; **~schlucker** dust shoot *(Br.)*, garbage chute (disposer) *(US)*; **~tonne** dustbin *(Br.)*, dust box *(Br.)*, orderly bin *(Br.)*, garbage box (barrel) *(US)*; **~verbrennung** waste incineration; **~verbrennungsanlage** municipal (garbage, *US*) incinerator, garbage burner *(US)*, garbage destructor *(US)*; **~verwertungsanlage** garbage plant *(US)*, reduction works; **~wagen** dumping (dump) car, dump waggon *(US)*, garbage truck (cart, waggon) *(US)*, dirt waggon *(US)*, sanitation van *(US)*, ash cart *(US)*; **~werker** dustman *(Br.)*, garbage man *(US)*; **~zerkleinerer** disposal unit, garbage destructor *(US)*.
mulmig precarious, rotten, *(Holz)* moldy, mouldy *(Br.)*;
~ aussehen to be somewhat fishy; **sich ~ fühlen** to feel uneasy, to have got butterflies in one's stomach;
~e Situation precarious situation.
multilateral multilateral, multipartite;
~es Verfahren multilateral treatment; **~er Verrechnungsverkehr** multilateral clearing system; **~es Zahlungssystem** multilateral system of payments.
Multimillionär multimillionaire.
Multimomentverfahren ratio delay studies.
multinational multinational;
~es Unternehmen multinational company, multicorporate enterprise *(US)*.
multiple | r Wechselkurs multiple exchange rate; **~s Wechselkurssystem** multiple rate system.
Multiplikation multiplication.
Multiplikationseffekt multiplier effect.
Multiplikator multiplier;
~wirkung multiplier effect.
multiplizierbar multiplicable.
Mumie mummy.
Mumm pep, go, kick, ginger *(coll.)*, vim, guts *(sl.)*, starch *(US sl.)*, true grit *(sl.)*;
~ haben to have pep, to have plenty of guts *(sl.)*, to be full of go; **keinen ~ haben** to lack gumption.
Mummelgreis doddery, dodderer.
Mummenschanz mumming play;
~ treiben to mum.
Mumpitz humbug, flimflam, bosh, rubbish, kibosh *(US sl.)*;
~ machen to play the fool; **~ reden** to talk rubbish.
Münchhausiade tall tale.
Mund, in aller ~e in everyone's mouth;
seiner Kinder wegen sich alles vom ~e absparen to pinch and scrape for one's children; **seinen ~ aufmachen** to speak up; **seinen ~ aufreißen** to talk big, to brag, to boast; **~ und Nase aufsperren** to be flabbergasted, to gape in amazement; **jem. über den ~ fahren** to jump down s. one's throat, to cut s. o. short; **etw. ständig im ~e führen** to be always talking about s. th.; **von ~ zu ~ gehen** to pass from mouth to mouth; **losen ~ haben** to have an unbridled tongue; **seinen ~ halten** to hold one's tongue, to hold one's peace, to keep one's mouth shut *(sl.)*, to pipe down *(coll.)*; **an jds. ~ hängen** to hang on s. one's lips; **jem. das Wort im ~e herumdrehen** to twist s. one's words; **j. mit offenem ~ stehen lassen** to leave s. o. with his jaw dropped; **von der Hand in den ~ leben** to live from hand to mouth; **jem. etw. in den ~ legen** to put s. th. into s. one's mouth; **jem. den ~ wäßrig machen** to make s. one's mouth water; **jem. das Wort aus dem ~e nehmen** to take the words right of s. one's mouth; **jem. den ~ öffnen** to make s. o. speak; **jem. nach dem ~e reden** to chime in with s. o.; **sich den ~ fusselig reden** to talk nineteen to the dozen; **in aller ~e sein** to be on the tongues of men, to be the talk of the town; **nicht auf den ~ gefallen sein** to have a glib tongue, to have an answer for everything; **wie auf den ~ geschlagen sein** to be speechless; **jem. den ~ stopfen** to stop s. one's mouth, *(bestechen)* to bribe s. o. to keep quiet; **sich den ~ verbrennen** to put one's foot in it.
mundartlich vernacular;
~ ausdrücken to vernacularize.
Munddiebstahl stealing of trifles, pilferage, petty theft, pickery *(Scot. law)*.
Mündel ward, pupil, child under guardianship, charge;
~ unter Amtsvormundschaft ward in chancery.
Mündelgeld trust fund (money), ward's money;
Anlage von ~ern in mit variablen Zinssätzen ausgestatteten Kommunalanleihen gestatten to authorize trustees to invest in local authority floating-rate papers; **~er unterschlagen** to embezzle the funds of a ward.
mündelsicher gilt-edged *(Br.)*, eligible *(US)*;
~e Anlage trustee *(Br.)* (eligible, *US*) investment, trust stock *(US)*; **~e Anlagewerte** gilt-edged securities *(Br.)*, trustee stocks *(Br.)*, trust (savings bank) investments *(US)*; **~e Kapitalanlage** gilt-edged *(Br.)* (high-grade, trustee, *US*) investment; **~e Sparkasse** trustee savings bank *(US)*; **~e Wertpapiere** gilt-edged securities *(Br.)*, trustee securities *(Br.)*, trust stock *(US coll.)*, trust investment *(US)*.
Mündel | sicherheit trustee status, eligibility; **~sicherheit genießen** to be gilt-edged *(Br.)*, to rank as trust stock *(US)* (trust investments, *US*, trustee securities, *Br.*); **~stand** pupilage; **~verhältnis** ward, guardianship; **~vermögen** trust fund; **~vermögen unterschlagen** to embezzle the funds of a ward.
mundgerecht | darbieten to dish up; **~ machen** to sweeten.
mündig of age, major;
für ~ erklären to declare of age; **~ werden** to come of age (to years of discretion), to reach majority.
Mündiger major.
Mündigkeit full age, majority.
Mündigkeits | alter age of consent; **~erklärung** emancipation from the authority of one's parents.
mündlich oral, verbal, parol, viva voce, by word of mouth;
~e Abmachung parol agreement; **~es Angebot** verbal offer; **~e Anweisung** verbal order; **~er Bericht** oral report; **~e Beweiserhebung** parol evidence; **~e Erklärung** verbal statement (explanation), deposition; **~e Erklärung unter Anwesenden** speaking to those present; **~es Examen** oral examination; **in ~er Form** verbally, orally, by word of mouth; **~ abgeschlossener Mietvertrag** parol lease; **~e Mitteilung** verbal communication; **~e Prüfung** oral examination, oral; **~es Testament** nuncupative will; **~e Überlieferung** verbal tradition; **~e Vereinbarung** oral agreement; **~es Verfahren** oral pleading; **~e Verhandlung** oral pleading; **~er Vertrag** oral (parol) contract.
Mündlichkeit orality.
Mund | raub petty larceny (theft), petit larceny, pilferage, pickery *(Scot.)*; **~stück** *(Zigarette)* tip; **mit ~stück** tipped.
mundtot machen to muzzle, to gag;
j. ~ to reduce s. o. to silence; **Opposition ~** to silence the opposition.
Mündung *(Fluß)* mouth, outlet, outfall, entry.
Mündungs | arm distributory; **~feuer** muzzle blast; **~gebiet** estuary.
Mundwasser mouthwash.
Mundwerk mouth, trap *(sl.)*;
gefährliches ~ spiteful tongue; **gutes ~** gift of the gab *(US)*; **loses ~** unbridled tongue;
enormes ~ haben to talk the hind leg off a donkey; **unverschämtes ~ haben** to be cheeky; **sein ~ halten** to shut one's trap; **j. aufs ~ hauen** to sock s. o. in the kisser *(sl.)*.
Munition ammunition;
scharfe ~ life ammunition;
~ ausgeben to munition; **seine ganze ~ verschießen** to fire away all one's ammunition.
Munitions | arbeiter ammunition worker; **~aufzug** *(Kriegsschiff)* ammunition hoist; **~bunker** blast-proof ammunition storage

side; ~**depot** ammunition depot; ~**fabrik** munition factory, arsenal; ~**karren** dolly; ~**lager** ammunition magazine (dump); ~**steuer** ammunition levy *(Br.)*; ~**verbrauch** ammunition expenditure; ~**verwaltung** control of ammunition; ~**vorräte** stocks of ammunition; **knappe** ~**vorräte** munition shortage; ~**wagen** ammunition carrier.

Munkelei rumo(u)rs, whispers.

munkel|n to whisper, to rumo(u)r; **man** ~**t** rumo(u)r has it.

munter lively, brisk, frisky;
gesund und ~ alive and kicking *(coll.)*; ~ **wie ein Fisch im Wasser** as fit as a fiddle;
~ **bleiben** to stay awake; **sich wieder völlig** ~ **fühlen** to be as fresh as a daisy; **j. wieder** ~ **machen** to wake s. o. up again; **äußerst** ~ **sein** to be full of beans; ~ **werden** to liven up;
~**e Farben** gay colo(u)rs; ~**er Knabe** jolly fellow; ~**es Lied** merry song; ~**e Unterhaltung** spirited conversation.

Münz|amt mint, bullion office; ~**anstalt** assay (bullion) office, mint; ~**automat** penny-in-the-slot (coin-operated) machine, coin-slot machine; ~**bestände eines Landes** gold and silver holdings of a country; ~**delikt** coinage offence; ~**direktor** warden of the mint.

Münze coin, money, bean *(sl.)*, *(Hartgeld)* specie, hard cash (money, *US*), *(Kleingeld)* change, coppers, *(Münzamt)* mint; **in klingender** ~ in hard (cash, good) money, in specie, in [ready] cash;
~**n** coinage, mintage, effective money;
abgegriffene (abgenutzte) ~ detrited (worn-out, defaced) coin; **echte** ~ genuine coin; **falsche** ~ fake (spurious, base, bad) coin; **fehlerhafte** ~**n** defective currency; **gangbare (gängige)** ~ common (current) coin; **gefälschte** ~ false coin; **gesetzliche** ~ legal (lawful, *US*) money; **kleine** ~ bit *(Br.)*; **klingende** ~ real money, hard cash, specie; **schlechte** ~ base coinage, bad coin; **untergewichtige** ~ light coin *(US)*; **vollgewichtige** ~ standard money (coin); **vollwertige** ~**n** undebased coinage;
~**n, deren Nominalwert den Metallwert übersteigt** token money; ~ **mit gesetzlich vorgeschriebenem Feingehalt** standard coin;
jem. eine falsche ~ **andrehen** *(fam.)* to unload a bad coin on s. o.; **sich in politischer** ~ **auszahlen** to deem pricy in political coinage; **in gängiger** ~ **bezahlen** to pay in hard cash; ~**n in den Verkehr bringen** to put a coinage in circulation; ~**n fälschen** to counterfeit coins; **einer** ~ **das richtige Gewicht geben** to adjust a coin; **es jem. mit gleicher** ~ **heimzahlen** to pay s. o. back in his own coin, to serve s. o. the same game, to give s. o. as good as one gets; **ein paar** ~**n aus der Tasche herausfischen** to fish a few coins out of one's pocket; ~ **fallen lassen** to drop a coin on the floor; **etw. für bare** ~ **nehmen** to take s. th. for gospel (at face value), to take s. th. for granted; ~ **auf das vorschriftsmäßige Gewicht prüfen** to test a coin for weight; ~**n schlagen** to mint (strike) coins; ~ **taxieren** to rate a coin; ~**n verfälschen** to debase the currency (coins); **in klingender** ~ **zahlen** to pay in specie; ~**n aus dem Verkehr ziehen** to retire coins from circulation; **jem. mit gleicher** ~ **zurückzahlen** to pay s. o. [back] in his own coin (in kind), to give as good as one gets, to repay s. o. in kind; **einem Bettler eine** ~ **zuwerfen** to toss a coin to a beggar.

Münz|einheit standard, monetary unit, denomination; ~**einwurf** coin slot.

münzen to coin, to mint, to strike.

Münzen|sammler collector of coins; ~**sammlung** numismatic collection; ~**umlauf** coins in circulation.

Münz|fälschung false coining, counterfeiting; ~**fälschung begehen** to counterfeit coins; ~**fernsehen** pay-as-you-see (coin, per channel, program(me) pay) television; ~**fernsprecher** coin *(US)* (public call, *Br.*) box, pay station (telephone, phone, *US*), public telephone, phonebooth *(US)*; **öffentlicher** ~**fernsprecher** coin-operated public telephone; ~**fuß** monetary standard, standard of coinage; ~**fuß festsetzen** to monetize; ~**gebühr** coinage, assay cost; ~**gehalt** standard of alloy; ~**geld** loose cash; ~**gepräge** mint stamp; ~**gerechtigkeit** monetary sovereignty, moneyage; ~**gesetz** Coinage Act *(Br.)*; ~**gewicht überprüfen** to test a coin for weight; ~**gewinn** seigniorage; ~**gold** monetary (standard) gold, bullion, gold specie; ~**hoheit** right of coinage, monetary sovereignty; ~**klo** pay toilet; ~**konvention** monetary convention; ~**kosten** coinage; ~**kunde** numismatics; ~**metallprüfanstalt** assay office; ~**parität** mint parity, mint par of exchange; ~**platz** mint; ~**prägeanstalt** Royal Mint *(Br.)*; ~**prägemaschine** coining press; ~**prägung** coinage, minting; ~**prägung und** ~**ausgabe** provision and issue of coins; **unentgeltliche** ~**prägung** gratuitous coinage; ~**preis** mint price; ~**prüfer** assayer; ~**recht** right of coinage; ~**regal** right of coinage, monetary sovereignty; ~**rohling** planchet; ~**sammlung** coin collection; ~**silber** standard silver, bullion; ~**sorten** foreign coins; ~**sortiermaschine** coin assorter; ~**standard** [monetary] standard; ~**stätte** mint; ~**stättenleiter** keeper of the touch *(Br.)*; ~**stempel** die, mint mark; ~**system** coinage; ~**tabelle** tariff of coins; ~**tankstelle** coin-operated petrol (gasoline, *US*) station; ~**tarif** standard of coinage; ~**toleranz** tolerance of the mint; ~**verbrechen,** ~**vergehen** coinage offence; ~**verfälschung** debasement of the currency; ~**verschlechterung** debasement of coinage, deficiency of the coin; ~**währung** standard; ~**wardein** master of the mint; ~**wäscherei** coin-operated laundry; ~**wechsler** coin changer; ~**wert** assay value, mint price; ~**wert erhöhen** to appreciate the coinage; ~**zähler** coin meter; ~**zeichen** mint-mark; ~**zusatz** alloy.

mürbe *(Fleisch)* tender, well-cooked, *(Gebäck)* crisp, friable, *(Stoff)* tender;
j. ~ **machen** to soften s. o. up, to break s. one's resistance; ~ **werden** to give way, to break down.

Murks botch, bungle, hash;
~ **machen** to mess up a business, to make a mess of a job, to make a hash of things; ~ **reden** to talk rubbish.

murksen to botch.

Murmeln, beifälliges murmur of approval.
~ **aus dem Nebenzimmer hören** to hear a murmur of conversation from the next room.

murmeln to mutter, to mumble, *(Bach)* to murmur, to purl;
etw. vor sich hin ~ to mumble to o. s.; **Fluch vor sich hin** ~ to mutter a curse under one's breath.

Murmeltier, wie ein ~ **schlafen** to sleep like a top.

Murren grumble, murmur, grouse, gripe *(US sl.)*;
etw. ohne ~ **tun** to do s. th. uncomplainingly; **höhere Steuern ohne** ~ **zahlen** to pay higher taxes without murmur.

murren to grumble over, to grouse about, to moan, to growl;
über die zu niedrige Bezahlung ~ to grumble at the low pay offered to one; **über das Essen** ~ to grumble about the food; **gegen höhere Steuern** ~ to murmur against higher taxes.

murrend, Rede ~ **unterbrechen** to interrupt a speech by groans of disapproval.

mürrisch morose, sullen, grumpy, cross, fretful;
~ **aussehen** to look glum; ~ **sein** to have the sullens, to be in the sulks; ~ **werden** to go crook *(Australia)*;
~**er Kerl sein** to be surly as a bear; ~**er alter Mann** grumpy old man; ~**e Stimme** gruff voice; ~**er Ton** surly tone of voice; ~**es Wesen** morose (surly) disposition.

museal|e Bestände museum holdings; **nur noch** ~**en Wert haben** to have only antiquarian value.

Museum museum;
~ **der Schönen Künste** art museum.

Museums|besucher führen to conduct the visitors through the museum; ~**direktor** conservator; ~**führer** guide to a museum, museum guide; ~**katalog** museum catalog(ue); ~**stück** period (museum) piece; ~**wärter** museum attendant.

Musical musical comedy.

Musik, elektronische electronic music; **ernste (leichte)** ~ serious (light) music;
moderne ~ **bevorzugen** to have a prejudice in favo(u)r of modern music;
~**abend** musical evening; ~**akademie** college of music.

Musikalienhandlung music shop (house, store, *US*).

musikalisch musical;
sehr ~ **sein** to have a fine ear for music;
~**e Abendunterhaltung** musical evening; ~**es Lustspiel** musical comedy; ~**e Untermalung** background music; ~**er Vortrag** recital; ~**es Wunderkind** musical prodigy.

Musik|aufnahme music recording; ~**automat** jukebox.

musikbegeistert keen on music.

Musikdrama music drama.

Musiker musician.

Musik|fetzen, aufpulvernde enlivening strains of music; ~**film** musical film; ~**freund** music lover; ~**freund sein** to be fond of music; ~**hochschule** conservatoire, conservatory *(US)*; ~**instrument** musical instrument; ~**kulisse** background music; ~**pavillon** bandstand; **volkstümliches** ~**programm** popular music program(me); ~**saal** music hall; ~**schrank** music cabinet; ~**sendung** musical program(me); ~**stück** music, musical composition (segment); **einleitendes** ~**stück** opener-upper *(sl.)*; ~**truhe** radiogram, radiogrammophone; ~**übertragung** transmission of music; **jem.** ~**unterricht geben** to teach s. o. music; ~**veranstaltung** musical event (performance); ~**verlag** music company; ~**werk** musical composition; ~**zeitschrift** musical periodical.

Muskel|kater Charley horse *(US coll.)*; **~kraft** muscle.
Muskeln, seine ~ spielen lassen to flex one's muscles.
Muskelprotz muscleman, muscle *(US sl.)*.
Muß compulsion, necessity, must *(fam.)*;
Englisch erwünscht, aber kein ~ *(Anzeige)* English is desirable, not a must; **für die Premiere ist Frack kein ~** evening dress is optional for the premiere.
Muße leisure time;
mit ~ leisurely;
etw. mit ~ betrachten to watch s. th. at one's ease; **in aller ~ frühstücken** to have a leisurely breakfast; **~ haben** to be at leisure; **selten Zeit zur ~ haben** to be seldom at leisure; **in der Eisenbahn ~ zum Lesen haben** to have a good read in the train *(Br.)*; **sich ~ für etw. nehmen** to do s. th. in a leisurely fashion; **~stunden, ~zeit** leisure (spare) time.
Mußheirat shotgun marriage.
müßig idle, leisured, *(sinnlos)* senseless, pointless;
~ herumstehen to idle about; **~ an den Straßenecken herumstehen** to be lounging at street corners; **~ sein** to be idle (at one's leisure); **~ sein, darüber zu reden** to be no use talking about it;
~e Frage superfluous question; **~es Gerede sein** to be empty (idle) talk; **~e Stunden** idle hours; **~er Versuch** futile attempt; **~e Zeit** spare time.
Müßiggang idleness, truancy, laziness;
~ treiben to eat the bread of idleness; **sein Leben in ~ verbringen** to drone one's life away;
~ ist aller Laster Anfang idleness is the root of all sin.
Müßiggänger saunterer, lounger, idler, loafer, fiddler.
Mußvorschrift mandatory clause *(US)*, mandatory provision *(US)*, peremptory provision.
Muster *(Form)* pattern, set form, device, shape, figure, *(Gebrauchsmuster)* design, pattern [sample], patterned sample, *(Modell)* model, copy, prototype, *(Norm)* norm, standard, *(Type)* type, *(Vorbild)* paragon, mirror, example, exemplar, *(Warenprobe)* sample, trial piece, specimen;
als ~ ohne Wert by sample post; **dem ~ entsprechend** up to sample; **laut ~, mit dem ~ übereinstimmend** true to specimen; **mit großem ~** large-patterned; **nach ~** according to pattern (sample), on the model, on the lines; **schlechter als das ~** inferior to sample; **streng nach ~** strictly up to sample;
auf Bestellung angefertigtes ~ custom design; **anhängende ~** annexed samples; **aufdringliches ~** loud pattern; **aufgedrucktes ~** printed design; **beigefügtes ~** attached sample; **eingetragenes ~** registered design *(Br.)*, registered pattern; **einheitliches ~** standard pattern; **entnommenes ~** picked sample; **fortlaufendes ~** consecutive pattern; **gängiges ~** conventional design; **gewerbliches ~** industrial design; **kostenloses ~** free sample; **kunstvolles ~** elaborate design; **übliches ~** conventional design; **ungeschütztes ~** open pattern; **unverkäufliches ~** free sample; **verschiedene ~** sundry samples; **verschlossenes ~** sealed sample; **vorgelegtes ~** sample displayed (shown); **wiederkehrendes ~** repeated pattern;
~ kostenlos auf Anfrage free samples on request; **~ von Selbstbeherrschung** model of self-control; **~ von einem Sozialisten** model socialist; **~ unter versiegeltem Verschluß** sealed sample; **~ ohne Wert** *(Postversand)* samples, no commercial value *(US)*, samples only, sample post, by pattern (sample) post, samples of no value *(Br.)*; **~ eines Wohlfahrtstaates** model of a welfare state;
~ abschneiden to cut off a sample; **mit ~n verschiedene Versuche anstellen** to put samples through a series of tests; **nach einem ~ arbeiten** to work from a pattern; **~ stichprobenartig auswählen** to select a specimen at random; **nach dem ~ bestellen** to order goods from sample; **als ~ dienen** to serve as a model; **~ einsehen** to have a look at the patterns; **dem ~ entsprechen** to correspond to pattern, to be up to (match the) sample; **dem ~ nicht entsprechen** not to be up to pattern; **neue ~ entwerfen** to create new styles; **sich auf ein ~ festlegen** to decide on a pattern; **nach ausländischen ~n gestalten** to foreignize; **~ bei sich haben** to carry samples of one's products; **als ~ hinstellen** to hold up as an example; **etw. nach dem ~ kaufen** to buy s. th. from sample; **~ für ein Kleid aus einer Zeitschrift kopieren** to copy a dress pattern out of a magazine; **~ nehmen** to draw samples; **sich j. zum ~ nehmen** to take a leaf out of s. one's book; **schlechter als das ~ sein** to be inferior to sample; **~ an Güte sein** to be kindness itself; **~ einer Hausfrau sein** to be a marvelous housewife; **~ an Höflichkeit sein** to be the pink of politeness; **als ~ ohne Wert senden (verschicken)** to send as samples of no value; **mit dem ~ übereinstimmen** to match the sample; **nach ~ verkaufen** to sell by sample; **mit ~n versehen** to pattern; **~ vorführen** to wait on with patterns; **~ vorlegen** to submit samples; **als ~ geschützt werden** to be registered as design; **~ in den Sand zeichnen** to draw figures in the sand; **~ ziehen** to draw (take) samples, to sample; **~ zusammenstellen** to make up a collection of samples, to arrange patterns, to assort samples;
~abänderung modification of a design; **~abkommen** model convention; **~abzug** film copy; **~anforderungskarte** sample request card; **~anfrage** request for pattern; **~angebot** sample offer; **~anmeldung** application for registration as design; **~arbeitsvertrag** model employment contract; **~auftrag** trial order; **~bedingungen** standard form contract conditions; **~beispiel** perfect specimen, prime example, test case; **~beispiel geben** to set a pattern; **~bericht** standard report; **~bestellung** sample order; **~betrieb** model enterprise (plant, workshop), pilot plant; **landwirtschaftlicher ~betrieb** model (demonstration) farm; **~beutel** mailing bag; **~bilanz** standard balance sheet; **~bogen** *(Schneider)* pattern sheet; **~brief** form (sample, standard, specimen) letter; **~buch** specimen (pattern, sample, design) book, book of patterns; **~dekoration** model display; **charakteristische ~eigenschaften** design requirements; **~eintragung** sample entry; **~entnahme** sampling; **~etat** guideline budget; **~exemplar** pattern, sample, specimen [copy], prototype, *(Prachtexemplar)* beauty; **~fall** test case, precedent; **~farm** demonstration (model) farm; **~flugzeug** prototype aircraft; **~formular** specimen form; **~galvano** mo(u)lder; **~gatte** exemplary husband; **~gemeinde** model community; **~gesetz** model act *(US)*.
mustergetreu according to pattern, true to specimen, *(Textilien)* true to shade;
nicht ~ not to sample;
~ sein to be up to (match the) sample.
Muster|größe sample size; **~gut** demonstration (model) farm.
musterhaft exemplary, model, as good as gold;
sich ~ betragen to behave perfectly; **etw. ~ verstehen** to be a capital hand at s. th.;
~es Betragen exemplary conduct, model behaviour; **~e Examensarbeit** brilliant paper; **in ~er Ordnung sein** to be in perfect order.
Muster|haus model house (dwelling); **~haushalt** guideline budget; **~heft** pattern (sample, specimen) book; **~inhaber** proprietor of a design; **~karte** show (sample, pattern) card; **~kasten** box of samples; **~klammer** paper fastener, mailing clasp *(US)*; **~knabe sein** to be the goody-goody *(coll.)*; **~koffer** sample bag (trunk, case); **~kollektion** set (variety, range, collection) of patterns, collection (line) of samples, range of models, assortment of patterns, sample stock (assortment), muster, *(Vertreter)* traveller's samples; **vollständige ~kollektion** full range of samples; **~kollektionssystem** model stock plan; **~kosten** cost of samples; **~kuvert** sample envelope; **~lager** sample stock (depot, room), showroom; **gewaltiges ~lager** huge collection of samples; **~lager unterhalten** to keep a stock of samples; **~leistung der Kraftfahrzeugindustrie** outstanding achievement of the motor industry; **~messe** sample (trade) fair.
mustern to examine, to look over, to scrutinize, to enrol(l) *(mil.)*, *(Stoff)* to pattern, to figure, to make a design;
j. genau ~ to inspect (scrutinize) s. o. closely; **j. kritisch von oben bis unten ~** to eye s. o. up and down; **jem. mißtrauisch ~** to look at s. o. suspiciously; **Rekruten ~** to call up conscripts.
Muster|nehmen sampling; **~nummer** sample number; **~paar** sample pair; **~patent** design patent *(US)*; **~produktion** prototype production; **~prozeß** test case, pattern and practice suit; **~prozeß zugunsten der Gesellschaft** *(Aktionär)* representative action; **~prüfung** sampling inspection; **~rabatt** discount on samples; **~reisender** pattern man, sampleman, commercial travel(l)er; **~reservat** showcase reserve; **~rolle** sample roll, *(Geschmacksmuster)* register of designs *(Br.)*, *(Schiff)* list of the crew, crew list, ship's articles, muster roll; **~sammlung** collection of samples, sampling; **~satzung** model set of articles, draft articles, *(AG)* Table A *(Br.)*; **~schule** demonstration (model) school; **~schüler** exemplary scholar, prig *(sl.)*; **~schüler sein** to be the goody-goody *(coll.)*; **~schutz** copyright in designs *(Br.)*, designs copyright *(Br.)*; **~schutz begehren** to apply for a design patent; **~sendungen** sample lots (parcels); **~-ohne-Wert-Sendung** parcel shipment, sample packet, fourth-class matter *(US)*; **~sohn** pattern son; **~sortiment** model stock, variety (collection, range) of patterns; **~stadt** model city; **~stück** sample item, pattern, sample, sampling, piece of one's work, specimen, model; **~tarifvertrag** master (pattern) agreement; **~text** standard text.

Musterung examination, survey, scrutiny, draft *(US)*, *(mil.)* muster, recruitment, first medical, *(Stoff)* pattern, design, *(der bisher Unabkömmlichen)* combing out *(Br.)*;
fünf Wochen nach der ~ einberufen to call up five weeks after the first medical.
Musterungs|bescheid decision by the recruiting (draft, *US*) board; **~kommission** *(mil.)* draft (examination) board; **~offizier** enrolling officer.
Muster|vereinbarung, **~vertrag** standard contract; **~verkaufsbrief** specimen sales letter; **~vertrag** prototype contract, standard [form] contract; **~vordruck** specimen form; **~vorlage** submission of samples; **~vorschriften** standard regulations; **~werbeanzeigen** sample advertisements; **~wirtschaft** model (demonstration) farm; **~wohnhaus** model dwelling; **~wohnung** housing prototype, show flat; **~zeichner** designer of patterns, pattern drawer (designer); **~zeichnung** pattern design, cartoon; **~zieher** sampler; **~ziehung** taking samples, sampling; **~zimmer** sample room; **~zusammenstellung** assortment of samples.
Mut courage, cheer, heart, pecker *(sl.)*, *(Schneid)* pluck, grit, guts *(sl.)*;
guten ~s in heart;
angetrunkener ~ Dutch courage, pot-valo(u)r; **sinkender ~** sagging spirits;
sich ~ antrinken to give o. s. some Dutch courage; **den ~ aufbringen** to get up the nerve; **dafür nicht den ~ aufbringen** not to find it in one's heart; **jem. ~ einflößen** to put s. o. in good heart, to catch s. one's spirit; **neuen ~ fassen** to take fresh heart; **viel ~ haben** to have plenty of courage; **seinen ganzen ~ verloren haben** to be utterly discouraged; **~ sinken lassen** to droop; **~ nicht sinken lassen** to keep up one's spirits; **jem. wieder ~ machen** to put new heart into s. o.; **sich guten ~es an die Arbeit machen** to set to work full of cheer; **frohen ~es sein** to be in a happy mood; **~ zeigen** to put a bold front on it; **seinen ganzen ~ zusammennehmen** to pluck up (muster up all one's) courage, to take one's courage in both hands; **jem. ~ zusprechen** to cheer s. o. up, to put fresh courage into s. o.; **einem Prüfling ~ zusprechen** to speak encouragingly to a candidate.
Mutation mutation.
Mütchen, an jem. sein ~ kühlen to take it out of s. o., to vent one's anger on s. o.
muten to apply for a mining concession.
mutig bold, courageous, plucky, spirited, game *(coll.)*, *(kühn)* audacious, daring;
einer Situation ~ begegnen to put a bold face on a matter; **sich dem Feind ~ entgegenstellen** to face the enemy courageously; **äußerst ~ sein** to have plenty of guts *(sl.)*; **sich ~ den Journalisten stellen** to bravely face the journalists; **sich ~ zeigen** to play the man;
~es Eingeständnis bold admission; **äußerst ~er Mann** heart of oak *(fam.)*; **~e Tat** gallant deed; **~es Unternehmen** bold enterprise.
mutlos discouraged, dispirited, disheartened, out of heart;
jem. ~ machen to break s. one's spirit.
mutmaßen to presume, to assume, to surmise;
~, daß der Minister zurücktreten wird to speculate that the minister will resign; **aus einer Tatsache eine andere ~** to presume a fact from another.
mutmaßlich assumed, probable, presumptive, putative, conjectural, implied, apparent;
~er Ankunftstag probable date of arrival; **~er Erbe** heir apparent, heir presumptive ; **~e Lebensdauer** anticipation of life, probable life; **~er Täter** presumed perpetrator; **~e Todesursache** probable cause of death; **~er Vater** putative father; **~er Verfasser** probable author.
Mutmaßlichkeit *(Statistik)* likelihood.
Mutmaßung conjecture, speculation, guess, *(Annahme)* presumption, assumption;
bloße ~en mere guesswork;
~en anstellen to make speculations; **zutreffende ~en anstellen** to be right in one's surmises; **~en über die Zukunft anstellen** to divine what will be the future; **reine ~ sein** to be idle speculations.
Mutter mother, *(techn.)* nut;
ledige ~ unmarried mother; **stillende ~** nursing mother; **werdende ~** expectant (prospective) mother;
~ der Kompanie *(mil.)* company sarge, topkick *(sl.)*;
~ anziehen to tighten a nut; **an ~s Rockschößen hängen** to be tied to mother's apron strings; **wie eine ~ sorgen** to mother; **bei ~ Grün übernachten** to sleep in the open.
Mütter|beihilfe maternity grant *(Br.)*; **~beratung** aid to mothers; **~beratungsdienst** maternity welfare service; **~beratungsstelle** maternity center *(US)* (centre, *Br.*), baby (health, *US*) station.
Mutterboden topsoil.
Mütterfürsorge maternal welfare.
Muttergesellschaft parent company (body, concern, enterprise, establishment, corporation).
Mütterhilfe home help.
Mutter|kompaß master gyrocompass; **~land** mother country, metropolitan territories (country), home country *(Br.)*, homeland; **sich vom ~land lösen** *(Kolonie)* to cut one's painter.
mütterlich|e Pflege maternal care; **~es Vermögen** maternal property.
mütterlicherseits verwandt related on the mother's side.
Mutter|mal birthmark; **~pause** reproducible copy; **~pflichten** maternal duty; **~platte** *(Rundfunk)* acetate; **~schaft** motherhood, maternity.
Mutterschafts|fürsorge maternity welfare; **~geld** maternity pay; **~urlaub** maternity leave; **~versicherung** maternity insurance.
Mutter|schiff mother ship *(Br.)*; **~schutzfrist** maternity period; **~söhnchen** mama's boy *(coll.)*, mollycoddle *(Br., dial.)*, milksop; **~sprache** mother tongue, national (original, native) language, vernacular; **~stelle bei jem. vertreten** to be like a second mother to s. o.
Müttersterblichkeit maternal mortality.
Mutter|tag Mother's day *(US)*, Mothering Sunday *(Br.)*; **~-Tochterverhältnis** *(Konzern)* parent-subsidiary relationship *(US)*; **~witz** mother wit.
Mutung claim, prospect, mining concession (licence);
regelrechte ~ clear title;
~ abstecken to peg out (stake off) a mining claim.
Mutungs|anspruch mining claim; **~anspruch aufteilen** to segregate a claim *(US)*; **~inhaber** claim holder; **~recht** mining claim; **~recht abstecken** to stake off (peg out) a mining claim; **~vorhaben** prospecting activities.
Mutwille sportiveness, frolicsomeness;
aus reinem ~n out of pure mischief.
mutwillig playful, wanton, wilful, *(absichtlich)* on purpose, deliberately;
~ zerstört werden to be destroyed senselessly;
~e Handlung wanton act; **~e Sachbeschädigung** wanton and wilful damage, wilful trespass; **~e Zerstörung** deliberate destruction.
Mutwilligkeit *(jur.)* wantonness.
Mütze cap, beret, hat;
etw. auf die ~ bekommen to be on the carpet, to get it in the neck.
mysteriös mystic;
~e Angelegenheit mysterious business.
Mystifikation mystification.
mystisches Testament mystic will.
Mythos myth.

N

Nabel der Welt hub of the universe.
nach | Ablauf der Frist on expiration of the term; ~ **Ankunft** on arrival; ~ **Bedarf** as requested; ~ **dato** after date; ~ **Erhalt** on receipt; ~ **deutschem Geld** in German money; ~ **bestehenden Gesetzen** under existing laws; ~ **dem Gewicht** by weight; ~ **den neuesten Methoden** according to the latest methods; ~ **zwei Monaten zahlbar** payable in two months; ~ **dem Muster** according to sample; ~ **der Reihe** in turn, by turns; ~ **jeder Richtung** in all directions; ~ **Sicht** at sight; ~ **und** ~ bit by bit, little by little, gradually, successively.
Nachabstimmung subsequent vote.
nach | addieren to check the addition; **j. ~äffen** to ape s. o., to take s. o. off; **Lehrer ~äffen** to mimic a teacher.
nachahmbar imitable.
nachahmen to imitate, to sham, *(fälschen)* to fake, to falsify, to counterfeit, *(kopieren)* to copy;
j. ~ to follow in s. one's footsteps; **j. täuschend ähnlich** ~ to imitate s. o. to the life, to take s. o. off to a T; **Patent** ~ to pirate a patent; **jds. Stil** ~ to imitate s. one's style; **Warenzeichen** ~ to pirate a trademark.
Nachahmer imitator, echo, repeater.
Nachahmung imitation, sham, mock, copy, echo, *(Fälschung)* counterfeit, fake, forgery, *(Plagiat)* plagiarism;
~en imitation goods;
täuschend ähnliche ~ colo(u)rable imitation; **betrügerische** ~ fraudulent imitation; **freie** ~ free imitation; **geringwertige** ~ inferior imitation;
~ **verboten** patent registered; **vor ~en wird gewarnt** beware of imitations (counterfeits);
~ **eines Patents** piracy of a patent; ~ **von Warenzeichen** imitation of trademarks.
nachaktivieren to revalue fixed assets.
Nach | aktivierung revaluation of fixed assets; **~anmelder** *(Patent)* subsequent applicant; **~anmeldung** supplementary registration, *(Patent)* subsequent application, *(Zoll)* further declaration; **~arbeit** [re]finishing, retouching, follow-up work, reoperation, *(zusätzliche Arbeit)* extra work, *(Ausbesserung)* repair, *(Wartung)* maintenance; **~arbeiten eines Werkstückes** reworking of a piece.
nacharbeiten to repeat, *(aufholen)* to catch up, *(ausbessern)* to repair, *(Muster nachbilden)* to copy, to work from a model (pattern), *(letzten Schliff geben)* to [re]finish, to retouch, to redo, to do over again, *(techn.)* to finish-machine;
mit der Hand ~ to hand-tool, to rework a piece; **am Wochenende** ~ to do extra work at the weekend; **verlorene Zeit** ~ to make up for lost time.
Nacharbeitung dressing, finish, finishing.
Nacharbeitungskosten rework expense, reoperation cost.
Nachbar, allernächster next-door neighbo(u)r; **leidiger (streitsüchtiger)** ~ vexatious neighbo(u)r; **unmittelbare ~n** next-door neighbo(u)rs;
seine ~n zu einem kleinen Schwatz aufsuchen to be visiting one's neighbo(u)rs and having a good gossip; **j. zum ~n begleiten** to walk s. o. over to the neighbo(u)r's house; **seine ~n belästigen** to make o. s. a nuisance to one's neighbo(u)rs; **angenehme ~n haben** to have good neighbo(u)rs; **mit den ~n Schritt halten** to keep up with the Joneses; **auf seine ~n herabsehen** to think small of one's neighbo(u)rs; **gute Beziehungen zu seinen ~n unterhalten** to be on friendly terms with one's neighbo(u)rs; **einem ~n die Aussicht verbauen** to stop a neighbo(u)r's light; **~bezirk** purlieu, outlying district; **~division** adjacent division; **~dorf** neighbo(u)rhood parish, adjacent (neighbo(u)ring) village; **~eigentümer** adjacent owner; **~einheit** *(mil.)* neighbo(u)ring unit; **~gebiet** adjacent territory; **~gefahr** *(Versicherung)* exposure hazard, surrounding risk; **~gemeinde** neighbo(u)ring community; **~grundstück** adjacent site (land), adjoining property (estate, lot), abutting (neighbo(u)ring) property; **~haus** adjoining (neighbo(u)ring) house; **im ~haus wohnen** to live next door; **~industrie** surrounding industry; **~kreis** neighbo(u)ring district; **~land** neighbo(u)ring country (nation); **in einem ~land intervenieren** to intervene in the affairs of a neighbo(u)ring country.
nachbarlich neighbo(u)ring, adjacent, adjoining, next-door;
~ **handeln** to act in a neighbo(u)rly way;
andauernde ~e Belästigungen constant vexations from neighbo(u)rs; **~er Verkehr** neighbo(u)rly intercourse.
Nachbarort neighbo(u)ring place (town, village).
Nachbarschaft neighbo(u)rhood, vicinity, proximity, contiguity, neck of the woods *(US coll.)*;
in unmittelbarer ~ in close vicinity;
gefahrerhöhende ~ *(Versicherung)* exposure hazard, surrounding risk; **gute** ~ *(pol.)* good neighbo(u)rliness;
wenig Verkehr mit der ~ haben to have little contact with one's neighbo(u)rs; **gute ~ halten** to be on friendly terms with one's neighbo(u)rs; ~ **wie seine Hosentasche kennen** to know every inch of the neighbo(u)rhood; **in unmittelbarer ~ leben** to live next door; **in unmittelbarer ~ liegen** to adjoin each other.
Nachbarschafts | gewinn *(Grundstück)* general benefit; **~heim** community center; **~hilfe** bee *(US)*; **~laden** neighbo(u)rhood shop; **~risiko** *(Feuerversicherung)* exposure hazard; **~verhältnisse** neighbo(u)rhood conditions; **~verkehr** communal intercourse.
Nachbars | junge boy next door; **~risiko** *(Feuerversicherung)* exposure hazard.
Nachbar | staat adjacent (neighbo(u)r) state; **~stadt** neighbo(u)ring town; **~verein** contiguous association; **~volk** neighbo(u)ring nation; **~weg** private way; **~zimmer** next (adjoining) room.
Nachbau reproduction, copying, *(unter Lizenz)* construction (manufacture) under licence, duplication;
unerlaubter ~ unlicensed construction.
nachbauen to manufacture (construct) under licence, *(unberechtigt)* to copy, to imitate.
nachbearbeiten to dress, to finish, to rework.
Nach | bearbeitung dressing, finishing, finish; **~beben** *(Erdbeben)* aftershock.
nachbehandeln to give further treatment, *(Patient)* to give aftertreatment.
Nachbehandlung aftertreatment, aftercare, follow-up care.
nach | bekommen to obtain later; **Ware ~bekommen** to get goods in replacement; **~belasten** to make an additional charge.
Nachbelastung additional (subsequent) charge *(Br.)*, *(Inserat)* short rate.
nachbelichten *(Vergrößerung)* to print up.
nachberechnen to make an additional charge;
Verpackungskosten ~ to charge subsequently for packing.
Nachberechnung afterreckoning, additional charge, *(Inserat)* short rate.
Nachbesitzer subsequent holder.
nachbessern to mend, to repair, to remedy defects, *(Foto)* to touch up.
Nachbesserung remedy of a defect.
Nachbesserungspflicht obligation to repair.
Nachbestellarbeit reordering work.
nachbestellen to [give a] reorder, to place a repeat order, to renew (repeat) an order, to repeat an article, to order again (a fresh supply).
Nachbestellung reorder, subsequent (second, repeat) order;
~ **vornehmen** to place a repeat order.
nachbesteuern to levy an additional tax.
Nach | besteuerung supplementary (subsequent) taxation; **~beten** mechanical repetition.
nachbeten to repeat blindly, to parrot;
alles ~ to be a mere parrot; **alle Worte ihres Führers** ~ to echo every word of their leader.
nachbewilligen to grant additionally.
nachbewilligte Gelder additional funds.
Nachbewilligung supplementary vote (grant), additional allowance.
nachbezahlen to make an additional (further, subsequent) payment, *(Zuschlag)* to pay extra.
Nachbezahlung subsequent payment.
nachbeziehen, ältere Zeitungsnummern to obtain back numbers of a newspaper.
Nach | bezug additional supply; **~bild** *(Marketing)* after-image.
nachbilden to pattern, to copy, to imitate, to reproduce, to duplicate, *(fälschen)* to fake, to counterfeit, to falsify, to forge, *(plagieren)* to plagiarize;
genau ~ to facsimile, to reproduce in (make a) facsimile; **etw. einem Modell** ~ to form s. th. on a model; **der Natur** ~ to copy from nature; **dem englischen System** ~ to pattern on the English system.
Nachbildung reproduction, copy, imitation, replica, *(Attrappe)* dummy, sham, *(Fälschung)* falsification, fake, forgery, counterfeiting, *(Plagiat)* plagiarism;

genaue (getreue) ~ facsimile, replica; offensichtliche ~ obvious imitation.
nachblättern, in seinen Aufrechnungen to leaf through one's notes.
nachbleiben *(bei Krankheit)* to have aftereffects;
~ müssen *(Schüler)* to have to stay in.
Nachbleibsel einer Krankheit aftereffect of an illness.
Nachbörse afterhours, *(Freiverkehr)* outside (street, *Br.*, unofficial, *Br.*) market, kerb [market] *(Br.)*, curb [market] *(US)*.
nachbörslich after [official] hours, [done] in the street *(Br.)*, street *(Br.)*, on the curb *(US)*;
~e Preise street (kerb) prices *(Br.)*, outside (curb, *US*) prices;
~er Wertpapierhandel secondary distribution of securities.
Nachbrenner *(Flugzeug)* afterburner.
nachbrüten, über etw. to brood (ponder) over s. th.
nachbuchen to post up, to make a subsequent entry;
Exportumsätze ~ to post up export sales; ausgelassene Posten ~ to record (book) omitted items.
Nachbuchung *(ergänzend)* supplementary entry, *(zeitlich)* subsequent entry, postentry, *(zusätzliche)* additional entry;
~ vornehmen to make a subsequent (supplementary) entry.
Nachbürge counterbail, second bail, surety for a surety, *(Wechsel)* subsequent endorser.
Nachbürgschaft countersurety, secondary security.
nachdatieren to postdate, to afterdate, *(Wechsel nachträglich vordatieren)* to antedate.
Nach|datierung postdate; ~deklaration postentry.
Nachdenken thought, reflection, consideration;
nach kurzem ~ after a pause for thought;
angestrengtes ~ hard thinking;
jem. Stoff zum ~ geben to give s. o. food for thought; in tiefes ~ versunken sein to be immersed in one's thoughts (in a brown study).
nachdenken to think about, to reflect, to consider, to ponder;
erst ~ und dann reden to think over well before speaking; scharf ~ to do some hard thinking; über etw. ~ to dwell upon s. th.; über seine Lage ~ to consider one's position; über ein Problem ~ to turn a problem over in one's mind; über die Zukunft ~ to think about the future.
nachdenklich reflective, speculative, pensive, contemplative, pondering;
~ gestimmt sein to be in a thoughtful mood; ~ werden to start wondering;
~er Blick pensive look; ~er Mensch reflective person; ~es Schweigen pondering silence; ~e Stimmung pensive mood.
nachdrängen to press forward.
Nachdruck reproduction, republication, reprint, *(fig.)* insistence, stress, *(Zeitschriften)* separate reprint;
mit ~ emphatically; mit großem ~ with great insistence;
betrügerischer ~ fraudulent impression; seitenweiser ~ paginal reprint; unberechtigter (unerlaubter) ~ counterfeited impression, piracy, piratic edition, pirate version; unveränderter ~ reprint;
~ nur mit Quellenangabe gestattet reproduction must include mention of the source; ~ verboten copyright (all rights) reserved, copyrighted in all countries; ~, auch auszugsweise verboten not to be reproduced in part or in whole;
Sache mit ~ betreiben to pursue a matter vigorously; mit ~ bessere Bedingungen fordern to make a forceful demand for better conditions; mit ~ darauf hinweisen to drive home a point; sich mit ganzem ~ auf eine Aufgabe konzentrieren to throw all one's energy into a task; besonderen ~ auf etw. legen to place emphasis (lay stress) on s. th.; einer Sache ~ verleihen to give effect to s. th.; seinen Worten ~ verleihen to give point to one's words.
nachdrucken to reprint, to reproduce, to republish, to reissue;
unerlaubt ~ to pirate, to counterfeit.
Nachdrucker copyist, plagiarist, reprinter, pirate.
Nachdruckerlaubnis reproduction permit, permission to reprint.
nachdrücklich insistent, vigorous, forceful, high-pressure, with emphasis;
~ betonen to emphasize, to stress a point; Sache ~ betreiben to pursue a matter vigorously; ~ auf die Notwendigkeit sorgfältig zu fahren hinweisen to emphasize the importance of careful driving;
~e Einwendungen erheben to object in strong language; ~ geäußerte Meinung emphatic opinion.
Nachdruck|recht copyright; zweites ~recht second serial rights; ~rechte für Zeitschriften magazine rights; ~verfahren reprinting process; ~vergütung reproduction fee; ~vermerk copyright notice *(US)*.
nach|dunkeln to darken; ~ehelich post-nuptial; ~eifern to strive for; jem. ~eifern to emulate s. o., to follow in s. one's tracks.
Nach|eiferung emulation; ~eile *(Handelsrecht)* right of stoppage, *(Völkerrecht)* hot pursuit.
nacheilen, jem. to hasten (rush) after s. o.
nacheinander one after another, consecutively, successively, in succession, *(abwechselnd)* in turns, alternately;
drei Tage ~ on three days running.
nachempfinden, jds. Gefühle to understand s. one's feelings; jds. Verlust ~ to sympathize in s. one's loss.
Nachempfindung sympathy, empathy.
nachentwickeln *(Foto)* to redevelop.
Nacherbe remainderman, reversioner, reversionary heir, substitute of an entail;
auf den ~n übergehen to pass to the remainderman; als ~ auf den Überlebenden eingesetzt werden to take the estate by way of remainder.
Nach|erbeneinsetzung executory devise; ~erbfolge reversionary succession; ~erbschaft estate in expectancy, expectant estate, limitation over, remaindership, limitation over; ~erbschaft festlegen to settle property; ~erbschaftsrecht revisionary interest, interest in expectancy; ~erbschaftswert value of a reversion.
nacherheben, Steuern to assess for additional payment.
Nach|erhebung additional assessment; ~erhebung von Zöllen subsequent levy of duties; ~ernte gleanings, *(zweite Ernte)* aftercrop, *(Heu)* aftermath; ~erwerber subsequent taker.
nacherzählen to retell, *(schriftlich)* to rewrite, to reproduce.
nacherzählt, dem Englischen adapted from the English.
Nacherzählung reproduction, *(Schule)* comprehension test.
nach|essen to eat later; ~exerzieren to do extra drill.
Nachfahre descendant.
nachfahren, Zug mit dem Auto to follow a train by car.
Nachfaß|aktion follow-up action, *(Interview)* follow-up on nonrespondents; ~brief follow-up letter.
Nachfassen follow-up, reminder, *(beim Essen)* second helping;
~ bei Nichtbeantwortung follow-up on correspondence.
nachfassen to follow up, to remind;
bei jem. ~ to approach s. o. again; beim Essen ~ to have a second helping.
nachfassende Tätigkeit follow-up.
Nachfaßwerbung follow-up (reminder) advertising.
Nach|feier subsequent (later) celebration; ~feststellung additional assessment; ~finanzierung supplementary financial assistance.
Nachfolge succession, descent;
direkte ~ lineal descent; rechtmäßige ~ legitimacy, legitimate descent;
~ im Amt succession in office; ~ im Erbschaftswege hereditary succession; ~ in gerader Linie lineal succession;
jds. ~ antreten to succeed to s. o., to become s. one's successor;
~ regeln to establish the right of succession;
~aktion follow-up; ~bank resulting bank; ~bedarf bei Instandsetzungsarbeiten maintenance backlog.
nachfolgeberechtigt sein to be entitled to succeed.
Nachfolge|firma successor in business, successor company; ~konferenz follow-up conference.
nachfolgen to follow suit, *(im Amt, Stellung)* to succeed;
jem. im Tode ~ to die shortly after s. o.;
einem Brief einen Zahlungsbefehl ~ lassen to follow up a letter with a summons.
nachfolgend subsequent, successive, following, *(nachbenannt)* named below;
im ~en hereinafter;
~e Beschreibung following description; ~e Entschließung following resolution; ~e Geschichte following story; ~e Hypothek subsequent mortgage; ~es Indossament subsequent endorsement; ~er Präsident incoming president; ~e Tätigkeit follow-up work.
Nachfolge|ordnung, vorherbestimmte entail; ~organisation successor organization.
Nachfolger successor, follower, *(Miet-, Pachtverhältnis)* incomer, *(Rechtsverhältnis)* representative, subsequent owner;
als ~ von in succession to;
j. zu seinem ~ ausersehen to designate s. o. as (for) one's successor; ~ bestimmen to appoint a successor; j. als geeigneten ~ erklären to vouch s. o. as a fit successor; sich zum ~ erklären to declare o. s. the successor; Geschäft seinen ~n übergeben to turn over a business to one's successors; als ~ für j. eingesetzt werden to replace s. o.; jds. ~ im Ministerium werden to succeed s. o. as minister.

Nachfolge|recht right of succession *(Br.)*; ~**staaten** succession states; ~**verpflichtungserklärung** *(Spediteur)* adoption notice.

nachfordern *(Aktieneinzahlung)* to call for additional payment, *(zeitlich)* to claim subsequently, *(zusätzlich)* to demand as extra, to claim in addition.

Nachforderung additional demand, supplemental (after, additional) claim, extra (back) charge, *(Steuer)* tax reappraisal.

Nachforderungs|bescheid additional assessment notice; ~**vorlage** supplementary budget.

nachforschen to inquire, to investigate, to search, to trace.

Nachforschung inquiry, investigation, search, research, tracing, inquest;
zwecks ~ for the purpose of inquiry;
amtliche ~**en** official inquiry; **genaue** ~**en** narrow (close) investigations; **polizeiliche** ~**en** investigations by the police;
~**en an Ort und Stelle** investigations on the spot; ~ **nach einem verlorenen Testament** search for a lost will;
~**en anstellen** to make (institute) inquiries (researches), to pursue an inquiry; **keine gründlichen** ~**en anstellen** to fail to make a reasonable investigation; ~**en auf zwei Personen einengen** to narrow the search down to two men; **sich den** ~**en der Polizei entziehen** to hide from the police.

Nachforschungsanweisung *(Bank)* tracing order.

Nachfrage demand, request, call, requisition, market, *(Bedarf)* demand, need, *(Erkundigung)* inquiry;
auf ~ on inquiry; **ohne** ~ not in demand;
abgeleitete ~ derived demand; **abnehmende** ~ decreasing (diminishing) demand; **anhaltende** ~ steady (persistent) demand; **anpassungsfähige** ~ adaptable demand; **aufgestaute** ~ pent-up demand; **plötzlich auftretende** ~ rush (immediate) demand; **bedeutende** ~ considerable demand; **beständige** ~ steady demand; **dringende** ~ pressing demand; **elastische** ~ elastic (adaptable) demand; **sich lebhaft entwickelnde** ~ freshly expanding demand; **fehlende** ~ deficiency of demand; **durch vorhandenes Bargeld gedeckte** ~ effectual demand; **geringe** ~ little (limited) demand; **gesamtwirtschaftliche** ~ overall economic (schedule) demand; **durch Kaufkraft und Kaufbereitschaft gestützte** ~ demand backed by the power and desire to buy; **gleichbleibende** ~ steady demand; **große** ~ great demand, run on; **recht gute** ~ quite a little run; **hektische** ~ keen demand; **inländische** ~ home demand; **laufende** ~ current demand; **lebhafte** ~ active (brisk, lively, keen, strong) demand; **äußerst lebhafte** ~ rush, run on; **lustlose** ~ sluggish demand; **mangelnde** ~ lack of demand; **nachlassende** ~ fall in demand, slackening demand; **reziproke** ~ reciprocal demand; **saisonbedingte** ~ seasonal demand; **schrumpfende** ~ contraction in demand; **schwache** ~ slack demand; **schwankende** ~ fluctuating market; **sinkende** ~ declining demand; **spärliche** ~ slack demand; **spekulative** ~ speculative demand; **stagnierende** ~ stationary (slack, stagnant) demand; **starke** ~ brisk (keen, strong) demand, run on, great run; **steigende** ~ increasing demand; **stürmische** ~ keen (strong) demand, run on; **tatsächliche** ~ effective demand; **träge** ~ sluggish demand; **überhöhte** ~ surplus (excess) demand; **unbedeutende** ~ insignificant demand; **unelastische** ~ inelastic demand; **ungeheure** ~ huge demand; **unvorhergesehene** ~ unprecedented market; **verbundene** ~ joint demand; **gesamte volkswirtschaftliche** ~ overall economic (schedule) demand; **ständig wachsende** ~ increase in (growing) demand; **zusammengesetzte** ~ composite demand;
Angebot und ~ supply and demand;
~ **nach Arbeitskräften** labo(u)r demand; ~ **nach Bankkrediten** bank-loan demand; ~ **nach Bauleistungen** orders for the building industry; ~ **nach Gütern des gehobenen Bedarfs** demand for luxuries; ~ **nach einem Markenartikel** brand demand; **starke** ~ **nach Montanaktien** rush on mining stocks; **ungeheure** ~ **nach Ölaktien** run on oil stocks; ~ **nach Personalkrediten** private demand for credit; ~ **nach allen Qualitäten** demand for every description; ~ **nach Verkehrsmöglichkeiten** traffic requirements, transportation needs;
von der ~ **abhängen** to be relative to demand; ~ **befriedigen** to meet (supply, satisfy) the demand; ~ **beleben** to stimulate demand; ~ **dämpfen** to curb demand; ~ **decken** to meet demand; ~ **für die kommende Saison decken** to order one's supplies for the season; **geringe** ~ **finden** to be in limited demand; **starke** ~ **finden** to come into great demand; **künstliche** ~ **nach Aktien hervorrufen** to make a market; ~ **nicht befriedigen können** to stay well ahead of supply; ~ **steigern** to increase demand; ~ **übersteigen** to outstrip (outpace) the demand;
~**abhängigkeit des Volkseinkommens** determination of national income; ~**abnahme** reduced demand; ~**analyse** demand analysis; **relative** ~**änderungen** proportionate changes in demand; ~**ankurbelung** boost to demand; ~**anstieg** growth of demand; ~**aussichten** expectation of demand; ~**ausweitung** extension in demand; ~**ballung** piling up of demand, accumulated demand.

nachfragebedingt demand-induced.

Nachfrage|bedürfnisse steuern to regulate the level of demand; ~**belebung** growth of (upturn in) demand; ~**boom** wave of demand; ~**dämpfung** damper on (dampening of) demand; ~**deckung** satisfaction of demand, commodity coverage; ~**druck** pressure (pull, push) of demand; **überhöhter** ~**druck** excessive demand pressure; ~**dynamik** demand pull, strength of market; ~**effekt** demand effect, impact on demand; ~**einbruch** decline in demand; ~**elastizität** elasticity of demand; ~**entwicklung** trend of the market, movement in demand, demand trend; ~**erhöhung** increase in demand; ~**ermächtigung** inquirendo; ~**expansion** expansion of demand; ~**faktor** demand factor; ~**flexibilität** market flexibility; ~**funktion** demand function; ~**impuls** stimulation of demand; ~**inflation** demand inflation; ~**instabilität** instability of demand; ~**intensivierung** intensified demand; ~**konjunktur** booming demand; ~**kredit** supplementary credit; ~**kurs** bid price; ~**kurve** demand curve; ~**kurve für Investitionskapital** investment demand curve; ~**lücke** hiatus in demand; ~**massierung** accumulated demand; ~**menge** quantity demanded; ~**monopol** buyer's monopoly, monopsony.

nachfragen *(im Laden)* to inquire for, to demand, *(nachforschen)* to make inquiries, to inquire about.

Nachfrage|rückgang decrease (decline, drop, fall) in (decreased, decreasing) demand; **plötzlicher** ~**rückgang** slump in demand; ~**rückstau** suppressed demand; ~**schöpfung** demand creation; ~**schrumpfung** contraction in demand; ~**schwäche** softness in demand; ~**schwankungen** fluctuations in demand; ~**seite** buyer's market; ~**sog** pressing demand, pressure of demand, demand pull; ~**soginflation** demand-pull inflation; ~**spitze** peak of demand; ~**stagnation** stagnation of demand; ~**stau** pent-up (piling up of) demand.

nachfragesteigernde|Maßnahmen demand-pull measures; ~ **Wirkung** demand-increasing effects.

Nachfrage|steigerung increase in demand; ~**steuerung** demand management; **zurückhaltende** ~**steuerung** restrictive demand-management policies; ~**stoß** run, rush, surge of demand; ~**struktur** demand structure; ~**tendenz** trend of demand; ~**theorie** theory of demand; ~**überhang** excess demand, surplus demand, buyers over *(Br.)*; ~**verlagerung** movement in demand; ~**verschiebung** shift in demand, demand shift; ~**wachstum** growth of demand; ~**wandel** change of requirement; ~**weckung** consumptionism; ~**welle** increase in (flood, wave of) demand; ~**wirkung** demand effect; **steigende** ~**wirkung** bandwaggon effect.

Nachfrist period (days) of grace, [additional] respite, *(zusätzliche Frist)* additional period, extension of time;
~ **gewähren** to give grace; ~ **setzen** to grant a delay for payment;
~**gewährung** extension (prologation) of time.

nachfüllen to fill up, to refill, to add to, to replenish;
Benzin ~ to refuel, to fill with petrol; **jds. Glas** ~ to fill up s. one's glass; **Öl** ~ to add oil; **Wasser** ~ to top up the water.

Nachgang, im ~ **zu unserem Brief** referring (further) to our letter.

Nachgeben give, yield, *(Zugeständnis)* concession, *(Kurse)* easing off, slackening, sagging;
beiderseitiges ~ reciprocal concessions;
~ **der Kurse** decline in prices; **anfänglich starkes** ~ **der Kurse** initial violent recession; ~ **des Pfundkurses** sagging of the pound; ~ **der Preise** slowdown in prices;
j. zum ~ **veranlassen** to cause s. o. to relent.

nachgeben to give (cave, *US*) in, to come round, to abate, to relent, *(klein beigeben)* to climb down, to cave in, to knuckle under, *(Konzessionen machen)* to make concessions, *(Kurse)* to [be on the] decline, to recede, to sag, to ease [off], to edge down, to slacken, to give way;
etw. ~ *(Kurse)* to ease off a fraction, to recede fractionally; **jds. Drängen** ~ to grant s. one's request; **Druck** ~ to yield to pressure; **in seinen Forderungen** ~ to moderate one's demands; **geringfügig** ~ to decline slightly; **einem Impuls** ~ to act on the impulse of the moment; **den Kindern** ~ to relent towards the children; **jds. Launen** ~ to indulge s. one's whims; **jem. in nichts** ~ to be equal (in no way inferior) to s. o.; **jem. in einem Punkt** ~ to yield (concede) a point to s. o.; **um einen Punkt** ~ *(Aktienkurs)* to recede a point; **unter der Schneelast** ~ *(Dach)* to sag under the weight of the snow; **stillschweigend** ~ to

acquiesce; **dem Vater** ~ to submit to the father; **der Versuchung** ~ to give way to temptation; **jem. vieles** ~ to close one's eyes to much that s. o. does.
nachgebend yielding;
~**e Aktienkurse** slackening share prices; ~**e Kurse** sagging (declining) market; ~**e Preise** receding prices.
nachgeboren puisne.
Nach|gebot later bid, afterbid; ~**gebühr** surcharge, excess (additional) postage, postage-due; ~**gebührenmarke** postage-due stamp.
nachgebührenpflichtig *(Postsendung)* subject to surcharge.
nachgedruckt reprinted;
unerlaubt ~ counterfeit, piratic;
~**e Ausgabe** reprint edition.
nachgehen *(Spur)* to trace, to trail, *(Uhr)* to be slow;
jem. ~ to follow after s. o.; **seiner Arbeit** ~ to pursue one's work; **einem Beruf** ~ to ply a trade, to pursue an occupation; **einem Gerücht** ~ to trace the source of a rumo(u)r; **seinen Geschäften** ~ to follow one's trade, to attend to one's work, to pursue one's business; **jedem Hinweis** ~ to follow up every scrap of information; **Kosten** ~ to keep track of costs; **immer der Nase** ~ to follow one's nose; **einer Sache** ~ to investigate (follow up, check upon) a matter; **jem. auf Schritt und Tritt** ~ to dog s. one's footsteps; **jds. Spuren im Schnee** ~ to follow s. one's track through the snow; **den Spuren eines Verbrechers** ~ to trail a criminal; **seinem Studium** ~ to pursue one's studies; **keiner geregelten Tätigkeit** ~ to have no regular work (occupation); **seinem Vergnügen** ~ to be out for a good time; **einem Vorfall** ~ to trace s. th. up, to check s. th.
nachgelassen posthumous;
etw. ~ **haben** to have gone down a bit;
~**e Werke** unpublished works.
nachgemacht ready-made, *(gefälscht)* counterfeit[ed], dud, fake, forged, queer, *(imitiert)* imitated, copied, *(unecht)* false, sham, fictitious, dummy, artificial, mock, bogus, phony *(US)*;
~**e Banknote** spurious (dud) bank note; ~**e Waren** imitation goods.
nachgeordnet subordinate, secondary, junior, puisne, lower;
jem. ~ **sein** to be inferior (subordinate) to s. o.;
~**e Dienststelle** subordinate authority; ~**es Gericht** inferior (lower) court; ~**e Stellen** subsidiary bodies.
nachgeraten sein, jem. to take after s. o.
nachgesandt *(Brief)* forwarded;
immer wieder ~ **worden sein** to have chased s. o. for weeks.
Nachgeschmack aftertaste;
üblen ~ **hinterlassen** *(fig.)* to leave a bad taste.
nach|gewiesen, nicht not proven *(Scot.)*; **schriftlich** ~**gewiesen** evidenced in writing; ~**gewiesenermaßen** as has been shown, evidently; ~**geworfen bekommen** to be a dozen a dime.
nachgiebig yielding, soft, compliant, flexible, acquiescent, relenting, placable, facile, pliable, compliant, waxy *(fig.)*, *(Kurse)* receding, yielding, declining, giving way, soft, *(nachsichtig)* forbearing, indulgent;
seine Mitmenschen ~ **behandeln** to show forbearance in dealing with people; **jem. gegenüber äußerst** ~ **sein** to grant s. o. every indulgence;
~**er Charakter** pliable character.
Nachgiebigkeit facility, compliance, flexibility, indulgence, pliability, forbearance, leniency, placability.
Nach|girant subsequent endorser; ~**giro** subsequent endorsement.
nachgrübeln to ponder, to muse;
über eine Bemerkung ~ to ponder over a remark; **über ein Problem** ~ to revolve a problem; **über die Vergangenheit** ~ to brood over the past.
Nachhall, starken ~ **im Publikum finden** to meet with a strong response in the public.
nachhaltig lasting, durable, enduring, persistent;
Hausfrieden ~ **stören** to invade the privacy of a home persistently; **Bewerber** ~ **unterstützen** to boost a candidate;
~**e Besserung** marked improvement; ~**e Erträge** *(Forstwirtschaft)* sustained yields; ~**er Protest** rigorous protest; ~**er Widerstand** strong resistance; ~**e Wirkung** lasting effect.
nachhängen, seinen Erinnerungen to muse over memories of the past; **seinen Gedanken** ~ to follow the thread of one's thoughts; **Illusionen** ~ to cherish illusions.
nachhängiger Erwerb *(Wertpapiere)* subsequent acquisition.
Nachhauseweg way home.
nachheizen to put more fuel on the fire.
nachhelfen, jem. to give s. o. a leg up, to lend s. o. a helping hand;
jem. im Englischen ~ to coach s. o. in English; **jds. Gedächtnis** ~ to prod (jog) s. one's memory; **dem Glück etw.** ~ to force the hand of fortune; **einer Sache** ~ to push up a scheme.
nachhetzen, jem. to hotfoot s. o. *(coll.)*; **jem. einen Hund** ~ to set a dog on s. o.
Nachhieb *(Forstwirtschaft)* secondary felling, relogging *(US)*.
Nachhilfe help, assistance, *(Förderung)* boost;
~**kursus** cramming (supplementary) course; ~**lehrer** family (private) tutor, coach; ~**stunden** private lessons, coaching; ~**unterricht** private tuition, coaching; ~**unterricht geben** to give private lessons, to coach, to tutor; ~**unterricht nehmen** to take private lessons, to go to a coach.
Nachhinken time lag;
~ **der öffentlichen Meinung** carryover in the public mind.
nachhinken to lag behind, to trail along;
jem. ~ to limp after s. o.; **hinter der allgemeinen volkswirtschaftlichen Entwicklung** ~ to be out of phase with the national economy; **der wirtschaftlichen Entwicklung** ~ to lag behind in its economic development; **mit seinen Zahlungen** ~ to be late with one's payments.
nachhinkende Entwicklung slow progress.
Nachhol|arbeit arrears of work; ~**bedarf** pent-up *(US)* (replacement, accumulated, backlog) demand; **in der psychiatrischen Behandlung einen großen** ~**bedarf haben** to be sadly lagging behind in the psychiatric treatment.
nachholen to make up, to recover, to retrieve, to catch up;
etw. ~ to pick up on s. th.; **rückständige Korrespondenz** ~ to work off (overtake) arrears of correspondence; **verlorenen Schlaf** ~ to catch up on one's sleep; **Versäumtes** ~ to recover lost (make up for) ground, to make up leeway;
erhebliche Rückstände ~ **müssen** to have considerable leeway to make up *(fam.)*.
Nach|holkonjunktur backlog boom; ~**holung verlorener Arbeitszeit** making up for lost time; ~**hut** *(mil.)* rearguard, rear; ~**hut heranführen** to bring up the rear; ~**hutgefecht** rearguard action; ~**impfung** revaccination; ~**indossament** indorsement after maturity, post indorsement; ~**indossent** subsequent indorser (endorser).
nachjagen to chase after, to run in hot haste;
dem Geld ~ to chase for money; **dem Glück** ~ to hunt after fortune; **jem. einen Hund** ~ to set a dog on s. o.; **jem. eine Kugel** ~ to fire a shot after s. o.; **einem Phantom** ~ to catch at shadows; **Reichtum** ~ to scramble for (hanker after) wealth; **jem. ein Telegramm** ~ to send a telegram after s. o.; **einem Verbrecher** ~ to follow a criminal in hot pursuit; **Vergnügungen** ~ to seek pleasure, to racket about.
nachjustieren to readjust, to true up.
Nach|kalkulation calculation of the historical costs; ~**kalkulator** costing statistician.
nachkalkulieren to calculate the historical costs.
nachkalkulierte Kosten post-mortem (historic) costs.
nachkauen, jem. alles to parrot s. one's words.
Nachkäufe repeat purchases.
nachkaufen to buy later;
Einzelstücke ~ to buy replacement pieces.
Nachklang reverberation, resonance, *(fig.)* aftereffect;
~ **im ganzen Lande haben** to have repercussions throughout the country.
nachklingen, im Gedächtnis to linger in one's mind.
Nachkomme descendant, legal issue;
ohne ~**n** without issue, issueless;
~**n** [legal] issue, offspring, progeny;
direkter ~ lineal (direct) descendant; **eheliche** ~**n** legitimate issue; **erbberechtigte** ~**n** inheritable descendants, issue in tail; **lebende** ~**n** living issue; **männliche** ~**n** male issue, worthiest of blood *(Br.)*;
~ **in gerader Linie** lineal descendant; ~ **in der Seitenlinie** collateral descendant;
zahlreiche ~**n haben** to leave a large posterity; ~**n hinterlassen** to leave (to die leaving) issue; **jds. direkter** ~ **sein** to be a direct descendant of s. o.; **ohne** ~**n sterben** to decease without heirs, to leave no descendants, to die without issue.
nachkommen to follow, to come later, *(befolgen)* to meet, to comply with, *(Schritt halten)* to keep up with;
mit seiner Arbeit nicht ~ to fall behind with one's work; **einer Bitte** ~ to grant a request; **den Forderungen des Klägers** ~ to satisfy a claimant; **einer Pflicht** ~ to fulfil (perform) a duty; **seinen Verbindlichkeiten** ~ to discharge (meet) one's liabilities; **seinen Verpflichtungen** ~ to meet one's commitments, to pay one's due; **einem Versprechen** ~ to keep a promise; **einem Vertrag** ~ to comply with the terms of a contract; **einer Vorladung** ~ to answer (obey) a summons; **Vorschriften** ~ to

follow directions; **Weisungen** ~ to follow instructions; **seinen Zahlungsverpflichtungen nicht** ~ to default in (fall behind with one's) payment; **einer Zusage fristgerecht** ~ to carry out within a given time;
Möbel ~ **lassen** to send for the furniture later.
Nachkommenschaft lawful issue, descendants, progeny, progeniture, begetting, posterity, issue, tail, offspring;
ohne ~ without (barren of) issue, issueless;
alleinige ~ unigeniture; **erbberechtigte** ~ issue in tail; **männliche** ~ male issue;
~ **hinterlassen** to leave issue; **ohne** ~ **sterben** to leave no descendants, to die without issue, to decease without heirs.
Nachkommensklausel words of procreation.
Nach|kömmling afterborn child, descendant, offspring; ~**konjunktur** delayed boom; ~**kontrolle** control, check, inspection, *(med.)* check-up.
nachkontrollieren to control, to check up.
Nachkosten subsequent charges, aftercost *(US)*.
nachkrähen, ihm wird kein Hahn no one will miss him.
Nachkriegs|aufgabe postwar issue; ~**bedürfnisse** postwar demands; ~**belastung** postwar burden; ~**entwicklung** postwar development; ~**epoche** postwar epoch; ~**höchststand** postwar peak; ~**jahre** postwar years; ~**kapitalismus** postwar capitalism; ~**konferenz** postwar conference; ~**konjunktur** postwar boom; ~**landschaft** postwar landscape; ~**möglichkeiten** postwar potentialities; ~**periode** period subsequent to the war; ~**planung** postwar planning; ~**rezession** postwar recession; ~**übergangszeit** postwar transitional period; ~**wirtschaft** postwar economy; ~**wirtschaftshilfe** postwar economic aid; ~**zeit** postwar (afterwar) period (era).
Nachkur aftertreatment.
Nachladen *(Batterie)* recharge.
nachladen, Batterie to recharge a battery; **Geschütz** ~ to reload a gun.
Nachlaß estate of [general] inheritance *(US)*, property left, deceased (decedent's, *US*) estate, *(Grundbesitz)* devise, *(Preisnachlaß)* allowance, abatement, rebate[ment], reduction, deduction, shrinkage, slash, *(Skonto)* discount, *(Steuern)* relief, *(Strafe)* remission;
aus meinem ~ out of my estate; **ohne** ~ without abatement; **unter** ~ **von** allowing, deducting;
von der Gesamtabnahme abhängiger ~ deferred discount *(US)*; **zur Schuldendeckung nicht ausreichender** ~ insufficient assets; **außergewöhnlicher** ~ abnormal discount; **zur Versilberung bestimmter** ~ blended fund *(Br.)*; **beweglicher** ~ personal assets (estate, property); **gesamter** ~ real and personal effects; **getrennter** ~ several inheritance; **herrenloser** ~ vacant estate (succession), estate without a claimant; **illiquider** ~ insolvent estate; **liquider** ~ solvent estate; **literarischer** ~ literary bequest, remains; **reiner** ~ net assets, residuary estate, clear residue; **restlicher** ~ residue, residuary property (estate); **steuerpflichtiger** ~ taxable estate; **überschuldeter** ~ insolvent estate; **umfangreicher** ~ large estate; **unbeweglicher** ~ immovable property, real property (estate); **unverteilter** ~ undivided estate; **frei verfügbarer** ~ dead's part *(Br.)*; **nur teilweise verfügter** ~ partial intestacy; **treuhänderisch verwalteter** ~ trust estate;
reiner ~ **nach Auszahlung aller Legate** net estate; ~ **bei Barzahlung** discount for cash, cash discount on sales; ~ **an der Jahresmiete** deduction from the yearly rent; **10%** ~ **auf den Listenpreis** 10% discount on the list price; ~ **bei Mengenabnahme** quantity discount; ~ **für Rechenfehler des Kassierers** allowance to cashier for errors; ~ **bei Serienbelegung** *(Inserate)* frequency discount; ~ **von 50% für das ganze Sortiment** reduction of five percent on all lines; ~ **bei Veranlagung der Erbschaftssteuer** succession relief; ~ **ohne letztwillige Verfügung** intestate estate; ~ **für vorfristige Zahlung** anticipation discount *(US)*; ~ **nach Zahlung aller Verbindlichkeiten** surplus, residuary estate, clear residue;
~ **abwickeln** to wind up an estate; ~ **beanspruchen** to lay claim to an estate; ~ **bewilligen** to allow an abatement (a discount); ~ **fordern** to demand an allowance (a reduction); ~ **gewähren** to allow a discount (remission), to grant a reduction; ~ **von 3% gewähren** to allow a discount of 3 per cent; ~ **von 3% bei Barzahlung gewähren** to allow 3% discount for cash; ~ **verkürzter Steuersätze in Anspruch nehmen können** to qualify for reduced rate relief; ~ **liquidieren (ordnen)** to wind up an estate; **seinen** ~ **regeln** to put one's affairs (set one's house) in order; ~ **eines Verstorbenen regulieren** to settle the estate of a deceased; ~ **sichern** to protect (preserve) an estate; ~ **zu Erbschaftssteuerzwecken veranlagen** to charge property to estate duty; ~ **verteilen** to distribute (settle, appropriate) an estate; ~ **verwalten** to be executor of an estate,to administer upon a decedent's estate *(US)*; **literarischen** ~ **verwalten** to act as literary executor; **als herrenloser** ~ **dem Staat zufallen** to pass to the Crown as goods vacated *(Br.)*;
~**abwicklung** probate proceedings, administration of decendent's estate *(US)*, *(ordnungsgemäße)* ordinary services; **zur** ~**abwicklung schätzen** to value for probate purposes; **frei verwertbare** ~**aktiva** legal assets; ~**aneignung** intromission; ~**angelegenheiten** estate affairs, probate matters, administrative business; ~**anspruch** claim against an estate; ~**anteil** share in an estate; ~**auseinandersetzung** distribution and partition of an estate; ~**begünstigter** residuary beneficiary; ~**berechtigter** distributee, beneficiary under a will; ~**beschränkung** benefit of inventory; ~**besitz** estate; **ungeteilter** ~**besitz** *(Grundstück)* parcenary; ~**bewertung** probate valuation; ~**einkünfte** estate income; ~**einsetzung** power of appointment.
Nachlassen slowdown, slackening, decrease, letup, wane, diminution, *(Diskont)* abatement, allowance, reduction, discount;
~ **der wirtschaftlichen Aktivität** shakeout; ~ **des Gedächtnisses** failure of memory; ~ **der Geschäfte** slackening of business; ~ **der Konjunktur** economic slowdown (slackening), softening of the economy; **plötzliches** ~ **der Konjunktur** abrupt downturn; ~ **der Kräfte** decline of strength; ~ **der Miete** remission of rent; ~ **der Spannung** relief of tension; ~ **des Sturms** lull in the storm; ~ **der Verstandeskräfte** decay of intellectual power; ~ **des Windes** abatement of the wind.
nachlassen to flag, to sag, *(bei der Arbeit)* to slow down, to let up *(US)*, *(Börse)* to ease off, to slacken, to fall off, to give way, to droop, *(Druck)* to ease off, to relax, *(Einfluß)* to weaken, to wane, *(Fieber)* to abate, *(Gedächtnis)* to fail, to deteriorate, *(Geschäfte)* to be slackening, *(Gesundheit)* to wane, to wither away, to weaken, *(hinterlassen)* to bequeath, to transmit, to leave [behind], *(Interesse)* to slacken, to subside, *(Konjunktur)* to move backwards, to wane, to soften, to slow down, to falter, *(im Preise)* to make an allowance, to allow, to reduce, to abate, *(Sicht)* to get dim, *(Strafe)* to mitigate, *(Sturm)* to lull, to calm, to subside, to abate, *(Verkaufsziffern)* to fall off, *(Wind)* to subside, to die down, to abate, to drop;
15 $ ~ to allow a discount of $ 15; **allmählich** ~ *(Schmerz)* to ease gradually; **mit zunehmendem Alter** ~ *(Reaktionsvermögen)* to slow down with age; **in seinen Anstrengungen (Bemühungen)** ~ to slacken (relax) in one's efforts; **in seiner Arbeit erheblich** ~ to fall off considerably in one's work; **Forderung** ~ to remit a claim; **mit seinen Fragen nicht** ~ to persist in questioning; **Geldstrafe** ~ to remit a fine; **an Geschwindigkeit** ~ to lose speed, to slow down; **am Kaufpreis** ~ to abate the purchase price, to make a reduction in price; **in seinen Leistungen** ~ *(Schüler)* to fall behind in one's studies; **merklich** ~ to deteriorate markedly; **nicht** ~ not to give up; **keinen Pfennig** ~ not to knock off a halfpenny (a cent, *US*); **soundso viel vom Preis** ~ to take so much off the price; **in der Qualität** ~ to fall off in quality; **jem. an der Strafe etw.** ~ to grant s. o. a remission; **Zügel ein wenig** ~ to slacken the reins.
nachlassende|Aufmerksamkeit slackening of attention; ~ **Geschwindigkeit** slackening (slowdown of) speed; ~**s Investitionstempo** slowdown in investment; ~ **Konjunktur** decline in (weakening) economic activity; ~ **Kurse** declining market; ~ **Nachfrage** slackening demand; ~ **Preise** slowdown in prices; ~ **Produktivität** diminishing productivity.
Nachlaß|feststellung probate of an estate; ~**finanzamt** estate duty office; ~**forderung** claim against an estate; **verschiedene** ~**forderungen** sundry moneys owing to the estate; ~**gegenstand** asset, heritable estate; **frei verwertbarer** ~**gegenstand** legal asset; **bei der allgemeinen Erbschaftssteuerberechnung ausgenommene** ~**gegenstände** aggregation exemption; ~**gegenstände, für die ratenweise Erbschaftssteuerbegleichung zulässig ist** instalment option assets; ~**gericht** parish (prerogative, *Br.*) court, register of probate, will and probate department, probate court *(US)* (division, *Br.*), surrogate's court *(New York)*, prefect's court *(New Mexico)*, orphans' court *(New Jersey, Pennsylvania, Maryland, Delaware)*; ~**gerichtsregister** probate court registry; ~**gewährung** allowance of a discount; ~**gläubiger** creditor of an estate; ~**grundstück** inherited real estate; ~**gut** heritable estate.
nachlässig neglectful, negligent, careless, slack, remiss, derelict *(US)*, unfaithful;
~ **im Bezahlen** slow of payment;
~ **arbeiten** to work carelessly; **seinen Amtspflichten** ~ **nachkommen** to be remiss in the performance of one's duties; ~

in seiner Arbeit sein to be slovenly (negligent) in one's work; **in seiner Erscheinung ~ sein** to be careless of one's attire (appearance); **in Geldsachen ~ sein** to be remiss in money matters; **seine Interessen nur ~ wahrnehmen** to be neglectful of one's interests; **bei der Arbeit ~ werden** to slacken in one's work; **sich ~ zurücklehnen** to lean back nonchalantly;
~ ausgeführte Arbeit sloppy (slipshod) work; **~ geführte Bücher** slovenly kept books; **~e Kleidung** sloppy dress; **~e Pflichterfüllung** laxity in one's duties; **~en Stil schreiben** to write a sloppy style.

Nachlässigkeit negligence, neglect, carelessness, *(in der Ausführung)* misfeasance, *(Schlampigkeit)* laxity, sloppiness, slovenliness, *(Ungenauigkeit)* irregularity;
grobe ~ gross negligence; **unglaubliche ~** piece of unbelievable carelessness;
~ in der Ausführung misfeasance;
jem. der ~ bezichtigen to charge s. o. with negligence; **auf jds. ~ zurückzuführen sein** to be due to s. one's negligence.

Nachlaß|inventar inventory; **~klage** administration suit, testamentary cause.

Nachlaßkonkurs insolvent estate, bankruptcy of a deceased;
~eröffnung decree of insolvency; **~verfahren** bankruptcy proceedings of a deceased; **~verwalter** trustee of a bankrupt's estate, receiver.

Nachlaß|kosten charges on an estate, administration (testamentary) expenses; **~liquidierung** winding up of an estate; **frei verfügbare ~masse** assets at hand (entre mains); **~ordnung** probate code, statute of distributions *(US)*; **~pacht** reversionary lease; **~papiere** estate security; **~pfändung** attachment of a hereditable estate, adjudication *(Scot.)*; **berechtigte ~pflege** *(Ehepartner)* necessary intromission; **~pfleger** collector of decedent's estate, curator, administrator of an estate; **gerichtlich eingesetzter ~pfleger** administrator with the will annexed; **~pflegschaft** administration of an estate; **auf einzelne Gegenstände beschränkte ~pflegschaft** special administration; **~pflegschaft anordnen** to grant administration; **~rechnungslegung** estate accounting; **~recht** probate law; **~regelung** estate planning; **~regelung vorsehen** to plan an estate; **~regulierung** settlement of an estate; **~rest für den ~verwalter** dead man's part *(Br.)*; **~rest nach Schuldendeckung** residuary estate *(Br.)*; **~richter** prerogative officer *(Br.)*, probate [court] judge *(US)*; **~sache** testamentary (probate) cause, probate matter; **~schätzer** district valuer *(Br.)*; **~schulden** debts of an estate, ancestral debts; **~schuldner** debtor of an estate; **~sicherung** protection of an estate; **~staffel** scale of discounts, *(Werbung)* sliding-scale discount.

Nachlaßsteuer succession *(US)* (estate, *Br.*, death, *US*, probate) duty, succession (inheritance, *Br.*, estate, *US*) tax;
~ für Verwandte in der Nebenlinie collateral inheritance tax;
~behörde estate duty office *(Br.)*; **~ersparnis** estate-tax savings *(US)*; **~experte** estate-planning tax man *(US)*; **~satz** estate-tax rate *(US)*.

Nachlaß|stiftung testamentary trust; **~teilung** division of an estate; **~treuhänder** settlement trustee; **~übernahme** accession to an estate, assumption of succession; **~überschuldung** insolvency of an estate; **~überschuß** surplus estate; **~unterlagen** *(Bank)* probate book; **~unterschlagung** expilatio; **~verbindlichkeit** heritable obligation, liability attaching to an inheritance; **~verfahren** administration suit, probate proceedings (action); **~verfügung** disposition of decedent's property; **~vergleich** voluntary partition; **~verkürzung** *(zu Steuerzwecken)* reduction in estate; **~vermögen** estate property, assets under will; **~vermögen festlegen** to tie up an estate; **Erbschaftssteuerraten unterliegendes ~vermögen** property with the instalment option; **~versteigerung** auction of an estate; **~verteilung** distribution of an estate, distribution and partition *(US)*, *(durch Testamentsvollstrecker)* appropriation of an estate; **~verteilung nach Stämmen** stipital distribution of property; **~verteilung vornehmen** to appropriate an estate; **~verteilungssystem mit freiem Verfügungsrecht** sprinkling mechanism; **~veruntreuung** subtraction of legacies.

Nachlaßverwalter administrator, general executor, personal representative, trustee of an estate, testamentary trustee (executor);
ausländischer ~ foreign administrator; **gerichtlich bestellter ~** public administrator *(US)*;
~ für einen Auslandsverstorbenen ancillary administrator; **~ eines Autors** literary executor; **behördlich bestellter ~ bei Nichtantritt von testamentarisch vorgesehenen Personen** administrator with the will annexed; **~ am letzten Wohnsitz des Erblassers** domestic administrator;
als ~ tätig sein to administer an estate;
~amt ausschlagen to renounce a probate; **~eid** oath for administrators *(Br.)*; **~in** administratrix; **~kaution** probate bond; **~konto** administrator's account; **~zeugnis** letters testamentary, letters of administration.

Nachlaßverwaltung administration of a decedent's estate *(US)*;
gerichtlich angeordnete ~ administration with the will annexed; **zeitlich begrenzte ~** limited administration; **gegenständlich beschränkte ~** special administration; **unbeschränkte ~** general administrations; **zusätzliche ~** ancillary administration;
~ von Bagatellsachen summary administration; **~ für die überlebende Ehefrau** surviving spouse settlement; **~ von Militärpersonen** regimental debts; **~ am Wohnsitz des Erblassers** domiciliary administration;
~ abgeben to resign control of an estate; **~ anordnen** to commit into administration; **~ ausschlagen** to renounce probate; **in ~ geben** to commit into administration.

Nachlaß|verwaltungskosten expenses of administration; **~verzeichnis** inventory; **~vorsorge** estate planning.

Nachlaßwert value of an estate;
~e estate assets (security);
reiner ~ clear value;
~ eines einzelnen Gegenstands probate value;
~ mit 100.000 $ angeben to swear an estate at $ 100.000.

Nachlaß|wesen administration of an estate; **~wohnsitz** domicile of succession.

nachlaufen, jem. to run after (follow) s. o.; **einem Mädchen ~** to dangle after a girl; **einem Trugbild ~** to pursue a phantom; **jem. überall ~** to tag after s. o.

nachlegen to mend the fire.

nachleiern, alles to be a mere parrot.

Nach|leistung subsequent (additional) performance; **~lese** gleaning; **beim ~lesen des Briefes** on reading the letter again.

nachlesen to read again, *(auf dem Feld)* to glean;
im Gesetz ~ to read up in the law; **in einem Nachschlagwerk ~** to consult a reference book; **Stelle ~** to look up a passage.

nachliefern to deliver subsequently, to supply later;
Nummern einer Zeitschrift ~ to supply back numbers of a magazine.

Nachlieferung additional (subsequent, renewed) delivery, renewed supply, completion;
zur ~ verpflichtet sein to be liable to replace the damaged goods; **~ verlangen** to demand goods in replacement.

nachlösen, Fahrkarte to take a supplementary ticket, to pay the additional fare.

Nachlöseschalter excess-fare window.

nachmachen to imitate, to copy, *(fälschlich)* to fake, to falsify, to forge;
Prüfung ~ to take a make-up; **jds. Stimme ~** to mimic s. one's voice; **j. täuschend ~** to imitate s. o. to the life; **Unterschrift ~** to forge a signature.

Nachmann subsequent holder, *(Wechsel)* subsequent endorser (indorser), second indorser;
potenter ~ substantial endorser.

Nachmieter new tenant.

Nachmietrecht haben to be renewable at the option of the tenant.

Nachmittag, freier afternoon off, half holiday, *(Schule)* remedy *(Br.)*;
an ihrem freien ~ am Mittwoch on their Wednesday half holiday;
~ mit geschlossenen Geschäften early closing day.

nachmittags post meridiam, p. m.

Nachmittags|aufführung matinée; **~kleid** tea gown; **~schicht** second shift; **~schluß der Geschäfte** early closing day; **frühe ~sendungen** *(Rundfunk)* Hank *(Br.)*; **~sitzung** afternoon session; **~unterricht** afternoon classes; **~vorstellung** afternoon performance; **~zeitung** afternoon paper.

Nachmonat subsequent month.

nachmustern *(mil.)* to reexamine.

Nachnahme cash (collect, *US*) on delivery (C.O.D.);
gegen ~ cash (collect, collection, *US*) on delivery, collect *(US)*;
unter ~ der Spesen charges forward *(Br.)*;
~ der Spesen collection (expenses charged) of charges;
mit einer ~ belasten to send cash-on-delivery; **~ einlösen** to meet a cash on delivery; **durch ~ erheben** to charge forward, to collect on delivery; **Paket per ~ schicken** to send a package collect on delivery *(US)* (cash on delivery, *Br.*); **Waren per ~ schicken** to send goods cash on delivery;
~begleitschein cash-on-delivery form; **~betrag** amount to be collected on delivery, trade charge *(Br.)*; **~brief** trade-charge

letter *(Br.)*; ~**gebühr** collection (collect-on-delivery, *US*) fee, charges to be collected; ~**karte** reimbursement card; ~**paket** cash-on-delivery parcel, C.O.D. parcel, collect-on-delivery package *(US)*; ~**postanweisung** trade-charge money order *(Br.)*; **eingeschriebene** ~**sendung** registered C.O.D. mail *(US)*, cash-on-delivery shipment (consignment); ~**spesen** cash- (collect-, *US*) on-delivery charges; ~**verfahren** collect-on-delivery system; ~**verkehr** cash- (collect-, *US*) on-delivery service.

Nachname surname, family (last, given) name.

nachnehmen to charge forward, to collect on delivery.

Nach|nennung post entry; ~**pächter** subsequent tenant; ~**pachtrecht haben** to be renewable at the option of the tenant; ~**patent** later-dated patent; ~**pfändung** second distress.

nachplappern to repeat automatically;
alles ~ to be a mere parrot.

Nachporto surcharge, extra (additional) postage, additional charges;
~**stempel** postage-due stamp.

nachprägen to recoin, to coin again.

Nachprägung repeated coining, *(Fälschung)* counterfeiting.

Nachprämie extra premium.

nachprüfbar verifiable, controllable, checkable;
nicht ~ **sein** not to be subject to review.

nachprüfen to check [up], to check off, to examine, to verify, *(Forderung)* to reconsider, *(kollationieren)* to collate, to tick off;
Angelegenheit ~ to check up on a matter; **jds. Behauptungen** ~ to check s. one's statements; **Echtheit einer Unterschrift** ~ to verify a signature; **erneut** ~ *(Konto)* to overhaul, to re-examine; **Kasse** ~ to verify the cash; **an Ort und Stelle** ~ to carry out an inspection on the spot; **Punkt für Punkt** ~ to examine item by item; **Rechnungsposten** ~ to dot accounts; **sorgfältig** ~ to examine carefully; **Urteil der Vorinstanz** ~ to review a judgment; **vergleichend** ~ to check against; **Wahlliste** ~ to scrutinize an election.

Nachprüfer controller, supervisor, *(Wahllisten)* scrutinizer.

Nachprüfung check[ing], inspection, checkover, countercontrol, verification, revision, re-examination, *(Gericht)* review, *(Schule)* make-up, *(Wahlliste)* scrutiny, recount;
bei nochmaliger ~ on second inspection;
genaue ~ careful examination; **öffentliche** ~ public inquiry; **richterliche** ~ judicial review;
~ **von Einfuhrgeschäften** control of imports; ~ **von Forderungen** reconsideration of claims; ~ **einer Kostenrechnung** review of costs; ~ **der gelieferten Mengen** verification of quantity; ~ **von Rechnungen** examination of business accounts; ~ **von Stimmen** scrutiny of votes; **richterliche** ~ **von Verwaltungsakten** judicial review of administrative actions *(US)*;
seine ~**en absolvieren** to work off one's conditions *(US)*; ~ **auferlegen** *(Universität)* to condition *(US)*; **jds.** ~ **unterliegen** to be subject to s. one's control (review); ~ **der Wahlergebnisse verlangen** to demand a scrutiny.

Nachprüfungs|antrag stellen to petition a review; ~- **und Berichtigungsbeschluß** surcharge and falsify.

nachprüfungspflichtig sein to be subject to review.

Nachprüfungs|recht right of review; ~**verfahren** auditing procedure.

nachrangig of subsequent rank, junior, inferior;
~**e Hypothek** junior (puisne, *Br.*) mortgage; ~**e Konkursforderungen** deferred debts.

nachrechnen to reckon over again, to go over the figures again, to recount, to check [an account], *(neu kalkulieren)* to verify a calculation, to recalculate, to recompute.

Nachrechnung examination, recalculation, checking, *(Konten)* verification, checking, control.

Nachrede, üble malicious gossip, defamation, slander, calumny, calumniation, malediction;
üble ~ **verbreiten** to calumniate, to slander.

nachreden, jem. Böses to cast a slur on s. one's character.

nachreichen to file subsequently.

Nachricht news, advice, letter of advice, intelligence, item, dispatch, wire, *(Auskunft)* information, *(Bericht)* report, account, *(Botschaft)* message, post, *(Kenntnis)* note, knowledge, *(Datenverarbeitung)* message, *(kurze Meldung)* notice, word, *(Mitteilung)* information, communication, *(Wink)* intimation, hint;
bis zum Erhalt einer neuen ~ until further notice; **mangels gegenteiliger** ~ unless countermanded; **ohne vorherige** ~ without prior notice; **von einer** ~ **wie gelähmt** stunned by the news;
eilige ~ urgent message; **große** ~ glad tidings; **irreführende** ~ canard; **rechtzeitige** ~ due notice; **schlechte** ~ a piece of bad news; **sensationelle** ~ sensational piece of news; **telefonische** ~ telephone message; **telegraphierte** ~ cable message; **unangenehme** ~ floorer; **unbestätigte** ~ whispered report; **verschlüsselte** ~ code message; **verspätete** ~ belated post; **zuverlässige** ~ reliable information;
~ **aus erster Hand** first-hand information;
~ **aufmachen** to feature a piece of news; ~ **bekommen** to hear from, to receive word; ~ **bestätigen** to confirm a report; ~ **chiffrieren** to write a message in cipher; ~ **erhalten** to receive notice; ~ **geben (erteilen)** to let know, to send (write) word, to inform, to advise, to inform, to notify, *(offiziell)* to notify; ~ **von jem. haben** to have news from s. o.; ~ **aus erster Hand haben** to have a piece of news first hand; ~ **herunterspielen** to soft-pedal a story; ~ **überall hinausposaunen** to carry the news to everyone in the village; **jem.** ~ **zukommen lassen** to send word to s. o.; **jem. eine** ~ **mitteilen** to put s. o. up to the news; ~ **überbringen** to deliver a message; **jem. eine** ~ **übermitteln** to deliver a message to s. o.; **jem. eine schlechte** ~ **übermitteln** to break the news to s. o.; ~ **telefonisch übermitteln** to send a message by telephone; **Teil einer** ~ **unterdrücken** to kill a passage; ~ **verbreiten** to circulate a report; ~ **veröffentlichen** to break an item of news; **j. auf eine schlechte** ~ **vorbereiten** to prepare s. o. for bad news; ~ **an j. unverbürgt weitergeben** to pass news on to s. o. for what it is worth; **jem. eine** ~ **zurücklassen** to leave a message for s. o.;
eine gute ~ **kommt stets gelegen** good news may be told at any time.

Nachrichten news, dispatches, intelligence, tidings, *(Rundfunk)* news items, newscast, broadcast news;
alarmierende ~ startling news; **allerletzte (nach Redaktionsschluß einlaufende)** ~ stop-press news *(Br.)*, very latest news, red-hot news *(coll.)*, news hot from the press; **angenehme** ~ welcome news; **bedrückende** ~ cold news; **beunruhigende** ~ disturbing (disquieting) news; **deprimierende (niederziehende)** ~ depressing news; **gerade eingetroffene** ~ fresh news; **nach Redaktionsschluß einlaufende** ~ stop-press news *(Br.)*; **erfreuliche** ~ pleasant news; **falsche** ~ hoax; **freudige** ~ exhilarating news; **gefärbte** ~ colo(u)red news; **geschäftliche** ~ business news; **katastrophale** ~ evil news; **letzte (neueste)** ~ latest intelligence, very latest news, stop-press news *(Br.)*; **kaum neue** ~ paucity of news; **schlechte** ~ evil (black) tidings, bad news, noise *(sl.)*; **schwerwiegende** ~ grave news; **sensationelle** ~ redhot news; **zur Verfügung stehende** ~ available information; **vermischte** ~ *(Zeitung)* miscellanies, miscellaneous items; **verschiedene** ~ various items of news; **verschlüsselte** ~ message in code, code message; **wichtige** ~ *(Rundfunk)* leading story; **wichtigste** ~ chief news, wrap-up; **widersprüchliche** ~ contradictiory news; **zusammenhanglose** ~ loose piece of information;
~ **für die Belegschaft** employee newsletter; ~ **aus dem Finanzleben** financial news; ~ **über den Geldmarkt** money article; ~ **aus dem Gerichtsleben** police intelligence; ~ **aus erster Hand** first-hand information; ~ **vom Hofe** court circular; ~ **in Kurzfassung** news summary, *(Rundfunk)* news headlines, news in brief, wrap-up of the news *(US)*; ~ **aus dem Universitätsleben** university intelligence; ~ **aus dem Wirtschaftsleben** industrial news service;
~ **für die Öffentlichkeit aufbereiten (aufmachen)** to edit news for the public, to angle (slant) news; **falsche** ~ **aufbringen** to forge news; ~ **sinnverfälschend aufmachen** to give a false colo(u)r to news; ~ **ausstrahlen** to flash news across the world by radio; ~ **auswerten** *(mil.)* to filter news; ~ **für sich behalten** to keep the news under one's hat; ~ **bei der Kursfestsetzung berücksichtigen** to discount news; ~ **beschaffen** to collect information; ~ **weitgehend nur vom staatlich kontrollierten Fernsehen beziehen** to depend mainly on government-controlled television for news; ~ **bringen** to carry news; ~ **unter die Leute bringen** to get the news across; ~ **durchgeben** to read the news; ~ **einziehen** to make inquiries, *(mil.)* to gather intelligence; ~ **frisieren** to slant (angle) news; ~ **von anderer Stelle haben** to have received news from other quarters; ~ **hören** to listen to the news; **von** ~ **sehr betroffen sein** to be much moved by the news; **von den** ~ **wie gelähmt sein** to be stunned by the news; ~ **senden** to broadcast news; ~ **verbreiten** to disperse (spread) news; **falsche** ~ **verbreiten** to circulate false news; ~ **über die ganze Welt verbreiten** to flash news across the world; ~ **ohne Nachprüfung veröffentlichen** to publish news without vouching for its accuracy; ~ **mit allem Vorbehalt veröffentlichen** to publish news with all reserve; **j. mit** ~ **versorgen** to

furnish s. o. with information; **ungeduldig auf ~ warten** to be eager for news; **~ weiterleiten** to hand on news; **von ~ beunruhigt werden** to feel alarm at the news; **~ zensieren** to exercise censorship over news;
~abteilung *(mil.)* intelligence department, signals battalion, *(pol.)* news department; **~abwehr** *(mil.)* intelligence; **~agentur** news agency, press agency (outfit), newspaper syndicate *(US)*; **~austausch** exchange of information, communicational exchange; **öffentlicher ~austausch** public correspondence; **~auswertung** *(mil.)* intelligence evaluation, filtering of news; **~beschaffung** collection of information; **~beschaffungssystem** news-gathering machine; **kleines ~blatt** news magazine, newssheet, bulletin, newsbill *(Br.)*; **~blätter von Untergrundbewegungen** underground newssheets; **~büro** news (newspaper) syndicate *(US)*, news (press) agency, news outfit; **~dienst** news bulletin (service), *(Geheimdienst)* intelligence (secret, *Br.*) service, military intelligence; **~durchsage** broadcasting of (reading the) news; **~einheit** *(mil.)* signals unit; **~einschätzung** *(Börse)* discounting of news; **~fluß** flow of news; **~freiheit** free communications; **~kommentar** news commentary; **~kommentator** news analyst, commentator; **~kompanie** signals company; **~magazin** news magazine, newsbill *(Br.)*; **~manipulation** news management (manipulation).
nachrichtenmäßige Bedeutung newsworthiness.
Nachrichten|material information; **geheimes ~material** clandestine intelligence; **~meldung** item of news, news item; **~mittel** news medium, *(pl.)* means (media) of communication; **~netz** network of communications; **~netz der Seestreitkräfte** marine communications; **~offizier** intelligence officer, *(Nachrichtentruppe)* signal officer; **~organe** information media, news business *(coll.)*; **~quelle** intelligence source; **gute ~quelle** good stock of information; **~redakteur** news editor; **~sammelstelle** message center *(US)* (centre, *Br.*), news desk; **~satellit** intelligence (communication) satellite; **~schutz** data secrecy; **~sendung** news bulletin (broadcast, broadcasting), news show, newscast, news program(me), radio newsreel *(Br.)*; **kurze ~sendung** news flash; **~sendung im Zeitraffertempo** speeded-up newsreel; **~sperre** news blackout (embargo); **unterlaufende ~sperre** broken embargo; **~sperre verhängen** to impose a blackout on information; **~sprecher** newscaster, news reader; **~stelle** news outlet, information center *(US)* (centre, *Br.*), *(mil.)* intelligence department; **~streifen** news slip; **~streuung** dissemination of news; **~technik** telecommunication, means of communication; **~träger, ~übermittler** message bearer; **~truppe** Royal Corps of Signals *(Br.)*, Signal Corps *(US)*; **~überbringer** intelligencer; **~übermittlung** transmission of news; **~übersicht** news headlines, wrap-up of the news *(US)*, news summary; **~überwachung** monitoring; **~unternehmen** communications company.
Nachrichtenverbindung intercommunication;
~en lines of communication;
mündliche ~ voice communication;
~en überwachen to monitor, to censor.
Nachrichten|verbreitung circulation of news; **~verkehr** telecommunication traffic; **~verkehrsmittel** communication facilities; **~verteilernetz** *(Agentur)* network distribution; **~weg** lines of communication, channel of communication; **~weltstadt** news capital; **~wesen** communications, communications system, traffic, *(mil.)* signal service; **~zensur** silken curtain *(Br.)*, censorship of the press; **~zentrale** information center *(US)* (centre, *Br.*), *(Zeitung)* newsroom; **~zentrum** staple of news, *(mil.)* communication center *(US)* (centre, *Br.*); **~zusammenstellung** newscast.
nachrichtlich for information, informational, informative, blind copy to.
nachrücken to fill a vacated post, to be promoted, *(mil.)* to close in, to move up, to pursue;
in ein aufgegebenes Gelände ~ to move on into a vacated territory; **in eine höhere Stelle ~** to be advanced to a higher post.
Nachruf *(Zeitung)* obituary [notice];
~ verfassen to write an obituary (a necrology).
nachrufen, jem. Schimpfwörter to shout after s. o. in the street.
Nachruhm posthumous fame, glory.
nachsacken *(Erdreich)* to subside, to settle.
nachsagen, jem. Schlechtes to cast obloquy upon s. o., to spread all sorts of falsehoods about s. o.
Nachsaison afterseason, off-season, late season, *(Bekleidungsindustrie)* pinockle season *(sl.)*;
~fahrschein off-season fare; **~geschäft** late-season business; **~tarif** *(Hotel)* afterseason rates.

Nach|schaden consequential damage; **~schätzung** additional assessment; **~schau** follow-up examination.
nach|schauen to gaze after, to follow with one's eyes; **j. Wein ~schenken** to refill s. one's glass of wine.
nachschicken *(Brief)* to reforward, to redirect;
Rest des Geldes ~ to send the remainder of the money later.
Nachschieben subsequent presentation;
~ von Ersatzteilen supply of spare parts; **~ von Kündigungsgründen** adducing reasons for dismissal.
nachschieben to adduce subsequentially;
Kündigungsgründe ~ to adduce reasons for dismissal.
nachschießen to add, to make an additional (supplementary) payment, to pay the remainder, *(auf Aktien)* to pay a further call, *(Effektendifferenzgeschäft)* to put up more margin (additional cover), to remargin *(US)*;
Kapital ~ to infuse fresh capital; **Rest einer Summe ~** to pay the balance of a sum.
Nachschlag *(mil.)* second helping.
Nachschlage|bibliothek reference library, *(öffentliche)* library for public reference; **~buch** handbook, reference book, wordbook.
Nachschlagen im Wörterbuch consultation of a dictionary.
nachschlagen, im Wörterbuch to consult (look up in) a dictionary.
Nachschlage|raum *(Bibiothek)* reference room; **~tabelle** reference table.
Nachschlagewerk reference book (work), handbook;
maßgebendes ~ authoritative research and reference work;
~ mit Anzeigenteil reference medium.
nach|schleichen, jem. to sneak stealthily after s. o.; **seine Füße ~schleppen** to drag one's feet; **schweren Koffer ~schleppen** to lug a heavy suitcase.
Nachschlüssel master (duplicate, false, skeleton) key, passkey, picklock.
nachschmeißen, jem. to throw (chuck) after s. o.; **gutes Geld schlechtem ~** to throw good money after bad.
nachschreiben, Arbeit to do a paper later; **Vorlesung ~** to take notes in a lecture.
Nachschrift postscript (P.S.), transcription, copy.
Nachschub fresh supply, *(mil.)* reinforcement;
ohne ~ unsupplied;
~ von Lebensmitteln supplying with provisions; **~ auf dem Luftwege** air supply; **~ und Rückschub** logistics;
~ sicherstellen to recruit supplies; **für ausreichenden ~ sorgen** to assure adequate supply;
~achse axis of supply; **~basis** supply base; **~bedarf** supply requirements; **~dienst** supply service; **~einheit** carrying party; **~gebiet** supply area; **~güter** supplies; **~kolonne** supply column; **einer ~kolonne Geleit geben** to convoy a supply column; **~kräfte** reinforcement troops; **~lager** supply store, magazine, general depot; **~linie** supply line; **~linien unterbrechen** to cut off supply; **~problem** logistical problem; **~schwierigkeiten** supply difficulties; **~straße** supply route; **~transport** transport of supplies; **~verteilungsstelle** supply center *(US)* (centre, *Br.*); **~verzögerungen** supply delays; **~wege** supply lines, communications; **~wesen** logistics, supply organization (system); **das ~wesen betreffend** logistic.
Nachschuß supplementary (additional) payment, *(Aktenemission)* further call, *(druckt.)* over copies, overs, *(Effektenlombard)* additional (further) cover, further margin, remargining *(US)*;
~ einfordern to call for additional payment, *(Effektenlombard)* to call for additional cover, to remargin *(US)*;
~aufforderung call for additional cover, margin call (notice) *(US)*, stock assessment *(US)*; **~frist** time allowed for additional payment; **~haftung der Aktionäre** stockholders' liability.
nachschüssig *(Zinsberechnung)* decursive.
Nachschuß|klausel *(bei Versicherungsvereinen auf Gegenseitigkeit)* safety clause; **~leistung** additional contribution.
Nachschußpflicht liability to contribute, *(Aktenmission)* liability to further call, *(Effektenlombard)* call for additional cover, *(Lebensversicherung)* reserve liability *(Br.)*;
mit beschränkter ~ limited by guarantee;
~ in doppelter Höhe double liability.
nachschußpflichtig assessable, *(Firmenkonkurs)* contributory;
nicht ~ nonassessable;
~ sein to be liable to contribute to the assets of a company *(Br.)*;
~e Aktien assessable stock *(US)*; **nicht ~e Vorzugsaktien** nonassessable preferred stocks *(US)*.

Nachschuß|pflichtiger *(Gesellschaftskonkurs)* contributory *(Br.)*; ~**prämie** additional premium; ~**summe** appoint; ~**summe aufbringen** to tender the exact amount; ~**verpflichtung** stock assessment *(US)*.
Nachschußzahlung fresh payment, *(Effektenlombard)* additional cover (margin), remargining *(US)*;
~ **auf Bankaktien** *(bei Sanierung)* assessment on bank stocks *(US)*;
~ **fordern** to call for additional payment; ~ **leisten** *(Aktenemission)* to make further payment on shares (stocks, *US*), *(Effektenlombard)* to put up more margin, to furnish (put up) additional cover, to remargin *(US)*.
nachschütten, Kohle to add (put on more) coal.
Nachsehen inspection, examination;
~ **der Rechnungsbücher** auditing the books; ~ **der Reifen** checking of tyres;
jem. das ~ **geben** to give s. o. the slip, to leave s. o. out in the cold; **das** ~ **haben** to go empty-handed, to get nothing.
nachsehen to look over, to examine, to inspect, *(Maschine)* to overhaul, *(Rechnungsbücher)* to audit, *(Schule)* to correct, *(überprüfen)* to verify;
Auto ~ to overhaul a car; **Bremsen** ~ to inspect (adjust) the brakes; **jem. seine Fehler** ~ to overlook s. one's faults; **gründlich** ~ to give a major overhaul, to overhaul thoroughly; **einem Kind zuviel** ~ to be too lenient with a child; **einem Schiff** ~ to watch a ship; **Schulhefte** ~ to correct exercises (exercise books); **in einem Wörterbuch** ~ to consult a dictionary.
Nachsende|anschrift forwarding address; ~**auftrag** redirection order; ~**gebühr** forwarding charges.
nachsenden to send on, to forward, to readdress, to redirect, to transmit;
bitte ~ please forward; **nicht** ~ to await arrival;
jem. einen Brief ~ to forward a letter to s. o.
Nachsendung forwarding, redirection, retransmission.
nachsetzen, einem Dieb to chase a thief.
Nachsicht indulgence, respite, forbearance, toleration, leniency;
j. um ~ **bitten** to ask (entreat) s. one's indulgence; ~ **mit jem. haben** to make allowances for s. o., to show forbearance with s. o.; **mit jds. Schwächen** ~ **haben** to bear with s. one's faults; **seinen Kindern gegenüber zuviel** ~ **walten lassen** to be too lenient with one's children; ~ **üben** to give fair quarter, to practise charity towards s. o.; **ohne** ~ **vorgehen** to proceed without mercy;
~**brief** letter of respite.
nachsichtig indulgent, forbearing, patient;
zu ~ over-indulgent;
j. ~ **behandeln** to show forbearance towards s. o.; ~ **sein** to indulge, to be indulgent (forbearing); **äußerst** ~ **gegenüber jem. sein** to grant s. o. every indulgence.
Nachsichts|frist period of grace; ~**tage** days of respite; ~**wechsel** time bill (draft), bill after sight, after-sight bill.
nachsinnen to mediate, to ponder, to reflect;
über seine Schicksalsschläge ~ to be meditating upon one's misfortunes; **über die Zukunft** ~ to muse on the future.
nachsitzen, Schüler ~ **lassen** to detain a pupil, to give a pupil detention; ~ **müssen** *(Schule)* to be kept in.
Nachsitzenlassen *(Schüler)* keeping in, detainment.
Nachsommer late summer.
Nachspiel aftermath, sequel;
gerichtliches ~ judicial sequel, sequel in court.
nach|spielen to replay, *(Theater)* to reenact; **jem.** ~**spionieren** to spy upon s. o.
nächstberechtigt next entitled;
~ **sein** to have the first title.
Nächstberufener next entitled.
nächstbeste Sorte next quality.
Nächste, jeder ist sich selbst der charity begins at home.
nächste|r nearest, closest, next;
der Wahrheit am ~**n kommen** to come closest to the truth; **am** ~**n wohnen** to live nearest;
~**r Anspruch auf die Erbschaft** first claim to an inheritance; **seine** ~ **Blutsverwandte** one's nearest of kin; **bei** ~**r Gelegenheit** at the earliest opportunity; ~**r Nachbar** next-door neighbo(u)r; **in** ~**r Nähe** in the immediate vicinity; **Waren mit der** ~**n Post schicken** to send goods by return of post; **im** ~**n Stock wohnen** to live on the floor above; ~**r Tagesordnungspunkt** next on the agenda; ~ **Tankstelle** nearest petrol station; ~ **Verwandte** closest relatives, immediate family.
nachstehen to be second (inferior), to take a back seat;
jem. in keiner Hinsicht ~ to be in no way inferior to (equal of) s. o.; **keinem** ~ to yield (be second) to no one; **jem. im Range** ~ to be second to s. o. in seniority; **jem. in vielem** ~ to be inferior to s. o. in many respects;
jem. ~ **müssen** to have to take second place to s. o.
nachstehend hereinafter, following, undermentioned, thereinafter;
im ~**en** as follows, thereinafter; **wie** ~ **angegeben** as indicated below;
~ **aufgeführte Preise** prices specified below.
nachsteigen, einem Mädchen to be after a girl.
nachstellbar adjustable.
nachstellen to readjust;
jem. ~ to set traps (lie in wait) for s. o.; **sein Privatleben seinem Pflichtenkreis** ~ to subordinate one's private life to one's duties; **Uhr** ~ to put back a watch.
Nachsteller giver of an option.
nachstellig junior.
Nachstellungen unwelcome advances, persecutions;
sich den ~ **eines Bewerbers nur schwer entziehen können** to have difficulty in repelling the advances of a suitor; **vor den** ~ **seiner Feinde sicher sein** to be safe from the persecutions of one's enemies.
Nächstenliebe, an die ~ **appellieren** to make an appeal to charity.
Nachsteuer additional tax, extra duty.
nächstliegend obvious, most likely;
~**es Problem** foremost problem.
Nächstliegende, das the most obvious thing.
nachstoßen *(mil.)* to follow on, to move up.
Nachsuchen request, petition.
nachsuchen to request, to petition, to solicit, to apply for;
um eine Audienz ~ to request an audience; **überall** ~ to search everywhere, to hunt high and low; **um finanzielle Unterstützung** ~ to ask for financial aid; **um Zulassung** ~ to seek admission.
Nachsuchung request, petition.
nachsynchronisieren to post-synchronize.
Nachsynchronisierung post-synchronization.
Nacht, bei Einbruch der at nightfall; **bis spät in die** ~ until all hours; **in tiefster** ~ at dead of night; **mit einbrechender** ~ at nightfall; **mitten in der** ~ in the depth of night; **unter dem Schutz der** ~ under the cover (mask) of night, under favo(u)r of the night;
die ganze ~ **geöffnet** open all night; **Tag und** ~ **geöffnet** open day and night; **die ganze** ~ **hindurch** all night long;
sternklare ~ starlit night;
ganze ~ **arbeiten** to work all night [long]; **bis spät in die** ~ **arbeiten** to burn the midnight oil; **Tag und** ~ **arbeiten** to work round the clock (day and night); **bei** ~ **und Nebel ausrücken** to shoot the moon; **jem. eine schlaflose** ~ **bereiten** to cause s. o. a sleepless night; **über** ~ **bleiben** to stay overnight; **sich bei** ~ **und Nebel davonmachen** to steal away under cover of darkness; **ganze** ~ **durchfeiern** to feast away the night; **ganze** ~ **durchschlafen** to sleep the whole night through; **bei** ~ **fliegen** to night-fly; **schlechte** ~ **hinter sich haben** to have had a poor night; ~ **zum Tag machen** to turn night into day; **sich die ganze** ~ **um die Ohren schlagen** to make a night of it; **häßlich wie die** ~ **sein** to be as ugly as sin; **so verschieden wie Tag und** ~ **sein** to be as different as chalk and cheese; **über** ~ **reich geworden sein** to wake up to find o. s. rich; **über** ~ **berühmt werden** to become famous overnight;
~**angriff** *(mil.)* night attack.
Nachtanken refuelling.
nachtanken to refuel.
Nacht|anschluß *(Telefon)* night number; ~**arbeit** nightwork, night shift, night employment, lamp oil; **in** ~**arbeit entstanden sein** to smell of the lamp; ~**arbeiter** night man; ~**arbeiter sein** to burn the midnight oil; ~**arbeitszuschlag** nightwork premium; ~**asyl** night refuge (shelter), cold harbo(u)r, common lodginghouse *(Br.)*.
Nachtat post-act.
Nacht|aufklärung *(mil.)* night reconnaissance; ~**aufnahme** night exposure; ~**ausgabe** late night final, extra special *(Br.)*.
nachtaxieren to re-assess.
Nachtbeleuchtung dimmed light.
nachtblind night-blind.
Nacht|blindheit night blindness; ~**bomber** *(mil.)* night bomber; ~**bummler** fly-by-night; ~**dienst** night duty (service); **heute** ~**dienst** *(Apotheke)* open all night; ~**dienstentschädigung** allowance for night duty.
Nachteil disadvantage, handicap, disinterest, harm, drawback, derogation, *(Schaden)* detriment, prejudice, damage, injury, *(Verlust)* loss, cost(s), damage;

ohne ~ für without prejudice for; **sehr im ~** out on a limb *(coll.)*; **zu jds. ~** to the injury (detriment, prejudice) of s. o.; **zum ~** to the prejudice (detriment) of;
finanzielle ~e pecuniary loss; **steuerpolitische ~e** fiscal deficiencies; **versteckter ~** nigger in the woodpile; **wesentlicher ~** material detriment; **wirtschaftliche ~e** economic handicaps; **zeitlicher ~** time handicap;
~e des Fortschritts penalty of progress;
zum ~ seiner Gesundheit zu lange arbeiten to work long hours to the detriment of one's health; **der Volkswirtschaft zum ~ ausschlagen** to be injurious to the national economy; **zum ~ gereichen** to be detrimental to, to derogate; **große finanzielle ~e haben** to be under a great financial handicap; **~e zur Folge haben** to affect prejudicially; **~e in Kauf nehmen** to put up with a disadvantage; **im ~ sein** to labo(u)r under a disadvantage; **durch seine Kurzsichtigkeit im ~ sein** to be handicapped by one's shortsightedness; **schwer im ~ sein** to have the cards stacked against one; **von ~ sein** to be a drawback; **sich zu seinem ~ verändern** to derogate from o. s.; **~e vergüten** to supply odds; **mit ~ verkaufen** to sell at a loss; **jem. ~e zufügen** to wrong s. o.
nachteilig derogative, detrimental, disadvantageous, prejudicial, injurious, harmful, pernicious, inimical, hurtful, *(abträglich)* derogatory, promiscuous, *(ungünstig)* adverse, unfavo(u)rable;
~ behandeln to prejudice, to discriminate; **sich als ~ für j. erweisen** to turn out to be bad for s. o.;
~e Folgen damaging consequences.
Nachteiliges, in allem nur ~ sehen to look for an evil intention in everything; **nichts ~ über jem. wissen** to know nothing to s. one's detriment.
Nachteiligkeit disadvantageousness.
Nachteinsätze fliegen to fly nighttime sorties.
Nachtest additional test.
Nacht|fahrt overnight drive; **~flug** night flight, night flying; **~flugausrüstung** night flying equipment; **~frost** night frost; **~gebühr** night rate; **~gewand** night attire (gown); **~glocke** night bell.
Nachtigall, was dem einen sin Uhl, ist dem anderen sin one man's food is another man's poison.
Nächtigung overnight stay.
Nachtisch dessert.
Nacht|jagd *(mil.)* night interception; **~jäger** night fighter.
Nachtklub night club, nighterie *(sl.)*;
eleganter ~ rug joint *(sl.)*; **mieser ~** mousetrap *(sl.)*; **passabler ~** right joint *(sl.)*;
~vorstellung floor show.
Nacht|lager shakedown, night's lodging; **~lampe** night lamp; **~landung** overnight stop; **~leben** night life.
nächtlich|er Anruf night call; **~es Dunkel** darkness of the night; **~e Reise** overnight journey; **~e Ruhe** night's rest; **~e Ruhestörung** disturbance by night; **~e Unterbringung** overnight stop; **~e Vision** night vision; **~e Vorbereitungen treffen** to make overnight preparations.
Nacht|licht night light; **~lokal** night club (spot), night trap *(sl.)*; **~mahl** dinner, supper; **~musik** serenade; **~portier** *(Hotel)* night porter; **~post** night mail; **~programm** night-time program(me).
Nachtquartier accommodation for the night, night's lodging, lodging place, shakedown;
einem Reisenden ein ~ geben to take a traveller in for the night; **bei jem. im ~ liegen** to be quartered with s. o.; **einem Freund ein ~ verschaffen** to fix (put) up a friend for the night.
Nachtrag addendum, supplement, additional clause, amendment, *(im Brief)* postscript (P.S.), *(Testament)* codicil, *(Versicherung)* endorsement, rider;
als ~ by way of a postscript, supplementary, *(im Testament)* codicillary;
~ zu einem Vertrag supplementary contract;
~ liefern to supplement.
Nachträge addenda.
Nachtragebuch *(Versicherung)* indorsement book.
nachtragen to add, to supply an omission, *(Bücher)* to bring up to date, to enter (post) up;
jem. etw. ~ to nurse (keep) a grudge against s. o.; **einige Bemerkungen ~** to add a few remarks; **in einer Liste ~** to add in a list; **jem. etw. nicht ~** to bear no ranco(u)r towards s. o.; **vergessenen Posten ~** to record (post) an omitted item;
jem. alles ~ müssen to have to keep running after s. o. with everything.
nachträglich additional, supplementary, subsequent, ulterior, *(Kurskorrektur)* additional, second, *(zeitlich)* later;
Einzelstücke ~ bestellen to order individual pieces later; **etw. ~ bezahlen** to pay for s. th. later; **jem. ~ gratulieren** to congratulate s. o. after the event; **~ hinzufügen** to add later;
~e Ansprüche subsequent claims; **~er Bedarf** additional requirements; **~e Belastung** supplementary charge; **~e Buchung** subsequent entry, postentry; **~es Geburtstagsgeschenk** belated birthday present; **~e Vereinbarung** additional agreement; **~e Zahlung** additional payment.
Nachtrags|abkommen supplementary agreement; **~anschlag** supplementary estimate; **~band** supplement, supplementary volume; **~bericht** supplementary report; **~bestimmung** subsequent condition, annex, *(Testament)* codicillary clause; **~bewilligung** supplemental appropriation, supplementary (deficiency) appropriation *(US)*; **~buchung** subsequent entry; **~budget** supplementary estimate; **~etat** supplementary budget, deficiency fund (bill) *(US)*; **~gesetz** amendment, novel.
Nachtragshaushalt supplementary budget (estimate), deficiency bill (fund) *(US)*;
~ vorlegen to supplement a budget.
Nachtrags|haushaltsvorlage Bill of Supply, deficiency bill *(US)*; **~kredit** supplementary credit; **~kreditbewilligung** supplementary vote; **~police** endorsement, additional (subsequent, supplementary) policy; **~urkunde** supplemental deed; **~verfügung** supplementary regulation; **~vertrag** supplementary agreement; **~voranschlag** supplementary estimate, deficiency bill *(US)*; **~zahlung** payment of arrears.
nachtrauern, der verlorenen Jugend to mourn for one's lost youth.
Nacht|reisender night tourist; **~ruf** *(Arzt)* night telephone number, *(Telefon)* night call; **~ruhe** night's rest; **~ruhe halten** to keep silence during the night.
nachts by (at) night, in the nighttime, nights *(coll.)*;
~ reisen to travel by night; **ganze Woche tags und ~ unterwegs sein** to travel night and day for a week; **~ zwischenlanden** to night-stop.
Nacht|safe night safe (depository); **~schalter** night counter.
Nachtschicht night (midnight) shift, *(Mehrschichtbetrieb)* third shift;
zweite ~ graveyard shift *(US sl.)*;
~arbeit nightwork; **~vergütung** nightshift bonus.
Nacht|schlaf dringend benötigen, längeren to do with a good night's sleep; **~schriftleiter** night editor; **~sitzung** all-night sitting; **~start** night take-off; **~streckenbefeuerung** *(Flugplatz)* route beacon for night-flying service; **~strom** off-peak electricity; **~stromspeicher** night storage heater; **~stromtarif** off-peak (time-of-the-day, *Br.*) tariff; **~tarif** night tariff (charge), night rate; **~tisch** bedside table; **~tischlampe** bedside lamp; **~tresor** night depository (safe); **~urlaubschein** *(mil.)* late pass; **~vogel** *(fig.)* fly-by-night; **~vogel sein** to keep late hours, to be accustomed to late nights, to burn the midnight oil; **~vorstellung** late-night show, nightly performance; **~wache** night watch; **~wache bei einem kranken Kind halten** to keep vigil over a sick child, to watch all night at the bedside of a sick child; **~wächter** watchman.
nachtwandeln to walk in one's sleep, to sleep-walk.
Nacht|wandler sonambulist, night walker, night prowler; **~zeit** nighttime; **~zeitgespräch** night call; **~zuschlag** overnight charge; **~zustellgebühr** late-letter fee.
Nach|übereignung zusätzlicher Rechte secondary conveyance; **~überlegung** afterthought; **~unternehmer** subcontractor; **~untersuchung** re-examination; **~urlaub** additional leave, prolongation (extension) of leave of absence.
nachveranlagen to make a subsequent assessment.
Nach|veranlagung additional (subsequent) assessment; **~verfahren** ancillary proceedings; **~vermächtnis** residuary bequest (legacy, residuary); **~vermächtnisnehmer** residuary legatee; **~vermessung** fresh survey; **~verpfändungsklausel** after-acquired clause.
nachversichern to reinsure, to insure for a larger amount.
nachversicherter Nichteigentümer *(Auto)* additional insured.
Nach|versicherung additional (subsequent) insurance; **~versicherungszeit** *(Sozialversicherung)* subsequent insurance period; **~versteuerung** subsequent taxation.
nachverzollen to pay additional duties, to pass a postentry.
Nachverzollung payment of additional duties, postentry;
~ durchführen to pass a postentry.
Nachwahl by-election *(Br.)*, special (sublimental) election *(US)*;
höhere ~beteiligung higher by-election turnout *(Br.)*; **~maßstäbe** by-election standards *(Br.)*; **~niederlage** by-election defeat *(Br.)*; **~sitzung** post-election session.

Nachweis proof, evidence, demonstration, *(Auskunft)* information, *(Unterlage)* [supporting] record, *(Zeugnis)* certificate, voucher;
als ~ des Anspruchs genügt die Police policy proof of interest; **bis zum ~ des Gegenteils** unless there is proof to the contrary; **mit lückenlosem ~ der bisherigen Tätigkeit** with full details of previous employment; **zum ~ seines Anspruches** in proof of one's claim; **zum ~ der Lieferung** in proof of delivery;
ausreichender ~ *(Versicherungsfall)* due proof; **buchmäßiger ~** evidence as shown by the books; **lückenloser ~** airtight case; **urkundlicher ~** documentation, proof by documentary evidence;
~ des Ablebens proof of death; **~ der Bedürftigkeit** proof of need; **~ der Befähigung** certificate of qualification, proof of competency; **~ für eine Behauptung** substantiation for a statement; **~ der Echtheit** proof of authenticity; **~ der erforderlichen Eignung** proof of competency (qualification); **~ einer Forderung** *(Konkurs)* proof of a claim; **~ der Identität** proof of identity; **~ der Konkursquotenberechtigung** proof for dividend; **~ der Merkfähigkeit** evidence (certificate) of memory; **listenmäßiger ~ einer Nachfrageentwicklung** market schedule; **~ über den Reingewinn** consolidated earnings statement *(US)*; **~ des eingetretenen Schadens** proof of loss; **~ der Staatsangehörigkeit** proof of nationality; **~ der Stimmberechtigung** *(Konkursverfahren)* proof for voting; **~ nichterfolgter elterlicher Unterstützung** *(Student)* claim of financial nonsupport *(US)*; **~ der Versicherungsfähigkeit** evidence of insurability satisfactory to the company; **~ der Vertretungsbefugnis** proof of authority; **~ der ordnungsgemäßen Zahlungsaufforderung** request for payment; **~ der Zahlungsunfähigkeit** evidence of insolvency; **~ gezahlter Zinsen** statement of interest paid; **~ der Zustellung** proof of service;
~ für jds. am-Leben-Gebliebensein bilden to prove s. o. still alive; **zufriedenstellenden ~ erbringen** to establish to satisfaction; **~ einer Forderung erbringen** to lodge a proof of debt, to prove a claim (debt); **~ führen** to prove, to furnish proof, to demonstrate; **~ seiner Ansprüche mittels Urkunden führen** to produce documents in proof of one's claims; **~ ausreichender Kaution führen** to justify bail; **~ der Schwangerschaft führen** to indicate pregnancy; **~ liefern** to adduce evidence.
nachweisbar ascertainable, detectable, provable, demonstrable, verifiable, *(offenbar)* manifest, *(verfolgbar)* traceable.
Nachweis|barkeit verifiableness, provableness, traceability; **~dienst** information service.
nachweisen to prove, to show proof, to demonstrate;
sein Alibi ~ to prove one's alibi; **seinen Anspruch ~** to substantiate a claim; **sein Eigentum ~** to establish a claim to a title; **einwandfrei ~** to establish beyond doubt; **als falsch ~** to prove false; **Forderung im Gesellschaftskonkurs ~** to prove a debt in liquidation; **Giftspuren ~** to find traces of poison; **seine Identität ~** to prove one's identity; **gute Kenntnisse auf einem Gebiet ~** to show sound knowledge in a field; **jds. Schuld ~** to prove s. one's guilt; **seine Staatsangehörigkeit ~** to give proof of one's nationality; **jem. eine Stellung ~** to find a post for s. o.; **jem. ein Zimmer ~** to get s. o. a room;
jem. etw. ~ können to have evidence against s. o.; **dreijährige Berufserfahrung ~ können** to have three years of professional experience; **sich mikroskopisch leicht ~ lassen** to be easily detected under the microscope.
Nachweiser index, pointer.
Nachweis|makler business transfer agent, *(Effektengeschäft)* half-commission man; **~pflicht** accountability.
nachweispflichtig accountable.
Nachweisung documentary proof.
Nachwelt posterity, ensuing ages, coming generations;
in die ~ eingehen to go down to posterity.
nachwerfen, gutes Geld schlechtem to throw good money after bad.
Nachwiegen check (test) weighing.
nachwiegen to reweigh.
nachwinken, jem. to wave goodbye to s. o.
nachwirken to produce an aftereffect;
in jem. ~ to linger in s. one's mind; **lange ~** *(Rede)* to have repercussions, *(Tablette)* to have a long-lasting effect.
Nachwirkung aftereffect, aftermath, backwash;
~en einer Krankheit aftereffects of an illness; **~en des Krieges** repercussions (aftermath) of the war;
~ erzielen to produce an aftereffect; **~en eines Unfalls fühlen** to feel the effects of an accident; **~en im ganzen Lande hinterlassen** to have repercussions throughout the country.

Nachwuchs rising (new) generation, *(Betrieb)* junior staff, trainees, *(Kind)* addition to the family, *(Theater)* young talents;
akademischer ~ rising generation of scientists; **hoffnungsvoller ~** white hope *(sl.)*;
~ ausbilden to train junior executives; **Schwierigkeiten haben, den entsprechenden ~ zu bekommen** to have serious recruitment problems; **redaktionellen ~ einstellen** to hire new editorial talents *(US)*; **~ erwarten** to be in the family way;
~ausbilder training manager; **~ausbildung, ~förderung** executive training, promotion of prospective managers, management education (training); **~ausbildungsplan** trainee plan; **~autor** promising author; **~bedarf** executive needs; **~jagd** manhunt; **~jäger** manhunter.
Nachwuchskraft junior executive, [management (executive)] trainee *(US)*;
erfolgreiche ~ up-and-coming executive; **hoffnungsvolle ~** white-haired boy *(US)*;
~ im Verkauf junior salesman;
systematisch zur ~ ausbilden to steer through the ranks; **dynamische ~ suchen** to have a career vacancy for a dynamic young man.
Nachwuchskräfte, erfolgreiche ~ laufend versetzen to rotate promising executives;
~bedarf decken to buy manpower resources; **~mangel** shortage of management executives.
Nachwuchs|parlamentarier, vielversprechender ~ young up-and-coming MP; **~reservoir** executive material; **~seminar** management seminar; **~sorgen** recruitment problems.
nachzahlen to pay in addition, to make an additional (supplementary) payment, *(später)* to pay later;
auf Aktien ~ to pay a further call on shares; **Fahrkarte ~** to pay the excess fare; **drei Monate Gehalt ~** to make a back payment of three months salary; **Porto ~** to pay a surcharge; **Rest des Geldes ~** to pay the remainder of the money later; **Steuern ~** to pay tax arrears.
nachzählen to recount, to count over, *(prüfen)* to check, to verify;
stückweise ~ to tally *(Br.)*;
Wechselgeld bitte nach Empfang ~ please check your change.
Nachzahlung supplementary (extra, subsequent, additional) payment, supply, *(Rückstand)* back payment, payment of arrears;
~ von Gehalt back payment of salary;
zur ~ auffordern to call; **~ leisten** to make an additional (further) payment; **~ an das Finanzamt leisten** to pay arrears to the tax office.
Nachzählung second counting, recount.
Nachzahlungs|aufforderung *(auf nicht eingezahlte Aktien)* call; **vollstreckbarer ~beschluß** *(Liquidationsverfahren)* balance order; **~pflicht** liability of a contributory.
nachzahlungspflichtig contributory *(Br.)*.
Nachzahlungs|veranlagung additional assessment *(US)*; **ohne ~verpflichtung** noncumulative; **~verpflichtung bei unterbrochener Pauschalreise** *(Flug)* open jaw.
nachzeichnen to draw from a model, *(kopieren)* to copy, *(pausen)* to trace;
auf Aktien ~ to subscribe for new shares (stocks, *US*); **Augenbrauen ~** to pencil one's eyebrows; **Entwicklung einer Stadt ~** to trace the development of a city.
Nach|zeichnung *(von Aktien)* subsequent subscription; **~zensur** post-publication censorship.
nachziehen to follow suit, *(Preise)* to go up accordingly, *(umziehen)* to move to the same place;
Linien eines Musters ~ to trace the lines of a pattern; **mit Preiserhöhungen ~** to follow suit by raising one's prices; **entsprechend der Preiserhöhung ~** *(Löhne)* to go up to keep pace with price increases.
Nach|zoll additional duty; **~zug** additional (special) train; **~zügler** late-comer, straggler; **~zugsaktie** deferred share *(Br.)* (stock, *US*); **~zugsaktienbesitz** deferred share ownership.
Nacken|beugen to knuckle down; **jem. den ~ beugen** to bend s. one's will; **Feind im ~ haben** to have the enemy hard on one's heels; **Schalk im ~ haben** to be a young imp; **steifen ~ haben** to be stubborn (obstinate); **j. am ~ packen** to seize s. o. by the scruff of the neck; **im ~ sitzen** *(Furcht)* to chill s. one's spine; **jem. im ~ sitzen** to be on s. one's back; **jem. im Nu im ~ sitzen** to be hot on s. one's trail; **Faust im ~ spüren** to feel the crunch *(fam.)*; **~ steifhalten** to keep a stiff upper lip; **jem. den ~ steifen** to give s. o. a backbone;
~kissen bolster, neck cushion; **geschäftliche ~schläge** business setbacks.

nackt naked, stripped, nude, *(Boden)* dry, plain;
~ **baden** to swim in the nude;
auf der ~en Erde schlafen to sleep on the bare ground; **~e Felsen** bare rocks; **mit ~en Füßen** barefooted; **~e Gier verraten** to betray sheer greed; **~er Kampf ums Dasein** struggle for life; **nur das ~e Leben retten** to escape with life and limb; **~en Lebensunterhalt verdienen** to earn a bare living; **wie zehn ~e Neger angeben** to be a terrible show-off *(coll.)*; **mit ~em Oberkörper** stripped to the waist; **~er Reaktor** bare reactor; **~e Tatsachen** naked (bare) facts; **~e Wahrheit** plain truth; **seine Augen vor der ~en Wirklichkeit verschließen** to close one's eyes to reality.
Nacktbadestrand nudist beach.
Nacktheit nakedness, nudity;
~ **des Bodens** bareness of the ground; ~ **einer Landschaft** baldness of a landscape.
Nackt|kultur nudism; **~tänzerin** stripteaser, stripper.
Nadel needle;
wie auf ~n sitzen to be on tenterhooks (on pins and needles); ~ **im Heuhaufen (Heuschober) suchen** to look for a needle in a bundle of hay (in a haystack);
keine ~ konnte zu Boden fallen people were packed like sardines;
~arbeit needlework, stitchwork; **~geld** pin money, allowance for necessities; **seiner Tochter ~geld zukommen lassen** to allow one's daughter a stipend; **~holz** softwood; **durch ein ~öhr gehen** to pass through a needle's eye; **jem. ~stiche versetzen** to pinprick s. o.; **mit ~streifen** *(Anzug)* pin-striped.
Nagel, jem. nicht das Schwarze unter dem ~ gönnen to begrudge s. o. everything; **Beruf an den ~ hängen** to chuck up *(sl.)*; **Uniform an den ~ hängen** to return to civvy street; **sich ein Buch unter den ~ reißen** to walk off with a book; ~ **zu jds. Sarg sein** to drive a nail in s. one's coffin; ~ **auf den Kopf treffen** to hit the nail [right] on the head, to hit it *(coll.)*, to ring the bell.
Nägel, Schuhe mit ~n beschlagen to nail (stud) shoes; **auf den ~n brennen** to be hard pressed; ~ **mit Köpfen machen** to make a good job of it.
nagel|neue Idee newfangled notion; **~sicher** puncture-proof.
nagen to gnaw, to bite;
an jds. Gesundheit ~ to be wearing down (undermining) s. one's health; **am Herzen** ~ to gnaw at the heart; **am Hungertuch** ~ to dine with Lord Humphrey; **an der Küste** ~ *(Meer)* to erode the coast line.
Nah|angriff close attack; **~aufklärung** *(mil.)* tactical reconnaissance; **~aufklärungsflugzeug** observation airplane; **~aufnahme** close-up, bust; **~beben** neighbo(u)ring earthquake; **~bedarfseinkommen** nonbasic income; **~beförderung** short-distance transport; **~bereich** close range, *(fig.)* immediate sphere of influence; **~bereichswaffe** close-range weapon.
nahe close, near, nearby *(US)*;
~ **am Bankrott** within measurable distance (on the verge, brink) of bankruptcy; ~ **bevorstehend** at hand, imminent; **ganz** ~ round the corner, at one's elbow; ~ **gelegen** nearby; **den Tränen** ~ on the verge of tears;
~ **bevorstehen** to be at hand; ~ **kommen** to approximate; ~ **der Stadt liegen** to lie close to the town; **dem Erfolg greifbar ~ sein** to come within a measurable distance of success; **einer Lösung ~ sein** to be well on the way to being solved; **dem Tode ~ sein** to be on the point of death; ~ **gelegen sein** to be no distance at all; ~ **verwandt sein** to be closely related; **jem. zu ~ treten** to hurt s. one's feelings;
ohne Ihnen zu ~ treten zu wollen without disparagement to you;
~ **Abreise** impending departure; **in ~n Beziehungen zu jem. stehen** to have close connections with s. o.; **~s Ende** approaching death; **jem. in ~r Freundschaft verbunden sein** to be a close friend of s. o.; **~r Osten** Near East; **~r Tod** imminent death; ~ **Verbindung** close relationship; ~ **Verkehrsbelegenheit** proximity to transportation; ~ **Verwandte** near relations; ~ **Verwandtschaft** proximity, close relationship; ~ **bevorstehende Wahlen** impending elections; ~ **gelegene Wohnung** nearby dwelling; **in der ~n Zukunft** in the near future.
Nähe contiguity, nearness, closeness, *(Umgebung)* vicinity, proximity, surroundings;
ganz in der ~ not a hundred miles from here *(hum.)*; **in der** ~ in the vicinity, up the road; **in der ~ der Stadt** near the town; **in allernächster** ~ at close quarters, within a stone's throw, in close proximity to; **in bequemer** ~ ready to hand;
~ **einer Fabrik** vicinity of a factory; ~ **eines lauten Flugplatzes** neighbo(u)rhood (proximity) of a noisy airport; ~ **des Todes** approaching death; ~ **der Verwandschaft** closeness of relationship;
sich in jds. ~ aufhalten to stay near (nearby, *US*) s. o.; **Protestkundgebung aus nächster ~ betrachten** to watch the demonstration from very close; **in unmittelbarer ~ leben** to live in the immediate neighbo(u)rhood; **in der ~ liegen** to be close by; **in greifbare ~ gerückt sein** to have come within reach; ~ **der Mutter suchen** to seek refuge with one's mother; **ganz in der ~ wohnen** to live near by (next door);
Haus, ~ München zu verkaufen house for sale, Munich area.
nahe|bringen, Menschen einander to bring people close together; **jem. die Werke eines Schriftstellers ~bringen** to make s. o. appreciate the works of an author; **jem. ~gehen** to affect (grieve) s. o. deeply.
nahegelegen near, nearby *(US)*, neighbo(u)ring;
~es Dorf nearby village; **~e Wasserversorgung** nearness to water supply.
nahegelegte Kündigung involuntary resignation.
Naheinstellung *(Foto)* short-range focus.
nahekommen, jem. to come close to s. o.; **einer Farbe** ~ to nearly match a colo(u)r; **der Wahrheit** ~ to come close to the truth.
nahelegen, jem. die Annahme eines Angebots to urge s. o. to accept an offer; **Dividendenbeschluß** ~ to recommend the amount of dividends; **dringend** ~ to recommend strongly; **jem. die Kündigung** ~ to urge s. o. to resign voluntarily.
naheliegen *(Vermutung)* to be obvious, to be very likely, to suggest itself.
naheliegend close to, likely, suggesting itself;
~ **sein** to seem very probable;
aus ~en Gründen for obvious reasons; **~er Schluß** obvious conclusion; **~er Verdacht** well-founded suspicion.
Naheliegendes, das the obvious thing to do.
Nah|empfang *(Rundfunk)* short-distance reception; **~empfangszone** primary service area.
nahen to approach, to draw near, *(Abschied)* to be approaching;
sich jem. mit einer Bitte ~ to approach s. o. with a petition.
nahend|e Gefahr imminent danger; **~es Gewitter** approaching thunderstorm.
Naher Osten Near East.
näher closer, nearer, *(genauer)* [more] specific, detailed;
~ **bekannt** intimately acquainted; ~ **verwandt** closely related;
sich ~ befassen (beschäftigen) to study up, to give a matter greater attention, to look into a matter more closely; ~ **beschreiben** to explain in greater detail; **mit jem. ~ bekannt werden** to become closely acquainted with s. o.;
~e Angaben detailed information, details; **~e Ansprüche** more valid claims; **um ~e Auskunft bitten** to ask for detailed information; **bei ~er Bekanntschaft** on closer acquaintance; **~e Beziehungen** closer links; **~e Einzelheiten** exact (further) details, further particulars; **~e Erkundigungen einziehen** to make further inquiries; ~ **bezeichneter Schuldner** designated debtor; **~e Umgebung** near surroundings; **~e Umstände** exact circumstances; ~ **bezeichnete Verschuldung** designated indebtedness; **in der ~en Zukunft** in the fairly near future.
Näheres full particulars, details;
~ **zu erfahren von ...** details can be obtained from ...
Naherholungsgebiet recreational area for half day.
näherkommen to get closer, *(Ferien)* to be approaching;
einander menschlich ~ to come closer to each other; **der Sache schon** ~ to be getting to the point; **der Wahrheit erheblich** ~ to come much nearer to the truth.
näherliegen to seem more likely, to be quite natural.
nähern *(math.)* to approximate;
sich ~ to approach, to draw (come) near; **sich 30%** ~ to nudge 30%; **sich jem. mit einer Bestechung** ~ to approach s. o. with a bribe; **sich dem Ende** ~ to draw to a close, to be drawing to an end; **sich einem brennenden Flugzeug** ~ to go near a burning aircraft; **sich den Grenzen guten Geschmacks bedenklich** ~ to overstep the bounds of good taste; **sich jem. langsam** ~ *(fig.)* to gradually confide in s. o.; **sich den Sechzigern** ~ to be going on for sixty; **verschiedene Standpunkte einander** ~ to reconcile different points of view.
nähertreten, jem. to get to know s. o. better; **einem Gedanken** ~ to get used to an idea; **einem Projekt** ~ to lock on a plan with favo(u)r.
Näherungs|fehler *(Statistik)* approximation error; **~rechnung** approximate calculation; **~rechnung der Kassenentwicklung vornehmen** to approximate the cash generation; **~verfahren** approximation method; **~wert** approximate value, approximation.
nahestehend close, intimate;
den Liberalen ~e Zeitung newspaper sympathizing with the liberals; **der Regierung ~e Zeitung** government newspaper.

Nahezu-Bargeld quasi-cash.
nahezu | hoffnungslose Angelegenheit wellnigh hopeless matter; ~ **unmöglich** next to impossible; ~ **zusammenbrechen** *(Verkehr)* to reach near-collapse.
Nah | fernverkehr *(tel.)* toll line, short-haul trunk circuit; ~**gespräch** *(Telefon)* local call; ~**güterverkehr** short-distance goods traffic, short-haul traffic; ~**güterzug** local train *(US)*.
Nahkampf *(mil.)* close combat, in-fighting;
brutaler ~ roughhouse, fighting at close quarters;
~**unterstützung durch Flugzeuge** close air support; ~**waffen** close-range weapons.
Nähkästchen sewing box;
aus dem ~ **plaudern** to blurt out a secret.
Nahost Near (Middle) East.
Nähr | bier near beer; ~**boden** fertile soil, *(fig.)* hotbed.
nähren to feed, to nourish;
Feuer seiner Leidenschaft ~ to add fuel to the fire of s. one's passion; **sich hauptsächlich von Fisch** ~ to live mainly on fish; **Flammen** ~ to feed the flames; **Groll** ~ to harbo(u)r a grudge; **sich von seiner Hände Arbeit** ~ to earn one's living by the sweat of one's brow; **Haß des Volkes** ~ to foster the people's hatred; **Hoffnung** ~ to nourish a hope; **Schlange am Busen** ~ to nourish a viper in one's bosom; **Verdacht** ~ to harbo(u)r a suspicion.
Nähr | gehalt nutritional contents; ~**kraft** nourishing power; ~**mittel** cereals; ~**präparat** alimentary preparation; ~**stoffeinheit** nutrition unit.
nährt, mühsam ~ **sich das Eichhörnchen** life is not all beer and skittles.
Nahrung food, fare, feed, eating, nurture, *(Kost)* diet, fare, nourishment, *(Unterhalt)* living, livelihood, subsistence;
flüssige ~ liquid food; **geistige** ~ nurture of the mind, intellectual (mental) food; **konzentrierte** ~ concentrate; **kräftige** ~ wholesome food; **leichte** ~ light diet; **vitaminreiche** ~ protective food;
jem. die ~ **entziehen** to deprive s. o. of food, to starve s. o.; **der Spekulation neue** ~ **geben** to revive speculation; **einem Verdacht gegen j. neue** ~ **geben** to throw fresh suspicion on s. o.; **jds. Zorn neue** ~ **geben** to serve to increase s. one's anger; ~ **zu sich nehmen** to take nourishment, to eat; **j. in** ~ **setzen** to employ s. o.; **für** ~ **sorgen** to be the breadwinner; **j. mit** ~ **versorgen** to feed s. o.; ~ **verweigern** to reject food, to refuse to eat; **einem Gerücht neue** ~ **zuführen** to strengthen a rumo(u)r.
Nahrungs | aufnahme intake of food; ~**bedarf** nutritional requirements; ~**entzug** denutrition; ~**mangel** food shortage.
Nahrungsmittel food[stuffs], provisions, victuals, consumables, edibles;
ekelerregende ~ nauseating food; **feste** ~ dry provisions; **hochwertige** ~ high-grade foodstuffs; **konzentrierte** ~ concentrated food; **saisonbedingte** ~ seasonal foods; **tiefgekühlte** ~ frozen food; **überflüssige** ~ spare food; **ungesunde** ~ unsound food; **verarbeitete** ~ processed food; **zollfreie** ~ duty-free food; ~ **und Genußmittel** food, beverages and tobacco;
dringend der ~ **und ärztlicher Versorgung bedürfen** to be suffering for want of food and medical supply; ~ **konservieren** to preserve foodstuffs; ~ **dem Tiefkühlverfahren unterziehen** to quick-freeze food; ~ **verfälschen** to adulterate food; ~ **verteilen** to dispense food; **jem.** ~ **vorenthalten** to deprive s. o. of food;
~**anzeige** food ad *(US)*; ~**bedarf** food requirements; ~**betrieb** food plant; ~**chemiker** food analyst, food chemist; ~**einfuhr** food imports; ~**fachmann** nutrition expert ~**fälschung** adulteration of food; ~**gesetz** National Food Bill *(US)*; ~**grundstoff** basic foodstuff; ~**gutschein** food stamp; ~**hilfe** food aid; ~**importe** food imports; ~**industrie** food (provisions) industry, food-processing industry; ~- **und Genußmittelindustrie** general and luxury food industry; ~**industrieaktien** food shares; ~**knappheit** food shortage; ~**krise** nutritional crisis; ~**kürzung** food cut; ~**lücke** food gap; ~**paket** food package; ~**preise** food prices; ~**preissteigerung** rise in food prices; ~**produkte** food products; ~**ration** food ration; ~**reserven** food reserve[s]; ~**sendungen** food shipments; ~**steuer** food tax; ~**überschüsse** food glut, food surplus; ~**verfälschung** adulteration of food; ~**vergiftung** food poisoning; ~**verpackungsbetrieb** food packers; ~**verschwendung** food waste; **schwächer werdende** ~**versorgung** diminishing food supplies; ~**verteilung** dispensation of food; **unzureichende** ~**vorräte** insufficient food supplies; ~**zubereitung** food preparation; ~**zuschüsse** food subsidies; ~**zuschußgebiet** food deficit area; ~**zuteilung** food allowance; **unzureichende** ~**zuteilung** short commons.
Nahrungs | suche quest for food; **auf der** ~**suche** on the feed; ~**verweigerung** rejection of food.
Nährwert nutritive (food) value, nutritional excellence.
Nahschnellverkehr rapid transit [from city to city] *(US)*.
Nahschnellverkehrs | linie rapid transit line *(US)*; ~**wesen** rapid transit system *(US)*; ~**zug** short-distance (rapid-transit, *US*) express.
Naht seam, *(Schweißnaht)* seam, weld, *(Wundnaht)* suture;
tüchtige ~ **Prügel bekommen** to get a good hiding; **eine** ~ **zusammenlügen** to be a downright liar.
Nähte, jem. auf die ~ **fühlen** to pump s. o.; **jem. auf den** ~**n knien** to breathe down s. one's neck; **aus allen** ~**n platzen** to burst one's buttons.
nahtlos *(Rohr)* seamless;
sich ~ **seiner Umgebung einfügen** to fit o. s. perfectly into one's surroundings; ~ **in eine Handlung eingefügt sein** to form an integral part of an action;
~**er Übergang** smooth transition.
Nahtransport short-distance transport (carriage, cartage).
Nahtstelle link, *(mil.)* boundary, coordinating line;
an den ~**n von Verantwortungsbereichen auftreten** to fall between the cracks of responsibility.
Nah | unterstützung durch Flugzeuge *(mil.)* close air support; ~**verbindung** local connection.
Nahverkehr suburban traffic, short-distance transport, local (way, *US*) traffic, commuting *(US)*, short hauls *(US)*, *(Flugzeug)* short-haul flights, *(Telefon)* junction service, toll traffic *(Br.)*;
im ~ **eingesetzt sein** *(Flugzeug)* to operate in or near midtown areas.
Nahverkehrs | amt *(tel.)* toll exchange *(US)*; ~**bahn** local railway, commuter railroad *(US)*; ~**bahnhof** commuter station *(US)*; ~**betrieb** short-distance passenger service, commuter service *(US)*; ~**bezirk** control zone, commuter area *(US)*; ~**fluggesellschaft** regional (commuter, *US*) airline; ~**gebiet** regional (commuter, suburban, *US*) area; ~**gewerbe,** ~**wirtschaft** local-service industry; ~**leitung** short-haul truck line, toll circuit (line) *(Br.)*; ~**linie** regional (commuter, *US*) line; ~**netz** commuter lines *(US)*; ~**schnellzug** local express, rapid transit train *(US)*, metroliner *(US)*; ~**strecke** commuter railroad line *(US)*; ~**teilnehmer** short-distance passenger; ~- **und Fernverkehrstransport** long and short hauls; ~**verbindung** intercity railway, commuter line *(US)*; ~**wagen** commuter car *(US)*; ~**zone** control zone, commuter zone *(US)*; ~**zug** local (intercity) train, commuter (way) train *(US)*.
Nahziel immediate objective;
hauptsächliches ~ **sein** to loom in the forefront.
naiv naive, *(arglos)* innocent, guileless;
auf ~ **machen** to act the innocent; **viel zu** ~ **sein** to be too easy a mark;
~**e Bemerkungen machen** to make naive remarks; ~**er Mensch sein** to be simple-minded; ~**e Rolle** *(Theater)* part of an ingenue.
Naivität naivety, simplicity, *(Arglosigkeit)* innocence, guilelessness.
Name name, style, *(Bezeichnung)* designation, denomination, *(Fabrikmarke)* trademark name, brand, *(Ruf)* reputation, repute, renown, *(Wertpapier)* title;
auf den ~**n lautend** registered, inscribed, nontransferable, *(Wechsel)* payable to order; **dem** ~ **nach** nominally; **im** ~**n des Gesetzes** in the name of the law; **im** ~**n meiner Regierung** on behalf of my government; **im** ~ **von** on behalf of; **im eigenen** ~**n** under one's own name; **im eigenen** ~**n und auf eigene Rechnung** in one's own name and on one's own account; **im eigenen** ~**n und für fremde Rechnung** on commission; **in fremdem** ~**n** as agent only; **nicht auf den** ~ **lautend** unregistered; **nur dem** ~**n nach** nominally; **nur auf einen** ~**n lautend** *(Stimmzettel)* uninominal; **ohne** ~**n** anonymous; **unter dem** ~**n von** by the name of, under the style of; **unter fremdem** ~**n** incognito;
altbekannter ~ old name; **angenommener** ~ assumed (feigned) name, alias; **voll ausgeschriebener** ~ name written in full; **handelsgerichtlich eingetragener** ~ **[einer Firma]** registered (trade, corporate, *US*) name, name of a company; **erfundener** ~ fancy name; **falscher** ~ fictitious name, pseudonym; **gesetzlich geschützter** ~ proprietary name; **gesetzlicher** ~ legal name; **irrtümlicher** ~ misnomer; **richtiger** ~ true name; **unbescholtener** ~ unblemished (untarnished) reputation; **vollständiger** ~ full name;
~ **des Ausstellers** name of the maker; ~ **des Inhabers** name of the bearer;
ein guter ~ **ist mehr wert als Silber und Gold** a good name is more worth than silver and gold.
Namen | [auf einer Liste] abhaken to put a tick against a name, to check off a name on a list; **seinen [vollen]** ~ **angeben** to give

one's [full] name; ~ **annehmen** to assume a name; **in jds. ~ auftreten** to go under the name of s. o.; **seinen ~ ausschreiben** to write one's name in full; **jds. guten ~ beflecken** to stain s. one's reputation; **sich einen ~ beilegen** to assume a name; **jds. ~ besudeln** to stain s. one's name; **j. um seinen guten ~ bringen** to blast s. one's reputation; **seinen ~ in ein Formular einsetzen** to fill in one's name on an official form; ~ **eintragen** to set down a name; ~ **in eine Liste eintragen** to enter a name on a list; **ohne ~ erscheinen** *(Buch)* to appear anonymously; **j. nach seinem ~ fragen** to ask (inquire) s. one's name; ~ **führen** to bear the name; ~ **geben** to name; **auf jds. ~ gehen** *(Rechnung)* to go to s. one's account; **auf den ~ der Ehefrau gehen** *(Geschäft)* to run under the wife's name; **guten ~ haben** to have a good reputation, to be of good report; **an der Börse einen guten ~ haben** to have a blue eye in the city *(US)*; **im eigenen ~ handeln** to act on one's own behalf; **in fremdem ~ handeln** to act as agent; **unter jds. ~ handeln** to assume s. one's character; **seinen ~ hergeben** to lend one's name; **seinen ~ zu einer Unternehmung hergeben** to endorse an enterprise with one's name; **j. dem ~ nach kennen** to know s. o. by repute (name); **im eigenen ~ klagen** to maintain an action, to sue in one's own name; **unter seinem handelsgerichtlichen ~ klagen** to sue in its corporate name; **unter dem ~ laufen** to pass by (go under, run by) the name of; **auf den ~ lauten** ot be made out in the name of; **von seinem guten ~ leben** to trade upon one's past reputation; **sich einen ~ machen** to make a name for o. s., to build up (earn) a reputation, to put o. s. on record; **sich als Anwalt einen ~ machen** to establish one's reputation as a lawyer; **jds. ~ mißbrauchen** to take s. one's name in vain, to abuse s. one's name; **j. seinen guten ~ neiden** to be jealous of s. one's good name; **j. mit ~ nennen** to name s. o.; **Kind beim richtigen ~ nennen** to call a spade a spade (a thing by its name); **um das Kind beim ~ zu nennen** not to put too fine a point on it *(coll.)*; **sich jds. ~ und Anschrift notieren** to take down s. one's name and address; ~ **registrieren** to enrol(l), to register in a list; **unter falschem ~ reisen** to travel under a false (assumed) name, to travel incognito; **unter dem ~ bekannt sein** to go by the name of; **in jds. ~ eingebracht sein** *(Antrag)* to stand in s. one's name; **auf jds. ~ eingetragen sein** to be in s. one's name; **nur dem ~ nach der Chef sein** to be the nominal head; **es dem ~ schuldig sein** to owe it one's reputation; **seinen ~ unter einen Brief setzen** to put (set) one's signature to a letter; ~ **als Notadresse auf einen Wechsel setzen** to place a name in case of need on a draft; **nur im eigenen ~ sprechen** to speak only for o. s.; **in der Zeitung auf jds. ~ stoßen** to come across s. one's name in the newspaper; **jds. ~ von einer Liste streichen** to remove (strike, expunge) s. one's name from a list, to scratch s. o. off a list; ~ **von der Mitgliederliste streichen** to take a name off the books; **mit seinem vollen ~ unterschreiben** to sign in full; ~ **verlesen** to call the roll, to roll-call; **etw. unter einem anderen ~ veröffentlichen** to publish s. th. under a pen name; **jds. ~ als Referenz verwenden** to use s. one's name as reference; **im ~ der Firma zeichnen** to sign on behalf of a firm; ~ **der Familie in den Schmutz ziehen** to drag the family's name through the mire; **sich einen anderen ~ zulegen** to give o. s. a different name; **in drei Teufels ~!** hang it all!

namenlos anonymous, nameless;
in ~em Elend leben to live in indescribable misery.

Namenloser unknown person.

namens on behalf of;
~ **und auftrags** in the name and on behalf of.

Namensaktie registered share (stock, *US*), personal share;
~n inscriptions *(Br.)*;
vinkulierte ~ restricted registered share;
~n mit Übertragungsvermerk assigned stocks *(US)*.

Namens|aktionär registered shareholder *(Br.)*, stockholder of record *(US)*; **~aktionäre registrieren** to inscribe the names of stockholders *(US)*; **~änderung** change in (alteration of) name; **~angabe** indication of name; **unrichtige ~angabe** misnomer; **~aufruf** call-over, roll-call, *(parl.)* call of the House; **durch ~aufruf abstimmen** to vote by calling the roll; **~bezeichnung** name, denomination, description; **~ehe** nominal marriage; **nicht begebbarer ~frachtbrief** straight bill of lading; **~führung** retention of a name; **unberechtigte ~führung** unlawful use of a name; **~gebung** naming, *(wissenschaftlich)* nomenclature; **kein ~gedächtnis haben** to have a bad memory for names.

namensgleich having the same name.

Namens|indossament special endorsement; **~irrtum** misnomer; **~lagerschein** nonnegotiable warehouse receipt; **~liste** list of names, roll, roster; **~liste herunterrasseln** to reel off a list of names; **~liste verlesen** to call the roll, to roll-call; **~mißbrauch** abuse of name; **~nennung** mentioning of a name; **ohne ~nennung** anonymously; **~obligation** registered debenture (bond, *US*); **~papier** registered share *(Br.)* (stock, *US*), straight note *(US)*; **~pfandbriefe** registered debentures (bonds, *US*), inscribed debentures *(Br.)*; **~police** named policy; **~register** register of names, *(Buch)* index of names; **~scheck** nonnegotiable check *(US)* (cheque, *Br.*); **~schild** nameboard, signboard, name plate (badge), escutcheon; **~schriftzug** logotype; **~schuldverschreibung** registered debenture *(Br.)* (coupon, bond, *US*), nonnegotiable (inscribed) bond *(Br.)*; **auswechselbare ~schuldverschreibungen** interchangeable bonds *(US)*; **~schutz** legal protection of names; **~stempel** stamped signature, facsimile stamp; **~tag** name day; **~test** *(Werbung)* name test.

Namensunterschrift signature, subscription to a document;
laut unseren ~en witness our hands;
eigenhändige ~ sign manual.

Namens|verlesung calling of names, roll-call; **~verwechslung** confusion of names; **~verzeichnis** list of names, nominal register, roll, index of names, *(Aktionäre)* shareholders' register, capital stock ledger *(US)*, stock book *(US)*, *(wissenschaftlich)* nomenclature; **~vetter** name son, namesake; **~wechsel** change of name; **~zertifikat** registered certificate; **mit ~zügen versehen** to personalize.

namentlich by name, nominally, individually;
~ **abstimmen** to vote by call-over; ~ **anführen** to mention individually; ~ **aufrufen** to call over, to roll-call; **j. ~ erwähnen** to refer to s. o. by name, to mention s. o. individually; **j. nur ~ kennen** to know s. o. by name;
~e Abstimmung roll-call vote, division *(Br.)*, vote by open ballot, *(parl.)* division, call of the House; ~ **eingetragener Aktionär** registered shareholder *(Br.)*, stockholder of record *(US)*; **beim ~en Aufruf** when the roll was called; **~e Erwähnung im Heeresbericht** mention in dispatches.

namhaft renowned, well-known, notable, *(beträchtlich)* substantial, considerable;
~ **machen** to name, to nominate, to find s. one's name;
~er Betrag considerable amount; **~er Künstler** celebrated artist; **~er Redner** notable speaker; **~er Unterschied** noteworthy difference.

Namhaftmachung naming, nomination, identification;
~ **der Revisionsgründe** specification of errors.

Nämlichkeit identity;
~ **des Versicherungsgegenstandes** identity of the subject matter.

Nämlichkeits|nachweis submission of proof of identity; **~prüfung** verification of s. one's identity; **~zeichen** identification mark; **~zeugnis** proof (certificate) of identity, identity certificate.

Nansenpaß Nansen passport.

Napalmbombe napalm bomb.

Narbe zurücklassen to leave a scar.

Narkotika narcotics, drugs;
gefährliche ~ dangerous drugs; **Süchtigkeit hervorrufende ~** habit-forming drugs;
~ **einnehmen** to load *(sl.)*; ~ **verabreichen** to administer drugs.

Narr fool, *(Spaßmacher)* buffoon, buff *(US fam.)*, jester;
hoffnungsloser ~ hopeless fool; **kompletter ~** out-and-out (positive) fool;
irgend so ein ~ unter den Politikern some fool of a politician *(coll.)*;
sich wie ein ~ aufspielen to make a fool of o. s., to play the giddy goat; **j. als ~en bezeichnen** to write s. o. down as a fool; **einen ~en an jem. gefressen haben** to be all over s. o. *(sl.)*; **j. zum ~en halten** to make a fool of s. o., to pull s. one's leg *(coll.)*; **die ~en werden nicht alle** there is a sucker born every minute; **ein ~ kann in einer Stunde mehr fragen, als zehn Weise in einem Jahr beantworten können** a fool may ask more questions in an hour than a wise man can answer in a year; **jedem ~en gefällt seine Kappe** every man thinks his own geese swans.

Narren|freiheit carnival licence; **~paradies** limbo of fools; **in einem ~paradies leben** to live in a fool's paradise; **~possen treiben** to play the fool.

närrisch foolish, funny, silly, potty *(sl.)*;
vor Freude ganz ~ sein to be mad with joy; **ganz ~ auf etw. sein** to be crazy about (infatuated with) s. th.

naschen, gern to have a sweet tooth, to be fond of titbits.

Näschereien goodies, sweets.

Nase, direkt vor jds. right under s. one's nose, before (under) one's very eyes;
mit langer ~ abziehen to come away disappointed; **Mund und ~ aufsperren** to be flabbergasted *(coll.)*; **sich die ~ begießen** to wet

one's whistle *(coll.)*; **jem. etw. auf die ~ binden** to pull a fast one on s. o. *(sl.)*; **jedem auf die ~ binden** to go round telling everyone; **jem. eine ~ drehen** to get up s. one's nose; **auf die ~ fallen** to fall on one's face; **sich an die eigene ~ fassen** to mind one's own business; **jem. eins auf die ~ geben** to give s. o. one on the nose *(fam.)*; **etw. direkt vor der ~ haben** to have s. th. right in front of o. s.; **~ für etw. haben** to have a nose for s. th.; **seine ~ in allem haben** to have a finger in every pie; **feine ~ für Gelegenheitskäufe haben** to have a flair for bargains; **~ zu tief ins Glas gesteckt haben** to have had one over the eight; **~ voll haben vom Krieg** to be fed up with (have a bellyful of) fighting; **gute ~ für junge Talente haben** to have a scent for young talents; **~ von etw. ziemlich voll haben** to be pretty sick of s. th.; **jem. etw. dauernd unter die ~ halten** to keep on at s. o., to rub it in; **j. an der ~ herumführen** to lead s. o. by the nose, to put it over s. o., to string s. o. along *(sl.)*, to lead s. o. up the garden path, to run a sandy on s. o. *(sl.)*; **j. ganz schön an der ~ herumführen** to lead s. o. a pretty dance; **j. auf der ~ herumtanzen** to do as one pleases with s. o.; **eins auf die ~ kriegen** to get a punch on the nose, to be hauled over the coals; **sich den Wind um die ~ wehen lassen** to see the world; **auf der ~ liegen** to be flat on one's back; **jem. eine lange ~ machen** to make a long nose at s. o.; **immer der ~ nachgehen** to follow one's nose; **seine ~ rümpfen** to rumple (screw up) one's nose, to pooh-pooh; **Zug vor der ~ wegfahren sehen** to miss a train by a second; **auf die ~ gefallen sein** *(fig.)* to have had bad luck; **alle ~n lang im Krankenhaus sein** to be always in and out of hospital; **seine ~ in anderer Leute Angelegenheiten stecken** to pry (put, thrust one's nose) into anothers' affairs (s. one's business), to nose; **jem. in die ~ steigen** to stink in s. one's nostrils *(coll.)*; **j. mit der ~ auf etw. stoßen** to rub s. one's nose in s. th. *(fam.)*; **seine ~ hoch tragen** to walk with one's head in the air, to hold one's head high; **jem. den Parkplatz vor der ~ wegschnappen** to nab s. one's parking place *(coll.)*; **einem anderen vor die ~ gesetzt werden** to be promoted over s. one's head; **jem. die Würmer aus der ~ ziehen** to worm a secret out of s. o.; **jem. die Tür vor der ~ zuschlagen** to slam the door in s. one's face.

nasenlang, alle again and again, repeatedly.

Nasenlänge, um eine by a short head, by a nose;
um eine ~ gewinnen to win by a neck, to win by a short head, to nose out *(sl.)*; **der Konkurrenz immer eine ~ voraus sein** to be one jump ahead of one's competitors.

Nasen|spitze, es jem. an der ~spitze ansehen to tell it by s. one's face; **~stüber** fillip; **~zähler** head counter.

Naseweis whippersnapper, smart aleck, pry.

naseweis saucy, pert, cheeky.

nasführen, j. to lead s. o. up the garden path.

naß dripping wet;
~ bis auf die Haut wet to the skin;
seine Kehle ~ machen to wet one's whistle *(coll.)*; **noch ~ hinter den Ohren sein** to be wet behind the ears *(coll.)*; **~ wie ein Pudel sein** to be soaked to the skin, to get a wetting;
mit ~en Augen with tears in one's eyes; **~-in-~-Druck** wet printing; **~e Füße bekommen** to get one's feet wet, *(fig.)* to get cold feet, to get the wind up *(coll.)*; **~es Grab** watery grave; **wie ein ~er Sack dastehen** to cut a sorry figure; **~e Stücke** unsold mortgage bonds.

Nassauer cadger, sponger, dead beat *(US sl.)*, free-loader *(US sl.)*, parasite.

nassauern to sponge, to cadge.

nass|forsch brazenfaced; **~kalt** damp and cold.

Naßverfahren wet process.

Nation nation, commonwealth, state, country;
englischsprechende ~ English-speaking people; **handeltreibende ~** mercantile nation;
in der ganzen ~ Widerhall finden to find a nation-wide response.

national national, *(innerstaatlich)* municipal;
~e Einheitsregierung national unity government; **~e Gesinnung** nationalism; **~es Kennzeichen** nationality plate; **~e Minderheit** national minority; **~er Notstand** national emergency; **~es Selbstverständnis** national identity; **~e Sicherheit** national safety.

National|anleihe national loan; **~banken** *(USA)* Federal Reserve Banks.

nationalbewußt national conscious, patriotic.

National|bewußtsein national consciousness; **~bibliothek** national library, Library of Congress *(US)*; **~budget** Economic Report, White Paper *(Br.)*; **~charakter** national character; **zum ~denkmal erklären** to proclaim a national memorial; **~eigentum** national property; **~einkommen** national income (dividend, revenue, *US*); **~farbe** national colo(u)rs; **~feiertag** national holiday; **~flagge** national flag (colo(u)rs), ensign, Union Jack *(Br.)*, Stars and Stripes *(US)*; **~fonds** national fund; **~galerie** national gallery; **~garde** militia; **~gefühl** national attachment, nationalism; **~haß** national hatred; **~hymne** national anthem.

nationalisieren to nationalize *(Br.)*.

Nationalisierung nationalization *(Br.)*.

Nationalismus nationalism.

Nationalist nationalist;
uneinsichtiger ~ out-and-out nationalist.

Nationalität nationality, national status;
doppelte ~ double nationality;
seine ~ aufgeben to expatriate; **~ eines Schiffes ausmachen** to identify a strange ship; **~ entziehen** to denationalize, to deprive of nationality.

Nationalitäten|frage problem of national minorities; **~staat** multinational state.

Nationalitäts|aufgabe expatriation; **~kennzeichen** *(Auto)* nationality plate, *(Flugzeug)* nationality mark.

National|konvent national convention; **~ökonom** political (public) economist; **~ökonomie** national (political, social) economy, economics.

nationalökonomisch economic.

National|park national park; **~produkt** national product; **~rat** national council; **~regierung** national government; **~schuld** [gross] national debt; **äußere ~schuld** external national debt; **~schuld verwalten** to manage the national debt; **~staat** national state; **~stiftung** National Trust *(Br.)*; **~trauer** national mourning; **~vermögen** national property; **~versammlung** National Assembly; **Verfassungsgebende ~versammlung** Constitutional Convention; **~währung** national currency.

Natodoppelbeschluß Nato deploy-and-talk decision.

Natur, aus seiner ureigensten ~ heraus by its very nature; **nach der ~** from life; **von monopolistischer ~** of monopolistic character; **eiserne ~** iron constitution; **freie ~** open countryside; **menschliche ~** human nature;
nicht jds. ~ entsprechen to be quite out of s. one's character; **der Stimme der ~ folgen** to follow one's natural instinct; **jem. gegen die ~ gehen** to go against s. one's grain; **kräftige ~ haben** to have a strong constitution; **in der freien ~ leben** to live an outdoor life; **in der ~ der Dinge liegen** to be in the nature of things; **entgegengesetzte ~en sein** to be opposite in temperament; **grundsätzlicher ~ sein** to be fundamental; **schöpferische ~ sein** to be creative; **Stück unberührter ~ sein** to be a bit of unspoilt countryside; **von ~ aus geizig sein** to be mean by nature; **von der ~ mit hervorragenden Anlagen bedacht worden sein** to be endowed by nature with great talents; **jem. zur zweiten ~ werden** to become second nature to s. o.; **der ~ seinen Tribut zahlen** to pay one's debt to nature.

natura, in in kind.

Natural|abgabe tax (levy) in kind; **~ausgleich** settlement in kind; **~bezüge** payment in kind; **~dividende** dividend payable in kind; **~einkommen** income received in kind; **~entschädigung** damage paid in kind; **~erfüllung** allowance in kind, specific performance, performance in kind; **~ersatz** replacement in kind; **~erträge** earnings in kind; **~geld** commodity standard; **~herstellung** specific performance.

Naturalien foodstuffs, victuals, tommy;
in ~ bezahlen to pay in kind.

Naturalisations|erklärung declaration of intention *(US)*; **~urkunde** certificate of naturalization.

naturalisieren to naturalize, to nationalize, to domesticate.

naturalisiert werden to become nationalized, to be admitted to citizenship by naturalization *(US)*.

Naturalisierung nationalization *(Br.)*, naturalization.

Natural|leistung specific performance, allowance (performance) in kind; **~lohn** allowance in kind, store pay *(US)*, *(Bergbau)* tribute system; **~nießbrauch** perfect usufruct; **~obligation** imperfect obligation; **~pacht** stated rental, sharecrop system *(US)*; **~pächter** share tenant *(US)*, sharecropper *(US)*; **~rente** food rent; **~restitution** restitution in kind; **~vergütung** allowance in kind, store pay *(US)*; **~wesen** metayer system *(Br.)*; **~wirtschaft** natural economy; **~zins** dry rent.

Natur|anbetung nature worship; **~anlage** temperament, nature; **~boden** uncultivated soil; **~bursche** child of nature, nature boy *(sl.)*; **~denkmal** natural monument.

Naturell, lebhaftes lively temperament;
glückliches ~ haben to be of a happy nature.

Natur|ereignis natural event, Act of God; **~erscheinung** phenomenon of nature; **~erzeugnis** produce (product) of the land.

naturfarben self-colo(u)r.
Natur|forscher scientist, naturalist; **~forschung** natural science; **~gabe** talent; **~gas** wet gas.
naturgegebene|Bedingungen natural conditions; **~ Vorteile** natural advantages.
Natur|genie natural; **~geschichte** natural history; **~gesetz** natural law, law of nature; **gegen ~gesetze angehen** to fly in the face of nature; **~gewalten** the elements; **~güter** original goods; **~haushalt** ecosystem; **~katastrophe** natural disaster; **~landschaft** natural landscape.
natürlich natural, *(echt)* real, genuine, actual, *(ungezwungen)* unforced, unstrained, unaffected;
ganz ~ sprechen to speak naturally; **ganz ~ zugehen** to be nothing strange about it;
das ist nicht mit ~en Dingen zugegangen there is s. th. odd behind it;
~es Absatzgebiet natural marketing area; **~e Auslese** natural selection; **~e Begabung** natural gift; **~e Grenze** natural boundary; **in ~er Größe** life-size; **~e Haltung** unstudied pose; **~es Kind** illegitimate child, bastard; **~er Maßstab** plain scale; **ganz ~er Mensch** unaffected person; **~es Monopol** natural monopoly; **~e Person** natural (physical) person; **eines ~en Todes sterben** to die a natural death; **~er Vormund** natural guardian; **~er Vorzug an** asset; **~e Zuneigung** natural affection.
Natur|notwendigkeit absolute necessity; **~produkte** products of the land; **~recht** natural right (law), law of nature (kind); **~reservat** nature reserve; **~schätze** natural resources; **~schönheit** beautiful scenery.
Naturschutz conservation;
~amt, ~behörde Civilian Conservation Corps, Nature Conservancy *(Br.)*; **~gebiet** nature (wild-life) reserve, protected area, preserve, national park *(US)*; **Internationale ~organisation** World Wild-Life Fund; **~park** national park *(Br.)*.
Natur|talent natural talent; **~theater** open-air theatre; **~treue** truth to nature; **~volk** primitive race.
Naturwissenschaft physical (natural) science;
allgemeine ~ general science; **angewandte ~** technology, applied science.
naturwissenschaftlich scientific, physical.
Natur|wunder wonder of nature; **im ~zustand** in the natural state, natural.
nautische|Ausrüstung navigational gear; **~s Jahrbuch** nautical almanac; **~ Meile** nautical mile.
Navigation navigation, sailing.
Navigations|fehler navigational error; **~hilfe** navigational aid; **~karte** navigational chart; **~kunde** navigation, shipmanship; **~lichter** navigation lights, *(Flugzeug)* position lights; **~offizier** navigation officer, navigator *(US)*; **~raum** chartroom, navigating room; **~satellit** navigation satellite; **~schule** naval academy, nautical school.
navigations|tüchtig in navigable condition; **~unfähig** out of control, unmanoeuvrable.
Navigator navigator.
Nebel fog, mist;
bei Nacht und ~ under the cover of darkness; **durch ~ aufgehalten** held up by fog; **in ~ gehüllt** wrapped in mist, enshrouded in fog;
dichter ~ thick (dense) fog, density of fog; **feiner ~** haze, mist; **feuchter ~** wet fog; **dichter gelber ~** peasouper; **künstlicher ~** *(mil.)* smoke screen; **typischer Londoner ~** a London particular *(fam.)*; **nässender ~** wet (whistle) fog; **jede Sicht nehmender ~** blind man's buff (bluff, *US*) of a fog; **nieselnder ~** drizzling fog; **undurchdringlicher ~** thick fog; **mit Rauch vermischter ~** smog;
~ auflösen to disperse (dispense) the fog; **sich bei Nacht und ~ davonmachen** to steal away under cover of darkness; **durch undurchsichtigen ~ fahren** to drive through a misty thickness; **in ~ hüllen** to fog; **etw. wie durch einen ~ sehen** to see s. th. as through a mist; **in ~ gehüllt sein** *(Affäre)* to be shrouded in mystery; **sich im ~ verirren** to get lost in the fog;
das fällt aus wegen ~s that won't take place;
~auflöser go fog; **~auflösung** dispersion of the fog, fog dispersal; **~bank** fog bank; **~bildung** formation of fog; **stellenweise ~bildung** local patches of fog; **~boje** fog buoy; **~bombe** *(mil.)* smoke bomb; **~decke** blanket of fog; **hinter einer dichten ~decke versinken** to become enshrouded in fog; **~dichte** density of fog; **örtliche ~felder** local patches of fog; **~frost** rime.
nebelhaft vague, hazy, foggy;
in ~er Ferne liegen to lie in the dim future; **~e Vorstellung haben** to have a vague (hazy) idea.
Nebelhorn foghorn.
nebelig foggy, misty, *(leicht)* hazy;
~ werden to become foggy, to fog;
~er Tag misty day; **~es Wetter** foggy weather.
Nebel|kerze *(mil.)* smoke candle; **~lampen** fog lights; **~landung** instrument landing; **~munition** *(Artillerie)* smoke ammunition; **~niederschlag** fog drip; **~regen** drizzling rain, drizzle; **~scheinwerfer** fog lights; **~schleier** veil (shroud) of mist; **~schlußleuchte** rear fog lamp; **~schwaden** wisp of fog; **~signal** fog signal (whistle); **~signale auflegen** *(Bahn)* to fog; **~sirene, ~horn** fog horn; **~streifen** misty cloud, streak of fog; **~treiben** drifting fog; **~tröpfchen** fog particle (droplet).
nebelverhangen shrouded in fog, wrapped in mist.
Nebel|wand curtain of mist, *(mil.)* smoke screen; **~warnung** fog alarm, fog signal (whistle); **~wetter** foggy weather.
Neben|abgaben, jährliche reprises; **~abkommen** additional (pocket) agreement; **~abrede** collateral agreement (covenant), subagreement, subsidiary (additional, pocket) agreement; **mündliche ~abreden** parol evidence; **wettbewerbseinschränkende ~abrede** ancillary restraint; **~abschnitt** *(mil.)* adjacent sector; **~absicht** by-end, secondary object; **~adresse** alternative address, *(Notadresse)* reference in case of need; **~amt** by-office, branch (subsidiary) office; **im ~amt** as a secondary occupation.
neben|amtlich extra-official; **~an** next door.
Neben|anlage subsidiary (additional) plant; **~anschluß[stelle]** *(Gleis)* siding, *(Telefon)* extension [line]; **~anspruch** secondary right, *(Patentrecht)* independent claim; **~antrag** ancillary relief; **~arbeit** spare-time work, bywork; **~arbeiten, um Geld zu verdienen** extra couple of job opportunities; **~artikel** sideline; **~ausgabe** subedition; **~ausgaben** incidental (miscellaneous) expense, incidentals, extras, contingencies; **~ausgang** side door; **~ausschuß** subsidiary committee; **alle ~auswirkungen dieser Politik** all the offshoots of the policy; **~bahn** side (branch) line, light railway (railroad, *US*); **~bedeutung** overtone, connotation, *(Warenzeichen)* secondary meaning *(US)*; **~bedingung** subordinate clause, collateral (additional) condition; **~befugnisse** *(Vertreter)* mediate powers.
nebenbei on the side;
sich ~ mit Juristerei beschäftigen to dabble in (at) law.
Neben|beklagter codefendant; **~bemerkung** incidental remark, aside *(Br.)*; **~beruf** bywork, avocation, sideline, minor occupation; **~beruf ausüben** to work part-time on the side; **~beruf während der eigentlichen Arbeit ausüben** to daylight *(US)*.
nebenberuflich avocational, as a secondary occupation, side-liner, side-line, spare- (part-) time.
Neben|beschäftigung avocation, bywork, sideline [employment], spare-time work (employment, job), minor occupation, side-bar job *(sl.)*; **keiner ~beschäftigung nachgehen** to have no occupation outside of one's office work; **~bestimmung** collateral (subordinate) clause; **~bestimmungen** incidental provisions; **~betrieb** subsidiary company, ancillary undertaking, *(Filiale)* branch office; **landwirtschaftlicher ~betrieb** part-time farm, small farming; **~beweis** additional (collateral) proof, adminicle, secondary evidence; **~bezüge** fringe benefits, perquisites *(Br.)*, perks *(Br., coll)*; **~börse** curb exchange; **~buch** auxiliary (subsidiary) book; **~buchkonto** secondary account; **~buhler** rival; **seinen ~buhler ausstechen** to cut out one's rival; **~bürge** additional bail, cosurety, coguarantor; **~bürgschaft** collateral guarantee; **~darsteller** supporting character; **~effekt** secondary consequence; **~eigenschaft** secondary qualities; **~einander** juxtaposition; **~einander von Gut und Böse** sandwich of good and bad.
nebeneinander|bestehend concurrent; **~ fahren** to drive side by side; **~ geschaltet** synchronized, parallel; **~ sitzen** to sit side by side.
Neben|einanderschaltung *(el.)* parallel connection; **~eingang** side entrance; **~einkünfte** incidental receipts, perquisites *(Br.)*, casual revenue, emoluments, additional (subsidiary, casual, outside, extra) income; **nicht koschere ~einkünfte** pickings and stealings; **~einnahmen** additional (outside) income, perquisities *(Br.)*, perks *(Br., sl.)*; **~erwerb** sideline, spare-time job, secondary calling (occupation); **~erwerbsbetrieb, landwirtschaftliche ~erwerbssiedlung** homecroft *(Br.)*, urban homestead *(US)*; **~erwerbstätigkeit** secondary calling; **~erzeugnis** by-product.
Nebenfach subsidiary (minor) subject, subsid *(fam.)*;
freiwilliges ~ optional subject; **notwendiges ~** tool subject *(US)*;
als ~ nehmen to minor in *(US)*.

Neben | figur *(Theater)* minor character, feeder; ~**film** supporting program(me); ~**flügel** *(Gebäude)* lateral wing; ~**fluß** subsidiary stream, tributory, creek *(US)*; ~**forderung** accessory claim; ~**frage** collateral (side, minor, by-) issue, secondary question; **untergeordnete ~frage** off issue; ~**front** *(mil.)* secondary front; ~**gebäude** dependency, annex, appendage, adjoining (outlying) building, *(Nachbarhaus)* attached building; ~**gebiet** side issue; **stagnierendes ~gebiet** backwater; ~**gebühren** extras, additional charges; ~**geräusch** *(Radio)* atmospherics, statics, interference, *(tel.)* background noise; ~**geschäft** sideline [business], collateral transaction, *(Filiale)* branch establishment; ~**gesellschaft** subsidiary company; ~**gesetz** special law; ~**gewässer** dependent seas; ~**gewerbe** ancillary trade; ~**gewinn** incidental (additional) profit, extra gain; ~**gleis** sidetrack, bytrack; **j. auf ein ~gleis abschieben** to sidetrack s. o.; **auf einem ~gleis abstellen** to sidetrack, to shunt; ~**handlung** underplot, secondary plot, subplot; ~**haus** adjoining (adjacent) house, house next door; **im ~haus** next door.

nebenhergehend additional, secondary, extra, minor.

Neben | information *(Statistik)* ancillary information; ~**interesse** private interest; ~**intervenient** intervener, third party, intervenant, interpleader; ~**intervenient werden** to become a third party to an agreement *(Br.)*; ~**intervention** intervention, notice to third party, interpleader; ~**interventionsverfahren** bill of interpleader, third-party claim (interpleader) proceeding; ~**kanal** sluice; ~**karte** inset; ~**kasse** petty cash; ~**klage** ancillary suit; ~**kläger** coplaintiff, prosecuting witness; ~**konto** companion (subsidiary) account; ~**kosten** additional (incidental) expense, incidentals, extras, extra (additional) charges, subsidiary costs, contingencies; ~**kostenstelle** departmental burden centre; ~**kriegsschauplatz** secondary theater; ~**leistung** secondary obligation; ~**leistungen** additional services, *(für Angestellte)* fringe benefits, perquisites *(Br.)*, *(Spediteur)* accessorial services; ~**linie** *(Bahn)* connecting (secondary, side, branch) line, loop [line], branch, *(Herkunft)* collateral line; ~**markt** secondary market; ~**nachlaßverwaltung** ancillary administration; ~**partei** joint suitor; ~**person** minor character; ~**pflicht** accessory obligation; ~**platz** by-place, *(Bankwesen)* branch, out-of-town point; ~**postamt** post office substation; ~**produkt** by-product, residual (joint, secondary) product, sideline; ~**produktgewinnung** by-product recovery, recovery of by-products; ~**programm** *(Film)* supporting program(me); ~**prozeß** ancillary suit; ~**raum** by-room; ~**rechnung** ancillary bill; ~**recht** right appendant; ~**rechte** additional rights; ~**redakteur** assistant editor; ~**regierung** collateral government; ~**register** *(Warenzeichen)* supplemental register *(US)*; ~**rolle** underpart; ~**rolle spielen** *(fig.)* to play the second fiddle; ~**sache** matter of secondary importance, minor point, subordinate matter; **Haupt- und ~sache** principal and costs; **Gehalt ~sache** *(Anzeige)* salary secondary consideration.

nebensächlich subordinate, collateral, secondary, accessory, incidental, *(Schulfach)* minor *(US)*;
über ~e Dinge sprechen to talk commonplaces; ~**e Einzelheiten** minor details; ~**e Rolle spielen** to be of secondary importance.

Neben | sächliches secondary; ~**sächlichkeiten** nonessentials, little things, trivialities, externals; ~**satz** accessory sentence, subordinate clause; ~**schaden** collateral damage; ~**schaltung** *(Kraftwerk)* synchronization; ~**schluß** *(el.)* shunt; ~**schlußstromkreis** *(el.)* derived circuit; ~**schuldner** codebtor; ~**sender** relay station, regional station *(Br.)*, affiliate; ~**sicherheit** subsecurity; ~**siegel** quarter seal *(Scot.)*; ~**speicher** branch warehouse; ~**spesen** incidental expense, incidentals, extra charges, extras; ~**sprechen** *(tel.)* cross talk; ~**stadtteil** neighbo(u)rhood center *(US)* (centre, *Br.*).

nebenstehend marginal, *(anbei)* annexed, subjoined;
~ **abgebildet** shown in the accompanying picture;
~**e Tabelle** adjoining table.

Neben | stelle branch office, *(Bank)* branch, suboffice, *(Post)* substation, *(Telefon)* extension, *(Vertretung)* agency; ~**stellenanlage** extension; ~**stellennummer** extension number; ~**steuer** minor tax; ~**stollen** lateral; ~**strafe** subsidiary sentence; ~**straße** by-pass, by-lane, byroad, by-street, side street, secondary (ancillary) road, sideline, crossroad, branch road *(US)*; **in eine ~straße einbiegen** to turn down a side street; ~**strecke** byroute, *(Bahn)* loop [line], branch line, branch railroad *(US)*; **kurze ~strecke** *(Bahn)* stub *(US)*; **konsumierte ~tat** *(Strafrecht)* lesser offence; ~**tätigkeit** subsidiary activity, sideline; ~**titel** subhead; ~**treppe** service stairs, backstairs; ~**umstand** incident; ~**unternehmer** subcontractor; ~**urkunden** documents in support, supporting documents; ~**ursache** secondary cause; ~**verbraucher** secondary consumer; ~**verdienst** incidental (subsidiary) source of income, incidental (subsidiary) earnings, additional income, perquisites *(Br.)*, perks *(Br., sl.)*, extra profit; ~**vereinbarung** subagreement, collateral covenant; **obligatorische ~vereinbarung** restrictive covenant *(US)*; ~**verfahren** ancillary (collateral) proceedings, ancillary bill, accessory action; ~**vergünstigungen** fringe (ancillary) benefits, perquisites *(Br.)*; ~**vergütung** fringe benefit; ~**verpflichtung** accessory obligation, deed of covenant; **schuldrechtliche ~verpflichtung** covenant in gross; ~**versicherung** collateral insurance; ~**vertrag** collateral (accessory, subsidiary) contract; **vom Hauptvertrag unabhängiger ~vertrag** separable contract; ~**vertrag abschließen** to subcontract; ~**vormund** joint guardian, coguardian; ~**vormundschaft** joint guardianship; ~**vorstellung** side show; ~**vorteil** incidental advantage; ~**weg** back (side) road, sidestreet; ~**werte** *(Kurszettel)* sundry securities; ~**wirkung** collateral (side) effect; ~**wohnung** apartment next door; ~**zentrum** neighbo(u)rhood center *(US)* (centre, *Br.*); ~**zimmer** adjoining room; ~**zweck** by-end, secondary (ancillary) object.

Necessaire toilet bag, travel kit *(US)*.

necken to tease, to banter, to needle, to kid, to rag, to chaff *(coll.)*, to razz *(US sl.)*.

Neckerei teasing, bantering, chaffing, ragging.

Neckwerbung teaser campaign.

Negativ *(Foto)* negative.

negativ negative, unfavo(u)rable;
sich ~ über j. äußern to drizzle over s. o.;
~**er Befund** negative result; ~**er Beweis** negative evidence; ~**e Dienstbarkeit** negative easement (servitude); ~**e Einkommensteuer** negative income tax; ~**e Kritik** destructive criticism; ~**e Reaktion** *(Absatzwirtschaft)* negative response; ~**e Steuern** negative taxes; ~**es Vorzeichen haben** to have a negative cast; ~**e Wachstumsrate** negative economic growth rate.

Negativ | attest elearance certificate; ~**ätzung** negative (reverse) plate; ~**bedingung** negative condition; ~**besteuerung** negative taxation; ~**beweis** negative evidence; ~**bild** *(Foto)* negative; ~**klausel** negative clause; ~**klischee** block white on black, negative (reverse) plate, reversed block; ~**liste** *(Zoll)* list of goods liable to pay customs; ~**vergrößerung** enlarged negative; ~**verpflichtung** negative covenant, *(Bankwesen)* covenant against encumbrances.

negatorische Einrede negative avernment.

Neger negro, black man *(US)*, nigger, Jim Crow *(US)*, *(Rundfunk, Fernsehen)* barn, cheese cutter;
wie zehn nackte ~ angeben to be a terrible show-off; **schwarz wie ein ~ sein** to be as black as the ace of spades *(Br.)*;
~**arbeitslosigkeit** nonwhite unemployment; ~**problem** colo(u)r problem; ~**viertel** black belt *(US)*.

Negligé negligee, informal dress, undress.

negoziierbar negotiable.

negoziieren to negotiate.

Negoziierung negotiation.

Negoziierungs | auftrag order to negotiate; ~**kredit** negotiation credit, drawing authorization.

Nehmen receiving, taking;
in-Zahlung-~ trading-in.

nehmen to take, *(kaufen)* to buy, to purchase, *(als Zahlung fordern)* to charge for;
Abdruck ~ to make an impression; **Abstand ~** to desist (refrain) from; **zu den Akten ~** to [place on] file; **in Anspruch ~** to have recourse to; **Anstoß ~** to take offence at; **Anwalt ~** to retain a lawyer; **Arbeit in Angriff ~** to set to work, *(sofort)* to have work started at once; **j. auf den Arm ~** to pull s. one's leg; **auf sich ~** to incur; **Aufschwung ~** to take an upward trend, *(Kurse)* to go up, to advance, to rise, to be booming; **sich ein Beispiel an jem. ~** to let s. o. be an example to o. s.; **Bezug ~** to refer to; **jem. die Binde von den Augen ~** to open s. one's eyes; **kein Blatt vor den Mund ~** not to mince matters, to speak (give s. o. a piece of) one's mind; **auf Bodmerei ~** to borrow on bottomry; **etw. buchstäblich ~** to take s. th. literally; **Dinge ~, wie sie sind** to take things in one's stride; **finanziellen Druck von j. ~** to relieve s. o. of financial pressure; **etw. auf seinen Eid ~** to take one's oath on s. th.; **in Empfang ~** to receive; **Festung im Sturm ~** to take a fortress by storm; **j. unter seine Fittiche ~** to take s. o. under one's wing; **Folgen auf sich ~** to bear the consequences, to face the music; **von seinen Forderungen Abstand ~** to withdraw one's claims; **Geld ~** to take bribes, to be bribable; **Gelegenheit beim Schopf ~** to take time by the forelock, to make hay while the sun shines; **gern ~** *(Effekten)* to take readily; **in Gewahrsam ~** to take charge of (into custody); **Gift ~** to poison o. s.; **alle Hindernisse ~** to clear all the hurdles; **jem.**

die Hoffnung ~ to destroy s. one's hopes; **j. fest an die Kandare** ~ to keep a tight rein on s. o.; **etw. in Kauf** ~ to put up with s. th.; **j. aufs Korn** ~ to draw a head on s. o. *(US)*, to put s. o. on the spot *(US)*, to seek s. o. out; **auf jds. Kosten einen** ~ to have a drink on s. o.; **auf Kredit** ~ to buy on credit; **Kredite in erhöhtem Maße in Anspruch** ~ to increase the borrowings; **Kurve zu schnell** ~ to take a corner too fast; **sich das Leben** ~ to take one's life, to commit suicide; **j. in die Lehre** ~ to apprentice s. o.; **Lehrling** ~ to take an apprentice; **fünfzehn Mark für die Stunde** ~ to charge DM 15 an hour; **aus dem Markt** ~ to take off the market; **Maschine in Betrieb** ~ to put a machine into operation; **jem. Maß** ~ to take s. one's measurements; **den Mund voll** ~ to talk big; **alles für bare Münze** ~ to take everything for gospel truth; **Nachhilfelehrer** ~ to engage a tutor; **in Pacht** ~ to lease; **Paket in Empfang** ~ to accept a parcel; **sich das Recht** ~ to arrogate to o. s.; **Reißaus** ~ to take to one's heels; **Rückgriff** ~ to have recourse to; **j. auf die Schippe** ~ to pull s. one's leg; **Schuld auf sich** ~ to take the blame; **etw. auf die leichte Schulter** ~ to make light of it; **j. in Schutz** ~ to speak up for s. o.; **j. auf die Seite** ~ to take s. o. aside; **Steigung im zweiten Gang** ~ to drive up a hill in second gear; **zu etw. Stellung** ~ to comment on s. th., to give one's opinion, to define one's attitude; **Straßenbahn** ~ to go by tram; **sich die besten Stücke** ~ to take the best of the bunch *(coll.)*; **zum Teilhaber** ~ to take into partnership; **Urlaub** ~ to take one's holiday, to go on leave; **j. ins Verhör** ~ to cross-examine s. o.; **in Verwahrung** ~ to take into safekeeping; **in Vormerkung** ~ to record; **Vorprämie** ~ to take for the call; **zum Vorwand** ~ to use as a pretext; **Waren auf Kredit** ~ to buy goods on credit; **Waren auf Lager** ~ to stock goods; **Waren aus dem Zollverschluß** ~ to take goods out of bond; **andere Wohnung** ~ to change one's quarters; **in Zahlung** ~ to receive in payment, to trade in; **Zimmer** ~ to rent a room; **jem. jeden Zweifel** ~ to relieve s. one's mind of all doubts;
leicht zu ~ to be pleasant to deal with, to be easy to get on with; **j. zu** ~ **wissen** to know how to manage s. o., to get round s. o.; **Kunden richtig zu** ~ **wissen** to have a way with (manage) customers; **jem.** ~ **wie er ist** to take s. o. in the rough;
~, was man in die Finger bekommt to take whatever one can lay hands on; **darauf kannst du Gift** ~ you can bet your life on it.

Nehmer *(Börse)* taker, buyer, purchaser, *(Empfänger)* payee, *(Kurszettel)* money, bid;
Geber und ~ givers and receivers.

Neid envy, jealousy;
blanker ~ pure envy *(coll.)*;
~ **hervorrufen** to excite (raise) envy; **j. vor** ~ **erblassen lassen** to make (turn) s. o. green with jealousy (envy).

neiden, jem. etw. to envy s. o. s. th.; **jem. seinen Erfolg** ~ to resent s. one's good fortune; **jem. seinen guten Namen** ~ to be jealous of s. one's good name.

neiderfüllter Blick envious look.

Neidhammel dog in the manger.

neidisch feign, jealous, envious;
~ **auf j. sein** to be jealous of s. o., to feel envy at s. th.;
~en Blick auf etw. werfen to cast an envious eye on s. th.

neidlos free from jealously, ungrudging;
~ **bewundern** to admire s. th. without envy.

Neige decline, end, close, slope, ebb;
an der ~ **des Lebens** at the sunset of life;
zur ~ **gehen** to be on the decline, to run short (low), *(Gefahr)* to be drawing to its close; **bis zur** ~ **leeren** to drink to the last drop; **Glas bis zur** ~ **leeren** to drain the cup to the dregs; **auf der** ~ **stehen** to be in the balance.

neigen to bend, to incline, *(Neigung haben)* to tend, to lean;
zu etw. ~ to feel inclined (tend, lean) towards s. th., *(Krankheit)* to have a propensity for s. th.; **zu Erkältungen** ~ to catch cold easily, to be susceptible to colds; **Faß** ~ to tilt a barrel; **zur Festigkeit** ~ to tend to a rise; **zur Flaute** ~ to incline to a fall; **zum Grübeln** ~ to be inclined to brood; **zu klassischer Musik** ~ to be fond of classical music; **zum Schuldenmachen** ~ to have a propensity for getting into debt; **zur Schwäche** ~ *(Börse)* to be inclined to weakness; **zu Übertreibungen** ~ to have a propensity to exaggerate; **noch immer zu der Überzeugung** ~ to be still convinced; **weitgehend dazu** ~ to have half a mind to do; **sich im Wind** ~ to sway in the wind.

Neigung propensity, inclination, tend, hang, habit, lurch, appetite, notion, ply, *(Abhang)* fall, slope, grade, tip, *(Beruf)* vocation, leaning, *(Markt)* trend, tendency, *(Straße)* gradient, incline, slope, *(Vorliebe)* preference, liking, penchant;
kriminelle ~ criminal leanings; **künstlerische ~en** artistic leanings; **steigende** ~ rising tendency;
~ **zum Fallen** falling tendency; ~ **zum Kauf** inclination to buy; **jds.** ~ **erwidern** to reciprocate s. one's affection; ~ **zu jem. fassen** to take a liking to s. o.; **seiner** ~ **frönen** to indulge one's taste; ~ **haben** to incline, to tend, to feel inclined; **sozialistische ~en haben** to lean towards socialism; **angeborene** ~ **für etw. haben** to have a natural tendency to do s. th.; **in seinen ~en schwanken** to be fickle with one's attentions.

Nein, kategorisches downright no;
mit ~ **stimmen** to declare o. s. not content;
Ja-~-Beobachtungen *(Statistik)* sensitivity data.

Neinstimme negative vote, vote against, *(parl.)* no, nays *(US)*;
~ **abgeben** to vote in the negative.

Nekrolog obituary.

Nennbetrag face (nominal) amount, face;
~ **einer Schuld** face of debt.

nennen to name, *(anführen)* to quote, to cite, *(betiteln)* to title, to style, *(bezeichnen)* to designate, to term, *(erwähnen)* to mention, *(Kandidat)* to nominate;
Beispiel ~ to give an example; **j. einen Lügner** ~ to call s. o. a liar; **namentlich** ~ to mention individually; **Preis** ~ to name a price; **Referenzen** ~ to quote references; **Zeugen** ~ to give the names of witnesses.

nennenswert significant, notable, mentionable, noteworthy;
kaum ~ not in any appreciable degree;
~ **gestiegen sein** to have risen significantly;
~er Betrag substantial amount; **keine ~en Einnahmen haben** to have no income to speak of; **kein ~er Fortschritt** no appreciable progress; **kein ~es Vermögen** no property worth mentioning.

Nenner, gemeinsamer common denominator;
auf einen gemeinsamen ~ **bringen** to reduce to a common denominator.

Nenn|gebühr, ~geld entrance (entry) fee; **~kapital** subscribed (nominal, *US*) capital; **~leistung** *(Maschine)* rated capacity.

Nennung naming, mention, *(Bezeichnung)* designation, *(Kandidat)* nomination, *(Sport)* entry;
ohne ~ **unseres Namens** without mentioning our name.

Nennungsgebühr entrance (entry) fee.

Nennwert nominal (face) value, denomination, face, *(Aktien)* [nominal] par, par value;
ohne ~ no par; **über dem** ~ above par, at a premium; **unter dem** ~ below par, at a discount; **zum** ~ at par;
~ **einer Hypothek** face of a mortgage; ~ **einer Police** face of a policy;
~aktie par value share *(Br.)* (stock, *US*).

nennwertlose Aktie no-par-value share (stock, *US*).

Nennwert|parität nominal parity; **~zertifikat** *(Investmenttrust)* face amount certificate.

Neon|beleuchtung neon light, strip lighting; **~lampe** neon lamp; **~licht** fluorescent (neon) light; **grelles ~licht** glaring neon lights; **~röhre** fluorescent light strip, neon tube; **~werbung** neon sign.

Nepotismus nepotism.

Nepp clip, gyp *(US)*.

neppen to fleece, to clip *(US sl.)*, to diddle *(sl.)*, to gyp *(US)*;
sich ~ **lassen** to pay through the nose.

Nerven, überempfindliche high-string nerves;
jds. ~ **beruhigen** to settle (soothe) s. one's nerves; **jem. auf die** ~ **gehen** to jump s. one's nerves, to be a trial to s. o., to get under s. one's skin (on s. one's nerves), to jar [on] the nerves, to wear on s. o., to give s. o. pains in the neck (the pip, needle); **eiserne** ~ **haben** to have nerves of steel (iron nerves); **mit seinen** ~ **am Ende sein** to have one's nerves on edge;
~anspannung jarring of the nerves, suspense of mind; **~arzt** mental specialist, psychiatrist, alienist.

nervenaufpeitschend highly exciting, stirring, nerve-cracking.

Nerven|beruhigungsmittel tranquilizer, sedative; **~bündel** jitterbug, nervous twitch, bag (bundle) of nerves; **reines ~bündel sein** to have one's nerves frayed at both ends, to be all nerves; **~gas** nerve gas; **~heilanstalt** mental asylum (hospital, *US*), mental home, lunatic (insane) asylum; **in eine ~heilanstalt zwangsweise einweisen** to admit to a mental hospital under compulsion; **zwangsweise in eine ~heilanstalt eingewiesen sein** to be compulsorily detained under the mental Health Act; **~kitzel** kick; **~kitzel bieten** to offer a thrill; **~kitzel verursachen** to titillate; **~kostüm** nervous system; **schlechtes ~kostüm haben** to be all of a jump; **~krieg** war of nerves; **~krise** nervous attack; **~leidender** nerve patient (case); **~nahrung** nerve food; **~säge** unpleasant jar to the nerves, handful; **~schaden** mental injury; **~schock** mental shock; **~schwäche** nervous debility; **~stränge eines Landes** nerves of a country; **~zerrüttung**

nervous derangement; ~**zusammenbruch** nervous (mental) breakdown; ~**zusammenbruch haben** to crack up; **jem. zum ~zusammenbruch treiben** to drive s. o. neurotic.

nervös nervous, on the jump, in a flurry, fussy;
leicht ~ high-keyed;
~ **auf und ab gehen** to nervously pace the floor; **j.** ~ **machen** to get in s. one's hair, to give s. o. the willies, to make s. o. jumpy, to flush s. o.; **j. total** ~ **machen** to set s. one's teeth on edge; **äußerst** ~ **sein** to be in a state of nerves; **nicht** ~ **werden** to play it cool.

Nervosität, unnötige fuss.

Nesseln, sich in die ~ **setzen** to get into hot water (in trouble), to look for trouble.

Nest nest, *(Diebesversteck)* hideout, den;
gemachtes ~ featherbed; **gottverlassenes** ~ god-forsaken hole, out-of-the-way spot, dead-and-alive place; **trostloses** ~ deadly dull hole; **unbedeutendes** ~ obscure retreat; **zweitrangiges** ~ one-horse town *(US)*;
sich ein ~ **bauen** to build a home for o. s.; **das eigene** ~ **beschmutzen** to blot one's own copybook *(coll.)*, to foul one's own nest, to cry stinking fish, to play the dozen *(sl.)*; ~ **leer finden** to find the hide-out empty; **nach einem nicht zu teuren** ~ **Umschau halten** to be looking for a little place that is not too expensive; **eigenes** ~ **reinhalten** to keep one's slate clean; **sich ins gemachte** ~ **setzen** to be as snug as a bug in a rug; **ins** ~ **steigen** to go between the sheets, to snuggle down in bed;
~**häkchen** pet of the family, youngest child, nestling; ~**wärme** *(fig.)* safety of the nest.

nett nice, pleasant;
j. ~ **behandeln** to be nice to s. o.; **j. ganz** ~ **zugerichtet haben** to have used s. o. badly; ~ **von jem. sprechen** to speak nicely of s. o.;
~**e Bescherung** a fine kettle of fish; ~**es Früchtchen** fine rascal; ~**es kleines Haus** tidy little house; ~**er Kerl** nice guy *(US)* (chap, *Br.*); ~**es Sümmchen auf der Bank** tidy little sum in the bank; ~**es Wochenende verbringen** to spend a pleasant weekend; ~ **eingerichtetes Zimmer** neatly furnished room.

netto net, neat, clear, *(Gewicht)* neat, *(ohne Verpackung)* without packing;
~ **Kasse [im voraus]** net cash [in advance]; **rein** ~ without any deduction; ~ **vor Steuerermäßigung** net of tax relief;
~ **bezahlen** to pay net; ~ **erbringen** to net; ~ **verdienen** to clear, to net.

Netto|abzug net reduction; ~**anlageeinkommen** net investment income; ~**anlageinvestition** net investment fixed assets, capital formation; ~**anteil** net worth *(US)*, equity; ~**anteil der Aktionäre** shareholders' equity; ~**anteil mit der Ausgabe von Gratisaktien verwässern** to dilute the equity with stock dividends; ~**aufwand** net expenditure; ~**aufwand für Investitionen** net revenue expenditure; ~**aufwand zur Befriedigung von Regreßforderungen** *(Versicherungsbilanz)* expenses net of recoveries; ~**auslandseinkünfte** net income from abroad; ~**auslandsposition** *(Währungspolitik)* net external monetary position; ~**ausschüttung** net relevant distribution; ~**austauschverhältnis** net barter terms of trade; ~**ausweis** *(Bank)* net return; ~**belastung von Sparguthaben** net withdrawal from savings account; ~**bestände** net holdings; ~**bestandsveränderung** *(volkswirtschaftliche Gesamtrechnung)* net change in business inventories; ~**bestandsveränderung des Betriebskapitals** net change in working capital; ~**betrag** net (clear) amount, net balance; ~**betrag der auf die Versicherung entfallenden Prämien** net level annual premium; ~**betriebserfolg** net operating income; ~**betriebsgewinn** net profit from (on) operations; ~**betriebsverlust** net operating deficit; ~**bezüge** net salary; ~**bezugskosten** net cost of purchase; ~**bilanz** net balance; ~**diensteinkommen** net remuneration; ~**dividende** net dividend; ~**eingänge** net receipts; ~**einkaufspreis** net purchase.

Nettoeinkommen net income (receipts, earnings), clear income, *(nach Steuerabzug)* net spendable income, disposable income *(US)*;
~ **nach Abzug der Steuerfreibeträge** surtax net income *(US)*; ~ **pro Kopf der Bevölkerung** per capita net income; ~ **nach Steuern** net income after taxes, disposable income *(US)*.

Netto|einkünfte net earnings; ~**einkünfte aus dem Ausland** net income from abroad; **während der Darlehnszeit erwartete** ~**einnahmen** prospected net profit expected to be earned over the period of the advance; ~**ergebnis** net result *(US)*; ~**erhöhung** net increase; ~**erlös** net yield (proceeds [of a sale], avails, *US*); ~**ersparnis** net savings; ~**ertrag** net proceeds (return, earnings, yield), *(Grundstück)* net rental; **zur Ausschüttung zur Verfügung stehender** ~**ertrag** net profit available for appropriation; ~**erträge** net earnings; ~**erträge nach Steuern** net income after taxes; ~**ertragswertberechnung** net earnings rule; ~**export** net exports; **verkaufsfähige** ~**förderung** net merchantable production; ~**fracht** clear freight, *(Seeschiffahrt)* net freight; ~**gehalt** nominal salary, take-home pay, pay after stoppage *(Br.)*; ~**gewicht** net (shuttle) weight; ~**gewinn** clear gain, net profits (gain, earnings); **erzielter** ~**gewinn** net realized gain; ~**gewinnspanne** net margin; ~**gewicht** net (shuttle) weight; ~**grenzprodukt** marginal net product; ~**guthaben** net holdings; **private** ~**inlandsinvestitionen** net private domestic investment; ~**inventarwert von Anteilen** net asset value of shares; **nach dem** ~**inventarwert ansetzen (veranschlagen)** to value on a net asset basis; ~**investition** net investment; ~**investitionsausgaben** net investment spending; ~**jahresertragswert** clear annual value.

Nettokapital|export net capital export; ~**gewinn** net capital gain; ~**import** net capital import; ~**wert** net capital gain.

Netto|kasse im voraus net cash in advance; ~**kosten** net cost; ~**kreditaufnahme** net borrowings; ~**kreditsaldo** net credit balance; ~**kurs** net price; ~**leistung** net flow; ~**liquidität** net liquidity; ~**lohn** take-home pay (packet, income, wages), nominal wage; ~**miete,** ~**pacht** net rental; ~**prämie** net (pure) premium; ~**preis** net price (cash), *(Selbstkosten)* net cost, *(Zoll)* short price *(US)*; **zum** ~**preis** straight; ~**produkt** net product; ~**produktion** net production; ~**produktionswert** net output; ~**produktionsziffer** net production rate; ~**provision** net commission; ~**raumgehalt** net tonnage; ~**rechnungswert** net invoice price; ~**registertonne** net register ton; ~**registertonnengehalt** net tonnage; ~**reichweite** *(Anzeige)* net unduplicated audience; **5%ige** ~**rendite auf das Anlagevermögen** 5% return on net assets employed; ~**renditesatz** net real rate of return; ~**rente** net revenue (income), *(Mietvertrag)* net rental *(Br.)*; ~**reserve** net reserve; ~**saldo** net balance; ~**satz** *(Darlehn)* face rate; ~**schöpfung** net value added; ~**sozialprodukt** social net product, net national income (product); ~**sozialprodukt zu Faktorpreisen** net domestic product; ~**sparzinssatz** net rate of interest on savings; ~**steueraufkommen** net tax receipts; ~**steuerbelastung** net burden of taxes; ~**steuerschuld** net tax liability; ~**tara** net tare; ~**tonnage** net tonnage; **reiner** ~**überschuß** net income (surplus); ~**überschußposition** *(Währungspolitik)* net creditor [limit] position; ~**umsatz** net sales; ~**verbindlichkeiten** net debts; ~**verbindlichkeiten nach Abzug der liquiden Aktien** net liabilities; ~**verdienst** net earnings; **beglaubigter** ~**verkauf** *(Zeitung)* certified net sale; ~**verkaufserlös** net profit on sales, net sales *(US)*; ~**verlust** net (clear, dead) loss; ~**vermögen** average net assets, *(Eigenkapital)* proprietary interest, net worth *(US)*; ~**vermögen eines Unternehmens** surplus of a corporation; ~**verschuldung** net indebtedness; ~**verzinsung** net value, net interest return, proprietary interest; ~**volkseinkommen** net national income; ~**wert** *(Unternehmen)* book value, net worth *(US)*; ~**wertschöpfung** net value added; ~**zinsen** net (pure, true) interest; ~**zinsfluß,** ~**zinssatz** net rate of interest, pure interest; ~**zoll** long duty; ~**zugang an liquiden Mitteln** cashflow.

Netz net, *(el.)* mains, *(Einkaufsnetz)* string (shopping) bag, *(Fadenkreuz)* reticule, reticle, *(Fallstrick)* meshes, *(Kartengitter)* grid, *(Koordinaten)* graticule, *(tel.)* telecommunication system, *(Verkehrsweg)* network, system;
weitgespanntes ~ far-flung network; **weltumfassendes** ~ global network;
gut ausgebautes ~ **von Eisenbahnlinien** well-developed network of railways; ~ **von Fluglinien** network of air routes; ~ **von Intrigen** network of falsehoods, meshes of intrigue; ~ **von Kanälen** network of canals; **zusammenhängendes** ~ **von Straßen** interlacing network of roads; ~ **mit Wählbetrieb** *(tel.)* automatic area;
Fluß nach einem verlorenen Kind mit ~**en absuchen** to drag a river for a missing child; **Wohnung ans** ~ **anschließen** to connect a house to the mains; **ohne** ~ **arbeiten** *(Artist)* to perform without a net; **seine** ~**e auswerfen** to cast one's nets; **Blitzgerät über das elektrische** ~ **betreiben** to operate a flash unit from the mains; **jem. ins** ~ **gehen** to walk into the net; **der Polizei ins** ~ **gehen** to be caught in the dragnet of the police; **j. ins** ~ **locken** to lure s. o. into a trap; **sich im** ~ **politischer Intrigen verfangen** to be entangled in the meshes of political intrigues; **über ein** ~ **von 550 Vertragshändlern verkaufen** to sell through a network of 550 dealers; **sich im** ~ **der eigenen Lügen verstricken** to become entangled in the web of one's own lies; **in sein** ~ **ziehen** to draw into one's meshes;
~**anschluß** mains input, current supply; **mit** ~**anschluß** *(Rundfunkgerät)* operating on the mains; ~**anschlußgerät**

power pack; ~**ausfall** mains (power) breakdown, line failure; ~**belastung** power load; ~**empfänger** mains receiving set; ~**entwurf** map projection; ~**gerät** mains-operated unit; ~**gruppenwähler** *(tel.)* code selector; ~**karte** *(Eisenbahn)* runabout *(Br.)* (rover, go-as-you-please) ticket, commutation ticket *(US)*, commuter fare *(US)*; ~**karte benutzen** to commute *(US)*; ~**karteninhaber** commuter *(US)*; ~**plantechnik** network technique; ~**stecker** mains plug; ~**teil** mains unit; ~**transformator** power transformer; ~**werk** web, network, *(Bahn)* gridiron.

neu new, fresh, *(neuartig)* original, newfangled, *(modern)* modern, *(Patentrecht)* novel;
fast ~ as good as new; **ganz ~** brand new; **wie ~** in new condition;
~ für alt *(Versicherungswesen)* new for old; **~ aufgelegt** reprinted; **~ ausgegeben** hot; **~ bereift** new-tyred; **~ eingeführt** new fashioned; **~ ernannt** newly appointed; **~ eröffnet** newly opened; **~ errichtet** new-built; **~ erschienen** recently published; **~ gewählt** reelected;
ganz ~ anfangen to start from scratch; **von ~em anfangen** to begin all over again; **~ anordnen** to rearrange, to reorganize; **~ anschaffen** to replace; **~ ausstatten, ~ ausrüsten** to re-equip, to retool; **~ auszeichnen** to reprice; **Buch ~ bearbeiten** to revise a book; **alte Tradition ~ beleben** to revive an old tradition; **~ besetzen** *(Rolle)* to recast; **~ bestellen** to reorder, to repeat an article; **~ bewerten** to reappraise, *(aufwerten)* to revalorize; **Effekten ~ bewerten** to mark down (up) securities; **Erzeugnis ~ auf den Markt bringen** to introduce a new product (launch a product) on the market; **sich ~ einkleiden** to refurnish one's wardrobe; **~ fassen** to redraft, to reword, *(Schmuck)* to reset; **~ finanzieren** to recapitalize; **~ gruppieren** to regroup, to reshuffle *(US)*; **~ inszenieren** to restage; **~ investieren** to reinvest; **etw. wieder ganz auf ~ machen** to do up s. th. like new; **Zaun ~ machen** to repair a fence; **Zimmer ~ machen** to redecorate a room; **Seite ~ schreiben** to retype the whole page; **offenbar völlig ~ für j. sein** to be apparently new to s. o.; **völlig ~ ausgestattet worden sein** to be completely re-equipped; **~ zugezogen sein** to be a newcomer to a community, to be new to a town; **~ tapezieren** to repaper the walls; **~ veranlagen** to reassess; **~ verteilen** to re-allocate, to redistribute;
~er Absatz fresh paragraph; **~e Aktien** junior stocks *(US)*; **~er Anfang** fresh start; **~en Anfang machen** to turn over a new leaf; **~e Aufträge** reorders, repeat orders; **ganz ~e Banknoten** brand-new bank-notes; **~e Besen kehren gut** new brooms sweep clean; **~e Besetzung** *(Theater)* new cast; **~e Beweise** fresh evidence; **~ entdecktes Beweismaterial** fresh evidence; **~er Bogen Papier** fresh sheet of paper; **~ erschienene Bücher** new publications; **sich mit ~em Eifer an die Arbeit machen** to set to work with renewed enthusiasm; **~e Entdeckungen machen** to make new discoveries; **~er Entwurf** new draft; **~e Firmengründungen** new entrants; **~er Gast** newcomer, arrival; **~e Generation** rising generation; **~e Geschichte** modern history; **~e Ideen** newfangled ideas; **~es Kapital** fresh (additional) capital; **~es Kapitel** fresh chapter; **~er Klagegrund** new cause of action; **~es Leben beginnen** to turn over a new leaf; **~ entdeckte Leidenschaft** new-born passion; **~e Linie** the new look; **~e Mitglieder werben** to recruit new members; **~e Mode** new fashion; **~e Möglichkeiten eröffnen** to open up new prospects; **~ entwickelter Motor** newly developed engine; **~en Mut schöpfen** to take fresh heart; **dem Gerede ~e Nahrung geben** to revive a rumo(u)r; **die ~e Perspektive** *(pol.)* the new look; **~e Sachlichkeit** new practicality; **~er Sachvortrag** new matter; **~ gefallener Schnee** freshly fallen snow; **~ eingetretener Schüler** new boy; **~e Schwierigkeiten** further difficulties; **~e Seite seines Wesens offenbaren** to reveal a very different side of one's nature; **~ere Sprachen** modern languages; **~er Stadtteil** new part of a town; **~e klagebegründende Tatsachen** new cause of action; **~e Truppen** fresh troops; **~e Unruhen** more disturbances; **~es Verfahren** new trial (process, method); **~e Version einer alten Geschichte** old parcel in a new string; **~er Versuch** another attempt; **~e Wendung nehmen** to take a new turn; **~e Zeile** new line; **~ere Zeit** modern times; **~e Zufuhren** fresh supplies.

Neu | abschlüsse new orders (business) ~**anfertigung** manufacture of new articles; ~**ankömmling** newcomer, arrival; ~**anlage** new installation, *(Investition)* reinvestment, new investment; ~**anlagengeschäft drosseln** to hold down investment in new facilities; ~**anmeldungen** new applications; ~**anpassung der Wechselkurse** readjustment of exchange rates; ~**anschaffungen** new acquisitions, renewals, *(Bibliothek)* accessions, *(Ersatzbeschaffung)* replacement; ~**anschaffung von Möbeln** purchase of new furniture; ~**anschaffungen machen** to lay in a fresh stock; ~**anschaffungskosten**, ~**anschaffungswert** replacement cost.

neuartig novel;
~es Verfahren novel method.

Neuaufführung revival.

neuaufgelegt reissued, re-edited, reprinted, republished.

Neuauflage new edition, reprint, reissue, republication, *(Anleihe)* refloating;
bearbeitete ~ revised edition;
~ herausbringen to publish a new edition; **kurz vor der ~ stehen** to be in the course of reprinting.

Neu | aufnahme admission of a new member, *(Film)* retake; ~**aufteilung** redistribution; ~**aufträge** new (repeat) orders; ~**ausfertigung** fresh copy; ~**ausgabe** new edition, reedition, reprint, reissue, republication, *(Aktien)* junior issues; ~**ausrichtung** readjustment; ~**ausstattung**, ~**ausrüstung** retooling, re-equipment; ~**auszeichnung** *(Waren)* repricing.

Neubau new building (construction), *(im Bau)* building under construction, *(Wiederaufbau)* rebuilding, reconstruction;
~ beziehen to move into a new house;
~beginn housing (new home) start; **~bewilligungen** new homes authorized.

Neu | bauten housing (new home) starts, new works (buildings); ~**bauwohnung** newly built flat (apartment, *US*).

neubearbeitet revised;
fürs Fernsehen ~ worden sein to be newly adapted for television.

Neu | bearbeitung *(Buch)* revised edition; ~**begebung** *(Anleihe)* new issue, refloating; ~**beginn** new deal *(US)*; ~**belebung der Außenpolitik** revival of foreign policy; ~**berechnung** revaluation; ~**besetzung** new appointment; ~**besetzung erledigter Stellen** filling of vacancies; ~**besitzer** *(Effekten)* junior bondholder; ~**bestellung** re-order, repeat order.

Neubewertung revaluation, new valuation, reappraisal, *(Aufwertung)* revalorization;
~ des Anlagevermögens revaluation of fixed assets; **~ von Effekten** markdown (markup) of securities;
~ verlangen to claim a reduction of assessment; **~ vornehmen** to revise one's estimates, *(aufwerten)* to revalorize.

Neubewertungs | gewinn revaluation surplus; ~**rücklage** special revaluation reserve.

Neu | bewilligung additional grant; ~**bildung** reorganization, reshuffle; ~**bruch** cleared (new, *US*) land; ~**bücherabsatz** new books turnover; ~**darstellung** restatement; ~**dekorierung** redecoration; ~**druck** reimpression, new edition; **unveränderter ~druck** reprint; ~**einrichtung** new institution, *(Möbel)* refurnishing, *(techn.)* new installations; ~**einstellungen** replacements, new employments, new hirings *(US)*; ~ **und Wiedereinstellungsprozentsatz** labo(u)r turnover; ~**einstellungszusagen** recruitment obligations *(US)*; ~**einstudierung** *(Theater)* restudy, reproduction; ~**einstufung** reclassification, *(gehaltlich)* regrading; ~**einstufung ohne Gehaltsänderung** ingrade classification change; ~**einteilung** reclassification, regrading; ~**einteilung der Wahlbezirke** redistriction of Congressional districts *(US)*; ~**eintragung** new registration, reincorporation; ~**einwanderer** new chum *(Australia)*; ~**emission** reissue, new issue; ~**emission im größeren Ausmaß übernehmen** to underwrite a large part of public issues; ~**engagement** *(Theater)* reengagement; ~**englisch** modern English; ~**erkrankungen** new cases; ~**erkrankungsziffer** attack rate.

neuerliche | Bestimmungen recent regulations; **nach ~n Versuchen** after repeated attempts.

Neuernennungsliste new hats department.

neueröffnet newly opened.

Neu | eröffnung reopening; ~**erscheinung** *(Buch)* new publication; ~**erscheinungen** *(Büchermarkt)* forthcoming books; ~**erscheinungs-Sofortdienst** immediate advice of new publications; ~**erteilung eines Patents** reissue of a patent *(US)*.

Neuerung novation, innovation, novelty, new tricks;
technische ~en technical innovations;
~en einführen to innovate, to make innovations, to introduce novelties.

Neuerwerbungen recent (new) acquisitions, *(Bibliothek)* accessions;
betriebliche ~ manufacturing acquisitions;
sich auf ~en stürzen to jump into new purchases.

Neues, etw. ganz ~ sein to be a wholly new ball-game; **auf etw. ~ stoßen** to find something new; **etw. ganz ~ unternehmen** to strike out a line of one's own way, to break fresh ground.

neuest newest, latest, most recent;
nach den ~en Meldungen according to the most recent reports; **~e Mode** all the vogue (kick); **nach der ~en Mode gekleidet** dressed like a dog's dinner; **~e Nachrichten** latest (stop-press, *Br.*) news.

Neufassung revision, rewrite, redrafting, revised text, *(Gesetz)* revision, new version, amendment, *(Schmuck)* resetting.

Neufestsetzung | des Einheitswertes reassessment of real property; **~ von Quoten** redetermination of quotas; **~ des Verkaufspreises** price alteration (change); **~ der Währungsparitäten** realignment (reestablishment) of parities; **~ von Warenpreisen** remarking of merchandise.

Neu | feststellung restatement; **~finanzierung** refinancing, recapitalization; **~formulierung** restatement, recording; **~fundierung** refunding.

neu | gebaut new-built; **sich wie ~geboren fühlen** to feel a new man; **~gedruckt** reprinted, reissued, republished; **~gegründet** recently formed; **~geprägtes Wort** new-coined word.

Neu | geschäfte erschließen to pick up new business; **~gesellschaft** new company; **~gestaltung** reorganization, reformation, *(baulich)* redevelopment, *(Film)* remake.

Neugier, Neugierde curiosity, inquisitiveness;
aus blanker ~ out of idle curiosity;
seine ~ bezähmen to restrain one's curiosity; **jds. ~ auf das Höchste erregen** to excite s. one's interest to the highest pitch; **seiner ~ die Zügel schießen lassen** to allow full play to one's curiosity; **vor ~ platzen** to be agog (eaten up) with curiosity.

neugierig | sein to be all question; **~ sein, zu erfahren** to be anxious to learn;
~er Blick inquisitive look; **vor ~en Blicken schützen** to protect from prying eyes; **~e Passanten** curious by-passers; **~e Person** pryer, rubberneck, Nosy Parker *(Br.)*, snooper.

Neu | gliederung reorganization, rearrangement; **~gliederung von Grund auf** top-to-bottom restructuring; **~gründung** reconstruction, reorganization, reestablishment; **~gruppierung** reclassification, regrouping, reshuffling.

Neuheit novelty [item], latest fashion, speciality, nouveauté *(US)*, *(Patentrecht)* novelty, new and useful;
letzte ~ all the kick; **mangelnde ~** want of novelty;
~ verneinen to negate the novelty.

Neuheiten fancy goods, novelties;
die letzten ~ the last cry.

Neuheits | aufkommen total of new inventions; **~beweis** proof of novelty; **~merkmal** novel feature; **~prüfung** *(Patent)* novelty search; **~reklame** novelty advertising.

neuheitsschädlich *(Patentrecht)* anticipatory;
~ sein to constitute a bar as to novelty.

Neuheits | schädlichkeit bar to novelty; **~wert** specialty value; **~wert verlieren** to wear off.

Neuigkeit piece of news;
mit ~en vollgestopft news-crammed;
abgestandene ~en stale news; **herzerfrischende ~en** heartening news;
~en auftreiben to pick up news; **auf ~en aussein** to pine after news; **~ bekanntgeben** to publish (tell) the news; **~ überall bekanntmachen** to blaze the news abroad; **~ erfahren** to hear a piece of news; **~en fabrizieren** to manufacture news; **von ~en platzen** to be full of the news; **neueste ~ sein** to be all the news; **immer über alle ~en im Bilde sein** to be posted up in recent affairs; **~ in der ganzen Stadt verbreiten** to cry the news all over the town; **~en verkaufen** to pitch *(sl.)*; **sich an den ~en weiden** to gloat over the news.

Neuigkeitswert newsworthiness, news value.

Neuinvestition reinvestment, dishoarding.

Neujahrs | ansprache New Year's message; **~geschenk** handsel; **~glückwünsche** new-year greetings; **~karte** new-year card; **~tag** New Year's day; **~wünsche** compliments of the season.

Neu | kalkulation recosting; **~kalkulation vornehmen** to revise one's estimates; **~kapitalisierung** recapitalization; **~konstruktion** reconstruction.

Neuland new territory (ground), virgin soil *(US)*, *(fig.)* new frontier;
~ betreten to enter unchartered seas, to break new ground; **~ erschließen** to reclaim soil, *(fig.)* to be groundbreaking; **~ kultivieren** to reclaim soil, to improve virgin land *(US)*; **~ öffnen** to open up new frontiers;
~gewinnung reclamation of land.

Neuling newcomer, fresh-comer, recruit, novice, upstart, probationer, new hire *(US)*, tiro *(Br.)*, tyro, greenhorn, stranger, neophyte, rooky, John Raw, jackaroo *(Australia)*;
unerfahrener ~ new chum *(Australia)*;
j. für einen ~ halten to make s. o. a newcomer; **~ auf einem Gebiet (in einer Sache) sein** to be a newcomer to a subject, to be a new (fresh) hand to s. th.

neumodisch fashionable, newfangled.

Neunmalkluger wisehead, wiseacre.

neuordnen to reorder, to realign.

Neuordnung rearrangement, reorganization, realignment, readjustment, reform;
~ des Geldwesens monetary (currency) reform; **~ der Politik** realignment of policy; **~ der Wechselkurse** realignment of exchange rates.

Neu | orientierung new course (departure), realignment, new course, *(Wirtschaft)* readjustment; **~philologie** modern languages; **~plazierung** placing securities with the public; **~prägung** restrike, new coinage; **~regelung** readjustment, reorganization, rearrangement.

Neu | reiche the new[ly] (vulgar) rich; **~reicher** parvenu, upstart.

neureiches Prozentum new-rich snobbery.

Neu | satz recomposition, reset; **~schätzwert** reappraisal value; **~schöpfung** new style; **~siedlung** new housing projects; **~silber** German silver, white metal, British plate; **~sprachler** modern linguist.

neutral neutral, noncommitted, nonaligned, on the fence, middle-of-the-road, colo(u)rless, *(Briefpapier)* plain, blank;
einbehaltene und ausgeschüttete Gewinne steuerlich ~ behandeln to be neutral as regards distributed and retained profits; **~ bleiben** to remain (stand, stay) neutral, to remain indifferent; **für ~ erklären** to neutralize; **liquiditätspolitisch ~ sein** to have no effect on liquidity; **sich ~ verhalten** to remain neutral, to maintain a neutral attitude, to sit on (ride, *US*) the fence; **sich dem Geldmarkt gegenüber strikt ~ verhalten** to take an apparently neutral line towards the money market;
~es Gebiet neutral territory; **~e Gewässer** neutral waters; **~er Hafen** neutrality of a port; **~es Schiff** free ship; **~er Status** neutrality; **~e Truppen** buffer force.

Neutraler *(pol.)* neutral [state].

neutralisieren to neutralize.

neutralisierte Zone neutralized zone.

Neutralisierung neutralization, counteraction.

Neutralismus neutralism, noncommittalism.

neutralistisch neutralistic.

Neutralität neutrality, neutral status;
bewaffnete ~ armed neutrality; **ewige ~** perpetual (permanent) neutrality; **freiwillige ~** voluntary neutrality; **ständige ~** permanent neutrality; **unbedingte ~** unconditional neutrality; **wohlwollende ~** friendly (benevolent) neutrality;
~ aufgeben to come off the fence; **~ bewahren** to remain neutral; **~ des Kanals garantieren** to preserve the canal's neutrality; **~ respektieren** to respect neutrality; **~ verletzen** to infract (infringe, violate) neutrality.

Neutralitäts | abkommen neutrality agreement; **~bruch** violation of neutrality; **~erklärung** neutrality proclamation, neutralization; **~gesetz** neutrality law; **~gesetzgebung** neutrality legislation; **~politik** policy of neutrality, neutralism, middle-of-the-road course; **~politik verfolgen** to observe neutrality; **~politiker** neutralist; **~rechte** rights of neutrality; **~status** neutral status; **~verletzung** violation (infringement) of neutrality.

neutralitätswidrige Dienste unneutral service.

Neu | veranlagung reassessment; **~veranlagung vornehmen** to revise an assessment; **~verfilmung** remake, retake; **~verhandlung** renegotiation, *(Gericht)* further hearing (proceedings); **~vermessung** fresh survey; **~vermietung** letting new premises; **~verpachtung** leasing for a next term; **~verplanung** expenditure budgeted for; **~verschuldung** new indebtedness; **staatliche ~verschuldung** new public debt; **~verteilung** reallocation, redistribution; **~verteilung der Parlamentssitze** redistribution of seats in Parliament; **~verteilung von Vorzugsaktien** readjustment of priorities; **~vortrag** carry forward.

Neuwagen | garantie new-car warranty; **~geschäft** new-car sales; **~knappheit** new-car shortage.

Neuwahl new election, re-election;
~en ansetzen (ausschreiben) to call a new election, to go (appeal) to the country *(Br.)*; **überraschend ~en ansetzen** to spring a surprise election; **~ des Aufsichtsrates vornehmen** to elect a new board; **zur ~ vorschlagen** to put up for election.

Neuwahlentermin bekanntgeben to name the day.

Neuwert original value, *(Versicherung)* replacement value, value as new.

neuwertig, fast hardly used; **Waschmaschine ~** *(Inserat)* washing machine, as new; **in ~em Zustand** in perfect condition.

Neuwert | leistung, ein Drittel für ~leistung abziehen to allow a deduction of one third new for old upon the balance; **gleitende ~police** floating policy; **gleitende ~versicherung** *(Feuerversicherung)* reinstatement insurance.

Neu | wortschöpfung new word formation; **~zeit** modern times.

neuzeitlich modern, up-to-date.

Neu | zugang new entrant; **~zugänge** *(Belegschaft)* accessions, *(Erkrankungen)* new cases, *(Versicherung)* fresh business; **~zugangsziffer** *(Kranke)* attack rate; **~zulassung von Kraftfahrzeugen** new-car registration; **~zuteilung von Einfuhrkontingenten** reallocation of import quotas.

nicht | abzugsfähig nondeductible, not deductible; ~ **akzeptiert** nonaccepted; ~ **ansässig** nonresident; ~ **befähigt** unqualified, ineligible; ~ **beitragspflichtig** noncontributory; ~ **berechtigt** unqualified, ineligible, unauthorized; ~ **berufsmäßig** nonoccupational; ~ **bevorrechtigt** nonprivileged; ~ **bewirtschaftet** nonrationed; ~ **mehr da** *(Restaurantgericht)* off; ~ **einklagbar** nonenforceable; ~ **einlösbar** inconvertible, *(Wertpapier)* irredeemable; ~ **gebraucht** unused; ~ **geliefert** short shipment; ~ **geschäftsfähig** incapable of acting in law; ~ **kommerziell** nonprofit, noncommercial; ~ **kommunistisch** noncommunist; ~ **konvertierbar** inconvertible; ~ **kündbar** noncallable; ~ **markengebunden** off-brand; ~ **nachschußpflichtig** nonassessable; ~ **negoziierbar** nonnegotiable; ~ **notiert** *(Börse)* unquoted, unlisted *(US)*; ~ **an Order** not [payable] to order, nonnegotiable; ~ **organisiert** nonunion; ~ **pfändbar** nonforfeitable, nonleviable; ~ **kaufmännisch tätig** nontrading; ~ **tilgbar** irredeemable; ~ **übertragbar** not transferable, *(Scheck)* nonnegotiable; ~ **verfügbar** unavailable; ~ **durch die Post versandfähig** nonmailable *(US)*; ~ **versichert** uninsured; ~ **versteuerbar** nontaxable; ~ **vollstreckbar** nonenforceable; ~ **vorbestraft** without previous conviction; ~ **wählbar** ineligible; ~ **wettbewerbsfähig** noncompetitive, not competitive;
~ **bezahlen** to make default;
~ **mitarbeitende Ehefrau** *(Steuer)* nonworking wife; ~ **entnommener Gewinn** undistributed (paid-in, *US*) profit.

Nicht | abgabe nondelivery, failure to deliver; **~abgabe einer Erklärung** nondeclaration; **~abkommensland** nonagreement country; **~abnahme** failure to take delivery; **schuldhafte ~abwendung einer bekannten Gefahr** concurrent contributory negligence; **~abzugsfähigkeit** nondeductibility; **~achtung** disregard, nonobservance; **~achtung des Gerichts** contempt of court; **~akzeptierung** nonacceptance; **~amerikaner** resident alien *(US)*.

nichtamtlich inofficial, unofficial, nongovernmental.

Nicht | anerkennung nonacknowledgment, nonrecognition, disallowance, disclamation, *(Schuld)* repudiation, disaffirmance; **~anerkennung eines Vertrages** repudiation of a contract; **~angabe** *(Versicherung)* nondisclosure; **~angriffspakt** pact of nonaggression, nonaggression pact (treaty); **~anklage eines Verbrechens** compounding a felony; **~anliegerstaat** nonriparian state; **~annahme** nonacceptance, *(Wechsel)* dishono(u)r by nonacceptance; **~ansässiger** nonresident person; **~ansässigkeit** nonresidence; **~antritt einer Erbschaft** laches of entry; **~anwendbarkeit** nonapplicability; **~anwendung** nonapplication, *(Gesetz)* dispensation, suspension; **~anwesenheit** absence, nonattendance, *(fortgesetzt)* absenteeism; **~anwesenheit bei der Namenverlesung** failure to answer the roll call; **~anzeige** *(Strafrecht)* negative misprision, *(Versicherung)* nondisclosure, failure to give notice, nonnotice; **~anzeige von Hochverrat** misprision of treason; **~ausfolgung** nondelivery; **~ausfolgung von Rechnungsbüchern** *(Konkurs)* failing to deliver up the books; **~ausführung** nonperformance, nonexecution; **~ausführung vereinbarter Reparaturen** nonrepair; **~aushändigung** nondelivery; **~auslieferung** nondelivery, *(Völkerrecht)* nonextradition; **~ausschüttung von Gewinnen** ploughing (plowing, *US*) back of profits.

Nichtausübung nonusage;
~ **einer Option** abandonment of an option; ~ **eines Rechtes** failure to enforce a right, nonuser; **vorübergehende ~ eines Rechts** suspension of a right.

Nicht | autofahrer nonmotorist; **~bankenkundschaft** nonbank customers; **~bankensektor** nonbanking sector; **~bankier** nonbanker; **~bankplatz** nonbank place; **~beachtung** inobservance, nonobservance; **~beachtung von Polizeivorschriften** breach of police regulations; **~beachtung eines Verkehrszeichens** failure to observe a traffic sign; **~beamter** outsider, nonofficial *(US)*.

nichtbeamtet nonestablished.

Nichtbeantwortung failure to give a reply, *(Umfrage)* nonresponse.

Nichtbefolgung noncompliance, inobservance, nonobservance; ~ **einer richterlichen Anordnung** constructive contempt; ~ **von Anweisungen** disobedience to orders; ~ **einer richterlichen Auflage** standing in contempt; ~ **eines Gesetzes** disregard of a law.

Nicht | beförderung *(Angestellter)* nonpromotion; **im Falle der ~beitreibbarkeit** in case of insolvency; **~beitritt im Falle der Streitverkündung** nonjoinder; **~beiwohnung** *(Eherecht)* nonaccess; **~benachrichtigung** nonnotification; **~benutzung** disusage, nonusage; **~benutzung von Warenzeichen** abandonment of trademarks; **~berechtigter** unauthorized person (party); **~berücksichtigung** disregard; **~berufsunfall** nonoccupational accident; **~beschäftigter** unemployed person; **~bestätigung** disaffirmance, *(Vertrag)* repudiation; **~bestehen** nonexistence; **~bestehen einer Steuerpflicht** nonliability; **~bestellung** *(Post)* nondelivery; **~besteuerung** nontaxation; **~bestreiten** true admission; **~beteiligung** nonparticipation; **~bewilligung** dissatisfaction; **~bezahlung** nonpayment; **~bezahlung eines Wechsels** dishono(u)ring of a bill of exchange, dishono(u)r by nonpayment; **~bezug** nonsubscription; **~diskriminierung** *(im Außenhandel)* fair trade *(US)*, *(Zoll)* nondiscrimination, nondiscriminatory treatment; **~diskriminierungsklausel** nondiscrimination clause; **~durchführung** nonaccomplishment, nonexecution; **~durchsetzbarkeit** nonenforceability; **~ehe** void marriage; **~ehelichkeit** illegitimacy; **~eigentümer** person not the owner, nonowner, nonproprietor; **versicherter ~eigentümer** *(Auto)* additional insured; **~eignung** nonqualification; **~eingeweihter** point-head *(sl.)*; **~eingreifen** nonintervention.

Nichteinhaltung failure to comply with, noncompliance, nonobservance, default;
~ **der Kündigungsfrist** leaving without notice; ~ **der Spielregeln** foul play; ~ **seiner Verpflichtungen** failure to meet one's obligations; ~ **eines Versprechens** failure to keep a promise.

Nicht | einigung nonagreement; **~einklagbarkeit** nonenforceability; **~einklagbarkeitserklärung** outlawry *(US)*; **~einlassung** nonappearance.

nichteinlösbar inconvertible.

Nicht | einlösbarkeit inconvertibility; **~einlösung** nonpayment; **~einlösung eines Wechsels** dishono(u)ring of a bill of exchange; **~einmischung** nonintervention, noninterference; **~einmischungsausschuß** nonintervention committee; **~einmischungspakt** nonintervention pact; **~einmischungspolitik** hands-off policy, policy of nonintervention; **~einreichung der Einkommensteuererklärung** failure to file a return; **~eintragung** nonregistration; **bei ~eintreffen kein Kaufzwang** no arrival no sale; **~eintreibung** failure to collect; **~eintritt einer Prophezeiung** failure of a prophecy; **~eisenmetalle** nonferrous metals; **~eisenmetallindustrie** nonferrous industry; **~engagement** noninvolvement.

Nichterfüllung failure to perform (of performance, to comply with), nonperformance, nonfulfil(l)ment, incompliance, nonexecution, *(Geldverpflichtung)* defaulting, failure, *(Lieferung)* nondelivery, failure to deliver;
schuldhafte ~ failure to meet one's obligations; **teilweise ~** failure in any part;
~ **eines Eheversprechens** breach of [a] promise [of marriage]; ~ **von Statuten** failure to observe a byelaw; ~ **einer Unterstützungsverpflichtung** nonsupport; ~ **einer Verbindlichkeit** default in an engagement; ~ **eines Vertrages** inexecution (breach) of a contract;
~ **zu vertreten haben** to make performance impossible; **wegen ~ verklagen** to sue for breach of contractual obligations.

Nicht | erneuerung nonrenewal; **~eröffnung des Konkursverfahrens mangels Masse** open insolvency.

Nichterscheinen nonattendance, *(Buch)* nonpublication;
im Falle seines ~s failing whom;
absichtliches ~ contempt of court, contumacy;
~ **am Arbeitsplatz** absence from work; ~ **vor Gericht** default of appearance, nonappearance, failure to appear;
wegen ~ verurteilen to default.

Nicht | erschienener nonattendant, *(vor Gericht)* defaulter; **~erstattung einer Meldung** failure to render a report; **~erwähnung** failure to mention; **~existenz** nonentity; **~fachleute** laity; **~fachmann** dilettante, layman, nonexpert, outsider, amateur; **~fertigstellung** noncompletion, failure to complete; **~fortsetzung** discontinuance; **~frankierung** nonprepayment; **~funktionieren des Handels** dislocation of trade; **~gebrauch** disuse, nonuser, nonusage; **bei ~gefallen Geld zurück** money back if not satisfied; **~genehmigung** nonapproval, dissatisfaction, *(Gesuch)* refusal.

nichtgewerblich noncommercial;
~es Unternehmen nonprofit corporation.

Nicht|gewerkschaftler nonunionist, nonunion worker, nonratification, free rider, papoose *(sl.)*; **~haftung** nonliability; **~haftung für durch Betriebsangehörige verursachte Schäden** fellow-servant rule; **~honorierung** dishono(u)r by nonpayment; **~honorierung eines Wechsels** failure to pay (hono(u)r) a bill.

nichtig void, invalid, null, insufficient, negatory, nugatory, inept, cancelled, moonshine, *(fig.)* idle, without worth, vain, insignificant;
von Anfang an ~ void ab initio; **teilweise ~** void in part; **null und ~** null and void, absolutely void;
für ~ erklären to make void, to cancel, to set aside, to annul, to void; **für null und ~ erklären** to declare null and void, to defeat, to invalidate; **Ehe für ~ erklären** to declare a marriage invalid; **Patent für ~ erklären** to nullify a patent; **Vertrag für null und ~ erklären** to nullify a contract, to invalidate a contract; **~ machen** to render void, to nullify; **Bestimmung ~ machen** to make a clause void; **von Anfang an ~ sein** to be void on its face; **aus ~em Anlaß entstehen** to arise from a trifle; **~e Einwände** insubstantial arguments; **~es Rechtsgeschäft** void transaction; **~es Urteil** void judgment; **~es Verfahren** void process; **~er Vertrag** void contract; **~er Vorwand** flimsy excuse.

Nichtigerklärung nullification.

Nichtigkeit futility, vanity, idleness, emptiness, mouthful *(sl.)*, *(jur.)* voidness, nullity, invalidity;
bei Gefahr der ~ under pain of being declared void;
~en trifles, trifling matters;
absolute ~ absolute nullity; **bedingte ~** voidability; **teilweise ~** partial nullity;
~ einer Ehe nullity of marriage;
sich mit ~en während einer Katastrophe beschäftigen to fiddle while Rome burns *(coll.)*; **Voraussetzungen der gesetzlichen ~ erfüllen** to be void under statute; **~en von sich geben** to let off hot air; **sich wegen einer ~ streiten** to quarrel about a trivial matter; **wegen ~ angefochten werden** to be voided.

Nichtigkeits|antrag *(Ehe)* nullity appeal, *(Patent)* application for revocation *(Br.)*; **~bescheinigung** certificate of forfeiture; **~beschwerde** writ in error, nullity appeal; **~einrede** plea in abatement (of nullity); **~erklärung** avoidance, cancellation, annulment, defeasance, nullification, *(Ehe)* decree of nullity, *(Urteil)* reversion of a sentence; **~erklärung von Patenten** declaration of patents nullified; **~grund** ground for nullity; **~gründe** *(Patentrecht)* grounds of revocation; **~klage** revocatory action, *(Ehe)* nullity suit; **~klausel** cancellation (irritant) clause; **~prozeß** nullity suit; **~senat** *(Patentrecht)* patent appeal court; **~urteil** *(Ehe)* decree of nullity, annulment of marriage; **~urteil erlassen** to declare an act a nullity; **~verfahren** invalidation (nullity) suit.

Nicht|inanspruchnahme von Abschreibungsmöglichkeiten disclaimer of allowance; **~intervention** nonintervention; **~jurist** layman; **~kämpfer** *(Völkerrecht)* noncombatant; **~käufer** walk *(sl.)*; **~kaufmann** nontrader; **~kenntnis** ignorance, absence of notice; **schuldhafte ~kenntnis** constructive notice; **~konvertierbarkeit** inconvertibility; **~kriegsführung** nonbelligerence; **~leistung** failure to perform, nonperformance; **bei ~leistung** on default; **~leiter** *(el.)* insulator, nonconductor; **~lieferung** failure to meet delivery, nondelivery; **~mitglied** nonmember, outsider; **~mitgliedsbank** nonmember *(US)* (outside) bank; **~mitgliedschaft** nonmembership; **~mitgliedsland** *(EG)* nonmember country; **~mitgliedstaat** nonmember government, *(ECA)* nonparticipating country; **~offenbarung** nondisclosure.

nichtöffentlich private, closed;
in ~er Sitzung in chambers (camera, closed session).

Nicht|raucher nonsmoker; **~raucherabteil** no-smoking area, nonsmoker.

nicht|rechtsfähiger Verein unincorporated society; **~rostender Stahl** stainless steel.

Nichtrückwirkung nonretroactivity.

Nichts nothing, blank, vacancy, nil;
aus dem ~ out of a chaos; **vor ~ zurückschreckend** stick-at-nothing;
~ von einem Nachthemd a mere wisp of a nightdress;
etw. aus dem ~ aufbauen to make bricks without straw; **sich in ~ auflösen** to vanish into thin air, to end up in smoke; **aus dem ~ auftauchen** to appear from nowhere; **mit fast ~ auskommen** to run s. th. on candle ends and bits of string; **dem ~ gegenüberstehen** to be faced with ruin.

nichts nix *(sl.)*;
fast ~ next to nothing, little or nothing; **~ von Bedeutung** nothing of note; **~ Interessantes in der Zeitung** nothing interesting in the newspaper; **~ zu machen** nothing doing, no soap *(US sl.)*; **~ wie raus** let's be off quick; **~ für ungut** no hard feelings; **~ Welterschütterndes** nothing to make a song about; **für ~ und wieder ~** for no reason at all; **mir ~ dir ~** without further ado (not so much as a by-your-leave);
~ Böses ahnen not to suspect anything wrong; **j. ~ angehen** to be none of s. one's business; **~ erbringen** to come to nothing; **so gut wie ~ essen** to eat practically nothing; **~ dabei finden** no to be able to see any harm in it; **mit ~ angefangen haben** to have started from scratch; **~ auf sich haben** to be of no consequence; **~ dagegen haben** to have no objections; **~ gegen j. haben** not to have got anything against s. o.; **~ zu lachen haben** to be no laughing matter; **~ zu sagen haben** to have no say in a matter, *(generell)* to be nobody; **mit jem. ~ zu tun haben** to have nothing to do with s. o.; **zu ~ kommen** to have no time for anything; **in einer Sache ~ tun können** to be helpless in a matter; **~ unversucht lassen** to leave no stone unturned; **~ entbehren müssen** to lack for nothing; **~ von Belang sein** to be nothing to write home about it; **~ daraus geworden sein** to have come to nought; **um ~ spielen** to play for love; **von ~ anderem sprechen** to talk of nothing else; **für ~ und wieder ~ streiten** to find quarrels in a straw; **~ taugen** to be no good; **sich von den anderen in ~ unterscheiden** to be in no way different from the others; **wie ~ vergehen** *(Zeit)* to be simply flying; **wie ~ verschwinden** to disappear in no time; **~ daraus werden** to come to naught; **~ hören und ~ sehen wollen** to be blind and deaf to everything.

Nichtschwimmer nonswimmer.

nichtseßhaft *(Volksstamm)* nomadic, vagabond.

Nichtsnutz good-for-nothing, waster;
kleiner ~ little rascal.

nichtsnutzig no-good, worthless;
~es Kind naughty child.

nichtssagend meaningless, trivial, colo(u)rless, empty, null, insignificant;
~e Antwort noncommittal reply; **~er Blick** vacant look; **~es Gerede** empty (idle) talk; **~es Gesicht** characterless face; **~e Redensarten** a few nothings, trivialities.

nichtstaatlich nongovernmental, private, independent;
~es Krankenhaus private (voluntary, *Br.*) hospital.

Nicht|stationierung *(Atomwaffen)* nondeployment; **~steuerpflichtiger** nontaxable person; **~streikender** nonstriker.

nichtstreitig noncontentious.

Nichtstuer drone, do-nothing, idler, loafer, lazybones.

Nichtstun do-nothingness;
süßes ~ delightful idleness, dolce far niente;
seine Tage mit ~ verbringen to laze away one's days, to spend one's days in idleness.

nichtswürdig contemptible, despicable, base, vile.

Nicht|tätigkeit benign neglect; **~teilhaber** nonpartner; **~teilnehmer** nonparticipant; **~teilnehmerland** *(ECA)* nonparticipating country; **~teilnehmerstaat** nonparticipating state; **~übereinstimmung** discrepancy, disaccord, nonconcurrence, *(Abweichung)* dissenting opinion, dissent, inconsistency, nonconformity; **~übereinstimmung von Klagebehauptung und Beweisergebnis** variance; **~übertragbarkeit** nonnegotiability; **~übertragbarkeitsvermerk** not negotiable crossing *(Br.)*, nonnegotiability notice; **~übertragung** nontransfer; **~umsetzbarkeit** inconvertibility; **~umwandelbarkeit** inconvertibility; **~unterzeichner** *(Preisvereinbarung)* nonsigner *(US)*; **~unterzeichnerregierung** nonsignatory government; **~unterzeichnungsstaat** nonsignatory state; **~verantwortlicher** nonresponsible person; **~verantwortlichkeit** unaccountability, irresponsibility; **~veräußerung** nonalienation; **~verfolgung** nonprosecution; **~verfügbarkeit** unavailability; **~verlängerung** nonrenewal; **~vermarktung** *(EG)* withholding from the market; **~vermögensschaden** nonpecuniary damage; **~versicherung** noninsurance; **~vertragsstaat** nonparticipating (noncontracting) country; **~verwendung** disuse, nonuser, nonusage; **~verwirkung** nonforfeiture; **~verwirkungsklausel** nonforfeiture clause; **~vollstreckbarkeit** nonenforceability; **~vollziehung** nonexecution.

nichtvollzogene Ehe unconsummated marriage.

Nicht|vorbestrafter person without a criminal record; **~vorhandensein** nonexistence; **~vorhandensein eines Wohnsitzes** nonresidence; **~vorlage** nonpresentment; **~vorzeigung** nonproduction; **~wählbarkeit** ineligibility; **~wähler** unpolled elector, nonvoter; **~weiterbetreiben eines Prozesses** abandonment of action; **~weitergabe** nonproliferation; **~weitergabevertrag** *(Atomsperrvertrag)* nonproliferation agreement; **~weiterkönnen** nonplus; **~wissen** ignorance; **bloßes ~wissen** mere ignorance; **schuldhaftes ~wissen** culpable ignorance, voluntary

ignorance *(US)*; **sich mit ~wissen entschuldigen** to plead ignorance; **durch ~wissen glänzen** to be conspicuous for one's ignorance; **~wisser** know-nothing.
nichtzahlender Kunde defaulting customer.
Nicht|zahlung nonpayment, failure to pay, default; **bei ~zahlung** upon default; **~zugehörigkeit** disaffiliation, nonmembership, extraneousness; **~zugestehen** nonadmission; **~zulassung** nonadmission, exclusion; **~zulassung zur amtlichen Notierung** nonquotation *(Br.)*, nonlisting *(US)*; **~zurechenbarkeit eines Schadens** remoteness of damage; **~zustandekommen** nonconclusion; **~zustandekommen eines Treuhandvertrages** failure of trust; **~zuständigkeit** incompetence; **~zustellung** nondelivery; **~zustimmung** nonconsent; **~zutreffendes bitte streichen** strike out (delete) words not applicable.
Nickel nickel;
frecher kleiner ~ naughty little devil;
~chromstahl nickel-chromium steel; **~legierung** nickel alloy.
nicken, mit dem Kopf to nod one's head; **zustimmend ~** to nod approval (one's assent), to give one's nod of approval.
Nickerchen nap, snooze, shut-eye *(sl.)*;
kleines ~ forty winks *(coll.)*;
~ machen to have (take) a nap, to take a snooze, to have forty winks.
nieder lower, *(Gesinnung)* mean, base, low;
im Zimmer auf und ~ gehen to pace the room;
~brennen to burn down (to the ground); **~brüllen** to cry (shout) down; **~donnern** *(Lawine)* to come thundering down.
Niederdruck low pressure;
~anlage low-heat hydropower station; **~dampfkessel** low-pressure steam boiler.
niederdrücken to depress, *(Zweige)* to weigh down;
j. sehr ~ *(Sorgen)* to weigh heavily on s. o.
Niederdruck|heizung low-pressure steam heating; **~pumpe** centrifugal pump.
Niedereinstufung, tarifliche in-grade salary decrease.
Niederfrequenz low frequency;
~verstärker audio frequency transformer.
Niedergang decline, fall, falling off, comedown, downcome, descent, decay, decadence, downdrag, downfall, breakup;
wirtschaftlicher ~ economic downturn (decline);
~ der Moral decay of moral principles; **~ eines Reiches** decay of an empire;
sich im ~ befinden to be on the downward path.
niedergebrannt, bis zu den Grundmauern burnt down to the ground.
niedergedrückt weighted down, depressed, down in the mouth, dejected;
j. völlig ~ antreffen to find s. o. in a state of deep depression; **~ nach Hause gehen** to go home in a state of depression;
~e Stimmung depressed spirits; **in ~er Stimmung sein** to be downcast, to have the blues *(coll.)*.
Niedergehen *(Ballon, Flugzeug)* descent.
niedergehen *(Flugzeug)* to touch (come) down, to descend, *(auf dem Wasser)* to splash down.
niedergelegt, schriftlich on record;
nicht schriftlich ~ unwritten.
niedergeschlagen depressed, crestfallen, downhearted, down in the mouth, blue;
~ sein to be cast down, to be in the dumps;
sehr ~en Eindruck machen to seem very depressed.
Niedergeschlagenheit depression, prostration, downheartedness.
nieder|geschmettert, von den Nachrichten ~ sein to be shattered by the news; **von einer Krankheit ~geworfen** prostrated by an illness; **~halten** to hold down; **Volk ~halten** to oppress the people, to hold the masses in subjection.
Niederkämpfen *(mil.)* neutralization.
niederkämpfen to subdue, to overcome;
aufkommende Angst ~ to fight down one's growing fear; **Feind ~** to neutralize the enemy; **seine Tränen ~** to hold back one's tears.
Niederkämpfungsfeuer neutralization fire.
nieder|knallen to shoot down; **~knüppeln** to truncheon, to bludgeon; **jeden Widerstand ~knüppeln** to break down all opposition; **~kommen** to give birth to, to be confined.
Niederkunft childbirth, confinement, delivery, accouchement, birth;
einer ~ beiwohnen *(Arzt)* to attend a confinement.
Niederlage storehouse, warehouse *(US)*, depot, magazine, depositary, repository, staple, *(Filiale)* branch, *(mil.)* defeat, licking;
vernichtende ~ thrashing (crushing) defeat, knockout;
jem. eine ~ beibringen (bereiten) to downgrade (defeat) s. o.; **~ ohne mit der Wimper zu zucken einstecken** to take one's licking like a man; **~ hinnehmen** to take a trimming; **bei den Wahlen eine ~ einstecken müssen** to meet with a heavy defeat at the polls; **~ hinnehmen müssen** to suffer defeat; **~ zugeben** *(Politik)* to concede;
~gebühren storage charges, warehouse rent *(US)*.
niederlassen, sich to set up for s. o., to settle down in business, to take up one's abode (domicile, residence), to localize, to locate *(US)*; **sich auch in Amerika ~** to open up branches in America; **sich als Anwalt ~** to set up as a lawyer, to settle down in the practice of law; **sich als Arzt ~** to put up one's shingle; **sich als Buchhändler ~** to establish o. s. (set up business) as a bookseller; **sich dauernd ~** to settle down for good; **Flagge ~** to haul down the flag; **sich geschäftlich ~** to establish o. s. as a businessman, to set up for o. s., to set up shop; **sich im Hauptgeschäftsviertel ~** to fix one's residence in the city; **sich häuslich ~** to hang up one's hat, to drive stakes, to make o. s. comfortable; **sich bei jem. häuslich ~** to park o. s. on s. o. *(fam.)*; **sich auf dem Lande ~** to make one's home in the country; **Sarg ins Grab ~** to lower the coffin into the grave; **sich an einem Seil ~** to let o. s. down on a rope; **sich in einen Sessel ~** to sink into an armchair; **sich ständig ~** to take up one's abode; **Vorhang ~** to drop a curtain; **sich widerrechtlich ~** to abate, to intrude unlawfully.
Niederlassung establishment of one's residence, branch, location, *(Bank)* branch, agency, *(Handel)* trading post, trading settlement, business establishment, *(Wohnsitz)* domicile, place of abode, foundation, lodgment;
ausländische ~ foreign agency; **eingetragene ~** registered office; **geschäftliche (gewerbliche) ~** business location, commercial establishment, place of business; **internationale ~** international concession (settlement); **örtliche ~** local office; **überseeische ~** overseas branch;
~ als Arzt putting up one's shingle *(coll.)*;
seine ~ aufgeben to give up one's trading station; **~en im Ausland gründen** to establish foreign branches; **neue ~ gründen** to found a settlement.
Niederlassungs|beschränkung restriction on freedom of establishment; **~bestimmungen** residence provisions; **~bewilligung** business licence; **~frage** question of establishment; **~freiheit** freedom to settle anywhere, freedom of movement, personal liberty, liberty to come and go, *(EG)* freedom of establishment; **~freiheit genießen** to have free choice of residence; **~leiter** branch manager; **~netz** network of branches; **~ort** place of business; **~recht** right of staple, law of establishment, right of settlement; **~vertrag** treaty of establishment; **~voraussetzungen** residence requirements; **~wesen** *(Banken)* branch-banking activities.
niederlegen to lay down, *(Waren)* to deposit, to warehouse *(US)*; **sein Amt ~** to retire from office; **Arbeit ~** to [lay] down tools, to stop work, to walk out *(US)*; **Bedingungen in einem Vertrag ~** to set out conditions in a contract; **in einem Bericht ~** to [make a] report; **Geschäftsführung ~** to resign from management; **Haus ~** to pull down (demolish) a house; **Kranz ~** to lay a wreath; **Krone ~** to abdicate; **sein Mandat ~** to vacate one's seat; **Regeln ~** to lay down rules; **schriftlich ~** to put down in writing, to place on record, to paper, to set down; **Verteidigung ~** to abandon the defence; **Vertretung ~** to resign the representation; **zur treuhänderischen Verwaltung ~** to bail, to deliver in trust *(US)*; **Waffen ~** to lay down arms; **Waren unter Zollverschluß ~** to bond goods, to put goods in bond; **Wertpapiere bei einer Bank ~** to deposit securities with a bank; **seinen letzten Willen ~** to put one's affairs in order.
Niederlegung *(Amt)* resignation, retirement, abdication, *(Waren)* deposition;
~ seines Abgeordnetenmandats vacation of one's seat; **~ der Arbeit** strike, walkout *(US)*; **~ eines Treuhänderamtes** disclaimer of a trustee; **~ der Verteidigung** abandonment of a defence (defense, *US*); **schriftliche ~ der geplanten Zeugenaussage** proof of witness *(Br.)*.
niedermetzeln to massacre, to slaughter, to butcher.
niederprasseln *(Hagel)* to rattle down.
niederreißen to demolish, to pull down, *(Haus)* to break (tear) down;
Schranken zwischen verschiedenen Gesellschaftsschichten ~ to pull down the barriers between different social classes; **ganze Stadtviertel ~** to demolish a whole district; **Wand ~** to peck down a wall.
Niederreißung demolition.
niederringen, Land to bring a country to its knees.

niederschießen, j. to shoot s. o. down.
Niederschlag *(nach Atomexplosion)* fallout, *(Bodenschatz)* sediment, *(Regen)* rainfall, precipitation, *(Schwitzwasser)* condensation;
erheblicher ~ quantities of rain; **jährlicher ~** annual precipitation;
~ bilden to precipitate; **in nachfolgenden Bestimmungen seinen ~ finden** to be embodied in the following regulations; **in einem Roman seinen ~ finden** to be reflected in a novel.
Niederschlagen | der Strafverfolgung gegen Entgelt stifling a prosecution; **~ eines Verfahrens** letters of abolition.
niederschlagen to beat (knock) down, *(Forderung)* to waive, to nol-pros;
j. ~ to cast s. o. down; **sich ~** *(Dampf)* to condense; **Anklage ~** to quash an indictment; **Anklage gegen Entgelt ~** to stifle a prosecution; **Aufstand ~** to quash a rebellion, to quell a riot, to crush a rising; **seine Augen ~** to cast one's eyes; **sich in der Bevölkerungsstatistik ~** to be reflected in the vital statistics; **Geldstrafe ~** to remit a fine; **sich in der Handelsbilanz ~** to be seen in the balance of trade; **Kosten ~** to cancel the charges; **Schulden ~** to cancel debts; **Steuern ~** to drop the tax; **sich als Tau ~** *(Nebel)* to settle as dew; **Verfahren ~** to quash proceedings.
niederschlagsarm of light precipitation;
~e Gegend dry area.
Niederschlagsdichte rainfall density.
niederschlagsfrei, im wesentlichen mainly dry.
Niederschlags | gebiet catchment area; **~häufigkeit** frequency of precipitation.
Niederschlagsmenge quantity of rain, amount of rainfall;
ergiebige ~ extensive rainfall; **ungewöhnliche ~** extraordinary rainfall;
~ messen to gauge the rainfall.
niederschlagsreich wet;
~e Gegend wet area.
Niederschlagsverteilung distribution of rainfall.
Niederschlagung *(Unterdrückung)* suppression, *(Verfahren)* quashing;
~ eines Aufstandes quashing a rebellion; **~ von Schulden** cancellation of debts.
niederschmettern to knock (dash) to the ground.
Baum ~ *(Blitz)* to fell a tree; **j. völlig ~** to shatter s. o. completely.
niederschmetternd crushing, shattering, staggering, devastating;
~e Nachricht shattering piece of news, knockdown.
niederschreiben to put down in writing, to write (mark, set) down, to paper;
in ungekürzter Form ~ to write out; **Protokoll ~** to draw up the minutes.
niederschreien, j. to clamo(u)r (shout) s. o. down.
Niederschrift record, writing down, notes, copy, transcript, *(Protokoll)* minutes;
gerichtliche ~ court record; **stenografische ~** stenographic record; **vereinbarte ~** minutes agreed upon; **wortgetreue ~** verbatim report;
~ seiner Gedanken anfertigen to commit one's ideas to paper; **~ der Konferenzergebnisse anfertigen** to make a record of the results of a conference; **~ einer Unterredung anfertigen** to take minutes of a conversation.
Niederspannung *(el.)* low tension (voltage).
Niederspannungsleitung low-tension line.
niedersten Stand erreichen *(Kurse)* to touch the bottom.
niederstimmen to vote down, to outvote.
niederstrecken, j. to floor s. o.
Niederstwert *(Bilanz)* cost or market value whichever is lower;
~prinzip *(Bilanz)* cost of market value whichever-is-lower principle *(US)*, lower of cost or market principle.
niedertourig low-revolving.
Niedertracht vileness, spite, baseness, meanness;
Bemerkung aus reiner ~ machen to make a remark out of sheer calculated malice.
niederträchtig mean, vile, low, ugly;
j. in der ~sten Weise hintergehen to deceive s. o. in the most despicable manner;
~e Gesinnung low mind; **~e Lüge** base lie; **~er Mensch** vile creature; **~er Schmerz** ghastly pain; **~er Schurke** scoundrel, rascal.
Niederträchtigkeit turpitude, vileness, maliciousness.
niedertrampeln to tread (trample) down.
Niederung lowland, flat;
~en des Lebens darker sides of life.
Niederwald coppice, copse, brushwood.
niederwerfen, Aufstand to crush a rising; **Feind in raschem Siegeszug ~** to overthrow the enemy in a rapid campaign; **sich flehend vor jem. ~** to throw o. s. at s. one's feet.
Niederwerfung suppression, crushing, prostration;
~ der Aufständischen subjection of the rebels.
niedlich ducky, sweet, pretty, cute *(US)*, cunning *(US)*;
sehr ~ angezogen sein to be very prettily dressed.
niedrig low, common, *(gemein)* low, mean, vulgar, *(Preis)* cheap, moderate, down, *(Qualität)* inferior, *(untergeordnet)* low, subordinate, inferior, humble;
~ bewertet low-priced; **künstlich ~ gehalten** artificially low; **~ im Preis** low-priced;
zu ~ angeben to understate; **~ von jem. denken** to have a poor opinion of s. o.; **~ fliegen** to fly low; **~ halten** *(Preise)* to keep down (at a low level); **Kosten ~ halten** to keep the lid on costs; **Unkosten ~ halten** to control expenditure; **Mauer ~ machen** to lower a wall; **zu ~ schätzen** to underestimate; **~ sein** *(Flut)* to be out; **im Preis ~ sein** to be cheap; **~ stehen** to be low;
~e Abstammung humble birth; **~e Arbeit** menial work; **~er Barometerstand** low barometer reading; **~e Beweggründe** base motives; **~er Charakter** vile nature; **~er Dienstgrad** subordinate rank; **~es Einkommen** low income; **nur ~e Einsätze riskieren** to play low; **~es Fahrgestell** low-built chassis; **in einen ~eren Gang schalten** to change into a lower gear; **von ~er Geburt sein** to be of humble birth; **~e Geburtenziffer** low birth rate; **von ~er Gesinnung** low-minded; **~e Instinkte** base instincts; **~er Kurs** low rate; **~er Lebensstandard** low standard of living; **~e Leidenschaften** vulgar passions; **~e Löhne** low wages; **~e Meinung von jem. haben** to have a low opinion of s. o.; **geistig ~es Niveau** low intellectual level; **~es moralisches Niveau einer Großstadt** low moral tone of a city; **sich weiterhin auf einem sehr ~en Niveau halten** to stay firmly in the bargain basement; **~er Ölverbrauch** low oil consumption; **~e Prämie** short premium; **~e Preise berechnen** to ask moderate prices; **~e Qualität** inferior quality; **zu einem ~en Satz** at a low rate; **~e Schätzung** low estimate; **~e Selbstkosten** low cost; **~e Stellung** inferior (subordinate) position, juniority; **~e Steuersätze** low tax rates; **auf einer sehr ~en Stufe stehen** to be at a very low level; **~e Versandkosten** low-cost transportation; **bei ~em Wasserstand** at low water; **~er Wechselkurs** low rate of exchange; **zu ~en Zinsen** at a low rate of interest.
niedriger lower, inferior, *(Kurse)* easier;
beträchtlich ~ sein *(Kurse)* to be appreciably lower; **um 3/4% ~ stehen** to be 3/4 per cent worse; **~ werden** *(Einkommen)* to shrink, *(Preise)* to decline, to sink;
~es Gebot lower bid; **~es Gericht** inferior court; **~ Kurs** low rate.
Niedrigkeit *(Preise)* low level, lowness, moderateness.
Niedrigmietengegend low-rent district.
niedrignotierend *(Kurse)* low-priced.
Niedrigpreis | angebot low-cost deal; **~grenze** lower-price limit; **~verkäufer** seller at bargain prices.
niedrigst lowest, bottom, knockdown;
~e Arbeiten verrichten müssen to have to do the most menial jobs; **~es Gebot** lowest bid; **~er Kurs** lowest quotation; **~en Kurs haben** to be at the lowest, to touch the bottom; **~er Preis** rock-bottom (minimum, lowest) price; **~es Preisniveau** lowest level of prices; **~er Punkt** at the lowermost (nethermost) point; **~er Stand** bottom (lowest) price, bargain level *(US)*; **~en Stand erreicht haben** to have touched rock-bottom.
niedrigstehend base, primitive, low-class.
Niedrigst | kurs lowest quotation; **~preise** bargain-[basement] prices; **~preisgeschäft** chain (one-price) shop *(Br.)*, dime store *(US)*; **~preisgrenze** lower-price limit; **~verkaufspreis** bargain price.
Niedrig | wasser, mittleres mean low tide; **~wassermarke** low watermark; **~zinspolitik** cheap money policy; **~zone** low level.
Niemandsland no man's land, no-rats land.
Nieren, jem. an die ~ gehen to upset s. o. very much, to put s. o. out; **j. auf Herz und ~ prüfen** to put s. o. through the mill.
nieseln to drizzle, to mizzle.
Nieselregen drizzle, mizzle;
in einen ~ übergehen *(Nebel)* to melt into a drizzle.
Nießbrauch usufruct, beneficial interest, *(Grundstück)* lifehold, life estate, use of land, *(Ehemann)* courtesy [of England] *(US)*; **lebenslänglicher ~** life status (estate, interest), liferent *(Scot.)*, *(an einem Grundstück)* tenancy for life, life tenancy; **potentieller ~** contingent use; **uneingeschränkter ~** perfect usufruct;

~ **für den überlebenden Ehegatten** life interest to survivor; ~ **an einem Grundstück** beneficial interest in land; ~ **des angelegten Kapitals** usufruct of investment; ~ **von verbrauchbaren Sachen** imperfect usufruct; ~ **an einem Vermögen** beneficial property; ~ **der Witwe** common-law dower, widow's tierce *(Scot.)*; ~ **bestellen** to create a life estate; ~ **haben** to [hold in] usufruct; **lebenslänglichen** ~ **haben** to own a life estate; **lebenslänglichen** ~ **an einem Haus haben** to hold a life tenancy of a house.

nießbrauchähnliches Verhältnis quasi usufruct.

Nießbrauchbelastung limited owner's charge *(Br.)*.

nießbrauchberechtigt sein to own beneficially.

Nießbrauch|berechtigter limited owner, usufructuary, beneficial occupant, tenant for life, cestui que use; **auf den lebens-länglich ~berechtigten übertragen** to vest in the tenant of life; **~besitzer** tenant for life; **unentgeltliche ~bestellung** voluntary settlement.

Nießbraucher beneficiary, beneficial owner, usufructuary; **lebenslänglicher** ~ life renter.

Nießbrauchrecht beneficial enjoyment (interest), usufructuary right;
auflösend bedingtes ~ qualified estate; **zeitlich beschränktes** ~ resulting use; **gesetzliches** ~ legal usufruct; **gestaffeltes** ~ shifting use; **lebenslängliches** ~ particular estate; **zukünftiges** ~ dead use;
~ **der Witwe am Mannesvermögen** jointure, common-law dower, dowry;
lebenslängliches ~ **im Erbwege erhalten** to take a life interest under a device.

Nießbrauchvermächtnis usufructuary legacy.

Niete *(fig.)* dropout, washout, flop, lame duck, dud, lemon *(sl.)*, slouch *(US sl.)*, *(Lotterie)* blank;
mit einer ~ **herauskommen** to turn up a blank; **eine** ~ **sein** to be a complete failure, to be a washout (dead loss); ~ **ziehen** to draw a blank.

Nietenhosen drain-pipe trousers.

niet- und nagelfest nailed down, clinched and riveted.

Nigger Jim Crow *(US sl.)*.

Nimbus nimbus, aura, halo, high reputation;
~ **der Heiligkeit** aura of sanctity; ~ **des Ruhms** halo of glory; ~ **des Tätigseins für eine gute Sache** glory in working for a good cause; ~ **der Unfehlbarkeit** reputation of infallibility;
j. seines ~ **entkleiden** to divest s. o. of his prestige, to debunk s. o.; **von einem** ~ **der Unbesiegbarkeit umgeben sein** to wear the mantle of invincibility.

Nimmerleinstag, St. Greek calends;
etw. bis zum St. ~ **verschieben** to put s. th. off till doomsday.

nimmermüde untiring;
~ **Hände** ever-busy hands; ~ **Sorge** unceasing care.

Nimmer|satt greedy-guts; **auf ~wiedersehen verschwinden** to vanish into thin air.

nippen, an einem Glas to sip from a glass.

Nippsachen bibelots, knick-knacks, rattletraps, trinkets, pretty-pretties.

Nische niche, recess, alcove.

Niveau horizontal plane, level, *(fig.)* level, standard, dignity;
auf dem gleichen ~ on the same plane; **auf höherem gesellschaftlichen** ~ on a higher social plane; **auf zu hohem** ~ **stehend** sophisticated; **unter dem** ~ not up to standard; **von hohem** ~ high-level;
akademisches ~ academic standards; **hohes sittliches** ~ high standard of ethics;
~ **vor der Ölkrise** pre-oil-crisis level; **hohes** ~ **einer Schule** high standard of a school; ~ **einer Zeitschrift** publication's standard;
~ **anheben** to upgrade the level; **soziales** ~ **der Flüchtlinge anheben** to raise the socio-economic status of the refugees; **sich jds.** ~ **anpassen** to descend to s. one's level; **sich dem** ~ **seines Publikums anpassen** to talk down to an audience; **altes** ~ **erreichen** *(Kurse)* to recover the old level; **jds. gesellschaftliches** ~ **erreichen** to rise to the level of s. o.; **zu einer raschen Senkung des wirtschaftlichen ~s führen** to lead to a rapid lowering of the economic level; ~ **haben** *(Buch)* to have class *(coll.)*; **hohes** ~ **haben** to be of high standard, to hold level; **ungleiches** ~ **haben** to be on different levels; ~ **halten** to maintain standards (level of education); **Preise auf dem gleichen** ~ **halten** to maintain the same level of prices; **auf ein tieferes** ~ **herabdrücken** to level down; **auf jds.** ~ **herabsteigen** to come down to s. one's level; **an das** ~ **heranreichen** to be up to the level; ~ **seiner Führungskräfte heraufsetzen** to upgrade one's executive personnel standards; **auf einem bescheidenen** ~ **leben** to do things on a humble scale; **über jds.** ~ **liegen** to be above s. o.; **über dem allgemeinen** ~ **liegen** *(Leistungen)* to be above the general standard; **im** ~ **sinken** to sink in the scale; **auf dem** ~ **eines Wilden stehen** to be on the same plane as a savage; ~ **wahren** to maintain the standard; **auf ein** ~ **zurücknehmen** to reduce to a level;
~grenzprodukt returns to scale; **~unterschied** difference in level.

nivellieren to level, to even up;
nach unten ~ to level down.

Nivellierung levelling, levelment.

Nivellierungs|kauf equalizing purchase; **~prozeß** levelling process.

nobel noble, noble- (high-) minded, handsome, *(freigiebig)* handsome, lavish, generous;
sich ~ **einrichten** to furnish one's home in grand style; ~ **gekleidet sein** to be stylishly dressed; **sich** ~ **zeigen** to show generosity;
~ **geht die Welt zugrunde** abundance, like want, ruins many.

Nobelpreis Nobel prize;
~träger Nobel prize winner, Nobel laureate, nobelist.

Nobelstiftung Nobel Foundation.

noble|Bewirtung handsome treatment; **~s Geschenk** generous (princely) gift; ~ **Gesinnung** generous mind; ~ **Passionen** fashionable foibles; **~r Vater** open-handed father.

Noblesse noble-mindedness.

Nochgeschäft *(Börse)* option to double, call of more *(Br.)*;
~ **in Käufers Wahl** buyer's option to double *(Br.)*; ~ **in Verkäufers Wahl** put of more, seller's option to double.

nochmalig, bei ~er Durchsicht on second inspection; **~e Vorlegung** *(Wechsel)* renewed presentation.

nochmals|überdenken to reconsider; ~ **vorlegen** to present again.

Nocken|antrieb cam drive; **~scheibe** cam disk; **~welle** camshaft.

Nomaden|gewohnheiten nomadic habits; **~leben** unsettled life; **~stamm** nomadic tribe.

Nomenklatur nomenclature.

nominal nominal, in terms of money.

Nominal|beteiligung nominal interest; **~betrag** nominal (face) amount, face value; **~einkommen** nominal income (wages); **~gewicht** standard weight; **handlungsfähige ~größe** *(Börse)* board lot; **~kapital** nominal *(US)* (subscribed, registered) capital, authorized capital, subscribed capital stock *(US)*; **~kurs** nominal (quoted) price; **~lohn** nominal (money) wages; **~nennwert** nominal value; **~parikurs** nominal par of exchange; **~partner** nominal partner; **~preis** nominal price; **~satz** nominal rate (price); **~teilhaber** nominal partner; **~verzinsung** nominal interest; **~wert** nominal (face) value, nominal amount, face, *(Aktie)* nominal par; **~zinsfuß, ~zinssatz** nominal rate of interest, nominal interest.

nominell nominal, by name, titular;
~er Kurs nominal price (rate); **~er Schaden** nominal damage.

nominieren to nominate;
j. für das Amt des Bürgermeisters ~ to nominate s. o. for mayor; **zum Botschafter** ~ to appoint ambassador; **als Kandidaten** ~ to name (nominate) as candidate.

Nominierter nominee.

Nominierung nomination;
gemeinsame ~ selection in common;
~ **als Botschafter** appointment as ambassador;
jds. ~ **bestätigen** to ratify s. one's nomination.

Nominierungskonvent nominating convention.

Nonchalance, mit ~ **tun** to do s. th. nonchalantly.

Nonkonfirmist nonconformist, dissenter, beatnik.

Non|pareilleschrift nonpareil; **~plusultra in Luxus** the ultimate in luxury; **~stopflug** nonstop flight; **~stopvorstellung** continuous performance; **~valeurs** *(Börse)* overdue and depreciated stocks *(Br.)*, defaulted and depreciated bonds *(US)*.

Nord-Süd-Dialog North-South dialogue.

Nordatlantik|rat North Atlantic Council; **~route** North Atlantic track.

Nordatlantische Verteidigungsgemeinschaft *(NATO)* North Atlantic Treaty Organization.

Norden, nach ~ **weisen** *(Magnetnadel)* to point to the north.

Nord|licht northern lights; **~pol** north pole; **geographisher ~pol** true north; **~polexpedition** arctic expedition; **~see** North Sea; **~seeölfelder** offshore oilfields.

Nörgelei faultfinding, grumble, nagging, carping, beet *(US sl.)*;
jds. ständige ~en nicht mehr ertragen können to be weary of s. one's constant grumble.

Nörgelfritze nagger.

Nörgeln nagging, carping.

nörgeln to niggle, to nag, to grumble, to kick *(coll.)*, to carp, to complain fussily, to beef *(US sl.)*.

nörgelsüchtig, nörglig peevish, querulous, nagging.
Nörgler stickler, grumbler, faultfinder, jackdaw, kicker *(US)*.
Norm norm, standard, mark, *(Arbeitsnorm)* rate, norm, quota, standards of performance, *(Regel)* rule, *(Normvorschrift)* standard specification, *(Regierungsvorschrift)* statutory rule; **unter der gesetzlich vorgeschriebenen ~** substandard; **anerkannte ~en** established standards; **arbeitsrechtliche ~en** labo(u)r standards; **staatlich festgelegte ~en** governmental standards; **gesetzlich festgesetzte ~** standard established by law; **in der Industrie geltende ~en** industry standards; **gewünschte ~** mark; **völkerrechtliche ~en** international standards; **zwingende ~en** mandatory rules;
~ für Luftqualität air quality standards; **~en und Typen** standards and types;
auf eine ~ bringen to standardize; **neue gesetzliche ~en zur Anwendung bringen** to apply a new legal standard; **der ~ entsprechen** to conform to standard specifications; **~ erfüllen** to fulfil its quota; **bestimmte ~ erreichen** to approach a certain standard; **als ~ gelten** to serve as a rule; **~en setzen** to standardize; **den Arbeitern eine ~ setzen** to set the workers a norm; **sich selbst ~en setzen** to write one's own ticket; **~ steigern** *(Akkordarbeit)* to raise the standard; **~en für Flugzeuge von 102 - 108 Phon zulassen** to establish maximum noise levels for airplanes between 102 and 108 decibles.
normal normal, nominal, regular, standard, ordinary;
geistig ~ sein to be in one's senses; **nicht ganz ~ sein** to be out of one's mind, not to be quite all there;
~e Abfertigung *(Bahn)* ordinary handling; **~e Abschreibung** ordinary depreciation; **~es Antragsformular** standard application form; **~e Arbeitsbedingungen** normal conditions; **~er Aufgabenkreis** normal operations; **~e Ausführung** standard design; **~e Berufsgefahr** ordinary hazard of occupation; **~er Beschaffungsweg** usual channels of trade; **~e Fehlerkurve** normal error curve; **~er Gebrauchszweck** ordinary use; **~e Geschäftsangelegenheiten** routine business; **~er Geschäftsverlauf** regular course of business; **mit ~er Geschwindigkeit fahren** to drive at a normal speed; **unter ~er Größe** undersized; **~es Leben führen** to follow standard lines; **~e Rechnung** ordinary bill; **~es Risiko** standard risk; **~e Schrift** standard type; **~es Verfahren** ordinary proceedings; **unter ~en Verhältnissen** normally.
Normal|abhebung ordinary withdrawal; **~absatzzahlen** standard figures of distribution; **~abschreibung** normal (ordinary) depreciation; **~abweichung** normal deviation, *(Statistik)* variation from standard, standard deviation; **höchstzulässige ~abweichung** maximum departure; **~arbeiter** normal worker (operator, *US*); **~arbeitstag** standard working day; **achtstündiger ~arbeitstag** standard eight-hour day; **~arbeitswoche** nominal workweek; **~arbeitszeit** nominal (regular) hours, regular time, standard labo(u)r (base) time, standard time for a given job; **achtstündige ~arbeitszeit** standard eight hours' day; **~ausführung** standard design (make), regular model, *(Auto)* standard car; **in ~ausführung** standard; **~ausführungszeit** standard performance time; **~ausgabe** standard edition; **~ausrüstung** standard equipment; **~ausstattung** *(Fabrik)* standby (standard) equipment; **~bedingungen** standard specifications; **~benzin** nonpremium (regular, *US*) grade gasoline, 2-star petrol *(Br.)*, 2-star fuel; **~bestand** *(an Waren)* basic inventory; **~bestand reduzieren** *(mil.)* to skeletonize; **~bezug** regular supply, *(Zeitung)* standard subscription; **~bezugsgröße** standard ratio; **~druck** normal pressure.
Normale, das the normal thing;
vom ~n abweichen to be off the beaten track.
Normal|eichmaß standard gauge; **~einheit** *(Anzeige)* standard unit, *(Börse)* regular lot; **~einkommen** straight (ordinary) income, transfer earnings, average pocket; **~erzeugung** normal output; **~fall** rule, usage; **im ~fall** normally; **~familie** standard family, family-of-five unit *(US)*; **~feuerpolice** ordinary (standard) policy; **gewinnberechtigte ~feuerpolice** ordinary with profits policy; **~film** standard-gauge film; **~flug** normal flight; **~flughöhe** cruising altitude; **~format** regular (standard) size; **~frachtsatz** standard rate; **~frequenz** standard frequency; **~gebühr** regular fee; **~gehalt** regular rate; **~geschwindigkeit** proper speed; **~gewicht** standard weight.
normalgroß standard-sized.
Normal|größe regular size, standard size (stock); **~höhe** ground level.
normalisieren to normalize, to rehabilitate;
sich ~ *(Lage)* to return to normal; **diplomatische Beziehungen ~** to normalize diplomatic relations; **Produkte ~** to standardize products.
Normalisierung normalization, rehabilitation;
~ von Produkten standardization of products.
Normalisierungsprozeß normalization process.
Normal|jahr common year; **~kalkulation** standard calculation; **~kapazität** normal capacity; **~käufer** full-price purchaser; **~konnossement** uniform bill of lading; **~kontenplan** standard scheme of accounts.
Normalkosten standard (predicted) cost;
anfängliche ~ basic standard cost;
~ per Einheit standard unit costs;
~plan standard cost budgeting; **~rechnung** standard (normal) cost system, standard costing.
Normal|kredit commercial credit; **~kurs** standard rate; **~leistung** standard output (production), normal performance, standard capacity, *(Maschine)* standard machine time; **~lohn** regular pay (rate, wage); **~lohnsatz** regular rate, general tariff; **~maß** standard measure; **über das ~maß hinaus** beyond the normal; **~papier** standard paper; **~post** surface mail; **~preis** regular (standard purchase, fair market) price; **~rechnung** standardized invoice; **~satz** standard rate, *(für Tiefdruckätzung)* scale rate; **~sätze des Krankengeldes** standards of benefit; **~schaden** normal loss; **~schrift** standard type; **~spur** *(Bahn)* standard gauge; **~stand** normal; **unter ~stärke** *(Alkoholgetränk)* underproof, *(mil.)* below strength; **~steuer** normal rate; **~steuersatz** standard rate; **~stunden** standard hours; **~stundentarif** standard time rate; **~tarif** general tariff, regular (standard) rates, *(Mietauto)* time and mileage tariff; **~typ** stock model; **~uhr** master clock, regulator; **~uhrsäule** public clock pillar; **~unterstützungssätze** relief standards; **~verbrauch** average (normal) consumption; **~verbraucher** average consumer, ordinary people; **~versteuerer** basic rate taxpayer; **~verteiler** *(Statistik)* normal distribution; **~verteilung** normal distribution; **~verteilungskurve** normal distribution curve; **~verzinsung** normal return, nominal yield, ordinary interest (return); **~wert** normal (standard) value; **~zeit** civil (mean, official, central, standard) time; **Greenwicher ~zeit** Greenwich Mean Time; **~zoll** general tariff; **~zustand** normality, normal condition; **~zuteilung** basic rations.
normative|Bestimmungen general rules, *(Tarifvertrag)* normative effect; **~ Kraft eines Vertrages** legal validity of a contract.
Norm|begriff normative concept; **~blatt** standard sheet.
Normen, die drei the three Fates.
normen, Produkte to standardize products.
Normen|ausschuß standardization committee, organization for standardization; **Internationaler ~ausschuß** International Standardization Organization **Amerikanisches ~büro** American Standard Association; **~festsetzung** establishment of standards, standard setting; **~kartell** standardization cartel; **~kollision** *(jur.)* conflict of laws; **~kontrolle** judicial review *(US)*; **~maße** standard measures; **~verband** standard institution; **Amerikanischer ~verband** American Standards Association; **~vertrag** standard contract; **~vordruck** standard printed form; **~vorschrift** standard specification; **~wert** standard value; **in ~werten ausdrücken** to standardize.
normenwidrig nonstandard.
normieren to standardize, to normalize.
Norm|satz standard rate; **abgeleitete ~setzung** delegated legislation; **~type** standard.
Normung standardization.
Norm|verbrauch standard consumption; **~vertrag** standard contract; **~vorschrift** standard specification; **in ~werten ausdrücken** to standardize; **~zeile** directive line.
Nostalgie nostalgia, homesickness;
von der ~welle erfaßt werden to be caught up in yesterday.
Nostro|geschäft business done for own account; **~guthaben** *(Bilanz)* due from (credit with other) banks, nostro balance, our account *(US)*; **~guthaben bei in- und ausländischen Banken** balances with home and foreign bankers; **~konto** our (nostro) account; **~transaktion** operation for own account; **~verpflichtungen** *(Bilanz)* due to banks, nostro liabilities.
Not need, want, *(Armut)* poverty, indigence, misery, destitution, privation, gripe, extremity, *(Bedrängnis)* distress, trouble, difficulty, scrape, *(Dringlichkeit)* urgency, exigency, *(Gefahr)* emergency, danger, *(Härtefall)* hardship, *(Sorge)* trouble, anxiety, worry;
für Zeiten der ~ for a rainy day; **im Falle der ~** in case of need, in an emergency; **in ~** distressed, in needy circumstances; **in größter ~** in sore distress; **mit knapper ~** by a fraction of an inch, by the skin of one's teeth *(fam.)*; **ohne ~** without real cause, *(nicht schwierig)* easily;

äußerste ~ utter destitution, necessity; **dringende** ~ extreme necessity; **drückende** ~ abject (deepest) misery, pressing need, pinching want;
~ **und Elend** destitution and misery; **große** ~ **der Flüchtlinge** miserable lives of refugees; ~ **und Gefahr** *(Schiff)* distress and danger;
sich in großer ~ **befinden** to be in dire want (distress, narrow straits); **in** ~ **bringen** to reduce to distress; **mit knapper** ~ **davonkommen** to have a narrow shave (squeak, *coll.*), to escape by the skin of one's teeth; **in** ~ **einlaufen** *(Schiff)* to put in in distress; **in** ~ **geraten** to get into a scrape, to fall on hard times; **seine** ~ **haben, mit dem Geld auszukommen** to find it difficult to make both ends meet; **seine liebe** ~ **mit etw. haben** to have no end of trouble with s. th.; **bittere** ~ **leiden** to be in necessity, to be in utter destitution, to undergo severe privation; **weiter** ~ **leiden** to remain in sufferance; **allgemeine** ~ **lindern** to relieve the common distress; ~ **der Armen lindern** to render aid to the poor; **aus der** ~ **eine Tugend machen** to make a virtue of necessity; **in** ~ **sein** to be in want, *(Schiff)* to be in distress; **in großer** ~ **sein** to be hard up, to be under the harrow (reduced to extremities); **jem. in der** ~ **zur Seite stehen** to stand by s. o. in time of need; **etw. der** ~ **gehorchend tun** to do s. th. out of necessity; **sich zu etw. in äußerster** ~ **verstehen** to do s. th. out of grim necessity; **für Zeiten der** ~ **zurücklegen** to put by for a rainy day;
Wechsel ~ **leiden lassen** to dishono(u)r a bill;
~ **kennt kein Gebot** necessity knows no law; ~ **macht erfinderisch** necessity is the mother of invention; **Freunde in der** ~ **gehen Tausend auf ein Lot** a friend in need is a friend indeed; **in der** ~ **frißt der Teufel Fliegen** any port in a storm.

Nota invoice, bill, note;
laut ~ as per note.

Not|abgabe capital levy; ~**abwurf** jettison; ~**adressat** referee (drawee) in case of need, emergency address; **als** ~**adressat intervenieren** to intervene in a case of need; ~**adresse** address in case of need, act of hono(u)r, notifying clause; **Namen als** ~**adresse auf einen Wechsel setzen** to place a name in case of need on a draft; ~**aggregat** standby unit; ~**akzept** collateral acceptance, acceptance in case of need; ~**anker** sheet anchor, *(fig.)* last refuge; ~**anzeige** *(Wechsel)* notice of dishono(u)r; **auf** ~**anzeige verzichten** to waive notice of dishono(u)r.

Notar notary [public], scrivener, greffier *(Kanalinseln)*;
beurkundender ~ conveyancing lawyer, attesting notary, conveyancer;
~ **von der Liste streichen** to strike a notary off the roll *(Br.)*.

Notariat notariate, notary's office.

Notariats|akt notarial deed; ~**angestellter** notary's clerk *(Br.)*; ~**beamter** conveyancing clerk; ~**befugnis entziehen** to strike a notary off the role *(Br.)*; ~**bescheinigung** notarial (notarized) certificate; ~**büro** notarial office, notary's office; ~**gebühren,** ~**kosten** notarial fees (charges, ticket), notary's fees, notarial expenses, *(Wechselprotest)* notarial ticket; ~**gebühren für die Auflassung** conveyancing cost (fee); ~**gehilfe** conveyancing clerk; ~**handlung** notarial act; ~**kanzlei** notary's office; ~**siegel** notarial (notary) seal; ~**stil** notarial style; ~**tätigkeit** notarial service; ~**urkunde,** ~**vertrag** notarial document, notarial deed, *(Grundstücksverkauf)* bargain and sale; ~**vertrag über die Änderung des Gesellschaftsvertrages** certificate of amendment; ~**vertrag unterzeichnen** to sign a legal agreement; ~**vertreter** deputy notary.

notariell notarial;
~ **beglaubigt** attested by a notary, certified, notarized;
~ **abschließen** to draw up before a notary; ~ **beglaubigen (bescheinigen, bestätigen)** to legalize, to certify, to attest, to notarize, to verify, to take acknowledgement of a deed, to acknowledge *(US)*;
~ **beglaubigte Abschrift** notarized (legalized) copy; ~**e Amtshandlung** notarial act (attestation); ~**e Beglaubigung** notarial attestation, *(Beurkundung)* notarial act, legalization; ~**e Bescheinigung** notarial (notarized) certificate; ~ **bekundeter Ehreneintritt** notarial act of hono(u)r; **in** ~**er Form** before a notary; **in** ~**er Form abgeschlossen werden** to be notarized (concluded before a notary); ~**e Gebühren** notarial fees; ~ **errichtetes Testament** notarial will; ~**es Testament errichten** to register a will; ~**er Vertrag** sealed contract, notarial deed; ~**e Vollmacht** authenticated power of attorney.

Notarztwagen emergency doctor's car.

Notaufnahme provisional accommodation, *(Krankenhaus)* emergency admission;
~**gebiet** reception area; ~**lager** reception camp; ~**zimmer** emergency room.

Not|ausgang emergency (fire) exit, emergency stairs; ~**ausrüstung** first-aid kit; ~**ausstieg** escape hatch; ~**ausstiegsrutsche** escape slide; ~**auswurf** *(Schiff)* jettison; ~**baracke** emergency barrack; ~**bedarf** emergency needs, necessaries.

Notbehelf expedient, makeshift, shift, apology *(coll.)*, stopgap;
als ein ~ as a shift;
zu ~**en greifen** to resort to expedients; **auf einen** ~ **verfallen** to pitch upon an expedient.

Not|beleuchtung emergency lights; ~**bett** emergency (improvised) bed, shakedown; ~**bremse** *(Bahn)* emergency brake (handle), communication cord, communicator *(Br.)*; ~**bremse ziehen** *(fig.)* to take emergency measures; ~**brücke** temporary (emergency) bridge; ~**diebstahl** pilferage; ~**dienst** emergency service, *(E-Werk)* breakdown service; **heute Nacht** ~**dienst haben** to be on emergency duty tonight.

notdürftig scanty, needy, poor, *(behelfsmäßig)* provisional, temporary, makeshift, rough-and-ready;
~ **bekleidet** scantily dressed; ~ **zusammengestoppelt** hastily improvised;
Schaden ~ **ausbessern** to repair a damage provisionally; **sein Leben** ~ **fristen** to eke out a scanty living;
~**e Ausbildung** rough-and-ready training; ~**e Beleuchtung** scanty illumination; ~**e Installierung** rough-and-ready installation; ~**e Reparatur** temporary repairs; ~**er Unterhalt** bare existence (necessaries of life).

Note note, memorandum, *(Banknote)* bank note *(Br.)* (bill, *US*), *(Eigenart)* touch, note, character, stamp, mark, *(Schule)* score, mark;
amtliche ~ note, memorandum; **besondere** ~ touch, characteristic; **diplomatische** ~ diplomatic note; **freundliche** ~ *(Werbung)* happy touch; **gemeinsame** ~ *(dipl.)* collective note; **gleichlautende** ~**n** parallel notes; **die goldene** ~ *(Werbung)* golden touch; **gute** ~**n** *(Schule)* high marks; **höchste** ~ *(Universität)* first [class] *(Br.)*; **menschliche** ~ human touch; **persönliche** ~ personal ring, individualism, personal touch; **ruhige** ~ *(Börse)* quiet trend; **schlechte** ~**n** *(Schule)* bad marks; **vertrauliche** ~ confidential note; **weibliche** ~ *(Werbung)* female touch;
~**n der amerikanischen Nationalbanken** bank currency *(US)*; **schlechte** ~ **fürs Zuspätkommen** *(Schule)* black mark for tardiness, late mark;
~**n austauschen** *(dipl.)* to exchange notes; ~**n decken** to back notes; **einer Sache eine persönliche** ~ **geben** to leave one's mark upon s. th., to give a personal touch to s. th.; **seine eigene** ~ **haben** to play tunes of one's own; **gute** ~**n haben** to have got (gotten, *US*) good marks; **wie nach** ~**n klappen** to go off without a hitch, to go like clockwork; **jds. persönliche** ~ **erkennen lassen** to carry the personal stamp of s. o.; ~**n außer Kurs setzen** to withdraw bank notes from circulation; **nach** ~**n spielen** to play from music; ~ **überreichen** to present (deliver) a note; **j. nach** ~**n verprügeln** to give s. o. a sound thrashing; **Annahme einer** ~ **verweigern** to refuse to accept a note; ~ **zurückweisen** to reject a note.

Nöte, seelische pangs of conscience;
~ **des Alltags** small worries of life; ~ **des Alters** infirmities of age;
jem. seine ~ **klagen** to pour out one's tale of misfortune; **in tausend** ~**n sein** to be in grave trouble.

Noteinsatzkommando emergency squad.

Notenaufruf withdrawal of bank notes.

Notenausgabe [new] issue of bank notes;
ungedeckte ~ fiduciary issue *(Br.)*;
ungedeckte ~**grenze** fiduciary limit; ~**recht** note-issuing privilege; ~**stelle** issue department *(Br.)*.

Notenaustausch *(pol.)* exchange of notes.

Notenbank note bank, bank of issue (circulation), central bank, Bank of England, United States Federal Reserve Bank;
~**ausweis** bank return *(Br.)* (statement, *US*); ~**behörde** central bank authority; ~**bericht** statement of a bank; ~**gesetz** Currency and Bank Notes Act *(Br.)*; ~**institut** bank of issue (circulation), central note-issuing bank; **abgestimmte** ~**interventionen** concerted central bank interventions; ~**liquidität** liquidity of the Federal Reserve System *(US)*; ~**maßnahmen,** ~**politik** central bank policy; **restriktive** ~**politik** restrictive central bank policy; ~**präsident** central banking governor, Governor of the Bank of England; ~**privileg** note-issuing privilege, privilege of note issue; ~**wesen** central banking.

Noten|deckung cover, backing of notes; ~**druck** printing of notes; ~**durchschnitt** *(Schüler)* average mark; ~**einlösung** conversion of bank notes; ~**emission** emission of bank notes; ~**folge** *(Musik)* melodic passage; ~**heft** music book;

~**kontingent** note issue *(Br.)*; ~**presse** printing press; ~**reserve** statutory reserve of bank notes; ~**schrank** music case; ~**ständer** music stand.

Notenumlauf circulation of bank notes, notes in circulation, paper currency;
tatsächlicher ~ active circulation; **ungedeckter** ~ uncovered (fiduciary, *Br.*) circulation, fiduciary currency;
~ **steigern** to increase paper circulation.

Notenwechsel *(dipl.)* exchange of notes.

Not|erbe lawful heir; ~**etat** emergency budget, contingent fund, deficiency fund *(US)*.

Notfall case of need, emergency, extreme case, push, exigency; **im** ~ in case of need (necessity), at a pinch (push); **im** ~ **stets zur Verfügung** a very present help in trouble;
äußerster ~ extreme case;
einem ~ **abhelfen** to meet an emergency; **nur im** ~ **benutzt werden dürfen** to be used only in an emergency; **für jeden** ~ **vorbereitet sein** to be ready for every emergency; **für einen** ~ **Vorsorge treffen** to provide for emergencies; **im** ~ **über 5000 Dollar verfügen** to command $ 5000 in an emergency; **für den** ~ **vorsorgen** to put away for a rainy day;
~**dienst** emergency service; ~**planung** contingency plan.

Not|feuer distress light; ~**flagge** distress flag, ensign hoisted union down; ~**fonds** contingency fund, deficiency account; ~**frist** peremptory term *(US)*.

notgedrungen necessitous, necessary, forced, compelled, compulsory, out of necessity;
etw. ~ **tun** to be forced to do s. th.

Not|geld emergency currency, money of necessity; ~**gemeinschaft** emergency organization; ~**gepäck** scram-bag *(US sl.)*; ~**gerät** standby; ~**gesetz** emergency bill; ~**groschen** nest egg, scram money *(sl.)*; **sich einen** ~**groschen als Reserve zurückgelegt haben** to have a sum put by to fall back upon; ~**groschen zurücklegen** to put aside for a rainy day; ~**hafen** port of refuge (distress, necessity, anchorage), emergency port; ~**helfer** rescuer; ~**hilfe** first aid; **Technische** ~**hilfe** Organization for the Maintenance of Supplies *(Br.)*, Salvage Corps *(US)*, protective department *(US)*; ~**hilfedienst** rescue service.

notierbar *(Börse)* quotable, listable *(US)*.

notieren to [make a] note, to take a note of, to put down in writing, to make a memorandum, to mark down, *(Anleihe)* to stand at, *(Börsenkurse)* to quote, to list *(US)*, *(bestimmtes Kursniveau haben)* to rule, *(in Liste aufnehmen)* to book, to list, to enter, to record, to item, *(notiert werden)* to be worth (quoted, listed, *US*), *(vormerken)* to book in advance;
sich etw. ~ to make a note of s. th.; **Aktien mit 800** ~ to quote shares (stocks) at 800; **amtlich** ~ *(Börse)* to quote (list, *US*) at the stock exchange; **flüchtig** ~ to jot down; **fortlaufend** ~ to quote consecutively; **hoch** ~ *(Wertpapiere)* to rule high; **weiterhin hoch (niedrig)** ~ to continue to rule high (low); **höher** ~ to be marked up; **bei Börsenschluß höher** ~ to close dearer; **Kurs** ~ to quote a price; **sich jds. Namen und Anschrift** ~ to take down s. one's name and address; **unter dem Nennwert** ~ to quote below par; **niedriger** ~ to mark down; **pari** ~ to quote at par; **Posten** ~ to enter an item in the books; **rasch** ~ to jot down; **unverändert** ~ to remain unchanged.

notiert noted, marketable, quoted, listed *(US)*;
amtlich ~ officially quoted, listed at the stock exchange *(US)*; **fortlaufend** ~ consecutively quoted, bunched *(US)*; **nicht** ~ not quoted (listed, *US*), unquoted, unlisted *(US)*, over the counter *(US)*;
~ **werden** to be quoted on the stock exchange; **niedriger** ~ **werden** to be marked down;
~**e Werte** quoted (listed, *US*) securities; **mit 8%** ~**e Wertpapiere** securities ruling at 8 per cent.

Notierung notation, *(Buchung)* booking, entry, *(Effekten)* [market] quotation, mark, listing *(US)*, market value, course; **ohne** ~ without official quotation, unquoted, unlisted *(US)*, not listed *(US)*; **unter der letzten** ~ **angeboten** offered down *(US)*; **zur** ~ **zugelassen** quoted (listed, *US*) on the stock exchange;
amtliche ~ official quotation *(Br.)*, listing *(US)*; **außerbörsliche** ~ unofficial quotation; **einheitliche** ~ regular quotation; **erste** ~ first call, opening quotation; **fortlaufende** ~ consecutive quotation; **genannte** ~ nominal quotation; **heutige** ~ today's quotation; **höchste** ~ highest quotation; **laufende** ~ consecutive quotation, consecutively quoted prices; **letzte** ~ previous (closing, final) quotation, *(Schlußkurs)* closing price; **mittägliche** ~**en** noon quotations; **uneinheitliche** ~ split quotation; **variable** ~ consecutive quotation; **zweite** ~ *(Börse)* second call;
~ **in Bruchteilen** split quotation; ~ **von Devisen** quotation of exchange rates; **zusammenfassende** ~ **aller Einzelbörsen der Länder** composite national tape for all markets; ~ **im Freiverkehr** unofficial quotation; ~ **für Industriewerte** industrial share prices; ~ **pro Stück** quotation per unit;
~ **aussetzen** to suspend a quotation; **zur** ~ **kommen** to be quoted officially *(Br.)* (listed on the stock exchange, *US*); **Antrag auf** ~ **an der Börse stellen** to apply for admission on the stock exchange; **zur** ~ **zulassen** to admit for quotation on the stock exchange.

Notierungs|art method of trading; ~**ausschuß** listing committee *(US)*; **letzter** ~**tag** previous day.

Notifikation notification, *(Wechsel)* notice of dishono(u)r.

Notifikations|pflicht obligation to disclose; ~**urkunde** instrument of notification; ~**vorschriften** notification orders.

notifizieren to notify.

Notifizierung notification.

Notifizierungswege, im on a notification basis.

nötig necessary, needed, needful, required, requisite;
unbedingt ~ absolutely essential, indispensible;
j. ~ **brauchen** to be in dire need of s. o.; ~ **haben** to want, to require; **etw. dringend** ~ **haben** to need s. th. badly;
~**ste Dinge zum Leben** bare necessities; ~**es Kleingeld** wherewithal, needful *(sl.)*; ~**e Mittel** necessary funds; ~**e Unterlagen** required documents.

nötigen to put under duress, to coerce, to force, to compel, to constrain;
j. zur Annahme eines Angebots ~ to urge s. o. to accept an offer; **Zeugen** ~ to intimidate a witness;
sich nicht lange ~ **lassen** not to stand on ceremony.

nötigenfalls in case of need.

Nötigste, sich auf das ~ **beschränken** to pinch o. s.

Nötigung coercion, constraint, duress, undue pressure, necessitation, intimidation, *(Erpressung)* blackmail, concession;
aufgrund einer ~ under duress;
~ **im Amt** oppression; ~ **der Ehefrau** marital coercion; ~ **durch körperliche Gewalt** physical duress; ~ **zur Unzucht** indecent assault; ~ **von Wählern** intimidation of voters *(US)*; ~ **von Zeugen** coercion (intimidation) of witnesses;
einer ~ **nachgeben** to surrender to intimidation.

Nötigungs|einwand plea of duress; ~**handlung** act of oppression.

Notiz note, memorandum, memo, jotting down, paragraph, minute *(Br.)*, *(Börse)* quotation, listing *(US)*, *(Zeitung)* news item, announcement;
kurze ~ chit *(Br.)*, memo;
~ **ohne Umsätze** *(Börse)* nominal quotation;
~ **über etw. anfertigen** to keep note of s. th.; **zur** ~ **aufgeben** *(Börse)* to give an order; **einige** ~**en aufheben** to retain some notes; **seine** ~**en durchsehen** to go over one's notes; **seine** ~**en heranziehen (konsultieren)** to consult one's notes, to refer to one's notes; **sich** ~**en machen** to take (keep) notes, to jot down; ~**en bei einer Vorlesung machen** to take lecture notes; ~ **nehmen** to take notice of; **von jem.** ~ **nehmen** to give s. o. a tumble; **keine** ~ **nehmen** to pass, to leave out; **von schlechten Nachrichten keine** ~ **nehmen** to shrug off bad news; ~ **von einer Sache nehmen** to take cognizance of s. th.; ~ **niederschreiben** to set down notes; **kurze** ~ **veröffentlichen** to cover s. th. in a few lines; ~**en in Kurzform zusammenfassen** to sum up in note form;
~**block** [copy] block, jotter, scribbling block *(Br.)*, memorandum (memo) pad, scratchpad *(US)*; ~**buch** scribbling block *(Br.)*, jotter, memorandum (memo, address, blank, memory, *US*) book, notebook, pocket book; **sich etw. in seinem** ~**buch notieren** to take a note of s. th. in one's pocket book.

Notizen|anfertigung note taking; ~**form** note form; ~**sammlung** collection of notes.

Notiz|kalender diary, tickler; ~**papier,** ~**zettel** scribbling *(Br.)* (scratch, *US*) paper.

Notklausel emergency clause, escalator clause.

Notlage [state of] need, calamity, distress, distressed condition, emergency, necessity, pinch, exigency, exigence, *(Geldverlegenheit)* embarrassment, fix, tight spot;
in Anbetracht meiner bitteren ~ in the lowness of my circumstances;
extreme ~ retreat to the wall; **landwirtschaftliche** ~ agricultural depression; **vorgetäuschte** ~ *(Schiff)* simulated distress; **wirtschaftliche** ~ economic distress;
sich in großer ~ **befinden** to be in great distress; ~ **beheben** to relieve an emergency; **jem. aus einer** ~ **helfen** to get s. o. out of a fix; **in einer** ~ **sein** to be in necessity, to be reduced to exigency (in necessity); **sich einer** ~ **voll gewachsen zeigen** to rise to the emergency.

Notlager shakedown.
notlanden to be forced down, to make a forced (emergency) landing, to force-land.
Not|landeplatz emergency landing field; ~**landestreifen** flight strip; ~**landung** forced (emergency) landing; ~**landung auf dem Wasser machen** to ditch one's plane; ~**landung vornehmen** to make an emergency landing, to force-land.
notleidend distressed, needy, indigent, destitute, necessitous, *(Brief)* unclaimed, *(Währung)* depreciated, *(Wechsel)* dishono(u)red, overdue;
~**e Aktie** nondividend-paying stock; ~**e Bevölkerung** suffering population; ~**es Depot** securities in abeyance; ~**e Gesellschaft** company in default; ~**e Obligationen** overdue stocks *(Br.)*, defaulted bonds *(US)*; ~**e Waren** distress merchandise; ~**er Wechsel** overdue (dishono(u)red) bill.
Not|leidender distressed person, sufferer; ~**lösung** makeshift, stopgap; ~**lüge** white (courtesy) lie, fib, ploy; ~**maßnahmen** emergency measures (actions), stopgap; ~**maßnahmen ergreifen** to take emergency steps; ~**mast** jury mast; ~**operation** emergency operation.
notorisch notorious, known;
~**er Betrüger** notorious swindler; ~**er Lügner** arrant liar.
Notpfennig savings, nest egg;
~ **zurückgelegt haben** to have a sum in reserve as standby; ~ **zurücklegen** to put aside for a rainy day.
Not|programm austerity (crash) program(me); ~**quartier** temporary lodging, shelter, crash pad *(sl.)*; ~**rakete** *(Schiff)* distress rocket; ~**ration** emergency (reserve) ration; ~**rücklage** contingency fund.
Notruf *(tel.)* emergency (hurry) call;
~**anlage** *(Autobahn)* emergency roadside telephone; ~**nummer** emergency number; ~**säule** call box; ~**welle** distress-call wavelength.
Not|schrei cry for help; ~**schüsse** minute guns; ~**sender** emergency transmitter; ~**signal** distress signal (call), *(Bahn)* washout signal *(sl.)*; ~**signal setzen** to fly a distress signal; **in jeder** ~**situation seinen Mann stehen** to be equal to any emergency; ~**sitz** *(Auto)* rumble (bucket) seat, dickey.
Notstand [state of] distress, state of national emergency;
kriegsbedingter ~ state of national emergency; **nationaler** ~ national emergency; **strafrechtlicher** ~ flagrant necessity, plea of necessity; **wirtschaftlicher** ~ economic distress;
übergesetzlicher ~ **im Kriegsfall** military necessity;
im ~ **handeln** to act under duress; ~ **über ein Gebiet verhängen** to proclaim a district.
Notstands|abgabe emergency tax; ~**ankündigung** emergency action notification; ~**anleihe** relief loan; ~**arbeiten** relief (emergency, remedial) works; ~**arbeiter** relief worker; **zentrale** ~**behörde** national emergency council, Office of Emergency Preparedness *(US)*; ~**beihilfe** emergency aid; ~**bestimmungen** emergency provisions; ~**büro** emergency board; ~**darlehn** emergency loan; ~**dienst** emergency relief service; ~**einsatz** emergency action; ~**ermächtigung** emergency powers; ~**fonds** emergency fund; ~**gebiet** depressed (distressed, *Br.*, special, *Br.*, stricken, *Br.*) area; **nahezu ständiges** ~**gebiet** semipermanently depressed area; ~**gebietsplan** area-development program(me); ~**gesetz** Emergency Power Act *(Br.)*, Special Areas Scheme *(Br.)*, Special Powers Act *(Ireland)*; **durch das** ~**gesetz gedeckt** under cover of emergency; ~**gesetzgebung** emergency legislation; ~**gesetzgebung abbauen** to dismantle the emergency; ~**gremium** emergency board; ~**herrschaft** emergency regime; ~**hilfe** depressed-area aid *(Br.)*; ~**kabinett** emergency cabinet; ~**kommission** emergency board, relief committee; ~**kredit** relief loan.
Notstandsmaßnahmen emergency measures (actions);
~ **für bedrohte Industriezweige** emergency protection for threatened industries;
~ **ergreifen** to take emergency steps; ~ **verhängen** to assume emergency powers.
Notstands|plan contingency plan; **militärpolitische** ~**planung** contingency planning; ~**programm** relief (emergency-aid, crash) program(me); ~**programm für die Wirtschaft** economic emergency plan; ~**quartier** poor housing; ~**regierung** emergency rule (regime), emergency coalition, emergency authorization rule; ~**sitzung** emergency session; ~**tarif** emergency rate; ~**verordnung** emergency decree; ~**verwaltung** emergency administration; ~**vorhaben** emergency facilities, *(Arbeitsbeschaffung)* unemployment relief project; ~**vorlage** emergency bill; ~**warnung** emergency action notification.
Not|steuervorrichtung dead-man control; ~**strom** emergency current; ~**testament** privileged will; ~**treppe** emergency stairs, exit staircase, fire escape; ~**unterhalt** *(geschiedene Ehefrau)* compassionate allowance; ~**unterkunft** makeshift dormitory, shelter; ~**unterkünfte** emergency barracks; ~**verband** preliminary dressing; ~**verbandskasten** first-aid outfit; ~**verkauf** emergency sale; ~**verkauf gepfändeter Gegenstände** distress sale; ~**verkäufe** necessitous selling, forced sales; ~**verordnung** provisional order, emergency enactment (order, decree), decree law *(Br.)*; ~**verordnungsbefugnisse** emergency powers; ~**verpflegung** emergency ration; ~**vorrat** emergency supply; ~**währung** emergency currency.
notwassern to ditch.
Notweg way of necessity.
Notwehr self-decence;
aus ~ in defence of life, self-defensive;
~**einwand** plea of necessity; **offensichtliche** ~**lage** apparent necessity; **sich in äußerster** ~**lage befinden** to flee to the wall; ~**recht** privilege of self-defence *(US)*.
notwendig necessary, requisite, essential;
~ **und zweckmäßig** necessary and expedient;
es ~ **finden** to be under the necessity; **etw. für** ~**halten** to judge it necessary to do s. th.; ~ **machen** to necessitate;
~**e Anschaffungen** necessary acquisitions; ~**e Ausgaben** necessary expenditure; ~**e Bedingung** necessary condition; ~**er Bestandteil** essential part; ~**e Bücher** essential books; ~**e Folge** logical consequence; **das** ~**e Geld beschaffen** to supply the needful *(sl.)*; ~**er Kosten** related costs; ~**er Lebensbedarf** necessaries; ~**e Reparaturen** emergency repairs; ~**e Streitgenossen** necessary parties; ~**e Voraussetzungen** basic requirements.
Notwendige, sich auf das unbedingt ~ **beschränken** to limit o. s. to strict necessities; **seinen Aufenthalt auf das unbedingt** ~ **beschränken** to stay no longer than is absolutely necessary; **nur das unbedingt** ~ **tun** not to do more than is absolutely necessary.
notwendigerweise necessarily, of necessity.
Notwendigkeit necessity, urgency, want;
absolute ~ a must; **dringende** ~ prime (dire) necessity, dire (pressing, extreme) necessity, urgent (crying) need, urgency; **sittliche** ~ moral necessity; **überragende** ~ paramount necessity; **unbedingte** ~ peremptory necessity; **unumstößliche** ~ imperative need; **zeremonielle** ~ pomp and circumstance; **zwingende** ~ must, stringent necessity;
seinen Schülern die ~ **hart zu arbeiten, eindringlich darlegen** to urge on one's pupils the importance of hard work; **auf die** ~ **zu sparen hinweisen** to urge the need of economy; ~ **vorsichtigen Fahrens unterstreichen** to emphasize the importance of careful driving; **in die** ~ **versetzen** to force to; ~ **vorschützen** to urge plea of necessity.
Not|wurf jettison; ~**zeichen** distress signal; **in** ~**zeiten** in times of need; ~**zeitung** temporary paper; ~**zucht** abuse, rape; ~**zucht an einer Minderjährigen** statutory rape.
notzüchtigen to violate, to commit rape.
Notzüchtigung violation, rape.
Notzucht|täter rapist; ~**verbrechen** assault with intent to commit rape.
Novation novation, merger of contract, substition of debt *(Scot.)*.
Novationsvertrag substituted contract.
Novelle short story, novel, *(Gesetz)* novel, amendment, amending law.
Novellensammlung collection of short stories.
Novellierung reenactment.
novellistisch novel.
Novität novelty, specialty.
Novitätenhändler specialty dealer.
Novize rookie;
~ **in einer Sache sein** to be a fresh hand at s. th.
Nu twinkle;
im ~ in a snap, in a flash (jiffy), on the instant, before one can say Jack Robinson;
im ~ **erledigen** to do it in a flash; **im** ~ **geschehen sein** to be the work of a moment; **im** ~ **weg sein** to be gone in wink; **sich im** ~ **wenden** to turn on a sixpence.
Nuance nicety, subtle distinction, *(Kurs)* shade.
nuancieren to shade, to tinge, to tint.
nüchtern levelheaded, hard-headed, dry, matter-of-fact, down-to-earth, bread-and-butter-minded, *(Geschmack)* without flavo(u)r, insipid;
wieder ~ above the weather;
j. wieder ~ **machen** to steady s. o. up; ~ **sein** to walk the chalk line;

~er Bericht dry account; **bei ~er Betrachtung** considered dispassionately; **~er Magen** empty stomach; **~ eingestellter Mensch** matter-of-fact person; **~er Raum** plain room; **~er Stil** vapid style; **~e Tatsachen** cold facts; **~es Urteil** sober judgment.
Nüchternheit sobriety, state of fasting, *(fig.)* prose, matter-of-factness.
Nudel, dicke fat creature; **komische ~** joker, card, character.
nuklear|e Abrüstung nuclear disarmament; **~e Energie** nuclear energy; **~e Erpressung** nuclear blackmail; **~es Gleichgewicht** nuclear parity; **zur ~en Kriegsausweitung zwingen** to put on the nuclear escalator; **~er Schaden** nuclear damage; **~er Schadensfall** nuclear incident; **~er Sprengsatz** nuclear explosive; **~e Überwachung** nuclear inspection; **[begrenzte] ~e Vergeltung** [limited] nuclear reaction.
Nuklear|anlagen nuclear facilities; **strategische ~bewaffnung** nuclear strategic armaments; **~krieg** nuclear war; **~macht** nuclear state; **~politik** nuclear policy; **~technik** nuclear engineering; **~verteidigung** nuclear defence; **für mittlere Entfernungen vorgesehene ~waffen** medium-range nuclear weapon.
Null zero, nil, nothing, *(Mensch)* nobody, nonentity, picayune, *(Ziffer)* cipher, naught;
gleich ~ next to nothing;
aufgeblasene ~ stuffed shirt *(US sl.)*; **eine ~** a simple nobody;
~ Komma nichts in a flash (jiffy), before one can say Jack Robinson;
~ anhängen to add a nought; **auf ~ einstellen** to zero; **gleich ~ sein** to be down to zero, *(Verhandlungsergebnis)* to come to nothing; **geschäftlich eine ~ sein** to be a mere cipher (simple nobody) in business; **gleich ~ setzen** to set at nought, to zero, *(Anlagewerte)* to amount to blank.
null null, nil;
~ und nichtig null and void, absolutely void;
für ~ und nichtig erklären to declare null and void, to negate;
~ Fehler *(Schularbeit)* no mistakes; **~ Uhr** midnight;
~-acht-fünfzehn pretty nondescript; **~-acht-fünfzehn Erscheinung** run-of-the-mill appearance.
Null|achse *(math.)* coordinate axis; **~ebene** *(Flut)* harmonic plane; **~eichung** rectification; **~einstellung** initial adjustment; **~grad** freezing point; **~grenze** freezing level; **~justierung** zero; **~last** no load; **~leiter** *(el.)* neutral wire; **~linie** zero line; **~nummer** *(Zeitschrift)* pre-launch issue.
Nullpunkt zero [point], freezing point, *(fig.)* scratch;
absoluter ~ absolute zero; **willkürlicher ~** *(Statistik)* arbitrary origin;
~ des Grenzertrages intensive margin;
vom ~ anfangen to start from scratch; **in der Geldpolitik den absoluten ~ erreichen** to zero in on appropriate monetary policy; **auf den ~ fallen** to drop to rock bottom; **auf dem ~ sein** *(Stimmung)* to be at its lowest ebb.
Null|sätze nil rates; **~serie** pilot lot; **~stellung** neutral position; **~stunde** *(mil.)* zero hour *(Br.)*; **~tarif** fare-free transport; **~wachstum** zero growth; **~wachstumsrate** nil (zero) growth rate; **~wachstumswirtschaft** no-growth economy; **fast ~werte erreichen** to be close to zero; **auf den ~wert setzen** to reduce to zero.
numerieren to number, to ticket, to label;
fortlaufend ~ to number consecutively.
numerierter Platz reserved seat.
Numerierung numeration, numbering;
fortlaufende ~ continuous numbering.
Numerierungsstempel numbering stamp.
numerisch|e Überlegenheit numerical superiority; **~er Wertkoeffizient** figure of merit.
Numismatik numismatics.
Nummer number, mark, *(Abkommen)* subitem, *(Fabriknummer)* serial, *(Größe)* size, *(Lotterie)* ticket, *(Person, coll.)* card, case, *(Programm)* item, *(Zeitung)* issue, copy, edition;
in einzelnen ~n serially, in serial parts;
~n *(Zinsnummern)* decimals *(Br.)*;
~ besetzt *(Telefon)* engaged, line busy *(US)*;
alte ~ *(Zeitschrift)* back number; **nicht mehr benutzte ~** dead number; **bestimmte ~** *(Auto)* distinctive number; **falsche ~** wrong number; **frühere ~** back number (issue); **gezogene ~** *(Los)* drawing number; **laufende ~** running (serial, progressive) number; **nächstgrößere ~** next in size; **rote ~** *(Autohändler)* dealer's licence number; **schwarze ~n** *(Zinszahlen)* black products; **tolle ~** live wire, humdinger *(US)*, crackerjack; **üble ~** nasty piece of work; **ulkige ~** funny character; **völlig unbedeutende ~** very small potato;
~ des Arbeitsausweises works number; **große ~ im Betrieb** big shot in a firm; **~ eines Lotterieloses** lottery number; **~ des Postzustellbezirks** postal district number; **~ des abgetretenen Wagnisses** *(Rückversicherung)* cession number; **~ des statistischen Warenverzeichnisses** statistical code number; **neue ~ einer Zeitschrift** most recent issue of a magazine; **vereinzelte ~n einer Zeitschrift** odd numbers;
tolle ~ abziehen to show off, to put it on; **~ angeben** to give a reference number; **auf ~ sicher bringen** to put under lock and key; **auf ~ sicher gehen** to play a safe game (for safety, cases), to choose the safest course; **~ 312 haben** *(Hotel)* to stay in room No. 312; **gute ~ bei jem. haben** to be in s. one's good books, to rate high with s. o., to have a good stand-in (be popular) with s. o.; **ruhige ~ schieben** to have a soft job; **nur eine kleine ~ sein** to have a petty position; **~ für sich sein** to be quite a character; **nach fortlaufenden ~n geordnet sein** to be arranged numerically; **auf ~ sicher sitzen** to be in clink *(fam.)*; **falsche ~ wählen** *(Telefon)* to dial a wrong number; **~ zuweisen** to assign a number.
Nummern|anzeige *(tel.)* call indicator disk; **~anzeiger** annunciator; **~aufgabe** numerical note; **~bezeichnung** numbering; **~folge** numerical order; **~konto** *(Bank)* numbered account.
nummernmäßig ablegen to file numerically.
Nummern|scheibe *(tel.)* dial, [finger] disk; **~schild** *(Auto)* number (licence, *US*) plate, registration plate *(Br.)*; **~serie** set of numbers; **~stempel** numbering stamp; **~sucher** *(Datenverarbeitung)* number detector; **einheitliches ~system** *(Bankwesen)* universal numerical system *(US)*; **~verzeichnis** specification of numbers.
Nuntiatur nunciature.
Nuntius nuncio.
Nurflügelflugzeug tailless airplane, flying wing, all-wing type aircraft.
Nürnberger Trichter [etwa] royal road to learning;
jem. etw. mit dem ~ beibringen to drum (cram) s. th. into s. o.
Nuß, doofe numbskull, fool, fathead *(coll.)*, nut *(US sl.)*; **harte ~** a hard nut to crack, teaser;
Muß ist eine harte ~ necessity is a hard master;
~kohle nut, egg (cob) coal; **~schale** nutshell, *(leichtes Boot)* walnut shell.
Nutz|anteil profit share; **~anwendung** practical application.
nutzbar useful, serviceable, *(produktiv)* profitable, productive, lucrative;
~ machen to utilize, to exploit, to turn to account, to take advantage of, to tap, *(Bodenschätze)* to develop, to utilize, to harness;
~er Laderaum payload space.
Nutzbarmachung utilization, use, exploitation, employment, *(Boden)* cultivation;
~ von Bodenschätzen utilization (development) of resources; **~ einer Erfindung** industrial application of an invention.
Nutzbarmachungskoeffizient utilization rate.
Nutzberechnung valuation of profit.
nutzbringend useful, profitable, lucrative;
~ anlegen to turn to account; **sein Geld ~ anlegen** to lay out one's money profitably; **~ machen** to turn to good purpose; **~ sein** to bring in profit; **~ verwenden** to put to good use; **seine Zeit ~ verwerten** to use one's time profitably;
~e Kapitalanlage profitable investment.
nütze, zu nichts of no use, no good, in vain;
zu nichts ~ sein to be absolutely hopeless.
Nutzeffekt useful work, *(Maschine)* commercial efficiency;
~ persönlicher Dienstleistungen service utility.
Nutzen use, *(Ertrag)* emolument, yield, proceeds, return, *(Gewinn)* good, capital, gain, profit, fruit, *(Hilfe)* service, *(Nützlichkeit)* usefulness, utility, *(Vorteil)* interest, advantage, benefit, behoof, avails *(US)*;
mit einem ~ von leaving a margin of; **ohne ~** profitless; **von geringem ~** of little use; **zum ~** for the benefit of; **zum eigenen ~** for one's own ends; **zum ~ der Gesellschaft** for the benefit of the company;
abnehmender ~ diminishing utility; **allgemeiner ~** common advantage, public interest; **bescheidener ~** modest profit; **gemeinsamer ~** mutual advantage; **geringer ~** small returns; **höchstmöglicher ~** utility optimum, maximum benefit; **mittelbarer ~** incidental profit; **negativer ~** disutility; **öffentlicher ~** public utility; **persönlicher ~** subjective utility; **schmaler ~** narrow profit margin; **verarbeitungsbedingter ~** form utility; **voller ~** full benefit; **wirtschaftlicher ~** economic value;

~ **abwerfen** to render (show) a profit; **geringen ~ abwerfen** to yield little; ~ **bringen** to benefit, to [yield a] profit; **jedermann zum ~ gereichen** to be to the common advantage; **nur geringen ~ von etw. haben** to get little out of it; **mit kleinem ~ realisieren** *(Börsengewinn)* to scalp *(US)*; **von ~ sein** to be useful; **jem. von großem ~ sein** to stand s. o. in good stead; **mit ~ verkaufen** to sell at a profit; ~ **ziehen** to derive advantage from, to find a transaction profitable, to realize profit (capital) from, to turn to advantage (profit), to make a profit out of (benefit, profit by); **nur geringen ~ ziehen** to get only a small profit (return) for one's money.

nutzen to utilize, to use, to make use of, *(Gewinn haben)* to benefit, to profit, *(nützlich sein)* to be useful (of advantage); **Gelegenheit ~** to avail o. s. of an opportunity; **Grund und Boden landwirtschaftlich ~** to use land for agricultural purposes.

nützen, jem. sehr to stand s. o. in good stead; **seine Zeit gut ~** to improve one's time.

Nutzen|kostenanalyse benefit cost analysis; **~skala** preference scale.

Nutz|ertrag, steigender improved value; **~fahrt** loaded run; **~fahrzeug** commercial vehicle (car, automobile); **~faktor** utilization coefficient; **~feuer** *(Versicherung)* friendly fire; **~fläche** useful area; **industrielle ~fläche** industrial floor space; **landwirtschaftliche ~fläche verpachten** to rent a field to a farmer; **~garten** kitchen garden; **~holz** commercial timber, wood, timber tree; **~holzversorgung** timber supply; **~ladefähigkeit** useful load; **~last** carrying capacity, useful (live) load, *(Flugzeug, Schiff)* payload, *(Waggon)* loading capacity; **~lastfahrzeug** load-carrying vehicle; **~leistung** effective output, *(Auto)* brake horsepower, *(Maschine)* duty, mechanical effect.

nützlich useful, serviceable, expedient, practicable, *(einträglich)* profitable, beneficial, *(vorteilhaft)* advantageous, wholesome; **seine Zeit ~ anwenden** to make good use of one's time; **sich ~ betätigen** to make o. s. useful; **Mittel ~ einsetzen** to employ funds usefully; **sich als ~ erweisen** to prove (come in) useful; **sich als ~ für jds. Laufbahn erweisen** to stand s. o. in good stead for his career; **sich äußerst ~ machen** to make o. s. very pleasant; **seine Begabungen für sein Land ~ machen** to turn one's talents to the service of one's country; **~ verwenden** to use to good advantage;
~e Einrichtung utility, useful thing; **~es Mitglied der menschlichen Gesellschaft** useful member of society.

Nützliche, das Angenehme mit dem ~n verbinden to combine business with pleasure.

Nützlichkeit usefulness, utility.

Nützlichkeits|erwägungen utilitarian considerations; **~prinzip** utilitarian principle; **~system** utilitarianism; **~wert** utility.

nutzlos useless, futile, of no avail, of no utility, unavailing;
ziemlich ~ no earthly use;
~ **sein** to be of no avail; **bei jem. völlig ~ sein** to be wasted on s. o.; **sein Leben ~ aufs Spiel setzen** to risk one's life unnecessarily; **seine Kräfte ~ vergeuden** to waste one's efforts in sheer futility; **als ~ weggeworfen werden** to be dumped into limbo;
~e Bemühungen vain endeavo(u)rs; **~e Geldausgabe** wasted money (expense); **~es Kapital** dead (unproductive, idle) capital; **~er Protest** demonstration of no avail.

Nutzlosigkeit nonutility, disutility, uselessness.

Nutzmasse payload.

nutznießen to [hold in] usufruct, to enjoy.

Nutznießer profit taker, usufructuary, user, appointee *(US)*, cestui que trust;
lebenslänglicher ~ life beneficiary, *(Grundstück)* life tenant;
~ **einer Grunddienstbarkeit** rent charger; **~ einer Stiftung (eines Stiftungsvermögens)** trust beneficiary, cestui que trust; **~ auf Zeit** termer.

nutznießerisch beneficial, usufructuary.

Nutznießung use, user, usufruct, beneficial interest;
gemeinschaftliche ~ common user, joint use; **kostenlose ~** beneficial service; **lebenslängliche ~** life interest;
~ **einer Domäne** domain of use; **~ des überlebenden Ehemanns** curtesy of England *(US)*; **~ zur gesamten Hand** undivided interest; **~ des angelegten Kapitals** usufruct of an investment; **~ haben** to hold in usufruct; **sich die ~ einer Sache vorbehalten** to reserve the use of s. th.

Nutznießungsrecht beneficial enjoyment, usufructuary right, freedom;
~ des Ehemanns am eingebrachten Gut apronstring tenure.

Nutz|pfandrecht Welsh mortgage, antichresis; **~pflanze** useful plant; **~schwelle** breakeven point; **~signal** *(Computer)* information signal; **~stromkreis** *(el.)* utilizable circuit.

Nutzung use, enjoyment, exploitation, utilization, *(Einkommen)* revenue, emolument, *(Ertrag)* profit, yield, proceeds;
mit gegenwärtigem Recht auf zukünftige ~ vested in interest; **~en** profit a rendre;
alleinige ~ entire use; **eigentumsähnliche beschränkte ~** determinable freehold; **fortgesetzte bestrittene ~** continuous adverse use; **industrielle ~** industrial use; **landwirtschaftliche ~** agricultural use; **lebenslängliche ~** life interest; **ungestörte ~** quiet enjoyment; **wiederkehrende ~en** recurring returns (benefits); **wirtschaftliche ~** commercial exploitation; **zwischenzeitliche ~** mesne profit;
friedliche ~ der Atomenergie peaceful use of atomic energy; **~ und Besitz** use and occupation; **~ des Eigenbesitzers** beneficial use; **gemeinsame ~ fremder Grundstücke** profit in common; **eigentumsähnliche ~ auf Lebenszeit** determinable freehold; **jahrweise zur landwirtschaftlichen ~ verpachten** to let on an annual agricultural tenancy; **~en ziehen** to draw the profit.

Nutzungs|änderung change of use; **~anschlag** profit estimate; **~anspruch** discovery claim; **~art einer Erfindung** application of an invention; **~aufgabe** desuetude; **~ausfall** loss of use; **~befugnis** usufructuary right; **~begünstigter** cestui que use; **~berechtigter** beneficiary; **~beschränkung** restrictive (restricted) covenant.

Nutzungsdauer useful (expected, economic) life, economic use, period of usefulness (enjoyment);
abschreibungsfähige ~ depreciable asset life; **durchschnittliche ~** average life; **steuerlich festgesetzte ~** deemed tax life; **gewöhnliche ~** *(Gerätepark)* expected life; **technische ~** physical life;
~ **einer Anlage** useful asset life;
steuerliche ~ von 25 Jahren haben to have a life for tax purposes of twenty-five years.

Nutzungs|entgelt, ~entschädigung compensation for use, hire, *(Grundstück)* ground rent, *(Wohnung)* rental fee; **doppeltes ~entgelt bei Räumungsverzug** double value *(Br.)*; **~entschädigung** compensation for use; **~ertrag** revenue, yield, return; **~genossenschaft** agricultural cooperation; **~geschwindigkeit** *(Schiff)* economical speed; **~grad** degree of utility; **~güter** income-yielding assets, durable goods; **~konzession** mining licence (license, *US*); **~mangel** lack of utility; **~maximum** utility optimum; **~möglichkeit** possible use; **von den vorhandenen ~möglichkeiten zuwenig konzentrierten Gebrauch machen** to spread a thing's use too thinly; **~pfand** antichresis.

Nutzungsrecht usufructuary right, privilege, use, easement;
alleiniges (ausschließliches) ~ exclusive use; **bedingtes ~** collateral limitation; **aufschiebend bedingtes ~** executory use; **zeitlich begrenztes ~** limitation in law; **beschränktes ~** qualified covenant; **gemeinsames ~** commonage; **auflösend bedingtes lebenslängliches ~** determinable life interest; **nachrangiges ~** secondary use; **unbeschränktes ~** positive covenant; **nicht mehr vorhandenes ~** expired utility;
~ **eines Grundstücks** right to enjoyment of a property; **~ auf Lebenszeit** life interest.

Nutzungs|schaden damage through loss of use; **~unwert** expired utility; **~vergütung** compensation for use.

Nutzungswert amount of revenue, value in use, utility, useful life;
anerkannter ~ established use value; **durchschnittlicher ~** expected value; **nicht mehr vorhandener ~** expired life;
~ **des eigengenutzten Einfamilienhauses** *(Steuererklärung)* notional income, net annual value *(Br.)*; **~ eines Grundstücks** real-estate utility.

Nutzungszeit *(Maschine)* machine time.

Nutzvieh domestic cattle.

Nylonprintverfahren nylon print process.

O

Oase oasis.
Obacht attention, care;
~ **geben** to pay attention to; ~ **auf j. haben** to take care of s. o.
Obdach shelter, cover, housing, covert, *(Wohnstätte)* lodging, dwelling, housing;
jem. ein ~ anbieten to offer harbo(u)rage to s. o.; **jem. ~ gewähren** to harbo(u)r s. o., to give shelter to s. o.; **ohne ~ sein** to be without shelter.
obdachlos harbo(u)rless, unhoused, homeless, houseless, roofless, unsheltered, without shelter;
~ **machen** to unhouse; ~ **werden** to be made homeless.
Obdachlosen|asyl casual ward, pauper asylum, night shelter, hostel for drifters, common lodginghouse, doss house *(sl.)*, poorhouse; **in ein ~asyl aufnehmen** to ward; **in einem ~asyl schlafen** to doss *(sl.)*; **~einweisung** assigment to a pauper asylum; **~fürsorge** relief for homeless persons.
Obdachloser homeless person, casual [pauper, *US*], dosser *(sl.)*.
Obdachlosigkeit homelessness.
Obduktion autopsy, post-mortem examination, necropsy;
gesetzlich angeordnete ~ judicial dissection.
Obduktionsbefund post-mortem findings.
obduzieren to hold an inquest, to hold a post-mortem examination.
oben above, aloft, *(im Haus)* upstairs, at the top, *(drucktechn.)* at the top, *(in leitender Stellung)* in high quarters;
~ **erwähnt** afore said; ~ **auf der Liste** at the top of the list; ~ **ohne** topless; **auf Seite 40** ~ at the top of page 40; **bis ~ zugeknöpft** *(fig.)* standoffish; **nach ~** upward; **von ~ herab** upstage, high-handed, with a high hand, on the high ropes; **jem. von ~ herab ansehen** to look down on s. o.; **Kopf ~ behalten** to keep one's presence of mind; **j. von ~ herab behandeln** to treat s. o. haughtily; **jds. Glas bis ~ füllen** to fill s. one's glass brimful; **das Reisen bis ~ hin stehen haben** to be sated to nausea with travelling; **mit den Rädern ~ in einem Graben landen** to land wheels uppermost in a ditch; **j. von ~ bis unten mustern** to look s. o. up and down; ~ **beliebt sein** to be popular with higher quarters; **bis ~ voll sein** to be full up; ~ **auf einer Liste stehen** to be at the top of a list; **sich ~ beliebt machen wollen** to curry favo(u)r with the boss;
~ **gelegenes Zimmer** upstairs room.
obenan bleiben to remain top of the table.
obenan stehen to top a list;
ganz ~ to take first priority; **bei den Verhandlungen ~** to be at the top of the agenda at the negotiations.
obenauf sein to be on top of the world;
wieder ~ to be up again, to be one's own self again.
obendrein into the bargain, in addition, to boot.
Obenerwähnte, das premises.
obengenannt above-mentioned, aforesaid;
wie ~ as previously mentioned.
oben|gesteuerter Motor overhead-valve engine; **~hin bemerken** to say casually.
Ober head waiter.
ober *(fig.)* superior, senior, leading, chief;
~e Behörde higher authority; **~e Ecke** upper corner; **~e Etage** upper stor(e)y; **~er Flur** upstairs corridor; **~er Goldpunkt** export point; **~e Instanz** superior court; **~e Klassen** upper classes (forms); **~e Ränge** higher ranks; **~es Stockwerk** upper (top) floor, upstairs; **die ~en Zehntausend** the upper ten (four hundred, *US*), high society.
Ober|amtmann chief inspector, bailiff; **~anspruch** overriding claim; **~aufseher** chief inspector, superintendent, *(Fabrik)* overseer, *(Gefängnis)* master warden; **~aufsicht** superintendence, inspectorship, supervisory control, supervision; **~aufsicht führen** to supervise, to superintend, to be in charge; **~bau** *(Bahn)* permanent way, roadbed, *(Brücke)* superstructure, *(Straße)* surface; **~bauleiter** site manager; **~befehl** *(mil.)* supreme command; **~befehl führen** to be commander in chief; **~befehlshaber** *(mil.)* commander-in-chief; **~begriff** *(ling.)* head, generic term, *(Patentschrift)* preamble; **~bekleidung** overclothes, outerwear; **~bergamt** Board of Mines; **~bett** eiderdown, quilt, *(Etagenbett)* upper bed; **~buchhalter** chief (senior) accoutant; **ehrenamtlicher ~bürgermeister** Lord Mayor *(Br.)*; **~bürgermeisterwahl** mayoral election; **~deck** upper deck.
oberfaul very fishy, queer;
~er Kunde rotten (shady) customer.
Ober|feldwebel staff sergeant *(Br.)*; **~finanzdirektion** inland revenue office, Regional Office *(US)*; **~finanzpräsident** [etwa] Chief Inspector of Taxes *(Br.)*.
Oberflächen|behandlung surface treatment; **~beschaffenheit** *(Papier)* finish; **~gestaltung** finish, finishing; **~schaden** surface damage; **~struktur** deep structure; **~wasser** surface water.
oberflächlich superficial, external, *(fig.)* sketchy, cursory, half, skin-deep, touch-and-go;
~ **betrachtet** on the surface;
Thema nur ~ berühren to touch on a subject; **etw. ~ durchgehen** to run over s. th.; **seine Arbeit ~ erledigen** to do one's work slapdash; **Buch ~ lesen** to skim through a book; **etw. nur ~ tun** to do s. th. after a fashion;
~e Arbeit slapdash; **~e Bekanntschaft** nodding (casual) acquaintance; **~e Berechnung** rough calculation; **~er Blick** hasty glance; **~e Kenntnisse** superficial knowledge, smattering; **~er Mensch** trifler, hollow character; **~e Nachforschungen** superficial investigations; **~e Prüfung** cursory inspection; **~e Schätzung** rough estimate; **~e Untersuchung** cursory inspection.
Oberflächlichkeit superficiality, cursoriness, slapdashness.
Ober|förster head forest ranger; **~gericht** court above, superior court, court of Session *(Scot.)*; **~gerichtsvollzieher** high bailiff *(Br.)*; **~geschoß** upper stor(e)y (floor), upstairs; **~gesellschaft** parent (controlling) company; **~gewerkschaft** parent union; **~grenze** upper limit; **~gutachten** resurvey.
Oberhand upper (whip) hand, predominance;
~ **über einen Feind behalten** to prevail over an enemy; ~ **bekommen (gewinnen)** to get the upper hand, to come uppermost, to wax *(US)*; **wieder die ~ bekommen** to recover the lost advantage; ~ **über j. gewinnen** to have the wind of s. o.
Ober|haupt head, chief; **~haus** upper house (Chamber), Gilded House *(Br.)*, House of Lords *(Br.)*, Senate *(US)*; **~hoheit** supremacy, suzerainty; **staatliche ~hoheit** eminent domain; **~in** mother superior; **~ingenieur** first engineer; **~inspektor** inspector general.
oberirdisch above ground;
~e Leitung overhead line.
Ober|kellner head-waiter, maitre; **~klassen** *(Schulen)* upper forms; **~kleidung** upper clothes; **~kommando** *(mil.)* high (supreme) command, general headquarters, Horse Guards *(Br.)*; **~kommissar** High Commissioner; **mit nacktem ~körper** stripped to the waist; **~land** upland; **~landesgericht** [etwa] appellate court; **~länge** *(drucktechn.)* ascender; **~lauf** *(Fluß)* headstream; **~lehrer** senior assistant master.
Oberleitung supervision, superintendence, chief (top) management, *(Bahn)* overhead line, *(Obus)* troll(e)y wire;
unter künstlerischer ~ von under the artistic direction of;
technische ~ technical direction;
~en legen *(tel.)* to erect poles.
Ober|licht fanlight, skylight, transom; **~lichtfenster** lantern light, raised skylight; **~lotse** chief pilot; **~mietverhältnis** concurrent lease; **~postdirektion** general post office *(Br.)*; **~prima** [etwa] six form; **~realschule** secondary grammar school *(Br.)*, high school *(US)*, secondary technical school; **~rechnungshof, ~rechnungskammer** audit office, board (commissioners, *Br.*) of audit; **~revisor** chief accountant, controller *(US)*; **~schicht** top drawer, stratum, upper crust, the upper (higher) classes, *(geologisch)* top layer; **geistige ~schicht** intelligentsia; **~schiedsrichter** umpire; **~schule** upper (grammar, *Br.*, secondary, high, *US*) school; **~schüler** high-school boy *(US)*, grammar-school pupil *(Br.)*, *(pl.)* college youths *(US)*; **~schulrat** superintendent of schools *(US)*; **~schwester** head nurse; **~sekretär** principal clerk.
oberst|e Aufsichtsbehörde supreme board of control; **~es Gebot sein** to be the order of the day; **~e Gehaltsgrenze** maximum salary; **~er Gerichtshof** High Court of Justice; **~e Gewalt** supreme power; **~er Grundsatz** leading (overriding) principle; **~e Heeresleitung** general headquarters; **~es Stockwerk** top floor.
Ober|staat, souveräner suzerain; **~staatsanwalt** director of public prosecution, attorney-general; **~stadtdirektor** town clerk *(Br.)*, city manager *(US)*.
Oberste, das ~ zuunterst drehen to turn everything upside down.
Ober|steiger mine foreman, captain; **~steuereinnehmer** receiver general; **~steuermann** first mate; **~stock** upper store(y); **nicht ganz richtig im ~stübchen sein** to be a little wrong in the upper

story (scratched in the noddle, *sl.*), to have got a kink in the brain, to have a tile loose *(sl.)*; ~**studiendirektor** headmaster principal *(US)*; ~**stufe** *(Schule)* higher grade, senior classes, senior high school *(US)*; ~**vormund** acting guardian; ~**wasser haben** to be in a strong position, to have the whiphand; ~**zahlmeister** chief purser; ~**zollamt** customhouse; ~**zollaufseher** landing surveyor *(Br.)*.

Obhut care, custody, charge, hands;
in der ~ von in charge of; **in sicherer ~** in good care;
jds. ~ anvertrauen to place in s. one's custody, to commit to s. one's trust, to consign to s. one's care, to leave s. th. to s. one's charge, to commit to the charge of s. o.; **sich in jds. ~ begeben** to put o. s. under s. one's care; **Kind in jds. ~ geben** to place a child under s. one's care; **Kind in die ~ des Jugendamtes geben** to commit a child to the charge of the child welfare department; **in seine ~ nehmen** to take charge of; **j. in seine ~ nehmen** to take s. o. by the hand; **in jds. ~ sein** to be in s. one's charge.

Obhuts|pflicht duty of care; ~**verhältnis** custodial relationship.

obige Anschrift address mentioned above.

Objekt object, thing, *(zu behandelnder Gegenstand)* subject matter, *(Grundstück)* property, *(mil.)* target;
abschreibungsfähige ~e items to be written off; **begehrenswertes ~** prize catch; **beliehene ~e** mortgaged properties; **bestimmtes ~** particular object; **betriebsfremdes ~** outside asset; **bevorzugtes ~** favo(u)rite target; **zu finanzierende ~e** transactions to be financed; **gewerbliche ~e** business and industrial property; **lohnendes ~** profitable transaction;
~ unbekannter Herkunft auf dem Radarschirm unidentified object on the radar screen;
~ gemeinsam finanzieren to finance a project jointly; **dankbares ~ für Werbefeldzüge sein** to be highly promotable; **größeres ~ verkaufen** to sell a major property;
detaillierte ~beschreibung particulars of sale; ~**besteuerung** property taxation.

Objektionist *(Kunst)* objectivist.

Objektiv, lichtstarkes high-speed lens.

objektiv objective, *(neutral)* disinterested, impartial, unbiassed, detached;
~ unmöglich physically impossible;
sich in einer Sache ~ verhalten to be impartial in a matter;
~**er Bericht** unbiassed report; ~**e Gefahr** actual danger; ~**e Meinung** candid opinion; ~**er Tatbestand** material (overt) facts; ~**e Unmöglichkeit** impossibility of performance; ~**e Untersuchung** impartial investigation; ~**er Wert** exchange value.

Objektiveinstellung focus.

objektivieren to objectify.

Objektivität objectiveness, *(Neutralität)* impartiality, detachment;
für einen Historiker unabdingliche ~ detachment essential to a historian.

Oblate wafer.

obliegen, jem. *(Beweislast)* to lie with (be incumbent upon) s. o.; **jem. als Pflicht ~** to be s. one's duty; **seinem Studium ~** to devote o. s. to one's studies.

Obliegenheit duty, business, function, obediential obligation;
zu jds. ~en gehören to be s. one's duty.

Obliegenheitsverletzung nonobservance of a duty.

Obligationär debenture holder, bondholder, loan holder;
schuldscheinberechtigter ~ debenture creditor.

Obligationen bonds, [debenture] stock *(Br.)*, debentures, debenture bonds *(US)*, obligations;
mit ~ belastet bonded;
Aktien und ~ stocks and shares;
hypothekarisch abgesicherte ~ mortgage-backed (secured) bond; **von Gewinnen in ihrer Verzinsung abhängige ~** income bonds *(US)*; **aufgerufene ~** called bonds; **ausgegebene ~ und Aktien** outstanding securities; **zwecks Ausbau eines Unternehmens ausgegebene ~** development bonds *(US)*; **von mehreren Gesellschaftern ausgegebene ~** joint and several bonds; **von einem Konkursverwalter ausgegebene ~** receiver's certificates *(US)*; **noch nicht ausgegebene ~** unissued debentures; **an Stelle von Zinsen ausgegebene ~** interest (income) bonds; **in Stücken ausgegebene ~** denominational bonds; **zur Verbesserung öffentlicher Anlagen ausgegebene ~** improvement bonds *(US)*; **ausgeloste ~** called (drawn) bonds; **mit Dividendenberechtigung ausgestattete ~** dividend bonds *(US)*; **mit attraktiven Steuervorteilen ausgestattete ~** bonds with attractive tax feature; **ausländische ~** foreign bonds; **auslosbare ~** redeemable bonds, bonds callable by lot; **auswechselbare ~** interchangeable bonds; **nicht mehr bediente ~** defaulted bonds *(US)*; **begebene ~** outstanding bonds; **am Sanierungsverfahren nicht beteiligte ~** nonassented bonds; **bevorrechtigte ~** preferred bonds; **eigene ~** own bonds; **endgültige ~** definitive bonds; **erstrangige ~** first debentures; **ertragssteuerfreie ~** tax-exempt (-free) bonds; **fällige ~** *(Bilanz)* bonds payable; **noch nicht fällige ~** outstanding securities; **festverzinsliche ~** fixed-interest bonds, active bonds *(Br.)*, debenture bonds *(US)*; **garantierte ~** guaranteed bonds (debentures); **durch die Muttergesellschaft garantierte ~** indorsed bonds; **überdurchschnittlich gehandelte ~** active bonds *(US)*; **dinglich gesicherte ~** debentures secured by a charge; **durch Effektenlombard gesicherte ~** collateral trust bonds; **erstrangig gesicherte ~** first-lien (senior-lien) bonds; **grundpfandmäßig (hypothekarisch) gesicherte ~** heritable bond *(Scot.)*, secured debentures, debenture stock *(Br.)*; **durch nachrangige Hypothek gesicherte ~** junior-lien bonds; **hypothekarisch nicht gesicherte ~** simple bonds (debentures); **durch besondere Vertragsbestimmungen gesicherte ~** stamped bonds *(US)*; **durch Vorranghypothek gesicherte ~** prior-lien (underlying, *US*) bonds; **getilgte ~** cancelled bonds; **gewinnberechtigte ~** profit-sharing bonds, participating bonds (debentures); **gezogene ~** drawn bonds; **gleichartige ~** similar bonds; **beim Treuhänder hinterlegte ~** escrow bonds; **hochverzinsliche ~** high-yield bonds; **indexgekoppelte ~** index-linked bonds; **kleingestückelte ~** fractional debentures, saving bonds *(US)*, baby bonds *(US)*; **kommunale ~** local government bonds *(Br.)*, municipal bonds *(US)*; **konvertierbare ~** convertible debentures; **jederzeit kündbare ~** callable (redeemable, optional, *US*) bonds, redeemable debentures; **nach festgelegten Terminen kündbare ~** indeterminate bonds *(US)*; **kurzfristige ~** short[-term] bonds (debentures); **langfristige ~** long[-term] bonds (debentures); **auf Dollar lautende ~** bonds denominated in dollars; **auf den Inhaber lautende ~** bearer (coupon, *US*) bonds, bonds to bearer, bearer debentures; **auf den Namen lautende ~** registered debentures (bonds, *Br.*); **mündelsichere ~** legal bonds *(US)*, trustee bonds *(Br.)*, gilt-edged stock *(Br.)*; **neue ~** new issue; **neufundierte ~** redemption bonds; **erststellig abgesicherte neufundierte ~** refunding first mortgage bonds *(US)*; **notleidende ~** defaulted bonds; **öffentlich-rechtliche ~** public bonds, bonds of state (public) corporations; **pfandgesicherte ~** secured bonds (debentures); **prolongierte ~** continued (extended, *US*, renewal) bonds; **zur Tilgung rückgekaufte ~** bonds purchased for cancellation; **rückkaufbare ~** redeemable debentures; **in Teilzahlungen rückzahlbare ~** instal(l)ment bonds *(US)*; **steuerfreie ~** tax-free (-exempt) bonds, tax-free obligations; **tilgbare ~** callable (redeemable) bonds; **nicht tilgbare ~** irredeemable debentures *(Br.)*; **nicht übertragbare ~** registered debentures (bonds, *Br.*); **uneingelöste ~** unpaid bonds; **ungesicherte ~** unsecured (naked) debentures; **ungetilgte ~** outstanding securities; **ungültige ~** disabled bonds *(Br.)*; **unkündbare ~** irredeemable bonds, irredeemable *(Br.)* (perpetual) debentures; **in Serien unterteilte ~** serial bonds; **unverzinsliche ~** noninterest-bearing bonds; **frei verfügbare ~** free bonds; **durch Wechsel verstärkte ~** endorsed bonds; **fest verzinsliche ~** fixed-interest bearing bonds; **vorläufige ~** temporary bonds; **in Währungen verschiedener Länder zahlbare ~** multiple-currency bonds *(US)*; **in gesetzlichen Zahlungsmitteln zahlbare ~** legal-tender bonds; **nur bei Gewinnerträgnissen zinspflichtige ~** adjustment bonds; **zinstragende ~** interest-bearing bonds; **zwecks Tilgung zurückgekaufte ~** bonds purchased for cancellation; **zurückgenommene ~** redeemed bonds; **in Raten zurückzahlbare ~** instalment bonds *(US)*; **zweitrangige ~** second debentures;
~ einer Aktiengesellschaft corporation bonds; **~, deren Besitzer einer Sanierung des Unternehmens nicht zustimmen** nonassented bonds; **~ einer Gebietskörperschaft** territorial bonds; **~ ausländischer Gesellschaften** foreign corporate bonds *(US)*; **~ mit zusätzlichem Gewinnbeteiligungsrecht** participating bonds (debentures); **~ der öffentlichen Hand** public stocks; **~ eines Immobilienfonds** real-estate bonds; **~, deren Kapitalbetrag und Zinsen in Währungen verschiedener Länder zahlbar sind** multiple-currency bonds *(US)*; **~ mit Kapital- und Dividendengarantie** guaranteed bonds *(US)*; **~ mit abgetrennten, noch nicht fälligen Kupons** ragged bonds *(US)*; **~ mit kurzer Laufzeit** short-term bonds (debentures); **~ mit langer Laufzeit** long-term bonds (debentures); **~ mit erst nach einer gewissen Laufzeit festgesetztem Rückzahlungstermin** indeterminate bonds *(US)*; **~ mit variabler Rendite** variable yield debentures; **~ in Stückelungen bis 500 Dollar** fractional debentures, small (savings) bonds *(US)*; **~ in Stückelungen zu mehr als 1000 Dollar** large bonds; **~ mit Tilgungsplan** sinking-fund bonds; ~

ohne Tilgungsraten irredeemable bonds (debentures); ~ öffentlicher Versorgungsbetriebe public-utility bonds; ~ mit aufgeschobener (allmählich ansteigender) Verzinsung noninterest-bearing discount (deferred, *Br.*) bonds; ~ mit gleichbleibender Verzinsung continued bonds *(US)*; ~ kommunaler Wasserwerke water bonds; ~ mit Wechselkursfreigabe floating-rate bonds; ~ mit gestaffeltem Zinssatz graduated interest debentures; ~ mit Zinsschein coupon bonds;
~ abrufen to call bonds; ~ ausgeben to issue bonds; ~ auslosen to draw bonds; ~ in großen Mengen auf den Markt bringen to put obligations on the market in large blocks; ~ einlösen to pay off (redeem) bonds; ~ auf den Namen eintragen to register bonds (debentures); ~ neu emittieren to reissue debentures; ~ kündigen to call in bonds; ~ tilgen to redeem bonds (debentures); ~ unterbringen to place bonds; ~ mit zweijähriger Laufzeit und einer 11%igen Rendite verkaufen to sell two-year bonds on yield of 11%;
~agio bond premium; ~anleihe loan on debentures, debenture loan; ~buch bond register (book); ~handel bond trading; ~kapital debenture capital; ~kündigung bond retirement; ~recht law of contract; ~schulden *(Bilanz)* bonded debts (indebtedness), bonds payable *(US)*; ~schuldner bond debtor, obligor *(US)*; ~tilgung redemption of bonds (debentures).

Obligations|anleihe debenture loan; ~ausgabe bond (debenture) issue, issue of debentures; ~besitz bondholdings; ~gläubiger bondholder, debenture holder, bond (debenture) creditor, obligee *(US)*; ~inhaber bondholder, debenture holder; ~markt bond market; ~schuld debenture (bonded, fixed) debt; ~schuldner bond debtor, obligor *(US)*; durch nachstehende Hypothek gesicherte ~serie junior issue; ~zinsen interest upon bonds, bond (debenture) interest *(US)*; ~zinsschein bond coupon.

obligatorisch obligatory, mandatory, personal, *(zwangsweise)* compulsory;
nicht ~ nonobligatory;
~ sein *(Teilnahme)* to be compulsory;
~er Anspruch chose in action, obligatory right; ~e Bestimmung compulsory clause, mandatory clause (provision) *(US)*; ~er Charakter eines Vertrages obligatory scope of a contract; ~e Klage personal action; ~e Meldepflicht obligatory registration; ~es Pensionsalter mandatory retiring age; ~e Richtlinien festsetzen to issue binding guidelines; ~e Versicherung compulsory insurance; ~er Vertrag consensual contract.

Obligo liability, engagement, commitment;
ohne ~ without prejudice (engagement), *(Wechsel)* without recourse; unter dem ~ früherer Zusagen committed by earlier promises;
~buch acceptance ledger (register), discount ledger; ~liste list of commitments; ~verzicht disclaimer of responsibility.

Obmann chairman, *(Betrieb)* shop steward, *(Geschworene)* foreman, *(Schiedsgericht)* umpire, *(Sprecher)* spokesman.

Obolus mite, contribution;
seinen ~ entrichten to give one's mite.

Obrigkeit government, magistracy, the authorities, powers that be.

obrigkeitlich magisterial, governmental, authoritarian, by high authority;
~e Verordnung decree issued by the authorities.

obrigkeitshörig subservient to authority.

Obrigkeitsstaat authoritarian state.

Observatorium observatory.

obsiegen to carry the day, to succeed;
in einem Prozeß ~ to win a lawsuit.

obsiegend victorious;
~e Partei successful party; ~es Urteil favo(u)rable decision (judgment).

obskur obscure, suspicious, doubtful, *(anrüchig)* notorious, disreputable;
~ klingen to sound ambiguous;
~e Angelegenheit fishy business; ~e Bedeutung *(Text)* obscure meaning; ~e Bekanntschaft discreditable acquaintance; ~e Forderungen doubtful accounts; ~e Geldquelle secret source of money; ~e Geschäftsmethoden improper practices; ~er Herkunft sein to be of obscure origin; ~e Kneipe disreputable bar; ~e Methoden dubious methods; ~e Umstände suspicious circumstances.

Obsorge, mangelnde ~ für die Erhaltung permissive waste.

Obst, ausländisches foreign-grown fruit; eingemachtes ~ preserved fruit;
~bau fruit growing; ~bauer fruit farmer; ~baum fruit tree; tragender ~baum fruiter; ~baumschule fruit-tree nursery; ~ernte fruit-time; ~farm, ~gut fruit ranch *(US)*; ~garten fruit garden, orchard; ~garten anlegen to plant land with fruit trees; ~glas fruit jar; ~handel fruit trade; ~händler fruit dealer (peddler); ~- und Gemüsehändler greengrocer; ~- und Gemüsehandlung greengrocery; ~konserve preserved (tinned, *Br.*) fruit; ~kultur fruit culture; ~kur machen to be on a fruit diet; ~pflücker fruit picker; ~plantage fruit farm.

Obstruktion obstruction[ism], ca'canny policy, *(parl.)* bloc, filibustering *(US)*, stonewalling *(Australia)*;
~ betreiben to practise obstruction, to obstruct, to ca'canny, *(parl.)* to block, to filibuster *(US)*, to stonewall *(Australia)*.

Obstruktions|antrag guillotine motion *(Br.)*; ~methoden obstructive tactics (measures); ~politik obstructionism, policy of obstruction, guillotine *(Br.)*, filibuster *(US)*, stonewalling *(Australia)*; ~politik betreiben to adopt a ca'canny policy, to stonewall *(Australia)*, to practise obstruction, to filibuster *(US)*; ~politiker obstructionist, obstructive, filibuster *(US)*, stonewaller *(Australia)*; ~taktik obstructionist tactics, guillotine *(Br.)*; ~verzögerung vexatious delay.

Obst|saft fruit juice; ~salat fruit salad; ~schwemme glut of fruit; ~stand fruit stand (stall); ~verkäufer fruit vendor; ~verwertungsbetrieb fruit-processing plant; ~waggon fruit car.

obszön obscene, pornographic, unclean, indecent, curious;
~e Geschichte smutty story; ~e Handlungen vile acts and gestures; ~e Reden filth; ~e Reden führen to talk obscenely; ~er Roman wanton novel; ~es Wort four-letter word; ~e Wörter foul words.

Obszönität obscenity;
~en sagen to talk obscenely.

Obus trolley car, trackless trolley;
~linie trolley line.

obwaltende Umstände prevailing circumstances.

Ochse ox, bullock, steer, *(Dummkopf)* donkey, blockhead, duffer;
bekannt wie ein bunter ~ sein to be known all over the place; ~n hinter den Pflug spannen to put the cart before the horse; wie der ~ am Berge stehen to be brought to a nonplus; wie der ~ zum Seiltanzen taugen to be good for nothing;
Du sollst dem ~n, der da drischt, nicht das Maul verbinden thou shalt not muzzle the ox when he treadeth out the corn.

ochsen *(fam.)* to cram, to dig away *(coll.)*, to swot, to stew *(sl.)*, to bone up *(US)*, to sap *(Br., sl.)*;
für ein Examen ~ to mug up for an examination *(Br.)*.

Öde, Ödland wasteland, wild desert.

öde waste, desolate, solitary, barren, *(unfruchtbar)* barren, waste, bleak;
~s Alltagsleben monotonous jogtrot of life; ~ Büroarbeit drab business routine; ~s Land bleak (barren) country; ~ und verlassene Stadt completely deserted town.

Odium odium, stigma;
dem ~ der Feigheit ausgesetzt sein to be exposed to the odium of cowardice.

Ofen stove, oven, furnace, kiln;
elektrischer ~ electric heater; sparsamer ~ fuel-saving stove; ~ mit Ölfeuerung oil burner (heater), oil-fired furnace;
~ beschicken to charge the furnace; Ziegel im ~ brennen to bake bricks in a kiln; Kohlen auf den ~ schütten to put coal on the fire;
jetzt ist aber der ~ aus! that's the last straw!;
~kachel oven tile; ~schlacke cinder, clinker, slag, dross.

offen open, unclosed, unshut, unlocked, overt, *(Ausschreibung)* unlimited, *(Auto)* opentop, *(nicht chiffriert)* uncoded, *(eisfrei)* open, clear, unblocked, *(geradezu)* outspoken, frank, downright, transparent, on the level *(coll.)*, up-and-down *(US coll.)*, flatfooted *(US sl.)*, *(nicht geregelt)* unsettled, outstanding, undecided, *(öffentlich)* public, *(sichtbar)* apparent, visible, *(Stelle)* vacant, running, *(Straße)* clear, *(nicht versiegelt)* unsealed;
~ und ehrlich fair and square; völlig ~ straight out; völlig ~ antworten to answer point-blank; seine Ansichten ~ äußern to speak one's mind; sich ~ zu einer Verpflichtung bekennen to make an open-ended commitment; Laden ~ halten to keep a shop open; ~ lassen to leave in abeyance; ~ zutage liegen to be obvious; ~ reden to speak candidly, to be outspoken; ~ sein *(Haus)* to be open; um ganz ~ zu sein to be perfectly candid; ~ stehen to stand open; Milch ~ verkaufen to sell unbottled milk; Wein ~ verkaufen to sell wine on draught; seinen Schmerz ganz ~ zeigen to make a great display of sorrow; seine Schuld ~ zugeben to admit one's guilt freely;
~e Absage point-blank refusal; ~e Antwort straight answer *(US)*; j. mit ~en Armen aufnehmen to receive s. o. open-armed;

mit ~en Augen ins Unglück rennen to be asking for trouble; **mit ~en Augen schlafen** to sleep with one's eyes open; **~e Aussprache mit jem. haben** to be quite frank with s. o.; **~e Bauweise** detached building; **~er Bestand** *(Abschreibungsmethode)* open-end account; **~er Brief** open letter; **in jem. wie in einem ~en Buch lesen** to read s. o. like an open book; **~es Depot** safe custody *(Br.)* (custodianship, *US*) account; **~er Dissens** patent ambiguity; **~es Fahrwasser** open fairway; **~e Feindseligkeit** overt hostility; **~e Feldschlacht** pitched battle; **~e Flanke** *(mil.)* exposed flank; **~er Funkspruch** radio message in clear; **~es Geheimnis** open (nobody's) secret; **~es Giro** blank indorsement (endorsement); **~er Güterwagen** platform carriage (car, *US*), flat (gondola) car *(US)*, goods truck *(Br.)*, lorry *(Br.)*; **~e Hand haben** to have an open hand, to give openhandedly.

Offene Handelsgesellschaft general (ordinary, *US*) partnership.

offen|es Haus haben to keep open house; **~er Himmel** *(Völkerrecht)* open skies; **~es Karree** hollow square; **mit ~en Karten spielen** to put all one's cards on the table; **~er und ehrlicher Kerl** honest fellow; **~er Kredit** open (blank, personal) credit; **~e Kreditlinie** unused credit line *(US)* (limit, *Br.*); **~er Laden** open shop; **Betreten mit ~em Licht verboten!** *(Tafel)* no naked lights!; **~er Markt** open (overt) market; **~e Police** floating (open, *Br.*, unvalued, *US*) policy; **~er Posten** unpaid item, uncovered amount; **~e-Posten-Buchführung** open-item system; **~e Rechnung** current (running) account, *(nicht bezahlt)* unsettled account; **~e Reede** open roadstead; **~e Reserven** declared (open) reserve; **~er Scheck** open cheque *(Br.)*; **~es Schuldeingeständnis** frank confession of one's guilt; **auf ~er See** in the open sea, in mid-ocean; **~e See gewinnen** to gain the open sea; **~e Sozialfürsorgestelle** relief center *(US)* (centre, *Br.*); **~e Stadt** *(mil.)* open (undefended) town; **zur ~en Stadt erklären** to declare an open city; **~e Stelle** vacancy, vacant post (situation), *(Lücke)* gap; **auf ~er Strecke** on the open road; **~er Stromkreis** open circuit; **Politik der ~en Tür betreiben** to pursue an open-door policy, *(international)* to open a door to agreements of international affairs; **~e Türen einrennen** to force an open door, to flog a dead horse; **~er Umschlag** unsealed envelope; **~e Verbindlichkeiten** outstanding debts; **~e Verkaufsstellen** retail establishments; **mit ~em Visier kämpfen** to be quite straightforward with it; **~ ausgelegte Ware** open display; **~er Wechsel** blank bill; **~er Wein** wine from the cask, draught wine; **in einer ~en Wunde herumwühlen** to keep rubbing it in; **~es Zahlungsziel** open terms; **~e Zession** absolute assignment, assignment of account.

offenbar bare, apparent, obvious, plain, overt, manifest, evident;
~ ohne Mängel fair on its face;
~ werden to become known;
~e Besserung evident improvement; **~er Irrtum** obvious mistake; **~e Mängel** apparent defects.

offenbaren to disclose, to discover, to manifest, to divulge, to unfold, to reveal;
sich jem. ~ to unbosom o. s. to s. o.; **Erfindung ~** to disclose an invention; **Geheimnis ~** to disclose a secret; **seine Vermögensverhältnisse ~** *(Konkurs)* to disclose one's assets; **seine Zukunftspläne ~** to unfold one's plans for the future.

Offenbarung disclosure, manifestation, revelation;
~ einer Erfindung disclosure of an invention; **unbefugte ~ fremder Geheimnisse** disclosure of secrets; **~ seiner Vermögensverhältnisse** discovery of one's assets.

Offenbarungs|eid poor debtor's oath, affidavit of means, oath of disclosure (manifestations, *US*); **~eid leisten** to swear a poor debtor's oath; **~eidverfahren** supplementary proceedings *(US)*; **~erklärung des Vollstreckungsschuldners** equitable garnishment; **~pflicht** duty to disclose, duty of disclosure, discovery of documents; **~pflicht in Sonderfällen** special facts rule.

offengelegt disclosed.

Offenhalten am Sonntag Sunday opening.

offenhalten to reserve, to leave open;
sich einen Ausweg ~ to leave o. s. a way out; **sich ein Hintertürchen ~** to leave a loophole for escape; **Laden ~** to keep a shop open; **sich eine Möglichkeit ~** to reserve a possibility; **auch nachts ~** to stay open during the night; **sich den Rücken ~** *(mil.)* to leave the getaway route clear; **Tür zu weiteren Verhandlungen ~** to keep (leave) the door open for further negotiations.

Offenheit sincerity, cando(u)r, unreserve, plain speaking;
schon bald an Beleidigung grenzende ~ frankness to the point of insult;
in aller ~ reden to speak with complete frankness.

offenherzig free- (open-) hearted, candid, frank;
zu ~ sein to wear one's heart upon one's sleeve.

Offenherzigkeit open-heartedness, cando(u)r, frankness;
in einem Anflug von ~ in an open-hearted moment.

offenkundig manifest, public, evident, overt, professed, patent, notorious, obvious;
~er Betrüger notorious swindler; **~e Mißwirtschaft** obvious mismanagement; **~e Tatsache** established (obvious) fact; **~e Ungerechtigkeit** manifest injustice; **~es Zeichen seines Mißfallens** clear indication of one's disapproval.

Offenkundigkeit notoriety, obviousness, evidence;
~ eines Skandals publicity of a scandal.

offenlassen to leave open (undecided);
Frage ~ to leave a question undecided; **Punkt noch ~** to leave open for further discussions; **Tür für weitere Verhandlungen ~** to leave the door open for further negotiations.

offenlegen to lay bare (open), to disclose, to reveal;
Fehler ~ to reveal a defect; **vertrauliche Geschäftsabschlüsse ~** to disclose secret transactions; **Kontostand ~** to divulge the state of an account; **Leitung ~** to expose a cable; **alle rechtserheblichen Tatsachen ~** to disclose all material facts; **Urkunden ~** to disclose documents.

Offenlegung discovery, *(in Fußnoten oder im Revisionsbericht)* disclosure;
fehlende (mangelnde) ~ failure to disclose, nondisclosure;
~ des Auftraggebers declaration of principal, *(Börse)* give-up; **~ finanzieller Beteiligungen** public declaration of financial interests; **~ einer Erfindung** *(Patentrecht)* disclosure of an invention; **~ seiner Informationsquelle** identification of source, disclosure of information; **~ des Schuldnervermögens** *(in Konkurs)* discovery of property; **~ aller rechtserheblichen Tatsachen** disclosure of all material facts; **~ durch den Versicherungsvertreter** disclosure by agent.

Offenlegungsbestimmungen rules of disclosure, disclosure provisions.

Offenlegungspflicht duty to disclose (of disclosure);
obligatorische ~ mandatory disclosure; **gesetzlich vorgeschriebene ~** compulsory disclosure, compulsion for disclosure, duty to disclose;
~en für Banken bank disclosure;
nicht der ~ unterliegen to be privileged from disclosure.

Offenlegungsschwelle disclosure threshold.

offenliegen to lie on the desk.

Offenmarkt open market;
~ausschuß open-market committee *(US)*; **~geschäfte** open-market operations (transactions); **~kredit** open-market loan; **~politik** *(Notenbank)* open-market policy; **~sätze** open-market rates; **~verkäufe** open-market sales.

offensichtlich manifest, apparent, obvious, self-evident, undisguised, open, palpable;
~ nicht kommen to be evidently not coming;
~e Besserung marked improvement; **~e Bestürzung** obvious dismay; **~er Fehler** apparent vice (error); **~e Lüge** loud lie; **~e Notwehrlage** apparent necessity; **~e Schwierigkeiten** visible difficulties; **~es Versagen der Regierung** manifest failure of the government; **~er Vorteil** obvious (patent) advantage.

Offensichtliche, das ~ erkennen to see through a ladder.

offensiv offensive, aggressive, attacking;
~ werden to become offensive;
~e Kriegsführung offensive warfare.

Offensivbündnis offensive alliance.

Offensive *(mil.)* offensive;
kraftvolle ~ *(mil.)* drive;
~ abwürgen to throttle an offensive; **~ ergreifen** to push forward to the attack; **~ starten** to mount (launch) an offensive.

Offensivkrieg war of offence, offensive war.

offenstehen to stand open;
jem. ~ to be up to s. o.; **in den Büchern noch ~** to be outstanding in the books; **noch ~** *(Rechnung)* to remain unpaid, to be outstanding (still unsettled), to be owing.

offenstehend *(Rechnung)* owing, open, unliquidated, unsettled, outstanding;
~es Konto unsettled account.

öffentlich public, in public, open, popular, to the view;
nicht ~ private, close, exclusive, intramural, intra muros, *(Gerichtssitzung)* in camera (chambers), *(Sitzung)* in closed session;
~ beglaubigt certified, notarized, legalized; **~ herausgestellt** highly publicized; **~ verhandelt** tried in open court;
~ anschlagen to post, to placard; **~ ausschreiben** to advertise;

Stelle ~ **ausschreiben** to advertise a post; ~ **beglaubigen** to certify, to notarize, to legalize; ~ **bekanntgeben** to announce publicly, to announce (make known) to the public, to publicize, *(amtlich)* to promulgate, to proclaim; **seine Pläne ~ bekanntgeben** to come out into the open with one's plans; ~ **bekanntmachen** to publicize, to announce publicly, to make known to the public; **Gesetz ~ bekanntmachen** to promulgate a law; ~ **Stellung nehmen** to make a public statement; ~ **sein** *(Handelsregister)* to be available for inspection; ~ **bekannt sein** to be a matter of common knowledge (known to the public); ~ **versteigern** to sell at (by, put up for) auction;
~**e Abgaben** rates and taxes; ~**es Amt** public appointment; ~**es Amt bekleiden** to hold a public office (official situation); ~**es Angebot** offer to the public; ~**e Angelegenheiten** matters of public concern, state affairs; ~**e Anhörung** public hearing; ~**e Ankündigung** public announcement, proclamation; ~**e Anlagen** public parks (gardens); ~**e Anleihe** public (government[al]) loan; ~**e Ansprache** public speaking; ~**e Anstalt** public institution; ~**e Arbeiten** public works; ~**es Ärgernis** public (common) nuisance; ~**es Ärgernis erregen** to offend public decency; ~**e Ausschreibung** public invitation to tender, bid invitation *(US)*; ~**er Bausektor** public sector building; ~**er Bedarf** public requirements; ~**es Bedürfnis** public convenience (necessity, want); ~**e Bedürfnisanstalt** public lavatory (convenience, *Br.*), comfort station *(US)*; **der ~en Beglaubigung bedürfen** to have to be legalized; ~**e Bekanntmachung** public notice (announcement), publication, proclamation; ~**e Belange** public policy; **sich ~en Belangen widmen** to enter public life; **Verkehrsweg zur ~en Benutzung freigeben** to open (dedicate, *US*) a highway; ~**er Bereich** public sector; ~**er Betrieb** public undertaking; ~**e Bibliothek** public library; ~**er Bücherrevisor** professional (public) auditor, chartered *(Br.)* (certified public, *US*) accountant; ~**er Dienst** civil (public, *US*) service, public employment; ~**e Dienststelle** public office; ~**er Durchgang** public thoroughfare; ~**es Eigentum** public property; **im ~en Eigentum stehen** to be owned publicly; ~**e Einrichtungen** public facilities (institutions, accommodations); ~**e Erklärung** public statement; ~**er Feiertag** public (legal, bank, *Br.*) holiday; ~**e Fernsprechzelle** telephone booth, public call box; ~**e Finanzen** public finances; ~**e Fürsorge** national *(Br.)* (public, social, *US*) assistance, public relief; ~**es Gebäude** public building; ~**e Gelder** public funds *(Br.)* (money); ~**e Gelder bestimmungsgemäß** used to use public money only for public purposes; **Maßnahmen zum Schutz der ~en Gesundheit treffen** to protect public health; ~**e Gesundheitspflege** public health [service]; ~**e Hand** public authorities, mortmain; **im Bereich der ~en Hand** in the public sector; ~**es Haus** house of ill repute, brothel; ~**e Hinterlegungsstelle** public trustee office *(Br.)*, legal custodian; ~**es Interesse** public policy (interest); **dem ~en Interesse dienen** to lie in the public interest; ~**e Körperschaft** public corporation; ~**es Krankenhaus** public hospital; ~**er Kredit** public loan; ~**e Lasten** public charges; ~**es Leben** public life; **ins ~e Leben eintreten** to enter public life; **im Brennpunkt des ~en Lebens stehen** to be very much in the public eye; ~**e Meinung** public opinion; ~**e Meinung beeinflussen** to influence public opinion; **sich die ~e Meinung dienstbar machen** to exploit public opinion; ~**e Meinungspflege** public relations; ~**e Mittel** public funds (means); ~**e Ordnung** public order; **gegen die ~e Ordnung verstoßen** to break the peace, to violate law and order; ~**er Parkplatz** public parking place; ~**er Platz** public place (square); ~**es Rechnungswesen** public accounts; ~**es Recht** public law; ~**es Register** public book; ~**e Ruhe und Ordnung** peace and quietude; ~**e Ruhe und Sicherheit** peace of the state, public peace and quiet; ~**e Schuld** public debt; ~**e Schulen** state (public, *US*) schools; ~**es Schulwesen** public education; ~**er Sektor der Wirtschaft** public sector of the economy; **Gefahr für die ~e Sicherheit darstellen** to be dangerous to the public; ~**e Sitzung** open session; **in ~er Sitzung** *(Gericht)* in open court; ~**er Sozialaufwand** public spending on the social services; ~**er Speicher** public warehouse *(US)*; ~**e Sprechstelle** telephone (call, *Br.*) box; ~**e Stelle** public authority; ~**es Transportunternehmen** common carrier; ~**er Umzug** public procession; ~**e Untersuchung** public enquiry; ~**e Urkunde** public (legal) document; ~**e Verhandlung** hearing in open court, public trial; **für den ~en Verkehr freigeben** open to traffic; ~**es Verkehrsmittel** public vehicle (transport, transportation, *US*); ~**es Verkehrsunternehmen** public transport undertaking; ~**es Verkehrswesen** public transport (transportation, *US*); ~**e Verlautbarung** public announcement; ~**e Versammlung** open (public) meeting; ~**er Versorgungsbetrieb** public utility [undertaking]; ~**es Versorgungsunternehmen** public supply undertaking; ~**e Versteigerung** public auction (outcry), open sale; ~**e Verwaltung** public administration; ~**e Vorlesung** open lecture; ~**es Vorratslager** public store; ~**er Wasserweg** public river; ~**er Weg** public way; ~**es Wohl** public welfare; ~**e Wohlfahrt** public charity; ~ **geförderter sozialer Wohnungsbau** federal financed low-cost housing *(US)*, council housing *(Br.)*; ~**e Zustellung** service by publication *(US)*, substituted service *(Br.)*.

öffentlich-rechtlich under public law;
~**e Anstalt** public institution, body corporate; **in eine ~e Gesellschaft umwandeln** to go public; ~**e Grunddienstbarkeit** public easement; ~**es Handelsunternehmen** public trading body; ~**e Körperschaft** public corporation, body corporate; ~**es Kreditinstitut** public-owned credit institution; ~**e Stiftung** public trust; ~**e Urkunde** public document.

Öffentlichkeit public, publicity, community, country;
außerhalb des Blickfelds der ~ off camera; **der ~ zugänglich** open to the public; **für die ~ geeignet** publishable; **im Lichte der ~** in the limelight; **in aller ~** openly, in public, on parade; **nicht für die ~ bestimmt** private, off the record; **ohne die ~ zu befragen** without public participation; **unter Ausschuß der ~** closed court, in camera (chambers), behind closed doors; **von der ~ gefordert** publicly demanded;
breitere (die breite) ~ the general public, public at large, the street, the open;
der ~ anpreisen to sell the public on s. th.; **Nachrichten für die ~ aufmachen** to edit news for the public, to angle (slant) news; **großangelegte Kampagne in der ~ aufziehen** to conduct a wide publicity campaign; **positive Reaktionen in der ~ auslösen** to create favo(u)rable publicity; ~ **ausschließen** *(Gericht)* to order the case (a trial) to be heard in closed session (in camera), to exclude the general public, to hear a case in chambers; **an (vor) die ~ bringen** to air, to bring (set) before the public, to publicize; **in die ~ dringen** to reach the public, to leak out; **günstige Aufnahme in der ~ erzielen (finden)** to create a favo(u)rable public opinion; **der ~ zur Last fallen** to become a charge on the public; **in der ~ Anklang finden** to catch the public imagination; **die ~ hinter sich haben** to carry public opinion with o. s.; ~ **hintergehen** to practise deception on the public; ~ **für etw. interessieren** to enlist public interest in a matter; **an die ~ kommen** to become generally known; **nicht an die ~ kommen lassen** to stash; **sich in der ~ sehen lassen** to show o. s. in public; **einem Roman breiteste Aufmerksamkeit in der ~ zukommen lassen** to give a novel wide publicity; ~ **auf etw. lenken** to bring a question before the public; **nicht für die ~ bestimmte Bemerkungen machen** to speak off the record; **in der ~ von sich reden machen** to be in the news (limelight); **etw. der ~ zugänglich machen** to let daylight into s. th., to dedicate *(US)*, to dispark; **Straße der ~ zugänglich machen** to open a road for traffic, to dedicate a highway *(US coll.)*; ~ **meiden** to shun publicity; **in den Blickpunkt der ~ rücken** to spotlight *(fam.)*; **der ~ bekannt sein** to be a matter of common knowledge; **im Brennpunkt der ~ stehen** to be in the public eye (limelight); **sein ganzes Leben im Scheinwerferlicht der ~ stehen** to live one's life in the full blaze of publicity; **der ~ zwangsweise zur Verfügung stellen** *(Patent)* to open to the public *(US)*; **unter Ausschluß der ~ tagen** *(Gericht)* to sit in closed session (camera, chambers); **den Wünschen der ~ Rechnung tragen** to please the public; **an (vor) die ~ treten** to come forward, to appear in public (publicly), to make a public appearance; **mit einem Plan an die ~ treten** to launch an idea; **in der ~ viel in Erscheinung treten** to be large in the public eye; **der ~ übergeben** to bring before the public, to publicize; **sich vor der ~ verbergen** to keep from the public; **unter Ausschluß der ~ verhandeln** to sit in chambers (closed session); **von der ~ nicht positiv aufgenommen werden** to offer resistance in the public; **in der ~ zunehmend positiv aufgenommen werden** to be rising in the estimation of the public; **in der ~ bekannt werden** to enter public life; **es darauf anlegen, in der ~ bemerkt zu werden** to like to be very much in evidence; **in der ~ notiert werden** to be in the news; **in der ~ unbeliebt werden** to fall from public favo(u)r; ~ **wiederherstellen** *(Gericht)* to restore publicity; **sich von (vor) der ~ zurückziehen** to withdraw one's tent.

Öffentlichkeitsarbeit public relations work, publicity;
gewerbliche ~ industrial information.

Öffentlichkeitsbeziehungen public relations.

offerieren to [make an] offer, to offer for sale, to make (put in, send in, submit) a tender, to tender, to bid *(US)*;
fest ~ to offer firm; **unverbindlich ~** to offer without commitment.

Offerte bid, offer, tender;
freibleibende ~ open (flat, *US*) offer, offer without commitment; **gültige** ~ valid offer; **unverbindliche** ~ open (flat, *US*) offer, offer without commitment; **verbindliche** ~ binding (firm) offer; **versteckte** ~ *(Anzeige)* hidden offer;
~ **abgeben** to [make an] offer, to tender, to bid *(US)*; **zur Angabe von ~n auffordern** to invite tenders; **~n unterbreiten** to submit tenders (offers).
Offertenbeurteilung bids evaluation.
Offizialverteidiger assigned counsel, public defender *(US)*;
~ **bestellen** to assign a counsel.
offiziell official, officiary;
~ **ankündigen** to announce publicly, to proclaim; **sich** ~ **entschuldigen** to make a formal apology; ~ **handeln** to act in one's official capacity; ~ **notiert werden** *(Börsenwerte)* to be quoted (listed, *US*) on the stock exchange; ~ **tätig werden (sein)** to act in one's official capacity; **nicht** ~ **zusammentreten** to meet informally;
~er Besuch formal call; **~e Bezeichnung** official nomenclature; **~e Biographie** authorized biography; **~er Charakter** official character; **~en Charakter haben** to be of an official nature; **~en Empfang geben** to give an official reception; **~e Erklärung abgeben** to make an official statement; **~es Essen** official dinner; **~e Kreise** official circles; **~e Notierung** *(Börse)* official quotation, listing *(US)*; **~es Organ** bulletin, gazette; **~e Rede** oration; **~e Verlautbarung** official statement, bulletin.
Offizier [commissioned] officer;
aktiver ~ serving officer, officer on the active list; **diensthabender** ~ orderly officer; **auf einem Überwasserfahrzeug diensttuender** ~ surface officer; **erster** ~ *(Handelsmarine)* mate; **zur Disposition gestellter** ~ half-pay officer; **aus dem Mannschaftsstand hervorgegangener** ~ ranker; **höherer** ~ senior officer; **pensionierter** ~ retired officer; **reaktivierter** ~ dugout *(Br., sl.)*; **technischer** ~ engineer officer; **wachhabender** ~ officer of the watch;
~ **des Beurlaubtenstandes** reserve officer; ~ **vom Dienst** official of the day, officer in charge, duty officer; ~ **im Generalsrang** general officer; **~e und Mannschaften** officers and crew; **~e und Mannschaften der Kriegsmarine** Maritime State *(Br.)*; **~e und Soldaten** officers and men;
~ **abordnen** to attach an officer; ~ **abstellen** to lend (detail, second) an officer; ~ **befördern** to prefer an officer; ~ **entlassen** to break an officer; **zum** ~ **ernennen** to commission; **j. aus der Liste der aktiven ~e streichen** to retire an officer from the active list; ~ **werden, zum** ~ **befördert werden** to receive (obtain) one's commission.
Offiziers|anwärter cadet; **~gruppe** officer group; **~kasino** officers' mess; **~messe** *(Schiff)* officers' mess, wardroom; **~patent** officers' commission (paper); **~patent verleihen** to commission; **~rang** officership; **im ~rang** commissioned; **~stelle** officership, commission.
offiziös semiofficial, officious, unofficial, not official;
~es Gehabe officiousness.
öffnen, Absatzmarkt to be the key to sales; **jem. die Augen** ~ to open s. one's eyes; **Grab** ~ to unseal a tomb; **Grenze** ~ to open up a frontier; **der Korruption Tür und Tor** ~ to open the door to corruption; **Laden** ~ to open a shop; **Leiche** ~ to perform a post-mortem; **neue Märkte** ~ to open new markets; **einer Sache Tür und Tor** ~ to open the door to s. th.; **Tür einen Spalt breit** ~ to inch open a door; **der Verleumdung Tür und Tor** ~ to lay o. s. open to calumny.
Öffnung opening, hole, gap, hiatus, vent;
~ **einer Höhle** mouth of a cave; ~ **nach links** *(pol.)* opening to the left.
Öffnungszeiten business (opening, official) hours, *(Kneipe)* time limit *(Br.)*.
Offsetdruck offset [lithography (printing)];
fotografischer ~ photo-offset.
Offset|druckerei offset printing office; **~druckfarben** offset printing inks; **~film** offset transparency; **~presse** offset press.
Offsetverfahren offset process;
im ~ **gedruckt** printed by offset;
im ~ **drucken** to offset.
Ohmzahl ohmage.
ohne|Arbeit out of work; ~ **Bericht** without advice; ~ **Bezugsrecht** without rights; ~ **Datum** undated; ~ **Dividende** ex dividend; ~ **Geld** hard up for money; ~ **Gewähr** without engagement; ~ **Gewährleistung** without guarantee, unwarranted; ~ **Kosten** without expense; ~ **Obligo** *(Wechselrecht)* without recourse; ~ **Protest** not to be noted *(Br.)*, protest waived *(US)*; ~ **Rückgriff** without recourse; **gar nicht so** ~ **sein** to know which side one's bread is buttered; ~ **Stellung** unemployed, out [of work]; ~ **Testament** intestate; ~ **Verbindlichkeit** not binding, subject to confirmation; ~ **Vorbehalt** unreservedly, without reservation; ~ **weiteres** ipso jure; ~ **mein Wissen** without my knowledge; ~ **Zinsschein** ex interest, without coupons.
Ohnmacht unconsciousness, faint, swoon;
~ **der Regierung** impotence of the government;
in ~ **fallen** to faint, to swoon, to pass out *(US sl.)*.
ohnmächtig|werden to faint, to fall into a fit, to throw a fit *(US)*, to pass out *(US sl.)*;
~e Anstrengungen helpless efforts; **~e Wut** impotent rage.
Ohnmachtsanfall fainting fit.
Ohr, jem. etw. ins ~ **flüstern** to whisper s. th. in s. one's ear; **leicht ins** ~ **gehen** to be a catchy tune; **von einem** ~ **zum anderen grinsen** to grin like a Cheshire cat; **sich aufs** ~ **gelegt haben** to pound the ear *(US sl.)*; **übers** ~ **hauen** to do (take) in, to do down *(Br., coll.)*, to pigeon *(sl.)*; **j. übers** ~ **hauen** to put across a fraud on s. o., to do s. o. in the eye *(coll.)*, to walk round s. o. *(US)*, to shortchange (dope) s. o. *(US)*, to diddle s. o. *(fam.)*; **einen Dummen übers** ~ **hauen** to pluck a pigeon; **beim einen** ~ **herein- und beim anderen herausgehen** to go in one ear and out of the other, to run off s. o. like water off a duck's back; **nur mit halbem** ~ **hinhören** to half-listen; **sich aufs** ~ **legen** to take forty winks (a nap), to kip down *(coll.)*; **jem. sein** ~ **leihen** to turn a sympathetic ear to s. one's request; **ganz** ~ **sein** to be all ears; **jem. einen Floh ins** ~ **setzen** to put a flea in s. one's ear *(US)*; **jem. sein** ~ **verschließen** to refuse to listen to s. o.; **der Wahrheit sein** ~ **verschließen** to turn a deaf ear on the truth; **j. übers** ~ **zu hauen versuchen** to try it on with s. o.
Ohren, bis über die (über beide) head over heels; **noch nicht ganz trocken hinter den** ~ not dry (wet) behind the ears, unripe; **verschlossene** ~ **finden** to find no hearing; **jem. ein paar hinter die** ~ **geben** to box s. one's ears; **es faustdick hinter den** ~ **haben** to be up to a dodge or two, to be as sly as a fox; **gute** ~ **haben** to have sharp ears; **viel um die** ~ **haben** to have a lot on one's hands (plate, *coll.*); **taube** ~ **für etw. haben** to turn a deaf ear to s. th.; **die** ~ **steif halten** to keep a stiff upper lip (one's chin up); **jem. zu** ~ **kommen** to come to s. one's ears (the knowledge of s. o.); **jem. die** ~ **langziehen** to tweak s. one's ears; **die** ~ **hängen lassen** to be cast down, to be down in the mouth; **jem. in den** ~ **liegen** to pester (tease) s. o.; **tauben** ~ **predigen** to preach to deaf ears; **über beide** ~ **verliebt sein** to be head over heels in love; **auf seinen** ~ **sitzen** to be as deaf as a post; **die** ~ **spitzen** to prick up one's ears; **bis über die** ~ **in der Arbeit stecken** to be up to the eyes in work; **auf taube** ~ **stoßen** to fall on deaf ears; **bis über beide** ~ **rot werden** to blush to the roots of one's hair;
Wände haben ~ walls have ears;
~bläser talebearer, whisperer; **~bläserei** talebearing; **~sessel** wing chair; **~stöpsel** ear plugs; **~zeuge** auricular (ear) witness.
Ohrfeige box on the ear;
jem. eine ~ **geben** to box s. one's ears, to slap s. one's face.
ohrfeigen, j. to box s. one's ears;
ich hätte mich ~ **können** I could have kicked myself.
Okkasion real bargain.
okkult occult;
~e Einflüsse hidden hand *(fam.)*.
Okkupations|gebiet occupied territory; **~heer** occupation army.
Ökologe ecologist.
Ökologie ecology.
ökologisch ecological.
Ökonom economist, *(Landwirt)* gentleman farmer, *(Wirtschaftsbetrieb)* steward.
Ökonometrie econometrics.
Ökonometriker econometrician.
ökonometrisch econometric.
Ökonomie economy, thrift, *(Landwirtschaft)* agriculture;
~gebäude farm building.
ökonomisch economic[al];
mit seinem Geld ~ **umgehen** to be thrifty with one's money; **mit seinen Kräften** ~ **umgehen** to use one's strength sparingly; **seine Mittel** ~ **verwenden** to use one's resources economically;
~es Gesetz economic law; **~e Größen** economic quantities; **~es Verhalten** economic behavio(u)r.
Oktanzahl octane number;
mit hoher ~ high-octane.
Oktav|band octavo volume; **~format** octavo.
oktroyieren *(Verfassung)* to force;
jem. seine Ideen ~ to thrust one's ideas upon s. o.
Öl, ätherische ~e volatile oils; **aus einem Bohrturm ausströmendes** ~ fugitive oil; **pflanzliches** ~ vegetable oil;

~ **ablassen** to discharge oil; **nach ~ bohren** to prospect for oil; ~ **aufs Feuer gießen** to pour oil on the flames (fire), to add oil to the fire, to heap fuel on the fire, to take oil to extinguish water; ~ **auf die Wogen gießen** to pour oil on troubled waters; ~ **durch eine Rohrleitung zur Raffinerie pumpen** to pipe the oil to the refinery; **mit ~ schmieren** to oil; **viel ~ verbrauchen** *(Auto)* to consume a lot of oil;
~**abflüsse** petroleum waste; ~**aktien** oil shares (stocks, *US*); ~**anzug** oilskin; ~**ausfuhrland** oil exporter; ~**bedarf** demand for oil; ~**behälter** fount; ~**boykott** oil sanction; ~**brenner** oil burner; ~**defizit** oil deficit.
öldicht oiltight.
Öl|dollarüberschüsse erneut anlegen to recycle petrodollars; ~**druckbremse** hydraulic brake; ~**einfuhren** oil imports, imported oil; ~**einfuhrquote** oil import quota.
ölen to lubricate.
Öl|export oil export; ~**exportland** oil exporter; ~**farben** oil colo(u)rs; **mit ~farben malen** to paint in oils; ~**faß** oil barrel; ~**feld** oil field; **in Küstennähe gelegene ~felder** offshore fields; ~**feuerung** oil firing (burning); ~**fladen** oil slick; ~**fleck,** ~**fläche** *(Meer)* oil slick; ~**fleck auf der Straße** patch of oil in the street; ~**förderung** oil production; ~**förderung einstellen** to shut in *(US)*; ~**fund** strike; **mit hohem ~gehalt** long in oils; ~**gelder** oil funds; ~**gemälde** oil painting; ~**gesellschaft** oil company; ~**gewinnung** oil production; ~**götze** tin god, dead pan *(US)*; **wie ein ~götze dastehen** to stand there like a stuffed dummy, to stand like a wooden image *(coll.)*; ~**hafen** oil port, tanker terminal.
ölhaltig oil-bearing.
Öl|händler oil merchant, oilman; ~**heizofen** oil heater; ~**heizung** oil heater; ~**heizung haben** to have oil heating.
Oligarchie oligarchy.
Oligopol oligopoly;
~**preis** oligopoly price.
Öl|industrie oil industry; ~**insel** oil platform; ~**interessen** oil interests; ~**kanister** oilcan, oiler; ~**keller** oil cellar; ~**konzession** oil concession; ~**krise** oil (fuel) crisis; ~**kuchen** oil cake; ~**lache** oil spill (slick); **auf ein ~lager stoßen** to strike oil; ~**laterne** oil lamp; ~**leitung** pipeline; ~**lieferungen** oil supply; ~**magnat** oil baron; ~**malerei** painting in oils; **auslaufende ~menge** spill; **zusätzliche ~mengen** surplus lot of fuel oil; **staatliches ~monopol** state oil monopoly; ~**motor** oil engine; ~**ofen** oil stove, oil heater; ~**peilstab** oil dipstick; ~**preis** oil price; ~**preis an Industrieproduktpreise koppeln** to index oil prices to industrial goods; ~**preisanstieg,** ~**preiserhöhung** oil price increase (rise, hike), increase in oil prices; ~**produktion steigern** to turn on the oil spigot; ~**produzent** oilman; ~**pumpe** oil pump; ~**quelle** oil spring (well); **sprudelnde ~quelle** gusher *(US)*; ~**quelle durch Sprengung löschen** to blow an oil well; ~**raffinerie** oil-refining plant, petroleum (oil) refinery; ~**raffinierung** oil refining; ~**sände** oil sands; ~**scheich** oil king; **ausgelaufene ~schicht** oil slick; ~**schlick** oil slick; ~**spur** patch of oil; ~**stand** *(Auto)* oil level; ~**standsmesser** oil gauge; ~**suche** prospecting for oil; ~**sucher** oil prospector; ~**tank** oil tank; ~**tanker** tanker, oiler; ~**tanklager** tank farm; ~**teppich** oil slick.
ölträchtiges Gebiet proven territory.
Ölüberschußland oil-surplus land.
ölundurchlässig oilproof.
Öl|verbrauch oil consumption; ~**verbraucher** oil consumer; ~**verbraucherland** oil-consuming nation; ~**verbrauchstest** oil consumption test; ~**verschmutzung** pollution of the sea by oil; ~**verschmutzungsabkommen** International Convention for the Prevention of Pollution of the Sea by Oil; ~**verseuchung** oil spill; ~**verwertungsanlagen** oil facilities; ~**vorkommen** oil field (reservoir, basin); ~**wanne** *(Auto)* oil pan; ~**wechsel machen lassen** to have the oil changed.
Olymp *(Theater)* nigger heaven, Ethiopian paradise, peanut gallery.
Olympische Spiele, Olympiade Olympic games.
Ölzuflußregler moderator.
Ombudsmann Parliamentary Commissioner for Administration *(Br.)*.
Omen, böses bad omen, writing on the wall.
ominös ominous, fatal;
~**e Stille** ominous silence.
Omnibus omnibus, autobus, [motor] coach, [motor]bus, barge *(dial.)*;
mit Liegemöglichkeiten ausgestatteter ~ restroom-equipped bus; **für den Pendelverkehr eingesetzter** ~ commuter bus *(US)*; **einstöckiger** ~ single-deck bus, single-decker; **in die Stadt fahrender** ~ up; **geräumiger** ~ roomy bus; **klimatisierter** ~ air-conditioned coach; **reservierter** ~ private bus; **vollgestopfter** ~ overcrowded bus; **behördlich nicht zugelassener** ~ pirate [bus] *(Br., coll.)*; **zweistöckiger** ~ double-decker bus, road car, two-decker;
~ **für Fernfahrten** motor coach; ~ **mit elektrischer Oberleitung** electric troll(e)y bus;
~ **benutzen** to ride on a bus; **mit einem ~ fahren** to go by (take a) bus, to ride on a bus; ~ **in Dienst stellen** to put a bus into service (on the road); ~ **aus dem Verkehr ziehen** to take a bus off the road;
~**bahnhof** bus terminal *(Br.)*, [omni]bus (coach) station; ~**benutzer** bus rider; ~**besitzer** omnibus proprietor; ~**fahren** omnibus driving, *(Fahrgast)* riding in a bus; ~**fahrer** omnibus (bus) driver, carman *(US)*, busman, bus driver.
Omnibusfahr|gast bus passenger; ~**geld** bus fare; ~**plan** bus guide, omnibus timetable, bus schedule *(US)*; ~**schein** bus fare (ticket), coach fare (ticket).
Omnibus|fahrt bus ride (trip); ~**fahrt machen** to ride on a bus; ~**führer** bus driver, busman; ~**gesellschaft** bus company; ~**haltelinie** bus lane; ~**halteplatz** bus area.
Omnibushaltestelle bus station (stop);
ganz in der Nähe der ~ conveniently near the bus stop;
geschützte ~ bus shelter.
Omnibus|karawane caravan of buses; ~**lenken** omnibus driving.
Omnibuslinie [motor]bus line, omnibus (bus, *US*) route;
öffentlich betriebene ~ publicly run bus;
~ **aufgeben (einstellen)** to discontinue a bus line; ~ **betreiben** to run a bus line; ~ **verlegen** to divert a bus route *(US)*.
Omnibus|park bus (coach) fleet; ~**parkplatz** bus parking; ~**plakat** car card; ~**route** omnibus route; ~**rundfahrt** motor-coach tour; ~**schaffner** bus conductor, busman; ~**station** bus (coach) station; ~**strecke** [motor]bus line (route, *US*); ~**unternehmen** bus company; **sich über ~verbindungen vorher genau orientieren** to assess bus connections efficiently; ~**verkehr** omnibus (bus) service, bus pool *(US)*; **regionaler ~verkehr** rural bus service; ~**versicherung** all-risk insurance; ~**werbung** bus advertising; ~**zulassungskarte** bus pass.
Onkel, angeheirateter uncle by marriage;
~**ehe** compassionate marriage.
Oper opera, *(Gebäude)* opera house;
komische ~ comic opera.
Operation *(med. und mil.)* operation, *(Börse)* transaction;
amphibische ~ amphibian landing; **größere (gefährliche)** ~ major operation; **harmlose** ~ minor operation; **kritische** ~ delicate surgical operation; **plastische** ~ plastic operation; **sofortige** ~ emergency operation;
militärische ~en in großem Ausmaß operating on a large scale *(mil.)*;
sich vor ~en fürchten to have a horror of the knife; ~ **überstehen** to go through a surgical operation; **sich einer ~ unterziehen** to undergo an operation.
Operations|ablauf, gesamter all phases of an operation; ~**abteilung** *(mil.)* operations section; ~**basis** base of operations, basis, base; ~**gebiet** *(mil.)* operations theater; **im ~gebiet der U-Boote liegen** to be within the zone of submarine activities.
Operationskosten *(med.)* surgical expenses;
~**versicherung** *(med.)* surgical fees insurance *(US)*; ~**zuschuß** *(med.)* surgical benefit.
Operations|linie *(mil.)* base of operations; ~**narbe** post-operation scar; ~**plan** plan of operations; ~**raum** *(mil.)* operating theater; ~**saal** *(med.)* operating room; ~**stab** *(mil.)* operations staff; ~**technik** *(med.)* operative technique; ~**tisch** operating table; **unbegründete ~verweigerung** *(verletzter Angestellter)* unreasonable refusal to submit to operation; ~**ziel** *(mil.)* point, operational objective.
operativ operative;
j. ~ behandeln to give s. o. a surgical treatment;
~ **unterstellte Kräfte** assigned forces.
Operette operetta, comic opera.
operieren *(med. und mil.)* to operate;
j. ~ to operate on s. o.; **mit größter Vorsicht und größtem Takt** ~ to move in one's most tactful way.
Opern|aufführung opera [performance]; ~**gebäude** opera house; ~**glas** opera glass; ~**glas auf seine Sichtweite einstellen** to focus opera glasses to suit one's sight; ~**haus** opera; ~**musik** operatic music; ~**singer** opertaic singer; ~**text** opera.
Opfer sacrifice, victim, *(an Toten)* toll;
unter schweren ~n at a great sacrifice; **unter schweren ~n an Geld** at heavy cost of money;
persönliches ~ personal sacrifice; **zufälliges** ~ unintended victim;

zahlreiche ~ **einer Bauernfängerei** numerous victims of a confidence trick; ~ **eines Fahrerfluchtvergehens** hit-and-run victim; ~ **des Mädchenhandels** white slave *(US)*; ~ **der Unterdrückungspolitik** victims of oppression; ~ **der Verhältnisse** creature (victim) of circumstances; ~ **eines Verkehrsunfalls** victim of a motor accident;
~ **beobachten** to pipe a victim *(sl.)*; **finanzielle** ~ **bringen** to make a sacrifice; **dem Feuer zum** ~ **fallen** to be destroyed by fire; **den eigenen Ränken zum** ~ **fallen** to be hoist with one's own petard; **viele** ~ **fordern** to claim many victims; **kein** ~ **scheuen** to spare no sacrifice; ~ **seiner Dummheit sein** to pay for one's folly; ~ **eines Schwindlers sein** to be the dupe of an impostor; ~ **einer Täuschung sein** to be duped; ~ **eines Sparsamkeitsprogramms werden** to fall victim to a cost-reduction program(me); ~ **der Verhältnisse werden** to fall a prey to circumstances; ~ **eines Verkehrsunfalls werden** to meet with an accident;
~**kasten** alms box (chest).

opfern, seine Gesundheit to sacrifice one's health; **sein Leben für seine Kinder** ~ to sacrifice one's life for one's children; **sein Leben für sein Vaterland** ~ to give one's life as a sacrifice for one's country; **seinen letzten Pfennig für eine gute Sache** ~ to give one's last penny for a good cause; **seine ganze Zeit** ~ to spend all one's time on s. th.

Opferteller alms basin (dish).

Opiumhöhle opium den, pad room *(sl.)*, smoke factory.

Opponent opponent, opposer, adversary, objector.

opponieren to oppose, to offer opposition, to buck;
heftig ~ to set one's face against.

opportun opportune, convenient.

Opportunismus opportunism, timeserving.

Opportunist opportunist, timeserver, henchman, trimmer *(Br.)*.

opportunistisch opportunist, temporizing, timeserving;
sich ~ **verhalten** to temporize, to trim.

Opportunitäts|denken opportunity reasons; ~**einkommen** transfer earnings; ~**kosten** opportunity costs; ~**politiker** temporizing politician, trimmer.

Opposition *(parl.)* opposition [benches, *Br.*], outs;
außerparlamentarische ~ extra-parliamentary opposition;
~ **vorher beruhigen** to pre-silence the opposition; ~ **zum Schweigen bringen** to extinguish opposition; ~ **hervorrufen** to roll up opposition; **zur** ~ **hinüberwechseln** to defect to the opposition, to cross the floor of the House *(Br.)*; ~ **gegen etw. machen** to come out against s. th.; **in der** ~ **sein** to be in opposition (out of office, out); **in** ~ **zur Regierung stehen** to oppose the government; **in** ~ **treten** to go into opposition, to buck the machine *(US sl.)*; **durch** ~ **verhindern** to ca'canny, *(parl.)* to block, to filibuster *(US)*; **Forderungen der** ~ **vorwegnehmen** to preëmpt opposition demands.

oppositionell oppositional, adversary;
~**e Haltung im Kongreß aufgeben** to recede from one's position *(US)*; ~**e Linke** opposition left.

Oppositions|bänke benches opposite, front opposition bench *(Br.)*; ~**bewegung** opposition movement; ~**blatt** opposition paper; ~**führer** leader of the opposition, opposition leader; ~**gruppe** opposition group; **starke** ~**kräfte mobilisieren** to run into a solid opposition; ~**kreise** opposition circles; ~**lager** opposition camp; ~**mehrheit** opposition party majority; ~**mitglieder** oppositionists, the outs *(Br.)*; ~**partei** opposition party, [Her Majesty's most loyal] opposition *(Br.)*; **zur** ~**partei übergehen** to defect to the opposition, to cross the floor of the House *(Br.)*; ~**politiker** opposition politician; ~**presse** opposition press.

Optant optant, person opting, taker of an option.

optieren to opt, to choose, to make a choice;
für eine Staatsangehörigkeit ~ to opt for a nationality.

Optik *(Fotoapparat)* optics.

optimal optimum, optimal, highest possible;
nicht ~ suboptimal;
~**e Bedingungen** optimal conditions; ~**e Betriebsgröße** optimum size firm; ~ **günstige Bevölkerungsgröße** optimum population; ~**e Ertragsfähigkeit** maximum output; ~**e Geldmenge** optimal quantity of money; ~**e Produktions- und Handelsstruktur** optimal pattern of production.

Optimal|betrieb optimum firm; ~**größe** optimum size; ~**isierung** optimalization; ~**leistung** *(Maschine)* optimum capacity; ~**planung** operations research *(US)*; ~**programmierung** optimum program(m)ing.

Optimierungsrechnung *(Produktionsmethode)* adaptive control.

optimistisch optimistic, upbeat, rosy *(sl.)*;
Leben ~ **betrachten** to see the bright side of things.

Optimum maximum, optimum.

Option optation, option [to put], first refusal, *(Bezugsrecht)* subscription, election, *(Vorkaufsrecht)* right of preemption;
gemeinsam ausgeübte ~ joint option; **gehandelte** ~**en** traded options;
~ **zum Festlegen der Auszahlung von Lebensversicherungsraten** settlement option; ~ **für eine Vertragsverlängerung** covenant to renew;
~ **aufgeben** to renounce an option; ~ **ausüben** to exercise an option; **seine** ~ **verfallen lassen** to let one's option slide; **nach Ausübung einer** ~ **seitens des Pächters verlängerbar sein** to be renewable at the option of the tenant.

Options|anleihe option bond, optional bonds *(US)*, convertible bond issue; ~**ausübung** exercise of an option, option exercise; ~**berechtigter** optionee; ~**börse** options exchange; ~**dauer** option period; ~**erklärung** granting of an option; ~**erwerb** buying an option; ~**frist** option period; ~**geber** giver of an option, optioner; ~**gebühren** option fees; ~**geld** option fees; ~**geschäft** option business, dealings in options, option dealings (trading); ~**geschäfte machen** to deal in options; ~**geschäft in Termindevisen** option forward *(Br.)*; ~**gewährer** optioner, giver of an option; ~**handel** trading in options; **schwindelhafter** ~**handel** bogus trade in options; ~**händler** option trader; ~**klausel** option clause, optional (first-refusal) clause; ~**nehmer** taker of an option; ~**provision** commission on options.

Optionsrecht option, right to opt, optional right, *(Bezugsrecht)* subscription right *(Br.)*;
nicht ausgeübtes ~ unexercised option;
~ **zur Festlegung der Auszahlung von Lebensversicherungsraten** settlement option;
~ **aufgeben (nicht ausüben)** to abandon an option; ~ **ausüben** to take up an option; ~ **einräumen** to [grant an] option; ~ **vereinbaren** to stipulate an option right; **auf ein** ~ **verzichten** to opt out.

Options|schein stock [purchase (allotment)] warrant *(US)*; ~**vertrag** option agreement; ~**vorzugsrechte** particulars of options; ~**zahlung** option payment; ~**zeit** option period.

optisch|er Entfernungsmesser optical range finder; **aus** ~**en Gründen** for show; ~**e Hilfsmittel** visual aids; ~**e Industrie** optical industry; ~**e Instrumente** optical instruments; ~**e Nachrichtenmittel** visual means of communication; ~**e Peilung** visual direction finding; ~**e Täuschung** optical illusion.

Orakel oracle;
in ~**n sprechen** to speak in riddles.

orakelhafte Äußerungen, Orakelspruch oracular utterance.

Orangensaft orange squash (juice);
~ **auspressen** to crush out the juice from oranges.

Orchester orchestra;
dem ~ **den Ton angeben** to give the orchestra the pitch; ~ **dirigieren** to lead an orchestra; **hinter dem** ~ **nachhinken** to drag behind the orchestra;
~**begleitung** orchestral accompaniment; ~**dirigent** director of music; ~**melodie** orchestra parts; ~**musik** orchestral music; ~**partitur** orchestra score; ~**pavillon** bandstand; ~**podium** concert platform; ~**versenkung** orchestra pit.

Orden order, medal;
~ **und Ehrenzeichen** medals and decorations;
einem ~ **angehören** to be in religion; **alle seine** ~ **tragen** to be wearing all one's orders, to sport all one's medals *(fam.)*; **jem. einen** ~ **verleihen** to award a medal to s. o.

Ordens|band cordon, ribbon; ~**gelübde ablegen** to profess o. s. in an order.

ordensgeschmückt bemedal(l)ed, laden with chest hardware *(US sl.)*.

Ordens|kette collar; ~**spange** palm frond; ~**zeichen** order.

ordentlich *(achtbar)* respectable, proper, decent, honest, *(aufgeräumt)* tidy, neat, shipshape, *(geregelt)* ordinary, orderly, regular, well, *(gewissenhaft)* thorough, diligent, accurate;
sich ~ **benehmen** to keep straight; **jem.** ~ **Bescheid sagen** to give s. o. a piece of one's mind; ~ **angezogen sein** to be neatly dressed; **ganz** ~ **verdienen** to earn good money, to be in a good way of business;
~**e Ausbildung** thorough education; ~**e Ausgaben** ordinary expenses; ~**es Benehmen** proper behavio(u)r; ~ **geführter Betrieb** well-run business; ~**e Generalversammlung** regular (statutory, *Br.*) meeting; ~**es Gericht** ordinary (law) court, regular court of law (justice); ~**es Gerichtsverfahren** ordinary proceedings, due process of law; ~**er Gesandter** ordinary ambassador; ~**e Hauptversammlung** stated meeting; ~**er Haushalt** ordinary budget; ~ **geführte Konten** straight accounts; ~**e Leute** respectable (honest) people; ~**es Mitglied**

full (ordinary, regular) member; ~**er Professor** full professor *(US)*, professor in ordinary; ~**en Rechtsweg beschreiten** to have recourse to law; ~**er Richter** regular judge; ~**en Schluck nehmen** to take a good swig; ~**e Sitzungsperiode** regular (ordinary) session; ~**e Summe** considerable (tidy, *fam.*) sum; ~**es Tagewerk** tidy day's work; ~**e Tracht Prügel beziehen** to get a good hiding; ~**es Verhalten** orderly behavio(u)r; **in** ~**en Verhältnissen leben** to live in decent conditions; **aus** ~**en Verhältnissen stammen** to belong to the respectable middle class; **ganz** ~**es Vermögen** decent (sizable) fortune; **sauberes und** ~**es Zimmer** clean and tidy room; **in** ~**em Zustand sein** to be in good condition.

Order order, commission;
an ~ to the order of; **an** ~ **ausgestellt** made out to order; **an** ~ **lautend** payable to order; **an unsere eigene** ~ to our own order; **an fremde** ~ to order of a third party; **auf** ~ **und Rechnung von** by order and on account of; **bis auf weitere** ~ until further orders; **gemäß Ihrer** ~ in conformity with your order; **laut** ~ as ordered, according to order; **nicht an** ~ nonnegotiable; **zahlbar an** ~ payable to order;
begrenzte ~ limit (stop-loss) order; **eigene** ~ own order; **feste** ~ firm order; **freibleibende** ~ conditional order; **nur für einen Tag gültige** ~ day order; **bis auf Widerruf gültige** ~ open order; **laufende** ~ standing order; **limitierte** ~ limited (stop-loss) order; **offene** ~ open order; **ständige** ~ standing order; **unbefristete (unlimitierte)** ~ unlimited (open) order, good till called for;
~ **annullieren** to cancel (revoke, withdraw) an order; ~ **ausführen** to execute (carry out) an order; **Wechsel an** ~ **ausstellen** to make a bill payable to order; ~ **erteilen** to [place an] order; **an** ~ **lauten** to be made out to order; **an jds.** ~ **zahlen** to pay to the order of s. o.;
~**buch** book of commission, order book, *(Makler)* blotter; ~**formular** order sheet (slip); ~**frachtbrief** order[-notify] bill of lading; ~**geber** orderer; ~**hafen** port of call; ~**klausel** order clause, negotiable words; ~**konnossement** order[-notify] bill of lading; ~**lagerschein** negotiable warehouse receipt; ~**liste** order book; ~**papier** negotiable instrument, instrument to order, bill payable to order, order bill; **unechtes** ~**papier** quasi-negotiable instrument; ~**police** policy to order; ~**scheck** check *(US)* (cheque, *Br.*) to order, order cheque *(Br.)*; ~**schuldverschreibungen** order bonds; ~**tratte** promissory note made out to order; ~**wechsel** order bill [of exchange]; ~**zettel** order sheet (slip).

ordinär common, vulgar, coarse, low;
~**es Benehmen** common manners; ~**es Parfüm** cheap and nasty perfume; ~**er Witz** vulgar joke.

Ordinariat professorial chair, full professorship *(US)*.

Ordinarius full professor *(US)*, professor in ordinary.

ordnen to [set in] order, to arrange, to settle, to regulate, *(klassifizieren)* to classify, to grade, *(mil.)* to array, to rally, *(Papiere)* to file;
alphabetisch ~ to arrange in alphabetical order; **seine Angelegenheiten** ~ to put (set) one's house in order, to arrange one's business affairs; **Begebenheiten chronologisch** ~ to arrange events in a chronological order; **sich zu einem Festzug** ~ to form into a procession; **seine Gedanken** ~ to get one's ideas into shape; **der Größe nach** ~ to arrange according to size; **Nachlaß** ~ to settle (wind up) an estate; **planmäßig** ~ to systematize; **nach Sachgebieten** ~ to arrange according to subjects; **Sicherheiten** ~ to marshal securities; **systematisch** ~ to arrange systematically, to systematize; **tabellarisch** ~ to tabulate, to tabularize; **Verbindlichkeiten** ~ to settle accounts; **seine Verhältnisse** ~ to settle one's affairs; **Vermögensmasse** ~ to wind up an estate.

Ordner organizer, regulator, *(Aktien)* file, *(Briefe)* sorter, *(Fest)* arranger, steward, *(Registrator)* filer *(US)*, *(Schule)* monitor, prefect *(Br.)*;
in einen ~ **einheften** to place on file, to file away.

Ordnung order, *(Anlage)* pattern, setup *(US)*, *(Anordnung)* arrangement, disposition, classification, *(Klasse)* class, rank, *(Reihenfolge)* succession, sequence, rank, order, *(System)* frame, system, setup *(US)*, *(Vorschrift)* rule, act, regulation, *(Zucht)* discipline;
außer ~ **geraten** out of line; **der** ~ **halber** for regularity's sake; **in** ~ in good working order, in key, in good trim, o. k., *(Konto)* straight, *(Paß)* valid, *(Scheck)* covered, *(Wechsel)* good; **in alphabetischer** ~ in alphabetical order; **in geöffneter** ~ *(mil.)* in open order; **in schönster** ~ as right as rain, in apple-pie order; **nicht in** ~ amiss, out of square, *(Maschine)* out of order; **zur** ~ *(parl.)* chair!; **zweiter** ~ secondary;
bestehende ~ present regime; **geschlossene** ~ *(mil.)* closed order; **häusliche** ~ domestic arrangement; **marktwirtschaftliche** ~ free enterprise system; **öffentliche** ~ public order, police; **politische** ~ polity; **sinnvolle** ~ sensible arrangement; **soziale** ~ social system; **verfassungsmäßige** ~ constitutional order (system); **wirtschaftliche** ~ economic system;
systematische ~ **der Bilanzposten** grouping of balance-sheet items; **staatliche** ~ **des Kreditwesens** banking regulations; ~ **der Sicherheiten** *(im Konkursfall)* marshalling securities;
in Geldsachen besonders auf ~ **achten** to be scrupulous in money matters; **als Menschen zweiter** ~ **ansehen** to regard as second-class citizens; **alles wieder in** ~ **ansehen** to cry quits; **öffentliche Sicherheit und** ~ **aufrechterhalten** to maintain law and order; ~ **in der Welt aufrechterhalten** to police the world; **Bücher in** ~ **befinden** to find the books straight; **in** ~ **bringen** to put to right (in order), to square, to straighten out, to clear up, to trim, to fix up *(US)*, to pipeclay, *(Apparat)* to repair, to put right; **in eine** ~ **bringen** to regiment into a system; **seine Angelegenheiten in** ~ **bringen** to get things square, to set (put) one's house (set one's affairs) in order; **seine Ausgabenwirtschaft in** ~ **bringen** to regulate one's expenditure; **seine Konten in** ~ **bringen** to get one's accounts square; **Briefzustellung total aus der** ~ **bringen** to cause a complete disorganization in the postal delivery; **sein Fahrrad in** ~ **bringen** to fix up one's bike; **seinen eigenen Hinterhof in** ~ **bringen** to clean up one's own back yard; **die Schweinerei in** ~ **bringen** to clear up the mess; **Unterlagen in** ~ **bringen** to sort out papers; **sein Zimmer in** ~ **bringen** to tidy up one's room, to set one's room straight; **zur Landstraße erster** ~ **erheben** to classify a road *(Br.)*; **sich nicht ganz in** ~ **fühlen** to feel off colo(u)r; **alles peinlich genau in** ~ **haben** to have everything dead straight and in order; **etw. tadellos in** ~ **halten** to keep s. th. spotless; **j. aus seiner gewohnten** ~ **herausreißen** to turn s. o. upside down; **alles in bester** ~ **hinterlassen** to leave one's affairs in perfect order; **zur** ~ **rufen** *(parl.)* to call to order, to name *(Br.)*; ~ **schaffen** to establish order; **in** ~ **sein** to be all settled; **in schönster** ~ **sein** to be in applepie order; **nicht in** ~ **sein** to be not up to the mark, to be out of whack, *(Maschine)* to be out of order; **Blödsinn erster** ~ **sein** to be too stupid for words; **für** ~ **in einer Schulklasse sorgen** to keep order in a classroom; **öffentliche Ruhe und** ~ **stören** to disturb peace and order, to disturb the peace; **soziale** ~ **stören** to be injurious to social order; **öffentliche Ruhe und** ~ **wiederherstellen** to restore public order (peace and order); **sich in guter** ~ **zurückziehen** to make good one's retreat.

Ordnungs|behörde regulatory agency (body, *US*); ~**dienst** maintenance of order and security; ~**dienst versehen** to act as stewards; ~**funktion** regulative function.

ordnungsgemäß proper, duly, in due form, orderly, right, according to regulations, regular;
~ **ausgestellt** duly drawn; ~ **bestellt** duly appointed; ~ **erhalten** duly received; ~ **unterschrieben** duly signed;
sich ~ **bei der Polizei anmelden** to duly register with the police; ~ **anzeigen** to give due notice; ~ **erledigen** to do in a businesslike way; **sich** ~ **angemeldet haben** to have duly registered with the police; ~ **abgeurteilt werden** to be brought to a legal trial;
~**e Aufbewahrung** proper custody; ~**er Erhaltungszustand** proper state of repair; ~**e Kündigung** due and proper (lawful) notice; ~**e Quittung** formal (proper) receipt; ~**es Verfahren** due course (process) of law; ~**es Verfahren sicherstellen** to regularize the proceedings; **in** ~**em Zustand** in proper condition, in apparent good order, in good order and condition; ~**e Zustellung** due service; ~ **durchgeführte Zustellung** fair sale.

Ordnungs|hüter guardian of the peace; ~**mäßigkeit** regularity, formality; ~**mäßigkeit einer Versammlung beanstanden** to attack the regularity of a meeting; ~**maßnahmen** regulatory measures; ~**norm** regulative standard; ~**nummer** reference number; ~**polizei** constabulary, civil police; ~**prinzip** regulating principle.

Ordnungsruf *(parl.)* call to order, naming of a member *(Br.)*;
~ **erhalten** to be called to order; **jem. einen** ~ **erteilen** to call s. o. to order, to name a member *(Br.)*.

Ordnungs|sinn orderly mind; ~**strafe** administrative fine, repressive measure, *(Disziplinarstrafe)* disciplinary punishment; **mit einer** ~**strafe belegen** to fine s. o.; ~**system** system of classifications; ~**vorschriften** administrative regulations, rules *(US)*.

ordnungswidrig contrary to public policy, disorderly, irregular;
~ **parken** to park against the regulations;
~**es Verhalten** disorderly conduct.

Ordnungswidrigkeit disorder, breach of the rules, irregularity, misdemeano(u)r, quasi crime;
~ **gegen das Straßenverkehrsgesetz** offence under the Road Traffic Act *(Br.)*.
Ordnungszahl ordinal number.
Ordonnanz *(mil.)* orderly;
~**dienst haben** to be on orderly duty; ~**offizier** orderly officer.
Organ organ, body, group, *(Behörde)* authority, agency, *(Blatt)* publication, paper, medium, organ, *(EG)* institution, *(Talent)* bump;
amtliches ~ official organ, gazette *(Br.)*; **ausführendes** ~ enforcement agency, executive body (branch), general executive *(US)*; **beratendes** ~ advisory body, consultative group; **halbwöchentlich erscheinendes** ~ semi-weekly publication; **führendes** ~ top publication; **geschäftsführendes** ~ managing body; **gesetzgeberisches** ~ legislative body; **lebenswichtige** ~e vital organs; **leitendes** ~ governing body; **offizielles** ~ official organ, bulletin, gazette; **staatliches** ~ national agency; **ständiges** ~ permanent (standing) body; **supranationales** ~ supranational body; **vollziehendes** ~ executive agent; **zuständiges** ~ regulatory agency *(US)*;
~**e der Europäischen Gemeinschaften** Institutions of the European Communities; ~**e einer Gesellschaft** executive bodies of a company (corporation); ~ **des Herausgebers** organ of the editor; ~ **der öffentlichen Meinungsbildung** organ of public opinion; ~**e der Vereinten Nationen** organs of the United Nations; ~ **der Werbung** advertising medium;
~**ausgleich** intercompany elimination (squaring); ~**ertrag** income from affiliates; ~**forderungen** intercompany claims; ~**gesellschaft** subsidiary company (corporation, *US*), organ company *(US)*; ~**gewinne** intercompany profits; ~**haftung** vicarious liability, *(Staat)* government (state) liability.
Organisation organization, entity, agency, economy, setup, front, *(pol.)* caucus, machine *(US)*;
funktionale ~ functional organization; **konfessionell gebundene** ~ denominational organization; **gemeinnützige** ~ nonprofit organization; **halbmilitärische** ~ quasi-military organization; **innerbetriebliche** ~ internal organization; **jämmerliche** ~ inadequate organization (arrangement); **linksstehende** ~ left-wing organization; **nichtstaatliche** ~ nongovernment organization; **rechtsradikale** ~ minutemen *(US)*; **regionale** ~ regional association; **unbedeutende** ~ fringe outfit; **unzureichende** ~ inadequate arrangement; **verwaltungsmäßige** ~ executive management; **vorläufige** ~ tentative organization; **zweistufige** ~ two-tier organization; **zwischenstaatliche** ~**en** intergovernmental bodies;
~ **für die Einheit Afrikas** Organization of African Unity; ~ **der Amerikanischen Staaten** Organization of American States (OAS); ~ **ohne Erwerbscharakter** nonprofit organization; ~ **der Erdöl exportierenden Länder** Organization of Petroleum Exporting Countries (OPEC); ~ **eines Unternehmens** business organization; ~ **der Vereinigten Nationen für industrielle Entwicklung** United Nations Industrial Development Organization; ~ **der Vereinten Nationen für Ernährung und Landwirtschaft** Food and Agricultural Organization of the United Nations; ~ **der Vereinten Nationen für Erziehung, Wissenschaft und Kultur** United Nations Educational, Scientific and Cultural Organization (UNESCO); ~ **für wirtschaftliche Zusammenarbeit und Entwicklung** Organization for Economic Cooperation and Development (OECD); ~ **für europäische wirtschaftliche Zusammenarbeit** Organization for European Economic Cooperation (OEEC);
aus einer ~ **ausschließen** to muscle out of a movement; **einer** ~ **beitreten** to join an organization; ~ **gründen** to set up an organization; ~ **ins Leben rufen** to call an organization into existence; ~ **unterwandern** to infiltrate an organization.
Organisations|abteilung administration department (division); ~**akt** foundation, establishment; ~**apparat** organizational machinery; ~**aufbau** organizational structure (setup); ~**aufgabe** organizational issue; ~**ausschuß** organizing *(US)* (steering) committee; ~**fachmann** organizational specialist; ~**fähigkeit** organizing (administrative, coordinating) ability; ~**fehler** faulty organization; ~**fonds** organization fund; ~**form** organizational form; **lose** ~**form** informal organization; ~**fragen** organizational matters; ~**gemeinschaft** *(Versicherungsgesellschaften)* bureau company; ~**klausel** *(Tarifabkommen)* closed-shop clause; ~**kosten** preliminary costs *(US)*; ~**mängel** organizational ineffectiveness; ~**plan** organization chart (arrangement); ~**planung** organization positioning; ~**problem** management problem; ~**programm** organization program(me); ~**schaubild** organization diagram; ~**schema** organization[al] chart (arrangement), organizational setup (structure); ~**schwierigkeiten** difficulties of organization; ~**struktur** oranizational chart; ~**stufe** level of organization; ~**talent** organizing genius, gift for organization, organizing (organizational, coordinating) ability, management; **an** ~**talent alles übertrefffen** to outgeneral; ~**typ** pattern of organization; ~**zwang** compulsory organization.
Organisator organizer, promoter, engineer, systematizer;
geborener ~ born organizer; **geschickter** ~ shunter *(sl.)*.
organisatorisch organizing, organizational;
~**e Einheit** organizational unity; ~**e Fähigkeit** organizing ability; ~**e Gründe** organizational grounds; ~**e Leitung haben** to hold the reins of an organization; ~**e Sanierungsmaßnahme** organizational realignment; ~**e Veränderungen** organizational changes.
organisch organic, natural;
~**e Chemie** organic chemistry; ~**es Ganzes** organic whole; ~**e Krankheit** organic disease; ~**es System** economy system of rules.
organisierbar organizable.
organisieren to organize, to manage, to arrange, to regiment, *(besorgen)* to commander, *(klauen)* to touch, to lay on *(fam.)*, to bag *(sl.)*, to snaffle *(sl.)*, to wangle, to find, to rustle up, to annex *(sl.)*;
Arbeiter und Angestellte in einer Fabrik ~ to organize a factory; **sich gewerkschaftlich** ~ to unionize; **Sache** ~ to quarterback *(sl.)*; **Wahlfeldzug** ~ to launch a campaign; **Werbefeldzug** ~to launch an advertising campaign.
organisiert organized, organic;
genossenschaftlich ~ cooperative[ly]; **gewerkschaftlich** ~ unionized; **nicht** ~ nonunion, unorganized;
völlig neu ~ **werden müssen** to need a thorough turnover;
gewerkschaftlich ~**er Arbeiter** unionist; **gewerkschaftlich** ~**e Arbeiterschaft** organized labo(u)r; **nicht gewerkschaftlich** ~**e Arbeitskräfte** free labo(u)r; **hoch** ~**e Lebensformen** highly organized forms of life; ~**e Streikposten** organisational picketing.
Organisierung organizing, regimentation.
Organismus, marktwirtschaftlicher free enterprise system.
Organ|konto intercompany account; ~**schaft** interlocking relationship; ~**schaftsverrechnung** intergroup elimination; ~**schaftsvertrag** intergroup agreement; ~**verhältnis** interlocking relationship; ~**verluste** intercompany losses.
Orgie orgy, debauch;
wilde ~**n** wild orgies.
Orient Eastern countries, East, Orient.
orientalisch oriental, eastern;
~**e Frage** Eastern question; ~**e Kultur** oriental civilization; ~**er Luxus** oriental luxury.
orientieren to orient[ate], to guide, *(benachrichtigen)* to inform;
sich ~ to take one's bearings, to orientate o. s., *(Nachrichten einziehen)* to gather information, to inform s. o. about s. th.;
sich an jem. ~ to be influenced by s. o.; **sich im Gelände** ~ to get an idea of the lie of the land; **sich nach der Küstenlinie** ~ to steer by the lay of the land; **seine Politik** ~ to fix one's policy; **sich in einer Stadt** ~ to find one's way about a town; **sich eingehend über jds. Verhältnisse** ~ to inquire into s. one's position; **Vertreter** ~ to instruct an agent; **sich weltweit** ~ *(Unternehmen)* to go multinational;
sich nicht mehr ~ **können** to have lost one's bearings.
orientiert oriented, orientated;
gut ~ well informed; **nicht** ~ unoriented; **vorwiegend wirtschaftlich** ~ with special emphasis on economics;
politisch ~ **sein** to be politically orientated; **sozialistisch** ~ **sein** to have a socialist slant.
Orientierung orientation, bearing, information;
zu Ihrer ~ for your guidance;
weltweite ~ *(Unternehmen)* multinationalization;
jem. die ~ **nehmen** to disorientate s. o.; **seine** ~ **verlieren** to lose one's bearings, to be (become) disorientated.
Orientierungs|daten *(Konjunkturpolitik)* wage-price guideposts;
~**daten für die Tarifpartner setzen** to indicate the maximum earnings increase compatible with growth and stable prices; ~**hilfe** guideline indication; ~**kursus** exploration course; ~**linie** datum line; ~**preis** *(EG)* guide price; ~**punkt** landmark, checkpoint *(US)*; ~**rahmen** guide lines; ~**richtlinien** *(Lohnverhandlungen)* pay guidelines; ~**schild** direction sign, signboard; **seinen** ~**sinn verlieren** to lose one's bearings; ~**system** reference system; ~**turm** *(Flugplatz)* pylon; ~**zahlen** reference value, guideline figure; ~**zeichen** bearings.
Orient|perle orient pearl; ~**teppich** Turkey carpet *(Br.)*.

Original original, institutional copy, original text, *(Druck)* first sheet, *(Type)* eccentric person, card *(fam.)*, caution *(coll.)*, archetype, *(Urschrift)* script, autograph;
mit dem ~ übereinstimmend corresponding to the original; **nach dem ~ bearbeitet** adapted from the original;
~ eines Maschinenmanuskripts first sheet; **~ einer Rechnung** original invoice;
sich eng an das ~ halten to keep close to the original; **Buch im ~ lesen** to read a book in the original; **vom ~ Abschrift nehmen** to copy [s. th. from] the original; **wahres ~ sein** to be quite a character; **Abschrift mit dem ~ vergleichen** to compare a copy with the original;
~abdruck original block; **~abfüllung** estate-bottled wine; **~auflage** first (original) edition; **~aufnahme** *(Radio)* spot pickup; **~ausfertigungen** concurrent writs; **~ausgabe** first (original) edition; **~band** original binding; **abgestempelter ~beleg** voucher stamp; **~buchung** original entry; **~einband** original binding; **~faktura** original invoice; **~fassung** original version; **~film** answer print; **~form** master mould; **~fracht** original freight; **~größe** same size; **~handschrift** original manuscript; **~klischee** original (master) block; **~kopie** *(Bild)* replica, *(Film)* master copy; **~manuskript** original manuscript; **~maß** standard measure; **~packung** original package (wrapping); **~papiere** proper papers; **~police** original policy; **~programm** *(Rundfunk)* package; **~quittung** original receipt; **~rechnung** original invoice; **~scheck** original check *(US)*; **~schrift** *(Handsatz)* foundry type; **~sendung** live broadcast; **~serie** original series; **~tara** original tare; **~testament** original will; **~text** original text; **~übertragung** live broadcast; **~unterschrift** true signature; **~urkunde** original instrument (document); **~verpackung** original package (packing, wrapping); **~vertrag abändern** to vary the original contract; **~wechsel** first bill of exchange, original bill *(US)*; **~werk** original title.
originär original, inborn, primary;
nicht ~ *(jur.)* derivative;
~e Ausstattung initial allocation; **~es Beweismaterial** original evidence; **~es Geld** primary money.
originell original, unusual;
sehr ~ schreiben to give an original touch to one's writing.
Orkan hurricane, tornado, whirlwind, wildwind, gale;
~ der Begeisterung roar of enthusiasm.
orkanartig tempestuous;
~er Beifall thunderous applause.
Orkanstärke gale force.
Ornament ornament, flower, garnish.
Ornat *(Universität)* robe, academic costume;
in vollem ~ with cap and gown.
Ort place, site, spot, locality, lieu, *(Bergbau)* working place (point), face, forefield, *(Dorf)* village, *(Ortschaft)* place, town, *(Schauplatz)* scene, site;
am ~ locally; **am angegebenen ~** loco citato (l. c.); **am unrechten ~** misplaced; **am ~ wohnend** resident; **an ~ und Stelle** on the spot (these premises), in situ; **frei ~ geliefert** delivered [on] site; **höheren ~es** by higher authority, in higher quarters; **vor ~** *(Bergbau)* in the drift, at the face;
abgelegener ~ remote spot, god-forsaken hole, one-horse town *(US)*; **geschichtlich bedeutsamer ~** historic spot; **berühmter ~** celebrated spot (place); **weit entfernter ~** Jericho *(coll.)*; **ein gewisser ~** lavatory, loo *(Br., coll.)*, John *(US coll.)*; **gleichnamiger ~** place of the same name; **kleiner ~** small place; **öffentlicher ~** public place; **sicherer ~** safe place, fort; **gänzlich unbekannter ~** obscure locality, nonplace; **vertraglich vereinbarter ~** place as provided in the contract; **vielbesuchter ~** much-frequented place; **allgemein zugänglicher ~** public place;
~ mit Asylrecht privileged place; **~ für Außenaufnahmen** *(Film)* location; **~ der Ausstellung** *(Wertpapier)* place of issue; **~ der tatsächlichen Geschäftsleitung** headquarters; **~ der Lieferung** place of delivery; **~ der Niederlassung** commercial domicile, domicile of corporation; **~ des steuerbaren Umsatzes** place of taxable transactions; **~ des Verbrechens** locality (scene) of the deed (crime); **~ und Zeit** place and time;
vor ~ arbeiten to work at the face; **an einem ~ bleiben** to continue at (in) a place; **etw. an einen sicheren ~ bringen** to put s. th. out of harm's way; **alles an ~ und Stelle haben** to have everything in its place; **aus meinem ~ kommen** to come from my place (hometown, *US*); **in einem ~ in der Nähe von London leben** to live in the neighbo(u)rhood of London; **sich an ~ und Stelle ein Bild machen** to build up an on-the-spot picture; **etw. gehörigen ~s melden** to notify the authorities; **sich an einem ~ niederlassen** to fix one's abode, to settle down for good; **an ~ und Stelle prüfen** to spot-check; **an ~ und Stelle schaffen** to bring to the spot; **vor ~ sein** to be at the coal face; **im ganzen ~ bekannt sein** to be known all over the town; **höheren ~s genehmigt sein** to be approved by higher quarters; **pünktlich an ~ und Stelle sein** to arrive on the spot; **an einem ~ wohnen** to dwell in a place; **an den ~ des Verbrechens zurückkehren** to go back to the scene; **an einem neutralen ~ zusammenkommen** to meet on neutral ground.
Örtchen Houses of Parliament *(Br.)*, loo *(Br.)*, John *(US coll.)*.
orten to locate, to navigate, *(mit Funk)* to radiolocate, *(Schiff)* to find (fix) the position, to take one's bearings.
Orter *(am Funkpeilgerät)* radiolocator.
orthodox orthodox, hard-shell *(US)*.
Orthographie orthography, correct spelling.
orthographischer Fehler spelling mistake.
örtlich local, regional, particular, topical;
~ begrenzen to localize; **~ beschränken** to localize; **~ verschieden sein** to vary from place to place;
~e Bedingungen local attachment; **~e Begrenzung** localization; **~e Beschaffenheit** local topography; **~e Besonderheiten** regional peculiarities; **~e Fachgewerkschaft** local industrial union; **~ zuständiges Gericht** local venue; **~e Interessen** local interests; **~ verbreitete Krankheit** endemic disease; **~er Verbrauch** local consumption; **~ begründete Vorurteile** local prejudices; **~ begrenzte Werbeaktion (Werbung)** local campaign (advertising); **~e Zuständigkeit** original (local) jurisdiction.
Örtlichkeit locality, place;
mit einer ~ nicht vertraut sein not to be familiar with a place.
Orts | abrechnung local clearing; **~abweichung** local alteration; **~amt** *(Telefon)* local exchange; **~angabe** address, indication of place; **~angelegenheiten** local concern; **~anruf** *(tel.)* local call; **~ansässiger** resident, resident person, local man, hometowner *(US)*; **~anschluß** *(tel.)* direct exchange line; **~anzeigenteil** local advertising; **~ausdruck** localism; **~ausgang** exit of a town; **~ausschuß** *(Gewerkschaft)* single branch union *(Br.)*, local [union] *(US)*; **~bauplan** street (development) plan *(Br.)*, zoning ordinance *(US)*; **~behörde** local council (authority, government), borough council, board of civil authority *(US)*.
ortsbekannt sein to be well known locally.
Orts | beschreibung topography; **~besichtigung** local inspection, *(Gericht)* judicial survey, visit to the scene, view; **~besichtigung durch Geschworene** view of an inquest; **~bestimmung** localization, *(Peilung)* bearing, radiolocation, *(Schiff)* position finding.
ortsbeweglich *(Maschine)* mobile, portable.
Orts | bewohner inhabitant, local people; **~bezeichnung** geographical (local) name.
Ortschaft locality, place, village;
geschlossene ~ built-up area; **nicht geschlossene ~** nonbuilt-up area; **größere ~** populous place.
Orts | dienst *(Post)* local *(Br.)*; **~durchfahrt** through road; **~einheit** local unit; **~einwohner** inhabitant, resident; **~empfang** *(Radio)* local reception.
orts | fest rigid, *(mil.)* permanent, fixed, stationary; **~fremd** nonresident.
Orts | gebrauch local customs, habit, usance, local usage; **~gebühr** local fee, *(tel.)* local charge.
ortsgebunden local, stationary;
nicht ~ transitory, mobile;
~er Ausdruck local expression.
Orts | gedächtnis bump of locality; **~gemeinde** parish community; **~geschwindigkeit** speed limit in built-up areas; **~gespräch** *(Telefon)* local call; **~gespräche** *(tel.)* local traffic; **~gewerkschaft** single branch union *(Br.)*, local *(US)*; **~größenklasse** town size group; **~gruppe** local branch, chapter *(US)*; **~kartell** *(Gewerkschaft)* local trade council *(Br.)*, city federation *(US)*; **~kenntnis** familiarity with a place, local knowledge; **~kenntnis haben** to know a place; **~kennzahl** *(Post)* postal area, *(tel.)* preselection number, prefix; **~kennzeichen** local sign; **~klassen[lohn]ausgleich** intercity wage differential; **~klassenunterschied** intercity wage difference; **~kommandant** town major *(Br.)*; **~kommandantur** army post; **~krankenkasse** sickness benefit fund; **~name** name of a place, place name; **~netz** local network; **~netzbereich** local exchange area; **~netzkennzahl** *(tel.)* trunk[-dialling] code; **~planungsbehörde** local planning authority *(Br.)*; **~planungsgebiet** development area *(Br.)*; **~polizeibehörde** local police; **~recht** local law; **~register** local record; **~satzung** municipal ordinance *(US)*; **~schild** place-name sign; **~sender** local station, local radio;

~**sendung** *(Post)* local mail; ~**sinn** sense of direction, bump of locality; ~**skizze** outline map; ~**spediteur** local shipper; ~**statut** local statute (act, byelaws, *Br.*), *(Baupolizei)* building byelaw, local housing law, zoning law (act) *(US)*, municipal charter (ordinance); ~**tarif** local agreement, *(Eisenbahn)* local (way, *US*) rates; ~**teilnehmer** *(Telefon)* local subscriber; ~**telegramm** local telegram; ~**termin** *(Gericht)* judicial survey.

ortsüblich in accordance with local custom, customary in a place; ~**er Lohn** local wage; ~**e Sätze** local rates.

Ortsüblichkeit local practice.

Orts|unterkunft *(mil.)* billet, cantonment; ~**veränderung** change of place (scene); ~**verband** *(Gewerkschaft)* single branch union *(Br.)*, local *(US)*; ~**verbandsausschuß** local labour party's general management committee *(Br.)*; ~**verbandstreffen** ranch meeting; ~**verbrauch** local consumption; ~**verbreitung** *(Zeitung)* city-zone circulation; ~**verbreitungsplan** *(Anzeigenwesen)* metropolitan plan; ~**verein** *(Gewerkschaft)* local [union] *(US)*; ~**verkehr** local (way, *US*) traffic, urban transport, *(Post)* local service, *(Telefon)* local calls; **dem ~verkehr dienen** to accommodate local traffic; ~**verkehrsbereich** local service area; ~**vermittlung** *(tel.)* local exchange; ~**vertreter** local representative, resident agent; ~**verwaltung** local self-administration; ~**verzeichnis** geographical dictionary, gazetteer; ~**vorsteher** chief magistrate; ~**wagen** *(Bahn)* destination car; ~**wechsel** change of scene; ~**zeit** zone (local) time; **mittlere ~zeit** [local] mean time; ~**zeitung** local paper; ~**zulage, ~zuschlag** residential allowance, local bonus; **vorübergehend gewährter ~zuschlag** unconsolidated allowance; **Londoner ~zuschlag** London weighting allowance; ~**zuschlag für das Zentrum von London** Inner London allowance; ~**zuschlagswesen** allowance system *(Br.)*; ~**zustellung** local delivery.

Ortung *(Funkortung)* radiolocation, *(Schiff)* navigation, position finding, location.

Ortungs|bake beacon; ~**gerät** position finder, localizer, locating device.

Oskar academy award.

Ost-Westhandel East-West trade.

Ostblock Eastern Bloc.

Osten East.

ostentativ den Saal verlassen to leave the room pointedly.

Osterferien Easter holidays.

osteuropäische Zeit East-European time.

östlicher Kurs eastern route.

Ouvertüre overture.

Ovation ovation, enthusiastic welcome;
im Stehen dargebrachte ~ standing ovation;
jem. eine ~ bereiten to give s. o. an ovation.

Ozean ocean, sea;
Stiller ~ Pacific [Ocean]; **unendlicher ~** limitless ocean;
~ überqueren to traverse (hop) the ocean;
~**dampfer** ocean liner (steamer), ocean-going steamer, ocean-going liner, transatlantic liner, greyhound *(sl.)*; ~**flug** transoceanic flight; ~**reise** ocean voyage; ~**transport** sea transport[ation]; ~**überfliegung** transoceanic flight.

ozeanisches Klima oceanic climate.

Ozon|gehalt ozone concentration; ~**schicht** ozone layer.

P

Paar pair, couple;
neu vermähltes ~ newly married couple;
ungleiches ~ **bilden** to make a poorly matched couple; **zu** ~**en treiben** to rout, to scatter; **ein** ~ **werden** to make a match.
paar, ein ~ **Brocken Spanisch** bit of Spanish; **ein** ~ **Bücher** a few books; **ein** ~ **Dutzend mal** dozens and dozens of time; **meine** ~ **Sachen** my bits and pieces; **jem. ein** ~ **Zeilen schreiben** to drop s. o. a line.
paaren, Güte mit Strenge to combine kindness with strictness.
Paarvergleich paired comparison.
paarweise in pairs, two by two;
~ **anordnen** to pair off.
Pacht lease, leasehold, landholding, tenancy, tenure, set *(Scot.)*, *(geldliche Gegenleistung)* rent, rental;
durch Verschulden des Vorgängers abgelaufene ~ lapse patent; **gleichzeitig abgeschlossene** ~ concurrent lease; **vertraglich ausbedungene** ~ contract rent; **zeitlich begrenzte** ~ tenancy for years; **billige** ~ low lease; **fünfzehnjährig festgelegte** ~ fair rent; **gemeinsame** ~ joint tenancy; **jederzeit kündbare** ~ tenancy at will; **landwirtschaftliche** ~ farm lease; **mäßige** ~ moderate lease; **unkündbare** ~ perpetual lease; **mit der Berufsausübung verbundene** ~ occupation lease; **mit Meliorationsauflagen verbundene** ~ improvement lease; **auf 28 Jahre vergebene** ~ homestead lease *(US)*; **von Jahr zu Jahr verlängerte** ~ estate from year to year; **wucherische** ~ rack rent *(Ireland)*; **in Naturalien zahlbare** ~ share tenancy;
~ **eines Bergwerkrechtes** mineral lease; ~ **mit Erhaltungspflicht** tenant-repairing lease; ~ **ohne Erhaltungsverpflichtung** landlord-repairing lease; ~ **eines Gewerbebetriebes** lease of trade; ~ **eines Hofes** farm tenancy; ~ **mit Instandhaltungs- und Reparaturpflicht des Pächters** tenant-repairing lease; ~ **auf Lebenszeit** lease for life, life land; ~ **und Rückverpachtung** demise and redemise; ~ **mit automatischer Steigerungsklausel** progressive rent; ~ **auf Zeit** lease for a term of years;
~ **aufheben** to cancel a lease; ~ **eingehen** to [take on] lease; ~ **erneuern** to renew (extend) a lease; **in** ~ **geben** to let on lease, to farm out; **in** ~ **haben** to hold under a lease; **in** ~ **nehmen** to take on lease, to farm;
~**abkommen** lease arrangement; ~**ablauf** expiration (determination) of a lease; ~**ablösung** leasehold enfranchisement; ~**abteilung** lease department; ~**abtretung** assignment of lease; ~**anschlag** estimate of a lease; ~**anspruch** leasehold interest; ~**aufkommen** rent-roll; ~**ausfallversicherung** leasehold insurance *(US)*.
pachtbar tenantable, leasable, to let.
Pacht|bedingungen terms of a lease (tenancy), letting conditions; ~**beendigung** [de]termination of a lease, ending of tenancy; ~**beginn** commencement of a lease.
Pachtbesitz leasehold [tenure], tenancy, rent *(US)*, *(Bilanz)* leasehold, land and building *(Br.)*;
zeitlich begrenzter ~ tenancy for years; **jederzeit kündbarer** ~ tenure at will; **landwirtschaftlicher** ~ agricultural holding; **nachgeordneter** ~ base estate;
~ **einräumen** to grant and demise; **in** ~ **haben** to hold under lease.
Pacht|besitzer tenant by the manner; ~**betrieb** farming, leasing out; ~**brief** lease; ~**dauer** duration of lease, tenancy, [life of] lease, term (period, life) of lease, leasehold tenure; ~**einleitungsklausel** yielding and paying; ~**einnahme[n]**, ~**einkünfte** rent income, property rents, rent-roll, rental; ~**einräumung** granting of a lease.
pachten to lease [out], to take on lease (at rent), to [let to] farm, to hire, to rent;
Grundstück ~ to take a lease on a piece of land; **Hof** ~ to rent a farm; **Lotterieunternehmen** ~ to farm a lottery.
Pächter tenant, lessee, leaseholder, renter, rent payer, occupier *(Br.)*, tacksman *(Scot.)*, *(Landwirtschaft)* tenant, farmer, holder, sharecropper *(US)*;
abgehender ~ waygoing tenant; **alleinberechtigter** ~ tenant in severalty; **jederzeit kündbarer** ~ tenant at will; **landwirtschaftlicher** ~ agricultural (farm) tenant; **neuer** ~ incoming tenant; **übernehmender** ~ ingoing tenant; **zur Barzahlung verpflichteter** ~ cash tenant *(US)*; **in Naturalien zahlender** ~ share tenant, sharecropper *(US)*;
~ **eines Domänengutes** tenant of a demesne; ~ **auf Geldbasis** cash tenant *(US)*; ~ **auf Lebenszeit** tenant for life; ~ **auf bestimmte Zeit** tenant for years;
~ **abmeiern** to turn out a farmer; **als** ~ **annehmen** to grant a lease; **als** ~ **besitzen** to hold on lease.
Pacht|erlaß remission of rent; ~**erneuerung** relocation; ~**ertrag** rental [return], rent-roll; **Miet- und** ~**erträgnisse** rents and profits from land.
Pächterverfügungen, zulässige innocent conveyances *(Br.)*.
Pacht|fläche leasable (leased) area; ~**fortfall durch Grundstückserwerb** extinguishment of rent.
pachtfrei rent-free.
Pacht|gebäude leasehold house (building); ~**gebiet** leasehold area, *(Völkerrecht)* leased (leasehold) territory; **jem. ein** ~**gebiet überlassen** to put s. o. into a farm; ~**gebühr**, ~**geld** [land] rent, premium on a lease, rental; **dem Pächter ungestörten** ~**genuß gestatten** to allow the lessee quiet enjoyment; ~**gesellschaft** leased company *(US)*; ~**gesetz** Agricultural Holding Act *(Br.)*; ~**- und Leihgesetz** Lend-Lease Act *(US)*; ~**gewährung** grant of a lease; ~**grundstück** leasehold, leased (leasehold) property, leasehold land, land out on lease, demised (leasehold) premises.
Pachtgut farm, leasehold, leased property, holding, agricultural holding *(Br.)*, copy *(Br.)*, *(klein)* croft, mailing *(Scot.)*;
~ **auf Lebenszeit** settled estate;
jem. ein ~ **überlassen** to put s. o. into a farm;
~**versicherung** leasehold insurance.
Pacht|häusler mailer, cotter; ~**herr** lessor, landlord; ~**hof** leased farm, ferm, barton; ~**inhaber** [sitting] tenant; ~**jahr** tenancy year; ~**kommissionär** lease broker; ~**kündigung** notice to vacate; ~**land** leasable area, leased (rented) land, leasehold land, agricultural holding *(Br.)*, manor *(US)*; ~**landbefreiung** enfranchisement of leaseholds *(Br.)*; **der Höhe nach bestimmte** ~**leistungen** certain services; ~**makler** lease broker, leasemonger; ~**minderung** reduction of rent; ~**nachlaß** remission of rent; ~**objekt** leased object; ~**-, Abgaben- und Steuerpflicht** obligation to pay rent, rates and taxes; ~**preis** rent, rental.
Pachtrecht leasehold interest;
auflösend bedingtes ~ reversionary lease;
~ **übertragen** to surrender a leasehold estate;
~**übertragung bei Zwangsveräußerung wegen rückständiger Steuern** tax lease.
Pacht|rückstände rent arrears, hanging gale *(Br.)*; ~**satz** tenancy, interest of a tenant, hanging gale *(Br.)*; ~**schutz** [etwa] Rent Act protection *(Br.)*; ~**schutz gewähren** to protect the tenant; ~**schutzverordnung** [etwa] Rent Restriction Act *(Br.)*; ~**summe** rent, rental; ~**system** tenancy system; ~**termin** rent day, gale day *(Br.)*; **kraft Gesetzes vorgenommene** ~**übertragung** surrender by operation of law.
Pachtung leasehold, holding, tenement, tenancy, *(Verpachtung)* leasing out, farming;
gemeinsame ~ cotenancy; **landwirtschaftliche** ~ lease of a farm, farm lease (tenancy); **mit Meliorationsauflagen vergebene** ~ improvement lease;
~ **in einer Hand** entire tenancy; ~ **auf Lebenszeit** lifehold, life leasehold (land).
Pacht|urkunde [covenant of] lease; ~**vereinbarung** agreement for a lease, lease agreement (arrangement); ~**verfallsklausel** forfeiture of a lease, irritant clause *(Scot.)*.
Pachtverhältnis tenancy, lease, [privity of] estate, tenurial relationship;
ohne ~ leaseless;
befristetes ~ determinable lease; **jederzeit kündbares** ~ estate at will; **landwirtschaftliches** ~ farm lease, agricultural tenancy; **sich monatlich verlängerndes** ~ month-to-month tenancy; **jährlich weiterlaufendes** ~ tenancy from year to year; **nach Ablauf der Pachtzeit jederzeit kündbar weiterlaufendes** ~ tenancy at sufferance;
~ **abschließen (begründen)** to enter into a lease; ~ **aufheben** to terminate a lease; ~ **kündigen** to terminate a lease.
Pachtverlängerung renewal (extension) of lease (of leasehold), holding over;
stillschweigende ~ tacit tack *(Scot.)*.
Pachtverlust loss in letting.
Pachtvertrag [covenant of] lease, agreement for a lease, lease contract, farm (farming) lease, indenture of lease, tack *(Scot.)*, articles of set *(Scot.)*;
mündlich abgeschlossener ~ leasehold parole, parole lease; **bedingter** ~ conditional lease; **kurzfristiger** ~ short lease; **landwirtschaftlicher** ~ farm lease; **langjähriger** ~ long-term

lease; **schriftlicher** ~ written lease; **unbefristeter** ~ general tenancy; **unkündbarer** ~ irrevertible lease; **ständig verlängerbarer** ~ perpetually renewable lease; **auf Option des Pächters verlängerbarer** ~ lease renewable at the option of the tenant; **zu gleichen Bedingungen verlängerter** ~ extended lease;
~ **mit Instandhaltungsklausel** repairing lease; ~ **für gewerblich genutzte Räume** commercial lease; ~, **der am Todestag des Verpächters endet** lease [de]terminable on the death of the lessor; ~ **für einen bestimmten Zeitraum** lease for a fixed period;
~ **aufsetzen** to draw up a lease; ~ **erneuern** to take on a lease; ~ **gewähren** to grant a lease; ~ **registrieren lassen** to record a lease; ~ **verlängern** to extend (renew) a lease; ~ **jeweils im letzten Augenblick provisorisch verlängern** to renew a lease on a hand-to-mouth basis.

Pachtvertrags|erneuerung relocation; ~**formular** printed lease form; ~**taxe** leasehold appraisal.

pachtweise on lease.

Pacht|wert rental (letting) value; ~**wirtschaft** tenant farm; ~**zahlung** lease payment, audit; **periodische** ~**zahlung** gale *(Br.)*.

Pachtzeit [term of] lease, tenancy, term of tenancy, rental period;
nach Ablauf der ~ when the lease expires;
noch nicht abgelaufene ~ unexpired term; **festgelegte** ~ periodical tenancy; **restliche** ~ outstanding term.

Pachtzins rental, quiet farm, rent, mailing *(Scot.)*;
angemessener ~ judicial rent; **fester** ~ dead rent; **symbolischer** ~ peppercorn rent *(Br.)*;
~ **für Bergwerksrechte** mining rent; ~ **für die Zeit nach der Aufkündigung** double rent;
zu hohen ~ **verlangen** to overrent;
~**quittung** ground-rent receipt.

Pachtzubehör tenant's fixtures.

Pack pile, *(Pöbel)* rabble, pack, mob;
mit Sack und ~ with bag and baggage;
elendes ~ riff-raff; **faules** ~ lazy lot; **verlogenes** ~ pack of liars;
~ **Wolle** pack of wool; ~ **von Zeitungen** stack of newspapers.

Päckchen parcel, [small] packet *(Br.)*, package;
~ **zurechtmachen** to do up a parcel;
~**gebühr** small packet rate *(Br.)*; ~**post** packet (halfpenny, *Br.*) post.

Packeis pack ice;
im ~ **festsitzen** to be ice-bound.

Packen pack, packing, package, bundle, pile, *(Ballen)* bale, *(Paket)* parcel, packet, *(Verpacken)* packing, packaging;
~ **Aufträge** bunch of orders; ~ **Briefe** bundle of letters; ~ **Bücher** pile of books; ~ **Geldscheine** bundle of bank notes, bank roll;
großen ~ **Arbeit vor sich haben** to have a load of work to do.

packen to pack, to do one's packing, to wrap (do) up, *(verstauen)* to stow;
j. ~ *(Entsetzen)* to seize (overcome, smite) s. o., *(erregen)* to enthral(l) s. o.; **j. ins Bett** ~ to put s. o. to bed; **in Bündeln** ~ to bundle, to make up in packages; **sich fest in eine Decke** ~ to wrap o. s. up in a blanket; **j. bei der Ehre** ~ to appeal to s. one's hono(u)r; **etw. endlich** ~ to get the hang of it; **j. an der Gurgel** ~ to grab s. o. by the throat; **seinen Koffer** ~ to pack one's trunks (traps); **Paket** ~ to roll up a parcel; **in Pakete** ~ to package; **Sache gerade noch** ~ to just make it; **j. beim Schlafittchen** ~ to seize s. o. by the scruff of the neck; **seine Siebensachen** ~ to pack up one's things; **Stier bei den Hörnern** ~ to take the bull by the horns; **Übel an der Wurzel** ~ to destroy evil practices root and branches; **Zeitungen in ein Bündel** ~ to bundle newspapers; **seine Zuhörer** ~ to grip one's audience.

packend gripping, enthralling, *(spannend)* exciting, thrilling, fascinating, breathtaking;
~**e Geschichte** gripping story; ~**er Roman** thriller; ~**e Szene** touching scene.

Packer packer, wrapper, storeman, shipping worker *(US)*, *(Umzug)* removal (moving, *US*) man.

Packerei packing department.

Packerlohn package, packing wage, charge for packing.

Pack|esel pack mule, *(fig.)* drudge, dogsbody *(sl.)*, wheel horse; **wie ein** ~**esel beladen** laden from head to foot; ~**film** film pack; ~**haus** packhouse, store (bonded, *US*) warehouse; ~**hof** dock, warehouse; ~**karton** packing cardboard (case); ~**kiste** packing case (box); ~**korb** basket, hamper; ~**lage** *(Straße)* bottoming; ~**leinwand** packcloth, canvas, packing sheet (paper), duck; ~**liste** packing note (list); ~**maschine** packing machine, packer; ~**material** packing, wrapping, wrappage; ~**meister** head packer; ~**papier** packing sheet, parcel (cap, shop, wrapping, packing, brown) paper; **starkes** ~**papier** manila paper, kraft [paper]; ~**presse** baler; ~**raum** packing (wrapping) room, *(Schiff)* stowage; ~**sattel** packsaddle; ~**schnur** twine, cord; ~**tier** pack animal; ~**tierkolonne** pack train *(US)*; ~**tisch** packing table; ~**tuch** packcloth.

Packung pack, parcel;
verlorene ~ expendable package; **weiterverwendungsfähige** ~ secondary-use package; **wiederverwendbare** ~ dual-use (reuse) package;
~ **im Original** original package;
~ **Zigaretten** pack of cigarettes.

Packungs|beilage package insert *(US)*; ~**bild** brand label; ~**gestalter** displayer; ~**spezialist** cardboard engineer.

Packwagen carriage for goods, luggage van *(Br.)*, baggage car *(US)*.

packweise by (in) parcels, in packages.

Pack|zettel packing slip (ticket), docket; ~**zwirn** pack twine.

Pädagoge educator, teacher, schoolmaster.

Pädagogische Hochschule teachers' college *(US)*, teachers' training college *(Br.)*.

Paddelboot canoe.

Page hotel messenger, callboy, button boy, footboy, bellboy *(US)*;
j. durch einen ~**n suchen lassen** to page s. o.

paginieren to paginate, to foliate, to folio, to page.

Paginierer pager.

Paginiermaschine paging machine.

paginiert, nicht unpaged.

Paginierung pagination, paging, foliation, folio.

Pagode pagoda.

Paket parcel, packet, pack, bundle, package *(US)*, *(Aktien)* block [of shares], parcel of shares;
als ~ by parcel post; **mit** ~**en überladen** overweighted with packages;
gewöhnliches ~ uninsured parcel; **kleines** ~ packet *(Br.)*; **postlagerndes** ~ parcel to be called for; **unversichertes** ~ uninsured parcel; **mit Luftpost versandtes** ~ air parcel *(Br.)*; **zusammenhängendes** ~ *(Wertpapiere)* considered package;
~ **von weniger als 100 Aktien oder von Obligationen unter 100 Dollar Nennwert** fractional lot *(US)*; ~ **üblicher Art und Größe** original package; ~ **mit Eilzustellung** express parcel; **ganzes** ~ **energiepolitischer Maßnahmen** energy package; **ganzes** ~ **geldmarktpolitischer Maßnahmen** package of monetary relief; ~ **von Verhandlungsangeboten** package offer; ~ **unter Wertangabe** insured (registered) parcel;
~ **von Vorschlägen zur Regelung der Beziehungen zwischen den Sozialpartnern ablehnen** to reject the industrial relations package; ~ **aufgeben** to send by parcel post, to dispatch (send off) a parcel; ~ **aufmachen** to undo a parcel; **seine** ~**e aufnehmen** to pick up one's parcels; ~ **ordnungsgemäß beschriften** to direct a parcel correctly; ~**e frankieren** to pay the carriage for a parcel; ~ **als Eilgut befördern lassen** to send a parcel express; ~**e numerieren** to put numbers on packages; ~ **packen** to parcel, to make [up] (roll up) a parcel; ~ **per Nachnahme schicken** to send a package cash *(Br.)* (collect, *US*) on delivery; ~ **setzen** *(drucktechn.)* to compose in companionship; **zu einem** ~ **verpacken** to packet; ~ **verschnüren** to tie up a parcel, to fasten up a box; ~ **fest verschnüren** to knot a parcel firmly;
~**adresse** label, facing slip *(US)*; ~**angebot** *(Kapitalanlagegesellschaft)* block offer; ~**annahmestelle** parcel office; **Brief- und** ~**annahmestelle** receiving house, express office *(US)*; ~**annahme- und** ~**ausgabestelle** parcels office *(US)*; ~**aufgabe** parcel-post window; ~**aufklebeadresse** parcel sticker, facing slip *(US)*; ~**ausgabe**, ~**beförderung** carriage of parcels; ~**beschriftung** directions on a parcel; ~**boot** packet boat (ship, vessel), mail steamer (boat), packet dispatch boat; ~**eingangszettel** parcel bill; ~**emission** block issue; ~**empfangsschein** parcel receipt; ~**gebühren** post-office parcels rates; ~**größe** package size; ~**handel** *(Effektengeschäft)* block transaction in share parcels, large-block trading [business], big-block business, secondary distribution of securities, block trade; ~**händler** large-lot (big-block) trader; ~**karte** parcel mailing form *(US)*; ~**liste** list of parcels; ~**lizenzen** compulsory package licensing; ~**papier** parcel paper; ~**police** packet (package) policy; ~**porto** parcel postage.

Paketpost parcel (parcels) post, fourth-class mail *(US)*;
als ~ parcel-post, by (in) parcels;
~ **im Ausland** foreign parcel post;
per ~ **schicken** to use the inland parcel service;
~**amt** parcel office; ~**briefmarke** parcel-post stamp; ~**dienst** parcel service; ~**dienst in die Gewinnzone bringen** to pull the

parcel service into profit; ~**gebühren,** ~**tarif** parcel-post rates; ~**marke** parcel-post stamp; ~**sätze** parcel-post rates; ~**schalter** parcel-post window; ~**sendung** parcel post; ~**versicherung** parcel-post insurance; ~**wagen** parcel[post] (luggage) van, mail van *(US)*; ~**wesen** parcel-post system; ~**zone** zone for parcels *(US)*; ~**zustellung** parcel delivery (cartage, *Br.*); ~**zustellungsdienst** parcel cartage service *(Br.)*.

Paket|satz *(drucktechn.)* piecework; ~**schalter** parcels desk (counter, window), parcel-post window; **[gewöhnliche]** ~**sendungen** surface parcels *(Br.)*; ~**stempel** parcel-post stamp; ~**verkauf** *(Effektenhandel)* block transaction in share parcels, large-block trading; ~**verkehr** parcel traffic; ~**verpackung** postal wrapping; ~**versand** parcel-post shipment; ~**versicherungsgebühr** insurance charge on a packet; ~**verteilungsstelle** post town *(Br.)*; ~**wagen** parcel carrier (van); ~**wert bei der Verzollung angeben** to declare the value of a parcel; ~**wert ersetzen** to reinstate the contents of a parcel; ~**zettel** label, dispatch note *(Br.)*; ~**zuschläge aushandeln** to negotiate prices on block trades; ~**zustelldienst** parcel delivery service; ~**zustellgebühr** portage; ~**zustellung** parcel delivery (cartage, *Br.*); ~**zustellwagen** parcel delivery truck, parcel van *(Br.)*.

Pakt pact, covenant, agreement, compact;
~ **zur gegenseitigen Hilfeleistung** mutual assistance pact;
~ **abschließen** to covenant, to sign (make) a pact.

paktieren to come to terms, to sign a pact;
mit jem. ~ to make a deal (come to terms) with s. o.

Palast palace;
~**revolte** palace coup; ~**revolution** palace revolution; ~**schätze plündern** to plunder a palace of its treasures; ~**wache** palace guard; ~**wache heraustreten lassen** to call out the state guard.

Palette palet, *(fig.)* range, spectrum, series, palette;
breite ~ varied assortment;
breite ~ **von Dienstleistungen auf dem Bank- und Finanzierungsgebiet** full range of banking and financial services; **bunte** ~ **von Varietévorstellungen** colo(u)rful selection in a variety show.

Palettenladung pallet loading.

Palisadenzaun palisade.

Palme, j. auf die ~ **bringen** to put s. one's monkey up, to get s. one's goat, to get s. o. worked up, to stroke s. o. the wrong way, to put s. o. in a paddy *(sl.)*; **auf die** ~ **gebracht werden** to get hot under the collar.

Pamphlet pamphlet, *(Schmähschrift)* lampoon.

pampig insolent, fresh *(US coll.)*, cheeky *(coll.)*.

Panaschieren split voting.

panaschieren to split one's vote.

Paneelwerk panel, wainscot.

Panier banner, standard;
etw. auf sein ~ **schreiben** to make s. th. one's aim.

Panik panic, stampede, scare;
von ~ **erfaßt** panic-striken;
~ **an der Börse** scare on the stock exchange;
in absolute ~ **geraten** to hit the panic button; ~ **verbreiten** to spread [a] panic; **in** ~ **versetzen** to panic; **politische Partei in** ~ **versetzen** to create a panic in a political party.

panikartig|fliehen to flee in panic-like fear;
~**e Angst** panic fear; ~**e Maßnahmen** panicky measures.

Panik|käufe panic buying; ~**kurse** panic prices; ~**mache** scaremongering; ~**macher** panicmonger, scaremonger, alarmist; ~**stimmung** athmosphere of panic; **in** ~**stimmung versetzen** to stampede.

panisch panic, panicky;
von ~**er Angst ergriffen** panic-stricken.

Panne breakdown, mishap, holdup, *(Maschine)* failure, burst *(US sl.)*, *(Reifen)* puncture, burst, flat, *(Schnitzer)* blunder, faux pas;
gesellschaftliche ~ gaffe; **kleine** ~ slight mishap; **technische** ~ bug *(US sl.)*;
~ **haben** to lay (break) down, *(Reifenpanne)* to malfunction, to have a flat; **in seiner Laufbahn mehrere** ~**n erlebt haben** to have had a few setbacks in one's career.

Pannen|auto car in distress; ~**dienst** breakdown service; ~**dienstversicherung** road service coverage; ~**hilfe** road patrol; ~**köfferchen** breakdown kit.

pannensicher fool-proof, *(Reifen)* puncture-proof.

Pannen|spur *(Autobahn)* hard shoulder; ~**warnschild** warning triangle.

Panoptikum waxworks.

Panorama|aufnahme panorama [photograph]; ~**blick** panoramic view, big-picture view; ~**kamera** panoramic camera; ~**kopf** *(Film)* panhead; ~**scheibe** panorama windshield *(US)*; ~**schwenk** *(Film)* movie panning.

panschen *(Wein)* to adulterate.

Pantoffel, unter dem hen-pecked;
j. unter dem ~ **haben** to have s. o. under one's thumb; **bei der Hitze aus den** ~**n kippen** to pass out in the heat; **unter dem** ~ **stehen** to be under petticoat government (tied to a woman's apron strings, wife-ridden, hen-pecked);
~**held** hen-pecked husband; ~**regiment führen** to wear the trousers, to rule the roost.

Panzer *(Hochofen)* steel jacket, *(mil.)* armo(u)r, *(Panzerwagen)* tank, *(Ummantelung)* casing;
schwerer ~ cruiser tank;
sich mit einem ~ **von Gleichgültigkeit umgeben** to surround o. s. with an armo(u)r of indifference;
~**abwehr** antitank device; ~**abwehrgeschütz** antitank gun; ~**angriff** tank attack; ~**armierung** tank armo(u)r; ~**auto** armo(u)red car; ~**bataillon** tank battalion; ~**besatzung** tank crew.

panzerbrechende|Munition armo(u)r-piercing ammunition; ~ **Waffe** tank buster.

Panzer|büchse bazooka; ~**deck** *(Schiff)* protective deck; ~**drehturm** revolving turret; ~**einheiten** mechanized forces; ~**fahrzeug** armo(u)red car, roller skate *(Br., sl.)*; ~**falle** tank trap; ~**faust** bazooka; ~**gefecht** tank battle; ~**gewölbe** strong room, safety vault; ~**glas** armo(u)r-proof glass; ~**grenadierdivision** armo(u)red division, mechanized division; ~**kabel** armo(u)red cable; ~**kampfwagen** armed combat car; ~**kette** tank track; ~**knacker** tank buster; ~**korps** tank corps; ~**kreuzer** armo(u)red cruiser; ~**landungsboot** tank landing craft; ~**motor** ironclad motor.

panzern to armo(u)r;
sich gegen den Haß seiner Mitmenschen ~ to become indifferent to the hatred of one's fellow men.

Panzer|nahkampf dogfight; ~**platte** steel plate; ~**regiment** tank regiment; ~**schiff** armo(u)r (turret) ship; ~**schlacht** tank battle.

Panzerschrank safe, strongbox;
feuersicherer ~ fire-protection steel filing safe (cabinet);
~**klausel** *(Feuerversicherung)* iron-safe clause.

Panzer|spähwagen armo(u)red (scout) car; ~**sperre** dragon's teeth; ~**spitze** armo(u)red spearhead; ~**transportfahrzeug** tank transporter; ~**turm** turret.

Panzerung durchdringen to penetrate armo(u)r.

Panzer|verband tank formation, armo(u)red unit; ~**wagen** armo(u)red car, land cruiser *(fam.)*.

Papier paper, *(Aktie)* share *(Br.)*, stock *(US)*, *(Scheck)* cheque *(Br.)*, check *(US)*, *(Schreibwaren)* stationery, *(Schuldverschreibung)* bond, *(Urkunde)* instrument, document, paper, *(Wechsel)* bill, *(Wertpapier)* instrument, paper, stock;
auf dem ~ on paper, *(fig.)* theoretically; **aus** ~ paper; **mit** ~ **durchschossen** interleaved; **mit falschen** ~**en versehen** mashed;
~**e** documents, papers, *(Arbeitspapiere)* working papers, *(Ausweispapiere)* indentity papers, *(Wertpapiere)* securities, stocks, effects;
leicht absetzbare ~**e** liquid securities; **ausgeloste** ~**e** drawn securities; **auf den Namen ausgestelltes** ~ straight note *(US)*; **bankfähiges** ~ bank paper (bill), bankable paper; **börsengängige** ~**e** realizable stock, quoted (listed, *US*) securities; **diskontfähiges** ~ discountable bill; **dreiprozentige** ~**e** three-percents *(Br.)*, threes; **durchsichtiges** ~ flimsy; **erstklassige** ~**e** high-quality stock, gilt-edged (fine) papers *(Br.)*, gilts *(Br.)*, blue chips *(US)*; **festverzinsliche** ~**e** fixed-interest securities, bonds; **fundierte** ~**e** consolidated stock *(Br.)*; **fünfprozentige** ~**e** fives *(US)*; **international gehandelte** ~**e** international stock, interbourse securities; **schlecht gehendes** ~ dull performer; **gekörntes** ~ grained paper; **geleimtes** ~ sized paper; **geripptes (gestreiftes)** ~ *(Banknoten)* laid paper; **gestempeltes** ~ stamped paper; **gestrichenes** ~ coated (enamel) paper; **getöntes** ~ colo(u)red paper; **glattes** ~ glazed paper; **gummiertes** ~ gummed paper; **handelsfähiges** ~ negotiable instrument (paper, note), instrument of credit, *(Aktiengesellschaft)* corporation paper *(US)*; **hartes** ~ *(Foto)* hard paper; **hochwertige** ~**e** high-grade issues; **holzfreies** ~ wood-free paper; **holzhaltiges** ~ wood-content paper; **indossables** ~ negotiable instrument; **kariertes** ~ cross-section paper; **konsolidierte** ~**e** consolidated stock; **kurzfristiges** ~ self-liquidating (short-sighted, short-dated, *Br.*) paper; **langfristiges** ~ long (long-dated, *Br.*) paper; **auf den Inhaber lautendes** ~ instrument payable to bearer; **auf den Namen lautendes** ~ registered stock; **lichtempfindliches** ~ sensitized paper; **liniertes** ~ ruled paper; **marktfähiges** ~ marketable securities; **maschinenglattes** ~ machine-finished paper; **mattes** ~ mat paper, unglazed paper; **mündelsichere** ~**e** gilt-edged securities

(stock) *(Br.)*, gilts *(Br.)*, trust stock *(US)*, trustee's bonds *(Br.)*; **nachgiebiges** ~ *(bei anziehenden Kursen)* soft spot *(US)*; **notleidende** ~e documents in default (sufferance); **prolongiertes** ~ lockup *(Br.)*; **rediskontfähiges und lombardfähiges** ~ eligible paper *(US)*; **hoch rentierliche** ~e securities yielding a high return; **satiniertes** ~ imitation art paper, glazed paper; **saugfähiges** ~ absorbent paper; **schlechte** ~e dubious stocks (securities); **sechsprozentige** ~e sixes *(US)*; **selbstdurchschreibendes** ~ self-duplicating paper; **sicheres** ~ first-rate stock; **übertragbares** ~ negotiable instrument; **unausgefülltes** ~ blank paper; **unbeschriebenes** ~ white paper; **ungesichertes** ~ straight paper; **ungestempeltes** ~ unstamped paper; **verpfändete** ~e pledged securities *(Br.)*, pawned (hypothecated) stocks *(US)*; **variabel verzinsliche** ~e determinable interest securities; **wasserdichtes** ~ waxed paper; **weißes** ~ clean paper; **wertloses** ~ worthless instrument, instrument of no effect, scrap of paper; **an verschiedene Zahlungsempfänger zahlbares** ~ instrument payable to joint payees; **zedierte** ~e assigned stocks; **zentralbankfähige** ~e approved securities, eligible papers *(US)*; **zerknülltes** ~ wad; **[nicht] zinstragende** ~e [non]dividendpaying stock; **zweitklassiges** ~ second-rate paper;
mündelsichere ~e **der ersten Auswahlstufe** narrower-range investments *(Br.)*; ~ **in Ballen** paper in reels; ~ **für den Druck von Obligationen** bond paper; ~e **mit schwankendem Ertrag** variable-yield securities; ~ **mit fester Laufzeit** time paper; ~ **mit bis zu fünfjähriger Laufzeit** shorts *(Br.)*, short-dated stocks; ~e **mit mittlerer und längerer Laufzeit** mediums *(Br.)*; ~ **mit Leinenstruktur** crash finish; ~ **mit Trauerrand** black-edged paper; ~ **mit nur einer Unterschrift** one-name paper *(US)*; ~ **mit zwei Unterschriften** double-name (two-name) paper; ~e **mit verschiedener Verfallzeit** papers with various periods to run; ~ **mit Wasserzeichen** filigreed (water-marked) paper; ~ **von zweifelhaftem Wert** dubious paper;
~e **aufrufen (einziehen)** to call in securities; ~e **auslosen** to draw securities by lot; **Schiff mit amtlichen** ~en **ausstatten** to document a ship; ~ **begeben** to deliver (give out) an instrument; **seine** ~e **bekommen** to get one's books (cards, *coll.*); ~e **mit einem Gewicht beschweren** to keep papers down with a weight; **zu** ~ **bringen** to reduce to writing, to [commit to] paper; **seine Gedanken schnell zu** ~ **bringen** to pop down one's ideas on paper; **seine** ~e **durcheinanderbringen** to muddle one's papers; ~e **durchwühlen** to forage among papers; **in** ~ **einschlagen (einwickeln)** to wrap up (fold) in paper; ~e **halten, um den Preis zu treiben** to go long of the market; ~e **hinauftreiben** to trump stocks *(Br.)*; ~ **liniieren** to line paper; **seine** ~e **mitbringen** to bring one's qualifications with one; **seine** ~e **realisieren** to liquidate one's securities; **ohne** ~e **reisen** to travel without identification papers; **Blatt** ~ **vermanschen** to spoil a sheet of paper; **mit den notwendigen** ~en **versehen** to furnish with documents, to document; ~e **über den ganzen Fußboden verstreuen** to litter papers about the floor; ~e **verwerten** to sell shares (stock, *US*); ~ **zerknüllen** to ruffle (crumple) paper; ~e **zusammenheften** to pin (clip) papers together;
~ **ist geduldig** paper won't blush;
~**abfälle** wastepaper; ~**bahn** web; ~**beschwerer** paperweight; ~**beutel** paper bag; ~**blockade** paper blockade; ~**bogen** sheet of paper; ~**brei** *(Papierherstellung)* pulp; ~**dollar** paper dollar; ~**drache** kite; ~**einband** paper cover; **mit** ~**einband** paper-covered; ~**einführung** inserting of paper; ~**einstampfung** reduction of old paper; ~**fabrik** paper mill (factory, works); ~**fabrikant** paper manufacturer; ~**fabrikation** papermaking, paper manufacturing; ~**falzmaschine** paper-folding machine, folder; ~**fetzen** scrap of paper; ~**flut** mounds of paper; ~**format** size of paper; **handelsübliches** ~**format** commercial note.

Papiergeld paper money (currency), notes *(Br.)*, bills *(US)*, representative (folding) money *(US)*, soft money *(US sl.)*, long green *(US sl.)*, lettuce *(sl.)*, fiduciary money *(Australia)*; **einlösbares** ~ convertible money (paper); **nicht einlösbares** ~ irredeemable money, inconvertible paper; **entwertetes** ~ rag money *(US)*; **gedecktes** ~ covered money *(US)* (paper); **teilweise durch Gold und Silber gedecktes** ~ credit currency; **ungedecktes** ~ uncovered paper (managed, fiat, *US*) money; ~ **ohne Deckung** uncovered (managed, fiat, *US*) paper money; ~ **mit Silber- oder Goldumtauschrecht** redeemable currency; ~ **einlösen** to redeem paper money;
~**ausgabe** issuance of paper money; ~**ausweitung** paper-money expansion; ~**inflation** paper-money inflation; ~**tasche** note (pocket, *US*) book; ~**umlauf** credit (note) circulation; ~**währung** paper currency, fiduciary standard.

Papier|geschäft stationery shop (store, *US*); ~**gewinn** paper profit (surplus); ~**handel** paper trade; ~**händler** stationer; ~**handlung** stationer's shop, stationery shop (store, *US*); ~**industrie** paper trade; ~**klammer** paper clip; ~**knäuel** wad; ~**korb** wastepaper basket, wastebasket *(US)*; **in den** ~**korb befördern** to throw into the wastepaper basket, to basket, to limbo; **das gehört in den** ~**korb** that's rubbish; ~**kosten** costs of paper; ~**kram** bumf *(Br., sl.)*; **von der Last des bürokratischen** ~**krams befreien** to dig the staff out from under the paperwork mountain; ~**krieg** red tape, paper warfare (work), bureaucracy; **langer** ~**krieg** pettifogging correspondence; ~**maché** papier-mâché; ~**macher** papermaker; ~**maschine** paper machine; ~**messer** paper knife; ~**mühle** paper mill; ~**reste** litter; ~**sack** paper sack (bag); ~**schere** paper scissors; ~**schlange** streamer; ~**schneidemaschine** paper cutter (-cutting machine); ~**schnitzel** scraps of paper; ~**serviette** paper napkin; ~**stau** *(Satzmaschine)* jam; ~**streifen** *(Lochstreifen)* tape, *(Telegrafie)* ticker tape; ~**strom** flow of paper; ~**tapete** wallpaper; ~**taschentuch** paper tissue, kleenex *(US)*; ~**tiger** paper tiger; ~**tüte** paper bag; ~**valuta** paper value (currency); ~**valuten** paper exchanges; ~**verluste durch Verkäufe in echte Verluste umwandeln** to turn paper losses into actual losses; ~**währung** paper (note, free) currency, paper (fiat) standard, inconvertible paper currency; ~**währung ohne Einlösungszwang** inconvertible paper currency; ~**waren** stationery; ~**warengeschäft** stationery shop (store, *US*); ~**wert** book value; ~**werte** paper assets; ~**wolf** shredder; ~**zeichen** watermark; ~**zoll** paper duty; ~**zuführung** paper feed.

Papp|band book in boards, pasteboard binding; ~**becher** paper cup; ~**deckel** paperboard, pasteboard, book in boards.

Pappe cardboard, paperboard, board, pasteboard;
in ~ **eingebunden** bound in boards;
starke ~ millboard;
nicht von ~ **sein** to be pretty tough;
das ist nicht von ~ that's not to be sneezed at.

pappen, Briefmarken auf einen Umschlag to stick stamps on an envelope.

Pappenheimer kennen, seine to know one's customers.

Pappenstiel *(coll.)* carfare;
kein ~ no trifling matter;
keinen ~ **wert sein** not to be worth a bean (twopence, a brass farthing); **für einen** ~ **verkaufen** to sell for a mere song.

Papp|kamerad *(Schießstand)* cardboard dummy; ~**karton** cardboard box; ~**rolle** mailing tube; ~**schachtel** cardboard box.

Papst Pope, Holy Father.

päpstlich papal, pontifical;
~**er Stuhl** Holy See.

Parabol|antenne dish antenna; ~**reflektor** dish.

Parade [military] review;
~ **in Galauniform** dress parade;
~ **abnehmen** to muster parade, to take muster of troops, to hold a review; **jem. in die** ~ **fahren** to snap off s. one's nose, to thwart s. one's plans;
~**aufstellung** review order; ~**investitionen** investment in show prices; ~**marsch** parade march; ~**pferd** show performer; ~**platz** parade ground; ~**rolle** star part; ~**schritt** parade (goose) step; ~**stück** showpiece, fat; ~**wagen** bandwaggon; ~**werte** *(Bilanz)* window-dressing figures.

paradieren, mit seinem neuen Auto to show off with one's new car.

Paradies auf Erden heaven on earth.

paradox klingen to sound paradoxical.

Paragraph *(Abschnitt)* paragraph, section, *(Artikel)* article, clause, *(Symbol §)* section mark, paragraph;
einzelne ~**en** loose paragraphs; **neuer** ~ fresh paragraph;
~**en einfügen** to insert a clause; **in** ~**en einteilen** to paragraph; **unter einen** ~**en fallen** to be covered by a clause; **in** ~ **5 geregelt sein** to fall within article 5; ~**en streichen** to cancel a paragraph; **in** ~**en zusammenstellen** to arrange articles in groups.

Paragraphen|gestrüpp meshes of the law; ~**reiter** Jack-in-office, pettifogger; ~**reiterei** officialism, red tapism, legalism; ~**zeichen** paragraph, section mark.

parallel *(el.)* multiple;
mit etw. ~ **laufen** to run parallel to s. th.; ~ **zur Eisenbahn verlaufen** to parallel the railway.

Parallel|ausgabe parallel edition; ~**buchung** parallel posting; ~**buchungsbeleg** posting reference.

Parallele ziehen to draw a parallel.

Parallel|fall parallel case; ~**gruppen** matched groups.

Parallelität parallel;
bewußte ~ **des Handels** *(Kartellrecht)* parallel conscious business behavio(u)r.

Parallel|markt *(Währungsverfall)* parallel (wildcat) market; **~rechner** *(Datenverarbeitung)* parallel computer; **~register führen** to rule a register similarly; **~schaltung** *(el.)* parallel connection, multiple; **~übertragungsbuchung** parallel posting; **~verhandlungen** parallel negotiations; **~verkehr** *(Schiene und Straße)* competing traffic; **~versammlung** overflow meeting; **~versuch** *(Statistik)* replication; **~währung** parallel standard; **~wertung** comparative valuation.
paralysieren to paralyse, to cripple.
paramilitärisch paramilitary.
Paraphe paraph, initial.
paraphieren to paraph, to initial, to append one's initials.
Paraphierung initialling.
Parasit parasite, sponger, leech, suck-egg;
~en der Gesellschaft caterpillars of society.
parat ready, prepared, on hand;
immer ~ always at your fingertips;
Antwort ~ haben to have a pat answer; **Verbandskasten immer ~ haben** to always keep a first-aid kit handy.
Pardon pardon, *(mil.)* quarter;
~ geben to grant pardon.
Parenthese parenthesis;
Satz in ~ setzen to put a sentence in brackets.
Parforce|jagd, an einer ~jagd teilnehmen to follow the hounds; **~leistung** tour de force.
Parfüm essence, perfume, scent.
Parfümerie scent shop, perfumery, cosmetic store *(US)*.
Pari par [value];
al ~ at par (parity); **über ~** above par, at a premium; **unter ~** below par, at a discount; **zu ~** at par;
Aktien über ~ ausgeben to issue shares at a premium; **Aktien unter ~ ausgeben** to issue shares at a discount; **~ begeben** to place at par; **über ~ kaufen** to buy at a premium; **zu ~ nehmen** to receive at par; **~ notieren** to quote pari; **unter ~ sinken** to fall below par; **~ stehen** to be at par (at a parity), to run (stand) at par, to be at a discount; **über ~ stehen** to be above par (at a premium), to sell at a premium; **unter ~ stehen (gehandelt werden)** to run (stand) at par, to stand (sell, be) at a discount; **zum Inventarwert unter ~ stehen** to sell at discount to its net asset value; **zu ~ umlaufen** to pass at par.
Pari|ausgabe issue at par; **~einlösungssystem** par redemption system; **~emission** issue at par, par emission.
parieren to knuckle under, to toe the line;
Schlag ~ to ward off a blow.
Pari|grenze parity; **~kurs** par of exchange, parity price; **~platz** par point *(US)*; **~rückzahlung** redemption at par; **~satz** par exchange rate.
Pariser|Seerechtsdeklaration Declaration of Paris on Maritime Warfare; **~ Verbandsübereinkunft über gewerblichen Rechtsschutz** Paris Convention for the Protection of Industrial Property; **~ Währungsklub** Group of Ten.
Parität par value, parity, equality;
feste ~ fixed parity; **künstlich gehaltene ~en** pegged exchange rates; **Londoner ~** London equivalent (parity); **rechnerische ~** calculated parity; **veränderliche ~** adjustable peg;
~ der Kaufkraft purchasing power parity; **~ der Währungen** parity value of currencies;
Wechselkurse in der festgelegten ~ halten to peg its exchange rates at par; **seine ~ langsam verändern** *(Währung)* to crawl its parity; **gegenseitige ~ wiederherstellen** to bring back to parity with each other.
Paritäten|änderung change of parity; **ermessensmäßig vorgenommene ~änderung** discretionary peg; **~liste** par (pari, *US*) list; **~tafel** table of parities, parity table.
paritätisch at par (parity), *(fig.)* on an equal footing, equal, *(Schulen)* undenominational;
~e Interessenvertretung parity representation; **~e Lohn- und Preiskommission** Joint Commission on Wages and Prices; **~e Mitbestimmung** codetermination; **~e Schule** nondenominational school; **~e Vertretung** representation in equal numbers; **~e Vertretung von Aktionären und Arbeitnehmern im Aufsichtsrat** parity representation of shareholders and workers on the supervisory board.
Paritäts|änderung change in the par values; **~freigabe** *(Wechselkurse)* floating of the exchange rate; **~gefüge** parity structure; **~klausel** parity clause; **~kurs** parity price; **~neuordnung** currency realignment; **~punkt** parity point *(US)*; **~rechte** parity rights; **~system** parity system; **~tabelle** par (pari, *US*) list, parity table; **~veränderung** parity shift; **~wechsel** bill at par (on a par point, *US*); **~wert** par value, parity.
Park park, grounds;
öffentlicher ~ commons *(US)*;
~ für die öffentliche Benutzung freigeben to open a park to the public.
Parkanlage public parks, lands, grounds, pleasure ground;
~ für transportable Häuser mobile home park.
Park|aufseher park-keeper; **~bank** park bench; **~bedürfnisse** parking demands; **~beschränkungen** parking limitation; **~bestimmungen** parking controls; **~bucht** lay by *(Br.)*, parking bay.
Parken, auf eine Seite beschränktes ~ unilateral parking; **~ verboten** parking prohibited, no parking; **wildes ~** unauthorized parking;
~ nur für Anlieger no parking except for residents access; **~ auf eigene Gefahr** all cars parked at owner's risk; **~ neben dem Gehsteig** curb parking; **~ nur für Kunden** for patrons only; **~ außerhalb der Ladenstadt** fringe parking; **~ im Parkverbot** parking in dangerous position; **~ auf der Straße** [on-]street parking; **~ in der Tiefgarage** underground parking.
parken to park;
neben einem abgestellten Fahrzeug ~ to double-park; **auf eigene Gefahr ~** to park at the owner's risk; **schräg ~** to angle-park.
Parkerschließung park development.
Parkett inlaid floor, parquet, parquetry, *(Börse)* floor, *(Theater)* orchestra *(US)*, stalls *(Br.)*;
auf diplomatischem ~ in diplomatic circles; **~ Mitte** centre (center, *US*) stalls;
ausverkauftes ~ *(Theater)* capacity crowd; **erstes ~** orchestra [stalls]; **hinteres ~** orchestra (parquet) circle *(US)*, back stalls *(Br.)*; **vorderes ~** parquet *(US)*, front stalls *(Br.)*; **zweites ~** pit; **Fußboden mit ~ auslegen** to parquet a floor; **sich auf dem besten ~ bewegen können** to feel at ease in high society;
~brett panel board; **~fußboden** parquet, parquetry, inlaid floor.
Parkettierung inlaying of floors.
Parkett|platz, ~sitz seat in the stalls, orchestra stall *(US)*.
Park|gebühr parking fee (charges); **monatliche ~gebühr** monthly parking; **~gelände** park, public parks; **keine ~gelegenheit** no place to park; **~[hoch]haus** multistor(e)y garage (car park, *Br.*), parking building; **~instandsetzung** *(mil.)* base maintenance; **~kino** drive-in cinema; **~kontrolleur** traffic warden *(Br.)*; **~leitlinien** parking lines; **~leuchte** parking lamp; **~licht** parking light; **~lücke** parking gap (space); **sich in eine ~lücke einrangieren** to park in a confined space.
Parkmöglichkeit|en parking facilities (lot, *US*), park spot;
beschränkte (eingeschränkte) ~en parking limitation, parking restraint; **kostenlose ~** free parking lot; **überdachte ~** rooftop parking; **unterirdische ~** underground parking;
billige ~en während der Nachtzeit low-cost night-time parking; **~en schaffen** to provide for parking.
Parkplatz parking site *(Br.)*, car park *(Br.)*, parking space (spot, lot, *US*), *(Autobahn)* parking area, roadside park, layby *(Br.)*; **bewachter ~** car park with attendant *(Br.)*, guaranteed parking lot *(US)*; **öffentlicher ~** public parking place; **reservierter ~** parking bay; **unbewachter ~** unattended car park;
~ nur für Anlieger no parking except for residents access; **~ für Omnibusse** bus parking;
sich einen ~ sichern to preempt a parking space;
~einnahmen income from a car park; **~politik** parking policy; **~vorschriften** parking regulations; **~wächter** parking attendant, car-park attendant *(Br.)*.
Park|problem car-park problem; **~randgebiete** fringe-area parking; **~raum** parking area; **~scheibe** parking disk; **~scheibensystem** disk parking; **~spur** parking lane; **~sünder** parking offender; **~uhr** parking meter (slot), parkometer *(US)*; **~uhrbereich** parking-meter zone; **~verbot** parking ban, no parking; **~verbotsgebiet, ~verbotszone** no-parking area (zone), clearway zone, two-away zone *(US)*, *(absolute)* pink zone *(Br.)*; **~verbotsschild** no-parking sign; **~verbotsstraße** restricted (no-waiting) street; **~vergehen** parking offence; **~vorschriften** parking regulations; **~wächter** park-keeper, traffic warden *(Br.)*, *(Parkplatz)* parking (car-park, *Br.*) attendant; **~zeit** parking time; **verbotene ~zeit** restricted hours; **~zeitüberschreitung** overtime parking, parking-meter violation; **~zettel** parking ticket; **~zone** parking area.
Parlament parliament, diet, The House *(Br.)*, *(einzelne Staaten der USA)* General Assembly *(US)*, legislature *(US)*;
dem ~ verantwortlich accountable to Parliament;
beschlußfähiges ~ quorum; **beschlußunfähiges ~** no House; **direkt gewähltes ~** directly assembly;
~ von Jasagern rubberstamp Parliament;

dem ~ angehören to sit in Parliament; **~ auflösen** to dissolve Parliament, to appeal to the country *(Br.)*; **im ~ bekanntgeben** to announce in a parliamentary answer; **~ einberufen** to summon (hold, convoke) Parliament; **~ eröffnen** to open Parliament; **~ informieren** to lay papers *(Br.)*; **für das ~ kandidieren** to run (stand) for Parliament; **sich dem ~ stellen** to meet the Parliament; **~ vollständig unterrichten** to lay complete information before the House *(Br.)*; **im ~ voll unterstützen** to give full parliamentary airing; **~ vertagen** to prorogue (adjourn) Parliament; **dem ~ zur Beratung vorlegen** to put before the House for consideration *(Br.)*; **dem ~ vorliegen** to be up before parliament; **ins ~ wählen** to return to Parliament; **ins ~ gewählt werden** to be returned (go into) to Parliament; **durch das ~ gestürzt werden** to be defeated in Parliament; **im ~ verwischt werden** to get lost in a parliamentary fog;
das ~ hat sich vertagt Parliament is up;

Parlamentarier parliamentarian, parliamentary, member of Parliament, representative;
alterfahrener ~ old parliamentary hand.

parlamentarisch parliamentary;
~e Anfrage interpellation, parliamentary question; **~e Anfrage unter den Tisch fallen lassen** to burke a parliamentary question; **~e Anfrage richten** to interpellate; **~e Ausdrucksweise** parliamentary language; **~er Ausschuß** parliamentary (House, *Br.*) committee; **~e Beratungen** parliamentary deliberations; **~e Beredsamkeit** parliamentary eloquence; **~er Berichterstatter** rapporteur; **~e Demokratie** parliamentarian democracy; **~e Einrichtungen** parliamentary institutions; **~e Genehmigung** parliamentary powers; **~e Geschäftsordnung** parliamentary law; **~e Immunität** parliamentary privilege; **~e Körperschaft** legislative body; **~e Mehrheit** majority in parliament; **~e Niederlage** parliamentary defeat; **~e Regierung** parliamentary government; **~e Regierungsform** parliamentary (representative) government; **~e Sitzungsprotokolle** parliamentary summary; **~ regierter Staat** parliamentary state; **~er Staatssekretär** Parliamentary Private Secretary; **~er Strafbeschluß** bill of attainder; **~es System** parliamentary system, parliamentary (representative) government; **~e Usancen** parliamentary practice; **~er Vertreter** parliamentary agent.

Parlamentarismus parliamentarism, parliamentary system.

Parlamentärs | flagge flag of truce; **~schiff** cartel ship.

Parlaments | abgeordneter member of parliament; **~abstimmung** parliamentary vote; **~akte** statute, Act of Parliament; **~anklage** articles of impeachment; **~ausschuß** parliamentary commission (committee), House committee *(Br.)*, *(zur Untersuchung einer Wahl)* electoral commission *(US)*; **~ausschuß für Verhaltensweise von Abgeordneten** house ethics committee; **~bannmeile** precinct; **gedruckte ~berichte** the journals, parliamentary debates *(Br.)*; **~beschluß** parliamentary order (act), Act of Parliament *(Br.)*; **~bezirk** parliamentary borough *(Br.)*; **~brauch** parliamentary practices; **~dauer** session; **~debatte** parliamentary (congressional, *US*) debate; **~debatte eines Gesetzentwurfes verlangen** to call up a bill before a legislative body; **~direktor** clerk of the House *(Br.)*; **~einberufung** summons *(Br.)*; **~eröffnung** opening of Parliament; **~eröffnungsrede** the Queen's speech; **~ferien** recess, congressional recess *(US)*; **~ferien beginnen** to rise for recess; **~fraktion** parliamentary group; **~gebäude** Parliament house, Houses of Parliament *(Br.)*, state house *(US)*; **~gesetz** House bill *(Br.)*, Act of Parliament; **~herrschaft** parliamentary rule; **~immunität** parliamentary immunity (privilege); **~kandidat** parliamentary candidate; **~kontrolle** parliamentary control; **~mandat** parliamentary mandate; **~mehrheit** parliamentary majority; **~mitglied** Member of Parliament *(Br.)*, parliamentary delegate, representative, deputy, member of congress *(US)*; **einfaches ~mitglied** private member; **~mitglied werden** to enter Parliament (The House, *Br.*); **~nötigung** obstructing proceedings of legislature, seditious assembly *(Br.)*; **~nötigung begehen** to obstruct the proceedings of legislature; **~ordnung** parliamentary practices; **erfahrener ~praktikus** old parliamentarian hand; **~präsident** president of the assembly, speaker; **~privilegien** parliamentary privileges; **~protokolle** parliament rolls *(Br.)*, official report, parliamentary (congressional, *US*) records; **~rede** parliamentary speech, *(erste)* maiden speech; **~schluß** prorogation; **~sekretär** clerk of the Assembly *(US)*.

Parlamentssitz seat [in Parliament], congressional seat *(US)*;
knapp gehaltener ~ marginal seat;
~ ohne Gegenkandidat uncontested seat;
~ aufgeben to vacate one's seat [in Congress] *(US)*; **sich um einen ~ bewerben** to put up for a seat, to contest (canvass for) a seat in Parliament; **seinen ~ verlieren** to lose one's seat in Parliament; **jem. einen ~ verschaffen** to seat a candidate; **~e neu verteilen** to redistribute the seats in Parliament.

Parlamentssitzung sitting (session) of Parliament, parliamentary proceeding;
einer ~ beiwohnen to attend the House;
es ist ~ there is a house *(Br.)*.

Parlaments | tagung session (sitting) of Parliament; **~vertagung** rising of Parliament; **~vorlage** bill in Parliament; **gedruckte ~vorlage** engrossed bill; **~vorrecht** privilege of the house; **~wachtmeister** serjeant; **~wahlen** general (parliamentary) election; **vorgezogene ~wahlen** early general election; **vorgezogene ~wahlen abhalten** to call for an early election; **~wahlkreis** borough, constituency.

Parodie parody, skit.

parodieren to parody, to burlesque.

parodistisch parodistic, burlesque;
in beinahe ~er Weise almost to the point of parody.

Parole *(mil.)* word, password, watchword, countersign, *(Parteipolitik)* rallying cry;
~buch orderly *(Br.)* (order) book.

Paroli bieten, jem. to stand up to s. o.

Partei *(parl.)* party, faction, camp, *(Clique)* clan, clique, *(Mietpartei)* tenant, lessee, *(Prozeß)* party, litigant, litigator, side;
keiner ~ angehörend nonpartisan; **der konservativen ~ angehörend** conservative;
abgewiesene ~ nonsuited party; **abwesende ~** defaulting party, defaulter; **antragstellende ~** petitioning party, claimant; **arme ~** *(jur.)* pauper, poor person; **an der Macht befindliche ~** governing (ruling) party, party in power; **im Verzug befindliche ~** party in default, defaulting party, defaulter; **beklagte ~** defendant, defence, party sued, party to be charged; **benachteiligte (beschwerte) ~** aggrieved party; **berechtigte ~** entitled party; **beteiligte ~en** parties concerned; **nicht beteiligte ~en** third parties; **betreibende ~** prosecuting party; **betroffene ~** person affected; **bürgerliche ~en** middle-class parties; **Demokratische ~** Democratic party *(US)*; **eigentliche ~** proper party; **erschienene ~** party present; **nicht erschienene ~** party in default, defaulting party; **erstgenannte ~** party of the first part; **fortschrittliche ~** progressive political party; **gegnerische ~** opponent; **geladene ~** party summoned; **gemäßigte ~** moderate party; **geschädigte ~** injured party; **interessierte ~** interested party; **klagende ~** claimant; **klägerische ~** prosecuting party, party suing, plaintiff; **Kommunistische ~** Communist[ic] Party, the Communists; **Konservative ~** Conservative Party; **kostenpflichtige ~** party liable for cost; **Labour ~** Labour Party *(Br.)*; **aktiv legitimierte ~** real party; **Liberale ~** Liberal party; **nachträglich mitverklagte ~** defendant added; **obsiegende ~** prevailing (winning, successful) party; **politische ~** political party; **radikale ~** extreme party; **rechtsgerichtete ~** right-wing party; **Republikanische ~** republican (Grand Old) party *(US)*; **säumige ~** defaulter, defaulting party; **sozialistische ~** Socialist party, the Socialists; **streitende ~** contestant; **die streitenden ~en** party and party, parties to a dispute, contending parties; **unterliegende ~** unsuccessful (aggrieved, defeated, losing) party; **verfassungswidrige ~** unconstitutional party; **verpflichtete ~** party under contract, party liable; **vertraglich verpflichtete ~** party under contract; **vertragsbrüchige ~** party in breach; **vertragsschließende ~en** parties to a contract, contracting parties (partners), parties to a agreement; **hohe vertragsschließende ~en** High Contracting Parties; **vertragstreue ~** nondefaulting party; **im Wahlkreis vertretene ~en** constituency parties; **wirkliche ~** party in interest *(US)*; **durch innere Streitigkeiten zerrissene ~** party turned by internal strife; **zum Armenrecht zugelassene ~** poor person, assisted party, pauper *(US)*;
~ im Armenrecht poor (assisted, *Br.*) person, poor litigant *(US)*; **~ der äußersten Linken** extreme left party; **~ in einem Zivilprozeß** party to a lawsuit, litigants at law;
von seiner ~ abfallen to desert one's party; **Staat als kriegführende ~ anerkennen** to recognize a government as a belligerent; **einer ~ als Mitglied angehören** to be affiliated to a party; **sich einer ~ anschließen** to adhere to (associate o. s. with) a party; **sich einer politischen ~ anschließen** to attach o. s. to a political party; **sich einer ~ wieder anschließen** to rejoin a party; **nicht genügend Begeisterung für seine ~ aufbringen** to lack the party spirit; **aus der ~ ausschließen** to purge from a party; **aus einer ~ ausstoßen** to expel s. o. from (read s. o. out of) a party, to drum out of a party; **aus einer ~ austreten** to secede from (leave) a political party; **einer ~ beitreten** to accede to (join) a

party; **seine ~ in den Griff bekommen** to establish a grip on one's own party; **~en belehren** to caution the parties; **aufrührerische Geister in der ~ besänftigen** to mollify the dissidents; **~ bilden** to constitute o. s. a party; **sich für eine ~ entscheiden** to vote for a side; **jds. (für j.) ~ ergreifen** to take the part of (side with) s. o., to take up the cudgels for s. o.; **~ der Regierung ergreifen** to side with the ministerial party; **~ des Siegers ergreifen** to come down on the right side of the fence; **~ führen** to lead a party; **konservative ~ führen** to lead the Conservatives; **~en Gelegenheit zur Stellungnahme geben** to hear the parties; **quer durch die ~en gehen** to cut across party lines; **~ gründen** to organize a political party; **es mit beiden ~en halten** to straddle *(US)*; **es mit keiner ~ halten** to sit on the fence; **bei Ernennungen auch Mitglieder der anderen ~ heranziehen** to cross the party line in making appointments *(US)*; **~ im Stich lassen** to rat a party; **zwischen den ~en lavieren** to temporize between parties; **~ nehmen** to stand up for; **von beiden ~en Geschenke nehmen** to take gifts with both hands; **sich zu keiner ~ schlagen** to sit on the fence, to remain neutral; **~ sein** to be interested (prejudiced); **mit der Führung der liberalen ~ einverstanden sein** to follow the Liberal Party; **in einer Frage in einer ~ verschiedener Meinung sein** to split a party on a question; **~ spalten** to split a party; **für die Republikanische ~ stimmen** to vote Republican; **zu einer anderen ~ übergehen** to cross the floor of the House *(Br.)*, to flop over *(US)*; **zur erfolgreichen ~ umschwenken** to climb aboard the bandwaggon; **politische ~ finanziell unterstützen** to support a political party; **~ verbieten** to ban a party; **~ verlassen** to break away, to desert (rat) a party; **~ überstürzt verlassen** to flounce out of a party; **~en vorladen** to notify the parties; **~ wählen** to give one's vote to a party; **Konservative ~ wählen** to go Conservative; **~ wechseln** to turn one's coat *(Br.)*; **in den Schoß der ~ zurückkehren** to return to the fold; **~abrede, ~absprache** deal between parties, stipulation; **~abstimmung** party ballot; **~abzeichen** party emblem (badge), *(für den Wahlkampf)* campaign button *(US)*.

parteiamtlich mitgeteilt werden to be announced by official party sources.

Partei|angehöriger, ~anhänger party follower (man), enrolled party member, partyist, partisan;
opportunistischer ~ party henchman; **treuer ~** loyalist, a true blue, regular *(US)*.

Partei|anklage partisan charge; **sich nach den ~anordnungen richten** to go with one's party; **~antrag** ex parte application; **~anwärter** candidate; **~anweisungen bei der Abstimmung folgen** to vote the straight ticket *(US)*; **~apparat** party *(US)* (political) machinery; **~appell** party appeal; **~archiv** party archive; **~aufgabe** party function; **~ausschluß im Schnellverfahren** summary expulsion; **~ausschuß** steering (district) committee, caucus; **~austritt** breakaway from a party, separation from a party; **~autonomie** party autonomy; **~basis** grassroots level; **~behauptung** *(jur.)* allegation; **~beitrag** party dues; **~beitragsfreiheit erreichen** to contract out *(Br.)*; **~beitritt** sign-up; **~beschluß** party vote; **~beschlüssen die Zustimmung versagen** to refuse to support the policy of one's party, to bolt *(US)*; **~blatt** party organ; **~buch** membership card; **~buchwirtschaft** spoils system *(US)*, nepotism; **~chef** party boss; **~clique** caucus; **~disziplin** party discipline *(Br.)*; **sich der ~disziplin fügen** to be loyal to one's party, to toe the line, to follow the party line, to act in a partisan spirit; **~dogmen** party lables; **~eid** suppletory (voluntary) oath, oath in litem, *(Schiedseid)* decisory (decisive) oath; **~einheit** party unity; **~einvernahme** *(Gericht)* examination of a party; **sich für ein ~emblem entscheiden** to run under a party's label.

Parteien|anklage partisan charge; **staatliche ~finanzierung** financial aid by the state to political parties; **~konflikt** party clash, partisan fight; **~system** political party system, partyism; **~wirtschaft** cliquishness, partisanship, spoils system *(US)*.

Parteierklärung vor Gericht entry on the roll.

parteifähig *(vor Gericht)* suable.

Partei|fähigkeit *(im Prozeß)* suability; **~flügel** fringe of a party; **militanter ~flügel** militant wing of a party; **~fonds** caucus fund; **~freund** party friend; **~führer** leader of a party, party chief *(US)*, party (floor) leader; **rückständiger ~führer** standpatter, mandarin *(US sl.)*; **~führer sein** to be the leader (at the head) of a party; **~führung** party leaders (leadership, executive); **~funktionär** party official (professional).

Parteigänger party man, partisan, follower, factionist, factionary, factious man, sider;
kein ~ sein to wear no man's collar;
unentwegte ~schaft stalwartism; **~tum** partisanship.

parteigebunden narrowly partisan.

Partei|geist factious spirit, spirit of faction, factiousness, factionism, partyism; **~genosse** enrolled party member, partisan, party man, friend; **~geschäft** deal between parties, party business (transaction); **~geschäftsführer** party manager; **~getriebe** factious doings; **~gezänk** party quarrels; **~gremium** caucus *(US)*; **über ~grenzen hinweg** across party lines; **~grundsätze** party lines, plank *(US)*; **sich an die ~grundsätze halten** to follow the party line; **gegen ~grundsätze verstoßen** to desert party principles; **~gruppe** section of a party, faction; **~gruppierung** party alignment, faction; **~handlung** act of a party; **~herrschaft** party rule (domination); **~hierarchie** party hierarchy; **~interessen dem öffentlichen Wohl unterordnen** to put public interests before party.

parteiinterner Berater party adviser.

Partei|kandidat sein, offizieller to have the party ticket *(US)*; **~kasse** party funds; **~konflikt** party clash; **~kongreß** [party] caucus *(US)*, meeting, conference of delegates *(Br.)*, party convention *(US)*; **~kontrolle** party control; **~kurs** party line; **~leben** party life; **~leiter** party leader (boss); **~leitung** party headquarters; **örtliche ~leitung** caucus.

parteilich, parteiisch interested, partial, *(voreingenommen)* biassed, unequal, unfair, factionary.

Parteilichkeit bias, partiality, prejudice;
Zeugen wegen ~ ablehnen to challenge a witness.

Parteilinie party line, keynote *(US)*;
~ festlegen to keynote *(US)*; **sich der ~ unterwerfen** to toe the line.

Parteiliste list of candidates, ticket *(US)*;
demokratische ~ democratic ticket *(US)*;
~ durch Streichungen abändern to scratch a ticket *(US)*; **auf die ~ eingeschworen sein** to vote the straight ticket *(US)*.

parteilos independent, unattached, nonparty, neutral, crossbench *(Br.)*.

Partei|loser neutral, free lance, independent, cross-bencher *(Br.)*; **~losigkeit** independence, neutrality; **~mann** party man, partisan, partyist; **einfache ~mitarbeiter** lower-ranking party workers.

Parteimitglied party member;
demokratisches ~ democrat *(US)*; **eingeschriebenes ~** enrolled party member; **hauptamtliches ~** party activist; **liberales ~** liberal; **treues ~** party man, true blue; **unzuverlässiges ~** mugwump;
~er des gemäßigten Flügels middle-of-the-roaders;
konservatives ~ sein to follow the Conservative Party; **~ werden** to join a party.

Partei|nahme espousal, *(pol.)* partisanship; **~organ** organ of a party, party organ; **~organisation** [party] organization, party machine (machinery, *US*); **~papier** party policy document; **~parole** party slogan, catchword; **~politik** party (partisan) politics.

Parteipolitiker party (partisan) politician;
führender ~ front bencher *(Br.)*; **reaktionärer ~** standpatter, mandarin *(Br., sl.)*.

parteipolitisch party-political;
~er Grund party-political reason; **~e Streitigkeiten** party warfare.

Parteiposten party post.

Parteiprogramm program(me), [party] platform, party doctrine, ticket *(US)*, plank *(US)*;
offizielles ~ party lines, regular ticket *(US)*; **republikanisches ~** Republican ticket *(US)*;
voll für das ~ eintreten to vote the straight ticket *(US)*.

Partei|programmatiker party-policymaker; **~rede** partisan speech, keynote *(US)*; **~revolte** party revolt; **~rivale** party rival; **~rücksichten** party considerations; **~sekretariat** party secretariat; **~spalter** factionalist; **~spaltung** split in a party, party split; **reaktionären ~standpunkt vertreten** to stand pat; **~statuten** party constitution, statutes of a party; **~stratege** party strategist; **~streitigkeiten** partisan fight, party warfare; **~sucht** factiousness.

parteisüchtig factious.

Partei|system party system, partyism; **~tag** party assembly, conference of delegates *(Br.)*, caucus *(US)*, convention *(US)*; **~umfrage** party poll; **~umlage** political levy; **~uniform** political uniform; **~unterstützung** party backing (support); **~utensilien** party accessories; **~verbot** ban of a party; **~verbundenheit** party affiliation; **~vereinbarung** agreement between the parties; **~vergleich** equitable arrangement between (compromise, agreement, settlement arrived at [by]) the parties; **~verhalten** behavio(u)r of the party, conduct of

parties; ~**verkehr** office hours; ~**verrat** *(Anwalt)* prevarication, *(pol.)* rattery; ~**verrat begehen** to prevaricate; ~**versammlung** party assembly (council), caucus *(US)*, rally; ~**versammlungsbeschluß** party resolution; ~**vertreter** representative; ~**volk** rank and file of a party.
Parteivorbringen argument, judicial declaration;
mutwilliges ~ sham pleading; **schriftliches** ~ pleadings *(Br.)*; **zusätzliches** ~ supplemental pleading.
Partei|vorsitzender chairman of a party, party chairman (president); **sich um das Amt des ~vorsitzenden bewerben** to run for party leadership; ~**vorstand** party executive, national executive committee; ~**vortrag** pleadings, tale; ~**wechsel** change of parties, defection; ~**wechsel vornehmen** to come over, to rat; ~**wille** *(jur.)* intention of the parties; **mutmaßlicher ~wille** implied intention; ~**zeitung** party paper; ~**zentrale** party headquarters; ~**zugehörigkeit** adherence to a party, party affiliation, party colo(u)r, membership; **direkte ~zuwendungen** direct subscriptions to a political party.
Parten|reeder joint owner, co-owner; ~**reederei** co-ownership of ships, co-partnership, part ownership.
Parterre ground (first, *US*) floor, *(Theater)* pit, ground, parterre *(US)*, orchestra (parquet) circle;
im ~ wohnen to live on the ground (first, *US*) floor;
~**akrobat** floor acrobate; ~**geschoß** high (English, *US*) basement; ~**loge** pit box *(Br.)*, parterre box *(US)*; ~**wohnung** apartment on the ground (first, *US*) floor, ground-floor flat *(Br.)*.
Partial|verlust, ~**schaden** partial loss, particular average.
Partie part, section, *(Buch)* passage, *(Buchhandel)* batch, lot, *(Fest)* party, *(Heiratsmöglichkeit)* match, *(Menge)* quantity, *(Teil)* part, section, *(Tennis)* set, *(Theater)* part, role, *(Ware)* parcel, lot;
in ~n in lots, by the bulk; **in großen ~n** in quantities; **in ~n von 5 bis 10 Stück** in lots of 5 to 10 units;
akzeptable ~ eligible; **große ~n** large parcels; **gute** ~ *(Ehe)* good match, eligible young man; **kleine ~n** small lots; **lyrische ~n** lyric passages; **reiche** ~ *(Ehe)* great catch; **zweitklassige** ~ cheap line;
schönste ~ eines Sees most beautiful part of a lake; ~ **Strümpfe** line of stockings;
erstklassige ~ abgeben to be a good prospect for any young girl; ~ **zu zurückgesetzten Preisen abgeben** to dispose of a lot at reduced prices; **Waren in ~n aufteilen** to lot out (do up) goods in parcels; ~ **von etw. kaufen** to buy as a job lot; **glänzende ~ machen** to make a brilliant marriage; **gute ~ machen** to make a good match, to marry a fortune (well); **mit von der ~ sein** to make (be) one of the party; ~ **verlieren** to lose a game;
~**artikel** *(Bücher)* remainder; ~**ergänzung** *(Buchhandel)* batch (lot) completion; ~**ergänzungszeitraum** batch (lot) completion period; ~**handel** spot business.
partiell partial, incomplete.
partienweise in lots (parcels), wholesale;
~ **verkaufen** to sell in lots.
Partie|preis wholesale price, *(Bücher)* special terms; ~**stück** *(Buchhandel)* lot item; ~**verkauf** sale in gross (by the bulk, by lots), partial sale; ~**ware** job goods (line, lot), dead stock, substandard goods; ~**warengeschäft** job-lot trade, junk shop; ~**warenhändler** jobber, middleman, junk dealer.
partieweise kaufen to buy as a job lot.
Partikularbestrebungen particularist tendencies.
Partikularismus particularism, sectionalism *(US)*.
Partikularist particularist, sectionalist *(US)*.
partikularistisch particularistic, sectional *(US)*.
Partisan partisan, irregular, guerilla, jaywalker.
Partisanen|ausbildung training of guerillas; ~**bekämpfung** guerilla fighting, counterguerilla war; ~**bewegung** partisan (guerilla) movement; ~**führer** guerilla chieftain; **rivalisierende ~führer** rival guerilla war lords; ~**gruppe** guerilla group; ~**gruppen vernichten** to fight guerilla campaigns; ~**kampfstil** frontier fighting style; ~**kräfte** partisan troops; ~**krieg** guerilla warfare; ~**streitmacht** guerilla forces (army); ~**tätigkeit** guerilla action; ~**unterschlupf** guerilla hide-out.
Partizipations|geschäft business for joint account, joint venture (adventure); ~**rechnung** joint account.
partizipieren to participate, to take part in, to have an interest (share);
j. zu den Gründungsbedingungen ~ lassen to let s. o. in on the ground floor; **j. an einer Sache ~ lassen** to give s. o. a joint interest in an affair.
Partner partner, copartner, party, *(pl.)* associates in office, companions;
ebenbürtiger ~ equal partner; **geschäftsführender** ~ acting partner;
als ~ aufnehmen to admit as partner; ~ **sein** to partner;
~**land** member country; ~**schaft** partnership, copartnership, association, cahoot *(US sl.)*.
Partnerschafts|familie colleague family; ~**verhältnis** partnership relation; ~**versicherung** partnership insurance.
Partnerstadt twinned town.
partout by all means, absolutely, simply;
~ **zu Hause bleiben wollen** to insist on staying at home.
Party party, *(improvisiert)* punch *(sl.)*;
~**dienst** take-away restaurant.
Parvenue upstart, parvenu, beggar on horseback, newly-rich, cocktail *(Br.)*.
Parzelle plot [of land], parcel, lot *(US)*, allotment *(Br.)*;
~ **abstecken** to mark out a plot of ground; **in ~n aufteilen** to plot, to parcel out into small holdings, to separate into small fields, to lot out *(US)*, to subdivide into lots *(US)*; **zwei ~n zusammenschreiben** to assemble two parcels of land.
Parzellen|besitzer, ~**inhaber** stake (allotment, *Br.*) holder; **im Wert gestiegene ~fläche** plottage; ~**vereinigung** assembling parcels of land, land assembly; **durch Zusammenlegung gestiegener ~wert** plottage increment (value).
parzellieren to partition, to divide into lots *(US)*, to lot out *(US)*, to parcel [out], to whack, to plot, to subdivide *(US)*;
Großgrundbesitz (große Grundstücksflächen) ~ to slice up large parcels of land, to parcel land into smallholdings; **Gut** ~ to crumble (cut) up an estate; **Land** ~ to parcel out land into small holdings, to subdivide into lots; **große Landgüter ~ und auf Bauernfamilien übertragen** to parcel estates out to small family farmers.
Parzellierung parcellation, parcel[l]ing out of land into small holdings, partition of a farm, subdivision *(US)*.
Parzellierungs|gesellschaft freehold land society; ~**plan** partition plan; ~**wesen** small-holding system.
Pascha pasha, bashaw;
j. wie einen ~ bedienen to wait on s. o. hand and foot; **sich wie ein ~ fühlen** to feel like a king; **wie ein ~ leben** to live like a lord;
~**allüren** pampered behavio(u)r.
Paß passport, *(Durchlaßschein)* pass, permit;
im Besitz eines ~es in possession of a passport;
abgelaufener ~ expired passport; **schwer zu erlangender** ~ hard-to-get passport; **gültiger** ~ valid passport; **internationaler** ~ *(Auto)* triptych;
~ **abstempeln** to stamp a passport; ~ **ändern** to amend a passport; ~ **ausstellen** to make out (issue) a passport; ~ **beantragen** to apply for a passport; **sich einen ~ beschaffen** to take out a passport; ~ **einziehen** to withdraw a passport; **jem. den ~ entziehen** to deprive s. o. of his passport; ~ **erneuern** to renew a passport; ~ **kontrollieren (prüfen)** to examine (inspect) a passport; **seinen ~ mit Sichtvermerk versehen lassen** to have one's passport viséed (visaed); **falsche Angaben zur Erlangung eines ~es machen** to make false statements for procuring a passport; ~ **vorübergehend außer Kraft setzen** to withhold tentatively passport privileges; ~ **verlängern** to extend a passport; **mit einem ~ versehen** to passport; ~ **mit Sichtvermerk versehen** to visa a passport; **seinen ~ vorzeigen** to exhibit (show) one's passport;
~**abfertigung** passport control (inspection).
passable|s Englisch sprechen to speak tolerable English; **ganz ~s Essen** guite good food; ~ **Straße** passable road.
Paßabteilung passport division.
Passage passageway, gangway, passage, *(Schiff)* passage money;
~ **in einem Buch abändern** to amend a passage in a book; ~ **erläutern** to eludicate a passage;
~**gebühr** toll rate, entry tax.
Passagier passenger, fare;
blinder ~ deadhead, stowaway, blind baggage; **zahlender** ~ revenue passenger;
~ **erster Klasse** first-class passenger; ~ **dritter Klasse** third-class (steerage) passenger;
~ **in der Touristenklasse** tourist (economy-class) passenger;
~**e absetzen** to put (set) down passengers; ~**e und Ladung aufnehmen** to embark passengers and cargo; ~**e einschiffen** to embark passengers; **sich als blinden ~ einschmuggeln** to stow away on board a ship; ~**e zum Flugzeug geleiten** to shepherd passengers to an airliner; ~**e aussteigen lassen** to set down passengers; **als blinder ~ mitfahren** to travel without a ticket, to hop the freight, to stow away; ~**e an Bord nehmen** to ship passengers; ~**e und Besatzung retten** to bring off the passengers and the crew;

~**aufkommen** total passenger transport; ~**bahnhof** passenger station (depot, *US*); ~**beförderung** passenger service; ~**dampfer** ocean liner, passenger steamer; ~**dichte** passenger density; ~**einschiffung** passenger boarding, embarkation; ~**fahrpreis** passenger rate; ~**flugverkehr** civil aviation; ~**flugzeug** passenger aircraft (plane), *(Düsenverkehr)* jet liner; ~**geld** fare; ~**gepäck**, ~**gut** passenger goods, luggage [in advance] *(Br.)*, baggage *(US)*; ~**kilometer** passenger mile; **neue ~linie in Betrieb nehmen** to launch a new passenger line; ~**liste** passenger list, list of passengers, waybill; ~**makler** runner; ~**maschine** passenger aircraft (plane); ~**räume** passenger accommodation; ~**schiff** passenger ship; ~**schiffahrt** passenger shipping; ~**verkehr** transportation of passengers, passenger traffic; ~**verkehrsdichte** passenger density; ~**verkehrskonto** passenger account.

Paßänderung amendment of a passport;
unberechtigte ~ alteration of passport.

Passant passer-by, pedestrian, transient visitor *(US)*.

Passanten|hotel transient hotel *(US)*, transit hotel *(Br.)*; ~**verkehr** pedestrian traffic.

Paß|antrag application for passport, passport application; ~**antragsformular** passport application form.

Passatwind trade wind.

Paß|aufnahme passport photograph; ~**aussteller** issuer of a passport; ~**ausstellung** issuance of a passport; ~**ausstellungsgebühr** passport fee; ~**beamter** passport officer; ~**besitzer** passport holder; ~**bestimmungen** passport provisions; ~**bild** passport photo[graph]; ~**büro** passport office; ~**eigentümer** passport holder; ~**einziehung** withdrawal of a passport.

passen to fit, *(genehm sein)* to suit, to accommodate;
jem. ~ to be convenient (congenial) for s. o., to suit s. o. (s. one's book), *(Benehmen)* to be fitting (seemly); **wie angegossen ~** to fit like wax (a glove); **wie die Faust aufs Auge ~** to fit like a square peg in a round hole; **jem. scharf auf die Finger ~** to keep a sharp eye on s. o.; **jem. glänzend ~** to fit s. o. to a nicety; **jem. gut ~** to do s. o. all right; **jem. voll in seinen Kram ~** to suit s. o. down to the ground; **jem. überhaupt nicht in den Kram ~** not to feel like it at all; **nicht ~** to misfit; **jem. nicht ~** not to suit s. one's book; **nicht in das übliche Schema diplomatischer Gepflogenheiten ~** not to follow the usual pattern of diplomatic convention; **nicht in eine Zeitschrift ~** not to be suitable for a magazine; **nicht zueinander ~** not to go well with each other, *(Farben)* not to tally (match).

passend appropriate, fitting, suitable, just, becoming, worthy, eligible, well, fit, proper;
bequem ~ easy-fitting; **zur vorliegenden Sache ~** pertinent to the matter in hand;
~ machen to tailor; **~ sein** to be suitable; **~ zusammenstellen** to match, to make equal;
schlecht ~er Anzug badly fitting suit; **zum Kostüm einen ~en Hut benötigen** to want a hat to go with the dress; **~e Lektüre** suitable reading matter; **~en Ton in einem Brief anschlagen** to write a letter in the appropriate style; **nicht der ~e Umgang sein** not to be quite the right company; **~e Umschläge** matching envelopes.

Paß|erleichterungen passport facilities; ~**erneuerung** renewal of a passport; ~**fälschung** fabrication (forgery) of a passport, passport forgery; **~fälschung begehen** to forge a passport; ~**förmlichkeiten** passport formalities; ~**foto** passport photograph; ~**freiheit** passport not required; ~**gebühr** passport fee.

passierbar *(Fluß)* passable, navigable.

passieren to pass, *(sich ereignen)* to occur, to happen, to take place, to come about, to turn up;
Brücke ~ to pass over a bridge; **glatt ~** to sail through; **Grenze ~** to cross the border; **Zensur ~** to pass the censor; **Zoll ~** to clear (pass) the customs; **zollfrei ~** to go through free of duty; **j. ungehindert ~ lassen** to let s. o. pass.

Passier|gewicht *(Münzen)* tolerance; ~**schein** [free] pass, transit pass, pass check *(US)*, permit, *(Schiff)* bill of permit (sufferance, *Br.*), *(Zollbegleitschein)* transire, *(Zollplombe)* docket; ~**scheinstelle** pass office.

passiert, jetzt ist es the fat is in the fire, that's torn it!

Passierzettel permit, *(Zoll)* docket *(Br.)*.

Paßinhaber bearer of a passport, passport holder.

Passion passion, hobby;
~ fürs Theater haben to be crazy (mad) about the theatre; **der ~ des Spielkasinos verfallen sein** to have become addicted to gambling.

Passions|woche Passion Week; ~**zeit** passiontide.

passiv passive, *(Bilanz)* unfavo(u)rable, showing a deficit, adverse, *(Vereinsmitglied)* supernumerary;
~ abschließen to show a debit balance; **~ legitimiert sein** to be capable of being (liable to be) sued; **sich ~ verhalten** to maintain a passive attitude;
~e Bilanz unfavo(u)rable (adverse, debit) balance; **~e Handelsbilanz** unfavo(u)rable balance of trade, adverse (passive, *US*) trade balance; **~es Mitglied** associate member; **~e Parteifähigkeit** passive title, suability, capacity (liability) to be sued; **~er Teilhaber** dormant (silent, sleeping, *Br.*) partner; **~es Wahlrecht** eligibility; **~er Widerstand** passive resistance, *(im Betrieb)* ca'canny; **~e Zahlungsbilanz** adverse balance of payments, balance-of-payments deficit.

Passiva liabilities, *(Bilanz)* debts *(Br.)*, accounts payable *(US)*;
antizipative ~ *(Bilanz)* accrued payables *(US)*, accrued income; **transitorische ~** *(Bilanz)* deferred [credits to] income *(US)*, deferred revenue (income) *(US)*, suspense liabilities, prepaid income;
Aktiva und ~ assets and liabilities, debts due and owing;
als ~ behandeln to carry as liabilities; **Aktiva und ~ übernehmen** to take over the receipts and expenditures.

Passiv|bereich deficit area; ~**bilanz** unfavo(u)rable (adverse) balance.

Passivenbestand commitments, liabilities.

Passiv|gelder borrowed funds, borrowings; ~**geschäft** *(Bankwesen)* deposit function; ~**handel** passive commerce (trade), import trade.

passivieren to carry as liabilities.

passivierte Einnahmen deferred liability.

Passivierung carrying as liabilities;
~ der Kapitalbilanz deterioration of the balance on capital account; **~ im Warenaußenhandel** negative trade balance.

Passivität passivism.

Passiv|konto liability account; ~**legitimation** passive title *(Scot.)*, liability (capacity) to be sued *(US)*; ~**masse** debts due to us, liabilities, accounts payable *(US)*; ~**obligationen** passive bonds; ~**posten** debit (liability) item; ~**posten der Rechnungsabgrenzung** deferred credits [to income] *(US)*, deferred income.

Passivsaldo debit balance, net liabilities;
~ im Außenhandel adverse foreign-trade balance, negative trade balance, [foreign] trade deficit, export deficit; **~ der Handelsbilanz** trade-balance deficit, deficit in the balance of trade; **~ im Waren- und Dienstleistungsverkehr** deficit on trade and services; **~ der Zahlungsbilanz** external deficit, balance-of-payments deficit.

Passiv|schulden debts due to us, debts *(Br.)*, liabilities, accounts payable *(US)*; ~**seite** *(Bilanz)* left[-hand] side, liability section, liabilities side; **auf der ~seite aufführen** to carry as liability.

Passivum *(gr.)* passive voice.

Passiv|wechsel bills payable; ~**wert** debtors' figure; ~**zinsen** interest payable (cost, due).

Paß|kontrolle passport control (inspection), examination of passports; ~**kontrolle für Engländer** British gate; **~prüfung durchführen** to examine a passport; ~**stelle** passport office; ~**straße** pass.

Passus *(Buch)* passage.

Paß|verlängerung extension (renewal) of passport; ~**vermerk** visa; ~**vorlage** submission of one's passport; ~**wesen** passport system; ~**zwang** passport requirement.

Pastor clergyman, parson.

Pate godfather, *(Rundfunksendung)* sponsor;
~ stehen to play one's part, *(Rundfunksendung)* to sponsor, to patronize; **bei einem Kind ~ stehen** to act as godfather to a child; **bei einem Projekt ~ stehen** to be one of the originators.

Paten|kind godchild; ~**onkel** godfather.

Patenschaft *(Rundfunkprogramm)* sponsorship;
~ für ein Rundfunkprogramm übernehmen to sign on as a sponsor; **~ für eine Stadt übernehmen** to adopt as a twin town.

Paten|schaftsabonnement für j. übernehmen to take out a subscription to a paper in favo(u)r of s. o.; ~**stelle** *(Rundfunksendung)* sponsorship.

Patent patent, *(Patenturkunde)* [letters] patent, *(mil.)* [officer's] commission, *(Kniff)* dodge, *(Schiff)* warrant;
~ angemeldet patent pending; **durch ein ~ geschützt** patented; **abgelaufenes ~** patent lapsed, expired patent; **noch nicht abgelaufenes ~** unexpired patent; **älteres ~** prior patent; **angefochtenes ~** patent sued on, contested patent; **angemeldetes ~** patent pending (applied for); **später angemeldetes ~** subsequent patent; **bahnbrechendes ~** pioneer patent; **nebeneinander bestehende ~e** coexistent patents; **früher eingereichtes ~** earlier patent; **einwandfreies ~** clean patent; **endgültiges ~** complete patent; **erloschenes ~** expired patent;

erteiltes ~ patent issued (granted); **gemeinsames** ~ joint patent; **grundlegendes** ~ pioneer (basic) patent; **gültiges** ~ patent in force, valid patent; **jüngeres** ~ subsequent patent; **laufendes** ~ pending patent; **mangelhaftes** ~ defective patent; **rechtsgültiges** ~ valid patent; **selbständiges** ~ independent patent; **späteres** ~ later-dated patent; **strittiges** ~ conflicting (litigious) patent; **umfassendes** ~ blanket patent; **verfallenes** ~ lapsed (expired) patent;
~ **in Aussicht** patent pending;
~ **anfechten** to attack (avoid) a patent; ~ **anmelden** to file an application (apply, put up) for a patent, to give notice of a patent; **Erfindung zum** ~ **anmelden** to patent an invention; ~ **aufgeben** to surrender a patent; ~ **aufrechterhalten** to maintain a patent; ~ **ausstellen** to issue a patent; ~ **ausüben** to work a patent; ~ **auswerten** to exploit a patent; ~ **beantragen** to seek a patent; ~ **berichtigen** to amend a patent; ~ **besitzen** to hold a patent; ~ **bewerten** to appraise a patent; **um ein** ~ **einkommen** to seek a patent; ~ **eintragen** to register a patent; ~ **enteignen** to acquire a patent compulsorily; ~ **erhalten** to take out a patent; ~ **in Geltung erhalten** to keep a patent in force (alive); ~ **für nichtig erklären** to revoke (annul, nullify) a patent; ~ **erlangen (erwerben)** to obtain (procure) a patent; ~ **erteilen** to grant (issue) a patent; ~ **ungenutzt lassen** to shelve a patent; ~ **verfallen lassen** to forfeit (abandon, drop) a patent; ~ **löschen** to cancel a patent; ~ **praktisch verwertbar machen** to reduce a patent to practice; ~ **mißbrauchen** to abuse a patent privilege; ~ **nehmen** to take out a patent; **zum** ~ **angemeldet sein** to be put up for patent; ~ **auf eine Basis stützen** to base an invention; ~ **übertragen** to assign a patent; ~ **umgehen** to circumvent a patent; ~ **verlängern** to extend a patent; ~ **verletzten** to infringe a patent; ~ **versagen (verweigern)** to refuse a patent, to withhold the grant of a patent; ~ **verwerten** to realize a patent, to use a patented product; **auf ein** ~ **verzichten** to drop (abandon) a patent; **auf ein unberechtigtes** ~ **verzichten** to surrender a patent; **erloschenes** ~ **wiederherstellen** to revive an expired patent; ~ **zurücknehmen** to revoke a patent;
~**abänderung** variance; **scheinbare** ~**abänderung zu Umgehungszwecken** colo(u)rable alteration; ~**abgabe** royalty; ~**ablauf** expiration (expiry) of a patent; ~**abteilung** patent department; ~**abtretung** assignment (assignation, conveyance) of a patent.

patentähnliche Tätigkeit patent-related work.

Patentamt Patent Office, Controller of Patents, Designs and Trademarks *(Br.)*, Commissioner of Patents *(US)*;
Internationales ~ International Patent Office at the Hague;
beim ~ **niederlegen** to deposit at (lodge with) the patent office; **beim** ~ **als Anwalt zugelassen sein** to be recognized to practise before the Patent Office.

patentamtliche Gebühr patent fee.

Patentamts|beglaubigung docket; ~**entscheidung** ruling of the patent office; ~**präsident** Commissioner of Patents *(US)*.

Patent|änderung amendment of a patent, variance; ~**änderungsgesetz** patent-law amendment; ~**angelegenheit** patent case (matter); ~**anmelder** patent applicant, intended patentee, *(mit dreimonatlicher Einspruchsfrist)* caveator *(US)*.

Patentanmeldung application for a patent, copyright notice;
~ **mit dreimonatiger Einspruchsmöglichkeit** caveat *(US)*; ~ **läuft** patent pending;
~ **einreichen** to file an application for a patent, to make application to the Commissioner of Patents *(US)*; ~ **im Ausland einreichen** to file an application for a patent abroad; **mit einer** ~ **kollidieren** to interfere with a patent application.

Patentanspruch claim for a patent, patent right (claim);
zusammenfassender ~ omnibus claim *(Br.)*;
~ **abtreten** to assign a patent; ~ **aufheben** to revoke a patent; ~ **aufrechterhalten** to maintain a patent in force; ~ **zu Fall bringen** to defeat the right to a patent; ~ **verteidigen** to assert a patent claim; ~ **verwirken** to invalidate a patent.

Patent|anteil part interest in a patent; ~**antrag** patent application; **abgeänderter** ~**antrag** memorandum of alteration; ~**antrag einreichen** to file an application for a patent, to make an application to the Commissioner of Patents *(US)*; **zugelassener** ~**anwalt** patent lawyer, chartered patent agent *(Br.)*, patent attorney *(US)*; **als** ~**anwalt zugelassen sein** to be recognized to practise before the patent office; ~**anwaltsbüro**, ~**anwaltskanzlei** patent law firm; ~**anwaltschaft** patent bar; ~**anwaltskammer** Chartered Institute of Patent Agents *(Br.)*; ~**aufhebung** revocation (cancellation, vitiation) of a patent; ~**ausdehnung** extension of the patent monopoly; ~**ausnutzung** licence, working of a patent; **unterlassene** ~**ausnutzung** nonuser of a patent; ~**austausch** cross licensing of patents; ~**austauschvertrag** patent exchange contract, cross licensing agreement; ~**beamter** examiner *(US)*; ~**beendigung** cesser; ~**begehren** patent claim; **mißbräuchliche** ~**benutzung** abuse of a patent; ~**berechtigter** claimant for a patent; ~**berichtigung** amendment of a patent, disclaimer; ~**berühmung** patent advertising; ~**beschreibung** disclosure, patent specification; **komplette** ~**beschreibung** complete specification; ~**besitz** patent property; ~**besitzer** patent owner; ~**bewerber** applicant for a patent; ~**blatt** Patent Office Journal; ~**bruch** infringement of a patent; ~**dauer** patent's life, life (duration, term) of a patent; ~**diebstahl** piracy of a patent; ~**einkünfte haben** to derive benefits from a patent; ~**einspruch** patent appeal, interference, opposition, *(gegen Patenterneuerung)* caveat; ~**einspruchsverfahren** interference proceedings, public use proceedings *(US)*; ~**einwand** anticipation; ~**einziehung** revocation of a patent; ~**entschädigungsamt** Patent Compensation Board *(US)*; ~**erfindung** patent invention; ~**erneuerung** renewal of a patent; ~**erneuerungsantrag** application for renewal of a patent; ~**erneuerungsgebühr** patent annuity; ~**erschleichung** surreptitious obtainment of a patent; ~**erteilung** grant (granting, issue) of a patent; ~**erteilung ablehnen** to refuse a patent; ~**erteilungsverfahren** patent-office procedure; ~**erträgnisse** royalties; **vereinnahmte** ~**erträgnisse** patent royalties received; ~**erwerb** purchase of a patent; ~**erwerbskosten** cost of patent right.

patentfähig patentable;
~ **sein** to achieve subject matter;
~**e Erfindung** patentable invention; ~**er Gegenstand** subject matter of patent.

Patent|fähigkeit patentability; ~**frist verlängern** to extend the term of a patent; ~**geber**, ~**gewährer** patentor; ~**gebiet** area of patents; ~**gebühr** patent (invention) royalty, fees payable on a patent, patent fee, *(Anmeldegebühr)* filing (patent) fee; ~**gegenstand** patented article (item); ~**gemeinschaft** patent (closed) pool; ~**gericht** Patent Appeal Tribunal *(Br.)*.

patentgeschützt covered by a patent, patented.

Patent|gesetz Patents Act *(Br.)*; ~**gesetzgebung** patent legislation; ~**gesuch** patent application; ~**gewährer** patentor; ~**gleichheit** identity of inventions; ~**grundlage abgeben** to form a sound basis for a patent; ~**gültigkeit** validity of a patent; ~**gutachten** patent award.

patentieren to grant (issue) a patent, to patent;
sich etw. ~ **lassen** to take out a patent for s. th.; **neue Erfindung** ~ **lassen** to take out a patent, to protect a new invention.

patentiert patented;
nicht ~ unpatented;
~**er Artikel** proprietary (patented) article; ~**es Erzeugnis** patented product; ~**es Verfahren** patented process.

Patentierung issuing of a patent.

Patent|ingenieur patent engineer; ~**inhaber** holder (proprietor, taker-out) of a patent, patent holder (owner), patentee; **alleiniger** ~**inhaber** sole patentee; **früherer** ~**inhaber** former (prior) patentee; ~**jahresgebühr** patent annuity; ~**kartell** patent pool *(US)*; ~**kennzeichnung** patent marking; ~**klage** patent (infringement) suit; ~**klage gegen jem. erheben** to sue s. o. for infringement of a patent; **internationale** ~**klassifikation** International Patent Classification; ~**kosten** patent charges; ~**lage** patent situation; ~**lizenz** [patent] licence; ~**lizenzabgabe** royalty; ~**lizenzvertrag** patent licensing agreement; ~**löschung** forfeiture of a patent; ~**löschungsklage** action for forfeiture of a patent; ~**lösung** quick fix, push-button way; ~**makler** patent broker, patent-right dealer; ~**mißbrauch** misuse of a patent, patent misuse, abuse of patent privilege; ~**mitinhaber** joint patentee; ~**monopol** patent monopoly; ~**nichtigkeitsklage** plea of nullity, nullity suit *(Br.)*; ~**nichtigkeitsverfahren** nullity proceedings; ~**nummer** patent number, number of a patent; ~**prozeß** patent (infringement) suit; ~**prüfer** patent examiner; ~**prüfung** patent examination.

Patentrecht patent right;
angemeldetes ~ inchoate right, patent pending; **ausschließliches** ~ exclusive privilege;
~**e aufheben** to remove patent rights; ~ **aufrechterhalten** to maintain a patent in force; ~ **verletzen** to infringe on a patent right.

patentrechtlich geschützt patented, covered by a patent.

Patentrechts|abtretung patent assignment; ~**spezialist** patent agent.

Patent|reform patent reform; ~**register** patent rolls *(Br.)*, patent register *(US)*; ~**rezept** nostrum, patent recipe; ~**rolle** patent register *(US)*, patent rolls *(Br.)*; **in die** ~**rolle eintragen** to record letters patent, to register a patent; ~**sachbearbeiterstelle** patent appointment; ~**sachen** patent matters; ~**schrift** letters patent, patent filing (specification); ~**schrift neu ausgeben** to reissue a patent *(US)*; ~**schriftenauszug** abridgment of patents.

Patentschutz protection of patents (inventions);
bestehender ~ alive patent;
~ **aufheben** to revoke a patent; ~ **gewähren** to observe patent rights;
~**frist** term of a patent; ~**gesetz** patent law; ~**recht** patent law; ~**verfahren** patent business.

Patent|spezialist patent agent (engineer); ~**steuer** patent tax; ~**streit** patent litigation; ~**sucher** intended patentee; ~**träger** patent holder (owner), patentee, proprietor of a patent; ~**übertragung** assignment (assignation, conveyance) of a patent; ~**umfang** scope of a patent; ~**umgehung** colo(u)rable alteration; ~**unkosten** cost of a patent; ~**unteranspruch** subclass; ~**untersuchung** examination; ~**urkunde** letters patent (overt); ~**verbesserung** improvement; ~**vereinbarung** patent convention; ~**verfahren** patented process, *(Patentamt)* patent-office procedure; ~**verfahren für etw. haben** to have a patent way of doing s. th. *(fam.)*; **nach einem** ~**verfahren hergestellt sein** to be manufactured by a patented process; ~**vergabe** patent licensing; ~**vergabe nur an bestimmte Außenseiter** *(Patentrecht)* closed pool; ~**verkauf** sale of a patent; ~**verkehr** patent transactions; ~**verlängerung [um sieben Jahre]** extension of the life of a patent; ~**verletzer** infringer of a patent.

Patentverletzung infringement of letters patent, patent infringement, privacy of copyright;
mittelbare ~ contributory infringement;
j. wegen ~ **verklagen** to bring an action for infringement of a patent against s. o., to sue s. o. for infringement of a patent.

Patentverletzungs|fall infringement case; ~**klage** action for infringement of copyright; ~**verfahren** patent infringement proceedings.

Patent|verpfändung charge on a patent; ~**versagung** withholding of a patent; ~**vertreter** patent agent; ~**verwaltungsabteilung** patent administration department; ~**verwertung** exploitation (utilization, working) of a patent; **erleichterte** ~**verwertungsmöglichkeit** easing of flow of patents; ~**verzeichnis** register of patents; ~**verzicht** abandonment of a patent; ~**voraussetzungen** conditions for patentability; ~**vorenthaltung** withholding of a patent; ~**vorgänger** former (prior) patentee; ~**vorwegnahme** anticipatory reference; ~**wert** patent value; ~**wesen** patent system; ~**widerspruch anmelden** to lodge an opposition to a patent; ~**widerspruchsklage** infringement action; ~**zeichnung** drawing of a patent, patent drawing; ~**zusammenfassung** consolidation of patents.

Paternoster paternoster, conveyor-type elevator, endless chain.

Patient patient, client;
ambulant behandelter ~ outpatient; **stationärer** ~ inpatient;
seine ~**en aufsuchen** to visit one's patients; ~**en behandeln** to cater patients; ~**en durchbringen** to bring through a patient; ~**en entlassen** to discharge a patient; ~**en geheilt aus einem Krankenhaus entlassen** to discharge a patient from a hospital as cured; ~ **sein** to be under medical treatment; ~ **einer Heil- und Pflegeanstalt sein** to be under care and treatment; **um einen** ~**en sehr besorgt sein** to be full of anxiety (apprehension) for a patient; ~**en zu nehmen wissen** *(Arzt)* to have good bedside manners; ~**en einem für die Kasse zugelassenen Arzt zuweisen** to place patients on a doctor's panel *(Br.)*.

Patientenwechsel in einem Krankenhaus, rascher rapid turnover of patients in a hospital.

patriotisch patriotic, national, public-spirited.

Patriotismus patriotism, public spirit;
übertriebener ~ chauvinism.

Patronat patronage, *(Rundfunksendung)* sponsorship *(US)*.

Patronats|firma *(Rundfunk)* commercial sponsor, scoutmaster *(sl.)*; **namentlich genannte** ~**firma** identified sponsor; ~**herr** lord of the manor; ~**sendung** sponsored broadcast (progra[me]), commercial *(US)*; ~**sendung übernehmen** to be sponsor to a program(me).

Patrone, scharfe live (ball) cartridge.

Patrouille *(mil.)* round, patrol.

Patrouillen|boot patrol vessel (boat); ~**fahrer** scout; ~**fahrzeug** scout car; ~**flug** patrol mission (flight); ~**flugzeug der Marine** patrol seaplane; ~**führer** patrol leader.

patrouillieren to patrol;
auf dem Bahnsteig ~ to pace up and down the platform.

Patsche sad (sorrow) pickle, fix, dilemma, mire, quagmire, hobble *(coll.)*;
in der ~ in trouble (the soup);
in eine ~ **geraten** to get into a jam (hot water), to come a howler; **jem. aus einer** ~ **helfen** to help s. o. out of a scrape, to get s. o. out of a hole; **in der** ~ **sitzen** to be in a hole (nice mess, plight, the cart, *Br., sl.*, grind); **sich aus der** ~ **ziehen** to save one's bacon.

Patt[situation] deadlock, stalemate.

Pauke kettledrum, timpano;
mit ~**n und Trompeten** with drums beating, *(fig.)* with might and main;
mit ~**n und Trompeten durchfallen** to be plucked *(Br.)*, to make a boss shot *(sl.)*; **j. mit** ~**n und Trompeten empfangen** to give s. o. a red-carpet reception; **auf die** ~ **hauen** to go on a spree (to town), to pub-crawl *(fam.)*, to kick over the traces; ~ **schlagen** to beat the drum.

pauken *(büffeln)* to cram, to grind, to swot *(sl.)*, to sap *(Br., sl.)*.

Paukenschlag *(fig.)* stunner, stunt.

Pauker crammer, coach.

Paukerei cramming, coaching, swot, grind.

pauschal in the lump, global, flat, overall, flat-rate, all-inclusive, on a flat-rate (lump-sum) basis;
~ **verurteilen** to condemn wholesale;
~**e Abfindungszahlung** lump-sum payment; ~**e Abgeltung** global settlement; ~ **übernommene Arbeit** lump-sum work; ~**e Berechnung** flat calculation; ~**e Erhöhung** flat increase; ~**er Kapitalbetrag** lump sum of capital; ~**er Lohnsteuerfreibetrag** flat-rate reduction; ~**e Preiserhöhung** overall increase of prices; ~**e Regulierung** lump-sum settlement; ~**e Steuer** all-in-one rate, lump-sum (composition) tax.

Pauschal|abdeckung all-inclusive cover; ~**abfindung** lump-sum settlement (indemnity, payout), *(Unterhalt)* alimony in gross; ~**abgabe** lump-sum levy; ~**abgeltung** global settlement; ~**abrechnung** lump-sum settlement; ~**abschlag** bulk-rate discount; ~**abschluß** bulk bargain; ~**abschreibung** lump allowance, overall depreciation; ~**absetzungen** flat-rate (lump-sum) deductions; ~**abzug** *(Lohnsteuer)* fixed (flat-rate) deduction; ~**abzug für Geschäftsunkosten** *(Einkommensteuer)* standard deduction *(US)*; ~**akkord** lump-sum work; ~**angebot** lump-sum investment; ~**arrangement** package deal; ~**ausgaben** lump-sum expenditure; ~**beitrag** flat-rate contribution; ~**besteuerung** flat-rate taxation; ~**betrag** flat-rate amount, lump (average) sum, global sum (amount); **abzugsfähiger (steuerfreier)** ~**betrag** *(Einkommensteuer)* basic abatement, standard deduction *(US)*, flat exemption *(US)*; **durch Zahlung eines** ~**betrages abgelten** to discharge by a lump-sum payment; ~**bezugspreis** bulk-order price; ~**bezugsvertrag** requirement contract; ~**delkredere** overall provisions for contingent losses.

Pauschale lump sum, flat charge, *(Hotel)* all-inclusive price, American plan *(US)*.

Pauschal|entgelt lump-sum remuneration; ~**entschädigung** lump indemnity, lump-sum payment (settlement); ~**erhöhung** flat-rate increase; ~**ertrag** flat yield; ~**ferienreise** package holiday; ~**fracht** lump-sum (lump, flat-rate, bulk) freight, freighting by contract; ~**freibetrag** *(Steuer)* basic abatement, standard deduction *(US)*, flat exemption *(US)*; ~**gebühr** lump-sum charge, comprehensive (lump) fee, flat rate (fee), *(Telefon)* fixed rental, lump fee; ~**gehalt** flat salary; ~**genehmigung** block permit; ~**honorar** general retainer, flat (lump-sum) fee.

pauschalieren to compound, to settle in bulk, to fix in the lump, *(Steuer)* to commute, to compound;
Rente ~ to commute an annuity into a lump sum; **Steuer** ~ to compound for a tax.

pauschaliert in the lump;
~**e Kosten** bunched costs; ~**e Pensionszahlung** lump-sum pension; ~**e Steuer** lump-sum (composition) tax, all-in-one rate.

Pauschalierung *(Abgaben)* composition, commutation, compounding.

Pauschal|kauf bulk purchase, purchase in the bulk, per aversionem *(lat.)*; ~**leistung** *(Sozialversicherung)* flat-rate benefit; ~**lizenz** *(Patentrecht)* block licence; ~**lohn** flat rate of pay; ~**miete** flat rent; ~**police** floating (block) policy, open cover (policy, *Br.*), unvalued policy *(US)*, *(Feuerversicherung)* blanket policy; ~**prämie** flat (flat-rate) bonus; ~**prämiensystem** flat-bonus system; ~**preis** flat rate (price), price in the lump, lump (blanket, bulk, all-round, inclusive, package) price; **zu** ~**preisen** on inclusive terms, by the job, for a lump sum; **dreiprozentige** ~**provision** flat 3% commission; ~**regulierung** lump-sum settlement; ~**reise** package (bulk, all-expense, *US*) tour; ~**reise unternehmen** to be packaged off; ~**reisesystem** package tourism; ~**rückstellungen** provision for contingencies; ~**satz** flat (lump-sum, overall) rate, *(Eisenbahn)* blanket rate, *(Versicherung)* flat (group risk, blanket, *US*) rate; ~**spesen**

global (lump-sum) charges; ~**steuer** lump-sum tax, all-in-one rate; ~**steuer für Kraftfahrzeuge** flat-rate car-licence fee; ~**subvention** lump-sum subsidy; ~**summe** lump (average) sum, flat yield, global sum (amount), composition; ~**summe entrichten** to compound; ~**tarif** flat rate, *(Autoverleih)* time and unlimited mileage tariff, *(Versicherung)* blanket rate *(US)*; ~**tarif incl. aller gefahrenen Kilometer** *(Autotarif)* special rates including free mileage; ~**tour** package (bulk, all-expense, *US*) tour; ~**urteil** sweeping generalization; ~**vereinbarung** package deal, lump-sum agreement; ~**vergabe** total package contracting; ~**vergütung** flat bonus, lump sum (payment), lump-sum allowance; ~**verkauf** wholesale (lumping) sale; ~**versicherung** all-in (global) insurance, floater [policy]; ~**versicherungsnehmer** composite insurer; ~**versicherungspolice** floater (floating, open matter, *Br.*, unlimited) policy; ~**versicherungspolice für Bauunternehmer** contractors' all-risk policy; **hochwertige** ~**versicherungspolice für die gesamte Familie** comprehensive high-ticket family policy; ~**vertrag** lump-sum contract (agreement); ~**wert** flat (overall) value; ~**wertberichtigung** global value adjustment; ~**zahlung** lump-sum payment, *(Pachtrecht)* fine; **Rente durch** ~**zahlung ablösen** to commute an annuity into a lump sum; ~**zoll** unascertained duty; ~**zuteilung** lump-sum allotment; ~**zuweisung** lump-sum appropriation.

Pausch|besteuerung flat-rate taxation; ~**betrag** lump (average) sum, flat yield, global sum (amount), *(EG)* standard amount, *(für Sonderausgaben)* standard deduction *(US)*, flat exemption *(US)*; **abzugsfähiger** ~**betrag** standard tax deduction *(US)*; ~**betrag für Werbungskosten** overall allowance for professional expenditure; ~**quantum** average quantity; ~**satz** flat (lump-sum, overall) rate.

Pause interval, intermission, pause, stop, vacation, rest, *(Absatz)* period, *(Atempause)* breather, *(im Betrieb)* rest pause (period), *(Börse)* lull, *(Kopie)* blueprint, tracing, *(Schule)* break, recess *(US)*, *(Theater)* interval;
ohne ~ right off the reel;
kleine ~ short break; **wohlverdiente** ~ well-earned rest;
einstündige ~ **für Mittagsessen** one hour's break for lunch; ~ **in der Preisbewegung** price pause; ~ **zum Tanken** fuel stop;
~ **einlegen** to take (make) a break; **sich eine** ~ **gönnen** to give o. s. a rest, to take a rest from work; **ohne sich eine** ~ **zu gönnen** to work without a break; **halbstündige** ~ **machen** to break off for half an hour.

pausen to blueprint, to trace.

Pausen|vorhang drop curtain; ~**zeichen** *(Rundfunk)* station announcement, theme, interval signal, signature, break; ~**zone** refreshment area.

pausieren to [make a] pause, to rest, to relax.

Pauspapier tracing (blue-print, pounce) paper.

Pavillon pavilion, kiosk, *(Musikpavillon)* bandstand, *(Sommerhaus)* summerhouse.

Pazifischer Sicherheitsvertrag Pacific Security Treaty.

Pazifismus pacifism.

Pazifist pacifist.

Pech pitch, *(Unglück)* hard lines, ill luck, deuce *(sl.)*;
~ **haben** to have bad luck, to come a howler; **laufend** ~ **haben** to fall on evil days; **vom** ~ **verfolgt sein (werden)** to be down on one's luck, to have a run of bad luck, to be dogged by misfortune; **wie** ~ **und Schwefel zusammenhalten** to be as thick as thieves.

pechschwarz as dark (black) as pitch.

Pechsträhne run of misfortune, bad luck, streak of hard luck *(US)*;
große ~ chapter of calamities;
~ **haben** to have a run of bad (be down on one's) luck, to strike a bad patch.

Pechvogel unlucky fellow, unfortunate man, jinks *(US sl.)*;
der geborene ~ **sein** to be born under an unlucky star.

Pedal pedal, treadle;
aufs ~ **treten** to step on the gas; **in die** ~**e treten** to tread the pedals of a bicycle.

Pedant pedant, hair splitter, purist, stickler.

Pedanterie pedantry, punctiliousness, fussiness.

pedantisch punctilious, prim, precise;
zu ~ **arbeiten** to work with too much finical detail; ~ **sein** to be pedantic, to split straws, to niggle; **bei seiner Arbeit sehr** ~ **sein** to be meticulous about one's work;
~**er Mensch** hairsplitter, stickler.

Pedell beadle, janitor, caretaker, poker *(Br., sl.)*, *(Universität)* protor's man, bulldog *(sl.)*.

Pegel water (tide) gauge, *(Öl)* level;
~**stand** water level, tidemark, watermark.

Peil|anlage direction finder; ~**antenne** direction-finding (directional) aerial (antenna); ~**bake** radio beacon; ~**empfänger** direction finder.

peilen to take a bearing;
über den Daumen ~ to give a rough (horseback, *US*) estimate; **um die Ecke** ~ to peer round the corner; **Flugzeug mit Radar** ~ to radiolocate an airplane; **die Lage** ~ to see how the land lies; **Wassertiefe** ~ to take soundings.

Peilfunk directional radio;
~**gerät** direction finder.

Peil|kompaß bearing compass; ~**linie** bearing [line], *(Radar)* cursor; ~**rahmen** loop aerial *(Br.)* (antenna); ~**richtung** bearing direction; ~**rufzeichen** code signal; ~**sender** radio beacon, directional transmitter; ~**sendung** directional message; ~**stock** *(Öltank)* sounding rod; ~**strahl** beam, radio-range beacon, beacon course.

Peilung bearing, fixing, *(Funkpeilung)* direction finding.

Peilzeichen code (directional) sign (signal).

Pein pain, suffering, agony, torment;
jem. ~ **verursachen** to inflict pain on s. o.

peinigen *(foltern)* to torment, to torture, to rack, *(Mücken)* to plague;
j. bis aufs Blut ~ to torment the life out of s. o.

peinlich embarrassing, awkward, trying, disconcerting;
Anordnung ~ **genau befolgen** to follow instructions meticulously; **j.** ~ **berühren** to embarrass s. o. greatly; **es** ~ **finden, sagen zu müssen** to be sorry to say; **es mit seiner Arbeit** ~ **genau nehmen** to be painstaking in one's work; **es** ~ **vermeiden** to carefully avoid it; ~ **wirken** to produce a painful expression;
~**e Befragung** interrogation under torture; ~**e Fragen stellen** to ask awkward questions; **in eine** ~**e Lage geraten** to be caught in a tight corner; ~**e Sauberkeit** *(mar.)* spit and polish; ~**es Schweigen** ominous silence; **mit** ~**er Sorgfalt** with meticulous care; ~**e Szene** embarrassing scene.

Peitsche, mit Zuckerbrot und with a stick and a carrot;
mit der ~ **knallen** to crack the whip.

peitschen to whip, to lash, to flagellate, to flog;
Gesetz durchs Parlament ~ to railroad a bill through Congress *(US)*, to rattle (rush) a bill through the House *(Br.)*; **gegen die Scheiben** ~ *(Regen)* to whip (splashs) against the window; **gegen den Strand** ~ *(Wogen)* to be lashing against the strand.

Peitschen|antenne whiplash antenna; ~**hieb** whip, lash of the whip; **j. wie einen** ~**hieb treffen** to cut s. o. like a knife; ~**schnur** whipcord.

pekuniär pecuniary, financial, monetary;
jem. ~ **gut gehen** to be in funds (well-off, fixed, *US*); ~ **schlecht dran sein** to be badly situated;
aus ~**en Gründen** for financial reasons, for pecuniary gain; **in** ~**er Hinsicht** financially; ~**e Schwierigkeiten haben** to be in low straits; ~**e Vorteile** pecuniary advantages.

Pelle *(Kartoffel)* peel, *(Wurst)* skin;
dicke ~ **haben** to be thick-skinned; **jem. auf die** ~ **rücken** to press s. o. hard, to intrude o. s. upon s. o.; **jem. auf der** ~ **sitzen** to pester s. o.

Pelz, in dicken ~**en vermummt** muffled up in thick furs;
Mantel mit ~ **füttern** to line a coat with fur; **mit** ~ **garnieren** to trim with fur; **sich die Sonne auf den** ~ **brennen lassen** to soak up the sun; **jem. auf den** ~ **rücken** to intrude o. s. upon s. o., to press s. o. hard; **jem. mit dem Messer auf den** ~ **rücken** to go at s. o. with the knife; **jem. eine Laus in den** ~ **setzen** to put a flea in s. one's ear *(US sl.)*; **jem. den** ~ **waschen** to give s. o. a good telling-off;
~**geschäft** fur (furrier's) shop (store, *US*); ~**händler** fur dealer, furrier; ~**macher** fur-dresser; ~**mantel** fur coat; ~**tierjäger** trapper; ~**tierzucht** fur farming; ~**werk** furs.

Pendant companion piece.

Pendel|der Preise price pendulum;
~**ausschlag** pendulum swing; ~**betrieb** shuttle [service], commuter service *(US)*; ~**bewegung** pendulum; ~**bus** shuttle bus; ~**dienst** shuttle [service], commuting business (traffic, *US*); ~**einzugsbereich** commuter zone *(US)*.

Pendeln *(Verkehr)* shuttle, commuting *(US)*, commutation *(US)*.

pendeln to pendulate, *(Verkehrsteilnehmer)* to shuttle, to commute to work *(US)*, to have a season ticket;
hin und her ~ *(Tachometernadel)* to flicker; **zwischen zwei Möglichkeiten** ~ to oscillate between two possibilities.

Pendel|tür swing door; ~**verkehr** shuttle [service], commutation *(US)*, commuting business (traffic) *(US)*; ~**zug** shuttle (commuter, *US*) train.

Pendler season-ticket holder *(Br.)*, daily breader *(Br.)*, commuter *(US)*;

~**bus** shuttle (commuter, *US*) bus; ~**einzugsbereich** commuter zone (suburban area) *(US)*; ~**entfernung** commuting distance *(US)*; ~**fahrplan** commuter schedule *(US)*; ~**strecke** shuttle (commuter, *US*) line; ~**strom** commuter flow *(US)*.

Pendlerverkehr shuttle [service], commuting business *(US)*, commuter traffic *(US)*, commutation *(US)*;
~ **von einem Ende des Kontinents zum anderen** coast-to-coast commuting *(US)*; ~ **in Spitzenverkehrszeiten** rush-hour commuting trip *(US)*;
j. im ~ befördern to shuttle s. o.

Pendlerzug shuttle (commuter, *US*) train.

penibel finical, finicking, prickly, overmeticulous, pernickety;
mit seiner Arbeit sehr ~ sein to be painstaking with one's work; **in Ehrensachen sehr ~ sein** to be particular on points of hono(u)r; **mit seiner Kleidung sehr ~ sein** to be very fastidious about one's dress; **in Kleinigkeiten sehr ~ sein** to be meticulous in little things.

penible Arbeit painstaking work.

Pennäler schoolboy.

Penne *(Herberge)* doss house, floghouse *(US sl.)*, *(Schule)* shop *(Br., sl.)*.

pennen gehen to go between the sheets, to sack in (out) *(sl.)*.

Pension *(Altersrente)* old-age pension, retiring (gratuitous, superannuation) allowance (benefit), retirement pension, *(Fremdenheim)* boarding (rooming, *US*) house, private hotel *(Br.)*, *(Kostgeld)* board, pension, *(Kostschule)* boarding school, *(mil.)* retired (half) pay, *(Unterkunft und Verpflegung)* room and board, board and lodging, *(ohne Verpflegung)* lodging (rooming, *US*) house;
in ~ retired [from service]; **in einer ~ bestehend** pensionary; **mit ~ verabschiedet** pensioned off;
~ **44 DM täglich** *(Hotel)* inclusive terms DM 44 a day;
auf das Einkommen angerechnete ~ pension charged on an income; **auskömmliche ~** satisfactory pension; **beitragsfreie ~** noncontributory pension; **beitragspflichtige ~** contributory pension; **vom Betrieb gewährte ~** company pension; **bei der Entlassung gewährte ~** retirement pension; **halbe ~** partial board; **lebenslängliche ~** life pension, pension for life; **staatliche ~** government (public-service) pension; **volle ~** board and residence, room and board (lodging), full board;
~ **auf Lebenszeit** life pension, pension for life;
jem. die ~ aberkennen to dock s. one's pension; **jem. eine ~ aussetzen** to make a pension for s. o.; **jem. eine jährliche ~ in Höhe von 10.000 DM aussetzen** to allow s. o. DM 10.000 a year; ~ **beantragen** to apply for a pension; **lediglich 2% zu einer sonst beitragsfreien und inflationssicheren ~ beitragen** to pay only 2% for an inflation-proofed noncontributory pension; ~ **bekommen** to receive a pension; **zu einer ~ berechtigen** to carry a pension; ~ **besitzen (betreiben)** to keep a boardinghouse (boarders); ~ **bewilligen** to grant a pension; ~ **beziehen** to draw (receive, be awarded) a pension; **staatliche ~ beziehen** to be pensioned on the government; ~ **in Höhe von 2/3 seines Gehalts beziehen** to have a pension of two-thirds salary; **jem. seine ~ entziehen** to cancel s. one's pension; **Voraussetzungen für die Gewährung einer ~ erfüllen** to qualify for a pension; ~ **erhalten** to receive a pension; **inflationssichere ~ erhalten** to have one's pension inflation-proofed; ~ **erhöhen** to put up the rate of a pension; **in ~ geben** to put out to board; **in ~ gehen** to retire on a pension, to go into retirement, to step down; **fünf Jahre vorzeitig in ~ gehen** to quit five years earlier than required; **in ~ gehen, aber noch beratend tätig bleiben** to retire to consultant status; **jem. eine ~ gewähren** to pension s. o. off, to grant s. o. a pension; **in ~ haben** to board; **zu seiner ~ hinzuverdienen** to supplement one's pension; ~ **kürzen** to retrench a pension; **in einer ~ leben** to live in a boardinghouse; **von seiner ~ leben** to live on a pension; **mit voller ~ mieten** to take full board and lodgings; **mit einer ~ auskommen müssen** to struggle along on a pension; **in ~ nehmen** to take as boarder; **in ~ sein** to be retired (pensioned off); **bei jem. in ~ sein** to board with s. o.; **mit ~ verabschieden** to pension off; **jem. seine ~ vorenthalten** to suppress s. one's pension; **in einer ~ wohnen** to live in a boardinghouse (pension); **jem. eine ~ zahlen** to grant a pension to s. o., to pension s. o. off; **jem. keine ~ mehr zahlen** to take a pension away from s. o.

Pensionär pensioner, retiree, pensionary *(Br.)*, *(Fremdenheim)* gentleman boarder, lodger, paying (pay) guest;
alter ~ retired oldster;
~**e annehmen** to keep boarders, to take in visitors.

Pensionärs|beratung retirement counsel(l)ing; ~**liste** retired list; ~**vertreter** pensioner delegate; ~**wohngegend** retirement community.

Pensionat boarding school *(Br.)*, pension, house, hall.

pensionieren to pension [off], to superannuate, to put on the retired list, to retire, *(mil.)* to put on half pay, to retire;
Beamten wegen Erreichung der Altersgrenze ~ to superannuate an official (civil servant, *Br.*);
sich ~ lassen to retire [on a pension, from active service], to go on a pension (into retirement), *(mil.)* to retire, to sell out and go on half pay; **jem. ermöglichen, sich ~ zu lassen** to enable s. o. to retire; **sich aus Altersgründen ~ lassen** to retire under the age limit; **sich frühzeitig ~ lassen** to retire early; **sich mit 60 vorzeitig ~ lassen** to choose early retirement at sixty.

pensioniert retired, in retirement, superannuated, pensionary, *(Beamter)* state-pensioned;
zwangsweise ~ compulsorily retired;
~ **sein** to be on the retired list; ~ **werden** to reach retirement, to retire on a pension, to be pensioned off (superannuated); **außerplanmäßig ~ werden** to retire out of turn; **entlassen und ~ werden** to be discharged with a pension; **unter Gewährung eines Ruhegehaltes mit 60 Jahren ~ werden** to retire on a pension at 60; **auf eigenen Wunsch ~ werden** to be placed on the retired list at one's own request; **zwangsweise ~ werden** to be compulsorily retired;
~**er Beamter** retired civil servant, pensionary on the government *(Br.)*.

Pensionierung retirement, retiring, pensioning off;
kurz vor der ~ nearing retirement;
freiwillige ~ optional (voluntary) retirement; **frühzeitige (vorzeitige) ~** early (premature) retirement; **zwangsweise ~** compulsory retirement;
~ **wegen Arbeitsunfähigkeit** disability retirement; ~ **wegen Erreichung der Altersgrenze** retirement on account of age, pensioning off due to retirement age, superannuation; ~ **mit vollem Ruhegehalt** retirement on full pension; ~ **auf eigenen Wunsch** optional (voluntary) retirement;
sich nach seiner ~ noch betätigen to spend an active retirement; **um seine ~ einkommen** to apply to be retired on a pension; **sich zur frühzeitigen ~ entscheiden** to opt for early retirement; **frühzeitige ~ ermöglichen** to enable s. o. to retire; **für die ~ reif sein** to qualify for a pension; **kurz vor der ~ stehen** to be nearing retirement age.

Pensionierungsalter pensionable (retirement, retiring) age, age of retirement;
festgesetztes ~ mandatory retirement age;
~ **nach der Pensionsordnung** pension-plan retirement age;
~ **erreichen** to superannuate; ~ **überschritten haben** to be past retirement age.

Pensionierungs|angelegenheiten retirement matters; ~**anspruch** right to pension, pension claim, retirement right; ~**grenze** retirement age limit, pensionable age; ~**grenze erreicht haben** to be due to retire; ~**termin** retiring date.

Pensionsalter pensionable (pension, retirement, retiring) age;
festgelegtes ~ mandatory retirement age;
~ **erreichen** to reach the retiring (retirement) age; ~ **überschritten haben** to be past retirement age; **ins ~ kommen** to be due to retire.

Pensions|angelegenheiten retirement matters; ~**anspruch** right to pension, pension right, retirement right, pension claim; **übertragbarer ~anspruch** portable pension; ~**ansprüche aberkennen** to cancel the pension rights; ~**ansprüche unter Berücksichtigung der langjährigen Militärdienstzeit stellen** to claim a pension by virtue of one's long military service; ~**anteil des Arbeitnehmers** *(Betriebspension)* pension; ~**anwartschaft** pension expectancy; ~**art** nature of pension; ~**ausschuß** pension committee, retiring (pension) board; ~**beitrag** superannuation money; ~**berechnung** determination of a pension.

pensionsberechtigt pensionable, entitled to (eligible for) a pension;
nicht ~ nonpensionable;
~ **sein** to qualify for a pension, to rank for pension, to be over pension age, *(Stellung)* to carry a pension, to be a participant in a pension scheme;
~**e Stellung anbieten** to offer employment on a pensionable basis.

Pensions|berechtigter pensioner, pensionary *(Br.)*, holder (recipient) of a pension; ~**berechtigung** pension right, retirement eligibility, qualification for a pension; ~**berechtigung gewähren** to carry a pension; ~**berechtigung haben** to be entitled (eligible) to a pension; ~**besitzer** boardinghouse (lodginghouse) keeper; ~**bestimmungen** pensionary (pension, superannuation) provisions; ~**betrag** pension, superannuation, retiring allowance;

~**bezüge** pensionable emoluments, retirement income (pay, benefits, *US*), income received from a pension; ~**dienstalter** pensionable age; ~**dienstalter erreichen** to superannuate; ~**einkommen,** ~**einkünfte** retirement income; ~**empfänger** pensioner, pensionary *(Br.)*, holder (recipient) of a pension, stipendiary; ~**entschluß** decision to retire; ~**erfüllungskasse** pension-plan trust fund; ~**ergänzungsversicherung** supplementary retirement pension insurance; ~**erhöhung** pension increment (increase, augmentation).

pensionsfähig pensionable, entitled to a pension, superannuable; **nicht** ~ nonpensionable;
~**es Alter** pension age, pensionable (retiring, retirement) age; ~**er Angestellter** superannuated employee.

Pensionsfestsetzungsbehörde pension board.

Pensionsfonds pension trust, pension (superannuation, staff pension, *Br.*, retirement) fund, pension plan;
aus Gratisaktien bestehender ~ employee stock bonus fund *(US)*; **400 DM Jahresbeitrag für den** ~ **erheben** to levy 400 DM a year for the pension fund; ~ **errichten** to fund a pension plan.

Pensions|garantiekasse Federal Pension Guarantee Corporation *(US)*; ~**gast** pensioner, paying guest, boarder, boarding-house guest; ~**gäste haben** to take in visitors; ~**gegenstände** *(Bankbilanz)* items assigned en pension; ~**geld** boarding-school fee; ~**geschäft** *(Börse)* carrying-over business; ~**gutschrift** pension credit; ~**höhe** rate of pension; ~**höhe festsetzen** to rate a pension; ~**inhaber** lodginghouse (boardinghouse) keeper; ~**jahre** retirement years.

Pensionskasse [old-age] pension (superannuation) fund, staff pension fund *(Br.)*, pension account (plan), retirement fund; **außerbetriebliche** ~ trust agreement pension plan; **beitragsfreie** ~ noncontributory (company-financed) pension plan; **beitragspflichtige** ~ contributory pension plan (scheme); **betriebliche (eigene)** ~ self-administrated pension plan, employees' pension fund, occupational pension fund; **gemeinsame** ~ **[mehrerer Betriebe]** pension pool *(US)*; **nicht an der staatlichen Altersversorgung partizipierende** ~ contracted-out pension scheme;
~ **für Betriebsangehörige** employees' pension fund; **gemeinsame** ~ **mehrerer Industriebetriebe** pension pool of several manufacturing establishments; ~ **der Post** post-office pension fund; ~ **und Unterstützungskasse** pension trust;
einer ~ **angehören** to be a participant in a pension scheme; ~ **einrichten** to fund a pension plan; **Jahresbeitrag von 100 Dollar für die** ~ **erheben** to levy 100 $ a year for the pension fund; **Beiträge zur** ~ **leisten** to make contributions to the pension trust.

Pensionskassen|beitrag, steuerlich anerkannter allowable contribution for superannuation benefits; ~**bestände** pension portfolio, pension-fund money; ~**mitglied sein** to belong to a pension scheme; ~**system mit Rechtsanspruch** defined benefit pension plan; ~**system ohne Rechtsanspruch** target benefit pension plan; ~**vereinigung** Association of Pension Funds.

Pensions|konto pension fund; ~**lasten** pension costs; ~**leistung** pension payment, retirement (fringe) benefit, retiring allowance; **verbesserte** ~**leistungen** pension improvements; ~**liste** retired list; ~**ordnung** pension law, *(Fonds)* pension (retirement) plan.

pensionspflichtig, über das ~**e Alter hinaus tätig bleiben** to stay on past retirement age.

Pensions|plan pension plan (scheme), retirement plan; **beitragspflichtiger** ~**plan** contributory pension plan; ~**preis** *(Fremdenheim)* board, room and board *(US)*; ~**regelung** superannuation provision.

pensionsreif due for retirement;
~ **sein** to superannuate;
~**er Vorstand** superannuated management.

Pensions|rente retirement benefit, retiring allowance; ~**richtlinien** pension guidelines; ~**rücklagenfonds** pension plan trust fund; ~**rückstellung** provision for pension, pension reserve; ~**sätze** pension rates; ~**sicherung** superannuation security; **in den** ~**stand treten** to be pensioned off, to retire on a pension.

Pensionssystem pensions system, pension plan (scheme), pension (retirement) plan;
beitragsfreies (allein vom Unternehmen finanziertes) ~ noncontributory pension plan, company-financed pension plan; **beitragspflichtiges** ~ contributory pension plan; **betriebliches** ~ occupational pension scheme; **gehaltsgebundenes** ~ definite benefit pension plan;
~ **mit feststehenden Lohnprozentsätzen** definite benefit pension plan; ~ **mit Zahlung von Überlebensrenten** joint annuity survivor pension plan.

Pensions|unterstützung retirement benefit, pension payment; ~**vereinbarung** pension-scheme arrangement, pension settlement; ~**verpflichtungen** pension obligations; ~**verwaltungsgesellschaft** pension management company; ~**vorsteher** boardinghouse manager, deputy *(Br.)*; ~**wechsel** bill on deposit; ~**zahlung** retirement (retired) pay, pension payment (paid), lump-sum pension, post-employment benefit; **festgesetzte** ~**zahlung** lump-sum pension; ~**zahlungen an j. einstellen** to stop s. one's pension; ~**zeit** retirement years; ~**zusage** pensioning warrant, pension commitment; ~**zuschuß** superannuation (pension) contribution, retirement benefit, retiring allowance; ~**zuschüsse** *(Bilanz)* pension payments, service apportionments *(US)*; ~**zusicherungsschein** pensioning warrant; ~**zuwendung** retirement benefit, pension benefit *(US)*.

Pensum stint, task, lesson;
großes ~ great deal of work;
~ **der Klasse erfüllen** to cover the syllabus; **sein tägliches** ~ **erledigen** to do one's daily stint; **sich ein** ~ **für jeden Tag setzen** to set o. s. a daily target.

per|Achse by road; ~ **Adresse** care of (c/o); ~ **Anhalter fahren** to hitchhike; ~ **Aval** *(Wechsel)* as guarantor for payment; ~ **Bahn** by rail; ~ **Eilboten** by express (special, *US*) delivery; ~ **Erscheinen** when issued; ~ **1. fällig** payable (due) on the first; ~ **Jahr** per annum; ~ **Medio** for settlement at the middle of the month; ~ **pedes apostolorum** *(fam.)* on foot; ~ **procura** per procuration; ~ **Saldo** by balance; ~ **sofort gesucht** *(Anzeige)* wanted immediately; ~ **Stück** apiece.

perfekt consummate, *(ausgebildet)* accomplished, down to the ground, right as nails, *(Vertrag)* settled;
alles ~ **beherrschen** to be perfect in everything; **sein Handwerk** ~ **beherrschen** to be a consummate master of one's craft; **Handel** ~ **machen** to clinch a deal; ~ **sein** to be settled; ~ **Englisch sprechen** to have an excellent command of English.

Perfektion perfection;
absolute ~ perfection itself;
es zur ~ **gebracht haben** to have attained perfection.

perfektionieren, sich to improve one's knowledge; **Erfindung** ~ to perfect an invention; **Geschäft** ~ to consummate (clinch) a deal.

perfektionierte Welt world of technical perfection.

Perfektionismus perfectionism.

perfid perfidious, treacherous, insidious.

perforiert *(Briefmarke)* perforate, perforated.

Pergament|band parchment binding; ~**papier** vellum (parchment) paper; ~**schrift** vellum; ~**streifen** label.

Periode period, cycle, spell, snatch;
rückläufige ~ sinking spell;
~ **erhöhter Gefahr** apprehensive period; ~ **erhöhter Kreditbeanspruchung** borrowing peak; ~ **schönen Wetters** spell of fine weather; ~ **der Wiederkehr** *(Statistik)* return period.

Perioden|bilanz periodic statement; ~**erfolg** result of the year; ~**erfolgsausweis,** ~**gewinnrechnung** statement of income *(US)*.

periodenfremde Erträge periodic income.

Perioden|gewinn accounting profit; ~**kosten** cost incurred in a stated period; ~**rechnung** periodic accounting; ~**reingewinn** *(Bilanz)* net profit for the year, surplus net profit *(US)*.

periodisch [wiederkehrend] periodical, recurrent, seasonal, at regular intervals of time, cyclical;
~ **erscheinend** serial;
~ **veröffentlichen** to serialize; ~ **wiederkommen** to cycle;
~**er Auftrag** repeat order; ~ **aufgestellte Bilanz** periodic statement; ~**e Veröffentlichung** periodical publication, serialization; ~ **erneuerte Werbung** periodical advertising; ~**e Zeitschrift** periodical, serial.

Peripherie outskirts.

Perle pearl, *(fig.)* gem, daisy *(sl.)*, jewel of a servant;
echte ~**n** genuine pearls; **unechte** ~ imitation pearl;
~**n vor die Säue werfen** to cast pearls before swine.

Perlen|fischer pearl diver (fisher); ~**glanz** lustre of pearls; ~**halsband** pearl necklace; ~**schimmer** lustre of pearls; ~**schnur** string (rope) of pearls.

Perl|leinwand glassbeaded screen; ~**schrift** pearl.

perplex bewildered, baffled, perplexed, flabbergasted;
~ **machen** to take to town *(sl.)*; ~ **sein** to be dumbfounded (flabbergasted).

Perron landing platform.

Persenning tarpaulin.

Perserteppich oriental rug, Persian carpet.

Persilschein ausstellen to whitewash.

Person person, individual, man, *(Theater)* role, part, *(im Vertrag)* party;

an der ~ haftend in the gross; **für meine ~** for my part; **ohne Ansehen der ~** without exception of persons; **pro ~** per man; **100 DM pro ~** DM 100 a head; **von ~ bekannt** of known identity;
ansässige ~ resident; **arbeitsscheue ~** idle and disorderly person *(Br.)*; **bedachte ~** beneficiary; **in Haft befindliche ~** arrested person, detainee; **befragte ~** interviewee; **bekannte ~** institution; **berechtigte ~** authorized person; **im Außendienst beschäftigte ~en** outdoor (field) staff; **bestimmte ~** person named; **beteiligte ~en** parties concerned, persons interested; **betroffene ~** afflicted person; **bevollmächtigte ~** authorized person; **dritte ~** third, third party; **die eigene ~** oneself; **einflußreiche ~** man with sway; **einzelne ~** individual; **nicht ermittelte ~** unascertained person; **erwerbstätige ~** gainful worker; **fiktive ~** fictitious person; **freiberufliche ~** self-employed person; **als Richter fungierende ~** judge de facto; **gebietsfremde ~** person not resident in a territory; **geisteskranke ~** person of unsound mind; **die genannten ~en** the said persons; **volljährige und geschäftsfähige ~** person of full age and capacity; **geschäftsunfähige ~** person under disability; **verständig und umsichtig handelnde ~** reasonable and prudent person; **hochgestellte ~** high-ranking personality, V.I.P.; **hochnäsige ~** blue nose *(US)*; **jugendliche ~en** adolescents, youths; **juristische ~** juristic (juridical, artificial, fictitious) person; **aus mehreren ~en bestehende juristische ~** aggregate corporation; **körperbehinderte ~** handicapped person; **maßgebende ~** person who matters; **natürliche ~** natural person, individual; **rauschgiftsüchtige ~** drug addict; **schwierige ~** tough nut *(coll.)*; **unter Alkoholeinfluß stehende ~** intoxicated person; **stumme ~** nonspeaking character; **Entscheidung treffende ~** decision maker; **übelbeleumdete ~** person of ill fame; **unbedeutende ~** nobody, small fry (beer); **unbefugte ~** unauthorized person; **unbekannte ~** unknown person; **unerwünschte ~** *(dipl.)* persona non grata; **unzuverlässige ~** unreliable person; **verläßliche ~** credible person; **verschleppte ~en** displaced persons; **versicherte ~** *(Versicherungswesen)* insured [person], risk; **vertrauenswürdige ~** trustworthy person; **wichtige ~** figure;
~ mit Auslandswohnsitz nonresident; **wichtige ~ des Betriebes** head cook and bottle washer *(fam.)*; **~en und ihre Darsteller** characters and performers; **~ mit verminderter Erwerbsfähigkeit** partly incapacitated person; **~ männlichen Geschlechts** male person; **~ am falschen Platz** horse-marine; **~ von Rang und Würden** worthy; **~en höchsten Ranges** persons of the best quality; **juristische ~ des öffentlichen Rechts** body corporate; **~ in fester Stellung** fixture; **~ mit Wohnsitz in den USA** denizen *(US)*, individual resident in the USA; **~ ohne festen Wohnsitz** transient person;
40 ~en fassen *(Bus)* to have room for forty people; **an eine bestimmte ~ girieren** to endorse specially; **sich in der ~ irren** to mistake s. one's identity; **j. von ~ kennen** to know s. o. personally; **Gärtner und Chauffeur in einer ~ sein** to serve as gardener and chauffeur; **Großzügigkeit in ~ sein** to be generosity itself; **Regisseur und Hauptdarsteller in einer ~ sein** to be both director and leading man; **der Teufel in ~ sein** to be the devil incarnate; **in höchsteigener ~ anwesend sein** to be personally present; **die eigene ~ stets in den Vordergrund stellen** to put o. s. in the foreground; **sich in einer ~ vereinigen** *(Rechte)* to merge in one person; **j. zur ~ vernehmen** to take down s. one's particulars; **steuerlich wie eine juristische ~ behandelt werden** to be treated as a corporate body for tax purposes.

Personal personnel, staff, crew, employees, *(Haushalt)* domestic staff, servants, attendants, establishment;
gut mit ~ versehen well-staffed;
ärztliches ~ hospital staff; **aufsichtsführendes ~** supervising staff; **erforderliches ~** staff required; **fliegendes ~** flying personnel; **geschultes ~** efficient (skilled, specialized, trained) personnel, *(Hotel)* good valeting service; **leitendes ~** executive personnel (staff); **ortsansässiges ~** local staff; **ständiges ~** permanent staff; **subalternes ~** subordinate personnel; **im Außendienst tätiges ~** field (outdoor) staff; **technisches ~** technical staff; **teilzeitbeschäftigtes ~** part-time employees; **überzähliges ~** redundant labo(u)r; **viel ~** large staff of servants;
~ der Hauptbuchhaltung ledger-keeping staff; **~ einer diplomatischen Vertretung** agency staff;
~ abbauen to reduce the staff; **~ anwerben (einstellen)** to appoint staff, to staff, to recruit personnel; **Büro mit ~ besetzen** to staff an office; **~ am Gewinn beteiligen** to give the staff a share in the profit; **~ einstellen** to engage (employ) staff, to recruit personnel; **sein ~ entlassen** to dismiss one's staff; **dem ~ einen Tag freigeben** to give the staff a day off; **zum ~ gehören** to be on the establishment, to be on the staff; **gutes ~ haben** to be well staffed; **zu viel ~ haben** to be overstaffed; **zu wenig ~ haben** to be understaffed; **~ reduzieren** to trim one's staff; **über leistungsfähiges ~ verfügen** to handle an efficient staff; **sein gesamtes ~ wechseln** to make a clean sweep of one's staff;
~abbau reduction of (decrease in) staff, staff reduction, staff cut, personnel cutback, retrenchment of employees; **vorübergehender ~abbau** employee layoff, laying off of personnel; **~abbau durchführen** to reduce the establishment; **~abteilung** personnel (appointments, staff) department, staff administration *(Br.)*, staff superintendent department *(Br.)*, personnel division *(US)*; **~abteilungsleiter** personnel officer; **~abwerbung** pirating, raiding, head hunting; **~akte** case history, personnel file (dossier, folder, jacket), record of service; **~akten** personnel records; **~amt** *(Kommunen)* establishment office *(Br.)*; **~anforderung** personnel requisition; **~angaben** personal data; **~angelegenheiten** personnel matters; **~aufgaben** personnel functions; **~aufwand** expenditure on personnel (staff, staff cost); **staatlicher ~aufwand** government payroll; **~- und Sachaufwand** staff and material expenses; **~aufwendungen** personnel expenses, *(Bilanz)* salaries and wages; **~ausbildung** staff (personnel) training; **~ausgaben** personnel budget (expenses, costs); **~ausschuß** establishment committee *(Br.)*; **~auswahl** selection of personnel, staff selection, recruitment *(US)*; **~auswahlgrundsätze** selection standards; **~auswahlprogramm** selection program(me); **~ausweis** identity card (papers), certificate of identity, pass; **zahlbar gegen Vorlage des ~ausweises** payable upon submission of proof of identity; **~bearbeiter** personnel assistant (technician); **~bedarf, ~bedürfnisse** manpower (staff, personnel, employment) requirements; **~berater** personnel counselor *(US)*; **spezialisierter ~berater** personnel specialist; **~beratung** employee counselling; **~beschaffung** engagement of staff, personnel recruiting *(US)*, recruitment *(US)*; **~beschreibung** personal particulars; **mit der ~beschreibung übereinstimmen** to answer to description; **~besetzung** staff-up, staffing; **~bestand** manpower establishment, strength of the staff, staff, personnel, manpower, labo(u)r force, *(dipl.)* size of a mission, *(mar.)* establishment; **~bestand des Beamtenkörpers** strength of the establishment *(Br.)*; **~bestand abbauen (verringern)** to cut manning level, to reduce the staff; **~bestandskontrolle** personnel inventory; **~beurteilung** performance appraisal, employee appraisal, personnel (merit, *US*) rating, personnel review, assessment of personnel *(US)*, efficiency report *(US)*; **~beurteilungsbogen** employee rating chart; **~bewegungen** staff changes (turnover); **~bogen** personal record, personnel (personal history) form, qualification (registration, *US*) card, history sheet *(US)*, *(Fragebogen)* questionnaire; **~buchhaltung** personnel accounting; **~büro** personnel department (division, *US*), appointments department, personnel office, staff administration *(Br.)*; **~chef, ~direktor** personnel manager (chief, director, officer), employment (staff) manager; **~einsparungen** staff savings; **~einstellung** engagement of staff, recruitment *(US)*; **~einstellungsstab** recruiting staff *(US)*; **~einstellungsverfahren** recruitment process *(US)*; **~ersparnis** saving of labo(u)r; **~etat** manpower budget; **~fachmann** personnel specialist; **~formblatt** personnel (personal history) form, history sheet *(US)*; **~fragebogen** questionnaire, application form; **~fragebogen erbitten** to write for a personal history form; **~fragen** personnel (staff) problems; **~führung** personnel management; **~fürsorge** staff welfare, personnel service *(US)*; **~gesellschaft** nontrading partnership (company); **~haushalt** manpower budget.

Personalien [name and] description, particulars, personal data, personalia, *(Verbrecher)* description signalment;
jds. ~ aufnehmen to establish the identity of s. o., to take down s. one's particulars.

Personal|investitionen investment in men; **~kartei** personal files, manpower inventory; **fachlich aufgegliederte ~kartei** manning table; **~knappheit** shortage of personnel (staff), staff shortage, manpower shortage; **~konto** personal account, *(Betriebskonto)* staff register *(Br.)*; **~kontrolle** personnel audit; **~konzession** individual licence.

Personalkosten personnel (staff) expenses, staff expenditure;
allgemeine ~ indirect (nonproductive, unproductive) labo(u)r;
anteilige ~ pro rata costs of labo(u)r;
~einsparung labo(u)r cost saving.

Personalkredit personal (private) credit, open (uncovered, personal, unsecured) loan;
ungesicherter ~ fiduciary loan;

~**abteilung** personal loan department; ~**geschäft** personal loan business; ~**gesellschaft** personal loan company *(US)*.

Personal|kürzung personnel cutback, retrenchment of employees; ~**leiter** personnel controller, establishment officer *(Br.)*; ~**mangel** shortage of personnel (staff, manpower), staff shortage; ~**mangel haben, an ~mangel leiden** to be understaffed (short of staff).

personalmäßig abgebaut laid off *(US)*.

Personal|nebenkosten incidental wages costs; ~**notiz** *(Zeitung)* personal; ~**ordnung** staff regulations, personnel statute; ~**papiere** identification papers; ~**planung** manpower planning, staff planning system; ~**politik** personnel (industrial) policy; **betriebliche ~politik** labo(u)r management; ~**probleme** personnel problems; ~**programm** personnel program(me); ~**prüfungen** employment test, personnel review (rating); ~**referent,** ~**sachbearbeiter** personnel (appointments) officer, staff manager; ~**schwierigkeiten** personnel difficulties; ~**stand** number of employees (persons employed); ~**stärke** strength of the staff, labo(u)r force, manpower; **vereinbarte ~stärke** personnel laid down in the agreement; ~**statut** personal statute, *(Betrieb)* staff regulations, personnel statute; ~**steuer** personal tax; ~**struktur** staff structure; ~**tabelle** personnel chart; ~**umbau,** ~**umbesetzung** shifting of personnel, personnel shift, staff transfer, shakeup; ~**union bei Verwaltungen verschiedener Gesellschaften** interlocking directorates; ~**unterlagen** personnel records; **laufend fortgeführte ~unterlagen** permanent history record *(US)*; ~**veränderungen** personnel changes; ~**verminderung** reduction of staff; ~**verringerung** decrease in staff; ~**versammlung** shopfloor meeting; ~**vertreter** employee (staff) representative; ~**vertretung** employee (staff) representation, staff association; ~**verwaltung** personnel (staff) administration (management), personnel (staff) organization; ~**verzeichnis** staff register; ~**wechsel** alteration in personnel, changes in the staff, staff turnover; ~**zusatzkosten** additional personnel costs.

personelle Umbesetzungen personnel transfer, personnel shakeup.

Personen|aufzug lift *(US)*, passenger elevator *(Br.)*; ~**ausweis** personal (identity) card, identification papers; ~**bahnhof** passenger station (depot, *US*).

Personenbeförderung conveyance of passengers, passenger transportation;

~ **gegen Entgelt übernehmen** to carry passengers for a consideration.

Personenbeförderungs|entgelt passenger fare; ~**steuer** transportation tax; ~**tarif** passenger tariff; ~**unternehmen** certified carrier; ~**vertrag** passenger contract.

Personen|beschreibung personal particulars, description, descriptive signalment *(US)*; ~**dampfer** passenger boat; ~**fahrkarte** ticket; ~**fahrpreis** passenger fare; ~**fahrzeug** passenger vehicle; ~**feststellung** identification; ~**gedächtnis** memory for faces; ~**gemeinschaft** association, combination of persons; ~**gesamtheit** body corporate; ~**gesamtheit mit eigener Rechtspersönlichkeit** aggregate corporation *(US)*; ~**gesellschaft** private company [with limited liability] *(Br.)*, partnership.

personengleich identical.

Personen|gleichheit identity; ~**gruppe** group of individuals, bunch; ~**hehlerei** harbo(u)ring of criminals; ~**kautionsversicherung** fidelity insurance; ~**kilometer** passenger kilometer *(US)* (kilometre, *Br.*) (mile), traffic mile; ~**kraftverkehr** line haul; ~**kraftwagen** [passenger] car, private motorcar *(US)*, automobile.

Personenkreis category of persons, circle;

befragter ~ panel, persons reviewed; **begünstigter ~** qualifying beneficiaries; **erfaßter ~** coverage; **werblich erreichbarer ~** exposed people; **geschlossener ~** panel; **nicht repräsentativer ~** *(Marktbefragung)* chunk;

~ **der Arrestanten festlegen** to designate the persons to be arrested.

Personen|kult cult of personality, personality cult; ~- **und Güterzugslokomotive** mogul locomotive *(US)*; ~**mehrheit** aggregate corporation; ~**name** personal name; ~**risiko** personal risk; ~**schaden** injury to person, personal (bodily) injury; ~**schäden** *(Versicherung)* personal damage; ~**sorgerecht** custody of the children; ~**stand** personal (civil, marital) status, status of a person.

Personenstands|änderung change of civil status; ~**aufnahme** census of population; ~**beamter** registrar *(Br.)*; ~**bücher** register of vital statistics (of births, deaths and marriages, *Br.*, of births, deaths, marriages and burials, *US*); ~**fälschung** false personation, impersonation; ~**fälschung begehen** to falsely impersonate; ~**klage** bastardy process; ~**register** register of births, marriages and deaths *(Br.)*, General Register *(Br.)*, register of vital statistics *(US)*; ~**urkunde** birth certificate, personal card; ~**wesen** family status.

Personen|steuer personal tax *(US)*; ~**tarif** passenger fares (rates, *US*); ~**transport** transportation of passengers; ~**vereinigung** combination of persons, association, society; ~**verkehr** movement of persons, *(Eisenbahn)* passenger transport, coaching traffic *(Br.)*; **freier ~verkehr** freedom of movement; **öffentlicher ~verkehr** public transport; ~**versicherung** personal accident insurance, *(Geschäftssparte)* long-term business *(Br.)*; ~**versicherungspolice** personal injury policy; ~**verwechslung** mistaken identity; ~**verzeichnis** register of persons, *(Theater)* dramatis personae.

Personenwagen passenger (railway) carriage *(Br.)*, [railroad] passenger car *(US)*, day car (coach, *US*), carport *(Br.)*;

~ **erster Klasse** first-class carriage; ~ **der Mittelklasse** economy car;

~ **durch Übergänge verbinden** to vestibule passenger cars; ~**herstellung** passenger-car production.

Personenzahl, beförderte traffic.

Personenzug stopping (passenger, omnibus, *Br.*, way, *US*, accommodation, *US*) train;

~ **mit ermäßigtem Fahrpreis** parliamentary train *(Br.)*; ~ **mit angehängten Güterwagen** mixed train;

~**lokomotive** passenger locomotive *(US)*; ~**verkehr** passenger train service.

Personifikation personification, embodiment, impersonation.

personifizieren to personify, to personalize, to impersonate.

personifiziert|er Geiz avarice personified; ~**e Unschuld** innocence incarnate.

Personifizierung personification, personalization, impersonation.

persönlich personal, in one's personal capacity, in person, intimate, direct, private, individually;

~! private and personal! *(Br.)*, special handling! *(US)*;

~ **haftbar** personally liable (answerable); ~ **zuzustellen** to be delivered to the addressee in person; **für Sie ~ bestimmt** for your private ear;

sich ~ bewerben to make a personal application; ~ **erscheinen** to appear in person, to make one's appearance; ~ **haften** to be personally liable (answerable); ~ **kennen** to know personally; **Brief als ~ kennzeichnen** to mark a letter private; **j. ~ verantwortlich machen** to hold s. o. personally liable; ~ **werden** to take to personalities, to make personal remarks;

~**e Angelegenheiten** private affairs; ~**e Anspielungen machen** to indulge in personalities; ~**e Aufwendungen** personal (out-of-pocket) expense; ~**e Ausstrahlung** personality impact; ~**e Bekanntschaft** personal acquaintance; ~**en Besuch abstatten** to make a personal call; ~**e Beziehungen** personal relations; ~**e Bindungen** personal ties; ~**er Brief** private letter; ~ **übernommene Bürgschaft** personal warranty; ~**e Dienstbarkeit** personal servitude; ~**er Dispositionskredit** drawing credit; ~**e Effekten** personal effects; ~**es Eigentum** private property; **unmittelbare ~e Empfängerbenachrichtigung** personal notice; ~**e Empfehlung** personal reference; ~**e Erklärung** *(Abgeordneter)* personal explanation; ~**es Erscheinen** personal appearance; ~**e Freiheit** individual freedom, *(Angestellter)* personal allowance; **zum ~en Gebrauch** for personal use; ~**e Gebrauchsgegenstände** personal articles (effects); ~ **gehaltener Geschäftsbrief** personal letter in business; ~ **haftender Gesellschafter** active (general) partner; **aus ~en Gründen** for personal reasons; ~**e Haftung** personal (private) liability; ~**e Initiative** private initiative; ~**es Interesse** private ends; ~**e Interessen verfolgen** to take care of number one, to have an axe to grind; ~**es Konto** private (personal) account; ~**er Kredit** open (blank, personal) credit; ~**er Lebensstil** personal style; ~**e Meinung** personal opinion; ~**e Note** individualism; **einer Sache eine ~e Note geben** to give a personal touch to s. th.; ~**er Referent** personal representative; ~**e Schulden** private debts, *(Gesellschafter)* individual debts; ~**er Steuerfreibetrag** personal exemption *(US)* (relief, *Br.*); ~**e Steuern** personal (direct) taxes; ~ **gehaltenes Tagebuch** intimate diary; ~ **haftender Teilhaber** responsible (general, associated, special, ordinary, *Br.*) partner; ~**e Umstände** particular circumstances; ~**e Unverletzbarkeit** *(dipl.)* personal inviability; ~**er Verkehr mit den Kindern** *(Geschiedene)* personal access to children; ~**es Vermögen** private property (means), *(Gesellschafter)* individual assets (estate); ~**e Verpflichtung** personal obligation; ~**er Vertreter** private agent, representative; ~**e Vorstellung**

erwünscht *(Anzeige)* personal attendance required; **~e Zusammenkunft** private interview; **~e Zustellung** personal service.

Persönliches *(Zeitung)* personals *(US)*.

Persönlichkeit personality, personage, character, figure, ego, individualism, identity;
schwer abzuschätzende ~ unpredictable quantity; **angesehene ~** man of prestige; **ausgereifte ~** mature individual; **bedeutende ~** person of prominence; **beherrschende ~** kingpin; **in der Öffentlichkeit bekannte ~** public character; **berühmte ~** front pager; **einflußreiche ~** man of influence, big wheel, name *(sl.)*; **unternehmerisch eingestellte ~** entrepreneurially-oriented person; **faszinierende ~** magnetic personality; **führende ~** captain, leading man, key community leader; **geistsprühende ~** sparkler; **gespaltene ~** dual consciousness (personality), split (dissociated) personality; **gewichtige ~** bigwig *(Br.)*, mogul, heavyweight *(US coll.)*; **hochgestellte ~** person of rank, cordon bleu, high-up *(coll.)*; **kraftvolle ~** vital (vibrant) personality; **die leitenden ~en** the leaders; **markante ~** man of mark; **meinungsbildende ~en** pacemakers in public opinion; **prominente ~** outstanding personality; **unternehmerische ~** enterprising personality; **vitale ~** vital personality; **wichtige ~en** people of importance;
berühmte ~en unseres Jahrhunderts great names of our century; **meinungsgebende ~en in der Kunstwelt** leading people (persons of, influence) in the world of art; **hervorragende ~ des Landes** first man in the country; **~en des öffentlichen Lebens** leaders in the community, public figures; **führende ~en des Wirtschaftslebens** policymakers of business; **führende ~en des Finanz- und Wirtschaftslebens** leading figures in finance, industry and trade; **führende ~ des Zeitgeschehens** public character;
sich auf die Beurteilung einer ~ positiv auswirken to prove a personality bonus; **wichtige ~ entlassen** to drop the pilot; **die ~ sein** to be the whole show; **einflußreiche ~ sein** to be a man with sway; **ideenreiche ~ sein** to be a man full of new ideas; **politische ~ sein** to be of influence in politics; **wichtige ~ sein** to be in the front rank; **ganz von der Bedeutung der eigenen ~ erfüllt sein** to be imbued with a sense of one's own importance.

Persönlichkeits|analyse personal analysis; **~aufbau** buildup; **~beurteilung** personality (merit) rating *(US)*; **~defekt** split personality; **freie ~entfaltung** pursuit of happiness; **~massage** ego-massage; **~recht** right of persons (privacy); **~spaltung** dual (dissociation of) personality, split of personality; **einem Unternehmen seinen ~stempel aufdrücken** to put one's personal stamp on a company; **~struktur bestimmen** to determine individual make-up; **~verletzung** violation of privacy; **aus seinen ~werten Kapital schlagen** to capitalize on one's personality assets.

Perspektive vista, perspective;
~ aus der Luft aerial perspective;
neue ~en eröffnen to open up new vistas; **etw. in der richtigen ~ sehen** to put s. th. into context.

Pessimismus gloom *(fig.)*.

Pessimist pessimist, sad apple *(sl.)*.

pessimistisch pessimistic;
alles immer nur ~ betrachten to look on the dark side of things.

Pest plague, *(fig.)* nuisance;
j. wie die ~ hassen to hate the sight of s. o.; **wie die ~ stinken** to stink to high heaven; **jem. die ~ an den Hals wünschen** to wish s. o. would drop dead;
~bazillus plague bacillus.

Petent petitioner, supplier.

Peter, Blauer Blue Peter;
jem. den Schwarzen ~ zuschieben to pass the buck to s. o. *(US)*, to lay the blame at s. one's door.

Petition memorial, petition;
~ überreichen to urge a petition.

Petitions|ausschuß receivers and triers of petitions; **~recht** right of petition; **auf dem ~wege** by way of a petition.

Petit[schrift] brevier.

Petitum request, prayer, petition.

Petrochemie petrochemistry.

petrochemische Industrie petrochemical industries.

Petroleum petroleum, paraffin oil, kerosene *(US)*;
~lampe oil (kerosene, paraffin) lamp.

Petschaft signet, seal.

petto, etw. in ~ haben to have a card up one's sleeve.

Petze *(Schule)* telltale, sneak *(Br., sl.)*.

petzen to tell tales, to sneak *(Br., sl.)*, to split, to peach.

peu à peu bit by bit, little by little.

Pfad path, lane, track, trace, trail;
ausgetretener ~ beaten path; **gewundener ~** tortuous course; **steiler ~** steep path;
~ der Freude primrose path;
vom ~ der Tugend abweichen to leave the straight and narrow *(fam.)*; **~ der Pflicht verlassen** to swerve from one's duty; **auf dem ~ der Tugend wandeln** to keep the narrow path of virtue;
~finder Boy Scouts; **~findertagung** jamboree.

Pfahl post, pole, pillar, pile, stake;
mit einem ~ abstützen to strengthen with a pile; **~ einrammen** to pile; **jem. ein ~ im Fleische sein** to be a thorn in s. one's flesh;
~bau pile dwelling; **~buhne** groyne, piled jetty.

Pfähle, mit ~n abstecken to picket.

Pfahlwerk pilework.

Pfand pledge, pledged property, pawn, gage *(Br.)*, charge, distress, hock *(US sl.)*, *(Bürgschaft)* surety *(US)*, security, bail, *(Flaschenpfand)* deposit, *(Handgeld)* deposit, earnest money, *(Pfandrecht)* lien, *(Sicherheit)* collateral [security];
als (zum) ~ as a pledge, in pawn;
uneingelöstes ~ unredeemed pledge; **verfallenes (verwirktes) ~** forfeit, forfeited pledge;
~ für seine guten Absichten earnest of one's good intentions;
als ~ annehmen to accept as pledge; **~ auslösen** to take out of (redeem a) pawn, to replevin *(US)*; **als ~ behalten (besitzen)** to hold in pawn (pledge); **als ~ bestellen** to create a lien, to pledge; **als ~ dienen** to serve as collateral; **~ einlösen** to recover a pledged article, to redeem a pledge (pawn), to take out of pawn; **sein Leben als ~ einsetzen** to stake one's life on it; **~ für verfallen erklären** to forfeit a pledge, to foreclose on a mortgage *(Br.)*; **~ geben** to pay a forfeit, to pawn, to collaterate, to [give as a] gage, to pledge; **als ~ halten** to keep as (in) pawn, to hold in pledge; **als ~ hinterlegen** to pledge, to pawn, to make a deposit *(US)*; **als ~ lassen** to leave for a pledge; **gegen ~ leihen** to lend against security (on collateral, *US*); **zum ~ nehmen** to take in pledge (pawn); **zum ~ setzen** to pawn; **als ~ verlieren** to forfeit; **~ verwerten** to realize a pledge;
~abstand return unsatisfied; **~abstandsbescheinigung** certificate of nulla bona.

Pfandauslösung redemption of a pledge, replevin;
~ behindern to clog the equity of redemption *(Br.)*.

Pfandauslösungsrecht equity of redemption.

pfändbar attachable, capable of attachment, distrainable, seizable, subject to execution, nonexempt, *(Grundstück)* mortgageable;
nicht ~ privileged from distress, nonattachable, nonforfeitable, judgment-proof, mace-proof *(US)*;
~ sein to be subject to distress;
ohne ~es Vermögen sein to be judgment- (mace-, *US*) proof.

Pfändbarkeit attachability, seizableness.

Pfand|benachrichtigung notice of lien; **~besitzer** pawnee, pledgee; **~besteller** pledgor, pawnor; **~bestellung** pawning, pledging, charge, creation of a lien, *(Hypothek)* mortgaging; **gegen ~bestellung Geld vorschießen** to advance money on pawns.

Pfandbrief bond, debenture *(Br.)*, *(Hypothekeninstrument)* mortgage bond (debenture), mortgage deed;
durch vorgehendes Pfandrecht an der hinterlegten Sicherheit gedeckte ~e first-lien collateral trust bonds; **zur Rückzahlung gekündigte ~e** bonds under notice of redemption; **erstrangig gesicherte ~e** senior lien bonds; **durch erststellige Hypothek gesicherte ~e** first mortgage bonds *(US)*; **hypothekarisch gesicherte ~e** mortgage bonds; **hypothekarisch nicht gesicherte ~e** simple debentures *(Br.)*; **vorrangiger ~** underlying bond;
~e einer landwirtschaftlichen Genossenschaft Federal Farm Loan bonds *(US)*;
~e zur Rückzahlung auslösen to redeem bonds by drawings; **~e unterbringen** to place bonds; **~e zeichnen** to subscribe bonds; **~e aus dem Verkehr ziehen** to retire bonds;
~agio bond discount; **~anleihe** mortgage loan; **~anstalt** land (mortgage) bank; **~ausgabe** issue of debentures *(Br.)*, bond issue; **~auslösung** redemption of bonds; **~besitz** bondholdings; **~besitzer** bondholder, debenture holder *(Br.)*; **~disagio** bond (unamortized debt) discount; **~disagio über die Jahre verteilen** to spread bond discount over the years; **~emission** bond issue, issue of debentures *(Br.)*; **~emission vornehmen** to float (launch) a bond issue; **~fonds** bond funds; **~inhaber** bond creditor, bondholder, debenture holder *(Br.)*; **~institut** land bank; **~kauf** purchase of mortgage bonds; **~markt** market for bonds, bond market; **~rendite** bond yieldings; **~schuldner** bond debtor; **~umlauf** bond circulation, total mortgage bonds outstanding.

Pfand|bruch breach of arrestment, breach of pound, pound breach (rescue) of goods distrained; ~**darlehn** loan against security, collateral loan *(US)*; ~**effekten** pledged securities; ~**einlösung** redemption of a pledge, taking out of pawn.

pfänden to levy, to attach, to lay attachment, to [levy a] distress, to distrain, to extend, to affix the seal, to seize, to make seizure, to take in execution, to garnishee, *(Vieh)* to pound, to impound;
etw. ~ to serve a writ of attachment upon s. th.; **Bankkonto** ~ to garnish (attach) a bank account; **jds. Eigentum** ~ to distrain upon s. one's belongings; **Forderung** ~ to arrest a debt; **Gehalt teilweise** ~ to attach part of a salary; **Konto[guthaben]** ~ to garnish (attach) an account; **Lohn** ~ to garnish wages; **jds. Möbel wegen Mietschulden** ~ to distrain upon s. one's furniture for rent;
j. ~ **lassen** to levy a distress upon (execution into) s. o.

Pfand|entstrickung release of a pawn; ~**erstreckung** spreading a lien; ~**forderung** hypothecary claim.

pfandfrei pledge-free, judgment- (mace-, *US*) proof.

Pfand|freigabe voluntary redemption, restoration of goods taken in distraint; ~**freigabe gegen Kautionsgestellung** replevin; ~**geber** chattel mortgager *(US)*, pledger, pledgor *(US)*, pawner; ~**gebühr** pawn money; ~**gegenstand** pawn, pawned object, pledge, pledged property (thing); **Vollstreckung gegen einen ~gegenstand betreiben** to levy against a pledged property; ~**gegenstand einlösen** to recover a pledged article; ~**gegenstände zurückgeben** to restore goods in distraint; ~**geschäft** pawnbroking, pawnbrokery, *(Laden)* pawnshop; ~**gläubiger**, ~**halter** bailee, lien creditor *(US)*, lienor, holder of a lien (pledge), pledgor's creditor, pledge keeper, distraining creditor, encumbrancer, holder of s. one's securities, pledgee, [chattel] mortgagee *(US)*; ~**gläubiger im Besitz des Pfandstücks** mortgagee in possession; ~**gläubiger sein** to hold property as a pledge, to hold a mortgage; ~**gut** pledged property, pledge.

Pfandhaus pawnshop, pawnbrokery, spout *(sl.)*;
im ~ in hock *(US sl.)*, up the spout *(coll.)*, in pop *(Br., sl.)*;
etw. ins ~ **tragen** to pawn (hock, *US sl.*) s. th.;
~**besitzer** pawnbroker.

Pfand|hinterlegung deposit, delivery of a pawn; ~**indossament** pledge indorsement; ~**inhaber** pawnee, pledgee, lien creditor, lienor, encumbrancer, mortgagee; ~**klage** action of replevin; ~**klausel mit voller Zahlung** mortgage clause with full contribution; ~**leihanstalt** pawnbrokery, pawn (loan, *US*) office, pawnshop; **gemeinnützige ~leihanstalt** remedial loan society *(Br.)*; ~**leihe** pawnbroking, pawnbroker's business, pawnbrokery; **auf der ~leihe sein** to be up the spout *(coll.)* (in pop, *Br., sl.*, in hock, *US sl.*); ~**leiher** pawnbroker, pawner, pawnor, lombard, uncle *(sl.)*; **beim ~leiher sein** to be in pawn (up the spout, *coll.*, in hock, *US sl.*, in pop, *Br., sl.*); ~**leihgeschäft** pawnbroking, pawnbrokery; **hochfeines ~leihgeschäft** high-class pawnbrokery; ~**leihgesetz** Pawnbroker Act *(Br.)*; ~**mißbrauch** abuse of distress; ~**nahme** pawntaking; ~**nehmer** pledge taker, pledgee, pawnee, chattel mortgagee.

Pfandobjekt pledged property (article, thing), pledge, lien;
keine ~e nulla bona;
sich aus dem ~ **eines Schuldners befriedigen** to distrain upon a debtor; ~**e erfassen** to marshal liens.

Pfandrecht lien, mortgage;
allgemeines ~ general lien; **älteres** ~ senior (first) lien; **im Prozeßwege begründetes** ~ judgment lien; **besitzloses** ~ equitable lien; **bevorrechtigtes** ~ prior lien; **eingetragenes** ~ lien of record; **gerichtlich entstandenes** ~ judicial mortgage *(Louisiana)*; **erstes (erststelliges)** ~ first lien; **gesetzliches** ~ statutory lien, lien by operation of law, judicial mortgage *(Louisiana)*; **gleichrangiges** ~ concurrent lien; **jüngeres** ~ junior lien; **nachrangiges, nachstehendes** ~ second lien, junior lien; **nächstrangiges** ~ subsequent mortgage; **ranghöheres (vorgehendes)** ~ prior (first) lien; **vertraglich vereinbartes** ~ conventional lien; **gesetzlich vermutetes** ~ implied lien; **vorrangiges** ~ paramount lien; **zweitrangiges** ~ second lien;
~ **auf alle Flugzeuge eines Unternehmens** fleet mortgage; ~ **des Frachtführers** carrier's lien; ~ **des Gastwirts** innkeeper's lien; ~ **an einem bestimmten Gegenstand** particular (special, specific) lien; ~ **des Handwerkers** mechanic's lien; ~ **am Konsignationslager** factor's lien; ~ **an Luftfahrzeugen** aircraft mortgage; ~ **an zweiter Rangstelle** second lien *(Louisiana)*; ~ **an beweglichen Sachen** chattel mortgage; ~ **aufgrund eines rechtskräftigen Titels** consummate lien; ~ **aufgrund eines noch nicht rechtskräftigen Titels** inchoate lien; ~ **des Vermieters** lessor's lien; ~ **am gesamten Vermögen** general mortgage;
~ **aufheben** to vacate a lien; ~ **ausüben** to exercise a lien; **sich aus einem** ~ **befriedigen** to distrain upon a debtor; ~ **begründen (bestellen)** to constitute (create) a lien, to create a pledge; **nachrangiges** ~ **bestellen** to submortgage; ~ **erweitern** to spread the lien; ~ **haben** to have a charge on; ~ **an den persönlichen Gebrauchsgegenständen des Schuldners haben** to have (lay) a lien on the personal property of the debtor; ~ **geltend machen** to enforce (lay) a lien upon s. one's property; **durch** ~ **gesichert sein** to have a lien; **einem** ~ **unterliegen** to be subject to a lien; ~ **verlieren** to lose a lien; ~ **verwerten** to enforce a lien; **auf ein** ~ **verzichten** to waive a lien.

pfandrechtlich hypothecary;
~ **gesichert sein** to be secured by a lien.

Pfand|rückgabe restoration of goods in distraint; ~**sache** pledged property, pawned object; ~**schein** pawn ticket, chattel mortgage note; ~**schuld** mortgage debt; ~**schuldner** lienee, pawner, pledger, pledgor *(US)*, *(Hypothek)* mortgager, mortgagor *(US)*, replevisor; ~**sicherheit** lien, pledged assets, collateral (hypothecary) security; ~**sicherheit verlieren** to lose a lien; ~**siegel** sheriff's seal; ~**stall** pound; ~**stück** pawn, pledge.

Pfändung levy of distress, attachment, seizure, distraint, distress, arrest[ment], distrainment, execution, extent, pounding *(Scot.)*;
im Wege der ~ by way of execution;
nicht beendete ~ uncompleted attachment; **im Gang befindliche** ~ execution in force and operating; **erneute** ~ fresh execution; **fruchtlose** ~ unsatisfied execution, nulla bona; **mehrfache** ~ multiple execution; **unberechtigt vorgenommene** ~ undue attachment; **vorläufige** ~ preliminary execution; **wiederholte** ~ reattachment;
~ **eines Bankkontos** attachment of a bank account; ~ **eines Drittschuldners** garnishee order, garnishment, factorizing; ~ **einer Forderung** arrest (attachment) of a debt, garnishee execution, garnishment; ~ **der Früchte auf dem Halm** seizure of crops; ~ **des Lohns** garnishment of wages, execution of wages; ~ **wegen Mietschulden (Mietrückstands)** distress for [nonpayment of] rent; ~ **beweglicher Sachen** seizure of movables; ~ **gegen Sicherheitsleistung** attachment against security; ~ **eines Staatsschuldners** extent in chief;
~ **aufheben** to lift the seizure, to replevin, to remove the seals, to vacate an attachment; ~ **ausbringen** to levy a distress, to distrain; ~ **gegen j. ausbringen** to issue an attachment against s. one's goods; ~ **beantragen** to sue a distraint; ~ **betreiben** to levy a distraint (distress), to distrain upon s. one's belongings; ~ **in das bewegliche Vermögen wegen nicht bezahlter Miete betreiben** to distrain chattels for nonpayment of rent; ~ **durchführen** to make a seizure; ~ **einer Forderung durchführen** to institute garnishee proceedings, to arrest a debt; **der** ~ **unterliegen** to be subject to attachment; **nicht der** ~ **unterliegen** to be exempt from execution, to be judgment- (mace-, *US*) proof; ~ **verhindern** to buy out the execution; ~ **vornehmen** to levy a distress, to put in an execution; ~ **wegen ausstehender Schulden vornehmen** to seize s. one's goods for payment of debts.

Pfändungs|anordnung writ of elegit (fiere facias); ~**anspruch** right to distrain; ~**anzeige** notice of lien; ~**auftrag** distress warrant; **zurückgestellter ~auftrag** dormant execution; ~**beamter** broker, executioner; ~**befehl** warrant of distress (attachment), distringas *(Br.)*, fieri facias *(lat.)*; ~**befehl erlassen** to execute a writ; ~**berechtigter** lien claimant; ~**bericht** return of writs; ~**bescheid zukommen lassen** to garnish.

Pfändungsbeschluß distress warrant, order of attachment *(US)*, attachment order *(US)*;
~ **gegen einen Drittschuldner** garnishee order (summons); ~ **über Gesellschaftsanteile** charging order *(Br.)*;
~ **aufheben** to cancel a garnishee order; ~ **erlassen** to levy an attachment order; ~ **zustellen** to give notice of distraint.

Pfändungs- und Überweisungsbeschluß writ of attachment, third-party order *(US)*, decree of forthcoming *(Scot.)*;
vorläufiger ~ garnishee order nisi;
~ **erlassen** to levy an attachment order.

Pfändungs|beschränkungen exemptions from execution; ~**erlös** proceeds of a distress; ~**forderungsverfahren durchführen** to institute garnishment proceedings.

pfändungsfrei exempt from execution, unattachable, judgment-proof, exempt from seizure, privileged from distress, mace-proof *(US)*;
~ **sein** to be exempt from execution (mace-proof, *US*);
~**er Betrag** mace-exempt amount *(US)*; ~**e Gegenstände** exemptions; ~**er Schuldner** poor debtor; ~**es Vermögen** exempt assets.

Pfändungs|freibetrag exemption from seizure (execution), *(Heimstättenbesitzer)* homestead exemption *(US)*; **~freigrenze, ~freiheit** exemption from seizure (execution); **~gebühren** cost of execution, sheriff's poundage; **~gläubiger** attaching (judgment) creditor, distrainer, distraining party; **~klage** proceedings of attaching property, attachment execution *(US)*; **~kosten** costs of levy (execution); **~liste** executive docket; **~ort** place of distraining; **~protokoll** fieri feci, sheriff's return; **~schuldner** judgment (execution) debtor, distrainee; **~schutz** exemption from seizure, exemption from execution; **~schutz genießen** to be exempt from seizure (liable to stay execution); **~schutzbestimmungen** exemption laws; **~verfahren** proceedings of attaching property, attachment proceedings *(US)*; **~verfügung** distress warrant, *(beim Drittschuldner)* garnishee order; **~versuch erfolglos** nulla bona, no goods.

Pfand|untergang extinguishment of a lien; **~unterschlagung** embezzlement of pledged articles; **~urkunde** letter of hypothecation, letter of lien *(Br.)*, mortgage deed, *(zur Schuldentilgung durch den Treuhänder)* trust deed.

Pfandverfall forfeiture of a bond;
endgültiger ~ nach einer Ausschlußfrist strict foreclosure.

Pfandverfalls|ankündigung notice of foreclosure *(Br.)*; **~beschluß** foreclosure order *(Br.)*; **endgültiger ~beschluß** foreclosure order absolute; **vorläufiger ~beschluß** foreclosure order nisi; **rechtskräftige ~erklärung** foreclosure order absolute; **~verfahren** foreclosure proceedings.

Pfand|verfügung distress warrant, garnishee order; **~verkauf** sale of pledge, distress sale (selling); **durch ~verkauf verwerten** to enforce the pledge by selling; **~verleiher** pawnbroker, pawnee, pledgee; **~verschleppung** removal of pledged property; **~verschreibung** bill of sale, letter of hypothecation; **verfallene ~verschreibung** foreclosed mortgage; **~verschreibungsurkunde** chattel mortgage; **~versteigerung** auction of pledged property; **~verstrickung lösen** to grant a replevin; **~vertrag** mortgage deed, pignorative contract; **~verwahrung** impoundage, sequestration; **~verwertung** enforcement of a lien; **~verwertung vornehmen** to enforce a lien upon s. one's property; **~verwirkung** forfeiture of bond.

pfandweise by way of pledge, on mortgage (pawn), as collateral *(US)*.

Pfanne pan, spider *(US)*, skillet, *(Dachpfanne)* pantile, *(zum Grillen)* broiler;
etw. auf der ~ haben to have s. th. up one's sleeve; **j. in die ~ hauen** to make mincemeat of s. o., to settle s. one's hash; **Essen in die ~ hauen** to knock up a meal; **Eier in die ~ schlagen** to break eggs into the pan.

Pfannkuchen pancake, flapjack;
wie ein ~ auseinandergehen to swell up like a balloon *(coll.)*; **Gesicht wie ein ~ haben** to be moon-faced.

Pfarr|amt clerical benefice, rectorate; **~bezirk** parish.

Pfarrer parson, rector, clergyman, vicar, *(katholisch)* priest, pastor *(US)*.

Pfarr|gehilfe curate; **~gemeinde** parish; **~haus** parish house, rectory, vicarage, parsonage; **~stelle** incumbency, rectorate.

Pfau, sich wie ein ~ aufputzen to dress o. s. to the nines, to doll o. s. up; **wie ein ~ daherstolzieren** to strut like a peacock; **eitel wie ein ~ sein** to be vain as a peacock; **sich wie ein ~ spreizen** to be puffed up with pride, to plume o. s.

Pfeffer, jem. ~ geben to hurry (egg) s. o. on; **~ im Hintern haben** to have ants in one's pants; **starker ~ sein** to be a bit too thick; **j. dahin wünschen, wo der ~ wächst** to wish s. o. would go to hell; **geh dahin, wo der ~ wächst** go to Jericho.

pfeffern, jem. eine to slap s. o. in the face; **seine Rede mit spitzen Bemerkungen ~** to salt one's speech with pungent remarks; **seine Stiefel in die Ecke ~** to fling one's boots into a corner.

Pfeife whistle, *(Raucher)* pipe;
sich in die ~ stopfen to fill one's pipe; **nach jds. ~ tanzen** to dance to s. one's pipe (tune), to dance after s. one's whistle.

Pfeifen *(Radio)* howler.

pfeifen, auf etw. not to care a fig for s. th.; **vor dem Bahnübergang ~** to whistle before reaching the level crossing; **bewundernd ~** to give a wolf whistle; **auf eine Einladung ~** not to give two hoots (a dam) for an invitation; **auf die ganze Geheimnistuerei ~** to throw discretion to the dogs; **ums Haus ~** *(Wind)* to shrill round the house;
die Spatzen ~ es schon von den Dächern it's the talk of the town.

Pfeifen|deckel nothing doing *(coll.)*; **~heini** stupid ass.

Pfeif|kessel whistling kettle; **~konzert** cat-calls; **~signal** whistle.

Pfeil, mit ~ und Bogen with bow and arrow;
~ für Linksabbieger arrow filter signal; **wie ein ~ davonschießen** to dart off; **noch einen ~ im Köcher haben** to have another card to play; **seine ~e verschossen haben** to be at the end of one's tether; **giftige ~e verschießen** to make caustic remarks.

Pfeiler pillar, pier.

Pfennig penny, farthing, stiver;
ohne einen ~ strapped, stony-broke; **von seinen Gläubigern um den letzten ~ gebracht** denuded by his creditors of every penny he has;
~e chickenfeed *(sl.)*;
sich jeden ~ vor dem Ausgeben zweimal ansehen to be very tight-fisted; **keinen ~ Geld von jem. bekommen** not to see the colo(u)r of one's money from s. o.; **mit jedem ~ im Haushalt geizen** to scrimp one's household; **keinen ~ haben** to have not a penny to bless o. s. with; **keinen ~ Courage haben** to have no guts; **mit dem ~ rechnen** to think of pennies; **keinen ~ wert sein** not to be worth tuppence (a plugged nickle); **seinen letzten ~ mit jem. teilen** to share one's last crust with s. o.; **jeden ~ zweimal umdrehen** to look at every penny twice; **~e verachten** to neglect the odd pence *(coll.)*; **jeden ~ zusammenkratzen** to have to pinch and scrape;
wer den ~ nicht ehrt, ist des Talers nicht wert who needs not a penny will never have many, take care of the pennies and the pounds will take care of themselves;
~absatz stiletto heel; **~artikel** catch-penny article; **~beträge** chickenfeed *(sl.)*; **~fuchser** scrapepenny *(Br.)*, pennypincher, pinchpenny; **sich selbst als ~fuchser bezeichnen** to be a self-proclaimed pennypincher; **~fuchserei** penny wisdom; **~sparen** penny deposit; **~ware** trinkets, trifles.

Pferd, zu on horseback; **zu ~e** *(mil.)* mounted;
~ anspannen to put a horse to the cart; **~ beim Schwanz aufzäumen** to put the cart before the horse; **sein ~ in einem Mietstall einstellen** to board one's horse at a livery stable; **mit jem. ~e stehlen können** to be game for anything; **seine ~ verschnaufen lassen** to wind one's horses; **~e scheu machen** to put the wind up s. o.; **bestes ~ im Stall sein** to be a regular brick; **wie ein ~ schuften** to work like a horse (dog, slave, nigger); **alles auf ein ~ setzen** to lump one's all on a horse; **aufs falsche ~ setzen** to back the wrong horse, to bring one's pigs (hogs, eggs) to the wrong market; **sich aufs hohe ~ setzen** to get on one's (ride the) high horse; **etw. von ~en verstehen** to be a judge of horse flesh; **~e mitten im Strom wechseln** to swap horses midstream;
das hält ja kein ~ aus that's more than flesh and blood can stand; **ihm gingen die ~e durch** he flew off the handle.

Pferde|arbeit backbreaking work; **~decke** quarter sheet *(Br.)*; **~droschke** cab; **~fuß** *(fig.)* rub, snag, fly in the ointment; **~fuß sehen lassen** to show the cloven hoof; **die Sache hat einen ~fuß** there's a snag in it; **~gespann** turnout; **~halter** horse holder; **~handel** horse trading; **~händler** horse coper (dealer); **~knecht** hostler; **~rennbahn** turf; **~rennen** horse race; **beim ~rennen wetten** to play the races; **~rennsport** turf; **~rücken** horseback; **~stall** stable; **~stärke** horsepower, *(Flugmotor)* soup *(sl.)*; **~verleiher** livery man; **~wagen** horse car; **~zucht** horse breeding; **~züchter** horse breeder.

Pfiff|des Erstaunens whistle of astonishment;
~ haben *(Kleid)* to be chic, to have style (punch, *fam.*); **~ raushaben** to know all the dodges, to have the knack of it; **der letzte ~ sein** to be the latest shake (all the kick).

Pfifferling tinker's damn, whoop *(coll.)*, rap, shuck, fig;
keinen ~ wert not worth a tinker's damn (curse, cuss, brass farthing, fillip, whoop, *coll.*, a pin, a button, a shuck, plugged nickle, *US*);
ein paar ~e a few coppers;
sich keinen ~ daraus machen not to care a fig (whoop, *US coll.*); **keinen ~ wert sein** not to be a halfpenny the worth of it, not to be worth a hoot.

pfiffig slick, smart, clever, bright, cheeky, shrewd;
~ sein to be on the ball *(fam.)*.

Pfiffikus slyboots, cunning fellow;
er ist ein richtiger ~ there are no flies on him.

Pfingstochse, geschmückt wie ein dressed fit to kill.

pflanzen to plant, *(in Topf)* to pot;
sich in einen Sessel ~ to plump o. s. into an armchair.

Pflanzen|dünger manure, *(künstlich)* fertilizer; **~öl** vegetable oil; **~saft** vegetable juice; **~schutz** plant protection; **~schutzmittel** pesticide; **~welt** vegetation, vegetable world; **wuchernder ~wuchs** wanton vegetation; **~zucht** plant cultivation.

Pflaster pavement, *(med.)* plaster;
abgetretenes ~ battered pavement; **holpriges ~** bumpy pavement; **teures ~** *(fig.)* high cost-of-living region;

~ anlegen to plaster; ~ aufreißen to tear up the pavement; nettes Sümmchen als ~ erhalten to get a tidy sum of money as compensation; jem. ein ~ zur Beschwichtigung seines Gewissens geben to do s. th. to salve s. one's conscience; jem. zu einem heißen ~ geworden sein to have become too hot for s. o.; ~ treten to pound the asphalt *(US fam.)*;
~decke block pavement *(US)*; ~maler pavement artist, screever *(sl.)*; ~stein paving stone; ~straße paved road; ~treter gadabout; ~werbung pavement advertising.

Pflege charge, care, nursing, fosterage, *(Kranke)* attendance;
dauernde ~ constant attendance; **schlechte ~** rough nursing; **sorgfältige ~** careful nursing;
Wartung und ~ eines Autos servicing (care) of a car; **~ von Baudenkmälern** preservation of monuments; **~ einer Freundschaft** cultivation of a friendship; **~ des Kapitalmarktes** nursing (cultivation of) the capital market; **~ und Wartung** *(Industrieanlagen)* upkeep and maintenance;
in ~ geben to give in charge; **Kinder gegen Bezahlung in ~ geben** to farm out children, to put children out to nurse; **in ~ haben** to have charge of s. th.; **jem. gute ~ angedeihen lassen** to take good care of s. o.; **seinen Vater im Alter in ~ nehmen** to take one's father in his old age; **bei jem. in ~ sein** to be in s. one's charge;
~anleitung *(Textilien)* care label; **~anstalt** nursing (foster) home, asylum.

pflegebedürftig needing care.

Pflege|bedürftiger person needing care and attention; **für das Wohlergehen seiner ~bedürftigen sorgen** to look after the welfare of one's charges; **~befohlener** charge, *(Mündel)* ward; **~beruf** nursing [profession]; **~beruf ausüben** to do nursing; **~beruf ergreifen** to go in for nursing; **~bruder** foster brother; **~dienst** nursing, *(Kraftfahrzeug)* service, servicing; **~dienst übernehmen** to service; **~eltern** foster parents; **~fall** person in need of care; **~geld** guardian's allowance; **~heim** foster home, charity house, convalescent house, *(Altenheim)* old people's home *(Br.)*; **~hinweis** *(Kleid)* care label; **~kind** foster (nurse) child, adoptee; **~kindschaftsverhältnis** fosterage; **~klasse** category; **~kosten** nursing fees; **~- und Instandsetzungskosten** upkeep and improvement.

pflegeleicht *(Kleid)* easy-care.

Pflege|mittel cosmetic, *(Fußboden)* preservative; **~mutter** foster mother.

pflegen to care, to tend, to foster, *(Fabrikanlagen)* to maintain, to keep up, to carry on, *(fördern)* to promote, to further, to foment, *(Kranke)* to attend, to do nursing, to nurse, *(Tiere)* to groom;
seinen Bauch ~ to do o. s. proud *(coll.)*; **jds. Bekanntschaft ~** to cultivate s. one's acquaintance; **Beziehung ~** to nurse a connection; **alte Bräuche ~** to retain old customs; **Geschäftsverbindungen mit einer Firma ~** to entertain business relations with a firm; **j. gesund ~** to nurse s. o. back to health; **Kapitalmarkt ~** to nurse (cultivate) the capital market; **Kontakt mit jem. ~** to keep in contact with s. o.; **Kunden ~** to keep in with a customer *(fam.)*; **Patienten ~** to tend a patient; **der Ruhe ~** to take a rest; **etw. zu tun ~** to be accustomed to doing s. th.; **Umgang mit jem. ~** to associate o. s. with s. o.; **Unterhandlungen ~** to carry on (conduct) negotiations, to be in treaty; **Verbindung ~** to nurse a connection; **gesellschaftlichen Verkehr mit jem. ~** to have social contact with s. o.

Pflegepersonal nursing staff.

Pfleger special guardian, *(für Entmündigte)* curator, *(Kranke)* caretaker, tender, receiver *(Br.)*, *(Nachlaß)* administrator, testamentary guardian, *(Vermögen)* trustee, curator, custodian;
vom Gericht (gerichtlich) bestellter ~ judicial factor (trustee), guardian by appointment of the court; **zugunsten der Gläubiger bestellter ~** assignee in insolvency;
~ bestellen to appoint a guardian; **jem. als ~ zugeteilt sein** to have care and oversight of s. o.

Pflege|satz *(Krankenhaus)* hospital allowance; **~sohn** foster son; **~station** sick station; **~stelle** foster home; **~tochter** foster daughter; **~vater** foster father; **~zulage** nursing allowance.

pfleglich behandeln to treat carefully;
Kapitalmarkt ~ to nurse (cultivate) the capital market.

Pflegling ward, charge, custodee, *(Mündel)* ward of court.

Pflegschaft guardianship, tutelage, tutorship, *(Entmündigte)* curatorship, custodial care, receivership *(Br.)*, *(Nachlaß)* administration, *(Treuhänder)* assigneeship;
mit besonderen Pflichten verbundene ~ special trust;
~ für einen Abwesenden curatorship for an absent person;
~ anordnen to grant a curatorship; **~ aufheben** to terminate a curatorship.

Pflegschaftseinsetzungsbeschluß letters of guardianship *(US)*.

Pflicht duty, *(Amt)* office, business, job, *(Verpflichtung)* [moral] obligation, liability, trust;
ausdrückliche ~ express obligation; **eheliche ~en** conjugal duties, marital obligations; **gesetzliche ~** legal (statutory) obligation; **lästige ~en** onerous duties; **moralische ~** moral consideration (obligation); **jem. obliegende ~** obligation incumbent on s. o.; **selbstverständliche ~** plain duty; **staatsbürgerliche ~** civic duty; **stillschweigende ~** implied obligation; **übertragene ~** commission; **mit dem Grundeigentum verbundene ~en** burden of a covenant; **vertragliche ~** obligation under a contract;
~ zur Abrechnung liability to render account; **~en eines Treuhänders** fiduciary duties; **~ zur Vorlage von Urkunden** liability to discover; **~en im eigenen Wirkungskreis** *(Kommune)* proprietary duties;
es als seine ~ ansehen to esteem it a duty; **jem. eine ~ auferlegen** to enjoin a duty on s. o., to fasten an obligation on s. o.; **~en eingehen** to enter into commitments; **j. von einer ~ entbinden** to exonerate s. o. from an obligation; **sich seiner ~ entziehen** to depart from one's (evade a) duty; **sich seinen ~en nie entziehen** never to flinch from one's duty; **seine ~ erfüllen** to fulfil(l) (discharge) one's duty (obligation), to do one's bit; **seine ~en getreulich erfüllen** to be faithful in the discharge of one's duties; **seine ~ nicht hinlänglich erfüllen** to fall short in one's duty; **etw. für seine verdammte ~ und Schuldigkeit halten** to consider s. th. one's bounden duty *(coll.)*; **j. an der Ausübung seiner ~en hindern** to obstruct s. o. in the execution of his duty; **seinen ~en wieder nachgehen** to resume one's duties; **seinen ~en nachkommen** to discharge one's duty (functions); **seine ~en nicht sehr ernst nehmen** to be lax in carrying out one's duties; **seinen ~en obliegen** to attend to one's duties; **~ sein** to be obligatory; **treu seine ~ tun** to stand to one's duty; **seine ~en vernachlässigen** to be slack in (derelict to, *US*) one's duty, to deviate (depart) from one's duty;
~ablieferung contingent delivery; **~aktien** *(Vorstand)* qualifying shares, qualification; **~altersversicherung** obligatory old-age insurance; **~andruck** imprint; **~anker** sheet anchor; **~anteil** contingent quota; **~assistent** intern *(US)*; **~aufenthaltszeit in der Zentrale** *(Diplomat)* home-office tour of duty; **hohe ~auffassung** high conception (sense) of one's duties; **kommunale ~aufgabe** statutory duty; **~ausbildung** formal training.

pflichtausgerüstet compulsorily fitted.

Pflicht|beitrag compulsory contribution; **~bekanntmachung** obligatory announcement; **~besuch** duty call.

pflichtbewußt mindful of one's duty;
stets sehr ~ sein to be always observant of one's duties.

Pflicht|bewußtsein sense of duty; **~blatt** official journal; **~eindruck** *(Bücher)* imprint; **~einlage** obligatory investment, contribution to capital, compulsory contribution.

Pflichten|erledigung, schlampige laxity in one's duties; **~festlegung** designation of s. one's duty; **~kodex** code of conduct; **~kollision** clash of responsibilities.

Pflichtenkreis responsibilities, duties;
häuslicher ~ domestic duties; **täglicher ~** one's daily tour of duty;
jem. seinem ~ entfremden to lure s. o. away from his duty; **~ festlegen** to define duties; **~ zuweisen** to allocate duties.

Pflichten|umfang extent of duty; **~wahrnehmung** exercise of duties; **~zuweisung** allocation of duties.

Pflicht|erfüllung performance (execution, discharge, observance) of one's duty; **~ergebenheit** devotion to duty; **~exemplar** *(Bibliothek)* presentation (deposit) copy; **~exemplare bei den Bibliotheken abliefern** to deposit duty copies of a book; **~exemplarbestimmungen** library tax; **~fach** compulsory subject; **~feuerwehr** fire brigade (company); **~gefühl** sense of duty; **angeborenes ~gefühl** inclination of duty.

pflichtgemäß due, mandatory;
nicht ~ optional.

Pflicht|interventionssystem *(EG)* compulsory intervention system; **~kartell** compulsory syndicate; **~lager** compulsory stock; **~landung** compulsory landing; **~leistung** performance of a duty; **~lektüre** must reading; **~mitglied** compulsory member; **~mitgliedschaft** compulsory membership; **~reserve, ~rücklagen** *(Bankwesen)* legal *(Br.)* (lawful, *US*) reserve, minimum cash reserve, required reserves *(US)*; **~schulalter** compulsory school age.

Pflichtteil *(Erbe)* statutory *(US)* (legal, lawful) share, legitimate (legal, hereditary, statutory, *US*) portion, statutory legacy *(Br.)*, appanage, legitim *(Scot.)*;

gerichtlich festgesetzter ~ family provision *(Br.)*;
~ **der Witwe** wife's part, widow's-bench, election dower; ~ **der Witwe und der Kinder** reasonable part *(Br.)*;
aufs ~ **setzen** *(Kinder)* to put (cut) off with a shilling.
Pflichtteils | anspruch forced heirship *(US)*; ~**anspruch der Witwe** widow right, widow-bench *(Br.)*, election dower, marital portion *(Louisiana)*; ~**ausstattung** advancement by portion; ~**berechtigter** forced heir *(US)*, legal distributee.
pflichtteilsberechtigter Erbe forced heir *(US)*.
Pflichtteils | eigenheim probate homestead; ~**entziehung** [etwa] disinheritance *(US)*; ~**festsetzung für jüngere Geschwister** raising of portions for younger children; ~**recht** forced heirship *(US)*; ~**vereinbarung** covenant to give a portion.
pflichttreu faithful;
seine Arbeit ~ **tun** to perform a task conscientiously.
Pflicht | treue faith, devotion to duty, faithfulness, fidelity, loyalty; ~**überstunden** compulsory overtime; **sich einer** ~**übung unterziehen** to go through the motions; ~**untersuchung** compulsory medical examination; ~**veranstaltung** command performance.
pflichtvergessen derelict to duty *(US)*, delinquent;
~ **sein** to be negligent of one's duty.
Pflicht | vergessenheit desertion, delinquency, delinquency of duty; ~**verletzung** breach of (lapse from one's) duty, neglect (evasion) of one's duties, *(im Amt)* malfeasance, *(Vertrauensbruch)* breach of trust; ~**versäumnis** evasion of one's duty, shortcoming, default; **jem.** ~**versäumnis vorwerfen** to tax s. o. with neglect of his work.
pflichtversichert sein *(Angestellter)* to be inside the scope of the national insurance system.
Pflicht | versicherter obligatorily insured person; ~**versicherung** compulsory (obligatory) insurance; ~**versicherungsgesetz** Compulsory Insurance Act *(Br.)*; ~**verteidiger** assigned counsel *(Br.)*, barrister appointed by the court *(Br.)*, assistance of counsel, public defender *(US)*; ~**vorlesungen belegen** to keep one's terms.
pflichtwidrig inofficious, unfaithful, disloyal;
~**es Unterlassen** neglect of one's duties.
Pflichtwidrigkeit disloyalty, breach of duty.
Pflock peg, picket;
Weidevieh an den ~ **binden** to stake cattle.
Pflöcke, mit ~**n befestigt** pegged;
einige ~ **zurückstecken müssen** to have to come down a peg or two.
pflücken to pick, to pluck;
Lorbeeren ~ to win laurels.
Pflücker, Pflückmaschine picker.
Pflug plough, plow *(US)*;
hinter dem ~ **gehen** to follow the plough; **Feld unter den** ~ **nehmen** to put the plough over a field.
pflügen to plough, to plow *(US)*;
mit dem Traktor ~ to plough (plow, *US*) with the tractor.
Pflugtiere beasts of the plow.
Pforte gate, door, entrance;
sich an der ~ **melden** to report at the reception; ~**n schließen** *(Ausstellung)* to close its doors; **vor der** ~ **des Todes stehen** to be at the point of death.
Pförtner gatekeeper, porter, doorkeeper, concierge, doorman *(US)*, janitor *(US)*, *(Gericht)* usher;
~**haus** gatehouse; ~**loge** porter's lodge.
Pfote, fürchterliche terrible scrawl *(coll.)*;
sich die ~**n verbrannt haben** to have burnt one's fingers; **eins auf die** ~**n kriegen** to get a wrap over the knuckles.
Pfründe benefice, prebend;
ohne ~ unbeneficed;
fette ~ lucrative office, fat living; **magere** ~ poor living;
j. in eine ~ **einsetzen** to institute s. o. into a benefice; **von einer mageren** ~ **leben** to live on a mere pittance; ~ **verwalten** to hold in commendam.
Pfründen | aufgabe resignation of a benefice *(Br.)*; ~**besetzungsrecht** advowson, advocacy; ~**besitz** incumbency; ~**besitzer** beneficed clergyman; ~**entzug** spoliation *(Br.)*; ~**handel** simony; ~**inhaber** prebendary, incumbent; ~**verleihungsrecht** patronage.
Pfund pound, *(Währung)* pound [sterling];
Zahlung erfolgt in ~ payment is in sterling;
mit Fremdwährungsmitteln erworbene ~**e** external sterling *(Br.)*;
~ **abwerten** to depreciate the pound; **mit seinem** ~**e wuchern** to have a talent for doing the right thing;
~**abgänge drosseln** to slow down the sterling outflow; ~**abwertung** devaluation of the pound; ~**anleihe** sterling loan; ~**aufwertung** revaluation of the pound; ~**block** sterling bloc; ~**erholung** pound strengthening; ~**guthaben** sterling-account balance; ~**konto** sterling account; ~**konvertibilität** convertibility of sterling; ~**krise** sterling crisis; ~**lücke** sterling gap; ~**note** pound note; ~**schwäche** weakness in sterling (of the pound).
Pfundskerl brick, sport, guy *(US sl.)*.
Pfund | sturz plunge in sterling; **langfristiger** ~**wechsel auf London** long sterling.
Pfusch, völligen ~ **geliefert haben** to have made a botch of the business;
~**arbeit** bad job, tinker, scamping, slapdash, malpractice.
pfuschen to tinker, to scamper, to slobber, to slapdash, to make a mess (a botch job);
bei der Arbeit ~ to bungle a piece of work; **in einem Examen** ~ to ride an examination *(sl.)*; **jem. ins Handwerk** ~ to meddle in s. one's affairs.
Pfuscher scamper, tinker, duffer *(Br., coll.)*, lobster *(US)*, tamperer, patcher, botcher, butcher *(US)*, dilettante, dabbler.
Pfuscherei bad job, tinker, slapdash, botched piece of work, malpractice.
Pfütze water hole, puddle, slop;
über die große ~ **fahren** to cross the herring pond.
Phänomen phenomenon, appearance, thing seen;
~ **außersinnlicher Wahrnehmungen** phenomenon of extrasensory perception.
phänomenales Gedächtnis phenomenal memory.
Phantasie fantasy, fancy, imagination, vision;
blühende ~ wanton imagination; **fieberische** ~ feverish hallucination; **lebhafte** ~ lively imagination, lively play of fantasy; **reine** ~ pure fabrication; **schöpferische** ~ fertile imagination; **üppige** ~ luxuriant imagination;
~ **anregen** to quicken the animation, to humo(u)r (tickle) s. one's fancy; **jds.** ~ **beflügeln** to fire s. one's imagination; **lebhafte** ~ **haben** to have a lively imagination; **seiner** ~ **die Zügel schießen lassen** to give free rein (play) to one's imagination;
~**bezeichnung** fanciful trade name; ~**gebilde** imaginary sight, day dream, act of the imagination, fantasy; **als** ~**gebilde abtun** to treat as delusion; ~**gebilde sein** to be a product of s. one's imagination; ~**land** never-never land.
phantasielos fanciless, lacking imagination, flatfooted *(Br.)*.
Phantasie | markenname coined brand name; ~**name** fancy name; ~**preis** fancy (sky-rocketing, *US*) price.
phantasieren to surrender to the play of one's imagination, to indulge in day dreams, *(med.)* to have delusions, to be delirious, to rave, *(Unsinn reden)* to talk nonsense (incoherently);
auf dem Klavier ~ to temporize (improvise) on the piano.
Phantasiewort *(Warenzeichen)* fancy word.
Phantast phantast, dreamer, castle-builder, notional man *(US)*.
Phantasterei chimera, day dream.
phantastisch fantastic, fanciful, visionary, whimsical, out of this world *(coll.)*, super-duper;
~ **angezogen sein** to be extremely well dressed; ~ **reich sein** to be rich as a Jew;
~**es Erlebnis** weird experience; ~**er Film** fantastic film; ~**e Geschwindigkeit** incredible speed; ~**e Ideen** high-flown ideas; ~**e Preise** fabulous prices; ~**es Wetter** marvel(l)ous weather.
Phantom phantom, phantasm, vapo(u)r, specter, spectre *(Br.)*;
einem ~ **nachjagen** to catch at shadows;
~**schaltung** *(tel.)* phantom circuit.
pharisäerhaft self-righteous.
Pharisäertum self-righteousness.
Pharmazeut druggist.
pharmazeutische Industrie pharmaceutical industry.
Phase phase, stage, grade;
in der ersten ~ **des Streikes** in a strike's early phase;
abklingende ~ passing phase; **wechselnde konjunkturelle** ~**n** alternating phases of the cyclical trend;
~ **konjunktureller Talfahrt** cyclical downswing phase; ~**n des Wachstums** growth phases, stages of growth;
in eine entscheidende ~ **eintreten** to enter a decisive stage.
Phasenangleichung phase adjustment.
phasengleich sein to be in phase.
Phasen | laufzeit *(tel.)* phase delay; ~**schreiber** phase recorder; ~**spannung** star voltage; ~**umsatzsteuer** all-stage turnover tax; ~**unterschied** phase difference, time lag; ~**verschiebung** phase shift, leads and lags; ~**verzerrung** phase distortion.
Philanthrop philanthropist, humanitarian.
philanthropische Einrichtungen philanthropic institutions.

Philatelie philately;
~**schalter** philatelic sales counter.
Philharmonische Gesellschaft philharmonic society.
Philippika gegen die Regierung halten to break out into a violent tirade against the government.
Philister philistine, Babbit *(US)*, square *(sl.)*.
philisterhaft philistine, narrow-minded, square *(sl.)*.
Philologie philology, textual criticism, language and literature.
Philosoph philosopher.
Philosophie philosophy.
philosophische Fakultät faculty of arts.
Phlegma, jds. ~ erschüttern to disturb s. one's equanimity.
Phon phon, decible;
Höchstwerte von 102 bis 108 ~ für Flugzeuge zulassen to establish maximum noise level for aircraft of between 102 and 108 decibles.
Phonetik phonetics.
Phonstärke decibel.
Phono|graph talking machine; ~**typistin** audiotypist.
Phrase phrase, trite remark, platitude;
abgedroschene ~ threadbare (common) phrase, cliché; **schön gedrechselte ~n** well-rounded periods; **hochtönende ~n** high-sounding phrases;
j. mit hohlen ~n abspeisen to fob s. o. off with empty talk.
Phrasen|drescher phrasemonger, platitudinarian, gasbag *(coll.)*; ~**drescher sein** to be a phrasemaker, to speak in a flowery language; ~**drescherei** phrasemongering.
Phraseologie phraseology, language.
phraseologisch phraseological.
Physik physical, science, physics.
physikalische Eigenschaften physical properties.
Physiognomie physiognomy, facial expression, face;
undurchdringliche ~ inscrutable expression.
physisch physical, corporeal;
~ unmöglich absolutely impossible.
picheln to booze, to tipple;
gern ~ to be fond of the bottle.
picken, immer die Rosinen aus dem Kuchen ~ wollen to always want the pick of the bunch.
Picknick picnic, junket, basket dinner (lunch) *(US)*;
Mittagessen auf dem ~ zu sich nehmen to take a picnic lunch; ~**abfälle einsammeln** to pick up one's litter after a picnic; ~**ausflug** picnic, junketing party, basket meeting *(US)*.
picknicken to picnic, to junket.
Picknick|korb picnic basket, box lunch *(US)*; ~**teilnehmer** picknicker; ~**wagen** chuck wagon *(US)*.
picobello|angezogen impeccably dressed; **~ sauber** spotlessly clean, spick and pan *(coll.)* .
Piedestal pedestal.
piekfein posh, spruce, dapper, snazzy *(US sl.)*, spiffy *(sl.)*, spiffed up *(sl.)*;
~ gekleidet sein to be dressed up to the nines.
pieksauber spick and span.
piepe, jem. völlig ~ sein not to care a damn (two hoots).
Piepen *(Geld)* dough, lolly, spondulicks *(US sl.)*, beans, dibs *(sl.)*;
für ein paar ~ arbeiten to work for a mere pittance; **seine letzten ~ ausgeben** to spend one's last penny;
das ist ja zum ~ that's a perfect scream.
Pieps, keinen ~ sagen not to say boo, not to open one's mouth.
Piepsen *(Zeitsignal)* pip.
piepsige Stimme squeaky voice.
Piepvogel haben to be nuts (slighty cracked).
Pier wharf, quay, dock *(US)*.
piesacken to heckle, to torment, to badger, to bug *(US sl.)*;
j. ~ to chip s. o.; **j. mit der Bitte um eine Vergünstigung ~** to badger s. o. into granting a favo(u)r; **j. in einem Examen ~** to grill s. o. in an exam; **mit Fragen ~** to pester with questions.
Pigment|druckverfahren pigment printing, carbon process; ~**papier** carbon paper.
pikant spicy, savo(u)ry, piquant, high-tasted;
~**es Abenteuer** amorous adventure; ~**es Buch** naughty book; ~**e Sauce** piquant sauce; ~**e Situation** piquancy of a situation; ~**es Thema** somewhat delicate subject; ~**er Witz** risqué joke.
Pike, von der ~ auf dienen to rise from the ranks, to start from scratch; **~ gegen j. haben** to take a pique (bear a grudge) against s. o.
pikiert *(fig.)* nettled, peeved;
~ reagieren to act in a pique; **~ sein** to be nettled (peeved), to feel huffed.
Pikkolo page[-boy], busboy *(US sl.)*.
Pilatus, von Pontius zu ~ laufen to run from pillar to post.
pilgern, von Wirtshaus zu Wirtshaus to go on a pub-crawl.
Pille, bittere bitter pill, dose;
bittere ~ schlucken müssen to put one's pride in one's pocket, to eat crow *(US)*; **~ nehmen** to take a pill; **die ~ schlucken** to swallow one's medicine *(US)*; **~ versüßen** to sugar the pill.
Pillen|dreher pharmacist; ~**schachtel** pillbox.
Pilot, automatischer autopilot; **geprüfter ~** sky pilot; **zugelassener ~** branch pilot; **zweiter ~** copilot;
~**en absetzen** *(fig.)* to drop the pilot.
Piloten|kanzel cockpit; ~**prüfung ablegen** to qualify as aviator; ~**prüfung abnehmen** to license a pilot; **seine ~prüfung machen** to get one's wings; ~**schein** pilot's licence; ~**schein ausstellen** to license a pilot; ~**sitz** cockpit, cabin.
pilz|artiges Anwachsen einer Vorstadt mushroom growth of a suburb; ~**förmig aus dem Boden schießen** to mushroom up, to shoot up like mushrooms.
Pilz|konstruktion mushroom construction; ~**lampe** mushroom desk lamp; ~**lautsprecher** mushroom loudspeaker.
pingelig fussy, pernickety, fastidious;
äußerst ~ sein to cross one's t's and dot one's i's; **in Geldsachen äußerst ~ sein** to be scrupulous in money matters; **was Kleidung angeht sehr ~ sein** to be very fastidious about one's dress; **nicht so ~ sein** not to stand upon niceties; **ein bißchen zu ~ sein** to be scrupulous to a degree.
Pinkel, feiner posh person, toff dandy *(Br.)*, dude *(US sl.)*.
Pinkepinke *(coll.)* dough *(sl.)*, brass *(sl.)*, spondulicks *(US sl.)*, nut *(US sl.)*;
keine ~ mehr haben not to have a bean left.
Pinsel paintbrush, *(fig.)* nincompoop, simpleton;
eingebildeter ~ conceited puppy (ass).
Pinte tavern, pub *(Br., coll.)*.
Pinunsen chink *(sl.)*, spondulicks *(US sl.)*.
Pionier pioneer, trail blazer, innovator, *(mil.)* engineer;
~**arbeit** pioneer work; ~**arbeit leisten** to pioneer, to blaze a trail *(US)*; **leichtes ~bataillon** engineer combat battalion *(mil.)*; ~**dienst** pioneering service; ~**park** engine park; ~**patent** pioneer (basic) patent; ~**tätigkeit** pioneering job; ~**truppe** field corps engineers, Corps of Engineers; **leichte ~truppe** field engineers *(Br.)*; ~**wesen** engineering.
Pirat sea robber, sea rover, freebooter, marooner, pirate, *(Flugzeugentführer)* hi[gh]jacker.
Piraten|akt begehen to commit piracy, to pirate; ~**flagge** blackflag, blackjack; ~**flugplatz** hi[gh]jacker's airfield; ~**flugzeug** hi[gh]jacker's plane; ~**schlupfwinkel** nest of pirates; ~**sender** pirate broadcasting station; ~**tum** piracy.
Piraterie piracy, hi[gh]jacking.
Piste runway, landing strip, track, *(Skifahrer)* ski run.
Pistole revolver, pistol, gun *(US)*, rod *(sl.)*;
wie aus der ~ geschossen like a shot;
jem. die ~ auf die Brust setzen to hold a pistol to s. one's chest;
~ ziehen to pull a gun.
Pistolen|schuß crack of a pistol, pistol shot; **in ~schußweite** within pistol shot; ~**tasche** holster.
Plackerei toil and moil, drudgery.
plädieren to plead, to count, to argue;
falsch ~ to misplead; **vor Gericht ~** to plead at the bar; **anstelle von Mord nur noch auf schwere Körperverletzung ~** to reduce a murder charge to aggravated assault.
plädierender Anwalt barrister *(Br.)*.
Plädoyer pleading, argument of council, counsel's speech *(Br.)*, submission, advocacy;
erneutes ~ repleader; **falsches ~** mispleading; **gegnerisches ~** adversary's speech;
~ des Staatsanwaltes statement declaration; **~ des Strafverteidigers** speech for the defence (defense, *US*);
sein ~ abschließen to rest the case *(US)*; **erneutes ~ anordnen** to award a repleader; **mit dem ~ beginnen** to open the pleadings; **sein ~ als Verteidiger halten** to address the court for the defence (defense, *US*).
Plafond upper limit, ceiling, *(Kreditrahmen)* borrowing limit, credit limit *(Br.)* (line, *US*);
genügend ~ für erhebliche Haushaltsbelebungen haben to have the headroom for substantial budget stimulus.
Plafondierung ceiling control.
Plage plague, nuisance, pest, affliction;
jem. das Leben zur ~ machen to make s. one's life miserable; **eine richtige ~ sein** to be a pain in the neck.
plagen to trouble, to afflict, to prick, to torment;
sich ~ to put o. s. about; **j. den ganzen Tag ~** *(Kinder)* to bother s. o. all day;
sich im Leben schwer ~ müssen to struggle hard to succeed.

Plagiat plagiarism, pirating, literary piracy;
~ **begehen** to commit a piracy, to pirate, to plagiarize.
Plagiator literary pirate, plagiarist, copyist.
plagiieren to lift, to plagiarize;
j. ~ to lift a passage from an author.
Plakat poster, placard, affiche *(US)*, posting bill, broadsheet; **beschädigtes** ~ torn poster; **farbiges** ~ picture poster; **grellfarbiges** ~ glaring (screaming) poster; **stockwerkgroßes** ~ floor-to-ceiling poster;
~ **ankleben (anschlagen)** to stick a bill [on a wall], to post (paste up) a placard, to bill; **durch** ~ **bekanntmachen** to bill, to poster; **mit ~en bekleben** to placard, to plaster;
~ **anschlagen verboten!** stick (post, *US*) no bills!;
~**ankleber** billsticker, billposter, placarder *(US)*; ~**anschlag** billposting, billsticking; **wilder** ~**anschlag** fly posting, sniping *(US)*; ~**anschläger** billsticker, placarder *(US)*; ~**anschlagfläche** outdoor advertising stand; ~**anschlagstelle** billboard (poster) hoarding, poster site; ~**anschlagunternehmen** poster plant, outdoor advertising firm, billposting agency; ~**buchstabengröße** heavy-face type; ~**entwurf** poster design.
Plakateur billsticker, billposter, placarder *(US)*.
Plakat|farbe poster colo(u)r; ~**fläche** hoarding *(Br.)*; ~**gestalter** poster artist.
plakatieren to placard, to bill, to post, to stick bills;
Wand ~ to post a wall with placards.
Plakatierung billposting, billsticking.
Plakatierungsauftrag billposting order.
plakative Darstellung slogan-like representation.
Plakat|maler poster artist; ~**säule** advertising pillar, billboard; ~**schild** show (advertising) placard; ~**schrift** heavy-face type, poster type; ~**ständer** stand; ~**tafel** billboard, placard, poster panel; ~**träger** sandwich man *(Br.)*, boardman *(US)*; ~**wand** boarding, billboard; ~**werbung** outdoor (billboard) advertising, poster display; ~**werbung durchführen** to placard; ~**zeichner** poster artist, designer.
Plakette plaque, badge, medal, plateau *(Br.)*.
Plan plan, arrangement, device, *(Absicht)* design, intent, intention, thought, *(grafische Darstellung)* diagram, *(Entwurf)* draft, design, drawing, plot, blueprint *(US)*, *(Karte)* map, *(Lageplan)* groundplan, layout, *(Tabelle)* chart, *(Vorhaben)* scheme, project, contrivance, *(Zeitplan)* timetable, schedule; **ohne** ~ without any plan[ning];
abänderungsfähiger ~ plan liable to modification; **gut ausgearbeiteter** ~ well-worked (mature) plan, well-worked scheme; **hinter den Kulissen ausgeheckter** ~ backstage plan; **ausgereifter** ~ mature plan; **durchführbarer** ~ workable scheme; **fester** ~ organized plan, schedule; **gedruckter** ~ prospectus; **Grüner** ~ farm program(me); **rechtsverbindlicher** ~ legally binding project; **umfassender** ~ master plan; **unüberlegter** ~ wild scheme; **utopischer** ~ utopian scheme; **verwässerter** ~ watered-down scheme; **wohlüberlegter** ~ deliberate plan;
~ **für die Beschaffung billiger Wohnungen** low-cost housing program(me); ~ **für vorgezogene Pensionierungen** early retirement scheme; ~ **in großen Umrissen** stretch plan;
~ **abändern** to modify a (depart from one's) plan; **nach** ~ **abfahren** *(Zug)* to start on time (after schedule, *US*); **ohne** ~ **und Überlegung arbeiten** to work on a piecemeal plan; ~ **aufgeben** to put s. th. out of one's head; ~ **völlig aufgeben** to throw a scheme overboard; ~ **ausarbeiten** to draw up (compose) a scheme, to plan; ~ **ausführen (durchführen)** to execute a plan; ~ **aushecken** to concoct a plan; **neuen** ~ **aushecken** to get a new tack; ~ **ausprobieren** to test out a scheme; ~ **beschleunigen** to step up a scheme; ~ **völlig durcheinanderbringen** to muddle a scheme completely; ~ **entwerfen** to draw up (frame) a plan; ~ **eines Hauses entwerfen** to design a building; **sich zu einem festen** ~ **entwickeln** to crystallize into a definite plan; ~ **fallenlassen** to abandon a scheme, to lump it *(sl.)*; **voreiligen** ~ **fassen** to be rather previous in forming a plan; **keinem festen** ~ **folgen** to follow no preconcerted plan; **jem. nicht in den** ~ **passen** not to suit s. one's book; **theoretisch ein guter** ~ **sein** to be a good scheme on paper; ~ **skizzieren** to outline a scheme; **auf den** ~ **treten** to enter the arena, to swing into action; **seinen** ~ **in die Tat umsetzen** to go ahead with one's plan; ~ **unterstützen** to promote a scheme; ~ **vereiteln** to thwart (upset) a plan; **sich einen** ~ **zurechtlegen** to work out a plan; **hinter einem** ~ **zurückbleiben** to fall behind schedule; **einem** ~ **von Herzen zustimmen** to give one's hearty approval to a plan;
~**abschnitt** budget period; ~**ansatz** budget estimate; ~**bestand** target inventory; ~**defizit** budget deficit.
Plane awning, tarpaulin, tilt, canvas.
Pläne, meine augenblicklichen my immediate plans; **noch im Anfangstadium befindliche** ~ plans in embryo; **nicht für die Öffentlichkeit bestimmte** ~ private plans; **langfristige** ~ long-range planning; **leicht veränderliche** ~ fluid plans; **verstiegene** ~ visionary plans;
~ **auf dem Papier** paper plans; ~ **zur Reform des Sozialwesens** welfare reform plan; ~ **auf lange Sicht** long-range planning; **seine** ~ **ändern** to alter one's plans; ~ **für die Bewässerung ausarbeiten** to work out a scheme for the irrigation; ~ **aushecken** to spin plots; **seine** ~ **bekanntmachen** to come out into the open with one's plans; **jds.** ~ **zum Scheitern bringen** to upset s. one's applecart *(coll.)*, to spike s. one's guns, to wreck s. one's plans; **feindliche** ~ **durcheinanderbringen** to upset the enemy's plans; **jds.** ~ **durchkreuzen** to cross (disconcert, discomfit, balk) s. one's (defeat s. o. in his) plans; **seine** ~ **enthüllen** to make one's plans known, to unfold one's design; **seine** ~ **erläutern** to show one's plans; ~ **in allen Einzelheiten erörtern** to talk over plans; **keine bestimmten** ~ **haben** to be uncertain about one's (have no fixed) plans; **ehrgeizige** ~ **haben** to fly high; **gleiche** ~ **haben** to be of council with; ~ **für den nächsten Urlaub machen** to make plans for the next holiday; **dunkle** ~ **schmieden** to put heads together; **jds. ~n im Wege stehen (hinderlich sein)** to be obstructive to (interfere with) s. one's plans; **jds.** ~ **vereiteln** to contravene (thwart, block) s. one's plans, to bring s. one's plans to nought; **seine** ~ **verwirklichen** to go ahead with one's plans; **sich jds. ~n widersetzen** to oppose s. one's plans.
planen to plan, to project, to scheme, to map out, to blueprint *(US)*, to calculate, *(entwerfen)* to concert, to devise, to design, *(zeitlich)* to time, to schedule, to phase;
gemeinsam ~ to concert (plan) together; **im Haushalt** ~ to budget for; **heimlich** ~ to plot; **Stadt** ~ to plan a city; **schon den nächsten Urlaub** ~ to be making plans for the next holiday; **Verrat** ~ to imagine treason *(Br.)*.
Planerfüllung performance of quotas.
Planerfüllungsindikator performance indicator.
Planeten|bahn track of a comet; ~**erforschung** exploration of planets; ~**sonde** planetary probe.
Plan|festsetzung, ~**feststellung** town planning, zoning *(US)*, *(mit Sonderbewilligungen)* incentive zoning *(US)*.
Planfeststellungs|ausschuß town-planning committee, zoning board (committee) *(US)*; ~**verfahren** zoning case *(US)*.
Planfilm flat (sheet) film.
plangerechte Fertigstellung completion on schedule.
planieren to grade, to level, to bulldoze;
Straße ~ to level a road down.
Planier|maschine road machine, [road] grader; ~**raupe** angledozer, bulldozer.
Planierung levelling, location.
Planimetrie plane geometry.
Plankarte plan chart.
Plänkelei *(mil.)* skirmish.
Plankengang *(Schiff)* strake of planks.
Plan|kommission planning commission; ~**kosten** budget (standard, target) costs; ~**kostenrechnung** budget accounting, budgeting.
planlos without plan (system), unsystematic, haphazard, random, desultory;
~ **umherlaufen** to wander aimlessly (forlornly); ~ **vorgehen** to proceed unsystematically.
planmäßig systematic, planned, methodical, according to plan, as scheduled *(US)*, normal;
~ **ankommen** to arrive on schedule *(US)*; ~ **ankommen sollen** to be due to arrive; ~ **verlaufen** to go according to plan;
~**e Abfahrt** scheduled departure *(US)*; ~**e Absatzförderung** sales drive; ~**er Ausbau des Straßennetzes** systematic extension of the road network; ~**er Beamter** regular official, established civil servant *(Br.)*; ~**e Fertigstellung** completion on schedule *(US)*; ~**er Luftverkehrsdienst** scheduled airline service *(US)*; ~**e Produktion** budget production; ~**e Tilgung** regular redemption.
Plannutzungsziffer speed factor.
plano *(drucktechn.)* unfolded.
Planobogen broadside.
Plan|pause blueprint, cyanotype; ~**quadrat** quarter section, grid; ~**quadratangabe** grid reference; ~**rechnung** estimates.
Planschbecken paddling pool.
Plan|schießen *(mil.)* predicted shooting; ~**skizze** sketch; ~**soll** target, quota; ~**spiel** *(Betrieb)* management game, *(mil.)* map exercise, experimental gaming; ~**spieldurchführung** *(Betrieb)* business gaming; ~**stärke** required strength.

Planstelle establishment, established (statutory) post;
in einer ~ on the establishment;
freie ~ vacancy;
~**n der Polizei auffüllen** to bring the police force up to strength;
jem. eine ~ **geben** to put s. o. on the establishment.
Plan|stelleninhaber established civil servant *(Br.)*, career civil servant *(US)*, fixture; ~**studie** planning study.
Plantage plantation.
Plantagen|besitzer planter; ~**wirtschaft** plantation system.
Planüberprüfung plan review.
Planung plan, planning, projection, blueprint *(US)*, *(Anlage)* layout, *(Haushalt)* budgeting, *(Städte)* city planning, zoning *(US)*; **betriebliche** ~ business (operational) planning; **einzelstaatliche** ~ state planning; **erfolgreiche** ~ productive planning; **grundlegende** ~ basic planning; **kommunale** ~ local (corporate) planning; **kurzfristige** ~ short-range planning; **langfristige** ~ long-range planning, long pull *(US)*; **regionale** ~ regional planning; **städtebauliche** ~ city (town, *Br.*) planning; **volkswirtschaftliche** ~ [etwa] national economic planning;
~ **der Entwicklung** development planning; ~ **auf sozialem Gebiet** social planning; ~**en für den Krankenhausbau** hospital planning; ~ **der Produktionsgebiete** product-line planning; **langfristige** ~ **der Produktionsgebiete** product line strategy; ~ **von Produktionsstätten** plant layout; ~, **Organisation, Durchführung und Kontrolle eines Projekts** project management; ~ **auf weite Sicht** long-range planning; **optimale** ~ **einer Wertpapieranlage** portfolio selection;
~ **durchführen** to accomplish planning; **in der** ~ **sein** to be being planned, to be in the blueprint stage.
Planungs|abteilung planning (layout) department, planning division; ~**amt** planning board; **an den** ~**arbeiten beteiligt sein** to be in on the planning; ~**aufgabe** planning function (job); ~**ausschuß** planning commission (committee); **städtischer** ~**ausschuß** town-plånning committee; ~**beamter** planning official; ~**behörde** planning agency (authority), economic planning board *(Br.)*, planning (conference) board; **kommunale** ~**behörde** local planning authority *(Br.)*; ~**behörde für neue Städte** new-town development agency; ~**bereich** planning sector; ~**bestrebungen** planning efforts; **staatliches** ~**büro** governmental planning agency; ~**einheit** planning unit; ~**forschung** operations research; ~**gebiet** planning area; **volkswirtschaftliches** ~**gebiet** economic planning region *(Br.)*; ~**grundsätze** planning principles; ~**gruppe** planning group; ~**hemmschuhe** obstacles to planning; ~**hoheit** planning competence; ~**ingenieur** production engineer, *(Städtebau)* master of city planning *(US)*; ~**instanz** planning board; ~**kosten** cost of planning; ~**minister** Planning Minister *(Br.)*; **staatliche** ~**politik** state planning; ~**programm** planning program(me); ~**raum** planning area; **interkommunaler** ~**raum** structure area *(Br.)*; ~**rechnung** cost budget, budgeting; **getrennte** ~**rechnung** separate program(m)ing; **lineare** ~**rechnung** linear program(m)ing; ~**region** [economic] planning region *(Br.)*; ~**sachverständiger** planning consultant; ~**sitzung** planning session; ~**stab** planning (plans) board, think-tank; ~**stabsprache** think-tank parlance; ~**stadium** thinking (planning) stage; **über das** ~**stadium hinausgelangen** to pass the planning stage; **noch im** ~**stadium sein** to be still on the drawing board; ~**stelle** planning board; ~**studie** study of planning; ~**system** planning methods; ~**tätigkeit** planning activity; **zentrale** ~**tätigkeit** central planning; ~**träger** governmental planning agency; ~**verband** planning group; ~**vereinbarung** planning agreement *(Br.)*; ~**verfahren** planning process.
planvoll methodical, systematical, well-planned, tactical.
Plan|wagen covered wag(g)on; ~**wagenzug** waggon train; ~**wirtschaft** planned (managed, draft, controlled, directed) economy, statism; **unternehmerische** ~**wirtschaft** industrial planning; ~**wirtschaftler** planner, statist.
planwirtschaftlich statist.
Plan|zahl target figure, standard; ~**zeichen** plotting; ~**zeichner** plotter; ~**ziel** target [area], *(Produktion)* planned output; ~**ziel nicht erreichen** to fall behind schedule (short of one's target); ~**zielindustrien** target industries; **für den Inlandsbedarf angesetzte** ~**ziffern erreichen** to bring domestic demand up to target.
Plappermaul chatterbox.
plappern to patter, to prate, to jabber, to jangle, to drivel.
Pläsierchen, jedem Tierchen sein every man to his taste.
Plastik|beutel plastic bag; ~**einband** plastic binding; ~**platte** *(Werbung)* button; ~**tüte** plastic bag.
plastisch plastic, *(anschaulich)* graphic, vivid, *(Figur)* three-dimensional;
Vorgang ~ **schildern** to give a vivid description;
~**e Chirurgie** plastic surgery; ~**es Sehen** stereoscopic vision.
Platin platinum.
Platitüden von sich geben to churn out a string of platitudes.
plätschern *(Bach)* to babble, to gurgle, *(Brunnen)* to splash;
gegen ein Boot ~ *(Wellen)* to lap against a boat.
plätschernde Unterhaltung drone of conversation.
platt flat, level, *(banal)* stock, *(Reifen)* down, flat;
~ **wie eine Flunder** flat as a pancake;
Nase an der Scheibe ~ **drücken** to press one's nose against the window; **Reifen** ~ **fahren** to get a flat tyre; ~ **auf der Erde liegen** to lie flat on the ground; **völlig** ~ **sein** to be flabbergasted, to be struck all of a heap *(coll.)*.
Platte plate, sheet, *(Ausziehplatte)* leaf, *(Druckplatte)* stereotype plate, *(Fliese)* tile, flag, *(Fotografie)* plate, *(Grammophon)* record, disk, *(aus Holz)* board, slab, *(Schüssel)* dish, *(aus Stein)* plate, slab, flag, *(Terrasse)* flag, slab;
kalte ~ cold cuts *(US)*; **lichtempfindliche** ~ sensitized plate; **lichthoffreie** ~ nonhalation plate;
übliche ~ **seiner Krankheiten abspielen** to reel off one's list of woes; ~ **auflegen** to put on a record; **Terrasse mit** ~**n auslegen** to flag a terrace; ~ **in eine Kassette einlegen** to load a slide; **jem. eins vor die** ~ **hauen** to bash s. o. over the head; **immer die gleiche** ~ **ablaufen lassen** to be always harping on the same string; ~**n legen** to lay flags; **die** ~ **putzen** to take to one's heels; ~**n spielen** to listen to records.
Plätteisen press iron, flatiron.
Platten|abzug stereotyped proof; ~**archiv** record cabinet; ~**automat** jukebox; ~**belag** flagging; ~**druck** stereotype; ~**fußboden** tile[d] floor; ~**hülle** sleeve; ~**hüllentext** sleeve note; ~**jockei** disk jockey; ~**koffer** record case; ~**legen** tiling; ~**leger** tile-layer; ~**panzerung** plate armo(u)r; ~**spieler** record player, gramophone, phonograph *(US)*; ~**ständer** record rack; ~**teller** turntable; ~**wechsler** auto-changer; ~**wischer** record cleaner.
Plattform *(fig.)* rostrum, *(pol.)* platform;
nach einer gemeinsamen ~ **suchen** to look for a common basis.
Plattfuß *(Auto)* puncture, flat *(sl.)*, *(mar.)* dog-watch.
Plattheiten trivialities, platitudes, banalities.
plattschlagen lassen, sich endlich to let o. s. be talked into it in the end.
Plattwagen *(Bahn)* flat *(US)*.
Platz place, spot, point *(US)*, *(Grundstück)* site, plot, lot *(US)*, location, *(Ort)* place, town, locality *(US)*, *(Schiff, Schlafwagen)* berth, *(Sitzplatz)* seat, *(Stellung)* post, position;
am ~**e** in the market, on the spot; **am dortigen** ~ in your town; **am hiesigen** ~ at this place; **bis auf den letzten** ~ **gefüllt** crowded to capacity;
abgelegener ~ remote place; **befestigter** ~ fortified place; **belegter** ~ seat taken; **bestellter** ~ reserved seat, reservation; **eingefriedeter** ~ yard; **erster** ~ *(Theater)* rear stalls, pit, first place; **fester** ~ *(mil.)* place of strength; **freier** ~ open spaces, area; **öffentlicher** ~ public square, public place; **reservierter** ~ reservation, reserved seat; **runder** ~ circus; **unbesetzter** ~ vacancy; **ungünstiger** ~ *(Laden)* dead spot; **verkehrsreicher** ~ busy square; **viel** ~ lots of room; **unendlich viel** ~ oceans of room *(sl.)*; **wichtiger** ~ center *(US)*, centre *(Br.)*; **zweiter** ~ *(Theater)* front stalls;
~ **des Angeklagten** bar; ~ **zum Parken** parking lot, stall *(US)*;
~ **anweisen** to locate; **jem. seinen** ~ **anweisen** to show s. o. to his seat; ~ **ausfüllen** to fill a position (bill); **seinen** ~ **gut ausfüllen** the fill the bill *(Br., sl.)*; **wenig** ~ **beanspruchen** to take up little room; **zuviel** ~ **beanspruchen** to occupy too much space; **sicheren dritten** ~ **behaupten** to run a strong third; ~ **belegen (bestellen)** to book space (a place), to reserve space, to secure (reserve, *US*) a seat, *(Schiff)* to book a passage; ~ **im Sekretariat bestellen** to file an application for a seat with the secretary; ~ **bestimmen** to situate; ~ **bieten** *(Auto)* to carry; **für hundert Personen bequem** ~ **bieten** *(Saal)* to easily accommodate 100 persons; **jds.** ~ **einnehmen** to substitute s. o. in his shoes; **besonderen** ~ **einnehmen** to fill a niche of its own; **ersten** ~ **einnehmen** to rank first; **festen** ~ **einnehmen** to occupy an established place; **seinen** ~ **einnehmen** to take up one's station, to take one's seat; **zweiten** ~ **einnehmen** to score second; ~ **einnehmen, der einem zukommt** to find one's level (own); ~ **freihalten** to keep a place; **j. zu seinem** ~ **geleiten** to guide (usher) s. o. to his place; ~ **greifen** to be gaining ground; **guten** ~ **haben** to have a ring-side seat; **überhaupt keinen** ~ **haben** to have not enough room to swing a cat in; **in einem Koffer** ~ **haben** to fit into a suitcase; **wenig** ~ **haben** to be cramped for space; **sich einen** ~ **reservieren lassen** to book a place (seat); **der Feuerwehr** ~ **machen** to make way for the fire-engine; **der**

rechte Mann am rechten ~ sein to be the right man for the job; **nicht am ~ sein** *(Äußerung)* to be out of place; **~ sparen** to save space; **am falschen ~ stehen** to be wasted; **auf dem letzten ~ auf der Tabelle stehen** to be bottom of the table; **j. an den richtigen ~ stellen** to position s. o.; **~ zur Verfügung stellen** to devote space; **~ mit jem. tauschen** to trade seats with s. o., to swop places with s. o.; **jem. seinen ~ überlassen** to give up one's seat to s. o.; **j. auf den ihm zustehenden ~ verweisen** to put s. o. in his place; **alle übrigen Teilnehmer auf den zweiten ~ verweisen** to beat all of the competitors into second place; **~ vorausbestellen** to book (reserve, *US*) a seat;
~abschluß spot contract; **~agent** local agent; **~akzept** local acceptance; **~angebot** spot offer; **~angst** claustrophobia; **~anweiser** usher; **~anweiserin** usherette; **ohne ~anweisung** *(Anzeige)* run-of-paper position, without spot notation; **~anzahl** seat availability; **~aufschlag** extra charge; **~bedarf** space required, *(Konsum)* local consumption (wants); **~bedingungen** local terms, *(Schiffsverkehr)* berth terms; **~befeuerung** airdrome (aerodrome, *Br.*) lighting; **~belegung** booking [space], seat reservation; **~bericht** local report; **~bestellung** reservation of seats, booking [space]; **~bestellung rückgängig machen** to cancel one's booking (reservation, *US*); **nicht ausgenutzte ~buchung** *(Flugzeug)* no-show.

Plätze, verfügbare seat availability;
~ zu volkstümlichen Preisen cheap seats; **freie ~ für Stenotypistinnen und Kontoristinnen** good vacancies for typists and clerks;
vorgebuchte ~ kontrollieren to make certain of one's seats; **~ tauschen** to change places with another, to exchange seats.

platzen to go pop, *(herauskommen)* to come to light, *(Projekt)* to come to naught, *(Reifen)* to burst, *(Spionagering)* to be disbanded, to blow out *(US)*, *(Versammlung)* to split [up], *(Wechsel)* to be dishono(u)red, to bounce *(fam.)*;
vor Lachen beinahe ~ to split one's sides with laughter; **aus Mangel an Beweisen ~** to be abandoned for lack of evidence; **aus allen Nähten ~** to burst one's buttons; **vor Neugier ~** to be bursting with curiosity; **vor Wut ~** to explode with rage.

Platz|feuer *(Flugplatz)* airport lights (lighting); **~gebrauch** local (special) custom; **~gedeck** *(Restaurant)* place mat; **~geschäft** local trade, spot business (transaction); **~geschäfte machen** to deal with the suppliers on the spot; **Artikel aus ~gründen zurückstellen** to crowd out an article for reason of space; **~halter** place holder; **~inkasso** walk bills *(US)*.

Platzkarte reservation, reserved seat (ticket);
nur gegen ~ all seats reserved;
~ bestellen to book seats in advance, to make one's seat reservations.

Platzkarten|formular reservation form; **~schalter** reservation office; **~zug** limited train.

Platz|käufe local (spot) purchases; **~kenntnis** local knowledge; **~kommandant** commandant; **~konsum** consumption on the spot, spot consumption; **~konzert** open-air concert; **~kostensatz** *(Buchungssystem)* machine-burden unit; **~kredit** local credit; **~kurs** spot-market price, spot rate, ready cable, exchange of the market; **~makler** local jobber, spot broker; **~mangel haben** to be pressed for space, to be cramped for room; **~miete** *(Messe)* space rental, *(Theater)* subscription; **~ordner** steward; **~patrone** *(mil.)* dummy charge; **~regen** pouring rain, downpour; **~reisender** town travel(l)er; **~reservierung** seat reservation, booking *(Br.)* (reservation of) space; **~reservierung rückgängig machen** to cancel a reservation (booking, *Br.*); **~runde** landing pattern; **~runde fliegen** to do a circuit [for a landing (on a landing platform)], to circle the field; **~scheck** local (walk) cheque *(Br.)*, town check *(US)*.

platzsparend space-saving.

Platz|spediteur switching carrier; **~spesen** local expenses (charges); **~überweisung** spot transfer; **~usancen** usage of the place, local customs; **~veränderung** *(versicherter Gegenstand)* removal; **~verbrauch** local consumption; **~verkauf** sales on the spot, impulse sale; **~verlust** loss on the spot; **~vertreter** local agent, agent on the spot, town travel(l)er; **~vorbestellungsgebühr** reservation fee; **~vorschrift** *(Anzeige)* appointed space; **~vorteil** advantage of location; **~wechsel** local bill (draft), town bill; **~wette** place bet; **~zahl** number of seats; **mit beschränkter ~zahl** *(Bahn)* limited.

Plauderei confabulation, chat, talk, visit *(coll.)*;
leichte ~ small talk.

plaudern to chat, to visit *(coll.)*;
aus der Schule ~ to tell tales out of school; **mit jem. ~** to have a talk (chat) with s. o.

Plauder|stündchen chat, coze; **~tasche** chatterbox, gossip, *(Klatschbase)* scandalmonger.

Plausch chat.

plausibel plausible, colo(u)rable;
~ klingen to sound credible; **~ machen** to give colo(u)r to; **jem. etw. ~ machen** to make s. th. clear to s. o.

plausible|Erklärung convincing explanation; **~ Geschichte** plausible story; **~r Grund** convincing reason.

Playback playback.

Plazet placet, approval.

plazierbar salable, negotiable, placeable.

plazieren to place, to position, to site, to invest, to bring out, *(Wechsel)* to negotiate;
Anleihe ~ to place a loan; **Anzeigen bei verschiedenen Werbeträgern ~** to place advertisements in various media; **Emission ~** to place (dispose of) an issue; **neben j. ~** to sit s. o. next to s. o.

plaziert placed, *(Emissionsgeschäft)* underwritten firm.

Plazierung *(Anzeige)* position, location, *(Gelder)* investment, placement, *(Wertpapiere)* negotiation, placing, sale;
besondere ~ special position, individual location; **bevorzugte ~** *(Anzeige)* preferred (full) position, *(Außenwerbung)* head-on location; **direkte ~** direct placement; **garantierte ~** *(Anzeige)* fixed positioning, guaranteed position; **vereinbarte ~** *(Anzeige)* fixed positioning, stated position; **vorgeschriebene ~** *(Anzeige)* stated position; **zugesagte ~** *(Anzeige)* guaranteed position;
~ einer Anleihe negotiation of a loan; **~ einer Anzeige** position of an advertisement; **~ ohne Berücksichtigung von Sonderwünschen** *(Anzeige)* ordinary position; **~ außerhalb des Publikumsverkehrs** tap issue *(Br.)*; **~ oben rechts** *(Anzeige)* top-right position; **~ von Wertpapieren beim Publikum** placing securities with the public; **~ eines Zeitungsartikels** putting in of an article.

Plazierungs|aufschlag *(Anzeige)* position charge; **~geschäft** investment banking (business); **~klima** *(Börse)* placement climate; **~konzept** placement concept; **~kosten** position costs, *(für werbliche Informationen)* publicity costs, *(für ein Produkt)* field costs; **~kraft** placing potential (power); **~vorschrift** prescribed position.

Plebejer pleb *(coll.)*.

plebejisch plebeian, non-U *(Br.)*.

Plebiszit plebiscite, referendum;
~ergebnis referendum plebiscit; **~erlaß** referendum decree; **~kampagne** referendum campaign.

plebiszitäre Demokratie direct democracy.

Pleite smash, bankruptcy, burst-up, bust *(US sl.)*, blowup *(US)*, the shorts, *(Fiasko)* fiasco, flop *(sl.)*, failure, fizzle *(coll.)*, washout *(sl.)*, turkey *(US sl.)*;
ausgesprochene ~ no end of a sell; **komplette ~** blue ruin *(sl.)*;
~ machen to go bust, to get the wall *(Br.)*.

pleite bankrupt, broke, bust, strapped, tapped out, cleaned out *(coll.)*, played out *(sl.)*, on the nut *(US sl.)*, gone up *(sl.)*, stonybroke *(sl.)*;
total (völlig) ~ melted out, flat broke *(US sl.)*, broke to the wide *(sl.)*, on one's uppers *(US sl.)*;
~ gehen to go down the drain (bust), to crash; **ohne Konjunkturaufschwung ~ gehen** to go under unless business improves; **jeden Tag ~ gehen können** to go any day; **~ sein** to be on the rocks (beam-ends, cracked); **völlig ~ sein** to end up broke, to be strapped for cash, to be broke to the wide *(coll.)*.

Pleitegeier, vom ~ bedroht sein to be on the brink (verge) of bankruptcy.

Pleitenfonds bank insurance pool.

plempern to splash, to tope, to lounge about;
mit seiner Zeit ~ to fritter one's time away.

plemplem, ein bißchen a bit cuckoo, plumb crazy *(US sl.)*.

Plenar|abstimmung floor vote; **~änderungen** floor amendments; **~ausschuß** committee of the whole house; **~entscheidung** *(Gericht)* ruling by the whole court; **~saal** floor of the house, house floor *(US)*; **~sitzung** full (plenary) session, *(Gericht)* court sitting in banc; **~versammlung** plenary meeting.

Plenum full assembly, plenum, full (plenary) session, house floor *(US)*, *(Gericht)* full (whole) court;
vom ~ entschieden per totam curiam;
das als Ausschuß zusammengetretene ~ committee of the whole House;
etw. im ~ behandeln to deal with s. th. in a plenary meeting; **Kandidaten im ~ vorschlagen** to make nominations from the floor.

Plombe seal, *(Motor)* lead seal, *(Zahn)* plug;
~ abnehmen to remove the seals.

plombieren to [seal with] lead, to [affix a] seal, to plumb, *(Zahn)* to plug.
plombiert sealed;
amtlich ~ plombé;
~**es Fahrzeug** sealed vehicle.
Plombierung sealing.
plötzlich sudden;
ganz ~ out of the blue [sky];
~ **in seiner Rede innehalten** to stop short;
~**e Wendung** unexpected turn;
nicht so ~! hang on!, hold your horses!
plump chubby, clumsy;
~**e Fälschung** clumsy forgery; ~**e Gestalt** plump figure; ~**e Lüge** blatant lie; ~**es Manöver** clumsy manoeuvre; ~ **vertrauliche Person** over-familiar person, backslapper *(US sl.)*; ~**e Vertraulichkeiten** bold familiarities.
Plunder dirt, rubbish, caboodle, junk, punk *(sl.)*, trash, trashery, lumber, plunder *(US coll.)*, tripe *(sl.)*;
alter ~ old plug; **der ganze** ~ the whole shebang, hogwash, deadwood, stuff.
Plünderer plunderer, pillager, ransacker, spoiler, despoiler, spoliator, looter, picaroon.
Plündern, vom ~ **leben** to live by plunder.
plündern to plunder, to loot, to pillage, to spoliate, to despoil, to liberate *(sl.)*, to ransack, to sack;
Haus ~ to ravage a house; **Kühlschrank** ~ to raid the fridge; **Laden** ~ to sack a shop; **Portokasse** ~ to raid the petty cash, to milk the till; **Stadt** ~ to loot a city.
plündernd predatory.
Plünderung plundering, pillage, sack, booty, plunder, despoliation, rapine.
Plünderungsgefahr risk of pilferage, pilferage hazard.
Pluralismus pluralism.
pluralistische Gesellschaft pluralistic society.
Pluralwahlrecht plural vote.
Plus plus, *(Vorteil)* asset, advantage, *(Überschuß)* surplus, increment;
zehn Grad über ~ **anzeigen** to show ten degrees above zero; **für sich als** ~ **buchen** to count it one's glory (a feather in one's cap); **im** ~ **sein** to be in the black *(US coll.)*.
Plüsch plush, pile.
Plus|korrektur upward adjustment; ~**pol** *(el.)* plus pole.
Pluspunkt additional asset, feather in one's cap;
~ **für seine Familie** credit to one's family;
jem. einen ~ **einbringen** to be a score in s. one's favo(u)r; **sich jds.** ~**e anzueignen suchen** to copy s. one's good points; **zu den** ~**en zählen** to be an asset.
Plus|seite plus angle; ~**zeichen** positive (plus) sign.
Pluto|krat plutocrat, plute *(sl.)*; ~**kratie** plutocracy.
Pöbel common (vulgar) herd, disorderly mob, rabble, riffraff, crew, hoi polloi, great unwashed *(coll.)*;
~ **anstacheln** to excite the mob; **sich mit dem** ~ **einlassen** to join the mob; **vom** ~ **attackiert werden** to be mobbed by the crowd.
pöbelhaft plebeian, vulgar.
Pöbel|haftigkeit vulgarity; ~**haufe** mob; ~**herrschaft** mob rule, mobocracy.
pochen to knock, to rap, *(Herz)* to pound, to thump;
auf sein Geld ~ to play upon one's wealth; **auf sein Recht** ~ to insist on one's rights; **an die Tür** ~ to knock (rap) at the door; **auf seine Verdienste** ~ to boast of having merits.
Pocken|epidemie smallpox epidemic; ~**impfung** smallpox vaccination; ~**impfzeugnis** vaccination certificate.
Podest landing, pedestal;
von seinem ~ **herunterkommen** to come off the high horse; **j. von seinem** ~ **stoßen** to knock s. o. off his pedestal.
Podium [raised] platform, rostrum, podium;
von einem ~ **aus sprechen** to platform; ~ **verlassen** to come down from the rostrum.
Podiumsdiskussion teach-in, panel discussion *(US)*.
poesielos prosaic, prosy, matter-of-fact, pedestrian.
poetische Ader haben to have a poetic streak (license).
Pogrom pogrom.
Pointe point, punch line, tag, snapper *(sl.)*;
~ **einer Geschichte** cream (point) of a story; ~ **eines Witzes** point of a joke;
~ **eines Witzes begreifen** to see the light of a joke; **keine** ~ **haben** to lack spice; **einer Anekdote die** ~ **nehmen** to take the point out of an anecdote.
pointiert *(Stil)* pointed.
Pokal goblet, tankard, *(Sport)* cup, plate;
um einen ~ **spielen** to compete for a cup.
Pokergesicht poker face, deadpan expression.
Pol, magnetischer magnetic pole;
jds. ruhender ~ **sein** to give s. o. a sense of stability; **ruhender** ~ **in einer Familie sein** to exert a calming influence in a family.
polare Kaltluft polar air.
Polar|eis polar ice; ~**expedition** polar expedition; ~**flug** transpolar flight; ~**forscher** polar explorer; ~**front** polar front; ~**gebiet,** ~**gegend** polar region (zone).
Polarität polarity.
Polar|kreis polar (Arctic) circle; ~**licht** polar (Northern) lights; ~**region** polar region; ~**route** transpolar route; ~**stern** pole star.
Polemik polemics, controversy, sharp dispute.
Polemiker controverser, controversialist, polemicist, polemist.
polemische Rede controversial speech.
polemisieren to polemize, to controversialize, to carry on a controversy.
Police policy, policy of insurance, *(Lebensversicherung)* life policy;
laut beigeschlossener ~ as per policy annexed;
abgelaufene ~ expired policy; **auf den Namen ausgestellte** ~ registered policy; **zeitlich befristete** ~ time policy; **beitragsfreie** ~ free policy; **benannte** ~ named policy; **mehrere verschiedenartige, dasselbe Versicherungsinteresse deckende** ~**n** nonconcurrent policies; **durchschnittliche** ~ standard policy; **nicht eingelöste** ~ policy not taken up; **eingetragene** ~ registered policy; **voll eingezahlte** ~ paid-up policy; **erneuerungsfähige** ~ renewable term policy; **mit einem sachverständig geschätzten Inventar gekoppelte** ~ policy based on an inventory and value; **gemischte** ~ mixed policy; **geschlossene** ~ closed policy; **gewinnberechtigte** ~ participating policy; **nicht gewinnberechtigte** ~ nonparticipation (nonparticipating) policy; **unwiderruflich gewordene** ~ incontestable policy; **laufende** ~ floating (paid-up, block, unvalued, *US*) policy, open matter policy *(Br.)*, standing policy; **nachschußfreie** ~ nonassessable policy; **nachschußpflichtige** ~ assessable police; **offene** ~ *(Seeschadensversicherung)* declared policy, floating (open, *Br.*) policy; **pauschale** ~ compound policy *(US)*; **prämienfreie** ~ free (paid-up) policy; **prolongierte** ~ extended-term policy; **taxierte** ~ valued policy; **verfallene** ~ lapsed policy; **auf den Tag der Antragsstellung vordatierte** ~ antedated policy;
ausschließliche ~ **für Berufstätige** commercial policy; ~ **mit Gewinnbeteiligung** participating policy; ~ **ohne Nachschußpflicht** nonassessable policy; ~ **mit begrenzter Prämienzahlung** limited payment policy; ~ **über eine aufgeschobene Rentenversicherung** deferred-annuity policy; ~ **mit beschränktem Risiko** limited policy; ~ **auf eine bestimmte Summe** value policy; ~ **über eine Überlebensversicherung** joint-life policy; ~ **über eine in Teilbeträgen zahlbare Versicherungssumme** instal(l)ment policy; **prämienfreie** ~ **mit gekürzter Versicherungssumme** paid-up policy of a reduced amount; ~ **mit Wertangabe** valued policy; ~ **ohne Wertangabe** open (unvalued) policy *(Br.)*, *(Seeschaden)* declared policy;
~ **abändern** to vary a policy; ~ **ausfertigen** to issue (effect) a policy; ~ **beleihen** to lend money (borrow) on a policy; ~ **ergänzen** to amend a policy; ~ **erneuern** to renew a policy; ~ **nehmen** to take out a policy; ~ **zurückkaufen** to redeem a policy;
als Nachweis der Versicherung genügt die ~ policy proof of interest.
Policen|abschrift, laut beigeschlossener as per copy of policy annexed; ~**abtretung** assignment of policy; ~**abwandlung,** ~**änderung** policy modification (variation); ~**ausfertigung** issue (execution) of policy, policy drafting; ~**ausstellungsbüro** policy signing office; ~**beleihung** policy loan (borrowing); ~**besitzer** policyholder; ~**buch** policy book; ~**darlehn** policy loan (borrowing); ~**datum** date of policy; ~**dauer** life of a policy, policy period; ~**erlös** proceeds of policies; ~**erneuerung** renewal of a policy; ~**form** policy document; ~**formular** blank policy, policy form; ~**gebühr** entrance fee; ~**inhaber** policyholder; ~**kürzung** cancellation of policy; ~**laufzeit** duration of policy; ~**nachtrag** rider, endorsement on an insurance policy; ~**nummer** policy number; ~**register** policy book; ~**rückkaufwert** surrender value of a policy; ~**verfall** lapse of a policy; ~**vermerk** endorsement on a policy; ~**vordruck** policy form, blank policy.
polieren to polish, to furbish;
Artikel ~ to polish (touch) up an article; **jem. die Fresse** ~ to bash s. o. in the jaw.
Polierer polisher.
Poliermittel polisher (s. th. used in polishing).

Poliklinik outpatient department, dispensary *(US)*.
Politbüro Political Bureau.
Politesse traffic warden *(Br.)*, metermaid *(US coll)*.
Politik politics, policy, polity, deal *(coll.)*;
abwartende ~ wait-and-see policy; **auf Erhaltung der Bodenschätze ausgerichtete** ~ resource policy; **auswärtige** ~ foreign politics (policy); **von zwei Parteien unterstützte auswärtige** ~ bipartisan foreign policy; **auf eigene Faust betriebene** ~ go-it-alone policy; **bewegliche** ~ activist policy; **doppelsinnige** ~ ambiguous policy; **einheitliche** ~ coordinated policy; **freundschaftliche** ~ good-neighbo(u)r policy; **gemäßigte** ~ deliberate policy; **auf Lohnstabilisierung und Preissenkung gerichtete** ~ wage-freezing and price-lowering policy; **gezielte** ~ deliberate policy; **hemdsärmelige** ~ hands-off policy; **kurzsichtige** ~ short-sighted policy; **reaktionäre** ~ standcat policy; **rechtseingestellte** ~ right-wing policy; **risikolose** ~ safe policy; **spaltungsgefährdete** ~ deeply divisive policy; **undurchsichtige** ~ ambiguous policy; **unnachgiebige** ~ policy of no compromise; **durch und durch vernünftige** ~ sound policy throughout; **Vogel-Strauß-**~ ostrich policy; **zurückhaltende** ~ policy of restraint;
~ **der von langer Hand vorbereiteten Anlagenstreuung** diversication strategy; **währungssichernde** ~ **der Ausgabenbeschränkung** austerity policy; ~ **des Ausgleichs** policy of compromise; ~ **der Blockfreiheit** neutralism; ~ **auf höchster Ebene** high-level policy; ~ **der Einkommensbeschränkung** new pay policy *(Br.)*; ~ **der verbrannten Erde** scorched-earth policy; ~ **des billigen Geldes** cheap-money policy, easy money policy *(US)*; ~ **des ungewöhnlich billigen Geldes** ultra-cheap money policy *(Br.)*; ~ **des Gewährenlassens** policy of inaction, masterly inactivity; ~ **der Härte** get-tough policy; ~ **der gegenseitigen Konzessionen** give-and-take policy; ~ **der Konjunkturbelebung** anti-recession policy; ~ **der Mitte** policy of the middle road; ~ **der Nadelstiche** policy of pinpricks; ~ **der gegenwärtigen Regierung** policy of the present government; ~ **der Risikoverteilung** diversification policy; ~ **der kleinen Schritte** [policy of] gradualism, step-by-step diplomacy; ~ **auf weite Sicht** long-range policy; ~ **der unverblümten Sprache** open-mouth diplomacy; ~ **der zurückhaltenden Tarifabschlüsse** pay-restraint policy; ~ **des sich Treibenlassens** policy of the drift (laissez-faire); ~ **der offenen Tür** open-door policy; ~ **der Unentschlossenheit** policy of scuttle; ~ **der Untätigkeit** won't-touch policy; ~ **des Untätigseins** do nothing policy; ~ **der gutnachbarlichen Verbindungen** good-neighbo(u)rhood policy; ~ **freigegebener Wechselkurse** currency float;
von seiner ~ **abweichen** to go out of one's way; **sich gänzlich von der** ~ **abwenden** to estrange o. s. from politics; ~ **aktivieren** to revive a policy; **sich nahtlos jds.** ~ **anpassen** to dovetail with s. one's policy; **Sache möglichst weit von der** ~ **ansiedeln** to put the least political face on s. th.; **seine** ~ **langfristig darauf ausrichten** to conduct a long-term campaign; **sich für jds.** ~ **aussprechen** to speak in support of s. one's policy; **sich mit** ~ **befassen** to deal (be engaged, dabble) in politics; **antikommunistische** ~ **betreiben** to adopt an anticommunist line; **harte** ~ **betreiben** to adopt a tough policy; **risikoreiche** ~ **betreiben** to tread a dangerous path; ~ **der verbrannten Erde betreiben** to adopt a scorched-earth policy; ~ **der kleinen Schritte betreiben** to take short steps; ~ **der offenen Tür betreiben** to open a door to agreements on international affairs; **sich um** ~ **drehen** *(Gespräch)* to run on politics; **neue** ~ **einleiten** to inaugurate a new policy; **in die** ~ **einsteigen** to launch into politics; **an einer** ~ **festhalten** to maintain a policy; **gemeinsame** ~ **festlegen** to define a common policy; **Partei auf eine** ~ **der Nichteinmischung in Verhandlungen der Tarifpartei festlegen** to rally a party round the free collective bargaining standard; **seine** ~ **bestätigt finden** to find one's policy vindicated; **in die** ~ **gehen** to enter politics; **von der** ~ **die Nase voll haben** to have done with politics; **seiner** ~ **die Treue halten** to implement a policy; **sich für** ~ **interessieren** to take an interest in politics; **sich kaum für** ~ **interessieren** to take no great interest in politics; **sich aus der** ~ **völliger Untätigkeit lösen** to swing away from a no-hands attitude; **seine** ~ **revidieren** to revise one's policy; **für die auswärtige** ~ **eines Landes verantwortlich sein** to run a country's foreign policy; **über** ~ **sprechen** to talk politics; ~ **unterstützen** to stand for a policy; ~ **verfolgen** to follow a policy; **bestimmte** ~ **verfolgen** to pursue a certain policy; **in die internationale** ~ **katapultiert werden** to be injected forcibly into international politics; **sich auf die** ~ **werfen** to engage in politics; **isolationistische** ~ **wiederaufnehmen** to retreat into isolationism.
Politikaster armchair (coffeehouse) politician.
Politiker politician, statesman, frock;
ämtersüchtiger ~ office-seeking politician; **aufgeschlossener** ~ forward statesman; **bedeutsamer** ~ political figure; **bestechlicher** ~ two-bit politician *(US)*; **durchtriebener** ~ tricky politician; **einflußreicher** ~ influential politician; **ernstzunehmender** ~ serious politician; **gerissener** ~ tortuous politician; **gewitzter** ~ shrewd politician; **käuflicher** ~ venal politician; **kommender** ~ rising politician; **machthungriger** ~ politico *(sl.)*; **radikaler** ~ radical politician; **unabhängiger** ~ independent in politics, maverick; **unbedeutender** ~ peanut politician *(US sl.)*; **unfähiger** ~ snollygoster *(sl.)*; **vielversprechender** ~ coming man;
~ **der vordersten Linie** front-rank politician; ~ **des gemäßigten Parteiflügels** middle-of-the roader(s); ~ **im Ruhestand** elderly statesman;
radikale ~**gruppe** ginger group *(Br.)*; **gefällige (schönklingende)** ~**reden** fair speeches of politicians.
Politikum political issue, matter of politics.
politisch political, state;
~ **gesehen** from a political point of view; ~ **interessiert** politically-minded;
sich ~ **positiv auswirken** to reap political gains; **sich** ~ **betätigen** to mix (dabble) in politics; **sich** ~ **profilieren** to win political points; ~ **interessiert sein** to take an interest in politics; ~ **tätig sein** to be engaged in politics; **sich** ~ **unterhalten** to talk politics; ~ **involviert werden** to get mixed up in politics;
~**e Alternative** policy alternatives; ~**e Aspekte** political aspects; ~**er Ausschuß** political panel; **seine** ~**e Begabung effektvoll einzusetzen wissen** to deploy one's best political skills; ~**es Bekenntnis** political belief; ~**er Beobachter** political observer; ~**er Berater** political consultant; ~**e Beratergruppe** policy-maker cluster; ~**e Direktive** policy directive; ~**e Ebene** political plane; ~**er Einfluß** pull; ~**e Einstellung** political opinion; ~**e Faktoren** policy factors; ~**e Flaute** political calm; ~**er Flüchtling** political refugee; **auf** ~**em Gebiet** in the field of politics; ~**er Gefangener** political detainee; **aus** ~**en Gründen** for political reasons; ~**e Grundrichtung** general policy line; ~**e Grundsatzfragen** basic political issues; ~**er Häftling** political prisoner; ~**e Haltung** policy stance; **in** ~**er Hinsicht** politically; ~**e Krise** political crisis; ~**es Leben** politics; ~**e Linie verfolgen** to follow a political course; ~**e Maßnahmen** political action; ~ **verschiedener Meinung sein** to argue in politics; ~**er Meinungsforscher** policy researcher; ~**e Meinungsverschiedenheiten** policy differences; ~**e Organisation** political organization; ~**e Partei** political party; ~**es Programm** platform, ticket *(US)*; ~**e Rechte** political rights; ~**es Rezept** policy prescription; ~**e Richtlinien** policy guidelines; ~**e Richtungsänderung** policy shift; ~**en Rückzieher machen** to make a politic retreat; ~**er Standpunkt** platform; ~**er Starrkopf** intransigent; ~**e Stellung** political office; ~**e Tätigkeit** political activity; ~**er Umschwung** political change; ~**e Verantwortung tragen** *(Minister)* to be answerable for policy; ~**es Verfahren** policy; ~**e Willenserklärung** political statement *(US)*; ~**e Wüste** political wilderness; ~**e Zurückhaltung** policy restraint; **für** ~**e Zwecke** for political purposes; ~**e Zweckmäßigkeit** political expediency.
politisieren to politicize, to talk (dabble in) politics.
Polizei, berittene mounted police; **motorisierte** ~ motorized police; **politische** ~ political police;
Verlustanzeige bei der ~ **abgeben** to notify the police of a loss; **sich bei der** ~ **anmelden** to register with the police; **j. bei der** ~ **anzeigen** to prefer a charge against s. o.; **sich bei der** ~ **beschweren** to pipe off *(sl.)*; **sich den Nachforschungen der** ~ **entziehen** to hide from the police; **mit der** ~ **in Konflikt geraten** to run foul of the police; ~ **direkt auf den Fersen haben** to have the police on one's heels; ~ **auf einen Einbruch aufmerksam machen** to alert the police of a break-in; **sich bei der** ~ **melden** to report to the police station *(Br.)*; **der** ~ **eine Straftat melden** to report an offence to the police; **sich der** ~ **stellen** to give o. s. up (surrender o. s.) to the police; **j. der** ~ **übergeben** to give s. o. into custody (charge) of the police, to turn s. o. in; ~ **von etw. unterrichten** to notify (inform) the police of s. th.; **j. der** ~ **vorführen** to bring s. o. before the magistrate; **von der** ~ **aufgegriffen werden** to be picked up by the police; **von der** ~ **gejagt werden** to have the police on one's heels; **von der** ~ **verhört (vernommen) werden** to be questioned by the police;
~**abteilung** police squad; ~**abzeichen** police badge; ~**agent** police agent; ~**akte** surveillance file; ~**aktion** police action (raid); ~**angelegenheit** police business (matter); ~**apparat** police force (services); ~**archiv** police records (morgue, *sl.*); ~**aufgebot** body (force) of police, police detachment, posse,

platoon; ~**aufsicht** police surveillance (supervision, *Br.*); ~**ausrüstung** equipment of the police; ~**ausweis** police pass; ~**auto** police car.

Polizeibeamter police constable, guardian of the peace, police officer (official);
höherer ~ chief inspector *(Br.)*;
~ **mit Nachtdienstfunktionen** night magistrate;
sich als ~ **ausgeben** to purport to be a police officer; ~ **sein** to serve in the police.

Polizei|beamtin policewoman, police matron; ~**bedeckung** police escort; ~**befugnisse** police powers; **innerstaatlich ausgeübte** ~**befugnisse** internal police *(US)*; ~**behörde** police, *(London)* hue and cry; **den** ~**behörden übergeben** to hand over to the police; ~**bericht** charge sheet, police blotter *(US)*; ~**bezirk** precinct; **örtlicher** ~**bezirk** constablewick; ~**boot** police boat, sloop; ~**chef** chief of police, police chief, law-enforcement officer, marshal; **örtlicher** ~**chef** petty constable, town sergeant, thirdborough *(Br.)*, sheriff *(US)*; ~**dezernat** police department; ~**dienst** police duty; ~**dienstkräfte** police troops; ~**dienststelle** police station; ~**direktion** headquarters; ~**direktor** chief commissioner; ~**distrikt** police division; ~**einheit** police unit, constabulary; **zwanzigköpfige** ~**einheit** posse of twenty police; ~**einsatz** police raid; ~**eskorte** police escort; ~**fahrzeuge** vehicles belonging to the police; ~**falle** speed trap, stake-out *(sl.)*; ~**funk** police radio; ~**funktionen** police service; ~**gefängnis** lockup; **ins** ~**gefängnis kommen** to get locked up by the police; ~**gewahrsam** police custody (detention); **im** ~**gewahrsam sein** to be in the hands of police authorities; ~**gewalt** police power; **Land unter** ~**gewalt haben** to police a country; ~**haft** detention by the police, ordinary imprisonment, imprisonment in the first division; ~**hauptmann** captain *(US)*; ~**hilfe in Anspruch nehmen** to ask the police for help; ~**hubschrauber** police helicopter; ~**hund** police dog; ~**inspektor** police inspector *(Br.)*; ~**knüppel** truncheon *(Br.)*, police baton *(Br.)*, club, night stick *(US)*, billy *(sl.)*; ~**kommissar** police inspector *(Br.)*; ~**kommissariat** police station; ~**kontingent** police contingent, posse; ~**kontrolle** police control; ~**kordon** cordon of police; ~**kordon durchbrechen** to break through a police cordon; ~**kräfte** police force; **uniformierte** ~**kräfte** uniformed police force; ~**kräfte in einer Stadt stationieren** to police a city; ~**krieg** police war.

polizeilich|verhört questioned by the police;
sich ~ **anmelden** to register with the police; ~ **beaufsichtigen** to police; ~ **überwacht werden** to be under police surveillance;
~**e Absperrkette** police line; ~**es Anmeldeformular** police form; ~**e Anmeldung** registration with the police; ~**e Anordnung** police ordinance; ~**e Aufgaben** police duties; ~**es Aufgabengebiet** police task; ~**e Auflage** police warning; **unter** ~**er Aufsicht stehen** to be under police surveillance; ~**er Ausweis** police pass; **unter** ~**er Bedeckung** in the care of policemen; ~**e Begleitmannschaft** police escort; ~**e Durchsuchung** police visit; **rücksichtsloses** ~**es Einschreiten herausfordern** to court tough police action; ~**e Ermittlungen** criminal investigation; ~**e Exzesse** outrageous behavio(u)r of the police; ~**es Kennzeichen** *(Auto)* licence number, number plate; ~**es Meldebuch** police blotter *(US)*; ~**es Meldeformular** registration form; ~**e Meldepflicht** obligatory registration; ~**e Nachforschungen konzentrieren** to concentrate police investigations; ~**e Nachwuchskräfte** police cadets; ~**e Razzia** police raid; ~**e Tätigkeit** police work; ~**e Untersuchung** police investigation; ~**e Vernehmung** police questioning; ~**es Vernehmungsprotokoll** police documents; ~**e Verordnung** police ordinance; ~**es Versagen** police failure; ~**e Verstärkung** police reinforcement; ~**e Verwahrung** police detention; ~**e Vollmachten** police powers.

Polizei|macht police force; ~**mannschaften** police troops; ~**marke** tin *(sl.)*; ~**melder** police alarm; ~**ordnung** police regulations; ~**organisation** police organization; ~**patrouille**, ~**streife** police picket; ~**posten** police picket; ~**präsident** police commissioner *(US)*, Chief Constable *(Br.)*, police chief *(US)*, chief of police *(US)*; ~**präsidium** police headquarters (office), Scotland Yard *(Br.)*; ~**rechte in einem Gebiet ausüben** to police a strip of land; ~**register** police record, charge sheet; ~**revier** [police] station *(Br.)*, precinct; ~**richter** police justice (magistrate), recorder *(US)*, judge of police *(Scot.)*; ~**schutz** police bodyguard, police protection; **ohne** ~**schutz** *(Bezirk)* wide open *(sl.)*; ~**spitzel** nark, police informer (agent), pathfinder *(US)*, setter *(sl.)*, nose *(sl.)*, split *(sl.)*, spotter, stool pigeon *(US sl.)*, slim *(sl.)*, trap, whistler *(sl.)*, pig *(sl.)*; ~**spitzel sein** to nose *(sl.)*; ~**staat** police state; ~**stärke** strength of the police; ~**station** police station; **Tag und Nacht geöffnete** ~**station** police station open day and night; ~**strafregister** police record; ~**streife** flying squad, police beat (ticket), raiding party, police patrol, *(Einzelpolizist)* patrolling policeman; **verstärkte** ~**streifen** strengthening of patrols; ~**stunde** curfew, *(Restaurant)* closing hours; **verlängerte** ~**stunde** extension night; ~**stundenverordnung** curfew order; ~**truppe** body of police, police force, constabulary; ~**verfügung** police ordinance; ~**verhör** police questioning; ~**verordnung** police ordinance; ~**verwaltung** police [administration]; ~**verwendung** police operation; ~**wache** [police] station, station house, factory *(sl.)*; **auf der** ~**wache enden** to end up in a police court; **j. auf die** ~**wache mitnehmen** to take s. o. to the police station; ~**wachtmeister** police sergeant; ~**wagen** prowl car *(sl.)*.

polizeiwidrig contrary to police regulations.

Polizei|widrigkeit nuisance; ~**zweck** police use.

Polizist policeman, police officer, constable *(Br.)*, bobby *(Br.)*, cop *(Br.)*, patrolman *(US)*, eye of the law, nab *(coll.)*;
berittener ~ mounted policeman; **in Ungnade gefallener** ~ sparrow cop *(sl.)*; **uniformierter** ~ harness cop *(US sl.)*;
~ **im Streifendienst** patrolman *(US)*; ~ **in Zivil** plain-clothes man.

Polizistenmord killing of a policemen.

Polizistin policewoman, police matron.

polnische Wirtschaft, hier herrscht eine this place is a shambles.

Polster pad, cushion, bolster, upholstery, wad;
~ **laufender Aufträge** cushion of orders on hand;
~ **von 100.000 DM als Reserve haben** to have DM 100.000 to fall back upon; **einem Industriekonzern ein** ~ **verschaffen** to bolster an industrial concern.

Polsterer upholsterer.

Polster|garnitur living-room suite; ~**klasse** *(Bahn)* first and second class; ~**material** upholstery.

polstern to upholster, to pad, to cushion.

Polstern, mit tiefen ~ **überzogen** overstuffed.

Polster|rolle cloth sausage; ~**sitz** cushioned seat.

Polsterung upholstery, padding, wadding.

Polsterwaren upholstered goods, upholstery furniture.

poltern to thump, to pound, to lumber;
auf dem Dachboden ~ to make a racket in the attic; **über das Kopfsteinpflaster** ~ *(Wagen)* to rumble over the cobble stones.

Poly|gamie polygamy, plural marriage; ~**graph** lie detector.

Polyp peeler *(Br., sl.)*, crusher, cop *(sl.)*, peeler *(Br.)*, blue-bottle *(Br., sl.)*, flatfoot *(US sl.)*, bull *(US sl.)*, fuzz *(US sl.)*, long arm *(sl.)*, shamus *(sl.)*, gumshoe *(US sl.)*, harness cop *(US sl.)*.

Poly|pol polypoly; ~**technikum** politechnic; ~**zentrismus** polycentrism.

Pomp pomp, splendo(u)r, display.

pompös pompous, splendid, gorgeous, flossy *(US sl.)*;
~**e Hochzeit** ostentatious wedding; **im** ~**en Rahmen** on palatial lines; ~**er Stil** pompous style; ~ **eingerichtetes Zimmer** pretentiously furnished room.

Pontius, j. von ~ **zu Pilatus schicken** to drive (send) s. o. from pillar to post, to give s. o. the runabout.

Ponton|brücke pontoon (floating) bridge; ~**kran** floating crane.

Pool pool, combination, combine;
~ **bilden** to pool;
~**bildung** pooling.

poolen, Aufträge to pool orders.

Pool|vereinbarung joint-purse arrangement; ~**vertrag** pooling (joint-purse) agreement.

Popanz bogey, bugbear, poker *(US coll.)*;
sich zu einem ~ **auswachsen** to have risen to a spectre.

populär popular, in vogue;
~ **machen** to popularize; **sich** ~ **machen** to win popularity; ~ **werden** to catch on, to acquire vogue;
~**e Darstellung** popular presentation; ~**e Preise** popular prices.

popularisieren to popularize, to vulgarize.

Popularisierung popularization, vulgarization.

Popularität popularity, vogue;
steigende ~ mounting popularity;
sich kurzfristiger ~ **erfreuen** to have a short-lived vogue; ~ **erlangen** to gain popularity; **etw. für seine** ~ **tun** to nurse one's public.

Popularitäts|analyse von Rundfunkprogrammen cooperative analysis of broadcasting ratings; ~**hascher** gladhander *(US)*; ~**hascherei** clutch at popularity; ~**liste anführen** to top the personal popularity poll; ~**umfrage** *(Filmgeschäft)* studio research; **jem. in den** ~**umfragen Auftrieb geben** to send s. o. soaring in the popularity charts.

Populärwissenschaft popular science.

populärwissenschaftlich popularized.
Pornographie pornography, obscenity.
pornographisch pornographic, obscene;
~**e Veröffentlichung** obscene book or paper; ~**e Veröffentlichungen** obscene publications.
Portal portal, main doorway, porch *(US)*.
Portefeuille investment portfolio, *(Minister)* portfolio;
breitgestreutes ~ diversified holdings;
~ **eigener Aktien** reacquired capital stock, treasury securities (stock, *US*), donated surplus *(US)*; ~ **von Anteilscheinen** unit holdings; ~ **eines Pensionsfonds** pension portfolio; ~ **an Wechseln** billholdings;
im ~ **behalten** to hold over *(Br.)*; **sein** ~ **zur Verfügung stellen** *(Minister)* to resign office;
~**aufgliederung** portfolio breakdown; ~**aufstellung** *(Investmentfonds)* portfolio description; ~**berater** investment analyst; ~**beratung** investment analysis; ~**erträge** portfolio income; ~**geschäft** portfolio deal; ~**investitionen** portfolio investment; ~**veränderungen** portfolio changes; ~**verwaltung** portfolio management; ~**wechsel** portfolio bill; ~**werte** *(Investmentfonds)* underlying securities *(Br.)*.
Portemonnaie purse, wallet;
dickes ~ heavy (long) purse; **leeres** ~ light (ill-lined) purse; **jds.** ~ **erleichtern** to ease s. one's purse; **sein** ~ **festhalten** to grip one's purse-strings tightly; **das** ~ **haben** to hold the purse-strings; **Daumen auf dem** ~ **halten** to tighten the purse-strings.
Portfolioinvestitionen investment securities.
Portier porter, doorkeeper, concierge, doorman, *(Hotel)* receptionist, desk clerk.
Portiersloge porter's lodge (office).
Portion portion, share, allowance, dose, *(Anteil)* share, portion, *(Kaffee)* pot, *(Mahlzeit)* go, *(mil.)* ration;
in kleinen ~**en** by drops;
eiserne ~ iron ration; **große** ~ large chunk; **halbe** ~ *(fig.)* half-pint, shrimp; **volle** ~ generous portion; **zweite** ~ *(Restaurant)* second helping;
gehörige ~ **Frechheit** good deal of impudence; **gute** ~ **Glück dabei** slice of good luck; ~ **gesunden Menschenverstandes** pile (a fund) of good (common) sense.
Portionspackung one-serving size.
portionsweise in portions.
Porto postage [rates, *US*], postal rate, *(Pakete)* carriage;
~ **bezahlt** postage paid; **einschließlich** ~ postage included; **zuzüglich** ~ postage extra;
gewöhnliches (normales) ~ ordinary postage (rate); **ungenügendes** ~ underpaid postage;
~ **für Auslandssendungen** overseas postage; ~ **für Kontoauszüge** statement postage;
~**anstieg** increase in postal charges, postal increase; ~**ausgleich** postage compensation; ~**auslagen** postage incurred, postal expenses; ~**auslagen vergüten** to reimburse for postage incurred; ~**buch** stamp book, schedule of postage; ~**einnahmen** postage and postal revenue; ~**erhöhung** raising of (increase in) postal (postage, *Br.*) rates; ~**ermäßigung** reduction of the postal tariff; ~**ersatz durch Freiexemplare** *(Buchhandel)* postage refunded by way of free copies; ~**erstattung** postage compensation.
portofrei postpaid, postage paid (free), prepaid, post-free *(Br.)*, free of postage *(US)*, official paid *(Br.)*, *(Dienstsache)* on Her Majesty's service *(Br.)*;
~ **machen** to frank; ~ **senden** to send prepaid;
~**e Dienstsache** on Her Majesty's service *(Br.)*.
Porto | freiheit frank, exemption from postage; ~**freiheit genießen** to be exempt from postage; ~**freiheitsprivileg** franking privilege *(US)*; ~**gebühren** postal (postage, *Br.*) rates, postage stamp rates, mailing expenses; **zusätzliche** ~**gebühr** fee payable in addition; ~**gebühr bezahlt der Empfänger** postage will be paid by licensee; **dem Kunden** ~**gebühren in Rechnung stellen** to charge the postage to the customer; ~**hinterziehung** defrauding postage; ~**kasse** petty cash, imprest fund *(Br.)*, office stamp-book; ~**kasse plündern** to raid the petty cash, to milk the till.
Portokassen | beleg petty-cash voucher; ~**buch** petty-cash journal, postage book; ~**fonds** petty-cash (imprest) fund; ~**führer,** ~**wart** petty cashier.
Porto | kosten expense for postage, postal (postage, *Br.*) charges; ~**nachnahme** postage to be collected; **unter** ~**nachnahme** postage to be collected.
portopflichtig liable (subject) to postage.
Porto | rechnung postage account; ~**rückvergütung** refunding of postage; ~**satz** rate of postage, postal tariff; **höchster** ~**satz** rate limit *(US)*; ~**spesen** expense for postage, postage cost, postal (postage, *Br.*) expenses (charges), petty charges (expenses); ~**spesen zurückvergüten** to refund the cost of postage; ~**tarif** postal tariff; ~**unkosten** postage cost; ~**vergünstigung** mail privilege *(US)*; ~**vergütung** refunding of postage; ~**verteuerung** increase in postal rates; ~**zuschlag** extra (additional) postage, surcharge.
Porträt | in Lebensgröße full-face portrait;
~ **auf die Leinwand werfen** to flash a portrait on the screen;
~**[aufnahme]** portrait; ~**aufnahme [eines Verbrechers]** mug shot *(sl.)*.
porträtieren, j. to take s. one's portrait;
sich ~ **lassen** to sit for an artist.
Porträtist portrait painter.
Porträt | linse portrait lens; ~**maler** portrait painter; ~**malerei** portrait painting.
Porzellan porcelain;
zerschlagenes ~ **kitten** to mend matters; **unnötig** ~ **zerschlagen** to do more harm than good;
~**manufaktur** manufacture of porcelain; ~**warengeschäft** china shop.
Posaunen von Jericho trumpets of Jericho.
Pose pose, attitude;
~ **einnehmen** to strike an attitude.
Position position, post, employment, job, *(in Aufstellung)* item, *(Buchung)* entry, *(Flugzeug, Schiff)* position, bearing, *(Radar)* plot, *(Rang)* standing, status, station, repute, *(Ruf)* standing; **jds.** ~ **entsprechend** suitable to s. one's station; **in einer hohen** ~ in a high place (position);
ausbaufähige ~ position with good prospects; **dominierende** ~ dominant position; **einflußreiche** ~ position of influence, purchase; **einträgliche** ~ lucrative position; **ertragreiche** ~ lucrative position; **führende** ~ leadership position; **gehobene** ~ advanced position; **geschäftliche** ~ station in business; **gesellschaftliche** ~ social position; **gesonderte** ~ separate item; **kostenvergütete** ~ pay item; **leitende** ~ policy-making (management, managerial) position; **offene** ~ open item; **verantwortliche** ~ position of responsibility; **vertragliche** ~ contractual position; **wirtschaftliche** ~ business standing;
~ **ohne Aufstiegschancen** dead-end job; ~**en unter dem Bilanzstrich** items below the line in the balance sheet; ~**en für Führungskräfte** management appointments; ~**en der Haussepartei** long positions; **bedeutende** ~ **in der Welt** world importance; ~ **gegenüber dem Weltwährungsfonds** position in the Fund; ~ **des Zolltarifs** tariff heading (item);
gewünschte ~ **angeben** to state the position desired; **nach** ~**en aufgliedern** to itemize; ~ **ausschreiben** to throw a post open to competition; **führende** ~ **in der Welt ausüben** to lead the world; **sich in einer abhängigen** ~ **befinden** to be in a subordinate position; **im Wirtschaftsleben eine verantwortliche** ~ **bekleiden** to hold a position of management responsibility in business; **gute** ~ **bekommen** to drop into a position; **j. in seiner** ~ **belassen** to maintain s. o. in his position; **sich mit allen nur denkbaren Mitteln um eine** ~ **bemühen** to jockey for position; ~ **durch Einschaltung einer Beratungsfirma besetzen** to fill a job through selection consultants; ~ **eines Schiffes bestimmen** to fix a ship's position, to take one's bearings; **sich um eine** ~ **bewerben** to go in for an appointment, to apply for a position; ~ **beziehen** to manoeuvre for position; **feste** ~ **beziehen** to define one's position, to take a hard line, to adopt a tough policy; **bescheidene** ~ **einnehmen** to occupy a humble station; **führende** ~ **einnehmen** to hold a high-level position; **verantwortungsvolle** ~ **erhalten** to move to a higher position (position of greater responsibility); ~ **eines Generaldirektors erhalten** to be given a post as general manager; **einflußreiche** ~ **erlangen** to make one's mark; **höchstmögliche berufliche** ~ **erreichen** to wind up in a top-policy position, to reach the top of the ladder; **an einer** ~ **festhalten** to stick to a job; **seine** ~ **festigen** to strengthen one's position; **innenpolitische** ~ **festigen** to improve one's stocks at home; **einflußreiche** ~ **gewinnen** to make one's mark; **starke** ~ **haben** to be in a strong position; **hohe** ~ **innehaben** to be high up the stick; **führende** ~ **in der Welt innehaben** to be a world leader; **als einziger für eine** ~ **in Frage kommen** to be the only possible man for a position; ~ **lösen** to liquidate an engagement; ~ **schwächen** to undermine a position; **in einer angesehenen** ~ **sein** to be in good standing; **für eine** ~ **nicht geeignet sein** to be ineligible for a position; **für eine** ~ **völlig ungeeignet sein** to be a square peg in a round hole; **einige** ~**en streichen** to cancel several items; **nach einer gesicherten** ~ **trachten** to desire status and security; **seine** ~ **seinen Beziehungen verdanken** to owe one's position to influence; **seine** ~ **Protektion verdanken** to get a job by push;

seine ~ mehr der Protektion als Verdiensten und Fähigkeiten verdanken to obtain one's position more by favo(u)r than by merit and abilities; **seine ~ verstärken** to strengthen one's hand, to dig o. s. in; **j. für eine ~ vorschlagen** to nominate s. o. for a post; **~ wechseln** *(mar.)* to fleet; **seine ~ häufig wechseln** to job-hop; **für eine ~ nicht zugelassen werden** to be excluded from a post.

Positions | anzeiger position indicator; **~auflösung** liquidation of commitments; **~laterne** navigation (position) lights; **~lichter** *(Flugzeug)* position (navigation, running, *US*) lights, *(Schiff)* top lights; **~meldung** *(Flugzeug)* position report; **~papier** position paper.

Positiv *(Foto)* positive [picture];
schnell fertiggestellte ~e *(Film)* rushes.

positiv positive, certain, sure, *(el.)* plus, positive, *(Kritik)* constructive, favo(u)rable;
~ antworten to answer in the affirmative; **sich ~ für die Beurteilung einer Persönlichkeit auswirken** to prove a personality bonus; **jem. ~ gegenüberstehen** to look on s. o. with a favo(u)rable eye; **einer Sache ~ gegenüberstehen** to be friendly to a cause;
~e Antwort favo(u)rable (positive, affirmative) answer; **~e Beurteilung** approval rating; **~er Beweis** positive evidence; **~es Ergebnis** positivity; **~e Lebenseinstellung** positivism; **~er Pol** *(el.)* plus (positive) pole; **~es Recht** positive law; **~e Vertragsverletzung** collateral negligence; **~es Vorzeichen** positive sign; **~e Zeugenaussage** positive statement; **~e Zusicherung** *(Versicherung)* affirmative warranty.

Positivismus positivism.

Positivist positivist.

Positivum plus, asset.

Positur pose, attitude;
theatralische ~ posture;
sich in ~ setzen to posture.

Posse frolic, trick, foolish action, *(Theater)* farce, low comedy, interlude;
~n fun and games;
derbe ~ knock-about farce;
~n reißen (treiben) to clown around, to play the fool.

Possenspiel farcial play, mockery.

possessorische Klage possessory action.

possierlich droll, funny, amusing.

Post post *(Br.)*, mail *(US)*, *(Postamt)* post office, *(Postdienst)* postal (mail) service, *(Postsachen)* letters, mail *(US)*;
durch die ~ by post; **mit der ersten ~** by the first mail *(US)* (delivery, *Br.*); **mit getrennter ~** under separate cover; **mit gewöhnlicher ~** by surface mail *(Br.)*; **mit gleicher ~** by the same mail; **mit der heutigen ~** by today's post (mail, *US*); **mit der nächsten ~** by the next mail *(US)*; **mit umgehender ~** by return of post *(Br.)* (mail); **ohne ~** letterless; **per ~** by post *(Br.)*, by mail *(US)*; **von der ~ befördert** mailed *(US)*;
abgehende ~ outgoing post (mail, *US*); **ausgebliebene ~** mail due *(US)*; **ausgehende ~** outgoing (departing) mail *(US)*; **beschädigte ~** damaged mail *(US)*; **betriebsinterne ~** interoffice mail *(US)*; **eingehende ~** incoming (arriving) mail *(US)* (post, *Br.*); **erste ~** morning delivery *(Br.)* (mail, *US*); **durch Freistempler freigemachte (freigestempelte) ~** metered mail *(US)*; **nicht durch Freistempler freigemachte ~** nonmetered mail *(US)*; **heutige ~** today's post (mail, *US*); **zugestellte ~** delivered mail *(US)*; **abends zugestellte ~** late-fee post; **noch nicht zugestellte ~** undelivered mail *(US)*;
~ abfertigen to dispatch (dispose of) the post (mail, *US*); **~ abholen** to pick up the mail *(US)*; **Brief bei der ~ aufgeben** to post (mail, *US*) a letter at the post office; **bei der ~ aufliefern** to post, to mail *(US)*; **~ aufmachen** to open the letters (mail, *US*); **~ befördern** to carry mail *(US)*; **mit der ~ befördern** to post *(Br.)*, to mail *(US)*; **~ bekommen** to receive mail *(US)* (letters); **mit der ~ bestellen** to order by mail *(US)*; **eingegangene ~ erledigen (durchsehen)** to attend to (go through) the correspondence; **~ expedieren** to forward the mail *(US)*; **zur ~ geben** to [send by] post *(Br.)*, to mail *(US)*; **zur ~ gehen** to go to the post office; **mit der zweiten ~ kommen** to come by the second delivery *(Br.)*; **~ öffnen** to open the mail *(US)* (letters); **mit der ~ senden (schicken)** to dispatch (forward, send) by post *(Br.)*, to mail *(US)*; **auf der ~ verlorengehen** to get lost in the mail *(US)*; **auf die ~ warten** to be waiting for the postman to pass; **bar in der ~ ausgezahlt werden** to be paid in cash at post offices; **mit der ~ zustellen** to deliver by mail *(US)*;
~abfertiger mailing *(US)* (dispatching) clerk, mailer *(US)*; **~abfertigung** dispatch of mail *(US)*; **~abfertigungssstelle** postal room, mailing room *(US)*; **~abholer** caller for the mail; **~abholung** collection of letters (mail, *US*); **~abkommen** postal agreement (treaty); **internationales ~abkommen** Postal Convention; **~ablage** postal rack; **~ablieferungsschein** certificate of posting; **~abonnement** postal subscription; **~abschnitt** coupon, stub, postal receipt; **~abteilung** mailing department *(US)*; **~adreßbuch** city (business) directory, post-office guide; **~adresse** post-office address; **~agentur** sub post office, post-office substation.

postalisch postal, post-office;
~ aufgegeben posted *(Br.)*, mailed *(US)*; **~ zu befördern** mailable *(US)*;
Aufträge ~ erledigen to do mail orders;
~e Anschrift post-office (postal, mailing, *US*) address; **~e Bestimmungen** postal regulations; **~e Verhältnisse** postal situation.

Postament pedestal.

Postamt post (letter) office, mail station *(US)*, *(Gebäude)* postal building;
betriebseigenes ~ self-service postal unit; **fliegendes ~** travelling post office; **zuständiges ~** delivery office;
~ für unzustellbare Postsendungen returned-letters office.

postamtlich postal, post-office.

Postamts | adreßbuch post-office directory; **~bedürfnisse** post-office supplies; **~vorsteher** postmaster.

Post | angelegenheit postal matter; **~angestellter** postal worker (employee, clerk, *US*), post-office worker; **~anleihe** post-office loan; **~annahmestempel** date stamp; **~anschluß** telephone connection; **~anschrift** mailing *(US)* (post-office, postal) address; **~anstalt** post office; **~antwortschein** reply coupon *(US)*.

Postanweisung money order *(Br.)*, post-office order *(Br.)*, postal order *(Br.)*, postal money order *(US)*, postal note *(US)*;
gebührenfreie ~ service money order; **internationale ~** foreign money order; **telegrafische ~** express money order; **verfallene ~** void money order;
jem. mittels ~ Geld schicken to send s. o. a sum of money by post.

Postanweisungs | dienst money-order service; **~formular** money-order form.

Post | arbeiter postal worker; **~arbeitergewerkschaft** postal trade union; **~arbeiterstreik** postal (mail, *US*) strike; **~aufbewahrungsstelle** poste restante *(Br.)*; **~aufgabe** posting *(Br.)*, mailing *(US)*; **~aufgabezeit** time of posting; **~auftrag** mail order; **im ~auftragswege** mail-order; **~ausgang** outgoing post, outgoing mail *(US)*; **~auslieferung** postal delivery, mail delivery *(US)*; **~auto** post-office (post, mail, *US*) car, mail van *(Br.)*; **~auto für den ländlichen Zustelldienst** rural delivery wag(g)on; **~barscheck** uncrossed postal check; **~beamter** post (post-office) official, post-office clerk, postal employee (official, clerk, *US*); **~bearbeitungsmaschine** mailing machine, mailer; **~bedienstete** postal staff; **~beförderung** postal transport of mail *(US)*; **normale ~beförderung** surface transportation *(Br.)*; **normale ~beförderung und Zustellung** ordinary course of post; **~begleitschein** post bill, dispatch note *(Br.)*; **~behörde** postal authorities; **~benutzer** postal user; **~bestimmungen für Drucksachen** printed paper conditions; **~bestimmungsort** office of destination; **~betrieb** postal plant; **~betrug** mail fraud; **~beutel** pouch, post bag *(Br.)*, mailbag *(US)*; **~bezieher** *(pl.)* subscriptions sold by mail; **einzelner ~bezieher** individual user of the mail service; **~bezirk** postal sector (district); **mit Abkürzungen versehener ~bezirk** code center; **~bezug** postal subscription (delivery); **bei ~bezug** if delivered by post *(Br.)* (mail, *US*); **~bezugspreis** postal subscription rate; **~boot** packet boat; **~bootroute** post line; **~bote** postman *(Br.)*, postboy, letter (mail, *US*) carrier, mailman *(US)*; **~briefkasten** pillar box *(Br.)*, mailbox *(US)*; **~buch** post-office guide; **~bus** mail coach *(US)*.

Pöstchen soft job;
fettes ~ fat living, snug berth; **ruhiges ~** snap, featherbed job; **~inhaber** placeman; **~jäger** pie (place) hunter, placeman *(Br.)*, carpetbagger *(US)*, spoilsman *(US)*, pork-chopper *(sl.)*; **~jägerei** carpetbaggery, carpetbaggism, spoils system *(US)*, rat-race *(sl.)*; **~politik** placemanship, spoils system *(US)*.

Post | dampfer packet (mail, *US*, post, *Br.*) boat, mail steamer; **~dezernat** postal section; **~diebstahl** mail theft (robbery) *(US)*; **~dienst** postal (mail, *US*) service; **~dienststelle für die Ausgabe von Postanweisungen** money-order office; **~direktion** General Post Office; **~eingang** incoming post (mail, *US*); **~einlieferung** posting, mailing *(US)*; **~einlieferungsbuch** postal receipt book; **~einlieferungsschein** certificate of posting *(Br.)*, post-office (postal) receipt, recorded delivery *(Br.)*.

Posten post, place, station, *(Abzahlung)* instal(l)ment, *(Amt)* office, *(Betrag)* sum, amount, *(Buchhaltung)* entry, item, *(dipl.)* assignment, *(Effektenpaket)* block, lot, *(mar.)* quarter, *(mil.)* outpost, sentry, warder, *(Minister)* portfolio, *(Scheck)* article *(Br.)*, item *(US)*, *(Stellung)* position, situation, job, berth *(Br.)*, billet, *(Streikposten)* picket, *(Ware)* parcel, lot, quantity, article, *(Wechsel)* article *(Br.)*, item *(US)*;
auf dem ~ up to par, on deck *(coll., US)*; **in kleinen** ~ by (in) parcels, in small lots;
absetzbarer ~ deductible item; **angenehmer** ~ featherbed *(fig.)*; **ausgetragene** ~ booted (retired) items; **ausschlaggebender** ~ post of commanding importance; **außergewöhnlicher** ~ extraordinary item; **ausstehender** ~ receivable item, outstander; **nicht auf Lager befindlicher** ~ out-of-stock item, item not in stock; **steuerlich begünstigter** ~ preference item; **nicht beitreibbarer** ~ uncollectable item; **bestreitbare** ~ debatable items; **betriebsfremde** ~ nonoperating items; **debitorischer** ~ debit item (entry), receivable item; **der Rechnungsabgrenzung dienende** ~ deferred charges [to expense]; **durchlaufender** ~ intransit item, item in transit, suspense (transitory) item; **einflußreicher** ~ post of authority; **eingetragener** ~ booked (recorded) item; **einmaliger** ~ nonrecurring item; **einträglicher** ~ remunerative post, snug berth *(Br.)*; **entstandene, noch nicht fällige** ~ accruing items, *(Bilanz)* deferred assets; **führender** ~ managerial post; **ohne Bewerber gebliebener** ~ post still unapplied for; **gebuchter** ~ entry, booked item; **großer** ~ large item; **guter** ~ good situation (berth, *Br.*); **innerbetrieblicher** ~ intercompany item; **irrtümlicher** ~ erroneous item; **kalkulatorischer** ~ imputed item; **kleiner** ~ small item; **kreditorischer** ~ credit item (entry); **leitender** ~ managerial (executive) position; **lukrativer** ~ lucrative position; **offener** ~ uncovered amount, unpaid item; **ruhiger** ~ soft job, snap; **nicht saldierter** ~ unbalanced entry; **selbständiger** ~ independent position; **sicherstehender** ~ sum safe in hand; **strittiger** ~ item in dispute; **transitorische** ~ *(Bilanz)* suspense (deferred, *US*) items, deferred (prepaid) assets, deferred charges [to expense], deferred expense (debit), prepaid expenses; **sich überschneidende** ~ overlapping items; **unbedeutender** ~ sidetrack; **unbeglichener** ~ item not squared; **unbesetzter** ~ unfilled post, vacancy, vacant position; **unbesoldeter** ~ honorary office; **sehr verantwortungsreicher** ~ post of great responsibility; **vorgeschobener** ~ *(mil.)* outguard; **im Haushaltsplan nicht vorgesehene** ~ unbudgeted appropriations; **vorgetragener** ~ amount carried forward; **vorläufiger** ~ suspense item;
~ **auf der Aktivseite** asset; ~ **für die Änderung des Gewinnvortrages** statement of earned surplus *(US)*; ~ **des Bestandsverzeichnisses** inventory item; ~ **als Buchhalter** situation as bookkeeper, accountantship; ~ **im Hauptbuch** ledger item; ~ **des Haushaltsplans** item included in the budget; ~ **im Journal** journal entry; **unsichtbare** ~ **der Leistungsbilanz** invisible items of trade; ~ **der Rechnungsabgrenzung** *(Bilanz)* deferred charges [to expense] *(US)*, deferred (prepaid) assets (expenses), deferred items *(US)*; ~ **des Umlaufvermögens** current assets items; ~ **des statistischen Warenkorbs** shopping-bag item; ~ **des Warenverkehrs** visible items of trade;
~ **abhaken** to check an entry; ~ **ablösen** *(mil.)* to relieve a sentry; ~ **abstreichen** to deduct an item, *(kontrollieren)* to check (tick off) an entry, to prick items; ~ **eines Ministers anbieten** to offer a cabinet office; **einzelne** ~ **angeben** to itemize accounts; ~ **aufführen** to list items; ~ **einzeln aufführen** to specify items; ~ **aufgeben** to resign a position, to throw up a post; **nach** ~ **aufgliedern** to itemize; ~ **in ein Verzeichnis aufnehmen** to enter an item in an index; ~ **aufnotieren** *(Buchhaltung)* to enter (post) up items; ~ **aufstellen** *(mil.)* to mount guards; ~ **austragen** to cancel an entry (item); ~ **[auf einem Konto] austragen** to tranfer entries; ~ **ausziehen** to take out an item; ~ **begleichen** to settle an amount; **bedeutsamen** ~ **bekleiden** to occupy an important position; **einflußreichen** ~ **bekommen** to make one's mark; **verantwortungsvollen** ~ **bekommen** to move to a position of greater responsibility; **Richter auf seinem** ~ **belassen** to continue a judge in his post; ~ **belasten** to debit an item; ~ **berichtigen** to adjust an entry; ~ **besetzen** to fill a position; ~ **neu besetzen** to fill a vacancy; **j. für einen** ~ **bestimmen** to appoint (assign) s. o. to a post; **sich um einen** ~ **bewerben** to run for a position, to apply for a situation, to throw one's hat into the ring; **auf seinem** ~ **bleiben** to remain at one's post; ~ **buchen** to make an entry, to post an item; **jeden** ~ **einzeln buchen** to post each entry singly; ~ **gleichlautend buchen** to pass an entry in conformity, to reciprocate an entry on the books; ~ **irrtümlich buchen** to make a false (wrong) entry; ~ **nachträglich buchen** to post an omitted item, to make a supplementary entry; **sich in einen** ~ **drängen** to push one's way into a job; ~ **eintragen** to post an item, to make an entry; ~ **im Hauptbuch eintragen** to enter an item in the ledger; **von seinem** ~ **entfernen** to unseat; **seines** ~**s entheben** to unmake, to depose from a rank; **j. für einen** ~ **erkennen** to carry (pass, place) an article to s. one's credit; ~ **etatisieren** to enter an amount in the budget; ~ **für j. finden** to fix s. o. up with a job; ~ **gutschreiben** to credit an item; **guten** ~ **haben** to have a good berth *(Br.)*; **gut bezahlten** ~ **gefunden haben** to have found a lucrative engagement; **auf verlorenem** ~ **kämpfen** to play a losing game; **an seinem** ~ **kleben** to stick to one's post; ~ **kreditieren** to credit an item; ~ **löschen** to cancel an item; ~ **nachtragen** to book an omitted item; ~ **notieren** to book an item; **sich für einen** ~ **qualifizieren** to qualify to hold a job; **auf dem** ~ **sein** to be on one's toes; **einem** ~ **gewachsen sein** to be equal to a position; ~ **spezifizieren** to enumerate items, to itemize; ~ **stehen** *(mil.)* to be on post, to be on sentry duty, to watch; ~ **stornieren** to cancel an item, to reverse an entry; ~ **streichen** to cancel (strike off) an item; ~ **tilgen** to cancel an entry; ~ **übertragen** to carry over an entry, to carry an item forward; **jeden** ~ **einzeln übertragen (verbuchen)** to post each entry singly; ~ **umbuchen** to carry out a product; **gegen einen** ~ **validieren** to set off *(Br.)*, to offset *(US)*; ~ **auf dem Kontokorrent verbuchen** to pass an item to the current account; **j. für einen** ~ **vorsehen** to put s. o. down for a job; ~ **vortragen** to carry forward an item; ~ **übereinstimmend vortragen** to reciprocate an entry; **auf einen** ~ **zurückkehren** to return to a position; **von seinem** ~ **zurücktreten** to relinquish one's appointment; ~ **zusammenwerfen** to lump items together;
~**aufgliederung** itemization; ~**gang** *(mil.)* sentry-go; ~**jäger** office seeker (hunter), job jockey, carpetbagger *(US)*, pie (place) hunter, placeman *(Br.)*, spoilsman *(US)*; ~**jägerei** carpetbaggery, spoils system *(US)*, huggery *(Br.)*; ~**kette** *(mil.)* sentry line.

Postentwertungsstempel postmark cancellation, mark of post office.

Postenumdrucker facsimile posting machine.

postenweise in lots, by items;
~ **aufführen** to itemize.

Post|fach post-office box; ~**fachnummer** post-office (box) number; ~**flugzeug** postal plane, mailplane.

postfrei postage paid, prepaid;
~ **machen** to frank, to prepay.

Postgebäude post-office building.

Postgebühren postage rates, charges for postal service, postal charges (fees, tariff, *US*), postage, rates *(US)*, mailing expenses (fees) *(US)*;
~**ermäßigung** reduction of postage; ~**freiheit** frank, exemption from charges; ~**heft** post-office guide; ~**tarif** postal tariff.

Post|geheimnis secrecy of correspondence; ~**gehilfe** post-office assistant; ~**gesetz** Post Office Act *(Br.)*; ~**gewicht** postal lot; ~**gut** mail matter; ~**halter** postmaster; ~**handbuch** Post Office Guide *(Br.)*; ~**hilfsstelle** sub post office *(Br.)*; ~**hoheit** postal principle *(US)*; ~**horn** post horn.

postieren to station, to post;
sich ~ to take a plant.

Postinspektor postal inspector.

Postkarte postcard *(Br.)*, postal card *(US)*, *(fam.)* postal *(US)*; **gewöhnliche** ~ plain postcard *(Br.)*; **vorgedruckte** ~ ready-printed postcard *(Br.)*;
~ **mit Rückantwort** reply-paid postcard *(Br.)*, double card *(US)*.

Postkarten|automat postcard automatic supply *(Br.)*; ~**größe** postcard size; ~**scheck** postcard check *(US)* (cheque, *Br.*).

Post|kasten letterbox, pillar box *(Br.)*, postbox, mailbox *(US)*; ~**konvention** Postal Convention; ~**kunde** post office user; ~**kutsche** *(hist.)* post coach *(Br.)*, postchaise, stagecoach.

postlagernd left till called for, general delivery *(US)*;
~ **aufbewahrt werden** to remain till called for.

Postlaufkredit mail credit *(US)*.

Postleit|vermerk post route; **mit** ~**vermerk versehen** to route; ~**vermerkverzeichnis** route list; ~**zahl** postal code *(Br.)*, postal zone (code, *Br.*) number, postcode *(Br.)*, zip number *(US)*; ~**zahlgebiet** postal zone, zip code area *(US)*; ~**zahlwesen,** ~**zahlsystem** postcode system *(Br.)*, system of postcoding, zip code *(US)*; ~**zone** zip code area *(US)*.

Post|liste post bill *(Br.)*, mailing list *(US)*; ~**marke** [postage] stamp; ~**meister** postmaster; ~**meisterstelle** postmastership; ~**minister** Postmaster General *(US)*; ~**ministerium** General Post Office *(Br.)*, Postmaster Generalship *(US)*, Post Office Department *(US)*; ~- **und Fernmeldeministerium** Ministry of

Post and Telecommunications *(Br., 1969)*; **~mißbrauch zu Betrugswesen** using mail to defraud *(US)*; **~monopol** postal principle *(US)*.
Postnachnahme postal cash order, cash (collect, *US*) on delivery, C.O.D.;
per ~ schicken to send cash (collect, *US*) on delivery;
~dienst cash (collect, *US*) on delivery service; **~sendung** collect-on-delivery mail *(US)*.
Post|nachsendung redirection of mail; **~nebenstelle** branch post-office, postal station *(US)*, sub post office *(Br.)*.
postnumerando|zahlbar payable later; **~ zahlen** to pay on receipt.
Post|omnibus mail coach *(Br.)*; **~ordnung** postal (post-office, *Br.*) regulations.
Postpaket parcel, postal packet *(Br.)*, package *(US)*;
als ~ schicken to send by parcel post;
~adresse label, dispatch note, facing slip *(US)*; **~dienst** parcel service.
Post|papier, hochwertiges bond paper; **~pferd** post horse; **~privileg** postal principle *(US)*; **~quittung** certificate of posting *(Br.)*, post-office receipt; **~raub** mail robbery; **~raum** mailroom *(US)*; **~reform** postal reform; **~reformgesetz** Postal Reform Act *(US)*; **~route** line of post, post route; **~route festlegen** to adopt a route of transportation of mail; **~sachen** postal matter (item), post *(Br.)*, mail matters *(US)*; **~sack** postbag, mailbag *(US)*, letter bag; **fehlgeleiteter ~sack** bag out of course; **versiegelte ~säcke im zwischenstaatlichen Durchgangsverkehr** close mail *(US)*; **~schaffner** mailguard *(Br.)*; **~schalter** post counter position, window *(US)*.
Postscheck postal giro *(Br.)*, national giro *(Br.)*, girocheque *(Br.)*, postal check *(US)*;
~ ausstellen to draw a postal cheque *(Br.)* (check, *US*); **~ einlösen** to cash a postal cheque *(Br.)* (check, *US*); **per ~ überweisen** to use the post office giro system *(Br.)*;
~abteilung giro department *(Br.)*; **~amt** postal giro office, National Giro Office *(Br.)*, giro administration *(Br.)*, National Giro Centre *(Br.)*, postal check office *(US)*; **~dienst** National Giro (Girobank) Service *(Br.)*, giro banking service *(Br.)*, national giro system *(Br.)*, postal giro system *(Br.)*, postal check system *(US)*; **~dienst betreiben** to operate the Giro; **~einlösung** encashment of postchecks; **~einrichtungen** giro (Girobank) service *(Br.)*; **~guthaben** giro account *(Br.)*, postal cheque *(Br.)* (check, *US*) account, balance on postal cheque *(Br.)* (check, *US*) account, balance on giro account *(Br.)*; **~karte** Giro Card *(Br.)*; **~konto** account of the national giro *(Br.)*, national giro account *(Br.)*, postal cheque account *(Br.)*, ordinary account *(Br.)*, postal checking account *(US)*; **~konto einrichten (eröffnen)** to open a giro account *(Br.)*; **~kontoinhaber** giro account holder *(Br.)*; **~system** postal cheque system *(Br.)*; **~überweisung** postal transfer, giro transaction *(Br.)*, giro transfer *(Br.)*; **mit ~überweisung** for use by national giro *(Br.)*; **~überweisungsformular** transfer deposit form; **~verkehr** post office giro system *(Br.)*, post office national giro *(Br.)*, postal giro system, giro service; **~wesen** National Giro System *(Br.)*, Post Office Giro *(Br.)*, postal giro system.
Post|schein post-office receipt; **~schiff** packet (post, mail, *US*) boat; **~-, Passagier- und Paketschiffahrt** mail, passenger and parcel service; **~schließfach** post-office box.
Postsendung post, mail *(US)*, item, postal packet *(Br.)*;
~en postal (mail, *US*) matter, post, mail *(US)*, postal items; **dringende ~en** urgent items; **eingeschriebene ~en** registered items; **fehlende ~en** missing items; **größere ~** a lot of mail *(US)*; **normale ~en** surface mail *(Br.)*; **unzustellbare ~** undeliverable mail *(US)*, nix *(US sl.)*; **versicherte ~** insured mail; **noch nicht zugestellte ~** undelivered mail *(US)*.
Postsortierer mail sorter *(US)*.
Postspar|buch post-office *(Br.)* (postal, *US*) savings book, deposit book *(Br.)*; **~einlagen** post-office *(Br.)* (postal, *US*) savings deposits, postal savings *(US)*; **~guthaben** postal savings account *(US)*; **~guthaben besitzen** to keep one's savings in the post office; **~karte** postal savings certificate *(US)*; **~kasse** post-office (postal, *US*) savings bank, national savings bank *(Br.)*, postal savings depository *(US)*.
Postsparkassen|amt ~behörde Director of Savings *(Br.)*, Department for National Savings *(Br.)*; **~buch** post-office *(Br.)* (postal, *US*) savings book; **~dienst** postal savings service *(US)*; **~einlage** postal savings deposit *(US)*; **~geschäft** post-office savings bank business *(Br.)*; **~gesetz** Post-Office Savings Bank Act *(Br.)*; **~schuldverschreibungen** postal savings bonds *(US)*; **~verkehr** post-office savings service *(Br.)*; **~vermögen** post-office savings bank fund *(Br.)*, postal savings fund *(US)*; **~wesen** postal savings system *(US)*.
Post|sparkonto post-office *(Br.)* (postal, *US*) savings account, National Savings Bank Account *(Br.)*, investment account *(Br.)*; **~sparmarke** postal savings stamp *(US)*; **~sperre** suspension of mail *(US)* (postal service); **~spesen** postage; **~station** posthouse; **~stempel** postmark, date stamp; **mit ~stempel versehen** to date-stamp; **~straße** post road; **~streuung** direct mail advertising *(US)*; **~tag** post day *(Br.)*; **~tarif** postal tariff *(US)*, rates of postage *(Br.)*, postage rates *(Br.)*; **zweistufiges ~tarifsystem** two-tiered mail system *(US)*; **~tasche** delivery bag; **~überwachung** postal control; **~überweisung** mail transfer *(US)*, post remittance *(Br.)*, *(im Bankauftrag)* bank post remittance *(Br.)*; **~überweisungsauftrag** mail transfer order *(US)*.
Postulat postulation.
Post|umschlagstelle schedule point *(US)*; **~union** Postal Union; **~unternehmer** postal transport contractor; **~verbindung** postal communication; **~verkehr** postal (mail, *US*) service; **~verkehr einstellen** to suspend postal (mail, *US*) service.
Postversand mail order, mailing, delivery of postal matters;
vom ~ ausgeschlossen nonmailable *(US)*; **zum ~ zugelassen** mailable;
~ zollpflichtiger Artikel green-label services *(Br.)*;
~abteilung outward mail department *(US)*; **~arten** mail classification; **~artikel** mailings, wrap-up; **~auftrag** mail order.
postversandfähig mailable.
Postversand|firma mail-order company; **~gebühr** outward fee; **~geschäft** mail-order business (concern, establishment, house, selling), postal trade; **~katalog** mail-order catalog(ue); **~liste** post-office (mailing) list; **j. in die ~liste aufnehmen** to add s. one's name to the mailing list; **~material** mailings, wrap-up; **~reklame** mail-order advertising; **~stelle für Sammlermarken** post-office philatelistic bureau *(Br.)*; **~unternehmen** mail-order establishment (house); **~verkauf** mail-order selling; **~verteilung** distribution of the incoming mail; **~werbung** mail-order publicity.
Post|-, Wasser- und Elektrizitätsversorgung unterbrechen to cut off post, water and electricity services; **~verteilungsstelle** post-distributing (-separating) office; **~vertrieb** mail-order marketing; **~verwalter** postmaster; **~verwaltung** postal authorities; **~vorschuß** post-office advance; **~wagen, ~waggon** post-office (postal, post, *US*) car, accelerator; **im ~wege verkaufen** to sell by mail.
postwendend by return of post (mail, *US*), by the returning mail *(US)* (post);
~ antworten to answer by return of post (mail, *US*);
~e Antwort immediate reply.
Post|werbung direct-mail (mail-order) advertising, direct-mail solicitation; **~werbungsexemplar** mailing shot.
Postwert|sendung insured item; **~versicherung** registered mail insurance.
Postwertzeichen [postage] stamp;
eingedrucktes ~ impressed stamp; **gummiertes ~** gummed postage stamp;
~ für Eilbestellung special delivery stamp.
Post|wesen postal matters (system); **~wurfprospekt** direct-mail literature; **~wurfsendung** house-to-house distribution, bulk mail, unaddressed mailing *(US)*, direct-mail advertising, *(Einzelstück)* envelope stuffer, mailing piece; **~zahlschein** postal order *(Br.)* (note, *US*); **~zeichen** [postage] stamp.
Postzeitungs|dienst postal newspaper service; **~gebührenordnung** post-office newspaper-charge regulations; **~gut** postal newspaper material; **~liste** post-office (mailing, *US*) list; **~ordnung** postal newspaper service.
Post|zensur censure of the mail, postal censure, postal censorship; **~zollordnung** post-office customs regulations; **~zug** mail [train]; **~zuschlag** surcharge; **~zustellbezirk** postal district (delivery zone, *US*); **~zusteller** postman, postboy, letter carrier, mailman *(US)*.
Postzustellung mail (postal) delivery (service), mail service *(US)*, post;
allgemeine (ortsübliche) ~ general post (delivery); **wetterbedingt verspätete ~** detention of the mail by bad weather.
Postzustellungs|adresse post-office address; **~dienst** postal (mail, *US*) service.
Postzwang postal principle *(US)*.
Potential potential[ity], capacity;
industrielles ~ industrial capacity; **militärisches ~** military potential; **wirtschaftliches ~** economic potential;
vorhandenes ~ an Arbeitskräften labo(u)r force available;
~ erschöpfen to exhaust a potential.

potentiell | er Ausstoß einer Volkswirtschaft potential output of the national economy; **~e Gefahr** possible danger; **~er Kunde** prospective customer, prospect *(US)*; **~er Markt** potential market.
Potenz *(math.)* power;
Taugenichts in höchster ~ sein to be a good-for-nothing of the first water.
potenzieren *(math.)* to raise a power;
Wirkung ~ to have an intensive effect.
potenzierte Faulheit utter laziness.
Potestativbedingung postetative condition.
Potpourri hotchpot, salmagundi, *(Musik)* potpourri, medley.
PR *(Öffentlichkeitsarbeit)* public relations;
~-Chef public-relations manager.
Präambel preamble, preface, caption, *(Policenformular)* recital clause;
falsche ~ misrecital;
~ schreiben to preamble.
Pracht pomp, splendo(u)r, magnificence, *(Luxus)* sumptuousness, luxury;
kalte ~ cold ostentation; **verschwenderische ~** extravagant splendo(u)r;
~ der Farben richness of colo(u)rs;
~ entfalten to display splendo(u)r; **der ~ und der Eitelkeit dieser sündigen Welt entsagen** to renounce the pomps and vanities of this wicked world; **wahre ~ sein** to be a real treat; **wahre ~ in seiner neuen Uniform sein** to be a gorgeous figure in one's new uniform;
~ausgabe edition de luxe, splendid edition; **~bau** magnificent edifice; **~einband** choice binding; **~entfaltung** pomp and circumstance; **~exemplar** beauty buster *(sl.)*.
prächtig splendid, magnificent, superb;
sich ~ amüsieren to have a gorgeous time;
~er Schmuck magnificent jewels; **~es Wetter** glorious (splendid) weather.
Pracht | kerl peach of a fellow; **~mensch** trump, crackerjack; **~straße** boulevard, avenue *(US)*; **~stück** finest specimen, showpiece, daisy.
prachtvoll splendid, magnificent, gorgeous;
~ ausgestatteter Raum magnificently furnished room; **~er Schmuck** magnificent jewels; **~es Wetter** splendid weather.
prädestiniert sein, seit Geburt für die militärische Laufbahn to be destined from birth for the army.
Prädikat grading, rating, marks;
Prüfung mit ~ bestehen to obtain first-class hono(u)rs; **niedrigstes ~ erhalten** *(Universität)* to be put in the gulf *(Br., sl.)*; **~ „wertvoll" erhalten** *(Film)* to be highly recommended; **jem. das ~ des schlechtesten Außenministers seit vielen Jahren geben** to label s. o. the worst foreign minister since many years.
Prädikatsexamen hono(u)rs' degree;
~ machen to obtain first-class hono(u)rs.
Präfekt prefect.
Präferenz preference, *(Zoll)* preferential *(Br.)* (most-favo(u)red-nation) treatment;
bekundete ~ revealed preference;
~ genießen to be given preferential treatment, to enjoy preferential (most-favo(u)red-nation) treatment;
~abgaben preferential levies; **~abkommen, ~abmachung** *(GATT)* preferential arrangement, preferential trade agreement; **~anspruch** preferential claim; **~bedingungen** preferential terms; **~gebiet** preference (preferential tariff) area; **~ordnung** scales of preference; **~politik** most-favo(u)red-nation policy; **mengenmäßige ~regelung** preferential quantitative arrangement; **~spanne** margin of preference, preference margin; **~system** preferentialism; **~zoll** preferential tariff (duty); **~zollsatz** preferential (most-favo(u)red-nation) rate.
Präge | anstalt mint; **~druck** relief printing, letterpress; **~form** coining die; **~gebühr, ~kosten** mintage, cost of coining, coinage; **~lohn** seigniorage, mintage.
prägen to take a cast, to emboss, to stamp, *(Blech)* to stamp, *(Buchbinderei)* to tool, *(Leder)* to emboss, *(Matern)* to press, to cut, *(Pappe)* to die-cut;
Charakter ~ to mould a character; **Falschgeld ~** to counterfeit (forge) money; **ins Gedächtnis ~** to imprint on one's memory; **Geld ~** to coin money, to strike coins; **Gesicht ~** to leave its mark on a face; **Namen auf eine Medaille ~** to stamp a name on a medal; **Silber in Münzen ~** to mint silver into coins; **neue Wörter ~** to coin new words; **sein Zeitalter ~** to leave an impress upon one's age.
Präge | ort mint; **~platte** *(Buchbinderei)* binder's block; **~presse** minting press, *(Blech)* screw press; **~recht** seign(i)orage, royalty; **unbegrenztes ~recht** free coinage; **~siegel** impressed seal; **~stempel** die, coin, stamp, puncheon, *(Buchbinderei)*, tool, block; **mit ~stempel pressen** to block, to tool.
pragmatisch | handeln to act in a practical way;
~e Geschichtsschreibung pragmatic historiography.
prägnant terse, precise, exact, trenchant;
um es ~ auszudrücken to put it concisely;
~e Bemerkungen pithy sayings; **~es Ereignis** pregnant event; **~er Stil** concise (terse) style.
Prägnanz terseness, conciseness.
Prägung mintage, coinmaking, coinage, *(Buchbinderei)* tooling, blocking;
~ eines Charakters moulding of a character;
Demokratie englischer ~ sein to be a democracy of English pattern; **Künstler eigenwilliger ~ sein** to be an artist with a highly individual style.
prahlen to show off, to brag, to put on the dog;
mit etw. ~ to pride o. s. on s. th., to plume o. s.; **mit seinem Auto ~** to parade with one's car; **mit seinen Heldentaten ~** to boast of one's exploits; **mit seinen Kenntnissen ~** to trot out one's knowledge; **mit seinem neu erworbenen Reichtum ~** to flaunt one's new riches.
Prahlerei bounce, jactation, blow *(US sl.)*, showing off, brag.
prahlerisch boasting, bragging, *(prunkend)* ostentatious.
Prahlhans braggart, blower, blow *(US sl.)*;
~ sein to pass gas *(sl.)*.
Präjudiz prejudice, preclusion, precedent.
Präjudizienrecht judge-made law.
präjudizieren *(jur.)* to prejudice;
Anspruch ~ to prejudice a claim; **Frage ~** to anticipate a decision.
Präklusion estoppage, foreclosure.
Präklusionswirkung preclusive effect.
Präklusivfrist time limit, deadline *(US)*.
praktikabel practicable, feasible, workable.
Praktikant practitioner, learner, improver, probationer, non-apprentice, on-the-job trainee *(US)*, *(Kanzlei)* articled clerk *(Br*;
~en ausnutzen to sweat probationers.
Praktikanten | ausbildung rotation training; **~lohn** learner wages; **~stelle** vacancy for a trainee.
Praktiken practices, machinations, tricks, dodges;
restriktive ~ restrictive practices; **unsaubere ~** manipulations, sharp practices, underhand dealings;
unsaubere ~ anwenden to resort to dodges (tricks).
Praktiker practised hand, practitioner;
alter ~ old hand, routinist;
alter ~ sein to know the ropes.
Praktikum practical [course];
sein ~ absolvieren to undergo a practical training.
Praktikus, alter old hand, routinist.
praktisch practical, in practice, applied, to all intents and purposes, virtually, *(sachlich)* matter-of-fact, down-to-earth;
~ durchführbar feasible, workable; **~ gesehen** for all practical purposes; **~ wertlos** of no practical value;
~ anwenden to reduce to practice; **~ die Kontrolle ausüben** to have practical control of; **~ funktionieren** to work in practice; **~ eingestellten Menschen gefallen** to appeal to practical minds; **~ veranlagt sein** to be able to turn one's hand to anything; **~ verwerten** to put into (reduce to) practice;
~e Anwendung practical application (experience); **~er Arzt** general (qualified medical) practitioner; **~e Ausbildung** on-the-job training; **~es Beispiel** working example; **~e Durchführung** practicability; **~e Erfahrung** practical experience; **~e Gebrauchseigenschaften** service properties; **in ~er Hinsicht** for all practical purposes; **~es Jahr** practical; **~e Kenntnisse** practical knowledge; **sich im ~en Leben bewährt haben** to have proved one's worth (shown one's mettle) in all situations; **nach ~en Lösungen suchen** to get down to practicalities; **~ veranlagter Mensch** practically-minded person; **~e Nationalökonomie** applied political economy; **~e Psychologie** applied psychology; **~er Unterricht** object lessons; **~e Veranlagung** practicality; **~er Versuch** field test; **~er Vorschlag** practical proposal.
praktizieren to be in practice, to practise;
freiberuflich ~ to free-lance; **jem. ein Geldstück in die Tasche ~** to slip a coin into s. one's pocket; **neue Methoden ~** to employ new methods; **als Rechtsanwalt ~** to practise the law (at the bar); **nur vormittags ~** to have consultation hours only in the morning.
praktizierender Anwalt legal practitioner, practising lawyer.
Präliminar | artikel preliminary article; **~friede** preliminaries of peace.

Präliminarien preliminaries;
~ **eines Vertrages** preliminary articles of a treaty.
Pralinenschachtel box of chocolates.
prall bulging, bursting, *(Glieder)* stout, sturdy, *(Kleidungsstück)* tightly fitting;
~ **gefüllt** crammed full;
~**e Backen** chubby cheeks; ~**er Beutel** plump bag; ~ **gefüllte Brieftasche** well-lined purse; ~ **gefüllte Speisekammer** larder crammed with food; **in der ~en Sonne** in the blazing sun.
prallen to bounce, to bound;
gegen ein anderes Auto ~ to collide with (crash, bump into) another car; **gegen einen Baum** ~ *(Auto)* to hit a tree; **auf die Felder** ~ *(Sonne)* to beat down on the fields; **hart auf das Pflaster** ~ to fall with a hard thud on the pavement.
Prämie premium [pay], consideration, *(Agio)* [exchange] premium, stock discount, *(Anreiz)* bonus, bounty, *(Belohnung)* reward, *(Buchklub)* free gift, *(Extradividende)* bonus, *(für Film)* award, *(Kaufmann)* giveaway *(US)*, goody, *(Lebensversicherung)* life insurance dividend, *(Prämiengeld)* option (forfeit) money, prime, *(Prämiengeschäft)* premium, option, privilege *(US)*, *(Preisverteilung)* award, prize, *(Sozialversicherung)* contribution, *(Verpackungsteileinsendung)* box-top offer *(US)*, *(Versicherung)* premium, rate, *(Wirtschaftsförderung)* bounty, *(Zollvergütung)* drawback, *(Zusatzlohn)* bonus, extra pay, premium pay *(US)*;
ohne ~ ex bonus;
abgekürzte ~ limited premium; **angegebene** ~ specified premium; **anteilige** ~ prorata rate; **ausbedungene** ~ stipulated premium; **ausstehende** ~ outstanding premium, premium due; **bedungene** ~ stipulated premium; **im Einzug befindliche** ~ premium in course of collection; **einheitliche** ~ flat bonus; **einmalige** ~ uniform premium; **erste** ~ opening premium; **fällige** ~ premium due; **noch nicht fällige** ~ *(Versicherung)* deferred premium; **feste** ~ fixed premium; **nach eigenem Ermessen festgesetzte** ~ *(Feuerversicherung)* judgment rate; **tariflich festgesetzte** ~ class rate; **gerechte** ~ equitable rate; **gleichbleibende** ~ level of premium; **gleitende** ~ sliding-scale premium; **höchstmögliche** ~ highest possible award; **hohe** ~ long (high) premium; **jährliche** ~ annual premium; **konstante** ~ level premium; **kostendeckende** ~ net premium; **monatliche** ~ monthly premium; **niedrige** ~ short premium; **pauschale** ~ flat premium, *(Betrieb)* flat bonus; **[nicht] produktionsgebundene (produktions[un]abhängige)** ~ [non]production bonus; **progressive** ~ step-rate premium; **rückständige** ~ premium in arrears; **rückvergütete** ~ return premium; **steuerfreie** ~ tax-free bonus; **veränderliche** ~ variable premium; **verdiente** ~ earned premium; **nicht verdiente** ~ unearned premium; **nachträglich zahlbare** ~ deferred premium; **zusätzliche** ~ additional (supplementary) premium; **zweischneidige** ~ double-option premium;
~ **für verringerte Abfallproduktion** waste-reduction bonus; ~ **für langjährige Betriebszugehörigkeit** longevity pay; ~ **für die Drosselung landwirtschaftlicher Produkte** domestic allowance *(US)*; ~ **für regelmäßige Einhaltung der Dienstzeit** regular attendance bonus; ~ **für einen Erfinder** award to inventor; ~ **zwecks Exportsteigerung** bounty [on exportation]; ~ **für unfallfreies Fahren** no-claim bonus *(Br.)*, preferred risk plan *(US)*; ~ **für gute Führung** *(Schule)* good-conduct prize; ~ **für Produktionsstillegung** nonproduction bonus; ~ **für besonderes Risiko** *(Betrieb)* bonus for special risk; ~ **bei Teileinsendung der Verpackung** box-top offer; ~ **frei von Unkosten** net premium; ~ **für Verbesserungsvorschläge** bonus for improvement suggestions; ~ **für erfolgreiche Verwaltungstätigkeit** management fee bonus; ~ **für Wiederausfuhr** drawback;
~ **abwerfen** to yield a premium; ~ **aussetzen** to put a prize (premium) on; ~**n für besondere Leistungen einschließen** to carry incentive arrangements; ~ **erhöhen** to raise the premium; ~ **erklären** *(Börse)* to declare an option; ~ **festsetzen** to assess (fix) a premium; **durch ~n fördern** to bonus; ~**n fortzahlen** to pay premiums to date; ~ **herabsetzen** to reduce a premium; ~ **vereinbaren** to arrange a premium; **auf ~n verkaufen** to sell at option; **zu einer niedrigen** ~ **versichern** to insure at a low premium; ~ **zum Ausgleich für geringe Pacht zahlen** to pay a premium as a setoff to a small rental; ~ **an eine Lebensversicherung zahlen** to pay a premium with an insurance company; ~ **zurückerstatten** to refund a premium.
Prämien|abrechnung premium statement; ~**abschlag** premium rebate; ~**akkordsystem** task bonus system; ~**änderung** rate change, changes in rates; ~**angleichung** adjustment of premium; ~**anleihe** lottery (premium) loan (bond), interest lottery; ~**anpassung an das konkrete Risiko** individual rating; **produktionsbezogener** ~**anreiz** output-oriented incentive; **verdienter** ~**anteil** prorata premium; ~**aufgabe** abandonment of option money; ~**aufkommen** *(Lebensversicherung)* premium income, earned premium; ~**aufschlag** loading; ~**aufwendungen** premium costs; ~**ausgabe** bond issue; ~**außenstände** outstanding premiums; **auf ~basis arbeiten** to go on a bonus, to work on a bonus system; ~**bedingungen** bonus terms; ~**befreiung** waiver of premium; ~**befreiung bei Tod oder Invalidität** *(Versicherung)* payer benefit.
prämienbegünstigt|sparen können to be eligible for state savings premium;
~**es Sparen** contractual saving *(Br.)*.
Prämien|begünstigung bonus advantage; ~**berechnung** calculation of premiums, premium computation, rating of premiums; ~**berechnungsstelle** rating office; ~**bestandteil** bonus element; ~**beteiligung** *(Lebensversicherung)* special settlement dividend; **fällige** ~**beteiligung** *(Lebensversicherung)* maturity dividend; ~**betrag** [amount of] premium; ~**bildung** rate setting; ~**bon** *(Sparen)* premium savings bond; ~**brief** confirmation of an option deal, option contract; ~**büro** rating bureau; ~**depot** *(Versicherung)* unearned reserve; ~**einkommen**, ~**einnahmen** earned (collected) premium, premium income (funds), *(Arbeiter)* premium pay, bonus earnings; ~**einzahlung** premium deposit; ~**einziehung** collection of premiums; ~**empfänger** bonusee; ~**entrichtung** payment of premium; ~**erhöhung** increase of premium, premium boost (increase); ~**erklärung** *(Börse)* declaration of options *(US)*; ~**erklärungstag** *(Börse)* carrying-over *(Br.)* (contango, *Br.*, making-up, *Br.*, option, *US*) day; ~**ermäßigung** premium reduction; ~**erträge** premium funds; **vorkalkulierter** ~**etat** budgeted expense plan; ~**fälligkeitstag** premium due-date; ~**festsetzung** *(Versicherungsgeschäft)* rate making (setting), rating; ~**festsetzungsausschuß** rate-making committee; ~**festsetzungssystem** *(Feuerversicherung)* system of rating, rating system; ~**fonds** bonus (prize) fund; **treuhänderisch verwaltete** ~**fonds** *(Lloyds)* Premium Trust Fund.
prämienfrei free of premium, paid up;
~**e Versicherung** paid-up insurance.
Prämien|geber *(Börse)* giver of option money; ~**geld** duty pay, *(Börse)* option money; **durch ~gelder flüssig sein** to be flush with new bonus money.
Prämiengeschäft premium bargain, *(Börse)* option business (deal), bonus transaction, optional (time) bargain, trading in puts and calls (privileges, *US*), day option *(Br.)*, spread *(US)*, *(Getreidehandel)* indemnity;
nicht ausgeübtes ~ unexercised option; **doppeltes** ~ compound option; **einfaches** ~ single option; **bis zum nächsten Tag 14.45 Uhr laufendes** ~ day-to-day option *(Br.)*;
~ **auf Geben** put; ~ **auf Nehmen** call; ~ **mit zweimal noch** call of twice more *(Br.)*; ~ **bis zum nächsten Tag** day option *(Br.)*;
~ **eingehen** to call an option; ~**e machen** to deal in options.
Prämien|gewährung allowance for bonus, bonus issue; ~**gleichheit** rate equity; ~**grundlage** rate basis; **in eine höhere ~gruppe einstufen** to rate higher (up); ~**handel** *(Börse)* option business, trading in puts and calls (in privileges, *US*); ~**händler** *(Börse)* option dealer; ~**herabsetzung** reduction of premium; ~**höhe** [amount of] premium, *(Versicherung)* rate level; ~**kauf** *(Börse)* purchase of an option; ~**käufer** *(Börse)* giver of option money, option buyer; ~**konkurrenz** rate competition; ~**konto** bonus account; ~**kosten** premium costs; ~**kurs** *(Börse)* option price; ~**leistung** premium payment; ~**leiter** scale of premiums.
Prämienlohn premium (incentive) pay, premium bonus (wage); ~**abkommen** incentive pay agreement; ~**satz** incentive (piece) rate; ~**system** premium (incentive wage) plan, premium wage system, piece-rate (reward) system, weir system.
Prämien|los lottery bond *(US)*; ~**lotterie** interest lottery; ~**makler** *(Börse)* privilege broker *(US)*; ~**marke** trading stamp; ~**markt** *(Börse)* options market; ~**mittel** premium funds; ~**nachlaß** premium rebate, discount; ~**nachlaß bei Gruppenversicherung** fleet discount; ~**nachlaß bei Schadensfreiheit** *(Kraftfahrzeugversicherung)* no-claim bonus *(Br.)*, preferred risk plan *(US)*; **ausgeloste** ~**nummer** prize-winning bond number; ~**obligationen** premium bonds (debentures); ~**pfandbriefe** lottery mortgage debentures *(Br.)* (bonds, *US*); ~**plan** premium (savings) plan; ~**programm** incentive (bonus) program(me); ~**prozentsatz** percentage premium; ~**quittung** premium receipt; ~**rabatt** premium rebate, discount; ~**rate** premium rate (instalment); ~**rechnung** *(Versicherung)* premium note, renewal notice; ~**recht ausüben** *(Börse)* to exercise an option, to declare options; ~**regelung** premium system; ~**regulierung** rate adjustment.

Prämienreserve unearned premium reserve, actuarial reserve, *(Deckungsstock)* premium reserve fund, *(Lebensversicherung)* reserve (life) fund, net value, insurance reserve;
~ **zum Jahresschluß** terminal reserve.

Prämienrück|erstattung reimbursement of premium; **~gewähr** return (refund) of premium; **~gewährpolice** return premium policy; **~stände** premium in arrears, arrears of premium, overdue premium, outstanding premiums.

Prämiensachverständiger rating engineer.

Prämiensatz premium rate, rate of insurance, rate of consideration *(US)*, insurance rate, *(Börse)* rate of option *(Br.)*, option rate (price) *(Br.)*;
ermäßigter ~ low premium;
~ **für Lebensversicherung** life rate; ~ **der Seetransportversicherung** marine rate; **erhöhter** ~ **für Versicherungen unter einem Jahr** short-period rate, short-period premium scale; ~ **für über ein Jahr ausgestellte Versicherungsprämie** long rate;
~ **erhöhen** to raise the premium; ~ **für ein Versicherungsrisiko festsetzen** to quote a premium rate for a risk; ~ **für eine Generalversicherung mitteilen** to quote a rate for an open policy; **jem. einen günstigen** ~ **zugestehen** to accord s. o. favo(u)rable rates.

Prämien|schatzanweisung premium treasury bond *(US)*; **~schein** premium bond (token), prize-drawing ticket; **aufgrund von Erfahrungen aufgestelltes ~schema** experience-rating plan; **~schuldverschreibungen** premium bonds (debentures); **~schwindel** premium dodge; **~senkung** lowering (reduction) of premiums, rate cutting; **~spareinlagen** contractual savings deposits *(Br.)*; **~sparen** contractual saving *(Br.)*; **~sparkonto** contractual savings account *(Br.)*; **indexgekoppeltes ~sparsystem** save as you earn *(Br.)*; **~sparvertrag** contractual saving agreement *(Br.)* (contract, *Br.*); **~spekulant** *(Börse)* option operator; **~staffelung** scale of premiums; **~stornierung** cancellation of premium; **in eine höhere ~stufe einstufen** to rate up; **~stundung** deferment of payment of a premium.

Prämiensystem *(Betrieb)* premium (bonus, wage-incentive) plan, bonus system, *(Exportförderung)* system of bounties;
beschleunigtes ~ accelerated bonus plan; **kollektives** ~ group bonus plan.

Prämien|tabelle scale of premiums; **~tarif** insurance tariff; **~tarif für Vorzugsplazierung** *(Anzeigenwesen)* premium rate; **~überhang** reserve for unearned premiums, unearned premium reserve; **~überschüsse** *(Lebensversicherung)* net premium income; **~unternehmen** gift enterprise; **~verdienst** premium pay, bonus earnings; **~vergütung** bonus payment; **~verkauf** *(Börse)* option sale, sale of an option; **~verkäufer** *(Börse)* taker of option money; **~versicherung** proprietary insurance, proprietary assurance *(Br.)*; **reine ~versicherung** nonparticipating insurance; **~versicherungsgesellschaft** proprietary insurance company; **~verteilung** distribution of prizes, bonus distribution; **~verzeichnis** premium catalog(ue); **~verzicht** abandonment of premiums; **~volumen** total of premiums collected; **~ware, ~werte** *(Börse)* securities dealt on the option market, stock on option *(Br.)*, option stocks *(Br.)*; **~wesen** incentive plan; **~wettbewerb** rate competition.

Prämienzahlung payment of premiums, premium payment;
abgekürzte ~ limited premium; **einmalige** ~ single payment; **laufende** ~ regular payment of premiums;
~ **mit weit auseinander liegenden Zeiträumen** *(Lebensversicherung)* ordinary business;
~en wiederaufnehmen to reinstate an insurance.

Prämien|zahlungszeit premium-paying period; **~zertifikat** bond unit; **~zettel** premium bond; **~ziehung** prize drawing (draw).

Prämienzuschlag extra (additional) premium, extra pay, *(Gefahrenzuschlag)* hazard bonus, *(Verwaltungskosten)* load;
~ **für Verwaltungskosten erheben** to load.

Prämienzuteilung bonus distribution.

prämiieren to award a prize, to reward with a premium, to place a premium on;
Verbesserungsvorschlag ~ to award suggested improvements.

prämiierter Roman prize novel.

Prämiierung awarding [of prizes], giving out the awards.

prangen, mit einem neuen Anzug to be resplendent in a new suit;
am Himmel ~ *(Sonne)* to glitter in the sky.

Pranger, am in the pillory;
j. an den ~ **stellen** to put s. o. into the pillory.

pränumerando zahlen to prepay, to pay in advance (by anticipation, beforehand), to make payments in advance.

Pränumerandozahlung payment in advance (by anticipation), prepayment.

Präparat, handelsübliches commercial preparation.

präparieren, sich to do one's homework, to prepare one's lessons.

Prärogativ prerogative, peculiar.

präsent|haben to have s. th. to hand; **das genaue Datum nicht** ~ **haben** not to be able to recall the exact date; **jem.** ~ **sein** to be fresh in s. one's mind.

präsentabler Erfolg respectable success.

Präsentant *(Scheck)* bearer, *(Wechsel)* party presenting, presenter.

Präsentation presentation, presentment, *(Wechsel)* sight;
~ **der Waren im Einzelhandelsgeschäft** retail merchandising of goods.

Präsentationsrecht right of nomination, *(Pfründe)* avowson.

präsentieren to present, *(Wechsel)* to sight, *(Zeitungsartikel)* to feature;
jem. die Rechnung ~ to present s. o. with the bill, *(fig.)* to make s. o. pay for it; **Wechsel zur Annahme** ~ to present a bill for acceptance.

Präsentierteller salver;
auf dem ~ **sitzen** to be on general show (the pan, *sl.*).

Präsentierung presentation, presentment, *(Wechsel)* sight;
beeindruckende ~ **statistischen Materials** imposing array of statistics.

Präsenz presence, attendance, *(Truppen)* present strength;
indirekte ~ constructive presence;
~bibliothek reference library; **~gelder** attendance fees; **~liste** attendance list (sheet); **~stärke** *(mil.)* effective strength.

Präsident president, chairman, chair, principal, presiding officer, governor, chief (first) magistrate, executive, *(College)* warden, *(Gericht)* chief justice, *(Institut)* warden, *(Kongreß)* speaker, *(Unternehmen)* president, chief executive [officer] *(US)*;
amtierender ~ acting president; **designierter** ~ president designate; **ehrenamtlicher** ~ honorary president; **geschäftsführender** ~ managing president; **gewählter (noch nicht eingeführter)** ~ president-elect *(US)*; **auf Lebenszeit gewählter** ~ permanent president; **neuer** ~ new president; **stellvertretender** ~ vice-president;
~ **der Anwaltskammer** Dean of Faculty *(Scotland)*; ~ **des statistischen Bundesamts** Director of Census *(US)*; ~ **des Bundesrechnungshofes** Comptroller and Auditor General *(Br.)*, Comptroller General *(US)*; ~ **des Geheimen Staatsrats** Lord President of the Council *(Br.)*; ~ **des Kassationshofes** Judge-Advocate-General; ~ **des Münzamtes** Director of the Mint *(US)*; ~ **des Patentamtes** Commissioner of Patents *(US)*, Comptroller General of Patents, Designs and Trademarks *(Br.)*; ~ **des Rechnungshofes** state comptroller; ~ **des Staatsschuldenregisters** Accountant and Comptroller General *(Br.)*; ~ **einer Universität** chancellor of a university;
als ~ **kandidieren** to run for the presidency; **schon** ~ **gewesen sein** to have passed the chair; **j. zum** ~ **wählen** to elect s. o. [to be] president, to vote s. o. into the chair.

Präsidenten|amt presidency, chairmanship; **~anwärter** presidential prospect; **~clique** palace guard; **~nachfolge** presidential succession *(US)*; **~platz** presidential chair; **~reise** presidential trip; **~schaft im Rat der Europäischen Gemeinschaft** Council presidency; **~schaft im Europäischen Ministerrat stellen** to hold the council presidency; **~stelle** presidency, presidentship; **~stuhl** presidential chair; **~stuhl besteigen** to take the chair; **~suite** presidential suite; **~wahl** election of a president, presidential election; **~wahl annehmen** to consent to being president; **kein ~wahljahr** off year *(US)*.

Präsidentschaft presidency, chairmanship, presidentship;
für die ~ **kandidieren** to run (stand) for the presidency *(US)*.

Präsidentschafts|jahr presidential year; **~kandidat** presidential candidate (nominee); **~kandidaten benennen** to nominate a man for the presidency; **~nachfolger** successor to the presidency; **endgültige ~vorwahl** runoff primary *(US)*; **~wahlen** presidential elections; **~zeit** presidential term.

Präsidialausschuß presidential committee;
geschäftsführender ~ executive board committee.

Präsidial|demokratie presidential system, presidential democracy; **~erlaß** presidential decree; **~kanzlei** presidential bureau; **~mitglied** board member; **~sitzung** board meeting; **~system** predidential system.

präsidieren to be in (occupy) the chair, to preside over, to act as chairman;
einem Ausschuß ~ to preside over (chair) a committee.

Präsidium presidency, chairmanship, chair, *(Direktorium)* board of directors, *(Verein)* house committee;
~ **übernehmen** to take the chair.

prasseln *(Fragen)* to be fired from all sides, *(Feuer)* to crackle, *(Regen)* to beat down, to rattle;
Schimpfworte auf j. ~ lassen to shower s. o. with abuses.
prasselnder Beifall thundering applause.
prassen to feast, to indulge o. s., to live in luxury;
mit seinem Geld ~ to scatter money broadcast, to fling one's money about.
Prasser spendthrift, squanderer.
Prasserei feast, gourmandizing;
nächtliche ~en genießen to have a night out *(fam.)*.
präsumptiv presumptive, *(Gesetz)* constructive.
Präsumptiverbe heir presumptive *(Br.)*.
Präventireaktionen *(mil.)* preemptive strike.
präventiv preventive, prophylactic.
Präventiv|angriff preemptive strike; **~behandlung** preventive treatment; **~krieg** preventive war; **~maßnahmen** preventive measures; **~zensur** pre-censorship.
Praxis *(Anwalt)* clientele, *(Anwalt, Arzt)* practice, *(Ausübung)* practice, application, *(Behandlungsraum)* consulting room, doctor's office *(US)*, *(Brauch)* usage, custom, *(Erfahrung)* [practical] experience;
in der ~ in practice, practically; **ohne [jede] ~** raw; **anwaltliche ~** practice of law; **ärztliche ~** practice of medicine, medical practice; **große ~** large practice; **handelsübliche ~** commercial (trade) practice, usage, custom; **langjährige ~** long personal experience; **lukrative ~** lucrative practice; **ständige ~** established practice;
~ der Gerichte court practice;
seine ~ aufgeben to retire from practice; **~ aufmachen** to put up one's shingle; **~ ausüben** to practise, to carry on a practice, *(Anwalt)* to practise at the bar *(Br.)* (as attorney, *US*); **ärztliche ~ ohne Approbation ausüben** to practise medicine without being qualified; **langjährige ~ auf einem Gebiet besitzen** to have long years of experience in a field; **Schwierigkeiten eines Planes bei der Umsetzung in die ~ bewältigen** to overcome the practical difficulties of a scheme; **seine ~ eröffnen** to put up one's shingle; **~ erwerben** to buy a practice; **~ haben** to be in practice; **seine ~ geöffnet haben** to have consulting hours; **sich eine ~ schaffen** to work up a practice as a physician; **~ übernehmen** to take over a practice; **Prinzip in die ~ umsetzen** to put a principle into practice; **über entsprechende berufliche ~ verfügen** to be an old hand at it; **seine ~ verkaufen** to sell one's practice;
~aufsuche office calls; **~ausübung** *(Anwalt)* practice of law.
praxisfremd sein to be out of step with practice.
Praxis|räume practising premises, consulting (waiting) room, *(Anwalt)* chambers; **~vergütung** practice allowance *(Br.)*; **~verwaltung** practice administration.
Präzedenzfall leading case (decision), [case in] precedent, leading (precedential) case, prejudication *(pol.)*, test case;
bindender ~ binding precedent; **nicht bindender ~** persuasive authority (precedent);
~ abgeben (bilden) to constitute a precedent (leading case); **~ anführen** to cite (quote, invoke) a precedent; **etw. als ~ betrachten** to take s. th. as a precedent; **~ vor die Gerichte bringen** to fight a test case in court; **sich über einen ~ hinwegsetzen** to overrule a precedent; **~ schaffen** to set a precedent.
Präzedenz|recht case law; **~streit** precedence question.
präzise precise, by the card;
ganz ~ sein to speak by the card.
präzisieren to state precisely, to specify.
Präzisierung precise statement.
Präzision precision, preciseness, accuracy;
mit der ~ eines Uhrwerks with clockwork precision;
ausreichende ~ fair accuracy;
~ einer Schätzung closeness of an estimation.
Präzisions|arbeit precision work, finest workmanship; **~instrument** precision instrument; **~kompaß** fair compass; **~technik** high-precision engineering; **~uhr** precision clock; **~waage** precision scale; **~werkzeug** precision tool.
Präziswechsel fixed bill *(Br.)*.
predigen, tauben Ohren to preach to deaf ears.
Prediger in der Wüste a voice in the wilderness.
Predigt sermon, *(Ermahnung)* talking-to;
jem. eine ~ halten to give s. o. a lecture, to preach s. o. a sermon, to give s. o. a good talking-to.
Preis price, *(Belohnung)* reward, premium, *(Fahrgeld)* fare, *(Gebühr)* charge, fee, *(Kosten)* cost, expense, price, *(Satz)* rate, figure, *(Summe)* amount, sum, *(Tarif)* rate, tariff, charge, *(Wert)* value, *(im Wettbewerb)* prize, award;
auf der Grundlage der ~e vom Jahr 1982 at 1982 survey prices; **bei sinkenden ~en** by declining prices, at prices dropping; **bis zum ~e von** as high as; **mit ~en versehen** priced, price-tagged; **mit festem ~** without discount, straight *(US)*; **niedrig im ~** low-priced; **um jeden ~** at any price, at all costs; **um keinen ~** not at any price, on no account; **unter [dem Selbstkosten] ~** priced below cost; **zu erhöhten ~en** at a higher price; **zu bedeutend ermäßigten ~en** at a sweeping reduction; **zu festem ~** at one price, at a firm rate; **zu herabgesetztem ~** at a reduced price, reduced, cut-price, at reduced rates, *(Taxpreis)* at a damaged valuation; **zu jedem ~** at any price (rate); **zu teuren ~en** at a high cost; **zu überhöhten ~en eingekauft** dear-bought, bought at excessive cost; **zu unerschwinglichen ~en** at prices beyond one's means; **zu dem verzeichneten ~** at price quoted; **zu zurückgesetztem ~** at a reduced price; **zum ~e von** at the charge (rate) of; **zum ermäßigten ~** at a lower rate; **zum festgesetzten ~** at the given price; **zum amtlich festgesetzten ~** at the established price; **zum gleichen ~** at a rate; **zum halben ~** at half price, for half the price; **zum niedrigsten ~** dirt-cheap; **zum vereinbarten ~** at the understood price;
~ freibleibend price subject to change without notice;
in verbindlichen Angeboten abgegebene ~e prices quoted in tenders; **abgemachter (abgesprochener) ~** settled price, price agreed upon, stipulated price; **abweichende ~e** diverging prices; **überhöhter, vom Kunden akzeptierter ~** class price; **allerniedrigster ~** rock-bottom price, lowest computation; **allgemeingültiger ~** allround price; **amtlicher ~** official price; **nicht amtlicher ~** *(Börse)* sidewalk price *(US)*; **angebotener ~** price offered; **angegebener ~** quoted price; **auf der Rechnung angegebener ~** invoice[d] price; **angehobener ~** advanced price; **angemessener ~** reasonable (fair, adequate, equitable) price; **angesetzter ~** quoted price; **annehmbarer ~** fair rate, reasonable price (terms); **anziehender ~** attractive price; **äquivalenter ~** making-up price; **knapp aufrechterhaltener ~** barely supported price; **augenblicklicher ~** market price; **vertraglich ausbedungener ~** price agreed upon, contract price; **ausgemachter ~** settled price; **ausgezeichneter ~** marked price; **auskömmlicher ~** remunerative price; **äußerster ~** rock-bottom (close) price, cut rate, lowest computation (possible price), *(Auktion)* knockdown price; **künstlich beeinflußter ~** manipulated price; **vor Verkaufsbeginn von der Konkurrenz bekanntgegebener ~** open price; **bescheidene ~e** moderate prices; **beweglicher ~** elastic (flexible) price; **bewirtschafteter ~** administered price; **billiger ~** budget (moderate, low) price; **bisheriger ~** previous rate; **Herstellungs- und Generalkosten deckender ~** overhead price; **nicht die Selbstkosten deckender ~** losing price; **stark divergierende ~e** wide prices; **doppelter ~** *(Anzeige)* double rate; **durchschnittlicher ~** average price; **echter ~** commercial price; **effektiver ~** real (actual) price; **eingefrorene ~e** frozen prices, price rigidity; **eingependelter ~** established price; **einheitlicher ~** uniform price; **empfohlener ~** reference (suggested, recommended) price; **über das Lohnniveau emporschnellende ~** prices outsoaring the wages; **enormer ~** huge (ruinous) price; **erhöhter ~** increased (inflated) price; **ermäßigter ~** reduced (short, cut) price; **Sicherungsvorschuß erschöpfender ~** *(Termingeschäft)* exhaust price; **erschwingliche ~e** prices suited to the average pocketbook; **[tatsächlich] erzielter ~** price obtained, actual price; **exorbitanter ~** exorbitant (outrageous) price; **fakturierter ~** invoiced price; **fallende ~e** dropping (sagging, declining, receding) prices; **feste ~e** standing (fixed, flat, steady) prices, *(Schaufenster)* no abatement (discount, reduction); **fester ~** fixed (firm, standing) price; **künstlich festgelegter ~** administered price; **festgesetzter ~** stated (fixed) price; **amtlich festgesetzter ~** administered (controlled) price, price as fixed by the authorities; **vertraglich festgesetzter ~** fixed contract price; **freibleibender ~** price subject to change without notice, open-matter price; **friedensmäßige ~e** prices at peace-time level; **früherer ~** previous price; **gängiger ~** salable price; **garantierter ~** guaranteed price; **gebotener ~** offer, bid (offered) price; **gebundener ~** fixed (fixed-selling, maintained, controlled) price, *(Kartell)* fixed cartel price, *(Einzelhandel)* fixed (minimum) resale price; **geforderter ~** asked price, charge; **gegenwärtiger ~** ruling (current, prevailing, actual, market) price; **künstlich gehaltener ~** pegged price; **gelenkter ~** controlled price; **augenblicklich geltender ~** ruling (present, prevailing, market, current) price; **in der ganzen Industrie geltender ~** industry-wide price; **genauester ~** nearest price; **genehmigter ~** approved price; **genormter ~** standardized price; **gepfefferte ~e** steep prices; **zu geringer ~** underrated price; **gestaffelter ~** graduated (scheduled) price; **in Rechnung**

gestellter ~ invoiced price; **gesteuerter** ~ manipulated price; **gestoppter** ~ stop price; **gestützter** ~ pegged (supported) price; **gesunkener** ~ reduced price; **gewöhnlicher** ~ customary charge, common price (charge); **für den Fortschritt gezahlter** ~ price paid for progress; **gleitender** ~ price subject to amendment, escalation (sliding-scale) price; **[augenblicklich] gültiger** ~ going (current, market) price; **allgemein gültiger** ~ allround price; **im internen Verrechnungsverkehr gültiger** ~ internal price; **günstige** ~**e** favo(u)rable terms (prices); **günstiger** ~ favo(u)rable (attractive) price; **sehr günstiger** ~ highly concessional price; **halber** ~ half price; **handelsüblicher** ~ market (ruling) price; **herabgesetzter** ~ reduced (marked-down) price, cut rate; **nicht herabgesetzter** ~ full price; **heraufgesetzter** ~ put-up (marked-up) price; **herrschender** ~ prevailing (ruling) price; **hochgestochener** ~ high-flying price; **höchster** ~ ceiling (maximum) price, price ceiling; **hoher** ~ long (high, advanced) price; **besonders hoher** ~ extra high price; **inflationistische** ~**e** inflationary prices; **inländischer** ~ domestic (home-market) price; **kalkulierter** ~ calculated price; **äußerst kalkulierter** ~ rock-bottom price; **niedrigst kalkulierter** ~ bargain level; **scharf kalkulierter** ~ price cut very fine, cut-rate (close) price; **knappheitsbedingter** ~ scarcity price; **konkurrenzfähiger** ~ competitive (keener) price; **nicht konkurrenzfähiger** ~ uncompetitive price; **konkurrenzloser** ~ unrival(l)ed (unmatched) price; **konstante** ~**e** constant prices, price stability; **kostendeckender** ~ price covering the costs of production; **laufender** ~ ruling price; **zugrunde zu legender** ~ price to be considered; **leidlicher** ~ fairly good price; **letzte** ~**e** previous rates; **letzter** ~ lowest limit; **limitierter** ~ limited price; **lohnender (lukrativer)** ~ remunerative (paying) price; **manipulierter** ~ managed (manipulated) price; **marktentscheidender** ~ key price; **marktgerechter** ~ *(Grundstück)* fair market price; **mäßiger** ~ moderate (reasonable) price; **mittlerer** ~ average price; **mörderischer** ~ cutthroat (ruinously high) price; **nachgebende** ~**e** easing prices; **niedriger** ~ low price, undercharge; **niedrigster** ~ bottom (lowest possible, minimum) price, bargain level; **nomineller** ~ nominal price; **notierter** ~ market (quoted, listed, *US*) value; **fortlaufend notierter** ~ consecutively quoted price; **obiger** ~ above quotation; **optischer** ~ charm price; **ortsüblicher** ~ customary (local) price; **reduzierter** ~ reduced (short, cut) price; **äußerst reduzierter** ~ lowest [possible] rate; **reeller** ~ fair (moderate) price; **regulärer** ~ regular price; **regulierter** ~ administered price; **richtiger** ~ adequate price; **rückgängige** ~**e** dropping (sagging, declining) prices; **rückläufige** ~**e** retrograde (receding, declining) prices; **ruinöser** ~ ruinous price; **saisonbedingter** ~ seasonal price; **in die Höhe schnellende** ~**e** soaring prices; **ganz schöner** ~ smart price; **schwacher** ~ weak price; **schwankende** ~**e** varying (fluctuating) prices; **sinkende** ~**e** sagging (declining, falling) prices; **solider** ~ moderate (fair) price; **spekulativer** ~ speculative price; **spottbilliger** ~ ridiculously low price, dead bargain; **stabiler** ~ steady (stable, settled, stationary, firm, sticky, *US*) price; **starrer** ~ rigid price; **stehender** ~ fixed price; **steigende** ~**e** increasing (rising, advancing) prices; **schnell steigende** ~**e** soaring (booming) prices; **subventionierter** ~ subsidized (support, pegged) price; **nicht subventionierter** ~ full economic price; **tatsächlicher** ~ actual price; **theoretischer** ~ nominal price; **überhöhter** ~ class (stiff, excessive, exaggerated) price; **künstlich überhöhte** ~**e** inflated prices; **übermäßiger** ~ exorbitant price; **übersetzter** ~ exaggerated (overcharged) price; **üblicher** ~ market (current, customary, usual) price, customer charge; **unabhängiger** ~ free price; **vom Lieferort unabhängiger** ~ uniform delivered price *(US)*; **unangemessener** ~ unreasonable price; **unbeschränkter** ~ unlimited price; **unelastischer** ~ rigid price; **unerhörter** ~ fabulous price; **unerschwinglicher** ~ prohibitive price; **ungebundener** ~ free (uncontrolled) price; **unterschiedliche** ~**e** discriminating prices; **unterschwelliger** ~ submarginal price; **unveränderte** ~**e** unchanged rates; **unverbindliche** ~**e** prices subject to alteration; **unverschämter** ~ steep (outrageous) price; **völlig unzulänglicher** ~ inadequate price; **verbindlicher** ~ operative price; **[vertraglich] vereinbarter** ~ price agreed upon (by arrangement), stipulated (agreed, contract) price; **volkstümlicher** ~ popular price; **voller** ~ full price; **vorgeschriebener** ~ administered price; **vorheriger** ~ previous price; **vorteilhafter** ~ attractive price; **weichende** ~**e** sagging (declining, retroactive) prices; **wettbewerbsfähiger** ~ competitive price; **willkürlicher** ~ arbitrary price; **wirtschaftlicher** ~ profitable price; **wucherischer** ~ usurious price; **zivile** ~**e** moderate (reasonable) prices, moderate charges; **auf den Höchstpreis zurückgesetzter** ~ rollback price *(US)*;

~ **bei der Anlieferung** landed cost; ~ **für eine doppelseitige Anzeige in Heftmitte** centerspread price; ~ **für vierfarbige Anzeigen** 4-colo(u)r rate; ~ **laut gültigem Anzeigentarif** rate-card price; ~ **bei Barzahlung** cash price; ~ **in Bausch und Bogen** allround (overhead) price; ~ **einschließlich Bedienung** terms inclusive of service; ~ **frei Bestimmungshafen** landed cost (price); ~ **zur Einführung eines Produktes** early-bird price; ~ **per Einheit** unit price; ~ **für den Endverbraucher** price to the ultimate consumer; ~**e für Endverbraucher incl. Mehrwertsteuer** prices inclusive of vat; **gebundener** ~ **auf der Stufe des Endverbrauchs** maintained minimum resale price; ~ **ab Erzeuger** factory price; ~**e der Erzeugnisse** product (producer's) prices; ~**e landwirtschaftlicher Erzeugnisse** agricultural (farm) prices; ~ **ab Fabrik** factory-gate price; ~ **des trockenen Gedecks** *(Hotel)* price of the dinner excluding wine; ~ **einschließlich Gemeinkosten** overhead price; ~ **frei Grenze** *(EG)* free-to-frontier price; ~ **für Güter und Dienstleistungen** cost of goods and services; ~ **zweiter Hand** secondhand price; ~ **frei Haus** delivered-in price, in-the-mail price; ~ **ab Hof** ex-farm price; ~ **einschließlich aller Kosten** allround price; ~ **incl. sämtlicher Kosten bis zum Schiff** FAS price; ~ **ab Lager** ex-store price; ~ **frei Längsseite Schiff** price free alongside ship; ~ **einschließlich Lieferkosten** delivered price; ~ **für künftige Lieferung** forward price; ~ **für letzte Lieferung** terminal price *(Br.)*; ~ **bei sofortiger Lieferung** price ex store, spot quotation; ~ **eines Markenerzeugnisses** brand price; ~**e verstehen sich einschließlich Mehrwertsteuer** prices include value-added tax; ~ **für greifbare Mengen** spot price; ~**e bei Mengenabnahme** prices shaded for quantities; ~ **einschließlich Porto und Verpackung** price inclusive of postage and packing; ~**e für eine Produktfamilie** price combination *(Br.)*; ~ **bei Ratenzahlung** hire-purchase *(Br.)* (time, deferred-payment, *US*) price; ~ **außerhalb der Saison** off-season price; ~ **ab Schacht** pithead price; ~ **ab Speicher** ex-warehouse price; ~ **für Stromverbrauch** electricity rate; ~ **pro Stück** unit price; ~**e nach dem Tarif** tariff rates; ~ **für Termingeschäfte** futures price *(US)*; ~ **für Übernachtung und Frühstück** price for bed and breakfast; ~ **unverzollt** price ex tax; ~ **ist Verhandlungssache** price is a matter for negotiation; ~ **ohne Verpackung** price excluding packing; ~ **ab Versandbahnhof** at-station price; ~**e für Vorsteuerabzugsberechtigte** prices exclusive vat; ~ **für unverzollte Ware im Zollager** in-bond price; **um keinen** ~ **der Welt** not for the life of me; ~ **auf dem Weltmarkt** world price; ~ **ab Werk** price ex works, trade price, factory price; ~ **unter dem Wert** underprice; ~ **für Wiederverkäufer** discount price; ~ **ab Zeche** pithead price; ~**e in Zeiten der Hochkonjunktur** boomtime prices;

~**e abbauen** to cut (reduce) prices; ~ **abflachen** to flatten prices; **vom** ~ **abhandeln** to obtain a reduction; ~ **absprechen** to settle a price; **jem. einen** ~ **für etw. abverlangen** to charge s. o. a price for s. th.; **auf die** ~**e abwälzen** to pass on prices; **vom** ~ **abziehen** to knock off the price; ~**e angeben** to quote (state) prices; **äußersten** ~ **angeben** to quote the outside price; ~**e angleichen** to adjust prices; ~**e schrittweise angleichen** *(EG)* to approximate prices progressively; ~**e anheben** to jack up (increase) prices *(coll.)*; ~**e anpassen** to adjust (align) prices; ~ **ansetzen** to price; ~ **aufrechterhalten** to keep up the price; **im** ~ **aufschlagen** to go (run) higher, to put on the price; **hohe** ~**e aufzwingen** to corner; ~ **aushandeln** to negotiate a price; ~ **ausmachen** to agree upon a price; ~ **aussetzen** to put a premium (prize) on; ~ **für jds. Kopf aussetzen** to put a price on s. one's head; **mit einem** ~ **auszeichnen** to distinguish with a prize; **mit einem höheren** ~ **auszeichnen** to mark up; ~**e beeinflussen** to influence prices; **seinen** ~ **beibehalten** to hold its price; **in einem Wettbewerb den ersten** ~ **bekommen** to obtain the first prize in a competition, to obtain first place; **etw. zu einem exorbitanten** ~ **bekommen** to obtain s. th. at a ransom price; ~ **benennen** to name a price; ~ **berechnen** to arrive at (calculate) a price; **alten** ~ **berechnen** to charge the old price; **jem. einen zu hohen** ~ **berechnen** to overcharge s. o.; **niedrige** ~**e berechnen** to ask moderate prices; ~ **bestimmen** to fix (go into, determine) a price; ~ **bieten** to offer a price; **angemessenen** ~ **bieten** to bid a fair price; ~ **davontragen** to carry the day (away the bell), to take the cake, to bring home the bacon *(US coll.)*; ~**e drücken** to bring (run, beat) down (bang) prices, to keep prices down; ~**e durcheinanderbringen** to put a crimp in prices *(sl.)*; ~**e einfrieren** to freeze prices; **sich auf einen** ~ **einigen** to agree upon a price; ~ **empfehlen** to recommend (suggest) a price; **sich durch überhöhte** ~**e den Markt entfremden** to price o. s. out of the market; ~ **erfragen** to enquire about the price; ~ **erhöhen** to advance (raise, put up, increase) a price, to jack up prices *(coll.)*; ~e **sprunghaft erhöhen** to jump prices; ~e **immer weiter erhöhen** to pyramid prices; **sich nach dem ~ erkundigen** to ask (enquire about) the price; ~e **ermäßigen** to bring down prices; ~ **ermitteln** to arrive at a price; ~ **erreichen (erzielen)** to realize (obtain, reach, fetch) a price; **bessere ~e erzielen** to secure higher prices; **enorme ~e erzielen** to fetch huge prices; **im ~ fallen** to sag in price, to depreciate; **um den ~ feilschen** to haggle over (about) the price; ~ **festlegen (festsetzen)** to price, to determine a price, to quote (make, arrive at, ascertain, name, fix, lay down) a price, to tariff; ~ **amtlich festsetzen** to establish a price; ~e **entsprechend dem amtlichen Preisindex festsetzen** to gear prices to formulas based on government price indexes; **als ~ fordern** to charge (name) a price, to tax *(US)*; **nach dem ~ fragen** to enquire about (ask) the price; ~e **freigeben** to release (decontrol) prices; ~ **genehmigen** to approve of a price; ~ **gewinnen** to obtain (win, bear away, capture) a prize; **höchste ~e bei einem Wettbewerb gewinnen** to win top hono(u)rs in a competition; **seinen ~ haben** to have a certain value; **Auswirkungen auf die ~e haben** to have repercussions on prices; **auf ~e halten** to stick to prices; **sich weitgehend an die festgesetzten ~e halten** to keep as near as possible to the prices quoted; **sich im ~ halten** to hold up its price; ~ **auf einer amtlich festgesetzten Höhe halten** to freeze a price *(US)*; ~e **niedrig halten** to keep prices down, to hold down prices; ~e **stabil halten** to hold the line on prices; ~ **herabdrücken** to bring (force) down (depress, send, squeeze down) the price; ~ **herabsetzen** to abate (sink) a price, to cheapen, to mark down; ~e **stark herabsetzen** to chop prices; ~e **stillschweigend herabsetzen** to cut prices on the quiet; ~ **heraufsetzen** to put up (increase) a price; ~e **herauftreiben** to jump up (boost, force up, drive up) prices; ~ **herunterbringen** to drive down a price; ~e **herunterdrücken** to bring (force, send) down (screw) prices, to squeeze down prices; **mit dem ~ heruntergehen** to reduce the price; ~ **herunterhandeln** to get a price reduced, to beat down a price; ~e **hinaufschrauben** to send (level, screw, send) up prices, to rig the market; ~e **hochhalten** to keep prices up; ~ **hochschrauben** to screw up (lift) prices; ~e **hochtreiben** to boost (puff up) prices, to bull (rig, *Br.*) the market; **sich einen ~ holen** to land a prize *(coll.)*; ~ **kalkulieren** to arrive at (make out, calculate) a price; ~e **schärfstens kalkulieren** to cut prices to the minimum; ~ **sehr vorsichtig kalkulieren** to establish a price at a low level; **zu festen ~en kaufen** to buy on the scale; **unter ~ kaufen** to underbuy; **völlig unsinnigen ~ kosten** to cost prohibitively high; ~e **lenken** to control prices; **unter dem ~ losschlagen** to sell under value, to let go under price; **zu jedem ~ losschlagen** to sell at a sacrifice; ~ **mindern** to reduce a price; **vom ~ nachlassen** to take off the (make an allowance upon, a reduction in) price, to abate a price; ~ **nennen** to indicate (name) a price; ~ **notieren** to quote a price; **mit der Ladenkasse den ~ notieren** to ring up the price; ~ **realisieren** to obtain a price; ~ **reduzieren** to lower (reduce) a price; ~ **regulieren** to control a price; **nicht auf den ~ sehen** not to consider the price; **mit einem ~ einverstanden sein** to be willing to pay a price; **im ~ konkurrenzfähig sein** to be competitively priced; ~ **senken** to lower (reduce) a price; ~ **drastisch senken** to slash a price dramatically; ~e **durch Subventionsmaßnahmen senken** to roll back prices; ~ **auf etw. setzen** to offer a prize for s. th.; **im ~e sinken** to look down[wards], to run off; ~e **stabilisieren** to stabilize (valorize, *US*) prices; **im ~ stehen** to be worth; **hoch im ~ stehen** to command a high price; **im ~ steigen** to increase (advance, enhance, go up) in price, to get (run) up, to bull; ~e **steigern** to raise prices; ~ **in die Höhe steigern** to bid up a price; ~e **stützen** to peg (buttress, support, *US*) prices; ~e **in die Höhe treiben** to drive up the prices, to bid up prices, to rig the market; **amtlich festgelegten ~ überschreiten** to sell s. th. above the established price; ~e **unterbieten (verderben)** to undercut (cut s. one's) prices; ~ **vereinbaren** to agree upon (negotiate) a price; **über einen ~ verhandeln** to negotiate a price; **zu ermäßigten ~en verkaufen** to sell at reduced prices; **zu einem festen ~ verkaufen** to sell at a fixed price; **zu höheren als den amtlich festgesetzten ~en verkaufen** to sell above the established prices; **etw. zum halben ~ verkaufen** to sell s. th. half-price; **zu herabgesetzten ~en verkaufen** to sell at slashed prices; **zu niedrigerem ~ verkaufen** to sell under value, to undersell; **über ~ verkaufen** to sell s. th. above the established price; **unter ~ verkaufen** to sell under price; **zu einem vernünftigen ~ verkaufen** to sell at a reasonable rate; ~ **verlangen** to demand a price; **zu hohen ~ verlangen** to overprice; **während der Saison enorm hohe ~e verlangen** to stick it on during the busy season; **zu hohe ~e für eine Lieferung verlangen** to overcharge goods; **mit einem ~ versehen** to price; ~e **verteilen** to distribute (present) the prizes; **im ~e niedriger werden** to decline in price; **zum ~ von 2 Dollar verkauft werden** to be priced at $ 2; **ermäßigte ~e durch große Umsätze wettmachen** to sell at a low price and recoup o. s. by large sales; **etw. um jeden ~ haben wollen** to buck for s. th. *(US sl.)*; **vollen ~ zahlen** to pay full fare; ~ **zuerkennen** to make an award, to adjudge a prize; **im ~ zurückgehen** to be on the decline; **der ~ spielt keine Rolle** price is no object; **die ~e sind ins Bodenlose gesunken** the bottom has fallen out of the market; ~e **ziehen heftig an** prices are rising sharply;

~**abbau** price cut, cut in (cutting of, fall in, decline in, reduction of, lowering of) prices; ~**abfall** decline in prices; ~**abkommen,** ~**abmachung** price[-fixing] agreement; **staatliches ~abkommen** price code *(Br.)*; ~**abnahme** fall (drop, decline) in prices; ~**abrede** price[-fixing] agreement, pricing arrangement; ~**abschlag** discount, allowance, price deduction (reduction), abatement; **durchschnittlicher ~abschlag von 3% bei hundert Grundnahrungsmitteln erzwingen** to trim 3% on average off the prices of some 100 basic items; **jem. einen ~abschlag einräumen (gewähren)** to allow a reduced price to s. o., to make an allowance on the (a reduction in) price; ~**abschwächung** easing (sagging) of prices, price weakness; ~**absprache** price agreement (arrangement, scheme), *(Kartell)* price fixing; ~**abstand** disparity in prices, margin; ~**abstufung** graduation of prices; ~**abweichung** price (value) variance, price difference; ~**aktion** price action; ~**änderungen** price changes, price variance (modifications, alterations); ~**änderungen vorbehalten** subject to alterations, prices subject to change without notice; **relative ~änderung** proportionate change in price; ~**änderungsklausel** repricing clause; ~**änderungsmitteilung** price change slip; ~**anfrage** inquiry as to price, price inquiry, request for quotation.

Preisangabe quotation [of a price], indication of price, statement of price, offer, price mark;
mit ~ versehen priced; **ohne ~** unpriced, not priced (marked); **mit ~n versehen** to mark out, to price.

Preisangebot quoted price, quote, quotation, [price] offer;
unverbindliches ~ prices without commitment; **verbindliches ~** firm quotation; **wettbewerbsfähiges ~** competitive quotation; ~ **machen** to offer a price; **niedriges ~ stellen** to quote a lower price.

Preis|angleichung price adjustment, adjustment of prices; ~**anhebung** raising of prices, price increase; ~**ankündigung** price announcement, *(Anzeigen)* rate announcement; ~**anpassung** adjustment of prices, price adjustment, *(an Lebenshaltungskosten)* price escalation; ~**anpassungsklausel** escalator clause; ~**anreiz** price appeal; ~**ansatz** quotation, fixing of a price (rate); ~**anschlag** quotation [of price].

Preisanstieg increase (rise) in prices, price increase (climb, hike, recovery), march of prices;
beschleunigter ~ price acceleration; **nachlassender ~** slowdown in price increase; **plötzlicher ~** price jump (speedup), upsurge in prices, spurt in prices; **40-prozentiger ~** 40% jump in prices; **prozentualer ~** percentage increase in value; **scharfer ~** sharp run-up in prices; **verlangsamter ~** slowing in prices, price slowdown;
~ **überwachen** to police the price increase.

Preis|äquivalent price equivalent; ~**aufblähung** price inflation; ~**aufgabe** prize question; ~**aufgliederung** breakdown of prices; ~**aufhebung** fixed-price lifting.

Preisaufschlag markup, mark-on, supplement, supplemental costs, additional price, *(Zuschlag)* extra cost (charge), additional charge, surcharge;
ohne ~ without extra charge;
~ **für Plazierungswünsche** *(Anzeige)* surcharge for special position.

Preis|aufschwung, plötzlicher sudden advance in prices; ~**aufsicht** price control (surveillance).

Preisauftrieb price increase, enhancement in prices, rise in (rising, upward trend, upward tendency of) prices, upsurge (uptrend, upturn) in prices, price uptrend (increase), price-raising tendency;
konjunkturbedingter ~ cyclical rise in price;
~ **bremsen** to curb the price increase; ~ **verlangsamen** to slow down the upward price trend.

preisauftriebsfördernd price-enhancing.

Preis|auftriebstendenz upward price movement, upward tendency of prices; ~**ausgleich** price adjustment (equalization, escalation); **automatischer ~ausgleich** price escalator; ~**ausgleichsstelle** Office of Price Stabilization, price adjustment board *(US)*; ~**ausschreiben** prize competition, prize contest;

~ausschreiben gewinnen to win a competition; an einem ~ausschreiben teilnehmen to go in for a competition, to compete for a prize; ~aussichten price outlook; ~austausch zwischen Konkurrenten open pricing; ~auswirkungen price effect.

Preisauszeichnung price marking (ticket), shopmark, tag, *(Tätigkeit)* pricing, price marking, label(l)ing;
höhere ~ markup on prices; **verdeckte** ~ pricing in code;
~ **für eine ganze Warenpartie** bulk marking.

Preisauszeichnungs|bestimmungen labelling provisions; **~maschine** marking machine; **~zettel** price tag.

Preis|barometer price barometer; **~basis** price basis.

preisbedingt price-induced.

Preis|bedingungen price conditions, terms; **~beeinflussung** influence on prices; **~befestigung** stiffening of prices; **~begrenzung** holding down prices; **~behauptung** maintenance of prices.

preisbeherrschend price-ruling (-deciding).

Preis|behörde price adjustment board *(US)*; **~- und Lohnbehörde** Prices and Income Board *(Br.)*; **~bemessung** price formation; **~berechnung** pricing, determination (calculation) of a price.

Preisberechnungs|grundlage basis of pricing; **~methode** pricing method (formulation); **~verfahren auf einheitlicher Frachtbasis** basing-point system *(US)*.

preisbereinigt adjusted for price.

Preis|bereinigung purge (adjustment) of prices; **~bereinigungsfaktor** deflator; **~bericht** prices current, market report; **~berichtigungen** price changes, rectification (revision) of prices; **~beruhigung** price stabilization; **~beschränkung** limitation of prices, price control; **~besserung** improvement in prices; **~beständigkeit** steadiness (stability) of prices; **~bestandteil** price element.

preisbestimmend price-ruling (-fixing, -deciding), pricing;
~e Faktoren pricing factors.

Preisbestimmung pricing, calculation (determination) of prices, price fixing, *(Preisbedingung)* price condition;
von der Kapitalverzinsung ausgehende ~ return-on-capital pricing; **pauschalierte** ~ flat pricing;
~ **durch die Konkurrenz** competitive determination of prices; ~ **nach dem Muster** sampling *(US)*.

Preisbestimmungs|grundlage basis of pricing; **~position** *(Großunternehmen)* discretionary market power; **~tabelle** pricing schedule.

Preis|bewegung price range (movement), movement of prices, fluctuation of prices; **rückläufige ~bewegung** downward movement of prices; **unterschiedliche ~bewegungen** disparities in price trend; **~bewerber** competitor, contestant *(US)*; **~bewerbung** competition, prize contest; **~bewertungsmethode** pricing method.

preisbewußt price-conscious.

Preisbewußtsein price consciousness.

preisbezogen linked (related) to prices.

Preisbildung pricing, price range (calculation, making), formation of prices, price formation;
freie ~ free adjustment of prices, freedom of price formation; **gebundene** ~ price fixing; **kostenorientierte** ~ cost-based pricing; **pauschalierte** ~ flat pricing;
~ **auf Durchschnittskostenbasis** average cost pricing; ~ **der zweiten Hand** retail price maintenance; ~ **im freien Wettbewerb** competitive determination of prices; ~ **nach Zonen** zone pricing *(US)*.

Preisbildungs|amt price adjustment board *(US)*; **~faktoren** price determinants, pricing factors; **~funktion** price-making function; **~mechanismus** pricing mechanism; **~system** pricing (delivered price, *US*) system.

preisbindend price-fixing;
~es Unternehmen fair trading firm *(US)*, fair trader *(US)*.

Preisbindung|[für Markenartikel] price maintenance (fixing, *Br.*), resale price fixing (maintenance, *Br.*), fair trade *(US)*; **unberechtigte** ~ unreasonable restraint of trade; **vertikale** ~ vertical price-fixing contract, fair trade [pricing] *(US)*;
~ **der zweiten Hand** resale (retail) price maintenance *(Br.)*, maintenance of resale prices [by local dealers], fair trade [pricing] *(US)*, quality stabilization *(US)*, vertical price-fixing contract, maintaining resale prices, collective enforcement of resale prices, resale price fixing *(Canada)*;
~ **der zweiten Hand aufheben** to abolish resale price maintenance; **aus der** ~ **herausnehmen** to release from the fixed-price obligation; ~ **der Wohnungsmieten lockern** to ease rent controls; **der** ~ **unterliegen** to be subject to a condition as to the price; ~ **verlangen** to maintain fixed resale prices.

Preisbindungs|abkommen, ~absprache *(Einzelhandel)* resale price (price maintenance) agreement, price arrangement scheme, fair trade agreement *(US)*; **~amt** office of fair trading *(US)*; **~bestimmungen** resale price conditions; **~gesetz** Resale Prices Act *(Br.)*; **~klausel** tying clause; **Waren mit ~klausel verkaufen** to sell goods subject to a condition as to the price.

preisbindungsmäßig fair-trade *(US)*.

Preisbindungs|maßnahmen fair trade practices *(US)*; **~stelle** office for fair trading *(US)*; **~system** delivered price system *(US)*; **~vereinbarungen** price arrangement scheme, price-fixing (price maintenance) agreement; **~verfahren** price-fixing proceedings; **~verordnung** price maintenance law; **~vertrag** resale-price agreement.

Preis|brecher price cutter, underseller, undercutter; **~brechergruppen anführen** to lead the price-cutting wave.

preisdämpfend price-curbing.

Preis|deflation price deflation; **~depression** temporary decline in prices, sag *(sl.)*; **~differenz, ~differenzierung** difference in prices, price difference (differential, differentiation), differential price system; **regional bedingte ~differenzierung** basing point pricing system, zone pricing *(US)*; **~differenzierung multinationaler Firmen** compensatory dumping; **~differenzkonto** price variance account; **~diskrepanz** discrepancy in prices, disparity (difference) in prices, price spread *(US)*; **~diskriminierung** price discrimination *(US)*; **~drosselung** price curb; **~druck** pressure of (raid on) prices, depression of the market.

preisdrückender Konkurrent cut-price competitor.

Preis|drücker cutting tradesman, close bargainer (bargainor), underseller, undercutter; **~drückerei** price cutting, undercutting, close bargaining; **~dumping** dumping; **~durchbruch** breakthrough in prices; **~durchschnitt** average price; **~einbruch** depression of prices, break in prices, slump; **~einflüsse** price influences.

preiseinschränkende Bestimmungen price-fixing restrictions.

Preis|einstufung graduation of prices; **~elastizität** price elasticity of demand; **~elastizität des Angebots** elastic supply; **~element** price element; **unverbindliche ~empfehlung** price recommendation, recommended price; **~empfehlung aussprechen** to recommend a price.

preisen to praise, to extol, to glorify, to laud;
j. glücklich ~ to call s. o. lucky.

preisentscheidend price-deciding (-ruling).

Preis|entscheidung pricing decision; **~entwicklung** development of prices, price development (trend, movement), course (trend) of prices; **rückläufige ~entwicklung** declining price trend, downturn in prices; **sich Kopf an Kopf mit der ~entwicklung bewegen** to be moving neck and neck with prices; **abgeschwächte ~entwicklungsprognose abgeben** to muffle one's forecast on prices; **~entzerrungen vornehmen** to straighten out foundered prices; **~erhebung** survey of prices.

Preiserhöhung price advance (increase, climb, hike, *fam.*), rise (increase, improvement) in prices, markup on prices, putting up (on) of prices, raising of prices, price raising, *(Grundstück)* improvement, appreciation;
auf ~en mit äußerster Empfindsamkeit reagierend ultrasensitive to price increases;
rasch um sich greifende ~ price boost *(US)*; **in der Öffentlichkeit gut vorbereitete** ~ well publicized price rise;
versteckte ~ **durch Qualitätsminderung** hidden price increase;
~ **erfahren** to experience a rise in prices; **~en rückgängig machen** to roll the price increases back; **~en so lange wie möglich vermeiden** to delay price increases as long as possible; **in der allgemeinen** ~ **vorangehen** to pace the general increase of living cost; **gegen ~en scharf vorgehen** to keep a lid on prices; ~ **vornehmen** to put up (increase) a price.

Preis|erhöhungstendenz price-rising tendency; **~erholung** recuperation of prices, comeback in prices; **~ermäßigung** price cut, reduction in prices, allowance, abatement, *(beim Bezug von zwei Zeitschriften)* clubbing offer; **~ermittlung** price determination (calculation), pricing; **~ermittlungsabteilung** marking department; **~erstarrung** price freeze (rigidity); **~erwartung** *(Verkäufer)* asking price, price outlook (expectation); **~etikett** price ticket *(US)* (tag); **~etikett feststecken** to pin on a price ticket *(US)*; **~fächer** scale of prices, wide range of prices, price range; **~faktoren** price factors, cost (pricing) factors; **~fall** price drop; **~feilscherei** haggling; **~festigkeit** price firmness; **~festlegung** fixing of prices, price condition, pricing regulation, pricing.

Preisfestsetzung pricing, price making, price determination (fixing), determination of price, fixing of a price, quotation;

neue ~ repricing;
~ **von Fall zu Fall** piecemeal price fixing *(US)*; ~ **nach Zonengebieten** area pricing, *(Fracht)* basing point pricing system, zone pricing *(US)*.
Preisfestsetzungs|ausschuß price-fixing committee *(US)*; ~**bestimmungen** *(EG)* price-fixing rules; ~**richtlinien** pricing rules; ~**wesen** price system.
Preis|feststellung pricing, calculation of prices, quotation; ~**flaute** flatation *(US)*; ~**flexibilität** flexibility of prices; ~**fluktuationen** price fluctuations; ~**folgewirkungen** price implications; ~**forderung** asked price, charge; ~**formel** price formula; ~**frage** prize (sixty-four thousand dollar, *US*) question; ~**freigabe** price decontrol; ~**front** price front; ~**führer** price setter, price leader *(US)*; ~**führerschaft** price setting (leadership, *US*); ~**führerschaft übernehmen** to become the leader in established pricing policies; ~**führerschaftspolitik** follow-the-leader price policy; ~**führerstellung** price setting (leadership) *(US)*.
Preisgabe relinquishment, disclosure, release, *(Schiff)* abandonment, *(Verzicht)* waiver, renunciation, abandonment;
~ **eines Geheimnisses** disclosure of a secret; ~ **vertraulicher Informationen** disclosure of confidential information; ~ **eines Rechtes** yielding (abandonment) of a right; ~ **der Sicherheiten** abandonment of securities.
Preisgarantie price guarantee;
~ **für Lagerbestände** inventory protection.
preisgeben to abandon, to give up, to expose, *(offenlegen)* to disclose;
Geheimnis ~ to reveal a secret; **unerlaubtes Informationsmaterial** ~ to disclose (divulge) information; **lebenswichtige Interessen** ~ to give up vital interests; **j. der Lächerlichkeit** ~ to expose s. o. to ridicule; **vertrauliche Mitteilung** ~ to disclose a confidence; **j. dem Pöbel** ~ to leave s. o. to the mercy of the mob; **j. der Schande** ~ to expose s. o. to shame; **Schüler dem Gespött der Klasse** ~ to expose a pupil to the mockery of the class.
Preisgebiet price area;
mittleres ~ medium-priced field.
preisgebunden price-controlled (-bound, -fixed, -linked), frozen;
~ **sein** to be subject to a condition as to the price;
~**e Artikel (Waren)** fixed-price lines, price-maintained goods.
Preisgefälle price gap (differential);
~ **ausebnen** to level out price differentials.
Preisgefüge price structure;
festes ~ stable price structure; **Lohn-**~ wage-price structure; **festes** ~ **der IATA angeschlossener Linienfluggesellschaften** tightly regulated airline industry;
~ **aufrechterhalten** to maintain prices.
preisgekrönt prize-winning, prize;
~ **werden** to be awarded a prize.
Preis|gericht jury; ~**gesetzgebung** price legislation.
Preisgestaltung pricing method, formation of prices, price formation;
diskriminierende ~ discriminatory prices; **freiheitliche** ~ price freedom.
preis|gestoppt price-controlled (-fixed), frozen; ~**gestützte Erzeugnisse** price-maintained goods.
Preis|gewinn price gain; ~**gewinner** prize winner; ~**gleichgewicht** equilibrium of prices, price equilibrium; ~**gleichung** price equation; ~**gleitformel** escalator formula; ~**gleitklausel** escalator (price-variation) clause, escalator formula.
Preisgrenze limit, price limit (barrier, ceiling);
feste (festgesetzte) ~ firm limit, price ceiling; **obere** ~ maximum price; **untere** ~ minimum price;
bestimmte ~ **einhalten** to observe a certain price limit; ~ **überschreiten** to exceed the price limit.
Preis|grundlage price basis; ~**gruppe** price category; **niedrige** ~**gruppe** low price group.
preisgünstig cheap, well priced, budget- (thrift-, economy-) priced *(US)*;
vergleichsweise ~ economy-priced;
~ **liegen** to meet the requirements of a competitive price.
Preisherabsetzung price reduction (decrease, slashing, shading, cut), lowering (shrinking) of (cut in, cutting of) prices, abatement, markdown *(US)*;
endgültige ~ net markdown *(US)*; **generelle** ~ rollback *(US)*; **5%ige** ~ **für das gesamte Sortiment** reduction of 5% on all lines; **in eine** ~ **einwilligen** to consent to a reduction in price.
Preis|herabsetzungskontrolle markdown revision *(US)*; ~**herabsetzungspolitik** lower-price policy; ~**hindernis** price obstacle; ~**höhe** level of prices, price level.
Preisindex, gewogener weighted price index;
~ **für die Lebenserhaltung** cost-of-living (consumer) price index; **langfristiger** ~ **für ausgewählte Produkte** statistical index *(Br.)*;
~**währung** tabular (isometric) standard; ~**zahl** price index number.
Preis|indikator price indicator; ~**inflation** price inflation; **sich überstürzende** ~**inflation** runaway inflation of prices; ~**informationsabrede** open-price agreement; ~**informationsstelle** open-price system; ~**instabilität** price instability.
Preiskalkulation pricing, calculation of prices, price calculation (estimate), *(Baukosten)* quantity surveying *(Br.)*;
an der Nachfrageelastizität orientierte ~ markup pricing;
~ **inklusive Gemeinkosten und Risikofaktor** full cost pricing; ~ **durch Gewinnzuschlag auf Herstellungskosten** cost-plus pricing;
steuerlich bedingten mißbräuchlichen ~**en Einhalt gebieten** to stop sharp practices on transfer pricing; ~ **vornehmen** to calculate a price.
Preis|kalkulator *(Baukosten)* quantity surveyor *(Br.)*; ~**kartell** price ring (association), market-price cartel, price[-fixing] agreement; ~**karussel** price merry-go-round, price carousel; ~**katalog** price list, priced catalog(ue).
Preisklasse price category, range of prices;
in der mittleren ~ medium-priced;
alle ~**n** full price range; **höchste** ~ *(Rundfunk)* class A rate.
Preis|klausel price condition; ~**klima** price atmosphere; ~**kode** price code; ~**koeffizient per Million Leser** million rate *(US)*; ~**kommissar** price administrator *(US)*; ~**konferenz** price-fixing meeting; ~**konjunktur** high-price period, upward trend of prices; **rückläufige** ~**konjunktur** price slowdown; ~**konkurrenz** price competition; ~**kontrolle** price control, *(absolut)* oligopoly; **dirigistische (staatliche)** ~**kontrolle** administrative price control; ~**kontrolle aufheben** to decontrol prices; ~**konvention** price[-fixing] agreement; ~**konzession** price concession; ~**korrektur** correction in prices, *(Anzeigenwesen)* short-rate adjustment; ~**krieg** price war; ~**krise** price crisis; ~**kritik** critical attitude towards prices.
preiskritisch price-conscious.
Preis|kurve, zyklische cyclical curve; ~**kürzung** price-cut; ~**kürzungsprogramm** price-cutting program(me).
Preislage range of prices, price range (bracket);
in derselben ~ within the limits of the price; **in jeder** ~ at all prices; **in niedriger** ~ low-priced;
feste ~**n** established price levels; **mittlere** ~ medium price range;
in der ~ **von 3000 DM aufwärts liegen** to be in the DM 3000 plus range.
Preis|lawine avalanche of price increases; ~**lenkung** price control (administration, *US*).
preislich|richtig liegen to be priced right; ~ **verschieden sein** to vary in price;
~**er Anreiz** price appeal; ~ **unterschiedliche Behandlung** price discrimination *(US)*; ~**er Unterschied** price difference; ~**er Vorteil** price advantage; ~**e Wettbewerbsfähigkeit** price competitiveness.
Preis|limit limited price, price limit, *(Auktion)* reserve price; ~**limit festsetzen** to limit a price; ~**limitierung** price fixing.
Preisliste prices current, price list (schedule, catalog[ue]), manufacturer's (trade, priced) catalog(ue), shop bill, statement of prices, prospectus, *(Anzeigen)* rate card (book), advertising rate, *(Restaurant)* tariff *(Br.)*;
auf der Auflage beruhende ~ circulation rate base; **illustrierte** ~ illustrated price list, trade catalog(ue).
Preis|lücke price gap; ~**manipulierung** manipulation of prices; ~**marke** price tag; ~**maßnahmen** price action; ~**mechanismus** price mechanism, pricing process; ~**medaille** prize medal; ~**meldestelle** open-price association *(US)*; ~**meßzahl**, ~**meßziffer** price relative (index); ~**minderung** reduction in (diminution of) prices; ~**minimum** minimum price, price floor *(US)*; ~**moratorium** moratorium on prices (price increase), price moratorium.
Preisnachlaß deduction from the price, price deduction (reduction, break), discount, abatement, [purchase] allowance, rebate, slash;
mit ~ at a reduced price, reduced; **ohne** ~ without abatement; **außergewöhnlicher** ~ abnormal discount;
~ **aus Konkurrenzgründen** price shading; ~ **von 10% auf Neuwagen** 10 per cent price slash on new cars;
~ **gewähren** to abate, to allow an abatement, to grant a reduction.

Preisnachlässe, außerhalb der Saison gewährte off-season price concessions;
~ **auf nicht preisgebundene Bücher einräumen** to give discount on non-net books; **erhebliche ~ bei Großaufträgen vorsehen** to make full allowance for large orders.
Preisnachlaßsystem für preisgebundene Bücher net book system.
preisneutral sein to have no effect on prices.
Preisniveau level of prices, price level;
doppeltes ~ two-price level; **niedriges** ~ low level of prices; **stabiles** ~ stability of price levels; **unterschiedliches** ~ difference in price levels;
~ **anheben** to raise the level of prices.
Preis|notierung quotation [of prices], prices quoted; **neueste ~notierungen** latest quotations; **~obergrenze** price ceiling; **~ordnung** price code; **~ortssystem** multiple basing point system *(US)*; **~pause** price pause; **~philosophie** pricing philosophy; **~piraterie** [open-]price piracy; **~plattform** price plateau; **~politik** price (pricing) policy; **zurückhaltende ~politik** price restraint; **~ und Lohnpolitik** Price and Incomes Policy *(Br.)*; **kombinierte Produktions- und ~politik** price-output policy; **~polster** price cushion; **~prüfer** regulator of market prices, pricer *(Br.)*; **~prüfung** price control (inspection); **~prüfungsamt** price adjustment board *(US)*; **~rahmen** range of prices, price range.
preisreagibel sensitive to prices.
Preis|reduktion price reduction (slashing, cut); **~reduzierung** diminution of a price; **~regelung, ~regulierung** price adjustment (regulation); **~regulierungspolitik** pricing and regulations policy; **~reihe** price indices; **~relation** price relationship (ratio).
Preisrichter umpire, judge, *(vereidigt)* juror;
als ~ fungieren to adjudicate upon;
~kollegium the judges' jury; **~kollegium auf einer Blumenschau** judges at a flower show.
Preis|richtlinien price guidelines, pricing lines; **~risiko** price risk.
Preisrückgang fall (drop, dip) in prices, price decline (dip, fall, recession);
beträchtlicher ~ considerable decrease in prices;
~ **erleiden** to be affected by a fall in prices.
Preis|rücknahme cutback in prices; **~ruhe** price stability; **~runde** across-the-board increase of prices; **~sanierung** price consolidation; **~schattierung** price shading; **~schema** price pattern; **~schere** price scissors; **~schild** price tag (ticket, *US*), label, price sticker, *(Theke)* counter card; **~schlager** bargain offer; **~schleuderei** price slashing (cutting), undercutting of prices; **~schraube** upward price pressure; **~schub** price push; **~schutz** price protection; **~schwäche** price weakness.
Preisschwankung price fluctuation (oscillation), variation in prices;
saisonal bedingte ~ seasonal price fluctuation;
zugestandene ~ pro Tag *(Warenbörse)* limit;
~en unterliegen to be subject to price fluctuations.
Preissenkung price fall (cut, cutting, reduction), decline in prices, depression (lowering) of prices;
allgemeine ~ rollback [of prices] *(US)*; **erhebliche** ~ price cutting;
~ **bewirken** to bring the prices down.
Preissenkungs|aktion price-cutting move; **staatliche ~aktion** [price] rollback *(US)*; **~programm** price-cutting program(me).
Preis|situation price situation; **angespannte ~situation** price-tight situation; **~skala** scale (range) of prices, price range (scale); **gleitende ~skala** escalator clause; **~sockel** price base; **~spaltung** discrimination in prices, price split; **~spanne** price spread *(US)* (range, scale, margin), margin (range) of prices, *(Spezialartikel)* price area; **~spektrum** price spectrum; **~spekulation** speculation on price; **~spiegel** price mirror; **Zusammenbruch des landwirtschaftlichen ~spiegels** slump in agricultural produce; **~spirale** vicious spiral of rising prices and wages; **~-Lohn-Spirale** price-wage spiral; **~sprünge** jump in prices, price jumps.
preisstabil stable in price;
~e Waren price-maintained goods.
preisstabilisierend price-stabilizing;
~e Maßnahmen holding the line.
Preisstabilisierung price stabilization, valorization *(US)*.
Preisstabilisierungs|abkommen price stabilization pact (agreement); **~politik** stabilizing policy; **~programm** price stabilization program(me); **~versprechen** price pledge.
Preisstabilität price stability (continuity), stability (steadiness, firmness) of prices.
preisstabilstes Land sein to have the most stable prices.

Preis|staffel differential price, sliding scale; **~staffelung** graduation of prices.
Preisstand level of prices, price level;
bei dem heutigen ~ at present prices;
hoher ~ high prices ruling; **niedriger** ~ *(Börse)* squeeze.
Preis|ständer poster; **~starre** rigidity of prices, price rigidity; **~statistik** price statistics.
preissteigernd price-raising;
~e Tendenz upward surge of prices.
Preissteigerung advance (enhancement, appreciation) in prices (value), price advance (increase, improvement, rise);
allgemeine ~ allround increase in prices; **lohnkostenbedingte** ~ wage-induced price increase; **nachfragebedingte** ~ demand-induced price increase; **plötzliche** ~ jump in prices, price boost *(coll.)*;
~en verhindern to keep prices down; **nur geringfügige ~en zulassen** to hold price rises to low level.
Preissteigerungs|rate rate of price increase, price-increase rate; **~rücklage** contingent reserve for price increases; **~tempo** price-increase pace; **~tendenz** tendency for prices to increase.
Preis|stellung quotation [of prices]; **tabellarisch angeordnete ~stellung** tabulated quotation; **~steuerung** price governance; **~stopp** price stop (freeze, ceiling, *US*), freezing of prices *(US)*; **~stopp durchführen (verhängen)** to freeze prices *(US)*; **~struktur** price structure.
Preissturz slump [in prices], break *(US)* (fall) in prices, collapse of price, price collapse, nose-dive, double bottom *(coll.)*;
jäher ~ steep fall in prices;
vom ~ betroffen werden to be affected by a fall of prices;
~periode überstehen to ride out the price slump.
Preisstützung support of prices, price support (relief, maintenance), maintenance (pegging) of prices, valorization *(US)*.
Preisstützungs|aktion price-support scheme; **~behörde für die Landwirtschaft** commodity credit corporation *(US)*; **~gesetz** price-maintenance law; **~maßnahmen** price-support activities, price-relief measures, valorization scheme *(US)*; **~programm** price-supporting program(me); **~stufe** price-support level.
Preis|subventionierung price subsidy; **gleitendes ~system** price-index escalator; **~tabelle** table of charges, scale of prices, price schedule; **~tafel** price board (list), *(Anzeigen)* rate card *(US)*; **~tafel aufhängen** to post up a price list; **~tarif** tariff card; **~tendenz** price trend, trend in prices, price-raising tendency; **rückläufige ~tendenz** price recession; **~theoretiker** price theorist; **statische ~theorie** equilibrium theory; **~träger** prize winner, prizeman, prizeholder, prizetaker, laureate; **zweiter ~träger** runner-up.
preistreibend price-enhancing (-raising).
Preis|treiber inflater, profiteer[er], booster *(US coll.)*, rigger, bull *(Br.)*, *(Auktion)* puffer; **~treiberei** boost *(US coll.)*, rigging the market, rig-up, forcing up the prices, puffing, bulling *(Br.)*; **~treiberei begehen** to rig the market; **~turbulenz** turbulent prices; **~übereinstimmung** uniformity of prices; **~übergangssystem** price-review system; **~überhöhung** excessive price quotation; **~überprüfung [durch staatliche Stellen]** [government] price review; **~überprüfungssystem** price-review system; **~überwachung** price control (surveillance, inspection, administration, *US*); **~überwachung aufheben** to lift price control.
Preisüberwachungs|bericht price commission report; **~gesetz** Price Commission Act *(Br.)*; **~gruppe** price-review team; **~ und Lohnüberwachungsstelle** National Board for Prices and Incomes *(Br.)*, Price Commission *(Br.)*, price adjustment board *(US)*; **~system** price-review system; **~vorschriften abbauen** to decontrol prices.
Preis|umschwung reversal in prices; **~unbeständigkeit** price volatility.
preisunelastisch price-inelastic.
Preisunterbieter undercutter, price cutter.
Preisunterbietung price cutting (undercutting), undercutting, underselling, *(im Ausland)* dumping;
ruinöse ~ predatory price cutting; **unlautere** ~ unfair price discrimination *(US)*;
gegen internationale ~ gerichtliche Maßnahmen herbeiführen to trigger antidumping measures.
Preisunterbietungs|plan, ~system price-cutting scheme.
Preisunter|grenze price floor, *(Verkäufer)* upset price; **~lagen** price data; **~scheidung** price differentiation.
Preisunterschied difference in prices, price difference (differential), disparity in prices, price spread *(US)*;
große ~e wide prices;
strittigen ~ teilen to split the price difference.

Preisverabredung price-fixing conspiracy.
Preisveränderung price (value) variance, price change, change in prices;
~ **vorbehalten** subject to price alterations;
~**en erfassen** to measure the change in prices.
Preis|verantwortung price responsibility; ~**verband** price combine; ~**verbilligung** price reduction; ~**verderber** cutting tradesman, price cutter, undercutter; ~**vereinbarung** price[-fixing] agreement; **vertikale** ~**vereinbarung** vertical price-fixing contract; ~**vereinbarung treffen** to agree about a price; ~**verfall** dip in prices, deterioration in prices, sharp fall in prices, price collapse (decline); ~**vergehen** offence against price regulations; ~**vergleich** comparing (comparison of) prices, price comparison; ~**vergleiche in den Läden anstellen** to shop around; ~**verhalten** price behavio(u)rism; ~**verhältnis** price relationship; ~**verständigung** price-fixing agreement.
Preisverteilung distribution of prizes, prize distribution, giving out (away) the awards, giving away the prizes;
offizielle ~ formal prize distribution;
~ **vornehmen** to give away the prizes.
Preis|verursacher price producer; ~**verzeichnis** prices current, price catalog(ue), manufacturer's (trade) catalog(ue), statement (schedule) of prices, price-list, premium catalog(ue), *(Restaurant)* tariff *(Br.)*; ~**verzerrung** price distortion; ~**vorbehalt** price reserve; ~**vorbehaltsklausel** clause reserving price; ~**vorschlag** expected (asking) price; ~**vorschriften** price control (regulations, rules); ~**vorteil** price advantage; ~**waffe** price weapon; ~**welle** wave of increasing prices; ~**wende** price turn.
preiswert cheap, moderately priced, good value, worth the money, at a cheap (low) rate, low-cost;
äußerst ~ excellent bargain;
in einem Restaurant ~ **essen** to get a good meal in a restaurant at a reasonable price; ~ **kaufen** to get good value for one's money; **sehr** ~ **kaufen** to buy for a mere song;
~**es Angebot** reasonable offer.
Preis|wettbewerb contending for a prize, prize competition; ~**widerstand** price resistance; ~**wucher** profiteering; ~**wucherer** profiteer[er].
preiswürdig worth the money, prizeworthy, moderate- (well-, economy-, budget-, *US*) priced;
~ **sein** to be good value for one's money.
Preis|würdigkeit cheapness, good value; ~**zeichen** mark, label, price tag.
Preiszettel price tag (mark, ticket, *US*, label);
mit ~**n versehen** to tag, to mark prices, to label for sale.
Preis|ziffern price figures; ~**zugeständnis** price concession; **außerhalb der Saison gewährte** ~**zugeständnisse** off-season price concessions; ~**zurückhaltung** price moderation; **gemeinsame** ~**zurückhaltung** price restraint cooperation; ~**zusagen** price commitments; ~**zusammenbruch** price collapse, collapse of prices; ~**zuschlag** supplemental cost, markup, markon, additional (extra) charge; ~**zuschläge und** ~**abschläge** sliding-scale differentials.
prekär precarious, delicate, awkward;
~**er Friede** uneasy peace; ~**e Gesundheit** delicate health; ~**e Lage** precarious situation.
Prellbock *(Bahn)* buffer, fender, bumping post *(US)*.
prellen to fleece, to cozen, to trick;
j. um etw. ~ to cheat (trick) s. o. out of s. th.; **j. um sein Geld** ~ to fleece s. o. of all his money, to trick money out of s. o.; **j. um seinen Lohn** ~ to trick s. o. out of his wages; **Taxifahrer ums Fahrgeld** ~ to bilk a taxi driver of his money; **Zeche** ~ to duck (dodge) payment of the bill.
Premiere first (initial) performance, first (opening, *US*) night;
~ **geben** to première; **bei einer** ~ **anwesend sein** to be present at the first performance of a play.
Premieren|abend first (opening, *US*) night; ~**besucher** first nighter; ~**kino** first-run cinema (movie, *US*); ~**publikum** opening-night audience *(US)*.
Premierminister Prime Minister;
stellvertretender ~ First Secretary *(Br.)*.
Preßbrett *(Buchmacherei)* pressing board.
Presse press, papers, journalism, newspaperdom, fourth estate, *(Kritik)* press review, *(Pressevertreter)* newspapermen, journalists, pressmen, press, *(Schule)* cramming establishment, cram shop, crammer, *(techn.)* power press;
durch die [Mitwirkung der] ~ through the medium of the press;
eben aus der ~ fresh from the press; **in der** ~ printing;
vorherige Besichtigung durch die ~ press view;
die ~ the prints *(US)*; **gesamte ausländische** ~ all foreign newspapers; **bezahlte** ~ kept (reptile) press; **deutschsprachige** ~ German-language press; **gedungene** ~ reptile press; **gute** ~ good press; **hydraulische** ~ hydraulic (water) press; **inländische** ~ national press; **käufliche** ~ corrupt press; **konservative** ~ press establishment; **örtliche** ~ local press; **regierungsfeindliche** ~ papers opposed to the government; **schlechte** ~ bad press; **sensationslüsterne** ~ yellow press; **überregionale** ~ national press;
~ **jeglicher Art** newspapers of every shade;
j. in der ~ **angreifen** to attack (run) s. o. down in the papers; **in der** ~ **über eine Hauptversammlung berichten** to cover a meeting of shareholders; ~ **bestechen** to subsidize the press; **gute Aufnahme in der** ~ **finden** to be favo(u)rably noticed in the press; **für die** ~ **freigeben** to release to the press; **in die** ~ **gehen** to go to press; **gute** ~ **haben** to have (receive) a good press; **schlechte** ~ **haben** to knock *(US sl.)*; **mit der** ~ **ständig Verbindung halten** to liaise with the press; ~ **knebeln** to muzzle the press; **frisch aus der** ~ **kommen** to come hot from the press; ~ **mundtot machen** to gag (suppress) the press; **Schüler auf die** ~ **schicken** to send a boy to the crammer's; **sich der** ~ **[nicht] stellen** [not] to be available for the press; **freie** ~ **unterdrücken** to suppress the press; **in der** ~ **erwähnt werden** to figure in the press, *(ausführlich)* to get a very substantial coverage; **etw. der** ~ **zuspielen** to leak s. th. into the press;
~**abkommen** press arrangement; ~**abteilung** press department, publication division; ~**agent** news agent, space bandit *(sl.)*; ~**agentur** press agency (association), news (press) service; ~**amt** Central Office of Information *(Br.)*, government information office; ~**ankündigung** press notice; ~**archiv** press archives; ~**artikel** newspaper article; ~**attaché** press secretary; ~**ausschnitt** press clipping *(Br.)* (cutting, *US*); ~**ausweis** press credentials; ~**bericht** press (newspaper) report, coverage, write-up *(US)*; **entstellte** ~**berichte** press distortions; ~**berichterstatter** newspaper (press) correspondent; ~**besichtigung** press view; ~**besprechung** press conference; ~**betreuung** press coverage; ~**bilderdienst** picture agency; ~**büro** pressroom, press office (bureau, agency); ~**chef** press-relations counsel, press (publications) officer; ~**chef des Weißen Hauses** White House Press Secretary; ~**dienst** news (press) service, news agency, press association; ~**einrichtungen** press facilities; ~**empfang** reception of the press; ~**enthüllung** press disclosure; ~**erklärung** press statement; ~**erklärung abfassen** to write a statement for the press; ~**erzeugnis** publication; ~**exemplar** press (review) copy; ~**fehde** paper warfare, press controversy; ~**feldzug** press campaign; ~**foto** press photo; ~**fotograf** press photographer; ~**freigabe** press release; ~**freiheit** liberty (freedom) of the press; ~**galerie** press gallery *(Br.)*; ~**gesetz** press law (bill); **fernsehübertragenes** ~**gespräch** televised conversation with the press; **vertrauliches** ~**gespräch** off-the-record press conference; ~**information** press briefing; **vertrauliche** ~**information** inside dope *(sl.)*; ~**interesse** press attention; ~**interview** press interview; ~**interview ablehnen** to refuse to give an interview to journalists; ~**kabine** press box; ~**kampagne** press campaign; ~**kampagne für etw. führen** to mount a press campaign in favo(u)r of s. th.; ~**karte** press credentials; ~**katalog** press guide; ~**klub** press club; ~**kommentar** press commentary; ~**konferenz** press (news) conference, press briefing; **durchs Fernsehen übertragene** ~**konferenz** live televised press conference; ~**konferenz ohne besonderen Anlaß** on-the-record press conference; ~**kontingent** press contingent; ~**kontrolle** control of the press; ~**kontroverse** press controversy; ~**kreise** segments of the press; ~**krieg** paper warfare; **lobende** ~**kritik** write-up; **negative** ~**kritik** hostile press reception; ~**liste** press list; ~**loge** press box; ~**mappe** press kit.
pressemäßige Betreuung press coverage.
Presse|material press material; **freigegebenes** ~**material** handout, press release; ~**meldung** press item; ~**mitarbeiter** press assistant; ~**mitteilung** press release, handout; ~**mitteilungen** press news (communications).
pressen to press, to squeeze, to jam, to stuff, to force, *(Kohlenstaub)* to briquette, *(Papier)* to press, *(Zitrone)* to squeeze;
j. zu etw. ~ to force s. o. to do s. th.; **sich in einen Aufzug** ~ to squash o. s. into a lift; **j. durch Foltern zu einem Geständnis** ~ to force a confession out of s. o.; **Kleider in einen Koffer** ~ to jam clothes into a suitcase; **zum Kriegsdienst** ~ to impress into war service; **sich in einen schon vollen Omnibus** ~ to squeeze (squash) o. s. into a crowded bus; **Schallplatten** ~ to mould records; **sich durch ein enges Tor** ~ *(Menge)* to jam themselves through a narrow gate.

Presse|nachrichten press news (items, communications); **letzte ~nachrichten** stop-press news; **~notiz** newspaper announcement, handout, press release (item), news release, press note (notice); **~notiz herausgeben** to release a text for publication; **~polemik** press controversy; **~programm** press program(me); **~rat** press council; **~referent** information (press, public-relations) officer, press-relations counsel; **~revision lesen** to read for the press; **sich durch die Mühlen des ~rummels drehen lassen** to put o. s. through all the publicity hops *(sl.)*; **~satzung** press charter; **~schau** press review; **~sprecher** official spokesman; **~stelle** press office; **~stenograf** news typist; **~stimmen** press quotations (comments); **ausländische ~stimmen** extract of foreign newspapers; **~stoff liefern** to get into the papers; **~syndikat** news syndicate; **~tätigkeit** press activities; **~telegramm** press message (telegram), flimsy; **~tribüne** press gallery *(Br.)*; **~überwachung** control of newspapers; **~unterrichtung** press orientation; **~verband** press association; **~verbindungen** press relations; **~verfassung** press charter; **~verlautbarung** press release, handout, *(für die Regionalpresse)* home-town release; **~verlautbarung herausgeben** to release a statement to the press; **~vertreter** representative (member) of the press, press agent (representative); **~viertel** *(London)* Fleet Street; **~vorschau** press preview; **~werbung** press publicity; **~wesen** journalism, press; **~zar** press tycoon, newspaper magnate, baron of Fleet Street; **~zeichner** cartoonist; **~zensur** censorship of the press, news censorship; **~zentrum** press center *(US)* (centre, *Br.*); **~zitate** press quotations.

pressieren to be urgent (pressing).

Pression pressure, compulsion;
~en aussetzen to put under the screw.

Preß|kohle patent fuel, briquettes; **~luft** compressed air; **~luftbohrer** pneumatic drill; **~lufthammer** pneumatic hammer; **~pappe** glazed cardboard; **~span** pressboard.

Prestige prestige, face, reputation, cachet;
soziales ~ social standing;
hohes ~ genießen to enjoy a great deal of prestige; **~ eines Landes ruinieren** to ruin the prestige of a country; **sein ~ verlieren** to lose face; **sein ~ wahren** to save one's face;
~artikel prestige merchandise.

prestigeempfindlich prestige-conscious.

Prestige|feldzug, in Zeitschriften durchgeführter prestige magazine campaign; **~frage** matter of prestige; **~gewinn** gain in prestige, prestige building; **aus ~gründen** in order to save one's face; **~konsum** conspicuous consumption.

prestigemäßig festlegen, sich to commit one's prestige.

Prestigepolitik prestige-seeking policy.

Prestigeverlust loss of face;
~ bedeuten to mean a loss of prestige; **~ vermeiden** to save one's face;
Vermeidung eines ~es face saver.

Prestige|werbung indirect-action (prestige, image) advertising; **~wert** prestige value.

Prickeln im Fuß haben to have pins and needles in one's foot.

prickeln, in der Nase to have a tickle in the nose; **auf der Zunge ~** to tickle (prickle) the tongue.

prickelnd prickling, tingling, tingly;
~er Reiz des Unbekannten titillating lure of the unknown; **~er Witz** spicy joke.

Priel tideway.

Priester priest, clergyman, minister;
~amt ministry; **~stand** clergy, frock; **~weihe** ordination, consecration.

Prima *(Schule)* sixth form, *(Wechsel)* first of exchange.

prima first-class (-rate), A 1, top-notch, first chop *(Br., coll.)*, excelsior, topflight, topping, crack, tiptop, bully *(US)*, prime *(US)*, up to the knocker *(sl.)*, crushing, nailing *(sl.)*, peachy *(sl.)*, smashing *(sl.)*, hunky *(sl.)*, top-hole *(Br., sl.)*, *(Wertpapiere)* gilt-edged *(Br.)*, fine *(Br.)*, high-grade *(US)*, swell *(sl.)*;
~ vista at sight, at first sight;
~ gelaufen sein to have gone off without a hitch; **sich ~ verstehen** to get on very well;
~ Bankakzept fine (prime, *US*) banker's acceptance; **~ Chef** marvel(l)ous boss; **~ Diskonten** first-class bills, prime banker's acceptances *(US)*; **~ Kerl** great bloke, good sort, swell guy *(US fam.)*; **~ Sache** peach *(sl.)*; **~ Ware** choice (high-quality) goods.

Prima|diskonten first-class bills, prime banker's acceptances *(US)*; **~facievoraussetzung** prima facie presumption.

Primaner six-former *(Br.)*.

primär primary, principal, prime, chief;
von ~er Bedeutung sein to be of prime importance.

Primär|daten primary data; **~einkommen** primary income; **~energie** primary energy; **~energieverbrauch** primary energy consumption; **~erhebung** *(Meinungsbefragung)* field research; **~farbe** primary colo(u)r; **~gruppe** primary group; **~güter** primary production; **~liquidität** liquid ratio, acid test; **~material** raw data; **~reserve** *(Weltwährungsfonds)* primary reserve; **~stromkreis** *(el.)* primary circuit; **~wechsel** primary (fine, *Br.*) bill, original bill *(US)*.

Primasorte prime (first) quality.

Primat der Außenpolitik priority of foreign policy.

Prima|ware article of first [first-class (-rate)] quality, first-rate (high-quality) goods; **~wechsel** first of exchange, fine *(Br.)* (prime, *US*) bill, primary (original, *US*) bill.

Primgeld primage, privilege, hat money.

primitiv primitive, rough, coarse, crude, *(unkultiviert)* uncultured, uncultivated;
~e Arbeit rough work; **~e Bedürfnisse** basic needs; **~er Bevölkerungsteil** rough element of the population; **~ste Grundbegriffe** basics; **~e Hütte** wretched hut; **~er Mensch** clumsy lout; **~e Unterbringung** rough accommodation; **~es Volk** savage (uncivilized) people; **~e Waffen** primitive weapons.

Primus head of the class, top of the form, dux *(Br.)*.

Primzahl prime (incommensurable) number.

Prinzgemahl prince consort.

Prinzip, im on principle;
leitendes ~ guide; **ökonomisches ~** economic principle;
~ gleitender Arbeitszeit flexible working hours scheme; **~ der Gegenseitigkeit** bilateralism; **~ der Gewaltenteilung** principle of separation of powers; **~ der freien Marktwirtschaft** free-enterprise principle; **~ der Meistbegünstigung** most-favo(u)red-nation principle; **~ der Preisunterschiedslosigkeit** law of indifference;
nach dem gleichen ~ arbeiten to work on the same principle; **auf einem einfachen ~ beruhen** *(Maschine)* to work on a simple principle; **etw. zum ~ machen** to make it a matter of principle; **~ zu Tode reiten** to flog a principle.

Prinzipal principal, proprietor [of a commercial establishment], head, employer, master, boss *(sl.)*.

prinzipiell dagegen sein to refuse on principle.

Prinzipien principles, lines;
~ der sozialen Anpassung economic harmonies;
seinen ~ treu bleiben to live up to one's principles; **in Außerachtlassung seiner ~ handeln** to do violence to one's principles; **auf seinen ~ herumreiten** to sit tight on one's principles; **~ vertreten, die man selbst nicht praktiziert** to profess principles which one does not practise;
~frage matter of principle; **~reiter** doctrinaire.

Priorität priority, rank in priority, precedence, preference, ranking;
~en priority bonds, first debentures, preference [income, *US*] bonds *(Br.)*, preferred stock *(US)*;
absolute ~en preëmptive priorities;
~en mit Ermessensspielraum discretionary priorities; **~ der Kapitalkonten** order of capital seniority; **~en zweiten Ranges** second debentures;
~ beanspruchen *(Patentrecht)* to claim priority; **~ genießen** to enjoy preference (priority); **höchste ~ genießen** to have the highest priority; **~ einer vorhergehenden Anmeldung in Anspruch nehmen** to take advantage of the priority of a previous claim; **~en setzen** to establish priorities; **~en in Frage stellen** to shake up priorities.

Prioritäten|liste priority table; **~liste neu zusammenstellen** to regroup priorities; **~rangfolge** order of priority.

Prioritäts|aktie priority (preference, *Br.*) share, preferred (preferential) stock *(US)*; **nicht kumulative ~aktien** non-cumulative shares *(Br.)*; **~aktien erster Emission** first preferred stocks *(US)*; **~ankündigung** priority notice; **~anleihe** preference (preferential, *Br.*) loan; **~anspruch** claim entitled to priority, priority claim; **~belege** *(Patentrecht)* priority documents; **~datum** priority date; **~dividende** preferred dividend *(Br.)*; **~folge** priority order; **~frist** *(Patentrecht)* priority period; **~gläubiger** prior (privileged, preferred, *US*) creditor; **~liste** priority table; **~obligationen** first debentures, priority (preferred, preference [income, *US*]) bonds *(Br.)*; **ertragsbedingte ~obligationen** preference income bonds; **~ordnung** ranking, priority, order of distribution; **~papiere** preference (preferred) stock *(US)*; **~recht** priority right (claim), preference; **sein ~recht geltend machen** *(Patentrecht)* to interfere *(US)*; **~streit** *(Patentrecht)* interference proceedings; **~termin** priority date.

Prise prize, capture;
für gute ~ erklärt condemned;
gute ~ lawful prize;
~ Schnupftabak pinch of snuff;
Schiff als ~ aufbringen to make prize of a ship; **~ in den Hafen einbringen** to bring the prize into port; **Schiff als gute ~ erklären** to condemn a ship as lawful prize; **als ~ nehmen** to make prize of.

Prisen|anteil prize money; **~geld** prize bounty (money); **~gericht[shof]** prize court, High Court of Admiralty *(Br.)*.

prisengerichtlich, aufgebrachtes Schiff ~ einziehen to condemn a captured vessel and her cargo.

Prisen|gut prize goods; **~kommando** prize crew; **einem ~kommando ein Schiff übergeben** to put a prize crew on board a vessel; **~nehmer** captor; **~offizier** prize master, boarding officer; **~ordnung** regulations governing prizes; **~recht** prize law; **~rückeroberung** rescue; **~sachen** *(Gerichtshof)* prize causes; **~verteilung** prize giving.

Pritsche *(Gefängnis)* plank bed, *(Geschütz)* barbette, *(Lastwagen)* platform, floor.

Pritschenwagen flatbed car, platform waggon, pickup, drop-side lorry *(Br.)*.

privat private, privately, *(persönlich)* personal, individual, intimate, *(vertraulich)* confidential, closed, intrinsic;
~ an j. herantreten to approach s. o. privately; **j. ~ sprechen** to talk to s. o. in privacy; **etw. ~ tun** to do s. th. in a private capacity;
~e Bautätigkeit private building; **~er Bereich** private sector of the economy; **in ~en Besitz übergehen** to pass into private hands; **~e Effektenplazierung** private placing *(Br.)* (placement, *US*); **~es Eigentum** private property; **~e Ersparnisse** personal savings; **~e Gesellschaft** proprietary company, private corporation; **~es Gespräch** private (confidential) talk; **~es Guthaben** private deposit; **in ~en Händen** privately owned; **~e Meinung** personal opinion; **~e Mitteilung** private communication; **~er Sender** private station; **~e Sphäre** privacy; **in jds. ~e Sphäre eindringen** to intrude on s. one's privacy; **~e Unfallversicherung** personal accident insurance; **~e Unkosten** private costs; **~e Zwecke** *(Kraftfahrzeugbenutzung)* social, domestic and pleasure purposes.

Privat|abhebungen personal drawings; **~abkommen, ~abmachung** private agreement (contract, arrangement); **~absatz** *(Wertpapiere)* direct sale; **~abteil** *(Bahn)* drawing room, stateroom *(US)*; **~akten** private files; **~angelegenheit** private concern (affair, business, interest), personal matter; **~anlagen** *(tel.)* private investment; **~anleger** private investor; **~anschluß** *(tel.)* private line; **~anschlußgleis** private siding; **~anschrift** private (home, residence) address.

privatärztliche Behandlung private medical treatment.

Privat|audienz private audience; **in ~audienz empfangen werden** to be received in private audience; **~ausgaben** personal spending (cost); **~auskunft** private information; **~bahn** private railway company *(Br.)*; **~bank[haus]** private bank, individual banker *(US)*; **~bankenbereich** private-sector banking; **~bankier** private (individual, *US*) banker; **im ~bereich** privately operated; **~besitz** private property (residence); **im ~besitz** privately owned; **kein ~besitz an der Küste** no property on the seashore.

Privatbetrieb private (privately owned) enterprise, private establishment (undertaking);
im ~ privately operated (owned);
kleiner ~ small private-sector company; **anerkannter mittelgroßer ~** medium-sized privately owned enterprise;
durch Austausch der an der Börse zugelassenen Fremdaktien wieder zum reinen ~ werden to revert to private status by buying out the quoted minority.

Privat|bibliothek private library; **~brief** private letter; **~brücke** occupation (private) bridge; **~buchhaltung** personal accounting; **~bucht** private bay; **~büro** private office; **~depositen** other deposits; **~detektiv** private detective (eye, *sl.*), inquiry agent *(Br.)*, sleuth *(US)*, spotter *(US)*, stool *(sl.)*, Pinkerton; **~diskont** market discount *(Br.)*, prime rate *(US)*; **~diskonten** prime banker's acceptances *(US)*; **~diskontsatz** market rate of discount *(Br.)*, private rate *(Br.)*, prime rate *(US)*; **[festangestellter] ~dozent** [senior] lecturer; **im ~druck erschienen** privately printed; **~eigentum** personal (private) property, personal effects, personalty; **~- und Gesellschaftseigentum** separate and common ownership; **im ~eigentum [stehend]** privately owned; **~eigentum an den Produktionsmitteln** private ownership of the means of production; **~eigentümer** private proprietor; **~einfahrt** private driveway; **~eingang** private door (entrance); **~einkünfte** individual (personal, private) income; **~einkünfte haben** to have an income of one's own; **~entnahmen** *(Teilhaber)* withdrawals, personal drawings; **~erziehung** private (home) education; **~fahrten** private motoring; **~fahrzeug** private motor car; **~firma** private business; **~flugzeug** private (privately owned) airplane; **~fluß** private river (stream); **zum ~gebrauch** for private use; **~gelehrter** independent scholar; **~geschäft** transaction for own account; **~gesellschaft** proprietary (privately-owned) company, private (close) corporation; **~gesetz** special statute (law); **~gespräch** *(tel.)* private call; **~gewässer** private water, posted waters; **~gläubiger** *(eines Gesellschafters)* private (individual) creditor; **~grenze** private boundary; **~grundstück** private premises (property); **~grundstücke für öffentliche Zwecke enteignen** to take private property for public use; **~guthaben** private account (deposit); **~haftpflichtversicherung** personal liability insurance; **~haftpflichtversicherungspolice** *(Auto)* private car comprehensive policy; **sich in ~hand befinden** to be privately owned; **in ~hand übergehen** to pass into private hands; **~haus** private [dwelling] house, domestic building; **für ein ~haus geeignet** residential; **teure ~häuser** privates *(sl.)*; **~haushalt** private household.

Privatier gentleman at large.

privatim privately;
jem. etw. ~ mitteilen to tell s. o. s. th. in strict confidence.

Privat|information private information, confidential report; **~initiative** private enterprise; **~interessen** private ends; **~interessen verfolgen** to take care of number one, to have an axe to grind.

privatisieren to be a gentleman of independent means, *(Unternehmen)* to denationalize;
ertragreiche Teilgebiete ~ to hive off profitable activities to the private sector.

Privatisierung *(Betriebe)* denationalization;
~ von Gemeindegrundstücken enclosure of common land; **~ verstaatlichter Industriebetriebe** hiving-off of state industries.

Privat|kapital private capital; **~kapitalismus** private capitalism; **~kasse** privy purse; **~klage** civil action; **~kläger** private prosecutor, accuser; **~klinik** nursing home *(Br.)*, hospital financed by voluntary efforts; **~kontenbuch** personal (private) ledger; **~konto** private (personal) account, drawing account; **~kontor** private office; **musikalisches ~konzert** musical evening; **~korrespondenz** private correspondence (communications); **~krankenhaus** pay hospital; **~kredit** personal credit; **~kunde** private customer, *(Bank)* personal borrower; **~kundschaft** private customers.

Privatleben private life, privateness, penetralia;
im ~ off parade;
in jds. ~ eindringen to intrude on s. one's privacy; **sich ins ~ zurückziehen** to go into retirement, to retire from the world (into private life).

Privat|lehrer family (private) tutor; **~mann** private individual (citizen); **~meinung** individual opinion; **~patient** private patient; **~pension** private boarding house, family hotel.

Privatperson private individual (person);
als ~ privately;
als ~ handeln to act in one's individual (personal) capacity.

Privat|pier private wharf; **~post** private mail *(US)*; **~praxis** private practice; **~quartier** private home; **~raum** closet; **~recht** private law; **internationales ~recht** private international law, law of conflict of laws *(US)*; **römisches ~recht** civil law.

privatrechtlich civil.

Privat|rücksichten, aus on personal grounds; **~sache** private affair; **sich in ~sachen einmischen** to intrude on privacy; **~sanatorium** nursing home *(Br.)*; **~schatulle** privy purse.

privatschriftlich private, handwritten, holographic;
~e Urkunde private deed.

Privatschulden *(Gesellschafter)* individual (separate) debts.

Privatschule independent (nonprovided, *Br.*) school;
staatlich anerkannte ~ direct-grant school *(Br.)*; **staatlich geförderte ~** aided school *(Br.)*;
~ mit staatlichem Lehrereinsetzungsrecht special-agreement school *(Br.)*; **~ für Mädchen** dame school *(Br.)*.

Privat|sekretär[in] private (confidential) secretary; **~sender** private commercial station; **~sphäre** privacy; **~station** *(Krankenhaus)* private ward; **~strand** private beach; **~straße** private (occupation) road, private street; **~stunden** private lessons (tuition); **~stunden geben** to pupilize, to tutor; **~telefon** subscriber's telephone, private line; **~unternehmen** private undertaking (enterprise, business corporation, company); **in ein ~unternehmen umgewandelt werden** to go private;

~**unternehmer** private proprietor, entrepreneur; ~**unterricht** private lessons (instruction, school, tuition), tutoring, coaching; **jem. ~unterricht erteilen** to tutor (pupilize) s. o., to give private lessons; ~**unterricht haben** to be educated at home; ~**urkunde** private document; ~**verbrauch** personal consumption; ~**verbraucher** ultimate buyer; ~**verhältnisse** private situation; ~**verkauf** private sale.

Privatvermögen private property (means, assets, capital), personal property, individual wealth (property), *(Gesellschafter)* individual (personal) assets, separate estate, *(Gemeinschuldner)* personal assets;
bankverwaltetes ~ personal (private) trust funds *(US)*;
~ **haben** to have an independent income; **von seinem ~ leben** to live on one's private means (capital).

Privat|versicherer private insurer; ~**versicherung** private insurance; ~**versicherungsunternehmer** private underwriter; ~**vertrag** private agreement; ~**vorstellung** *(Theater)* invitation (command, private) performance; ~**wagen** private car; ~**wagen ins Geschäft einbringen** to introduce a private car into the business; ~**wagenbesitzer** private car motorist; ~**waggon für Stückgutladungen** ferry car *(US coll.)*; ~**weg** private way (road), occupation road; ~**weiher** private pond.

Privatwirtschaft private business [sector], private economy (industry), private enterprise system;
in die ~ eingreifen to interfere with private business; **der ~ vor der Zwangswirtschaft den Vorzug geben** to prefer private enterprise to government control; **in die ~ zurückführen** to denationalize, to hive off state industries.

privatwirtschaftliche|Aktivitäten private enterprise; ~ **Machtstellung** private economic power; ~ **Unternehmen** private sector companies.

Privat|wohnung private dwelling (quarters, residence), residential flat; ~**zimmer** cabinet, closet, retired apartment; ~**zwecke** private ends.

Privileg privilege, prerogative, liberty, indulgence, peculiar, patent, *(Bank)* charter, statute, *(Gläubiger)* preference, priority, favo(u)r, *(Immunität)* immunity, *(Sonderrecht)* licence *(Br.)*, license *(US)*, franchise *(US)*, *(Vorteil)* benefit;
mit offiziellen ~ien ausgestattet patent;
althergebrachte ~ien vested rights; **ausschließliches** ~ exclusive privilege; **königliches** ~ royal prerogative; **wirtschaftliche ~ien** economic privileges; **zweifelhaftes** ~ questionable privilege;
~**ien aufheben** to retrench privileges; **mit einem ~ ausstatten** to privilege, to franchise, to license, to [grant a] charter; **verfassungsmäßig garantierte ~ien beschränken** to abridge privileges of the citizens; **jds. ~ einschränken** to curtail s. one's privileges; **auf sein ~ verzichten** to yield one's privilege.

privilegieren to privilege, to charter, to license, to franchise.

privilegiert privileged, chartered, granted;
~**e Bank** chartered bank; ~**e Forderung** privileged (preferred, *US*, preferential) debt; ~**e Gesellschaft** corporate franchise; ~**er Gläubiger** specialty (privileged) creditor; ~**e Stände** privileged classes.

Privilegiertenklasse genteel class.

Privilegierter privileged person, exempt, grantee, franchiser.

Privilegium privilege, prerogative.

pro|Jahr annually, per annum (year); ~ **Kopf (Person)** per head (capita); **5 Mark ~ Stück** 5 marks a piece; ~ **Stunde** per hour.

probates Mittel effective remedy.

Probe *(Beweis)* proof, evidence, *(drucktechn.)* proof, specimen, *(Erprobung)* test, trial, experiment, tryout *(US)*, *(Kontrollberechnung)* proof, *(Metall)* assay, *(Muster)* sample, pattern, *(Nachprüfung)* verification, check, *(Probezeit)* probation, *(Prüfstück)* specimen, *(Theater)* rehearsal;
auf ~ on approbation, *(Warensendung)* on approval; **auf ~ angestellt** probationary; **der ~ entsprechend** answering the (to) pattern, up to sample; **laut beiliegender** ~ as per pattern enclosed; **nach** ~ on (upon the authority of) sample, according to pattern; **streng nach der** ~ strictly up to sample; **zur** ~ on trial (approbation);
unsortierte, nicht ausgewählte ~n unpicked samples; **entnommene** ~ picked sample; **bewußt gewählte** ~ purposive sample; **kostenlose** ~ free trial (sample); **kurze** ~ *(Theater)* run-through; **vorgelegte (vorgezeigte)** ~ sample displayed (shown);
~ **auf Feinheit** assay; ~ **liegt bei** enclosed please find a sample;
~**n abhalten** *(Theater)* to have rehearsals; **j. auf ~ anstellen** to engage s. o. on probation, to give s. o. a trial; ~ **bestehen** to stand the test (trial), to come up to scratch; ~ **entnehmen** to [take a] sample, to draw samples; **der ~ entsprechen** to be up to (match the) sample; ~ **seines Könnens geben** to prove one's skill; **zur ~ gebrauchen** to have on trial; **etw. auf ~ kaufen** to buy s. th. on trial; **es auf eine ~ ankommen lassen** to challenge a proof; **zur ~ laufen** *(Motor)* to be given a test run; ~ **aufs Exempel machen** to put s. th. to the test (touch); ~ **auf eine Rechnung machen** to check an invoice; ~ **nehmen** to draw samples, to retain a sample; **Maschine kostenlos zur ~ schicken** to send a machine for free trial; **auf ~ angestellt sein** to be [employed] on probation; **j. auf die ~ stellen** to put s. o. to the test, to try s. one's mettle; **jds. Geduld auf eine harte ~ stellen** to tax s. one's patience severely; **einer ~ unterziehen** to put to trial;
~**n versenden** to send out samples;
~**abdruck** proof [sheet], pull; ~**abdruck für zweite Korrektur** revised proof; ~**abonnement** trial subscription; ~**abschluß** *(Bilanz)* [preclosing] trial balance; ~**abstimmung** test ballot, preliminary (straw, *US*) vote; ~**abzug** *(Briefmarkenserie)* essay, *(drucktechn.)* proof impression, pull, *(Foto)* proof; ~**abzug machen** to proof; ~**abzüge** repro proofs; ~**alarm** *(Feuerwehr)* fire drill; ~**anfertigung** sample; ~**angebot** trial offer; ~**angestellter** probationer, probationary employee; ~**anstellung** probation[ary] employment (appointment), trial engagement; ~**anwärter** probationer; ~**arbeit** test paper; ~**arbeitsverhältnis** probationary employment; ~**aufnahme** *(Film)* screen test; ~**auftrag** trial (sample) order; ~**auftrag plazieren** to place a trial order; ~**auftritt einer Sängerin** trial hearing of a singer; ~**ballon** pilot balloon; ~**band** dummy copy; ~**befragung** pilot study, pretest; ~**belastung** *(Maschine)* proof (testing) load; ~**benutzung** trial use; ~**beschäftigung** trial (probationary) employment; ~**bestellung** sample (trial) order.

Probebilanz rough (preclosing trial) balance, tentative balance sheet;
bereinigte ~ closing trial balance; **nach Gruppen geordnete** ~ classified trial balance.

Probe|bild proof; ~**bogen** proof [sheet]; ~**bohrung** exploratory drilling, test bore, exploration; ~**bühne** rehearsal stage; ~**dienstzeit** probationary arrangement; ~**druck** proof sheet, specimen volume; ~**entlohnung** probationary [wage] rate; ~**entnahme** sampling, taking a sample; ~**entwurf** tentative draft; ~**erhebung** *(Statistik)* exploration (pilot) survey, pilot study; ~**exemplar** complimentary copy, specimen [copy], sample copy; ~**fahrt** *(Auto)* trial run (trip, drive), test run (drive), road test, *(auf See)* maiden trip, sea trial, shakedown cruise; ~**fahrt unternehmen** to test-drive; **einer ~fahrt unterzogen werden** to be test-run; ~**fall** trial (test) case; ~**flug** trial (test, shakedown, demonstration) flight, test flying; **zum ~flug vorgesehen sein** to be scheduled for its first flight; ~**flugzeug** prototype aircraft; ~**gehalt** entrance (trial) rate, probationary wage rate.

probe|gelaufen *(Maschine)* tested; ~**gemäß** up to pattern.

Probe|gold standard gold; ~**heft** specimen; ~**interview** pretest interview; ~**jahr** year of probation, probation (trial) year; ~**kandidat** probationer; ~**karte** sample card; ~**kauf** sale on approval; ~**kiste** sample box; ~**lauf** dummy run, *(Auto)* run-up, *(Produktion)* witness assembly; ~**lauf einer Fabrik** trial run of a plant, *(mit voller Kraft)* full-power run; ~**leiter** *(Theater)* rehearser; ~**lektion** trial lesson; ~**lieferung** trial delivery; ~**lohnsatz** probationary [wage] rate; ~**mitgliedschaft** trial membership; ~**mobilmachung** defence test; ~**modell** pattern design; ~**münze** proof coin; ~**muster** check (trial, reference) sample, market (reference) pattern, *(Münzen)* assay sample.

proben, Theaterstück to rehearse a play.

Probe|nahme sampling; ~**nummer** specimen number, *(Zeitung)* trial issue; ~**packung** trial package; ~**prozeß** test action; ~**schacht** prospecting shaft; ~**seite** specimen page; ~**sendung** trial package (consignment, shipment, *US*, lot), goods sent on trial, sample sent on approval, pattern parcel; ~**stück** specimen [copy], pattern [sample], patterned sample, trial [piece]; ~**termin** trial day; ~**untersuchung** pilot study (test), pretest; ~**vertrag** tentative agreement; ~**verzollung** trial (test) shipment; ~**vorführung** showcase; ~**vorstellung** *(Theater)* tryout.

probeweise on trial (probation), *(Waren)* on approval;
Zeitung ~ abonnieren to take a newspaper on trial; **j. ~ anstellen (einstellen)** to give s. o. a trial, to engage s. o. on probation; **Maschine ~ laufen lassen** to give a machine a trial;
~ **beschäftigter Angestellter** probationary employee, probationer.

Probezeit qualifying (trial) period, testing period, *(Angestellter)* time of probation, probation[ary term];
seine ~ abmachen to be on probation; **j. mit ~ anstellen** to engage s. o. on probation, to take s. o. on trial; **mit einer zweijährigen ~ anstellen** to engage s. o. on two years probation;
~ **nicht bestehen** to be found on trial to be incompetent.

Probieren geht über Studieren the proof of the pudding is in the eating.

probieren to try, to test, to attempt, to give a run, *(kosten)* to taste;
es noch einmal mit jem. ~ to give s. o. another chance; **neue Methode** ~ to try out a new method.

Probier|gewicht assay ton; **~waage** assay balance.

Problem problem, difficulty, *(Geschichte)* proposition, knot;
eigentliches ~ real issue; **entscheidendes** ~ vital problem; **geschäftspolitische** **~e** business policy issues; **heikles** ~ thorny problem; **innenpolitisches** ~ home-front problem; **juristisches** ~ legal problem; **kompliziertes** ~ overriding problem; **schwieriges** ~ hard problem (nut to crack); **ungelöstes** ~ unresolved problem; **vielschichtiges** ~ complex problem; **vorrangiges** ~ weighty matter; **wichtige** **~e** great issues; **wirtschaftspolitisches** ~ economic[-policy] problem;
~e der Anlagenstreuung diversification problem; **~e der Betriebsführung** managerial problems, business-policy issues; ~ **der richtigen Zeitwahl** timing problem;
~ **angehen (sich mit einem ~ auseinandersetzen)** to get down to (deal, grapple) with (wade into) a problem; **~en ausweichen** to straddle issues; ~ **behandeln** to handle a problem; **kein ~ darstellen** to pose no problem; **einem ~ gegenüberstehen** to face an issue; **geschäftliche ~e haben** to run into trouble; **jds. ~ lösen** to meet s. one's case; ~ **zusammen mit den zuständigen Abteilungen lösen** to solve a problem between the departments concerned; ~ **ohne Rücksicht auf die Folgen lösen** to force issues; ~ **nicht loslassen** to worry out a problem; **schwieriges ~ aus einer Sache machen** to make it tough; ~ **meistern** to lick a problem *(US)*; ~ **wälzen** to roll a problem round in one's head.

Problematik problematic nature;
über die ~ des modernen Verkehrs sprechen to give a talk on modern traffic problems.

Problem|dickicht, in ein ~dickicht geraten to run into bushy problems; **~gebiet** problem area; **~kreis** complex of problems.

problemlos problem-free.

Problemstück *(Theater)* problem (thesis) play.

Procedere procedure.

Produkt produce, product[ion], making, *(Arbeitsergebnis)* work, *(Ergebnis)* result, outcome, *(Handelsware)* commodity;
ausländisches ~ product of foreign make; **fertiges** ~ finished product; **geistiges** ~ product of one's brain, progeny; **gekoppeltes** ~ tying product *(US)*; **gesamtwirtschaftliches** ~ national product; **gewerbliches** ~ industrial (manufactured) product; **halbfertiges** ~ half-finished product; **homogenes** ~ homogeneous product; **verfälschtes** ~ adulteration;
~ **jahrelanger Arbeit** result of several years' work.

Produkte *(Agrarwirtschaft)* produce, *(Industrie)* manufactures, products, *(Waren)* wares, commodities, goods;
abgepackte ~ packaged goods; **chemische** ~ chemical products; **im Markt eingeführte** ~ established products; **einheimische** ~ home (inland) manufactures; **industriell gefertigte** ~ industrial (manufactured) products; **maschinell hergestellte** ~ machine-made products; **serienmäßig hergestellte** ~ serial manufactures; **hochqualifizierte** ~ high-quality (sophisticated) products; **landwirtschaftliche** ~ agricultural products (produce); **minderwertige** ~ inferior products, irregulars; **modische** ~ fancy articles; **anerkannte pharmazeutische** ~ ethical products; **nicht preisstabile** ~ nonprice-maintained products, nonfair items *(US)*; **teure** ~ high-priced commodities; **tierische** ~ animal products; **leicht verderbliche** ~ highly perishable products;
~ **des gehobeneren Bedarfs** high-quality products; ~ **mit stabilen Preisen** price-maintained articles (goods, merchandise, *US*); ~ **erstklassiger Qualität** high-grade goods, first-class quality;
seine ~ billig abgeben to sell one's wares cheaply; **Verhandlungen über einzeln aufgeführte ~ führen** to carry out negotiations on a selective product-by-product basis; ~ **maschinell herstellen** to produce goods by machinery; **neue ~ vorführen** to showcast new products.

Produkt|absatz, schleppender poor market; **~analyse** product analysis; **~aussage** product endorsement; **~auswahl** product choice; **~bekanntmachung** product endorsement (exposure); **~beschreibung** product specifications; **~bündel** product grouping; **~differenzierung** diversification of products, product differentiation; **~eigenschaften** product features; **~einführung** product training; **~einheit** unit labo(u)r costs; **letzte ~einheit** marginal unit; **~einteilung** product category.

Produkten|basis product base; **~börse** produce (goods) exchange, commodity market, commodity exchange; **~großhandelsbörse** wholesale product market, pit *(US)*; **~handel** trade in domestic produce, produce trade; **~händler** produce merchant (dealer); **~kartell** producer cartel; **~kenntnis** product information; **~makler** produce (merchandise, commercial) broker, produce middleman; **selbständiger ~makler** pit trader *(US)*; **~markt** produce market; **~werbung** product advertising.

Produkt|etat product budget; **~familie** product family; **~gestalter** product designer; **~gruppe** product class (line); **~kategorie** product category.

Produktion production, producing, output, manufacture, manufacturing, outturn, make;
in ~ *(Film)* on the floor;
abnehmende ~ ebbing production; **mit hohen Kosten arbeitende** ~ high-cost production; **bedarfsgerechte** ~ production on demand; **billige** ~ low-cost production; **durchschnittliche** ~ average production; **einheimische** ~ home (domestic) production; **erhöhte** ~ increased production; **fabrikmäßige** ~ mass (series) production; **gedrosselte** ~ curtailed production; **gekoppelte** ~ combined production; **gelenkte** ~ controlled production; **genormte** ~ standardized production; **geplante** ~ budgeted production; **gesamtwirtschaftliche** ~ overall economic output; **patentamtlich geschützte** ~ copyrighted production *(US)*; **gewerbliche** ~ factory (economic, industrial) production; **gleichmäßige** ~ steady production; **großbetriebliche** ~ large-scale (wholesale) production; **handwerkliche** ~ manual production; **mit geringen Unkosten (niedrigen Selbstkosten) hergestellte** ~ low-cost production; **industrielle** ~ industrial production; **inländische** ~ domestic (home) production; **jährliche** ~ annual (yearly) production; **landwirtschaftliche** ~ agricultural (farm) production, farm output; **laufende** ~ current production; **innerhalb der Rentabilität liegende** ~ marginal production; **literarische** ~ literary output; **maschinelle** ~ machine production; **minderwertige** ~ irregulars; **mittelbare** ~ indirect production; **monatliche** ~ monthly production; **nachhinkende** ~ lag in production; **rückläufige** ~ falling (declining, receding) production; **saisonbedingte** ~ seasonal production; **schrumpfende** ~ contracting (falling) production; **serienmäßige** ~ serial (series, volume) production, production in bulk; **stetige** ~ settled production; **stillgelegte** ~ nonproduction; **tägliche** ~ daily output; **teure** ~ high-cost (expensive) production; **überschüssige** ~ surplus production; **verbundene** ~ joint production; **vergesellschaftete** ~ socialized production; **verminderte** ~ curtailed production; **volkswirtschaftliche** ~ gross national production; **volle** ~ full production; **vorübergehende** ~ changeover production; **wirkliche** ~ genuine production;
~ **vor Auftragseingang** speculative production; ~ **am laufenden Band** moving-band production, assembly-line technique, line (belt-system of) production; ~ **je Beschäftigtenstunde** production per man-hour; ~ **bei voller Beschäftigung** capacity output; ~ **nur auf Bestellung** intermittent manufacturing; ~ **mit großen Exportmöglichkeiten** output of high export potential; ~ **schnell verbrauchter Güter** soft-goods production; ~ **an der Kostengrenze** marginal production; ~ **von Massengütern** large-scale (wholesale) production, production of manufactured goods; ~ **von Siemens-Martin-Stahl** output of open-hearth steel;
~ **abbremsen** to put a check (brake) on production; ~ **ankurbeln** to crank up production; ~ **den Absatzmöglichkeiten anpassen** to match production to the absorption capacities; ~ **der Nachfrage anpassen** to tailor (gear) production to demand; ~ **anregen** to stimulate production; **in der ~ arbeiten** to work on the assembly line; **bei geringerer ~ wirtschaftlicher arbeiten** to work economically at a lower output; ~ **aufnehmen** to go into production; **wesentlichen Teil der ~ ausmachen** to form the bulk of production; **mit der ~ beginnen** to go on stream *(US)*; **sofort wieder mit der ~ beginnen** to rush into production; ~ **beschränken** to curtail production; ~ **auf den Höchststand bringen** to raise production to a maximum; ~ **drosseln (einschränken)** to reduce the output, to restrain (curb, curtail, cut, slash, check, restrict) production; ~ **künstlich einschränken** to ca'canny; ~ **einstellen** to discontinue the manufacture, to fold up, to phase out [production]; ~ **erhöhen** to step up production; ~ **fördern** to stimulate (promote) production; ~ **in Gang halten** to keep industry going (production wheels humming); ~ **hochtreiben** to gear up production; ~ **programmieren** to scale production; **in der ~ begriffen sein** to be in process of production; ~ **steigern** to step (speed) up (increase) production; ~ **stillegen** to halt production lines; ~ **umstellen** to convert production; ~ **verlangsamen** to slow down production; ~ **verringern** to reduce production.

Produktions|abfall drop (decline) in production, production slump; ~**abkommen** agreement between producers.

Produktionsablauf production flow, production run (operations), manufacturing process;
gleichmäßiger ~ even flow of production; **normaler** ~ regular course of manufacture;
~ **festlegen** to schedule production *(US)*.

Produktions|abnahme dwindling production; ~**abschreckung** production disincentive; ~**abschwächung** productive weakening; ~**abteilung** manufacturing (production) division, productive (manufacturing) department; ~**anfang** startup of production; ~**angleichung** adjustment in production; ~**angleichung vornehmen** to adjust production; ~**ankurbelung** cranking-up of production; ~**anlage** production machinery, plant, manufacturing establishment; ~**anlagen** productive assets (facilities, machinery), manufacturing (producing) facilities; ~**anlauf** starting of production; ~**anlaufkosten** start-up costs of production; ~**anstieg** increase (jump) in production, uptick; **mengenmäßiger** ~**anstieg** increase in the volume of production; **rasanter** ~**anstieg** upsurge in production; ~**anstrengungen** productive efforts; ~**anteil** share of output; ~**apparat** production network (facilities), productive (production) apparatus *(US)*; ~**auffächerung** product diversification; **erfolgreich durchgeführte** ~**auffächerung** diversification record; ~**aufgabe** production function, *(Stillegung)* closing down, shakeout; ~**aufnahme** going into production, *(erneute)* resumption of manufacturing operations; ~**aufteilung** product split; ~**auftrag** production order (contract), manufacturing order.

Produktionsaufträge, lawinenartige ~ **auslösen** to mushroom into production orders; ~ **erst nach positiv verlaufenen Modellversuchen erteilen** to fly before you buy; ~ **teilweise bei Fremdbetrieben herstellen lassen** to hive off production, to sublet part of its production.

Produktions|aufwand production (product) cost; ~**ausdehnung** expansion of production; ~**ausfall** loss (lack) of production, shortfall in production; ~**ausschuß** production committee; ~**ausstattung** productive (production) equipment.

Produktionsausstoß manufacturing output;
beschleunigter ~ speedup of production;
~ **erhöhen** to step (speed) up production; ~ **eines Verkaufsschlagers erhöhen** to step up production of a fast-moving line; ~ **durch bessere Fertigungsmethoden steigern** to increase production by better methods.

Produktionsausweitung expansion of production;
erfolgreich durchgeführte ~ diversification record; **im Inland vorgenommene** ~ home-based productive expansion;
~ **eines Unternehmens** company diversifications.

Produktions|barometer commerce's (composite) index of indicators; ~**basis** manufacturing basis; ~**bedingungen** manufacturing conditions; ~**beginn** startup of production; ~**beginn sofort aufnehmen** to rush into production; ~**begrenzung** restriction of output, limitation upon production; ~**belebung** stimulation of production; ~**bereich** product, production diversifications; ~**bericht** production report; ~**beschränkung** restriction (curtailment) of (limitation upon) production, output restriction; ~**betrieb** productive enterprise (establishment), manufacturing plant; **billiger** ~**betrieb** lower-cost manufacturer; ~**betrieb für Fernsehgeräte** television-set manufacturer; ~**bilanz** production (manufacturing) statement; ~**bild** production picture; ~**breite** product diversification; **zu einer wohlgepolsterten** ~**breite Zuflucht nehmen** to fall back on a broad cushion of diversification; ~**dauer** production period; ~**differenzierung** diversification of products; ~**dispositionen** production plan (budget); ~**drosselung** reduction (dampening) of output, cut in production, cutback of production, production cutback, curtailment of production; ~**drosselung vornehmen** to cut (slash) production; ~**durchschnitt** production average; ~**einheit** producing (production) unit, unit of output (production); **gleichartige** ~**einheiten** equivalent units; ~**einrichtungen** productive (production) facilities (equipment).

Produktionseinschränkung restriction (slashing) of (contraction in) production (output), production cut, *(Volkswirtschaft)* disinvestment *(US)*, diminution of capital goods;
künstliche ~ ca'canny.

Produktions|einstellung phase-out, closing down, shake-out, termination of production; **neue** ~**einstellung vornehmen** to reschedule production; ~**elastizität** elasticity of production; ~**engpaß** bottleneck in production; ~**entfaltung** expansion of production; ~**entscheidung** production decision; ~**entscheidung treffen** to finalize; ~**entwicklung der Industrie** development of industrial output; **industrielle** ~**erfahrungen** industrial (manufacturing) know-how; **statistische** ~**erfassung** census of production; ~**ergebnis** output, production; **erste** ~**ergebnisse** initial production; ~**erhöhung** increase in production (output); **beschleunigte** ~**erhöhung** speedup of production; ~**erlaubnis** production permit, licence; ~**erlös** factory proceeds; ~**ertrag** output; ~**etat** production budget; ~**fächer** range of production; ~**fachmann** mechanical production man; ~**fähigkeit** productive (producing) capacity (efficiency), production rate, service capacity; ~**faktoren** factors (agents) of production, productive factors, production agents; **jederzeit auswechselbare** ~**faktoren** nonspecific factors of productions; **nicht auswechselbarer** ~**faktor** specific factor of production; ~**fehler** manufacturing defect; ~**finanzierung** production financing; ~**fläche** factory space; ~**flexibilität** flexibility in production; ~**förderung** promotion of production; ~**funktion** production function; ~**gang** production process, flow of production; **normaler** ~**gang** regular course of manufacture; ~**gebiet** production (producing) area, area of production, *(Herstellungszweig)* product (production) line; **verändertes** ~**gebiet** diversification area; **unrentable** ~**gebiete aufgeben** to eliminate unprofitable operations; **breites** ~**gefüge** diversified structure; ~**geheimnis** manufacturing secret; ~**gemeinkosten** indirect (overhead) cost, factory overheads; ~**gemeinschaft** collective; ~**genossenschaft** productive (production) cooperation, co-operative association for production, producer cooperative; **landwirtschaftliche** ~**genossenschaft** collective farm; ~**gesellschaft** manufacturing company (corporation, *US*); **ziemlich einseitige** ~**gesellschaft** little-diversified company (corporation); ~**gewinn** manufacturing profit; ~**gliederung** distribution of production; ~**größe** level of production; ~**grundlagen** productive apparatus *(US)*; ~**gutachten** production expertise; ~**güte** quality of production.

Produktionsgüter production (producer, capital, auxiliary, instrumental, manufacturers') goods, goods of the second order;
~**betrieb** manufacturing establishment; ~**hochkonjunktur** boom of production goods; ~**industrie** producer (production) goods industry; ~**marktforschung** industrial market research; ~**werbung** industrial advertising.

Produktionshöchst|grenzen festlegen to set production ceilings; ~**leistung** maximum capacity; ~**stand** peak of production, all-time production record; ~**ziffer** production limit figure.

Produktions|höhe rate of production, production rate; ~**index** index of industrial production, industrial production index; **bereinigter** ~**index** adjusted production index; ~**interessen** producing interest.

Produktionskapazität production (productive, output) capacity, producing power;
hundertprozentig ausgenutzte ~ full capacity production;
betriebliche ~ **voll ausfahren** to gear production to the capacity of a plant; ~ **erweitern** to expand one's production facilities; ~**en überanstrengen** to overstrain production capacity.

Produktions|kapazitätskurve production indifference curve; ~**kapital** productive capital; ~**kartell** producers' association, production combination; **kündbares** ~**kartell** terminable association; **spezielle** ~**kenntnisse** manufacturing know-how; ~**kennziffer** production index, index of industrial production; ~**koeffizient** production (input) coefficient; **fester** ~**koeffizient** fixed production coefficient; ~**kontingent** production quota; ~**konto** production (manufacturing) account; ~**kontrolle** control of production, production control; ~**kontrolleur** dispatcher; ~**konzession** industrial (manufacturing) licence.

Produktionskosten cost of manufacturing (production, goods manufactured, manufacture), manufacturing (product, production, factory, output) cost, manufacturer's (separable) costs, *(Rundfunk)* talent cost, *(Selbstkosten)* cost price;
einmalige ~ sunk cost; **durchschnittlich niedrigste** ~ normal costs; **reine** ~ mere costs of production; **unterschiedliche** ~ difference in costs of production; **volle** ~ total production costs;
~ **von Produkten, die zusammen hergestellt werden** joint costs;
~ **teilweise übernehmen** to contribute in part to the expense of production;
~**aufstellung** manufacturing cost sheet; ~**kontrolle** manufacturing cost control; ~**senkung** manufacturing economics; ~**theorie** cost-of-production theory of value.

Produktions|kraft productive force (capacity), producing power; ~**kräfte** factors of production; ~**kredit** production (productive) credit; ~**kreditgenossenschaft** production credit corporation; ~**kreislauf** production cycle; ~**kreuzzug** production crusade; ~**kurve** production curve; ~**kürzung** cutting back of production, production cut (cutback); ~**kürzung vornehmen** to slash production; ~**land** producing (manufacturing) country.

Produktionsleistung production rate (capacity), manufacturing efficiency, producing power, output, productivity;
inländische ~ domestic (home) production; **volkswirtschaftliche** ~ national product, the country's output;
~ **eines Kartells** cartel output; **erhöhte** ~ **einer Maschine** increased rate of production of a machine;
zu um 40 - 50% verkürzten ~en im Rahmen der Planung der letzten beiden Jahre führen to keep output down 40 - 50% of budgeted levels for the past two years.

Produktions|leiter production (plant) manager (supervisor), superintendent engineer, chief engineer in charge of production, director of production, production chief, line executive, executive producer; ~**leitung** plant (production) management, production planning; ~**lenkung** production control; **kriegsbedingte** ~**lenkung** production allocation program *(US)*; ~**lizenz** production permit, manufacturing licence; ~**löhne** manufacturing wages, productive labo(u)r; ~**material** direct material; ~**maximum** peak output; ~**menge** flow, amount of output, output in volume, make, amount (quantity) of production, *(Landwirtschaft)* output, yield; **monetär bewertete** ~**menge** money output; ~**methode** method of production, production method; **kostensparende** ~**methoden** cost-saving production methods; ~**minderung** reduction of output; ~**minimum** minimum output; ~**mittel** means of production, productive equipment, capital (producer) goods; ~**mittelindustrie** capital-goods industry; ~**möglichkeiten** productive (production) facilities, productive resources; ~**monopol** production (manufacturing) monopoly; ~**nachweis** production record; ~**niveau** level of production; ~**norm** production standard; ~**optimum** maximum capacity (output), production optimum.

produktionsorientiert production-oriented.

Produktions|pause production pause; ~**periode** working period; ~**plan** production scheme (schedule, budget, plan); ~**planung** planning of production, budgeted production, production planning, *(Kommunismus)* state planning; ~**politik** production policy; ~**potential** output potential, productive capacity (potential); ~**prämie** output bonus, production (piece-rate) bonus, production grant *(Br.)*; ~**preis** cost of production; ~**probelauf** field test.

Produktionsprogramm production budget (plan, schedule), manufacturing program(me) (schedule), product lines, plant program(me);
breites (breit gestreutes) ~ broad diversification, broadly diversified product lines; **gemischtes** ~ product mix; **reichhaltiges (weitgestreutes)** ~ product diversification, diversification program(me) into manufacturing;
sein ~ **abrunden** to round off one's production, to round up its product lines; ~ **auffächern** to diversify production; **einseitig auf Bedürfnisse der Raumfahrtindustrie abgestelltes** ~ **auffächern** to diversify out of aerospace industry; ~ **erweitern** to broaden its line of products; **der allgemeinen Tendenz breitgestreuter** ~**e folgen** to jump on the diversification bandwaggon; **seinen Erfolg einem breitgefächerten** ~ **verdanken** to owe one's performance to diversification.

Produktions|programmierer production scheduler *(US)*; ~**programmierung** production scheduling *(US)*; ~**prozeß** manufacturing (production, productive, industrial) process, process of manufacture; ~**qualität** product quality; ~**quote** production quota, quota of production; ~**rahmen** range of products; **alleinige** ~**rechte haben** to have the exclusive production rights.

produktionsreif sein to be ready to go into production.

Produktions|reife finished product stage; ~**reserve** idle capacity; ~**risiko** risk of production, producer's risk.

Produktionsrückgang falling (fall in, setback, decline in, drop in) production, production decline, downturn in manufacturing; **saisonbedingter** ~ seasonal drop in production; **scharfer** ~ slump in production.

Produktions|schrumpfung in der Schiffahrtsindustrie new shake-out in the shipbuilding industry; ~**schwankungen** fluctuations in production; ~**schwelle** shutdown point; ~**schwerpunkt verlagern** to divert production, to shift product emphasis; ~**schwierigkeiten** production difficulties; ~**sektor** sector of production, manufacturing sector; ~**senkung** restriction (curtailment) of production; ~**serie** series; ~**skala** range of production; ~**soll** production target; ~**sparte** line of production; ~**spezialisierung** specialization of production; ~**spezifikation** product specification; ~**spitze** alltime production record; ~**stab** production staff; ~**stadium** stage of production; ~**stand** level of production (output), production level, industrial output; ~**standard** standard of production, production standard, norms; ~**stätte** manufacturing establishment (plant, factory), producing unit (factory), productive establishment, production facility; **ausländische** ~**stätte errichten** to build up production plant abroad; ~**stätten unterhalten** to manufacture; ~**steigerung** increased (rise in) production, production increase; ~**steigerung herbeiführen (hervorrufen)** to increase (encourage) production; ~**stelle** producing (production) unit, manufacturing establishment; ~**steuer** fabrication tax; ~**steuerung** production control (management, planning); **vorübergehende** ~**stillegung** shutdown in production; ~**stopp** shutdown in production; ~**stopp vornehmen** to tie production; ~**streuung** diversification of product lines, diversifying; **optimale** ~ **und Handelsstruktur** optimal pattern of production; ~**stufe** production step, stage of production; ~**system** production system; ~**tätigkeit** productive occupation, manufacturing (production) activity; **saisonbedingte** ~**tätigkeit** seasonal production; ~**technik** production engineering.

produktionstechnische Anforderungen manufacturing requirements.

Produktions|tempo tempo of production, production rate; ~**termin** production date; ~**test** product test; ~**theorie** theory of production; ~**überschuß** production surplus, surplus products; ~**überschüsse beseitigen** to trim excess production; ~**übersicht** production return; ~**überwacher** production controller; ~**überwachung** production control (supervision), control of production; ~**umfang** production volume; ~**umstellung** conversion of production; ~**umwege** round-about methods of production; ~**unternehmen** manufacturing concern, productive undertaking; ~**verbot** prohibition to produce; **geplante** ~**verbreitung** diversification planning; ~ **und Konsumverein** industrial and provident society *(Br.)*; ~**verfahren** technique of production, production technique, production (manufacturing) method, manufacturing service (process), manufacturing know-how; **rationalisiertes** ~**verfahren** production rationalization; **veraltetes** ~**verfahren** method obsolescence; ~**vergleich der gesamten Industrieerzeugung** comparison of total industrial output; **günstige** ~**verhältnisse** low-cost production facilities; ~**verlagerung** diversion of production; **schwerpunktartige** ~**verlagerung** major switch to different industries; ~**verlangsamung** throttling back of assembly lines, production slowdown; **absichtliche** ~**verlangsamung** ca'canny strike; ~**verlauf** production schedule (run); ~**verlust** loss of production (output), production loss; ~**vermögen** productive property; ~**vertrag** production (manufacturing) contract; ~**verzögerung** production delay; ~**volumen** production volume, volume of industrial production; ~**vorgang** productive (manufacturing) process (operations); ~**vorschau** production outlook; ~**vorschriften** production prescriptions, manufacturing directions; ~**wachstum** growth of production, output growth; ~**weise** method of production; ~**wert** production (cost) value, value of production; ~**wirtschaft** economics of production, producing industry; ~**zahlen** output (production) figures; ~**zeit** period of production, production time; ~**zentrum** center *(US)* (centre, *Br.*) of production, production (manufacturing) center *(US)* (centre, *Br.*); ~**ziel** production goal, output target, production schedule; ~**ziel nicht erreichen** to fall short of production goal; **effektive** ~**ziffer** real output; ~**ziffern** output figures, production figures (rates), rates (data) of production; **schwankende** ~**ziffern** unsteady output; ~**zunahme** production increase, output growth; ~**zuschüsse** production grants; ~**zuwachs** output growth; **für** ~**zwecke** for manufacturing purposes; ~**zweig** production line, manufacturing branch; **auftragsloser** ~**zweig** empty production line; **einzelne** ~**zweige stillegen** to halt certain (some) production lines; ~**zyklus** cycle of production.

produktiv productive, fertile, *(Schriftsteller)* prolific;
~**e Anlage** paying investment; ~**e Aufgabe** productive function; ~**e Löhne** productive wages; ~**er Schriftsteller** prolific author.

Produktiv|genossenschaft producer cooperative, productive trading society; ~**güter** productive goods.

Produktivität productivity, productiveness, productive capacity, *(Schriftsteller)* fertility, prolificacy, prolificness;
betriebliche ~ plant productivity; **potentielle** ~ idle overhead; **schöpferische** ~ creativeness; **volkswirtschaftliche** ~ national productive capacity.

Produktivitäts|abkommen productivity deal (agreement) *(Br.)*; **~abnahme** diminishing productivity; **rasanter ~anstieg** productivity surge; **~ausschuß** commission on productivity; **~beraterstab** productivity team; **~bild** productivity showing; **~bindung** productivity linking; **~entwicklung** trend of productivity, productivity trend; **erstklassige ~ergebnisse aufweisen** to turn in the best productivity performance; **~feldzug** productivity drive; **~fortschritte** process in (advance in, increase of) productivity; **~gefälle** productivity differential.

produktivitätsgekoppelter Lohnanstieg productivity-related pay hike.

Produktivitäts|gewinn gain in productivity; **~grad steigern** to increase productivity; **~grenze** margin of productivity, marginal productivity; **~index** productivity index; **~niveau** level of productivity; **~normen** productivity standards; **~politik** policy for productivity; **~prämie** productivity bonus; **~programm** productivity incentive program(me); **~rate** rate of productivity; **Lohnerhöhungen an die ~rate koppeln** to peg wage increases to the rate of productivity; **~rente** productivity-linked pension; **~spanne** margin of productiveness; **~stand** level of productivity.

produktivitätssteigernder Maschinenpark productivity-boosting machinery.

Produktivitäts|steigerung increase of productivity, productivity raise *(US)* (rise, *Br.*, boost, hike); **~studie** study of productivity; **~theorie** marginal productivity theory of wages; **~theorie des Zinses** productivity theory of interest; **~verbesserungen** improvements in productivity, productivity improvements; **tarifliche ~vereinbarung** productivity agreement *(Br.)*; **~wachstum** productivity growth; **~wert** productivity value; **~zunahme** increased productivity, growth in productivity; **~zunahme wettmachen** to outrun increases in (return to) productivity; **~zuwachs** increase in productivity, productivity gain (increase, boost, hike); **Tariferhöhungen auf ~zuwächse abstellen** to settle for rises based on a productivity rate; **~zuwachsrate** productivity growth rate; **~zweck** productive purpose.

Produktiv|kapital productive (auxiliary, instrumental) capital; **~kategorie** product category; **~kräfte** productive facilities (resources), forces of production; **~kredit** production credit; **~kreditgenossenschaft** production credit corporation; **~vermögen** productive property.

Produkt|manager brand (product) manager; **~test** product testings.

Produzent producer, manufacturer, maker, operator, outputter *(US)*, *(Film)* producer, play craftsman;
mit hohen Kosten arbeitender ~ high-cost producer; **mit geringen Selbstkosten arbeitender ~** low-cost operator; **freier ~** entrepreneur;
~ landwirtschaftlicher Erzeugnisse agricultural producer;
~en und Konsumenten producers and consumers.

Produzenten|bereich manufacturer's sphere; **~gewinn** producer's rent (surplus); **~haftung** product liability, manufacturer's warranty (liability); **~handel** direct distribution; **~kredit** producer credit; **~preis** producer price; **~rente** *(Marshall)* quasi-rent; **~verband** producer association.

produzieren to produce, to manufacture, to make, to turn out; **sich ~** to show off, to trot out, to make an exhibition of o. s.; **jährlich 600.000 Lastwagen ~** to roll out 600.000 trucks a year; **in Massen ~** to mass-produce; **Mist ~** to make a mess of things, to make a hash of it; **Waren verschiedenster Qualität ~** to manufacture goods in various qualities; **sich als Witzbold ~** to act the fool.

produziert|werden *(Film)* to be on the floor;
~es Einkommen produced income.

profan profane, secular;
~es Ende einer Laufbahn undistinguished end of a career.

Profanbau profane building.

profanieren to desecrate.

Profanierung desecration, violation of a church.

Profession vocation, profession, trade.

professionell in a professional way, professional;
~er Spieler professional gambler.

Professor professor, reader *(Br.)*;
angehender ~ prospective professor; **außerordentlicher ~** extraordinary (associate, *US*, adjunct, *US*) professor, lecturer with temporary appointment; **mit Teilaufgaben betrauter ~** assistant professor *(Br.)*; **emeritierter ~** emeritus [professor]; **ordentlicher ~** full professor *(US)*, professor in ordinary, lecturer with permanent appointment; **als freier Forscher tätiger ~** research professor;
~ mit Lehrauftrag supernumerary professor; **~ der Rechtswissenschaft** professor in law *(Br.)*;
j. zum ~ ernennen to appoint s. o. to a professorship; **als ~ lehren** to profess *(Br.)*.

professorenhaft professorial.

Professoren|schaft professoriate; **~stelle erhalten** to be appointed to a professorship; **~stelle innehaben** to hold a professorship (a chair).

professorial, im ~en Bereich liegen to be within the professorial range.

Professur professorship, lectureship, lecture, professorial (professor's) chair;
gestiftete ~ endowed professorship; **ordentliche ~** full professorship *(Br.)*; **volkswirtschaftliche ~** chair in economics;
~ für Handelswissenschaften chair of commerce;
~ ablehnen to refuse a professorship; **~ annehmen** to accept a professorship; **~ ausschreiben** to declare a professorial chair vacant; **~ erhalten** to be appointed to a professorship; **~ gründen** to endow a professorship; **~ innehaben** to be a professor, to hold a professorship; **~ niederlegen** to vacate a professorship; **jem. eine ~ übertragen** to appoint s. o. to a professorship.

Profi pro.

Profil profile, outline, contour, *(fig.)* personality, *(Reifen)* tread;
im ~ side-face; **mit flachem ~** low-profile;
abgeriebenes ~ thin thread; **markantes ~** striking profile;
~ eines Produkts product personality;
j. im ~ aufnehmen to photograph s. o. side-face; **~ haben** *(Zeitung)* to stand out; **kein ~ haben** to be colo(u)rless; **an ~ gewonnen haben** to have done one's image a great deal of good; **kein ~ mehr haben** *(Reifen)* to have no tread left;
~abrieb tread abrasion; **~eisen** profile (structural, figured) iron.

profilieren, sich to make a name for o. s., to make one's personality felt; **sich für das Amt des Parteivorsitzenden ~** to render o. s. eligible for the job of party leader; **sich in einer Rolle ~** to stand out in a part; **sich bei Verhandlungen ~** to distinguish o. s. during negotiations.

Profil|neurose image neurosis; **~reifen** nonskid tire (tyre, *Br.*); **~stahl** structural steel.

Profit profit, gain, advantage, turn, makings, clean-up *(US sl.)*;
kleiner ~ thin profit, peanuts;
~ aus einem öffentlichen Amt spoils of office; **guter ~ für wenig Mühe** money for jam *(Br., sl.)*;
~ bringen to bring grist to the mill; **~ erzielen** to make one's hand, to turn to advantage, to have a rake-off on s. th.; **~e durch optimale Auftragsgrößenordnungen erzielen** to reap economies of scale; **10 Pfund ~ machen** to be ten pounds to the good; **auf ~ aus sein** to have an eye to the main chance.

profitabel pay, remunerative, lucrative.

Profit|geier profiteer, percentage worker *(sl.)*; **~geschäft** job; **~gier** greed of gain (profit); **gemeine ~gier** filthy lucre.

profitgierig money-grubbing.

profitieren to profit by, to gain, to benefit;
von etw. persönlich ~ to benefit privately from s. th.; **an einem Geschäft ~** to profit by a bargain, to study to one's profit, to find one's account in a business, to make on an action; **10 £ ~** to be £ 10 in pocket; **vom Reiseergebnis ~** to share a voyage; **von den konkursrechtlichen Schutzbestimmungen ~** to take the benefit of the bankruptcy laws; **steuerlich ~** to benefit tax-wise; **von einem Streik ~** to capitalize on a strike; **aus einem Vortrag ~** to benefit from a lecture.

Profit|jäger profiteer[er], profitmonger, percentage worker *(sl.)*; **~macherei** profiteering.

profitsüchtig profit-seeking.

pro forma pro forma, as a matter of form, *(zum Schein)* simulated, sham, feigned;
nur noch ~ zustimmen to assent merely as a matter of form.

Proforma|anteil *(Vorstandsmitglied)* dummy (qualifying, *US*) share; **~bezüge** nominal income; **~bilanz** pro-forma balance sheet; **~direktor** dummy director; **~faktur** pro-forma invoice; **~geschäft** pro-forma transaction (purchase); **~indossament** straw name; **~rechnung** pro-forma invoice, pro-forma (simulated) account; **~verfahren** sham trial; **~verkauf** fictitious (sham) sale; **~verkaufsrechnung** pro-forma account sales; **~wechsel** pro-forma (accommodation, fictitious) bill.

profundes Wissen profound knowledge.

Prognose prognosis, forecast, forecast[ing];
entgegen allen ~n beyond all forecasts;
konjunkturelle ~ economic forecast, business outlook;
langfristige ~ long-range forecasting;

~ **wirtschaftlicher Entwicklungen** economic forecasting; **günstige ~ der wirtschaftlichen Entwicklung** favo(u)rable prognosis of the economic development; **~n für die Zukunft** prognostications for the future;
in seiner ~ auf eine Preisabschwächung setzen to muffle one's forecast on prices; **sehr ernste ~ stellen** to give a very serious prognosis; **der Konjunktur eine ~ stellen** to forecast the course of business; **~n des Finanzministeriums übertreffen** to overshoot treasury forecasts; **wirtschaftliche ~ vornehmen** to to forecast the course of business;
~abteilung forecasting division; **~änderung** forecast amendment; **~branche** forecasting business; **miserable ~erfolge** poor forecasting records; **~fehler** forecasting (projection) error; **~irrtum** forecasting error; **~korridor** prediction corridor; **~methode** forecasting method; **~stelle** forecasting body; **~tätigkeit** forecasting service; **~verfahren für kurzfristige Bedarfsvorhersage** *(Statistik)* exponential smoothing; **~zeitraum** forecast period.
prognostische Dispositionsberatung advisory prognostic.
prognostizieren to forecast, to prognosticate.
Programm program(me), plan, *(Fernsehen)* program(me), channel, *(Theater)* program(me), paybill, *(Unternehmen)* product line;
mit einem neuen ~ *(Partei)* under a new label;
abendfüllendes ~ full-length program(me); **auf Dose (Tonband) aufgenommenes ~** recorded program(me); **in allen Einzelheiten ausgearbeitetes ~** package *(US)*; **von verschiedenen Fernsehanstalten gemeinsam ausgestrahltes ~** television linkup; **beliebtes ~** *(Fernsehen)* high-rated program(me); **ferngesteuertes ~** *(Fernsehen, Rundfunk)* remote *(US)*; **konjunkturpolitisches ~** [anti]cyclical program(me); **kopflastiges ~** head-start program(me); **langfristiges ~** long-term program(me); **von Menschen lesbares ~** *(Datenverarbeitung)* source language; **parteipolitisches ~** party platform; **politisches ~** political program(me), platform, ticket *(US)*, policy lines; **steuerpolitisches ~** fiscal policy (tax) program(me); **umfassendes ~** comprehensive program(me); **ganze Skala umfassendes ~** full-scale program(me); **im einzelnen vorbereitetes ~** kit; **wirklichkeitsnahes ~** bread-and-butter program(me);
~ für die Beschaffung billiger Mietwohnungen low-cost housing program(me); **das ~ gilt als Eintrittskarte** entrance is by program(me); **~ zur Energieeinsparung** energy-saving program(me); **~ mit zwei Hauptfilmen** double feature program(me); **~ für technische Hilfe an Entwicklungsländer** Expanded Program(me) of Technical Assistance; **umfangreiches ~ an Küchenmöbeln** wide range of kitchen furniture; **~ zur Leistungsbeurteilung** appraisal program(me); **~ der vereinigten Linken** left-wing program(me); **~ zur Schaffung von Arbeitsplätzen** job placement program *(US)*; **~ für Schulung ungelernter Arbeiter** manpower training program *(US)*; **~ staatsverbürgter Studentendarlehen** Federal Insurance Loan Program *(US)*; **~ zur Umsiedlung von Industriearbeitern** Resettlement Transfer Scheme *(Br.)*; **umfassendes ~ zusätzlicher Vergünstigungen** overall compensation program(me); **~ eines Verlages** list of publications; **~ für die Weiterbildung von Führungskräften** executive development program(me);
vom ~ absetzen to take off a program(me); **~ ankündigen** to bill; **ganzes ~ ansehen** to go through the whole program(me); **~ auflockern** to disseminate a program(me); **~ aufstellen** to formulate (draw up) a program(me); **~ ausschmücken** to flourish a program(me); **~ für die breiten Massen ausstrahlen** *(Fernsehprogramm)* to cater for the masses; **als erster ein neues politisches ~ beantragen** to initiate a new policy; **~ gestalten** to program(me); **sich streng an ein ~ halten** to adhere strictly to a program(me); **~ kaufen** to buy a program(me); **~ kürzen** to pare a program(me); **jem. nicht ins ~ passen** not to suit s. one's book; **sein ~ skizzieren** to outline one's program(me); **mit einem breiteren ~ vor die Öffentlichkeit treten** to speak from a broader national platform; **scharfe Einsparungsmaßnahmen eines ~s verhindern** to spare a program(me) from meat-axe cuts; **~ vertreten** to support a program(me); **ins ~ eingestreut werden** to be thrown into the program(me); **~ zusammenstellen** to arrange a program(me);
~ablaufplan program(me) flow; **~absage** *(Fernsehen)* closing announcement; **~agentur** *(Rundfunk)* agency; **~analyse** program(me) analysis; **~analysegerät** *(Fernsehen)* program(me) analysis; **~änderung** change in the program(me); **~änderung in der letzten Minute** eleven-hour change in the program(me); **~ankündigung, ~ansage** program(me) (broadcast) announcement.
Programmatik declared intentions.
Programmatiker *(Partei)* keynoter *(US)*.
programmatisch programmatic[al];
~e Rede keynote address.
Programm | auflockerung dissemination of program(me)s; **~ausgabe** *(Computer)* information output; **~auswahl** *(Fernsehen)* television viewing; **~berichtigung** *(Lochkarten)* debugging; **~beschneidung** paring a program(me); **~bibliothek** library of program(me)s; **~direktor** *(Rundfunk)* program(me) director; **~dokumentation** *(Computer)* program(me) documentation; **~durchführung** program(me) management; **~durchlauf** *(Computer)* run; **~einblendung** fading-in, blurb; **~eingabe** *(Datenverarbeitung)* information input; **~einheit** program(me) unit; **~fehler** *(Datenverarbeitung)* program(me) bug; **~füller** *(Radio)* filler.
programmgemäß as arranged, according to plan;
~ verlaufen to go off according to schedule;
nicht ~er Zwischenfall unforeseen incident.
Programm | gestalter program(m)er; **~gestaltung** making of program(me)s, program(m)ing.
programmgesteuert computer-controlled.
Programm | heft program(me), playbill; **~hersteller** program(me) producer program(me) planner.
Programmiereinrichtung program(m)ing device.
Programmieren information.
programmieren to [enter in a] program(me);
Produktionsprozeß ~ to program(me) a production process.
Programmierer *(Computer)* program(m)er;
~sprache program(m)ing language.
Programmierhilfe *(Datenverarbeitung)* software.
programmierter Unterricht program(m)ed instruction.
Programmierung program(m)ing, information;
ganzzahlige ~ integer program(m)ing; **mehrfache ~** multiple program(m)ing; **[nicht]lineare ~** [non]linear program(m)ing.
Programmierungs | ablauf program(m)ing flowchart; **~fehler** program(m)ing error; **~verfahren** program(m)ing method.
Programm | kode function code; **~kredit** personal credit; **~kürzung** paring a program(me); **~leiter** *(Rundfunk)* program(me) director, editor; **~musik** program(me) music; **~nummer** number of a program(me), turn *(Br.)*, package *(US)*; **erste ~nummer** first item on a program(me); **~paket** software packet; **~punkt** item, *(Politik)* plank; **parteipolitische ~punkte** main lines of a party's policy; **entscheidende politische ~punkte** keynote of a policy; **~redaktion** program(me) planning department; **~rede** address, keynote speech; **~redner** *(pol.)* keynoter *(US)*; **~schritt** *(Computer)* program(me) step; **~steuerung** program(me) control; **~streckung** stretchout of program(me); **~taste** *(Fernseher)* channel (program[me]) selector; **~umsetzer** *(Datenverarbeitung)* assembler; **~verkäufer** program(me) seller; **~versammlung** *(Partei)* caucus; **~verzeichnis** *(Rundfunk)* schedule; **~vorschau** *(Rundfunk)* program(me) parade; **~wahl** choice of program(me)s; **~wähler** program(me) (channel) selector; **~wechsel** change of program(me); **~zeitplan** *(Rundfunk)* schedule.
Progression progression;
arithmetische ~ arithmetical progression; **geometrische ~** geometrical progression; **steile ~** steep progression.
Progessions | satz rate of progression; **~steuer** progressive (graduated) tax; **~stufe** stage of progression; **höher besteuerte ~zonen** higher-rate tax bands.
progressiv progressive;
~ eingestellt sein to hold progressive views;
~e Abschreibung sinking-fund method of depreciation *(US)*; **~e Krankheit** progressive disease; **~e Steuer** progressive (graduated) tax; **~er Steuersatz** progressive scale of tax rates; **~er Zinssatz** progressive rate.
Progressivität der Besteuerung progressivity of taxation.
Progressiv | lohn progressive wage rate; **~steuer** progressive tax[ation], graduated tax.
Prohibitionsanhänger prohibitionist.
prohibitionsfreundlich in favo(u)r of prohibition.
Prohibitionsgesetz prohibition (dry, *US*) law.
prohibitive Steuer prohibitive tax.
Prohibitiv | satz discriminating rate; **~system** prohibitive system, prohibitionism; **~zoll** discriminatory (prohibitive) duty.
Projekt project, scheme, design, plan;
technologisch aufwendiges ~ high-technology project; **in der Planung befindliches ~** project in the planning stage; **aus Steuermitteln finanziertes ~** project supported by taxes; **gemeinsames ~** joint project; **lebensfähiges ~** viable scheme; **zur Diskussion stehendes ~** project now under discussion **unter einem Unglücksstern stehendes ~** ill-fated project;

~ **zur Unterbringung entlassener Arbeiter** statutory redundancy scheme *(Br.)*;
politisches ~ **aufgeben** to withdraw from a political project; ~ **ausarbeiten** to plan a scheme; ~ **befürworten** to favo(u)r a scheme; ~ **zu Fall bringen** to upset a project; ~ **in Gang bringen** to get a plan under way; ~ **durchführen** to run (carry out, engineer) a scheme; ~ **lediglich mit eigenen Mitteln finanzieren** to bet its own resources fully on a project; **jem. ein** ~ **schmackhaft machen** to sell s. o. a project; ~ **vorantreiben** to push a scheme; **sich aus einem** ~ **zurückziehen** to withdraw from a project;
~**abkommen** project agreement; ~**auswahl** project identification, choice of project; ~**bearbeiter** project officer; ~**berater** project analyst; ~**bericht** project report; ~**bewertung** project evaluation (appraisal); ~**bewilligungsverfahren** project procedure; ~**bindung** project tying; ~**durchführung** project execution (performance).
Projektemacher castle-builder.
Projekt | finanzierung project financing; ~**fortschrittsplanung** program(me) evaluation and review technique.
projekt | freie Wirtschaftshilfe untied aid; ~**gebundene Hilfe (wirtschaftliche Unterstützung)** *(Entwicklungsländer)* commodity (tied) aid.
Projektgruppe project team.
projektieren to project, to plan, to schedule;
neue Eisenbahn ~ to project a new railway.
projektierter Zusammenschluß planned amalgamation.
Projektierung | einer neuen Eisenbahnlinie projection of a new railway line; ~ **einer neuen Straße** projection of a new road.
Projektil *(mil.)* projectile.
Projektingenieur project engineer.
Projektion projection, projected image.
Projektions | apparat projector, projection apparatus; ~**bild** projected image, lantern slide; ~**fläche** projection area; ~**gerät** projection machine; ~**leinwand** [projection] screen; ~**raum** projection room, *(Kino)* projection booth; ~**vorrichtung** projection system; ~**wand** projection screen.
Projekt | kontrolle project control; ~**leiter** project leader (manager), director of operations; ~**leitung** project management; ~**mittel** project funds; ~**reife** pre-production stage; ~**steuerung** project control; ~**studie** feasibility study, blueprint *(US)*; ~**vorschlag** draft scheme.
projizieren to screen.
projizierte Entwicklung forecasted (predicted) development.
Projizierung screening.
Proklamation proclamation, declaration, manifesto *(US)*;
~ **erlassen** to issue (launch) a proclamation.
proklamieren to proclaim;
Streik ~ to declare a strike.
Prokura procuration, agency, proxy;
per ~ per procuration (per proc.), by proxy;
ausdrücklich erteilte ~ express procuration; **gemeinsame** ~ joint procuration;
~ **entziehen** to cancel procuration; ~ **erteilen** to confer (give) procuration; ~ **haben** to hold procuration; **per** ~ **zeichnen** to sign by (per) procuration (p. proc., p. p.);
~**entziehung** cancellation of a procuration; ~**indossament** indorsement by procuration (in representative capacity); ~**unterschrift** signature by procuration, per procuration signature.
Prokurist [etwa] authorized (confidential, managing) clerk, manager;
erster ~ first-class clerk.
Prolet proletarian, grub.
Proletariat proletariate.
Proletarier proletarian.
proletarisch proletarian.
proletarisieren to proletarianize.
Proletarisierung proletarianization.
Prolog prologue.
Prolongation renewal, extension, prolongation, *(Reportgeschäft)* carryover, carrying over, continuation *(Br.)*;
stillschweigende ~ tacit renewal;
~ **eines Wechsels** renewal of a bill of exchange;
in ~ **geben** to give on *(Br.)*, to give on stock *(US)*; **in** ~ **nehmen** to carry over *(Br.)*, to take in *(Br.)*, to continue, to take in stock *(US)*; ~**en zum Kurs von 8% tätigen** to put through renewals at 8 per cent; **einer** ~ **zustimmen** to agree (assent) to a renewal.
Prolongations | abkommen extension agreement; ~**akzept** renewal bill; ~**bedingungen** terms of continuation.
prolongationsfähig renewable, continuable.
Prolongations | gebühr contango *(Br.)* (carrying-over, continuation, *Br.*) rate, rate of contango *(Br.)*, respite money, backwardation *(Br.)*, back *(Br., coll.)*, *(Tagesgeld)* renewal rate; ~**geschäft** contango *(Br.)* (prolongation, continuation, *Br.*, carrying-over, *Br.*) business; ~**gewährung** granting of renewals; ~**klausel** renewal clause, continuation clause *(Br.)*, *(Versicherung)* nonforfeiture clause; ~**kosten** renewal cost, contango money *(Br.)*; ~**preis** making-up price; ~**provision** renewal commission; ~**recht** right of renewal; **mit** ~**recht** renewed if required; ~**satz** continuation rate *(Br.)*, *(Tagesgeld)* renewal rate; ~**tag** continuation day *(Br.)*; ~**wechsel** renewal (continuation, *Br.*) bill.
prolongierbar renewable, continuable.
prolongieren to extend, to renew, to prolong, *(Effektenengagement)* to carry forward (over, *Br.*), to continue *(Br.)*;
Darlehn ~ to continue a loan; **Wechsel** ~ to grant a renewal of (renew) a bill, to extend a bill, to accord a respite for the payment of a bill; **Zahlungstermin** ~ to extend the time of payment.
prolongierter Schuldschein renewed note.
Prolongierung prolongation.
Promemoria memorandum, memo.
Promenade promenade, walk, parade *(Br.)*, parkway *(US)*, walkway, avenue *(US)*.
Promenaden | deck promenade (hurricane) deck; ~**konzert** open-air concert; ~**mischung** mongrel, Heinz fifty-seven dog *(US)*.
promenieren to take a stroll, to promenade.
Promesse promissory note, due bill;
kurzfristige ~ short note *(US)*.
Promille per thousand, permillage;
~**gehalt** pro mille content.
prominent prominent, outstanding, notable, grand;
~ **sein** to outstand; **in letzter Zeit** ~ **geworden sein** to have come to the fore recently; ~ **werden** to cut it fat, to cut a shine;
~**e Bürger** top people, civic heads, headliners *(US)*; ~**e Persönlichkeit** outstanding personality; ~**e Rolle im Leben der Stadt spielen** to play a prominent part in civic life.
Prominente well-known (top) people, civic heads.
Prominenten | almanach social register; ~**jäger** lion hunter; **jem.** ~**rechte zuerkennen** to make a lion of s. o.; ~**suite bestellen** to engage a stateroom; ~**tribüne** distinguished strangers' gallery.
Prominenter lion, big shot, heavyweight *(US coll.)*, top sawyer *(coll.)*, socialite *(US)*, v.i.p.
Prominenz greatness, *(Prominente)* top people, civic heads, headliners *(US)*;
zur ~ **gehören** to be in the front rank; **auf seinem Gebiet zur** ~ **gehören** to be a leading figure in one's field.
Promotion taking one's degree, graduation.
Promotions | examen degree examination; ~**feier** commencement [day]; ~**gebühr** degree fee; ~**schrift** dissertation; ~**tag** degree day, commencement [day]; ~**verleihung** degree conferring; ~**voraussetzung** degree-level qualifications.
promovieren to take one's [doctor] degree, to doctor, to doctorize, to commence *(Br.)*, to proceed *(Br.)*, to graduate at (from, *US*).
promoviert graduate;
in Oxford ~ **haben** to have received one's degree in Oxford; ~ **werden** to obtain a doctor's degree.
Promovierter graduate, postgraduate *(Br.)*.
prompt prompt, ready, pat, expeditious, *(pünktlich)* punctual, *(sofort)* quick, with dispatch;
~ **in Erfüllung seiner Pflichten** punctual in the performance of one's duties;
~ **antworten** to answer like a shot; ~ **bezahlen** to make ready payment; ~ **in eine Falle gehen** to fall straight into a trap; ~ **liefern** to deliver promptly;
~**e Antwort** immediate answer; ~**e Bedienung** prompt service; ~**e Erledigung** prompt discharge (attention); ~**e Lieferung** *(Börse)* spot delivery; ~**er Zahler** good payer.
Prompt | geschäft prompt transaction; ~**heit** promptitude, promptness, dispatch.
prononciert decided, definite;
sich ~ **zu einem Thema äußern** to express o. s. strongly on a subject; **Wort** ~ **aussprechen** to enunciate a word clearly;
~**e Ansichten** pronounced ideas; ~**e Eleganz** pointed elegance.
Propaganda propaganda, *(Kunden)* canvassing, *(Werbung)* publicity, boost, sales promotion *(US)*, plug *(US)*;
aufdringliche ~ puff *(Br.)*, ballyhoo *(US)*; **politische** ~ stump speaking *(US)*; **staatsgefährdende** ~ seditious literature; **unauffällige** ~ silent propaganda; **verstärkte** ~ intensive propaganda;

sich mit ~ beschäftigen to propagandize; **politische ~ betreiben** to go on the stump *(US)*; **~ aus etw. machen** to make propaganda capital out of s. th.; **für etw. ~ machen** to set up propaganda for s. th.; **für j. ~ machen** to canvass for s. o., to build s. o. up;
~abteilung publicity (advertising) department; **~apparat** propaganda apparatus; **~ballon** propaganda balloon; **~bewegung** propaganda; **~feldzug** advertising (sales, publicity) campaign, canvass, detailing; **~film** propaganda film; **~fonds** publicity fund; **aus ~gründen** for propaganda purposes; **~krieg** mind campaign; **~leiter** advertising manager; **~material verteilen** to disseminate material; **~ministerium** Ministry of Information; **~mittel** vehicle of (for) propaganda; **~offensive** propaganda offensive; **~organisation** propaganda organization; **politische ~rede** stump speech *(US)*; **~redner** *(pol.)* stumper *(US)*; **politische ~reise unternehmen** to go on the stump *(US)*; **~rummel** ballyhoo, *(pol.)* buildup; **~schrift** pamphlet, propaganda writing; **~sendungen des Rundfunks** propaganda broadcasts; **~stück** propaganda play, stunt; **~trick** trick, bluff; **~unternehmen** propaganda organization; **~veranstaltung** pep rally *(sl.)*; **~wert** propaganda value; **~wesen** propagandism; **~zweck** propaganda purpose.
Propagandist propagandist, propagator, shouter, publicity man.
Propagandistenwerbung detailing.
propagandistisch propagandistic;
~ ausnutzen to harvest a propaganda feast;
~e Fähigkeit propagandism, propaganda.
propagieren to propagate, to publicize, to promote, to push, to make publicity for, to advertise;
Artikel ~ to make publicity for an article.
Propagierung propagation, promotion.
Propatriapapier foolscap.
Propeller propeller, airscrew *(Br.)*;
~düsentriebwerk propjet; **~flügel** vane of a propeller; **~flugzeug** prop[eller] plane; **~triebwerk** propjet engine.
proper aussehen to look neat and tidy.
Prophet oracle, prophet;
der ~ gilt nichts in seinem Vaterlande a prophet is not without hono(u)r save in his own country.
Prophetengabe gift of prophecy.
prophezeien to forebode;
Erdbeben ~ to predict that there will be an earthquake.
Prophezeiung prophesy, foreboding, prognostic.
prophylaktisch prophylactic, preventive;
aus ~en Gründen as a precautionary measure.
Proportion proportion;
richtige ~en haben to have a perfect figure.
proportional proportional, prorata;
umgekehrt ~ in inverse ratio;
~ verkleinern to scale down;
~e Häufigkeit *(Statistik)* proportional frequency; **~er Steuertarif** proportional schedule of tax rates.
Proportional | bereich, unterer ~bereich der Einkommensteuertabelle basic rate (threshold) of personal tax; **~besteuerung** proportional taxation; **~satz** proportional rate; **unterer ~satz des Einkommensteuertarifs** standard rate of income tax, basic rate of personal tax; **~system** proportional (proportionate) scale; **~wahl** proportional vote; **~wahlrecht** proportional representation.
proportioniert sein, gut to have a perfect figure.
Proporz proportional representation;
Ministersitze nach dem ~ verteilen to distribute the ministries in proportion to the seats polled;
~politik denominationalism.
proppenvoll *(Bus)* packed to the door, *(Saal)* crowded to capacity.
Propre | geschäft business for own account, *(Makler)* broker's market; **~händler** trader for own account; **~handlung** separate trade.
prorata[risch] prorata, in proportion, proratable *(US)*.
Prorektor *(Universität)* prorector, vice chancellor.
prosaisch *(fig.)* pedestrian, down-to-earth, bread-and-butter, matter-of-fact.
Prosit cheers, cheerio *(Br.)*, your health, mud in your eye *(US sl.)*.
Prospekt catalog(ue), brochure, broadsheet, pamphlet, leaflet, literature, circular, booklet, handout, *(Aktien)* prospectus, circular note;
kostenlos angeforderte ~e literature sent gratis on request; **ausführliches ~** descriptive catalog(ue); **eingelegter ~** cover fold; **vom Vertreter überreichter ~** salesman's folder; **von Hand zu Hand verteilter ~** handbill; **zusammengelegter ~** folder;
~ über die Ausgabe von Obligationen bond circular; **~ für den Handel** trade folder; **~ für die Zulassung zum Börsenhandel** prospectus for admission to the stock exchange;
~e hier erhältlich prospectuses sold here; **~ wird zugeschickt** literature on request;
~ lancieren to issue a prospectus; **~ verschicken** to circularize, to send out a prospectus; **~e verteilen** to hand out leaflets;
~angebot circular offer (letter); **~anzeige** Dutch door; **~blatt** broadsheet; **~gesellschaft** prospectus company *(Br.)*; **~haftung** prospectus liability; **~herausgabe** issue of a prospectus; **~material** [advertising] literature, handout material; **~umschlag** prospectus cover; **~versand** circularization; **~versand durchführen** to send out a prospectus; **~verteilung** distribution of circulars; **~zwang** prospectus method.
prosperieren to prosper, to flourish, to thrive.
Prosperität [business] prosperity;
anhaltende ~ continuance of prosperity, boom.
Prosperitätszeit wave of prosperity, boom time.
prostituieren, sich to prostitute o. s.
Prostituierte prostitute, streetwalker, whore, unfortunate.
Prostitution social evil, street walking.
Proszenium *(Theater)* proscenium, frontispiece.
Proszeniumsloge proscenium (stage) box, dress box.
Protegé protegé, white-haired boy *(US sl.)*.
protegieren to patronize, to protect, to take under one's wing.
protegiert patronized, protected;
von höchster Stelle ~ werden to be well in at headquarters.
Protegierter protected person, protegé, white-haired boy *(US sl.)*.
Protektion *(Schirmherrschaft)* sponsorship, auspices, protection, patronage, push, pull *(US sl.)*, drag *(US)*, *(pol.)* pie *(US sl.)*;
jds. ~ erlangen to win s. one's favo(u)r; **~ genießen** to have friends at court (influential friends); **seine Beförderung der ~ verdanken** to owe one's promotion to favo(u)ritism, to get a job by push.
protektionieren to protect, to patronize, to push;
j. ~ to give s. o. a helping push, to boost s. o. into a position.
Protektionismus protectionism;
wachsender ~ protectionist sentiment;
~ im Schach halten to keep protectionism at bay; **sich immer mehr dem ~ zuwenden** to edge towards protectionism.
protektionistisch protectionist;
~en Einflüsterungen widerstehen to resist the protectionist side;
~e Maßnahmen protectionist activities.
Protektionswirtschaft favo(u)ritism, protectionism, spoils system *(US)*;
~ bei Beförderungen favo(u)ritism in promotion.
Protektor protector, *(Rundfunksendung)* sponsor.
Protektorat protectorate, protected territory, dependency, *(Förderung)* patronage;
unter dem ~ von under the auspices of.
Protektoratsvertrag treaty of protectorate.
Protest protest[ation], *(dipl.)* protest, representation;
als ~ as a protest; **mangels ~s** in the absence of protest; **nach ~** supra protest; **ohne ~** no protest, protest waived, not to be noted; **sofort zum ~** to be protested at once; **ungeachtet unserer ~e** notwithstanding our remonstrances; **unter ~** under protest; **zu ~ gegangen** protested; **zum ~ vorgemerkt** *(Wechsel)* noted for protest;
eindringlicher ~ vigorous protest; **energischer ~** sharp protest; **zu spät erhobener ~** past-due (retarded) protest; **feierlicher ~** solemn protest; **öffentlicher ~** public protest; **rechtzeitiger ~** due protest; **scharfer ~** sharp protest; **schriftlicher ~** written protest; **verspäteter ~** retarded protest; **voreiliger ~** forward protest;
~ mangels Annahme protest for nonacceptance; **~ zwecks weiterer Sicherheiten bei Zahlungsunfähigkeit des Akzeptanten** protest for better security; **~ mangels Zahlung** protest for nonpayment;
unter ~ akzeptieren to accept under protest; **~ anzeigen** to give notice of a protest; **~ aufnehmen** to draw up a protest; **~e auslösen** to spark off protest; **~ beschließen** to pass a resolution of protest; **~ bei der Regierung einlegen** to protest to a government; **~ erheben** to lodge a protest, to take objection; **formellen ~ erheben** to enter (lodge, raise, extend) a protest; **zu ~en Anlaß geben** to give rise to protests; **zu ~ gehen** to go to protest; **zahlreiche ~e hervorrufen** to call forth numerous protests; **~ hinausschieben** to delay (defer) a protest; **sich über alle ~e hinwegsetzen** to ride over all protests; **~ aufnehmen lassen** to have a bill noted; **Wechsel zu ~ gehen lassen** to dishono(u)r a bill; **Wechsel zwecks weiterer Sicherheitengestel-**

lung zu ~ gehen lassen to protest a bill for better security; **mit ~ zurückgehen lassen** to return under protest; **Sitzung unter ~ verlassen** to leave a meeting under protest;
~aktion protest activities; **~anzeige** note (notice) of protest, notification of protest, notice of dishono(u)r; **~aufnahme** protestation, protesting; **nachträgliche ~aufnahme** extending a protest; **~benachrichtigung** notice of dishono(u)r; **allgemeine ~bewegung** general protest of the people; **~demonstration** protest demonstration, teach-in, sit-in; **~erhebung** protestation, lodgement of a protest, noting; **Wechsel unter ~erhebung einlösen** to pay a bill under protest.
protestfähig protestable.
Protest|frist time for protesting; **~gebühr** protest fees; **~geschrei** howl of protest; **~gläubiger** protester.
protestieren to [enter a] protest, to object;
gegen Gewaltanwendung ~ to act under protest; **gegen getroffenen Maßnahmen ~** to protest against measures;
Wechsel ~ lassen to have a bill protested (noted).
Protestierender protester *(US)*.
protestierter Wechsel bill noted for protest, dishono(u)red bill.
Protest|kosten *(Wechsel)* cost of protest, protest fees; **~kundgebung** protest demonstration, remonstrance, opposition (indignation, *US*) meeting; **~marsch** banner march; **~note** note (notice) of protest; **~ort** place of protest; **~schreiben** remonstrative letter, written protest; **sich einem ~schritt anschließen** to join in a protest; **~spesen** *(Wechsel)* protest fees (charges); **~streik** protest strike; **~sturm hervorrufen** to bring a storm about one's ears; **~urkunde** note (notice) of protest, protest certificate, deed of protest; **~vermerk** *(Wechsel)* notation on a bill of exchange; **~versammlung** opposition (protest, indignation, *US*) meeting; **~verzichtserklärung** waiver of protest; **~wechsel** bill protested, dishono(u)red bill; **~zahlung** payment under protest.
Protokoll record, register, minute book, minutes, *(Diplomatie)* protocol, proces verbal, *(Verkehrsteilnehmer)* ticket *(US)*, warning and fee *(Br.)*;
aus dem ~ gestrichen struck out (stricken from, *US*) the record; **für das ~** for the record *(US)*;
amtliches ~ official record; **gedrucktes ~** printed report; **gerichtliche ~e** public records; **polizeiliches ~** police report;
~ über den Austausch von Ratifikationsurkunden protocol of ratification; **~ über die Beweisaufnahme** recording of evidence; **~e einer Gesellschaft** proceedings of a society; **~ einer Hauptversammlung** corporate minutes, minutes of a corporate meeting; **~ der Vorstandssitzung** minutes of the board of directors, board minutes;
~ abfassen to draft (draw up, take, keep) the minutes; **~ abzeichnen** to sign minutes; **~ aufnehmen** to draw up (enter) the minutes, to [draw up a] protocol, to enter on the record, *(Polizei)* to take down the evidence; **~ aufsetzen** to draw up a protocol, to protocolize, *(Polizei)* to take down the evidence; **~ ausgeben** to [issue a] protocol; **einander genau dem ~ entsprechend behandeln** to act with extreme punctiliousness towards one another; **~ beifügen** to attach the minutes; **~ bekommen** *(Verkehrsteilnehmer)* to get a ticket *(US)*; **~ der letzten Sitzung bestätigen** to confirm (adopt) the minutes of the last (preceding) meeting; **im ~ festhalten** to spread on the record *(US)*; **~ führen** to [record in a] protocol, to keep (take) the minutes, to keep the register (rolls), to record; **in einer Sitzung ~ führen** to minute a meeting; **zu ~ geben** to place on (in the) record, to have a report made, *(bei Gericht)* to depose; **Stellungnahme zu ~ geben** to put (place, go) on record *(US)*; **~ genehmigen** to approve the minutes; **~ herausgeben** to issue a protocol; **zu ~ nehmen** to take down in writing, to record, to take down [the minutes], to put on record, *(Gericht)* to minute, to take down the evidence; **eidliche Aussagen zu ~ nehmen** to take depositions; **im ~ vermerkt sein** to stand on record; **~ verlesen** to read the minutes; **für das ~ verlesen** to read in the record; **im ~ vermerken** to enter in the minutes, to put on record; **gegen das ~ verstoßen** to break the rules of protocol; **mit dem zustehenden ~ empfangen werden** to be received with due ceremonies; **zu ~ genommen werden** to go on record;
aus dem ~ geht hervor according to the minutes;
~abfassung minute writing; **~abschrift** copy of the proceedings; **~abteilung** *(dipl.)* Protocol Service (section); **~änderung** alteration of the minutes; **für ~änderungen stimmen** to vote for amendment of the minutes.
Protokollant recorder, clerk.
protokollarisch on record, recorded, entered in the minutes, *(dipl.)* protocolary, ceremonial;
~ festhalten to state in a protocol;
~e Bestimmungen ceremonial rules, rules of protocol; **den ~en Bestimmungen entsprechen** to be according to protocol; **sich streng an die ~en Bestimmungen halten** to stick closely to protocol; **übliche ~e Grußadresse** protocol greeting; **~es Procedere** ceremonial procedure; **~e Verhaltensregeln** protocol.
Protokoll|aufbewahrung keeping of minutes; **~aufnahme** recording, entry in the minute book (into the minutes), *(Gericht)* recording of evidence; **~auszug** extract of the minutes; **~auszüge dem Vollstreckungsbeamten übergeben** to estreat; **~berichtigung** correction of the minutes; **~buch** record (minute) book, act book *(Scot.)*, blotter *(US)*, *(parl.)* the journals *(Br.)*, Hansard *(Br.)*; **~chef** Chief of Protocol, Protocol Chief, Marshal of the Diplomatic Corps; **~eintragung** entry, minute *(Br.)*; **~fehler** misprision; **~fragen** points of protocol; **es mit ~fragen übergenau nehmen** to stand upon punctilios; **~führer** recording clerk, protocolist, recording secretary, recorder, *(Gericht)* court registrar, court stenographer, clerk of the court, reporter, recording clerk.
protokollgemäß according to protocol, protocolary.
Protokollgenehmigung approving the minutes.
protokollieren to enter in (keep) the minute book, to minute, to take down [the minutes], to draft a report, to [draw up a] protocol, to protocolize, to record;
amtlich ~ to [place on] record;
jds. Aussage ~ to take s. one's deposition;
~ lassen to leave on record, *(Richter)* to enter up;
bitte nicht ~! this is off the record!
protokolliert sein to stand on record.
Protokollierung recording, entry in the minute books, registration, protocolization, *(gerichtlich)* record of the court.
Protokollierungsgebühr registration fee.
Protokoll|muster specimen minutes; **handschriftliche richterliche ~notizen** judge's minutes (notes); **~prüfungsausschuß** Committee for the Journals *(Br.)*; **~verfahren** ceremonial practice; **~verlesung** reading the minutes.
Prototyp archetype, prototype;
~ des Reaktionärs prototypical reactionary; **~ des Unternehmers** archetype of a manager.
Protz show-off, braggart, swank, flaunter.
Protze *(mil.)* limber.
protzen to show off, to boast, to talk large, to swank;
mit seinem neuen Auto ~ to parade one's new car; **mit seinem Reichtum ~** to flaunt one's wealth; **mit seinem Wissen ~** to make a display of one's knowledge.
Protzentum, neureiches new-rich snobbery.
Protzerei swank, show;
~ mit seinem Reichtum obscene flaunting of wealth.
protzig flaunty, flashy, swanky, purse-proud, large.
Provenienz provenance, origin.
Proviant provisions, supplies, victuals, food, viands, stores, commissaries *(US)*;
ohne ~ unvictualled;
mit ~ versehen to provision, to supply; **sich mit ~ versorgen** to supply o. s. with provisions;
~amt supply depot, store (victualizing, *Br.*) office; **~ausgabe** issue of rations; **~beutel** haversack, knapsack; **~boot** supply boat.
proviantieren to provision, to victual, to supply;
frisch ~ to reprovision.
Proviant|kammer *(Schiff)* provision (issue) room; **~kolonne** supply depot; **~korb** food basket, hamper *(Br.)*; **~lager** supply depot, cache, *(mil.)* magazine, victualling yard *(Br.)*; **~meister** steward, *(Marine)* caterer *(Br.)*, *(mil.)* quartermaster; **~raum** storeroom; **~schiff** supply (victualling, *Br.*) ship, storeship, victualler *(Br.)*; **~tasche** *(mil.)* haversack; **~wagen** supply waggon, chuck wagon *(US sl.)*; **~zug** supply train.
Provinz province, country;
aus der ~ provincial, parochial; **in der ~** in the province, down in the country;
finsterste (hinterste) ~ backwater, stick *(US)*;
in der ~ gastieren to tour the province; **in die ~ gehen** to go down into the country; **in der hintersten ~ leben** to live at the back of beyond;
~arbitrage shunting *(Br.)*.
Provinzausgabe regional edition;
inkomplett vorab versandte ~ bulldog edition *(US)*; **vorgezogene ~** early-bird issue *(US)*.
Provinz|bank country (interior, *US*) bank; **~behörden** provincial authorities; **~bewohner** provincial, rustic, *(pl.)* upstates *(US)*; **~hauptstadt** provincial center *(US)* (centre, *Br.*).

Provinzial | abgaben provincial taxes; ~**ismus** provincialism, localism; ~**verband** county borough.
provinziell provincial, suburban, *(fig.)* parochial;
~**e Aufführung** mediocre performance; ~**e Denkungsweise** parochialism, provincialism.
Provinzler provincial, rustic, country jack, yokel, bumpkin, clodhopper, backwoodsman.
provinzlerisch provincial, *(rückständig)* yokelish, backwoodsy, parochial, hick *(sl.)*;
~**en Charakter geben** to provincialize; ~**e Einstellung** parochial spirit, provincialism.
Provinz | nest jerkwater town, one-house (hick) town *(US)*, tank town *(sl.)*, rhubarb *(sl.)*, wide place in the road *(sl.)*; **spendabler** ~**onkel** visiting fireman *(sl.)*; ~**presse** provincial newspaper (press, *Br.*), regional newspapers; ~**regierung** regional government; **kleine** ~**schule** freshwater college *(US coll.)*; ~**stadt** provincial city (town), country town *(Br.)*, jerkwater (one-horse, hick, *US*) town, courthouse *(US, local)*, noplace ville *(sl.)*; ~**vertretung** provincial agency; ~**zeitungen** provincial press *(Br.)*; ~**zentrum** provincial center *(US)* (centre, *US*); ~**zug** country (down, *Br.*) train.
Provision commission, compensation, rake *(US)*, rake-off *(US sl.)*, *(Makler)* brokerage, *(Prozentsatz)* percentage;
franko ~ free of commission; **gegen eine** ~ **von** subject to a commission of, on a percentage basis; **nach Abzug unserer** ~ allowing for our commission; **ohne** ~ no commission; **unter Abzug Ihrer** ~ deducting your commission;
angemessene ~ reasonable commission; **vertraglich ausgehandelte** ~ contract percentage; **erzwungene** ~ kickback; **von der Bank in Ansatz gebrachte** ~ commission charged by the bank; **geteilte** ~ split commission; **halbe** ~ *(Börse)* half commission; **unberechtigte** ~ rake-off *(US sl.)*; **vorbehaltlose** ~ straight commission;
~ **des Auktionators** auctioner's fee; ~ **des Befrachters** address commission; ~ **aus Konsortialbeteiligungen** underwriting commission; ~ **für Überziehungskredite** overdraft commission;
~ **bekommen** to draw (receive) a commission; **3%** ~ **berechnen** to charge 3 per cent commission; ~ **aus einem Geschäft beziehen** to draw a commission on a transaction; ~ **gewähren** to accord a commission; ~ **sparen** to save on commission, to save middlemen's profit; **einer** ~ **unterliegen** to be subject to a commission; ~ **auf den Gesamtumsatz zugestehen** to allow a percentage on all transactions; ~ **zurückvergüten** to return a commission; ~**en zuschustern** to deal out provisions.
Provisionierungssystem commission plan.
Provisions | abrechnung commission statement; ~**agent** commission merchant (agent), delcredere agent, factor *(US)*; ~**anspruch** accrued commission; ~**anspruch haben** to be entitled to (have earned) a commission; **der** ~**anspruch entfällt** no commission shall be paid; ~**anteil** commission percentage, slice of a commission; **dem Generalvertreter verbleibender** ~**anteil** overriding commission; ~**aufstellung** commission note; ~**aufteilung** division of commission, commission splitting; ~**aufwendungen** expenditure on commission, commision paid.
Provisionsbasis commission basis;
j. auf ~ **anstellen** to appoint s. o. as buyer on commission; **auf** ~ **arbeiten** to sell on commission; **Effektengeschäfte auf** ~ **durchführen** to execute orders in listed securities on a commission basis *(US)*.
Provisions | belastung beim Ersterwerb von Investmentzertifikaten front-end load; ~**beleg** commission note (slip); ~**belegbuch** order book; ~**berechnung** statement of commission.
provisionsberechtigt sein to have earned one's (be entitled to a) commission.
Provisions | bestimmungen compensation provisions; ~**beteiligung durch den Versicherungsmakler** rebate; ~**einnahmen**, ~**einkünfte** commission earnings (income, revenues), commissions received; ~**forderungen** accrued commission.
provisionsfrei free of commission.
Provisionsgebühr commission, rate to be charged for commission, commission charge (fee), factorage *(US)*, compensation, *(Finanzmakler)* brokerage, finder's fee;
hohe ~ *(Ausgabe von Investmentzertifikaten)* front-end fee;
~ **für die Durchführung des Aktiensplits** split commission;
~ **sparen** to save on commission.
Provisions | geschäft transaction on a commission basis, *(Kapitalanlagegesellschaft)* mutual fund brokerage; ~**geschäfte abwickeln (machen)** to buy and sell on commission, to go marketing, to sell goods on commission; ~**gewährung** brokerage payment.
provisions | gierig, ~**hungrig** commission-starved.
Provisions | grundlage commission basis; **auf** ~**grundlage arbeiten** to operate on a commission basis, to sell goods for a commission; ~**guthaben** accrued commission; ~**gutschrift** commission note; ~**höhe** commission cost; ~**konto** drawing (commission) account; ~**makler** commission broker *(US)*; ~**nachlaß** *(Versicherungswesen)* commission rebate.
provisionspflichtig commissionable, subject (liable) to a commission.
Provisions | rechnung commission note (account); ~**reisender** commercial traveller, travel(l)ing salesman; ~**reisender schwer verkäuflicher Artikel** tinge; ~**rückgewähr** refunding of the commission; ~**satz** rate of commission, commission rate; **fester** ~**satz** fixed percentage fee; **vertraglich ausgehandelter** ~**satz** contract percentage; ~**sätze der Banken** bank charges; ~**schema**, ~**system** commission plan; **gleitende** ~**staffel** sliding scale of commissions; ~**tabelle** schedule of commissions, commission schedule; ~**teilung** division of commission, commission splitting; **erzwungene** ~**teilung** kickback; ~**überweisung** remittance of commission; ~**vergütung** commission, compensation, factorage *(US)*; ~**verkauf** commission sales; **üblicher** ~**vertrag** straight commission arrangement.
Provisionsvertreter commission (del-credere) agent, travelling salesman, factor *(US)*;
als ~ **arbeiten** to be paid on a commission basis; **j. zum** ~ **ernennen** to commission s. o. to act as agent; ~ **sein** to sell goods for a commission.
Provisions | vertretung agency coupled with an interest; ~**vorschuß** drawing account.
provisionsweise on commission.
Provisions | wesen commission system; ~**zahlung** payment of commission; **mit** ~**zahlungen abgefunden** remunerated by commission.
provisorisch provisional, provisory, temporary, makeshift, temporarily, ad interim, stopgap;
~ **ernannt** provisionally appointed;
Amt ~ **bekleiden** to occupy a post temporarily;
~**er Abschluß** provisional booking; ~**e Ernennung** temporary appointment; ~**es Konto** interim (provisional) account; ~**e Maßnahmen** temporary measures; ~**e Regierung** provisional (caretaker) government, interim administration; ~**e Reparatur** temporary repairs.
Provisorium provisional (temporary) arrangement, makeshift arrangement, stopgap solution.
Provokateur provocateur, provoker;
~ **bei Lohnstreitigkeiten** goon *(US sl.)*.
Provokation provocation, challenge;
beabsichtigte ~ calculated provocation;
schuldmindernde ~**en der Gegenseite** adequate provocation;
aufgrund von ~**en handeln** to act under provocation.
provokative Fragen stellen to ask provocative questions.
provozieren, j. aufs Äußerste to provoke s. o. to the highest pitch of resentment; **Krieg** ~ to trigger (spark) off a war; **Streit** ~ to pick a quarrel.
provozierende Reden provoking speeches.
provoziert, nicht unprovoked;
~ **werden** to do (act) under provocation.
Provozierung einer strafbaren Handlung entrapment.
Prozedur procedure, routine;
langwierige ~ lengthy business;
~ **abkürzen** to shorten the procedure; ~ **über sich ergehen lassen** to suffer an ordeal, to put up with s. th.; ~ **überstehen** to survive an ordeal.
Prozent per cent, percentage, *(Gewinnanteil)* share of profit, *(Provision)* commission, *(Rabatt)* rebate, discount, *(Tantieme)* royalty;
gegen ~**e** on a percentage basis; **in** ~**en [ausgedrückt]** expressed (shown) as a percentage, percentaged, percentable; **zuzüglich 10** ~ **Bedienung** plus 10 per cent for service;
5 ~ a shilling in the pound *(Br.)*;
~**e abwerfen** to yield a percentage; **auf Rundfunkgeräte 4** ~ **bekommen** to get 4 per cent discount on wireless receivers; **Steuern um 5** ~ **erhöhen** to raise taxes by 5 per cent; **mit 8** ~ **verzinslich sein** to bear interest at 8 per cent;
~**bruchteil** fraction in per cent; ~**gehalt** percentage; ~**gewinn** per cent gain.
prozentig per cent;
4-~ bearing 4 per cent;
10-~**e Lohnerhöhung** 10 per cent increase in wages.
Prozent | notierung quotation in percentage; ~**rechnung** interest account.

Prozentsatz percentage rate, *(Zinsen)* rate of interest;
fester ~ fixed percentage fee; **hoher** ~ large (high) percentage; **beunruhigend hoher** ~ **an Fehlern** disquietingly high percentage of errors; ~ **der Invalidität** degree of invalidity; ~ **eines voll in der Ausbildung befindlichen Jahrgangs** enrolment rate; ~ **der Kranken** sick rate; ~ **von Laden- oder Nettopreis** percentage of the retail or net price; **hoher** ~ **alter Leute** high ratio of old people; ~ **der Schulschwänzer** truancy rate; ~ **freistehender Wohnungen** vacancy ratio *(US)*;
~- **oder Kostensatzmethode** *(Anzeigenetat)* percentage-or-sales method; ~**zunahme** percentage increase.

prozentual in percent;
~ **am Gewinn beteiligt sein** to receive a percentage of the profit; ~**er Anstieg** percentage of increase; ~**er Anteil** percentage; ~**e Verteilung** percentage distribution; ~**e Zunahme** percentage of increase.

Prozentverteilung *(Statistik)* percentage distribution.

Prozeß action (suit, *US*) at law, [law] case, lawsuit, suit, cause, litigation, plea, *(Prozeßverfahren)* procedure, legal proceedings, *(Strafverfahren)* criminal proceedings, penal suit, trial, *(technisches Verfahren)* process;
ohne ~**e** *(Anwalt)* briefless; **während der Dauer des** ~**es** during the pendency of a suit, pendente lite;
anhängiger ~ pending lawsuit (litigation); **frühere** ~**e** earlier proceedings; **vom Konkursverwalter geführter** ~ controversy arising in bankruptcy proceedings; **geschickt geführter** ~ bolstered-up case; **kostspieliger** ~ expensive lawsuit; **laufender** ~ pending case; **politischer** ~ state trial; **schikanöser** ~ vexatious lawsuit; **schwebender** ~ case pending, pending lawsuit; **streitiger** ~ adversary suit;
~ **vor dem Bundesverfassungsgericht** state trial; ~ **zur Klärung einer Rechtslage** fictitious action; ~ **gegen den Staat** suit against the state; ~ **als Streitgenossen** joint action (law suit); ~ **androhen** to threaten a suit; ~ **anfangen** to commence (engage in) a lawsuit; **jem. einen** ~ **anhängen** to clap a writ upon s. one's back; ~ **anstrengen** to institute legal proceedings, to file a bill, to have recourse to law; ~ **gegen j. anstrengen** to commence an action (suit) against s. o., to initiate proceedings (institute legal proceedings, bring a lawsuit, commence an action) against s. o.; ~ **aufgeben** to drop a suit; ~ **aufnehmen** to take cause; ~ **neu aufrollen** to reopen a case; ~ **aussetzen** to stop a suit, to stay (suspend) the proceedings; **einem** ~ **beitreten** to join an action; ~ **beschleunigen** to speed up a judicial business; **sich an einem** ~ **beteiligen** to become party to an action; ~ **betreiben** to prosecute an action; **mit einem** ~ **drohen** to threaten legal action; ~ **durchführen** to sustain an action; **sich in einen** ~ **einlassen** to enter an appearance; ~ **einleiten** to institute legal proceedings; ~ **einstellen** to abate an action, to discontinue a suit; ~ **zu jds. Gunsten entscheiden** to give judgment in favo(u)r of s. o.; ~ **fortsetzen** to hold an action, to maintain a suit; ~ **führen** to be at law, to maintain an action, to carry on (conduct) a lawsuit, to conduct a suit, to lawyer; ~**e führen** to prosecute a suit *(US)*, to conduct law business; ~ **als Beklagter führen** to defend a suit; ~ **für einen Mandanten führen** to conduct a lawsuit for a client; ~ **im eigenen Namen führen** to maintain an action in one's own name; ~ **im Namen eines Prozeßbeistandes führen** to sue a plaintiff to one's next friend; ~ **gewinnen** to win a lawsuit (case); **seinen** ~ **gewinnen** to recover in one's suit, to win (gain) one's case; ~ **durch ein Versäumnisurteil gewinnen** to win a case by default; **mit j. einem** ~ **haben** to have a lawsuit with s. o.; ~ **zu gewärtigen haben** to be faced with a lawsuit; **j. in einen** ~ **hineinziehen** to bring s. o. into an action; ~ **einfach hinnehmen** to suffer judicial proceedings; **es auf einen** ~ **ankommen lassen** to venture a lawsuit; **Beklagten einen** ~ **verlieren lassen** to cast the defendant; ~ **leiten** to conduct a trial; **jem. den** ~ **machen** to put s. o. on (bring s. o. up for) trial; ~ **anhängig machen** to institute legal proceedings, to raise an action, to litigate a cause, to bring in; **kurzen** ~ **mit etw. machen** to make short work with (shrift of) s. th.; **in einen** ~ **verwickelt sein** to be involved in a lawsuit; ~ **unterbrechen** to discontinue an action; **in einem** ~ **unterliegen** to lose a case, to be defeated in a lawsuit; ~ **verhandeln** to deal with a case; ~ **verhindern** to duck a lawsuit; ~ **verlieren** to fail (be cast) in a suit (lawsuit), to lose a case, to lose a court battle, to go without day; ~ **durch Versäumnisurteil verlieren** to lose a case by default; ~ **verschleppen** to delay the proceedings, to protract a lawsuit; **sich in einem** ~ **verteidigen** to fight an action at law; **zu den Kosten eines** ~**es verurteilt werden** to be condemned in (ordered to pay) the costs; ~ **wiederaufnehmen** to revive an action, to resume the proceedings;
formloser und schneller ~**ablauf** informal and speedy procedure; ~**akten** case records, minutes of a case, issue rolls, records of a lawsuit, demurrer book, *(Anwalt)* pleadings, brief, judicial documents (records, *US*); **einschlägige** ~**akten** documents pertaining to a case in court; ~**androhung** threats action *(Br.)*; ~**anstifter** common barrator; ~**antrag** formal motion, interlocutory application, counsel's brief *(Br.)*; ~**anwalt** barrister[-at-law] *(Br.)*, *(Strafprozeß)* trial lawyer *(US)*; ~**anwalt beauftragen (instruieren)** to deliver a brief to a barrister *(Br.)*; ~**auslagen** mise; ~**aussetzung** suspension (stay) proceedings, discontinuance; **gute** ~**aussichten haben** to have a good case; ~**beendigung** close of a case, nonsuit; ~**begehren** prayer of process; ~**beginn** inception, litiscontestation, beginning of a suit in court.

Prozeßbehauptung, nicht zur Sache gehörige impertinent averment; **unerhebliche** ~ immaterial averment; **wesentliche** ~ material allegation.

Prozeß | beistand counsel *(US)*; ~**beistand eines Minderjährigen** next friend; ~**beitritt** joinder of issue, intervention; ~**beratungsgebühr** retaining fee; ~**beschleunigung** speeding up of a judicial business; ~**beteiligter** party in a case; ~**betrug** deceitful plea.

Prozeßbevollmächtigter procurator *(US)*, pleader, attorney of record *(US)*, plaintiff's counsel *(Br.)*, mandatary;
~ **für die beklagte Partei** counsel for the defence *(Br.)*;
als ~ **für den Kläger auftreten** to appear for the plaintiff; ~ **beider Parteien plädieren lassen** to hear counsel on both sides *(Br.)*.

Prozeß | dauer duration of the proceedings; ~**eid** oath in litem; ~**einstellung** abatement of an action; **rechtskräftige** ~**entscheidung** complete determination of cause; ~**eröffnungsbeschluß** writ of summons.

prozeßfähig liable to be sued, actionable, personable, suable;
nicht ~ **sein** to be under some personal incapacity to sue.

Prozeßfähigkeit legal capacity to sue, right of (to bring) action;
passive ~ capacity to be sued;
keine ~ **besitzen** to be under personal incapacity to sue.

Prozeß | fall court issue; **geschickt geführter** ~**fall** bolstered-up case; ~**forderung** liquidated claim; **seine** ~**forderung zurückziehen** to withdraw from litigation (one's claim); ~**form** form of action.

prozeßführende Parteien parties to a suit.

Prozeßführer litigant, plaintiff.

Prozeßführung conduct of a case, conducting law business *(US)*;
schikanöse ~ vexatious proceedings; **vernachlässigte** ~ default;
~ **übernehmen** to undertake the defence *(Br.)* (defense, *US*) of a lawsuit.

Prozeß | führungsbefugnis right to bring a suit; ~**gebühr** docket fee; ~**gegenstand** subject of litigation, matter of dispute; ~**gegner** opposite (adverse) party, adversary, opposing party, opponent; **dem** ~**gegner einen Schriftsatz zustellen** to serve a writ on the other party; ~**gericht** trial court; **dem zuständigen** ~**gericht überstellen** to commit for trial; ~**gewinn** recovery; ~**gewinn in letzter Instanz** final recovery *(US)*; ~**handlung** pleadings.

prozeßhängig litigious, subject to litigation.

Prozeßhilfe legal aid.

prozeßhindernde Einrede common law estoppel, general demurrer, plea in bar, conclusion;
~ **erheben** to put in a plea in bar.

Prozessieren litigation;
durch ~ by legal process;
mutwilliges ~ malicious prosecution, barratry.

prozessieren to maintain an action, to sue, to carry on a lawsuit (legal proceedings), to be at (go to, have recourse to) law, to litigate;
gegen j. ~ to go to law with s. o., to commence an action (carry on a suit, *US*, initiate proceedings) against s. o.

Prozeßinhalt main issue of a suit.

Prozession procession, train;
~ **veranstalten** to [go in a] procession.

Prozeß | kaution security for costs; ~**klausel** suability clause.

Prozeßkosten [law] costs, court (litigation, legal) costs, cost of an action (of a suit, litigation), mise, *(Verhandlungskosten)* costs of the day, common fund costs *(Br.)*;
erstattungsfähige ~ taxable costs; **festgesetzte** ~ taxed costs *(US)*; **gesamte** ~ final costs;
~ **auferlegen** to order (condemn) to pay the costs; ~ **festsetzen** to tax the costs *(US)*; **zu den** ~ **verurteilt sein** to be condemned in (ordered to pay) the cost;
~**aufstellung** bill of costs *(US)*; ~**sicherheit** security for costs; ~**vorschuß [für die Ehefrau]** *(Scheidung)* suit money.

Prozeß|lage stage of proceedings; ~**lawine** flood of lawsuits.
prozeßleitende Verfügungen side-bar rules.
Prozeßliste docket [book], docket (caution) list;
inoffizielle ~ bar docket;
in die ~ **eintragen** to docket.
Prozeß|mandat counsel's brief; ~**material** grounds for litigation; ~**mißbrauch** malicious prosecution, abuse of process; ~**ordnung** procedural rules, standing rules of the court.
Prozeßpartei party to a case (litigation, dispute, lawsuit), contending party, litigant at law, suitor;
fiktive (fingierte) ~ fictitious plaintiff, John Doe; **im Armenrecht klagende** ~ pauper *(US)*, assisted person *(Br.)*; **unterlegene** ~ unsuccessful party; **wirkliche** ~ real party in interest *(US)*;
~ **sein** to be party to a (in the) suit *(US)*.
Prozeß|pfleger guardian (administrator, curator) ad item, receiver pendente lite, solicitor to the suitor's fund, *(eines Minderjährigen)* next friend; ~**praxis** practice of the courts; ~**protokoll** docket; ~**rechner** process computer; ~**recht** adjective (procedural) law, law of procedure; ~**regeln** general (standing) rules of court; ~**register** [judgment] docket (book), cause list, calendar, roll, register of writs; ~**sache** contentious business; ~**schriftsätze** pleadings; ~**serie** string of law suits; ~**standsschaftsklage** class suit, derivative action *(US)*; ~**stoff** subject matter of an action, cause of litigation; ~**sucht** litigiousness.
prozeßsüchtig litigious;
~ **sein** to vitiligate.
Prozeßtätigkeit litigation work.
prozeßtechnisch procedural.
Prozeß|teilnehmer contestant in legal proceedings; **außenstehender** ~**treiber** maintenor *(Br.)*; ~**trennung** severance of an action.
prozessual procedural, processal;
~**er Mangel** mistrial; ~**e Schwierigkeiten beseitigen** to iron out procedural difficulties; ~**e Voraussetzungen** procedural requirements; ~**e Vorschriften** procedural provisions.
prozessualistisch processual.
prozeßunerhebliches Vorbringen irrelevant allegation.
Prozeß|unfähigkeit incapacity (disability) to sue; ~**unterbrechung** discontinuance; ~**unterlagen** papers in a case; ~**urteil** judgment on the merits; **klageabweisendes** ~**urteil** peremption; ~**verbindung** joinder (consolidation) of actions.
Prozeßverfahren legal (judiciary, judicial) proceedings;
schikanöses ~ vexatious proceedings;
neue ~ **in Gang bringen** to bring fresh court suits; ~ **gegen j. einleiten** to proceed (institute legal proceedings) against s. o.
Prozeß|vergleich consent decree (judgment); ~**verlauf** course of a lawsuit; ~**verlauf beobachten** to watch (follow the trail of an action); ~**verschleppung** protraction of a lawsuit; ~**verschleppungseinwand vorbringen** to plead laches as a defense (defence, *Br.*) to a suit; ~**vertreter** counsel; ~**verzeichnis** litigation (trial) list; ~**verzögerung** circuity of action; ~**vollmacht** power (warrant, letter, *US*) of attorney, warrant to sue and defend, mandate; ~**voraussetzungen** procedural requirements; ~**vorbereitung** background preparation; **ausreichende** ~**vorbereitung** adequate preparation; ~**vorschriften** general (procedural) rules; ~**wesen** legal procedure.
Prüf|anlage test facility; ~**anstalt** testing laboratory; ~**attest** test certificate; ~**aufnahme** *(Zeitstudie)* check study; ~**beamter** inspector; ~**befund** test result; ~**belastung** testing load; ~**bericht**, ~**bescheid** test report; ~**einrichtungen** testing facilities.
prüfen to prove, *(besichtigen)* to inspect, to survey, *(eichen)* to assay, *(erforschen)* to examine, *(erproben)* to try, to test, *(heimsuchen)* to afflict, to try, *(Maschine)* to overhaul, *(nachprüfen)* to verify, to check, *(Polizei)* to investigate, to screen *(US)*, *(überprüfen)* to control, to look over, to review, to audit;
j. ~ to subject s. o. to a test; **sich** ~ to examine one's conscience; **von Amts wegen** ~ to consider without application; **Anwesenheit** ~ to roll-call; **Bericht** ~ to verify a report; **Bilanz** ~ to audit a balance sheet; **Bücher** ~ to audit (inspect, examine) the books; **Dokumente** ~ to verify documents; **eingehend** ~ to go into, to examine closely; **flüchtig** ~ to glance at s. th., to give the once-over *(US sl.)*; **Grundbuchunterlagen** ~ to inspect the documents of title; **gründlich** ~ to scrutinize, to canvass, to probe, to sift to the bottom; **auf Herz und Nieren** ~ to vet, to bolt to the bran; **j. auf Herz und Nieren** ~ to put s. o. through his paces (it, a searching examination, his facings), to pierce s. o. to the head *(fam.)*; **Kandidaten** ~ to screen candidates; **Konto** ~ to audit (verify, check) an account; **Kredit** ~ to check a credit; **zu Kreditzwecken** ~ to audit for credit purposes; **laufend** ~ to have under constant examination; **alle Möglichkeiten** ~ to look round; **Möglichkeiten einer Einigung** ~ to sound the possibilities of reaching an agreement; **j. mündlich** ~ to examine s. o. orally, to quiz s. o. *(US)*; **Münze auf das vorgeschriebene Gewicht** ~ to test a coin for weight; **nochmals** ~ re-examine; **seine Notizen** ~ to consult one's notes; **Qualität** ~ to check quality; **Rechnung** ~ to audit (examine, check) an account, to check (look over) a bill; **Rechnungsposten** ~ to verify the items of a bill; **Richtigkeit eines Kontoauszugs** ~ to verfiy an account (statement); **in aller Ruhe** ~ to study at one's leisure; **Sache erneut** ~ to look into a matter again; **Schüler** ~ to examine a pupil; **sorgfältig** ~ to sift, to go over s. th. with a fine tooth comb; **ständig** ~ to have under constant examination; **Tatsachen noch gründlicher** ~ to investigate the facts more thoroughly; **Testament** ~ to prove a will; **Unterschrift auf ihre Echtheit** ~ to authenticate a signature; **Vorschlag näher** ~ to consider the details of a proposal; **Ware** ~ to inspect goods; **wohlwollend** ~ to consider favo(u)rably; **Zahlenwerk** ~ to verify the figures; **Zusammenstellung** ~ to examine a statement.
prüfend searching, scrutinizing;
j. ~ **ansehen** to scrutinize s. o., to give s. o. a searching look.
Prüfer examiner, searcher, *(Abnahme)* inspector, *(Gesellschaft)* auditor, visitor, accountant, *(Patent)* tester, checker, *(Wahlen)* scrutinizer, scrutineer, canvasser *(US)*;
aufsichtführender ~ accountant in charge; **betriebseigener** ~ private accountant, internal auditor; **öffentlich bestellter chemischer** ~ public analyst *(Br.)*; **externer** ~ independent auditor; **zollamtlicher** ~ jerquer *(Br.)*;
~**bericht** auditor's report.
Prüfergebnis test result.
Prüferstab auditing staff.
Prüf|feld testing ground; ~**feldingenieur** testing engineer; ~**gerät** testing intrument (apparatus), trier; ~**irrtum** miscasting; ~**kabel** measuring cable *(el.)*; ~**kosten** inspection costs; ~**last** testing load.
Prüfling examinee, candidate, *(Leistungsprüfung)* ratee *(US)*;
~ **bestehen lassen** to pass a candidate; **alle** ~**e durchfallen lassen** to slaughter candidates wholesale; **Hälfte der** ~**e durchfallen lassen** to fail half the candidates.
Prüf|liste check list; ~**maß** test statistic; ~**nummer** check number; ~**objekt** test object; ~**platz** *(tel.)* monitor position; ~**siegel** seal of approval; ~**stab** auditing staff; ~**stand** test bench, testing stand, *(für Motoren)* test block; ~**stein** acid test, touchstone, trier; ~**stelle** *(Patentbüro)* examination department; ~**stempel** control stamp; ~**stück** specimen.
Prüfung examination, *(Abnahme)* inspection, *(Bilanz)* audit[ing], *(Durchlesen)* perusal, *(Durchsicht)* revisal, *(Erprobung)* trial, test, *(Konkursforderungen)* examination, *(Konto)* verification, reconcilement, check[ing], *(Kontrolle)* supervision, checking [operation] *(US)*, checkup *(US)*, *(Maschine)* overhaul, *(Metallprobe)* assay, *(Nachforschung)* investigation, research, *(Probezeit)* probation, *(Testfragen)* quiz *(US)*, *(Untersuchung)* investigation, analysis, studies, examination, *(Urteil)* review, *(Versuch)* experiment;
bei ~ on examining (examination); **bei** ~ **Ihres Kontoauszuges** upon reconcilement of your abstract of account; **bei nochmaliger** ~ on re-examination; **nach erfolgter** ~ on cause shown, on consideration; **nach genauer** ~ after further consideration; **nach** ~ **des Sachverhalts** on ascertaining the facts; **vor Beendigung der** ~ before the close of the audit;
abgebrochene ~ curtailed inspection; **abgekürzte** ~ limited audit; **akademische** ~ academic examination; **amtliche** ~ official control; **betriebseigene (betriebsinterne)** ~ internal audit; **betriebsfremde** ~ external audit; **zum Jahresende durchgeführte** ~ complete audit; **laufend durchgeführte** ~ continuous (periodic) audit; **eingehende** ~ detailed audit; **flüchtige** ~ look-over, once-over *(US sl.)*, quick-over *(sl.)*; **gemeinsame** ~ assembled examinations; **genaue (gründliche)** ~ close examination (going-over), scrutiny; **innerbetriebliche** ~ internal audit (checkup, *US*); **kritische** ~ scan; **mündliche** ~ oral examination, viva-voce examination; **nochmalige** ~ re-examination, reconsideration; **planmäßige** ~ routine testing; **schriftliche** ~ written examination, paper; **schwere** ~ hard examination; **ziemlich schwere** ~ stiffish examination; **sorgfältige** ~ careful examination, close going-over; **äußerst sorgfältige** ~ hard-nosed scrutiny; **stichprobenartige** ~ audit test, sampling; **überörtliche** ~ auditing above local level; **zollamtliche** ~ customs examination;

übliche ~ **bei der Abfertigung** *(Bahn)* ordinary inspection; ~ **der Arbeitsabläufe** operational auditing; ~ **am Aufstellungsort** test on site; ~ **der Auszahlungsbelege (Buchungsunterlagen)** voucher audit; ~ **des Betriebspersonals** personnel test; ~ **der Betriebstätigkeit** operational auditing; ~ **der Bilanz** balance-sheet audit; ~ **der Buchungsunterlagen** voucher audit; ~ **der Echtheit** verification of authenticity; ~ **der Eigentums- und Grundpfandrechte (Belastungsverhältnisse)** investigation of title; ~ **der Eigentumsverhältnisse** investigation of ownership; ~ **des Erfindungsanspruchs** patent examination; ~ **der Ertragsfähigkeit** determination of earning power; ~ **der Finanzverhältnisse auf Herz und Nieren** financial vetting; ~ **einer Flagge** *(Völkerrecht)* verification of a flag; ~ **der Geschäftsbücher** inspection of the books; ~ **der Grubensicherheit** inspection of mines; ~ **auf der Handelsschule** trade test; **regelmäßige** ~ **von Instrumenten** regular check of instruments; ~ **des Jahresabschlusses** general (annual) audit; ~ **der Kasse** verification of the cash, cash audit; ~ **der Konten** auditing of accounts; ~ **eines Kontoauszugs** reconcilement of bank statement *(Br.)*, verification of an account; ~ **der Liquidität** acid (liquidity) test; ~ **an Ort und Stelle** spot check; ~ **der Qualität** checking of quality; ~ **eines Rechtsfalles** investigation of a case; ~ **einer Sache** inquiry into s. th.; ~ **von Unterlagen** perusal of documents; ~ **der wirtschaftlichen Verhältnisse** examination of financial conditions; ~ **am Versandort** shipping-point inspection *(US)*; ~ **von Vollmachten** verification of credentials; ~ **durch selbständige Wirtschaftsprüfer** professional audit;
~ **abhalten** to hold an examination; ~ **ablegen** to undergo an examination; ~ **der mittleren Reife ablegen** to graduate from high school *(US)*, to get an ordinary general certificate of education *(Br.)*; ~ **abschließen** *(Revisor)* to conclude an audit; **j. zu einer** ~ **anmelden** to put in (register) s. o. for an examination; **sich zu einer** ~ **anmelden** to apply for admission to an examination; ~ **bestehen** to pass (take) an examiantion, to obtain a pass, *(fig.)* to stand the racket *(coll.)*; **mündliche** ~ **bestehen** to pass the oral; ~ **mit Auszeichnung bestehen** to pass an examination with hono(u)rs; ~ **mit befriedigend bestehen** to satisfy the examiners; ~ **nicht bestehen** to fail (flunk, *US*) in an examination; **j. durch eine** ~ **bringen** to put s. o. through an examination; ~ **durchführen** *(Revisor)* to make (prosecute) an audit; **j. durch ~en durchhetzen** to race s. o. through examinations; **in einer** ~ **durchrasseln** *(fam.)* to be plucked; **bei einer** ~ **gerade noch durchrutschen** to shave through an examination; **durch eine** ~ **fallen** to fail an examination; **schwere ~en zu bestehen haben** to pass through (have to meet with) heavy trials; **auf eine** ~ **hinarbeiten** to go (prepare) for an examination; ~ **machen** to sit for an examination; **sich erneut zu einer** ~ **melden** to re-enter an examination; **sich durch eine** ~ **qualifizieren** to qualify o. s.; **bei einer** ~ **durchgefallen sein** not to appear in the class list; **in eine** ~ **steigen** to go up for one's examination *(Br.)*; **der** ~ **unterliegen** to be subject to review; **einer** ~ **unterworfen (unterzogen) werden** to come under review, to undergo a test; **sich einer** ~ **unterziehen** to sit for (subject o. s. to) an examination; **j. auf eine** ~ **vorbereiten** to coach s. o. for an examination; **sich auf eine** ~ **vorbereiten** to prepare o. s. for an examination; **zu einer** ~ **zugelassen werden** to be permitted to sit for an examination.

Prüfungs|ablauf *(Revision)* audit procedure; **~abschnitt** *(Revision)* period under audit; **~abteilung** *(Abnahme)* inspection department, *(Revision)* auditing department (division); **~akten** examination records; **hohe ~anforderungen** high standard of an examination; **~antrag** application for an examination; **~anweisung** *(Revision)* audit instructions; **~arbeit** examination paper; **schriftliche ~arbeit** examination paper, script *(Br.)*, test paper.

Prüfungsaufgabe examination paper;
schriftliche ~ test paper;
~n beantworten to answer the questions; **~n bekanntgeben** to give out the examination papers; **neue ~n stellen** to set fresh papers.

Prüfungs|auftrag *(Abnahme)* inspecting order, *(Revision)* auditing order (engagement); **~ausschuß** examination board, examining body, review board *(US)*, screening jury (panel) *(US)*, *(Revision)* auditing commission; **~ausschuß für Zollfragen** tariff commission *(US)*; **~beamter** *(Abnahme)* inspecting officer, test clerk, *(Revisor)* auditor, accountant, examiner; **~bedingungen** testing conditions; **~behörde** examining board; **~bericht** inspector's report, examination report, *(Revisor)* auditor's (audit) report; **eingeschränkter ~bericht** qualified certificate (report); **schriftlicher ~bericht** auditor (auditor's) certificate; **~bescheinigung** examination certificate, *(Abnahme)* inspection certificate, certificate of analysis (inspection), *(Revision)* accountant's (audit) certificate; **~bogen** examination paper, *(Revision)* working papers; **~diagramm** inspection diagram; **~einrichtungen** testing facilities; **~ergebnis** examination results, test result, examination (test) score, findings; **Englisch als fremdsprachliches ~fach wählen** to offer English as [one of] one's foreign language(s); **~fahrt** trial run; **alle ~fragen beantworten** to floor a paper *(Br., fam.)*; **~gang** *(Revision)* audit routine; **~gebühr** examination fee, *(Abnahme)* inspection fee, *(Revision)* audit (auditing) fees; **~gebührenbefreiung** remission of examination fees; **~gehilfe** junior accountant; **~gesellschaft** auditing company, auditors; **~gremium** examination board (authorities), examining body (board), board of examiners, review board *(US)*; **~grenze** *(Statistik)* control limit; **~grundsätze** *(Revision)* principles of accounting; **~handlungen** *(Revision)* features of audit; **~jahr** *(Revision)* audit year; **~kandidat** examinee, candidate, questionist; **~kommission** examination board, board of examiners, examining body, review board *(US)*, *(Abnahme)* inspection committee (commission), *(Revision)* auditing commission; **~kosten** examination fees, *(Abnahme)* inspection cost, *(Revision)* audit fees; **~leistung** test performance; **~leiter** chief examiner; **~maßstab** test; **~methode** examination technique, testing method; **~muster** specimen; **~noten** examination marks; **~personal** inspection personnel, *(Buchprüfer)* auditing staff; **~pflicht** obligatory inspection.

prüfungspflichtig *(Abnahme)* subject to inspection;
~e Fächer examination schools *(Br.)*.

Prüfungs|plan *(Revision)* audit program(me); **~posten** *(Abnahme)* inspection lot; **~programm** testing program(me), *(Revision)* audit program(me); **~protokoll** test certificate, *(Revision)* accountant's certificate, *(Warenbeschaffung)* certificate of inspection; **~recht** *(Revision)* audit privilege; **~richtlinien** *(Revision)* audit standards; **~schein** *(Lagerei)* certificate of inspection; **~siegel** inspection stamp; **~stelle** control office, *(Examen)* examining board, *(Spediteur)* inspection bureau; **~termin** time of examination, *(im Konkurs)* public examination, *(Revision)* audit date; **nicht vorbereiteter ~test** *(Übersetzung)* unseen *(coll.)*; **~umfang** *(Abnahme)* amount of inspection, *(Revision)* audit scope, scope of audit.

Prüfungsverfahren examination system, inspection (screening) process, *(Revision)* auditing procedure, *(Statistik)* test;
gemeinsames ~ assembled examination;
~ **gut bestehen** to undergo a test successfully.

Prüfungsvermerk test note, *(Revisor)* accountant's (audit, auditor's) certificate;
einschränkender ~ qualified report (certificate);
Bilanz mit ~ **versehen** to certify a financial statement.

Prüfungs|voraussetzungen qualifying requirements, qualifications for an examination *(US)*; **~voraussetzungen erfüllen** to qualify for an examination; **~vordruck** *(Schule)* test blank; **~vorschriften** examination requirements, *(Qualitätsprüfung)* acceptance specifications, *(Revision)* audit standards; **~vorsitzender** presiding examiner; **~wesen** *(Revision)* auditing, audit system; **~zeichen** mark; **~zeit** probationership; **~zeit um die Jahresmitte** midyear *(US)*; **~zeitraum** *(Revision)* audit period; **~zeugnis** certificate, diploma, *(Abnahme)* certificate of inspection; **~zimmer** examination room; **~zweck** *(Revision)* purpose of auditing.

Prüf|verfahren testing method; **~vorrichtung** checking device; **~wesen** testing engineering; **~zeichen** test mark, *(Gütezeichen)* certification mark.

Prügel thrashing, hiding, whipping, flogging, *(Knüttel)* cudgel, club;
~ **austeilen** to deal out blows; ~ **bekommen** to cop it; **ordentliche Tracht** ~ **bekommen** to get a sound thrashing, to come in for a good licking *(coll.)*; **jem. eine Tracht** ~ **verabreichen** to give s. o. a little strap oil.

Prügelei brawl, scrap *(sl.)*;
knapp vor einer ~ **stehen** to be within an inch of fight.

Prügelknabe whipping boy, scapegoat.

prügeln to whip, to thrash;
sich ~ to have a scrap, to come to blows; **j. krumm und lahm** ~ to beat s. o. black and blue.

Prügel|strafe corporal punishment, whipping, flogging, fustigation, lash.

Prunk splendo(u)r, magnificence;
bei der Parlamentseröffnung entfalteter ~ pomp of State Opening of Parliament;
großen ~ **entfalten** to make a great display.

prunken to be resplendent, to flaunt, to show off;
mit seinen Kenntnissen ~ to parade one's knowledge; **mit einem neuen Kleid** ~ to show off with one's new dress; **mit seinem Reichtum** ~ to flaunt one's new riches.
Prunk | gemach state room; ~**karosse** state carriage; ~**saal** state room; ~**stück** showpiece, set piece, spectacular.
prunksüchtig sein to like pomp.
Prunkzimmer state apartment.
Pseudoaristokratie shoddy aristocracy.
Pseudonym pseudonym, fictitious (assumed) name, alias, *(Schriftsteller)* pen name;
unter einem ~ **reisen** to travel under an alias; **unter einem** ~ **schreiben** to write under a pseudonym.
Psychiater alienist, psychiatrist, trick cyclist *(Br., mil., sl.)*.
psychiatrische Behandlung psychiatric treatment.
psychischer Zwang mental duress.
Psycho | analyse psychoanalysis; ~**analytiker** psychoanalyst.
Psychologe psychologist, head shrinker *(sl.)*;
Psychologie, gerichtliche forensic psychology.
psychologische Folter psychological torture.
Psychopath psychopath[ist], alienist, wrong number *(sl.)*.
Psychose psychosis.
Psycho | therapie mind cure (healing); ~**thriller** whodunit.
publik | machen to publicize, to make generally known; ~ **sein** to have become public [knowledge].
Publikation publication;
~ **im voraus bestellen** to subscribe for a publication; ~ **vorübergehend einstellen** to suspend a publication; ~ **für November vorsehen** to schedule the publication for November.
Publikations | organ newssheet, gazette; ~**pflicht** compulsory disclosure; **alleinige** ~**rechte** sole right of publication.
Publikum public, turnout, gallery, visitors, *(Hörer)* audience, *(Kundschaft)* clientele, patronage, *(Leser)* readers, reading public, *(Rundfunk)* audience, listeners, *(Sportveranstaltung)* crowd, onlookers, spectators, *(Theater)* audience, house;
dem ~ **zugänglich** open to the public;
aus Studenten bestehendes ~ undergraduate audience; **das breite** ~ the public at large, the general public; **breiteres** ~ wider public; **geladenes** ~ selected audience; **das große** ~ the public at large; **kauflustiges** ~ crowd of eager shoppers; **ländliches** ~ agricultural clientele; **Anlage suchendes (interessiertes)** ~ prospective (capital-seeking) investors, general investing public; **sympathisches** ~ sympathetic audience; **verständnisvolles** ~ appreciative audience; **vorgesehenes** ~ stand-in audience; **wohlsituiertes** ~ high-income audience;
das ~ **in seiner Gesamtheit** the public at large;
beim ~ **ankommen** to get across with an audience; ~ **anlocken** to pull (draw) an audience (in the crowds); ~ **gefühlsmäßig ansprechen** to appeal to the feelings of an audience; ~ **begeistern** to bring down the house; **dem** ~ **empfehlen** to merchandise; **sein** ~ **fesseln** to hold one's audience; **beim** ~ **Anklang finden** to take the fancy of the public; **vornehmes** ~ **haben** to have a select patronage; ~ **zur Begeisterung hinreißen** to kindle the interest of an audience; ~ **langweilen** to tire the audience; **Sammlung dem breiten** ~ **zugänglich machen** to put a collection on show to the general public; **sein** ~ **mit sich (von den Sitzen) reißen** to take one's audience by storm, to electrify an audience; **vor einem großen** ~ **spielen** to play to a large audience; **sein** ~ **überfordern** to be over the heads of an audience; **seine Aktien im** ~ **unterbringen** to go public; **sich vor dem** ~ **verbeugen** *(Theater)* to take a bow; **beim** ~ **sehr gut aufgenommen werden** to take the public fancy; ~ **zufriedenstellen** to please an audience.
Publikums | analyse audience (readership) analysis; ~**anlage** popular investment; ~**beteiligung** *(Rundfunk)* audience turnover (participation); ~**erfolg** hit, box-office draw *(US)*; ~**fonds** public fund, fund open to the general public; ~**geschmack** audience taste; ~**geschmack treffen** to hit the taste of the public; ~**gesellschaft** publicly owned company (corporation, *US*); **in eine** ~**gesellschaft umwandeln** to convert into a public company, to go public; ~**interesse** audience interest; ~**liebling** idol of the public; ~**liebling sein** to be very popular with the audience; ~**programm** participation program(me); ~**tribüne** public gallery; ~**umfrage** *(Rundfunk)* listener research; ~**verhalten** crowd behavio(u)r; ~**verkehr** official (opening) hours; ~**verkehr haben** to deal directly with the public.
publikumswirksam with public appeal, *(Film)* attractive;
~ **sein** to appeal to the public.
Publikums | zeitschrift consumer publication; ~**zusammensetzung** audience profile.
publizieren to publish, to publicize.
Publizist publicist, journalist.
Publizistik journalism.
publizistisch publicistic, journalistic.
Publizität publicity, *(Gesellschaft)* disclosure;
mangelnde ~ lack of publicity.
auf ~ **bedacht sein** to be publicity-minded.
Publizitäts | erfordernisse disclosure requirements; ~**kampagne** prestige magazine (publicity) campaign; ~**prinzip** compulsion for disclosure, compulsory disclosure; ~**umfang** volume of publicity.
Pudel, wie ein begossener with one's tail between one's legs;
des ~**s Kern** gist (very essence) of the matter;
wie ein begossener ~ **dastehen** to look like a dying duck in a thunderstorm;
~**mütze** ski-cap.
pudel | naß dripping wet; ~**wohl** as snug as a bug in a rug.
Puder | beutel powder bag; ~**dose** puff box.
Puff dig, poke, pop, *(Hurenhaus)* brothel, whorehouse, crib *(US)*, *(für Wäsche)* basket, box;
jem. einen ~ **in die Seite geben** to give s. o. a poke in the ribs; ~ **vertragen können** to be able to take a lot.
Puffer buffer, cushion;
~**batterie** *(el.)* floating battery; ~**gebiet** buffer zone; ~**sendung** *(Rundfunk)* cushion; ~**speicher** *(Datenverarbeitung)* buffer; ~**staat** buffer state; **freie** ~**zeit** *(Netzplantechnik)* [early] free float; **unabhängige** ~**zeit** *(Netzplantechnik)* independent float; ~**zone** buffer zone.
Pullmannwagen pullman car *(US)*.
pulsierendes Leben einer Großstadt city throbbing with business activity.
Pult desk;
~**dach** lean-to roof.
Pulver, das nötige the wherewithal (needful, *sl.*);
das ~ **nicht erfunden haben** not to be able to set the Thames on fire; **sein ganzes** ~ **verschossen haben** to have shot one's last bolt; **keinen Schuß** ~ **wert sein** not to be worth one's salt; **das** ~ **nicht wert sein** not to be worth one's keep;
wie auf einem ~**faß sitzen** to sit on top of a volcano.
pulverisieren to pulverize.
Pulver | kaffee instant coffee; ~**magazin** *(mil.)* powder magazine; ~**schnee** powdery snow.
Pump, auf ~ **kaufen** to buy on credit (tick, *Br.*, pump, *sl.*, touch, *sl.*, mace, *sl.*), to take on cuff *(US)*.
pumpen to pump, *(leihen)* to take on tick *(Br.)* (cuff, *US*);
von jem. ~ to touch s. o.; **jem. Geld** ~ to lend (borrow) s. o. money; **von seinen Freunden hemmungslos Geld** ~ to feel no qualms about borrowing from one's friends; **Luft in die Reifen** ~ to pump air into the tyres.
Pumpen | antrieb vangee *(Br.)*; ~**haus** pump house, pump room; ~**hebel** pump lever; ~**schwengel** pump brake.
Pump | station pumping station; ~**werk** pumping plant.
Punkt point, dot, place, *(Anklage)* count, *(Bewirtschaftung)* point, ration coupon, *(Börsennotierung)* point, *(Einzelheit)* detail, item, point, *(Frage)* matter, subject, point, topic, *(I-Tüpfelchen)* dot, tittle, *(Interpunktion)* full stop, period *(US)*, *(Parteiprogramm)* item, plank *(US)*, *(Posten)* item, article, *(Vertrag)* term, clause, *(Zeugnis)* mark;
in vielen ~**en** in many respects;
dunkler ~ heel of Achilles, *(in der Familie)* skeleton in the cupboard; **offen gebliebene** ~**e** points of difference; **halber** ~ *(drucktechn.)* hair space; **heikler** ~ delicate matter, subtle point, punctilio; **höchster** ~ tip, summit; **kritischer** ~ juncture, *(Zollwesen)* hinge, peril point; **springender** ~ the point, salient (crucial) point; **strittiger** ~ point of issue, moot point; **toter** ~ dead point, deadlock, stalemate; **unerledigte** ~**e [der Geschäftsordnung]** unfinished business; **für die Entscheidung unwesentlicher** ~ immaterial issue; **wesentliche** ~**e** essential elements, essentials; **wichtiger** ~ important item, high spot *(US)*; **strategisch wichtiger** ~ strategic point; **wunder** ~ tender spot, sore point;
~ **für** ~ clause by clause, in detail, point by point;
der ~**, um den sich die ganze Frage dreht** the pivot on which the whole question turns; ~**e, über die wir uns nicht einigen konnten** points on which we agreed to differ;
wunder ~ **der Beweisführung** weak point in the evidence; **dunkler** ~ **in der Familie** skeleton in the cupboard (closet), family skeleton; **tiefster** ~ **der Konjunkturkrise** low of the cycle; **dunkler** ~ **in jds. Leben** shady point in s. one's life; ~**e auf der Tagesordnung** items on the agenda (of business); **einzelne** ~**e eines Wirtschaftsabkommens** details of a business contract; ~ **zwölf** twelve o'clock sharp;

Kurs zwei ~e nach Westen abändern to alter the course two points to the west; **auf dem toten ~ anlangen** to come to a deadlock; **sich nur zu bestimmten ~en äußern** to confine one's remarks to specific points; **ganze Reihe neuer ~e behandeln** to cover a great deal of new ground; **einige ~e in einem Bericht gesondert behandeln** to treat a few points in a report separately; **weiteren ~ der Tagesordnung behandeln** to proceed to the next business; **in einem bestimmten ~ recht bekommen** to gain a point; **kitzligen ~ berühren** to touch a delicate matter; **sich auf zwei ~e beschränken** to restrict one's matter to two points; **strittige ~e ausdrücklich bestreiten** to join issue; **~ für ~ durchgehen** to examine item by item, to discuss point for point; **auf einen wichtigen ~ eingehen** to labo(u)r a point; **~ erledigen** *(Tagesordnung)* to discuss a point; **~ für ~ erledigen** to do s. th. with minute detail; **zehn ~e fallen** *(Kurs)* to drop (slump, decline) ten points; **seinen Gegner auf einen ~ festnageln** to pin one's opponent down to a point; **auf ~e freigeben** *(Bewirtschaftung)* to release on points; **~ gewinnen** to gain a point; **etwa 10 ~e gewinnen** *(Aktie)* to push ahead about ten points; **mit jem. die gleichen ~e haben** to tie with s. o.; **sich in den wesentlichen ~en geeinigt haben** to be in substantial agreement; **drei ~e tiefer liegen** *(Kurs)* to be off three points; **in einem ~ nachgeben** to concede (yield) a point; **um 5 ~e nachgeben** *(Kurs)* to decline five points; **ohne ~ und Komma reden** to talk nineteen to the dozen; **j. nach ~en schlagen** to beat s. o. on points; **um fünf ~e gefallen sein** *(Kurs)* to be down by 5 degrees; **bis zu einem gewissen ~ richtig sein** to be correct up to a point; **~ setzen** to put a period; **auf der acht-~ Times setzen** to set up in eight-point; **einen halben ~ niedriger stehen** *(Börse)* to be half a (a half, *US*) point less; **um einen ~ steigen** *(Kurs)* to rise (move up, push ahead) a point; **um mehrere ~e steigen** *(Lebenshaltungskosten)* to go up several points; **um 13 ~e auf 567 steigen** *(Kurs)* to forge ahead 13 points to 567; **einige ~e übergehen** to slip over some items; **zum nächsten ~ der Tagesordnung übergehen** to proceed to the next business; **toten ~ überwinden** to overcome a deadlock, to get one's second wind; **auf ~e verkaufen** to sell on points (under the point system); **um zwei ~e zurückgehen** *(Kurs)* to drop (recede) two points;
~**anstieg** point rise.

Punktationszeichen punctuation marks.

Punkt | bewertung factor credit; ~**bewertungssystem** *(Angestellte)* point [rating] system.

punkt | frei point-free, coupon-free; ~**gleich** equal in points.

punktiert | e Linie dotted line; ~**er Rand** stippled frame.

Punktlandung *(Flugzeug)* precision landing.

pünktlich punctual, to the minute, on the nose (dot), prompt, sharp, on the stroke, clockwork, *(genau)* accurate;
auf die Sekunde ~ on the dot (tick); **~ wie die Uhr** as regular as clockwork, as punctual as the clock;
~ ankommen to arrive on the minute (as scheduled, *US*); **auf die Sekunde ~ ankommen** to come on the dot; **~ sein** to keep one's day; **~ zahlen** to pay promptly;
~**e Lieferung** promptness of delivery; ~**e Lieferung garantieren** to warrant punctual delivery.

Pünktlichkeit promptitude, promptness, punctuality, readiness; **etw. mit militärischer ~ erledigen** to do s. th. army fashion; **für seine ~ bekannt sein** to have a name for punctuality;
~ ist die Höflichkeit der Könige punctuality is the politeness of princes.

Punkt | licht spotlight; ~**linie** dotted line; ~**lohnsystem** point wage system; ~**schraffierung** stipple; ~**schweißung** spot welding; ~**system** *(Angestelltenbeurteilung)* point plan, *(Bewirtschaftung)* point system; ~**wert** points value, score; ~**wertung** point estimation, classification by points; ~**zahl** score; **bei gleicher ~zahl** in case of equality in points; ~**zahl herabsetzen** to downpoint; ~**ziel** pinpoint target *(US)*.

Puppen, bis in die ~ feiern to revel into the small hours of the morning; **~ tanzen lassen** to paint the town red;
~**theater** puppet theater, toy theater (theatre, *Br.*).

pur | es Gold pure gold; ~**e Wahrheit** nothing but the truth.

Puritaner Puritan, blue nose *(sl.)*.

Putsch uprising, riot, coup d'etat.

Putzfrau charwoman, cleaner *(US)*, scrubwoman *(US)*, Mrs. Mop *(fam.)*.

putzmunter fit as a fiddle.

Putz- und Flickstunde *(mil.)* spit and polish, make and mend *(mil., Br.)*.

Putzträger und Putz lath and plaster.

Pyramide *(Altersaufbau)* pyramid structure.

Pyrrhussieg Pyrrhic victory.

Q

Quacksalber quack, charlatan, mountebank.
quacksalbern to play the quack (mountebank).
Quacksalbertum charlatanry, quackery, mountebankery.
Quader ashlar, square stone;
~**bauten** pre-cast concrete blocks.
Quadrat | latschen beetle crushers, clodhoppers; ~**meile** square mile; ~**netz** *(Karte)* graticule.
Quadratur des Kreises versuchen to be trying to square the circle.
Quadrat | wurzel square root; ~**zahl** square number.
Quadruplik *(jur.)* rebutter.
Quäker Quaker, *(pl.)* Society of Friends.
Qual torment, pain, agony, distress, grief;
~**en des Gewissens** pangs of conscience;
~**en ertragen** to bear (stand) pains; **jds. Aufenthalt zur ~ machen** to make s. one's stay an ordeal; **jds. ~en mildern** to alleviate (mitigate) s. one's pain; **unter furchtbaren ~en sterben** to die in terrible agony.
quälen to torment, to prick, to vex, to lacerate, to heckle, to worry, to wring;
j. mit seiner Eifersucht ~ to cause s. o. anguish by one's jealousy; **j. mit blödsinnigen Fragen** ~ to torment s. o. by asking silly questions; **j. zu Tode** ~ to torture o. s. to death; **sich mit einer Übersetzung** ~ to be struggling with a translation.
quälend torturing, tormenting, painful, worrying;
~**er Durst** raging thirst; ~**e Hitze** tormenting heat; ~**er Hunger** gnawing hunger; ~**e Ungewißheit** agonizing uncertainty; ~**e Zahnschmerzen aushalten müssen** to suffer torments from an aching tooth.
Quälerei cruelty, torture, torment.
Quälgeist nuisance, pest, trial, plague *(coll.)*;
~ **seiner Eltern** positive torment of his parents.
Qualifikation qualification, competence, *(Befähigungsnachweis)* qualifying certificate, certificate of competency, *(Eignung)* capacity, fitness, eligibility;
fachliche ~ professional qualification;
~ **zum Richteramt** qualification to hold the office of a judge; ~ **zum Treuhänder** trustee capacity;
fachliche ~ auf dem Gebiet des Rechnungswesens mit sich bringen to hold a professional qualification in accountancy; **notwendige ~ besitzen** to have the necessary qualifications, to measure up to one's position *(US)*.
Qualifikations | aktien *(Vorstandsmitglied)* qualification shares *(Br.)*; ~**wettbewerb** qualifying contest.
qualifizieren to qualify, to fit, to capacitate, to specify, *(Straftat)* to aggravate;
sich ~ to qualify, to be suitable, to become eligible; **sich für ein Amt** ~ to render o. s. eligible to fill an office; **j. zum gefährlichen Gewohnheitsverbrecher** ~ to designate s. o. as a dangerous habitual criminal; **sich für einen Posten** ~ to qualify to hold a job.
qualifiziert qualified, eligible, fitted, fit, capable, specified, *(ermächtigt)* authorized, entitled, *(erstklassig)* first-class, excellent;
beruflich ~ eligible for an occupation; **gut** ~ well qualified; **nicht** ~ ineligible, unfit, not qualified; **für einen Posten** ~ eligible for a post;
~ **für etw. sein** to be fit for (entitled to do) s. th.; **fachlich ~ sein** to be qualified in one's subject;
~**e Annahme** qualified acceptance, acceptance under reserve; ~**er Arbeiter** efficient (capable) worker; ~**e Arbeitskräfte** skilled workers; ~**er Bewerber** eligible candidate; ~**e Mehrheit** qualified majority; ~**er Mehrheitsbeschluß** extraordinary resolution; ~**es Vergehen** aggravated offence.
Qualifizierung qualifying, qualification, eligibility;
mangelnde ~ nonqualification.
Qualifizierungsnachweis qualifying experience.
Qualität *(Art)* kind, *(Güte)* quality, grade, class, *(Marke)* brand, description, mark, *(Sorte)* sort, type, run;
abweichend von der üblichen ~ off standard; **erster** ~ first-rate, of finest grade; **in jeder** ~ of every description; **von ausgesuchter (bester)** ~ choice, of first (prime) quality; **von durchschnittlicher** ~ of ordinary quality; **von erstklassiger** ~ of high (top) quality; **von geringer** ~ low-class, poor; **von höchster** ~ excelsior; **von minderer** ~ low-grade, third-rate; **von schlechter** ~ off, poor;
abfallende ~ inferior quality; **gut abgelagerte** ~ well-conditioned quality; **allererste** ~ sterling quality, extra fine (unrivalled) quality; **ausbedungene** ~ stipulated quality; **auserlesene** ~ prime quality; **ausgesuchte (ausgezeichnete)** ~ choice quality, class; **ausreichende** ~ acceptable quality level; **nicht ausreichende** ~ poor quality; **bessere** ~ superior quality; **beste ~ für geringsten Preis** best buy; **bestimmte** ~ concrete (definite) quality; **durchschnittliche** ~ standard (average) quality; **beste englische** ~ of best English make; **erforderliche** ~ required quality; **erlesene** ~ choicest quality; **erste** ~ choice quality, *(Brillant)* first water; **erstklassige** ~ first-rate (first-class, finest, top[-grade]) quality, prime; **besonders feine** ~ selected quality; **feinste** ~ superior quality; **gangbare** ~**en** fair assortment; **gängige** ~ current quality; **geringere** ~ inferiority, inferior quality; **gute** ~ good (fair) quality; **handelsübliche** ~ merchantibility, merchantableness, commercial standard; **hervorragende** ~ transcendent quality; **mangelnde** ~ non-quality, lacking quality; **marktübliche** ~ merchantable quality; **minderwertige** ~ quality falling short, cheap, low (low-grade, poor) quality; **mittlere** ~ medium quality (goods, sorts); **schlechte** ~ poor (inferior) quality; **schlechtere** ~ quality not up to standard; **schlechteste** ~ lowest (bottom) quality; **unzureichende** ~ unsatisfactory quality; **vereinbarte** ~ agreed quality; **vorzügliche** ~ prime (superior) quality; **zugesicherte** ~ promised quality, warrant of merchantibility; **zweite** ~ second[-class] quality;
gute ~ und Beschaffenheit good merchantable quality and condition; ~ **eines Erzeugnisses** product quality; ~ **laut Muster** quality as per sample; **beste ~ für geringsten Preis** best buy; ~ **eines Schuldners** standing of a debtor;
j. nicht entsprechend seinen ~en bezahlen to overlook s. one's services; **nicht der ~ entsprechen** to be off standard; **mehr auf Quantität als auf ~ gehen** to seek size rather than quality; **dieselbe ~ liefern** to match s. one's grade; **nach ~en ordnen** to grade; ~ **prüfen** to check quality; ~ **steigern** to enrich (upgrade) a quality; **mit der vorgezeigten Probe in der ~ übereinstimmen** to correspond in quality to (match) the sample; **über ~en verfügen** to have one's good points;
~ **setzt sich durch** quality will tell in the end.
qualitativ qualitative;
~ **verschieden ausfallen** to vary in quality;
~**e Analyse** qualitative analysis; ~**e Angaben** qualitative data; ~**er Unterschied** difference in quality.
Qualitäts | abnahmeschein certificate of inspection; ~**abweichung** variation in quality; ~**anforderungen** exacting standards of quality; ~**angabe** quality mark; **allen ~ansprüchen genügen** to be up to standard in every way; ~**ansprüche stellen** to promote high standards; ~**arbeit** quality workmanship; **hochwertige ~arbeit** superior (first-class) workmanship, work of high quality; **für ~arbeit garantieren** to guarantee the finest workmanship; ~**arbeiter** qualified worker, experienced (master) craftsman; ~**artikel** high-quality products, branded goods; ~**auflage** quality circulation; ~**benzin** high-grade fuel (petrol); ~**bescheinigung** certificate of quality, kite *(Br.)*; ~**bestimmung** quality grading (designation); ~**beurteilung** quality rating; ~**bewertung** evaluation of products; ~**bezeichnung** quality description; ~**bild** quality picture; ~**differenz** *(Statistik)* variation in quality; ~**erzeugnisse** high-quality products, high-grade goods; **überall bekannte ~erzeugnisse** national brands *(US)*; **sich auf teure ~erzeugnisse spezialisieren** to feature high-priced items; ~**fehler** defective quality; ~**garantie** warrant of merchantibility; **jem. eine ~garantie für gelieferte Waren geben** to give s. o. a warranty of quality of goods; ~**grad** degree of quality; ~**gruppierung festverzinslicher Effekten** bond rating; ~**gütezeichen** quality mark; ~**hinweis** certification mark; ~**kennzeichnung** grade labelling, grading of commodities; ~**klasse** grade.
Qualitätskontrolle process (statistical quality) control, quality assurance analysis, *(Nahrungsmittel)* inspection;
ausreichende ~ satisfactory control; **statistische** ~ acceptance sampling;
Fabrik auf Vorlage ihrer Unterlagen über ~ verklagen to subpoena a company's records on quality control.
Qualitäts | kontrollverfahren quality-control practice; ~**lage** quality range; ~**leistung** quality performance; ~**leistungen anstreben** to aim at quality; ~**leistungen eines neuen Autos bestätigen** to bear witness to the quality of a new car; ~**mangel** breach of warranty; ~**marke** brand; ~**markt** quality market; ~**minderung** deterioration in quality.

Qualitätsniveau quality level, standard;
toleriertes ~ acceptable quality level;
durchschnittliches ~ **der herausgehenden Lieferungen** average outgoing quality level.
Qualitätsnormen standards of quality, quality standards;
~ **festlegen** to establish standards of quality.
Qualitäts|papier good-quality paper; ~**probe** sample, pattern; **laut beiliegender** ~**probe** as per pattern enclosed; ~**produkt** high-quality line; ~**produktion** reproduction quality.
Qualitätsprüfung quality control;
~ **vorbehalten** quality subject to approval;
~ **vornehmen** to check the quality.
Qualitäts|rüge complaint concerning quality, quality complaint; ~**schutz** quality protection; ~**schwankungen** fluctuations in quality; ~**sorte** superior grade; ~**stempel** stamp; ~**stufe** quality grade; **in eine höhere** ~**stufe eingereiht werden** to be upgraded in the scale of selection; ~**übereinstimmung** quality conformance; **statistische** ~**überwachung** statistical quality control; ~**unterschied** *(Warenbörse)* difference; ~**verbesserung** improvement in quality; ~**verschlechterung** deterioration in quality; ~**vorschriften** quality rules, quality specification *(Br.)*; ~**wagen** quality car; ~**ware** high-quality products, choice (quality) commodities (merchandise, goods), articles of high quality, superior articles, firsts, branded goods, value; ~**zeichen** quality mark, kite mark *(Br.)*; ~**zertifikat** certificate of quality; **vom Käufer anzuerkennendes** ~**zeugnis** certificate to be final; ~**zuschlag** *(Lohnsystem)* step bonus; ~**zusicherung** quality assurance; ~**zuwachs** *(Forstwirtschaft)* quality increment.
qualitätvoller Film quality film.
Qualm smoke, smother.
qualmen to smoke, *(Vulkan)* to send out clouds of smoke;
durch die Gegend ~ *(Zug)* to puff slowly through the countryside; **wie ein Schlot** ~ to smoke like a chimney.
qualvoll agonizing, painful, tormenting;
~ **sterben** to die in agony;
~**e Enge** cramped discomfort.
Quantentheorie quantum theory.
Quantität quantity, *(große Anzahl)* bulk, lot, *(Betrag)* amount, number;
in kleinen ~**en** in small lots.
quantitativ quantitative, quantity-wise *(US)*;
sich ~ **unterscheiden** to differ in quantity;
~**e Analyse** quantitative analysis; ~**e Angaben** quantitative data.
Quantitäts|angaben quantitative data; ~**bestimmung** quantitative determination, quantification; ~**gleichung** quantity equation; ~**mangel** deficiency, shortage; ~**theorie des Geldes** *(Finanzwissenschaft)* quantity theory of money.
Quantum quantum, quantity, *(Anteil)* share, quota, portion;
sein tägliches ~ **an Bier** one's daily ration of beer; **geringes** ~ **Gift** small amount of poison;
sein ~ **beitragen** to contribute one's share; **über ein gehöriges** ~ **Frechheit verfügen** to have got a lot of cheek.
Quarantäne, in under quarantine;
~ **aufheben** to remove (take off) the quarantine; ~ **durchmachen** to perform one's quarantine; **aus der** ~ **entlassen** to discharge (release) from quarantine; **in** ~ **gehen** to go into quarantine; ~ **hinter sich haben** to be out of quarantine; ~ **halten** to ride at quarantine; **in** ~ **legen** to put into quarantine; **in** ~ **liegen,** ~ **machen** to ride at (be in) quarantine; ~ **halten müssen** to be subject to quarantine; **unter** ~ **stellen** to quarantine; ~ **verhängen** to quarantine; ~ **verletzen** to break quarantine regulations;
~**arzt** quarantine (health, *US*) officer, healthguard *(Br.)*; ~**beamter** quarantine officer; ~**bestimmungen** quarantine regulations; ~**dienst** quarantine service; ~**flagge** quarantine (sick, yellow) flag, flag of quarantine; ~**gelder** quarantine expenses; ~**hafen** quarantine harbo(u)r; ~**lazarett** isolation (detention) hospital; ~**maßnahmen** quarantine.
quarantänepflichtig sein to be subject to quarantine.
Quarantäne|prüfung quarantine inspection; ~**risiko** quarantine risk; ~**sperre** quarantine, sanitary cordon; ~**station** quarantine station; ~**verletzung** breaking quarantine regulations; ~**vorschriften** quarantine law (regulations); ~**zeit** quarantine period.
Quark, sich über jeden ~ **aufregen** to scream easily *(sl.)*; **alten** ~ **aufrühren** to rake old quarrels; **sich um jeden** ~ **kümmern** to waste one's time with trifles; ~ **reden** to talk rubbish (rot); **seine Nase in jeden** ~ **stecken** to poke one's nose in everything; **keinen** ~ **davon verstehen** to know beans about it *(sl.)*.
Quartal quarter, quarterly period, *(Schule, Zahltag)* quarter day;
angefangenes ~ broken quarter.
Quartals|abrechnung quarterly account (statement); ~**abschluß** quarterly settlement; ~**bericht** quarterly statement; ~**dividende** quarterly dividend; **zum** ~**ende kündigen** to give notice at the end of the quarter; ~**geld** quarterly allowance; ~**medio** half quarter; ~**miete** quarter's rent; ~**rechnung** quarter bill, quarterly account; ~**säufer** incurable drunkard; ~**schluß** end of quarter; ~**tag** quarter day *(Deutschland und USA: 1. 1., 1. 4., 1. 7., 1. 10., England: 25. 3., 24. 6., 19. 9., 25. 12.)*; ~**termin** quarter day, term *(Br.)*; ~**verrechnung** quarterly account.
quartalsweise every (by the) quarter, quarterly.
Quartalszahlung quarterly (quarter's) payment, quarterage, *(Zinsen)* quarterly disbursement.
Quartawechsel fourth [bill] of exchange.
Quartformat quarto.
Quartier quarters, lodging, quartering, accommodation, *(mil.)* quarterage, billet, digs *(Br., coll.)*;
verkommenes ~ dilapidated abode;
~ **für die Nacht** accommodation for the night, night's lodging, shakedown;
sein ~ **aufschlagen** to take up one's quarters; ~ **beschaffen (besorgen, machen)** to arrange for accommodation; ~ **beziehen** to take up quarters; **neues** ~ **in einem anderen Stadtteil beziehen** to move to another part of a town; **bei jem. im** ~ **liegen** to be quartered (billeted) upon s. o.; ~ **nehmen** to take one's lodgings; **Sommergäste ins** ~ **nehmen** to take summer visitors;
~**amt** billeting office; ~**beschaffungsstelle** lodging bureau; ~**macher** billeting party; ~**meister** *(mil.)* billet master, quartermaster; ~**meisterabteilung** q department *(Br.)*; ~**schein** billeting paper; ~**wirt** host; ~**zettel** billet.
Quarz|steuerung crystal control; ~**uhr** quartz clock.
Quasi|delikt quasi delict; ~**geld** near money *(US)*; ~**monopol** semi-monopoly; ~**rente** quasi-rent.
Quasselbude *(Parlament)* talking shop.
Quasselei jabbering, chatter, babble, gabble.
Quasselkopf blatherer, blatherskite, gasbag.
quasseln to blather, to babble, to jabber;
zu viel ~ to run off the money *(sl.)*; **dummes Zeug** ~ to talk drivel (rubbish).
Quassel|strippe *(Mensch)* wind-bag, gasbag, *(tel.)* phone, blower *(Br., sl.)*; ~**wasser getrunken haben** to be in a talkative mood.
Quästur *(Universität)* bursary.
Quatsch nonsense, twaddle, trumpery, rigmarole, piffle, fiddle-faddle, rot *(Br., sl.)*, poppycock *(US sl.)*, *(wertloses Zeug)* trash, rubbish, junk;
völliger ~ a lot of poppycock *(US sl.)*;
~ **mit Soße!** nuts!;
~ **machen** to do a silly thing, to play the fool; ~ **reden** to talk through one's hat (out of the back of one's neck, *fam.*).
quatschen to piffle, to chaff, to waffle, to rot *(Br., sl.)*;
stundenlang am Telefon ~ to be nattering for hours on the telephone; **über ein Thema** ~, **von dem man nichts versteht** to prate about a subject of which one knows nothing; **dummes Zeug** ~ to talk rubbish, to talk through one's hat, to shoot the bull *(sl.)*.
Quelle fountain, well [spring], head, spring, *(Gewährsmann)* source, origin, quarter, grassroots, authority, informant, mother, parent;
an der ~ **abgezogen** *(Steuer)* at the (deducted at) source; **aus einwandfreier** ~ from an unimpeachable source; **aus erster** ~ at first hand, straight from the horse's mouth *(sl.)*; **aus guter** ~ on good (the best) authority; **aus halbamtlicher** ~ from a semi-official source; **aus sicherer (zuverlässiger)** ~ from a reliable source, on good authority, from a safe quarter; **aus unzuverlässiger** ~ from an unreliable source; **aus vertraulicher** ~ through private channels; **von der** ~ **bis zur Mündung** from the source to the mouth;
authentische ~ reliable source; **benutzte** ~**n** sources used; **einwandfreie (sichere)** ~ trustworthy source; **finanzielle** ~**n** financial resources; **heiße** ~ thermal (boiling) spring; **unverbürgte** ~ unaccredited source; **wohlunterrichtete** ~**n** well-placed sources; **zuverlässige** ~ straight tip;
~ **ständigen Verdrusses** constant source of annoyance; ~ **allen Wissens** fountainhead of all knowledge;
seine ~**n angeben (aufführen)** to quote one's authorities; **sich auf eine** ~ **berufen** to refer to an authority; **Einkommen an der** ~ **besteuern (erfassen)** to tax income at the source, to withhold a tax *(US)*; **aus verläßlicher** ~ **erfahren** to have it from a reliable source; ~ **eines Bühnenstücks erforschen** to trace the source of a play; **neue** ~**n erschließen** to open up (tap) new sources; ~

fassen to impound a source; **von einer zuverlässigen ~ haben** to have s. th. from a reliable source; **an der ~ kaufen** to buy at first hand; **seine ~ nennen** to name the source of one's information; **über geheime ~n verfügen** to have secret sources of information; **Steuerabzug an der ~ vornehmen** to deduct tax at source; **etw. aus sicherer ~ wissen** to know s. th. from a good source.

Quellen|abzug *(Steuer)* deduction at source; **~abzugsverfahren** pay-as-you-earn principle; **~angabe** quotation of one's authorities, source notes, sources used, references; **~beleg** historical record; **~belegung** source documentation; **~besteuerung** collection of tax at source, tax deduction at source; **der ~besteuerung unterliegen** to suffer tax at source; **~besteuerung vornehmen** to levy by deduction at source; **~buch** source book; **~forschung** original research; **~hinweis** credit; **~kritik** historical criticism; **~material** source material; **~nachweis** source documentation, indication of sources used; **~prinzip** system of collection of tax at source, pay-as-you-go system *(US)*; **~staat** country of origin, *(Doppelbesteuerung)* state of source.

Quellensteuer tax deducted at source, withholding tax *(US)*, pay-as-you-go tax *(US)*;
~ entrichten to pay a tax at the source, to pay as you go; **~ erheben** to tax income at the source, to withhold a tax *(US)*; **~abzug** deduction of tax at source.

Quellenverzeichnis sources used, bibliography.

Quell|fluß headstream; **~gebiet** headwaters.

Quengelei carping, grumbling.

Quengelfritze, Quengler grizzler, whiner, pester.

quengelig fretful, crabbed, grizzling.

quengeln to carp, to grumble, *(Kind)* to whine, to grizzle, to pester;
ganzen Tag ~ to be whining all the day.

Quentchen drop, pinch, knob, bit, pinch, grain, iota;
kein ~ Verstand not an ounce of common sense.

quer crosswise, crossways;
~ über eine Straße gehen to cross a road; **Stoff ~ nehmen** to cut the fabric on the weft; **seinen Namen ~ über einen Scheck schreiben** to write one's name across a check *(US)* (cheque, *Br.*); **~ zur Hauptstraße verlaufen** to run at right angles to the main road;
~er Rohrdurchschnitt cross sectional diameter of a pipe.

Quer|addition cross addition; **~bahnsteig** underpass.

Quere, jem. in die ~ kommen to cross s. one's path, to queer s. one's pitch, *(fig.)* to get in s. one's way, to thwart s. one's plans, to upset s. one's applecart;
ihm ist etw. in die ~ gekommen things have gone wrong with him.

querfeldein cross-country.

Quer|folio folio oblong; **~format** broadside, cross size; **~gang** traverse, gangway *(Br.)*; **~heftung** side stitching; **~kurs** cross rate; **~linie** *(drucktechn.)* space rule; **~ruder** *(Flugzeug)* aileron.

Querschnitt cross section, sample;
repräsentativer ~ typical embodiment; **wirtschaftlicher ~** industrial cross section;
~ durch die Bevölkerung cross section of the people; **~ durch die Verbraucherschaft** cross section of the consumers;
repräsentativen ~ der gesamten Wirtschaft darstellen to represent every facet of business.

Querschnittsuntersuchung cross section study.

Querschreiben *(Wechsel)* crossing.

querschreiben *(Wechsel)* to cross.

Quer|straße crossroad; **~summe** sum of the digits; **~träger** cross beam (girder); **~treiber** intriguer, thwarter, obstructionist, pettifogger, kicker *(US)*; **~treiberei** obstructionism, pettifoggery, intrigues; **~treibereien veranstalten** to pettifog.

Querulant querulous (litigious) person, crab, pettifogger.

querulierender Matrose sea lawyer *(sl.)*.

Querverbindung cross connection, *(Lehrfach)* interconnection;
~ zwischen zwei Städten direct route between two towns;
~ zwischen zwei Themen herstellen to establish a correlation between two subjects.

Quer|verbund intercommunication; **~verweis** cross reference; **~wand** traverse.

quetschen to squeeze, to squash, to compress;
sich in einen Bus ~ to squash o. s. into a bus; **sich den Finger ~** to get one's finger jammed; **seine Sachen in einen Koffer ~** to cram one's things into a suitcase; **zu Tode ~** to crush to death; **sich an eine Wand ~** to flatten (press) o. s. against a wall.

Quetschkommode squeeze-box *(sl.)*, squiffer *(Br., sl.)*.

Quetschung bruise, contusion.

quietschen to squeak, *(Bremse)* to screech, to squeal.

quietschend, mit ~en Bremsen with a screech of brakes; **mit ~en Reifen** with squealing tyres (tires, *US*); **~e Tür** squeaking door.

quietschvergnügt as fit as a fiddle, merry as the day is long.

Quintessenz quintessence, fifth essence, *(Werbetext)* story;
~ einer Erklärung pith and marrow of a statement.

Quintuplik *(jur.)* surrebutter.

quitt square, even, upsides *(Br., coll.)*;
Schuld ~ machen to settle a debt; **~ sein** to be all square; **mit jem. ~ sein** to be quits (even, upside, finished, done, through, *US*) with s. o.

quittieren to receipt, to put one's receipt on, to acknowledge receipt of, to give a discharge;
Bemerkungen mit einem Lächeln ~ to meet a remark with a smile; **Dienst ~** to leave service, to quit the place; **Empfang von Waren ~** to acknowledge receipt of goods; **Rechnung ~** to receipt a bill; **per Saldo ~** to give receipt in full; **Urteil mit einem Achselzucken ~** to receive a verdict with a shrug of one's shoulders.

quittiert, dankend received with thanks; **doppelt für einfach ~** in duplicate; **nicht ~** unreceipted;
~e Rechnung receipted bill.

Quittung receipt, acknowledgment, acquittance, quittance, bill, discharge, *(Beleg)* voucher, *(Einzahlungsbeleg)* deposit slip;
gegen ~ on (against) receipt; **laut beiliegender ~** as per receipt enclosed;
doppelte ~ double (duplicate) receipt; **einzelne ~** itemization *(US)*; **endgültige ~** receipt in full; **förmliche ~** formal receipt; **gestempelte ~** stamped receipt; **gültige ~** good (valid) receipt; **doppelt für einfach gültige ~** double receipt for single; **löschungsfähige ~** *(Grundbuchrecht)* satisfaction piece *(US)*, deed of release, statutory receipt *(Br.)*; **ordnungsgemäße ~** receipt in due form; **rechtsgültige ~** proper (effectual) receipt; **unausgefüllte ~** receipt in blank; **unvollständige ~** receipt that is not in order; **vollständige ~** discharge in full; **vorbehaltlose ~** clean receipt; **vorläufige ~** interim (provisional) receipt;
~ mit Angabe des Zahlungsgrundes receipt with consideration for payment stated; **~ über den gesamten Betrag** receipt in full; **~ des Gerichtsvollziehers** seizure note; **~ über eingelagerte Güter** warehouse-keeper's certificate *(Br.)*; **~ über die Restzahlung** receipt for the balance; **~ ohne Unterschrift** receipt not signed;
~ ausstellen to [give (make out) a] receipt; **löschungsfähige ~ erteilen** to enter a memorandum of satisfaction *(US)*.

Quittungs|abschrift duplicate; **~aussteller** receiptor; **~bescheinigung** accountable receipt; **~blankett** receipt form; **~block, ~buch** receipt (slip) book; **~duplikat** duplicate (double) receipt; **~formular** receipt form; **~formular für Barabhebungen** counter check *(US)* (cheque, *Br.*); **~heft** *(Bank)* receipt book, chequelet *(Br.)*; **~inhaber** receipt holder; **~karte** receipt card; **~marke, ~stempel** receipt stamp; **mit ~stempel versehen** to receipt; **~stempelgebühr** receipt stamp duty *(Br.)*; **~vordruck** receipt form.

Quivive, auf dem ~ sein to be on the alert (lookout);
er ist stets auf dem ~ there are no flies on him *(coll.)*.

Quiz|master quizmaster; **~sendung** quiz program(me).

quotal in proportion, proportionate, on a quota basis, pro rata, proratable *(US)*.

Quote quota, proportional allotment (share), allocation, *(Anteil)* share, [pro]portion, *(Konkurs)* liquidation dividend, *(Rückversicherung)* quota share, *(Verhältniszahl)* ratio, *(Verlustanteil)* contribution;
mit gleichen ~n pari passu; **nach ~n** proportionally, pro rata, proratable *(US)*;
anteilsmäßige ~ contribution pro rata, pro-rata share; **erschöpfte ~** exhausted quota; **vorgesehene ~** quota provided for;
voraussichtliche ~ ungesicherter Gläubiger possible dividend to unsecured creditors;
seine ~ aufbringen to pay one's share; **~n beseitigen** to eliminate quotas; **~ erhöhen** to raise (increase) a quota; **~ festsetzen** to fix a quota; **hohe ~ haben** to rate high in; **~ kürzen** to reduce a quota; **seine ~ übernehmen** to contribute one's quota; **unausgenutzte ~n ins nächste Jahr übertragen lassen** to allow unfilled quotas to carry into next year; **über seine ~ verfügen** to dispose of a quota; **~ zuteilen** to [assign a] quota, to apportion a quota.

Quoten|abdeckung quota cover; **~abrechnung** quota accountancy; **~aktie** no-par value share *(Br.)* (stock, *US*), unvalued stock *(US)*; **~anteil** quota share; **~aufstockung** *(Weltwährungsfonds)* quota increase; **~aufteilung** division of quotas;

~**aushandlung** quota bargaining; ~**auswahl** quota selection (sample); ~**auswahlverfahren** quota sampling; ~**berechnung** *(Treuhänder)* calculation of dividends; ~**berichtigung** adjustment of quotas; ~**beschränkung** quota restriction; ~**beseitigung** elimination of quotas; ~**einwanderer** quota immigrant *(US)*; ~**erhöhung** increase in quotas, quota increase; ~**festsetzung** fixing of a quota; ~**kürzung** reduction of a quota, quota cut; ~**kürzung eines Betrages** deduction of a sum from a quota.

quotenmäßig quotational, pro rata;
~**es Miteigentum** proportionate ownership; ~**e Verteilung** prorata distribution.

Quoten|rückversicherung reinsurance by quota cession, quota share reinsurance; ~**stichprobe** quota sample; ~**system** quota system; ~**träger** quota agent; ~**überschreitung** exceeding the quota; ~**urteil** distributive finding of the issue; **sich innerhalb der freiwilligen ~vereinbarung bewegen** to stay within the quota voluntarily agreed on; ~**verteilung** distribution of the quotas; ~**vertrag** *(Rückversicherung)* quota share treaty.

Quotient quotient.

quotieren to allot, to allocate, *(Preis)* to quote a price.

Quotierung quotation.

Quotitätssteuer percentage tax.

R

R-Gespräch *(Telefon)* reverse *(US)* (transfer, *Br.*) charge call;
~ **führen** to make the call collect *(US)*.

Rabatt abatement, rebate[ment], allowance, deduction [from the price], reduction, markdown *(US)*, *(für Händler)* dealer's discount, *(Skonto)* discount, anticipation;
abzüglich ~ less rebate[ment] (discount); **auf** ~ on rebate[ment], at a discount, with a deduction of; **mit** ~ at a discount; **mit einem** ~ **von** subject to a deduction of; **ohne** ~ without abatement, straight;
25%iger ~ a 25 per cent rebate[ment];
von der Gesamtabnahme abhängiger ~ deferred discount *(US)*; **besonderer** ~ special allowance; **dem Händler eingeräumter** ~ dealer's discount; **erhaltener** ~ discount received; **nicht in Anspruch genommener** ~ lost (missed) discount; **gestaffelter** ~ adjusted discount; **kein** ~ no deductions;
Retouren und ~**e** returns and allowances;
~ **bei Barzahlung** cash discount on sales; **bei Barzahlung3%** ~ three per cent discount for cash; **besonderer** ~ **bei Belegung mehrerer Regionalausgaben desselben Blattes** *(Anzeige)* combined edition discount; ~ **bei gleichzeitigem Bezug von ...** rebate for simultaneous purchase of...; ~ **für den Bucheinzelhandel** rebate for book retail trade; ~ **für Einzelhändler** discount earned, retail discount; **kumulativer** ~ **für wiederkehrende Käufe** deferred rebate; ~ **für Ladenangestellte** employee discount; ~ **bei Mengenabnahme (für Mengenkäufe)** quantity discount, quantity rate (rebate, deduction), space (volume, mass) discount; ~ **bei Serienbelegung** frequency discount; ~ **für Stammkunden** patronage discount; ~ **für regelmäßige Verlader** deferred rebate; ~ **für Wiederverkäufer** trade discount (allowance);
~ **abziehen** to deduct a discount; ~ **von 4% in Abrechnung bringen** to take off 4%; ~ **geben** to allow an abatement, to grant a reduction, to make an allowance; **4%** ~ **genießen** to be subject to 4 per cent discount; ~ **gewähren** to allow an abatement (a discount), to make an allowance, to grant a reduction; **5%** ~ **gewähren** to make a reduction of 5 per cent; **bei Barzahlung** ~ **gewähren** to allow a discount for cash; **bei Bezug von 100 Stück 5%** ~ **gewähren** to allow a discount of five per cent with orders of 100; **üblichen** ~ **gewähren** to allow the usual discount; **mit** ~ **kaufen** to buy at market discount; **mit einem** ~ **verkaufen** to sell at market discount (a reduction); ~ **zugestehen** to rebate, to grant a reduction;
nach ~**abzug** ultra reprisal; ~**anspruch von 50% haben** to be entitled to a 50 per cent discount on purchases; ~**bedingungen** discount terms; ~**berechnung** calculating a discount; ~**bestimmungen** discount terms; ~**betrag** discount, discount sum.

rabattfähig subject (liable) to discount.

Rabatt|geschäft discount shop (store, house, *US*), cut-price shop; ~**gewährung** discount allowance; ~**gewährung bei Inzahlungnahme** trade-in allowance; ~**gutschrift** discount credit.

rabattieren to give a reduction (discount).

Rabatt|kunde *(Anzeigenwesen)* rate holder; ~**laden** thrift store, discount house *(US)*; ~**marke** premium, patronage dividend, discount ticket, savings stamp *(Br.)*, trading (trade) stamp, green stamp *(US)*; ~**markengesetz** Trading Stamps Act *(Br.)*; ~**markensystem** trading-stamp scheme; ~**methoden** discount practices; ~**preis** discount price; ~**rechnung** discount; ~**rückbelastung** *(Werbung)* short rate; ~**satz** discount (anticipation) rate; **gewährte** ~**sätze** reductions allowed; **gestaffelte** ~**sätze anbieten** to offer allowances on a sliding scale; **übliche** ~**sätze gewähren** to allow the usual discount; ~**schinder** *(Inserat)* rate holder; ~**spanne** margin of discount allowed; ~**staffel** *(Anzeigenwesen)* scale of discounts (rebates), sliding-scale discount; ~**system** *(Frachten)* rebate system; ~**tarif** *(Anzeigenwesen)* sliding scale, short rate *(US)*; ~**vereinbarung zwischen Verlagen und dem Sortiment** net book agreement; **alle** ~**vorteile und Vorzugsplazierungen aufheben** to nullify rate and position protection.

Rabatz din, row, rumpus;
~ **machen** to kick up a row, to make a din (hell of a racket).

Rabauke tough, guy, lout, rough, boor.

Rabe crow, raven;
weißer ~ *(fig.)* white crow, black swan, rarity;
gefräßig wie ein ~ **sein** to be greedy as a swine; **wie ein** ~ **stehlen** to be thievish as a magpie.

Raben|aas bitch *(coll.)*; ~**eltern** cruel parents.

rabenschwarze Nacht pitch-black night.

rabiat ruthless, raving, mad;
~ **werden** to become furious;
~**er Bursche** rude fellow.

Rabulismus pettifoggery.

Rabulist pettifogger, hairsplitter.

Rache revenge, vengeance;
~ **des Schicksals** nemesis;
~ **brüten** to brood on revenge; **nach** ~ **dürsten** to lust for revenge; ~ **für etw. nehmen** to take revenge for s. th.; **an jem.** ~ **nehmen** to wreak one's vengeance on s. o.; **jem.** ~ **schwören** to swear vengeance against s. o.;
~**akt** act of revenge; ~**ankündigung** denunciation of vengeance; ~**durst** particular malice.

rachedurstig thirsting for revenge.

Rache|gedanken verbannen, alle to dismiss all thoughts of revenge; ~**gefühle hegen** to nurse feelings of revenge.

Rachen throat, *(Tier)* mouth, jaws;
~ **aufreißen** *(fig.)* to talk big; ~ **nicht voll genug bekommen können** to have an ever open door; **jem. einen Brocken in den** ~ **werfen** to throw a sop to Cerberus; **jem. Geld in den** ~ **werfen** to waste money on s. o.

rächen to revenge;
sich jetzt ~ *(Fehler)* to come home to roost;
sich an jem. für eine Beleidigung ~ to revenge o. s. on s. o. for an insult; **sich an seinen Feinden** ~ to avenge o. s. on one's enemies;
sich überlegen zu ~ **wissen** to repay an injury with interest *(fam.)*.

Rachgier lust for revenge.

rachsüchtiger Charakter vengeful character.

Racker, kleiner little rascal.

Rad wheel, *(Fahrrad)* bicycle, bike;
fünftes ~ **am Wagen** fifth wheel on (of) the coach;
ins ~ **der Geschichte eingreifen** to change the course of history; **sich aufs** ~ **setzen** to get on one's bike; ~ **wechseln** to change a wheel; ~ **der Geschichte zurückdrehen** to reverse the march of time.

Radar radar;
mit ~ **ausgerüstet** radar-equipped; **vom** ~ **erfaßt** painted *(sl.)*;
~**anlage** radar installation; **vollgepfropft mit** ~**anlagen** radar-ridden; ~**anpeilung** radiolocation; ~**antenne** radar antenna (aerial), scanner; ~**aufklärer** radar reconnaissance aircraft; ~**ausrüstung** radar equipment; ~**bake** radar beacon; ~**beobachtung** radar interception; ~**bereich** radar coverage; ~**bild** blip; **zum** ~**bild gehörig** video; ~**blindlandung** ground-controlled approach; ~**echo** radar echo (response); ~**einrichtung,** ~**gerät** radar equipment; ~**empfänger** radar receiver; ~**entfernungsmesser** range-finding radar; ~**erdstation** ground radar; ~**falle** radar trap (speedmeter), speed trap; ~**flugzeug** radar aircraft; ~**frühwarnsystem** early warning radar; ~**frühwarnkette** defense (defence, *Br.*) early warning line.

radargelenkt radar-guided.

Radar|höhenmesser radar altimeter; ~**kontrolle** police radar control; ~**landehilfe** radar landing aid; ~**lotse** radar controller.

radarmäßig erfassen to pick up by radar installation.

Radar|mast radar mast; ~**meßwagen** radar control trailer; ~**nase** radome; ~**navigation** radar navigation; ~**ortung** radarlocation; ~**ortungsempfänger** radiolocator; ~**schiff** flighthouse, radar picket; ~**schirm** radar screen; **Flugzeug auf dem** ~**schirm verfolgen** to follow the flight of an aircraft by radar.

radarsicher radarproof.

Radar|spiegel *(Weltraum)* radar disk; **mit einem auf dem Dach angebrachten** ~**spiegel ausgestattet sein** to be topped with a revolving radar disk; ~**station** radar station; ~**steuerung** radar guidance; ~**störflugzeug** radar jammer; ~**störfolie** chaff; ~**störgerät** radar jamming equipment; ~**störung** radar jamming; ~**strahl** radar beam; ~**suchgerät** search-radar set; ~**techniker** radarman; ~**turm** radar tower; ~**überwachungsnetz** radar surveillance network; ~**warnsystem** radar warning system; ~**ziel** radar target; ~**zielpunkt** radar spot.

Radau racket, rumpus, uproar, tumult;
~**bruder** roudy, boor, lout, tough *(coll.)*.

Radbremse wheel brake.

Rädchen im Getriebe cog in the machinery.

Raddampfer paddle steamer, side wheeler *(US)*.

radebrechen to smatter, to murder a language;
Englisch ~ to speak broken English.

Radeinzelaufhängung independent suspension.
Rädelsführer agitator, principal, principal actor, ringleader, riot leader, leader of a gang.
Räder, auf ~n on wheels, rattling;
unter die ~ kommen to be run over by a car *(fig.)*, to go to the bad (dogs, *fam.*);
~kettenfahrzeug track-laying vehicle, caterpillar, half-track; **~spur** trace, prints of a wheel; **~übersetzung** gear transmission.
Räderwerk wheelwork, machinery;
~ der Verwaltung wheels of government;
ins ~ der Gesetze fallen to be caught in the meshes of the law.
Radfahren verboten *(Schild)* no cycling.
radfahren to ride (go) by bicycle, to bicycle, to bike *(coll.)*, *(Katzbuckeln)* to heel, to bootlick, to toady, to apple-polish.
Rad | fahrer cyclist, bicyclist, pedal cyclist, *(fig.)* sneak; **~fahrweg** cycle path.
radieren to erase, to rub out.
Radier | gummi eraser, rubber; **~messer** desk knife; **~stelle** erasure.
Radierung print, lithography, etched plate, *(radierte Stelle)* erasure.
Radieschen, sich die ~ von unten besehen to push up the daisies.
radikal radical, extreme, intransigent;
Vorschlag ~ ablehnen to reject a proposal absolutely; **sich ~ ändern** to undergo a radical change; **~ vereinfachen** to carry out an extreme simplification;
~e Ansichten vertreten to hold extreme opinions; **~e Maßnahmen** drastic (radical) measures; **~e Partei** radical (extremist) party; **~er Politiker** radical politician, extremist.
Radikaler radical, extremist;
extremer ~ too-too radical.
Radikalinski leftist, lefty, rightist.
radikalisieren to radicalize, to become extreme in one's views.
Radikalismus radicalism, extremism, intransigence.
Radikalkur drastic cure.
Radio wireless, broadcasting, radio *(US)*;
durch das ~ over the radio; **im ~** on the wireless (air); **mit ~ ausgestattet** wireless-equipped;
~ und Fernsehen mass media *(Br.)*;
~ anstellen to switch (put) the radio on; **~ ausstellen** to turn off a wireless set; **~ einstellen** to tune in the radio; **~ hören** to listen to the radio (in on a broadcast); **Nachrichten im ~ senden** to read the news, to wireless (radio) a message; **im ~ sprechen** to go on the air.
radioaktiv radioactive;
~ machen to activate, to cook;
~e Kriegsführung radioactive warfare; **~er Niederschlag** atomic fallout; **~e Schäden** radioactive losses; **~e Verseuchung** radioactive contamination; **~er Zerfall** radioactive decay.
Radio | aktivität radioactivity; **~amateur** ham; **~apparat** wireless (radio, *US*) set; **~apparat mit Plattenwechsler** autoradiogram; **~durchsage** spot announcement, spot *(US)*; **~durchsage hören** to monitor a call; **~empfang** wireless (radio) reception; **~empfänger, ~gerät** wireless set, broadcast receiver, radio *(US)*, box *(coll.)*; **~geschäft** radio shop; **~gramm** radiogram, aerogram; **~kompaß** radio compass; **~programm finanzieren** to sponsor a program(me); **privatwirtschaftliche ~programmfinanzierung** commercial sponsoring of program(me)s; **~reklame** radio advertising; **~sendung** broadcast; **~sonde** radiosonde; **~station** wireless (broadcasting) station; **~techniker** radio engineer; **~telefonie** wireless telephony, radiotelephony; **~telegramm** wireless telegram, radiogram; **~teleskop** radio telescope; **~übertragung** radio transmission, broadcast; **~uhr** combination clock radio; **~welle** radio wave; **~werbesendung** commercial *(US)*; **~werbung** broadcast advertising.
Radius radius, range.
Rad | nabe hub; **~scheibe** web; **~weg** cycle track.
raffen to scratch, to grab;
Geld ~ to amass (accumulate) money.
Raffer grasper.
Raffgier greediness, avarice, rapacity.
raffgierig greedy, avaricious.
Raffinement refinement, subtlety.
Raffinerie refinery;
~einrichtungen refining equipment; **~kapazität** refinery capacity; **~kapazität pachten** to hire refinery capacity.
Raffinesse ingenuity, cunning, shrewdness, slyness;
~ des Luxus refinements of luxury;
mit allen ~ ausgestattet sein to be fitted with all the trappings.
raffinieren to refine, to purify, to try.
raffiniert refined, purified, *(fig.)* sly, cunning, crafty, tricky, wily, slick *(US)*;
nicht ~ unrefined;
~ eingefädelt sein to be a clever move; **nicht ~ genug sein** to be too easy a mark;
~er Anwalt slick (Philadelphia, *US*) lawyer; **~er Betrug** artful dodge; **~er Einbruch** well-devised burglary; **~er Geschmack** refined (sophisticated) taste; **~er Luxus** subtile extravagance.
Raffke money-grubber, go-getter.
Raffprobe *(Statistik)* chunk sampling.
Rage, in ~ geraten to get hot under the collar.
Rahm abschöpfen to skim the cream.
Rahmen *(Auto)* chassis, *(Bereich)* frame, scope, limits, skeleton, environment, *(Gefüge)* framework, structure, *(Zeitung)* box; **aus dem ~ fallend** out of the ordinary; **außerhalb des ~s von** beyond the measure of; **außerhalb des ~s von jds. Vertretungsmacht** beyond the scope of s. one's express authority; **im ~ von** within the limits (scope) of; **im kleinen ~** small-scale; **im ~ eines Abkommens** under an agreement; **im ~ des Festes** in the course of the celebration; **im ~ des Möglichen** within the range of possibility; **im ~ seiner Tätigkeit** during the carrying out of his duties; **im ~ seiner Vollmacht** within the scope of one's authority; **im ~ der Vorjahresentwicklung** about the same as in the previous year; **in engerem ~** within narrow bounds;
geplanter ~ budgeted level; **gerasterter ~** backed (shaded) frame; **gesetzlicher ~** legal framework;
~ einer Erzählung framework of a story; **~ eines Gesetzes** scope of a law;
im würdigen ~ ablaufen to go with proper decorum; **~ des Gemeinschaftslebens bestimmen** to set the life pattern of the community; **prunkvollen ~ bieten** to provide a magnificent setting; **als ~ dienen** to serve as the setting; **sich in den ~ seiner neuen Umgebeung einfügen** to adapt o. s. to one's new surroundings; **aus dem ~ fallen** to be out of place (line, *US*), to be the odd one; **sich im ~ seiner Befugnisse halten** to keep within the bounds (scope) of one's authority; **sich im ~ der üblichen Gesellschaftertätigkeit halten** to act in the ordinary course of partnership; **im ~ der Schlüsselgewalt handeln** *(Ehefrau)* to pledge her husband's credit for necessaries; **im ~ seiner Vertretungsbefugnisse handeln** to act within the scope of one's authority; **im ~ seiner Vollmachten handeln** to act intra vires; **im ~ seiner Arbeit liegen** to fall within the scope of s. one's work; **im ~ des üblichen Geschäftsverkehrs liegen** to be incidental to the normal activity of a business; **im ~ des Möglichen liegen** to lie within the scope of possible events; **im ~ von jds. finanziellen Möglichkeiten liegen** to be within the reach of s. one's pocket; **im ~ seiner Tätigkeit liegen** to fall within the scope of one's work; **~ eines Aufsatzes sprengen** to go beyond the scope of an essay; **~ des Üblichen sprengen** to go beyond the limits of established practice;
~abkommen skeleton (master, basic) agreement; **~antenne** frame aerial, coil (loop) antenna *(US)*; **~frachtabkommen** master freight agreement; **~gebühr** skeleton due (fee); **~geschichte** frame story; **~gesetz** skeleton bill (law), omnibus act; **~kredit** credit limit *(Br.)* (line, *US*); **~kreditvertrag** underlying agreement, working plan; **~lizenz** open licence; **~organisation** skeleton organization, cadre; **~personal** skeleton staff; **~plan** strategic plan; **~police** *(Lebensversicherung)* master policy; **festes ~programm** *(Rundfunk)* across-the-board program(me); **~strafe** indeterminate sentence; **~tagesordnung** skeleton agenda; **~tarif** skeleton tariff, *(Lohnabkommen)* skeleton wage agreement; **~tarifvertrag** industry-wide (master, model) agreement; **~verbot** *(Gerichtsanordnung)* blanket injunction; **~vereinbarung** outline agreement; **~verfassung** framework constitution; **~vertrag** skeleton (basic) agreement, basic contract, general pact; **~vertragsergänzung** *(Zollwesen)* blanket tariff supplement; **~vorschrift** general rule; **~werk** framework.
räkeln, sich to loll.
Rakete rocket, ballistic missile;
von U-Booten abgefeuerte ~n submarines' missiles; **dreistufige ~** three-stage rocket; **ferngesteuerte ~** guided missile; **gesteuerte ~** controlled rocket; **interkontinentale ~** intercontinental rocket;
~ mit Atomsprengkopf nuclear-tipped missile; **~ auf U-Bootbasis** submarine-launched ballistic missile;
~ abbrennen *(Feuerwerk)* to let off a rocket; **~ abschießen** to launch a rocket; **mit ~n beschießen** to rocket; **~ ins Ziel steuern** to guide a missile to its target.
Raketen | abfeuerung, ~abschuß missile (rocket) launching.

Raketenabschuß|basis rocket launching (missile) site; ~**gelände** rocket field; ~**platz** launching range for rockets; ~**stelle** missile base, missile site.

Raketen|abwehranlagen antimissile defence; ~**abwehrsystem** safeguard missile system; ~**antrieb** rocket propulsion; **mit ~antrieb** rocket-powered; ~**flugzeug** rocket[-driven] airplane (plane); ~**forscher** rocketeer; ~**konstrukteur** rocket builder; ~**prüfgelände** missile testing centre (center, *US*); ~**silo** missile silo; ~**spitze** nose cone; ~**start zum Mond** moon shot; ~**startplatz** missile base; ~**stufe** stage of a rocket; ~**technik** rocketry; ~**treibsatz** rocket composition; ~**triebwerk** rocket engine; ~**-U-Boot** missile submarine; ~**verschiebungen** missile movements; ~**versuchsgelände** rocket range; ~**werfer** *(mil.)* rocket launcher; ~**wesen** rocketry; ~**zeitalter** missile age.

Rammbock, Ramme rammer, pile driver, ram.

rammdösig giddy, dazed;
j. ~ machen to make s. one's head swim.

rammen to ram, *(Schiff)* to run down;
Pfähle in die Erde ~ to drive piles into the ground.

Rampe platform, ascent, elevated approach, rising ground, *(Schiff)* landing place.

Rampenbeleuchtung footlights.

Rampenlicht footlights, floats, *(Öffentlichkeit)* limelight, spotlight *(US)*, *(Theater)* floodlights;
im vollen ~ in the full blaze of publicity;
~ der Öffentlichkeit scheuen to shun the limelight; **im ~ der Öffentlichkeit stehen** to be in the limelight.

ramponieren to damage, to spoil.

ramponiert spoilt;
ziemlich ~ aussehen to look the worse for wear;
~**er Ruf** clouded reputation; ~**er Teppich** worn carpet.

Ramsch trumpery, junk (job) goods, refuse, rubbish, jumble, rummage *(Br.)*;
im ~ kaufen to bulk, to buy in the lump (in lots); **im ~ verkaufen** to sell as a job lot, to sell in bulk;
~**geschäft** junk shop; ~**handel** petty trade; ~**händler** junk dealer, slaughterer; ~**kauf** job-lot buying; ~**laden** junk (jumble, *Br.*) shop, job-goods shop; ~**markt** *(Buchhandel)* oddments market; ~**partie** job lot, trumpery; ~**verkauf** jumble *(Br.)* (rummage) sale; ~**ware** job goods (line, lot), junk (sale) goods, oddments, trumpery, rummage *(Br.)*, duffer *(sl.)*.

Rand edge, border, confine, fringe, rim, brink, *(drucktechn.)* margin;
am ~e on the margin; **am ~e des Bankrotts** on the brink of ruin (verge of bankruptcy); **am ~e bemerkt** by the way; **am ~e der Stadt** on the outskirts of the town; **am ~ des Verderbens** on the verge of ruin; **auf den ~ gedruckt** marginal; **außer ~ und Band** completely out of hand; **bis zum ~ gefüllt** filled to the brim; **bis an den ~ eines Krieges** short of war;
aufgeschnittener ~ opened margin; **bis in die Schrift hinein beschnittener ~** bleed margin; **zu stark beschnittener ~** cropped margin; **breiter ~** *(Schreibmaschine)* wide margin; **goldener ~** *(Teller)* gold rim (border); **schwarzer ~** black frame (border); **unterer ~** foot margin; **oberer weißer ~** head margin, top margin; **unterer weißer ~** bottom margin, tail margin;
~ abschneiden *(Anzeige)* to bleed; **Fehler am ~ anstreichen** to mark a mistake in the margin; **am ~e bemerken** to remark in passing; **nur am ~e berühren** to touch the fringes of; **j. an den ~ des Abgrunds bringen** to bring s. o. to the brink of ruin; **Land an den ~ des Krieges bringen** to get a country on the brink of war; **an den ~ der Verzweiflung bringen** to drive s. o. to the verge of despair; **bis an den ~ eines Verbrechens gehen** to go to the length of crime; **außer ~ und Band geraten** to run out of control, to get crazy about s. th.; **mit etw. nicht zu ~e kommen** not to be able to manage it; **am ~e der Armut leben** to skirt the edge of poverty; **am ~e miterleben** to be a bystander; **am ~e des Grabes stehen** to be on the brink of the grave; **am ~e vermerken** to write on the margin; **mit einem ~ versehen** to margin; **sich am ~e verstehen** to go without saying.

randalieren to kick up a fuss (shindy), to raise the roof.

Randalierer disorderly person, rowdy, roisterer.

Rand|auslösung *(Schreibmaschine)* margin stop (release); ~**befeuerung** *(Flugplatz)* boundary lighting; ~**bemerkungen** marginal notes, sidenote, gloss; **mit ~bemerkungen versehen** to marginalize, to [write on the] margin, to admarginate; **Buch mit ~bemerkungen versehen** to make marginal notes in a book; ~**bevölkerung** fringe population; ~**bezirk** fringe; ~**bezirke einer Stadt** suburbs of a town; ~**breite** *(drucktechn.)* marginal space; ~**breite festsetzen** to make margin; ~**einteilung** marginal classification; ~**erscheinung** side issue; ~**figur** second-stringer, *(Strafrecht)* accomplice; ~**form** *(drucktechn.)* key plate.

Randgebiet fringe area, *(Stadt)* outskirts, suburbs, *(Staat)* borderland;
~**e** *(fig.)* fringe activity;
~ der Wissenschaft borderland of science;
~**e eingemeinden** to absorb border areas.

Rand|geschäfte aufgeben to sell off one's peripheral activities; ~**glosse** marginal gloss (note), sidenote; **militante ~gruppen** fringe militants; ~**klasse** *(Statistik)* marginal category; ~**kommentar** happenstance note; ~**landschaft** rimland; ~**leiste** border; ~**meer** marginal sea (belt); ~**persönlichkeit** *(soziol.)* marginal man; ~**platte** *(drucktechn.)* key plate; ~**siedlung** suburban settlement; ~**spur** *(Autobahn)* verge; ~**staat** border (peripheral) state; ~**stein** curbstone; ~**steller** *(Schreibmaschine)* margin stop; ~**streifen** *(Straße)* shoulder, nearside (inside) lane; ~**tätigkeit** fringe activity; ~**tief** *(Wetter)* secondary depression.

randvolles Glas glass full to the brim.

Rand|wetterbedingungen marginal weather conditions; ~**zeche** marginal mine; ~**zone der Zivilisation** fringes of civilization.

Rang rank, degree, mark, *(Besoldungsskala)* rate, rating, grade, *(Güteklasse)* quality, grade, *(Stellung)* rank, echelon, standing, status, state, position, station, estate, condition, *(Stellung eines Unternehmens)* rating, standing;
dem ~ nach in order of merit, according to priority; **ersten ~es** primary, first-rate (-class); **gleichen ~es** with rank equal to; **ihrem ~ entsprechend** according to their rank; **im gleichen ~ zu** with rank equal to; **im ~ höher** senior, superior; **im ~ vorgehend** of prior rank; **von hohem ~** of a high order; **zweiten ~es** secondary;
älterer ~ prior rank, priority; **dritter ~** *(Theater)* gallery; **einfacher ~** *(Matrose)* rating; **erster ~** *(Theater)* dress circle, first balcony *(US)*; **gesellschaftlicher ~** social standing (status), class; **gleicher ~** equality of rights; **hoher ~** high degree, dignity, eminence, greatness; **niederer ~** mean rank, *(mil.)* lower rank; **oberster ~** *(Theater)* gallery; **ehrenhalber verliehener ~** honorary rank; **zweiter ~** *(Theater)* upper circle *(Br.)*, second balcony *(US)*;
~ nach dem Dienstalter seniority [in rank]; **~ einer Forderung** rank of debt; **~ der Gläubiger** ranking of creditors; **~ einer Hypothek** rang of a mortgage;
jem. den ~ ablaufen to get the jump on (get the better off, fly at a higher pitch than) s. o.; **hohen ~ bekleiden** to attain a high place, to occupy a high position, *(mil.)* to hold a high rank; **bescheidenen ~ einnehmen** to occupy a humble station; **ersten ~ einnehmen** to rank first [in priority]; **gesellschaftlich einen hohen ~ einnehmen** to occupy a high position in society; **höheren ~ einnehmen** to rank *(US)*, to have priority; **besseren ~ einräumen** *(Grundbuch)* to grant prior rank; **jem. unmittelbar im ~ folgen** to rank next to s. o.; **zu ~ und Würden gelangen** to rise to eminence; **gleichen ~ haben** to rank alike, *(Konkursgläubiger)* to rank equally (pari passu); **im ~ nachgehen** to rank after; **jem. im ~e nachgehen** to be second to s. o. in seniority; **jeden entsprechend seinem ~ plazieren** to give each a place according to his deserts; **mit einer Belastung im ~e rücken** *(Grundbuch)* to postpone a charge; **ohne ~ und Namen sein** to be a nobody; **jem. im ~ untergeordnet sein** to be inferior in rank to s. o.; **im gesellschaftlichen ~ sinken** to sink in the social scale; **im gleichen ~ stehen** to take rank with (among), to range among, to be on the same footing, *(Aktien)* to rank pari passu; **mit jem. im gleichen ~ stehen** to be even with s. o. (rank equally), to be on equal footing with s. o.; **im ~ eines Hauptmanns stehen** to hold the rank of a captain; **jem. im ~e vorgehen** to outrank (have priority over) s. o.;
~**abzeichen** insignia of rank, badge.

rangälter superior, senior;
~**er Offizier** elder officer.

Rang|ältester senior, superior, *(mil.)* senior [officer]; ~**änderung** alteration of priority.

rangbesser *(Grundbuch)* of prior rank.

Rang|bestimmung von Gläubigern marshalling of creditors; ~**dienstalter** *(mil.)* standing.

Ränge, niedere *(mil.)* lower echelons;
vor leeren ~n spielen to play to empty benches.

Rang|einräumung postponement of priority; ~**einteilung** rating, ranking.

Rangelei tussle, wrangling.

rangentsprechend ausschütten to distribute according to priority.

Rangerhöhung increase (elevation) in rank;
~ ohne Gehaltssteigerung Mexican promotion *(sl.)*.

Rangfolge order of preference (rank, precedence, merit), sequence, *(Konkurs)* priority, *(Rangordnung)* ranking;

~ **von Forderungen** priority of debts; ~ **von Gläubigern** ranking of creditors; ~ **von Konkursforderungen** arrangement of claims; ~ **von Konkursgegenständen** ranking (marshalling) of assets; ~ **von Pfandrechten** marshalling of liens; ~ **von Sicherheiten** marshalling of securities.

Rangfragen, mit jem. über ~ streiten to contend for precedence with s. o.

ranggleich of equal rank.

Ranggleichheit equality of rights;
~ **von Gläubigern** equality of rank of creditors.

ranghöher *(mil.)* senior, superior.

Rangier|bahnhof shunting (train-order) station, railway (marshalling) yard, switchyard *(US)*; ~**betrieb** switching movement (operation); ~**dienst** switching service.

Rangieren *(Bahn)* shunt, shunting, *(Forderungen)* marshalling.

rangieren *(Auto)* to manoeuvre, *(Eisenbahn)* to marshal, to shunt, to switch *(US)*, to shuffle up *(sl.)*, *(einstufen)* to rate, to rank, to range, to classify, *(Gläubigerforderungen)* to rank, to marshal;
sich ~ to range o. s., to settle one's debts; **sein Auto in eine Parklücke** ~ to manoeuvre one's car into a narrow parking space; **an erster Stelle** ~ to rank foremost; **erst an zweiter Stelle** ~ to play second fiddle.

Rangierer shunter, switchman *(US)*, berther *(US)*.

Rangier|gebühr switching charge; ~**gelände** switch limits; ~**gleis** siding, shunting track *(US)*, switching track; ~**lokomotive** shunter, switching (shunting) locomotive *(US)*, switcher *(US)*, pony engine *(US)*; ~**meister** yardman, yardmaster.

rangjünger *(Pfandrecht)* puisne.

Rang|klasse class, category; ~**liste** list of precedents, ranking list, *(mil.)* Army List, *(mar.)* Navy List *(Br.)*; ~**loge** tier box, first balcony box *(US)*; ~**mannschaft** shunting (switching, *US*) crew.

rangmäßig einstufen to classify according to rank.

Rangordnung ranking, order of ranks, rank order, classification, echelon, *(Protokoll)* [order of] precedence, table of precedence *(Br.)*;
berufliche ~ job ranking; **betriebliche** ~ managerial ranks; **festgelegte** ~ determinate order of precedence; **protokollarische** ~ ceremonial precedence;
~ **der Ansprüche** ranking of claims; ~ **der Gläubiger** ranking (priority) of creditors; ~ **von Hypotheken** ranking of mortgages; ~ **der Nachlaßgläubiger** discussion *(Scot. law)*; ~ **von Pfandrechten** priority (ranking, ordering, marshalling) of liens; ~ **der Sicherheiten** *(Konkursverfahren)* marshalling of assets; ~ **der diplomatischen Vertreter** classification of diplomatic agents;
~ **eines Gläubigers bestimmen** to rank (marshal) a creditor; ~ **der Pfandrechte feststellen** to marshal liens; **in der ~ dem Ausgabedatum unterliegen** to rank in the order of issue.

Rangordnungs|grad *(Statistik)* grade; ~**maßnahmen** *(Statistik)* rank order; ~**meßzahlen** rang order statistics; ~**nummer** *(Statistik)* rank.

Rang|rücktritt *(Grundbuch)* postponement of priority; ~**rücktritt einer Belastung** postponement of charge; ~**rücktritt gewähren** *(Hypothekengläubiger)* to postpone; ~**rücktrittserklärung** deed (written notice, letter) of postponement; ~**stelle** position on the promotion roster; ~**stellenvermerk** *(Grundbuch)* priority notice *(Br.)*; ~**stufe** order, class, degree, range, rank, stick, *(mil.)* step, degree of rank; ~**unterschied** distinction of rank; **auf ~unterschieden bestehen** to pull rank; ~**verhältnis der Gläubiger** ranking of creditors; ~**verlust** forfeiture of a seniority right, loss of priority, *(mil.)* reduction in rank (to a lower grade, *US*), degradation; ~**verlust erleiden** to lose priority; ~**vorbehalt** reservation of priority; ~**vormerkung** *(Grundbuch)* priority caution; ~**vorrang erreichen** *(Pfandrecht)* to tack.

Ränke intrigues, tricks, deceit;
jds. ~ durchschauen to be up to s. one's tricks; **seinen eigenen ~n zum Opfer fallen** to be hoist with one's own petard; ~ **schmieden** to make intrigues;
~**schmied** plotter, schemer, intriguer, designer; ~**spiel** practice, intrigue, frame-up *(US sl.)*; **jds. ~spiel durchschauen** to see through s. one's little game.

rankriegen, j. to make s. o. sit *(coll.)*.

Ranzen knapsack, haversack, wallet, bag;
sich den ~ vollschlagen to eat one's fill, to fill one's belly.

ranzige Butter rancid butter.

rapide rapid, fast;
~ **abwärts gehen** to go downhill;
~**n Aufschwung nehmen** to improve rapidly; ~ **Fortschritte machen** to make rapid progress.

Rappel tantrum, bonkers, *(Verrücktheit)* craze, fad, freak;
einen ~ bekommen to be off one's head (nuts), to blow one's top *(fam.)*; ~ **haben** to have a bee in one's bonnet.

rappelig irritated, fidgety;
heute ganz ~ sein to be on edge today.

rappeln to rattle, to clatter;
sich ~ to get back on one's feet, to pick up.

Rappen, auf Schusters ~ reisen to go on Shanks' mare, to beat the hoof.

Rapport *(mil.)* report;
zum ~ bestellen to warn for duty; **sich bei jem. zum ~ melden** to report to s. o.

rar rare, scarce;
sich ~ machen not to let o. s. seen very much.

Rarität fly in an amber, curiosity, rarity, rare specimen.

Raritäten|kabinett cabinet of curiosities; ~**laden** curiosity shop.

rasant headlong, wild;
~**e Erscheinung abgeben** to cut a dashing figure; ~**e Frau** smashing woman, smasher; ~**e Geschwindigkeit** breakneck speed; ~**er Sportwagen** swish sports car.

rasch quick, speedy, swift;
Auftrag ~ erledigen to meet an order promptly; **mit seinem Urteil zu ~ bei der Hand sein** to be too rash in one's judgment; ~**e Antwort** snappy answer; ~**e Auffassungsgabe haben** to be quick in the uptake; ~**e Erholung** speedy recovery; **in ~er Folge** in close succession.

rascheln, mit der Zeitung to rustle the newspaper.

raschlebige Zeit fast-moving age.

Rasen lawn, grass, turf, *(Wut)* rage;
gepflegter ~ well-kept lawn;
j. zum ~ bringen to make s. o. furious.

rasen to scorch, to race (tear) along, *(wütend sein)* to rage, *(Wind)* to storm;
mit dem Auto in die Stadt ~ to rush one's car to the city; **zum Bahnhof** ~ to race to the station; **vor Begeisterung** ~ to be wild with enthusiasm; **in eine Mauer** ~ *(Auto)* to career into a wall.

Rasenbank grass bank.

rasend *(wütend)* raging, frenzied, frantic;
~ **teuer** terribly expensive;
~ **verliebt sein** to be madly in love; **etw. ~ gern tun** to love to do it; ~ **werden** to go mad, to see red, to fly off the handle;
mit ~em Beifall empfangen werden to be greeted with tumultuous applause; ~**e Eifersucht** violent jealousy; ~**e Geschwindigkeit** breakneck speed; ~**er Hunger** agonizing hunger; ~**e Kopfschmerzen** splitting headache; ~**er Schneesturm** raging blizzard; **in ~em Tempo reden** to talk terribly fast.

Rasender madman.

Rasen|mäher lawn mower; **kleiner ~platz** pocket-handkerchief lawn; ~**sprenger** sprinkler; ~**streifen** strip of park, terrace *(US)*.

Raser *(Auto)* scorch, roadhog, jehu *(sl.)*.

Raserei raving, rage, tantrum, *(Autofahrer)* scorch, reckless (furious) driving, scorch;
j. zur ~ bringen to drive s. o. wild; **in ~ geraten** to fly off the handle.

Räson|annehmen to listen to reason; **j. zur ~ bringen** to bring s. o. to reason.

raspeln, Süßholz to whisper sweet nothings.

Rasse, aussterbende vanishing species; **menschliche** ~ the human kind; **weiße** ~ white race;
~ **haben** to have class.

Rasselbande noisy lot, boisterous children.

rasseln to rattle, to clank, to jangle, *(Wecker)* to go off noisily;
durch eine Prüfung ~ to flunk an examination; **mit dem Säbel** ~ to rattle one's saber (sabre, *Br.*); **mit dem Schlüsselbund** ~ to jangle one's bunch of keys; **durch die Straßen** ~ to rattle through the streets.

Rassenangehöriger coracialist.

rassenbewußt race-conscious.

Rassen|bewußtsein, übertriebenes racialism *(US)*; ~**diskriminierung** colo(u)r bar, racial discrimination, racialism, Jim Crowism *(US sl.)*; ~**diskriminierung betreiben** to discriminate racially; ~**fanatiker** racist *(US)*, segregationist; ~**fanatismus** racism; ~**feindschaft** racial hostility; ~**frage** colo(u)r (racial) problem; ~**gegensätze** racial antagonism; ~**gemisch** blend of different races; ~**gesetzgebung** racial legislation; ~**gleichheit** racial equality; ~**haß** race (racial) hatred; ~**kampf** racial conflict; ~**komplex** racial complex; ~**konflikt** interracial strife; ~**krawall** race riot, racial troubles (unrest); ~**kreuzung** cross breeding; ~**kunde** ethnology; **hervorragende ~merkmale** outstanding features of a race; ~**mischmasch** medley of races;

~mischung miscegenation, amalgamation *(US)*; **~politik** racial policy, racism; **~politiker** racist *(US)*; **~problem** race problem; **~schranken** racial barriers, colo(u)r bar (line), segregation; **~schranken aufheben** to desegregate; **~selbstmord** race suicide; **~spannungen** racial tensions; **~toleranz** racial tolerance; **~trennung** segregation; **~trennung aufheben** to desegregate; **~unruhen** racial troubles (unrest, riot); **~unterschied** racial distinction, race difference; **~verfolgung** racial persecution, racialism; **~vermischung** racial mixing; **~vorurteil** racial (colo(u)r) prejudice; **~zwiestreit** racial dissention.

rassig thoroughbred, mettlesome, striking, good-looking.

Rassismus racism, racialism.

Rast rest, stop, repose, *(mil.)* halt;
ohne ~ und Ruhe arbeiten to work without a letup; **kurze ~ einlegen** to take a short break, to have a short rest, *(mil.)* to make a halt.

rast ich so rost ich if you rest you rust.

rasten to rest, to [make a] stop, to take a break.

Raster screen, *(Fernsehen)* scanning device, scanner;
grober ~ coarse screen;
~ für Zeitungsdruck screen for newspaper printing;
~ätzung half-tone etching, autotype; **~bild** frame; **~druck** autotype; **~frequenz** *(Fernsehen)* scanning frequency; **~linie** grid line; **~platte** scanned area; **~schirm** scanning screen; **~tiefdruck** rotogravure; **~tönung** tints.

Rasthaus roadhouse, rest house, roadside inn.

rastlos ceaseless, restless;
~es Leben hectic life.

Rastplatz halting (stopping) place, watering hole, *(Autobahn)* lay-by *(Br.)*;
auf einen ~ fahren to pull into a lay-by *(Br.)*.

Raststättengebiet service area.

Rasur erasure, blot.

Rat advice, counsel, council, *(Anregung)* suggestion, *(Ausschuß)* advisory board, *(Ausweg)* way out, remedy, *(Empfehlung)* recommendation, *(Person)* counsel(l)or, adviser;
unabhängiger fachmännischer ~ proper independent advice; **gesetzgeberischer ~** legislative council; **gutgemeinter ~** well-meaned advice; **juristischer ~** legal advice; **kostenloser ~** gratuitous advice; **schlechter ~** bad piece of advice;
~ der Europäischen Gemeinden Council of European Municipalities; **~ der Europäischen Gemeinschaften** Council of Ministers; **~ der europäischen Industrieverbände** Council of European Industrial Federations; **~ für gegenseitige Wirtschaftshilfe** Council of Mutual Economic Aid (COMECON);
~ annehmen to be open to (follow s. one's) advice; **j. um seinen ~ bitten** to ask consultation of s. o.; **~ einholen** to ask for advice; **jds. ~ einholen** to take s. one's advice; **~ erteilen** to give counsel; **fachmännischen ~ erteilen** to give expert advice; **jds. ~ folgen** to listen to s. o.; **um ~ fragen** to ask for advice; **j. um ~ fragen** to consult (ask consultation, counsel of) s. o.; **auf jds. ~ nichts geben** to put no value on s. one's advice; **mit sich selbst zu ~e gehen** to hold counsel with one's own heart; **sich rechtlichen ~ holen** to hire legal counsel; **auf einen ~ hören** to listen to reason; **in einer Angelegenheit keinen ~ erteilen können** to be incompetent to advise on a matter; **ärztlichen ~ in Anspruch nehmen** to take medical advice; **sich nach jds. ~ richten** to follow s. one's advice; **~ schaffen** to find a way out; **~ in den Wind schlagen** to throw advice to the winds, to set advice at naught; **vom ~ eines Freundes abhängig sein** to lean on a friends' advice; **jem. mit einem ~ dienlich sein** to help s. o. with one's advice; **immer ~ wissen** to be never at a loss; **sich keinen ~ mehr wissen** to be at one's wit's end (at the end of one's tether); **~ von jem. haben wollen** to come (go) to s. o. for advice; **zu ~e ziehen** to consult, to seek advice; **j. zu ~e ziehen** to take counsel with s. o.; **Experten zu ~e ziehen** to call in an expert;
guter ~ kommt über Nacht night is the mother of counsel.

Rate instal(l)ment, part payment, *(Aktie)* call on shares, *(Konkurs)* dividend, *(Satz)* rate, *(Verhältniszahl)* ratio, proportion;
auf ~n in part payment, on the instal(l)ment (hire-purchase) system *(Br.)*, on deferred terms *(US)*; **in ~n** by (in) instal(l)ments; **in festgelegten ~n** by stated instal(l)ments; **in monatlichen ~n** in monthly instal(l)ments; **in vierteljährlichen ~n** paid quarterly; **in ~n zahlbar** payable by instal(l)ments;
erste ~ *(Anzahlung)* deposit, first instalment, downpay *(US)*; **fällige ~** instal(l)ment due; **geringfügige ~n** petty instal(l)ments; **letzte ~** final instal(l)ment, payoff; **rückständige ~** instal(l)ment in arrears; **überfällige ~** past due instal(l)ment;
~ des Preisanstiegs rate of price rush; **~ der aufgeklärten Straffälle** detection rate;
in kleinen ~n abbezahlen to pay in (clear off by) small instal(l)ments; **in ~n bezahlen** to make part payments; **mit einer ~ im Rückstand bleiben** to fall behind with an instal(l)ment; **auf ~n kaufen** to buy by instal(l)ments, to buy on the instal(l)ment plan; **Möbel auf ~n kaufen** to buy furniture on the hire-purchase system *(Br.)* (on deferred terms, *US*); **auf ~n verkaufen** to sell on the deferred-payment *(US)* (hire-purchase, *Br.*) system; **~n auf mehrere Monate verteilen** to spread instal(l)ments over several months; **in ~n zahlen** to pay by (in) instal(l)ments, to buy (pay) on the instal(l)ment (hire-purchase, *Br.*, deferred-payment, *US*) system.

raten to advise, to give advice, to counsel;
zu einem frühen Aufbruch ~ to counsel an early start; **Kreuzworträtsel ~** to solve a crossword puzzle; **zur Vorsicht ~** to recommend caution;
sich nicht ~ lassen not to listen to reason.

Raten|einkauf instal(l)ment buying, hire purchase *(Br.)*; **~hypothek** repayment mortgage; **~kauf** instal(l)ment business (purchase), hire-purchase [sale] *(Br.)*, purchase on deferred terms *(US)*; **~kredit** hire-purchase *(Br.)* (instal(l)ment, deferred-payment, *US*) credit; **~preis** instal(l)ment price; **~rückstände** arrears of instal(l)ments; **~sparen** deferred savings; **~system** instal(l)ment (hire-purchase, *Br.*, deferred-payment, *US*) system; **~vereinbarung** instal(l)ment contract; **~verzug** failure to pay an instal(l)ment.

ratenweise by instal(l)ments;
Kredite ~ bewilligen to vote credits in instal(l)ments.

Ratenzahler, als ~ besitzen to hold on hire purchase *(Br.)*.

Ratenzahlung instal(l)ment [payment], payment by instal(l)ments, part (partial, deferred, *US*, spaced) payment;
in ~en hire-purchase *(Br.)*, on the instal(l)ment (deferred-payment) system;
jährliche ~ annual instal(l)ment; **letzte ~** terminal payment *(US)*; **vierteljährliche ~** quarterly instal(l)ment;
~en einhalten to meet the payments; **~en nicht einhalten** to default; **auf ~ kaufen** to buy on hire purchase *(Br.)*, to buy on the deferred payment system *(US)*; **~ leisten** to pay an instal(l)ment.

Ratenzahlungs|bedingungen part-payment terms; **~beschluß** instal(l)ment order; **~geschäft** deferred-payment *(US)* (hire-purchase, *Br.*) sale, instal(l)ment business, *(Laden)* instal(l)ment store *(US)*; **~gesetz** Hire Purchase Act *(Br.)*; **~kauf** conditional sales agreement (contract), hire-purchase *(Br.)*; **~kredit** deferred-payment credit *(US)*, hire-purchase credit *(Br.)*; **~system** instal(l)ment (hire-purchase, *Br.*, deferred-payment, *US*) system, instal(l)ment plan; **~verkauf** hire-purchase sale *(Br.)*; **~vertrag** instal(l)ment [sales] contract, hire-purchase *(Br.)* (deferred-payment, *US*) agreement, contract of hire purchase *(Br.)*, hire-purchase contract *(Br.)*; **~vertrag [für 5 und mehr Raten]** credit sale agreement *(Br.)*; **~verträge** *(Bilanz)* instal(l)ment receivables *(US)*; **~wechsel** hire-purchase paper *(Br.)*.

Räteregierung Soviet Government.

Raterei guesswork.

Raterteilung giving advice.

Rätesystem soviet system.

Ratgeber counsel(l)or, counsel, adviser, mentor, advisor, director, guide, *(Zeitschrift)* lonely hearts column;
unaufgeforderter törichter ~ guardhouse lawyer *(sl.)*; **unerbetener ~** kibitz *(US sl.)*;
~gruppe *(Präsident, US)* kitchen cabinet *(US)*.

Rathaus town hall, city (common) hall *(US)*, *(London)* guildhall.

Ratifikation ratification, confirmation, establishment;
der ~ bedürfen to be subject to ratification.

Ratifikations|urkunde instrument of ratification; **~urkunde hinterlegen** to deposit the ratification; **~verfahren** ratification proceedings.

ratifizierbar confirmable.

ratifizieren to confirm, to ratify.

Ratifizierender ratifier.

ratifiziert, noch nicht unratified;
~ sein to stand approved.

Ratifizierung ratification;
nachfolgende ~ subsequent ratification;
~ durch den Kongreß congressional ratification.

Ratifizierungsgesetz validating statute.

Ration ration, *(Anteil)* portion, *(Schiff)* allowance;
auf niedrigsten ~en *(Marine)* on whack *(sl.)*;
eiserne ~ emergency ration, iron ration; **eiserne ~ von 3500 Kalorien** C ration; **knappe ~** short allowance; **volle ~** *(Schiff)* full allowance;

~en ausgeben to dispense rations; ~en bewilligen to ration, to allowance; ~en beziehen to draw rations; ~en kürzen to cut (slash, shorten) the rations; mit gekürzten ~en auskommen müssen to be on short (live on lean) rations; auf kurze ~en setzen to put on [short] rations; in ~en zuteilen to ration.

rational veranlagter Mensch rational person.

rationalisieren to rationalize.

Rationalisierung rationalization;
betriebswirtschaftliche ~ industrial rationalization; **innerbetriebliche ~** internal economy; **technische ~** value engineering.

Rationalisierungs|anstrengungen efforts to rationalize, rationalization efforts; **~aufwand** rationalization expenditure; **~effekt** influence of rationalization; **~erfolge** success in greater efficiency; **~fachmann** efficiency engineer (expert); **~investition** investment for increased efficiency; **~kartell** cartel for rationalization; **~konjunktur** rationalization boom; **~kuratorium** rationalization board; **~maßnahmen** rationalization measures; **~möglichkeiten** opportunity to rationalize; **~prüfung** efficiency audit; **~studium** efficiency engineering; **~vorteile** rationalization advantages; **zu ~zwecken** for rationalization purposes.

rationell rational, *(wirtschaftlich)* efficient, *(sparsam)* economical;
~e Ausnutzung rational employment; **~es Verkaufsargument** rational sales.

Rationenkürzung cutting of rations.

rationenweise in (by) rations.

rationieren to ration, to allocate, to allowance, to freeze.

rationiert rationed, couponed;
~ sein to go on points;
~er Artikel rationed item; **~e Waren** allocated (rationed, quota, coupon) goods.

Rationierung rationing, allocation, allotment, points scheme;
preisbezogene ~ value rationing;
~ durch Karten card rationing; **~ von Produktgruppen** point rationing; **~ nach dem Punktsystem** points system;
~ für etw. aufheben to take s. th. off the ration, to deration s. th.

Rationierungs|karte ration[ing] card; **~maßnahmen** rationing arrangements; **~programm, ~system** rationing system; **~vorschriften** rationing regulations; **~wesen** rationing system.

Rations|kürzung ration cut, cut in rations; **~kürzung durchführen** to slash rations; **~sätze** ration rates, travel rations.

ratsam advisable, prudent.

Ratsbeschluß council's resolution.

ratschen to chatter, to gossip.

Ratschlag [piece of] advice, counsel;
taub für einen ~ dead to advice;
freundschaftlicher ~ friendly piece of advice; **nützlicher ~** profitable advice; **unangebrachter ~** a word out of season;
~ nicht beachten to make light of an advice; **~ befolgen** to put advice to use, to pursue (act on s. one's) advice; **jds. ~ keinerlei Wert beimessen** to put no value on s. one's advice; **bereitwillig einen ~ erteilen** to be free with one's advice; **viel auf jds. ~ geben** to set a high value upon s. one's advice; **sich einen ~ bestens dienen lassen** to profit by s. one's advice.

Ratschläge für Hausfrauen hints for housewives;
fremde ~ nicht befolgen to take one's own way; **jem. nicht erbetene ~ erteilen** to put in s. one's oar; **viel auf jds. ~ geben** to value s. one's advice; **sich nach jds. ~n richten** to be guided by s. one's advice.

Ratsdiener beadle.

Rätsel puzzle, riddle, puzzler, problem *(fig.)*
jem. ein ~ aufgeben *(fig.)* to be a mystery for s. o.; **Lösung eines ~s finden** to puzzle out; **~ lösen** to solve a riddle; **vor einem ~ stehen** to be mystified, to be confronted with a mystery;
~ecke *(Zeitung)* puzzle corner.

rätselhaft puzzling, mysterious, mystic.

Rätsel|heft puzzle book; **passionierter ~löser** puzzler; **~reklame** teaser advertisement *(US)*.

Rats|entscheidung council decision; **~herr** [city] councilman, municipal, [town] council(l)or, burgess, borough councillor *(Br.)*, alderman *(Br.)*, magistrate *(Scot.)*; **aus ~kreisen verlautet** council sources said; **~mitglied** councillor, [fellow] counsel(l)or; **~mitglieder zusammenrufen** to summon a council; **freigewordener ~sitz** council vacancy; **~sitzung, ~versammlung** guildhall sitting, council [meeting (board)]; **~sitzung anberaumen** to call a council; **~tisch** council board (table); **~treffen** council meeting.

Ratsversammlung council [meeting (board)], consistory;
parteilose ~ nonparty council;
~ abhalten to meet in council, to hold council (counsel).

Rats|vorsitzender council chairman, convener *(Scot.)*; **~zimmer** council room (chamber).

Ratten|fänger rat catcher, *(fig.)* Pied Piper; **~gift** rat poison; **~könig** *(fig.)* entanglement; **~nest** wretched hole of a place *(fam.)*, a rat's nest; **ganzer ~schwanz von Fragen** string of questions; **~vertilgung** extermination of rats; **~vertilgungsmittel** raticide.

Rattern rumble.

rattern *(Fahrzeug)* to jolt, to rumble, to rattle, to chatter.

ratzekahl aufessen to lick the platter clean *(coll.)*.

Raub robbery, rapine, spoliation, holdup, grab raid, *(Beute)* loot, booty, prey, *(Urheberrechtsverletzung)* piracy;
versuchter ~ assault with intent to commit robbery;
~ aufteilen to divide the loot; **auf ~ ausgehen** to prey; **~ begehen** to commit robbery.

Raubbau wasteful exhaustion, exhaustive cultivation, predatory exploitation, spoliation of the soil, extirpation, waste;
~ mit seiner Gesundheit betreiben to abuse one's health, to burn the candle at both ends; **~ treiben** to exhaust the soil, to overcrop.

Raubdruck pirated edition, fraudulent impression, pirate version (copy).

rauben to rob, to commit robbery, to spoil, to spoliate, to plunder;
jem. die Ehre ~ to defame s. o.; **Kuß ~** to steal a kiss; **jem. den Schlaf ~** to deprive s. o. of his sleep.

Räuber robber, highwayman, spoiler, despoiler, marauder, picaroon, raider, stickup *(sl.)*;
unter die ~ fallen to fall among thieves;
~bande band of robbers, lay, expedition of thieves, predatory band; **sich einer ~bande anschließen** to join a band of robbers; **~höhle** den of robbers; **wie eine ~höhle aussehen** to be a regular pigsty.

räuberisch|e Methoden predatory practices; **~er Überfall** armed robbery.

räubern, in der Speisekammer to raid the larder.

Räuber|pistole *(Geschichte)* cock and bull story; **~unwesen** banditry; **~zivil** tatty get-up.

Raub|gut stolen property, loot; **~mord** murder and robbery; **~mörder** murderous robber; **~platte** pirated record; **~tier** wild beast, predatory animal, beast of prey; **~tierinstinkt** predacious instinct; **~tierschau** wild-beast show.

Raubüberfall robbery with violence, holdup, grab raid, mugging *(fam.)*, stick-up *(US sl.)*, knock-over *(US sl.)*;
bewaffneter ~ armed robbery;
sich an einem ~ beteiligen to take part in a gang robbery, to trigger *(sl.)*.

Raubüberfälle durchführen to undertake plundering raids, to hi[gh]jack, to mug *(US sl.)*.

Raub|überfallversicherung robbery insurance; **~zug** depredation, incursion, forage; **~züge durchführen** to undertake plundering raids; **~züge ins Feindgebiet unternehmen** to make incursions into an enemy's country.

Rauch smoke, vapo(u)r;
kein ~ ohne Feuer there's no smoke without fire;
sich in ~ auflösen to come to nothing, to end in smoke; **~ ausstoßen** *(Vulkan)* to vomit;
~abzug vorsehen to provide an outlet for the smoke; **~bekämpfungsvorschriften** smoke control; **~belästigung** smoke nuisance; **~boje** smoke buoy; **~bombe** smoke bomb.

Rauchen|ist in der Garage nicht gestattet the public are forbidden to smoke in the garage;
mit dem ~ aufhören to leave off smoking.

Rauchentwicklung smoke emission.

Raucherabteil smoking area (compartment).

Räucher|kammer smoking chamber, smokehouse *(US)*; **~kerze** pastille.

Raucherwagen smoking car *(US)* (carriage, *Br.*).

Rauch|fahne trail (plume) of smoke; **~fang** flue, chimney, vent; **~fetzen** wisp of smoke; **~glas** tinted glass; **~nebel** smaze; **~säule** pillar of smoke; **~schleier** *(mil.)* smoke screen; **~verbot** no smoking; **~vergiftung** smoke poisoning; **~versicherung** smoke insurance; **~verzehrer** smoke consumer; **~waren** tobacco products, *(Pelze)* hides and furs; **~warenhändler** tobacconist; **~wolke** pall of smoke; **dicke ~wolke** dense smoke.

räudiges Schaf *(fig.)* black sheep.

Raufbold brawler, hoodlum *(US sl.)*.

Raufe hack, crib.

Rauferei knockdown, fist fight, scuffle, turnup *(coll.)*, tussle, mix, knockabout *(US sl.)*;
allgemeine ~ free-for-all.

Raufhandel chance-medley, brawl.
rauh coarse, rough, uneven, *(Stimme)* harsh, hoarse, husky;
j. ~ anfassen to treat s. o. roughly;
~en Hals haben to have a sore throat; **~es Klima** harsh climate; **~es Papier** rough-textured paper; **guter Kern in einer ~en Schale** rough diamond; **~er Winter** severe (hard) winter; **~e Wirklichkeit** harsh reality (facts).
Rauhbein rough diamond, *(streitsüchtig)* rowdy, roughneck *(US sl.)*
ein ~ sein to be somewhat gruff.
rauhbeinig unrefined, crusty, gruff.
Rauh|fasertapete oatmeal wallpaper; **~putz** daub; **~reif** hoarfrost, white frost, rime.
Raum room, space, *(Fläche)* area, *(Gebiet)* district, area, zone, territory, range, *(Laderaum)* hold, *(Platz)* space, *(Rauminhalt)* volume, capacity, *(Unterbringung)* accommodation;
im politischen ~ in the realm of politics;
abgeschirmter ~ screened room; **begrenzter ~** confined space; **vom Feuer bestrichener ~** *(mil.)* covered area, beaten zone; **dreidimensionaler ~** three-dimensional space; **enger ~** narrow space; **in Anspruch genommener ~** space occupied; **gewerblicher ~** business premises; **leerer ~** void space, blank [space], white line, *(unbedruckt)* vacancy, empty space; **luftleerer ~** vacuum; **schalldichter ~** dead room; **beschränkt zur Verfügung stehender ~** limited space at s. one's disposal; **umbauter ~** enclosed space;
~ für Außenwerbung location; **~ für die Beine** *(Auto)* leg-room; **~ für letzte Meldungen** fudge; **~ für öffentliche Veranstaltungen** place of public resort;
~ bieten to accommodate, *(Auto)* to carry; **weiten ~ in einer Diskussion einnehmen** to occupy a large part in a debate; **einem Punkt in einem Referat breiten ~ einräumen** to give a point much attention in a paper; **einer eitlen Hoffnung ~ geben** to indulge a vain hope; **einer Vorstellung ~ geben** to take an idea into consideration; **~ lassen** *(drucktechn.)* to letterspace; **~ für die Unterschrift lassen** to leave a blank for the signature; **auf engstem ~ zusammen leben** to live on top of one another; **Bemerkung in den ~ stellen** to make a statement; **~ für j. vorsehen** to consign a room to s. one's use;
~anordnung disposition of rooms in a building; **~aufteilung** floor plan; **falsche ~aufteilung** *(Anzeige)* faulty spacing; **~aufteilungsplan** floor plan.
raumbeanspruchend land-using.
Raum|bedarf room (space) required; **~benutzer** space user; **~bild** stereogram, stereoscopic photograph.
Räumboot mine sweeper.
Raum|charter affreightment; **~einheit** unit of space (volume); **~element** spatial unit.
räumen *(Mieter)* to surrender possession, *(Wohnung)* to quit, to evict, to evacuate, to vacate, to remove, to oust;
Geschirr vom Tisch ~ to clear the dishes; **Lager ~** to sell off, to clear (push, *coll.*) off old stock; **Lokal ~** to vacate the premises; **den Platz für j. ~** to give up one's seat to s. o.; **aus dem Wege ~** to put away, to do in *(sl.)*.
Raum|ersparnis economy of space; **~fähre** space shuttle, orbital ferry; **~fahrer** astronaut, spaceman; **~fahrerhelm** space helmet; **~fahrerschutzanzug** space suit.
Raumfahrt space flight (travel), space navigation;
interplanetare ~ interplanetary aviation;
~anteil aerospace part; **~auftrag** aerospace contract (work); **~ausschuß** space committee; **~behörde** space agency; **~beteiligungen** aerospace interests; **~etat** space budget; **~experte** space expert; **~forschung** space research; **~gebiet** aerospace side (activities); **~gesellschaft** aerospace company (corporation); **Luft- und ~industrie** space (aerospace) industry; **~ingenieur** aerospace engineer; **~konzern** aerospace conglomerate; **~projekt** aerospace project; **~station** space station (platform); **bemannte ~station** manned orbiting laboratory, skylab, spacelab; **~unternehmen** aerospace manufacturer, space contractor; **unbemanntes ~vorhaben** unmanned space project; **~wissenschaften** astrogation; **~zeitalter** space age; **~zentrum** aerospace components.
Raum|fahrzeug space vehicle, spaceship, spacecraft; **~fahrzeugträger** space vehicle launcher; **~flug** space flight; **bemannter ~flug** manned space flight; **~flugkörper** unmanned spacecraft.
raumfremde Interessen outside interests.
Raum|gestalter interior designer; **~gestaltung** architectural design, interior decoration; **~heizgerät** convector (space) heater; **~heizung** room heating; **~inhalt** cubic content, volume; **~kapsel** space capsule; **~-Zeitkontinuum** space-time continuum.
räumlich spatial;
~ sehr beengt sein to be cramped for space;
~es Sehen stereoscopic vision; **~e Verteilung** spatial distribution.
Räumlichkeit locality;
~en premises, accommodation.
Raum|mangel restricted space; **~maß** dimensions, cubic measure; **~meter** cubic meter (metre, *Br.*); **~nebenkosten** incidental expenses on accommodation; **~ordnung** regional policy (planning).
Raumordnungs|behörde regional economic planning board *(Br.)*; **~plan** regional policy plan; **~programm** regional planning program(me), regional strategies.
Räumpanzer *(mil.)* tank dozer.
Raum|pflege domestic service; **~pflegerin** charwoman *(US)*, chorewoman, [daily] cleaner, cleaning woman *(Br.)*, domestic servant.
Räumpflug bulldozer.
Raum|pilot space pilot, astronaut; **~planung** area (regional) planning; **~planungsgesetzgebung** planning legislation *(Br.)*; **~satellit** regional satellite; **~schiff** spaceship, space vehicle; **~schiff ankoppeln** to dock a space vehicle; **~schiffahrt** astronautics, aerospace, space travel; **~schiffstart** space launch; **~sonde** space capsule; **unbemannte ~sonde** space probe.
raumsparende Verladung commercial loading.
Raum|station space platform, skylab; **~struktur** spatial structure; **~tiefe** depth of a room; **~ton** stereophone sound; **~toneffekt** binaural effect; **~tonhören** binauralty; **~tonne** measurement (measured) ton; **~transporter** space unit; **wiederverwendbarer ~transporter** space shuttle.
Räumtrupp demolition squad.
Räumung vacation, *(Lager)* clearance, clearing, *(Wohnung)* evacuation, removal *(Br.)*, removing, *(zwangsweise)* eviction, ejection, ejectment, dispossession, ousting;
verzögerte ~ holding over;
~ eines Gebiets abandonment of a territory; **~ eines Hauses** vacating of a house; **~ eines Lagers** *(mil.)* decampment;
~ der Galerie beantragen to spy strangers *(Br.)*; **auf ~ klagen** to sue for eviction (ejection, *US*, possession, *Br.*); **~ verzögern** to hold over; **zur ~ zwingen** to evict, to eject *(US)*, to oust, to dispossess.
Räumungs|anerkenntnis, gerichtliches consent rule; **~anordnung** eviction order; **~anspruch** right to possession; **~aufschub** stay of eviction; **~ausverkauf** clearance (closing-down) sale; **von den Verwaltungsbehörden erlassenen ~befehl durchführen** to enforce an administrative eviction decree; **~befehl, ~beschluß** dispossess warrant *(Br.)*, order for possession *(Br.)*, possession order *(Br.)*, eviction notice (order), writ of ejectment *(US)*, order to quit *(Br.)*; **~beschluß aussetzen** to suspend an order of possession *(Br.)*; **~beschluß gegen einen Mieter durchführen** to dispossess a tenant *(Br.)*, to evict a tenant for nonpayment of rent; **einem Mieter eine ~frist von 14 Tagen setzen** to give a tenant two weeks notice to surrender possession; **~gläubiger** ejector; **~klage** action of ejectment *(US)*, ejectment bill *(US)*, writ of entry, dispossess proceedings *(Br.)*, action to recover land, equitable ejectment *(Louisiana)*; **~klage erheben** to sue for eviction (ejection), to take legal proceedings for ejectment *(US)*; **fiktiver ~kläger** casual ejector *(Br.)*; **~kosten** cost of eviction; **~schlußverkauf** clearance (closing-down) sale; **gesetzlicher ~schutz** statutory tenancy; **~schutzanspruch** right not to be evicted; **~urteil** eviction order, order of possession *(Br.)*, writ of ejectment *(US)*, clearance order *(Br.)*; **~urteil gegen einen Mieter erwirken** to warn a tenant out of the house; **~verfahren** justice ejectment *(US)*, eviction proceedings, dispossess (possession) proceedings *(Br.)*; **~verfahren durchführen** to enforce an administrative eviction decree, to dispossess *(Br.)*; **~verkauf** clearance (closing-down, winding-up) sale; **~verzug** delay in vacating premises.
Raum|verhältnisse abschätzen to take the measurements of a room; **~verschwendung** waste of space; **~verteilung** disposition of rooms in a building; **~verteilungsplan** floor plan; **~wirtschaftslehre** spatial economics.
Raupe caterpillar, track-laying vehicle;
jem. ~n in den Kopf setzen to put ideas into s. one's head.
Raupen|antrieb tracklaying drive; **~fahrzeug** tracked (wheeled) vehicle, caterpillar truck, full-track vehicle, tracklayer; **~schlepper** crawler tractor, tracklayer, caterpillar.
Rausch drunkenness, intoxication;
im ~ while drunk;
~ der Begeisterung frenzy of enthusiasm;

sich einen ~ **antrinken** to get tight; **seinen ~ ausschlafen** to sleep off one's liquor; ~ **bekommen** *(Drogen)* to get high; **gehörigen ~ haben** to be dead drunk (drunk as a lord); **vom ~ der Geschwindigkeit erfüllt sein** to be exhiliarated by speed.

Rauschen *(Radio)* noise, *(Schallplatte)* needle scratch.

rauschen *(Bach)* to burble, to bubble, to murmur, *(Radio)* to noise, *(Wind)* to rush;
beleidigt aus dem Zimmer ~ to sweep offended out of the room.

rauschend|er Beifall enthusiastic (thundering) applause; ~**e Feste** magnificent parties, sumptuous feasts.

Rauschgift narcotics, dangerous drugs, dope *(sl.)*;
~ **nehmen** to drug *(coll.)*; ~ **verabreichen** to administer narcotic drugs;
~**abteilung** Narcotics Division; ~**aufklärung** drug education; ~**bande** narcotics (dope) ring; ~**behörde** Bureau of Narcotics and Dangerous Drugs *(US)*; ~**dezernat** drug authority; ~**ermittler** drug investigator; ~**handel** drug traffic, dope peddling (running, selling), narcotics traffic; ~**händler** drug pedlar (dealer, pusher, trafficker), dope merchant (pedlar, seller), doper, connection *(US sl.)*; ~**schmuggel** narcotics (dope) smuggling; ~**sucht** drug addiction, drug habit.

rauschgiftsüchtig addict, on the needle *(sl.)*.

Rauschgift|süchtiger drug addict (fiend), narcotic, junkie, dope, dope addict (fiend), narcotics addict *(US)*; ~**vergehen** drug trafficking offence.

Rauschmittel intoxicant, narcotic;
~**steuer** narcotic tax.

rausgeworfen werden to be out on one's neck *(coll.)*, *(aus der Stellung)* to be sacked (fired, *sl.*).

rauslassen, versehentlich to spill the beans *(coll.)*.

räuspern, sich to clear one's pipe.

rausschmeißen to kick out, to bounce *(US sl.)*, to brush off *(US sl.)*, to can *(US sl.)*, *(kündigen)* to fire *(sl.)*, to sack *(sl.)*, to give the order of the boot, to rif *(sl.)*.

Raus|schmeißer *(Lokal)* chucker-out, bouncer *(US)*, strong-arm man *(US)*; ~**schmiß** kick-out *(US sl.)*, letout *(sl.)*, *(Kündigung)* bounce *(US sl.)*, sack, boot *(sl.)*.

Rayon district.

Rayonierungskartell sales cartel.

Razzia police raid, razzia, roundup, battue;
überraschende ~ tip-over *(sl.)*;
~ **durchführen (veranstalten)** to make a raid, to conduct a roundup, to crack down *(US)*, to pull *(sl.)*, to lean against *(sl.)*, to tip over *(sl.)*;
~**durchführung** raiding; ~**teilnehmer** raider.

Reagenzglas test tube.

Reagibilität des Marktes sensitiveness of the market.

reagieren to react, to respond;
blitzschnell ~ to know how to take a hint; **auf eine Einladung nicht** ~ to fail to answer an invitation; **falsch** ~ to get one's wires crossed, to get one's signals mixed; **mit Gelassenheit** ~ to roll with punches; **heftig** ~ *(Börse)* to move violently; **mit einem Lächeln** ~ to answer with a smile; **völlig natürlich auf etw.** ~ to take s. th. like a duck to water; **überhaupt nicht** ~ to take not the least notice; **positiv** ~ to react with favo(u)r; **auf etw. sauer** ~ to be peeved at s. th.; **sofort** ~ to take immediate action; **auf veränderte Verhältnisse** ~ to respond to changing conditions.

Reaktion *(Politik)* reaction, *(Werbung)* response;
geteilte ~ mixed reaction; **Ja-Nein-~** *(Befragung)* quantal response; **negative** ~ negative response; **staatliche** ~ government response; **übliche** ~ standard reaction; **unwiderstehliche** ~ *(Strafrecht)* uncontrollable impulse;
~ **der Arbeiterklasse** blue-collar reaction *(US)*; ~ **der Geschäftswelt** business reactions; ~ **beim Käufer** buyer reactions; ~ **auf eine Nachricht** reaction to a piece of news; ~ **auf einen Vorschlag** reaction to a proposal; ~ **der Wähler** electorate's response;
positive ~en in der Öffentlichkeit auslösen to create favo(u)rable publicity.

Reaktionär reactionist, reactionary, rightist, Philistine, stick-in-the-mud, white, blimp *(Br.)*, mossback *(US)*, hunker *(US sl.)*;
hartnäckiger ~ diehard.

reaktionär reactionary, standpat, stick-in-the-mud, rightist, white, tory, hard-shell *(US)*, hunkerous *(US sl.)*;
~**e Kräfte** forces of reaction; ~**e Maßnahmen ergreifen** to put the clock back.

reaktionsfähig reactive, responsive.

Reaktionsfähigkeit power of reaction.

reaktionsschnell quick-off-the-mark *(coll.)*.

Reaktions|training sensitivity training; ~**zeit** reaction (thinking) time.

reaktivieren *(mil.)* to recommission;
Anlagen ~ to revalue assets; **Offizier** ~ to restore an officer to full pay.

Reaktivierung *(Bilanz)* revaluation of assets, *(mil.)* recommissioning.

Reaktor [nuclear] reactor;
~**technik** reactor technology.

real real, actual, *(jur.)* corporeal, tangible, *(stofflich)* substantial, material;
ganz ~e Gründe practical reasons; ~**e Kaufkraft** purchasing power in real terms; ~**e Lagebeurteilung** realistic assessment of the situation; ~**e Vermögensgüter** tangible assets; ~**es Wachstum** increase in real terms; ~**er Zinssatz** real interest rate.

Real|abteilung *(Schule)* modern school *(Br.)*; ~**angebot** tender; ~**ausgaben** real outlays; ~**besteuerung** real taxation.

Realeinkommen real income (earnings);
frei verfügbares ~ real personal disposable income;
~ **nach Steuern** real after-tax income.

Real|einkommenssteigerung increase in real income; ~**großhändler** rack jobber *(US)*; ~**gymnasium** secondary modern school.

Realien real estate (properties).

Realinjurie assault and battery.

Realisation realization, sale, liquidation;
ausländische ~en foreign liquidations.

Realisations|konto realization and liquidation account; ~**prinzip** *(Bilanz)* retail method of valuation, *(Lagerbewertung)* first-in, first-out, fifo; ~**verkauf** liquidating sale; ~**welle** wave of selling; ~**wert** salvage value.

realisierbar realizable, liquidatable, convertible, *(Effekten)* marketable;
kurzfristig ~ realizable at short notice; **leicht** ~ commanding a ready sale, easily marketable; **nicht** ~ unrealizable; **sofort** ~ readily convertible into cash, liquid;
sofort ~e Aktiva liquid (fluid, *US*) assets; **nicht sofort ~e Aktiva** frozen assets; **nicht ~e Vorschläge** impracticable suggestions.

Realisierbarkeit realizability.

realisieren to carry into effect, to materialize, *(zu Geld)* to realize, to cash, to sell off (out), to convert [into cash], to bank, *(verkaufen)* to effect a sale;
Kapitalanlage ~ to realize an investment; **Preis** ~ to obtain a price.

realisiert realized, *(Kursgewinn)* earned;
nicht ~ *(Kursgewinn)* unearned;
sich nicht ~ haben to have come unstuck;
~**er Gewinn** realized revenue (profit); **noch nicht ~e Gewinne** paper profits *(US)*.

Realisierung realization, liquidation, disposal, sale;
~ **von Vermögenswerten im Ausland** disinvestment abroad.

Realisierungs|verkäufe profit-taking sales; ~**wert** liquidation value, *(bei sofortigem Verkauf)* salvage value.

Realismus *(Kunst)* objectivism.

Realist realist, objectivist.

realistisch realistic, tough (practically) -minded, hard-headed;
außerordentlich ~ schildern to describe with extraordinary reality;
~**es Denken** realism of intellect.

Realität, in der in the flesh;
wirtschaftliche ~en economic reality;
~**en anerkennen** to see s. th. in its true colo(u)rs; **der ~ anpassen** to tailor to reality; **den politischen ~en nicht entsprechen** to be insensitive to political realities; **weit hinter der ~ zurückbleiben** to fall short of reality.

Realitätenmakler land broker *(Br.)*, estate agent *(Br.)*, realtor *(US)*.

Real|kapital tangible assets; ~**katalog** *(Bibliothek)* subject-matter catalog(ue); ~**kauf** executed sale; ~**konkurrenz** *(Strafrecht)* cumulation; **in ~konkurrenz** cumulative; ~**kosten** actual costs; ~**kredit** credit on landed property, credit on real estate, real-estate loan; ~**kreditinstitut** mortgage (land) bank, farm mortgage company *(US)*; ~**last** real burden *(Scot.)*, ground rent *(Br.)*, land charge; **eingetragene ~last** registered charge *(Br.)*; **städtische ~last** municipal lien; ~**leistung** real obligation; ~**lexikon** encyclopedia, practical lexicon; ~**lohn** actual (real) wages, real earnings; ~**lohnanstieg** real wage growth; ~**lohnerhöhung** rise (increase) in real earnings; ~**politik** realistic (practical) politics; ~**politiker** realistic politician; ~**rechte** appurtenances; ~**schule** [etwa] secondary technical school, modern school *(Br.)*, high-school *(US)*; ~**schüler** high-school boy *(US)*; ~**servitut** easement, real servitude; ~**statut** real statute; ~**steuer** real tax, property tax; ~**union**

(Völkerrecht) real union; ~**vermögen** real estate (property); **reproduzierbares ~vermögen** reproduceable assets; ~**vertrag** executed contract; ~**wert** actual (tangible) value; ~**wert der Einkommensteuerfreibeträge den Inflationsauswirkungen anpassen** to restore the real value of income tax allowance; ~**zeit** *(Datenverarbeitung)* real time; ~**zinssatz** real interest rate.

Rebbach plunder *(sl.)*, clean-up *(US sl.)*;
~ **machen** to make a pile of money.

Rebell rebel, insurgent, insurrectionist, revolter;
~**en unterwerfen** to bring under rebels.

Rebellen | führer sein to head a rebellion; ~**gruppe** rebel group; ~**heer** insurgent army; ~**regierung** rebel government; ~**truppen** insurgent forces.

rebellieren to rebel, to rise in rebellion, to revolt, to insurrect.

rebellierende Studenten student rebels.

Rebellion rebellion, insurgence, insurrection, revolt.

rebellisch rebellious, insurgent, up in arms, wild;
ganzes Haus ~ machen to have the whole house in arms; **ganzes Land ~ machen** to cause a nation-wide uproar.

Rechen *(Croupier)* rake;
~**anlage** computer, data processing machine; **digitale ~anlage** digital computer; ~**anlage anwählen** to dial a computer; ~**aufgabe** arithmetical problem, sum; ~**aufgabe lösen** to do a sum; ~**automat** computer; ~**beispiel** arithmetical sample; ~**bildgerät** automatic aerial camera; ~**brett** abacus; ~**buch** arithmetical book; ~**fehler** error of calculation, mistake in the figures, miscount, miscalculation, computational error; ~**gerät** data computer; ~**kniff** arithmetical shortcut; ~**künstler** arithmetical genius; ~**maschine** calculator, calculating (computing, counting) machine; **blindschreibende ~maschine** blind calculator; ~**pfennig** counter, marker.

Rechenschaft [rendering an] account;
~ **ablegen** to account (answer) for, to render account; **sich ~ ablegen** to take stock; ~ **über seine Vermögensverwaltung ablegen** to give an account of one's stewardship; **von jem. ~ fordern** to call s. o. to account; **keine ~ geben können** *(Treuhänder)* to default; **jem. ~ ablegen müssen** to be accountable to s. o.; ~ **schuldig sein** to be accountable; ~ **verlangen** to demand an explanation; **zur ~ gezogen werden** to be on the mat *(sl.)*; **j. zur ~ ziehen** to call (bring) s. o. to book.

Rechenschaftsbericht statement, account rendered, *(AG)* report and accounts, director's report;
abgelegter ~ account stated; **jährlicher ~** annual report (return); **öffentlicher ~** public accounting; **vorläufiger ~** flash report;
~ **über die Generalversammlung** company report, corporation report *(US)*.

Rechenschafts | legung rendering an account, accounting, *(fig.)* audit; ~**pflicht** accountability, responsibility.

rechenschaftspflichtig accountable, liable to render account, responsible;
nicht ~ not accountable.

Rechen | schieber slipstick, slide rule; ~**stift** slate pencil; ~**stift ansetzen** to make a critical appraisal of expenses; ~**tabelle** ready reckoner; ~**tafel** calculator; ~**werk** arithmetic and logical unit, alu; ~**werk eines Unternehmens** accountancy of an enterprise; ~**zentrum** computer (computing) center *(US)* (centre, *Br.*), data processing center *(US)* (centre, *Br.*).

Recherche investigation, inquiry, search;
~**n anstellen** to investigate, to make investigations.

Recherchengebühr search fee.

Rechercheur investigator.

recherchieren to make inquiries;
nach j. ~ to be out after s. o.

Rechnen reckoning, calculation, calcuting, numeration, *(Schule)* arithmetic;
kaufmännisches ~ business (commercial) arithmetic.

rechnen to reckon, to compute, to calculate, *(anrechnen)* to charge, to debit, *(sparsam sein)* to be economical, to economize, *(veranschlagen)* to estimate, to value, *(zusammenzählen)* to count, to sum (add, cast) up;
auf etw. ~ to rely on (reckon upon) s. th.; **mit jem. ~** to count on s. o.; **mit einem guten Abschluß ~** to calculate on a good trade; **mit allem ~** to be prepared for anything; **mit jds. früher Ankunft ~** to figure on s. o. arriving early; **Aufgaben ~** to do sums; **mit Beförderung ~** to calculate on preferment; **in Dollars ~** to calculate in dollars; **elektronisch ~** to compute; **falsch ~** to miscalculate, to misreckon; **mit den Fingern ~** to count on one's fingers; **j. zu seinen Freunden ~** to count s. o. as one of one's friends; **mit seinem Geld ~** to watch one's spending, to budget carefully; **nicht genau ~** to be free with one's money; **auf jds. Hilfe ~** to count (reckon) upon s. one's help; **zu knapp ~** to cut it too fine; **im Kopf ~** to reckon (work out) in one's head; **zu seiner Kundschaft ~** to number among one's customers; **mit Mark und Pfennig ~** to stretch one's money; **maschinell ~** to compute; **mit dem Pfennig ~** to think of pennies; **in Schillingen ~** to calculate in shillings; **mit dem Schlimmsten ~** to be prepared for the worst; **mit vier Stunden Fahrzeit ~** to calculate on four hours of a journey; **nach Stundeneinheiten ~** to count by the hour;
gut ~ können to be smart (good) at figures.

Rechner reckoner, calculator, computer;
guter ~ sein to be good (smart) at figures.

rechnerisch arithmetical, mathematical;
~ **ausschalten** to eliminate statistically;
~**er Fehlbetrag** numerical shortage; ~**es Geldvolumen** statistical volume of money; ~**e Parität** calculated parity; ~**er Überschuß** book surplus; ~**er Wert** absolute (arithmetical) value.

Rechnung account, note, tally, *(Beleg)* voucher, *(Berechnung)* calculation, reckoning, count, *(Waren)* invoice, *(Zeche)* reckoning, bill, check *(US)*, score;
auf ~ on account, to be carried; **auf jds. ~** to s. one's account; **auf alte ~** on former account; **auf feste ~** at a fixed price; **auf gemeinsame (gemeinschaftliche) ~** at common cost, on (for) joint account; **auf Ihre ~ und Gefahr** for your account and risk; **auf meine alleinige ~** for my sole account; **auf neue ~** on new account; **auf neue ~ vorgetragen** carried forward to new account; **für fremde ~** for foreign (third) account, for account of a third party; **gemäß beigefügter ~** as per invoice enclosed; **im Auftrag und für ~ von** by order and for account of; **in ~ gestellt** billed; **in ~ zu stellen** *(fig.)* on the map; **laut ausgestellter ~** as per account [rendered]; **laut beiliegender ~** as indicated in enclosed invoice; **laut eingeschickter (erhaltener) ~** as per account rendered; **laut umstehender ~** as per invoice on the other side; **nach meiner ~** according to my calculation; **nicht in ~ gestellt** uncharged; **zum Ausgleich unserer ~** in full discharge of our accounts;
abgeänderte ~ amended invoice; **alleinige ~** sole account; **alte ~** *(fig.)* score; **ausgestellte ~** account rendered; **ausstehende ~en** *(Bilanz)* accounts receivable *(US)*, *(nicht bezahlte)* accounts payable *(US)*; **lang ausstehende ~** long outstanding account; **im Rückstand befindliche ~** account in arrears; **beglaubigte ~** certified invoice; **beglichene ~** settled account, paid invoice; **nicht beitreibbare ~** uncollectable account; **berichtigte ~** corrected invoice; **bezahlte ~en** paid bills, clear accounts; **detaillierte ~** specified (itemized) account; **nicht einziehbare ~** uncollectable account; **endgültige ~** final invoice; **längst fällige ~** past-due account; **falsche ~** *(Kalkulation)* misreckoning; **fingierte ~** simulated (pro-forma) account; **formale ~** ordinary bill; **fremde ~** third-party account; **frisierte ~** doctored account; **gemeinsame ~** joint account, half share; **gepfefferte ~** *(fam.)* swinging bill, salt account; **getrennte ~** separate account, Dutch treat; **große (hohe) ~** long bill; **laufende ~** current (continuing, running, open, *US*) account, open book account *(US)*; **monatliche ~** monthly account; **nächste ~** next account; **offene (offenstehende) ~** outstanding (running, unsettled, open, *US*) account; **provisionsfreie ~** account free of commission; **quittierte ~** accountable receipt; **regulierte ~** settled account; **spezifizierte ~** minute (itemized, detailed, specified, stated) account, bill of parcels; **tägliche ~** current account; **überfällige ~** bill overdue; **überhöhte ~** stiff bill; **total überhöhte ~** exorbitant bill; **überschlägliche ~** rough calculation; **unbeglichene (unbezahlte) ~en** outstandings, back bills, unpaid invoices; **ungefähre ~** approximate calculation; **unquittierte ~** unreceipted bill; **vordatierte ~** postdated invoice; **vorgelegte ~** account rendered; **vorläufige ~** provisional invoice; **in Pfund zahlbare ~** sterling invoice; **quittierte ~en in doppelter Ausfertigung** duplicate receipted bills; **~ und Gegenrechnung** debit and credit;
~ **ablegen** to [render] account; ~ **abschließen** to close the books, to settle (wind up) an account; **für eigene ~ abschließen** to trade for own account; ~**en abzeichnen** to initial accounts; ~ **addieren** to reckon up a bill; ~ **anfechten** to debate an account; **auf eigene ~ arbeiten** to go (be in business) for o. s., to work on one's own, to open up one's own account; **gepfefferte ~ aufmachen** to salt an account; ~ **aufsetzen (ausfertigen)** to make out a bill; ~ **ausgleichen** to settle (balance) an account, to strike a balance; **alte ~en völlig ausgleichen** to wipe off old scores; ~ **ausstellen (ausschreiben)** to [make out an] invoice (an account), to prepare an invoice, to bill; ~ **ausziehen** to make an extract of account; ~**en bearbeiten** to handle invoices; ~ **in**

Ordnung befinden to pass an account; ~ **begleichen** to pay the reckoning, to settle (balance) an account, to settle (meet, take up, foot, *US*) a bill; **jds.** ~ **begleichen** to put paid to s. one's account; **seine** ~ **begleichen** to pay one's score; ~ **bei jem. begleichen** to settle up with s. o.; ~ **pünktlich begleichen** to settle an account on time; **für eigene** ~ **behalten** to keep for one's own account; ~ **belasten** to debit an account; **jds.** ~ **belasten** to charge s. one's account; **mit ~en belegen** to verify by invoices; ~ **bereinigen** to settle an account; ~ **durch Nachrechnen berichtigen** to correct an account; **auf** ~ **bestellen** to order against invoice; **auf eigene** ~ **betreiben** to operate on one's own account; ~ **bezahlen** to clear (pay) an account, to foot the (tab a) bill *(US)*; ~ **für j. bezahlen** to settle for s. o.; **in** ~ **bringen** to carry (put, pass) to account, to count; **auf neue** ~ **bringen** to place to new account; ~ **in Ordnung bringen** to put an account right, to straighten an account; **~en in Übereinstimmung bringen** to agree accounts; ~ **durchgehen (durchsehen)** to go (look) over an account; **seine ~en durchsehen** to go through one's bills; **in einem Geschäft auf** ~ **einkaufen** to run an account with a shop; ~ **nicht einlösen** to leave a bill unpaid; **für neue** ~ **erkennen** to carry forward to new account; ~ **eröffnen** to open an account; ~ **erteilen** to render (give) account; ~ **führen** to keep accounts; **Arbeit auf feste** ~ **geben** to job; ~ **genehmigen (gutheißen)** to pass an account (invoice); **getrennte** ~ **haben** to keep separate accounts, to pay one's own way; **über einen Geldbetrag** ~ **abzulegen haben** to be accountable for a sum of money; **mit jem. eine alte** ~ **zu bereinigen haben** to have some old scores to settle with s. o.; **dem Gericht** ~ **zu legen haben** to be responsible to the court; **für fremde** ~ **handeln** to act on behalf of a third party; **ausstehende ~en hereinbekommen** to get in bills; ~ **unter einem Stoß von Briefen hervorziehen** to root out a bill from under a pile of letters; ~ **hochschrauben** to pile up the costs; **auf** ~ **kaufen** to purchase on account, to buy on credit, to run up a score; **etw. auf eigene** ~ **kaufen** to buy s. th. on one's own account; **für feste** ~ **kaufen** to buy firm; **auf fremde** ~ **kaufen** to buy for third account; **auf zukünftige** ~ **kaufen** to take on future account; **auf seine** ~ **kommen** to get one's money's worth; ~ **anwachsen lassen** to run up a score (bill); **~en auflaufen lassen** to chalk it up; ~ **legen** to render account; **getrennte** ~ **machen** to go Dutch; **große** ~ **machen** to run up a bill; ~ **für j. fertig machen** to get s. one's bill ready; ~ **ungültig machen** to cancel an invoice; ~ **ohne den Wirt machen** to reckon without one's host, to count one's chickens before they are hatched; ~ **nachrechnen** to pass an account; ~ **prüfen** to audit (verify, examine) an account, to check a bill; ~ **quittieren** to receipt a bill; ~ **saldieren** to balance an account; **jem. eine** ~ **schicken** to bill s. o.; ~ **schließen** to close the books, to settle an account; ~ **schreiben** to [make out an] invoice; **auf** ~ **schreiben** to debit an account; **jem. eine** ~ **schreiben** to bill s. o.; **auf die** ~ **setzen** to charge on the bill, to enter in the invoice, to include in the bill, to score; **auf jds.** ~ **setzen** to set down to s. one's account; **auf neue** ~ **setzen** to charge (place) to new account; ~ **spezifizieren** to state an account, to itemize a bill *(US)*, to extend an invoice; **auf einer** ~ **stehen** to appear in an account; **in laufender** ~ **stehen** to have a current (running, open, *US*) account; **in** ~ **stellen** to bill, to charge, to invoice, *(Konto belasten)* to debit, to pass (carry, place, put) to account; **jem. in** ~ **stellen** to pass (put) to s. one's account, to enter to the debit of s. o.; **Gefahr in** ~ **stellen** to reckon with a danger; **etw. zu hoch in** ~ **stellen** to overcharge on an account; **zu niedrig in** ~ **stellen** to undercharge; **dem Kunden Portogebühren in** ~ **stellen** to charge the postage to the customer; **sich mit jem. in die** ~ **teilen** to stand in with s. o.; ~ **tragen** to pay due regard, to bear in mind; **den Umständen** ~ **tragen** to accommodate o. s. to circumstances; **den Wünschen** ~ **tragen** to comply with s. one's wishes; ~ **überfliegen** to run through an account; **ausstehende** ~ **einem Anwalt übergeben** to place an account with an attorney; **Arbeit auf feste** ~ **übernehmen** to job; **~en überprüfen** to check invoices, to audit accounts; **auf neue** ~ **übertragen** to carry forward to new account; **~en überwachen** to follow up invoices; **für jds.** ~ **10 $ überweisen** to remit $ 10 for s. one's account; **auf** ~ **verkaufen** to sell for the account of; **spezifizierte** ~ **verlangen** to demand an itemized bill; **~en verschicken** to send out accounts; ~ **vorlegen** to present an account, to send in one's bill; **auf neue** ~ **vortragen** to bring (carry forward, place) to new account; **für fremde** ~ **tätig werden** to act in s. one's interest; ~ **als unrichtig zurückweisen** to disallow an account; ~ **zusammenrechnen** to add up an account.

Rechnungsabgrenzung *(Bilanz)* deferral, accrued expenses and deferred income *(US)*;
aktive ~en deferred charges [to expense] *(US)*; **passive ~en** deferred credits [to income] *(US)*;
~ **zum Jahresultimo** end-of-year adjustment;
als ~en behandeln to defer.

Rechnungsabgrenzungsposten extraordinary (transitory, deferred, *US*, suspense) item, *(pl.)* accrued expenses and deferred income *(US)*;
aktive ~ **prepaid expenses, deferred charges to operation (expense); passive** ~ deferred credits to income *(US)*.

Rechnungs|ablage invoice filing, *(Rechnungslegung)* rendering of account, statement; **~abnahme** audit[ing]; **~abnehmer** auditor.

Rechnungsabschluß final settlement, rest *(Br.)*, windup of an account, balance, balancing (closing) an account, *(Bilanz)* balance sheet, annual statement;
anerkannter ~ settled account; **festgestellter** ~ accounts agreed upon; **vierteljährlicher** ~ quarterly accounts;
~ **machen** to make out the balance sheet.

Rechnungs|abschnitt accounting period; **~abteilung** accounting (accounts, billing) department; **~alter** age of billing; **~amt** audit office; **~anteil** quota; **~art** method of computation; **~aufstellung** accounting (accounts, *Br.*) statement, statement (rendering) of accounts, account rendered; **spezifizierte ~aufstellung** *(Einkäufer)* bill of parcels; **~ausschuß** audit commission; **~ausstellung** making out an account (invoice), billing; **spezifizierte ~ausstellung** *(Einkünfte)* bill of parcels; **über den Monat verteilte ~ausstellung** cycle billing; **~austausch** substitution of invoices.

Rechnungsauszug extract (abstract, statement) of account;
fehlerhafter ~ faulty statement; **spezifizierter** ~ itemized statement.

Rechnungs|beamter accountant, auditor; **~begleichung** settlement of an account (invoice).

Rechnungsbeleg|e accounting records, vouchers in support of an account;
~ **anfertigen** to prepare a voucher for billing.

Rechnungs|bericht auditor's report; **~betrag** face (amount) of invoice, invoiced amount (price), invoice, total, *(Kosten vor Abzug des Bardiskonts)* billed cost; **~bogen** tally sheet; **~buch** invoice (account) book, book of accounts, ledger; **gesetzlich vorgeschriebene ~bücher** statutory books; **~bücher aufheben** to preserve books; **~bücher führen** to keep accounts; **~datum** billing date *(US)*, date of invoice; **~defizit** accounting deficit; **~doppel** duplicate invoice; **~durchschlag** copy of invoice; **~einheit** accounting unit, unit of account, money of account; **~einzugsverfahren** direct debiting service, direct debiting system; **~empfang** receipt of invoice; **~empfänger** debtor; **~entlastung** final discharge; **~ergebnis** result of calculation; **~erstellung** invoicing of accounts, billing; **~erteilung** rendering an account; **gedrucktes ~formular** billhead; **~führer** accountant, bookkeeper, *(mil.)* pay clerk *(US)*, *(Zahlungsabkommen)* accounting agency *(US)*; **~führer einer Kirchengemeinde** vestry clerk *(Br.)*.

Rechnungsführung accountancy, accounting, keeping of accounts, keeping books, *(AG)* corporation accounting;
ständig fehlerfreie ~ consistently maintained sound accounting practices;
~ **der Hauptgeschäftsstelle** head-office accounting;
~ **prüfen** to audit the accounts.

Rechnungs|gebühren accounting charges; **~geld** money of account, fiat money *(US)*; **~gewicht** billed weight; **~grundlage** basis of calculation; **~gutschrift** credit memorandum; **~höchstbetrag** account limit; **oberster ~hof** Commissioner of Audits *(Br.)*, General Accounting Office *(US)*; **~jahr** current (account, accounting, trading, working) year; **staatliches ~jahr** financial *(Br.)* (fiscal, *US*) year; **~kammer** chamber of accounts, audit office; **~kauf** purchase on account; **~kontrolle** accounts control; **~kontrolleur** comptroller, controller, checker; **~kopie** copy [of] invoice; **beglaubigte ~kopie** certified copy of invoice; **~kosten** *(vor Abzug des Bardiskonts)* billed cost; **~lage** account; **~leger** accountable person.

Rechnungslegung rendering of account, presentation of (giving-in) accounts;
abschließende ~ full account; **anerkannte** ~ settled account;
~ **der Hauptgeschäftsstelle** head-office accounting; ~ **über den Nachlaß** residuary account; ~ **eines Treuhänders** charge and discharge statement;
zur ~ **verpflichtet sein** to be accountable.

Rechnungslegungs|beschluß order for an account; **~klage** action for an account (for accounting).

Rechnungslegungspflicht liability to render account, accountability;
~ **über ein Vermögen** property accountability.

rechnungsmäßig in accordance with the books;
~**er Wert** actuarial value.

Rechnungs|münze money of account; ~**nachlaß gewähren** to allow a rebate on an account; ~**nachweis** accounting evidence; ~**nummer** invoice number; ~**periode** account period, accounting (fiscal) period; **am Schluß der ~periode** at the close of the period.

rechnungspflichtig accountable, liable to render account, responsible;
nicht ~ unaccountable;
~ **sein** to be accountable.

Rechnungs|plan accounting plan; ~**position** accounting position, item on the account.

Rechnungsposten accounting unit, head, item [of a bill], entry, post;
einmaliger ~ nonrecurring item;
~ **einer Organgesellschaft** intercompany items;
~ **abhaken (abstreichen)** to tick off items in (dot articles of) an account; ~ **abziehen** to deduct an item from an account; ~ **anerkennen** to allow an item in an account; **einzelne** ~ **angeben** to itemize an account; ~ **aufaddieren** to sum up the items of a bill; ~ **fälschen** to falsify an item in an account; ~ **kontrollieren (nachprüfen)** to verify the items of a bill; ~ **streichen** to scratch an item from an account.

Rechnungspreis invoiced amount, invoice price.

Rechnungsprüfer auditor, comptroller of accounts, controller, accountant;
betrieblicher ~ internal (staff, operational, management) accountant; **staatlicher** ~ government accountant, expenditure controller, state auditor; **vereidigter** ~ chartered *(Br.)* (certified public, *US*) accountant;
~**amt** auditorship.

Rechnungsprüfung audit, auditing [of accounts], invoice auditing, checking of (examination of business) accounts (books);
bei der ~ when auditing (examining) the accounts (books); **betriebliche** ~ industrial accounting, management accountancy; **ständige fehlerfreie** ~ consistently maintained sound accounting practices;
~ **vornehmen** to audit accounts.

Rechnungsprüfungs|amt Commissioner of Audits *(Br.)*, audit[ing] office; ~**ausschuß** auditing committee, Public Accounts Committee *(Br.)*; ~**wesen** audit system.

Rechnungs|rest residue, rest, remainder of account; ~**revisor** auditor, comptroller (controller) of accounts; ~**rückstand** remainder of account, account in arrears; ~**sachverständiger** accounting expert.

Rechnungssaldo balance, rest;
festgestellter ~ balance of accounts agreed upon;
~ **bezahlen** to pay (settle) a balance.

Rechnungs|stelle accounting office (department); ~**stellung** making out an account (an invoice); ~**summe** sum owing, amount payable; ~**system** accounting classification; ~**tag** billing date; ~**überschlag** rough estimate; ~**überschuß** balance, surplus; ~**übersicht** statement of accounts; ~**übertrag** invoice continued; ~**überwachung** invoice supervision; ~**unterlagen** accounting records; ~**vierteljahr** quarter of a financial year; ~**vordruck** billhead; ~**vorgang** accounting operation; ~**vorlage** submission of account; **bei ~vorlage** upon presentation of the invoice; ~**währung** money of account; ~**werk** the accounts; ~**wert** value as per invoice, invoice value.

Rechnungswesen accountancy, accounting;
betriebliches ~ cost (manufacturing) accounting, costing; **dezentralisiertes** ~ departmental accounting; **industrielles** ~ industrial accounting; **inflationsbezogenes** ~ accounting for changing price levels; **kaufmännisches** ~ merchant's accounts; **kommunales** ~ municipal accounting; **öffentliches** ~ public accounts; **staatliches** ~ government accounts; **volkswirtschaftliches** ~ economic accounting;
~ **einer Aktiengesellschaft** corporate accounting; ~ **für besondere Betriebsführungsbedürfnisse** management accounting; ~ **einer Konzerngesellschaft** entity accounting.

Rechnungs|zeit account (accounting) period; ~**zettel** slip, check *(US)*.

Recht law, *(Anspruch)* right, claim, interest, title, *(Befugnis)* power, authority, *(rechtliches Gehör)* due process of law, *(Gerechtigkeit)* justice, *(Rechtsstudium)* jurisprudence, law, *(Vorrecht)* privilege;
alle ~e vorbehalten copyright entered at Stationer's Hall, reservation of all rights, all rights reserved; **aus eigenem** ~ in one's own right; **ausschließlich aller ~e** *(Wertpapier)* ex all; **mit** ~ **der Partieergänzung** *(Buchhandel)* with right to batch (lot) completion; **mit dem** ~ **des Substanzeingriffs** *(Pächter)* without impeachment of waste; **mit** ~ **oder Unrecht** rightly or wrongly; **mit dem Anschein des ~s** under the colo(u)r of law; **mit Fug und** ~ by good rights; **nach** ~ **und Billigkeit** according to law and justice; **nach englischem** ~ under English law; **nach geltendem** ~ under the existent law (the law in force); **nach materiellem** ~ upon the merits; **ohne das geringste (jeden Schein von)** ~ without any colo(u)r of right; **sehr auf die Wahrung seiner ~e bedacht** jealous of one's rights; **von ~s wegen** as of rights, according to (by operation of) law, in virtue of law, in justice, ipso jure, in duty bound;
hiermit wird zu ~ **erkannt** it is hereby ordered and adjudged;
abdingbare ~e disposable rights; **abgetretenes** ~ assigned right; **absolutes** ~ absolute rights; **abstraktes** ~ bare right; **abtretbares** ~ transferable right; **akzessorisches** ~ incidental (secondary) right; **alleiniges** ~ sole right; **älteres** ~ prior right, *(Sachenrecht)* paramount title; **anerkanntes** ~ primary (vested) right; **allgemein anerkanntes** ~ common right; **angeborenes** ~ inherent right; **angestammtes** ~ birthright; **nicht mehr angewandtes** ~ law fallen into disuse; **anwachsendes** ~ accruing right; **anwendbares (anzuwendendes)** ~ law which applies, governing (relevant) law; **ausländisches** ~ foreign law; **ausschließliches** ~ exclusive right (privilege), *(Monopol)* monopoly; **bedingtes** ~ contingent interest; **schwach begründetes** ~ inchoate right; **vertraglich begründetes** ~ contractual right; **mit Mängeln behaftetes** ~ defective title; **auf früheren Entscheidungen beruhendes** ~ case law, law of the case; **beschränktes** ~ qualified title; **besseres** ~ outstanding title; **bestehendes** ~ established law; **nebeneinander bestehende ~e** concurrent interests; **bindendes** ~ binding law; **bürgerliches** ~ common (civil, private) law; **dienstbarkeitsähnliches** ~ quasi easement; **dingliches** ~ real right, right in rem; **aufschiebend bedingtes dingliches** ~ executory interest; **subjektiv dingliches** ~ right in rem; **nur gerichtlich durchsetzbares** ~ litigious right; **eheliches** ~ conjugal (marital) rights; **einklagbares** ~ enforceable right, pertinent right; **einwandfreies** ~ clear title; **einzelstaatliches** ~ *(EG)* national law, *(US)* state law; **daraus sich ergebende ~e** rights ensuing from; **erloschenes** ~ lapsed law; **ersessenes** ~ prescriptive right; **erworbene ~e** rights accrued, vested rights; **durch Ersitzung erworbenes** ~ prescriptive right (title); **durch Geburt erworbenes** ~ inherent right, birthright; **gutgläubig erworbenes** ~ bona-fide acquired law; **formelles** ~ law adjective, procedural law; **früheres** ~ prior claim; **verfassungsmäßig garantiertes** ~ constitutional right *(US)*; **an Besitz gebundenes** ~ chose in possession; **gegenwärtiges** ~ existing right; **geltendes** ~ existing (established) law, law in force; **subsidiär geltendes** ~ subsidiary law; **nicht geltend gemachtes** ~ unclaimed right; **gemeines** ~ common law; **geschriebenes (gesetztes)** ~ statute (statutory, written) law, statute; **widerruflich gewährtes** ~ precarious right; **auf den ersten Anschein hin glaubhaftes** ~ color *(US)*; **grundlegendes** ~ fundamental right; **grundstücksunabhängiges** ~ right in gross; **gültiges** ~ law in force; **nicht aus dem Eigentum hergeleitetes** ~ nonproprietary rights; **höchstpersönliches** ~ right of persons; **immaterielles** ~ intangible right; **inländisches** ~ national law; **innerstaatliches (inländisches)** ~ internal (domestic, national) law, territorial law *(US)*; **internationales** ~ international law, law of nations; **kodifiziertes** ~ codified (statute, written) law; **kriegführende ~e** belligerent rights; **künftige ~e** future rights; **lebenslängliches** ~ life interest; **lokales** ~ local law; **mangelhaftes** ~ defect of title; **materielles** ~ substantive law; **nachgewiesenes** ~ proved claim; **nachgiebiges** ~ flexible law; **natürliche ~e** natural rights; **obligatorisches** ~ right in personam, personal right; **öffentliches** ~ public law; **originäres** ~ natural right; **persönliches** ~ private (personal) law; **positives** ~ positive right; **resultierende ~e** resulting powers; **römisches** ~ Roman law, civil course; **staatsbürgerliche ~e** political (civil) rights; **stärkeres** ~ title paramount; **strenges** ~ cogent law; **subsidiäres** ~ subsidiary law; **genau umschriebene ~e** definite rights; **unabdingbares** ~ peremptory law; **unangreifbares** ~ unimpeachable right; **unantastbares** ~ indefeasible interest; **unbestrittenes** ~ clear title; **uneingeschränktes** ~ absolute law; **ungeschriebenes** ~ unwritten law; **unübertragbares** ~ inalienable right; **unveräußerliches** ~ inalienable right; **unverjährbares** ~ imprescriptible right; **unverzichtbares** ~ indefeasible right; **unvollkommene ~e** imperfect rights; **veräußerliches** ~ alienable right; **verbriefte ~e** vested (chartered) rights; **mit einem Grundstück verbundene ~e** rights that run with the land; **verfassungsmäßig verbürgtes** ~ constitutional right; **vererbliche ~e** incorporeal hereditaments;

vergleichendes ~ comparative law; **verjährtes** ~ statute-barred right; **gesetzlich vermutetes** ~ implied lien; **vertragliches** ~ contractual right; **vertragsähnliches** ~ quasi-contractual right; **verwirktes** ~ forfeited right; **vollkommenes** ~ perfect right; **im Rang vorgehendes** ~ senior title; **wechselseitige** ~**e** relative rights; **unbeschränkt wirksames** ~ absolute right; **wohlerworbene** ~**e** vested interests, *(Verfassung)* vested rights *(US)*; **zukünftiges** ~ future right; **zustehendes** ~ appendant; **zwingendes** ~ binding law, cogent law; **zwischenstaatliches** ~ law of nations, international law;

~ **des Aberntens** *(Pächter)* right to emblement; ~ **auf Abtretung der Ersatzansprüche** right of subrogation; ~ **auf Ämterbesetzung** patronage; ~ **auf Arbeit** right to work, employment right; ~ **auf Ausschluß der Öffentlichkeit** right of privacy; ~ **auf Aussicht** right of view; ~ **zur Banknotenausgabe** note-issuing privilege *(Br.)*; ~ **auf vorzugsweise Befriedigung im Konkursverfahren** priority (preference) claim; ~ **auf Beibehaltung des Arbeitsplatzes bei Entlassungen** bumping right; ~ **der Benennung** right to name; ~ **auf Benutzung** usufructuary right; ~ **der Berufung auf das Anwaltsgeheimnis** legal professional privilege; ~ **auf ausschließlichen Besitz** right to exclusive possession; ~ **und Billigkeit** right and equity; ~**e Dritter** third-party rights; ~**e gutgläubiger Dritter** rights of innocent purchasers; ~ **am geistigen Eigentum** intellectual property; ~ **auf Einsichtnahme** right to inspect; ~ **auf Einsichtnahme in die Geschäftsbücher** right of access to the books; ~ **auf Entnahme** right of withdrawal; ~ **des Erben auf Inventareinrichtung** benefit of inventory; ~ **auf die Ernte [auch nach Beendigung der Pachtzeit]** right to emblement; ~ **der Erstgeburt** primogeniture; ~**e gutgläubiger Erwerber** rights of innocent purchasers; ~ **auf Flaggenerkundung** *(Völkerrecht)* right of approach (to visit and research); ~ **auf Freizügigkeit** freedom of movement; ~ **auf Gegendarstellung** right of reply; ~ **auf Gegenseitigkeit** law of reciprocity; ~ **der Gesetzgebung** legislative power, legislation; ~ **auf Gestellung eines Pflichtverteidigers** benefit of counsel; ~**e der Gewerkschaft** union rights; ~ **auf Grenzabstützung** right to support; ~**e an einem Grundstück** legal interests in land, chattels real; ~ **auf Handel** commercial rights; ~ **der Handelsvertreter** agency law; ~ **der unerlaubten Handlungen** law of torts; ~ **des Heimathafens** law of the flag; ~ **auf Heirat und Familiengründung** right to marry and found a family; **sachenrechtsähnliches** ~ **an Immobilien** equitable estate; ~ **auf Inanspruchnahme des Hauptschuldners** right of relief *(Scot.)*; ~ **auf Inbesitznahme** right of entry; ~ **auf Inventareinrichtung** *(Erbe)* benefit of inventory; ~ **der Kapitalgesellschaften** company law *(Br.)*; ~ **des Kaufvertrags** law of sales, right of emption; ~ **auf Klageerhebung** right of action; ~ **auf Lebenszeit** life interest; ~ **auf ungehinderten Lichtzutritt** ancient lights; ~ **auf saubere Luft** right to air; ~ **auf Luftraum** right to air space; ~**e der Mehrheit** majority rights; ~ **auf freie Meinungsäußerung** freedom of speech, right to speak (of free speech); ~ **der persönlichen Meinungsbildung** private judgment; ~**e der Minderheit** minority rights; ~ **auf Mithaftung des zweiten Pfands** right to consolidate; ~ **auf Nachlaßbeschränkung** *(Erbe)* benefit of inventory; ~ **der Niederlassung** right of settlement; ~ **auf ungestörte Nutzung** right to enjoyment of a property; ~ **auf ein Patent** title of a patent; ~**e einer juristischen Person** corporate rights; ~**e und Pflichten** rights and liabilities; **ehe[männ]liche** ~**e und Pflichten** marital rights and duties; ~ **der Richterablehnung** right of objection; ~**e an Sachen** right of things; ~ **der belegenen Sache** law of the place where property is situated, lex situs; ~ **an beweglichen Sachen** chattel interest; ~ **an unbeweglichen Sachen** title in real property; ~ **des Schadensersatzes** law of damages; ~ **der Schuldverhältnisse** law of contract; ~ **auf Schutz der Intimsphäre** right of privacy; ~ **auf Selbstverwaltung** right of local self-government; ~ **auf Seßhaftigkeit** *(Unterstützungsempfänger)* status of irremovability *(Br.)*; ~**e eines kriegführenden Staates** belligerent rights; ~ **des Stärkeren** club law; ~ **auf Stellvertretung** law of agency; **nachgeordnetes** ~ **an einem Teilgrundstück** derivative estate; ~ **des freihändigen Verkaufs** power of sale; ~**e und Verpflichtungen aus einem Vertrag** rights and obligations arising under a contract; ~ **der ersten Wahl** first choice; ~**e des Wechselinhabers** holder's right; ~ **auf Wiederinbesitznahme** right of re-entry; ~ **der freien Zufahrt** ingress, egress and regress;

jem. ein ~ **aberkennen** to divest (deprive) s. o. of a right; **auf ausländisches** ~ **abstellen** to refer to foreign law; ~ **abtreten** to assign (cede) a right; **sich ein** ~ **anmaßen** to arrogate (assume) a right to s. o.; **sich jds.** ~**e anmaßen** to usurp s. one's rights; ~ **anwenden** to apply the law, to administer justice; ~ **aufgeben** to discontinue (abandon, resign, yield) a right; ~ **in unberechtigter Weise auslegen** to stretch law; ~ **des Hypothekenschuldners auf Grundstücksübertragung für immer ausschließen** to foreclose the mortgagor's right of redemption; ~ **ausüben** to exercise a right; ~ **auf den Bezug junger Aktien ausüben** to exercise the right to subscribe for new shares (stocks, *US*); ~ **beanspruchen** to vindicate a claim; ~ **aufgrund von Ersitzung beanspruchen** to claim a right by prescription; **jds.** ~**e beeinträchtigen** to prejudice (commit an offence against, encroach upon) s. one's rights; ~**e einer Partei beeinträchtigen** to abridge a party of its rights; **für** ~ **befinden** to hold, to find; **sich eines** ~**es begeben** to abandon (surrender) a right, to put o. s. out of court, to divest o. s. of one's right; ~ **begründen** to constitute a right; **sein** ~ **begründen** to establish one's claim; **auf seinem** ~ **beharren** to stand on (assert) one's right; **sein** ~ **bekommen** to carry the day; **j. eines** ~**es berauben** to divest s. o. of his right; **sich auf ein** ~ **berufen** to assert a right; ~**e berühren** to affect the rights; **auf seinem** ~ **bestehen** to insist on one's right; **zu** ~ **bestehen** to be valid (in force), to be good (valid) in law; ~ **bestreiten** to question a right; ~ **beugen** to stretch law, to pervert the course of (deviate from) justice; **sein gutes** ~ **beweisen** to establish one's right; **seine** ~**e gerichtlich durchsetzen** to enforce (assert) one's rights; **in fremde** ~**e eingreifen** to trespass, to infringe upon s. one's rights; **in vertragliche** ~**e eingreifen** to impair the obligations of a contract; **jem. ein** ~ **einräumen** to grant s. o. a privilege; **in jds.** ~**e eintreten** to succeed to s. one's rights; **wieder in seine** ~**e eintreten** to reenter in one's rights; ~ **entziehen** to defeat a right; **für** ~ **erkennen** to hold, to adjudge, to adjudicate, to find; **j. eines** ~**es für verlustig erklären** to interdict s. o.; ~ **ersitzen** to prescribe to (for) a right; ~ **erwerben** to acquire a right; **sein** ~ **fordern** to claim one's right; **eines** ~**es verlustig gehen** to forfeit a right; ~ **genießen** to enjoy a right; **kein** ~ **haben** to have no business; ~ **auf etw. haben** to be entitled (have a title) to s. th.; ~ **auf eigene Meinung haben** to be entitled to one's opinion; ~ **auf seiner Seite haben** to have a strong case; ~ **innehaben** to hold a right; **bestimmte** ~**e innehaben** to possess certain rights; **zu seinem** ~ **kommen** to come into one's rights; ~ **erlöschen (verfallen) lassen** to allow a right to lapse; **von seinem guten** ~ **Gebrauch machen** to exercise one's perfectly valid right; **seine** ~**e geltend machen** to vindicate(assert, uphold) one's rights, to claim one's due; **jem. ein** ~ **streitig machen** to contest (contend) s. one's right; **j. zur Ausübung eines** ~**s unfähig machen** to disqualify s. o.; **seine** ~**e mißbrauchen** to exceed one's rights, to act in excess of one's rights; ~ **für sich in Anspruch nehmen** to claim the right to do s. th.; **sein** ~ **in Anspruch nehmen** to push one's demands; **es mit dem** ~ **nicht so genau nehmen** to stretch law; **jds.** ~**e schmälern** to curtail (entrench, encroach upon, restrain) s. one's rights; **seine** ~**e geschmälert sehen** to be curtailed in one's right; **im** ~ **sein** to have the law on one's side, to be within one's right; **auf der ganzen Linie im** ~ **sein** to be right in every point; ~ **sprechen** to dispense (deal out, administer) justice, to exercise jurisdiction, to adjudicate, to judge; **j. im Genuß seines** ~**es stören** to disturb s. o. in the lawful enjoyment of a right; **die** ~**e studieren** to take up law, to study for the bar; **jedermann zu seinem** ~ **zu helfen trachten** to be always fighting other people's quarrels; ~ **mit Füßen treten** to fly in the face of the law; ~ **übertragen** to assign (transfer) a right; **auf j. ein** ~ **übertragen** to transfer (confer) a right to s. o., to grant s. o. a right; **auf jem. die** ~**e eines anderen übertragen** to subrogate s. o. to the rights of another; ~**e verbriefen** to secure by charter; **j. aus seinem** ~ **verdrängen** to thrust s. o. from his right; ~ **verdrehen** to pervert the course of justice, to twist the law; **jem. zu seinem** ~ **verhelfen** to right s. o.; ~**e auf Verfilmung eines Buches verlangen** to ask for an option on the film rights of a book; ~ **verleihen** to grant a right; **jem. ein** ~ **verleihen** to confer a right upon s. o.; **dem** ~ **Wirksamkeit verleihen** to make the law effective; ~ **verletzen** to infringe a right; **jds.** ~**e verletzen** to trespass on s. one's rights; ~ **verschaffen** to relieve; **sich selbst** ~ **verschaffen** to right o. s., to take the law into one's own hands; **in jds.** ~ **Übergriffe verüben** to invade s. one's rights; **auf ein** ~ **verzichten** to relinquish (renounce, disclaim) a right; **auf Ausübung eines** ~**es verzichten** to renounce (waive) a right; **sich ein** ~ **vorbehalten** to reserve a right for o. s.; ~ **vormerken** to note a right on the record; ~ **wahren** to safeguard a right; **seine** ~**e wahren** to maintain (preserve) one's rights; **nach dem** ~ **des Wohnsitzes beurteilt werden** to be governed by the law of domicile; **j. in seine** ~**e wiedereinsetzen** to reinstate s. o. in his rights; **j. ein** ~ **zugestehen** to make a concession of a right to s. o.; **den Arbeitern ein verbrieftes** ~ **auf Grundkapitalbeteiligung zugestehen** to give workers a recognized right to a bit of the equity.

recht just, right, *(rechtmäßig)* lawful, legitimate;
~ **und billig** just (fair) and equitable;
auf dem ~en Flügel stehen *(pol.)* to be on the right wing; **~e Hand** *(fig.)* right-hand man; **zur ~en Zeit** in due time.
Rechte, äußerste *(pol.)* extreme right; **gemäßigte** ~ right center *(US)* (centre, *Br.*).
Rechtens lawfully, by law.
rechtfertigen to justify, to exculpate, to warrant;
zu ~ vindicable;
sich ~ to clear (explain) o. s.; **seine Beurteilung** ~ to vindicate one's judgment; **sich vor Gericht** ~ to purge o. s. of a charge; **sein Verhalten** ~ to speak in vindication of one's conduct.
rechtfertigend exculpatory, vindicatory.
Rechtfertigung justification, exculpation, apology, warranty, *(Entlastung)* exoneration, clearing;
zu seiner ~ on his own defence;
~ **einer unerlaubten Handlung** purging a tort; ~ **des eigenen Verhaltens** self-justification;
überhaupt keine ~ **haben** not to have a leg to stand on.
Rechtfertigungsgrund [defence of] justification, defence of privilege;
absoluter ~ conditional (absolute, qualified) privilege; **ohne** ~ without lawful excuse.
Rechtfertigungs|schrift apology; **~vorbringen unter Anerbieten des Wahrheitsbeweises** plea of justification.
rechtgläubig orthodox, sound;
nicht ~ infidel.
Rechthaber disputant.
rechtlich lawful, legal, judicial, juridical, legitimate, *(gültig)* valid;
bürgerlich-~ civil-law; **materiell-~** substantial; **öffentlich-~** under public law; ~ **und tatsächlich** in fact and in law; ~ **unmöglich** legally impossible; ~ **verpflichtet** bound by law; ~ **zulässig** good in law;
~ **als Träger von Rechten und Pflichten gelten** to be treated in one's own law; ~ **und sachlich begründet sein** to be good in law and in fact;
~e Ausführungen legal arguments; **ohne ~e Bedeutung** irrelevant, not supporting the issue; **~es Ermessen** legal discretion; **~es Gehör** full hearing, due process of law; **aus ~en Gründen** for legal reasons; **~e Verpflichtung** legal obligation; **~e Wirkung** legal effect.
rechtlos lawless, outlawed, without rights.
rechtmäßig lawful, legal, legitimate, rightful, true, as of right, apparent;
~ **besitzen** to hold in due course; **für** ~ **erklären** to legitimate; ~ **erwerben** to obtain lawfully; ~ **gehören** to belong s. o. by right; ~ **handeln** to act by right;
~er Anspruch legal demand; **~er Besitz** lawful possession; **~er Besitzer** legal possessor; **~er Eigentümer** holder in due course; **~e Entscheidung** fully justified decision; **~er Erbe** rightful (lawful, true) heir; **~e Inbesitznahme** lawful entry; **~es Verfahren** legal (legitimate) proceedings; **~er Vertreter** legal (lawful) representative.
Rechtmäßigkeit lawfulness, warrantableness, legality, legitimacy, justice, justifiability, validity;
~ **eines Anspruchs** justice of a claim; ~ **einer Berufung** force of an appeal; ~ **eines Verfahren** legitimate proceedings;
~ **amtlicher Maßnahmen nachprüfen lassen** to challenge the legality of official actions.
rechts fahren to drive on the right side.
Rechts|abbiegen verboten no right turn; **~abbieger** vehicle turning right; **~abteilung** law (solicitor's, legal) department (division), legal branch, *(Gericht)* side, *(Versicherung)* disputed-claims office; **~abtretung** cession, assignment of a right; **~abweichler** right-wing devationist; **~akademie** law school *(Br.)*; **~änderung** change of title; **~angelegenheit** legal case, law business; **~angleichung innerstaatlicher Rechtsvorschriften** *(EG)* approximation of municipal laws; **~anmaßung** usurpation of franchise; **~anschauung** legal view; **~anschein** color *(US)*.
Rechtsanspruch [legal] right, title, claim, legal demand;
ohne ~ untitled;
abgeleiteter ~ derivative title; **besserer** ~ superior title; **durchsetzbarer** ~ marketable title; **einwandfreier** ~ clear record title; **fehlender** ~ lack of title; **gültiger** ~ valid title; **allgemein gültiger** ~ existing right; **klägerischer** ~ plaintiff's title; **mangelnder** ~ lack of title; **ruhender** ~ dormant title; **unanfechtbarer** ~ root of good title; **unverzichtbarer** ~ indefeasible right; **unwirksamer** ~ invalid claim; **verjährter** ~ statute-barred right; **zweifelhafter** ~ doubtful title;
sich eines ~s begeben to waive a claim; **eines ~s berauben** to disentitle; ~ **bestreiten** to dispute a claim; ~ **auf etw. haben** to be entitled to s. th.; ~ **geltend machen** to enter a claim; ~ **überprüfen** to clear a title; ~ **verlieren** to derogate from a right; **auf einen** ~ **verzichten** to abandon a legal title; ~ **vorbehalten** to reserve the right of.
Rechtsanwalt lawyer, solicitor *(Br.)*, barrister [at law] *(Br.)*, attorney at law *(US)*, counsel *(Br.)*, counsel(l)or at law *(US)*, writer to the signet *(Scot.)*;
mit der ständigen Vertretung beauftragter ~ general (standing) lawyer; **bedeutender** ~ leading counsel *(Br.)*; **beratender** ~ chamber counsel *(Br.)*, counsel in chambers, special pleader, consulting barrister *(Br.)*, office lawyer *(US)*; **engagierter** ~ paid attorneys *(US)*; **erfahrener** ~ case lawyer; **sehr erfahrener** ~ lawyer of wide experience; **gegnerischer** ~ opposing lawyer (counsel, *Br.*); **gerissener** ~ Philadelphia lawyer *(US fam.)*; **klägerischer** ~ plaintiff's counsel *(Br.)*, counsel for the plaintiff *(Br.)*; **plädierender** ~ pleader, barrister *(Br.)*, attorney at law *(US)*; **praktizierender** ~ practising lawyer; **prozeßbevollmächtigter** ~ attorney of record *(US)*; **prozeßführender** ~ senior counsel *(Br.)*; **auf Schadenersatz bei Verkehrsunfällen spezialisierter** ~ ambulance chaser *(US)*; **auf Versicherungssachen spezialisierter** ~ insurance lawyer; **versierter** ~ full-fledged barrister *(Br.)*; **zugelassener** ~ authorized counsellor *(US)*;
~ **des Beklagten** counsel for the defendant;
Tätigkeit als ~ **aufgeben** to retire from the bar *(Br.)*; **für j. als** ~ **auftreten** to act as counsel for s. o. *(Br.)*; **sich als** ~ **ausgeben** to pass o. s. off as counsel *(Br.)*; ~ **aus der Anwaltschaft ausschließen** to disbar a barrister *(Br.)*; ~ **beauftragen** to engage the service of a lawyer, to brief a barrister *(Br.)*; ~ **befragen** to take counsel's opinion *(Br.)*; ~ **beiordnen** to assign a counsel *(Br.)*; **j. als** ~ **beraten** to act as counsel for s. o. *(Br.)*; **sich mit seinem** ~ **beraten** to confer with one's counsel *(Br.)*; ~ **beschäftigen** to employ a solicitor *(Br.)*; ~ **bestellen** to instruct (brief) a counsel *(Br.)*, to brief instructions to a barrister *(Br.)*; **j. zu seinem** ~ **bestellen** to constitute s. one's attorney; ~ **dirigieren** to direct (brief) a counsel *(Br.)*; ~ **zur laufenden Beratung engagieren** to retain a lawyer; **seinen Fall durch einen** ~ **vortragen lassen** to be heard by counsel *(Br.)*; **sich einen** ~ **nehmen** to retain (brief) a barrister (counsel, *Br.*), to brief instructions to a barrister *(Br.)*; **sich als** ~ **niederlassen** to set o. s. up as a lawyer, to settle down in the practice of law; **als** ~ **nicht reüssieren** to be a failure as a lawyer; **als** ~ **tätig sein** to be in (practise the) law, to lawyer, to practise at the bar; **durch einen** ~ **vertreten sein** to be represented by counsel *(Br.)*; **Angelegenheit einem** ~ **übergeben (übertragen)** to put (place) a matter in the hands of a lawyer (solicitor, *Br.*); ~ **mit Weisungen versehen** to give instructions to a solicitor (barrister) *(Br.)*; **sich an einen** ~ **wenden** to apply to a solicitor *(Br.)* (lawyer); ~ **werden** to go to the bar; **als** ~ **zugelassen werden** to be admitted (come) to the bar, to qualify as a solicitor *(Br.)*; ~ **zu Rate ziehen** to call in the aid of an attorney *(US)*; **als** ~ **zulassen** to call to the bar; ~ **zuziehen** to consult an attorney *(US)*, to employ a counsel *(Br.)*.
Rechtsanwältin advocatress, woman barrister.
Rechtsanwaltsanderkonto solicitor's trust account *(Br.)*.
Rechtsanwaltsberuf legal profession, bar, lawyer's office;
~ **ausüben** to practise law; **sich auf den** ~ **vorbereiten** to study for the bar, to eat one's dinner *(Br.)*.
Rechtsanwaltsbüro barrister's [writing] chamber *(Br.)*, law office.
Rechtsanwaltschaft bar, attorneyship, solicitorship *(Br.)*.
Rechtsanwalts|firma firm of solicitors *(Br.)*; **~gebühren** counsel's *(Br.)* (lawyer's retaining) fee, general retainer; **~gutachten** counsel's opinion *(Br.)*; **~kammer** Bar Council, Faculty of Advocates; **~kanzlei** barrister's [writing] chamber *(Br.)*, law office *(US)*; **~sozietät** law firm.
Rechts|anwendung application of a law, dispensation of justice, practice of a court; **~auffassung** judicial (legal) conception; **~auffassung der Minderheit** minority opinion; **~aufgabe** waiver of rights; **~ausdruck** legal term (phrase); **~ausführungen** legal arguments, pleadings, law memorandum *(US)*; **~auskunft** legal information; **~auslegung** legal interpretation; **~ausschließung** foreclosure; **~ausschluß** exclusion of a right; **~ausschuß** judicial panel (committee), judiciary (legal) committee; **~ausübung** enjoyment (exercise, user) of a right; **~ausübung verhindern** to prevent the exercise of a right; **~basis** legal basis; **~beflissener** graduate in law, law student; **~befugnis** competence, authority; **~begehren** petition, prayer of process; **~begriff** legal term (phrase), legal expression.
rechtsbegründend|es Ereignis law-creating event; **~e Wirkung** constitutive effect.

Rechtsbehelf defense, defence *(Br.)*, appeal, legal remedy, *(Gegenvorstellung)* remonstrance, *(Rechtseinwand)* plea, demurrer;
ausreichender ~ adequate remedy; **außergerichtlicher** ~ extrajudicial (extraordinary) remedy; **kein** ~ no recourse to law; **summarischer** ~ speedy remedy; **ungeeigneter** ~ inadequate remedy; **vorläufiger** ~ provisional remedy; **zusätzlicher** ~ cumulative remedy;
~ **in bürgerlichen Rechtsstreitigkeiten** civil remedy; ~ **des unbezahlt gebliebenen Verkäufers** remedies of the unpaid sellers; ~ **in Verwaltungsangelegenheiten** administrative remedy;
von einem ~ **Gebrauch machen** to resort to a remedy.

Rechtsbeistand legal (law) adviser, solicitor, legal agent, counsel(l)or at law *(US)*, advocate *(Scot.)*;
unentgeltlicher ~ free legal aid *(US)*, legal aid *(Br.)*; **zugelassener** ~ enrolled law agent *(Scot. law)*.

Rechtsbelehrung *(Geschworene)* summing up, instruction *(US)*;
bindende ~ peremptory instruction; **erbetene** ~ special charge; **fehlende** ~ nondirection; **unrichtige** ~ **von Geschworenen** misdirection of a jury; **verbindliche** ~ binding instruction.

Rechts|berater legal (law) adviser, counsel *(US)*, chamber counsel *(Br.)*, counsel(l)or of law *(US)*, syndic; ~**berater der Regierung** law officer of the crown *(Br.)*; ~**beratung** legal advice; **unentgeltliche** ~**beratung** free legal aid *(US)*, legal aid system *(Br.)*; ~**beratungsstelle** legal-aid office *(Br.)*; ~**beschwerde** appeal on points of law; ~**beschwerdeverfahren** appellate procedure.

rechtsbeständig valid, lawful.

Rechts|beständigkeit *(Patent)* validity; ~**bestimmungen** provisions of the law; ~**betreuung** legal assistance; ~**beugung** maladministration, perversion (miscarriage) of justice, circumvention of the law; ~**beugung durch die Geschworenen** false verdict; ~**beugung begehen** to pervert the course of justice; ~**beziehungen** legal relations; **in** ~**beziehungen eintreten** to enter into privity; ~**beziehungen herstellen** to create legal relations; ~**bezirk** jurisdiction; ~**bibliothek** law (county) library; ~**brauch** legal custom *(US)*.

Rechtsbrecher lawbreaker, transgressor, offender, criminal;
flüchtiger ~ fugitive from justice, fugitive criminal; **mutwilliger** ~ defiant trespasser *(US)*.

Rechts|bruch breach of the peace, violation of the law; ~**buch** law book.

rechtschaffen uncorrupted, honest, straight, good, righteous, white *(US coll.)*.

Recht|schaffenheit probity, virtue, equity; ~**schreibewettbewerb** spelling bee; ~**schreibung** spelling, orthography; **keine Schwierigkeiten mit der** ~**schreibung haben** to be able to spell backward.

Rechts|darstellung statement of law, brief; ~**dokument** legal document (instrument); **politischer** ~**drall** right-wing political leaning; ~**durchsetzung** law enforcement; ~**eingestellter** rightist; ~**einrichtung** legal institution; ~**eintritt** subrogation of rights; ~**eintrittsklausel** subrogation clause; ~**einwand** common bar, demurrer at law, estoppel, traverse; **auf Formfehler gegründeter** ~**einwand** special demurrer; ~**einwand erheben** to impose a demurrer, to demur, to traverse, to put in a plea; ~**einwendung** general plea; ~**empfinden** sense of justice; **gesundes** ~**empfinden** [etwa] natural equity; **gegen das** ~**empfinden gerichtet** against good conscience; ~**entscheidung** legal decision.

rechtserheblich relevant in law, material;
~**er Einwand** relevant plea.

Rechts|erheblichkeit relevance in law; ~**erklärung** statement of law; **einseitige** ~**erklärung** deed poll; ~**erwerb** acquisition of title.

rechtserzeugende Wirkung constitutive effect.

Rechts|experte legal expert; ~**extremist** right-wing extremist, hardline right-winger.

rechtsfähig [legally] capable, personable, capable to act in law;
~ **sein** to have legal status;
~**er Verein** incorporated society, registered association (club).

Rechtsfähigkeit capability, legal capacity (status);
mangelnde ~ legal incapacity; **staatlich verliehene** ~ general franchise; **völkerrechtliche** ~ international personality;
~ **verleihen** to grant a charter.

Rechtsfakultät faculty of law.

Rechtsfall law (court) case;
berühmter ~ famous case; **erstmaliger** ~ first impression; **schwebender** ~ pending case; **erstmalig vorgetragener** ~ original bill; **vorliegender** ~ case at bar.

Rechts|fehler error in law; **offensichtlicher** ~**fehler** error apparent of record; **unerheblicher** ~**fehler** harmless error; ~**figur** legal entity; ~**fiktion** fiction of law, legal fiction; ~**findung** findings of the court; ~**folge** legal sequence (consequence); ~**folgen ausschließen** not to accept legal responsibility; ~**folgerung** implication of law; ~**form** legal form; **öffentliche** ~**form annehmen** *(Firma)* to go public; ~**formalismus** legalism; ~**formalität** legal formality; ~**formularbuch** precedent book.

Rechtsfrage legal issue (dispute, question), matter of law;
schwierige ~ nice point of law;
~ **aufwerfen** to raise an issue; **j. während einer Verhandlung in** ~**n beraten** to advise s. o. in legal points during a hearing; ~ **entscheiden** to adjudge a question (decide a point) of law; ~ **erörtern** to argue a point of law; ~**en klären** to settle points of law.

Rechts|frieden law and order; ~**früchte** civil fruits; ~**gang** practice, legal procedure, course of law; ~**gebiet** field of law; ~**gedanke** legal conception; ~**gefühl** sense of justice; **unkörperlicher** ~**gegenstand** legal chose in action; ~**gelehrsamkeit** law, jurisprudence; ~**gelehrter** student of law, jurisconsult, jurist, legal scholar, legist; ~**gemeinschaft** privity; ~**- und Interessensgemeinschaft** community of rights and interests; ~**genuß** enjoyment of a right.

rechtsgerichtet *(pol.)* right-wing, right, rightward.

Rechtsgeschäft legal act (transaction);
anfechtbares ~ voidable transaction; **konkursrechtlich anfechtbare** ~**e** transactions not protected; **angefochtenes** ~ voided transaction; **bedingtes** ~ conditional legal transaction; **entgeltliches** ~ transaction for value; **genehmigtes** ~ authorized act; **genehmigungsbedürftiges** ~ transaction subject to permission; **kaufähnliches** ~ quasi-purchase; **kausales** ~ underlying transaction; **nichtiges** ~ void transaction; **sittenwidriges** ~ unconscionable bargain (transaction), constructive fraud, transaction contra bones mores (contrary to the policy of the law; **steuerpflichtiges** ~ taxable transaction; **unerlaubtes** ~ illicit transaction; **der Konkursanfechtung unterliegende** ~**e** unprotected transactions; **nicht der Konkursanfechtung unterliegende** ~**e** protected transactions; **verbotenes** ~ prohibited transaction; **zweiseitiges** ~ bilateral transaction;
~**e unter Lebenden** transactions inter vivos; ~ **von Todes wegen** transaction mortes causa;
~ **abschließen** to enter into a transaction; ~ **anfechten** to avoid a transaction; ~ **beurkunden** to record a deed.

rechtsgeschäftlich|begründen to constitute completely;
~**e Erledigung** disposal of a piece of business; ~**e Verfügung** voluntary disposition.

rechtsgestaltende Worte operative words.

Rechts|gewohnheit legal custom; ~**gleichheit** equality of rights, isonomy.

Rechtsgrund legal ground, title, claim, legal consideration;
ohne ~ without lawful title;
einheitlicher ~ unity of title;
~ **einer Forderung** consideration of a debt.

Rechtsgründen, aus for legal reasons.

Rechtsgrund|lage legal (jurisdictional) basis; ~**satz** maxim (axiom) of law, legal principle; **feststehende** ~**sätze** established principles of law.

rechtsgültig valid in law, legal, sufficient (good) in law, good and valid, lawful, in force, *(Unterschrift)* authentic, genuine;
~ **ausgestellt und bestätigt** authentic;
Urkunde ~ **ausstellen** to execute a deed; **für** ~ **erklären** to validate; ~ **sein** to be good in law (in force);
~**er Anspruch** legal title; ~**es Testament errichten** to execute a will; ~**e Urkunde** title deed; ~**er Vertrag** binding contract.

Rechtsgültigkeit validity, legal force, legality, lawfulness, *(Unterschrift)* authentication, genuineness;
~ **einer Forderung** validity of a claim; ~ **eines Testaments** validity of a will; ~ **einer Unterschrift** authenticity of a signature; ~ **eines Vertrages** validity of a contract (deed);
~ **eines Verfahrens bestreiten** to object to the regularity of the proceedings; **volle** ~ **haben** to be valid in law; ~ **eines Vertrages herbeiführen** to make a contract binding; ~ **verleihen** to legalize.

Rechts|gut object of an action; ~**gutachten** [counsel's] opinion *(Br.)*, opinion of counsel *(Br.)*, advisory opinion, law memorandum *(US)*, *(Gericht)* certificate into chancery *(Br.)*; **immaterielle** ~**güter** choses in action; ~**handel** litigation, lawsuit, action; **in einen** ~**handel verwickelt sein** to be involved in a lawsuit; ~**handlung** lawful (legal) act, legal transaction, juristic act.

rechtshängig pending at law (in court), litigious, sub judice.
Rechtshängigkeit commencement of procedings, pendency, litigiosity *(Scot.)*;
während der ~ pending the decision of the court.
rechtshemmender Einwand estoppel.
Rechtshilfe legal aid (remedy), relief;
innerstaatliche ~ domestic remedy; **kostenlose** ~ free legal aid *(US)*, legal aid *(Br.)*;
~ **erhalten** to get relief at law;
~**ersuchen** letters rogatory *(US)*, writ of commission, *(betr. Zeugenvernehmung)* commission to take depositions (examine witness) *(US)*; ~**richter** commissioner; ~**system** system of legal aid *(Br.)*; ~**verkehr** judicial assistance.
Rechts|hindernis legal bar; ~**hypothek** legal hypothec; ~**inhaber** holder of a right; **materieller** ~**inhaber sein** to be beneficially interested; ~**institut** legal institution.
rechtsirrig erroneous in point of law.
Rechtsirrtum error in law, judicial error, mistake of law;
grundlegender ~ fundamental error;
~ **begehen** to err on a point of law.
rechtsirrtümlich erroneous in point of law.
Rechts|kenntnisse knowledge of the law, legal attainments; **rudimentäre** ~**kenntnisse** horn-book law; ~**kniff** chicanery; ~**koalition** right-wing coalition; ~**kollision** conflict of laws; ~**kommission** law commission *(Br.)*; ~**konsulent** procurator, solicitor [at law], legal adviser; ~**korrespondenz** legal correspondence; ~**kosten** legal costs *(Br.)*, law costs.
Rechtskraft legal force (sufficiency), validity, *(Urteil)* nonappealableness;
mit Erlangung der ~ when a judgment becomes final; **mit materieller** ~ with prejudice;
formelle ~ nonreversibility; **materielle** ~ law of the case;
~ **erlangen** *(Gesetz)* to become final (valid, effective, absolute), to pass into law, to obtain legal force, *(Urteil)* to become final (definite); ~ **haben** to be in force, to run; **einem Gesetz** ~ **verleihen** to give effect to a law;
~**einrede** former adjudication.
rechtskräftig *(Gesetz)* legal, valid in law, of legal force, *(Urteil)* final and conclusive, unappealable, sentential, nonappealable, good;
formell ~ nonreversible; **noch nicht** ~ pending appeal;
~ **machen** to pass into law; ~ **sein** to have legal force; ~ **werden** *(Gesetz)* to become valid (absolute), to pass into law, *(Urteil)* to become final;
~**e Entscheidung** final decision; ~**es Scheidungsurteil** decree absolute; ~**es Urteil** final decree (judgment); ~**e Verurteilung** final sentence.
Rechtskunde jurisprudence.
rechtskundig wise in the law.
Rechts|kundiger legal practitioner, legist; **in eine** ~**kurve gehen** to right-bank; ~**lage** legal position; ~**lehrbuch** law book; ~**lehre** jurisprudence; ~**lehrer** law teacher; ~**literatur** legal literature; ~**lücke** gap in the law.
Rechtsmangel flaw in a (lack of) title, defective title;
arglistiger ~ fraud in law;
~ **beseitigen** to remove cloud from title; ~ **heilen** to cure a defect.
Rechtsmängel|beseitigung removing cloud from title; ~**garantie**, ~**gewähr** covenant of warranty (for title), warranty (guaranty) of title; **übliche** ~**gewährleistung** usual covenant; ~**gewährleistungsversicherung** guaranty of title insurance *(US)*; ~**haftung** warranty of title, title warranty.
Rechts|maxime legal maxim; ~**mißbrauch** misuser, unauthorized assumption of a right, *(Völkerrecht)* abuse of rights.
Rechtsmittel legal remedy (redress), relief, appeal;
durch ~ **anfechtbar** appealable, appellate; ~ **ausgeschlossen** without appeal;
voll ausgeschöpfte ~ exhausted remedies; **außerordentliches** ~ prerogative writ *(US)*; **innerstaatliches** ~ local remedy; **zur Wahl stehendes** ~ alternative relief;
~ **der Berufung** right of appeal; ~ **der Revision** appeal with the Supreme Court;
mit einem ~ **nicht durchkommen** to fail to obtain relief; ~ **einlegen** to resort to a remedy, to appeal a suit *(US)*, to appeal a case *(US)*, to lodge an appeal; ~ **gegen ein Urteil einlegen** to appeal against a decision; ~ **ergreifen** to resort to a remedy; **von seinen** ~**n Gebrauch machen**, ~ **in Anspruch nehmen** to pursue one's legal remedies; **einem** ~ **unterliegen** to be subject to an appeal; ~ **zurücknehmen** to withdraw an appeal;
~**begründung** reasons for appeal; ~**belehrung** caution; ~**einlegung** appeal at law.
rechtsmittelfähig appellate, appealable, with possible appeal;
nicht ~ nonappealable.
Rechtsmittel|fähigkeit appealability; ~**frist** time for appeal; ~**gebühr** appeal fee; ~**gericht**, ~**instanz** reviewing (appellate) court; ~**instanz sein** to have appellate jurisdiction; ~**verfahren** appeal (appellate) procedure, proceeding in error; ~**weg erschöpfen** to exhaust the remedies; ~**zulassung** writ of review.
Rechtsnachfolge subrogation, *(Erbrecht)* [legal] succession, succession in title, devolution upon death;
auf Leibeserben beschränkte ~ general tail;
~ **durch Erbgang** devolution upon death (of inheritance, *US*);
~**klausel** subrogation clause.
Rechts|nachfolger assign, assignee, cessionary, successor in title, *(Erbrecht)* legal (personal) representative, *(pl.)* heirs and assigns; ~**nachteil** legal detriment (prejudice, disadvantage); ~**nachweis** proof of a right; ~**norm** legal rule, rule of law; **geltende** ~**normen** law of the land; **neue** ~**normen zur Anwendung bringen** to apply a new legal standard; ~**objekt** chose in action; ~**opposition** right-wing opposition; ~**ordnung** legal system.
rechtsorientiert right-wing.
Rechts|partei right-wing party; ~**persönlichkeit** legal entity (personality), body corporate; ~**persönlichkeit haben** to be a subject of law (incorporated); ~**persönlichkeitsverleihung** franchise of corporation *(US)*.
Rechtspflege judicial system, administration of justice, judicature;
völkerrechtliche ~ international justice;
~ **ausüben** to dispense (administer) justice; **in den Gang der** ~ **eingreifen** to impede the course of justice.
Rechtspfleger master in chancery (at common law, *Br.*);
~ **einer Hinterlegungsstelle** receiver.
Rechtspflicht legal obligation (duty), judicial duty;
ohne Anerkennung einer ~ without prejudice;
gesetzliche ~ statutory obligation.
Rechts|philosophie philosophy of law; ~**politik** policy of the law; ~**politiker** rightist; ~**position** legal situation (status); ~**position erlangen** to acquire legal status; **bessere** ~**position haben** to have firmer legal ground; ~**praktikant** articled clerk; ~**praxis** practice of the courts.
Rechtsprechung administration of justice, jurisdiction, judicature;
die ~ **betreffend** jurisdictional; **nach geltender** ~ stare decisis; **abweichende** ~ prospective ruling *(US)*; **ausländische** ~ foreign jurisdiction; **höchstrichterliche** ~ supreme court practice; **ständige** ~ judicial declaration of law, established practice, practice (holding) of the courts;
~ **der Berufsinstanz** appellate jurisdiction; ~ **zu einem Fall** precedents of a case.
Rechts|presse rightist press; ~**prinzip** legal principle; ~**punkte festsetzen** to settle points of law; ~**quelle** source of the law; ~**quellen** books of authority; ~**radikaler** rightist, extreme right-winger, high tory *(Br.)*; ~**rat erteilen** to render legal advice; ~**reform** law reform; ~**regierung** right-wing government; **kräftigen** ~**ruck machen** to swing sharply to the right.
Rechtssache action, cause, legal (court) case, lawsuit, controversy, judicial (law) business;
anhängige ~ pending case; **nicht streitige** ~ noncontentious business;
~ **gütlich erledigen** to settle a lawsuit amicably; ~ **führen (vertreten)** to be counsel in a case *(Br.)*.
Rechts|satz legal rule; **allgemein anerkannter** ~**satz** settled law; ~**satz der Auslegung gegen den Urkundenaussteller** contra proferentem rule; ~**schein** colo(u)r of law; ~**scheinanspruch** colo(u)rable title; ~**scheinvollmacht** estoppel by representation, agency by estoppel; ~**schlüsse ziehen** to make submissions to the law.
rechtsschöpferische Entscheidung lawmaking decision.
Rechtsschöpfung lawmaking;
~ **durch die Gerichte** judicial legislation.
Rechtsschutz legal aid *(Br.)* (protection), free legal aid *(US)*;
gewerblicher ~ protection of inventions; **vorläufiger** ~ interlocutory relief;
~**anerkennung nur für redliche Kläger** unclean hands principle; ~**begehren** general relief, prayer of process; ~**verein** legal-aid society *(Br.)*, Civil Liberties Union *(US)*; ~**versagung** nonenforceability; ~**versicherung** legal protection insurance.
Rechts|sicherheit law and order; ~**sprache** law (legal) language, legal parlance; ~**spruch** legal (judicial) decision, judgment, adjudication, award, sentence; ~**staat** constitutional state.
rechtsstaatlich constitutional.

Rechts|staatlichkeit rule of law, maintenance of law and order; **für ~staatlichkeit eintreten** to grow more on the side of law and order; **~standpunkt** legal viewpoint; **~status** legal status; **~statut** statute.

rechtsstehend right-wing.

Rechts|stehender right-winger; **~stellung** position in law, legal position (status); **~stellung einnehmen** to succeed to s. one's rights.

Rechtsstreit suit (dispute) at law, lawsuit *(US)*, process, action, cause, court litigation, controversy, contest, plea;
anhängiger ~ pending action (lawsuit); **bürgerlicher ~** civil action (case), common-law action; **schwebender ~** pending action;
~ vor dem Handelsgericht [etwa] commercial cause;
einem ~ beitreten to intervene in an action, to join a lawsuit; **sich in einen üblen ~ einlassen** to engage in a dishonest lawsuit; **~ fortsetzen** to maintain a suit; **~ führen** to litigate; **identisch mit einem früheren ~ sein** to be on all fours; **in einen ~ verwickelt sein** to be involved in a lawsuit; **zu den Kosten eines ~s verurteilt werden** to be ordered (condemned) to pay the costs.

Rechtsstreitigkeit suit [at law], lawsuit *(US)*, justifiable controversy, cause, case, action;
~en cases and controversies;
bürgerliche ~ civil dispute, civil (common-law) action, common plea; **dingliche ~** proceeding in rem.

Rechts|streitverweisung remover; **~student** law student, jurist *(Br.)*; **~studium** study for the bar, law studies; **~studium abbrechen** to leave off studying law; **~subjekt** legal subject; **~system** legal (judicial) system, system of justice; **~tendenz** drift towards the right.

Rechtstitel [legal] title, judicial entitlement, *(Eigentumstitel)* title deed;
absoluter ~ just title; **besserer ~** elder title; **einwandfreier ~** good (perfect, sound) title; **formell nicht einwandfreier ~** title defective in form; **mangelhafter ~** unmarketable title; **nicht originärer ~** derivative title; **unangreifbarer ~** clear (good) title; **urkundlicher ~** muniments, clear title of record; **vollgültiger ~** marketable (merchantable, limitation) title; **zweifelhafter ~** doubtful title;
~überprüfung title search; **~versicherung** title insurance *(US)*; **~versicherungsgesellschaft** title company *(US)*; **~versicherungspolice** title guarantee policy.

Rechts|tod civil death *(US)*; **~träger** legal entity.

Rechtsübergang subrogation, assignment, *(im Erbwege)* devolution of title;
gesetzlicher ~ transmission by operation of law, subrogation arising from statute; **ungültiger ~** erroneous assignment;
~ kraft Gesetzes legal subrogation; **~ auf den Versicherer** subrogation for the benefit of the insurer.

Rechtsübergangsklausel subrogation clause.

Rechtsübertragung transmission (assignment, subrogation) of a right;
gesetzliche ~ transfer by operation of law, legal subrogation.

rechts|unerheblich irrelevant; **~unfähig** incapable, [legally] disabled; **~unfähig machen** to disable.

Rechtsunfähigkeit legal disability (incapacity, incapability).

rechtsungültig invalid, void, insufficient, illegal;
~ machen to annul; **~ sein** to lie under a disability.

Rechts|ungültigkeit invalidity, illegality; **~unkenntnisse vorschützen** to plead ignorance of the law.

rechtsunkundig not versed in law.

Rechts|unsicherheit legal uncertainty; **~unterricht nach Präzedenzfällen** case system.

rechtsunwirksam ineffective, invalid, without (of no) legal force, *(nichtig)* [null and] void;
~ machen to outlaw, to invalidate, to annul, to nullify.

Rechts|unwirksamkeit ineffectiveness, invalidity, *(Nichtigkeit)* voidness; **~urkunde** legal document.

rechtsverbindlich obligatory, legally binding, authorized;
für alle Gläubiger ~ binding upon all creditors;
~ für j. sein to be binding upon s. o.

Rechts|verbindlichkeit legal force; **~verdreher** prevaricator, pettifogging shyster *(US)*, pettifogger; **~verdrehung** prevarication, pettifoggery, chicanery, strain of the law; **mit ~verdrehungen arbeiten** to pettifog; **~vereinheitlichung** unification of law.

Rechtsverfahren legal process, lawsuit *(US)*, action, claim procedure, course of law;
ordnungsgemäßes ~ due process of law; **summarisches ~** summary proceeding, Halifax law.

Rechts|verfahrensregeln forms of legal procedure; **~verfassung** judiciary; **~verfolgung** prosecution of an action; **böswillige ~verfolgung** malicious prosecution; **~vergleich** juridical comparison; **~vergleichung** comparitive jurisprudence; **~verhältnis** legal relationship; **vertragsähnliches ~verhältnis** quasi-contractual relationship; **~verhältnis begründen** to create legal relations; **~verkehr** legal relations, *(Straßenordnung)* right-hand traffic; **~verleihung** granting of a right; **~verletzer** infringer, lawbreaker; **~verletzung** legal offence, violation of a law, lawbreaking, legal injury, infringement of a right, transgression; **mittelbare ~verletzung** relative injury; **~verlust** loss (forfeiture) of a right; **~verluste eines Konkursschuldners** disqualifications of a bankrupt; **~verlust durch Zeitablauf** extinctive prescription.

Rechtsvermutung general presumption of law, legal presumption (fiction);
unwiderlegbare ~ conclusive (irrebuttable) presumption; **widerlegbare ~** rebuttable (refutable, inconclusive) presumption.

Rechts|verordnung decree law, statutory order (instrument) *(Br.)*; **~verpflichtung** legal obligation; **gesetzliche ~verpflichtung** privity in law; **~vertreter** law agent, counsel, legal representative, proxy, attorney [in fact]; **~verweigerung** refusal of justice; **~verwirkung** forfeiture of a right; **~verzicht** disclaimer (release, relinquishment, renunciation, resignation, waiver) of a right; **~verzicht auf eine Konkursvorzugsstellung** surrender of a preference; **~vorbehalt** reservation, reserve of right, saving; **~vorgang** legal matter, judicial business; **~vorgänger** predecessor in interest (title).

Rechtsvorschrift rule of law, legislative (statutory) provision;
aufgehobene ~en enactments repealed; **geltende ~en** legislation in force;
innerstaatliche ~en angleichen *(EG)* to approximate municipal laws.

Rechts|vorteil legal benefit, benefit of the law; **~vortrag** legal argument.

Rechtsweg process of law;
auf dem ordentlichen ~ in due course of law, by legal process; **unter Ausschluß des ~es** admitting of no legal appeal;
~ ausschließen to bar legal proceedings, to oust the jurisdiction of a court; **~ beschreiten** to go (have recourse) to law, to take legal action; **Zahlungen auf dem ~e betreiben** to enforce payment by legal proceedings; **seine Ansprüche auf dem ~ verfolgen** to enforce one's claims by suit; **~ zulassen** to allow legal action.

Rechtswesen judicial (legal) system.

rechtswidrig illegal, illicit, unlawful, contrary to law;
~e Handlung illegal (tortious, unlawful) act.

Rechtswidrigkeit wrong, illegality, unlawfulness.

rechtswirksam valid, operative, legally effective, *(Urteil)* final, of legal force.

Rechtswirksamkeit validity, legal force.

Rechtswirkung legal effect;
ohne ~ invalid;
~en eines Konkurses beilegen to attach the incidents of a bankruptcy case; **einem Gesetz ~ geben** to sign a bill into law.

Rechtswissenschaft jurisprudence, science of law;
vergleichende ~ comparative jurisprudence;
~ studieren to read (study) law, to study (read) for the bar.

rechtswissenschaftlich jurisprudential;
~e Fakultät faculty of law.

Rechtswohltat benefit of the law;
~ der Inventarerrichtung benefit of inventory; **~ des Zweifels** benefit of the doubt.

Rechts|wörterbuch legal dictionary (lexicon); **~zug** legal process; **~zuständigkeit** competence.

rechtzeitig in [good, due] time, in good term, in due course, prompt, at the right time, early, in due course, well-timed;
~ avisieren to advise in due course;
~e Kündigung legal notice to quit.

Redakteur editor;
festangestellter ~ full-time editor; **juristischer ~** legal editor; **stellvertretender ~** subeditor; **verantwortlicher ~** responsible (managing) editor; **für den Anzeigenteil verantwortlicher ~** publicity editor; **zweiter ~** sub-editor, copyreader *(US)*;
~ des Börsenteils city editor *(Br.)*; **~ vom Dienst** news desk; **~ des kulturellen Teils** cultural editor; **~ des lokalen Teils** local (city, *US*) editor; **~ des Wirtschaftsteils** city *(Br.)* (financial, *US*) editor.

Redaktion editorial staff (board, management), editors, desk *(US)*, *(Büroräume)* editorial department (office, bureau),

editor's office, *(Fassung)* editing, wording, drafting, *(Tätigkeit)* editing, editorship, editorial work;
unter der ~ **von** under the editorship of;
~ **einer Zeitung** editorial conduct of a newpaper;
einer ~ **angehören** to be on [the staff of] a newspaper.
redaktionell editorial;
~ **Stellung nehmen** to editorialize, to write (run) an editorial; ~ **aufgemachte Anzeige** editorial advertisement; ~**e Aufbereitung** editorial preparation; ~**er Aufgabenbereich** editorial duties; ~**e Durchsicht** editorial preparation; ~**e Freiheiten** editorial freedom; ~**er Inhalt** editorial content; ~**er Kommentar** editorial comment; ~**e Leitung** editorship; ~**e Meinungsäußerung** editorial opinion; ~**en Nachwuchs anwerben** to hire editorial talents; ~**er Teil** reading matter, editorial space (part); ~**e Tendenz** editorial policies; ~**er Text** editorial matter; ~**e Unterstützung** editorial assistance; ~ **aufgemachte Werbung** editorialized advertisement.
Redaktions|abteilung editorial department; ~**arbeit** editorial work; ~**assistent** assistant editor; ~**ausschuß** draft (drafting) committee; ~**bote** copy boy; ~**büro** editorial board (bureau), editorial (editor's) office; ~**entwurf** tentative editorial outline; ~**gemeinschaft** joint editorial board; ~**konferenz** editorial conference; ~**leitung** editorial management; ~**mitarbeiter** editorial worker; ~**mitglied** staff writer (member), staffer, subeditor, rewrite (desk, *US*) man; **weitverzweigtes** ~**netz** editorial network; ~**politik** editorial policies; ~**räume** editorial rooms.
Redaktionsschluß press day (date), editorial close (closing), deadline *(US)*;
vor ~ before going to press.
Redaktions|stab editorial unit (staff), staff of a newspaper, editors; **im** ~**stab sein** to be on the staff of a newspaper; ~**tätigkeit** editing (editorial) work; ~**tisch** copy desk; ~**ziel** editorial object.
Rede *(Ansprache)* address, *(Redeweise)* language, *(Vortrag)* speech, lecture;
am Ende seiner ~ at the conclusion of one's speech; **in freier** ~ viva voce, off the cuff *(US)*; **in gewöhnlicher** ~ in common parlance;
in ~ **stehende Personen** persons in question;
auf Band aufgenommene ~ canned speech; **ausgezeichnete** ~ capital speech *(coll.)*; **beeindruckende** ~ telling speech; **bombastische** ~ high-flown speech; **chauvinistische** ~ chauvinistic *(Br.)* (spread-eagle, *US*) speech; **deplazierte** ~ inappropriate speech; **direkte** ~ direct discourse; **einschläfernde** ~ narcotic speech; **energische** ~ trenchant speech; **erfolgreiche** ~ effective speech; **erste** ~ maiden speech; **fließende** ~ eloquent address; **nicht gehaltene** ~ undelivered speech; **gepfefferte** ~ good talking-to; **grundlegende (grundsätzliche)** ~ platform (keynote) speech **herausfordernde** ~**n** provoking speeches; **indirekte** ~ indirect speech; **inhaltlose** ~ flat speech; **katastrophale** ~ unlucky speech; **hübsche kleine** ~ neat little speech; **langatmige** ~ screed; **leere** ~**n** empty phrases; **leidenschaftliche** ~ harangue; **miserable** ~ miserable speech; **mitreißende** ~ stirring speech; **programmatische** ~ keynote address; **scharfe** ~ salt speech; **schwülstige** ~ bombastic (high-flown) speech; **überschwengliche** ~ rhapsody; **umstrittene** ~ controversial speech; **unflätige** ~**n** dirt, obscene words; **ungebundene** ~ prose; **völlig unvorbereitete** ~ offhand speech; ~ **und Gegenrede** address and rejoinder, dialogue; ~ **zur Lage der Nationen** Union message *(US)*; ~ **nach Tisch** postprandial (after-dinner) speech;
~ **abkürzen** to curtail a speech; **seine** ~ **abschließen** to end off one's speech; ~ **abstimmen auf** to pitch a speech on; ~ **abstottern** to fluff one's lines *(Br., sl.)*; ~ **aufbauschen** to pad a speech; **jds.** ~ **ungünstig aufnehmen** to give s. one's speech a hostile reception; ~ **aufsetzen** to frame a speech; ~ **ausarbeiten** to make up a speech; **über eine** ~ **in zusammenfassender Form berichten** to report a speech; **seine** ~ **beschließen** to wind up one's speech; ~ **zu einem Abschluß bringen** to round off a sentence (by saying); **in seine** ~ **Verse einflechten** to tag one's speech with verses; **sich zu einer** ~ **entschließen** to nerve o. s. to make a speech; ~ **entwerfen** to draft a speech; **Versammlung durch seine** ~ **fesseln** to spellbind one's audience, to hold the floor of the house; **in seiner** ~ **fortfahren** to proceed with one's speech; **große** ~**n führen** to talk big (tall); **respektlose** ~**n führen** to speak disrespectfully; **schlüpfrige** ~**n führen** to be somewhat free in one's conversation; **wirre** ~**n führen** to talk wild; ~ **halten** to make (deliver) a speech, to give an address, to declaim; **bombastische** ~ **halten** to harangue; **kurze** ~ **halten** to deliver a short address; **lange** ~ **halten** to spiel *(US sl.)*; **öffentliche** ~ **halten** *(Politiker)* to go on the stump *(US)*; **patriotische** ~ **halten** to spread-eagle; ~ **stehend halten** to be on one's legs; ~ **herunterrasseln** to run off a speech; ~ **mitstenografieren** to take down a speech in shorthand; ~ **schwingen** to hold forth; **kaum der** ~ **wert sein** to be hardly worth mentioning; **zu einer** ~ **verdonnert worden sein** to have been let in for a speech; **in einer** ~ **steckenbleiben** to get stuck in the middle of a speech; **in** ~ **stehen** to be under discussion; ~ **und Antwort für etw. stehen** to answer (give a clear accounting) for s. th.; **zur** ~ **stellen** to take to task, to call to account; ~ **durch Rundfunk übertragen** to broadcast a speech; **jds.** ~ **unterbrechen** to interrupt s. o. in his speech; ~ **mit Beifallsrufen unterbrechen** to punctuate a speech with cheers; ~ **verfassen** to compose a speech; ~ **mit Humor würzen** to needle a speech with humo(u)r.
rede- und stimmberechtigt sein to be entitled to vote and to speak.
Rede|duell battle of words; **erbittertes** ~**duell** slanging match; **lautstarkes** ~**duell** shouting match; ~**duell austragen** to passage; ~**entwurf** draft for a speech; ~**floskeln** flowers of speech; ~**fluß** ceaseless flow of talk, flow of words; **jds.** ~**fluß stoppen** to dam up the torrent of s. one's eloquence; **direkte** ~**form** quotation form.
Redefreiheit liberty (freedom) of speech;
~ **und Versammlungsfreiheit** freedom of expression and assembly;
~ **behindern** to suppress freedom of speech; ~ **beschränken** to lay an embargo on free speech; ~ **unterdrücken** to throttle free speech.
Redegabe eloquence.
redegewandt eloquent;
~ **sein** to be a good speaker, to have a silver tongue.
Rede|gewandtheit command of language, eloquence, facility in speaking; ~**kunst** rhetoric, speaking.
reden to speak, to talk;
heute ganz anders ~ to have changed one's tune today; **Blech** ~ *(fam.)* to talk rubbish; **Böses von j.** ~ to speak ill of s. o.; **emphatisch** ~ to thump the cushion; **fesselnd** ~ to hold spellbound; **j. ins Gewissen** ~ to appeal to s. one's conscience; **in Grund und Boden** ~ to outtalk; **j. in Grund und Boden** ~ to talk one's head off to s. o., to talk the hind leg off a donkey *(fam.)*; **Kohl** ~ to talk through one's hat; **sich um Kopf und Kragen** ~ to talk away one's life; **frei von der Leber weg** ~ not to put too fine an edge upon it; **wie ein Maschinengewehr** ~ to have a ready flow of language; **zur Menge** ~ to harangue the mob; **nicht mehr miteinander** ~ not to be on speaking terms any longer; **sich den Mund fusselig** ~ *(fam.)* to talk one's head off; **jem. nach dem Munde** ~ to chime in with s. o.; **offen** ~ to be outspoken, to speak one's mind; **ganz offen mit jem. über etw.** ~ to be quite plain with s. o., to tackle s. o. about a matter; **öffentlich** ~ to speak in public; **über Politik** ~ to talk politics; **zur Sache** ~ to talk to the purpose; **aus Schüchternheit nicht** ~ to have lost one's tongue; **sich etw. von der Seele** ~ to get s. th. off one's chest, to make a clean breast of it; **keine Silbe** ~ to speak not a word; **unter den Tisch** ~ to talk down; **umsonst** ~ to waste one's breath; **zu leeren Wänden** ~ to preach to deaf ears; **wie ein Wasserfall** ~ to talk nineteen to the dozen; **in den Wind** ~ to spend one's breath, to talk to the wind;
~**, wie einem der Schnabel gewachsen ist** to speak one's mind; **sich gern** ~ **hören** to like to hear o. s. talk; **mit sich** ~ **lassen** to be open to conviction; **viel von sich** ~ **machen** to give rise to much comment, to be very much in the news; **volksnah zu** ~ **verstehen** to be at home with idioms;
sonderbare Art zu ~ queer way of talking.
Redensart expression, phrase, idiom, saying;
abgedroschene ~**en** well-worn phrases; **alltägliche** ~ common expression; **bloße** ~ mere figure of speech; **feste** ~ stock phrase, tag line; **leere** ~**en** blarney; **nichtssagende** ~**en** empty phrases, a few nothings; **stehende** ~ byword, tag line, stock phrase.
Rede|recht right to speak, floor *(US)*; **sein** ~**recht mißbrauchen** to hog the floor *(US sl.)*; ~**ritis haben** to be in a talkative mood; ~**schlacht** battle of words; ~**schwall** torrent of words, word flow; ~**tempo** speech tempo; ~**unterricht** elocution lessons; ~**verbindung** context; ~**verbot auferlegen** to put to silence; ~**verpflichtung** speaking engagement; ~**versuch** attempt to speak, parlance.
Redeweise tongue, talk, mode of speaking;
unanständige ~ improper language; **unparlamentarische** ~ unparliamentary language; **unverblümte** ~ plain talk; **zweideutige** ~ double talk;
Heuchler an seiner ~ **erkennen** to know a hypocrite by his tongue.

Redewendung figure of speech, locution, phrase;
bevorzugte ~ favo(u)rite phrase; **feststehende ~en** set phrases; **idiomatische** ~ idiom; **schwülstige** ~ flourish; **veraltete** ~ obsoletism;
idiomatische ~en gebrauchen to express o. s. idiomatically.
Redezeit debating time;
~ **beschränken** to limit the time allotted to each speaker; **seine ~ einhalten** to keep to alloted time; ~ **von vornherein festlegen** to fix the limit of the debate beforehand; ~ **mißbrauchen** to hog the floor *(US)*; ~ **überschreiten** to overrun the allotted time.
redigieren to edit, *(Entwurf)* to draw up, *(überarbeiten)* to revise, to copyread *(US)*.
redigiert edited;
gut ~ well-edited; **nicht** ~ inedited.
Redigierung drafting, editing.
Rediskont rediscount;
~antrag application for rediscount.
rediskontfähig eligible for rediscount, rediscountable.
Rediskont|fähigkeit rediscount facility, eligibility for rediscount **unbeschränkte ~fazilitäten in Anspruch nehmen** to borrow freely at the discount window *(US)*.
rediskontierbar rediscountable.
rediskontieren to rediscount.
Rediskontierung rediscounting;
~ **ablehnen** to decline to lend at the discount window.
Rediskont|kontingent rediscount quota; **~kontingente zur Verfügung stellen** to act as a lender of last resort; **~kredit** rediscount credit; **~linie, ~plafond** rediscount line *(US)* (limit, *Br.*); **~möglichkeiten** rediscount facilities; **~politik** rediscount policy; **~richtlinien** eligibility rule; **~satz** rediscount rate; **~zusage** rediscount promise.
redlich honest, good, aboveboard, on the square *(coll.)*, with clean hands, white *(US coll.)*;
sich ~ durch das Leben schlagen to make an honest living; **Strafe ~ verdienen** to thoroughly deserve a punishment;
~e Leute honest folk; **sich ~e Mühe geben** to take great pains.
Redlichkeit probity, fidelity, truth, good faith, uprightness.
Redlichkeitserklärung, eidliche oath of calumny.
Redner speaker, talker, debater, discourser, ventilator;
aufgeblasener ~ spread-eagle orator; **faszinierender** ~ finished (luminous) speaker, stump orator *(US)*, spellbinder *(US)*; **geistreicher** ~ smart speaker; **gewandter** ~ fluent speaker; **glänzender** ~ brilliant speaker; **öffentlicher**~ platformer, stump orator *(US)*, stumper *(US)*; **schlechter** ~ poor orator (talker); **wirkungsloser** ~ ineffective speaker;
~ **auf politischen Versammlungen** platform speaker, stump orator *(US)*, soapbox orator *(US sl.)*;
dem ~ beipflichten to concur with the speaker; ~ **aus dem Konzept bringen** to throw out an orator; ~ **durch Scharren zum Schweigen bringen** to scrape down a speaker; **Aufmerksamkeit des ~s erlangen** to catch the speaker's eye; **keine Erfahrung als öffentlicher ~ haben** to be unaccustomed to speaking in public; **sich für einen guten ~ halten** to fancy o. s. as a speaker; ~ **niederschreien** to howl down a speaker; **sich um den ~ scharen** to pack round the speaker; **sich als ~ aufgeführt sehen** to see o. s. down for a speech; **zugkräftiger ~ auf politischen Versammlungen sein** to be a good draw at political meetings; **als ~ zugelassen sein** to have the floor; ~ **unterbrechen** to catch up (stop) a speaker;
~begabung faculty of speech.
Rednerbühne platform, tribune, rostrum, hustings, speaker's stand;
improvisierte ~ soapbox *(sl.)*;
~ **in einer Massenveranstaltung** mass-media platform;
~ **besteigen** to go up to the rostrum, to take the floor; **auf eine ~ stellen** to platform.
Redner|folge order of speech (speaking); **~gabe** faculty of speech.
rednerisch rhetorical, oratorical;
~e Glanzleistung vollbringen to rise to oratorical height.
Redner|kurs speech course; **~liste** list of speakers; **j. in die ~liste eintragen** to put s. one's name on the list of speakers; **auf der ~liste stehen** to be inscribed as a speaker; **~pult** [speaker's] desk; **von einem improvisierten ~pult sprechen** to soapbox *(sl.)*; **~schlacht** round of oratory, *(auf Wahlveranstaltungen)* soapbox campaign *(US sl.)*; **~stuhl** chair; **~tribüne** tribune, platform, rostrum, hustings; **~tribüne besteigen** to go up to the rostrum; **auf eine ~tribüne stellen** to platform.
redselig talkative, loquacious.
reduzierbar reducible, diminishable.
reduzieren to reduce, to diminish, to cut, to abate, to shorten;
Ausgaben ~ to reduce (cut one's) expenses; **Brüche auf einen gemeinsamen Nenner** ~ to reduce fractions to a common denominator; **Forderung** ~ to cut a claim; **Preise um die Hälfte** ~ to reduce prices by half; **seine Stabskräfte** ~ to trim one's staff; **Unkosten drastisch** ~ to slash costs.
reduziert curtate;
anteilmäßig ~ scaled down;
~e Preise reduced prices.
Reduzierung reduction, cut, cutback *(US)*, diminution;
~ **auf ein Minimum** minimization.
Reede roads, roadstead;
auf der ~ at the roads;
geschlossene ~ safe (good) roads; **offene** ~ open roadstead;
auf der ~ ankern to remain off the harbo(u)r;
Schiff auf die ~ fahren to put out a vessel at the roads; **auf der ~ liegen** to lie (be) in (ride at) the roads.
Reeder shipowner, shipping operator, shipper, freighter, fitter out;
~ **und Befrachter** owner and charterer.
Reederei shipping business, freighting, *(Büro)* shipowner's office, *(Firma)* shipping company (firm, house, office, *Br.*);
~ **betreiben** to be in the shipping line;
leitender ~angestellter shipping executive; **~betrieb** shipping trade (interest); **~brief** certificate of registry; **~flagge** house (merchant) flag; **~geschäft** shipping interest; **~haftpflicht** liability of a shipowner; **~haftpflichtversicherung** protection and indemnity insurance; **~haftung** liability of a shipowner; **~versicherungsverein auf Gegenseitigkeit** ship-owner's club; **~vertrag** contract with the shipowner; **~vertreter** shipping agent.
reell *(angesehen)* respectable, *(anständig)* fair, fair-dealing, *(ehrlich)* honest, straight, *(finanziell gesund)* solid, *(vorsichtig)* conservative, *(Ware)* genuine, good, sound, *(Wert)* real, *(zuverlässig)* reliable;
~ **bedient werden** to get good value for one's money;
~es Angebot reasonable offer; **~e Bedienung** reliable service; **~e Firma** sound (solid) business firm; **~es Gewicht** full weight; **~es Muster** reliable sample; **~e Preise** fair (moderate, reasonable) prices; **~e Qualität** sound quality; **~e Ware** good articles; **~er Wert** actual (real) value.
Reexport re-export.
REFA-Studie time and motion study.
Refaktie tret, shrinkage, allowance for loss, breakage.
Referat lecture, paper, *(Abteilung)* department, division, *(Bericht)* report, *(Buch)* review;
~ **halten** to give (deliver) a lecture, to read a paper.
Referatsleiter head of a department.
Referendum plebiscite, referendum.
Referent referee, reporter, *(Behördenleiter)* department head, *(Kritiker)* reviewer, lecturer, *(Sachbearbeiter)* desk officer, *(Sachverständiger)* adviser, consultant, expert, *(Vortragender)* reader of a paper;
persönlicher ~ personal representative (aide), *(Minister)* private secretary;
~ **für freie Mitarbeiter** *(Werbeagentur)* art buyer.
Referentenentwurf draft bill.
Referenz reference, credentials, *(Auskunft)* information;
erstklassige ~en first-class references; **persönliche ~en** character reference;
~ **einer Bank** banker's reference;
~en angeben to quote (furnish) references; **j. als ~ angeben** to give s. o. (use s. one's name) as a reference; **jem. seinen letzten Arbeitgeber als ~ angeben** to give s. o. a reference to one's last employer; **über j. ~en einholen** to take up s. one's references; **gute ~en haben** to have good references, to bear high credentials; ~ **überprüfen** to follow up (track down, check) s. one's reference;
~jahr year reported on; **~menge** datum quantity; **~periode** period reported on; **~preis** posted price, *(EG)* reference price, *(Stahleinfuhren)* trigger price *(Br.)*; **~preissystem** trigger price system *(US)*; **~überprüfung** reference checking.
referieren to [make a] report, *(Vorlesung halten)* to give a lecture, to read a paper;
über den Stand der Verhandlungen ~ to report on the stage negotiations have reached.
refinanzieren to refinance.
Refinanzierung refinancing;
~ **bei der Landeszentralbank** access to the discount window *(US)*; ~ **von Teilzahlungswechseln** rediscount of instal(l)ment finance bills;
~ **sicherstellen** to secure refinancing.

Refinanzierungs|aufgabe refinancing task; ~**gesellschaft** refinancing agency; ~**kosten** refinancing costs; ~**kredit** *(Landeszentralbank)* rediscount credit; ~**limit** rediscount quota; ~**möglichkeiten durch die Bundesnotenbank** lender of last resort, federal borrowing requirements *(US)*; **seine ~möglichkeiten bei der Landeszentralbank verlieren** to lose access to the discount window *(US)*; ~**satz** federal borrowing rate *(US)*; ~**system** refinancing plan; ~**zusage** refinancing arrangement.
Reflation reflation.
Reflations|maßnahmen reflationary measures; ~**runde** reflationary round.
Reflektant prospective (potential, intending) buyer, prospect *(US)*, *(auf eine Stellung)* prospective candidate;
ernsthafte (ernstliche) ~en genuine purchasers, serious inquirers.
reflektieren to reflect, *(interessiert sein)* to intend to purchase, to be interested;
ernsthaft ~ to have in view, to mean business *(fam.)*; **steigende Nachfrage** ~ to show the rising demand; **auf einen Posten** ~ to have one's eye on a position.
Reform reform;
durchgreifende ~ sweeping reform; **einschneidende** ~ trenchant reform; **längst fällige** ~ overdue reform;
~ **der Abschreibungsrichtlinien (Abschreibungssätze)** depreciation reform; ~**en des Gesetzgebers** legislative reforms; ~ **an Haupt und Gliedern** root-and-branch reform; ~ **des Kommunalwesens** municipal reform; ~ **des Postwesens** post office reform; ~ **der Sozialversicherung** social security reform *(US)*; ~ **des Sozialwesens** welfare reform;
auf ~en brennen to be hot for reforms; ~ **der Verwaltung durchführen** to reform administration; ~**en einführen** to inaugurate reforms; ~**en einleiten** to initiate (inaugurate) a reform; **für soziale ~en eintreten** to agitate for social reforms; **gegen ~en eingestellt sein** to work against reform; **durchgreifende ~en verlangen** to demand sweeping reforms;
~**bestrebungen** reform efforts; ~**bewegung** reform movement; ~**bewegung ins Leben rufen** to originate a reform.
reformfeindlich hostile to reform.
Reform|flügel reform wing; ~**gesetz** reform act *(Br.)*; ~**haus** health food store.
reformieren to reform.
Reformierung reformation.
Reformismus reform.
Reform|kleidung rational dress; ~**maßnahmen** reformatory measures; ~**paket** reform package; **überzeugter ~politiker sein** to be all out for reform; ~**vorhaben** intended reform.
Regal royalty, royal prerogative, Royal Privilege, *(Gestell)* storage rack, stack *(US)*, shelf, stand;
unterstes ~ bottom shelf;
~ **mit Schreib- und Korrespondenzunterlagen** stationery cupboard;
~**e ausräumen** to clear from the shelves; **Buch aufs ~ stellen** to place a book on the shelf;
~**fläche** amount of shelf space; ~**großhändler** rack jobber; ~**schild** shelf label; ~**streifen** shelf strip.
rege active, bustling, busy;
geistig ~ sein to be alert;
~**n Absatz finden** to sell very well; ~ **Anteilnahme** keen concern; ~ **Beteiligung** good attendance; ~**r Briefwechsel** lively correspondence; ~ **Diskussion** lively discussion; ~ **Geschäftigkeit** great hustle and bustle; ~**s gesellschaftliches Leben** busy social life; ~ **Nachfrage** brisk (active) demand; ~ **Phantasie** lively imagination; ~ **Unterhaltung** animated conversation; ~**r Verkehr** busy traffic; ~ **Wahlbeteiligung** good turnout at the polls.
Regel rule, canon, precept, routine, *(Norm)* norm, standard, *(Vorschrift)* observance;
in der ~ as a rule, ordinarily; **nach der** ~ according to the rules; **unbedingt einzuhaltende ~n** hard and fast rules; **feststehende** ~ fixed (standing) rule; **ausnahmslos geltende** ~ universal rule; **starre ~n** rigid rules; **unabänderliche** ~ standing rule; unumstößliche ~ iron-clad rule;
~**n für die Auslegung handelsüblicher Vertragsformeln** incoterms; ~**n einer ordnungsgemäßen Bewirtschaftung** rules of good husbandry *(Br.)*; ~**n der gesetzlichen Erbfolge** canons of descent; ~**n über das Führen von Telefongesprächen** telephone regulations; ~**n der Rechtschreibung** rules of orthography; ~**n des Seerechts** sealaws;
~ **anwenden** to apply a rule; ~ **aufstellen** to state (establish, make) a rule; **allgemein gültige ~n aufstellen** to lay down general rules; ~ **beachten** to observe a rule; ~**n befolgen** to adhere to rules; **j. nach allen ~n der Kunst betrügen** to jockey s. o. out of his money; ~ **festlegen** to state a rule; **sich an die ~n halten** to stick to the rules; **etw. zur ~ werden lassen** to make routine of s. th.; **etw. zur festen ~ machen** always to make s. th. one's policy; **etw. nach allen ~n der Kunst machen** to do s. th. in a workmanlike manner; **die ~ sein** to be routine; **jem. zur ~ geworden sein** to have become a habit with s. o.; ~ **verletzen** to break a rule; **gegen eine ~ verstoßen** to transgress a rule; **zur ~ werden** to become the rule;
die Ausnahme bestätigt die ~ the exception proves the rule;
~**abweichung** deviation from the rules; ~**anwendung** application of a rule, operation of rule; ~**ausführung** standard model; ~**fall** normal case; **im ~fall** normally; ~**leistung** minimum benefit.
regellos *(Markt)* irregular, unsettled;
~**e Anordnung** irregular arrangement; **in ~er Flucht** in a stampede; ~**es Leben führen** to lead a disorderly life.
regelmäßig regular, frequent, orderly, *(Markt)* settled;
~ **tun** to make it a rule;
~**e Beschäftigungen** regular occupation; ~**e Bestandteile** essential elements; ~**er Besucher** regular customer; ~**es Einkommen** regular (assured) income; ~**es Muster** geometric pattern; ~**e Wahlen** regular election; ~ **wiederkehrende Zahlungen** regular payments; **in ~en Zeitabständen** periodically, at regular intervals.
Regelmäßigkeit regularity.
regeln to regulate, to regularize, to order, *(erledigen)* to arrange, to settle;
es mit jem. ~ to fix it up with s. o.; **Angelegenheit** ~ to wind up an affair; **seine Angelegenheiten** ~ to arrange one's business affairs; **außergerichtlich** ~ to settle out of court; **endgültig** ~ to clinch; **mit dem Finanzamt** ~ to sort out at the tax office *(coll.)*; **seine Finanzen** ~ to adjust one's finances, to put one's financial affairs in order; **Gang einer Maschine** ~ to regulate the working of a machine; **gütlich (in Güte)** ~ to settle amicably, to compound; **etw. intern** ~ to settle s. th. privately; **Lautstärke** ~ to control the volume; **Nachlaß** ~ to wind up an estate *(Br.)*; **Rechnung** ~ to meet (pay) a bill; **seine Schulden** ~ to settle one's debts; **sich von selbst** ~ to take care of itself; **sich selbsttätig** ~ to adjust itself automatically; **durch Vergleich** ~ to settle by compromise; **Verkehr** ~ to direct (control, regulate) the traffic; **vertraglich** ~ to stipulate in writing.
Regelnachweis *(auf Vordruck)* records.
regelnd regulatory.
regelrecht regular, normal, *(korrekt)* proper, correct;
~ **unverschämt** downright rude.
Regel|sätze *(Unterhalt)* relief standards; ~**spannung** control voltage; ~**spur** *(Eisenbahn)* normal gauge.
Regelung regulation, control, *(Erledigung)* settlement, arrangement, adjustment, *(von Gehältern)* determination, *(Geschäftsabwicklung)* winding up, *(Richtlinie)* ruling, *(Vertragsbestimmungen)* provision;
abweichende ~ regulation to the contrary; **außergerichtliche** ~ arrangement out of court; **befriedigende** ~ acceptable settlement; **bundesgesetzliche** ~ regulation under federal law; **devisenpolitische** ~ foreign-exchange regulation; **einstweilige** ~ interim solution; **endgültige** ~ clinch; **friedensvertragliche** ~ peace settlement; **zur Abwendung der Produzentenhaftung getroffene** ~ product liability settlement; **gütliche** ~ private settlement, amicable composition; **interne** ~ internal arrangements; **frei vereinbarte schiedsgerichtliche** ~ voluntary arbitration; **vergleichsweise** ~ compromise; **vertragliche** ~ contract settlement; **vollständige** ~ overall settlement; **vorläufige** ~ provisional arrangement (regulation);
~ **des Absatzwesens** marketing control; ~ **von Angelegenheiten** regulation of affairs; ~ **des Fußgängerverkehrs** pedestrian-crossing regulation; ~ **der Grenzfrage** settlement of the border question; **großzügige** ~ **des Heimaturlaubs** generous arrangement for home leave; ~ **eines Kontos** regulation of an account; ~ **von Rechtsstreitigkeiten** settlement of disputes; ~ **im Fall von Sozialabfindungen** redundancy payments scheme *(Br.)*; **endgültige** ~ **einer Streitigkeit** final concord *(Br.)*; **vergleichsweise** ~ **vor Urteilsverkündung** settlement before judgment; ~ **des Verkehrs** traffic control (regulation, duty); ~ **eines Versicherungsfalles** claim settlement; ~ **des Zahlungsverkehrs** regulation of payments;
~ **erzielen** to get a settlement; **gütliche ~ herbeiführen** to reach an amicable settlement; **vergleichsweise ~ treffen** to make a composition; **einer vergleichsweisen ~ zustimmen** to agree to a compromise.
Regel|ventil regulating valve; ~**vorschriften** regulations.

regelwidrig abnormal, contrary to the rules (regulations), irregular, informal;
für ~ erklären to rule s. th. out of order.
Regelwidrigkeit abnormality, irregularity.
Regen, bei strömendem in the pouring rain; **vom ~ in die Traufe** from bad to worse, from smoke to smother, out of the frying pan into the fire;
anfallender ~ constant rain; **drohender ~** threat of rain; **ergiebiger ~** fruitful rain; **feiner ~** drizzle; **kurzer ~** short fall of rain; **strichweiser ~** scattered showers; **strömender ~** teeming rain; **zeitweiser ~** occasional rain;
~ von Vorwürfen shower of reproaches;
vom ~ in die Traufe kommen to go from bad to worse, to jump out of the frying pan into the fire;
auf ~ folgt Sonnenschein every cloud has a silver lining.
regen, sich to move, to stir, *(fig.)* to wake; **sich nicht ~** to give no sign of life;
sich ~ bringt Segen of idleness comes no good.
regenarm arid.
Regen|bö rain squall; **~bogenfarben** hues of the rainbow; **~dichte** rainfall intensity.
Regeneration regeneration, new birth.
regenerieren to regenerate, *(Reifen)* to reclaim, to recycle.
Regenerierung regeneration, *(Reifen)* reclaim, recycling.
Regen|fälle heavy fall of rain; **~fluten** floods of rain; **~gebiet** rain area; **~guß** heavy shower; **~häufigkeit** rain frequency; **~himmel** watery sky; **~macher** rainmaker; **synthetischer ~mantel** plastic raincoat; **~menge** precipitation, rainfall; **bisher nie aufgetretene ~menge** unprecedented rainfall; **~periode** rain spell; **~plane** water plane; **~rinne** gutter; **~schauer** shower [of rain], flurry; **~schirm** umbrella; **gespannt wie ein ~schirm sein** to be all agog (on tenterhooks).
Regent regent, sovereign, ruler, governor.
Regentonne rainwater tub, water butt.
Regentschafts|rat, ~zeit regency.
Regen|versicherung rainfall (pluvious) insurance; **~versicherungspolice** pluvious policy; **~wasser** rain-water; **~wetter** rainy (foul) weather; **~zeit** rainy (wet) season.
Regie management, administration, *(Fernsehen)* master control, *(Film)* direction, production, stage managership, *(Staatsmonopol)* state (government) monopoly;
in eigener ~ betreiben to operate for one's own account; **in einem Film ~ führen** to direct a film; **Arbeit in ~ geben** to put out a job on commission;
~anstrengung directing effort; **~anweisung** *(Film)* producer's direction; **~arbeiten** scheduled work; **~assistent** *(Film)* assistant director, *(Theater)* assistant producer; **~auslagen** overhead, oncost *(Br.)*; **~betrieb** quasi-public corporation, governmental (government-owned, state) enterprise, *(Gefangenenarbeit)* public-account (state-use, *US*) system; **~buch** *(Theater)* prompt book; **~fehler** flaw in the production; **~fehler sein** not to be exactly according to plan; **~führung** *(Theater)* stage managing; **~kosten** overhead [charges, costs, expenses], oncost *(Br.)*; **~pult** *(Rundfunk)* mixing table; **~raum** control room.
regierbar governable.
Regieren eines Landes running of a country.
regieren to govern, to rule, *(herrschen)* to reign, to sit on the throne, *(Hosen anhaben)* to rule the roost, *(Minister)* to be at the head of affairs, *(Partei)* to be in [power], to hold office; **j. ~** to have s. o. under one's thumb; **mit eiserner Hand ~** to rule with an iron hand, to rule with a rod of iron; **j. mit leichter Hand ~** to go easy with s. o.; **konservativ ~** to govern on conservative lines; **Land ~** to run a country; **im Notverordnungswege ~** to govern by injunctions, to rule by decree; **schlecht ~** to misgovern; **Stadt mit harter Hand ~** to clap an iron lid on a city;
Wagen nicht mehr ~ können to have lost control of a car.
regierend ruling, governing;
sich selbst ~ autonomic[al], self-governing;
~er Bürgermeister governing mayor; **~e Partei** party in power.
regiert werden, von seiner Frau to be tied to one's wife apron strings; **von seiner Sekretärin ~** to be run by one's secretary.
Regierung government, ministry, power, authority, the authorities, cabinet, administration *(US)*, Downing Street *(Br.)*, *(Herrscher)* reign, throne, rule, court, rulership;
an der ~ in [power]; **in den Reihen der ~** in the government ranks; **mit der ~ unzufrieden** malcontent; **ohne Einwilligung der ~** without governmental consent; **unter der ~ von** *(Herrscher)* under the reign of; **während der ~** *(Herrscher)* during the rule of;
Amerikanische ~ White House *(US)*; **anerkannte ~** government de jure; **vom Militär gestützte rechts angesiedelte ~** military-based right-wing civilian government; **rechts von der Mitte angesiedelte ~** right-of-centre government; **aufständische ~** insurgent government; **ausscheidende ~** outgoing (lame-duck, *US*) administration; **mit der Ausarbeitung einer Verfassung beauftragte ~** constitution-drafting government; **aus Mittelmäßigkeiten bestehende ~** government of mediocrities; **schon bestehende ~** established government; **nur aus Zivilisten bestehende ~** all-civilian cabinet; **Britische ~** Court of St. James, Whitehall *(Br.)*, Downing Street *(Br.)*; **demissionierende ~** outgoing (lame-duck, *US*) ministry; **demokratische ~** responsible government; **ersuchte ~** requested government; **feindliche ~** hostile government; **feste ~** stability of government; **gegenwärtige ~** present cabinet; **geschäftsführende ~** caretaker government; **handlungsunfähige ~** lame-duck administration *(US)*; **jeweilige ~** government of the day; **konservative ~** Tory government; **konstitutionelle ~** limited government; **neue ~** incoming government; **parlamentarische ~** parliamentary (representative) government; **provisorische ~** provisional (caretaker) government; **rechtmäßige ~** legal (legitimate) government; **stabile ~** stable government; **keine Sonderansprüche stellende ~** no-frills government; **verfassungsmäßige ~** constitutional government; **vertragsschließende ~en** contracting governments; **vorläufige ~** provisional government;
~ politischer Abenteurer carpet government; **~ auf breiter Grundlage** broader-based government; **~ mit geteilter Machtausübung** power-sharing government; **~ eines Mitgliedstaates** member government; **~ mittels Notverordnungen** emergency rule; **~ der nationalen Sicherheit** government of national safety;
~ völkerrechtlich anerkennen to recognize a government; **der ~ angehören** to have a seat in the cabinet; **bestehende ~ angreifen** to interfere with (lash out against) the established government; **aus der ~ ausscheiden** to quit (resign from) the cabinet; **zum Sturz der ~ beitragen** to contribute to the government's downfall, to lead to the fall of the government; **~ im Amt belassen** to sustain the government in office; **~ in Fragen der Währungspolitik beraten** to advise the government on monetary policy; **~ der Selbstzufriedenheit beschuldigen** to accuse the government of complacency; **~ bilden** to form (make up) a government (cabinet, administration, *US*), to establish a government, to form a ministry; **neue ~ bilden** to erect a new government; **~ einsetzen** to institute a government; **in die ~ eintreten** to enter a government; **in der ~ folgen** *(Herrscher)* to succeed to the throne; **zur ~ gelangen** to come to power; **~ aus einer Krise heraussteuern** to pull the government out of the mess; **Sturz der ~ herbeiführen** to lead to the fall of the government; **von der ~ abhängig machen** to governmentalize; **dem Wunsch der ~ nachkommen** to be responsive to the government's appeal; **~ niederlegen** to resign; **an der ~ sein, in der ~ sitzen** *(Partei)* to be in power (office); **wie selbstverständlich an der ~ sein** to be a natural governing party; **für die ~ stimmen** to vote for the government; **~ stürzen** to overthrow (upset, turn out) the government *(Br.)*, to put a government out of office; **~ aus etatpolitischen Gründen stürzen** to bring down the government on the budget issue; **der ~ den letzten Nerv töten** to set government nerves almost everywhere on edge; **~ übernehmen** to take over the government, *(Partei)* to come into power; **~ umbilden** to reshuffle (revamp) the government, to shuffle the cabinet, to make changes in the cabinet; **Schritte bei einer ~ unternehmen** to approach a government; **aus der ~ vertreiben** to throw out of power; **~ zusammenstellen** to organize a government.
Regierungs|abkommen executive (intragovernmental, state) agreement; **~abteilung** ministry; **~amt** office; **~angestellter** government clerk; **~anhänger** partisan of the present government; **~anleihe** government loan; **kurzfristige ~anleihen der Bank von England** deficiency bills *(Br.)*; **~ansicht widerspiegeln** *(Zeitungsartikel)* to reflect the approach of the government; **~antritt** entry upon office, accession to power, *(König)* accession to the throne; **~anweisung** government order; **~apparat** machine of government; **umfangreich konzipierter ~apparat** big government; **~art** mode of a government; **~aufgaben** business of government, governmental duties; **fetten ~auftrag erhalten** to be awarded a juicy government contract; **~ausgaben** government spending, governmental expenditure; **~ausschuß** governmental (governing, cabinet) committee, governing commission; **~ausübung durch Notverordnungen** government by injunctions; **~bank**

Treasury (front, *Br.*) bench *(Br.)*, ministerial benches *(Br.)*; ~**beamter** official, government clerk (officer, employee, agent), civil servant *(Br.)*, governmental officer *(US)*; ~**beauftragter** governmental agent; ~**behörde** administrative body, governmental authority (agency, unit); **örtliche** ~**behörde** regional (local) government; ~**beihilfe** governmental grant; ~**beratungen** government consultations; ~**bereich** government sector; ~**bezirk** governmental (federal, *US*) district, administrative area; ~**bildung** cabinet-making, formation (organization, fabrication) of government; **mit der** ~**bildung beauftragt werden** to be called upon to make up a cabinet; **offizielles** ~**blatt** government newspaper, bulletin, gazette; ~**büro** [government] office; ~**chef** head of the government, chief magistrate *(Scot.)*; **nicht mehr** ~**chef sein** to be out of office; **wieder zum** ~**chef gewählt werden** to be swept back into office; ~**ebene** government level; **auf** ~**ebene** on cabinet-level, at governmental level; ~**einrichtungen** government instrumentalities; ~**entwurf** government bill; ~**erfahrung** government experience; ~**erklärung** government communiqué (proclamation), announcement of the government, state-of-the-union message *(US)*; ~**erlaß** government notice *(Br.)*, statutory rule (instrument) *(Br.)*.

regierungsfeindlich anti-government, oppositional;
~**e Presse** opposition press.

Regierungsflugzeug government aircraft.

Regierungsform form of government (administration), government, regime, polity, governance;
absolute ~ absolutism; **demokratische** ~ democratic government; **gemischte** ~ mixed government; **monarchische** ~ monarchy; **parlamentarische** ~ responsible (parliamentary) government; **republikanische** ~ republicanism, republican government; **totalitäre** ~ totalitarianism, totalitarian government; **verfassungsmäßige** ~ constitutionalism.

regierungsfreundlich pro-government.

Regierungs|funktion governmental function; ~**gebäude** government office (house), governmental facility, public building; ~**gegner** member of the opposition; ~**geschäfte** business of government; **etw. vom** ~**geschäft verstehen** to have a knowledge of government; ~**geschäfte führen (wahrnehmen)** to administer the government, to mind the store *(US)*.

Regierungsgewalt governance, govermental power, supreme authority;
auf mehrere Ministerien aufgeteilte ~ coordinated government; **von einem Ministerium ausgeübte** ~ consolidated government; **zentrale** ~ big government *(US)*;
~ **ausüben** to exercise authority; ~ **erringen** to force one's way into government; ~ **innehaben** to run the government, to be in power.

Regierungs|handlung governmental act, cabinet action; ~**herrschaft** governance; **alleinige** ~**herrschaft der weißen Minderheit** white minority rule; ~**hilfe** government aid; ~**jahr** *(König)* regnal year; ~**koalition** coalition government, coalition in power; ~**kommissar** state commissioner; ~**kommission** government commission; ~**konferenz** intergovernmental conference; ~**kontakter** influence peddler, lobbyist; ~**konten** state funds; ~**kreise** government circles, government quarters; ~**krise** cabinet (government) crisis; ~**kunden** government clients; ~**kunst** statesmanship, king-craft, policy; **vergleichende** ~**lehre** comparative government; ~**maschinerie** government apparatus; ~**maßnahmen** governmental action (operations, *US*); ~**maßnahmen rechtfertigen** to justify the action of the government; ~**mehrheit** government's majority; ~**methode** policy; ~**mitglied** cabinet officer *(US)*, cabinet minister, member of the government; ~**mitteilung** government communication; ~**niederlage** government defeat; ~**organ** organ of the government, governmental body *(US)*, *(Zeitung)* official newspaper; ~**partei** governing party, party in power, ins, administration; ~**partei werden** to get in; ~**partei und Opposition** the ins and outs; ~**partner** coalition partner.

Regierungspolitik government's policy;
~ **unterstützen** to support the government; ~ **einstimmig unterstützen** to be unanimous in support of the government's policy; **der** ~ **im großen und ganzen zustimmen** to approve at large of the government's policy.

Regierungs|posten cabinet job; ~**programm** government plan (program[me]); ~**rücktritt** resignation of the cabinet; ~**sachverständiger** government expert; ~**sitz** seat of the government, Federal District *(US)*; ~**spitzel** creature of the government; ~**sprecher** government spokesman (speaker).

Regierungsstelle governmental agency, government department *(Br.)*;
höchste ~**n** highest quarters; **nachgeordnete** ~ governmental subdivision; **untätige** ~ deadhead agency.

Regierungs|studie government study (survey); ~**sturz** subversion (overthrow, abolition, collapse, fall) of the government; ~**sturz herbeiführen** to result in the fall of the government.

Regierungssystem framework of a government, governmental system, system (form) of government;
autoritäres ~ authoritarianism; **bürokratisches** ~ system of bureaucracy; **kompliziertes** ~ complex system of government; **parlamentarisches** ~ parliamentary regime, parliamentarianism.

Regierungstätigkeit governmental action (activity).

regierungstreu loyal.

Regierungs|treuer loyalist; ~**truppen** governmental (government) forces; ~**übereinkommen** intergovernmental agreement; ~**übernahme** accession to power; ~**umbildung** reshuffle of the government, general post in the cabinet; **formlose** ~**vereinbarung** intergovernmental arrangement; **stabile** ~**verhältnisse** stable government; ~**verlautbarung** government communiqué; ~**vertreter** government delegate, government agent *(US)*, minister resident; ~**viertel** center *(US)* (centre, *Br.*) of government; ~**vorlage** ministerial (government, *Br.*, public) bill, command paper *(Br.)*, administration bill *(US)*; ~**vorschlag** administration proposal; ~**wechsel** change in the cabinet, change of government; ~**weise** government, form of administration; ~**zeit** period of rule, *(Monarch)* regency; **behinderte** ~**zeit** lame-duck term *(US)*; ~**zentrum** center *(US)* (centre, *Br.*) of government; ~**zugehörigkeit** membership of the cabinet; ~**zügel führen** to hold the whip hand; ~**zusage** administration's commitments *(US)*; ~**zuschuß** [government] grant, grant-in-aid *(US)*; **staatswirtschaftliche** ~**zweige** economic branches of government.

Regie|tätigkeit directorial work; ~**vertrag** schedule contract; ~**verwaltung** excise office *(Br.)*; ~**zettel** time sheet.

Regime regime, governance;
~ **der Manager** managerial revolution.

Regiment, zu einem ~ **abkommandieren** to attach to a regiment; **ein ganzes** ~ **ersetzen** to be a host in o. s.; **das** ~ **führen** to rule the roost; **strenges** ~ **führen** to rule with a heavy hand, to wear the breeches, to boss it, to rule with a rod of iron.

Regiments|befehl regimental orders; ~**offizier** regimental officer; ~**stück** *(mar.)* mess.

Regimewechsel change of regime.

Region local area, region, territory;
in höheren ~**en schweben** to be in the clouds.

regional regional, local, provincial;
~ **geleitet werden** to be operated under a regional system; ~**e Arbeitsplatzprämie** regional employment premium *(Br.)*; ~**e Erschließung** regional development; ~**es Listensystem** regional list system; ~ **bestimmter Lohnunterschied** regional wage differential; ~**es Selbstverwaltungssystem** regional system; ~**e Streuung** *(Anzeigen)* regional dispersal; ~**e Struktur** regional structure; ~**e Strukturforschung** regional research; ~**er Verrechnungsverkehr** provincial clearing; ~**e Wirtschaftsförderungsstelle** regional industrial development board *(Br.)*.

Regional|abkommen regional pact, area agreement; ~**anzeigen** regional ads; ~**anzeigenkampagne** regional advertising campaign; **billigere Anzeigenpreise für** ~**ausgaben berechnen** to run ads at lower local rates *(US)*; ~**bank** regional (provincial, interior, *US*) bank, country bank *(Br.)*; ~**bankscheck** country cheque *(Br.)*; ~**bedürfnisse** regional needs; ~**börse** provincial stock exchange *(Br.)*, regional exchange, local stock exchange *(US)*, out-of-town market *(US)*; ~**büro** regional office; ~**clearing** country (provincial) clearing *(Br.)*; ~**fernsehen** regional television; ~**fonds** *(EG)* regional fund; ~**gliederung** regional organization; ~**grenze** parochial boundary; ~**handel** regional trade; ~**haushalt** *(EG)* regional budget; ~**hilfe** regional help (aid); ~**hilfemittel** regional aid funds; ~**institut** regional institution; ~**markt** regional market, provincial market *(Br.)*; ~**ökonomie** regional economics; ~**organisation** regional organization; ~**pakt** regional pact; ~**planung** regional planning, town and country planning; ~**politik** regional policy; ~**presse** regional press; ~**programm** *(Rundfunk)* regional program(me); ~**statistik** regional statistics; ~**steuer** regional tax; ~**streik** sectional strike; ~**struktur** divisionalized structure; ~**studie** regional study; ~**tarif** local agreement (rate, tariff); ~**treffen** regional meeting; ~**untersuchung** regional study; ~**verband** regional association; ~**versammlung mit Gesetzgebungsbefugnissen** regional legislative assembly; ~**vertretung** provincial agency; ~**wahlen** regional elections; ~**wechsel** country note *(Br.)*; ~**werbung** regional advertising; ~**wirtschaft** regional economics.

regionalwirtschaftliche Gesamtrechnung regional accounts.
Regionalzeitungen regional papers, provincial newspapers (press) *(Br.)*.
Regisseur stage manager (director), *(Film)* producer *(Br.)*, manager, director *(US)*.
Register register, registry [books], record, roll, roster, *(Inhaltsverzeichnis)* table of contents, index, register, *(Katalog)* catalog(ue), *(Liste)* list, schedule;
amtliches (öffentliches) ~ office book, public register (book); ~ **für Aktienverkäufe** register of transfers *(Br.)*; ~ **einer Bank über die von ihr an die Kunden ausgegebenen Kontobücher** passbook register; ~ **über alle für Einzahlungen auf Depositenkonten ausgegebenen Quittungen** deposit register *(Br.)*; ~ **der Staatspapiere** register of annuities *(Br.)*;
~ **für ein Buch anlegen** to index a book; **zum** ~ **anmelden** to apply for registration; ~ **bereinigen** to rectify a register; **in ein** ~ **eintragen** to [make an entry in the] register, to enrol(l); ~ **führen** to keep a register; ~ **parallel zu einem anderen führen** to rule a register similar to another; **im** ~ **löschen** to strike off the register (roll); **alle** ~ **ziehen** *(fig.)* to go all out; **andere** ~ **ziehen** to employ hard measures; **alle** ~ **seines Könnens ziehen** to bring the whole range of one's abilities into play; ~ **zusammenstellen** to compile an index;
~**abschrift,** ~**auszug** certificate of registration (incorporation); ~**beamter** registrar; ~**einsicht** inspection of register; ~**eintragung** entry made in the registry; ~**führer** recorder, keeper of the records, registrar; ~**führung** keeping of the records; ~**gebühr** registration fee; ~**hafen** port of register; ~**löschung** cancellation of a registration; ~**pfandrecht** lien of record; ~**schiff** register[ed] ship; ~**schiffsraum,** ~**tonnage** registered (register, net) tonnage; ~**tonne** register ton.
Registrator registrar, recorder, calendarer, actuary, greffier, filing clerk, file clerk *(US)*, filer *(US)*.
Registratur registry, register (registration, enrol(l)ment) office, depository [for records], *(Akten)* old records, *(Schrank)* filing cabinet, *(Versicherung)* record (filing) department;
~ **nach Orten** geographical filing; ~ **nach Sachgebieten** subject filing;
~**angestellter** file *(US)* (filing, *Br.*) clerk; ~**einrichtungen** filing equipment; ~**leiter** file *(US)* (filing, *Br.*) clerk; ~**system,** ~**verfahren** filing (classification) system.
Registrier|- und Übertragungsabteilung registry and transfer department *(US)*; ~**apparat** recorder, recording apparatus, totalizator; ~**ballon** sounding (meteorological) balloon.
registrieren to [enter in the] register, to record, to enrol(l), to incorporate, to bill, to calendar, to list, to index, to inscribe, to tally *(Br.)*;
sich ~ to check in; **amtlich** ~ to enter in an official list, to make an official entry; **Arbeitsbeginn** ~ to clock in; **Betrag** ~ *(Kasse)* to ring up the sale; **nur eine Darstellung** ~ *(Presse)* to confine itself to a simple statement; **gerichtlich** ~ to enrol(l), to register on records of a court; **auf Karten** ~ to card; **Mietverträge mit Mieterschutzbestimmungen** ~ to register contracts of premises *(Br.)*; **Tatsachen** ~ to state the facts; **höchste Temperatur des Jahres** ~ to record the highest temperature of the year;
sich ~ **lassen** to report for registration; **Buch gegen unerlaubten Nachdruck** ~ **lassen** to enter a book at Stationers' Company *(Br.)*.
registrierfähig recordable, registrable.
Registrier|fähigkeit eligibility for registration; ~**gerät** recording instrument; ~**kasse** cash register, damper *(US sl.)*; ~**kasse bedienen** to operate a cash register; ~**kassenstreifen** audit slip; ~**stelle** register office.
registriert on record, registered, incorporated, listed, inscribed;
nicht ~ unregistered;
als vorbestraft ~ **sein** to have a police record; ~ **werden** to enter the record;
~**es Schiff** registered ship.
Registrierung registry, register, registration, record, recording, entering, incorporation, listing, recordation *(US)*, *(Ablage)* filing, *(Mitglied)* enrol(l)ment;
unterlassene ~ nonregistration;
~ **von Ausländern** aliens' registration; ~ **des Firmennamens** registration of business name *(Br.)*; ~ **einer Gesellschaft** incorporation of a company; ~ **von zum Verkauf stehendem Grundbesitz** listing of real estate *(US)*; ~ **von Namenspapieren** inscription of securities; ~ **eines Schiffes** enrol(l)ment of a ship; ~ **eines Siedlungsanspruchs** homestead entry *(US)*; ~ **des Urheberrechts** copyright registration; ~ **von Verträgen** *(Völkerrecht)* registration of treaties;
~ **verbindlich vorschreiben** to make registration compulsory.
Registrierungs|angaben registration statement; ~**ausweis** registration card; **amtliche** ~**bescheinigung** certificate of registration, registration certificate; ~**bezirk** registration district; ~**gebühren** registration (enrol(l)ment) fees; ~**land** country of registration; ~**mitteilung** notice of registration; ~**pflicht** obligation (duty) to register; **von der** ~**pflicht ausnehmen** to provide an exemption from registration.
registrierungspflichtig sein to require one's registration, to be eligible for registration.
Registrierungs|stelle für wettbewerbsbeschränkende Kartellvereinbarungen Registrar of Restrictive Trading Agreement *(Br.)*; ~**system** recording system; ~**unterlagen** enrol(l)ment records; ~**verfahren** registration proceedings, process of registration; ~**wirkung** effect of registration; ~**zwang** compulsory registration; ~**zweck** registration purpose.
reglementieren to bring under regulation, to regularize, to officialize, to regiment, to governmentalize;
Wirtschaft eines Landes ~ to regulate the industries of a country.
Reglementierung regimentation, bringing under regulations, regularization, governmentalization;
fortschreitende ~ regulatory process;
eskalierende ~ **der Wirtschaft** escalating business registration;
staatliche ~ **des Verkehrswesens aufheben** to free the entry into the transportation market; ~ **der Wirtschaft eskalierend vorantreiben** to escalate business regulation.
Regler regulator, *(el.)* controller.
regnen, Bindfäden to rain cats and dogs; **fein** ~ to drizzle, to mizzle; **stark** ~ to pour down; **drei Tage hintereinander** ~ to rain for three whole days.
regnerisch rainy, showery, pluvious.
Regreß recourse, regress, *(Schadenersatz)* recovery of damages, remedy over, recovery over *(US)*;
mit ~ with recourse; **ohne** ~ without recourse;
~ **beim Indossanten** recourse to the endorser; ~ **mangels Zahlung** recourse in default of payment;
~ **nehmen** to recourse, to recover [over, *US*], to seek recovery, to go back; ~ **bei jem. nehmen** to recoup o. s. for injury, to obtain regress from (have recourse against) s. o.;
~**anspruch** right of recourse, right of relief; ~**anspruch gegen j. haben** to have a comeback against s. o.; ~**anspruch verlieren** to forfeit the right of relief; ~**ansprüche stellen** to seek recourse; **sich** ~**ansprüche vorbehalten** to reserve the right of relief; ~**haftung** liability to recourse.
Regression, fehlerfreie *(Statistik)* true regression.
Regressions|analyse regression analysis; ~**schätzwert** regression estimate.
Regreß|klage common recovery; ~**möglichkeit** recourse basis; **ohne** ~**möglichkeit** without recourse; ~**nahme** recovery over *(US)*; ~**nehmer** recoverer, claimant; ~**pflicht** third-party indemnity, liability over *(US)*, liability to recourse, endorser's liability.
regreßpflichtig liable to recourse;
j. ~ **machen** to have recourse against s. o.; ~ **sein** to be liable to recourse.
Regreß|pflichtiger recoveree, indemnitor *(US)*; ~**recht** right of recourse; ~**recht wahren** to preserve recourse; ~**risiko** third-party risk; ~**schuldner** party liable to recourse, indemnitor *(US)*; ~**urteil** judgment over *(US)*; ~**vereinbarung** recourse agreement; ~**versicherung** third-party indemnity insurance; ~**verzichtsabkommen** *(Versicherungsgesellschaften bei Unfällen* knock-for-knock agreement; **auf dem** ~**wege** by way of recovery.
regulär regular, normal;
~**e Abfahrtszeit** normal (scheduled, *US*) train departure; ~**e Arbeitszeit** set working time; ~**er Beschaffungsweg** usual channels of trade; **nicht ganz** ~**e Methoden** methods not quite above board; ~**er Preis** regular price; ~**e Truppen** regular forces (troops).
Regularien regulatory matters.
Regulativ regulatory [tool].
regulierbar *(Versicherung)* adjustable.
regulieren to regulate, to regularize, *(Ansprüche)* to settle, *(an der Börse)* to even up, to liquidate, to settle, *(el.)* to control, *(modulieren)* to modulate, *(Preise)* to administer, to control;
leicht zu ~ manageable;
Geschwindigkeit einer Maschine ~ to regulate the speed of a machine; **Kompaß** ~ to correct the compass; **Konto** ~ to place an account in funds; **Nachlaß** ~ to settle an estate; **Preis** ~ to control a price; **Schaden** ~ to make good a damage; **Versicherungsanspruch** ~ to settle (adjust) an insurance claim.

reguliert adjusted, settled;
noch nicht ~ unadjusted;
~**es Konto** settled account; ~**er Schaden** settled claim.
Regulierung regulation, regularization, *(Abstimmung)* modulation, *(Ansprüche)* settlement, *(Börse)* evening up, liquidation, settlement, *(el.)* control, *(Versicherungsansprüche)* adjustment, settlement;
offizielle ~ formal settlement; **pauschale** ~ global (lump-sum) settlement;
~ **von Angebot und Nachfrage** supply-demand adjustment; ~ **eines Anschreibungskontos** charge-account payment; ~ **in bar** cash settlement; ~ **eines Kontos** regulation of an account; ~ **eines überzogenen Kontos** remittance of cover; ~ **von Preisen** price adjustment (control); ~ **eines Schadens** settlement of a claim (loss); ~ **eines Versicherungsfalles** adjustment of an insurance claim, claim settlement;
umfangreichen ~**en unterworfen sein** to come in for heavy liquidations.
Regulierungs|abkommen settlement agreement; ~**aufgabe** regulatory job; ~**beamter**, ~**beauftragter** *(Versicherung)* [claim] adjuster, claims inspector, loss adjuster (assessor); ~**diskont** settlement discount; **staatlichen** ~**fesseln entgehen** to escape from the shackles of state regulation; ~**kosten** *(Versicherung)* claim costs (expenses); ~**kurs** settling (liquidation) rate; ~**mechanismus** regulating mechanism; **ganztägig beschäftigtes** ~**personal** full-time claims staff; ~**prozeß** regulatory (adjustment) process.
Regung motion, movement, stir;
einer plötzlichen ~ **folgend** on a sudden impulse;
den ~**en seines Herzens folgen** to follow the promptings of one's heart; **menschliche** ~ **spüren** to feel a touch of human sympathy.
Rehabilitation comeback, *(Konkursschuldner)* whitewash *(Br.)*.
rehabilitieren to rehabilitate, to clear, *(Konkursschuldner)* to whitewash *(Br.)*, to discharge;
sich ~ to right o. s., to make one's comeback; **Beamten** ~ to whitewash an official *(Br.)*.
rehabilitiert|werden to be whitewashed *(Br.)*;
~**er Beamter** whitewashed official *(Br.)*; ~**er Konkursschuldner** certificated bankrupt *(Br.)*.
Rehabilitierung rehabilitation, whitewash *(Br.)*, comeback;
~ **eines Konkursschuldners** discharge (whitewash, *Br.*) of a bankrupt (in bankruptcy);
berufliche ~ vocational rehabilitation.
Rehabilitierungs|antrag *(Konkursschuldner)* application for discharge; ~**bescheinigung**, ~**schein** *(Gemeinschuldner)* bankrupt's certificate *(Br.)*, certificate of misfortune; ~**beschluß** order of discharge *(Br.)* (for discharge, *US*).
Reibach plunder *(sl.)*, clean-up *(US sl.)*;
~ **machen** to make a pile of money.
reiben *(Schuh)* to chafe, to pinch;
sich an etw. ~ to take offence at s. th.; **sich an jem.** ~ to pick a quarrel with s. o., to have a tiff with s. o.; **sich die Hände** ~ to rub one's hands; **jem. etw. unter die Nase** ~ to rub it in.
Reibereien friction, tiff.
Reibung friction, *(fig.)* clash.
Reibungs|flächen bieten to cause friction; **wirtschaftlicher** ~**koeffizient** economic friction.
reibungslos smoothly;
~ **ablaufen** to go off without a hitch;
~ **ablaufender Verkehr** smooth traffic.
Reibungslosigkeit smooth handling.
Reich empire, commonwealth;
neues ~ **begründen** to erect a new commonwealth; ~ **zerstören** to lay low an empire.
reich rich, wealthy, well-to-do, opulent, pecunious, moneyed, *(Vorräte)* well-stocked;
~ **begütert** propertied; ~ **illustriert** richly illustrated;
~ **belohnen** to reward richly; ~ **beschenken** to load with gifts, to shower presents on; ~ **heiraten** to marry a fortune; ~ **beschenkt nach Hause kommen** to come home laden with gifts; ~ **sein** to be on easy street; **enorm** ~ **sein** to have pots of money; ~ **an Bodenschätzen sein** to abound with mineral resources; ~ **an Ideen sein** to be a man full of new ideas, to have a wealth of ideas; **über Nacht** ~ **geworden sein** to have become a rich man overnight; ~ **werden** to grow rich; **durch gutes Wirtschaften** ~ **werden** to thrive by good husbandry; **für** ~ **gehalten werden** to pass for rich;
~**e Auswahl** wide selection; **Kind** ~**er Eltern sein** to be born with a silver spoon in one's mouth; ~**e Erbschaft machen** to come into a fortune; ~**e Erfahrungen** ample experience; ~**e Ernte** heavy crop; **in** ~**er Fülle** in abundance; ~**er Knopp** *(fam.)* moneybag; ~**e Leute** moneyed people; ~**e Partie machen** to marry money; ~**e Phantasie** fertile imagination.
Reiche und Arme haves and have-nots.
reichen to offer, to hand, to pass, *(ausreichend sein)* to suffice, to last;
fast bis an die Decke ~ to reach almost up to the ceiling; **Erfrischungen** ~ to serve refreshments; **mit seinem Gehalt gut** ~ to manage very well on one's salary; **Hand fürs Leben** ~ to give one's hand in marriage; **gerade zum Leben** ~ to make both ends meet; **für die Oberschule** ~ to be bright enough to go to a grammar school; **bis zum Wald** ~ *(Grundstück)* to stretch as far as the wood;
jem. nicht das Wasser ~ **können** not to be able to hold a candle to s. o.; **eine Woche** ~ **müssen** to have to last for a week.
reichhaltig rich, ample, abundant, plentiful, well-stocked;
~ **dekoriert** profusely illustrated;
~**e Auswahl** rich selection; ~**e Mahlzeit** substantial meal; ~**es Material** wealth of material; ~**es Programm** varied program(me).
Reichhaltigkeit des Produktionsprogramms diversification of products.
reichlich plentiful, abundant, abounding, affluent, ample, enough and to spare, galore, fat, thick, plump, unsparing, like water, precious *(coll.)*, *(Verbrauch)* liberal;
~ **langweilig** rather boring; ~ **versehen mit** flush of;
~ **fließen** to run freely; ~ **zu essen haben** to have food galore; ~ **gerechnet sein** to be a generous reckoning; ~ **mit etw. versehen sein** to have plenty of s. th.; ~ **mit Mitteln versehen sein** to have ample means at one's disposal; ~ **entschädigt werden** to be amply awarded;
~**es Angebot** plentiful supply; ~**es Auskommen haben** to make a good living; ~ **ausgestattete Bibliothek** extensive library; ~**es Einkommen** comfortable income; ~**e Mahlzeit** sumptuous meal; ~**e Mittel** ample means; ~**es halbes Pfund** good half pound; ~**er Vorrat** copious supply; ~ **Zeit haben** to have ample time.
Reichtum wealth, riches, fortune, golden calf, plenty, gold, money, abundance, affluence, amplitude, ful(l)ness, treasure;
vom Himmel gefallener ~ windfall wealth; **märchenhafter** ~ untold wealth; **sagenhafter** ~ fabulous wealth; **unwahrscheinlicher** ~ fabulous wealth; **üppiger** ~ exuberance, luxuriance;
~ **an Erfahrungen** range of experience; ~ **an Ideen** wealth of ideas;
~ **anbeten** to worship the golden calf, to make an idol of wealth; **Atmosphäre von** ~ **atmen** to smell rich; **dem** ~ **nachjagen** to scramble for wealth; ~ **eines Landes reduzieren** to diminish a country's wealth; **seinen neu erworbenen** ~ **zur Schau stellen, seinen** ~ **öffentlich zeigen** to flaunt one's new riches, to make a display of one's wealth.
Reichtümer, natürliche natural resources, land;
alle ~ **dieser Welt** all the wealth of the Indies;
~ **ansammeln** to treasure (heap) up (rake together) wealth *(Br.)*, to amass great riches.
Reichweite range, scope, grasp, reach, sweep, *(Aktionsradius)* cruising range, *(Bericht)* coverage, *(mil.)* firing range;
in ~ within reach (touch);
akustische ~ voice range;
~ **eines Werbeträgers** media penetration;
etw. in ~ **haben** to have s. th. within one's grasp; **außerhalb jds.** ~ **sein** to be beyond s. one's reach; ~ **feindlicher Geschütze übertreffen** to outrange the enemy guns.
Reif frost, hoar[frost], silver thaw, rime;
mit ~ **überziehen** to frost.
reif ripe, mellow, *(fig.)* mature;
~ **für die Irrenanstalt** ready for the lunatic asylum; ~ **fürs Krankenhaus** fit for the hospital;
für eine gehörige Tracht Prügel ~ **sein** to be in for a sound thrashing; ~ **werden** *(fig.)* to draw to a head; ~**er und erfahrener werden** to cut one's wisdom teeth;
~**es Alter** ripe age, age of maturity; ~**e Arbeit** competent piece of work; **jem. wie eine** ~**e Frucht in den Schoß fallen** to drop into s. one's lap; **in** ~**eren Jahren** middle-aged; ~**e Leistung** finished performance; ~**e Persönlichkeit** mature individual; ~**es Urteil** ripe (mature) judgment.
Reife perfection, *(Frucht)* ripeness, *(Wein)* maturity;
mittlere ~ *(Schulabgang)* Ordinary General Certificate of Education *(Br.)*, higher school certificate *(US)*;
~ **des Alters** maturity of age;
zur ~ **bringen** to bring to maturity; **von mangelnder** ~ **zeugen** to show lack of maturity.

Reifen tyre *(Br.)*, tire *(US)*;
abgefahrener ~ worn-out tire; **geplatzter** ~ burst tyre;
~ **mit ungenügendem Druck** deflated tyre; ~ **mit Matsch- und Schneeprofil** mud-and-snow tire *(US)*, town-and-country tyre *(Br.)*;
~ **aufpumpen** to pump up (air into) a tyre; ~ **aufziehen (montieren)** to fit on (fix) a tyre; **Profil eines ~s erneuern** to retread a tyre (tire, *US*); ~ **wechseln** to change a wheel (flat tyre, tire, *US*); ~ **zerstören** to perish tyres;
~**abnutzung** tyre wear (use); ~**decke** cover; **abgefahrene ~decke** smooth tyre casing; ~**defekt** puncture, blowout *(US)*, flat tyre; ~**druck** tyre pressure; ~**ersatzbeschaffung** tyre replacement; ~**fabrik** tyre factory; ~**firma**, ~**hersteller** tyremaker, tiremaker; ~**garantie** tyre guarantee; ~**heber** tyre lever; ~**industrie** tyre industry; ~**lager** tyre store; ~**panne** puncture, blowout *(US)*, flat tyre, flat *(sl.)*, tire trouble *(US)*; ~**panne haben** to have a puncture; ~**preis** tyre price; ~**profil** tread, track; ~**schaden** injury to the tyre, burst; ~**schaden beheben** to repair a puncture; ~**spur** tyre track; ~**übergröße** oversize in tyres; ~**verschleißwert** tyre wear rate; ~**wechsel** tyre replacement.

Reife | prozeß durchmachen to mature during the years; ~**prüfung** examination for the general certificate *(Br.)*, A-levels *(Br.)*, finals *(US)*; ~**prüfungszeugnis** school (leaving) certificate, general matriculation certificate of education *(Br.)*, graduation *(US)*; **volkswirtschaftlicher ~zustand** economic maturity.

reiflich überlegen, sich eine Sache to give a question mature deliberation.

Reihe row, train, *(Anzahl)* run, series, *(Menschenschlange)* queue, line *(US)*, *(mil.)* file, rank, *(Obligation)* issue, *(Skala)* gamut;
aus der ~ **der Mitglieder** from among the members; **aus der obersten** ~ from the top row; **außer der** ~ out of turn; **bevor man an der** ~ **ist** before one's turn; **der** ~ **nach** in turn; **in** ~ **und Glied** in rank and file; **in vorderster** ~ **des Kampfes** in the front line of the battle;
dichte ~**n** close ranks; **geometrische** ~ geometric progression; **geordnete** ~**n** *(Statistik)* ordered series; **senkrechte** ~ column; **unendliche** ~ infinite series; **vordere** ~**n** front benches; **vorderste** ~ forefront;
lange ~ **von Autos** string (stream) of cars; ~ **Briefmarken** strip of stamps; ~ **guter Ernten** sequence of good harvests; ~ **von Fragen** string of questions; ~ **frachtgleicher Häfen** range of ports; ~ **von Jahren** vista of years; ~ **von Namen** number of names; ~**n der Opposition** opposite benches; ~ **von Rundfunksendungen** serial; ~ **von Unfällen** series of accidents; ~ **von Vorträgen** series of lectures; ~ **von Zimmern** suite of rooms;
ganze ~ **abnehmen** to purchase the whole series; ~**n einer Kompanie abschreiten** to pass down the ranks of a company; **in einer** ~ **anstehen** to queue (line, *US*) up; **lange** ~ **von Beispielen aufführen** to give a long series of examples; **außer der** ~ **befördern** to promote ahead of s. one's turn, to prepromote; **Probleme der** ~ **nach behandeln** to take the problems one by one; **außer der** ~ **erhalten** to jump the queue; ~ **der Ansprachen eröffnen** to make the first speech; **der** ~ **nach erzählen** to tell from the beginning; **aus der** ~ **fallen** to cause some embarrassment; **in einer** ~ **zu vieren gehen** to walk four abreast; **nicht alle in der** ~ **haben** to be a bit touched; **Sitz in der ersten** ~ **haben** to have a front-row seat; **Verräter in den eigenen** ~**n haben** to have a traitor in our ranks; ~**n lichten** to thin the ranks; **in geschlossenen** ~**n marschieren** to march in close ranks; **an der** ~ **sein** to be one's turn; ~**n schließen** to close up; **aus der** ~ **tanzen** to step out of line *(US)*; **außer der** ~ **befördert werden** to be promoted by selection (ahead of one's turn), to be picked out.

Reihen | abwurf *(mil.)* stick (salvo) bombing; ~**anfertigung** serial (series, flow, mass) production, serialization; ~**anschlag** series posting; ~**arbeit** repetition work; ~**aufnahme** sequence shot; ~**bauten** terraced houses; ~**bild** *(Flugwesen)* mosaic; ~**eigenheim** semidetached house, terraced house *(Br.)*, row house *(US)*; ~**fabrikation**, ~**fertigung** serial (series, flow, mass) production (manufacture).

Reihenfolge order, sequence, turn, graduation, succession, *(math.)* ordinal succession, *(Schuldentilgung)* collocation;
in alphabetischer ~ in alphabetical order; **in chronologischer** ~ in order of date; **in der richtigen** ~ in due succession; **in umgekehrter** ~ in reverse order, *(Auflassung)* in inverse order; **geregelte** ~ regular turn; **zeitliche** ~ chronological order;
~ **der Aufführung** *(Bilanzposten)* order of presentation; ~ **der Eintragung** order of registration; ~ **der Pfandrechte** marshalling of liens; ~ **der Regelung von Nachlaßverbindlichkeiten** order of administration; ~ **der Wichtigkeit** order of merit; ~**planung** jobshop sequencing.

Reihen | haus semidetached (row, *US*) house, serial (terraced, *Br.*) house, *(am Stadtrand gelegen)* ribbon building *(Br.)*; ~**häuser** block *(Br.)*; ~**motor** in-line engine; ~**untersuchung** mass examination.

reihenweise in series (rows);
~ **desertieren** to desert in large numbers.

Reihenwurf *(Flugzeug)* stick (salvo) bombing.

Reim rhyme;
sich keinen ~ **auf etw. machen können** not to be able to make head or tail of it.

reimen, sich to rhyme, to jingle.

rein plain, pure, *(ehrlich)* straight, square, transparent, *(Gewicht)* neat, *(Gewinn)* net, clear, *(Gold)* genuine, pure, fine, *(Luft, Wasser)* fair, *(makellos)* white, *(Papierbogen)* blank, *(unverfälscht)* unmixed, unmingled;
~**er Alkohol** undiluted (absolute) alcohol; **aus** ~**er Bosheit** out of pure malice; ~**e Familienangelegenheit** purely a family matter; ~**e Formalität** mere (empty) formality; ~**en Gewinn ergeben haben** to have netted; ~**es Gewissen** clear conscience; ~ **netto Kasse** net cash; ~**er Kursunterschied** net change; ~**e und angewandte Mathematik** pure and applied mathematics; **aus** ~**em Mitleid** out of sheer compassion; ~**er Nachlaß** clear residue; ~**er Nachlaß nach Auszahlung der Legate** net estate; ~**en Tisch machen** to make a clean sweep of it; ~**er Überschuß** net profit; **kein** ~**es Vergnügen** not at all beer and skittles *(Br.)*; ~**er Verlust** dead loss; **aus** ~**er Verzweiflung** out of utter despair; ~**er Wahnsinn** sheer madness; ~**e Wahrheit** unvarnished truth; **Diamant von** ~**stem Wasser sein** to be a diamond of first water; **Sozialist** ~**sten Wassers sein** to be a dyed-in-the-wool socialist; **jem.** ~**en Wein einschenken** to make a clear breast of it, to talk cold turkey *(US)*; ~**e Weste haben** to have a clean sheet, to be without a spot on one's reputation; **keine** ~**e Weste haben** to have a blot on one's escutcheon; ~**er Zeitverlust** sheer (pure) waste of time; **alten Freund aus** ~**em Zufall treffen** to run into an old friend.

Rein | abzug clean proof; ~**ausgaben** net expenditure; ~**bilanz** neat balance; ~**dividende** net dividend *(Br.)*; ~**druck** clean impression.

Reine, Geschäft ins ~ **bringen** to clear a business; **mit jem. ins** ~ **kommen** to get even (come to terms) with s. o.; **ins** ~ **schreiben** to [make a clear] copy, to write out fair, to engross; **mit sich im** ~**n sein** to be at peace with o. s.

Rein | einkommen net income; ~**einkommen zugrunde legen** to measure income net of tax; ~**einnahme** net income (revenue); ~**einnahmenschätzung** net profit calculation.

Reinemachefrau charwoman, [daily] cleaner *(US)*, scrubwoman *(US)*, cleaning woman *(US)*;
als ~ **arbeiten** to char.

Reinemachen charing, spring-cleaning;
großes ~ **in einer Partei** extensive purge within a party.

Rein | erhaltung der Luft maintenance of unpolluted air; ~**erlös** net proceeds, *(Abbruchwert)* net salvage, *(Diskontierung)* net avails *(US)*; ~**ertrag** net (clear, clean, pure) profit, net yield, net income (proceeds, produce), net, clear amount; **betriebsfremder** ~**ertrag** net nonproperty profit; ~**ertrag geringer als im Vorjahr** *(Börsenbericht)* net off.

Reinertrags | lage cashflow position; ~**übersicht** statement of net proceeds; ~**verwendung** disposition of net profit (income).

Reinfall bust, fiasco, fizzle *(coll.)*, comedown, mucker, flop *(sl.)*, washout *(sl.)*, lead balloon *(sl.)*, frost *(sl.)*;
kompletter ~ blue ruin *(sl.)*; **totaler** ~ dead frost;
~ **erleben** to draw a blank; **totalen** ~ **erleben** *(Unterhalter)* to lay a bomb (an egg) *(sl.)*; **glatter** ~ **sein** to turn out a frost.

reinfallen to come a cropper, to be diddled (taken in, sold);
auf j. ~ to be duped by s. o.; **leicht** ~ to be easily taken in; **auf einen Schwindel** ~ to swallow the bait.

Rein | fracht dead freight; ~**gewicht** weight allowed free.

Reingewinn clear (clean, pure, net) profit, clear (net) gain, net proceeds (earnings), profit and loss surplus, net margin, surplus net profit;
ausgewiesener ~ reported net earning; **ausschüttungsfähiger (unverteilter)** ~ unappropriated retained earnings *(US)*; **auf Neubewertung beruhender** ~ surplus arising from revaluation; **im Betrieb erzielter** ~ net profit from operation; **für das Börsengeschäft zur Verfügung stehender** ~ trading cashflow; **unverteilter** ~ undivided profits, undistributed net profit, unappropriated earned surplus *(US)*, surplus profit (earnings) *(US)*; **verfügbarer** ~ surplus available; **frei verfügbarer** ~ free surplus; **verwendeter** ~ appropriated surplus; **nicht verwendeter** ~ undistributed net profit, unappropriated earned surplus *(US)*;

~ **einer Aktiengesellschaft** company's surplus; ~ **nach Ausschüttung der Dividende** net surplus *(US)*; **Verhältnis des ~s zum Eigenkapital** net profit to net worth ratio *(US)*; ~ **vor Eintragung ins Handelsregister** initial surplus *(US)*; ~ **eines Geschäftsjahres** operating surplus; **unverteilter** ~ **bei Geschäftsübernahme** acquired surplus at date of acquisition; ~ **einschließlich Vortrags** net profit including balance;
~ **abwerfen (erzielen)** to net, to clear a profit; **400 £** ~ **erzielen** to net (clear) £ 400; **keinen** ~ **erzielen** to leave a zero net; ~**beteiligung** participation in earnings (surplus); ~**beteiligungsvertrag** net-money receipts pool; ~**konto** earned-surplus account *(US)*; ~**verwendung** distribution of profit (surplus), disposition of net income (profit).

Reinheit purity, pureness, white;
~ **garantiert** warranted free from adulteration.

reinigen to clean, to cleanse, to purge, to scour, *(pol.)* to expurgate, *(Schiff)* to clean down, *(waschen)* to wash, *(Zimmer)* to do out *(coll.)*;
Atmosphäre ~ *(fig.)* to clear the air; **Buch von unanständigen Stellen** ~ to purge a book; **chemisch** ~ to dry-clean; **gründlich** ~ to clean down; **Partei von unerwünschten Mitgliedern** ~ to purge a party of undesirable members; **Teppich chemisch** ~ to wash a carpet; **j. von jedem Verdacht** ~ to clear s. o. from any suspicion; **Zimmer gründlich** ~ to give a room a thorough cleaning;
Anzug ~ **lassen** to have a suit cleaned, to send a suit to the cleaners.

Reinigung cleanup, *(pol.)* purge;
chemische ~ dry cleaning;
zur ~ **schicken** to send to the cleaners.

Reinigungs|anstalt cleaners, cleaning company; **chemische** ~**anstalt** dry cleaners; ~**dienst** police *(mil., US)*; ~**maschine** cleaner.

Reinkorrektur clean sheet.

reinlegen to diddle, to do in, to do up brown *(sl.)*;
j. ~ to walk round s. o., to shortchange (beat) s. o. *(US)*; **j. schwer** ~ to do s. o. badly.

reinlich clean, tidy, neat;
~ **gekleidet** immaculately dressed.

Rein|machefrau charwoman *(US)*, [daily] cleaner *(Br.)*, cleaning woman *(Br.)*; ~**nachlaß** residuary; ~**saldo** net balance; ~**schiff** clean ship.

Reinschrift fair (clean, final) copy, engrossment;
~ **anfertigen** to engross; ~ **von einem Brief anfertigen** to make a fair copy of a letter; ~ **von einer Urkunde anfertigen** to extend a deed; ~ **herstellen** to enrol(l), to engross, to make a fair copy.

Rein|überschuß net balance, earned surplus *(US)*; ~**umsatz** net sales; ~**verdienst** net earnings; ~**verlust** net (clear) loss; ~**vermächtnis** residuary gift; ~**vermögen** financial worth, net (actual) assets; ~**vermögen einer Aktiengesellschaft** corporate proprietorship *(US)*; ~**verschuldung** net indebtedness.

reinvestieren to reinvest, to plough (plow, *US*) back.

Reinvestition reinvestment, ploughing (plowing, *US*) back of earnings (profits).

reinwaschen, sich *(fig.)* to purge (whitewash) o. s.; **j. von einem Verdacht** ~ to clear s. o. from any suspicion.

Rein|waschung exculpation, whitewashing; ~**zeichnung** finished drawing (art), final artwork.

Reise journey, course, *(kurze Fahrt)* trip, walk, tour, excursion, *(längere Fahrt)* travel, *(Rauschgiftsüchtiger)* down trip, *(Seereise)* voyage, passage;
auf ~**n** travelling, on the wing (a voyage), *(Vertreter)* on the road; **auf seinen** ~**n durch die Welt** on one's walk through the world;
mühsame ~ miserable journey; **verbilligte** ~ bargain tour; **versicherte** ~ voyage insured; **vollbezahlte** ~ all-expense trip; **weite** ~ long journey; **zusammengestellte** ~ conducted tour;
~ **ins Ausland** journey (travel, trip) abroad; ~ **im Auto** motoring tour; ~ **in Etappen** leisure journey; ~ **im Pendelverkehr** commuter trip *(US)*; ~ **auf Schusters Rappen** journey on Shank's mare; ~ **ohne Unterbrechung** nonstop journey; ~ **um die Welt** trip around the world; ~ **mit zahlreichen Zwischenfällen** journey full of incidents;
~ **antreten** to start on a journey; **sich auf eine** ~ **begeben** to set out on a journey; **seine** ~ **fortsetzen** to continue (resume, proceed on) one's journey; ~ **mit größter Beschleunigung fortsetzen** to prosecute a journey with the utmost dispatch; ~ **machen** to go on a journey; ~**n machen** to travel; ~ **um die Welt machen** to take a trip round the world; **sich zu einer** ~ **rüsten** to gird up one's loins; **j. auf** ~**n schicken** to send s. o. on tour (on a voyage); **auf** ~**n sein** to be away from home, to be travelling; **viel auf** ~**n sein** to get about a great deal, to be away a lot; **seine** ~ **unterbrechen** to interrupt one's journey, to stop over *(US)*; ~ **unternehmen** to go on a journey, to voyage, to take a trip; **gefahrvolle** ~ **unternehmen** to venture on a perilous journey; **Ferien auf** ~**n verbringen** to spend one's vacation in travel; ~ **vorbereiten** to arrange for a journey; **zu einer** ~ **eingeladen werden** to be invited to tour; **jem. glückliche** ~ **wünschen** to wish s. o. a pleasant journey, to bid s. o. good-speed; ~ **in Etappen zurücklegen** to travel in brief stages;
~**abenteuer** adventure; ~**abkommen** travel agreement; ~**agentur** travel agent (agency), passenger agent *(US)*; ~**akkreditiv** traveller's letter of credit *(US)*; ~**andenken** travel souvenir; ~**anhänger** travel trailer; ~**anstrengungen** burden of travel; ~**antritt** setting out on a journey, *(Schiff)* embarkation; ~**anzug** travel(l)ing dress; ~**apotheke** medicine chest; ~**artikel** travelling requisites; ~**auftrag** traveller's order; ~**ausgaben,** ~**auslagen** travel(l)ing expenses, travel spending; ~**ausrüstung** equipment for a voyage, travel(l)ing equipment; ~**ausweis** travel document; ~**beamter** *(Versicherung)* travel(l)ing inspector; ~**bedürfnisse** travel necessities; **für seine** ~**bedürfnisse ausreichen** to cover the needs of a journey; ~**begleiter** travelling companion, fellow traveller, *(Gesellschaftsreise)* tourist guide, travel(l)ing agent, courier *(Br.)*, companion of a journey, bear leader; ~**begleiterin** [air] hostess; ~**beilage** *(Zeitung)* travel supplement; ~**bekanntschaft** chance acquaintance, pickup; ~**bereitschaft** availability to travel; ~**bericht** travelog(ue); ~**berichte** travels; ~**bericht verfassen** to write an account of a journey; ~**beschränkungen** restrictions on travel(l)ing, travel(l)ing restrictions; ~**beschreibung** itinerary, voyage, book of travel, travelog(ue) *(US)*; ~**bezirk** travel(l)ing territory; ~**bibliothek** travel(l)ing library; ~**buchhandel** guidebook trade; ~**büro** travel agent (agency), travel(l)ing bureau *(Br.)*, ticket agent, tourist agency (bureau) *(US)*; **zentral gelegenes** ~**büro** downtown ticket office *(US)*; ~**bus** [motor] coach; ~**decke** travelling rug; ~**devisen** tourist exchange; ~**dienst** travel service; ~**diplomatie** shuttle diplomacy; ~**entschädigung** travel allowance; **seine** ~**erinnerungen in Buchform veröffentlichen** to write a book about one's travels; ~**erleichterungen** tourist accommodations, travelling facilities; ~**ersatz** substitute for travel.

reise|fähig fit to travel; ~**fertig** ready to start (sail).

Reise|flasche pocket flask (pistol, *sl.*); ~**flughöhe** cruising altitude; ~**fracht** voyage freight.

Reiseführer travel book (guide), handbook, guidebook, itinerary;
amtlicher ~ official guide;
~ **für Autofahrer** roadbook, blue book *(US)*;
als ~ **fungieren** to function as [act as] guide.

Reise|gefährte fellow traveller (passenger); ~**gefolge** suite; ~**geld** viaticum, *(Urlaub)* travel funds, *(Zeuge)* conduct (marching) money *(Br.)*; ~**geldpauschale** *(Abgeordnete)* travelling allowance, constructive mil(e)age *(US)*; ~**genehmigung** travel permit, clearance.

Reisegepäck luggage *(Br.)*, baggage *(US)*, things;
~**versicherung** luggage insurance *(Br.)*, tourist baggage insurance *(US)*, personal floater *(US)*, *(Handlungsreisende)* commercial (drummer) floater *(US)*; **globale** ~**versicherung** tourists' baggage floater insurance *(US)*; ~**versicherungspolice** tourist floater policy *(US)*.

Reise|geschwindigkeit *(Flugzeug, Kraftwagen)* cruising speed; ~**gesellschaft** touring company (party), coach party, excursion, itinera[n]cy, outfit *(US)*, *(betreute)* conducted tour, guided package tour *(US)*; ~**gesellschaften** tourism; ~**gesellschaftstarif** *(Flugzeug)* group charter rate; ~**gewerbe** itinerant trading, itinerant peddling; ~**gewerbekarte** hawker's licence; ~**gewerbetreibender** itinerant dealer (trader, merchant); ~**handbuch** travel book, guidebook, *(Auto)* roadbook, blue book *(US)*; ~**hinweis** traveller tip; ~**inspektor** travel(l)ing (walking) inspector; ~**journalist** travel editor; ~**koffer** travel(l)ing case, trunk; ~**komfort** travel(l)ing conveniences; ~**konjunktur** tourist boom; ~**korb** hamper.

Reisekosten travel (tourist) expenses (expenditures), travel(l)ing charges (expenses), expenses of a journey, *(Zeugen)* conduct money *(Br.)*;
~ **abziehen** to deduct the travel(l)ing expenses; ~ **eines Journalisten übernehmen** to pay the expenses of a newspaper reporter to travel; ~ **veranschlagen** to calculate the costs of a journey; ~ **vergüten** to reimburse travel(l)ing expenses;
~**abrechnung** account of travelling expenses *(Br.)*, travel-expense report *(US)*; ~**beleg** note of travel(l)ing expenses *(Br.)*; ~**entschädigung** travelling (transport) allowance; ~**erstattung** refund of travel expenses; ~**pauschale** travelling allowance;

~**vergütung** travel (travel(l)ing) allowance, *(Gewerkschaft)* travel(l)ing benefit; ~**vorschuß** travel advance *(US)*; ~**zuschuß** travel(l)ing allowance, travel subvention, assisted passage.

Reise | krankheit travel (railway, railroad, *US*) sickness; ~**kreditbrief** travel(l)er's (circular) letter of credit, circular note; **überall gültiger** ~**kreditbrief** world-wide letter of credit; ~**leiter** travel(l)ing agent, tour manager, courier *(Br.)*; ~**leiter sein** to engineer a party; ~**lektüre** travel literature; ~**lust** travel urge, itchy feet *(coll.)*; **bequeme** ~**möglichkeit** comfort ride; ~**muster** sample of merchandise.

Reisen travel(l)ing, touring;
~ **im Wohnwagen** caravan(n)ing.

reisen to travel, to make (go on) a journey, to go, *(mit Auto)* to be touring, *(mit dem Schiff)* to sail, to voyage;
über M. ~ to go via M.; **ins Ausland** ~ to travel abroad; **in die Ferien** ~ to go for one's holiday; **für seine Firma** ~ to travel for one's business house; **per Flugzeug** ~ to travel by air; **mit wenig Gepäck** ~ to travel light; **geschäftlich** ~ to travel on business; **erster Klasse nach New York** ~ to travel first-class to New York; **aufs Land** ~ to go into the country; **unter fremdem Namen** ~ to travel incognito; **von Ort zu Ort** ~ to travel from town to town; **mit einer Reisegesellschaft** ~ to join a conducted tour; **für eine Staubsaugerfirma** ~ to travel in vacuum cleaners; **auf die dumme Tour** ~ to play the innocent; **auf die sanfte Tour** ~ to try the soft approach; **zum Vergnügen** ~ to travel for pleasure, to go places *(US)*.

reisend itinerant, travelling.

Reisende | absetzen (aussteigen lassen) to discharge (off-load) passengers; ~ **in eine höhere Klasse überwechseln lassen** to transfer passengers from one class to another; ~ **nächtigen** to put up travel(l)ers.

Reisender travel(l)er, voyager, tourist, journeyer, *(Fahrgast)* passenger, *(für ausstehende Forderungen)* collector, *(Vertreter)* travel(l)ing agent (salesman) *(US)*, sales representative, commercial travel(l)er, drummer *(US)*, road agent *(US)*;
festangestellter ~ professional salesman; **nicht seefester** ~ bad sailor;
~ **auf der Eisenbahn** railway travel(l)er *(Br.)*; ~ **in der ersten Klasse** first-class passenger; ~ **der zweiten Klasse** second-class passenger; ~ **dritter Klasse** steerage passenger; ~ **auf Spesenkonto** expense-account travel(l)er.

Reise | necessaire dressing (toilet) case; ~**omnibus** [motor] coach; **klimatisierter** ~**omnibus** air-conditioned coach; ~**omnibus benutzen** to travel by coach; ~**paß** passport; ~**paß ausstellen** to make out (issue) a passport; **jem. den** ~**paß entziehen** to deprive s. o. of his passport; ~**plan** itinerary; ~**planung** trip planning, scheduling; ~**police** voyage policy; ~**prospekt** [travel] folder, tourist pamphlet; ~**proviant** viaticum, travel ration; ~**rabatt für Bestellungen beim Verlagsvertreter** traveller rebate for orders placed with publisher's representative; ~**revisor** travel(l)ing auditor.

Reiseroute line of travel, route, itinerary;
~ **aufstellen** to draw up an itinerary; **feste** ~ **befolgen** to be on a tight schedule; ~ **festlegen** to mark out a course, to map out a route; **sich ein paar** ~**n überlegen** to think up some routes for a trip.

Reise | sack travelling bag; ~**scheck** travel (travel(l)er's) check *(US)* (cheque, *Br.*), circular cheque *(Br.)*, international check *(US)*; ~**scheckheft** travel check *(US)* (cheque, *Br.*) book; ~**schreibmaschine** portable typewriter; ~**sperre** travel ban.

Reisespesen travel expenses (expenditure, cost, allowance), travel(l)ing charges (expenses), subsistence for travel;
~ **ersetzt bekommen** to get one's travel(l)ing (be reimbursed for travel) expenses; ~ **in einer bestimmten Höhe bewilligen** to vote a sum for travel(l)ing expenses;
~**abrechnung** billing on travel expense, travel-expense report *(US)*; ~**konto** travel(l)ing expenses account; ~**pauschale** travel allowance; **doppelte** ~**rechnung** double billing on travel expenses; ~**tagessatz** per-diem allowance.

Reise | statistik tourist statistics; ~**stipendium** travel(l)ing fellowship (scholarship); ~**strapazen nicht gewöhnt sein** to be unequal to the exertions of travelling; ~**strecke** line of travel, route, route to be followed; **unterbrochene** ~**strecke** jump; ~**tag** day of departure; ~**tasche** travel(l)ing (carpet) bag, carrybag, overall, carryall, wallet, gripsack *(US coll.)*; **ausziehbare** ~**tasche** telescope bag; ~**tätigkeit für eine Sammelaktion** fund-raising circuit.

reiseüblich incidental to a journey.

Reise | unfallversicherung travel(l)er's accident insurance; ~**unkosten** travel(l)ing charges (expenses); ~**unterbrechung** discontinuance of travel, break of a journey, travel break, interruption in a voyage, stopover *(US)*; **unabhängig geführtes** ~**unternehmen** independently listed tour operator; ~**utensilien** travel(l)ing requisites; ~**verbot** travel ban; ~**vergütung** travel(l)ing allowance; ~**verkehr** tourist travel (traffic), touring, travel service; **grenzüberschreitender** ~**verkehr** international passenger traffic; **zunehmender** ~**verkehr** travel (touristic) growth; **positive** ~**verkehrsbilanz** favo(u)rable balance of payments in tourism; ~**vermittlung betreiben** to arrange tourist booking; ~**versicherung** travel (voyage) insurance; ~**versicherungspolice** voyage (tourist) policy; ~**versicherungsprämie** voyage premium; ~**vertreter** travel(l)ing agent (salesman), sales representative, commercial travel(l)er, drummer *(US)*; ~**volumen** volume of travel; ~**vorbereitungen** travel arrangements, arrangements for a journey; ~**vorbereitungen treffen** to arrange for a journey; ~**wagen** touring car; ~**wecker** travel(l)ing clock; ~**weg** route, itinerary, line of travel; ~**welle** wave of tourists; ~**wesen** travel field; ~**wetterversicherung** tourist-weather insurance; ~**zahlungsmittel** travel fund; ~**zeit** traveltime, *(Saison)* tourist season; ~**ziel** destination, objective; **sein** ~**ziel erreichen** to reach one's journey's end; ~**zuschuß** travel grant; ~**zwischenfälle** incidents of a journey.

Reisigbündel faggot.

Reißbrett drawing board;
~**stadium** blue-print stage; ~**stadt** paper city.

reißen *(Papier, Seil)* to break, *(Telefonverbindungen)* to be cut off, *(zerren)* to wrest, to pull;
an sich ~ to monopolize, to engross, to usurp; **mit sich** ~ *(Welle)* to carry away; **alles mit sich** ~ to bear all before one; **sich um etw.** ~ to scramble for s. th.; **sich um eine Arbeit gerade nicht** ~ not to be keen on doing a job; **jem. einen Brief aus der Hand** ~ to snatch a letter from s. one's hand; **Gespräch an sich** ~ to monopolize a conversation; **j. aus seinen Illusionen** ~ to disillusion s. o.; **sich die Kleider vom Leib** ~ to rip off one's clothes; **Loch in seine Ersparnisse** ~ to make a large hole in one's savings; **Loch in die Mauer** ~ *(Explosion)* to blow a hole into the wall; **Lücke** ~ to leave a gap; **Macht an sich** ~ to seize power; **j. aus unserer Mitte** ~ to snatch s. o. from our midst; **sich etw. unter den Nagel** ~ to walk off with s. th.; **Possen** ~ to play the fool; **Seite aus einem Buch** ~ to tear a page out of a book; **j. rechtzeitig zur Seite** ~ to pull s. o. to the side in time; **in Stücke** ~ to tear into pieces; **Tapete von der Wand** ~ to strip the wall; **j. aus seiner gewohnten Umgebung** ~ to drag s. o. from his accustomed environment; **j. mit ins Verderben** ~ to drag s. o. down with one; **Worte aus dem Zusammenhang** ~ to take words out of context; **Ziegel vom Dach** ~ to rip the tiles from the roof; **Zuhörer von den Sitzen** ~ to sweep the audience off its feet; **wenn alle Stricke** ~ if the worst comes to the worst.

reißend | abgehen (Absatz finden) to have a quick draft, to be of quick sale, to sell rapidly (like hot cakes, dogs, *US*);
~**e Geschäfte machen** to do a roaring trade; ~**er Strom** raging torrent; ~**es Tier** wild animal.

Reißer *(Erfolgsstück)* big draw, box-office success, *(Film)* thriller, *(Buch)* best-seller.

reißerische Aufmachung sensational getup.

Reiß | feder drawing (ruling) pen; ~**festigkeit** breaking strength; ~**grenze** tensile strength; ~**leine** *(Fallschirm)* release cord; ~**verschluß** zip (slide, *US*) fastener, zipper; **mit einem** ~**verschluß schließen** to zip; ~**verschlußtasche** zipper bag; ~**wolf** opener, shredding machine, shredder, devil, wool mill; ~**zwecke** drawing pin *(Br.)*, thumbtack *(US)*.

reiten, vor Anker *(Schiff)* to be riding at anchor; **j. über den Haufen** ~ to ride s. o. down; **Idee zu Tode** ~ to ride an idea to death; **Prinzipien** ~ to harp on one's principles; **auf Schusters Rappen** ~ to ride on Shank's mare; **sein Steckenpferd** ~ to start on one's hobby horse; **j. in die Tinte** ~ to land s. o. in a tricky situation; **keine krummen Touren** ~ to be perfectly straight in one's dealings.

reitende Artillerie mounted artillery.

Reiter rider, horseman, trooper *(mil.)*;
spanische ~ barbed wire barrier; **spanischer** ~ cheval-de-frise; ~**abteilung** troop.

Reit | pferd saddle horse; ~**schule** riding school; ~**wechsel** accommodation bill, kite *(Br.)*, windmill *(Br.)*; ~**wechsel ausstellen** to [fly a] kite *(Br.)*; ~**weg** bridle path.

Reiz *(Anreiz)* stimulus, incentive, impulse, *(Kitzel)* tickle, *(Verlockung)* enticement, lure, temptation;
~ **exotischer Länder** fascination of exotic countries; ~**e eines Landes** attractions of a country; ~ **des Neuen** charm of novelty; ~ **der See** lure of the sea; ~ **des Verbotenen** attraction of forbidden fruits;

geringen ~ ausüben to have little attraction; **großen ~ auf j. ausüben** to appeal greatly to s. o.; **keinen ~ mehr ausüben** to pall; **jds. ~en zum Opfer fallen** to fall victim to s. one's lure; **seine ~e spielen lassen** to play off graces.

reizen to irritate, to stimulate, *(ärgerlich machen)* to annoy, to nettle, to rile;
j. bis zum Äußersten ~ to provoke s. o. beyond endurance; **zum Beschmieren ~** to tempt to scribble on it; **Gaumen ~** to tickle one's palate; **Hund ~** to tease a dog; **zur Nachahmung ~** to encourage imitation; **j. bis zur Weißglut ~** to make s. one's blood boil; **zum Widerspruch ~** to invite contradiction; **j. zum Zorn ~** to provoke s. one's anger.

reizend delightful, attractive, charming, engaging;
~ von jem. sein to be sweet of s. o.; **sich ~ unterhalten** to have a most delightful chat;
~e Bescherung pretty kettle of fish; **~es kleines Dorf** charming little village.

Reiz|klima bracing climate; **~partie** *(Buchhandel)* attractive batch (lot); **~schwelle** stimulus threshold, *(Werbung)* boundary.

reizvoll attractive, charming;
~e Aufgabe fascinating job.

Reizwäsche French lingerie, flimsies *(coll.)*.

Rekapitulation recapitulation, summing up.

rekapitulieren to recapitulate, to sum up.

Reklamation reclamation, claim, *(Einspruch)* protest, objection, *(Mängelrüge)* complaint;
berechtigte ~ legitimate complaint; **spätere ~** subsequent claim;
~ annehmen (anerkennen) to admit a claim; **~ berücksichtigen** to consider a complaint; **zwecks ~ einschicken** to write in *(US)*; **~en entgegennehmen** to receive complaints; **~ vorbringen** to bring one's complaints to attention; **~ zurückweisen** to reject a claim.

Reklamations|abteilung claim (complaints) department; **~brief, ~schreiben** complaint letter; **~frist** time for complaint; **~stelle** complaint department; **~verfahren** complaints procedure.

Reklame advertisement, advertising, publicity, propaganda, puff *(Br.)*, claptrap, boost *(US)*, promotion *(US)*, *(im Schaufenster)* window dressing;
durch ~ verschandelt disfigured by advertisement; **mit ~ übersät** plastered with advertisements;
ausgefallene ~ off-beat advertising; **im ganzen Land durchgeführte ~** national advertisement; **einwandfreie ~** clean advertisement; **ganzseitige ~** full-page advertisement; **gemeinsame ~** association advertising; **hochtönende ~** high-pressure advertising; **irreführende ~** misleading advertisement; **kolossale ~** big boom; **laute ~** ballyhoo, puff; **marktschreierische ~** flaming (puffing, *Br.*) advertisement, puff *(Br.)*; **täuschende ~** deceptive advertising; **überregionale ~** national (nation-wide) advertisement; **übertriebene ~** puffery *(Br.)*; **wirksamste ~** advertising getting the best results;
~ innerhalb des Ladens point-of-purchase advertising; **~ in den Zeitungen** newspaper advertisement;
gute ~ abgeben to serve as good propaganda; **~ machen** to advertise, to boom, to write up, to promote, to boost, to publicize, to cry up, to push, to set up propaganda; **in ~ machen** to be in the advertising game; **für sich selbst ~ machen** to advertise o. s. (one's work); **für seine Erzeugnisse ~ machen** to advertise one's wares; **mit ~ übersät sein** to be covered with advertisements; **Stadt mit ~ überschütten** to bill a town; **großzügige ~ veranstalten** to advertise widely;
offiziell überprüfte ~ankündigungen guaranteed advertising; **wilder ~anschlag** fly posting; **~anzeige** advertising, advertisement; **zweiseitige ~anzeige** center spread *(US)*; **~artikel** advertised article (product), leading line; **~auslage** advertising display, layout; **~ballon** propaganda balloon; **~beigabe** dealer help; **~beilage** *(Zeitung)* inset, stuffer *(US)*; **~beitrag** advertising contribution; **~beleuchtung** advertising lights; **fachmännische ~beratung** expert advertising advice; **~bild** advertising picture; **~broschüre** promotional brochure, leaflet; **~drucksache** advertising matter; **~feldzug** advertising campaign; **~feldzug durchführen** to run an advertising campaign; **~fläche** advertising space, hoarding, billboard *(US)*; **bewilligter ~fonds** appropriation for advertising, advertising appropriation; **~gerüst** signboard *(US)*; **~geschenk** advertising article, free gift; **~gestaltung** copywriting; **aus ~gründen** for propaganda advantage; **~idee** advertising idea; **~kärtchen [zur Beschreibung der Ware]** store sign (card); **~kosten** advertising expenditure (cost, outlay), costs for advertising; **~löscher** advertising blotter; **~macher** booster; **~masche** public-relations stunt; **~material** advertising (advertisement) material; **~material für Postwurfsendungen** direct mail literature; **~mätzchen** advertising stunts; **~plakat** advertising poster; **~preis** knockdown (early-bird, cut-rate) price, loss leader; **~prospekt** handbill, leaflet, throwaway, dodger *(US)*; **~rummel** ballyhoo, publicity stunt, boom *(US)*; **~rundschreiben** circular; **~sachen** dealer aids, advertising material; **~schild** publicity sign; **helleuchtendes ~schild** sky sign; **~schild im Schaufenster** window card; **~schlager** stunt; **~schlepp** air-poster towing; **~schönheit** glamo(u)r girl; **~schrift** advertising type; **~schriften** propaganda writings; **ganzseitige ~seite** bleed; **~seiten** advertising pages, pages of advertising; **~sendung** *(Rundfunk)* commercial, plug, soap opera *(US)*; **~steuer** advertising tax, tax on advertising; **~streifen** *(Buch)* blurb; **~stück** showpiece; **~tätigkeit** advertising activity; **~technik** advertising technique; **~teil** *(Zeitung)* advertising columns (part); **~text** advertising copy; **~texter** copywriter; **~träger** medium; **~trick** stunt, bluff, gimmick *(US)*; **~trommeln rühren** to drum up business *(fam.)*; **~überschrift** advertising headline; **~unkosten** advertising expenses (charges); **~unternehmer** advertising agency; **~verbot** ad ban *(US)*; **~verfasser** copywriter; **~verkauf** bargain sale; **~wagen** advertising van; **~wand** advertisement hoarding, billboard *(US)*; **~wert** attention value; **~woche** propaganda week; **~wort** slogan; **~zeichner** advertising artist (designer), signwriter; **~zettel** handbill, throwaway, leaflet, dodger *(US)*; **~zettel verteilen** to scatter handbills; **~zweck** advertising end, show purpose.

reklamieren *(Anspruch erheben)* to claim, *(beanstanden)* to complain, *(Einspruch erheben)* to protest, to object, *(zurückverlangen)* to reclaim;
Paket bei der Post ~ to enquire at the post office about a parcel; **schriftlich ~** to lodge a complaint; **Sendung beim Hersteller ~** to make enquiries with a manufacturer about the goods ordered.

rekognoszieren reconnoitre, to find out.

rekonstruieren, Verbrechen to reconstruct a crime.

Rekonstruktion eines Verbrechens reconstruction of a crime.

Rekonvaleszent convalescent.

Rekonvaleszentenheim convalescent home.

Rekonvaleszenz convalescence.

Rekonzentration reconcentration, regrouping.

Rekord *(Kurs)* record, all-time high *(US)*;
unübertroffener ~ unbroken record;
~ aufstellen to set up a record; **~ brechen** to break (beat) a record, to cut a record; **alle ~e schlagen** to reach an all-time high *(US)*;
~absatzziffern record-breaking sales; **~aufträge** record orders; **~besuch** record attendance; **~ergebnisse zeitigen** to run a record pace; **nahezu ~ergebnisse zeitigen** to enter at close to record rates; **~ernte** bumper crop *(fam.)*; **~gewinn** record profit (earnings); **~gewinne verzeichnen** to notch up record profits; **~höhe** peak level, record level (peak, high); **~höhe der Gewinne** profit record; **~höhen erreichen** to climb to record levels; **~inhaber** record holder; **~jahr** record year; **~leistung** record performance; **unerreichte ~leistung** all-time high *(US)*; **~mehrheit** record majority; **~preis** record price; **~produktion** record production (output); **~satz** record rate; **~sparleistung** record savings volume; **~stand** record level; **~tiefstand** record low; **~überschuß** record surplus; **~verbrauch** consumption record; **~zeit** record time; **~ziffern** record figures.

Rekrut recruit, rooky *(sl.)*, dogface *(US sl.)*, *(mar.)* boot *(US)*;
ausgehobener ~ conscript, enlisted man *(US)*, enlistee *(US)*;
~en bimsen to lick a recruit into shape; **~en drillen** to set up recruits; **~en einziehen** to conscribe (enlist) recruits, *(bisher Unabkömmliche)* to comb out *(Br., sl.)*; **~en werben** to beat up for recruits.

Rekruten|ausbildung basic training; **~aushebung** levy; **~jahrgang** class.

rekrutieren to recruit, to enlist, to conscribe, to enroll;
Mitarbeiter nur aus Universitätsabsolventen ~ to recruit one's staff exclusively from university undergraduates.

rekrutiert enlisted [in the army], drafted.

Rekrutierter enlisted man *(US)*, enlistee *(US)*, conscript, draftee *(US)*.

Rekrutierung recruiting, recruitment, *(mil.)* enlisting, enlistment, draft *(US)*, enrol(l)ment.

Rekrutierungs|büro recruiting office (firm); **~feldzug** recruiting campaign; **~gesetz** Draft Act; **~gesetz für Ausländer** Foreign Enlistment Act *(Br.)*; **~liste** draft record *(US)*.

Rekta|giro, ~indossament restrictive endorsement (indorsement); **~klausel** clause not to order, restrictive clause;

~**konnossement** straight bill of lading *(US)*; ~**lagerschein** nonnegotiable warehouse receipt; ~**papier** nonnegotiable instrument, instrument not to order, *(Aktie)* registered security; ~**scheck** nonnegotiable check *(US)* (cheque, *Br.*), cheque not to order *(Br.)*; ~**schuldverschreibung** registered debenture; ~**wechsel** nonnegotiable bill of exchange.

Rektifikationsposten valuation item.

Rektor *(Schule)* headmaster, principal *(US)*, *(Universität)* university chancellor *(US)*, rector, president *(US)*, master *(US)*, warden *(Br.)*, *(schottische Universitäten)* Lord Rector.

Rektorat headmastership, *(Universität)* rectorship, principalship.

Rekultivierung recultivation.

Rekurs *(Regreß)* recourse.

Relais *(el.)* relay;
~ **ansprechen lassen** to operate a relay;
~**betrieb** relay operation; ~**sender** repeater station, *(Fernsehen)* satellite television relay; ~**station** relay (booster) station; **Nachrichten durch** ~**stationen übertragen** to relay news; ~**übertragung** rebroadcast, relay transmission, repeater; ~**wähler** *(tel.)* relay-type selector.

Relation relation[ship];
~ **von Anzeigen zum Text** quota of advertising to editorial.

Relationsprinzip *(Inventur)* first-in, first-out principle.

relativ relative, comparative;
~ **gut gehen** to go reasonably well;
~**e Häufigkeit** *(Statistik)* relative frequency; ~**e Konterbande** conditional contraband; ~**e Kosten** relative cost; ~**e Mehrheit** relative majority; ~**er Wert** relative value.

Relativitätstheorie principle of relativity.

Relegation *(Universität)* rustication, expulsion, suspension;
mit der ~ **rechnen müssen** to be under threat of expulsion.

relegieren *(von der Universität)* to expel, to suspend, to drop, to rusticate, to send down *(Br.)*.

relevant relevant, pertinent, material.

Relief|druck relief [printing]; ~**karte** relief map.

Religion religion, denomination, belief, confession, creed.

Religions|bekenntnis profession; ~**freiheit** religious liberty; ~**gemeinschaft** community of religion, religious community (body, society); **der gleichen** ~**gemeinschaft angehören** to be of the same persuasion; ~**unterricht** religious education; ~**zugehörigkeit** religious affiliation.

religiös religious;
streng ~ pious, devout.

Reling des Schiffes ship's rail.

Rembours|abteilung commercial credit department; ~**bank** commercial bank, merchant bank[er]; ~**geschäft** merchant banking, documentary credit operation; ~**kommission** documentary provision.

Rembourskredit commercial (acceptance, draft, documentary, reimbursement) credit, commercial letter of credit;
~ **abschließen** to arrange for an acceptance credit;
~**geschäft** commercial (merchant) banking; ~**institut** commercial bank, merchant bank[er].

Rembourstratte documentary (reimbursement) draft.

Remedium *(Münze)* remedy, tolerance.

Remise shed, coach, carriage house.

Remissier intermediate broker.

Remission *(Buchhändler)* return;
körperlose ~ token return.

Remissionsrecht right to return.

Remittende returned article, returner.

Remittenden unsold (surplus) copies, goods returned, overrun;
~**bearbeitung** handling of unsold copies; ~**exemplar** return copy; ~**rückgabe** return of unsold copies.

Remittent remitter, payee of a bill of exchange, *(Waren)* consignor;
fingierter ~ fictitious payee; **wahlweise** ~**en** alternative payees.

remittieren to make (send, provide for) remittance, *(Waren)* to return;
zum Abrechnungstag ~ to return by settlement date.

Rendant treasurer, accountant.

Rendezvous appointment, tryst, date *(coll.)*;
~**platz** trysting place.

Rendite revenue, investment (net) return, lucrativeness, profit, *(Wertpapier)* [interest] yield, income basis, return income *(US)*;
angemessene ~ fair return on investment; **äußerst attraktive** ~ mouth-watering return; **effektive** ~ net yield, effective interest yield; **feste** ~ fixed rate of return; **geringe** ~ low rate of return; **gute** ~ good rate of return; **sinkende** ~ disminishing yield;
~ **einer Anlage** yield of an investment; ~ **einer Obligation unter Zugrundelegung der Gesamtlaufzeit** maturity basis; ~**n auf dem Rentenmarkt** bond market yields; **gegenwärtige** ~ **mündelsicherer Wertpapiere** going rate on gilts *(Br.)*;
geringe ~ **abwerfen** to yield little; **gute** ~ **abwerfen (bringen)** to be a lucrative business, to give a good return on an investment; **effektive** ~ **von 6% bringen** to yield an effective sum of 6 per cent; **hohe** ~ **erbringen** to yield high interest (returns); ~ **ergeben** to yield; **gute** ~ **erwirtschaften** to put on a profitable track, to bring in a good income, to get a good return on an investment; **so viel** ~ **aus einem Vermögen erwirtschaften** to get so much out of a property; **geringe** ~ **erzielen** to yield little; **hohe** ~ **erzielen** to yield high interest; **wieder** ~ **bei einem Unternehmen erzielen** to put a company in the black *(US coll.)*;
~**basis** profitability, profit basis; **auf** ~**basis betreiben** to run for profit; **umgekehrtes** ~**gefälle** reverse yield gap; ~**haus** tenement (apartment, *US*) house; ~**kalkulation** rate-of-return calculation; ~**konzeption** return-on-investment concept; ~**kurve** yield curve; **hochverzinsliches** ~**objekt** high-rent building; ~**satz** rate of investment (return, *US*); ~**verantwortung** profit responsibility; ~**verhältnis** bond-stock ratio.

Renegat renegade, turncoat.

Renn|bahn *(Motor)* race course (track), speedway *(US)*; ~**boot** speedboat, race (racing) boat.

Rennen race;
totes (unentschiedenes) ~ deadhead;
gut im ~ **liegen** *(Kandidat)* to be in the running (run, *US*); **das** ~ **machen** to breast the tape.

Renn|fahrer race (racing, *Br.*) driver, racing motorist, racer; ~**fahrzeug**, ~**wagen** racing car, racer; ~**leitung** race committee, stewards; ~**pferd** race horse; ~**pferde halten** to be on the turf; ~**platz** race course; ~**platzbesucher** racegoer; ~**programm** race card; ~**sportwelt** the turf; ~**stall** stable; ~**stallbesitzer** racehorse owner; ~**strecke** race track (circuit), race, *(Autorennen)* motor-racing track, speedway; ~**tip** racing tip, drum *(sl.)*; ~**wagen** racing car; ~**wagen der Formel I** Formular 1 racing (grand prix) car; ~**wagenhersteller** racing-car builder; ~**wettsteuer** betting (race-betting) tax; ~**woche** race week.

Renommee reputation, fame, renown;
gutes ~ **haben** to be held in high repute, to gain a good reputation; **sein** ~ **verbessern** to improve one's safety record.

Renommieren swash[buckling], splurge, showing off.

renommieren to draw the long bow, to talk big.

Renommierer braggart, swaggerer, boaster, swashbuckler.

renommiert, gut of good repute, renowned.

renovieren to repair, to renew, to renovate, to refurbish, *(Innenraum)* to redecorate, to do up;
Haus ~ to renovate a house.

Renovierung renovation, repair, face-lifting, *(Innenraum)* redecoration;
sich in der ~ **befinden** to be under repair; ~**en vornehmen** to carry out repairs.

Renovierungs|arbeiten, kostspielige costly renovations; **während der** ~**arbeiten geschlossen sein** to be closed during repair; ~**auftrag** repair order; ~**kosten** repair costs; ~**vorhaben** renovation scheme.

rentabel lucrative, profitable, paying, remunerative, payoff, profit-earning, worth-while, payable;
knapp ~ marginal; **nicht mehr** ~ submarginal; **wirtschaftlich** ~ commercially (economically) viable;
sein Geld ~ **anlegen** to invest one's money to good account; **Geschäft** ~ **gestalten** to put a business on a payable basis; ~ **produzieren** to produce at an economic figure; ~ **sein** to be a lucrative business, to pay its way, to be in the black *(US coll.)*.

Rentabilität earnings (profit-earning) capacity, earning power, remunerativeness, profitability;
normale ~ fair return;
~ **des Eigenkapitals** profitability of net worth; ~ **einer Werbesendung** program(me) turnover;
~ **im folgenden Jahr nur schwer garantieren** to run into more earning troubles next year; ~ **eines Geschäfts sicherstellen** to put a business on a paying basis.

Rentabilitäts|analyse analysis of surplus; ~**aussichten** profit-earning prospects; ~**berechnung** calculation of profits, cost accounting (system), costing; ~**bild** survey of productiveness; ~**chancen durch Investitionen auf bisher vernachlässigten Gebieten verbessern** to generate additional earnings through investments in special undervalued situations; ~**darstellung** rental figure; **bei reinem** ~**denken** on a strictly commercial rate-of-return calculation; ~**diagramm** profitability graph; ~**faktor** markup *(US)*; ~**gesichtspunkte** profit aspects; ~**grenze** margin of productiveness (profitableness), marginal profit, break-even point; ~**grundlage** cost basis of accounting; ~**prüfung** break-even analysis; ~**rechnung** cost accounting, costing; ~**schätzung** cost accounting (system), costing, assessment of profitability; ~**schätzung einer Investition** investment appraisal; ~**schwelle** marginal profit, break-even point, profitability level; ~**schwelle erreichen** to break even; **an die ~schwelle heranbringen** to put on a profitable track; ~**situation rapide verschlechtern** to send earnings into a dive; ~**standpunkt** profit motive; ~**steigerung** earnings increase; ~**tabelle** break-even chart; ~**trend** profitability trend; ~**untersuchung** economic study; ~**verbesserung** earnings improvement (recovery); ~**vergleich** earnings comparison; ~**zeitpunkt** break-even date; ~**ziffer** break-even figure, *(Kurzversicherung)* rental figure; ~**ziffer des Warenlagers** profitability index of stock held.

rentable|s Geschäft paying (profitable) business (enterprise), paying concern, lucrative business (transaction); ~ **Kapitalanlage** profitable (remunerative) investment; ~**s Unternehmen** remunerative undertaking.

Rentamt bursar's office.

Rente *(Altersrente)* [retiring] pension, old-age pension, *(Einkommen)* income, revenue, *(Ertrag)* profit, return, *(Jahresrente)* annuity, *(Kapitalertrag)* yield, unearned (investment) income, *(Miete)* rent, *(Sozialversicherung)* benefit, social security benefit *(US)*, *(Unterstützung)* [old-age] benefit, *(Zinsertrag)* interest;

~**n** *(Staatsanleihen)* funds, governmental bonds;

abgekürzte ~ terminable (temporary) annuity; **auf den Lebenshaltungsindex (Anlagenwertzuwachs) abgestellte** ~ variable annuity; **ablösbare** ~ redeemable annuity; **aufgeschobene** ~ deferred annuity; **aufgewertete** ~ revalorized annuity; **testamentarisch ausgesetzte** ~ barren rent; **ausländische** ~**n** *(Börse)* external bonds; **bedingte** ~ annuity certain; **zeitlich befristete** ~ termed annuity; **beitragsfreie** ~ noncontributory annuity (pension); **beitragspflichtige** ~ contributory pension; **dynamische** ~ index-linked pension; **ewige** ~ perpetuity, irredeemable bond, perpetual annuity; **sofort fällige** ~ immediate annuity; **in der Zukunft fällige** ~ deferred (reversionary) annuity; **festverzinsliche** ~**n** *(Börse)* fixed-interest bearing securities; **gekürzte** ~ reduced annuity; **gleichbleibende** ~ level annuity; **immerwährende** ~ perpetuity; **kleine** ~ small competence; **kündbare** ~ terminable annuity; **lebenslängliche** ~ life pension, perpetual (whole life) annuity, annuity for life (in perpetuity); **sofort fällige, lebenslängliche** ~ immediate annuity; **nachschüssige** ~ ordinary annuity; **nominelle** ~ nominal (peppercorn, *Br.*) rent; **stetige** ~ continuous annuity; **steuerfreie** ~ clear annuity, nontaxable pension; **temporäre** ~ temporary annuity; **trockene** ~ rent seck; **umwandlungsfähige** ~ convertible annuity; **unablösbare** ~ irredeemable annuity; **verkürzte** ~ reduced annuity; **vorschüssige** ~ annuity due; **wirtschaftliche** ~ economic (ordinary) rent; **zeitliche** ~ termed annuity;

~ **mit Barausschüttung nicht erschöpfter Prämienzahlungen** cash-refund [life] annuity; ~ **ohne Beitragspflicht** noncontributory pension; ~ **mit vollem Betrag nach dem Todesjahr** complete annuity; ~ **mit nicht vollem Betrag im Todesjahr** curtailed (curtate) annuity; ~ **im Fall einer Berufskrankheit** industrial injury benefit *(Br.)*; ~ **mit bestimmter Laufzeit** annuity certain; ~ **mit unbestimmter Laufzeit** contingent annuity; ~ **für Mutter und Kind** mothers' pension *(US)*; ~ **aus der Sozialversicherung** old-age (retirement) pension, social security benefit *(US)*; ~ **auf den Überlebensfall** reversionary annuity; ~ **einer Versicherung über verbundene Leben** two-life annuity;

~ **ablösen** to redeem an annuity; ~ **durch Pauschalbezahlung ablösen** to commute an annuity for (into) a lump sum; **in** ~**n anlegen** *(Börse)* to place in funds; ~ **während der Beschäftigungszeit laufend dem Bruttolohn anpassen** to revalue a pension pre-retirement in line with earnings; ~ **nach Ausscheiden aus dem Berufsleben laufend dem Preisniveau anpassen** to revalue a pension pre-retirement in line with prices; ~**n der Preisentwicklung anpassen** to equalize social security benefits to price movements *(US)*; **lebenslängliche** ~ **aussetzen** to liferent; **jem. eine jährliche** ~ **von 5000 Dollar aussetzen** to settle $ 5000 a year on s. o.; **seiner Schwester eine jährliche** ~ **von 4000 Dollar aussetzen** to make one's sister an allowance of $ 4000 a year; ~ **auswerfen** to settle an annuity; **zu einer** ~ **berechtigen** to carry a pension; ~ **beziehen** to hold an annuity, *(Pension)* to draw a pension; **sich in lebenslängliche** ~**n einkaufen** to invest one's fortune in life annuities; **in** ~ **gehen** to retire on a pension; **jem. eine** ~ **gewähren** to pay s. o. an annuity; ~ **kapitalisieren** to capitalize an annuity; **von einer** ~ **leben** to live on a pension; **in** ~ **sein** to be retired (pensioned off); ~ **tilgen** to redeem an annuity; ~**n umstellen** to recalculate pensions; **jem. eine** ~ **zahlen** to pay s. o. an annuity.

Renten|ablösung commutation (liquidation, redemption) of an annuity; ~**absatz** annuity sales; ~**abteilung** annuity department; ~**anleihe** annuity bonds, *(unkündbar)* perpetual loan; ~**anpassung** revaluation of a pension; ~**anspruch** retirement right; ~**ansprüche haben** to be entitled to a pension; ~**anstalt** life-annuity company; **gestaffelter** ~**anteil** *(Sozialversicherung)* graduated pension part *(Br.)*; ~**anwartschaft** pension expectancy; ~**aufbesserung** increase in pensions, pension increase; ~**ausgleichsforderung** pension equalization claim; ~**ausschließungsgrund** disqualification from benefit; ~**auszahlung** pension (rent) payment; ~**auszahlung sicherstellen** to service an annuity; ~**auszahlung wählen** to select an instal(l)ment option; ~**baisse** slump on the bond market; ~**bank** mortgage bank; ~**barwert** annuity value; ~**basis** annuity basis; ~**beginn** beginning receiving a pension; ~**beitragseingänge** cash inflow on the pension side; ~**bemessung** valuation of a pension; ~**bemessungsgrundlage** valuation basis; ~**berater** retirement counsel(l)or; ~**beratung** retirement counselling; ~**berechnung** annuity computation.

rentenberechtigt|sein to become entitled to benefit, to begin receiving a pension, to qualify for a pension under national insurance *(Br.)*;

~**es Alter** pension age.

Renten|berechtigter annuitant, holder (grantee) of an annuity, annuity holder, beneficiary; ~**bescheid** pension approval certificate; ~**bestellung** settlement of annuity; ~**besteuerung** taxation of pensions; ~**bewilligung** granting of a pension; ~**bezieher** holder of an annuity, annuitant, recipient of a pension, beneficiary; ~**bezüge** income received from a pension, pensions; ~**bezugsdauer** perpetuity period; ~**brief** annuity bond; ~**depot** bond deposit; ~**dienst** bond service; **versicherungspflichtige** ~**einheit** pension unit; ~**einkommen** rental income; ~**empfänger** annuitant, holder (grantee) of an annuity, *(Altersversorgung)* holder (recipient) of a pension, pensioner, rentier, [primary] beneficiary; ~**entziehung** forfeiture of a pension; ~**erhöhung** pension increase; ~**erhöhung vornehmen** to put up the rate of a pension; ~**erwartung** expected pension; ~**fachmann** bond analyst; ~**fonds** annuity trust, alimentary trust, *(Kapitalanlagegesellschaft)* bond fund; ~**formel** *(Sozialversicherung)* benefit formula; ~**gewährung** granting of a pension; ~**haus** tenement house, apartment house *(US)*; ~**hausbaustelle** apartment-house site *(US)*; ~**höchstsätze** benefit limits; ~**höhe** pension level; ~**höhe festsetzen** to rate a pension; ~**kurs** bond price; ~**last** pension costs; ~**leistungen** pension payments; ~**leistungen im Invaliditätsfall** long-term disability benefits.

Rentenmarkt bond (gilt-edged, *Br.*) market;

~ **inspirieren** to buoy the bond market;

~**renditen** bond-market yields; ~**schwäche** bond-market weakness.

Renten|mehrbetrag pension increase; ~**nachzahlung** supplementary pension; ~**neufestsetzung** revaluation of a pension; ~**niveau** pension level; ~**papiere** bonds, government annuities; **langfristige** ~**papiere** long gilts *(Br.)*; ~**pfändung** garnishment of a pension; ~**police** annuity policy; ~**reform** pension reform; ~**rendite** government bond yield; ~**rückstand** arrears of annuity; ~**sachbearbeiter** disablement resettlement officer; ~**sachbearbeiter für Umschulungsfälle** disablement resettlement officer; ~**schein** annuity certificate; ~**schuld** annuity charge; ~**schuldverschreibung** annuity bond; ~**steigerungsbetrag** pension increment; ~**stiftung** annuity gift; ~**system** pensions system; ~**titel** annuity bonds; ~**verschreibung** annuity bond.

Rentenversicherung old-age pension insurance, *(Leibrente)* annuity insurance, *(kollektiv)* group rent insurance;

sich in eine ~ **einkaufen** to invest (sink) money in (buy) an annuity.

Rentenversicherungs|berechtigter pension policy holder, *(Leibrente)* annuity holder, annuitant; ~**police** annuity policy; **private gewinnbeteiligte** ~**police** personal pension with profits policy; ~**police zugunsten eines überlebenden Dritten** survivorship annuity policy; ~**vertrag** refund (insurance) annuity contract.

Renten|vertrag contract of annuity, annuity contract; ~**verzeichnis** rentroll, rental; ~**wahlrecht** annuity option; ~**werte** bonds, gilts *(Br.)*; ~**werte erwerben** to buy funds; ~**witwe** widow pensioner.

Rentenzahlung annuity [benefit] payment, pension benefit (payment);
auf das letzte Gehalt abgestellte ~ *(Pensionsplan)* final pay; **von Kursschwankungen abhängige** ~ variable annuity; **wöchentliche** ~ weekly rate of pension;
~ **bei Gliederverlust** dismemberment benefit.
Rentenzusammensetzung elements of a pension.
Rentier annuitant, pensioner, rentier, gentleman of independent means, private gentleman, gentleman boarder, scissorbill *(sl.)*;
im Ausland lebender ~ remittance man.
rentieren, sich to pay [one's way (for costs)], to give good returns, *(Betrieb)* to be profitable, *(Ware)* to leave a margin, to answer well; **sich gut** ~ to yield good profits, to pay well; **sich nicht** ~ not to be worthwhile; **sich noch** ~ break even; **sich gerade noch** ~ to wash its face *(Br., sl.)*; **sich in zehn Jahren** ~ to pay its way in ten years.
rentierlich profitable, remunerative;
~**er Betrieb** economic operation, profitable business.
Rentierlichkeit profitability;
~ **einer kostspieligen Fabrikeinrichtung sicherstellen** to make the installation of expensive plant pay.
Rentner annuitant, old-age (retired) pensioner *(US)*, rentier, private gentleman, gentleman of independent means, senior citizen;
~**krankenversicherung** social health insurance for pensioners.
Reorganisation reorganization, readjustment, reconstruction *(Br.)*, revampment *(coll.)*;
mit Entlassungen verbundene ~ house cleaning *(US sl.)*;
~ **einer Gesellschaft** reorganization (refloating) of a company;
~ **der Kommunalverwaltung** local government reorganization;
~ **einer Partei** party reorganization; ~ **eines Unternehmens** reconstruction of a company *(Br.)*, reorganization of a corporation *(US)*.
Reorganisations|aufgabe remodel(l)ing job; ~**ausschuß** reorganization committee; ~**plan**, ~**programm** reorganization program(me), reconstruction plan *(Br.)*.
Reorganisator reorganizer.
reorganisieren to reorganize, to reconstruct *(Br.)*, to refloat, to remodel, to revamp *(coll.)*.
Reparationen leisten to make reparations.
Reparations|abgabe reparation levy *(Br.)*; ~**abkommen** reparation agreement; ~**anleihe** reparation loan; ~**ausschuß** reparation (transfer) committee; ~**forderungen** reparation claims (demands); ~**konto** reparation account; ~**leistungen** payment of reparations; ~**liste** reparation list; ~**programm** reparation program(me); ~**verpflichtung** reparation obligation; ~**zahlungen** reparations.
Reparatur repair, recondition, mending, refection;
in ~ under repair, *(Auto)* in dock;
zur ~ **geben** to hand in for repair.
Reparaturen, üblicherweise anfallende ordinary repairs; **aufgeschobene** ~ deferred maintenance; **bauliche** ~ building repairs; **am Betriebsgebäude durchgeführte** ~ repair of premises; **unterwegs erforderliche** ~ road-side repairs; **zu Lasten des Eigentümers gehende** ~ repairs chargeable to the owner; **geringfügige** ~ minor repairs; **größere** ~ major repairs; **kleine** ~ slight repairs; **laufende** ~ running repairs; **bei der Pachtbeendigung notwendige** ~ dilapidations; **regelmäßig notwendige** ~ ordinary repairs; **unbedingt notwendige** ~ emergency repairs; **dem Mieter obliegende** ~ tenant's repairs; **provisorische** ~ temporary repairs; **umfangreiche** ~ extensive repairs; **unvermeidliche** ~ *(Schiff)* necessary repairs; **zurückgestellte** ~ arrears of repairs;
laufender ~ **bedürfen** to be in need of constant repairs; ~ **durchführen** to carry out repairs; **zur Vornahme von** ~ **in den Hafen einlaufen** to put into port for repairs; **für alle** ~ **aufzukommen haben** *(Pächter)* to be responsible for all dilapidations; ~ **vornehmen lassen** to undergo repairs; **Schiff in** ~ **nehmen** to lay up a ship for repairs; **an einem Mietshaus die notwendigen** ~ **vornehmen** to keep one's tenant house in habitable repair; ~ **an Ort und Stelle vornehmen** to effect repairs on the site.
Reparatur|abteilung repair department; ~**angebot** offer to repair goods; ~**anlagen** repair facilities; ~**anstalt** repair shop; ~**arbeiten** repair activity; **zu** ~**arbeiten einlaufen** to put in for repairs; **während der** ~**arbeiten geschlossen sein** to be closed during repair; ~**auftrag** repair order; ~**aufwand** repair expenditure; ~**ausrüstung** repairing outfit.
reparaturbedürftig out (in need) of repair, out of fix, reparable;
dringend ~ **sein** to be in bad disrepair (in pressing need of repair), to go on the blink *(sl.)*.
Reparatur|bedürftigkeit disrepair, unrepair; ~**dienst** repair service; ~**dock** navy yard.
reparaturfähig reparable, repairable.
Reparatur|fähigkeit reparableness; ~**fahrzeug** repair vehicle; ~**halle** maintenance hall.
Reparaturkosten repairs, repairing charges, cost of (expenditure on) repair(s);
aufgeschobene ~ deferred maintenance (repairs); **zu Ausgleichszwecken über das ganze Jahr verteilte** ~ equalization account;
~ **eines Gebäudes veranschlagen** to estimate the repair of a building;
~**aufwand** expenditure on repairs; **vom Schiffseigner getragenes** ~**drittel** thirds off *(US)*; **Bauunternehmer zu einer** ~**kalkulation auffordern** to ask a contractor to estimate for the repair of a building.
Reparatur|lager service depot; ~**liste** list of repairs (dilapidations, *Br.*); ~**mannschaft** repair crew; ~**möglichkeiten** repair facilities; ~**rechnung** repair bill; ~**rücklage** provision for repair; ~**schein** repair permit; ~**schiff** floating workshop; ~**vereinbarung**, ~**verpflichtung**, ~**vertrag** obligation to repair, repair covenant; ~**werft** ship-repairing company, repair shipyard; ~**werkstatt** repair (repairing, repairman) shop, overhaul workshop, *(Auto)* service station (centre), garage; ~**werkzeuge** repair kit.
reparierbar repairable;
nicht ~ beyond repair.
reparieren to repair, to refit, to mend, to overhaul, to fix up *(US)*, to vamp up *(coll.)*;
nicht mehr zu ~ **sein** to be beyond repair.
repariert werden to be under repair;
nicht mehr ~ **können** to be out (incapable) of repair; ~ **müssen** to want a repair.
repartieren *(Aktien)* to apportion, to reallot, to distribute equally, to scale down an allotment.
Repartierung *(Aktien)* apportionment, [re]allotment;
scharfe ~ heavy scaling down.
Repartitionssteuer apportioned (rated) tax.
repatriieren to repatriate, to relocate.
repatriierte Anleihen repatriated bonds.
Repatriierung repatriation, relocation.
Repatriierungs|abkommen repatriation agreement; ~**beihilfe** relocation assistance; ~**kosten** cost of relocation; ~**prämie** go-home bonus; ~**system** go-home scheme.
Repertoire repertoire, repertory, stock, *(Orchester)* book;
das ganze ~ the whole bag of tricks;
~**stück** stock play.
Repetent repeater, holdover.
repetieren to repeat, to review.
Repetitor tutor, crammer, coacher, coach;
als ~ **tätig sein** to coach.
Repetitortätigkeit coaching.
Replik answer, reply, counterplea *(US)*, replication;
rasch in der ~ quick to answer back;
unbegründete ~ sham reply;
auf die ~ **erwidern** to rejoin; ~ **vorbringen** to deliver a replication.
Report *(Kursabschlag)* premium, contango rate *(Br.)*, over spot *(Br.)*, *(Prolongationsgebühr)* continuation (carrying-over) rate;
in ~ **geben** to give in continuation (pension); **in** ~ **nehmen** to take in continuation (in stock, *Br.*), to continue *(Br.)*, to carry over.
Reportage [news] reporting, on-the-spot account, coverage *(US)*, rewrite *(US)*;
laufende ~ running commentary;
~ **aufgrund von Recherchen** investigative reporting;
~**mannschaft** *(Rundfunk)* broadcasting team.
Reporter reporter, correspondent, pressman *(Br.)*, legman *(US)*;
unerfahrener ~ cub reporter;
einem ~ **einen anonymen Tip zukommen lassen** to give a tip to a reporter on a no-name basis;
~**gruppe** panel of reporters.
Report|geber rate payer of contango, person carried over *(Br.)*; ~**gebühr** continuation *(Br.)* (carrying-over, contango, *Br.*) rate; ~**geld** contango money *(Br.)*; ~**geschäft** continuation business *(Br.)*, carrying over, speculation (jobbing) in contangos *(Br.)*, contango business, trading on margin *(US)*; ~**geschäfte machen** to carry over, to continue, to [lend money on] contango *(Br.)*.
reportieren to carry over, to continue *(Br.)*, to contango *(Br.)*, to trade on margin.

Reportierung carrying over, continuation business *(Br.)*, jobbing in contangos *(Br.)*, trading on margin *(US)*.

Report|kommission commission on contangos *(Br.)*; **~nehmer** person carrying over, giver; **~prämie** contango *(Br.)*; **~provision** commission on contangos *(Br.)*; **~satz** *(Kursabschlag)* contango rate *(Br.)*, *(Prolongation)* continuation *(Br.)* (carrying-over, carryover) rate; **~tag, ~termin** continuation *(Br.)* (carrying-over, making-up, contango, *Br.*) day; **~- und Lombardvorschüsse** advances and loans on security of negotiable stock.

Repräsentant representative, *(Anzeigen)* newspaper (advertising) representative, space salesman *(US coll.)*, *(einer Partei)* exponent, agent;
~en aller Bevölkerungsschichten representative men from all classes; **~ eines souveränen Staates** public person; **~en der Wirtschaft** business representatives.

Repräsentantenhaus House of Representatives *(US)*.

Repräsentanz representation.

Repräsentation representation, official display.

Repräsentations|anzeige prestige announcement; **~aufwand** expenditure of (accruing from) representation; **~erhebung** sample statistic.

repräsentationsfähig representable, institutional.

Repräsentations|fähigkeit representativeness; **~figur** figurehead; **~fonds** representation (office, entertainment) allowance, *(Diplomat)* outfit; **~gelder** *(mil.)* table money; **~inserat** display (institutional, image) advertisement; **~kosten** cost of entertainment; **~pflicht** social function; **ganz gegen ~pflichten eingestellt sein** to have a horror of display; **seine ~pflichten verstärkt wahrnehmen** to bring about a better program(me) of representation; **~tätigkeit** representational activity; **~werbung** image (prestige) advertising; **~zulage** extra pay (sums) for entertainment, allowance for professional expenditure (representation), *(Diplomat)* allowance; **~zulage gewähren** to allow for representation.

repräsentativ representative, functional, *(beeindruckend)* prestigious, imposing, impressive, distinguished;
nicht ~ unrepresentative;
für die USA ~ all-American;
~e Auswahl representative selection; **~es Auswahlverfahren** representative sampling; **~er Charakter** representativeness; **~e Erscheinung** distinguished-looking man; **~e Feier** impressive ceremony; **~e Meinungsumfrage** public opinion poll; **~e Polstergarnitur** handsome three-piece suite; **~er Querschnitt** *(Statistik)* representative conglomeration (selection); **~en Querschnitt der gesamten Wirtschaft darstellen** to represent every facet of business; **in ~em Rahmen stattfinden** to take place in imposing surroundings; **~e Stichprobe** representative sample; **~es Unternehmen** representative firm; **~e Verbrauchergruppe** consumer panel; **zu ~en Zwecken** for purposes of display.

Repräsentativ|auswahl sampling; **~befragung** sample inquiry; **~erhebung** controlled sampling; **~geld** *(Geldsurrogat)* representative money *(US)*.

repräsentieren to represent, to stand for, to typify, *(gesellschaftlich)* to carry out social functions;
seine Firma auf Messen ~ to act as a representative of one's firm at trade fairs; **Zehntel der Gesamtstimmrechte ~** to represent one tenth of the total voting rights.

Repressalien retaliation, retorsion, reprisal, counter (retaliatory) measures;
wirtschaftliche ~ economic reprisals;
~ ergreifen to make reprisals, to exercise (inflict) retaliation.

Reprise *(Film)* repeat, re-issue.

reprivatisieren to reprivatize, to turn over to private managers, to revert to private enterprise *(Br.)*, to hive off, to denationalize;
Industriebetriebe teilweise ~ to return parts of industry to private hands; **Staatsbetriebe ~** to hive off state industries; **ertragreiche Teilgebiete ~** to hive off profitable activities to the private sector.

Reprivatisierung reprivatization, reversion to private ownership *(Br.)*, hiving off, hive-off, denationalization;
~ verstaatlichter Industriegebiete hive-off of state industries.

Reprivatisierungsmaßnahme hiving-off operation.

Reproduktion reproduction, replica, copy[print], *(Vervielfältigung)* multiplication.

Reproduktions|kamera process camera; **~technik** reproduction technique; **~verfahren** reproduction process; **~vorlage** *(Werbeagentur)* copy; **~wert** reproduction cost value.

reproduzierbar reproducible.

Reproduzierbarkeit reproducibility.

reproduzieren to reproduce, to copy.

Reprovorlage artwork.

Reptilienfonds secret service (slush, *US*) fund.

Republik republic, republican government;
~ ausrufen to proclaim a republic.

Republikaner republican;
überzeugter ~ out-and-out republican.

republikanisch republican.

Republikanische Partei Republican Party *(US)*.

Repudiation repudiation.

requirieren to impress, to [put in a] requisition, to commandeer, to intend.

Requirierung requisition;
im Wege der ~ erheben to lay under requisition.

Requisiten *(Theater)* props;
mit ~ ausstatten to set;
~kammer property room, wardrobe; **~raum** scene dock.

Requisiteur *(Theater)* property man (master).

Requisition, einer Gemeinde ~en auferlegen to make requisitions upon a community.

Reservat land reserved, reserve, reservation *(US)*, preserve *(Br.)*.

Reserve reserve[s], reserve fund, bank, *(Bank)* reserve, rest *(Br.)*, *(Lager)* stockpile, *(Leistung)* idle-plant capacity, *(mil.)* reserves, ready reserve *(US)*, *(Rückstellung)* provision, *(Zurückhaltung)* distance;
in ~ in reserve (store), on a string; **mit ~n angereichert** flush with reserves;
abnehmende ~n reserves running short; **angemessene ~** reserve adequacy; **angesammelte ~n** accumulated reserves; **ausgewiesene ~** declared (disclosed) reserve, *(Versicherungsgesellschaft)* underwriting reserve; **ausreichende ~** adequate reserve, reserve adequacy; **nicht ausreichende ~n** reserve deficiency; **außerordentliche ~** provident reserve fund, excess *(US)* (surplus, *US*, true, *US*) reserve; **bare ~** cash reserve; **eingesetzte ~** reserve set up; **freie ~n** available reserve, reserve at disposal, *(Bank)* excess reserves, *(Versicherung)* free surplus; **gesetzliche ~** statutory (legal, *Br.*, lawful, *US*) reserve, *(Bank)* bank (legal) reserves, fractional reserves *(US)*; **über die gesetzlichen Bestimmungen hinausgehende ~n** excess (surplus, *US*) reserves; **hinreichende ~n** adequate reserve, reserve adequacy; **Ist-~** actual reserve, *(Bank)* reserves maintained; **letzte ~** *(fig.)* shot in the locker; **liquide ~n** liquid reserves; **nutzbare ~n** productive resources; **offene ~** declared (disclosed, visible, open, official) reserve; **sofort realisierbare ~n** *(Bankwesen)* liquid reserves; **rückläufige ~n** running down of reserves; **satzungsgemäße ~** statutory reserve; **sichtbare ~n** visible reserves; **stille ~n** secret (latent, hidden, concealed, undisclosed, inner, passive) reserve, hidden (concealed) assets; **strategische ~** *(mil.)* mass of manoeuvre *(Br.)*; **taktische ~n** *(mil.)* reserve forces; **überschüssige ~n** surplus reserve *(US)*; **unerschöpfliche ~n** unfailing resources; **unnütze ~n** sterile reserves; **unzureichende ~n** reserve deficiency; **frei verfügbare ~n** available (general) reserves; **gesetzlich vorgeschriebene ~** statutory (legal, *Br.*, lawful, *US*) reserve, *(Bankwesen)* bank (lawful, fractional, *US*) reserves; **vertraglich vorgesehene ~n** reserve required by contract; **zweckbedingte ~n** reserve for special purposes;
~ an Arbeitskräften labo(u)r reserve; **~ für unvorhergesehene Ausgaben** margin for unforeseen expenses; **~n einer Bank** bank (fractional, required, *US*) reserves; **~ im Fall der Liquidation** reserve capital; **~ für besondere Fälle** contingency fund, working margin; **~n für zweifelhafte Forderungen** bad-debt *(US)* (doubtful, *Br.*) reserve; **~n für zurückkommende Verpackung** return-package reserve; **~n für schwebende Versicherungsfälle** reserves for claims pending;
der ~ angehören *(mil.)* to be on the reserve list; **~n angreifen** to raid (draw on) the reserves; **~n anlegen** *(Bilanz)* to make provisions; **finanzielle ~n irgendwo im Ausland anlegen** to build up a financial nest-egg somewhere abroad; **unzureichende ~n anreichern** to rebuild inadequate reserves; **~ ansammeln (aufbauen)** to build up (accumulate) reserves; **~ auffüllen** to replenish the reserves; **~ auflösen** to release a reserve; **~n bilden** to create reserves; **große ~n bilden** to put large sums to reserve; **Unangemessenheit der ~n darlegen** to disclose a material inadequacy of reserves; **seine ~n offen darlegen** to disclose one's reserves; **~n einberufen** *(mil.)* to conscript reserves; **alle ~n einsetzen** to be working flat out *(coll.)*; **noch ~n haben** still to have some money on hand, to have on ice *(US)*; **unzureichende ~n haben** to be short in one's reserves; **alle ~n aufgebraucht haben** to have exhausted every resource; **~n einzusetzen haben**

to have much at stake; **finanzielle ~n als Rückhalt haben** to have recourse to financial reserves; **aus seiner ~ heraustreten** to depart from one's reserve, to thaw; **~n schwinden lassen** to draw on one's reserves; **~n in immer stärkerem Maße in Anspruch nehmen** to dip even deeper into reserves; **sich keinerlei ~n schaffen** to put all one's goods in the shopwindow; **stille ~n schaffen** to build up a secret reserve fund; **~n unterhalten** to maintain reserves; **über ausreichende stille ~n verfügen** to be well padded with hidden reserves; **den ~n zugerechnet werden** to be classifiable as reserve; **von den ~n zehren** to draw on the reserves; **~n aus dem Verkehr ziehen** *(Weltwährungsfonds)* to cancel reserves; **auf seine ~n zurückgreifen** to fall back on (draw [up]on) one's reserves; **Betrag den ~n zuweisen** to carry an amount to reserve;
~anker spare anchor; **~anlage** stand-by plant; **industrielle ~armee** reserve army of enemployed labo(u)r; **~ausweis** reserve statement *(US)*; **~batterie** spare battery; **~betrag** appropriated (reserved) surplus; **~betrag für unvorhergesehene Fälle** contingency fund, working margin; **~einheit** *(mil.)* reserve echelon, reserve forces *(Br.)*; **kollektive ~einheit** *(Weltwährungsfonds)* collective reserve unit; **~einrichtungen** standby facilities; **~exemplar** spare copy; **~fahrer** emergency man; **~forderung** *(Weltwährungsfonds)* reserve claim; **~gerät** stand-by; **~guthaben** *(Weltwährungsfonds)* reserve holding; **~kanister** jerry can; **~kapazität** industrial plant reserve; **gesetzlich nicht erforderliches ~kapital** nonstatutory capital reserves.

Reservekonto reserve (contingent, *Br.*) account;
dem ~ überweisen, auf ~ verbuchen to place (put) to reserve.

Reserve|kräfte emergency hands; **~lager** reserve stock, buffer warehouse, *(Rohstoffe)* buffer stock; **~lazarett** reserve hospital; **~lokomotive** stand-by locomotive; **~meldung** reserve statement *(US)*.

Reservenabbau raid on the reserves;
~ verursachen to draw on one's reserve.

Reserven|anhäufung, ~ansammlung pyramiding (build-up) of reserves; **~auflösung** disposition of (reduction in) reserves.

Reservenberechnung *(Versicherung)* valuation;
~ nach dem Bruttowert der Prämien gross valuation; **~ nach dem Nettowert der Prämien** net valuation.

Reserven|bestimmungen reserve requirements; **~bildung** creation (accumulation) of reserves, appropriations of surplus *(US)*; **~charakter haben** to have the character of reserves; **~einsatz** reserves maintained; **~erhöhung** increase of reserves; **steuerfrei gebildete ~grenze für die Rückstellung ungewisser Schulden seitens der Bankwelt** tax-free bad-debt reserve level allowed to banks; **~höhe** amount of reserves; **~zunahme** growth of reserves.

Reserve|offizier reserve officer; **~offizier sein** to hold a commission as a reserve officer; **~pilot** backup pilot *(US)*; **~position** *(Weltwährungsfonds)* reserve position; **~posten** reserve position, surplus item; **~rad** spare (extra) wheel; **~reifen** spare tyre; **~satzstaffel** *(Bankwesen)* legal reserve ratio *(US)*; **~schiff** support vessel; **~soll** reserve required by contract, *(Bankwesen)* legal *(Br.)* (lawful, *US*, fractional, required, *US*) reserves, legal reserve requirements *(US)*; **~stellung** allocation to reserves; **~tank** *(Auto)* storage tank; **~teil** spare [part]; **~truppen** reserves, line of support, reserve forces; **~vorschriften** reserve requirements; **~währung** reserve currency; **~währungsguthaben** reserve currency balance.

reservieren to reserve, to set aside (apart), *(vorausbestellen)* to book [in advance], to make reservations;
für zweifelhafte Forderungen ~ to make due allowance for doubtful *(Br.)* (bad, *US*) debts; **Platz ~** to reserve (book, *Br.*) a seat; **für sich selbst ~** to earmark for o. s.;
Tisch ~ lassen to make a reservation for a table.

reserviert *(besetzt)* reserved, occupied, *(Börse)* cautious, inactive, flat, dead, dull, *(Käufer)* reluctant, cautious, *(zurückhaltend)* standoffish, distant, uncommunicative;
für eine ausländische Bank ~ earmarked for a foreign bank *(coll.)*; **für persönliche Zwecke ~** reserved for private use;
j. ~ behandeln to be distant to s. o.; **in eigenen Angelegenheiten sehr ~ sein** to be very private about one's affairs; **sich ~ verhalten** to sit on the hedge, *(Käufer)* to hold back; **sich jem. gegenüber sehr ~ verhalten** to be cool towards s. o.;
~er Anzeigenplatz reserved position; **~er Platz** reserved-seat ticket; **~er Tisch** reserved table.

Reserviertheit standoffishness, distance, ice.

Reservierung reservation, booking;
feste ~ confirmed reservation;
~ rückgängig machen to cancel a reservation.

Reservierungs|gebühr reservation (booking) fee; **~stelle** reservation office; **~system** reservation system.

Reservist *(mil.)* reservist.

Reservoir reservoir, base.

Residenz residence, *(Hauptstadt)* capital, court, *(Präsident der USA)* White House.

Residenzpflicht residence, *(Inserat)* residence is required;
seiner ~ nachkommen to reside.

residenzpflichtig residentiary.

Residenzstadt residence, capital.

residieren to reside, to be in residence, to hold state.

Resignation resignation, acquiescence.

resignieren to give up, to resign, to acquiesce;
völlig ~ to resign to one's fate.

resigniert resigned, discouraged.

resolut determinate, resolute, determined, vigorous.

Resolution resolution, vote, act, resolve *(US)*, determination;
~ des Haushaltsausschusses ways and means resolution *(Br.)*;
~ ablehnen to reject (rescind) a resolution; **~ annehmen** to pass (adopt, carry) a resolution (vote); **~ durchbringen** to engineer a resolution; **~ in einer Versammlung einbringen** to bring up (move) a resolution in a meeting; **verabschiedete ~en in Protokollform übertragen** to convert successful resolutions into draft minutes; **~ vorlegen** to table a resolution.

Resolutions|annahme passing (adoption) of a resolution; **~ausschuß** resolution committee; **~entwurf** (study) draft resolution; **~entwurf vorbereiten** to draft (offer) a resolution.

Resolutivbedingung resolutive (resolutory) condition.

Resonanz *(fig.)* echo, response;
keine ~ finden to meet with no response; **auf ~ bei jem. stoßen** to appeal to s. o.;
~boden soundboard.

resozialisieren to rehabilitate.

Resozialisierung rehabilitation, social adjustment;
~ ländlicher Gebiete rural rehabilitation.

Respekt respect, regard, hono(u)r, comity, esteem;
mit allem gehörigen ~ with all due submission (respect, deference, reverence);
tiefer ~ high respect;
jem. ~ bezeigen to pay hono(u)rs to s. o.; **einem Richter ~ bezeugen** to show deference to a judge; **jem. ~ einflößen** to inspire s. o. with respect; **jem. ~ eintragen** to earn s. o. respect; **keinen ~ vor Persönlichkeiten haben** to be no respecter of persons; **es jem. gegenüber an ~ fehlen lassen** to fail in respect for s. o.; **seinem Vater ~ schulden** to owe respect to one's father; **seinen Vorgesetzten den ~ versagen** to defy one's superiors; **dem Gesetz ~ verschaffen** to enforce obedience to the law.

respektabler Betrag respectable amount.

Respekt|blatt *(drucktechn.)* flyleaf, half-title page; **~frist** *(Wechsel)* period of grace.

respektieren to be regardful, to respect;
jds. Meinung ~ to respect s. one's opinion; **Neutralität ~** to respect neutrality; **Vertragsklausel ~** to respect a clause in a contract.

respektiert respected;
von seinen Kollegen voll ~ werden to be in high credit with one's colleagues.

respektlos disrespectful, irreverential;
j. ~ behandeln to treat s. o. with disrespect; **ein bißchen ~ von jem. sprechen** to take s. one's name in vain.

Respektlosigkeit disrespect.

Respektspersonen respectabilities;
keine Achtung vor ~ haben to be no respecter of persons.

Respekttage *(Wechsel)* days of grace (respite).

respektvollen Abstand halten to stand at a respectful distance.

Ressentiments resentment, ill-feeling, hard feeling[s];
~ gegen Ausländer prejudices against foreigners.

Ressort *(Fachgebiet)* field of study, *(pol.)* portfolio, department, division, ministry, *(im Schattenkabinett)* shadow portfolio *(Br.)*, *(im Vorstand)* group, desk, *(Zuständigkeit)* province, purview;
zu jds. ~ gehören to come (fall) within s. one's province; **nicht zu jds. ~ gehören** to be out of s. one's line; **zum ~ des Innenministeriums gehören** to come within the purview of the Home Office *(Br.)*; **kein besonderes ~ haben** *(Minister)* to be without portfolio; **nicht in jds. ~ liegen** to be outside the sphere of s. one's activities (of s. one's purview), not to be within s. one's province; **Fragenkreis zwischen den zuständigen ~s lösen** to solve a problem between the departments concerned; **neues ~ schaffen** to create a new department; **Leiter des ~ Politik sein** to be the political editor of a newspaper;

~abkommen interdepartmental agreement; ~ausschuß interdepartmental committee; ~bearbeiter desk officer; ~bedenken departmental objection; ~besprechung interdepartmental conference; ~chef head of a department, *(Zeitung)* editor; ~leiter group executive.

ressortmäßig interdepartmental.

Ressortminister departmental minister, holder of a portfolio.

Rest rest, holdover, remainder, residue, rump, remnant, remanet, *(math.)* difference, *(Rückstand)* residue, *(Saldo)* balance due, remainder, *(Überschuß)* surplus, *(Zahlungen)* arrears;
ohne ~ aufgehend aliquot;
~e leavings, odds and ends, oddments, remnants, *(Effekten)* leftover stocks, leftovers;
nicht aufteilbarer ~ residue; **letzter ~** tag end *(coll.)*; **sterbliche ~e** mortal remains; **unverwertbare ~e** scraps;
verbilligte ~e im Ausverkauf remnants at reduced prices in a clearance sale; **der ~ meines Geldes** all the money I have left; **~e und Gelegenheitskäufe** remnants and oddments; **~e einer früheren Kultur** vestiges of an earlier civilization; **~ eines großen Vermögens** overplus of a great fortune, remnants of a large property;
ohne ~ aufgehen to work out exactly; **~ begleichen** to pay the balance; **~e des Grabenkriegs beseitigen** to mop up the trenches; **~ von Anständigkeit besitzen** to have a spark of decency left; **jem. den ~ geben** to finish s. o. off, *(beruflich)* to put paid to s. one's career.

Restanten leavings, odd lots, *(Buchhaltung)* suspense items, *(Effekten)* leftovers, leftover stocks.

Restauflage billig abstoßen to remainder.

Restauflagen|angebot remainders offer; **~buchhandel** remainders book trade.

Restaurant restaurant, tavern, refreshment house *(Br.)*, *(Hotel)* dining room;
alkoholfreies ~ coffee tavern; **billiges ~** chophouse; **an der Landstraße gelegenes ~** roadside inn (establishment), roadhouse; **vornehmes ~** class restaurant;
~ mit Lieferungen frei Haus caterer; **~ mit Plattenautomat** juke joint; **~ mit Selbstbedienung** self-service restaurant, cafeteria;
~ betreiben to run *(Br.)* (operate, *US*) a restaurant, to keep an inn;
~angestellter restaurant worker, pan-jerker *(sl.)*; **~besitzer** restaurant owner, restaurateur; **~kette** restaurant chain; **~rechnung** restaurant bill.

Restaurateur restaurateur, caterer, catering establishment, *(für Gemälde)* picture restorer, traiteur *(Fr.)*.

Restauration restaurant, refreshment house *(Br.)*, *(Künstler)* restoration, renovation;
~ neben dem Schwimmbad pool-side buffet; **~ mit Selbstbedienung** self-service restaurant, cafeteria.

Restaurations|arbeiten restaurative work; **~betrieb** catering establishment, caterer; **~maßnahmen in großem Stil** large-scale restoration.

restaurieren to renovate, to restore, to rehabilitate.

Restaurierung *(Gebäude)* restoration, rehabilitation;
~ eines Gemäldes restoration of a painting.

Restbestand balance, remaining stock, remainder [of stock], *(Arbeitslosigkeit)* hard core, *(Effekten)* remainder of stocks;
unverkaufter ~ remainder line; **nicht versicherungsfähiger ~** *(Autoversicherung)* residual market;
~ der Arbeitslosigkeit residual unemployment, hard core;
als ~ übrigbleiben to remain on the shelf.

Restbetrag remainder, remaining (residual) amount, residue, *(ausstehende Forderungen)* outstanding amount, *(Konto)* balance;
noch nicht ausgezahlter ~ undisbursed balance; **geschuldeter ~** remainder of a debt, balance due (owing); **unbezahlter ~** arrearage; **innerhalb einer Woche zu zahlender ~** balance to be paid within one week;
~ einer Rechnung balance of an account;
~ auszahlen to pay out the balance; **~ bezahlen** to pay the balance.

Rest|betragsrente modified refund annuity; **~buchwert** residual cost (value), net book value, depreciated costs.

Restchen|an Kraft last ounce of strength; **letztes ~ Mut** last shred of courage.

Reste|buchhandel remainders book trade; **~händler** piece broker; **~inzahlungsverpflichtung** uncalled capital; **~laden** outlet store; **~lager aus Konkursen** bankrupt stocks, stock of remnants; **~partie** odd lot; **~verkauf** remnant sale; **~waren** remnants, oddments, rummage goods.

Rest|forderung outstanding amount, residual claim *(Br.)*; **~gewinn** residue of profit; **~größe** *(Statistik)* residual; **~gut** remnants of an estate; **~guthaben** remaining credit balance.

restieren to be left over, to remain.

restituieren to restitute, to refund, to restore.

Restitution restitution, restoration.

Restitutions|anspruch, ~recht claiming back, restitution claim, restitutory right; **~prozeß** restitution case.

Restkaufgeld balance of purchase price;
~darlehen purchase-money loan; **~hypothek** purchase-money mortgage *(US)*, vendor's lien; **~rente** purchase annuity; **~schuldschein** purchase-money bond; **~versicherung** house purchase insurance.

Rest|kosten residual costs; **~laufzeit** residual term.

restlich remaining, residuary, vestigial;
~e Arbeiten rest of the work; **~er Betrag** remaining amount, balance due; **~es Guthaben** remaining credit balance; **~er Teil** residue.

Restlieferung back order.

restlos complete, perfect, utter, without a remainder;
~ erledigt fagged out, done up; **~ glücklich** perfectly happy; **etw. ~ beherrschen** to do s. th. to perfection; **sich ~ für etw. einsetzen** to go all out for s. th.; **~ ausverkauft sein** *(Theater)* to be fully booked; **jem. ~ vertrauen** to trust s. o. unreservedly; **~er Einsatz** utter devotion; **zu meiner ~en Zufriedenheit** to my entire satisfaction.

Rest|masse remaining assets, *(Nachlaß)* residue [estate]; **~nachfrage** resudiary (residual, *US*) demand; **~nachlaß nach Zahlung aller Verbindlichkeiten** residuary (residual) estate; **~nutzungsdauer** remaining life; **~nutzungswert** scrap value *(US)*; **~partie** odd lot; **~posten** residual item, closed (remaining) stock; **~quote** final payment (dividend).

Restriktion restriction, limitation;
~en abbauen to remove controls.

Restriktions|bündel restrictive package; **~erleichterungen** easing of restrictions; **~grad** degree of restrictions; **~maßnahmen** restrictive measures; **~politik** restrictive policy.

restriktiv|e Kreditpolitik restrictive (tight) credit policy; **~er Kurs** restrictive line; **~e steuerpolitische Maßnahmen** restrictive fiscal policy.

Rest|saldo remaining balance; **~schuld** surviving (remaining, residual) debt; **~schuld in Raten abzahlen** to pay the balance in instal(l)ments; **~staat** remnant of a state; **~summe** balance, remainder, arrearage, *(Konto)* balance account; **~varianz** residual variance; **~vermächtnis** residuary gift; **~vermögen** remaining property, residual assets; **von der Haftung nicht erfaßtes ~vermögen** general balance; **~waren** rummage; **~wert** *(Schrottwert)* scrap value, salvage *(US)*; **~wertabschreibungsmethode** reducing-fraction method of depreciation; **~zahlung** payment of the balance, *(Rate)* final instal(l)ment (payment).

Resultat result, issue, outcome;
~e fleißigen Studiums fruit of much study;
gutes ~ zeitigen to lead to a good result; **negative ~e zeitigen** to come in negative colo(u)rs.

resultieren to result to issue.

Resümee summary, conspectus.

resümieren to sum up, to resume, to summarize.

Retorsion *(Völkerrecht)* retorsion, *(Zoll)* retaliation.

Retorsions|maßnahmen retaliatory measures; **~recht** law of marque; **~zoll** retaliatory duty; **~zölle erheben** to retaliate.

Retortenkind test-tube baby.

Retourbillet return ticket.

Retouren|buch returns book; **~journal** sales (purchase) returns journal; **~konto** purchase returns account; **~- und Nachlaßkonto** returned sales and allowance account.

Retour|fahrkarte return ticket; **~fracht** cargo homeward, returned shipment *(US)*; **~frachtsatz** returned shipment rate *(US)*; **~kutsche** tit for tat, nifty *(US sl.)*.

retourniert returned.

Retour|provision return commission; **~rechnung** return account, banker's ticket; **~scheck** returned check *(US)* (cheque, *Br.*); **~sendungen** returned shipments *(US)*, cargo homeward; **~spesen** back charges; **~waren** sales returns, goods returned; **~wechsel** returned (dishono(u)red) bill, redraft.

retten to rescue, to salvage, to recover, to save;
seine Ehre ~ to retrieve one's hono(u)r; **j. vor dem Ertrinken ~** to save s. o. from drowning; **aus dem Feuer ~** to rescue from the fire; **sich vor einem Gewitter ~** to take shelter from a thunderstorm; **seine eigene Haut ~** to save one's hide; **sich vor Journalisten ~** to get away from journalists assailing one with questions; **sein Leben ~** to run for one's life; **jem. das Leben ~**

to save s. one's life; **Mannschaft eines untergehenden Schiffes ~** to rescue the crew of a sinking ship; **sich vor seinen Verfolgern ~** escape from one's pursuers;
j. mit allen Mitteln zu ~ versuchen to pull out all the stops to save s. o.; **sich vor Telefonanrufen nicht zu ~ wissen** to be swamped with telephone calls;
~, was zu ~ ist to make the best of a bad job (bargain);
du bist nicht mehr zu ~ you must have lost your senses.
rettend|er Einfall fortunate flash of inspiration; **~er Engel** guardian angel.
Retter rescuer, saver, *(biblisch)* Saviour;
~ der Nation savio(u)r of the nation;
~ in der Not spielen to pick up the bits.
Rettung rescue, recovery, salvage, saving;
~ als Schiffbrüchiger escape from shipwreck;
zu jds. ~ herbeieilen to gallop to s. one's rescue; **sich Hoffnung auf eine ~ machen** to cling to a hope of being rescued.
Rettungs|aktion rescue operation; **~aktion in Gang setzen** to mount a salvage operation; **~anker** *(fig.)* sheet anchor, life line; **jem. einen ~anker hinwerfen** to come to s. one's rescue; **~arbeiten** salvage, rescue work, *(sozial)* welfare work; **~bohrung** escape shaft; **~boje** life (safety) buoy; **~bojensignal** life signal; **~bombe** *(Bergbau)* rescue torpedo; **~boot** rescue vehicle, lifeboat, crash boat, salvage craft, *(vom Flugzeug)* life raft; **in die ~boote gehen** to take to the boats; **letzte ~chance** last clear chance *(US)*; **~dienst** lifesaving service, rescue (salvage) service, *(Gesellschaft)* first-aid association; **~fahrzeug** rescue vehicle, crash truck (wagon) *(US)*; **~floß** life raft; **~flugzeug** rescue (ambulance) plane; **~geld des neuen Nehmers** prize salvage; **~gerät** *(Schiff)* lifesaving gun, rocket apparatus; **~gürtel** life belt (preserver, *US*), lifesaver, float; **~hubschrauber** rescue helicopter; **~kolonne** search party, rescue team (squad); **~leine** life line; **~lohn** salvage money.
rettungslos beyond help;
~ verfahren sein to be in a hopeless mess.
Rettungs|mannschaft wrecking crew, rescue party (squad, team); **~manöver** saving maneuver *(US)* (manoeuvre, *Br.*); **~maßnahmen** salvage (rescue) operations; **~medaille** lifesaving medal; **~mission** rescue mission; **~plan** rescue plan; **~plan fünf Minuten vor zwölf** last-ditch rescue plan; **~rakete** life (escape) rocket; **~ring** life preserver, life belt *(Br.)*; **~schacht** escape shaft; **~schiff** rescue ship; **~schwimmen** lifesaving; **~schwimmer** lifesaver; **~station** lifeboat station *(Br.)*, first-aid room, emergency hospital; **~trupp** rescue party (squad, team); **~unternehmen** rescue operation, rescue attempt; **~versuch** rescue (escape) attempt; **~wache** *(an der See)* lifeguard *(US)*; **~wagen** ambulance car, meatwaggon *(sl.)*, *(mar.)* life car, *(Feuerwehr)* hook-and-ladder truck *(US)*; **~weg** road to salvation, *(Bergbau)* escape way, *(bei Feuer)* fire exit; **~wesen** rescue.
Retusche retouching, *(Foto)* masking out, *(mit Messer)* knifing.
retuschieren to touch up, to retouch, *(Foto)* to mask out.
Reue repentance, penitence, remorse, contrition;
tiefe ~ empfinden to feel deep remorse;
~gefühl contrition.
reuen, j. to feel remorse;
das wird dich noch ~ you will live to regret it.
Reufracht dead freight.
Reugeld atonement (forfeit, smart) money, fine, *(Prämiengeschäft)* option money, premium, *(Steuer)* conscience money;
~ zahlen to pay the forfeits.
reumütig penitent, repentant, remorseful;
~es Lächeln apologetic smile.
reüssieren to succeed, to have success, to be successful;
als Anwalt nicht ~ to be a failure as a lawyer; **geschäftlich nicht ~** to fail in business.
Revalidierungsanspruch right of indemnity.
revalorisieren to restore the currency.
Revanche an jem. nehmen to pay s. o. out for s. th. *(Br.)*, to square accounts with s. o.
revanchieren, sich to strike back; **sich für eine Beleidigung ~** to revenge o. s. on s. o. for an insult; **sich für eine Einladung ~** to return an invitation; **sich für jds. Freundlichkeiten ~** to repay s. one's kindness; **sich für eine Ungerechtigkeit ~** to revenge an injustice;
sich zu ~ wissen to have s. one's guts for garters.
Revers [counter]bond, *(Garantieerklärung)* undertaking, *(Jacke)* lapel, *(Münze)* reverse, back side, *(Vertrag)* pocket agreement;
~ ausstellen to give a written declaration.
reversibel reversible.
revidieren to audit, to examine, *(Ansicht)* to reconsider, *(Entscheidung)* to review, *(überprüfen)* to check, *(untersuchen)* to examine, to investigate, *(verbessern)* to work over, to revise, to correct;
Bücher ~ to audit the books (accounts); **Gepäck ~** to inspect the luggage *(Br.)* (baggage, *US*); **Kasse ~** to verify the cash; **seine Meinung ~** to change one's mind (opinion).
Revidierung *(Ansicht)* revision, revisal, *(Besichtigung)* inspection, investigation, *(Buchführung)* examination, auditing.
Revier district, quarter, *(Briefträger)* round, walk, *(Förster)* forest range, beat, *(Jagdrevier)* shooting ground, hunt, preserve *(Br.)*, *(Kellner)* area, *(Krankenstube)* infirmary, *(mil.)* quarters, sick room, *(Polizei)* beat, ward, police station, precinct *(US)*, station house *(US)*;
j. ins ~ bringen to take s. o. to the police station; **ins ~ kommen** *(mil.)* to be put on the sick list; **im ~ liegen** to be in the sick bay; **~briefträger** postman of the walk *(Br.)* (for the district, *US*); **~dienst** *(mil.)* light duty; **~förster** district (forest, *US*) ranger; **~stube** *(mil.)* infirmary, sickroom, dispensary; **~stunde** *(mil.)* sick call; **~wachtmeister** station sergeant.
Revirement shake-up, *(Kabinett)* reshuffle.
revisibel reviewable, revisable, *(jur.)* reversible, subject to judicial review;
nicht ~ not subject to review;
~ sein to be susceptible of revision.
Revisibilität reviewability, revisableness.
revisibles Urteil appealable judgment.
Revision *(Abänderung)* amendment, modification, revision, *(Berufung)* appeal, revision, *(Bücherprüfung)* audit[ing], *(drucktechn.)* revise, *(Prüfung auf Richtigbefund)* verification review, *(Überprüfung)* examination, checking, *(Untersuchung)* investigation, examination, inspection, *(Urteil)* review, *(Vertrag)* reviewal, revisal;
bei der ~ when auditing the books; **nicht von der ~ erfaßt** unaudited;
außerbetriebliche ~ external audit (auditing); **außerplanmäßige ~** special audit; **betriebseigene ~** internal audit (auditing); **betriebsfremde ~** external audit; **laufend durchgeführte ~** periodic audit; **zum Jahresabschluß durchgeführte ~** completed audit; **eingehende ~** detailed audit; **konzerneigene ~** group internal audit; **nochmalige ~** re-examination; **überraschende ~** surprise audit; **in der Berichtszeit vorgenommene ~** interim audit; **zollamtliche ~** customs examination, examination of the luggage *(Br.)* (baggage, *US*);
~ im Armenrechtsverfahren appeal in forma pauperis; **~ einer Bank durch den Vorstand** director's examination; **~ der Bilanz** balance-sheet audit; **~ der Geschäftsbücher** inspection of the books; **~ der Kasse** cash audit; **~ der Lohnbuchhaltung** payroll audit *(US)*;
~ gegen das Urteil einer niederen Instanz ablehnen to refuse to review a lower court decision; **~ abschließen** to conclude an audit; **sich einer ~ anschließen** to cross-appeal; **~ durchführen** to prosecute an audit; **~ einlegen** to lodge an appeal with [the Supreme Court], to give notice of an appeal; **einer ~ stattgeben** to allow (uphold) an appeal; **der ~ unterliegen** to be susceptible of revision; **einer ~ unterziehen** to review; **seine Politik einer ~ unterziehen** to revise one's policy; **über eine ~ verhandeln** to hear an appeal from a decision; **~ verwerfen (zurückweisen)** to dismiss an appeal; **~ vornehmen** to investigate, to inspect, to examine, to audit; **~ zulassen** to grant leave to appeal.
Revisionist *(pol.)* revisionist.
Revisions|abteilung auditing department (division); **betriebseigene ~abteilung** internal audit group (department), *(Bundeswehr)* Financial Department *(US)*; **~abzug** foundry proof; **~antrag** appeal, motion on appeal, bill of certiorary; **abgelehnter ~antrag** certiorary denied *(US)*; **~anweisungen** audit instructions; **~arbeiten** audit work; **laufende ~arbeiten** continuous audit; **~arten** types of audit; **~auftrag** audit engagement (program[me]), auditing order; **~ausschuß** board of audit, auditing commission; **~beamter** general accountant, [official] auditor; **innerbetrieblicher ~beamter** corporate controller, internal auditor; **selbständiger ~beamter** senior accountant; **~begründung** reasons of appeal, assignment of error; **~behörde** commission of review; **~beklagter** respondent, defendant in error, appellee *(US)*.
Revisionsbericht accountant's report, report of the auditors, audit (auditor's) certificate (report), auditor's statement, inspector's report, accounting statement, audited accounts;
detaillierter ~ long-form report;
~ in abgekürzter Form short-form report;
~ beanstanden to take exception to an auditor's report.

Revisions|beschluß writ of error; ~**bestimmungen** provisions as to audits; ~**bogen** *(drucktechn.)* revise [proof], clean proof; ~**buch** audit book; ~**büro** auditor's office; ~**einlegung** lodging an appeal, appeal with (to) the Supreme Court; ~**entscheidung** decision of the Supreme Court; ~**ergebnisse** *(Berufungsgericht)* findings; ~**erwiderung** *(Strafrecht)* joinder of error; ~**exemplar** reviewer's copy.

revisionsfähig reviewable, revisable, *(jur.)* appealable;
~ **sein** to be susceptible of revision.

Revisions|fähigkeit reviewability; ~**fehler** reversible error, *(Revisor)* auditing error; ~**firma** auditing company, accounting firm, auditors; ~**frist** time for appeal; ~**gebühren** *(Buchprüfung)* audit (auditing) fees; ~**gericht** appellate court, Supreme Court of Appeal, court for the correction of errors, Court of Errors and Appeal *(New Jersey)*; ~**gericht für Strafsachen** Court of Justiciary *(Scot.)*; ~**gesellschaft** auditors, audit office, auditing company.

Revisionsgrund reversible error;
absoluter ~ fundamental error; **anerkannter** ~ common error; ~**lage** basis of revision; ~**sätze** principles of accounting.

Revisions|instanz stages of appeal; **in die** ~**instanz gehen** to lodge an appeal; ~**jahr** audit year; ~**kläger** plaintiff in error, appellant; ~**lage** audit situation; ~**leiter** accountant in charge; ~**plan** audit program(me); ~**politik** revisionism; ~**protokoll** audit certificate; ~**recht** audit privilege; ~**richter** appellate judge; ~**richtlinien** audit standards; ~**sache** appealed case, case stated *(Br.)*; ~**schrift** motion in error; ~**tätigkeit** audit services; ~**technik** auditing technique; ~**termin** audit date; ~**umfang** scope of audit; ~**unterlagen** audit notebook; ~**urteil** judgment in error; ~**verfahren** proceedings to appeal, appeal procedure, certiorari, *(Buchprüfung)* auditing (accounting) procedure; ~**verhandlung** hearing of an appeal; ~**vorschriften** audit standards; **gesetzlich vorgeschriebene** ~**vorschriften** statutory audit requirements; ~**wesen** auditing, audit system; ~**zeitraum** auditing period; ~**zulassungsbeschluß** writ of error; ~**zyklus** accounting cycle.

Revisor auditor, auditing expert, visitor, examiner, supervisor, controller of accounts;
betriebseigener ~ private accountant *(US)*, internal auditor; **öffentlich zugelassener** ~ chartered *(Br.)* (certified public, *US*) accountant;
zum ~ **geeignet sein** to qualify for the appointment as auditor.

Revisoren|amt office of auditors; ~**beruf** accountantship, auditing profession.

Revokationszoll contractual tariff.

Revolte revolt, riot, insurrection, insurgence;
~ **des linken Flügels** left-wing revolt;
~ **unterdrücken** to put down a revolt.

revoltieren to riot, to rise, to revolt.

revoltierende Studenten student rebels.

Revolution revolution;
~ **der Technik** technological revolution; ~ **unseres gesamten Verkehrssystems** revolution in our ways of travelling.

Revolutionär revolutionary, revolutionist, destructionist, Red.

revolutionäre|Gesellschaft revolutionary society; ~ **Politik** firebrand politics; ~ **Prinzipien** revolutionary principles; **Klima für** ~ **Verhältnisse schaffen** to create a revolutionary climate.

revolutionieren to revolutionize.

Revolutions|gericht revolutionary tribunal; ~**plan** design for a revolution; ~**regierung** revolutionary government; ~**zustand** revolutionism.

Revolver revolver, gun *(US)*, persuader *(sl.)*;
schnell mit dem ~ **bei der Hand sein** to be quick on the draw; ~ **bei sich tragen** to pack a revolver *(US sl.)*;
~**attrappe** dummy gun; ~**bank** turret lathe; ~**blatt** hedge press, gutter paper; ~**drehbank** turret lathe; ~**duell** shootout *(sl.)*; ~**film** blood-and-thunder film; ~**held** gunman *(US)*, trigger, bad man *(US sl.)*; ~**journalismus** claptrap (sidewalk, *US*) journalism; ~**schnauze** loud mouth; ~**schnauze haben** to talk the hind leg off a donkey.

revolvierendes Konto revolving account.

Revolvingabkommen revolving-credit agreement (arrangement).

Revue revue, [musical] show, *(Zeitschrift)* magazine, review, periodical;
etw. im Geist ~ **passieren lassen** to go over s. th. in one's mind; **sein Leben** ~ **passieren lassen** to pass one's life in review; **Vergangenheit** ~ **passieren lassen** to run back over the past; ~**film** musical film; ~**girl** show girl, hoofer *(US sl.)*; ~**theater** vaudeville theatre, variety show.

Rezensent book reviewer, critic.

rezensieren to review, to criticize.

Rezension review[al], critique, notice;
neues Buch einer unfairen ~ **aussetzen** to contain unfair censures of a new book; **günstige** ~ **über ein Buch schreiben** to review a book favo(u)rably; ~**en für Zeitschriften schreiben** to write reviews for magazines.

Rezensionsexemplar review (free) copy.

Rezentralisierung recentralization.

Rezept physician's prescription, recipe;
kein allgemeines ~ no general rule;
kein ~ **gegen die Arbeitslosigkeit** no way against unemployment; ~ **gegen Langeweile** remedy for boredom;
auf ~ **abgeben** to dispense; ~ **ausstellen** to make up a (dispense, fill a doctor's) prescription; ~ **für j. ausstellen** to write out a prescription; **dem gleichen** ~ **folgen** to follow the same pattern; ~**block** prescription pad; ~**buch** prescription book, formulary; ~**formel** prescription formula; ~**gebühr** prescription charge; ~**gebühren** cost of a prescription.

Rezeption reception office (hall), desk *(coll.)*, *(Krankenhaus)* admittance;
~ **des römischen Rechts** adoption of the Roman law.

rezeptiv veranlagt sein to have a receptive mind.

rezeptpflichtig obtainable only on prescription.

Rezession recession, business decline;
ganze Wirtschaft erfassende ~ full-fledged business recession; **der Ölkrise folgende** ~ post-oil-crisis recession; **industrielle** ~ industrial slump; **tiefgreifende** ~ far-reaching recession; **wirtschaftliche** ~ economic recession;
~ **in der Textilindustrie** textile slump;
Zeitraum als ~ **definieren** to put a recession tag on a period; ~ **gerade hinter sich gebracht haben** to come out of a recession; **aus einer** ~ **herausführen** to steer out of a recession; ~ **nicht hochkommen lassen** to buck the recession; **in einer tiefen** ~ **stecken** to be in a deep recession; **sich mit allen Mitteln gegen eine** ~ **stemmen** to buck the recession; **in eine heftige** ~ **stürzen** to topple into a severe recession.

Rezessionsangst recession fear.

rezessionsbedingt recession-induced, recessional;
~**en Sturz erleben** to slump in the recession.

Rezessions|befürchtungen fear of recession; ~**bekämpfung** fight against recession.

rezessions|empfindlich vulnerable to recession; ~**gesteuert** recession-borne.

Rezessions|himmel, unter einem bedeckten recession-clouded; ~**jahr** year of recession, recession year; ~**loch,** ~**lücke** recession gap; ~**mulde** recession trough; ~**periode ansteuern** to head into a recession; ~**phase** stage (phase) of recession, recession period; **tiefster** ~**punkt** bottom of a recession; **immer noch auf der** ~**sohle sein** to be still at a recession level; **einer Wirtschaftsepoche den** ~**stempel aufdrücken** to put a recession tag on a period; ~**tief** recession trough.

rezessionsunempfindlich recession-proof.

Rezessionszeit period of recession, recession times (period);
noch immer ~**en entsprechen** to be still at a recession level.

Reziprozitätsversicherung reciprocal insurance.

Rezitation recital, reading.

rezitieren, Stück to say one's piece.

Rhetorik oratory.

rhetorische Frage rhetorical question.

Richt|antenne directional antenna; ~**betrieb** consulting (fact-finding, guiding) establishment; ~**blei** plummet.

richten, sich to tend; **sich danach** ~ to act up to; **sich ganz nach jem.** ~ to bestow one's attention upon (fit in with) s. o.; **sich selbst** ~ to take one's life; **Bett** ~ to get a bed ready; **Bitte an j.** ~ to ask a favo(u)r of s. o.; **Dach** ~ to erect the roof timbers; **sich gegen die staatliche Einkommenspolitik** ~ to be levelled against the government's incomes policy; **alles für einen Empfang** ~ to prepare everything for a reception; **seine Familie zugrunde** ~ to ruin one's family; **Frage an j.** ~ to put a question to s. o.; **Funkantenne auf einen Sender** ~ to direct the aerial (antenna) towards a station; **seine Geschütze gegen den Feind** ~ to aim one's guns at the enemy; **Grußbotschaft** ~ to send a congratulary message; **seine Krawatte** ~ to straighten one's tie; **sich nach der Mode** ~ to follow the fashion; **Pistole gegen j.** ~ to point a pistol at s. o.; **sich nach einer Uhr** ~ to go by a clock; **seinen Verdacht auf j.** ~ to suspect s. o.; **sich nach den Weisungen seines Auftragsgebers** ~ to comply with one's principal's instructions; **sich nach jds. Wünschen** ~ to comply with s. one's wishes; **Zimmer** ~ to tidy up a room;
seine Uhr ~ **lassen** to have one's watch regulated; **sich nach den Kundenwünschen** ~ **müssen** to have to be guided by one's client's wishes.

Richter judge, justice, judicial officer;
abgelehnter ~ challenged judge; **amtierender ~** judge sitting in court; **aufsichtführender ~** supervising judge; **ausscheidender ~** retiring judge; **beauftragter ~** judge delegate, official referee *(Br.)*, commissioner; **mit der Vernehmung beauftragter ~** special examiner; **beigeordneter ~** associate judge; **beisitzender ~** associate judge; **berichterstattender ~** reporting judge; **bestechlicher ~** corrupt (venal) judge; **dienstältester ~** senior judge; **erkennender (erstinstanzlicher) ~** trial judge; **ersuchter ~** commissioner; **gelehrter ~** learned judge; **Herr ~** Your Lordship *(Br.)* (Honor, *US*); **herumreisender ~** circuit judge; **hoher ~** justice; **käuflicher ~** corrupt (venal) judge; **milder ~** indulgent judge; **oberster ~** master of the Rolls *(Br.)*; **ordentlicher ~** regular (ordinary, *US*) judge, ordinary *(US)*, judge delegate; **stellvertretender ~** alternate judge; **strenger ~** severe (harsh) judge; **untergeordneter ~** puisne judge; **unvoreingenommener ~** impartial judge; **voreingenommener ~** partial judge; **vorsitzender ~** judge sitting in court, presiding judge; **zuständiger ~** competent judge;
~ und Anwälte bar and bench; **~ kraft Auftrags** commissioned judge; **~ in einem Bürotermin** judge in chambers; **~ während der Ferienzeit** vacation judge *(Br.)*; **~ am Obersten Gerichtshof** Associate Justice *(US)*; **~ auf Lebenszeit** judge for life; **~ in Nachlaßangelegenheiten** probate judge; **~ in der Rechtsmittelinstanz** appellate judge; **~ in Steuersachen** Special Commissioner *(Br.)*;
~ wegen Befangenheit ablehnen to challenge (recuse) a judge; **~ von der Ausübung des Richteramtes ausschließen** to disqualify a judge; **vor den ~ bringen** to bring to justice; **j. als ~ einsetzen** to constitute s. o. as judge; **sich dem irdischen ~ entziehen** to commit suicide; **j. zum ~ ernennen** to make s. o. a judge; **als ~ fungieren** to adjudicate; **vor den ~ kommen** to come before the judge; **~ sein** to sit (be) on the bench; **dem ~ vorführen** to bring up before the court; **zum ~ ernannt werden** to be appointed judge, to be raised to the benches (elected to the bench, *Br.*); **dem ~ vorgeführt werden** to be brought before the magistrate; **~ablehnung** challenge of a judge, declination *(Scot. law)*.
richterähnlich quasi-judicial.
Richteramt office of a judge, judicial office (function, post), judgeship, judicature, justiceship;
vom ~ ausschließen to disqualify a judge; **Befähigung zum ~ haben** to qualify as a judge; **~ innehaben** to hold a judicial office.
Richter | anklage impeachment of a judge; **~bank** judicial bench, bank; **~bestechung** judicial corruption (bribery); **~kollegium** bench.
richterlich judicial, judiciary, judicatory, magisterial;
~ entscheiden to adjudicate, to adjudge;
~er Akt judicial act; **~er Augenschein** judicial inspection; **~e Auslegung** judicial construction; **~er Eid** judicial oath; **~e Entscheidung** [judicial] decision, judgment; **auf ~er Entscheidung beruhend** judge-made; **~es Ermessen** judicial discretion; **dem ~en Ermessen überlassen bleiben** to be left to the discretion of the court; **~e Frist** regular term; **~e Funktionen** judicial functions; **~e Funktionen ausüben** to discharge judicial functions; **~e Funktionen übernehmen** to assume the role of a judge; **~e Gewalt** judicial authority, judicatory power, judiciary *(US)*; **~e Gewalt ausüben** to be invested with judicial powers; **~e Tätigkeit** judicial action (act); **~e Verfügung** ruling of the court, judge's order, judicial order; **aufgrund ~er Verfügung** by order of the court.
Richter | recht judge-made law; **~schaft** magistracy; **~sitz** judgment seat, bench; **~sitz einnehmen** to bench; **~spruch** judgment, judicial decision, sentence; **~stand** judicature, justice box, judiciary *(US)*; **dem ~stand angehören** to be on the bench; **~stuhl** judgment seat, chair, *(fig.)* tribunal; **~stuhl der öffentlichen Meinung** tribunal of public opinion; **~talar anlegen** to don the toga of a judge; **~vorlage** case stated *(Br.)*; **~würde** justiceship; **~zimmer** camera, chambers.
Richt | fernrohr *(Geschütz)* telescopic sight; **~fest** topping-out ceremony; **~feuer** *(mar.)* leading light.
Richtfunk directional radio;
~bake radio beacon; **~sender** directional transmitter; **~sendung** directional message; **~verbindung** microwave link.
Richtgeschwindigkeit recommended speed.
richtig just, correct, due, right, proper, *(angemessen)* appropriate, adequate;
~ erhalten duly received; **ganz ~** right as nails; **nicht mehr ganz ~** touched, crackbrained;
Sache ~ anfassen to tackle s. th. the right way; **sich ~ ausschlafen** to have a really good sleep; **~ befinden** to find correct; **sich als ~ herausgestellt haben** to have proved correct; **es für ~ halten** to deem it right to do so; **~ liegen** *(Börse)* to be on the right side; **hundertprozentig ~ liegen** to make a lucky guess; **nicht ganz ~ sein** to have a screw loose; **j. ~ zu nehmen wissen** to rub s. o. the right way;
~e Abschrift true copy; **~e Adresse** proper address; **im ~en Augenblick** at the right moment; **~e Aussprache** correct pronunciation; **keinen ~en Beruf haben** to have no regular occupation; **~er Engländer** trueborn Englishman; **~es Geld** good money; **~er Geschäftsmann** shrewd businessman; **~e Information** correct information; **~er Kerl** plucky fellow *(coll.)*; **der ~e Mann am ~en Platz** the right man in the right place; **etw. auf das ~e Maß zurückbringen** to cut s. th. to the just proportions; **~er Name** real name; **das ~e Parteibuch haben** to be siding with the right people; **auf das ~e Pferd setzen** to back the right horse; **kein ~er Sommer** no summer at all; **~e Tracht Prügel** sound thrashing, good hiding; **~en Zeitpunkt verpassen** to miss the right moment.
Richtigbefund verification, approval, acknowledgement;
nach ~ after (on) verification;
~ eines Kontos anzeigen to return a signed reconcilement blank.
Richtige, genau das just the [right] thing, the ticket *(coll.)*, quite the potato *(sl.)*;
genau der ~ sein to be the ticket *(fam.)*; **für j. genau das ~ sein** to be s. one's cup of tea; **nicht gerade das ~ sein** not to be quite the potato *(sl.)*; **genau das ~ tun** to touch the spot.
Richtigkeit correctness, exactness, *(Aussage)* truth, justice, justness, verity;
für die ~ correct attest; **~ der Abschrift wird beglaubigt** certified true copy;
~ einer Rechnung anerkennen to approve an account; **~ einer Aufstellung bestätigen** to verify a statement; **~ eines Kontoauszuges bestätigen** to verify an account; **~ von jds. Aussage bestreiten** to discredit s. one's evidence; **~ einer Behauptung bestreiten** to controvert a statement; **~ einer Feststellung beweisen** to prove the truth of a statement; **~ einer Aussage bezweifeln** to challenge the accuracy of a statement.
richtigstellen to correct, to rectify, to adjust, to verify;
Aussage ~ to rectify a statement.
Richtigstellung correction, rectification, adjustment, reclamation, *(in der Presse)* dementi;
~ veröffentlichen to publish a correction.
Richt | kosten standard cost; **~kreisel** directional gyro.
Richtlinien instructions, directives, guiding lines (rules), guidelines, working guides, code of standards;
den anerkannten ~ entsprechend classic; **nach diesen ~** along these lines;
einheitliche ~ uniform rules; **gegebene ~** lines laid down; **grundsätzliche ~** basic policy; **internationale ~** international standards; **staatliche ~** government guidelines; **standesrechtliche ~** professional standards;
~ für die Abwicklung von Schiedssachen arbitration rules; **~ zur Berechnung der zusätzlichen Einkommensteuer** surtax directions *(Br.)*; **~ zur Berechnung der Steuer** rules of taxation; **~ für die Einkommensteuerveranlagung** rules of assessment; **~ für die Festsetzung von Pensionen** rules of pensions; **~ über die Führung von Anderkonten** Solicitors' Trust Account Rules *(Br.)*; **einheitliche ~ und Gebräuche für Dokumenten-Akkreditive** Uniform Customs and Practices for Documentary Credits; **einheitliche ~ für das Inkassogeschäft** Uniform Rules for the Collection of Commercial Papers; **~ der Politik** lines of policy; **~ für die Spesenabrechnung** rules on expense-account spending;
~ aufstellen to set standards, to adopt (lay down) rules; **allgemeine ~ ausarbeiten** to hammer out policies; **~ genau befolgen** to stick to the rules; **sich außerhalb der staatlich festgelegten ~ bewegen** to act outside the guidelines laid down by the government; **als ~ dienen** to serve as a guidance; **strenge ~ für seine Lebensführung festlegen** to order one's life according to strict rules; **obligatorische ~ festsetzen** to issue binding guidelines; **~ geben** to lay down lines; **den Geschworenen ~ geben** *(Richter)* to charge the jury; **sich innerhalb der ~ halten** to keep within the guidelines; **~ mißachten** to defy the rulings; **~ überholen** to revamp rules;
~änderung rule change; **~ausschuß** policy (general purpose) committee; **~ausschuß für Lohn- und Gehaltsfragen** Pay Board *(Br.)*; **~entwurf** draft directive; **~erlaß für steuerabzugsfähige Ausgaben** expense rules *(Br.)*; **~grenze** guideline limit; **~katalog** catalog(ue) of guidelines; **~rede** policy speech; **~satz** standard rate; **~ziffern** guideline figures.

Richt | maß gauge, standard; ~**mikrophon** directional microphone; ~**preis** standard [purchase] price, administered (guiding, leading) price, *(EG)* target price; **empfohlener ~preis** suggested (recommended) price; ~**preis festsetzen** to administer a price; ~**rohr** telescope sight; ~**satz** rule *(US)*, standard rate, rate base; ~**satzmiete** controlled rent.
Richtschnur guideline, guiding principle, directory, direction, instruction, rule *(US)*;
politische ~ line of policy;
als ~ dienen to serve as a rule (guidance); **zur ~ guter Verwaltung gehören** to be the principle of good government; **sich j. zur ~ nehmen** to take one's cue from s. o.; **~ von jds. Politik sein** to govern s. one's policy.
Richt | sendung beam transmission; ~**stätte** place of execution; ~**strahl** radio beam; **auf dem ~strahl anfliegen** to come in on the beam; ~**strahler** beam aerial (antenna); ~**strahlsystem** beam system.
Richtung direction, line, drive, movement, ply, *(Konjunktur)* trend, *(Tendenz)* tendency, trend, slant, drift, *(Lehrsystem)* school, *(Weg)* course, route, way;
aus wechselnden ~en *(Wind)* variable; **in entgegengesetzter ~** in the opposite direction;
allgemeine ~ trend, tendency; **neuere ~en** modern methods; **neue ~ im Erziehungswesen** new direction in education;
~ ändern to veer; **allgemeine ~ angeben** to set the trend; **derselben politischen ~ angehören** to be of the same political stripe; **verschiedenen politischen ~en angehören** to belong to different political camps; **sich einer extremen ~ anschließen** to fall into an extreme camp; **nach allen ~en davonlaufen** to scatter in all directions; **~ einnehmen** to take one's ply; **andere ~ einschlagen** to change one's tack; **in eine nördliche ~ (nach Norden) fliegen** to fly in a northerly direction; **dem Gespräch eine neue ~ geben** to start a hare; **~ haben** to trend, to tend; **seine ~ nehmen** to tend; **extreme ~ vertreten** to hold extreme views; **in die gleiche ~ weisen** to make in the same direction; **in eine ~ zeigen** to point to a direction.
Richtungs | änderung shift of direction; **politische ~änderung** shift in policy; **plötzliche ~änderung einer Straße** sudden turn in the road; ~**anzeige** directional sign; ~**anzeiger** *(Auto)* direction (traffic) indicator, *(Flugzeug)* turn indicator; ~**empfang** direction reception; ~**kämpfe** domestic struggles; ~**sinn** sense of direction; ~**sucher** *(Radio)* direction finder; ~**verkehr** one-way traffic; **überwiegender ~verkehr** unbalanced traffic; ~**wechsel** break in one's course, veer; ~**weisender** trend setter; ~**weiser** *(Auto)* direction (traffic) indicator.
richtungweisend indicative, policy-making.
Richtwert approximate (target) value, standard;
~e *(Zeitstudie)* standard time data;
~e für die Fertigung production standards; **~e für die Lohn- und Preisentwicklung** wage-price guidelines.
Richtzahl coefficient, guiding figure, index.
riechen to smell, to have an odo(u)r (scent);
den Braten ~ *(fig.)* to smell a rat; **Lunte ~** to get wind of s. th.; **nach Verrat ~** to smack of treachery; **nach Vetternwirtschaft ~** to smell of nepotism;
zu ~ beginnen *(Lebensmittel)* to smell tainted; **j. nicht ~ können** not to be able to stand s. o., not to like the cut of s. one's jib; **kein Pulver ~ können** to be chicken-hearted.
Riecher haben, guten to have a good nose, to be keen-nosed.
Riegel bar;
hinter Schloß und ~ sitzen to be behind bars; **~ vorschieben** to shoot the bolt; **einer Sache einen ~ vorschieben** to put an end to s. th.;
~schloß dead lock.
Riemen strap, thong;
sich in die ~ legen to put one's shoulder to the wheel (nose to the grindstone); **sich am ~ reißen** to pull o. s. together;
aus fremdem Leder ist gut ~ schneiden men cut large thongs of other men's leather;
~antrieb belt drive; **~fußboden** wood-block floor.
Rieselfeld sewage farm (plant).
rieseln to ripple, to trickle, *(Regen)* to drizzle;
jem. über den Rücken ~ *(Angst)* to run up and down s. one's spine; **von den Wänden ~** to trickle off the wall.
Riesen | auftrag tall order; ~**berg von Arbeit bewältigen** to knock off a lot of work; ~**düsenflugzeug** jumbo jet; ~**erfolg** smash hit, buster *(sl.)*; ~**erfolg haben** to go off with a bang; ~**erfolg sein** *(Film)* to be a box-office draw *(US)*; ~**fehler** colossal blunder; ~**fete** a real bash *(US sl.)*; ~**format** blow-up; **als ~format herausbringen** to blow up; ~**gewinnauszahlung** melon cutting; ~**gewinne einstreichen** to reap big gains, to make huge profits.
riesengroß jumbo *(US)*.
Riesen | konzern mammoth business enterprise; ~**krach machen** to make so much din, to kick up a row (shindy), to whoop it (things) up *(US sl.)*; ~**laster** juggernaut; ~**menge** enormous (huge) amount, whale of a lot; ~**packung** giant package; ~**plakat** thirty-two sheet poster; ~**reklame** gigantic publicity; **sich seinem Untergang mit ~schritten nähern** to rush headlong to one's ruin; **mit ~schritten vorankommen** to progress by leaps and bounds; ~**spaß haben** to have a ball *(sl.)*; ~**spektakel** flare-up, pandemonium; ~**stapel** slacks and stacks; ~**summe an Löhnen zahlen** to have a huge payroll; ~**transporter** juggernaut; ~**tumult hervorrufen** to put the cat among the pigeons; ~**vergrößerung** *(Foto)* photomural; ~**verluste** mammoth losses.
riesig colossal, gigantic, giant, enormous, immense;
sich ~ freuen to be terribly pleased;
~e Ausmaße annehmen to assume gigantic proportions; **~er Betrug** fraud on a vast scale; **~er Blödsinn** utter nonsense; **~er Geldbetrag** enormous sum of money; **~e Gemeinheit** really dirty trick; **~e Kräfte** Herculean strength; **~es Truppenaufgebot** huge force of troops.
rigoros rigorous, drastic, vast, exact;
Gesetz ~ anwenden to put the law into operation in all its rigo(u)r; **j. ~ behandeln** to treat s. o. rigorously; **~ durchgreifen** to take drastic measures;
~e Bestrafung severe punishment; **~e Maßnahmen** rigorous measures.
Rikambio redraft, re-exchange;
~nota account of re-exchange; **~rechnung** cross account *(Br.)*; **~wechsel** redraft, re-exchange.
Rimesse remittance, *(Rückzahlungen)* returns of payment, *(Wechsel)* bills receivable *(US)*;
dokumentarische ~ documentary remittance; **einfache ~** clean remittance;
~ machen to remit, to make (send, provide for) remittance.
Rimessen | brief letter of remittance; ~**buch** book of remittances; ~**konto** bills receivable account *(US)*.
Rinder neat cattle;
~weidung im Wald staff herding; **~zucht** cattle breeding.
Rindvieh neat cattle.
Ring *(Aufkäufergruppe)* corner, *(Kettenlied)* link, *(Ringstraße)* circular ring, boulevard, *(Syndikat)* ring, circle, syndicate, pool, combine, combination, trust *(US)*;
kostbarer ~ precious ring;
dunkle ~e unter den Augen dark circles around the eyes; **~ von Händlern** *(Auktion)* ring of dealers; **~ von Rauschgifthändlern** dope ring;
~ bilden to pool, to corner the market; **~ um eine Stadt bilden** to encircle a town; **~ auffliegen lassen** to break up a ring; **in den ~ steigen** to enter the arena;
~bahn belt line *(US)*, circular railway *(Br.)*; **~bildung** *(bei Auktionen)* knockout *(Br.)*; **~buch** loose-leaf (ring) binder.
ringen to wrestle, to wrench, to contend, to fight;
um etw. ~ to struggle (grapple) with s. th.; **nach Atem ~** to gasp for breath; **die Hände ~** to wring one's hands; **um die Nachfolge ~** to fight for the succession; **mit einem Problem ~** to wrestle with a problem; **mit dem Tode ~** to be in the throes of death; **mit den Tränen ~** to fight back one's tears; **mit jem. um die Vorherrschaft ~** to contend with s. o. for predominance.
Ring | kampf wrestling; **etw. im ~kauf verkaufen** to sell s. th. at a knockout price *(Br.)*; ~**linie** *(U-Bahn)* circle line *(Br.)*; ~**mappe** spring-back binder; ~**mitglied** *(Auktion)* ringster; ~**sendung** *(Rundfunk)* chain broadcast, hookup; ~**straße** boulevard, circular (ring) road; ~**tausch** bartering; ~**verkehr** circular traffic.
Rinne trough, gutter, gully, *(Fahrrinne)* channel.
rinnen *(Zeit)* to pass, to run, to flow, to pour;
einem durch die Finger ~ *(Geld)* to slip through one's fingers.
Rinn | sal tricklet, streamlet, rivulet; ~**stein** gutter, gully, groove, kennel stone.
Rippe rib;
jem. alle ~n brechen to break every bone in s. one's body; **sich etw. aus den ~n schneiden** to conjure it up out of thin air; **j. in die ~n stoßen** to give s. o. a nudge (poke in the ribs);
bei ihm kann man alle ~n zählen he is nothing but skin and bones.
Rippenstoß dig in the side;
jem. einen ~ geben to give s. o. a poke in the ribs.
Risiken, ausgeschlossene hazards not covered; **noch bestehende ~** *(Versicherungsgesellschaft)* unexpired risks; **gesundheitliche ~** health hazards; **handelsübliche ~** customary risks; **laufende ~**

pending (current) risks; **vom Erwerber übernommene** ~ risks assured by the buyer; **übliche** ~ usual (ordinary) risks; **ungedeckte** ~ uninsured risks; **unvermeidbare** ~ unavoidable hazards; **versicherbare** ~ fair risks; **nicht versicherbare** ~ prohibited class risks;

von allen ~ **freihalten** to safeguard against all risks; **voller** ~ **stecken** to be full of risks.

Risiko risk, hazard, jeopardy, venture, peril, throw;

auf eigenes ~ at one's own risk; **auf** ~ **des Käufers** let the buyer beware, caveat emptor; **kein** ~ **eingehend** safe, cautious;

von der Lebensdauer abhängiges ~ life contingency; **nicht abzuschätzendes** ~ expectable risk; **akutes** ~ imminent risk; **anomales** ~ substandard risk; **ausgeschlossenes** ~ excluded risk; **außerordentliches** ~ extraordinary risk; **berufliches** ~ risk of occupation, risk incident to employment; **auf einen Einzelfall beschränktes** ~ particular risk; **unmittelbar bevorstehendes** ~ imminent risk; **erhebliches** ~ substantial risk; **erhöhtes** ~ abnormal (substandard, aggravated) risk, *(Lebensversicherung)* impaired life; **durch andere Arbeitnehmer erhöhtes** ~ extraordinary hazard; **klar erkennbares** ~ obvious risk; **finanzielles** ~ financial risk; **gedecktes** ~ risk covered; **nicht gedecktes** ~ uncovered risk; **geschäftliches** ~ commercial risk; **besonders hohes** ~ substandard risk; **juristisches** ~ legal hazard; **normales** ~ standard risk; **offensichtliches** ~ obvious risk; **noch nicht plaziertes** ~ *(Versicherung)* balance of risk; **subjektives** ~ *(Versicherung)* moral hazard; **tätigkeitsbedingtes** ~ special risk; **tatsächliches** ~ physical hazard; **übersehbares (überschaubares)** ~ perceivable risk; **unbekanntes** ~ unknown risk; **ungedecktes** ~ uninsured (uncovered) risk; **unkalkulierbares** ~ expectable risk; **unterdurchschnittliches** ~ *(Lebensversicherung)* substandard risk; **unternehmerisches** ~ risk of an undertaking; **unübersehbares** ~ perceivable risk; **versicherbares** ~ insurable risk, hazard; **nicht versicherbares** ~ uninsurable risk; **versichertes** ~ contingency risk; **nicht versichertes** ~ uncovered risk; **wirtschaftliches** ~ commercial risk; **wohlabgewogenes** ~ calculated risk; **zweifelhaftes** ~ bad risk;

~ **falscher Angaben des Versicherten** moral hazard; ~ **höherer Gewalt** fundamental risk; ~ **im engeren Sinn** pure risk; ~ **zweifachen Strafverfahrens** twice in jeopardy;

~ **trägt der Käufer** caveat emptor, let the buyer beware;

~ **abdecken** to cover a risk; ~ **abwägen** to calculate the risk; **sein Geld mit verteiltem** ~ **anlegen** to diversify one's investments; ~ **ausschalten** to eliminate risk; **sich einem** ~ **aussetzen** to incur (run) a risk; **unnötigem** ~ **aussetzen** to expose to unnecessary risks; **sich dem** ~ **der Verhängung einer Geldstrafe aussetzen** to make o. s. liable to a fine; **von einem** ~ **befreien** to relieve of a risk; **überdurchschnittliches** ~ **darstellen** to be an above-average risk; ~ **drehen** to cover a risk; ~ **eingehen** to take (incur, undertake, run) a risk, to run a hazard; **ziemlich aussichtslose** ~**s eingehen** to take long-shot risks; **großes** ~ **eingehen** to take close chances; **höchstes** ~ **eingehen** to go nap; **kalkuliertes** ~ **eingehen** to take a calculable gamble; **kein** ~ **eingehen** to take no risks, not to take any chances, to play for safety, to keep up one's head tucked in *(fam.)*; **zum besonders hohen** ~ **erklären** to class as high risk; ~ **laufen** to run a risk; ~ **auf sich nehmen** to take upon o. s. the (run a) risk; **hohes** ~ **auf sich nehmen** to chance a high risk; **erheblichem** ~ **ausgesetzt sein** to be exposed to considerable risk; ~ **tragen** to bear the (incur a) risk; ~ **übernehmen** to accept (assume, incur, entertain, undertake) a risk; **volles** ~ **übernehmen** to assume all risks; ~ **der Selbstbelastung vermeiden** to avoid the risk of incriminating o. s.; ~ **versichern** to underwrite a risk; ~ **verteilen** to spread a risk;

~**abgrenzung** risk limitation; ~**abschätzung** calculation of risk, risk appraisal; ~**absicherung** coverage of a risk; ~**abteilung** *(Versicherung)* underwriting department; ~**abwälzung** shifting (passing) of risk; ~**analyse** risk (venture) analysis; ~**änderung** change of risk; ~**arten** types of hazard (risks); ~**ausgleich** spreading the risk; ~**auslese** selection of risks; ~**ausschluß** exception; ~**ausschluß bei Gebäudeeinsturz** falling building clause; ~**ausschlußklausel** excepted peril clause; ~**auswirkung** effects of risk; ~**beginn** attachment of risk; ~**begrenzung** risk limitation; ~**begrenzung bei Katastrophen** catastrophe limit; ~**beherrschung** risk management, *(pol.)* brinkmanship.

risikobereit ready to take a risk.

Risiko|bereitschaft readiness to take risks; ~**beschreibung** *(Versicherung)* representation; ~**beseitigung** elimination of a risk; **Versicherung unter** ~**beteiligung übernehmen** to underwrite a risk; ~**betrag** *(Lebensversicherung)* net amount at risk; ~**beurteilung,** ~**einschätzung** assessment of risk; ~**deckung** insurance against (covering) a risk; ~**einstufung** classification of risks; ~**elemente** essentials (elements) of risk; ~**erhöhung** aggravation of risk, increase of hazard, added risk; ~**erklärung** *(Schiffskapitän)* bill of adventure; ~**faktor** risk factor; ~**formular** running (reporting) form.

risikofreudig prepared to take a risk.

Risiko|funktion *(Statistik)* risk function; ~**garantie** indemnity; ~**gattungen** types of risk (hazard); ~**geschäft** speculative enterprise, adventure, *(Lebensversicherung)* substandard business; ~**häufung** accumulation of risks; ~**herabsetzung** reduction in hazard; ~**investition** investment in venture capital; ~**kapital** risk (venture) capital; **neues** ~**kapital auftreiben** to raise fresh venture capital; ~**klasse** category (class) of risk, *(Transportversicherung)* rate; ~**klassifizierung** hazard classification; ~**lebensversicherung** term life insurance; **verlängerungsfähige** ~**lebensversicherung [ohne ärztliche Untersuchung]** renewable term life insurance; ~**lebensversicherungsschutz** term-life coverage; **verlängerungsfähiger** ~**lebensversicherungsvertrag** renewable term contract.

risikolos risk-free;

nicht ganz ~ attended by some risk.

Risiko|marge margin of risk; ~**merkmale** particulars of a risk; ~**mischung** spreading of risks; ~**prämie** hazard[ous-work] bonus, bonus hazard, risk premium; **hohe** ~**prämie bei Anlageinvestitionen** high-risk premium on capital investment; ~**quelle** source of danger; ~**rückstellung** contingency (risk) reserve.

risikoscheu risk-averse.

Risiko|schwelle perilous point; ~**steigerung** increase of hazard; ~**streuung** spreading (spread, distribution) of risk, *(bei Kapitalanlage)* diversification; ~**streuung betreiben** *(Kapitalanlage)* to diversify; ~**summe** net amount at risk; **nicht rückversicherter** ~**teil** retained risk; **Versicherung unter** ~**teilung übernehmen** to underwrite a risk; ~**träger** risk bearer (taker); ~**tragung** risk carrying (taking); ~**übergang** passing of risk; ~**übernahme** assumed (assumption of) risk, risk taking, taking (acceptance of) a risk; **gemeinschaftliche** ~**übernahme** cooperative risk carrying; **volle** ~**übernahme** full risk, full coverage; ~**übertragung** transfer of risk; ~**umfang** degree of risk; ~**umtauschversicherung** convertible term insurance (assurance, *Br.*); ~**unternehmen** venture capital company; ~**verbindung** *(Versicherung)* linkage of risks; ~**vergütung** compensation for risk incurred; ~**vermeidung** avoidance of a risk; ~**verminderung** risk improvement; ~**versicherung** hazardous insurance, *(Lebensversicherung)* term insurance, term assurance *(Br.)*; ~**versicherung abschließen** to insure against a risk; **globale** ~**versicherungspolice** all-risks insurance policy; ~**verteilung** diversification (spread, spreading, distribution) of the risk, risk venture; ~**verteilung (innerhalb eines Unternehmens)** pooling of risk; ~**vertrag** hazardous (aleatory) contract; ~**zulage** danger money; ~**zuschlag** risk surcharge.

riskant risky, dangerous, aleatory, adventurous, venturesome, insecure, touch-and-go;

~**e Angelegenheit** risky business; ~**es Geschäft** touch-and-go business; **äußerst** ~**e Lage** touch-and-go sort of a situation; ~**e Spekulation** hazardous (risky) speculation; ~**es Unternehmen** risky undertaking, [ad]venture, wildcat enterprise; ~**e Veränderungen** *(Meinungsforschung)* risky shifts.

riskieren to [run the] risk, to [put to the] venture, to [run a] hazard, to jeopardize;

etw. ~ to put the boat out, to chance one's arm *(coll.)*, to run hazard; **alles** ~ to stake one's bottom dollar, to play double or quits, to go one's death; **ein Auge** ~ to steal a glance; **Bemerkung** ~ to venture a remark; **Kopf und Kragen** ~ to risk one's neck; **sein Leben** ~ to risk one's neck, to venture (hazard) one's life; **Prozeß** ~ to venture a lawsuit; **seinen guten Ruf** ~ to risk one's reputation; **geschäftliche Verluste** ~ to jeopardize one's business; **sein Vermögen in einem Unternehmen** ~ to venture one's fortune in an enterprise.

Riß fissure, crack, breach, rift, *(im Eis)* split, crack, *(Entwurf)* draft, sketch, *(im Papier)* tear;

tiefer ~ **zwischen zwei Anschauungen** deep gulf between two views;

~ **bekommen** *(Freundschaft)* to break up.

Risse|in einer Partei dissensions between rival groups in a party;

~ **bekommen** to crack, *(in Haut)* to chap; ~ **in einer Freundschaft flicken** to patch the rifts in a friendship; ~ **verkleben** *(fig.)* to paper over the cracks.

rissig cracked, full of cracks, *(Stoff)* threadbare.

ristornieren *(Buchhandlung)* to reverse a contra entry;

Versicherung ~ to cancel an insurance.

Ristorno reverse of a contra entry.

Riten rites;
vorgeschriebene ~ einhalten to maintain the customary observance.
Ritt ride on horseback;
auf einen ~ in one go.
Ritter | ohne Furcht und Tadel knight without fear and without reproach;
~gut manor.
Rittergüter aufteilen to slice an estate into farms.
Rittergutsbesitzer lord of the manor, seignior.
ritterlich | er Mann chivalrous man; **~e Tat** knight service.
Ritual ritual;
leeres ~ durchspielen to go through the motions;
~mord ritual murder.
Ritze crevice, crack, chink;
neugierig durch eine ~ schauen to peep through a crack.
Rivale rival, competitor.
rivalisieren to rival, to be rivals, to compete.
Rivalität rivalry.
Robe *(Anwalt)* gown, robe.
Roboter robot.
robust sturdy, strong, robust.
röcheln to breathe stertorously, to give the death rattle.
Rock coat, jacket, *(Amtstracht)* robe, gown;
abgetragener ~ threadbare coat; **ausrangierter ~** discarded coat;
bunten ~ anziehen to don one's uniform;
an Mutters ~zipfel hängen to be tied to mother's apron strings.
roden to clear, *(kultivieren)* to make arable, to cultivate.
Rodung deforestation, clearing, cleared woodland.
roh *(brutto)* gross, *(Buch)* in sheets, *(Entwurf)* rough, *(Frucht)* crude, *(unbearbeitet)* unwrought, raw, in native state, crude, coarse, gross, *(ungebildet)* uncivilized, *(ungefähr)* roughly;
~ bearbeitet roughly dressed;
Gefangenen ~ behandeln to treat a prisoner brutally;
~e Behandlung harsh treatment; **~er Betrag** gross amount; **~e Dielen** bare floor; **~e Gewalt** brute force; **~er Kostenüberschlag** rough estimate.
Roh | abzug first proof; **~bau** skeleton, carcass, shell of a building; **im ~bau anfertigen** to skeletonize; **im ~bau fertiggestellt sein** to be finished in the rough; **~baumwolle** cotton wool; **~betrag** gross amount.
Rohbilanz trial (rough) balance, work sheet *(US)*;
berichtigte ~ adjusted trial balance;
~ ohne Aufwand und Ertrag postclosing trial balance;
~ aufstellen to take a trial balance.
Roh | diamant uncut (rough) diamond; **berichtigtes ~einkommen** adjusted gross income; **~einkünfte** gross revenue; **~einnahme** gross income (receipts); **~eisen** pig iron; **~eisenwerk** mill; **~energie** basic energy; **~entwurf** rough copy (sketch), *(erster)* scribble; **~ertrag** gross proceeds (receipts, produce), *(Pacht)* gross rental; **~ertragsaufstellung** trading report; **~erzeugnisse** raw products; **~fassung** *(Film)* work print; **~gewicht** gross weight.
Rohgewinn gross profit, balance of revenue;
~ für 1980 trading profit for 1980;
~analyse gross-profit analysis.
Rohgewinnaufschlag gross profit extra;
~ auf den Einstandspreis markup on cost; **~ auf den Inventarwert** inventory markup; **~ auf den Verkaufspreis** markup on retail; **~ auf das Warenlager** inventory markup.
Rohgewinn | quotient gross profit ratio; **~satz** gross profit rate, markup percentage; **~spanne** gross margin.
Roh | gummi crude (India) rubber; **~heit** brutality, vulgarity; **~kost** uncooked vegetables, rude fare, rabbit food *(sl.)*; **~last** total (gross) load; **~material** raw material (produce), crude material, staple; **~materialeinkäufe** [raw-]material purchases; **~materialien** unmanufactured materials; **~metall** crude metal; **~öl** crude oil; **~ölquellen** sources of crude oil; **~preis** gross price; **~produkte** raw produce (products), primary products (commodities), natural products; **~putz** rough (first) coat, daub.
Rohr pipe, tube;
nahtloses ~ seamless tube; **schwankendes ~** *(fig.)* reed;
im heißen ~ backen to bake in a hot oven; **Haus mit ~ decken** to reed a house; **einem ~ entströmen** to gush from a pipe; **wie ein ~ im Winde schwanken** to be like a reed before the wind;
~bruch *(Ölleitung)* pipe failure, pipeline break (fault), *(Wasser)* burst in the water mains.
Röhrchen *(Alkoholtest)* test tube;
ins ~ blasen to take a breath-analyser test.
Röhre pipe, tube, *(el.)* valve;
in die ~ gucken *(fig.)* to be left in the cold.
Röhrenblitzgerät electronic flash unit.
röhrenförmig tubular.
Röhren | herstellung tubing; **~kupplung** union joint; **~sockel** valve base; **~verkaufsvertrag gegen Gasabnahmeverpflichtung** gas-for-pipe deal; **~werk** pipe plant.
Rohr | erzeugnisse tubular products; **~kupplung** pipe joint.
Rohrleitung trunk, pipeline, tubing *(coll.)*;
~ zum Transport pulverisierter Kohle coal slurry pipeline;
Öl in durch die Wüste verlegten ~en transportieren to carry oil across the desert in pipelines; **~en verlegen** to lay pipes, to pipeline.
Rohrleitungs | bau pipeline engineering; **~bruch** pipeline break (fault); **~konstruktion** piping; **~netz** system of pipelines, pipeline system; **~tarif** pipeline tariff; **~verlauf** pipeline route.
Rohr | möbel wicker (cane) furniture; **~muffe** pipe socket; **unter der Erde verlegtes weitverzweigtes ~netz** network of underground pipes; **~netz mit Wasserbrausen** network of sprinkler valves.
Rohrpost blow post *(Br.)*, pneumatic postal system, pneumatic dispatch (post, *Br.*);
~anlage, ~einrichtung pneumatic dispatch; **~büchse** pneumatic dispatch carrier; **~sendungen** pneumatic tube items.
Rohr | produktion tube (pipe) production; **~schelle** pipe clip; **wie ein ~spatz schimpfen** to scold like a fishwife; **~verbindung** union; **~verleger** pipelayer, pipeliner; **~verstopfung** block in a pipe.
Roh | saldo rough balance; **~schnitt** *(Film)* rough out; **~seide** raw silk; **~skizze** scribble, layout; **~skizze machen** to scribble, to block in; **~stahl** natural steel; **~stahlproduktion** output of crude steel; **~stoff** raw material.
rohstoffarm poor in raw materials.
Rohstoff | ausfuhr exportation of raw materials; **~ausgleichslager** buffer stock; **~ausschuß** raw-material board; **über keinerlei ~basis verfügen** to be lacking entirely in raw materials; **~bedarf** raw-material requirements; **~bedarf decken** to meet the requirements of raw materials; **~beschaffungskosten** cost of raw materials, preprocess cost; **~bestände** raw-materials inventory.
Rohstoffe raw materials (products), primary materials (commodities, products), basic commodities, staple, unwrought goods;
per Termin gehandelte ~ *(Börse)* commodity; **zollfreie ~** duty-free material;
~, Hilfs- und Betriebsstoffe *(Bilanz)* raw materials and supplies;
einer Maschine ~ zuführen to feed a machine with raw materials.
Rohstoff | eindeckungsplan material analysis; **~einfuhr** imports of raw material, raw-material imports; **~ersparnis** economy in raw materials; **~erzeugung** primary production, production of raw material; **~exporte** commodity exports; **~gebiet** raw-material producing area; **~gehalt** raw-material content; **~handel** commodity trade (trading); **~hortung** stockpiling of raw materials; **~käufe** purchases of raw materials, material purchases; **~knappheit** scarcity of raw materials, raw-material shortage; **~lager** stock of raw materials, raw-materials inventory; **beweglich geführtes ~lager** buffer stock; **~land** raw-material (primary-) producing country; **~mangel** scarcity of raw materials, raw-material shortage; **~markt** raw-material market; **Richtwerte setzender ~markt** primary market *(US)*; **~preis** commodity price; **~preisbewegungen** commodity price movements; **~preisprognose** commodity price forecasting; **~probe** specimen; **~produzent** primary producer; **~quellen** material (natural) resources; **~stadium** raw-material stage; **~verarbeitung** processing of raw materials; **~verbrauch** raw materials used; **~verknappung** limit on resources; **~versorgung** supply of raw materials; **~vorkommen** raw materials deposit.
Roh | überschuß gross supply; **~übersetzung** rough translation; **~verlust** gross loss; **~vermögen** gross assets; **~zucker** crude sugar; **~zustand** rough, crude condition, *(Metall)* crude state, crudeness.
Rolladen venetian blind;
stählerner ~ steel shutter.
Roll | bahn *(Flugplatz)* runway, airstrip, lead, taxiway, taxi strip, landing track; **~dach** *(Auto)* slide-back roof.
Rolle roll, register, scroll, list, *(Funktion)* rôle, role, *(Geld)* roll, *(Papierfabrikation)* reel, *(Stammrolle)* muster roll, *(Theater)* part, character, cue, *(Walze)* trundle, *(Zylinder)* cylinder, roller;

führende ~ leading part, *(Theater)* leadership, lead; **kleine** ~ bit, *(Theater)* small part; **stumme** ~ thinking part; **tragische** ~ heavy part;
~ **der Angeklagten** calendar; ~ **Banknoten** bundle of notes, bankroll *(US)*; ~ **von Dokumenten** wad, collection of documents; ~ **Druckpapier** roll of printing paper; ~ **des Friedensstifters** peacekeeping role; ~ **Garn** spool of thread; ~ **auf einer Konferenz** part in a conference; ~ **eines Menschenfreundes** rôle of a philanthropist; ~ **Pergament** scroll of parchment; ~ **Tapeten** piece (roll) of wallpaper;
sich mit seiner ~ **abfinden** to become reconciled with one's role; **sich eine** ~ **anmaßen** to usurp a role; ~ **ausspielen** to play out; **sich in der** ~ **des Züngleins an der Waage befinden** to be in the position to tip the scales; **seine** ~ **beherrschen** to be sure of one's lines; ~ **mangelhaft beherrschen** to fluff *(Br., sl.)*; **seine** ~ **perfekt beherrschen** to be letter- (word-) perfect in one's part; ~ **zugewiesen bekommen** to be cast as; ~ **besetzen** to cast the parts; ~ **darstellen** to interpret a role; **seine** ~ **noch einmal durchgehen** to run over one's part again; ~ **einstudieren** to get up a role; ~ **ergattern** to land an assignment; **aus der** ~ **fallen** to drop a brick; **seine** ~ **herunterspielen** to walk through one's part; **über** ~**n laufen** to run on rollers; **seine** ~ **auswendig lernen** to study one's part (lines); **Stück mit verteilten** ~**n lesen** to do a play-reading; ~ **mitübernehmen** to double a part; **in jds.** ~ **schlüpfen** to inherit s. one's mantle; ~ **spielen** to be of importance, to count, *(Theater)* to play a role (part), to act a part; **armselige** ~ **spielen** to cut a poor figure; **bedeutende** ~ **spielen** to cut a dash (splash, shine); **große** ~ **spielen** to figure large; **in der Wirtschaft eine große** ~ **spielen** to make o. s. a great factor in the economy; **herausragende** ~ **spielen** *(Schauspieler)* to hit the high spots; **historische** ~ **spielen** to figure in history; **klassische** ~**n spielen** to do the classics; **keine** ~ **in der Gesellschaft spielen** to occupy an insignificant place in society; **seine** ~ **glänzend spielen** to act one's part well; ~ **gut spielen** to fill a part well; ~ **in einem Theaterstück spielen** to perform in a play; ~ **übernehmen** to take a part; ~ **des Gastgebers übernehmen** to perform the part of host; ~**n vertauschen** to turn the tables; ~**n in einem Stück verteilen** to cast the parts in a play;
Geld spielt keine ~ *(Anzeige)* money is no object.

Rollen *(Donner)* rumble, roar, *(Schiff)* rolling, lurch;
Stein ins ~ **bringen** to start the ball rolling.

rollen to roll, *(Donner)* to rumble, to roar, *(Flugzeug)* to taxi, *(im Rollstuhl)* to wheel, *(schlingern)* to lurch;
auf die Startbahn ~ to taxi onto the runway.

Rollen|besetzung cast [of parts]; ~**buch** *(Theater)* script, continuity.

rollend rolling, on track;
~**es Material** *(Eisenbahn)* rolling stock.

Rollen|darsteller role performer; ~**darstellung** role performance.

rollenfest sein to be letter- (word-) perfect, to be sure of one's lines.

Rollen|interpretation playing; ~**verteiler** casting director; ~**verteilung** cast [of parts]; **unpassende** ~**verteilung** miscasting; **ausdrucksvolle** ~**wiedergabe** full-blooded interpretation of a part.

Roller scooter.

Roll|erlaubnis taxi clearance; ~**feld** *(Flugplatz)* landing ground (track, strip), taxiway; ~**film** roll film; ~**filmspule** film cartridge.

Rollfuhr|dienst cartage service, freight delivery, pick-up [and delivery] service, trucking service, *(Firma)* carting agent; **bahnamtlicher** ~**dienst** door-to-door service, rail express agency *(US)*; ~**geschäft** carrier's business; ~**mann** carter, [common] carrier, teamster *(US)*; ~**tarif** cartage rates; ~**unternehmen** carter, carting agent, trucking agency (company); ~**unternehmer** carting (cartage) contractor (agent), [common] carrier, haulage contractor, road haulier; **bahnamtlicher** ~**unternehmer** door-to-door service, rail express agency *(US)*.

Roll|geld cartage, carriage, portage, rolling charges, porterage, truckage, haulage, wheelage, drayage *(US)*; ~**gut** carted goods, rolling freight, cases and casks; ~**gutverkehr** local freight; ~**jalousie** roller blind; ~**kommando** raiding squad; ~**kutscher** drayman, carter, carrier, teamster *(US)*; **als** ~**kutscher tätig sein** to dray; ~**laden** roll top, window blind; ~**schrank** roll-front cabinet; ~**schreibtisch** roll-top desk; ~**split** loose chippings; ~**strecke** *(Flughafen)* run, taxiway; ~**stuhl** invalid (rolling) chair; ~**treppe** moving (travel(l)ing) staircase, escalator; ~**treppe benutzen** to escalate; ~**verdeck** *(Auto)* roller roof; ~**wagen** light waggon, van *(Br.)*; **kleiner** ~**wagen** trundle.

Roman novel, fiction;
soeben erschienener ~ fresh novel; **gängiger** ~ straight novel; **gewöhnlicher** ~ straight novel; **historischer** ~ historical novel; **klassischer** ~ standard novel; **spannender** ~ exciting novel; ~ **für gehobenere Ansprüche** sophisticated novel;
wie ein ~ **anmuten** to read like a novel; **an einem neuen** ~ **arbeiten** to have a new novel on the stocks, to be working on a new novel; ~ **in Fortsetzungen erscheinen lassen** to serialize a novel; ~ **in England spielen lassen** to lay a novel in England; ~**e in einer Zeitschrift rezensieren** to do the fictions in a magazine; ~ **verfassen** to write a novel; ~ **für die Verfilmung vorsehen** to intend a novel for the screen; **jem. einen** ~ **zuschreiben** to mother a novel on s. o.;
~**abteilung** fiction department; ~**autor** novel (fiction) writer, fictioner, novelist; **nachträgliche** ~**fassung erfolgreicher Filme** novelization of successful films; ~**figur** fiction character, fictitious characters of a novel; **lebensfremde** ~**figuren darstellen** to overdraw characters in a novel; ~**folge** serial; **in** ~**form darstellen** to novelize; ~**leser** novel reader; **leichte** ~**literatur** light fiction.

romantisch romantic;
~ **eingestellt sein** to lean to romance;
~**es Abenteuer** romantic adventure; ~**e Landschaft** wild scenery; ~**es altes Schloß** romantic old castle; ~**e Vorstellungen** romantic visions.

Romanvorwurf, erstklassiger knockout plot for a fiction story.

Romanze romance, love affair.

Römische Verträge Treaty of Rome.

röntgen to x-ray.

Röntgen|aufnahme, ~**bild** radiograph, x-ray; ~**bild machen** to take a x-ray; ~**durchleuchtung** fluoroscopy; ~**film** x-ray film; ~**reihenuntersuchung** mass radiography; ~**schirm** fluorescent screen; ~**strahl** x-ray; ~**verfahren** radiography.

rosarote Brille *(fig.)* rose-colo(u)red spectacles.

Rose *(Kompaß)* compass rose (card);
er ist nicht auf ~**n gebettet** his life is no bed of roses.

Rosen|montag Shrove Monday; ~**muster** *(Tapete)* pattern of roses.

rosig rose-colo(u)red, *(verheißungsvoll)* rosy, favo(u)rable;
im günstigsten Fall nicht sehr ~ **sein** to be at best far from bright;
~**e Aussichten** fine prospects; **alles in** ~**sten Farben sehen** to see things through rose-colo(u)red spectacles; **in** ~**ster Laune sein** to be in high spirits.

Rosine *(fig.)* plum;
dicke ~ prize plum;
große ~**n im Kopf haben** to have big ideas, to fly high; **sich die** ~**n aus dem Kuchen herauspicken** to take the pick of the bunch, to skim the cream off.

Roß, von seinem hohen ~ **heruntersteigen** to come off one's perch (high horse), to climb down; **j. von seinem hohen** ~ **heruntersteigen lassen** to knock s. o. off his perch; **sich aufs hohe** ~ **setzen** to mount (ride) the high horse; **auf einem hohen** ~ **sitzen** to ride the (get on one's) high horse, to perk it.

Rost rust, *(Bratrost)* grid, grill, *(an Öfen)* grate;
vom ~ **befreien** to clean of rust; **vom** ~ **zerfressen** rust-eaten; ~ **angesetzt haben** *(Sprachkenntnisse)* to have become a bit rusty;
~**ansatz** first signs of rust; ~**beständigkeit** rust-resisting property; ~**fänger** rust trap; ~**fleck** rust stain.

rostfrei rust-proof, rust-resisting;
~**er Stahl** stainless steel.

rostig rusty.

Rost|schutz rust prevention; ~**schutzmittel** rust preventive; ~**stab** fire bar.

Rot *(Verkehrsampel)* red light;
bei ~ **fahren** to run a red light; **bei** ~ **die Straße überqueren** to cross against the red light;
~**es Kreuz** Red Cross.

rot *(pol.)* red;
~ **ankreuzen** to red-letter; **Tag** ~ **im Kalender anstreichen** to mark as a red-letter day; ~ **sehen** to see red *(sl.)*; ~ **angehaucht sein** *(fig.)* to have red leanings; **bis über beide Ohren** ~ **werden** to blush right up to one's ears;
~**e Gefahr** Communist menace; ~**en Kopf bekommen** to flush, to blush; ~**es Licht überfahren** to run a red light; ~**e Nummer** *(Auto)* dealer's licence number; ~**en Teppich auslegen** to lay (roll) out the red carpet; **für j. den** ~**en Teppich ausrollen** to spread out the welcome mat for s. o.; ~**es Tuch für einen Bullen** red rag to a bull; **wie ein** ~**es Tuch wirken** to act like a red rag to a bull; ~**e Welle** *(Verkehr)* one red light after the other; ~**e**

Zahlen *(Bilanz)* red figures; ~**e Zahlen ausweisen** to show red ink *(US coll.)*; **in die** ~**en Zahlen geraten** to run in the red *(US)*, to fall into red ink *(US)*; **aus den** ~**en Zahlen herauskommen** to climb (come, get) out of the red *(US)*.
Rotaprint rotary printing, multilith.
Rotations|druck rotary printing, web; ~**maschine** rotary-printing machine; ~**papier** newsprint; ~**presse** rotary (rolling, web) press, cylinder printing machine; ~**tiefdruck** rotary photogravure, rotagravure.
Rotbuch *(pol.)* Red Book.
Röte red, redness, blush;
jem. die ~ **ins Gesicht steigen lassen** to make s. o. blush.
röten to redden, to turn red;
sich vor Verlegenheit ~ to blush with embarrassment.
Rotfilter *(Foto)* red filter.
rotierend rotary.
Rotkreuz|flagge Red Cross flag; ~**krankenhaus** Red Cross hospital; ~**schwester** field hospital nurse.
Rotstift red pencil.
Rotte gang, band, *(mil.)* file, platoon, *(Verbandsflug)* two-ship formation.
Rotten|arbeiter tracklayer, platelayer *(Br.)*; ~**führer** foreman, ganger, gang boss *(US)*.
Rotwelsch thieves' patter.
Rotzjunge whipper-snapper, saucy (fresh, *US*) youngster.
Rouleau [window] blind, spring curtain, curtain roller, window shade *(US)*.
Roulett roulette;
~**tisch** roulette table.
Route route, journey;
kürzeste ~ direct route; **tägliche** ~ milk round; **übliche** ~ course of the voyage;
~ **festlegen** to route.
Routenfestlegung für die Verkäufer routing of salesman.
Routine routine, rote, groove, practice, versedness;
~ **sein** to be routine; **zur** ~ **werden** to fall into a groove;
~**anfrage** routine request; ~**angelegenheit** cut-and-dried affair, matter of routine; ~**antwort** routine reply; ~**arbeit** daily dozen, routine work (business, chores), journeyman (donkey, repetitive) work; ~**aufgaben** routine duties; ~**auftrag** routine order; ~**bericht vorlegen** to furnish a routine report; ~**besuch** routine visit; ~**buchung einer Geschäftstransaktion** entry in the regular course of business; ~**einsatz,** ~**flug** routine flight; ~**frage** question of routine.
routinemäßig routine, by rote, groovy;
~ **erledigen (tun)** to routinize, to do as a matter of routine; **Pflichten** ~ **erledigen** to perform duties by rote;
~**e Aufklärungsflüge** routine reconnaissance flights; ~**e Erledigung** routinization; ~**e Prüfung** routine testing.
Routine|sache routine matter, cut-and-dried affair; ~**sitzung** usual meeting; ~**verfahren** routine procedure; ~**verfügungen** *(mil.)* special orders; ~**verlauf** trivial round; ~**zwang** trammels of routine.
Routinier professional, experienced person;
alter ~ old hand at work.
routiniert practised, experienced, versed, smart;
sehr sicher und ~ **sein** to be fully articulate; ~ **im Umgang mit Kunden sein** to know how to deal with customers from experience;
~**e Übersetzung** expert translation.
Rowdy rowdy, rough, roughneck *(coll.)*, hoodlum *(US sl.)*.
Rowdytum vandalism, hooliganism.
Rübe turnip, *(Kopf, coll.)* pate, noddle;
eins auf die ~ **bekommen** to get a bash in the face.
Rubrik rubric, column, category, *(Steuerklasse)* bracket, *(Überschrift)* head, heading, title, *(Zeitung)* special section;
mit ~**en versehen** rubricated; **unter derselben** ~ under the same title;
~ **Leserbriefe** section letters to the editor; ~ **in einem Sachregister** subject heading;
in die gleiche ~ **einordnen** to bracket; **unter eine besondere** ~ **fallen** to come under a separate heading; **unter die** ~ **gehören** to fall under the headline; ~ **für Bücherrezensionen zur Verfügung stellen** to devote a column to book criticism; **mit** ~**en versehen** to rubricate, to head.
Rubrizierung rubrication.
Rubrum heading, caption, premises, recital, title.
ruchbar known;
~ **geworden sein** to have got abroad; ~ **werden** to take wind, to get around;
es wurde ~ it transpired (leaked out) that.
ruchlos odious, wicked, flagrant;
~**es Gewerbe** nefarious trade.
Ruchlosigkeit profanity, heinousness.
Ruck jerk, jolt, flounce, tug;
mit einem ~ at one go;
~ **nach links** *(Wahl)* swing to the left; ~ **am Zügel** pull on the reins;
mit einem ~ **anhalten** *(Zug)* to stop with a jerk; **jem. einen** ~ **geben** to shock s. o.; **sich einen** ~ **geben** to pull o. s. together, to force o. s.
Rück|abtretung reconveyance, recession, reassignment, reassignation, retrocession; ~**abtretungsempfänger** retrocessionary; ~**abwicklung** reversed transaction; ~**ansicht** back view; ~**anspruch** counterclaim.
Rückantwort reply, answer;
bezahlte ~ reply paid, prepaid reply;
~ **eines Telegramms vorausbezahlen** to prepay a reply to a telegram;
~**karte** business reply (self-addressed) card, reply-paid postcard *(Br.)*; ~**schein** reply coupon; ~**telegramm** prepaid telegram.
ruckartig jerky, jolting, flouncy, all of a sudden;
~ **anhalten** to stop with a jerk.
Rück|assekuranz reassurance, reinsurance; ~**auflassung** reconveyance; ~**äußerung** reply; ~**beeinflussung** *(Soziologie)* feedback; ~**behaltungsrecht** retention; ~**belastung** return debit; ~**belastungsaufgabe** return debit voucher; ~**berufung** avocatory letter, recall; ~**beziehung** relation back; ~**bildung** *(ling.)* backformation; ~**blende** *(Film)* flashback, flash *(Br.)*, cutback; ~**blick** retrospective, review, retrospect.
rückbuchen to write back, to reverse an entry.
Rück|buchung reversal, reverse entry, storno; ~**buchung eines überzogenen Betrags** overdraft; ~**bürge** countersecurity, surety for a surety, attestor of a cautioner.
rückbürgen to countersecure.
Rückbürgschaft backdown, backbond, surety for a surety, countersurety *(Br.)*, countersecurity, counterbond.
rückdatieren to date back, to backdate, *(nachdatieren)* to antedate.
Rückdatierung dating back, postdate, postdating, *(Nachdatierung)* antedating.
Rückdatierungsbestandteil backdated element.
rückdecken to buy back, to repurchase, *(Versicherung)* to reinsure.
Rück|deckung reinsurance; ~**einfuhr** reimportation.
Rücken *(Buch)* back;
mit dem ~ **gegen die Wand** with one's back to the wall;
gebeugter ~ bent back; **verlängerter** ~ posterior;
~ **an** ~ back to back;
hinter jds. ~ **agieren** to go behind s. one's back; **jem. die Hände auf den** ~ **binden** to tie s. one's hands behind his back; **sich den** ~ **decken** to play it safe; **jem. den** ~ **decken** to take s. o. under one's wing; **jem. in den** ~ **fallen** to stab s. o. in the back, to attack s. o. from the rear; **breiten** ~ **haben** *(fig.)* to have a strong back; **Feind im** ~ **haben** to have the enemy in one's rear; **hundert Jahre auf dem** ~ **haben** to have reached the age of a hundred; **reichen Vater im** ~ **haben** to have a rich father behind one; **Wind im** ~ **haben** to have the wind behind one; **einem kalt und heiß den** ~ **herunterlaufen** to go hot and cold all over; **seiner Heimat den** ~ **kehren** to leave one's home for good; **einer Sache den** ~ **kehren** to turn one's back on s. th.; **der Welt den** ~ **kehren** to die to the world; **krummen** ~ **vor jem. machen** to cringe before s. o.; **hinter dem** ~ **reden** to backbite; **hinter jds.** ~ **über ihn reden** to say s. th. behind s. one's back; **jem. den** ~ **stärken** to stiffen (stay) s. o., to back s. o. up, to give s. o. moral support; **mit dem** ~ **zur Wand stehen** to be with one's back to the wall.
rücken, jem. auf die Bude *(fam.)* to blow in on s. o., *(drängen)* to press s. o. hard; **höher** ~ to rise in rank; **Komma einer Dezimalstelle zwei Stellen weiter** ~ to move the decimal two places; **an jds. Stelle** ~ to take s. one's place.
Rückendeckung backing, support;
finanzielle ~ financial backing;
jem. ~ **geben** to give s. o. cover, to close one's ranks behind s. o.
Rücken|einlage *(Buch)* stiffener; ~**flug** inverted flight.
rückenfrei *(Kleid)* low-backed.
Rücken|lage *(Flugzeug)* upside-down position; ~**lehne** back rest, *(Auto)* squab; ~**plakat** sandwich board; ~**stärkung** moral support; ~**stempel** *(Buchbinderei)* creaser; **zu jds.** ~**stützung** at s. one's back.
Rück|entflechtung reconcentration, decartelization; ~**entwicklung** backwards motion.

Rückenwind tailwind;
~**landung** downwind (Chinese, *sl.*) landing.
Rück|erbittung request for return; **unter ~erbittung** please return, to be returned; ~**erinnerung der heute noch Lebenden** living memory.
rückerstatten to restitute, to replace, to redeliver, to give back, *(Auslagen)* to refund, to reimburse.
Rückerstattung reimbursement, refund, refunding, refundment, compensation, drawback, *(Rückgabe)* restitution, restoration, return, returning, redelivery, *(Rückzahlung)* repayment;
~ **von Auslagen** compensation for outlay incurred; ~ **in bar** cash refund; ~ **eines zuviel gezahlten Betrages** return of an amount overpaid; ~ **irrtümlich eingezahlter Gelder** restitution of an overpaid amount; ~ **des Kaufpreises** restitution of money paid; ~ **von Steuern** reimbursement (refund) of taxes; ~ **von Vermögen** restitution of property.
Rückerstattungs|angebot refunding offer; ~**anspruch** restitutory right; ~**antrag** drawback application; ~**berechtigter** restitutee; ~**beschluß** restitution order.
rückerstattungsfähig refundable, restorable, repayable.
Rückerstattungspflicht obligation to repay.
rückerstattungspflichtig liable to refund;
~ **sein** to be liable to make restitution.
Rückerstattungs|prozeß restitution case; ~**urteil** restitution order; ~**verpflichteter** restitutor.
Rückerwerb repurchase, reacquisition, true recovery;
~ **von Investmentanteilen** redemption of units *(Br.)*.
rückerwerben to repurchase;
Investmentzertifikate ~ to redeem units *(Br.)*.
Rückerwerber reacquirer.
Rückfahrkarte return [ticket, fare], round-trip ticket *(US)*;
verbilligte ~ cheap-day return;
~ **mit eintägiger Gültigkeit** day ticket; ~ **mit viertägiger Gültigkeit** return ticket valid (available) for four days;
~ **erster Klasse nach X lösen** to take a first-class return to X.
Rückfahrkartenabschnitt return half.
Rückfahrschein return [ticket];
~ **mit eintägiger Gültigkeit** day ticket.
Rückfahrt return [journey], return passage, *(Auto)* drive back, *(Schiff)* inward passage, *(Zug)* return run;
auf der ~ on the way home;
Hin- und ~ round trip;
~ **belegen** to book the return ticket;
~**ermäßigung** return-ticket reduction, round-trip discount *(US)*.
Rückfall backslide, *(Heimfall)* reversion, *(Krankheit)* relapse, recrudescence, *(Rückschlag)* setback, relapse, *(Verbrecher)* recidivism;
im ~ in case of a repeated (second, *US*) offence;
~ **bekommen** to suffer a relapse;
~**anspruch** reversionary interest; ~**diebstahl** stealing as a repeated offence; ~**gut** revision estate.
rückfällig *(Heimfall)* revertible, relapsing, *(Verbrecher)* recedevist, recidivous;
~ **werden** to relapse, *(Verbrecher)* to be a recidivist, to recidivate;
~**er Täter** repeater, second offender *(US)*.
Rückfälliger repeater *(US)*, backslider, recidivist, relapser, second offender *(US)*.
Rückfall|recht reversion, reverter, reversionary interest; ~**tat** repeated (second, *US*) offence; ~**täter** repeater, second offender *(US)*; ~**vergehen** recidivism, repeated offence, second offence *(US)*.
Rückfenster *(Auto)* rear window.
Rückflug flight (plane, trip) home, return flight;
auf dem ~ homebound;
~**buchung** return plane reservation; ~**geld** return air passage; ~**karte** return air ticket (fare); ~**zeug** return plane.
Rück|fluß *(Geld)* efflux, reflux; ~**fluß heißen Geldes** reflux of hot money; ~**forderung** reclaim, redemand, *(Gegenforderung)* counter-demand, counterclaim, reclamation; **abgetretene** ~**forderungen** assigned book accounts.
Rückforderungs|anspruch restitutory right; ~**anspruch gegen j. geltend machen** to claim s. th. back from s. o.; ~**klausel** recapture (recovery) clause.
Rückfracht cargo homeward, return cargo, return freight *(Br.)*, reshipment *(US)*, back carriage (freight), home freight;
durch Verkauf (Tausch) der Hinfracht erworbene ~ proceeds of a cargo; **langsame** ~ slow return freight *(Br.)*;
als ~ **senden** to reship *(US)*;
~**faktor** return load factor; ~**tarif** returned shipment rate *(US)*.
Rückfrage query, inquiry;
angebotsbezogene ~ request for further information;
~ **halten** to inquire, to [make a] query, to check.
rückfragen, bei jem. to check with s. o.
rückführen to repatriate.
Rückführung repatriation;
~ **eines Abzahlungsvertrages** hire-purchase *(Br.)* (deferred-payment, *US*) repayment; ~ **von Kapital** repatriation of capital; ~ **eines Mietwagens** dropoff of a rented car; ~ **von Öldollarströmen** recycling of petro-dollars; ~ **der kurzfristigen Verbindlichkeiten** reduction in current liabilities.
Rückführungs|betrag redemption sum; ~**gebühr** *(Mietwagen)* return charge, dropoff charge (fee); ~**plan** *(Schuldenabbau)* redemption plan; ~**soll** redemption rate agreed upon.
Rückgabe giving back, return, redelivery, restitution, surrender, restoration, *(an früheren Eigentümer)* revesting;
~ **an den Eigentümer** return to the owner; ~ **gestohlener Gegenstände** restitution of stolen goods, kickback *(sl.)*, blowback *(sl.)*; ~ **von Pfandgegenständen** restoration of goods in distraint; ~ **eines konfiszierten Vermögens** restoration of confiscated property; ~ **eines bestimmten Vermögensgegenstandes** specific restitution of property;
langfristige ~**möglichkeit** *(Buchhändler)* long-term possibility of return.
rückgabepflichtig returnable.
Rückgabeprämie return premium.
Rückgaberecht return privilege, *(Investmentfonds)* repurchase privilege;
mit ~ on sale and return; **Kauf mit** ~ memorandum buying;
mit ~ **verkaufen** to send (ship, *US*) on memorandum.
Rückgang fall, falling off, decline, drop, downward movement, letdown, *(Kurse)* decline, recession, retreat, *(Umsatz)* decrease;
ausgeprägter ~ marked decline; **beträchtlicher** ~ material (considerable) recession; **konjunkturbedingter** ~ cyclical downswing; **leichter** ~ slight falling off; **saisonbedingter** ~ seasonal slump;
~ **der Aktienkurse (Börsenkurse)** decline in stock prices, stock-market decline; ~ **der Arbeitslosigkeit** decline (drop) in unemployment; ~ **der Auslandsaufträge** falling off of export orders; ~ **der Einnahmen** decline (shortfall) in revenue; ~ **der Erträge** drop (decline) in earnings; ~ **der Geburtenrate** decline (fall) in (falling of) the birth rate; ~ **der Gewinne** dropoff (drop, fall) in profits, profit decline (dip); ~ **der Kurse** fall (drop, decrease) in prices; ~ **der Mitgliederzahl** reduction of members; ~ **der Nachfrage** drop (decline) in demand; ~ **der Preise** fall (dip, drop) in prices, price decline (recession); ~ **der Produktion** production decrease, dwindling production; ~ **des Touristenstroms** dropoff in tourists; ~ **des Umsatzes** drop in sales;
~ **erfahren** to experience a decline; **leichten** ~ **erfahren** to suffer a slight reaction.
rückgängig declining, falling, *(Konjunktur)* downward, *(Kurse)* reactionary, retrograde, drooping;
~ **machen** to countermand, to annul, to cancel, to revoke, to declare off, to unmake, to undo, to rescind;
Auftrag (Bestellung) ~ **machen** to cancel (rescind, countermand, annul, withdraw) an order; **Handel** ~ **machen** to call off a bargain; **seine Verlobung** ~ **machen** to break off one's engagement; **Vertrag** ~ **machen** to rescind a contract; **leicht** ~ **sein** to suffer a slight reaction (decline);
~**e Bewegung** downward (retrograde) movement; ~ **gemachter Kauf** countermanded sale; ~**e Kursbewegung** retrograde movement of prices; ~**e Tendenz** drooping of prices, downward trend (tendency).
Rückgängigmachung recission, cancellation, cancel, reversal, cancellation;
~ **von Bestellungen** withdrawal of orders; ~ **eines Kaufs** redhibition *(US)*.
rückgewähren to restitute, to restore.
Rück|gewährpflicht obligation to refund; ~**gewährung** restitution, restoration; ~**gewinnung verlorenen Gebietes** recovery of lost territory; ~**gewinnung von Wüstengebiet** desert reclamation.
rückgliedern to reintegrate, to reincorporate.
Rückgliederung reintegration, reincorporation.
Rückgrat *(fig.)* spine, mainstay, backbone, fibre;
moralisches ~ moral fibre;
~ **der städtischen Finanzen** mainstay of the city's finances; ~ **eines Geschäftes** mainstay of a business; ~ **eines Staates** backbone of a country;

einer Firma das ~ **brechen** to break the back of a firm; **kein ~ haben** to have weak knees (no backbone), to be spineless; **j. das ~ stärken** to back s. o. up, to stiffen s. o.; ~ **zeigen** to stand up straight.

Rückgriff recourse;
~ **gegenüber Dritten** recourse against third parties; ~ **auf die Hilfsquellen** hold on the resources; ~ **auf den Indossanten** recourse to the endorser; ~ **auf die Reserven (Rücklagen)** drawing on the reserves; ~ **mangels Zahlung** recourse for want of payment;
~ **nehmen** to recourse.

Rückgriffs|haftung liability to recourse; **mit ~haftung** with recourse; **~möglichkeit** recourse basis, backup facilities; **~recht** right of recourse, *(Bürge)* right of relief; **~schuldner** party liable upon recourse.

Rückgut returns, goods returned.

Rückhalt support, backing, stay, shot in the locker;
ohne jeden ~ without any organization behind it;
finanzieller ~ financial backing; **moralischer** ~ moral support;
zahlenmäßiger ~ numerical support;
~ **seiner Familie** chief stay of one's family;
~ **an jem. haben** to have s. o. to fall back upon; **keinerlei finanziellen ~ haben** to have no resources to fall back upon; **finanzielle Reserven als ~ haben** to have recourse to financial reserves.

rückhaltlos without reserve, unreserved, straight, down-the-line, without stint;
sich einer Bewegung ~ anschließen to join a movement wholeheartedly; ~ **sprechen** to speak without control; **einem Vorschlag ~ zustimmen** to approve a suggestion without reservation.

Rückkauf repurchase, buyback, buying back, *(Einlösung)* redemption;
vorzeitiger ~ anticipated redemption;
~ **von Gewinnanteilen** surrendering of bonuses *(Br.)*; ~ **einer Lebensversicherung** surrender of policy.

rückkaufbar repurchasable, redeemable.
~e Vorzugsaktien redeemable preference shares *(Br.)*.

Rückkäufer repurchaser.

Rückkaufs|ankündigung notice of redemption; **~berechtigung** *(Versicherung)* surrender privilege; **obligatorische ~bestimmungen** nonforfeiture provisions; **~frist** repurchase period; **~garantie** *(Grundstück)* lease back; **~gebühr** *(Lebensversicherung)* surrender penalty; **~kurs** redemption price; **~prämie** redemption premium; **~preis** redemption (buy-back) price; **~projekt** buy-back project.

Rückkaufsrecht right (equity, option, power) of redemption (to redeem), legal revision, redemption right;
mit ~ with option for repurchase.

Rückkaufs|satz retirement rate; **~vereinbarung** buy-back arrangement; **~verlust** redemption loss; **~vertrag** repurchase agreement; **~vorschlag** request for repurchase; **~wert** redemption (repurchase, nonforfeiture) value, *(Lebensversicherung)* cash [surrender] value, paid-up value, valuation; **~wert eines Sparvertrages** repayment value of a savings contract.

Rückkehr return, comeback;
bei meiner ~ on my return home;
~ **einer Epidemie** fresh outbreak of an epidemic; ~ **zum Goldstandard** return to the gold standard; ~ **in den Kreis der Wirtschaftsmächte** economic comeback; ~ **zur Zivilverwaltung** derequisition *(Br.)*;
~möglichkeit comeback vehicle.

Rück|koppelung *(Radio)* feedback, **~kunft** return; **bei meiner ~kunft** on my return; **~ladeort** point of reshipment *(US)*; **~ladung** return (homeward) cargo, reshipment *(US)*; **~lageguthaben** reserve balance.

Rücklagen reserve[s], reserve fund, appropriations *(US)*, surplus *(US)*, *(Ersparnisse)* savings;
allgemeine ~ general [purpose contingency] reserve, unappropriated surplus *(US)*; **ausgewiesene** ~ declared reserves; **bilanzmäßig ausgewiesene** ~ balance-sheet reserves; **bei der Liquidation ausschüttbare** ~ reserve capital; **nicht ausschüttbare** ~ capital reserve; **außerordentliche** ~ extraordinary reserves, provident reserve fund, *(Versicherung)* catastrophe reserves; **besondere** ~ naked reserve *(US)*, special contingency reserves; **aus Geschäftssanierung entstandene** ~ recapitalization surplus; **aus Kapitalherabsetzung entstandene** ~ recapitalization surplus, reduction surplus *(US)*; **freie** ~ available (voluntary) reserves, reserve at disposal, uncommitted reserves, free reserves *(US)*, voluntary reserve fund, nonstatutory capital reserves, free surplus, discretionary appropriations *(US)*, *(Bank)* excess reserves, *(Versicherung)* free surplus; **aus Höherbewertung von Anlagegütern gebildete** ~ revaluation (appraisal, *US*) surplus; **gesetzliche (gesetzlich vorgeschriebene)** ~ legal *(Br.)* (lawful, *US*) reserves, statutory reserve [fund], nondisposable capital, legal appropriations *(US)*, *(AG)* [etwa] accumulated earnings *(US)*, earned surplus *(US)*; **offene** ~ declared (disclosed, published, surplus) reserves, reserves as shown in the balance sheet; **satzungsmäßige** ~ reserve provided by the articles, statutory reserves, contractual (statutory) appropriations *(US)*; **stille** ~ undisclosed (hidden) reserves (assets); **unzureichende** ~ reserve deficiency; **versicherungstechnische** ~ actuarial reserves; **zweckgebundene** ~ appropriated (reserved) surplus, surplus reserve *(US)*;
~ **für Abschreibungen** reserve for depreciation (wear, tear, obsolescence or inadequacy), depreciation fund; ~ **zur Abschreibung langfristiger Anlagegüter** amortization reserves; ~ **für den Ankauf eigener Aktien** reserve for purchase of treasury stock *(US)*; ~ **für Arbeitnehmerabfindungen** employee compensation reserves, redundancy fund *(Br.)*; ~ **einer Bank** bank's (banking) reserves; ~ **für Beteiligungen an Banken und Bankfirmen** reserve against shareholding interests in foreign banks; ~ **für Betriebserneuerungen** reserve for additions, betterments and improvements; ~ **für Betriebserweiterungen** reserve for plant expansion *(US)*; ~ **für das Betriebskapital** operating-cash reserve; ~ **für Erneuerungszwecke** reserve for additions, betterments and improvements; ~ **für Erweiterungsbauten** reserve for expansion *(US)*; ~ **für zweifelhafte Forderungen** bad-debts *(US)* (doubtful, *Br.*) reserve; ~ **für Gewährleistungsansprüche** warranty reserves; ~ **für Katastrophenfälle** *(Versicherung)* reserve for catastrophes; ~ **für Kursverluste** reserve for loss on investment; ~ **für Notfälle** contingency reserves; ~ **für laufende Risiken** *(Versicherungsgesellschaft)* loss reserves; ~ **für den Rückkauf von Vorzugsaktien** reserve for retirement of preferred stocks *(US)*, capital redemption reserve fund *(Br.)*; ~ **für Steuern** tax reserves; ~ **für den Tilgungsfonds** reserve for sinking fund;
~ **angreifen** to draw on the reserves; **seine ~ auffüllen** to replenish one's reserves; **seine ~ aufzehren** to overrun one's reserves, to be a draw on one's reserves; ~ **bilden** to create (form, accumulate, build up) reserves; **seine ~ offen darlegen** to disclose one's reserves; **in die freien ~ einstellen** to appropriate to free reserves; **in die offenen ~ einstellen** to allocate to the published reserves; **unzureichende ~ haben** to be short in one's reserves; ~ **in immer stärkerem Maße in Anspruch nehmen** to dip even deeper into reserves; ~ **in Kapital umwandeln** to capitalize its reserves; **nicht offen angelegte Beträge in den stillen ~ verstecken** to shunt undisclosed sums into inner reserves; **im Geschäft als ~ verwenden** to retain in business; **den ~ zugerechnet werden** to be classifiable as reserves; **den ~ zuführen (zuweisen)** to add (transfer, place) to the reserve fund; **Betrag den ~ zuweisen** to carry an amount (put a sum) to reserves;
~anstieg growth of reserves; **~bildung** creation of reserves, appropriations of surplus *(US)*; **zur ~bildung verwenden** to set aside as reserve; **~charakter haben** to have the character of reserves; **~einstellung** appropriation to free reserve; **~entwicklung** development of reserves.

Rücklagenfonds guarantee *(Br.)* (guaranty, *US*, reserve, safety, emergency, general fund, surplus, *US*) fund, end money, treasury stock, rest capital *(Br.)*;
in langfristig verzinslichen Wertpapieren angelegter ~ funded reserve; **außerordentlicher** ~ contingent account *(Br.)* (fund), contingency (provident-reserve, surplus, *US*) fund;
~ **einer Lebensversicherungsanstalt** life-insurance reserve; ~ **für drohende Verluste** *(Versicherung)* specific reserve fund; ~ **für mögliche Verluste** surplus contingency reserve;
~ **auflösen** to release a reserve; ~ **dotieren** to allocate the reserve fund; **dem ~ zufließen** to go to the reserve fund; **dem ~ zuführen** to place (put) to reserve, to transfer (carry) to the reserve fund; **größere Beträge dem ~ zuführen** to put large sums to reserve; **dem ~ zuweisen** to add to the reserve fund.

Rücklagen|konto reserve (contingent, *US*) account, capital (earned-) surplus account *(US)*; **auf das ~konto übertragen** transferred to rest account *(Br.)*; **dem ~konto zuweisen** to add to the reserve fund; **~polster** reserve position; **~reduzierung** cancellation of reserves; **~satz** reserve ratio; **~soll** required reserves; **~vermögen** reserve fund (assets); **~verringerung** running down of reserves; **~vortrag in einer Gewinn- und Verlustrechnung** income statement charges to reserve;

~**zuführung** transfer (allocation) to reserves (the reserve fund); ~**zuführung bewilligen** to approve the amounts set aside to reserve; ~**zuweisung** allocation to reserve.

Rücklauf reverse movement, backward travel, *(Tonbandgerät)* rewind, *(Wähler)* homing;
~ **von Leergut** empty return running.

rückläufig on the decrease, *(Konjunktur)* recessional, downward, *(Kurse)* declining, falling off, drooping, retrograde, retroactive;
~ **sein** to be downward, to be on the decrease;
~**e Bewegung** downward (retrograde) movement; ~**e Bewegung der industriellen Fertigung** decline in industry; ~**es Geschäft** declining business; ~**e Konjunktur** business slump; ~**e Konjunkturbewegung** decline in business activity, business (economic) downturn; ~**e Konjunkturphase** depression (slump) period; ~**er Konjunkturzyklus** down cycle; ~**e Kurse** declining market; ~**e Marktbewegung** downturn in the market; ~**e Ölbezüge** decline in oil purchases; ~**e Preise** falling (drooping) prices; ~**e Produktion** falling production; ~**e Tendenz** downward tendency; ~**er Umsatz** drop in sales.

Rückläufigkeit decline, decrease.

Rücklauf|servoantrieb *(Auto)* reverse servo unit; ~**taste** *(Tonbandgerät)* rewind key.

Rücklicht rear lights, tail lamp, tail-light;
~**schalter** tail-light switch.

rückliefern to redeliver, to return.

Rücklieferung redelivery, return, *(Rückgabe)* restitution;
~**en der Kundschaft** property returns.

Rück|lieferungsauftrag return shipping order *(US)*; ~**lizenz** grant-back license *(US)*; ~**marsch** retreat, countermarch.

Rücknahme taking back, withdrawal, repurchase, *(Lizenz)* revocation, *(Wertpapiere)* redemption, repurchase, *(Widerruf)* revocation;
~ **eines Angebotes** revocation of an offer; ~ **eines Auftrags** withdrawal of an order, countermanding; ~ **einer Beleidigung** withdrawal of an insult; ~ **einer Berufung** abandonment of an appeal; ~ **einer Bewerbung** withdrawal of an application; ~ **einer Erklärung** withdrawal of a statement; ~ **von Investmentzertifikaten** redemption (repurchase) of units *(Br.)*; ~ **einer Klage** abandonment (discontinuance) of an action; ~ **einer Konzession** withdrawal of an authorization to operate; ~ **der Kündigung** withdrawal of a notice; ~ **einer auf Teilzahlung gekauften Sache** repossession of goods bought on hire purchase (the deferred-payment system, *US*); ~ **eines Strafantrags** withdrawal of a charge; ~ **eines Vermächtnisses** redemption of a legacy; ~ **einer Vollmacht** withdrawal of a power of attorney;
~**anspruch** right of repurchase; ~**antrag** motion to withdraw, withdrawal request; ~**garantie** repurchase guarantee; ~**klausel** *(Konzession)* escape clause *(US)*, *(Obligationen)* redemption clause; ~**kurs** redemption price; ~**preis** *(EG)* reserve price, *(Investmentgesellschaft)* redemption price, current bid price, price of redemption, repurchase price; **von einer Kapitalanlagegesellschaft festgelegter** ~**preis** price calculated in accordance with the terms of the Agreement of Trust; ~**recht** right to redeem (of redemption); ~**sätze für Geldmarktpapiere** repurchase rates for money-market papers; ~**spesen** *(Investmentfonds)* redemption charges; ~**verpflichtung** obligation to repurchase.

Rück|porto return postage; ~**prämie** premium on redemption, [premium for the] put, put premium, seller's option; ~**prämie kaufen** to take for the put; ~**prämie verkaufen** to give for the put; ~**prämiengeschäft** option deal for the put, trading in puts, put premium operation (transaction); ~**prämienkurs** price of put, put [and call] price; ~**rechnung** account of return, return account, *(Wechsel)* reaccount, account of redraft, banker's ticket.

Rückreise return (home) journey, return voyage *(Br.)*;
auf seiner ~ on his way home;
auf der ~ **begriffen** homeward bound; **auf meiner** ~ on my way back;
Hin- und ~ out and home voyage;
~ **antreten** to start on the return voyage; **auf der** ~ **sein** *(Schiff)* to be homeward bound; **sich selbst die** ~ **verdienen** to work one's passage back;
~**fahrkarte** return (round trip, *US*) ticket.

Rückruf *(tel.)* recall;
~ **von Konditionsgut** *(Verlag)* recall of qualified items;
automatische ~**anlage** *(Atombomber)* fail-safe device; ~**recht** right of stoppage in transit.

Rucksack rucksack, knapsack, haversack, packsack.

Rück|schaffung von Kriegsgefangenen repatriation of prisoners of war; ~**schau** review, retrospect; ~**scheck** returned cheque (check, *US*); ~**schein** notice (advice) of delivery, counterbond, reply coupon, *(Post)* return receipt; **gegen** ~**schein** return requested; ~**scheinwerfer** reversing (backup, *US*) light.

Rückschlag setback, backset, throwback, *(Börse)* relapse, reaction, smasher *(Br.)*, *(med.)* relapse, setback, *(pol.)* swingback *(US)*;
konjunktureller ~ economic setback; **scharfer** ~ sharp reaction; **vorübergehender** ~ temporary setback; **wirtschaftlicher** ~ economic dip, business (trade) recession, commercial setback; **im Ansehen der Öffentlichkeit einen dramatischen** ~ **erleben** to suffer a dramatic drop in public support; ~ **erleiden** to have a setback, to relapse, to get a smack in the eye; **geschäftlichen** ~ **erleiden** to have a setback in one's business; **leichten** ~ **erleiden** *(Börse)* to suffer a slight reaction; **mit einem** ~ **in seiner beruflichen Entwicklung fertig werden** to live down an incident in one's career.

rückschleusen *(Geld)* to recycle.

Rückschleusung *(Geld)* recycling.

Rück|schluß conclusion, inference; ~**schlüsse ziehen** to draw conclusions; ~**schlußwahrscheinlichkeit** *(Statistik)* inverse probability; ~**schreiben** reply, answer; ~**schritt** *(fig.)* setback, regression, step back.

rückschrittlich *(pol.)* reactionary, standpat, stick-in-the-mud, hard-shell *(US)*, hunkerous *(US sl.)*;
~**e Tendenz** downward tendency.

Rückseite *(Buch)* back page, off board, *(Buchhaltung)* off side, *(Haus)* rear, *(Münze)* reverse, tail, *(Zeitschrift)* back cover;
siehe ~ see back (overleaf);
~ **eines Gebäudes** rear of a building;
auf der ~ **eines Wechsels einen Teilbetrag quittieren** to endorse a sum of money on a bill of exchange; **auf die** ~ **schreiben** to endorse, to indorse.

Rückseiten|druck backup; ~**vermerk** indorsement.

rücksenden to return, to send back.

Rücksendeporto return postage;
~ **trägt der Empfänger** return postage guaranteed.

Rücksendung return, returning, sending back, reconsignment, redelivery, reshipment *(US)*;
~ **der Verpackung** return of empties.

Rücksendungsgebühr reconsignment (return) charges.

Rücksicht regard, respect;
aus ~ **auf** in deference to; **aus** ~ **auf seinen Gesundheitszustand** for reasons of health; **aus geschäftlichen** ~**en** for business reasons; **mit** ~ **auf** considering, in consideration of; **mit** ~ **auf die Kosten** in deference to (view of) the cost; **ohne** ~ **auf** regardless, irrespective of, notwithstanding; **ohne** ~ **auf etwa anderslautende Bestimmungen** notwithstanding anything to the contrary in the provisions; **ohne** ~ **auf Kosten** regardless of cost; **ohne** ~ **auf die Preise** regardless of prices (expenses); **ohne** ~ **auf Verlust der Ladung** *(Versicherungsrecht)* lost or not lost; **finanzielle** ~**en** financial reasons; **gehörige** ~ due regard;
~ **walten lassen** to use discretion; ~ **nehmen** to take into account, to pay attention, to be tender of; **gebührende** ~ **nehmen** to give due consideration; **auf die Gefühle anderer keine** ~ **nehmen** to have little regard for the feelings of others; **auf andere Leute etw. mehr** ~ **nehmen** to be a thought more considerate of other people;
~**nahme** consideration, regard.

rücksichtslos regardless, ruthless, callous, unregardful, inconsiderate, heedless;
~ **fahren** to drive recklessly, to road-hog; ~ **gegen andere vorgehen** to ruin others with a light heart;
~**e Ausbeutung** ruthless exploitation; ~**er Fahrer** reckless driver, roadhog; ~**es Verhalten** ruthless (callous) behavio(u)r.

Rücksichtslosigkeit lack of consideration, inconsideration, devil-may-care attitude.

rücksichtsvoll considerate, regardful;
sich ~ **verhalten** to show consideration;
~**es Verhalten** thoughtfulness, consideration.

Rück|siedler repatriated settler, repatriate; ~**siedlung** repatriation, relocation, resettlement; ~**siedlungsbeihilfe** resettlement aid; ~**siedlungszuschuß** relocation allowance; ~**sitz** back seat, *(Auto)* reverse (rumble, *US*) seat, dickey; ~**spesen** return (back) charges; ~**spiegel** driving mirror, rear-view mirror; ~**spieleinrichtung** playback unit; ~**spielen** playback.

Rücksprache consultation, conference;
nach ~ after consulting; **nach** ~ **mit meinen Mitarbeitern** after consultation with my colleagues;
~ **mit jem. halten (nehmen)** to confer with (consult) s. o.

Rückstand arrears, arrearage, shortfall, lag, remanet, *(Abfall)* waste, refuse, *(Aufträge)* backlog, arrears, *(Lücke)* gap, *(Rest)* remainder, remnant, *(Saldo)* balance, *(Schulden)* arrears, outstanding debts;
im ~ in arrears, behind, back;
technischer ~ technological gap;
im ~ bleiben to remain in arrears; **mit der Zahlung im ~ bleiben** to default on (fall behind with) one's payments; **~ eintreiben** to collect outstanding debts; **in ~ geraten** to fall (get) into arrears; **mit seinen Zahlungen in ~ geraten** to fall behind with one's payments; **im ~ sein** to be in arrears, to fall behind; **mit seinem Arbeitspensum im ~ sein** to be behind with one's schedule (work); **mit den Aufträgen im ~ sein** to be behind on orders; **mit der Miete im ~ sein** to be behind[hand] with (back in) one's rent; **mit einer Rate im ~ sein** to be one instalment behindhand, to fall behind with an instalment; **mit seinen Verpflichtungen im ~ sein** to be in default with one's obligations; **mit den Zahlungen im ~ sein** to be behind[hand] with one's payment (delinquent in payment, in arrears).
Rückstände arrears, rests, *(Schulden)* outstanding debts;
verlorene ~ lost debts;
~ bei der Begleichung von Exportrückständen export payment lags;
~ aufarbeiten to make up (clear off) arrears [of work], to work off arrears (backlogs down); **~ begleichen** to make good (pay up) arrears; **~ eintreiben** to collect (recover) outstanding debts; **~ auflaufen (entstehen) lassen** to let the arrears run on.
rückständig residuary, *(altmodisch)* not up-to-date, obsolete, old-fashioned, fusty, old-hat, behind the times, behindhand, upstage, *(Land)* back, backward, undeveloped, underdeveloped, *(Rate)* delinquent, *(schuldig)* unpaid, outstanding, in arrears, behind[hand], *(überfällig)* overdue;
~ sein to be outstanding, to be in arrears, *(altmodisch)* to be behind the times (a back number, *coll.*); **mit den Zahlungen ~ sein** to be behind[hand] with one's payment; **~ werden** to fall behind[hand];
~e Ansichten stuffy views; **völlig ~e Ansichten haben** to live in an intellectual backwater; **~er Betrag** overdue amount; **~e Beträge** arrears; **~e Dividende** dividends in arrear; **~es Gehalt** back salary; **~es Land** backward country; **~er Lohn** back pay; **~e Löhne** arrears of wages; **~er Mensch** back number, oldtimer, old-fashioned person, backwoodsman; **~e Miete** rent [in] arrears, back rent; **~e Raten** outstanding instalments; **~e Steuern** arrears of taxes, tax arrears, delinquent taxes *(US)*; **~er Steuerzahler** taxpayer in arrears; **~er Zahler** defaulting debtor; **~e Zahlung** overdue payment, payment in arrears; **~e Zinsen** arrears of interest, overdue (unpaid) interests.
Rückständigkeit backwardness.
Rückstands|gebiete backward areas; **~öl** residual oil; **~rechnung** statement of accounts; **~zahlung** payment of arrears.
Rückstellen *(Schreibmaschine)* backspacing.
rückstellen *(Reserven)* to allocate to the reserve, to allow, to make allowance (provision), *(Schreibmaschine)* to space back, to backspace.
Rückstelltaste *(Schreibmaschine)* backspace.
Rückstellung provision, reserve[s], transfer (allocation) to reserves, reservation, deduction, *(Dienstpflicht)* draft deferment, *(Rückstellungsbetrag)* reserve allowance, sum reserved;
nach ~ für unvorhergesehene Ausgaben after provision for contingencies; **ohne ~** without deduction;
außerbetriebliche ~en nonoperating reserves; **besondere ~** special (provident) reserve, *(Bundesnotenbank)* adjusted reserve *(US)*; **langfristige ~en** long-term provisions; **steuerfreie ~en** untaxed reserves; **zweckgebundene ~en** appropriated reserves;
~ für Abnutzungen (Abschreibungen) allowance (provision) for depreciation, depreciation reserve (allowance), reserved property *(Br.)*, reserve for wear, tear, obsolescence or inadequacy; **~ für Abschreibung langfristiger Anlagegüter (Anlagenerneuerung)** amortization reserve, reserve for amortization; **~ für Anlagenwertverminderung** provision for depreciation of investment; **~en für Anlageveränderungen** reserve for investment fluctuations; **~ für Anschaffung hochwertiger Wirtschaftsgüter des Anlagevermögens** reserve for high replacement cost; **~ für Auffüllung der Lagerbestände** provision for replacement of inventories *(US)*; **~ für genehmigte Ausgaben** reserve for authorized expenditures; **~ für unvorhergesehene Ausgaben** reserve (provision) for contingencies, contingent reserve; **~ für Ausgleichsforderungen** equalization reserve; **~en für Betriebskostenerhöhungen** operating reserve; **~en für Betriebsunfälle** industrial accident reserve; **~ für erschöpfte Bodenschätze** depletion reserve; **~ für Devisenschwankungen** allowance for exchange fluctuations; **~ für Dividendenausschüttungen** reserve for dividends voted; **~ für Dividendennachzahlung** reserve for deferred dividends; **~ für Dubiose** allowance for doubtful *(Br.)* (bad, *US*) debts, bad-debts reserve *(US)*, reserve for contingent liabilities *(Br.)*, doubtful-debts provision *(Br.)*; **~ für Eigenversicherung** insurance reserve; **~ für Einkommensteuer** provision (reserve) for income tax; **~ für Ersatzbeschaffungen** replacement reserve, provision for renewals *(Br.)*; **~ für Eventualverbindlichkeiten (Eventualverpflichtungen)** provision for contingencies, contingency reserves, reserve for contingent liabilities, liability reserve; **~en für strittige Forderungen** bad-claim reserve *(US)*; **~ für zweifelhafte (dubiose) Forderungen** provision (reserve) for doubtful accounts *(Br.)*, bad-debt reserve *(US)*; **~ für Gebäudereparaturen** provision for building repairs; **~ für Generalunkosten** reserve for overhead; **~en von Gold** earmarking of gold; **~ für Grundstücksbelastungen** reserve for encumbrances; **~ für Grundstücksentwertungen** reserve for depreciation of real-estate owned; **~ für Inventarergänzungen** provision for inventory reserve; **~ für mögliche Inventarverluste** reserve for possible inventory losses; **~ für Konsolidierungsaufgaben** funding provision; **~ für Kontonachlässe** reserve for discounts; **~ für Kosten eines schwebenden Prozesses** reserve for payments to be made under a pending lawsuit, reserve for claims in litigation; **~en im Kreditgeschäft (für Kreditausfälle)** provisions for possible loan losses; **~ für faule Kunden** provision for doubtful accounts *(Br.)*, bad-debt provision (reserve) *(US)*; **~en für Kursverluste** reserve for loss on investment; **~ für Lagerabwertungen** *(Bilanz)* inventory reserve; **~ für Mietausfälle** allowance for vacancies; **~ für Mindereinnahmen** deficiency reserve; **~ für Neubewertungen** revaluation reserve; **~ für Nichtvorgesehenes** contingent reserve; **~ für besondere Notfälle** *(Bundesnotenbank)* naked reserve *(US)*; **~ für Pensionsverpflichtungen** reserve for retirement allowances; **~ für Produktionsausfall** deficiency reserve; **~ für Prozeßkosten** reserve for litigation costs (expenses, *US*); **~en für nicht vermietete Räume** allowance for vacancies; **~ für einzelne Rechnungsposten** allowance for items in an account; **~ für erforderliche Reparaturen** reserve for repairs; **~en für zurückgestellte Reparaturen und Neuanschaffungen** reserve (provision) for deferred repairs and renewals; **~ für noch nicht feststehende Risiken** *(Bilanz)* contingencies; **~ für Ruhegeldverpflichtungen** pension reserve; **~en für noch nicht regulierte Schadensfälle** *(Bilanz einer Lebensversicherungsgesellschaft)* reserve for outstanding claims (claims pending), claim reserves; **~ für zweifelhafte Schulden** allowance for doubtful *(Br.)* (bad, *US*) debts, [reserve for] contingent liabilities *(Br.)*, bad-debts reserve *(US)*; **~ für Schuldentilgung** reserve for debt redemption; **~ für Sonderfälle** provident reserve; **~en für Steuern** deduction (reserve) for taxes, provision for taxation (taxes), taxation reserve; **~ für Steuernachzahlungen** deferred tax provision; **~ für Steuerzahlungen auf nicht entnommene Gewinne** provision for taxation on unrealized surpluses; **~ für Substanzverminderung** reserve for depletion; **~ für Überalterung** provision for obsolescence; **~ für Umstellungskosten** reserve for conversion cost; **~ für Unfälle** reserve for accidents; **~ für Unterhaltungskosten** maintenance reserve; **~ für eingegangene Verbindlichkeiten** liability reserve; **~en für ungewisse Verbindlichkeiten** contingency reserve; **~ für Verluste** loss reserve; **~en für drohende Verluste** *(Versicherung)* technical reserves; **~ für eventuelle Verluste im Kreditgeschäft** reserve for possible loan losses; **~en für mögliche Verluste am Reingewinn** surplus contingency reserve; **~ für zurückkommende Verpackung** return-package reserve; **~ für schwebende Versicherungsfälle** reserve for claims pending; **~ zur Verteilung des Reingewinns** reservation for earned surplus *(US)*; **~ für Währungsausgleich** reserve for currency equalization; **~en und Wertberichtigungen** revaluation and reserves, evaluation reserves; **~ für Wertminderung** provision for depreciation; **~ für Wertminderungen der Vorräte** reserve for future decline in inventories; **~ für Wiederbeschaffung** replacement reserve;
gewaltige ~en für Steuernachzahlungen in der Bilanz ansammeln to accumulate mountainous deferred tax provisions in the balance sheet; **~en auflösen** to write back provisions; **~ bilden** to create (set up) a reserve, to make provision for; **~en für Steuernachzahlungen bilden** to provide for deferred taxes; **~en für Steuernachzahlungen zur Pflicht machen** to make provisions for deferred tax compulsory; **~en vornehmen** to set aside as reserve, to make provisions, to create

reserves; **hohe ~en vornehmen** to put large sums to reserve; **~en für Devisenschwankungen vornehmen** to allow for exchange fluctuations; **~en für Dubiose (dubiose Forderungen) vornehmen** to allow for bad *(US)* (doubtful, *Br.*) debts, to make due allowance for doubtful *(Br.)* (bad, *US*) debts; **ausreichende ~en für Pensionsverpflichtungen vornehmen** to make proper provisions for pension liabilities; **~en für Steuern vornehmen** to make provisions for taxation.

Rückstellungs|betrag sum reserved, reserve item; **~bildung** creation of reserves; **~fonds** reserve fund; **~konto** reserve (appropriation) account; **~konto für unvorhergesehene Verpflichtungen** contingencies account; **~posten** reserve item; **~richtlinien** *(mil.)* draft deferment rules; **~zuweisung** allocation to reserve fund, reserve allocation; **~zweck** reserve purpose.

Rück|strahler mirror, *(Fahrrad)* reflector, *(Katzenauge)* cat's-eye; **~strahlung** reflection, *(Film)* bloom; **~taste** *(Schreibmaschine)* backspacer; **~transport** return transportation; **~tratte** redraft, reexchange; **~trift** lag.

Rücktritt resignation, withdrawal, demission, rescission, retirement, vacating an office, *(Minister)* going out of office, *(Thronfolger)* abdication, *(von einer Verpflichtung)* withdrawal;

freiwilliger ~ voluntary quit; **nahegelegter ~** involuntary resignation;

~ der Regierung resignation of the cabinet; **~ von einer Treuhanderrichtung** revocation of a trust; **~ vom Versuch** abandonment of attempt; **~ vom Vertrag** rescission (cancellation, repudiation, revocation) of contract; **einseitiger ~ eines Vertragsteiles** rescission by one party;

seinen ~ anbieten to tender one's resignation; **j. zum ~ auffordern** to call for s. one's resignation; **seinen ~ einreichen, um seinen ~ einkommen** to hand in (send in, tender) one's resignation, to vacate office, to declare one's withdrawal, to recede from one's position; **seinen ~ erklären** to announce one's resignation, *(Minister)* to step down; **kurz vor dem ~ stehen** *(Regierung)* to be wavering on the edge of collapse; **auf den ~ zusteuern** *(Minister)* to ride for a fall; **j. zum ~ zwingen** to drive s. o. to resign;

das wird den ~ einiger Minister bedeuten some heads will roll in the government.

Rücktritts|absicht intention to resign; **~alter** age of retirement, retiring age; **~angebot** tender of resignation; **~aufforderung an den Minister** demands for the minister to resign; **~bedingungen** *(Vertrag)* conditions of avoidance; **~bestimmung** escape clause; **~bremse** *(Fahrrad)* coaster brake, back-pedal(l)ing brake *(Br.)*; **~drohung** threat of resignation; **~erklärung** resignation; **schriftliche ~erklärung** written notice of withdrawal; **~ersuchen** resignation request; **~frist** escape period; **~gesuch** [letter of] resignation, resignation request, resignation letter; **sein ~gesuch einreichen** to hand in one's resignation; **~grund** cause for leaving (resignation), *(vom Vertrag)* cause for rescission; **~klage** rescissory action; **~klausel** clause protestative, escape clause; **~mitteilung** notice of revocation; **~recht** right of rescission (to rescind, of cancellation), right of avoidance; **~schreiben** resignation letter; **sein ~schreiben an X richten** to address one's resignation to X; **~termin** retiring date; **~versuch** attempt to quit; **~vorbehalt** reservation of the right to rescind.

rückübereignen *(Grundstück)* to reconvey.

Rück|übereignung reconveyance; **~übereignungsanspruch des Sicherungsgebers** equitable interest.

rückübersetzen to retranslate.

Rück|übersetzung retranslation; **~übertragung** redemise, reassignation, retransfer, retrocession, *(Grundstück)* reconveyance; **notarielle ~übertragung** reconveyance under seal.

Rückübertragungs|klausel grant-back clause; **~preis** reconveyance price; **~verpflichtung** counterletter.

Rück|überweisung return remittance, retransfer; **adressierter ~umschlag** self-addressed envelope; **~umwandlung** reconversion; **~valutierung** retrospective valuation; **~verflechtung** recartelization; **~verfügung** return disposal.

rückvergüten to refund, to reimburse, to replace;

Portospesen ~ to refund the cost of postage; **jem. seine Spesen ~** to reimburse s. o. for his costs.

Rückvergütung refund, reimbursement, drawback, repayment, *(Agentur)* patronage, dividend, *(Versicherung)* short return of interest, *(Zinsen)* rebate[ment];

~ für Exporte reimbursement for exports; **~ von Provisionen** return commission; **~ von Spesen** reimbursement of charges; **~ von Steuern** refunding of taxes.

Rück|vergütungsgarantie bei Nichtgefallen money back if not to satisfaction; **~verkehr** heavy stream of returning traffic; **~verschiffung** reshipment.

Rückversicherer reinsurer, coinsurer, reinsurance (direct-working) carrier, reassurer *(Br.)*, accepting company;

reiner ~ specialist reinsurer;

auf den ~ übertragen to transfer part of one's insurance to another insurer, to cede *(coll.)*.

rückversichern to reinsure, to coinsure, to retrocede, to reassure;

sich ~ to take out a reinsurance, to lay off a risk.

Rückversicherung reinsurance, counterinsurance, counter-assurance *(Br.)*, reassurance *(Br.)*;

individuelle ~ facultative reinsurance; **unbegrenzte ~** excess of loss reinsurance; **unkündbare ~** flat reinsurance; **automatisch wirksame ~** treaty reinsurance;

~ mit Festlegung des maximalen Selbstbehalts surplus treaty reinsurance; **~ für Katastrophenfälle** catastrophe reinsurance; **~ für einen Spitzenbetrag** excess reinsurance;

~ abschließen, sich durch ~ decken to take out a reinsurance, to lay off a risk; **~ automatisch annehmen** to accept reinsurance automatically.

Rückversicherungs|angebot request note; **~anstalt** reinsurance company; **~anteil** reinsurance share, cession; **~auftrag** reinsurance order; **~bestand** reinsurance business; **~fonds** reinsurance pool; **~geschäft** reinsurance business (broking), *(einzelnes)* reinsurance transaction; **~gesellschaft** direct-working carrier, direct-writing company, reinsurance company (carrier); **~konsortium** reinsurance syndicate; **~konzern** reinsurance group; **~makler** reinsurance broker; **~markt** surplus line market; **~option** facultative reinsurance; **~police** reinsurance policy; **~pool** reinsurance pool; **~prämie** reinsurance premium; **~risiko atomisieren** to spread the risk; **~schutz** reinsurance protection; **~träger** reinsurance company, reinsurer; **~vereinbarungen** reinsurance arrangements; **~vertrag** reinsurance agreement (contract, treaty, pool, *Br.*); **zusätzlicher ~vertrag** second layer treaty; **~vertrag zur verhältnismäßigen Begrenzung des Versicherungsrisikos** excess of loss ratio treaty, stop loss treaty.

Rück|verweisung reference back, *(Parlament)* recommittal, recommitment, *(Register)* cross reference; **~verweisungsantrag** reference-back motion; **~wanderung von Anleihen** repatriation of funds; **~waren** returns, return goods, returned goods *(US)*; **~warenbuch** sales return journal.

rückwärtig|es Armeegebiet base of operations; **~e Verbindungen** rear communications; **~es Zimmer** room at the back.

rückwärts fahren, Auto to back a car.

Rückwärts|bewegung backward (downward) movement, back-up, decline, falling off; **~fahren** backing, reversing.

rückwärtsfahrend in reverse.

Rückwärts|fahrt *(Schiff)* stemway; **~gang** *(Auto)* reverse [gear].

rückwärtsgehen *(Geschäft)* to decline, to fall off.

Rückwechsel redraft, unpaid (returned) bill, reexchange *(Br.)*, *(pl.)* returns *(Br.)*.

~rechnung return of exchange; **~spesen** redraft charges.

Rückweg way back, return journey;

~ antreten to set out for home.

ruckweise by jerks, by fits and starts.

rückwirken to have repercussions, to react, *(Gesetz)* to be retroactive, to relate back.

rückwirkend retroactive, with retroactive effect, retrospective;

nicht ~ prospective;

~ vom 4. März gelten to have relation to March 4th; **~ in Kraft treten** to become retroactive;

~es Gesetz ex-post-facto (retroactive) law; **~e Kraft eines Gesetzes** retrospective effect of statute; **mit ~er Kraft** retroactively; **~e Kraft haben** to relate back; **~e Lohnerhöhung** retroactive pay.

Rückwirkung reaction, *(Gesetz)* retroactive effect, retroaction, *(pol.)* repercussion, *(Veräußerung)* relation back;

mit ~ von with retroactive effect from;

~ auf den Effektenmarkt reaction on the stock market; **~en einer Klage** consequential effects of an action.

rückzahlbar repayable, reimbursable, returnable, terminable, to be paid back, *(Anleihe)* redeemable;

auf Abruf ~ repayable on demand; **in Gold ~** to be redeemed (redeemable) in gold; **in Jahresraten ~** repayable by annual instalments; **gegen Kündigung ~** subject to notice of withdrawal; **kurzfristig ~** repayable at short notice; **über dem Nennwert ~** repayable above par; **nicht ~** irredeemable; **pari ~** repayable at par; **auf Verlangen ~** repayable on demand; **innerhalb 24 Stunden ~er Kredit** overnight loan *(US)*.

rückzahlen to repay, to refund, to reimburse, *(amortisieren)* to amortise, *(Anleihe einlösen)* to redeem.
Rückzahler refunder.
Rückzahlung paying back (off), repayment, reimbursement, return, *(Amortisation)* amortization, *(Einlösung von Anleihen)* redemption, retirement, amortization;
zur ~ fällig due for repayment;
~en returns of payment;
teilweise ~ part repayment; **vorzeitige ~** anticipated (premature) repayment;
~ vor Fälligkeit redemption before due date; **~ in Gold** redemption in gold; **~ in voller Höhe** full repayment; **~ einer Hypothek** mortgage payment, redemption (discharge, repayment) of a mortgage; **~ von Investmentanteilen** redemption of units; **~ des Kapitalbetrags** return of a capital sum (the principal); **~ eines Kredits** repayment of a loan (credit); **~ zum Nennwert** redemption at par; **~ in Raten** repayment by instal(l)ments; **~ zuviel erhobener Steuern** refund (repayment) of taxes; **~ in Teilbeträgen** repayment by instalments; **~ zu den festgelegten Terminen** scheduled repayment; **~ eines Vorschusses** repayment of an advance;
Obligationen zur ~ anmelden to give notice of withdrawal of bonds; **zur ~ anstehen** to be eligible to be paid; **zur ~ aufrufen** to call in (for redemption); **zur ~ auslosen** to redeem by lot; **~ einer Anzahlung im Klagewege fordern** to sue for the return of a deposit; **für die ~ einer Schuld einzustehen haben** to be responsible for the repayment of a debt; **zur ~ kommen** to be repaid; **~ von Obligationen kündigen** to give notice of withdrawal of bonds; **~en auf einen Kredit leisten** to make payments on a loan; **~ eines Kredits verlangen** to ask for the return of a loan; **zur ~ ausgelost werden** to be redeemed by lot.
Rückzahlungs|agio premium payable on redemption; **~angebot** tender of money; **~anspruch (wegen Überforderung)** repayment due (claim), overclaim, right to redeem; **~anweisung** repayment order; **~aufforderung** demand for repayment; **~bedingungen, øbestimmungen** terms of repayment (redemption); **~betrag** repayable amount; **~frist** repayment period, time for repayment; **~klausel** proviso for redemption, redemption clause; **~kurs** rate of redemption, redemption price; **~pflicht** obligation to repay; **~plan** redemption scheme; **mittelfristiger ~plan** medium-term repayment program(me); **~prämie** redemption premium; **~preis** redemption price; **~provision** redemption commission; **~tabelle** repayment table; **~termin** date of redemption, redemption (repayment) date; **~verfügung** repayment order; **~vorschlag** repayment proposal; **~weise** repayment method; **~wert** redemption value; **~zeitraum** repayment period, time for repayment.
Rückzieher backing down, retraction, climb-down *(coll.)*, flunk *(US sl.)*;
~ machen to climb down *(coll.)*, to abate one's demands, to backpedal, to backtrack, to walk back, to draw in one's horns, to flunk *(US sl.)*.
Rückzinsen interest returned.
Rückzoll drawback, rebate[ment], long duty, customs penny *(Br.)*, *(Wiederausfuhrprämie)* bounty on reexportation;
als ~ bekommen to draw back.
rückzollberechtigt debentured.
Rückzoll|bescheinigung debenture; **~buch** debenture book; **~güter** debenture[d] goods; **~schein** debenture bond *(Br.)*; **~scheingebühren** charges of debenture.
Rückzug retreat, withdrawal, *(Bahn)* back train, *(Rückzieher)* drawing back, climb-down *(coll.)*, flunk *(US sl.)*;
im ~ in a jiffy (flash), before you can say Jack Robinson *(Br.)*; **geordneter ~** orderly retreat; **hastiger ~** precipitate retreat; **ungeordneter ~** skedaddle *(sl.)*;
~ auf die Hauptstadt retreat on the capital;
dem Feind den ~ abschneiden to cut off the enemy's retreat; **~ anordnen** to order the retreat; **~ antreten** to beat a retreat.
Rückzugs|gefecht *(mil.)* rearguard action, battle of retreat, running fight; **~linie** line of retreat.
rüde|Antwort rude answer; **~ Gesellen** rough characters; **sich einer ~n Sprache bedienen** to use coarse language.
Rudel herd, flock, *(U-Boote)* pack;
~ von Kindern swarm of children.
rudelweise in flocks (gangs, swarms).
Ruder rudder, *(fig.)* helm, wheel, power, control, *(Steuerung)* helm, wheel;
am ~ *(pol.)* at the wheel, to the fore; **nicht mehr am ~** out;
am ~ bleiben *(pol. Partei)* to remain in power; **~ des Staates führen** to be at the helm of the state; **~ aus der Hand geben** to give up the leadership; **dem ~ gehorchen** *(Schiff)* to obey the helm; **~ fest in der Hand haben** to be master of the situation; **ans ~ kommen** to come to the fore, to come into power, to rise to ascendancy; **sich kräftig ins ~ legen** to put one's shoulder to the wheel; **am ~ sein** to be in (at the helm), to be at the head of affairs, to be in power; **schon lange am ~ sein** to have had a long innings; **nicht mehr am ~ sein** to be out;
~boot rowboat, pulling boat, *(leicht)* whiff *(local, Br.)*; **~haus** pilothouse.
rudern, Boot to pull a boat.
Rudimente rudiments, remains.
Ruf call, shout, *(Ansehen)* repute, reputation, face, character, distinction, respect, name, *(gesellschaftliches Ansehen)* credit, standing, record, escutcheon, odo(u)r, *(Ernennung)* call, appointment;
dem ~ nach by repute; **in gutem ~ stehend** well-thought of; **von untadeligem ~** without a stain;
anfeuernde ~e shouts of encouragement; **angreifbarer ~** vulnerable reputation; **beeinträchtigter ~** impaired credit; **festbegründeter ~** established credit; **guter ~** established reputation, renown, good record, high standing; **kaufmännischer ~** credit standing (status); **lauter ~** shout, whoop; **makelloser ~** undamaged (spotless) reputation, unblemished character; **miserabler ~** unsavo(u)ry reputation; **schlechter ~** disrepute, discredit, bad (evil) reputation, bad name, black eye, evil report, bad will; **tadelloser (untadeliger) ~** unimpeachable (stainless) reputation; **ungeschmälerter ~** unimpaired credit; **zweifelhafter ~** doubtful standing, clouded reputation;
bewährter ~ einer Firma standing of a commercial house; **~ in der Geschäftswelt** standing in industry;
jds. guten ~ angreifen to assault s. one's reputation, to fling dirt at s. o.; **jds. guten ~ ankratzen** to pick a hole in s. one's reputation; **~ annehmen** *(Professor)* to accept a chair; **jds. guten ~ attackieren** to assault s. one's reputation; **jds. guten ~ beeinträchtigen** to cast a slur upon s. one's reputation, to spoil s. one's fair name; **seinen guten ~ behaupten** to maintain one's reputation; **jds. guten ~ beschmutzen** to foul s. one's name; **guten ~ besitzen** to be of good report, to bear a good character; **seinen guten ~ bewahren** to keep up one's credit, to keep one's reputation intact, to underprop one's reputation; **j. um seinen guten ~ bringen** to discredit s. o., to ruin s. one's reputation; **j. in einen üblen ~ bringen** to run down s. one's character, to disrepute s. o.; **~ erhalten** *(Professor)* to be offered a chair (professorship), to receive a call; **sich einen ~ erwerben** to make o. s. a name; **in den ~ der Kühnheit gelangen** to earn a character for audacity; **guten ~ genießen (haben)** to be judged good (in good savo(u)r), to enjoy a good reputation, to be of a good repute; **schlechten ~ genießen** to have a bad name; **neuen ~ durch besseren Lebenswandel gewinnen** to unlive one's reputation; **makellosen ~ haben** to be without a spot on one's reputation; **sich überhaupt nicht um seinen ~ kümmern** to hold one's reputation cheap; **jem. den guten ~ nehmen** to take away s. one's character; **seinen guten ~ retten** to save one's reputation; **seinen guten ~ riskieren** to risk (mortgage) one's reputation; **jds. ~ schaden** to detract from s. one's reputation; **seinem ~ schaden** to do damage to one's reputation, to blot one's escutcheon; **~ schmälern** to deflate the reputation; **auf seinen guten ~ bedacht sein** to be mindful of one's good name; **im ~ stehen** to have one's name up; **in gutem ~ stehen** to be in estimation; **bei jem. in gutem ~ stehen** to be in s. one's good books; **bei jem. in schlechtem ~ stehen** to be in ill odo(u)r with s. o.; **im ~ eines Gelehrten stehen** to enjoy the reputation of being a scholar; **im ~ eines Strebers stehen** to have the character of a place hunter; **jds. gutem ~ Abbruch tun** to injure (prove injurious to) s. one's reputation; **jds. ~ durch Lügen untergraben** to lie away s. one's reputation; **seinen guten ~ verlieren** to grow out of estimation, to forfeit one's credit; **jds. ~ durch höhnische Bemerkungen verunglimpfen** to sneer away s. one's reputation; **seinen guten ~ wahren** to defend one's good name; **jds. guten ~ restlos zerstören** to tear s. one's reputation to shreds (tatters).
rufen, sich ein Ereignis wieder ins Gedächtnis to recall an event to one's mind; **um Hilfe ~** to call for help; **ins Leben ~** to set up, to call into being, to organize; **zur Ordnung ~** to call to order; **j. auf den Plan ~** to bring s. o. to the scene; **mit höchster Stimmstärke ~** to shout at the pitch of one's voice;
j. ~ lassen to send for s. o.
Rüffel rebuke, wigging *(Br., coll.)*, telling-off;
jem. einen ~ erteilen to give s. o. a ticking-off; **~ einstecken müssen** to catch it hot.
rüffeln to tick off, to give a wigging *(Br., coll.)*.

Rufmord character assassination, smearing campaign;
~ **an jem. begehen** to ruin (impair, damage) s. one's reputation, to take away s. one's character, to fling mud at s. o.;
~**begehung** mudslinging.

Ruf|name first *(US)* (Christian) name; ~**nummer** telephone number; ~**nummerngeber** drum information assembler and dispatcher; ~**schädiger** detractor; ~**schädigung** damage to (destruction of) reputation, detraction, defamatory statement, injurious falsehood; ~**schädigung der Konkurrenz** defamation of a competitor's reputation, disparagement of a competitor; ~**taste** ringing key; **in ~weite** within call (cry); ~**zeichen** call signal, ring, *(Erkennungszeichen)* identification signal, *(Schiff)* signal (code) letters.

Rüge censure, reprimand, animadversion, rebuke, reprehension, wigging *(Br., coll.)*, *(beim Kauf)* claim, complaint, *(Prozeß)* plea, exception, objection;
~ **mangelnder Schlüssigkeit** speaking (general) demurrer; ~ **der mangelnden Substantiierung** common bar; ~ **der Unzuständigkeit** jurisdictional plea;
~ **aussprechen** to animadvert; ~ **erhalten** to be rebuked (reprimanded); **jem. eine ~ erteilen** to reprove s. o., to tick s. o. off, *(parl.)* to pass a vote of censure on s. o.;
~**frist** period (time limit) for claims.

rügen to reprimand, to reprove, *(Mängelanzeige)* to make a claim, to make a complaint, to notify a defect, *(parl.)* to censure, to rebuke;
jds. Nachlässigkeit ~ to rebuke s. o. for his carelessness; **öffentlich ~** to denounce; **jds. Verhalten ~** to reprove s. one's conduct.

Ruhe rest, repose, quiet, quietude, *(Erholung)* recreation;
absolute ~ complete silence; **ewige ~** eternal rest; **innere ~** tranquil(l)ity, serenity; **nächtliche ~** night's rest; **unbedingte ~** strict silence; **wohlverdiente ~** well-earned rest;
öffentliche ~ und Ordnung public order, public peace; **unnatürliche ~ auf den Straßen** unnatural quiet of the streets; **sich etw. in ~ ansehen** to look at s. th. at leisure; **der ~ bedürfen** to need rest; **sich zur ~ begeben** to go to roost *(coll.)*; **j. zur letzten ~ betten** to lay s. o. to rest; **~ bewahren** to keep one's temper, to keep one's cool; **um ~ bitten** to ask for silence; **erregte Menge zur ~ bringen** to calm the excited crowd; **der Zukunft in ~ entgegensehen** to face the future calmly; **j. zur letzten ~ geleiten** to pay s. o. the last hono(u)rs; **vollkommene ~ genießen** to enjoy perfect peace and quiet; **keinen Augenblick ~ haben** to have a hectic time; **die ~ weg haben** not to be easily ruffled; **zur ~ kommen** to come to anchor, to find peace of mind; **nach den politischen Verwirrungen zur ~ kommen** to quieten down after political disturbances; **sich zur ~ setzen können** to be all right for the rest of one's life; **j. in ~ lassen** to leave s. o. in peace; **jem. keine ~ lassen** to give s. o. no peace; **die ~ selbst sein** to be cool as a cucumber; **sich zur ~ setzen** to go into retirement, to give up one's (quit) business; **für Aufrechterhaltung von ~ und Ordnung sorgen** to maintain internal peace; **jds. ~ stören** to disturb s. one's peace; **öffentliche ~ und Ordnung stören** to disturb (break) the peace; **seine ~ wiederfinden** to cool down *(coll.)*;
~**bett** day bed.

Ruhegehalt [retiring (retirement)] pension, retired (retirement) pay, pension benefit *(US)*, gratuitous (retiring) allowance, superannuation allowance (benefit), *(mil.)* half-pay;
betriebliches ~ occupational pension;
~ **wegen Dienstunfähigkeit** invalidity pension;
jem. das ~ aberkennen to deprive s. o. of his pension; ~ **aussetzen** to settle a pension; ~ **beziehen** to draw a pension; ~ **in Höhe von 2/3 des Gehalts beziehen** to have a pension of two thirds of the salary; **jem. ein ~ gewähren** to pension s. o. off.

Ruhegehälter *(Bilanz)* income received from pensions.

Ruhegehalts|aberkennung deprivation of a pension; ~**alter** retiring age; ~**anspruch** pension right; **unentziehbarer ~anspruch** vested pension plan; ~**anspruch aberkennen** to cancel the pension rights; ~**ansprüche haben** to be entitled to a pension; ~**ansprüche verlieren** to forfeit the right to a pension.

ruhegehaltsberechtigt pensionable.

Ruhegehalts|berechtigung eligibility for a pension; ~**bezüge** retirement income, benefit pension, pensionable emoluments, pension income (payments); ~**bezüge eines Gehaltsempfängers** employment retirement income; ~**bezüge kürzen** to retrench a pension; ~**empfänger** pensioner, retiree, recipient of a pension, pensionary *(Br.)*; ~**erhöhung** pension increase.

ruhegehaltsfähiges Einkommen pensionable income.

Ruhegehalts|verlust forfeiture of pension; ~**zahlung** pension benefit.

Ruhegeld retirement (pension, *US*) benefit, gratuitous allowance, superannuation allowance (benefit), pension, *(mil.)* half-pay;
betriebliches ~ occupational pension;
jem. das ~ aberkennen to deprive s. o. of his pension;
unentziehbare ~anwartschaft vested pension plan; ~**bestimmungen** superannuation provisions; ~**bezüge** retirement income; ~**empfänger** pensioner, retiree, recipient of a pension.

ruhegeldfähiges Einkommen pension income.

Ruhegeld|ordnung occupational pension scheme (plan); ~**system für selbsttätig Erwerbstätige** self-employment retirement plan; ~**verpflichtungen** pension obligations; ~**verwaltungsgesellschaft** pension management company.

Ruhe|genüsse retirement benefits; ~**lage** rest, *(Zeiger)* neutral position.

ruhelos unquiet, restless, without rest, wandering;
~ **im Zimmer auf und ab gehen** to pace up and down in a room;
in dieser ~en Zeit in this hectic age.

Ruhen suspense;
~ **der Geschäfte** suspension of dealings; ~ **eines Strafverfahrens** stay of prosecution; ~ **der Verjährung** suspension of the statute of limitations; ~ **der Versicherung** suspension of an insurance.

ruhen to [have a] rest, *(basieren)* to be based on, *(Geschäft)* to be at a standstill, *(Recht)* to fall into abeyance, *(in der Schwebe sein)* to be in abeyance, *(Verfahren)* to stay, *(Verhandlungen)* to have been interrupted, to be at a standstill, *(Versicherung)* to be suspended;
auf Pfeilern ~ to rest on (be supported by) pillars;
Sache ~ lassen to let a matter rest, to drop a matter.

ruhend *(Kapital)* idle, uninvested;
~**e Belastung** steady load; **auf einem Hof ~e Schulden** debts encumbered on a farm; ~**er Verkehr** stationary vehicles; ~**er Vulkan** dormant volcano.

Ruhepause rest, pause (period) interval, break, breather, spell, relaxation allowance, recreation time;
kurze ~ a minute's rest;
~ **nach den Wahlen** period of quiet after the elections;
~ **einschieben** to take a rest (time out, *US*, an ease, a break); **sich eine ~ gönnen** to take a rest (time out, *US*); **längere ~ verordnen** to prescribe a long rest.

Ruhe|platz resting place, home of rest; ~**posten** sinecure, soft (cushy) job, snap; ~**sitz** vacation retreat; ~**sitz in den Bergen** mountain retreat.

Ruhestand retirement;
im ~ retired, pensionary, pensioned off, *(mil.)* on half-pay, *(Professor)* emeritus; **in den ~ versetzt** superannuated;
einstweiliger ~ *(mil.)* half-pay;
im ~ leben to live in retirement (retired); **im ~ sein** to be on the retired list; **in den ~ treten** to retire from service (active life), to go (retire) on a pension, to superannuate, to pension, to retire; **j. in den ~ versetzen** to place (put) s. o. on the retired list, to pension s. o. off, to retire s. o.; **j. in den zeitweiligen ~ versetzen** *(mil.)* to put s. o. on half-pay; **in den ~ versetzt werden** to be superannuated (pensioned off).

Ruheständler retiree, retired person, pensioner.

Ruhestands|alter, obligatorisches mandatory retiring age; ~**beamter** retired civil servant; ~**jahre** retirement years; ~**liste** retired list; ~**versicherung** retirement insurance; ~**versorgung** retirement pension.

Ruhe|stätte resting place; **letzte ~stätte** last resting place, the grave; ~**störer** disturber of the peace, rioter, disorderly person; ~**störung** noisemaking, disorder, brawling *(Br.)*, *(der öffentlichen Ordnung)* disturbance (breach) of the peace; ~**strom** *(el.)* closed circuit; ~**stromkreis** closed-circuit current; ~**stunde** leisure hour; ~**tag** rest day, day of rest, holiday, day off; **öffentlicher ~tag** public holiday; ~**zeit** rest pause (period), hours of repose, *(Flugzeugbesatzung)* layover, *(Geschäftswelt)* off season.

ruhig quiet, equal, tranquil, *(Börse)* quiet, lifeless, flat, easy, at ease, calm, dull, *(umsatzlos)* featureless;
ganz ~ bleiben to play it cool; **dem Tode ~ entgegengehen** to face death calmly; ~ **laufen** *(Motor)* to run smoothly; ~ **liegen** *(Börse)* to be easy, *(Haus)* to be in a quiet area; **sich ~ verhalten** to hold one's peace; ~ **verlaufen** to run smoothly, to go off without a hitch;
~**e Börse** dull market; ~**e Fahrt** smooth steering; ~**er Gang einer Maschine** silent running of an engine; **mit ~em Gewissen** with a clear conscience; ~**e Kugel schieben** to have a soft (cushy) job; ~**es Leben führen** to lead an easy life, to live a secluded life; ~**er Mieter** quiet lodger; ~**er Posten** cushy job; **in einer ~en Straße wohnen** to live in a quiet street; ~**er Ton** steady

voice; ~**e Überfahrt** calm passage; **in ~er Umgebung** in peaceful surroundings; ~**e Zeit im Büro haben** to have a quiet time at the office;
man kann ~ darüber sprechen there is no harm in talking about it.
Ruhm fame, distinction, glory, hono(u)r, nimbus, kudos *(coll.)*;
auf ~ erpicht eager for fame;
für seinen ~ arbeiten to work with the object of earning fame; **sich mit ~ bedecken** to cover o. s. with glory; **nach ~ dürsten** to follow the path of glory; **~ einbüßen** to suffer an eclipse; **mit den Auswirkungen seines ~es fertig werden müssen** to pay the penalty of fame; **auf seinen ~ bedacht sein** to look to one's laurels; **auf dem Gipfel seines ~es stehen** to be in the heyday of one's glory.
rühmen, sich to praise o. s., to boast; **j. wegen seiner Zuverlässigkeit ~** to speak highly of s. one's reliability.
Ruhmes | blatt glorious chapter; **für alle Beteiligten gerade kein ~blatt sein** to be an action disgraceful for all concerned; ~**halle** pantheon; ~**weg für j. vorbereiten** to pave the way to fame for s. o.
rühmlich | e Ausnahme noteworthy exception; ~**es Ende nehmen** to die a glorious death; **kein ~es Ende nehmen** to come to a bad end.
ruhmloses Ende eines Feldzugs inglorious end of a campaign.
Ruhmsucht hankering after fame, itch for praise.
ruhmsüchtig insatiable of glory;
~ sein to hunt after glory.
Rühren fühlen, ein menschliches to feel a touch of sympathy.
rühren to move, to stir;
sich ~ *(fig.)* to wake, to stir a leg; **nicht daran ~** let sleeping dogs lie; **keinen Finger ~** not to move hand or foot; **ohne einen Finger dafür zu ~** without lifting a finger; **sich nicht vom Fleck ~** not to budge an inch; **alle Kräfte ~** to leave no stone unturned; **an einen schmerzlichen Punkt ~** to touch a sore point; **j. zu Tränen ~** to move s. o. to tears; **an die Vergangenheit ~** to stir up the past; **Werbetrommel ~** to make propaganda, to drum *(US)*;
sich nicht ~ können to be in low straits; **sich vor Schreck nicht ~ können** to be rooted to the spot with fright;
bitte nicht an die Ausstellungsstücke ~ please do not touch the exhibits.
rührend moving, touching, heart-rending;
~ um j. besorgt sein to be concerned about s. o. in a touching way;
~**e Geschichte** moving story; ~**er Vater** devoted father.
rührig active, busy, bustling, alert, painstaking, enterprising, up-and-coming *(US)*;
~ sein to display activity, to be on the job;
~**er Beamter** go-ahead official; ~**er Mensch** hustler *(coll.)*.
Rührigkeit activity, enterprise;
~ zeigen to display activity.
rührselig maudlin, sentimental, lachrymose;
~**er Film** tearjerker *(sl.)*, weepie *(sl.)*; ~**e Geschichte** sob stuff *(sl.)*.
Ruin ruin, decay, downfall, perdition, *(Konkurs)* bankruptcy, breakup;
jds. ~ beschleunigen to precipitate s. one's ruin; **sein Vermögen vor dem ~ bewahren** to save one's fortune from wreck (ruin); **jds. ~ herbeiführen** to bring about s. one's ruin; **seinen eigenen ~ herbeiführen** to draw ruin upon o. s., to be on the downward path; **kurz vor dem ~ stehen** to be on the brink of (faced with) ruin; **sich zu jds. finanziellem ~ zusammentun** to conspire to ruin s. o.
Ruine wreck, debris, *(fig.)* physical wreck;
völlige ~ old crock *(fam.)*;
nur noch eine ~ sein to be a mere shadow of one's former self;
zur ~ werden to fall into ruin.
Ruinieren wrecking.
ruinieren to ruin, to spoil, to shipwreck, to drive to the dogs, to mar, to undo, to do up *(US sl.)*;
Ernte ~ to ruin the crop; **finanziell ~** to smash, to drive to the wall *(Br.)*; **seine Gesundheit ~** to undermine (ruin) one's health; **Handelsfirma ~** to wreck a commercial house; **Kleid ~** to spoil a dress; **sein Leben ~** to wreck one's life; **seinen Ruf ~** to mar one's reputation; **Teppich ~** to spoil a carpet; **jds. Zukunft ~** to ruin s. one's fortune.
ruiniert lost, broken down, smashed up, up the tree, pegged out *(US)*, washed out (-up) *(sl.)*, *(Handel)* gone, bankrupt, broke, broken;
~ sein to be ruined (in ruins), to go to smash (the wall, *Br.*), to be smashed up, to come a cropper;
~**e Bank** wrecked bank.
ruinös ruinous, cutthroat;
~**er Aufwand** ruinous expenditure; ~**e Bedingungen** ruinous terms; ~**e Folgen** disastrous consequences; ~**er Preis** cutthroat (ruinous) price; ~**e Steuern** ruinous taxes; ~**er Wettbewerb** cutthroat competition.
Rummel hubbub, row, racket, whoopee, hoopla *(US sl.)*, *(Reklamerummel)* ballyhoo *(coll.)*;
~ auf den Straßen hustle and bustle in the streets;
ganzen ~ satt haben to be fed up with it; **den ~ kennen** to know the ropes; **großen ~ um j. machen** to make a big fuss of s. o.;
~**platz** amusement park, fairground, fun fair *(Br.)*.
rumoren to make a noise, to fumble (rumble) about;
im Kopf ~ to cause a stir in one's head; **in der Küche ~** to be pottering about in the kitchen; **im Volk ~** to be simmering in the people's mind.
Rumpel | kammer box (lumber) room, limbo, glory hole *(coll.)*;
~**kasten** rattletrap.
rumpeln *(Fuhrwerk)* to bump, to rumble, to lumber;
über eine Brücke ~ to jolt over a bridge.
Rumpf *(Flugzeug)* body, fuselage, *(Schiff)* hull, shell;
~**abwurfbehälter** bellytank; ~**belegschaft** skeleton staff.
rümpfen, seine Nase über etw. to turn up one's nose; **seine Nase über j. ~** to sneer at s. o.
Rumpf | geschäftsjahr part of an accounting year; ~**gruppierung** rump grouping; ~**jahr** abbreviated financial year; ~**kabinett** rump cabinet; ~**parlament** rump parliament; ~**versammlung** rump caucus.
Run veranstalten to run.
rund round, globular, globose, *(pummelig)* plump, *(Zahl)* in round numbers, *(ungefähr)* approximately, about;
sich dick und ~ essen to eat one's fill;
~**e Augen machen** to gaze wide-eyed with astonishment; ~**es Dutzend** round (full, good) dozen; ~**es Fest** rollickings; ~**e Klammern** curved brackets, parentheses; ~**e Leistung** finished performance; ~**e Million verdient haben** to have earned a good million; ~**e tausend Pfund kosten** to cost easily a thousand pounds; ~**e Summe** good round sum; **in ~en Zahlen** in round figures.
Rund | bau rotunda; ~**blick** panorama.
Runde patrol, round, beat, *(Lage)* round [of drinks], *(Platzrunde)* circle, landing pattern;
weitere ~ zur Rettung nutzloser Betriebe another round of lame duckery;
~ ausgeben to stand treat (a drink to all); **etw. über die ~n bringen** to bring s. th. to a successful conclusion; **seine ~ gehen** to make a circuit, to be on patrol; **alle Stunden seine ~ gehen** to make one's round every hour; **~ durch den Garten gehen** to take a stroll in the garden; **über die ~n kommen** to tide over; **gerade noch über die ~n kommen** to make both ends meet; **mit wenig Geld über die ~n kommen** to manage with little money; **im Dorf schnell die ~ machen** to take the round of the village; **seine ~ machen** to [walk one] round, *(Flasche)* to pass round, *(Gerücht)* to be going around, to traverse one's beat *(US)*; **überall die ~ machen** to spread from mouth to mouth; **durch die ganze Verwandtschaft die ~ machen** to pass round to all members of the family; **~ unter den Gästen machen** to circulate among the guests; **~ durch die Lokale machen** to go on a pub crawl; **in einer gemütlichen ~ sitzen** to be sitting in convivial company; **~ spendieren** to pay for a round of drinks, to call for glasses all round, to stand treat.
Runderlaß circular [note].
runderneuern *(Reifen)* to retread, to cap.
runderneuerter Reifen retread.
Runderneuerung retread, full cap.
Runderneuerungsgummi camel-back.
Rundfahrt circular (sightseeing) tour, round trip;
~ durch die Stadt circuit of the city;
~ unternehmen to be on tour;
~**autobus** sightseeing bus, rubberneck bus *(US)*.
Rundflug air trip, circuit, flip *(Br.)*;
~**karte** tour fare; ~**karte mit variablem Endflugplatz** open-jaw.
Rundfrage inquiry, poll.
Rundfunk broadcast[ing], wireless, aircast *(US)*, radio *(US)*;
durch ~ by wireless *(Br.)*, on the air; **im ~** over the wireless *(Br.)*, on the air (radio, *US*);
gebührenpflichtiger ~ toll broadcasting;
~ und Fernsehen sound and television broadcasting *(US)*, the instant media;
im ~ gastieren to star on the air; **~ hören** to listen in; **durch ~ senden** to radio *(US)*, to wireless *(Br.)*, to flash, to put on the air; **im ~ sprechen** to talk over the radio *(US)*; **alle**

Parlamentssitzungen im ~ übertragen to broadcast Parliament permanently; **Rede durch ~ übertragen** to broadcast a speech; **durch ~ verbreiten** to broadcast, to put on the air; **durch ~ übertragen werden** to be put on the air;
~abteilung broadcast division (section); **~anlage** wireless installation; **~ansage** broadcast announcement; **~ansager** announcer, broadcaster; **~ansprache** broadcast (radio, *US*) address (speech), broadcast talk, *(informell)* fireside chat *(US)*; **~ansprache über alle Sender** coast-to-coast radio speech *(US)*; **~ansprache am Tage vor der Wahl** election-eve radio appeal *(US)*; **~anstalt** broadcasting corporation; **private ~anstalt** commercial radio; **~antenne** antenna, aerial; **~apparat** wireless set *(Br.)*, radio [receiver] *(US)*; **~bearbeiter** producer; **~bericht** broadcast account (report); **~berichterstatter** radio commwntator; **~einnahmen** broadcast revenues; **~empfang** wireless (broadcast) reception; **~empfang stören** to black out, to jam; **~empfänger** [wireless] set, radio [receiver] *(US)*; **~empfangsanlage** radio installation; **~frequenz** broadcast frequency, radio circuit; **~gebiet** broadcasting front; **~gebühr** radio receiver fee *(US)*, radio (wireless, *Br.*) tax, shilling tax on wireless sets *(Br.)*, wireless licence fee *(Br.)*; **~genehmigung** wireless licence *(Br.)*, broadcast receiving license *(US)*; **~gerät** wireless (radio, *US*) receiver, [wireless] set, broadcasting (radio) equipment; **~gerät abschalten** to turn off the radio; **~gesellschaft** broadcasting company (corporation); **~gruppe** broadcasting network; **~hören** listening-in; **~hörer** broadcast listener, listener-in; **~industrie** broadcasting business; **~journalist** radio journalist; **~kampagne starten** to go on the air; **~kommentar** [running] commentary; **~kommentator** broadcaster, news (radio) commentator; **~manuskript** radio (broadcast) script; **~meldung, ~nachricht** broadcast news, wireless communication.

Rundfunkprogramm broadcast (wireless, radio, *US*) program(me), *(Werbung)* guide sheet;
auf Tonband aufgenommenes ~ recorded program(me); **überseeisches ~** overseas broadcast program(me);
~ ohne Reklameanteil sustaining program(me), sustainer.

Rundfunk|rat broadcasting council (commission); **~reklame** radio advertising; **~reportage** running commentary; **~reporter** broadcast journalist; **~röhre** radio valve; **~sendefolge** wireless program(me).

Rundfunksender broadcast (wireless) station, broadcasting transmitter;
im Interesse der Allgemeinheit errichteter ~ general public service station;
~ errichten (installieren) to fix up a wireless station;
~netz broadcasting network.

Rundfunksendung broadcast[ing], broadcast (wireless) transmission, radio, broadcast, wireless program(me);
bestochene ~ payola *(US sl.)*;
~ mitschneiden to take down a broadcast on tape.

Rundfunk|sprecher broadcaster, announcer; **~station** broadcasting (radio) station, wireless transmitter, broadcaster; **~station für Werbesendungen** commercial station; **~störung** interference, *(feindlicher Sender)* jamming; **~stunde** wireless talk; **~techniker** radio engineer; **~übertragung** radio broadcast, broadcasting, broadcast (wireless) transmission, transmission by radio; **~unterhalter** disk jockey; **~veranstaltung mit Telefonanfragen** call-in radio show; **~versorgung** broadcast coverage; **~verwaltungsrat** broadcasting commission; **~welle** broadcasting wave; **~werbesendung** broadcast production, commercial.

Rundfunkwerbung broadcast (radio, *US*) advertising, broadcast publicity;
regional beschränkte ~ spot broadcasting;
~ betreiben to go on the air; **wiederholt ~ betreiben** to plug.

Rundfunkzeit radio time *(US)*;
zugeteilte ~ für politische Sendungen political broadcasting time.

Rundgang turn, *(Führung)* guided tour, *(Polizist)* round, beat;
~ durch den Garten tour of the garden;
seinen ~ machen to walk one's round, to traverse one's beat *(US)*; **~ durch ein Museum machen** to go round a museum.

Rund|gemälde cyclorama *(US)*; **~gespräch** panel discussion.

rundheraus point blank, bluntly;
~ verweigern to refuse flatly.

Rund|holz logs; **~kopfmarkierung** *(Straße)* button.

Rundreise [circular] tour, round trip (tour, voyage, *US*), round, circuit;
~ im Düsenflugzeug round-trip jet;
auf ~ gehen to go on circle, to tour the country;
~ausflugspreise excursion fares; **~billet** tourist (circular, *Br.*, round-trip, *US*) ticket; **~dauer** turn-around; **~fahrkarte** tourist (round-trip, *US*) ticket; **~flugkarte** round-trip air fare *(US)*, point-to-point ticket; **~heft** combination ticket; **~karte** round-trip fare (ticket) *(US)*; **~preise** excursion fares; **~tarif** round-trip excursion fare *(US)*; **~verbilligung** reduction for round trips; **~zug** cruise train.

Rundschau *(Zeitung)* review, survey.

Rundschreiben circular [note], newsletter, *(Partei)* whip *(Br.)*;
~ verfassen (verschicken) to issue (send out) a circular, to circularize;
~versand sending out of circulars, circularization.

Rund|sicht panorama; **~sichtscheibe** *(Auto)* panorama windshield; **~sprechanlage** public-address system; **~suchgerät** panorama equipment.

Rundum|beschriftung *(Omnibus)* solus bus site; **~licht** rotating lights; **~verteilung** allround defence.

Rundverkehr roundabout traffic, merry-go-round.

Runenschrift rune[s], runic.

Rungenwagen platform car *(US)*, (carriage, *Br.*), flat car *(US)*, open carriage *(Br.)*, lorry, truck *(Br.)*;
~ für überhängende Ladung idler car.

Runzel wrinkle.

rupfen *(übers Ohr hauen)* to fleece, to pigeon *(sl.)*;
ein Hühnchen mit jem. zu ~ haben to have a crow to pluck (bone to pick) with s. o.

Ruß soot, coal, dust, smut;
~ und Schmutz einer Industriestadt soot and grime of a manufacturing town.

rüsten to arm, to equip.

rustikal rustic.

Rüstung armament;
in voller ~ full-armed.

Rüstungs|anleihe defence loan (bonds), armament credit *(Br.)*; **~arbeit** war (defence-plant) work; **~arbeiter** war worker; **~auftrag** military (war) order, war (defence) contract, military contract, offshore order; **für die Ausführung von ~aufträgen benutzen** to use its defence production lines; **~auftragsvergabe** defence award; **~ausgaben** expenditure (outlay) on armament; **~begrenzung** restriction of armaments, arms limitation; **~begrenzungsabkommen** agreement on arms control, *(Atomwaffen)* SALT; **~beschränkung** limitation of armaments; **~betrieb** armament company, war (defence) plant, defence contractor (factory); **~etat** expenditure of money on armaments; **~fabrik** munition factory, war factory, armament plant *(Br.)*; **~geschäft** military business; **sich aus dem ~geschäft teilweise zurückziehen** to reduce its reliance on defence contracts; **~gewinn** war (defence) profit; **~gewinnsteuer** war-profits tax *(US)*; **~gleichheit** equality of armaments; **~güter** war goods, armament supplies; **~hausse** war boom; **~hilfsaufträge** offshore orders *(US)*; **~hochkonjunktur** armament boom; **~industrie** armament (war) industry; **~industrieller** armament magnate; **~käufe** military sales, defence (offshore) purchases; **~kommission** war control commission; **~konjunktur** armaments boom; **~kredit** armament credit *(Br.)*; **~lenkung** arms control; **~ministerium** War Board *(US)*; **~politik** armaments policy; **~potential** war potential; **~produktion** production of armaments, war (defense, *US*) production; **~programm** armaments program(me); **~verminderung** arms reduction; **~vorlage** defence bill; **~werte** armament issues; **~wettlauf** arms (armament) race; **~wirtschaft** armament (war) industry; **~zentrum** war production center *(US)* (centre, *Br.*); **~zulieferungsbetrieb** defence supplier; **~zuschuß** war grant.

Rüstzeug, geistiges plant;
~ für die Berufsausbildung tools of trade.

Rutschen *(Auto)* side-slip, skid[ding].

rutschen *(Auto)* to skid, to slide;
seitwärts ~ to broadside.

rutschenden Wagen abfangen to get out of (correct) a skid.

rutschfest *(Reifen)* nonskidding, skid-proof.

Rutsch|gefahr risk of skidding; **~spur** skid mark.

S

S-Kurve S (reverse) curve.
Saal hall, saloon, ball room;
~ **verlassen** to walk out; **aus dem** ~ **weisen** to expel from the hall;
~**dienst** ushers; ~**miete bezahlen** to pay for the hire of a hall; ~**ordner** usher, steward.
Saat seed;
die ~ **steht gut** the crops are promising;
~**händler** corn chandler *(Br.)*.
Säbel, mit dem ~ **rasseln** to rattle one's sabre, to swash about with one's sword;
~**rasseln** sabre rattling, swash buckling; ~**rassler** arms shaker, sabre rattler, swashbuckler, swaggerer.
Sabotage sabotage, rattening, *(Kommunismus)* diversionism;
~ **im Betrieb** plant wrecking; ~ **eines Planes** frustration of a plan;
~ **treiben** to [practise] sabotage, to ratten; **durch** ~ **verursacht werden** to be caused by sabotage;
~**abwehr** countersabotage, counterintelligence; ~**akt** sabotage; **fortgesetzte** ~**akte** continual acts of sabotage.
sabotageanfällig vulnerable to sabotage.
Sabotage|ausbildungslager training camp for saboteurs, saboteur camp; ~**drohung** sabotage threat; ~**gruppe** *(pol.)* Trojan horse; ~**kommando** sabotage squad, demolition team; ~**politik** wrecking policy; ~**verdacht** suspicion of sabotage; ~**versuch** attempt to sabotage.
Saboteur saboteur, rattener, *(Kommunismus)* diversionist.
sabotieren to [practise] sabotage, to ratten *(sl.)*;
Plan ~ to torpedo a plan of action, to frustrate a plan; **jds. Plan** ~ to upset s. one's applecart, to put the skids under s. o. *(sl.)*.
Sachangaben statement of facts *(US)*, stated case.
Sachanlagen tangible (fixed) assets, real investments, *(Bilanz)* land, buildings, plant and machinery *(Br.)* (and equipment);
~ **der Rüstungsindustrie** emergency facilities *(US)*;
~**abschreibung** depreciation on fixed assets; ~**erneuerung** replacement of fixed assets; ~**investitionen** investment in fixed assets; ~**konto** fixed-assets account; **feststehender** ~**posten** fixed-assets unit.
Sach|anlagevermögen physical (fixed capital, tangible) assets; ~**antrag** action for relief, motion for judgment *(Br.)*; ~**antrag stellen** to apply to the court for relief; ~**aufklärung** stating the case, *(detailliert)* amplification; ~**aufruf** *(Gericht)* calendar call, calling the docket; ~**aufwendungen** material expenditure (expenses, cost); ~**ausschüttung** distribution in kind.
Sachbearbeiter official (officer) in charge, clerk, *(Sozialpflege)* caseworker;
zuständiger ~ desk officer, *(Werbeträger)* media man;
~ **für Fragen der Jugendarbeit** youth employment officer; ~ **für Funkwerbung** *(Agentur)* time buyer; ~ **für Öffentlichkeitsfragen** public relations executive, publicity officer; ~ **eines Werbeetats** account executive.
Sach|behandlung handling of an affair; ~**bericht** report, feature.
Sachbeschädigung destruction of (damage to) property;
mutwillige (vorsätzliche) ~ malicious (wilful) trespass, malicious mischief *(US)*, vandalism; **schwere** ~ criminal damage.
Sach|besitz effects; ~**beweis** relevant (material) evidence; ~**bezeichnung** physical description; ~**bezüge** payment (allowance, benefits) in kind, perquisites *(Br.)*; ~**buch** nonfiction [book].
Sachdarstellung stating a case, statement (representation) of facts *(US)*;
einleitende ~ recital; **falsche** ~ misstatement of facts; **kurze** ~ brief account, brief *(Br.)*, concise statement; **objektive** ~ factual statement.
sachdienlich expedient, pertinent, relevant, to the point, *(geeignet)* suitable, appropriate, *(nützlich)* useful, helpful, serviceable;
~**e Angaben** relevant details; ~**er Beweis** pertinent evidence; ~**e Mitteilungen** pertinent information.
Sachdienlichkeit expediency, relevance, pertinence.
Sachdividende property (commodity, *US*) dividend, dividend payable in kind.
Sache affair, matter, business, job, line, kind, pidgin *(Br., coll.)*, *(Betreff)* concern, *(Ereignis)* event, show, *(Gegenstand)* object, thing, article, *(Geschichte)* proposition *(coll.)*, baby *(sl.)*, *(Punkt)* point, *(Rechtsfall)* case, cause, action, lawsuit, matter, *(Streitfrage)* issue, *(Tatsache)* fact, *(Thema)* point, subject, *(Umstand)* circumstance;
in eigener ~ on one's own behalf; **in gerechter** ~ in a good quarrel; **nach Lage der** ~ as things stand, *(jur.)* upon its merits; **neben der** ~ **liegend** irrelevant; **nicht jedermanns** ~ not everybody's cup of tea; **nicht zur** ~ **gehörig** beside the point (mark); **zur** ~! question!; **zur** ~ **gehörig** to the point, pertinent, relevant;
abgekartete ~ regular plant, put-up job *(US)*; **anrüchige** ~ shady business; **zur Entscheidung (Verhandlung) anstehende** ~ case before the court (on the court list); **aufgegebene** ~ derelict; **ausgemachte (beschlossene)** ~ foregone conclusion; **mit dem Grundstück verbundene bewegliche** ~ local chattel; **dumme** ~ silly business, foolish thing, rum go; **eilbedürftige** ~ immediate matter; **keine einfache** ~ not at all plain sailing; **entscheidungsreife** ~ case ripe for judgment; **rechtskräftig entschiedene** ~ ruled case, res judicata; **fragliche** ~ matter in question; **fremde** ~ property of (belonging to) another; **gut funktionierende** ~ going concern; **vor ein anderes Gericht gehörige** ~ foreign matter; **gemeinsame** ~ joint (common) cause; **gerechte** ~ rightful cause; **geschäftliche** ~ business matter; **gewagte** ~ touched-and-go; **große** ~ big affair; **größere** ~ no mean affair; **halbe** ~ half measure; **handelsrechtliche** ~ commercial cause; **heikle** ~ delicate point, ticklish situation; **herrenlose** ~ derelict; **kinderleichte** ~ child's play, a boy's job; **klare** ~ plain sailing; **komplizierte** ~ gimmick; **öffentliche** ~ public property; **ortsfeste** ~ local chose; **schwebende** ~ pending case; **schwierige** ~ difficulty; **sichere** ~ a sure card; **nicht streitige** ~ nonlitiguous case; **strittige** ~ matter in issue; **tolle** ~ hot stuff, clipper *(sl.)*, snorter, rattler *(sl.)*; **unangenehme** ~ a bad business; **unerledigte** ~ outstanding matter; **einseitig zu verhandelnde** ~ undefended suit; **verlorengegangene** ~ lost article; **dem Obergericht zur Entscheidung vorgelegte** ~ case certified; **vorliegende** ~ matter in hand, [subject] matter;
~ **des Geschmacks** question of taste; ~ **auf Leben oder Tod** question of life and death; ~ **für die Polizei** police matter; ~ **für sich** a matter apart; **keine** ~ **zum Spaßen** no jesting matter; **einer** ~ **die beste Seite abgewinnen** to put the best face on s. th.; ~ **als erfolglos abtun** to give s. th. up as a bad job; **sich einer** ~ **annehmen** to take a matter in hand; **sich eine** ~ **ansehen** to look into a matter; **die** ~ **X gegen Y ansetzen** to docket the case of X vs. Y; ~ **aufrufen** to call a case (cause); **sich zur** ~ **äußern** to refer to the merits of a case; **seine** ~ **begründen** to make out one's case; ~ **im Auge behalten** to keep track of a matter; **über eine** ~ **beraten** to discuss a matter; ~ **beschlafen** to consult one's pillow; **bei der** ~ **bleiben** to stick to the point; ~ **in Schwung bringen** to make things hum; ~ **deichseln** to wangle a matter; **sich auf eine gefährliche** ~ **einlassen** to skate on thin ice; **in einer** ~ **entscheiden** to pronounce on a subject, *(Gericht)* to give a judgment; **über eine** ~ **erkennen** to cognosce a case; ~ **fallenlassen** to drop a plan; **einer** ~ **auf den Grund gehen** to get to the bottom of a matter; **j. für eine** ~ **gewinnen** to enlist s. o. in support of a case; **j. für seine** ~ **gewinnen** to win s. o. to one's party; ~ **völlig satt haben** to be sick of the whole show; ~ **bis oben hin stehen haben** to be fed up to the teeth with a business; **mit einer** ~ **nichts zu tun haben** to have no concern in a matter, to have no hand in an affair; **sich in einer** ~ **auf dem laufenden halten** to keep o. s. up to date on a matter; **unverrichteter** ~ **heimgehen** to go home empty-handed; **um eine** ~ **herumreden** to beat about the bush; **aus einer** ~ **siegreich hervorgehen** to come out of s. th. with flying colo(u)rs; **j. in eine unangenehme** ~ **mit hineinziehen** to involve s. o. in a sorry business; **für eine gute** ~ **kämpfen** to fight for a just cause; **in einer** ~ **klarsehen** to see clearly in a matter, to know one's way about; **zur** ~ **kommen** to get down to business (tin tacks, brass tacks, *sl.*), to come to the point (down to cases, *US*), to proceed (get down) to business, to touch ground; ~ **lancieren** to set an undertaking on foot; **sich eine** ~ **angelegen sein lassen** to make it one's business; ~ **laufenlassen** to let things slide; **außerhalb einer** ~ **liegen** to be extrinsic to s. th.; **gemeinsame** ~ **mit jem. machen** to make common cause with s. o., to act in common (join interests) with s. o.; ~ **gegen jem. anhängig machen** to take judicial proceedings against s. o.; **seine** ~ **gut machen** to acquit o. s.; ~ **noch schlimmer machen** to add insult to injury; ~ **in Angriff nehmen** to take on s. th.; **der** ~ **den Reiz nehmen** to take the gilt off the gingerbread; ~ **pressieren** to crowd a matter *(US)*; **die** ~ **schon schaukeln** to turn the cat in the pan; **mit Leib und Seele bei der** ~ **sein** to put one's heart and soul into one's work, to be in it with one's whole heart; **nicht bei der** ~ **sein** to be absent-

minded; **an einer ~ beteiligt sein** to play a part in the business; **einer ~ nicht sicher sein** to be uncertain of s. th.; **einer ~ überdrüssig sein** to be sick of a matter; **in eine unangenehme ~ verwickelt sein** to be mixed up in an unpleasant affair; **einer ~ völlig sicher sein** to be positive about s. th.; **für und wider eine ~ sprechen** to cut both ways; **zur ~ sprechen** to speak (answer) to the point (purpose, matter); **hinter der ganzen ~ stecken** to be at the bottom of a business; **sich wegen einer ~ nicht schlecht stehen** to be none the worse for s. th.; **Kern der ~ treffen** to get to the core; **~ übernehmen** to take charge of a matter; **~ genau untersuchen** to look closely (narrowly) into an affair; **~ verhandeln** to hear (try, sit on, proceed with) a case; **über eine ~ schiedsrichterlich verhandeln** to arbitrate a case; **einer ~ neuen Schwung verleihen** to give fresh impetus to s. th.; **Zeugen zur ~ vernehmen** to question a witness; **sich einer ~ verschreiben** to apply o. s. to a task; **~ mit Substanz versehen** to put meat around the bone; **einer ~ einen schweren Stoß versetzen** to throw a severe jolt into s. th.; **seine ~ verstehen** to know the ropes (a thing or two); **~ vertreten** to uphold a cause, to plead a case, to be in counsel; **~ verweisen** to remit a case; **sich eine ~ vorbehalten** to reserve a th. to o. s.; **~ vorbringen** to state a case; **große ~ vorhaben** to have big plans; **~ flüssig vortragen** to make out one's case; **sich eine ~ unrechtmäßig zueignen** to take and carry away; **auf eine ~ noch einmal zurückkommen** to come back to a matter; **~ zurückweisen** to remand a case; **einer ~ zustimmen** to give one's fiat to s. th.;
das ist Ihre ~ that's your pigeon; **man kann in eigener ~ nicht Richter sein** no man ought to be judge in his own cause.

Sach|eigentum tangible assets (property); **~einlage** contribution in kind, assets in kind brought in.

Sachen things, belongings, effects, chattels, goods, *(Gepäck)* luggage *(Br.)*, baggage *(US)*, *(Möbel)* furniture, stuff;
in ~ A gegen B in re A versus B;
alte ~ junk; **zur Verhandlung anstehende ~** cases on the cause list; **beschlagnahmte ~** attached property; **zum persönlichen Gebrauch bestimmte ~** personal chatters; **bewegliche ~** choses in possession, goods and chattels, choses transistory (transportable); **eigene ~** stuff *(coll.)*; **von Natur aus gefährliche ~** things dangerous in themselves; **gestohlene ~** stolen property; **körperliche ~** corporeal property; **persönliche ~** personal effects; **schöne ~** pretties; **unbestimmte ~** unspecific goods; **unbewegliche ~** things immovable; **unerledigte ~** arrears of work; **unkörperliche ~** intangible property; **unpfändbare ~** nonattachable (mace-proof, *US*, exempt) property; **untergegangene ~** goods destroyed; **verbrauchbare ~** consumption (consumer) goods; **leicht verderbliche ~** perishable goods; **verkehrsfähige ~** marketable goods; **verlorene ~** lost property; **vertretbare ~** fungible things, fungibles;
~ zur Erledigung im Schnellverfahren short causes, summary matters;
verschiedene ~ berücksichtigen to take various points into consideration; **mit 100 ~ um die Ecke brausen** to come round the bend at sixty miles; **sich in fremde ~ einmischen** to meddle in another people's affairs; **sich um seine ~ kümmern** to tend to one's own business; **sich um seine eigenen ~ kümmern** to keep one's own counsel; **keine krummen ~ mehr machen** to go straight; **seine ~ packen** to pack up; **~ zurücknehmen** to take goods back;
~recht law of property *(Br.)*, property *(Br.)* (real) law.

sachenrechtsähnliches Recht an Immobilien equitable state.

Sach|entscheidung decision on the merits; **~entziehung** removal of property; **~erörterung zurückstellen** to postpone consideration of a subject; **~frage** question of merit; **~früchte** natural fruits.

Sachgebiet subject, area, field, province;
spezielles ~ area of specialization;
nach ~en ablegen to file by subject matter; **sich in jds. ~ einmischen** to trespass on s. one's preserves.

Sachgebiets|ablage subject filing, classified file; **~aufteilung** subject heading; **~bezeichnung** subject label.

Sachgegenstand subject matter.

sachgemäß pertinent, appropriate, proper, suitable, reasonable.

Sach|gemäßheit reasonableness; **~gesamtheit** impersonal entity; **~gruppe** category; **~gruppenindex** classified index; **~güter** material goods; **~hehlerei** receiving stolen goods; **~herrschaft** possession; **~inbegriff** aggregate; **~index** subject index; **~information** factual information; **~investition** real investment; **~kapital** fixed (real) capital, permanent assets; **~kapitalbildung** capital investment; **~katalog** subject catalog(ue) (index); **~kenner** competent person, expert, authority, *(Kunstsachverständiger)* connoisseur; **~kenntnis** expert (factual) knowledge; **genaue ~kenntnis** intimate knowledge; **~kontenbuch** impersonal ledger; **~konto** inventory (property, impersonal, *Br.*, furniture and fixtures, nominal, *Br.*) account; **~kosten** material cost (expenses); **~kostenersparnis** saving of material cost; **~kredit** collateral credit; **~kunde** proficiency, expert knowledge, experience; **ausreichende ~kunde** fair knowledge or skill.

sachkundig acquainted with a matter, competent, versed, experienced;
~e Beratung expert guidance.

Sachlage state of affairs, circumstances, surrounding [state of] facts, lie of the land *(Br.)*;
bei dieser ~ under these circumstances; **je nach ~** as the case may be;
~ richtig beurteilen to view the matter in the right light; **~ darlegen** to state the facts; **nach ~ entscheiden** to decide (judge) a case on its merits; **sich mit der ~ vertraut machen** to acquaint o. s. with the facts.

Sachleistung payment (performance, benefit, allowance) in kind, specific performance, store pay *(US)*;
als ~ zahlen to pay in kind.

Sachleistungsvertrag contract for work and labo(u)r service.

sachlich real, actual, material, *(einschlägig)* pertinent, relevant, *(gegenständlich)* factual, technical, *(nüchtern)* businesslike, matter-of-fact, *(objektiv)* objective, *(vorurteilslos)* unprejudiced, unbiassed, impartial, *(wesentlich)* material, essential;
ganz ~ all business, businesslike, no-nonsense, matter-of-fact;
~ bleiben to keep to the point;
~e Ausgaben material cost; **aus ~en Gründen** for technical reasons; **~er Zusammenhang** factual relationship; **~e Zuständigkeit** jurisdiction in rem.

Sachlichkeit reality, functionalism, *(Architektur)* utility, *(Objektivität)* objectivity, *(Unvoreingenommenheit)* impartiality.

Sach|lieferung performance in kind; **~lohn** allowance in kind; **~mangel** defect of quality, redhibitory defect *(US)*; **~mängelausschuß** all faults; **~mängelgewähr, ~mängelhaftung** express warranty, *(für besondere Zwecke)*, warranty of fitness (in the contract of goods, *US*); **~miete** hire; **~mittel** noncash resources; **~nießbrauch** perfect usufruct; **~register** table of contents, subject index; **mit ~register und Anmerkungen versehen** indexed and annotated; **~registerrubrik** index (subject) heading; **~rüge** assignment of error; **~schaden** material (property) damage, damage (injury) to property, actual loss; **versicherter ~schadensgrundbetrag** basic limit for property damage; **~schadensversicherung** property damage liability insurance; **~spende** donation in kind; **~steuern** impersonal taxes; **~urteil** judgment on the merits, judgment on verdict; **~vergütung** allowance (earnings) in kind.

Sachverhalt facts of the case, statement of facts, issue in fact, bearings, circumstances, actual situation;
unter eingehender Darstellung des ~s giving a detailed account of the facts;
Zuständigkeit begründender ~ jurisdictional facts; **im Urteil festgestellter ~** findings of the facts; **glaubhaft gemachter ~** prime facie case; **für den Beklagten sprechender ~** case for the defendant; **unstreitiger ~** case agreed on; **unwesentlicher ~** immaterial facts; **vorstehender ~** foregoing facts; **wahrer ~** true bearing;
ganzen ~ anschneiden to raise the whole issue; **dem wahren ~ ausweichen** to beg the question; **wahren ~ kennen** to know the rights of a case; **jem. den ~ im einzelnen vortragen** to lay before s. o. all the facts of a case.

Sachverhaltsdarstellung stating part of a bill, premises.

Sach|vermögen tangible property (assets), tangibles; **bewegliches ~vermögen** movables, movable property; **~versicherung** insurance of property, property insurance, general business *(Br.)*.

Sachversicherungs|aktien property insurance stocks; **~geschäft** general business *(Br.)*; **~markt** property insurance market.

sachverständig competent, expert, prudential;
~e Beratung expert advice; **~er Schätzer bei Zollwertfestsetzungen** merchant appraiser; **~e Zeugenaussage** expert evidence.

Sachverständige|r expert, authority, competent judge (party, person), specialist, *(Versicherung)* surveyor;
nach Ansicht der ~n according to [the opinion of] the experts;
nach dem Urteil des ~n according to expert advice;
amtlicher ~r official referee; **beeidigter ~r** expert, sworn appraiser; **amtlich bestellter ~r** qualified expert; **gerichtlich bestellter ~r** expert appointed by the court; **nüchtern denkender**

~r no-nonsense expert; **halber ~r** quasi expert; **juristischer ~r** legal expert; **kaufmännischer ~r** appraiser; **landwirtschaftlicher ~r** agricultural expert;
~r in Fragen der Leistungskontrolle efficiency expert *(US)*; **~r für Schiffahrtsfragen** nautical assessor *(Br.)*; **~r des Wirtschaftsministeriums** Commerce-Department expert;
sich als ~n ausgeben to pose (set up, represent o. s.) as an expert, to claim to be an expert; **~n beiziehen (zuziehen)** to call in (consult) an expert; **~n bestimmen** to appoint an expert; **als ~r fungieren** to [serve as an] expert; **~r für etw. sein** to be an expert in a matter.

Sachverständigen | aussage expert testimony; **~ausschuß, ~beirat** committee (panel) of experts; **~beirat für Steuerveranlagungen** board of referees *(Br.)*; **~bericht** expert opinion, surveyor's report; **~beweis** expert evidence; **medizinischer ~beweis** medical evidence; **~eigenschaft** expert capacity; **~entscheidung** expert advice, reference; **~gebühren** expert's fees; **~gremium** expert committee, committee (panel) of experts; **~gruppe** expert group, panel of experts.

Sachverständigengutachten expert opinion (evidence), expertise, referee's report;
übereinstimmende ~ concurrent views of several experts; **widerstreitende ~** conflicting views of several experts; **gerichtlich ein ~ veranlassen** to have goods officially surveyed by order of the court.

Sachverständigen | honorar professional (expert's) fee; **~konferenz** meeting of experts; **~kosten** cost of appraisal; **~rat** board (panel) of experts; **~untersuchung** expert inquiry; **~urteil** expert advice, reference; **~vergütung** expert's fee.

Sach | verweis subject reference; **~verzeichnis** subject index, table of contents, *(Inventar)* inventory.

Sachvortrag stated matter, statement of a case, argument, averment, *(Kläger)* allegation of fact, recital, opening, *(Verleumdungsklage)* colloquium;
erster ~ first pleading, complaint; **neuer ~** new matter; **gegnerischen ~ anerkennen** to give colo(u)r.

Sachwalter agent, procurator, mandatary, receiver, proctor, *(Anwalt)* private attorney, attorney [in fact], counsel, *(Treuhänder)* trustee, *(Verwalter)* administrator;
sich zum ~ für etw. machen to act as advocate for s. th.

Sachwert commodity (real) value;
~e tangible (material) assets, physical resources; **persönliche ~e** personal effects;
~anleihe loan on collateral securities; **~dividende** property (commodity, *US*) dividend.

sachwertgesichert secured by mortgage.

Sach | wertklausel escalator clause; **~wort** appellative; **~wörterbuch** technical (specialized) dictionary, encyclopaedia; **~zusammenhang** connexity of facts; **~zuwendung** payment in kind.

Sack sack, bag;
in ~ und Asche in dust and ashes; **inklusive ~** sack included; **mit ~ und Pack** lock, stock and barrel, bag and baggage, neck and crop; **~ voller Neuigkeiten** a budget of news;
wie ein nasser ~ dastehen to cut a sorry figure; **etw. im ~ haben** to have it in the bag *(sl.)*; **Katze im ~ kaufen** to buy a pig in a poke; **Katze aus dem ~ lassen** to let the cat out of the bag; **wie ein ~ schlafen** to sleep like a top; **voll wie ein nasser ~ sein** to be drunk as a lord; **j. in den ~ stecken** to nonplus (get the better of) s. o.; **in ~ und Asche trauern** to mourn in sackcloth and ashes;
~bahnhof terminus *(Br.)*, terminal *(US)*.

sacken *(Gebäude)* to sag, to subside, to sink.

Sackgasse blind alley, dead end (street), no through road, cul-de-sac, impasse, *(fig.)* stalemate, deadlock;
berufliche ~ blind-alley job;
Ausweg aus einer ~ finden to find a way out of a deadlock; **in eine ~ geraten** to come to a dead end, *(fig.)* to reach a deadlock; **beruflich in eine ~ geraten** to be at a dead end in one's job; **jem. in eine ~ treiben** to corner s. o.

Sack | gut bag cargo; **~landung** pancake (stalled) landing; **~leinwand** sackcloth, *(grobe)* hop sacking; **~träger** sack carrier.

säen to sow, to seed;
Haß ~ to sow the seed of hatred.

Safe safe, safe deposit [box], strongbox, peter *(sl.)*;
feuer- und diebessicherer ~ fire and burglar-resisting safe;
~ aufbrechen to break open a safe; **~ knacken** *(sl.)* to pop a peter; **~ mieten** to rent a safe (safe-deposit box);
~aufbewahrung safe custody, safekeeping, safe-deposit keeping *(US)*; **~einrichtungen** safe-deposit facilities *(US)*; **~gebühr** safe-custody fee; **~klausel** iron-safe clause; **~knacker** safebreaker, safeblower, safecracker; **~kombination** combination used to open a safe; **~miete** hire of a safe, safe hiring.

Saft juice, sap, *(Benzin)* sauce *(sl.)*;
~ einer Zitrone auspressen to press the juice out of a lemon; **jem. im eigenen ~ schmoren lassen** to let s. o. stew in his own juice; **ohne ~ und Kraft sein** to be sapless, to lack energy.

saftig mellow, juicy, succulent;
~er Brief strongly worded letter; **~e Forderung** steep demand; **~es Grün** lush green; **~e Ohrfeige** resounding box (cuff) on the ear; **~e Rechnung** stiff (swinging) bill; **~er Witz** spicy joke.

Saftladen sheebang *(US sl.)*.

Sage legend, myth.

Sagen haben, das to be top dog.

sagen to say, to state, to express, to make known;
jem. geradeheraus ~ to tell s. o. straight out; **jem. Grobheiten ~** to make rude remarks to s. o.; **etw. vor sich hin ~** to mumble to o. s.; **seine Meinung ~** to say (speak) one's mind; **jem. etw. ins Ohr ~** to whisper s. th. in s. one's ear; **die reine Wahrheit ~** to tell the plain truth;
~ wie es ist to call a spade a spade;
mehr zu ~ haben to gain a greater say; **nichts zu ~ haben** to be nobody; **wenig zu ~ haben** to play second fiddle.

sagenhaft legendary, mythological, fabulous;
~e Geldbeträge ausgeben to spend incredible sums of money;
~er Reichtum fabulous wealth.

Sagenschatz legend, legendry.

Sägewerk saw mill, lumbermill *(US)*.

Saison season;
außerhalb der ~ in the off-season; **für die ~ passend** seasonable; **fortgeschrittene ~** advance of the season; **kommende ~** opening season; **stille (tote) ~** dead (dull) season, off-season, slack period;
sich für die ~ verpflichten to engage o. s. for the season.

saisonabhängig seasonal.

Saisonabschlag seasonal deduction.

saisonal | bedingt sein to be due to seasonal factors;
~e Faktoren seasonal factors.

Saison | anforderungen seasonal pressure; **~arbeiter** seasonal labo(u)r (worker), itinerant worker; **landwirtschaftlicher ~arbeiter** itinerant agricultural worker; **~arbeitslosigkeit** seasonal unemployment; **~artikel** seasonal goods (articles, commodities, items); **~aufschlag** seasonal price increase; **~aufschwung** seasonal upswing (upturn); **~ausgleich** seasonal adjustment; **~auslage** seasonal display; **~bedarf** seasonal consumption (supply).

saisonbedingt seasoned, seasonal, seasonally, on seasonal grounds;
~e Absatzmulde seasonal trough; **~er Anstieg** seasonal upswing (upturn); **~e Arbeit** seasonality of work; **~e Arbeitslosigkeit** seasonal unemployment; **~er Bedarf** seasonal demand; **~e Belieferung** seasonal supply; **~e Entlassungen** seasonal layoffs; **~er Geldbedarf** seasonal demand for cash; **~er Geschäftsrückgang** seasonal slump; **~e Gewerbe** seasonal industries; **~er Konjunkturaufschwung** seasonal upward trend; **~e Nichtbeachtung von Tarifbestimmungen** seasonal tolerance; **~e Produktionstätigkeit** seasonal production; **~e Schwankungen** seasonal fluctuations; **~er Tarif** seasonable rate, *(el.)* seasonal tariff *(Br.)*; **~e Tendenz** seasonal trend; **~es Tief** seasonal low.

Saisonbedingtheit seasonality, seasonal nature.

Saisonbedürfnisse seasonal requirements (demands).

saisonbereinigt, saisonberichtigt adjusted to seasonal variations, seasonally adjusted;
~e Größe deseasonalized item.

Saison | beruf seasonal occupation; **~beschäftigung** seasonal employment; **~betriebe** seasonal enterprises; **~einflüsse** seasonal influences; **~entlassungen** seasonal layoffs; **~eröffnung** commencement of the season; **~erzeugnisse** seasonal goods (products).

saison | gebundener Verbrauch seasonal consumption; **~gemäß** seasonal.

Saison | geschäft seasonal trade (business), *(einzelnes)* [early-] season business; **~gesellschaft** seasonal corporation; **~gewerbe** seasonal trade; **~industrie** seasonal industry; **~kredit** seasonal loan (advance).

saisonmäßig seasonal.

Saison | produktion seasonal production; **~rabatt** seasonal allowance; **~sätze** seasonal rates; **~schlußverkauf** seasonal closing-out *(Br.)* (end-of-season, seasonal clearance, *US*) sale; **~schwankungen** seasonal fluctuations (variations); **~spitze** seasonal booster; **~tarif** *(für bestimmte Waren)* seasonable rate; **~tendenz** seasonal trend; **~tief** seasonal low.

saisonüblich seasonal.

Saison|verbrauch seasonal consumption; ~**verkauf** seasonal sale; ~**wanderung** seasonal migration; ~**werbung** seasonal advertising; ~**werte** season's stocks.
Saite string, chord;
richtige ~ **anschlagen** to touch the right chord; **strengere** ~**n aufziehen** to change one's tune.
Sakkoanzug lounge suit.
Sakrileg begehen to commit a sacrilege.
säkularisieren to secularize.
Säkularisierung secularization.
Salär salary.
Salat, ganzen ~ **satt haben** to be fed up with the whole show.
Salbaderei slobber.
salbadern to slobber a bibful *(sl.)*.
Salden|abstimmung balance reconciliation; ~**abtretung eines Kundenkontos** assignment of a customer's credit balance; ~**anerkenntnis** reconciliation statement; ~**auszug bestätigen** to verify a statement; ~**bestätigung** verification statement; ~**bilanz** trial (rough) balance; ~**liste** balance ledger; ~**spalte** residual column; **durchschnittlicher** ~**stand der Kundschaft** average customer balance in a year; ~**verrechnung** clearing-house settlement.
Saldierbuch balance book.
saldieren to balance, to square, to settle, *(aufrechnen)* to set off *(Br.)*, to offset *(US)*, *(Bank)* to net out, *(Girozentrale)* to clear;
Konto ~ to balance (liquidate) an account.
saldiert [counter-]balanced, settled.
Saldierung striking of a balance, balancing, settlement.
Saldo balance, *(Rest)* remainder;
per ~ in full, on balance;
aufgestellter ~ balance struck; **beglichener** ~ account settled; **berichtigter** ~ adjusted balance; **debitorischer** ~ debit balance; **derzeitiger** ~ current balance; **effektiver** ~ actual balance; **fälliger** ~ account payable; **der Höhe nach feststehender** ~ liquidated account; **kassenmäßiger** ~ cash balance; **kreditorischer** ~ credit balance; **täglicher** ~ daily balance; **ungedeckter** ~ uncovered balance; **ungenutzter** ~ dormant balance; **verfügbarer** ~ available (disposable) balance; **vorgetragener** ~ balance carried forward, carry-forward;
~ **zu Ihren Gunsten** your credit balance, balance in your favo(u)r; ~ **der Kapitalbilanz** balance of capital transactions; ~ **zu Ihren Lasten** your debit balance; ~ **nicht erfaßbarer Posten und Fehler** errors and omissions; ~ **aus letzter Rechnung** balance brought forward from last account; ~ **auf neue Rechnung** balance carried forward; ~ **der Transferzahlungen** net current transactions;
~ **anerkennen** to accept a statement of account; ~ **aufstellen** to strike a balance; ~ **aufweisen** to show (turn out) a balance; ~ **von 100 Dollar zu Ihren Gunsten aufweisen** to present a balance of $ 100 to your credit; ~ **von 100 Dollar zu Ihren Lasten aufweisen** to leave (present) a balance of $ 100 to your debit; ~ **ausgleichen** to balance an account, to settle (clear) a balance, to make up the even money; ~ **auszahlen** to pay over the balance; ~ **festhalten** to strike a balance; **jem. einen** ~ **gutschreiben** to balance in favo(u)r of s. o.; **per** ~ **quittieren** to receipt (give receipt) in full; ~ **remittieren** to remit in full; **per** ~ **trassieren** to draw per appoint; ~ **übertragen** to extend a balance; ~ **von 100 £ übertragen** to cover the balance of £ 100; ~ **eines Kontos auf ein anderes übertragen** to close the balance of an account into another account; ~ **überweisen** to remit the balance; ~ **vergleichen** to ascertain a balance; ~ **vortragen** to carry over (forward) a balance; ~ **auf neue Rechnung vortragen** to carry a balance forward to new account; ~ **ziehen** to [strike a] balance, to cast accounts;
~**abdeckung** payment of a balance; ~**anerkennung** account stated; ~**anschaffung** remittance [for the amount payable]; ~**ausgleich** settlement of an (payment per) account; ~**auszug** balance, extract (statement) of account; ~**barabdeckung** remittance in cash; ~**betrag** [amount of] balance; ~**bilanz** net balance; ~**guthaben** balance in favo(u)r (carried down), credit balance, amount carried forward; ~**rest** remainder, residue; ~**rimesse** remittance per account; ~**schuld** balance due; ~**übertrag**, ~**vortrag** balance brought (carried) forward, balance of former (passed to new) account, carryforward; ~**wechsel** balance bill, appoint; ~**zahlung** payment per (settlement of) account.
Salon salon, drawing room, parlor *(US)*, *(Schiff)* saloon, *(Schönheitssalon)* beauty shop (parlor, *US*);
~**bolschewist** parlo(u)r radial, drawing-room bolshevist *(Br.)*, parlor Red *(US)*, pink *(US sl.)*; ~**dampfer** saloon steamer; ~**deck** saloon deck.
salonfähig reputable, respectable;
nicht ~ *(Witz)* blue, risqué, off-colo(u)r.
Salon|löwe parlo(u)r snake *(sl.)*, tea-hound *(coll.)*, big-time operator *(sl.)*, carpet knight, squire of dames, cookiepusher *(US)*, lounge lizard *(Br.)*, socialite *(US)*; ~**stück** *(Theater)* drawing-room drama; ~**wagen** drawing-room car, saloon carriage *(Br.)* (car, *US*), club car *(US)*, state (pullman, *US*, palace, chair, parlor, *US*) car.
salopp casual, slipshod, sloppy;
~ **gekleidet** casually dressed.
Salto somersault, tumble, flip.
salutieren to salute.
Salutschießen salute.
Salve volley, salvo, *(Schiff)* broadside;
~ **abgeben** to deliver a broadside.
salvieren to get off without a loss.
Salzsteuer salt duty.
Samariterkrankenhaus charitable hospital.
Sammelabrechnungen im Sinne des Steuerrechts periodic clearing in accordance with tax regulations.
Sammelaktion drive [to raise funds], fund-raising activity, purse;
~ **für Altmaterial** salvage campaign; **große** ~ **zugunsten der Blinden** drive to raise money for the blind;
~ **starten** to launch a fund-raising drive, to launch an appeal, to pass the hat round, to put up a drive (purse); **große** ~ **für 5000 Dollar unternehmen** to make a great drive to raise $ 5000.
Sammel|album scrapbook; ~**analyse** clustering analysis, ~**anschluß** *(gemeinsames Telefon)* party line, collective number *(US)*, *(Zentrale)* private branch exchange; ~**anzeige** composite advertisement; ~**aufgabe** *(Versicherung)* bordereau; ~**aufgabeformular** *(Bankwesen)* listing form; ~**aufwendung** collective expenditure; ~**auskunftsbuch** rating book; ~**auslieferung** consolidated delivery system; ~**ausweis** collective permit; ~**ballen** *(Buchhandel)* collective pack; ~**band** omnibus volume; ~**becken** catchment basin, reservoir; ~**becken für radikale Elemente** reservoir for radical elements; ~**begriff** generic term, collective name; ~**bestand** total orders on hand; ~**bestellung** omnibus order; ~**bezeichnung** collective title (name); ~**bezirk** collecting zone; ~**bogen** combination sheet, *(Materialausgaben, Löhne)* recapitulation sheet; ~**buch** scrapbook; ~**büchse** collection (money) box; **mit der** ~**büchse klappern** to rattle the begging bowl; ~**buchung** compound journal entry; ~**depot** collective (general) deposit, custody held in joint names (for joint deposition), *(Versicherung)* corporate bonding; ~**druck** *(Werbung)* combination run; ~**einbürgerung** group naturalization; ~**einkauf** group (collective) buying; ~**fahrschein** party (block, collective) ticket; ~**ferienreise** group-rate travel; ~**fonds** fund pool; ~**form** *(drucktechn.)* gang; ~**formel** collective formula; ~**fracht** general commodity shipment, carload freight *(US)*; ~**frachtbrief** collective consignment note; ~**frachtsatz** general commodity rate, mixed carload rate *(US)*; ~**garage** open garage; ~**gebiet** catchment area, *(Geldsammler)* collecting zone; ~**gesetz** hodge-podge act; ~**gespräch** *(tel.)* conference call; ~**gesprächsschaltung** conference call hookup; ~**girokonto** omnibus deposit account; ~**graben** drainage canal.
Sammelgut mixed consignment, miscellaneous goods, general commodities, packed parcels;
~**ladung** general commodity shipment, consolidated carload freight *(US)*; ~**transport** general commodities trucking, carload loadings *(US)*; ~**verkehr** collective traffic.
Sammel|heizung district heating system; ~**journal** general journal; ~**kabel** coaxial cable; ~**karte** *(Bahn)* party ticket; ~**kasse** consolidated cashier; ~**käufe** bulk buying; ~**klausel** omnibus clause, *(Tarifwesen)* dragnet clause; ~**konnossement** omnibus (grouped, consolidated, collective) bill of lading; ~**konto** omnibus *(Br.)* (summary, summarizing) account; ~**ladung** mixed (general) cargo (commodity, collective, composite) shipment, collective consignment, truckload, [mixed (consolidated)] carload freight *(US)*, mixed consignment, aggregated (consolidated, *Br.*, pooled) shipment *(US)*; ~**ladung zusammenstellen** to assort collective consignments, to consolidate shipments *(US)*.
Sammelladungs|spedition pool car service; ~**tarif** general commodity rate, mixed carload rate *(US)*; ~**tarif zur Anwendung bringen** to handle a shipment as a carload *(US)*; ~**verkehr** grouped traffic; **vom unrentierlichen** ~**verkehr abgehen** to pull out of unprofitable wag(g)onload service.
Sammel|lager general depot, collecting point *(US)*, *(Flüchtlinge)* refugee camp; ~**lagerung** collective storage; ~**lebensversicherung** group life insurance; ~**leitung** *(el.)* omnibus wire; ~**liste** subscription list; ~**mappe** file, folder, looseleaf booklet.

Sammeln collection, *(Anhäufung)* accumulation, amassment; ~ **von Antiquitäten** curio hunting; ~ **zerstreuter Truppen** reassembly of scattered troops;
zum ~ blasen to sound the recall;
in diesem Haus ist ~ nicht gestattet no solicitors allowed in this building.

sammeln to collect, to hive, *(Geld)* to gather (raise) a subscription (funds), to raise for collection, *(horten)* to stock, to hoard, to accumulate, to pile up, *(Stimmen)* to canvass, to muster;
sich ~ to gather, to assemble, to troop up, *(fig.)* to concentrate, to collect one's thoughts, *(Lichtstrahlen)* to focus; **sich um j.** ~ to cluster (gather) round s. o.; **für j.** ~ to pass the hat round (make a purse) for s. o.; **Antiquitäten** ~ to collect curios; **für die Armen** ~ to collect for the poor; **Aufträge** ~ to solicit orders; **Auskünfte** ~ to check up on information; **Erfahrungen** ~ to gain experience; **Geld für wohltätige Zwecke** ~ to canvass in *(US)* (on, *Br.*) behalf of charity; **Inserate** ~ to canvass advertisements; **seine Kräfte** ~ to rally one's strength; **leidenschaftlich** ~ to be a passionate collector; **sich vor dem Rathaus** ~ to meet in front of the townhall; **Reichtümer** ~ to amass great riches, to hoard (heap) up treasures; **Stimmen** ~ to canvass votes; **Stoff für einen neuen Roman** ~ to gather material for a new novel; **zerstreute Truppen wieder** ~ to rally scattered troops; **Wörter** ~ to compile words.

Sammel|name collective name; **~nummer** *(Telefon)* party line, collective call (number, *US*), multiple telephone number *(US)*; **~objekt** collector's item; **~paket** package parcel; **~partei** omnibus party; **~paß** collective passport; **~plakat** collective advertising sign; **~platz** rallying point, meeting place, *(Güter)* collecting point *(US)*, depot; **~police** group (package) policy, *(Firmenfahrzeug)* fleet policy; **~posten** compound item, *(mil.)* alarm post; **~prozeß** class action; **~punkt** rallying (collecting) point; **~revers** *(Buchhandel)* collective undertaking; **~rückstellung** general contingent reserve; **~ruf** *(mil.)* assembly; **~rufzeichen** collective call; **~schaltung** *(el.)* omnibus circuit; **~schau** collective show; **~schiene** bus bar, omnibus bar; **~schuldverschreibungen** general mortgage bonds; **~schutzraum** airraid shelter; **~sendung** collective consignment (shipment, *US*), combined items, commodities trucking, carload loadings *(US)*; **~spediteur** keypoint operator; **~stelle** *(mil.)* depot, collecting point *(US)*, *(für Geldspenden)* fund-raising booth; **~stelle für Beutegut** collecting point for captured goods; **~stimme** block vote; **~stück** collector's item; **~surium** kit, hodgepodge, hotchpotch, medley; **~tag für wohltätige Zwecke** flag day *(Br.)*; **~tarif** joint tariff, group (mixed, carload, *US*) rate, *(Fernverkehr)* blanket (class, group) rate; **kombinierter ~tarif** joint combination rate; **~tarifreise** group-rate travel; **~tasse** fancy cup; **~tätigkeit** collectorship, fund-raising activity (efforts); **~transport** collective transport, full truckload shipment *(US)*, carloading *(US)*; **~überschrift** general heading; **~überweisung** summary transfer, collective remittance; **~unfallversicherung** group disability insurance; **~urkunde** certificate of stock *(US)*, stock certificate *(US)*, collective deed; **~verladung** block loading; **~vermessung** block of survey; **~versicherung** group (collective, global) insurance, *(Kfz)* fleet insurance; **~versicherungsvertrag** master group contract; **~verwahrung** general (collective) deposit; **~visum** collective visa; **kurzer ~werbefilm** budget film *(Br.)*; **~werk** compilation, contributed work; **~wert** assemblage value, *(gr.)* collective; **~wertberichtigung** global value adjustment, overall adjustment; **~wut** rage for collecting things; **~zahlungsauftrag** combined payment orders.

Sammler collector, gatherer, picker-up, *(el.)* storage (accumulator) battery, *(drucktechn.)* carrier, *(Geld)* fund raiser, collector;
~ausgabe *(philat.)* speculative issue; **~ausweis** collecting card; **~batterie** storage battery (accumulator); **~eldorado** happy hunting ground for collectors; **~ladegerät** battery charger; **~stück** collector's piece.

Sammlung gathering, collecting, *(Auslese)* selection, digest, *(Gedichte)* anthology, *(Geld)* collection, subscription, fund-raising, drive to raise a fund, purse, whip-round *(Br., coll.)*, *(Hortung)* accumulation, hoarding, *(Kunstgegenstände)* collection, *(Sammelband)* miscellany, *(Zusammenstellung)* compilation;
im Wege einer öffentlichen ~ by public subscription;
grafische ~ *(Museum)* print room; **zweckbestimmte ~** collection in aid of an undertaking;
~ **höchstrichterlicher Entscheidungen** summary of leading cases and decisions; ~ **vermischter Gegenstände** miscellanea; ~ **von Gerichtsentscheidungen** table of cases, law reports; ~ **von Gesetzen und Verordnungen** compiled statutes; ~ **von Inseraten** canvassing of advertisements; ~ **von Vorschriften** body of regulations; ~ **für wohltätige Zwecke** collection (gathering of money) for charitable purposes, charity collection;
~ **ins Leben rufen** to get up a subscription; ~ **veranstalten** to start a fund, to raise a collection, to put up a drive (purse), to pass the hat round; **seine ~ vervollständigen** to make up the missing number [of a publication].

Samstag, langer late-closing Saturday.

Samt velvet, pile;
j. mit ~handschuhen anfassen to hand s. o. with velvet gloves.

sämtlich all and singular;
~e Anwesende all people present.

Samt|methode velvet-glove approach, kid-glove method; **~papier** velvet paper; **~stickerei** velvetwork; **~stoff** pile fabric; **~tapete** flock paper.

Sanatorium sanatorium, sanitarium *(US)*, convalescent home (hospital).

Sand, auf ~ gebaut built on sand; **wie ~ am Meer** as thick as peas; ~ **im Getriebe** grit in the machinery;
auf ~ bauen *(fig.)* to build on sand; **Schulden wie ~ am Meer haben** to be head over heels in debt; **auf ~ laufen** *(Schiff)* to run aground, to strike the sand; **j. auf den ~ setzen** to nonplus s. o.; **auf dem ~ sitzen** to be at the end of one's tether; **jem. ~ in die Augen streuen** to throw dust in one's eyes, to pull the wool over s. one's eyes; ~ **ins Getriebe streuen** to throw sand (a monkey wrench, spanner) into the works; **im ~e verlaufen** *(Fluß)* to peter out in the sand, *(fig.)* to fizzle out, to come to (end in) nothing, to go up in smoke;
wer Gott vertraut hat nicht auf ~ gebaut god provides for him that trusteth;
~bank port bar; **auf eine ~bank geraten** to strike the sands; **~grube** sandpit; **~hose** sand spout, dust devil, twister *(coll., US)*; **~kasten** *(mil.)* sand table; **~papier** sandpaper, abrasive (emery) paper; **~sack** sandbag; **~strahlgebläse** sandblast unit; **~strand** sandy beach; **~sturm** dust storm; **~uhr** *(mar.)* hourglas, watchglass; **~verwehung** sand drift; **ungeheure ~wüste** vast wilderness (desert) of sand.

sanft soft, gentle, mild, meek;
~ **und selig schlafen** to sleep blissfully;
~e Brise gentle breeze; **~en Druck ausüben** to apply gentle pressure; **ein gutes Gewissen ist ein ~es Ruhekissen** a quiet conscience sleeps in thunder; **~er Tadel** gentle rebuke; **etw. auf die ~e Tour versuchen** to try the soft sell.

Sang und Klang, mit ~ durchfallen to be plucked.

sang- und klanglos without much ado;
~ **abziehen** to sneak off; ~ **verschwinden** to disappear unceremoniously.

sanieren to reorganize, to reconstruct *(Br.)*, to refloat, to rehabilitate, *(Stadtbezirke)* to redevelop;
j. ~ to put s. one's finances on a healthy basis; **sich** ~ to reestablish one's affairs, to line one's pockets, to clean up *(sl.)*; **Elendsgebiete** ~ to clear (redevelop) slums, to upgrade slum housing; **durcheinandergeratenen Etat** ~ to set up the budget on its feet again; **Finanzen einer Gesellschaft** ~ to rehabilitate a company financially, to reconstruct *(Br.)* (reorganize) a company; **Industriezweig nach kaufmännischen Gesichtspunkten** ~ to reorganize an industry on commercial lines; **Konto versuchsweise** ~ to nurse an account *(Br.)*; **Land wirtschaftlich** ~ to put a country economically on its feet again; **ganze Stadtteile** ~ to improve whole sections of a town; **Währung** ~ to restore (re-establish) a currency.

Sanierung reconstruction *(Br.)*, reorganization, reorganizing, debt readjustment, financial recovery, re-establishment, rescue, *(Regionalplanung)* renewal *(Br.)*, rehabilitation;
finanzielle ~ reorganization of finances; **steuerfreie** ~ tax-free reorganization;
~ **von Elendsgebieten** clearing (redevelopment) of slums, upgrading of slum housing, slum clearance; ~ **einer Firma (Gesellschaft)** reorganization of a company (corporation), company reorganization *(Br.)*, refloating of a company, reconstruction of a company *(Br.)*; **versuchsweise ~ eines Kontos** nursing an account *(Br.)*; **allgemeine ~ ganzer Stadtteile** general improvement of whole sections; ~ **der Währung** restoration (re-establishment) of the currency, monetary rehabilitation;
~ **durchlaufen** to pass through a reorganization.

Sanierungs|aktion, einer ~aktion Rückenwind (Rückendeckung) geben to back a rescue; **umfassendes (gekoppeltes) ~angebot** rescue package; **~ausschuß** *(Gläubiger)* reorganization committee; **~bericht** reorganization report; **~bezirk** Improvement

Act District *(Br.)*; ~**darlehen** reorganization (reconstruction, *Br.*) credit; ~**feldzug** slum-clearance campaign; ~**fonds** reorganization fund; ~**gebiet** [slum-]clearance (inner, improvement, *Br.*) area; **für Hausmodernisierungen bestimmtes** ~**gebiet** general improvement area *(Br.)*; **städtische** ~**gebiete** redevelopment areas; **industrielle** ~**gebiete schaffen** to set up industrial improvement areas; ~**gewinn** rehabilitation gain; ~**konto** reorganization account; ~**kredit** reorganization credit, reconstruction credit *(Br.)*; ~**maßnahmen** reconstruction (austerity, reorganization) measures, organizational realignment, *(Stadt)* urban renewal; ~**phase durchlaufen** to pass through a reorganization; ~**plan** plan of readjustment (reorganization), reorganization (rehabilitation) plan, *(Stadtbezirke)* redevelopment (improvement, slum-clearance) plan; ~**programm** reorganization (reconstruction, *Br.*) program(me), *(Staat)* austerity (civil reorganization) program(me); **staatliches** ~**programm durchführen** to put the finances of a country on a healthy footing; ~**prospekt** reorganization prospect; ~**schuldverschreibungen** reorganization bonds; ~**spezialisten** reorganization bar *(US)*; ~**umgründung** reconstruction and reorganization, company reorganization, company reconstruction *(Br.)*; **Vergleichs- und** ~**verfahren** reorganization proceedings *(US)*; **Vergleichs- und** ~**verfahren durchführen** to reorganize under chapter X *(US)*; **Antrag auf ein Vergleichs- und** ~**verfahren stellen** to file a petition for reorganization under chapter X *(US)*; ~**viertel** [slum-]clearance (inner, improvement, *Br.*) area; ~**vorschlag** reconstruction proposal; ~**zeitraum** readjustment phase.

sanitär sanitary, hygienic;
~**e Anlagen** hygienic facilities; ~**e Bedingungen** sanitary conditions; ~**e Einrichtungen** sanitary installations (arrangements); ~**e Mängel** sanitary deficiencies; ~**e Maßnahmen** sanitary measures; ~**e Maßnahmen treffen** to sanitate; ~**e Verhältnisse** hygienic conditions.

Sanitäter ambulance man, sanitarian, *(mil.)* aid man, orderly, corpsman.

Sanitäts|abteilung hospital battalion *(mil.)*; ~**auto** ambulance; ~**behörde** Board of Health *(US)*, public health authority *(Br.)*; ~**dienst** sanitary engineering; ~**fahrzeug** ambulance; ~**flugzeug** ambulance plane, air ambulance, medical aircraft; ~**hund** ambulance dog; ~**kolonne** fleet of ambulances, sanitary squad; ~**kompanie** *(mil.)* bearing (clearing) company; ~**korps**, ~**truppe** Royal Army Medical Corps *(Br.)*; ~**material** medical stores; ~**soldat** hospital orderly *(mil.)*; ~**tasche** first-aid kit; ~**trupp** sanitary squad; ~**wache** first-aid post, ambulance station; ~**wagen** ambulance; ~**wesen** sanitary affairs; ~**zelt** hospital tent.

Sanktionen sanctions, *(Kartellgesetz)* remedies *(US)*;
wirtschaftliche ~ economic sanctions;
~ **auferlegen** to impose sanctions; ~ **zur Anwendung bringen** to apply sanctions; ~ **erlassen** to put sanctions into motion; ~ **fallenlassen** to recede from sanctions; ~ **gegen einen Angreiferstaat verhängen** to apply sanctions against an aggressor.

sanktionieren to sanction, to approve, to countersign.

sanktioniert, durch langen Gebrauch authorized (sanctioned) by usage.

Sanktionierung eines Brauchs sanction by usage.

Sanktions|bestimmungen sanctions; ~**bestimmungen eines Gesetzes** vindicatory parts of a law; ~**gebiet** territory affected by sanctions; ~**maßnahmen** sanctions, peaceful pressure; ~**maßnahmen nur zögernd einleiten** to move slowly on sanctions; ~**maßnahmen in Gang setzen** to put sanctions into action; ~**umgehung** evasion of sanctions.

Saphirstift stylus.

Sarg coffin, burial case;
hinter jds. ~ **hergehen** to pay the last hono(u)rs to s. o.; **Toten in den** ~ **legen** to coffin a body;
jds. ~**nagel sein** to drive a nail into s. one's coffin, to be the death of s. o. *(coll.)*; ~**träger** pallbearer, bearer; ~**tuch** pall.

Sarkasmus, beißender keen sarcasm.

sarkastisch, j. leicht ~ **behandeln** to have a light dig at s. o.;
~**e Bemerkung** dig, cutting remark.

Satellit, feststehender stationary satellite;
~**en abschießen** to launch a satellite.

Satelliten|abschuß satellite launching; ~**fernmeldegesellschaft** communication satellite corporation; ~**fernmeldesystem** satellite telecommunication system; ~**fernsehen** satellite television; ~**kanal** satellite channel; ~**kopfstation** satellite terminal; ~**nachrichtenübermittlung** satellite communication; ~**nachrichtenwesen** satellite communication system; ~**projekt** satellite project; ~**regime** *(pol.)* satellite regime; ~**rundfunk** satellite broadcasting; ~**sender** satellite relay; ~**staat** satellite state; ~**stadt** satellite suburb (township); ~**station** satellite station; ~**system** satellite system; ~**übertragung** satellite transmission; ~**verbindungen** satellite communications; ~**verteilungssystem** satellite distribution system.

Satinieren glazing, pressing.

satinieren *(Papier)* to calender, to glaze.

satiniertes Papier calendered (imitation art) paper.

Satinpapier glazed paper.

satt satisfied, replete, full, *(Farbe)* vivid, *(großartig)* smashing, gorgeous, *(selbstzufrieden)* complacent;
etw. ~ **bekommen** to get fed up with s. th.; **sich** ~ **essen** to eat one's fill; **eine Sache** ~ **haben** to be sick and tired of s. th., to be cheesed off;
~**es Bürgertum** sated bourgeoisie; **mit** ~**em Lächeln** with a complacent smile.

Sattel, sich im ~ **halten** to stay in the saddle; **j. in den** ~ **heben** *(fig.)* to launch s. o.; **j. in den** ~ **helfen** *(fam.)* to give s. o. a leg up; **fest im** ~ **sitzen** to be firmly in office (in the saddle);
~**dach** span roof.

sattelfest in etw. sein to be well up (versed) in a subject, to know the ropes *(sl.)*.

Sätteln, in allen ~ **gerecht sein** to be an allround man.

Sattel|schlepper semitrailer; ~**trunk** stirrup cup.

sättigen *(Markt)* to saturate, to satiate, *(überschwemmen)* to glut.

sättigend satiating, substantial.

Sättigung saturation, satiation;
~ **des Inlandmarktes** saturation of the home market.

Sättigungs|grad degree of saturation; ~**grad des Verbrauchs** margin of consumption; ~**koeffizient** saturation coefficient; ~**punkt** *(Markt)* absorption (saturation) point.

sattsam bekannte Tatsache well-known fact.

saturieren to saturate, to satisfy.

Satz jump, leap, bound, *(Betrag)* amount, rate, *(Dokumente)* set, file, *(drucktechn.)* setting, typesetting, composition, copy, matter, *(Garnitur)* suite, set, *(Gebühr)* fee, *(Gesetzesbestimmung)* clause, *(ling.)* sentence, period, *(festgesetzte Menge)* limit, rate, *(Preis)* price, rate, *(Setzen)* composing, setting, typesetting, *(Sortiment)* assortment, lot, *(Spieleinsatz)* stake, *(Sprung)* jump, leap, *(Tarif)* rate, *(Waren)* lot, parcel, assortment;
zu einem ~ **von 4%** at a rate of 4 per cent; **zu einem bestimmten (festen)** ~ at a fixed rate; **zu einem ermäßigten** ~ at a reduced rate; **zum günstigsten** ~ at the best possible rate; **zum herabgesetzten** ~ at a modified rate;
abgelegter ~ *(drucktechn.)* dead matter; **ausgeschlossener** ~ *(drucktechn.)* justified composition; **druckfertiger** ~ *(drucktechn.)* live matter; **durchschnittlicher** ~ average rate; **durchschossener** ~ *(drucktechn.)* open matter; **eingerückter** ~ *(drucktechn.)* hanging indent; **einheitlicher** ~ flat (standard, uniform) rate; **ermäßigter** ~ reduced rate; **fester** ~ fixed price, *(Tarif)* fixed rate; **fetter** ~ *(drucktechn.)* heavy-faced type, boldface; **geltender** ~ current rate; **gemischter** ~ *(drucktechn.)* mixed matter, mixture; **gesperrter** ~ *(drucktechn.)* open-spaced setting; **gestaffelter** ~ graduated (scale, *Br.*) rate; **glatter** ~ *(drucktechn.)* run-on (straight, plain, solid) matter; **halbfetter** ~ *(drucktechn.)* semi-bold type; **handelsüblicher** ~ normal commercial rate; **höchster** ~ maximum rate; **kompresser** ~ *(drucktechn.)* solid matter; **endlos langer** ~ stringy sentence; **lichter** ~ *(drucktechn.)* open matter; **niedriger** ~ low rate; **ortsüblicher** ~ local rate; **perlender** ~ *(drucktechn.)* open-spaced setting; **schlechter** ~ *(drucktechn.)* lean work; **stufenförmiger** ~ step rate; **unvollständiger** ~ odd set; **vorgeschriebener** ~ prescribed rate;
~ **für briefliche Auszahlung** rate for mail transfer *(US)*; ~ **Briefmarken** set of stamps; **kein vollständiger** ~ **[Briefmarken]** some odd stamps; **voller** ~ **Dokumente** full set of documents; **kompletter** ~ **von Eigentumsurkunden** bundle of titled deeds; ~ **für tägliches Geld (Tagesgeld)** rate on interbank loans, call money rate *(Br.)*; ~ **Gewichte** set of weights; ~ **für Kabelauszahlungen** rate for cable transfers, cable rate; **vollständiger** ~ **Konnossemente** complete set of bills of lading; ~ **für Sichtwechsel** sight rate; ~ **Wechsel** bills in a set, set of bills of exchange; ~ **Werkzeuge** kit of tools;
~ **ablegen** *(drucktechn.)* to diss *(Br.)*; ~ **abrunden** to turn a sentence; ~ **auflösen** to break up a sentence; ~ **von 5% in Anwendung bringen** to apply a rate of 5 per cent; **mehr** ~ **als berechnet ergeben** *(drucktechn.)* to run out; ~ **formulieren** to frame a sentence; **in** ~ **geben** to give to the printer; **bestimmten** ~ **an Geld pro Tag haben** to have a certain travel allowance per

diem; ~ **herabsetzen** *(Tagesgeld)* to mark the rate down; ~ **für tägliches Geld heraufsetzen** to mark up call money *(US)*; **zu viel ~ herstellen** *(drucktechn.)* to overset; ~ **stehen lassen** *(drucktechn.)* to keep the composition standing; **im ~ sein** *(Buch)* to be being set; ~ **spationieren** *(drucktechn.)* to lead out a matter; ~ **strecken** *(drucktechn.)* to white out the matter; ~ **umstellen** to invert a sentence.

Sätze | für langfristiges Geld long-term interest rates; ~ **für Handelswechsel** commercial paper rates *(US)*.

Satz | abzug letter-set proof; **~akzent** stress; **~anordnung** typographical arrangement; **~anweisung** type layout, composition pattern; **~arbeit** job work, composing; **~arbeiten vergeben** to farm out composing; **~bau** construction; **~befehl** *(Satzmaschine)* typographic instruction; **~bild** setting; **~block** block composition; **~breite** composing area; **~brett** *(drucktechn.)* composition board; **~entwurf** typographical layout; **~fehler** setting mistake; **~gefüge** complete sentence; **rationelle ~herstellung** rationalized composition; **~höhe** depth of page; **~konstruktion** structure of a sentence, composition; **~kosten** costs of composition, cost of type, composition costs; **~kosten bezahlen** to pay for the composition; **~länge** sentence length; **~lehre** syntax; **weiteres ~manuskript benötigen** to wait for more copy; **~maschine** type-setting (composing) machine; **~muster** composition pattern; **~preis berechnen** to calculate the cost of setting; **~probe** specimen of type; **~skizze** type layout; **~spalte** column; **~spiegel** type area, printing space; **~stellung** order; **~stil** sentence style; **~teile** parts of speech; **~type** type; **~typengröße** size of type; **~umfangberechnung** casting off copy, character count *(Br.)*.

Satzung statute, charter, byelaw, regulations, covenant, *(Gesellschaft)* memorandum and articles of association *(Br.)*, corporate articles (bylaws) *(US)*, articles of incorporation *(US)*, *(Verein)* standing rules of procedure;
im Rahmen der ~ intra vires; **in den ~en der Gesellschaft vorgesehen** provided by the articles of the association *(Br.)*; **städtische ~** rules and byelaws;
~en einer Aktiengesellschaft articles of association (incorporation), charter *(US)*; ~ **der Vereinten Nationen** United Nations Charter;
~ **ändern** to alter the conditions contained in the memorandum; ~ **aufheben** to release (sever) a statute; **~en erfüllen** to comply with the statutes (rules); ~ **erlassen** to make bylaws; ~ **geben** to create a charter; ~ **verleihen** to grant a charter; ~ **zurücknehmen** to vacate a charter.

Satzungs | änderung alteration in (modification of) the articles of an association, alteration of memorandum (articles), alteration (change) in the constitution, charter amendment; **~befugnisse einer juristischen Person** corporate powers; **~befugnisse erweitern** to extend a charter; **~berichtigung** rectification of the articles of association; **~bestimmungen** clauses in (provisions of) a memorandum, charter provisions; **~bestimmung über die Kapitalstruktur einer Gesellschaft** capital clause; **den ~bestimmungen genügen** to observe the articles of association; **~erfordernisse** statutory (charter) requirements.

satzungsgemäß statutory, regular, according to statute, according to the articles, intra vires;
~ **bestellt** appointed by the articles;
~ **vorgeschriebene Reserve** statutory reserve; **~e Verpflichtung** liability created by statute; **~e Voraussetzungen** statutory requirements.

Satzungs | recht statutory (positive) law; **~rücknahme** vacation of a charter; **~verstoß** infringement of the articles.

satzungswidrig contrary to statute (articles, regulations), against the articles.

Satzungs | zweck, ~ziel object of a statute, statutory object.

Satz | vorlage manuscript, layout, schedule; **~zeichen** punctuation mark.

Sau, wie eine gesengte ~ fahren to drive like mad; **j. zur ~ machen** to read the Riot Act to s. o.; **unter aller ~ sein** to be lousy;
~arbeit drudgery, *(schlechte Arbeit)* rotten (lousy) work.

sauber tidy, clean, white, *(Atomwaffe)* clinical, *(Bilanz)* uncooked, unfaked;
j. ~ reinlegen to play a dirty trick on s. o.;
~e Abschrift fair copy; **~e Arbeit** neat work; **~e Arbeit leisten** to do a decent job of work; **~e Geschäftsmethoden** fair practices, fair trade *(US)*; **~e Handschrift** neat (legible) handwriting; **~e Luft** clean (unpolluted) air; **~er Patron** bad egg; **~e Weste haben** to have a clean slate, to come with clean hands.

Sauberkeit cleanliness, neatness, *(Luft)* cleanness, purity;
geschäftliche ~ business integrity.

säuberlich verpackt meticulously packed.

saubermachen to clean out.

säubern to clean, to do out, to scour, to cleanse, *(mil.)* to mop up, *(pol.)* to purge, to expurgate.

Säuberung cleaning, cleanup, *(pol.)* purge, expurgation;
~ **eines Gebietes** mopping up of an area; ~ **der Stadtrandgebiete** environmental cleanup; ~ **eines Textes** expurgation of a text.

Säuberungsaktion *(mil.)* mopping-up action, *(pol.)* [political] purges.

saublöd damned stupid;
~e Situation awkward situation.

saudämlich *(fam.)* dead from the neck up.

sauer sour, *(fig.)* sore;
es sich ~ werden lassen to choose the hard way; ~ **reagieren** to react sour; ~ **sein** *(fam.)* to be fed up with; **über j. ganz schön ~ sein** to be pretty sore at s. o.; ~ **werden** to go crook *(Australia)*;
~ **verdientes Geld** hard earned money, tough buck *(sl.)*.

saures Gesicht machen to put on a peeked face.

säuerliches Lächeln sourish smile.

Sauerstoff | flasche oxygen cylinder; **~gehalt** oxygen content; **~maske** oxygen mask.

Sauertopf sour old man.

saufen, wie ein Loch to drink like a fish; **j. unter den Tisch ~** to drink s. o. under the table.

Säufer drunkard, tippler, boozer, guzzler, lush *(US sl.)*;
ausgekochter ~ three-bottle man; **notorischer ~** notorious drunkard;
~wahnsinn delirium tremens, blue devil, the jumps *(sl.)*, jimjams; **an ~wahnsinn leiden** to have the jumps *(sl.)*.

Sauf | gelage bum, razzle, spree, jamboree *(sl.)*; **~lokal** boozer.

Sauftour pub crawl, spree, drinking bout, soak, painting the town red *(sl.)*, reeler *(sl.)*, toot;
auf ~ on the town (roof, *sl.*);
auf eine ~ gehen to go to town, to pub-crawl, to have a binge, to go on a spree (bend, *sl.*), to paint the town red *(sl.)*.

saugen to suck, *(Staub)* to hoover;
sich eine Geschichte aus den Fingern ~ to cook up a story.

saugfähiges Papier absorbent (manifold) paper.

Säugling nursling, nursing infant.

Säuglings | alter infanthood, babyhood, infancy; **~fürsorge** infant welfare, childbirth care; **~heim** resident nursery, baby farm (nursery); **~nahrung** infant food; **~schwester** dry nurse; **~sterblichkeit** infant mortality.

Saug | papier, ~post mimeograph (manifold, absorbent) paper; **~- und Druckpumpe** lift and force pump.

Säule post, pillar, *(el.)* pile;
~ **der Wissenschaft** pillar of science;
durch Pfeiler und ~n stützen to pillar.

Säulen | diagramm block diagram, bar chart, histogram; **~gang** portico.

saumäßig beastly, awful, lousy;
j. ~ behandeln to treat s. o. like dirt; ~ **frieren** to freeze to the marrow; **sich ~ fühlen** to feel lousy (off colo(u)r);
~es Glück haben to be damned lucky; **~es Wetter** rotten weather.

säumen, die Straßen to line the streets.

säumig defaulting, in default, behindhand, tardy, delinquent, dilatory, negligent, *(saumselig)* dilatory, slow, remiss;
~er Kunde delinquent customer; **~e Partei** defaulting party, defaulter; **~er Schuldner (Zahler)** slow (tardy, defaulting) debtor, defaulter; **~er Zahler sein** to be behindhand with (tardy in) one's payments, to be remiss in paying one's bills.

Säumnis default;
~gebühr default fee (fine); **~urteil** default judgment; **~zuschlag** surcharge, *(Einkommensteuer)* delinquent tax due.

Saum | pfad mule track, packway; **~pferd** packhorse; **~sattel** packsaddle.

saumselig slow, tardy, dilatory, laggard;
~ **arbeiten** to work sluggishly.

Sauregurkenzeit silly season.

Saus, in ~ und Braus leben to live high on the hog (at rack and manger, *Br.*).

säuseln to murmur, to sigh, *(flüstern)* to whisper.

sausen to rush, to dash, to shoot, to scoot *(coll.)*, *(Geschoß)* to whiz, to whistle;
in den Graben ~ to be ditched; **durch eine Prüfung ~** to get ploughed in an exam *(Br.)*, to flunk an exam *(US)*;
j. ~ lassen to give s. o. the brush-off, *(Prüfling)* to flunk s. o. *(US)*.

Saustall pigsty;
~ **anrichten** to make an awful mess; ~ **sein** to be in a shamble.

Sauwetter rotten (dirty, filthy) weather.
sauwohl fühlen, sich to feel as snug as a bug in a rug (like a million dollars, *US*).
Schabe|karton scratchboard; ~**manier** scratch drawing, mezzotint technique.
Schabernack prank, hoax, mockery, monkey business;
jem. einen ~ spielen to play a hoax on s. o.; ~ **treiben** to be a practical joker, to monkey.
schäbig treadbare, out at elbow, shoddy, rusty, heel, seedy, tacky *(US)*, *(geizig)* mean, shabby, stingy;
~ **angezogen** shabbily dressed;
sich ~ benehmen to make o. s. cheap; **sich ~ vorkommen** to feel mean; **allmählich ~ werden** to begin to look the worse for wear;
~**e Belohnung** meagre reward; ~**e Hütte** tumble-down hut; ~**er Teppich** threadbare carpet.
Schablone pattern [design], mould, mold *(US)*, stencil, groove, form, cutout, model, *(fig.)* stereotype;
nach der ~ by routine (rote), mechanically;
mit einer ~ arbeiten to work with a stencil; **nach der ~ arbeiten** to work mechanically (by routine); **mittels ~ aufmalen** to stencil; **nach der ~ machen** to do according to pattern.
schablonenhaft by routine, routine-like, stereotyped, hackneyed, groovy, mechanical;
~**er Ausdruck** stereotyped expression.
Schablonenhaftigkeit routinism, conventionality.
schablonenmäßig|erledigen, etw. to do s. th. as a matter of routine;
~**e Herstellung** stencil production.
Schablonen|mensch werden to get into a groove; ~**papier** stencil (pattern) paper; ~**vervielfältiger** stencil duplicator.
Schach, jem. ~ bieten to defy s. o.; **in ~ halten** to keep in check, to hold at bay, *(mit dem Revolver)* to hold at gunpoint.
Schacher[ei] haggling, haggle, chaffer.
politischer ~ political jobbery, horse trading, spoils system *(US)*;
~ **treiben** to huckster.
Schacherer haggler, chafferer, bargainer, bargainor, huckster.
schachern to chaffer, to hagger, to haggle, *(knickern)* to polter, to bargain, to barter for, to dicker *(US)*, *(pol.)* to job.
Schachfigur *(fig.)* figurehead.
schachmatt checkmate, *(erschöpft)* dead-beat, exhausted;
~ **setzen** to checkmate.
Schacht trunk, *(Bergbau)* pit, shaft;
feuersicherer ~ fire tower; **fündiger ~** *(Ölbohrung)* completed well;
~ **befahren** to descend into a shaft;
~**abteufung** sinking of a shaft; ~**anlage** colliery; **stillgelegte ~anlage** disused workings; ~**arbeiter** pitman, shaftsman; ~**ausbau** shaft lining.
Schachtel box, case, *(Beteiligung)* intercorporate stock holdings *(US)*, interlocking interest;
in ~n verpackt boxed;
alte ~ old frump;
~ **Streichhölzer** box of matches; ~ **Zigaretten** packet (pack, *US*) of cigarettes;
~**aufsichtsrat** overlapping (interlinked) directorship *(Br.)*, interlocking directorate *(US)*; ~**besitz**, ~**beteiligung** interlocking interest, intercorporate stockholdings *(US)*; ~**gesellschaft** subsidiary (interrelated) company, consolidated corporation; ~**privileg** interlocking rights, intercorporate privilege *(US)*; **das von der Steuergesetzgebung vorgesehene ~privileg genießen** to be eligible for the dividend received exclusion provided by the Internal Revenue Code *(Br.)*; ~**satz** involved period; ~**unternehmen** interrelated (subsidiary) company, consolidated corporation; ~**wort** portmanteau word.
Schachtförderung hoisting.
Schachzug *(fig.)* maneuver *(US)*, manoeuvre *(Br.)*, well-timed measure;
meisterhafter diplomatischer ~ master stroke of diplomacy; **kluger ~** clever move.
schade, für j. viel zu ~ sein to be a long sight too good for s. o.
Schädel skull, noodle *(sl.)*, nut *(sl.)*;
eins über den ~ bekommen to get one over the head; **sich den ~ einrennen** to run one's head against a brick wall; **jem. den ~ einschlagen** to blow s. one's brains out;
~**bruch** fractured skull.
Schaden damage, loss, hurt, evil, *(jur.)* tort, *(Kosten)* costs, *(Nachteil)* prejudice, detriment, disadvantage, mischief, nuisance, *(Verletzung)* injury, harm, *(Versicherung)* loss, casualty, claim;
mit ~ at a sacrifice; **ohne ~** without prejudice; **zu meinem ~** at my expense; **zum ~ von** to the detriment of;
abschätzbarer ~ estimable loss; **in Geld abzulösender ~** constructive loss; **allgemeiner ~** general damage; **durch Vieh angerichteter ~** cattle damage; **lang anhaltender ~** protracted loss; **außergewöhnlicher ~** exceptional loss; **auf Brandstiftung beruhender ~** incendiary loss; **auf Unfall beruhender ~** accidental injury; **beträchtlicher ~** considerable damage, substantial harm; **eigentlicher ~** actual loss; **bereits eingetretener ~** detriment already incurred; **noch nicht eingetretener ~** unaccrued damage; **einklagbarer ~** actionable loss, civil injury; **empfindlicher ~** serious loss; **entstandener ~** loss incurred; **durch einen Autounfall entstandener ~** accidental collision damage; **bei der Brandbekämpfung entstandener ~** fire-fighting damage; **durch Feindeinwirkung entstandener ~** queen's enemies; **durch Feuer entstandener ~** damage by fire, fire loss; **tatsächlich entstandener ~** actual damage; **auf dem Transport entstandener ~** damage in transit; **durch Vertragsbruch entstandener ~** loss occasioned by breach of contract; **erlittener ~** damage suffered, sustained loss; **ernstlicher ~** serious loss; **ersetzbarer ~** compensable injury; **nicht ersetzbarer ~** irreparable injury; **erstattungsfähiger ~** recoverable loss; **fahrlässiger ~** accidental injury; **festgestellter ~** ascertained (proved, observed) damage, *(Spediteur)* known damage; **in Geld feststellbarer ~** pecuniary damage; **nicht in Geld feststellbarer ~** general damage; **finanzieller ~** money damage, pecuniary loss; **fingierter ~** constructive injury; **formaler ~** petty damage; **durch die Versicherung voll gedeckter ~** loss fully covered by insurance; **geldwerter ~** pecuniary damage (loss); **als Totalverlust geltender ~** constructive total loss; **geringer ~** slight injury; **geringfügiger ~** nominal (small) damage; **durch Schadensersatz nicht gutzumachender ~** inadequate damage; **immaterieller ~** nominal damage; **indirekter ~** remote damage; **konkreter ~** special damage; **körperlicher ~** bodily injury (harm); **materieller ~** material (physical) damage; **mittelbarer ~** indirect (prospective, consequential) damage (loss); **nachgewiesener ~** proved damage; **nomineller ~** nominal damage; **psychischer ~** mental injury; **radioaktiver ~** radioactive losses; **regulierter ~** *(Versicherung)* settled claim; **schätzungsbedürftiger ~** unliquidated damage; **schwerer ~** serious (substantial) damage; **seelischer ~** mental distress; **substantiierter ~** substantiated damage; **tatsächlicher ~** actual (special) damage; **unbedeutender ~** nominal (negligible) damage; **uneinbringlicher ~** irretrievable loss; **unersetzbarer ~** irrecoverable (irretrievable) loss; **unmittelbarer ~** direct damage (loss), positive injury; **versicherter ~** direct (insured) loss; **nicht versicherter ~** uninsured loss; **von Ihnen zu vertretender ~** damage chargeable to you; **verursachter ~** damage done; **durch Wasser verursachter ~** damage caused by water; **vorausberechneter ~** speculative damage; **nicht voraussehbarer ~** remote damage; **nicht wiedergutzumachender ~** injury past redress; **zufälliger ~** accidental loss; **nicht zurechenbarer ~** remote damage; **nur auf die versicherte Gefahr zurückzuführender ~** loss from insured peril only;
~ **jeder Art** loss or damage; ~ **wirtschaftlicher Art** material damage; ~ **im Einzelfall** special damage; ~ **an der Ladung** damage to cargo; ~ **durch inneren Verderb** damage by intrinsic defects; ~ **durch Wasser** damage caused by water;
~ **abschätzen** to estimate (assess, value) the damage, to assess a loss; ~ **auf fünfzig Pfund abschätzen** to value the damage at fifty pounds; ~ **abwenden** to avert damage; ~ **anmelden** to give notice of claim; ~ **anrichten** to [cause] damage; **großen ~ anrichten** to do great harm; **schweren ~ anrichten** *(Unwetter)* to cause havoc; **für einen ~ aufkommen** to indemnify, to compensate; ~ **aufnehmen** to assess damage; ~ **ausbessern** to repair a damage; ~ **beheben** to repair damage; ~ **berechnen** to compute the damage; ~ **besichtigen** to inspect the extent of damage; ~ **auf 1000 £ beziffern** to put the loss at £ 1000; ~ **decken** to make good a deficiency, *(Versicherung)* to recover a loss; **zu seinem ~ erfahren** to learn to one's cost; **sich von einem ~ erholen** to recover one's losses; ~ **erleiden** to suffer damage, to sustain (incur, meet with) a loss; ~ **durch unzulässige Staatseingriffe erleiden** to suffer from undue regulations; ~ **ermitteln** to estimate (assess) damage; ~ **ersetzen** to make good (up for) a loss; **jem. seinen ~ ersetzen** to make good the damage done to s. o.; **jem. den ~ in voller Höhe ersetzen** to pay full indemnity to s. o.; ~ **feststellen** to estimate the loss; ~ **haben** to suffer a loss; ~ **zu vertreten haben** to be answerable (responsible, liable) for damages; **für einen ~ haften (haftbar sein)** to be responsible (liable) for a damage, to be liable for a

loss; **zu ~ kommen** to come to grief; **bei einem Unfall zu ~ kommen** to be injured in an accident; **j. für den ~ verantwortlich machen** to hold s. o. responsible for the damage; **seinen ~ mindern** to mitigate one's damage (loss); **für einen ~ aufkommen müssen** to be liable for a loss; **seinen ~ nachweisen** to prove one's damage; **auf dem Transport ~ nehmen** to suffer damage in transit; **~ regeln (regulieren)** to settle a loss (claim); **einem Kunden in Höhe des entstandenen ~s haftbar sein** to be liable to a customer in extent of a loss; **~ tragen** to be liable for (bear) a loss; **~ vergüten** to make good a loss; **mit ~ verkaufen** to sell at a loss; **Ersatz des mittelbaren ~s verlangen** to claim constructive damages; **gegen ~ versichern** to insure against loss; **~ verursachen** to cause damage; **~ wiedergutmachen** to redress an injury; **~ zufügen** to damage, to damnify, to injure, to do (inflict) an injury, to hurt, to wrong, to cause a (inflict) damage;

durch ~ wird man klug once bitten twice shy; **wer den ~ hat braucht für den Spott nicht zu sorgen** the laugh is always the loser.

Schäden, geringfügige small damage;

~ nicht zu unseren Lasten free of damage;

~ beseitigen to redress injuries; **alle ~ decken** to cover all losses.

schaden to damage, to injure, to be an injury, *(nachteilig sein)* to be derogatory (prejudicial), to prejudice;

mehr ~ als nützen to do more harm than good; **sich selbst ~** to stand in one's own light; **jds. Ruf ~** to do damage to (compromise) s. one's reputation.

schadenanrichtend damaging, damage-feasant.

Schadenersatz amends, indemnification, indemnity, reimbursement, *(Abfindung)* paying off, buying out, *(in Geld)* damages, compensation for damage, compensatory damages *(US)*, *(Wiedergutmachung)* reparation of the damage *(US)*, redress; **~ leistend** compensatory; **zum ~ verpflichtet** liable to pay (respond in) damages, bound to allow indemnity;

adäquater ~ compensatory damages; **angemessener ~** adequate (fair) damages; **durch Verzögerung der Zuerkennung entstehender ~** intervening damages; **fahrlässigkeitsunabhängiger ~** compensation irrespective of negligence; **vertraglich festgesetzter ~** liquidated damages; **für Folgeschäden vorsorglich festgesetzter ~** speculative damages; **festgestellter ~** proved damages; **der Höhe nach noch nicht feststehender ~** unliquidated damages; **formaler ~** contemptuous damages; **geltend gemachter ~** affirmative damages; **gesetzlicher ~** damages at law; **pauschalierter ~** agreed damages; **üblicher ~** general damages; **unbezifferter ~** indeterminate (unliquidated) damages; **vertraglich vereinbarter ~** liquidated damages; **verschärfter ~** exemplary (punitive) damages, retributive damages *(US)*; **zuerkannter ~** *(Versicherung)* awarded damages, award; **doppelt zuerkannter ~** double damages; **im Ermessungswege zuerkannter ~** discretionary damages; **rechtlich zuerkannter ~** legal award;

~ wegen Annahmeverweigerung damages for nonacceptance; **~ für Betriebskrankheiten** compensation for industrial diseases; **~ für Betriebsunfälle** workmen's compensation; **~ wegen verspäteter Fertigstellung** damages for delay in finishing; **~ für Folgeschäden** special damages; **~ in Geld** pecuniary damages; **~ für entgangenen Gewinn** consequential damages; **unbezifferter ~ wegen unerlaubter Handlung** unliquidated damages for tort; **~ wegen widerrechtlicher Kündigung** damages for wrongful dismissal; **~ wegen ausgebliebener Lieferung** damages for nondelivery; **~ für Mehraufwendungen** out-of-pocket loss rule; **~ wegen Nichterfüllung** damages for nonfulfilment; **~ für tatsächlich eingetretenen Schaden** substantial damages; **~ für Spätfolgen** remote damages; **~ wegen arglistiger Täuschung** damages for the tort of deceit or fraud; **~ des Verkehrswertes** commercial indemnity; **~ für Verschlechterung der Wohngegend** compensation for loss of amenities;

~ aberkennen (nicht anerkennen) to disallow compensation; **gleichwertigen ~ anbieten** to offer an equivalent for damage done; **~ ausschließen** to exclude any damages claim; **~ beanspruchen** to claim damages, *(bei der Versicherung)* to place a claim; **~ beantragen** to make a claim for damages; **grundsätzliche Feststellung der Verpflichtung zum ~ beantragen** to sue for damages at large; **j. wegen ~es belangen** to come upon s. o. for damages; **~ berechnen** to lay damages; **~ dem Grunde nach einklagen** to sue for unliquidated damages; **zwei Millionen Dollar ~ einklagen** to seek 2-million in damages; **~ einreichen** to advance a claim for indemnification; **~ erhalten** to recover (obtain) damages; **Anspruch auf ~ erhalten** to be awarded entitlement to damages; **~ im Wege der Gegenklage erhalten** to recoup; **auf ~ erkennen** to award damages against; **~ erlangen** to recover damages; **~ wegen unerlaubter Handlung erlangen** to obtain damages in tort; **~ feststellen** to lay (liquidate) damages; **~ der Höhe nach feststellen** to assess the damages; **~ fordern** to claim damages; **auf ~ haften** to be liable for (respond in) damages, to be responsible for [a loss]; **auf ~ klagen** to bring an action for damages, to sue for damages; **~ leisten** to pay (respond in, *US*) damages, to make amends (reparations) for an injury, to redeem, to compensate, to pay compensation, to make reparation for an injury *(US)*; **einem Arbeiter ~ für einen Betriebsunfall leisten** to compensate a workman for his injuries; **~ wegen Körperverletzung leisten** to make amends for an injury; **j. auf ~ in Anspruch nehmen** to claim damages from s. o.; **auf ~ verklagen** to sue for damages; **~ verlangen** to lodge a claim for (demand) compensation, to claim damages, to claim as compensation [for a loss], to demand (collect) damages, to seek recovery; **vor Gericht ~ wegen Betruges verlangen** to sue damages in tort for deceit; **~ wegen unerlaubter Handlungen verlangen** to sue in tort; **~ für geringe Lebenserwartung verlangen** to claim damages for loss of expectation of life; **~ wegen Nichterfüllung verlangen** to sue in tort for conversion; **~ auf dem Regreßwege verlangen** to sue for damages by way of recovery; **vollen ~ vom Spediteur verlangen** to hold the carrier responsible for the full value; **~ wegen Vertragsbruchs verlangen** to claim damages for breach of contract; **zur Leistung von ~ verurteilen** to award (order) damages; **~ verweigern** to disallow damages; **auf ~ verklagt werden** to be defendant in an action for damages; **zum ~ verurteilt werden** to be cast in damages; **~ zahlen** to pay damages; **~ zuerkennen (zusprechen)** to give (adjudge) damages, to award a sum for damages.

Schadenersatzanspruch damage (compensation) claim, claim for indemnity (to compensation, for damages), [remedy of] damages, recovery right, right of recovery (indemnity);

vertraglich anerkannter ~ liquidated damages, admitted claim; **eingetretener (entstandener) ~** damages sustained (accrued); **durch Verzögerung der Zuerkennung entstandener ~** intervening damages; **vertraglich der Höhe nach festgelegter ~** liquidated damages; **vertraglich nicht festgesetzter ~** unliquidated damages; **festgestellter ~** proved damages; **gesetzlicher ~** damages at law; **verschärfter ~** retributive (punitive) damages; **bedingt zuerkannter ~** contingent damages *(US)*; **nachzuweisender zusätzlicher ~** special damages;

~ aus unerlaubter Handlung claim founded in (unliquidated damages for) tort, tort claim; **~ bei Nichtannahme** action for damages for nonacceptance; **~ für festgestellte Schäden** claim for damages observed; **~ wegen unbestrittenen Verlustes der Fracht** known-loss claim; **~ gegen die Versicherung** loss claimable on insurance; **~ wegen positiver Vertragsverletzung** damages for breach of contract;

~ begründen to sound in (lay one's) damages; **~ beschränken** to abridge damages; **~ feststellen** to adjust damages; **~ haben** to have a case at law for damages; **~ regulieren** to adjust damages; **~ stellen** to claim damages; **auf einen ~ verzichten** to waive (renounce) a claim to indemnity;

~aufwand compensation costs.

schadenersatzberechtigt sein to be entitled to damages.

Schadenersatz|berechtigter party entitled to damages, indemnitee, loss payee, injured party; **~bestimmungen** compensation provisions; **~betrag** amount (quantum) of damages; **gerichtlich festgestellter ~betrag** judgment limit; **~betrag [der Höhe nach] feststellen** to assess damages; **~erlangung** recovery of damages; **~folge** corollary of indemnity.

Schadenersatzforderung demand for compensation;

auf Produzentenhaftung gegründete ~en product liability claims;

~ für unmittelbaren zugefügten Schaden indirect claim; **~ im Wege der Gegenklage** counterclaim for damages;

~ der Höhe nach geltend machen to lay one's (sound in) damages.

Schadenersatzhöhe measure of damages.

Schadenersatzklage action for (sounding in) damages, liability claim, remedial action, damage suit, loss claim;

auf arglistige Täuschung gegründete ~ writ of deceit;

~ wegen widerrechtlicher Aneignung action for conversion; **~ für fahrlässige Handlungen** trespass on the case *(US)*; **~ wegen Hausfriedensbruchs** trespass wherefore he broke the close; **~ wegen Kreditschädigung** action for damages to credit; **~ wegen Nichterfüllung** action for damages for nondelivery, action for assumpsit, general assumpsit, action at law for damages caused by nondelivery; **~ für Nutzungsentzug** *(Mieter, Pächter)*

trespass for mesne profits; ~ **wegen Rufschädigung** action for tort of libel; ~ **für aus unmittelbarer Gewaltanwendung eingetretenen Schäden** *(Gericht)* trespass on the case ~ **wegen Schiffszusammenstoßes** collision and damage action; ~ **wegen Substanzverschlechterung** *(Pächter)* impeachment of waste; ~ **wegen arglistiger Täuschung** action for damages for deceit; ~ **wegen fahrlässigen Verhaltens** action for negligence; ~ **aus vertragsähnlichem Verhältnis** common (general) assumpsit; ~ **wegen Verletzung der Gewährleistungspflicht** action for damages for breach of warranty; ~ **wegen Vertragsverletzung** breach-of-contract action; ~ **wegen widerrechtlicher Wegnahme** trespass for goods carried away;
~ **einreichen** to advance a claim for indemnification; ~ **erheben** to sue for damages, to make (put in) a claim for damages, to bring an action for damages.

Schadenersatzklausel loss-payable clause.

Schadenersatzleistung indemnification, compensation [payment], compensatory damages *(US)*, condemnation money; **der Form halber festgesetzte geringe** ~ nominal damages; **überhöhte ~en** excessive damages;
zur ~ verurteilen to order to pay for damages.

Schadenersatzpflicht liability for damages (compensation);
~ **ablehnen** to disclaim liability for a loss.

schadenersatzpflichtig answerable (held, liable) for damages, liable for compensation (to be sued for, to respond in damages), liable to make good a loss, accountable;
gemeinsam ~ jointly liable for damages;
j. ~ machen to recoup s. o. for injury; ~ **sein** to be liable (responsible, answerable) for (to pay) damages, to be liable in damages, to respond in damages *(US)*.

Schadenersatz|pflichtiger tortfeasor; **~prozeß** sounding in damages, action for damages, damages suit; **~prozeß aufgrund geleisteter Nothilfe** rescue case; **~prozeß wegen Patentverletzung** infringement suit; **~recht** civil damages law; **~vereinbarung** compensation agreement.

Schadenersatzverpflichtung liability for damages;
allgemeine ~ general assumpsit;
~ **für Fahrlässigkeit von Erfüllungsgehilfen** liability for negligence of servants, vicarious liability;
j. von einer ~ freistellen to hold s. o. harmless from a loss.

Schadenersatz|versicherung liability insurance; **~vorschlag** offer to make amends; **fortlaufende ~zahlungen** continuing damages; **der Form halber festgesetzte geringe ~zahlung** nominal damages.

Schadenfeuer *(Versicherung)* unfriendly fire.

Schadens|abfindung indemnification, compensation; **~abrechnung als große Havarie** average adjustment; **~abschätzer** claim adjuster, loss expert, loss assessor *(Br.)*; **selbständiger ~abschätzer** independent adjuster; **~abschätzung** appraisal (adjustment) of damage, loss assessment; **~abteilung** *(Versicherungsgesellschaft)* claims department; **~abwälzung** redistribution of loss; **~abwicklung** claims settlement, adjustment of an insurance claim; **~anfall** incidence (occurrence) of loss; **~anspruch** claim for damages, damages claim; **~anzeige** damage report, *(Versicherungsfall)* notice of claim (loss), notification of claim (loss), complaint, loss advice; **sofortige ~anzeige** immediate notice; **~anzeige erstatten** to give notice of loss; **~aufstellung** damage report, statement of damage; **~aufteilung** distribution of losses; **~ausgleich** compensation for damage, claims settlement, *(Havarie)* extraordinary average; **~ausgleichmaßnahmen** adjustment action; **~ausmaß** extent of damage; **~bearbeiter** appraiser, claims inspector, loss assessor *(Br.)*; **~bearbeitung** claims management; **~begleichung** claim payment; **~begrenzung** loss limitation; **~begutachtung** appraisal of loss; **~bekämpfung** minimizing of losses; **~bemessung** measure (assessment) of damages; **~berechnung** appraisal (assessment, estimate) of damages; **~bericht** damage report, report of loss; **~besichtigung** damage survey; **~beteiligung** *(Versicherung)* contribution; **proportionaler ~beteiligung im Fall der Unterversicherung unterworfen** subject to average.

Schadensbetrag amount of loss, compensation costs, damages;
der Höhe nach nicht festgestellter ~ unliquidated damages;
~ **anteilmäßig aufgliedern** to average a loss; ~ **[der Höhe nach] feststellen** to assess the damages.

Schadens|bevorschussung advance compensation; **~bewertung** ascertainment of a loss; **~büro** *(Versicherung)* claims department, *(Warenhaus)* adjustment bureau; **~eintritt** occurrence (incidence) of a loss; **~erfahrung** loss experience; **~ergebnisse** *(Versicherung)* claims results; **~erledigung** claims settlement, adjustment of an insurance claim; **~erwartung** expectation of loss; **~experte** surveyor, claim adjuster; **~fall** event of loss, *(Versicherung)* claim, loss; **im ~fall** in case (the event) of loss; **nach Eintritt des ~falles** after loss; **noch nicht regulierte ~fälle** *(Versicherung)* unsettled reported claims; **~fälle bearbeiten** to handle claims; **~festsetzer** insurance (claim) adjuster; **~festsetzung** fixing of damages, determination of compensation; **freiberuflicher ~feststeller** professional claims investigator; **~feststellung** ascertainment of loss, assessment (adjustment, settlement) of damage, loss assessment; **~feststellungsantrag** claim tracer; **~folgen** consequential damages; **~folgenversicherung** consequential loss (damage) insurance; **~forderung** claim for damages, damages claim; **unbezifferte ~forderung** unliquidated damages; **~formular** claim form (blank, *US*).

schadensfreie Versicherungsjahre previous claim-free years.

Schadensfreiheitsrabatt *(Autoversicherung)* no-claim (discount) bonus *(Br.)*, preferred risk plan *(US)*;
Anspruch auf ~ haben to be entitled to no-claim discount *(Br.)*; **~system** no-claim bonus system.

Schadens|haftung liability for losses (damages); **anerkannte ~haftung** *(Grundstück)* permanent damages; **~häufigkeit** frequency (incidence) of loss, loss frequency, *(Autoversicherung)* bad claims record; **~höhe** extent (amount) of loss (damage); **~höhe festsetzen** to assess the damage; **~kommission** claims commission; **~leistungsvertrag** *(Rückversicherung)* quota treaty; **~liquidation** liquidation of damage; **~meldung** damage report, report of a loss, *(Versicherungsfall)* notice of claim (loss); **sofortige ~meldung** immediate notice; **~merkmal** element of a damage; **~minderung** mitigation (reduction) of damage (loss), minimizing of losses; **~minderungsklausel** sue and labour clause *(Br.)*; **~nachweis** proof of loss (damage), establishment of damage; **erster ~nachweis** *(Versicherung)* preliminary proof; **~ort** place of loss; **~protokoll** certificate of damage; **~prüfung** ascertainment of damage, *(Havarie)* damage survey; **~quote** *(Versicherung)* loss ratio; **~rechnung** statement of damage; **~referent** claims agent; **~regelungsvereinbarung** *(Versicherung)* claim agreement; **~regulierer** *(Versicherung)* appraiser, claims inspector, claim agent (adjuster), loss assessor *(Br.)*; **~regulierung** adjustment of damages (a loss), settlement of a loss (claim), loss adjustment (settlement), claim settlement (payment); **im Ausland erfolgte ~regulierung** foreign adjustment; **~rente** accident (injury, *Br.*) benefit; **~reserve** *(Versicherung)* liabilities on outstanding claims, policy (claim, loss) reserve, provision for outstanding losses, net surplus *(US)*; **~- und Exzedentenrückversicherung** excess loss insurance; **~sachverständiger** [claim] adjuster, claim agent, insurance adjuster; **~schätzung** appraisal (assessment) of damage; **~stelle** place of loss; **~stifter** tortfeasor; **~summe** [amount of] damage; **vertraglich festgesetzte (festgestellte, vorausgeschätzte) ~summe** liquidated damages; **~teilungsverband** interinsurance exchange *(US)*; **~umfang** extent of damage; **~umschichtung** redistribution of loss; **~unterlagen** claim papers, *(Seeschadenversicherung)* average documents; **~untersuchung** damage survey; **~ursache** cause of loss; **unmittelbare ~ursache** proximate cause of loss; **gesamtes ~verhältnis im Verhältnis zum Prämienaufkommen** complete claims ratio; **~verhütung** prevention of loss, loss (claim) prevention; **~verlauf** loss experience; **~verlustversicherung** property damage (liability) insurance; **spezielle ~versicherung** more specific insurance; **~versicherung auf Gegenseitigkeit** mutual indemnity insurance; **der Aufsichtsbehörde gegenüber den Nachweis einer ~versicherung erbringen** to file an indemnity policy with the department; **~versicherungssumme** insurance cover; **~verteilung** distribution of losses; **~wahrscheinlichkeit** probability of damage (loss); **~zertifikat** *(Schiff)* survey report; **~zufüger** damage faisant (feasant); **~zufügung** infliction of damages, *(verbrecherisch)* criminal damage.

schadhaft defective, damaged, imperfect, faulty, *(Gebäude)* dilapidated, out of repair, *(verdorbene Ware)* spoiled, spoilt; **~es Buch** hurt book; **einige ~e Stellen haben** to be worn out in places; **~e Straßendecke** damaged road surface; **~e Teile auswechseln** to replace defective parts.

Schadhaftigkeit damaged condition, defectiveness, *(Gebäude)* disrepair, dilapidated condition.

schädigen to damnify, to [cause] damage, *(Abbruch tun)* to prejudice, *(Rechte)* to impair, *(verletzen)* to injure, to hurt, to infringe;
jds. Gesundheit ~ to affect s. one's health; **einige Industriezweige schwer** ~ to cause serious losses to some branches of industry; **Interessen** ~ to impair interests; **jds. guten Ruf** ~ to injure s. one's reputation.

schädigend injurious, damaging.
Schädiger wrong doer, tortfeasor.
Schädigung damage, damnification, injury, *(Funktionsstörung)* lesion, *(Nachteil)* detriment, prejudice, *(Rechte)* impairment, infringement;
vorsätzliche ~ wilful and malicious (wanton) damage; **nicht wiedergutzumachende** ~ injury past redress.
Schädigungsabsicht intention to damage, express (actual) malice, malice in fact.
schädlich injurious, harmful, detrimental, destructive, pernicious, prejudicial, disadvantageous, hurtful, *(Frucht)* bad, *(Luft, Nahrung)* noxious;
~ **für die Gesundheit** injurious to health;
~**er Einfluß** bad influence; ~**e Immissionen** noxious air.
Schädlichkeit injuriousness, *(für die Gesundheit)* noxiousness.
Schädling pest, parasite, *(fig.)* weed, vermin.
Schädlingsbekämpfung verminicide, pest control, *(biologische)* biological control.
Schädlingsbekämpfungs|aktion, konzentrierte pesticide blitz; ~**flugzeug** crop duster; ~**mittel** pest-destruction agent, pesticide.
schadlos free from loss, indemnified;
~ **halten** to compensate, to recoup, to refund, to indemnify; **sich** ~ **halten** to recover one's loss, to recoup (indemnify) o. s.; **sich bei jem.** ~ **halten** to distrain upon (recover damages from) s. o.; **j.** ~ **halten** to save s. o. harmless.
Schadlos|bürgschaft collateral guaranty, guaranty of collection *(US)*, indemnity bond *(US)*, fidelity guaranty (bond); ~**erklärung** indemnity, compensation; ~**haltung** damages, damage indemnification, indemnity, compensation, recourse, recoupment, amends; ~**haltung zusagen** to indemnify; ~**haltungssumme** indemnity, sum paid as compensation; ~**haltungsvereinbarung** indemnification agreement.
Schadstoffe pollutants.
Schaf, schwarzes ~ **der Familie** black sheep (reprobate) of the family, skeleton in the cupboard; ~**e und Rinder** flocks and herds;
~**e von den Böcken trennen** to separate the sheep from the goats; **verlorenes** ~ **in den Schoß der Familie zurückführen** to bring back the stray sheep to the social fold.
Schäfchen, sein ~ **ins Trockene bringen** to feather one's nest, to line one's pockets; **sein** ~ **im Trockenen haben** to have made one's pile;
~**wolken** fleecy clouds, mackerel sky.
Schäfer flockman.
Schäfer|ei sheep breeding; ~**spiel** *(Theater)* pastoral.
Schaffen creation;
künstlerisches ~ art;
geistiges ~ **einer Epoche** intellectual activity of an era.
schaffen to create, to produce, to work, *(beschaffen)* to procure, to provide;
es ~ to come (manage) it *(coll.)*, to make it *(US)*; **j.** ~ to take it out of s. o.; **Abhilfe** ~ to remedy, to redress; **Angelegenheit aus der Welt** ~ to drive the nail home; **neue Arbeitsplätze** ~ to create new jobs; **zur Bahn** ~ to bring to the station; **Bedarf** ~ to create a demand; **beiseite** ~ to take away, to hide, to put aside, *(unterschlagen)* to embezzle; **Fonds** ~ to set up (establish) a fund; **vom Halse** ~ to get rid of; **Hindernisse aus dem Weg** ~ to clear obstacles; **Kapitalgüter** ~ to create capital goods; **Kommission** ~ to set up a committee; **Linderung** ~ to have a soothing effect; **mit Mühe und Not** ~ to barely manage it; **es gerade noch** ~ to cut it fine; **Ordnung** ~ to tidy up; **an Ort und Stelle** ~ to bring to the spot; **Pakete zur Post** ~ to take the parcels to the post office; **Rat** ~ to find a way out; **Schande aus der Welt** ~ to wipe out a disgrace; **tüchtig** ~ to do a good job; **j. aus dem Weg** ~ to get rid of s. o., *(umbringen)* to remove s. o. out of the way;
jem. sehr zu ~ **machen** to be a handful for s. o.; **sich etw. zu** ~ **machen** to busy o. s. with s. th.; **sich im Haus zu** ~ **machen** to be pottering about in the house; **sich an einer Urkunde zu** ~ **machen** to tamper with a document.
schaffend creative, productive;
~**e Bevölkerung** working classes.
Schaffender, geistig professional man.
Schaffens|drang creative urge; ~**kraft** creative (productive) power.
Schaffner guard *(Br.)*, [ticket] conductor *(US)*, *(Schlafwagen)* attendant, porter *(US)*, *(Verwalter)* steward.
Schaffnerin conductorette *(US)*, clippie *(US)*.
Schaffung creation, production, organization;
~ **neuer Arbeitsplätze** creation of new jobs.
Schafott scaffold.
Schafskopf old buffer *(fam.)*.
Schaf|zucht woolgrowing; ~**züchter** woolgrower, sheep farmer, flock master.
schal flat, stale, insipid.
Schale skin, *(Schüssel)* bowl, dish, vessel;
rauhe ~ *(fig.)* rough diamond;
sich richtig in ~ **geworfen haben** to be dressed up to the nines; **sich in** ~ **werfen** to put on one's best bib and tucker.
Schalk wag, joker, *(Kind)* rascal, imp;
der ~ **sitzt ihm im Nacken** he is full of fun.
Schall|dämpfer *(Auto)* muffler, exhaust box, *(Pistole)* silencer; ~**dämpfung** sound absorption, deadening.
schalldicht soundproof.
Schalldose soundbox, pickup.
schallendes Gelächter peals of laughter.
Schall|fortpflanzung sound propagation; ~**frequenz** acoustic frequency; ~**geschwindigkeit** velocity of sound, *(doppelte)* twice the speed of sound, Mach two; ~**isolierung** acoustic insulation; ~**mauer** sound (sonic) barrier; ~**mauer durchbrechen** to break the sound barrier; ~**meßgerät** sonometer, sound ranger; ~**minderung** noise reduction; ~**platte** record, disk *(US)*, disc, phonogram; ~**platte auflegen** to put on a record; **auf** ~**platte aufnehmen** to record, to wax.
Schallplatten|album record album; ~**ansage** disk jockeying; ~**ansager** disc *(US)* (disk) jockey; ~**archiv** record cabinet; ~**- und Tonbandarchiv** transcription program(me) library; ~**aufnahme** recording session; ~**aufnahme machen** to do a recording; ~**firma** recording company; ~**hülle** record sleeve; ~**industrie** record industry; ~**methode** disk *(US)* (disc) system; ~**musik** recorded music; ~**reszensent** record writer; ~**sammlung** collection of records; ~**sendung** recorded program(me); ~**verzeichnis** discography; ~**werbung** record advertising.
Schallschutz sound-absorbing device, *(Mikrofon)* gobo;
~**haube** *(Kamera)* blimp; ~**meßgerät** sound-ranging instrument.
Schall|trichter speaking trumpet; ~**übertragung** conveyance of sound; ~**welle** sound wave; ~**zone** sound shadow.
schaltbar, geräuschlos synchromesh.
Schalt|bild hookup; ~**brett** switchboard, plugboard, panel board, *(Auto)* dashboard; **vom** ~**brett aus** push-button.
Schalten switch, shift, move, operation, manipulation;
~ **der Gänge** changing of gears.
schalten to switch, *(Gänge)* to shift, to change, *(Hebel)* to shift, to move, to operate, *(Maschine)* to operate;
falsch ~ *(fig.)* to get the wrong idea; **in den ersten Gang** ~ to engage the first gear; **zu hart** ~ to ram the gears; **Kraftwerk auf das Netz** ~ to connect a power station to the mains; **in den Leerlauf** ~ to put the lever into neutral; **schnell** ~ *(fig.)* to be quick on the uptake;
nach Belieben ~ **und walten können** to do as one pleases; **j.** ~ **und walten lassen** to give s. o. plenty of rope.
schaltend, blitzschnell quick-witted, needle-witted.
Schalter counter, desk *(Br.)*, window *(US)*, *(Eisenbahn)* booking (ticket, *US*) office, *(Elektrizität)* switch, circuit breaker, *(Flugplatz)* check-in counter, *(Theaterkasse)* box office;
am ~ over the counter; **am** ~ **zahlbar** payable over the counter; ~ **geschlossen** *(Postamt)* position closed; **mehrstufiger** ~ multiple-point switch;
am ~ **abgeben** to hand across the counter; **am** ~ **aufgeben** to post at the counter; ~ **ausknipsen** to turn off a switch; **am** ~ **auszahlen (bezahlen)** to pay over the counter (window, *US*); ~ **betätigen** to operate (flick) a switch; ~ **schließen** to close the doors;
~**auszahlung** payment over the counter; ~**beamter** booking *(Br.)* (counter, window, *US*) clerk, passenger (ticket) agent *(US)*, windowman *(US)*, *(Bank)* cashier, teller *(US)*; ~**beamter für den Inkassoverkehr** collection teller *(US)*; ~**dienst** counter service, window delivery *(US)*; ~**fenster** wicket, grilled window; ~**geschäft** over-the-counter trade (business) *(US)*; ~**halle** *(Bank)* banking hall, *(Eisenbahn)* booking hall, ticket hall *(US)*, *(Post)* central hall; ~**öffnung** grille, *(Bank)* bank's opening hours; ~**personal** counter staff; ~**schluß** *(Bank)* closing time; ~**stunden** hours of attendance, *(Bank)* banking hours, *(Post)* post-office hours; ~**system** array of switches; ~**verkauf**, ~**verkehr** over-the-counter (window) *(US)* trading.
Schalt|hebel gear lever; ~**hebel ziehen** to pull the levers; ~**jahr** leap (bissextile) year; ~**kasten** *(el.)* switch box, panel; ~**kreis** circuit, circuitry; **integrierter** ~**kreis** integrated circuit; ~**pause** *(Rundfunk)* switching pause; ~**plan** switch diagram, distribution map, hookup; ~**pult** operator's desk; ~**schema** circuit

diagram, circuitry drawings; ~**stöpsel** switch plug; ~**tafel** panel [board], plugboard, switchborad, instrument board; ~**tag** odd (intercalary, leap) day, bissext, bissextile day; ~**uhr** *(Lichtregelung)* time switch.
Schaltung connection *(el.)*, *(Gänge)* gear change, switching;
automatische ~ automatic transmission.
Schalt | vorrichtung tripping device; ~**zeit** operating time; ~**zentrale** *(el.)* central station.
Scham, ohne jede devoid of all shame.
schämen, sich to feel ashamed.
Schamgefühl sense of shame;
sich über jegliches ~ **hinwegsetzen** to throw off all sense of shame; ~ **verletzen** to offend against decency.
schamhaft lächeln to smile bashfully.
schamlos shameless, unashamed, unabashed, indecent, lewd, flagrant;
j. ~ **ausnutzen** to take a mean advantage of s. o.; ~ **lügen** to tell a brazenfaced lie;
~**e Forderung** steep demand; ~**e Korruption** unblushing corruption; ~**e Lüge** whopping lie.
Schamröte ins Gesicht treiben, jem. die to make s. o. blush all over.
Schamotte fire clay;
~**stein** firebrick.
Schampus pop *(coll.)*.
Schandblatt gutter paper, rag.
Schande dishono(u)r, disgrace, ignominy, contempt;
~ **für die ganze Familie** reprobate of (discredit to) one's family;
~ **für die Nation** dishono(u)r to the nation;
seiner Familie ~ **bereiten** to disgrace the family name.
schänden to ravish, to rape, to disgrace, *(Heiligtum)* to profane, to desecrate.
Schandfleck blemish, blot, blur, scar, brand, taint, dark spot;
~ **einer Stadt** plague spot of a city, disgrace to the city authorities.
Schand | frieden ignominious (ignoble) peace; ~**geld** paltry sum.
schändlich shameful, dishono(u)rable, disgraceful, flagrant;
~ **verdienen** to work for a mere pittance;
~**e Gedanken** vile thoughts; ~**e Lüge** whopper; ~**e Tat** atrocity.
Schand | lohn, für einen ~**lohn arbeiten** to work for a mere pittance; ~**mal** stigma, brand; ~**maul** loose tongue, *(Person)* scandalmonger; ~**preis** scandalous (outrageous) price; **etw. für einen** ~**preis verkaufen** to sell s. th. dirt-cheap (for a mere song); ~**tat** foul deed; **gegen Bezahlung zu allen** ~**taten bereit sein** to be game *(sl.)*, to do anything for a consideration.
Schändung rape, violence, abuse, *(Kirche)* profanation, desecration.
Schank | bier beer on tap (draught); ~**erlaubnis** excise *(US)* (liquor, publican's, *Br.*) licence; ~**erlaubnissteuer** licence (license, *US*) fee; ~**gesetz** licensing law, excise law *(US)*; ~**gewerbe** licensed trade; ~**kellner** barman *(Br.)*, bartender, tapster, barkeeper; **als** ~**kellner arbeiten** to tap, to act as tapster; ~**kellnerin** barmaid.
Schankkonzession excise *(US)* (liquor, publican's, *Br.*, justice's, *Br.*) licence, licence for the sale of alcoholic drinks, liquor tax certificate *(US)*;
mit unbeschränkter ~ fully licensed; **ohne** ~ nonlicensed;
beschränkte ~ occasional licence;
jem. eine ~ **erteilen** to license s. o. to sell drinks; ~ **haben** to be licensed to sell drinks.
Schank | lokal licensed premises *(Br.)*, bar, saloon *(US)*; ~**raum** taproom, saloon, bar-room; ~**recht im eigenen Betrieb** on-licence *(Br.)*; ~**recht über die Straße** off-licence *(Br.)*; ~**steuer** tax on beverages; ~**stube** saloon *(US)*, bar *(Br.)*, bar (tap) room; ~**wirt** licensed victualler *(Br.)*, publican *(Br.)*, saloonkeeper *(US)*; ~**wirtschaft** licensed premises *(Br.)*, public house *(Br.)*, pub *(Br.)*, tap, tavern, saloon *(US)*.
Schanzarbeit fieldwork, trenchwork, entrenchment.
Schanze *(mil.)* fieldwork, entrenchment;
sein Leben in die ~ **schlagen** to risk one's life.
Schar crowd, swarm, flock, posse, assemblage, band, gang;
~**en** numbers, loads *(coll.)*;
glänzende ~ galaxy;
~ **schutzzöllnerisch eingestellter Anhänger** protectionist pack;
~ **von Leuten** crowd of people; ~ **junger Mädchen** bevy of girls;
~ **von Schulkindern** troop of schoolchildren; ~**en von Urlaubern** holiday crowds, loads of tourists;
in hellen ~**en herbeiströmen** to come in crowds (flocks), to flock; **in** ~**en in ein Kino strömen** to swarm into a cinema.
scharen, sich to troop up (together); **sich um j.** ~ to rally to the support of s. o.

scharf sharp, *(abrupt)* abruptly, sharply, *(Geschmack)* hot, spicy, peppery, *(Munition)* live, *(Säure)* acrid, corrosive, mordant;
~ **eingestellt** *(Fotoapparat)* in focus;
~ **wie ein Rasiermesser** sharp as a razor; ~ **im Urteil** judicial, critical;
Kind ~ **anfassen** to be very strict with a child; **j.** ~ **bewachen** to watch s. o. closely; ~ **bremsen** to jam on the brakes; ~ **durchgreifen** to take drastic measures; ~ **herausarbeiten** to work out clearly; ~ **kalkulieren** to calculate closely; **j.** ~ **rannehmen** to put s. o. through the mill; ~ **schießen** to shoot with live ammunition; ~ **auf j. sein** to be keen on s. o.; **auf etw.** ~ **sein** to be turned on (nuts) about s. th.; **sich** ~ **senken** *(Straße)* to dip sharply; ~ **verurteilen** to condemn strongly;
~ **begrenzte Befugnisse** clearly defined powers; ~**e Bemerkung** cutting remark; ~**er Beobachter** keen observer; **gestochen** ~**es Bild** well-focussed picture; ~**e Gegenmaßnahmen** drastic countermeasures; ~**er Gegner** strong opponent; ~**er Geruch** pungent smell; ~**e Kalkulation** close calculation; ~**e Kälte** stinging cold; ~**er Konkurrenzkampf** keen (cutthroat) competition; ~**e Kritik** severe (scathing) criticism; ~**e Kurve** sharp curve; ~**e Ohren haben** to have quick ears; ~**er Polizist** tough copper; ~**en Protest einlegen** to raise a strong protest; ~**e Schnäpse** hard drinks; ~**es Verhör** grill; ~**en Verstand haben** to have a keen mind; ~**er Verweis** severe reprimand; ~**er Wind** biting wind; ~**es Zeug** hot stuff.
Scharf | abstimmung sharp tuning; ~**blick** sharp eye, *(fig.)* discernment, discrimination; ~**blick bei der Menschenbeurteilung zeigen** to be a keen judge of men.
Schärfe sharpness, *(Beweisführung)* stringency, *(Bitterkeit)* virulence, *(Fernsehbild)* sharpness, *(Foto)* distinction, sharpness, *(Kritik)* sting, bite, pungency, *(Prüfung)* strictness, toughness, *(Ton)* edge;
~ **des Konkurrenzkampfes** competitive edge; ~ **der Unterscheidung** nicety of distinction.
Scharfeinstellungsvorrichtung focusing mechanism.
schärfen to sharpen, *(Bombe)* to prime.
Scharf | macher *(pol.)* firebrand, rabble-rouser; ~**macherei** rabble-rousing; ~**richter** headsman, executioner; ~**schießen** live shooting (firing); ~**schütze** sharpshooter, marksman, sniper; ~**sinn** acumen, penetration, acuteness; **über** ~**sinn verfügen** to have a keen mind.
scharfsinnig knowing, penetrant, keen-witted, clear-headed;
~ **sein** to have a keen mind.
Scharlatan charlatan, impostor, quack, mountebank.
Scharlatanerie charlatanry, mountebankery.
Scharmützel *(mil.)* skirmish, brush.
Scharte *(Messer)* notch, *(mil.)* embrasure, loophole;
~ **auswetzen** to repair a mistake, to patch up.
Schatten shadow, shade, *(Verfolger)* plaster, tail;
nicht der ~ **eines Verdachts** not a breath of suspicion; **nicht der** ~ **eines Zweifels** without a shadow of doubt; **ohne den** ~ **eines Beweises** without a shadow of proof; **von den Leistungen seines Sohnes in den** ~ **gestellt** dimmed by the deeds of his son;
jem. wie ein ~ **folgen** to shadow s. o.; **im** ~ **des Wirtschaftswunders leben** to live on the seamy side of the economic miracle; **nur ein** ~ **seines früheren Ichs sein** to be only a shadow of one's former self; **in den** ~ **stellen** to cast in the shade, to eclipse, to outshine, to overshadow; **j. in den** ~ **stellen** to be head and shoulders above s. o.; **jds. Verdienste in den** ~ **stellen** to cast (throw) s. one's merits in the shade; ~ **auf etw. werfen** to cast a cloud (shadow) on s. th.; ~ **auf die Ferientage werfen** to cast a damp over the holidays;
man kann nicht über seinen ~ **springen** the leopard cannot change his spots; **wo Licht ist, ist auch** ~ strong lights cast deep shadows;
~**betrieb** *(mil.)* shadow factory; ~**bild** *(Radar)* echo; ~**boxen** shadow-boxing (show); **nur ein** ~**dasein führen** to lead a drab existence, to retire into obscurity; ~**druckanzeige** shadow print advertisement.
schattenhaft shadowy, indefinite, indistinct;
~**e Eindrücke** vague impressions.
Schatten | kabinett shadow government *(Br.)*, government in waiting; ~**könig** phantom of a king, mock king; ~**land** shadowland; ~**organisation** shadow organization; ~**preis** shadow (imputed, accounting) price; ~**seite** dark side *(fig.)*, drawback; **auf der** ~**seite des Lebens stehen** to be on the seamy side of life; ~**stelle** *(Radio)* blind spot; ~**temperatur** shade temperature.
schattieren to shade, to tone.
Schattierung tone, *(Börsenkurs)* shade, shading;
ohne ~ *(Foto)* flat.

Schatulle box, cabinet, casket, cashbox, strongbox, *(Herrscher)* privy purse.
Schatz treasure, spoil, riches, wealth, jewel, *(Liebhaber)* sweetheart, boyfriend, *(Liebling)* one and only, honey *(US)*; **aufgefundener** ~ treasure trove; **verborgener** ~ buried treasure; ~ **an Erfahrungen** rich store of experience; **unerschöpflicher** ~ **amüsanter Geschichten** fund of amusing stories; **verborgenen** ~ **finden** to come upon a hidden treasure; ~ **heben** to dig up a treasure; **verborgenen** ~ **heben** to unearth a buried treasure; **auf einen** ~ **stoßen** to come across a treasure; ~ **verbergen** to hide away a treasure.
Schatzamt public treasury, Exchequer *(Br.)*, chamber *(Br.)*, Treasury [Department] *(US)*.
Schatz|amtsquittungen, verzinsliche treasury deposit receipts *(Br.)*; ~**anleihe** treasury loan, exchequer stock *(Br.)*.
Schatzanweisung [treasury] warrant *(Br.)*, exchequer bond *(Br.)*, treasury bond *(US)* (obligation), warrant check; **kurzfristige** ~ treasury certificate of indebtedness *(US)*, United States Certificate of indebtedness, exchequer bill *(Br.)*; **langfristige** ~ *(an finanzschwache Gemeinden)* Exchequer *(Br.)* (treasury, *US*) bond; **mittelfristige** ~**en** treasury notes; **unverzinsliche** ~**en** short-term treasury bills, noninterest-bearing treasury bonds *(US)*; **verzinsliche** ~**en** exchequer bills *(Br.)*.
schätzbar appreciable, estimable, computable, ratable.
Schätzbarkeit estimableness, ratability.
Schätz|beamter appraiser, assessor; ~**betrag** estimated amount.
Schätze wealth; ~ **ansammeln** to hoard, to treasure up (amass) riches; ~ **aus alten Büchern heben** to quarry treasures from old books.
schätzen *(anerkennen)* to appreciate, to esteem, *(berechnen)* to compute, to calculate, *(bewerten)* to rate, to value, to evaluate, to [form an] estimate, *(steuerlich)* to assess, to rate, *(Versicherung)* to appraise, to make an appraisal, to prize; **Einheitswert eines Grundstücks** ~ to value (assess) an estate; **Gebäude für die Versicherung** ~ to rate a building for insurance purposes; **Gebäudewert zwecks Steuerveranlagung** ~ to assess a building; **jeden Gegenstand einzeln** ~ to value each object; **Grundstückswert** ~ to estimate the value of land (an estate); **zu hoch** ~ to overvalue, to overestimate, to overrate; **von neuem** ~ to revaluate; **zu niedrig** ~ to underestimate, to underrate, to undervalue; **Reparaturkosten eines Hauses** ~ to estimate the repair of a building; **Schaden auf 100 Pfund** ~ to value the damage done at £ 100; **zu Steuerzwecken** ~ to assess for taxable value; **seine Verluste auf 1000 £** ~ to compute one's losses at £ 1000; **jds. Vermögen auf 400.000 Dollar** ~ to rate s. one's fortune at $ 400.000; **im voraus** ~ to anticipate, to forecast; **Wert** ~ to make an appraisal (a valuation); **Wert eines Hauses auf 500.000 £** ~ to value a house at £ 500.000.
schätzenswert estimable, valuable.
Schätzer appraiser, appreciator, valuer, valuator, estimator, *(Steuerwesen)* assessor, *(Zollbescheidverfahren)* merchant appraiser, liquidator *(US)*; **amtlicher** ~ official appraiser, professional valuer; **beeidigter** ~ sworn appraiser, licensed valuer *(Br.)*; ~ **des Finanzamtes** crown assessor *(Br.)*; ~**firma** appraisal company.
Schätzfehler error in estimating.
Schatzfund treasure trove, recovery of a lost treasure.
Schätz|funktion estimator; ~**gebühr** valuation (appraisal) fee; ~**gleichung** *(Statistik)* estimating equation.
Schatzgräber treasure seeker.
Schätz|größe estimator; ~**gutachten** valuer's report.
Schatz|kammer treasure room, treasure (jewel) house, treasure, coffers, *(Schatzamt)* Exchequer *(Br.)*, Treasury Department *(US)*, Department of the Treasury *(US)*; ~**kanzler** Chancellor of the Exchequer *(Br.)*, Secretary of the Treasury Department *(US)*; ~**kästlein** *(Buch)* treasury.
Schatzmeister treasurer, bursar, thesaurier; **umsichtiger** ~ vigilant treasurer; ~ **der Partei** party treasurer; ~**amt** treasureship, bursary.
Schätzpreis estimated price, assessed value (price).
Schatzschein government note *(Br.)*, treasury note *(US)*.
Schatz|suche treasure hunt; ~**sucher** treasure hunter; ~**truhe**, ~**kasten** treasury box (coffers, chest).
Schätzung estimate, estimation, valuation, pricing, *(Berechnung)* computation, calculation, *(Hochachtung)* esteem, *(Steuerwesen)* rating, assessment, *(Versicherung)* appraisal, appraisement, *(Voranschlag)* estimate, rough calculation, *(Wert)* price, value, *(steuerlicher Wert)* assessed value (valuation, *US*); **bei roher (vorläufiger)** ~ at a venture (rough estimate, rough computation); **nach der niedrigsten** ~ at the lowest estimate; **amtliche** ~ official appraisement (estimate), professional valuation; **angemessene** ~ fair estimate; **annähernde** ~ approximate calculation, approximation; **erneute** ~ revaluation, reassessment; **falsche** ~ incorrect estimate, misestimation; **möglichst genaue** ~ outside estimate; **gerichtliche** ~ judicial valuation; **grobe** ~ guesstimate *(sl.)*; **gutachtliche** ~ expert appraisal; **zu hohe** ~ overestimation, overestimate, overvaluation; **irrtümliche** ~ error in estimating; **marktgerechte** ~ market valuation; **zu niedrige** ~ low estimate, underestimate, undervaluation; **rohe (ungefähre)** ~ rough estimate, guess; **ungeprüfte** ~ uncritical estimate; **unsichere** ~ long guess; **vorsichtige** ~ conservative (safe) estimate; ~ **zwecks hypothekarischer Beleihung** rating of the entire mortgage pattern; ~ **zu Erbschaftssteuerzwecken** appraisal for inheritance taxation purposes; ~**en des Finanzministeriums** treasury forecasts; ~ **eines Geschäftsgrundstücks** business property appraisal; ~ **der Grundsteuer** rating valuation *(Br.)*; ~ **eines Grundstücks** real-estate appraisal; ~ **der Herstellungskosten** estimate of the cost of construction; ~ **der Sozialproduktentwicklung** forecast of the national product; ~ **der Unterhaltungskosten** maintenance cost estimate; ~ **nach dem höchsten Wahrscheinlichkeitswert** maximum likelihood estimation; ~ **des Wertes festverzinslicher Effekten** bond rating; **durch** ~ **feststellen** to ascertain by valuation; **vorsichtige** ~ **zugrunde legen** to employ a more conservative estimate; ~ **im Blitzverfahren vornehmen** to evaluate on a hurry-up basis; **zu niedrige** ~ **vornehmen** to pitch an estimate too low.
Schätzungs|ausschuß appraisement committee; ~**beamter** valuation officer, *(Zoll)* merchant appraiser, liquidator *(US)*; ~**befugnis** valuation function; ~**bericht** appraisal report; ~**betrag** estimated amount, appraisement; ~**fehler** error in estimating; ~**grundlage** basis of valuation, valuation basis; ~**kommission** appraisal committee; ~**kosten** appraiser's fees, cost of appraisal, valuation expense; ~**methode** valuation method; ~**richtlinien** assessment principles; ~**sache** valuation case; ~**skala** appraisal profile; ~**tabelle** rating (valuation) table; ~**verfahren** valuation process.
schätzungsweise it has been estimated.
Schatzwechsel government note *(Br.)*, bill of exchequer *(Br.)*, Exchequer (treasury) bill *(Br.)*, treasury note *(US)*; **laufend ausgegebene** ~ tap treasury bills *(Br.)*; **wöchentlich ausgegebene** ~ market treasury bills *(Br.)*; **kurzfristiger** ~ Exchequer (treasury) bill *(Br.)*, treasury's short-term bill *(US)*, treasury certificate *(US)*; **mittelfristiger** ~ treasury note; **noch nicht plazierter** ~ hot treasury bill *(Br.)*; **unverzinsliche** ~ short-time treasury bills *(Br.)*; ~ **neuester Ausgabe** hot treasury bills *(Br.)*; ~ **mit dreimonatiger Laufzeit** tender treasury bill *(Br.)*; ~ **einlösen** to fund government notes; ~**agio** discount on treasury bills *(Br.)*; **verbilligter** ~**ankauf** *(Notenbank)* back-door operation; ~**diskontgeschäft** treasury's short-term bill borrowing; **angestrebter** ~**diskontsatz** treasury's target discount rate; ~**emission** treasury issue; ~**finanzierung** treasury financing; ~**kurs** treasury bill price (rate, *Br.*); ~**offerte von regionalen und ausländischen Börsen** outside tender *(Br.)*; ~**satz** treasury bill rate *(Br.)*.
Schätzwert estimated price (value), *(Steuer)* assessed value (valuation, *US*), *(Versicherung)* appraised (objective, expert) value, appraisement. **unverzerrte** ~**e** estimates free from bias; **verzerrte** ~**e** biassed estimates; **voller** ~ full extended value.
Schau show, exhibition, exposition, *(Angabe)* splurge, splash; ~ **industrieller Erzeugnisse** industrial display; **große** ~ **abziehen** to make a splash, to cut a dash, to splurge, to be a play actor; **sich die ganze** ~ **stehlen lassen** to give the whole show away; **zur** ~ **gestellt sein** to be featured; **jem. die ganze** ~ **stehlen** to steal a march upon s. o.; **zur** ~ **stellen** to sport, to parade, to lay out, to display, to exhibit, to trot out; **sein Elend zur** ~ **stellen** to make a parade of one's misery; **seine Gefühle zur** ~ **stellen** to parade one's feelings, to wear one's heart on one's sleeve; **seine Kenntnisse zur** ~ **stellen** to show (parade) one's knowledge; **Waren zur** ~ **stellen** to set out goods on a stall, to display one's goods for sale; ~**bild** chart, graph, flowsheet, *(Diagramm)* diagram; ~**bild der Verantwortungsbereiche** responsibility chart; ~**bude** booth, stall; ~**budenbesitzer** [itinerant] showman, shower, grifter *(US sl.)*; ~**bühne** stage, theater; **politische** ~**bühne** political scene; ~**burg** picture palace.
Schauder shudder, creeps *(coll.)*.

schauderhaft horrifying, ghastly, terrible;
~**es Englisch sprechen** to murder the King's (Queen's) English.
schaudern to shudder, to shiver, to chill;
j. ~ lassen to give s. o. the creeps.
Schau|effekt visual impact; ~**effekte** gimmickry.
schauen, auf j. to look (gaze) at s. o.; **sich die Augen nach jem. aus dem Kopf** ~ to strain one's eyes to make s. o. out; **zu tief ins Glas** ~ to have a drop too much; **dem Tod ruhig ins Auge** ~ to face death calmly; **besorgt in die Zukunft** ~ to have a gloome view of the future.
Schauer *(Entsetzen)* shudder, shiver, thrill;
gewittrige ~ thundershowers; **vereinzelte** ~ occasional precipitation;
~**drama** blood-and-thunder melodrama; ~**geschichte** horror yarn, atrocity story, penny dreadful *(Br.)*; ~**leute** stevedores.
schauerlich hair-raising, bloodcurdling.
Schauer|mann stevedore, lumper, docker *(Br.)*, longshoreman *(US)*, roustabout *(US)*; ~**roman** penny dreadful *(Br.)*, shilling shocker *(Br., sl.)*, dime (horror) novel *(US)*, bloodcurdler; ~**wetter** showery weather.
Schaufel shovel, scoop, *(Dampfer)* paddle, *(Förderband)* loading bucket;
~**bagger** dipper dredger.
schaufeln, sich sein eigenes Grab to dig one's own grave.
Schaufelrad water wheel.
Schaufenster shopwindow, shopfront *(Br.)*, show (store, *US*) window;
~ **ansehen** to window-gaze, to window-shop, to go window-shopping; **im ~ ausstellen** to display in the window; ~ **dekorieren** to dress (trim, *US*) a [shop]window, to display for sale;
~**anlagen ansehen** to go window-shopping, to window-shop, to window-gaze; ~**arrangement** window dressing; ~**artikel** articles shown in the window; ~**auslage** display in the shopwindow, [window] display; ~**auslagen ansehen** to window-gaze, to go window-shopping; **bei jeder ~auslage stehenbleiben** to pause at every shopwindow; ~**beleuchtung** shopwindow lighting; ~**bummel** larry *(sl.)*; ~**bummel machen** to window-shop, to go window-shopping; ~**bummler** window-shopper; ~**dekorateur** window dresser (decorator, display man), display builder; ~**dekoration** window dressing (display, decoration), display work; ~**einbruch** smash-and-grab raid; ~**gestaltung** window dressing; ~**hintergrund** background; ~**karton** blank board; ~**plakat** window (show) card; ~**puppe** display (lay) figure, dummy; ~**reklame** [shop]window display (advertising); ~**scheibe** shopwindow pane; ~**schmuck** window dressing, trim *(US)*; ~**ständer** prop, bracket; ~**streifen** window streamer; ~**ware** displayed goods; ~**werbung** shopwindow advertising, window advertising; ~**wert** showpiece value; ~**wettbewerb** window-display competition.
Schau|fliegen stunt flying; ~**flug** air display; ~**geschäft** show business; ~**kampf** rodeo; ~**karton** display box; ~**kasten** showcase, display case, glass case.
schaukeln to swing, to seesaw, *(Schiff)* to roll, to rock, *(Omnibus)* to jolt;
das Kind schon ~ to wangle (manage) it somehow.
Schaukelpolitik seesaw policy.
Schau|linie *(Statistik)* curve; ~**loch** inspection hole.
schaulustige Menge crowd of rubbernecks *(US sl.)*.
Schaum foam, *(auf Getränken)* froth;
~ **schlagen** *(fig.)* to lay it on with a trowel; **zu ~ werden** to come to nothing;
~**bad** bubble bath.
schäumen, vor Wut to foam with rage.
Schaum|feuerlöscher foam extinguisher; ~**gummi** sponge (foam) rubber; ~**gummimatratze** foam rubber mattress; ~**krone** white cap, head; ~**schläger** braggart, boaster, gasbag *(coll.)*; ~**schlägerei** swagger, bragging, boasting.
Schaumünze medal.
Schaumwein sparkling wine.
Schaupackung dummy [pack], sham (display) package.
Schauplatz arena, scene, *(Roman)* scene, site, *(Verbrechen)* scene, venue;
vom ~ abtreten to quit the scene; ~ **verlegen** to shift the scene; ~ **eines Romans nach England verlegen** to lay a novel in England.
Schauprozeß show (sham) trial.
Schauspiel stage play, *(fig.)* spectacle, scene;
klägliches ~ pitiful scene; **kurzes** ~ playlet;
~ **bieten** to put on a show; **den Leuten ein ~ geben** to make a spectacle of o. s.;
~**direktor** stage manager.
Schauspieler actor, player, histrionic;
zweitklassiger ~ second-rate actor;
als ~ auftreten to tread the boards; ~ **auspfeifen** to give an actor the bird; ~ **herausrufen** to call for the actor; ~ **sein** to be on the stage; ~ **werden** to go upon the boards (on the stage).
Schauspieler|ei masquerade, play-acting; ~**gruppe** troupe.
Schauspielerin herausbringen to produce an actress.
schauspielerische Leistung theatrical performance.
Schau|spielerkarriere acting career; ~**spielertruppe** theatrical company; ~**spielhaus** theater, theatre *(Br.)*, playhouse; ~**spielkunst** histrionic art; ~**steller** exhibitor, shower, showman; ~**stellung** display, exhibition; ~**stück** exhibit, exhibited article, showpiece, show-off piece, *(Glanzstück)* feat, stunt *(coll.)*; ~**tafel** display board, diagram, chart, broadside, graph; ~**werbegestalter** display man, window dresser.
Scheck cheque *(Br.)*, check *(US)*;
abgerechneter ~ cleared cheque (check); **noch nicht abgerechneter** ~ uncleared cheque *(Br.)*; **annullierter** ~ cancelled check *(US)* (cheque, *Br.*); **nicht fertig ausgefüllter** ~ inchoate check; **von einem Nichtkaufmann ausgestellter** ~ personal check; **als Sicherheit ausgestellter** ~ memorandum cheque *(Br.)*; **auswärtiger** ~ out-of-town cheque *(Br.)*; **avisierter** ~ advised check; **im Einzug befindliche** ~**s** checks in process of collection, float *(US)*; **von einer Bank beglaubigter (bestätigter)** ~ marked (guaranteed) cheque *(Br.)*, certified check *(US)*; **beschädigter** ~ mutilated cheque *(Br.)*; **durchkreuzter** ~ crossed check; **eigener** ~ house item *(Br.)*, own check *(US)*, home debit *(US)*; **insgesamt bei einer Verrechnungsstelle eingehende** ~**s** inclearing *(Br.)*, incoming exchanges *(US)*; **eingelöster** ~ paid check; **nicht eingelöster** ~ unpaid (dishono(u)red) check; **noch nicht eingelöster** ~ outstanding cheque *(Br.)*; **am Schalter eingelöster** ~ check cashed over the counter; **der Verrechnungsstelle eingereichte** ~**s und Wechsel** bank clearings (exchanges, *US*); **entwerteter** ~ cancelled check; **fehlerhafter** ~ defective check; **nicht firmierter** ~ uncrossed cheque *(Br.)*, open check *(US)*; **gefälschter** ~ false (forged, bogus, cold, *US*) check; **durch Erhöhung des Betrages gefälschter** ~ raised check *(US)*; **zum Ausgleich eines Anspruchs gegebener** ~ cheque in full settlement of a claim *(Br.)*; **gekennzeichneter** ~ certified cheque *(Br.)*, marked check *(US)*; **abhanden gekommener** ~ lost check; **gekreuzter** ~ crossed cheque *(Br.)*; **nicht in Anspruch genommener** ~ unclaimed cheque *(Br.)*; **auf Echtheit der Unterschrift geprüfter** ~ initialled cheque *(Br.)*; **zum Einzug gesandte** ~**s** checks in process of collection; **insgesamt an andere Verrechnungsstellen gesandte** ~**s** outclearing *(Br.)*; **gesperrter** ~ stopped (blocked) check; **girierfähiger** ~ negotiable cheque *(Br.)*; **girierter** ~ endorsed check; **nicht girierter** ~ unendorsed cheque *(Br.)*; **nicht ordnungsgemäß girierter** ~ cheque irregularly endorsed *(Br.)*; **zum Einzug hereingegebene** ~**s** checks paid in for collection; **nicht indossierter** ~ unbacked check; **auf Dollar lautender** ~ dollar check; **auf den Namen lautender** ~ nonnegotiable check; **auf den Überbringer lautender** ~ check [payable] to bearer; **limitierter** ~ limited cheque *(Br.)*; **nachdatierter** ~ postdated check; **protestierter** ~ protested check; **retournierte** ~**s** returned checks, returns *(Br.)*; **überfälliger** ~ state (overdue) check; **zum Einzug übersandter** ~ check sent for collection; **unausgefüllter** ~ blank check; **der Höhe nach unbegrenzter** ~ unlimited cheque *(Br.)*; **unbezahlter** ~ returned cheque *(Br.)*; **undatierter** ~ undated check; **uneingelöster** ~ unpaid (uncleared, dishono(u)red) check; **ungedeckter** ~ flash (dud, bad, uncovered) check, worthless cheque *(Br.)*, check without provision, rubber check *(US)*, bouncer, kite *(Br.)*, stumer *(Br., sl.)*, bad check *(US)*, cheque without sufficient funds *(Br.)*; **unvollständiger** ~ invalid check; **verfallener** ~ overdue cheque *(Br.)*; **verjährter** ~ stale cheque *(Br.)*; **auf dem Postwege verlorengegangener** ~ cheque lost in the post *(Br.)*; **verspätet vorgelegter** ~ overdue check; **noch nicht verrechnete** ~**s** uncleared effects *(Br.)*; **vordatierter** ~ antedated check, check dated ahead; **vorgekommener** ~ presented check; **zur Einlösung noch nicht vorgelegter** ~ outstanding check;
~ **auf die Londoner City** town cheque *(Br.)*; ~ **ohne Deckung** flash check; ~ **auf Groß-London** metropolitan cheque *(Br.)*; ~ **mit angehefteter Quittung** cheque with receipt form attached *(Br.)*; ~ **mit Rechnungsvermerk** check voucher *(US)*; ~ **auf sich selbst** cashier's check *(US)*; ~ **mit geprüfter Unterschrift** initial(l)ed check; ~ **nur zur Verrechnung** nonnegotiable check, crossed cheque *(Br.)*, clearinghouse check *(US)*; **am nächsten Tag eingelöste** ~**s und Wechsel** holdovers *(US)*;
gekreuzten ~ in einen Barscheck abändern to open a crossing *(Br.)*; ~ **vom Scheckheft abtrennen** to tear a check out of the

book; ~ **annehmen** to accept a cheque *(Br.)*; **zu jds. Gunsten einen ~ ausfüllen** to write out a cheque *(Br.)* (check, *US*) in s. one's favo(u)r; ~ **ausschreiben** to write (make) out a check; ~ **ausstellen** to draw a cheque *(Br.)*; **gegenseitig ~s ausstellen** to kite *(Br.)*; **ungedeckte ~s ausstellen** to issue bad checks; ~ **auf j. ausstellen** to oblige s. o. with a check, to make out a check to s. o.; **~s auf London ausstellen** to value cheques on London *(Br.)*; ~ **auf den Schatzmeister ausstellen** to draw a cheque in favo(u)r of the treasurer *(Br.)*; ~ **auf den Überbringer ausstellen** to make a cheque payable to bearer *(Br.)*; **zum Rechnungsausgleich einen ~ beifügen** to enclose a cheque in settlement *(Br.)*; **ungedeckte ~s benutzen** to lay paper *(sl.)*; ~ **bestätigen** to mark a cheque *(Br.)*, to certify a check *(US)*; **ungedeckten ~ bestätigen** to overcertify *(US)*; **mit ~ bezahlen** to remit (pay) by check *(US)* (cheque, *Br.*); ~ **höher beziffern** to raise a check *(US)*; **gefälschten ~ in Verkehr bringen** to pass a forged cheque *(Br.)*; ~ **einlösen** to cash (collect, pay in) a cheque *(Br.)*, to hono(u)r a check; ~ **bei der Bank einlösen** to pay a check into (get the check cashed at) the bank; ~ **nicht einlösen** to dishono(u)r a cheque *(Br.)*; ~ **einreichen** to lodge a check; ~ **zum Einzug einreichen** to pay in a check for collection; ~ **zur Gutschrift einreichen** to deposit a check; ~ **einziehen** to collect a cheque *(Br.)*; ~ **entgegennehmen** to accept a check; ~ **fälschen** to forge (alter) a check; ~ **girieren** to endorse a check; ~ **vor Einreichung gutschreiben** to credit a cheque as cash before clearance *(Br.)*; ~ **honorieren** to pay a check; ~ **für j. kassieren** to cash a check for s. o.; ~ **kreuzen** to cross a cheque *(Br.)*; **sich einen ~ vom Konto auszahlen lassen** to draw a check upon an account; ~ **platzen lassen** to bounce a check; ~ **sperren lassen** to stop payment on a check, to place a stop on a cheque *(Br.)*; ~ **zurückgehen lassen** to dishono(u)r a cheque *(Br.)*; ~ **durch Streichungen ungültig machen** to obliterate the writing of a check; ~ **sperren** to earmark a cheque *(Br.)*; ~ **stornieren** to cancel a check; ~ **einer Bank zum Einzug übergeben** to lodge a check with a bank for collection; ~ **zum Ausgleich übersenden** to send a check in settlement; ~ **verfolgen** to trace a check; ~ **verrechnen** to clear a check *(US)* (cheque, *Br.*); ~ **bei der Girozentrale verrechnen** to pass a cheque through the clearinghouse *(Br.)*; ~ **mit Verrechnungsvermerk versehen** to cross a cheque *(Br.)*; ~ **vor[aus]datieren** to date a check ahead, to antedate (date forward) a check; ~ **zur Bestätigung vorlegen** to present a cheque for certification *(Br.)*; ~ **zur Einlösung vorlegen** to cash (collect) a check, to present a check for payment; **per ~ zahlen** to pay by check; ~ **auf ein Guthaben ziehen** to issue a check against (draw a check upon) an account; ~ **an den Aussteller zurückgeben** to refer a check to the drawer; ~ **zurückweisen** to return (dishono(u)r) a check, to reject a cheque *(Br.)*;

~abrechnung cheque clearance *(Br.)* (clearing); **~abrechnungssatz** clearinghouse exchange rate *(US)*; **~abrechnungsstelle** clearinghouse; **~abrechnungsverkehr** cheque clearing *(Br.)*; **~abschnitt** counterfoil of a check, stub *(US)*; **~anforderung** request for a check; **~außenstände** outclearing *(Br.)*; **~aussteller** drawer (maker) of a check; **~ausstellung** making out (drawing, issuance, issue of) a check, check writing; **vereinbartes ~ausstellungslimit** agreed limit for a check; **~austausch innerhalb einer Stadt** intercity check clearing service; **~austauschstelle** clearinghouse; **~bestand** checks in hand; **~bestätigung** *(durch Bank)* certifying of a check *(US)*, marking of a cheque *(Br.)*, certification of a check, advice of fate; **~betrag fälschen** to kite (raise) a check *(US)*; **~betrug** cheque fraud *(Br.)*, issuing bad checks *(US)*; **~betrug begehen** to issue bad checks *(US)*; **~betrüger** cheque trickster *(Br.)*; **~betrügereien** cheque cheats *(Br.)*; **~bezogener** drawee; **~buch** cheque book *(Br.)*, checkbook *(US)*; **~buch anfordern** to make application for a checkbook *(US)*; **sein ~buch zücken** to pull out one's cheque book *(Br.)*; **~bündel** package of checks; **~bürgschaft** check guarantee; **vereinfachter ~dienst** personal cheque service *(Br.)*; **~duplikat** duplicate check; **~einlagen** demand deposits subject to check *(US)*; **~einlösung** cashing of a check, check cashing; **~einlösung im Lastschriftinkassoverfahren** payment of a cheque under advice *(Br.)*; **~einreichung** lodging of a check; **~einreichungsformular** credit slip for checks; **~einziehung** (cashing) collection of cheques *(Br.)* (checks, *US*), cheque collection *(Br.)*; **~empfänger** payee of a check; **~fälscher** check forger, fake check customer *(US)*, paper hanger *(sl.)*; **~fälschung** fraudulent alteration of checks, forgery on checks, check alteration (forgery), paper hanging *(sl.)*; **~formular** blank check, check form; **kombiniertes ~- und Quittungsformular** combined cheque and receipt form *(Br.)*; **~gesetz** Cheques Act *(Br.)*; **~guthaben** demand deposit, current account *(Br.)*, drawing account *(US)*; **~handelssatz** clearinghouse exchange rate, cash rate *(Br.)*; **~heft** cheque book *(Br.)*, checkbook *(US)*; **~inhaber** endorsee (bearer, holder) of a check; **rechtmäßiger ~inhaber** bona-fide holder for value without notice; **~inkasso** collection of checks *(US)* (cheques, *Br.*), check collection, check cashing; **am vereinbarten ~- und Lastschrifteninkasso teilnehmen** to claim the protection of the Cheques Act *(Br.)*; **~inkassospesen** check-collection charges; **~karte** banker's card, cheque card *(Br.)*, check card *(US)*; **~karteninhaber** holder of a cheque card *(Br.)*, check card holder *(US)*; **~konto** cheque account *(Br.)*, drawing (checking) account *(US)*; **gebührenpflichtiges ~konto** special checking account *(US)*; **~kontoinhaber** cheque account depositor *(Br.)*; **~kontrollabteilung** certification department *(US)*; **besondere ~kreuzung** special crossing *(Br.)*; **~kreuzung rückgängig machen** to open a crossing *(Br.)*; **~kurs** cash rate *(Br.)*, clearinghouse exchange rate *(US)*; **~leiste** counterfoil, stub *(US)*, check (cheque) register; **~merkmale** data of a check; **~nummer** number of a check, check number; **~rechnung** check account; **~schutzvorrichtung** device for protection of checks *(US)* (cheques, *Br.*), check protection device; **~sperre** stopping [payment of] a check *(US)* (cheque, *Br.*), stop [payment] order; **~stempel**, **~steuer** duty on checks, check stamp, stamp duty on cheques *(Br.)*; **~stornierung** countermand of payment of a cheque *(Br.)*; **~summe** amount of a check; **~system** check system; **~umlauf** checks in circulation; **~unterschrift** signature on cheques (checks, *US*); **~- und Wechselverkäufe** cheque and bill transactions *(Br.)*; **~verkehr** check transactions, clearing-house business; **~- und Wechselverkehr** check and bill transactions; **~verrechnung** clearing of checks, check clearing; **regionale ~verrechnungsstelle** regional clearinghouse; **~verrechnungssystem** clearinghouse system; **~versicherung** check alteration and forgery insurance *(US)*; **~verzeichnis** check register; **~vordruck** check form, blank check; **~zahlung** payment by cheque *(Br.)*; **~ziffern in betrügerischer Absicht erhöhen** to raise a check *(US)*; **~zurückweisung wegen nicht ausreichenden Guthabens** returning a cheque for lack of funds *(Br.)*.

Scheffel, sein Licht unter den ~ stellen to hide one's light under a bushel.

scheffeln, Geld to be simply coining money.

scheffelweise in stacks (loads, *coll.*);
~ **Geld ausgeben** to be off on a spending spree, to spend money like water.

Scheibe disk, disc, *(Fenster)* [window] pane, *(Schießscheibe)* target, *(Wählscheibe)* dial;
~ **Brot** slice of bread;
sich von jem. eine ~ abschneiden to take a leaf out of s. one's book; **jem. die ~ einschmeißen** to smash s. one's window; ~ **einsetzen** to pane, to furnish with panes; ~ **beschlagen lassen** to blur the window.

Scheiben|belüfter demister; **~bremse** disk brake; **~bremssystem** disc-drum braking system; **~eis** pancake ice; **~gardinen** short blinds; **~glas** sheet (window) glass; **~kupplung** disc clutch (coupling); **~rad** disk wheel; **~schießen** target practice; **~signal** *(Bahn)* disk signal; **~stand** shooting range; **~waschanlage** windshield *(US)* (windscreen, *Br.*) washer; **~wasserstand** screen wash level; **~wischer** windscreen wiper *(Br.)*, windshield wiper *(US)*; **langsam laufender ~wischer** delayed-action wiper; **~wischergummi** wiper blade.

Scheide|anstalt refinery; **~geld** subsidiary (token) coin; **~münze** change, fractional currency, base (minor, subsidiary, fractional, divisional) coin.

scheiden to depart, *(Bergbau)* to separate, to sort, *(Eheleute)* to divorce, *(raffinieren)* to try;
aus dem Dienst ~ to retire from office, to resign; **als Freunde ~** to part friends; **aus dem Leben ~** to depart this life, *(Selbstmörder)* to take one's life; ~ **von Tisch und Bett** to separate from bed and board;
sich ~ lassen to [seek a] divorce, to get (obtain) a divorce, to divorce one's husband (wife).

Scheide|wand barrier; **~weg** crossroads; **am ~weg stehen** to be at the parting of the ways, *(fig.)* to come to the crossroads; **~wert** dividing value.

Scheidung|im gegenseitigen Einvernehmen divorce by mutual consent; ~ **wegen Verschuldens** divorce on grounds of guilt;
~ **aussprechen** to grant a divorce; ~ **beantragen** to petition for a divorce, to seek divorce; ~ **einleiten** to start divorce proceedings; **auf ~ erkennen** to grant a divorce; ~ **erlangen** to get a divorce; **auf ~ klagen** to petition for a divorce; **der ~ widersprechen** to oppose the divorce.

Scheidungs|antrag, ~begehren petition for a divorce, divorce petition; **~beklagter** respondent; **~gericht** divorce court; **~grund** ground for a divorce, divorcer *(US)*; **~klage** divorce petition; **~klage einreichen** to sue (file a petition) for [a] divorce; **~kläger** divorcer, petitioner *(Br.)*; **~prozentsatz** divorce rate; **~prozeß, ~sache** divorce case (suit); **~richter** divorce judge.

Scheidungsurteil decree of divorce;
ausländisches ~ foreign divorce; **bedingtes ~** decree nisi *(Br.)*; **rechtskräftiges ~** decree absolute;
~ erwirken to obtain (get) a divorce; **~ verkünden** to grant a divorce.

Scheidungs|vereinbarung divorce settlement; **~verfahren** divorce proceedings (suit); **~ziffer** divorce rate.

Schein certificate, bill, *(Anschein)* air, outward appearance, colo(u)r, shade, mask, sham, *(Formular)* form, blank, *(Leuchten)* shine, *(Papiergeld)* bill, [bank] note, *(Quittung)* receipt, acquittance, *(Urkunde)* document, deed, instrument, voucher, *(Vortäuschen)* pretence, mock, sham, *(Zettel)* slip, *(Zeugnis)* certificate, attestation;
beim trüben ~ einer Kerze in the dim light of a candle; **dem ~ nach** apparently; **gegen doppelten ~** on double receipt; **laut beiliegendem ~** as per certificate enclosed; **nur zum ~** only for show; **unter dem ~** under the mask (cloak) of;
schwacher ~ gleam;
Rechnung nur zum ~ ausstellen to write out a proforma bill; **auf seinem ~ bestehen** to demand one's pound of flesh; **dem ~ nach zu urteilen** to judge by appearances; **den ~ wahren** to keep up appearances, to put up a front *(US)*; **um den ~ zu wahren** for appearance's sake;
~adoption fictitious adoption; **~angebot** rigged bid, dummy tender; **~angriff** *(mil.)* feint, mock (false, holding) attack; **~angriff durchführen** to feint; **~anlage** *(mil.)* dummy work, decoy; **~anleger** dummy investor; **~anspruch** colo(u)rable title; **~antrag** sham plea; **~argument** seeming (spurious, specious) argument, sophism; **~auktion** mock (sham) auction, knockout [auction] *(Br.)*; **~autorität** phantom of authority.

scheinbar quasi, apparent, seeming, ostensible, bogus, mock, fictitious, specious, would-be;
~er Anspruch specious claim; **~es Interesse** feigned interest; **~e Vertretungsmacht** apparent (ostensible) authority; **~er Widerspruch** apparent contradiction.

Schein|beantwortung sham answer; **~beweis** seeming (spurious) argument, specious (sham) proof; **~bieter** mock (straw, *US*) bidder, by-bidder, white bonnet *(fam.)*, *(für den Grundeigentümer)* puffer; **~bilanz** fictitious balance sheet; **~blüte** specious (sham, *US*) boom; **~dividende** sham (fictitious) dividend; **~ehe** mock (shift, sham, fictitious) marriage, marriage in name only; **~einwand** sham plea; **~faktura** proforma invoice; **~filiale** dummy branch; **~firma** bogus firm (company); **~flugplatz** decoy airport; **~forderung** bogus (specious) claim; **~freundschaft** professed friendship; **~friede** hollow peace; **~gebot** sham (rigged, feigned) bid, straw bid *(US)*; **~gebot abgeben** to puff; **~gefecht** sham fight, *(mil.)* sham (mock) battle; **~gericht** mock trial, kangaroo court *(US sl.)*; **~geschäft** colo(u)rable (bogus, dummy, fictitious, pro-forma, simulated, sham) transaction, fictitious bargain, sham business, dummy activity; **~gesellschaft** quasi partnership, dummy corporation *(US)*; **~gesellschafter** ostensible (apparent, nominal) partner, holding-out partner *(Br.)*; **~gewinn** apparent (imaginary, fictitious, illusory, paper) profit; **~grund** pretence; **~handel** phantom trade; **~heiliger** devil dodger, snuffer, hypocrite.

scheinheiliges Gerede cant.

Schein|herrschaft mock rule; **~kauf** mock (feigned, proforma, sham, fictitious) purchase; **~käufer** button *(sl.)*; **~klage** false action; **~konjunktur** quasi prosperity, specious (sham, *US*) boom; **~konto** fictitious account.

scheinkrank malingering.

Schein|kranker malingerer; **~krieg** mimic warfare; **~manöver** *(mil.)* demonstration, stratagem; **~pistole** imitation firearm, dummy pistol; **~prozeß** feigned (fictitious) action, mock trial; **~quittung** pro-forma receipt; **~tod** asphyxia, apparent death; **~transaktion** simulation; **~unternehmen** dummy concern; **~urteil** simulated judgment; **~verfahren** feigned issue (action), mock trial; **~verkauf** simulated (fictitious, sham, pro-forma) sale; **~ankauf und ~verkauf von Börsenpapieren** wash sale *(US)*, washing *(US)*; **~verkäufe vornehmen** *(Börse)* to wash sales of stock *(US)*; **~vertrag** simulated (feigned, fictitious, sham) contract, simulation; **~vertreter** ostensible agent, agent by estoppel; **~vertretung** ostensible (dummy) agency; **~vollmacht** agency by estoppel, apparent authority; **~vorbringen** deceitful plea, sham answer; **~wahl** mock (sham) election; **~wechsel** bogus (pro-forma) bill, fictitious bill *(Br.)*, kite *(Br.)*.

Scheinwerfer searchlight, reflector, *(Auto)* headlight, *(Theater)* floodlight projector;
von ~n angestrahlt flood-lit;
abgeblendete ~ nondazzle headlight;
~abblendung dimming of lights.

Scheinwerferlicht floodlight, spotlight;
im ~ der Öffentlichkeit in the full glare of publicity; **im vollen ~** full in the beam of a searchlight;
gegen die Versuchungen des Lebens im ~ ankämpfen to stem the temptations of public life; **im ~ stehen** to be in the limelight.

Schein|wert apparent (fictitious, imaginary) value; **~zahlung** feigned (fictitious, sham) payment.

Scheitel, vom ~ bis zur Sohle from tip to toe, from top to bottom.

Scheitelpunkt summit, zenith, pinnacle, peak, crest;
~ der Investitionsanstrengungen peak investment; **~ der Macht** zenith of power.

Scheiterhaufen funeral pile, pyre, stake;
auf dem ~ at the stake;
vor einem ~ stehen to have stranded upon the rocks.

Scheitern failure, miscarriage, breakdown, flop, *(Schiff)* grounding, stranding;
~ einer Ehe irretrievable breakdown of a marriage; **~ seiner Hoffnungen** shipwreck of one's hopes; **~ der Verhandlungen** breakdown of negotiations;
zum ~ bringen to shipwreck, to wreck; **jds. Pläne zum ~ bringen (über den Haufen werfen)** to upset s. one's applecart, to frustrate (thwart) s. one's plans; **zum ~ verurteilt sein** to be doomed to failure, to be bound to fail, to be a dead duck.

scheitern to miscarry, to fall to the ground, to run upon the rocks, to break down, to flop, to founder, *(im Geschäftsleben)* to fail, *(Schiff)* to ground, to run aground, to be stranded (wrecked);
an der Abschlußprüfung ~ to fail (flunk, *US*) in the finals; **auf den Klippen ~** to run on the rocks;
~ lassen to blow up *(sl.)*; **Verhandlungen ~ lassen** to frustrate negotiations.

Schelle bell.

schellen, bei jem. to ring at s. one's door.

Schelm wag, rascal, rogue.

Schelmenroman picaresque novel.

Schelmereien begehen to play loosely (tricks).

Schelte talking-to, scolding, telling-off, wig *(Br., coll.)*.

schelten to scold, to take to task.

Schema form, scheme, schedule, system, array, formula, *(Anordnung)* table, arrangement, diagram, system, *(Muster)* pattern, model;
nach ~ F according to pattern, stereotyped;
festes ~ set pattern;
nach ~ F behandeln to do s. th. as a matter of routine; **an ein ~ gebunden sein** to have to stick to a pattern;
~brief form letter.

schematisch schematical, systematic;
~ arbeiten to work mechanically; **Vorgang ~ darstellen** to present a process by means of a schematic diagram;
~e Anordnung schematic arrangement; **~e Darstellung** diagram, chart, schematic arrangement; **~e Zeichnung** skeleton sketch.

schematisieren to schematize, to standardize, to systemize.

Schematisierung standardization, systemization.

Schematismus schematism.

Schemel footrest.

Schemen blur, shadowy figure.

schemenhaft phantom, ethereal.

Schenke tavern *(US)*, pub *(Br.)*, taphouse, pothouse.

schenken to give, to make a present, to gift, to grant, *(vermachen)* to endow, to donate *(US)*;
jem. etw. ~ to give a present to s. o., to present s. o. with s. th.; **jem. seine ganze Aufmerksamkeit ~** to listen to s. o. with profound interest; **sich einen Besuch ~** to skip a visit; **jem. die Freiheit ~** to bestow freedom on s. o.; **jem. etw. zum Geburtstag ~** to give s. o. a birthday present; **jem. drei Monate Gefängnis ~** to remit s. o. three months of imprisonment; **jem. Gehör ~** to listen to s. o.; **einer Propaganda Gehör ~** to fall victim to propaganda; **jem. das Leben ~** to spare s. one's life, to pardon s. o.; **einem Kind das Leben ~** to bring a child into the world; **sich gegenseitig nichts ~** *(Gegner)* not to pull one's punches; **sich selbst nichts ~** not to spare o. s.; **jem. Vertrauen ~** to place confidence in s. o.;
sich nichts ~ lassen wollen not to want special treatment.

Schenker donator, giver, benefactor;
in ~laune sein to be in a giving mood.
Schenkung donation, gift, charitable disposition, benefaction, bestowal, *(schriftliches)* grant, *(Stiftung)* foundation, dotation, endowment;
juristisch nicht abgeschlossene ~ imperfect gift; **bedingungslose ~** outright gift; **großzügige ~** liberal gift; **karitative ~** charitable gift; **letztwillige ~** testamentary gift; **notarielle ~** gift under seal; **steuerfreie ~** tax-free gift; **steuerpflichtige ~** taxable gift; **unentgeltliche ~** gratuitous donation, voluntary gift; **mit einer Auflage verbundene ~** onerous donation; **vollgezogene ~** vested gift; **widerrufene ~** revoked donation; **wohltätige ~** gift to charity;
~ in Anerkennung geleisteter Dienste remunerative donation; **~ unter Auflage** onerous gift; **~ beweglicher Gegenstände** gift of chattels; **~ unter Lebenden** absolute (lifetime) gift, gift during life (inter vivos); **~ an einen bestimmten Personenkreis** gift to a class of persons, class gift; **~ von Todes wegen** testamentary gift, gift by will, donation mortis causa *(US)*; **~ auf dem Totenbett** deathbed bequest;
~ nicht annehmen to repudiate a gift; **~ machen** to make a present, to donate; **~ widerrufen** to demand the return of a gift, to revoke a donation.
Schenkungs|absicht intention to make a gift; **~annahme** acceptance of gift; **abzugsfähiger ~aufwand** deductible donation costs; **steuerfreie ~beträge** net gifts; **~brief** deed of gift [for a nominal sum]; **~empfänger** receiver of a gift, donee, presentee; **~land** bounty lands.
Schenkungssteuer gift tax *(US)*;
Erbschafts- und ~ capital transfer tax *(Br.)*;
vermiedene ~ gift-tax exclusion *(US)*;
der ~ unterliegen to be subject to gift tax *(US)*;
~freibetrag gift-tax exemption *(US)*; **~freibetrag für Gegenstände unter DM 2000** small-gift relief *(Br.)*.
schenkungssteuerpflichtig sein to be accountable for duty on a gift, to be subject to gift tax *(US)*.
Schenkungssteuer|satz gift-tax rate *(US)*; **~vergünstigungen** gift-tax benefits *(US)*.
Schenkungs|urkunde gift by deed; **~vermutung** presumption of a gift (advancement, *Br.*); **~versprechen** promise to make a gift, executory gift; **~vertrag** gift deed, deed of gift, deed of donation, charitable contract; **etw. im ~wege erwerben** to acquire s. th. by free gift.
schenkungsweise by way of donation, as a free gift.
Schenkungswiderruf revocation (return) of a donation (gift).
Scherbe piece, fragment;
in ~n gehen to fall to pieces.
Scherbengericht ostracism.
scheren *(Flugzeug)* to yaw;
sich den Teufel um etw. ~ to not to care a button about s. th., to let things go hang.
Scherenfernrohr telescope, periscope.
Scherereien trouble, bother;
gerichtliche ~ vexation, harassment by process of law;
allerhand ~ haben to be subjected to many vexations; **jem. erhebliche ~ machen** to cause s. o. a lot of trouble.
Scherflein mite, alms, penny, two-cents worth *(US coll.)*;
sein ~ für eine gute Sache beitragen to give one's mite for a good cause.
Scherge bum, bailiff *(Br.)*;
~ des Gerichts myrmidon of the law.
Scherz frolic, joke, jest, pleasantry;
~ beiseite all kidding aside *(US)*, joking apart;
improvisierter ~ *(Theater)* wheeze *(sl.)*;
~e und Streiche quips and cranks;
sich einen ~ mit jem. erlauben to play a joke on s. o.; **sich einen schlechten ~ mit jem. erlauben** to play a nasty trick on s. o.;
seine ~e mit jem. treiben to poke fun at s. o.
scherzhaft gemeint sein, nur to be meant only as a joke.
Scheu shyness, bashfulness, *(Abneigung)* aversion;
ohne ~ sprechen to express o. s. freely.
scheu shy, bashful, timid.
scheuen to shrink, to shun, *(Pferd)* to shy, to skit;
Arbeit ~ to shirk one's share of work; **sich vor neuen Bekanntschaften ~** to shrink from meeting strangers; **keine Kosten ~** to spare no expense; **keine Mühe ~** to leave no stone unturned; **Öffentlichkeit ~** to shun publicity.
Scheuerleiste washboard.
Scheuklappe *(Pferd)* winker;
sich ~n aufsetzen to put on the blinkers.
Scheune barn.

Scheunen|drescher, wie ein ~drescher essen to eat like a horse; **~tor** barndoor.
Scheusal monster, *(hum.)* beast.
scheußlich monstrous, hideous, repulsive;
~ kalt awfully cold;
~es Geräusch hideous noise; **~e Geschichte** dreadful story; **~es Verbrechen** atrocious (beastly) crime; **~es Wetter** abominable weather.
Scheußlichkeit monstrosity, beastliness, atrocity.
Schicht shift, spell, bout, *(Arbeitskolonne)* shift, gang, *(Arbeitszeit)* shift, turn, work period, swing *(coll.)*, *(Bergbau)* stint, *(Foto)* emulsion, *(geol.)* zone, *(der Gesellschaft)* rank, class, layer, *(Gruppe)* bracket, *(Ölschicht)* film, *(Pause)* break, rest, off-time, *(Straßenbau)* layer, bed, *(Überzug)* coat;
aus allen ~en der Bevölkerung from all walks of life; **in einer ~** uninterruptedly, without a break;
abwechselnde ~ rotating shift; **Mitternacht beginnende ~** graveyard (midnight) shift; **bürgerliche ~** middle class; **drei ~en täglich** three tours a day; **nicht durchgehende ~** split shift; **erste ~** first shift; **führende ~** leading class; **gebildete ~** educated classes; **gesellschaftliche ~** social ladder *(fam.)*; **gleichbleibende ~** fixed shift; **halbe ~** half time; **herrschende ~en** governing (ruling) classes; **die oberen ~en** the higher classes; **periodische ~** rotating shift; **soziale ~** social status, stratum; **die unteren ~en** the lower classes; **verarmte ~** shabby genteel; **verfahrene ~** shifts worked; **verlorene ~en** men shifts lost; **zusätzliche ~** relief (swing) shift *(US)*;
~ der gehobenen Angestellten ranks of middle management; **~ der leitenden Angestellten** executive class; **breite ~en der Bevölkerung** wide sections (great masses) of the population; **alle ~en der Gesellschaft** all ranks and classes;
in ~en abwechseln to rotate shifts; **~ arbeiten** to work staggered hours (in shifts, by stints); **halbe ~ arbeiten** to work short time; **~en auswechseln** to rotate shifts; **~ machen** to close down, to knock off (down, *sl.*), to make (take) a break *(fam.)*; **sich für die führende ~ qualifizieren** to match the executive suite;
~arbeit daywork, shift [operation (work)]; **~arbeit verrichten** to work in shifts (staggered hours); **~arbeiter** shift worker, dayworker; **~ausfall** shifts not worked; **~ausgleich** shift differential; **~betrieb** [multiple] shift operation; **im ~betrieb laufen** to run full time; **~holz** stacked wood; **~leistung** *(Bergbau)* output per manshift; **normale ~leistung** standard output per shift; **~lohn** shift (basic, base) wage (pay); **~meister** shift boss, shifter *(US)*, *(Bergbau)* purser; **~prämie** shift premium; **~staffelung** *(Verkehr)* staggering of shifts; **~umsetzung** shift transfer.
Schichtung, gesellschaftliche social stratification.
Schicht|unterricht *(Schule)* shift work (differential); **~verkürzung** *(Arbeitslosigkeitsbekämpfung)* staggering of shifts; **~wechsel** changeover; **~wechsel bei der Bahnabfertigung** trick in a railroad dispatch office.
schichtweise by shifts.
Schicht|zeit shift hours; **~zettel** shift slip; **~zulage** shift premium; **~zuschlag** shift allowance (differential).
Schick chic, style, elegance.
schick stylist, smart, knowing *(US)*, chic *(coll.)*, keen *(sl.)*, posh *(fam.)*, nifty *(US sl.)*;
nicht ~ out of line;
für ~ gehalten werden to become chic;
~es Restaurant smart restaurant.
schicken to send, *(absenden)* to dispatch, to forward, *(Brief)* to post *(Br.)*, to mail *(US)*, *(Güter expedieren)* to consign, to convey, *(Telegramm)* to dispatch;
sich ~ to accommodate o. s., *(geziemen)* to befit; **nach einem Arzt ~** to send for a doctor; **mit der Bahn ~** to rail, to forward by rail, to transport by railroad *(US)*; **jem. einen Boten ~** to send a messenger to s. o.; **als Drucksache ~** to send by book post *(Br.)* (printed matter, printed papers, book, *Br.*) rate; **Geld ~** to remit (transfer) money; **jem. j. auf den Hals ~** to set s. o. on s. o.; **Mädchen auf die Straße ~** *(Zuhälter)* to make a girl walk the street; **per Nachnahme ~** to send cash (collect, *US*) on delivery; **ins Parlament ~** to return to Parliament; **mit der Post ~** to send by post *(Br.)* (mail, *US*); **seine Rechnung ~** to send in one's bill; **j. auf Reisen ~** to send s. o. on a tour; **auf dem Seeweg ~** to send by sea, to ship, to convey by water; **sich in das Unvermeidliche ~** to submit to the inevitable; **Vertreter ~** to send one's agent; **Waren mit der Post ~** to forward goods by post (mail, *US*);
sich die Ware ins Haus ~ lassen to have the goods sent by free delivery.
schicklich becoming, decorous, decent, proper.

Schicklichkeit decency, decorum, propriety, good breeding.
Schicksal fortune, fate, destiny, lot, doom, portion, cross; **grausames ~** hard fate; **unentrinnbares ~** inevitable fate; **unglückliches ~** adverse fortune; **nicht verdientes ~** hard luck; **jds. ~ besiegeln** to seal s. one's fate; **seinem ~ in Ruhe entgegensehen** to meet one's fate calmly; **jds. ~ entscheiden** to determine (dispose of) s. one's fate; **~ seiner Vorgänger erfahren** to suffer the same fate as one's predecessors; **sich in sein ~ ergeben** to submit to one's lot; **gleiches ~ haben** to be embarked on the same boat; **mit seinem ~ hadern** to quarrel with one's lot; **sein ~ in den eigenen Händen halten** to hold the key of one's own fate; **~ herausfordern** to ask for trouble, to tempt one's fate; **sein ~ in jds. Hände legen** to place one's fate in s. one's hands; **von jds. ~ nicht beeindruckt sein** to show indifference to s. one's fate; **jds. ~ teilen** to cast in one's lot with s. o.; **sein ~ tragen** to beat one's cross; **j. seinem ~ überlassen** to abandon s. o. to his fate; **vom ~ ereilt werden** to meet one's destiny.
schicksalhaft fatal, providential.
Schicksals|fügung luck; **~prüfung** trial; **~schlag** blow (reverse) of fortune, buffet; **katastrophaler ~schlag** catastrophe.
Schicksalsschläge vicissitudes of fortune;
~ geduldig hinnehmen to be patient of adversity; **von ~n heimgesucht sein** to be proved by adversity.
Schicksalswende, plötzliche sudden turn of the wheel.
Schiebe|bühne *(Bahn)* travelling platform, traverse table; **~dach** *(Auto)* sliding roof; **~fenster** slide window, window sash; **~kulissen** slips.
Schieben *(Börse)* carrying over.
schieben to work the oracle, to profiteer, to traffic, to wangle, to manipulate, to job, to graft *(US)*, *(Börse)* to carry over *(Br.)*, to continue *(Br.)*, *(Schieber)* to push, *(schmuggeln)* to smuggle, *(Schwarzhandel treiben)* to sell on the black market, *(stoßen)* to thrust;
Auto in die Garage ~ to slip the car into the garage; **auf die lange Bank ~** to table, to put off (into cold storage), to shelve; **Knast ~** to be in clink; **sich durch die Menge ~** to push one's way through the crowd; **Riegel vor die Tür ~** to slide the bolt across the door; **jem. etw. in die Schuhe ~** to lay the blame at s. one's door; **Schuld von sich ~** to deny one's guilt; **etw. von einem Tag auf den anderen ~** to postpone from one day to another; **sich in den Vordergrund ~** to push o. s. forward; **Zug auf ein Nebengleis ~** to shunt a train on a sidetrack.
Schieber bolt, bar, *(Geschäftemacher)* profiteer, trafficker, wangler, grafter *(US)*, racketeer *(US)*, shyster *(US)*, five-percenter *(US)*, jobber, *(Schmuggler)* smuggler, *(Schwarzmarkthändler)* black marketeer;
großer ~ big-time operator *(US)*.
Schiebergeschäft illegal transaction, profiteering [job], graft *(US)*, racket *(US)*;
~e machen to profiteer, to job, to graft *(US)*.
Schiebetür sliding door.
Schiebung sharp practices, underhand dealing, profiteering, wangling, put-up job *(sl.)*, jobbery, graft *(US)*, trade *(US)*, racket *(US)*, *(im Amt)* manoeuvre, manipulation, *(pol.)* backstairs politics, pull, gravy *(sl.)*, *(Wahlschiebung)* gerrymandering, spoils *(US)*;
~ bei Wettbewerben setup *(US sl.)*;
~en machen to job, to manipulate, to graft *(US)*.
Schiebungs|geschäft *(Börse)* carrying over *(Br.)*, continuation *(Br.)*; **~satz** *(Börse)* continuation (carrying over, *Br.*) rate.
schiedlich by arbitration.
Schieds|abkommen arbitration agreement; **~abrede** arbitral clause; **~amt** court (board) of conciliation, arbitration board *(US)*; **~angelegenheit** arbitral case; **~antrag** request for arbitration; **~ausschuß** board of arbitration, arbitration committee (commission, panel), conciliation (arbitration, *US*) board; **~bestimmung** arbitration condition; **~einrichtungen** arbitral facilities; **~gebühren** arbitration charges.
Schiedsgericht arbitration [board, tribunal], board (court) of arbitration, arbitral tribunal, referee's court, *(Mietstreitigkeit)* tribunal;
Haager ~ Hague Tribunal; **internationales ~** international arbitration; **kaufmännisches ~** court of arbitration of the chamber of commerce *(New York)*;
~ in arbeitsrechtlichen Auseinandersetzungen National Industrial Relations Court *(Br.)*, industrial court [for trade disputes] *(Br.)*; **~ in Lohnstreitigkeiten** wage arbitration; **~ für Streitigkeiten zwischen Betrieben und Gewerkschaften** industrial relations court *(Br.)*; **~ für Tarifkonflikte im öffentlichen Dienst** civil service arbitration tribunal;
einem ~ angehören to sit upon a tribunal; **in einer Sache ein ~ anrufen** to submit a dispute (have recourse) to arbitration; **vor ein ~ gehören** to belong to an arbitration court; **~ in Anspruch nehmen** to appeal to arbitration; **durch ein ~ regeln** to settle by arbitration; **sich einem ~ unterwerfen** to go to arbitration; **an ein ~ verweisen** to refer to arbitration; **von einem ~ beigelegt werden** to be settled by arbitration.
schiedsgerichtlich arbitral, arbitrational, by arbitration;
~ beilegbar arbitrable;
~ beilegen (regeln) to settle by arbitration; **Streitigkeit ~ beilegen lassen** to refer a dispute to arbitration;
~e Beilegung settlement by arbitration; **~e Einrichtungen** arbitration institution; **~e Entscheidung** arbitrament, arbitrator's award; **~e Entscheidung einholen** to go to arbitration; **Sache ~er Erledigung überlassen** to leave a matter to arbitration; **~e Gesetzgebung** arbitral legislation; **frei vereinbarte ~e Regelung** voluntary arbitration; **~es Verfahren** arbitration proceedings (process); **sich einem ~en Verfahren unterwerfen** to submit to arbitration; **in einem ~en Verfahren tätig werden** to arbitrate between parties to a suit.
Schiedsgerichts|abkommen für die gewerbliche Wirtschaft trade arbitration agreement; **~antrag** appeal to arbitration.
Schiedsgerichtsbarkeit arbitral jurisdiction;
betriebliche ~ labo(u)r arbitration; **gewerbliche ~** industrial arbitration; **frei vereinbarte ~** voluntary arbitration; **wirtschaftliche ~** commercial arbitration;
~ in arbeitsrechtlichen Streitigkeiten labo(u)r arbitration.
Schiedsgerichts|bestimmungen provisions of arbitration; **~entscheidung** decree arbitral *(Scot.)*.
schiedsgerichtsfähig arbitrable.
Schiedsgerichts|gebühren arbitration charges; **~hof** court of arbitration, arbitration (arbitral) court, arbitral tribunal; **Haager ~hof** Hague Tribunal, Permanent Court of Arbitration.
Schiedsgerichtsklausel arbitration clause;
obligatorische ~ jurisdiction clause; **vertraglich vereinbarte ~** contractual arbitration clause;
~ aufheben *(Gericht)* to break an arbitration clause.
Schiedsgerichts|kosten cost of arbitration; **zukünftige Auseinandersetzungen ausschließlich englischer ~tätigkeit unterstellen** to refer future disputes exclusively to English arbitration; **~vereinbarung** submission to arbitration, agreement of submission; **schriftlich anerkannte ~vereinbarung** arbitration bond; **~verfahren** arbitration proceedings (process); **abschließendes ~verfahren** terminal arbitration; **~verpflichtung** submission bond; **~vertrag** contract of arbitration, arbitration treaty; **~wesen** arbitral jurisdiction, conciliation service; **gewerbliches ~wesen** industrial arbitration; **wirtschaftliches ~wesen** commercial arbitration.
Schieds|gremium arbitration panel; **~gutachten** arbitrator's award (finding); **~gutachter** adjudicator, arbitrator; **~instanz** court of arbitration, arbitral body; **~klausel** arbitration (arbitral) clause; **~kommision** arbitration committee (commission); **gemischte ~kommission** Mixed Claims Commission; **~[ob]mann** umpire, arbiter, [third] arbitrator; **~[ob]mannstellvertreter** alternative arbitrator; **~ordnung** arbitration statute, Arbitration Act *(Br.)*; **~organ** arbitral body, arbitration medium; **~parteien** parties to arbitration; **~recht** arbitration law.
Schiedsrichter arbiter, arbitrator, moderator, adjudicator, *(Handelsgericht)* referee, *(Sport)* umpire;
von einer Partei benannter ~ party-appointed arbitrator; **industrieller ~** industry-union arbiter; **vereinbarter ~** special referee;
sachverständige ~ ausbilden to train experts in arbitration; **als ~ benennen** to constitute as arbitrator; **als ~ einsetzen** to appoint an arbitrator; **als ~ fungieren** to arbitrate, to umpire; **als ~ zwischen zwei Parteien fungieren** to umpire between two parties, to arbitrate between parties to a suit; **~ sein** to act as arbitrator; **an einen ~ verweisen** to refer to an arbitrator; **~ vorschlagen** to nominate an arbitrator;
~amt arbitratorship, umpireship; **~ausschuß** panel of arbitrators; **~kollegium** board of arbitration.
schiedsrichterlich arbitral, arbitrational, arbitrative, by arbitration;
~ beilegen to settle by arbitration; **~ entscheiden** to arbitrate; **~ tätig sein** to act as arbitrator, to arbitrate between two parties to a suit; **über eine Sache ~ verhandeln** to arbitrate a case;
~e Entscheidung arbitrator's award (finding), umpirage; **~e Entscheidung einholen** to go to arbitration; **mit ~en Funktionen ausgestattet** arbitrative; **frei vereinbarte ~e Regelung** voluntary

arbitration; ~e **Vereinbarung** arbitration bond; ~**es Verfahren** arbitration [procedure]; **sich einem ~en Verfahren unterwerfen** to submit to arbitration.
Schiedsrichter|liste panel of arbitrators; ~**spruch** arbitrator's award (finding); **sich einem ~spruch unterwerfen** to accept a finding as binding; ~**tätigkeit** activities of an arbitrator.
Schiedssache arbitral case.
Schiedsspruch arbitrament, arbitration [award] board decision, arbitrage, arbitrator's award (finding), final disposition, decree arbitral, arbitral award;
ausländischer ~ foreign award; **parteiischer** ~ partial award; **alles endgültig regelnder** ~ final disposition; **staatlicher** ~ state award; **tarifrechtlicher** ~ industrial award; **allgemein verbindlicher** ~ commonly binding award;
~ **in einem gewerblichen Schiedsverfahren** industrial award;
~ **anerkennen** to abide by an [arbitral] award; ~ **aufheben** to set aside an award; ~ **befolgen** to abide by an arbitral award; **Angelegenheit durch** ~ **erledigen** to settle a matter by arbitration; ~ **fällen** to make (pronounce) an award, to arbitrate; ~ **geltend machen** to abide by an arbitral award; **durch** ~ **schlichten** to arbitrate; **sich einem** ~ **unterwerfen** to accept a finding as binding; ~ **vollstrecken** to enforce an award; **durch** ~ **zuerkennen** to award; ~ **zur nochmaligen Beratung an die Schiedsrichter zurückverweisen** to remit an award for the reconsideration of the arbitrators.
Schieds|stelle arbitral body, arbitration board *(US)*; ~**stelle für Bahn- und andere Beförderungstarife** Transport Tribunal *(Br.)*; ~**stelle für Enteignungsentschädigungen** Agricultural Land Tribunal *(Br.)*; ~**tätigkeit** arbitration service; ~**urteil** award; ~**vereinbarung** arbitration agreement; ~**verfahren** arbitration procedure (proceedings); **obligatorisches ~verfahren** compulsory arbitration; ~**verfahren wegen strittiger Entlassungen** arbitration procedure governing disputed firings; ~**vertrag** arbitration [treaty], arbitration agreement, arbitration bond, submission to arbitration; **inländischer ~vertrag** domestic arbitration agreement; ~**vertrag eingehen** to compromise to an arbitration; **auf dem ~wege** by arbitration.
schief crooked, slanting;
jem. ~ **ansehen** to look askane at s. o.; **Sache** ~ **darstellen** to give a distorted account;
~**e Ebene** inclined plane; **auf die ~e Ebene geraten** to go to the bad, to be on the downgrade *(US)*; ~**es Gesicht ziehen** to pull a wry face; **in eine ~e Lage bringen** to put s. o. in a bad spot; ~**es Licht auf etw. werfen** to cast an unfavo(u)rable light upon s. th.; ~**e Treppenstufen** lobsided steps.
Schiefer|dach slate roof; ~**tafel** slate.
schief|gehen to turn out crabs, to go crosswire (haywire, all wrong); ~**gewickelt sein** to be mistaken; **sich ~lachen** to double up with laughter; ~**liegen** *(Börse)* to be on the wrong side; ~**stehend** *(Buchstaben)* off its feet.
schielen, auf etw. to take a side-glance; **auf das Heft des Nebenmannes** ~ to peer at one's neighbour's book.
Schiene rail, *(Schienenstrang)* track, rails;
auf ~n on rails; **frei** ~ free on rail; **ohne** ~ trackless;
~ **und Straße** road and rail;
aus den ~n springen to run off the rails; **mit ~n versehen, ~n verlegen** to track *(US)*, to lay rails, to metal.
Schienen|bahn railway, railroad *(US)*, *(Gleis)* track; ~**bus** railway omnibus *(Br.)*, business (private) car, multiple-unit train; ~**fahrzeug** rail car; ~**fahrzeuge** rolling stock.
schienengleicher Bahnübergang level *(Br.)* (grade, *US*) crossing.
Schienen|kartell rail trust; ~**keil** key; ~**kreuzung** crossing, crosspoint *(Br.)*; ~**leger** platelayer; ~**netz** railway (railroad, *US*) system; ~**omnibus** private car, railway omnibus *(Br.)*; ~**räumer** *(an Lokomotive)* obstruction guard, pilot *(US)*, cowcatcher *(US)*; ~**strang**, ~**strecke** track, line, *(Straßenbahn)* tram, tramway rail; ~**transport** rail transport[ation]; ~**übergang** level crossing; ~**verkehr** rail traffic, fixed-track transport; ~**verkehrsmittel** rail transportations; ~**verlegung** platelaying, tracking, laying of trails, metal(l)ing; ~**weg** track, iron road, railway, railroad *(US)*; ~**weite** gauge.
Schießbude *(Jahrmarkt)* shooting gallery.
Schießbudenfigur target doll, *(fig.)* scare-crow.
Schießeisen shooter *(coll.)*, shooting cron *(sl.)*.
Schießen firing, fire, shoot, discharge of a gun;
~ **eröffnen** to open fire; **zum** ~ **sein** to be too funny for words.
schießen to shoot, to fire, to gun;
wütenden Blick auf j. ~ to dart an angry look at s. o.; **Bock** ~ to make a blunder, to drop a clanger; **direkt auf j.** ~ to fire pointblank at s. o.; **aus der Erde** ~ *(Saat)* to spring up; **über den Haufen** ~ to gun down; **aus dem Hinterhalt** ~ to snipe; **in die Höhe** ~ to upspring, *(Kurse)* to go through the roof, to skyrocket *(US)*, *(Preise)* to be shooting up; **mit Kanonen auf Spatzen** ~ to break a butterfly upon a wheel; **auf die Menge** ~ to fire upon the crowd; **wie Pilze aus dem Boden** ~ to shoot (spring up) like mushrooms; **Rakete zum Mond** ~ to launch a rocket to the moon; **scharf** ~ to shoot with live ammunition;
seinem Zorn die Zügel ~ **lassen** to give vent to one's anger.
schießenlassen, Bürgschaft to jump bail.
Schießerei shooting of revolvers, shoot-up, shooting [incident], shootout *(sl.)*, gunfight, gunplay *(US sl.)*.
Schieß|hund, wie ein ~hund aufpassen to watch like a lynx; ~**platz**, ~**stand** shooting gallery (range); ~**scharte** embrasure, loophole.
Schiff ship, vessel, *(Dampfschiff)* steamer, steamship, *(drucktechn.)* galley, *(Kahn)* barge, *(kleineres)* boat, *(Küstendampfer)* coaster, coasting vessel;
auf dem ~ on board ship; **frei** ~ free on board, free on steamer; **frei ab** ~ ex ship; **frei Längsseite** ~ free alongside the vessel (ship);
abgehendes (abfahrendes) ~ outgoing boat; **abgetakeltes** ~ ship in ordinary; **aktionsunfähiges** ~ crippled ship; **alleinfahrendes** ~ single-cruising ship; **atomangetriebenes** ~ nuclear-powered ship; **aufgebrachtes** ~ prize; **aufgegebenes** ~ derelict (abandoned) ship; **ausfahrendes (auslaufendes)** ~ outgoing ship, outward bounder; **hilflos dem Meer ausgesetztes** ~ ship under the sea; **ausländisches** ~ foreign ship, foreigner; **nicht besteuertes ausländisches** ~ free ship *(US)*; **im Bau befindliches** ~ ship under construction; **in Gefahr (Seenot) befindliches** ~ ship in distress; **voll beladenes** ~ full (fully laden) ship; **nach X bestimmtes** ~ ship bound for X; **für den Heimathafen bestimmtes** ~ inbound (homeward-bound) ship; **eingelaufene** ~**e** arrivals; **im Überseeverkehr eingesetztes** ~ foreign-going ship; **unter amerikanischer Flagge fahrendes** ~ American-flag ship; **in Kiellinie fahrende** ~**e** column; **nicht regelmäßig fahrendes** ~ transient ship; **fahrplanmäßiges** ~ scheduled ship *(US)*; **feindliches** ~ enemy ship; **nur teilweise fertiggestelltes** ~ partly completed ship; **gechartertes** ~ chartered ship; **gekapertes** ~ captured ship, prize; **gerammtes** ~ ship collided with; **in Seenot geratenes** ~ ship in distress; **außer Dienst gestelltes** ~ laid-up vessel; **gestrandetes** ~ wreck; **havariertes** ~ ship under average; **auf Reede liegendes** ~ ship anchored in a roadstead; **manövrierunfähiges** ~ ship not under control; **neutrales** ~ neutral (free) ship; **schiffbrüchiges** ~ wrecked ship; **schnelles** ~ flyboat; **seetüchtiges** ~ sound ship, seaworthy vessel; **seeuntüchtiges** ~ unseaworthy ship; **stilliegendes** ~ idle vessel; **überfälliges** ~ missing ship; **unbeladenes** ~ light (empty) ship (vessel); **auf einer bestimmten Route verkehrendes** ~ constant trader; **verlassenes** ~ wreck; **vorfahrtberechtigtes** ~ privileged vessel; **wrackes** ~ wrecked ship, shipwreck; **zurückfahrendes** ~ homeward-bound ship; **zusammengebautes** ~ fabricated ship;
~ **auf Auslandsfahrt (großer Fahrt)** foreign-going ship (vessel); ~ **mit voller Bemannung** fully-manned ship; ~ **unter fremder Flagge** foreign vessel; ~ **mit Kernenergieantrieb** nuclear-powered ship; ~ **erster Klasse** class ship, a first rater *(Br.)*; ~ **einer fremden Nation** foreigner; ~ **in Seenot** ship in distress; ~**e neutraler Staaten** free (neutral) ships; ~ **des Wetterdienstes** weather ship; ~ **der Wüste** ship of the desert, camel;
~ **abtakeln (abwracken)** to dismantle (unrig, break up, strip) a ship; ~ **anbohren** to scuttle a ship; ~ **anhalten und durchsuchen** to stop and examine a ship; **an ein** ~ **anlegen** to come alongside a ship; ~ **aufbringen** to bring up a ship; ~ **aufgeben** to abandon (surrender) a ship; ~ **ausklarieren** to clear the ship; ~ **ausrüsten** to equip (fit, furnish) a ship, to man and supply a ship; ~ **für eine lange Reise ausrüsten** to fit a ship out for a long journey; ~ **mit amtlichen Papieren ausstatten** to document a ship; ~**e bauen** to build (fabricate) ships; ~**e auf Vorrat bauen** to build ships on stock; ~ **beflaggen** to flag a ship; **durch ~e befördern** to ship; ~ **befrachten** to take a ship to freight, to lade goods to a vessel; ~ **mit Stückgütern befrachten** to load a ship on the berth; ~ **beidrehen** to bring a ship to; ~ **als verloren bekanntgeben** to post a ship missing; ~ **mit Beschlag belegen** to arrest a ship; ~ **seiner Besatzung berauben** to unman a ship; ~ **ins Dock bringen** to bring a ship into dock; ~ **chartern** to freight (hire) a ship; ~ **durchschleusen** to lock a ship; ~ **durchsuchen** to search a ship; ~ **in den Hafen einbringen** to put a ship into port; ~ **einklarieren** to clear inwards; ~ **in ein Dock einschleusen** to pass a ship into dock; ~ **wieder einstellen** to recommission a ship; **aufgebrachtes** ~ **und Ladegut prisengerecht einziehen** to condemn a captured vessel; ~ **entern** to board a ship; ~ **entladen** to clear a ship of her cargo, to unload a ship; ~ **für**

seeuntüchtig erklären to condemn a ship; **zu ~ fahren** to sail; **~ festmachen** to make a ship fast; **an Bord eines ~es gehen** to board a ship; **versunkenes ~ heben** to raise a sunken vessel; **~ aus einem Flottenverband herauslösen** to detach a ship from a fleet; **~ aus dem Hafen hinauslotsen** to pilot a ship out of the harbo(u)r; **~ zum Gefecht klarmachen** to clear the decks for action; **~ auflaufen lassen** to beach (strand) a ship, to run a ship aground, to pile up *(mar., sl.)*; **~ unter falscher Flagge laufen lassen** to mask a ship under a neutral flag; **~ vom Stapel laufen lassen** to launch a ship; **~ auf Strand laufen lassen** to force a ship on shore; **~e auf Halde legen** to stockpile ships; **~ auf Kiel legen** to lay a ship on the keel, to lay down a ship, to dry-dock; **~ wieder flott machen** to get a ship afloat again; **~ manövrieren** to handle a ship; **~ in Reparatur nehmen** to lay up a ship for repairs; **~ gewerblich nutzen** to trade with a ship; **~ auf einem Gegenkurs passieren** to pass a ship on an opposite course; **~ pfänden** to arrest a ship; **mit dem ~ reisen** to travel by sea; **~ auf den Felsen schleudern** to drive a ship upon the rocks; **~ auf den Strand setzen** to force a ship on shore; **~ außer Dienst stellen** to lay up (disable) a ship, to put a vessel out of commission; **~ in Dienst stellen** to put a ship into service (in commission); **~ zum Hafen steuern** to lead a ship for the harbo(u)r; **~ leewärts steuern** to pay off the ship's head; **~ teeren** to pitch a ship; **~ überführen** to remove a ship; **~ seinem Schicksal überlassen** to let a ship go down the wind; **~ den Versicherern überlassen** to abandon the property covered by a policy; **~ umtaufen** to change the name of a ship; **seine ~e hinter sich verbrennen** to burn one's boats (bridges, *US*); **~ verchartern** to freight out a ship; **~ verlassen** to abandon (surrender) a ship; **~ verpfänden** to bottomry, to make prize of a ship; **~ verproviantieren** to store a ship with provisions; **~ verschrotten** to break up an old ship; **~ mit Treibstoff versehen** to fuel a ship; **Waren per ~ versenden** to ship goods; **~ versenken** to scupper a ship; **~ auf der Hin- und Rückreise versichern** to insure a ship out and home; **~ vertäuen** to moor a ship; **~ zur Verladung vormerken** to put up a vessel for freight; **~ auf die Felsen werfen** to throw a ship on the rocks; **~ als Prise wegnehmen** to make prize of a ship; **~ aus der Fahrt ziehen** to lay up a ship; **mit einem ~ zusammenstoßen** to run foul with a ship;
~ muß schwimmend löschen discharge afloat.

Schiffahrt navigation, shipping;
~ behindern to obstruct navigation; **der ~ schweren Schaden zufügen** to do much mischief to shipping.

Schiffahrts|abkommen treaty of navigation, shipping (navigation) agreement; **~agentur** shipping agency; **~aktien** shipping shares *(Br.)* (stocks, *US*, issues); **~angelegenheiten** maritime affairs (matters); **~angestellter** shipping clerk; **~bedürfnisse** shipping needs; **~behinderung** obstruction to navigation; **~behörde** shipping board (authorities); **~berichte** shipping news; **~gefahren auf den großen Seen** perils of the lakes; **~gericht** naval court; **~gesellschaft** steamship (shipping) company; **~gesetz** Navigation Act *(Br.)*; **~industrie** merchant marine industry; **sein Geld in der ~industrie angelegt haben** to be interested in shipping; **~interessen** shipping interests; **~kalender** shipping directory; **~kanal** canal for navigation, ship canal, ship (shipping) channel; **~katastrophe** maritime disaster; **~konferenz** maritime (shipping) conference; **~konferenz der Trampschiffahrt** Baltic and International Maritime Conference; **~kontor** shipping agency; **~kunde** navigation, nautics; **~linie** shipping [steamship] line, sailing line, *(Route)* seaway, waterway, *(Flußmitte)* thread; **~linie subventionieren** to subsidize a steamship line; **~nachrichten** shipping intelligence (news), ship news; **Zwischenstaatliche Beratende ~organisation** Intergovernmental Maritime Consultative Organization; **~politik** shipping policy; **~recht** maritime (admiralty) law; **internationale ~regeln** rules of navigation; **Lloyds ~register** Lloyds Register of Shipping; **~rinne** midchannel; **~risiko** dangers (risk) of navigation; **~route** shipping route (lane), navigation route, ocean lane, *(für Vergnügungsreisen)* cruiseway; **~saison** shipping season; **~sperre** close of navigation, embargo on shipping; **~straße** shipping (navigation) route, ocean lane; **~subvention** shipping subsidy; **~unternehmen** shipping company; **~verkehr** waterborne traffic, shipping service; **~versicherung** maritime insurance; **~vertrag** maritime contract, treaty on navigation; **~weg** shipping route, ocean lane, seaway, waterway; **~werte** *(Börse)* shipping issues (shares, *Br.*, stocks, *US*); **~wesen** maritime affairs; **~zeichen** seamark.

schiffbar navigable, boatable, passable;
nicht ~ nonnavigable, unnavigable;
~er Fluß navigable river; **~es Gewässer** navigable waters.

Schiffbarkeitsgrenze navigation head.

Schiffbau construction of a vessel, naval construction, shipbuilding;
~ beginnen to lay down a ship;
~auftrag shipbuilding order.

Schiffbauer shipbuilder, shipwright.

Schiffbau|fachmann naval constructor *(US)*; **~gesellschaft** shipbuilding company; **~industrie** shipbuilding (shipping) industry; **sein Geld in der ~industrie angelegt haben** to be interested in shipping; **~ingenieur** naval architect; **~kapazität** shipbuilding capacity; **~konjunktur** shipbuilding boom; **~konstrukteur** shipbuilding draughtsman; **~krise** shipbuilding slump; **~markt** shipbuilding market; **~meister** shipbuilder; **~programm** shipbuilding program(me); **~technik** naval engineering.

Schiffbruch wreck, shipwreck, *(fig.)* bankruptcy;
dem ~ entgehen to be saved from wreck; **~ erleiden** to be cast away (wrecked), to suffer wreck, to make shipwreck, *(fig.)* to split, to run upon the rocks, to fall down, *(finanziell)* to be ruined, to go bust; **~ in allen Einzelheiten schildern** to detail a story of the shipwreck; **~ verursachen** to shipwreck.

schiffbrüchig wrecked, shipwrecked, castaway;
~ werden to be cast away;
~es Schiff shipwreck, wrecked ship.

Schiff|brüchiger shipwrecked person, castaway; **~bruchsgüter** shipwrecked goods, flotsam and jetsam; **~dunstschaden** sweat damage.

Schiffer [ship]master, master mariner, skipper;
~ausdruck nautical term; **~jacke** pilot jacket; **~klavier** concertina, accordion, squeeze-box *(sl.)*; **~patent** master's certificate; **~patent für kleine Fahrt** mate's patent.

Schiffs|abgaben shipping (navigation) dues; **~abladeplatz** wharf, port of discharge; **~agent** ship's husband, ship broker, shipping agent; **~agentengebühr** husbandage; **~agentur** shipping agency, *(Linienschiffahrt)* liner agency; **~angelegenheiten** shipping (maritime) affairs; **~anlegeplatz** landing stage; **~anteil** interest (share) in a vessel; **~arrest** restraint of a ship; **~arrest anordnen** to lay embargo; **~artikel** ship's articles; **~artillerie** naval artillery; **~arzt** ship's surgeon; **~aufgabe an die Versicherungsgesellschaft** abandonment of a ship to the underwriters; **~aufkäufer** ship breaker; **~auftrag** ship order; **~aufzug** shiphoist; **~ausdruck** nautical term; **~ausrüstung** equipment (furniture) of a ship, fitting out of a vessel, ship chandlery; **~ausschlachter** ship breaker, knacker; **~ausschlachtung** shipbreaking; **~ausstattung** outfit; **~barometer** marine barometer; **~bedarfsgeschäft, ~bedarfshandlung** ship chandlery, marine store *(Br.)*; **~bedarfslieferant** marine store dealer *(Br.)*; **~bedarfsmagazin** marine stores *(Br.)*, ship chandlery; **~befrachter** charterer, freighter; **~befrachtung** freighting, chartering; **~befrachtungsvertrag** charterparty, contract of affreightment; **~behälter** shipboard container; **~beladung** shiploading; **~belastung** charge on ship; **~bergung** salvage; **gesamte ~besatzung** ship's company, full (ship's) complement, crew; **erstklassige ~beschaffenheit** A 1 at Lloyd's; **~beschlagnahme** arrest of a vessel; **~besichtiger** marine surveyor; **~besichtigung durch das Aufsichtsamt** survey of a vessel; **~bestand** shipping; **~beteiligung** interest (share) in a vessel; **~bewegungen** movement of ships; **~bewuchs** underwater growth; **~boden** bulge, bottom; **bewachsener ~boden** foul bottom; **~brief** ship's passport, ship letter; **~brücke** floating (pontoon, flying) bridge; **~brücke abbrechen** to withdraw a pontoon bridge; **~bücher** ship's papers; **~charter erteilen** to grant and to freight let; **~deck** deck; **~dokumente** ship's papers; **~durchsuchung** search of a ship; **~eigentümer, ~eigner** shipowner; **~eigentümervereinigung** chamber of shipping; **~eintragung** enrol(l)ment of vessel *(US)*; **~eisenbahn** ship railway; **~empfangsschein** ship's (mate's) receipt; **~finanzierung** ship financing; **~flagge** flag, ensign.

Schiffsfracht shipload, shipping (ship's) freight, cargo;
~brief bill of lading; **~gewerbe** shipping freight service;
~vertrag charterparty, affreightment.

Schiffs|führer captain, shipmaster; **~funker** wireless operator, sparks *(sl.)*; **~garnierung** dunnage; **~gefährdung** jeopardizing a ship; **~gefängnis** hulks; **~gelegenheit** shipping opportunity; **~geleit** convoy; **~gerippe bauen** to frame a ship; **~geschütz** naval gun; **~gläubiger** bottomry bondholder; **~gläubigerrecht** maritime lien; **~glocke** watch bell; **~haftpflicht** protection and indemnity; **~haftpflichtversicherung** protection and indemnity insurance; **im ~handel sein** to be in the shipping business; **~hebewerk** ship elevator; **~herr** shipmaster, patron, shipowner; **~hypothek** mortgage over a ship, ship mortgage;

vorrangige ~hypothek preferred ship mortgage *(US)*; **~hypothekenbestellung** creation of mortgages over ships; **~hypothekenregister** register book; **~industrie** maritime industry; **sein Geld in der ~industrie angelegt haben** to be interested in shipping; **~ingenieur** engineer of a ship, marine (naval) engineer; **~inspektion** survey of a vessel; **~inspektor** *(Versicherung)* marine inspector; **~inventar** ship's inventory; **~journal** logbook, log; **~junge** shipboy, ship's (cabin) boy; **~kapitän** master, skipper, sea captain; **~karte** passenger ticket; **seine ~karte lösen** to book one's passage; **~kasko** hull; **~kaskoversicherung** hull insurance; **~katastrophe** disaster at sea; **~klasse** class, category of ships; **~klassenregister** classification register; **~klassifizierung** classification (rating) of ships; **~kollision** collision between two vessels; **seitliche ~kollision** allision; **zufallsbedingte ~kollision** fortuitous collision; **~kompaß** mariner's compass; **~konstruktion** ship's construction; **~konzern** shipping group; **äußerer ~körper** outer hull; **~kran** derrick; **~kreisel** gyrostabilizer; **~küche** galley, caboose; **~kurs** course of a vessel; **~kurs auf der Karte abstecken** to prick off a ship's position on the chart; **~kurs behindern** to foul a ship's course.

Schiffsladung shipload, boatload, freight, loading, load of a ship, shipment *(US)*, cargo;
unverpackte ~ bulk cargo;
~ befördern to haul cargo; **~ deklarieren** to enter a cargo.

Schiffs|ladungsverzeichnis manifest, freight list; **~landeplatz** quay; **~last** shipload; **~laterne** top light; **~lazarett** sick bay; **~leiter** ship (accommodation) ladder; **~lieferant** ship chandler; **~liegeplatz** loading berth, *(im Fluß)* lay-by; **~liste** shipping list; **~logbuch** ship's log; **~löschplatz** discharging berth; **~luke** hatch; **~maat** shipmate.

Schiffsmakler ship broker, ship's agent (husband), shipping agent (master, *Br.*), freight (chartering) broker;
~büro shipping office *(US)*; **~geschäft** ship (shipping) brokerage.

Schiffs|mannschaft ship's company, crew; **gesamte ~mannschaft** all hands, full complement; **~mannschaft für eine Weltreise anheuern** to ship a crew for a voyage round the world; **~maschinenbau** marine engineering; **~maschinist** marine engineer; **~mast** mast; **~meldung** ship's report; **~meßschein** tonnage certificate; **~miete** charter money, freight; **~mieter** charterer; **~mietvertrag** charterparty; **~motor** marine engine; **~musterrolle** muster roll, ship's articles; **~name** name of a ship; **~notsignal** ship's distress signal; **~ort** position; **~ort bei der Abfahrt bestimmen** to take a departure; **~ortung** position finding, bearing; **~packraum** storage room; **~papiere** ship's (shipper's, shipping) papers, shipping documents; **falsche ~papiere** false papers; **~park** floating equipment; **~part** interest (share) in a vessel; **~partner** part owner; **~paß** ship's passport, sea letter (pass), sea-brief; **~passagekosten** passage money; **~passagier** ship's passenger; **~pech** common black pitch; **~pfandbrief** bottomry bond; **~pfandrecht** charge on a ship, maritime lien (hypothecation, *US*); **~pfändung** arrest of a vessel; **~planke** plank; **~police** ship's policy; **~position** ship's position; **~profos** master-at-arms.

Schiffsraum space on board a vessel, *(Laderaum)* ship's hold, shipping space, *(Rauminhalt)* tonnage;
im ~ befindlich inboard;
leerer ~ waste stowage (tonnage), light displacement; **verfügbarer ~** freight (shipping) space; **zuviel vorhandener ~** overtonnage;
im ~ untergebracht sein to be loaded in the hold;
~ausnutzung ship utilization; **~mangel** scarcity of tonnage.

Schiffs|reeder owner of a ship, shipowner; **~reederei** shipping office.

Schiffsregister register of shipping, Lloyd's Register of Shipping *(Br.)*, Registrar of the Treasury *(US)*;
~amt register *(US)*, marine registry office *(Br.)*; **~auszug** certificate of registry (enrol(l)ment), registry; **~brief** ship's register; **~eintragung** marine registry *(Br.)*.

Schiffs|registrierung registry of a ship, enrol(l)ment of vessels *(US)*; **~reise** sea journey (trip); **~reise machen** to travel by sea; **~reling** rail; **~reparaturwerft** repair yard; **~reservierung** ship reservation; **~rettung** salvage; **~rolle** quarter bill; **~rumpf** hull, body of a ship; **~rundreise** round voyage; **amtlich bestellter ~sachverständiger** nautical assessor, marine surveyor; **~schaden** ship damage; **~schraube** screw; **~schweiß** [ship's] sweat; **~seite** board; **an ~seite** shipside; **über ~seite** overside; **~sicherheit** safety of lives at sea; **irreführende ~signale** false lights and signals; **~spediteur** ship deliverer; **~tagebuch** ship's logbook, official logbook; **~tank** ship's tank; **~taufe** launching ceremony, *(an Bord)* ducking; **~tonnage** tonnage; **~tonnage feststellen** to measure the tonnage of a ship; **~trümmer** wreckage; **~überführungsgebühr** address commission; **~unfall** collision at sea, foul; **~untergang mit der gesamten Besatzung** loss of a ship with all hands; **~verkaufsurkunde** grand bill of sale; **~verkehr** shipping [traffic], navigation; **~verkehr im Hafen** inward traffic of a port; **~verkehr zwischen England und dem Festland** cross-channel service; **~verladung** shiploading; **~verlust** loss of a ship at sea; **~verlustliste** *(Lloyds)* casualty book; **~vermessung** measurement of a ship; **~vermieter** charterer; **~vermietung** chartering, freighting; **~verpackung** stowage; **~verpfändung** bottomry; **~verschollenheit** presumptive loss of a ship; **~verschrottung** shipbreaking; **~versicherung** hull (ship) insurance; **gemischte ~versicherung** mixed policy; **~versicherungsmakler** marine insurance broker; **~verzeichnis** shipping list; **halbjährliches ~verzeichnis** Navy Register *(US)*; **~verzollung** clearance; **~vorräte** naval (ship's, marine) stores; **~vorräte auffüllen** to replenish a ship's stores; **~wache** watch, lookout; **~wand** bulwark; **~wechsel** bottomry bond; **~werft** shipbuilding yard, shipyard, dockyard; **~wrack** shipwreck, wreck, carcass; **~wrack markieren** to buoy a wreck; **~wracks in einem Kanal mit Baken versehen** to mark the wrecks in a channel; **~zahlmeister** purser; **~zertifikat** ship's register, certificate of registry (enrol(l)ment), registry; **~zettel** shipping note *(Br.)*, shipping order *(US)*; **~zimmermann** ship's carpenter; **~zoll** tonnage lastage; **~zubehör** equipment of a ship; **~zubehörhändler** ship chandler; **~zusammenstoß** collision of ships, foul; **~zwieback** ship biscuit, hardtack, pilot biscuit.

Schikane chicanery, vexation, *(Rechtsverdrehung)* pettifogging;
~n *(Sonderaustattung)* refinements, gadgets, frills;
mit allen ~n slap-up *(Br.)*, bang-up, crack; **mit den neuesten ~n ausgestattet** with all modern conveniences;
~ und Belästigung annoyance and inconvenience; **laufende ~n des Nachbarn** constant vexations from one's neighbo(u)r;
mit ~n arbeiten to pettifog; **etw. nur aus ~ tun** to do s. th. out of spite;
~prozeß vexatious suit.

Schikanieren chicanery, vexation, victimization, tail twisting, hazing *(US)*.

schikanieren to chicane, to pettifog, to victimize, to vex, to play tricks upon, to haze *(US)*;
als Kommunisten ~ to red-bait *(US sl.)*; **j. immer weiter ~** to keep on at s. o. *(fam.)*.

schikanös pettifogging, vexatious, spiteful, annoying;
~e Einwendungen pettifogging objections; **~es Prozeßverfahren** vexatious proceedings; **~e Zahlungsverweigerung** vexatious refusal to pay.

Schild *(Auto)* plate, *(Etikett)* tally, label, tag, ticket, *(Firmenschild)* name plate, shingle, *(Gepäckträger)* badge, *(Koffer)* luggage (baggage, *US*) tag, *(Laden)* signboard, sign, panel, facia, *(Straßenschild)* road sign, *(Türschild)* doorplate, *(Wappen)* coat of arms;
~ mit Preisangabe price tag (ticket);
im ~e führen to compass; **Böses (nichts Gutes) im ~e führen** to be up to no good (mischief); **j. auf den ~ heben** to bring s. o. to the forefront; **sein ~ heraushängen** to hang out one's shingle; **mit einem ~ versehen** to ticket;
~beschriftung sign writing.

Schildbürger wise man of Gotham, Gothamist;
~streich foolish action.

Schilder|haus watch box; **~hersteller** signpost maker; **~maler** sign writer.

schildern to give an account, to depict, to describe, to narrate, to paint;
anschaulich ~ to give a graphic picture (vivid description); **in leuchtenden Farben ~** to paint in bright colo(u)rs; **Sachverhalt in allen Einzelheiten ~** to give a detailed account of the facts.

Schilderträger sandwich man *(Br.)*.

Schilderung description, depiction, representation, picture;
bildhafte ~ word picture; **lebhafte ~** vivid description;
~ in allen Einzelheiten detailed description; **~ des Sachverhalts** recital of the facts;
keine ausreichende ~ bieten to be not the word for it.

Schilderwald jungle of traffic signs.

Schild- und Schwertstrategie *(NATO)* shield and sword strategy.

Schildwache sentinel, watch.

schillern to be iridescent, to play from one colo(u)r into another.

schillernd sparkling, glittering, scintillating;
~er Charakter ambiguous character.

Schimmel mould, mold *(US)*, *(Wand)* mildew;
~bogen *(Buchhandel)* mildewed sheet; **~fleck** mildew stain.

schimmeln to mould, to mold *(US)*, to mildew.
Schimmer shimmer, glimmer, gleam, gloss, blink, *(Spur)* trace, flicker, gleam;
rötlicher ~ reddish tinge;
kein ~ von Hoffnung not a flicker of hope; ~ **eines Lächelns** trace of a smile;
keinen ~ haben not to have the faintest idea, to have no clue *(coll.)*.
schimmern to glimmer, to shimmer, to gleam;
rötlich ~ to have a tinge of pink.
Schimpf insult, abuse, ignominy, *(Demütigung)* affront, injury;
mit ~ und Schande davonjagen to chase s. o. out of the house in disgrace; **j. mit ~ und Schande entlassen** to dismiss s. o. ignominiously; **j. mit ~ überschütten** to pour abuse upon s. o.
schimpfen to scold, *(beklagen)* to grumble, to grouse, to gripe about *(US sl.)*;
j. einen Betrüger ~ to call s. o. a swindler; ~ **und fluchen** to curse and swear; **über die hohen Steuern** ~ to grumble about high taxes; **über das schlechte Wetter** ~ to complain about the bad (inveigh against the) weather.
Schimpfkanonade broadside, torrent of abuse.
schimpflich disgraceful, discreditable, dishono(u)rable, ignominious;
~e Bedingungen opprobrious terms; **~e Behandlung** scandalous treatment; **~er Friede** inglorious peace.
Schimpf|lied lampoon; **j. mit ~namen belegen** to call s. o. names; **~reden** abusive (injurious) language.
Schimpfwort abusive (buzz) word, invective;
~e abuse of (abusive, bad) language;
j. mit ~en belegen to call s. o. names; **~e gebrauchen** to use bad language; **j. mit ~en überschütten** to vituperate s. o.
Schindanger bone yard *(US)*.
Schindeldach shingle roof.
schinden to maltreat, to ill-treat, *(Arbeitskräfte)* to sweat, to grind, to exploit;
j. ~ to keep s. one's nose to the grindstone; **sich** ~ to work like a nigger; **Arbeitskräfte** ~ to sweat (grind, exploit) workers; **Eintrittsgeld** ~ to dodge (duck, *US*) paying the entrance fee; **bis zur Erschöpfung** ~ to overdrive; **Motor** ~ to flog the engine; **Zeilen** ~ to pad one's lines; **Zeit** ~ to play for time, to temporize.
Schinder slave driver, *(Ausbeuter)* sweater, grinder, driver *(coll.)*, *(mil.)* taskmaster, rawhider *(US coll.)*.
Schinderei drudgery, fag *(Br.)*, toil, moil, grind *(coll.)*;
gehörige ~ tough going *(coll.)*.
Schindluder, mit etw. ~ treiben to handle s. th. carelessly; **mit jem. ~ treiben** to make cruel sport of s. o., to play the deuce with s. o., to guy the life out of s. o. *(US)*; **mit jds. Gefühlen ~ treiben** to juggle with (play on) s. one's feelings, to play with s. one's affections; **mit seiner Gesundheit ~ treiben** to abuse one's health, to burn the candle at both ends.
Schirm umbrella, *(Fernsehen)* screen, brolly *(Br., coll.)*, bunkershoot *(US sl.)*, *(Lampe)* shade, *(Mütze)* peak, visor, *(Schutz)* shelter, protection;
~ **aufspannen** to put up an umbrella;
~bild *(Fernsehen)* screen image, *(Radar)* display pattern, image; **~bildgerät** terminal, display; **~dach** marquee, awning; **~gitter** screen grid; **~herr** protector, patron, sponsor.
Schirmherrschaft patronage, sponsorship, protectorship;
unter der ~ von sponsored by, under the auspices of; **unter der ~ des Oberbürgermeisters** under the umbrella of the mayor;
~ **durch die Regierung** state patronage.
Schirm|hülle umbrella case (cover); **~ständer** umbrella stand.
Schlacht battle;
blutige ~ red battle; **heiße** ~ hard-fought field; **unentschiedene** ~ drawn battle; **verlorene** ~ losing battle;
~ **gewinnen** to gain the battle;
~abfälle offal; **~aufstellung** martial array; **~bank** slaughtering block, butchery.
schlachten to slaughter, to butcher;
sein Sparschwein ~ to break open one's piggy bank.
Schlachten|bummler camp follower; **~maler** military painter.
Schlächter butcher, killer, slaughterer, packer.
Schlächterei butchery, slaughterhouse.
Schlachtfeld battlefield, *(fig.)* shambles;
wie ein ~ aussehen *(Zimmer)* to be all at sixes and sevens; ~ **behaupten** to carry the day; **in ein ~ verwandeln** to turn into a shambles.
Schlacht|fleisch butcher's meat; **~flotte** battle fleet; **~flugzeug** attack plane, battleplane; **~getümmel** confusion of battle, affree, skirmish, melee; **mitten ins ~getümmel** in the thick of the battle; **~hausmeister** packer; **~hof** slaughterhouse, meat house *(fam.)*; **~kreuzer** battle cruiser; **~linie** front; **~ordnung** battle array, battle formation; **in offener ~ordnung** in open formation; **Truppen in ~ordnung aufstellen** to marshal troops; **~plan** plan of action.
schlachtreif killable.
Schlacht|ruf battle cry; **~schiff** battleship; **marktfähiges ~schwein** hog; **~vieh lebend erwerben** to buy cattle on the hoof; **~zeit** killing time.
Schlacke dross, slag, tap cinder.
Schlacks hobbledehoy.
Schlaf, fester fast sleep; **gestörter** ~ broken sleep; **unruhiger** ~ unsound sleep;
~ **vor Mitternacht** beauty sleep;
festen ~ haben to be a sound sleeper; **aus dem ~ hochfahren** to wake up with a start; **etw. im ~ können** to know s. th. backwards; ~ **nachholen** to make up for sleep; **Mütze ~ nehmen** to have forty winks, to snatch an hour's sleep; ~ **des Gerechten schlafen** to sleep the sleep of the just; **im ~ sterben** to pass away in one's sleep;
~abteil sleeping compartment; **~baracke** bunkhouse *(US)*; **~bursche** night lodger.
Schläfchen nap, snooze *(coll.)*;
~ **halten** to have forty winks (a snooze).
Schlafen, sich zum ~ legen to lay o. s. down.
schlafen, mit offenen Augen to daydream; **wie ein Murmeltier** ~ to sleep like a top; **bis in die Puppen** ~ to sleep till all hours; **volle zwölf Stunden** ~ to sleep the clock round; **unregelmäßig** ~ to keep inordinate hours;
j. nicht ~ lassen to give s. o. no rest; **Kind ~ legen** to put a child to bed.
schlafender Riese slumbering giant.
schlaff limp, languid, weary, droopy, *(Haut)* flabby, *(Börse)* dull, slack, *(Disziplin)* lax.
Schlaf|gel" lodging (doss, *Br.*, flophouse, *US sl.*) money; **~gelegenheit** sleeping accommodation.
Schlafittchen, j. am ~ nehmen to grab s. o. by the collar, to walk s. o. Spanish *(sl.)*.
Schlaf|kabine *(LKW)* sleeping cabin; **~kamerad** bed fellow; **~koje** sleeping cabin, *(Schlafwagen)* sleeperette, *(Schiff)* berth, bunk; **in ~kojen mittschiffs untergebracht werden** to be berthed amidship; **~kojeneinrichtung** sleeperette service; **~krankheit** sleeping sickness; **~losigkeit** sleeplessness, vigilance; **~mittel** sleeping drug; **~mütze** nightcap, *(fig.)* sleepyhead, stick-in-the-mud; **~quartier** sleeping quarter; **~ratte** sound sleeper, doormouse, sack artist (rat) *(sl.)*; **~saal** dormitory; **~sack** sleeping (body) bag, flea bag *(sl.)*; **~sitz** *(Flugzeug)* slumberette; **~stadt** dormitory suburb, bedroom town *(US)*; **~stätte** roost *(coll.)*; **jem. eine ~stätte bieten** to sleep s. o.; **~stelle** sleeping place (accommodation), lodging place, *(Schiff)* berth; **~tablette** sleeping draught (pill); **~trunk** nightcap.
Schlafwagen sleeping car *(US)* (carriage, *Br.*), compartment (Pullmann, *US*) car, sleeper *(US)*;
~abteil sleeping compartment, section of a sleeper *(US)*; **~betrieb** operating of sleeping cars, sleeper-train service *(US)*; **~gesellschaft** sleeping-car company; **~kabine** roomette, sleeperette; **~karte** berth (sleeping-car) ticket; **~karte lösen** to book a sleeping car (sleeper, *US*); **~platz** *(Schiff)* berth, bunk, *(Zug)* sleeperette; **~platz bestellen** to book a sleeping car (sleeper, *US*); **~schaffner** sleeping-car attendant, [Pullmann] porter *(US)*; **~verkehr** operating of sleeping cars, sleeper-train service *(US)*; **~zug** sleeping-car (compartment) train, sleeper train *(US)*.
Schlaf|wandler sleepwalker, somnambulist; **~zeit** sack duty *(mil., sl.)*; **~zimmer** chamber, bedroom.
Schlag blow, beat, pat, jerk, pelt, pound *(Br.)*, *(Schlaganfall)* stroke;
~ **auf** ~ in quick succession; **mit einem** ~ at one sweep (swoop), *(plötzlich)* all at once; **vom gleichen ~e** of the same stamp; **von ganz anderem** ~ of quite different stripe; **wie ein ~ aus heiterem Himmel** like a bolt from the blue;
elektrischer ~ electric shock; **fürchterlicher** ~ crushing punch; **kalter** ~ *(Blitz)* cold stroke; **schwerer** ~ *(fig.)* great shock; **tödlicher** ~ deathblow;
~ **ins Gesicht** smack in the eye; **dumpfer ~ der Kirchturmuhr** deep sound of the church-tower clock; ~ **gegen jds. Stolz** dent in one's pride; ~ **zwölf Uhr** on the stroke (dot) of 12 o'clock; ~ **ins Wasser** fiasco, flop *(sl.)*, washout *(sl.)*;
schweren finanziellen ~ abbekommen to take the knock *(sl.)*; ~ **gegen j. führen** to aim a blow at s. o.; ~ **auf ~ gehen** to go like

clockwork; **sich einen zweiten ~ holen** to go for a second helping; **Diener vom alten ~ sein** to be an old-fashioned servant; **von ganz anderem ~ sein** to be of another paste; **vom gleichen ~ sein** to be birds of the same feather; **vom richtigen ~e sein** to be of the right kidney; **schwerer ~ für j. sein** to be a heavy blow for s. o.; **mit einem ~ berühmt werden** to become famous over night;
~abtausch exchange of blows; **~anfall** stroke; **beim Anblick der Rechnung um ein Haar einen ~anfall bekommen** to almost have a fit when seeing the bill.
schlagartig all of a sudden, in the twinkling of an eye;
~ aufhören to come to a dead stop; **~ berühmt werden** to become famous over night.
Schlagbaum tollgate, barrier, [turn]pike, toll bar;
~pfosten barpost.
schlagen to beat, to strike, to defeat, to knock, *(Uhr)* to strike; **Augen zu Boden ~** to cast one's eyes down; **j. zu Boden ~** to knock s. o. down; **zu Brei ~** to knock into a cocked hat; **Brücke ~** to throw a bridge; **sich an die Brust ~** to be full of regret; **bei jem. auf den Busch ~** to pump s. o.; **sich in die Büsche ~** to make one's escape; **in jds. Fach ~** to be (lie in) s. one's line, to come within s. one's province; **nicht in jds. Fach ~** to be out of s. one's line; **mit der Faust auf den Tisch ~** to bang one's fist on the table; **gegen die Felsen ~** *(Wellen)* to wash against the rocks; **gegen die Fenster ~** *(Regen)* to be beating against the windows; **j. in die Flucht ~** to put s. o. to flight; **j. ins Gesicht ~** to smack s. o. in the face; **j. grün und blau ~** to beat s. o. black and blue (to a mummy); **Hände vors Gesicht ~** to cover one's face with one's hands; **Kapital aus etw. ~** to make propaganda capital out of s. th.; **sich etw. aus dem Kopf ~** to dismiss s. th. from one's thoughts; **kurz und klein ~** to make matchwood of s. th.; **sich durchs Leben ~** to make a living; **j. mit Leichtigkeit ~** to beat s. one's hands down; **j. auf den Magen ~** to make s. o. feel sick; **sich die Nacht um die Ohren ~** to make a night of it; **Nagel in die Wand ~** to drive a nail into the wall; **Notiz ans Schwarze Brett ~** to put up a notice on the board; **wie rasend ~** *(Puls)* to be throbbing like mad *(coll.)*; **jem. ein Schnippchen ~** to outwit s. o.; **j. auf die Schulter ~** to slap s. o. on the shoulder; **Steuern auf eine Ware ~** to tax an article; **über die Stränge ~** to kick over the traces; **sich tapfer ~** to stand one's ground; **Unkosten auf den Preis ~** to add the cost onto the price; **j. mit seinen eigenen Waffen ~ schlagen** to beat s. o. at his own game; **Warnung in den Wind ~** to make light of a warning; **wild um sich ~** to lash out wildly; **j. windelweich ~** to beat the lights (living hell) out of s. o. *(sl.)*; **Wurzeln ~** to strike root.
schlagend | er Beweis conclusive evidence; **~e Wetter** firedamp.
Schlager novelty item, box-office draw *(US)*, hit, corker *(sl.)*, puller *(sl.)*, *(Buch)* bestseller, *(Musik)* hit, popular tune, pop, *(Reklameartikel)* loss leader, stunt;
bekannter ~ popular song; **sentimentaler ~** tearjerker *(US coll.)*, croon [song];
Schlägerei affray, brawl, fight, struggle, mix-up, melee, turnup *(coll.)*, free-for-all;
zu einer ~ kommen to proceed to blows.
Schlager | erfolg song hit; **~festival** pop-song festival; **~komponist** pop-song writer; **~parade** hit parade; **~preis** record (rock-bottom) price; **~sänger** crooner; **~werbung** novelty advertising.
schlagfertig quick at repartee;
äußerst ~ as sharp as a needle;
~ antworten to make a lightning retort; **~ sein** to have quick wits, to have a ready wit, to give tit for tat, to be quick-witted;
~e Antwort repartee, snappy comeback *(US sl.)*.
Schlagkraft combat effectiveness;
~ erhöhen to lift effectiveness.
schlagkräftig *(mil.)* strong, effective.
Schlag | licht auf etw. werfen to spotlight s. th.; **~loch** road hole, pothole; **mit ~löchern übersät sein** to be strewn with potholes; **~ring** brass knuckles, knuckle duster; **~seite** *(mar.)* list; **leichte ~seite haben** to be a sheet in the wind's eye, to be half-seas over *(coll.)*; **~wetter** *(Bergbau)* firedamp.
schlagwetterreich gassy.
Schlagwort catchword, catch phrase, slogan, *(pol.)* rallying cry;
~e gebrauchen to sloganize;
~katalog subject catalog(ue); **~verzeichnis** catchword index.
Schlagzeile headline, slogan;
ganzseitig fettgedruckte ~ front-page splash; **sensationelle ~** scare headline, screamer *(US sl.)*; **ungeschickte ~** blind headline;
~ auf der ersten Seite front-page headline; **~ über die ganze Seite** banner [line], streamer;
~n machen to be headlined; **seinen Weg in die ~n machen** to kick one's way into (hit) the headlines; **~n für sich in Anspruch nehmen** to get (take) the headlines; **mit ~n versehen** to headline.
Schlagzeilen | verfasser headliner; **~werbung** display advertising.
Schlag | zeug drums, timpani, battery, traps; **~zeuger** drummer.
Schlamassel trouble, razor's edge, scrape, fix, mess, jam, wheel and wheel, caboodle, warm corner, plight;
in einem ~ in bad bread (hot water), in the soup;
sich selbst aus dem ~ helfen to work out one's own salvation.
Schlamm mud, mire, slob;
im ~ steckengeblieben fast stuck in the mud;
in den ~ fahren to mire; **im ~ steckenbleiben** to get stuck in the mud; **im ~ versinken** to get bogged in the mud;
~kur mud cure; **~loch** mudhole; **~schicht** warp.
Schlampe slob, slut, slattern, trollop, dowdy, faggot.
schlampen to slobber.
Schlamperei sloppiness, sloppy work, slovenliness, shoddiness.
schlampig *(Arbeit)* slovenly, sloppy, slipshod, shoddy, *(Aussehen)* sluttish;
~ erledigt negligently done;
~e Arbeit slipshod (shoddy) work, careless job.
Schlange snake, *(beim Anstehen)* queue, line *(US)*, tail, *(Stellenbewerber)* hiring line, *(Währungsverbund)* currency snake;
floatende ~ *(Devisenhandel)* water snake;
~ von Arbeitslosen unemployment line *(US)* (queue, *Br.*); **~ Bedürftiger** bread line; **~ von Bewerbern** queue of applicants, *(Br.)* hiring line; **~ von Fahrzeugen** queue of cars; **~ wartender Kinobesucher** line of people waiting to go to the cinema; **~ vor einem Lebensmittelladen** food queue;
~ an seinem Busen nähren to nourish a viper in one's bosom; **listig wie eine ~ sein** to be as wily as a weasel; **~ stehen** to form (stand in) a queue *(Br.)*, to stand in (wait in a) line *(US)*, to queue up *(Br.)*, to line up *(US)*.
schlängeln, sich to wind, to twist; **sich durch die Menge ~** to corkscrew one's way through the crowd.
Schlangen | beschwörer snake charmer; **~linie** wiggle, wiggly line; **~mensch** contortionist; **~währungen** snake currencies.
schlank slim, slender, lank;
auf seine ~e Linie achten to watch one's figure.
Schlankheitskur slimming (reducing) cure, dieting;
~ machen to slim.
schlankweg point-blank.
schlapp weary, listless, languid, lethargic, droopy;
~er Händedruck wet sock *(sl.)*.
Schlappe reverse, rout, discomfiture;
jem. eine ~ beibringen to foil s. o.; **~ einstecken müssen** to take a trimming (hiding).
schlappmachen to collapse, to swoon, to pass out, to flag, to wilt.
Schlappschwanz weakling, milksop, jellyfish *(coll.)*, chicken *(sl.)*.
Schlaraffenland land flowing with milk and honey, land of plenty, fool's paradise;
wie im ~ leben to live in peace and plenty (a fool's paradise).
schlau shrewd, clever, cute, quick-witted, sharp, sliek *(coll.)*, *(verschlagen)* sly, wily, artful;
aus jem. nicht ~ werden können not to be able to make head or tail of s. o.; **viel zu ~ sein** to be too clever by half; **~er als alle anderen sein** to outsmart everybody; **genauso ~ sein wie zuvor** to be none the wiser;
~er alter Fuchs sly old fox; **~er Schachzug** clever move.
Schlau | berger, ~meier slyboots, knowing one, smarty *(sl.)*;
~ sein to be a cute one.
Schlauch flexible pipe, *(Anstrengung)* tough job, slog, fag *(Br.)*, *(Auto, Fahrrad)* inner tube, *(Gartenschlauch)* hose;
~boot inflatable (rubber) boat, *(Notwasserungen)* airraft, *(Rettungsboot)* life raft.
schlauchen, j. to take a lot out of s. o., to fag (wear) s. o. out.
Schlauchventil inner tube valve.
Schlauheit cleverness, shrewdness, cunning, cuteness, wiliness.
schlecht bad, ill, lousy *(coll.)*, *(abgestanden)* bad, stale, *(abscheulich)* foul, rotten, *(Aktie)* inferior, dubious, *(Börse)* heavy, *(Fleisch)* gone off, tainted, *(Geld)* base, inferior, hedge, *(verdorben)* rotten, unsound, tainted, spoilt, spoiled, decayed, *(Wasser)* foul;
~ abgestimmt ill-timed; **~ begründet** ill-founded; **~ beraten** badly (ill-) advised; **~ beschaffen** ill-conditioned; **~ bewirtschaftet** ill-managed; **~ bezahlt** underpaid; **~er gestellt** worse off; **finanziell ~ gestellt** financially depressed; **gar nicht so ~** not half so bad *(coll.)*; **~ und recht** after a fashion, of sorts; **mehr ~ als recht** in a rough-and-ready manner; **~ verkäuflich** slow of sale;
~ ausfallen to miscarry; **~ gehen** *(Artikel)* to drag, *(Geschäft)* to

be in a bad way (on the downgrade); ~ **geschlafen haben** to have had a poor night; **es sich ~ leisten können** to ill afford it; ~ **landen** to make a bad landing; **bei jem. ~ angeschrieben sein** to be in s. one's bad books; ~ **dran sein** to be badly (poorly) off, to be in a fix *(coll.)*; **finanziell ~ gestellt sein** to be badly situated (in a weak financial situation); ~ **weggekommen sein** to have fared badly; ~ **über j. sprechen** to backbite s. o., to run s. o. down; **sich ~ stehen** to fare badly; **jem. ~ stehen** to sit badly on s. o.; ~ **verkaufen** to come to a bad market; ~ **verwalten** to mismanage; **einem ~ werden** to turn one's stomach;
~**er Abdruck** foul impression; ~**er Absatz** slow (poor, heavy) sale; ~**e Arbeit** poor workmanship; ~**e Aussichten** poor prospects; ~**e Bezahlung** poor payment; ~**en Dienst erweisen** to do s. o. a disservice (bad turn); ~**en Eindruck hinterlassen** to leave a bad impression; ~**e Ernte** poor crop; ~**e Erziehung** ill breeding; ~**es Essen** bad food; ~**e Finanzlage** financial embarrassment; ~**e Führung** misconduct; ~**es Gedächtnis** poor memory; ~**es Geld** counterfeit money, base coin; ~**es Geschäft** losing (bad) bargain; ~**e Geschäftsführung** poor management; **sich in ~er Gesellschaft befinden** to be in bad company; **in ~em Gesundheitszustand** in poor health; ~**e Kapitalanlage** poor investment; **sich in ~er Lage befinden** to be in a fix; ~**e Laune haben** to be in a bad temper (mood); ~**e Luft** tainted air; ~**es Manuskript** bad manuscript; ~**e Meinung von jem. haben** to have a poor opinion of s. o.; ~**er Mensch** wicked person; ~**e Münze** base coinage; ~**e Nachrichten** bad news, black tidings; ~**e Noten** poor marks; ~**e Papiere** *(Börse)* dubious stocks; ~**e Qualität** inferior (poor) quality, quality not up to standard, lowest quality; ~**e Regierung** misgovernment; ~**er Ruf** bad reputation, ill fame; ~**e Schrift haben** to write a bad hand; ~**ere Stellung** inferior position; ~**e Übersetzung** incorrect translation; ~**e Umgangsformen haben** to have bad manners, to be ill-mannered; **in ~er Verfassung sein** to be in bad form, to be in bad fettle (out of the whack, *US*); ~**e Verwaltung** mismanagement, maladministration; ~**e Ware** inferior products (goods); ~**es Wetter** rotten (bad) weather; ~**er Witz** off-colo(u)r (dirty, poor) joke; ~**e Zeiten** slack (hard) times; **in ~em Zustand** ill-conditioned, in poor condition.

Schlechten, sich zum ~ wenden to take a turn for the worse.

Schlechterfüllung malperformance, misperformance.

Schlechtergestellter discriminated (underprivileged) person, underdog.

Schlechterstellung discrimination;
finanzielle ~ für j. bedeuten to be worse fixed financially.

schlechtgläubig mala fide, in bad faith.

schlechtmachen, j. to run s. o. down, to speak ill of s. o.

Schlechtwetter|flug all-weather flight; ~**flugbetrieb** all-weather operation; ~**front** bad-weather front; ~**gebiet** bad-weather zone; ~**geld** bad-weather allowance; ~**periode** spell of bad weather; ~**versicherung** weather insurance; ~**zeit** wet time; ~**zulage** wet-time pay.

schleichen to sneak, to slink, to steal, to pussyfoot, to cat-foot *(US)*, *(Zeit)* to wear away;
sich in jds. Vertrauen ~ to worm o. s. into s. one's confidence; **auf Zehenspitzen durch den Korridor ~** to tiptoe through the corridor.

Schleicher creeper, pussyfoots.

Schleichhandel illegal (clandestine) trade, illegal traffic, trafficking, underhand dealings, *(Schmuggel)* smuggling, contrabandism, *(Schwarzhandel)* black market;
~ **betreiben** to run contraband.

Schleichhändler trafficker, clandestine trader, interloper, *(Schmuggler)* smuggler, contrabandist, *(Schwarzhändler)* black marketeer.

Schleichweg secret path;
etw. auf ~en erreichen to achieve s. th. by oblique ways; **alle ~e kennen** to be up to all the dodges.

Schleichwerbung masked (camouflaged) advertisement.

Schleier screen, twilight, *(Fernsehen)* snow, *(Foto)* fog;
~ **lüften** to lift a curtain (veil); ~ **des Vergessens über das Nachfolgende ziehen** to draw a veil over what followed.

schleierhaft wrapped up in mystery, mystic, baffling, puzzling;
jem. völlig ~ sein to be a complete mystery to s. o.

Schleife bow, tie, *(Straße)* bend, *(el.)* loop, winding.

schleifen to polish, to grind;
j. ~ to put s. o. to the grind; **über den Boden ~** *(Kleid)* to trail on the ground; **Festung ~** to dismantle (demolish) a fortress; **j. in eine Gesellschaft ~** to drag s. o. into going to a party; **j. vor den Richter ~** to bring s. o. to justice; **j. zu Tode ~** to club s. o. to death;
Kupplung ~ lassen to let the clutch slip.

Schleifer polisher, *(mil.)* taskmaster.

Schleifstein grindstone.

Schleifung *(Festung)* dismantlement, demolition.

schleimig *(Mensch)* fawning, cringing.

schlemmen to feast, to regale.

Schlemmer glutton, gourmet, epicure, free liver;
~**leben** high life, sumptuous living; ~**leben führen** to live high on the hog; ~**mahl** gourmet meal.

schlendern to stroll, to wander, to rove at pleasure;
durch die Straßen ~ to saunter through the streets.

Schlendrian jog-trot, humdrum, rut, groove, routine;
alten ~ aufgeben to leave the beaten track; **am alten ~ festhalten** to travel in the same groove; **j. aus seinem ~ herausholen** to lift s. o. out of the rut.

Schlepp, Schiff in ~ nehmen to take a ship in tow;
~**anker** drag anchor; ~**antenne** trailing aerial; ~**boot** tugboat, tow boat *(US)*; ~**dienst** towage service.

Schleppen hauling, haul, *(Auto)* towage, towing.

schleppen to [have in] tow, to haul, to lug, *(Schiff)* to tug;
j. zu einer Gesellschaft ~ to drag s. o. into going to a party; **sich ins fünfte Jahr ~** *(Prozeß)* to be dragging on into the fifth year; **j. vor den Kadi ~** to bring s. o. to justice; **Kunden ~** to tout customers;
an einem Koffer zu ~ haben to have to struggle with a suitcase; **sich ~ lassen** to take tow.

schleppend *(Geschäft)* dragging, slow, *(Markt)* languid, sagging, sluggish, slack;
~ **eingehen** to come in slowly;
~**er Geschäftsgang** slack business, slackness of the market; ~**e Nachfrage** slack demand; ~**e Sprechweise haben** to speak with a drawl; ~**er Warenabsatz** poor market.

Schlepper motor tractor, mule, hauler, haulier *(Br.)*, *(Abschleppwagen)* recovery vehicle, wrecker *(US)*, breakdown van, tow truck *(US)*, *(Kunde)* runner, tout *(US sl.)*, steerer *(sl.)*, *(Schiff)* barge, tug[boat], *(Spielhölle)* roper;
~**dienste leisten** *(sl.)* to steer; ~**verkehr** barge traffic.

Schlepp|fischer trawler skipper; ~**fischerei** trawling; ~**flug** aerotow flight; ~**flugzeug** [tug] glider; ~**gebühr** towing charges, towage; ~**gebührenzuschlag** extra towing charges; ~**geld** streaming; ~**kahn** canal boat, barge; ~**kosten** towage charges; ~**lohn** towage.

Schleppnetz dragnet, trawl;
~**fahndung** dragnet technique; ~**fischer** trawlboat, trawler; ~**fischerei** trawling.

Schlepp|schiff lighter, tug, tugboat; ~**schiffahrt** towing, towage; ~**schiffahrtsunternehmen** towage contractor; ~**seil** towline, tow-rope, tow, hauling rope, *(Flugzeug)* dragline; ~**start** towed start.

Schlepptau dragrope, guide rope, tow-rope, tow;
im ~ haben to have in tow; **immer gleich die ganze Familie im ~ haben** to have one's family in tow; **ins ~ nehmen** to take into tow; **Schiff ins ~ nehmen** to tow a ship; **in jds. ~ segeln** to ride on s. one's coat-tails.

Schlepp|transport haul; ~**trosse** tow; ~**weg** towpath; ~**zug** tow.

Schleuder sling, catapult *(Br.)*, slingshot *(US)*;
~**angebot** cut-rate offer; ~**arbeit** slovenly (badly finished) work, slopwork; ~**artikel** job line, catchpenny [article], *(im Ausland)* dumping goods; ~**ausfuhr** dumping; ~**bahn** catapult; ~**bewegung abfangen** *(Autofahrer)* to get out of a skid; ~**flugzeug** catapult plane; ~**gefahr** *(Verkehrszeichen)* slippery road; ~**geschäft** cutting trade.

Schleudern skid, skidding, side-slip, *(um die eigene Achse)* spin, *(Werfen)* throw;
ins ~ geraten to get into a skid (side-slip).

schleudern to swerve, to throw, to hurl, to toss, *(Auto)* to [get into a] skid (side-slip), *(Wäsche)* to centrifuge, to spin-dry;
um die eigene Achse ~ to spin; **jem. eine Anklage ins Gesicht ~** to hurl an accusation into s. one's face; **Auto über die Straße ~** to send a car spinning across the road; **j. Beleidigungen ins Gesicht ~** to fling out at s. o.

Schleuderpreis giveaway (cutting, cutthroat, wretched, ruinous, slaughtered) price, underprice, flingaway *(fam.)*, drive *(US)*, *(Anzeige)* cut rate, *(im Ausland)* dumping price;
zu ~en verkaufen to sell dirt-cheap (at a sacrifice); **im Ausland zu ~en verkaufen** to dump goods on a foreign market.

schleudersicher *(Reifen)* antiskid, nonskidding.

Schleuder|sitz *(Flugzeug)* catapult (hot, *sl.*, ejection, ejector, panic, *sl.*) seat; ~**spur** skid mark; ~**start** catapult start; ~**verkauf** sale below cost, sale at giveaway price, sacrifice sale, *(im Ausland)* dumping; ~**ware** job line (goods), catchpenny [article].

Schleuse sluice, lock, gate;
die ~n des Himmels the window of heaven;
durch ~n absperren to lock off; **in die ~ gehen** to lock in; **~n seiner Leidenschaft öffnen** to open the floodgates of one's passion.
schleusen to sluice, to lock;
Frachtschiff durch einen Kanal ~ to lock a freighter through a canal; **j. durch die Paßkontrolle ~** to channel s. o. through the passport inspection.
Schleusen|bau system of locks; **~dock** tret dock; **~geld** lockage, lock dues (charges); **~hafen** wet dock; **~kammer** canal lock; **~kanal** sluiceway; **~meister** lockman, lockkeeper, sluicer; **~preis** *(EG)* sluice-gate price; **~tor** sluice (flood, head, lock) gate, drawgate; **~wärter** lockman, lock keeper, sluicer.
Schlich dodge, trick, doubling, gadget, device, knack, lurk *(Br., sl.)*;
jem. die ~e beibringen to show s. o. the ropes; **alle ~e kennen** to know a trick or two, to know the ropes; **jem. auf die ~e kommen** to be up to s. one's tricks, to see through s. one's game.
schlicht plain, simple, unpretending, homespun, unsolemn;
~e Feier unceremonious festivity; **~e Lebensweise** plain living; **~e Leute** simple (plain, homely) people; **~e Wahrheit** unvarnished (plain) truth.
schlichten to settle amicably, to arbitrate, to accommodate, to adjust, to arrange, to mediate, to smooth, to palliate, to intervene, to compromise;
Streit durch Schiedsspruch ~ to settle a dispute by arbitration.
schlichtend eingreifen to intervene in a dispute.
Schlichter arbiter, friendly arbitrator, conciliator, mediator, troubleshooter *(US)*;
amtlicher ~ referee; **gemeinsamer ~** joint arbiter; **staatlicher ~** government mediator (conciliator); **ständiger ~** conciliation commissioner;
als ~ tätig sein to act as arbitrator, to arbitrate a case, to settle by arbitration.
Schlichtung reconciliation, reconcilement, mediation, accommodation, adjustment, arrangement, settlement, *(durch Schiedsspruch)* arbitration;
~ von Arbeitsstreitigkeiten labo(u)r arbitration; **~ von Streitigkeiten** adjustment of differences.
Schlichtungs|abkommen arbitration (reconciliation) agreement; **~amt** arbitration board *(US)*, board of arbitration *(US)*, bureau of conciliation *(US)*, *(Gewerbe)* industrial court *(Br.)*, *(Löhne)* National Wage Board *(US)*; **~angebot** offer of mediation; **~aufgabe** mediation function; **~ausschuß** conciliation (adjustment) committee, council (court) of conciliation *(Br.)*, arbitration committee (commission, board, *US*), *(Gewerbe)* industrial conciliation court (board) *(Br.)*; **vor einen ~ausschuß kommen** to come before a conciliation court; **~befugnisse haben** to imparl; **oberste ~behörde** Federal Mediation and Conciliation Service *(US)*; **~einrichtungen** conciliation facilities; **neutrale ~einrichtungen in Anspruch nehmen** to bring a complaint before an outside mediation service; **~kammer** conciliation board; **~kommission** conciliation (arbitration) committee, adjustment board.
Schlichtungsstelle arbitration agency, arbitration *(US)* (conciliation) board, Bureau of Conciliation, conciliation court;
staatliche ~ government's conciliation service, mediation agency of the government; **zentrale ~** Central Arbitration Committee *(Br.)*;
~ für arbeitsrechtliche Streitfragen trade board *(Br.)*.
Schlichtungs|tätigkeit conciliation services; **~vereinbarung** reconciliation agreement, conciliation scheme, arbitration board; **~verfahren** grievance procedure (arbitration), *(gewerblicher Streitigkeiten)* arbitration (conciliation) proceedings, [industrial] arbitration; **~verfügung** order to arbitrate; **~verhandlungen** conciliation negotiations, arbitration proceedings; **~versuch** attempted conciliation; **~vertrag** arbitration agreement; **~vorschlag** offer of mediation, conciliatory proposal; **~wesen** arbitral jurisdiction, *(in der Wirtschaft)* industrial conciliation.
Schlick warp.
schließen to close [down], to shut, to lock, *(Abkommen)* to negotiate, *(Ausstellung)* to close its doors, *(Betrieb)* to shut down, *(Börse)* to close, to finish, *(Geschäft)* to close, to be closing, *(schlußfolgern)* to conclude, to draw conclusions, to infer, to reason, to presume, *(Schule)* to break up, to end, *(Stromkreis)* to make;
mit 185 1/2 gegen 185 ~ *(Börse)* to close 185 1/2 against 185; **bei gängigen Aktien mit höheren Schlußkursen ~** to close higher in active trading; **von sich auf andere ~** to measure another man's foot by one's own last; **dem Ansehen nach zu ~** judging from appearance; **Antwort in sich ~** *(Frage)* to imply an answer; **j. in seine Arme ~** to clasp s. o. in one's arms; **behördlich ~** to interdict the use of, to padlock *(US)*, to close operations; **neue Bekannschaft ~** to make a new acquaintance; **Bergwerk ~** to lay in a coal mine; **Betrieb aufgrund von Sparmaßnahmen ~** to close its doors for reasons of economy; **Betrieb vorübergehend ~** to close down temporarily, to shut down a factory; **Beweisaufnahme ~** to close (rest) a case; **Brief ~** to conclude a letter; **Bücher ~** to close the books; **Bündnis ~** to form an alliance; **Debatte auf Antrag ~** to close a debate; **Ehe ~** to consummate a (contract s. one's hand in) marriage; **Fabrik wegen Auftragsmangels ~** to close down a factory because of lack of orders; **fest ~** *(Börse)* to close firm, to finish higher; **Filiale ~** to close down a branch office; **flau ~** *(Börse)* to leave off flat; **Freundschaft ~** to strike up a friendship; **Frieden ~** to make (conclude) peace; **Geschäft ~** to close up a shop, to close down, to put up the shutters, to shut up shop *(US)*; **Gläubigervergleich ~** to compound with one's creditors; **Koffer ~** to lock a suitcase; **Konto ~** to close an account; **mit kleinen Kursaufbesserungen ~** *(Börse)* to emerge with small advances; **Laden ~** to shut up (close a) shop; **Lücke ~** to close a gap; **Rede mit den Worten ~** to conclude (wind up) by saying; **Schalter vorübergehend ~** to close a counter temporarily; **schwächer ~** *(Börse)* to finish lower; **sich von selbst ~** *(Tür)* to shut automatically; **Sitzung ~** to close (break up) a meeting; **Subskriptionsliste ~** to close a subscription list; **von der Ursache auf die Wirkung ~** to infer the effect from the cause; **Vergleich mit jem. ~** to come to terms (an arrangement) with s. o.; **Verhandlung ~** to close the court; **mit einem Verlust ~** to close (result) in a loss, to run in the red *(US coll.)*; **Versammlung ~** to break up a meeting; **Versammlung mit einem kurzen Schlußwort ~** to wind up a meeting with a short speech; **Vertrag ~** to come to (enter into, conclude) an agreement; **Vorlesung ~** to conclude a lecture; **in eine Zelle ~** to lock up in a cell.
Schließer doorkeeper, porter, *(Hausmeister)* caretaker, janitor *(US)*, *(Schließgesellschaft)* locker.
Schließfach locker, *(Bank)* safe-[deposit box (vault, *US*)], *(Gepäck)* luggage locker *(Br.)*, *(Post)* post-office (private) box;
~ mieten to rent a safe[-deposit box]; **~ zur Verfügung stellen** to provide safe custody for valuables;
~aufbewahrung safe-deposit keeping; **~einrichtung** safe-deposit institution; **~gebühr** safe[-deposit] fee; **~gesellschaft** safe-deposit company *(Br.)*; **~klausel** *(Versicherung)* safe clause; **~miete** safe-deposit rent, safe hiring, box rent *(US)*; **~nummerinserat** box-number ad *(US)*; **~vermietung** renting of safes, safe-deposit facilities; **~versicherung** safe-deposit insurance; **~vorrichtung** safe-deposit institution.
schließlich in the end, after all, finally.
Schließung closing, closure, *(Betrieb)* shutdown;
bei ~ unserer Bücher on closing our books;
behördlich angeordnete ~ padlock *(US)*; **saisonbedingte ~** seasonal shutdown; **zeitweilige ~** temporary suspension;
~ der Aktienumschreibebücher closing of transfer books; **~ eines Betriebes** closing down of a factory; **~ eines veralteten Betriebes** closure of an antique plant; **~ in der Ferienzeit** holiday (vacation, *US*) shutdown; **~ der Grenze** closure of the frontier; **~ eines Hafens** closing of a port; **umfassende ~en von Industriebetrieben** plant-wide shutdowns; **~ des Parlaments** rising of Parliament; **~ einer Versammlung** breaking up of a meeting.
Schließungs|anweisung, ~verfügung shutdown order, closing order, padlock injunction *(US)*; **~jahr** year of cessation.
Schliff *(Edelstein)* cut, *(fig.)* polish;
letzter ~ master touch;
jem. den ~ beibringen to teach s. o. manners, to lick s. o. into shape; **den letzten ~ geben** to finish, *(fig.)* to add the finishing touches, to act as a fine hone; **einer Arbeit den letzten ~ geben** to polish up a piece of work; **keinen ~ haben** to lack polish.
schlimm bad, dreadful;
~ dran sein to be in a bad way, to be ill (badly) off;
~es Ende nehmen to come to a bad end; **~e Erfahrungen** unpleasant experiences; **~e Folgen** serious consequences; **~e Gedanken** wicked thoughts; **jem. einen ~en Streich spielen** to play a nasty trick on s. o.; **~e Vorbedeutung** bad omen; **~e Zeiten** hard times.
schlimmer worse;
um so ~ so much the worse;
Sache noch ~ machen to add fuel to the fire; **immer ~ werden** to go from bad to worse.

Schlimmeres folgte worse followed.
Schlimmste, das ~ hinter sich haben to ride out a storm, to break the back of s. th., to be out of the woods *(US)*; **sich auf das ~ gefaßt machen müssen** to be for the high jump *(sl.)*; **das ~ überstehen** to break the neck of s. th.
schlimmstenfalls if the worst comes to the worst.
Schlinge loop, *(fig.)* cob, trap, snare;
~**n** meshes, toils;
sich in der eigenen ~ fangen to be caught in one's own trap; **in die ~ gehen** to walk into a trap; ~**n legen** to snare; **jem. die ~ um den Hals legen** to put a noose around s. one's neck; **in die ~n des Gesetzes verstrickt sein** to be caught in the meshes of the law; **Arm in der ~ tragen** to wear one's arm in a sling; **Kopf aus der ~ ziehen** to get o. s. out of a snare, to have a lucky escape.
schlingen, sein Essen to gobble one's food, to gormandize.
Schlingerbewegung *(Schiff)* rolling.
Schlingern toss, *(Schiff)* labo(u)r.
schlingern to lurch, to toss, *(Schiff)* to labo(u)r, to wallow in the water.
Schlingertank antiroll device.
Schlips, j. beim ~ erwischen to catch s. o. by the scruff of one's neck; **sich einen hinter den ~ gießen** to wet one's whistle; **j. auf den ~ treten** to tread on s. one's toes.
Schlitten sled, sledge *(Br.)*, toboggan, *(altes Auto)* flivver *(sl.)*;
mit jem. ~ fahren to wipe (mop) the floor with s. o. *(sl.)*, to walk (ride roughshod) over s. o.; **unter den ~ geraten** to go off the rails;
~**kufe** sled (sledge) runner, *(Flugzeug)* skid; ~**spur** trace of a sleigh.
schlittern to slip, to slither, *(Auto)* to skid.
Schlitz slit, slot, *(Kühlerhaube)* louver;
~**verschluß** *(Foto)* focal plane shutter.
Schloß castle, palace, manor house, *(Verschluß)* lock, padlock, mortise lock;
hinter ~ und Riegel under lock and key, behind bars;
verfallenes ~ ruined castle;
~ **im Mond** castle in Spain;
~ **mit einem Dietrich aufbrechen** to pick a lock; **j. hinter ~ und Riegel bringen** to take s. o. into custody; **ins ~ fallen** *(Tür)* to slam shut; **jem. hinter ~ und Riegel halten** to keep s. o. in prison (under lock and key); **jem. ein ~ vor den Mund hängen** to stop s. one's mouth; **in ein ~ passen** to fit a lock;
er hat ein ~ vor dem Mund his lips are sealed;
~**aufseher** castellan.
Schlosser locksmith, fitter.
Schlosserei locksmithery.
Schloß|führung guided tour of a castle; ~**hof** castle yard; **wie ein ~hund heulen** to cry one's eyes out; ~**vogt** castellan.
Schlot chimney, *(Fabrik)* smokestack;
wie ein ~ qualmen to smoke o. s. sick;
~**baron** tycoon, business baron.
schlottern to shake, to tremble, to wobble;
vor Kälte ~ to shiver with cold.
schlotternd, mit ~en Knien with shaking knees.
Schlucht gorge, ravine, chasm, canyon, gulf, abyss.
Schluck mouthful, swallow, swig, *(kleiner)* sip;
~ **Alkohol** load *(sl.)*; ~ **Bier** draught of beer; ~ **Wasser** piece (drink) of water; **ein ~ zuviel** one too many.
schlucken, etw. to swallow s. th., *(fig.)* to gulp it down, to eat up *(sl.)*, to take it on the chin *(sl.)*; **seine Arznei ~** to take one's medicine; **kleinere Betriebe ~** to absorb splinter operations (small industries); **seine ganzen Einkünfte ~** to swallow up more than one's earnings;
bittere Pille ~ müssen to have to swallow the bitter pill.
Schlucker, armer lack-all, empty-pocket, poor devil.
Schluckimpfstoff oral vaccine.
Schluderarbeit slapdash (slovenly) work.
schludern, bei der Arbeit to scamp, to skimp, to do one's work slapdash.
schludrig botched, slipshod, slapdash;
~ **im Bezahlen seiner Rechnungen** remiss in paying one's bills;
~**e Arbeit** slapdash, slovenly work, slopwork.
schlummern to slumber, to doze;
weiterhin ~ *(Verdacht)* to lurk in s. one's mind.
schlummernde Talente dormant talents (gifts).
Schlummertrunk nightcap.
Schlund chasm, abyss, yawn.
schlüpfen, durch die Finger to slip through one's fingers; **in eine andere Haut ~** to change one's role; **schnell in die Kleider ~** to pop into one's clothes; **durch die Maschen des Gesetzes ~** to find a loophole in the law.
Schlupfloch bolthole, let-out, out *(coll.)*.
schlüpfrig loose, *(Pflaster)* slippery, *(Roman)* risqué, lewd;
~**er Witz** off-colo(u)r joke.
Schlupfwinkel lurk, haunt, cache, covert, lurking place, nook, nest, hiding;
verteidigungsfähiger ~ hold-up.
schlurfen, über die Straße to shuffle across the street.
Schluß finish, windup, termination, *(Abschluß)* conclusion, close, closure, *(Abschlußeinheit im Börsengeschäft)* unit of trade, trading unit, board (full) lot *(US)*, *(Ende)* close, end, *(Ergebnis)* result, issue, upshot, *(Redaktionsschluß)* deadline, *(Schlußfolgerung)* conclusion, consequence, deduction, inference, *(Schule)* break-up;
am ~ der Rechnungsperiode at the close of the period; **nach ~ der Vorstellung** after the end of the performance; **zum ~ eines Jahres** at the end of a year;
~**!** domino!
~ **fest** *(Börse)* close (closing) firm;
fester ~ *(Börse)* steady closing; **unvermeidbarer ~** foregone conclusion; **zusammenfassender ~** *(Rede)* peroration; **zwingender ~** violent presumption;
~ **eines Abenteuers** end of an adventure; ~ **auf Abruf** *(Börse)* negotiation on (at) call; ~ **der Beweisführung** close of argument; ~ **der Debatte** *(parl.)* closure, cloture *(US)*, *(Abwürgen)* gag; ~ **einer Rede** winding up of a speech; ~ **einer Sitzung** end of a meeting; ~ **einer Sitzungsperiode** conclusion of a session; ~ **der Verladung** closure of cargo;
~ **der Debatte beantragen** to move the closure, to put the question; ~ **bilden** *(Kolonne)* to bring up the rear; **Verhandlungen zu einem glücklichen ~ bringen** to bring negotiations to a satisfactory conclusion; **zum ~ gelangen** to arrive at the conclusion; **schwachen ~ haben** *(Roman)* to have a weak ending; ~ **machen** *(Arbeit beenden)* to knock off; **für heute ~ machen** to call it a day *(coll.)*; **mit dem Rauchen ~ machen** to stop smoking; **beim ~ dabei sein** to be in at the finish; ~ **der Debatte verlangen** *(parl.)* to be calling for the question; ~ **vermitteln** *(Börse)* to negotiate (do) a deal; ~ **ziehen** to draw a conclusion; **voreiligen ~ ziehen** to jump (leap) to a conclusion;
~ **folgt** *(Fortsetzungsgeschichte)* to be concluded;
~**abnahme** *(Bau)* final architect's certificate; ~**abrechnung** final account (bill, statement), account of settlement, *(Nachlaßverwalter)* final settlement; ~**abrechnungstag** *(Börse)* settling (settlement) day, day of account; ~**absatz** closing paragraph; ~**abschnitt** concluding section; ~**abstimmung** final vote; ~**agonie** final throes; ~**akte** final act; ~**alter** *(Versicherung)* final age; ~**ansprache** final speech (address); ~**antrag** *(Plädoyer)* conclusion; ~**antrag stellen** *(parl.)* to put the question, *(Prozeß)* to conclude one's argument; ~**ausführungen** concluding statements; ~**aussage** *(Anzeige)* base line; ~**ausschüttung** final distribution; ~**band** final volume; ~**bearbeitung** finish; ~**bemerkungen** concluding (closing) remarks, final observation; ~**bericht** final report; ~**besprechung** concluding conference; ~**bestand** closing inventory (stock); ~**bestimmungen** concluding (final) provisions, conclusion; ~**bilanz** final balance, *(Jahresbilanz)* annual balance sheet; ~**börse** terminal market; ~**brief** *(Warenverkehr)* sales note *(Br.)*, sold note *(US)*; ~**buchung** closing entry; ~**dividende** liquidation (liquidating, final) dividend.
Schlüsse ziehen to make inferences, to draw conclusions;
voreilige ~ to jump at (rush to) a conclusion.
Schlüssel key, *(Entzifferung)* cryptograph, *(fig.)* clue, key, *(für Telegramm)* cable code, cipher, *(Verteilungsschlüssel)* quota;
falscher ~ skeleton key; **fester ~** specified formula;
~ **zum Erfolg** secret of (key to hit) success; ~ **zur politischen Lage** key to the political situation;
~ **abziehen** to take out the key; ~ **zum Erfolg in der Tasche haben** to be on the highway to success; ~ **des Rätsels kennen** to hold the key to the puzzle; ~ **von einem ~bund losmachen** to detach a key from a key ring; ~ **steckenlassen** to leave the key in the lock; **Geld nach dem gleichen ~ verteilen** to distribute money at an equal ratio;
~**arbeit** key job; ~**barometer** key indicator; ~**bart** key bit; ~**bedingung** key provision; ~**beruf** priority job; ~**beteiligungen** key holdings; ~**betrieb** key plant; ~**betriebe** key economics; ~**blatt** code sheet; ~**brett** keyboard; ~**bund** bunch of keys, key ring; ~**dienst** key service; ~**faktor** key factor.
schlüsselfertig on a turn-key basis;
~ **abliefern (übergeben)** to turn it over ready to turn a key;
~**er Anlagenvertrag** turn-key job; ~**er Auftrag** turn-key contract.

Schlüssel|figur key figure (roll); ~**figur im Parlament darstellen** to play a key part (role) in Parliament; ~**gemeinkosten** prorated expenses; ~**gerät** privacy scrambler, converter; ~**gewalt** *(Ehefrau)* wife's expenditure, agency of necessity; ~**gewalt ausüben** to pledge the husband's credit for necessaries *(Br.)*; ~**gruppe** cipher (code) group; ~**industrie** key (pivotal) industry, basic trade (industry); ~**industrien** pivotal trades; ~**katalog** code sheet; ~**kind** latch-key (door-key) kid; ~**kosten** apportionable costs; ~**kraft** key aid (man, executive); ~**kraft wegengagieren** to tempt a keyman away from his employer; ~**kräfte** key employees (executives, people, personnel); **internationale** ~**kräfte** key international executives; **durchs** ~**loch gucken** to peep through the keyhole; ~**maschine** privacy scrambler, converter, cryptomechanism; ~**material** key facts.

Schlüssel|offizier cipher officer; ~**organ** key body; ~**personal** key personnel (executives).

Schlüsselposition key position (post), leading position;
hohe ~ high slot; **strategische** ~ key (strategic) position;
~**en im Kabinett** key cabinet posts;
~ **im Verteidigungsprogramm einnehmen** to be a keystone in the defence program(me).

Schlüssel|punkt, ~**stellung** *(mil.)* keypoint; ~**ring** key ring; ~**rolle** pivotal role; ~**rolle darstellen** to play a key role; ~**roman** roman à clef.

Schlüsselstellung key position (post, office), key center *(US)* (centre, *Br.*), priority (key) job, pivotal position, *(mil.)* keypoint;
wirtschaftliche ~ key industrial emporium;
für eine ~ **ausersehen** to earmark for a key position; ~ **für die politische Zukunft eines Landes besitzen** to hold the key to a country's political future.

Schlüssel|telegramm cipher telegram; ~**text** cryptotext, code (cipher) text; ~**übergabe** hasp and staple *(Scot. law)*; ~**unterlagen** encoding and decoding chart; ~**verfahren** code system; ~**währung** key currency; **statistische** ~**werte für die Wirtschaft** economic indicators; ~**wesen** cryptography; ~**wort** key (code) word; ~**zahl** code figure, key factor (figure, ratio), index number, *(Safe)* combination; **mittels** ~**zahl bestätigen** to authenticate by keyword; ~**zentrale** code centre *(Br.)* (center, *US*); ~**ziffern** key data; ~**zuweisung** rate support grant *(Br.)*.

Schluß|ergebnis final result, upshot; ~**etappe** final leg.

Schlußexamen terminal examination;
im ~ in the schools *(Br.)*;
juristisches ~ bar final;
sein ~ **machen** to take one's finals.

Schlußfeier closing ceremony, *(Schule)* speech day *(Br.)*, commencement *(US)*.

schlußfolgern to reason, to conclude, to deduct.

Schlußfolgerung argumentation, conclusion, inference, reasoning, finding;
falsche ~ fallacy; **rechtliche** ~ conclusion of law; **tatsächliche** ~ conclusion of fact;
~**en ziehen** to draw conclusions, to put two and two together; **übereilte** ~**en ziehen** to rush to conclusions, to jump to a hasty conclusion; **vorläufige** ~ **ziehen** to come to a tentative conclusion; ~**en aus einer Vertragsbestimmung ziehen** to infer a term.

Schluß|formeln *(Brief)* [formal] ending, complimentary close (closure); ~**frist für beiderseitiges Parteivorbringen** term to conclude; ~**gebühr** final tax; ~**haltung** *(Börse)* final tone.

schlüssig conclusive, convincing, issuable, *(folgerichtig)* logical;
nicht ~ inconclusive, *(Klage)* demurrable;
~ **begründen und glaubhaft machen** to establish a prima facie case; **nicht** ~ **sein** *(Klage)* to have no merits; **sich** ~ **werden** to make up one's mind.

Schlüssigkeit conclusiveness;
mangelnde ~ inconclusiveness;
~ **eines Anspruchs prüfen** to examine the merits of a claim.

Schluß|inventur ending (final, closing) inventory, final stocktaking; ~**kapitel** final chapter; ~**klausel** *(Urkunde)* testimonium; ~**kundgebung** final manifestation; ~**kurs** *(Börse)* final quotation, closing price, *(Devisen)* closing rate; **in gängigen Aktien höhere** ~**kurse erzielen** to close higher in active trading; **bei ruhigen** ~**kursen liegen** to close in quiet markets; ~**leiste** *(drucktechn.)* tailpiece; ~**licht** *(Auto)* taillight, tail lamp, *(Allerletzter)* tail ender *(US)*; ~**licht abgeben** to be at the bottom of the table; ~**licht bilden** *(mil.)* to bring up the rear; ~**markt** terminal market; ~**note** *(Kauf)* bought note *(Br.)*, *(Makler)* call, stockbroker's contract *(Br.)*, contract note *(Br.)*, broker's memorandum (note) *(Br.)*, purchase contract, *(Verkauf)* sale (sales) note *(US)*, sold note *(Br.)*.

Schlußnoten|register bargain book; ~**stempel** contract stamp *(Br.)*, transfer tax *(US)*.

Schlußnotierung *(Börse)* closing (last, final, terminal) quotation, closing price;
gestrige ~ yesterday's closing rates.

Schluß|plädoyer closing address, final submission, summing up, summation; ~**protokoll** final record, *(dipl.)* final protocol; ~**protokoll erstellen** to finalize an agreement; ~**prüfung** terminal examinations, finals; **sich einer** ~**prüfung unterziehen** to take one's finals; ~**quittung** receipt in full (for the balance), *(Grunderwerb)* final receiver's receipt; ~**quote** final dividend, *(Konkursverfahren)* liquidation dividend; ~**rate** final instal(l)ment; ~**rechnung** final (terminal) accounts, account of settlement, *(Nachlaßverwalter)* final settlement; ~**redakteur** night editor; ~**rede** closing speech; ~**satz** concluding sentence; ~**sätze** concluding lines; ~**schein** *(Makler)* broker's note, call, contract note *(Br.)*, *(Kauf)* bought and sold note, bought note *(Br.)*, *(Verkauf)* sale (sales) note *(US)*, sold note *(Br.)*; ~**scheinbuch** contract book; ~**semester** final term; ~**sitzung** final (closing) session; ~**spalte** last column; ~**stein** key; ~**stempel** contract stamp *(Br.)*, transfer tax *(US)*; ~**strich unter eine Rechnung ziehen** to settle a matter for good; ~**szene** close (final) scene; ~**tag** last (closing) day; ~**termin** latest (cut-off, closing, ending) date, deadline *(US)*, *(Gericht)* final hearing; ~**termin Mitternacht** midnight deadline *(US)*; ~**urteil** final judgment (determination); ~**vereinbarung** final accord; ~**verfahren** final process; ~**verfügung** final order (decree); ~**vergütung** *(Lebensversicherung)* terminal bonus; ~**verhandlung** final negotiation (meeting), *(Gericht)* final hearing; ~**verkauf** close-out (clearance) sale, *(Frühjahr)* spring sales, *(Inventurausverkauf)* inventory sale, *(Räumungsverkauf)* closing-down sale, *(Saisonausverkauf)* [seasonal] sale; ~**versammlung** final meeting; ~**verteilung** *(Konkurs)* distribution of assets of the bankrupt estate, *(Nachlaß)* final settlement (distribution); ~**vignette** tailpiece; ~**vortrag** final address; ~**waggon** end carriage *(Br.)*; ~**wort** summary, *(Angeklagter)* last word; ~**worte** concluding (last) words, summary; ~**zahlung** terminal payment *(US)*, final instal(l)ment; ~**zeile** catch line; ~**zettel** broker's (contract, *Br.*, sales, *US*) note, delivery ticket.

Schmach dishono(u)r, disgrace, shame, ignominy, contempt;
~ **und Schande über j. bringen** to bring shame and disgrace upon s. o.

schmachten to suffer, to languish;
vor Durst ~ to be parched with thirst; **im Kerker** ~ to languish in prison.

Schmachtfetzen pop, croon song, corn *(sl.)*, tearjerker *(US coll.)*, sob stuff *(US sl.)*, weeper *(sl.)*.

schmächtig slight, slender, slim.

schmachvoll disgraceful, ignominious, dishono(u)rable, shameful.

schmackhaft|machen to add zest to s. th.; **dem Kunden** ~ **machen** to style for the customer *(US)*; **Speise** ~ **zubereiten** to make a dish tasty.

Schmähbrief defamatory (libel(l)ous) letter.

schmähen to calumniate, to vilify, to revile;
jem. ~ to disparage s. o., to run s. o. down.

schmählich disgraceful, shameful, dishono(u)rable;
j. ~ **im Stich lassen** to leave s. o. in the lurch;
~**es Ende nehmen** to come to a wretched end.

Schmäh|lied abusive song; ~**rede** invective, calumny, defamatory words; ~**schrift** lampoon, libel(l)ous publication; **aufrührerische** ~**schrift** seditious libel *(Br.)*.

Schmähungen abusive language, invectives, calumny, revilement, vilification;
jem. mit ~ **überhäufen** to bombard s. o. with invectives, to heap insults (obloquy) upon s. o.

schmal *(Buch)* thin, slender, *(Gewinn)* narrow;
~**es Einkommen** small income; ~**e Gewinnspanne** narrow [profit] margin; ~**e Kost** slender diet; **jem. auf** ~**e Kost setzen** to put s. o. on short commons; ~**e Schrift** lean type.

schmäler werden to narrow.

schmälern to diminish, to encroach, to impair, to disparage, *(Ausgaben einschränken)* to retrench, to curtail, to reduce, to cut down, *(Ruf)* to derogate;
j. in seinen Rechten ~ to curtail (encroach upon) s. one's rights;
jds. Verdienste ~ to detract from s. one's merits.

schmälernd derogatory.

Schmälerung *(Ausgaben)* curtailment, cut, retrenchment, *(Rechte)* impairment, encroachment, entrenchment, *(Ruf)* disparagement, derogation, defamation, belittlement;
~ **von jds. Verdiensten** detraction from s. one's merits.

Schmal|film narrow film, cinefilm; ~**filmkamera** cine-camera; **bei ihnen ist ~hans Küchenmeister** they are on short commons; ~**schrift** *(Druck)* condensed type; ~**seite** *(Haus)* gable; ~**spur** *(Bahn)* narrow gauge; ~**spurbahn** narrow-gauge (light) railway.
schmalspurig narrow-gauge.
Schmalspurorganisation smalltime organization.
schmalzig sloppy, trashy, corny *(US sl.)*.
schmarotzen, bei jem. to sponge (mooch, *US*) on s. o. *(fam.)*.
Schmarotzer parasite, sponger, drone, sluggard, hanger-on, shark, freeloader, passenger *(sl.)*;
~**leben** parasitical life, life of a parasite; ~**tum** parasitism.
Schmarren *(fig.)* rubbish, trash;
das geht dich einen ~ an that's none of your business.
Schmaus junket, banquet, spread, feast.
schmausen to eat heartily, to banquet, to feast, to tuck in *(Br.)*.
Schmauser merrymaker.
schmecken to taste, to relish, *(kosten)* to try, to taste;
schal ~ to taste flat;
jem. die Rute zu ~ geben to give s. o. a taste of the rod.
Schmeichelei flattery, fair words, flattering compliments, soft soap *(sl.)*, butter *(sl.)*, taffy *(US coll.)*;
leicht zu durchschauende ~ transparent flattery; **unaufrichtige ~** cheap flattery;
jem. etw. durch ~en abluchsen to wheedle s. th. out of s. o.; **keine ~en sagen können** not to have the gift of pleasing; **jem. die ~en in Dosen verabreichen** to give s. o. a dose of flattery.
schmeichelhaft flattering;
nicht ~ uncomplimentary; **wenig ~** unflattering;
~**e Bemerkungen machen** to make flattering remarks.
Schmeichelkatze sly minx.
schmeicheln to flatter, to make fair weather, to soft-soap *(sl.)*, *(unterwürfig)* to toady, to bootlick *(US)*;
jem. ~ to do s. o. proud *(fam.)*, to eat s. one's toad, to sweet-talk to s. o. *(sl.)*; **jds. Eitelkeit ~** to tickle s. one's vanity; **kriecherisch ~** to cringe; **sich ins Ohr ~** *(Melodie)* to be pleasing to the ear; **ungern ~** not to be given to praise.
Schmeichelworte flattering (honeyed) words.
Schmeichler flatterer, cajoler, wheedler, coax;
glattzüngiger ~ mealy-mouthed flatterer.
schmeichlerisch flattering, wheedling, fawning, cajoling, coaxing, well-oiled.
schmeißen, Betrunkenen aus dem Lokal to chuck a drunken man out of a pub; **Geld aus dem Fenster ~** to fling one's money out of the window, to throw money down the drain; **mit dem Geld nur so um sich ~** to play ducks and drakes with one's money; **sich jem. an den Hals ~** to fling o. s. into s. one's arms; **Laden ~** to run the show, to boss it, to swing it *(US)*; **Lage ~** to stand a round of drinks; **Vorstellung ~** to make a mess of a performance.
schmelzen to melt, to dissolve, *(auftauen)* to thaw, *(Sicherung)* to blow, *(Vorräte)* to dwindle, to decrease, to melt away;
in jds. Händen wie Schnee in der Sonne ~ *(Geld)* to melt in s. one's hands; **vor Mitleid ~** to melt with pity.
Schmelz|käse soft cheese; ~**ofen** furnace; ~**punkt** *(Eis)* melting point; ~**sicherung** *(el.)* thermal cutout; ~**tiegel** *(fig.)* melting pot; ~**wasser** melted snow (water).
Schmerz pain, torment, *(Kummer)* grief;
heftiger (großer) ~ violent pain; **rasender ~** wild pain; **seelischer ~** mental anguish; **stechender ~** pang, tinge, stab, piercing pain;
jem. ~ bereiten to give s. o. pain; **~ ertragen** to suffer pain of body; **sich vor ~ krümmen** to double with pain; **~ lindern** to alleviate pain;
geteilter ~ ist halber ~ two in distress make sorrow less;
~**empfinden** sense of pain.
schmerzen to [cause] pain, to hurt, to ache, to grieve.
Schmerzensgeld exemplary damages, smart money, damages for pain and suffering *(Br.)*, compensation for pain and suffering *(US)*;
jem. ~ zahlen lassen to make s. o. smart.
Schmerzerleichterung ease from pain.
schmerzlich painful, distressing;
jem. ~ vermissen to miss s. o. badly;
~**e Trennung** wrench; ~**er Verlust** severe loss; ~**er Verzicht** bitter sacrifice.
Schmerz|linderungsmittel palliative; ~**tablette** pain killer.
schmerzunempfindlich sein to be insensible to pain.
schmettern, zu Boden to hurl to the ground; **einen ~** to wet one's whistle; **in Stücke ~** to dash to pieces; **Tür ins Schloß ~** to slam a door.
Schmied smith, blacksmith;
~ des eigenen Glücks architect of one's own fortune.
Schmiede blacksmith's shop, *(Fabrik)* forge;
~**eisen** wrought iron.
schmieden to forge;
das Eisen ~, solange es heiß ist to strike while the iron is hot; **Pläne ~** to make plans.
Schmiedeofen forging furnace.
schmiegsam *(Material)* pliable, flexible.
Schmierblock scribbling block, memo pad, scratch pad *(US)*.
Schmiere slush, smire, *(Wanderbühne)* barnstormers, penny gaff *(Br., sl.)*;
auf der Straße eine gefährliche ~ bilden to form a dangerous greasy spot on the road; **~ stehen** to keep cave *(Br., sl.)*, to lay chickie *(sl.)*.
Schmieren lubrication, *(Bestechen)* bribery.
schmieren to lubricate, *(bestechen)* to fee, to bribe, to palm *(US)*, to grease the palm, *(unleserlich schreiben)* to scribble, to scrawl;
j. ~ to cross s. one's hand with a piece of money, to oil (grease) s. one's palm *(fam.)*, to smear (square, *sl.*) s. o., to oil (cross, grease) s. one's hand; **Butter aufs Brot ~** to spread a slice of bread with butter; **Butterbrote ~** to butter slices of bread; **jem. eine ~** to paste s. o. one *(sl.)*; **sich die Kehle ~** to wet one's whistle; **die richtigen Leute ~** to grease the right palms.
Schmierenkomödiant barnstormer.
Schmiererei quill driving, scribbling, scrawling.
Schmierfink messy fellow *(coll.)*.
Schmiergelder secret commission, palm oil (grease) *(sl.)*, soap *(sl.)*, sweetener, payola *(sl.)*, soak *(US sl.)*, slush money *(US)*, graft *(US)*, *(des Arbeiters für Vorarbeiter)* kickback *(US)*, *(Bestechung)* bribe, fee, *(pol.)* slush fund *(US)*, hush money;
durch ~ in Schwung bringen to grease the wheels, to placate *(US)*;
~**fonds** bribery (slush, *US*) fund; ~**unwesen** corruption, grafting *(US)*.
schmierig smeary, greasy, *(Geschäft)* filthy, dirty;
~**er Kerl** oily fellow.
Schmier|loch oilhole; ~**mittel** lubricant, lubricator; ~**öl** lubricating (machine) oil; ~**papier** scribbling paper *(Br.)*, scratch paper *(US)*; ~**seife** yellow soap; ~**skizze** sketch, rough; ~**stelle** *(Drucker)* monk.
Schminke grease paint.
schminken, sich to paint one's face.
Schmirgelpapier abrasive (emery) paper.
Schmiß pep, go zip, snap;
~ haben to have pep, to zip; **keinen ~ haben** to have no go.
schmissig full of go (pep), peppy *(sl.)*.
Schmöker yellowback.
schmollen to be sulky;
mit jem. ~ not to be speaking to s. o.
schmoren, in der Sonne to roast in the hot sun;
jem. ~ lassen to let s. o. stew in his own juice.
Schmonzes tittle-tattle, trash, rubbish;
~ verzapfen to be right of it *(sl.)*.
Schmu swindle, cheat.
Schmuck jewellery, jewelry, *(Verzierung)* ornament, adornment, embellishment, decoration, pennyweight *(sl.)*, garnish;
kitschiger ~ cheap finery; **unechter ~** sham jewellery, trinkets, bijouterie.
schmuck spruce, trim, neat, dinky *(coll.)*.
Schmuckblattelegramm greetings (decorative) telegram.
schmücken to ornament, to embellish, to adorn, to decorate, to garnish;
sich ~ to spruce (smarten) o. s. up; **sich wie ein Pfingstochse ~** to dress up to the nines.
Schmuck|farbe accompanying colo(u)r; ~**gegenstände** jewellery, jewelry, bijouterie, pretties; ~**geschäft** jeweller, jewelry store *(US)*; ~**kassette** jewellery box; ~**leiste** printer's flower.
schmucklos plain, without ornament;
~**er Bericht** unvarnished account; ~**e Fassade** plain front.
Schmuck|sachen jewels, jewelry, pretties; ~**stück einer Sammlung** gem of a collection; ~**truhe** jewel case; ~**versicherung** jewellery insurance; ~**waren** jewellery, trinkets; ~**warenindustrie** jewelry industry.
Schmuggel smuggling, illegal (contraband) trade, contrabandism;
bandenmäßiger ~ organized smuggling;
~ von Kunstgegenständen art smuggling;
~ betreiben to [run] contraband, to smuggle;
~**fahrt** smuggling run.

schmuggeln to smuggle, to [run] contraband, *(Alkohol)* to bootleg;
Geschenke ins Haus ~ to sneak presents into one's house; **etw. außer Landes ~** to smuggle s. th. out of the country; **Rauschgift ~** to traffick in narcotic drugs.
Schmuggel|tätigkeit smuggling activities; **~ware** prohibited articles, smuggled (undeclared, prohibited) goods, contraband [articles (goods)].
Schmuggler smuggler, contrabandist, *(Alkohol)* rum-runner *(US)*, bootlegger *(US)*;
~bande gang of smugglers; **~schiff** smuggler, runner, contraband vessel.
Schmus blarny, butter *(sl.)*, flattery, soft soap *(sl.)*, eyewash *(sl.)*, *(leere Phrasen)* empty talk, prattle;
~ reden to prattle, to babble.
schmusen to cuddle, to spoon, to pet.
Schmuser spooner, *(Schönredner)* wheedler, cajoler.
Schmutz filth, *(Straße)* mud, dirt, mire, slush, garbage;
~ der Elendsviertel squalor of the slums; **Ruß und ~ einer Industriestadt** the soot and grime of a manufacturing town; **~- und Schundliteratur** trashy and obscene literature;
j. mit ~ bewerfen to sling mud (fling dirt) at s. o.; **im ~ herumrühren** *(fig.)* to muckrake; **voller ~ sein** to be muddy; **im ~ steckenbleiben** to get stuck in the mud; **in den ~ ziehen** to spot, to trail, to drag into the dust, to disparage;
~betrieb polluter; **~blatt** *(Buch)* flyleaf, gutter paper; **~bogen** spoiled (offset, slip) sheet.
schmutzempfindlich sein to spoil easily.
Schmutz|fänger dust trap, filter, *(Auto)* mudguard; **~farbe** *(mil.)* olive drab; **~fink** dirty, slob, hog, *(Kind)* grubby urchin; **~fleck** smear, stain, spot; **durch Finger verursachter ~fleck** finger mark; **~flecken** spots (splash) of mud, splotch; **~geld** dirty money *(Br.)*.
schmutzig dirty, unclean, unwashed, foul, impure, *(abgegriffen)* thumb-marked, *(Straßen)* dirty, muddy, miry, *(unausstehlich)* obscene, gross, vile;
j. ~ behandeln to treat s. o. like dirt;
~er Abzug smudged (uneven) proof; **~e Arbeit** dirty work; **~e Banknoten** soiled bank notes; **~e Elendsgebiete einer Großstadt** sordid slums of a big city; **~e Fensterscheibe** dingy windowpane; **~er Geizhals** stingy old skinflint; **~es Geschäft** dirty business; **~es Gewerbe** no lawful trade; **~e Hände** black hands; **~e Kneipe** filthy dive; **~e Lüge** monstrous lie, whopper; **~e Phantasie** nasty mind; **~e Redensarten gebrauchen** to use foul language; **~e Straßen** streets full of mud; **seine ~e Wäsche in der Öffentlichkeit waschen** *(fig.)* to wash one's dirty linen in public; **~er Witz** smutty joke.
Schmutz|kittel smock; **~konkurrenz** sharp practices, mean (cutthroat) competition, underselling; **~lappen** rag, clout; **~literatur** obscene literature, pornography; **~presse** gutter press; **~seite** *(Buch)* sham (foul) page; **~titel** *(Buch)* bastard (half) title, sham title page; **~zulage** dirty money *(Br.)*.
Schnabel *(Mund)* mouth, gob, [potato] trap *(sl.)*;
~ aufreißen to talk big, to brag; **~ halten** to shut up; **jem. den ~ stopfen** to silence s. o.; **seinen ~ an anderen Leuten wetzen** to have a sharp tongue;
reden, wie einem der ~ gewachsen ist not to mince matters.
Schnake mosquito, gnat *(Br.)*.
schnallen, Gürtel enger to tighten one's belt; **sich an einen Sitz ~** to fasten one's seat belt.
schnappen to snap, *(Feder)* to spring, to shoot, *(Verbrecher)* to catch;
j. ~ *(Polizei)* to pull up s. o.; **Dieb ~** to nail a thief *(sl.)*; **Luft ~** to gasp for breath, *(fig.)* to be flabbergasted (speechless).
Schnapp|messer flick knife; **~schloß** snap lock; **~schuß** *(Foto)* snapshot; **~schüsse machen** to make desultory pictures, to snapshot.
Schnaps intoxicating liquor, brandy, strong drink, booze *(coll.)*, tape *(sl.)*, *(Fusel)* rotgut;
~brenner distiller; **~brennerei** stillhouse, distillery; **verbotene ~brennerei** grog-shop; **~bude** joint *(sl.)*, jerry shop *(Br.)*, speakeasy *(US)*, dive *(US sl.)*, gin mill *(sl.)*, groggery *(US sl.)*.
Schnäpschen whet, pick-me-up, appetizer, snort *(US)*, quick-one, sniffer *(sl.)*.
Schnaps|fahne haben to reek of alcohol; **~flasche** brandy (gin, whisky) bottle; **rückfälliger ~händler** common liquor dealer; **~idee** nutty (wet, crazy, crackpot) idea.
schnattern *(schwatzen)* to prate, to chatter, to jabber, to clatter.
schnauben, nach Rache to breathe revenge.
Schnaufer, seinen letzten ~ getan haben to have given one's last gasp *(coll.)*.
Schnauferl vintage (antique) car, kemp *(US sl.)*.
Schnauze snout, mouth, trap *(sl.)*, mug *(sl.)*, yap *(US sl.)*;
jem. eins auf die ~ geben to give s. o. a sock on the jaw; **große ~ haben** to have a big mouth; **~ von etw. voll haben** to be pretty sick about (fed up with) it; **frei nach ~ machen** to do s. th. by guesswork; **sich die ~ verbrennen** to burn one's fingers.
Schnecke conveyer;
j. zur ~ machen to tell s. o. what is what; **langsam wie eine ~ sein** to go at a snail's pace.
Schnecken|antrieb worm gear; **~tempo** snail's gallop (pace).
Schnee snow, *(Kokain)* cocaine, crystals, snow *(sl.)*;
vom ~ eingeschlossen snowbound; **vom ~ verschüttet** buried in the snow;
frisch gefallener ~ new-fallen snow;
im ~ liegenbleiben *(Auto)* to be stuck in the snow; **wie ~ in der Sonne schmelzen** *(Geld)* to melt in one's hands; **durch den tiefen ~ stapfen** to pick one's way through deep snow.
Schneeball|system snowball system; **~systembriefe** snowball letters *(Br.)*; **~verkaufssystem** pyramid selling.
Schnee|bruch *(Wald)* snowbreak; **~decke** snow; **~dichte** density of snow; **~fall** snowfall.
schneefrei free of snow.
Schnee|gestöber snowstorm; **~grenze** snow line; **~höhe** depth of snow; **~ketten** snow (skid) chains; **sich wie ein ~könig freuen** to be pleased as Punch; **märchenhafte ~landschaft** wonderland of snow; **riesige ~massen** vast quantities of snow; **~matsch** slush; **~pflug** snow plough; **~räumer** snow sweeper; **~räumkommando** snow-clearing team; **~räumung** snow removal; **~schauer** snow shower (flurry, *US*); **~sturm** snowstorm, blizzard; **~treiben** blowing snow; **~verwehung** snowdrift, snow drift; **~wächte** snow pinnacle; **~wasser** melted snow; **~wüste** waste of snow.
Schneid zip, vim, devil *(coll.)*, pep, go, ginger *(coll.)*, pluck, guts *(sl.)*;
jem. den ~ abkaufen to make s. o. sing small; **~ haben** to have plenty of guts (sand) *(sl.)*, to zip; **keinen ~ haben** to have no gumption.
Schneide, auf des Messers razor-edge;
auf des Messers ~ stehen to be a touch-and-go situation.
schneiden to cut, *(Kälte)* to bite;
j. ~ *(beim Überholen)* to cut in on s. o.; **sich ~** *(Linien)* to intersect; **Film ~** to cut a film; **sich ins eigene Fleisch ~** to bite off one's nose, to cut one's throat; **Grimassen ~** to pull faces; **Kupons ~** to clip coupons; **Kurve ~** to cut a corner; **Stoff in Streifen ~** to cut cloth into pieces; **j. in auffälliger Weise ~** to give s. o. the cut direct (go-by).
schneidend|e Bemerkung caustic remark; **~e Kälte** biting (piercing) cold; **~er Schmerz** cutting (keen, sharp) pain.
Schneider tailor;
wie ein ~ frieren to be shivering with cold; **aus dem ~ sein** *(Frau)* not to be a spring chicken any longer *(sl.)*, *(finanziell)* to be out of the wood.
Schneideraum *(Film)* cutting room.
Schneider|meister master tailor; **~werkstatt** tailor's shop, tailory.
schneidig plucky, brave, courageous.
schneien to snow, to be snowing;
jem. ins Haus ~ *(Brief)* to blow in *(coll.)*, *(Mensch)* to pop in, to drop in on s. o.
Schneise drive.
schnell quick, fast, speedy, rapid, like the wind, speedy, prompt, *(Verkauf)* brisk, ready;
~ wie der Blitz as quick as lightning; **~ entschlossen** quick to make up one's mind; **~ lieferbar** for ready delivery; **sehr ~** at a great speed; **so ~ als möglich** at full pelt, ride hell for leather; **etw. ~ erledigen** to rush through s. th.; **~ fahren** to drive fast; **~ vergriffen sein** to be taken up rapidly; **~ sinken** *(Kurse)* to decline rapidly; **~ steigen** *(Kurse)* to move briskly ahead; **zu ~ urteilen** to jump to conclusions; **~ vergehen** *(Zeit)* to fly; **sich ~ verkaufen** to be quick of sale; **~er werden** to gather (pick up, gain) speed; **~ bedient werden** to be given prompt service; **sehr ~ verkauft werden** to sell like hot cakes; **~ wütend werden** to fly off the handle;
~en Absatz finden to find a ready market; **~e Antwort** speedy reply; **~er Aufbruch** hasty departure; **~e Auffassungsgabe haben** to be quick on the uptake; **~es Auto** fast car; **~er Brüter** fast breeder; **~er Entschluß** quick decision; **~e Erledigung** speedy dispatch, speedy attention, quick way of doing; **zu ~es Fahren** speeding; **in ~er Folge** in rapid succession; **~e Fortschritte machen** to make quick progress; **~es Handeln erfordern** to call for prompt action; **in ~em Tempo** at a quick

pace; **auf die ~e Tour** in a hurry; **~e Truppen** mobile troops; **~er Umsatz** quick turnover; **~er Verkauf** brisk (ready) sale; **~er Wechsel** sudden change; **~e Zahlung** prompt payment.

Schnell|ablage speed filing; **~abschreibung** rapid depreciation; **verteidigungsbedingte ~abschreibung** fast write-off for defence (defense, *US*) facilities; **~amt** *(Telefon)* no-delay service, toll exchange *(US)*; **~amtsverkehr** toll traffic *(US)*; **~arbeiter** speedball *(coll.)*; **zur ~auffindung** for ready reference; **~aufzug** high-speed lift, express elevator *(US)*; **~ausbildung** crash training; **~auslösung** quick-action release; **~bahn** high-speed railway, rapid-transit railroad *(US)*; **~bahnverkehr** rapid transit; **~bauweise** rapid-erection method; **~bericht** cursory report; **~betrieb** speed service; **~boot** speedboat, express (mosquito, motor torpedo) boat; **~bus** flier; **~dampfer** fast steamer, clipper, ocean greyhound, express liner *(US)*; **~dienst** express service, *(Telefon)* toll *(US)* (no-delay) service; **~dienstgebühr** expressage; **~drucker** high-speed printer.

schnellfahrend fast moving.

Schnell|fahrer speeder, speedster *(US)*, speed merchant; **~fahrspur** fast lane; **~feuer** quick fire; **~feuergeschütz** quick firer; **~frachtgüterzug** expedited freight train *(US)*, fast goods train *(Br.)*; **~gang** *(Auto)* quick-change gear, overdrive, supercharge, high [gear]; **~gang einschalten** *(Auto)* to let in the supercharge; **~gaststätte** fast-food restaurant, luncheonette, cafeteria; **~gericht** fast food, quick lunch, snack, short order, snatch food, *(Aburteilung)* magistrates *(Br.)* (magistrate's, *US*, traffic, police) court, summary court of jurisdiction; **~gerichtsbarkeit** summary jurisdiction; **~gut** speed goods *(Br.)*, fast freight *(US)*; **~güterzug** expedited (fast) freight train *(US)*, fast goods train *(Br.)*; **~guttarif** expressage *(US)*, express goods tariff *(Br.)*; **~gutverkehr** fast goods traffic *(Br.)*; **~hefter** letter file, file holder, flat file; **~hinweis** speedy reference.

Schnelligkeit quickness, rapidity, *(Fahrzeug)* speed, velocity.

Schnelligkeitsrekord speed record.

Schnell|imbiß snack, snatch food; **~imbißhalle, ~imbißstube** fast-food (quick) restaurant, quick-lunch bar, snack bar (counter); **~kocher** pressure cooker; **~kochplatte** hot (fast-heating) plate; **~kochtopf** pressure cooker; **~kran** high-speed crane; **~kursus** blitz training *(US)*, accelerated (crash) course; **~laster** high-speed truck; **~lesen** speed reading; **~leser** *(Computer)* high-speed reader; **~lösung** quick fix; **~nachweis** speedy reference; **~nahverkehr** rapid transit from city to city; **~paket** express parcel *(Br.)*, special handling parcel *(US)*; **~postgut** express postal delivery *(Br.)*; **~presse** fly press; **~rechner** high-speed computer; **~reinigung** express cleaners; **~restaurant** fast-food restaurant, quick lunch bar, luncheonette, cafeteria *(US)*; **~restaurantpächter** fast-food franchiser; **~richter** police judge *(US)* (justice), magistrate; **vor den ~richter kommen** to be up befor the magistrate; **~rücklauf** *(Tonband)* high-speed rewind; **~schalter** quick-break switch; **~scheibenwischer** speed wiper; **~schreiben** rapid writing; **~schrift** shorthand; **~schuß** priority (rush) job; **~speicher** *(Datenverarbeitung)* high-speed memory; **~sperre** hasty obstacle; **~stopp** quick cut; **~straße** road carrying fast-moving traffic *(Br.)*, express highway (route) *(US)*, motorway *(Br.)*, expressway *(US)*, speedway *(US)*; **einbahnige ~straße mit wechselnder Fahrtrichtung** reversible express lane; **~taste** *(Telegraf)* curb key; **~tauchen** *(U-Boot)* crash dive; **~transport von Massengütern** rapid mass transport; **~triebwagen** high-speed rail car; **~verband** first-aid dressing; **~verbindung** express service; **~verfahren** speed-up, *(Gericht)* speed (speedy) trial, summary proceedings (process); **im ~verfahren abgeurteilt** summarily sentenced; **~verhör** rapid cross-examination.

schnellverkäuflicher Artikel fast-selling item.

Schnellverkehr fast-moving traffic, high-speed operation, rapid transit from city to city *(US)*, *(Spediteur)* express business, *(Telefon)* no-delay service, toll traffic *(US)*.

Schnellverkehrs|amt *(Telefon)* no-delay traffic office, toll exchange *(US)*; **~anruf** toll call *(US)*; **~flugzeug** express airliner; **~linie** express (rapid-transit) line; **~schiff** express liner; **~straße** road carrying fast-moving traffic *(Br.)*, express highway (route) *(US)*, expressway *(US)*, motorway *(Br.)*; **~weg** express (fast) lane, motorway *(Br.)*, expressway *(US)*, speedway *(US)*; **~wesen** rapid transit system; **~zug** high-speed train.

Schnell|verschluß *(Flasche)* stopper; **~wählsystem** *(tel.)* speed calling; **~wäscherei** launderette, laundromat *(US)*; **~weg** express lane, motorway *(Br.)*, expressway *(US)*, speedway.

Schnellzug express [train], quick (fast) train, red ball *(sl.)*, meat run *(sl.)*;
mit dem ~ fahren to travel express;
~lokomotive express engine; **~station** fast station; **~verbindung** fast route; **~zuschlag** excess charge.

Schnippchen schlagen, jem. to outwit s. o., to take s. o. in, to steal a march upon s. o.

Schnitt *(am Buch)* edge, *(Durchschnitt)* cross section, average, *(Film)* cutting, *(Gewinn)* profit, *(Gravur)* intaglio, *(Heu)* cut, *(Muster)* dressmaker's (paper) pattern, *(Vorteil)* turn, advantage, *(Zeichnung)* sectional view;
im ~ on the whole, on the average; **nach dem neuesten ~** in the latest fashion;
~ eines Rockes cut of a coat;
guten ~ fahren to make a good time; **eleganten ~ haben** to be elegantly cut; **guten ~ machen** to make a packet (one's pile), to make a good thing of *(coll.)*, to scoop a large profit, to cut a melon *(US)*;
~ansicht sectional view; **~blumen** cut flowers.

Schnittholz saw-timber.

schittiger Wagen streamlined (stylish) car.

Schnitt|meister *(Film)* cutter; **~muster** dressmaker's (dressing, paper) pattern; **~muster ausradeln** to pink out a pattern; **~punkt** point of intersection; **~waren** piece (dry, *US*) goods, drapery, smallware *(Br.)*; **~warengeschäft** mercery, mercer's shop, drapery, dry-goods store *(US)*; **~warenhändler** mercer, draper, drygoodsman *(US)*; **~zeichnung** sectional drawing.

Schnitzel chop [of meat];
~jagd hare and hounds, paper chase.

Schnitzer *(fig.)* blunder, stumble, gaffe, slip-up, slip, balk *(Br.)*;
grober ~ serious blunder, howling mistake, howler *(sl.)*, boner *(US)*;
~ machen to blunder, to slip a cog, to make a butt.

schnöde mean, filthy, vile;
j. ~ behandeln to be mean to s. o.;
~r Geiz base avarice; **~r Mammon** filthy lucre; **~r Undank** base ingratitude; **~s Verhalten** contemptible conduct; **~r Verrat** shameless betrayal.

Schnörkel flourish, squiggle, tag;
~ gebrauchen to flourish, to be flowery; **alle unnötigen ~ streichen** to prune away all flourishes.

schnorren to cadge *(coll.)*, to sponge *(coll.)*, to panhandle, to bum *(US sl.)*.

Schnorrer cadger *(coll.)*, sponger *(sl.)*, scrounger, panhandler, load of hay *(sl.)*, bum *(US sl.)*, freeloader *(US sl.)*, dead beat *(US sl.)*, schnorrer *(sl.)*.

Schnösel silly fellow, fop;
eingebildeter ~ conceited snot; **junger ~** snotty kid *(sl.)*.

schnüffeln to nose around, to snoop, to pry;
in jds. Privatangelegenheit ~ to nose about in s. one's private affairs.

Schnüffeltätigkeit, politische political snooping.

Schnüffler peeper, spy, dick *(sl.)*, smeller *(sl.)*, snooper *(US)*, stool pigeon *(US sl.)*.

Schnulze tearjerker *(US coll.)*, croon song, pop, corn, novelette *(Br.)*, sob stuff *(US sl.)*.

Schnulzensänger tearjerker *(US coll.)*, crooner.

schnulzig sentimental, corny *(sl.)*, schmaltzy *(sl.)*.

Schnupfen auskurieren to nurse a cold.

schnuppe, einem völlig ~ sein not to care a cuss (two hoots).

Schnur band, cord, twine, twist, string, line, *(el.)* flexible lead;
~ und Packpapier string and brown paper;
Paket mit einer ~ umwickeln to tie up a parcel with string.

Schnürboden *(Theater)* gridiron, rigging loft, *(Werft)* mould (mold, *US*) loft.

Schnürchen, am like clockwork;
etw. wie am ~ können to have s. th. at one's finger-tips (ends), to have it [off] pat; **seine Aufgaben am ~ können** to have one's lessons perfect.

schnüren to tie with string (cord);
sein Bündel ~ to pack up one's kit (things).

schnurgerade as straight as a die;
~ stehen to be lined up as a die; **~ auf j. zusteuern** to go straight for s. o.; **~ auf die nächste Kneipe zusteuern** to make a beeline for the next pub.

Schnürsenkel shoe-laces.

schnurstracks point-blanck.

Schober stack, stackyard.

Schock sixty, *(med.)* shock, *(Menge)* dozens, lots;
seelischer ~ traumatising shock;
ein ganzer ~ Kinder crowds (lots) of children;
~behandlung shock treatment.

schockieren to shock, to scandalize;
j. mit etw. ~ to sting s. o. with s. th.

schockierendes Benehmen shocking manners.
Schockpunkt, psychologischer *(Einkommensteuer)* psychological breaking point.
schockweise by the dozen.
Schock|wirkung impact; ~**wirkung zeitigen** to react with shock; ~**zustand** state of shock.
schofel shabby, mean, dingy, *(knauserig)* stingy, mean;
j. ~ behandeln to treat s. o. shabbily.
Schöffe juryman, juror, jurat;
~ **ablehnen** to challenge a juror; ~**n auslosen** to call the jury; **als ~ erfassen** to empanel a juror; **zu den ~n gehören** to serve on the jury.
Schöffen|auslosung calling of the jury; ~**bank** the jury; ~**gericht** common jury, quarter (general) sessions; ~**gericht in Strafsachen** trial jury; ~**liste** panel; **nicht auf die ~liste setzen** to exempt from jury duty.
schön beautiful, delightful, nice;
ganz ~ pretty *(coll.)*; **so ~ wie gemalt** as pretty as a picture; **unbeschreiblich ~** beautiful beyond description; **zu ~, um wahr zu sein** to good to be true;
es ~ bleibenlassen to do nothing of the kind; **~ daherreden** to talk a lot of hot air;
jem. ~e Augen machen to give s. o. the glad eye; ~**e Aussicht** lovely view; ~**e Bescherung** nice state of affairs, pretty kettle of fish *(US)*; **das ~e Geschlecht** the fair sex; **in ~ster Harmonie** in perfect harmony; ~**e Künste** fine arts; **in ~ster Ordnung** in apple-pie order; ~**e Stange Geld kosten** to cost a pretty penny; **eines ~en Tages** one fine day; ~**es Wetter** fine weather; **j. mit ~en Worten abspeisen** to put s. o. off with fair words;
~**e Leute haben ~e Sachen** nice people have nice things.
Schonbezug slip, cover.
Schöndruck first run, primer, outer form;
~**seite** upper side.
schonen to take care of;
sein Geld ~ to husband one's money; **jds. Leben ~** to spare s. one's life.
schonend careful, gentle;
jem. eine Nachricht ~ beibringen to break the news gently to s. o.; **j. ~ behandeln** to treat s. o. with indulgence; **Maschine ~ behandeln** to handle a machine with care.
Schoner *(Polstermöbel)* cover, antimacassar.
Schönes anrichten, etw. to make a nice mess of it.
Schönfärberei window dressing, sugar coating;
moralische ~ moral whitewashing.
Schon|frist period of grace; ~**gang** *(Auto)* overdrive.
Schöngeist wit, bel esprit, high-brow.
schöngeistig high-brow.
Schönheit, gefeierte celebrated beauty; **landschaftliche ~en** scenic beauties.
Schönheits|chirurgie cosmetic surgery; ~**fehler** beauty spot; ~**königin** beauty queen; ~**pflege** beauty culture, cosmetic treatment; ~**pflegemittel** beauty aid; ~**pfleger** beautician *(US)*; ~**pflegestätte** beauty farm; ~**reparaturen** house improvements; ~**reparaturen durchführen** to decorate a house; ~**salon** beauty shop (parlo(u)r); ~**tänzerin** stripper, stripteaser; ~**wettbewerb** beauty contest.
Schon|klima relaxing climate; ~**kost** diet; ~**reifen** rubbing strip.
Schönschrift calligraphy.
Schonung nursery of young trees.
Schönwetter|periode interval (spell) of fair weather; **dazwischenliegende ~periode** interludes of bright weather; **ruhige ~tage** halcyon days.
Schonzeit closed (close) season, fence month *(Br.)*.
Schopf, Gelegenheit beim ~ nehmen to make hay while the sun shines; **j. beim ~ packen** to seize s. o. by the scruff of his neck.
Schöpf|becherwerk bucket conveyor; ~**brunnen** draw well.
schöpfen, wieder Kraft to recover one's strength; **neuen Mut ~** to get up fresh courage; **Verdacht ~** to smell a rat; **aus dem vollen ~** to draw upon unlimited resources; **Wasser aus einem Boot ~** to bail (bale) out a boat; **Eimer Wasser ~** to scoop a bucket of water.
Schöpfer *(Erfinder)* originator, creator.
schöpferisch creative, fertile, productive, pregnant in ideas;
~ **veranlagt sein** to have a creative mind;
~**e Denkweise** creative thought; ~**er Geist** creative mind; ~**e Jahre eines Schriftstellers** productive period of an author; ~**e Kraft** creative power, creativeness; ~**e Pause einlegen** to pause for inspiration.
Schöpfer|kraft creative power; ~**tätigkeit** creative imagination.
Schöpfung *(Erfindung)* creation;
~**en seines Geistes** products of one's brain.
Schoppen Wein trinken gehen to go for a glass of wine.
Schoppenwein open wine.
Schornstein chimney;
hoher ~ stalk; **verrußter ~** foul chimney;
Geld zum ~ **herausjagen** to throw one's money down the drain; **in den ~ schreiben** to whistle for it;
~**brand** chimney fire; ~**feger** chimney sweeper, chimney-sweep.
Schoß, im ~e der Familie in the bosom of one's family; **im ~e des Glücks** in fortune's lap; **im ~e der Götter** on the knees of the gods; **im ~e der Kirche** within the pale of the church;
j. in den ~ fallen to fall into s. one's lap;
~**hund** toy dog; **Mutters ~kind** mother's pet.
Schott bulkhead, compartment;
wasserdichte ~en watertight compartments.
Schotten|deck bulkhead; ~**ladelinie** subdivision load line.
Schotter broken (crushed) stone;
~**bett** *(Bahn)* ballast bed; ~**decke** metal(l)ed surface, macadam; ~**haufen** stock pile; ~**lager** hard core.
Schottern macadamization.
schottern, Straße to macadamize a road.
Schotterstraße metal(l)ed (unpaved) road, macadam[ized road].
schräg slanting, diagonal;
j. ~ ansehen to look askance at s. o.; **~ über die Straße gehen** to cross the road at an angle; **~ parken** to angle-park;
~**e Musik** hot music; ~**er Vogel** queer character.
Schräg|lage slant, tilt; **Flugzeug in eine ~lage bringen** to bank an aircraft; ~**luftaufnahme** *(mil.)* oblique aerial photograph; ~**parken** angle parking; ~**schrift** slanting hand; ~**stollen** slope; ~**streifen** *(Kleidung)* bias; ~**strich** oblique stroke.
Schramme scar, scratch, scrape;
bei einem Unfall mit ein paar ~n wegkommen to get off with a few scratches in an accident.
schrammen, jds. Auto to scratch s. one's car.
Schrank closet, cupboard *(Br.)*;
begehbarer ~ walk-in closet;
~ **von einem Mann** big hulking creature;
nicht alle Tassen im ~ haben *(fam.)* to have a screw loose, to be screwy.
Schranke bar, barrier, wall, *(Begrenzung)* limit, *(Börse)* counter, *(Eisenbahn)* gate, *(für Fußgänger)* level-crossing gate;
innerhalb der ~n des Gesetzes within the bounds of the law; **vor den ~n der öffentlichen Meinung** at the bar of public opinion; **von der Verfassung errichtete ~n** constitutional barriers;
~**n der Konvention** limits of convention;
sich ~n auferlegen to set o. s. limits; ~**n durchbrechen** to overflow the barriers; **seine ~n einhalten** to keep within limits; ~ **errichten** to set up a barrier; **vor den ~n des Gerichtes erscheinen** to appear before the court; **in ~n halten** to bound; ~ **herunterlassen** to close the gates; **sich über alle ~n hinwegsetzen** to know no bounds; ~ **hochziehen** to open the gates; **gegen j. in die ~n treten** to enter the lists against s. o.; **j. in seine ~n weisen** to show s. o. (put s. o. in) his place, to tell s. o. where to get off.
schrankenlos *(Bahnübergang)* unguarded, unbounded, without limits;
~ **Geld verleihen** to lend money without limits;
~**er Ehrgeiz** unbridled ambition.
Schrankenwärter gateman, gatekeeper, cross keeper.
Schrankfach compartment, shelf, *(Ablage)* pigeonhole, *(Bank)* safe [deposit box];
~**miete** renting of safes.
Schrankkoffer wardrobe, trunk.
Schraube screw, *(mit Mutter)* bolt;
~ **ohne Ende** perpetual screw;
~**n anziehen** to tighten up the screws.
schrauben, seine Forderungen höher to raise one's claims; **sich in die Höhe ~** *(Auto)* to wind its way up, *(Flugzeug)* to spiral up.
Schrauben|antrieb, mit propeller-driven; ~**dampfer** screw steamer; ~**mutter** nut; ~**schlüssel** wrench; **verstellbarer ~schlüssel** tommy; ~**zieher** turnscrew.
Schrebergarten small-holding allotment;
in Kriegszeiten angelegter ~ victory garden;
~**land** [cottage] allotment *(Br.)*; ~**system** allotment system.
Schrebergärtner small allotment holder.
Schrecken horror, terror, fright;
~ **des Krieges** horrors of war; ~ **der Nachbarschaft** terror of the neighbo(u)rhood;
jem. einen gewaltigen ~ einjagen to frighten s. o. out of his wits; **j. mit ~ erfüllen** to scare s. o., to freeze s. one's blood; ~ **hervorrufen** to cause alarm; **von panischem ~ erfaßt werden** to be seized with panic (terror-stricken).

Schreckens|botschaft terrifying news; ~**herrschaft** reign of terror; ~**herrschaft einführen** to terrorize; ~**tat** atrocity; ~**welle** flood of terror; **absolute** ~**zeit durchmachen** to live through sheer horror.

Schreckgespenst specter, spectre *(Br.)*, nightmare, poker *(US coll.)*;
~ **eines Krieges heraufbeschwören** to conjure the nightmare of war.

schrecklich terrible, dreadful, horrible, awful, frightful, vicious *(coll.)*;
~ **lange dauern** to take ages;
~**er Anblick** horrible sight; ~**e Angst haben** to be scared stiff (in a blue funk); ~**e Drohungen** dreadful threats; ~ **viel Geld kosten** to cost a packet of money; ~**e Geschichte** grim story; ~**e Handschrift** awful handwriting; **in einer** ~**en Lage sein** to be in a terrible situation; **unter** ~**en Schmerzen sterben** to die in terrible agony; **eines** ~**en Todes sterben** to die an awful death; ~**er Unfall** terrible accident; ~**e Unordnung** frightful (terrible state of) disorder; ~**es Verbrechen** horrible crime; ~**es Wetter** dreadful (abominable) weather.

Schrecksekunde reaction period (time).

Schrei cry, shout, scream, exclamation;
gellender ~ piercing shriek; **der letzte** ~ all the kick (cry, *US*), the last word; **markerschütternder** ~ bloodcurdling scream;
~ **der Entrüstung** cry of indignation;
der letzte ~ **sein** to be all the go now.

Schreib|abteil *(Bahn)* writing compartment; ~**arbeit** clerical (paper, desk) work; **mit** ~**arbeiten beschäftigt sein** to be busy with writing; ~**auslagen** clerical expenses; ~**automat** word processor; ~**bedarf** writing materials, stationery; ~**block** writing block (pad); ~**büro** typewriting bureau.

Schreibe, farbige colo(u)rful style of writing.

Schreiben letter, writing, *(Kurznachricht)* note, *(Mitteilung)* communication;
bezugnehmend auf Ihr ~ with reference (referring) to your letter; **im Besitz ihres geschätzten** ~**s** in receipt of your favo(u)r; **amtliches** ~ official letter, writ; **anliegendes (beigefügtes)** ~ attached (enclosed, covering) letter; **beleidigendes** ~ libel(l)ous letter; **fingiertes** ~ fictitious letter; **Ihr geschätztes** ~ your esteemed lines; **kurzes** ~ note; **undatiertes** ~ undated letter;
~ **und Rechnen** standards of literacy and numeracy;
das ~ **von Danksagungsbriefen satt haben** to be weary of writing letters of thanks; **mit dem** ~ **fertig sein** to have done writing.

schreiben to write, *(mitteilen)* to inform, to communicate, to deliver a message, *(schriftstellern)* to be engaged in literature; **für einen anderen anonym** ~ to ghost; **Aufsatz** ~ to do a composition; **nach Diktat** ~ to write from dictation; **bei zugesicherter Diskretion** ~ to write in confidence; **einander** ~ to correspond; **falsch** ~ to misspell; **gewandte Feder** ~ to wield a skilful pen; **ganz gelöst** ~ to write at ease; **gut** ~ to write a good hand, to write well; **mit der Hand** ~ to write by hand; **schlechte Handschrift** ~ to have a bad hand; **regelmäßig nach Hause** ~ to write home regularly; **hochgestochen** ~ to write in a high-flown style; **sich seit Jahren mit jem.** ~ to be corresponding with s. o. for years; **als freier Journalist** ~ to be a free-lance writer; **j. krank** ~ to put s. o. on the sick list, to give s. o. a medical certificate; **Kurzschrift** ~ to write shorthand; **mit der Maschine** ~ to type, to typewrite; **Namen** ~ to sign one's name; **seinen Namen schnell auf ein Blatt Papier** ~ to jot one's name on a piece of paper; **sehr originell** ~ to give an original touch to one's writings; **Rechnung** ~ to make out a bill, to draw (make) out an account; **auf Rechnung** ~ to debit an account; **ins reine** ~ to engross, to make a fair copy; **richtig** ~ to spell; **in den Schornstein** ~ to whistle for it; **mit der Schreibmaschine** ~ to typewrite, to type; **schwungvoll** ~ to write with punch; **ungekünstelt** ~ to write without frills; **ins unreine** ~ to [make a] draft; **sich die Finger wund** ~ to write one's arm off *(coll.)*; **jem. ein paar Zeilen** ~ to drop s. o. a line; **für Zeitungen** ~ to journalize, to write for the papers, to contribute newspaper articles.

Schreiber clerk, secretary, underclerk;
~ **dieses Briefes** the undersigned.

Schreiberei paperwork.

Schreiberling hack, hedge writer, quill driver, inkslinger *(sl.)*;
~e grubstreet.

Schreiberstelle clerkship.

schreibfaul sein to be a bad correspondent.

Schreib|feder writing pen, nib; ~**fehler** clerical mistake, spelling (clerical, scribal) error, lapse (slip) of the pen, *(Tippfehler)* typing error; ~**garnitur** inkstand, standish, desk appointments; ~**gebühren** clerk's (copying) fee; ~**gerät** writing utensils (set); ~**heft** writing (exercise) book, *(mit Vorlage)* copybook; ~**hilfe,** ~**kraft** secretarial help, clerk (copy) typist, writer *(Br.)*, girl-Friday *(Br.)*, clerk; ~**kräfte** clerical staff (force); ~**krampf** writer's cramp; ~**mappe** portfolio, writing (blotting) case.

Schreibmaschine typewriter, [type]writing machine;
mit der ~ **geschrieben** typewritten;
elektrische ~ electric typewriter; **geräuschlose** ~ silent typewriter;
~ **mit Lochstreifensteuerung** automatic typewriter; **elektrische** ~ **mit Tabulatorvorrichtung** electric typewriter suitable for tabulating;
Brief auf der ~ **schreiben** to type a letter.

Schreibmaschinen|arbeiten pro Seite berechnen to charge typing by piece rate; ~**artikel** typewriting supplies; ~**büro** typewriting office; ~**hülle** dust cover; ~**katalog** typewriter catalog(ue); ~**kenntnisse** ability to type; ~**kursus** typing course; ~**manuskript** typescript, typewritten matter; ~**papier** typewriter paper; ~**prüfung** typewriting examination; ~**schreiber** typist; ~**schrift** typewritten type, typescript; **vier** ~**seiten umfassen** to hold four typewritten pages; ~**stuhl** typist's chair, *(mit Rückenstütze)* posture chair; ~**tisch** typewriter table (desk), typist's desk; ~**unterlage** typewriter pad; ~**zeugnis** certificate of typewriting.

Schreibmaschineschreiben typewriting;
Zeit beim ~ **sparen** to save typing time.

Schreib|materialien writing materials, correspondence supplies, stationery; ~**papier** writing (note) paper; ~**papier mit eingedrucktem Briefkopf** letterhead; ~**pult** [writing] desk; ~**saal** typing pool; ~**schrank** secretaire, bureau, writing desk; ~**schrift** cursive script, handwriting; **gewöhnliche** ~**schrift** long hand; ~**stube** office, *(mil.)* orderly room.

Schreibtisch writing table, [writing] desk;
an den ~ **gefesselt** chained to one's desk;
nicht aufgeräumter ~ disorderly desk;
~ **mit kleinem Aufbau** flat-top desk; ~ **mit Rollvorrichtung** roll-top desk;
seinen ~ **aufräumen** to clear [up] one's desk;
~**arbeit** desk work; ~**arbeiter** desk-bound executive; ~**bulle** *(mil.)* penguin *(sl.)*; ~**einkäufer** armchair shopper; ~**forschung** desk research; ~**garnitur** standish, inkstand, desk appointments; ~**lampe** desk lamp; ~**mörder** humane killer; ~**stratege** desk-bound executive, *(pol.)* armchair politician; ~**unterlage** desk pad.

Schreib|übungen writing exercises; ~**unkundiger** marksman *(US)*; ~**unterlage** writing (blotting) pad; ~**unterricht** writing lesson; ~**utensilien** writing utensils; ~**verpflichtungen** writing duties; ~**vorlage** copy [slip]; ~**vorlagen geben** to set copies; ~**waren** writing material, stationery; ~**warenhändler** stationer; ~**warenhandlung** stationery (stationer's, *Br.*) shop, stationery store *(US)*; ~**weise** [way of] writing, style, *(Rechtschreibung)* spelling; **entwickelte** ~**weise** explicit form; **andere** ~**weise eines Wortes** variant spelling of a word; ~**werkzeug** writing utensils; ~**wut** urge to write; ~**zentrale** typing pool; ~**zeug** pen and ink, desk set, writing case, inkstand; ~**zimmer** writing room (chamber).

schreien to scream, to shout, *(jammern)* to wail;
gellend ~ to yell, to scream; **zum Himmel** ~ to be a crying shame; **aus Leibeskräften** ~ to shout at the top of one's voice; **wie am Spieß** ~ to be crying blue murder *(coll.)*.

schreiend shouting;
~**e Farben** loud (gaudy) colo(u)rs; ~**e Ungerechtigkeit** crying injustice.

Schreier brawler, grumbler, troublemaker.

Schreiner joiner.

schreiten to stride, to stalk along;
zur Abstimmung ~ to put a question to the vote; **über den Laufsteg** ~ to parade across the platform; **zur Tat** ~ to proceed to action; **im Zimmer auf und ab** ~ to pace the room.

Schrift writing, *(Abhandlung)* paper, *(Broschüre)* pamphlet, booklet, brochure, *(Druckschrift)* type, characters, text, *(Drucktype)* type, character, text, face, *(Handschrift)* handwriting, hand, *(Urkunde)* roll, *(Veröffentlichung)* publication, work;
in lateinischer ~ in Roman characters; **in schräger** ~ in italics; **abgenutzte** ~ worn-out type; **breite** ~ extended letter; **fette** ~ full face, boldface, extrabold; **flüssige** ~ current handwriting; **gestochene** ~ book hand; **halbfette** ~ blank face; **kleine** ~ small text; **kursive** ~ italics; **laufende** ~ condensed type; **leserliche** ~ legible handwriting; **magere** ~ lightface type; **obszöne** ~**en** obscene publications; **Pariser** ~ agate *(US)*; **sämtliche** ~**en [eines Autors]** complete edition; **schmallaufende** ~ condensed

type; **schräge** ~ italics; **staatsgefährdende** ~**en** seditious literature; **unleserliche** ~ illegible writing; **vermischte** ~**en** miscellaneous writings, miscellanies;
Sprache in Wort und ~ **beherrschen** to master a language; **seine** ~ **verstellen** to disguise one's handwriting;
~**art** type [face], letter, fount *(Br.)*, font *(US)*; ~**bildträger** image master; ~**block** column; ~**charakter** type style.

Schriften|nachweis bibliograph, list of references; ~**weite** series of publications.

Schrift|form writing, written form; **in einfacher** ~**form** under hand, written, in writing; ~**form vorgeschrieben** writing obligatory; ~**führer** recording secretary, clerk, reporter, recorder; **einstweiliger** ~**führer** secretary for the time being; ~**garnitur** font *(US)*, fount *(Br.)*; ~**gattung** type family; ~**gießer** type (letter) founder; ~**gießereiabzug** foundry flimsy; ~**grad** body; **sehr kleiner** ~**grad** gem; ~**gradunterschied** remove; ~**größe** size of type; **in** ~**größe** type-high; ~**größenbereich** size range; ~**guß** letter founding; ~**gutachten** graphological expertise; ~**höhe** height-to-paper; ~**kegel** body, shank; ~**leiter** editor, journalist; ~**leiter einer wissenschaftlichen Beilage** science editor; ~**leiter des Wirtschaftsteils** city editor *(Br.)*, financial editor *(US)*; ~**leitung** editorial staff (management, board), editors, *(Büro)* editorial department (office).

schriftlich written, in writing, on paper, in black and white, under one's own hand, *(brieflich)* by letter;
~ **abfassen** to draw up, to draft, to compose, to confirm in writing; ~ **anfragen** to inquire in writing; ~ **berichten** to send in a written notice; ~ **bestätigen** to confirm in writing; **etw.** ~ **darlegen** to explain s. th. on paper; **Fall** ~ **darlegen** to submit a written statement of a case; ~ **festhalten** to record on note paper; ~ **niederlegen** to put down in (put into) writing, to put on record; ~ **abgefaßt sein** to be in writing; ~ **vereinbaren** to stipulate (agree upon) in writing;
~**e Abmachung** written agreement; ~**e Arbeit** [examination] paper, written exercise; ~**e Arbeiten** paper work; ~**e Beantwortung** answer to a letter; ~**e Benachrichtigung** written communication; ~**e Bestätigung** written confirmation; ~**er Entwurf** composition, draft; ~**es Examen** written examination; **in** ~**er Form** in writing; ~**e Kündigung** written notice; ~**e Prüfung** written examination; ~**e Prüfungsaufgabe** paper; ~**es Schuldanerkenntnis** written evidence of debt; ~**e Vereinbarung** written agreement; ~**er Vertrag** written contract; ~**er Verweis** written censure; ~**es Zeugnis** testimonial; ~**e Zustimmung** written consent.

Schrift|linie, unter der inferior; ~**montage** paste-up; ~**muster** type specimen; ~**probe** specimen (sample) of one's handwriting, *(Druckschrift)* specimen of type, type specimen; ~**probenvergleich** comparison of handwritings; ~**rolle** scroll; ~**sache** written matter, writing; ~**sachverständiger** expert in handwriting, handwriting (graphological) expert, graphologist.

Schriftsatz bill, [written] pleadings, declaration, brief *(US)*, *(drucktechn.)* composition, composing, font *(US)*, fount *(Br.)*, type, *(UNO)* memorial;
ergänzender ~ bill of particulars, supplemental pleadings *(US)*; **erweiterter** ~ supplemental bill; **fehlerhafter** ~ mispleading; **gefertigter** ~ filed proceedings; **mit der Hand gesetzter** ~ hand composition; **mit der Maschine gesetzter** ~ machine composition; **vorbereiteter** ~ brief, pleadings *(Br.)*;
~ **vorläufiger Verfahrenseinreden** skeleton bill of exceptions;
~ **aufsetzen** to draw a pleading; ~ **einreichen** to submit (file) a brief; **neuen** ~ **einreichen** to replead; ~ **vorbereiten** to draw up a writ; ~ **zusammenstreichen** to abridge a pleading; **jem. einen** ~ **zustellen** to serve a writ on s. o.;
~**ablage** distribution; ~**zustellung** notice of motion.

Schrift|scheibe *(Fotosatz)* type disk; ~**schreiben** lettering; ~**seite** *(Münze)* reverse; ~**setzen** *(drucktechn.)* composition, typesetting; ~**setzer** compositor, overseer of the machine room; ~**sprache** literary language; ~**spiegel** type face.

Schriftsteller writer, author, publicist, literary man, man of letters, composer, pen, *(Journalist)* journalist, newspaperman;
erfolgreicher ~ penmaster; **freier** ~ free lance; **phantasievoller** ~ imaginative writer; **unbedeutender** ~ small-fry writer;
sich als ~ **erschöpfen** to write o. s. out; ~ **sein** to be engaged in literature, to write, to be a writer; **berühmter** ~ **sein** to be booming as a novelist;
~**agent** ten-percenter; ~**beruf** profession of letters, literary profession.

Schriftstellerei literary profession, penmanship, writing, desk;
sich für die ~ **entschließen** to take to writing; **von der** ~ **leben** to make a living by writing (one's living by one's pen).

Schriftstellerhonorar copy money, royalty, honorarium.

Schriftstellerin woman writer.

schriftstellerisch literary;
sich ~ **betätigen** to be a writer (engaged in literature), to sling ink *(sl.)*;
~**e Begabung** writing ability; ~**es Konzept** writing formula; ~**e Tätigkeit** literary profession (activity, work).

Schriftstellermetier writing profession.

schriftstellern to write, to make one's living by one's pen, to be engaged in literature (a writer), to sling ink *(sl.)*;
nebenbei ~ to dabble in writing.

Schriftsteller|name pen name, pseudonym; ~**ruhm** literary fame; ~**tantieme** royalty; ~**tätigkeit** creative writing.

Schriftstil literary style;
seinen ~ **nach guten Beispielen entwickeln** to form one's style on good models.

Schriftstück writing, writ, paper, bill, *(Entwurf)* composition, draft, *(Urkunde)* deed, document, instrument;
amtliches ~ official document (paper), diploma; **eigenhändiges** ~ holograph; **maschinengeschiebenes** ~ typescript; **vertrauliche** ~**e** confidential documents;
vervielfältigte ~**e für internen Gebrauch** subliterature;
~ **abfassen** to write, to draw up, to word.

Schrift|tum literature, documentation, bibliography; ~**vergleich** comparison of handwritings; ~**verkehr** correspondence; ~**verkehr abbrechen** to discontinue the correspondence; ~**wahl** choice of type; ~**wart** secretary; ~**wechsel** correspondence, exchange of letters; ~**wechsel führen** to attend to the correspondence; ~**werk** literary work; ~**zeichen** character, letter, graphic symbol; **phonetisches** ~**zeichen** phonotype; ~**zug** duct, stroke, flourish; **sonderbare** ~**züge** strange characters.

Schritt step, footstep, tread, measure, remove, degree, *(Aktion)* move, step;
mit gemessenen ~**en** with measured steps;
~ **für** ~ step by step, by inches, inchmeal; ~ **vor** ~ pace for pace; **erste berufliche** ~**e** first steps in one's career; **diplomatischer** ~ demarche, diplomatic action; **einleitende** ~**e** introductory (initial) steps; **erforderliche** ~**e** remedial measures; **erste** ~**e** preliminaries; **erster** ~ initiative, gambit; **gemeinsame** ~**e** *(pol.)* common steps; **juristische** ~**e** legal measures; **unkluger** ~ indiscreet step; **der Gründung vorangehende** ~**e** preliminary steps for an establishment;
~**e zur Ausweitung des Leistungsprogramms** diversification moves; ~ **von entscheidender Bedeutung** key step; **erster** ~ **zum Erfolg** first step to success; ~**e zur Streikbeendigung** move towards settling a strike; ~ **nach vorn** progressive step; **wesentlicher** ~ **nach vorn** major step forward;
gerichtliche ~**e androhen** to threaten proceedings; **jds.** ~**e beflügeln** to lend wings to (wing) s. one's steps; **seinen** ~ **beschleunigen** to mend one's pace; **Politik der kleinen** ~**e betreiben** to take short steps; **gerichtliche** ~**e einleiten** to initiate judicial proceedings; **alle erforderlichen** ~**e ergreifen** to take all due measures; **umgehend** ~**e ergreifen** to take immediate steps; ~ **fahren** to drive slowly, to drive at walking pace; **jem. auf** ~ **und Tritt folgen** to tail [after] s. o., to shadow s. o.; ~ **halten** to keep abreast; **mit jem.** ~ **halten** to get up to s. o., to go hand in hand with s. o.; **mit der modernen Entwicklung** ~ **halten** to keep pace with modern invention; **mit den Nachbarn** ~ **halten** to keep up with the Johnes's; **mit der Zeit** ~ **halten** to keep up with (abreast of) the times; **sich j. drei** ~**e vom Leibe halten** to keep s. o. at arm's length; **seine** ~**e heimwärts lenken** to set one's face for (direct one's steps towards) home; **erste** ~**e eines Kindes lenken** to guide a child's first steps; **große** ~**e machen** to take long strides; ~ **planen** to have a step in mind; **jem. stets einen** ~ **voraus sein** to stay one jump (hop) ahead of s. o.; ~**e tun** to take action (steps); **entscheidenden** ~ **tun** to take a decisive step, to take the plunge; **ersten** ~ **tun** to make the first move (advances), to take the initiative; **unüberlegte** ~**e unternehmen** to rock the boat; ~**e bei einer Regierung unternehmen** to approach a government; **erforderliche** ~**e veranlassen** to take the necessary steps.

Schrittfahren driving at a walking pace.

Schrittmacher pacemaker, pioneer;
~ **für die europäische Einheit** pacemaker for European unity;
~ **abgeben** *(Börse)* to pace the market; ~ **sein** to pioneer;
~**dienste** pacemaking; **jem.** ~**dienste leisten** to pace s. o., to pave the way for s. o.

Schrittempo dead slow.

schrittweise gradual, progressive, step by step, stepwise, by inches (steps);
Beschränkungen ~ **aufheben** to lift restrictions gradually.

schroff precipitous, abrupt, steep, *(fig.)* brusque, gruff;
~ **ablehnen** to refuse flatly; ~ **sein** to have an abrupt manner; ~**e Ablehnung** blunt refusal; ~ **abfallende Felswände** precipitous rock faces; **in** ~**em Gegensatz stehen** to contrast sharply.
schröpfen, j. to fleece s. o., to milk (clean out, *sl.*) s. o, to bleed s. o. white.
Schrot pellet, buckshot;
von echtem ~ **und Korn** full of mettle;
Mann von echtem ~ **und Korn sein** to be a man of the right sort;
~**säge** pit (crosscut) saw.
Schrott scrap [iron, metal], junk;
~**anfall** scrap material; ~**angebot** supply of scrap; ~**auto** junk[ed] car (auto), auto scrap, junk heap *(sl.)*; ~**beseitigungsgebühr** junk car tax; ~**eisen** scrap iron; ~**erlös** scrap proceeds; ~**firma** scrap company; ~**handel** scrap trade; ~**händler** scrap (junk) dealer (merchant), scrap-steel dealer; ~**handlung** junk shop; **auf den** ~**haufen werfen** to throw onto the scrap heap, to scrap; ~**markt** junk (scrap-steel, scrap-metal) market; ~**platz** junk (scrap) yard; ~**preis** scrap price; ~**verarbeitung** scrap processing; ~**verhüttung** scrap melting; ~**verkäufe** scrap sales; ~**verwertungsanlage** scrapping facility; ~**wagen** junk auto, knockdown kit; ~**wert** scrap (junk, breakup, salvage) value; ~**wertanrechnung** *(Autoversicherung)* salvage.
Schrulle fancy, whim, kink, whimsy, fad, crotchet.
schrullenhaft whimsical, kinky, crotchety, cranky.
schrumpfen *(Partei)* to dwindle away, *(Umsätze)* to diminish, to shrink, to dwindle.
schrumpfend dwindling, shrinking, diminishing;
~**e Erträge** diminishing returns; ~**es Geschäft** contracting business; ~**es Kapital** dwindling assets, shrinking capital; ~**e Produktion** contraction of production; ~**e Umsätze** *(Börse)* light trading.
Schrumpfung diminution, dwindling, shrinkage, contraction;
~ **des Exports** shrinkage of the export trade; ~ **des Geschäftsvolumens** decline in business; ~ **der Gewinnmenge** shrinkage in the profit margin; ~ **der Lagerbestände** shrinkage of stocks; ~ **der Umsätze** decrease in sales, diminishing returns.
Schub push, shove;
j. per ~ **an die Grenze bringen** to take s. o. to the frontier for deportation; **mit dem letzten** ~ **kommen** to come with the last batch;
~**karren** barrow, wheelbarrow, pushcart, trolley; **oberste** ~**lade** top drawer; **Papiere in eine** ~**lade stopfen** to cram papers into a drawer.
Schubs *(fig.)* shove, push;
jem. einen ~ **geben** to give s. o. a push.
Schubschiff pusher barge.
Schubverarbeitung *(Datenverarbeitung)* batch processing.
schubweise in batches, gradually, by degrees.
schüchtern timid, shy, coy, bashful;
über die Maßen ~ **sein** to be unable to say bo to a goose.
Schuft blackguard, scoundrel, rogue, villain, rascal, heel *(US sl.)*.
schuften to toil, to plod away, to push, to plug, to grind, do drudge, to work o. s. to the bone, *(Schüler)* to skull-drag *(sl.)*; **bis zur Erschöpfung** ~ to fag; **wie ein Pferd** ~ to work like a horse (slave, Trojan); **unablässig** ~ to toil without respite; **schwer** ~ **müssen** to be chained to the oars; **im Leben tüchtig** ~ **müssen** to plod along through life.
Schufterei plodding, drudgery, grind, elbow grease.
Schuh, jem. etw. in die ~**e schieben** to stick (pin) s. th. on s. o., to lay the blame at s. one's door; **nicht in jds.** ~**en stecken wollen** not to like to be in s. one's shoes;
wissen, wo der ~ **drückt** to know where the shoe pinches;
~**creme** boot (shoe) polish; ~**industrie** boot and shoe industry; ~**karton** shoe box; **zu kleine** ~**nummer für eine Position** a square peg in a round hole; ~**werk** footwear; ~**wichse** shoe (boot) polish; ~**zeug** footgear.
Schulabgang school-leaving, leaving school.
Schulabgangs|alter school-leaving age; ~**klasse** graduating class *(US)*; ~**zeugnis** leaving certificate *(Br.)*, school certificate *(US)*.
Schul|abzeichen school badge; ~**alter** legal school age; ~**amtsleiter** director of education *(Br.)*; ~**anfänger** beginning pupil; ~**anmeldung** school enrol(l)ment; **im Herbst erfolgende** ~**anmeldungen** fall registration at the school *(US)*; ~**anstalt** educational establishment, school; ~**arbeit** lesson, work, task, school exercise, schoolchildren's work; **seine** ~**arbeiten machen** to prepare (learn) one's lessons; ~**arzt** school doctor, medical officer; ~**aufgaben** homework, task, home lessons; **seine** ~**aufgaben machen** to learn one's lessons (homework); ~**aufsatz** composition; ~**aufsichtsbehörde** board of governors (education, *US*), school board, inspectorate of schools *(Br.)*; ~**ausflug** school treat, school excursion (party), field trip; ~**ausschuß** school (education) committee; ~**bank** school bench, form; **noch die** ~**bank drücken** to be still at school; ~**behörde** school authorities, board of governors (education, *US*); ~**beispiel** test case; ~**besuch** attendance at school; ~**bezirk** school district; **selbständiger** ~**bezirk** excepted district; ~**bibliothek** school library.
Schulbildung education;
mit schlechter ~ ill-educated;
höhere ~ central school education;
abgeschlossene höhere ~ **besitzen** to have been educated to general certificate standards *(Br.)*, to be a high-school graduate *(US)*.
Schulbuch schoolbook, classbook, *(Leitfaden)* textbook, manual, educational book;
~**verlag** school (educational) publisher, educational book company.
Schul|bücher herausgeben to edit books for school use; ~**bus** school bus.
Schuld debt, claim, *(geschuldeter Betrag)* sum due, money owing, *(Fehler)* fault, blame, *(Ursache)* cause, *(Verbindlichkeit)* liability, obligation, due, charge, *(Vergehen)* guilt, culpability, offence, *(Verschuldung)* indebtedness;
abgetragene ~ paid-up (assigned) debt; **angekreidete** ~ chalk *(Br.)*; **antizipative** ~ accrued liability, liability accrual; **aufgelaufene** ~ accumulated debt; **äußere** ~ foreign debt; **beglichene** ~ paid (settled) debt; **beitreibbare** ~ recoverable debt; **nicht beitreibbare** ~ nonrecoverable debt; **schon lange bestehende** ~ debt of old standing; **bevorrechtigte** ~ privileged debt; **bezahlte** ~ liquidated debt; **nicht bezahlte** ~ undischarged (unliquidated) debt; **buchmäßige** ~ book debt; **dingliche** ~ real obligation; **drückende** ~ pressing (heavy-weighing) debt; **einklagbare** ~ debt enforceable at law; **nicht einklagbare** ~ debt dead in law; **nicht eintreibbare** ~ irrecoverable debt; **erloschene** ~ extinct claim; **fällige** ~ existing debt, debt owing (due); **noch nicht fällige** ~ future debt; **faule** ~ bad debt; **frühere** ~ antecedent debt; **fundierte** ~ funded (bonded, consolidated, permanent) debt, funded indebtedness; **hypothekarisch gesicherte** ~ mortgage debt; **getilgte** ~ discharged debt; **innere (interne)** ~ internal debt; **konsolidierte** ~ funded (consolidated, unified) debt; **kurzfristige** ~ short-term debt (liability); **langfristige** ~ long-term debt (liability); **nachrangige** ~ subordinate debt; **obligatorische** ~ civil debt; **öffentliche** ~ public (national, government) debt; **persönliche** ~ *(Gesellschafter)* personal obligation; **rechtsgültige** ~ just debt; **reine** ~ net indebtedness; **restliche** ~ surviving debt; **rückständige** ~ debt in arrears; **schwebende** ~ floating debt (charge, *Br.*); **städtische** ~ municipal debt; **in Raten zu tilgende** ~ instal(l)ment debt; **überwiegende** ~ predominance of guilt; **unablösliche** ~ perpetual debt; **der Höhe nach unbestimmte** ~ unliquidated debt; **uneinbringliche** ~ irrecoverable debt; **unfundierte** ~ floating debt; **ungedeckte** ~ unsecured debt; **ungetilgte** ~ uncrossed debt; **unsichere** ~ doubtful *(Br.)* (bad, *US*) debt; **unteilbare** ~ indivisible obligation; **unverbriefte** ~ nonbonded debt; **unverzinsliche** ~ passive (noninterest-bearing) debt; **verbriefte** ~ debt secured by a document, specialty debt; **verjährte** ~ barred (prescriptive, stale) debt, debt barred by the statute of limitations; **verzinsliche** ~ interest-bearing debt; **vollgültige** ~ just debt; **evtl. zu zahlende** ~ contingent debt; **unbedingt zu zahlende** ~ debt certain; **zinstragende** ~ interest-bearing debt;
~ **älteren Datums** old (old-standing) debt;
~ **abarbeiten** to work off (out) a debt; ~ **abführen** to settle a debt; ~ **ablösen** to redeem a debt; ~ **hypothekarisch absichern** to secure a debt by mortgage; ~ **durch Pfandbestellung absichern** to collaterate a debt; ~ **abtragen** to compound (redeem, sink) a debt; ~ **abverdienen** to work off a debt; ~ **von sich abwälzen** to clear o. s. of a guilt; **seine** ~ **abzahlen** to discharge one's debt; ~ **anerkennen** to acknowledge (admit, confess, recognize) a debt; ~ **nicht anerkennen** to renounce a debt; ~ **auswechseln** to substitute a debt; ~ **avalieren** to stand security for a debt; ~ **begleichen** to discharge (sponge out) a debt; **jem. die** ~ **beimessen** to attribute the fault to s. o.; ~ **beitreiben** to recover a debt; **jds.** ~ **beschönigen** to extenuate s. one's guilt; ~ **bestreiten** to dispute a claim; ~ **bezahlen** to liquidate (answer, discharge, satisfy, pay off) a debt; ~ **nicht bezahlen** to default on a debt; **für eine** ~ **bürgen** to stand [as] security for a debt; ~ **einfordern** to claim a debt; ~ **einklagen** to sue for a debt; **für eine**

~ **einstehen** to answer for a debt; ~ **entrichten** to discharge a debt; ~ **erlassen** to release from a debt (an indebtedness), to relinquish (waive, cancel, forgive) a debt, to remit a claim; ~ **fundieren** to fund a debt; **jem. die ~ geben** to blame s. o., to put the blame upon s. o.; ~ **dem wirklich Schuldigen geben** to put the shoe on the right foot; ~ **haben** to be responsible (liable); **keine ~ haben** to be free from fault; **an einem Unfall ~ haben** to be at fault in (blame for) an accident; **für eine ~ haften** to be responsible for a debt; ~ **konsolidieren** to fund discharge (bond, a debt); ~ **anwachsen lassen** to run up debts; ~ **verjähren lassen** to outlaw a debt; **seine ~ leugnen** to plead not guilty; ~ **löschen** to cancel a debt; **j. für die ganze ~ haftbar machen** to hold s. o. liable for the whole debt; ~ **für etw. auf sich nehmen** to take the blame for s. th., to shoulder the guilt; ~ **reduzieren** to scale a debt; **jds. ~ sein** to be on s. one's head; **jem. die ~ in die Schuhe schieben** to lay a charge at s. one's door; **tief in jds. ~ stehen** to be deeply indebted to s. o.; ~ **tilgen** to redeem (pay [off]) a debt, to strike off; **sich für eine ~ verbürgen** to guarantee (answer for) a debt, to stand security for a debt; **j. auf Bezahlung einer ~ verklagen** to summons s. o. for debt; ~ **wiedergutmachen** to right a wrong; **seine ~ zugeben** to admit one's guilt; ~ **zurückzahlen** to pay off a debt; ~ **innerhalb der vereinbarten Zeit zurückzahlen** to discharge a liability within the agreed period; **jem. die ~ zuschieben** to put the blame (fasten a crime) upon s. o., to lay the blame at s. one's door; **~ablösung** discharge (liquidation, refunding, repayment) of a debt; **~abtretung** expromission, transfer (assignment) of a debt; **~abwägen** comparative rectitude.

Schuldanerkenntnis debt by special contract, express assumpsit, new promise, I.O.U. (I owe you), bill of debt, debenture, *(gegenüber einer Behörde)* recognizance, *(beim Kontoauszug)* account stated confession;
abstraktes ~ express (special) assumpsit, naked promise; **schriftliches ~** acknowledgment of a debt (indebtedness) in writing, debtor's acknowledgment, written evidence of debt, *(im Prozeß)* cognovit note *(US)*;
jem. ein ~ schicken to send s. o. a statement of the amount owing to him;
~klage special assumpsit; **~schein mit Unterwerfungsklausel** cognovit *(US)* (judgment) note.

Schuld|arrest committal for debts; **~aufnahme** borrowing, debt issue, *(Weltwährungsfonds)* drawings; **~aufnahme zu gleichbleibenden Zinssätzen** fixed-interest borrowing; **~ausschließungsgrund** legal excuse; **~ausspruch** verdict of guilty; **~auswechslung** substitution of a debt; **~begleichungsurkunde** *(Hypothek)* satisfaction piece; **~beitreibung** collection of a debt; **~bekenntnis** admission of guilt; **~bescheinigung** certificate of indebtedness; **~betrag** amount owing (due), sum payable, indebtedness; **verschiedene ~beträge** *(Bilanz)* sundry moneys owing; **~beweis** proof (evidence) of guilt, inculpatory evidence; **~beweis nicht erbracht** not proven.

schuldbewußtes Verhalten guilty behavio(u)r.

Schuldbewußtsein guiltiness.

Schuldbuch debt register (ledger, book) *(Br.)*, *(Hauptbuch)* ledger [book];
~eintragung entry in the debt register; **~forderung, ~titel** registered debt, debt register claim; **~giroforderungen** inscribed (uncertificated) stock *(Br.)*.

Schuldeingeständnis, freimütiges frank concession of one's guilt; **praktisch ein ~ darstellen** to amount to a confession of guilt.

Schulden debts, liabilities, *(Aktivschulden)* due from customers, accounts receivable *(US)*, *(Dubiose)* contingent liabilities, *(Passivschulden)* due to customers, accounts payable *(US)*, *(Schuldenlast)* indebtedness;
bis über die Ohren in ~ over head and heels (up to the eyes) in debt; **frei von ~** free from debts, *(Haus)* unencumbered; **mit ~ belastet** bonded, debted, encumbered with debts; **nach Abzug der ~** clear after debts paid; **ohne ~** in the black *(US coll.)*, afloat;
antizipative ~ *(Bilanz)* accrued liabilities *(US)*; **aufgelaufene ~** accumulative debts; **aufgenommene ~** borrowings, debts incurred; **ausstehende ~** outstanding debts; **bedenkliche ~** staggering debts; **vor der Masseverteilung zu begleichende ~** preferential (preferred) debts; **im Nebenprozeß begriffene ~** debts on mesne process; **schon bestehende ~** pre-existing debts; **bevorrechtigte ~** preferential (preferred, *US*) debts; **vor Fälligkeit bezahlte ~** dues paid in advance; **drückende ~** pressing debts; **eingefrorene ~** frozen debts; **eingegangene ~** debts contracted; **vor Konkurseröffnung eingegangene ~** debts contracted before bankruptcy; **als Minderjähriger eingegangene ~** debts contracted during infancy; **[nachträglich] eingetriebene ~** debts recovered; **nach dem Ausscheiden eines Gesellschafters entstandene ~** post-retirement debts; **faule ~** bad debts *(US)*, doubtful debts *(Br.)*; **gerichtlich festgestellte ~** debts of record, judgment debts, debts owed under court orders; **nicht zum Gewerbebetrieb gehörige ~** nonbusiness debts; **gemeinschaftliche ~** *(Ehepaar)* community debts; **gesamtschuldnerische ~** joint and several debts; **gestundete ~** deferred liabilities; **vor Fälligkeit gezahlte ~** dues paid in advance; **laufende ~** current (running) debts; **persönliche ~** *(Gesellschafter)* private (individual) debts; **riesige ~** staggering debts; **kurzfristig rückzahlbare ~** quick liabilities; **unbezahlbare ~** insolvable debts; **unbezahlte ~** unsettled (unsatisfied) debts; **uneinbringliche ~** irrecoverable debts; **unverzinsliche ~** passive debts; **voreheliche ~** antenuptial debts; **zweifelhafte ~** doubtful debts *(Br.)*, bad debts *(US)*;
~ **einer Aktiengesellschaft** corporation debts *(US)*; ~ **einer Firma** partnership (company) debts; ~ **von Gebietskörperschaften** local debts; ~ **des Gemeinschuldners** bankrupt's debts; ~ **der öffentlichen Hand** national debt *(Br.)*, public debt *(US)*; ~ **aus einer Pflichtteilsvereinbarung** portion debts; ~ **aufgrund eines Treuhandverhältnisses** fiduciary debts; ~ **vor der Währungsreform** prestabilization debts;
~ **abbauen** to reduce debts; **seine ~ abbezahlen** to pay off one's debts; ~ **abdecken** to cover debts; **zweifelhafte ~ abschreiben** to write off doubtful *(Br.)* (bad, *US*) debts; ~ **abtragen (abzahlen)** to wipe (pay) off debts; ~ **anerkennen** to acknowledge liabilities; ~ **anhäufen** to pile up debts; ~ **annullieren** to wipe off debts; ~ **aufnehmen** to contract debts, to borrow; **sich von seinen ~ befreien** to pay up one's debts; **alle ~ begleichen** to pay one's debts down the line (all that is owing); **alte ~ begleichen** to pay off old scores; **seine ~ begleichen** to meet (settle, discharge) one's debts; ~ **beitreiben** to recover debts; **sich mit ~ belasten** to encumber o. s. with (involve o. s. in) debts; **sich vor ~ bewahren** to pay one's way (debts), to discharge one's liabilities, to meet one's engagements; **alle ~ bezahlen** to pay all that is owing; **alte ~ bezahlen** to pay off old scores; **jds. ~ bezahlen** to clear s. o. of debts; **seine ~ bezahlen** to pay (settle) one's debts, to discharge one's liabilities, to get clear of debts, to meet one's engagements, to ante up *(US sl.)*, *(Gläubiger befriedigen)* to satisfy one's creditors; **seine ~ nicht bezahlen** to neglect to pay one's (default on) debts; **seine ~ auf Heller und Pfennig bezahlen** to pay twenty shillings in the pound *(Br.)*, to pay one's debt to the last penny; **seine ~ voll bezahlen** to discharge one's liabilities in full; ~ **decken** *(Nachlaß)* to be solvent; **j. zur Begleichung seiner ~ drankriegen** to bind s. o. to pay his debts *(sl.)*; ~ **eingehen** to contract (make) debts; ~ **einkassieren** to gather in debts; ~ **einklagen** to take legal proceedings for the recovery of debts; ~ **eintreiben** to recover (call in, enforce payment of) debts; ~ **bei jem. eintreiben** to exact payment of a debt from s. o.; **ausstehende ~ einziehen** to collect outstanding debts; **sich seinen ~ entziehen** to escape one's liabilities; ~ **[teilweise] erlassen** to abate debts; **in ~ geraten** to get (fall, run) into (incur) debts; **bei jem. in ~ geraten** to run into s. one's books; ~ **haben** to have bills, to be in financial difficulties, to be indebted (in the red, *US coll.*); **1000 Dollar ~ haben** to be indebted to a thousand dollars; **hohe ~ haben** to be deep in the books (in debt); **riesige ~ haben** to be over head and heels in debt; **überall ~ haben** to be in debt to everybody; **noch ~ auf seinem Haus haben** to owe for one's house; ~ **hereinbekommen** to get in debts; **sich um die Bezahlung seiner ~ herumdrücken** to evade payment of one's debts; **nichts als ~ hinterlassen** to leave nothing but debts; ~ **kassieren** to gather in debts; ~ **anwachsen lassen** to pile up debts; **seine ~ loswerden** to get out of debt; ~ **machen** to contract (incur, make, run into) debt, to run up a score, to score up debts; **bei jem. ~ machen** to get in s. one's books; **für die ~ der Ehefrau aufkommen müssen** to be liable for one's wife's debts; ~ **regulieren** to settle debts; **in ~ verwickelt sein** to be involved in debt; **bis an die Ohren in ~ stecken** to be over head and heels (up to the eyes) in debt; **faule ~ streichen** to credit bad *(US)* (doubtful, *Br.*) debts; **sich in ~ stürzen** to plunge (plump, involve o. s., run) into debt, to outrun the constable; ~ **tilgen** to redeem (pay off, strike off, discharge) debts; ~ **übernehmen** to assume (shoulder) debts, to take over liabilities; **sich in ~ verstricken** to encumber o. s. with (involve o. s. in) debts; **seine ~ zurückführen** to clear up one's indebtedness.

schulden to owe, to be indebted;
jem. einen großen Betrag ~ to be indebted to a large amount to s. o.; **jem. großen Dank ~** to be greatly indebted to s. o., to owe s. o. a deep debt of gratitude; **jem. eine Erklärung ~** to owe s. o. an explanation; **jem. Gehorsam ~** to owe allegiance to s. o.; **aus**

Giroverbindlichkeiten ~ to be contingently indebted; **keinen roten Heller** ~ to have not a scrap of debts; **hundert Pfund** ~ to be down for £ 100; **seinen Eltern Respekt** ~ to owe respect to one's parents.

Schulden|abbau debt retirement, reduction of debts, debt reduction; ~**abdeckung** debt redemption; ~**ablösung** debt conversion; ~**abtragung** wiping off debts; ~**abzahlung** [re]payment of debts; ~**annullierung** abolition of debts; ~**anwachs** growing debts; ~**art** category of debts.

Schuldenaufnahme borrowing, contraction (incurrence) of debts;
staatliche ~ government borrowing;
~**beschluß** borrowing resolution.

Schulden|aufstellung statement of liabilities; ~**aufteilung** distribution of debts; ~**begleichung** liquidation of debts; ~**begleichung im Legatswege** satisfaction of debts by legacies; ~**beitreibung** collection of debts, debt collecting.

schuldenbelastet indebted, burdened (encumbered) with debts, deep in debt.

Schulden|belastung indebtedness; ~**bereinigung** debt retirement; ~**berg** mountain of debts; ~**bezahlung** payment of debts; ~**deckung** debt coverage; ~**dienst** debt service; ~**dienstbelastung** burden of debt service; ~**dienstverpflichtungen von über 5 Mio. Dollar haben** to service over $ 5 m in debts; ~**eintreibung** collection of debts, debt collecting (collection); ~**einziehung** recovery of debts; ~**erhöhung** increased debts; ~**erlaß** release from (remission of) debts, debt relief; **stillschweigend gewährter** ~**erlaß** implied release.

schuldenfrei debtless, clear, even, free of debt, not indebted, unindebted, unembarrassed, afloat, *(Grundstück)* unencumbered, free from encumbrances;
sich ~ **halten** to keep out of debt; **sich** ~ **machen** to free o. s. from debt, to get clear of debts; ~ **sein** to be out of debt; ~ **werden** to free o. s. from debt.

Schuldenhaftung liability for contracted debts.

schuldenhalber owing to debts.

Schulden|herabsetzung reduction of debts; ~**konferenz** debt conference; ~**konsolidierung** consolidation of indebtedness, debt consolidation (funding); ~**konto** debt balance; ~**last** indebtedness, burden of debts, *(Grundstück)* encumbrance; **große** ~**last** heavy debts; ~**last tragen** to owe debts; ~**machen** running into debt; ~**machen im großen Maßstab** wholesale borrowing; ~**macher** contractor of debts; ~**macher sein** to have a propensity for running into debt; ~**masse** *(Konkurs)* liabilities; ~**moratorium** moratorium on debt, letter of licence; ~**nachweis** proof of debt; ~**pyramide** debt pyramid.

Schulden|regelung, ~**regulierung** settlement of debts, debt readjustment, liabilities adjustment *(Br.)*;
~ **im Vereinbarungsweg** partial payment of debts; **vergleichsweise** ~ **aufheben** to annul a scheme of arrangements, *(Br.)*; ~ **vornehmen** to liquidate.

Schulden|regelungsplan scheme of arrangement (composition); ~**rückführung** debt reduction (redemption); ~**rückstand** debts in arrears; ~**rückzahlung** repayment (settlement) of debts; ~**saldo** debt balance; ~**seite** red *(US coll.)*; ~**senkung** reduction of debts, debt reduction; ~**situation** debt situation.

Schuldentilgung extinction (sale, satisfaction, liquidation, repayment, sinking) of debts, redemption, discharge, wiping off, wiping [out] of debts, debt redemption (retirement, liquidation), *(Amortisierung)* amortization;
bis zur ~ until discharged in full;
massierte ~ **vornehmen** to service its massive debt.

Schuldentilgungs|aufwand debt service costs; ~**dienst** servicing one's debt, debt service (servicing); **Belastungen des** ~**dienstes erfüllen** to meet debt-service charges; ~**fonds,** ~**kasse** sinking (redemption) fund; ~**last** debt servicing burden; ~**maßnahmen** meeting debt repayment; ~**plan** redemption plan, scheme of arrangement; ~**rate** sinking-fund (redemption) instalment; ~**rücklage** sinking-fund (debt-redemption, debt-reduction) reserve.

Schulden|übertragung transfer of liabilities; ~**umwandlung** conversion of debts, debt conversion; ~**verwaltung** debt administration (management); ~**verzeichnis** schedule of liabilities, recital of debts; ~**vorauszahlung** dues advances *(US)*; ~**zahlung** payment of debts; **von** ~**zahlungen entlasten** *(Gemeinschuldner)* to discharge, to whitewash *(Br.)*; ~**zunahme** growing debt, debt expansion.

Schulderlaß debt relief, release from (remission of) debts, acquittance;
ausdrücklicher ~ conventional remission; **beabsichtigter** ~ intention to release a debt; **teilweiser** ~ abatement of debts.

Schuldforderung claim, active debt, demand;
~**en** *(Bilanz)* debts due, debts receivable *(US)*;
uneintreibbare ~ irrecoverable debt;
~ **abtreten** to delegate (assign) a debt; ~ **abweisen** to reject a proof of debt; ~ **belegen (beweisen)** to prove debts; ~ **übertragen** to transfer a debt.

Schuld|frage *(Unfall)* blame for an accident; ~**gefängnis** sponging house *(Br.)*; ~**gefühl loswerden** to shake off the guilt; ~**geständnis** plea of guilty, confession (admission) of guilt; **bei der Polizei ein** ~**geständnis ablegen** to admit one's guilt to the police; ~**haft** committal for debts.

schuldhaft culpable;
~**e Nichterfüllung** failure to meet one's obligations; ~**e Nichtkenntnis** constructive notice.

Schuldhöhe amount of indebtedness, *(AG)* debt-equity ratio.

Schul|diener school caretaker; **im** ~**dienst sein** to be in the teaching profession.

schuldig *(Betrag)* due, owing, payable, *(strafrechtlich)* guilty, culpable, *(verantwortlich)* liable, responsible, answerable;
nicht ~ not guilty;
j. des Mordes für ~ **befinden** to convict s. o. on a charge of murder; **sich** ~ **bekennen** to plead guilty; ~ **bleiben** to remain due; **jem. nichts** ~ **bleiben** to give s. o. tit for tat, to pay s. o. back in his own coin; **jem. die Antwort nicht** ~ **bleiben** to hit back, not to be at a loss for an answer; **seit drei Monaten die Miete** ~ **bleiben** to owe for three months rent; **für** ~ **erkennen (erklären)** to return (deliver a verdict of) guilty, to convict, to find s. o. guilty of a charge; **sich für** ~ **erklären** to declare o. s. guilty; **j. für** ~ **halten** to hold s. o. culpable; **j. als** ~ **erscheinen lassen** to point s. o. out as guilty; **sich eines Betruges** ~ **machen** to commit a fraudulent act; ~ **sein** to owe, to be indebted to; **jem. großen Dank** ~ **sein** to be under a great obligation to s. o.; **jem. eine Erklärung** ~ **sein** to owe s. o. an explanation; **es seinem Namen** ~ **sein** to owe it to one's reputation; **jem. nichts mehr** ~ **sein** to be even with s. o.; **jem. Rechenschaft** ~ **sein** to owe s. o. an explanation; **zu gleichen Teilen** ~ **sein** *(Versicherungsrecht)* to be equally to blame; ~ **sprechen** to bring in a verdict of guilty; **j.** ~ **sprechen** to find s. o. guilty; **in allen Anklagepunkten für** ~ **befunden werden** to be found guilty on all counts;
~**er Betrag** sum payable (owing); **bei allem** ~**en Respekt** with all due reference.

Schuldiger culprit, *(Unfall)* party at fault in an accident.

Schuldig|erklärung nolo contendere; ~**keit** duty, obligation; **seine** ~**keit tun** to do one's part; ~**sprechung** conviction.

Schul|direktor headmaster, principal *(US)*; ~**disziplin** school discipline.

Schuld|kapital borrowed capital; ~**klage** action of debt; ~**komplex** feelings of guilt; ~**konto** debit balance; ~**konto anwachsen lassen** to run up debts (a score, *Br.*).

schuldlos clear, clean-handed, innocent, clear [from guilt];
~ **geschieden** divorced as the innocent party.

Schuld|losigkeit white hands, innocence; ~**lossprechung** compurgation; ~**nachlaß** partial remission of debt.

Schuldner debtor, debitor, party liable, *(Hypothekenschuldner)* mortgagor, *(Verpflichteter)* obligor, obligator *(US)*, *(säumiger Zahler)* defaulter;
schwer bedrängter ~ hard-pressed debtor; **in Schwierigkeiten befindlicher** ~ embarrassed debtor; **in Verzug befindlicher** ~ cessor; **flüchtiger** ~ absconding (fugitive) debtor; **gemeinsame** ~ joint debtors; **gepfändeter** ~ attached debtor; **sekundär haftender** ~ secondary debtor; **säumiger** ~ dilatory (slow, tardy) payer, debtor in arrears, defaulter, defaulting debtor; **schlechter** ~ bad (dubious) debtor; **solventer** ~ solvent debtor; **unsicherer** ~ dubious debtor; **unzulässiger** ~ irresponsible debtor; **unbekannt verzogener** ~ absconding debtor, skip *(US)*; **zahlungsunfähiger** ~ poor (bad, insolvent) debtor, defaulter; ~ **zur gesamten Hand** joint and several debtors; ~ **in laufender Rechnung** debtor in account current, *(Bilanz)* advance to customers and other accounts; ~ **im Verzug** defaulter;
Zahlungsunfähigkeit eines ~**s bei Gericht anzeigen** to strike a docket; ~ **ausklagen** to discuss a debtor; ~ **auspfänden** to inquire into the assets of a debtor; ~ **bedrängen** to crowd a debtor; **seine** ~ **laufend bedrängen** to harry one's debtors; ~ **von seinen Schulden befreien** to free a debtor of his debts; **einem** ~ **Zahlungsfrist gewähren** to allow a debtor time to pay, to indulge a debtor; ~ **vor Gericht laden** to summon[s] a debtor; ~ **mahnen** to give notice to a debtor; **vom** ~ **die gesamte Summe verlangen** to hold s. o. for the whole debt; **dem** ~ **zustellen** to serve upon the debtor; **gegen einen** ~ **zwangsvollstrecken** to distrain upon a debtor;

förmliche ~benachrichtigung formal notice to the debtor; **~entlastung** whitewashing *(Br.)*; **~firma, ~gesellschaft** obligor (obligator) company, debtor corporation (company); **~gefängnis** Queen's prison; **~gruppe** class of debtors, debtor group.

Schuldnerin debtor company (corporation), obligator company.

Schuldner|land debtor nation (country), borrowing country; **~mitteilung** notice by a debtor; **~rolle** role as debtor; **~seite** debtor side; **~staat** debtor nation; **~stellung** debtor position; **~vergleich** liabilities adjustment *(Br.)*; **Gläubiger-~-Verhältnis** creditor-debtor relation; **~vermögen** property of a debtor, debtor's property; **~vermögen verwalten lassen** to commit a debtor; **~vernehmung** *(Konkursausfall)* preliminary examination *(Br.)*; **~verpflichtung** debtor's duty; **~verzeichnis** defaulter's book; **~verzug** debtor's delay.

Schuld|papiere debt securities; **~posten** debit (liability) item, debt, debit account, sum due, score, tick *(Br.)*; **~recht** law of obligations (contract), contract law.

schuldrechtlich contractual;

~er Anspruch contractual (debt) claim; **~e Beziehungen** consensual relations; **~e Verpflichtung** contractual obligation.

Schuld|rest balance due (owing); **~saldo** debit [balance].

Schuldschein bond [of indebtedness], I.O.U. (I owe you), loan receipt, obligation, writing obligatory, bill of debt, bill obligatory, dog *(US)*, *(Aktiengesellschaft)* corporate bond, certificate (bond) of indebtedness, *(Kommunalschuldschein)* municipal (county) warrant, *(Schuldverschreibung)* bond, debenture, note, warrant *(US)*;

durch ~ gesichert debentured, bonded;

erstklassig abgesicherter ~ iron-clad note; **ausstehende ~e** warrants payable *(US)*; **bedingter ~** conditional (double) bond; **beim Tod eines Dritten fälliger ~** post-obit bond *(Br.)*; **durch Gestellung von Sicherheiten gedeckter ~** secured (collateral, *US*) note; **dinglich gesicherter ~** borrower's note against ad rem security, collateral note *(US)*; **hypothekarisch gesicherter ~** principal note; **durch Lombardierung von Wertpapieren gesicherter (lombardgesicherter) ~** secured note, stock note *(US)*; **kurzfristige ~e** interim bonds, short[-term] notes *(US)*; **persönlicher ~** individual bond; **steuerfreier ~** tax-exempt note; **überfälliger ~** past-due note; **uneingeschränkter ~** absolute bond; **ungesicherter ~** plain (unsecured) bond, unsecured note; **kurzfristiger durch Makler verkaufter ~** street paper *(US)*; **verlängerter ~** renewed note; **vorläufiger ~** interim bond;

~ mit gleichbleibenden Bedingungen closed bond; **~ mit Unterwerfungs~, Zwangsvollstreckungsklausel** judgment (instalment, *US*) note; **~ für einen Vorschuß** advance note;

~ ausstellen to make a promissory note, to sign a bond; **~ bezahlen** to lift a promissory note; **~ einlösen** to discharge a bond;

~aussteller recognizor; **~besitzer** warrant creditor; **~darlehn** loan against borrower's note, open-market credit; **kommunales ~darlehn** registered warrant; **~darlehnsurkunde** open-market paper; **~forderung** bonded debt; **~inhaber** noteholder, *(Kommunalwesen)* warrant (certificate) creditor; **~markt** commercial paper (note) market; **~verpflichtungen** *(Bilanz)* notes payable *(US)*, *(Kommunalwesen)* net bonded debt; **bezahlte ~zinsen** debenture interest paid.

Schuldspruch verdict of guilty;

~ aufheben to quash a conviction; **~ bestätigen** to uphold a conviction; **~ verkünden** to find a verdict of guilty.

Schuld|summe amount of a debt, indebtedness; **gesamte ~summe** total debt, gross debt *(US)*, entire debenture; **~tilgung** repayment (redemption) of a debt, debt redemption; **~titel** evidence (proof) of indebtedness, *(Wertpapier)* debt instruments (securities); **kurzfristiger ~titel** short-term debt instrument; **vollstreckbaren ~titel haben** to have a writ of execution for service.

Schuldübernahme promise to pay the debt of another, assumption of indebtedness, assumed liability, expromission, delegation, *(Novation)* novation;

befreiende ~ perfect delegation; **nicht befreiende ~** imperfect delegation;

~vertrag indemnity contract.

Schuld|übernehmer substituted debtor; **~übertragung** assignment of a debt; **~umwandlung** conversion of debt, novation.

Schuldurkunde evidence of indebtedness, proof of debt, debt instrument, *(Konventionalstrafe)* double bond *(Scot.)*;

deckungsstockgesicherte ~n blue notes; **dinglich gesicherte ~** heritable bond; **hypothekarisch gesicherte ~** mortgage note; **wiedereingelöste ~** redeemed debenture;

~ in der gesetzlich vorgeschriebenen Form statutory bond; **~ mit festgesetzter Konventionalstrafe** penal bill; **~ eines Treuhänders** debenture trust deed *(Br.)*;

~formular debenture form.

Schuldverhältnis contractual obligation;

gesetzliches ~ constructive contract; **ursprüngliches ~** original liability; **vererbliches ~** heritable obligation;

~ zur gesamten Hand joint and several obligation;

~ begründen to create an obligation; **~ zum Erlöschen bringen** to extinguish an obligation.

Schuldvermutung presumption of guilt.

Schuldverpflichtung liability, [contractual] obligation;

persönliche ~ individual bond, personal obligation; **durch Verkauf von Schuldnereigentum realisierte ~** secured liability; **übernommene ~** *(einer fusionierten Gesellschaft)* assumed bond;

~ unter Eid zurückweisen to forswear a debt.

Schuldverschreibung bond [of obligation], obligation, debenture stock *(Br.)*, debenture [bond] *(US)*, *(Bankier)* delegation, *(Schuldschein)* handbill, promise to pay, writing obligatory, note, promissory note, I.O.U.;

durch ~ gesichert debentured, bonded;

vollstreckbare ~ pocket judgment.

Schuldverschreibungen debenture bonds *(US)* (stocks, *Br.*), obligations;

in Serien abgestufte ~ classified bonds; **ablösbare ~** redeemable bonds; **zur Rückzahlung (Tilgung) aufgerufene ~** redeemed (called) bonds; **ausgegebene ~** issued (outstanding) bonds, *(Bilanz)* bonds payable *(US)*; **noch nicht ausgegebene ~** unissued bonds (debentures); **über dem Nennwert ausgegebene ~** bonds issued above par; **zu Sanierungszwecken ausgegebene ~** reorganization (adjustment) bonds; **in verschiedenen Serien ausgegebene ~** classified (class) bonds; **in Stücken ausgegebene ~** denominational bonds; **ausgeloste ~** drawn bonds; **mit Dividendenberechtigung ausgestattete ~** dividend bonds *(US)*; **mit Kapital- und Dividendengarantie ausgestattete ~** guaranteed bonds; **mit attraktiven Steuervorteilen ausgestattete ~** bonds with attractive tax features; **zugunsten einer Bank ausgestellte ~** bank debentures; **ausländische ~** foreign currency bonds *(US)*; **ausstehende ~** outstanding bonds; **auswechselbare ~** interchangeable bonds; **bereits begebene ~** already issued debentures; **bevorrechtigte ~** priority (preferential, preferred) bonds; **börsennotierte ~** bonds listed *(US)* (quoted) on the stock exchange; **eigene ~** treasury bonds *(US)*; **eingetragene ~** registered bonds; **jederzeit einlösbare ~** optional bonds *(US)*; **endgültige ~** definitive bonds; **erstrangige ~** first debentures; **ertragssteuerfreie ~** tax-exempt bonds; **festverzinsliche ~** coupon (obligatory, fixed-interest bearing) bonds, debenture bonds *(US)*; **firmeneigene ~** treasury bonds *(US)*; **durch Effektenlombard gedeckte (gesicherte) ~** collateral trust bonds *(US)*; **außer Kurs gesetzte ~** invalidated bonds; **dinglich gesicherte ~** debentures secured by a charge, debenture stock *(Br.)*; **durch Ersthypothek gesicherte ~** first-mortgage bonds; **erstrangig gesicherte ~** first-lien bonds, consolidated first mortgage bonds *(US)*; **durch Gesamthypothek gesicherte ~** consolidated bonds *(US)*, general mortgage bonds *(US)*; **durch erste Gesamthypothek gesicherte ~** consolidated first-mortgage bonds *(US)*; **durch Hypothek gesicherte ~** backed (mortgage) bonds; **durch nachstellige Hypothek gesicherte ~** overlying (junior) bonds; **durch eine im Range vorgehende Hypothek gesicherte ~** underlying bonds *(US)*; **hypothekarisch gesicherte ~** backed (mortgage, *Br.*) debentures, secured debentures, fixed debentures, mortgage (open-end) bonds *(US)*, collateral mortgage bonds, debenture stock *(Br.)*; **hypothekarisch nicht gesicherte ~** simple debentures (bonds); **durch Pfandbestellung gesicherte ~** backed bonds; **durch im Range nachstehendes Pfandrecht gesicherte ~** junior lien bonds; **gesiegelte ~** writing obligatory; **gestückelte ~** fractional bonds; **getilgte ~en** redeemed bonds; **gewinnberechtigte ~** participating (profit-sharing) bonds, parliamentary debentures; **industrielle ~** internal (industrial) bonds, corporate bonds *(US)*; **kleingestückelte ~** fractional debentures, savings bonds *(US)*; **kommunale ~** local bonds *(Br.)*, municipal (special assessment) bonds *(US)*, general obligation bonds, municipal stocks *(Br.)*; **konsolidierte ~** consolidated stocks; **konvertierbare ~** convertible bonds; **kündbare ~** callable (redeemable) bonds, optional bonds *(US)*; **nach festgelegtem Termin kündbare ~** indeterminate bonds; **nicht vorzeitig kündbare ~** noncallable (nonredeemable) bonds; **kurzfristige ~** short-term debentures; **langfristige ~** long-term debentures; **auf den Inhaber lautende ~**

bearer bonds, debentures (bonds) to bearer; **auf den Namen lautende** ~ registered bonds *(Br.)*; **auf englische Pfund lautende** ~ sterling bonds; **lieferbare** ~ good-delivery bonds; **mündelsichere** ~ trustee bonds *(Br.)*, legal bonds *(US)*; **nennwertlose** ~ no-par debentures; **neue** ~ new-issue bonds; **öffentlich-rechtliche** ~ public (government) bonds, civil stocks (bonds, *US*); **prolongierte** ~ renewal bonds, extended bonds *(US)*; **durch jährliche Auslosung rückzahlbare** ~ bonds repayable by annual drawing; **nicht rückzahlbare** ~ irredeemable bonds; **übertragbare** ~ negotiable bonds; **ungesicherte** ~ unsecured (naked) debentures *(Br.)*, simple bonds; **mittelfristig ungesicherte** ~ notes *(US)*; **ungültige** ~ disabled bonds *(Br.)*; **unkündbare** ~ irredeemable bonds, perpetual debentures *(US)*; **unverzinsliche** ~ passive bonds, noninterest-bearing obligations *(US)*; **verbriefte** ~ documented debentures; **verbürgte** ~ guaranteed debentures; **verkehrsfähige** ~ negotiable bonds; **verlängerte** ~ extended bonds; **verzinsliche** ~ interest-bearing obligations *(US)*; **gewinnabhängige verzinsliche** ~ income debentures *(Br.)*; **nur bei Gewinnerzielung verzinsliche** ~ adjustment bonds; **im Range vorangehende** ~ senior-lien bonds; **vorläufige** ~ provisional (temporary) bonds; **gleichzeitig fällig werdende** ~ term bonds; **in englischen Pfunden zahlbare** ~ sterling bonds; **in gesetzlichen Zahlungsmitteln zahlbare** ~ legal-tender (currency, *US*) bonds; **zinslose** ~ passive bonds, noninterest-bearing obligations *(US)*; **zinstragende** ~ active bonds, interest-bearing obligations *(US)*; **zur Tilgung zurückgekaufte** ~ bonds purchased for cancellation; **zweitrangige** ~ second debentures;

~ **zur Ablösung ungültig ausgegebener Garantien** rescission bonds; ~ **von Aktiengesellschaften** corporate bonds *(US)*; ~ **des Amortisationsfonds** sinking-fund bonds; ~ **über eine breit gestreute Anlagesumme** managed bonds; ~ **mit zusätzlicher Bürgschaftsurkunde** bonds with surety; ~ **zur Finanzierung von Bewässerungsprojekten** irrigation bonds *(US)*; ~ **zur Finanzierung für Eisenbahnbedarf** equipment bonds *(US)*; ~ **für bevorrechtigte Forderungen** trust bonds (debentures); ~ **einer Gebietskörperschaft** territorial bonds; ~ **mit Gewinnbeteiligung** participating (profit, profit-sharing) bonds; ~ **der öffentlichen Hand** public securities, civil stocks (bonds, *US*); ~ **eines Immobilienfonds** real-estate bonds *(US)*; ~ **mit Kapital- und Dividendengarantie** guaranteed bonds *(US)*; ~ **von Kapitalgesellschaften** corporate bonds *(US)*; ~ **von Kommunen** municipal bonds *(US)*; ~ **zweiten Ranges** second debentures; ~ **mit hoher (variabler) Rendite** high- (variable-) yield bonds; ~ **des Staates** government (state) bonds *(US)*, public stocks, funds *(Br.)*; ~ **in kleiner Stückelung** small bonds *(US)*; ~ **ohne Tilgungsverpflichtung** perpetual bonds; ~ **öffentlicher Versorgungseinrichtungen** public-utility bonds; ~ **mit gleichbleibender Verzinsung** continued bonds; ~ **ohne Zinsgarantie** debenture income bonds; ~ **mit Zinsschein** coupon bonds; ~ **mit aufgeschobener Zinszahlung** noninterest-bearing discount bonds;

~ **ablösen** to discharge debentures; ~ **ausgeben** to float a bond issue, to put out (issue) bonds; ~ **erneut ausgeben** to reissue debentures; ~ **unter dem Nennwert ausgeben** to issue bonds below par; ~ **ausstellen** to [enter into] bond; **mit** ~ **belasten** to bond; ~ **auf den Markt bringen** to float bonds; ~ **in den Verkehr bringen** to issue debentures; ~ **einlösen** to retire (pay off) bonds; ~ **an der Börse handeln (notieren)** to trade bonds at the stock exchange; ~ **im Freiverkehr handeln** to trade bonds over the counter *(US)*; ~ **kündigen** to call in (redeem) bonds; **durch** ~ **sichern** to bond; ~ **in Aktien umwandeln** to convert debentures into shares; ~ **im Depot verwahren** to keep bonds in safe custody; ~ **zurückkaufen** to repurchase bonds (debentures).

Schuldverschreibungs|agio bond premium; ~**art** bond category; ~**darlehn** debenture loan; ~**inhaber** bondholder, debenture holder, bond creditor; ~**kapital** debenture capital (stock, *US*); ~**serie** series of debentures; ~**umlauf** circulation of bonds; ~**urkunde** definitive bond; ~**zinsen** bond interest.

Schuldversprechen promise, common (general) assumpsit, note, marker *(sl.)*;

abstraktes ~ naked (bare) promise; **mündliches** ~ parole promise; **schriftliches** ~ promissory note; **unbedingtes schriftliches** ~ unconditional promise in writing.

Schuld|wechsel *(Bilanz)* notes (bills) payable *(US)*; ~**wechselbuch** bills-payable book; ~**zinsen** interest costs.

Schule school, educational establishment, *(Schulhaus)* schoolhouse, school building, *(Unterricht)* lessons;

durch Zusammenlegungen entstandene ~ consolidated school; **staatlich geförderte** ~ publicly-supported school, grant-aided school *(Br.)*; **im Elendsviertel gelegene** ~ slum school; **hohe** ~ university; **höhere** ~ grammar (secondary, upper, collegiate) school *(Br.)*, senior high school *(US)*; **öffentliche** ~ county *(Br.)* (common, public, *US*) school; **praktische** ~ modern-secondary school *(Br.)*; **private** ~ private (public, *Br.*) school; **staatliche** ~ county (state) school *(Br.)*; **kommunal unterhaltene** ~ maintained school *(Br.)*; **öffentlich unterhaltene** ~ public school *(Br.)*; **weiterbildende** ~ further education college; **weiterführende** ~ secondary school;

~ **für Fernunterricht** learn-by-mail school *(US)*; ~ **für beide Geschlechter** mixed school *(Br.)*; ~ **mit Internat** boarding school; ~ **für schwer erziehbare Kinder** training school; ~ **ohne Rassentrennung** integrated school; **staatlich geförderte** ~ **ohne Religionsunterricht** public elementary school *(Br.)*;

von der ~ **abgehen** to leave school; ~ **abhalten** to keep school; **an der** ~ **das Abschlußexamen ablegen** to take one's finals, to graduate from school *(US)*; **zu einer** ~ **anmelden** to register for a school; **von der** ~ **ausschließen** to expel from school; ~ **besuchen** to go (attend a) school; ~ **ein weiteres Jahr besuchen** to continue at school for another year; ~ **mit Ach und Krach durchlaufen** to scrape up the school; **in der** ~ **fehlen** to be absent from school; **bei jem. in die** ~ **gehen** to go to school to s. o.; **durch eine harte** ~ **gehen** to stand a severe test, to go through the mill; **in der** ~ **zu den Besten gehören** to be high up in school *(Br.)*; ~ **gründen** to set up a school; ~ **machen** to come into vogue, to catch on, to be imitated; **von der** ~ **nehmen** to take from school; **aus der** ~ **plaudern** to tell tales out of school, to spill the beans; **zur** ~ **schicken** to school; **j. in eine harte** ~ **schicken** to put s. o. through the mill; ~ **schließen** to break up school; ~ **schwänzen** to play truant (hooky, *US*), to miche *(sl.)*; **mit der** ~ **fertig sein** to leave school; **sich für die** ~ **vorbereiten** to prepare (learn) one's lessons.

Schul|einrichtung school furniture (equipment); ~**eintritt** entrance to a school; ~**einzugsbereich** school catchment area.

schulen to school, to teach, to instruct, to tutor, to train, to indoctrinate;

j. politisch ~ to give s. o. a political education.

Schulentlassener graduate, school leaver *(Br.)*.

Schulentlassung school leaving, graduation *(US)*.

Schulentlassungs|alter school-leaving age; ~**feier** speech day *(Br.)*, commencement *(US)*; ~**zeugnis** school-leaving certificate.

Schüler [school] pupil, schoolboy, disciple, *(Anfänger)* novice, rookie *(sl.)*;

auswärtiger ~ extern; **ehemaliger** ~ old boy; **höherer** ~ school graduate; **leistungsschwacher** ~ underachieved *(US)*; **sitzengebliebener** ~ holdover, repeater;

~ **mit unterdurchschnittlichen Leistungen** underachiever *(US)*; ~ **einer Tagesschule** day boy *(Br.)*; ~ **der Unterstufe** lower boy *(Br.)*;

~ **mit Arrest bestrafen** to keep a pupil in; ~ **fördern** to bring forward (push on) a pupil; ~ **nicht fördern** to retard a pupil; ~ **zurückfallen lassen** to put a pupil back; ~ **[eines Professors] sein** to sit under; **einem** ~ **eine Strafe verpassen** to hand a boy a punishment *(US fam.)*;

~**ausschuß** student council *(US)*; ~**austausch** exchange of pupils; ~**beirat** student council; ~**bibliothek** school library.

schülerhafte Ansichten immature views.

Schulerholungslager school camp.

Schüler|jargon schoolboy (students', *US*) slang; ~**-Lehrer-Verhältnisziffer** student-faculty ratio; ~**lotse** lollipop man; ~**lotsendienst** lollipop (road-crossing) service; ~**monatsfahrkarte** scholar's season ticket *(US)*; ~**treffen veranstalten** to organize a reunion of former pupils; ~**zeitung** school paper (magazine).

Schul|fach subject; ~**fall** test case; ~**ferien** school holidays, [school] vacation *(US)*; ~**fernsehen** education television; ~**fest** school treat; ~**fibel** primer; ~**flugzeug** training plane, trainer; ~**französisch** school French.

schulfrei|haben to have a holiday;

~**er Nachmittag** half holiday; ~**er Tag** holiday, playday, liberty.

Schul|freund schoolfellow, schoolmate; **alter** ~**freund** old pupil; ~**freundschaft** school friendship; ~**funk** educational broadcasting; **ärztliche** ~**fürsorge** school health service; ~**fürsorger** visiting teacher; ~**gebäude** schoolhouse, school building (premises), campus *(US)*, *(Mädchen)* lyceum; **für den** ~**gebrauch** for use in schools; ~**geld** school (tuition) fees, school tax, terms.

schulgeldfrei tuition-free;

~**e Anstalt** charitable school.

Schul|grundstück school site (lands); ~**haus** schoolhouse; ~**heft** exercise book; ~**hof** school yard, playground; ~**inspektor** school inspector.

schulisch schoolish;
~**e Angelegenheiten** school affairs; ~**e Eignung** school aptitude.
Schul|jahr school (academic) year, school term, unit *(US)*; ~**junge** schoolboy; ~**kamerad** schoolmate, school chum *(coll.)*, schoolfellow, bookmate, stable companion *(Br.)*; ~**kantine** school canteen; ~**kind** school child.
Schulklasse school form *(Br.)*, class, grade *(US)*;
höhere ~n higher forms; **oberste ~** senior class *(US)*; **überfüllte ~** overcrowded class; **unterste ~** petty form *(Br.)*; **vierte bis sechste ~n** intermediate grades *(US)*;
~ aus dem Unterricht entlassen to dismiss a class; **~ wiederholen** to stay down in a class.
Schul|kommission school committee; ~**konto** school account; ~**lehrer** schoolmaster, [school] teacher; ~**lehrerin** school mistress; ~**leiter** schoolmaster, preceptor, headmaster, school principal *(US)*; **stellvertretender ~leiter** submaster *(Br.)*; ~**leiterin** school mistress; ~**mädchen** schoolgirl; ~**mappe** schoolbag, satchel.
schulmäßig formal, methodical.
Schulmeister schoolmaster.
schulmeisterlich schoolmasterly, pedantic.
schulmeistern, j. to schoolmaster (lecture) s. o.
Schul|milch school milk; ~**neubauten** new school buildings; ~**omnibus** school bus (omnibus); ~**ordnung** school rules; ~**pause** break, recess *(US)*; **in einer ~pause** during a break in school; **allgemeine ~pflicht** compulsory education (schooling).
schulpflichtig schoolable;
~**es Alter** schoolable (compulsory school) age; ~**e Kinder** school-age children.
Schul|preise gewinnen, alle to carry off all the school prizes; ~**pult** school desk; ~**rat** school supervisor (inspector, superintendent, *US*); ~**raum** classroom; ~**reform** educational reconstruction; ~**reife** school age; ~**rektor** headmaster, school principal *(US)*, tack (school, *sl.*); ~**schießen** *(mil.)* target practice; ~**schiff** practice (training, cadet) ship; ~**schluß** end of school, breakup; ~**schwänzer** truant, wag *(Br., sl.)*; ~**sparen** school savings; ~**sparkasse** school savings bank; ~**speisung** school lunch (meals); ~**stiftung** foundation school, educational trust; ~**stunde** school hour, lesson; ~**tafel** blackboard; ~**tag** school day; **erster ~tag** Black Monday *(sl.)*; **letzter ~tag** final day of a school term; ~**tasche** schoolbag, satchel.
Schulter, kalte coldshoulder; **wattierte ~n** padded shoulders;
j. über die ~ ansehen to look down on s. o.; **j. auf die ~n heben** to hoist s. o. shoulder-high; **jem. auf die ~ klopfen** to pat (tap) s. o. on the back; **vertraulich auf die ~ klopfen** to backslap; **auf die leichte ~ nehmen** to take (treat) a thing lightly, to make light of; **auf jds. ~n ruhen** to rest on s. one's shoulders; **den Mantel auf beiden ~n tragen** to blow hot and cold; **kalte ~ zeigen** to snub, to give the cold shoulder;
~**kissen** *(Gepäckträger)* porter's knot.
Schulung training, schooling, instruction, *(Erziehung)* education, *(pol.)* indoctrination, *(Übung)* practice;
berufliche ~ professional (industrial) training; **betriebliche ~** in-plant (-service) training; **politische ~** political education; **praktische ~** on-the-job (job-instruction) training;
~ von Führungskräften training of management, executive (management) training; **~ von Nachwuchskräften** cold-storage training *(US)*.
Schulungs|dauer training period; ~**gruppe für Verkäufer** sales training group; ~**kurs** [training] course, training session, refresher course; ~**lager** training camp; ~**leiter** training coordinator (director); ~**programm** training program(me); ~**stätten** training facilities; ~**woche** one-week training course.
Schul|unterricht schoolteaching, school; **unentgeltlicher ~unterricht** free school; ~**veranstaltung** school exhibition; ~**verlag** school publisher; ~**versager** school dropout; ~**versäumnis** nonattendance at school; ~**vorstand** school committee *(US)*; ~**vorsteher** headmaster, school principal *(US)*; ~**vorsteherin** schooldame *(Br.)*; **ziemlich langer ~weg** some distance to the school; ~**weisheit** scholastic philosophy, scholasticism, book knowledge; ~**werdegang** school career; ~**wesen** educational system, education; **höheres ~wesen** post-primary education; **öffentliches ~wesen** public education; ~**wettkampf** scholastic competition; ~**wörterbuch** collegiate dictionary.
Schulze tungreve.
Schul|zeit school life, schooltime, termtime; ~**zeugnis** school certificate, report, record; ~**zimmer** classroom, schoolroom; **freier ~zugang** liberal system of public schools; ~**zwang** compulsory school attendance, compulsory education; **gemeiner ~zweckverband** consolidated school district.
schummeln to cheat, *(Klatsche benutzen)* to pony *(US)*.
Schund trash, muck, tripe *(sl.)*, punk *(sl.)*, rubbish, offal, garbage, refuse, *(Ausschußware)* low-class goods, trashy goods, catchpenny articles *(Br.)*;
~**blatt** gutter paper, hedge press; **~- und Schmutzgesetz** Harmful (Obscene) Publications Act *(Br.)*; ~**literatur** shoddy (blood-and-thunder, obscene) literature, pulp *(US)*; ~**roman** penny-dreadful *(Br.)*, shilling shocker *(Br.)*, dime novel *(US)*, potboiler *(US)*, pulp *(US coll.)*; ~**ware** trash, trashery, catchpenny articles *(Br.)*, slopmade goods, waste; ~**zeitschrift** gutter paper, pulp [magazine] *(US)*.
schunkeln, mit der Musik to sway with the music.
Schupo bobby *(Br.)*, cop *(US)*.
Schuppen shed, barn, hovel, cote, hut, shack *(US)*, *(Flugzeug)* hangar, *(Lagerschuppen)* storehouse, warehouse, *(Lokomotive)* engine house, round house *(US)*, *(Omnibus, Straßenbahn)* depot.
schüren to poke, to stir up, to rake;
absichtlich ~ to fan deliberately;
Aufstand ~ to work up a rebellion; **allgemeine Unzufriedenheit ~** to add fuel to the general discontent.
Schürf|anspruch placer claim; ~**betrieb** prospecting operations.
Schürfen prospecting.
schürfen to prospect, to win, to explore, to dig for, to costean;
nach Gold ~ to prospect for gold.
Schürfer prospector.
Schürf|ergebnisse versprechen, gute to prospect well; ~**erlaubnis** prospecting license; ~**feld** diggings; **zugewiesenes ~feld** location; ~**gesellschaft** prospecting party *(US)*; **~- und Abbaukonzession** exploration and mining lease; ~**recht** common of digging, prospect, royalty, drilling (mineral) rights, prospecting licence; **vorweggenommene ~rechte** claim jumping; ~**schacht** trial (test, *US*) pit; ~**stelle** prospect, location; ~**vertrag** prospecting contract; ~**vorhaben** prospecting activities.
Schürhaken poker, fire hook.
Schurke villain, rogue, scoundrel, scamp, rascal, bad man *(US sl.)*, hound, heel *(US sl.)*, *(Theater)* heavy;
abgefeimter ~ out-and-out rogue; **absoluter ~** absolute (unmitigated) scoundrel; **ausgemachter ~** accomplished villain; **gewissenloser ~** unconscionable rascal; **niederträchtiger ~** mean rascal; **skrupelloser ~** unscrupulous rascal;
sich als ~ entpuppen to appear in the light of a scoundrel.
Schurkenstreich devilment, roguery, rascality.
Schürzen|jäger dangler, skirt-chaser, ladykiller, a lady's man, wolf; ~**jäger sein** to be always after a petticoat; **an Mutters ~zipfel hängen** to be tied to one's mother's apron-strings.
Schuß shot, pop, *(Injektion)* shot *(sl.)*;
~ ins Blaue shot in the dark, wild (random) shot; **~ Ironie** touch of irony; **~ Munition** round of ammunition;
~ abgeben to shoot, to fire a shot; **~ ins Blaue abgeben** to shoot at rovers (random); **etw. in ~ bringen** to straighten out, to put in order; **~ Leichtsinn im Blut haben** to have a touch of recklessness in one's blood; **~ Negerblut haben** to have some Negro blood; **sein Auto gut im ~ halten** to keep one's car in good working order; **nicht zum ~ kommen** not to have a chance; **gut im ~ sein** to be going strong, to have one's hand in; **wieder im ~ sein** to be out and about (up to the mark) again; **keinen ~ Pulver wert sein** not to be worth powder and shot *(coll.)*;
~**bereich** covered area.
Schüssel dish;
hübsch angerichtete ~ well-prepared dish;
vor leeren ~n sitzen to live at hunger's door.
schusseln, bei etw. to scamp at s. th.
Schußlinie line of fire;
in jds. ~ geraten to draw blasts from s. o.
schußsicher bulletproof.
Schuß|waffe firearm; ~**waffengebrauch** use of firearms; ~**weite** firing range, carry; **in ~weite** in gunshot; **wirksame ~weite** effective range.
Schuster shoemaker, cobbler;
~ bleib bei deinem Leisten the cobbler must stick to his last; **~s Rappen reiten** to ride Shank's mare *(sl.)*.
Schute dump barge *(Br.)*, lighter.
Schutentransport lighterage.
Schutt rubbish, refuse, garbage *(US)*, tip, hard dirt, *(Trümmer)* debris, detritus, rubble;
feiner ~ crumble;
~ abladen to dump, to tip, to shoot rubbish; **in ~ und Asche legen** to lay in ruins; **in ~ und Asche liegen** to be reduced to ashes;

~abladen dumping, tipping; ~abladen verboten no rubbish may be dumped here, tipping prohibited; ~abladeplatz, ~abladestelle dumping ground (place), garbage (trash) dump *(US)*, shoot; ~aufräumung rubble clearance.

Schüttel | fahrt in einem Omnibus jerky ride in a bus; **~frost** chills and fevers.

schütteln, aus dem Ärmel to play it off the cuff *(coll.)*; **sich vor Ekel** ~ to shudder with disgust; **aus dem Handgelenk** ~ to do off one's own bat; **seinen Kopf** ~ to shake one's head.

schütten *(Regen)* to pour down;
in den Ausguß ~ to empty into the sink; **auf einen Haufen** ~ to heap into a pile.

Schüttgut bulk materials (goods, cargo), carloading *(US)*;
als ~ shipped in carloads *(US)*;
als ~ **verladen** to bulk;
~flotte bulk fleet; **~ladung, ~sendung** bulk cargo, carload (carlot) shipment *(US)*; **~tarif** bulk rate, carload rate *(US)*; **~transporter** bulk cargo carrier.

Schutt | halde dump [heap], spoil bank; **~haufen** dump heap (pile), rubbish heap; **Stadt in einen ~haufen verwandeln** to raze a town to the ground, *(Fliegerangriff)* to coventrize a town.

Schütt | ladung, ~massengut bulk cargo, carloading *(US)*.

Schutt | platz dump; **~ramme** bulldozer.

Schutz protection, defence, security, covering, *(Abwehr)* ward, *(Bollwerk)* bulwark, *(Fürsorge)* care, *(Geleit)* safeguard, escort, *(mil.)* cover, convoy, screen, *(Obdach)* shelter, harbo(u)rage, *(Obhut)* custody, safety;
im ~ der Dunkelheit under the veil of darkness; **unter dem** ~ under the lee; **unter dem ~ der UNO** under the umbrella of the UNO; **zum ~ der Gesundheit** for the protection of health; **konsularischer** ~ consular protection; **persönlicher** ~ bodyguard; **vorläufiger** ~ provisional protection;
~ **vor feindlichen Angriffen** defence against enemies; ~ **vor steuerlichen Belastungen** tax shelter; ~ **der internationalen Beziehungen** functional protection; ~ **gutgläubiger Dritter** protection of third parties acting in good faith; ~ **geistigen Eigentums** protection by copyright; ~ **vor inflationären Entwicklungen** inflation shelter; ~ **von Gebrauchsmusterrechten** protection of registered designs *(Br.)*; **gleicher ~ durch die Gesetze** equal protection of the law; ~ **kultureller Güter** protection of cultural goods; ~ **der Intimsphäre (von Persönlichkeitsrechten)** right of privacy; **gegenseitiger ~ von Kapitalanlagen** reciprocal protection of investments; ~ **von Minderheiten** protection of minorities; ~ **durch Patente** protection of inventions; ~ **gegen die Sonne** protection from the sun; ~ **gegen Umweltverschmutzung** environment protection; ~ **von Warenzeichen** protection of trademarks;
~ **der Gesetze anrufen** to claim the protection of the law; **sich jds.** ~ **anvertrauen** to place o. s. under s. one's protection; **sich in jds.** ~ **begeben** to take refuge with s. o.; **dem** ~ **der Öffentlichkeit vor Verbrechern dienen** to protect the public from criminals; **j. unter seinem ~ einführen** to patronize s. o.; ~ **gewähren** to provide with cover, *(Patent)* to afford protection; **einem ge-flohenen Gefangenen** ~ **gewähren** to shelter an escaped prisoner; **j. in ~ nehmen** to stand up for s. o., to take s. one's side; **Freund gegen Tadel in ~ nehmen** to shield a friend from censure; **unter dem** ~ **des Bürgermeisters stehen** to be under the patronage of the mayor; ~ **suchen** to seek refuge, to take shelter; ~ **zusichern** to promise safety;
~ablauf *(Patent)* expiration; **~anordnungen** protective directions, safety regulations; **~anstrich** *(mil.)* camouflage paint; **~anzug** overall; **~aufsicht** protective detention, *(Jugendlicher)* surveillance, *(Strafgefangener)* probation; **unter ~aufsicht stellen** to place on probation; **~befohlener** charge, custodee, protegé, *(Mündel)* ward; **~behandlung** remedial treatment; **~behauptung** self-serving declaration; **~bekleidung** protective clothing; **~bereich** *(mil.)* covered (restricted) area; **~bereich eines Patents** scope of a patent; **~bestimmung** protective clause.

Schutzbestimmungen safeguarding provisions;
vertragliche ~ contractual safeguards;
~ **für die Minderheit** minority safeguards;
von den konkursrechtlichen ~ Gebrauch machen to take the benefit of the bankruptcy laws; ~ **der Mieterschutzgesetzgebung in Anspruch nehmen** to claim the protection of the Rent Acts *(Br.)*.

Schutz | blatt *(Buchbinderei)* end paper; **~blech** mudguard, splashboard, splasher, guard plate; **~brief** letter of safe conduct, *(Satzung)* charter; **~brille** goggles, blinkers; **~bündnis** defensive alliance; **~- und Trutzbündnis** offensive and defensive alliance; **~dach** canopy, *(zum Unterstellen)* shelter; **vorspringendes ~dach** marquee; **~damm** dike; **~dauer** *(Buch)* term (duration) of copyright; **~dauerverlängerung** *(Patent)* extension of a patent.

Schütze marksman, shot, *(mil.)* rifleman.

schützen to protect, to defend, to guard, to safeguard, to save, to vindicate, *(abschirmen)* to shield, to screen, *(Kreditbrief)* to provide with due protection, *(sichern)* to secure;
Aussteller durch Ehreneintritt ~ to protect a signature; **gegen inflationäre Entwicklungen** ~ to guard against inflationary tendencies; **einheimische Erzeugnisse durch Erhebung von Schutzzöllen** ~ to protect domestic products from foreign competition by trade barriers; **sich gegen eine Gefahr** ~ to protect o. s. against a danger; **jds. Interessen** ~ to safeguard s. one's interests; **vor Nässe ~!** keep dry!; **patentrechtlich** ~ to patent; **Tratte** ~ to hono(u)r (protect) a bill; **gegen Unfälle** ~ to guard against accidents; **urheberrechtlich** ~ to copyright, to patent; **sich gegen einen Verlust** ~ to secure (safeguard) o. s. against a loss; **Vormarsch durch Artilleriefeuer** ~ to cover the advance by artillery fire; **etw. vor Wetterunbilden** ~ to protect s. th. from the weather;
gesetzlich ~ lassen to register, to trademark.

schützend protective.

Schutzengel guardian angel.

Schützengraben fire, trench, line;
im vordersten ~ in the firing line.

Schützengräben, vorderste tail of the trenches;
~ **besetzen** to mount the trenches.

Schutzersuchen wegen Bedrohung swearing the peace.

schutzfähig *(Patent)* patentable, *(Urheberrecht)* copyrightable;
~e Erfindung patentable invention; **~es Interesse** legitimate interest.

Schutzfähigkeit *(Buch)* copyrightability, *(Patent)* patentability.

Schutz | farbe protective paint; **~flagge** distinctive flag.

Schutzfrist term (duration, period) of copyright, copyright period, *(Patent)* term of a patent;
~ablauf *(Buch)* extinguishment of copyright.

Schutz | gatter barrier, *(Wehr)* floodgate; **~gebiet** protectorate, reserve, dependent territory, dependency; **~gebühr** nominal price, *(Verbrecher)* protection money; **~geländer** *(Brücke)* guardrail; **~geleit** safe conduct, escort, *(Schiff)* convoy; **~gerüst** rigger; **~gesetz** remedial statute; **~gesetz für Minderjährige** Infants Relief Act *(Br.)*; **~gitter** fireguard, fire screen, grid, *(Auto)* radiator grille; **~glas** safety glass; **~gürtel** protective belt; **~hafen** harbo(u)r of refuge; **~haft** detention under demand, protective detention (custody, *Br.*), preventive protection; **~heiliger** patron saint; **~helm** helmet, crash helmet; **~herr** patron, *(pol.)* protector, protecting prince *(Br.)*.

schutzherrlich protectoral.

Schutz | herrschaft protectorship; **~hoheit** suzerainty; **~hülle** *(Buch)* slipover cover, dust jacket, wrapper, *(Fahrzeug)* tarpaulin, *(eingemottetes Gerät)* cocoon; **~hütte** mountain hut, refuge, cold harbo(u)r; **~impfung** preventive vaccination (inoculation); **~insel** *(Verkehr)* street island; **~karton** carton, *(Bücher)* slipover cover; **~klausel** protective hedge (safeguarding) clause; **~klausel gegen Mitgliederverlust** *(Gewerkschaft)* union-security clause; **~kleidung** protective clothing.

Schützling protected person, protegé, charge, nursling, *(Mündel)* ward.

schutzlos unprotected, defenseless;
jem. ~ ausgeliefert sein to be at s. one's mercy; **dem Unwetter ~ ausgesetzt sein** to be left without shelter in a storm.

Schutz | losigkeit unprotectedness, nakedness; **~macht** protecting state (power), protector; **~mann** policeman, constable *(Br.)*, patrolman *(US)*, bobby *(Br.)*, cop *(US)*; **~mantel** mantle; **~mantel eines Patents** shield of patent.

Schutzmarke trademark, mark, brand, label;
eingetragene ~ registered trademark; **gewerbliche** ~ industry label; **überregionale ~n** national brands *(US)*.

Schutzmarken | gesetzgebung trademark legislation; **~inhaber** owner of a registered trademark, trademark owner, registrant; **~recht** trademark rights; **~verletzung** infringement of trademarks.

Schutz | maske face guard, protective mask; **~maßnahmen** safety precautions, protective umbrellas; **handelspolitische ~maßnahmen** protective trade measures; **~mauer** protecting wall, *(fig.)* rampart, bulwark, *(Ufer)* embankment; **~mittel** preventive; **~plane** tarpaulin; **~platte** *(Tür)* finger plate; **~polizei** police, constabulary; **~polizist** policeman, police officer, constable *(Br.)*, bobby *(Br.)*, patrolman *(US)*, cop *(US)*; **~raum** shelter; **~recht** protective right; **~rechte** *(Patent)* patent rights; **verwandtes ~recht** neighbo(u)ring right;

~**rechtsinhaber** registered propietor, *(Patent)* patent owner; ~**rechtsverletzung** infringement of registered design *(Br.)*, *(Patent)* infringement of letters patent; ~**schild** protective screen; **polizeilicher ~schild** riot shield; ~**staat** protecting state, protector; ~**stätte** sanctuary; ~**truppen** protective troops, constabulary; ~**umfang eines Patents** scope of a patent; ~**umschlag** book (protection) cover, dust cover (jacket); ~**verband** *(Gläubiger)* trade protection society; ~**vereinigung** protective association; ~**vereinigung von Wertpapierinhabern** investors' protection society; ~**vermerk für ungültig erklären** to cancel a copyright; ~**vorkehrungen** safety devices; ~**vorrichtung** safeguard, safety (protective) device, fender; ~**vorrichtungen für Maschinenanlagen** guarding of machinery; **nicht für genügend ~vorrichtungen für die Arbeiter sorgen** to endanger the safety of the workers; **vertragliche ~vorschriften** contractual safeguards; ~**wache** escort; ~**wall** *(mil.)* rampart, revetment, blast wall; ~**wirkung** *(Zolltarif)* protective aspect.

schutzwürdiges Interesse legitimate interest.

Schutz|zeichen trademark, brand; ~**zelt** shelter tent; ~**zoll** protective tariff, protective (protecting) duty, safeguarding duty *(Br.)*; ~**zollabkommen** protective agreement; ~**zollanhänger** prohibitionist, restrictionist *(Canada)*.

Schutzzölle, durch ~ abgesichert tariff-protected;
~ für einen Industriezweig festsetzen to safeguard an industry.

Schutzzollgesetzgebung prohibitory legislation.

Schutzzöllner prohibitionist, restrictionist *(Canada)*.

schutzzöllnerisch protectionist, protective;
~**e Maßnahmen** protectionist activities.

Schutzzoll|politik pro-tariff policy, protectionism, protective system, tariff reform *(Br.)*; ~**politiker** protectionist; ~**system** safeguarding of industry, protective (prohibitive) system, prohibitionism, protectionism, tariff protection.

schwach weak, feeble, languid, *(Batterie)* low, *(Börse)* poor, weak, slack, languid, feeble, infirm, *(Brücke)* slight, light, *(drucktechn.)* feint *(Br.)*, *(Farbe)* faint, distant, *(mäßig)* moderate;
~ bemannt *(Schiff)* shorthanded, undermanned; **~ besucht** poorly attended; **ganz ~** weak as water;
weiterhin ~ liegen *(Börse)* to continue to rule low; **~ sein** *(Börse)* to rule low, to be in a dull condition; **~ auf den Beinen sein** to be shaky on one's legs; **~ bemannt sein** to be undermanned (shorthanded); **~ besucht sein** to be poorly attended; **~ auf der Brust sein** *(fig.)* to be low in cash (hard up for money); **~ werden** *(Börse)* to develop weakness, to turn weak, to sag;
~**er Abglanz der einstigen Schönheit** faint traces of former beauty; ~**e Ähnlichkeit** remote resemblance; ~**es Argument** feeble argument; ~**er Beifall** slight applause; ~**er Besuch** poor attendance; ~**e Bevölkerung** sparse population; **nur ein ~es Echo finden** to meet with a faint response; ~**e Erinnerung** dim recollection; **auf ~en Füßen** *(Behauptung)* to be unfounded; **auf ~en Füßen stehen** *(Firma)* to be financially weak (strapped for capital); ~**es Geschäft** little doing, dull trade; ~**e Hoffnung** slender hope; ~**er Jahrgang** poor vintage; **tun, was in seinen ~en Kräften steht** to do one's little best; ~**er Kredit** small credit; ~**er alter Mann** decrepit old man; ~**e Majorität** bare majority; ~**er Markt** weak market; **auf Gewinnrealisationen hin ~er Markt** heavy market; ~**e Mittel** limited resources; ~**e Nachfrage** slack demand; ~**er Preis** weak price; ~**e Seite** blind side; ~**e Stelle** weak point, blind spot; **j. an seiner ~en Stelle treffen** to hit s. o. on his weak spot; ~**e Stunde** frailty of a (weak) moment; ~**er Trost** cold comfort; ~**e Vorstellung** faint idea, remote conception; ~**e Währung** soft (weak) currency.

Schwäche weakness, feebleness, faintness, *(Alter)* debility, *(Börse)* infirmity, weakness, dullness, languor, *(Unvollkommenheit)* imperfection;
menschliche ~n frailties of human nature, human foibles; **verborgene ~** feet of clay;
~ der Beweisführung weak point in the evidence; **~ den eigenen Kindern gegenüber** partiality for one's children; **~ des Pfundes** weakness in sterling; **~ eines Systems** drawback of a system; **jds. ~ ausnutzen** to exploit s. one's weakness; **jds. ~ erkennen** to put one's finger on s. one's weak spot; **~ für etw. haben** to have a weakness for s. th.; **~ für j. haben** to be partial to s. o., to have a soft spot for s. o.; **große ~ für j. haben** to be filled with passion for s. o.; **~ fürs Theater haben** to have a fancy for the theatre; **jds. ~ genau kennen** to know the length of s. one's foot; **zur ~ neigen** *(Börse)* to be likely to fall, to be inclined to weakness (to fall);
~**anfall bekommen** to come over faint; ~**gefühl** sinking feeling.

schwächen to weaken, to dilute, to cripple, to impair, to diminish.

schwächer|liegen *(Kurs)* to decrease, to be sagging; **~ werden** to waste away, *(Börse)* to fade, to decrease, to weaken, to develop weakness, to sag, *(Konjunktur)* to move backwards, to wane, to slow down, to falter, *(Licht)* to fade, to grow dim, *(Nachfrage)* to fall off, to recede, to slacken, *(Patient)* to lose in strength, to sink; **immer ~ werden** to be wasting away;
~**e Tendenz** weaker tendency.

Schwachkopf featherbrain.

schwächlich infirm, weakly, feeble, delicate.

Schwächling weakling, feebling, softy, sissy.

Schwachsinn weak-mindedness, feeblemindedness, dementia.

schwachsinnig feebleminded, soft-headed, weak-minded, imbecile, mentally deficient, half-witted, demented.

Schwachsinniger feeble-minded person, moron, idiot, fatuous person, imbecile, cretin, fool, natural;
von Geburt an ~ natural idiot.

Schwachstrom weak (minute) current.

Schwaden fume, vapo(u)r;
in ~ über dem Moor hängen *(Nebel)* to hang in patches over the moor.

Schwadron *(mil.)* squadron, troop.

Schwadroneur swashbuckler, braggart, gasbag *(coll.)*.

Schwadronieren swashbuckling, swash.

schwadronieren to boast, to talk big, to brag.

Schwager brother-in-law.

Schwägerin sister-in-law.

Schwägerschaft connection by marriage.

Schwägerschaftsgrad degree of affinity.

Schwall volley, burst, flow, volume, diction;
~ von Fragen barrage of questions; **~ von Worten** volley of words;
~ von Beschimpfungen ausstoßen to pour out volumes of abuse.

Schwamm sponge, *(Gebäude)* dry rot;
~ drüber! let bygones be bygones!

schwanen, nichts Gutes to have misgivings (forebodings).

Schwanengesang swan song.

schwanger pregnant, quick with child;
mit großen Plänen ~ gehen to fly high; **~ werden** to conceive, to become pregnant.

schwängern, Mädchen to get a girl in trouble.

Schwangerschaft pregnancy, utero-gestation;
~ unterbrechen to perform an abortion.

Schwangerschafts|abbruch induced abortion; ~**test** pregnancy test; **unerlaubte ~unterbrechung** illegal abortion.

Schwängerung insemination, impregnation.

Schwank prank, farce, light comedy.

Schwanken *(Gefühl)* oscillation, pendulation, *(im Gehen)* teeter, stagger, *(Vibration)* vibration, *(Zögern)* hesitation, quaver, unsteadiness, falter;
~ des Charakters vacillation of the character; **~ der Kurse** range, fluctuation of the market;
ins ~ geraten sein *(Vertrauen)* to have been shaken.

schwanken to vacillate, to sway, to waver, to totter, to yaw, to whiffle, to wobble, to back and fill *(US)*, *(Kurse)* to move irregularly, to range between, to fluctuate, to waver, *(Magnetnadel)* to oscillate, to flicker, *(Meinungen)* to be divided, *(pol.)* to trim, *(Preise)* to vary, to fluctuate, to change about, *(zögern)* to falter, to hesitate;
keinen Augenblick ~ not to hesitate for a moment; **in seiner Entscheidung ~** to be shilly-shally; **zwischen Furcht und Hoffnung ~** to vacillate between hope and fear; **unter seinen Füßen ~** *(Boden)* to rock beneath one's feet; **zwischen zwei Meinungen ~** to be in two minds, to waver (vibrate) between two opinions; **in seinen Neigungen ~** to be fickle with one's attentions; **saisonal ~** *(Preise)* to vary with the season; **über die Straße ~** to lurch across the street; **zwischen 10 und 20 ~** to range between 10 and 20.

schwankend wavering, dotty, unbalanced, unballasted, undecided, wayward, *(Börse)* irregular, fluctuating, variable, unsettled, unsteady, unstable, wide, *(unbeständig)* inconsistent fickle, vacillating;
in seinem Entschluß ~ werden to waver in one's resolution;
~**e Brücke** swaying bridge; **mit ~em Ertrag** with variable yield; ~**er Gang** faltering gait; ~**e Gesundheit** precarious state of health; **in ~er Haltung verkehren** to fluctuate; ~**e Kurse** fluctuating quotations (rates); ~**e Lohnabzüge** variable deductions; ~**e Normen** variable standards; ~**e Preise** fluctuating (varying) prices; ~**e Produktionsziffern** unsteady output; **wie ein ~es Rohr sein** to be like a reed bent by the wind; ~**er Wähler** floater.

Schwankung fluctuation, variance, range.

Schwankungen *(Radio)* drift;
konjunkturelle ~ market fluctuations, cyclical fluctuations in business; **saisonbedingte ~** seasonal variations (fluctuations); **zufallsbedingte ~** chance fluctuations;
~ der Beschäftigungsziffer ups and downs of employment; **~ am Effektenmarkt** fluctuations in the stock market; **~ im Exporthandel** export fluctuations; **~ des Geldmarktes (der Geldmarktsätze)** fluctuations in the money market; **~ im Handelsverkehr** leads and lags in the trade; **~ der Kurse** price fluctuations; **~ in der öffentlichen Meinung** variations in public opinion, swing of the pendulum; **~ auf dem Nachfragesektor** fluctuations in demand; **~ von zwei Pence auf das Pfund** variations of twopence in the pound; **häufige ~ in der Stimmung** frequent change of mood; **~ der Wechselkurse** fluctuations in the rate of exchange; **konjunkturbedingte ~ der Wirtschaft** industrial fluctuations;
~ auffangen to cushion fluctuations; **geringe ~ aufweisen** *(Kurs)* to move in a narrow range; **~ unterworfen sein** to undergo variations; **preislichen ~ unterworfen sein** to be subject to price fluctuations; **saisonellen ~ unterworfen sein** to vary with the season; **für Druckausgleich saisoneller ~ sorgen** to ease seasonal pressure.
Schwankungs|bereich range, limits of variation; **~breite** margin of fluctuation, fluctuation margin, spread; **~spitze** maximum fluctuation; **~werte** variable-price securities.
Schwanz tail;
kein ~ not a living soul;
mit hängendem ~ abziehen to slink away like a whipped cur *(coll.)*; **Pferd beim ~ aufzäumen** to put the cart before the horse; **~ der Prozession bilden** to tail the procession; **~ einziehen** to have one's tail between one's legs, to draw in one's horns, to come down a peg or two; **sich auf den ~ getreten fühlen** to feel offended; **jem. auf den ~ treten** to tread on s. one's corns.
Schwänze *(Börse)* corner, ring.
schwänzeln, um j. to toady (fawn) upon s. o.
Schwänzen truancy, cut.
schwänzen, Schule to play truant, to skip school, to wag *(Br., sl.)*, to cut *(sl.)*.
Schwanzlandung tail landing.
schwanzlastig tail-heavy.
Schwarm drove, flock, troop, swarm, cluster, crush *(sl.)*, *(Ideal)* heartthrob, dreamboat, crush, *(Verbandsflug)* flight;
~ von Ausflüglern drove of excursionists; **~ von Journalisten** tail of journalists.
schwärmen to swarm, to flock, to gush;
für etw. ~ to take a fancy to s. th., to be enthusiastic about (dream of) s. th., to go into raptures about s. th.; **für j. ~** to go for s. o. *(US coll.)*, to go for (be in raptures about) s. o.
Schwärmer daydreamer, *(Begeisterter)* fan, *(Eiferer)* zealot, fanatic, *(Feuerwerk)* cracker;
politischer ~ utopian[ist].
Schwärmerei slush.
schwärmerisch enthusiastic, visionary, swooning;
~ von etw. sprechen to go into raptures about s. th.
Schwarte skin, rind;
alte ~ *(Buch)* old tome; **dicke ~** fat volume;
arbeiten, daß einem die ~ kracht to work one's fingers to the bone.
Schwarz black;
das ~e *(Zielscheibe)* bull's-eye; **~er** black, black man *(US)*, negro;
jem. nicht das ~e unter den Nägeln gönnen to begrudge s. o. everything; **ins ~e treffen** to ring up the bell;
am ~en Brett anschlagen to put up on the notice board *(Br.)* (bulletin, *US*); **jem. den ~en Peter zuschieben** to pass the buck to s. o. *(US sl.)*.
schwarz *(ohne Marken erhältlich)* black;
~ auf weiß in black and white, in cold print;
sich ~ ärgern to fly into a blue rage; **etw. ~ auf weiß nach Hause tragen** to have s. th. down in black and white; **einem ~ vor den Augen werden** to have a blackout;
~es Bild von etw. malen to paint a gloomy picture; **~e Börse** black bourse, bucket shop; **~e Devisenkurse** black exchange rates; **~es Geld** black money; **~e Liste** black (stop) list, unfair list *(US)*; **Politik der ~en Listen betreiben** *(Gewerkschaft)* to use the blacking technique; **auf die ~e Liste setzen** to blacklist; **der Gewerkschaft nicht genehmen Betrieb auf die ~e Liste setzen** to black a shop; **auf der ~en Liste stehen** to be blacklisted; **~er Markt** black market; **~er Rand** black (thick) frame; **~es Schaf der Familie** black sheep of the family *(Br.)*; **~e Straßendecke** blacktop; **~e Tafel** blackboard; **~e Ware** smuggled goods.
Schwarzarbeit illicit (scab) work, *(während der Dienstzeit)* moonlighting *(US coll.)*.
schwarzarbeiten to do scab work, *(während der Dienstzeit)* to moonlight *(US coll.)*.
Schwarz|brauerei wildcat brewery; **~brenner** illicit distiller; **~brennerei** illicit distillery; **~fahren** *(Fahrer)* driving while disqualified.
schwarzfahren to jump a train *(US)*, to dodge the fare, *(Fahrer)* to drive without a licence, *(Vergnügungsfahrt)* to joy-ride.
Schwarz|fahrer deadhead, joy-rider *(coll.)*, *(Omnibusfahrer)* pirate *(Br., coll.)*; **~fahrt** joy ride (riding) *(coll.)*; **~geldkonto** black money account; **~handel** clandestine (underhand) trade, trafficking, black-market operations, *(in Devisen)* black bourse; **im ~handel** on the black market; **~handel treiben** to black-market; **~handelsgeschäft** black-market operation; **~händler** blacketeer, black marketeer, black-market operator, profiteer, clandestine (illicit) trader, interloper, trafficker, spiv *(Br.)*, *(Theaterkarten)* ticket speculator (scalper); **sich als ~händler betätigen** to operate the black market, to black-marketeer; **~händlertyp** barrow boy *(Br.)*; **~hörer** radio (wireless) pirate; **~kauf** black-market purchase; **~marktgeschäft** black-market operation, illicit transaction; **~markthandel** black marketing; **~marktpreis** black-market price; **~schlachtung** unlawful slaughtering; **~seher** alarmist, calamity howler *(US)*, *(Fernsehen)* television pirate; **~seher sein** to take a gloomy (pessimist) view; **~sender** nonlicensed (pirate) transmitter.
Schwärzung *(Foto)* density.
Schwarzverkauf illicit sales.
Schwarzweiß|anzeige black-and-white advertising; **doppelte ~anzeige** two-page black-and-white spread; **~seite** black-and-white advertising page; **~zeichnung** wash drawing.
Schwatz chat, chin-wag *(Br., coll.)*;
~bude talking shop.
Schwatzen chat, visit *(coll.)*.
schwatzen to chat, to patter, to prate, to visit *(US coll.)*, to spiel *(US sl.)*, to wag the chin *(Br., coll)*;
dummes Zeug ~ to talk rubbish (rot, *sl.*); **pausenlos ~** to talk nineteen to the dozen, to put at *(US local)*.
Schwätzer[in] tattle, pratter, chatterbox, windbag, gasbag *(coll.)*, *(Aufschneider)* braggart, bouncer *(Br., coll)*, blow *(US sl.)*.
Schwatzveranstaltung talkfest *(US sl.)*.
Schwebe abeyance, poise, suspense, dependence;
in der ~ in the balance (air), trembling in the balance, abeyant, in abeyance, in dependence, pendent;
sich in der ~ befinden to hang at poise; **in der ~ bleiben** to be left in abeyance; **in der ~ lassen** to leave hanging, to hold in suspense, to leave in abeyance; **Frage in der ~ lassen** to let a question stand over; **in der ~ sein** to be (hang) in the balance, to be (hang) in suspense, to depend, to lie at issue, to tremble, to pend, to be pendent;
~bahn aerial (suspension) railway; **~bühne** suspended platform.
Schweben *(Rechtshängigkeit)* pendency;
während des ~s des Prozesses pendente lite; **während des ~s der Verhandlungen** pending negotiations.
schweben to float, to drift along, to hang, to pend, to depend, to be pending, *(Ballon)* to float, *(Hubschrauber)* to hover, *(Prozeß)* to float, *(unentschieden sein)* to be in abeyance, *(Wolken)* to hang;
in tausend Ängsten ~ to be in a blue funk; **dauernd ~** to impend; **zwischen Furcht und Hoffnung ~** to waver between hope and fear; **in tödlicher Gefahr ~** to be in mortal danger; **in Illusionen ~** to harbo(u)r illusions; **in Lebensgefahr ~** to be in jeopardy; **in größten Nöten ~** to get hot under the collar; **in höheren Regionen ~** to live in the clouds; **lange Zeit in Ungewißheit ~** to be held in suspense for a long time; **einem auf der Zunge ~** to be on the tip of one's tongue.
schwebend pending, in suspense (abeyance), *(nicht geregelt)* unadjusted, unsettled, *(gesetzliche Regelung)* in abeyance, abeyant, *(unfundiert)* floating, unfunded;
~e Anmeldung *(Patent)* pending application; **~es Engagement** forward deal not yet completed; **~er Prozeß** pending action (lawsuit, *US*); **~e Schuld** floating (running, pending, unfunded, *Br.*) debt, floating charge *(Br.)*; **~e Transaktionen** pending transactions; **~e Verhandlungen** pending negotiations; **~e Verrechnung** suspense items.
Schwebe|schiff hovercraft; **~zeit** transitional period, period of transition, *(Prozeß)* pendency; **~zustand** abeyance, dependence.

Schwede, alter old chap (fruit, *Br., sl.*).
Schweige|geld hush (slush, *US*) money, palm oil (grease) *(sl.)*; **jem. 100 Pfund ~geld zahlen** to pay s. o. a hundred pounds to hold his tongue; **~marsch** silent march.
Schweigen silence, hush, mum;
eisiges ~ stony silence; **nachdenkliches ~** pondering silence; **spannungsgeladenes ~** electric silence; **unheilvolles ~** ominous silence;
~ bedeutet Zustimmung silence gives consent;
dem ~ anheimfallen to lapse into silence; **~ bewahren** to observe silence, to hold one's peace, to keep mum; **diskretes ~ bewahren** to maintain a discreet silence; **j. zum ~ bringen** to snub (reduce) s. o. into silence; **feindliche Batterien zum ~ bringen** to silence the batteries of the enemy; **sich in ~ hüllen** to wrap o. s. in silence; **Angelegenheit mit ~ übergehen** to pass over an affair with silence; **j. zum ~ verpflichten** to tie s. one's tongue; **jds. ~ als Ablehnung werten** to interpret s. one's silence as refusal.
schweigen to be silent, to keep one's tongue (mum);
darüber ~ *(Gesetz)* to be silent; **wie ein Grab ~** to be as silent as the grave; **zu allen Vorwürfen ~** to make no reply to all the reproaches.
schweigende Mehrheit silent majority.
Schweige|pflicht, berufliche professional (business) discretion, professional secrecy; **~system** *(Strafhaft)* silent system.
Schwein pig, *(fig.)* lewd fellow;
armes ~ poor soul;
~ haben to have the devil's own luck.
Schweine|fleisch pork; **~geld** hoard (mint) of money; **~geld verdienen** to be simply coining money; **~hund** son of a bitch, bastard, blighter *(Br., sl.)*, swine.
Schweinerei awful mess, *(Gemeinheit)* dirty trick, *(Sauerei)* crying shame;
~en erzählen to tell smutty jokes.
Schweinezucht pig farm, pig breeding, piggery.
Schweiß, in ~ gebadet all of a sweat;
im ~e seines Angesichts arbeiten to work in the sweat of one's brow; **in ~ geraten** to break out in perspiration; **in ~ gebadet sein** to be in a muck of a sweat *(fam.)*.
schweißen to weld.
Schweißerei welding shop.
Schweißstahl wrought steel.
schwelen *(pol.)* to smoulder.
schwelgen to regale, to feast, to banquet;
in Erinnerungen ~ to relish one's memories; **in Klatschgeschichten ~** to revel in gossip; **im Luxus ~** to luxuriate in opulence, to live on the fat of the land.
Schwelgerei gluttony, indulgence.
schwelgerisch luxurious, voluptuous.
Schwelle threshold, flood, confine;
an der ~ zum Mannesalter on the threshold of manhood; **an der ~ des Todes** on the confines (at the point) of death;
kritische ~ *(Zoll)* peril point *(US)*;
jds. ~ nicht betreten not to darken s. one's door; **an der ~ des Todes stehen** to be at death's door; **j. von der ~ weisen** to turn s. o. from the door.
schwellen *(Fluß)* to swell, to rise.
Schwellenpreis *(Agrarmarkt, EG)* threshold price.
Schwemmdelta fan delta.
Schwemme watering place, *(Fülle)* glut, overabundance, oversupply, *(Geldmarkt)* glut of money.
schwemmen, an Land to wash ashore.
Schwemmland alluvial [soil], bottom lands *(US)*.
Schwengel *(Pumpe)* lever, handle.
Schwenk *(Kamera)* pan shot.
schwenken to wave, *(Fahne)* to flourish, *(Kamera)* to pan;
ins andere Lager ~ to cross the line, to change sides.
Schwenkflügelflugzeug swing-wing aircraft.
Schwenkung turn, swing, *(Meinungswechsel)* about-face, *(mil.)* traverse, *(pol.)* shunt, changing sides.
schwer heavy, *(drückend)* onerous, oppressive, burdensome, *(gewichtig)* weighty, *(Prüfung)* hard;
~ zu befriedigen hard to please; **~ von Begriff** slow in the uptake; **~ beladen** heavily laden (loaded); **~ bewaffnet** heavy armed; **~ wie Blei** heavy as lead; **~ krank** dangerously ill; **~ verkäuflich** hard to sell, slow of sale, not moving; **~ zugänglich** difficult of access;
~ arbeiten to work hard, to be hard at it; **j. ~ beleidigen** to insult s. o. gravely; **j. ~ bestrafen** to punish s. o. severely; **es ~ haben** to have a sticky job; **sich ~ verkaufen lassen** to go off heavily, to be hard to sell (a drug on the market); **es jem. ~ machen** to put s. o. to it; **jem. ~ zu schaffen machen** to give s. o. a lot of trouble; **etw. ~ büßen müssen** to have to pay dearly for s. th.; **~ verdienen** to rack up big sales, to make huge profits, *(Anwalt)* to pocket large fees; **sich sein Brot ~ verdienen** to work hard for one's living;
~es Amt burdensome office; **~es Amt übernehmen** to assume onerous duties; **~e Artillerie** heavy artillery (armament); **~e Aufgabe** difficult task; **~e Belastungsprobe** severe test; **~er Beruf** hard job; **~er Boden** heavy soil; **~er Diebstahl** grand larceny; **~e Fahrlässigkeit** gross negligence; **~er Fehler** serious mistake; **~ verdientes Geld** hard-earned money; **~es Geld kosten** to cost a lot (pot) of money; **~es Geld verdienen** to make money hand over fist, to earn big money, to line one's pockets; **~en Herzens** reluctantly; **~er Junge** hard case, thug; **~e Krankheit** severe illness; **~e Last** heavy load; **~e Last tragen** to bear a burden; **~ verdauliche Lektüre darstellen** to be heavy (hard) reading; **~ zu behandelnder Mensch sein** to be a difficult man to get on with; **~e Papiere** *(Börse)* blue chips *(US)*; **~e Pflichten** onerous duties; **~en Schaden anrichten** to cause serious damage; **~e Strafe** severe punishment; **~es Stück Arbeit** difficult task; **~e Verantwortung** heavy responsibility; **~e Verletzung** serious injury; **~er Verlust** heavy loss; **~e Verluste haben** to lose heavily; **~ zu erfüllende Verpflichtung** onerous obligation; **~er Wein** full-bodied wine; **~e Zeiten** hard times.
Schwerarbeit hard (heavy) work.
schwerbeschädigt badly injured, seriously disabled.
Schwerbeschädigteneigenschaft disablement.
Schwerbeschädigter disabled man, invalid.
Schwere heaviness, weightiness, *(Strafe)* severity;
ganze ~ der Verantwortung full weight of responsibility; **~ eines Vergehens** gravity of an offence.
schwerelos weightless.
Schwerelosigkeit, sich an die ~ in einem Raumschiff gewöhnen to become accustomed to weightlessness in a spacecraft.
Schwerenöter ladies' man, lady-killer, rogue.
schwerer superior in weight;
durch Beimischungen ~ machen to weight, to increase by adding inferior quantities.
schwererziehbares Kind problem child.
schwerfällig ponderous, clumsy, awkward, flatfooted *(Br.)*, *(geistig)* dense, slow.
Schwerfälligkeit ponderosity, awkwardness.
Schwer|gewicht preponderance, emphasis; **~gewicht der Nachfrageentwicklung** main force of demand; **~gut** heavy lift, weight (heavy) goods; **~gutaufschlag** heavy-lift charge; **~gutladefähigkeit** deadweight capacity.
schwerhörig|sein to be hard of hearing; **sich ~ stellen** to feign deafness.
Schwer|industrie heavy industries; **Entstehung der ~industrie begünstigen** to foster the growth of heavy industries; **~industrieller** heavy industrialist; **~kraft** force of gravity, gravitation; **~kraftfeld** gravitational field; **~krankenliste** danger list; **~kriegsbeschädigter** war-disabled man, invalid; **~lastkran** heavy-lift crane, goliath crane; **~maschinenindustrie** heavy engineering industry; **~metall** heavy metal; **~mut** melancholy, the blues *(coll.)*; **in ~mut verfallen** to be cast into gloom.
schwermütig sein to be melancholic, to have the blues *(coll.)*.
Schweröl heavy oil.
Schwerpunkt keypoint, crucial (focal) point, focus, *(Radar)* center *(US)* (centre, *Br.*) target;
~ einer Beweisführung strong point of an argument; **~ der Ereignisse** focal point of events; **~ der Interessen** focus of attention; **~ der Nachfrage** chief demands;
~ bei etw. ansetzen to concentrate one's efforts on s. th.;
~bildung concentration of efforts; **~industrie** key industry; **~politik** mainstream policy; **~programm** priority program(me); **~streik** pinpoint strike; **~verlagerung** *(Betrieb)* diversification step; **~werbung** zone plan.
schwerreich tinny *(Br., sl.)*.
Schwerstreitkräfte retaliatory forces.
Schwert|des Damokles sword of Damocles;
zum ~ greifen to draw one's sword; **mit Feuer und ~ zerstören** to destroy by fire and sword.
Schwer|transporter heavy commercial vehicle, heavy-duty truck; **~verbrecher** felon; **~verletzter** seriously injured person.
schwerverständlich hard to understand, obscure.
Schwerwasser heavy water.
schwerwiegend serious, grave;
~e Bedenken serious objections; **~e Nachrichten** grave news.

Schwester *(Krankenhaus)* nurse, sister;
diensthabende ~ nurse on duty; **leibliche** ~ full sister;
~**anstalt** affiliated institution; ~**firma,** ~**gesellschaft** related (associated, affiliated, sister) company (corporation); ~**schiff** sister ship; ~**unternehmen** associated house.
Schwestern|beruf ergreifen to take up nursing as a career; ~**verband** sister (nurses') union.
Schwieger|mutter mother-in-law; **zukünftiger** ~**sohn** prospective son-in-law; ~**tochter** daughter-in-law; ~**vater** father-in-law.
schwierig difficult, hard, complex, tough;
alles noch ~**er machen** to complicate matters even more; ~**es Alter** awkward age; ~**e Aufgabe** tough job; ~**e Frage** knotty (puzzling, sixty-four dollar, *US*) question, poser; ~**es Gelände** broken country; ~**es Kind** problem child; ~**e Lage** predicament, fix, awkward situation; **sich in einer** ~**en Lage wiederfinden** to be placed in difficult circumstances; ~**es Problem** knotty (thorny) problem; ~**e Prüfung** stiff examination; **sich im** ~**sten Stadium befinden** to be at their most delicate; ~**es Unternehmen** delicate enterprise; ~**e Verhältnisse** trying circumstances; ~**e Verhandlungen** complicated negotiations.
Schwierigkeit difficulty, complexity, complicacy, hurdle, nut.
Schwierigkeiten difficulties, quandaries, woes, rub;
in ~ under hatches, reduced to great straits, on a lee shore, in the creek *(sl.)*, in the nine holes *(US)*; **mit großen** ~ **verbunden** attended with great difficulties; **um** ~ **zu vermeiden** with a view to saving trouble;
plötzlich auftretende ~ facer; **zu erwartende** ~ trouble in store; **finanzielle** ~ financial difficulties (pressure, straits), pecuniary difficulties; **fiskalische** ~ fiscal difficulties; **geringfügige** ~ petty troubles; **offensichtliche** ~ visible difficulties; **zeitweilige** ~ temporarily difficult situation;
sich in finanziellen ~ **befinden** to be in low (financial) straits; **jds. finanzielle** ~ **weitgehend beheben** to go far towards overcoming s. one's financial troubles; **plötzlich** ~ **bekommen** to run up against difficulties; ~ **bei der Absatzplanung bekommen** to run into marketing headaches; ~ **bereiten** to present difficulties, to make trouble; **jem.** ~ **bereiten** to cause s. o. trouble; **in** ~ **bringen** to straiten, to mire; **j. in** ~ **bringen** to put s. o. in a hole *(coll.)*; **in politische** ~ **bringen** to plunge into political embarrassment; **sich selbst in** ~ **bringen** to put o. s. out of the way; **sich** ~ **einbrocken** to involve o. s. in troubles; ~ **entgehen** to land like a cat; **unendlichen** ~ **gegenüberstehen** to be faced with a host of difficulties; **in** ~ **geraten** to encounter (fall into) difficulties, to get (run) into trouble (a fix), to swap; ~ **haben** to be in a bad way, to have a bad time with *(coll.)*; **erhebliche** ~ **haben** to be in serious trouble; **nicht enden wollende** ~ **haben** to have trouble without end; **mit** ~ **zu rechnen haben** to see rocks ahead; **jem. aus** ~ **heraushelfen, jem. über** ~ **hinweghelfen** to pull s. o. through, to see s. o. through difficulties; **mit** ~ **kämpfen** to grapple with a difficulty; **mehr und mehr in** ~ **kommen** to grow more beleaguered; ~ **machen** to make trouble, to kick up a fuss; **j.** ~ **machen** to put obstacles in s. one's way; **künstliche** ~ **machen** to create imaginary difficulties; ~ **nicht ernst nehmen** to laugh at difficulties; **in** ~ **sein** to have one's back to the wall, to be bunkered; **in finanzielle** ~ **geraten sein** to be pinched for money; **auf** ~ **stoßen** to meet with (experience) difficulties; ~ **überbrücken** to bridge over a difficulty; **in** ~ **verwickeln** to dip to *(coll.)*, to cause trouble; **nur unter** ~ **vorankommen** to make heavy weather; ~ **voraussehen** to foresee trouble; **mit unvorhergesehenen** ~ **fertig werden** to deal with unforeseen difficulties; **mit den wachsenden** ~ **fertig werden** to tackle the mounting troubles; **seiner** ~ **Herr werden** to tide over one's difficulties; **sich erhebliche** ~ **zuziehen** to land o. s. in great difficulties.
Schwimm|bad swimming bath; **wärmebindende** ~**badabdeckung** heat-retaining cover for swimming pools; ~**bagger** dredge; ~**becken** swimming pool; ~**dock** floating (wet, hydraulic) dock.
schwimmen to swim, *(Ware)* to float;
im Gelde ~ to be rolling in cash (money); **in jds. Kielwasser** ~ to follow in the wake of s. o.; **in einem Meer von Seeligkeit** ~ to swing from chandeliers; **obenauf** ~ to be at the top of the ladder; **bei einer Prüfung** ~ to be at sea in an examination; **gegen den Strom** ~ *(fig.)* to swim against the tide; **im Überfluß** ~ to live in the lap of luxury.
schwimmend afloat, above water, *(Börse)* floating;
sich ~ **in Sicherheit bringen** to swim to safety;
~**e Ladung** cargo afloat; ~**es Material** *(Börse)* floating supply; ~**es Strandgut** waveson *(Br.)*, flotsam; ~**e Waren** goods afloat, venture.
Schwimmer *(Flugzeug)* float;
~**flugzeug** floatplane; ~**gestell** float; ~**nadel** *(Vergaser)* float needle.
schwimmfähig floatable.
Schwimm|fahrzeug amphibian vehicle; ~**flugzeug** float plane, hydroplane, seaplane; ~**gürtel** life belt; ~**halle** indoor pool; ~**kran** floating crane; ~**lastkraftwagen** amphibian truck; ~**weste** life (air) jacket, life preserver *(US)*.
Schwindel swindle, quackery, imposture, farce, sharp business, bubble *(Br., sl.)*, spoof *(Br., sl.)*, graft *(US)*, gold brick *(US)*, humbug, sham, rouser, eyewash, shuffle, phony, mace *(sl.)*, have *(Br., sl.)*, cross *(sl.)*;
~**aktien an der Börse unterbringen** to push shares; ~**auktion** mock auction; ~**bank** wildcat (bogus) bank.
Schwindelei, kleine fib, fiddle *(US sl.)*; **die übliche** ~ the old army game *(sl.)*.
Schwindel|firma bogus (bubble, long, *Br.*, wildcat, *US*) firm; ~**geschäft** swindle, fraudulent (bogus) transactions, monkey business; ~**gesellschaft** bubble *(Br.)* (bogus [stock], wildcat) company.
schwindelhaft bogus, wildcat, crooked;
~**e Gründung** bubble company *(Br.)*, bogus concern.
Schwindel|makler bucket shop, [bucket] swindler, bucketeer *(US)*; ~**methode** confidence trick (game); ~**unternehmen** fraudulent device, bubble scheme *(Br.)*, bubble *(Br., sl.)*, wildcat enterprise *(US)*, swindling (bogus, long, *Br.*) firm.
Schwinden shrinkage, dwindling, *(Ton)* fading;
~ **der geistigen Kräfte** decay of intellectual power.
schwinden *(Einfluß)* to wane, *(Flüssigkeit)* to leak, *(Kaufkraft)* to decrease, to diminish, *(Ton)* to fade, *(Vorräte)* to dwindle [away], to diminish, to shrink.
schwindend dwindling, shrinking, diminishing, decreasing, wasting, *(Lautstärke)* fading;
~**e Vorräte** shrinkage of stocks.
Schwindler imposter, swindler, sharper, gammoner *(coll.)*, wangler, crook, cheater, deceiver, trickster, humbugger, doer *(sl.)*, con man *(US)*, grafter *(US)*;
gewerbsmäßiger ~ *(Börse)* confidence man *(US)*;
erstklassigen ~ **abgeben** to make a hell of a con man *(US)*; **j. als** ~ **bloßstellen** to denounce s. o. as an imposter.
schwindlig dizzy, giddy;
leicht ~ **werden** not to have a head for heights.
schwingen to swing, to oscillate, to sway;
sich auf sein Fahrrad ~ to get on one's bike; **große Klappe** ~ to bray, to talk big, to blow *(US)*; **Knüppel** ~ to brandish a club; **Pantoffel** ~ to rule the roost; **Rede** ~ to deliver (bounce off, *US*) a speech; **Tanzbein** ~ to shake a leg; **unter den Tritten der marschierenden Soldaten** ~ *(Brücke)* to quiver under the marching soldiers.
Schwingung swing, oscillation, *(Brücke)* vibration;
durch jeden Lastwagen in ~**en versetzt werden** to vibrate whenever a heavy lorry passes.
Schwips jag, load, kick *(US sl.)*;
~ **haben** to be tipsy (tight, half-seas over).
schwirren, jem. durch den Kopf to be going round in s. one's head;
durch die Stadt ~ *(Gerüchte)* to be rife with rumo(u)rs.
schwitzen, bei der Arbeit to sweat while working; **Blut und Wasser** ~ to sweat blood;
j. ~ **lassen** to keep s. o. on tenterhooks, to sweat s. o. *(sl.)*.
Schwof hap *(sl.)*.
schwören to swear, to take an oath;
auf die Bibel ~ to swear on the Bible, to kiss the book; **falsch** ~ to swear falsely, to forswear; **jem. Rache** ~ to swear vengeance against s. o.; **Stein und Bein** ~ to swear by all that's holy;
j. ~ **lassen** to put s. o. on his oath.
schwül sultry, oppressively warm, sticky.
Schwüle sultriness, oppressive weather, mugginess.
Schwulitäten jam, hot water, scrape, mess, fix, trouble;
j. in ~ **bringen** to get s. o. into a fix; **in** ~ **sein** to be in a stew.
schwülstig bombastic, pompous, fustian, florid;
~ **sprechen** to flourish, to be flowery;
~**e Sprache** high-falutin (pompous) language.
Schwülstigkeit inflation, pomposity.
schwummerig giddy, dizzy.
Schwund shrinkage, reduction, wearing away, *(Gewicht)* loss in weight, ullage, *(Lager)* inventory shrinkage, *(durch Lecken)* leakage, *(Radio)* fading, fade-out;
natürlicher ~ normal (natural) loss;
~ **des Eigenkapitals** dwindling assets; ~ **durch Einsickern** soakage;
~ **haben** to fade;

~**ausgleich** *(Radio)* fading control, antifading; **selbsttätiger ~ausgleich** automatic volume control; ~**erscheinung** fading effect; ~**geld** scalage, scrip money *(US)*.
schwundmindernde Antenne fading-reducing aerial.
Schwund|satz rate of waste; ~**vergütung** leakage; ~**zone** *(Radio)* fading area; ~**zulage** allowance for shrinkage.
Schwung pep, go, stimulus, push, zip, punch, drive, go-ahead, impetus, impulse, *(Anzahl)* batch, bunch, *(Tempo)* hustle, demon *(Br., coll.)*;
in vollem ~ at full tear; **ohne** ~ lackadaisical, pedestrian;
~ **neuer Kleider** a batch of new clothes; ~ **der Phantasie** flight of fancy (imagination);
geringen ~ **aufweisen** to show little zip; **etw. in** ~ **bringen** *(fig.)* to make a thing go, to get going (in full swing); **j. auf** ~ **bringen** to put some pep into s. o., to get s. o. going; **keinen** ~ **haben** to have no sting in it, *(Buch)* to lack pep; **j. in** ~ **halten** to make s. o. tick; **in** ~ **kommen** to get up steam (into one's stride), *(Verhandlungen)* to get under way; **langsam in** ~ **kommen** to be getting in full swing; **mit** ~ **darauf losgehen** to go to it; **mit** ~ **in Angriff nehmen** to jump to it *(sl.)*; ~ **hinter seine Arbeit setzen** to put spirit into one's work; **einer Sache neuen** ~ **verleihen** to give fresh impetus to s. th.; **Rede mit großem** ~ **vortragen** to deliver a speech with great vivacity.
schwunghaft prosperous, thriving, flourishing, booming;
~**er Handel** roaring (flourishing) trade.
schwunglos inanimate, listless, lifeless, without drive (pep, zip).
schwungvoll flowing, full of drive (pep, life), lively, punchy, snappy, humming;
~**e Rede** vivacious speech; ~**e Werbung** dynamic advertising.
Schwur oath;
vorsätzlich falscher ~ perjury;
~ **leisten** to swear (take) an oath;
~**gericht** court of assizes, assize trial, jury; **vor ein ~gericht gehörig** in pais.
Schwurgerichts|sache indictable offence *(Br.)*; ~**urteil** finding of the jury; ~**verfahren** jury trial, trial by jury (the country); **ergebnisloses ~verfahren** mistrial *(US)*; ~**verhandlung beantragen** to apply for one's case to be heard by a jury.
Schwurhand uplifted hand.
See sea, ocean;
auf ~ at sea, ashore; **auf hoher** ~ on the open (high) seas, on the main; **auf offener** ~ in mid-ocean; **zur** ~ on the water;
gefährliche ~ nasty sea; **grobe** ~ rough sea; **hohe** ~ high sea; **kurze** ~ choppy sea; **offene** ~ open [sea], main sea; **schwere** ~ heavy sea; **spiegelglatte** ~ smooth sea;
an die ~ **gehen** to go to the seaside (seashore, *US*); **offene** ~ **gewinnen** to gain the open sea; **in** ~ **stechen** to put out (launch out into) sea, to bear to (make for the open) sea, to set sail; **in schwerer** ~ **treiben** to make heavy weather; **zur** ~ **befördert werden** to sail;
~**amt** maritime (naval) court (commission, *US*), Trinity House *(Br.)*; ~**assekurant** maritime insurer; ~**assekuranz** marine (maritime) insurance; ~**bad** seaside resort, watering place *(Br.)*; ~**bäderschiff** seaside excursion vessel; **alter ~bär** old salt; ~**beben** seaquake, waterquake; ~**beförderung** sea transport, ocean transportation *(US)*; ~**beförderungsvertrag** marine contract.
seebeschädigt averaged.
See|blockade naval (long-distance) blockade; ~**chronometer** watch chronometer.
seefahrend seafaring, maritime.
See|fahrer seafarer, navigator, sailor, mariner; ~**fahrervolk** maritime nation; ~**fahrt** navigation, shipping, seafaring, *(Seereise)* ocean voyage.
Seefahrts|angelegenheit nautical matter; ~**buch** discharge book; ~**schule** merchant marine (nautical) school.
seefertig ready for sea.
seefest seaworthy;
~ **sein** to be a good sailor; ~ **werden** to get one's sea legs.
See|feuer sea light; ~**fischerei** maritime (deep-sea) fishing; ~**flughafen** seadrome, seaplane base; ~**flugzeug** seaplane; ~**flugzeug an Bord nehmen** to hoist in a seaplane.
Seefracht ocean (maritime) freight, cargo, freight *(Br.)*;
~ **und Landfracht** freight and carriage *(Br.)*;
~ **oder Landfracht bis A bezahlt** freight or carriage paid to A; ~**brief** [ocean] bill of lading; ~**fahrer** water (marine) carrier, carrier by sea; ~**führer** marine carrier; ~**geschäft** affreightment, carriage of goods by sea; ~**gut** sea cargo; ~**handel** floating (ocean, *US*) trade; ~**satz** ocean freight (floating) rate; ~**vertrag** voyage charterparty, maritime contract of affreightment.
See|funk marine radio; ~**funkempfänger** marine band receiver; ~**funkwelle** marine band; ~**gang** heave of the sea, seaway, swell; **hoher ~gang** heavy sea; ~**gebiet** waters; ~**gebiet laufend überwachen** to patrol the line; ~**gebräuche** uses and customs of the sea; ~**gefahr** dangers (risks and perils, hazards) of the sea, risk of navigation, sea risks, marine perils (risk, adventure); ~**gefecht** sea fight, naval action (engagements); ~**geleitschein** navy certificate; ~**gericht** naval (marine, admiralty) court, admiralty; ~**gerichtsbarkeit** maritime (Admiralty, *US*) jurisdiction.
seegestützt *(mil.)* sea-based.
See|gewohnheiten uses and customs of the sea; ~**hafen** seaport, maritime harbo(u)r (port); **an die Flußmündung vorgelegter ~hafen** outport; ~**hafenbahnhof** harbo(u)r station; ~**handel** seaborne (maritime, marine) trade, maritime commerce, merchant service (shipping, *Br.*), shipping business.
Seehandels|gesellschaft shipping company; ~**güter** seaborne goods; ~**recht** sea laws, shipping law.
See|handlung shipping house; ~**herrschaft** naval supremacy, ownership (control) of the sea, maritime reign; ~**herrschaft behalten** to keep the sea; ~**hoheitsgebiet** maritime sovereignty, territorial waters; ~**kabel** submarine (transatlantic) cable; ~**kadett** naval cadet; ~**kanal** interoceanic canal; ~**karte** marine (hydrographic) map, [ocean, nautical] chart.
seeklar ready for sea.
See|klima maritime climate; ~**konnossement** ocean (marine) bill of lading.
seekrank|sein to feed the fishes *(sl.)*; ~ **werden** to be liable to sea sickness, to be overcome with nausea; **leicht** ~ **werden** to be a bad sailor.
See|kriegsschule naval college; ~**küste** sea-shore.
Seele soul, heart;
aus tiefster ~ from the bottom of one's heart;
gequälte ~ soul in torment; **treue** ~ trump; **verwandte ~n** kindred natures;
zwei ~n und ein Gedanke two minds with but a single thought; ~ **eines Geschäfts** soul of an enterprise;
jem. mit Leib und ~ **gehören** to belong to s. o. with one's whole heart; **sich einer Sache mit Leib und** ~ **verschrieben haben** to have put one's heart and soul in a work; **jem. auf der** ~ **herumtrampeln** to tread (trample) on s. one's corns (feelings); **jem. schwer auf der** ~ **liegen** to weigh heavily (prey) on s. one's mind; **sich etw. von der** ~ **reden** to make a clean breast of it, to unburden one's heart; **ein Herz und eine** ~ **sein** to be bosom friends; ~ **von einem Menschen sein** to be a perfect dear; ~ **eines Unternehmens sein** to be the prime mover of an enterprise; **jem. aus tiefster** ~ **zuwider sein** to utterly detest s. o.; **in der** ~ **weh tun** to hurt to the quick.
Seelen|arzt psychologist, physician of the soul; **jds. ~frieden stören** to disturb s. one's peace of mind; ~**größe** nobility (dignity) of soul; ~**konflikt** mental conflict; ~**massage** tug at s. one's heart strings, *(Konjunkturpolitik)* moral suasion, ear bashing; ~**ruhe** ease (peace) of mind; **in aller ~ruhe** as cool as a cucumber; ~**stärke** fortitude, strength of mind; ~**verkäufer** *(fam.)* cockleshell, sieve *(sl.)*, tub *(sl.)*, crimp *(sl.)*; ~**wanderung** transmigration of the soul.
Seeleute seafarers.
seelisch emotional, mental, psychical, inner;
~**e Belastung** mental stress; **sein ~es Gleichgewicht wiederfinden** to recover one's balance.
Seelsorge, telefonische telephone service (lifeline).
seelsorgerische Zwecke pious uses.
See|luft sea air; ~**lufthafen** seadrome; ~**luftstreitkräfte** naval air force; ~**macht** maritime power.
Seemann seaman, mariner, navigator, shipman;
bordflüchtiger ~ deserter; **erfahrener** ~ shellback *(sl.)*; **unerfahrener** ~ inexperienced (fresh-water) sailor;
~ **anheuern** to enter a seaman on the ship's books; ~ **werden** to follow (use) the sea.
seemännisch naval, seamanlike.
Seemanns|amt seamen's employment agency; ~**amtsleiter** shipping commissioner *(US)* (master, *Br.*); ~**ausdruck** sea (seaman's) term; ~**beruf ergreifen** to use (follow) the sea; ~**brauch** maritime custom; ~**erfahrung** seamanship; ~**garn** nautical yarn *(fam.)*; ~**garn spinnen** to spin a yarn, to yarn; ~**handwerk verstehen** to know the ropes; ~**heim** sailor's home (rest); ~**heuer** seamen's wages; ~**leben** life afloat, maritime life; **Internationale ~ordnung** International Seaman's Code; ~**schule** navigation school.
seemäßig|verpackt sea-packed;
~**e Verpackung** seaworthy packing.

Seemeile nautical (sea) mile, marine league;
englische ~ Admiralty mile *(Br.)*; **internationale ~** international nautical mile;
~ pro Stunde knot.

Seenot distress;
größte ~ *(Schiff)* extreme hazard;
einem in ~ geratenen Schiff Hilfe leisten to assist a ship in distress;
~dienst salvage service; **~flugzeug** sea rescue plane; **~ruf** distress call, SOS.

See|offizier naval officer; **~paß** ship's passport, sea letter; **~pfandrecht** maritime lien (hypothecation, *US*); **~police** policy of marine insurance, maritime-insurance policy (certificate, *US*), *(für eine bestimmte Ladung)* voyage policy; **mit dem Namen des zu befördernden Schiffes versehene ~police** named policy; **~prämie** marine-insurance premium; **~promenade** marina, seaside promenade; **~protest** extended (ship's) protest; **~räuber** pirate, marooner, rover, sea robber, freebooter, buccaneer; **~räuberei** piracy.

seeräubern to maroon.

Seerecht marine (maritime, shipping, Admiralty, *US*) law.

seerechtlicher Vertrag marine contract.

Seerechts|deklaration, Pariser Declaration of Paris; **~fall** maritime cause; **Genfer ~konferenz** Geneva Conferences on the Laws of the Sea.

See|reise sea journey, seagoing, ocean voyage, cruise; **~reise unternehmen** to voyage, to cruise; **~rettungsdienst** Lifesaving Service, salvage service (business); **~risiko** marine risk (peril, adventure), dangers (risks and perils) of the sea; **~route** sea route (road, *US*), ocean lane; **~rückbehaltungsrecht** maritime lien (hypothecation, *US*); **~sack** duffel (kit) bag; **~schaden** ship (sea) damage, damage by sea water, average, deficiency of a ship's cargo; **~schadensberechnung** average adjustment (statement), adjustment of average; **~schadenssumme** maritime claim; **~schiff** ocean-going vessel (ship, liner); **~schiffahrt** maritime navigation (shipping), maritime commerce, merchant service; **~seite** sea front; **~spediteur** water carrier; **~staat** maritime power; **~straße** sea route (road, *US*), ocean lane; **~straßenordnung** international rules of the road, Regulation for Preventing Collisions at Sea; **~streitkräfte** naval forces, sea force, marine forces; **~stützpunkt** naval base.

Seetransport shipment (carriage) by sea, transit by sea, oversea shipment, sea (maritime, marine) transport;
auf dem ~ seaborne;
~gefahr maritime (marine) peril (risk); **~geschäft** shipping business (trade), marine transport; **~gesellschaft** marine transportation company; **~risiko** sea risks; **~schein** Admiralty bond; **~versicherer** marine [insurance] underwriter; **~versicherung** marine (maritime) insurance.

Seetransportversicherungs|gesetz Marine Insurance Act *(Br.)*; **~police** marine policy; **~vertrag** contract of marine insurance, marine insurance contract.

See|transportvolumen total sea transport; **~trift** flotsam.

seetüchtig seaworthy, *(Seeschadensversicherung)* well;
Schiff ~ machen to render a ship seaworthy;
~e Verpackung seaproof packing.

See|tüchtigkeit seaworthiness; **~ufer** waterside; **~uferanlage** sea bank; **~unfall** accident (disaster) at sea; **~unfallversicherung** accident-at-sea insurance.

see|untauglich, ~untüchtig unseaworthy, disabled, condemned;
für ~ erklären to condemn.

Seeuntauglichkeitserklärung condemnation.

See|untüchtigkeit unseaworthiness; **~verbindung** sea route, ocean line, shipping line; **~vermessung** hydrographic survey.

seeverpackt sea-packed, packed for ocean shipment.

Seeverpackung sea-proof (seaworthy) packing;
in ~ sea-packed, packed for ocean shipment.

See|verschollenheit presumption of death at sea; **~versicherer** maritime (marine) insurer, marine [insurance] underwriter; **~versicherung** marine (maritime) insurance; **normale ~versicherung** general insurance.

Seeversicherungs|geschäft underwriting; **~gesellschaft** marine insurance company; **~makler** marine insurance broker; **~police** marine insurance policy; **~recht** marine insurance law.

See|völkerrecht international law of the sea; **~warte** Hydrographic Office; **~wasserschwimmbad** sea-water swimming pool; **~wechsel** respondentia.

Seeweg sea route, ocean lane;
auf dem ~ [befördert] sea-borne;
~ benutzen (nehmen) to travel by sea, to voyage; **auf dem ~ schicken** to send by sea.

See|wesen marine, maritime affairs; **~wetterbericht** marine weather report; **~wetterdienst** marine weather service; **~wind** on-shore wind; **~wurf** ligan, jetsam, jettison; **~zeichen** seamark, buoy; **landfestes ~zeichen** landmark, beacon; **~zollhafen** port of entry; **~zollinspektor** tides-surveyor.

Segel, mit vollen ~n running free;
jem. den Wind aus den ~n nehmen to take the wind out of s. one's sails; **kampflos die ~ streichen** to go down without a fight;
~boot sailing boat, sailboat, yacht; **~fliegen** gliding.

segelfliegen to glide, to soar.

Segel|flieger glider; **~flug** motorless flight; **~flugzeug** sailplane, glider; **~flugzeug mit Hilfsmotor** motor glider; **~jacht** yacht; **kleine ~jacht** knockabout.

segeln, durch ein Examen to flunk in an examination; **unter falscher Flagge ~** to sail under false colo(u)rs; **in seichtem Gewässer ~** to make foul water.

Segel|schiff sailing vessel; **~schiffahrt** sailing; **~schiffahrtslinie** sailing line; **~schulschiff** training sailship.

Segen blessing, benediction, *(Reichtum)* abundance, riches;
zum ~ der Menschheit for the prosperity of mankind;
der ganze ~ the whole lot; **wahrer ~** real blessing;
ein ~ Gottes a gift of God;
jem. ~ bringen to bring good luck to s. o.; **jem. seinen ~ geben** to give s. o. one's blessing;
sich regen bringt ~ industry is fortune's right hand.

Sehbereich visual range.

Sehen, plastisches three-dimensional vision;
j. vom ~ her kennen to know s. o. by sight.

sehen to see, to look, to view, *(beobachten)* to observe, to watch, *(erleben)* to experience, *(feststellen)* to find out;
jem. ähnlich ~ to resemble s. o.; **einfach alles ~** to have eyes at the back of one's head; **sich schon als berühmten Arzt ~** to already imagine o. s. as a famous doctor; **alles durch eine rosarote Brille ~** to see the world through rose-colo(u)red spectacles; **jem. durch die Finger ~** to turn a blind eye on s. o.; **sehr aufs Geld ~** to be keen on moneymaking; **Gespenster ~** to be seeing ghosts; **j. ziemlich häufig ~** to see quite lot of s. o.; **sehr auf seine Kleidung ~** to be particular about one's dress; **weiße Mäuse ~** to see pink elephants; **in einer Sache klar ~** to see clear in a matter; **Sache von einem anderen Standpunkt aus ~** to look differently at it; **zu spät ~** to realize too late; **dem Tod ruhig ins Auge ~** to face death calmly; **Wald vor lauter Bäumchen nicht ~** not to see the wood for trees; **sich wieder ~** to meet again;
j. einfach nicht mehr ~ können not to be able to bear s. o. any longer; **kaum aus den Augen ~ können** to hardly be able to keep one's eyes open; **seine Hand nicht vor den Augen ~ können** not to be able to see beyond one's nose; **sich nicht satt ~ können** to glut one's eyes on s. th.; **sich ~ lassen können** to bear inspection; **sich ~ lassen** to show [up]; **nicht ~ wollen** to close one's eyes, to wink at;
~, wie der Hase läuft to see which way the cat jumps, to see how the land lies.

Sehenswürdigkeit spectacle, sight, place of interest;
attraktive ~ beauty mark.

Sehenswürdigkeiten|eines Platzes lions of a place; **~ einer Stadt** sights of a city, lions of a place;
~ besichtigen to see the sights, to lionize; **jem. die ~ zeigen** to show s. o. the lions; **jem. bis zum Umfallen die ~ zeigen** to trot s. o. off his legs.

Sehlinse viewing lens.

sehnen, sich nach etw. to long (hanker, yearn, languish) for s. th.

Sehnsucht desire, craving, languishing;
sich vor ~ nach jem. verzehren to pine for s. o.

sehnsüchtig longing, yearning, hankering;
j. ~ erwarten to be longing to see s. o.

Seh|rohr *(U-Boot)* periscope; **~störung** impaired vision; **~vermögen** vision, sight.

seicht shallow, shoaly, *(Buch)* thin, *(Stil)* wishy-washy;
~e Redensarten banalities, trivialities, shallow phrases.

Seide, empfindliche fine silk; **reine ~** pure silk.

Seiden|druck silk print; **~papier** tissue (silk) paper; **~talar** silk gown.

Seifenblase *(fig.)* bubble;
wie eine ~ platzen to vanish into thin air.

Seil rope, cord, line, tether, twist, *(Abschleppseil)* drag rope;
~e einer Hängebrücke cables of a suspension bridge;
Platz mit ~en absperren to rope off a square; **mit ~en am Kai festmachen** to moor to the quay; **auf einem ~ tanzen** to tightrope;

~**absperrung** rope barrier; **Zuschauer durch ~absperrung ausschließen** to rope out the spectators; ~**bahn** ropeway, cableway; ~**fähre** cable ferry; ~**tänzer** rope (tightrope) dancer, wire walker.

Seine, jedem das ~ geben to give the devil his due.

seinesgleichen one's peers;
~ **finden** to meet one's match.

Seite side, *(Buch)* page, *(fig.)* aspect, *(Folio)* folio, *(Gebäude)* flank, *(Konto)* side, *(Partei)* side, part, camp, *(Quelle)* quarter, source, *(Richtung)* direction;
am Fuße einer ~ bottom of page; **auf der ersten ~ [einer Zeitung]** first page; **auf der gegenüberliegenden ~** on the opposite page; **auf jeder ~** on every hand; **auf umstehender ~** overleaf; **von allen ~n** from all sides (directions); **von maßgeblicher ~** ex cathedra; **von gut unterrichteter ~** on good authority, from a safe quarter (reliable, well, well-informed source); **von meiner ~ aus** for my part;
[druck]angeschnittene ~ *(Anzeigen)* bleed-off page; **eng beschriebene ~n** closely written pages; **dazwischenliegende ~n** intervening pages; **erste ~** front (first) page; **ganze ~** whole (full) page; **leere ~** white (blank) page; **letzte ~** last (back) page; **linke ~** left-hand page, left; **menschliche ~** human factor; **obere ~** upside; **schwache ~** soft spot, weak (side) point; **starke ~** forte, strong point; **vordere ~** front page; **etw. über 200 ~n** 200 odd pages; **zweispaltige ~** page of two columns;
~ **einer Angelegenheit** aspect of a matter; **alle ~n einer Frage** the ins and outs of a question; **die angenehmen ~n des Lebens** niceties of life; **andere ~ der Medaille** back side of the coin; **rechte ~ einer Straße** right-hand side of a street;
allem die beste ~ abgewinnen to make the best of everything; **von der ~ angreifen** *(mil.)* to attack from the flank; **beide ~n anhören** to hear both sides; **von beiden ~n Geschenke annehmen** to take gifts with both hands; **neue ~ aufschlagen** to turn over a new leaf; **nach allen ~n auseinanderlaufen** to run in all directions; **auf beiden ~n bedrucken** to perfect; **Angebote von mehreren ~n bekommen** to get several offers; ~ **in einer Zeitschrift belegen** to place a page in a magazine; **Frage von allen ~n beleuchten** to view a question from all sides, to study every aspect of a question; **Leben von der angenehmen ~ betrachten** to look on the bright side of things; **auf die ~ bringen** to put aside, *(heimlich)* to pocket; **j. auf die ~ bringen** to do away with s. o.; **über die ganze erste ~ gehen** to be spread across the front page; **Recht auf seiner ~ haben** to have the law on one's side; **es mit beiden ~n halten** to run with the hare and hunt with the hounds; **von allen ~n herbeiströmen** to flock in from all directions; ~ **frei lassen** to leave a page blank; **sich auf die ~ legen** *(Schiff)* to heel; **etw. Geld auf die ~ legen** to put money by, to put away for a rainy day; **Eselsohr in eine ~ machen** to fold down a corner of a page; **sich auf die andere ~ schlagen** to change front (sides), to cross the floor of the house *(Br.)*, to rat; **j. von der schlechtesten ~ sehen** to see s. o. at his worst; **auf jds. ~ stehen** to belong to s. one's party *(fam.)*; **auf der ersten ~ stehen** to be printed on the front page; **auf der falschen ~ stehen** to be in a false position; **jem. hilfreich zur ~ stehen** to support s. o., to give a helping hand to s. o., to be on s. one's side; **auf ~n der Regierung stehen** to support the government; **sich auf jds. ~ stellen** to take the part of (side with) s. o.; **j. zur ~ stoßen** to jostle s. o. out of the way; **Buch mit ~n versehen** to side a book; ~ **vollschreiben** to write a sheet full; **sich von der besten ~ zeigen** to be on one's best behavio(u)r, to put one's best foot forward; **j. auf seine ~ ziehen** to win s. o. over to one's side; **der väterlichen ~ zufallen** to fall to the heirs of the father's side;
diese ~ nach oben! this side up!

Seiten|abstammung collateral descent; ~**abstand** lateral distance; ~**abstimmung** reconciliation of numbers; ~**abzug** page proof; ~**angabe** indication of page; ~**ansicht** side (lateral) view; ~**ausgang** side exit; ~**bahn** branch line, light railway.

seitenbeherrschende Anzeige page dominance.

Seiten|bestimmung *(Funkpeilung)* sense finding; ~**bezeichnung** paging; ~**bordmotor** sideboard engine; ~**deckung** flank guard; **umgeschlagene ~ecke** turnover; ~**eingang** side entry; ~**ende** foot of a page; ~**erbe** collateral heir; ~**flügel** *(Gebäude)* wing; ~**format** size of page, page size; ~**gasse** lane, back alley *(US)*; ~**gebäude** wing, outhouse; ~**gesamtbetrag** columnar total; ~**gewehr** bayonet; ~**gleis** siding; ~**hieb** rub; **jem. einen ~hieb verpassen** to have a dig at s. o.; ~**kanal** distributory canal, by-channel; ~**kulisse** *(Theater)* wing; ~**lampe** sidelight.

seitenlang pages of.

Seiten|layout page layout, location of page; ~**leuchten** side lamps; ~**licht** sidelight; ~**linie** sideline, transversal line, *(Eisenbahn)* branch line, collateral line, *(Verwandtschaft)* lateral branch, branch of a family, offshoot; **in der ~linie verwandt** collateral; ~**loge** side box; ~**mitte** centre *(Br.)* (center, *US*) of a page; ~**numerierung** pagination, folio[ing]; ~**nummer** page number; ~**preis** *(Anzeige)* page (one-time) rate; **voller ~preis** full-page rate; ~**rand** margin.

seitenrichtig right reading.

Seiten|ruder rudder; ~**sprung** *(fig.)* side slip, escapade; ~**steg** side reglet; ~**straße** byroad, by-lane, side street (road), crossroad; **aus einer ~straße hervorschießen** to swing out of a side street; ~**streifen** *(Straße)* shoulder; ~**stück** tally, companion piece; ~**tarif** *(Anzeigen)* page rate; ~**teil** lateral.

seitenteilige Anzeige space advertisement.

Seiten|überschrift headline; ~**umbruch** paging.

seitenverkehrt reversed, left to right, mirror-inverted.

Seiten|verwandter collateral relative; ~**verwandtschaft** collateral degree of kindred; ~**verweise** paginal references; ~**waffen** side arms *(mil.)*; ~**wagen** *(Motorrad)* sidecar; ~**weg** byway, sideway; ~**wege gehen** to engage in illicit transactions.

seitenweise paginal.

Seiten|wind crosswind; ~**zahl** page number; **ohne ~zahlen** unpaged; **mit ~zahlen versehen** to folio, to page, to paginate; ~**zweig** offshoot.

Sekretär secretary, clerk, *(Schreibtisch)* writing desk, secretaire, bureau;
ehrenamtlicher ~ honorary secretary;
~ **der Liberalen Partei** Liberal Whip *(Br.)*;
j. als ~ beschäftigen to employ s. o. as secretary; **als ~ fungieren, ~ sein** to perform the office of (act as) a secretary.

Sekretariat secretariat[e], secretaryship, secretary's office;
straff organisiertes ~ professional secretariat;
im ~ tätig sein to perform the office of (act as) a secretary.

Sekretariats|arbeit secretarial work; ~**aufgaben** secretarial duties; ~**ausbildung** secretarial training; ~**ausbildung absolvieren** to train for secretarial work; ~**bereich** secretarial area; ~**erfahrung** secretarial practice; ~**gestellung** secretarial assistance; ~**hilfskraft** secretarial help; ~**kenntnisse** secretarial competence; ~**kräfte** secretarial staff; ~**kursus** secretarial course; ~**posten** secretarial position; ~**tätigkeit** secretarial job; ~**zuschuß** secretarial allowance.

Sekretärin [lady] secretary;
deutschsprachige ~ German-language secretary; **tüchtige ~** efficient secretary;
für eine gute ~ halten to value as secretary; **sich eine ~ nehmen** to take a secretary; **j. an die ~ verweisen** to refer s. o. to the secretary; **seine Wünsche der ~ vortragen** to state one's business to the secretary.

Sekretärinnenangebot secretarial supply.

Sekretärposten post of a secretary, secretaryship.

Sekte sect, confraternity, denomination.

Sektfrühstück champagne breakfast.

Sektion section, compartment, dissection *(med.)*, *(Zweigverein)* branch society.

Sektionschef departmental head.

Sektor sector;
auf dem politischen ~ on the political side; **in ~en eingeteilt** sectoral;
industrieller ~ industrial sector; **kommunaler ~** local authorities; **öffentlicher ~** public sector; **privater ~** private sector; **produktiver ~** wealth-creating sector;
billigen ~ des Marktes gewinnen to move down the market.

Sektoren|bildung sectoring; ~**gliederung** breakdown by sectors; ~**grenze** sector boundary; ~**übergang** checkpoint.

Sekunda *(Wechsel)* second [of exchange], *(Schule)* fifth form *(Br.)*;
girierte ~ second in course;
~**qualität** medium (middling) quality.

sekundär derivative, secondary.

Sekundär|bahn secondary railway; ~**bereich** capital goods industries; ~**energie** secondary fuel; ~**erhebung** desk research; ~**gruppe** *(Soziologie)* secondary group; ~**güterproduktion** secondary production; ~**haftung** secondary liability *(US)*; ~**liquidität** *(Banken)* secondary reserve, *(EEC)* secondary liquidity; ~**reserve** *(Weltwährungsfonds)* secondary reserve; ~**stadtteil** neighbo(u)rhood center *(US)* (centre, *Br.*); ~**wirkung** secondary effect; ~**zentrum** neighbo(u)rhood center *(US)* (centre, *Br.*).

Sekundawechsel second [of exchange], duplicate.

Sekunde, auf die on the dot *(coll.)*;
auf die ~ pünktlich kommen to come on the dot, to be there on the stroke.

Sekunden|bruchteil split second; **für einen ~bruchteil** for the small fraction of a second; **in ~schnelle** in a flash (two shakes of a duck's tail); **~zeiger** second hand.
Selbst self, ego;
zweites ~ alter ego.
selbst self, in person;
~ veranlagungspflichtig self-assessable;
~ Vermögen besitzen to have s. th. in one's own right; **an sich ~ denken** to consult one's own interest; **nur an sich ~ denken** to take care of number one; **von ~ kommen** to come on one's own initiative; **sich auf sich ~ verlassen können** to be self-reliant; **sich ~ richten** to commit suicide; **für sich ~ die Werbetrommel rühren** to be self-advertising; **auf sich ~ gestellt sein** to shift for o. s.; **für sich ~ sprechen** to be self-explanatory; **sich von ~ verstehen** to be obvious;
jeder ist sich ~ der Nächste charity begins at home.
Selbstabholung collection by the customer, self-service;
~ gegen Kasse cash-and-carry *(US)*.
selbständig independent, in an independent capacity, free, on one's own, self-employed, *(autark)* autarcic, self-supporting, *(freiberuflich tätig)* free-lance, *(Maschine)* self-contained, *(Staat)* autonomous, sovereign;
~ erwerbstätig self-employed; **noch nicht ~** unsettled;
sich ~ gemacht haben to be on one's own hook; **~ machen** to emancipate; **sich ~ machen** to establish o. s. as a businessman, to set up (go into business) for o. s., to cut the painter *(fig.)*; **~ sein** to be working on one's own, to be self-supporting (on one's own, in business on one's own account), to stand on one's own legs, to be one's own master; **~ werden** to find one's feet, *(Kolonie)* to hive off;
an ~es Arbeiten gewohnt sein to be used to working independently; **~er Beweis** independent proof; **~er Denker** independent thinker; **~e Einheit** self-contained unit; **~es Einzelhandelsgeschäft** independent retail shop (store, *US*); **~er Einzelhändler** independent retailer; **~e Forschung** original research; **~er Freiberufler** self-employed person; **~er Gewerbetreibender** independent businessman; **~er Kaufmann** established merchant; **~es Land** substantive nation; **~es Patent** independent patent; **in ~er Position sein** to be in an established position; **~er Schadensabschätzer** independent adjuster; **~e Tätigkeit** self-employment, independent activities; **~es Tätigkeitsgebiet** free field of operations; **~er Unternehmer** independent contractor, self-employer; **~er Vertrag** independent contract.
Selbständigeneinkommen resources of self-employed.
Selbständiger self-employed (independent) person.
Selbständigkeit independence, self-reliance, *(Land)* autonomy, sovereignty.
Selbständig|machen setting up in business; **~machen mit eigenem Wohnsitz** express emancipation; **~werden** *(Kolonie)* hive-off.
Selbst|anfertigung own make; **~anklage** self-accusation; **~anlasser** self-starter, automatic starter; **~anleger** *(drucktechn.)* automatic feeder; **~anschlußamt** automatic exchange; **~anschluß[betrieb]** *(Telefon)* automatic telephone (dial(l)ing); **~auflösung** voluntary liquidation (winding up); **~aufopferung** self-sacrifice; **~ausbildungsverfahren** pickup method; **~auskunft** disclosure of one's financial conditions; **~auslöser** *(Foto)* delayed-action device; **~auslöser einstellen** to set the shutter to delayed action; **~ausschalter** automatic circuit-breaker; **~bedarf** personal requirements; **~bedienung** self-service.
Selbstbedienungs|ampel zigzag; **~geschäft** *(Lebensmittel)* riggly-wiggly store *(US)*; **~großhandel** self-service wholesale trade; **~laden** self-service shop *(Br.)* (store, *US*), groceteria *(US)*, supermarket *(US)*, *(Lebensmittel)* riggly-wiggly store *(US)*; **kleiner ~laden** superette *(US)*; **~restaurant** self-service restaurant, cafeteria; **~system** self-service system; **~tankstelle** self-service petrol station *(Br.)*, gaseteria *(US)*.
Selbst|befreiung prison breaking; **~behalt** *(Autoversicherung)* collision damage responsibility, own risk, policy excess, *(Versicherung)* franchise, deductible average, net retention, *(bei Unterdeckung)* coinsurance; **~behalt in festgelegter Höhe übernehmen** to assume a specified amount of each loss.
Selbstbehalts|bestimmung deductible provision; **~betrag** *(Rückversicherungsgeschäft)* retention figure; **~klausel** deductible (sue-and-labour, *Br.*, suing and laboring, *US*) clause, *(Unterdeckung)* coinsurance (franchise) clause; **~übernahme in festgesetzter Höhe** assumption of a specified amount of each loss.
Selbstbeherrschung self-control, self-possession, retenue, possession, nerve;
über ~ verfügen to have command over one's temper; **nicht über genügend ~ verfügen** to have a short temper; **seine ~ verlieren** to lose control of o. s., to let one's temper get out of hand.
Selbst|bekenntnis voluntary confession; **~belastung** self-incrimination.
Selbstbeschränkung self-restraint, austerity;
freiwillige ~ voluntary restriction, social contract *(Br.)*;
~ des Bundesverfassungsgerichts judicial self-restraint *(US)*; **~ bei Lohnforderungen** voluntary wage restraint.
Selbst|beschränkungsabkommen *(internationaler Handel)* orderly marketing; **~beschuldigung** self-accusation; **~bestimmung** self-determination; **~bestimmungsprinzip** principle of self-determination; **~bestimmungsrecht** right of self-determination; **~beteiligung** own risk, self-retention; **~beteiligung bei Bagatellschäden** policy franchise; **~beteiligungsklausel bei verringerter Prämienzahlung** reduced-rate average clause; **~bewirtschaftung** *(Hof)* self-government; **~bezichtigung** self-incrimination; **~biographie** autobiography; **~einschätzung** self-assessment, self-rating (-appraisal); **~eintritt** self-contracting; **unzulässiger ~eintritt** *(Makler)* cross sale; **~eintrittsangebot** crossed order; **~entlader** railway hopper; **~entleibung** self-destruction; **~entzündung** spontaneous combustion.
selbsterhaltend self-supporting.
Selbst|erhaltung self-preservation; **~erhaltungstrieb** sense of survival; **~erhitzung** self-heating.
selbsternannt self-proclaimed (-appointed, -styled).
Selbst|fahrer owner-driver, *(Invalide)* invalid carriage; **für ~fahrer** self-drive *(Br.)*; **Autovermietung für ~fahrer** self-drive car for hire; **~finanzierung** self-financing, own financing, ploughing (plowing, *US*) back of earnings; **~finanzierungsquote** self-financing ratio.
Selbstgefährdung, bewußte unnötige voluntary exposure to unnecessary danger.
selbstgefahrener Lastwagen self-drive car.
selbstgefällig complacent, smug.
Selbstgefälligkeit conceit, complacency.
Selbstgefühl, übersteigertes overdeveloped ego;
jds. ~ verletzen to put s. one's nose out of joint.
selbst|gemacht self-made, home-made; **~genügsam** self-sufficient, autarchic.
Selbstgenügsamkeit self-sufficiency, autarchy, austerity.
selbstgerecht self-righteous, pharisaical;
~er Mensch stiff-neck.
Selbstgerechtigkeit self-righteousness, pharisaism.
selbstgeschrieben autograph.
Selbstgespräche führen to talk to o. s.
selbst|haftend on one's own risk; **~herrlich** arbitrary, with a high hand, positive.
Selbst|herrschaft autocracy; **~herrscher** autocrat.
Selbsthilfe self-defence (-help), self-redress;
zur ~ schreiten to take the law into one's own hands;
~methode do-it-yourselfism; **~programm** self-help program(me); **~unternehmen** self-help enterprise; **~verkauf** intromission *(Br.)*, resale, replevin, emergency sale; **im ~wege verkauft** sold without resort to legal process.
Selbst|infektion auto-infection; **~interesse** self-interest; **~kontrahent** principal; **~kontrahieren** self-dealing, self-contraction.
selbstkontrahieren to contract with o. s., to act as principal and agent.
Selbstkontrolle self-control;
~ der Presse press watchdog group.
Selbstkontrollinstitut der Funkwerbung network clearance bureau.
Selbstkosten enterprise (direct, actual, own, first, original, prime) cost, cost price, *(Verkäufer)* selling costs;
nachträglich errechnete ~ historical cost;
~ plus prozentualer Aufschlag cost-plus;
gerade die ~ decken to operate on a marginal basis; **~ einer Ware veranschlagen** to cost;
~berechnung cost accounting, costing.
Selbstkostenpreis flat (prime, first, net) cost, cost price, *(Hersteller)* manufacturer's costs;
zum ~ at cost, at cost price, marginal;
bereinigter ~ *(Einkommensteuer)* adjusted cost basis;
~ einer Ware feststellen to cost an article; **unter dem ~ verkaufen** to sell under cost price; **zum ~ verkaufen** to sell at prime cost;
~rechnung costing, cost accounting.
Selbst|kritik self-criticism; **~ladepistole** automatic pistol; **~läufer** fast-selling item; **~losigkeit** disinterestedness; **~machen** do-

it-yourself; ~**mord** self-murder, suicide; ~**mord begehen** to commit suicide, to die by one's own hand, to cut one's throat, to lay violent hands on o. s.; ~**mordabsicht** suicide intent; ~**mörder** self-murder, felo-de-se, suicide.

selbstmörderisch, in ~er Absicht with suicidal intention.

Selbstmord|klausel *(Lebensversicherung)* suicide clause; ~**vereinbarung** suicide pact; ~**verhütung** suicide prevention; ~**versuch** attempted suicide.

Selbst|potenzierung snowball growth; ~**prüfung** introspection; ~**reflektanten erwünscht** *(Anzeige)* no agents need apply; ~**regierung** autonomy, autarchy, home-rule, self-government; ~**schuldner** primary obligor; **als ~schuldner haftbar sein** to be primarily liable.

selbstschuldnerisch|er Bürge absolute guarantor, paying surety, primary obligor *(US)*; ~**e Bürgschaft** guaranty of payment *(US)*, absolute guaranty; ~**e Haftung** primary liability.

Selbst|schuß spring gun; ~**schutz** self-protection.

selbstsicher self-possessed, positive;
übertrieben ~ cocksure.

Selbstsicherheit self-possession, self-confidence, assurance;
seine ~ wiederfinden to regain one's nerve.

Selbst|steuergerät automatic pilot, robot pilot, autopilot; ~**steuerung** automatic regulation; ~**studium** self-study; **pure ~sucht** lump of selfishness.

selbstsüchtig selfish, egoistical.

selbsttätig self-acting, automatic;
~**er Schwundausgleich** automatic volume control.

Selbst|tätigkeit automatism; **sich ~täuschungen hingeben** to delude o. s. with false hopes.

selbsttragend self-supporting;
~**e Brücke** cantilever.

Selbst|tragung von Kostenerhöhungen, teilweise absorption of part of the cost increase; ~**überhebung** egoism; ~**unterbrecher** automatic circuit breaker; ~**unterricht** self-tuition, self-instruction, self-study; ~**veranlagung** self-assessment.

selbstveranlagungspflichtig self-assessed.

Selbst|verbrauch private (internal) consumption; ~**verbraucher** private consumer; ~**verbrennung** self-cremation; ~**verkäufer** manufacturer and retailer; ~**verlag** author and publisher; **im ~verlag des Verfassers** published by the author; ~**verleugnung** self-denial; ~**verleugnung üben** to deny o. s.; ~**verpflegung** self-cooking; ~**verschulden** one's own fault; ~**versicherer** co-insurer, self-insurer, private (own) insurer; ~**versicherung** self-insurance, co-insurance, own insurance; ~**versicherungsklausel** co-insurance clause; ~**versicherungsrücklage** insurance reserve.

selbstversorgend autarchic.

Selbst|versorger self-supporter; ~**versorger sein** to be self-sufficient (-supporting); ~**versorgung** self-support (-sufficiency), direct production, *(Land)* national self-sufficiency, autarchy; ~**versorgungsgrad** degree of self-sufficiency.

selbstverständlich obvious, self-evident;
das ist doch ~ don't mention it;
etw. als ~ hinnehmen to take s. th. in one's stride; **~ sein** to go without saying; **jem. ganz ~ vorkommen** to come to s. o. by nature.

Selbstverständlichkeit foregone conclusion, truism, matter of course.

Selbst|verständnis, nationales national identity; ~**verstümmelung** *(mil.)* mayhem, self-inflicted wound; **kollektive ~verteidigung** collective self-defence; ~**verteidigungsrecht** right of self-defence.

Selbstvertrauen self-confidence;
sein nationales ~ finden to begin to feel its feet; **~ haben** to feel sure of o. s.; **kein ~ haben** to be distrustful of o. s.; **~ stärken** to boost confidence.

selbst|verwaltend self-governing; ~**verwaltet** self-governed.

Selbstverwaltung self-government (administration), autonomy, home rule;
kommunale ~ local self-government; **städtische ~** municipalism;
~ der Wirtschaft industrial self-government;
~ beseitigen to suspend autonomy; **~ haben** to self-administer.

Selbstverwaltungs|angelegenheiten county affairs; ~**körper** self-governing body; ~**organisation** quasi corporation *(US)*; ~**prinzip** communalism; ~**recht** [right of local] self-government; **regionales ~system** regional system.

Selbstwähl|amt *(Telefon)* automatic exchange; ~**anschluß** *(Telefon)* automatic telephone; ~**betrieb** *(Telefon)* dial system.

Selbstwähler dial(l)ing apparatus, dial telephone, dialphone.

Selbstwähl|fernsprecher dial(l)ing apparatus, dial telephone; ~**fernverkehr** *(Telefon)* intercity (subscriber-trunk, *Br.*) dial(l)ing, toll-line dial(l)ing *(US)*; ~**system** dial telephone system; ~**verkehr** automatic operation, dial (direct inward-dial(l)ing) system; **internationaler ~verkehr** international subscriber (direct) dial(l)ing; **400 Millionen Telefonapparate in 85 Ländern an den ~verkehr anschließen** to put 400 million phones in 85 countries within self-dial reach.

Selbst|zerfleischung blood-letting; ~**zerstörung** self-destruction; ~**zucht üben** to discipline o. s.; ~**zweck** end in itself; **als ~zweck** for its own sake.

Selektionstafel select mortality table.

selektive Absatzpolitik selective sales policy.

Selenzelle photoelectric cell.

selig blissful, delightful, happy;
jeder soll nach seiner Fasson ~ werden every man to his taste.

Seligkeit, voller ~ sein to be blissful.

Seltenheit rarety, white crow.

Seltenheits|gut rare commodity; ~**wert** scarcity (curiosity) value.

seltsam odd, strange, peculiar, queer;
jem. ~ vorkommen to strike s. o. as being strange;
~**er Brauch** quaint custom; ~**es Gefühl** strange feeling.

Semester term, session, half, semester *(US)*;
im letzten ~ in the last term; **während des ~s** during the term;
älteres ~ senior man *(Br.)*, upper classman *(US)*; **erstes ~** freshman; **jüngeres ~** lower classman *(US)*; **zusätzliches ~** by-term *(Br.)*;
klinische ~ absolvieren to walk the hospitals; **~ belegen** to enrol(l) for a course of lectures; **~ studieren** to keep a term *(Br.)*;
zum ~anfang wieder erscheinen to go up *(Br.)*; ~**beginn** beginning of the term; ~**belegung** enrol(l)ment; ~**provision** six-months' commission; ~**prüfung** term examination, collection *(Br.)*; ~**schluß** close of term, break-up; **letzte ~tage** fag end of the term.

semesterweise terminally.

Semester|wochenstunde unit *(US)*; ~**zeit** termtime.

Seminar seminar, lecture with discussion, training college, workshop;
~ abhalten to run a seminar; **an einem ~ teilnehmen** to attend a tutorial;
~**arbeit** term paper; ~**bibliothek** institute library; ~**leiter** tutor; ~**raum** seminar room; ~**übung** tutorial exercise; ~**zeit** classroom time.

Senat senate, *(Gericht)* division, *(Universität)* council;
im ~ angenommen werden to pass the senate.

Senator senator *(US)*;
~**würde** senatorial dignity, senatorship.

Senats|ausschuß senate committee; **~- und Sitzungsberichte** Books of Council and Session; ~**beschluß** senatorial vote; **durch ~beschluß** by grace of the Senate; ~**bezirk** senatorial district; ~**gebäude** senate house; ~**mandat** senatorial seat; ~**mitglied** senator, member of the senate; ~**sitzung** session of senate, *(Universität)* council; ~**wahlen** senatorial election; ~**zustimmung** senate confirmation.

Sende|anflug *(Flugzeug)* homing; ~**anlage** transmitter; ~**antenne** transmitting aerial (antenna); ~**beginn** sign-on; ~**bereich** service (listening, broadcasting) area.

sendebereit sein to stand by.

Sende|energie transmitting power; ~**erlaubnis** broadcast transmitting licence; ~**erlaubnis erteilen** to clear a number.

sendefertig *(Tonkonserve)* pre-recorded.

Sendefolge wireless program(me).

sendefreie Zeiten nonbroadcasting hours.

Sende|frequenz broadcast frequency; ~**gebiet** broadcasting front; ~**gerät** transmitting set; **~- und Empfangsgerät** transceiver; ~**leistung** transmitting power; ~**leiter** program(me) director, producer.

senden *(absenden)* to send, to dispatch, *(expedieren)* to consign, to forward, *(Fernsehen)* to telecast, to transmit, *(Geld)* to remit, *(mit der Post)* to post *(Br.)*, to mail *(US)*, *(Rundfunk)* to transmit, to broadcast, to radio, to be on the air, *(übermitteln)* to communicate;
zur Ansicht ~ to send on approval; **mit der Bahn ~** to forward (send) by rail; **Baugenehmigung an das Gemeindeamt ~** to submit a plan to the city council; **Betrag sofort ~** to remit an amount at once; **etw. als Frachtgut ~** to send s. th. by freight (goods train, *Br.*); **auf der Kurzwelle ~** to broadcast on the short wave; **mit Luftpost ~** to send by airmail; **per Nachnahme ~** to send cash on delivery; **Nachrichten ~** to broadcast the

news; **nicht** ~ *(Rundfunkstation)* to be off the air; **Notruf** ~ to radio an urgent appeal; **Programm in französischer Sprache** ~ to broadcast a program(me) in French; **mit Rückstrahl** ~ to beam; **gleichzeitig über Rundfunk und Fernsehen** ~ to simulcast; **Waren an jds. Adresse** ~ to consign goods to s. one's address; **Waren mit der Bahn** ~ to send goods by rail; **weiterhin** ~ to stay on the air.

Sende|pause dead air; **~pause ansagen** to discontinue transmitting, to sign off *(US)*; **~plan** guide sheet; **~programm finanzieren** to sponsor a program(me); **~qualität überwachen** to monitor the transmission.

Sender transmitter, transmitting set, sender, broadcasting (wireless) station, radio broadcaster;
alle ~ **umfassend** coast-to-coast *(US)*;
angeschlossener ~ repeater station; **fahrbarer** ~ mobile radio; **privater** ~ private station; **programmgestaltender** ~ key station *(US)*;
~ **und Empfänger** transceiver; ~ **ohne Werbeprogramm** noncommercial station;
~ **einstellen** to dial a broadcasting station; ~ **finanzieren** to sponsor a radio program(me); ~ **hereinbekommen** to pick up a broadcasting station; **über alle** ~ **sprechen** to go on the air nationally, to speak over a country-wide hookup;
~anlage transmitting set, radio installation; **~ansage** broadcasting announcement, station identification.

Sende|raum [broadcasting] studio, broadcasting room; **~rechte** broadcasting rights; **~reihe** broadcast series, *(Werbung)* serial, block.

Sender|einstellung station selector; **~frequenz** radio frequency (circuit); **~gruppe** basic (broadcast, broadcasting) network; **~gruppenprogramm** full net program(me); **~netz** radio network, web.

Senderöhre power tube.

Sender|programm broadcast (wireless) program(me), log; **~standort** transmitter site; **~wahl** station memory.

Sende|schluß sign-off; **~stärke** transmitting power; **~stelle** transmitting station (set).

sendestille Zeiten nonbroadcasting hours.

Sende|streifen *(Funk)* transmitting tape; **~streifen nochmals senden** to rerun a tape; **~studio** transmitting studio; **~tag** broadcasting day; **normale ~tätigkeit** normal broadcasting; **~unterbrechung [zwecks Werbedurchsagen]** break; **~verlust** transmitting loss; **~welle** carrier wave.

Sendezeichen call letters, station announcement, interval, signature;
bildmäßiges ~ video;
~ **während des Programms** middle break.

Sendezeit air (station) time;
noch verfügbare ~en availability;
~ **belegen** *(Werbung)* to buy time; ~ **überziehen** to overrun the allotted time.

Sendschreiben message.

Sendung sending, *(Absendung)* forwarding, dispatch, *(Fernsehen)* telecast, television, *(Geld)* remittance, *(Lieferung)* delivery, *(Postversand)* posting *(Br.)*, mailing *(US)*, *(Rundfunk)* trans-mission, broadcast [talk], program(me), *(Waren)* consignment, invoice, lot, shipment;
beliebte ~ high-rate program(me); **eingeschriebene** ~ registered letter (item); **fehlgeleitete** ~ misrouted freight; **pauschalverkaufte fertige** ~ package; **feststehende** ~ script show, hour; **gemeinschaftliche** ~ *(Werbefunk)* cooperative program(me); **gemischte** ~ mixed shipment; **kleine ~en** small consignments; **Muster-ohne-Wert-**~ sample shipment (packet), parcel shipment; **nachgebührenpflichtige ~en** items liable to surcharge *(Br.)*; **nochmalige** ~ reconsignment; **portofreie** ~ prepaid remittance, free delivery; **rundfunkeigene** ~ sustained program *(US)*; **unfrankierte** ~ unpaid remittance; **unverlangte ~en** *(Buchhandel)* unsolicited deliveries; **unverpackte** ~ unpacked consignment; **unzustellbare** ~ dead (undeliverable) letter; **verspätete** ~ delayed delivery; **zollfreie** ~ duty-free delivery; **noch nicht zugestellte ~en** parcels (letters) awaiting delivery; **zugkräftige** ~ audience builder; **zuschlagspflichtige ~en** items liable to surcharge *(Br.)*;
~ **gegen Barzahlung** cash consignment (on delivery); ~ **von Belegexemplaren** sending of vouchers; ~ **als Frachtgut** consignment by goods train *(Br.)*; ~ **eines Geldbetrages** remittance of funds; ~ **eines Konkurrenzprogramms** opposite program(me); ~ **gegen Nachnahme** cash (collect, *US*) -on-delivery; ~ **von Nachrichten** newscast, news broadcast (bulletin), radio newsreel *(Br.)*; ~ **des Werbefunks** commercial broadcast;
~ **abrufen** to call forward a shipment; ~ **ausstrahlen** to broadcast a program(me); ~ **beenden (einstellen)** *(Rundfunk)* to go off the air; ~ **beginnen** to go on the air; ~ **unterbrechen** to interrupt the program(me).

Sendungsbewußtsein sense of mission.

Senf dazugeben, seinen to chime (chip) in, to have an oar in everyman's boat, to put in one's oar.

Senge beziehen to get a hiding (thrashing).

sengen und brennen to burn and to ravage.

sengende Hitze parching (scorching) heat.

senil senile;
~ **sein** to be in one's dotage.

Senior senior, elder;
~ **der Anwaltschaft** father of the bar;
~chef senior chief, chief (senior) partner.

Senioren|verein old-age pensioners club; **~wohnheim** old folk's (people's, *Br.*) home, asylum for the aged.

Senioritätsprinzip seniority rule.

Senke low ground, depression, *(gemächliche)* gradual descent.

senken to lower, to reduce, to depress;
sich ~ *(Boden)* to give way, *(Fundament)* to settle, to sag, *(Preis)* to reduce, to lower, to take off, to cut, *(Straße)* to dip, to drop, to descend; **Blick** ~ to lower one's eyes; **Diskontsatz** ~ to lower (cut, reduce) the bank *(Br.)* (discount, rediscount, *US*) rate; **Fahne** ~ to dip the colo(u)rs; **um die Hälfte** ~ to cut (reduce) by half; **Mieten** ~ to lower the rents; **sich stark** ~ to descend steeply; **Steuern** ~ to reduce (cut, lighten) taxes; **Unkosten** ~ to reduce costs; **Zinssätze** ~ to lower the rate of interest, to reduce interest; **Zollsätze** ~ to reduce the customs duties.

Senk|grube sump, draining (waste) well, cesspool; **~kasten** caisson.

senkrecht perpendicular, vertical, plumb, upright;
~ **abfallen** to drop sheer;
~ **abfallender Felsen** vertical cliff; **~e Linie** vertical line.

Senkrecht|start direct (vertical) take-off; **~starter** vertical take-off aircraft, *(fig.)* flyer.

Senkung cut, reduction, lowering, *(Abhang)* falling off, decline, hang, *(Kurse)* downward movement, depression, *(Preise)* reduction, lowering;
~ **der Ausgaben** retrenchment of expenses; ~ **des Diskontsatzes** lowering (reduction) of the discount (bank, *Br.*) rate, lowering of the rate of rediscount *(US)*; ~ **der Kosten** cost reduction (cutting); ~ **der Miete** reduction of rent; ~ **der Mindestreserverhaltung** reduction of the minimum reserves; ~ **der Preise** price cut, cut (cutback) in prices; ~ **der Steuern** tax reduction (cut); ~ **der Straße** dip in the road; ~ **der Unkosten** cutting down the expenses; ~ **der Zinssätze** reduction of the interest rate; ~ **der Zollsätze** customs reduction, reduction in duty.

Sensation splash, scorcher, sensation;
kurzlebige ~ a nine days' wonder;
große ~ **hervorrufen** to create (cause) a great sensation; **auf ~en aus sein** to be out for sensation.

sensationell sensational, hot, sensay *(sl.)*;
~ **aufgemacht** sensationalized;
~e Nachrichten sensational piece of news, hot stuff, redhot news *(coll.)*; **~e Überschrift** scare headline, screamer *(US sl.)*;
~e Werbung stunt advertising, gimmick *(US)*.

Sensations|bedürfnis hunger for excitement; **~blatt** sensational newspaper, yellow journal *(US)*, tabloid paper, rag; **~gier** hunger for excitement; **~hascherei** sensationalism; **~journalismus** sensational (yellow, *US*) journalism; **sich der ~lust der Öffentlichkeit beugen** to cater to the public demand for the sensational; **aus ~lust übertreiben** to pile on the agony.

sensationslüstern sensationalistic, *(Presse)* yellow.

Sensations|lustiger, übersättigter jaded thrillseeker; **~nachricht, ~meldung** sensational news, hot stuff *(US)*; **~nachricht abgeben (darstellen)** to make good copy; **vorwiegend ~nachrichten verbreiten** to deal largely in sensations; **~presse** yellow *(US)* (stunt) press, tabloid journalism; **~roman** sensational novel; **~rummel** ballyhoo *(coll.)*; **~schau** monkey act; **~stück** tank drama, thriller, shocker, spine-chiller *(sl.)*; **~sucht** sensationalism.

sensationssüchtig agog for news.

Sensationswerbung stunt advertising, gimmick *(US)*.

Sensitivitätsanalyse sensitivity analysis.

Sensoreinstellung, computergesteuerte electronic control touch-turning system.

sentimental sentimental, mawkish, maudlin, mushy, sloppy, soppy *(Br.)*;
~er Film pop, corn, tearjerker *(US coll.)*; **~es Gerede** slush; **~er Schlager** croon song; **~es Zeug** sob stuff.

Sentimentalität sentimentality;
ohne falsche ~ as hard as nails;
kommerziell ausgenutzte ~ schmaltz *(sl.)*.
separat separate, apart, self-contained, *(zusätzlich)* additionally;
~ **wohnen** to have a self-contained flat (apartment);
~**er Eingang** private entrance; ~**es Zimmer** separate room.
Separat|abdruck special impression, offprint; ~**anzeige** special advice; ~**eingang** private entrance; ~**friede** separate peace.
Separatismus separatism.
Separatistenprogramm separatist ticket.
separatistische Wünsche separatist urge.
Separat|konto special (separate) account; ~**vertrag** special agreement, separate treaty.
Sequester sequestrator of land, administrator, stakeholder, trustee, official receiver *(Br.)*, *(während der Prozeßdauer)* receiver pendente lite;
aufgrund einer Globalverpfändung eingesetzter ~ receiver under a floating charge;
~**vermögen** sequestered property; ~**verwaltung** sequestration, temporary receivership.
sequestrieren to sequester, to sequestrate.
Sequestrierung des Vermögens sequestration of property.
Serie series, line, run, set, cycle, batch, lot, nest, *(Anleihe)* issue, series, *(Ausgabe)* issue, *(Satz)* set, suit;
in ~**n hergestellt** mass-produced, manufactured; **nicht in** ~**n hergestellt** nonmanufactured;
erste ~ first issue; **gezogene** ~**n** *(Lotterie)* series drawn; **kleine** ~ short run; **neue** ~ fresh issue; **zweite** ~ second issue;
~ **von Ereignissen** consecution of events; **durch nachstehendes Pfandrecht gesicherte** ~ **von Obligationen** junior issue of bonds; ~ **von Prozessen** string of lawsuits; **großangelegte** ~ **von Verkaufsbriefen** campaign series of sales letters;
in ~**n herstellen** to serialize, to mass-produce.
Serien|anleihe serial bonds; ~**anzeige** serial (flowing-on) advertisement; ~**arbeit** serial (repetition) work; ~**artikel** mass-produced article, standard line; ~**ausführung** standard model (make); ~**ausgabe von Pfandbriefen** serial issue of bonds; ~**auslosung** series drawing; ~**auto** volume (mass-production) car, stock model (car) *(US)*; ~**bauprogramm** mass-production program(me); ~**emission** serial issue of bonds; ~**erzeugnis**, ~**fabrikat** standard item, set work, mass-produced article; ~**fabrikant** mass producer; ~**fabrikation**, ~**fertigung** continuous manufacturing, serial production, wholesale manufacture; ~**güter** mass-produced articles; ~**haus** prefabricated house; ~**herstellung** large-scale manufacture, repetition work, mass- (multiple, machine, series, batch) production, serial construction (manufacture), wholesale manufacture; ~**kalkulation** job-order cost accounting; ~**lotterie** serial lottery; ~**marke** associated trademark.
serienmäßig in series, standard, regular, production-line;
~ **hergestellt** manufactured wholesale;
~ **herstellen** to mass- (volume-) produce, *(Verleger)* to serialize; ~ **hergestellt werden** to be manufactured wholesale;
~**e Herstellung** mass (volume) production, wholesale manufacture, *(Verlag)* serialization.
Serien|modell standard (stock, *US*) model, *(Auto)* mass-production (-volume) car, stock car (model) *(US)*; ~**muster** representative sample; ~**nummer** serial number; ~**obligation** serial bond; ~**preis** serial price; ~**preisgeschäft** chain (one-price) shop *(Br.)*, dime store *(US)*; ~**produktion** mass (quantity, large-sale, batch, standardized) production, quantity manufacturing; **in** ~**produktion hergestellt** mass-produced; **mit der** ~**produktion beginnen** to start full production; ~**rabatt** fre-quency discount; ~**rabatt innerhalb eines Jahres** *(Werbung)* time rate *(US)*.
serienreif ready to go in mass production.
Serien|reife production stage; ~**schalter** *(el.)* multibreak, sequence switch; ~**umfang** batch size; ~**verarbeitung** *(Datenanlage)* serial processing; ~**wagen** production (mass-production, stock, *US*) car; ~**ware** stock articles.
serienweise in series;
~ **anordnen** to seriate.
Serienziehung *(Lotterie)* serial drawing.
seriös serious, reliable, trustworthy, respectable;
~ **wirken** to make a serious impression;
~**er Eindruck** serious appearance; ~**e Firma** respectable firm; ~**es Geschäft** sound business house; ~**er Geschäftsmann** trustworthy businessman; ~**er Käufer** serious buyer; ~**e Quelle** reliable authority (source).
Serpentine switchback;
in ~**n heraufführen** to switchback up; **in** ~ **verlaufen** to zigzag.
Serpentinenstraße serpentine (ribbon) road, switchback, zigzag [road].
Service service, *(Auto)* maintenance service, *(Auto)* service station;
erstklassiger ~ first-class service;
üblichen ~ **bieten** to provide the usual amenities; **nutzbringenden** ~ **leisten** to provide with intelligent service.
Servierbrett tray, salver.
Servieren eines Abendessens waiting at a dinner.
servieren to dish up the dinner.
Servier|mädchen waitress; ~**platte** platter; ~**tisch** sideboard; **fahrbarer** ~**tisch** dining-room table; ~**wagen** trolley table *(Br.)*, *(Flugzeug)* food cart.
Serviette napkin.
servil servile, cringing, toadyish, obsequious.
Servitut easement, servitude.
Servo|bremse servo (power) brake; ~**lenkung** power-assisted steering [wheel]; ~**motor** booster.
Sessel easy chair, armchair;
~**lift** chair lift; ~**rückstellknopf** seat recline button.
seßhaft permanent, established, stationary, sedentary, *(ansässig)* domiciled, resident;
sich ~ **machen** to settle in life.
Seßhaftigkeit domestication, settlement.
Setzen typesetting, composition;
beim ~ **auslassen** to make an omission.
setzen to set, to place, to put, *(Schrift)* to set in type, to compose, *(wetten)* to wager, to bet, to stake;
sich ~ *(Erde, Haus)* to settle, to sag, *(Staub)* to settle; **mit Abständen** ~ *(drucktechn.)* to keep out; **alles daran** ~ **eine Stelle zu bekommen** to do one's utmost to get a job; **in Anführungsstriche** ~ to put in converted commas; **auf etw.** ~ to stake (bet) on s. th.; **sich vor ein anderes Auto** ~ to put o. s. in front of another car; **in Betrieb** ~ to start running, to put into operation, to set to work; **sich in Bewegung** ~ to start; **Himmel und Hölle in Bewegung** ~ to move heaven and earth; **zu breit** ~ *(drucktechn.)* to overset; **j. auf Diät** ~ to put s. o. on a diet; **j. unter Druck** ~ to exert pressure on s. o.; **fortlaufend** ~ *(drucktechn.)* to run on; **Frist** ~ to lay down a time limit, to appoint a day; **in Gang** ~ to set going; **außer Gefecht** ~ to put out of action; **Gerücht in die Welt** ~ to spread (circulate) a rumo(u)r; **gesperrt** ~ *(drucktechn.)* to space out; **Grenzen** ~ to limit; **Holz** ~ to stack wood; **alles auf eine Karte** ~ to put all one's eggs into one basket; **auf die falsche Karte** ~ to back the wrong horse; **j. von etw. in Kenntnis** ~ to inform s. o. of s. th., to serve notice to s. o.; **kompreß** ~ *(drucktechn.)* to close up, to set solid; **sich etw. in den Kopf** ~ to get an idea in one's head; **außer Kraft** ~ *(Gesetz)* to repeal, *(Vertrag)* to annul, to cancel, to rescind, to avoid; **außer Kurs** ~ to withdraw from circulation; **sich ins rechte Licht** ~ to put o. s. in a good light; **j. auf halben Lohn** ~ to put s. o. on half-pay; **j. an die frische Luft** ~ to chuck s. o. out, *(kündigen)* to fire *(coll.)*, to sack *(coll.)*; **Manuskript** ~ to cast off (set up) a manuscript; **Maschine in Gang** ~ to start a machine; **seinen Namen unter einen Brief** ~ to put one's signature to a letter; **jds. Namen auf eine Liste** ~ to put s. one's name on a list; **jem. einen anderen vor die Nase** ~ to make s. o. some's superior; **neu** ~ *(drucktechn.)* to recompose, to reset; **j. obenan** ~ to put s. o. at the head of the table; **aufs falsche Pferd** ~ to back the wrong horse; **Pünktchen aufs I** ~ to dot the i; **auf jds. Rechnung** ~ to charge to s. one's account; **neue Rechtsnormen** ~ to establish new legal standards; **sich zur Ruhe** ~ to retire; **j. schachmatt** ~ to checkmate s. o.; **aufs Spiel** ~ to risk, to hazard; **Stück auf den Spielplan** ~ to stage a play; **j. auf die Straße** ~ to throw (chuck) s. o. out; **sich in Szene** ~ to put o. s. in the limelight; **auf die Tagesordnung** ~ to place on (include in) the agenda; **Banknoten in Umlauf** ~ to issue bank-notes, to put bank-notes in circulation; **Falschurkunde in Umlauf** ~ to utter a forged document; **sich ins Unrecht** ~ to put o. s. in the wrong; **seine Unterschrift unter eine Urkunde** ~ to sign a document; **sich mit jem. in Verbindung** ~ to contact (communicate with) s. o.; **Vertrauen in j.** ~ to place confidence in s. o.; **sich in seinen Wagen** ~ to get into one's car; **in die Zeitung** ~ to insert into a paper, to put into the papers; **sich hohe Ziele** ~ to fly high;
etw. zu ~ **vergessen** *(drucktechn.)* to make an out.
Setzer typesetter, form setter, composer, printing worker.
Setzerei composing (case) room.
Setzer|lehrling apprentice compositor, printer's devil; ~**saal** composing (case) room.
Setz|fehler typographical error, error in composition, misprint, setting mistake; ~**kasten** letter case; ~**keil** key; ~**ling** nursing

plant; ~**linie** setting rule; ~**maschine** typesetting (composing) machine, *(für Einzelbuchstaben)* monotype; **computergesteuerte ~maschine** computer-based typesetter; ~**maschinenzeile** slug; ~**schiff** [makeup] galley; ~**stein** press stone.

Seuche epidemic (contagious) disease, contagion, plague; **rasch um sich greifende ~** rapidly spreading epidemic; **meldepflichtige ~** notifiable disease;
~ ausrotten to eradicate a disease.

seuchenartig epidemic.

Seuchen|gebiet epidemic area; ~**lazarett** isolation hospital; ~**opfer** victim of a plague.

Seufzerspalte *(Zeitung)* lonely hearts column, agony column *(Br.)*.

Sex|boutique sex shop; ~**film** sex film, nudic, skin flick *(sl.)*.

Sexual|aufklärung birds-and-bees talk; ~**verbrechen** sex crime; ~**werbung** indecent advertising.

sezieren to dissect, to perform an autopsy.

Sichausgeben als Gesellschafter holding out *(Br.)*.

Sichaustoben fling.

Sicher, auf Nummer ~ sitzen to be out of harm's way, to be safe.

sicher secure, unfailing, *(Anlage)* safe, *(befestigt)* fast, *(bestimmt)* definite, certain, *(Kredit)* secured, *(kreditwürdig)* reliable, trustworthy, sound, good, *(Seeschadensversicherung)* well, *(stabil)* stable, solid, *(Urteil)* sure, reliable, *(Wertpapier)* first-class (-rate), gilt-edged *(Br.)*, prime *(US)*, *(zuversichtlich)* confident, positive;
absolut ~ as safe as houses; **fast ~** *(Statistik)* almost certain; **so ~ wie das Amen in der Kirche** as sure as eggs is eggs;
~ anlegen to invest safely; **etw. ~ aufbewahren** to keep s. th. safe; **~ auftreten** to act with assurance; **sich nicht ganz ~ auf den Beinen fühlen** to feel a bit shaky; **auf Nummer ~ gehen** to be on the safe side, to play for safety; **~ Erfolg haben** to be sure to succeed; **j. bis zu einem Kredit von 5000 Dollar für ~ halten** to consider s. o. trustworthy to the extent of $ 5000; **~ sein** to make no doubt; **gesellschaftlich völlig ~ sein** to be at home in society; **seiner Sache völlig ~ sein** to be sure of one's ground (certain of s. th.); **sich eines Parlamentssitzes völlig ~ sein** to be safe to win a seat;
mit ~en Absatzmöglichkeiten certain to sell; ~**er Arbeitsplatz** safe place to work; ~**e Aufbewahrung** safekeeping; ~**es Auftreten** assurance, aplomb; ~**e Außenstände** good debts; ~**er Beweis** positive proof; ~**er Bürge** substantial bail; ~**es Ergebnis** trustworthy result; ~**e Existenz** secure existence; ~**er Fahrer** safe driver; ~**e Forderungen** good debts; ~**e Garantie** reliable guarantee; **~ angelegtes Geld** safely invested money; ~**es Geleit** safe conduct; ~**es Geschäft** trustee business; ~**er Gewahrsam** safekeeping, safe custody; ~**er Gewährsmann** reliable authority; **mit ~em Griff** with a practised hand; ~**e Informationsquelle** reliable source; ~**e Kapitalanlage** safe investment; ~**er Kunde** loyal customer, good man; **j. an einen ~en Ort verbringen** to take s. o. to a safe place; ~**e Papiere** gilt-edged *(Br.)* (trustee, *US*) stock; **aus ~er Quelle** from a safe quarter, on good authority; ~**e Sache** safe business (bet, *coll.*), a cinch *(sl.)*; ~**e Tatsache** certainty; ~**er Tip** reliable tip; ~**e Valuta** sound currency; ~**er Verladeplatz** safe loading place; ~**er Wechsel** fine bill *(Br.)*, first-class paper *(US)*, prime bill *(US)*; ~**e Zusage** binding promise.

sichergehen to err on the safe side.

sichergestellt secured;
nicht ~ unsecured;
~**e Forderung** secured debt; ~**er Gläubiger** secured creditor; ~**er Kredit** secured credit.

Sicherheit security, *(Auftreten)* assurance, aplomb, *(Bürgschaft)* bail, surety, guarantee *(Br.)*, guaranty *(US)*, warranty, *(Deckung)* cover, *(Garantie)* warranty, *(Gefahrlosigkeit)* safety, *(Gewißheit)* certainty, surety, *(Kreditdeckung)* security, collateral *(US)*, *(mil., pol.)* security, *(Pfand)* pledge, security, surety *(US)*, *(Schadloshaltung)* indemnity, *(Selbstvertrauen)* confidence, *(Zuverlässigkeit)* trustworthiness, reliability;
durch eine ~ gedeckt covered by a guarantee; **gegen ~** by way of security; **in ~** safe, secure, out of harm's way; **mit einiger ~** with a degree of certainty; **mit hinreichender ~** with reasonable certainty; **mit tödlicher ~** sure as eggs is eggs; **nur zur ~** *(auf Wechseln)* for deposit only; **zur ~** by way of security; **zur ~ bestellt** pledged;
~**en** *(Bank)* securities, collateral *(US)*;
angemessene ~ fair security; **ausreichende ~** ample (sufficient) security; **auswechselbare ~** floating (shifting) security; **bankmäßige (bankübliche) ~** banking collateral; **dingliche ~** material (real, *US*) security, heritable (underlying) security, security on property *(US)*; **erstklassige ~en** first-class (gilt-edged, *Br.*, trustee, *US*) securities; **nicht durch Dokumente gedeckte ~** personal security; **geeignete ~** eligible security; **gemeinsame ~** joint collateral *(US)*; **von dritter Seite gestellte ~** third-party security; **gewährte ~en** guarantees furnished; **zusätzlich gewährte ~en** *(Grundstücksübertragung)* collateral assurance; **gültige ~** valid security; **hinreichende ~** sufficient security; **hinterlegte ~** security deposited; **hochwertige ~** high-grade security; **hypothekarische ~** mortgage, real security *(US)*, security by mortgage, security on property *(US)*; **kaufmännische ~** trading security; **kollektive ~** *(pol.)* collective security; **nationale ~** national security (safety); **öffentliche ~** public security; **ordnungsgemäße ~** reliable security, peace; **persönliche ~** personal security, security of person; **nicht realisierbare ~** dead security; **scheinbare ~** rope of sand; **soziale ~** social security; **statistische ~** confidence coefficient; **auf einen Treuhänder übertragene ~** debenture trust deed *(Br.)*; **unbedingte ~** absolute safety; **vertragliche ~** contractual security; **vorhandene ~** security owned, underlying security; **vorrangige ~en** prior-ranking securities; **weitere ~** collateral warranty; **wertlose ~** dead security, straw bail; **zusätzliche ~** additional (collateral, *US*) security; **zweifache ~** double security; **zweitrangige ~** junior security;
~ über alles safety first; **~ am Arbeitsplatz** safe working conditions, employee security; **~ des Flugverkehrs** airline security; **~ für eine Forderung** security for a debt; **~ in Form von an der New Yorker Börse gehandelten Effekten** stock-exchange collateral *(US)*; **~ durch Hinterlegung handelsüblicher Effekten** regular collateral *(US)*; **~ durch Hinterlegung von Industrieaktien** industrial collateral *(US)*; **~ für einen Kredit** security (collateral) for a loan; **~ für Prozeßkosten** security for costs; **~ zur See** maritime safety;
~ anbieten to offer bail; **sein Haus als ~ anbieten** to offer one's house as guarantee; **~en aufteilen** to marshal securities; **mit großer ~ auftreten** to have plenty of assurance; **Schuldschein mit zusätzlicher ~ ausstatten** to secure a note by the pledge of collateral security; **~ auswechseln** to float a security; **zur ~ gegebene Effekten auswechseln** to commute collateral; **~ bestellen** to register (give, charge, afford) a security, to perform a warranty, to collaterate, to give bonds; **öffentliche ~ bewahren** to keep the peace; **~ bieten** to offer security; **etw. in ~ bringen** to put s. th. in a safe place; **Wertsachen in ~ bringen** to secure valuables; **Gefahr für die öffentliche ~ darstellen** to be dangerous for the public; **als ~ dienen** to serve as cover (collateral, *US*); **~ für verfallen erklären** to forfeit security; **als ~ gegebene Schuldverschreibungen für verfallen erklären** to escheat bonds; **~en fordern** to ask for a guarantee; **~en freigeben** to release securities; **~ geben** to secure; **öffentliche ~ gefährden** to endanger the maintenance of public order; **öffentliche ~ beim Autofahren gefährden** to drive to the public danger; **~ eines Landes gefährden** to jeopardize the security of a country; **gegen ~ Kredit gewähren** to lend on security, to loan on collateral *(US)*; **zusätzliche ~ für einen Kredit gewähren** to replenish a loan; **~ des Vaterlandes gewährleisten** to keep the home fires burning; **als ~ hingeben** to turn over as security; **als ~ hinterlegen** to post a bond *(US)*, to lodge (turn over) as security, to leave as a guarantee, to deposit as underlying security *(US)*; **~ leisten** to provide security, to become (stand) surety, to put up (post) a bond *(US)*, *(für Kredit)* to furnish security (collateral, *US*); **doppelte ~ leisten** to give (furnish) collateral security; **zusätzliche ~en leisten** to furnish collateral *(US)*, to margin up; **~ in Anspruch nehmen** to call up a guarantee; **mangels ~ protestieren** *(Wechsel)* to protest for want of security; **in ~ sein** to be on the pavement *(fam.)*; **um jds. ~ besorgt sein** to be concerned about s. one's safety; **durch ~en gedeckt sein** to be in possession of pledges; **für größere ~ im Straßenverkehr sorgen** to promote greater safety in road traffic; **~ stellen** to supply collateral, *(Bürgschaft)* to offer (find) bail, to post (put up) a bond *(US)*, *(Kredit)* to afford (furnish) security; **erstklassige ~en stellen** to sweeten a loan *(sl.)*; **geeignete ~en stellen** to provide with acceptable securities; **sein Vermögen als ~ stellen** to pledge one's property; **zusätzliche ~en stellen** to replenish a loan; **~ bei Gericht stellen** to file a bond; **öffentliche ~ und Ordnung stören** to break (disturb) the peace; **~ überprüfen** *(mil.)* to vet; **gegen ~ verkaufen** *(Effektengeschäft)* to sell on margin; **~[en] verlangen** to want a security; **~en verwerten** to realize securities; **auf eine ~ verzichten** to surrender a security; **öffentliche ~ und Ordnung wiederherstellen** to restore public order (law and order); **in ~ wiegen** to rock in security; **~ zurückkaufen** *(Treuhänder)* to redeem a security; **~ zurückziehen** to revoke a guarantee; **~en zusammenfassen** to tack securities.

Sicherheiten|bewertung valuation of securities; ~**empfänger** security holder; ~**formular** *(Bank)* security form; ~**mappe** *(Kreditakte)* loan envelope; ~**verpfändung** pledge of securities; ~**verwertung** realization of securities; **auf ~verwertung verzichten und den Gesamtbetrag als Konkursforderung anmelden** *(Aussonderungsberechtigter)* to surrender the security and to prove the whole debt.

Sicherheits|abkommen *(pol.)* security agreement, defensive alliance; ~**abstand** *(Fahrzeug)* safe distance; ~**anforderungen** security requirements; ~**arrest** preventive custody; ~**aspekt** security aspect; ~**aufzug** safety hoist; ~**ausschuß** security (vigilance, *US*) committee, National Security Council *(US)*; ~**ausweis** safety card; ~**beamter** security guard, security officer, spook *(US sl.)*; **leitender ~beauftragter** security director; ~**bedürfnis** need for security, security interest; ~**berater** adviser on national security, [national] security adviser; ~**bereich** sensitive area.

Sicherheitsbestimmungen safety regulations (provisions, conditions);
unter strengen ~ arbeiten to work in tight security; ~ **sorgfältig beachten** to be safety-conscious; **sorgfältige Einhaltung der ~ gewährleisten** to promote safety consciousness; **in die ~ eingewiesen werden** to receive security briefing.

Sicherheitsbetrag caution money *(Br.)*;
~ **für unvorhergesehene Fälle** *(Börse)* working margin.

sicherheitsbewußt sein to be security conscious.

Sicherheits|depot guarantee *(Br.)* (contingency) fund; ~**dienst** secret (intelligence) service; **staatlicher ~dienst** Bureau of State Security; ~**einrichtungen** safety features (equipment); ~**empfänger** warranty (security) holder; ~**erfordernisse** *(Börse)* margin requirements; ~**erklärung** guaranty bond; ~**erwägungen** security considerations; ~**faktor** safety factor, margin of safety, backstop; ~**film** nonflammable film; ~**fonds** safety (collateral) fund, *(Garantiefonds)* guarantee *(Br.)* (contingency, provident reserve) fund; ~**garantie** *(pol.)* security guarantee; ~**geber** warrantor; ~**glas** safety glass; ~**grad** level of reassurance; ~**gründe** security reasons; ~**gurt** safety belt (harness), *(Flugzeug)* seat belt, scare strap *(sl.)*; ~**gurt anlegen** to buckle one's seat belt.

sicherheitshalber for safety's sake, preventively, to be on the safe side;
~ **übereignen** to pledge as security.

Sicherheits|hinterlegung guarantee deposit; ~**interesse** security interest *(US)*; ~**kette** safety (door, guard) chain; ~**klausel** safeguard, escape (savings) clause; ~**koeffizient** margin of safety; ~**konferenz** security conference; ~**kontrolle** safety supervision; ~**kräfte** security force (guards); **seine gesamten ~kräfte in Alarmzustand versetzen** to put one's security services on full alert; ~**lage** security situation; ~**lampe** *(Bergbau)* miner's lamp; ~**leck** security leak; ~**leine** grab rope.

Sicherheitsleistung lodging of security, *(Bürgschaft)* bail, *(bei Gericht)* cost bond, *(Kreditunterlage)* [collateral] security, *(Pächter)* security deposit, *(Prozeß)* recognizance, cost (judiciary, court) bond, *(Seeversicherung)* bail, *(Sicherheit)* security bond (deposit), *(Treuhänder)* official bond;
~ **zur Abwendung der Vollstreckung** replevin bond; ~ **im Berufungsverfahren** appeal bond; ~ **bei Gericht** judicial (court) bond; ~ **für Gerichtskosten** security (bond) for costs; ~ **des Nachlaßverwalters (Testamentsvollstreckers)** administration (administrator's) bond; ~ **des Revisionsklägers** bail in error; ~ **des Submittenden** performance bond; **gerichtliche ~ für eine einstweilige Verfügung** attachment bond *(US)*; ~ **des Vollstreckungsschuldners** forthcoming bond;
~ **ablehnen** to refuse to grant bail; **gegen ~ ankaufen** *(Börse)* to purchase on margin; ~ **anordnen** to grant bail; **j. gegen ~ entlassen** to release s. o. on bail; ~ **erhöhen** to enlarge bail; ~ **für verfallen erklären** to forfeit security; **j. gegen ~ freilassen** to admit s. o. to bail; **gegen ~ kaufen** *(Börse)* to buy on margin; **gegen ~ verkaufen** *(Börse)* to sell on margin; **gepfändete Sachen gegen ~ zurückerhalten** to replevy, to recover goods.

Sicherheits|marge safety margin; ~**maßnahmen** protective (precautionary, safety, security) measures, safety performance, measures of public security; ~**maßnahmen treffen** to take precautions; ~**nadel** safety pin; ~**nehmer** chattel mortgagee, warrantee, guarantee; ~**netz** safety net; ~**normen** safety standards, standards of safety; ~**pakt** security pact; ~**pfand** pledge, pawn, security; ~**polizei** security police; ~**position** collateral position; ~**programm** safety program(me); ~**rat** *(pol.)* National Security Council *(US)*, *(UN)* Security Council; **dingliches ~recht** security interest *(US)*; ~**reifen** safety tyre; ~**riegel** safety bolt; ~**risiko** safety hazard; ~**schloß** safety (guard, check) lock, Yale lock; ~**spanne** *(Börse)* safety margin; ~**stufe** *(Statistik)* significance level; ~**summe** *(Börse)* margin, retention money *(Br.)*; ~**system** security apparatus; ~**truppen der UN** United Nations peacekeeping forces; **aus ~überlegungen** on safety aspects; ~**überprüfung** *(mil.)* security clearance, vetting; ~**urteil** cautionary judgment; ~**ventil** escape (overpressure, alarm, safety, priming) valve; **politisches ~ventil** political escape valve; ~**vereinbarung** collateral agreement; ~**versprechen** security pledge; ~**vertrag** security treaty; ~**verwahrung** preventive custody; ~**vorkehrungen** security (safety) precautions, security arrangements, protective (precautionary) measures; ~**vorkehrungen verstärken** to tighten security; ~**vorrichtung** fail-safe device, safety catch (device, appliance), *(gegen Diebstahl)* theft prevention device; ~**vorschriften** security (safety) regulations; **den neuen ~vorschriften entsprechen** to qualify under the new safety regulations; ~**wechsel** guaranteed bill of exchange; ~**wechsel geben** to deposit a bill as collateral *(US)*; ~**zone** safety [control] zone; ~**zuschlag** excess charge, *(Lebensversicherung)* loading, *(Versicherung)* excess clause.

sicherlich and no mistake.

sichern to secure, to safeguard, to bring into safety, *(gewährleisten)* to guarantee, to guaranty, *(schadlos halten)* to indemnify, *(Kredit)* to secure, to cover, to collaterate, *(Stellung)* to make good, *(Straße)* to cover, to protect;
sich ~ to secure o. s., to put on ice *(US)*, *(rückversichern)* to hedge; **durch vertragliche Bestimmungen** ~ to guard (hedge in) by clauses; **Frieden** ~ to ensure peace; **hypothekarisch** ~ to secure by mortgage; **sich Importe** ~ to book for imports; **Kurs** ~ to hedge (cover) a rate; **sich einen größeren Marktanteil** ~ to secure a better share of the market; **Nachlaß** ~ to preserve (protect) an estate; **sich einen Parkplatz** ~ to preempt a parking place; **sich eine Vertretung** ~ to secure an agency; **durch Vorposten** ~ *(mil.)* to picket.

sicherstehender Betrag safe sum in hand.

sicherstellen to secure, to safeguard, to insure, to put on ice *(US)*, *(durch Deckung)* to cover, to impound, *(gewährleisten)* to guarantee, to guaranty, to warrant, *(schadlos halten)* to indemnify;
sich ~ to secure o. s.; **Gläubiger** ~ to secure a creditor; **hypothekarisch** ~ to cover by a mortgage, to mortgage; **Forderung hypothekarisch** ~ to secure a debt by mortgage; **gegen Verluste** ~ to safeguard (protect) against losses; **Versorgung der Bevölkerung** ~ to provide the population with food; **gestohlenen Wagen** ~ to put a stolen car in safekeeping; **Zahlung** ~ to secure payment.

Sicherstellung safeguard, *(durch Deckung)* cover, *(Garantie)* guarantee, guaranty, assurance, *(Kredit)* security, collateral *(US)*, *(Schadloshaltung)* indemnification, indemnity;
gegen ~ against security;
hypothekarische ~ security by mortgage;
~ **der Familie** family protection.

Sicherstellungs|depot security (collateral, *US*) deposit; ~**fonds** guarantee *(Br.)* (contingency) fund; ~**konto** guaranty account *(US)*.

Sicherung *(el.)* safety fuse, *(Interessen)* protection, safeguard, *(Kredit)* security, furnishing of collateral *(US)*;
zur ~ des Friedens in order to protect peace;
durchgebrannte ~ blown fuse;
~ **des Arbeitsplatzes** safe working conditions, employee security; ~ **der Umweltbedingungen** environmental safety; ~ **gegen Verlust** cover against loss;
zur ~ gegebene Effekte auswechseln to commute collateral *(US)*; **neue ~ einsetzen** to put in a new fuse.

Sicherungs|abtretung assignment of accounts receivable *(US)*; ~**auftrag** *(pol.)* security performance; ~**automat** *(el.)* automatic circuit breaker; ~**bereich** security zone; ~**draht** fuse wire; ~**geber** lienee, principal, chattle mortgagor *(US)*; ~**gegenstand** collateral; ~**geschäft** hedge, secured transaction *(US)*; ~**geschäft abschließen** to hedge; ~**gut** equitable lien, pledged goods; ~**hypothek** conventional mortgage; ~**kauf** conditional sales contract; ~**klauseln** safeguards, safeguard clauses; ~**maßnahmen** security transactions; ~**maßnahmen auf einem Flugplatz** airport security precautions; ~**nehmer** chattel mortgagee *(US)*, lienor *(US)*; ~**pfandrecht** charging lien; **hypothekenähnliches ~recht** equitable mortgage; ~**recht in wechselnder Höhe** floating lien *(US)*; ~**recht für eine Restkaufpreisforderung** purchase money security interest *(US)*; ~**schein** letter of trust *(Br.)*, trust letter *(Br.)*; ~**stöpsel** safety plug; ~**truppen** protecting troops, covering forces.

sicherungsübereignen to give in security.

sicherungsübereignet pledged as security;
~e Gegenstände equitable lien; **~er Wechsel** pawned bill of exchange.

Sicherungsübereignung [etwa] field warehousing *(US)*, mortgage of goods, chattel mortgage, trust receipt transaction *(US)*;
~ zur Absicherung des Restkaufpreises purchase-money chattel mortgage *(US)*, *(am Warenlager mit wechselndem Bestand)* statutory factor's lien *(US)*; **~ von Kapitalanteilen** mortgage of shares;
~ aufheben to release from trust.

Sicherungsübereignungs|gesetz [etwa] Bill of Sale Act *(US)*; **~schein** field warehouse receipt *(US)*; **~urkunde** trust (field warehouse, *US*) receipt; **~verfahren** trust receipt device *(US)*; **~vertrag** fiduciary contract, letter of lien *(Br.)*, field warehouse receipt *(US)*, trust agreement *(US)*.

Sicherungs|vereinbarung, schriftliche memorandum of equitable mortgage under hand; **~verkauf** hedge selling;
~verwahrung restraint, preventive custody, *(Straftäter)* preventive detention; **zu ~zwecken** pledged as security; **zu ~zwecken übereignen** to pledge as security.

Sicht sight, *(Flugwetter)* visibility;
auf kurze ~ at short sight, short-dated; **auf kürzere ~** in the shorter term; **auf lange ~** at a long date, long-dated, over the long pull (term); **auf längere ~ gesehen** on the longer view; **auf weite ~** on a long-term basis; **aus dieser ~** from this angle; **aus meiner ~** from my point of view; **bei ~** on presentation; **bei ~ zahlbar** payable at sight; **mit kurzer ~** at short sight, short-dated; **nach ~** after sight; **60 Tage nach ~** at sixty day's sight; **noch nicht in ~** still unsighted;
vertikal und horizontal begrenzte ~ *(Flugwetter)* zero conditions; **beschränkte ~** constricted outlook; **gute ~** high visibility; **kurze ~** short date; **schlechte ~** obscure view, *(Flugwetter)* low visibility;
in ~ kommen to heave in sight; **~ nehmen (verbauen)** to obstruct (shut out) the view, to block up the window; **auf lange ~ planen** to make plans on a long-term basis; **~ trüben** to dim the sight; **einem Nachbarn die ~ verbauen** to stop a neighbo(u)r's light; **~ versperren** to blot out (blur) the view; **bei ~ fällig werden** to mature on (upon) presentation;
~anweisung sight (demand) bill.

sichtbar visible, viewable, visual, open, external, perceptible, *(offenkundig)* obvious, conspicuous, manifest, plain, distinct, clear;
deutlich ~ in evidence, evident; **gut ~** plain to view;
~ sein to meet the eye; **für alle ~ sein** to be on public parade; **~ erfreut sein** to be obviously pleased;
als Zeichen meiner ~en Anerkennung as a token of my appreciation; **~e Ausfuhr** visible exports; **~e Besserung** marked improvement; **ohne ~en Erfolg** without noticeable success; **~e Gegenstände** visual objects; **~e Posten der Leistungsbilanz** visible items of trade; **~e Reserve** open (declared) reserves; **~er Unterschied** marked difference; **äußerlich ~e Verletzung** visible injury.

Sicht|barkeitsmesser visibility meter; **~barmachung** *(einer Werbeidee)* visual, visualization; **~bedingungen** conditions of visibility; **~behinderung** obstructing the view; **~bereich** range of vision; **durch Bäume geschaffene ~blende** screen of trees; **~einlagen** current account deposits, deposits on current account, sight (demand, *US*) deposits, deposits at call *(Br.)*, call deposits *(Br.)*, checking deposits *(US)*; **verzinsliche ~einlagen** [etwa] negotiated order of withdrawal accounts *(US)*.

sichten to sight, *(sortieren)* to sift, to sort;
Land ~ to make landfall; **Material für eine Arbeit ~** to sift material for a scientific work.

Sicht|feld field of vision; **~flug** contact flight; **~geschäft** forward transaction; **~grenze** limit of visibility; **~guthaben** *(Bilanz)* credit balance maintained; **~höhe** height of eye; **~kartei** visible card index; **~kurs** *(Devisen)* sight (demand, *US*) rate; **~papier** sight item, demand paper (instrument) *(US)*; **~tage** days of grace; **~tratte** sight bill (draft), draft payable at sight, demand bill (draft), promissory note payable on demand *(US)*, cash order *(Br.)*; **~verbindlichkeiten** liabilities due on presentation, sight liabilities, liabilities payable on demand; **~verhältnisse** *(Flugwetter)* visibility conditions; **wegen schlechter ~verhältnisse zurückfliegen** to turn back because of poor visibility.

Sichtvermerk *(Paß)* consular visa;
Wechsel mit ~ versehen lassen to procure acceptance of a bill; **Paß mit ~ versehen** to visé a passport; **Wechsel mit ~ versehen** to sight a bill.

Sichtwechsel draft (bill) payable on sight, sight bill (draft), bill (draft) at sight, demand bill (draft) *(US)*, bill payable on demand *(US)*, demand note (paper), presentation draft *(US)*;
~ auf London demand Sterling;
~ auf j. ziehen to draw on s. o. at sight.

Sichtwechselkurs sight exchange;
laufender ~ current rate of exchange on sight drafts.

Sichtweite visibility, range of vision;
außer ~ out of sight; **in ~** within range of vision (eyeshot); **in ~ eines Beamten** *(Straftat)* in the presence of an officer;
behinderte ~ obscured vision.

Sichtzielflug visual homing flight.

Sicker|graben drain trench; **~grube** cesspool; **~loch** drainage pit.

sickern to ooze, to soak, to seep, to percolate.

Sickerwasser percolating waters.

Sieb sieve, strainer, screen;
j. wie ein ~ durchlöchern to riddle s. o. with bullets; **Gedächtnis wie ein ~ haben** to have a memory like a sieve;
~druck silk-screen printing.

sieben, Bewerber to screen candidates.

Sieben|jahresvertrag lease determinable at the end of seven years; **~meilenstiefel** seven-league boots; **~sachen** duds, traps, possibles *(US)*; **meine ~sachen** my bits and pieces, all my belongings.

Siebschablonendruck silk-screen printing.

Siechtum lingering illness, decline, languishing state.

Siedeln homecrofting *(Br.)*, homesteading *(US)*.

siedeln to settle, to colonize, *(Arbeiter)* to homestead *(US)*, to homecroft *(Br.)*;
wild ~ to squat.

siedend heiß boiling hot.

Siedepunkt boiling point, *(Wahlkampf)* hottest part.

Siedler settler, colonist, colonizer, *(Arbeiter)* smallholder *(Br.)*, homesteader *(US)*, homecrofter *(Br.)*, *(ohne Rechtstitel)* squatter *(US)*;
~gemeinde settler community; **~stelle** homecroft *(Br.)*, homestead *(US)*; **~strom** flow of settlers.

Siedlung settlement, colony, housing project (estate, development), council estate *(Br.)*, *(Kleinsiedlung)* smallholding;
abgelegene ~ backwoods settlement; **am Stadtrand gelegene ~** suburban colony (housing estate), ribbon development *(Br.)*; **geschlossene ~en** self-contained developments.

Siedlungs|anspruch headright *(US)*; **~bauten** housing estate (project); **~behörde** resettlement administration *(US)*; **~brei** urban sprawl; **~entwicklung** settlement development; **~fläche, ~gebiet** area of a scheme of development, development area; **landwirtschaftliches ~gebiet** settlement; **neuentstandenes ~gebiet** built-up area; **~gefüge** settlement structure; **~gelände** development area, housing (council, *Br.*) estate; **~genossenschaft, ~gesellschaft** land settlement society; **gemeinnützige ~gesellschaft** homestead corporation *(US)*; **~gesetz** Homecraft Scheme *(Br.)*, Homestead Act *(US)*; **~grenze** American frontier; **~grundstück** freehold land *(Br.)*; **~haus** cooperative apartment house *(US)*; **~kredit** loan for development purposes; **~netz** settlement pattern; **~programm, ~projekt** land settlement scheme, scheme of development, building development scheme, land development project; **~raum** development area; **~struktur** settlement structure, system of cities; **~weise** settlement type; **~wesen** land settlement.

Sieg victory, winning;
entscheidender ~ substantial victory; **teuer erkaufter ~** dearly purchased victory; **leichter (leicht errungener) ~** walkover, facile victory; **trügerischer ~** hollow victory *(fam.)*; **überwältigender ~** overwhelming victory;
~ nach Punkten victory on points;
~ ausnutzen to follow up a victory; **~ davontragen** to carry (gain) the day, to bear away the palm, to sweep the board, to get the best of it, to win the plume; **leichten ~ davontragen** to win hands down, to walk over the course; **alle Kräfte für den ~ einsetzen** to fight tooth and nail; **~ erringen** to win a victory, to win the day (field); **glänzenden ~ erringen** to come off with flying colo(u)rs; **hundertprozentigen ~ erringen** to sweep the board; **mit den Truppen einen ~ erringen** to lead the troops on to victory; **glänzenden ~ über seine Feinde erringen** to score a resounding triumph over one's enemies; **jem. den ~ streitig machen** to dispute the victory to s. o.

Siegel seal, signet, wafer;
unter dem ~ der Verschwiegenheit under the seal of secrecy; **erbrochenes ~** broken seal; **intaktes ~** intact seal; **privatrechtliches ~** private seal; **unverletztes ~** unbroken seal;

~ **abnehmen** to take off the seals; ~ **anbringen** to affix a seal; ~ **auf einem Gesetz anbringen** to append a seal to an act; **sein** ~ **aufdrücken** to set (impress) one's seal; ~ **entfernen** to unseal; ~ **erbrechen** to break a seal; **unter** ~ **legen** to place under seal; **jem. etw. unter dem** ~ **der Verschwiegenheit mitteilen** to tell s. o. s. th. in strict confidence, to let s. o. into the secret; **mit einem** ~ **versehen** to seal; **Urkunde mit einem** ~ **versehen** to put one's seal on a document;
~**abdruck** impression of a seal; ~**abnahme** removal of (taking off) the seal, unsealing; ~**anlage** affixing of a seal; ~**beamter** sealer; ~**bruch** breaking the seals; ~**fälschung** forging seals; ~**führung** use of a seal; ~**lack** sealing wax; ~**marke** paper seal, wafer.
siegeln to [affix a] seal;
Urkunde ~ to seal a document.
Siegelring seal (signet) ring.
Siegelung affixing a seal.
Siegelwachs sealing wax.
siegen, bei einem Wettbewerb to carry the day (off the prize).
Sieger, voraussichtlicher probable winner;
als ~ **hervorgehen** to be first past the post; **bei den Wahlen als knapper** ~ **hervorgehen** to win an election with a narrow margin; **auf den** ~ **setzen** to pick a winner.
Siegespalme palm, garland;
~ **davontragen** to carry off the prize.
siegessicher confident of victory.
Siegestrophäe scalp.
siegreich zurückkehren to return home in triumph.
Siele, in den ~n sterben to die in harness.
Siemens-Martin-Ofen open-hearth furnace.
Signal signal, sign, *(Anzeichen)* indication;
~ **für Linksabbieger** left-turn signal;
~ **aussenden** to [make a] signal; ~ **zum Rückzug blasen** to give the signal for retreat; ~ **festlegen** to lock a signal; ~ **überfahren** *(Zug)* to pass a signal that is at danger;
~**anlage** light signal; ~**arm** *(Bahn)* signal arm, semaphore; ~**bake** signal beacon; ~**buch**, ~**code** signal book, *(mar.)* naval code; **internationales** ~**buch** International Code [of Signals]; ~**dienst** signal service; ~**feuer** signal fire, watch fire; ~**flagge** signal (red) flag; ~**gast** *(Schiff)* signalman, signal(l)er, wigwagger; ~**geber** flagman; ~**glocke** signal bell; ~**horn** horn.
Signalisieren flagwagging, signal(l)ing.
signalisieren to flag, to wigwag, to [flag-]signal, to telegraph;
politische Veränderung ~ to signal a change in policy.
Signal|lampe signal lantern, *(Bahn)* target (signal) lamp; ~**laterne** signal lantern; ~**licht** signal light; ~**maat** yeoman of signals; ~**mast** *(Bahn)* signal mast, semaphore; ~**pfeife** signal whistle; ~**rakete** signal rocket; ~**reiz** *(Werbung)* appeal; ~**schuß** signal gun; ~**stellwerk** *(Bahn)* signal box; ~**tafel** *(Hotel)* teleseme; ~**vorrichtung** signalling apparatus; ~**wärter** signalman, towerman *(US)*; ~**wirkung** announcement effect.
Signatarmacht convention country, signatory power.
Signatoren eines Vertrages subscribers to a document (an agreement).
Signatur signature, *(drucktechn.)* signature [mark], groove;
~**rinne** nick.
signieren to sign, to initial, to mark, to brand, to designate, *(mit Anfangsbuchstaben)* to initial.
Signierstift marking pencil.
Signifikanzgrad *(Statistik)* level of significance.
Silbe, [un]betonte [un]stressed syllable;
keine ~ **verraten** not to breath a word of it.
Silben|trennprogramm *(Satzmaschine)* language module, hyphenation program(me); ~**trennung** word division.
Silber, feuervergoldetes vermeil; **gediegenes** ~ solid silver; **geringhaltiges** ~ silver of base alloy; **legiertes** ~ alloyed silver; **ungemünztes** ~ silver bullion;
~**agio** silver agio; ~**barren** bar (bullion) silver; ~**bergwerk** silver mine; ~**bestand** silver coin and bullion; ~**besteck** silver knife, fork and spoon; ~**dollar** silver dollar *(US)*; ~**gehalt** percentage of silver; ~**geld** silver money.
silberhaltig sein to carry silver.
Silber|hochzeit silver wedding; ~**kleingeld** loose silver.
silberlegiert white.
Silber|legierung silver alloy; ~**münze** silver coin, piece of silver; ~**münzen** silver money; ~**notierungen** silver quotations; ~**papier** silver paper; ~**produktion** silver production; ~**schmied** silversmith; ~**standard** silver standard; ~**streifen** *(fig.)* silver lining; ~**währung** silver currency (standard, basis); ~**währungsland** silver-standard country; ~**waren** silver goods, silverware; ~**zertifikat** silver certificate *(US)*.
Silhouette silhouette, outlines, *(Stadt)* skyline;
sich als ~ **gegen den Himmel abheben** to be outlined against the sky.
Silo silo, elevator *(US)*;
Futter im ~ **einlagern** to ensilage fodder;
~**futter** ensilage.
simpel simple, plain, *(einfältig)* simple-minded, stupid;
es an den ~sten Voraussetzungen fehlen haben not to know the ABC of s. th.
Simulant simulator, malingerer, dissembler.
Simulation an Modellen policy simulation.
Simulieren simulation, malingering.
simulieren to simulate, to feign, to malinger;
Krankheit ~ to sham illness.
simuliert feigned.
simultan simultaneous.
Simultan|betrieb *(tel.)* simultaneous working; ~**kauf und** ~**verkauf** *(Börse)* wash sale *(US)*, washing *(US)*; ~**leitung** *(el.)* phantom circuit, *(tel.)* composite line; ~**schule** undenominational school; ~**sendung** *(Rundfunk)* simulcast *(US)*; ~**übersetzung** simultaneous interpretation (translation).
Sinekure sinecure;
reine ~ featherbed job *(US)*.
Sinfonieorchester symphony orchester.
singen *(Verbrecher)* to squeal, to peach, to squeak, to come clean *(sl.)*, to pipe *(sl.)*;
immer das alte Lied ~ to harp on the same string.
Sinken *(Kurse)* fall, falling, decline, easing off, drop, *(gesamte Tendenz)* depression;
scharfes ~ break, slump *(Br.)*, smash *(US)*;
~ **der Aktienkurse** drop in share prices; ~ **der Arbeitslosigkeit** drop in unemployment; ~ **der Beschäftigung** reduction of employment, employment decline; ~ **der Erträge** drop in earnings; ~ **der Preise** falling (drop) of prices, price decline; **im** ~ **begriffen sein** to be on the decline.
sinken to sink, to fall, to drop, *(Einfluß)* to diminish, to decrease, *(Kurs, Preise)* to fall, to drop, to go down, to [be on the] decline (on the downgrade, on the fall), to dwindle, to slip back, to be falling (on the fall), to give way, to ease off (down), to sag, to look downwards, *(Luftdruck)* to fall, *(Schiff)* to sink, to founder, to touch ground, *(sich senken)* to descend;
allmählich ~ *(Kurse)* to shade; **ins Grab** ~ to sink into the grave; **auf Null** ~ *(Stimmung)* to sink to rock bottom; **in Ohnmacht** ~ to faint, to pass out, to swoon; **plötzlich** ~ *(Kurse)* to slump, to break; **um zwei Punkte** ~ to drop two points; **schnell** ~ *(Kurse)* to decline rapidly; **in Schutt und Asche** ~ to be reduced to ashes.
sinkend declining, falling;
~**e Kurse** sagging (falling) prices; ~**e Nachfrage** drop in demand; **bei ~en Preisen** with declining prices.
Sinkkasten gully, sinkstone.
Sinn sense, mind, *(Auslegung)* construction, interpretation, interest, *(Bedeutung)* significance, signification, purport, meaning, effect, tenor, *(Gesetz)* intent, *(Grundgedanke)* basic idea;
dem ~ **nach** in spirit; **im Besitz seiner** ~**e** in one's right senses; **im eigentlichen** ~ in the proper (literal) sense; **im juristischen** ~**e** in the legal sense; **im strengen** ~ in the strict sense; **im weitesten** ~ in the broadest sense; **im** ~ **des Gesetzes** in the intendment (within the meaning) of the law; **im** ~ **des Uhrzeigers** clockwise; **in bestätigendem** ~ confirmatively; **in bildlichem** ~ figuratively; **in übertragenem** ~ figuratively; **ohne** ~ **und Verstand** without rhyme or reason;
~ **eines Briefes** purport of a letter; ~ **eines Gesetzes** intention of a law; ~ **einer Rede** tenor of a speech; ~ **eines Verfahrens** point of an exercise; ~ **und Zweck** essence and purpose;
alle fünf ~**e beisammenhaben** to be in possession of all one's faculties; **seine fünf** ~**e beisammenhaben** to have one's wits about one; **seine fünf** ~ **nicht beisammenhaben** not to have one's wits about one; ~ **eines Textes enträtseln** to pick out the meaning of a passage; ~ **eines Textes entstellen** to distort the meaning of a text; **keinen** ~ **ergeben** to make nonsense; **wahren** ~ **eines Textes nicht erkennen** to miss the true meaning of a text; **nichts Böses im** ~ **haben** to intend no harm; **nichts Gutes im** ~ **haben** to be up to no good; **einen praktischen** ~ **haben** to have a practical turn of mind; **nur** ~ **fürs Geldverdienen haben** to be keen on money-making only; **in jds.** ~ **handeln** to enter into s. one's ideas; ~ **einer Textstelle herausfinden** to pick out the meaning of a passage; **falschen** ~ **aus einer Passage herauslesen** to read into a sentence what is not there; **jem. in den** ~ **kommen** to occur to s. o.; **jem. plötzlich in den** ~ **kommen**

to cross s. one's mind; **über alle fünf ~e verfügen können** to be in the enjoyment of all one's senses; **sich etw. aus dem ~ schlagen** to put s. th. out of one's mind; **von ~en (seiner ~e beraubt) sein** to be out of one's mind, to have taken leave of one's senses; ~ **eines Gesetzes verhöhnen** to flout the spirit of the law; **doppelten ~ aus jds. Worten herauszulesen versuchen** to go behind s. one's words; **anderen ~es werden** to change one's mind; **jem. etw. dem ~ nach wiedergeben** to tell s. o. the gist of it;
aus den Augen aus dem ~ out of sight, out of mind; **der langen Rede kurzer ~** the long and the short of it;
~bild emblem, symbol, allegory.
sinnen, auf Mittel und Wege to devise ways and means; **auf Rache ~** to scheme revenge.
Sinnes|täuschung mental delusion; **~trick** illusion; **~werkzeug** sense organ.
Sinngebung interpretation.
sinngemäß analogous, correspondent, accordingly;
~ Anwendung finden to apply analogously; **jds. Worte ~ wiederholen** to tell the gist of what s. o. said.
sinnieren to muse, to brood, to ponder.
sinnlich sensual, voluptuous.
sinnlos senseless, meaningless, insensible, useless;
völlig ~ sein to make no sense at all; **~ betrunken sein** to be drunk as a lord;
in ~er Wut in frenzied rage; **~es Zeug reden** to talk rubbish.
sinnvoll meaningful, significant;
wenig ~ sein to make a modicum of sense.
sinnwidrige Auslegung misinterpretation.
Sintflut the Flood;
~ von Briefen flood of letters.
Sippe kin, tribe, clan *(Scot.)*, family, name.
Sippenangehöriger kinsman.
Sippschaft kinship, kindred, clan, tribe, clique, set;
die ganze ~ kit and caboodle *(US sl.)*, the whole and boiling kit *(sl.)*, the whole lot (kit, boiling, *sl.*).
Sirene hooter, hoot, siren;
mit heulenden ~n durch die Straßen rasen to race through the streets with wailing sirens.
sistieren to arrest, to apprehend, *(anhalten)* to stop, to inhibit, *(Verfahren)* to suspend, to stay;
Zahlungen ~ to stop payments.
Sistierung apprehension, arrest;
~ eines Verfahrens stay of proceedings; **~ einer Zahlung** stoppage of (stopping) payment.
Sisyphusaufgabe haben to paint the Forth Bridge.
Sitte custom and usage, practice, morality;
tief eingewurzelte ~ strong custom; **lockere ~n** lax (loose) morals;
~n und Gebräuche manners and customs, established customs; **~ und Gewohnheit** use and wont;
gegen die guten ~n contrary to good morals, contra bonos mores; **gegen die guten ~n verstoßend** immoral;
mit einer alten ~ brechen to break with an old custom; **gegen die guten ~n verstoßen** to offend public policy, to act contrary to the moral sentiment of the community.
Sitten|dezernat *(Polizei)* vice department (squad); **~gesetz** moral law; **~kodex** moral code; **starrer ~kodex** inflexible code of morals; **~lehre** ethics, morals, moral science; **~lehrer** moralist.
sittenlos immoral, dissolute, profligate, libertine.
Sitten|losigkeit immorality, profligacy, dissolution, depravity; **~polizei** vice squad; **~richter** Grundyite; **sich als ~richter aufspielen** to constitute o. s. a judge of conduct, to set o. s. up as a moral censor; **~roman** study in manners; **übertriebene ~strenge** Grundyism; **~strolch** sex molester *(coll.)*.
sittenverderbend filthy.
Sitten|verderbnis demoralization; **~verfall** deterioration in morals, moral decay.
sittenwidrig against public policy, immoral, contra bonos mores, unethical;
~ herbeigeführt collusive;
~e Bereicherung filthy lucre; **~es Geschäft** constructive (equitable, legal) fraud; **~e Handlung** public indecency; **~es Verhalten** immoral conduct; **~er Vertrag** illegal contract; **in ~er Weise** for a corrupt purpose.
Sitten|widrigkeit immorality, undue influence; **~zeugnis** good-conduct certificate.
sittlich moral, ethical;
~ gefährdet sein to be in moral danger;
~e Grundlagen der Erziehung ethical basis for education; **~e Grundsätze** ethical principles; **~e Kraft** moral force; **hohes ~es Niveau** high moral standards; **~e Notwendigkeit** moral necessity; **~e Verfehlungen** immoral conduct; **~es Verhalten** moral conduct, morality; **~ einwandfreies Verhalten** irreproachable conduct; **~er Wert** moral value.
Sittlichkeit public decency, morality.
Sittlichkeits|empfinden, gegen das allgemeine ~empfinden verstoßen to offend against public morals; **~gefühl** moral faculty (sense); **allgemeines ~gefühl anheben** to raise the moral standard of the community; **~verbrechen** immoral offence, sex crime; **~verbrecher** immoral offender.
Situation situation, position, *(Kreditwürdigkeit)* standing, credit rating;
heikle ~ hot sea; **kreditpolitische ~** credit situation; **prekäre ~** touch-and-go; **schwierige ~** predicament, squeeze, pickle; **unangenehme ~** trying situation; **verfahrene ~** fouled-up situation *(US)*; **verworrene ~** troubled waters; **wirtschaftliche ~** economic situation;
~, in der alles möglich ist situation full of potentialities; **~ der Arbeiter** conditions of the workers;
sich der neuen ~ anpassen to adjust o. s. to the new circumstances; **~ auflockern** to break the ice; **~ ausnutzen** to make the most of a situation; **~ voll beherrschen** to have a good grip of the situation; **~ in den Griff bekommen** to cope with a situation; **verfahrene ~ bereinigen** to break deadlocks; **~ bessern** to help matters; **~ sofort erfassen** to take in the scene at a glance; **~ voll erfassen** to embrace a situation; **~ noch schrecklicher machen** to invest the situation with additional horrors; **schwierige ~ meistern** to come to terms with a difficult situation; **der ~ nicht gewachsen sein** not to be equal to the situation; **~ sofort überblicken** to keep one's wits about one; **die ~ verschlimmern** to make things worse; **sich einer ~ gewachsen zeigen** to cope with a situation, to be equal (rise) to an occasion.
Situations|bericht report on the situation, sitrep; **~erkenntnis** situational judgment; **~komik** humo(u)r of the situation; **~plan** site (situation) plan.
situiert, gut (wohl) wealthy, well-to-do, well-off, on one's legs, comfortably off, well fixed *(US)*; **schlecht ~** badly off (situated).
Sitz chair, seat, bank, bench, *(Geschäftsleitung)* headquarters, situs, head (registered) office, location of the registered office, commercial domicile, seat, *(Parlament)* bench, *(Wohnort)* abode, domicile, residence;
auf einen ~ at one go; **mit dem ~ in** located in; **mit dem ~ in England** incorporated in the United Kingdom;
freier ~ vacant seat; **schlecht gepolsterter ~** poorly cushioned seat; **juristischer ~** *(Gesellschaft)* registered office *(Br.)*, location of the registered office; **ständiger ~** permanent abode; **steuerlicher ~** taxable (business) situs; **verstellbarer ~** *(Auto)* adjustable seat;
~ im Aufsichtsrat seat on the board, board seat; **~ einer Behörde** headquarters of an agency; **~ der Geschäftsleitung** place of management, location of office, headquarters; **eingetragener ~ einer Gesellschaft** registered office *(Br.)*, location of the registered office; **~ der Hauptniederlassung** headquarters; **~ einer Industrie** site of an industry; **~ der Kreisverwaltung** county site; **~ einer Landeszentralbank** Federal Reserve City *(US)*; **~ der gewerblichen Niederlassung** commercial domicile, *(Firma)* domicile of corporation; **~e der unabhängigen Parlamentsmitglieder** cross benches; **~ der Regierung** seat of the government; **~ des Schiedsgerichts** place of arbitration; **~ und Stimme in der Spitze des Weltwährungsfonds** seat on the top table at the International Monetary Fund; **~ eines Unternehmens** business situs;
seinen ~ in A aufschlagen to settle down (take up residence) in A; **~ belegen** to occupy a seat; **~ neu besetzen** to fill a vacancy; **~ eines Stuhls neu beziehen** to reseat a chair; **sich in die vordersten ~e drängen** to crush into the front seats; **~ im Parlament erringen** to be returned to parliament; **den Arbeitern ~ und Stimme im Aufsichtsrat geben** to give workers a seat in the boardroom; **seinen ~ in A haben** to be domiciled (located, incorporated) in A; **sein Publikum von den ~en reißen** to bring down the house, to knock them in the aisles *(US sl.)*; **~ reservieren** to reserve a seat; **über fünf ~e verfügen** *(Auto)* to hold five seats; **~ verlegen** to relocate headquarters;
~anordnung seating arrangement (plan); **~arbeit** sedentary work; **~badewanne** hip bath, bidet.
sitzen to sit, to be seated, *(Behörde)* to have its seat, *(Firma)* to have its headquarters, to reside, *(Gefangener)* to do time;
wie angegossen ~ to fit like a glove;

in mehreren Aufsichtsräten ~ to sit on various supervising boards; in einem Ausschuß ~ to sit on a committee; im gleichen Boot ~ to row in the same boat; über seinen Büchern ~ to pore over one's books; im Bundestag ~ to be a member of parliament; im Examen ~ to sit for an examination; in der Fahrtrichtung ~ to sit facing the engine; im Finanzamt ~ to have a job in the tax office; gedrängt wie die Heringe ~ to be packed like sardines; genau ~ *(Bemerkung)* to go home; auf seinem Geld ~ to take care of one's pennies; zu Gericht ~ to be sitting; über j. zu Gericht ~ to sit in judgment on s. o.; gut ~ to be comfortable; auf einem Hof ~ to be settled on a farm; im Kittchen ~ to be in clink; wie die Made im Speck ~ to be as snug as a bug in a rug; jem. auf der Pelle ~ to dog s. one's footsteps, to pester s. o.; direkt an der Quelle ~ to have the news straight from the horse's mouth; auf dem hohen Roß ~ to be on one's high horse, to perk it *(US)*; hinter Schloß und Riegel ~ to be behind prison bars; tief in der Tinte ~ to be deep in the mire; auf dem Trockenen ~ to be stranded (in low water);
einen ~ haben to have a drop in one's eye *(coll.)*, to have a kick *(US sl.)*, to be merry in one's cups.

sitzenbleiben to keep one's seat, to remain seated, *(Schüler)* to stay down in a class;
mit seiner Ware ~ to be left over with stocks, to hold the bag *(US)*; auf guten Werten ~ to maintain a position in sound stocks.

sitzenlassen, j. to leave s. o. flat (in the lurch), to stand s. o. up, to walk out on s. o.; seine Frau ~ to leave one's wife; Schüler ~ to make a pupil repeat a year; Vorwurf nicht auf sich ~ not to take a reproach lying down.

Sitz|fläche seat; kein ~fleisch haben to be always on the move; ~gelegenheiten seating facilities (accommodation, arrangement); ~komfort seating convenience; ~krieg phony war; ~ordnung seating plan, seat chart; ~platz seat, sitting place; ohne ~platz seatless; ~plätze seating capacity; sechs ~plätze haben *(Auto)* to hold six people; ~redakteur dummy (prison) editor; ~reihe row [of seats]; hintere ~reihe back benches; von den hinteren ~reihen from the rear; ~streik sit-down strike, *(Bergbau)* stay-down strike; mehrtägiger ~streik prolonged stay-in strike; ~streik veranstalten to sit down.

Sitzung sitting, meeting, conference, *(Gericht)* sitting, session, *(Parlament)* parliamentary session *(Br.)*, *(Zahnarzt)* appointment;
auf der ~ at the session; in einer ~ at a (one) sitting; in öffentlicher ~ in full session, *(Gericht)* in open court; in nicht öffentlicher ~ in chambers *(Br.)* (camera); während der ~ in session;
abschließende ~ final (tidying-up) session; außerordentliche ~ special session; sofort einberufene ~ on-the-spot meeting; entscheidende ~ field night *(Br.)*; feierliche ~ formal meeting; nach der Vertagung fortgesetzte ~ adjourned meeting; ganztägige ~ all-day meeting; gemeinsame ~ joint session (meeting), *(von Kongress und Senat)* joint convention *(US)*; geschlossene ~ closed-door meeting; nächste ~ forthcoming session; nichtöffentliche ~ private meeting (sitting), closed session, meeting not open to the public, *(Gericht)* hearing (sitting) in camera, hearing in chambers *(Br.)*; öffentliche ~ public meeting, *(Gericht)* hearing in court; turnusmäßige ~ regular session; verlängerte ~ overtime session; vertagte ~ adjourned meeting, *(Gericht)* deferred hearing; zwanglose ~ informal meeting;
~ des Aufsichtsrates meeting of the board of directors, board meeting; ~ unter Ausschluß der Öffentlichkeit closed session, hearing in camera (chambers, *Br.*); ~ eines Ausschusses committee meeting; vollständige ~ des Kongresses general term *(US)*; ~ eines Krisenstabes emergency session; ~ des Notstandskabinetts emergency cabinet meeting (session); ~ des Parlaments parliamentary session; ~ der Schlangenmitgliedsstaaten snake meeting; ~ hinter verschlossenen Türen closed-door hearing; ~ im Vorbeigehen on-the-run session; ~ des Vorstandes board-of-directors meeting;
~ abhalten to hold a meeting (conference), *(Gericht)* to sit, to be sitting, *(parl.)* to be in session; rasch aufeinanderfolgende ~en abhalten to hold meetings at short intervals; jeden Freitag eine ~ abhalten to sit on Fridays; geheime ~ abhalten to sit in conclave; nicht öffentliche ~ abhalten to sit in private; ~en im Betriebsgelände abhalten to hold meetings on the factory floor; ~ anberaumen (ansetzen) to appoint a day (fix a date) for a meeting; ~ aufheben to leave (vacate) the chair, to rise, to dissolve a meeting; ~ gewaltsam auflösen to break up a meeting; ~ mit einem Schlußwort beenden to wind up a meeting with a short speech; einer ~ beiwohnen to attend a sitting, to summon a conference; über die ~en der UNO berichten to cover United Nations sessions; ~ einberufen to convene (call) a meeting, *(parl.)* to convoke a session; ~ auf 12 Uhr einberufen to fix a meeting (session) for twelve o'clock; zu einer ~ zu viel Teilnehmer einladen to overstaff a meeting; ~ für beendet erklären to declare proceedings at an end; ~ eröffnen (für eröffnet erklären) to open a meeting, *(Gericht)* to open a court, to declare a court in session; beiderseits einer ~ fernbleiben *(Parlamentsabgeordneter)* to pair off; Zeit und Ort für die nächste ~ festsetzen to arrange time and place for the next meeting; Vorsitz in einer ~ führen to preside over a meeting; in einer ~ das Wort haben to be in possession of the house; ~ leiten to preside at a conference, to run a meeting; Verhandlungsführung in einer ~ an sich reißen to monopolize a meeting; ~ schließen to dissolve (close) a meeting, to declare a meeting closed; in einer ~ sein to be in conference; bei einer ~ anwesend sein to attend (be present at) a meeting; an einer ~ teilnehmen to take part in a conference, to attend a session; ~ unterbrechen to adjourn a meeting, *(Gericht)* to adjourn a case, *(parl.)* to be in recess; ~ für eine Stunde unterbrechen to recess for an hour; ~ unter Protest verlassen to leave a meeting under protest; ~ in ein Hotel verlegen to shift a meeting to a hotel; ~ vertagen to adjourn a meeting; Angelegenheit bis zur nächsten ~ zurückstellen to hold over a matter until the next meeting; zu regelmäßigen ~en zusammenkommen to meet in regular sessions; zu einer ~ zusammentreten to meet.

Sitzungs|abend *(parl.)* business night; bei ~beginn at the opening of the meeting; ~benachrichtigung notice of meeting.

Sitzungsbericht minutes, protocol, account of gathering, symposion, conference paper, report of a meeting, *(Gericht)* [record of] proceedings, judgment record, procès verbal, *(Verein)* transactions;
Senats- und ~e Books of Council and Session;
~e des Kongresses congressional reports;
für Abänderung des ~es stimmen to vote for amendment of the minutes; dem ~ zustimmen to vote for approval of the minutes.

Sitzungs|dauer time of holding, *(parl.)* term *(US)*; ~einladung requisition for a meeting *(Br.)*; ~gebühr, ~geld attendance (sitting) fee *(Br.)*; ~gewalt *(Gericht)* police powers; ~kalender *(parl.)* calendar *(US)*; ~leiter conference leader; ~liste paper of cases (causes, *Br.*); ~liste der Kammer für Handelssachen commercial list; ~liste verlesen to call the docket; ~mitglied sitting (conference) member; ~niederschrift minutes, conference paper, *(Gericht)* trial transscript (record); ~ort place of a meeting; ~pause einlegen to take a recess; ~periode sitting term, legal session, *(Gericht)* law term, *(Parlament)* session *(US)*; verlängerte ~periode adjournment term; ~programm notice (order) paper, agenda, program(me) of a meeting.

Sitzungsprotokoll record (minutes) of a meeting, face of record, *(AG)* corporate minutes, *(Gericht)* judgment record, record of the court (trial), trial record (transscript);
dem ~ beifügen to attach to the minutes; ~ bestätigen to confirm the minutes of the last meeting; ~ führen to keep the minutes of a meeting; ~ ohne Verlesung genehmigen to take the minutes as read.

Sitzungs|raum cabinet room; ~saal meeting room, assembly (conference) hall, [council] chamber, floor, *(Gericht)* court room; ~schluß close (end) of meeting, *(Gericht)* conclusion of the session period; ~tag meeting day, *(Gericht)* lawful (judicial) day, term of court; ~tage paper days, *(Gericht)* days in banc; ~tagegelder sessional expense allowance, sitting fees *(Br.)*; ~teilnehmer participant of a meeting, meeting participant; ~teilnehmer sein to attend a sitting (meeting); ~termin auf den 15. anberaumen to set down a meeting for the 15th; ~termin festlegen to settle a day (fix, determine a date) for a meeting; ~unterbrechung adjournment of a meeting; ~unterlagen documentation for a meeting; ~verlängerung prolongation of a meeting; ~vertagung adjournment of a meeting; ~vorbereitungen premeeting preparations; ~zimmer committee (board, conference, cabinet) room, *(parl.)* chamber, floor *(US)*; ~zimmer des Stadtrats common council chamber; ~zwang compulsory meeting.

Sitz|verstellung seat adjustment; ~verteilung allotment of mandates.

Skala scale, dial, gamut, *(Einteilung)* graduation, division, *(Farbskala)* colo(u)r chart;
direkt ablesbare ~ direct-reading scale; beleuchtete ~ illuminated scale; gleitende ~ sliding scale;
ganze ~ der Gefühle whole gamut of feelings; breite ~ von Produkten wide range of items;
ganze ~ durchlaufen to run the whole gamut of.

Skalen|ablesung scale reading; ~**analyse** scale analysis; ~**beleuchtung** dial light; ~**einteilung** graduation of scale, scale graduation; **konstante** ~**erträge** constant returns to scale; ~**faktor** *(Computer)* scale factor; ~**scheibe** *(Radio)* dial.

Skandal scandal, shame, disgrace, nuisance;
widerlicher ~ unsavo(u)ry scandal;
~ **auslösen** to create a scandal; ~ **öffentlich bekanntmachen (enthüllen)** to publish a scandal, to blow the lid off *(sl.)*; ~ **erregen** to scandalize; ~ **hervorrufen** to cause an outrage; ~ **machen** to kick up a row; ~ **für eine Partei sein** to be a disgrace to a party; ~ **vertuschen** to hush up a scandal;
~**affäre** scandalous affair; ~**blatt** gutter paper, rag; ~**blatt mit heißen Nachrichten** red-hot newsy journal *(sl.)*; ~**blätter** gutter (yellow, hedge) press; ~**chronik** chronique scandaleuse; ~**fall** scandalous matter.

Skandalgeschichte scandalous (unsavo(u)ry) story, sizzle *(sl.)*; **sich** ~**n erzählen** to talk about *(coll.)*; ~**n mit dem größten Vergnügen hören** to keep one's ears open for scandals; ~**n wittern** to have a nose for scandal.

Skandal|journalismus gutter journalism; ~**kolporteur** muckraker.

skandalös|e Behandlung scandalous treatment; ~**es Verhalten** shocking behavio(u)r; ~**e Zustände** scandalous conditions.

Skandalpresse gutter (yellow) press, hedge press, rag.

skandalumwittert scandal-ridden.

Skelett skeleton, framework, *(Schiff)* bone;
zum ~ **abgemagert sein** to be worn to a shadow; **im** ~ **vorliegen** *(Plan)* to be in the rough;
~**bauweise** skeleton construction; ~**schrift** skeleton face.

Skepsis scepsis, scepticism;
etw. mit ~ **betrachten** to take a dim view of s. th., to be wary of, to eye with raised eyebrows.

Skeptiker, ewiger confirmed sceptic.

Ski|ausrüstung skiing kit; ~**lift** ski lift; ~**urlaub** ski vacation; ~**urlaubsort** ski resort.

Skizze sketch, drawing, [rough] draft, outline, layout, *(Ideenskizze)* scribble, skeleton, *(mil.)* croquis.

Skizzenblock sketch block.

skizzieren to sketch, to design, to outline, to touch;
Haus in groben Umrissen ~ to make a sketch of a house; **Plan** ~ to outline a scheme; **Plan für eine neue Straße** ~ to sketch out proposals for a new road; **in groben Umrissen** ~ to make a rough sketch.

skizziert in outline.

Sklave|der modernen Technik slave of modern technology;
wie ein ~ **arbeiten (schuften)** to sweat blood, to work like a nigger; **jahrelang wie ein** ~ **an seinem Wörterbuch arbeiten** to slave away on one's dictionary for years; **sich zum** ~**n machen** to enslave o. s.

Sklaven|arbeit slave work, drudgery; ~**handel** slave trade (trading, dealing, traffic); ~**händler** slave trader (dealer), blackbirder *(sl.)*, slaver; ~**markt** slave market.

Sklaverei|abschaffen to abolish slavery; **in die** ~ **geraten** to fall into slavery.

sklavisch slavish, servile;
in ~**e Abhängigkeit von seinen Hausangestellten geraten** to make o. s. a slave to one's servants; **in** ~**er Abhängigkeit von Konventionen leben** to be a slave to conventions; ~**e Nachahmung** slavish imitation.

skontieren to allow a cash discount.

Skontierung allowance of cash discount.

Skonto [trade] discount;
abzüglich ~ less (deducting) discount; **mit** ~ at a discount; **nach Abzug des** ~**s** allowing for discount;
echter ~ primary discount; **einbehaltener** ~ retained discount; **nicht in Anspruch genommener** ~ discount lost;
~ **bei Barzahlung** cash discount on sales; **3%** ~ **für Barzahlung** 3% for cash; **2 1/2%** ~ **bei Rechnungsbegleichung innerhalb eines Monats** with 2 1/2% discount allowance for settlement within one month; ~ **für Vorauszahlung** discount for early payment;
~ **für vorzeitige Rechnungsbegleichung abziehen** to discount a bill for early payment; ~ **ausnutzen** to take cash discounts; ~ **gewähren** to allow a discount; **3%** ~ **gewähren** to take 3% off the price;
~**abzug** discount deduction, allowance for cash discount; ~**aufwendungen** discounts allowed; ~**bedingungen** discount terms; ~**betrag** discount sum; ~**ersuchen** discount request; ~**erträge** discounts earned; ~**gewährung** allowance of a discount; ~**schinderei** discount piracy; ~**verlust** lost (missed) discount; ~**zeitraum** discountable period.

skontrieren to square, to clear, to settle.

Skontrierung settling of accounts, settlement *(Br.)*.

Skontrierungstag settling (settlement) day, ticket (name) day *(Br.)*.

Skontrozettel [balance] ticket.

skribbeln to block in.

Skripdollar dollar scrip *(US)*.

Skriptgirl continuity (script) girl.

Skrupel scruple, qualm;
von stärksten ~**n gepeinigt** scrupulous to a fault;
keinerlei ~ **bei einer Tätigkeit empfinden** to have no qualms about doing s. th.

skrupellos unscrupulous, unconscionable, without scruples, stick-at-nothing.

Skulptur sculpture.

Skylla, zwischen ~ **und Charybdis** on the horns of a dilemma.

Slang|ausdruck slang expression; ~**ausdrücke aus einem Aufsatz entfernen** to eliminate slang words from an essay.

Slogan slogan, jingle, catchword.

Slumbesucher slummer.

Slums slums.

Smoking dinner jacket, tuxedo *(US)*.

Snob snob, pretentious man, prig.

Snobismus snobism, snobbery, tufthunting.

Sockel foundation, basis, *(Ausstellung)* block, *(el.)* base, *(Maschine)* setting, *(Motoren)* pedestal;
~**betrag** basic allowance (amount), *(Ruhegehalt)* basic benefit; ~**geschoß** basement; **vermögenspolitisch motivierte** ~**prämie** property-motivated basic premium.

Socken, sich auf die ~ **machen** to stir one's stumps, to foot it, to shake a leg (it up, *sl.*).

Sodawasser soda water.

Sofa couch, sofa, day bed.

Soffitten *(Theater)* flies, fly loft;
~**lampen** tubular (festoon) lamp; ~**lichter** border lights.

sofort instantly, on the instant, immediate, outright, forthwith, at a word, with dispatch, quick, on the nail, in short order *(US)*;
~ **bezugsfähig** with immediate possession; **ab** ~ **gesucht** *(Anzeige)* wanted immediately; ~ **gültig** immediately effective; ~ **lieferbar** for immediate delivery, *(Effekten)* spot;
~ **bezahlen** to pay on the nail; ~ **entlassen** to dismiss without notice; ~ **erledigen** to deal promptly with it; ~ **reagieren** to take immediate action; ~ **tot sein** to be killed on the spot; ~ **wirksam werden** to become immediately effective;
~ **fällige Rente** immediate annuity; ~ **lieferbare Stücke** *(Börse)* spot parcels, spots; ~ **lieferbarer Weizen** spot wheat.

Sofort|abschreibung initial allowance; ~**abzug** *(Steuer)* deduction at source; ~**aktion** instantaneous action; ~**antwort bedingen** to demand an immediate answer; ~**auftrag** crash job, rush order (job); ~**bedarf** immediate demand; ~**bezug** immediate occupation; ~**druckerei** instant print shop; ~**einlagen** deposits at call, demand *(US)* (sight) deposits; ~**entscheid** on-the-spot decision; ~**hilfe** spot (emergency) aid; ~**hilfsprogramm** emergency aid (crash) program(me).

sofortig immediate, prompt, instantaneous;
~**e Antwort** immediate reply; ~**e Auftragserledigung** prompt attention to an order; **gegen** ~**e Barzahlung** for prompt cash; ~**e Bedienung** prompt service; ~**e Benachrichtigung** *(beim Eintritt des Versicherungsfalls)* immediate notice; ~**e Entlassung** summary (instant) dismissal, kick-off *(US sl.)*; ~**e Entscheidung** prompt decision; ~**e Entwicklung** *(Foto)* instantaneous exposure; ~**e Erledigung** quick way of doing; ~**e Erleichterung** instant relief; ~**er Hilfe bedürfen** to be in instant need of help; ~**e Kasse** cash down, spot cash; **gegen** ~**e Kasse** for prompt cash; ~**e Lieferung** prompt, immediate (spot, prompt) delivery; **gegen** ~**e Lieferung kaufen** to buy outright *(US)*; ~**e Schadensanzeige** immediate notice; ~**er Versand** prompt forwarding (shipment, *US*); ~**er Versicherungsschutz** immediate benefit; **mit** ~**er Wirkung** immediately effective; ~**e Zahlung** prompt (immediate) payment.

Sofort|käufe tätigen to spot-buy; ~**kontrolle** verification on the spot; ~**kredit** emergency loan; ~**maßnahmen** emergency measures, immediate steps, immediate (instantaneous) action, speedy action, fire-brigade measures; ~**maßnahmen einleiten** to take prompt action; ~**programm** crash program(me), fire-brigade measures; ~**sache** *(Gericht)* urgent case, immediate matter; ~**übersetzung** sight translation; ~**verfahren** summary proceedings; ~**verkehr** *(Telefon)* no-delay (toll, *US*) service; ~**zahlung** cash (down, *Br.*) payment; **einmalige** ~**zahlung** once-off payment.

Sog undertow, *(fig.)* whirlpool, maelstrom, *(Luftstrudel)* wash;
starker ~ auf die Dollarbestände strong drive on the dollar holdings;
in den ~ geraten to get into the wake.
Sohle *(Bergbau)* floor, wall *(Br.)*;
auf leisen ~n softly, noiselessly; **vom Scheitel bis zur ~** from top to toe;
sich die ~n nach etw. ablaufen to run one's legs off after s. th.;
kesse ~ aufs Parkett legen to shake a leg;
es brennt mir unter den ~n I'm pressed for time.
Sohlenstrecke main gangway.
Sohn, der verlorene the prodigal son;
~ in der Universitätsausbildung college-age son;
seinen ~ zum Juristen ausbilden lassen to educate one's son for the bar; **~ studieren lassen** to send a son to the university; **auf den ältesten ~ übergehen** to go to the eldest son.
Söhne aus gutem Hause youth of good social position.
Soiree soirée, evening party (performance).
Solawechsel promissory (negiotable) note, single bill (name paper, *US*);
diskontierter ~ discounted note; **gesamtschuldnerischer ~** joint and several promissory note; **zusätzlich girierte ~** approved indorsed notes; **nicht honorierter ~** returned note;
~kredit loan against borrower's note.
Sold pay, salary;
betrügerisch weiterbezogener ~ deadpay;
~ und Kostgeld *(mil.)* ordinary pay and allowance;
~ beziehen to draw one's pay; **j. in ~ nehmen** to hire s. o.; **in jds. ~ stehen** to be in s. one's pay, to be s. one's pensioner.
Soldat soldier, [military] man, enlisted man;
altgedienter ~ battered veteran; **in Strafhaft einsitzender ~** general prisoner *(US)*; **entlassener ~** ex-serviceman, veteran *(US)*, separatee; **fronterfahrener ~** seasoned soldier; **gedienter ~** ex-service-man, veteran *(US)*; **gemeiner ~** private; **gezogener ~** draftee; **pensionierter ~** army pensioner; **unbekannter ~** unknown soldier;
~ mit Druckposten goldbrick *(US)*;
~en anwerben to recruit (enlist, enrol(l)) soldiers; **~en ausrüsten** to field soldiers; **zehn Jahre als ~ gedient haben** to have served ten years as a regular; **sich als ~ anwerben lassen** to take the Queen's shilling *(Br.)*; **~ sein** to be in the army; **für ~en verboten sein** to be out of bounds for soldiers *(Br.)*; **~ werden** to enter (enlist, join in) the army, to join up (the colo(u)rs), to follow the drum *(coll.)*, to get into khaki; **als ~ entlassen werden** to be discharged from the forces.
Soldaten|beruf military profession; **~eskorte** escort of soldiers; **~gepäck** military kit; **zügelloser ~haufen** licentious soldiery; **~heim** soldier's recreation center *(US)* (centre, *Br.*); **~leben** military life; **~stand** military state (order); **~testament** privileged will; **~zeitung** forces newspaper.
soldatisch military, martial;
~e Aufgaben *(Pflichten)* duties of a soldier.
Sold|auszahlung distribution of pay; **~buch** military pay book; **~einbehaltung** deferred pay; **in der ~liste streichen** to redline *(sl.)*.
Söldner mercenary, hired gun, hireling;
~truppen hired troops.
Solidar|bürge joint surety (warrantor); **~bürgschaft** joint security (warranty), collateral guaranty; **~gläubiger** co-creditor; **~haftung** joint and several liability, joint warranty; **~haltung** joint liability (guaranty, warranty).
solidarisch solidary, corporately, *(jur.)* joint and several, jointly and severally;
sich mit jem. ~ erklären to identify o. s. (throw in one's lot) with s. o.; **sich mit einer neu gegründeten Partei ~ erklären** to identify o. s. with a new political party; **~ haften** to be jointly and severally liable; **~ haftbar machen** to render jointly liable;
~e Haftung joint and several liability; **~es Vorgehen** concerted action.
Solidarität solidarity, unity;
~ der Belegschaft staff solidarity;
aus ~ streiken to strike in sympathy.
Solidaritäts|beweis show of solidarity; **~gefühl** solidarity feeling; **~kampagne** solidarity campaign; **~streik** sympathetic (sympathy, loyalist) strike.
Solidar|schuld joint and several debt; **~schuldner** joint debtors; **~verpflichtung** joint and several obligation, obligation binding on all parties.
solide *(echt)* genuine, bona fide, *(finanziell gesund)* good, substantial, solvent, solid, sound, well-established, *(haltbar)* durable, *(Preis)* reasonable, moderate, fair, stable, *(in gutem Ruf stehend)* respectable, trustworthy, of good standing, *(Stoff)* durable, hard-wearing, *(zuverlässig)* creditable, reliable;
~ gebaut sturdily constructed;
~ geworden sein to have become respectable;
~ Aktien sound stock; **~ Finanzgebarung** sound finance (financial position); **~ Firma** solid business firm, house of good standing; **~s Geschäft** trusty business; **~ Grundlage** solid (steady) foundation; **~ finanzielle Grundlage** sound economic basis; **~ Handwerksarbeit** sound workmanship; **~ Kapitalanlage** sound investment; **~s Leben führen** to lead a steady life; **~ Mahlzeit** substantial (square) meal; **~ Tracht Prügel** good hiding; **~s Unternehmen** solid (substantial) business firm; **in ~n Verhältnissen leben** to live in easy circumstances.
Solidität *(Festigkeit)* solidity, steadiness, stability, firmness, *(guter Ruf)* respectability, standing, trustworthiness, *(Sicherheit)* safeness, *(Zahlungsfähigkeit)* soundness, solvency, *(Zuverlässigkeit)* reliability, responsibility.
Solitär *(Brillant)* solitaire;
hundertkarätiger ~ paragon.
Soll debit [account], *(Buchführung)* debit (debtor's) side, *(Liefersoll)* delivery quota, *(Produktion)* target;
~ und Haben debit and credit, account;
im ~ buchen to enter on (carry to) the debit side, to debit; **sein ~ erfüllen** to fulfil one's quota; **im ~ stehen** to be on the debit side; **hinter dem ~ zurückbleiben** *(Produktion)* to fall short of the target;
~arbeitsstunden nominal manhours; **~aufkommen** budgeted yield; **~ausgaben** budgeted expenditure; **~bestand** calculated number, *(Lager)* target inventory, nominal balance; **~betrag** nominal amount; **~buchung** debit balance (entry), *(Bank)* bank debit; **~einnahmen** supposed (estimated) receipts; **~etat** estimates, budgeted receipts, progr
gungszeit standard labo(u)r time; **~frequenz** assigned frequency; **~gewicht** standard weight; **~kosten** budget (estimated, target) costs; **~kostenrechnung** budget accounting; **~leistung** standard of performance, standard output, planned target; **~menge** *(Produktion)* target; **~miete** rent receivable; **~posten** debit item, entry on the debit side; **~saldo** debit balance; **~saldo abdecken** to cover a short account; **~seite** debit, debit side; **~spalte** debit column; **~spanne** target rate of return; **~stärke** establishment, *(mil.)* effective (authorized) strength; **~vorgabe** target; **~vorgaben im Verkauf** sales (marketing) quota; **~vorschrift** directory statute; **~wert** nominal amount; **~zahlen** target figures; **~zeit** required time; **~ziffer** standard; **~zinsen** interest on debit balance, debt (debit, red) interest, debtor interest rates; **~- und Habenzinsen** interest pro and contra; **~zinsnummern, ~zinszahlen** red numbers, debit products *(Br.)*; **~zinssatz** debit (debtor) interest rate.
solo solo, on one's own, by oneself.
Solo|geschäft outright purchase; **~vorstellung** solo.
solvent solvent, sound, good, able to pay, responsible, in the black *(US coll.)*.
Solvenz ability to pay, solvency, soundness;
~erklärung bei Gesellschaftsauflösung declaration of solvency *(Br.)*.
Sommer, im heißesten in the heat of summer;
~abend summer evening; **~aufenthalt** summer stay (abode); **~ausflug** summer outing; **~beschäftigung** summer job; **~bevorratung** stockpiling during the summer; **~fahrplan** summer timetable; **~ferien** summer holidays (vacations, *US*); **~frische** summer resort; **~frischler** holidaymaker, holidayer, vacationist *(US)*; **~gäste** summer visitors; **~halbjahr** summer term; **~haus** summerhouse, summer home, lodge, bungalow, cottage *(US)*; **~hitze** heat of summer; **~kleidung** summer clothes (wear); **~kurort** summer resort (spa); **~kurse an einer Universität durchführen** to run a summer camp; **~lager** summer stock, *(Ferienlager)* summer campus (camp); **~mode** summer fashion; **~pause** *(Parlament)* summer recess, *(Werbung)* hiatus; **~saison** summer season; **~schlußverkauf** seasonal sale, summer sales *(US)*; **~semester** summer session *(US)*; **~sitz** summer residence, country house, cottage *(US)*; **einmonatigen ~urlaub machen** to take a month's holiday in summer; **~weg** soft shoulder; **~wetter** summer weather; **~wohnsitz** summer residence; **~zeit** summer (daylight-saving, *US*, monkey, *sl.*) time; **~zeit einführen** to alter the time to the summer.
Sonde probe.
Sonder|abdruck extra reprint, separate print, offprint; **~abgabe** special levy (assessment, charge, contribution); **~abgabe für Schutt und Müll** nuisance abatement assessment *(US)*;

~**abhandlung** special section; ~**abkommen** separate treaty (agreement), special agreement; ~**abrechnung** special settlement; ~**abreden** special clauses.

Sonderabschreibung special (additional, extraordinary) depreciation;
erhöhte ~ additional capital allowance, initial allowance *(Br.)*;
verkürzte ~ accelerated writeoff *(US)*;
~ **für Neuanschaffungen** initial allowance *(Br.)*.

Sonder|abteilung special branch, built-in department, *(Krankenhaus)* specialized ward; ~**aktion** special action; ~**anfertigung** special make, one-off production, manufacture to customer's specification, *(Auto)* private (custom) car[riage]; ~**angebot** special (introductory, preference, exceptional, preferential) offer, *(günstiges Angebot)* special bargain, premium, featured articles, *(Wertpapiermarkt)* special offering; **billige** ~**angebote für die Urlaubszeit** money-saving holiday package; ~**angebot machen** to make a special feature; ~**ankläger** special prosecutor; ~**anlagefonds** special assessment fund; ~**artikel** *(Zeitung)* special feature; ~**artikel herstellen** to manufacture specific items, to scare up *(sl.)*; ~**aufgabe** specific function; ~**auftrag** special mission, *(Anfertigung)* specific (special) order, *(Anwalt)* special retainer, *(mil.)* detail; **jem. mit einem** ~**auftrag betrauen** to retain s. o. specially; ~**aufwendungen** extra expense (costs); ~**ausbildung** special schooling (training), *(Führungskräfte)* additional (cold-storage, *US*) training; ~**ausführung** special make.

Sonderausgabe *(Buch)* extra (special, separate) edition, commemorative issue, *(Zeitung)* extra edition, extra special *(Br.)*;
~**n** special expenditures, extras, *(Einkommensteuererklärung)* class B deductions *(US)*, special deductions *(Br.)*;
pauschalierte ~ flat exemption *(US)*, standard tax deduction;
~**n bei Gericht** extra costs;
~**n anderweitig ausgleichen** to absorb the extras; ~ **der Werke eines Autors veranstalten** to make a selection of an author's works.

sonderausgabenberechtigt sein to qualify for special deductions *(Br.)*.

Sonderausgaben|erhöhung personal exemption increase *(US)*; ~**freibetrag** expenditure relief; ~**pauschale** standard tax deduction.

Sonder|ausrüstung special (extra, *US*) equipment; ~**ausschuß** special commission *(Br.)*, ad-hoc (special) committee, *(parl.)* select (secret) committee *(Br.)*, Special Senate Committee *(US)*; **in** ~**ausschüssen beraten** to go into committees; ~**ausschüttung** melon *(US)*, plum *(sl.)*; ~**ausstattung** special (extra, *US*) equipment, *(Auto)* optional equipment; ~**ausstellung** special exhibition; ~**ausverkauf** bargain sale; ~**ausweis** special pass; ~**bataillon des Grenzschutzes** antiterrorist force, commando squad; ~**beauftragter** commissioner general, special agent (administrator, commissioner, representative, *US*), special deputy; ~**bedingungen** special terms; ~**befreiungsvorschriften** exemption provisions; ~**begünstigte** special interests *(US)*; ~**behandlung** preferred treatment; ~**behörde** specialized agency; ~**beilage** [special] supplement, *(Zeitung)* insert; ~**beitrag** special contribution; ~**belastung** extra charge; ~**berater** special assistant; **als** ~**berater engagieren** to retain as special counsel; **gegen** ~**berechnung** at extra cost; ~**bereich** individual area; ~**berechtigung** special permit, extra; ~**bericht** special report; ~**berichterstatter** special correspondent, specialist writer, special; ~**berichterstattung über eine AG** corporation story; ~**bestellung** specific (special) order; ~**besteuerung** special assessment; ~**bestimmung** special rule, exceptional provision, special condition; ~**bestimmungen** special conditions, special terms (provisions); **gesetzliche** ~**bestimmungen** special rules of law, saving clauses; ~**bestrebungen** *(pol.)* separatism; ~**bevollmächtigter** special agent (deputy), attorney in fact (ad hoc), plenipotentiary; ~**bilanz** special-purpose financial statement; ~**bonus** golden handshake; ~**botschafter** ambassador extraordinary, ambassador-at-large, special emissary; ~**delegation** [special] mission; ~**depot** special *(US)* (specific) deposit; ~**dividende** extraordinary dividend, melon *(US)*, plum *(sl.)*; **am Schluß des Jahres gezahlte** ~**dividende** year-end dividend *(US)*; ~**druck** limited publication, special impression, separate print, reprint; ~**einheit** *(mil.)* special force; **polizeiliche** ~**einheit** task force *(Br.)*; [**etwa**] ~**einheit des Bundesgrenzschutzes** commando squad, antiterrorist force; ~**einkünfte** extraordinary income; **überprozentuale** ~**einkünfte** excess preference income; ~**einnahmen** extraneous (extraordinary) income, *(Staat)* special revenue; ~**einsatz** emergency assignment; ~**einsatzgruppe** task force, flying squad *(Br.)*; ~**eintragung** special registration; ~**einwendung** special issue (exception); ~**entschädigung** extra allowance; ~**erlaubnis** special permission, occasional licence; ~**ermächtigung** special power; ~**ermäßigung** special price reduction; ~**erzeugnisse** specialities; ~**erziehung** special educational treatment; ~**fach** extra; ~**fahrbahn für Omnibusse** bus (priority) lane; ~**fahrt** excursion, tour; ~**fall** exceptional circumstances, particular (exceptional, special, isolated) case; ~**fenster** *(Buchhandlung)* special window display; ~**flug** extra flight; ~**flugzeug** special plane.

Sonderfonds special (revenue, contingency, separate) fund;
politischer ~ separate political fund, slush fund *(US)*;
~ **für zweckgebundene Steuern** trust fund *(US)*;
~ **einrichten** to set apart funds for a purpose; **einem** ~ **zufließen** to be placed in a special fund.

Sonder|freibetrag *(Einkommensteuer)* excess deduction; ~**freibetragskonto** excess deductions account; ~**friede** separate peace; ~**funktion** specific function; ~**gebiet** *(fig.)* demesne, province, preserve; ~**gebühr** specific duty, extra fee, special charge; ~**gefahren** *(Versicherung)* extraneous perils; ~**genehmigung** special licence (permit, authorization), *(Einzelgenehmigung)* individual licence; ~**genehmigung des Finanzministeriums** treasury licence; ~**gericht** special (legislative, *US*) court; ~**gericht der Besatzungsmacht** provisional court *(US)*; ~**gerichtsbarkeit** special jurisdiction, jurisdiction of an exceptional court; ~**gesetz** special act (statute); ~**gesetzgebung** special legislation; ~**gewinn** excess profit; ~**gewinnsteuer** excess profits duty *(Br.)* (tax, *US*); ~**gut** own (separate, *US*) property, *(Ehefrau)* separate estate, paraphernalia; ~**gutachten** minority report; ~**gutschein** special voucher; ~**haushalt** extraordinary budget; ~**heft** special edition (number); ~**heiratserlaubnis** special licence *(Br.)*; ~**honorar** special retainer, extra fee; ~**information** special information, lowdown *(sl.)*; ~**interessen** special interests, by-interests, preserve; ~**interview** exclusive interview; ~**kasse** special fund; ~**kenntnisse** specialized knowledge; ~**klasse** extra class; ~**kommando** special squad, *(mil.)* detachment, detail; **polizeiliches** ~**kommando** special police unit, task force *(Br.)*; ~**kommission** special commission; ~**konditionen** special terms; ~**konjunktur** special boom; ~**kontingent** special quota; ~**konto** separate (segregated, *US*, special) account; ~**konto für Emissionsagio** share premium account; ~**konten nach Portokassenrichtlinien überwachen** to control special accounts on an imprest-fund basis; ~**konzession** special concession, *(Alkoholausschank)* high licence; ~**kosten** extra charge; ~**kredit** special credit, *(Weltwährungsfonds)* special credit operation; ~**leistung** extra performance, extra.

sonderlich particular, special;
etw. ~ **sein** to be a little peculiar;
keine ~**e Lust haben** not to be keen on; **kein** ~**es Vergnügen** not much of a treat.

Sonderling odd (peculiar, strange) person, queer bird, screwball *(sl.)*, oddball *(US)*, singular man.

Sonder|liquidation *(Börse)* special settlement *(Br.)*; ~**liquidationstag** special settling day *(Br.)*; ~**lohnsatz** temporary rate; ~**marke** special stamp; ~**meldung** *(Rundfunk)* special announcement; ~**minister** minister without portfolio; ~**mission** [special] mission; ~**mittel** extra funds; ~**monopol** special privilege, monopoly; ~**müll** special refuse; ~**munition** express bullet; ~**nachfolger** subrogee; ~**nachlaß** special discount (reduction); ~**nummer** special edition (number), *(Zeitschrift)* extra; ~**nutzung** separate use; ~**omnibus** extra bus; ~**organisation** special agency, *(UNO)* specialized agency; ~**pachtverhältnis** special lease; ~**packung** special package; ~**parteitag** party conference; ~**plazierung** *(Inserat)* preferred position, individual location; ~**polizeieinheit** special police unit; ~**postamt** special post-office; ~**posten** separate (extraordinary) item; ~**posten mit Rücklageanteil** special item including reserves, special reserve; ~**prämie** extra premium.

Sonderpreis special (exceptional, out) price, *(Anzeigen)* special rate;
~ **für Daueranzeigen** multiple insertion rate;
jem. einen ~ **machen** to give s. o. special terms; ~**e vereinbaren** to secure special prices.

Sonder|privileg exemption; ~**programm** special; ~**provision** overriding commission; **verbotene** ~**provision** secret commission; ~**prüfung** special audit; ~**rabatt** extra (additional, special) discount, special reduction (allowance); **gestaffelten** ~**rabatt anbieten** to offer a special allowance on a sliding-scale basis; **hochkonzentrierte** ~**ration** *(mil.)* k ration; ~**recht** liberty, immunity, special privilege (law); ~**recht einschränken** to limit a privilege.

Sonderrechts|klausel subrogation clause, *(Befrachtungsvertrag)* liberties clause; **gewillkürte ~nachfolge** subrogation arising out of contract; **vereinbarte ~nachfolge** conventional subrogation; **~nachfolger** subrogee, special occupant.

Sonder|referat *(bei Behörde)* special branch; **~regel** special rule; **~regelung** separate settlement; **verfahrensmäßige ~regelung** special rule; **~revision** special audit; **~richter** special referee *(Br.)*; **~risiko** *(bei Industrieversicherungen)* special hazard; **~rücklage** contingency (provident, special, excess) reserve; **~rücklage für Emissionsagio** statutory capital reserve; **~rückstellung** extraordinary reserve, *(Versicherung)* specific reserve; **~rückstellungen für einzeln ausgewiesene Schulden** specific provisions against particular debts; **~schau** special show; **~schicht** extra (swing, *US*) shift; **~schichten machen** to work overtime; **~schreiben** separate letter; **~schuldverschreibung** special bond; **~schule** special school; **~seite** special page; **~sitzung** special meeting, *(Gericht)* extra (special) session; **~status** special status; **~statut** special statute; **~stelle** special agency, *(Inserat)* preferred position, individual location; **~stellung** exceptional position, privilege, franchise; **~stempel** commemorative postmark; **~steuer** specific (special, privilege, *US*) tax; **~strafmaß** special term *(US)*; **~studium** private study, special course of study; **~tarif** *(Bahn)* special service tariff, exceptional rate, *(Spediteur)* class rate, *(Versicherung)* specially favo(u)rable rate, preferred risks, *(Werbung)* special rate, *(Zoll)* specific (preferential) tariff; **~tarifangebot für Geschäftsreisende** *(Fluggesellschaft)* business package; **~termin** special session; **~umlage** *(Anliegerkosten)* special assessment; **~umlage der Industrie** special contribution *(Br.)*; **~urlaub** special (short, compassionate, *Br.*) leave; **~veranstaltungen** *(Einzelhandel)* special promotions; **~vereinbarung** special arrangement (composition, agreement), separate (special) covenant; **~verfahren** special proceedings; **~vergünstigung** special favo(u)r, extra benefit, *(für leitende Angestellte)* executive fringes; **umfassende ~vergünstigungen** comprehensive benefits; **mit Spitzenpositionen dieser Art verbundene übliche ~vergünstigungen** top-level benefits associated with appointments of this nature; **~vergütung** extra (special) allowance, bonus, gratuity, *(Angestellter)* fringe benefit, premium pay *(US)*, perquisite; **massierte ~vergütungen für leitende Angestellte** executive compensation package; **tarifliche ~vergütung** package benefit; **~verkauf** bargain sale.

Sondervermögen separate estate (property, *US*), severalty;
treuhänderisch gebundenes ~ settled estate, settlement property, settled property *(Br.)*; **kommunales ~** special revenue fund, general rate fund *(Br.)*; **zweckgebundenes ~** working-capital fund;
~ des Bundes state-operated fund; **~ der Bundesanstalt für Arbeitslosenversicherung** [etwa] unemployment fund; **~ der Ehefrau** paraphernalia, paraphernal property; **~ öffentlicher Versorgungswerke** utility fund.

Sonder|verpackung special wrapping; **~versicherungstarif** specially favo(u)rable rate, preferred risks; **~vertrag** separate covenant (agreement); **~vertretung** special agency; **~verwahrung** specific deposit, special deposit *(US)*; **für eine ~verwendung bestimmt sein** to be used for a specific purpose; **~vollmacht** specific authority (power), particular power, power of attorney in a specific act, *(Anwalt)* special retainer; **~vordruck** special form; **~vorrecht** special privilege; **~vorschriften** special provisions; **~vorschüsse** special advances; **~vorstellung** special performance; **~vorteil** exceptional advantage; **~vorzugsaktie** prior preference (preferred, *US*) stock; **~waggon anhängen** to put on an extra coach; **~widerruf** special revocation; **~wünsche** special requirements; **auf alle ~wünsche eines Geschäftsmannes eingestellt sein** to cater for all the special needs of a businessman; **~zahlung** extra payment; **~ziehungskonto** *(Weltwährungsfonds)* special drawing account; **~ziehungsrechte** *(Weltwährungsfonds)* special drawing rights, paper gold *(coll.)*; **~ziehungsrechte aus dem Verkehr ziehen** *(Weltwährungsfonds)* to cancel special drawing rights; **~ziehungsrechte zuteilen** to allocate special drawing rights; **~zoll** specific (additional) duty; **~zuführung zur Pensionsrückstellung** allocation to the pension reserve; **~zug** special (extra, excursion) train, special; **~züge einsetzen** to run (put on) extra trains, to lay on special trains; **~zulage** *(Leistungszulage)* merit increase, *(Produktionsprämie)* bonus payment, special bonus, incentive wage; **~zulagen für erschwerte Arbeitsbedingungen** salary differential; **~zulagensystem** incentive-wage plan; **~zuschlag** extra (special) charge; **~zustellung** special service; **~zuteilung** special allowance, extra ration; **~zuweisung** special allocation; **~zweck** specific purpose.

sondieren to sound, to beat about the bush, to explore, to probe, *(Wassertiefe)* to plumb, to plumb-line, to fathom;
j. ~ to pump s. o.; **auf dem diplomatischen Wege ~** to take diplomatic soundings; **Geschäftsführer wegen der Ferienregelung ~** to sound the manager on the question of holidays.

Sondierung soundings, probe;
~en explorations, exploratory talks, soundings, probe, probing.

Sondierungsgespräche talks about talks *(US)*.

Sonnabend, verkaufsoffener late-closing Saturday;
~e, bei denen man auf die Pauke haut devil-may-care Saturday nights.

Sonne, aufgehende rising sun;
in jds. Händen wie Schnee in der ~ schmelzen to melt in s. one's hands;
die ~ bringt es an den Tag murder will out.

Sonnen|aufgang sunrise; **~batterie** *(Raumschiff)* solar battery; **~blende** sunshade, *(Auto)* sun visor, *(Foto)* lenshood; **~blendscheibe** antiglare windshield (windscreen, *Br.*); **~brille** dark glasses; **~dach** *(Schaufenster)* awning, sunshade; **~deck** sun deck; **~einstrahlung** insolation; **~energie** solar power (energy); **durch ~energie betrieben** solar-powered; **~flecken** sun spots.

sonnengebräunt sun-tanned.

Sonnenheizungssystem solar-heating system.

sonnenklar as plain as plain can be (as a pikestaff).

Sonnen|kollektor solar collector; **~schein** sunshine, queen's weather; **~scheindauer** duration of sunshine; **~schutz** sunshade; **~segel** tilt; **~strahlung** solar radiation; **~system** solar system; **~terrasse** sun terrace; **farbenprächtiger ~untergang** purple sunset.

sonnige Lage sunny position.

Sonntag, freier free Sunday; **Weißer ~** Low Sunday;
~e und Feiertage nonbusiness days;
~ heiligen to keep Sunday.

sonntäglich|e Briefkastenleerung Sunday collection; **~e Kleidung** Sunday clothes; **~er Ladenverkauf** Sunday store opening *(US)*.

sonntags geschlossen bleiben not to open on Sundays.

Sonntags|anzug Sunday (meeting) clothes; **~arbeit** Sunday working; **erlaubte ~arbeiten** work of necessity; **~ausflug** weekend trip; **~ausflug machen** to go for an outing on Sunday; **~ausgabe** Sunday edition; **~beilage** Sunday supplement; **~blatt** Sunday paper; **~dienst haben** to be on duty on Sunday; **~fahrer** Sunday driver; **puritanische ~gesetze** blue laws *(Br.)*; **~kind sein** to be born under a lucky star; **~kleider** holiday (Sunday) clothes; **in seiner ~kleidung** in one's Sunday best, in one's Sunday go-to-meeting clothes, in one's best bib and tucker; **~kluft** Sunday clothes, glad rags *(sl.)*; **~rückfahrkarte** weekend (excursion) ticket.

Sonntagsruhe Sunday observance, *(der Geschäfte)* Sunday closing;
~ im Geschäftsleben practice of closing shops on Sundays;
Verletzung der ~ Sabbath breaking;
~ einhalten to keep the Sunday (blue, *Br.*) laws; **~ verletzen** to break the Sabbath.

Sonntags|schule Sunday school; **~staat** Sunday regalia (go-to-meeting clothes); **seinen ~staat anlegen** to put on one's best bib and tucker; **~verkauf** Sunday trading; **~verkehr** Sunday traffic; **~zeitung** Sunday newspaper.

sonstige|Auslagen other assets, sundry expense, sundries; **~ Erträge** other income (revenue); **~ Verpflichtungen** *(Bilanz)* other liabilities.

sonstiges miscellaneous, *(Buchungsrubrik)* other expenses, *(Tagesordnung)* any other business.

Sophisterei word splitting.

Sore score, loot.

Sorge concern, grief, heartache, vexation, custody, care, tuition, charge, worry, *(Sorgerecht)* custody, tutorship, curatorship;
~n woes;
ernste ~ the devil to pay;
mit ~ erfüllen to distress, to cause anguish;
jem. ~ für etw. anvertrauen to confide s. th. to s. one's care; **seine ~n im Alkohol ertränken** to drown one's sorrows in drink; **keine ~n haben** to be free from care; **jem. ~ machen** to give s. o. trouble; **sich ~n machen** to worry (be worried) abouth s. th.; **sich unnötige ~n machen** to borrow trouble; **~ los sein** to be quit of a trouble; **~ tragen** to take care, to see about; **für j. ~ tragen** to have the care of s. o., to cater for s. o.; **für jds. Wohlbefinden ~ tragen** to look after s. one's well-being.

sorgeberechtigt entitled to custody.

Sorgeberechtigter tutor, curator, custodian, guardian.

sorgen to take care, to cater, to attend, to provide for;
für j. ~ to take care of s. o.; **für jds. Ausbildung** ~ to pay for s. one's schooling; **für jds. leibliche Bedürfnisse** ~ to supply s. one's bodily wants; **für Deckung** ~ to provide for payment; **nicht** ~ to neglect; **für ein Taxi** ~ to arrange for a taxi; **für Unterhalt** ~ to provide maintenance for s. o.;
für sich selbst ~ **müssen** to housekeep for o. s.
Sorgen|falten, mit down-faced; **~kind** problem child; **~kinder** handicapped children; **~last** load of care; **jem. eine ~last abnehmen** to take s. one's mind off his sorrows.
sorgenvoll worried, anxious;
~ **in die Zukunft sehen** to look into the future with concern.
Sorgerecht custody, tutorship, curatorship;
gerichtlich angeordnetes ~ tutorship by appointment of the judge; **testamentarisch bestimmtes** ~ tutorship by will; **gesetzliches** ~ tutorship by the effect of the law; **natürliches** ~ tutorship by nature;
~ **für die Kinder** custody of the children; ~ **für eine Person** care and custody of a person;
~ **beantragen** to apply for custody; ~ **für die Kinder zugesprochen erhalten** to be awarded custody of the children; **zur Ausübung des ~s für j. bestimmt sein** to be appointed to have the care of s. o.
sorgerechtlich beim Vater bleiben to remain in the custody of the father.
Sorgerechtsverfahren custody procedure.
Sorgfalt care, carefulness, diligence, heed, prudence;
mit der erforderlichen ~ with all due diligence; **mit gebührender** ~ with due [amount of] care;
angemessene ~ reasonable care; **außerordentliche** ~ extraordinary diligence; **besondere** ~ special diligence; **erforderliche** ~ necessary diligence; **im Berufsleben erforderliche** ~ reasonable care and skill; **im Verkehr erforderliche** ~ reasonable care and diligence, legal diligence, ordinary care and prudence, due diligence; **im gewöhnlichen Verkehr erforderliche** ~ diligence usual in ordinary business; **erhöhte** ~ increased care; **gehörige** ~ due diligence, ordinary (reasonable) care (diligence); **geringe** ~ low diligence; **größte** ~ greatest diligence; **größtmögliche** ~ highest degree of diligence; **handelsübliche** ~ **[bei der Versendung]** customary dispatch; **hinreichende** ~ proper care; **höchste** ~ utmost care; **mangelnde** ~ lack of care (due diligence); **übertriebene** ~ overcare; **im Verkehr übliche** ~, **verkehrsübliche** ~ ordinary care; **zumutbare** ~ reasonable diligence;
~ **wie in eigenen Angelegenheiten** diligence exercised in regard to any and all of one's affairs; ~ **eines ordentlichen Kaufmanns** attention of a conscientious businessman; **mangelnde** ~ **des Spediteurs** carrier negligence;
~ **anwenden** to observe (exercise, use, expend) care, to employ diligence; **besondere** ~ **anwenden** to exhibit a greater degree of skill; **erforderliche** ~ **anwenden** to do one's (give, use) diligence; **die im Verkehr erforderliche** ~ **anwenden** to exercise the required degree of skill and diligence; **gehörige** ~ **anwenden** to exercise reasonable skill and care; **große** ~ **anwenden** to bestow great diligence; ~ **eines ordentlichen Kaufmanns anwenden** to use the care and caution of an ordinary man of business; **notwendige** ~ **außer acht gelassen haben** to have been guilty of negligence; **mit der im Verkehr erforderlichen** ~ **handeln** to act with reasonable care and diligence; ~ **außer acht lassen** to dissipate care; **mangelnde** ~ **erkennen lassen** to show want of care; **im branchenüblichen Verkehr erforderliche** ~ **walten lassen** to be reasonably prudent in circumstances where one is; **gehörige** ~ **verwenden** to use due diligence; **große** ~ **verwenden** to bestow great diligence.
sorgfältig careful, diligent, scrupulous, nice, painstaking, ingoing;
sehr ~ by rule and line;
~er arbeiten to be a bit more careful; ~ **auswählen** to make a careful choice; ~ **behandelt werden müssen** *(Frage)* to require to be aired; **Beweismaterial** ~ **prüfen** to sift the evidence; **in Geldsachen sehr** ~ **sein** to be scrupulous in money matters;
~e Arbeit conscientious piece of work; **bei ~er Behandlung** if treated with care; **~e Prüfung** careful examination, close going-over; ~ **angelegte Schützengräben** deliberate trenches; **nach ~er Überlegung** upon careful consideration.
Sorgfaltsgrad degree (measure) of care;
hoher ~ high standard of diligence.
Sorgfaltspflicht diligence, care;
allgemeine ~ common duty of care; **äußerste** ~ high degree of care and diligence; **erhöhte** ~ great (high) diligence, great care; **von einem Fachmann erwartete** ~ special diligence; **geringe** ~ slight care, slight (low) diligence; **gesetzliche** ~ necessary diligence; **gewöhnliche** ~ ordinary (reasonable) care (diligence); **höchste (außergewöhnlich hohe)** ~ extraordinary diligence; **verkehrsübliche** ~ ordinary diligence, ordinary (reasonable) care;
~ **des Reisenden** caveat viator, let the wayfarer beware;
~ **üben** to exercise ordinary care; **wegen der Außerachtlassung der im Berufsleben erforderlichen** ~ **verklagen** to sue for professional negligence.
sorglos careless, inadvertent, easy in one's mind;
~es Leben führen to lead a life of ease.
Sorglosigkeit inadvertence, carelessness;
jds. ~ **zuzuschreiben sein** to be owing to s. one's carelessness.
sorgsam attentive, solicitous;
Fehler ~ **zu vermeiden suchen** to be anxious not to make a mistake;
~ **gehütetes Geheimnis** carefully kept secret.
Sorte *(Art)* sort, kind, description, denomination, class, order, variety, *(Gattung)* type, species, stripe *(US)*, *(Güte)* quality, grade, run, *(Marke)* brand, line, make, mark;
in allen ~n und Preislagen of all sorts and at all price levels; **von feinster** ~ of first (prime) quality; **von jeder** ~ of every description; **von der schlimmsten (übelsten)** ~ of the worst description, of the deepest dye;
ausländische ~n foreign notes and coins (cash, currency); **gut eingeführte** ~ well recognized grade; **erste** ~ best quality; **erstklassige** ~ top-grade quality; **feinste** ~ choicest brand, superior quality, grade A; **gangbare** ~ current description; **geringe** ~ inferior quality; **mittlere** ~ medium (average) quality; **nächstbeste** ~ next quality; **prima** ~ first (prime) quality; **schlechtere** ~ inferior quality; **vertraglich vereinbarte** ~ contract grade; **vorzügliche** ~ choice brand;
milde ~ **Zigaretten** mild brand of cigarettes;
Waren nach ~n einteilen to grade goods; **nur eine** ~ **führen** to stock only one quality; **zu den Schwindlern der übelsten** ~ **gehören** to be a fraud of the worst kind; **nur gängige ~n auf Lager haben** to have only conventional designs in stock; **nur in sehr begrenztem Umfang ausländische ~n zur Verfügung halten** to carry minimal supplies of foreign notes.
Sorten|abteilung foreign currency (money) department; **~bezeichnung** quality description; **~einlieferung** delivery of coin; **~geschäft**, **~handel** *(Bank)* transaction of notes and coins, dealings in foreign coins and notes; **~händler** exchange jobber, money dealer; **~konto** specie account; **~kurs** rate of exchange for notes and coins; **~- und Devisenkurse auf europäischen Plätzen** continental rates *(Br.)*; **~kurszettel** bill of specie; **~provision** foreign exchange commission; **~verzeichnis** note of specie; **~wahl** grading; **~zettel** bordereau, bill of specie.
sortierbar sortable.
Sortieren sorting, grading;
~ **nach Güteklassen** grading of commodities.
sortieren to sort, assort, to grade, *(ordnen)* to arrange, *(sichten)* to sift;
Akten chronologisch ~ to file papers in order of date; **Briefe** ~ to sort [out] letters; **nach Größen** ~ to [grade by] size; **nach Klassen** ~ to classify; **nach Qualitäten (Sorten)** ~ to grade goods.
Sortierer sizer, sorter, selector, stapler.
Sortiermaschine sorting machine, sorter.
sortiert assorted;
gleichmäßig ~ equally graded; **nach Größen** ~ graded by size; **nicht** ~ of sorts;
reich ~es Lager well-assorted stock.
Sortierung assorting, assortment, *(Anordnung)* arrangement;
~ **nach Größen** sizing; ~ **nach Klassen** classification; ~ **nach Qualitäten** grading of commodities.
Sortiment assortment, collection, choice, range of goods, line of products, product line, sales mix *(US)*, *(Satz)* set;
breites ~ varied assortment; **gemischtes** ~ mixed assortment; **gesamtes** ~ full line; **weit gestreutes** ~ wide variety of product lines; **großes** ~ wide ranges of items, large (rich) assortment; **hereingenommenes** ~ line of goods taken in stock; **kleines** ~ little stock in hand; **unvollständiges** ~ broken assortment; **verwandtes** ~ complementary line; **vollständiges** ~ whole range of articles;
großes ~ **neuer Bücher** wide selection of new books; ~ **des Einzelhandels** retail line; **großes** ~ **an Mustern** wide range of samples; **breites** ~ **an Waren** diversification (wide range) of products;
größtmögliches ~ **anbieten** to hold the widest possible range of stock.

Sortimenter retail bookseller;
~-Kommittent retail bookseller customer; **~rabatt** retail bookseller discount.

Sortiments|abteilung new book department; **~ausweitung** increase in range of goods, expansion of assortment, product line extension; **~breite** variety, buying choice, diversification; **~buchhandel** general booksellers; **~buchhändler** general (retail, discount) bookseller; **~buchhandlung** retail bookshop (bookstore, *US*); **~geschäft** single-line store *(US)*; **ähnliche ~gruppen dazunehmen** to diversify into complementary fields; **~marken** associated trademarks; **~vereinfachung, ~verkleinerung** product line simplification.

Souffleur *(Theater)* prompter;
sich ganz auf den ~ verlassen to wing;
~kasten prompter's box.

soufflieren to prompt.

Souffliergerät, optisches teleprompter.

Souterrain basement;
im ~ downstairs;
~geschäft basement shop (store, *US*); **~räume** underground rooms; **~wohnung** underground dwelling, basement flat (apartment).

Souvenir [travel] souvenir, remembrance, keepsake;
~laden souvenir shop.

Souverän sovereign, throne, crown *(Br.)*.

souverän imperial;
Situation ~ beherrschen to be in full command of a situation; **~ siegen** to win in a superior style;
~e Beherrschung mastery; **mit wenigen ~en Pinselstrichen** with a few masterly strokes; **~er Staat** sovereign state.

Souveränität sovereignty, statehood;
parlamentarische ~ parliamentary sovereignty;
~ erringen to become a sovereign.

Souveränitäts|rechte sovereign rights; **~rechte ausüben** to exercise sovereign rights; **~verletzung** violation of sovereign rights.

sowjetisieren to sovietize.

Sowjetisierung sovietization.

sozial social;
~ abgesunken declassé; **~ eingestellt** welfare-minded, social-minded;
~ absinken to sink in the social scale; **~ denken** to be social-minded;
~e Abgaben old-age benefit taxes, social [security] contributions; **~e Aufgaben** social duties; **~e Aufwendungen** social cost, welfare expenditure; **~e Aufwertung** social advancement; **~e Beitragsleistungen** social contributions; **~e Belastung** welfare load; **~e Berufe** social [welfare] work; **~e Dienstleistungen** social services; **~e Einrichtungen** social services, welfare organization (centre, *Br.*, center, *US*); **~e Entwicklung** social evolution; **~e Erträge** social benefits; **~e Fesseln** social fetters; **~er Fortschritt** social progress (advance); **~e Frage** social question; **Zeit für die Lösung ~er Fragen aufwenden** to spend one's time in social involvement; **~e Fürsorge** welfare work, social service; **auf ~em Gebiet** in the social field; **~e Gegebenheiten** social structure; **~e Gerechtigkeit** social legislation; **~e Gesamtrechnung** social accounting; **~es Gewissen** social conscience; **~es Gleichgewicht** social stability; **~e Hilfestellung** welfare assistance; **~es Hilfswerk** welfare association; **in ~er Hinsicht** socially; **~e Kosten** *(Volkswirtschaft)* social cost; **~e Leistungen** *(freiwillige)* fringe benefits (payments), *(Arbeiterrentenversicherung)* welfare expenditure *(US)*, *(gesetzliche)* social-security contributions; **~e Marktwirtschaft** free-enterprise system; **~e Ordnung** social order; **~e Schicht** social category (class); **~e Sicherheit** social security; **~e Stellung** social position (standing), walk; **Einbußen in seiner ~en Stellung hinnehmen müssen** to sink in the social scale; **~e Tätigkeit** social welfare activity; **~es Übel** social ill; **~e Umwelt** social environment; **~e Unterschiede** social distinctions; **~e Verantwortlichkeit** social responsibility; **~e Verhältnisse** social conditions; **~e Versorgung** social service; **~e Wohlfahrt** social welfare *(US)*; **~e Wohlstandsfunktion** social welfare function; **~er Wohnungsbau** low- (moderate-) income housing, federally-financed low-cost housing *(US)*.

Sozial|abfindung redundancy payment *(Br.)*, severance allowance (benefit, pay) *(US)*; **~abfindungsgesetz** Redundancy Payments Act *(Br.)*; **~abgaben** *(Arbeiterrentenversicherung)* old-age benefit taxes *(US)*, social [security] contributions (payments), social security tax *(US)*; **~abteilung** welfare department, *(Betrieb)* employee benefit and service division; **~amt** social security office *(Br.)*, health and welfare department *(US)*, welfare agency *(US)*, Public Assistance Authority *(US)*, poor-law parish *(Br.)*, overseer of the poor *(Br.)*, social services department; **seine zusätzlichen ~ansprüche abtreten** to transfer one's service credits; **~arbeit** welfare *(US)* (charity, social) work, casework; **~arbeiter** caseworker, slum (welfare) worker; **~attaché** labo(u)r attaché; **~aufwand** social service spending (expenditure), cost of social security, welfare expenditure (spending) *(US)*; **öffentlicher ~aufwand** public spending on the social services; **gesetzliche ~aufwendungen** social expenditure (security contributions); **freiwillige ~aufwendungen** fringe benefits (payments); **~ausgaben** social (welfare, *US*) expenditure, social service expenditure, welfare benefits *(US)*; **zusätzliche ~ausgaben** fringe benefits; **im Vorjahr 10,8 Mio. Dollar geringere ~ausgaben haben** to save $ 10,8 m last year on the welfare budget; **~ausschuß** public *(US)* (national, *Br.*) assistance committee, public welfare committee, committee on social questions; **Wirtschafts- und ~ausschuß** *(EG)* Economic and Social Council; **~beamter** social (welfare) worker; **~behörde** social (welfare) agency *(US)*; **betriebliche ~beihilfen** company (fringe) benefits; **~beihilfe beantragen** to claim social security *(Br.)*; **~beiträge** old-age benefit taxes *(US)*, social [security] contributions; **~belastung** welfare load; **~bericht** social survey, social [welfare] work; **~bestimmungen** welfare provisions; **~betreuer** welfare worker; **~betreuerin** lady almoner *(Br.)*; **~bewußtsein** social consciousness; **~bilanz** social-economic balance sheet; **~bonus** discount for low-income subscribers; **~demokrat** social democrat, socialist; **~demokratie** Social Democracy; **~diagnose** social analysis; **~einkommen** social service payments, supplementary security income *(US)*; **~einrichtungen** welfare institutions (facilities), social services; **~etat** social budget; **~fonds** welfare fund, *(Unternehmen)* employee benefit trust; **Europäischer ~fonds** European Social Fund; **~forscher** social investigator; **~forschung** social research (investigation).

Sozialfürsorge social casework, social security *(Br.)*, social welfare *(US)*, social (parish) relief *(Br.)*;
betriebliche ~ industrial welfare (welfare work), welfare management;
der ~ anheimfallen to be put on public assistance rolls *(US)*, to come upon the parish *(Br.)*; **in der ~ tätig sein** to do welfare work.

Sozial|fürsorger social (welfare) worker, welfare officer, social (welfare) caseworker, relieving officer *(Br.)*, warden the poor *(Br.)*; **~fürsorger für Geisteskranke** mental welfare officer; **~gericht** Local Appeal Tribunal *(Br.)*, Pension Tribunal *(Br.)*; **~gerichtsverfahren** procedure in a local appeal tribunal *(Br.)*; **~geschichte** social history; **~gesetzgebung** social (welfare) legislation; **~gesetzgebung neu fassen** to rewrite the welfare system; **~haushalt** social budget; **~helfer** caseworker, reliever of the poor *(Br.)*.

Sozialhilfe social relief, social (public) welfare *(US)*, social security benefits *(Br.)*, supplementary benefits *(Br.)*, out-relief *(Br.)*, poor (parish, outdoor) relief *(Br.)*, outrelief *(Br.)*;
~ public (social, *US*, national, *Br.*) assistance, social welfare *(US)*, welfare aid *(US)*, state assistance *(US)*;
~ für den Lebensunterhalt von Familienangehörigen supplementary benefits for one's dependants *(Br.)*;
Betrügereien beim Bezug von ~ abstellen to crack down on welfare cheats; **der ~ anheimfallen** to come upon the parish *(Br.)*, to be put on public assistance rolls *(US)*; **~ beantragen** to claim social security, to apply for relief under the poor law *(Br.)*, to apply for outdoor relief *(Br.)*; **keine ~ mehr bekommen** to go off welfare *(US)*; **~ beziehen** to be on welfare *(US)* (upon the parish, *Br.*), to be in receipt of national *(Br.)* (public, *US*) assistance, to be on local public relief *(Br.)*; **~ an beitragsfreie Angehörige gewähren** *(Sozialversicherung)* to award supplementary benefits on a noncontributory basis *(Br.)*;
~abteilung Supplementary Benefits Commission *(Br.)*; **~anspruch** claim for national *(Br.)* (public, *US*) assistance; **~ausschuß** public *(US)* (national, *Br.*) assistance committee; **j. auf die ~basis herunterdrücken** to put s. o. virtually into a poverty-trap; **~beratungsstelle** Citizen's Advice Bureau *(Br.)*.

sozialhilfeberechtigt sein to be eligible for welfare *(US)* (national assistance, *Br.*).

Sozialhilfeberechtigte, Kreis der ~n ausweiten to expend the welfare rolls.

Sozialhilfeempfänger public charge, welfare beneficiary, assisted person *(Br.)*;
nicht ortsansässiger ~ casual pauper *(US)* (poor, *Br.*);
~ sein to live on national *(Br.)* (public, *US*) assistance;
~liste public assistance roll *(US)*.

Sozialhilfe|gesetz National Assistance (Supplementary Benefits) Act *(Br.)*; **~leistungen** social benefits, public assistance benefits *(Br.)*, social welfare benefits *(US)*; **~niveau** supplementary benefit level *(Br.)*; **~politik** national *(Br.)* (public assistance, *US*) policy; **~recht** welfare legislation; **~satz** national assistance rate *(Br.)*.

Sozial|interventionismus Fair Deal *(US)*; **~investitionen** investment in human capital.

sozialisieren to socialize, to nationalize *(Br.)*, to communize.

Sozialisierung socialization, nationalization *(Br.)*, communization.

Sozialisierungsentschädigung nationalization indemnity *(Br.)*.

Sozialismus, gemäßigter pink socialism;
sich zum ~ bekennen to profess o. s. a socialist.

sozialistisch socialist[ic], social, leftist;
~e Errungenschaften socialist achievements; **~es Lager** socialistic camp; **~e Marktwirtschaft** market socialism.

Sozial|kapital employee benefit trust; **allgemeines ~kapital** social overhead capital; **~kontrakt** social contract (compact); **~kosten** social costs (expenditure); **~kredit** social credit; **~kritik** criticism of society; **~lasten** social cost (charges), social service costs, welfare expenditure (spending); **~leistungen** *(Sozialversicherung)* social service (security) payments, social benefits (expenditure), social service expenditure, social expenditure *(US)*, welfare benefits (services); **freiwillige ~leistungen** voluntary social contributions *(US)*, employee (voluntary social) services, voluntary social security services *(US)*, marginal benefits (perks, *Br., sl.*), *(für gehobene Angestellte)* fringe benefits (payments) *(US)*; **~lohn** social wages; **~miete** council tenancy *(Br.)*; **~mieter** council tenant *(Br.)*, council house tenant *(Br.)*; **~minister** Social Service Secretary *(Br.)*, Secretary of State for Social Services *(Br.)*, Minister of Social Security *(Br.)*, Social Welfare Minister *(US)*; **~ministerium** Ministry of Social Security, Ministry of National Insurance *(Br.)*, Department of Social Security *(Br.)*; **~ökologie** human ecology; **~ökonomie** social economics; **~ordnung** social order (system); **~pädagogik** educational sociology; **~paket** package of social measures and benefits; **~partner** management and labo(u)r; **~partnergesetz** Industrial Relations Act; **~pfleger** caseworker, social worker, welfare assistant, warden (guardian) of the poor *(Br.)*, community worker, almoner *(Br.)*, poormaster *(US local)*; **~pflegerin** visiting nurse, lady almoner *(Br.)*; **~plan** *(bei Personalabbau)* severance scheme *(US)*, redundancy payments scheme *(Br.)*; **~politik** social (welfare) policy.

sozialpolitisch politico-social.

Sozial|produkt national product (dividend, income), social dividend; **marginale ~produktivität** social marginal productivity.

Sozialprodukt|rechnung national product accounts; **~volumen** national productivity capacity; **~zuwachs** national productivity increase.

Sozial|psychologie social psychology; **Wirtschafts- und ~rat der Vereinten Nationen** United Nations Economic and Social Council; **~recht** social legislation; **~referent eines Betriebes** factory welfare worker; **~reform** social (welfare) reform; **sich für ~reformen aussprechen** to profess o. s. to be a social reformer; **~reformer** social reformer; **~rente** old-age (retirement, social-security) pension, National Insurance retirement pension *(Br.)*, *(Sozialhilfe)* national asssistance allowance *(Br.)*, public assistance benefit *(US)*; **zusätzliche ~rente** supplementary allowance *(Br.)*; **~rente für bedürftige Mütter mit minderjährigen Kindern** mothers' aid (allowance, pension, compensation); **abgestuftes ~rentensystem** graduated pension scheme *(Br.)*; **~rentner** public charge, assisted person *(Br.)*, social-security recipient *(US)*, annuity holder, pensioner; **~richter** Local Appeal Tribunal judge *(Br.)*; **~staat** social (welfare) state; **~statistik** national income statistics, social accounting; **~struktur** social structure; **~umfrage** social issue poll; **freiwilliger ~unkostenaufwand** fringe cost; **~unterstützung** payment of benefits, *(staatlich)* public *(US)* (national, *Br.*) relief (assistance); **~unterstützung empfangen** to go on public assistance (relief) rolls *(US)*, to be upon the parish *(Br.)* (on welfare, *US*); **~untersuchung** social investigation; **~verbindlichkeiten** social service liabilities; **~vereinbarung** social contract *(Br.)*; **~vergütung im Fall der Notwendigkeit von Dauerpflegschaft** constant attendance allowance *(Br.)*; **~verhalten** social behavio(u)r; **~vermögen** social wealth.

sozialversichert, nicht ~ sein to be outside the scope of the national insurance system *(Br.)*, to be relieved from security payments *(US)*.

Sozialversicherung social insurance (security) *(US)*, old age and survivor's insurance *(US)*, national insurance *(Br.)*;
sich nicht an der ~ beteiligen to contract out *(Br.)*; **Beiträge in die ~ einzahlen** to pay contributions into the scheme.

Sozialversicherungs|amt social security office *(Br.)*; **~ansprüche** national *(Br.)* (public, *US*) assistance claims; **vom Arbeitgeber bezahlter ~anteil** social security payroll tax *(US)*, employee benefits paid by the company; **vom Arbeitnehmer bezahlter ~anteil** employee benefit; **~anteil zahlen** *(Arbeitgeber)* to pay employer's national insurance contribution *(Br.)*; **~aufsichtsamt** Social Security Board *(US)*, National Insurance Commission *(Br.)*; **~ausgaben** social insurance expenditure *(US)*; **~ausschuß** insurance committee; **~behörde** Bureau of Employment Security *(US)*, Ministry of Pensions and National Insurance *(Br.)*.

Sozialversicherungsbeitrag social insurance (security) contribution;
angerechneter ~ contribution credited; **gestaffelter ~** graduated contribution;
~ des Arbeitgebers employers' national insurance contribution.

Sozialversicherungsbeiträge social insurance (security) contributions *(US)*, national insurance contributions *(Br.)*, social security taxes *(Br.)*;
nach Lohnstufen gestaffelte ~ graduated contributions;
~ für j. abführen to stamp s. one's national insurance card *(Br.)*; **keine ~ zahlen müssen** to be relieved from security payments *(US)*, to be outside the scope of the national insurance system *(Br.)*.

Sozialversicherungs|belastungen social security taxes *(US)*; **~bestimmungen** National Insurance Regulations *(Br.)*, social security provisions *(US)*; **~einnahmen** social security revenue *(US)*; **~empfänger** social security *(US)* (national insurance, *Br.*) recipient; **~fonds** establishment fund *(Br.)*; **~freiheit** exemption from social security payments; **~gesetz** National Insurance Act *(Br.)*, Social Security (Federal Insurance Contribution) Act *(US)*; **~gesetzgebung** social security *(US)* (national insurance, *Br.*) legislation; **über der ~grenze liegen** to be outside the scope of national insurance *(Br.)* (relieved from security payments, *US*); **~karte** national insurance (contribution) card *(Br.)*, social security card *(US)*; **~karte abstempeln** to stamp the employed person's card; **~kosten** cost of social security, *(Staat)* social security bill *(US)*.

Sozialversicherungsleistungen social security (insurance, *US*, national insurance, *Br.*) benefits, social insurance services *(US)*, *(bei Arbeitsunfällen)* industrial injuries benefits *(Br.)*;
angepaßte ~ social security adjustments; **lohnabhängige ~** earnings-related benefits; **pauschale ~** flat-rate social security benefits.

Sozialversicherungs|marke national insurance stamp *(Br.)*; **~nummer** national *(Br.)* (social, *US*) insurance number.

sozialversicherungspflichtig inside the scope of the national insurance *(Br.)*;
nicht ~ sein to be outside the scope of the national insurance system *(Br.)* (relieved from security payments, *US*);
~es Jahr contribution year.

Sozialversicherungs|pflichtiger national insurance contributor *(Br.)*; **normalbeschäftigter ~pflichtiger** class I contributor *(Br.)*; **~politik** social security policy *(US)*; **~reform** social security reform; **~rente** old-age (retirement) pension, National Insurance retirement pension *(Br.)*, social security pension *(US)* (benefit, *Br.*); **übliche ~rente** standard National Insurance retirement pension *(Br.)*; **~rente bei Vollinvalidität** industrial pension; **~stock** National Insurance Fund *(Br.)*, social security [trust] fund *(US)*; **~system** social security *(US)* (national insurance, *Br.*) system, *(bei Unfällen)* industrial injuries scheme; **betriebliches ~system** social security benefit plan *(US)*; **~träger** social *(US)* (national, *Br.*) insurance institution; **~vermögen** social security [trust] fund *(US)*, National Insurance Fund *(Br.)*; **~versorgung** social security service *(US)*; **~wesen** social *(US)* (national, *Br.*) insurance system, National Insurance Scheme *(Br.)*; **~zahlung** social security check *(US)*, national insurance cheque *(Br.)*; **~zuschläge für Kinder** national insurance dependency benefits.

Sozial|-, Alters- und Hinterbliebenenversorgung old-age, survivor's and liability insurance *(US)*; **~verwaltung** social [security] administration; **~wesen** social matters; **~wirtschaft** social economics (economy).

sozialwirtschaftlich socio-economic.

Sozial|wirtschaftsrat social science research council *(Br.)*; **~wissenschaft** sociology, social science, social economics; **~wissenschaftler** social scientist, sociologist.

sozialwissenschaftlich sociological.
Sozialwohnung publicly financed dwelling, council home (flat, house) *(Br.)*.
Sozialzulage family allowance (benefit);
betriebliche ~n fringe benefits (payments); **einer Bedürftigkeitsüberprüfung unterliegende ~** means-tested benefit;
~system [social security] benefit plan *(Br.)*; **betriebliches ~wesen** employee benefit plan (system, program[me]); **umfassendes ~wesen** comprehensive benefit program(me).
Sozial|zuschläge für Kinder National Insurance Dependency Benefits *(Br.)*; **~zuschuß** welfare grant, National Assistance grant *(Br.)*; **~zuwendung** welfare payment.
Sozietät professional practice, association, nontrading partnership, copartnership.
Sozietätsvertrag partnership agreement (deed).
Soziologe social student, sociologist, social scientist.
Soziologie social science, sociology;
Bindestrich-~ applied sociology.
soziologisch sociological.
Sozius copartner, law partner;
~fahrer pillion passenger (rider); **~sitz** pillion seat; **auf dem ~sitz mitfahren** to [sit on a] pillion, to ride on a pillion.
spähen to spy, to pry;
durch eine Zaunlücke ~ to peep through a gap in the fence.
Spähtrupp reconnaissance party, patrol;
~führer patrol leader; **~tätigkeit** patrol (reconnaissance) activity.
Spalier guard of hono(u)r, *(für Blumen)* trellis;
~ bilden to line the streets (route), to form a lane; **durch ein ~ von Menschen gehen** to pass through a lane of people; **am Bürgersteig ~ stehen** to line the kerb;
~obst espalier (wall, fan-trained) fruit.
Spalt gap, opening, crack, chink, *(Geldeinwurf)* slit, slot, *(Kluft)* gulf, chasm;
tiefer ~ zwischen zwei Ideologien deep gulf between two ideologies; **tiefer ~ in der Mauer** gaping crack in the wall.
spaltbares Material fissionable material.
Spaltbildkamera one-shot camera.
Spalte cleft, split, rift, fissure, *(Buch, Zeitung)* column;
in ~n columnar;
besondere ~ feature; **nebenstehende ~** adjoining column;
~ für Todesanzeigen obituary column;
~n füllen to fill the columns; **über vier ~n gehen** *(Artikel)* to take up four columns; **in ~n setzen** to compose in slips (galleys); **~ für Bücherrezensionen zur Verfügung stellen** to devote a column to book criticism.
spalten to split, to disunite, to divide, *(Erdöl)* to crack, *(Land)* to rend;
sich ~ *(Partei)* to split; **Goldmarkt in einen freien und offiziellen Markt ~** to split the gold market into a free and an official market; **sich in mehrere Lager ~** to split up into several groups; **Partei in zwei Lager ~** to divide the party into two camps; **jem. den Schädel ~** to split s. one's skull.
Spalten|breite column width, width of column; **~höhe** column depth, depth of column.
spaltenlang covering several column.
Spalten|linie dividing rule; **~maß** column inch, single column measure; **voller ~satz** full measure; **~überschrift** column heading.
spaltenweise setzen to compose in slips (galleys).
Spalter|gewerkschaft breakaway union; **~gruppe** fraction.
Spaltmaterial fissionable material.
Spaltung disruption, dissociation, division, *(Aktien)* splitting, *(Erdöl)* cracking, *(pol.)* division, split, disunion;
~ in einen rechten und linken Flügel splitting into a right and left wing; **~ des Goldmarktes** splitting of the gold market; **~ einer Partei** split of a party.
Spaltungsbewegung disunionism.
Spaltwache dogwatch.
Späne, wo gehobelt wird, fliegen ~ omelets are not made without breaking eggs.
Spanferkel sucking pig.
spanisch, das kommt mir ~ vor there's s. th. fishy about it.
Spann|band banner; **~beton** prestressed concrete; **~brücke** prestressed concrete bridge.
Spanne margin, range, spread *(US)*;
geringe ~ narrow margin;
~ von dreißig Jahren space of thirty years; **~ des Lebens** span of life; **große ~ zwischen den Preisen** wide range of prices; **~ in Renditen** yield spread; **~ in den Zinssätzen** gap in interest rates, margin [between the rates] of interest.
spannen to stretch, to string [up];
etw. ~ to grasp s. th., to catch on; **auf eine Erbschaft ~** to wait for a dead man's shoes; **seine Erwartungen hoch ~** to pitch one's expectations high; **j. auf die Folter ~** to put s. o. on tenterhooks; **Ochsen ins Joch ~** to yoke an oxen; **Zeltschnüre ~** to tighten the guy ropes.
spannend thrilling, exciting, breath-taking, dramatic, juicy *(coll.)*, wool(l)y *(US coll.)*;
etw. ~ für j. machen to keep s. o. on tenterhooks; **nicht gerade ~ sein** to lack a certain kick;
~er Roman thriller, exciting novel.
Spann|kraft resilience, elasticity; **geistige ~kraft** spring, tone, healthy elasticity; **seine geistige ~kraft verlieren** to lose one's elasticity of mind (tone); **~plakat** wall banner; **~schloß** tightener; **~teppich** wall-to-wall carpet.
Spannung tension, friction, strain, excitement, *(Druck)* pressure, *(Buch)* thrill, *(el.)* voltage, *(pol.)* tension, friction, strained relations;
unter ~ *(el.)* live;
atemlose ~ atmosphere of breathless suspense; **inflationäre ~** inflationary pressure; **innerpolitische ~en** internal strain; **konjunkturelle ~en** cyclical tensions; **nervöse ~** nervous tension; **niedrige ~** *(el.)* low voltage; **politische ~** political tension; **soziale ~en** social strains;
politische ~en zwischen zwei Ländern political friction between two countries;
~ abbauen to lessen (reduce) tension; **in größter ~ bleiben** to remain on tenterhooks; **~ erhöhen** *(el.)* to assist the voltage; **Tag voller ~ erwarten** to await a day in a flutter of expectation; **jem. in ~ halten** to keep s. o. on his toes *(fam.)*; **Publikum in ~ halten** to hold the audience; **ernste ~en hervorrufen** to create a serious strain; **Buch mit wachsender ~ lesen** to read a book with growing excitement; **~ lockern** to slack[en] off a tension; **Brief voller ~ öffnen** to open a letter full of suspense; **in großer ~ sein** to be all agog; **~en vermindern** to ease strains.
Spannungs|abfall *(el.)* fall of potential, drop in voltage, line drop; **~abnahme** *(pol.)* relaxation of tension; **~anzeichen** *(pol.)* notes of tension; **~feld erzeugen** *(pol.)* to charge the air with tension; **~gebiet** *(pol.)* area of tension (friction).
spannungsgeladen tense;
~ sein *(Geschichte)* to tingle with interest.
Spannungsverlust *(el.)* line drop.
Spannweite *(Brücke)* width, *(Flugzeug)* wingspread, *(Statistik)* range;
geistige ~ intellectual range.
Spar|anlage savings account; **~anlagenverlust** savings loss; **~anleihe** savings bonds *(US)*; **erhebliche ~anstrengungen machen** to save at a higher rate; **~anreiz** incentive for saving; **~aufkommen** savings volume; **~bank** savings bank; **~begünstigung** promotion of savings; **~betrag** saved amount.
sparbewußt savings-conscious.
Spar|bildung savings; **~bon** saving bond, savings certificate *(Br.)*, national savings stamp *(Br.)*; **~brenner** pilot light.
Sparbrief savings certificate (bond, *US*);
staatlicher ~ national savings certificate *(Br.)*;
~absatz sales of savings certificates; **~konto** savings certificate account.
Spar|buch savings bank [deposit] book, passbook *(Br.)*; **~bucheintragung** entry in the passbook, passbook entry; **~büchse** thrift box, money box; **~buchzinsen** interest on deposit account *(Br.)*; **~eckzins** standard savings interest rate; **~einlage** savings account, deposit in a savings bank (account).
Spareinlagen savings [deposits], thrift deposits *(US)*;
sofort fällige ~ demand savings deposits; **längerfristige ~** longer-term savings deposits; **mündelsichere ~** trustee savings; **~ mit gesetzlicher Kündigungsfrist** savings deposits at statutory notice;
~abgänge savings withdrawals; **~bestand bei Bausparkassen** savings put into building and loan associations; **~bestand bei Kreditinstituten** savings placed in loan institutes; **~entwicklung** development of savings; **~konto** savings account; **~verzinsung** return on savings; **~zinssatz** interest rate for savings deposits; **~zunahme, ~zuwachs** accumulation of savings, increase in savings accounts, growth in savings deposits.
Spareinleger savings-bank depositor.
Sparen saving, moneysaving, *(Sparsamkeit)* thrift, economy, economizing;
freiwilliges ~ planned savings; **staatlich gefördertes ~** government-approved save-as-you-earn scheme *(Br.)*; **indexgekoppeltes (inflationssicheres) ~** index-linked saving; **kollektives ~** social savings; **langfristiges ~** long-term savings;

prämienbegünstigtes ~ premium (contractual, *Br.*) saving; **privates** ~ individual savings; **steuerbegünstigtes** ~ tax-favo(u)red saving, deferred savings plan, national savings scheme *(Br.)*; **steuerfreies** ~ save as you earn *(Br.)*; **unsystematisches** ~ unplanned saving;
~ **über vermögensbildende Leistungen** [etwa] contractual saving;
~ **fördern** to encourage saving.

sparen to save, to spare, to set by, to lay by (up), *(Einsparungen machen)* to practise economy, to economize, to retrench, to cut down expenses, *(knausern)* to be stingy, to skimp, to stint, to scrimp;
durch automatische Abbuchung vom Lohnkonto ~ to save as you earn *(Br.)*; **für sein Alter** ~ to save up for one's old age; **kleine Beträge** ~ to save little by little; **am falschen Ende** ~ to be penny-wise and pound-foolish; **Geld** ~ to save money; **Geld im Strumpf** ~ to sock *(sl.)*; **Hälfte seines Monatsgehalts** ~ to save half of one's salary each month; **beim Hausbau überhaupt nicht** ~ to build a house without regard to cost; **am Haushaltsgeld** ~ to scrimp one's household; **keine Kosten** ~ to spare no expenses; **seine Kräfte** ~ to reserve one's forces; **im Laufe der Jahre ein Vermögen** ~ to save a packet over the years; **keine Mühe** ~ to go over backwards, to leave no stone unturned; **für Notfälle** ~ to put away (provide) for a rainy day; **Omnibusfahrkarte** ~ to save spending money for the bus fare; **Produktionskosten** ~ to cut down on production costs; **Provision** ~ to save middleman's profit; **für später** ~ to save for the future; **steuerbegünstigt** ~ to take savings in deferred form; **Steuern** ~ to save tax (on income taxes); **in größerem Umfang** ~ to save at higher rates; **für den Urlaub** ~ to save for one's holiday; **auf dem Versicherungssektor** ~ to save via an insurance scheme; **Zeit** ~ to save time, to be economical of time; **für schlechte Zeiten** ~ to put away for a rainy day;
nicht ~ **können** not to know how to save money; **zu** ~ **versuchen** to study economy.

Sparentwicklung development of savings.

Sparer [money] saver, depositor, economizer, penny-saver;
institutioneller ~ institutional saver;
~**genossenschaft** thrift society *(US)*, deposit society *(Br.)*;
~**gewinn** saver's surplus.

Spar|fähigkeit saving capacity; ~**feldzug** economy campaign (drive); ~**flamme** pinpoint flame; **auf** ~**flamme kochen** *(fig.)* to run flat, to go easy with one's funds; ~**förderung** savings promotion; **betriebliche** ~**förderung** company saving plan (system); ~**förderungsmaßnahmen ergreifen** to encourage saving; ~**freudigkeit** propensity to save; **an der Grenze liegende** ~**freudigkeit** marginal propensity to save; ~**ganggetriebe** *(Auto)* overdrive; ~**gemisch** lean mixture.

Spargelder savings (thrift) deposits;
langfristige angelegte ~ term deposits;
~ **mit gesetzlicher Kündigungsfrist** savings deposits at statutory notice;
~**strom** flow of savings.

Spar|gewohnheiten saving habits; ~**groschen** savings, nest egg; ~**guthaben** savings account (balance), savings account deposit, savings deposits, deposit with a trustee savings bank *(Br.)*, stock of savings, thrift deposit *(US)*; ~**gutmarken** national savings stamps *(Br.)*.

Sparkapital [stock of] savings, savings capital;
noch nicht angelegtes ~ fluid savings; **neues** ~ fresh savings; ~**bildung** accumulation of savings; **private** ~**bildung** private savings capital formation.

Sparkasse savings (provident) bank;
nicht aufsichtspflichtige ~ voluntary savings bank *(US)*; **gemeinnützige** ~ trustee bank (savings bank, *US*); **genossenschaftliche** ~ cooperative (mutual, *US*) savings bank; **städtische** ~ municipal savings bank;
~ **nach Art einer Aktiengesellschaft** stock savings bank *(US)*; ~ **auf Gegenseitigkeit** mutual savings bank *(US)*; ~ **für Schulkinder** school savings bank;
Geld zur ~ **tragen** to put money into a savings bank.

Sparkassen|abteilung savings (thrift, special interest, *US*) department; ~**angestellter** savings-bank official; ~**bereich** savings deposit industry; ~**betriebswirtschaft** savings banking; ~**buch** savings bank [deposit] book, National Savings Bank Ordinary Account Book *(Br.)*, passbook *(Br.)*; ~**buchbesitzer** savings-account owner; ~**buchkonto** ordinary deposit account with a National Savings Bank *(Br.)*; ~**einlagen** savings deposits; ~**einleger** savings depositor; ~**einrichtungen** savings facilities, facilities for saving.

sparkassenfähige Wertpapiere savings-bank securities.

Sparkassen|fonds savings fund; ~**funktionen** functions of savings institutions; ~**gelder** savings-bank money; ~**geschäft** savings business; ~**gesetz** Trustee Savings Bank Act *(Br.)*; ~**gesetzgebung** savings bank legislation; ~**guthaben** savings bank deposit; ~**gutschein** national savings certificate *(Br.)*; ~**institut** savings institution; ~**konto** savings bank ordinary account; ~**kredit** savings-bank credit; ~**leiter** savings-bank manager; ~**verband** National Association of Saving Banks *(US)*; ~- **und Darlehnskassenverein** savings and loan association; ~**wesen** savings banking (bank system).

Spar|kommissar cost cutter; ~**kommission** savings commission, cost cutters, axe *(Br.)*; **rückläufige** ~**konjunktur** decline of the savings boom; ~**konten annehmen** to accept savings accounts.

Sparkonto savings (deposit, *Br.*) account, thrift account *(US)*, *(bei Sparkasse)* savings-bank ordinary account *(Br.)*;
mit einer Lebensversicherung gekoppeltes ~ life-insured savings account *(US)*;
~ **mit gesetzlicher Kündigungsfrist** savings deposit at statutory notice;
Geld auf ein ~ **einzahlen** to place money on deposit; **Betrag auf ein** ~ **übertragen** to move an account into a savings account;
~**inhaber** savings bank depositor.

Sparleistungen passbook savings;
seine ~ **laufend dem Einzelhandelspreisindex anpassen (inflationsmäßig absichern)** to adjust one's contributions in line with the general index of retail prices; **monatliche** ~ **der Preisinflation anpassen** to adjust saving contributions in line with any change in prices.

spärlich scarce, scant, scanty;
nur über ~**e Kenntnisse der englischen Sprache verfügen** to have only a smattering of English; ~ **bevölkerter Landstrich** sparcely populated region; **nur über** ~**e Mittel verfügen** to be scarce of money; ~**e Nachfrage** slack demand, ~**e Rationen** short allowances; ~**er Rest** scanty remainder; ~ **beleuchtete Straße** poorly lit street; ~ **besuchte Veranstaltung** meagre attendance at a meeting.

Spar|marke money-saving (thrift) stamp, *(Sparkasse)* savings stamp *(Br.)*; ~**maßnahmen** measures of economy, saving measures, economy (economizing) measures, austerity measures, economies; ~**menge** volume of saving; ~**methode** saving method; ~**mittel** savings deposits; ~**modell** economy model; ~**möglichkeiten** means of (opportunity for) saving, savings facilities, way of saving; **erhebliche** ~**möglichkeiten gewähren** to provide a substantial margin for saving; **durchschnittliche** ~**neigung** average propensity to save; ~**organisation** savings institution; ~**paket** economy pack; ~**paradoxon** paradox of thrift; ~**pfennig** nest egg, money put by for a rainy day; ~**pfennig zurückhalten** to put by for a rainy day; ~**plan** thrift plan; **vertraglicher** ~**plan** contractual savings *(Br.)*; ~**politik** policy of economy; ~**potential** savings capacity; ~**prämie** savings premium, premium savings bond, *(Lebensversicherung)* initial reserve.

Sparprämien|anleihe lottery loan; ~**briefe** lottery saving bonds *(Br.)*; ~**gesetz** Savings Act; ~**los** premium bond; ~**obligationen** premium saving bonds *(Br.)*; ~**versicherung** salary deduction (savings) insurance; ~**vertrag** contractual savings contract.

Spar|programm cost-cutting drive, thrift (retrenchment) program(me), *(Staat)* austerity program(me); **privater** ~**prozentsatz** rate of private saving; **volkswirtschaftliche** ~**quote**, ~**rate** rate of saving, savings ratio (rate); ~**quote der privaten Haushaltungen** personal savings ratio; **monatliche** ~**rate** monthly saving contribution.

Sparren rafter;
~ **zuviel im Kopf haben** to have a screw loose.

Sparrücklagen, größere savings amounting to a large sum.

sparsam saving, sparing, thrifty, provident, near, economizing, economical, managing;
nicht ~ uneconomical, not thrifty;
~ **in Kleinigkeiten** penny-wise;
~ **anwenden** to economize; ~ **leben** to economize, to live near; ~ **umgehen** to be economical, to spare; **mit seinem Geld sehr** ~ **umgehen** to be very near with one's money, to think of pennies; **mit dem Haushaltsgeld äußerst** ~ **umgehen** to scrimp one's household; **mit Lob** ~ **umgehen** to be sparing with praise; ~ **wirtschaften** to be careful of one's small savings;
~**es Angebot** *(Börse)* few offerings; ~**er Kunde** economy-minded customer; ~**e Nachfrage** slack demand; ~**er Verwalter** saving manager; ~**e Verwaltung** economical administration; ~**es Wirtschaften** belt-tightening.

Sparsamkeit economy, economization, providence, thrift, thriftiness, sparing, retrenchment;

mangelnde ~ want of economy; **strengste** ~ rigid economy; **übertriebene** ~ cheese-paring economies, scrimpiness;
~ **am falschen Platz** irrational economy;
sich äußerster ~ **befleißigen** to practise rigid economy; **jem.** ~ **vorschreiben** to enjoin on s. o. the necessity for economy.
Sparsamkeits|gründe, etw. aus ~**gründen aufgeben** to do away with s. th. as a measure of economy; **Opfer eines** ~**programms werden** to fall victim to a cost-reduction program(me); **aus** ~**rücksichten** for reasons of economy; ~**wirtschaft** economy of scarcity, austerity.
Sparschwein piggy bank;
sein ~ **schlachten** to break one's piggy bank.
Spar|system savings scheme; ~**tabelle** savings schedule.
spartanisches Leben führen to live a Spartan life.
Spartätigkeit saving (savings) activity;
intensive ~ intensive period of saving; **laufende** ~ current savings; **private** ~ personal savings; **übermäßige** ~ oversaving; **zunehmende** ~ increase in savings;
sich hemmend auf die ~ **auswirken** to be disincentive to savings;
~ **ermutigen (fördern)** to promote (encourage) saving.
Sparte branch, field, sphere, line;
auf verschiedenen ~**n** in a wide selection of fields;
sich in allen ~**n seines Berufs auskennen** to be at home in all sections of one's profession; **nicht in jds.** ~ **fallen** to be outside of s. one's field; **sich in einer** ~ **spezialisieren** to specialize in a line.
Spar|vereinigung savings association, savers' (shop) club, thrift institution, thrift society *(US)*, deposit society *(Br.)*; ~**vergaser** economy carburettor; ~**versicherung** capital redemption insurance; ~**versicherungspolice** capital redemption policy; ~**vertrag** savings plan; ~**vertrag mit monatlichen Raten** *(Kapitalanlagegesellschaft)* monthly investment plan; **fünfjährigen** ~**vertrag mit 60 Monatsraten abschließen** to make 60 regular monthly contributions over five years; ~**volumen** volume of savings; ~**vorgang** saving [process], long-term saving; **beim** ~**vorgang beratend tätig sein** to specialize in savings service; ~**vorteil** advantage of saving; ~**wachstumsrate** growth rate in savings; ~**welle** economy wave; ~**wesen** savings system; **steuerbegünstigtes** ~**wesen** tax-favo(u)red savings scheme; ~**zertifikat** treasury savings certificate *(US)*; ~**ziel** object of saving; **übliche** ~**zinsen** interest on ordinary deposits; ~**zinssätze** savings-bank interest rates; ~**zugang** accumulation of savings, growth of saving deposits; ~**zwang** compulsory saving.
Spaß fun, jest, trick;
~ **beiseite** joking apart; **nur zum** ~ just for kicks (fun); **weil es** ~ **macht** for the pleasure of it;
sich einen ~ **mit jem. erlauben** to pull s. one's leg, to poke fun at s. o.; **nur** ~ **machen** to be only kidding; **ziemlich teurer** ~ **sein** to cost a pretty penny; **jem. dem** ~ **verderben** to be a bad sport (spoilsport, wet blanket); **keinen** ~ **verstehen** to have no sense of humo(u)r.
spaßen, damit ist nicht zu that's no joking matter.
Spaß|macher, ~**vogel** jester, clown, buffoon, humo(u)rist.
spät late, tardy *(US)*;
ein bißchen ~ late in the day; **fast zu** ~ at the eleventh hour;
j. ~ **benachrichtigen** to give s. o. short notice.
Spät|abend later part of the evening; ~**ausgabe** evening edition, late-night final; ~**aussiedler** post-war resettled person; ~**briefkasten** late-mail bag *(US)*; ~**einkäufer** late shopper; ~**einlieferungsgebühr** late fee *(Br.)*.
Spatenstich tun, ersten to break ground, to lay the corner stone.
Spätentwickler slow developer.
später subsequent, posterior, ulterior;
j. auf ~ **vertrösten** to put s. o. off;
~**e Generationen** future generations; ~**er Girant** subsequent endorser; ~**e Lieferung** forward delivery; **zu** ~ **Stunde** at a late hour of the day.
Spatienkeil *(drucktechn.)* spaceband.
Spätindikator lagging indicator.
spationieren *(drucktechn.)* to space (white, lead) out.
Spationierung spacing out, letter spacing.
Spatium *(drucktechn.)* break, space.
Spät|kapitalismus late capitalism; ~**phase der Hochkonjunktur** late phase of a boom; ~**schalter** *(Bank)* night safe deposit, *(Zoll)* outside service; ~**schicht** night (swing, *US*) shift; ~**schichtarbeiter** swing shifter *(US)*; ~**schließungstag** late closing day; ~**sommer** Indian (late) summer.
Spatz, frech wie ein as cheeky as a parrot;
wie ein ~ **essen** to nibble at one's food; **mit Kanonen auf** ~**en schießen** to break a butterfly on the wheel;
der ~ **in der Hand ist besser als die Taube auf dem Dach** a bird in the hand is better than a bird in the bush; **die** ~**en pfeifen es von den Dächern** it is all over the town.
Spatzengehirn nitwit.
Spät|zünder late starter, *(fig.)* slow developer; ~**zünder sein** to be slow on the uptake; ~**zündung** retarded (delayed) ignition, *(fig.)* double take; ~**zustellung** late delivery.
spazierenfahren to drive out.
spazierengehen, mit jem. to take s. o. for a walk.
Spazierfahrt drive, joy ride.
Spaziergang walk, airing, *(leichte Sache)* easy task;
gemütlicher ~ lounge; **kurzer** ~ turn; **reinster** ~ walkover;
~ **machen** to go (out) for a walk, to stretch one's legs; **reinster** ~ **sein** to be as easy as shelling peas.
Spazier|gänge favo(u)rite walks in the neighbo(u)rhood; ~**gänger** walker, stroller, pedestrian, ~**weg** walk.
Speck, durchwachsener streaky bacon;
~ **ansetzen** to put on weight; **wie die Made im** ~ **leben** to live like a fighting cock;
mit ~ **fängt man Mäuse** good bait catches fine fish;
~**gummi** soft rubber.
Spediteur carrier [and forwarding agent], motor (transportation, *US*) carrier, hauler, haulier *(Br.)*, carrying (forwarding) agent, [freight] forwarder, forwarding merchant (house) *(US)*, transport agent, shipper *(US)*, shipping agent (clerk) *(US)*, *(Möbel)* [furniture] remover;
auf Gefahr des ~**s** at carrier's risk; **mit Hilfe (unter Inanspruchnahme) eines** ~**s** through the medium of a goods agent;
bahnamtlicher ~ railway express agency *(Br.)*, express agent *(US)*, common carrier *(US)*, *(Rollfuhrunternehmen)* contract carrier, haulage contractor; **gewerbsmäßiger** ~ professional carrier; **ländlicher** ~ country shipper *(US)*; **örtlicher** ~ local shipper *(US)*; **übernehmender** ~ receiving (on-) carrier; **zustellender** ~ delivery carrier;
Ware dem ~ **übergeben** to deliver the goods into custody of the carrier;
der ~ **trägt das volle Risiko** carrier's risk;
~**bescheinigung** carrier's receipt; ~**geschäft** carrier's business; ~**haftpflichtversicherung** common carrier's legal liability insurance; ~**haftung** carrier's liability, liability of a common carrier; ~**konnossement** forwarder's bill of lading; ~**offerte** carrier's quotation; ~**pfandrecht** carrier's lien; ~**übernahmeschein** shipping and forwarding receipt, forwarder's receipt, forwarding agent's certificate of receipt (FRC).
Spedition forwarding, carrying, dispatch, transport, conveyance, consignment, transmission of freight *(US)*, haulage *(US)*, shipment *(US)*, *(Speditionsgeschäft)* forwarding (freight) business, [common] carrier, carrying company, shipping trade *(US)*;
internationale ~ international forwarding.
Speditions|abteilung forwarding department, dispatching office; ~**agent** forwarding agent, shipper's representative; ~**angestellter** freight clerk; ~**auftrag** dispatch (shipping, *US*) order, forwarding note; ~**beruf** traffic work; ~**bestimmungen** forwarding instructions; ~**betrieb** forwarding house (firm), haulage firm, trucking company, carriers, shipping agency *(US)*; ~**bücher** books of conveyance; ~**buchführung** transportation accounting; ~**büro** forwarding (shipping, *US*) office; ~**firma** forwarding house, transportation agency (company) *(US)*, haulage firm, trucking company, carriers, shipping agency *(US)*, shipper *(US)*; ~**gebühren** forwarding charges (expenses, commission), carrier's charges, shipping charges *(US)*, haulage *(US)*, drayage; **besondere** ~**gebühr bei abgeändertem Frachtziel** stop-off rate; ~**geschäft** carrying (carrier's, freight) business, motor carrier industry, carrying and forwarding trade, shipping trade (agency) *(US)*, *(Firma)* forwarding firm (agency, business), carrying establishment, transport company, common carrier *(US)*, shipper *(US)*, express business *(US)*; ~**gesellschaft** forwarding (shipping, transport, *Br.*, transportation, *US*) agency, shipper *(US)*, transfer (forwarding, transportation, *US*) company, *(Kraftwagentransport)* common trucking company, carriers; ~**gewerbe** road haulage industry, carrying (forwarding, shipping, *US*) trade; ~**güter** goods to be forwarded; ~**handel** carrying (shipping, *US*) trade; ~**kasse** cash of conveyance; ~**konto** account of conveyance, shipping-expenses account *(US)*; ~**konzession** operator's license *(US)*; ~**kosten** forwarding expenses, carrying charges, trucking costs, shipping charges *(US)*; **kombinierte** ~**leistung** single-carrier service; ~**lizenz** contract carrier permit; ~**niederlassung** agency station; ~**personal** wheelers; ~**provision** forwarding commission;

~rechnung bill of conveyance, forwarder's note of charges; ~satz, ~tarif tariff rate, agency tariff; ~unternehmen forwarding (shipping, *US*) agency, common trucking company, haulage firm, carrier's business, carriers; ~verkehr carrying (forwarding, shipping, *US*) trade; ~versicherung forwarder's risk insurance; ~vertrag contract of carriage, shipping contract *(US)*; ~vertreter forwarding agent, shipper's representative *(US)*; ~wagen carrying van; ~wesen motor carrier (road haulage) industry.

Speichellecker flunkey, bootlick, toadeater, crawler, truckler, lackey;
j. als ~ bezeichnen to qualify s. o. as a toady.

Speichelleckerei flunkeyism, toadeating, cringe.

Speicher store, storehouse, warehouse, magazine, depot, entrepot, dump, *(Computer)* memory, memo unit, storage, *(Dachboden)* garret, attic, loft *(US)*, *(Möbel)* furniture depository (repository), storage, warehouse, *(Trinkwasser)* reservoir, storage basin;
öffentlicher ~ public warehouse (store);
auf den ~ bringen to store in a warehouse, to warehouse *(US)*, to deposit in a warehouse *(US)*; **Möbel auf den ~ bringen** to store furniture;
~adresse *(Computer)* memory address; **~arbeiter** warehouseman, warehouse labo(u)rer; **~batterie** storage battery; **~eingabe** read-in storage; **~gebäude** storage building, loft building *(US)*; **~gebühren** warehouse rates, warehousing charges (expenses), *(Eisenbahn)* elevating charge; **~geld** storage; **~größe, ~kapazität** *(Datenverarbeitung)* memory capacity; **~miete** warehouse rent, loft rental *(US)*; **~möglichkeiten** storage accommodation.

speichern to lay (treasure) up, to store, to warehouse, *(Computer)* to store, *(im Silo)* to ensile, to silo;
häufig gebrauchte Telefonnummern auf einem Band ~ to store frequently called telephone numbers on tape; **Trinkwasser ~** to store drinking water in a reservoir; **Wärme für die ganze Nacht ~** *(Ofen)* to accumulate heat for the whole night.

Speicherprogramm *(Datenverarbeitung)* stored program(me).

speicherprogrammierte Rechenanlage stored-program(me) computer.

Speicher|raum warehouse space (room), storage area, loft space *(US)*; **~sachen** stored goods, goods in warehouse; **~system** storage system.

Speicherung *(el.)* storage, storing.

Speicher|verwalter warehouse keeper; **~werk** *(Computer)* storage unit; **~zugriff** memory access; **~zugriff veranlassen** to access.

speien, Feuer und Lava to belch fire and lava.

Speise food, nourishment, fare, dish, eating, *(Imbiß)* snack;
warme und kalte ~n hot and cold dishes;
~n und Getränke food and drink;
~n austeilen to dish out;
~automat snack-vending machine; **~haus** eating (victual(l)ing) house; **billiges ~haus** hash house *(US sl.)*; **~karte** menu [card], bill of fare; **nicht mehr auf der ~karte stehen** to be off the menu; **~lokal** eating (victual(l)ing) house.

speisen to eat, to have luncheon (dinner);
außerhalb ~ to take one's meals out of doors, to be dining out; **fantastisch ~** to eat high on the hog; **auf goldenem Geschirr ~** to eat off gold plate; **Kraftwerk mit Strom ~** to feed (supply) a power station with current.

Speisen|aufzug plate carrier, dumb-waiter *(US)*; **~folge** menu; **~lieferung ins Haus** catering and takeout business.

Speise|raum dining room, *(Schiff)* dining saloon; **~saal** dining hall (room); **~wagen** luncheon (refreshment, buffet, *US*, restaurant, *US*, hotel, *US*, dining, café, *US*) car, diner *(US)*; **~wagenangestellter** dining-car worker; **~zimmer** dining room.

Spektakel row, din, noise, racket, hullabaloo, kick-up *(US sl.)*;
schrecklichen ~ machen to kick up a terrible row.

Spektrum spectrum;
gesamtes ~ von links bis rechts umfassen to span the entire left-right spectrum.

Spekulant speculative dealer, gambler, adventurer, projector, boomer *(US)*, racketeer *(US)*, prospector *(sl.)*, wildcatter, *(Baisse)* bear *(Br.)*, *(Grundstück)* jobber, *(Hausse)* bull *(Br.)*;
bankrotter ~ lame duck *(US)*; **berufsmäßiger ~** market operator, professional speculator; **kleiner ~** dabbler, piker *(US sl.)*; **ruinierter ~** lame duck *(US)*; **unerfahrener ~** lamb; **waghalsiger ~** plunger; **wilder ~** wildcatter *(US)*; **windiger ~** shady speculator;
~ auf dem grauen Markt gray- (grey-) market operator; **~ in Staatspapieren** fund monger.

Spekulantengruppe zur Herbeiführung einer Baisse (Hausse) bear (bull) pool.

Spekulation speculation, jobbing, gamble, gambling, venture, adventure, enterprise, flyer *(coll.)*, flutter *(sl.)*, wildcatting *(US)*;
geglückte ~ successful speculation; **gemeinsame ~** co-adventure; **gewagte ~** risky piece of business, hazardous speculation, flier *(US sl.)*; **gewinnbringende ~** profitable speculation; **mißglückte ~** bad (wrong, unlucky) speculation; **ungesunde ~** wildcat finance; **verfehlte ~** unlucky speculation, unsuccessful gamble; **zügellose ~** unbridled speculation, wildcatting *(US)*; **zweifelhafte ~** gold brick *(US)*;
~ auf Baisse speculation for a fall, bear transaction *(Br.)*, bearish operation *(Br.)*; **~ in Eisenbahnaktien** speculation in railroad stocks *(US)*; **~ mit Grundstücken** speculation in real estate; **~ auf Hausse** speculation (operation) for a bull *(Br.)*, bull[ish] operation (transaction) *(Br.)*; **~ in Staatspapieren** fund mongering; **~ in Terminpapieren** speculation in futures; **sich auf eine ~ einlassen** to embark on a project; **sich auf eine gewagte ~ einlassen** to engage in a risky speculation; **sich als erfolgreiche ~ erweisen** to turn out to be a good speculation; **auf ~ kaufen** to buy for speculative account (on speculation); **durch ~en verlieren** to lose by speculation; **sich in ~en verlieren** to be absorbed in speculations.

Spekulations|aktie speculative share (stock, *US*); **~bauplatz** accommodation land; **~betrieb** mushroom enterprise; **~bewegungen** flutters; **~buch** book of adventure; **~druck** speculative pressure; **~firma** firm of speculators, speculative enterprise; **~gebiet** venture capital field; **~gelder** speculative money.

Spekulationsgeschäft adventure, speculative business (transaction, enterprise, undertaking, trading), hazardous speculation, privilege, speculating transaction (operation);
~e speculations, stockjobbery *(Br.)*;
noch nicht abgeschlossenes ~ open trade; **vorteilhaftes ~** profitable speculation;
~e finanzieren to finance speculation; **kurzfristige ~e machen** to speculate for differences.

Spekulationsgewinn speculative profit (gain);
hoher ~ scoop *(US)*, killing *(coll.)*;
überhöhte ~e im Immobilienhandel profiteering in land;
hohe ~e in festverzinslichen Papieren erzielen to make a killing in bonds *(coll.)*.

Spekulations|interesse speculative interest; **~kapital** venture (risk-bearing) capital; **~kauf** purchase on speculation, speculative purchase; **~kauf eines Außenseiters** flier *(US)*; **~käufe** purchases on speculations, speculation (speculative) purchases (buying); **~kredit** speculative credit; **~kurs** speculative price; **~lust** speculativeness, speculative spirit; **~manöver** manoeuvre, gambling; **~möglichkeiten** highways of speculation; **~moment, ~motiv** speculative motive; **~objekt** venture, flutter *(sl.)*; **~papiere** speculative securities (descriptions), floating stock; **unsichere ~papiere** fancy stocks *(US)*; **~preis** speculative price; **~ring** corner; **~risiko** speculative risk; **~steuer** capital gains tax; **~sucht** proneness to speculation; **~tätigkeit** speculation, playing the market *(coll.)*; **~unternehmen** adventure, risky undertaking, fly-by-night corporation *(US)*; **~verkäufe** speculative selling; **~verlust** gambling loss; **~versicherung** speculative underwriting.

spekulationsweise on speculation.

Spekulations|wert speculative value; **~werte** speculative securities (stocks); **~zweck** speculative purpose; **zu ~zwecken aufkaufen** to corner the market, to buy s. th. on (as a) speculation; **zu ~zwecken sich häufen lassen** to pyramid *(US)*.

spekulativ speculative, speculatory;
~er Charakter speculative character; **~e Kapitalanlagen** speculative investments; **~e Papiere** speculative securities (stocks), fancy stocks *(US)*; **~es Unternehmen** venture, adventure, risky undertaking, fly-by-night corporation *(US)*.

Spekulativ|händler scalper *(US)*; **~zwischenhändler** wholesale middleman.

Spekulieren speculating, speculation.

spekulieren to speculate, to operate;
in Aktien ~ to play the stock market, to job; **ein bißchen mit Aktien ~** to make a little deal with stocks as a feeler; **auf dem Aktienmarkt ~** to play the stock market; **in Atomaktien ~** to speculate in atomic shares; **auf Baisse ~** to operate (speculate) for (gamble on) a fall, to bear *(Br.)*, to sell short *(US)*; **ein bißchen ~** to make a little deal in stocks as a feeler; **an der Börse ~** to gamble (trade) on the stock exchange, to play the stock market; **ein bißchen an der Börse ~** to dabble on the stock exchange; **ohne kapitalmäßige Deckung ~** to overtrade; **auf eine**

Erbschaft ~ to reckon on an inheritance, to wait for a dead man's shoes; **falsch** ~ to speculate on the wrong side; **auf Hausse** ~ to buy (speculate, operate) for a rise, to bull *(Br.)*; **mit Kursunterschieden** ~ to speculate for differences; **waghalsig** ~ to plunge; **wild** ~ to gamble.

Spelunke speak-easy *(US sl.)*, dump *(sl.)*, shabby house, jerry shop *(Br.)*, saloon *(US)*, juke joint *(US sl.)*, scatter *(sl.)*, slop *(sl.)*, crib house *(US)*, snake ranch *(sl.)*, crip *(US)*, dive *(US sl.)*, barrel house *(US sl.)*;
schäbige ~ rub joint *(sl.)*.

Spende charitable disposition (contribution), subscription (contribution) to charity, dole, *(Almosen)* alms, almsgiving, *(Beitrag)* contribution, *(Gabe)* gift, present, donation, *(Stiftung)* endowment, benefaction;
im Wege öffentlicher ~n by public subscription;
eingegangene ~n contributions which came in; **freiwillige** ~ unasked (voluntary) contribution, voluntary efforts; **kleine** ~ widow's mite; **politische** ~ political contribution (subscription); **steuerabzugsfähige** ~ tax-deductible contribution (subscription); **wohltätige** ~ charitable subscription, contribution (subscription) to charity, alms;
~ **für die Armen** contribution for the poor; **~n aus der Großindustrie** big-business contributors; ~ **für das Rote Kreuz** donation to the Red Cross; ~ **für eine politische Partei** subscriptions to a political party; ~ **für einen Unterstützungsfonds** contribution to a relief fund; ~ **für politische Zwecke** political donation; ~ **für wohltätige Zwecke** distribution of money in charity, charitable subscription; **verbriefte ~n für wohltätige Zwecke** covenanted donations of charity;
durch eine kleine ~ **für eine gute Sache beitragen** to give one's mite for a good cause; **um ~n bitten** to solicit donations; **~n in jeder Höhe entgegennehmen** to accept contributions of any size; **durch ~n finanzieren** to finance by private subscription; **dem Roten Kreuz eine** ~ **zukommen lassen** to contribute to the Red Cross; **von ~n leben** to live on alms; **~n sammeln** to go round with the hat; ~ **zusammentrommeln** to whip round for subscriptions.

spenden to contribute, to subscribe, to donate, to bestow alms, to deal out;
Beifall ~ to applaud; **Geld zur Unterstützung der Armen** ~ to spend money on alms; **für das Rote Kreuz** ~ to contribute to the Red Cross; **reichlich** ~ to give freely, to lavish; **überreichlich** ~ to give with a profuse hand; **Verpflegung und Bekleidung für die Flüchtlinge** ~ to contribute food and clothing for the refugees; **viel Wärme** ~ *(Ofen)* to give off a great deal of heat; **für wohltätige Zwecke** ~ to subscribe to charity, to dispense charity; **sein Vermögen für wohltätige Zwecke** ~ to leave one's money to charity.

Spenden|abzug deductions allowed for gifts to charity; **~aktion** gift-parcel program(me); **Rede mit einem ~appell anschließen** to tack an appeal for money onto a speech; **~appell an die Öffentlichkeit richten** to make a public appeal for funds; **~aufruf** appeal on behalf of charity; **~beitrag** contribution of alms; **kleiner ~beitrag** alms-penny, mite; **politischer ~beitrag** contribution for political purposes; **anvisierten ~betrag hereinbekommen** to meet an appeal target; **~empfänger** donatory *(Br.)*; **~fonds** charity fund; **~gelder persönlich verwenden** to divert campaign funds to one's personal use; **steuerfreier ~höchstbetrag** maximum tax exemption for gifts to charity; **~konto** subscription account; **~strom** flood of donations; **~strom aus der Großindustrie** big-business contributors; **~strom für wohltätige Zwecke** charitable subscription; **~zahlungen beenden** to discontinue a subscription to charity.

Spender subscriber to charity, contributor, giver, donor, *(Wohltäter)* benefactor, almsgiver;
~ **aus der Großindustrie** big-business contributors.

spendieren to lavish, to shout *(sl.)*;
jem. etw. ~ to treat (stand) s. o. s. th.; **jem. eine Flasche Wein** ~ to treat s. o. to a bottle of wine; **jem. ein Glas Bier** ~ to stand s. o. a glass of beer; **Kasten Bier** ~ to chip in with a case of beer *(coll.)*; **Lage (Runde)** ~ to serve a round of drinks, to stand treat all round.

Spendierhosen anhaben to be in a spending mood.

Sperenzchen machen to make a fuss about, to resort to tricks.

sperrangelweit|offen stehen to stand wide open; **Mund** ~ **aufreißen** *(fig.)* to talk big, to brag.

Sperr|auftrag *(Aktie)* stop order, *(Scheck)* stop [payment]; **~ballon** *(mil.)* barrage balloon; **~betrag** blocked amount; **~bezirk** restricted (closed) area; **~depot** blocked account (deposit); **~druck** *(drucktechn.)* space type.

Sperre bar, barrier, blocking, ban, *(Bahnsteig)* gate, platform, barrier, *(Elektrizität, Gas, Wasser)* cutoff, *(geistig)* blackout, *(Gesundheitsbehörde)* quarantine, *(Hafen)* closing, *(Handel)* embargo, blockade, *(Hindernis)* obstacle, impediment, *(mil.)* boom, blockade, *(Kartellrecht)* boycott, *(Schranke)* barrier, gate *(US)*, *(Polizei)* cordon, barrier, *(Scheck)* stop, *(Stilllegung)* stoppage, *(Verbot)* ban, inhibition, *(Zoll)* toll bar, tollgate, turnpike;
telefonisch angeordnete ~ stop by telephone;
~ **für Einwanderer** ban on immigrants; ~ **eines Kontos** blocking (freezing) of an account; ~ **eines Schecks** stopping a check *(US)* (cheque, *Br.*); ~ **des Vermögens** blocking of property; **vollständige** ~ **des Wirtschaftsverkehrs** outright economic embargo;
zweistündige ~ **des Flughafens anordnen** to order the closure of the airport for two hours; ~ **aufheben** to lift an embargo (a blockade); **j. mit einer** ~ **für einen Monat belegen** *(Sport)* to suspend s. o. for one month; ~ **durchbrechen** to break through a barrier; ~ **errichten** to set up a roadblock; ~ **fliegen** to fly on interception patrol; ~ **verhängen** to block, to impose an embargo; **seine Fahrkarte an der** ~ **vorzeigen** to show one's ticket at the barrier.

Sperren *(drucktechn.)* letter-spacing.

sperren to block, *(durch Absperrmannschaften)* to bar, to cordon off, *(Datenverarbeitung)* to space, *(Grenze)* to shut, *(Hafen)* to blockade, to lock, *(Warenverkehr)* to embargo, to blockade;
sich gegen etw. ~ to resist (oppose, balk) against s. th.; **Auszahlung** ~ to stop payments; **Einfuhr von Luxusartikeln** ~ to ban the import of luxuries; **Gebiet** ~ to forbid an area; **j. ins Gefängnis** ~ to lock s. o. up, to put s. o. in prison; **Gehälter** ~ to freeze wages; **Gold für ausländische Zahlungen** ~ to earmark gold for foreign account; **Grenze (Grenzübergang)** ~ to close (shut) the frontier; **Konto** ~ to block (freeze) an account; **für Lastwagenverkehr** ~ to close for heavy motor traffic; **weitere Lieferungen** ~ to withhold supply of goods from a dealer; **polizeilich** ~ to cordon off; **Scheck** ~ to stop payment of a check; **mit einem Seil** ~ to rope off; **dem Sohn den Wechsel** ~ to cut off a son's allowance; **einer Stadt die Lebensmittelzufuhr** ~ to cut off a town's food supply; **offene Stellen** ~ to freeze vacancies; **Straße** ~ to close a road, to bar a street, to block a street to traffic; **Straße mit Barrikaden** ~ to obstruct (barricade) a road; **Urlaub** ~ to stop leave; **Wasserzufuhr** ~ to cut off the water supply; **Wechsel** ~ to stop a bill; **Zahlung** ~ to stop payment; **zeitweilig** ~ to close temporarily; **Zufuhr** ~ to cut off supplies;
~ **lassen** to register a stop, to stop payment.

Sperr|feuer *(mil.)* [umbrella] barrage, rolling barrage, accompanying line; **~feuer schießen** to barrage; **~flug** patrol flight; **~fort** *(mil.)* outer fort; **~frist** period of embargo, blocking period, *(Versicherung)* waiting period, *(Wertpapiere)* period of nonnegotiability; **~gebiet** closed (prohibited, blocked, restricted, *US*, military) area, forbidden (operational, prohibited, danger, *mil.*) zone; **militärisches ~gebiet** closed military zone, exclusion zone; **zum ~gebiet erklären** to place out of bounds *(Br.)*, to declare off limits *(US)*; **~geld** blocked funds, *(Zoll)* tolerance; **~gürtel** *(Polizei)* cordon; **~gut** bulky (measured, cumbersome) goods, goods shipped in bulk, measurement cargo (goods), long, heavy or bulky articles; **~guthaben** blocked account (balance), blocked credit balance, *(durch Forderungspfändung)* garnishee account; **~holzkiste** plywood box.

sperrig bulky, voluminous;
~e Güter bulky (cumbersome) goods, long, heavy or bulky articles; **nicht ~e Güter** goods of small bulk; **~e Ladung** bulky (measurement) cargo, measurement goods.

Sperr|jahr one-year waiting period; **~kette** cordon, *(mil.)* boom; **~klausel** saving (restrictive) clause; **~klinke** pawl; **~konto** blocked account, *(des Drittschuldners)* garnishee account; **~kreis** *(el.)* block (rejector) circuit, eliminator, *(Rundfunkgerät)* wave trap; **~liste** *(Scheck)* stop card; **~mark** blocked mark; **~markguthaben** blocked-mark account; **~maßnahmen aufheben** to defrost; **~mauer** concrete dam; **~minorität** blocking (vetoing) minority; **~minorität in einem Unternehmen erwerben** to acquire a controlling interest in a concern; **~müll** bulky refuse; **~patent** blocking-off patent; **~riegel** safety bolt; **~satz** spaced composition; **~sitz** *(Theater)* orchestra stall *(Br.)*, orchestra seat *(US)*, parquet *(US)*; **vorderste ~sitzreihe** baldheaded row *(US sl.)*; **~stunde** closing hour, *(mil.)* curfew.

Sperrung stop, stoppage, stopping, blocking, *(drucktechn.)* letter spacing, *(Hafen)* blockade, embargo, *(Verbot)* prohibition, ban;

~ **eines Kontos** blocking (freezing) of an account; ~ **eines Schecks** stopping [payment of] a check *(US)* (cheque, *Br.*); ~ **einer Straße** closing a road;
~ **einer Straße aufheben** to reopen a road to traffic; ~ **eines Kontos verfügen** to block an account; **Auftrag zur ~ eines Kontos zurückziehen** to cancel a stop *(Br.)* (payment, *US*) order.

Sperr|ventil stop (check) valve; ~**vermerk** blocking note, *(Wertpapier)* nonnegotiability notice; ~**vermerk [im Grundbuch] eintragen** to vacate a registration; ~**vermerksbeschluß erlassen** to make an order vacating a registration; ~**vorrichtung** blocking mechanism; ~**zeit** closing hour (time); ~**zoll** prohibitive duty; ~**zone** restricted (prohibited, sensitive, military, danger, closed) area, exclusion zone.

Spesen charges, expenses [incurred], out-of-pocket expenses *(Br.)*, expenditure, *(Gebühren)* fees, *(Kosten)* cost[s];
ab an (abzüglich der) ~ charges to be deducted; **einschließlich aller** ~ including all charges; **franko** ~ free of charges; **gegen Erstattung der** ~ with out-of-pocket expense; **nach Abzug aller** ~ all deductions made; **nach Abzug Ihrer** ~ after deducting your charges; **unter Einschluß der** ~ including the expenses; **unter Inbegriff sämtlicher** ~ all charges included; **unter Nachnahme der** ~ charges forwarded *(Br.)*, expenses to be collected; **zuzüglich Ihrer** ~ by adding your charges;
abzugsfähige ~ charges to be deducted; **aufgelaufene** ~ accrued expenses; **diverse** ~ sundries, sundry expense; **einmalige** ~ nonrecurring expenses; **erwachsene** ~ cost involved (accrued); **feste** ~ fixed charges; **fremde** ~ *(Bank)* cost of our correspondent; **geschätzte** ~ estimated charges; **kleine** ~ petty charges (expenses), small charges; **laufende** ~ current (standing) expenses; **übliche** ~ *(Bank)* normal service charges; **verausgabte** ~ out-of-pocket expenses; **vereinbarte** ~ agreed costs; **verschiedene** ~ sundries, petties; **wiederkehrende** ~ fixed charges;
~ **für Noteneinlösung** demurrage *(Br.)*;
seine ~ abrechnen to account for one's expenses; **Mittagessen über ~ abrechnen** to justify a lunch as business expenses; ~ **absetzen** to deduct expenses; **jem. 40 $ und den Ersatz der ~ anbieten** to offer s. o. 40 $ and expenses; ~ **aufschlüsseln** to break down expenditure (expenses); ~ **begleichen** to refund the expenses; **fast alle ~ ersetzt (erstattet) bekommen** to get a good percentage on one's outlay; **gerechtfertigte ~ erstattet bekommen** to recover one's expenses properly incurred; **für ~ belasten** to expense; **Konto mit sämtlichen ~ belasten** to charge an account with all the expenses; **jds. ~ bestreiten** to defray s. one's expenses; ~ **mit argwöhnischen Augen betrachten** to eagle-eye expenses; **sich für den Betrag seiner ~ erholen** to recover expenses; **jem. die (seine) ~ ersetzen** to reimburse s. o. for his costs, to allow s. o. his expenses, to indemnify s. o. for expenses incurred; ~ **erstatten** to refund the expenses; ~ **niedrig halten** to hold (keep) down expenditure (expenses); **jds. ~ herabsetzen** to cut down s. one's allowances; **hohe ~ aushalten können** to stand the racket *(US sl.)*; ~ **nachnehmen** to charge expenses forward; **doppelte ~ in Rechnung stellen** to double-bill; ~ **genauestens überwachen** to keep a strict account of expenses; ~ **umlegen** to apportion the expenses; ~ **vergüten** to reimburse expenses incurred, to reimburse travelling expenses; ~ **verringern** to cut down expenses; ~ **zurückerstatten** to refund the expenditure;
~**abrechnung** statement of expenses, expense sheet (bill, record, report), note (account) of travelling expenses *(Br.)*; ~**abrechnungen lasch behandeln** to be lax in handling expenses; **nach ~abzug** ultra reprisal; ~**abzüge** expense-account deduction; ~**anschlag** expense budget, cost account; ~**anteil** share of the expenses, cost rate; ~**aufgliederung** expense classification, breakdown of expenses; ~**aufstellung** statement of expenses, specification of disbursements; ~**aufwand begrenzen** to put a stop to expenditures; ~**aufzeichnung** costs records; ~**ausgaben** expense-account spending; ~**belastung** *(Versicherung)* expense loading; ~**belastungsformular** sundries debit form.

Spesenbeleg expense voucher;
gefälschter ~ swindle sheet;
~**e einreichen** to submit expense reports; ~**e sammeln** to keep a record of one's expenses.

Spesen|beteiligung cost sharing; ~**einschränkungen** expense-account restrictions; ~**einsparung** cost saving; ~**erstattung** reimbursement of expenses incurred.

Spesenetat expense budget;
~ **niedrig halten** to hold down expenses; ~ **kürzen** to cut down expenditure (expenses), to whittle down expenses.

Spesen|faktor expense factor; ~**fonds** testimonial (expense) fund; ~**forderungen** accrued expenses.

spesenfrei free of charge (all charges, expenses), clear (exempt from) charges.

Spesen|konto expense (sundries, cost, imprest, *Br.*, drawing) account; **auf ~konto gehen** to go on expenditure (expense) account; **zu Lasten des ~kontos verreisen** to travel on expense account; ~**kontrolle** expense control; ~**nachnahme** charges to be collected, collection of charges, carriage (charges, *Br.*) forward; ~**nachweisbuch** travel and entertainment diary; ~**note** charges note; ~**posten** expense item; ~**posten genehmigen** to pass an item of expenditure; ~**rechnung** expense account (bill, sheet), note of expenses *(Br.)*, scandal sheet *(sl.)*; **doppelte ~rechnung** dual billing; ~**reisender**, ~**ritter** expense-account travel(l)er; ~**richtlinien** expense-account rules, rules on expense-account spending; ~**rückerstattung** expense-report reimbursement; ~**satz** expense ratio; **höchstzulässiger ~satz** expenditure (cost) rate; ~**tabelle** schedule of expenses; ~**tarif** schedule of fees; ~**umlegung** apportionment of costs; ~**vergütung** reimbursement of expenses incurred, reimbursement charges; ~**vorschuß** advance on costs (expenses), advanced expense, imprest fund *(Br.)*, expense prepayment; ~**wirtschaft im Auge haben** to keep tabs on the expenses; ~**zettel** cost record, expense voucher; ~**zuschuß** expense allowance.

Spezi pal *(sl.)*.

Spezial|abteilung special branch, *(Krankenhaus)* specialized ward; ~**agentur** subagency; ~**anfertigung** manufacture to customer's specification, *(Auto)* custom car; ~**anlage** special installation; ~**anwalt für Grundstücksfragen** conveyancer; ~**arbeiter** qualified worker; ~**arbeitskolonne** flying squadron; ~**artikel** speciality, *(pl.)* special lines, speciality goods; ~**artikelgeschäft** one-line business, stockist *(Br.)*, speciality store *(US)*; **hochwertiges ~artikelgeschäft** high-class speciality store *(US)*; ~**arzt** specialist; ~**auftrag** special mission; ~**ausbildung** special schooling (training), *(Führungskräfte)* additional (cold-storage, *US*) training; ~**ausdruck** technical expression, particulars; ~**ausführung** custom design; ~**bericht** detailed report; ~**berichterstatter** special correspondent, specialist writer; ~**beruf** skilled trade; ~**bestimmungen** special provisions; ~**bibliothek** special[ized] library; ~**brot** fancy bread; ~**depot** special deposit *(US)*; ~**erfahrung** specialized experience; ~**erzeugnis** speciality product; ~**fach** special line (subject), speciality, specialism, bailiwick, major subject *(US)*; **als ~fach betreiben** to specialize, to major in a subject *(US)*; ~**fach für eine Prüfung vorbereiten** to get up a subject for an examination; ~**fahrzeug** special-purpose vehicle; ~**fall** special case; ~**fonds** specialized (restricted) fund; ~**forderung** special claim; ~**gebiet** special subject, bailiwick, specialism, metier, speciality work; ~**geschäft** one-line business (shop), speciality store *(US)*, stockist *(Br.)*; **hochwertiges ~geschäft** high-class speciality store *(US)*; ~**geschäft für Radio und Fernsehen** radio and television specialist; ~**gesetz** special law; ~**großhändler** specialty jobber *(US)*; ~**güter** specialties; ~**gütermesse** specialized fair; ~**handel** specialized trade; ~**hersteller** specialty manufacturer; ~**indossament** special indorsement.

spezialisieren, sich auf etw. to specialize in (on) (become a specialist in) s. th., to specialize one's studies, to make a special feature of s. th., to major in a subject *(US)*.

Spezialisierung specialization;
berufliche ~ job specialization.

Spezialist specialist, specialized (qualified) worker, master hand, functional expert;
~ **für Feuerversicherungen** insurance engineer; ~ **für ausländische Währungsarbitrage** cambist;
~**en zuziehen** to call in an expert (a specialist).

Spezialistentum specialism, professionalism.

Spezialität speciality *(Br.)*, specialty *(US)*, special branch (subject), branch of business, major subject *(US)*, *(Stärke)* forte.

Spezialitäten|geschäft speciality shop (store, *US*), stockist *(Br.)*; ~**großhändler** speciality jobber *(US)*; ~**makler** privilege broker *(US)*, specialist *(US)*; ~**verkäufer** speciality salesman.

Spezial|karosserie *(Auto)* custom body; ~**karte** local map; **erforderliche ~kenntnisse** *(Fertigung)* manufacturing knowhow, *(Zeitungsanzeige)* special knowledge required; ~**konto** separate account; ~**kraft** specialized worker, specialist; ~**kräfte** specialized labo(u)r, technical personnel, skilled labo(u)r, specialist staff; ~**krankenhaus** special hospital; ~**literatur** trade literature; ~**papiere** specialities, special stocks *(US)*; ~**preis** cut price, *(Anzeige)* special rate; ~**produkt** specialty product;

~**rechenanlage** special-purpose computer; ~**risiko** special risk; ~**rückversicherungsvertrag** facultative insurance treaty; ~**schule für Piloten** ground school; ~**sortiment** model stock; ~**stelle** *(Anzeige)* individual location; ~**studium** professional studies, specialized study; ~**tarif im Rahmen des Flughafenzubringerdienstes** special airport feeder service rates; ~**teilbetrieb** job shop; ~**transportunternehmen** specific commodity carrier; ~**truppe** rapid-deployment force; ~**verfahren** special process; ~**verpackung** special packing; ~**versandkatalog** flyer; ~**versicherung** special insurance; ~**vollmacht** special (particular) power; ~**warengeschäft** speciality shop (store, *US*), single-line store *(US)*, stockist *(Br.)*; ~**werte** *(Börse)* specialities *(Br.)*, special stocks *(US)*, specialties *(US)*; ~**wissen** expert knowledge; ~**wörterbuch** technical (special) dictionary, glossary.

speziell special, particular, individual;
zu ~ too detailed;
Thema ~ **behandeln** to deal with a subject separately;
~**er Fall** particular case; **für einen** ~**en Zweck anfertigen** to make for a special purpose.

Spezielles, auf Ihr to your health.

Spezies|kauf sale of ascertained goods; ~**sachen** ascertained (specified) goods; ~**schuld** determinate (specific) obligation; ~**verkauf** sale of specific goods; ~**vermächtnis** specific legacy.

Spezifikation specification, detailed statement, statement of particulars, itemization *(US)*;
~**en nach Menge, Gewicht sowie Maß und Größe** specification as to quantity, weight, measurement and size.

Spezifikationskauf sale at a valuation (to specification).

spezifisches Gewicht specific weight.

spezifizieren to specify, to particularize, to detail;
Rechnung ~ to state an account, to itemize a bill *(US)*.

spezifiziert specified, itemized *(US)*;
nicht ~ unspecified;
~**e Klageschrift** bill of particulars; ~**e Rechnung** detailed (itemized, *US*) account; ~**e Rechnung verlangen** to demand an itemized bill *(US)*.

Spezifizierung specification, particularization, itemization *(US)*;
~ **von Patentansprüchen** notice of opposition; ~ **einer Rechnung** stating an account, itemization of a bill *(US)*.

Sphäre element, natural sphere;
in jds. private ~ **eindringen** to intrude upon s. one's privacy; **in höheren** ~**n schweben** to live in the clouds.

spicken *(bestechen)* to palm *(Br.)*, to tip, *(Schule)* to crib *(Br.)*, to ride *(sl.)*;
seine Rede mit Zitaten ~ to interlard one's speech with quotations.

Spickzettel cue card, crib.

Spiegel mirror;
auf dem Kotflügel installierter ~ wing mirror;
~ **eines Stausees** level of a reservoir;
~ **der öffentlichen Meinung abgeben** to be a reflex of public opinion;
~**bild** mirror image; ~**bild seiner Zeitgenossen sein** to hold up a mirror to one's contemporaries; ~**fechter** bluffer, juggler; ~**fechterei** jugglery, make-believe, fencing, bluff, eyewash; ~**fechterei treiben** to fence; ~**glas** plate glass; ~**glasversicherung** plate-glass insurance.

spiegelglatt| sein to be as smooth as a mirror;
~**e Straße** slippery road.

Spiegellandesystem mirror-landing system.

Spiegeln *(Redaktion)* copy fitting.

spiegeln to reflect, to mirror, *(glänzen)* to shine, to sparkle, *(Zeitung)* to copy-fit.

Spiegel|reflexkamera reflex camera; ~**schrift** mirror writing; **in** ~**schrift** written in reverse.

Spiegelung reflex, reflection, *(Luft)* mirage, fata morgana.

spiegelverkehrt mirror-inverted.

Spiegelvisier mirror sight.

Spiel game, *(Hasard)* gambling;
auf dem ~ **[stehend]** upon the die; **mit klingendem** ~ with drums beating;
abgekartetes ~ calculated game, put-up job *(sl.)*, frame-up *(US)*; **freies** ~ *(Preise)* free working; **leichtes** ~ walkover, child's play;
~ **der Kräfte** play of forces; **seltsames** ~ **der Natur** a freak of nature; **ausdruckvolles** ~ **eines Schauspielers** expressive performance of an actor;
das ~ **aufgeben** to throw up one's cards, to chuck (toss) in the sponge; **doppeltes** ~ **betreiben** to play a double game; **aus dem** ~ **bleiben** to keep one's fingers out of the pie; **ins** ~ **bringen** to start a hare, to bring into play; **sein Vermögen im** ~ **durchbringen** to gamble (game) away one's fortune; **jds.** ~ **durchschauen** to be up to s. one's tricks, to see through s. one's game; **sich in das** ~ **einschalten** to get in on the act; ~ **verloren geben** to throw in (up) the sponge; ~ **haben** *(techn.)* to have play; **seine Finger im** ~ **haben** to have a finger in the pie; ~ **gewonnen haben** to be home and dry; ~ **in der Hand haben** to have the ball on one's feet *(Br.)*; **ins** ~ **kommen** to become involved; **j. aus dem** ~ **lassen** to keep s. one's name out; **bei etw. mit im** ~ **sein** to have a hand in s. th., to be mixed up in an affair; **leichtes** ~ **für j. sein** to be an easy game for s. o.; **dem** ~ **verfallen sein** to be addicted to gambling; **aufs** ~ **setzen** to hazard, to jeopardize, to venture, to [put to the] stake, to risk; **alles aufs** ~ **setzen** to risk everything, to put all one's eggs into one basket; **ganzen Gewinn aufs** ~ **setzen** to play on the velvet *(US)*; **sein Leben aufs** ~ **setzen** to take one's life into one's hands, to set one's life on a game; **seinen Ruf aufs** ~ **setzen** to risk one's reputation; **für ein ehrliches** ~ **sorgen** to see fair play; **auf dem** ~ **stehen** to be at stake, to be involved; **böses** ~ **mit jem. treiben** to play the deuce with s. o.; **doppeltes** ~ **mit jem. treiben** to double-cross (juggle with) s. o.; **ehrliches** ~ **treiben** to play fair; **falsches** ~ **mit jem. treiben** to play s. o. false; **gefährliches** ~ **treiben** to go near the margin, to play a dangerous game, to run a great risk, to steer a dangerous course, to skate on thin ice; **sein** ~ **mit jem. treiben** to play fast and loose with s. o.; **jem. das** ~ **verderben** to queer s. one's pitch, to thwart s. one's plans; **Vermögen im** ~ **verlieren** to gamble away a fortune; **sein Glück im** ~ **versuchen** to try one's luck at gambling;
~**anweisung** *(Theater)* stage direction; ~**art** variety, version; ~**automat** gambling device, fruit machine *(Br.)*, slot machine, one-armed bandit *(US)*; ~**ball** shuttlecock; ~**ball des Schicksals** sport of fortune; ~**bank** casino, gambling resort, gambling (gaming) house; ~**bank halten** to hold the bank; **großen** ~**bankgewinn machen** to win a large sum at the casino.

Spielchen, ein paar ~ **machen** to have a little flutter; **mit jem. sein** ~ **treiben** to take s. o. for a ride, to lead s. o. up the garden path.

Spiel|dauer *(Film)* box-office life; ~**dauer feststellen** to time the picture; ~**dose** musical box, music box *(US)*; ~**einsatz** stake, venture; ~**einwand erheben** to plead the gaming out.

spielen to gamble, *(Theater)* to play, to act, to represent;
ganzen Abend ~ *(Radio)* to be on all evening; **gegen die Bank** ~ to punt; **vor leeren Bänken** ~ *(Theater)* to play to empty benches; **den Beleidigten** ~ to put on the offended; **an der Börse** ~ to play the stock market; **um die Ehre** ~ to play for love; **um große Einsätze** ~ to play for high stakes; **falsch** ~ to cheat at cards; **mit dem Feuer** ~ to play with edged tools, to play with fire, to court disaster; **Film** ~ to show a film; **mit dem Gedanken** ~ to toy with the idea; **zweite Geige** ~ to play second fiddle; **um Geld** ~ to play for money (keeps), to game; **einander in die Hände** ~ to play into one another's hands; **den großen Herrn** ~ to lord it, to give o. s. airs; **hoch** ~ to play for high stakes; **mit offen Karten** ~ to put one's cards on the table; **in der Lotterie** ~ to have a stake in the lottery; **Lotto** ~ to play at lotto (policy, *US*); **reichen Mann** ~ to pretend to have money; **Rolle** ~ to act a part; **jem. einen Streich** ~ to play a trick on s. o., to play s. o. up; **jem. einen bösen Streich** ~ to play s. o. a dirty trick, to put s. one's nose out of joint, to do s. o. an ill turn; **den Unschuldigen** ~ to play the innocent; **sich in den Vordergrund** ~ to thrust o. s. into the foreground; **wochenlang** ~ *(Film)* to run for weeks; **mit Worten** ~ to juggle with words; **in der Zeit des ersten Weltkriegs** ~ *(Stück)* to be set at the time of world war one;
seine Beziehungen ~ **lassen** to pull strings; **alle seine Künste** ~ **lassen** to make full use of one's talents; **seine Muskeln** ~ **lassen** to flex one's muscles; **seine Reize** ~ **lassen** to play off graces.

spielend hands down, very easily, nonchalantly;
j. ~ **besiegen** to walk over s. o.; **Kurve** ~ **nehmen** to take a bend with ease.

Spieler gambler, *(Theater)* actor, performer;
leidenschaftlicher ~ passionate gambler;
~ **vom Platz verweisen** to order a player off the field.

Spielerei *(Fummeln)* fooling, fiddling, *(Zeitvertreib)* hobby;
aus reiner ~ out of mere play;
technische ~**en** gimmicky, gadgetry, trinkets.

Spiel|film feature [film]; **abendfüllender** ~**film** feature length picture; ~**folge** program(me); ~**geld** play money; ~**gewinn** gambling profit (winning); ~**gewinne teilen** to whack up; ~**halle** amusement center *(US)* (centre, *Br.*); ~**höhle,** ~**hölle** gambling hell (den, *coll.*), disorderly house, bucket shop; ~**höllenbesitzer** keeper af a gambling den; ~**kamerad** playmate, playfellow; ~**karte** playing card; ~**kasino** gambling resort (house), casino; ~**klub** gaming club; ~**leidenschaft** indulgence in gambling; ~**leiter** stage manager, *(Film)* producer, *(Quiz)* quizmaster; ~**leitung** stage management, *(Film)* direction; ~**lokal** gaming house; ~**marke** chip, jetton, counter, fish; **seine ~marken eintauschen** to pass in one's checks; ~**omnibus** playbus; ~**pause** *(Theater)* intermission.

Spielplan *(Theater)* program(me), repertory, repertoire;
auf dem ~ bleiben to hold the boards, to be kept in the schedule; **auf den ~ setzen** to schedule; **vom ~ streichen** to remove from the program(me).

Spielplatz playground, play area, recreation ground, campus, *(Sport)* playing field.

Spielraum range, scope, latitude, circle, swing, reach, elbow room, leeway, play, rope, safety value, *(Marge)* margin, *(techn.)* free play;
aus Loyalität gewährter ~ faithful grace; **großer ~** wide margin, ample scope; **kein ~** not room to swing a cat in; **zulässiger ~** permissible clearance;
~ gewähren to leave (reserve) a margin; **genügend ~ haben** to have considerable leeway; **~ lassen** to give full play, to leave (reserve) a margin; **jem. ~ lassen** to give s. o. plenty of rope.

Spielregeln, diplomatische diplomatic standards;
~ zu seinen Gunsten auslegen to bend the rules; **auf parlamentarischen ~ bestehen** to enforce order; **sich [nicht] nach den ~ richten** [not] to play the game according to the rules; **~ verletzen** to fight foul.

Spiel|saal gaming room; ~**salon** gaming house; ~**schuld** gambling (game, play) debt, debt of hono(u)r; **vom ~teufel besessen** given to gambling; ~**tisch** gaming (gambling) table, green cloth; **gewerbliches ~unternehmen** common gambler; ~**verderber** spoilsport, killjoy, party pooper, wet blanket; ~**verlust** gaming loss; ~**vertrag** gambling (gaming, wager, aleatory) contract.

Spielwaren|geschäft toy shop (store, *US*); ~**händler** toyman; ~**industrie** toy industry; ~**messe** toy fair.

Spielzeit *(Theater)* [theatrical] season;
~ von zwei Stunden haben *(Film)* to last for two hours.

Spielzeug plaything, toy;
~**eisenbahn** clockwork railway, toy train; ~**laden** toyshop; ~**pistole** cap pistol; ~**warenhersteller,** ~**warenhändler** toyman.

Spieß *(drucktechn.)* blacks, pick, work-up, *(mil.)* top kick *(sl.)*;
vom ~ roasted, barbecued;
wie am ~ schreien to cry blue murder, to scream one's head off;
~ umdrehen to turn the tables.

Spießbürger bourgeois, Philistine, square *(sl.)*, Babbit *(US)*, mossback *(US sl.)*;
typischer ~ out-and-out bourgeois;
~ erschrecken to flutter the dove-cotes.

spießbürgerlich provincial, narrow, square, philistine, parochial, stuffy;
~**e Ansichten haben** to have narrow-minded views.

Spießbürgertum Philistinism.

Spießer Philistine, bourgeois, Babbit *(US)*, mossback *(US sl.)*;
die ~ suburbia;
altmodischer ~ square *(sl.)*.

Spießgeselle fellow rogue, accomplice, pal *(sl.)*.

spießig parochial, stuffy, philistine, provincial, square.

Spießigkeit parochialism.

Spießruten laufen to run the gauntlet (gantlet, *US*).

Spießrutenlaufen gantlet *(US)*, gauntlet *(Br.)*.

Spillage spillage, waste.

Spind *(mil.)* locker.

spindeldürr as thin as a rake *(sl.)*.

Spindrevision kit inspection.

Spinne *(Straßenbau)* road junction, spider.

spinnefeind sein, jem. to hate s. o. like poison.

spinnen *(fig.)* to yarn, to have lost a button;
Lügennetz ~ to spin a web of lies; **Ränke ~** to hatch a plot.

Spinnengewebe meshes of a spider's web.

Spinner crackbrain, crackpot, screwball *(US sl.)*.

Spinnerei spinning (cotton) mill.

spintisieren to brood, to muse.

Spion spy, ferret, beagle, intelligence agent, intelligencer, smeller *(sl.)*, plant *(Br., sl.)*, nark *(sl.)*, gumshoe [man] *(US)*, *(in der Tür)* window mirror;
vom Gegener als ~ bezahlt in the pay of the enemy;
bezahlter ~ pensionary spy; **von der Arbeitgeberseite bezahlter ~** labor spy *(US)*.

Spionage spying, espionage, *(mil.)* intelligence;
~ begehen to spy, to commit espionage; **jem. der ~ beschuldigen** to denounce s. o. as a spy;
~**abwehr** counterintelligence, secret service, counter-espionage; ~**abwehrdienst** Counterintelligence Corps, counterintelligence organization, M.I. 5 *(Br.)*; ~**abwehrgesetz** Espionage Act *(US)*; ~**affäre** espionage affair; ~**anklage** spy charge; ~**anschuldigung** charge of espionage; ~**bekämpfung** spy-catching operations; ~**delikt begehen** to combat espionage; ~**dienst** military intelligence; ~**fall** instance of espionage; ~**film** spy film; ~**flug** intelligence flight; ~**flugzeug** spy plane; ~**geschäft** business of spying, espionage; ~**geschichte** spy serial; ~**gruppe** Trojan horse; ~**handwerk betreiben** to be a professional spy; ~**netz** spy network; ~**organisation,** ~**ring** spy (espionage) ring; ~**prozeß** spy trial; ~**ring auffliegen lassen** to smash a spy ring; ~**roman** spy thriller; ~**satellit** spy satellite; ~**schiff** spy ship; ~**skandal** spy scandal; ~**system** spy system; ~**tätigkeit** espionage (intelligence) work (activity), spying activities.

spionageverdächtig suspected of espionage.

Spionage|verfahren espionage proceedings, spy trial; **auf dem ~wege** by espionage means; ~**zentrum** spy center (centre, capital), espionage basis.

Spiralantenne coil antenna.

spiralartig ansteigende Lohnkosten spiral(l)ing wage costs.

Spiritist spiritualist, spirit rapper.

Spirituosen spirits, alcoholic beverages;
geschmuggelte ~ bootleg *(US)*;
~**geschäft** liquor shop (store, *US*); ~**handel** traffic in liquor, liquor trade, the trade *(Br.)*; ~**händler** liquor dealer; **konzessionierter ~händler** licensed victualler *(Br.)*; ~**handlung** liquor store *(US)*; ~**verkauf** liquor selling.

Spiritus sprit.

Spital spital, spittle, almshouse, infirmary;
~**vorsteher** infirmarian.

spitz|e Bemerkung pointed remark; ~**e Feder schreiben** to wield a sarcastic pen; **etw. mit ~en Fingern anfassen** to set about s. th. gingerly; ~**er Gegenstand** prick; ~**e Zunge** sharp tongue.

Spitz|boje conical buoy; ~**bube** rascal, scoundrel, rogue; ~**dach** pointed roof.

Spitze remaining margin, head, extremity, *(Anzeige)* leading (lead) story, *(Bemerkung)* hit, edge, *(Bleistift)* point, *(Börse)* fractional amount, remainder, odd lot *(US)*, *(Führung)* lead, *(Höchstwert)* top, peak, summit, *(Rückversicherung)* excess, surplus, *(Textil)* lace, *(Unternehmen)* head, *(Zipfel)* tip;
an der ~ in front, at the top (head) of affairs, at the wheel, paramount, at the top of the ladder;
~**en** *(Börse)* fractional shares, odd lots *(US)*;
einsame ~ head and shoulders above the others; **frei verfügbare ~** free balance;
~ der Behörden top-ranking officials, the leading authorities, heads of government, civic headliners *(US)*; ~**n des Finanz- und Wirtschaftslebens** policy-makers of business; ~**n der Gesellschaft** cream of society, leading people, leaders of society, elite society, upper crust *(coll.)*; **südliche ~ einer Insel** southern tip of an island; **~ einer Liste** head of a list; ~**n der Ministerialbürokratie** administration's top leaders; ~**n der Regierung** heads of government; ~**n der Stadt** principal men of a city, leaders in the community;
einem Argument die ~ abbrechen to take the point out of an argument; **~ anführen** to lead the van; **~ des Inflationsberges beseitigen** to knock the top off its inflation mountain; **jem. die ~ bieten** to defy s. o.; **kaum verhüllte ~n gegen die Regierung enthalten** *(Rede)* to comprise scarcely disguised hits against the government; **~ erreichen** *(Verkaufszahlen)* to reach the peak; **in der ~ vier Prozent erreichen** to peak at 4 per cent; **160 km ~ fahren** *(Auto)* to do a hundred miles; **an die ~ gelangen** to reach the top of the ladder, to zoom to the top; **gemeinsam an der ~ liegen** to come out joint top; **sich an die ~ schieben** to shoot ahead; **an der ~ sein** to be up; **gemeinsam an die ~ der Liste setzen** to bracket together at the top of the list; **an der ~ eines Unternehmens stehen** to have control (be the head, on top) of an undertaking, to head a firm; **Scherz auf die ~ treiben** to carry a joke too far; **an die ~ treten** to take the lead; **zu den ~n der Behörde zählen** to form the top echelon in civic activities; **es steht auf Knopf und ~** it's a touch and go.

Spitzel common informer, feigned accomplice, snooper, ferret, noser, nark *(sl.)*, gumshoe *(US sl.)*, nightingale *(sl.)*, *(Lockspitzel)* stool pigeon, undercover man;
berufsmäßiger ~ finger *(sl.)*;
~ der Regierung creature of the government;
~ sein to nose, to ferret, to nark;
~**gelder** undercover payment; ~**wesen** in former system.

spitzeln to nark, to ferret, to nose.

spitzen, auf etw. to be keen on (eager to get) s. th.; **seine Ohren ~** to prick up one's ears.

Spitzen|angebot marginal supply; **~anlage** first-class investment; **~arbeit** lacework; **~aufsichtsrat** top board; **~ausgleich** surplus settlement, clearing transfer, *(Börse)* evening up; **~beamter** top-ranking official *(US)*; **~beanspruchung** peak load; **~bedarf** peak [of the] demand; **vordringlicher ~bedarf** top-priority needs; **winterlicher ~bedarf** winter peak in demand; **~belastung** maximum (permissible) load, *(el.)* peak load; **mit dem Problem der saisonalen ~belastung fertig werden** to handle the seasonal peak problems; **~belastungszeit** peak (rush) hours; **außerhalb der ~belastungszeit** off-peak; **~berater** top adviser; **~betrag** maximum (residual) amount, *(Kredit)* balance, *(Börse)* fractional (uneven) amount, odd lot *(US)*; **~beträge erwerben** to buy shares in odd lots *(US)*; **~betrieb** top plant; **~bewertung erzielen** to hit top ratings; **~einkommen haben** to be in the highest income brackets; **~ergebnis** record level; **~erzeugnisse** choice articles (goods), high-quality products; **~erzeugnis der Markenindustrie** top-selling brand; **~fahrzeug** leading vehicle; **~film** first-class film; **~finanzierung** peak financing; **~funktionär** top-level official; **~funktionäre** *(Partei)* establishment; **gewerkschaftliche ~funktionäre** key union leaders; **~gehalt** top[-level] salary (pay), maximum salary, ceiling; **~gehalt beinhalten** to command a very substantial salary; **~geschwindigkeit** top speed; **~geschwindigkeit von 160 km erreichen** to do a hundred miles; **~gewinn** *(Börse)* top gain; **~gremium** board of supervisors, top-team *(US)*; **~hilfskraft** top aid; **~industrie** leading industry; **~jahr** peak year, *(Gewinn)* vintage year of profits; **~journalist** top-notch reporter; **~kandidat** top candidate, frontrunner, shoo-in *(US)*; **zahlenmäßig hinter dem ~kandidaten liegen** to stand a close second; **~klasse** top grade, top of ranks; **~kosten** topmost cost; **~kraft** top[-level] executive *(US)*, top talent (aid), blue-eyed (fair-haired) boy *(sl.)*; **~kraft für Wertpapieranlagen** top analyst.

Spitzenkräfte top management (executives, officials, levels) *(US)*;
~ auf dem Gebiet der Steuerumgehung top tax-avoidance experts; **~ der Wirtschaft** top business executives *(US)*;
über zu wenig ~ verfügen to be too thin in its top managerial ranks *(US)*.

Spitzen|kreditbedürfnis peak advance requirements; **~leistung** record, peak performance (output), *(Höchstleistung)* top efficiency (work), *(Maschine)* maximum capacity, *(Produktion)* maximum capacity; **~lohn** peak (maximum, top) wages; **~manager** top manager; **~manager von Staatsbetrieben** top state people; **~mannschaft** top team; **~marke** brand leader; **~modell** top-of-the-line model; **~nachfrage** maximum demand, *(Restnachfrage)* residual demand; **~organisation** head (central) organization; **~papiere** leading (glamo(u)r, *US*) stock, favo(u)rites, gilt-edged shares *(Br.)*; **~politiker** front-rank politician.

Spitzenposition senior appointment, top, top spot *(US)*, top executive position *(US)*, top-level management status *(US)*, top management post (position, appointment);
~en top echelons *(US)*;
~ in der Beamtenhierarchie top mandarin post; **~ im Verkäufermarkt** top seller position;
knapp unter der ~ liegen to be off only slightly from their peak.

Spitzen|preis top price; **~produktion** maximum (top, peak) output; **~produzent** top producer; **~publikum** top audience *(US)*; **~qualität** prime, top (star) quality; **~regulierung** settlement of fractional amounts, evening-up; **~reiter** *(Börse)* star performer, market leader, frontrunner; **~reiter unter den Investmentgesellschaften** top-performing mutual fund; **~reiterposition im Arbeitslosenbereich** unemployment peaking; **~satz** record rate; **~schlager** number one hit; **~stand** *(Kurse)* peak level, all-time high; **~stellung** top position (job, appointment); **~stellung erreichen** to reach the top; **~steuersatz, ~steuertarif** top [marginal] tax rate, marginal rate of taxation; **~umsatz** top (record) sales; **~unterhändler** top negotiator.

Spitzenverband head (umbrella, top, summit) organization, *(Gewerkschaft)* trades council;
kommunaler ~ Association of County Councils *(Scotland)*;
~ amerikanischer Arbeitgeber National Industrial Conference Board *(US)*; **~ Britischer Arbeitgeberverbände** British Employers' Confederation; **örtlicher ~ der Gewerkschaft** trade (union) council.

Spitzen|verbrauch maximum consumption; **~verdiener** top earner; **~verkäufer** star (top) salesman; **~verkaufszahlen** peak sales; **~verkehr** peak hours, rush-hour peak, peak traffic, rush-hour traffic; **~verkehr umgehen** to beat the rush hours; **~versorgung** *(el.)* standby supply; **~wein** vintage wine; **~wert** peak (prime) value; **~werte** *(Aktien)* gilt-edged (leading) shares *(Br.)*, high-quality stocks *(US)*, favo(u)rites, leaders, glamor stocks *(US)*, glamors *(US)*, blue chips *(US)*; **industrielle ~werte** top industrials; **~zeitbedarf** peak period demand.

spitzfindig critical, hypercritical, subtle, cavil(l)ing, sophistical.

Spitz|findigkeit sophism, quibble, sophistry, refinement, nicety, subtlety; **juristische ~findigkeit** pettifogging; **~giebel** pointed hood; **~hacke** pick.

spitzkriegen to become aware of, to tumble to *(US sl.)*.

Spitzname nickname.

Spleen whim, fad, crotchet;
~ haben to have a bee in one's bonnet.

Split *(Börse)* split, splitup, share bonus *(Br.)*, reserve splitup *(Br.)*, *(Straßendecke)* broken stone.

Splitter splinter, chip;
~aktionär smallholder; **~bombe** splinter (fragmentation, anti-personnel) bomb; **~box** *(Flugzeug)* revert.

splitterfrei splinter-proof.

Splitter|graben split trench; **~gruppe** split; **sich in ~gruppen auflösen** to split into petty factions; **~partei** splinter (fringe) party, faction; **~schutz** splinterproof protection; **~siedlung** scattered housing; **~stimmen** scattered votes; **~wirkung** fragmentation.

Splitting *(Einkommensteuer)* splitting.

spontan voluntary, spontaneous, on the spur of the moment, unprompted, impromptu, offhand, off the cuff, extempore;
~ handeln to act on the impulse of the moment;
~er Einfall freak, sudden whim; **~es Hilfsangebot** spontaneous offer of help; **~ gekaufte Waren** impulse goods.

Spontan|kauf impulse buying; **~käufer** impulse buyer.

sporadisch, sich nur ~ sehen to see each other only now and then;
~ auftretende Krankheit sporadic case of a disease.

Sporen, sich die ~ verdienen to win one's spurs; **sich in einem Anwaltsbüro die ~ verdienen** to serve a hitch with a law firm.

Sporn spur, *(Flugzeugheck)* skid, *(Kriegsschiff)* ram.

spornstreichs whip and spur.

Sport|anlagen sports facilities; **~artikelgeschäft** sports-wear department, sporting goods store *(US)*; **~ausrüstung** sporting equipment; **~berichte im Fernsehen** sports coverage (reporting) in television; **besondere ~berichterstattung haben** to make a feature of sport.

Sporteln emoluments, appointments, perquisites *(Br.)*.

Sport|ereignis, beliebtes popular event; **spektakuläres ~ereignis** sporting spectacular; **~fanatiker** devotee of sport; **~feld** sports field; **~fliegerei** amateur flying; **~flugzeug** sporting plane; **~halle** gymnasium; **~journalist** sports writer; **~kinderwagen** push-chair; **~kleidung** sport clothes, sportswear; **~lehrer** games master; **~minister** minister for sport *(Br.)*; **~redakteur** sports editor (columnist); **~reportage** sportcast; **~seite** sporting page; **~stadion** sport stadium; **~veranstaltung** sports event; **~veranstaltung mit Eintrittspreis** gate meeting; **~veranstaltung im Freien** outdoor sports event; **~wagen** sports car (model); **~warengeschäft** sporting goods shop (store, *US*); **~zweisitzer** roadster, two-seater, runabout car.

Spott mockery, scorn, ridicule, derision, scoff;
sich dem allgemeinen ~ aussetzen to lay o. s. open to ridicule; **j. zur Zielscheibe seines ~es machen** to bring s. o. into derision; **seinen ~ mit jem. treiben** to make a mock of s. o., to hold s. o. to ridicule; **j. mit ~ und Hohn überschütten** to pour scorn on s. o.; **Zielscheibe des allgemeinen ~es werden** to become the laughingstock (scoff) of the town.

spottbillig dirt-cheap, dog-cheap, at a knockout price *(Br.)*;
etw. ~ kaufen to get a thing dead bargain, to buy (pick up) for a mere (a, an old) song; **~ sein** to be a dozen a dime;
~e Ware sacrificed goods, dead bargain.

spötteln to mock, to scoff, to chaff, to banter.

spotten to pass derisive remarks;
über j. ~ to mock (make fun) of s. o.; **jeder Beschreibung ~** to be beyond description.

Spötter scoffer, scorner, mocker, flouter, sneerer.

Spott|figur laughingstock, butt; **~gedicht** satirical poem; **~geld** paltry sum, ridiculously low price; **um ein ~geld** for a (an old) song.

spöttisch derisive, mocking, scoffing, scornful;
etw. mit ~em Gelächter abtun to laugh s. th. to scorn; **~es Lächeln** mocking smile.

Spottpreis [real] bargain, dead bargain, ridiculously low price, knockdown (bargain) price;

für einen ~ zugeschlagen knocked-down for a song;
zu einem ~ kaufen to get s. th. as a real bargain, to buy s. th. for a mere song.

Sprach|akademie linguistic academy; ~**angewohnheiten** peculiarities of speech; ~**armut** poverty of expression; ~**atlas** dialect atlas, linguistic map.

sprachbegabt sein to have a good head (flair) for languages.

Sprach|begabung gift for language; ~**begabung haben** to have great facility in learning languages; ~**beherrschung** command of a language; ~**bereicherung** addition to a language.

Sprache language, parlance, talk, *(Ausdrucksweise)* term, *(Stil)* diction, style;
der ~ nach zu urteilen judging from s. one's accent; **in offener ~** *(Telegramm)* in plain language, plain, not coded;
blumenreiche ~ flowery style; **schwer zu erlernende ~** hard (difficult) language; **fremde ~** foreign language; **gemäßigte ~** moderate language; **gesittete ~** decent language; **gesprochene ~** primary language; **gewählte ~** choice of language; **kultivierte ~** educated diction; **lebende ~** modern (living) language; **maßvolle ~** temperate language; **parlamentarische ~** parliamentary language; **schwülstige ~** inflated language; **tote ~** dead language; **noch unbekannte ~** sealed language; **unflätige ~** filth; **unzweideutige ~** downright language; **verschlüsselte ~** coded language; **verwandte ~n** related (kindred, cognate) languages; **vulgäre ~** vile (bad) language;
~ der Diplomaten language of diplomacy; **~ der Juristen** legal language;
mehrere ~n beherrschen to have a command (an understanding, a knowledge) of several languages, to possess (master) several languages; **seine ~ beherrschen** to know one's grammar; **~ völlig beherrschen** to have great command of a language; **zur ~ bringen** to come up with; **Thema zur ~ bringen** to broach (raise) a subject; **Thema mit Gewalt zur ~ bringen** to drag a subject in; **sich in eine ~ einlesen** to read o. s. into a language; **j. an seiner ~ erkennen** to know s. o. by his speech; **~ erlernen** to acquire a language; **gemäßigte ~ gebrauchen** to speak in a measured tone; **einige Kenntnisse in einer ~ haben** to have a working knowledge of a language; **mit der ~ herausrücken** to own up, to come clean *(sl.)*; **zur ~ kommen** to come up for discussion; **in der nächsten Woche der Vereinten Nationen zur ~ kommen** to come before the United Nations Assembly next week; **sehr leicht ~n lernen** to have great facility in learning languages; **sich mit einer ~ vertraut machen** to make o. s. familiar with a language; **deutliche ~ mit jem. reden** to talk turkey with s. o., to talk United States, *(Tatsache)* to speak for themselves; **auf der gestrigen Sitzung zur ~ gekommen sein** to have been raised at yesterday's meeting; **~n studieren** to go in for (read) languages; **aus der französischen in die deutsche ~ übersetzen** to translate from French into German; **jem. die ~ verschlagen** to strike s. o. dead (dump), to leave s. o. speechless; **viele ~n verstehen** to be multilingual (polyglot); **es einmal mit der spanischen ~ versuchen** to have a dig at Spanish; **in die ~ aufgenommen werden** to arrive linguistically; **~ wiedergewinnen** to recover one's speech; **nicht mit der ~ herausrücken wollen** to hum and haw.

Spracheigentümlichkeit idiom, idiomatic expression;
amerikanische ~ Yankeeism.

Sprachen|atlas linguistic map, dialect atlas; ~**bedürfnis** language need; ~**dienst** language department; ~**gemisch** hodgepodge (medley) of languages; ~**gewirr** babble (confusion) of tongues; ~**gleichberechtigung** language equality; ~**gruppe** stock; ~**karte** linguistic map; ~**klasse** language class; ~**lernen** learning of languages; ~**problem** linguistic problem; ~**regelungsgesetz**, ~**verordnung** language bill (law); ~**zulage** language allowance.

Sprach|familie linguistic stock; ~**fehler** speech defect, solecism; ~**fehler haben** to have an impediment in one's speech; ~**fernsehen** foreign-language course in television; ~**forscher** linguist; ~**führer** phrase book; **englischer ~führer** guide to English; ~**gebiet** linguistic (speech) area; ~**gebrauch** grammar usage; **im alltäglichen ~gebrauch** in everyday language; **englischer ~gebrauch** English usage; ~**gefühl** flair for languages.

sprachgewandt sein to be a good linguist.

Sprach|gewandtheit proficiency in languages; ~**grenze** language border; ~**gruppe** family of languages, speech community; ~**hindernis** language barrier; ~**insel** linguistic enclave, speech island.

Sprachkenntnisse linguistic attainments;
annehmbare englische ~ passable knowledge of English; **ausreichende englische ~** competent knowledge (sufficient command) of English; **einige ~** working knowledge of a language; **fließende englische ~** fluent knowledge of English; **gründliche (gute) ~** thorough command of a language; **zusätzliche ~** additional language capability;
~ auffrischen to polish up a language; **seine französischen ~ bei jem. ausprobieren** to practise one's French on s. o. **englische ~ erwerben** to pick up a knowledge of English.

Sprach|klinik speech clinic; ~**korrektur** speech correction.

sprachkundig languaged, polyglot.

Sprach|kursus language course; ~**labor** language laboratory; ~**lehrer** professor of languages, language teacher (master, *Br.*).

sprachlich linguistic;
j. ~ ausbilden to train s. o. in a language;
~e Eigenheiten pecularities of a language; **~e Minderheit** linguistic minority.

sprachlos speechless, mute, dumb;
vor Wut ~ inarticulate with rage;
j. völlig ~ machen to knock s. o. all of a heap; **völlig ~ sein** to be flabbergasted.

Sprach|lücke language gap; ~**minderheit** linguistic minority; ~**niveau** level of language; ~**raum** speech area; ~**regelung** official version; **von der allgemeinen ~regulierung abweichen** to speak out of turn; ~**rohr** megaphone, speaking trumpet, vocal proponent, *(fig.)* mouthpiece, spokesman, voice, speaker, *(Zeitung)* organ; **sich zum ~rohr einer Sache machen** to appoint o. s. a spokesman of a cause; ~**schatz** vocabulary; ~**schnitzer** blunder, flaw, solecism; ~**schranke** language barrier; ~**schule** language school; ~**störungen haben** to have an impediment in one's speech; ~**studium** study of languages; ~**talent besitzen** to be a good linguist, to have great facility for learning languages; ~**ungenauigkeit** incorrect expression; ~**unterricht** language instruction; **englischer ~unterricht** English lessons; **dem ~unterricht besondere Bedeutung zumessen** to lay special emphasis on language study; ~**verschlüsselung** cryptophony; ~**verwandtschaften** language relationship; ~**verwirrung** confusion of tongues; **vergleichende ~wissenschaft** comparative study of languages; ~**wissenschaftler** linguist; ~**zentrum** language center *(US)* (centre, *Br.*).

Sprech|anlage intercommunication system, intercom, chatter box *(sl.)*; ~**blase** bubble, [speech] balloon; ~**brief** phonopost.

Sprechen, j. zum ~ bringen to make s. o. find his tongue, to unseal s. one's lips; **sich zum ~ erheben** to get on one's feet.

sprechen, für j. ~ speak in favo(u)r of s. o., *(eintreten für j.)* to put in a good word (speak) for s. o.; **für sich ~** to tell one's own tale; **mit jem. ~** to talk (speak) to (converse with) s. o.; **mit einem englischen Akzent ~** to speak with a British accent; **anerkennend von jem. ~** to speak highly of s. o.; **mit seinem Anwalt ~** to see (consult) one's lawyer; **ausführlich ~** to discuss at some length; **auf Band ~** to record one's voice; **Bände ~** to speak volumes; **befürwortend ~** to plead; **besser nicht darüber ~** no good talking about it; **gebrochen Englisch ~** to speak broken (murder King's) English; **aufgrund eigener Erfahrungen~** to speak from one's own experience; **in glühenden Farben von jem. ~** to speak in glowing terms of s. o.; **fernmündlich ~** to telephone; **frei (ohne Manuskript) ~** to speak offhand (without notes, without book, off the cuff, *coll.*); **gebildet ~** to speak in a refined manner; **geringschätzig ~** to speak disdainfully, to be derogatory (disparaging), to cheapen, to make low; **von Geschäften ~** to talk shop; **zur Geschäftsordnung ~** *(parl.)* to rise to order; **Gutes über j. ~** to speak well of s. o.; **kurz mit jem. ~** to have a word with s. o.; **lauter ~** to elevate (raise) one's voice; **leise ~** to whisper; **nicht mehr miteinander ~** to be no longer on speaking terms; **in Rätseln ~** to talk in riddles; **rückhaltlos ~** to speak without restraint; **über den Rundfunk ~** to be on the air, to talk over the radio; **zur Sache ~** to speak to the point; **über ganz bestimmte Sachen ~** *(fam.)* to get down to brass tacks; **schlecht über j. ~** to speak evil (talk ill) of s. o.; **j. schuldig ~** to find s. o. guilty; **jem. aus der Seele ~** to express s. one's innermost feelings; **für sich selbst ~** to be selfexplanatory, to speak for itself; **aus dem Stegreif ~** to speak extempore (off the cuff, *coll.*), to improvise; **stundenlang ~** to talk for hours on end; **Tischgebet ~** to say grace; **undeutlich ~** to mumble, to speak indistinctly; **ganz ungeniert ~** to have a direct way of speaking; **zögernd ~** to speak with a halt; **zurückhaltend ~** to sing low;
vor Aufregung nicht ~ können to have a lump in one's throat; **geläufig Französisch ~ können** to express o. s. with ease in French; **für j. nicht zu ~ sein** not to be at home for (shut the door on) s. o.

sprechend spelling, revealing;
seinem Vater ~ ähnlich sein to be the spit of one's father;
~e Ähnlichkeit striking resemblance.

Sprecher *(Auswärtiges Amt)* [public] speaker, public orator *(Br.)*, spokesman, voice, discourser, prolocutor, *(Film)* commentator, *(Geschworene)* foreman, *(Lobby)* advocate, *(Nachrichten)* newsreader, newscaster, *(Rundfunk)* announcer, narrator, broadcaster;
autorisierter ~ publicity spokesman; **tonangebender ~** keynote speaker;
~ des Auswärtigen Amtes foreign-office spokesman; **~ auf handelsrechtlichem Gebiet im Schattenkabinett** shadow trade spokesman *(Br.)*; **~ einer großen Mehrheit** protagonist of a great majority; **~ des Unterhauses** leader of the House of Commons;
~kabine commentator's booth.
Sprech|erlaubnis *(Gefängnis)* visitor's permit; **~fehler** *(Rundfunk)* fluff; **~fenster** grilled opening, grating; **~film** talking film, talkie, talky.
Sprechfunk radiotelephony;
durch ~ by radio;
mit ~anlage ausgestattet radio-equipped; **~gerät** radiotelephone, *(tragbar)* walkie-talkie; **~verkehr** radiotelephone traffic.
Sprech|kanal telephone channel; **~kreis** *(tel.)* speech circuit; **gewöhnliche ~leitung** voice telephone line; **~maschine** talking machine; **~muschel** mouthpiece; **~pause** *(tel.)* quiet period; **~probe** *(Rundfunk)* audition; **~stelle** *(tel.)* call (telephone) station; **~stunden** calling hours, office (business) hours, *(Arzt)* hours of attendance, consulting hours; **~stundenhilfe** receptionist; **~taste** microphone key; **~verbot** speaking prohibited; **~verkehr** intercommunication; **verschlüsselter ~verkehr** cryptophony; **~zeit** speaking time; **reservierte ~zeit** *(tel.)* reservation; **~zimmer** parlo(u)r, consulting room.
spreizen, sich to give o. s. airs, to strut.
Sprengbombe explosive (demolition) bomb.
Sprengel parish, diocese.
sprengen to dynamite, to explode, to blow up, *(aufbrechen)* to break open;
Bank ~ to break the bank; **Brücke ~** to blow up a bridge; **Koalition ~** to disrupt a coalition; **Rahmen eines Aufsatzes ~** to go beyond the scope of an essay; **Rasen ~** to sprinkle (water) the lawn; **Schiff ~** to blow up a ship; **Versammlung ~** to break up (dissolve) a meeting.
Spreng|kammer mine chamber; **~kapsel** percussion cap, detonator; **~kommando** *(Bomben)* demolition party, bomb-disposal squad; **~kopf** *(Rakete)* warhead; **~körper, ~ladung** explosive charge; **~kraft** explosive force; **~meister** blaster; **~mittel** exploder; **~patrone** torpedo; **~pulver** black (miner's) powder; **~satz** demolition charge, blasting composition.
Sprengstoff, hochexplosiver high explosive;
~ heimlich anbringen to plant explosives;
~anschlag bomb attempt; **~anschlag auf ein Haus verüben** to blow up a house; **~attentäter** dynamiter.
Sprengtrichter mine crater.
Sprengung explosion;
~ einer Koalition disruption of a coalition; **~ einer Versammlung** breakup of a meeting.
Spreng|wagen street sprinkler, watering cart *(Br.)*; **~wirkung** explosive effect; **~zünder** fuse.
Spreu *(fig.)* deadwood;
~ vom Weizen trennen to winnow the chaff from the wheat, to pick out the good from the bad.
Sprichwort proverb;
zum ~ geworden sein to be proverbial for.
sprichwörtlich proverbial.
sprießen to sprout, to shoot, to spring up.
Springbrunnen bunt anstrahlen to play colo(u)red lights on a fountain.
springen to jump, to leap, *(Glas)* to burst, to crack;
in die Augen ~ to strike the eye; **für j. in die Bresche ~** to help s. o. out of a tight corner, to pinch-hit for s. o. *(US)*; **aus den Gleisen ~** to jump of the metals, to derail; **über einen Graben ~** to leap over (clear) a ditch; **jem. an die Gurgel ~** to fly at s. one's throat; **in tausend Stücke ~** to break into thousand pieces; **von einem Thema zum anderen ~** to jump from one topic to another; **auf einen fahrenden Zug ~** to jump a train;
etw. ~ lassen to cough up (fork out) s. th.; **an seinem Geburtstag etw. ~ lassen** to stand a treat on one's birthday; **j. über die Klinge ~ lassen** to put s. o. to the sword; **alle Minen ~ lassen** to leave no stone unturned.
springender Punkt crucial (salient) point.
Springer *(Berufsleben)* jobhopper.
Spring|flut spring (flood) tide; **~insfeld** harum-scarum, tomboy.
springlebendig full of beans.
Sprinkleranlage sprinkler system.
Sprit commercial alcohol, petrol, juice *(sl.)*;
hochwertiger ~ soup;
~kanister jerrycan.
Spritze syringe, shot, injection, *(für die Konjunktur)* stimulous, fillip, boost, shot in the arm, needle *(sl.)*;
an der ~ sein to have the say.
spritzen to squirt, to spurt, *(Garten)* to sprinkle, *(Straße)* to water;
nach allen Seiten ~ to splash in all directions;
Wagen ~ lassen to have the car sprayed.
Spritzenhaus enginehouse, firehouse.
Spritzer splash, *(kleine Menge)* dash, *(Tour)* trip, spin, joy ride.
spritzig witty, sparkling;
~ geschriebener Bericht wittily written report; **~er Wagen** flashy car.
Spritz|lack spraying varnish; **~pistole** paint sprayer, airbrush, spraygun; **~technik** airbrush technique.
Spritztour jaunt, running spree, spin, trip, joy ride (riding);
~ an die See trip to the seaside;
~ machen to jaunt, to go for a trip, to joy-ride.
spröde coy, standoffish, reserved, *(Glas)* brittle;
~ tun to simper;
~ Art standoffish manner.
Sproß scion, issue.
Sprosse, höchste ~ seiner Laufbahn erklimmen to reach the top of the ladder.
Sprößling son, junior;
hoffnungsvoller ~ young hopeful.
Spruch *(Ausspruch)* saying, adage, *(Funkspruch)* message, *(Geschworene)* assize, verdict, sentence, conviction, deliverance, *(Schiedsgericht)* award;
~ fällen to pronounce a sentence, *(Schiedsgericht)* to make an award;
~ausschuß grievance committee; **~band** banner.
Sprüche machen to brag, to talk big.
Spruchkammer board of arbitration, conciliation court.
Sprüchlein sagen, sein to say one's piece.
Sprudel mineral (tonic) water;
~ mit Geschmack flavo(u)red soda water.
sprudeln to gush, to bubble, to spout;
von Ideen ~ to bubble with ideas.
sprudelnd bubbling, *(Getränk)* fizzy, effervescent;
in ~er Laune in high spirits.
Sprühdose aerosol can.
sprühen *(Edelstein)* to scintillate, to sparkle, *(Funken)* to emit sparks.
sprühender Witz sparkling wit.
Sprühregen drizzle, mist *(US)*.
Sprung leap, jump, breach, pounce, *(im Glas)* crack, *(Kurse)* leap, spurt, *(mil.)* dash;
nur ein ~ bis zur Bushaltestelle a stone's throw to the bus stop; **~ in einem Edelstein** flaw in a gem; **~ ins Ungewisse** leap in the dark;
j. auf einen ~ besuchen to drop in on s. o., to pay s. o. a flying visit; **zum ~ in einer Freundschaft führen** to cause a rift between two friends; **großen ~ nach vorn machen** to take a big step forward; **immer auf dem ~ sein** to be always on the go; **schon auf dem ~ sein** to be coming; **der Konkurrenz immer einen ~ voraus sein** always to be one jump ahead of one's competitors; **~ wagen** to take the plunge;
~abtastung *(Fernsehen)* interlaced scanning.
sprungbereit ready to go.
Sprungbrett diving board, *(fig.)* stepping stone, take-off, springboard.
Sprünge, jem. auf die ~ helfen to give s. o. a helping hand, *(einheizen)* to give it hot to s. o., to give s. o. hell; **jem. auf die ~ kommen** to be up to s. one's dodges; **keine großen ~ machen können** to live in narrow circumstances.
Sprungfedermatratze spring mattress.
sprunghaft *(Kurse)* erratic, by leaps and bounds, by fits and starts, *(Markt)* jerky, spasmodic, buoyant, *(Stimmung)* volatile, fickle;
~ ansteigen to rise by leaps and bounds; **Preise ~ erhöhen** to jump prices; **~ steigen** to leap up; **~ steigen und einen Höchststand erreichen** to jump into new high ground, to skyrocket *(US)*;
~es Anziehen der Kurse upward spurts; **~er Einkommensanstieg** jump in incomes; **~e Entwicklung auf dem Börsenmarkt** erratic development on the stock market; **~er Ertragsanstieg** jump in

earnings; ~er **Preisanstieg** jump in prices, price speedup; ~e **Steigerung** buoyancy; ~er **Stil** jerky style; ~es **Wesen** erratic behavio(u)r; ~e **Zunahme der Kriminalität** jump in crime.
Sprung|kosten semi-variable cost; ~**regreß** recourse to prior endorser; ~**revision** leapfrogging; ~**tuch** *(Feuerwehr)* life net.
sprungweise *(Kurse)* by fits and starts, by leaps [and bounds].
Spucke, mir blieb die ~ weg I was flabbergasted.
spucken *(Motor)* to spit, *(Ofen)* to be heating well;
in die Hände ~ to buckle down to work; **jem. in die Suppe ~** to thwart s. one' plans, to upset s. one's applecart; **immer große Töne ~** to be always bragging, to draw the long bow.
Spuk spook, haunting;
dem ~ ein Ende bereiten to put paid to s. th. *(sl.)*; **viel ~ um etw. machen** to make a great fuss about it; **wie ein ~ vorbeijagen** to flit past like a ghost.
spuken to haunt, to walk;
im Kopf ~ *(Idee)* to possess s. o.
Spuk|geschichte ghost story; ~**haus** haunted house.
Spül|automat dishwasher; ~**becken** sink, *(WC)* closet bowl.
Spule spool, reel, bobbin, *(el.)* coil.
spülen to wind, to reel, to spool;
über Bord ~ to sweep overboard; **über den Damm ~** *(Hochwasser)* to wash over the dam; **Geschirr ~** to wash [up] dishes; **Wäsche ~** to rinse the washing.
Spül|küche scullery, pantry *(Br.)*; ~**lappen** dish cloth; ~**maschine** dishwasher; ~**mittel** detergent; ~**stein** sink.
Spülung *(WC)* flush.
Spül|vorrichtung *(WC)* plug; ~**wasser** dishwater, wash, waste liquid.
Spur scent, clue, vestige, *(Anzeichen)* sign, indication, smell, *(Bahn)* track, *(für Fahrzeuge)* lane, strip of roadway, *(Fußabdruck)* tread, footprint, *(Kleinigkeit)* shadow, streak, suggestion, touch, trace, slit, shade, colo(u)r, breath, foil *(Br.)*, particle, tincture, *(Kriminalistik)* clue;
auf einer heißen ~ hot on the trail; **ohne ~en zu hinterlassen** traceless;
ausgefahrene ~ beaten track; **frische ~** *(Fahndung)* hot scent; **keine ~** no sign (trace) of;
~ von Fanatismus strain of fanaticism; **~en von Grausamkeit in jds. Charakter** streaks of cruelty in s. one's character; **~en einer alten Kultur** remains (traces) of an ancient civilization; **~ für Linksabbieger** filter lane; **keine ~ von Müdigkeit** no trace of fatigue; **~ von Vernunft** show of reason; **keine ~ eines Zweifels** without a shadow of doubt;
von der ~ abbringen to throw off the scent; **~ aufnehmen** to pick up a track; **auf die ~ bringen** to put on the scent; **jds. ~en folgen** to track s. one's trail; **seine ~ halten** *(Autofahrer)* to keep one's lane; **~en bei jem. hinterlassen** to tell on s. o.; **keine ~en hinterlassen** to leave no traces behind; **auf die ~ kommen** to get on (strike) the track, to find a clue; **einer Sache auf die ~ kommen** to get wind of s. th.; **keinerlei ~en eines Diebes auffinden können** to be unable to find any traces of a thief; **den ~en nachgehen** to walk the tracks; **auf der ~ sein** to have in the wind; **auf der falschen ~ sein** to be on the wrong track; **~en sichern** to preserve traces; **~ verfolgen** to hunt a trail; **falsche ~ verfolgen** to bark up the wrong tree; **jds. ~ im Schnee verfolgen** to follow s. one's track through the snow; **~ verlieren** to lose the scent; **seine ~en verwischen** to remove one's traces, to cover up one's tracks; **seine ~ wechseln** *(Autofahrer)* to change from one lane to another, to straddle the lane; **ständig die ~ wechseln** to weave between the lanes; **keine ~ von Reue zeigen** not to show the slightest regret; **~ eines Verbrechers bis A zurückverfolgen** to trace a criminal to A.
spürbar marked, percepticle, sensible;
~e Erleichterung noticeable relief; **~e Preiserhöhung** considerable increase in prices.
spüren to take the hint, *(Politik)* to toe the mark;
Gefahr ~ to sense a danger; **es in allen Knochen ~** to feel s. th. in one's bones;
deutlich zu ~ sein *(Tendenz)* to be strongly marked.
Spuren|beseitigung removal of traces; ~**nachweis** detection of traces; ~**sicherung** preserving traces; ~**vereinheitlichung** *(Bahn)* standardization of gauge.
Spürhund tracker dog, sniffler dog, trackhound, *(fig.)* beagle.
spurlos traceless, trackless;
~ verschwinden to vanish into thin air; **nicht ~ vorübergehen** to leave one's mark.
Spürnase nose, scent, flair;
~ für Skandalgeschichten haben to have a nose for scandal.
Spürsinn nose, scent;
über einen guten ~ verfügen to have a gift for nosing things out.

Spur|stange tie rod; ~**wechsel** lane straddling; ~**weite** *(Bahn)* gauge, gage *(US)*.
sputen, sich to hurry up, to get a hustle on *(US fam.)*.
Staat state, nation, country, commonwealth, power, crown *(Br.)*, *(Allgemeinheit)* the public, *(Fiskus)* fisc, *(Pomp)* display, pomp, show, trim, wampum *(US sl.)*, *(Regierung)* government;
in vollem ~ in full feather (wig); **vom ~ finanziert** state-financed;
abhängiger ~ dependent state; **kürzlich neu entstandene afrikanische ~en** recently emerging countries of Africa; **nicht anerkannter ~** unrecognized state; **nicht der Währungsschlange angehörender ~** nonsnake country; **anspruchstellender ~** claiming state; **antragstellender ~** applicant state; **assoziierter ~** associated country; **ausländischer ~** foreign country; **autarker ~** self-supporting nation; **autoritärer ~** authoritarian state; **befreundeter ~** friendly state (nation); **in Entstehung begriffener ~** inchoate state; **beitrittswilliger ~** applicant state; **auf freiheitlicher Gesellschaftsordnung beruhender ~** country based on a free social order; **beschützter ~** protected state, protectorate; **dicht besiedelter ~** densely populated country; **besteuernder ~** taxing state; **an Verrechnungsabkommen beteiligter ~** clearing country; **blockfreier ~** nonaligned nation; **führender ~** banner state; **geschädigter ~** injured state; **Wirtschaftshilfe gewährender ~** aid donor; **halbsouveräner ~** semi-sovereign state; **hochindustrialisierter ~** highly industrialized nation; **junger ~** infant state; **kriegführender ~** belligerent power; **mit kriegführender ~** cobelligerent; **unter Nahrungsmittelmangel leidender ~** food-short country; **um Auslieferung nachsuchender ~** requesting state; **neutraler ~** neutral [nation]; **von einer weißen Minderheit regierter ~** white-run country; **selbständiger ~** independent state; **souveräner ~** sovereign state, public person; **nach Rechts tendierender ~** right-wing country; **totalitärer ~** totalitarian (police) state; **unabhängiger ~** independency; **Vater ~** Whitehall *(Br.)*, Uncle Sam *(US)*; **vertragschließende ~en** contracting powers; **zollfreier ~** tariff-free country;
~ als Erbe last heir *(Br.)*; **~ mittlerer Größe** medium-ranking state; **~ mit aktiver Handelsbilanz** creditor nation; **~ mit passiver Handelsbilanz** debtor nation; **~ mit mehreren Rassen** multiracial country; **~ eines Staatenbundes** confederated state; **~ der dritten Welt** third-world country;
~ von einem Staatenbund abtrennen to detach a state from a confederation; **dem ~ anheimfallen** to revert to the state; **dem ~ dienen** to serve the country; **~ einem anderen einverleiben** to incorporate a state into another; **dem ~ gehören** to be government-owned, to be owned by the state; **~ mit etw. machen** to flaunt (parade) s. th.; **mit einem neuen Kleid ~ machen** to cut a dash with a new dress; **mit seinen Kleidern ~ machen** to make a parade of one's apparel; **einem ~ ein Mandat übertragen** to confer a mandate on a power; **vom ~ finanziert werden** to be financed by the government; **vom ~ konfisziert werden** to be forfeited by the state; **vom ~ unterhalten werden** to live at the common expense;
damit kannst du keinen ~ machen that is nothing to write home about it.
Staaten|bildung establishment of a new state; ~**bund** commonwealth of nations, federation, federacy, confederation (confederated) states, union; ~**bund bilden** to federalize.
staatenbündisch confederal.
Staaten|gemeinschaft commonwealth; ~**liga** league of states.
staatenlos stateless, without a nationality.
Staaten|loser stateless person; ~**losigkeit** statelessness; ~**nachfolge** succession of states (of a state).
staatlich national, governmental, state, public;
~ anerkannt state-registered; **~ besteuert** state-taxed; **~ finanziert** state-paid, bounty-fed; **~ gefördert** government-sponsored; **~ gelenkt** state-controlled; **~ unterstützt** state-aided, state- (bounty-) fed;
~ subventioniert sein to be subsidized by the state;
~e Aktiengesellschaft state corporation *(US)*; **~e Altersversorgung im Betrieb einführen** to integrate with the state pension system; **~e Anerkennung** state recognition; **unter ~er Aufsicht** state-controlled; **~er Ausbildungsvertrag** government training contract; **~e Ausfuhrversicherung** government export credit insurance; **~es Ausgabenprogramm** government spending program(me); **~es Ausschreibungsverfahren** government bidding process; **~ konzessionierte Bank** state bank; **~e Beihilfe** state aid, subsidy, subvention, state grant; **~es Beschaffungswesen** government procurement; **~e Beteiligung** government participation; **~ subventionierter Betrieb** government-subsidized enterprise, taxeater; **~e Bewirtschaftung** governmental

(state) planning; ~e **Dienstbarkeit** *(Völkerrecht)* state servitude; ~er **Dirigismus** planned economy; **in ~er Eigenschaft** in its governmental capacity; ~er **Eingriff** state interference; ~e **Einkaufsgesellschaft** state-buying organization; ~e **Einnahmen** public revenue; ~e **Einrichtungen** state (government) facilities; ~e **Entziehungsanstalt** state inebriate reformatory; ~e **Erlaubnis** government permission; ~e **Finanzhilfe** government aid; ~e **Finanzierung** government spending; ~e **Förderungsmaßnahmen** government promotion; ~e **Funktion** government function; ~e **Fürsorge** national *(Br.)* (public, *US*) assistance; ~es **Gehalt** government salary; ~es **Gemeinwesen** body politic; ~e **Genehmigung** government clearance; ~er **Gesundheitsdienst** state medicine, National Health Service *(Br.)*; ~er **Grundbesitz** crown *(Br.)* (state, *US*) lands; ~e **Handelsgesellschaft** state-trading company (enterprise); ~er **Hoheitsakt** act of state; ~e **Initiative unterstützen** to participate in a government drive; ~e **Intervention** state intervention; ~e **Kapitalsammelstelle** government depository; ~e **Kontrolle** government (state) control; ~e **Kreditaufnahme** government borrowing; ~e **Kredithilfe** government financial credit; ~e **Kreditmittel** state loans; ~e **Mittel** public funds; ~e **Monopolverwaltung** state monopoly; ~er **Personalaufwand** government payrolls; ~e **Planungsbehörde** state-planning agency; ~e **Preisüberwachung** price control (administration, *US*); ~er **Rechnungsprüfer** state auditor; ~es **Rechnungswesen** government accounts; ~e **Richtlinien** government guidelines (directives); ~er **Schiedsspruch** state award; ~er **Schlichter** government mediator; ~e **Schlichtung** state conciliation; ~e **Schlichtungsstelle** government conciliation board; ~e **Schulen** state-maintained schools; ~e **Stelle** government agency; **vom Bundestag bewilligte ~e Stelle** govermental instrumentality *(US)*; ~ **geprüfter Übersetzer** certified translator; ~es **Umschulungslager** government training center *(US)* (centre, *Br.*); ~es **Unternehmen** government-owned enterprise, government corporation; ~e **Unterstützung** state subsidy (aid, *US*), government assistance (support); ~es **Unterstützungsprogramm** state-aid program(me); ~er **Untersuchungsausschuß** government affairs committee; ~er **Verbrauch** government consumption; ~e **Versicherung** state insurance; ~e **Vollmachten** government powers; ~es **Vorratslager** buffer stock; ~ **gelenkte Wirtschaft** controlled (guided) economy; ~e **Wirtschaftslenkung** government economic manipulation, planned economy; ~ **geförderter Wohnungsbau** federally financed low-cost housing *(US)*; ~e **Zuschüsse** governmental grants (subsidy), grants-in-aids *(US)*; ~**em Zwang unterworfen** state-enforced.

Staats|abgaben government (state) taxes, fiscal dues; ~**abkommen** convention, treaty; ~**affäre** affair of state; ~**akt** government act, act of state; ~**akten** state papers; ~**aktion aus etw. machen** to make a fuss about it; ~**amt** government appointment, state office *(US)*.

Staatsangehöriger national, subject *(Br.)*, citizen *(US)*, national resident *(US)*;
ausländischer ~ foreign national; **britischer** ~ U.K. (British) resident, Crown subject *(Br.)*; **neutraler** ~ neutral;
~ **kraft Geburt** national-born subject (citizen, *US*).

Staatsangehörigkeit nationality, national status, citizenship *(US)*;
erworbene ~ acquired nationality; **durch Geburt erworbene** ~ nationality (citizenship, *US*) at birth; **ursprüngliche** ~ original nationality;
jem. die ~ **aberkennen** to deprive s. o. of his nationality, to denaturalize s. o.; **seine** ~ **aufgeben** to renounce one's citizenship *(Br.)* (nationality, *US*); **britische** ~ **beantragen** to register for greatness *(Br., sl.)*; **seine** ~ **beibehalten** to retain one's citizenship *(US)*; **britische** ~ **erlangen** to become great *(Br., sl.)*; ~ **erwerben** to acquire nationality (citizenship), to become naturalized; **für eine** ~ **optieren** to opt for a nationality; ~ **verleihen** to confer citizenship, to citizenize; ~ **verlieren** to become denationalized; **seine** ~ **wiedererwerben** to reacquire one's nationality.

Staatsangehörigkeits|ausweis certificate of citizenship (nationality, *US*); ~**beschränkungen für seine Mitglieder festsetzen** to place nationality restrictions on its members; ~**gesetz** nationality law *(Br.)*; ~**option** option of nationality; **mit ~rechten ausgestattet** patrial *(Br.)*; ~**urkunde** certificate of naturalization.

Staats|angelegenheit state (public) affair, public concern, matter (business) of state; ~**angelegenheiten führen** to manage the affairs of state; ~**angestellter** public (state, government, *US*) employee.

Staatsanleihe government *(US)* (public, *Br.*) bonds, public stocks, government stocks *(US)* (annuities) *(Br.)*, government papers, funds *(Br.)*, state securities *(US)*, public (state, government[al]) loan, federal funds *(US)*;
5%ige ~ national development bonds *(Br.)*; **sechsprozentige** ~ **von 1970** 6% Exchequer stocks *(Br.)*; **ausländische ~n** foreign government bonds; **britische ~n** treasury stocks *(Br.)*; **einmalige** ~ single loan; **fundierte (konsolidierte) ~n** consolidated annuities, funded debt (loan) *(Br.)*; **hochverzinsliche** ~ high-coupon stocks *(Br.)*; **langfristige** ~ long-term debt; **südamerikanische** ~ South Americans *(Br.)*;
Geld in ~ **anlegen** to invest money in funds *(Br.)*;
~**papiere** gilt-edged stocks *(Br.)*; ~**schein** consols certificate *(Br.)*; ~**verzeichnis führen** to keep a register of government stocks.

Staats||anstellung situation under government, government appointment (situation), public office (appointment); ~**anwalt** public prosecutor, prosecuting (State's, *US*) attorney, prosecuting counsel, district (circuit, county, public) attorney *(US)*, crown solicitor *(Br.)*, procurator fiscal *(Scotland)*, impectator, silk *(Br.)*; ~**anwaltschaft** Director of Public Prosecution *(Br.)*, crown office *(Br.)*.

staatsanwaltschaftliche Ermittlung criminal investigation.

Staats|anzeiger bulletin, gazette *(Br.)*, official gazette *(US)*, Federal Register *(US)*; ~**apparat** government (state) machinery; ~**apparat einsetzen** to use government muscles; ~**archiv** national archives, the Public Records, The Rolls, Public Record Office *(Br.)*; ~**aufgaben** governmental duties.

Staatsaufsicht government (state) supervision, state inspectorship, government control, state control;
unter ~ **stehen** to be state-controlled;
für bestimmte Zwecke gesetzlich vorgesehene ~ standby control;
Industriezweige unter ~ **stellen** to bring industries under state control.

Staats|aufsichtsbehörde supervisory authority; ~**auftrag** government order (contract, business); **fetten ~auftrag erhalten** to be awarded a juicy government contract; **an größeren ~aufträgen mitarbeiten** to work on a large public scale; **sich auf ~aufträge konzentrieren** to focus on the government market; **mit ~aufträgen beschäftigt sein** to hold government contracts.

Staatsausgaben expenses of the state, public spending, state spending, government outlay, expenditure of the state, national (government[al], state) expenditure;
~ **ausdehnen** to expand government spending;
~**kürzung** public spending cuts; ~**vorschlag** public expenditure estimate.

Staats|bahn state (government, *Br.*) railway; ~**bank** central bank, national bank *(US)*, Bank of England; ~**bankabrechnung** Fifth Teller *(US)*; ~**bankett** solemn state dinner; ~**bankpräsident** governor of the Central Bank, Federal Reserve Chairman *(US)*; ~**bankrott** national bankruptcy (insolvency); ~**bauten** public works; ~**beamter** government (state, public) officer, crown official *(Br.)*, civil servant *(Br.)*, civil (governmental) officer *(US)*, public servant, public functionary *(US)*, officeholder *(US)*, jobholder *(US)*; **festangestellter ~beamter** established civil servant *(US)*, officer de jure; **höherer ~beamter** senior civil servant *(Br.)*; ~**beamten ablösen** to displace a government official; ~**beamten entlassen** to remove a civil servant *(Br.)*; ~**beauftragter** public agent, appointee of the government, Royal Commissioner *(Br.)*; ~**bediensteter** civil officer *(US)*, government employee *(US)*, person holding office under Her Majesty *(Br.)*; **erweiterte ~befugnisse** state expansion; ~**begräbnis** state *(Br.)* (national, *US*) funeral; ~**behörde** authority, governmental agency; ~**beihilfe** governmental grant (assistance), state grant, grant-in-aid *(US)*; ~**besitz** government property, state property (ownership); **im ~besitz** state- (government-) owned; **in ~besitz überführen** to transfer to state ownership, to nationalize *(Br.)*; ~**besuch** state visit; ~**beteiligungen an Aktiengesellschaften** government equity shareholdings; ~**betrieb** public business (ownership), state (government-owned, government) enterprise (corporation), nationalized undertaking *(Br.)*, state-owned industry, government-operated plant, public (governmental) undertaking, government corporation, state-run company, publicly-owned enterprise (corporation, *US*); **nicht mit Finanzierungsaufgaben befaßter ~betrieb** nonfinancial public enterprise; ~**budget** national budget.

Staatsbürger national, subject *(Br.)*, citizen *(US)*;
~ **mit Wohnsitz im Ausland** nonresident citizen *(US)*;
letzter ~antrag second papers *(US)*; ~**kunde** civics *(US)*.

staatsbürgerlich civic, public, political;
~e Freiheit political liberty; **~e Pflichten** civil duties; **~e Rechte** civil rights.

Staatsbürger|rechte civil rights; **~schaft** citizenship *(US)*, nationality; **doppelte ~schaft** dual citizenship, intercitizenship; **j. der ~schaft verlustig erklären** to deprive s. o. of his nationality.

Staats|bürgschaft government guarantee; **~chef** head (chief) of a state; **~darlehen** public (government) loan; **~defizit** government's (budget) deficit; **~defizite mittels der Notenbank beseitigen** to finance government deficits by printing money; **~depositen** public deposits.

Staatsdienst public employment, government service, civil service *(Br.)*, officeholding *(US)*, public (state) service *(US)*; **höherer ~** higher grades of the civil service *(Br.)*;
in den ~ eintreten to become a civil servant *(Br.)*; **Qualifikation für den ~ erwerben** to qualify for a civil service position *(Br.)*; **im ~ angestellt sein** to be on civil service *(Br.)*; **sich auf den ~ vorbereiten** to train for public service *(US)*; **in den ~ übernommen werden** to become a civil servant *(Br.)*.

Staats|diplom national diploma, certificate; **~dokumente** state (government) papers; **~domäne** Royal Estate *(Br.)*, crown land *(Br.)*, public land *(US)*; **~druckerei** public printing, Her Majesty's Stationery Office *(Br.)*, Government Printing Office *(US)*.

staatseigener Betrieb state-owned enterprise.

Staatseigentum demesne of the state, public (state) domain, state (government, public) property (ownership, *US*), national property, internal wealth, property of state *(US)*;
im ~ government-owned, state- (public-) owned;
~ sein to belong to (be owned by) the state; **in ~ überführen** to transfer to state ownership *(US)*, to nationalize *(Br.)*.

Staats|eingriff in die Wirtschaft state interference; **durch unnötige ~eingriffe Schaden nehmen** to suffer from undue regulations; **~einkommen** public revenue, governmental income.

Staatseinkünfte national revenue *(US)*, inland revenue [receipts] *(Br.)*, state revenue, government revenue *(Br.)*, governmental income;
nicht aus Steuern herrührende ~ nontax revenue; **ordentliche ~** ordinary receipts *(US)*; **nicht verplante ~** uncommitted revenue;
Steuern und sonstige ~ general fund;
~ aus inländischen Steuern und Abgaben internal revenue *(US)*.

Staatseinmischung state interference.

Staatseinnahmen state (national, *US*, government, *Br.*) revenue;
~ und -ausgaben state's revenue and expenditure;
nicht aus Steuern herrührende ~ nontax revenue *(US)*;
~ in Tagespreisen ausdrücken to put revenue figures in current prices; **~ zu konstanten Preisen berechnen** to calculate revenue figures in constant prices.

Staats|einrichtung national institution, state (government) facilities; **~empfang** state reception, red carpet; **~empfang geben** to lay (roll) out the red carpet; **auf höchster Ebene getroffene ~entscheidung** top-level government decision; **~etat** national (fiscal) budget, estimates *(Br.)*; **~examen** state examination, *(Aufnahmeprüfung)* civil service examination *(Br.)*; **~fehlbetrag** government's (budget) deficit; **~feind** anarchist, enemy of the people, public enemy *(US)*.

staatsfeindlich anarchistic;
~e Umtriebe subversive activities.

Staats|finanzen finances [of a state], a country's finance, state (national, public) finance; **~finanzen in Ordnung bringen (sanieren)** to purge the finance of a country, to put the finances of a country on a healthy footing; **~finanzierung** government spending; **~finanzwirtschaft** governmental finance; **~flagge** national flag; **~fonds** national fund, government appropriation; **konsolidierter ~fonds** Excise Account *(Br.)*.

Staatsform form (system) of government, polity;
konstitutionelle ~ constitutional government; **monarchistische ~** monarchical government, monarchism; **republikanische ~** republican government;
~ ändern to alter the form of government.

Staats|forst national forest; **~führung** statecraft, statesmanship; **~funktionär** government functionary; **~garantie** government guarantee; **~gebäude** public building, premises owned by the Crown *(Br.)*; **~gebiet** national territory, territory of a state; **außerhalb amerikanischen ~gebiets** without the state *(US)*; **vorübergehendes ~gebilde** interim state; **~gefangener** prisoner of state, political (state) prisoner; **~gefängnis** state prison *(US)*, big school *(sl.)*; **~geheimnis** secret of state, state (official) secret; **~geheimnisse enthüllen** to betray the secrets of a government; **~gelder** state funds, public funds, public money; **durch ~gelder unterstützen** to subsidize; **~gemach** state apartment; **~gerichtshof** state security court; **~geschäfte** state affairs, official business; **~geschäfte führen** to carry on (hold the reigns of) government *(Br.)*; **~geschenke** government handout; **~gewalt** supreme (governmental) power; **~gläubiger** state (public) creditor; **~grenze** border, national boundary (border); **außerhalb der ~grenzen** out of the state; **~grenzen zementieren** to cement the territorial status; **~grundsatz** political maxim; **~gründung** formation of (establishment of a new) state; **~gut** royal demesne *(Br.)*, domain *(US)*; **~guthaben** state funds; **~haftung** government (state) liability; **~handelsländer** state-trading nations (countries).

Staatshaushalt public accounts, national (fiscal) budget, estimates *(Br.)*;
ausgeglichener ~ balanced budget; **außerordentlicher ~** extraordinary budget; **ordentlicher ~** government ordinary expenditure and revenue;
~ unter Vollbeschäftigungsbedingungen full employment budget;
~ einbringen to bring in the estimates *(Br.)*, to introduce the budget; **~ einhalten** to keep to the budget; **für den ~ verantwortlich sein** to run the nation's budget.

Staatshaushalts|führung public budgeting; **~gesetz** Appropriation Act *(Br.)*, revenue bill *(US)*; **~plan** state budget.

Staats|hilfe government help, state aid *(US)*, grant-in-aid *(US)*; **~hoheit** sovereignty; **~hoheitsgebiet** territorial property; **~interesse** interests of the state, national interests; **das ~interesse hinreichend gewährleisten** to be on balance expedient in the national interest; **~intervention** government intervention; **~interventionismus** social control of business, state interference; **~kapital** government capital; **~kapitalismus** state capitalism; **~karosse** state carriage (coach).

Staatskasse treasury, Consolidated Fund *(Br.)*, The Exchequer *(Br.)*, Federal Treasury *(US)*;
in die ~ eingezahlt covered into the treasury *(US)*;
Kosten der ~ aufbürden to award the costs against the state; **~ erschöpfen** to deplete the treasury.

Staats|kirche national church; **~kommissar** state commissioner; **~konkurs** national bankruptcy; **~konto** public account; **~kontrolle** government (state) control; **~konzern** state conglomerate; **~konzession** license, *(Bank)* charter; **auf ~kosten** at public expense, on government funds; **~kredit** government credit, public loan; **sich um einen ~kredit bemühen** to tender the government for a loan; **~kunde** politics; **~kunst** statesmanship, politics, statecraft; **~kutsche** state coach (carriage); **~ländereien** public lands (domain) *(US)*, government lands, crown land *(Br.)*; **~lasten** public burden; **~lenkung** government control; **~lieferant** contractor to the government (Crown, *Br.*); **~lotterie** state lottery.

Staatsmann statesman, politician;
aufgeschlossener ~ forward statesman; **erfahrener ~** elderly statesman; **führender ~** leading statesman; **hervorragender ~** eminent statesman; **an Bedeutung zunehmender ~** rising statesman;
~ der ersten Garnitur front-rank statesman.

staatsmännisch statesmanlike, political.

Staats|maschinerie machinery of government, government machinery, governmental machine; **~maxime** political maxim; **~mechanismus** mechanism of government; **erster ~minister** cabinet (government) minister, Minister (Secretary, *US*) of State; **~ministerium** ministry; **~mittel** state (public) funds, public moneys, Exchequer money *(Br.)*; **~monopol** government (state, national, fiscal) monopoly; **~notstand** national emergency, state of national emergency *(US)*; **~oberhaupt** chief head of state, *(Herrscher)* sovereign; **~obligationen** public stocks (securities), government bonds (obligations), government securities (funds, *Br.*); **~ordnung** system of government; **~organ** government organ (agency).

Staatspapiere government funds (bonds, *US*, stocks, *Br.*, papers, securities, *US*), public securities, public funds *(Br.)* (stocks), *(Renten)* annuities *(Br.)*, consols *(Br.)*;
in [fundierten] ~n angelegt funded;
ausgeloste ~ redeemed bonds; **fundierte ~** government (governmental, public, *Br.*) funds, federal funds *(US)*; **konsolidierte ~** consolidated stocks (funds, *Br.*), consols *(Br.)*, consolidated government bonds *(US)*; **unverzinsliche ~** dead weight; **in ausländischer Währung zahlbare ~** external bonds; **börsengängige ~ mit über 10jähriger Laufzeit** long-dated gilts *(Br.)*;

tausend Pfund in ~n anlegen to invest 1000 pounds in government stock (public fund); **aus ~n bestehen** to consist of consols *(Br.)*; **10.000 DM in ~n angelegt haben** to have DM 10.000 in the funds.
Staats|pension public (state) pension, public service pension *(US)*; **~pensionär** state pensioner; **~politik** state policy.
staatspolitisch national.
Staats|polizei state (secret, political, *US*) police, special branch *(Br.)*; **~präsident** president of a state; **~projekt** government project; **~prozeß** state trial; **~prüfung** civil service examination *(Br.)*; **~quote** state's share; **aus Gründen der ~räson** for reasons of state; **~rat** Privy Council *(Br.)*, Council of State *(US)*; **~rechnungswesen** governmental accounting; **~recht** public (political) law; **~regierung** national government; **~religion** official (established) religion; **~renten** government *(Br.)* (consolidated) annuities, stocks, consols *(Br.)*; **~rentner** state pensioner; **~ruder** helm of state; **~rundfunk** state radio, state-run radio; **~säckel** public purse; **~schatz** public purse (treasury), coffers of the state, state coffers, national treasury, The Exchequer *(Br.)*; **~schiff** public vessel; **~schiff leiten** to be at the helm of state.
Staatsschuld public (government) debt, Federal *(US)* (National) Debt;
aufgeschobene ~ deferred funds; **äußere ~** external national debt; **fundierte ~** stocks *(Br.)*, consols *(Br.)*, federal funds *(US)*, funded debt; **nicht fundierte ~** unfunded debt; **innere ~** internal national debt; **konsolidierte ~** consolidated funds; **kurzfristige ~** floating debt;
durch Vermögenswerte gedeckter Teil der ~ reproductive debt; **~ nicht anerkennen** to repudiate the national debt; **~ konsolidieren** to fund the floating debt;
~buch National Debt Register *(US)*, Great Ledger *(Br.)*.
Staatsschulden|aufnahme state borrowing; **~dienst** servicing of the national debt *(US)*, consolidated fund services *(Br.)*; **~register** Accountant's Department *(Br.)*; **~tilgung** redemption of the national debt; **~tilgungsfonds** sinking fund; **~verwaltung** administration (management) of the national debt, National Debt Commissioner *(Br.)*; **~verwaltung leiten** to manage the national debt.
Staatsschuld|schein state note; **~verschreibungen** state (public, *US*) bonds, governmental obligations *(US)*; **langfristige ~verschreibungen** long-term bonds (notes).
Staatsschutz state security.
Staatssekretär State (Permanent, *Br.*) Secretary, Undersecretary *(US)*, [etwa] assistant deputy minister;
parlamentarischer ~ parliamentary secretary, junior minister, parliamentary Secretary of State *(Br.)*; **ständiger ~** permanent secretary *(Br.)*; **stellvertretender ~** deputy secretary;
~ im Finanzministerium Financial Secretary to the Treasury *(Br.)*.
Staatssicherheit national (state) security;
~ gefährden to imperil national security.
Staatssicherheits|dienst state security organization (branch); **~gerichtshof** state security court; **~polizei** special branch *(Br.)*, state (political, *US*) police.
Staats|siegel broad seal; **großes ~siegel** Great Seal *(Br.)*; **durch das ~siegel beglaubigt werden** to pass the seal; **~sozialismus** state socialism; **~sozialist** state socialist; **~stellung** government situation (job), government appointment, officeholding *(US)*; **~stellung durch die Beeinflussung eines Kabinettsmitgliedes erhalten** to obtain a government position through interest with a cabinet minister; **hohe ~stellung innehaben** to be high up in the civil service *(Br.)*; **~steuer** state (national, imperial, *Br.*) tax; **~stipendium** state scholarship.
Staatsstreich coup d'état;
drohender ~ threat of a coup; **mißlungener ~** abortive coup; **~ durch das Heer** army coup.
Staats|streik public sector strike; **~subvention** subsidy; **rückzahlbare ~subvention** revolving fund *(US)*; **~symbol** national emblem; **~system** governmental system; **~telegramm** government telegram; **~titel** government securities, public funds; **~trauer** state (national) mourning.
staatstreu loyal.
Staats|umwälzung revolution, upheaval; **~unternehmen** government business (corporation), governmental undertaking, state corporation, state-owned enterprise, state-run company; **~unterstützung** state aid, subsidy, [export] bounty; **~urkunden** state (government) papers; **~verbrauch** government consumption; **~verbrechen** political crime; **~verfassung** state constitution; **~verleumdung** defamation of a state; **~vermögen** national domain, public (crown) property *(Br.)*; **~verschuldung** state indebtedness; **~verschuldung im Ausland** external (public) debt; **~versicherung** state insurance, *(Krankenversicherung)* National Health Insurance *(Br.)*; **~versicherungsfonds** state insurance fund.
Staatsvertrag contract between states, treaty, protocol, convention;
~ abschließen to sign a treaty; **~ aufkündigen** to denounce (withdraw from) a treaty; **einem ~ beitreten** to accede to a treaty.
Staats|verwaltung government, conduct of the state, civic administration; **~voranschlag** state budget, Estimates *(Br.)*; **~wappen** national coat of arms; **~werft** state shipyard, naval yard *(US)*; **~wesen** state, commonwealth, *(System)* political system; **~wirtschaft** *(Lehre)* public sector of the economy, political (national) economy.
staatswirtschaftlich economic.
Staats|wirtschaftslehre [applied] political economy **~wirtschaftsprinzip** statism; **~wissenschaft** political science, politics, policy; **~wissenschaftler** political scientist.
staatswissenschaftlich politico-scientific.
Staats|wohl public weal; **~zeitung** government newspaper; **~zimmer** state room; **~zugehörigkeit** nationality, citizenship; **~zugehörigkeitszeichen** *(Flugzeug)* nationality mark.
Staatszuschuß state (government, governmental) grant (subsidy), Treasury subsidy *(Br.)*, grant-in-aid *(US)*;
ohne ~ without government support;
~ zum Einkommen income supplement *(US)*;
~ erhalten to be subsidized, to receive a state grant.
Staatszuschüsse governmental subsidies, grants-in-aid *(US)*;
durch ~ unterstützt subsidized, bountyfed;
politisch bedingte ~ pork barrel *(US sl.)*;
~ für den Ankauf landwirtschaftlicher Betriebe farm subsidies *(Br.)*; **~ an die Kommunen** rate support grant *(Br.)*, *(bis 1959)* exchequer equalization grants *(Br.)*; **~ zur Sozialversicherung** Exchequer Supplements(Br.); **~ für Teilzeitbeschäftigte** temporary employment subsidy *(Br.)*;
durch ~ unterstützen to pay a subsidy.
Staatszuweisungen government allocations.
Stab staff, personnel, *(Minister)* suite, aide, *(Sachverständige)* panel, *(Stange)* pole, rod, bar;
diensttuender ~ duty team; **diplomatischer ~** diplomatic staff; **rückwärtiger ~** *(mil.)* rear echelon; **technischer ~** engineering staff (force);
~ von Lektoren staff of readers; **~ von tüchtigen Mitarbeitern** efficient staff; **~ von Sachverständigen** panel of experts;
~ über j. brechen to condemn s. o. utterly; **übersetzten ~ durchkämmen** to comb out a department;
~antenne rod antenna; **~batterie** torch battery *(Br.)*.
Stäbchen *(Zigarette)* fag *(sl.)*, pill *(US sl.)*, gasper *(Br., sl.)*.
Stab|diagramm bar chart; **unter der ~führung von** conducted by.
stabil stable, *(Kurs)* steady, *(solide)* solid, strong, *(im Wert)* standard;
~ gebaut solidly built; **nicht ~** unstable, slippery;
Preise ~ halten to keep prices on an even keel, to hold the line on prices; **~ werden** *(Markt)* to grow steady;
~e Arbeitsmarktlage employment stabilization; **~e Börse** steady market; **~e Preise** firm (stable) prices; **~e Regierung** stable government; **~e Währung** stable currency.
Stabilisator stabilizing device, stabilizer, *(Auto)* harmonic balance.
stabilisieren to stabilize, to peg;
sich ~ to become stable, to grow steady;
Preise ~ to stabilize (peg) prices.
stabilisiert, sich ~ haben to have found its feet again;
~e Preise pegged prices; **~e Währung** stabilized currency.
Stabilisierung stabilization;
~ der Beschäftigungslage employment stabilization; **~ der Bevölkerungszunahme** population stabilization; **~ der Konjunkur** economic stabilization; **~ der Rohstoffpreise** raw-material price stabilization; **~ der Währung** re-establishment of the currency; **~ der Wechselkurse** re-establishment of the currency, currency stabilization.
Stabilisierungs|anleihe stabilization loan; **~faktor** stabilization factor of the market; **~fonds** stabilization fund; **~gesetz** stabilization law; **~maßnahmen** stabilization measures; **antizyklisch wirkende ~mechanismen** built-in stabilizers; **~politik** stabilization (stabilizing) policy; **~programm** stabilization program(me).
Stabilität stability, *(Markt)* steadiness;
finanzielle ~ financial stability;
~ des Geldwertes monetary stability.

Stabilitätsabgabe stabilization levy.
stabilitätsorientiert stability-oriented.
Stabilitäts|politik, staatliche management of the economy; ~**vorsprung** stability advantage.
Stablinienprinzip line-and-staff principle.
Stabs|abteilung staff department (division), *(mil.)* staff, section; ~**angehöriger** staff member, staffer; ~**arbeit** staff work (activity); ~**aufgaben** staff duties; ~**befehl** headquarters order; ~**besprechung** staff conference (session); ~**funktionen** staff functions; ~**gruppe** staff group; **seine ~kräfte reduzieren** to trim one's staff; ~**leiter** staff manager; ~**mitglied** staff member, staffer; ~**offizier** field officer; ~**personal** front-office personnel; ~**personal ausländischer Vertretungen stellen** to staff overseas posts; ~**quartier** headquarters; ~**sekretariat** staff secretariat; ~**sitzung** staff session; ~**stellung** staff position.
Stachel, wider den ~ löcken to kick against the pricks; ~**draht** barbed wire; ~**drahtzaun** barbed-wire fence.
Stadium stage, phase;
neuestes ~ der auswärtigen Politik latest developments in foreign policy; **~ der Verhandlungen** stage of negotiations; **entscheidendes ~ bei Verhandlungen** turning point in the negotiations;
in ein kritisches ~ eintreten to reach a turning point; **in ein neues ~ treten** to enter upon a new phase.
Stadt town, city, *(Stadtgemeinde)* municipality;
am Rande der ~ on the outskirts of a city; **auf Kosten der ~** at city expenses; **in die ~** to town, up *(Br.)*; **in der ~ aufgewachsen** city- (town-) bred; **innerhalb einer ~** within the walls; **nicht in der ~** out of town;
aufstrebende ~ boom town; **mit vielen Sehenswürdigkeiten ausgestattete ~** town possessed of many objects of interest; **befestigte ~** walled town; **betriebseigene ~** company town *(US)*; **dicht bevölkerte ~** crowded town; **bombardierte ~** blitzed city; **gastgebende ~** host town; **an der Grenze gelegene ~** border town; **aus dem Boden geschossene ~** mushroom town, boom city (town); **kreisangehörige ~** [etwa] noncounty borough *(Br.)*, municipal borough *(Br.)*, urban district *(Br.)*; **kreisfreie ~** corporate town, county borough *(Br.)*, county town *(Br.)* (seat, *US*), administrative county *(Br.)*, burgh *(Scot.)*, incorporated city; **im Nahverkehrsbereich liegende ~** commuting town; **mittelgroße ~** medium-sized city; **offene ~** *(mil.)* open city, undefended (unfortified) town; **tote ~** dead city; **übervölkerte ~** overspill town; **verlassene ~** ghost city *(US)*; **gut verwaltete ~** well-managed town;
~ von einiger Bedeutung no mean city; **~ mit Grüngürtel** greenbelt town; **~ mit Marktrecht** market town *(Br.)*; **~ mit Selbstverwaltung** municipal town; **~ an der Siedlungsgrenze** front town *(US)*;
~ als Vertreter bearbeiten to canvass in (work) a town; **~ völlig einebnen** to raze a town to the ground; **~ eingemeinden** to incorporate a town; **~ einnehmen** to take a town; **in eine ~ einrücken** *(mil.)* to enter a city; **~ fest einschließen** *(mil.)* to invest a town closely; **belagerte ~ entsetzen** to relieve a besieged town; **Ort zur ~ erheben** to incorporate a town; **seine Einkäufe in der ~ erledigen** to do one's shopping in town; **~ auf der grünen Wiese errichten** to start a town from scratch; **in die ~ gehen** to go to town (downtown, *US*); **einer ~ politische Rechte gewähren** to enfranchise a city; **~ gründen** to found a new city; **j. in der ~ herumführen** to show s. o. around the town; **in die ~ hineinfahren** to enter the city limits; **~ kanalisieren** to improve the sanitation of a town; **~ wie seine Hosentasche kennen** to know a town inside out (like the back of one's hand); **sich um eine ~ konzentrieren** to center in a town; **bei der ~ angestellt sein** to be a municipal employee; **in der ganzen ~ bekannt sein** to be known all over the place; **aus einer ~ stammen** to be a native of a town; **aus derselben ~ stammen** to be from the same place; **ganze ~ auf den Kopf stellen** to paint the town red; **sich in ~ und Land verbreiten** to spread up and down the country; **~ mit Gas versorgen** to serve a town with gas; **~ in einen Trümmerhaufen verwandeln** to turn a town into a shambles; **von der ~ getragen werden** to be defrayable by the town; **nicht in der ~ wohnen** to live out of town;
~**abgaben** town dues, municipal taxes (rates).
stadtähnlich citied.
Stadt|anleihe municipal (corporation, *Br.*) loan, city bonds, municipal bonds (stock, *US*); ~**anzeiger** home-town newspaper; ~**archiv** town records; ~**asyl** district asylum; ~**ausdehnung** town extension, urban sprawl (growth); ~**ausgabe** city edition; ~**ausrufer** town crier; ~**ausschuß** city committee; ~**autobahn** urban freeway (motorway, *Br.*), urban expressway *(US)*; ~**bad** municipal swimming pool; ~**bahn** interurban railway, metropolitan railway *(Br.)*; ~**bank** municipal bank.
Stadtbau|amt surveyor's office, town planning department *(Br.)*; ~**ordnung** building (zoning, *US*) code; ~**platz** city lot *(US)*, town property; ~**rat** town surveyor.
Stadtbebauungs|plan development plan, zoning ordinance *(US)*; ~**wesen** town planning system.
Stadtbehörde city (municipal) authorities, municipal corporation *(Br.)*, municipality.
stadtbekannt known all over the place.
Stadt|bevölkerung urban population, cityfolk, townspeople, the town; ~**bewohner** city (town) dweller, inhabitant of a town, *(pl.)* cityfolk, townsfolk, townspeople; ~**bezirk** borough *(Br.)*, municipal district, town district, neighbo(u)rhood ward, township; ~**bibliothek** free (town) library; ~**bild** townscape, cityscape; ~**brief** local letter; ~**brücke** town bridge; ~**bücherei** public library; ~**bummel machen** to go to town (on a spree, *sl.*); ~**büro** city office.
Städtchen townslet.
Stadtdirektor city *(US)* (council, town, *US*) manager, town clerk, town commissioner, city's managing director *(US)*.
Städte|ausdehnung town extension, urban sprawl; ~**ballung** conurbation; ~**bau** city *(US)* (town, *Br.*) planning.
städtebauliche Entwicklung town (city) planning, urban development;
~ steuern to control urban growth.
Städte|bauministerium Ministry of Town and Country Planning *(Br.)*; ~**berater** urban counsellor; ~**erneuerung** urban renewal; ~**führer** city guide.
Stadteinteilung division of a city.
Städte|modernisierung urban modernization; ~**ordnung** Municipal Corporation Act *(Br.)*; ~**planer** town *(US)* (city *Br.*, urban) planner; ~**planung** city *(Br.)* (town, urban, *US*) planning; ~**programm** urban programm(me).
Städter city dweller, urban, townsman, *(pl.)* cityfolk, townspeople.
Stadterschließung town development, civic development.
Städte|sanierung slum clearance; ~**tag** congress of municipalities; ~**verkehr** *(Bus)* stage line; ~**verschmutzung** spoliation of towns; ~**wachstum** urban growth; ~**wesen** city (town, *US*, urban) planning.
Stadt|fahrt town driving; ~**filiale** city branch; ~**flucht** urban outmigration *(US)*; ~**form** cityscape; ~**gärtner** city gardener; ~**gas** town gas; ~**gas legen** to serve a town with gas; ~**gebiet** urban (built-up) area, corporation, city area, city zone *(US)*, township *(Br.)*; ~**gefängnis** town jail, town pound; ~**gegend** neigho(u)rhood; ~**gemeinde** township *(Br.)*, borough *(Br.)*, incorporated city, burgh *(Scot.)*, *(Verwaltungsbezirk)* municipality, municipal corporation; **Stadt zur ~gemeinde erheben** to incorporate a town; ~**gespräch** common talk, talk of the town, *(Telefon)* local call; ~**graben** moat; ~**grenze** municipal border, city boundaries (limits), corporate limit *(US)*; **innerhalb der ~grenze** within the limits of the city; ~**grenze erweitern** to extend the city boundaries; ~**grundstück** town property *(Br.)*; ~**guerilla** urban terrorists (guerilla); ~**guerillawesen** urban terrorism; ~**halle** city (guild, assembly, town, *Br.*) hall; ~**haus** burgage, town house; ~**inkassi** city (walk, *Br.*) collections; ~**inkassoabteilung** walk department *(Br.)*; ~**inspektor** city inspector.
städtisch municipal, urban, metropolitan, civic;
~ verwaltet werden to be municipally run;
~**e Abgaben** town dues, urban rates, municipal taxes; ~**es Amt** municipal office; ~**e Angelegenheiten** urban affairs; ~**er Angestellter** municipal (city, *US*) officer; ~**er Ausschuß** city commission; ~**es Ballungsgebiet** urban center *(US)* (centre, *Br.*); ~**er Beamter** municipal officer; ~**e Behörden** municipal authorities; ~**e Beleuchtung** urban lighting; ~**e Bevölkerung** urban population, townspeople, cityfolk; ~**en Charakter verleihen** to urbanize; ~**e Dienstbarkeit** urban servitude; ~**e Dienstleistungen** city services; ~**es Eigentum** municipal (city) property, property of a corporation; **im ~en Eigentum** municipally owned; ~**e Einrichtungen** city institutions, municipal services; ~**es Einzugsgebiet** shopping hinterland; ~**e Gasversorgung** town (city) gas; ~**es Gebäude** municipal building; ~**es Gefängnis** town jail (pound); ~**er Grundbesitz** city property (real estate); ~**es Grundstück** town lot *(US)* (property); ~**er Haushaltsplan** city budget; ~**er Konzessionär** city concessionaire; ~**es Krankenhaus** city hospital; ~**er Planungsausschuß** town planning *(Br.)* (zoning, *US*) committee; ~**e Probleme** civic problems; ~**e Reallast** municipal lien; ~**es Rechnungswesen** municipal accounting; ~**e Selbstverwal-**

tung municipalism; ~e **Sparkasse** municipal savings bank; ~er **Steuereinnehmer** town (city tax, *Br.*) collector; ~es **Steuerwesen** municipal taxation; ~e **Straßenbahn** urban tramway; ~e **Szenerie** urban landscape; ~e **Umlage** city levy; ~es **Unternehmen** municipal enterprise (undertaking), civil enterprise; ~e **Verkehrsbetriebe** city transport *(Br.)* (transportation, *US*); ~e **Verordnung** city regulation; ~e **Verwaltung** municipal government (authorities); ~e **Wählerversammlung** town meeting; ~e **Wasserversorgung** municipal water supply; ~e **Zahlungsunfähigkeit** municipal default; **für** ~e **Zwecke** for town purposes.

Stadt|jugendamt Childrens' Officer *(Br.)*, youth welfare center; ~**kämmerei** city tax collector *(US)*, treasurer's office *(Br.)*, town clerkship *(Br.)*; ~**kämmerer** municipal accountant (treasurer) *(Br.)*, city treasurer, chamberlain *(Scot.)*, city chamberlain *(US)*; ~**kern** center (heart) of the town, city core; ~**kind** townsman; ~**klatsch** talk of the town; ~**kleidung** town clothes, townwear; ~**koffer** attaché case; ~**kommandant** town mayor *(Br.)*; ~**kreis** town circle (circuit, district); ~**küche** catering department; ~**kunde** city customer; ~**lager** up-town warehouse; ~**leben** town life; ~**leute** cityfolk, townspeople; ~**mauer** town wall; ~**mitte** center *(US)* (centre, *Br.*) of the town, city [center], midtown, downtown *(US)*; ~**müll** town refuse; **in** ~**nähe** in proximity of a town; ~**netz** metropolitan railway system; ~**park** town (city) park; ~**parlament** town (city) council; ~**plan** town plan *(Br.)*, city map (plan); ~**planer** city planner; ~**planung** city *(US)* (town) planning; ~**planungsamt** town planning department; ~**polizei** metropolitan police.

Stadtrand outskirts of a town, suburbia;
am ~ **wohnen** to skirt;
~**gebiet** suburban [housing] estate, environmental area, outer fringe of a city; ~**geschäft** out-of-town store; ~**siedlung** outer suburb, ribbon (string) development *(Br.)*, suburban zoning housing *(US)*, housing estate; ~**vorort** outer suburb.

Stadtrat municipal (town, local, city) council, borough council *(Br.)*, corporate authority, board of eldermen *(Br.)*, common council *(London)*, *(Mitglied)* city council *(US)*, common (city, *US*) councilman, burgess, borough councillor *(Br.)*, alderman *(Br.)*;
paralysierter ~ deadlocked council;
im ~ **sitzen** to chair the city council *(US)*.

Stadtrats|ausschuß select council *(US)*; ~**mitglied** burgess, common councilman, town (borough, *Br.*) councillor, alderman *(Br.)*, selectman *(US)*; ~**mitglieder** city fathers, town officers; ~**mitglied sein** to chair the council; ~**sitzung** council (parish, *Br.*, town, *US*) meeting; ~**wahlen** city elections.

Stadt|rechte privileges granted a town; **einer Stadt das** ~**recht verleihen** to incorporate a community; ~**region** city region; ~**reinigungsamt** cleansing department; ~**reisender** city salesman, town traveller *(Br.)*; ~**richtungsweiser** town circuit *(US)*; ~**rundfahrt** circuit of a city, sight-seeing tour; **auf** ~**rundfahrt** on the town; ~**säckel** borough fund; ~**sanierung** slum clearance, urban development; ~**sanierungsplan** slum clearance plan; ~**schlüssel ausliefern** to give up the keys of a city; ~**schulamt** board of the town; ~**silhouette** cityscape; ~**sparkasse** municipal savings bank; **autonomer** ~**staat** city state; ~**steueramt** city tax collector *(US)*, rate collector's office; ~**streicher** street loafer; ~**syndikus** city clerk (attorney, *US*), city recorder.

Stadtteil part of a town, quarter, district, ward, neighbo(u)rhood center *(US)* (centre, *Br.*);
im oberen ~ uptown; **in mehreren** ~**en gelegen** interborough;
zu eng bebauter ~ overbuilt part of a town; **belebter** ~ busy section; **übel beleumdeter** ~ low part of a town;
~ **mit Geschwindigkeitsbeschränkung** restricted area.

Stadt|telegramm local telegram; ~**tor** city port; ~**tore bewachen** to keep the gates of a town; ~**väter** city fathers *(coll.)*; ~**verkehr** city (town) traffic, municipal transit; ~**verkehrsplaner** city traffic planner; ~**verordnetenversammlung** town council, parish (town) meeting, board of aldermen *(Br.)*, court of aldermen *(Br.)*; ~**verordneter** town councillor *(Br.)*, city *(US)* (common) councilman, bailie *(Scotland)*, councilman *(US)*, municipal councillor *(Br.)*; ~**verordnung** city regulation; ~**vertreter** town agent, city salesman; ~**vertretung** town agency; ~**verwaltung** city government (authorities), municipal administration, corporation *(Br.)*, municipal corporation (government) *(US)*, urban administration, city cabinet; **von einem Ausschuß ausgeübte** ~**verwaltung** commission plan *(US)*; ~**verwaltung leiten** to manage a town; ~**viertel** part of a town, quarter, district, ward, neighbo(u)rhood, section *(US)*; **reiches** ~**viertel** wealthy neighbo(u)rhood, silk-stocking district *(US)*; **vornehmes** ~**viertel** westend; ~**volk** urban nation; ~**wald** town forest; ~**wappen** city arms (crest); ~**werke** municipal undertakings; ~**wohnung** town residence (house, apartment), city apartment *(US)*; ~**zentrum** urban (town, city) center *(US)* (centre, *Br.*), center *(US)* (centre, *Br.*) of the town; **seinen Laden ins** ~**zentrum verlegen** to move one's store uptown; ~**zweigstelle** sub-branch.

Staffel scale, bracket, *(Flugzeuge)* squadron, *(Steuern)* taper, *(mil.)* echelon;
~**anleihe** graduated-interest loan; ~**auszug** equated abstract of account; ~**begünstigung** *(Steuer)* taper relief; ~**besteuerung** progressive (graduated) taxation; ~**bestimmungen** *(Steuer)* tapering provisions; ~**bild** *(Statistik)* histogram; ~**flug** staggered flight, echelon; **im** ~**flug fliegen** to fly in echelon.

staffelförmig|anordnen to echelon; ~ **aufgestellt** in echelon.

Staffel|gebühren differential duties; ~**lohn** differential wage, *(Leistungslohn)* payment by results, incentive pay (wage), efficiency pay *(US)*; ~**methode** scaling method.

staffeln to scale, *(Arbeitszeit)* to stagger, *(Löhne, Steuern)* to graduate, to differentiate, *(mil.)* to echelon;
Löhne nach der Leistung ~ to pay by results.

Staffel|preis sliding-scale (graduated, differential) price; ~**rechnung** *(Zinsen)* equated interest account; ~**sätze** progressive rates; ~**skonto** adjusted discount; ~**steuer** graduate (progressive) tax; ~**tarif** sliding scale, flexible (differential, graduated) tariff, *(Einkommensteuer)* tapering rate, *(Anzeigenwesen)* rate scale *(US)*, *(Löhne)* sliding scale of wages; **tageszeitlicher** ~**tarif** *(el.)* time-of-day tariff *(Br.)*.

Staffelung graduation, grading, progression, differentiation, *(mil.)* echelon, *(Steuern)* progression;
~ **der Arbeitszeit** staggering of hours; **jahreszeitliche** ~ **von Preisen** seasonal graduation of prices; ~ **der Steuersätze** progressive rates of taxation, tapering of rates; ~ **des Tarifs** scale graduation.

Staffelvergünstigung *(Steuern)* taper relief.

staffelweise on a sliding scale, in echelons.

Staffel|zinsen sliding rate of interest, compensatory (compound, graduated, equated) interest; ~**zinsrechnung** equated calculation of interest.

Stagnation *(Markt)* stagnation, stagnancy, standstill, inactivity, sluggishness;
wirtschaftliche ~ lull in business, economic stagnation.

Stagnations|erscheinungen symptoms of stagnation; ~**zeit** period of stagnation.

stagnieren to stagnate, to be at a standstill (stagnant), to be (remain) stationary.

stagnierend stagnant, sluggish, dull, slackening;
~**er Markt** stagnant (dull, trading, *US*) market; ~**e Nachfrage** slackening demand.

Stahl, so hart wie as hard as adamant;
rostfreier ~ stainless steel;
~ **abschrecken** to quench steel;
~**aktien** steel shares *(Br.)* (stocks, *US*); ~**arbeiter** steel worker; ~**arbeitergewerkschaft** steelworkers union; ~**band für Verpackungskisten** box strapping; ~**baumonteur** ironworker; ~**bauweise** skeleton construction; ~**bedarf** steel demand; ~**beton** armo(u)red (reinforced, ferro) concrete; ~**block** ingot of steel; ~**drahtgewebe** fabric, reinforcement of concrete; ~**einfuhrstrom** steel import surge; ~**einfuhrunternehmer** steel importer; **totales** ~**einfuhrverbot** banning of all steel imports; ~**erzeugung** steel production; ~**expansion** steel expansion; ~**fabrikant** steelmaker.

Stahlfach strongbox, safe deposit box (vault, *US*);
~ **mieten** to rent a safe;
~**abteilung** safe-deposit department; ~**aufbewahrung** safe custody, safe deposit keeping *(US)*; ~**mann** steel technician; ~**miete** safe-deposit facilities *(US)*, safe custody facilities *(Br.)*; ~**verwahrungsgesellschaft** safe deposit company *(Br.)*.

Stahl|firma steelmaker, steel producer; ~**gerippe** steel skeleton; ~**großhandel** steel service center *(US)*; ~**gürtelreifen** steel radial tire.

stahlhart as hard as adamant.

Stahl|helm steel helmet; ~**herstellungsverfahren** process of steelmaking; ~**hochstraße** fly-over; ~**hütte** steel foundry; ~**industrie** steel industry, *(Börse)* steel group; ~**kammer** steel vault, safe deposit vault *(US)*, strong room; ~**kammeraufbewahrung** safe-deposit keeping; ~**kapazität** steelmaking capacity; ~**karosserie** steel automobile body; ~**kartell** steel cartel; ~**kassette** strongbox; ~**knappheit** steel shortage; ~**konjunktur** steel boom; ~**konsortium** steel consortium; ~**konstruktion** steel frame (work); ~**kontingent** steel quota; ~**konzern** steel concern (trust); **mit der ~krise fertig werden** to ride out the steel crisis; **~lagerhaus** steel-service center *(US)*; **~lieferungen** steel supplies (shipments); **~mantelrohr** steel-lined pipe; **~platte** steel plate; **~preisgefüge** steel price structure; **~produktion** steel output (production); **~produzent** steel producer (manufacturer); **~rezession** steel recession; **~rohr** tubular steel; **~rohrmöbel** tubular-steel furniture; **~schrank** steel cabinet, safe, safety vault; **feuerfester ~schrank** fire-resisting steel cabinet; **~skelett** steel skeleton; **~sonde** steel probe; **~stich** steel engraving; **~tresor** strong room; **~trust** steel trust.

stahlverarbeitende Industrie steel-using industry.

Stahl|verbrauch steel consumption; **~verbraucher** steel user, user of steel; **~weiterverarbeitung** steel processing; **~werk** steel works (mill, plant); **~werte** steel shares (stock, *US*).

Staketenzaun paling.

Stall stall, stable, cote, barn;
~ von Kindern hordes of children;
~ ausmisten *(fig.)* to make a clean sweep of it;
~bursche groom.

Ställe, umgebaute converted mews.

Stall|fütterung im Winter wintering; **~gefährte** companion; **~knecht** groom, ostler.

Stamm trunk, *(Abstammung)* stock, lineage, family, house clan, *(Belegschaft)* permanent staff, *(Grundstock)* cadre, skeleton, stock, *(feste Kundschaft)* steady customers, custom, goodwill, *(mil.)* skeleton, cadre, *(Volk)* tribe, race;
aus königlichem ~ of royal blood;
männlicher ~ male line;
~ von Facharbeitern permanent staff of skilled workers;
Holz auf dem ~ kaufen to buy timber standing; **der Letzte seines ~es sein** to be the last of one's family.

Stammaktie ordinary share *(Br.)* (stock, *US*), common share *(Br.)* (stock, *US*), common stock certificate *(US)*, senior share *(US)*, senior stock *(US)*;
~n ordinaries *(Br.)*, equity shares *(Br.)*, equities *(Br.)*; **dividendenberechtigte ~n** consent stocks; **stimmrechtslose ~n** nonvoting ordinary shares *(Br.)*;
~n mit großem Anteil an Vorzugsaktien leverage stock.

Stamm|aktionär original subscriber, ordinary shareholder *(Br.)* (stockholder, *US*), common stockholder *(US)*; **~anteil** common share *(Br.)* (stock, *US*), equity share; **~arbeiter** permanent labo(u)rer, regular worker; **~auflage** *(Zeitung)* guaranteed minimum circulation; **~bank** parent bank; **~baum** descent, family tree, *(Materialbegleitschein)* flowsheet; **genealogischer ~baum** genealogical table (tree), family tree, pedigree; **seinen ~baum zurückverfolgen** to retrace one's family; **~belegschaft** regular workforce, backbone, permanent staff; **~besatzung** *(Schiff)* nucleus crew; **~betrieb** parent plant; **~buch** album, family register, *(Züchter)* herdbook, studbook; **mein ~café** my usual café; **~dividende** ordinary dividend.

Stämme, nach ~n *(Erbrecht)* per stirpes, stipital;
wandernde ~ errant tribes.

Stamm|einheit *(mil.)* parent unit; **~einlage** original share, contribution to capital, capital contribution, initial contribution.

stammeln to stammer, to falter, to stutter;
Entschuldigung ~ to blunder out an apology, to falter forth an excuse.

stammen|von to descend (originate, stem, spring, proceed) from;
aus A ~ to hail from A; **aus einer guten Familie ~** to come from a good family, to spring from a noble stock; **von der Großmutter ~** to belong to the grandmother; **aus dem Krieg ~** to date from the war; **aus einem Lande ~** to originate from a country; **vom Lande ~** to hail from the country; **aus der Land- und Forstwirtschaft ~** *(Einkünfte)* to issue out of land; **aus dem Lateinischen ~** to be derived from Latin; **aus einer zuverlässigen Quelle ~** to come from a reliable source; **aus einfachen Verhältnissen ~** to stem from humble stock.

Stammentschädigung basic compensation.

Stammes|angehöriger tribesman; **~anhänger** tribal follower; **~bewußtsein** family pride; **~bräuche** tribal customs; **~fehde** tribal strife; **~gebiet** tribal homeland; **~häuptling** tribal chief; **~recht** tribal law; **~streitigkeiten** tribal disputes.

Stamm|firma parent firm; **~folge** line of descent; **~gast** regular (standing, steady) customer, patron, patronizer, habitué; **~gast in einem Hotel sein** to patronize a hotel; **~gast in einem Lokal sein** to frequent a public house; **~gericht** regular dish; **~geschäft** parent store; **~gut** family estate, entail; **~haus** parent company (establishment, concern, corporation, enterprise), parent store, principal establishment (house), head office, headquarters.

stämmiger Bursche sturdy fellow.

Stammkapital *(Aktiengesellschaft)* ordinary share capital *(Br.)*, equity share capital, common equity, joint stock, *(Bank)* fund *(Br.)*, *(Grundkapital)* authorized (nominal, share) capital *(Br.)*, capital stock *(US)*, original capital *(US)*, corpus;
mit kleinem (geringem) ~ in a small way;
dividendenberechtigtes ~ consent stock;
zu hohen Nennwert für das ~ angeben to overcapitalize;
~konto common stock account *(US)*.

Stamm|karte master card; **~kneipe** favo(u)rite pub *(Br.)*; **~kompanie** *(mil.)* skeleton, home battalion; **~konto** head-office account; **~kunde** regular (registered, standing, steady, local) customer, regular patron; **einem ~kunden Lagerreste aufschwätzen** to palm off old stock on a client; **~kundenrabatt** patronage discount; **~kundschaft** steady customers, patronage, goodwill; **~leitung** *(Telefon)* trunk line; **~leserschaft** steady readership; **~lieferant** regular supplier; **~miete** charter money, *(Theater)* subscription; **~mitglied** charter member; **~organ** parent body; **~organisation** cadre; **~patent** pioneer (basic, original) patent; **~personal** permanent (regular) staff, backbone, skeleton [crew], *(Schiff)* nucleus crew; **~platz** prescriptive place, *(Theater)* subscribed seat; **~rolle** roll, register, *(mil.)* muster (nominal) roll; **in die ~rolle eingetragen** *(mil.)* on the strength; **in die ~rolle eintragen** to put on the roll; **~rollenauszug** registration card; **~schloß** ancestral castle; **~sitz** family seat, *(Theater)* subscribed seat; **~tafel** table of descent.

Stammtisch the regulars' table in a pub;
~politiker armchair politician, tinker, dabbler in politics;
~runde group of regulars; **~stratege** armchair strategist.

Stamm|truppenteil parent unit; **~vater** stirpes, ancestor, parent; **~vermögen** capital stock, original assets; **~werk** parent establishment (plant); **~wert** original value; **~wort** stem.

Stampfbeton rammed concrete.

Stampfen *(Schiff)* labo(u)r, pitching, pounding.

stampfen *(Schiff)* to labo(u)r, to heave and set, to pitch, to pound;
aus dem Boden ~ to conjure a rabbit out of a hat, to throw up;
vor Wut auf den Boden ~ to stamp with rage.

Stand rank, order, *(Barometer)* reading, *(Gewerbe)* calling, profession, vocation, *(Klasse)* class, estate, social standing, rank, station, condition, *(Konto)* balance, *(Kurs)* rate, quotation, level, *(Lage)* situation, status, *(Marktplatz)* stand, booth, stall *(Br.)*, *(Stellung)* position, standing, *(Taxi)* taxi stand, *(Wasser)* level, *(Zeitungskiosk)* kiosk, newsstand *(US)*, *(Zustand)* state, condition;
auf dem höchsten ~ at the highest level; **auf dem neuesten ~** up to date; **aus niederem ~e** lowborn; **beim jetzigen ~ der Dinge** in the present state of affairs, as things are at the moment; **nach dem neuesten ~** according to the latest news; **~ vom ...** position as per ...;
allerhöchster ~ *(Kurse)* all-time high; **bürgerlicher ~** middle class, commoners; **der Dritte ~** *(historisch)* the commons, the Third Estate; **höchster ~** highest (peak) level; **jetziger ~** present position; **lediger ~** single state; **niedrigster (tiefster) ~** bottom, lowest (bargain, *US*) level, hardpan; **der Vierte ~** *(fam. für den Journalismus)* The Fourth Estate;
~ am 1. 1. 1981 balance as (at, *US*) Jan. 1, 1981; **~ der Aktiven und Passiven** statement of assets and liabilities *(US)*; **~ der Arbeiter** the working classes; **derzeitiger ~ der Aufträge** reserve of unfilled orders; **gegenwärtiger ~ des Außenhandels** current foreign-trade figure; **~ des Barometers** barometer reading; **~ oder Beruf** profession or business; **~ der Dinge** state (position) of affairs; **~ am Jahresende** financial position at the end of the year; **~ der Technik** level of technology, *(Patentrecht)* state of the art, prior art; **hochentwickelter ~ der Technik** sophistication; **~ des Verfahrens** stage of proceedings; **~ der Verhandlungen** stage of negotiations; **erhöhter ~ des Verkehrsschutzmannes** traffic policeman's raised platform; **~ im Vorjahr** year-ago level;
dem geistlichen ~ angehören to be in holy orders; **über den ~ der Angelegenheit berichten** to report progress; **Konten auf den neuesten ~ bringen** to bring accounts up to date, to update accounts; **Liste auf den neuesten ~ bringen** to bring a list up to date; **höchsten ~ erreichen** to reach the peak; **niedrigsten ~ erreichen** *(Kurse)* to touch (hit) the bottom; **festen ~ haben** to have a firm foothold; **keinen leichten ~ haben** to have no easy time of it; **bei jem. keinen leichten ~ haben** to be in bad odo(u)r with s. o.; **mit jem. einen schweren ~ haben** to have a great deal of trouble with s. o.; **~ auf dem Jahrmarkt haben** to have a booth at the fair; **schweren ~ gegen die Konkurrenz haben** to meet with stiff competition; **mit dem neuesten ~ der technischen**

Entwicklung Schritt halten to be in keeping with the latest technological developments; **unter seinem ~ heiraten** to marry below one's station; **seinem ~ gemäß leben** to live up to one's reputation; **ledigen ~es sein** to be unmarried; **j. in den ~ setzen** to enable s. o.; **in den vorherigen ~ setzen** to restore the state of things; **in den heiligen ~ der Ehe treten** to be joined in holy matrimony; **hinter dem ~ des Vorjahres zurückbleiben** to remain below year-before levels.

Standard standard, mark, *(Währung)* monetary standard; **~abmachung** regular arrangement; **~abweichung** standard deviation, *(Statistik)* variance; **~aktien** representative shares (stocks, *US*), gilt-edged shares *(Br.)*, barometer (representative) stocks *(US)*, blue chips *(US)*; **~artikel** standard line; **~ausführung** standard make, standard model (design), conventional type, *(Auto)* standard car, stock model *(US)*; **~ausgabe** standard edition; **~ausrüstung** standard equipment; **~aussprache** standard of pronunciation; **~bevölkerung** standard population; **~brief** standard letter; **~briefdrucksachen** surface printed papers *(Br.)*; **~briefe** *(Post)* surface letters *(Br.)*; **~bücherzettel** standard book slip; **~drucksachengebühr** surface mail printed paper full rate *(Br.)*; **~erzeugnis** standard item, standardized product; **~fabrikat** *(Auto)* standard car, stock model *(US)*; **~fehler** *(Statistik)* standard error; **~form** standard form; **~format** standardized sheet size, *(Anzeige)* standard unit (size); **~gewicht** agreement weight; **~größe** stock (standard) size; **internationale ~größe** standard international size; **~herstellungskosten** standard cost.

standardisieren to standardize.

Standardisierung standardization.

Standard|klauseln standard clauses (conditions); **~kopie** *(Film)* standard print; **~kosten** standard (specification, predicted) costs; **optimale ~kosten** ideal standards; **~kostenrechnung** standard cost accounting; **~lohn** standard rates; **~lohnsatz** regular amount of pay rate; **~modelle der Autoindustrie** car standards; **~muster** standard pattern; **~normstempel** kite mark *(Br.)*; **~preis** standard price; **~qualität** standard quality, stock lines; **~satz** standard rate; **~sendungen** surface mail *(Br.)*; **~sprache** *(Datenverarbeitung)* machine language; **~type** *(Auto)* conventional type, standard car, stock model *(US)*; **~vertrag** standard form contract; **~ware** staple articles, uniform quality; **~werbeprogramm** *(Rundfunk)* open-end transcription, standard media rates; **~werk** standard work; **~wert** standard value; **~werte** established shares, gilt-edged shares *(Br.)*, glamor stocks *(US)*, glamors *(US)*, representative (standard) stocks *(US)*, blue chips *(US)*; **~werte für die Ermittlung der Markttendenz** barometer stocks *(US)*.

Standarte standard, banner.

Standartenträger standard bearer.

Stand|bild statue; **~bremse** parking brake.

Stände, höhere higher orders; **privilegierte ~** privileged classes.

Stander *(Auto)* banner, pennant, burgee;
~ führen to carry a banner.

Ständer rack, *(Bücher)* bookstand, bookrack, *(Werbung)* prop, bracket.

Standesamt [General] Register Office *(Br.)*, vital statistics office *(US)*, marriage licence bureau *(US)*.

standesamtlich, sich ~ trauen lassen to be married at a registry (registrar's office, *Br.*);
~ geschlossene Ehe civil marriage; **~e Trauung** civil marriage.

Standesamts|bezirk registry district; **~register** register of births, marriages and deaths *(Br.)*; **~wesen** vital statistics *(US)*.

Standesbeamter registrar *(Br.)*, registrar of vital statistics *(US)*;
stellvertretender ~ deputy registrar;
~ für Eheschließungen marriage registrar.

standesbewußt class-conscious.

Standes|bewußtsein class consciousness, pride of rank; **~bezeichnung** social rank; **~erhebung** elevation; **~ethik** professional morals; **~gefühl** pride of rank.

standesgemäß according to one's station in life;
~ leben to live up to one's reputation;
~es Verhalten ethical behavio(u)r.

Standes|genosse equal, coequal, compeer; **~kennzeichen** status symbol; **~neid** jealousy of rank; **~ordnung** code of ethics; **ärztliche ~ordnung** medical code; **~person** person of rank, notability, personage; **~person sein** to be a person of [high] rank; **~pflichten** *(Anwalt)* legal ethics, etiquette of the bar; **~pflichten eines Berufs** professioanl duties (ethics), ethics (ethical standards) of a profession; **~pflichten eines Prüfers** accountant's responsibility; **~regeln** etiquette of the profession, professional etiquette, canons of professional ethics; **~sprache** jargon.

Ständestaat corporative state.

Standes|unterschied class distinction; **~vereinigung** professional association; **~vergehen** misconduct, malpractice; **~vorurteil** class prejudice.

standeswidrig unethical, unprofessional;
~es Verhalten unethical conduct, malpractice, misconduct, *(Anwalt)* conduct discreditable to a barrister.

Standeswidrigkeit unethical conduct, malpractice.

Stände|tag diet; **~versammlung** *(historisch)* diet; **~vertretung** corporative representation.

Stand|festigkeit staying power; **~foto** still, movie film clip; **~gebühren** market dues; **~geld** toll, stallage *(Br.)*, stall money (rent), *(Auto)* garage fee, *(Eisenbahn)* demurrage [charges].

Standgericht *(mil.)* summary court martial;
vor ein ~ stellen to try by martial law.

Standgestaltung stand design.

standhaft firm, unshaken.

standhalten to maintain (hold) one's ground;
einer Belagerung ~ to hold out against a siege; **jeder Belastung ~** *(Brücke)* to hold any load; **Belastungen des modernen Lebens nicht ~** to suffer from the strain of modern life; **dem Feinde ~** to withstand the enemy; **einer näheren Untersuchung nicht ~** not to bear closer scrutiny.

ständig constant, regular, standing, permanent, steady, daily;
~ zunehmen to be steadily increasing;
~e Adresse permanent address; **in ~er Angst leben** to live in constant fear; **~er Aufenthaltsort** fixed place of abode, permanent abode; **~er Ausschuß** standing (permanent) committee; **~er Begleiter** running mate, appanage; **~er Beirat** permanent advisory board; **~e Bemühungen** sustained efforts; **in ~er Bereitschaft sein** to lie ready; **~er Beruf** regular occupation; **~es Büro** permanent office; **~es Einkommen** fixed (regular) income.

Ständig|er Internationaler Gerichtshof Permanent Court of Justice; **~e Kommission zur Sicherung der Luftfahrt** Permanent Commission for the Safety of Air Navigation.

ständig|er Korrespondent resident correspondent; **~er Lärm** constant noise; **~es Mitglied** permanent member; **~e Nachfrage** steady demand; **~e Niederschläge** continual rain; **~es Organ** permanent body; **~es Personal** regular (permanent) staff; **~er Produktionsanstieg** steady increase of production; **~e Rechtsprechung** established practice.

Ständiger Schiedsgerichtshof Permanent Court of Justice.

ständig|er, in ~er Verbindung sein (stehen) to be in close touch, to communicate regularly; **~e Versammlung** permanent assembly; **~er Vertreter** permanent representative, regular agent; **~er Wohnsitz** permanent residence (abode); **~e Zunahme** steady increase.

Stand|inhaber stall holder; **~licht** *(Auto)* parking light[s]; **~linie** *(Landvermessung)* base; **~miete** *(Messe)* space rental; **~motor** stationary engine.

Standort location, fixed locality, *(Flugzeug, Schiff)* position, fix, *(mil.)* post, garrison, headquarters, *(Radar)* plot;
günstiger ~ vantage point, desirable location; **ungünstiger ~** ineligible location;
~ einer Industrie site (location) of an industry;
seinen ~ angeben to indicate one's position; **~ eines Flugzeuges anpeilen** to pinpoint the location of an airplane; **~ für eine Fabrik auswählen** to locate a factory; **~ bestimmen** *(Schiff)* to fix the position; **günstigen ~ haben** to be in a desirable (pleasant) location; **seinen ~ in A haben** to be stationed in A;
~ältester, ~kommandant station (garrison) commander; **~analyse** location analysis; **~bedingungen** local conditions; **~belegenheit** location of business assets; **~bestimmung** *(Industrie)* industrial development certificate *(Br.)*, *(Schiff)* position finding; **~bestimmungsgerät** direction finder; **~faktor** location factor *(US)*.

standortgebundene Industrie foot-loose industry.

Standortgunst locational advantage.

Standort|katalog *(Bibliothek)* shelf list; **gute ~lage für neue Fabriken** suitable location for new factories; **~lazarett** post hospital, station hospital *(US)*; **~meldung** *(Flugzeug)* position report; **~modell** location model; **~nachteile** site disadvantages; **~nummer** *(Bibliothek)* call number *(US)*; **~politik** industrial location policy, *(EG)* regional economic policy; **~präferenz** location preference; **~verlegung eines Betriebes** relocation of an industry; **~verzeichnis** site list; **~vorteil** locational advantage; **~wahl** locational choice.

Stand|pauke dressing-down, telling-off, talking-to, yaw *(sl.)*; **jem. eine ~pauke halten** to give s. o. a talking-to, to read the Riot Act to s. o.; **~platz** *(Taxi)* stand, taxi rank.

Standpunkt standpoint, side, stand, stance, ground, point of view, position, outlook;
vom ~ des Gesetzes aus in the eyes of the law; **vom wissenschaftlichen ~ aus** from a scientific point of view; **banktechnischer ~** banking point of view; **politischer ~** platform; **überwundener ~** exploded idea;
~ des Arbeitnehmers employee attitude;
seinen ~ vollkommen ändern to make an aboutface; **seinen ~ begründen** to drive one's point home; **seinen ~ behaupten** to maintain one's point; **seinen ~ darlegen** to define one's position; **seinen ~ durchsetzen** to play the ego game; **individuellen ~ einnehmen** to take a unique stand; **jem. seinen ~ klarmachen** to give s. o. a piece of one's mind; **sich jds. ~ zu eigen machen** to adopt s. o. view; **~ vertreten** to take up a position, to be of the opinion; **anderen ~ vertreten** to take a different view; **sich widersprechende ~e vertreten** to issue;
welchen ~ man auch einnimmt by any measure.

Standrecht martial (military) law;
~ verhängen to proclaim martial law.

standrechtlich erschießen lassen, j. to have s. o. court-martialled and shot.

Stand|seilbahn inclined railway *(US)*; **~uhr** pendulum (grandfather) clock.

Stange pole, post, stick, bar;
von der ~ gekauft reach-me-down, ready-made, off the hook (peg);
schöne ~ Geld tidy fortune, mint of money;
~ angeben to talk big, to show off; **bei der ~ bleiben** to stick to business; **jem. die ~ halten** to back s. o., to take s. one's part; **j. bei der ~ halten** to bring s. o. up to scratch, to keep s. o. to the point; **Anzug von der ~ kaufen** to buy a suit off the rack, to strip a peg; **fertig von der ~ kaufen** to buy ready-made (off the rack, off the peg), to strip a peg; **schöne ~ Geld kosten** to cost (run to) a pretty penny; **dünne ~ sein** to be as thin as a rake.

Stangen|geländer barrier; **~gold** ingot gold, gold ingots; **~leiter** rung ladder; **~silber** ingot silver, silver in ingots; **~wähler** *(tel.)* panel switch.

Stänkerer troublemaker, mischief-maker.

stänkern to make mischief (trouble).

Stanniol tin foil;
mit ~papier ausschlagen to tin-foil; **~streifen** *(Radarstörung)* chaff.

Stanzpresse stamping press.

Stapel *(Haufen)* pile, heap, mass, cluster, *(Lager)* staple, stack, stock[pile], *(Schiff)* stock;
~ von Briefen pile of correspondence, stack of letters; **~ Bücher** heap of books; **~ von Rechnungen** swarm of bills;
vom ~ lassen to launch; **Rede vom ~ lassen** to deliver (run off, rattle off) a speech; **Witz vom ~ lassen** to crack a joke; **vom ~ laufen lassen** to launch; **vom ~ laufen** *(Schiff)* to take the water, to be launched; **auf ~ legen** to lay down;
~ablage *(drucktechn.)* pile delivery; **~artikel** staples; **~gerechtigkeit** staple privilege (right); **~gut, ~güter** staple commodity (goods), staples; **~hafen** staple port; **~handel** staple trade; **~kaufmann** stapler; **~lauf** *(Schiff)* launch[ing].

stapeln to pile up, *(mil.)* to dump, *(einlagern)* to store, to warehouse.

Stapelplatz staple, entrepot, emporium, settled market, depository;
~ für Wolle wool staple.

Stapelungsgewicht stacking weight.

Stapel|verarbeitung *(Daten)* batch processing; **~ware** staple commodity (goods, articles).

Star star, feature;
~allüren star trappings; **höchst gerissener ~anwalt** legal eagle *(sl.)*; **~auftritt** star turn; **~besetzung** all-star (star-studded) cast; **~journalist** feature writer.

stark strong, potent, powerful, mighty, *(Getränk)* stiff, *(Maschine)* powerful, *(schwungvoll)* humming;
~ besetzt crowded, packed; **~ betrunken** dead drunk;
~ regnen to rain heavily; **50.000 Mann ~ sein** *(Heer)* to number 50.000; **~ vom Wetter abhängig sein** to be sensitive to the weather; **~ benachteiligt sein** to be badly handicapped; **~ gesucht sein** to be in great demand; **~ verschuldet sein** to be head over heels in debt;
~e Armee strong army; **~e Auflage** *(Buch)* large edition; **~er Band** big volume; **~e Erkältung** bad cold; **~er Esser** big eater; **~er Frost** severe frost; **~ bevölkertes Gebiet** densely populated area; **~e Kopfschmerzen** splitting headache; **~ befahrene Linie** heavily travelled line; **~er Mann in einem Verband sein** to be the strong man in an organization; **~er Motor** powerful engine; **~e Nachfrage** keen (strong) demand; **~e Nerven haben** to have strong nerves; **~e Organisation** powerful organization; **~es Polizeiaufgebot** large force of police; **~er Raucher sein** to be a heavy smoker; **jds. ~e Seite** s. one's strong point; **~e Übertreibung** gross exaggeration; **~er Verkehr** heavy traffic; **~e Verschuldung** heavy indebtedness; **~e Wand** thick wall; **~er Wind** stiff (violent) wind; **~e Worte gebrauchen** to use strong language.

Starkbier heavy (double) beer.

Stärke strength, power, force, might, forte, *(Blech)* gauge, *(Farbe, Licht)* intensity, *(Fieber)* height, *(mil.)* strength, *(Wind)* force, strength;
von gleicher ~ equal in strength;
finanzielle ~ financial strength (muscle); **nicht gerade jds. ~** not s. one's strong point; **moralische ~** morale force; **wirkliche ~** true strength;
~ der Belegschaft personnel strength; **~ der Nachfrage** keenness of demand; **~ auf dem Papier** *(mil.)* paper strength; **~ eines Unternehmens** corporate vigo(u)r, market power of a corporation;
jds. ~ sein to be s. one's long suit; **seine ~ zeigen** to show one's muscle;
~meldung *(mil.)* state.

stärken to strengthen, to fortify;
sich ~ to refresh o. s.; **moralisch ~** to fortify; **jem. den Rücken ~** to stiffen (back) s. o., to give s. o. moral support; **sein Selbstvertrauen ~** to boost one's confidence.

stärkendes Mittel tonic, restorative.

stärker geworden sein to have put on weight.

Stärkerer, sozial top dog.

Stärkeverhältnis voting strength.

starkmotorig high-powered.

Starkstrom power (heavy) current;
~anlage power plant; **~kabel** power cable; **~leitung** power line; **~sperre** electrified obstacle.

Stärkung refreshment, *(Trost)* consolation, comfort;
zur ~ seiner Gesundheit for the good of one's health;
kleine ~ anbieten to provide refreshments; **~ zu sich nehmen** to refresh o. s.

Stärkungs|getränk refresher, pick-me-up *(coll.)*, reviver *(sl.)*, bracer *(US coll.)*; **~mittel** restorative, tonic, roborant.

starr rigid, stern, ironclad, *(Preise)* hard, stiff, *(System)* rigid, inflexible, *(unnachgiebig)* unbending, adamant, inflexible, rigid;
~ vor Kälte numb with cold; **~ vor Schreck** paralysed with fright;
j. ~ ansehen to stare at s. o.;
~e Etikettevorschriften rigid rules of etiquette; **~e Grundsätze** rigid principles; **~e Haltung** unbending attitude; **~es Luftschiff** rigid airship; **~e Preise** rigid (pegged) prices; **~e Regeln** rigid rules; **~er Sittenkodex** inflexible code of morals.

Starreklame star billing *(US)*.

starren to stare, to glare;
von Fehlern ~ to be teeming with mistakes; **jem. ins Gesicht ~** to stare s. o. in the face; **vor Schmutz ~** to be full of dirt; **von Waffen ~** to bristle with weapons.

Starr|kopf bullhead, mule, wronghead, pigheaded fellow; **~luftschiff** rigid airship; **~sinn** stubborness, obstinacy.

starrsinnig obstinate, bullheaded, stubborn, mulish.

Starrummel star billing *(US)*.

Start start, *(Anfang)* beginning, *(Flugzeug)* start, take-off, get-off, *(Marineflugzeug, Rakete)* launching;
glatter ~ smooth take-off;
~ ins Leben start in life; **~ mit Radarhilfe** radar-assisted take-off;
~ freigeben to clear for take-off; **schlechten ~ haben** *(Geschäft)* to muddle at the start; **keinen guten ~ gehabt haben** to have made a poor start in one's new post; **zum ~ rollen** to taxi to the take-off; **am ~ durch Nebel verhindert sein** to be grounded by fog; **einem Flugzeug den ~ verbieten** to ground a plane;
~anlagen *(Rakete)* launching facilities; **~automatik** automatic choke.

Startbahn launching site, *(Flugzeug)* runway;
~ und Landebahn strip of runway;
~befeuerung runway lights; **~länge** take-off distance.

Start|band *(Film)* leader; **~bedingungen** starting conditions; **~befehl** order to take off.

startbereit ready to start, cranked up, *(Flugzeug)* in flying condition, ready to take off.

Start|bereitschaft *(Flugzeug)* readiness to take off, *(mil.)* ground alert; **~brett** take-off.

Starten *(Flugzeug)* start, take-off, get-off, *(Wasserflugzeug, Rakete)* launching.

starten to start, to pull up, *(Flugzeug)* to take the air (off), to get off;

Aktion ~ to launch (start) a drive; **Auto** ~ to start a car; **Flugzeug** ~ to launch an airplane into the air; **mit nichts** ~ to start from scratch; **Rakete** ~ to launch a rocket; **zu einer Reise** ~ to set out on a journey; **Sammelaktion** ~ to launch an appeal, to put up a fund-raising drive; **stündlich** ~ to start at intervals of an hour (hourly intervals); **neues Unternehmen** ~ to launch a new business enterprise; **Werbefeldzug** ~ to launch an advertising campaign.

Starter *(Sport)* flagman;

~**klappe** choke [throttle], starter knob, starter choke (lever) *(Br.)*.

Starterlaubnis *(Flugzeug)* clearance;

keine ~ **haben** to be grounded; **auf** ~ **warten** to wait for take off.

Start|fehler *(Datenverarbeitung)* inherent error; ~**fonds** starter fund; ~**gebiet** *(Raumschiff)* launching area; ~**geld** *(Wette)* entrance stake; ~**geschwindigkeit** take-off speed; ~**gleichheit** even odds.

Starthilfe initial aid, seed money, pump-priming *(US)*, *(Flugzeug)* assisted take-off;

~ **bei Feuchtigkeit** damp start;

~ **erhalten** to get a start in business; **jem. eine** ~ **geben** to aid s. one's recovery, *(nach Pleite)* to give s. o. a start.

Start|jahr startup year; ~**kapital** startup money, initial capital.

startklar all set, *(Flugzeug)* ready to take off, in flying condition.

Start|kommando *(Raumschiff)* launching team; ~**kosten** startup (launching) costs, cost to launch; ~**länge** take-off distance; ~**leitzentrum** ground control center *(US)* (centre, *Br.*); ~**möglichkeit** start in life; ~**plattform** launching platform; ~**platz**, ~**position** *(Ballon)* point of ascent, *(Flugzeug)* take-off point; ~- **und Landeplatz für Hubschrauber** heliport; ~**problem** start-up problem; ~**rakete** booster rocket; ~**rampe** *(Rakete)* launching pad; ~**schwierigkeiten** starting trouble; ~**strecke** take-off run; ~- **und Landestreifen** landing strip; ~**stufe** *(Rakete)* launcher stage; ~**triebwerk** booster engine; ~**verbot** suspension, *(Flugzeug)* take-off restriction, grounding; **einem Flugzeug** ~**verbot erteilen** to ground an airplane; ~**vermögen** pickup, acceleration; **gutes** ~**vermögen haben** to be quick off the mark; ~**zählung** *(Raketenabschuß)* countdown; ~**zählung durchführen** to countdown; ~**zeichen** start, *(Raumschiff)* launch time.

Starunwesen star system.

Statik statics;

~**berechnung** static calculation.

Station *(Bahn, Rundfunk)* station, *(Haltepunkt)*, halt, stopover, *(Krankenhaus)* ward, *(Teilstrecke)* stage;

frei ~ free station;

ambulante ~ outpatient department (clinic, *US*); **bemannte** ~ attended station; **freie** ~ board and lodging found, all found, room and board *(US)*; **meteorologische** ~ meteorological office;

gegen freie ~ **arbeiten** to work for one's keep, to work au pair *(Br.)*; **aus der** ~ **dampfen** to puff out of the station; **in die** ~ **einfahren** to draw into the station; **auf jeder** ~ **halten** to call at every station; ~ **machen** to have a rest, to stop over *(US)*, to break one's journey.

stationär stationary, firm, fixed, rigid;

~**e Behandlung** inpatient treatment; ~**e Bevölkerung** stationary population; ~ **behandelter Patient** inpatient.

stationieren to station, to locate, to site, *(mil.)* to position, *(Atomwaffen)* to deploy;

Truppen in Kasernen ~ to settle troops in barracks, to garrison troops.

stationiert located, stationed, based;

nicht in Washington ~ out in the field *(US)*.

Stationierung *(mil.)* stationing;

~ **von Atomwaffen** deployment of nuclear weapons; ~ **von Beamten** location of officials.

Stationierungskosten support costs.

Stations|ansage *(Rundfunk)* station identification; ~**arzt** ward physician; ~**gebäude** railway station; ~**schwester** ward sister, *(Schiff)* hospital apprentice; ~**vorsteher** stationmaster, station agent *(US)*.

statische|Berechnung static calculation; ~ **Verhältnisziffer** static ratio.

Statist supernumerary, dummy, extra, walk-on, walker-on.

Statisten|publikum studio audience; ~**rolle** walk-on, walking part; ~**rolle spielen** to have a walking part.

Statistik statistics;

nach der letztgreifbaren ~ **des Jahres 1979** at 1979 survey prices;

amtliche ~ government statistics; **beschreibende** ~ descriptive statistics; **demographische** ~ population statistics; **theoretische** ~ statistical method; **nicht enden wollende** ~**en** never-ending (yards of) statistics;

~**en angleichen** to harmonize statistics; ~ **aufstellen** to make up (compile) statistics, to record statistically; ~ **auswerten** to interpret statistics; ~ **zusammenstellen** to record statistically, to make up statistics, to statisticize.

Statistiker statistical expert, statistician.

statistisch|bereinigt statistically adjusted;

~ **erfassen** to record statistically, to statisticize;

~**e Abteilung** statistical department; ~**e Abweichung** statistical discrepancy; ~**es Amt** statistical bureau; ~**e Angaben** statistical data; ~**er Angestellter** census employee; ~**e Aufstellung** statistical statement (table); ~**er Ausschuß** statistical committee; ~**e Berechnung** structural analysis; ~**e Berichte** statistical returns.

Statisches Bundesamt Bureau of Statistics, [etwa] central statistical office *(Br.)*, Census Bureau *(US)*, National Bureau of Economic Research *(US)*.

statistisch|e Einheit statistical unit; **erfaßte** ~**e Einheit** census information; ~**e Entscheidungsfunktionen** statistical decision functions; ~**e Ergebnisse auswerten** to interpret statistics; ~**e Erhebung** statistical inquiry (investigation); ~**e Gesamtmasse** statistical universe; ~**e Güterüberwachung** quality control; ~**e Hypothese** statistical hypothesis.

Statistisches Jahrbuch Annual Abstract (Digest, *Br.*) of Statistics, statistical abstract *(US)*.

statistisch|es Material statistical data, statistics; ~**es Material über die Geldversorgung** money supply figures; ~**es Material zusammenstellen** to collect statistical information; ~**e Meßzahl** statistic; ~**e Preistheorie** equilibrium theory; ~**e Qualitätsüberwachung** quality control; ~**e Sicherheit** confidence coefficient; ~**e Tabelle** statistical table, data sheet; ~**e Unterlagen** statistics, statistical data; ~**es Verfahren** census procedure; ~**e Wertermittlung** statistical evaluation; ~**e Zusammenstellung** statistical compilation (information).

Stativ *(Foto)* tripod, stand, support;

~**fahrwagen** dolly; ~**kamera** stand camera *(Br.)*.

Stätte place, site, location;

geweihte ~ consecrated place;

~ **der Ausgrabungen** site of excavations; ~ **des Grauens** place of horror;

keine bleibende ~ **haben** to have no fixed abode.

stattfinden to occur, to take place, to happen, to come off;

nächste Woche ~ to come on next week;

Reise nicht ~ **lassen** to cancel a journey.

Stattgabe einer Berufung allowance of an appeal.

stattgeben to allow, to permit, to grant;

einem Antrag ~ to grant a petition, to sustain a motion; **einer Forderung** ~ to allow a claim; **einem Gesuch** ~ to grant a request (suit); **einer Klage** ~ to sustain an action, to find for the plaintiff; **nicht** ~ to overrule.

statthaft admissible, permitted, permissible, *(rechtlich)* legal, lawful.

Statthalter governor, locum tenens.

stattlich handsome, presentable, dignified, commanding;

~**es Sümmchen** tidy sum of money.

statuieren, ein Exempel an jem. to make an example of s. o.

Status state of affairs, status, *(Finanzlage)* financial status (statement), *(Vermögensaufstellung)* statement of affairs, *(Vermögensstand)* statement of assets and liabilities;

ehelicher ~ status of legitimacy; **erworbener** ~ achieved status; **gesellschaftlicher** ~ social standing (status), rank; **rechtlicher** ~ legal status;

~ **von Aktionären** status of members; ~ **eines Beamten** government situation; ~ **eines Konkursschuldners** bankrupt's balance sheet; ~ **quo** status quo; ~ **eines Territoriums** territoriality;

miserablen ~ **aufweisen** to have a poor financial showing; **im** ~ **quo lassen** to leave things as they are; **seinen** ~ **verlieren** to lose one's footing;

~**gewinn** status-plus; ~**kampf** rat race; ~**prüfung** status enquiry; ~**symbol** symbol of status; ~**verlust** loss of status; ~**zahlen** figures of a financial statement.

Statut statute, charter, institute;

~**en** regulations, rules and byelaws, *(Aktiengesellschaft)* articles of association (incorporation), *(Verein)* standing rules; ~**en der Vereinten Nationen** charter of the United Nations;

~en aufsetzen to lay down the regulations; ~ einhalten to comply with a statute; ~ nicht einhalten to fail to observe a bylaw.
Statutenänderung alteration of the articles of association.
statutengemäß statutory, according to regulations (the rules).
Statutenkonflikt conflict of laws.
statutenwidrig contrary to the regulations (articles).
Stau traffic jam (block), congestion of traffic;
~**attest** certificate of stowage.
Staub dust, powder;
radioaktiver ~ radioactiv dust;
viel ~ aufwirbeln to kick up (raise) a dust (shindy); **sich aus dem ~ machen** to sling one's hook, to take it on the lam (*US sl.*), to make off with, to make one's getaway, to make away, to show a clean pair of heels, to run for it, to whistle off (*coll.*), (*mil.*) to give leg bail, to decamp; **sich schnellstens aus dem ~ machen** to cut and run (*coll.*); ~ **saugen** to vacuum-clean; ~ **von seinen Füßen schütteln** to shake the dust from one's feet.
staubbedeckt thick with dust.
Staubecken reservoir.
Staubgehalt dust content.
staubig machen (werden) to dust.
Staub|lawine drift avalanche; ~**loch** dust bowl; ~**mantel** dust coat; ~**sauger** vacuum cleaner; ~**schicht** film of dust; ~**teilchen** particles of dust; ~**tuch** dustcloth, wiper; ~**wolke** cloud of dust.
Staudamm river dam.
stauen (*Fluß*) to dam, to stem, (*Fracht*) to stow, to trim;
sich ~ (*Menschenmenge*) to pile up, (*Verkehr*) to be jammed (congested), (*Wut*) to build up;
seemäßig ~ to trim the hold, to stow cargo in a ship's hold.
Stauer trimmer, stevedore;
~**lohn** [rate of] stowage.
Stau|höhe (*Wehr*) surface level; ~**holz** dunnage; ~**lage** trimming; ~**lücken** broken stowage; ~**material** dunnage; ~**mauer** dam.
Staunen amazement, astonishment.
staunen to wonder, to be amazed (astonished), to marvel;
Bauklötze ~ to be bowled over.
Stau|plan stowage plan; ~**raum** stowage capacity, (*Schiff*) hold; ~**schein** stevedore's certificate; ~**strahltriebwerk** ramjet engine.
Stauung (*Fracht*) stowage, estivage, (*Verkehr*) congestion, traffic jam.
Stauwasser backwater.
Stechen, sich mit jem. auf Hauen und ~ stehen to be at daggers drawn with s. o.
stechen (*Biene*) to sting, (*Kontrolleur*) to punch, (*Mücken*) to bite, (*Sonne*) to burn, to beat down, (*Zeituhr*) to check in (out), to clock in (out);
jem. den Dolch in den Rücken ~ to stab s. o. in the back; **in Kupfer** ~ to engrave in copper; **Löcher in etw.** ~ to pierce (prick) holes in s. th.; **mit einer Nadel** ~ to prick with a needle; **in See** ~ to put [out] to sea, to make for the open sea, to sail, to stand for the offing; **in ein Wespennest** ~ to stir up a nest of hornets.
stechend (*Geruch*) pungent, keen, acrid, (*Sonne*) scorching, burning;
~**er Schmerz** acute (sharp) pain.
Stech|karte clock card, timecard, time ticket; ~**uhr** time (watchman's) clock (recorder), telltale (*Br.*); ~**zirkel** dividers.
Steck|anschluß plug and socket connection; ~**brief** warrant of arrest (apprehension); ~**brief gegen j. erlassen** to issue a warrant of apprehension, to raise a hue and cry against s. o.
steckbrieflich gesucht werden to be wanted by the police, to have a warrant out against one.
Steckdose socket, electric outlet (plug) box, jack.
stecken, jem. etw. to give s. o. a hint; **Abzeichen an den Mantel** ~ to pin a badge on one's coat; **mitten (tief) in der Arbeit** ~ to be stuck in one's work, to be up to one's neck in work; **voller Bosheiten** ~ to be full of malice; **in Brand** ~ to set on fire; **Brief in den Briefkasten** ~ to post (*Br.*) (mail, *US*) a letter; **voller Fehler** ~ to be full of (teeming with) mistakes; **j. ins Gefängnis** ~ to shut s. o. up in prison; **etw. Geld zu sich** ~ to take some money along with one; **Geld in ein Unternehmen** ~ to embark on a new business undertaking; **Geldscheine unbemerkt in seine Manteltasche** ~ to slip bank notes into one's coat pocket; **Gewinn in die eigene Tasche** ~ to line one's pockets; **seine Hände in die Tasche** ~ (*fig.*) to twiddle one's thumbs; **seine Nase in anderer Leute Angelegenheiten** ~ to poke one' nose into other people's business; **in tausend Nöten** ~ to be up to one's neck in trouble; **hinter der ganzen Sache** ~ to be at the bottom of a business; **im Schlamm** ~ (*Räder*) to be stuck in the mud; **tief in Schulden** ~ to be head over heels (up to the ears) in debt; **Schwert in die Scheide** ~ (*fig.*) to sheathe one's sword; **j. in die Tasche** ~ to be more than a match for s. o.; **jem. etw. tüchtig** ~ to talk to s. o. like a Dutch uncle.
Steckenbleiben fizzle.
steckenbleiben to break down, to be mired (bogged down), (*Redner*) to break down, (*Verhandlungen*) to come to a dead stop (end), to come to a standstill, to fizzle out;
in der Rolle ~ to dry; **in einer Schneeverwehung** ~ to get stuck in a snowdrift.
steckenlassen, Schlüssel im Schloß to leave the key in the lock.
Steckenpferd hobby, hobby-horse, toy, fad, whim;
vorübergehendes ~ passing fad;
sein ~ reiten to ride a hobby-horse (one's pet hobby).
Stecker (*el.*) point, connecting plug, connector;
dreiteiliger ~ three-pin plug; **passender** ~ mating connector;
~ **herausziehen** to pull a plug out;
~**kabel** attachment cable; ~**vorrichtung** plug-in apparatus.
Steck|kontakt plug (outlet) box; ~**ling** cutting, layer, shoot; **wie eine ~nadel suchen** to search high and low; ~**nadelkopf** pinhead.
stecknadelkopfgroß pinhead-sized.
Steckschloß mortise lock.
Steg footpath, foot log (*US*), trail, (*über Bahnlinie*) overpass, (*Brille*) bridge, nosepiece, (*über Brücke*) footbridge, (*drucktechn.*) reglet, furniture, quotation;
Weg und ~ kennen to know every hill and dale;
~**hose** strapped trousers.
Stegreif, aus dem off (out of) hand, impromptu, extempore, extemporaneous, unpremeditated;
aus dem ~ sprechen to speak offhand (extempore, off the cuff, *coll.*), to extemporize;
~**ansprache** extempore address; ~**dichter** improviser, improvisator; ~**interview** informal interview; ~**rede** improvised speech, impromptu; ~**vorstellung** impromptu performance, play in progress.
Steh|ablage lateral filing; ~**aufmännchen** roly-poly, never-say-die fellow; ~**bierhalle** refreshment bar; ~**bild** slide; ~**empfang** standing reception.
Stehen, Mahlzeit im ~ einnehmen to have a stand-up meal; **zum ~ kommen** to come to a halt; **zum ~ gebracht werden** to be brought to a stand[still].
stehen to stand, (*Kurse*) to rule, to remain, (*Maschine*) to have stopped;
auf j. ~ to be fond of s. o.; **bei jem. ~ zu entscheiden** to be up to s. o. to decide; **hinter jem.** ~ to back s. o.; **geschlossen hinter jem.** ~ to go solid for s. o.; **über jem.** ~ to be s. one's superior; **zu jem.** ~ to take s. one's part; **am Anfang seiner Karriere** ~ to be at the beginning of one's career; **am Anfang einer Liste** ~ to head a list; **unter Anklage** ~ to stand one's trial; **in Arbeit** ~ to be employed; **vor dem Bankrott** ~ to be on the verge of bankruptcy; **vor seiner Beförderung** ~ to be down for promotion; **mit beiden Beinen fest auf der Erde** ~ to have both feet on the ground; **sich die Beine in den Leib** ~ to cool one's heels; **mit jem. in Briefwechsel** ~ to correspond with s. o.; **zu Buch** ~ to stand at cost; **zur Debatte** ~ to be on the carpet; **nicht zur Debatte** ~ to be out of the question; **im Debet** ~ to be on the debit side; **auf Empfang** ~ (*Rundfunkgerät*) to stand by; **in Flammen** ~ to be on fire; **außer Frage** ~ to be beyond doubt; **mit jem. auf gutem Fuß** ~ to be on good terms with s. o.; **mit einem Fuß im Grabe** ~ to have one foot in the grave; **auf eigenen Füßen** ~ to stand on one's feet, to play off one's own bat; **auf schwachen Füßen** ~ to be financially weak, (*Beweisführung*) to have a shaky basis; **vor Gericht** ~ to stand one's trial; **in Geschäftsbeziehungen mit jem.** ~ to transact business with s. o.; **in einem Gesetz** ~ to be embodied in a law; **in jds. Gunst** ~ to be in s. one's good books; **günstig** ~ to be in good train; **gut** ~ (*Aktien*) to be at a favo(u)rable price, (*Ernte*) to look promising, (*Sache*) to be in a fair way; **jem. gut** ~ to suit s. o.; **sich gut** ~ to be well off (situated); **sich gut miteinander** ~ to get along well, to be on good terms with s. o.; **sich finanziell gut** ~ to be in funds (well-off, fixed, *US*); **sich mit seinem Kollegen gut** ~ to hit it off with one's colleague; **sich mit seinem Vorgesetzten gut** ~ to stand well with one's chief; **hoch** ~ (*Kurse*) to rule high; **weiterhin hoch** ~ to continue to rule high; **hoch im Preis** ~ to command a high price; **um einen halben Punkt höher** ~ (*Kurse*) to be 1/2 higher; **höher denn je** ~ to be at an all-time high (*US*); **sich auf 80.000 DM im Jahr** ~ to have an income of 80.000 DM a year; **mit jem. in Konkurrenz** ~ to be in competition with s. o.; **Kopf an Kopf** ~ to stand shoulder to shoulder; **hinter dem Ladentisch** ~ to be behind the counter; **leer** ~ (*Wohnung*) to

stand empty, to be vacant; **unter jds. Leitung** ~ to be directed by s. o.; **auf einer Liste** ~ to appear (figure) in a list; **bei jem. in Lohn und Brot** ~ to be in s. one's employ; **nicht in jds. Macht** ~ not to be within s. one's power; **auf des Messers Schneide** ~ to be a touch-and-go situation; **jem. näher** ~ to be much closer to s. o.; **niedrig** ~ *(Aktien)* to be down, *(Kurse)* to be low; **sehr niedrig** ~ *(Kurse)* to stand at a minimum; **niedriger** ~ *(Kurse)* to rule lower; **um 4 Punkte niedriger** ~ to be 4 points worse (less); **über Pari** ~ *(Anleihe)* to sell at a premium; **unter Pari** ~ *(Anleihe)* to sell at a discount; **Pate** ~ to stand godfather, *(Rundfunk)* to sponsor a program(me); **auf einer Rechnung** ~ to appear on (figure in) an account; **in laufender Rechnung** ~ to have a running account; **in schlechtem Ruf** ~ to be in bad repute, to have a bad reputation; **vor dem Ruin** ~ to be faced with ruin; **hinter einer Sache** ~ to be at the back (bottom) of s. th.; **Schlange** ~ to stand in line, to line (queue, *Br.*) up; **schlecht** ~ to look bad; **schlechter** ~ to fare badly; **Schmiere** ~ to keep a lookout; **vor Schwierigkeiten** ~ to be confronted with difficulties; **auf jds. Seite** ~ to side with s. o., to support s. o.; **ein gutes Stück über j.** ~ to be a cut above s. o. else; **auf der Tagesordnung** ~ to be on the agenda; **vor vollendeten Tatsachen** ~ to be confronted with accomplished facts; **unveränderlich** ~ *(Kurse)* to remain steady; **mit jem. in Verbindung** ~ to be in touch (have contact) with s. o.; **in Verdacht** ~ to be under suspicion; **jem. zur Verfügung** ~ to be at s. one's disposal; **zum Verkauf** ~ to be up for sale; **vor der Verwirklichung** ~ to be about to be realized; **Wache** ~ to be on guard; **unter Waffen** ~ to be under arms; **jem. im Wege** ~ to be in s. one's way; **zu seinen Worten** ~ to stand by one's words;

Geld bei jem. ~ haben to have money lodged with s. o.; **Geld in der Bank ~ haben** to have a banking account; **etw. bis zum Hals ~ haben** to be fed up with s. th.; **DM 2000 auf dem Sparbuch ~ haben** to have 2000 DM in one's savings account; **Wasser bis zum Halse ~ haben** to be in deep waters; **zu ~ kommen** to cost; **zu hoch zu ~ kommen** to bear too high a price; **auf 5 Pfund pro Kopf zu ~ kommen** to work out at five pounds a head.

Stehenbleiben *(Auto)* pull-up.

stehenbleiben to pause, to stop, to [come to a] halt, *(Auto)* to pull up, *(Kurs)* to remain steady, *(Motor)* to die, *(Satz)* to remain in type.

stehend standing, *(stereotyp)* stock, stereotyped;
~**en Fußes** immediately, straightaway; ~**es Kapital** fixed capital; ~**e Redewendung** stock phrase; ~**e Schuld** consolidated (funded) debt.

stehenlassen *(Satz)* to keep the type standing, *(Schuldbetrag)* to leave on tick.

Steh|imbiß stand-up buffet; ~**kragenberuf** black-coated *(Br.)* (white-collar, *US*) job; ~**kragenproletariat** white-collar *(US)* (black-coated, *Br.*) proletariat; ~**lampe** floor (standard, *Br.*) lamp; ~**leiter** stepladder.

stehlen to purloin, to commit larceny, to steal, to take by stealth, to lift, to palm *(US sl.)*;
Geld aus der Ladenkasse ~ to steal money from the till; **jem. eine Idee** ~ to lift a passage from an author; **jem. die Schau** ~ to steal a march upon s. o.; **sich in jds. Vertrauen** ~ to sneak into s. one's confidence; **jem. die Zeit** ~ to make inroads upon s. one's time; **dem lieben Gott die Zeit** ~ to eat the bread of idleness; **mit ihm kann man Pferde** ~ he is game for anything.

Steh|platz standing space; **nur** ~**plätze** standing room only; ~**platzinhaber** straphanger *(coll.)*, standee *(US coll.)*; ~**platzkarte** hard-wood *(sl.)*; ~**pult** desk; ~**satz** *(drucktechn.)* standing (live) matter (type), retained composition; ~**satzanweisung** hold; ~**vermögen** standing power, stamina.

steif stiff, *(Benehmen)* stilted, homebred, trig, starchy, *(vor Kälte)* numb;
~ **und fest behaupten** to persist in saying; **sich sehr ~ benehmen** to be as stiff as a poker; ~ **und fest daran glauben** to believe in it firmly; **die Ohren ~ halten** to keep a stiff upper lip;
~**e Atmosphäre** formal atmosphere; ~**e Brise** stiff breeze; ~**er Empfang** stiff reception; ~**es Lächeln** wooden smile.

Steig path, trail;
~**bö** rising gust; **jem. den ~bügel halten** to give s. o. a legup.

Steigen *(Börse, Preise)* increase, climb, improvement, advance, rise, rising, upward movement, recovery, upturn, lift, hike *(US coll.)*, *(Flugzeug)* climb, soar, zoom, *(Grundstückswert)* appreciation, betterment, unearned increment, *(starker Kursanstieg)* boom, *(Straße)* rise, ascent, ascension;
im ~ begriffen on the rise;
~ **und Fallen** fluctuation, up and down; ~ **der Kurse** upward movement of stocks, strength in the market; ~ **der Preise** price advance, increase (appreciation) of prices;
~ **aufweisen** to show a rise; **im ~ begriffen sein** to be on the rise (rising); **auf das ~ der Kurse spekulieren** to buy for a rise, to bull.

steigen *(Diskontsatz)* to be advanced, *(sich ereignen)* to take place, *(Flugzeug)* to climb, to soar, to zoom, *(Flut)* to be at the flood, to swell, *(Kurse)* to rise, to advance, to improve, to move up (higher, upward), to be on the (show a) rise, to harden, *(Nebel)* to lift, to rise, *(Preise)* to go (get, mount, pick) up, to be on the upgrade, to increase, to rise, to hike *(US)*, *(Straße)* to rise, to ascend, to climb, *(Tachometer)* to creep up;
von 388 auf 410 ~ *(Kurs)* to jump up from 388 to 410; ~ **und fallen** to rise and fall, to fluctuate; **weder ~ noch fallen** to be in a sidewise price movement; **an der Börse** ~ to jump on the stock exchange; **aus dem Bus** ~ to alight from a bus; **jem. auf das Dach** ~ to haul s. o. over the coals; **um das Doppelte** ~ to rise by 100 per cent; **auf der Erfolgsleiter eine Stufe höher** ~ to move up a step on the ladder; **ins Examen** ~ to go in (up) for an examination; **aufs Fahrrad** ~ to get on one's bicycle; **durchs Fenster** ~ to climb through the window; **in ein Flugzeug** ~ to emplane, to get into (board) a plane; **auf breiter Front** ~ *(Kurse)* to rise widely; **hausseartig** ~ to rise sharply; **raketenartig in die Höhe** ~ to skyrocket; **jährlich um 28%** ~ *(Inflation)* to run at about 28% a year; **im Kurs** ~ to advance in price, to be on the rise, to experience a rise in prices, to be a rising market; **an Land** ~ to get ashore; **langsam** ~ *(Preise)* to creep; **langsamer** ~ to slow; **immer noch** ~ to go on increasing, to be still going up; **plötzlich** ~ *(Kurs)* to go up with a jump, to surge ahead, to jump up, to have a sudden rise, to spurt; **auf das Podium** ~ to mount the platform; **im Preis** ~ to enhance (increase) in price; **um drei Punkte** ~ to move (go) up three points; **um 13 Punkte auf 567** ~ to forge ahead 13 points to 567; **raketenhaft** ~ to zoom upward, to skyrocket; **rasch** ~ to move briskly ahead; **sprunghaft** ~ to soar, *(Hausse)* to surge forward; **sprunghaft ~ und einen neuen Höchststand erreichen** to jump into new high ground; **übermäßig** ~ to inflate; **über seine Ufer** ~ to rise above its banks; **ganz unerwartet** ~ to soar; **weiter** ~ to continue to rise; **im Wert** ~ to improve in value; **wieder** ~ to recover; **in einen Zug** ~ to board a train;
Grundstückswerte ~ lassen to enhance the value of land; **Rede ~ lassen** to deliver (launch) a speech.

steigend increasing, advancing, upward, improving, flowing, *(Kurse)* rising, buoyant, bull, bullish;
schnell ~ runaway;
~**e Aktien** advancing stocks; ~**e Ausgaben** growing expenditure; ~**es Interesse** increasing interest; ~**e Kosten** rising (increasing) costs, advancing prices; ~**e Kurse** rising market; **ständig ~e Nachfrage** increasing demand; ~**e Popularität** mounting popularity; ~**e Preise** rising (advancing) prices; **sprunghaft ~e Preise** soaring prices; ~**e Tendenz** upward tendency, bullish proclivities; ~**e Unkosten** increasing costs.

Steiger *(Bergwerk)* overman, captain.

Steigerer bidder, auctioneer.

Steigern bid.

steigern to mark up, to advance, to heighten, *(Auktion)* to bid [up], to outbid, *(Preis)* to increase, to enhance, to force up, *(verbessern)* to improve, to better;
sich ~ to increase, to heighten, to augment, to intensify; **Auflage** ~ *(Zeitung)* to increase the circulation; **Ausstoß** ~ to increase the output; **um das Doppelte** ~ to double; **Geschwindigkeit** ~ to accelerate; **hoch** ~ *(Auktion)* to run up; **künstlich** ~ *(Geldumlauf)* to inflate the currency; **Kurse** ~ to bull the market; **j. mit der Miete** ~ to raise a lodger's rent; **Notenumlauf** ~ to increase paper circulation; **Produktion** ~ to step up production; **Qualität** ~ to heighten a quality.

Steigerung progression, *(Kurse, Preise)* rise, increase, advance, improvement, upward trend, enhancement, upward movement, *(mil.)* escalation, *(im Wert)* appreciation, increment, increase in value;
jährliche ~ *(Gehalt)* annual increase; **leichte** ~ slight increase; **plötzliche** ~ boom; **sprunghafte** ~ rise by leaps and bounds, jump in prices;
~ **von 12%** upward gradient of 12%; ~ **auf einen neuen Höchstkurs** advance to a new high; ~ **der Kapitalintensität** capital deepening; ~ **des Sozialprodukts** economic growth;
~ **aufweisen** to show a rise (an increase, an uptick), to be on the increase; ~ **erfahren** to show a rising tendency, to undergo a rise; **bedeutende ~ erfahren** to improve considerably; **unerwartete ~ erfahren** to soar; **in rascher ~ neue Höchstkurse erzielen** to shoot into new high ground; **der ~ der Lebenshaltungskosten Einhalt gebieten** to control the rise in the cost of living; **schnellen ~en unterworfen sein** to move briskly ahead; ~ **verzeichnen** to experience (show) a rise.

Steigerungs|betrag rate of advance (increase); **jährlicher ~betrag** *(Gehalt)* annual increment; **~faktor** increment factor; **~klausel** *(Lohn)* escalator clause; **~rate, ~satz** rate of increase; **~tendenz** upward tendency.
Steig|geschwindigkeit rate of ascent; **~leistung** *(Auto)* hill-climbing efficiency; **~leitung** uptake, riser; **~rohr** ascending pipe, rising, main, riser.
Steigung grade, gradient, rising, slope.
Steigungs|fähigkeit hill-climbing efficiency; **~winkel** pitch angle.
steil steep, precipitous;
~ ansteigen *(Flugzeug)* to zoom, to ascend (rise) sharply (steeply), *(Preise)* to soar;
~e Karriere career of resounding progress; **~e Steigung** steep gradient; **~es Ufer** bluff, steep bank.
Steil|feuer *(mil.)* plunging fire; **~flug** nosedown; **im ~flug niedergehen** to nose down; **~hang** precipice, steep slope; **~küste** cliff, bluff; **~wand** precipice.
Stein stone, brick, *(Lithographie)* stone;
~ des Anstoßes stumbling block;
~ ins Rollen bringen to start the ball rolling; **zu ~ erstarren** to petrify; **einen ~ zum anderen fügen** to dot and carry; **~ vom Herzen haben** to be a weight off one's mind; **keinen ~ auf dem anderen lassen** to leave not a stick standing; **jem. ~e in den Weg legen** to put a spoke in s. one's wheel; **jem. einen ~ vom Herzen nehmen** to take a load off s. one's mind; **jem. alle ~e aus dem Weg räumen** to pave the way for s. o.; **~ und Bein schwören** to swear by all that's holy; **nur ein Tropfen auf dem heißen ~ sein** to be only a drop in the bucket (ocean); **ersten ~ auf j. werfen** to cast the first stone.
steinalt as old as the hills.
Stein|bruch quarry; **im ~bruch arbeiten** to quarry; **~druck** lithography.
steinern|er Blick stony stare; **~e Brücke** stone bridge; **~es Herz** heart of stone.
Stein|gut pottery, crockery; **~hagel** volley (shower) of stones.
steiniger Boden stony soil (ground).
Steinkohle mineral (pit) coal.
Steinkohlen|bergbau pit (hardcoal) mining; **~einheit** energy equivalent; **~förderung** pit-coal production.
Stein|mauer stone wall; **~packung** pitched work; **~pflaster** block pavement *(US)*; **~platte** flag, slab, tile.
steinreich made of money, rich as a Jew, stone rich *(sl.)*;
~ sein to have oceans of money, to be worth a mint of money *(coll.)*.
Stein|schlag falling rocks; **in ~wurfweite** within a stone's throw.
Stellage privilege, put and call;
~geber seller of a spread, seller of a put and call; **~geschäft** put and call, pac, double option, spread *(US)*, straddle *(sl.)*; **~kurs** put and call price; **~nehmer** buyer of a spread.
Stelldichein rendezvous, tryst, date *(coll.)*;
jem. ein ~ geben to date s. o. *(coll.)*.
Stelle place, spot, stead, lieu, *(Abschnitt)* patch, *(Baustelle)* site, location, *(Beruf)* position, post, appointment, situation, place, berth *(Br.)*, quarter, *(Buchstelle)* passage, *(Dezimalstelle)* decimal, digit, *(Dienststelle)* agency, authority, charge, office, unit;
an ~ von in place of, in lieu of, in substitution for, vice; **an autorisierter ~** in responsible quarters; **an dieser ~** at this juncture; **an einer empfindlichen ~** between wind and water; **an erster ~** first and foremost, in the first instance (place); **an oberster ~** topside; **an zuständiger ~** in responsible quarters; **an zweiter ~** in the second place; **auf der ~** offhand, at once, on the nail (spot); **in ungekündigter ~** not under notice; **von amtlichen ~n** from official quarters; **von kompetenter (zuständiger) ~** on good authority;
~n gesucht *(Inserat)* situations wanted;
amtliche ~n official authorities; **ausführende ~** enforcement agency; **ausgewählte ~n** *(Buch)* selected passages; **beratende ~** advisory body; **sofort zu besetzende ~** immediate opening; **nicht am Postscheckverkehr beteiligte ~n** non-Giro outlets; **buchführende ~** accounting department; **gut dotierte ~** well-paid position; **eingeklammerte ~** parenthesis; **einträgliche ~** good berth (situation); **entscheidende ~** decision-making unit; **erledigte (freie) ~** opening, vacancy, vacant office; **fachliche ~** technical agency; **Zoll festsetzende ~** tariff maker; **freie ~n** *(Zeitung)* unfilled vacancies; **freiwerdende ~** expected vacancy; **aus dem Zusammenhang gerissene ~** out-of-context excerpt; **von der Zensur gestrichene ~** censored passage; **durch Pensionierung frei gewordene ~** retirement vacancy; **gleichlautende ~** parallel passage; **gute ~** good situation (berth, *Br.*); **höchste ~** highest place, head; **höhere ~** higher (upper) reaches; **informierte ~n** informed sources; **kreditgewährende ~** lending institution; **kurspflegende (kursstützende) ~** price-supporting agency; **leitende ~** managerial post; **lohnsteuerabzugspflichtige ~** withholding agency; **maßgebende ~** powers that be; **nachgeordnete ~n** subsidiary bodies; **nichtstaatliche ~** nongovernmental body; **offene ~** vacancy, vacant situation, job opening, *(Inserat)* help wanted, unfilled vacancies, jobs offered; **offene ~ bei einer Bank** opening in a bank; **öffentliche ~** public authority; **örtliche ~** local authority; **politische ~n** political authorities; **radierte ~** erasure; **sachkundige ~n** competent bodies; **schadhafte ~** defect, flaw; **schwache ~** foible, weak spot; **unbesetzte ~** vacant position, vacancy, vacant situation, open position; **undichte ~** *(fig.)* leak; **unschöne ~** eyesore; **untergeordnete ~n** subordinate bodies; **verbrannte ~** burn; **verwischte ~** blur; **wasserundichte ~** leak; **weiche ~** underbelly; **zensierte (von der Zensur gestrichene) ~** censored passage; **zitierte ~** quotation; **zuständige ~** proper quarter, competent office;
~ als Buchhalter accountantship; **zweite ~ hinter dem Komma** second place after the decimal point; **schwache ~ in der Landesverteidigung** weakness of a country's defences; **schadhafte ~ im Straßenbelag** damaged area on the road surface; **unanständige ~ in einem Theaterstück** warm scene in a play; **freie ~ in einem Werbebüro** opening in an advertising agency;
~n abstreichen to point off places; **jds. schwache ~ angreifen** to catch s. o. on the hip; **~ annehmen** to take a post; **an gut sichtbarer ~ anschlagen** to post in a conspicuous place; **~ antreten** to take up one's duties, to enter a post, to start on a job; **~ auffinden** to localize a quotation; **~ aufgeben** to throw up a situation (one's job), to vacate an office, to leave one's job; **in eine höhere ~ aufrücken** to rise to a better position; **~ ausfüllen** to supply (fill) a vacancy; **leere ~n ausfüllen** to fill in blank spaces; **~ in unberechtigter Weise auslegen** to strain the meaning of a passage; **[freie] ~ ausschreiben** to advertise a post (vacancy), to invite applications for a position; **sich in seiner ~ behaupten** to hold one's position; **~ bekleiden** to occupy a post; **~ bekommen** to get an appointment; **freie ~ besetzen** to fill a post, to fill (supply) a vacancy; **sich um eine freie ~ bewerben** to seek employment, to apply for a vacant position (a job); **jds. ~ einnehmen** to step into s. one's shoes, to take (fill) s. one's place, to replace s. o.; **hervorragende ~ einnehmen** to fill the bill *(Br.)*; **leitende ~ einnehmen** to lead; **gute ~ erhalten** to secure a good appointment; **an Ort und ~ erledigen** to do it now (right away); **an die falsche ~ geraten** to bark up the wrong tree; **~ haben** to be in (hold) a situation; **gute ~ haben** to be in a good position, to have a good berth *(Br.)*; **~ innehaben** to hold a job (an appointment); **bedeutende ~ innehaben** to take a prominent place; **~ auf Lebenszeit innehaben** to hold a post (office) for life; **~ einige Zeit innehaben** to fill a post for some time; **~ zeitweilig innehaben** to be in office pro tempore; **nicht von der ~ kommen** *(Verhandlungen)* to be at a deadlock, to make no headway; **an letzter ~ auf eine Liste kommen** to rank last on a list; **von dieser ~ auf keinen Pfennig hoffen können** to expect no help from that quarter; **j. in eine ~ aufrücken lassen** to promote s. o. to an office; **seine Schritte zu einer ~ lenken** to incline one's steps towards a place; **weit abgeschlagen an zweiter ~ liegen** to trail a distant second; **sich zur ~ melden** to report o. s. present; **zwei ~n weiter rücken** to move the decimal point two places; **~ schaffen** to cause a vacancy; **an jds. ~ sein** to be in s. one's skin; **zur ~ sein** to be on the scene; **pünktlich zur ~ sein** to arrive on the dot; **j. an eines anderen ~ setzen** to subrogate s. o. in the place of another; **seinen Namen an die freigelassene ~ setzen** to write one's name in the space indicated; **an der richtigen ~ sitzen** *(Bemerkung)* to go home; **an erster ~ stehen** to rank (come) first, to take precedence; **~ streichen** to abolish a post; **nach einer passenden ~ für eine Fabrik suchen** to look for a suitable site for a factory; **j. an einer empfindlichen ~ treffen** to touch a sensitive nerve in s. o., to touch s. one's tender spot (s. o. on the raw, to the quick), to flick s. o. on the raw; **an jds. ~ treten** to succeed (replace, supersede) s. o.; **in einer Diskussion auf der ~ treten** to mark time in a discussion; **~ übernehmen** to undertake a post; **sich um eine ~ umtun** to be looking for a job, to apply for a situation; **sich an jds. ~ versetzen** to imagine o. s. in another's position; **sich an die zuständige ~ wenden** to apply to the proper quarter; **an erster ~ genannt werden** *(Schauspieler)* to get top billing; **~ zitieren** to refer to (quote) a passage;
solange er die ~ innehatte during his occupancy of the post.
stellen to place, to put, *(beisteuern)* to contribute, *(liefern)* to supply, *(zuweisen)* to allocate, to assign;

j. ~ to hunt s. o. down; **sich** ~ to accept a challenge, *(Kurse)* to rule, *(mil.)* to enlist, to join up; **sich [im Preis auf]** ~ to amount (come) to, to run up to, to be priced at; **in Abrede** ~ to deny, to disavow; **sein Amt zur Verfügung** ~ to tender one's resignation; **bescheidene Ansprüche** ~ to have simple tastes; **übertriebene Ansprüche** ~ to exaggerate one's claims; **Antrag** ~ to file an application, *(in Sitzung)* to bring forward a motion; **Antrag auf Konkurseröffnung** ~ to file one's petition (a declaration of bankruptcy); **Antrag auf Schließung der Debatte** ~ to move closure; **Auto in die Garage** ~ to garage a car; **Bedingungen** ~ to make (stipulate) conditions; **seine Bedingungen** ~ to make one's terms; **jem. eine Belohnung in Aussicht** ~ to promise s. o. a reward; **bereit** ~ to get ready, to prepare, *(Geld)* to appropriate, *(Geld für bestimmten Zweck)* to earmark; **unter Beweis** ~ to prove one's case; **sich billiger** ~ *(Kurse)* to rule lower; **Bürgen** ~ to put up bail; **jem. hinreichende Deckung zur Verfügung** ~ to furnish s. o. with (put s. o. in) funds; **in Dienst** ~ *(Schiff)* to put into commission; **sich in den Dienst einer guten Sache** ~ to devote o. s. to a good cause; **jem. seine Dienste zur Verfügung** ~ to place o. s. at s. one's disposal; **zur Diskussion** ~ to open a discussion; **sich dumm** ~ to play the idiot, to pretend ignorance; **in jds. Ermessen** ~ to leave to s. one's discretion; **Ersatz für j.** ~ to substitute (supply) s. o.; **Frage zur Diskussion** ~ to submit a question to the debate; **dumme Fragen** ~ to ask silly questions; **sich freiwillig** ~ *(Rechtsbrecher)* to give o. s. up (surrender to the police); **die meisten Gastarbeiter** ~ to supply most of the foreign workers; **Geld für ein Unternehmen zur Verfügung** ~ to put up the money for an undertaking; **jem. einen Geldbetrag zur Verfügung** ~ to place a sum at s. one's disposal; **sich dem Gericht** ~ to give o. s. up to the law; **j. vor Gericht** ~ to bring s. o. up for trial; **sich gut mit jem.** ~ to get on good terms with s. o.; **sich hinter j.** ~ to back s. o.; **sich recht hoch** ~ *(Preis)* to come rather high; **sich höher** ~ *(Kurse)* to rule higher; **sich den Journalisten zu einer Pressekonferenz** ~ to present o. s. to the journalists at a press conference; **sich zum Kampf** ~ to accept combat; **Kaution** ~ to put up (furnish) bail; **Kind unter Vormundschaft** ~ to place a child under s. one's guardianship; **sich krank** ~ to malinger; **Kreditantrag** ~ to apply for a credit line *(US)*; **sich der allgemeinen Kritik** ~ to face the music; **seinen Mann** ~ to be up to the mark; **sich zum Militärdienst** ~ to join up; **j. in den Mittelpunkt** ~ to make s. o. the center *(US)* (centre, *Br.*) of attention; **auf Null** ~ to set a zero; **niedrigeres Preisangebot** ~ to quote a lower price; **auf die Probe** ~ to put to the test; **j. vor ein Problem** ~ to confront s. o. with a problem; **Problem in den Mittelpunkt seiner Rede** ~ to focus a problem in one's speech; **Radio leiser** ~ to turn the radio down; **j. vor ein Rätsel** ~ to puzzle s. o.; **in Rechnung** ~ to put (pass) to account, to charge, to debit; **zur Rede** ~ to take to task, to call to account; **Schadenersatzansprüche** ~ to put in a claim for damages; **j. in den Schatten** ~ to put s. o. in the shade, to wipe s. one's eyes *(sl.)*; **etw. zur Schau** ~ to display (exhibit) s. th.; **Schiff außer Dienst** ~ to take a ship off the active list; **schlechter** ~ to discriminate; **Sicherheiten** ~ to provide cover; **Signal auf Halt** ~ to switch a signal to stop; **sich auf den Standpunkt** ~ to hold the view; **unter Strafe** ~ to make punishable; **sich stur** ~ to stall *(US sl.)*; **Termin** ~ to fix a date; **Ultimatum** ~ to deliver an ultimatum; **zum Verkauf** ~ to expose for sale, *(Grundstück)* to list *(US)*; **Vertrauensfrage** ~ to ask for a vote of confidence; **Weichen für j.** ~ to pave the way for s. o.; **neue Wohnung in Aussicht** ~ to hold out the prospect of a new flat; **zahlbar** ~ to make payable, *(Wechsel)* to domicile, to domiciliate; **Zeugen** ~ to produce a witness; **Zug auf ein Nebengleis** ~ to switch a train onto a siding.

Stellen|abbau reduction of staff; **~angebot** job offer (opening), position available, offer of appointment, *(Inserat)* position offered, situation vacant, help wanted, unfilled vacancies, want ads *(US)*; **~anzeigen** advertisements of appointments (for positions), unfilled vacancies, help-wanted ads *(US)*, ad placements *(US)*; **~aufkündigungsmitteilung** redundancy notice *(Br.)*; **~ausschreibung** advertisement of a vacancy; **~beschreibung** job description; **~besetzung** filling of vacancies, staffing, placement; **~besetzungsplan** organizational chart, manning table, employee roster, staffing schedule *(US)*, job pattern; **kopflastiger ~besetzungsplan** top-heavy organizational chart; **~besetzungsplan für Führungskräfte** management inventory; **~bewerber** candidate for a post, applicant for an employment, applicant for a position, [employment (job)] applicant; **~bewerbung** application for a position (job, employment), application; **~börse** job centre *(Br.)* (center, *US*); **~einsparung** abolition of an office; **~gemeinkosten** departmental burden; **~gesuch** application for a position (job), *(Zeitung)* situation (employment) wanted, want ads *(US)*; **~gesuche kostenlos veröffentlichen** to run free ads for job seekers *(US)*; **~inhaber** jobholder, incumbent, occupant of a post, officeholder *(US)*; **~jäger** office (place) hunter; **~jägerei** office (place) hunting; **~kürzung** job slash; **~leiter** agency head.

stellenlos unemployed, [thrown] out of employment, unengaged, out of place (situation, *Br.*), unplaced.

Stellen|markt labo(u)r (employment, job) market; **~markt für Raumfahrtspezialisten** aerospace job market; **~nachweis** employment bureau *(Br.)*, labo(u)r exchange, placement agency *(US)*; **staatlicher ~nachweis** employment exchange *(Br.)*, public employment office *(US)*, government placement center *(US)*; **~netz** holding of outdoor advertising sites; **~plan** classification plan, manning table, organizational chart, establishment in a budget, staff planning, staffing schedule *(US)*, establishment plan; **~rotation** job rotation; **auf der ~suche sein** to be looking for a job; **rein politisch begründete ~vergabe** spoils system *(US)*; **für die ~vergabe zuständig sein** to be in s. one's gift; **~vergaberecht** patronage; **~vermittler** employment (placement, *US*) agent, placement officer *(US)*.

Stellenvermittlung employment (domestic) agency (bureau), placement agency *(US)*, job placement *(US)*, registry office *(US)*;
staatliche ~ government placement center *(US)*;
amtliche ~ **für Führungskräfte** appointments board *(Br.)*; ~ **für Hausangestellte** servants' registry.

Stellenvermittlungs|büro appointments board *(Br.)*, employment agent (agency, bureau, *Br.*), registry office *(US)*, placement agency *(US)*, *(Hausangestellte)* servants' registry; **gemeinsames ~büro von Arbeitgeber und Arbeitnehmer** joint hiring hall; **~dienst** placement *(US)* (employment) service; **~möglichkeiten** placement facilities *(US)*.

Stellen|verzeichnis site list; **geregelter ~wechsel** rotation; **~wert** *(Computer)* digit value.

stellenweise in places (patches, spots, *US*), here and there.

Stell|fläche shelf (standing, charging) space; **~geld** premium for double option (spread, *US*); **~geschäft** privilege, put and call, pac *(Br.)*, spread *(US)*; **~macher** wheelwright; **~platz** parking space; **~schild** portable panel.

Stellung position, post, place, job, employ[ment], engagement, station, occupation, level, berth *(Br.)*, assignment, billet, *(Anordnung)* arrangement, *(Ansehen)* [social] standing, position, rank, status, state, level, walk, *(Funktion)* character, capacity, *(Haltung)* pose, stance, *(Hausangestellte)* service, *(Platz)* place, position, location;
in amtlicher ~ in commission; **in angesehener** ~ of good position; **in aufsichtführender** ~ in a supervisory capacity; **in führender** ~ at executive level, in the highest flight; **in einer guten** ~ well-positioned, in good bread; **in einer hohen** ~ in a high position; **in leitender** ~ in a managerial capacity, at executive level; **in meiner** ~ **als Botschafter** in my capacity as ambassador; **in seiner** ~ **als ...** in his character of ...; **in sitzender** ~ in a sitting posture; **in ungekündigter** ~ not under notice; **in unsicherer** ~ unsettled; **ohne** ~ unplaced, out-of-situation *(Br.)*, out of a job, unemployed; **unter Mißbrauch seiner amtlichen** ~ under colo(u)r of one's office;
~ **gesucht** *(Zeitung)* [situations] wanted;
amtliche ~ official position, public function; **angesehene** ~ reputable employment, well-established position; **ausbaufähige** ~ position with good prospects, developable position; **ausschlaggebende** ~ post of commanding importance; **beamtenähnliche** ~ quasi-official position; **beruflich bedeutsame** ~ career position; **befestigte** ~ *(mil.)* fortified position, lodgment; **begehrenswerte** ~ plum; **beherrschende** ~ commanding (dominating) position, controlling power; **bequeme** ~ fat job; **berufliche** ~ business standing (position); **besoldete** ~ salaried position; **gut bezahlte** ~ well-paid position; **schlecht bezahlte** ~ badly paid situation; **voll bezahlte** ~ full-time job; **einflußreiche** ~ post of authority, position of influence; **feste** ~ stable position, permanent position (job), perch; **finanzielle** ~ capital rating; **führende** ~ managerial occupation, head; **geachtete** ~ respectability; **gehobene** ~ advanced position; **gehobenere** ~ elevated (senior) position, high-level job *(US)*; **gesellschaftliche** ~ social standing (position, status), station of life, position in society, conditions; **günstige** ~ advantageous position; **gute** ~ good place (billet); **hochdotierte** ~ high-paying position, highly paid job; **hohe** ~ high position, eminence; **leitende** ~ key position (post), policy-making (senior, executive, leading, managerial, *US*, management, managing) position, administrative post; **marktbeherrschende** ~ [dom-

inant] market power; **nichtamtliche** ~ private station; **niedrige** ~ inferior (subordinate) position, juniority; **obrigkeitliche** ~ magisterial rank; **passende** ~ suitable employment; **pensionsberechtigte** ~ pensionable employment, pensionable post; **prozessuale** ~ legal standing in court; **rechtliche** ~ legal status; **rückwärtige** ~ *(mil.)* reserve position; **selbständige** ~ occupation of a professional nature; **senkrechte** ~ upright; **sichere** ~ sound position, foothold, footing; **soziale** ~ social station (position, standing), status, walk of life, rank, class; **unkündbare** ~ permanent tenure; **untergeordnete** ~ subordinated (lower, inferior) position, juniority; **verantwortungsvolle** ~ responsible position, position of responsibility (authority); **gesellschaftlich verbesserte** ~ improvement in one's social condition; **hervorragend verteidigte** ~ *(mil.)* best defended box; **vorgeschobene** ~ *(mil.)* advance position, outpost; **vorteilhafte** ~ weather gauge; **vorübergehende** ~ temporary position (post);

~ **eines Antrags** filing of an application; ~ **als ungelernter Arbeiter** labo(u)ring job; ~ **ohne Aufstiegsmöglichkeiten** blind-alley job; **höchste ~en in einer Berufssparte** prizes of a profession; ~ **in der Betriebshierarchie** relative position within the organizational chart; **führende** ~ **in der Gemeinde** local influence, position of community leadership; ~ **mit Härtezulage** hardship post; ~ **in der Raumfahrtindustrie** aerospace job; ~ **des Verbrauchers** consumer's role; ~ **unter Vormundschaft** placing under guardianship;

~ **ablehnen** to turn down a job; ~ **annehmen** to accept (take) a position, to take a job; ~ **außer Haus annehmen** *(Hausangestellte)* to go out; ~ **wieder annehmen** to re-enter an employment; ~ **einer Kaution anordnen** to hold to bail; ~ **antreten** to enter upon (take) office, to start on a job, to take up one's post (a position); **neue** ~ **antreten** to take a new situation (position); ~ **bei jem. antreten** to enter into s. one's service; **seine** ~ **aufgeben** to leave (give up) one's position (job), to relinquish one's appointment, to throw up (quit, *US*) one's job, to turn one's job in, to fling (pack) up one's job, to step out *(US)*; **feindliche** ~ **aufrollen** to turn the enemy's flank; **seine** ~ **ausbauen** to consolidate one's position; **selbständige** ~ **gewissenhaft ausfüllen** to handle a large degree of independence with great accuracy; **bedeutende** ~ **im Leben ausfüllen** to occupy a high station in life; **seine gesellschaftliche** ~ **ausnutzen** to pull rank *(sl.)*; **seine** ~ **befestigen** to strengthen one's position; **seine** ~ **behalten** to retain one's position, to hold down a job *(US)*; **seine** ~ **behaupten** to hold one's own; ~ **beibehalten** to stay on the job; ~ **bekleiden** to fill a position, to hold an office; **hohe** ~ **bekleiden** to be high in office; ~ **bekommen** to obtain a position; **gute** ~ **bekommen** to drop into a position; ~ **durch Beziehungen bekommen** to secure an office through one's pull; **j. in seiner** ~ **belassen** to maintain s. o. in a position; **sich mit allen Mitteln um eine** ~ **bemühen** to make every effort to get a job; **vorhandene Einrichtungen zur Befestigung der sozialen** ~ **benutzen** to use facilities as status conveniences; **j. seiner** ~ **berauben** to turn s. o. out of his position; **j. in eine** ~ **berufen** to appoint s. o. to an office; ~ **für j. besorgen** to find a post for s. o. (s. o. a job), to land s. o. a job, to fix s. o. up with a job; **sich um eine** ~ **bewerben** to try (apply) for a post (position), to put in for a job (post), to run for an office; ~ **beziehen** to take one's stand; **feste** ~ **beziehen** to dig o. s. in; **feste** ~ **zu einer Frage beziehen** to adopt a definite position on a question; **Geschütz in** ~ **bringen** to bring a gun into the firing position; **j. um seine** ~ **bringen** to do (kick) s. o. out of a job; **sich für eine** ~ **in Vorschlag bringen** to offer o. s. for a post; ~ **einnehmen** to rank high; **bescheidene** ~ **einnehmen** to occupy a humble position; **feindliche** ~ **einnehmen** to carry the enemy's position; **führende** ~ **einnehmen** to hold a high-level position; **hohe** ~ **einnehmen** to rank high; **führende** ~ **bei Hörerbefragungen einnehmen** to hold a lead in program(me) ratings; **j. wieder in seine frühere** ~ **einsetzen** to reinstate s. o. in his former office; **j. seiner** ~ **entheben** to dismiss s. o. from a post; ~ **ergattern** to grab a job *(fam.)*; ~ **erhalten** to get a situation; **gute** ~ **erlangen** to drop into a position; **seine eigene** ~ **erschüttern** to do s. th. derogatory to one's position; **sich hilfreich bei der Beschaffung einer gutbezahlten** ~ **für einen Freund erweisen** to be instrumental in finding a well-paid job for a friend; **jds.** ~ **festigen** to assure s. one's position; **seine** ~ **festigen** to consolidate one's position, to raise one's reputation; ~ **finden** to find work, to land a job; **im Ausland eine** ~ **finden** to find a situation abroad; **bequeme** ~ **finden** to find a snug berth; **leicht eine** ~ **finden** to be jumped at; **vorteilhafte** ~ **finden** to find a lodgment; ~ **für j. finden** to fix s. o. up with a job; **in eine führende** ~ **gelangen** to move up to an executive position; ~ **haben** to have a situation; **angesehene** ~ **haben** to be in good standing; **erstklassige (glänzende)** ~ **haben** to have a first-rate position, to have a fine job; **gute** ~ **haben** to be in good position, to have a snug berth *(Br.)*; **keine** ~ **haben** to be out of a situation (unemployed); **stärkere** ~ **haben** to be in the driver's seat *(US)*; ~ **im Ausland haben** to work on assignment; ~ **in Aussicht haben** to have a job in prospect; **beherrschende** ~ **über einen Talzugang haben** *(Festung)* to command the entrance to a valley; **seine** ~ **als Handelsplatz eingebüßt haben** to have lost its dominating position as a trading center; ~ **halten** to hold the fort; **seine** ~ **halten** to hold the pass (down a job, *US*), *(mil.)* to stand to one's colo(u)rs; ~ **offen halten** to keep a job open; **seine** ~ **an den Nagel hängen** to chuck up *(sl.)*; **sich in eine** ~ **hineindrängen** to edge one's way into a job; **sich in eine gute** ~ **hineinmogeln** to manoeuvre for position *(fam.)*; ~ **innehaben** to occupy a post; **bedeutsame** ~ **innehaben** to hold a prominent position; **dominierende** ~ **innehaben** to dominate (over) others by force of character; **zufällig zu einer guten** ~ **kommen** to step into a good job; **seine** ~ **kündigen** to give notice to one's employer; **den Erfordernissen einer** ~ **Genüge leisten** to have the necessary qualifications for a post; ~ **ausfindig machen** to scent a job; ~ **nehmen** to adopt an attitude, to express (take) a view, to give one's opinion, to define one's attitude, to comment; **ausführlich zu etw.** ~ **nehmen** to spread o. s.; **zu einer Frage** ~ **nehmen** to take position on a question, to square up to a problem; **zu einem Problem als Steuerzahler** ~ **nehmen** to view a matter from the taxpayer's standpoint; **redaktionell** ~ **nehmen** to editorialize; **befestigte** ~ **im Sturm nehmen** to jump a stronghold; **sich eine** ~ **schaffen** to gain a position; **nicht mehr in der alten** ~ **sein** not to be on one's old lay; **auswärts in** ~ **sein** to live out *(US)*; **ohne** ~ **sein** to be out of a job, to be thrown out of employment; **in untergeordneter** ~ **sein** to be in an inferior position; **für seine** ~ **geeignet sein** to be fit for one's job, to be fitted for a post; **feindliche** ~ **stürmen** to storm the enemy's position; ~ **mit guten Aufstiegsmöglichkeiten suchen** to seek a situation with a future; ~ **dem Feind überlassen** to abandon a position to the enemy; **jem. eine** ~ **übertragen** to assign a post to s. o.; **sich nach einer** ~ **umsehen** to look for a job (situation), to set one's bag for an office *(Br.)*; **j. in einer** ~ **unterbringen** to find a situation for s. o.; **sich in einer** ~ **verankern** to establish o. s. in a secure position; **seine** ~ **verbessern** to improve one's situation; **seine** ~ **Beziehungen (Protektion) verdanken** to owe one's position to influence, to get a job by push; **bessere** ~ **verdienen** to be too good for one's situation; **j. aus seiner** ~ **verdrängen** to edge s. o. out of a job; **jem. zu einer besseren** ~ **verhelfen** to assist s. o. in advancing his position; **seine** ~ **verlieren** to lose (fall from) one's position (job), to be thrown out of employment, to forfeit one's place; **seine gesellschaftliche** ~ **verlieren** to lose one's caste; **sich durch Beziehungen eine** ~ **verschaffen** to pull the wires for office; **sich durch List und Tücke eine** ~ **verschaffen** to push one's way into a job; **jem. durch unlautere Machenschaften eine** ~ **verschaffen** to create a job for s. o.; **sich die für eine** ~ **notwendigen Kenntnisse verschaffen** to fit o. s. out for a post; **jem. eine gute** ~ **versprechen** to ensure s. o. a good post; **seine** ~ **wechseln** to change one's position, *(häufig)* to jobhop; **in eine** ~ **mit höherem Verantwortungsbereich befördert werden** to be promoted to heavier responsibilities; **den Feind aus der** ~ **werfen** to dislodge the enemy; ~ **wiederaufnehmen** to re-enter an employment; **einem Angestellten seine alte** ~ **wiedergeben** to restore an employee to his old post.

Stellungnahme *(Antwort)* answer, *(Beurteilung)* endorsement, *(Entscheidung)* decision, *(Erklärung)* declaration, statement, commentary, *(Meinung)* [advisory] opinion, comment, attitude, approach, [point of] view;

in einer kritischen ~ **zu den Vorfällen** in a critical comment to the incidents; **zu Ihrer** ~ for your observation;

abweichende ~ dissenting opinion; **gutachtliche** ~ advisory opinion; **keine** ~ no comment; **positive** ~ favo(u)rable opinion; **mit Gründen versehene** ~ reasoned opinion; **vorsichtige** ~ reserved judgment; **vorurteilslose** ~ large attitude;

~ **zu einem Thema** approach to a subject;

~ **abgeben** to express an opinion, to make a statement, to declare one's attitude; ~ **ablehnen** to decline to comment; ~ **einholen** to ask for an opinion; **sich jeder** ~ **enthalten** to refrain from comments; **Gelegenheit zur** ~ **geben** to afford s. o. the opportunity to give his opinion; ~ **veröffentlichen** to publish a statement; **sich seine** ~ **vorbehalten** to reserve one's view, to be noncommittal; ~ **vorbringen** to offer an opinion.

Stellungs|ausbau consolidation of field fortification; **~befehl** calling up, enlistment (induction) order *(US)*; **~gesuch** application for a position; **~krieg** trench warfare.

stellungslos out of a job (employ), unemployed;
~ **sein** to be thrown out of employment.
Stellungs|suche job hunting; **auf ~suche sein** to be looking for a job; **~suchender** [employment] applicant, job seeker (candidate), job hunter, place seeker; **~verlust** loss of office, job loss; **~wechsel** change of position, *(mil.)* evolution; **häufiger ~wechsel** job-hopping.
stellvertreten to represent, to act as deputy, to deputize.
stellvertretend substitutional, representative, vicarious, acting, vice, deputy;
Amt ~ ausüben to hold an office as deputy; **~ für j. sprechen** to speak for and on behalf of s. o.;
~er Abteilungsleiter assistant department head; **~er Direktor** assistant manager (director), vice manager; **~er Geschäftsführer** deputy (active) manager; **~er Kassierer** assistant paying teller; **~er Kommandeur** second-in-command; **~er Leiter** acting manager; **~ ausgeübte Vollmacht** vicarious authority (power); **~er Vorsitzender** deputy (acting) chairman, vice-chairman (president).
Stellvertreter *(Aktienstimmrecht)* proxy [holder], *(Bevollmächtigter)* agent, representative, attorney in fact, locum tenens, *(Ersatzmann)* substitute, supply, secondary, alternate *(US)*, *(mil.)* second in command, *(Vertreter)* deputy, delegate, surrogate;
Botschafter ~ Ambassador's deputy; **selbstkontrahierender ~** procurator in rem suam;
~ des Polizeichefs deputy sheriff;
seine Stimme durch einen ~ abgeben *(Hauptversammlung)* to vote by proxy; **als ~ auftreten** to act as deputy; **j. zu seinem ~ einsetzen** to appoint s. o. one's deputy; **als ~ fungieren** to appear by proxy, to stand proxy for; **als ~ für j. fungieren** to act as a deputy (substitute) for s. o.; **als jds. ~ handeln, ~ für j. sein** to deputize for s. o.; **zu jds. ~ bestimmt sein** to be appointed s. one's substitute;
~ebene number-two level.
Stellvertretung representation [of persons], proxy, agency, substitution, deputyship, principal and agent.
in ~ by deputy;
gewillkürte ~ agency created by conduct of parties; **verdeckte ~** undisclosed agency; **wirkliche ~** actual agency;
~ für j. ausüben to stand proxy for s. o.
Stellwerk *(Bahn)* signal box, cabin *(Br.)*, switch tower *(US)*.
Stellwerksweiche interlocking points.
Stelzen, auf on stilts.
stemmen to lift, to heave, to hoist;
sich ~ to oppose, to resist; **sich gegen etw. ~** to resist (oppose) s. th.; **sich gegen alle Neuerungen ~** to be dead set against every innovation; **sich mit allen Mitteln gegen die Rezession ~** to buck the recession *(US)*.
Stempel impress, imprint, *(Datum)* [dated] stamp, postmark, *(Gold)* hallmark, *(Lochstempel)* punch, *(Post)* postmark, *(Prägezeichen)* mark, stamp, *(Stempelabdruck)* stamp, *(Stempelsteuer)* stamp duty *(Br.)* (tax, *US*), *(auf Waren)* brand, *(Werbeaufdruck)* cachet, publicity impression, postmark ad *(US)*;
mit einem ~ versehen *(Waren)* branded;
eingedrückter ~ impressed stamp;
~ der gesellschaftlichen Anerkennung stamp of social approval;
~ der Unaufrichtigkeit mark of insincerety;
~ aufdrücken to print, to stamp, to affix a stamp, to impress; **dem Leben eines Volkes seinen ~ aufdrücken** to make one's mark on the life of a country; **seiner Zeit seinen ~ aufdrücken** to leave one's mark upon one's time; **mit einem ~ bestätigen** to vouch; **~ der Armut tragen** to bear every mark of poverty; **~ vom 10. Juli tragen** to bear the postmark of July 10th.; **mit einem ~ verziehen** *(Buchbinderei)* to tool;
~abgabe stamp duty *(Br.)* (tax, *US*); **~amt** stamp office *(US)*; **~beidrückung** stamping; **~bogen** stamped [sheet of] paper; **~bruder** dole drawer *(Br.)*; **~farbe** stamping ink; **~freiheit** exemption from stamp duty; **~gebühr** stamp duty *(Br.)* (tax, *US*), *(Aktien)* transfer duty; **~gebühr bezahlt** stamp collected; **~geld** stamp duty, *(Arbeitslosenbeitrag)* unemployment tax; **~kissen** stamp (ink) pad.
Stempelmarke inland-revenue (duty, finance, adhesive) stamp;
~ aufkleben to affix a stamp; **Antrag auf Erstattung beschädigter ~n stellen** to make a claim for allowance of spoiled stamps.
Stempelmaschine *(Post)* stamping (cancelling) machine.
stempeln to seal, to stamp, *(brandmarken)* to brand, to stigmatize, *(Gold)* to mark, *(Kontrolluhr)* to clock in (out), *(Silber)* to hallmark;
Adresse auf den Briefumschlag ~ to stamp an address on an envelope; **bei Arbeitsanfang (Arbeitsende) ~** to clock in (out); **mit dem Datumsstempel ~** to datestamp; **j. zum Demagogen ~** to label s. o. as a demagogue; **Urkunde ~** to stamp a document; **~ gehen** to be on unemployment rolls, to be on (draw) the dole *(Br.)*.
Stempelpapier stamp[ed] paper.
Stempelsteuer stamp duty *(Br.)* (tax, *US*), *(Effekten)* issue stamp;
~ bezahlen to stamp.
stempelsteuerfrei exempt from stamp duty.
Stempelsteuer|gesetz Stamp Act *(Br.)*; **~marke** inland revenue stamp; **~marke aufkleben** to affix a stamp; **Antrag auf Erstattung beschädigter ~marken stellen** to make a claim for allowance of spoiled stamps; **~pauschalierung** composition for stamp duty.
stempelsteuerpflichtig subject (liable) to stamp duty;
~ sein to incur stamp duty.
Stempel|uhr time clock; **~zeichen** countermark.
Stengel, nicht gleich vom ~ fallen to keep one's skirt on;
ich bin fast vom ~ gefallen you could have knocked me down with a feather.
Stenoblock shorthand pad, notebook.
Stenograf stenographer *(US)*, shorthand writer.
Stenografendienst shorthand (stenographic, *US*) service.
Stenografie stenography, shorthand [writing].
Stenografieren shorthand writing.
stenografieren to write (take down in) shorthand.
Stenografiermaschine stenotype.
stenografiert in shorthand.
stenografisch stenographic[al], shorthand;
~ aufnehmen to write (take down in) shorthand; **Rede ~ aufnehmen** to take down a speech in shorthand;
sich ~e Aufzeichnungen machen to take notes in shorthand; **~e Niederschrift** shorthand, stenographic record; **~e Notizen** shorthand notes.
Stenogramm shorthand note, stenograph;
~ aufnehmen to take dictation in shorthand; **aus dem ~ übertragen** to write down from dictation, to transcribe;
~aufnahme taking down shorthand notes; **~block** shorthand notebook; **fehlerhafte ~übertragung** mistranscription in shorthand.
Steno|kontoristin shorthand clerk; **~sekretärin** shorthand secretary; **~typist** stenotypist, [shorthand] typist; **~typistin** lady (girl) typist, female stenotypist.
Steppdecke quilt, comfort *(US)*.
Steppenbrandkrieg bushfire war.
Sterbe|alter age of death; **~beihilfe** death benefit, funeral allowance, death grant *(Br.)*; **~bett** death bed; **~buch** register of deaths.
Sterbefall death, decease, exitus;
~ anzeigen to notify a death; **~ beurkunden** to register a death;
~geld funeral costs insurance contribution; **~versicherung** funeral cost insurance.
Sterbegeld death benefit, death grant *(Br.)*, funeral allowance (benefit);
~ für Betriebsunfälle industrial death benefit;
~verein mit Umlageverfahren assessment company; **~vorsorge** death benefit protection.
Sterbe|glocke passing (death) bell; **~häufigkeit** mortality; **~hilfe** euthanasia; **~jahr** year of death; **~kasse** funeral society, friendly society, burial club (fund, society); **~kurve** mortality curve.
Sterben death;
etw. zum ~ langweilig finden to be bored to death; **zum Leben zu wenig und zum ~ zu viel sein** to keep the wolf from the door.
sterben to die, to decease, to pay one's debt to nature;
aus Altersschwäche ~ to die of old age; **in Ausübung seines Berufes ~** to die in harness; **als Bettler ~** to die a beggar; **feige ~** to die the dunghill; **wie die Fliegen ~** to die like flies; **im Geruch eines Heiligen ~** to die in the odo(u)r of sanctity; **gleichzeitig ~** to die simultaneously; **Hungers ~** to die of hunger; **kämpfend ~** to die the game; **kinderlos ~** to die without issue; **infolge (an) einer Krankheit ~** to die of an illness; **vor Neugier fast ~** to be dying with curiosity; **reich ~** to cut up well *(sl.)*; **in den Sielen ~** to die in harness; **ohne ein Testament zu hinterlassen ~** to die intestate; **eines gewaltsamen Todes ~** to die a violent death; **eines natürlichen Todes ~** to die a natural death (in one's bed); **bei einem Unfall ~** to be killed in an accident; **tief verschuldet ~** to die deeply in debt; **völlig verwahrlost ~** to die in total neglect.
sterbend dying.
Sterbender dying man.

sterbenslangweilig terribly dull.
Sterbens | seele, keiner ~seele etw. erzählen not to tell a soul; **kein ~wörtchen** not a syllable (single word).
Sterbe | pfleger *(Krankenhaus)* terminal ward; **~register** register of deaths; **~statistik** mortality statistics; **~stunde** fatal hour; **~tafeln** mortality (survival, select, mortuary, *US*) tables; **~urkunde** certificate of death, death certificate; **~verein** friendly society *(Br.)*; **~versicherung** burial insurance; **~wahrscheinlichkeit** *(Versicherung)* probable death rate; **~worte** dying words; **~ziffer** death rate; **~zuschuß** funeral grant.
sterblich mortal;
sich ~ blamieren to make an absolute fool of o. s.;
~e Hülle dust, earthly (mortal) remains.
Sterblicher, gewöhnlicher ordinary mortal.
Sterblichkeit mortality;
eingetretene ~ actual mortality; **hohe ~** high mortality.
Sterblichkeits | erwartung force of mortality; **~kontrolle** mortality control; **~kurve** survivor-life (mortality, retirement) curve; **~quotient** mortality ratio; **nach Altersgruppen aufgegliederte ~rate** age-specific mortality rate; **~risiko** mortality risk, risk of death; **~rückgang** decline in mortality, mortality reduction; **~tabelle** life (select, mortality, mortuary, *US*) table; **~tafeln** actuarial (experience, expectation of life) tables; **amtliche ~tafeln** American Experience Tables *(US)*; **~überhang** excess mortality; **~ziffer** mortality rate, death rate, rate of mortality; **nicht aufgegliederte ~ziffer** crude death rate; **hohe ~ziffer** high (heavy) mortality.
Stereo high fidelity, stereo, hi-fi;
~anlage stereo equipment (set); **~aufnahme** stereo[phonic] pickup (recording); **~bandgerät** stereo tape recorder; **~box** stereophonic loudspeaker box; **~eindruck, ~effekt** stereo illusion; **~empfang** stereo reception; **~empfang auf mehreren Kanälen** multichannel stereo; **~gerät** stereo unit, stereophonic record player; **~grammophon** high-fidelity gramophone; **~kamera** stereoscopic camera; **~klang** high fidelity; **~kopfhörer** stereo compatible headphone; **~lautsprecher** stereophonic loudspeaker box.
Stereophonie stereophony.
stereophonisch stereo[phonic];
~e Tonwiedergabe stereophonic sound, stereo.
Stereo | -, Galvano- und Nyloprintplatten für den Hochdruck stereotype, electrotype and nylo printing plates for relief prints; **~rundfunkgerät** stereo radio set; **~sendung** stereo[phonic] broadcast.
stereoskopisches Bild stereograph.
Stereoton stereophonic sound.
stereotyp stereotyped, cliché-ridden;
~ wiederholen to stereotype;
~e Antwort cliché answer; **~e Redenswendung** stock phrase.
Stereo | typdruckverfahren stereotypography; **~wiedergabe** stereo reproduction.
steril sterile, barren, unproductive, infertile;
~e Atmosphäre atmosphere of sterility; **~e Diskussion** sterile discussion.
sterilisieren to sterilize.
Sterilisierung sterilization.
Sterling | block sterling bloc *(Br.)*; **~gebiet** sterling area; **~krise** sterling crisis; **~obligationen** sterling bonds; **~saldo** sterling balance.
Stern, in den ~en geschrieben in the lap of the gods;
die ~e befragen to question the stars; **nach den ~en greifen** to cry for the moon; **fünf ~e im Hotelführer haben** to be a five-star hotel; **~e sehen** *(fig.)* to see stars; **seinem guten ~ vertrauen** to follow one's star;
~antenne star aerial.
Sternchen *(*)* asterisk, *(Film)* starlet.
Sterndeuter astrologer, star-gazer.
Sternen | banner stars and stripes, Star-spangled Banner *(US)*; **~licht** starlight, starry light; **~zelt** firmanent.
sternhagelvoll drunk as a lord, whole-seas over, sloshed, sozzled, canned *(US sl.)*;
~ sein to have three sheets in the wind.
sternklare Nacht starlight night.
Stern | schnuppe shooting star; **~tafel** star map; **~warte** observatory.
stetig continual, *(Markt)* steady, continuous, stable;
~e Produktion settled production; **~e Zunahme** steady increase.
Stetigkeit continuance *(Markt)* continuity, steadiness, stability;
~ in der Geschäftsführung consistent business policy.

Steuer tax, *(Abgabe)* impost, imposition, assessment, levy, lot *(Br.)*, rate *(Br.)*, *(Auto)* [steering] wheel, *(Schiff)* rudder, helm, *(Zoll)* customs duty;
abzüglich ~n less taxes; **einschließlich ~** tax included; **frei von ~n** tax-exempt, tax-free; **mit ~n überladen** tax-ridden; **nach Abzug der ~n** after [deduction for] taxes, tax[es] paid; **nach Bezahlung der ~n** tax[es] paid; **vor ~** pretax, less taxes; **vor Berücksichtigung (Abzug) der ~n** prior to deduction of taxes, less tax; **zuzüglich ~** plus tax;
da man gerade von ~n spricht talking of taxes;
auf den Verbraucher abgewälzte ~ tax shifted onto the consumer; **abzuziehende ~** tax to be deducted; **allgemeine ~n** general taxes; **angefallene ~n** accrued taxes; **anrechenbare ~** imputable tax; **anteilmäßige ~** pro rata (proportional) tax; **aufgeteilte ~** apportioned tax *(US)*; **ausgewiesene ~n** declared taxes; **mit einem höheren Satz berechnete ~** higher-rate tax; **im Abzugswege zu bezahlende ~** tax payable by deduction; **zuviel bezahlte ~** excess tax; **degressive ~** degressive tax; **direkte ~n** tax payable direct, assessed taxes; **doppelte ~** double tax; **drückende ~n** oppressive taxes; **einbehaltene ~n** taxes withheld ; **vom Parlament eingeführte ~n** parliamentary taxes; **nicht eingegangene ~n** tax-collection shortage; **einheitliche ~** uniform tax; **einmalige ~** nonrecurring tax; **einzige ~** single tax; **entstandene ~n** taxes incurred; **erhobene ~n** taxes levied; **fortlaufend erhobene ~** tax by stages; **jährlich erhobene ~** annual tax; **im Veranlagungswege erhobene ~n** assessed taxes; **erträgliche ~n** reasonable taxation; **fällige ~n** matured taxes, *(Bilanz)* accrued taxes payable; **geschätzte ~** estimated tax; **gesparte ~** duty saved; **gestaffelte ~** progressive tax; **gestundete ~** deferred tax; **gewinnabhängige ~n** taxes subject to profit; **zuviel gezahlte ~** excess tax; **harmonisierte ~n** *(EG)* harmonized taxes; **harte ~n** grievous taxes; **hinterzogene ~** defrauded (evaded) tax; **hohe ~n** heavy taxes; **indirekte ~n** expenditure taxes, indirect (outlay, excise) taxes, excise [duty]; **innerstaatliche ~n** internal taxes; **kettenladenfeindliche ~** anti-chain store tax *(US)*; **kommunale ~n** county rates *(Br.)*, local (municipal) taxes *(US)*; **laufende ~n** U.K. taxation *(Br.)*; **negative ~n** negative taxes; **örtliche ~n** local rates (taxes, *US*); **pauschalierte ~** composition tax; **persönliche ~** personal tax; **progressive ~** progressive (graduated) tax; **prohibitive ~** prohibitive tax; **regressive ~** tax on a descending scale; **rückläufige ~** recurrent duty; **rückständige ~n** tax [in] arrears, delinquent *(US)* (back) taxes; **rückwirkende ~** regressive tax; **sonstige ~n** taxes other than federal income *(US)*; **staatliche ~** state (public) tax; **städtische ~n** rates *(Br.)*, local (municipal) taxes; **vom Pächter zu tragende ~n** taxes payable by the tenant; **übermäßige ~n** excessive taxes; **überzahlte ~** excess (overpaid) duty; **umfassende ~** blanket tax; **unwirtschaftliche ~** nuisance tax; **parlamentarisch verabschiedete ~n** parliamentary taxes; **veranlagte ~** assessment, assessed (scheduled) tax; **vereinnahmte ~** tax suffered; **verschleierte (versteckte) ~** hidden tax; **völkerrechtswidrige ~** illegal tax; **im Abzugswege zahlbare ~n** tax payable by deduction; **in Raten zahlbare ~** duty payable on instalment; **zu zahlende ~** assessment, rating *(Br.)*; **in Naturalien zu zahlende ~** tax in kind; **zurückvergütete ~** refunded tax; **zusätzliche ~** additional tax; **zweckgebundene ~n** apportioned taxes;
~n und Abgaben taxes and dues; **inländische ~n und Abgaben** internal revenue taxes; **~n und sonstige Einkünfte** general fund; **~n und Umlagen** rates and taxes; **Zölle und ~n** customs and excise entries; **~n, Zölle und Abgaben** taxes, duties, imposts and excises *(US)*;
~n für Ausgaben im privaten Bereich private expenditure taxes; **~ auf Bodenerzeugnisse** severance tax; **~ für Devisenausländer** nonresident tax; **~n vom Einkommen, vom Ertrag und vom Vermögen** taxes on income and property; **~n auf im Ausland angefallene Einkünfte** tax on foreign earnings; **~n auf Einkünfte aus selbständiger Arbeit** tax on income or profits from trade, profession or vocation; **~ auf alkoholische Getränke** alcoholic beverage tax *(Br.)*, liquor excise *(US)*; **~ auf nicht ausgeschüttete Gewinne** undistributed profits tax, accumulated earnings tax *(US)*; **~ auf Grundbesitz** general property tax *(US)*; **~ auf kurzfristige Kursgewinne** short-term capital gains tax; **~ mit höherem Satz** higher-rate tax; **~ mit normalem Steuertarif** basic tax rate; **~ auf selbständige Tätigkeit** tax in respect of any profession or vocation; **~n vom Vermögen** tax on capital; **~ auf das bewegliche (persönliche) Vermögen** personal tax *(US)*; **~n auf den Wertzuwachs** *(Doppelbesteuerungsabkommen)* taxes on capital appreciation; **~ auf Wettgewinne** tax on racing bets;
~n abführen to pay taxes; **~ gleich vom Ertrag abführen** to pay a

tax at the source; ~n an die Finanzverwaltung abführen to hand over a tax to the commissioners of the Inland Revenue *(Br.)*; ~ abschaffen to abolish a tax; ~ in Etappen abschaffen to phase out a tax; von der ~ absetzen to deduct from the tax; ~ auf den Kunden abwälzen to pass on (shift) a tax to the customer; ~ anrechnen to impute a tax, *(Doppelbesteuerungsabkommen)* to credit taxes; in USA gezahlte ~ in der Bundesrepublik anrechnen to allow United States taxes as credit against Federal Republic taxes; neue ~ aufbrummen to crack on another tax *(US)*; ~ auferlegen to [impose a] tax; jem. eine ~ auferlegen to assess s. o. with a tax *(US)*; neue ~ auferlegen to impose a new tax on the people; ~ aufschlüsseln to break down a tax; ~n ausschreiben to levy taxes, to tax *(US)*; von der ~ befreien to frank (exempt, relieve) from a tax; Öffentlichkeit von einer ~ befreien to relieve the people of a tax; ~n einfach als Geschäftsunkosten behandeln to treat taxes simply as business expense; ~n beitreiben to collect taxes; mit ~n belasten (belegen) to lay (impose, burden) taxes upon; Höhe einer ~ berechnen to assess (fix, compute the amount of) a tax; ~ zum Satz des unteren Proportionalbereichs berechnen to deduct tax at the basic rate; ~n bereitstellen to allow (make provisions) for taxation; sich über zu hohe ~n beschweren to grumble at high taxation; ~ beseitigen to abolish a tax; ~n bezahlen to return taxes to the treasury, to pay one's taxes; seine ~n mit Straßenarbeiten bezahlen to work out one's taxes on the road; ~n nach dem Vermögen bezahlen to pay scot and lot *(Br.)*; bei der ~ in Abzug bringen to relieve; ~ zum Normalsatz in Abzug bringen to deduct income tax at the standard rate from payment; ~ einbehalten to retain a tax; ~ bei der Lohnzahlung einbehalten to withhold a tax from wage payment *(US)*; ~ an der Quelle einbehalten to deduct a tax at source; ~ einführen to impose a tax on the people; sich für niedrigere ~n einsetzen to fight for lower taxes; ~n eintreiben to collect (exact) taxes; ~n einziehen to collect taxes; ~n erheben to raise revenue, to levy (lay) a tax, to tax; ~n von jem. erheben to assess s. o.; ~ an der Quelle erheben to levy a tax at the source; ~n erhöhen to increase (raise) the taxes, to raise tax rates; ~ erlassen to remit (abate) a tax; ~ ermäßigen to reduce (lower, cut down) a tax; ~ erstatten to repay (refund) a tax; ~n festsetzen to assess (graduate) taxes upon; dem ~ gehorchen to feel the helm; ~ in Pacht haben to farm a tax; ~ herabsetzen to reduce (lower, abate, cut down) a tax; j. zu einer ~ heranziehen to assess (tax, *US*) s. o.; ~n hereinholen to get in taxes; ~ herumwerfen to swing right round; ~n hinterziehen to evade a tax, to defraud the revenue; ~n kassieren to gather taxes; j. ans ~ lassen to let s. o. drive; ~ auf etw. legen to impose (levy) a tax on s. th., to put (lay) a duty [up]on s. th.; größere Geldbeträge für die ~ aufbringen müssen to have to fork out a lot of money to the collector of taxes; ~ niederschlagen to drop a tax; ~ pauschalieren to compound for a tax; ~ rückvergüten to refund a tax; von ~n befreit sein to be exempt from taxes; von der ~ erfaßt sein to be in the tax net; von der ~ schon erfaßt sein to have suffered tax; mit ~n verbunden sein to involve taxes; ~n senken to lighten (lower, cut) the taxes; ~n sparen to save on [income] taxes; ~ stunden to defer payment of taxes; ~ übernehmen *(Boot)* to take the helm; ~ überwälzen to shift (pass on) a tax; ~ umgehen to dodge a tax, to avoid payment of a tax; ~n umlegen to apportion taxes; der ~ unterliegen to be taxable (liable to a tax); nicht der ~ unterliegen to be tax-exempt; der ~ unterwerfen to fiscalize; nur in der Stadt selbst getätigte Umsätze der ~ unterwerfen to allocate only receipts from sales within the city for tax purpose; ~ veranlagen to assess a tax; ~ verlangen to charge duty; ~ vermeiden to avoid (dodge) taxes; ~n verpachten to farm out taxes; ~ wiederaufheben to withdraw (abandon, back down, eliminate) a tax; ~ zahlen to pay taxes; 1000 DM an ~n zahlen to pay DM 1000 in taxes; höhere ~n zahlen to write bigger tax cheques *(Br.)* (checks, *US*); zu niedrige ~n zahlen to underpay taxes; höhere ~n ohne Einspruchserhebung zahlen to pay higher taxes without a murmur; überzahlte ~ zurückerstatten to refund an excess of a tax; für ~n zurückstellen to allow (make provisions) for taxation; in Amerika fällige ~n auf ausländische Einkünfte bis zur Transfermöglichkeit zurückstellen to defer tax on income from abroad until it is repatriated;

~-ABC taxation primer; ~abfindung tax settlement; ~abgabe levy.

steuerabgabepflichtig taxable, assessable, ratable.

Steuer|abkommen tax convention (conventional treaty, *US*); ~ablieferung tax payment; ~ablösung commutation of taxes; ~abschaffung abolition of a tax; ~abschätzung eines Geschenkes gift valuation; ~abschlag tax abatement; ~abschluß machen to close its fiscal books; ~abschlußmeldung final declaration; ~abschnitt fiscal period; ~abschreibung tax write-off; ~abteilung tax division (department), *(Behörde)* Commissioners of Taxation; ~abwälzung shifting of (passing on) a tax, tax shifting; ~abwehr tax dodging.

Steuerabzug deduction for taxes, tax deduction, *(Einkommensteuer)* income-tax relief *(Br.)*, tax credit *(US)*, *(Lohn-, Kapitalertragssteuer)* tax withholding *(US)*;

vor (nach) ~ before (after) taxes;

gesetzlich anerkannter ~ statutory deduction; zulässiger ~ deduction for exemption *(US)*;

~ für Abschreibung auf Anlagegüter relief for capital allowance *(Br.)*; ~ für unter Abschreibungswert veräußerte Anlagen balancing allowance; erster ~ für Anschaffungskosten initial allowance; ~ für das eigene Büro im Haus office-at-home deduction; ~ an der Quelle deduction of tax at source; ~ für Sonderausgaben special deduction;

~ an der Quelle vornehmen to deduct tax at source.

Steuerabzüge detailliert aufführen to itemize one's deductions.

Steuerabzugs|bescheid withholding tax notice; ~betrag amount qualifying for relief *(Br.)*; anerkannter ~betrag business deduction.

steuerabzugsfähig admitted as deduction, tax-deductible;

~e Beträge tax deductibles; ~e Beträge in früheren Bilanzen prior-period deductions; ~e Spende tax-deductible contribution.

Steuerabzugs|karte tax-deduction card; ~verfahren *(Lohnsteuer)* pay-as-you-earn system, tax deduction at source, withholding system (tax principle) *(US)*.

Steuer|akte tax file (matter), taxpayer's files, tax papers; ~amnestie tax amnesty; allgemeine ~amnestie general release; städtisches ~amt city tax collector *(US)*, rate collector's office; ~analyse tax analysis; ~änderung tax amendment (change); ~änderungsbescheid notice of amended assessment; ~anfall incidence of taxation, incidence of a duty, tax incidence, *(Ertrag)* tax yield; ~anfangsbetrag tax threshold; ~angelegenheit tax affair (matter), taxation affair (matter); ~angleichung *(EG)* harmonization of taxation; ~anmeldung tax return; ~anordnung tax instruction; ~anpassung *(EG)* coordinating taxation; ~anrechnung imputation of a tax, allowance as a tax credit *(US)*; indirekte ~anrechnung indirect tax credit *(US)*; ~anrechnungsbetrag quantum of relief; ~anrechnungsmethode tax credit system *(US)*; ~anreiz fiscal stimulus, tax incentive; besonderen ~anreizen entgegenwirken to contradict extra fiscal stimulus; ~anreizvorschläge fiscal stimulus package; ~anschlag assessment; ~anspruch tax claim; keinerlei ~anspruch ausweisen to show a zero net tax accrual; ~anstieg boost in taxes; ~anteil revenue quota, lot; ~anwalt tax attorney *(US)* (lawyer); ~anwendungsgebiet ambit of a tax; ~arrest distress for nonpayment of taxes; ~aspekte taxation aspects; erneute ~auferlegung reimposition; ~aufgliederung breakdown of a tax; ~aufhebung abolition of a tax.

Steueraufkommen taxation, revenue (tax) receipts, revenue from taxation, tax revenue, tax yield, inland *(Br.)* (internal, *US*) revenue;

rasant angestiegenes ~ fiscal boost; erhöhtes ~ tax revenue gains; gesamtes ~ tax levy, total sum raised by a tax (treasury receipts); indirektes ~ indirect revenue *(Br.)*; unzureichendes ~ revenue shortage;

~ pro Kopf der Bevölkerung pro-capita tax revenue;

geringes ~ erzielen to produce less revenue; ~ der Wirtschaft wieder zuführen to feed the revenue back into the economy.

Steuer|aufkommensschätzungen revenue forecast; ~aufschlag surtax; ~aufschub tax deferment (deferral); ~aufsicht fiscal control; ~aufsichtsbehörde levy court *(Delaware)*; ~aufstellung tax statement; ~aufteilung tax distribution, apportionment of a tax *(US)*; ~aufwand tax expenditure; ~ausfall tax deficit, deficit in revenue, revenue deficit, shortfall in tax revenue; rezessionsbedingter ~ausfall recession-induced loss of revenue; ~ausfallkalkulation jeopardy assessment.

Steuerausgleich equalizing assessment of taxes, *(Länder)* Exchequer Equalization grant *(Br.)*, revenue sharing;

~ für fälschlich mit Sätzen des unteren Proportionalbereichs besteuerte Einkünfte excessive basic rate adjustment *(Br.)*.

Steuerausgleichs|betrag compensatory relief *(Br.)*; ~prinzip compensatory principle of taxation; ~rücklage *(Bilanz)* taxation equalization reserve *(Br.)*.

Steuer|auskunft tax information; ~ausschreibung imposition of taxes; ~ausschuß tax[-writing] committee (commission, *US*), commission on taxation, board of customs, fiscal committee; ~aussetzung deferral; ~ausetzungsantrag application to postpone payment of tax; ~ausweichung tax dodging;

~ausweis tax statement; **~ausweitung** fiscal expansion; **~auswirkungen** tax effects, tax consequences; **~bandbreite** tax band; **~banderole** stamp *(Br.)*, revenue stamp.

steuerbar taxable, assessable, *(Fahrzeug, Schiff)* manoeuvrable, steerable, *(Sache)* dutiable, *(umlagepflichtig)* ratable;
~ **sein** to be liable to pay taxes, to reach taxable level;
~er Wert taxable (ratable, *Br.*) value, assessed value (valuation, *US*).

Steuerbarkeit taxability, liability to pay taxes, *(Umlagepflicht)* ratability.

Steuer | basis tax (rate) base, basis of taxation; **~beamter** assessor of taxes, tax collector (official, man), fiscal officer, revenue officer (agent) *(US)*, Inland Revenue Official *(Br.)*; **~beauftragter** tax representative; **~bedürfnisse** fiscal requirements; **Veränderungen der ~bedürfnisse Rechnung tragen** to meet changing fiscal requirements.

steuerbefreit tax-exempt (-free);
~e Anleihe tax-free loan.

Steuerbefreiung exemption from taxation, tax exemption;
50% ~ composition of ten shillings in the pound *(Br.)*;
~ **gewähren** to give a dispensation, to grant an exemption.

steuerbegünstigt entitled to tax relief, tax privileged, tax supported;
~ **sein** to enjoy tax privileges;
~e Einkünfte tax preference income; **~es Geschäft** tax-shelter deal; **~es Sparen** tax-favo(u)red savings, deferred savings plan.

Steuerbegünstigung tax privilege;
~ **für gezahlte Hypothekenzinsen** mortgage-tax relief.

Steuerbegünstigungsprogramm tax incentive program(me).

Steuerbehandlung, unterschiedliche tax discrimination.

Steuerbehörde taxing (taxation, fiscal) authority, inland revenue office *(Br.)*, Internal Revenue Authorities *(US)*;
kommunale ~ rating authority *(Br.)*; **oberste** ~ Internal Revenue Service *(US)*.

Steuer | beitreiber tax collector; **~beitreibung** tax recovery (collection).

steuerbelastet tax-ridden *(US)*.

Steuerbelasteter person suffering duty.

Steuerbelastung pressure of taxation, tax load (burden, incidence, impact, *Br.*), taxation charge, charge to duty, fiscal burden;
effektive ~ real tax load; **erhöhte** ~ increased taxation; **unberechtigte** ~ tax grab;
~ **durch zu hoch vorgenommene Abschreibungen** balancing charge;
~ **so niedrig wie möglich halten** to minimize the charge to duty.

Steuer | bemessungsgrundlage tax (taxable) base, basis of taxation; **~benachrichtigung** tax notice; **~berater** tax expert (adviser, consultant, preparer, planner, practitioner, *Br.*); **seine Dienste als ~berater anbieten** to offer one's tax service; **~beratung** tax service (consulting, consultation, business).

Steuerberatungs | dienst tax-preparation service; **~dienst anbieten** to offer tax service; **~firma** tax-service wholesaler; **~gewerbe** tax-service (-preparation) business; **~heft** tax guide; **~kosten** tax consultant's fee; **~wesen** tax-preparation (-service) business.

Steuerberechnung tax calculation (computation), tax assessment, duty computation.

Steuerberechnungsgrundlage basis of taxation, tax base.

steuerbereinigt adjusted for taxation.

Steuerbescheid tax demand (bill, *US*), demand note *(Br.)*, bill of taxes *(US)*, notice of assessment *(US)*, assessment (tax) notice *(US)*, tax assessment note *(Br.)* (notice, *US*);
gegen einen ~ Einspruch einlegen to appeal against a tax assessment; **nachträglichen ~ erlassen** to charge back tax; ~ **in Abweichung von der Steuererklärung festsetzen** to raise an estimated assessment.

Steuerbeseitigungsverfahren *(Kommunalabgaben)* derating system *(Br.)*.

Steuerbestimmungen tax [law] provisions;
~ **über den Beginn eines Gewerbebetriebs** commencement provisions; ~ **für betriebseigene Fahrzeuge** company-car tax rules;
nicht den ~ unterliegen not to be within the taxing sections.

Steuerbetrag tax amount, assessment;
abgezogener ~ amount of tax deducted; **veranlagter** ~ assessment.

Steuer | betrug defraudation of the revenue, fiscal (tax) fraud; **~bevollmächtigter** tax representative; **~bewertung** assessment, assessed valuation *(US)*; **~bewilligung** *(parl.)* grant of supply; **~bewilligungsausschuß** Committee of Ways and Means *(Br.)*; **~bezirk** assessment (taxing, *US*, tax collector's, *Br.*) district, area of assessment, assessment area, *(Kommunalabgaben)* rating area; **~bilanz** tax statement, tax status, tax report (balance sheet, *US*); **für ~bilanzzwecke** for tax reporting; **~bord** starboard, right; **~bremse** fiscal break (drag); **~buchhaltung** tax accounting; **~bürger** taxpayer; **~debatte** tax debate; **~defizit** revenue (tax, fiscal) deficit, deficit in taxes; **~delikt** offence against a Revenue Statute, revenue offence, fiscal offence; **~depot** excise warehouse; **~differenzierung** fiscal differentiation; **~diskriminierung** tax discrimination, discriminative taxation; **~distrikt** taxing area (district), area of assessment; **~druck** tax burden, pressure of taxation, impact of a tax; **~drückeberger** tax dodger; **~durchführungsgesetz** Tax Management Act *(Br.)*; **~effekt** tax incidence; **~einbehaltung** deduction of tax, withholding of a tax *(US)*, tax withholding *(US)*; **~eingänge** tax receipts, tax collections; **geschätzte ~eingänge** estimated taxes; **laufende ~eingänge sicherstellen** to ensure a continuing flow of taxes; **~einheit** taxing unit; **~einkommen** *(Einzelperson)* taxable income, *(Ertrag einer Steuer)* yield of a tax, *(Staat)* public (inland, *Br.*) revenue; **~einkommen aufspalten** to split the income *(US)*; **~einkünfte** *(Staat)* taxation, public (inland, *Br.*, internal, *US*) revenue, *(Eingänge)* tax (inland revenue, *Br.*) receipts.

Steuereinnahmen *(Staat)* taxation, public (inland, *Br.*, internal, *US*) revenue, *(Eingänge)* tax (revenue, *Br.*) receipts;
erhöhte ~ revenue gains, tax take; **staatliche** ~ government tax take;
~ **für ein Krankenhaus zweckbestimmen** to dedicate certain tax revenues to a hospital.

Steuereinnahme | prognose revenue projection; **hauptsächliche ~zeit** tax-gathering season.

Steuereinnehmer taxgatherer, collector of taxes *(Br.)*, tax collector *(Br.)* (receiver, taker), exciseman *(Br.)*;
amtlicher ~ receivers general of the public revenue *(Br.)*, receiver of taxes *(US)*.

Steuereinschätzung tax assessing (assessment, *Br.*), *(Kommunalsteuern)* rating;
zu hohe ~ overassessment.

Steuer | einsparung tax saving; **~einsparungsmöglichkeit** potential tax saving; **~einspruch** notice of appeal, tax appeal (query); **komplizierter ~einspruch** highly technical appeal; **~einspruch begründen** to state the grounds of a tax appeal; **~einspruchsverfahren** *(Steuerrecht)* appeal hearing; **~einstufung** tax classification; **~eintreibung** exaction (collection) of taxes.

Steuereintreibungsverfahren tax-collection system;
beschleunigtes ~ speedup of tax collection, tax-collection speedup;
~ **modernisieren** to streamline a tax-collection system.

Steuer | einzieher tax collector, collector of taxes; **~einziehung** tax collection, taxgathering, collecting a tax, levy of taxes.

Steuereinziehungs | bestimmungen tax-collection regulations; **~stelle** tax-collection office; **~verfahren** tax-collection procedure; **beschleunigtes ~verfahren** tax-collection speedup.

Steuer | elastizität elasticity of a tax; **~entrichtung** payment of taxes; **~entscheidung** tax judgment; **~erfordernisse** fiscal requirements; **~ergänzungstabelle** cumulative tax table; **~ergebnis** tax result; **~erheber** tax layer; **städtischer ~erheber** town (city, *US*) tax collector, taxgatherer; **~erhebung** establishment (imposition) of a tax, tax levy (collecting, collection), collection of taxes, taxgathering, raising of revenues, assessment; **~erhebung genehmigen** to authorize the levy of a tax; **~erhebungsstelle** precepting authority *(Br.)*.

Steuererhöhung tax rise (increase), increase in taxes (taxation);
lineare ~ linear increase of taxation; **zehnprozentige** ~ increase in taxation of 10 per cent;
~ **vornehmen** to raise a tax.

Steuererklärung return of tax, income-tax return (declaration);
beeidigte ~ Inland Revenue Affidavit *(Br.)*; **gemeinsame** ~ joint return; **getrennte** ~ separate return; **jährliche** ~ annual return; **konsolidierte** ~ consolidated tax return *(US)*; **unrichtige** ~ false return; **vierteljährliche** ~ quarterly return;
~ **eines Konzerns** consolidated return *(US)*;
~ **abgeben** to file a tax declaration (one's income-tax return); **gemeinsame ~ abgeben** to file a joint return; **keine ~ abgeben** to fail to file a return.

Steuererklärungs | formular tax form; **~pflicht** period for filing a tax return; **~tag** tax-filing date; **~vordruck** tax form.

Steuer | erlaß abatement of a tax, remission of a tax, tax remission; **~erlaßanspruch** claim in abatement.

Steuererleichterung relief from taxation (duty), tax relief (benefit, shelter), revenue (tax) concession, reduction of a tax;

~en **für gezahlte Abstandsbeträge** relief against premium received *(Br.)*; ~ **für kleine Einkommensbezieher** small-income relief *(Br.)*;
~en **gewähren** to lighten taxes; **auf kleine ~en hoffen** to hope for a small diminution of taxes.
Steuererleichterungsbestimmungen, von ~ Gebrauch machen to exploit tax shelters.
Steuerermäßigung reduction of taxes (in tax rates, of taxation), remission (abatement) of a tax, lowering of taxation, tax reduction;
begrenzte ~ registered relief; **degressive** ~ graduated tax relief; ~ **für Arbeitseinkommen der Ehefrau** wife's earned income relief *(Br.)*; **gestaffelte** ~ **für kleine Einkommen** reduced-rate (small-income) relief *(Br.)*; ~ **in Grenzfällen** marginal relief *(Br.)*; ~ **für eine Hausangestellte** housekeeper relief *(Br.)*; ~ **bei erhöhter Lagerbewertung** stock appreciation relief; ~ **für Lebensversicherungen** life-insurance relief *(Br.)*; ~ **für überhöhte im Ausland gezahlte Steuersätze** overspill relief; ~**en für Verluste** allowance for losses;
~ **beantragen** to claim relief *(Br.)*; ~ **bei der Kapitalertragssteuer gewähren** to grant relief from capital gains tax; ~ **für Verluste gewähren** to allow for losses.
Steuerermäßigungsbetrag amount qualifying for relief *(Br.)*.
Steuer|ermittlung tax assessment, *(Untersuchung)* tax investigation; ~**ersparnis** saving of duty, tax saving; ~**ersparnisse machen** to save on [income] taxes; ~**erstattung** refund (repayment) of a tax, tax refund (replacement); ~**erstattung vornehmen** to repay (refund) a tax.
Steuererstattungs|anspruch claim for tax refund, tax repayment due; ~**formular** form for claiming repayment of tax; ~**scheck** tax refund cheque *(Br.)* (check, *US*); ~**verfahren** tax-refund proceedings.
Steuer|ertrag tax proceeds (yield), *(Einzelsteuer)* yield of a tax; **der ~ertrag ist gut** the tax draws well; **schwankende ~erträge** swing in taxes; ~**erträgnisse** *(Gesamtaufkommen)* public revenue; ~**experte**, ~**fachmann** tax expert (man, technician), fiscal expert, taxation specialist.
steuerfähig taxable, ratable, leviable;
~ **bleiben** *(Schiff)* to maintain steerageway.
Steuer|fähigkeit taxability, ratability; ~**fahnder** tax ferret; ~**fahndung** tax ferrets (investigation); ~**fall** taxation matter; ~**fehlbetrag** shortfall in tax revenue, tax (revenue) deficit; ~**festsetzung** determination of a tax, tax assessment *(Br.)*, taxing; ~**festsetzungsbestimmungen** methods of assessing taxable property; ~**flucht** tax avoidance (evasion, *US*); ~**flüchtling** tax exile; ~**folgen** tax implications.
Steuerforderung tax claim;
fällige ~en accrued taxes, tax accruals *(US)*; **uneinbringliche ~en** uncollectable taxes; **zusätzliche ~en** additional revenue requirements;
~ **unter Einlegung von Widerspruch zahlen** to pay a tax demand under protest.
Steuer|formular tax form; ~**frage** tax question (matter), problem of taxes; **unerledigte ~frage** unsettled tax dispute.
steuerfrei free of taxes, tax-exempt (-free), exempt from taxes (taxation), net of tax, nontaxable, nonassessable, taxless, untaxed, scot-free, *(Waren)* duty-free;
~ **anlegen** to convert into nontaxable form; ~ **sein** to be tax-exempt;
vom Nettoeinkommen abzugsfähige ~e Beträge credits allowed against net income *(US)*; ~**es Einkommen** tax-exempt income; ~**er Gehaltsanteil** tax-free element; ~**er Pauschalbetrag** flat exemption *(US)*; ~**e Rente** clear annuity; ~**e Schenkung** tax-free gift; ~**er Schuldschein** tax-exempt note *(US)*; ~**e Stellung** tax-exempt status *(US)*; ~**er Tag** tax holiday; ~**e Wertpapiere** tax-exempt bonds *(US)*, tax exempts *(US)*; ~**es Wertpapiergeschäft** tax-free transaction.
Steuerfreibetrag basic abatement, tax-[free] allowance *(Br.)*, tax exemption *(US)*, tax-exempt amount *(US)*, exemption (tax) credit *(US)*, tax relief *(Br.)*;
angerechneter ~ tax-credit relief *(US)*; **allgemein gewährter** ~ outright (flat) exemption *(US)*; **höchster** ~ maximum allowance *(Br.)*; **persönlicher** ~ personal allowance (relief, *Br.*, exemption, *US*), personal-income tax exemption *(US)*; **üblicher persönlicher** ~ ordinary personal allowance *(Br.)*;
~ **für Dubiose** recovery exclusion; ~ **des Ehemanns** married man's allowance *(Br.)*; **zusätzlicher** ~ **für Einkünfte der Ehefrau aus freiberuflicher Tätigkeit** wife's earned-income allowance *(Br.)*; ~ **für Einkünfte aus gewerblicher Tätigkeit** earned income credit *(US)*; ~ **für den Erwerb eines Bergwerks** mineral depletion allowance *(Br.)*; ~ **für erwerbsunfähige Familienangehörige** allowance *(Br.)* (credit, *US*) for dependents, income-tax allowance for wife and child *(Br.)*, dependency exemption *(US)*, dependent relative allowancee *(Br.)*; ~ **für Grundstücksmeliorationen** tax exemption on land improvement *(US)*; ~ **für Hausangestellte** housekeeper allowance (relief, *Br.*); ~ **für Kinder** tax allowance for children, child tax allowance *(US)* (relief, *Br.*), child exemption *(US)*, children's exemption *(US)*, credit for dependants *(US)*; ~ **für Lebensversicherung** life-insurance relief *(Br.)*; ~ **für Ledige** single allowance *(Br.)*; ~ **zur Stärkung der Eigenmittel in Höhe von 25% des Produktionserlöses** resource allowance of 25% production income; ~ **für werterhöhende technische Verbesserungen** tax exemption on capital improvement *(US)*; ~ **für Verheiratete** married allowance *(Br.)*; ~ **für karitative Zuwendungen** deduction allowed for gifts to charity; ~ **für wohltätige Zwecke** exemption for charities (charitable purposes) *(US)*;
~ **aufteilen** to split an allowance; ~ **gewähren** to grant exemption *(US)*; ~ **nicht mehr gewähren** to phase out an exemption *(US)*; **Anspruch auf einen ~ haben** to be eligible for exemption *(US)*; ~ **in Anspruch nehmen** to claim an allowance *(Br.)*.
Steuerfreibeträge taxation allowances;
sonst gewährte ~ allowance given against other income; **in das vorangegangene Veranlagungsjahr zurückgebuchte** ~ allowances related back;
~ **für Arbeitgeber bei Ausbildungslehrgängen** tax exemptions to employers for training *(US)*; ~ **für die Bewirtung von Geschäftsfreunden** business entertaining expenses allowance; ~ **zur Förderung von Forschungs- und Entwicklungsarbeiten** tax exemptions to encourage research and development *(US)*; ~ **für Sozialabfindungen** redundancy rebate *(Br.)*; ~ **für Umweltschutzmaßnahmen** pollution control tax credits *(US)*; ~ **einräumen** to rule in favo(u)r of credits *(US)*; ~ **praktisch voll indexieren** to set tax allowance short of full indexation; ~ **in Anspruch nehmen können** to qualify for tax relief.
Steuerfreigrenze exemption limit *(US)*.
Steuerfreiheit exemption from taxation *(US)*, tax exemption *(US)*, immunity from taxes, freedom from tax, fiscal immunity, nontaxability, chartered exemption *(Br.)*;
~ **einer Aktiengesellschaft** immunity of corporation tax; ~ **bis zur Anlagenabschreibung** free depreciation; ~ **für staatliche Einrichtungen** government immunity;
~ **gewähren** to relieve (free) from taxes, to grant an exemption *(US)*.
Steuer|fuß basis of taxation; ~**gebiet** taxing district; **auf dem ~gebiet große Anstrengungen machen** to make strong tax efforts; ~**gefährdung** jeopardy of taxation; ~**gefälle** tax difference; ~**gefüge** tax structure; ~**gegenstand** taxable unit; ~**geheimnis** tax secrecy; ~**gelder** tax money (dollars, *US*), taxpayer's cash (money); **mit ~geldern äußerst vorsichtig umgehen** to be tight with public money; ~**gemeinde** land-tax parish; ~**gerechtigkeit** tax justice, equal distribution of taxes.
Steuergesetz tax (taxation) law, finance (revenue) bill *(Br.)*, Finance Act *(Br.)*, Revenue Law (Act) *(US)*;
~**antrag** money bill *(Br.)*, revenue bill *(US)*; ~**geber** tax writer; ~**gebung** tax (revenue) laws, Internal Revenue Code *(US)*; **ausländische ~gebung** foreign taxation.
Steuer|gesichtspunkt tax angle; ~**gewinn** taxable profit (gain), revenue gain; ~**gläubiger** tax creditor; ~**gleichheit** equal distribution of taxes; ~**gründe** tax reasons; **aus ~gründen erworben** tax-bought *(US)*; **aus ~gründen als getrennt lebend behandelt werden** to be treated as separated for tax purposes; ~**grundlage** basis of taxation, taxable basis; ~**gruppe** [income] tax bracket; **zur unteren ~gruppe gehörend** lower-bracket; ~**guthaben** tax credit *(US)*; ~**gutschein** tax-anticipation bond (warrant, certificate, *US*), tax remission (reserve, *Br.*) bill, rebate certificate, tax bond *(US)*, *(kleingestückelt)* treasury tax anticipation certificate, tax anticipation note *(US)*; **hochverzinslicher ~gutschein** high-yielding certificate of tax deposit; ~**gutscheinausgabe** treasury borrowing; ~**gutschrift** tax credit *(US)*; ~**harmonisierung** fiscal harmonization; ~**haus** *(mar.)* wheelhouse; ~**hebebezirk** taxing district; ~**hebeliste** tax book (roll, *US*), assessment roll; ~**helfer** tax expert (preparer); ~**hemmschuh** fiscal drag; ~**herabsetzung** diminution (reduction) of taxes, tax reduction, tax (taxation) cut *(US)*, lowering of taxes; ~**herabsetzungsantrag** request for diminution of taxes; ~**hinterzieher** tax dodger, tax evader *(US)*; ~**hinterziehung** tax evasion *(US)* (dodging), fiscal fraud, tax (revenue) fraud; ~**hinterziehung begehen** to evade a tax *(US)*, to defraud the revenue; ~**hinterziehung verhindern** to prevent fraud; ~**hinterziehungsvertrag** contract to defraud the revenue;

~höchstgrenze tax limit; **~höchstsatz** maximum (marginal, top) tax rate, tax-rate limit, maximum taxation; **~höchstsatz für Spitzenverdiener** top marginal tax rate; **~höchstsatz von 98%** marginal tax rate of 98%; **~höhe berechnen** to compute the amount of a tax; **~hoheit** tax sovereignty, fiscal jurisdiction, power of taxation, taxing power *(US)*; **~immunität** immunity from taxes; **~index** tax index; **~indexierung** indexation of taxes, tax indexation; **gesamte ~indexierung** indexation package; **~inflation** tax inflation; **~inspektor** tax inspector; **~interesse** fiscal interest.

Steuerjahr financial *(Br.)* (fiscal, *Br.*, taxable, *US*) year;
laufendes ~ current tax year; **vorangehendes ~** prior taxable year *(US)*;
~ 1980 income tax year 1980, fiscal 1980 *(US)*.

Steuer|jurist tax lawyer; **~kalender** tax calendar; **~karte** tax sheet (card), notice of coding *(Br.)*; **~kasse** general revenue fund; **~kataster** tax roll *(US)* (book); **~katastrophe** tax debacle; **~kenntnisse** tax knowledge.

Steuerklasse tax group, income-tax bracket, scale of taxation, schedule *(Br.)*;
höchste ~ highest scale of taxation;
die drei höchsten ~n gewerblich versteuerten Einkommens abschaffen to abolish the top three earned-income tax rates; **j. in eine höhere ~ einstufen** to put s. o. into a higher tax bracket.

Steuer|kniffe tax wrinkles; **~knüppel** *(Flugzeug)* control column, control (joy, *sl.*) stick; **~kommission** tax-writing commission; **~kraft** taxability, taxable capacity; **~kurs** *(Wertpapiere)* taxable value; **~kürzung** tax evasion; **~lage** tax position; **~lager** excise warehouse; **~last** tax burden (load), fiscal charge, burden of taxation; **verminderte ~last** reduced taxation; **~lastquote** per capita tax load; **allgemeine ~lehre** theory of taxation; **~leistung** treasury rate; **~leistungsfähigkeit** taxing capacity; **~leistungsprinzip** faculty principle of taxation, ability-to-pay principle.

steuerlich fiscal, taxable, taxative;
~ absetzbar deductible from income tax; **~ attraktiv** tax-incentive; **~ begünstigt** tax-supported; **~ belastet** tax-ridden (-laden, -burdened); **~ berichtigt** adjusted for taxation; **~ leistungsfähig** taxpaying; **~ subventioniert** taxeating;
~ als Kapital zu behandeln attributable to capital;
~ bevorzugt behandeln to benefit (credit) tax-wise; **höhere Angestellte im verstärkten Maße ~ beraten** to reinforce its tax services at senior management level; **Gebäude ~ bewerten** to assess a building; **~ erfassen** to impose (levy) a tax upon; **Einkommen ~ an der Quelle erfassen** to tax income at the source, to withhold taxes; **~ profitieren** to benefit tax-wise; **~ voll abgeschrieben sein** to be written off against taxes; **~ abzugsfähig sein** to be available for relief; **~ endgültig anerkannt sein** *(Unkosten)* to be closed by the statute of limitations; **j. ~ so hoch veranlagen** to assess s. o. in (at) so much; **~ zu niedrig veranlagen** to charge too little tax; **Einkommen ~ verteilen** to spread income over the years, to average income; **~ als Devisenausländer behandelt werden** to be resident for exchange-control purposes outside the Scheduled Territories *(Br.)*; **~ als Deviseninländer behandelt werden** to be regarded as resident; **~ wie eine juristische Person behandelt werden** to be treated as a corporate body for tax purposes;
~ zulässige Abschreibungen tax writeoffs *(US)*, capital allowance *(Br.)*; **hundertprozentige ~e Abschreibung im ersten Jahr** 100% first year tax allowance; **~e Absetzung der Zinsen** interest deduction; **~e Änderungen** tax changes; **~e Anrechnung übermäßiger Belastungen** relief for excess charges *(Br.)*; **~e Anrechnung im Ausland gezahlter Steuern** double taxation relief *(Br.)*; **~er Anreiz** tax incentive, fiscal stimulus; **~es Aufgabengebiet** tax function; **~e Aufstellung** tax statement (status); **~er Ausgleichsposten** tax-equalization item; **~e Auswirkungen** tax effects (implications), taxation consequences; **~e Begünstigung** tax privilege; **~e Behandlung** tax (taxation) treatment; **~e Behandlung bei der Einkommensteuerveranlagung** income-tax treatment; **~e Behandlung von Lebensversicherungsprämien** life assurance arrangements *(Br.)*; **~e Behandlung von Veräußerungsgewinnen** treatment of capital gains; **~e Belastung** tax burden (load, charge), pressure of taxation, tax impact *(Br.)*, incidence (impact, *Br.*) of a tax, fiscal drag (charge); **einer ~en Belastung ausweichen** to create a tax shelter; **~e Beratungstätigkeit** tax-saving service; **~ subventionierter Betrieb** taxeater; **~e Diskriminierung** taxation discrimination; **~er Einheitswert** *(Grundstück)* site value; **~ begünstigte Einkommenspositionen** tax preference items; **~e Einkünfte** tax receipts, internal (inland, *Br.*) revenue; **~ begünstigte Einkünfte** tax preference income; **~e Einstufung** tax classification; **~e Entlastung** tax relief; **~e Erfassung** taxation, assessment; **~e Erleichterungen** tax relief [measures]; **~e Erwägungen** tax considerations; **~e Folgewirkungen** tax implications; **~er Gewinn** taxable gain (profit); **~er Gewinnfaktor** revenue producer; **~e Gründe** tax reasons; **~e Haftung des Grundbesitzers** tax lien; **~es Hintertürchen** tax loophole; **~e Illusionen** fiscal illusions; **~es Interesse** fiscal concern; **~e Lage** taxation position; **~e Lasten** fiscal burden; **~e Maßnahmen** tax practices (measures); **~er Mietwert** assessed rental; **~e Möglichkeit** fiscal opportunity; **~e Privilegien** fiscal privileges; **~e Progressionszone** tax band; **~er Ratgeber** tax guide; **~e Selbsteinschätzung** self-assessment; **~er Spitzensatz** top (maximum, marginal) tax rate; **~e Überlegungen** tax considerations; **~e Untersuchung** tax investigation (probe, *US*); **~e Veränderungen** tax changes; **~e Veranlagung** assessed valuation; **~e Vergünstigungen** tax privileges (benefits, *Br.*, concession, break, *US*, credit, *US*), taxation benefits; **~e Vergünstigungen für wohltätige Stiftungen in Anspruch nehmen können** to qualify for a charity's favo(u)rable tax treatment; **~er Verlustfaktor** revenue drain; **~es Verlustgeschäft** tax-loss selling; **~e Verpflichtungen** tax obligations; **~er Vorteil** tax advantage (break, *US*); **~es Zugeständnis** tax concession; **~e Zuständigkeit** tax jurisdiction; **~er Zwangsverkauf** tax sale of property *(US)*.

Steuer|liste assessment list, list of taxable persons, assessment roll (list), tax book (roll), *(Kommunalsteuern)* rate book, *(säumiger Zahler)* tax list; **~lücke** tax loophole; **~mahnschreiben, ~mahnung** deficiency letter, tax reminder; **~mahnzettel** tax reminder; **~manipulation** fiscal manipulations; **~mann** helmsman, steerman, *(Handelsmarine)* mate, navigator.

Steuermanns|empfangsschein mate's receipt; **~maat** quartermaster; **~patent** mate's certificate; **~quittung** mate's receipt.

Steuer|marke stamp *(Br.)*, revenue stamp *(US)*; **~maßnahmen** tax measures (practices); **~maßstab** standard of taxation; **~mehrbetrag** increased tax rate; **~mehrertrag** increased treasury receipts; **~merkmal** tax (taxing) feature; **~meßbescheid** basic assessment notice; **~meßbetrag** ratal, tax rate; **~meßwert** ratable value *(Br.)*; **~methode** taxation method, method of assessing taxable property; **~milderung** remission (diminution, mitigation) of a tax, tax abatement (mitigation); **~minderaufkommen** tax-collection shortages; **~minderung** tax reduction; **~mindestsatz** minimum taxation; **~mittel** tax (taxpayer's) money, general fund, *(Maßnahme)* fiscal instrument; **~monopol** fiscal monopoly; **~moral** tax morale; **~motiv** fiscal motive.

steuern to navigate, to steer, to head, *(Auto)* to drive, to be at the wheel, *(Flugzeug)* to pilot, *(leiten)* to direct, to engineer, to control, *(Maschine)* to control, *(Ton)* to modulate;
schwer zu ~ *(Schiff)* wild;
Gesetzesvorlage durchs Parlament ~ to steer (engineer) a bill through parliament; **nach dem Kompaß ~** to steer by the compass; **Kurs ~** to steer a course; **auf dem gefunkten Kurs ~** to fly [on] the beam; **einem Mißstand ~** to remedy a grievance; **Schiff in den Hafen ~** to head a ship to the harbo(u)r; **direkt in sein Unglück ~** to be heading straight for disaster.

Steuernachforderung additional tax demand.

Steuernachlaß tax reduction (abatement, rebate, forgiveness), abatement of [income] tax, refunding of duties;
~ für unterhaltsberechtigte Angehörige allowance for dependants; **~ für Betriebsanteile** relief under the business scale *(Br.)*; **~ für Betriebsverluste** relief for trading losses *(Br.)*; **~ im Konzernverband** group relief *(Br.)*; **~ bei schneller Todesfolge** quick succession relief *(Br.)*;
~ gewähren to abate income tax;
~antrag claim for abatement; **~verteilung** allocation of relief.

Steuer|nachteile taxation disadvantages; **~nachveranlagung** tax reappraisal; **~nachzahlung** payment of tax arrears; **anonyme ~nachzahlung** conscience money; **~nachzahlungsbetrag** additional assessment; **~nachzahlungspflicht** back duty.

steuerneutral behandeln, einbehaltene und ausgeschüttete Gewinne to be neutral as regards distributed and retained profits.

Steuer|normen tax provisions; **~nöte** fiscal difficulties; **~novelle** revenue bill; **~nummer** tax-office reference number; **~oase** tax haven; **~objekt** tax base, taxing unit, taxable article (unit); **~ordnungswidrigkeit** offence under the tax regulations.

steuerorientiert influenced by tax considerations.

Steuer|paket tax package; **~paradies** tax haven; **~pauschale zahlen** to compound for a tax; **~pauschalierung** lump-sum taxation; **~pauschalsatz** lump-sum tax; **~periode** fiscal (taxable) period; **~pfandrecht** tax lien; **~pfändung** distress for nonpayment of taxes, tax foreclosure.

Steuerpflicht liability to pay taxes, tax liability;
beschränkte ~ limited taxability, limited tax liability; **unbeschränkte ~** unrestricted tax liability;
der ~ unterliegen to be taxed (liable to pay taxes).

steuerpflichtig taxable, assessable for tax, liable to pay taxes (to a tax, to taxation), subject to a tax (to taxation), leviable, *(Kommunalsteuern)* ratable;
beschränkt ~ subject to limited taxation; **nicht ~** nonassessable, nontaxable, nontaxed; **voll ~** wholly liable to pay tax; **~ machen** to make taxable; **~ sein** to be taxed, to be subject (chargeable) to tax, to reach the taxable level, to incur a duty; **~es Anfangseinkommen** tax threshold; **~er Betrag** taxable portion; **~er Betrieb** taxpayer corporation; **~es Einkommen** assessable (taxable) income; **~e Erbmasse** taxable estate; **~er Ertrag** taxable profit; **~er Gewinn** taxable profit; **~er Gewinnanteil** assessable share of profit; **~er Grundbesitz** ratable property *(Br.)*; **~es Jahr** taxable year; **~er Kapitalgewinn** revenue reserve *(Br.)*; **~er Nachlaß** taxable estate; **~es Roheinkommen** adjusted gross income *(US)*; **~er Umsatz** taxable turnover (transaction); **~es Vermögen** taxable property, ratable estate; **~er Vorgang** taxable transaction; **~e Waren** taxable class of goods.

Steuerpflichtigen veranlagen, jeden to extend a tax.

Steuerpflichtiger taxpayer, taxable person, ratepayer;
beschränkt ~ nonresident taxpayer; **inländischer ~** resident taxpayer; **normaler ~** standard-rate taxpayer; **säumiger ~** taxpayer in arrears, dilatory taxpayer; **unbeschränkt ~** resident taxpayer; **im Ausland wohnhafter ~** absentee taxpayer;
~ mit niedrigem Einkommen low-income taxpayer; **~ im unteren Proportionalbereich** basic-rate taxpayer; **~ in der Spitzenklasse** top-rate taxpayer.

Steuer|pflicht[igkeit] liability to pay taxes, tax liability, taxability, *(Kommunalsteuern)* ratability; **~plan** fiscal system; **~politik** policy of taxation, taxation policy, tax practices (policies), *(Geldpolitik)* fiscal (financial) policy, fiscality, revenue policy; **langfristige ~politik** long-range tax strategy; **zurückhaltende ~politik** fiscal restraint.

steuerpolitische|Initiativen fiscal policy initiatives; **~ Maßnahmen** tax measures, fiscal-monetary policy; **ausgeuferte ~ und geldmarktpolitische Maßnahmen** overexpansive fiscal and monetary policies; **~ Nachteile** fiscal deficiencies.

Steuer|position tax position; **~posten** tax item; **~prinzip** principle of taxation; **~privileg** tax privilege; **~programm** tax (fiscal) program(me); **~progression** tax progression; **expansionsbedingte ~progression** fiscal drag; **~prozeß** tax procedure; **~prüfdienst** tax service; **~prüfer** income tax investigator, tax inspector *(Br.)* (auditor, *US*); **~prüfung** tax inspection *(Br.)* (audit, *US*, auditing, *US*); **~prüfungsdienst** tax service; **~pult** *(Datenverarbeitung)* control panel; **~quelle** source of taxation (revenue), revenue source; **~quittung** tax bond *(US)*; **~quote** per capita tax load; **~rabatt** tax rebate; **~rad** *(Auto, Schiff)* steering wheel; **~rakete** *(Raumschiff)* control rocket; **~rate** assessment (tax) instal(l)ment; **~recht** revenue law, law of taxation, *(Steuerhoheit)* taxing power *(US)*.

steuerrechtlich financial, fiscal;
~e Bestimmungen tax regulations; **laut den ~en Bestimmungen** under tax law.

Steuerrechts|änderung change of tax law; **~verfahren** tax procedure.

Steuerreform tax (fiscal) reform;
~arbeiten work on tax reform; **~bündel** tax-reform package; **~gesetz** tax-reform bill (act, *US*); **~gesetzgebung** tax-reform legislation; **~vorlage** tax-reform bill; **~vorschlag** tax-reform proposal; **~werk** tax reform.

Steuer|regelung tax regulation; **~register** register of taxes; **~relais** control relay, pilot relay; **~revision** tax inspection *(Br.)* (audit, *US*, auditing, *US*); **~revisor** tax inspector (auditor, *US*); **~richtlinien** rules of taxation (assessment), tax rules, revenue ruling; **~rolle** tax book (roll, *US*), assessment roll, *(Kommunalsteuern)* rate book; **~rückerstattung** refund (repayment) of a tax, tax refund (replacement); **~rückgang** decreasing treasury receipts; **~rücklage** reserve for taxation, taxation reserve; **~rücklagenfonds** special revenue fund; **~rückstände** back taxes, arrears of taxes, delinquent taxes, delinquency amount *(Br.)*, tax arrears (deficiency, delinquency, *US*), *(Bilanz)* due for taxes, taxes receivable *(US)*; **~rückstände mit Nachsicht eintreiben** to ease tax arrears; **~rückstellungen** allowance for tax, reserve (provision, deduction) for taxes, tax provision, tax (taxation) reserve, *(Bilanz)* future taxation *(Br.)*; **~rückstellung für nicht entnommene Gewinne** provision for taxation on unrealized surpluses; **~rückstellungen vornehmen** to allow for tax, to make provision (allow) for taxation; **~rückvergütung** tax refund (replacement, rebate), reimbursement of taxes, bonification, drawback; **sofortige ~rückvergütung** on-the-spot tax refund; **~rückvergütungsschein** tax-refund certificate; **~rückzahlung** tax refund (repayment), repayment of duty (tax); **~sache** revenue case, fiscal matter, taxation matter; **~sachverständiger** tax expert (counsel(l)or), taxation specialist.

Steuersatz tax rate, rate of assessment (taxation), levy, *(Zoll)* rate of customs (duty, *Br.*);
anwendbarer ~ applicable rate; **einheitlicher ~** flat rate; **ermäßigter ~** rate of relief; **gestaffelter ~** progressive rate of taxation; **höchster ~** top (maximum) tax rate; **normaler ~** ordinary tax; **tatsächlicher ~** effective tax rate; **verkürzter ~** reduced rate of tax;
~ nach Anrechnung der Doppelsteuer net U. K. rate *(Br.)*; **ermäßigter ~ für die untersten Einkommensteuergruppen** marginal relief *(Br.)*; **verkürzter ~ für Klein- und Mittelbetriebe** small companies rate *(Br.)*; **~ im unteren Proportionalbereich** basic rate (threshold) of personal tax, standard rate of income tax;
~ anheben to put up the rate of a tax; **~ anwenden** to apply the tax rate; **höheren ~ anwenden** to tax at a higher rate; **niedrigen ~ anwenden** to charge a tax at a lower rate; **für den größeren Teil des Einkommens den normalen ~ anwenden** to shove more of the earned income into the ordinary tax bracket; **nur den halben ~ auslösen** to attract income tax on only 50%; **einer Bestrafung gleichkommender Kombination hoher Inflationsraten mit progressivem ~ ausweichen** to avoid a punitive combination of high inflation and progressive taxation; **höheren ~ bezahlen müssen** to be liable to tax at a higher rate; **dem normalen ~ (dem ~ des unteren Proportionalbereiches) unterliegen** to be taxable as ordinary income; **mit einem niedrigen ~ veranlagt werden** to be taxed at lower income rates; **nur mit dem halben ~ versteuert werden** to be eligible for the earned income ceiling rate of 50%; **niedrigsten ~ zahlen** to be at the bottom of the tax pile.

Steuer|sätze, sich über hohe ~sätze beklagen to grumble at high taxation; **~säule** tax pile, *(Auto)* steering column (post), *(Flugzeug)* control column; **~säumnis** tax delinquency *(US)*; **~säumniszuschlag** tax penalty; **~schätzer** tax assessor; **~schätzung** tax assessment, rating, *(Grundsteuer)* real-estate appraisal; **fünfjährige ~schätzung von landwirtschaftlichen und Wohngrundstücken** quinquennial valuation *(Br.)*; **~schein** customhouse bond; **~schema** tax scheme; **~schlacht** tax battle; **~schraube** tax screw, oppressive taxation; **~schraube anziehen** to put the tax bite (screws) on, to increase taxation; **~schuld** tax liability, liability to pay taxes, charge to duty, tax delinquency *(US)*, *(Bilanz)* accrued taxes, taxes payable *(US)*, *(geschuldete Steuer)* tax due (delinquency, *US*); **rückständige ~schuld** arrears of taxes; **tatsächliche ~schuld** actual tax liability; **~schuldner** tax debtor, taxpayer.

steuerschwach|sein to produce less revenue;
~er Monat month with low revenue receipts.

Steuerschwelle tax (duty) threshold.

Steuersenkung reduction in taxation (of taxes), tax reduction (cut);
gestaffelte ~ graduated tax reduction; **lineare ~** flat tax reduction.

Steuer|senkungsvorschlag tax-cut proposal; **~situation** tax position; **~sitz** taxable situs; **~skala** scale of taxation, tax scale; **~skandal** tax scandal; **~soll** tax due (liability).

steuersparend|e Tätigkeit tax-saving service; **übliches ~es Verfahren** tax-saving pattern.

Steuer|spezialist taxation specialist; **~staffelung** graduated taxation; **~status** tax status (statement); **~stempel** revenue stamp; **~strafe** tax (fiscal) penalty, surcharge, fine; **~strafsatz** tax penalty rate; **~straftat** tax offence; **~strafverfahren nach sich ziehen** to result in a tax procedure; **~streik** taxpayer's strike, civil disobedience; **~streitfrage** tax argument (dispute); **~struktur** tax structure.

Steuerstufe tax bracket;
~n bands of taxable income;
höchste ~ top bracket;
~n der inflationellen Entwicklung anpassen to lift tax bands in line with inflation; **in einer höheren ~ sein** to be in the higher income brackets.

Steuer|stundung tax deferment (deferral, *US*); **~stundungserfordernisse** deferred tax needs; **~subjekt** subject for taxation, taxing unit; **~sünderfonds** conscience fund *(US)*.

Steuersystem tax plan (scheme, structure), taxation, financial *(Br.)* (fiscal, *US*) system, assessment system;
abgestuftes ~ graduated taxation; **gespaltenes** ~ two-tier scheme of taxation; **proportionales** ~ proportional tax system; **vereinheitlichtes** ~ unified tax structure; **zyklisches** ~ incentive taxation.

Steuer|systematik tax planning; **~systematiker** tax planner; **~tabelle** tax table, tax (tax-rate) schedule.

Steuertarif scale of taxation, tax scale, tax-rate schedule, assessment;
progressiver ~ progressive scale of tax rates; **proportionaler** ~ proportional schedule of tax rates; **regressiver** ~ regressive scale of tax rates.

steuertechnische|Maßnahmen fiscal techniques; ~ **Methode** taxation method.

Steuer|termin tax payment (-filing, *US*) date (deadline); **~theorie** tax theory; **~träger** subject for taxation, ultimate taxpayer; **~transparenz** transparency of a tax system; **~überlegungen** revenue considerations; **zur ~überprüfung dran sein** to land s. o. on the audit pile *(US)*; **~überschuß** surplus in taxes, revenue surplus; **~überwälzung** shifting of a tax, tax shifting; **~überzahlung** overpayment of tax.

steuerumgehend tax-avoiding (-dodging).

Steuerumgeher tax avoider.

Steuerumgehung tax avoidance, *(unerlaubte)* fiscal evasion *(Br.)*, tax evasion (dodging);
~ **begehen** to avoid payment of a tax; **~en einen Riegel vorschieben** to crack down on tax evasion.

Steuer|umgehungsprojekt, ~umgehungssystem tax-avoidance scheme; **~umlage** tax levy; **~unbedenklichkeitsbescheinigung** clearance certificate.

Steuerung steering, *(Auto)* driving, *(Flugzeug)* piloting, control, *(Leitung)* direction, control;
automatische ~ *(Flugzeug)* robot pilot, George *(sl.)*;
~ **eines gesunden Durchschnittkurses** middle-of-the-road conduct; ~ **von Engpaßwaren** channel(l)ing of scarce materials; **elastische** ~ **des Geldmarktes** flexible control of the money market; ~ **der Konjunktur unter Eingehung von Risiken** economic brinkmanship; **direkte** ~ **von Produktion und Verbrauch** physical control; ~ **von Vertrieb und Verkauf** merchandising.

Steuerungssystem control system.

steuerunschädlich sein to be neutral as regards taxation.

Steuer|unterlagen tax papers, *(Finanzamt)* tax digest, books of a tax receiver; **jem. seine ~unterlagen zur Erledigung übergeben** to hand over one's tax affairs to s. o.; **~unterschied** tax difference; **~untersuchung** tax investigation (probe, *US*); **~urteil** tax judgment.

Steuerveranlagung taxation, assessment of taxes, tax assessment *(Br.)*, assessor's (assessed) valuation, levy, precept, *(Kommune)* rating;
zu hohe ~ excessive assessment; **ordnungsgemäße** ~ fair and proper legal assessment;
~ **einer Handelsgesellschaft** partnership assessment; **sofortige** ~ **wegen befürchteten Steuerausfalls** jeopardy assessment; ~ **verschiedener Steuerpflichtiger** extending a tax; **wahlweise** ~ **nach den Steuertabellen** optional tax table;
neue ~ **beantragen** to reopen an assessment; ~ **durchführen** to prepare an assessment; **um getrennte** ~ **einkommen** *(Eheleute)* to apply (claim) for a separate assessment; **falsche** ~ **vornehmen** to assess incorrectly.

Steuerveranlagungs|ausschuß valuation *(Br.)* (tax-writing) committee, tax commission *(US)*; **~beamter** tax assessor; **~behörde** tax-writing (valuation, *Br.*) committee, tax commissioner *(Br.)*; **~bezirk** assessment (taxing) district; **~einrichtungen** assessment machinery; **~gesetz** assessment committee act; **~prinzipien** methods of assessing taxable property; **~stelle** assessment office, tax (crown, *Br.*) assessor; **~zeitraum** assessment period.

Steuer|verbindlichkeiten tax obligations (liabilities); **~vereinbarung** tax convention, tax treaty *(US)*; **zweifelhafte ~verfahren** debatable tax practices; **~verfügung** tax instruction; **~vergehen** tax-evasion (revenue) offence, fiscal offence, tax fraud; **~vergleich** tax comparison.

Steuervergünstigung tax benefit (break, *US*, credit, *US*, privilege, concession, favo(u)r), taxation (tax) relief *(Br.)*;
angerechnete ~ tax-credit relief *(Br.)*; **nach fünf Jahren auslaufende ~en** tax tapers to zero after five years; **auf 5 - 7 Jahre beschränkte** ~ tax tapers for five-to-seven years deferral (deferment); **für Hypothekenzinsen gewährte** ~ mortgage interest relief *(Br.)*; **stufenweise gewährte** ~ graded tax; **vorübergehend gewährte** ~ transitional relief *(Br.)*; **unberechtigte ~en** excess relief *(Br.)*;
~ **für bezahlte Bausparzinsen** relief for interest paid to building societies *(Br.)*; ~ **für Berufstätige** earned income relief *(Br.)*; ~ **für Betriebskredite** business credit relief *(Br.)*; ~ **für im Ausland erzielte Einkünfte** foreign tax relief *(Br.)*; ~ **für Einkünfte aus Gewerbetätigkeit** earned income credit *(US)* (relief, *Br.*); ~ **für Investitionen** investment tax credit *(US)*, investment allowance; **~en für langfristige Kapitalanlagen** capital investment tax credits *(US)*; **~en bei Maschinenanschaffungen** tax exemption on equipment or machinery *(US)*; ~ **für Schuldenrückzahlung** relief for debts *(Br.)*; **~en für bezahlte Zinsen** tax relief in interest payments *(Br.)*, relief allowable in respect of interest paid *(Br.)*;
~en und Erleichterungen nicht voll ausschöpfen to derive less than full benefit of tax reliefs and allowances *(Br.)*; **~en für gezahlte Zinsen beantragen** to claim relief for interest paid on debt *(Br.)*; **~en beseitigen** to remove tax perks; **~en für Kapitalgewinne drastisch einschränken** to cut back drastically on the tax bands for capital gains; **~en ermöglichen** to offer beneficial taxation; **~en auslaufen lassen** to phase out tax allowances; **~en in Anspruch nehmen** to claim (qualify for) tax relief *(Br.)*.

Steuervergünstigungs|anspruch begründen to establish a claim for relief of tax *(Br.)*; **~richtlinien** tax credit rules *(US)*.

Steuer|vergütung tax refund (rebate); **~verhältnis** fiscal relationship; **~verkürzung** tax reduction, reduction in duty, *(unerlaubt)* fiscal evasion *(Br.)*; **~verlagerung** tax deferral *(US)*.

Steuerverlust loss of tax, taxable (revenue) loss;
~e kompensieren to soak up tax losses; ~ **über fünf Jahre verteilen** to spread the impact of a tax loss over five years; ~ **vortragen** to declare a tax loss against future earnings;
~vortrag tax-loss carry-forward *(Br.)* (carryover, *US*).

Steuer|vermehrung increase in taxes; **~vermeidung** tax avoidance (mitigation); **~verpachtung** *(historisch)* tax farming; **~verschuldung** fiscal indebtedness; **~verteilung** apportionment of taxes, allocation of revenue; **~verwaltung** administration of taxes, tax administration, fiscal (taxes) management, *(Behörde)* Board of Inland Revenue *(Br.)*, Internal Revenue Service *(US)*; **~verwaltungsakt** tax measure, fiscal action; **~verwaltungsbezirk** taxing district; **~vollmacht [des Steuereinnehmers]** tax warrant; **~voranschlag, ~vorausschätzungen** revenue estimates; **~vorauszahlung** prepayment of taxes, tax prepayment, advance tax payment, *(Einkommensteuer)* tax (assessment) instalment *(US)*; **~vorgriff** tax anticipation; **~vorgriffsschein** tax-anticipation bond *(US)*; **~vorlage** finance (money) bill *(Br.)*, revenue bill *(US)*; **gegen neue ~vorschläge Sturm laufen** to raise a hue and cry against new tax proposals; **~vorschriften** tax regulations; **~vorteil** tax advantage, taxrelief advantage; **attraktive ~vorteile** attractive tax features; **~vortrag nicht ausgenutzter Abschreibungsmöglichkeiten** carry-forward of access allowance *(Br.)*; **~vorzugssätzen unterliegen** to be subject to preferentially low rates of tax; **~werk** *(Datenverarbeitung)* control unit; **~wert** assessed (taxable, ratable, assessable, *Br.*) value, assessed valuation *(US)*; **nach dem ~wert abschätzen** to assess for taxable value; **~wesen** taxation, taxation system, tax business, fiscal matters; **örtliches ~wesen** local taxation; **~widerstand** resistance to taxation, civil disobedience; **~willigkeit** tax confidence; **~wirkung** tax effect; **~wohnsitz** fiscal domicile, ordinary residence *(Br.)*, residence status for tax purposes, residential status for a tax.

Steuerzahler taxpayer, *(Kommunalsteuer)* ratepayer *(Br.)*;
auf Kosten des ~s at public expense;
die ~ tax-paying public; **normaler** ~ standard-rate taxpayer; **rückständiger** ~ ratepayer (taxpayer) in arrears; **säumiger** ~ dilatory taxpayer;
~ **mit niedrigem Einkommen** low-income taxpayer; ~ **im unteren Proportionalbereich** basic-rate taxpayer; ~ **in der Spitzenklasse** top-rate taxpayer;
Angelegenheit aus der Sicht des ~s sehen to view a matter from the taxpayer's standpoint.

Steuerzahlung payment of taxes (duty), tax payment, taxpaying, *(kommunal)* ratepaying *(Br.)*;
anonyme ~ conscience money; **zu niedrige** ~ undercharge of tax; **pauschalierte ~en** unascertained duties; **rückständige ~en** tax unpaid for earlier years; **verspätete** ~ tax delinquency *(US)*; **pauschalierte vorzeitige** ~ commutation of taxes; **zurückgestellte ~en** *(Bilanz)* deferred taxes;
sich vor der ~ **drücken** to evade paying taxes; **von ~en befreit sein** to be exempt from taxes; **~en vermeiden** to avoid paying taxes; **mit ~en belastet werden** to carry the burden of taxes.

Steuerzahlungstermin hinausschieben to defer a duty.
Steuer|zeichen revenue stamp *(US)*, tax-paid; ~**zeichenfälschung** forgery of revenue; ~**zettel** tax paper (bill, *US*).
Steuerzuschlag extra duty, additional tax (duty), *(für höhere Einkommen)* surcharge, surtax;
~ **für Einkünfte aus Kapitalvermögen (Kapitalerträgen)** investment income surcharge *(Br.)*;
~ **zahlen** to pay extra duty.
Steuer|zuschuß, zehnprozentiger ~**zuschuß für Investitionsvorhaben** 10% investment tax credit *(US)*; ~**zwangsverkauf** tax sale of property *(US)*, tax selling; **zu** ~**zwecken** for taxation purposes, for the purpose of taxation.
Steven *(Schiff)* stem.
Steward steward, porter *(US)*.
Stewardeß stewardess, airline (air) hostess.
stibitzen to filch, to lurch, to pilfer.
Stich prick, stab, thrust, *(Gravur)* engraving, *(Kartenspiel)* trick, *(Kummer)* pang, sting, wrench, *(Mücke)* bite, *(Stichelei)* gibe, thrust, passing shot;
~ **ins Makabre** a touch of the macabre; ~ **ins Rote** tinge of red; **jem. einen** ~ **geben** to cut s. o. to the quick; ~ **haben** *(Nahrungsmittel)* to have gone off, *(verrückt sein)* to be touched (cracked); ~ **halten** to withstand; **nicht** ~ **halten** not to hold water; **im** ~ **lassen** to desert, to forsake, to let down, to leave in the lurch; **j. im** ~ **lassen** to turn one's back on s. o., to go back on s. o. *(coll.)*; **Freund in der Not im** ~ **lassen** to betray (throw over) a friend; **im** ~ **gelassen sein** to be left holding the baby *(fam.)*; **jem.** ~**e versetzen** to gibe at s. o.;
~**bahn** branch line.
Stichelei wisecrack, pinprick, rub, shy, fling, tease, *(witzige Bemerkung)* wisecrack, drive *(US)*.
sticheln to needle, to gibe, to taunt;
gegen j. ~ to make gibs (jibs) at s.o.
Stichentscheid second (casting) vote, tie-break *(US)*.
stichhaltig cogent, watertight, valid, solid, sound-proof, founded on facts;
[nicht] ~ **sein** [not] to hold water;
~**es Argument** sound argument; ~**er Grund** valid reason.
Stichhaltigkeit soundness, validity;
~ **eines Argumentes** validity of an argument.
Stichmonat relevant month.
Stichprobe random test (sample), spot (snap, *US*) check;
mittels ~**n** by means of a test;
angepaßte ~ balanced sample; **subjektiv ausgewählte** ~ judgment sample; **einseitig betonte** ~ biassed sample; **entnommene** ~ picked sample; **doppelt erhobene** ~ duplicate sample; **festgelegte** ~ fixed sample; **gemischte** ~ mixed sample; **geschichtete** ~ stratified sample; **berechtigt (bewußt) gewählte** ~ purposive sample; **zufällig gewählte** ~ random sample; **gewichtete** ~ balanced sample; **gezielte** ~ precision sample; **zu große** ~ oversample; **kontrollierte** ~ controlled sample; **mehrstufige** ~ multistage sample; **repräsentative** ~ representative (adequate) sample; **unkontrollierte** ~ haphazard sampling; **unpräzise** ~ bias; **unvollständige** ~ defective sample; **unvorbereitete** ~ sample taken offhand; **verknüpfte** ~**n** linked samples; **verzerrte** ~ biassed sample; **zweistufige** ~ two-stage sample;
~ **von Haushalten** sample of households; ~**n mit Parallelfällen** matched samples; ~ **aus einer Personengesamtheit** sample of persons;
~**n entnehmen** to take samples at random.
stichprobenartige|Marktuntersuchung accidental (haphazard) sampling; ~ **Überprüfung** audit test, snap check, spot checking.
Stichprobenauswahl random sample selection;
planlose ~ chunk sampling; **systematische** ~ systematic sample; **ungleichartige** ~ mixed sampling; **zufallsgesteuerte** ~ probability sample;
~ **nach Gruppen** stratified sample.
Stichproben|basis sample basis; ~**befragung** haphazard sampling; ~**einheit** sample unit.
Stichprobenentnahme bulk sampling;
planlose ~ chunk sampling; **ungleichartige** ~ mixed sampling; **unmittelbare** ~ unitary sampling;
~ **bei der Abnahme** acceptance sampling; ~ **aus der Masse** bulk sampling.
Stichproben|erhebung sample survey, random sample, poll; ~**fehler** sampling error; ~**mittelwert** sample mean; ~**netz** network of samples; ~**plan** sample design (plan); ~**prüfung** sampling inspection; ~**punkt** sampling point; ~**raum** sample room; ~**schema** sampling scheme; ~**umfang** sample size.
Stichprobenverfahren spot-check system, *(Statistik)* sampling; **einfaches** ~ simple sampling; **gemischtes** ~ mixed sampling; **geschichtetes** ~ stratified sampling; **mehrstufiges** ~ multistage sampling; **ungeschichtetes** ~ simple sampling; **zufallsähnliches** ~ quasi-random sampling; **zweistufiges** ~ double sampling;
~ **im Gittermuster** lattice sampling.
Stichproben|vergleich test comparison; ~**verteilung** sampling distribution.
Stichtag appointed day, fixed (key, crucial, closing, target) date, deadline *(US)*, *(Bankbuchung)* value (valuation, *US*) date, *(Börse)* settling day, *(Erhebung)* date of survey, *(Fälligkeit)* due (accrual, maturity) date;
~ **für den Dividendenanspruch** accrual of a dividend; ~ **für die Wahlberechtigung** qualifying date.
Stichwaffe thrust weapon.
Stichwahl second (additional) ballot, casting (runoff) vote, tie-break *(US)*;
~**wettbewerb** tie-break competition *(US)*.
Stichwort catchword, test word, *(Bibliothek)* entry word, *(Schlüsselwort)* key word, *(Telegramm)* code word, *(Theater)* cue, feed, *(Wörterbuch)* entry, head word;
~ **aufnehmen** to enter a head word; **sich ein paar** ~**e aufschreiben** to jot down a few notes; **sein** ~ **verpassen** to miss one's cue;
~**aufführung,** ~**eintragung** catchword (subject) entry; ~**geber** *(Rundfunk)* stooge *(US)*; **erweitertes** ~**register** extended catchword register; ~**verzeichnis** subject catalog(ue), index, catalog(ue) raisonné; ~**zeile** catch line; ~**zettel** cue card.
Stichzahl *(Produktionskontingent)* quota, *(Telegrammverkehr)* test number.
Stiefbruder stepbrother.
Stiefel boot;
sich einen ~ **einbilden** to think no small beer of o. s.; **ziemlichen** ~ **vertragen** to be able to take a lot of alcohol; **seinen alten** ~ **weiterarbeiten** to travel in the same groove; **ziemlichen** ~ **zusammenquatschen** to talk a lot of rubbish *(coll.)*;
~**putzer** shoe-black *(Br.)*, boot-black *(US)*.
Stief|eltern stepparents; ~**kind** stepchild; ~**mutter** stepmother; ~**vater** stepfather.
Stiege staircase, stairs.
Stiel, mit Stumpf und neck and crop.
Stielaugen, gewaltige eyes popped like organ-stops (chaped hatpegs);
~ **machen** to rubber *(US sl.)*.
Stier bei den Hörnern packen to take the bull by the horns, to grasp the nettle.
stier|geradeaus straight ahead;
~**er Blick** vacant stare.
stieren to stare, to gaze.
Stier|hetze bull run; ~**kampf** bullfight, corrida *(US)*; ~**kampfarena** bull ring.
Stiesel bore, flat tire *(US sl.)*, drip *(sl.)*.
Stift pin, plug, *(Altersheim)* [charitable] foundation, *(Knirps)* squirt *(coll.)*, nipper *(Br., coll.)*, *(Lehrling)* apprentice.
stiften to found, to institute, to establish, to set up, *(dotieren)* to endow, to donate *(US)*, *(im Erbwege)* to bequeath, *(spendieren)* to donate, to shout *(sl.)*;
100 Dollar ~ to subscribe $ 100; **Ehe** ~ to bring about a marriage, to make a match; **Kasten Bier** ~ to chip in with a case of beer *(coll.)*; **Krankenhausbett** ~ to endow a bed in a hospital; **Majorat** ~ to found an entail; **Preis** ~ to offer a prize; **Schule** ~ to found a school; **Stipendium** ~ to found a scholarship; **Unheil** ~ to cause disaster; **Verwirrung** ~ to make havoc; **für wohltätige Zwecke** ~ to contribute for a work of charity, to put one's hand in one's pocket; **Zwietracht** ~ to sow discord.
stiftengehen to take to one's heels, to bolt.
Stifter founder, institutor, organizer, donor *(US)*, donator *(US)*, sponsor *(US)*, *(Rente)* settler, *(Treuhandverhältnis)* trustor *(US)*, grantor *(US)*.
Stiftsschule foundation (endowed, public, *Br.*) school, charitable educational constitution;
~ **errichten** to found a school.
Stiftung *(Anstalt)* foundation, endowed institution, trust, settlement, benefice, erection, plantation, *(Dotation)* endowment, grant, dotation, donation *(US)*, *(Gründung)* establishment, *(an Museum)* benefaction;
ausländische ~ foreign charity; **reich dotierte** ~ richly endowed foundation; **entgeltliche** ~ trust for value; **zu Lebzeiten errichtete** ~ inter vivos trust; **rechtsgeschäftlich errichtete** ~ voluntary trust (settlement); **rechtsgültig errichtete** ~ perfect trust; **testamentarisch errichtete** ~ testamentary trust; **auf**

unbegrenzte Zeit errichtete ~ perpetual trust; in den Grundzügen festgelegte ~ directory trust; in allen Einzelheiten festgesetzte ~ completely voluntary (constituted) trust; in das Belieben des Erben gestellte ~ executory trust; kirchliche ~ fabric fund; kündbare ~ revocable trust; milde (mildtätige) ~ charitable foundation (trust), charitable endowment, endowed charity, eleemosinary corporation, charitable donation; öffentlich-rechtliche ~ public trust; private ~ private foundation, express trust; Rockefeller ~ Rockefeller Foundation; wohltätige ~ charitable institution (trust, use, establishment, foundation), charity, complex trust, eleemosynary corporation, trust for charitable purposes;
~ für eine Bildungsanstalt educational trust; ~ zugunsten eines Dritten savings-bank (Totten, *US*) trust; ~ zugunsten der Ehefrau oder der Kinder settlement for the wife or children; ~ für Entwicklungsländer Overseas Development Institute; ~ mit festgesetzten Ersatzberechtigten shifting trust; ~ zum Zwecke der Familienversorgung sheltering (spendthrift) trust;
~, die nur Zinsen ausschüttet simple trust;
~ errichten to create a trust (foundation); von einer ~ leben to be on a foundation; ~ für das Rote Kreuz machen to make a donation to the Red Cross; ~ verwalten to act as trustee.

Stiftungs|[aufsichts]amt foundation board, Charity Commissioner *(Br.)*; ~aufsicht supervision of a foundation; ~beirat board of trustees; ~berechtigter trust beneficiary, cestui que trust; ~einkünfte foundation (trust) income; ~errichtung setting up of a trust; ~feier, ~fest anniversary, commemoration day; ~fonds endowment (trust) fund; ~gebäude foundation building; ~gelder trust fund (money, endowments); ~kapital settlement capital; ~rat board of trustees, foundation board; ~register führen to maintain a register of charities *(Br.)*; ~treuhänder charity trustee; ~urkunde charter, trust deed, settlement deed, deed of donation (gift, settlement); ~vermögen trust property (estate), trust fund, endowment fund, charity estate; ~vermögen im Ausland foreign charity; ~vertrag trust settlement (deed); ~verwalter settlement trustee; ~vorstand foundation executives; ~zuwendungen einstellen to turn off the faucet of funds.

Stil style, diction, language, writing, manner, make;
im ~ von after the fashion (in the vein) of; im großen ~ in a big way; in gutem ~ in style;
bombastischer ~ inflated style; charakteristischer ~ individual style; flüssiger ~ even-running (smooth, easy) style; gekünstelter ~ forced style, mannerism; geschraubter ~ bookish style; gespreizter ~ pretentious style; gewandter ~ clever style; gotischer ~ pointed style; hochtrabender ~ stilted style; klarer ~ lucid literary (transparent) style; knapper ~ close (terse) style; kraftvoller ~ virile style [of writing]; kümmerlicher ~ inadequate style; pompöser ~ pompous style; prägnanter ~ concise style; richtiger ~ correct style; schlechter ~ vicious style; schwerfälliger ~ clumsy style; schwülstiger ~ inflated style; seichter ~ washy style; trockener ~ dull style; umständlicher ~ ponderous style; uneleganter ~ hard style; unverständlicher ~ obscure style; verbesserter ~ polished style;
~ der neuen Sachlichkeit functional style;
~ eines Buches bestimmen to set the tone of a book; in großem ~ leben to live in great style; Betrügereien in großem ~ machen to commit frauds on a large scale; beißenden ~ schreiben to give an edge to one's style; seinen ~ verfeinern to refine (polish up) one's style;
~art manner, style; ~blüte bloomer; ~bruch lapse (corruption) of style; ~flüssigkeit reading ease.

stilgerecht gekleidet appropriately dressed.

Stilgleichheit bei der Verpackung family likeness.

stilisieren to ward, to formulate, to compose, to be stylistic, to frame.

stilistisch stylistic;
~e Feinheiten subtleties of style.

still silent, quiet, *(flau)* dull, flat, dead, slack, *(inaktiv)* dormant, inactive, *(ruhig)* calm, quiet, passive, *(stagnierend)* stagnant;
sich ~ davonmachen to steal away secretly, to take French leave; sich ~ verhalten to keep quiet;
~e Beteiligung silent partnership; Forderungsabtretung in ~er Form vornehmen to operate on a nonnotification basis; ~es Geschäft slack business; ~e Gesellschaft dormant (sleeping, silent, *Br.*) partnership; ~er Gesellschafter dormant (sleeping, silent, *Br.*) partner; ~e Gewässer quiet waters; ~e Jahreszeit dull (dead) season; ~e Liquidation voluntary liquidation; ~es Örtchen the loo *(Br.)*, the john *(US)*; ~er Ozean Pacific; ~e Reserven latent (inner, hidden, secret, passive) reserves, hidden assets; sich dem ~en Suff ergeben to drink deep, to be on the drink *(coll.)*; ~er Teilhaber dormant (latent, secret, silent, *US*, sleeping, side, *US*) partner; ~e Teilhaberschaft silent *(US)* (sleeping) partnership; ~e Übereinkunft tacit (implied) agreement; ~er Verehrer secret admirer; ~er Vorbehalt mental reservation; ~e Vorbehalte gegen j. hegen to harbo(u)r inner reservation against s. o.; ~es Wasser sein to be a deep one; ~er Winkel quiet nook;
~e Wasser sind tief still waters run deep.

Stille silence, quiet, tranquil(l)ity, mum, hush, *(Markt)* dullness, flatness, deadness, stagnancy;
im ~n within o. s.; in aller ~ secretly, on the quiet; in der nächtlichen ~ in the silence of the night;
absolute ~ dead silence, *(Rundfunk)* dead air *(sl.)*;
eindrucksvolle ~ impressive silence; unheimliche ~ deathly silence;
die ~ vor dem Sturm the hush before the storm;
in aller ~ heiraten to get married on the quiet; sich in aller ~ vollziehen to take place unnoticed.

stillegen *(Auto)* to lay up, *(Betrieb)* to shut down, to close, *(Geld)* to immobilize, to neutralize, *(Schiff)* to put out of commission, *(Verkehr)* to stop, to paralyse;
Eisenbahnlinie ~ to close down a railway line; Fabrik wegen Auftragsmangels ~ to close down a factory because of lack of orders.

Stillegung *(Auto)* lay-up, *(Betrieb)* shutdown, shutting down, closing down, cessation, *(Geld)* immobilization, neutralization, tying up, locking up, *(Verkehr)* stoppage, paralysation;
umfassende ~en plant-wide shutdowns;
~ eines veralteten Betriebs closure of an antique plant; ~ einer Eisenbahnlinie (Eisenbahnstrecke) abandonment of a railway (railroad, *US*), rail closure; ~ unrentabler Eisenbahnstrecken elimination of unprofitable lines; ~ in der Ferienzeit holiday shutdown; ~ eines Geschäftsbetriebes cessation of a business; ~ der gesamten Industrie general tie-up of industry; ~ von Nebenlinien branch-line abandonment.

Stillegungs|bestimmungen cessation provisions; ~verfügung shutdown (closing) order; ~vergütung bonus for closing down.

stillen *(Durst)* to appease, *(Neugier)* to satisfy, *(Säugling)* to nurse;
Wissensdurst eines Kindes ~ to gratify a child's thirst for knowledge.

Stillgeld nursing benefit.

stillgelegt *(Betrieb)* shut-down, closed, *(unproduktiv)* dead, idle;
~ sein to be at a standstill, to run idle;
~er Betrieb nonoperating property; ~es Geld tied (locked, *Br.*) -up money, lock-up *(Br.)*.

Stillhalte|abkommen standstill agreement, blocking arrangement, blocking agreement, moratorium, moratory; ~anordnungg standstill order; ~ausschuß standstill commission; ~erklärung *(Gläubiger)* letter of licence; ~gläubiger standstill creditor; ~konsortium supporting syndicate; ~kredit frozen (standstill) credit.

stillhalten *(Kreditgeber)* to grant a moratory, to defer payment, *(Prämiengesellschaft)* to sell at an option *(Br.)* (a privilege, *US*), *(Staat)* to refrain from interference.

Stillhalter *(Prämiengeschäft)* seller of an option *(Br.)* (a privilege, *US*).

Stillhalte|schulden frozen (standstill) debts; ~vereinbarung standstill (blocking) agreement, moratorium; ~verfügung standstill order; ~zusage standby facilities.

Stillhaltung eines Kredits prolongation (freezing) of a credit.

Stilliegekosten idle-plant expenses.

Stilliegen *(Betrieb)* standing idle, down period.

stilliegen *(Betrieb)* to run (stand) idle, to be at a standstill (shut down), *(festgelegtes Geld)* to be immobilized (tied up, locked up, *Br.*), *(Geschäft)* to be dormant, *(Verkehr)* to be paralysed (suspended).

stilliegende Betriebsanlagen idle facilities.

Stilliege|risiko *(Schiff)* lay-up risk; ~zeit lay days.

Stillschweigen silence, secrecy;
durch ~ tacitly;
verabredetes ~ conspiracy of silence;
jem. ~ auferlegen to impose (enjoin) silence on s. o.; ~ als Ablehnung auslegen to interpret s. one's silence as refusal; während der Verhandlungen ~ bewahren to maintain secrecy during negotiations; sich in ~ hüllen to wrap o. s. up in silence, to keep one's counsel; Sache mit ~ übergehen to pass over an affair with (in) (maintain a discreet) silence; j. zum ~ verpflichten to enjoin s. o. to secrecy, to shut s. one's mouth;
~ bedeutet Zustimmung silence shows (gives) content.

stillschweigend silent, tacit, by implication, implied;
~ **einbegriffen** implicit; ~ **geduldet** on sufferance;
~ **über etw. hinwegsehen** to pass s. th. over in silence; ~ **verlängert werden** to be renewed automatically;
~**e Anerkennung** implicit recognition; ~**e Annahme** silent (tacit) acceptance; ~**e Bedingung** implied condition; ~**e Bewilligung** tacit approval; ~**es Einverständnis** tacit agreement (understanding); ~**e Folgerung** implication; ~ **gewährte Garantie** implied warranty; ~**e Pachtverlängerung** tacit relocation; ~ **eingeschlossene Pflichten des Arbeitnehmers** implied duties; ~**e Übereinkunft (Vereinbarung)** tacit (implied) agreement; ~**e Verlängerung** tacit renewal; ~ **anerkannte Verpflichtung** implied obligation; ~ **geschlossener Vertrag** tacit agreement; ~ **angenommenes Vertragsverhältnis** implied contract; ~ **vorgenommene Vertragsverlängerung** tacit renovation; ~**er Verzicht** implied waiver; **mit der ~en Voraussetzung** under the tacit understanding; ~**er Vorbehalt** mental reservation; ~**e Zustimmung** implied (silent) consent.

Stillstand standstill, stillstand, stoppage, arrest, *(Betrieb)* shutdown, standstill, *(Flaute)* dullness, deadness, *(Pause)* cessation, *(Stagnation)* stagnancy, stagnation, slackness, *(Untätigkeit)* inactivity, *(Verkehr)* breakdown, suspension, tie-up;
völliger ~ dead stop, deadlock;
~ **im Fortschritt** stalemate in progress; ~ **des normalen Geschäftsverkehrs** suspension (stoppage) of business; ~ **der Rechtspflege** recess of the courts;
zum ~ **bringen** to bring to a standstill, *(Auto)* to stop; **etw. abrupt zum** ~ **bringen** to stop s. th. dead in its tracks; **zum völligen** ~ **bringen** to deadlock; **zum** ~ **kommen** to come to a standstill, *(Verhandlungen)* to reach a deadlock; **fast zum** ~ **kommen** to slow down to a crawl; **knirschend zum** ~ **kommen** to grind to a halt; **völlig zum** ~ **kommen** to come to a full stop *(coll.)*, to be paralyzed.

Stillstands|bericht idle-time report; ~**kosten** idle-plant expenses; ~**periode** down period; ~**versicherung** business interruption (use and occupancy, *US*) insurance.

stillstehen *(Betrieb)* to run (lie) idle, to be closed (shutdown, at a standstill), *(Geschäft)* to be stagnant, *(Verkehr)* to be blocked (jammed);
fast ~ *(Verkehr)* to be reduced to a crawl; **völlig** ~ *(Betriebe)* to be paralyzed.

stillstehend *(Betrieb)* idle, closed, shut down.

stillvergnügt inwardly happy.

Stillzeit, in der during the nursing time.

Stil|möbel period furniture; ~**veränderung** style change.

stilvoll, Dinge ~ **zu erledigen wissen** to do things in style.

Stilwörterbuch dictionary of style.

Stimmabgabe vote, voting, *(Wahl)* poll, polling, election;
beim Beginn der ~ at the opening of the poll;
betrügerische ~ fraudulent voting; **freie** ~ freedom of election; **geheime** ~ vote by secret ballot; **geschlossene** ~ block vote; **geteilte** ~ split vote; **kumulative (mehrfache)** ~ cumulative voting; **namentliche** ~ roll-call vote, division *(Br.)*; **offene** ~ voting by open ballot; **schriftliche** ~ vote by correspondence;
~ **durch Erheben von den Sitzen** voting by rising and sitting; ~ **durch Handaufheben** vote by show of hands; ~ **in Kästchen** box sorting; ~ **durch einen Stellvertreter** vote (voting) by proxy; ~ **durch Zuruf** vote by acclamation;
sich der ~ **enthalten** to withhold one's voice; ~ **überwachen** to superintend an election; ~ **einstimmig vornehmen** to carry a vote unanimously.

stimmberechtigt qualified (entitled) to vote, with voting power, votable, enfranchised;
nicht ~ nonvoting, unqualified to vote, voteless, voiceless;
~ **sein** to be qualified to vote, to have a vote, *(Aktien)* to carry voting rights; **rede- und** ~ **sein** to be entitled to vote and to speak;
~**es Aktienkapital** voting capital stock; **nicht** ~**es Aktienkapital** nonvoting capital stock; ~**er Kapitalanteil** voting pool stock; ~**es Mitglied** voting member; ~**e Wertpapiere** voting securities (stock).

Stimmberechtigte electorate.

Stimmberechtigter voter, vote;
ausschlaggebender ~ casting voter.

Stimmberechtigung right to vote, vote, voting power (privilege), *(Wahlrecht)* suffrage, franchise;
eingeschränkte ~ contingent voting power;
~ **der Gläubiger** creditors' voting rights.

Stimm|berechtigungsschein voting-trust certificate *(US)*; ~**bevollmächtigter** proxyholder; ~**bevollmächtigung** proxy; ~**bezirk** electoral district; ~**bindungsvertrag** voting trust agreement; ~**bindungszertifikat** voting-trust certificate *(US)*.

Stimme voice, *(Meinung)* opinion, *(Wahl)* vote, voice;
mit einer Mehrheit von 11 ~**n** by a majority of eleven votes; **mit beleidigter** ~ in an injured voice, in an offended tone of voice; **mit schwacher** ~ in a feeble pipe; **mit zorniger** ~ in an angry tone; **ohne** ~ without a vote;
abgegebene ~**n** votes cast (recorded, polled); **akkumulativ abgegebene** ~ plumper; **von der Mehrheit abgegebene** ~**n** majority vote; **schriftlich abgegebene** ~ written vote; **abweichende** ~ dissentient; **ausschlaggebende** ~ casting (decisive) vote; **beratende** ~ deliberative voice; **entscheidende** ~ casting vote; **gültige** ~ valid vote; **innere** ~ inner voice; **Ja-**~ *(parl.)* consent; **kumulierte** ~**n** cumulative votes; **vergeblich mahnende** ~ voice in the wilderness; **auf anderen Kandidaten übertragene** ~ transferable vote; **ungültige** ~ invalid (spoiled) vote, invalid ballot, spoiled voting paper; **unsichere** ~**n** floating vote; **wahlberechtigte** ~**n** eligible votes *(Br.)*; **zersplitterte** ~**n** scattered votes;
~ **des Gewissens** voice (the dictates) of conscience; ~**n der Landbevölkerung** rural vote; ~**n der Presse** press comments; ~**n durch Stellvertreter** vote by proxy; ~ **der Umweltschützler** environmental vote; ~ **der Vernunft** the dictates of common sense; ~ **des Volkes** the popular cry, vox populi;
Ja- und Nein-~**n** ayes and noes;
~**n dafür** votes cast in favo(u)r, *(parl.)* content; ~**n dagegen** votes cast against; ~**n für und wider** yeas and nays;
mehr als eine ~ **abgeben** to repeat *(US)*; **Ja-**~ **abgeben** to vote in the affirmative; **Nein-**~ **abgeben** to vote in the negative; **seine** ~ **abgeben** to cast one's vote, *(Wahlen)* to poll, to elect, to vote; **seine** ~ **für etw. abgeben** to vote in favo(u)r of s. th.; **seine** ~ **für j. abgeben** to vote for s. o., to give s. o. one's vote; ~ **für die Regierungsparteien abgeben** to vote for the pro-government parties; **seine** ~ **für die Vorschläge des Präsidenten abgeben** to cast a vote for the presidency; **Antrag mit 14 gegen 9** ~**n ablehnen** to reject a motion by 14 votes to 9; **Antrag mit einer Mehrheit von** ~**n annehmen** to adopt a motion by a majority of votes; ~**n auszählen** to count the votes; **sich der** ~ **enthalten** to abstain from voting (in a vote); **hundert** ~**n erhalten** to poll a hundred votes; **Mehrheit der abgegebenen** ~**n erhalten** to poll a majority of votes cast; **fast alle** ~**n in einem Wahlbezirk erhalten** to sweep a constituency; **weiterhin seine** ~ **erheben** to keep on roaring; **j. an seiner** ~ **erkennen** to recognize s. one's voice; ~**n erlangen** to roll up votes; **25% der abgegebenen** ~**n bei einer Wahl erzielen** to poll as much as 25% of the vote; **jem. seine** ~ **geben** to give one's vote to (vote for) s. o.; **alle** ~**n einem Kandidaten geben** to plump for a candidate *(coll.)*; **beratende** ~ **haben** to act in an advisory capacity; **in einer Sache keine** ~ **haben** to have no say in a matter; **die meisten** ~**n haben** to head the poll; **in einer Versammlung Sitz und** ~ **haben** to have seat and vote in an assembly; **wenigste** ~**n erhalten haben** to be at the bottom of the poll; ~**n verschwinden lassen** *(Radio)* to fade out a conversation; ~**n sammeln** to collect the votes; ~**n für einen Abgeordneten sammeln** to canvass for a candidate; **seine** ~ **schonen** to nurse one's voice; **mit leiser** ~ **sprechen** to speak in a low voice; **Mehrheit der abgegebenen** ~**n auf sich vereinigen** to poll the majority of votes cast; ~**n der Gewerkschaftsmitglieder verlieren** to lose the trade-union vote; **jem. seine** ~ **versagen** to turn one's thumb down on s. o.; **seine** ~ **auf mehrere Kandidaten verteilen** to split the vote (one's ticket, *US*); **um** ~**n werben** to canvass for votes; **in einem Wahlbezirk** ~**n werben** to canvass a district; **mit 8 gegen 5** ~**n abgelehnt werden** to be rejected by 8 votes to 5; **mit allen** ~**n gegen eine angenommen werden** to pass (be resolved) with one dissentient voice; ~**n zählen** to cast (count, tell, scrutinize) votes.

stimmen *(abstimmen)* to cast one's vote, *(Instrument)* to tune, *(optieren)* to opt, *(in Ordnung sein)* to be in order, *(Rechnung)* to be correct, *(übereinstimmen)* to tally, *(wählen)* to [go to the] poll, to vote, to elect;
für etw. ~ to vote in favo(u)r of s. th.; **für j.** ~ to give one's vote to s. o.; **gegen jds. Aufnahme** ~ to blockade (blackball) s. o.; **für einen Bewerber** ~ to vote for a candidate; **j. ernst** ~ to make s. o. serious; **j. fröhlich** ~ to put s. o. in a cheerful mood; **gegen etw.** ~ to vote against s. th.; **nicht genau** ~ *(techn.)* to be out of truth; **geschlossen für etw.** ~ to vote solidly for s. th.; **mit Ja** ~ to vote in the affirmative; **j. nachdenklich** ~ to make s. o. think; **mit Nein** ~ to vote in the negative; **nicht** ~ *(Kasse)* not to be correct (balance); **für die Republikanische Partei** ~ to vote Republican; **gegen einen Vorschlag** ~ to vote down a proposal.

Stimmenabgabe vote, voting, *(Wahl)* poll, polling, election;
bei Beginn der ~ at the opening of the poll.

Stimmenanteil percentage of votes;
hoher ~ chunk of votes; ~ **der Labourpartei** labour vote *(Br.)*; ~ **der liberalen Wähler abschmetzen** to pick the liberal vote apart; **seinen** ~ **nur geringfügig vergrößern** to make only a limited advance on the share of the vote.

Stimmen|anzahl number of votes; ~**auszählung** counting the votes; ~**auszählung verlangen** to call a count; **geringe** ~**differenz** closeness of the vote; ~**einheit** unanimity of votes; **mit** ~**einheit** without a dissentient voice; ~**fang** vote hunting (getting), catching votes; ~**fang betreiben** to play the sovereign *(US)*; ~**fänger** vote getter (hunter, catcher); ~**fängerei** vote getting (hunting), vote-catching manoeuvre; ~**gemurmel** hum of voices; ~**gewinne verzeichnen** to pick up votes; ~**gewirr** hubble-bubble, riot of sounds.

stimmengleich enden to end in a tie.

Stimmen|gleichheit parity (equality) of votes, equally divided, tie; **annähernde** ~**gleichheit** closeness (close-up) of a vote; **bei** ~**gleichheit entscheiden** to have the casting vote, to cast the tie-breaking vote *(US)*; ~**häufung** cumulative voting; ~**jäger** vote hunter (getter); ~**kauf** traffic in votes; ~**kontrolle** vote checking, voting control.

Stimmenmehrheit voting majority, majority vote, plurality of votes;
mit ~ by a majority of voices;
der wertmäßigen ~ **entsprechend** reckoned on the majority in value;
einfache ~ base (simple) majority; **qualifizierte** ~ qualified (special) majority; **relative** ~ plurality *(US)*;
Beschluß mit ~ **annehmen** to pass a resolution by a majority of votes; **durch** ~ **besiegen** to outvote; ~ **haben** to have the majority on one's side; **über eine** ~ **verfügen** to control a majority of votes.

Stimmen|minderheit minority of votes, minority vote; ~**prüfer** scrutator; ~**prüfung** scrutiny of votes; ~**teilung** splitting, division; ~**verlagerung** shift of votes; **abgegebene** ~**zahl** number of votes cast; ~**zählung** vote counting, scrutiny of votes, *(Versammlung)* poll rate.

Stimmenthaltung abstinence (abstention) from voting;
angegebene ~ declared abstention;
~ **üben** to abstain from voting.

Stimmen|übergewicht haben to preponderate in voting; ~**unterschied** difference of votes cast; ~**unterstützung erlangen** to obtain voting support; ~**vereinigung** pooling of votes; ~**verhältnis** proportion of votes; ~**verlust erleiden** to lose votes; ~**vertreter** proxy, voting trustee; ~**werber** canvasser, electioneerer, solicitor of votes, vote getter (hunter); ~**werbung** canvass[ing], solicitation of votes, vote getting (hunting); ~**werbung betreiben** to solicit votes, to tout; ~**werbung für einen Abgeordneten treiben** to canvass for a candidate.

Stimmenzahl number of votes, voting strength, *(Wahl)* poll;
abgegebene ~ number of votes recorded; **genügende** ~ sufficient number of votes.

Stimmen|zähler vote counter, teller, scrutineer, tally clerk *(US)*; ~**zählung** vote counting (count), counting of votes, poll, scrutiny of votes, division *(US)*; ~**zuwachs erlangen** to roll up votes.

stimmgebundener Aktionär voting trust certificate holder *(US)*.

Stimm|karte voting paper; ~**kauf** traffic in votes; **hohe** ~**lage haben** to speak in a high key; ~**liste** electoral register.

Stimmrecht voting power (privilege), right to vote, individual vote, *(Wahlrecht)* suffrage, franchise;
ohne ~ nonvoting;
allgemeines ~ universal suffrage; **doppeltes** ~ double vote; **einfaches** ~ individual vote; **eingeschränktes** ~ contingent voting power; **erhöhtes** ~ *(Aktionär)* weighted voting rights; **größere** ~**e** bigger voice; **kumulatives** ~ cumulative voting; **mehrfaches** ~ card vote, plural voting; **übertragbares** ~ transferable vote;
~ **der Grundstücksbesitzer** occupation franchise; ~ **des Haushaltvorstandes** household franchise *(Br.)*;
~ **aberkennen** to disqualify from voting; **sein** ~ **ausüben** *(Aktionäre)* to vote [on, *Br.*] the stock; **sein** ~ **durch einen Bevollmächtigten dagegen (dafür) ausüben** to send in proxies against (in favo(u)r); ~ **beschränken** to restrict the right to vote; **sich des** ~**s enthalten** to abstain from voting; ~ **entziehen** to take away the right to vote; **seines** ~**s verlustig gehen** to be deprived of voting power; ~ **haben** to have a (be entitled to) vote; **volles** ~ **haben** to be entitled to speak and to vote; **jem. an der Ausübung seines** ~**s hindern** to bar s. o. from voting his stock; ~ **durch einen Vertreter (Bevollmächtigten) ausüben lassen** to vote by proxy; **sich das** ~ **übertragen lassen** to act as proxy; **von seinem** ~ **Gebrauch machen** to exercise one's voting rights; **ohne** ~ **sein** to be deprived of voting power; **sein** ~ **übertragen** to transfer one's voting shares; ~ **verleihen** to enfranchise; **sein** ~ **verlieren** to be disfranchised; **sein** ~ **verwirken** to forfeit one's voting rights.

Stimmrechts|abgabe voting; ~**abgabe durch Vertreter** proxy voting; ~**aktie** voting share (stock, *US*); ~**aussteller** proxy giver.

Stimmrechtsausübung, mehrfache multiple voting;
~ **durch Stellvertretung** proxy voting; ~ **durch einen Treuhänder** voting trust.

Stimmrechts|beschränkung limitation of voting power (right of vote); ~**bevollmächtigter** proxy.

Stimmrechtsermächtigung instrument appointing a proxy;
auf zwei Personen ausgestellte ~ two-way proxy; **auf eine Hauptversammlung begrenzte** ~ special proxy; **schriftliche** ~ form of proxy;
~ **ohne Bindung** two-way proxy form;
~ **zurückziehen** to revoke a proxy.

Stimmrechtsermächtigungswiderruf revocation of proxy.

Stimmrechts|formular form of proxy, proxy form; ~**formular hinterlegen** to deposit a proxy form; ~**gebrauch** use of one's voice; ~**kampf** proxy contest (fight, *US*); ~**karte** *(Hauptversammlung)* proxy card; ~**kontrolle** voting list.

stimmrechtslos nonvoting;
~**e Aktie** nonvoting share; ~**es Aktienkapital** nonvoting stock; ~**e Vorzugsaktien** nonvoting preference shares *(Br.)*.

Stimmrechts|mißbrauch abuse of voting rights; ~**nachweis** voting trust record *(US)*; ~**treuhänder** proxy, voting trustee *(US)*; ~**übertragung** voting pool; ~**urkunde** proxy paper; ~**vereinbarung** voting-trust agreement; ~**vertretung** proxy; ~**vollmacht** proxy paper (rights); **sich um** ~**vollmachten bemühen** to solicit proxies *(US)*.

Stimmschein ballot, ticket;
~**wähler** outvoter *(Br.)*.

stimmt das auch? no kidding?

Stimmung disposition, temper, feel, atmosphere, spirit, colo(u)r, fit, humo(u)r, cue, vein, whim, mood, *(Börse)* tone, tendency, sentiment, *(mil.)* morale;
in gehobener ~ in high spirits (feather), on a jolly pin; **in melancholischer** ~ in a melancholic vein; **in mieser** ~ in the doldrums; **in trauriger** ~ in a minor key;
allgemeine ~ general tone; **deprimierte** ~ black day *(coll.)*; **deutschfeindliche** ~ anti-German sentiment; **feste** ~ buoyancy, buoyant performance; **festliche** ~ festivity, festive mood; **flaue** ~ bearish tone; **gedrückte** ~ depressed spirits, gloom, *(Börse)* depressed state, gloomy tone; **geteilte** ~ mixed (divided) tendency; **nachdenkliche** ~ thinking cap; **vorherrschende** ~ prevailing tone; **wechselnde** ~**en** mercurial moods; **zurückhaltende** ~ dull (reserved) tendency, tone of restraint;
flaue ~ **auf dem Aktienmarkt** dull tone in the stock market; ~ **unter den Arbeitern** worker sentiment; ~ **der Börse** mood of the market, market sentiment; ~, **Geld auszugeben** spending mood; ~ **in der Öffentlichkeit** public mood; ~ **der Versammlung** feeling of the meeting;
~ **aufbessern** to buoy up spirits; **in** ~ **bringen** *(Publikum)* to panic *(US sl.)*; **gedrückte** ~ **in einem Dorf hervorrufen** to cast a gloom over a village; ~ **der Wählerschaft ausfindig machen** to feel the pulse of the electorate; **in fröhlicher (gehobener)** ~ **sein** to be in high spirits; **in gedrückter** ~ **sein** to have the blues *(US)*; **leicht gedrückter** ~ **sein** to be easily depressed; **in gereizter** ~ **sein** to be on the war path; **in der richtigen** ~ **sein** to be in the right vein; ~**en unterworfen sein** to have an uneven temper (moods); **für gute** ~ **sorgen** to keep things pleasant.

Stimmungs|barometer der öffentlichen Meinung barometer of public opinion; ~**bericht** *(Zeitung)* background story; **kriminalistischer** ~**effekt** *(Werbung)* Hitchcock appeal; ~**kanone sein** to be the life and soul of a party; ~**käufe** impulse buying; ~**lokal** place of amusement; ~**mache betreiben** to boom; ~**mensch sein** to be a man of moods; ~**musik** background music; ~**umschwung** turnover of sentiment, *(öffentliche Meinung)* swing of the pendulum, mood swing *(US)*; ~**wechsel** change of mood, *(Börse)* change of tendency.

Stimm|vieh easily fooled voter; ~**zählapparat** voting machine.

Stimmzettel voting paper, *(Wahl)* ballot, ticket;
unausgefüllter ~ blank voting paper; **ungültiger** ~ void voting paper, mutilated ballot;
~ **abgeben** to cast the ballot; **leeren** ~ **abgeben** to return a blank voting paper; **durch** ~ **abstimmen** to [go to the] ballot; ~ **einwerfen** to deposit a voting paper *(Br.)*; **mit gefälschten** ~**n füllen** *(Wahlurne)* to stuff *(US sl.)*.

Stimmzwang compulsory voting;
durch ~ gebunden sein to be under the party whip *(Br.)*.
stimulierend stimulant, reflationary.
stinkbesoffen beastly drunk.
Stinkbombe stink-bomb, stinker.
stinkegeizig sein to whip the cat *(Br.)*.
stinken, nach Geld to stink of money *(sl.)*; **wie die Pest ~** to stink like hell; **nach Verrat ~** to smack of treachery.
stinkend stinking, foul, sour, rank;
~es Gewässer foul water.
stink|faul bone-idle; **~langweilig** dull as ditch water; **~langweilig sein** to be an awful bore; **~reich** up in the bucks *(sl.)*, well heeled *(sl.)*.
Stinkreiche the moneyed pack.
stinkt, etw. ~ an der Sache there's s. th. fishy about it.
stinkvornehm swanky, posh, swish.
Stinkwut towering rage;
~ bekommen to get the hump *(fam.)*.
stinkwütend mortally angry.
Stint, sich wie ein ~ freuen to be as happy as a sandboy.
Stipendiat fellow, foundationer *(Br.)*, stipendiary, beneficiary [student], bursary holder *(Scot.)*, exhibitioner *(Br.)*, sizar *(Br.)*, *(Schule)* bursar, scholar of a foundation;
~en grant-aided students;
~ sein to be on a foundation.
Stipendiatssystem fellowship scheme, scholarship system.
Stipendien|und Preise scholarships and exhibitions *(Br.)*;
~fonds fellowship; **~staffel** scale of stipends; **~wesen** scholarship system.
Stipendium scholarship, fellowship, grant, sizarship *(Br.)*, foundation, stipend, studentship *(Br.)*, exhibition *(Br.)*, bursary *(Scot.)*, burse *(Scot.)*;
ausgeschriebenes ~ open scholarship *(Br.)*; **nur an bestimmte Kandidaten verteiltes ~** close scholarship *(Br.)*;
~ ausschreiben to exhibit a foundation; **sich um ein ~ bewerben** to compete (try) for a scholarship; **~ einrichten** to establish (found) a scholarship, to exhibit a foundation; **~ erhalten** to gain (win) a scholarship; **jem. ein ~ gewähren** to put s. o. on a foundation; **~ haben** to be on a foundation; **~ stiften** to found a scholarship; **~ zuerkennen** to award a scholarship.
Stipendiums|inhaber bursary holder *(Scot.)*; **~prüfung** scholarship examination.
Stipp|angriff hit-and-run raid; **~visite** flying visit; **bei jem. eine ~visite machen** to pay s. o. a flying visit, to drop in on s. o.
Stirn forehead, brow;
mit eiserner ~ brazen-faced;
~ bieten to confront; **jem. die ~ bieten** to affront s. o., to make head against (resist) s. o., to show s. o. a bold front; **dem Feind die ~ bieten** to face the enemy; **die ~ haben** to have the face (cheek, impudence), to have the effrontery; **mit eiserner ~ leugnen** to deny brazenly; **~ runzeln** to knit one's brow; **jem. auf der ~ geschrieben sein** to be written all over s. one's face;
~runzeln frown; **~wand** front wall.
stöbern to rummage, to root;
in den Akten ~ to search through the files.
stochern, in seinem Essen to pick at one's food; **in der Glut ~** to poke (stoke) the fire.
Stock bat, stick, wand, *(Etage)* storey *(Br.)*, story, floor;
im dritten ~ gelegen three-pair *(Br.)*;
über ~ und Stein up hill and down dale;
erster ~ first floor, second floor *(US)*;
am ~ gehen to use a stick, *(finanziell)* to be in financial straits;
jem. mit dem ~ verprügeln to give s. o. a good flogging.
stock|besoffen blinddrunk *(sl.)*, plastered *(coll.)*, blotto *(sl.)*;
~dumm blockheaded, dim-witted; **~dunkle Nacht** pitch-black night.
Stocken stagnancy, stagnation, *(Arbeit)* standstill, *(in der Rede)* hesitation, inactivity, tie-up *(US)*;
ins ~ geraten to stagnate, to slacken, *(Export)* to fall off, to decline, *(Redner)* to begin to falter, *(Verhandlungen)* to make no progress, to [come to a] deadlock, *(Verkehr)* to be blocked (held up), to become congested, *(vollständig)* to have come to a standstill (reached a deadlock); **fast gänzlich ins ~ geraten** *(Verkehr)* to be reduced to a crawl; **ohne ~ lesen** to read fluently.
stocken *(Handel)* to stagnate, to be stagnant (slack), to slacken, to grow flat, to languish, *(Motor)* to stall, to conk *(coll.)*, *(Papier)* to turn mouldy (moldy), *(Verhandlungen)* to be at a deadlock (standstill), *(Verkehr)* to be congested (jammed, blocked, held up), *(Zahlungen)* to be in arrears, *(zögern)* to hesitate, to falter;
in einer Erzählung plötzlich ~ to stop short in the middle of a story.
stockend *(Geschäft)* slack, stagnant, dull, sluggish;
mit ~er Stimme in a faltering voice.
Stock|engländer trueborn Englishman; **~fisch** *(fig.)* blockhead, stick; **~fleck** dampstain.
stock|fremde Leute utter (complete) strangers; **~konservativ** fogyish, diehard, blue *(Br.)*, hunkerous *(US sl.)*.
Stockkonservativer diehard, hunker *(US sl.)*.
stock|nüchtern sober as a judge; **~steif** stiff as a poker; **~taub** deaf as an adder (a doorpost).
Stockung *(Handel)* stagnation, stagnancy, dullness, slackness, blockade, *(Hemmung)* arrest, blockade, *(Pause)* break, pause, *(Stillstand)* standstill, tie-up *(US)*, lock, deadlock, stalemate, *(Unterbrechung)* interruption, *(Verkehr)* block, congestion [of traffic], traffic jam (delay), stoppage of traffic, holdup, *(Verzögerung)* delay, holdup;
~ im Güterverkehr congested state of the goods traffic, freight congestion; **ernsthafte ~ in den Verhandlungen** serious hitch in the negotiations;
~ erfahren *(Verkehr)* to be congested; **~ hervorrufen** to delay the traffic; **~ überwinden müssen** to be locked in the doldrums;
~ überwinden *(Verhandlungen)* to break a deadlock.
Stockwerk story, storey *(Br.)*, floor, *(Wohnung)* flat;
ein ~ tiefer downstairs; **im ~ darüber** overhead; **im oberen ~** upstairs; **in einem höheren ~** abovestairs, upstairs;
erstes ~ first (second, *US*) floor (storey); **oberstes ~** top floor, *(Bus)* upper (top) deck; **zweites ~** second floor *(Br.)*, third floor *(US)*;
neues ~ aufsetzen to add a storey to a house; **das ganze erste ~ bewohnen** to occupy the whole of the first (second, *US*) floor.
Stockwerks|anzeiger floor indicator; **~eigentum** freehold flat *(Br.)*, condominium *(US)*; **~eigentumsbürogebäude** condominium office building *(US)*; **~eigentumssystem** condominium principle of ownership *(US)*; **~garage** parking garage; **~verteilungsplan** floor plan; **~wohnung** flat, apartment.
Stoff material, matter, substance, *(Alkohol)* lush, *(Gegenstand)* subject, matter, *(Rauschgift)* stuff, *(Textilien)* fabric, material, cloth, textile;
~e goods *(US)*;
bedruckte ~e printed fabrics (goods, *US*); **gelesener ~** matter read; **pflegeleichter ~** treatable fabric; **spaltbarer ~** fissionable substance (material);
~ für Auseinandersetzungen food for controversy; **~ für einen Bericht** copy; **~ zum Nachdenken** food for thought, s. th. to think about, matter of reflection; **~ für eine Rede** topic of a speech; **~ für die Unterhaltung** food (subject matter) for [the] conversation;
seinen ~ beherrschen to master one's subject; **~ sammeln** to collect material; **aus härterem ~ gemacht sein** to be made of a sterner stuff; **~ zuschneiden** to cut out a pattern;
~abteilung *(Warenhaus)* textile department; **~bahn** width of material, *(Luftschiff)* panel; **~ballen** ball of cloth; **~bespannung** cloth skin; **~druck** fabric printing.
Stoffel bore.
Stoff|handel drapery *(Br.)*, dry goods business *(US)*; **~händler** dealer in cloths (dry goods, *US*), draper *(Br.)*; **~handschuhe** fabric gloves.
stoffliche Veränderungen material changes.
Stoff|muster pattern, design; **~puppe** lay figure; **~rest** remnant; **~sammlung** collection of material; **~verbindung** *(Patentrecht)* composition of a matter.
Stöhnen der Verwundeten groans of the injured men.
stöhnen to moan, to groan;
über die schwere Arbeit ~ to complain about the heavy work.
Stollen drift, gallery, heading, adit;
~ vortreiben to drive a mine passage, to tunnel;
~betrieb drift mining.
Stolperdraht *(mil.)* trip wire.
stolpern to stumble, to trip up, to miss one's footing;
über j. ~ to come across (run into) s. o.; **durchs Dunkle ~** to blunder through the dark; **über einen Strohhalm ~** to stumble over a straw; **über ein Wort ~** to be puzzled at a word.
Stolperstein stumbling block.
Stolz pride;
vor ~ geschwellt inflated with pride; **vor ~ platzend** puffed up with pride;
falscher ~ false pride; **gekränkter ~** wounded feelings;
~ seines Vaters apple of one's father's eye;
jds. ~ demütigen to bring down s. one's pride; **seinen ~ fahrenlassen** to cast pride to the winds; **vor ~ platzen** to be

eaten up with pride; **in seinem ~ getroffen sein** to be hit in one's pride *(fam.)*; **jds. ~ verletzen** to wound (injure) s. one's pride.
stolz | wie ein Pfau as proud as a peacock (as Punch);
~ auf seine Arbeit sein to take pride in one's work;
~er Anblick splendid sight.
stolzgebläht puffed up with pride.
stolzieren to strut, to stalk, to promenade;
aus dem Zimmer ~ to stalk out of the room.
stopfen to darn, to mend;
ins Auto ~ to cram (pack, stuff) into the car; **Loch ~** to plug a leak; **ein Loch ~ und das andere aufreißen** to rob Peter to pay Paul; **jem. den Mund ~** to shut s. o. up; **seine Habseligkeiten in eine kleine Tasche ~** to stuff one's belongings into a small bag.
Stopfstelle mend.
Stopp stop, halt, *(Einfuhren)* ban, *(Preise)* stop, freeze.
Stoppen der Löhne wage freeze, freezing (pegging) the wages.
stoppen to stop, to pull up, to halt;
Fahrzeug durch Gongsignale ~ to gong a vehicle *(Br.)*; **Löhne ~** to peg (freeze) wages.
Stopp | kurs ceiling quotation; **~licht** stoplight, *(Ampel)* red light; **~lohn** ceiling wage; **~preis** ceiling (stop, controlled, blocked, frozen) price; **~signal** stop signal; **~straße** stop street; **~strecke** measured distance; **~uhr** stopwatch.
Stöpsel plug, *(Knirps)* humpty-dumpty.
Störaktion planned disruption.
störanfällig *(Auto)* susceptible to breakdown.
Stör | anfälligkeit breakdown susceptibility; **~einsatz** *(mil.)* nuisance operation.
stören to disturb, to plague, to annoy, to interrupt, to interfere with, to be intruding, *(überlagern)* to blanket;
Arbeitsfrieden ~ to cause labo(u)r troubles; **Besitz ~** to trespass; **j. in seinem Besitz ~** to disturb s. one's lawful enjoyment, to interfere with s. one's possessions; **Feierlichkeit ~** to disturb a ceremony; **j. im Genuß seines Rechtes ~** to disturb s. o. in the lawful enjoyment of his right; **j. laufend ~** to bother s. o. all the time; **öffentliche Ordnung ~** to break (disturb) the peace; **Redner ~** to heckle (interrupt) a speaker; **feindlichen Rundfunksender ~** to jam the enemy's station; **Verkehr ~** to dislocate the traffic; **Vorlesung ~** to interrupt a lecture.
störend interfering, in the way, annoying, disturbing;
~er Eingriff interference, disturbance; **~e Eingriffe in die Handelsbeziehungen** disturbance of trade.
Störenfried mischief-maker, troublemaker, intruder, spoilsport, killjoy, gadfly.
Störer disturber, intruder, troublemaker, nuisancer.
Stör | feuer harassing fire; **~filter** *(Radio)* wave trap; **~flugzeug** nuisance raider; **~frequenz** interference frequency; **~funk** jamming transmission; **~gebiet** *(Radio)* mush area; **~geräusch** *(Radio)* background noise, mush, statics, *(tel.)* cross fire.
stornierbar to be cancelled;
nicht ~ noncancellable.
stornieren to cancel, to counterenter, to counterorder, to countermand, to counterpass, to write back, to kill;
Auftrag ~ to revoke (cancel, countermand) an order; **Buchung ~** to reverse (cancel) an entry.
storniert cancelled.
Stornierung cancellation, writing back, revocation, *(Auftrag)* cancellation, countermanding, counterorder;
~ einer Buchung reversing of an entry, reversal; **~ einer Eintragung** cancellation of an entry; **~ der Prämie** cancellation of a premium; **~ eines Zahlungsauftrages** stop payment, freezing of payments.
Stornierungs | buchung, ~eintrag reversing of an entry, counterentry, reversal; **~gebühr** cancellation fee, counterbalance commission; **~gesuch** request for cancellation; **~satz** cancellation rate; **im ~wege** as counterbalance.
Störniveau *(Radio)* noise level.
Storno cancellation, countermand of payments, *(Buchung)* cancellation of an entry, offsetting entry, *(Versicherung)* return;
~buchung writing back, counterentry, reversing (cross) entry; **~buchung vornehmen** to reverse an entry, to write back; **~gebühr** cancellation fee, counterbalance commission.
Störpegel noise level.
störrisch stubborn, obstinate, pigheaded;
sich ~ zeigen to take the bit between one's teeths.
Stör | schutz noise suppression; **~sender** jammer, jamming transmitter; **~sendung** radio jamming; **~signal** interfering signal; **~streifen** *(Fernsehen)* interference pattern.
Störung disturbance, *(Behinderung)* obstruction, *(Betriebsstörung)* failure, breakdown, defect, *(Eindringen)* intrusion, *(Einmischung)* interference, hitch, *(el.)* trouble, failure, fault, *(Funktionsstörung)* malfunction, *(mil.)* harassment, *(Rauschen)* noise, mush, *(Rundfunksender)* jam, interference, *(Unterbrechung)* interruption, *(Verkehr)* dislocation;
atmosphärische ~en atmospherics *(Br.)*, statics *(US)*; **geistige ~** mental alienation, disorder of the mind; **gewittrige ~en** thundery disturbances; **nervöse ~** nervous disorder; **rechtserhebliche ~** actionable nuisance; **rechtswidrige ~** nuisance at law (per se); **technische ~** technical fault, trouble; **tropische ~en** tropical disturbances; **vorübergehende ~en** temporary difficulties;
~ in der freien Ausübung des Wahlrechts disturbance of franchise; **~ im Besitz** disturbance of possession, trespass; **~ der Brotversorgung** dislocation of bread supplies; **komplette ~ des Eisenbahnverkehrs** breakdown of the railway; **krankhafte ~ der Geistestätigkeit** mental deficiency (aberration, derangement); **vorübergehende ~ der Geistestätigkeit** temporary mental derangement; **~ im Genuß eines Rechtes** disturbance of s. o. in lawful enjoyment of his right; **~ des Gleichgewichts** disequilibrium; **~ des Gottesdienstes** disturbance of public or religious worship; **~ eines Kanals** spot jamming; **~ der Mieter** disturbance of tenants; **~ der Nachtruhe** disturbance of repose; **~en im Postverkehr** irregularities in the mail service; **~ der Rechtspflege** criminal contempt; **~ der öffentlichen Ruhe und Ordnung** breach (disturbance) of the peace, public nuisance; **~ des Rundfunkempfangs** disturbance of broadcast reception; **~ durch ausländische Rundfunksender** interference from foreign broadcasting stations, jamming; **~ der Sonntagsruhe** sabbath breaking; **ernsthafte ~ der Verhandlungen** serious hitch in the negotiations; **~ des Verkehrs** traffic block, holdup, jam in the street, dislocation (interruption) of traffic; **~ von Wahlen** interference with elections; **~en der Zahlungsbilanz** maladjustments in the balance of payments;
~ abstellen (beseitigen) to remedy a fault, to abate a nuisance; **~ auffinden und beseitigen** *(tel.)* to trouble-shoot *(US)*; **~ hervorrufen** to disorder; **geistige ~ bei jem. hervorrufen** to derange s. o.; **ohne ~en verlaufen** to go off without a hitch (swimmingly); **~ verursachen** to cause a disturbance.
Störungsdienst *(Telefon)* breakdown service, trouble shooting, faultfinder.
störungsfrei *(Rundfunkempfang)* static-free, *(tel.)* trouble-free.
Störungs | suche *(tel.)* troubleshooting; **~sucher** *(tel.)* fault localizer, troubleshooter, lineman *(US)*, faultsman, troubleman; **~trupp** *(Telefon)* repair gang.
Stör | welle jamming wave; **~widerstand** jam resistance.
Stoß push, knock, blow, concussion, dig, jog, jolt, poke, pound, thrust, *(Auto)* bump, *(Papier)* package, knock, bundle, pile, stack;
plötzlicher ~ jerk;
~ Akten bundle of files; **~ Arbeit** stacks of work; **~ Briefe** packet (batch, bundle) of letters; **~ von Büchern** pile of books; **~ abwehren** to ward (fend) off a blow; **auf einen ~ kommen** to come in a batch; **~ vertragen können** to have broad shoulders; **jem. einen erheblichen ~ versetzen** to come as quite a shock to s. o.; **seinem Herzen einen ~ versetzen** to find it in one's heart; **jem. Selbstbewußtsein einen ~ versetzen** to shake s. one's self-confidence;
~aktion one-shot promotion; **~angebot** *(Börse)* concentrated offer; **~arbeiter** shock worker.
stoßartiger Verkauf *(Börse)* unloading.
Stoß | auftrag rush order; **~bedarf** deferred (pent-up) demand; **~betrieb** intermittent working; **~brigade** shock brigade *(US)*; **~dämpfer** shock absorber (eliminator), crash pad, cushion; **~dämpfung** shock absorption.
stoßen to knock, to thrust;
sich ~ to bump o. s.; **sich an jds. Äußerem ~** to take exception to s. one's appearance; **direkt auf den Bahnhof ~** to come straight to the station; **jem. Bescheid ~** to tell s. o. what is what; **Boot ins Wasser ~** to shove a boat into the water; **auf Erdöl ~** to strike oil; **ganz unerwartet auf einen alten Freund ~** to run into an old friend; **j. mit der Nase darauf ~** to give s. o. a broad hint; **an einen Park ~** to border on a park; **j. in die Rippen ~** to dig s. o. in the ribs; **auf unerwartete Schwierigkeiten ~** to meet with unexpected difficulties; **zur Truppe ~** *(Nachhut)* to join the main body; **zufällig auf j. ~** to drop across s. o.
Stoßfänger *(Lokomotive)* fender.
stoßfest shockproof.
Stoß | festigkeit shock resistance; **~kraft** *(Anzeige)* impact; **~lücke** *(Schienen)* expansion gap; **~stange** bumper; **~stangenaufkleber** bumper sticker; **~verkehr** rush hour, peak traffic; **~verkehr umgehen** to beat the rush hours.

stoßweise *(unregelmäßig)* by jerks, by fits and starts, intermittently;
~ **arbeiten** to work by fits and starts; ~ **fließen** *(Ölquelle)* to flow by heads.
Stoß|werbung impact advertising; ~**wirkung** *(Nachfrage)* impact effect; ~**zeit** rush hour, peak [time]; ~**zeit in der Saison** seasonal peak.
Stottern *(Abzahlungssystem)* never-never *(Br., sl.)*;
auf ~ on the never-never;
auf ~ **kaufen** to buy on the hire purchase *(Br.)* (deferred-payment, *US*) system.
stottern to stammer, to stutter, *(Automotor)* to splutter, to falter, *(Flugzeugmotor)* to pack up *(sl.)*.
Straf|akten case records, adjournal *(Scot.)*; ~**aktion unternehmen** to take punitive action; **sich für nicht die Freiheit beschrän-kende** ~**alternativen aussprechen** to endorse non-custodial alternatives to prison; ~**änderung** commutation; ~**änderungsgesetz** Criminal Law Amendment Act.
strafandrohend comminatory.
Strafandrohung commination;
unter ~ under penalty;
j. unter ~ **vorladen** to subpoena s. o.
Straf|anspruch, verwirkter former jeopardy; ~**anstalt** prison, convict (penal) establishment, penitentiary *(US)*; ~**antrag stellen** to institute criminal proceedings; ~**antritt** commencement of a sentence; ~**anzeige** criminal complaint (information), charge; ~**anzeige erstatten** to prefer an information, to inform, to denounce; ~**anzeige gegen j. erstatten** to bring a charge against s. o., to report s. o. to the police, to denounce s. o.; ~**arbeit** *(Schule)* extra work (task), pensum, imposition *(Br.)*; ~**arrest** *(mil.)* personal arrest.
Strafaufschub suspension of execution, reprieve;
~ **zur Bewährung** suspension of sentence on probation;
~ **gewähren** to reprieve; ~ **zur Bewährung zubilligen** to grant suspension on probation.
Strafaussetzung interruption of sentence;
bedingte ~ **zur Bewährung** parole, probation; **unbefristete** ~ permanent suspension; **vorübergehende** ~ temporary suspension;
auf ~ **zur Bewährung erkennen** to make a probation order, to put s. o. on parole.
Strafaussetzungsbeschluß zur Bewährung probation order.
strafbar punishable, criminal, penal, guilty, liable to prosecution, *(disziplinarisch)* disciplinable;
gesetzlich ~ punishable by law; **nicht** ~ unpunishable;
sich ~ **machen** to be liable to prosecution, to incur punishment, to render o. s. liable to proceedings; ~ **sein** to be subject to penalty;
~**e Beleidigung** criminal libel; ~**e Fahrlässigkeit** criminal negligence; ~**e Handlung** public wrong, criminal (punishable, penal) act, criminal offence (offense, *US*); **jem. eine** ~**e Handlung anhängen** to pin an accusation on s. o.; ~**e Handlung begehen** to commit an offence; ~**e Handlung darstellen** to constitute an offence; **sich zu** ~**em Tun verabreden** to conspire; ~**es Verhalten** criminal conduct.
Straf|befehl fine; ~**befugnis** punitive power; ~**beginn** commencement of a sentence; ~**bemessung** assessment of a penalty; ~**bestimmung** penal clause (statute), penalty provision, *(Testament)* comminatory clause; ~**buch** default book; ~**buchauszug** *(Soldat)* defaulter sheet, conduct sheet; ~**dauer** length of a prison term.
Strafe punishment, penalty, disciplinary sentence, *(Geldstrafe)* fine;
bei ~ **von** under penalty (upon pain) of;
angemessene ~ adequate punishment; **auferlegte** ~ sentence imposed; **auf Bewährung ausgesetzte** ~ suspended sentence, probation; **empfindliche** ~ severe punishment; **exemplarische** ~ exemplary punishment; **geringfügige** ~ slight penalty; **grausame** ~ cruel and unusual punishment; **harte** ~ severe (smart) punishment; **hohe** ~ heavy penalty; **übermäßig hohe** ~ excessive sentence; **körperliche** ~ corporeal punishment; **lebenslängliche** ~ life sentence, lifer; **leichte (milde)** ~ light punishment (penalty), lenient sentence; **schwere** ~ heavy penalty (sentence); **strenge** ~ stern penalty; **verschärfte** ~ increased penalty; **wirksame** ~ effectual punishment, operative penalty; **gesetzlich zulässige** ~ lawful punishment;
~ **für übermäßige Arbeit** forfeit paid for overworking; ~ **von unbestimmter Dauer** independent sentence *(US)*; ~ **nach freiem Ermessen** arbitrary punishment;
von ~ **absehen** to refrain from punishment; **seine** ~ **absitzen** to serve a sentence of imprisonment, to do one's time, to take the rap *(sl.)*; ~ **androhen** to threaten with punishment; **jem. eine** ~ **auferlegen** to inflict punishment on s. o.; ~ **aussetzen** to respite, to reprieve; **jds.** ~ **zur Bewährung aussetzen** to put s. o. on parole, to bind a sentence over on probation; **mit einer** ~ **belegen** to penalize; **sich einer** ~ **beugen** to kiss the rod; **der gerechten** ~ **für seine Verbrechen entgegensehen** to be brought to punishment for one's crimes; **der** ~ **entgehen, sich der gerechten** ~ **entziehen** to escape punishment, to cheat justice (the gallows); **seine gerechte** ~ **erhalten** to receive one's just deserts; **auf** ~ **erkennen** to award a sentence; ~ **erlassen** to remit a penalty; **jem. eine** ~ **erlassen** to let s. o. off a penalty, to let s. o. off; ~ **herabsetzen** to reduce a sentence; **seine** ~ **hinnehmen** to take one's medicine; ~ **mildern** to lighten a sentence, to relax (mitigate) a penalty; **in** ~ **nehmen** to penalize; **mit** ~ **bedroht sein** to carry a penalty; **Entscheidungen über Aussetzung der** ~ **örtlichen Bewährungsausschüssen überlassen** to delegate more parole decisions to local review committees; ~ **umwandeln** to commute a sentence; **seine** ~ **voll verbüßen** to complete one's sentence, to do one's time; ~ **verdienen** to deserve punishment; ~ **verhängen** to inflict (impose) a penalty (punishment); **adäquate** ~ **verhängen** to make the punishment fit the crime; **zusätzliche** ~ **verhängen** to superimpose a punishment; ~ **verwirken** to incur a penalty; ~ **vollstrecken** to execute a punishment; ~ **zumessen** to mete out punishment; ~ **zahlen** to pay a fine.
strafen to punish, to sentence, to avenge, to correct, *(züchtigen)* to chasten.
strafend punitive, vindicatory.
Strafenhäufung cumulative sentence.
Straf|entlassene wieder eingliedern to rehabilitate offenders; ~**entlassener** discharged prisoner; ~**entlassung** discharge from prison; **bedingte** ~**entlassung** ticket-of-leave, release on parole; ~**erhöhung beim Rückfalltäter** cumulative punishment.
Straferlaß pardon, remission of penalty, *(pol.)* oblivion;
allgemeiner ~ amnesty; **bedingter** ~ conditional pardon; **teilweiser** ~ partial pardon.
Straf|ermäßigung remission (commutation) of sentence;
~**erschwerungsgrund** aggravating circumstance; ~**exerzieren in Gefechtsausrüstung** pack drill *(mil.)*.
strafexerzieren lassen, j. to put a man on extra fatigue.
Strafexpedition punitive expedition.
Straffall criminal case.
straffällig punishable, delinquent, liable to a penalty, amercable, culpable;
~ **werden** to incur a penalty.
Straf|fällige wieder eingliedern to resettle offenders; ~**fälliger** delinquent, misdemeanant, offender; **jugendlicher** ~**fälliger** juvenile delinquent, delinquent minor; ~**fälligkeit** guilt; ~**festsetzung** infliction of a penalty.
straffrei ausgehen to go unpunished (scot-free), to be free of prosecution.
Straf|freiheit immunity from punishment (prosecution), impunity; ~**gefangener** person imprisoned, prisoner, convict; **entlassener** ~**gefangener** ex-convict; ~**gefangenen abschieben** to transport a criminal; ~**gefängnis** convict prison; ~**gericht** criminal court, general session *(Br.)*; ~**gerichtsbarkeit** criminal jurisdiction (justice); ~**gerichtsprotokolle** book of adjournal *(Scot.)*; ~**gesetz** criminal (penal) statute, punitive statute; ~**gesetzbuch** criminal (penal) code; ~**gesetzgebung** crime (penal) legislation; ~**gewalt** punitive power; ~**haft** confinement, imprisonment in the second degree; **aus der** ~**haft entlassen** discharged from prison; ~**haftentschädigung** compensation for false imprisonment; ~**häufung** cumulative sentence; ~**höhe festsetzen** to determine the sentence; ~**kammer** criminal court *(Br.)*; ~**klage** penal action (suit, *US*); ~**klausel** penal clause (provision, statute), *(Testament)* comminatory clause; ~**kolonie** convict settlement, penal colony, labo(u)r camp; ~**lager** prison (detention) camp.
Sträfling prison inmate, prisoner, convict, criminal, lag;
alter ~ gaol bird;
~ **mit Vergünstigungen** trusty *(Br.)*;
einem entsprungenen ~ **Unterschlupf gewähren** to harbo(u)r an escaped prisoner.
Sträflings|arbeit convict labo(u)r; ~**kolonie** convict settlement, penal colony.
straflos with impunity, unpunished;
~ **ausgehen** to go unpunished (scot-free).
Strafmandat [traffic] ticket *(US)*, warning and fee *(Br.)*.
Strafmaß sentence;
zu niedriges ~ inadequate sentence;
~ **aussprechen** to sentence; ~ **herabsetzen** to lighten a sentence.

Strafmaßnahmen punitive measures;
einträgliche ~ remunerative sanctions; **wirtschaftliche ~** economic (punitive) sanctions.
Strafmaßpolitik sentencing policy.
strafmildernd berücksichtigen to consider in mitigation.
Strafmilderung mitigation of punishment, extenuation, commutation;
für ~ plädieren to plead in mitigation; **Armut als ~ für einen Diebstahl vorbringen** to plead poverty in extenuation of a theft.
strafmündig werden to become amenable to criminal law, to come to the years of discretion.
Straf|mündigkeit discretion, criminal responsibility, criminal liability; **~mündigkeitsalter** age of discretion (criminal responsibility); **~nachlaß** reduction (remission) of a sentence; **~norm** penal provision; **~porto** penalty (extra, excess) postage, postage due, surcharge; **~predigt** sermon, jaw *(sl.)*; **jem. eine ~predigt halten** to read s. o. a lecture; **~prozeß** criminal proceedings, criminal process, penal suit; **~prozeßordnung** Federal Rules of Criminal Procedure *(US)*; **gewöhnlicher ~rahmen** ordinary term *(US)*; **~recht** criminal (penal, criminal justice, crown, *Br.*) law.
strafrechtlich|verfolgen, j. to prosecute (start a prosecution against) s. o.;
~e Verantwortlichkeit criminal liability (responsibility).
Strafrechts|gesetz Criminal Law Act *(Br.)*; **~lehre** penology; **~notstand** plea of necessity.
Straf|reform penal reform; **~register** register of convictions, criminal (police) record, *(mil.)* crime sheet; **~registerauszug** extract of the police record; **~richter** magistrate, recorder *(US)*; **nicht vor ein Geschworenengericht gehörende ~sache** nonjury case; **~sachen** criminal cases, crown cases *(Br.)*; **~sanktionen** punitive sanctions.
strafschärfend aggravating.
Straf|schärfungsgründe aggravating circumstances; **~summe** fine; **~tabelle für Verkehrsüberschreitungen** motorist's penalty chart; **~tarif** *(Steuer)* penalty rate.
Straftat indictable offence, crime, criminal action (act), tort, tortious act;
bereits abgeurteilte ~ same offence; **auslieferungsfähige ~** extraditable crime; **gemeinsam begangene ~** joint offence; **aus politischen Gründen begangene ~** political offence; **im Rausch begangene ~** crime committed while under the influence of intoxicating liquor; **in Realkonkurrenz begangene ~** cumulative offence; **mit Geldstrafe belegte ~** pecuniary offence; **ehrenrührige ~** infamous crime; **fahrlässige ~** negligent offence; **fortgesetzte ~** continuing offence; **zur Last gelegte ~** offence charged with; **nicht kautionsfähige ~** nonbailable offence; **gesetzlich normierte ~** statutory crime; **unvollendete ~** inchoate crime; **vollendete ~** accomplished crime;
~ eines Ersttäters first offence; **~ mit Haftverschonung gegen Kaution** bailable offence; **~en gegen die öffentliche Ordnung** offenses against public order *(US)*; **~en und Ordnungswidrigkeiten auf öffentlichen Straßen** offences under the Road Traffic Acts *(Br.)*; **~ im Rückfall** second offence; **~ mit geringer Strafandrohung** petty offense *(US)*;
~ anzeigen to report an offence; **~ begehen** to offend against the law, to commit an offence; **~ eingestehen** to admit an offence; **~ verschärfen** to aggravate an offence;
auf Analogie fußender ~bestand constructive crime; **gesetzlich normierter ~bestand** statutory offence (crime).
Straftäter criminal (indictable) offender, convict;
flüchtiger ~ fugitive offender; **geisteskranker ~** criminal lunatic; **jugendlicher ~** juvenile offender (delinquent), youthful offender.
Straf|tenor accusatory part; **~terminliste** crown paper *(Br.)*; **~tilgung** extinction of previous convictions; **~umwandlung** commutation (remission) of a sentence.
strafunmündig incapable of crime.
Straf|unmündigkeit criminal insanity, incapability to commit a crime; **~urlaub erhalten** to be allowed out on parole.
Strafurteil sentence, *(Geschworene)* verdict;
abschließendes ~ final sentence; **zur Bewährung ausgesetztes ~** suspended sentence; **zusätzliches, zunächst ausgesetztes ~** accumulative judgment;
~ bestätigen to uphold a conviction; **~ fällen** to pass a sentence, *(Geschworene)* to render (return) a verdict; **~ kassieren** to quash a verdict.
Straf|verbüßung serving of a sentence; **sich der ~verbüßung entziehen** to evade punishment; **~vereitelung** obstructing criminal justice.
Strafverfahren criminal suit, penal suit (action), criminal trial (action), criminal (penal) proceeding;
abgekürztes ~ speedy trial; **anhängiges ~** pending criminal procedure, pending prosecution; **gemeinsames ~** joint trial;
~ einleiten to institute criminal proceedings; **~ einstellen** to withdraw a prosecution, to lapse criminal proceedings *(Br.)*; **~ über sich ergehen lassen** to stand trial; **~ nach sich ziehen** to result in prosecution.
Strafverfahrens|ablauf beschleunigen to speed up trial proceedings; **~recht** law of criminal procedure.
Strafverfolgung criminal proceedings, penal prosecution;
abermalige ~ double jeopardy;
~ einleiten to put a prosecution under way; **~ einstellen** to drop a charge, to withdraw a prosecution; **sich der ~ entziehen** to avoid prosecution, to cheat justice (the gallows), to flee from justice; **~ niederschlagen** to stifle prosecution; **~ unterbrechen** to bar the initiation of prosecution; **~ unterdrücken** to quash an indictment; **~ veranlassen** to authorize prosecution.
Strafverfolgungs|ankündigung notice of intended prosecution; **~beamter** prosecutor, prosecuting officer *(US)*; **~behörde** prosecution, Director of Public Prosecutions *(Br.)*; **~verjährung** limitation of criminal proceedings.
Straf|verhandlung trial of an action; **~verjährung** limitation of time; **~vermerk auf dem Führerschein** endorsement of a driving *(Br.)* (driver's, *US*) licence.
Strafverschärfung increase of penalty.
strafversetzen to transfer for disciplinary reasons.
Straf|versetzung disciplinary transfer, transfer for disciplinary reasons; **~verteidiger** trial *(US)* (defence, criminal) lawyer, counsel for the defence *(Br.)*, defending counsel *(US)*, mouthpiece *(sl.)*; **~verteidigung übernehmen** to assume the defence; **~vollstreckung** execution of sentence; **~vollstreckung aussetzen** to suspend a sentence; **~vollstreckungsaufschub** reprieve *(Br.)*; **~vollzug** execution of punishment (sentence); **~vollzug im Zuchthaus** close jail execution.
Strafvollzugs|anstalt penal institution (establishment); **~beamter** prison guard (officer); **~behörde** prison commissioners; **~ordnung** prison regulations; **~system** prison system.
Strafvorschriften penal provisions.
strafwürdig punishable, indictable;
~es Fehlverhalten criminal misconduct.
Straf|zeit prison term, penal time, stretch; **verlängerte ~zeit** extended term *(US)*; **~zelle** prison cell.
Strafzettel [traffic] ticket *(US)*, warning and fee *(Br.)*;
~ für Geschwindigkeitsüberschreitung speeding ticket *(US)*, ticket for speeding *(US)*; **~ für ordnungswidriges Parken** parking fine, parking ticket *(US)*;
~ für j. ausstellen to give s. o. a ticket *(US)*; **~ bekommen** to get a ticket; **~ wegen Überschreitung der Höchstgeschwindigkeit erhalten** to be booked for speeding, to get a green stamp *(US sl.)*; **jem. wegen rücksichtslosen Fahrens einen ~ verpassen** to book s. o. for reckless driving; **~ wegen unerlaubten Parkens verpassen** to pass a fine for illegal parking.
Straf|zoll penal duty; **~zumessung** determination of penalty; **zusätzliche ~zumessung** accumulative sentence *(US)*; **~zuschlag** surcharge; **~zuständigkeit** criminal jurisdiction.
Strahl ray, beam, *(Luft, Wasser)* jet, stream;
schädliche ~en noxious rays;
~antrieb jet propulsion.
strahlen to beam, to radiate, to ray, *(funkeln)* to flash, to sparkle;
über beide Backen ~ to beam all over one's face.
Strahlenbehandlung ray treatment.
strahlend|e Augen sparkling eyes; **~es Lächeln** beaming smile; **in ~er Laune sein** to be in high spirits.
Strahlen|dosis radiation dose; **zulässige ~dosis** permissible dose; **~gefährdung** radiation hazard; **~geschädigter** radiation victim; **~messung** radiometry; **~schaden** radiation injury; **~schädigung** irradiation injury; **~schutz** radiation protection; **~schutzanzug** frog suit *(coll.)*.
strahlensicher radiation-proof.
Strahl|flugzeug jet aircraft (plane); **~triebwerk** fan jet engine.
Strahlung radiation.
Strahlungs|abschirmung radiation barrier; **~dosis** radiation level; **~gürtel** Van Allen radiation belt; **~intensität** irradiation; **~krankheit** radiation sickness.
strahlungssicherer Behälter heavily shielded container.
Strahlungswaffe, verstärkte enhanced radiation weapon.
stramm tight, close, *(mil.)* straight;
~ arbeiten to work hard; **~ stehen** to stand to attention;
~e Arbeit strenuous work; **~er Bursche** sturdy fellow; **~e Disziplin** strict discipline; **~er Soldat** smart soldier.

Strand beach, shore, foreshore, strand, foreside *(US)*;
steiniger ~ stony beach;
Schiff auf den ~ auflaufen lassen to run a ship on the beach, to beach a ship; **auf den ~ laufen** to run ashore, to strand;
~anzug beach suit; **~arbeiter** beachman; **~auto** dune buggy.
Stranden eines Schiffes beaching a ship.
stranden to run (be driven) ashore, to strike the sand, to founder, to pile up, *(fig.)* to founder, to go to wreck.
Strand|gebiet beach area; **~gut** salvage goods, floatages *(Br.)*, flotsam and jetsam, waif, stranded property, wrecked goods, wreck, wreckage; **~gutjäger** beach-comber; **blau wie eine ~haubitze** drunk as a lord; **~hotel** seaside hotel; **~promenade** seaside promenade, front *(Br.)*, boardwalk *(US)*; **~vogt** wreck commissioner *(Br.)*, receivers of wrecks *(Br.)*, wreck master *(US)*; **~wächter** lifeguard, lifesaver *(Br.)*.
Strang rope, cord;
toter ~ *(Bahn)* dead track;
j. zum Tod durch den ~ verurteilen to sentence s. o. to death by hanging; **am gleichen ~ ziehen** to be in the same boat, to join forces, to play with s. o.
Stränge, über die ~ schlagen to overshoot the mark, to kick over the traces (up one's heels, *US sl.*).
Strangguß|anlage continuous caster; **~verfahren** continuous casting process.
strangulieren to strangle.
Strangulierung strangulation.
Strapaze strain, drag, exertion, fatigue;
richtige ~ sein to be an awful strain.
strapazieren to strain, to overtax;
jds. Geduld zu sehr ~ to overtax (exercise) s. one's patience; **sein Gewissen ~** to overstrain one's conscience; **j. ungemein ~** to take an awful lot out of s. o.
strapazierfähig *(Anzug)* knockabout, hard-wearing, durable.
strapaziert weary, overtaxed;
bis aufs Äußerste ~ sein to reach breaking point.
Straß imitation diamond.
Sträßchen streetlet, alley.
Straße street, *(breite Allee)* lane, avenue, broadway *(US)*, boulevard *(US)*, *(Fernstraße)* highway, highroad, route *(US)*, *(Landstraße)* road, *(Weg)* way;
an der ~ wayside; **auf der ~** on the road, in the street; **auf offener ~** in a public thoroughfare, in broad daylight; **auf die ~ gehend** fronting the street; **die ~ hinauf** up the street; **von ~n durchzogen** streeted;
~ gesperrt road closed (up);
abgelegene ~ back road (street); **ansteigende ~** uphill road; **armselige ~n** mean streets; **aufgerissene ~** corrugated road; **ausgefahrene ~** heavy road; **nur auf einer Seite bebaute ~** one-sided road; **befahrbare ~** vehicular road, road fit for traffic (practicable for vehicles); **nicht befahrbare ~** impassable road; **nur für Omnibusse befahrbare ~** exclusive bus lane; **befahrene ~** frequented road; **schwer zu befahrene ~** heavy road; **belebte ~** busy street; **kümmerlich beleuchtete ~** poorly lighted street; **ungenügend beschilderte ~** inadequately sign-posted road; **ebene ~** level road; **eingesunkene ~** depressed roadway; **enge ~** bottleneck; **erstklassige ~** first-class road; **feste ~** covered road; **freie ~** clear road; **für den öffentlichen Verkehr freigegebene ~** road open to traffic; **mit öffentlichen Mitteln gebaute ~** land-grant road *(US)*; **gebührenfreie ~** free road; **gebührenpflichtige (mautpflichtige) ~** toll (turnpike, *US*) road; **gepflasterte ~** paved road, pavement *(US)*, surface street; **gesperrte ~** pent-road; **für den Autoverkehr gesperrte ~** road closed to motor traffic; **wegen Instandsetzungsarbeiten gesperrte ~** road under repair; **gewundene (kurvenreiche) ~** twisty (winding, *Br.*) road; **aus der Stadt herausführende ~** outward road; **holprige ~** bumpy road, rough street; **LKW-~** truckway; **lärmende ~n** loud (noisy) streets; **nichtöffentliche ~** private road; **öffentliche ~** public road (thoroughfare); **parkfähige ~** unrestricted street; **ruhige ~** quiet street; **schmutzige ~** muddy road; **staubfreie ~** hard-surface road; **steile ~** hilly road; **überfüllte ~n** crowded streets; **unbefestigte (ungepflasterte) ~** rough road, dirt road *(US coll.)*; **unebene ~** rough street; **vom Kommunalverband unterhaltene ~** adopted road *(Br.)*; **von der Stadt unterhaltene ~** township road *(US)*; **unterirdische ~** underground road; **für Parker verbotene ~** no-waiting street; **vereiste ~** icy (frozen) road; **verkehrsreiche ~** congested street, road carrying a great deal of traffic; **parallel zur Autobahn verlaufende ~** frontage road *(US)*; **verstopfte ~** congested (jammed) street; **vorfahrtberechtigte ~** major highway; **eine ~ weiter** a block further on; **zollpflichtige ~** toll road; **allgemein zugängliche ~** open road; **~ mit zwei Fahrbahnen** two-lane road; **~ mit zwei getrennten Fahrbahnen** double *(Br.)* (dual, *US*) carriageway; **~ mit Gegenverkehr** two-way street; **~ ohne Geschwindigkeitsbeschränkung** decontrolled (derestricted) road; **~n voll von Menschen** densely crowded streets; **~ erster Ordnung** main highway, classified road *(Br.)*; **von Polizisten umsäumte ~** road lined with police; **~ mit Schnellverkehr** road carrying fast-moving traffic *(Br.)*, expressway *(US)*; **~ mit Vorfahrtsrecht** major road;
~ absperren to bar a street; **an eine öffentliche ~ angrenzen** to touch a public road; **~ bauen** to build (make, construct) a road; **~ befestigen** to settle a road; **~ blockieren** to obstruct a highway, to beset a street; **in die nächste ~ einbiegen** to take the next turning; **~ einziehen** to abandon a road; **~ erweitern** to widen a road; **bergige ~ im Schnellgang fahren** to take the hill in top gear; **~ mit Kommunalobligationen finanzieren** to bond a road; **~ für den öffentlichen Verkehr freigeben** to open a road for traffic, to dedicate a highway; **auf die ~ gehen** to make a demonstration, to take to the streets; **direkt auf die ~ herausführen** *(Tür)* to open directly onto the street; **auf die richtige ~ kommen** to hit the right road; **~n austrocknen lassen** to harden the roads; **abseits der ~ liegen** to lie remotely (be away) from the road; **~ dem öffentlichen Verkehr öffnen** to dedicate a highway; **~ neu pflastern** to relay the pavement of a road; **~n säubern** to clear the streets; **durch die ~n schlendern** to stroll the streets; **j. auf der ~ schneiden** to give s. o. the go-by in the street; **auf die ~ setzen** to chuck out, to turn out onto the street; **Arbeiter auf die ~ setzen** to put the workers onto the street; **~ instand setzen** to fit a road for traffic; **~ sperren** to block a road; **~ überqueren** to cross a street; **~ verkehrswidrig überqueren** to jaywalk; **~ unterhalten** to keep a road in repair; **~ unterspülen** to wash out a road; **über die ~ verkaufen** to sell for consumption off the premises; **~ versperren** to obstruct a highway; **~ verstopfen** to obstruct the street; **sein Geld auf die ~ werfen** to throw one's money out of the window; **durch die ~n ziehen** to parade.
Straßen|abgaben highway rates, road taxes; **~abschnitt** road section; **~absperrung** closing of a road; **~anlieger** frontager; **~anliegerbeitrag** frontage assessment; **~anzug** lounge suit *(Br.)*, business suit *(US)*, undress; **~arbeiten** road labo(u)r *(Schild)* road under repair.
Straßenarbeiter road worker, roadman, road mender, roader, road repairer (labo(u)rer), highwayman *(Br.)*, shockworker; **~kolonne** itinerant gang of roadsmen.
Straßen|atlas road map, roadbook; **~auflauf** roadside crowd, street brawl; **~aufschließung** street improvement; **~aufseher** road inspector (surveyor); **~aufsicht** traffic control; **~ausbesserung, ~ausbesserungsarbeiten** road repairs (mending).
Straßenbahn tram[way], street railway *(Br.)*, electric *(coll.)* streetcar *(US)*, trolley car (coach, *US*);
städtische ~ corporation tramway;
mit der ~ fahren to go by tram, to travel by trolley car *(US)*, to trolley *(US)*; **mit der ~ zur Arbeit fahren** to ride to work on a streetcar *(US)*; **~ in Betrieb setzen** to tram *(Br.)*;
~angestellter tramwayman *(Br.)*, employee of a streetcar *(US)*; **~betrieb** tramway service *(Br.)*; **~depot** tramyard *(Br.)*, tramway depot *(Br.)*; **~führer** conductor, tramwayman *(Br.)*, motorman, carman *(US)*; **~gesellschaft** tramway company *(Br.)*; **~haltestelle** tram (streetcar, *US*) stop; **~linie** tramway *(Br.)*, tramline *(Br.)*, streetcar line *(US)*, tramroad *(US)*; **~netz** tramway system *(Br.)*; **~plakat** car card; **~reklame** streetcar advertising *(US)*; **~schaffner** tram guard *(Br.)*, clippie *(sl.)*, trolley attendant *(US)*; **~schuppen** tram shed *(Br.)*; **~unfall** streetcar accident *(US)*, tramway accident *(Br.)*; **~verkehr** streetcar *(US)* (tramway, *Br.*) traffic; **~wagen** tram *(Br.)*, tramcar *(Br.)*, tramway car *(Br.)*, electric car, trolley car (coach) *(US)*, streetcar *(US)*; **~werbung** streetcar *(US)* (tramway) advertising; **~wesen** trolley line *(US)*.
Straßenbankett embankment.
Straßenbau road building, roadmaking, road construction, highway construction (engineering);
~amt overseers of highways, highways department, Road Board *(Br.)*; **~behörde** highway authority, responsible authorities for roads; **~bezirk** highway parish.
Straßenbauer roadbuilder, highway builder.
Straßenbau|etat road budget; **~fonds** road fund *(Br.)*, road-building fund; **~ingenieur** highway engineer; **~kosten** cost of roadbuilding; **~maschine** road-building machinery; **~meister** road builder; **~programm** road program(me); **~trupp** road [construction] gang; **~unternehmen** road builder (contractor); **~verband** road district; **~wesen** highway engineering.

Straßen|begrenzungsstreifen singing shoulder *(US)*; **~behinderung** forestalling, obstructing the highway; **~behörde** highway authority; **~bekanntschaft** pickup; **~belag** road surface; **~beleuchtung** street illumination (lighting); **~benutzer** road user; **~benutzung** use of a road; **verkehrsübliche ~benutzung** ordinary traffic; **~benutzungsgebühr** road-using (road, *Br.*) tax, road-use fee, highway-user fee *(US)*, highway tax, road toll; **~beschaffenheit** condition of a road, going; **~beschotterung** road metal; **~bezirk** highway district; **~biegung** turn, turning, bend; **~block** square block; **~blockierung** obstruction of the highway; **~böschung** slope; **~breite** width of a road; **~café** sidewalk café; **~damm** roadway, causeway, embankment; **~darbietung** street performance; **~decke** paving of streets, road metal (surface); **schwarze ~decke** blacktop; **~demonstrationen** street demonstration; **~dichte** density of the road system; **~dienstkarte des ADAC** a year's free roadside assistance from the AA *(Br.)*; **~ecke** street corner; **gefährliche ~ecke** awkward corner; **unübersichtliche ~ecke** obscure (blind) corner; **~einmündung** road junction; **~erneuerung, ~erschließung** improvement in roads, street improvement; **~erweiterung** road widening; **~erweiterungsvorhaben** road-widening scheme; **~fahrzeug** road vehicle; **~falle** *(Polizei)* speed trap; **~fläche** road surface; **~floh** pillbox *(sl.)*; **~flucht** building line; **~freigabe** dedication of a highway.

Straßenfront road frontage, facade;
in ~ stehen to range with the street.

Straßengabelung bifurcation, fork of a road.

straßengebunden road-bound.

Straßen|gewerbe street industry; **~gewirr** warren of narrow streets; **~glätte** *(Schild)* slippery road; **~graben** ditch, gutter; **im ~graben landen** to be ditched; **~handel** street sale (trading), hawking, huckstery; **~händler** street trader (seller, vendor), pedlar *(Br.)*, peddler, hawker, huckster, costermonger, handseller, roadman, curbstoner *(US)*, pitchman *(US coll.)*; **~händler mit Billigware** fakir *(US)*; **~hindernis** road block; **~inspektor** highway surveyor; **~instandhaltung, ~instandsetzung** street repair, road maintenance (mending); **~instandsetzungsarbeiten** road repairs; **~junge** guttersnipe, street Arab *(Br., sl.)*; **~kämpfe** street fighting; **~kampfwaffe** riot gun; **~karte** road (street) map; **~kehre** bend, sharp turn; **~kehrer** street cleaner, orderly *(Br.)*, roader; **~kehricht** street sweepings; **~kehrmaschine** street cleaner, scavenger; **~kleid** walking dress; **~kleidung** outdoor garments; **~kontrolle** road check; **~kontrollpunkt** checkpoint; **~kostenbeitrag** paving rate, *(Anlieger)* frontage assessment; **~kreuzer** battleship *(coll.)*; **~kreuzung** road junction, street crossing, crossroads, intersection *(US)*; **~kreuzung mit Haltesignalen** boulevard stop *(US)*; **~kundgebung** street demonstration; **~kurve** curve in a road; **~lage** *(Auto)* roadability, road-holding facilities (grip); **gute ~lage haben** to hold the road well; **höhere ~lage haben** to ride higher off the ground; **~lärm** noise of the street; **~lärm unterbinden** to stop the noise in the street; **~laterne** lamp standard, street lamp (lantern); **~leuchtnagel** reflector stud; **voller ~löcher sein** to be full of holes; **~lümmel** plug-ugly *(US sl.)*; **~mädchen** streetwalker, prostitute; **~markierung** road marking; **~meister** surveyor of highways *(Br.)*; **~meisterei** highway depot; **~name** street name; **~netz** road system (net, network), grid, highway network; **~neubau** construction of new streets; **~niveau** street level; **~pflaster** pavement, paving; **~pfütze** pool on the road; **~quadrat** block [of buildings]; **am ~rand** roadside, wayside, at the roadside, by the wayside; **nahegelegener ~rand** near side of the road; **ungepflasterter ~rand** shoulder; **~raub** highway robbery, latrocinium; **gewaltsamer ~raub** street mugging; **~raub betreiben** to hijack; **~räuber** highway robber, highway ganger, hi[gh]jacker, footpad, padder, gentleman of the road (pad), knight of the road, holdup man *(US)*; **~redner** soapbox orator; **~reiniger** street cleaner, flusher; **~reinigung** cleaning of streets, street cleaning, scavengery; **~reinigungsmaschine** street cleaner, scavenger; **~reklame** outdoor advertising (publicity); **~rennen** road race (racing); **~restaurant** roadside establishment; **~rinne** gutter, ditch, drain; **~sammlung** street collection; **~schild** highway (yellow road, street) sign; **~schlacht** street battle (rioting); **~schmutz** dirt; **~schreck** road hog.

Straßenseite roadside, wayside;
auf der anderen ~ over the street; **auf der linken ~** on the left-hand side of the street;
andere ~ opposite side of the road; **falsche ~** wrong side of the pavement *(US)*;
auf der falschen ~ fahren to drive on the wrong side of the road;
auf der anderen ~ wohnen to live across the way.

Straßen|senkung depression in a road; **~sicherheit** road safety; **~sperre** road block, barricade; **militärische ~sperre** army roadblock; **~sperrung** blocking (closing, obstructing) a road, obstruction of a highway; **~spinne** multiple road junction; **~stand** roadside stand *(US)*; **holprige ~stellen** jolts of a road; **~system** road system, street pattern; **zusammenhängendes ~system** interlocking network of roads.

straßentauglich roadworthy.

Straßentauglichkeitsprüfung roadworthiness test.

Straßentransport road transport, carriage by road, haulage;
im ~ by road; **zum ~ geeignet** roadable.

Straßen|überfall holdup; **~überführung** crossover, viaduct, dry bridge *(US)*, fly-over; **~übergang** crossover, pedestrian crossing, crosswalk *(US)*; **~überquerung** crossing the road; **verkehrswidrige ~überquerung** jaywalking; **~umleitung** diversion, detour *(US)*; **~unebenheit** hump in the road; **~unkostenbeitrag** paving rate; **~unterführung** fly-under, underpass, undercrossing, *(Fußgänger)* [pedestrian] subway; **~unterhaltsabgabe** highway rate *(Br.)*; **~unterhaltszuschüsse** road maintenance grants; **~unterhaltung** upkeep of roads, road maintenance; **~verbesserung** improvement in roads, road improvements; **~verbreiterung** road widening; **~verhältnisse** road conditions; **~verkauf** hawking, peddling, street sale, huckstery; **~verkäufer** huckster, street trader (seller, vendor), frontsman *(Br.)*; **~verkaufsstand** kiosk, roadside stand *(US)*.

Straßenverkehr street (road) traffic, road transport, highway traffic;
starker ~ great deal of (much) traffic on the roads;
~ behindern to forestall (obstruct) the highway.

Straßenverkehrs|amt Bureau of Public Roads *(US)*; **~aufsicht** traffic management; **~betrieb** road-transport undertaking; **~delikt** traffic (motoring, *Br.*) offence, moving violation *(US)*; **~gesetz** Road Traffic Act *(Br.)*, traffic law; **~gewerbe** road-transport services; **~lage** road conditions; **~ordnung** Highway Code *(Br.)*, Uniform Traffic Code *(US)*; **~planung** transport planning in road sectors, traffic planning; **~recht** law of the road; **~regeln** rules of the road *(US)*, traffic rules; **~schild** traffic sign; **~sicherheit** road (traffic, *US*) safety; **der ~sicherheit genügen** to meet the demands of road safety; **~statistik** traffic statistics; **~teilnehmer** road user; **~vorschriften** rules of the road, road regulations; **~walze** steam roller; **~wesen** traffic management (highway) system; **~zeichen** road (direction) sign; **~zulassungsstelle** traffic commissioner *(Br.)*.

Straßen|verstopfung traffic jam, congestion of traffic, road congestion; **~verwaltung** public road administration *(US)*; **~verzeichnis** street directory; **~vorschriften** road regulations; **~walze** road (steam) roller; **~wärter** traffic warder, waywarden *(Br.)*; **auf dem ~weg** by road; **~- und Eisenbahnwesen** road and rail system; **~zoll** turnpike money; **~zustand** road conditions; **schlechter ~zustand** defect in highway; **~zustandsbericht** motoring report on road conditions.

Stratege strategist, general.

Strategie|der kleinen Schritte gradualism;
~ für die Wahlen festlegen to settle strategy for election.

strategisch strategic;
~e Bomberflotte strategic bomber force; **~ wichtige Erzeugnisse** strategic goods (items); **~es Luftwaffenkommando** Strategic Air Command; **~er Plan** strategic plan; **~ wichtiger Punkt** strategic point; **~er Rückzug** strategic retreat.

Stratosphärenflugzeug stratoliner, stratocruiser.

sträuben, sich mit Händen und Füßen to kick against it;
da ~ sich einem ja die Haare that's enough to make your hair stand on end.

Strauchdieb bushranger, prowler, foodpad.

straucheln to stumble, to stagger, to flounder, *(auf Abwege geraten)* to go astray.

Strauchwerk brush.

Strauß mit jem. ausfechten to have it out with s. o.

Strazze foul paper, blotter, scroll, waste book *(Br.)*.

Streb *(Bergbau)* face.

Strebe prop, shore, *(Flugzeug)* strut, stay.

Streben pursuit, endeavo(u)r, push;
~ nach Glück pursuit of happiness; **~ nach Wissen** pursuit of knowledge.

streben strive, to aspire, to aim, to tend;
nach Hohem ~ to reach high; **nach mehr Macht ~** to seek greater power; **nach Ruhm ~** to look to one's laurels.

Streber swot, careerist, mothball *(sl.)*, grind *(US)*, pusher *(coll.)*, dig *(US sl.)*, climber *(US)*, sap *(Br., sl.)*, smug *(Br., sl.)*;
gesellschaftlicher ~ social climber;
im Rufe eines ~s stehen to have the character of a place hunter.

streberhaft pushing, grinding, swotting.
Strebertum grind, swot *(Br.)*.
strebsam industrious, assiduous, diligent.
Strecke route, road, track, stretch, *(Bahn)* line, track, section, roadway, *(Bergbau)* gallery, gangway, passage, drift, *(Buch)* passage, part, *(Entfernung)* distance, *(Jagd)* kill, killing, *(tel.)* line, cable, *(Zeitungsverkäufer)* paper route *(US)*;
auf freier ~ on the line;
angegebene ~ advertised route; **gut ausgebaute** ~ well-built stretch of a road; **stark befahrene** ~ heavily travelled line; **regelmäßig beflogene** ~ regular route; **eingleisige** ~ single track; **elektrifizierte** ~ electrified track; **kurze** ~ short way, spell *(US)*; **kürzeste** ~ direct route; **landschaftlich schönste** ~ top scenic route; **weite** ~ long haul (distance); **zurückgelegte** ~ distance covered; **zweigleisige** ~ double track;
~ **von London** down line *(Br.)*; **lange** ~**n eines Romans** long patches of a novel; **kurze** ~ **Weges** little way; **tüchtige** ~ **Weges** quite a stretch;
~ **abgehen** to pace off a distance, *(Bahn)* to inspect the tracks; ~ **abstecken** to lay out the line; **auf freier** ~ **anhalten** to stop in the middle of nowhere; ~ **zweigleisig ausbauen** to double an existing track; **auf der** ~ **bleiben** to drop out, *(im Konkurrenzkampf)* to fall by the wayside, to be put out of business; ~ **blockieren** to block the line; **j. zur** ~ **bringen** to shoot (hunt) s. o. down; ~ **frei machen** *(Bahn)* to set up; ~ **zurücklegen** to cover a distance; ~ **in Etappen zurücklegen** to cover a distance by stages, to travel by easy stages; ~ **zu Fuß zurücklegen** to walk a distance; **gesamte** ~ **in acht Tagen zurücklegen** to make the whole distance in a week.
strecken to stretch, to extend, *(Arbeit)* to protract;
Artikel ~ to pad out an article; **j. zu Boden** ~ to knock s. o. down; **sich nach der Decke** ~ to make both ends meet, to cut one's coat according to one's cloth; **sein Geld bis zur nächsten Gehaltszahlung** ~ to make one's money spin out until next payday; **seine Kohlenvorräte** ~ to eke out one's coal; **seinen Kopf aus dem Fenster** ~ to pop one's head out of the window.
Strecken|abschnitt fare stage, section *(US)*; ~**arbeiter** tracklayer, platelayer, lineman, navy *(Br.)*, section hand (man) *(US)*, maintenance-of-way employee, *(pl.)* section gang *(US)*; ~**aufseher** trackwalker *(US)*, lineman; ~**ausbau** completion of the road system, *(Bergbau)* roadway supports; ~**ausfall** line break; ~**bau** construction of a railway *(Br.)*, railroading *(US)*; ~- **und Pfeilerbau** board and pillar work; ~**begehung** *(Bahn)* line inspection *(Br.)*, trackwalking; ~**belastung** volume of traffic, *(Eisenbahn)* load on section; ~**benutzungsgebühr** trackage; ~**betrieb** *(Bergbau)* drift mining, driving; ~**förderung** *(Bahn)* transport, *(Bergbau)* roadway haulage; ~**fracht** distance (interline) freight; ~**führung** routing; ~**geher** line walker; ~**geschwindigkeit** *(Bahn)* speed; ~**karte** route map; ~**markierung** marking, *(Bahn)* signal(l)ing system; ~**meister** trainmaster; ~**meldung** *(Flugwesen)* airway weather report; ~**pfeiler** *(Bergbau)* post; ~**plakat** railroad bulletin *(US)*; ~**prüfer** *(Bahn)* spotter *(US)*; ~**signal** block signal; ~**stillegung** abandonment of a railway (railroad, *US*), rail closure; ~**tarif** line haul rate, hauling rates, basing tariff; ~**unterhaltung** maintenance of way; ~**verkehr** local traffic; ~**vorhersage** *(Flugverkehr)* route forecast; ~**wärter** lineman, surfaceman, trackwalker *(US)*.
Streckmaschine stretching machine.
Streckung stretching;
~ **der Arbeit** spreading of work, work (employment) spreading; ~ **eines Programms** stretch-out of a program(me).
Streich blow, slap, smack, *(Schabernack)* trick, prank, jig *(sl.)*; **lustiger** ~ frolic; **törichte** ~**e** extravagances; **übler** ~ dirty (nasty) trick, booby trap;
jem. einen ~ **spielen** to pull s. one's leg (a fast one on s. o., *sl.*), to play a trick (practical joke) on s. o.; **jem. einen tödlichen** ~ **versetzen** to deal s. o. a fatal blow; ~**e verüben** to play pranks.
Streichen deletion, obliteration, expurgation, *(Disqualifikation)* disqualification;
~ **eines Absatzes** cancellation of a paragraph; ~ **von der Anwaltsliste** striking off the roll; ~ **eines Auftrags** cancellation of an order; ~ **der Kriegsschulden** cancellation of war debts; ~ **von einer Liste** withdrawal from a list; ~ **von der Mitgliederliste** expurgation of a member; ~ **in der amtlichen Notierung** removal from the stock-exchange list; ~ **einer Stelle** abolition of a post.
streichen *(ausstreichen)* to cross out, to delete, to obliterate, to strike through, to expunge, *(disqualifizieren)* to disqualify, *(mit Farbe)* to paint, to coat, *(Mörtel)* to fill, *(Zensur)* to black out;
j. von der Anwaltsliste ~ to strike s. o. off the roll; **Artikel** ~ to cancel (kill, *coll.*) an article; **Auftrag** ~ to cancel (countermand) an order; **Buchstelle** ~ to strike a passage out of a book; **Butter auf ein Brötchen** ~ to spread butter onto a roll; **jem. aus seinem Gedächtnis** ~ to erase s. one's name from one's memory; **von der Mitgliederliste** ~ to drop a member from the rolls; **Namen von der Liste** ~ to strike a name from the list; **jds. Namen in einem Verzeichnis** ~ to take s. one's name from a register; **Nichtzutreffendes** ~ delete what does not apply; **Posten** ~ to cancel (strike off) an item; **Punkt von der Tagesordnung** ~ to withdraw an item from the agenda; **Rechnungsposten** ~ to scratch an item from an account; **faule Schulden** ~ to credit doubtful *(Br.)* (bad, *US*) debts; **durch die Stadt** ~ to roam through the streets;
seine Ferienreise ~ **müssen** not to be able to afford to go away on a holiday;
Nichtzutreffendes bitte ~ strike out words not applicable.
Streich|holz, abgebranntes spent match; ~**hölzchenheft** matchbook; ~**hölzerholz** matchwood.
Streichholz|fabrikant match manufacturer; ~**fabrikation** match manufacture; ~**schachtel** matchbox.
Streichsatz deleted matter;
zu ~ **erklären** *(drucktechn.)* to cancel.
Streichung deletion, obliteration, erasure, elimination, expurgation, *(Kürzung)* cut, reduction, *(Szene)* cut, *(drucktechn.)* cancel, *(Zensur)* blacking;
~ **einer Schuld** cancellation of a debt;
Scheck durch ~**en ungültig machen** to obliterate the writing of a cheque *(Br.)* (check, *US*); ~**en in einem Auftritt vornehmen** to cut a scene.
Streifband [newspaper] wrapper;
unter ~ by book post;
~**depot** general deposit; ~**zeitung** newspaper wrapper; ~**zeitungen** all-up newspapers.
Streife patrol, beat, *(mil.)* round;
motorisierte ~ patrol (squad, *US*, prowl, *US*) car, cruiser;
~ **gehen** to go on patrol, to walk one's round; **auf** ~ **sein** to be on patrol (on one's beat).
Streifen stripe, streak, strip, *(Fernsehen)* striation, *(Film)* motion picture, *(Kondensstreifen)* trail, *(Telegrafie)* tape;
weißer ~ **in der Fahrbahnmitte** white line in the middle of the road;
jem. nicht in den ~ **passen** not to suit s. one's books; **Tuch in** ~ **schneiden** to cut a cloth into strips.
streifen *(wandern)* to wander, to touch, to brush against;
Baum ~ *(Auto)* to graze a tree; **durch die Felder** ~ to roam the fields; **Ort auf seiner Reise nur** ~ to glance at a place on a journey; **Thema nur kurz** ~ to touch a subject; **Wasseroberfläche** ~ *(Flugzeug)* to skim the water surface;
seinen Blick über die Zuhörer ~ **lassen** to skim over the audience.
Streifen|anzeige continuity panel, streamer, strip, banner, band; ~**boot** watchboat; ~**dienst** patrol duties; ~**dienst auf den Straßen durchführen** to patrol the streets; ~**drucker** *(Telegrafenapparat)* perforator; ~**fahrzeug des ADAC** [etwa] A.A. patrol; ~**flug** patrol mission; ~**führer** patrol leader; ~**gänger** *(Polizei)* roundsman, patrolman *(US)*; ~**leser** tape reader; ~**locher** tape punch, keypunch; ~**polizist** cop on the beat; ~**polizist mit Radargerät** picture taker *(US sl.)*; ~**wagen** police patrol (squad, *US*, prowl, *US*) car, cruiser *(US)*; **zusätzliche** ~**wagen eingesetzt haben** to have extra patrols on the prowl; ~**zuführung** tape feed.
Streif|licht sidelight; **spannende** ~**lichter** fascination notes; ~**licht auf etw. werfen** to provide incidental information about s. th.; ~**schuß** graze, grazing; ~**zug** raid, incursion, forage, wander, ~**zug durch die Kneipen machen** to go on a binge, to pub-crawl.
Streik strike, tie-up, work stoppage, turnout *(Br.)*, walk-out *(US coll.)*;
vom ~ **betroffen** strike-bound;
von der Gewerkschaft nicht anerkannter ~ outlaw strike; **rechtzeitig angemeldeter** ~ strike with due notice; **aus politischen Gründen begonnener** ~ political strike; **örtlich (zeitlich) begrenzter** ~ sectional strike; **bundesweiter** ~ industry-wide strike; **ordnungsgemäß durchgeführter** ~ legal strike; **schwerpunktartig durchgeführter** ~ selective strike; **aufgrund von Lohnverhandlungen entstandener** ~ contract strike; **von der Gewerkschaft nicht genehmigter** ~ illegal (quickie, *US*) strike; **massierte** ~**s** spate of strikes; **mittelbarer** ~ secondary strike; **organisierter** ~ official strike; **örtlicher** ~ local strike; **spontaner** ~ lightning strike, walkout *(US)*;

symbolischer ~ token strike; **unangekündigter** ~ wildcat (quickie, *US*) strike; **unbefristeter** ~ unlimited strike; **vertragswidriger** ~ unconstitutional strike; **widerrechtlicher** ~ illegal strike; **wilder** ~ wildcat (flash, illegal, outlaw, quickie, *US*, hit-and-run, wanton) strike;
~ **ohne vorherige Ankündigung** lightning strike; ~ **gegen schlechte Arbeitsbedingungen** strike against bad working conditions; ~ **der Autoarbeiter** car strike; ~ **der im öffentlichen Dienst Beschäftigten** public-sector strike; ~ **der Führungskräfte** management strike; ~ **innerhalb eines ganzen Industriezweiges** industry-wide strike; ~ **für höhere Löhne** strike for higher pay; ~ **von Polizeibeamten** police strike; ~**, Aufruhr und bürgerliche Unruhen** strike, riots and civil commotion; ~ **durch Verlangsamung der Arbeit** slow-down strike, go-slow *(Br.)*; ~ **der öffentlichen Versorgungsbetriebe** public-utility strike; ~ **zwecks Wiedereinstellung eines entlassenen Arbeiters** one-man strike;
~ **abblasen (abbrechen, absagen)** to call off a strike; ~ **abwenden** to avert a strike; ~ **anordnen** to order a strike; ~ **auslösen** to trigger off a strike; ~ **ausrufen** to call (proclaim) a strike; ~ **beenden** to terminate (call off) a strike; **sich im** ~ **befinden** to [be on] strike; ~ **brechen** to break a strike, to rat; ~ **vom Zaun brechen** to trigger a strike; **von der Gewerkschaft genehmigten** ~ **durchführen** to strike with the approval of the union; **bundesweiten** ~ **durchführen** to strike on a nation-wide basis; **in einen** ~ **eintreten** to [go on] strike, to stop work; ~ **fortsetzen** to continue a strike; ~ **organisieren** to stage a strike; ~ **proklamieren** to call (declare, proclaim) a strike; ~ **schlichten** to settle a strike; **in den** ~ **treten** to [go on] strike, to come out on strike, to go out, to [lay] down tools *(Br.)*, to walk out *(US)*; ~ **unterbrechen** to suspend a strike; ~ **untersagen** to bar a strike; ~ **durch Regierungsbeschluß verbieten** to prohibit a strike by government decree; ~ **verkürzen** to shorten a strike; ~ **vermeiden** to avoid a strike;
~**abkommen** strike pact; ~**absicht** intent to strike; ~**abstimmung** strike vote (ballot); ~**abwendung** prevention of a strike.

streikähnliche Maßnahmen strike-like tactics.

Streik|aktion strike campaign; ~**androhung** threat of a strike.

streikanfällig strike-prone.

Streik|anführer durch Entlassung bestrafen to victimize a strike leader; ~**ankündigung** strike notice; ~**anordnung** cease-work instruction; ~**anweisungen** strike orders (instruction); ~**arbeit** black-leg (scab, *US*) work; ~**arten** types of strike; **massiertes** ~**aufgebot** mass picketing; ~**aufhebung** calling off a strike; ~**aufruf** strike call; **einem** ~**aufruf der Gewerkschaft nicht Folge leisten** to give a union the bird over a strike call; ~**ausschuß** strike committee; ~**aussichten** strike outlook; ~**beendigung** cessation from strike, strike cancellation (deadline); **Abkommen zur** ~**beendigung** strike settlement; ~**befehl** strike order, cease-work instruction; ~**beginn** onset of a strike; ~**beihilfe** strike aid (pay); ~**beilegung** settlement of a strike; ~**bekämpfung** crackdown on strikes; ~**beschluß** strike resolution; ~**bestimmungen** strike provisions; ~**bewegung** strike movement; ~**bilanz** strike record.

streikbrechende Maßnahmen strikebreaking activities.

Streikbrecher strikebreaker, nonstriker, knobstick, blackleg *(Br., sl.)*, blacksheep *(Br.)*, rat, scab *(US)*;
berufsmäßiger ~ fink *(US sl.)*, missionary worker *(sl.)*; **gewalttätiger** ~ goon *(US sl.)*;
~ **sein** to scab *(US)*.

Streikbrechertum blackleggery *(Br.)*.

Streik|dauer duration of a strike; ~**drohung** strike threat; ~**einstellung** calling off a strike; ~**einstellungsbeschluß** vote to end a strike.

Streiken going on strike.

streiken to [be (go) on] strike, to come out on strike, to withdraw one's labo(u)r, to down tools *(Br.)*, to go (come, be) out, to leave (stop) work, to walk out *(US)*, *(Motor)* to conk [out] *(sl.)*, *(sich weigern)* to refuse, to balk;
für Gehaltserhöhung ~ to be on strike for more pay; **für höhere Löhne** ~ to strike for higher wages.

streikend on strike;
~**er Angestellter** striking employee; ~**es Gewerkschaftsmitglied** striking member.

Streikende strike deadline.

Streikender striker, striking workman.

Streik|enthaltungsabkommen no-strike agreement; ~**finanzierung** financing a strike; ~**fonds** strike (fighter) fund, strike-benefit fund; ~**fonds auffüllen** to beef up the strike fund; ~**fortsetzung** continuation of a strike; ~**führer** strike leader; ~**führung** strike committee; ~**gefahr** danger of a strike; ~**geld[er]** strike pay (benefits); ~**gruppe** band of pickets; ~**hetzer** strikemonger; ~**jahr** strike year; ~**kasse** strike (sustentative) fund, war chest; ~**klausel** strike clause; ~**leiter** strike leader; ~**leitung** strike committee; ~**lohn** strike pay.

streiklustig strike-prone.

Streik|maßnahmen, verfassungsmäßig erlaubte constitutional strike actions; ~**maßnahmen einleiten** to take strike action; ~**nachteile** strike toll; ~**parole** strike slogan; **in der ersten** ~**phase** in a strike's early phase; ~**plan** strike plan.

Streikposten picket;
betriebsfremde ~ stranger (secondary, *US*) picketing; **bewaffneter** ~ gunman; **organisierte** ~ organizational picketing; **mit den gesetzlichen Vorschriften in Einklang stehende** ~ peaceful picketing;
~ **von Betriebsfremden** stranger (secondary, *US*) picketing; **durch** ~ **absperren** to picket; ~ **aufstellen** to throw a picket line, to place strikers on picket (duty); ~ **vor einer Fabrik aufstellen** to picket a factory; ~ **nicht beachten** to cross the picket line; ~ **beziehen** to walk the picket lines; ~ **stehen** to picket;
großes ~**aufgebot** mass picketing; ~**aufstellung durch zwei Gewerkschaften** cross picketing; ~**einteilung** picket assignment; ~**kette,** ~**linie,** ~**sperre** picket line, picketing row; **nicht aggressiv durchgeführtes** ~**stehen** peaceful picketing; **unerlaubtes** ~**stehen** unlawful picketing.

Streik|recht freedom (right) to strike; ~**schutzkräfte** strike protection force; ~**statistik** strike record; ~**tätigkeit** strike activity; ~**termin** strike date; ~**unterstützung** strike benefit; ~**verbot** strike ban; ~**verbot verhängen** to bar a strike; ~**verbotsklausel** no-strike clause; ~**vereinbarung** strike settlement; ~**verhalten** picketing conduct; ~**verhütungsmittel** strike deterrent; ~**versammlung** strike-vote meeting; ~**versicherung** strike insurance; ~**wache** picket; ~**welle** wave of strikers; ~**ziel** strike target.

Streit difference, disagreement, dispute, controversy, fight, warfare, *(Prozeß)* litigation, lawsuit, action;
im ~ **mit** at odds with; **im** ~ **befangen** litigious, in action (litigation); **noch im** ~ **befangen** unadjudged;
mühsam beigelegter ~ patched up quarrel; **juristischer** ~ legal dispute;
~ **um des Kaisers Bart** dispute about trifles;
~ **mit jem. austragen** to pick a bone (have it out) with s. o.; ~ **mit den Fäusten austragen** to come to fisticuffs; ~ **beenden** to terminate a controversy, to make up a quarrel; ~ **begraben** to bury the hatchet; ~ **beilegen** to fix up a quarrel, to make one's peace with, to sink a controversy, to compose a difference; ~ **mit jem. bekommen** to run up against s. o.; ~ **vom Zaun brechen** to pick a quarrel; ~ **durch Schiedsspruch erledigen** to settle a dispute by arbitration; ~ **mit jem. haben** to have words with s. o.; ~ **heraufbeschwören** to make the furs fly; **j. in einen** ~ **hereinziehen** to involve s. o. in a quarrel; **mit jem. im** ~ **liegen** to be at variance (loggerheads, warfare) with s. o.; ~ **schlichten** to settle a dispute, to make up (accommodate) a difference, to pour oil on troubled waters; ~ **schüren** to blow up a quarrel, to foment strife; ~ **mit jem. suchen** to try to pick a quarrel with s. o.; ~ **in eine Familie tragen** to bring division into a family; ~ **verhindern** to head off a quarrel; ~ **verkünden** *(Zivilprozeß)* to interplead, to implead *(US)*, to give third-party notice *(US)*; ~ **wegen mitwirkenden Verschuldens verkünden** to serve notice of contribution and indemnity; **in einem** ~ **vermitteln** to interpose in a dispute; **sich in einen** ~ **mit jem. verwickeln** to embark upon a quarrel with s. o.; **bis zur Austragung des** ~**es zurückgestellt werden** *(Patentrecht)* to go into interference.

streitbar aggressive, militant, quarrelsome;
~ **wie ein Zinshahn sein** to have a chip on one's shoulder.

streitbefangen in litigation, pendent.

Streitbefangenheit pendency.

streiten to contend, to argue, to dispute, to wrangle, to pull caps, *(vor Gericht)* to litigate;
sich mit jem. über etw. ~ to be at issue (odds) with s. o.; **sich über Kleinigkeiten** ~ to wrangle over trifles; **miteinander** ~ to quarrel with each other; **sich nicht mehr darüber** ~**, daß man verschiedener Meinung ist** to agree to differ; **um den Sieg** ~ to compete for victory;
über Geschmack läßt sich nicht ~ there is no accounting for taste.

streitend litigant;
~**e Parteien** litigants at law, parties to a suit.

Streiter fighter, combatant, advocate.

Streitfall dispute, contest, controversy, *(Prozeß)* action, lawsuit, litigation, case, issue;
im ~ in case of litigation;

~ **behandeln (bearbeiten)** to process (deal with) a case; ~ **beilegen** to settle (accommodate) a dispute; ~ **gütlich beilegen** to settle a dispute amicably; ~ **auf dem Verhandlungswege beilegen** to settle a dispute by negotiation; ~ **darlegen** to set out the issue; ~ **einem Schiedsrichter unterbreiten** to submit a difference (refer a dispute) to an arbitrator; **dem Gericht einen ~ vorlegen** to submit a question to the court.

Streitfrage controversial subject, controversy, case at issue, controversial subject, contentious (point at) issue, issue, argument;
große ~ a much debated question; **hypothetische ~** feigned issue; **juristische ~** issue at law;
sich über eine ~ erhitzen to grow warm over an argument.

Streitgegenstand matter in controversy (issue), debating point, bone of contention, shuttlecock;
am ~ beteiligt united in interest;
~ **festsetzen** to define the issue.

Streitgenosse third party, co-plaintiff, co-defendant;
notwendige ~n indispensable (necessary) parties, privies in law;
~ **ohne eigenes Prozeßinteresse** nominal party;
als ~ klagen to join as plaintiff; **als ~n haftbar machen** to render jointly liable; **als ~n mitverklagen** to join as a party to an action.

Streit|genossenschaft joinder of parties; **unzulässige ~genossenschaft** misjoinder of parties; **~hahn, ~hammel** fire-eater, quarrelsome type, squabbler, brawler; **~hammel sein** to be always ready for a row; **~helfer** intervening party, intervener.

streitig contentious, questionable, *(kontradiktatorisch)* contentious, *(streitbefangen)* at issue, contestable, contested, contradictory, litigious, litigable;
~ **entscheiden** to decide a case; **jem. das Eigentum ~ machen** to dispute s. one's title; **jem. die Erbfolge ~ machen** to contest s. one's right to succeed; **jem. den Rang ~ machen** to rival s. o.; ~ **sein** to be in issue; ~ **verhandeln** to hear a case;
~e Gerichtsbarkeit contentious jurisdiction; **~er Punkt** case (point) at issue; **~e Sache** matter in dispute, contentious issue; **~es Urteil** contradictory judgment; **in ~em Verfahren** in action (litigation).

Streitigkeit dispute, quarrel, controversy;
arbeitsrechtliche ~ labo(u)r conflict (dispute); **seerechtliche ~en** admiralty actions; **vermögensrechtliche ~** pecuniary causes; **zukünftige ~** future disputes;
~ **beilegen** to accommodate (adjust, settle) a dispute, to sink an issue; **in nachbarliche ~en eingreifen** to take up the quarrel of one's neighbo(u)rs; **lediglich ~en hervorrufen** to be productive only of quarrels; **~en durch ein Schiedsgericht beilegen lassen** to settle disputes by arbitration; **~en schlichten** to adjust differences.

Streitkräfte armed (military) forces, armed services;
alliierte ~ allied forces; **ausländische ~** foreign forces; **im Ausland stationierte ~** forces stationed abroad; **im Inland stationierte ~** home forces (army); **überlegene ~** superior forces; **feindliche ~ umgehen** to turn the hostile powers; **~ vereinigen** to join forces with; **feindliche ~ vernichten** to cut up the enemy's forces.

Streit|macht, multilaterale multilateral force; **~objekt** subject matter, matter in issue, **~punkt** debating (contentious) point, *(Politik)* [point at] issue, disputed point.

Streitsache case under dispute, matter in issue, *(Prozeß)* litigation, lawsuit, law case;
~ **aufrufen** to call the calendar.

Streitschrift pamphlet.

streitsüchtig quarrelsome, contentious, pugnacious, cantankerous.

Streit|summe value of the matter in dispute, jurisdictional amount *(US)*; **~verfahren** contentious business; **~verkünder** applicant of interpleader, person giving notice *(US)*; **~verkündung** citation *(Br.)*, interpleader, impleader *(US)*, notice to third party, third-party notice (complaint, *US*); **~verkündigungsverfahren** third-party claim procceeding.

Streitwert amount in controversy (dispute), amount involved, jurisdictional amount *(US)*;
~ **der befangenen Sache** value of matter in controversy;
sich nach dem jeweiligen ~ richten to be based on how much is in the dispute;
~festsetzung assessment of value in issue.

streng hard, severe, stern, exacting, exact, rigorous;
~ **verboten** strictly prohibited; ~ **vertraulich** in strict confidence, strictly confidential;
~ **bis zur Grausamkeit** severe to the point of cruelty; **j. ~ ansehen** to give s. o. a stern look; **Gesetz ~ anwenden** to execute a law with rigo(u)r; **Bestimmung ~ beachten** to adhere strictly to a clause; ~ **bestrafen** to punish severely; **j. ~ bewachen** to keep a strict watch on s. o.; **Vertragsbestimmung ~ einhalten** to adhere strictly to a clause; **sich ~ an die Vorschriften halten** to adhere closely to the regulations; **~ zu jem. sein** to be hard on s. o.;
in ~er Abgeschlossenheit leben to live in seclusion; **j. zu ~em Arrest verurteilen** to sentence s. o. to close confinement; **~e Auslegung** rigo(u)rous definition, strict construction; **~e Bestrafung** severe punishment; **~ durchgeführte Blockade** close blockade; **~e Diät halten** to observe a strict diet; **~e Disziplin** stern (stringency of) discipline; **~e Einhaltung** strict observance; **mit ~er Geheimhaltung behandelt werden** to rate for top-secret treatment; **~es Gesetz** strict (rigo(u)rous) law; **~e Grundsätze** rigid principles; **~e Maßnahmen ergreifen** to take drastic measures; **~e Prüfung** stiff examination; **~es Regiment führen** to rule with a heavy hand; **~er Richter** severe judge; **im ~en Sinne** in the strict sense; **~e Sparsamkeit** rigid economy; **~e Strafe** severe punishment; **~e Untersuchung** close investigation; **~e Verfahrensweise** stringent code of procedure; **~e Verordnung** stringent regulation; **~er Verweis** severe reprimand; **~er Vorgesetzter** rigid disciplinarian; **~er Winter** hard (severe) winter; **~e Zensur** strict censorship.

Strenge severity, rigo(u)r, stringency, strictness;
~ **des Gesetzes** rigo(u)r (stringency, strictness) of the law;
Gesetz mit aller ~ zur Anwendung bringen to put the law in operation in all its rigo(u)r.

Streu|abdeckung coverage; **~bereich** *(Werbefeldzug)* dispersion area; **~besitz** diversified holdings; **~bild** *(Statistik)* scatter diagram; **~breite** coverage, dispersion area; **~diagramm** scatter diagram; **~dichte** coverage, *(Werbemedien)* density of circulation.

streuen *(Risiko)* to spread, *(Strahlen)* to disperse, to scatter, *(Stroh)* to litter, *(Werbewesen)* to distribute, to disperse;
Kies auf eine vereiste Straße ~ to scatter gravel (spread grit) on an icy road; **jem. Sand in die Augen ~** to cast dust in s. one's eyes; **sein Vermögen risikomäßig ~** to diversify one's capital.

Streu|kosten *(Werbung)* coverage cost, space charge; **~ladung** buckshot.

streunen to stray, to roam about.

streunend|er Hund stray dog; **~e Kinder** waifs.

Streuner vagabond, strayaway, tramp, *(Kind)* waif.

Streu|plan spreadover, space (media) schedule; **~planer** media man (director); **~planung** media strategy (planning); **~prüfung** *(Anzeigenwesen)* media evaluation; **~siedlung** scattered settlement.

Streuung *(Anlagen)* diversification, dispersal, *(Kompaß)* deviation, *(mil.)* diversion, *(Risiko)* spread, *(Werbung)* coverage, frequency distribution, dispersion, spread, media allocation;
lineare ~ *(Kompaß)* mean deviation; **regionale ~** *(Anlagen)* regional dispersion; **überlappende ~** *(Werbung)* overlapping circulation;
~ **der Aktienbesitzer** diversification of shareholders; **weite ~ des Eigentums** wide dispersion of ownership; ~ **industrieller Fertigungsstätten** distribution of industry.

Streuungs|breite range [of dispersion]; **~erfassung** census of distribution; **~fachmann** media man; **überschneidendes ~gebiet** overlapping situation; **~koeffizient** scatter coefficient; **~kosten** coverage cost, space charge.

Streuzeichnung spot drawing.

Strich stroke, line, *(Dirne)* prostitution, street walking, *(Land)* stretch, tract;
auf dem ~ *(Prostituierte)* on the streets, on the turf; **gegen den ~** against the wool (grain); **nach ~ und Faden** right and left; **unter dem ~** *(Bilanz)* below the line;
j. nach ~ und Faden betrügen to cheat s. o. right, left and center *(US)* (centre, *Br.*); **auf den ~ gehen** to sell one's bacon *(coll.)*, to walk the streets; **jem. gegen den ~ gehen** to go against s. one's grain; **j. auf dem ~ haben** to have a grudge against s. o.; **keinen ~ Arbeit getan haben** not to have done a stroke of work; **jem. einen ~ durch die Rechnung machen** to thwart s. one's plans, to settle s. one's hash; **unter dem ~ sein** *(Examensarbeit)* not to be up to the mark; **nur ein ~ in der Landschaft sein** to be nothing but skin and bone; **Situation mit wenigen ~en umreißen** to outline a situation broadly; **j. nach ~ und Faden verprügeln** to give s. o. a good hiding (sound thrashing); **~ unter etw. ziehen** to turn over a new leaf; ~ **unter Vergangenes ziehen** to let bygones be bygones;
~ätzung line block *(Br.)*, line cut (etching, engraving, *US*).

stricheln *(Linie)* to draw a broken line.

Strichelverfahren tally-sheet method.
Strich|klischee line cut; ~**linie** shaded (hatched) rule; ~**liste** check list, tally; ~**mädchen** cruiser *(sl.)*, streetwalker; ~**markierung** tally, bar code; ~**regen** local rain; ~**skala** graduated scale; ~**zeichnung** line drawing.
Strick rope, cord, *(Schelm)* little beggar, rascal;
am ~ baumeln to swing on the gallows; **jem. einen ~ daraus drehen** to hang a rap on s. o., to hang s. o. with s. th.;
wenn alle ~e reißen if the worst comes to the worst;
~**arbeit** knit; ~**leiter** ladder; ~**waren** knitted goods.
strikt strict, stern, severe;
~ ablehnen to refuse flatly;
~**er Befehl** strict order; ~**e Einhaltung** strict adherence; ~**e Maßnahmen ergreifen** to take stringent measures; ~**e Neutralität** strict neutrality.
Strippe string, *(Telefon)* phone;
j. fest an der ~ haben to keep a tight rein on s. o.; **ganzen Tag an der ~ hängen** to be on the phone all day.
Stripteaselokal striptease theater (theatre, *Br.*).
strittig *(im Streit befangen)* litigious, at issue, *(bestreitbar)* disputable, in dispute, debatable, *(streitig)* contentious, contested, *(umstritten)* controversial, in contestation, moot;
~ sein to be in issue (dispute);
~**e Forderung** litigious claim; ~**e Frage** controversial question; ~**er Punkt** point at issue, disputed (contentious) point; ~**es Recht** litigious right; ~**es Thema** controversial subject.
Stroh, dem Vieh frisches ~ aufschütten to litter the cattle; **wie ~ brennen** to burn like straw; **Haus mit ~ decken** to thatch a house; **leeres ~ dreschen** to thresh over straw, to pluck a crow, to flog a dead horse; **nur ~ im Kopf haben** to be empty-headed; **wie ~ schmecken** to have no taste;
~**ballen** bale of straw; ~**dach** thatched roof; ~**feuer** flash in the pan; ~**halm** straw; **nach einem ~halm greifen** to catch (clutch) at a straw; **sich um einen ~halm zanken** to find quarrels in a straw; ~**kopf** empty-headed fellow, fathead.
Strohmann man of straw, straw man, stalking horse, front, dummy, ostensible partner, *(Börse)* fictitious operator, *(Effektentransfer)* nominee, *(Kläger)* nominal plaintiff, *(Repräsentationsfigur)* figurehead, pawn;
als Aktionär vorgeschobener ~ nominee shareholder;
~**aktie** nominal share; ~**beteiligung** nominee's shareholdings; ~**gesellschaft** dummy corporation *(US)*, nominee company.
Stroh|puppe jackstraw; ~**sack** mattress, donkey's breakfast *(sl.)*; ~**schuppen** straw house; ~**witwe[r]** grass widow[er].
Strolch vagabond, tramp, bum *(sl.)*, hoodlum *(US sl.)*.
Strom stream, river, jet, *(el.)* current, electricity, power, *(Schwall)* volley, burst;
mit dem ~ with the stream; **unter ~ stehend** *(el.)* live, hot; **elektrischer ~** electric current (power); **reißender ~** torrent; **schiffbarer ~** navigable river;
~ von Auswanderern stream of emigration; **~ von Besuchern** flood of callers; **~ von Flüchtlingen** stream of refugees; **~ von Menschen** flood of people; **~ von Tränen** flood of tears; **~ des Verkehrs** flow (stream) of traffic;
jem. den ~ abschalten to stop s. one's supply of electricity; **~ im ganzen Land abschalten** to black out the country; **~ einschalten** to turn (switch) on the current, to make contact; **~ von Flüchen vom Stapel lassen** to pour out a torrent of abuse; **sich vom ~ der Menge treiben lassen** to drift with the crowd; **elektrischen ~ in eine Fabrik legen** to furnish a factory with current; **gegen den ~ schwimmen** to strive against the stream, to swim (row, *sl.*) against the tide; **mit dem ~ schwimmen** to go with the tide; **~ sparen** to save electricity; **~ unterbrechen** to break the current; **mit ~ versorgen** to supply with electricity.
stromab down the river, downstream.
Strom|abfall current drop; ~**abgabe** current output, power supply; ~**ableser** electricity-meter reader; ~**abnehmer** consumer of electricity, *(Ableser)* electricity-meter reader, collector, *(Gerät)* brush, tap, *(Straßenbahn)* trolley arm, collector; ~**abnehmerrolle** trolley; ~**abschaltung** power cut, cut-off of power.
stromabwärts down the river, downstream.
Strom|anliegerstaat riparian state; ~**anschluß** connection to the mains; ~**anschlußkosten** power installation costs.
stromaufwärts upstream, upward, up the river.
Strom|ausfall power (current) failure, [power] blackout; ~**ausschalter** contact breaker; ~**bedarf** power requirements; ~**belastung** power load; **~- oder Gasberechnung für Mieter** supplying electricity or gas to tenants; ~**bett** water course; ~**bilanz** net position on electricity; ~**durchgang** passage of current.
Ströme von Whisky lashings of whisky, whisky galore;
in ~n regnen to be raining cats and dogs.
Strom|einheit power unit; ~**einschränkung** power rationing; ~**einsparung** power cut.
strömen to stream, to flow, to gush.
strömender Regen pouring rain, downpour of rain.
Strom|entnahme consumption of electricity; ~**erzeuger** generator; ~**erzeugung** electricity generation, generation (production) of electricity.
stromführend *(el.)* live.
Strom|gebiet water system; ~**impuls** current impulse.
Stromkreis electrical (power, current) circuit;
geschlossener ~ loop; **offener ~** open circuit;
~ überlasten to overcharge an electric current; **~ unterbrechen** to break contact.
Strom|kürzung brownout; ~**leistung** power output; ~**lieferung** current (electric power) supply; ~**linienform** *(Auto)* streamline design (shape).
stromlinienförmiges Auto streamlined car.
Stromlinien|karosserie streamlined body; ~**wagen** streamlined car; ~**zug** streamliner *(US)*.
stromlos dead.
Strom|messer current (electricity) meter, power-factor meter; ~**mitte** midstream; ~**netz** power-supply system, mains; ~**polizei** river police; ~**polizist** water bailiff *(Br.)*; ~**preis** electricity rate; ~**rationierung** power rationing, brownout; ~**rechnung** electricity bill; ~**schiene** third (live) rail; ~**schiffahrt** river navigation; **kleine ~schnelle** ripple *(US)*; ~**schwankungen** fluctuations of current; ~**sicherung** fuse; ~**spannung** voltage, tension.
stromsparend power-saving.
Strom|sperre power cut (shutdown), blackout, electricity cut; ~**spitze** peak current; ~**spule** current coil; ~**stärke** current intensity (strength); ~**störung** current interference (failure); ~**stoß** jolt of electric current, current impulse; ~**tarif** electricity rate *(Br.)* (tariff, *US*); **gemischter ~tarif** two-charge rate.
Strömung current, flood, flow, stream, *(fig.)* current, trend, drift, tendency, drive, direction;
fortschrittliche ~en progressive tendencies; **revolutionäre ~** revolutionary trend;
von der ~ fortgerissen werden to be swept away by the current.
Strom|unterbrecher circuit (contact, current) breaker; ~**unterbrechung** power interruption; ~**unterbrechungsversicherung** power interruption insurance; ~**verbrauch** consumption of electricity, electric power supply, electricity sales; ~**verbraucher** consumer of electricity; ~**verhältnisse** river conditions; ~**versorgung** electric power (current) supply.
Stromversorgungs|anlage generating plant; ~**bezirk** public power district *(US)*; ~**kabel** power cable; ~**netz** electric grid system.
Strom|verteilung distribution of current; ~**weg** path of current; ~**wirtschaft** power industry; ~**zähler** electricity (power-factor) meter, current (demand, electricity) meter; ~**zölle** river dues; ~**zufuhr** supply of electricity; ~**zufuhr unterbrechen** to break the current, to black out the supply of electricity.
strotzen, vor Dreck to be thick with dirt; **von Fehlern ~** to be teeming with mistakes; **vor Gesundheit ~** to be in rude health.
Strudel whirlpool, vortex, *(Geschäft)* crush;
~ der Ereignisse whirligig (whirlpool) of events; **~ gesellschaftlicher Veranstaltungen** whirlpool of social engagements;
in einen ~ geraten to be caught up in a whirlpool; **in einen politischen ~ gezogen werden** to be drawn into the vortex of politics.
Struktur formation, arrangement of parts, structure, pattern, make-up, setup, constitution, *(Stoff)* fabric, texture;
demographische ~ audience composition; **gesellschaftliche ~** structure of society; **soziale ~** social structure (fabric);
~ des Kreditgeschäfts structure of the lending business; **wirtschaftliche ~ eines Landes** economic setup of a country;
~**analyse** structural analysis; ~**anpassung** structural adjustment.
strukturbedingte Arbeitslosigkeit structural (technological) unemployment.
strukturell structural;
~**e industrielle Abhängigkeit** structural interdependence; ~**e Arbeitslosigkeit** structural (technological) unemployment; ~**e Fehlentwicklung** structural distortion; ~**e Kapitalknappheit** fundamental shortage of capital; ~**e Tendenz** structural tendency; ~**e Unterschiede** structural disparities; ~**e Veränderungen** structural changes; ~**e Verschiebungen** structural shifts.

Struktur|fehler structural error; ~**hilfe** structural aid; ~**karte** structure map; ~**krise** structural crisis; ~**krisenkartell** rationalization cartel; ~**plan** structure plan *(Br.)*; **sektorale ~politik** industrial (regional economic) policy; ~**unterschied** structural discrepancy; ~**veränderung** structural change (alteration); ~**verbesserung** structural improvement, regional development; ~**verbesserungsbezirk** Economic Planning Region *(Br.)*; ~**verbesserungsprojekt** structural improvement scheme; ~**wandel** structural change; ~**wandel im Wohnungsbau** structure of housing tenure.

Strumpf, Geld in den ~ stecken to put aside for a rainy day; **im ~ sparen** to sock.

Strümpfe, sich auf die ~ machen to take to one's legs, to get a move on *(sl.)*.

Strumpf|fabrik hosiery factory; ~**industrie** hosiery manufacture.

Stübchen, behagliches snuggery.

Stube room;
gute ~ parlo(u)r;
immer in der ~ hocken to be a stay-at-home (stick-indoors), to frowst *(Br.)*.

Stuben|ältester *(mil.)* senior soldier; ~**appell** *(mil.)* bunk inspection; ~**arbeit** indoor work; ~**arrest** confinement to quarters, chamber arrest; ~**arrest haben** to be confined to one's quarters; ~**belegschaft** room complement; ~**dienst** barracks duty; ~**genosse** room-mate; ~**hocker** stick-indoors, stay-at-home *(US)*, homebody; ~**hocker sein** to frowst *(Br.)*; ~**mädchen** parlo(u)r maid, *(Hotel)* chambermaid; ~**nachbar** fellow lodger.

stubenrein *(Hund)* housebroken.

Stuck plaster of Paris.

Stück piece, unit, item, *(Abschnitt)* segment, slice, *(Bruchstück)* fragment, bit, shred, *(Buchauszug)* passage, patch, extract, *(Buchexemplar)* copy, *(Holz)* log, piece, *(Probestück)* specimen, *(Teil)* part, portion, article, *(Theater)* play, *(Weg)* distance, stretch, way, bit;
alle aus einem ~ all of one piece; **aus dem ~ genommen** taken from the bulk; **aus einem ~** of a piece, in one piece; **aus freien ~en** of one's own accord, of one's own free will, voluntarily, willingly; **in ~en zu zehn Dollar** issued in denominations of $ 10; **nach dem ~** by the tally; **pro ~** a (by the) piece, each;
~e *(Wertpapiere)* securities, stocks, shares, debentures, bonds; **albernes ~** silly thing; **einwandfreies ~** *(Wertpapier)* good delivery; **extravagantes ~** piece of extravagance; **fehlerfreies ~** effective unit; **fehlerhaftes ~** rejective, defective unit; **freches ~** cheeky brat; **sofort lieferbare ~e** *(Börse)* spot parcels; **miserables ~** rotten play; **nicht passendes ~** misfit; **seltenes ~** treasure, valuable stock, fly in an amber; **T-~** tee; **überarbeitetes ~** adaptation; **unverschämtes ~** piece of impertinence; **verloste ~e** drawn bonds (debentures); **winziges ~** morsel; **zugkräftiges ~** *(Theater)* box-office success *(US)*, popular play, drawing card *(US)*;
~e einer Anleihe individual bonds; **schweres ~ Arbeit** honest piece of work, hard row to hoe, difficult task, tough job; **~ Butter** lump of butter; **jedes ~ für einen Dollar** a dollar a piece; **~ Garten** garden plot; **schönes ~ Geld** nice little sum, nice piece of change *(sl.)*; **~ blauen Himmels** patch of blue sky; **~ Land** plot (nook) of land, lot *(US)*, tract (spot, strip, spread, parcel, slice, piece) of land; **abgestecktes ~ Land** location *(US)*; **nur ein ~ Papier** only a scrap of paper; **~ einer Rede** part of a speech; **~ Rindvieh** head of cattle; **schönstes ~ einer Sammlung** finest piece (gem) of a collection; **~ Seife** cake (tablet) of soap; **~ Stoff** piece of cloth; **kleines ~ die Straße hinunter** a spell down the road; **~ für ~** bit by bit, piecemeal, piece by piece, part by part, one at a time;
neues ~ aufführen to produce a new play; **in ~en zu 10.000 Dollar ausgeben** to issue in denominations of $ 10.000; **j. ein ~ begleiten** to set s. o. on his way; **wie ein ~ Dreck behandeln** to treat like dirt; **~ neu besetzen** to recast a play; **sich große ~e einbilden** to think no small beer of o. s.; **in tausend ~e gehen** to go into splinters; **jem. in vielen ~en gleichen** to take after s. o. in many ways; **schönes ~ Geld gespart haben** to have saved a nice bit of money; **große ~e von jem. halten** to think well (a great deal) of s. o.; **große ~e von sich halten** to fancy o. s., to think no small beer of o. s.; **Käse in einem ~ kaufen** to buy cheese unsliced; **mehrere ~e auswendig können** to know several parts by heart; **schönes ~ Geld kosten** to cost a pretty penny, to take plenty of dough; **sich für j. in ~e reißen lassen** to go through fire and water for s. o.; **sich ein tolles ~ leisten** to make a hash of s. th.; **j. ein ~ im Auto mitnehmen** to give s. o. a lift; **in ~e reißen** to tear (pull) to pieces; **in ~e schlagen** to dash to pieces, to knock into a cocked hat *(sl.)*; **etw. aus freien ~en tun** to do s. th. of one's own volition; **schönes ~ Geld verdienen** to make pots of money; **nach dem ~ verkaufen** to sell by the piece, to retail; **fünftausend ~ von einem Buch verkaufen** to sell 5000 copies; **gutes ~ vorankommen** *(Verhandlungen)* to make headway (progress); **gutes ~ Weges zurücklegen** to cover a fair distance;
~**akkord** job work, piece price; ~**arbeit** piecework, taskwork, jobbing, job work; ~**arbeiter** pieceworker, taskworker, job worker, jobber.

Stückchen particle;
~ blauen Himmels patch of blue sky.

Stück|dividende dividend per share; ~**einzelspanne** markup.

Stückekonto stock (securities) account, safe-deposit *(Br.)* (custodianship, *US*) account.

stückeln to cut into pieces, *(Anleihe)* to denominate, *(Börse)* to divide into shares.

Stückelung *(Aktien)* division (subdivision) into shares, *(Anleihe)* denomination;
in der ~ von in denominations of; **in kleiner ~** in small denominations;
vorläufige ~ temporary denomination.

Stückemangel scarcity (want) of securities.

Stückerfolgsrechnung job-order cost accounting.

Stückeschreiber playwright.

Stückeverzeichnis dispatch note, *(Inventar)* inventory, *(Sortenzettel)* bill of specie, numerical statement, *(Wertpapiere)* statement of securities deposited;
namentliches ~ specification.

Stückezuteilung allocation of shares.

Stück|fertigung job production *(US)*, manufacture to customer's specification; ~**fracht** mixed (general) cargo *(Br.)*, less-than-carload freight *(US)*; ~**gedinge** *(Bergbau)* lump bargain; ~**geld** notes and coins; ~**gewicht** individual weight, weight per unit.

Stückgut mixed (general) cargo *(Br.)*, small consignments, goods in parcels, astray freight, part loads, mixed carload *(US)*, less-than-carload (truckload) freight *(US)*, less-than-carload lot *(US)*, *(im Stück verkauft)* piece goods;
als ~ [versandt], mit ~ befrachtet freighted by parcels, less-than-car-load *(US)*, shipped in carloads *(US)*, laden in parcels; **Schiff mit ~ befrachten** to load a ship on the berth; **~ laden** to freight by (load in) parcels; **als ~ versenden** to convey (forward, ship, *US*) by goods (freight, *US*) train;
~**auftrag** less-than-carload order *(US)*; ~**bahnhof** parcels station; ~**befrachtung** berth freighting, loading on the berth, liner freighting, freighting by the case; ~**begleitschein** astray freight waybill; ~**dampfer** general cargo liner.

Stückgüter mixed (general) cargo, parcel goods, parcels, mixed carload *(US)*, mixed carload (freight) *(US)*, less-than-carload (truckload) freight *(US)*, *(im Stück verkauft)* piece goods.

Stückgut|fracht general (astray, less-than-carload, *US*) freight, liner freight, general merchandise, berth cargo; ~**frachtdienst** less-than-carload service *(US)*; ~**frachtgeschäft** berth freighting, less-than-carload business *(US)*; ~**ladung** general (mixed, *Br.*) cargo, mixed consignment, astray freight, parcels, mixed carload [freight] *(US)*, less-than-carload (truckload) *(US)*, consolidated carload freight *(US)*; ~**lieferung** drop shipment delivery, less-than-carload delivery *(US)*; ~**markt** piece market *(Br.)*; ~**mindestgewicht** minimum carload weight *(US)*; ~**sendung** packed parcels, general (mixed, *Br.*) cargo, mixed carload *(US)*, small-lot consignment, less-than-carload (truckload) shipment *(US)*; ~**sendungen** package freight, less-than-carload lots *(US)*, less-than-carloads *(US)*; ~**spediteur** general freight carrier; ~**tarif** all-commodity rate *(Br.)*, berth rate, mixed cargo rate *(Br.)*, less-than-carload rate *(US)*, less-than-truckload rate *(US)*, less-than-carload freight charges (rate) *(US)*, LCL-rates *(US)*, package freight *(US)*; ~**verkehr** berth freighting, retail traffic, part load traffic, less-than-carload business (traffic) *(US)*; ~**verpackung** less-than-carload packages *(US)*; ~**versand** less-than-carload (truckload) shipment *(US)*, less-than-carload business (traffic) *(US)*, berth freighting, packed parcels; ~**zustellung** less-than-carload delivery *(US)*.

Stück|kalkulationskarte product cost card; ~**kaufpreis** unit price; ~**kohle** lump coal.

Stückkosten unit (product) cost, cost per item (unit);
niedrigere ~ lower per-unit costs;
~**rechnung[ssystem]** job-order cost accounting, job-order costing.

Stück|kurs price per share; ~**leistung** *(Maschine)* output, capacity; ~**liste** piece list, bill of materials, specification; ~**lizenz** per-unit royalty.

Stücklohn task wages, piece (unit, job) wage, basic piece rate, piece-rate wages, piecework pay, wage on piece-work basis;
im ~ by the job;
reiner ~ straight piece rate;
~ mit garantiertem Mindestbetrag piecework with base guarantee;
im ~ arbeiten to [work by the] job; **j. im ~ beschäftigen** to put s. o. on piecework; **etw. im ~ bezahlen** to pay for by the piece; **~ erhalten** to be paid by the piece;
~arbeiten taskwork, piecework, jobbing, job work; **~arbeiter** jobber, job worker, pieceworker, taskworker, jobbing workman; **~berechnung** computation of piece-rate earnings; **~berechnungsformel** piece-rate formula; **~bezahlung** piece-work pay; **~ordnung** piece scale, piece price system; **~satz** job (piece) rate; **~system** straight (differential) piece-rate plan; **~verdienst** piecework (taskwork) earnings; **~verfahren** multiple piecework (differential piece rate) system, *(Gefangenenarbeit)* piece-price system; **~ware** bargain *(Br.)*.
Stück| muster sample; **~notiz** *(Börse)* unit quotation; **~nummer** serial number; **~pforte** cargo port; **~preis** piece (unit) price, throw *(sl.)*; **~rechnungssystem** job-order cost accounting, job-order costing; **~schuld** determinate obligation; **~steuer** specific tax; **~tarif** piece rates; **~verkauf** retail sale; **nur im ~verkauf** sold only by the piece; **~verzeichnis** inventory specification; **~ware** piece goods.
stückweise piecemeal, piece by piece, by the piece, in bits and pieces, by (in) parcels, by retail, by the job;
~ einkaufen to buy piecemeal; **~ nachzählen** to tally; **Waren ~ verkaufen** to sell goods by the piece; **Waren ~ versenden** to send goods in small units.
Stückwerk piecework, patchwork.
Stückzahl piece number, piece, *(Anzahl, Einheiten)* number of units, quantity;
nach der ~ by the piece;
börsenübliche ~ marketable parcel; **rationelle ~** economic lot size.
Stück| zeichnung detail drawing; **~zeit** job (individual production, machining) time; **~zeitakkord** job work, taskwork, piecework.
Stückzinsen accrued interest, *(zusätzliche Zinsen)* additional interest;
ausschließlich ~ ex[cluding] interest; **einschließlich ~** cum (with) interest.
Stückzoll specific duty (tariff).
Student [university] student, college boy (man), undergraduate, colleger *(US)*, *(früherer)* alumnus *(US)*;
auf die ~en beschränkt intramural;
auswärtiger ~ extramural student *(Br.)*; **in der Ausbildung befindlicher ~** preparatory student; **ehemaliger ~** alumnus; **meine ehemaligen ~en** my former students; **ewiger ~** skull *(sl.)*; **fleißiger ~** close student; **mit Mitteln des Bundesausbildungsgesetzes geförderter ~** student in receipt of a grant from public funds; **gegängelte ~en** spoonfed-students; **intelligenter ~** smart student; **knickriger ~** sofa lizard *(sl.)*; **leistungsschwacher ~** under-achieved *(US)*;
~ mit höchstem Ausbildungssatz student on full grant; **~ im dritten Jahr** junior *(US)*; **~ im zweiten Jahr** sophomore *(US)*; **~ im ersten Semester** first-year man, freshman, fresher *(Br., sl.)*; **~ im Vorbereitungsdienst** preparatory student; **~ auf Zeit** part-time student;
unterdurchschnittlich begabte ~en haben to have poor students in a year; **~en immatrikulieren** to enter a student at a university, to matriculate a student; **~en relegieren** to expel (rusticate) a student, to send a student down *(Br.)*.
Studenten| abonnement student subscription; **~ausschuß** student council; **~austausch** exchange of students, student exchange; **~ausweis** identification card *(US)*, student's union card *(Br.)*; **~beihilfe** *(Bafög)* student grant; **~bude** digs *(coll.)*; **~demonstration** student demonstration; **~förderungsprogramm** Work-Study Program *(US)*; **~führer** campus leader; **~gemeinschaft** fellowship of students; **~generation** campus generation; **~heim** [student] hostel *(Br.)*, hall of residence *(Br.)*, dormitory *(US)*; **~jahre** university years, college time; **~jahrgang** class *(US)*; **~leben** student life; **~liebchen** college widow *(US)*; **~proteste** campus protests; **~publikum** audience of students; **~schaft** students, student body; **~unruhen** student riots (disturbances, unrest), campus disorders; **~vereinigung, ~verbindung** fraternity; **~viertel** student's quarter; **~werk** student welfare organization; **~wohnheim** hall of residence *(Br.)*, hostel *(Br.)*, dormitory *(US)*.
Studentin woman student.
studentisch undergraduate.
Studie study, sketch, essay.
Studien studying, studies, pursuits;
seine ~ beenden to finish one's studies; **seine ~ fortsetzen** to continue one's studies;
~anstalt secondary school, grammar school *(Br.)*, high school *(US)*; **~ausgabe** textbook edition; **~ausschuß** study commission; **~beihilfe** student aid, study grant, scholarship, studentship *(US)*; **~berater** student (faculty, *US*) adviser, councellor *(US)*; **~bescheinigung** student's union card *(Br.)*, identification card *(US)*; **~direktor** headmaster, principal *(US)*; **~einrichtungen** facilities for study; **~fach** study; **fakultative ~fächer** optional studies; **soziologische ~fächer** social studies; **~fahrt** field trip; **~freund** college friend; **umfassendes ~gebiet** wide field of studies; **~gebühren** university fees, tuition; **~gebühr für Nichtansässige** nonresident tuition; **~geldversicherung** endowment insurance; **~genosse** fellow student, bookmate; **~gruppe** study group; **~jahr** session *(Br.)*; **~jahre** years of study; **~kollege** fellow student, bookmate; **~kommission** study commission; **~kreis** study group; **~lehrgang** course of study; **~leiter** principal lecturer; **~mittel** sabbatical funds; **~objekt** study; **am ~ort** up *(Br.)*; **in den Ferien am ~ort bleiben** to stay up for the vacations *(Br.)*; **~plan** syllabus, curriculum; **zentrale ~platzvergabe** The Universities Central Council on Admissions (UCCA, *Br.*); **~professor** professional fellow; **~quartal** quarter *(US)*; **~rat** master; **~reform** educational reform; **~reise** study tour, field trip; **~richtung** study side *(Br.)*; **~seminar** seminar; **~semester** term *(Br.)*, session; **~stiftung** scholarship; **~urlaub** sabbatical leave; **bezahlten ~urlaub haben** to be on sabbatical; **~zeit** preparation *(Br.)*, college years; **nach beendigter ~zeit** postgraduate; **~zweig** study life *(Br.)*.
studieren to study, to go to college, to read *(Br.)*;
eifrig ~ to pore over, to pound the books *(sl.)*; **Frage eingehend ~** to make a detailed investigation (close study) of a problem; **Materie eingehend ~** to read up on a matter; **mit Erfolg ~** to study profitably; **gründlich ~** to study up; **als Hauptfach ~** to major in a subject *(US)*; **anstelle von Medizin jetzt Jura ~** to leave medicine for the law; **Rechtswissenschaft ~** to read for the bar, to eat one's terms *(Br.)*; **auf der Universität ~** to keep one's terms *(Br.)*;
Sohn an der Universität ~ lassen to maintain a son at the university; **~ wollen** to go on to higher education.
studiert educated, lettered;
~ haben to have had a university education, to be a university man, to have been through the university.
Studierter graduate, egg head *(US sl.)*.
Studierzimmer study, cabinet, sanctum, library.
Studio studio, lot, atelier;
außerhalb des ~s *(Filmaufnahme)* on location;
fahrbares ~ mobile study; **schalldichtes ~** soundproof broadcasting studio;
~einrichtungen studio facilities; **~gelände** studio real estate, location; **~leiter** *(Fernsehen, Rundfunk)* stage manager; **~redakteur** presenting editor; **~sendung** studio broadcast.
Studium study, studies, university (college) education, undergraduate work, *(Forschung)* research work;
abgeschlossenes ~ academic qualification; **eingehendes ~** deep (comprehensive) study; **fakultatives ~** elective *(US)*; **fortgeschrittenes ~** advanced studies; **mit praktischer Ausbildung gekoppeltes ~** corporative education; **~ generale** general science; **gründliches ~** detailed study; **intensives ~** intense study; **kostenloses ~** free university education; **nächtliches ~** lamp oil; **regelrechtes ~** formal study; **übermäßiges ~** overstudy; **ununterbrochenes ~** continuous studies;
~ mit zwischenzeitlicher praktischer Ausbildung corporative plan (education); **~ der Betriebsführung** management study; **~ der einschlägigen Fachliteratur** studying the relevant literature; **~ der Rechtswissenschaft** reading for the bar;
sein ~ abschließen to pursue one's studies to the end, to finish one's studies; **ganztägiges ~ absolvieren** to receive full-time instruction at a university; **sein ~ in M absolvieren** to graduate from the M university; **sich sein ~ vom Munde absparen** to pinch and spare for one's study; **langjähriges ~ bedingen** to presuppose long years of study; **sich mit dem ~ von etw. befassen** to work professionally on s. th.; **mit dem ~ der Rechtswissenschaften beginnen** to take up law; **staatswissenschaftliches ~ ergreifen** to study politics; **jds. ~ finanzieren** to finance s. one's education; **sein ~ fortsetzen** to continue one's studies; **abgeschlossenes ~ haben** to have a university degree; **sein ~ gerade beendet haben** to come fresh from college; **dem ~**

nichts abgewinnen können to have no taste for study; seinem ~ obliegen to prosecute one's studies; eifrig seinem ~ obliegen to be a hard reader; für jds. ~ äußerst wertvoll sein to be of great value to s. o. in his studies; sich sein ~ als Werkstudent verdienen to work one's way through college; mit seinem ~ vorankommen to progress (get on) with one's studies; sich seinem ~ widmen to give one's time to study.

Studiums|abschluß, mit university-trained; ~**kosten** student expenses; ~**zuschuß** study grant.

Stufe step, stair, *(Grad)* grade, degree, remove, *(Niveau)* level, standard, *(Rakete)* stage, step, *(Rang)* rank, echelon, *(Schule)* standard *(Br.)*, grade *(US)*;
auf gleicher ~ on a level; **auf der höchsten** ~ at the top of the ladder;
~**n des Beschaffungsprozesses** purchasing level; **erste** ~ **zum Erfolg** first stepping-stone to success; **höchste** ~ **des Glücks** height of happiness; **kritische** ~ **einer Krankheit** critical stages of an illness; **nächste** ~**n seiner Laufbahn** next rank of one's career; ~ **in der gesellschaftlichen Rangordnung** steps in the social scale;
~**n abtreten** to wear away the steps; ~**n des Erfolgs emporklimmen** to climb the ladder to success; **höchste** ~**n des Ruhms erreichen** to reach the pinnacle of one's fame; **mit jem. auf gleicher** ~ **stehen** to be on the same level (equality) with s. o.; **auf einer niedrigen** ~ **stehen** *(Volk)* to be of a low order; **auf die gleiche** ~ **stellen** to equate, to treat as equivalent.

Stufenakkord step bonus.

stufenartig angeordnet gradually.

Stufen|ausbildung in-service training; ~**flexibilität** *(Wechselkurse)* crawling (floating) peg; ~**folge** graduation, progression; ~**landschaft** terraced landscape; ~**leiter** gradation, gamut, stair; ~**leiter zum Erfolg** ladder to success; ~**leiterverfahren** *(innerbetriebliche Leistungsverrechnung)* step-ladder system; ~**plan** graduated plan, *(Werbung)* cream plan; ~**preise** shaded prices; ~**rabatt** chain discount; ~**rakete** step rocket; ~**satz** *(Versicherung)* step rate; ~**tarif** graded (flexible) tariff; **ökonomische** ~**theorie** theory of economic stages.

stufenweise by progressive stages, gradually, by degrees;
~ **Anpassung** gradualism; ~ **Wechselkursänderung** dynamic peg; ~**r Zollabbau** gradual reduction of tariffs.

Stuhl, vor dem ~ **des Richters** before the judge;
elektrischer ~ [death] chair *(US)*;
jem. einen ~ **anbieten** to offer s. o. a seat; **jem. den** ~ **vor die Tür setzen** to show s. o. the door, to turn s. o. out, to give s. o. the sack *(sl.)*.

Stühle, sich zwischen zwei ~ **setzen** to fall between two stools.

stumm mute, dumb;
~ **wie ein Fisch** mute as a fish; **vor Schreck** ~ speechless with terror;
auf alle Fragen ~ **bleiben** to remain silent to all questions; **jem.** ~ **einen Brief reichen** to hand s. o. a letter without saying a word;
~**er Diener** dump waiter; ~**e Person** *(Theater)* walking part; ~**es Spiel** pantomime; ~**er Verkäufer** counter display, dummy salesman, container.

Stummabstimmung quiet automatic volume control.

Stummel *(Zigarette)* fag end, stub, butt *(US)*.

Stummfilm silent film (movie).

Stumpen *(Zigarre)* cheroot, stogie *(US)*.

Stümper tamperer, dilettante, patcher, vamper, duffer *(Br., coll.)*, butcher, amateur, lobster *(sl.)*.

Stümperei patchery, tinker, botch, bungle, amateur work.

stümperhaft dabbling, botchy, dilettantish, hashed, blunkeye;
~**e Arbeit** bad job, bungle, slopwork, slipshod work, hash *(Br., coll)*.

stümpern to boggle, to bungle, to hash, to make a mess.

Stumpf, mit ~ **und Stiel ausrotten** to destroy s. th. root and branch.

stumpf dull, edgeless, blunt, *(teilnahmslos)* apathetic, stolid, dull;
j. ~ **anblicken** to look at s. o. impassively.

Stumpfsinn dullness, stolidity, apathy.

stumpfsinnig dull, apathetic, tedious, drab, vegetable;
Arbeit ~ **finden** to find work deadly dull;
~**e Arbeit** tedious (drab, monotonous) work; ~**es Leben führen** to lead a drab existence.

Stunde hour, *(Unterricht)* lesson, session;
in einer schwachen ~ in a weak moment; **in vorgerückter** ~ late at night; **zu der bezeichneten** ~ at the hour indicated; **zu später** ~ at a late hour of the day; **zu einer unpassenden** ~ at an unreasonable (ungodly) hour; **zur rechten** ~ at the right time; **zur verabredeten** ~ at the appointed time;
aktuelle ~ live broadcast; **anrechenbare** ~ *(Universität)* hour; **freie** ~ off (loose) hour; **geschlagene** ~ solid hour; **knappe** ~ short hour; **verkehrsarme** ~**n** slack hours; **verkehrsreichste** ~**n** peak (rush) hours;
~**n nach Mitternacht** the early hours; ~ **um** ~ hour by hour; **nach der** ~ **bezahlen** to pay by the hour; ~**n geben** to give lessons; ~**n nehmen** to take lessons; **jede** ~ **verkehren** to run every hour; **auf eine** ~ **vorbeikommen** to drop in for an hour; **eine** ~ **vorgehen** to move an hour ahead; **Gunst der** ~ **wahrnehmen** to take time by the foreclock; **geschlagene** ~ **warten** to wait a full hour;
seine ~ **ist gekommen** his sands are running low.

stunden to [grant a] respite, to indulge a debtor, to respite payment, to time, to give time, to allow [a] time, to hold over; **Zahlung** ~ to extend the term of (allow a respite in) payment.

Stunden|begrenzung hours limit; **24-~-Dienst** round-the-clock service; ~**durchschnitt** *(Auto)* average speed per hour; **tatsächlich geleisteter** ~**durchschnitt** actual hours; ~**durchschnittslöhne** average hourly earnings; ~**geben** giving lessons (tuition); **sich mit** ~**geben durchbringen** to teach for a living; **sich durch** ~**geben Geld verdienen** to earn a living by teaching; ~**geld** [coaching] fee; ~**hotel** house of ill fame; ~**kilometer** mile per hour; **140** ~**kilometer fahren** to go a hundred miles an hour; **auf 50** ~**kilometer heruntergehen** to throttle down a car to thirty miles an hour.

stundenlang|benötigen to take hours over s. th.; ~ **erzählen** to talk for hours on end.

Stunden|leistung *(Maschine)* output per hour, hourly output, *(Mensch)* hourly efficiency, output per man-hour; ~**liste** time sheet.

Stundenlohn hourly wage (rate), wage per hour, pay by the day;
durchschnittlicher ~ average hourly earnings; **garantierter** ~ clock-card rate; **tariflicher** ~ standard hourly wage; **üblicher** ~ occupational rate;
im ~ **arbeiten** to be paid by the hour; **jem. einen** ~ **von 4 Dollar zahlen** to pay s. o. at the rate of 4 dollars an hour;
~**arbeit** time work; ~**kosten** hourly employment costs; ~**satz** hourly rate of pay; **garantierter** ~**tarif** guaranteed hourly rate; ~**vergütung** hourly compensation.

Stunden|plan timetable, syllabus, schedule *(US)*; ~**platte** *(Briefkasten)* notice plate; **im 24-~rhythmus** round the clock; ~**satz** hourly (time) rate; **mit dem** ~**schlag** on the stroke; ~**verdienst** hourly earnings.

stundenweise|berechnen to charge by the hour; **j.** ~ **einstellen** to employ s. o. by the hour; ~ **verkehren** to run every hour;
~ **bezahlt werden** to be paid by time;
~ **bezahlter Arbeiter** hourly employee; ~ **Beschäftigung** casual employment; ~ **Bezahlung** pay by the hour.

Stunden|zeiger hour hand; ~**zettel** time card (ticket, *US*).

Stündlein, sein letztes his last hour.

stündlich hourly, every hour;
j. ~ **erwarten** to expect s. o. any minute; ~ **verkehren** to run every hour;
~**er Zugverkehr** hourly train service.

Stundung respite [for payment], letter of respite, time to pay, allowance of time, delay in payment, postponement, forbearance, extension agreement, *(Wechsel)* indulgence;
~ **einer Geldstrafe** time to pay a fine;
~ **beantragen** to apply for a term of respite; ~ **gewähren** to [grant a] respite, to respite payment; **sich mit seinen Gläubigern wegen einer** ~ **verständigen** to arrange with one's creditors for an extension of time.

Stundungs|antrag request for respite; ~**frist** days of grace, respite, period of extension; ~**gesuch** request (application) for respite; ~**gesuch stellen** to apply for a respite; ~**vereinbarung**, ~**verlängerung** letter of licence (respite), extension agreement; ~**zinsen** interest for delay.

Stunk hullabaloo, rumpus;
~ **machen** to kick up a row, to raise hell *(sl.)*.

stupid stupid, dull, thick;
Arbeit ~ **finden** to find a work deadly dull.

stur stubborn, obstinate, pigheaded, mulish, dogged, cussed *(coll.)*;
~ **und steif behaupten** to swear black and blue; ~ **an seiner Meinung festhalten** to stick (cling) obstinately to one's opinion;
seine ~**e Haltung nicht aufgeben** not to move an inch; ~**er Mensch** wronghead, pighead, mule.

Sturm storm, blast, gale *(Br.)*, *(Gefühle)* flush, rush, *(mil.)* assault, charge, onset, attack;
von einem ~ **überrascht** overtaken by a storm;

abklingender ~ tail of a storm; **gewaltiger** ~ violent storm, whole gale; **ungewöhnlich heftiger** ~ freak storm; **innerer** ~ turmoil, commotion; **verheerender** ~ destructive storm;
~ **auf die Banken** run on the banks; ~ **und Drang** storm and stress; ~ **der Entrüstung** storm of anger, outcry of indignation; ~ **auf Erdölaktien** run on oil stocks; ~ **auf den Feind** dash at the enemy; ~ **auf die Geschäfte** wild rush (run) on the shops; ~ **von Protesten** storm of protest; ~ **auf die Sitzplätze** rush for seats; ~ **im Wasserglas** storm in a teacup;
~ **in einem Lande entfachen** to stir up a political storm in a country; **jds. Herz im** ~ **erobern** to take s. one's heart by storm; **gegen die Parteiorganisation** ~ **laufen** to run against the political machine; **gegen eine neue Steuererhöhung** ~ **laufen** to be up in arms against the increase of taxes; **gegen neue Steuervorschläge** ~ **laufen** to raise a hue and cry against new tax proposals; ~ **läuten** to ring the doorbell vehemently; **im** ~ **nehmen** *(mil.)* to carry by assault, to take by storm; **Festung im** ~ **nehmen** to assault a fortress; **den Gewalten des** ~**s ausgesetzt sein** to be exposed to the fury of the elements; ~ **überstehen** to weather (live through) a storm;
das Thermometer steht auf ~ *(fig.)* there is a storm brewing;
~**angriff** assault, charge, attack; ~**anzeichen** indication of storm; ~**bahn** track of a storm, storm track; ~**bataillon** assault battalion; ~**bö** white squall; ~**boot** assault boat; ~**deck** hurricane (weather) deck.

stürmen to storm, to rage, *(mil.)* to [to take by] storm, to assault;
~ **und schneien** to be storming and snowing;
Bank ~ to make a run on a bank; **Boote** ~ to rush the boats; **Geschäfte** ~ to make a rush on the shops; **gegnerische Stellung** ~ to take the enemy's position by assault.

Sturm|fahne warning flag; ~**feld** storm area.

sturmfest stormproof.

Sturm|flut flood tide; ~**gepäck** combat pack; ~**gewehr** automatic rifle; ~**glocke** storm bell.

stürmisch stormy, tempestuous, windy, *(heftig)* violent, vehement, turbulent;
nicht so ~ take it easy;
~**er Aufschwung** boom; ~**er Beifall** round of applause, roaring (frenzied) applause; **bei teilweise** ~**em Geschäft** with dealings brisk at times; ~**er Kursanstieg** skyrocketing *(US)*; ~**er Liebhaber** passionate lover; ~**es Meer** rough sea; ~**e Nachfrage** huge demand; ~**e Überfahrt** stormy crossing, rough passage; ~**e Versammlung** stormy (tempestuous, tumultuous) meeting; ~**es Wachstum** rapid expansion; ~**er Wind** fresh gale.

Sturm|laterne storm lantern, hurricane lamp; ~**läuten** sounding the alarm, tocsin; ~**lücke** breach; ~**schäden** damage caused by storm, storm damage; ~**schädenversicherung** storm and tempest insurance, tornado insurance *(US)*; **im** ~**schritt** at (on, *US*) the double; ~**signal** storm signal; ~**trupp** *(mil.)* storming party, storm troops; ~**warnung** notice of a storm, storm (gale, *Br.*) warning; ~**wind** wind; ~- **und Drangzeit** salad days *(sl.)*; ~**zentrum** storm center *(US)* (centre, *Br.*); ~**zone** storm zone, eye of the storm.

Sturz fall, precipitation, plunge, *(Kurse, Preise)* drop, slump, crash, collapse, decline, tumble, heavy fall, *(Minister)* fall, overthrow, *(Temperatur)* drop, fall, sudden change, *(Ungnade)* disgrace, *(Untergang)* downfall, downcome, ruin;
größter je gezeitigter ~ **der Aktienkurse** worst-ever slump in share prices; ~ **des Frankenkurses** slump in the franc; ~ **der Regierung** collapse of ministry, overthrow (fall, subversion) of the government; ~ **eines Reiches** fall of an empire;
neuen ~ **erfahren** *(Aktien)* to experience a fresh decline; ~ **der Aktienkurse ins Gegenteil umkehren** to reverse a nose-dive in share prices;
~**acker** new-ploughed (-plowed, *US*) field; ~**bach von Worten** torrent of words; ~**bomber** dive bomber.

stürzen to fall, to overthrow, *(Flugzeug)* to nose-dive, to power-dive, *(Kurse, Preise)* to tumble, to collapse, to drop, to plunge downward, to plummet, to slump;
j. ~ to bring s. o. down, to force s. o. to resign; **sich in etw.** ~ to go to town on s. th.; **sich in ein Abenteuer** ~ to rush into an undertaking; **sich in die Arbeit** ~ to plunge into business; **sich in jds. Arme** ~ to fling o. s. into s. one's arms; **sich in extravagante Ausgaben** ~ to launch out into extravagance; **j. ins Elend** ~ to be the death of s. o.; **über die eigenen Fehler** ~ to perish by one's own mistakes; **sich auf den Feind** ~ to swoop down on the enemy; **ans Fenster** ~ to rush to the window; **sich aus dem Fenster** ~ to throw o. s. out of the window; **sich blindlings in die Gefahr** ~ to rush headlong into danger; **von einem Gerüst** ~ to fall from a scaffold; **sich wieder ins Getümmel** ~ to jump back into the fray; **Kasse** ~ to make up the cash; **Land in einen Krieg** ~ to plunge a country into war; **ins Meer** ~ *(Flugzeug)* to crash into the sea; **Minister** ~ to unseat a minister; **Monarchie** ~ to subvert the monarchy; **sich auf die wenigen leeren Plätze** ~ to make a beeline for the few empty seats; **Regierung** ~ to overthrow (upset) the government, to throw out of power; **sich tief in Schulden** ~ to plunge into debt; **auf die Straße** ~ to dash onto the street; **sich in Unkosten** ~ to launch out into (go to) expenses, to spend a lot of money; **sich in große Unkosten** ~ to incur heavy expenses; **ins Zimmer** ~ to pounce (plunge) into a room;
nicht ~! This side up! Keep upright!

Sturzflug nose-dive;
~ **abfangen** to pull out of a nose-dive; ~ **machen** to dive, to power-dive, to nose-dive.

Sturzgüter bulk (loose) goods, goods laden in bulk;
~ **laden** *(Schiff)* to load in bulk;
~**befrachtung** loading in bulk; ~**sendung** bulk shipment; ~**verlust** shortage of bulk.

Sturz|helm motorcycle helmet, crash helmet, skid lid *(Br., sl.)*; ~**see** surge, roller, breakers.

Stuß footle, nonsense.

Stützbalken shore, prop, bracket, principal rafter.

Stütze foothold, prop, crutch, *(fig.)* keystone, support, backing, arm, asset, mainstay, buttress, easer, stay, *(Gehilfe)* subsidiary;
mächtige ~ tower of strength;
~ **seines Alters** mainstay of one's old age; ~ **seiner Familie** chief stay (support) of one's family; ~ **für das Gedächtnis** aid to memory, memory aid, *(Werbung)* aided recall; ~**n der Gesellschaft** pillars (props) of society; ~ **der Hausfrau** lady help *(Br.)*; ~ **der Regierung** pillars of government;
feste ~ **in jem. finden** to rely heavily on s. o.

Stutzen pipe connection, fitting.

stutzen to become suspicious, to hesitate.

stützen to support, to back, *(Anspruch)* to base on, to predicate, *(Kurs)* to peg, *(Theorie)* to base, to found;
sich ~ to rest upon; **Ansicht auf etw.** ~ to found an opinion on s. th.; **sich auf jds. Arm** ~ to lean on s. one's arm; **seine Beweisführung auf Tatsachen** ~ to ground one's arguments on facts; **Franken** ~ to give support to the Franc; **Konjunktur** ~ to underpin the economy; **Preise** ~ to maintain (peg, uphold, buttress, valorize) prices; **seine Theorie auf das Buch eines berühmten Gelehrten** ~ to base one's theory on a famous scholar; **Währung** ~ to back the currency; **englische Währung** ~ to peg the rate of sterling exchange; **sich auf eine Zeugenaussage** ~ to be based on the evidence of a witness.

Stutzer pink, jackanapes, nut, buck, dandy, fashionmonger, Johnny *(Br., sl.)*, heavy swell *(Br.)*.

stutzig machen, j. to boggle s. one's mind, to make s. o. hesitate.

Stütz|kurs pegged (supported) price; ~**mauer** retaining (sustaining, breast) wall; ~**pfahl** prop; ~**pfeiler** buttress, abutment; ~**pfeiler der Konjunktur** support for economic activity; ~**preis** support[ed] (cushioning) price; ~**punkt** base; **schwimmender** ~**punkt** floating base.

Stützung support, backing;
~ **der Agrarpreise** farm price support *(US)*; ~ **des Klagevorbringens auf Vertrag anstelle von unerlaubter Handlung** waiver of tort; ~ **eines Kurses** support of a price, price support; ~ **der Währung** backing of currency; ~ **des Wechselkurses** pegging the exchange; **ermessensmäßig vorgenommene** ~ **des Wechselkurses** discretionary crawling peg *(US)*;
~ **des Marktes durchführen** to peg the market.

Stützungsaktion support measures;
~ **durch die Banken** banking support;
~**en für den Pfundkurs durchführen** to support the sterling rate of exchange; ~ **unternehmen** to rescue (hold) the market.

Stützungsauftrag supporting order.

stützungsbedürftig deserving support.

Stützungskäufe support, support buying, backing, supporting orders (purchases), *(Notenbank)* back-door operation *(Br.)*;
infolge von ~**n der Haussepartei** on bull support;
~ **durch ein Konsortium** pool support;
~ **für Aktien durchführen** to support stocks.

Stützungs|kredit emergency (stand-by) credit; ~**kurs** pegged price; ~**kurs des Franken** rate at which the franc has been established; ~**maßnahmen** support measures; ~**operation** pegging operation; ~**politik** support policy; **angebotsbeschränkende** ~**politik** valorization scheme; ~**preis** pegged (supported) price; ~**syndikat** supporting syndicate; ~**vereinbarung** support arrangement.

Stützwerk underpinning.
subaltern subaltern, subordinate, obsequious, underling.
Subalternbeamter subordinate (inferior) officer, underling.
Subalterner sub *(sl.)*.
Subhastation judicial sale, *(Grundstück)* foreclosure.
Subjekt subject, individual, legal entity;
übles ~ bad lot, blackguard, nasty individual; **verdächtiges** ~ suspicious individual (character); **verkommenes** ~ reprobate.
subjektiv subjective;
~**er Tatbestand** mental element of an offence.
Submission invitation for tenders, contractor's offer, invitation to bid *(US)*, bid invitation *(US)*, bidding;
in ~ by contract;
bei einer ~ **leer ausgehen** to lose out on a bidding; ~ **ausschreiben** to invite tenders (bids) for a subscription; **sich an der** ~ **für eine neue Autobahn beteiligen** to tender for the construction of a new motorway; **an einer** ~ **teilnehmen** to participate in a tender; ~ **veranstalten** to put out to tender; **in** ~ **vergeben** to put out work, to give out by contract.
Submissionsangebot tender, contractor's estimate (award);
versiegeltes ~ sealed tender (bid, *US*);
~ **machen** to tender, to make a tender for a contract; **niedrigeres** ~ **machen** to outbid; **an das niedrigste** ~ **vergeben** to allocate to the lowest tender.
Submissions|anzeiger contract journal; ~**aufforderung** call for tenders; ~**bedingungen** specification [of work to be done], terms of tender, tender instructions; ~**bewerber** contractor, tenderer, bidder; ~**bogen**, ~**formular** form of tender; ~**frist** bidding (tender) period; ~**garantie** guarantee of tender, bid (performance) bond *(US)*; ~**gebot** tender; ~**kartell** bidding cartel; ~**lieferant** contractor; ~**offerte** tender; ~**preis** contract (tender, offering) price; ~**termin** submission date; ~**unterlagen** tender documents; ~**verfahren** competitive bidding, bidding process (procedure); ~**vergebung** allocation by tenders, award of contract; ~**verkauf** sale by sealed tender (bids); ~**versicherung** contract insurance; ~**vertrag** contract; **sich um einen** ~**vertrag bemühen** to tender for a supply of goods.
Submissionswege, auf dem by tender;
Arbeit im ~ **ausschreiben** to invite tenders (bids) for a subscription; **im** ~ **vergeben** to allocate by tender, to put work out to contract.
Submittent tenderer, bidder.
Subrogationsrechte subrogation rights.
subsidiär subsidiary, subordinate.
Subsidien subsidy, subsidies;
durch ~ **unterstützt** state-fed, bounty-fed;
~ **gewähren** to grant a subsidy, to subsidize; **einem Verbündeten** ~ **gewähren** to grant a subsidy to an ally; **durch** ~ **unterstützen** to subsidize; ~ **zahlen** to give (pay) a subsidy;
~**bedarf** subsidy requirements; ~**fonds** subsidy fund; ~**vertrag** subsidiary treaty.
Subskribent subscriber;
~**en sammeln** to canvass subscribers, to solicit subscriptions.
Subskribentenliste subscription list;
sich in eine ~ **eintragen** to enrol(l) as subscriber;
Subskribentensammler book canvasser (agent), solicitor *(US)*.
subskribieren to subscribe, to enrol(l) as subscriber;
auf ein Buch ~ to subscribe for a book.
Subskription subscription;
~ **in Raten bezahlen** to pay a subscription in instal(l)ments.
Subskriptions|abteilung subscription department; ~**angebot** subscription offer (solicitation); ~**ankündigung**, ~**anzeige** prospectus, proposal for subscriptions; ~**anteil** subscription share; ~**anzeige einer neuen Gesellschaft** company prospectus; ~**aufforderung für eine Anleihe** invitation to the public to subscribe to a loan; ~**auftrag** subscription order; ~**ausgabe** subscription edition; ~**bedingungen** terms of subscription; ~**buch** subscription book; ~**dauer** period of subscription; ~**dienst** subscription service; ~**einladung** invitation to subscribe, bid invitation *(US)*; ~**erneuerung** renewal of subscription; ~**formular** subscription form; ~**frist** subscription period; ~**gebühr** subscription fee (charge).
Subskriptionsliste subscription list, list of subscribers;
~ **auflegen** to open a subscription list, to start a fund; **jds. Namen in eine** ~ **mit 20 Dollar einsetzen** to put s. o. down for $ 20; ~ **erweitern** to swell the number of subscribers; ~ **schließen** to close a subscription list.
Subskriptions|preis subscription price (fee), prepublication price; ~**recht** subscription privilege; ~**scheck** subscription check *(US)* (cheque, *Br.*); ~**schein** subscription warrant *(US)*; ~**summe** subscription, amount subscribed; ~**verein** proprietary club; ~**verfahren** subscription method, bidding process; ~**vertrag** subscription contract; ~**vordruck** subscription blank *(US)*; **im** ~**wege** subscriptive; **Buch im** ~**wege vertreiben** to canvass a territory for a subscription book.
substantiell substantial, material;
~**e Abnutzung** depletion.
substantiieren to state full particulars, to detail;
Anspruch ~ to substantiate a claim; **Klage** ~ to substantiate an action.
Substantiierung substantiation, statement of particulars;
hinreichende ~ particularity; **mangelnde** ~ insufficiency;
~ **einer Forderung** substantiation of claim.
Substanz substance, material, body, *(Kapital)* principal, *(Vermögen)* property, total assets, resources;
moralische ~ moral fiber (fibre, *Br.*);
in der ~ **abschreibbar** depletable;
~ **eines Vorrats angreifen** to draw heavily on the stocks; **wenig** ~ **haben** to be of little substance; **von der** ~ **leben** to live on (off) the capital;
vorsätzliche ~**beschädigung** active waste; ~**erhaltung** conservation of assets; **für** ~**schäden haften** *(Pächter)* to be impeachable for waste; ~**schadenersatz** *(Grundstück)* fee damages.
Substanzschädigung commissive waste;
unzulässige ~ equitable waste; **vorsätzliche** ~ voluntary (positive) waste.
Substanz|schwund dwindling assets; ~**steuer** capital levy; **werterhöhende** ~**veränderung** ameliorative waste; ~**verlust** loss of substance; ~**vernichtung von Bodenschätzen verlangsamen** to slow the depletion of resources; **entstandene** ~**verringerung** accrued depletion; ~**verringerungskosten** depletion expenses; **doppelte** ~**verschlechterung** double waste; **gewöhnliche** ~**verschlechterung** natural waste; ~**verschlechterung eintreten lassen** to waste; ~**verzehr** consumption, depletion; **dem** ~**verzehr unterworfen** depletable; **dem** ~**verzehr unterliegen** to be of a wasting character; ~**wert** assets value, *(Wertpapiere)* breakdown value; ~**zerstörung** destruction of the substance, abuse.
substituieren to substitute;
j. ~ to act as substitute for s. o.
Substituierung substitution.
Substitut substitute, assistant.
Substitutions|effekt substitution effect; ~**güter** substitute articles; ~**kostentheorie** theory of opportunity costs; ~**prinzip** principle of substitution.
subtil subtle, delicate;
~**e Unterscheidung** subtle distinction.
substrahieren to substract.
Substraktion substraction.
Subtraktionszeichen subtraction sign (mark).
subtropisch subtropical.
Subvention subvention, subsidy, grant, *(an Industrie)* bonus;
im Wege der ~ state-fed, bounty-fed;
~**en** subsidies, grants-in-aid *(US)*;
öffentliche (staatliche) ~ state (government) subsidy, government grant, grant-in-aid *(US)*; **versteckte** ~ under-the-counter subsidy;
~ **zum Ausgleich für Konstruktionskosten** *(Schiffahrt)* construction differential subsidy *(US)*; ~ **zum Ausgleich für höhere Unterhaltungskosten** operating differential subsidy *(US)*; ~ **für die Exportindustrie** subsidy to exports, bounty on exportation;
~ **für Preisherabsetzungen** rollback subsidies *(US)*;
~ **erhalten** to be subsidized (bounty-fed); ~ **gewähren** to give (pay) a subsidy, to extend financial aid.
subventionieren to subventionize, to subsidize, to extend financial aid, to bonus, to pay (give) a subsidy;
Schiffahrtslinie ~ to subsidize a steamship line; **landwirtschaftliche Überschußprodukte** ~ to subsidize farm surpluses.
subventioniert subventioned, subsidized, bounty-fed;
nicht ~ unsubsidized; **staatlich** ~ subsidized by government, state-fed (-aided), taxeating;
staatlich ~ **sein** to be subsidized by the state;
~**er Export** subsidized export; ~**e Industrie** subsidized industry; **nicht** ~**er Preis** full economic price; ~**er Wohnungsbau** subsidized housing.
Subventionierung subsidization, subsidizing, payment of subsidies;
~ **des Exports** subsidy of exports, bounty on exportation; ~ **der Landwirtschaft** featherbedding of the farmers; ~ **von Preisen** price subsidy.
Subventionsbedarf subsidy requirements.
subventionsbedürftig subsidizable.

Subventions|empfänger taxeater; **~fonds** subsidy fund; **Preise durch ~maßnahmen senken** to roll back prices *(US)*; **~system** subsidy system; **~wesen** bounty feeding; **~wettlauf** subsidy race; **~zahlungen** subvention payments.
subversive Tätigkeit subversive activity.
Suchaktion search;
~ nach einem überfälligen Flugzeug search for a missing aircraft;
~ nach einem verlorenen Kind starten to go in search of a missing child.
Such|anzeige wanted, want ad *(US)*; **~auftrag** tracing order; **~dienst** tracing service; **~- und Rettungsdienst** search and rescue service.
Suche hunting, search, tracing, quest;
auf der ~ nach Wahrheit in pursuance of truth;
hektische ~ mad search;
~ nach Arbeitskräften job hunting; **~ nach Minen** sweep for mines; **~ nach Nahrung** quest for food; **~ nach einem verlorenen Testament** search for a lost will;
etw. nach langer ~ finden to find s. th. after a long hunt; **sich auf die ~ nach etw. machen** to go in search of s. th., to be off on the trail of; **auf der ~ sein** to be on the trundle looking for *(fam.)*; **auf der ~ nach einem Hotel sein** to be looking for a hotel.
Sucheinrichtung *(Computer)* search feature.
suchen to search, to seek, to look;
großindustrielle Abstützung ~ to seek shelter with conglomerates; **in allen Ecken und Winkeln danach ~** to look up and down for it; **nach Gold ~** to quest for gold; **sein Heil in der Flucht ~** to seek safety in flight; **überall nach einem verlorengegangenen Kind ~** to search far and wide for a missing child; **nach Minen ~** to sweep mines; **Schutz vor dem Regen ~** to take shelter from the rain; **nach jem. wie nach einer Stecknadel ~** to hunt for s. o. high and low; **nach einer Stellung ~** to seek employment, to look about for a job; **Streit ~** to be out for a quarrel; **überall nach einem verlorengegangenen Testament ~** to hunt (search) high and low for a missing will; **Tod ~** to court death; **unaufhörlich ~** to keep on searching; **nach einem Verbrecher ~** to hunt a criminal; **stets den eigenen Vorteil ~** to know on which side one's bread is buttered; **sich einen Weg durch die Menge ~** to pick one's way through the crowd; **das Weite ~** to take to one's heels, to make off; **nach Worten ~** to be at a loss for words; **durch die Zeitung ~** to advertise.
Sucher *(Foto)* finder.
Such|gebiet area of search; **~gerät** *(Radar)* search radar; **~kartei** tracing file (index); **~licht** searchlight; **~meldung** *(Radio)* radio call; **~scheinwerfer auf einen Gegenstand richten** to focus a searchlight on an object.
Sucht greed, maniac, craze, itch;
~ nach Machtpositionen pursuit of office;
bei jem. zur ~ geworden sein to have become a craze with s. o.
süchtig manic, mania, *(Drogen)* addicted;
~ auf etw. sein to become hooked on s. th. *(sl.)*.
Suchtrupp search party *(Br.)*.
Suchtstoffkommission Commission on Narcotic Drugs.
Südbahn southern line.
Sudelei mess, slapdash work.
Südfrüchte tropical and subtropical fruits *(Br.)*.
Südlage southern exposure;
mit ~ with southern aspect;
~ haben *(Haus)* to head south.
Süd|pol South Pole; **~seeparadies** south-sea island paradise; **~seite** south side; **~staatler** *(USA)* secessionist *(US)*; **warme ~winde** warm winds from the south.
Suff boozing, drinking;
dem ~ ergeben sein to take to the bottle.
süffeln to tipple, to peg.
süffisant self-satisfied.
suggerieren to suggest.
Suggestionskraft power of suggestion.
Suggestiv|frage leading (biassed) question, leader; **einem Zeugen ~fragen stellen** to lead a witness; **~wirkung** sympathy effect; **auf ~wirkung beruhen** to be suggestive.
Sühne expiation, atonement, conciliation, *(Schmerzensgeld)* smart (atonement) money, *(Wiedergutmachung)* recompense, reparation;
~gericht conciliation court.
sühnen to atone, to expiate;
Verbrechen mit dem Tod ~ to pay for one's crime with death.
Sühne|termin conciliation hearing; **~verfahren** conciliation (conciliatory) proceedings; **~versuch** attempt at reconciliation; **~vorschlag** conciliatory proposal.

Suite retinue, suite.
sukzessiv successively, gradually, in stages, bit by bit.
Sukzessiv|lieferung delivery by instalments, multiple delivery; **~lieferungsvertrag** multiple delivery contract.
Summa (Sa.) total.
summarisch, Thema ~ behandeln to treat a subject cursorily;
~es Verfahren summary proceedings.
Sümmchen, hübsches pretty penny.
Summe sum, amount, stock, value, *(Gesamtsumme)* total;
bis zu einer ~ von up to an amount of; **in einer ~** in one amount; **in einer runden ~** in round figures;
abgerundete ~ amount rounded up; **ausgesetzte ~** amount allowed, granted amount; **bedeutende ~** respectable amount; **berechenbare ~** liquidated sum; **bestimmte ~** given (definite) sum; **doppelte ~** double the amount, twice the sum; **einbehaltene ~** amount retained; **eingeklagte ~** face of a judgment; **einmalige ~** lump sum; **erhebliche ~** large chunk; **errechnete ~** sum arrived at; **fällige ~** amount due; **fehlende ~** missing amount, deficit, deficiency; **feste ~** stationary sum; **doppelt gebuchte ~** amount entered twice; **geringfügige ~** paltry amount, insignificant sum; **gesamte ~** total amount; **geschuldete ~** sum payable, amount owing; **glatte ~** good round sum; **große ~** large (considerable) amount, a king's ransom; **hinterlegte ~** deposited amount; **kleine ~** pittance; **notwendige ~** requisite money; **restliche ~** residual amount; **überschüssige ~** surplus, amount in excess; **überwiesene ~** remittance; **veranschlagte ~** estimated amount; **verfügbare ~** amount at disposal; **zusätzliche ~** additional sum;
~ der Aktiva total assets; **volle ~ einer Forderung** principal and charges; **enorme ~ Geldes** vast amount of money;
~ abführen to pay over a sum; **von einer ~ abgehen** to be deducted from a sum; **~ abrunden** to round off a sum; **~ zur Zahlung aus der Staatskasse anweisen** to make an expense payable out of public funds; **mit einer ~ aufrechnen** to settle a debt per contra; **~ auswerfen** to allow an amount; **beträchtliche ~ darstellen** to make up a considerable amount; **fehlende ~ ergänzen** to make up the requisite sum, to make good (up) a deficiency; **~ guthaben** to have a balance in one's favo(u)r; **~ gutschreiben** to credit an amount; **~ bei einem Dritten hinterlegen** to deposit a sum in the hands of a third party; **jdm. eine ~ zur Verfügung stellen** to place a sum at the disposal of s. o.; **~ von ... übersteigen** to exceed the sum of ...; **~ überweisen** to remit a sum of money; **~ validieren** to place a sum against; **~ verdoppeln** to double a sum; **ungeheure ~n verschlingen** to cost a tremendous amount of money, to cost the earth; **große ~ Geld veruntreuen** to embezzle a large sum; **fehlende ~ vollmachen** to make up the off money (requisite sum); **~ ziehen** to compute (run up) the total; **~ der Rechnungsspalten ziehen** to extend an invoice; **~ zusammenrechnen** to compute a sum.
Summen hum, drone, monotonous tone;
~bilanz turnover balance; **~depot** irregular deposit; **~rabatt** quantity rebate; **~tabelle** cumulative table; **~vermächtnis** monetary proceeds of assets of the estate *(US)*; **~versicherungspolice** valued policy; **~verwahrung** irregular deposit; **~zuwachs durch stehengelassene Prämien** *(Lebensversicherung)* paid-up (reversionary) additions; **~zuwachs feststellen** to declare a reversionary bonus.
Summer buzzer, hummer, howler;
~zeichen *(Telefon)* dial tone, buzz.
summieren to sum (add, tot, cast) up, to totalize;
sich ~ to run up.
Summierung addition, summing up.
Summierungsmethode *(Bewertung)* summation method.
Sumpf swamp, mire, estuary, wash *(Br.)*;
in einen ~ geraten *(fig.)* to fall into bad company; **~ trockenlegen** to drain a swamp;
~boden marshy ground.
Sumpf|gegend marshy district; **~land** marshland.
Sünde, Öffentlichkeit wie die ~ meiden to shun publicity like the plague.
Sündenbock scapegoat, goat *(US sl.)*, fall guy *(US sl.)*;
den ~ abgeben to carry the can (baby) *(sl.)*.
Sündenregister list of sins.
Sünder, alter old offender; **hartgesottener ~** hardened sinner;
alter ~ sein to be old in sin.
sündhaft|teuer shockingly expensive;
~es Geld kosten to cost a wicked amount of money.
Super|benzin four-star petrol *(Br.)*; **~benzin tanken** to use super; **~dividende** super (extraordinary, surplus, *US*) dividend, bonus, melon *(US)*, *(Bardividende)* cash surplus; **~fernsehschau** spectacular.

super|geheimer Gegenstand big hush-hush object; **~gescheit** too clever by half.
Super|het heterodyne receiver; **~kraftstoff** four star petrol *(Br.)*; **in ~lativen sprechen** to speak in superlatives; **~macht** superpower; **~markt** supermarket *(US)*; **kleiner ~markt** superette *(US)*; **~miete** premium rent, rackrent *(Ireland)*; **~provision** supercommission, *(Generalvertreter)* overwrite, *(Konsortialführer)* overriding commission; **~provision zahlen** to overwrite; **~staat** superstate; **~tanker** supertanker.
Suppe soup, *(Fleischbrühe)* broth, bouillon, consommé; **heiße ~ zum Auslöffeln** the devil to pay; **~ auslöffeln, die man sich eingebrockt hat** to face the music; **sich eine schöne ~ einbrocken** to make a nice mess of it; **sich eine schöne ~ eingebrockt haben** to have a deuce to pay; **jem. die ~ versalzen** to spoil s. one's fun.
supranational supranational; **~e Organisation** supranational organization.
Supranationalität supranationality.
Surrogat substitute, *(Geld)* token money, auxiliary currency, representative money *(US)*, *(Notbehelfe)* makeshift.
suspendieren to suspend, to stay; **j. vom Dienst ~** to order s. o. suspended.
suspendiert held in suspension.
Suspendierung suspension, stay; **~ von Satzungsbestimmungen** suspension of rules.
Suspensiv|bedingung suspensive (suspensory) condition; **~wirkung** suspensive condition, suspensory effect.
süß sweet, *(Wein)* mellow; **~es Lächeln** sugary smile; **das ~e Leben** dolce vita.
Süßholzraspelei whispering sweet nothings, mealy-mouthed flattery.
Süßigkeiten confectionery, sweets, candies *(US)*, goodies *(US)*; **~ lieben** to have a sweet tooth.
süßsauer lächeln to smile sourly.
Süß|speise sweet dish, dessert; **~warenabteilung** sweet department; **~warengeschäft** confectioner's shop, sweetshop *(Br.)*, candy store *(US)*, tuckshop *(Br., sl.)*; **~wasser** fresh water; **~wasserfisch** fresh-water fish; **~wasserschaden** fresh-water damage.
Swap|abkommen swap arrangement; **~bedingungen** swap terms; **zu ~bedingungen Geld aufnehmen** to borrow on swap; **~engagement** swap commitment; **~fazilitäten** swap facilities; **~geschäfte** swap transactions; **~linien** swap lines; **~satz** swap rate.
Swinggeschäft *(Devisen)* swing.
Switchgeschäft switch; **~ machen** to switch.
Symbol symbol, emblem; **~ für etw. sein** to stand for s. th.; **~charakter** representativeness; **~figur** status symbol.
symbolische Übergabe symbolic delivery.
symmetrisch symmetrical, *(el.)* balanced.
Sympathie sympathy, attachment, affection, good feeling; **~ empfinden** to take a liking; **~aussperrung** sympathetic lockout; **~bezeugung** expression of sympathy, *(Diplomatie)* handsome gesture.
Sympathiestreik sympathy (sympathetic) strike; **in einen ~ treten** to strike (walk out, *US*) in sympathy.
Sympathiewerbung prestige advertising.
Sympathisant sympathizer, fellow traveller, fringe supporter.
Sympathisanten|gruppe fringe group; **~kreis** outer ring of sympathisers.
sympathisch sympathetic, likable, prepossessing; **~es Lächeln** pleasant smile; **~er Mensch** prepossessing (likable) person; **~es Publikum** sympathetic audience.
sympathisieren, mit jem. to sympathize with s. o., to lean (tend) to s. o., to enter into s. one's feelings.
Sympathisierender sympathizer.
Symphonieorchester symphony orchestra.
Symptom, schwerwiegendes serious manifestation.
Synchron|bahn *(Raumschiff)* synchronous orbit; **mit ~blitzlicht** synchroflash; **~gangschaltung** synchronized shifting; **~getriebe** synchromesh gear.
Synchronisation synchronization, voice over, dubbing.
synchronisieren *(el.)* to phase, *(Film)* to synchronize, to dub, to voice over.
synchronisierte Uhr sympathetic clock.
Synchronisierung *(Film)* synchronization, dubbing, voice over; **~ von Zollsenkungen** phasing-in of tariff reductions.
Synchron|lauf *(Film)* synchronous running; **~rechner** synchronous computer; **~schaltung** *(Auto)* synchronized shifting.
Syndikalismus syndicalism.
Syndikalist syndicalist.
Syndikat syndicate, association, ring, consortium; **sich zu einem ~ zusammenschließen** to [form a] syndicate.
Syndikats|anteil underwriting share; **~beteiligung** underwriting share; **~mitglied** underwriting member; **~preis** underwriting price; **~vertrag** underwriting agreement.
Syndikus syndic, trustee, general (standing) counsel *(US)*, corporation lawyer, corporation counsel *(US)*; **als ~ tätig sein** to syndicate, to serve as syndic.
Synode synod.
Synthese synthesis; **schematische ~** topic[al] sentence.
synthetisch artificial, synthetic, plastic; **~ hergestellt** man-made.
System system, plan, body, form, frame, framework; **gut funktionierendes ~** efficient system; **kapitalistisches ~** capitalistic (profits) system; **metrisches ~** metric system; **parlamentarisches ~** parliamentary system of government; **~ der Analyse von Beamtengehältern** pay research system *(Br.)*; **~ der Ausgabe von Belegschaftsaktien** employees' shares plan; **~ zur Erforschung der Kundenmeinung** image-rater system; **~ der mehrfachen Führungsgremien** multiple management; **~ der Gefangenenarbeit** contract (state-use) system; **~ des gespaltenen Goldpreises** two-tier gold-price system; **~ automatischer Lohnangleichung** automatic system of pay settlements; **~ der freien Marktwirtschaft** free-enterprise system; **~ vorgeschriebener Mindestreserven** safety-fund system *(US)*, fractional reserve banking system; **~ der gespaltenen Preise** two-price system; **~ der differenzierten Preisfestsetzung für Auslieferungsstellen** basing-point pricing system; **~ mit voll wirksamer Preisgleitklausel für Lebenshaltungskosten** full cost-of-living escalator plan; **~ des Privateigentums** private ownership; **~ zur beschleunigten Prüfung von Eingängen am Kassenschalter** batch system; **~ betrieblicher Sozialzulagen** employee-benefit plan; **~ gegenseitiger Überwachung** *(Politik)* system of check and balance; **umfassendes ~ zusätzlicher Vergünstigungen** overall compensation program(me); **~ flexibler (gespaltener) Wechselkurse** flexible exchange-rate system, multiple rate system, adjustable peg system *(US)*; **~ des sozialen Wohnungsbaus** National House-Building Council Scheme *(Br.)*; **~ der Zulassung aller Versicherungsarten bei einer Gesellschaft** multiple line system of insurance; **bestehendes ~ ablehnen** to reject the establishment; **nach einem ~ arbeiten** to have system in one's work; **~ befolgen** to follow a system; **in ein ~ bringen** to reduce to a system, to systemize, to systematize; **neues ~ einführen** to supersede (adopt, introduce) a new system; **kein ~ haben** to lack system; **~analytik** systems engineering; **~analytiker** systems engineer.
Systematik systematics, taxonomy; **~ der Betriebsstätten** Standard Industrial Classification *(Br.)*.
Systematiker systematizer.
systematisch systematic, orderly, organic; **~e Anordnung** orderly arrangement; **~e Marktuntersuchung** systematic sampling; **~e Stichprobe** systematic sample.
systematisieren to systemize, to systematize; **seine Arbeit ~** to organize one's work.
systembedingt systematic.
System|berater systems engineer; **~beratung, ~forschung** systems engineering (research); **~theorie** general system theory.
Szene scene, *(Film)* sequence; **auf offener ~** during the act; **hinter der ~** off-stage; **vom fahrenden Kamerawagen gedrehte ~** tracking shot; **häusliche ~n** domestic scenes; **herausgeschnittene ~** *(Film)* cutout; **eine ganz neue ~** a whole new ball game *(US)*; **schreckliche ~n beim Ausbruch des Erdbebens** distressing scenes when the earthquake occured; **rührendste ~n eines Buches** most touching passages of a book; **gemütliche ~ am häuslichen Kamin** homely fireside scene; **~ aus dem täglichen Leben** life story; **in ~ gehen** to be staged; **~ machen** to make a scene *(coll.)*; **~ proben** to rehearse a scene; **sich in ~ setzen** to put o. s. in the limelight.
Szenen|applaus applause during the action; **~aufbau** set; **~aufnahme** *(Film)* take, shot; **~bild** *(Theater)* scenery, set; **~übergang** *(Film)* interscene; **~wechsel** shifting of scenes, sceneshifting.
Szenerie scenery; **städtische ~** urban landscape; **~ konkurrenzlos beherrschen** to loom over a scene unrival(l)ed.

T

T-Eisen tee.
Tabak, das ist starker that's a bit thick;
~**geschäft** tobacco store *(US)*, cigar store *(US)*, tobacconist's store *(Br.)*; ~**händler** tobacconist, tobacco dealer *(US)*; ~**industrie** tobacco industry; ~**monopol** tobacco monopoly.
Tabaksbeutel tabacco pouch.
Tabak|steuer tobacco [manufacturer's] excise (tax) *(US)*, tax on cigarettes, cigarette tax; ~**steuer einführen** to establish a tax on tobacco; ~**waren** tobacco goods, smokes *(coll.)*; ~**warengeschäft,** ~**laden** tobacconist, tobacco (cigar) shop (store, *US*).
tabellarisch tabular, schedular;
~ **angeordnet** tabulated;
~ **anordnen** to tabulate, to tabularize, to arrange in tabular form, to schedule;
~**e Anordnung (Aufstellung, Zusammenstellung)** tabulation, tabularization, schedule, table.
Tabelle table, scale, schedule *(US)*, *(Diagramm)* chart, graph, diagram, *(Inhaltsverzeichnis)* index, *(Verzeichnis)* record, *(Zusammenstellung)* tabulation, tabularization, scroll, diagram;
amtliche ~ official scale; **genealogische** ~ genealogical chart; **mathematische** ~**n** mathematical tables; **nebenstehende** ~ adjoining table; **statistische** ~ data sheet; **synoptische** ~ synoptic table, synopsis; **versicherungsstatistische** ~ actuarial table;
~ **zur Berechnung der Lohnsteuer** pay-as-you-earn schedule *(Br.)*, wage-tax table *(US)*; ~ **zur Berechnung des Nettoertrages von festverzinslichen Papieren** bond-value table; ~ **zur Berechnung der Zinsen** table of interest; ~ **lohnsteuerfreier Beträge** free-pay table *(Br.)*; ~ **über die Herstellungskosten** cost-process chart; ~ **der unbedingt Nachschußpflichtigen** list of contributories; ~ **der Verbrauchergewohnheiten** scale of preferences;
~ **anführen** to head a table, to be at the top of the scale; ~ **anlegen** to table; **in** ~**n anordnen** to tabulate; ~**n aufbereiten** to prepare tables; ~ **aufstellen** to compile (dress) tables; **statistische** ~ **aufstellen** to make a table of statistics; **an der Spitze der** ~ **stehen** to be at the top of the scale, to head a table.
Tabellen|buch table book; ~**form** tabular form; **in** ~**form anordnen** to tabulate, to tabularize.
tabellenförmig [angeordnet] tabulated.
Tabellen|kopf boxhead; ~**punkte** *(drucktechn.)* leaders; ~**satz** tabular composition, table; ~**wert** tabular value.
Tabelliermaschine tabulator, tabulating machine.
tabelli[si]eren to tabularize, to tabulate.
Tabellisierung tabulation, tabularization.
Tableau tableau, indicator board.
Tablett server, tray, waiter, salver.
Tablette tablet, tabella, troche;
schmerzlindernde ~ pain-killer.
Tabu taboo, touch-me-not;
etw. für ~ **erklären** to [put s. th. under] taboo.
Tabulator tabulator.
Tachometer tachometer, speedometer, *(Fahrrad)* cyclometer; ~**stand** odometer reading.
Tadel blame, rebuke, reprimand, reproach, correction, upbraiding, *(Kritik)* criticism, censure, blame, *(Schule)* bad mark;
ohne ~ blameless, irreproachable; **über jeden** ~ **erhaben** above reproach;
sanfter ~ gentle rebuke;
jem. einen ~ **erteilen** to give s. o. a reprimand (lecture), to censure s. o.; **sich jds.** ~ **zuziehen** to incur s. one's condemnation.
tadellos irreproachable, blameless, above reproach, *(Charakter)* flawless, sterling;
sich ~ **benehmen** to behave irreproachably; **seine Aufgaben** ~ **erfüllen** to be perfect in the performance of one's duties; ~ **laufen** *(Motor)* to run perfectly;
~**e Ausführung** excellent workmanship; ~**er Charakter** unimpeachable character; **in** ~**em Englisch antworten** to answer in faultless English; ~**e Kleidung** impeccable clothes; **in** ~**em Zustand** in perfect conditon.
tadeln to blame, to censure, to find fault with, to reprimand, to rebuke, to condemn, to correct, to criticize;
j. wegen eines Zwischenfalls ~ to blame s. o. for an accident; **an allen etw. zu** ~ **finden** to find fault with everything.
tadelnswert reproachable, culpable, rebukable, reprehensible, exceptionable.
Tadels|antrag *(parl.)* motion of censure; ~**antrag stellen** to move a censure; ~**debatte** censure debate; ~**punkt** censure count; ~**resolution** censure resolution (vote); ~**sucht** faultfinding; ~**verfahren** censure proceedings (hearing); ~**votum** vote of censure, censure vote (resolution).
Tafel table, scale, schedule *(US)*, *(für Anzeigen)* bulletin, poster boarding *(Br.)* (hoarding), notice board *(Br.)*, billboard *(US)*, *(Buchillustration)* figure, *(Schule)* blackboard, chalkboard *(US)*, *(Tabelle)* index, list;
festlich geschmückte ~ festive board;
~ **Schokolade** bar of chocolate; ~ **der ankommenden und abfahrenden Züge** timetable of trains, train sheet, schedule of arrivals and departures *(US)*;
~ **abwischen** to clean (wipe) the blackboard; ~ **an einem Haus anbringen** to fix a plaque on the wall of a house; ~ **aufgeben** to rise from the table; **an die** ~ **schreiben** to write on the blackboard;
~**berg** table mountain; ~**besteck** flatware; ~**druck** block print; ~**geschäft** over-the-window business *(Br.)* (counter trade, *US*); ~**geschirr** dinner set (service); ~**glas** sheet (plate) glass; ~**methode** table (actuarial) method.
tafeln to feast, to banquet, to feed at the high table;
gern gut ~ to be fond of good living.
Tafel|runde round table; **ganze** ~**runden unterhalten** to keep the table amused; ~**silber** flat silver, table (silver) plate.
Täfelung matchboarding, panel, panelling.
Tafel|wasser table water; ~**wein** table wine; ~**ziffer** actuarial rate.
Tag day, date;
alle acht ~**e** once a week; **am festgesetzten** ~ on the set day; **am hellichten** ~**e** in broad daylight, in the very face of day; **am** ~**e vor seiner Abreise** on the day before his departure; **an einem bestimmten** ~ on a given day; **an dem betreffenden** ~**e** on the day in question; **an festgesetzten** ~**en** on stated days; **bis auf den heutigen** ~ to date; **den ganzen** ~ **über** around-the-clock; **eines schönen** ~**es** one fine day; **heute in acht** ~**en** a week from today; **im Laufe des** ~**es** in the daytime, during the course of the day; **in guten und schlechten** ~**en** through good and evil report; **in vierzehn** ~**en** in a fortnight *(Br.)*, in two weeks *(US)*; **pro** ~ per diem; **seit Jahr und** ~ for many years; **über** ~**e** surface, *(Bergbau)* aboveground; **unter** ~**e** *(Bergbau)* below ground, down the pit, underground; **vom gleichen** ~**e** of the same date; **während des** ~**es** in the daytime; **zahlbar 30** ~**e nach Sicht** payable at thirty days' sight; **zur Feier des** ~**es** to mark the occasion;
10 ~**e nach dato** 10 days date (sight) ...; **drei** ~**e nacheinander** three days running;
~ **und Nacht geöffnet** open day and night;
arbeitsreicher ~ very busy day; **aufreibender** ~ a trying day; **bessere** ~**e** better days; **bestimmter** ~ fixed (certain, appointed) day; **denkwürdiger** ~ day of account, red-letter day; **dienstfreier** ~ blank day; **ereignisreicher** ~ field day; **festgesetzter** ~ term day; **freier** ~ free (open, leave) day, day off, holiday *(US)*; **gerichtsfreier (geschäftsfreier)** ~ dies non, nonjudicial day; **gestriger** ~ yesterday; **heutiger** ~ present day; **bald kommender** ~ odd-come shortly; **regnerischer** ~ fine day for ducks *(coll.)*; **für Haushaltssitzungen reservierte** ~**e** allotted days *(Br.)*; **schöner** ~ pleasant day; **schwarzer** ~ unfortunate day; **sitzungsfreier** ~ *(Gericht)* nonjudicial day; **trüber** ~ overcast day; **volle** ~**e** *(Kündigung)* clear days; **wetterabhängige** ~**e** weather-working days; **jeder zweite** ~ every other day;
~ **des Außerkrafttretens** termination date; ~ **der Besitzübertragung** vesting date; ~ **des persönlichen Erscheinens [vor Gericht]** return day; ~ **des Jüngsten Gerichts** Judgement Day, Day of Judgment (Reckoning); ~ **des Inkrafttretens** effective date, rule-day; **letzte** ~**e des Jahres** closing days of the year; ~ **der Rechnungsausstellung** date of invoice; ~**e nach Sicht** days after sight; ~ **der offenen Tür** open-door invitation, open house *(US)*;
sich einen ~ **rot [im Kalender] anstreichen** to make a mark in the calendar, to chalk up, to mark a red-letter day; **über** ~**e arbeiten** to do pithead work; **unter** ~**e arbeiten** to work underground; ~ **und Nacht arbeiten** to work day and night (round the clock); **den ganzen** ~ **über arbeiten** to work all day long; **Verhandlung für drei** ~**e aussetzen** to adjourn a case for

three days; ~ **festlich begehen** to celebrate a day; **sich für einen anderen ~ bescheiden** to appoint a day to meet again; **seine ~e beschließen** to end one's days; ~ **bestimmen (festsetzen)** to agree upon a day; **etw. an den ~ bringen** to bring to light; **lustlosen ~ hinter sich bringen** *(Börse)* to meander through a listless day; **jem. einen ~ freigeben** to give s. o. a day off (a holiday, *US*); **sich einen ~ freinehmen** to arrange to take a day off, to take a holiday *(US)*; **seinen faulen ~ haben** to have a fit of laziness; **schlechten ~ haben** to be in a bad mood; **bessere ~e erlebt haben** to come down in the world; **jem. in guten und bösen ~en die Treue halten** to go through thick and thin with s. o.; **in den ~ hineinleben** to live for the day; **in den ~ hineinreden** to talk at random; **sich einen guten ~ machen** to make a day of it; **nicht jeden ~ anzufinden sein** not to grow on every hedge; **ganzen ~ auf den Beinen sein** to be on the trot all the day; **ganzen ~ geöffnet sein** to be open throughout the day (all day long); **dem lieben Gott den ~ stehlen** to laze all day; ~ **vereinbaren** to agree upon a day; ~ **und Nacht verkehren** *(Züge)* to run day and night; **pro ~ verlangen** to charge a day; **für ein paar ~e verreisen** to go away for a few days; **jem. einen guten ~ wünschen** to pass the time of day with s. o.;

die Sonne bringt es an den ~ truth will out; **man soll den ~ nicht vor dem Abend loben** dont't halloo before you are out of the wood;

~- **und Nachtarbeit** double shift.

tagaus, tagein day in, day out, day after day.

Tag|- und Nachtbetrieb, durchgehender continuous operations; ~- **und Nachtdienst** 24-hour service.

Tag[e]bau *(Bergbau)* opencast (open, surface) working, open-work, open-day (opencast) mining, open pit, strip mining *(US)*;

im ~ open-worked; **im ~ ausgebeutet** opencast;

im ~ abbauen (gewinnen) to strip *(US)*, to surface-mine.

Tageblatt daily paper, journal.

Tagebuch diary, journal, daybook, book of original entry, date (journal) book, *(einfache Buchführung)* blotter, *(Schiff)* log;

persönliches ~ intimate diary;

sein ~ aufs laufende bringen to write up one's diary; **im ~ eintragen** to diarize; **in ein ~ eintragen** to journal; ~ **führen** to keep a diary;

~**blatt** record sheet; ~**eintragung** entry into a diary; ~**führer** keeper of diary; ~**schreiber** diarist.

Tage|dieb sluggard, idler, layabout; ~**geld** attendance (daily) fee, per diem (daily, travelling) allowance, per diem pay, subsistence allowance, *(als Zeuge)* conduct (appearance) money.

Tagelohn daily wages (pay), a day's wage;

im ~ arbeiten to work by the day; **in ~ nehmen** to hire by the day.

Tage|löhner day labo(u)rer, dayman, jack, jobber, jobbing man, hack, hackney, coolie, hired man *(US)*; **literarischer** ~**löhner** penny-a-liner, devil, grub; ~**löhnerfamilie** sharecropping family *(US)*; ~**lohnsatz** rate of pay, day rate.

tagen to meet, to hold a meeting, *(beraten)* to deliberate, to confer, to sit in conference *(US)*, *(Gericht)* to sit, to be sitting, *(Parlament)* to be in session;

bis in den frühen Morgen ~ to sit into the small hours of the morning; **hinter verschlossenen Türen** ~ to sit behind closed doors (in camera, *Br.*).

Tages|ablauf daily routine, day-to-day operation, schedule *(US)*; **morgigen** ~**ablauf festlegen** to make one's plans for the next day; ~**abrechnung** *(Spediteur)* daily cash settlement; ~**abschluß** daily balance; ~**abschlußbuch** daily balance book; ~**anbruch** daybreak, dawn; **bei** ~**anbruch** at the peep of day; **vor** ~**anbruch** before day; ~**anforderung** stores requisition; ~**angriff** daylight attack; ~**anzug** business *(US)* (lounge, *Br.*) suit; ~**arbeit** day labo(u)r, daywork, a day's (journey) work; ~**auflage** daily circulation; ~**auftrag** order valid to day, day order *(US)*; ~**ausflug mit dem Wagen** day's outing in a car; ~**ausweis der Bank von England** daily bullion return *(Br.)*; ~**auszug** bank deposit, daily statement; **auf** ~- **und Spesenbasis beschäftigen** to retain on a per-diem-plus expense basis; ~**bedarf** [daily] ration; ~**befehl** *(mil.)* order of the day, routine order, general orders, detail; ~**bericht** daily report, bulletin, *(Versicherungsvertreter)* daily; ~**bestand** daily balance; ~**besuch** day attendance; ~**betreuung** day care; ~**betrieb** *(Bergbau)* surface mining (working); ~**bulletin** [daily] bulletin; ~**creme** vanity cream; ~**decke** bedspread; ~**durchschnitt** day's average; ~**einnahme[n]** daily sales (receipts, takings, turnover, returns), day's receipts; ~**einnahmen nachprüfen** to check the day's takings; ~**ereignisse** current events (affairs), passing events; ~**ereignisse laufend verfolgen** to keep track of current events; ~**erholung** day-trip recreation; ~**fläche** *(Bergbau)* bank; ~**flug** day flight; ~**förderung** daily output; ~**fragen** issues (questions) of the day; **politische** ~**fragen** political discussion of the day; **wirtschaftliche** ~**fragen** bread-and-butter economic issues; ~**gage** daily fee; ~**gast** day guest; ~**gebühr** day rate.

Tagesgeld *(Bankwesen)* call money (loan) *(Br.)*, demand loan (money) *(US)*, daily loan (money) *(Br.)*, overnight loan *(US)*, day-to-day money *(Br.)*, money at (on) call, *(für Makler)* day-to-day loan, morning loan *(US)*, *(Sitzungsgeld)* per diem, money at (on) call;

~**er** money at call and short notice *(Br.)*;

abgewickelte (ausgeglichene) ~**er** adjusted demand deposits *(Br.)*;

~ **anlegen** to lend day-to-day money *(Br.)*; ~ **um 2% herabsetzen** to mark down call money to 2 per cent *(Br.)*;

~**aufnahme** overnight borrowing *(US)*; ~**markt** call (overnight, *US*) market; ~**satz** call loan (money) rate *(Br.)*, rate on interbank loans; ~**satz um 2% heruntersetzen** to mark down call money to 2 per cent *(Br.)*.

Tages|gericht *(Restaurant)* special dish; ~**geschäft** daily return; ~**gespräch** topic of the day, talk of the town, *(Telefon)* daytime call; ~**grundpreis** *(Automiete)* daily rate; ~**heimschule** all-day school; ~**hilfe** day servant, daily; ~**karte** day ticket, *(Netzkarte)* rover ticket; ~**kasse** *(Theater)* box office [receipts]; ~**kauf** cash purchase; ~**kellner** day waiter; ~**kilometerzähler** tripodometer; ~**kindergarten** day care center *(US)*, (centre, *Br.*), kindergarten; ~**kino** nonstop performance; ~**kladde** scratcher *(US)*; ~**kollekte** collect of the day; ~**kommentar** daily commentary; ~**kopie** live letter; ~**kopiebuch** live-letter book, float file; ~**kosten** current cost.

Tageskurs *(Devisen)* current rate [of exchange], day's (today's) rate, rate (quotation) of the day, market rate *(US)*, *(Wertpapiere)* market price (quotation, value), current quotation, today's (current, ruling) price, transfer price (rate) *(Br.)*;

berechnet nach dem ~ von calculated at the rate of exchange ruling on; **zum** ~ *(Börse)* at current market prices, at value, at the present quotation, *(Devisen)* at the current rate;

~ **für Sichtwechsel auf London** current rate of exchange for sight drafts on London; ~ **für Staatsanleihen** federal funds rate *(US)*;

zum ~ kaufen to buy at the current rate of exchange;

~**zettel** official quotations.

Tagesleistung daily output (produce);

maschinelle ~ daily capacity; **normale** ~ an ordinary day's work.

Tageslicht daylight;

bei ~ by day; **in vollem** ~ in broad daylight;

künstliches ~ artificial daylight;

ans ~ bringen to bring to light (forth), to dig up, to unearth; **ans ~ kommen** to come to light; ~ **scheuen** to shun the light of day; ~ **vergeuden** to burn daylight;

~**aufnahme** daylight shot; ~**kassette** daylight loading magazine; ~**lampe** daylight lamp; ~**papier** *(Foto)* daylight paper; ~**schirm** *(Radar)* bright display screen; ~**zeit** daylight hours.

Tages|literatur journalistic literature; ~**lohn** day's pay; ~**lohnsatz** daily wage rate; ~**lohnsystem** day rates system; ~**losung** over-the-counter receipts, drawings, *(mil.)* password, parole; ~**meldung** daily report; ~**nachrichten** news of the day; ~**notierung** daily quotation.

Tagesordnung order of the day, agenda [paper], business before the meeting, memorandum sheet, *(Gericht)* docket, *(parl.)* order of business;

in Übereinstimmung mit der ~ agreeable to the order of the day; **zur** ~ on a point of order, order! order!;

endgültige ~ approved agenda; **festgelegte** ~ order of the day *(Br.)*; **konjunkturpolitische** ~ economic-policy agenda; **neue** ~ fresh business; **schriftliche** ~ order (agenda) paper; **übliche** ~ *(Hauptversammlung)* ordinary business; **vorgesehene** ~ business to be transacted; **vorläufige** ~ provisional agenda;

~ **einer Kabinettssitzung** cabinet business; ~ **einer Sitzung** conference business (agenda);

von der ~ absetzen to remove (delete, cut out) from the agenda; ~ **anerkennen** to adopt the agenda; **in die ~ aufnehmen** to include in the agenda; ~ **aufstellen** to draw up (fix) the agenda; ~ **behandeln** to proceed with the business of the day; ~ **einhalten** to preserve the order of business; **in die ~ eintreten** to proceed to business, to come to order; **in eine neue ~ eintreten** to deal with fresh business; **wieder in die ~ eintreten** to resume business; **Einwendungen gegen die ~ erheben** to raise a point of order; ~ **festlegen** to draw up (fix) the agenda; **zur ~ gehören** to be the order of the day; **auf die ~ kommen** to come up for discussion; **auf die ~ einer Versammlung setzen lassen** to bring forward at a meeting; **zur ~ schreiten** to proceed to the agenda; **an der ~ sein** to be nothing out of the ordinary; **auf die ~ setzen** to call up, to place on (put down, include in) the agenda, *(parl.)* to raise to the point of order; **Antrag auf die ~ setzen** to put a resolution on record; **außerhalb der ~ sprechen** to travel out of the record; **zur ~ sprechen** to speak on a point of order; **auf der ~ stehen** to be on the agenda; **Frage von der ~ streichen** to withdraw an item from the agenda; **zur ~ übergehen** to pass (proceed) to the order of the day; **~ überladen** to overload an agenda; **~ verlesen** to read the agenda; **~ vorher versenden** to send the agenda in advance; **Punkt für die ~ vorschlagen** to raise a point of order.

Tagesordnungs|ausschuß sifting (agenda) committee, *(parl.)* Senate Rules Committee; **~entwurf** draft agenda.

Tagesordnungspunkt item on the agenda (of business);
behandelte ~e business transacted; **besondere ~e** non-routine business, special business; **noch nicht erledigte ~e** carryover business; **nächster ~** next on the agenda; **normale ~e** ordinary business items;
übrige ~e erledigen to transact any other ordinary business; **zum nächsten ~ übergehen** to proceed to the next business (item of the agenda); **~e zusammenstellen** to draw up a list of items of business.

Tages|pendler commuter *(US)*, daily-breader *(Br.)*; **sein ~pensum erledigen** to do one's daily stint; **~politik** day-to-day policy, current affairs; **~post** post, daily mail *(US)*; **~preis** market (going, current, today's) price, *(Börse)* latest (ruling) price, last quotation; **unter dem ~preis** under today's quotation; **angemessener ~preis** clear market price; **~presse** daily newspaper (press), dailies; **~produktion** daily output (production); **~programm** daily schedule, *(Rundfunk für die Hausfrau)* steam radio *(coll.)*, order paper; **~ration** daily ration, *(einer militärischen Einheit)* day of supply; **~raum** dayroom, restroom; **~redakteur** day editor; **~reise** day's journey; **~rückfahrkarte** day ticket; **~saldo** daily balance; **~satz** *(Börse)* day rate, *(Geldbeschaffung)* daily rate, *(Spesensatz)* travel allowance, per diem charges; **~schau** television news show (bulletin, broadcast); **~schicht** day (first) shift; **~schule** dayschool; **~schüler** day scholar (boarder, boy, *Br.*); **~schwester** day nurse; **~- und Nachtsender** full-time station; **~spesen** travel(l)ing allowance, per diem charges, dieta; **~stempel** postmark, date stamp, dater; **~stunde** day hour; **bis in die frühen ~stunden** until (into) the small hours; **~umsatz** daily returns (turnover, sales), return of the day; **~umsätze** *(Börse)* markings; **~urlaub** one-day leave; **~verbrauch** daily consumption; **~verdienst**daily wages (earnings); **voller ~verdienst** full-time earnings; **~verpflegung** *(mil.)* daily ration; **~versand** daily loadings (shipment, *US*); **~versandmeldung** daily loading list; **~vorrat** day supply; **~wert** present (sound, market, current, today's) value, going price, *(bei Inzahlungnahme)* trade-in value *(US)*.

Tageszeit daytime;
zu jeder ~ at any time; **zu einer unmöglichen ~** at an ungodly hour;
übrige ~ remainder of the day; **zumutbare ~** reasonable hour.

Tageszeitung daily [paper];
~en today's newspapers, daily prints *(US)*;
führende ~en leading dailies; **regionale ~** provincial daily;
für ~en schreiben to journalize.

Tages|zinsen daily interest; **~zufuhren an den Hauptgetreidemärkten** primary receipts *(US)*; **~zulage** daily extra pay.

tageweise by the day.

Tagewerk day task (labo(u)r), day's work, *(Arbeitseinheit)* man-day, *(Bergbau)* stint, *(Schicht)* shift;
ordentliches ~ tidy day's work.

täglich daily, per day, per diem;
~ erscheinen to appear daily;
~es Angebot floating supply; **~er Arbeitsbericht** daily performance report; **~er Bedarf an Lebensmitteln** daily food requirements; **sein ~es Brot verdienen** to earn one's daily bread; **~ kündbares Darlehn** call loan, loan repayable on demand; **~er Einkauf** daily shopping; **~er Flugzeugverkehr** daily emplanement; **~es Geld** call loan, call *(Br.)* (demand, *US*, day-to-day, *Br.*) money; **~ fällige Gelder** sight (demand, *US*) deposits; **auf ~e Kündigung** at call; **~e Kursdepesche** daily telegraphic quotation; **im ~en Leben** in everyday life; **~e Lohnauszahlungen** daily payroll; **~ fälliges Maklerdarlehn** day-to-day loan *(Br.)*, morning loan *(US)*; **~es Saldo** daily balance; **der ~e Trott** the daily round, trut.

tagtäglich daily, day-to-day, day in, day out.

Tagung conference, meeting, congress, sitting, symposion, *(parl.)* session, convention *(US)*, *(Parteiversammlung)* gathering, rally, caucus, *(Versammlung)* assembly;
bevorstehende ~ forthcoming conference; **sofort einberufene ~** on-the-spot meeting; **geschäftspolitische ~** policy meeting; **öffentliche ~** public meeting;
~ der Minister ministerial session; **~ des Parlaments** parliamentary session;
~ abhalten to hold a meeting (conference, congress), to be (sit) in conference; **~ einberufen** to convene a meeting; **zu einer ~ zu viel Teilnehmer einladen** to over-staff a meeting; **~ eröffnen** to open a meeting; **~ leiten** to preside at a conference; **an einer ~ teilnehmen** to attend a congress (session); **~ veranstalten** to arrange a meeting; **zu regelmäßigen ~en zusammenkommen** to meet in regular sessions.

Tagungs|ablauf conference proceedings; **~ausweis** conference ticket; **~bericht** conference paper (report), symposion; **~botschaft** meeting message; **~dauer** session; **~einrichtungen** convention facilities; **~flug** convention trip; **~halle** meeting hall; **~heft** conference plan (handbook, *US*); **~leiter** conference leader; **~mitglied** conference member (delegate); **~ort** meeting place, place of meeting, convention resort, venue; **~programm** conference program(me), conference plan (handbook, *US*); **~raum, ~saal** conference (meeting, board) room; **~teilnehmer** conference member (delegate), meeting participant, conferee *(US)*; **~unterlagen** documents for the meeting; **~wesen** convention business; **~zentrum** convention center *(US)* (centre, *Br.*).

Taifun typhoon.

Taille waist, waistline, *(Kleidung)* bodice, corsage;
auf ~ gearbeitet waisted.

Takt tact, *(fig.)* discretion, delicacy, tact, *(Fließbandproduktion)* phase, cycle, *(tel.)* cadence;
politischer ~ diplomacy;
~ angeben *(fig.)* to be a leader in a field; **j. mit ~ behandeln** to use tact in dealing with s. o.; **Angelegenheit mit ~ behandeln** to handle an affair with delicacy; **j. aus dem ~ bringen** to disconcert (discomfit) s. o.; **~ erfordern** to require careful handling; **aus dem ~ kommen** to be put out of one's stride; **den notwendigen ~ vermissen lassen** to be wanting in tact; **über ~ verfügen** to show tact.

Taktgefühl tact, delicacy;
über großes ~ verfügen to have great tact; **gegen jds. ~ verstoßen** to outrage s. one's delicacy.

Taktieren, hinhaltendes dilatory defence.

taktieren to proceed tactically, to manoeuvre;
hinhaltend ~ to use delay.

Taktik tactics, policy;
seine ~ ändern to shuffle the cards; **neue ~en anwenden** to resort to new tactics; **raffinierte ~ anwenden** to use subtle means.

Taktiker tactician, manoeuvrer;
ungewöhnlich erfolgreicher politischer ~ superb parliamentary tactician.

taktisch|e Atomwaffen tactical atomic weapons; **~er Fehler** tactical error; **~e Luftunterstützung** tactical air support; **~es Manöver** delaying tactics.

taktlos lacking tact, tactless, crude, inconsiderate, indelicate;
völlig ~ sein to have no sense of delicacy;
~e Bemerkung indelicate remark.

Taktlosigkeit lack of tact, indelicacy, bad taste, tastelessness, brick *(Br., coll.)*;
~ begehen to drop a brick.

Taktstraße conveyor line.

taktvoll with tact, diplomatic, discreet, well-judged;
Menschen ~ behandeln to show great tact in dealing with people; **über etw. ~ hinweggehen** to pass s. th. over with tact; **sehr ~ behandelt werden müssen** to need tactful handling.

Tal valley;
über Berg und ~ wandern to hike cross-country.

talabwärts down the valley.

Talar robe, *(Richter)* gown, court dress;
~ anlegen to gown.

Talent talent, gift, endowment, faculty, ability, aptitude, bump;
erstklassige (hervorragende) ~e talents of the first order; **gesellschaftliche ~e** parlo(u)r tricks *(fam.)*; **ungenutztes ~** wasted talent;
~ günstiger Selbstdarstellung gift for presentation;
auf sein eigenes ~ angewiesen sein to be left to one's own resources;
~suche talent hunt (scout); **~sucher** talent scout.

Talfahrt slide, sliding, *(mit Auto)* downhill drive, *(fig.)* downswing, downtrend;
konjunkturelle ~ downtrend in economic activity.
Talisman talisman.
Talmi pinchbeck, goldbrick *(US coll.)*, sham, duffer *(sl.)*;
~**ware** imitation (fake) goods.
Talon talon, apron, stub, countertally, counterfoil, counterstock, *(Erneuerungsschein)* renewal coupon (certificate);
~**buch** counterfoil book; ~**steuer** coupon (talon, *Br.*) tax.
Tal|sohle *(Konjunktur)* trough; ~**sperre** reservoir, barrage, river dam; ~**station** *(Seilbahn)* valley station; ~**weg** downway.
Tamtam fuss, ado, to-do, ballyhoo;
ohne jedes ~ without further ado;
~ **machen** to ballyhoo; **viel** ~ **um jem. machen** to make great fuss of s. o.
Tand tinsel, glitter, *(Trödel)* junk, trash, trumpery.
Tandem tandem [bicycle];
~**flugzeug** tandem aircraft.
Tangente *(Städteplanung)* tangential truck road.
tangieren, j. to touch s. o.
Tangojüngling dandy, playboy.
Tank tank, *(Auto)* petrol *(Br.)* (gasoline, *US*) tank, *(mil.)* tank, *(Wasser)* rain-water tank, cistern;
~ **auffüllen (vollmachen)** to fill up a tank, to tank *(sl.)*;
vom Hubschrauber abgefeuerte ~**abwehrraketen** helicopter-borne antitank missile; ~**abwehrwaffen** antitank weapons;
~**anhänger** trailer; ~**anlage** petrol *(Br.)* (gasoline, *US*) tank;
~**attrappe** dummy tank; ~**aufenthalt** fuel stop; ~**ausweis** fuel permit; ~**dampfer** [oil] tanker.
Tanken [re]fuelling.
tanken to fuel, to refuel, to fill up with petrol *(Br.)*;
in der Luft ~ to refuel in flight; **frische Luft** ~ to get a breath of fresh air; **zu viel** ~ *(fig.)* to have one too many, to get tanked-up *(sl.)*.
Tanker|auftrag tanker order; ~**fahrer** tank driver; ~**markt** tanker market.
Tank|flugzeug tanker plane; ~**inhalt** tank capacity; **unterirdisches** ~**lager** underground tank; ~**lastzug** tank truck;
~**reeder** tanker owner; ~**säule** gasoline *(US)* (petrol, *Br.*) pump; ~**scheck** filling station check *(US)* (cheque, *Br.*); ~**schiff** tanker, tank ship.
Tankstelle petrol *(Br.)* (filling, gasoline, *US*, service, fuelling, *US*) station;
freie ~ independent filling station;
~ **mit Restauration** transport café, truck shop *(US)*;
an der nächsten ~ **halten** to stop at the next petrol station *(Br.)*;
~ **renovieren** to face-lift a service station *(US)*.
Tankstellen|besitzer gasoline *(US)* (petrol, *Br.*) station owner, service station dealer *(US)*; ~**hinweis** gas sign *(US)*; ~**wärter** petrol-station *(Br.)* (gasoline, *US*) attendant; ~**zubehör** service station equipment *(US)*.
Tank|uhr fuel (petrol, *Br.*, gasoline, *US*) gauge; ~**verschluß** filler-cap; ~**wagen** tanker lorry, road tanker, tank truck, *(Bahn)* tank car (wag(g)on); ~**wart** gasoline *(US)* (petrol station, *Br.*) attendant.
Tantalusqualen torments of Tantalus;
~ **ausstehen** to go through hell *(coll.)*.
Tante Emma Emily Post.
Tante-Emma-Laden pop and mom shop;
~ **führen** to deal in goods of all kinds.
Tantieme *(Aufsichtsrat)* director's percentage (royalty), *(Autor)* royalty, author's fee, seigniorage, *(Gewinnanteil)* share, percentage, bonus, premium, gratuity, poundage, *(Ölindustrie)* override, *(Vorstand)* bonus, director's fee, percentage of profit;
dem Verantwortungsbereich voll entsprechende ~ bonus fully equated to the levels of responsibilty; **leistungsbezogene** ~ performance-related bonus; **produktionsgebundene** ~ production bonus, accelerating premium; **nicht produktionsgebundene** ~ nonproduction bonus;
~ **leitender Angestellter** executive bonus;
Autor unter Mißachtung des Urheberrechts um seine ~ **bringen** to defraud an author of his royalties by ignoring copyright; ~ **erhalten** to get a royalty; **seine** ~ **kassieren** to draw one's fees.
tantiemeberechtigt sein to be entitled to a bonus.
Tantiemen|abgabe royalty tax; ~**abrechnung** royalty statement;
~**anteil** royalty interest, *(Ölindustrie)* over-riding royalty interest; ~**aufteilung** fee splitting; ~**einkünfte** bonus income;
~**forderung** accrued royalty, royalty demand; ~**gewährung** bonus issue; ~**regelung** bonus scheme; ~**regelung für leitende Angestellte** management cash-incentive scheme; ~**steuer** tax on allocated portion of profits; ~**transfer** royalty remittance;
~**vereinbarung** bonus arrangement; ~**vergütung** payment of a royalty, *(Angestellte)* bonus payment; ~**verteilung** percentage distribution; **fortentwickeltes** ~**wesen** bonus trend.
tantiemepflichtig subject to payment of royalties.
Tanz dance;
~ **um das goldene Kalb** worship of the golden calf;
~ **aufführen** to kick up a fuss; ~ **aussetzen** to sit out a dance; ~ **mit jem. haben** to have a quarrel with s. o.;
~**bein schwingen** to shake a leg; ~**café** coffeehouse.
tanzen, nach jds. Pfeife to dance to s. one's tune (after s. one's whistle); **aus der Reihe** ~ to step out of line; **auf dem Seil** ~ to walk the tightrope; **auf einem Vulkan** ~ to sit over a volcano *(coll.)*.
Tanz|fest dancing party, dance; ~**fläche** dancing floor; ~**kapelle** dance band (orchestra); ~**lehrer** dancing master; ~**lokal** dance (dancing) house (hall), dancing room, shine box *(sl.)*, juke [house], joint; **öffentliches** ~**lokal** dancing hall *(US)*, dancing saloon *(US)*; ~**musik** dance music; ~**orchester** dance band (orchestra); ~**paar** courting couple; ~**partner** dancing partner;
~**saal** ballroom; ~**schule** dancing school; ~**stunde** dancing lesson; ~**tee** tea dance; ~**vergnügen** ball.
Tapet, aufs ~ **bringen** to bring upon the tapis, to broach a subject;
bei jem. etw. aufs ~ **bringen** to break a matter to s. o.; **aufs** ~ **kommen** to come into question (up for discussion); **auf dem** ~ **sein** to be on the carpet.
Tapete wallpaper, paper hangings;
bedruckte ~**n** printed wallpaper;
~ **anbringen** to hang wallpaper.
Tapeten|druckerei printworks; ~**geschäft** wallpaper shop (store, *US*); ~**rolle** roll of wallpaper; ~**tür** jib door; ~**wechsel** change of scene; **zwecks** ~**wechsels ins Ausland verreisen** to go abroad for the change of scene.
Tapezieren paper hanging, papering.
tapezieren to hang wallpaper, to [wall]paper, to decorate, to upholster;
Zimmer ~ to paper a room.
Tapezierer paperhanger, paperer, upholsterer, decorator.
tapfer brave, courageous, gallant, heroic;
sich ~ **halten** to keep a stiff upper lip; ~ **zugreifen** to tuck in;
~**en Widerstand leisten** to resist bravely.
Tapferkeit courage, bravery, pluck.
tappen, im Dunkeln to grope in the dark, to be at sea.
Tara, vom Zoll angenommene tare assumed by the customs;
durchschnittliche ~ average tare; **geschätzte** ~ estimated tare;
handelsübliche ~ customary tare; **reine** ~ net (clear) tare; **am Empfangsort umgerechnete** ~ converted tare; **zusätzliche** ~ additional allowance for tare, super tare;
~ **und Gutgewicht** tare and tret;
~ **in Abzug bringen (berechnen)** to rate the tare; ~ **vergüten** to allow (make an allowance) for tare;
~**gewicht** tare weight; ~**rechnung** tare account (note, rate);
~**vergütung** [allowance for] tare; **zusätzliche** ~**vergütung** supertare.
tarieren to [state the] tare, to ascertain (allow for) tare.
Tarif tariff, scale, rate, statement, *(Anzeigenwesen)* advertising charges, space (advertisement, *Br.*) rate, rate card *(US)*, series rate, *(Eisenbahn)* rates, rating, *(el.)* electricity tariff, rate *(US)*, *(Gas)* gas tariff, rate *(US)*, *(Gebührenordnung)* scale (list, schedule) of charges, *(Gebührentarif für die Börse)* schedule of commissions, *(Löhne)* scale of wages, wage scale (schedule), collective bargaining agreement, *(individueller Lohntarif)* pay scale, *(Post)* postal rates, *(Steuern)* scale of taxation, tax scale, *(Transportgewerbe)* freight tariff, [transportation] rate, *(Versicherung)* premium rate, rates, *(Zoll)* customs rate, customs tariff;
laut ~ as per tarif;
tatsächlich abgerechneter ~ *(Anzeigenwesen)* earned rate;
gesetzlich anerkannter ~ *(Eisenbahn)* lawful (legal) rate; **den Lebenshaltungskosten angepaßter** ~ cost-of-living sliding scale;
anzuwendender ~ tariff applicable, applicable (relevant) rate;
nach wissenschaftlichen Prinzipien aufgestellter ~ scientific tariff; **ausgehandelter** ~ conventional tariff; **ausgehender** ~ *(Seeschiffahrt)* outward tariff; **autonomer** ~ *(Zoll)* single tariff;
besonderer ~ exceptional tariff *(Br.)*, *(Bahn)* class rate, *(Versicherung)* specific rate; **degressiver** ~ sliding-scale tariff;
einheitlicher ~ standard rate, *(Löhne)* standard wage rate;
erhöhter ~ advanced rate; **ermäßigter** ~ reduced tariff (rate, *Br.*), *(Anzeigenwesen)* short rate *(US)*; **fehlender** ~ nontariff;
festvereinbarter ~ *(Verkehr)* arbitrary; **wechselweise in Ansatz gebrachter** ~ alternative rate; **gekoppelter** ~ coupled rate;

geltender ~ rate in force; **gemischter** ~ mixed tariff; **genehmigter** ~ rate authorized; **staatlich genehmigter** ~ state-approved (official) rate; **gestaffelter** ~ differential tariff, graduated rate (tariff), rate scale *(US)*, *(Steuer)* tapering rate; **degressiv gestaffelter** ~ *(Strom)* block rate; **gleichmäßiger** ~ *(Bahn)* freight-of-all-kinds rate; **gleitender** ~ *(Löhne)* sliding wage scale; **gültiger** ~ applicable rate; **allgemein gültiger** ~ general purpose rate, general tariff, tariff (rates) in force; **örtlich gültiger** ~ local rate; **halber** ~ half rate; **hereinkommender** ~ *(Seeschiffahrt)* homeward tariff; **kombinierter** ~ combination tariff, *(Anzeigenwesen)* combined (combination) rate, *(tel.)* two-part tariff; **pauschaler** ~ flat (blanket, *US*) rate; **saisonbedingter** ~ seasonal tariff; **nur auf dem Papier stehender** ~ *(Bahn)* paper rate; **übersetzter** ~ exorbitant rate; **von der Mengeneinheit unabhängiger** ~ any-quantity rate *(US)*; **vom Verbrauch unabhängiger** ~ *(el.)* straight-line rate; **ungekürzter** ~ full tariff; **vergleichbarer** ~ comparable rate; **jahreszeitlich verschiedener** ~ seasonal tariff; **gesetzlich zulässiger** ~ lawful (legal) rate; **zweispaltiger** ~ two-column tariff; **zwischenstaatlicher** ~ intrastate tariff *(US)*;

Tag- und Nachtstrom~ night and day tariff;

unterdurchschnittlicher ~ **für Behinderte** substandard rate; **verbilligter** ~ **für Durchgangsgüter** transit rate; ~ **für Einzelinsertion ohne Rabatt** transient rate; ~ **für Expreßgüter** spot rate; **ermäßigter** ~ **bei beschränkter Haftpflicht des Spediteurs** released rate *(US)*; ~ **für Mustersendungen** sample rate; ~ **für den Personenverkehr** passenger rates, table of fares; ~**e außerhalb der Saison** off-season fares; ~ **mit begrenztem Sonderangebot** *(Liniendienst)* stand-by tariff; ~ **für Stückgüter** all-commodity rate, less-than-carload rate *(US)*, mixed carload rate *(US)*, mixed cargo rate *(Br.)*; ~ **für später zugestellte Telegramme** deferred rate; ~ **nach normalem Verbrauch** load-rate tariff, *(el.)* meter rate; ~ **für Werbesendungen** time charge;

~ **aufstellen** to tariff; ~ **erheben** to levy a rate; ~ **erhöhen** to raise a tariff; ~ **festsetzen** to [fix the] tariff, to list (schedule) the tariff value; ~ **nach Teilstrecken festsetzen** to zone; ~**e freigeben** to deregulate rates; ~ **herabsetzen** to cut rates; ~ **senken** to lower a tariff; **jem. einen günstigen** ~ **zugestehen** to accord s. o. a favo(u)rable rate;

~**abbau** cut in rates, rate cutting; ~**abkommen** *(Lohnabkommen)* trade (industrial, joint) agreement, wage settlement, union contract, bargaining agreement, *(Zollwesen)* tariff treaty; **ganzen Industriezweig umfassendes** ~**abkommen** collective (labo(u)r) agreement; ~**abkommen in der Bauindustrie** construction agreement; ~**abschluß** *(Gewerkschaft)* pay settlement, collective bargaining agreement; **neuer** ~**abschluß** [settlement] package; ~**abschlüsse im Rahmen einer zehnprozentigen Steigerung halten** to keep pay settlements down to within the 10% margin; ~**abschlußvollmacht** *(Gewerkschaft)* bargaining power; **nicht an** ~**absprachen gebunden sein** to be outside the trade-union system; ~**änderung** *(Eisenbahn)* exception to classification, *(Löhne)* modification of a bargaining agreement, *(Zoll)* duty (rate) change, change in rates, tariff revision; ~**änderungsbescheid** exception sheet; ~**angebot** pay offer; **gebündeltes** ~**angebot** pay package; **der Belegschaft ein an die Produktivität gekoppeltes** ~**angebot zur Abstimmung vorlegen** to ballot the workforce on a productivity deal; ~**angestellter** standard wage earner; ~**angleichung** *(Löhne)* wage adjustment, *(Zoll)* standardization of tariffs; ~**anhänger** tariff advocate; ~**anhebung** *(Bahn)* raising of railway rates *(Br.)*, *(Zoll)* tariff increase (hike, raising); ~**anpassung** *(Zoll)* adjustment of rates; ~**anpassung in Grenzfällen** marginal adjustment; ~**ansätze** collectively agreed wage rates; ~**anwendung** application of rates; ~**anwendungsgebiet** *(Eisenbahn)* classification territory; ~**arbeit** *(Arbeiter)* bargain work; ~**aufschlag** surcharge on goods; ~**auseinandersetzung** collective dispute; **harte** ~**auseinandersetzungen** rough rounds of collective bargaining; **sich mit einer** ~**auseinandersetzung nach kurzer Stellungnahme nicht mehr beschäftigen** to dismiss a tariff issue with a brief reference; ~**ausgangspunkt** *(Spediteur)* common (basing) point; ~**ausnahme** exemption; ~**ausschuß** tariff commission (committee), *(Arbeitsplatzbewertung)* merit-rating committee, *(Arbeitsverträge)* wages council; ~**autonomie** *(Löhne)* wage autonomy, *(Zoll)* autonomous tariff system; ~**begrenzung** pay control; ~**begünstigung** *(Zollwesen)* tariff (imperial, *Br.*) preference, *(Verkehrspolitik)* closed door; ~**behörde** rate-making body; ~**berechner** rate maker; ~**berechnung** rate (tariff) making.

tarif|besteuert *(Wertpapiere)* subject to standard tax; ~**bestimmend** tariff-regulating, rate-fixing (-making).

Tarifbestimmung rate setting;
~**en** tariff regulations, *(Lohntarif)* provisions of a collective bargaining agreement;
einschränkende ~ restrictive article of a tariff;
~**en unterworfen sein** to be subject to tariff.

Tarif|betrieb mit Beitrittszwang agency shop *(Br.)*; ~**bevollmächtigter** *(Löhne)* [collective] bargaining agent; ~**bezirk** *(Lohnabkommen)* collective bargaining area, *(Versicherungswesen)* rating area; ~**bildung** tariff (rate) making; ~**bindungen** tariff commitments; ~**bruch** infringement of rates in force, *(Lohnabkommen)* violation of a bargaining agreement; ~**buch** *(Anzeigen)* rate book; ~**büro** rating bureau, *(Autoversicherung)* tariff office *(Br.)*; ~**differenzierung**, ~**diskriminierung** discrimination in rates, tariff discrimination.

Tarifeinstufung *(Angestellter)* wage classification, classification rating, *(Eisenbahn)* class rating;
höhere ~ *(Angestellter)* upgrading; **niedrigere** ~ *(Angestellter)* demotion, demotional classification change, downgrading.

Tarifentgelt rate of remuneration.

tariferhöhend tariff-raising, rate-raising.

Tarif|erhöhung rate raising (hike), increase (upsurge) in rates, interim (rate) increase, tariff raising, *(Löhne und Gehälter)* increase in pay rates, *(Zoll)* increase in tariff, tariff hike (increase, raising); ~**erhöhungen auf Produktivitätszunahmesätze abstellen** to settle for rises based on a productivity rate; ~**erhöhung vornehmen** to raise a tariff; ~**erhöhungsantrag** application for increase; ~**ermäßigung** reduction of tariff, reduction in rate, rate cutting, rate (tariff) reduction; ~**fächer** rate range; ~**fähigkeit** *(Löhne)* bargaining power; ~**faktoren** rate factors; ~**festsetzer** rate fixer; ~**festsetzung** rating, fixing of rates, rate fixing (setting), tariff (rate) making *(US)*, tariffication; ~**festsetzung durch Betriebsführung und Betriebsrat** joint rate setting; **differenzierte** ~**festsetzung nach Gebieten** territorial rating; ~**festsetzungsmethode** rate-making method; ~**forderung** tariff request, *(Gewerkschaft)* contract bargaining demand; ~**formel** *(Löhne)* wage (tariff) formula; ~**frage** *(Zoll)* tariff question, *(Löhne)* wage matter; ~**freigabe** rate deregulation; ~**freiheit** *(Versicherungsgeschäft)* rating freedom; ~**gebiet** *(Eisenbahn)* zone; ~**gebühr** *(Telefon)* tariff charge for calls.

tarifgebunden tariff-bound.

Tarif|gefälle rate differential; ~**gehalt** flat rate of pay, scale salary *(US)*; **diszipliniertes und geordnetes** ~**gehaltsverhandlungssystem** disciplined and ordered pay bargaining system; ~**gemeinschaft** rate association; ~**gesetzgebung** tariff law; ~**grenze** *(Eisenbahn)* fare stage; ~**grundlage** rate basis; ~**grundsätze** tariff plank.

Tarifgruppe bargaining unit, wage class (group), job rate, *(Zoll)* tariff category;
~**n bei der Einkommensteuer** income brackets;
in eine höhere ~ **einstufen** to upgrade; **in eine niedrigere** ~ **einstufen** to downgrade.

Tarif|herabsetzung *(Löhne)* reduction in rate, rate cutting, *(Zoll)* tariff reduction; ~**hoheit** collective bargaining prerogative.

tarifieren to [fix the] tariff, to fix rates, to list (schedule) the tariff value, to classify.

Tarifierung tariffing, tariffication, rating, fixing of rates, tariff classification.

Tarifierungsausschuß rate-fixing (-setting, *US*) committee.

Tarif|kampf tariff war, rate war *(US)*, *(Löhne)* wage dispute; ~**klage** rate filing; ~**klasse** wage class, *(Rundfunk)* rate class, *(Zoll)* tariff category; ~**klassenbeschreibung** grade description; ~**klausel** *(Löhne)* wage clause, *(Zoll)* tariff provision; ~**kombination** rate combination; ~**kommission** *(Eisenbahn)* railroad commission *(US)*, *(Gewerkschaft)* collective bargaining commission, Wages Council *(Br.)*, *(Zoll)* tariff commission *(US)*; ~**konferenz** conference bargaining; ~**krieg** tariff war, rate war *(US)*, *(Löhne)* wage (labour) dispute; ~**kündigung** collective contract termination *(US)*; ~**kürzung** *(Frachten)* rate reduction, *(Löhne)* rate cutting (cut), *(Zoll)* tariff reduction.

tariflich *(Löhne)* on the collectively agreed scale, *(Zoll)* tariff-wise;
~ **belastet** tariff-ridden; ~ **entstanden** tariff-born; ~ **geschützt** tariff-protected; ~ **subventioniert** tariffed;
~ **aushandeln** *(Löhne)* to bargain collectively; ~ **verankern** to bargain on a collective basis;
~ **festgelegte Arbeitszeit** nominal (standard) hours; ~**er Stundenlohn** standard hourly wage; ~**er Urlaub** holiday with pay, on-leave *(US)*.

Tariflohn wage tariff, union rate, standard wages, agreed scale salary, contractual (scale) wages *(US)*;

gewerkschaftlich ausgehandelter ~ union wage; **vereinbarter** ~ negotiated wage;
~ **für ungelernte Arbeiter** common labo(u)r rate;
unter ~ **arbeiten** to scab it *(sl.)*;
~**bestimmung durch Betriebsrat und Vorstand** joint rate setting; ~**erhöhung** scale wage increase *(US)*; ~**gruppe** wage-rate bracket; ~**kosten** standard labo(u)r cost; ~**satz** standard wage rates; ~**vereinbarung** collective bargaining (wage) agreement.
tarifmäßig tariff-wise, in accordance with (by) the tariff;
~ **profitieren** to benefit from a duty advantage;
~**e Gebühr** official rate.
Tarif|mauern gegen ausländische Produkte errichten to raise tariff walls against foreign goods; ~**nomenklatur** nomenclature; ~**nummer** tariff item, position, *(GATT)* item; ~**ordnung** regulations of pay scale, wage pattern, Wages Order *(Br.)*; **betriebliche** ~**ordnung** single-plant bargaining; ~**paket** contract package; ~**partner** bargaining agent, collective bargainer, *(pl.)* management and labo(u)r; **alleiniger** ~**partner** exclusive bargaining agent; ~**politik** *(Löhne)* pay (wage) policy, *(Verkehr)* rate policy, *(Zoll)* tariff policy.
tarifpolitische Auseinandersetzung wage dispute.
Tarif|position tariff item (heading); **unter eine** ~**position einreihen** to classify under a tariff item; ~**posten** tariff line; ~**prämie** tabular premium, premium pay, schedule rate, *(Grundlohn im Akkordsystem)* class rate, base pay; ~**preis** scale rate, standard price; **betriebliche** ~**probleme** plant bargaining problems; ~**progression** progressive scale of tax rate; ~**rechte** bargaining rights; ~**reduktion** tariff reduction, *(Löhne)* rate cutting; ~**reform** tariff reform; ~**regelung** rate treatment, *(Löhne)* wage regulation; ~**regulierung** regulation of rates; ~**revision** tariff revision; ~**rubrik** rating column; ~**runde** wage round.
Tarifsatz *(Löhne)* standard rate [of wages], *(Spediteur)* class (freight) rate, *(Zoll)* tariff rate (charge);
zum ~ at the proper rate;
geltender ~ rate in force;
anderthalbfacher ~ **für Überstunden** overtime rate of time and a half.
Tarif|schema *(Zoll)* tariff scheme (nomenclature); ~**schiedsgericht** wage arbitration; ~**schiedsspruch** wage award; ~**senkung** *(Löhne)* rate cutting, downshift in rates, *(Zoll)* tariff reduction (cut, rollback); ~**sitzung** *(Löhne)* bargaining session; ~**spanne** rate range; ~**staffel** differential price system; ~**staffelung** scale graduation; ~**statistik** tariff statistics; ~**streitfrage**, ~**streitigkeit** tariff issue (case), *(Löhne)* wage (bargaining, labo(u)r) dispute; ~**struktur** rate structure, *(Löhne)* wage bargaining structure, *(Zölle)* tariff structure; ~**stufe** *(Bahn)* zone, *(Besoldung)* salary grade *(Br.)*, *(Einkommensteuer)* tax band; ~**stufen der inflationellen Entwicklung anpassen** to lift tax bands in line with inflation; ~**stunden** standard hours; ~**stundenlohn** standard hourly wage; ~**system** *(Frachten)* rating system, *(Löhne)* wage schedule (setting), *(Zoll)* tariff system; **für mehrere Linien geltendes** ~**system** *(Eisenbahn)* multiple tariff system; ~**tabelle** class tariff, scale of wages, pay scale; ~**überwachung** wage control; ~**unterbietung** rate cutting, *(Versorungsunternehmen)* price cutting; ~**unterschied** *(Anzeigen)* differential, *(Löhne)* wage (pay) differential; **regional bedingter** ~**unterschied** regional wage differential; ~**urlaub** holiday with pay, on-leave *(US)*; ~**verband** *(Kfz-Versicherung)* tariff organization, *(Löhne)* collective bargaining (rate-making) association, *(Versicherungen)* tariff bureau, *(Zölle)* tariff association; ~**verbesserung** improvement in rates; ~**verbilligung** rate decrease; ~**verdienst** standard earnings.
Tarifvereinbarung collective bargaining (association, bargained) agreement, *(Frachtsätze)* rating agreement, *(Zoll)* tariff agreement;
ausgehandelte ~ contractual bargaining agreement; **am Produktivitätszuwachs orientierte** ~ *(Löhne)* productivity bargaining;
~ **im öffentlichen Bereich** public-sector pay settlement; ~ **für einen Einzelbetrieb** single-plant bargaining; ~ **über Lohnabzüge durch den Betrieb** checkoff agreement; ~ **zum Zweck der Festlegung von Zwangsbeiträgen** approved closed-shop agreement *(Br.)*;
Idol freier ~ **zwischen den Sozialpartnern anbeten** to worship before the free collective-bargaining totem pole.
Tarif|vereinheitlichung *(Frachten)* standardization of freight charges, *(Zölle)* standardization of tariffs; ~**vereinigung** *(Löhne)* collective-bargaining association; ~**vergleichstabelle** comparative rate schedule; ~**vergünstigungen** *(Zoll)* tariff preferences, discriminations.
Tarifverhandlungen *(Löhne)* collective bargaining, wage (pay) negotiations, contract negotiations *(US)*, *(Zölle)* tariff negotiations;
unter Streikdruck stehende ~ pressure bargaining;
~ **in der Autoindustrie** auto bargaining; ~ **für einen gesamten Industriebereich** industry-wide bargaining; ~ **auf Verbandsebene** multi-employer bargaining;
sich gegen eine Politik der Zurückhaltung bei ~ **aussprechen** to line up against wage restraint; ~ **führen** to bargain collectively; **globale** ~ **führen** to negotiate en bloc; ~ **in überschlagenden Einsatz führen** to leapfrog bargaining.
Tarifverhandlungs|bevollmächtigter *(Löhne)* [collective] bargaining agent; ~**methode im überschlagenden Einsatz** *(Löhne)* leapfrogging bargaining; ~**partei**, ~**partner** *(Löhne)* collective bargainer, bargaining agency *(US)*; ~**rechte** *(Löhne)* bargaining rights; **ausschließliches** ~**recht** sole bargaining; ~**struktur** pay bargaining structure; ~**verfahren** *(Löhne)* bargaining process.
Tarif|veröffentlichung publication of rates; ~**verstoß** violation of a collective bargaining agreement.
Tarifvertrag *(Handel)* trade agreement, *(Löhne)* collective (bargaining, union, wage) agreement, collective bargaining (labo(u)r) contract, labo(u)r (wage) agreement, *(Zoll)* tariff treaty;
auf enge Zusammenarbeit abgestellter ~ sweetheart agreement *(US)*;
~ **mit Indexklausel** threshold agreement; ~ **mit Lohngleitklausel** open-end wage contract;
~ **aushandeln** to bargain collectively; **örtlich begrenzten** ~ **aushandeln** to bargain on a local basis.
Tarifvertrags|bestimmung collective agreement (bargaining) provision; ~**bevollmächtigter** [collective] bargaining agent; ~**bruch darstellen** to constitute an unfair industrial practice; ~**freiheit** free collective bargaining; ~**gesetz** Industrial Relations Act *(Br.)*; ~**partei** bargaining unit, collective-bargaining agency *(US)*; ~**partner** collective bargainer (representative), *(pl.)* management and labo(u)r; ~**recht** law of collective bargaining; **ausgehandelte** ~**vereinbarung** contractual bargaining agreement; ~**verhandlungen** *(Löhne)* collective bargaining; ~**verhandlungen für den Gesamtbetrieb** company-wide bargaining; ~**vollmacht** *(Gewerkschaftsvertreter)* bargaining power, authorization card; ~**wesen** *(Löhne)* collective bargaining, wage system.
Tarif|vertreter bargaining agent; ~**vertretung** bargaining unit, collective-bargaining agency *(US)*; ~**vorschlag** wages regulation proposal; ~**vorschriften** tariff regulations; ~**vorteil** *(Zoll)* tariff advantage; ~**wert** *(Zoll)* tariff value; ~**wert festsetzen** to schedule (list) the tariff value, to tariff; ~**wesen** tariffism; ~**wettbewerb** *(Spediteur)* market competition; ~**zoll** tariff duty; ~**zone** *(Paketpost, Telefon)* zone *(US)*; ~**zugeständnis** tariff concession; **landwirtschaftliche** ~**zugeständnisse** farm concessions; **zu** ~**zwecken** for rate purposes.
Tarn|anstrich *(mil.)* pattern (camouflage) painting, *(Schiff)* dazzle paint, ~**bezeichnung** code word, cover name.
tarnen to camouflage, to mask, to screen, to cover, to conceal.
Tarn|farbe camouflage paint, *(Schiff)* dazzle; ~**maßnahmen** camouflage measures; ~**name** cover name; ~**netz** camouflage net; ~**organisation** cover organization; ~**scheinwerfer** masked headlamp; ~**tafel** code table.
Tarnung camouflage, mask, cloak, screen, concealment, *(mil.)* screening, camouflage.
Tarnzahl code number.
Tasche pocket, *(Aktentasche)* briefcase, portfolio, *(Geldtasche)* purse, *(Handtasche)* [ladies'] handbag, bag, *(Reisetasche)* travelling bag, holdall, gripsack *(US)*, grip *(US)*, *(Schultasche)* schoolbag, satchel;
aus eigener ~ out of one's own purse (pocket);
~**n voller Geld** pockets full of money, lousy with cash *(sl.)*; ~ **des Steuerzahlers** taxpayer's pocket;
in die eigene ~ **arbeiten** to line one's pockets; **jem. die** ~**n ausräumen** to pick s. one's pocket; **j. aus eigener** ~ **bezahlen** to pay s. o. from one's own pocket; **jem. die** ~ **entreißen** to snatch (grab) s. one's bag; **in die** ~ **greifen** to loosen the purse strings; **tief in die** ~ **greifen** to fork out (up, *sl.*), to dig one's hand into one's pocket; **in der** ~ **haben** to be in the bag *(sl.)*; **j. in der** ~ **haben** to have s. o. just where one wants him; ~**n voller Geld haben** to have one's pockets full of money; **die Hand auf der** ~ **halten** to tighten the purse strings; **Stadt wie die eigene** ~ **kennen** to know the town like the back of one's own hand; **j. in die** ~ **stecken können** to be more than a match for s. o.; **in die** ~ **langen** to dive into one's pocket; **jem. auf der** ~ **liegen** to live on

s. one's income; **schwer in die ~ greifen müssen** to have to pay through the nose; **in die ~ stecken** to pouch, to pip; **j. in die ~ stecken** to put s. o. in one's pocket, to buy and sell (run rings around) s. o., to be more than a match for s. o.; **Hälfte des Gewinns in die eigene ~ stecken** to pocket half of the profits; **Hände in die ~n stecken** *(fig.)* not to stir a finger; **nach einem Schlüssel in seinen ~n tasten** to fumble in one's pockets for a key; **jem. das Geld aus der ~ ziehen** to juggle s. o. out of his money.

Taschenausgabe pocketbook, pocket edition.

Taschenbuch paperback, pocketbook, notebook, *(Almanach)* annual, gift book *(US)*, *(Volksausgabe)* paperback;
~ausgabe paperback (pocket) edition, pocketbook edition (volume); **~format** paperback size; **~führer** pocket guide; **~laden** pocket-edition bookshop; **~verlag** pocket-book publishers.

Taschen|dieb snatcher, pickpocket, diver *(Br., sl.)*, dipper *(fam.)*, knuck *(US sl.)*, wire *(sl.)*; **vor ~dieben wird gewarnt** beware of pickpockets; **~diebstahl** larceny from the person, pocket-picking, dip *(sl.)*; **~diebstähle begehen** to pick, to pilfer, to manticulate; **~fahrplan** pocket timetable; **~feuerzeug** pocket lighter; **~flakon** hip flask; **~format** pocket size; **im ~format** pocket-size[d]; **~geld** pocket (spending) money, allowance; **wöchentliches ~geld** weekly allowance; **~kalender** pocket almanac; **~lampe** pocket lamp, flashlamp *(Br.)*, flash[light] *(US)*, torchlight *(Br.)*, electric torch; **~messer** pocket knife; **~pfändung** body execution; **~rechner** pocket calculator, pocket computer; **~schirm** collapsible (telescopic) umbrella, telescopic brolly; **~spieler** knockabout comedian, legerdemainist, warlock, juggler; **~spielertrick** juggle, sleight-of-hand; **~tuch** handkerchief; **~uhr** watch, ticker *(coll.)*, kettle *(US sl.)*; **~wörterbuch** pocket dictionary; **~wörterbuch zu einem Großlexikon umarbeiten** to expand a pocket dictionary into a large volume.

Tasse, trübe wet blanket;
nicht alle ~n im Schrank haben to have bats in the belfry (a slate loose), to be wrong in the garret (upper stor(e)y).

tassenfertig *(Getränk)* instant.

Tastatur *(Computer)* keyboard, *(Schreibmaschine)* bank;
~belegung keyboard layout; **~eingabe** keyboard entry.

Taste *(Computer)* button, *(Schreibmaschine)* key;
mit ~n versehen keyed;
~ bedienen to operate a key.

tasten to key, to keyboard;
nach jds. Hand ~ to feel for s. one's hand; **nach dem Lichtschalter ~** to grope for the light switch.

Tastenanschlag keystroke.

tastend tentative.

Tasten|feld *(Schreibmaschine)* keyboard; **~geber** transmitter; **~reihe** keybank.

Tastfehler keying error.

Tat action, deed, act, work, *(Straftat)* offence, offense *(US)*, criminal (penal) act;
auf frischer ~ in the very act, red-handed;
zur Last gelegte ~ alleged offence; **geschichtliche ~** historic deed; **gute ~** kind (moral) act; **verbrecherische ~** criminal act; **versuchte ~** attempted crime; **vollendete ~** offence committed, accomplished crime; **vorsätzliche ~** criminal intent;
~ der Verzweiflung act of despair;
jem. mit Rat und ~ beistehen to stand by s. o. whatever happens; **j. auf frischer ~ entdecken** to detect s. o. in the act; **auf frischer ~ ergreifen** to catch in the act (red-handed); **zu einer ~ ermuntern** to string up to a deed; **den Worten ~en folgen lassen** to suit the action to the word; **jeden Tag eine gute ~ tun** to do a good deed every day; **j. einer ~ überführen** to convict s. o. of a criminal act; **in die ~ umsetzen** to put into practice, to carry into effect; **große ~en vollbringen** to perform feats of valo(u)r; **~bericht** charge report.

Tatbestand state of affairs, facts of the case, statement of facts *(US)*, *(Gericht)* finding of fact, general finding, *(Strafrecht)* elements of an offence;
objektiver ~ overt act, actual facts; **subjektiver ~** culpability, mental element;
~ eines besonderen Gerichtsstandes venue facts; **~ einer strafbaren Handlung** statutory crime;
~ aufnehmen to establish the facts of a case; **~ der Exportsubventionierung erfüllen** to constitute unfair bounty; **~ einer strafbaren Handlung erfüllen** to constitute an offence; **~ eines strafbaren Versuchs erfüllen** to amount to an attempt; **~ ermitteln** to ascertain the facts; **Darstellung des ~s geben** to state the facts.

Tatbestands|angaben particulars of a charge; **~aufnahme** statement of facts, fact finding; **~irrtum** error of fact; **~merkmal** constituent fact, criterion, characteristic feature; **~merkmale** *(Verbrechen)* merits of a case, elements of an offence, operative facts *(US)*; **~urkunde** *(Schiffzusammenstoß)* preliminary act.

Tat|beweis proof of the fact; **in ~einheit mit** in coincidence with.

Tatendrang enterprising spirit;
voller ~ energetic;
voller ~ stecken to buzz with activity.

tatendurstig full of go, enterprising;
plötzlich äußerst ~ werden to have sudden fits of energy.

tatenlos inactive, idle, passive.

Täter delinquent, perpetrator, offender, culprit, committer, principal in the first degree;
jugendlicher ~ delinquent minor, juvenile (youthful) offender; **rückfälliger ~** persistent offender, recidivist; **unbekannter ~** some unknown person; **nicht vorbestrafter ~** first offender;
~ beherbergen to comfort the felon; **~ feststellen** to discover the culprit; **j. als den ~ erscheinen lassen** to point to s. o. as the culprit; **wie der ~ bestraft werden** to be punished as principal.

Täterschaft perpetration of a crime;
seine ~ ableugnen to plead not guilty.

Täterwille intention to commit a crime.

Tat|frage point (matter, question, issue) of fact; **~gehilfe** aider and abettor, art and part *(Scot.)*.

tätig active, acting, operative, busy, *(energisch)* energetic, efficacious, up-and-doing, stirring, *(fleißig)* industrious, busy;
beruflich ~ having a job; **freiberuflich ~** professional, freelance; **als Kaufmann ~** engaged in commerce;
~ sein to work, to operate *(US)*, to act, *(amtieren)* to function, to officiate; **für j. ~ sein** to serve with (be employed by) s. o.; **anwaltlich ~ sein** to be a lawyer by profession, to serve as solicitor *(Br.)*, to solicit *(Br.)*; **ehrenamtlich ~ sein** to be employed in an honorary capacity, to work without recompense; **erstinstanzlich ~ sein** to have original jurisdiction; **bei einer Firma ~ sein** to be in the employ of a firm; **freiberuflich ~ sein** to act as a free-lance; **geschäftlich ~ sein** to carry on (be engaged in) business; **nicht mehr geschäftlich ~ sein** to be out of business; **gewerblich ~ sein** to follow (carry on, ply) a trade, to carry on a trade or business; **in der Industrie ~ sein** to work in industry; **journalistisch ~ sein** to write for the press (in the papers); **offiziell ~ sein** to act in one's official capacity; **als Vermittler ~ sein** to act as an intermediary; **weltweit ~ sein** to cover the globe; **auf verschiedenen Plätzen im Außendienst ~ gewesen sein** to have a background in various parts of the world; **amtlich ~ werden** to act ex officio; **weitgehend in einer Angelegenheit ~ werden** to be largely instrumental in a matter; **auf höchster Ebene persönlich ~ werden** to operate personally at high levels; **aus eigennützigen Motiven ~ werden** to act from interested motives; **von sich aus ~ werden** to do s. th. on one's own initiative;
~en Anteil nehmen to take an active part; **~er Gesellschafter** working (active) partner.

tätigen to effect, to transact, to carry out;
Abschluß ~ to transact a deal, to conclude a bargain; **Abschlüsse auf London ~** to effect exchange deals on London; **Devisenabschlüsse ~** to effect foreign exchange transactions; **Effektengeschäfte auf Provisionsbasis ~** to execute orders in quoted (listed, *US*) securities on a commission basis; **Geschäfte ~** to do (transact) business; **Großeinkäufe ~** to wholesale, to buy in large quantities; **Verkauf ~** to execute (effect) a sale; **Versicherungsabschluß ~** to effect an insurance.

Tätiger, ehrenamtlich für die Regierung dollar-a-year man; **freiberuflich ~** professional [man], free-lancer, practitioner.

Tätigkeit activity, agency, *(Arbeit)* work, *(Aufgabe)* function, *(Beruf)* profession, vocation, job, *(Beschäftigung)* occupation, business, employment, pursuits, play *(Scot.)*, *(Betrieb)* operation, *(Handlung)* action, *(Laufbahn)* career;
in voller ~ in full swing;
angemessene ~ suitable work; **anstrengende ~** trying work; **anwaltliche ~** practice of law, attorneyship, *(nach Bedarf)* general retainer; **regelmäßig ausgeübte ~** regular occupation; **außerberufliche ~** outside activities; **auswärtige ~** field work; **bankfremde ~** nonbanking activity; **beratende ~** advisory function (capacity, service), *(Anwalt)* chamber practice; **berufliche ~** professional employment (activity), occupation; **bisherige ~** previous career; **ehrenamtliche ~** honorary position (service), unpaid position; **entgeltliche ~** paid work; **erhöhte ~** increased activity; **fördernde ~** promotional activity; **freiberufliche ~** occupation of a professional nature, professional employment; **führende ~** executive capacity;

gefährliche ~ hazardous employment; **geistige** ~ brainwork, mental work, black-coated work *(Br.)*; **geschäftliche** ~ business activity, activity in trade; **gewerbliche** ~ industrial activity, business occupation (activity), pursuit of a trade; **auf Gewinnerzielung gerichtete gewerbliche** ~ *(Doppelbesteuerungsabkommen)* trade or business carried on for purpose of profit; **gewerkschaftliche** ~ union activity; **gewinnbringende** ~ gainful occupation, productive activity; **handwerkliche** ~ handicraft trade; **hauptberufliche** ~ full-time job; **häusliche** ~ housework; **industrielle** ~ industrial employment; **intensive** ~ extensive activities; **karitative** ~ good works; **kaufmännische** ~ mercantile (commercial) pursuits; **landwirtschaftliche** ~ farming operations; **langweilige** ~ dull occupation, mean job *(US)*; **läppische** ~ fiddling little jobs; **leitende** ~ executive work (action, capacity); **außerhalb meines Büros liegende** ~ occupation outside of my work; **mechanische** ~ routine job; **mehrjährige** ~ activities over several years; **nebenberufliche** ~ sideline employment; **pflichtversicherte** ~ covered job *(US)*; **primitive** ~ rough work; **produktive** ~ productive activity; **richterliche** ~ judicial act; **schöpferische** ~ creative work; **schriftstellerische** ~ literary profession (work); **selbständige** ~ independent activities, self-employment; **sitzende** ~ sedentary profession; **staatswichtige** ~ work of national importance; **streikfreie** ~ strike-free work; **subversive** ~ subversive activity; **treuhänderische** ~ fiduciary activity; **überwiegende** ~ *(Steuerrecht)* paramount occupation; **unbedeutende** ~**en** fiddling little jobs; **unbefugte** ~ unauthorized act; **unselbständige** ~ payroll employment, employment work; **verantwortungsvolle** ~ responsible post; **nicht vergütete** ~ *(Beamter)* extra services; **vervollständigende** ~ follow-up work; **wirtschaftliche** ~ economic activity; **beratende wissenschaftliche** ~ scientific advisory work; **zumutbare** ~ reasonable act;
~ **in einer Branche** line activity; ~ **im Dienst der Öffentlichkeit** public occupation (calling); ~ **außerhalb der Dienststunden** work out of hours; ~ **als Führungskraft** managerial (executive) work; ~ **für die Gewerkschaft** union business; ~ **in der Industrie** industrial occupation; ~ **am Jugendgericht** juvenile court work; ~ **in der Landwirtschaft** agricultural occupation; ~ **im Ministerium** service in a ministry; **wissentschaftliche** ~ **nach der Promotion** postgraduate work; ~ **auf Vorstandsebene** working at board level;
anwaltliche ~ **aufgeben** to retire from the bar; **schriftstellerische** ~ **aufgeben** to give up writing; ~ **aufnehmen** to engage in an activity, to enter upon one's duties; **seine** ~ **wieder aufnehmen** to resume one's activity; **seine** ~ **über das ganze Land ausdehnen** to sell one's services country-wide; ~ **ausüben** to be engaged in an activity, to carry on a profession; **keine bestimmte** ~ **ausüben** to have no regular work (occupation); **stabilisierende** ~ **ausüben** to serve as a stabilizing force; **seine** ~ **beenden** to relinquish one's place, to complete action; ~ **entfalten** to be active; **fieberhafte** ~ **entwickeln** to display great activity; **sich an eine geregelte** ~ **gewöhnen** to get used to regular work; **einer** ~ **nachgehen** to pursue an occupation; **in** ~ **sein** *(Vulkan)* to be active; **im Rahmen seiner** ~ **beruflich viel unterwegs sein** to travel much in one's job; **Alarmanlage außer** ~ **setzen** to stop the alarm system; **Schauplatz seiner** ~ **verlegen** to shift the scene of one's activities; **sich zur Nichtausübung einer** ~ **verpflichten** to undertake not to perform a particular act; ~ **wiederaufnehmen** to resume activity.

Tätigkeits|analyse job analysis; ~**bereich** way, province, business, line, field (radius) of activity, activities, sphere of action, area of operation, purview; **geschäftlicher** ~**bereich** field of business activity; ~**bericht** progress (action, activity) report, *(Geschäftsbericht)* business (annual) report; ~**beschreibung** job specification (description, *US*); **sich lähmend auf jds.** ~**drang auswirken** to act as a brake on s. one's activities; ~**feld** line, purview; **freies** ~**feld** free field of operations; **sein** ~**feld ausdehnen** to extend the scope of one's activities; ~**gebiet** line, purview, field of action (operation), province, business; ~**kreis** sphere of activity.

Tat|irrtum mistake of fact; ~**kraft** push, energy, go, pep.

tatkräftig energetic, vigorous, active.

tätliche Beleidigung assault [and battery].

Tätlichkeit battery, assault *(US)*;
zu ~**en schreiten** to proceed to violence.

Tat|mehrheit joinder of offences; ~**mensch** man of action; ~**motiv** inducement.

Tatort venue, scene of crime, place of tort;
beteuern, nie in der Nähe des ~**s gewesen zu sein** to protest that one has never been near the scene of the crime;
~**besichtigung** viewing scene of crime.

Tatsache fact, matter of (issue in) fact;
als ~ **angenommen** habit and repute; **angesichts der** ~**n** in view of the facts;
~**n** facts, data *(US)*;
anerkannte ~ admitted fact; **für die Zuständigkeit bedeutsame** ~ jurisdictional fact; **belastende** ~ incriminatory fact; **beweiserhebliche** ~**n** probative (evidentiary) facts; **bereits bewiesene** ~ proven fact; **vom Versicherungsvertreter bei der Besichtigung nicht entdeckte** ~**n** facts which the insurer's representative fails to notice on a survey; **entlastende** ~**n** exculpatory (informative) facts; **erfundene** ~ simulated fact; **für die Entscheidung erhebliche** ~**n** facts in issue; **vorgespiegelte falsche** ~ fabricated fact; **festgestellte** ~ accomplished (ascertained) fact; **feststehende** ~**en** known facts, established facts; **aktenmäßig feststehende** ~ matter of record; **gegebene** ~ datum; **gerichtsnotorische** ~**n** jurisdiction notice; **grundlegende** ~**n** basic facts, fudamental data; **klagebegründende** ~**n** facts constituting the cause of action; **neue klagebegründende** ~**n** new cause of action; **nachgewiesene** ~**n** evidentiary facts; **urkundlich nachweisbare** ~ matter in deed; **nackte** ~**n** hard (cold, glaring, nude, crude) facts; **offenkundige** ~ obvious fact; **rechtsbegründende** ~**n** dispositive (constitutive, investive) facts; **risikoherabsetzende** ~**n** *(Feuerversicherung)* facts which improve the risk; **simulierte** ~ false fact; **strittige** ~**n** facts in issue; **nicht zu übersehende** ~**n** striking facts; **unbestreitbare** ~ irrefutable facts; **für die Entscheidung unerhebliche** ~ immaterial fact; **ungeschminkte** ~**n** crude (dry, sober) facts; **unstreitige** ~**n** *(Prozeß)* collateral facts; **umumstößliche** ~**n** hard (frozen, *US*) facts; **unwesentliche** ~**n** immaterial facts; **verbürgte** ~ matter of record; **vollendete** ~ accomplished fact, fait accompli; **vorgebrachte** ~**n** material allegations; **sinnlich wahrnehmbare** ~ physical fact; **wesentliche** ~**n** material facts; **für das Versicherungsrisiko wesentliche** ~**n** facts material to risk; **zugestandene** ~**n** conceded facts;
~, **die den Verlust eines Rechtes nach sich zieht** divestitive fact; **sich mit den** ~**n abfinden** to come round to the facts; ~**n anführen** to state (adduce) facts; **von der** ~ **ausgehen** to start from the fact; **Ausschuß mit den** ~**n bekanntmachen** to lay facts before a committee; **auf** ~**n beruhen** to be founded on facts; ~ **bestätigen** to testify to a fact; **sich der Macht der** ~**n beugen** to acknowledge the evidence of facts; ~ **beweisen** to establish a fact; **einige neue** ~**n zu Tage bringen** to develop some new facts; ~**n feststellen** to ascertain the facts; **sich mehr an die** ~**n halten** to be more factual; ~ **leugnen** to blink a fact; ~**n mitteilen** to make discovery; ~**n noch gründlicher prüfen** to investigate the facts more thoroughly; **eine** ~ **aus einer anderen schließen** to presume one fact from another; **den** ~**n ins Gesicht sehen** to face the facts; ~**n ins richtige Licht setzen** to put the record straight; **sich auf den Boden der** ~**n stellen** to face the facts; **wichtige** ~ **unterdrücken** to suppress an important fact; **mit** ~**n untermauern** to prove with facts; ~**n verdrehen** to pervert the facts; ~**n verkennen** to misapprehend the facts; **sich den** ~**n verschließen** to blind o. s. to the facts; **falsche** ~ **vorspiegeln** to make false pretences, to fraudulently misrepresent; **sich mit den** ~**n nicht abfinden wollen** to fly in the face of facts; ~**n zusammenstellen** to piece together; ~**n zusammentragen** to gather (glean) facts.

Tatsachen|angaben machen to state the facts; ~**behauptung** statement (allegation) of facts, averment; ~**bericht** first-hand account, factual (relevant) statement (report); ~**enthüllung** discovery of facts; **unrichtige** ~**erklärung** misrepresentation of facts; ~**feststellung** *(Gericht)* finding of fact, fact finding; **einleitende** ~**feststellung** inducement; ~**film** documentary; ~**geständnis** admission of facts; ~**irrtum** error (mistake) of facts; ~**material** factual evidence, data *(US)*; ~**schilderung**, ~**vortrag** recital of facts; ~**schlußfolgerung** conclusion of fact; ~**unterdrückung** concealment (misrepresentation) of facts; ~**verdrehung** distortion of facts; ~**verkennung** misapprehension of facts; ~**vermutung** presumption of fact; ~**vortrag** submission of the facts; **gelangweilten Schülern** ~**wissen eintrichtern** to pump facts into the heads of dull pupils.

tatsächlich actual, factual, based on fact, in effect, virtual, true, real, in [point of] fact;
~ **und rechtlich** in fact and in law;
~**es Angebot** real offer; ~**e Arbeitsstunden** actual hours; ~**er Bedarf** effective demand; ~**er Besitz** naked possession; ~**er Bestand** actual amount, real stock; ~**e Beweisführung** real evidence; ~**e Einigung** factual consent; ~**es Einkommen** real income; ~**e Einnahmen** actual takings; ~**e Feststellungen** statement of facts; ~**es Gehalt** effective pay rate; ~**er Gesamtverlust** actual total loss; ~**er Gewinn** actual profit; ~

eingezahltes **Kapital** paid-up capital; **~e Kosten** actual costs; **~er Notenumlauf** active circulation; **~er Preis** real price; **~e Sachlage** real state of affairs; **~ entstandener Schaden** actual damage; **~er Verdienst** actual earnings; **~er Wert** real (effective, true) value.

Tattergreis totterer, dodderer *(coll.)*.

Tatumstände set of circumstances, facts of the case;
Darstellung der ~ geben to state the facts.

Tatverdacht suspicion;
wegen dringenden ~s on strong suspicion;
kein ausreichender ~ not found; **hinreichender ~** reasonable and probable cause;
dringenden ~ bestätigen to find an indictment; **mangels ~s freisprechen** to pronounce an hono(u)rable acquittal; **unter ~ stehen** to be under suspicion.

Tat|verdächtiger person under suspicion, suspected person; **~vorsatz** premeditated design; **~waffe** murderous weapon; **~zeit** time of tort; **~zeuge** witness to a crime.

Tau dew, *(Seil)* line, rope;
~ losmachen to unbend a rope.

taub deaf, *(vor Kälte)* numb;
sich ~ stellen to feign deafness;
~en Ohren predigen to talk to deaf ears.

Taube *(pol.)* dove.

Taubenschlag dovecote;
wie im ~ zugehen to be like a railway station.

taubstumm deaf and dumb.

Taubstummen|alphabet deaf-and-dumb alphabet; **~lehrer** oral teacher; **~sprache** finger alphabet, deaf-and-dumb signs (language).

Tauchboot submarine.

Tauchen diving, dive.

tauchen *(U-Boot)* to dive, to submerge;
nach Perlen ~ to dive for pearls.

Taucher diver;
~anzug diving suit (dress); **~ausrüstung** diving equipment, skin-diving gear; **~brille** diver's goggles; **~glocke** diving bell; **~helm** diving helm; **~kugel** bathosphere, bathysphere.

Tauch|fahrt dive; **~sieder** immersion heater; **~station** diving station; **auf ~station gehen** to dive, *(fig.)* to keep shady *(sl.)*, to go bush; **~tank** *(U-Boot)* ballast tank; **~tiefe** diving depth; **~versuch** trial dive.

tauen to be thawing, to melt.

Taufe baptism, christening;
etw. aus der ~ heben to stand sponsor for s. th.; **Verein aus der ~ heben** to inaugurate (found, initiate) an association.

taufen to baptize, to christen, *(Äquatortaufe)* to duck.

Tauf|name Christian (given, *US*) name; **~register** baptism register.

taufrisch fühlen, sich to feel as fresh as a daisy.

Taufschein certificate of baptism.

taugen to be good (fit) for, to be suited (suitable);
etw. ~ to be worth one's salt; **zu nichts ~** to be fit (good) for nothing; **überhaupt nichts ~** to be up to no good; **nicht zum Rechtsanwalt ~** not to be cut out to be a lawyer; **in der Schule überhaupt nichts ~** to be no earthly good at school.

Taugenichts reprobate, never-do-well, ne'er-do-well, good-for-nothing, no-good, waster, wastrel, rip.

tauglich fit, capable, qualified, able, apt, *(brauchbar)* serviceable, *(mil.)* able-bodied, *(Schiff)* seaworthy;
~ zum Dienst mit der Waffe fit for active service; **nicht ~** unfit; **~ befunden werden** *(mil.)* to be passed fit, to pass muster.

Tauglichkeit capacity, competence, fitness, qualification, capableness, *(Brauchbarkeit)* serviceableness, *(mil.)* ablebodiedness, fitness for service, *(Schiff)* seaworthiness;
körperliche ~ physical fitness;
~ zum vertragsmäßigen Gebrauch fitness for a particular purpose.

Tauglichkeits|bescheinigung certificate of fitness; **~grad** degree of fitness; **~zeugnis** certificate of fitness, qualifying certificate.

Taumel giddiness, dizziness, grogginess;
im ~ der Begeisterung in the whirl of excitement;
~ der Freude rapture of joy.

taumeln to totter, to stagger, to teeter;
über die Straße ~ to lurch across the street.

Tausch barter, trading, truck *(US)*, *(Austausch)* change, exchange, *(Börse)* swap, swop;
neuen Posten durch ~ erhalten to exchange into a new post; **in ~ geben** to give in exchange, to barter, to truck; **in ~ nehmen** to trade in, to take in exchange; **~ vornehmen** to make an exchange; **im ~ weggeben** to barter away;
~abkommen barter agreement (deal); **~angebot** exchange offer; **~anzeige** barter (exchange) advertisement; **~befugnis** authority to barter; **~einheit** barter unit.

tauschen to exchange, to merchandise, to trade, to barter, to truck *(US)*, *(Börse)* to swap;
Arbeitsplätze ~ to trade jobs; **ausländische Briefmarken ~** to swop foreign stamps; **Plätze ~** to exchange seats; **Rollen ~** to exchange parts;
um keinen Preis mit jem. ~ wollen not to like to be in s. one's shoes.

täuschen to deceive, to delude, to fraud, to mislead, to double-cross *(sl.)*, *(hinters Licht führen)* to fool, to bamboozle, to hoodwink, *(Schüler)* to cheat;
sich ~ to deceive o. s.; **j. über seine Absichten ~** to mislead s. o. as to one's intentions; **j. in seinen Erwartungen ~** to frustrate s. one's expectations; **durch eine Finte ~** to feint; **Öffentlichkeit ~** to practise deception on the public;
leicht zu ~ deceivable.

täuschend delusive, misleading, deceptive, illusory;
seinem Vater ~ ähnlich sein to be the spit and image of one's father;
~e Ähnlichkeit striking resemblance; **~e Nachahmung** remarkable good imitation; **~e Werbung** misleading advertising.

Tausch|er barterer; **~exemplar** exchange copy.

tauschfähig exchangeable, barterable.

Tausch|gegenstand exchange, barter; **~geschäft** exchange [transaction, deal], barter [transaction], bartering, trading operation, *(Börse)* swap, swop; **~geschäfte machen** to barter, to trade, to dicker *(US)*, to truck *(US)*, *(Börse)* to swap, to swop.

Tauschhandel exchange, bartering, barter [trade], permutation, dicker *(US)*, truck *(US)*;
~ treiben to interchange, to trade, to [carry on] barter, to truck *(US)*.

Tauschhandels|abkommen barter (bartering) agreement; **~geschäft** barter transaction; **fingiertes ~geschäft** dry exchange.

Tausch|händler barterer, trucker *(US)*; **~kredit** barter credit; **~mittel** circulating (exchange) medium, medium of exchange, barter; **~objekt** exchange, barter; **als ~objekt annehmen** to take in exchange; **~produkte** barter[ing] (exchangeable) goods.

Täuschung deception, disguise, cheat, deceit, camouflage, mirage, mystification, *(Betrug)* fraud;
zum Zwecke der ~ with intent to deceive;
arglistige ~ wilful deception, positive (actionable, moral) fraud, *(Vertragsabschluß)* false (fraudulent) misstatement, fraudulent (wil(l)ful) misrepresentation, deceit; **bewußte ~** wilful deception, deceit; **landesverräterische ~** treacherous forgery; **optische ~** optical illusion; **vorsätzliche ~** *(Betrug)* false (fraudulent) representation;
~ zur Umgehung der Wehrpflicht fraudulent draft evasion *(US)*, attempt to avoid conscription *(Br.)*;
arglistige ~ begehen to be liable to deceit; **sich einer ~ hingeben** to cherish an illusion.

Täuschungs|absicht intentional deceit, intention to deceive; **~angriff** feint attack; **~handlung** deception; **~manöver** diversion, artifice; **~manöver durchführen** to draw a red herring across the trail; **~versuch** attempted deceit, try-on *(sl.)*.

Tausch|vertrag barter agreement; **~waren** barter goods; **~wert** exchange (exchangeable) value; **~wert für Inzahlungnahme** trade-in value; **~wirtschaft** barter (truck, *US*) economy.

Tausend, glatte ~ in der Woche verdienen to clear a cool thousand a week.

tausend, in ~ Ängsten schweben to be scared out of one's senses.

Tausenddollargrenze überschritten haben to have turned the thousand dollar point.

Tausenderpreis *(Anzeigenpreis)* cost-per-thousand, milline *(US)*.

Tausend|sassa allround man, Jack-of-all-trades; **~satz** permillage, *(Anzeigenwesen)* cost-per-thousand, milline *(US)*.

Tau|wetter *(pol.)* thaw; **~ziehen** tug-of-war.

Taxameter taximeter.

Taxamt valuation board.

Taxator appraiser, valuer, valuator, appreciator, taxer, assessor, rater, liquidator *(US)*;
amtlicher ~ professional valuer, general appraiser; **vereidigter ~** sworn valuer.

Taxe valuation, appraisement, appraisal, rate, estimate, *(Abgabe)* duty, *(Auktion)* knock-down price, *(Gebühr)* charge, valuation fee, *(Tarif)* tariff, *(Taxi)* cab, taxicab, motorcab, hack *(US)*;
nach der ~ as per tariff;

~ **eines Geschäftsgrundstücks** business property appraisal; ~ **über dem Wert** overvaluation; ~ **unter dem Wert** undervaluation;
~ **aufstellen** to draw up a valuation; ~ **bestellen** to call (order) a cab (a taxi); **mit der** ~ **fahren** to [ride in a] taxi; **sich über die Höhe einer** ~ **nicht einig werden können** to disagree about a valuation; ~ **zum Bahnhof nehmen** to [take a] taxi to the station; **einer** ~ **unterliegen** to be subject to a tax; **nach** ~ **verkaufen** to dispose at a valuation; **unter der** ~ **verkaufen** to sell at a reduced price (discount).
Taxenstand taxi stand (rank), cabstand.
Tax|gebühren [appraiser's] fees, valuer's charges; ~**gewicht** appraised weight.
Taxi cab, taxicab, motorcab, hack *(US)*;
freies ~ empty taxi, taxi with the flag up, crawler *(Br.)*; **vereinzeltes** ~ stray taxi;
~ **benutzen** *(fam.)* to cab [it]; ~ **bestellen** to call (order) a cab (taxi); **sich für ein System gemeinsam benutzter** ~**s entscheiden** to opt for a share-a-cab system; **mit dem** ~ **nach Hause fahren** to cab it home; ~ **heranwinken** to hail a taxi; ~ **nehmen** to take a taxi; **sich in ein** ~ **stürzen** to jump into a taxi; **j. in ein** ~ **verfrachten** to bundle s. o. into a taxi;
~**besitzer** taxi operator.
taxierbar assessable, appreciable, taxable, rat(e)able.
Taxieren rating, appraisal, valuation.
taxieren to appraise, to appreciate, to value, to evaluate, to estimate, to prize, to gauge *(steuerlich)* to assess, to rate;
j. ~ to sum s. o. up; **Gebäude zu hoch** ~ to set too high a valuation on a building; **Grundstück** ~ to estimate an estate (the value of land); **zu hoch** ~ to overrate, to overvalue; **j. auf etwa dreißig Jahre** ~ to put s. o. down at about thirty; **zu niedrig** ~ to undervalue, to underrate; **Schaden auf fünf Pfund** ~ to value the damage [done] at five pounds; **Waren** ~ to value goods.
Taxierer appraiser, prizer.
taxiert|auf valued at;
zu hoch ~ rated too high; **nicht** ~ unprized; **zu niedrig** ~ underrated.
Taxierung appraisal, appraisement, valuation, rating, evaluation;
~ **des Anlagevermögens** fixed-asset valuation; ~ **zu Steuerzwecken** appraisal for taxation purposes, assessment.
Taxi|fahrer cab (taxi) driver, cabby *(Br.)*, cabman *(Br.)*; **auf Kundschaft wartender** ~**fahrer** taxi driver plying for hire; ~**fahrergewerkschaft** taxi-drivers' union; ~**fahrerin** cabette *(Br.)*; ~**fahrt** taxi ride, run; ~**flotte** fleet of cars; ~**haltestelle** taxi rank *(Br.)* (stand), cabstand, taxistand; ~**konzession** brief, hack licence *(US)*; ~**preis für hin und zurück** return taxi fare; **hohe** ~**rechnung anzeigen** to tick up a huge fare; ~**stand** cabstand, hack stand *(US)*, taxi stand (rank, *Br.*), cab *(Br.)* (taxi, *US*) rank; ~**verleih** cab company.
Tax|kurs estimation price, *(Wertpapiere)* estimated quotation, appraisal value; ~**ordnung** scale of fees.
Taxpreis appraisal (assessed) value, set-up (assessed) price, *(Auktion)* put-up price;
zu einem ~ **von** at a valuation of;
über ~ **verkaufen** to sell at a figure above valuation.
Taxwert appraisal (assessed, estimated) value, appraisal, appraisement.
Team team, line-up;
~ **zur Aufspürung von Führungsnachwuchs** executive search unit;
~**mitglied** team member.
Technik technics, engineering, *(Fertigkeit)* workmanship, skill, *(Verfahren)* technique, practice, *(Wissenschaft)* technology, technical science;
auf dem neuesten Stand der ~ **sein** to be the latest technical development; **über eine brillante** ~ **verfügen** to be an excellent technician.
Techniker [technical] engineer, *(Spezialist)* technician, *(Wissenschaft)* technologist.
Technikolorverfahren technicolo(u)r.
Technikum technological school.
technisch technical, engineering;
~**e Abteilung** engineering department; ~ **bedingte Arbeitslosigkeit** technological unemployment; ~**e Ausbildung** technical training; ~**er Ausdruck** technical term; ~**e Ausführung** technique; ~**e Ausstattung** machinery; ~**er Berater** technical consultant (adviser); ~**er Beruf** technical profession; ~**e Beschaffenheit** technicality; ~**e Betriebsabteilung** technical (engineering) department; ~**er Betriebsleiter** chief engineer; ~**es Büro** engineering department, technical office; ~**e Chemie** engineering chemistry; ~**e Dimensionen** technical potential; ~**er Direktor** technical director (manager); ~**e Einrichtungen** engineering facilities; ~**er Einwand** technical estoppel; ~**e Einzelheiten** technicalities, technical details; ~**e Errungenschaft** technical feat; ~**e Fächer** engineering fields; ~**es Fachwörterbuch** technological dictionary; ~**e Formalitäten** legal formalities; ~**er Fortschritt** technological progress (advance), technical progress; ~**es Geschick** technical skill, technique; **aus** ~**en Gründen** for practical reasons; ~**e Hilfeleistungen** technical aid; ~**e Hochschule** engineering college (school), technical college, school of technology; ~**e Kapazitäten** industrial capacities; ~**er Kaufmann** sales engineer; ~**e Kenntnisse** technical knowledge; **bedeutende** ~**e Leistungen** brilliant feats of engineering; ~**er Leiter** technical manager (director); ~**e Messe** engineering fair; ~**e Neuerungen** technical innovations; ~**e Normenvorschriften** engineering standards; ~**e Nothilfe** Organization for the Maintenance of Supplies *(Br.)*, Office of Emergency Preparedness *(US)*; ~**es Personal** engineering (technical) staff; ~**e Produktionsanlagen** production facilities; ~**er Rückstand** technological gap; ~**e Schwierigkeiten** technical difficulties; ~**er Stab** engineering force (staff); ~**er Überwachungsverein** technical control board; ~**e Unterlagen** technical data; ~**e Verbesserung** technical improvement; ~**es Verfahren** technical process; ~**er Verkäufer** technical sales representative, salesman engineer; ~**es Versagen** breakdown; ~**e Voraussetzungen** technical prerequisites; ~**e Vorschau** technological forecasting *(US)*; ~**er Zeichner** tracer, draughtsman, draftsman; ~**e Zeitschrift** engineering journal, technical publication; ~**e Zusammenarbeit** technical collaboration; ~**er Zustand** technicality; ~**e Zuverlässigkeitsbescheinigung** roadworthiness test certificate.
Technisierung technicalization.
Technologie technology.
technologisch technological;
~ **bedingte Arbeitslosigkeit** technological unemployment; ~**e Entwicklung** technological progress; ~**er Fortschritt** technological advance; ~**e Lücke** technological gap; ~**er Rückstand** technological backwardness.
Tee, dünner weak (husband's) tea;
abwarten und ~ **trinken** wait and see;
~**beutel** tea-bag; ~**gebäck** tea biscuit; ~**geschirr** tea-things; ~**händler** tea merchant; ~**haus** tea house; ~**kiste** tea chest; ~**pflanzung** tea garden.
teeren und federn to tar and feather.
Teer|jacke jack-tar; ~**pappe** tarred felt.
Tee|service tea-service; ~**stube** tea-room, café; ~**wagen** tea-trolley, tea waggon, trolley table *(Br.)*; ~**zeit** tea-time.
Teich pond, *(künstlich)* pool;
der große ~ the herring pond *(sl.)*.
Teil part, *(Abschnitt)* section, segment, division, *(Anteil)* lot, share, portion, quota, *(Bauteil)* [structural] member, *(Bestandteil)* component, element, *(Ersatzteil)* spare [part], *(Prozentsatz)* percentage, *(Stück)* piece, *(Zubehör)* accessory;
aus allen ~**en der Welt** from all over the world; **aus einzelnen** ~**en bestehend** sectional; **in allen** ~**en** throughout; **zu gleichen** ~**en** share alike, in equal parts (shares, portions), fifty-fifty; **zum** ~ in part;
ausgewechselte ~**e** replaced parts; **auswechselbare** ~**e** interchangeable (interceptable) parts; **beide** ~**e** both sides; **beklagter** ~ defending party, defendant; **beleidigter** ~ party offended; **bildwichtiger** ~ *(Foto)* center of interest; **einleitender** ~ *(Urkunde)* recital; **innerhalb eines Jahres fälliger** ~ *(Obligation)* current maturity; **geschäftlich genutztes** ~ *(Grundstück)* business proportion; **geschädigter** ~ injured party; **größerer** ~ bulk, major part, majority; **innerster** ~ heart, center *(US)*, centre *(Br.)*; **klagender** ~ plaintiff; **literarischer** ~ *(Zeitung)* literary supplement; **lokaler** ~ *(Zeitung)* local section; **pfändbarer** ~ judgement- (mace-proof, *US*) portion; **redaktioneller** ~ editorial matter; **risikoreicherer** ~ *(Kapitalanlagegesellschaft)* aggressive portion *(US)*; **risikoschwächerer** ~ **[der Effektenanlage]** defensive portion *(US)*; **schuldige** ~**e** *(Scheidung)* guilty party, *(Unfall)* party at fault in an accident; **schwenkbarer** ~ *(Maschine)* traverse; **überlebender** ~ *(Versicherung)* surviving party; **unbedruckter** ~ blind part; **frei verfügbarer** ~ *(Erbe)* disposable portion; **vertragschließender** ~ contracting party, contractant; **vorderer** ~ *(Zeitung)* front section; **wesentlicher** ~ essential (substantial) part, part and parcel;
wesentlicher ~ **einer Beschwerde** sum and substance of a complaint; **großer** ~ **der Einwohner** large number of the

inhabitants; **wesentlicher ~ eines Gesetzes** operative part of an act; ~ **einer Maschine** section of a machine; ~ **einer Parzelle** piece of parcel ground, pendicle *(Scot.)*; **nicht rückversicherter ~ des Risikos** retained risk; **ungedeckter ~ der Staatsschuld** deadweight debt *(Br.)*; **schönster ~ der Stadt** most beautiful part of a town; ~ **einer Strecke** section of a road; **einleitender ~ einer Urkunde** whereas clauses; **größerer ~ des Vermögens** bulk of the property; **~e mit hoher Verschleißquote** high-mortality parts; ~ **einer Versuchsgruppe** *(Marktforschung)* subsample; **größter ~ der Zuschauer** majority of the spectators;
seinen ~ abbekommen to come in for one's share; **seinen ~ beitragen** to do one's share (bit), to stand one's corner *(sl.)*, to pay one's share, to pull one's weight; ~ **bilden** to form a part; **sich seinen ~ denken** to have one's own opinion about s. th.; **an der Verschwörung keinen ~ haben** to have nothing to do with the conspiracy; **Roman zum großen ~ gelesen haben** to have read the greater part of a novel; **beide ~e hören** to hear both parties (sides); **jeden ~ sorgfältig prüfen** to check each piece carefully; **~e reprivatisieren** to hive off parts; **nur ein ~ des Jahres befahrbar sein** to be passable only part of the year; **zu gleichen ~en beteiligt sein** to go shares (share and share alike, fifty-fifty); **ein gut ~ größer sein** to be a good deal greater; **besseren ~ wählen** to make the better bargain; **in einzelne ~e zerlegen** to dismantle; ~ **eines Nachlasses zweckbestimmen** to set off a portion of an estate.

teilabgeschrieben sein to be partly depreciated.

Teil|abhebung partial withdrawal; **~abkommen** *(Völkerrecht)* partial agreement; **~abladung** partial shipment; **~abrechnung** *(Testamentsvollstrecker)* partial account; **~abschnitt** subjection, *(Abzahlung)* instal(l)ment, *(Anleihe)* fractional lot *(US)*, *(Autobahn)* section; **~abtretung** partial assignment; **~aktie** stock scrip; **~akzept** partial acceptance; **~anmeldung** *(Patent)* partial application; **~annahme** partial acceptance; **~ansicht** sectional view; **~anspruch** part interest; **~anspruch einklagen** to split a cause of action; **~arbeitskräfte** part-time workers; **~arbeitslosenunterstützung** partial unemployment benefit; **~arbeitslosigkeit** partial unemployment; **~aufhebung eines Gesetzes** derogation of a law; **~ausbau** partial extension; **~ausführung** partial execution; **~ausgabe** *(Anleihe)* slice; **~ausverkauf** closeout *(US)*, clearance sale.

teilbar divisible, partable, *(abtrennbar)* severable.

Teil|barkeit divisibility; **~baugenehmigung** partial building permit; **~befrachtung** partial freighting; **~befriedigung** partial satisfaction; **~bereich** subregion; **~beschäftigter** part-time worker; **~beschäftigung** part-time employment; **~bescheid** interim decision; **~besitz** part ownership; **~besitzer** part owner; **~betrag** fractional amount, *(Abzahlung)* instal(l)ment, *(Anleihe)* part, slice, *(Quote)* quota; **in Gold zahlbarer ~betrag** *(Weltwährungsfonds)* gold tranche; **auf der Rückseite eines Wechsels den Empfang eines ~betrages quittieren** to endorse a sum of money on a bill; **in ~beträgen** in denominations; **~betrieb** part of a business; **~beweis** partial evidence; **~bilanz** section of a balance sheet; **~bild** *(Fernsehen)* frame, field *(US)*; **~charter** part-charter.

Teilchen particle.

Teil|diebstahl partial theft; **auf ~einkünfte verzichten** to relinquish one's right to part of the income.

teilen to divide, to halve, *(abteilen)* to separate, to part, to partition off, *(Aktien)* to split, *(aufteilen)* to allocate, to apportion, *(Gewinne)* to pool, to share, to take part;
sich ~ *(Partei)* to split, to splinter, *(Straße)* to branch out, to fork; **sich in etw. ~** to go shares (halves, snacks), to share s. th.; **Ansicht ~** to share a view; **Anwaltshonorar ~** to split a fee; **sich die Beute gleichmäßig ~** to split even on a swag; **Büro mit jem. ~** to share an office with s. o.; **Erlös ~** to distribute the proceeds; **Gewinn untereinander ~** to divide the profit among themselves; **Gewinne und Verluste zu gleichen Teilen ~** to share and share alike; **letzten Groschen mit jem. ~** to share one's last penny with s. o.; **sich ein Hotelzimmer mit jem. ~** to share a hotel bedroom with a stranger; **sich mit jem. in die Kosten ~** to share (go shares) with s. o. in the costs, to bear the expenses in equal shares; **sich den Preisunterschied ~** to split the difference; **Verlust ~** to share a loss; **Wohnung mit jem. ~** to share an apartment (flat, *Br.*) with s. o.

Teil|entschädigung partial indemnification (indemnity); **~erfolg** partial success; **~erfüllung** part performance; **~erhebung** *(Statistik)* sample statistics, partial data, incomplete census; **~erneuerung** partial renovation; **~ersatz** partial replacement; **~finanzierungskredit** instal(l)ment credit; **~fläche** piece of parcel ground; **~fracht** part cargo; **~frage** *(Tagesordnung)* point; **~freispruch** partial verdict; **~gebiet** subregion, section, branch, *(Stadt)* zone; **ertragreiche ~gebiete wieder reprivatisieren** to hive off profitable activities to the private sector; **~gesellschaft** subsidiary; **~geständnis** partial admission; **~grundstück** piece of parcel ground; **~gültigkeitsklausel** separability clause; **~gutschriftskonto für ausländische Wechsel** marginal deposit account *(Br.)*.

teilhaben to participate, to partake, to be sharer (a partner) in, to share in, to take a share, to have a part in.

Teilhaber [joint] partner, copartner, [business] associate, fellow, fellow partner, companion, consociate, *(Beteiligter)* participant, participator, partaker, sharer, shareholder, party, *(Maklerfirma)* floor partner *(US)*, *(Miteigentümer)* joint proprietor (owner), *(pl.)* associates in office;
~ gesucht *(Anzeige)* partnership wanted;
abwickelnder ~ liquidating partner; **aktiver ~** working partner; **älterer ~** senior partner; **ausgeschiedener ~** past partner; **ausscheidender ~** retiring (withdrawing, outgoing) partner; **vom Konkurs nicht betroffener ~** solvent partner; **neu eintretender ~** incoming partner; **Gesellschaftsverhältnis fortsetzender ~** surviving partner; **geschäftsführender ~** active (acting, managing, working) partner; **nicht geschäftsführender ~** silent (sleeping) partner; **beschränkt haftender ~** limited (special) partner; **persönlich (unbeschränkt) haftender ~** responsible (general, associated, unlimited, ordinary, *Br.*) partner; **nicht persönlich haftender ~** subordinate partner *(Br.)*; **jüngerer ~** junior partner; **minderjähriger ~** infant partner; **staatlicher ~** state-run partner; **stiller ~** sleeping *(Br.)* (dormant, latent, secret) partner, merchant dormant, silent partner *(US)*; **tätiger ~** active owner (partner), acting, (working) partner; **nicht tätiger ~** inactive partner; **verbleibender ~** continuing partner; **verstorbener ~** deceased partner; **zahlungsunfähiger ~** partner in default;
~ abfinden to buy out a partner; **[als] ~ aufnehmen** to take in a (admit as) partner, to take into partnership, to make a party to an undertaking; **j. als ~ ausgeben** to hold s. o. out as a partner; **als ~ ausscheiden** to leave (withdraw from) a partnership; **als ~ eintreten** to join a firm (be admitted) as partner, to become partner in a firm, to enter a firm as partner, to connect o. s. as partner with a house, to go into copartnership with; **als ~ persönlich haften** to be personally liable as a partner; **sich als ~ qualifizieren** to reach partnership level; **als ~ aufgenommen werden** to join a partnership; **jds. ~ in einem Unternehmen werden** to associate o. s. with s. o. in an undertaking.

teilhaberähnliches Interesse partner-like stake.

Teilhaber|anspruch auf das Gesellschaftsvermögen zur Schuldendeckung equity of partners; **~chancen** prospects of partnership; **~konto** partnership account.

Teilhaberschaft [joint] partnership, associateship, participating rights, parcenary, copartnership;
mit der Aussicht späterer ~ with a view to partnership; **auf mündlicher Vereinbarung beruhende ~** oral partnership; **jederzeit kündbare ~** partnership at will; **stille ~** dormant (secret, sleeping, *Br.*, silent, *US*) partnership;
~ durch Erwerb von Aktien contributory copartnership;
~ auflösen to dissolve a partnership; **~ eingehen** to enter into partnership.

Teilhaberschaftsverhältnis begründen to organize a partnership.

Teilhaber|spedition participating carrier; **~vergütung** partner's salary; **~verhältnis** partnership relation; **~versicherung** partnership insurance, partnership assurance *(Br.)*; **~vertrag** partnership agreement, copartnery, contract of partnership, copartnership contract.

Teil|haftung partial liability; **~havarie** petty (particular) average; **~index** subindex; **~indossament** partial endorsement (indorsement); **~invalidität** partial disability (incapacity); **dauernde ~invalidität** permanent partial disability; **~inventur** departmental stocktaking, *(Stichprobenprüfung)* test inventory; **~kasko** comprehensive coverage *(US)*; **~kaskoversicherung** comprehensive automobile and property damage *(US)* (motorcar, *Br.*) insurance; **~käufe machen** to buy on a scale; **~klage** splitting a cause of action; **~kostenrechnung** direct costing *(US)*, marginal costing *(Br.)*; **~krise** localized crisis; **~ladung** partial shipment; **in ~ladungen verschiffen** to export in sections, to ship goods by instal(l)ments; **~lagerschein** part warrant; **~leistung** part performance; **~lieferung** short (part) delivery, consignment in parts, delivery by instal(l)ments, instal(l)ment, partial shipment *(US)*, *(Buch)* fascicle; **angemessene ~lohnvergütung** quantum meruit; **~markt** market segment; **~markt für kurzfristige (langfristige) Papiere** the short (long) end of the market *(Br.)*; **~mobilmachung** partial mobilization.

teilmöbliert partly furnished.
Teil|monopol partial monopoly; ~**montage** subassembly.
teilmotorisierte Einheit semimobile unit.
Teilnachlaßpfleger administrator de bonis non.
Teilnahme participation, share, *(Anwesenheit)* attendance, *(Interesse)* interest, concern, *(Mitarbeit)* cooperation;
in aufrichtiger ~ in sincere sympathy;
aktive ~ active part; **regelmäßige** ~ regular attendance;
~ **am Gemeindeleben** community responsibilities; ~ **an einer strafbaren Handlung** participation in committing an offence, partnership in crime; ~ **an einer Sitzung** participation in a meeting;
seine ~ **ausdrücken** to condole with s. o.; ~ **erwecken** to interest; **von der** ~ **ausgeschlossen sein** to be disqualified; **j. seiner** ~ **versichern** to commiserate with s. o.; **der** ~ **an einem Verbrechen beschuldigt werden** to be charged with partnership in crime; ~ **an jds. Schicksal zeigen** to show sympathy in s. one's lot;
~**bedingungen** entry conditions.
teilnahmeberechtigt entitled to attend, eligible for admission.
Teilnahme|berechtigter entitled person; ~**berechtigung** eligibility to attend (for admission), *(Wettbewerb)* entry qualification.
Teilnahmeland attending country.
teilnahmslos unconcerned, indifferent, dry, pasive, without feeling, listless, stolid.
Teilnahmslosigkeit indifference, passivism, stolidity.
teilnehmen to partake in, to take part, to participate, to assist, to go into, *(anwesend sein)* to be present at, to attend, *(Interesse haben)* to take an interest, to be interested, *(mitwirken)* to cooperate, to collaborate;
gemeinsam ~ to share jointly; **nicht** ~ to stand out;
an einer Aussprache (Diskussion) ~ to take a hand in a debate, to take part (participate) in a discussion; **an den Ereignissen seiner Umwelt nicht mehr** ~ to be past caring what happens; **an einem Essen** ~ to partake in a meal; **an jds. Freude** ~ to share in s. one's joy; **am Gewinn** ~ to partake of the profits; **an einer Handlung** ~ to be privy to an act; **an einer strafbaren Handlung** ~ to participate in committing an offence; **an einem Kursus** ~ to attend a course; **an einem Kursus für Fortgeschrittene** ~ to take part in a course for advanced students; **an einer Sache** ~ to play a part in a business; **an einer Sitzung** ~ to attend a session, to be present at a meeting; **an einem Wettbewerb** ~ to enter into a competition, to enter the lists.
teilnehmend taking part, participating.
Teilnehmer participant, partaker, partner, participator, *(Lehrgang)* student, *(Nachlaßverteilung)* distributee, *(pl.)* those present, *(strafbare Handlung)* accessary, accomplice, *(Telefon)* [telephone] subscriber, *(Versammlung)* attendant, attendee, *(Wettbewerb)* competitor, contestant, rival, entrant;
angerufener ~ *(Telefon)* called subscriber, wanted party; **anrufender** ~ calling subscriber; **ausscheidender** ~ outgoing partner; **regelmäßiger** ~ constant attendant;
~ **einer Demonstration** demonstrator; ~ **an einer strafbaren Handlung** partner in crime, joint tortfeasor (offender); **völkerrechtswidrige** ~ **an Kampfhandlungen** unlawful belligerents *(US)*; ~ **bei einem Quizprogramm** panel(l)ist; ~ **an einer Reise** member of a trip; ~ **einer Sitzung** participant of a meeting; ~ **an einem Volkshochschulkursus** extension student;
~**anschluß** *(Telefon)* subscriber's line; ~**frequenz** attendance at meetings; ~**karte** admission ticket; ~**land** *(Sonderziehungsrechte)* special drawing rights participant; ~**liste** list of participants, entry list; ~**nummer** telephone (subscriber's) number; ~**quote** *(Volkshochschule)* student quota; ~**regierung** participating government; ~**staat** participating state; ~**versammlung** meeting of members; ~**verzeichnis** list of participants, attendance list, roster, *(Telefon)* telephone directory; ~**zahl** number of participants, attendance figure, audience turnover.
Teil|nichtigkeitsklausel separability clause; ~**obligation** divisible obligation, participation certificate *(US)*; ~**offerte** partial offer; ~**pacht** share tenancy; ~**pächter** share tenant, sharecropper *(US)*; ~**pension** partial board, European plan *(US)*.
teilprivatisieren to denationalize partially, to hive off parts.
teilprivatisierte Fragmente hive-off fragments.
Teil|privatisierung hive-off of parts; ~**prüfung** sampling inspection; ~**quantum** quota; ~**quittung** receipt in part, *(Bankwesen)* marginal note for receipt; ~**rechnung** marginal costing; ~**rechtsnachfolge** partial succession; ~**region** subregion; ~**revision** partial audit; **sofortige** ~**revision** spot audit; ~**risiko übernehmen** *(Versicherungsgesellschaft)* to write a line; ~**rückzahlung** partial repayment; ~**schaden** *(Seeversicherung)* partial loss (damage to goods), particular average.
Teilschuld|schein partial bond *(Br.)*; ~**verhältnis** part[ial] obligation; ~**verschreibung** fractional bond (debenture), partial debenture (bond) *(Br.)*.
Teil|sendung consignment in part, partial (split) shipment *(US)*; ~**staat** constituent part; ~**stichprobe** subsample; ~**stillegung** partial cessation; ~**storno** partial reverse; ~**strecke** *(Eisenbahn)* zone, section of a line, fare stage, *(Flugzeug)* leg *(US)*, *(Straße)* section, stretch; **Reise in** ~**strecken zurücklegen** to travel by brief (easy) stages.
Teilstrecken|aufteilung apportionment distribution; ~**einnahmen** interline revenues; ~**fahrkarte** zone (interline) ticket; ~**fahrpreis** interline fare; ~**gebühr** intermediate toll; ~**personenverkehr** interline passenger service.
Teil|streik sectional strike; ~**streuung des Vermögens eines Pensionsfonds zur Auflage machen** to make some diversifying of pension funds mandatory; ~**strich** scale line, division mark; ~**stück** fragment.
Teilung division, partition, separation, *(Aktien)* splitting, split, *(Grundstück)* parcelling out, *(Nachlaß)* distribution, *(Partei)* split;
~ **der Kosten** distribution of costs (expenses); ~ **eines Nachlasses** division (severance) of an estate, partition of a succession *(US)*; ~ **des beweglichen und unbeweglichen Nachlasses** distribution and partition *(US)*; ~ **eines Vermögens** separation of property;
jem. bei der ~ **zufallen** to fall to s. one's share.
Teilungs|ausschuß commission of partition; ~**klage** action of partition; ~**masse** *(Konkurs)* [bankrupt's] estate, *(Nachlaß)* residuary estate; ~**plan** *(Nachlaß)* scheme of inheritance; **schriftliche** ~**vereinbarung** deed of partition; ~**verfahren** action of partition; ~**vertrag** deed of separation, partition (repartition) treaty; ~**zeichen** division sign.
Teil|untergang *(Sachen)* partial destruction; ~**unwirksamkeit** partial invalidity; ~**verantwortlichkeit** reduced responsibility; ~**veräußerung** part disposal; ~**verkauf** partial sale, breaking bulk, less-than-lots sale; ~**verladung** partial shipment; ~**verlust** *(Seeversicherung)* partial loss, particular average; ~**versand** consignment in parts.
teilversichert partially insured.
Teil|versicherung partial insurance; ~**waggonladung** part truckload *(Br.)*, less-than-truckload *(US)*.
teilweise partially, partly, in part;
ganz oder ~ in whole or in part;
~ **abgeschrieben sein** to be partly depreciated; ~ **ganz gut sein** not to be bad in parts; **Produktionskosten** ~ **übernehmen** to contribute in part to the expenses of production;
~ **Bezahlung** part payment.
Teilwert fractional value;
versicherungsmathematisch ermittelter ~ actuarially computed part value.
Teilzahlung payment in part, part (partial) payment, *(Rate)* instal(l)ment [payment];
als ~ **auf den geschuldeten Betrag** as an instal(l)ment against the balance due; **auf** ~ by instal(l)ments;
geringfügige ~**en** petty instal(l)ments; **monatliche** ~**en** monthly instal(l)ments;
~ **in Anerkennung einer Verpflichtung** token payment;
als ~ **annehmen** to take in part payment; ~**en einhalten** to meet the payments; **auf** ~ **kaufen** to buy on the instal(l)ment plan (system); **Möbel auf** ~ **kaufen** to buy furniture on the hire-purchase *(Br.)* (deferred-payment, *US*) system; ~**en leisten** to make part payments, to pay in parts (by instal(l)ments); ~ **auf Aktien leisten** to pay a [further] call on shares; **auf** ~ **verkaufen** to sell on the deferred-payment *(US)* (hire-purchase, *Br.*) system.
Teilzahlungs|aktie partly paid stock; ~**bank** hire-purchase finance house *(Br.)*, consumer finance company *(US)*; **auf** ~**basis** on the instal(l)ment plan; ~**bedingungen** hire-purchase terms *(Br.)*, part-payment (deferred-payments, *US*) terms; ~**beschränkungen** instal(l)ment restrictions; ~**darlehn** instal(l)ment credit, consumption loan; ~**finanzierung** instal(l)ment[-plan] financing, hire-purchase finance *(Br.)*; ~**geschäft** instal(l)ment buying (credit business), hire purchase [transaction] *(Br.)*, deferred-payment sale *(US)*; ~**kauf** budget payment, hire purchase *(Br.)*; ~**kredit** instal(l)ment credit, deferred-payment credit *(US)*, hire-purchase credit *(Br.)*; ~**kredit mit Eigentumsvorbehalt** instal(l)ment equipment loan *(US)*; ~**kreditbank** instal(l)ment finance company; ~**kunde** charge-account customer; ~**plan** instal(l)ment plan; ~**preis** instal(l)ment (hire-purchase, *Br.*, deferred-payment, *US*) price; ~**system** instal(l)ment (hire-purchase, *Br.*, deferred-payment, *US*) system,

instalment (hire-purchase, *Br.*) plan; ~**verkauf** instal(l)ment sale (selling), deferred-payment sale *(US)*; ~**verpflichtungen** instal(l)ment obligations, hire-purchase debts (commitments) *(Br.)*; ~**vertrag** instal(l)ment contract, hire-purchase agreement (contract) *(Br.)*; ~**verträge** *(Bilanz)* instal(l)ment receivables *(US)*; ~**wechsel** instalment sale finance bill; **im ~weg** by instal(l)ments, on the deferred-payment plan *(US)*.

Teilzeichnung detail drawing.

Teilzeit | arbeit part-time work; ~**beschäftigter** half- (part-) time worker, half-timer; ~**beschäftigung** part-time (employment) commitment, half-time job *(US)*; **angebotene ~beschäftigung** part-time vacancy; **in einem ~beschäftigungsverhältnis stehen** to be on half time *(US)*; ~**beschäftigungswesen** half-time system *(Br.)*; ~**job haben** to be on half time; ~**kraft** part- (half-) time worker.

teilzerlegt semi knocked-down.

Teilzone *(Bahn)* stage, subzone.

Telefon telephone;

~ **mit Lautsprecherverstärkung** speaker telephone;

~ **zwanzig Minuten blockieren** to engage the line for 20 minutes; ~ **haben** to be on the telephone; **ans ~ kommen** to come on the line; **ans ~ rufen** to call up;

~**aktien** telephone shares (stocks, *US*); ~**anlage** telephone installation, call system; ~**annahme** telephone desk.

Telefonanruf telephone call, blast *(sl.)*, tinkle *(sl.)*;

gebührenfreier ~ toll-free number;

~ **entgegennehmen** to answer the telephone [bell]; ~ **überprüfen** to screen a call.

Telefonanschluß subscriber's telephone line, telephonic connection (connexion, *Br.*), telephone extension;

mit ~ connected by telephone;

gemeinsamer ~ party line;

~ **auf dem Zimmer** *(Hotel)* room telephone;

~ **erhalten** to get a connection (connexion, *Br.*); ~ **haben** to be on the telephone (phone).

Telefon | anschlüsse, mit zu wenig ~anschlüssen ausgestattet telephone-starved; ~**anzapfung** wire tap; ~**apparat** telephone [set]; **umsteckbarer ~apparat** plug-in telephone.

Telefonat [telephone] call.

Telefon | auftragsdienst telephone answering service; ~**auskunft** directory inquiries; ~**auskunftsdienst** telephone enquiries service; ~**bedienung** answering the telephone, *(Person)* telephone attendant; ~**befragung** *(Rundfunk)* coincidental; ~**benutzer** telephone user; ~**benutzung** telephone usage; ~**besitzer** subscriber; ~**buch** telephone directory (book), phone-wide directory; ~**dienst** telephone service; ~**diktieranlage** teledictation unit; ~**einrichtungen** telephone equipment; ~**fräulein** [telephone] operator, hullo girl *(fam.)*, hello girl *(US coll.)*; ~**gebühren** telephone charges (rate, tax); ~**gebühren in der gesprächsarmen Zeit** off-peak telephone rates; ~**gebührenrechnung** telephone bill; ~**gesellschaft** telephone company.

Telefongespräch [telephone] call, conversation by telephone, telephone conversation, telecon *(US)*;

in Bestätigung unseres ~s confirming our telephone conversation;

abgehörtes ~ taped telephone conversation; **auswärtiges ~** outside call; **unterbrochenes ~** broken connection;

~**e in der verbilligten Tarifzeit** off-peak calls;

~ **mit jem. abbrechen** to cut s. o. off; ~ **abhören** to listen in, to wiretap, to intercept a telephone call; ~**e ohne richterliche Genehmigung abhören** to wiretap without a court order; ~ **abnehmen** to answer (take) a call; ~ **anmelden** to place *(US)* (book, *Br.*) a call; ~ **annehmen** to accept a call; ~ **beenden** to get off the line; ~ **brieflich bestätigen** to confirm a telephone message by letter; ~ **führen** to carry on a telephone conversation; ~ **unterbrechen** to leave the line; **in einem ~ unterbrochen werden** to be cut off during a telephone call.

Telefon | grundgebühr telephone subscription (rate), line charge; ~**handel** *(Börse)* telephone trade, over-the-counter market *(US)*; ~**hörer** telephone receiver; ~**hörer auflegen** to cradle the telephone receiver.

Telefonie, drahtlose wireless (radio) telephony.

telefonieren to [tele]phone, to call, to ring up, to give s. o. a ring, to talk on the phone;

mit jem. ~ to be speaking with s. o. on the telephone; **mit der Privatsekretärin ~** to be on the line to the private secretary; **den ganzen Tag ~** to dial all day; **von einer Telefonzelle aus ~** to call from a telephone booth.

Telefonierender telephonist.

telefonisch telephonic, over the telephone;

~ **anfragen** to inquire by telephone; ~ **anmelden** to telephone ahead; ~ **anrufen** to ring up, to call; **j. ~ benachrichtigen** to inform s. o. by telephone; ~ **durchgeben** to telephone a message; ~ **erreichbar sein** to be on the telephone (phone); ~ **verlangt werden** to be wanted on the telephone;

~**e Befragung** telephone interview; ~**e Benachrichtigung** telephone message; ~ **aufgegebene Bestellung** telephone order; ~**e Bestellung bestätigen** to confirm a telephone message; ~**e Durchsage** telephone announcement; ~**e Erreichbarkeit** telephone contact; **jederzeitige ~e Erreichbarkeit** phone-in program(me); ~**e Kundenwerbung** telephone solicitation; ~**e Mitteilung** telephonic message; ~**e Nachricht übermitteln** to send a message by telephone; ~ **zugestelltes Telegramm** telegram by telephone; ~**e Unterredung** conversation over the telephone; ~**e Verbindung herstellen** to put through a call.

Telefonist [telephone, switchboard, *US*] operator, telephonist.

Telefon | kabel telephone cable; ~**klingel** telephone bell; ~**konferenz** conference telephone call.

Telefonleitung [telephone] line;

angezapfte ~ tapped line;

~ **anzapfen** to tap a telephone wire, to tap a line; ~ **überprüfen** to check up on a line; ~ **unterbrechen** to disconnect a telephone line.

Telefon | möglichkeit telephone privilege; ~**netz** telephone network; **direkt geschaltetes ~netz** interoffice communication; ~**notruf** emergency number.

Telefonnummer [telephone (call)] number;

falsche ~ wrong number; **gebührenfreie ~** toll-free number; **jds. ~ aufschreiben** to take s. one's number; **häufig gebrauchte ~n auf einem Band speichern** to store frequentely called phone numbers on tape; ~ **wählen** to dial a number.

Telefon | rechnung telephone bill; **von der Firma bezahlte private ~rechnung** home-telephone bill paid by the office; ~**schalter** telephone counter; ~**schaltung** telephone hookup; ~**spesen** telephone expense; ~**tarif** telephone rates; ~**teilnehmer** telephone customer; ~**tischchen** telephone stand (table).

Telefonverbindung telephone connection (connexion, *Br.*);

unterbrochene ~ broken line;

unmittelbare ~en abschalten to dismantle direct telephone links; ~ **herstellen** to establish a telephone connection.

Telefon | verkehr telephone service (traffic), telephoning, *(Börsenverkehr)* interoffice dealings; **im ~verkehr gehandelt werden** to be dealt with after hours; ~**verzeichnis** telephone index; **automatischer ~wähler** magic dialler; ~**werbung** telephone solicitation; ~**zelle** call *(Br.)* (telephone) box, telephone booth (kiosk); ~**zelle blockieren** to tie up a telephone booth.

Telefonzentrale chief operator, telephone switchboard (desk, exchange), call station;

betriebliche ~ business switchboard; **eigene ~** private business exchange;

~ **anrufen** to call the operator; ~ **einrichten** to set up a switchboard.

Telegraf telegraph.

Telegrafen | agentur dispatch agency; ~**amt** telegraph office; ~**arbeiter** telegraph wireman, lineman; ~**beamter** telegraph operator, *(am Schalter)* telegraph clerk; ~**bote** telegraph messenger (boy); ~**büro** dispatch agency; ~**dienst der Wirtschaft** commercial telegraph service; ~**draht** telegraph wire; ~**kabel an Bord nehmen** to pick up a telegraph cable; ~**leitung** telegraph line; ~**mast** telegraph post (pole, *Br.*); ~**netz** wire; ~**schlüssel** figure code; ~**stange** telegraph post *(Br.)* (pole).

Telegrafie telegraphy;

drahtlose ~ radiotelegraphy *(US)*.

Telegrafieren wiring, cabling.

telegrafieren to telegraph, to telegram, to [send a] wire, to cable.

telegrafisch telegraphic, by telegram, per wire, by cable;

~ **anfragen** to inquire by telegram; ~ **antworten** to reply by telegram; ~ **benachrichtigen** to telegraph; ~ **beordern (bestellen)** to [send an] order by wire; **Auftragsangebot ~ bestätigen** to cable one's acceptance; ~ **Geld überweisen** to transfer money by cable;

~**e Antwort** reply by telegram; ~**e Auszahlung** telegraphic (cable) transfer; ~**e Geldanweisung** telegraphic money order (remittance); ~**e Mitteilung** telegraphic message (communication); ~**e Notierung** tape quotation; ~**e Postanweisung** telegraphic money order; ~**e Überweisung** telegraphic (cable) transfer; **auf ~em Weg** by telegram.

Telegramm telegram, message, wire *(US)*, telegraphic dispatch, *(Kabel)* cable, cablegram;

vom Empfänger bezahltes ~ telegram sent collect *(US)*; **chiffriertes ~** cipher telegram; **nicht chiffriertes ~** telegram in

plain language; **dringendes** ~ urgent telegram, urgent wire; **gebührenfreies** ~ deadhead; **gewöhnliches** ~ ordinary (deferred) telegram; **kollationiertes** ~ repetition-paid telegram; **langatmiges** ~ wordy telegram; **nachgesandtes** ~ forwarded telegram; **nachzusendendes** ~ telegram to follow (to be redirected); **offenes** ~ plain-language cable; **postlagerndes** ~ telegram to be called for (addressed poste restante); **unchiffriertes** ~ telegram in plain language; **verglichenes** ~ collated telegram; **verschlüsseltes** ~ cipher (code) telegram (dispatch); **verstümmeltes** ~ multilated telegram; **vervielfältigtes** ~ multiple telegram; **zugesprochenes** ~ phonogram; **telefonisch zugestelltes** ~ telegram by telephone;
~ **mit Empfangsbenachrichtigung** telegram with notice of delivery; ~ **im Fernverkehr** interurban telegram; ~ **zu Lasten des Empfängers** cash-on-delivery telegram; ~ **ohne Leitvermerk** unrouted telegram; ~ **im Ortsverkehr** local telegram; ~ **mit bezahlter Rückantwort** reply-paid (prepaid) telegram, wire collect *(US)*; ~ **mit Wiederholung** repetition-paid telegram;
~ **abfangen** to intercept a telegram; ~ **absenden** to telegraph, to wire; ~ **aufgeben** to send [off] (deliver, hand in, dispatch, file, *US*, tender, *US*) a telegram; ~ **beschleunigt aufgeben** to hurry up the dispatch of a telegram; ~ **befördern** to dispatch (transmit) a telegram; ~ **chiffrieren** to code a telegram; ~ **telefonisch durchsagen** to telephone a wire (telegram); ~ **expedieren** to send off a wire; ~ **kollationieren** to repeat back a telegram; ~ **schicken** to [send a] wire, to telegraph, to send [off] a telegram, to cable; ~ **weiterleiten** to transmit (translate) a telegram; ~ **widerrufen** to recall (kill) a wire (telegram); ~ **zustellen** to deliver a telegram;
~**adresse**, ~**anschrift** telegraphic (telegram, cable) address; ~**annahme[schalter]** telegram reception.

telegrammartige Kürze telegraphic brevity.

Telegramm|aufgabe handing in (filing of, *US*) a telegram, dispatch of a telegram; ~**austausch** exchange of telegrams; ~**beförderung** transmission of telegrams; ~**bote** telegraph messenger *(US)* (boy, *Br.*); ~**fahrzeug** telecar; ~**formular** telegraph (message) form; ~**gebühr** telegram rate, telegraphic charges, cable expenses; ~**kode** cipher (cable) code; ~**schalter** telegraph office, telegrams counter *(Br.)*; ~**schlüssel** telegraph code, cipher (cable) code; ~**spesen** cable expenses; ~**sprache** telegraphic English; ~**stil** telegraphese; **im** ~**stil sprechen** to speak in telegraphic (clipped) sentences; ~**übermittlung** telegraphic (cable) transfer; ~**übertragung** telegraph repeater; ~**verkehr** telegraph service; ~**verstümmelung** multilation of a telegram; ~**verzögerung** drag; ~**zusteller** telegraph boy *(Br.)* (messenger, *US*); ~**zustellung** delivery of a telegram.

Telekopiergerät telecopier.

Teleskopleiter extension ladder.

Telex|anschrift telex address; ~**nummer** telex number; ~**teilnehmer** telex subscriber.

Teller plate;
bunter ~ plate of assorted delicacies;
für j. mit dem ~ **sammeln gehen** to pass round the hat for s. o.; ~ **waschen** to wash the dishes;
~**mine** *(mil.)* antitank mine; ~**sammlung** whip round for subscription; ~**untersatz** place mat; ~**wäscher** dishwasher, pot walloper *(sl.)*, pearl diver *(sl.)*.

Telquelkurs *(Börse)* tel quel rate *(Br.)*.

Tempel temple, sanctuary, pagoda;
j. zum ~ **herauswerfen** to turn (throw) s. o. out.

Temperament temperament, disposition, *(Schwung)* fire, spirits, vivacity;
impulsives ~ impulsive nature; **lebhaftes** ~ quicksilver; **ungezügeltes** ~ violent temper;
~ **haben** to be full of spirits; **sein** ~ **zügeln** to control (govern, hold in) one's temper, to keep a check on one's temper.

temperament|los spiritless, lifeless; ~**voll** full of spirits, vivacious; ~**volle Rede** fervent speech.

Temperatur|abnahme decrease in temperature; ~**anstieg** rise of temperature; ~**gefälle** temperature gradient, lapse rate; ~**kurve** temperature curve; **plötzlicher** ~**rückgang** sudden drop of temperature; ~**schwankungen** variations in temperature, swinging temperature, fluctuations of temperate, thermal fluctuations; **extreme** ~**schwankungen** extremes of temperature; ~**schwankungen messen** to measure changes of temperature; ~**sturz** fall in temperature; ~**unterschied** difference in temperature; **höchster bisher aufgezeichneter** ~**wert** maximum temperature recorded.

Temperenzler abstainer, teetotaller, blue ribboner.

Tempo speed, pace, tempo, drive, demon *(Br., coll.)*, *(Filmgeschichte)* pace;
in gemächlichem ~ leisurely; **in höchstem** ~ at full lick *(sl.)*; **in hohem** ~ at a great pace; **in langsamem** ~ at a slow rate; **in schnellem** ~ at a great speed, at a quick pace;
gemächliches ~ leisurely pace; **halsbrecherisches** ~ breakneck speed; **mörderisches** ~ killing pace;
~ **angeben** to set the pace, *(fig.)* to make the running, to stand the pace; ~ **beschleunigen** to force the pace; ~ **durchhalten** to stand the pace; **auf** ~ **fahren** to drive in double-quick time; **mörderisches** ~ **fahren** to drive like mad (flat out, *coll.*); **in vollem** ~ **gegen einen Baum fahren** to crash into a tree at full speed; **im** ~ **nachlassen** to slacken the time; ~ **steigern** to speed up; ~ **vermindern** to reduce speed, to decelerate, to slow down; **tolles** ~ **vorlegen** to step on it;
~**laden** partial self-service; ~**regulierung** timing; ~**verminderung** slowdown.

Tendenz trend, tend, drift, drive, direction, leaning, *(Börse, Konjunktur)* tendency, trend, course, movement, drive, run, bearing, slant *(US)*, *(Wetter)* outlook;
~ **gehalten** steady market; ~ **hinzu** advance toward;
abschwächende ~ sagging tendency; **allgemeine** ~ prevailing tone, general tendency; **ausgeprägte** ~ distinct tendency; **zum Umsatz disproportionale** ~ leverage; **einheitliche** ~ general tendency; **fallende** ~ bearish tendency, downward trend (tendency); **stark fallende** ~ strong downtrend; **feste** ~ firm tendency; **generelle** ~ overall tendency; **an der Börse herrschende** ~ prevailing tone of the market; **heutige** ~ present trend, present-day tendency; **inflationistische** ~ inflationary tendency; **kollektivistische** ~ trend to collectivism; **konjunkturelle** ~ cyclical (business) tendency, economic trend; **kurserholende** ~ rallying tendency; **kurstreibende** ~ price-rising tendency; **lebhafte** ~ brisk tendency; **lustlose** ~ dull tone; **monopolistische** ~ monopolistic tendency; **preissteigernde** ~ price-raising tendency, upward surge of prices; **protektionistische** ~ tendency towards protectionism; **redaktionelle** ~ editorial policy; **rückgängige** ~ downward [business] trend; **rückläufige** ~ downward (bearish) tendency (trend, movement); **saisonbedingte** ~ seasonal trend; **schwache** ~ despondent note; **deutlich spürbare** ~ strongly marked tendency; **steigende** ~ upward trend, uptrend, bullish (upward) tendency, buoyancy; **uneinheitliche** ~ unsteady tendency; **unterschwellige** ~ undercurrent; **weichende** ~ softening tendency; **zurückhaltende** ~ tone of restraint, dull tendency;
~ **der Aktienkurse** stock trend; ~ **zur Einführung von Tantiemeregelungen** bonus trend; ~ **der öffentlichen Meinung** set of public opinion; **politische** ~ **einer Zeitung** political (colo(u)r) of a journal;
uneinheitliche ~ **aufweisen** to make a mixed showing; ~ **ausnutzen** to profit by the tendency; ~ **beibehalten** to maintain the tone; **der allgemeinen** ~ **breitgestreuter Produktionsprogramme folgen** to jump on the diversification bandwaggon; ~ **in der Politik der Geldmarkterleichterungen fortsetzen** to continue their run towards ease in money rates; **steigende** ~ **erkennen lassen** to show a tendency to improve; **fallende** ~ **zeigen** to tend downward; **steigende** ~ **zeigen** to show a tendency to rise;
~**angabe** indication of tendency; ~**blatt** tendentious paper; ~**buch** tendential book.

tendenziös tendentious, biassed, painted;
Thema ~ **behandeln** to be biassed on a subject;
~**er Bericht** tendentious report.

Tendenz|roman purpose novel; ~**stück** thesis play; ~**umschwung** trend reversal, change of tendency; ~**veränderer** trend-breaker; **konjunkturelle** ~**wende** cyclical turnaround.

Tenderlokomotive tank engine.

tendieren to tend towards, to lean, to show (have a) tendency;
fest ~ to show a stronger tendency; **zur Hausse** ~ to be on the upgrade; **nach oben** ~ to take an upward trend, to tend upwards; **schwach** ~ to show a weaker tendency; **schwächer** ~ to edge down; **uneinheitlich** ~ *(Kurse)* to show an irregular (uneven) tendency, to show an uneven trend, to make a mixed showing.

tendierend, nach rechts right-wing.

Tenor tenor, substance;
~ **einer Gerichtsverfügung** exigency of a writ; ~ **eines Urteils** operative provisions.

Teppich carpet, *(klein)* rug;
roter ~ *(fig.)* red carpet, welcome mat; **samtartiger** ~ velvet carpet;
~ **mit samtartigem Flor** velvet pile;
roten ~ **auslegen** to lay (roll) out the red carpet, to give s. o. a

red-carpet reception; **Zimmer mit ~em auslegen** to carpet a room; **auf dem ~ bleiben** to draw it mild; **unter den ~ kehren** to sweep under the carpet (rug); **unerfreuliche Tatsachen unter den ~ kehren** to sweep some gloomy facts under the bonnet (carpet);
~**bombenwurf** carpet bombing; ~**kehrmaschine** carpet sweeper; ~**schoner** drugget.

Termin term, *(Datum)* date, clear day, *(Endtermin)* appointed day, time limit, deadline *(US)*, *(Gericht)* hearing [of a case], day of hearing, term day, *(Mietzahlungen)* quarter day, term, *(Verfallzeit)* term, maturity, *(Zahlungstermin)* respite, *(festgesetzter Zeitpunkt)* appointed date (time), terminal date, fixed day (time);
auf kurzen ~ *(Geldausleihung)* for short credit; **im ~ von** at the hearing on; **zu einem bestimmten ~** at a set time; **zu einem früheren ~** at an earlier date; **zum festgesetzten (vorgesehenen) ~** at the stated time, at term;
~ **abwarten** *(Werbung)* wait order;
abgelaufener ~ expired term; **äußerster ~** time limit, final date, deadline *(US)*; **auswärtiger ~** out-of-town appointment; **festgesetzter ~** time appointed; **laufender ~** present quarter; **letzter ~** target date, time limit, deadline *(US)*; **letztvorhergehender ~** next preceding date; **mittlerer ~** average date; **nächstfolgender ~** succeeding date; **neuer ~** *(Gericht)* adjournment day; **planmäßiger ~** target date; **vereinbarter ~** date agreed upon; **vertraglich vereinbarter (vorgesehener) ~** time as provided in the contract, contract date; **verstrichener ~** due date;
~ **vor dem Einzelrichter** date of reference; **frühester ~ für die Fertigstellung** earliest date of completion; ~ **zur Hauptverhandlung** day of appearance, hearing in court; ~ **für die Invasion** target date for the invasion; ~ **für die Rücksendung einer Klageschrift** return day; ~ **für die Zustellung eines Schriftstücks** return day;
~ **absetzen** to adjourn a hearing; ~ **anberaumen** to appoint a day; ~ **zur mündlichen Verhandlung anberaumen** to assign a day for a hearing in court, to set down a case for trial; ~ **für eine Sache ansetzen** to docket a case, to set a case down for hearing; ~ **aussetzen** to postpone a term; ~ **bestimmen** to fix a time, to target for *(US)*; **um einen ~ bitten** to ask for an appointment; **sich zum festgesetzten ~ einfinden** to present o. s. by appointment; ~ **einhalten** to comply with (observe) a time limit, to keep one's time; **sich über einen ~ einigen** to fix (decide) on a date; **rechtzeitig zum ~ erscheinen** to surrender to one's bail; **in einem ~ nicht erscheinen** to fail to appear, *(bei Gericht)* to default; ~ **festlegen (festsetzen)** to set (settle, fix) a date, to appoint a date (day, time), to decide upon (set up) a day, to set a term; **am nächsten Tag ~ haben** to be summoned to appear on the next day; **auf ~ kaufen** to purchase (buy) forward *(Br.)* (for future delivery, *US*); **an feste ~e gebunden sein** to be made on fixed dates; ~ **setzen** to fix a time; ~ **überschreiten** to exceed a term (time limit); ~ **vereinbaren** to settle a day; ~ **für die Zahlung vereinbaren** to agree on a date; **auf ~ verkaufen** to sell for future delivery *(US)* (forward, *Br.*); ~ **verlängern** to extend a term; ~ **verlegen** to postpone a date, to adjourn a hearing; ~ **versäumen** to fail to observe a time limit, to lose a term, *(bei Gericht)* to fail to appear, to nonappear, to default, to make default of appearance; ~ **wahrnehmen** to keep an appointment;
~**abschluß** forward (futures, *US*) contract (deal), time bargain; ~**abteilung** *(Börse)* option department, *(Werbeagentur)* traffic department; ~**akten** papers in the case; ~**anberaumung** assigning a day for a hearing in court, setting down a cause for trial; **neue ~anberaumung** adjourned summons; ~**anzeige** fixed-date advertisement; ~**arbeit** scheduled work; ~**auftrag** forward order, *(Börse)* order for the account (settlement, *Br.*), *(Werbeagentur)* wait order; ~**bearbeiter** progress clerk, chaser, *(Werbeagentur)* traffic manager, accelerator; ~**bestimmungen** time clauses; ~**börse** forward market, market for futures (future delivery) *(US)*, futures market (exchange) *(US)*; ~**devisen** forward exchanges (currency), foreign exchange futures *(US)*; ~**devisensatz** outright rate of exchange; ~**dollar** forward dollar; ~**effekten** forward stocks; ~**einlagen** fixed deposit, time (long-term) *(US)* deposits, deposits at short notice, restricted cash, deposit accounts *(US)*; ~**engagement** commitment for future delivery *(US)*, forward deal *(Br.)*; ~**festsetzung** *(Gericht)* assigning a day for a hearing in court.

termingebunden scheduled.

Termin|geld, ~gelder time money, term deposits, time *(US)* (fixed) deposits, restricted cash;
~**konto** deposit account, time deposit account *(US)*.

termin|gemäß, ~gerecht on the agreed date, in due time, on schedule, in good time, terminal;
~ **bezahlt** paid at maturity;
~ **ausführen** to carry out within a given time; ~ **fertig werden** to be finished on schedule.

Termingeschäft transaction for future delivery, forward business (contract, operation, transaction, deal) *(Br.)*, time bargain (purchase), contract trade, dealing for the account, dealings for the settlement *(Br.)*, settlement bargain, trading (business) in futures *(US)*, futures dealing (trading, contract) *(US)*;
~**e** option dealings, option business (trading), transactions on credit, puts and refusals *(Br.)*, futures *(US)*;
~**e in Devisen** forward-exchange deals *(Br.)* (operations, *US*), forwarded exchange deals *(Br.)*, futures exchange *(US)*;
~**e abschließen (betreiben)** to trade (call) in futures *(US)*.

Termin|gründe, aus ~n owing to previous engagements;
~**guthaben** term (time, *US*) deposit, *(Börse)* time balance.

Terminhandel option business (trading), forward operations *(Br.)*, puts and refusals *(Br.)*, [trading in] futures *(US)*, futures trading *(US)*;
~ **in Devisen** forward exchange operations (dealings, transactions) *(Br.)*, futures exchange *(US)*; ~ **in Wertpapieren** forward transactions in securities, trading in security futures *(US)*.

Terminhändler option writer (trader).

terminieren to time, to schedule.

terminiert timed, scheduled;
~**e Einlagen** long-term deposits, deposits at short notice, restricted cash, time deposits *(US)*; ~**e Verbindlichkeiten** long-term liabilities, time liabilities *(US)*.

Terminierung timing.

Terminkalender tickler, letter (desk) calendar *(US)*, date block, appointments book (schedule, *US*), engagement book, *(Gericht)* schedule of cases, roll, docket, calendar *(US)*, cause list *(Br.)*, *(Strafsachen)* trial docket (list) *(US)*;
~ **ausstehender Strafsachen** calendar of causes in trial *(US)*; ~ **einer Werbeaktion** advertising schedule;
~ **aufeinander abstimmen** to coordinate one's schedule *(US)*; **vollbesetzten ~ haben** to have numerous engagements for the next week; **mit seinem ~ herumjonglieren** to juggle one's schedule *(US)*; **etw. in seinem ~ unterbringen** to fit s. th. into one's schedule *(US)*.

Terminkauf purchase on forward (future, *US*) delivery, put and call *(Br.)*, forward purchase (buying) *(Br.)*, purchase for the settlement (account, *Br.*), future delivery, *(Warenbörse)* purchase for future delivery *(US)*, futures purchase *(US)*, sale on delivery;
~ **von Devisen** forward exchange operation *(Br.)*, futures exchange *(US)*; ~ **und -verkauf** double option.

Termin|käufer forward (future, *US*) buyer; ~**kaufoption** stock call; ~**kommissionär** future commission man *(US)*; ~**konto** forward account, time account; ~**kontrolle** *(Anzeigen)* progress control, *(Warenlager)* inventory control; ~**kurs** *(Devisen)* forward exchange rate, future price *(US)*, *(Effekten)* liquidating (making up, *Br.*) price, price for the settlement (account) *(Br.)*.

terminlich, aus ~en Gründen owing to previous engagements.

Termin|lieferung forward (future) delivery; ~**lieferungsauftrag** order for futures *(US)*; ~**liste** *(Gericht)* docket calendar *(US)*, *(Rechnungen)* list *(Br.)*, aging schedule; ~**mappe** tickler (calendar, suspense, follow-up) file; ~**markt** forward (options, *Br.*, settlement, *Br.*, contract, *US*) market, market for futures [delivery] *(US)*; ~**markt für Devisen** forward exchange market *(Br.)*, market for forward (futures, *US*) exchange (future delivery), futures market *(US)*; ~**monat** futures month *(US)*; ~**notierung** forward quotation *(Br.)*, quotation for futures *(US)*, *(Effekten)* liquidating (making-up, *Br.*) price; ~**notierung für Devisen** forward exchange quotation.

Terminologie terminology, nomenclature, language;
nationalökonomische ~ economist's terminology; **verschwommene ~** muddy terminology.

Termin|papiere securities dealt in for account (for future delivery, *US*), forward securities; ~**pfund** forward pound; ~**plan** time (aging) schedule *(US)*, date plan, appointments card; ~**plan einhalten** to catch up with (meet a) schedule *(US)*; ~**planung** scheduling, *(Markeneinführung)* product timing; ~**preis** price for forward (future, *US*) delivery, delivery (settlement, forward, *Br.*) price, futures price *(US)*; ~**sätze** *(Devisen)* forward (future, *US*) rates, rates of exchange for future delivery *(US)*; ~**schluß** deadline; **wegen ~schwierigkeiten absagen** to decline owing to previous engagements; ~**sicherung**

forward cover, hedging transaction; ~**spekulation** speculation in futures *(US)*; ~**tag** *(Mietzahlungen)* quarter day, term; ~**überprüfung** calendar inspection; ~**überschreitung** noncompliance with a time limit; ~**überwacher** expediter, progress clerk, chaser, *(Werbeagentur)* traffic manager, accelerator; ~**überwachung** follow-up of orders; ~**verfolgungsplan** follow-up chart; ~**verkauf** time (forward, future) sale, sale for the settlement *(Br.)*, sale for forward (future, *US*) delivery, short sales *(US)*; ~**verkauf von Devisen** forward (future, *US*) sale of exchange; ~**verkäufe** selling forward; ~**verkäufer** forward seller; ~**verlängerung** extension of time, *(Verbindlichkeiten)* extension of payment, delay, prolongation; **um ~verlängerung bitten** to ask for time; ~**verlängerung zugestehen** to grant a delay; **um ~verlegung bitten** to petition for adjournment; ~**verpatzer** deadline misser *(US)*; ~**versäumnis** *(Gericht)* default of appearance, nonappearance, failure to appear; ~**vertagung beantragen** to apply for deferment of a hearing; ~**vertrag** forward contract, contract for futures *(US)*, futures contract *(US)*; ~**vertretungen übernehmen** to devil; ~**vorschrift** fixed date; ~**wechsel** time draft.

terminweise by terms (instal(l)ments).

Termin|werte forward securities *(Br.)*, futures *(US)*; ~**zahlung** payment in due time; ~**zeit** hour of cause *(Scot.)*; ~**zettel** appointments card.

Terrain terrain, ground, *(Grundstück)* plot of land, building site; **sich auf unbekanntem ~ bewegen** to be on unfamiliar ground; ~ **gewinnen** to gain ground; ~ **sondieren** to reconnoitre the ground, to see how the land lies; ~ **verlieren** to lose ground; ~**aufklärung** topographical reconnaissance; ~**aufnahme** surveying, topographical survey; ~**beschreibung** topographical description, description of property, real-estate picture, parcel; ~**eigenarten** features of the ground; ~**gesellschaft** real-estate trust (company, corporation, firm, syndicate, *US*), land speculation company; ~**spekulation** speculation in real estate; ~**verhältnisse** ground conditions.

Terrasse terrace, *(Dachterrasse)* roof garden.

Terrassendach terrace (roof) garden.

terrassenförmig terraced;
~ **anlegen** to terrace.

territorial|e Ansprüche territorial claims; ~**e Ausdehnung** territorial expansion.

Territorial|armee territorial army *(Br.)*; ~**gebiet** territorial property; ~**gerichtsbarkeit** territorial jurisdiction; ~**gewässer** territorial waters; ~**grenzen** territorial limits; ~**hoheit** territorial sovereignty.

Territorialität territoriality.

Territorialitätsprinzip territorial principle.

Territorial|regierung territorial goverment; ~**system** territorial system.

Territorium territory, territorial property.

Terror, organisierter organized terror;
~ **hervorrufen** to spread terror; ~ **unterdrücken** to suppress terror;
~**akt** terrorist act; ~**aktion** terror campaign, terrorist action; ~**angriff** terror attack; ~**bande** terrorist band, network of terrorists; ~**drohungen** terroristic threats; ~**herrschaft** reign of terror.

terrorisieren to terrorize, to bulldoze.

Terrorisierung terrorization.

Terrorismus, stadtguerilla-ähnlicher brutaler brutal urban guerilla-style terrorism.

Terrorist, verdächtiger terrorist suspect.

Terroristenangriff terrorist raid.

Terroristenbekämpfungs|einheit antiterrorist squad; ~**maßnahmen** counterterroristic policy; ~**politik** counterterrorist policy.

Terroristen|gruppe terrorist group, guerilla group; ~**netz** guerilla network, network of terrorists; ~**organisation** terrorist organization; ~**unterschlupf** guerilla hide-out.

terroristisch terrorist;
~**e Gewaltakte** terrorist violence; ~**e Kampfmaßnahmen** terrorist acts; ~**e Vereinigung gründen** to set up a terrorist communication system.

Tertiawechsel third [of exchange], triplicate.

Tesa|band Scotch tape; ~**film** cellophane tape, Sellotape.

Test test, trial;
bestmöglicher ~ optimum test; **nichtparametrischer** ~ distribution-free test; **psychologischer** ~ mental test; **zuverlässiger** ~ valid test;
~ **eines Befragtenkreises** sampling test; ~ **am Verkaufsort** instore test;
~ **durchführen** to conduct a test; **sich mit Erfolg einem** ~ **unterziehen** to pass a test; **Maschine weiteren ~s unterziehen** to put a machine to further trials; **einem** ~ **unterzogen werden** to undergo a test.

Testament testament, last will, devise, *(letztwillige Verfügung)* testamentary paper (instrument);
kraft ~es by will; **nach dem ~ seines Vaters** under his father's will;
später abgefaßtes ~ later will; **von der Bestätigung durch einen Dritten abhängiges** ~ third-person will; **für gültig anerkanntes** ~ proved will; **anfechtbares** ~ flaw in a will; **gesetzliche Erbrechte (Pflichtteilsberechtigte) ausschließendes** ~ unofficious will; **bedingtes** ~ conditional will; **nicht beglaubigtes** ~ unattested will; **notariell beglaubigtes** ~ notarial will, secret (closed) testament; **Berliner** ~ [etwa] double (reciprocal, *US*, mutual) will; **eigenhändiges** ~ holographic will (testament); **entgegenstehendes** ~ alternative will; **zugunsten der Familie errichtetes** ~ officious will; **mündlich und vor Zeugen errichtetes** ~ nuncupative will; **notariell errichtetes** ~ notarial will; **ordnungsgemäß errichtetes** ~ properly executed will; **in zwei Urschriften errichtetes** ~ duplicate will; **fehlerhaftes** ~ flaw in a will; **formloses** ~ privileged (informal) will; **früheres** ~ previous will; **gefälschtes** ~ surreptitious will; **gegenseitiges** ~ double (counter, reciprocal, mutual) will, mutual testament; **gemeinschaftliches gegenseitiges** ~ joint and mutual will; **notariell beglaubigtes** ~ notarial will, secret (closed) testament; **gemeinsames** ~ conjoint will; **eigenhändig geschriebenes (handschriftliches)** ~ holographic (privileged) testament (will); **gültiges** ~ valid will; **jüngeres** ~ later will; **öffentliches** ~ notarial will; **ungültiges** ~ invalid will; **untergeschobenes** ~ forged will; **von Zeugen unterschriebenes** ~ attested will; **unwirksames** ~ inofficious testament; **verlorengegangenes** ~ lost will; **mit Ausführungen über die Vollstreckung versehenes** ~ modal will; **wechselbezügliches** ~ joint and mutual (reciprocal, *US*) will; **widerrufenes** ~ cancelled will; **widerrufliches** ~ ambulatory will; **willkürliches** ~ unofficious will;
~ **eines Ausländers** foreign will; ~ **ohne Bestimmung eines Testamentsvollstreckers** unsolemn will; ~ **zugunsten der gesetzlichen Erben** officious will;
~ **gerichtlich abändern** to vary the terms of a will; ~ **anfechten** to dispute (contest, oppose) a will; ~ **aufheben** *(Gericht)* to revoke a will, *(mittels Gerichtsverfahren)* to break a will; ~ **aufsetzen** to make (draw up) a will; **Erfordernisse eines ~s aufweisen** to constitute a will; **unvollständiges** ~ **auslegen** to construe an unskilfully drawn will; **j. in seinem** ~ **bedenken** to mention (include, remember) s. o. in one's will; **j. bei der Abfassung seines ~s beeinflussen** to use undue influence with the maker of a will; **Gültigkeit eines ~s bestätigen** to prove a will; **Urkunde als rechtsgültiges** ~ **bestätigen** to probate a paper as a will; ~ **gerichtlich bestätigen** to probate (grant probate of) a will, to have a will proved; **Gültigkeit eines ~s bestreiten** to dispute (contest) a will; **Gültigkeit eines ~s beweisen** to establish a disputed will; ~ **zur Ausführung bringen** to administer a will; ~ **einreichen** to file a will; **aufgrund eines ~s erben** to take by (under) a will; ~ **für kraftlos (ungültig) erklären** to invalidate a will, to set a will aside; ~ **eröffnen** to open (read out) a will; ~ **errichten** to make (execute) a will, to testament *(Scot.)*; **notarielles** ~ **errichten** to register a will; **rechtsgültiges** ~ **errichten** to execute a will; ~ **fälschen** to fabricate a will; ~ **hinterlegen** to deposit a will; ~ **durch das Nachlaßgericht eröffnen lassen** to have a will proved; **widerrufenes** ~ **wiederaufleben lassen** to revive a will; ~ **machen** to make a testament; **sein** ~ **machen** to write (make) one's will, to put one's affairs in order; **Gültigkeit eines bestrittenen ~s nachweisen** to establish a disputed will; **ohne ein** ~ **zu hinterlassen sterben** to die without making a will, to die intestate; ~ **umstoßen** to revoke a will; ~ **unterschieben** to forge a will; ~ **unterschlagen (unterdrücken)** to suppress a will; **durch** ~ **vermachen** to bequeath; **jem. im** ~ **1000 Dollar vermachen** to have s. o. down in one's will for 1000 Dollars; **einem** ~ **richterliche Anerkennung versagen** to reduce a will; ~ **vollstrecken** to carry out the provisions of (administer) a will; **gefälschtes** ~ **vorlegen** to produce a forged will; ~ **zur Bestätigung (zwecks Erbscheinerteilung) vorlegen** to admit a will to probate, to propound a will; **in einem** ~ **bedacht werden** to benefit by a will; ~ **widerrufen** to cancel (countermand, revoke) a will.

testamentarisch testamentary, by will;
Haus für seine Tochter ~ **bestimmen** to mean a house for one's daughter; ~ **hinterlassen** to will; ~ **bedacht sein** to benefit under a will; ~ **verfügen (vermachen)** to leave (dispose) by will, to bequeath, *(Grundbesitz)* to devise (leave) by will;

~e **Auflage** testamentary burden; ~ **bestimmter Erbe** heir of provision; ~e **Erbfolge** testamentary succession; ~e **Verfügung** testamentary disposition, disposition by will; ~e **Zuwendung** legacy, bequest.

Testaments|abänderung adjustment of a will; ~**abfassung** making a will; **beglaubigte** ~**abschrift** probate, fascimile probate *(Br.)*; ~**änderung** alteration to a will; **gerichtliche** ~**änderung** variation of a will; ~**anfechtung** breaking a will, caveat to will; ~**anfechtungsverfahren** will contest; ~**anhang** codicil, addition to a will; ~**aufhebung** revocation of will; ~**auslegung** construction of a will.

Testamentsbestätigung, einfache ~ probate in common form *(Br.)*; **verweigerte** ~ probate denied; **wortgetreue** ~ fascimile probate *(Br.)*;
gerichtliche ~ **erwirken** to obtain probate.

Testamentsbestimmung clause of a will, testamentary clause, devise;
~**en** terms of a will;
~ **über Einsetzung der Haupterben** residuary clause;
~ **anfechten** to defeat the provision of a will; ~**en durchführen** to administer a will.

Testaments|entwurf draft of a will, script *(Br.)*; ~**erbe** testate estate, testamentary heir, heir of provision, next devisee; ~**erfordernisse** formalities of a will; ~**ergänzung** little will, codicil; ~**eröffnung** opening (reading) of a will, *(Gericht)* proving (proof, probate) of [a] will; ~**errichtung** establishment (making, execution) of a will; **zur Zeit der** ~**errichtung** at the time of making a will; ~**gesetz** Will Act *(Br.)*; ~**hinterlegung** depositing of a will; ~**klausel** testamentary clause; **aufhebende** ~**klausel** derogatory clause; ~**kosten** testamentary expenses; ~**nachtrag** codicil, label; **als** ~**nachtrag** codicillary; ~**recht** probate law; ~**sache** probate action; ~**schluß** end of a will; ~**unkosten** testamentary expenses; ~**urkunde** testamentary instrument (paper).

Testamentsvollstrecker executor of a will, legal (personal) representative, trustee testamentary *(US)*;
alleiniger ~ sole executor; **nicht autorisierter** ~ executor de son tort; **befreiter** ~ general executor; **gegenständlich beschränkter** ~ special executor; **gerichtlich bestellter** ~ executor [to an estate], executor dative; **testamentarisch bestellter (eingesetzter)** ~ executor nominate (named in a will), instituted executor; **ordnungsgemäß eingesetzter** ~ rightful executor;
~ **mit beschränkten Befugnissen** limited executor;
~ **bestellen (einsetzen)** to nominate an executor of a will, to appoint an executor, *(Nachlaßgericht)* to grant letters of administration; **sich zum** ~ **bestellen lassen** to take out letters of administration; **als** ~ **[im Testament] eingesetzt sein** to be appointed as executor [under a will]; **als** ~ **verwalten** to administer;
~**amt** executorship; **auf sein** ~**amt verzichten** to renounce to act as executor of an heir; ~**bestätigung** confirmation of an executor; ~**bestellung** executor's decree, decree dative, grant of letters of administration; ~**bestellung durch das Gericht** letters of administration with the will annexed; ~**einsetzung** appointment of an administration; ~**fähigkeit** executorial duties.

Testamentsvollstreckerin executrix.

Testamentsvollstrecker|kaution executor's bond; ~**konto** executorship account; **debitorisch geführtes** ~**konto** executor's debit account; ~**kosten** testamentary expenses; ~**recht** executorship law; ~**zeugnis** grant of probate, letters of administration, letters testamentary *(US)*, *(Abschrift hiervon)* office copy probate *(Br.)*; ~**zeugnis vorlegen** to prove a will in common form.

Testaments|vollstreckung administration of a will; ~**vorlage** insinuation of a will.

Testamentswiderruf cancellation (countermand, revocation) of a will;
auslegungsfähiger ~ dependent relative revocation;
~ **durch Errichtung eines neuen Testaments** revocation by another will; ~ **durch Vernichtung** revocation of a will by destruction.

Testaments|zeuge witness to will; ~**zusatz** codicil, little will, addition to a will; ~**zusatz anfertigen** to annex a codicil.

Testat certificate, testimonial, *(Wirtschaftsprüfer)* opinion, confirmation, approval;
negatives ~ negative confirmation; **positives** ~ positive confirmation;
einschränkendes ~ **eines Wirtschaftsprüfers** audit qualifications.

Testator testator.

Testbericht survey, study.

Testen|eines Produkts product test; ~ **der Werbewirkung** copy testing.

testen to test, to survey;
Produkt ~ to test a product.

Test|ergebnis test result; ~**fall** test case; ~**flug** test flight; ~**frage** probing question.

testierbar devisable, bequeathable.

testieren to make (write) a will, *(bescheinigen)* to attest, to certify, *(bezeugen)* to testify, to testate, *(vermachen)* to bequeath;
jem. den Besuch einer Vorlesung ~ to certify s. one's attendance at a course of lectures.

testierfähig capable of disposing, competent to dispose by will, able to make a will, of sound and disposing mind *(US)*;
nicht ~ intestable, incompetent to make a will;
~ **sein** to be of sound and disposing mind *(US)*.

Testierfähigkeit testamentary capacity, disposing capacity (mind) *(US)*, ability (capacity) to make a will, sound and disposing mind and memory *(US)*, testator's capacity, testacy, power of testation, liegepoustie.

testierunfähig disqualified from (incapable, incompetent of) making a will;
~ **machen** to disqualify from making a will.

Testierunfähigkeit incapacity to (incapability of) making a will, testamentary incapacity.

Test|kampagne launching test, test campaign; ~**kopie** *(Film)* rush print; ~**laden** audit store; ~**methode** experimental method; ~**packung** bread-board model; ~**pilot** test pilot; ~**sendung** *(Rundfunk)* pilot program(me); ~**serie** test series; ~**strecke** test track, control road; ~**streuung** *(Werbung)* test campaign; ~**vereinbarung** test arrangement; ~**verfahren** test.

teuer dear, expensive, costly, high-priced, long-priced, at a high cost (figure, rate), pricy, high, at great cost, *(wertvoll)* valuable;
außergewöhnlich ~ outrageously expensive; **schamlos** ~ shockingly expensive;
~ **bezahlen** to pay dearly; **etw. zu** ~ **bezahlen** to pay through the nose; **jem.** ~ **zu stehen kommen** to cost s. o. dearly, to be a heavy pull upon s. one's purse; ~ **sein** to be (come) expensive, to cost dearly, to be at a high rate; **sehr** ~ **sein** to cost money, *(Hotel)* to have steep prices; **unverschämt** ~ **sein** to cost an exorbitant price; ~ **verkaufen** to sell at a high price; **sein Leben** ~ **verkaufen** to sell one's life dearly; **zu** ~ **vermieten** to overrent; **sehr** ~ **werden** to run into a lot of money;
das wird dich ~ **zu stehen kommen** you will smart for it.

teure|r werden to get dearer, to become more expensive, to increase (advance) in price;
~**s Geld** close (dear) money; **sündhaft** ~**s Kleid** exorbitantly expensive dress; ~**s Pflaster** *(fig.)* high cost-of-living region; ~**s Vergnügen sein** to cost a pretty penny.

Teuerung dearness, high prices, general price increase, *(Knappheit)* dearth, scarcity;
künstliche ~ artificial dearness;
gestiegene ~ **abbremsen** to slow down the rising cost of living.

Teuerungs|druck pressure of increasing prices; ~**periode** era of scarcity; ~**rate** rate of price increase; ~**welle** wave of high prices; ~**wert** increment value; ~**zulage** cost-of-living (high-cost) bonus, dearness allowance *(US)*, dearness pay *(US)*, cost-of-living allowance, equalization pay; ~**zuschlag** price increment; ~**zuwachs** price increment.

Teufel devil, old Harry, the old gentleman;
wie der ~ like the devil;
armer ~ poor wretch;
auf ~ **komm raus arbeiten** to be working like the devil; **sich wie der** ~ **im Weihwasser benehmen** to hit out blindly; **weder Tod noch** ~ **fürchten** to be afraid of nothing; **zum** ~ **gehen** to go to blazes, *(Auto)* to be smashed to pieces; **in des** ~**s Küche geraten** to get into a mess; **wie der** ~ **das Weihwasser hassen** to shun s. th. like plague; **j. zum** ~ **jagen** to send s. o. packing (to the devil); **sich einen** ~ **darum kümmern** not to give a hang (care a hoot) about; **wie der** ~ **rennen** to run like blazes; **vom** ~ **begünstigt sein** to have the devil's own luck; **zum** ~ **gegangen sein** *(Geld)* to have gone down the drain; **wie der** ~ **hinter etw. her sein** to be hell-bent on s. th.; **wie der** ~ **hinter dem Geld her sein** to be keen on money-making; **mit dem** ~ **fertig werden** to beat the Dutch;
der ~ **ist los** fat's in the fire; **in der Not frißt der** ~ **Fliegen** any port in a storm; **man soll den** ~ **nicht an die Wand malen** talk of the devil and his horns will appear.

Teufels|bande devilry; **etw. in** ~**eile erledigen** to do s. th. in a harum-scarum way; ~**kerl** devil of a fellow, demon; ~**kreis**

vicious circle; ~**spiel** devil on two sticks; **mit jem. ein ~spiel treiben** to play the deuce (devil) with s. o.; ~**weib** a devil in petticoats; ~**werk** work of the devil.

teuflisch devilish, fiendish, satanic, diabolic;
~**e Sache** a devil of a business; ~**e Zeit hinter sich bringen müssen** to have the devil of a time.

Text text, tenor, body matter, *(Druck)* letterpress, *(Filmuntertitel)* caption, *(ohne Präambel)* body, *(Wortlaut)* wording; **dem ~ nach** textual; **gegenüber ~** *(Anzeige)* next to editorial (reading) matter, facing text; **in dreisprachigem ~** in three languages;
~ **und Kontext stimmen nicht überein** *(Wechsel)* words and figures differ;
abgekürzter ~ abridged text; **abweichender ~** different wording; **aktueller ~** news story; **authentischer ~** authentic (received) text; **diktierter ~** dictation; **Klischee einschließender ~** run-around; **fehlerhafter ~** incorrect text; **genauer ~** exact wording; **gleichbleibender ~** *(Anzeige)* same text; **hinzuzusetzender ~** addendum; **illustrierter ~** illustrated text; **kommentierter ~** annotated text; **korrigierter ~** clean proof; **maschinegeschriebener ~** typescript; **maßgeblicher ~** authentic text; **offizieller ~** official text; **redaktioneller ~** editorial matter; **schwerer ~** stiff course of reading; **verbesserter ~** revised text, revise; **verbindender ~** *(Rundfunk)* continuity; **verderbter ~** corrupt text; **verschlüsselter ~** coded text, encodement;
~ **voller Fehler** corrupt text; ~ **eines Wechsels** tenor of a bill; **im ~ abweichen** to read differently; ~ **auslegen** to open a text; ~ **frei auslegen** to take liberties with a text; ~ **auszeichnen** to display text matter; **j. aus dem ~ bringen** to interrupt s. one's train of thought, to put s. o. out, *(durch Zwischenrufe)* to heckle;; ~ **kritisch durchsehen** to amend a text; ~ **entstellen** to torture a text; **sich genau an den ~ halten** to stick to the text; **zu viel in einen ~ hineinlesen** to read too much into a text; ~ **interpretieren** to interpret a text; **aus dem ~ kommen** to lose the thread, *(Redner)* to break down; ~ **kommentieren** to write notes on a text; **seinen ~ können** *(Schauspieler)* to have learned one's lines; **jem. gehörig den ~ lesen** to call (haul) s. o. over the coals; ~ **rekonstruieren** to restore a text; ~ **in Umrahmung stellen (umranden)** *(Anzeige)* to box in; ~ **umarbeiten** to rewrite a text; ~ **verfälschen** to tamper with a text; ~ **mit Anmerkungen versehen** to make comments (comment) on a text; ~ **verzerren** to torment a text; ~ **frei wiedergeben** to paraphrase a text;
~**abbildung** illustration of the letterpress; ~**abfassung** drafting of a text, *(Reklame)* copywriting; ~**abschnitt** passage; ~**abteilung** *(Werbeagentur)* copy department; ~**analyse** copy research; ~**anmerkungen** textual notes on a work.

textanschließend *(Anzeige)* following matter.

Text|anzeige *(im redaktionellen Teil)* reading notice, reader advertisement, advertorial, *(kleine)* short article (paragraph); ~**aufhänger** copy approach; ~**ausgabe** *(Schulunterricht)* text edition; ~**auszählen** copy casting; ~**berichtigung** emendation of a text; ~**blase** balloon, bubble; ~**block** *(Anzeige)* bold type; ~**buch** *(Oper)* wordbook, *(Theater)* playbook, libretto; ~**buchrevisor** play doctor; ~**dichter** *(Oper)* librettist; ~**durchsicht** emendation of a text; **betonter ~einsatz** *(Anzeige)* lead-off; ~**einschub** insertion.

texten *(Fernsehen, Rundfunk)* to script, *(Werbung)* to copywrite.

Text|entstellung torture of a text; ~**entwurf** draft text.

Texter *(Fernsehen, Rundfunk)* scriptwriter, scripter, *(Werbeagentur)* copywriter.

Text|erfassung, Daten- oder data caption; ~**fälschung** interpolation; ~**fehler** textual error.

textgemäß textual.

Textil|arbeiter textile worker; ~**erzeugnisse** textile (dry, *US*) goods; ~**fabrik** textile mill; ~**fabrikant** textile maker (manufacturer); ~**faser** fibre *(Br.)*, fiber *(US)*; ~**firma** textile company; ~**geschäft** drapery shop, dry-goods store *(US)*; ~**handel** drapery, drapery business, dry-goods business *(US)*.

Textilien textiles, textile (dry, *US*) goods, drapery *(Br.)*;
~ **und verwandte Produkte** soft goods *(US)*.

Textil|industrie textile industry; ~**kaufmann** draper *(Br.)*; ~**laden** draper's shop *(Br.)*, drapery shop *(Br.)*, dry-goods store *(US)*; ~**messe** textile goods fair; ~**punkt** clothing coupon; ~**sektor** textile sector; ~**verarbeitung** textile processing; ~**veredelung** textile finishing.

Textilwaren textiles, dry *(US)* (textile) goods, drapery *(Br.)*, soft goods *(US)*;
nach dem Stück verkaufte ~ piece goods;
~ **nach dem Meter** dry goods *(US)*;
~**abteilung** soft goods department *(US)*.

Textilwirtschaft textile industry.

Text|interpolierung interlineation of a text; ~**interpretation** paraphrase; ~**korrekturen** author's alterations; ~**kritik** textual (verbal) criticism; ~**prüfung** *(Anzeigen)* copy testing; ~**schreiber** copywriter; ~**seite** text page; ~**stelle** passage; **einer ~stelle eine Bedeutung beimessen** to attribute a meaning to a passage; ~**stelle ins Englische übertragen** to translate a passage into English; ~**teilanzeige** textual advertisement.

Textur fibre.

Textverarbeitung *(Computer)* word processing.

Textverarbeitungsanlage editing typewriter.

textverbessernd emendatory.

Text|verbesserung emendation of a text, castigation of a text; ~**verdrehung** strain upon (distortion of) a text; ~**vergleichung** collation; ~**werbung** advertisement to the reader, reader advertisement; ~**zeile** caption; ~**zusätze** textual additions.

Theater theater, theatre *(Br.)*, *(Bühne)* stage, *(Getue)* farce, fanfare, masquerade, *(Rampe)* footlights;
im ~ at the theater;
durchgehend geöffnetes ~ grind house; **reines ~** mere pose; **staatlich subventioniertes ~** state-subsidized (national) theater (theatre, *Br.*);
~ **mit einem Fassungsvermögen von 2000 Personen** theater (theatre, *Br.*) capable of seating two thousand; ~ **mit Staatszuschuß** national (state-subsidized) theatre (theater);
im ~ auftreten to play in a theater; ~ **durch Freikartenausgabe füllen** to dress the house, to paper a theatre *(sl.)*; **ins ~ gehen** to go to the theater; **nach dem Feierabend ins ~ gehen** to finish up the evening at the theatre; **zum ~ gehen** to go on the stage; **zum ~ gehören** to belong to the profession *(fam.)*; ~ **machen** to carry on, *(fig.)* to make a fuss; **beim ~ sein** to be on the stage; ~ **spielen** to play; **aus dem ~ strömen** to pour out of the theatre;
~**abonnement abschließen** to buy a season ticket; ~**agent** theatrical promoter (agent), ten percenter; ~**agentur** booking agency; ~**amateure** theater-minded people; ~**aufführung** theatrical performance, show, house; ~**bericht** theater (theatre, *Br.*) review; ~**beruf** stage.

theaterbesessen stage-struck.

Theater|besuch theatergoing, playgoing; ~**besucher** theatergoer, playgoer, visitor; ~**coup** textbook coup; ~**direktor** producer; ~**domäne** theater land; ~**gebäude** theatre *(Br.)* (theater, *US*); ~**jargon beherrschen** to know the jargon of the stage; ~**karte** theater [admission] ticket; ~**karten schriftlich bestellen** to make a theater booking by post; **verbilligte ~karten verkloppen** to leblang *(sl.)*; ~**kasse** booking office, box office; ~**klatsch** greenroom; ~**konzession** theater (theatre, *Br.*) licence; **in ~kreisen** in theatrical circles; ~**kritik** dramatic criticism; ~**kritiker** dramatic critic, aisle-sitter *(US)*; ~**kulissen machen** to paint the scenery for a play; ~**laufbahn einschlagen** to go upon the boards (on the stage); ~**loge** box; ~**plakat** theater poster; ~**probe** rehearsal; ~**programm** theater program(me); ~**publikum** theater audience (business), patrons of the drama business; **aus vielen Freikarteninhabern bestehendes ~publikum** paper house *(sl.)*; ~**requisiten** stage properties, props *(coll.)*; ~**rezensent** dramatic editor; ~**ring** circuit; ~**rolle** actor's lines.

Theaterstück play, piece;
durchgefallenes ~ flop; **geistreiches ~** sophisticated play;
~ **auf den Geschmack des Publikums abstellen** to tailor a play for the audience; ~ **ansehen** to see a play; ~ **aufführen** to present (put up) a play; ~ **auszischen** to hoot a play off the stage; ~ **zur Aufführung freigeben** to license a play; **an einem ~ schreiben** to write for the stage, to have a play on the stocks; ~ **verbieten** to ban a play; ~ **vorführen** to give a play.

Theater|truppe theatrical company; ~**viertel** Great White Way *(US)*; ~**vorstellung** house, theatrical performance; ~**welt** stage; ~**werbung** program(me) advertising, theater publicity; ~**zettel** playbill.

theatralisch theatrical.

Theke counter, bar;
unter der ~ verkaufen to sell under the counter.

Thekenaufsteller counter card (display) [piece].

Thema subject, theme, topic, story, text, heading;
nicht zum ~ gehörig immaterial to the subject; ~ **wechselnd** discursive;
aktuelles ~ topical subject; **nicht angeschnittenes ~** unbroached (untouched-upon) subject; **in Vorbereitung befindliches ~** subject to come; **fachmännisches ~** professional subject; **heikles ~** touchy (slippery, delicate) subject, touch-me-not; **taktisches ~** *(mil.)* tactical problem; **vorgesehenes ~** subject prescribed;
~ **abhandeln** to treat of (deal with) a subject; ~ **ganz abhandeln** to cover the whole subject; **vom ~ abkommen** to wander from

the point (subject), to travel out of the record, to glance off a subject; **völlig vom ~ abkommen** to get totally off the point; **vom ~ abschweifen** to deviate (digress) from the question; **vom ~ abweichen** to depart from one's subject; **~ völlig unvoreingenommen angehen** to be open-minded on a subject; **heikles ~ äußerst vorsichtig angehen** to touch lightly on a delicate matter; **~ anschneiden** to raise an issue, to strike a theme; **~ nur antippen** to go easy on a subject *(US)*; **j. über ein ~ aushorchen** to sound s. o. on a subject; **sich weit und breit über ein ~ auslassen** to linger over a subject; **sich zu einem ~ äußern** to let s. o. have one's thoughts in a matter; **sich umfassend zu einem ~ äußern** to speak at large on a subject; **sich unüberhörbar zu einem ~ äußern** to express o. s. strongly on a subject; **sich dezidiert zum ~ gleichen Lohns äußern** to express strong views on the subject of equal pay; **sich zu einem ~ uneingeschränkt äußern** to let o. s. go on a subject; **~ behandeln** to handle a subject; **~ detaillierter behandeln** to dilate upon a subject; **~ erschöpfend behandeln** to treat exhaustively of a subject, to treat a subject fully; **~ in der gebotenen Ausführlichkeit behandeln** to treat a subject with the fulness due; **gleiches ~ von allen Seiten beleuchten** to dish up the same subject in every shape; **~ flüchtig berühren** to glance at a subject; **sich mit einem ~ beschäftigen, das nichts hergibt** to be at work on a meagre subject; **sich auf sein ~ beschränken** to confine o. s. (keep) to the subject; **beim ~ bleiben** to stick to the point; **nicht beim ~ bleiben** to make irrelevant remarks; **j. auf ein ~ bringen** to get s. o. upon a subject; **~ zur Sprache bringen** to raise a subject; **sich an einem ~ festbeißen** to hold forth at length on s. th.; **dauernd auf einem ~ herumreiten** to harp upon the same string; **sich mit einem ~ vertraut machen** to read up a subject; **zum ~ sprechen** to speak to the matter; **~ zur Diskussion stellen** to bring up a subject for discussion; **auf ein anderes ~ überleiten** to swing the talk to another topic; **von einem ~ zum anderen überspringen** to run (leap) from one topic to the other; **sich eingehend über ein ~ verbreiten** to speak at some length on a subject; **am ~ vorbeigehen** to be beside the point; **~ wechseln** to proceed to another (shift, change the) subject.

thematisch thematic.

Themen|behandlung, umfassende large treatment of a subject; **breiter ~kreis** wide range of topics.

Theoretiker theorist.

theoretisch theoretical, speculative, armchair, on paper;
rein ~ betrachtet in the abstract;
~ ein guter Plan sein to be a good scheme on paper.

Theorie, in der armchair, on paper;
abgelehnte ~ exploded theory; **entgegengesetzte ~** counter-theory; **kaum haltbare ~** theory hardly tenable; **überholte ~** obsolete theory; **unhaltbare ~** untenable theory;
~ der Grenzproduktivität marginal theory of distribution; **~ der reinen Metallwährung** bullionism; **~ des reinen Überflusses** clear surplus theory; **~ der außenwirtschaftlichen Wertübertragung** transfer theory;
~ aufstellen to put forward (elaborate, erect, come up with, frame) a theory; **~ ausarbeiten** to construct a theory; **~ darlegen** to set forth a theory; **~ erhärten** to sustain a theory; **~ in die Praxis umsetzen** to reduce a theory to practice; **~ verfechten** to advocate a theory; **~ vortragen** to advance a theory; **~ zerpflücken** to pick a theory to pieces.

Therapie therapy.

Thermal|bad spa, baths; **~brunnen** thermal water; **~quelle** thermal (hot) spring.

Thermometer thermometer;
~skala scale of a thermometer.

Thermosflasche thermos flask, vacuum bottle.

Thermostat thermostat (regulator).

thesaurieren to store up, to hoard, *(Gewinn)* to retain;
Einkünfte ~ to accumulate income; **Erträge ~** to retain income; **Kapital ~** to accumulate capital.

thesaurierender Investmentfonds cumulative (accumulating) fund.

thesaurierter Gewinn retained income.

Thesaurierung accumulation, hoarding, storing;
unzulässige ~ *(Treuhänder)* excessive accumulation;
~ von Gewinn retaining of income; **~ von Kapital** accumulation (amassing) of capital.

Thesaurierungs|fonds restricted fund, accumulating (cumulative) trust, nonexpendable [trust] fund; **~treuhand** accumulating trust; **~verbot** rule against accumulation; **~vollmacht** *(Treuhänder)* power to accumulate; **~zeitraum** accumulation period.

Thomas|eisen basic iron; **~stahl** basic steel.

Thron throne, crown;
seinen ~ behaupten to remain upon one's throne; **sich des ~es bemächtigen** to usurp the throne; **~ besteigen** to come to (mount, ascend, accede to) the throne; **dem ~ entsagen** to renounce one's rights to the throne, to abdicate the throne; **auf den ~ erheben** to raise to the throne; **auf dem ~ folgen** to accede to the throne; **auf den ~ setzen** to enthrone; **~ usurpieren** to seize the throne; **seinen ~ verlieren** to lose one's throne;
~anwärter heir to the throne, pretender; **~besteigung** accession (elevation) to the throne, enthronement; **~bewerber** claimant to the throne, pretender [to the throne]; **~bewerbung** pretendership; **~entsagung** abdication; **~erbe** successor (heir) to the throne, heir apparent; **~folge** succession to (demise of, devolution of) the throne (crown); **~folgegesetz** Act of Settlement *(Br.)*; **~folger** successor to the throne; **~niederlegung** abdication of the throne; **~prätendent** pretender [to the throne]; **~raub** usurpation of the throne; **~rede** King's (Queen's) Speech, royal speech; **~saal** presence chamber (room) *(Br.)*; **~verzicht** disclaimer to the throne.

Tick, auf j. einen ~ haben to bear a grudge against s. o.; **einen kleinen ~ haben** to be soft-headed (a bit crazy).

Ticken ticktock, tick, ticking.

Ticker *(Börse)* stock ticker;
~dienst ticker service.

Tief *(Konjunktur)* depression, low, *(Wetter)* low-pressure area, depression, low, cyclone;
abziehendes ~ departing low;
sich in einem seelischen ~ befinden to be in a state of depression.

tief *(extrem)* utter, deep, extreme, *(Land)* low, *(Wasser)* deep;
~ gekränkt deeply hurt;
bis ~ in die Nacht arbeiten to burn the midnight oil, to study deep into the night; **~ gehen** *(Schiff)* to draw much water; **zu ~ ins Glas geschaut haben** to have had one too many; **j. ~ hineinreiten** to get s. o. in an awful mess; **~ blicken lassen** to speak volumes; **~ empört sein** to be scandalized; **~ im Schlamm stecken** to be stuck deep in the mud; **~ in jds. Schuld stecken** to be deeply indebted to s. o.; **~ in den Schulden stecken** to be over head and heels in debt;
~er Ausschnitt low neckline; **~er Fall** *(fig.)* grave fall; **im ~en Wald** deep in the woods.

Tiefätzung deep-etching.

Tiefbau civil engineering;
~ an der Universität studieren to do civil engineering at the university;
~arbeiten engineering operations; **~arbeiter** engineering worker, pick and shovel man, excavator, navvy *(sl.)*; **~auftrag** engineering contract; **~ingenieur** civil engineer.

Tief|bunker underground shelter; **~decker** low-wing aircraft.

Tiefdruck intaglio (copperplate) printing, rotogravure, *(Wetter)* low pressure;
~gebiet minimum depression low, area of low pressure, low area, depression; **~rinne** trough of a low barometric pressure;
~rotationsmaschine photogravure [rotary] press.

Tiefe deep, depth;
unergründliche ~ unplumbed depth;
Höhen und ~n des Lebens ups and downs of life; **~ des Ozeans** bosom of the ocean, ocean deep; **~n des Weltraums** interstellar space;
bei einer Erörterung in die ~ gehen to probe deeper into a subject.

Tiefebene low country, lowland.

tiefempfundener Dank hearty thanks.

Tiefen|analyse in-depth analysis; **~gliederung** *(mil.)* distribution on (deployment in) depths; **~interview** depth (qualitative) interview; **~lot** depth finder, deep-sea lead, bathometer, fathometer; **~messung** sounding; **~psychologe** depth psychologist; **~psychologie** depth psychology; **~schärfe** depth of focus; **~schärfebereich** belt of sharpness; **~verteidigung** *(mil.)* defence in depth; **~wirkung** *(Bühnenbild)* stereoscopic effect.

Tiefereinstufung, tarifliche ingrade salary decrease, demotional classification change.

Tief|flieger strafer, hedgehopper *(sl.)*; **~fliegerangriff** low-level attack, strafing; **~flug** low-level flight, hedge-hopping.

Tiefgang *(Bergbau)* dip, *(Schiff)* gauge, draught, draft *(US)*, *(leeres Schiff)* light draught;
mittlerer ~ mean draught (draft, *US*);
~ des beladenen Schiffs load draught;
Schiffe ohne Rücksicht auf den ~ aufnehmen to accommodate vessels of any draught; **15 Fuß ~ haben** to draw 15 feet of water; **großen ~ haben** to draw deep; **ohne ~ sein** *(Roman)* to be lacking in depth.

Tief|gangsmarke high watermark; ~**garage** basement garage; ~**garage mit zwei Etagen** two-level underground car park.
tief|gefrieren to deepfreeze, to quick-feeze; ~**gehend** *(Schiff)* deep-drawing, *(Untersuchung)* thorough, intensive; ~**gekühlt** deep-frozen, quick frozen; ~**gekühlte Lebensmittel** frozen food.
Tiefgeschoß mit Sonderangeboten bargain basement.
tiefgründig recondite, deep, profound;
~**er Denker** profound thinker.
Tief|konjunktur cyclical (trade) depression; ~**kühlaufbewahrung** deep-freeze locker plant.
tiefkühlen to quick-freeze, to refrigerate, to deepfreeze.
Tiefkühl|fach deep freeze; ~**gemüse** frozen vegetables; ~**industrie** refrigeration industry; ~**kost** frozen food; ~**lastwagen** lorry freezer; ~**nahrungsmittelbetrieb** frozen-goods manufacturer; ~**schiff** reefer; ~**schrank** deep freezer; ~**truhe** food (home) freezer; ~**verfahren** quick-freezing, freezing (refrigerating) process; ~**waggon** reefer.
Tief|ladeanhänger low-bodied trailer; ~**ladearbeiter** trammer; ~**parterre** basement.
Tiefpunkt bottom, low watermark, nadir;
~ **der Konjunktur** depression low;
~ **erreichen** *(Zinssatz)* to ground; **weit unter den letzten** ~ **fallen** to break far below the previous low level; **ausgesprochenen** ~ **haben** to be down in the dumps, to have the blues *(coll.)*.
Tief|schlaf deep sleep; ~**schlag** blow below the belt.
tiefschürfend|schreiben to write in depth;
~**es Buch** profound book.
Tiefsee deep sea;
~**fischerei** deap-sea fishery; ~**forscher** underwater explorer; ~**forschung** deep-sea research; ~**kabel** submarine cable; ~**taucher** deep-sea diver.
tiefst, im ~**en Elend leben** to live in misery and want; **im** ~**en Frieden** in the midst of peace; **aus** ~**em Herzen** from the bottom of one's heart; ~**es Mittelalter** absolutely medieval; **in** ~**er Nacht** in the dead of the night; ~**er Rezessionspunkt** bottom of a recession.
Tiefstand ebb, low watermark, *(fig.)* depression, slump, nadir, *(Kurse)* low level (point), bottom;
absoluter ~ *(Börse)* the lowest level ever, all-time low; **äußerster** ~ *(Börse)* double bottom *(US)*; **neuer** ~ *(Börse)* bottom dropped out;
~ **bei Anlageinvestitionen** investment slump;
Kurse auf einen neuen ~ **bringen** to carry the prices to a new low level; ~ **erreichen** to hit the bottom; **absoluten** ~ **erreichen** to hit an all-time low, to run down to rock bottom; **neuen** ~ **erreichen** to reach a new low; **zu einem neuen** ~ **der Kurse führen** to carry the prices to a new low level; ~ **erreicht haben** to have touched rock bottom; ~ **überschreiten** to bottom out.
Tiefstapelei understatement.
tiefstapeln to make understatements.
Tiefstpreis bottom (bottom-of-the-line) price.
Tiefstpunkt bottoming-out pattern;
am ~ **von jds. Mißgeschick** at the lowest pitch of s. one's fortune;
weit unter den letzten ~ **fallen** to break far below the previous low levels; **immer noch auf dem** ~ **verharren** *(Kurse)* to be still bumping along near its low.
Tiefst|stand lowest level; ~**zinspolitik** ultra-cheap money policy.
Tief|tonlautsprecher low-frequency loudspeaker, woofer; ~**wasserzeichen** low watermark.
Tier animal, beast;
ausgestorbenes ~ extinct animal; **hohes (großes)** ~ big shot (bud, *US*), vip, great gun, high up *(coll.)*, top sawyer *(coll.)*, worthy, mugwump *(US)*, pumpkin *(US coll.)*, large charge *(sl.)*, bigwig *(sl.)*; **hohe** ~**e** the top, top brass *(US sl.)*; **ganz hohes** ~ nob of the first water *(sl.)*; **jagdbare** ~**e** game; **lebendes** ~ entire animal; **streunendes** ~ waif, stray; **zahmes** ~ tame animal;
hohes ~ **in der Politik** swell in politics;
~ **halten** to keep an animal;
~**arzt** veterinary surgeon, vet.
tierärztlich veterinary;
~ **untersuchen (behandeln)** to vet.
Tier|asyl animal home (shelter); ~**buch** book about animals; ~**haftung** liability for animals; ~**halter** keeper of an animal; ~**handlung** pet shop; ~**heilkunde** veterinary medicine.
tierisch beastly, brutal, bestial;
mit ~**em Ernst** deadly earnest, dead seriously.
Tier|klinik veterinary hospital; ~**körper** dead animal, carcass; ~**körperverwerter** knacker *(Br.)*.
tierlieb kind to animals.
Tier|öl animal oil; ~**pflegeanstalt** banian hospital; ~**quälerei** cruelty to animals; ~**reich** animal world; ~**reservat** wildlife sanctuary; ~**versicherung** livestock insurance; ~**welt** animal life.
Tiger, sich wie ein ~ **auf die Arbeit stürzen** to set to work like a madman.
Tilde tilde, tittle.
tilgbar redeemable, subject to redemption, amortizable;
nicht ~ irredeemable, not payable; **vorzeitig** ~ redeemable in advance.
Tilgbarkeit redeemableness, redeemability, annullability, amortizableness.
tilgen *(amortisieren)* to amortize, *(auslöschen)* to efface, to wipe off, to extinguish, *(Buchung stornieren)* to reverse, to cancel, *(drucktechn.)* to delete, *(einlösen)* to redeem, *(Eintragung)* to strike out, to expunge, to blur out, *(Schuld)* to cancel, to acquit, to clear off, to compound, to discharge, to liquidate, to pay off (up), *(vernichten)* to exterminate, to extirpate;
Anleihe ~ to retire a loan; **anteilmäßig** ~ to pay off pro rota; **Eintragungen** ~ to strike out entries; **unliebsame Erinnerungen aus dem Gedächtnis** ~ to efface unpleasant memories of the past; **Hypothek** ~ to extinguish (wipe off) a mortgage; **Posten** ~ to delete an item; **im Strafregister** ~ to delete in the criminal record.
Tilgung *(Amortisation)* amortization, *(Ausstreichung)* deletion, effacement, extinguishment, erasement, *(Einlösung)* redemption, sinking, *(Hypothek)* extinction, satisfaction, *(Schulden)* discharge, acquittal, paying off, repayment, clearance, liquidation, wiping off (out);
planmäßige ~ regular redemption; **teilweise** ~ partial extinction; **vertraglich vereinbarte** ~ solicited redemption; **vorzeitige** ~ previous (prior, priority) redemption;
~ **einer Anleihe** amortization of a loan, retirement (withdrawal) of a loan, bond redemption; ~ **eines Darlehns** redemption of a loan; ~ **vor Fälligkeit** redemption before due date; ~ **in voller Höhe** full payment; ~ **einer Hypothek** extinguishment (redemption, discharge, paying off) of a mortgage; ~ **über (unter) dem Nennwert** redemption above (below) par; ~ **von Obligationen** bond redemption; ~ **in Raten** payment by instal(l)ments; ~ **der öffentlichen Schuld** retirement of the public debt *(US)*; ~ **von Schuldverschreibungen** bond amortization; **frühzeitige** ~ **unkündbarer Schuldverschreibungen** redemption before maturity of noncallable bonds; ~ **von Verbindlichkeiten** discharge of liabilities; ~ **vertraglich eingegangener Verpflichtungen** payment under deed of covenant; ~ **einer Wechselverbindlichkeit** discharge of a bill;
zur ~ **aufrufen** to call up for redemption.
Tilgungs|abkommen redemption agreement; ~**anleihe** redemption (sinking-fund, amortization) loan; ~**aufforderung** *(Anleihe)* call for redemption of a loan; ~**bedingungen** terms of amortization (redemptions); ~**beihilfe** redemption grant; ~**bescheinigung,** ~**bestätigung** certificate of redemption, acquittance; ~**bestimmungen** terms of amortization (redemption); ~**betrag** redemption money (capital); ~**darlehn** redemption (redeemable, amortizing) loan; ~**dauer** period of repayment, redemption period; ~**dienst** redemption service; ~**eingänge** incoming redemption; ~**eintragung** *(Grundstückslast)* registration of satisfaction; ~**fälligkeit** redemption date; ~**fonds** sinking (liquidation, amortization, redemption, *US*) fund; ~**fonds zweckentfremden** to raid the sinking fund.
tilgungsfrei redemption-free;
~**e Zeit** *(Kredit)* grace period.
Tilungs|frist pay-off period, time of redemption; ~**gebühr** redemption charge; ~**hypothek** redemption (amortization) mortgage, sinking-fund mortgage loan; ~**kapital** redemption capital; ~**kasse** redemption office, sinking fund; ~**klausel** redemption clause; ~**konto** redemption account; ~**kredit** redemption (amortization) loan; ~**kurs** price of redemption, redemption price (rate); ~**plan** redemption table, amortization schedule (plan), sinking-fund instal(l)ment plan; ~**prämie** redemption premium; ~**protokoll** redemption record; ~**quote** amortization quota, redemption rate (instal(l)ment); ~**rate** rate of repayment, amortization rate (quota), sinking-fund instal(l)ment; ~**raten leisten** to pay amortization; ~**recht** right of redemption (to redeem); ~**rente** amortizable (redeemable) annuity; ~**rücklage** reserve for redemption, redemption (sinking-fund) reserve, retirement reserve fund, amortization reserve; ~**rückstand** arrears of payment; ~**satz** redemption (amortization) rate; ~**schein** certificate of redemption, bill of

amortization; ~**schema** sinking-fund (redemption) table, redemption plan; ~**schuld** indemnity (amortization, redemption) loan; ~**schuldverschreibungen** redemption bonds; ~**stock** sinking-fund (amortization, redemption) fund; ~**termin** redemption date; ~**vereinbarung** redemption agreement; ~**verpflichtungen** redemption commitments; ~**wert** redemption value; ~**zeitplan** redemption table; ~**zeitraum** time of redemption, payoff period *(US)*.

Tingeltangel low drinking resort, cheap saloon, honky-tonk *(US)*.

Tinktur tincture.

Tinnef trash, junk, rubbish.

Tinte writing ink;
in der ~ *(fig.)* in trouble (a tight corner);
unsichtbare ~ invisible ink;
in der ~ **sitzen** to be in a plight; **gleichfalls in der** ~ **sitzen** to be in the same predicament.

Tinten|faß ink glass, inkpot; ~**klecks** blot, splotch, ink stain; ~**kleckser** inkslinger *(sl.)*; ~**klecksereien** inkslinging *(sl.)*; ~**radiergummi** ink eraser; ~**stift** copying (indelible) pencil.

Tip tip, hint, point, pointer *(US)*, office *(sl.)*, shady *(sl.)*, *(Foto)* round;
der richtige ~ the straight tip; **sicherer** ~ reliable tip;
~ **befolgen** to take the hint (office, *sl.*); **jem. einen** ~ **geben** to give s. o. a hint (wrinkle, the office, *sl.*).

Tippelbruder *(fam.)* tramp, hobo, piker *(US sl.)*.

Tippelei trapes *(coll.)*, traipse *(coll.)*.

tippeln to traipse, to trapes, to tramp.

tippen to type, to typewrite, *(Lotto spielen)* to play at lotto (policy, *US*), *(raten)* to guess, to suppose;
an einen wunden Punkt ~ to touch a sore point; **j. auf die Schulter** ~ to tap s. o. on the shoulder.

Tipp|fehler *(fam.)* error in typing, typing error; ~**geber** tipster *(US)*.

tipptopp tiptop, bang-up *(sl.)*, galumptious *(sl.)*;
~ **gekleidet** immaculately dressed.

Tippzettel policy slip (ticket) *(US)*.

Tirade tirade, harangue;
sich in ~**n ergehen** to deliver a long harangue.

Tisch, am grünen armchair;
ausziehbarer ~ extension (draw-leaf, sliding) table; **bestellter** ~ reserved table; **grüner** ~ council board (table);
~ **und Bett** bed and board;
zwei Parteien an einen ~ **bringen** to initiate conciliatory talks between two parties; ~ **decken** to spread the table; **etw. am grünen** ~ **entscheiden** to make an armchair decision; **unter den** ~ **fallen** to go to the board, to be dropped; **zu** ~ **führen** to take in (out, *US*); **zu** ~ **gehen** to sit down to dinner; **mit der Faust auf den** ~ **hauen** to bang one's fist on the table; **Problem auf den** ~ **legen** to bring a question into the foreground; **reinen** ~ **machen** to clean the slate; **Beine unter einen fremden** ~ **stecken** to sponge upon other people; ~ **und Bett miteinander teilen** to share bed and board; **j. unter den** ~ **trinken** to drink s. o. under the table; **bar auf den** ~ **zahlen** to pay money down, to plank down *(US sl.)*;
~**apparat** desk telephone; ~**besteck** knife, fork and spoon; ~**decke** table cover; ~**empfänger** table set; ~**feuerzeug** table cigarette lighter; ~**gast** diner; ~**geschirr** tableware; ~**gesellschaft** company at table; ~**gespräch** table talk; ~**glocke** call (hand, dinner) bell; ~**herr** dinner partner, partner at table; ~**kalender** table calendar; ~**karte** place (dinner, guest) card; ~**klopfen** spirit rapping; ~**lampe** table (desk) lamp.

Tischleindeckdich easy street *(US sl.)*.

Tischler carpenter.

Tisch|nachbar neighbo(u)r at dinner; ~**ordnung** table plan, seating plan; ~**ordnung machen** to seat people at dinner, to marshal a company at table; ~**rechner** desktop calculator; ~**rede** after-dinner speech; ~**rücken** table lifting (rapping, turning); ~**telefon** desk telephone; **das** ~**tuch zwischen sich und jem. zerschneiden** to cut all connections with s. o.; ~**wäsche** table linen.

Titel title, style, appellation of dignity, predicate, *(Anrede)* style, *(Anspruch)* claim, title, *(Film)* caption, *(Leitfaden)* slogan, motto, *(Rechtstitel)* title deed, *(Rubrik)* rubric, title, *(Überschrift)* heading, title, caption, *(Wertpapiere)* securities, *(Wertpapiername)* title, *(Zeitung)* head, flag, *(Zoll)* position, item;
auf Kundenfang angelegter ~ catch-penny title; **unberechtigt angenommener** ~ sham title; **durchgehender** ~ *(Zeitung)* running head; **erloschener** ~ extinct title; **falscher** ~ bogus title; **nur im Lager und Katalog geführte** ~ *(Buchhändler)* only titles held in stock and listed in catalog(ue); **hochtrabender** ~ high-sounding title; **rollender** ~ *(Inserat)* roller caption; **verliehener** ~ honorary title; **ehrenhalber verliehener** ~ title by courtesy, courtesy title; **vollstreckbarer** ~ enforceable judgment, executory decree;
~ **einer Gesetzesvorlage** bill heading; ~ **des Haushaltsplans** item of the budget;
jem. einen ~ **aberkennen** to deprive s. o. of a title; **j. mit einem** ~ **anreden** to address s. o. by his title, to entitle s. o.; **sich einen** ~ **beilegen** to assume a title; ~ **erwirken** to procure judgment; ~ **führen** to hold (bear) a title, to have a handle to one's name *(coll.)*; **sich mit einem falschen** ~ **schmücken** to parade a false title; ~ **im Haushaltsplan streichen** to cancel a budget item; ~ **tragen** *(Buch)* to be entitled; ~ **verleihen** to confer a title; **seinen** ~ **verschweigen** to sink one's title; **mit einem** ~ **versehen** to head; **Buch mit einem** ~ **versehen** to title a book;
~**änderung** alteration of title; ~**anfertiger** *(Film)* caption artist; ~**angebot** *(Buchhändler)* title offer; ~**aufführung** *(Buch)* title entry, *(Film)* credit titles; ~**auflage** reissue under a new title; ~**aufnahme** *(Buchhandel)* list of titles, *(Film)* caption shooting; ~**bild** frontispiece, *(Zeitschrift)* cover picture; ~**bildfigur** front pager; ~**bildschönheit** cover girl; ~**blatt** front (title) page, cover; ~**bogen** title sheet, preliminaries.

Titelei oddments, front matter *(US)*.

Titel|feld *(Buchbinderei)* panel; ~**figur** front pager; **unberechtigte** ~**führung** unauthorized assumption of a title; ~**geschichte** cover (feature) story; ~**geschichtenverfasser** feature writer; ~**herstellung** *(Foto)* titling; ~**inhaber** title bearer; ~**insert** caption; ~**kopf** *(Druck)* headline, heading, head, rubric; ~**leiste** masthead; **erste Seite für** ~**meldungen freihalten** to hold the front page; ~**melodie** theme tune; ~**nachricht** front-page news; ~**nachricht abgeben** to make the feature; ~**rolle** *(Theater)* name part, title role (part); ~**schönheit** cover girl; ~**schrift** *(Druck)* display type; ~**schutz** copyright; ~**seite** front (title) page, *(Buch)* face of book; **auf die** ~**seite bringen** to carry on the front page; **namentliche** ~**seitenerwähnung verlieren** *(Berühmtheit)* to lose one's cover spot; ~**träger** title bearer, titleholder; **nomineller** ~**träger** titulary; ~**überschrift** newspaper headline; ~**verleihung** conferment of title; ~**vorspann** opening (credit) titles, credits; ~**wort** *(Wörterbuch)* head word, catchword; ~**zeile** headline, masthead; **hervorgehobene** ~**zeile** displayed line; ~**zeile abgeben** to make the papers.

Titular|professor honorary professor; ~**rang** nominal rank.

Titulatur styling.

titulieren to style, to address.

Toast toast, *(Rede)* rouse;
~ **auf j. ausbringen** to give a rouse (toast) to s. o.;
~**röster** toast rack.

Tobak, starker strong stuff.

toben *(Kinder)* to romp, to caper, to frolic, *(Sturm)* to rave, to rage;
vor Begeisterung ~ to be wild with enthusiasm.

tobende See tempestuous sea.

Tobsuchtsanfall raving fit;
~ **bekommen** to hit the roof, to blow one's top.

Tochter, seine ~ **ausstatten** to endow (settle) one's daughter;
~**anstalt** branch establishment; ~**betrieb** subsidiary plant.

Tochtergesellschaft affiliate, affiliated company (corporation, society), allied company, subsidiary, subsidiary company (corporation), controlled (constituent, related) company, subcompany *(US)*;
abhängige ~ underlying company *(US)*; **vollständig abhängige (hundertprozentige)** ~ wholly-owned subsidiary company; **ausländische** ~ foreign affiliation (subsidiary); **für den Aktienhandel gegründete** ~ share trading subsidiary; **[bilanzmäßig] konsolidierte** ~**en** consolidated subsidiaries; **durch Mehrheitsbesitz kontrollierte** ~ majority-owned subsidiary; **lizenzierte** ~ franchise satellite *(Br.)*; **selbständige** ~ unaffiliated company;
~ **einer Bank** banking subsidiary;
~**en hundertprozentig besitzen** to own subsidiaries outright; ~ **in die Gewinn- und Verlustrechnung mit einbeziehen (bilanzmäßig konsolidieren)** to consolidate the subsidiary's financial statement with one's own.

Tochter|sendestation affiliate *(US)*; ~**sprache** derivative language; ~**unternehmen** subsidiary company (corporation).

Tod death, decease, demise, exit;
an der Schwelle des ~**es** at the point of death; **angesichts des** ~**es** in contemplation of death; **gelegentlich seines** ~**es** on the occasion of his death; **im Zeitpunkt des** ~**es** at the time of death; **von** ~**es wegen** mortis causa; **zu** ~**e erschöpft** utterly exhausted; **zu** ~**e gelangweilt** bored to death;

bürgerlicher ~ civil death; **gewaltsamer** ~ violent death; **gleichzeitiger** ~ simultaneous death; **natürlicher** ~ natural death; **sofortiger** ~ instantaneous death;
~ **der Demokratie** end of democracy; ~ **durch gewaltsame äußere Einwirkung** death through external, violent and accidental means; ~ **durch Erfrieren** death by exposure; ~ **durch Fahrlässigkeit** negligent homicide; ~ **durch den Strang** rope; ~ **durch Unfall** accidental death; ~ **durch Unglücksfall** death by misadventure;
sich zu ~e arbeiten to kill o. s. with (the) work, to flog o. s. to death; **sich zu ~e ärgern** to fret one's life away; **wie der leibhaftige ~ aussehen** to look like death warmed up; **jds. ~ beschleunigen** to hasten s. one's death; **Verbrechen mit dem ~e bestrafen** to punish crime with death; **dem ~e ruhig entgegensehen** to meet death calmly; **mit knapper Not dem ~ entgehen** to narrowly escape death, to escape death by a narrow margin; **j. dem ~ entreißen** to snatch s. o. from the jaws of death; **j. zu ~e erschrecken** to frighten s. o. out of his wits, to make one's blood freeze, to give s. o. the shock of his life; ~ **bei jem. feststellen** to pronounce s. o. dead; **bei einem Unfall den ~ finden** to be killed in an accident; **um ~ und Leben gehen** to be a matter of life and death; **etw. auf den ~ nicht ausstehen können** to hate s. th. like poison; **j. fast zu ~e prügeln** to beat s. o. within an inch of his life; **langsam zu ~e quälen** to kill by inches; **zu ~e reiten** to do to death; **in den sicheren ~ rennen** to rush into certain death; **j. vom ~e retten** to deliver s. o. from death; **j. in den ~ schicken** to send s. o. to his doom; **zwischen ~ und Leben schweben** to hover between life and death; **zu ~e erschrocken sein** to be scared stiff; **zum ~e verurteilt sein** to lie under (a) sentence of death; **an der Schwelle des ~es stehen** to be at death's door; **eines gewaltsamen ~es sterben** to die a violent death (in one's shoes); **eines jämmerlichen ~es sterben** to die a dog's death; **eines natürlichen ~es sterben** to die a natural death; **eines sanften ~es sterben** to die an easy death; **zum ~e verurteilen** to doom to death; **j. zum ~e verurteilen** to pass a sentence of death on s. o.; **j. zum ~ durch Erhängen verurteilen** to be condemned (sentenced) to be hanged; **mit dem ~e bestraft werden** to be sentenced to death;
gegen den ~ ist kein Kraut gewachsen there is no medicine against death.

todbringend fatal.

Todes|ahnung presentiment of death; ~**angst** fear of death, mortal fear; **in ~ängsten** in fear of one's life; ~**ängste ausstehen** to be frightened out of one's wits, to die; **jem. ~ängste einjagen** to put s. o. in fear of his life; ~**anzeige** obituary notice, death announcement (notice), announcement of death, funeral letter *(US)*; ~**beweis** proof of death; ~**datum** deathday; ~**dosis** lethal dose; ~**erklärung** dying declaration.

Todesfall death, decease, fatality;
im ~ on the occurrence (in case) of death; **im Hinblick auf den ~** in contemplation of death;
~ **anzeigen** to notify death; **beim ~ übergehen** to pass on death.

Todesfalle death trap.

Todesfälle, angenommene *(Versicherungswesen)* expected deaths; **eingetretene ~** *(Versicherung)* actual deaths.

Todesfallprämie *(Lebensversicherung)* mortuary *(US)* (post-mortem) dividend.

Todesfallversicherung whole life insurance;
abgekürzte ~ temporary assurance *(Br.)*, term insurance (assurance, *Br.*); **unredlich erworbene ~** graveyard insurance; **normale ~** old-line life insurance, whole life assurance *(Br.)*, assurance payable at death *(US)*.

Todesfallziffer fatality rate.

Todes|feststellung ohne Angabe des Grundes *(Schwurgericht)* open verdict; **mit ~folgen** with a fatal result.

Todesgefahr peril of one's life;
in ~ in danger of death;
j. aus ~ retten to save s. one's life; **in ~ schweben** to be in mortal danger.

Todes|jahr year of death; ~**kampf** agony; ~**kandidat** death-marked person, doomed man; ~**krankheit** last sickness, last illness; ~**lager** death camp; ~**marsch** death march; ~**nachrichten** obituary notice; **in ~nöten sein** to be in peril of death; ~**opfer** death, casualty, fatality; ~**opfer auf der Landstraße** toll of the roads; **viele ~opfer fordern** to result in a great loss of life; ~**ort** death place; ~**qualen** death pangs; ~**risiko eingehen** to carry one's life in one's hands; ~**röcheln** death rattle; ~**schrecken bekommen** to be frightened out of one's wits (in a blue funk, *sl.*); ~**stoß** death blow, finishing (fatal) blow; **einem Unternehmen den ~stoß versetzen** to sign the death warrant of an enterprise *(Br.)*.

Todesstrafe capital sentence (punishment), death sentence (penalty, *US*), extreme penalty of the law;
nicht zu vollstreckende ~ sentence of death recorded;
~ **abschaffen** to abolish capital punishment; **auf ~ erkennen** to pronounce a sentence of death; ~ **wiedereinführen** to revive the death penalty.

Todes|stunde mortal hour, hour of death; ~**tag** date of death, deathday; ~**urkunde** death certificate; ~**ursache** cause of death; ~**ursache unbekannt** *(Leichenbeschauer)* open verdict; ~**ursache angeben** to state the cause of death.

Todesurteil death warrant, death sentence;
~ **bedeuten** to spell the doom; ~ **fällen** to pronounce a sentence of death; ~ **unterzeichnen** to sign a death warrant.

Todes|verachtung contempt of death; ~**vermutung** presumption of (presumptive) death; **gleichzeitige ~vermutung** *(Versicherung)* common calamity; **gleichzeitige ~vermutungsklausel** *(Versicherung)* common (calamity) disaster clause; **zufällige ~verursachung** killing by misadventure; ~**warnung** knell.

todeswürdiges Verbrechen capital crime.

Todes|zeitpunkt, zum *(Testament)* now; ~**zelle** death row; ~**ziffer**, ~**zoll** death toll, toll of death; ~**zone** zone of death.

Tod|feind deadly (mortal, sworn) enemy; ~**geweihter** moribund.

tod|krank sein to be on the danger list; ~**langweilig** mortal *(coll.)*.

tödlich deadly, mortal, fatal;
~ **erschrocken** scared stiff *(coll.)*; **nahezu ~** near-fatal;
~ **verunglücken** to be killed in an accident;
~ **ausgehen** to have a fatal end; **sich ~ langweilen** to be bored out of one's mind; **j. ~ treffen** to strike s. o. a mortal blow;
~**e Beleidigung** mortal offence; ~**er Betriebsunfall** industrial fatality; **mit ~er Sicherheit** as sure as death; ~**er Unfall** fatal accident, accidental death; ~**e Verletzungen** fatal injuries.

tod|müde dead tired, done, dead *(coll.)*, tired to the world; ~**schick** very stylish, classy, swell *(coll.)*, snazzy *(US sl.)*.

todsicher as safe as houses, as sure as eggs is eggs, as sure as fate, cocksure, six to one;
~**er Fall** airtight case; ~**e Methode** foolproof method; ~**e Sache** dead certainty, sure thing, sitter *(sl.)*.

Tohuwabohu chaos, helterskelter, topsy-turvy, juggermugger;
sich in ein ~ verwandeln to turn into a mess.

Toilette water closet, lavatory, toilet, washroom, rest room *(US)*;
in großer ~ erscheinen to appear in full dress; **auf die ~ gehen** to spend a penny *(Br.)*; ~ **machen** to do o. s. up.

Toiletten|artikel toilet articles; ~**frau** lavatory attendant; ~**papier** toilet paper, bumf, loo paper *(fam.)*; ~**wärter** lavatory attendant.

Toleranz tolerance, toleration, margin, *(Kompaß)* permissible deviation, *(Münzen)* remedy allowance *(Br.)*, mint remedy *(US)*, remedy of the mint *(US)*;
zulässige ~ *(Qualitätskontrolle)* total tolerance;
unter Berücksichtigung üblicher ~abweichungen subject to any tolerance; ~**breite** range; ~**faktor** tolerance factor; ~**grenze** boundary, tolerance requirements, tolerance limit; ~**klausel** deviation clause.

toll mad, crazy, *(rasend)* wild, raging, raving, *(verwegen)* daring, bold;
wie ~ arbeiten to work at white-hot speed; **nicht so ~ sein** not to be so hot;
~**es Auto** smashing car; ~**e Frau** smasher *(sl.)*; ~**es Gedränge** frightful crowd; ~**e Gerüchte verbreiten** to spread wild rumo(u)rs; ~**e Geschwindigkeit** breakneck speed; ~**er Hecht** daredevil; ~**en Lärm veranstalten** to kick up a row; ~**e Sache** topper *(coll.)*, humdinger, hummer *(sl.)*, knockout *(US)*; ~**es Wetter** marvel(l)ous weather; ~**e Zeit** wild time.

tollkühn reckless, rash, foolhardy;
~**es Unternehmen** risky undertaking.

Tolpatsch clumsy fellow.

Tölpel ninny, dupe, sap *(US sl.)*, mug *(US)*.

Tombola tombola, charity lottery, raffle;
~ **verlosen** to raffle off.

Ton tone, sound, note, voice, chord;
in einem beleidigenden ~ in an offensive tone; **in mürrischem ~** in a querulous tone; **in ganz sachlichem ~** in a matter-of-fact voice;
entschlossener ~ decisive tone; **gemäßigter ~** measured language; **ungezwungener ~** free and easy tone;
~ **eines Briefes** sound of a letter;
seinen ~ ändern to change one's note (tune); ~ **angeben** to give the lead *(fam.)*; **anderen ~ anschlagen** to sing another tune; **besorgten ~ anschlagen** to sound a note of alarm; **richtigen ~ anschlagen** to adopt the right tone, to strike the right note (tone), to touch the right key; **passenden ~ in einem Brief**

anschlagen to write a letter in appropriate style; ~ **aussteuern** to modulate; **sich eines groben ~s bedienen** to speak in a rude fashion; **seiner Stimme einen leicht nörgelnden ~ geben** to strike a querulous note; **nicht zum guten ~ gehören** not to be done; **gleichen ~ haben** to be of the same shade; **sich im ~ mäßigen** to relax one's tone; **in scharfem ~ sprechen** to speak in a sharp key; **in herablassendem ~ mit j. sprechen** to talk down to s. o.; **richtigen ~ treffen** to hit the right note; ~ **treffen, der beim Publikum ankommt** to strike a responsive chord among the audience; ~ **unterlegen** to dub sound;
~**abnehmer** reproducer, pickup, cartridge; ~**abnehmer mit Magnetsystem** magnetic pickup.

tonangebend leading [the fashion], rampant, topnotch;
~ **sein** to rule the roost (roast);
~**e Valuta** dominating currency.

Ton|angeber fashion leader; ~**arm** tone arm, reproducer; ~**art** key; **andere ~art anschlagen** to change one's tone, to sing another tune; **j. in allen ~arten loben** to break into praise for s. o.; ~**assistent** sound operator; ~**atelier** recording (soundproof) studio; ~**aufnahme** take, tape (sound) recording, *(Sendung)* electrical transcription; ~**aufnahmen machen** to make transcriptions; ~**aufnahmegerät** sound-recording device; ~**aufzeichnung** sound recording; ~**ausblendung** fade; ~**ausfall** sound breakdown; ~**bad** *(Foto)* toning bath.

Tonband [magnetic] ribbon, [magnetic recording] tape, *(Film)* sound tape;
auf ~ aufgenommen recorded, canned, on tape; **nicht auf ~ aufgenommen** unrecorded;
auf ~ aufnehmen to tape[-record], to can;
Schallplatten- und ~archiv transcription program(me) library;
~**aufnahme** taped recording; ~**diktat in die Schreibmaschine übertragen** to transcribe from s. one's reel; ~**gerät** tape recorder (player), sound-recording device; ~**gerät einschalten** to turn on a tape recorder; ~**kassette** recording tape cassette; ~**kopie** tape transcript; ~**spule** recording tape spool; ~**übertragung** electrical transcription.

Ton|bildschau film strip; ~**blende** fader; ~**dichtung** tone poetry.

Töne, in den höchsten ~n von jem. sprechen to speak of s. o. in lofty strains (high, flattering, terms); **große ~ spucken** to put it on, to splurge, to talk big, to brag.

Ton|effekt sound effect; ~**einblendung** dub-in.

tönen to sound, to ring, *(Glocke)* to chime, to ding, *(schattieren)* to tinge, to tone;
groß ~ to lay it on thick.

tönende Worte empty words.

tönern, auf ~en Füßen stehen to have a shaky basis.

Tonfall expression, intonation, modulation;
ausländischer ~ foreign accent.

Tonfilm talking film, talkie, sound motion picture *(US)*, speakie;
~**streifen** combine track; ~**vorführgerät** sound projector.

Ton|filter tone filter; ~**frequenz** audio frequency; ~**galgen** microphone boom; ~**gemälde** tone picture; ~**höhe** pitch; ~**ingenieur** audio control engineer, monitoring operator; ~**kapsel** sound box; ~**kopf** pickup cartridge; ~**kopie** sound print, ~**kunst** musical art, music; ~**lage** pitch level; ~**malerei** tone painting; ~**mischpult** [sound] mixer, monitoring desk.

Tonnage tonnage, *(Schiff)* displacement;
aufgelegte ~ idle tonnage (shipping); **eingetragene ~** enrol(l)ed tonnage *(US)*; **im Krieg verlorene ~** war-lost tonnage;
~**kontingent** *(Stahleinfuhren)* tonnage quota; ~**rekord** tonnage record; ~**verlust** loss of tonnage.

Tonne tun, cask, *(Boje)* buoy, *(Faß)* barrel, vat, butt, *(Gewicht)* ton, long ton *(Br.)*, short ton *(US)*;
metrische ~ metric (long, *Br.*) ton;
~ **der Fracht** freight ton.

Tonnen|boje can buoy; ~**brücke** floating bridge; ~**fracht** freight by the ton, ton freight; ~**gehalt** displacement ton[nage], measurement, capacity, burden; ~**geld** tonnage, tonnage rent *(US)*, beaconage, warpage; ~**kilometer** ton mile; ~**leger** buoy-laying vessel; ~**meile** ton mile.

tonnenweise by tons (barrels).

Tonnen|zahl, verarbeitete tons processed; ~**zoll** tonnage duty.

Ton|platte tint block; ~**regisseur** sound engineer; ~**rohr** tile; ~**röhrenkanal** tile drain; ~**schnitt** cut; ~**spur,** ~**streifen** sound track; ~**störung** audio interference; **schalldichtes ~studio** soundproof studio; ~**technik** sound engineering; ~**techniker** sound man; ~**treue** high fidelity; ~**übertragung** electrical transcription; ~**untermalung** background sound (music); ~**wagen** recording car, sound truck; **stereophonische ~wiedergabe** stereo, high fidelity; ~**wiedergabegerät** sound reproducing instrument.

Topf, goldener pot of gold;
~ **heißen Geldes verwalten** to run a hot fund; **alles in einen ~ werfen** to lump things together, to measure everything with the same yardstick;
jeder ~ findet seinen Deckel there's a nut for every bolt.

Töpfe, nur auf drei ~n laufen to be firing on only three cylinders.

Töpfer potter;
~**waren** pottery.

Topf|kratzer wire wool; ~**pflanze** indoor pot plant.

Topographie eines Landes national features of a country.

Toppflagge masthead flag;
~**n hissen** to dress ship.

topplastig *(Schiff)* top-hampered, tender.

Tor door, entrance, gate;
vor den ~en der Stadt outside the town;
wie die Kuh vorm neuen ~ dastehen to be completely at a loss;
der Unmoral Tür und ~ öffnen to open the door to immorality;
~ **schießen** to kick a goal;
~**durchfahrt** archway, passageway; ~**einfahrt** gateway.

Torf|gerechtigkeit common of turbary, profit à prendre; ~**kohle** peat coal.

Tor|heit folly, silliness, foolishness, unreason; ~**hüter** gatekeeper.

töricht foolish, silly, unwise;
sich ~ benehmen to make a fool of o. s.; ~ **handeln** to footle.

torkeln to totter, to wobble, to swagger, to sway.

Tornado tornado, twister *(US coll)*.

Tornister *(mil.)* pack, knapsack;
~ **abnehmen** to remove the pack.

torpedieren, Verhandlungen to torpedo negotiations.

Torpedo torpedo;
~ **abschießen** to torpedo, to launch a torpedo, to squirt a mould *(Br., sl.)*;
~**bahn** torpedo wake; ~**boot** torpedo boat; ~**bootzerstörer,** ~**bootjäger** torpedo-boat destroyer; ~**flugzeug** torpedo aircraft (bomber, plane); ~**rohr** torpedo tube; ~**schutznetz** torpedo net (netting).

Torschluß, knapp vor ~ kommen to arrive at the fag end (eleventh hour);
~**panik** eleventh-hour panic.

Torso torso, *(fig.)* basket case.

tosen to roar, to thunder.

tosender|Beifall thunderous applause; ~ **Sturm** roaring storm.

tot dead, deceased, departed, defunct, *(abgestorben)* numb, benumbed, *(nicht angelegt)* uninvested, idle, dormant, *(erloschen)* extinct, *(total erschöpft)* done *(coll.)*, dead beat, fagged out, *(Gewässer)* stagnant, standing, *(leblos)* lifeless, dead, *(Straße)* deserted, dead;
bürgerlich ~ dead; **physisch ~** actually dead; **sofort ~** killed instantly;
sich ~ arbeiten to work o. s. to death (one's fingers to the bone); **j. für ~ erklären** to declare s. o. [legally] dead; **sofort ~ sein** to be killed on the spot; **sich ~ stellen** to play possum;
~**e Bahnlinie** disused line; ~**er Gang** *(Auto)* play; ~**es Gebirge** *(Bergbau)* exhausted mine; ~**es Gewicht** *(Fahrzeug)* deadweight; ~**es Gleis** dead track; ~**e Hand** mortmain, dead hand; **an die ~e Hand verkaufen** to alienate in mortmain, to amortize; ~**es Inventar** dead stock; ~**es Kapital** idle money (funds), unemployed (dead) capital, dead stock; ~**es Konto** *(Depot)* securities ledger, *(Sachkonto)* impersonal (nominal, *Br.*) account, *(unbewegliches Konto)* dead account; ~**e Last** tare; ~**e Leitung** *(tel.)* dead line; ~**er Punkt** deadlock, hitch; **auf einem ~en Punkt angelangt sein** to rest in deadlock; ~**es Rennen** deadhead; ~**e Saison** off (dead) season; ~**e Sprache** dead language; ~**e Stadt** dead city; ~**er Vulkan** extinct volcano; ~**er Winkel** *(Auto)* blind corner; ~**e Zeit** dull season; ~**e Zone** *(Radar)* blind zone, *(Rundfunk)* blind (dead) spot.

total total, outright, all-out, utter, complete, positive, from hub to tire *(US)*, plumb *(US coll.)*, six ways to Sunday *(sl.)*;
~ **betrunken** drunk to the world;
~**er Krieg** total war.

Total|ansicht general view; ~**ausfall** total loss; ~**ausverkauf** clearance (going-out-of-business, close-out, *US*, winding-up) sale; ~**betrag** sum total; ~**bilanz** overall balance; ~**erlös** total proceeds; ~**fracht** lump-sum freight; ~**fusion** total merger; ~**invalidität** total and permanent invalidity.

Totalisator totalizator, totalizer *(Br.)*, tote, parimutual, pool;
am ~ wetten to totalize.

totalitär totalitarian;
~**e Staatsform** totalitarianism.

Totalitarismus totalitarianism.

Totalitätsprinzip totalitarian principle.
Total|leistung *(Maschine)* gross effect; ~**liquidation** purchase and liquidation.
Totalschaden total loss, *(Auto)* complete breakdown (write-off), worthless wreck;
nur bei ~ total loss only;
haftet nur bei ~ *(Schiffsversicherung)* warranted free of all average;
fingierter ~ *(Schiff)* constructive total loss.
Totalverlust actual total (dead, *sl.*) loss, *(Flugzeug)* complete write-off, *(Schiff)* total wreck (loss);
nur bei ~ total loss only;
durch Aufgabe des Schiffs entstandener ~ constructive total loss;
Waren als ~ **reklamieren** to abandon the goods as a constructive total loss.
Tote|r dead person, deceased, defunct, *(Leiche)* body, corpse;
viele ~ heavy casualties;
~**n in die Heimat überführen** to take the body to his native country.
töten to kill, to put to death, to end;
sich ~ to take one's own life; **j. mit Gift** ~ to poison s. o.; **jem. den letzten Nerv** ~ to drive s. o. mad (scatty, *coll.*); **in Notwehr** ~ to commit homicide in self-defence; **j. auf der Stelle** ~ to kill s. o. outright.
Totenacker churchyard.
totenähnlicher Schlaf deathlike sleep.
Toten|bahre bier; ~**bestattung** burial; ~**bett** deathbed; ~**blässe annehmen** to take on the hue of death; ~**feier** exequies; ~**gewand** grave clothes; ~**glocke** funeral (death, passing) bell; ~**gräber** grave digger; ~**halle,** ~**haus** morgue *(US)*, mortuary *(Br.)*, funeral home (parlor) *(US)*; ~**kopf** *(Gefahrenquelle)* skull and cross bones; ~**licht** watch candle; ~**liste** obituary, bill of mortality, *(mil.)* death roll; ~**marsch** dead march; ~**maske** death mask; ~**messe** office for the dead; ~**register** register of deaths; **amtliche** ~**schau** coroner's inquest; ~**schein** certificate of death, death certificate; ~**starre** rigor mortis *(lat.)*; ~**stille** dead (deathful) stillness; ~**urne** funerary urn; ~**wache** death watch; ~**wache halten** to wake a corpse.
tot|ernst sein to be in sober (dead) earnest; ~**fahren** to knock down and kill; ~**geboren** stillborn, deadborn.
Totgeburt deadborn child, stillbirth.
totkrank sein to be sick to death.
totlachen, sich to die with laughter.
Totlast dead load, deadweight.
totlaufen, sich to run its course, to peter out.
totmachen, Konkurrenz to eliminate a competitor.
Toto [etwa] pools, policy *(US)*, sweepstake, tote *(Br., sl.)*;
beim ~ **ein Vermögen machen** to win a fortune on the pools; ~**ergebnis** tote board result *(Br., coll.)*; **blühendes** ~**geschäft** flourishing tote scheme *(Br., sl.)*; ~**gewinner** pools winner; ~**schein** sweepstake card, pools coupon *(Br.)*, pools entry blank *(US)*, policy slip *(US)*; ~**spieler** pool filler.
totschießen, j. to blow s. one's brains out.
Totschlag felonious (culpable) homicide, manslaughter, manslaying, murder in the second degree *(US)*;
versuchter ~ assault with intent to commit manslaughter;
~**aus Notwehr** chance medley;
jem. von der Anklage des ~**s freisprechen** to acquit s. o. of manslaughter; ~ **verüben** to commit homicide.
totschlagen to kill, to slay;
Zeit ~ to kill time;
sich dafür ~ **lassen** to stake one's life on it.
Totschläger killer, slayer, manslayer, *(Knüppel)* bludgeon, life preserver, leather-covered club, blackjack *(US)*.
tot|schweigen to hush up, to keep mum, to pass over in silence, to blanket; ~**sicher** as safe as houses, as sure as eggs is eggs; **sich** ~**stellen** to feign death, to play possum.
Tötung killing, kill, dispatch, homicide;
fahrlässige ~ involuntary (negligent, *US*) manslaughter; **gerechtfertigte** ~ justifiable homicide; **rechtlich notwendige** ~ homicide by necessity; **unverschuldete** ~ casual homicide, killing by misadventure; **versuchte** ~ homicidal attempt; **vorsätzliche** ~ wilful (malicious) killing, voluntary manslaughter, homicide; **zufällige** ~ involuntary manslaughter; ~ **im Affekt** chaud-medley; ~ **des Ehemanns** petit treason *(Br.)*; ~ **der Leibesfrucht** feticide; ~ **in Notwehr** excusable homicide, homicide in self-defence; ~ **auf Verlangen** mercy killing; ~ **bei Vorliegen von Rechtfertigungsgründen** justifiable homicide; ~ **bei Vorliegen von Schuldausschließungsgründen** excusable homicide.
Tötungs|absicht, ~**vorsatz** premeditated malice; ~**delikt** culpable homicide; ~**versuch** homicidal attempt.
Tour tour, trip, round, excursion, walking, walk, *(Bus, Straßenbahn)* run, *(Kundenbesuch)* business round, *(Motor)* turn, revolution, *(Runde)* turn, round, *(Strecke)* way, *(Trick)* trick, dodge, *(Wanderung)* hike;
auf vollen ~**en laufend** high-flying; **in einer** ~ in a stretch, without a break;
krumme ~ tortuous policy, funny business; **weiche** ~ soft sell; **zusammengestellte** ~ conducted tour;
von der üblichen ~ **seiner Politik abweichen** to go out of one's way; **auf** ~**en bringen** *(Motor)* to speed up, to rev up an engine; **j. auf** ~**en bringen** to jack s. o. up; **auf** ~ **gehen** *(Vertreter)* to go out on business (commerce-destroying), *(Zirkus)* to go on the road; **heute seine** ~ **haben** to be in one of one's moods; **auf** ~**en kommen** *(Motor)* to gather (pick up) speed, to rev up; **richtig auf** ~**en kommen** *(fig.)* to hit one's stride; **auf volle** ~**en kommen** to get into top gear; **mit 3000** ~**en laufen** *(Maschine)* to run at 3000 revolutions per minute; **auf niedrigen** ~**en laufen** *(Konjunktur)* to run flat; **auf vollen** ~**en laufen** *(Betrieb)* to go full blast (a humdinger, *US sl.*), to be in full swing, *(Motor)* to run at full speed; **5000** ~**en in der Minute machen** to run at 5000 revolutions per minute; **in einer** ~ **reden** to talk nineteen to the dozen; **auf die dumme** ~ **reisen** to con people; **keine krummen** ~**en reiten** to be perfectly straight in all one's dealings; **auf** ~ **sein** *(Vertreter)* to be out (on the road); ~ **unternehmen** to make an excursion, to tour; **jem. die** ~ **vermasseln** to thwart s. one's plans, to queer s. one's pitch; **etw. auf alle** ~**en versuchen** to ring the chances *(US)*; **es bei jem. auf die krumme** ~ **versuchen** to try one's tricks on s. o.
Touren|fahrt touring competition; ~**schreiber** gyrograph; ~**wagen** touring car, tourer; ~**zahl** number of revolutions, revs; ~**zahl pro Minute** revolutions per minute, rpm; ~**zähler** speed (revolution) counter, gyrograph.
Tourismus tourism, tourist traffic;
hauptsächlich vom ~ **leben** to be mainly dependent for one's living on tourism;
~**geschäft** travel agency business; ~**konto** travel account; ~**zunahme** tourist growth.
Tourist tourist, travel(l)er, excursionist;
von ~**en überlaufen** tourist-haunted (-ridden);
ausländischer ~ transient foreigner; **gewöhnlicher** ~ ordinary tourist; **mit dem Flugzeug reisender** ~ air tourist; **sparbewußter** ~ budget-minded tourist; **neugieriger** ~ rubberneck *(US)*;
~**en zum Anfang der Saison** beginning-of-season tourists; ~ **der mittleren Einkommensklasse** medium-income travel(l)er;
wohlhabende ~**en anlocken** to catch the summer's Jaguars; **von** ~**en überlaufen sein** to be full of tourists.
Touristen|abteil economy cabin; ~**attraktion** tourist attraction, hot spot; ~**ausgaben** tourist expenditure; ~**betreuung** guidance of travellers; **positive** ~**bilanz** favo(u)rable balance of payments in tourism; ~**bus** charabanc; ~**dollar** tourist dollar; ~**fahrzeug** tourist car; ~**fluggast** air tourist (passenger); ~**flugkarte** economy fare; ~**flugschein** economy fare; ~**flugzeug** economy plane, air coach *(US)*; ~**förderungsbüro** development office; ~**führer** tourist guide; ~**gepäckversicherung** tourist floater policy; ~**gruppe** party of holidaymakers, itinerancy; ~**gutschein** tourist voucher; ~**herberge,** ~**hotel** travel(l)er's rest (hotel), hostel, inn; ~**invasion** invasion of tourists; ~**kabine** deck cabin; ~**karte** excursion ticket; ~**klasse** deck cabin, *(Flugzeug)* economy class, *(Omnibus)* coach class *(US)*, *(Schiff)* tripper class, tourist (cabin, deck) class; ~**konjunktur** tourist boom; ~**land** tourist country; ~**menü** economy menu; **staatliche** ~**organisation** government tourist organization; ~**ort** tourist destination; **beliebter** ~**ort,** ~**paradies** tourist haven; ~**passagier** tourist (deck) passenger; ~**platz** economy seat; ~**quartier** tourist accommodation; ~**ranch** dude ranch *(US)*; ~**rundreise in einer Linienmaschine** scheduled economy round trip *(US)*; **übliche** ~**rundreise machen** to make the tour of a country; ~**saison** tourist season; ~**straße** tourist road, scenic road *(US)*; ~**strom** flow (drove, inundation, inrush) of tourists; **aufdringliche** ~**ströme** invasive tourists; ~**tarif** excursion rates; ~**tum** tourism; ~**verkehr** tourist travel, tourism; ~**visum** tourist visa; ~**werbung** tourist advertising; ~**wesen** tourism; **sich vorratsmäßig auf die** ~**zeit einstellen** to stock up for the holiday trade; ~**zentrum** tourist center *(US)* (centre, *Br.*), tourist area, motoring center *(US)* (centre, *Br.*), much-travel(l)ed part of the country.
Touristik|branche travel business; ~**unternehmen** tour operator, travel business; **unabhängig geführtes** ~**unternehmen** independent listed tour operator.

Tournee route, tour, *(Schauspieler, Zirkus)* road;
auf ~ on the road; **auf ~n konzipiert** travel(l)ing;
auf ~ gehen to open, to go on (take) the road; **mit einem Stück auf ~ gehen** to tour a play;
~agentur booking agency; **~festlegung** routing plan; **~gruppe** touring company.
Trab, auf ~ gebracht *(fig.)* on one's mettle; **immer auf ~** on the run;
j. auf ~ bringen to prod s. o. on; **etw. in ~ bringen** to set s. th. going; **j. in ~ halten** to keep s. o. on the go (jump, *coll.*); **immer in ~ sein** to be always on the move.
Trabant satellite.
Trabanten|siedlung satellite colony; **~stadt** satellite suburb, *(Raumplanung)* new town, expanded town *(Br.)*.
Tracht traditional costume, *(Amtstracht)* garb;
akademische ~ academic gown;
~ einer bestimmten Epoche period costumes; **~ Holz** load of wood; **~ Prügel** cudgelling, hiding, flogging *(coll.)*, jacketing *(coll.)*; **jem. eine gehörige ~ Prügel verabreichen** to dust s. one's jacket, to tan s. one's hide, to mop the floor with s. o. *(coll.)*.
Trachten endeavo(u)r, aspiration, aim.
trachten to endeavo(u)r, to aspire, to aim;
nach Ruhm ~ to strive for fame.
Tradition, ganz in alten ~en aufgehen to be devotedly attached to tradition; **gewisse ~en beibehalten** to preserve certain traditions; **alte ~ neu beleben** to revive an old tradition; **mit der ~ brechen** to break with tradition.
traditionell old-age (-line).
traditionsbewußte politische Partei traditional political party.
Traditions|bewußtsein traditionalism; **~gebundenheit** old school tie; **~papier** negotiable instrument; **~papier an beweglichen Sachen** document of title to goods.
Tragbahre stretcher, litter.
tragbar portable, *(Kandidat)* acceptable, *(Preis)* reasonable;
nicht mehr länger ~ sein to have become unbearable; **für alle Parteien ~ sein** to be acceptable for all parties;
~er Fernseher portable [television set].
Tragdrehflügelflugzeug rigid helicopter.
träge idle, inert, laggard, lazy, *(Börse)* dull, slack, stagnant, sluggish;
geistig ~ sein to have a torpid (dull) mind; **~ werden** *(Geschäft)* to stagnate;
~r Fluß sluggish river; **~r Mensch** sluggard, poke *(US)*; **~ Nachfrage** sluggish demand.
Trage|balken structural beam; **~kissen des Gepäckträgers** porter's carrying pad.
tragen *(befördern)* to carry, to convey, *(Rendite)* to yield, to bear;
sich mit der Absicht ~ to contemplate; **aus der Bahn ~** *(Auto)* to fling off its course; **keine Bedenken ~** to have no scruples; **Brief zur Post ~** to take a letter to the post office, to mail a letter *(US)*; **Datum ~** to bear the date, to be dated; **Eulen nach Athen ~** to carry coals to Newcastle; **mit Fassung ~** to keep one's balance; **Folgen ~** to bear the consequences, to face the music; **sich mit Heiratsabsichten ~** to have marriage in mind; **Kosten ~** to defray (meet the) expenses; **schwere Lastwagen ~** *(Brücke)* to carry heavy lorries; **Nase hoch ~** to give o. s. airs; **Neuigkeiten von Haus zu Haus ~** to spread news from door to door; **Rechnung ~** to take into account; **Risiko ~** to bear (take) a risk; **Schaden ~** *(Versicherung)* to pay for the damage; **sich [selbst] ~** to leave a margin, to yield, *(Unternehmen)* to pay its way; **sich gerade noch ~** to break even, to wash its face *(Br., sl.)*; **sich nicht ~** to be unprofitable, to leave no margin; **Sorge dafür ~** to see about; **Unterschrift ~** to bear a signature; **Verantwortung ~** to take (bear) the responsibility, to be responsible; **Verlust ~** to stand (bear) a loss; **Waffen ~** to bear (carry) arms; **Zinsen ~** to yield (bear) interest.
Trageplatz carry.
Träger bearer, *(Bahnhof)* porter, *(jur.)* subject, *(Institution)* agency, institution, *(Titel)* holder, bearer, *(Vertreter)* representative;
gemeinnütziger ~ nonprofit institution;
~ der Konjunkturentwicklung promoter of the cyclical trend; **~ von Rechten und Pflichten** subject of rights and duties; **~ der Sozialversicherung** social insurance institution;
rechtlich als ~ von Rechten und Pflichten gelten to be treated by law as a person in his own right;
~brücke girder bridge; **~flugzeug** carrier-borne (carrier-based) aircraft.
Trägerfrequenz *(Telefon)* radio (carrier) frequency;
~telefonie carrier telephony; **~telegrafie** carrier telegraphy; **~übertragung** carrier transmission.

Träger|gebühr porter's fee, porterage; **~gerüst** supporting structure; **~gesellschaft** carrier; **~organisation** sponsoring agency; **~rakete** carrier rocket, booster; **~welle** carrier wave.
Trage|tasche bag, catchall *(US)*, holdall *(Br.)*; **~tier** pack animal; **~tierkolonne** pack train; **~tüte** carrier (paper) bag.
tragfähig load-carrying.
Tragfähigkeit burden, carrying (load) capacity, *(Nutzlast)* payload, *(Schiff)* deadweight tonnage, *(Soziologie)* population capacity;
freitragende ~ cantilever;
~ für Ballast deadweight capacity; **~ eines Stockwerks** floor-weight capacity.
Tragfläche *(Flugzeug)* plane, wing, deck;
linke ~ port plane; **weit zurückversetzte ~n** set-back wings.
Tragflächen|abstand *(Flugzeug)* gap; **~belastung** wing loading; **~kufe** wing skid.
Trag|flügel wing; **~flügelboot** hydrofoil; **~gestell** *(Fahrrad)* carrier.
Trägheit rust, indolence, inertia, *(Markt)* sluggishness, dullness;
j. aus seiner ~ reißen to provoke s. o. out of inertia.
Trägheits|effekt *(Konsum)* ratchet effect; **~faktor** inertia factor.
tragisch, alles ~ nehmen to take things tragically;
~es Ereignis tragic event.
Tragkraft carrying power.
Tragöde tragic actor.
Tragödie aufführen to play a tragedy.
Trag|rad trailing wheel; **~rippe** web; **~schraube** rotor; **~schrauber** rotor, rotodyne, autogiro, gyroplane; **~seil** supporting cable, *(Schwebebahn)* suspension cable.
Tragung|der Kosten payment of cost;
zur ~ der Kosten verurteilt werden to be ordered (condemned) to pay the costs.
Tragweite purport, bearing, implication, range, moment, reach;
volle ~ von Worten full implication of words;
~ eines Ereignisses begreifen to realize the importance of a decision; **~ haben** to carry an implication.
trainieren to train, to coach.
Trainings|anzug track suit; **~platz** exercise station; **~spiel** knockup; **~zeit** workout.
Trajekt ferry bridge;
~schiff seatrain, train ferry, steam ferryboat.
Trakt *(Gebäude)* wing, tract, *(Straße)* stretch, run.
Traktandenliste agenda paper.
Traktat tract, treatise.
traktieren, j. to maltreat s. o.; **j. mit Fragen ~** to pester s. o. with questions; **j. mit Schlägen ~** to beat s. o. up.
Traktor motor tractor, mule;
~fabrik tractor works; **~fahrer** tractor driver; **~reifen** tractor tire (tyre, *Br.*).
Tramp tramp, hitchhiker, thumb-pusher, hobo *(US)*;
~dampfer tramp (mushroom) steamer, tramp (transient) ship.
trampeln, Weg durch den Schnee to tread a path through the snow.
Trampelpfad beaten path, broadwalk.
Trampen tramp, hitchhiking.
trampen to tramp it, to hit the road, to hitchhike, to thumb a lift, *(Schiff)* to tramp.
Tramper hitchhiker, tramp, hobo *(US)*, thumber *(US)*, *(Schiff)* tramp (transient) ship.
Tramp|reeder tramp shipowner; **~schiffahrt** occasional navigation, tramping, tramp shipping.
Tranche tranche, part, portion, slip;
fällige ~ maturing portion;
~ einer Anleihe portion (slice, tranche) of loan;
Anleihe in ~n aufteilen to split a loan in tranches.
Träne, den ~n nahe on the verge of tears, verging on tears; **zu ~n gerührt** touched to tears;
keine ~ mehr in der Flasche no drop left in the bottle;
zu ~n gerührt sein to melt into tears.
Tränen|drüsen, auf die ~drüsen drücken to put on the sentimental stop, *(Film)* to be a tearjerker; **~gas** tear gas; **~gasgranate** tear-gas grenade; **~säcke** pockets under the eyes.
Tranfunzel wretched lamp, *(fig.)* slow coach.
tranig *(fig.)* sluggish, dawdling.
Tränke watering place;
Vieh zur ~ führen to water cattle.
Tränken watering.
tränken to water.
Transaktion transaction, operation, bargain, deal, dealing, business;
abgeschlossene ~ executed transaction; **banktechnische ~en**

banking transactions; **im Verwaltungswege durchgeführte ~en** administrative-managerial transactions; **finanzielle ~** financial transaction (operation); **geschäftliche ~en** trade transactions, commercial operations; **marktglättende ~en** operations to smooth the market; **schwebende ~en** pending operations; **unerlaubte ~** illegal proceedings; **unsichtbare ~en** invisible transactions; **zusammenhängende ~en** associated operations; **~en in verschiedenen Effekten** spreading operations *(Br.)*; **~en in einer Höhe von mehreren Millionen Pfund** transactions amounting to several million pounds; **~ gegen sofortige Kasse** cash transaction; **~en am offenen Markt** open-market credit transactions; **~en zur Wiederanlage von Ölgeldern** downstream operations;
~ durchführen to effect a transaction; **unerlaubte ~en tätigen (vornehmen)** to indulge in illicit transactions; **ungedeckte ~en vornehmen** to operate without cover.

Transatlantik|flug transatlantic flight; **~fracht** ocean freight; **~frachtsatz** ocean freight rate; **~interview** ship-shore telephone interview; **~kabel** transatlantic cable; **~verkehr** ocean transport.

transatlantisch transatlantic.

Trans-Europa-Express Trans-European Express (TEE).

Transfer transfer;
bargeldloser ~ cashless money transfer;
~ von Devisen foreign exchange transfer, transfer of foreign exchange; **~ von Kapital** transfer of capital; **~ von Vermögenswerten** resources transfer;
~abkommen transfer agreement; **~agent [für die Umschreibung von Wertpapieren]** transfer agent; **~aufschub** delay in transit; **~begünstigter** transferee, remittee; **~beschränkungen** transfer restrictions; **Zahlungs- und ~beschränkungen** exchange restrictions on payments and transfers; **~bewilligung** transfer permit; **~dienst** transfer service; **~einkünfte** transfer income.

transferfähig transferable.

Transfer|garantie transfer guarantee; **~gebühr** *(Wertpapiere)* transfer (registration) fee, cost of transfer; **~genehmigung** transfer permit.

transferierbar transferable;
frei ~ freely transferable;
frei ~es Devisenkonto transferable account *(Br.)*.

transferieren to transfer, to transmit;
Gewinne in Länder mit niedrigen Steuersätzen ~ to transfer profits to low-tax countries; **auf ein anderes Konto ~** to transfer to another account; **Vermögen ~** to transfer property.

Transferierung transfer;
~ von Vermögenswerten transfer of resources.

Transfer|konto transfer account; **~kosten** transfer expense; **~leistung** transfer; **~lockerungen** relaxations of transfer restrictions; **~moratorium** transfer moratorium; **~problem** transfer problem; **~risiko** currency risk; **~spesen** transfer expense; **~verpflichtung** obligation to transfer; **~zahlungen** transfer to foreign countries, transfer remittances (payments, *US*); **laufende ~zahlungen** current transfers; **staatliche ~zahlungen** official transfers.

Transformator transformer;
~spannung transformer voltage.

transformieren *(el.)* to convert, to change.

Transistor, mit ~en ausstatten to transistorize;
~gerät transistor radio; **~zündung** electronic ignition.

Transit transit;
im ~ durchlaufen to pass in transit;
~abfertigung transit clearance; **~abgabe** transit duty (charge); **~ausfuhr** third-country export; **~bahnhof** transit station; **~bescheinigung** transit bond (certificate); **~dauer** duration of transit; **~deklaration, ~erklärung** transit entry, entry for warehousing; **~erlaubnis** transit permit; **~fracht** transit freight; **~frachtsatz** transit (through) rate; **~gebühr** transit charges; **~genehmigung** transit permit; **~geschäfte** merchanting transaction *(Br.)*; **~gut** goods in transit; **Waren als ~gut deklarieren** to enter goods as transit; **~güter** transit goods, goods in transit; **~hafen** intermediate port, port of transit; **~handel** transit (merchanting, *Br.*) trade, trade with transit goods; **~handelsland** merchanting country *(Br.)*; **~händler** transit agent; **~klausel** transshipment clause; **~konnossement** through bill of lading; **~konto** transit account; **~kosten** transit costs; **~ladung** transit cargo; **~lager** bonded warehouse *(US)*, transit storehouse (entrepot); **~land** transit country.

transitorisch transitional, transient, transitory, deferred;
~e Aktiva prepaid expenses, deferred charges [to expense] *(US)*; **~e Buchungen** suspense entries; **~e Klage** transitory action; **~es Konto** suspense account; **~e Passiva** suspense liabilities, prepaid income, deferred charges [to income] *(US)*, deferred income *(US)*; **~e Posten** *(Bilanz)* deferred charges [to expenses], suspense (transitory) items, deferred items *(US)*; **~e Zinserträge** *(Bilanz)* unearned interest.

Transit|papiere der Europäischen Gemeinschaft community transit documents; **~preis** transit rate; **~recht** right of transit; **~schein** permit of transit, transit permit (bond); **~sendung** through shipment; **~spediteur** transit agent; **~spesen** transit charges; **~straße** transit road; **~tarif** transit rate; **~vergünstigung** transit privilege; **~verkehr** transit, through (transit) traffic; **internationaler ~verkehr** international transit; **Waren im ~verkehr abfertigen** to convey goods in transit; **~versand** transit dispatch; **~versicherung** insurance in transit; **~visa** transit visa; **~waren** transit goods, goods in transit; **~warenverkauf** sale to arrive; **~warenversand** transit dispatch; **~zoll** transit duty; **~weg** transit route.

Transparent translight, *(bei Umzügen)* banner;
~papier glassine.

Transparenz transparency;
~ der Bilanz transparency in business practices; **~ des Steuersystems** transparency of the tax system.

Transport transport, carriage, carrying, conveyance, portage, haul, transportation *(US)*, *(Versand)* freightage, forwarding, dispatch, shipping;
auf dem ~ in transit; **auf dem ~ verlorengegangen** lost in transit; **beim ~ beschädigt** knocked about in transit;
Konterbande gleichgesetzter ~ contraband by analogy; **verbilligter ~** reduced-cost transportation *(US)*;
~ per Achse road transport, haulage; **~ von Arbeitskräften** deadheading; **~ per Bahn** rail (railway, railroad, *US*) transport, transport (conveyance) by rail; **~ im Binnenschifffahrtsverkehr** inland water transport; **~ mit dem nächsten Dampfer** shipment with the first steamer; **~ per Flugzeug (auf dem Luftwege)** aircraft (air) transport, conveyance by aircraft, transportation by air *(US)*, carriage by air; **~ auf Güterwagen** truckage *(Br.)*, shipment *(US)*, freight service *(US)*; **~ mit dem Kraftfahrzeug (per LKW)** road transport *(Br.)*, haulage, motor-truck transport *(US)*, transport of goods by road *(Br.)*, highway transportation *(US)*; **~ auf dem Landwege** transport by land, land transport; **~ auf dem Land- und Seeweg** surface transportation; **~ auf dem Seewege** carriage by sea, sea (marine, maritime) transport; **~ im Überseeverkehr** ocean transport; **~ auf dem Wasserwege** transport (conveyance) by water, waterborne transportation *(US)*; **~ nur auf dem Wasserwege** all-water;
~e abwickeln to handle shipments; **~ bezahlen** to pay the carriage; **auf dem ~ Schaden nehmen** to suffer in transport; **beim ~ verrutschen** to shift in transport; **auf dem ~ beschädigt werden** to be damaged in transit;
~abteilung forwarding (shipping, *US*) department; **~agentur** transport agent (agency), transportation agency *(US)*; **~anlage** conveyor plant, transportation equipment *(US)*; **~anweisungen** forwarding (shipping, *US*) instructions; **~arbeiter** transport (maritime, *US*) worker; **~arbeitergewerkschaft** [etwa] Transport and General Workers Union *(Br.)*; **~arbeiterstreik** strike of transport workers, trucking strike *(Br.)*; **~art** mode of conveyance; **~auftrag** forwarding (shipping, *US*) order; **~ausstattung** conveyor plant, transportation equipment *(US)*; **~band** production line, band conveyor, conveyor belt; **~bedingungen** terms of transport, shipping terms *(US)*; **~behälter** container; **angemessene ~beschaffenheit** suitable shipping conditions *(US)*; **~bilanz** net position on transport; **~dampfer** transport ship (vessel); **~dokument** transport document; **~einrichtung** conveyer, transportation means (facility); **~empfangsschein** transportation receipt *(US)*; **~erfahrungen** shipping experience *(US)*.

Transporteur transport (express, *US*) agent, transportation agency *(US)*, common carrier.

transportfähig transportable.

Transport|fähigkeit transportability; **~fahrzeug** transport vehicle, goods vehicle *(US)*, transportation *(US)*, means of conveyance; **~firma** haulage firm, conveyor, common carrier; **~flugzeug** commercial (cargo) airplane, transport aircraft (plane), freight carrier, transporter, freight plane, sky plane, sky truck *(US)*; **~gefährdung** endangering public transport; **~gefahren** transport risk, perils of transportation *(US)*, *(zur See)* marine perils, risk of navigation; **~gefahren im Straßenverkehr** perils of the street; **~gelegenheit** transport facility, transportation *(US)*; **~genehmigung** transport permit; **~geschäft** carriage, carrying (shipping, *US*) trade, truck operation, forwarding business; **~gesellschaft** forwarding (shipping, *US*, transport) company, common carrier, transportation agency *(US)*; ~**gesellschaft für Langstreckenflüge** long-haul carrier; ~**gewerbe** carrying trade, transport industries (trade), road haulage industry, shipping business *(US)*, business of transportation *(US)*; **den Belastungen des ~gewerbes gewachsen sein** to cope with the transportation burden *(US)*; ~**gut** cargo, shipment; **gefährliches ~gut** dangerous goods; ~**haftung** carrier's liability; ~**hindernis** obstacle to transportation.

transportierbar conveyable, transportable, removable.

transportieren to transport, to convey, to carry, to ship *(US)*, *(Buchführung)* to carry (post) forward, *(Fuhrwerk)* to cart, to carry, to haul;
Film ~ to wind on (advance) a film; **Güter** ~ to transport goods by truck; **Waren** ~ to convey goods.

transportiert werden, von englischen Schiffen to go in British bottom.

Transport|kapazität transport capacity; ~**kette** conveyer chain; ~**kolonne** motor convoy; ~**koordinierung** coordination of transport (transportation, *US*).

Transportkosten carriage (running, transport, transportation, *US*) expenses, portage, carrier's (carriage, carrying, forwarding) charges, [cost of] transportation *(US)*, transportation (shipping) charges *(US)*, *(Bahn)* cost of carriage, freight [expenses], *(Straße)* cartage, haulage, waggonage *(US)*;
inklusive aller ~ inclusive of all transport costs;
anfallende ~ earned freight; **fiktive** ~ phantom freight; **sich nicht tragende** ~ absorbing freight;
~ **vom Gewinn absetzen (in Abzug bringen)** to deduct the cost for transport[ation] from the profit;
~ **bezahlt** carriage paid; ~ **gehen zu Lasten des Empfängers** carriage forward; ~ **trägt der Absender** carriage paid home;
~**berechnung vom Ausgangsort** basing-point system; ~**rechnung** freight account.

Transport|leistungen transport services; ~**linie** freight route; ~**makler** forwarding (shipping, *US*, transport) agent, freight broker, transportation agency *(US)*.

Transportmittel means of transport (transportation, conveyance), means of carriage, conveyance, transportation *(US)*;
mit öffentlichem ~ by public transport (common carrier, *US*);
fehlende ~ shortage of transport; **öffentliche** ~ public conveyance (transportation, *US*);
notwendige ~ **bereitstellen** to provide the necessary transport;
~ **zuteilen** to assign transport vehicles.

Transport|möglichkeiten means (facilities) of transport, means of conveyance, transport convenience (facilities), transportation *(US)*; **fehlende (mangelnde) ~möglichkeiten** shortage of transport, lack of transport, lack of sufficient transportation *(US)*; ~**monopol** transport (transportation, *US*) monopoly; ~**papiere** accompanying documents, shipping documents (papers) *(US)*; ~**police** certificate, *(Schiff)* marine policy; ~**politik** transport (transportation, *US*) policy; ~**problem** handling (transportation, *US*) problem; ~**raum** freight space, shipping (transportation) space *(US)*, *(Schiff)* cargo space; ~**risiko** transportation risk *(US)*, risks of carriage, transport risk, perils of transportation *(US)*; ~**sachverständiger** transportation expert *(US)*; ~**schaden** transport loss, damage (loss) in transit; ~**schadensforderung** loss and damage claim; ~**schein** waybill, consignment note; ~**schiff** transport ship (vessel) transporter; ~**schnecke** conveying spiral; ~**schwierigkeiten** transport difficulties; ~**spediteur** [common] carrier; ~**spesen** carriage, transport charges; ~**steuer** (mil(e)age) transportation tax *(US)*; ~**stockung** transport holdup; ~**strecke** haul; ~**system** transport system; ~**tarif** hauling (transport, transportation, *US*) rates; ~**unfähigkeit** unfitness for transportation; ~**unternehmen** carrying (carrier's) business, land carrier, trucking company (agency) *(US)*, transportation agency *(US)*; **betriebliches ~unternehmen** industrial carrier; ~**unternehmen leiten** to run a transport business; ~**unternehmer** [common] carrier, conveyor, land carrier, haulage (road, transport) contractor, teamster *(US)*, transportation agency *(US)*.

Transportversicherung *(Seetransport)* transport (transportation, shipping, *US*) insurance, *(See und Land)* marine insurance, insurance of goods in transit;
vollständige ~ warehouse-to-warehouse insurance.

Transportversicherungs|formular marine-insurance form; ~**geschäfte erledigen** to underwrite; ~**gesellschaft** transport insurance company, *(Seeversicherung)* marine insurance company; ~**klausel** warehouse-to-warehouse clause *(US)*; ~**police** *(Seefracht)* transport insurance policy.

Transport|vertrag contract of carriage, transportation (shipping) contract *(US)*; ~**verzögerung** delay in transit; ~**verzögerung erfahren** to be delayed in transit; ~**volumen** total transports; ~**vorrichtung** transporter; ~**vorschriften** forwarding (shipping, *US*) instructions; ~**wagen** van *(Br.)*, truck; ~**weg** way of transportation *(US)*, haul, route; ~**weg einer Warensendung** route to be followed by a shipment of goods; ~**wesen** transport matters, transportation *(US)*, transportation system *(US)*, forwarding business; **öffentliches ~wesen** public transport service, public transportation *(US)*.

Trapez|flügel trapezed wing; ~**künstler** trapezist; ~**vorführung** trapezing.

Trara tantara, *(Aufhebens)* ado, fuss;
mit großem ~ with fanfare.

Trassant drawer of a bill.

Trasse *(Bahn)* alignment.

Trassenführung profile of an alignment.

Trassieren drawing a bill of exchange.

trassieren *(Bahn, Straße)* to plot out a line, to trace, *(Wechsel)* to draw a bill of exchange, to value;
in blanko ~ to make out in blank; **per Saldo** ~ to draw per appoint; **Wechsel al pari** ~ to draw a bill at par.

trassierter Wechsel draft, drawn bill of exchange.

Trassierung *(Bahn, Straße)* location, drawing (issue of) a bill of exchange.

Trassierungs|kredit drawing (acceptance) credit; **dokumentarisch gesicherter ~kredit** documentary credit; **nicht dokumentarisch gesicherter ~kredit** clean (open, *Br.*) credit; ~**provision** drawing commission.

Tratsch gossip, tittle-tattle.

tratschen to wag one's tongue, to jabber, to jangle, to gossip, *(schwatzen)* to prattle, to chat.

Tratte draft, bill [(letter) of exchange];
angezeigte ~ addressed draft; **nicht angezeigte** ~ nonadvised (nonaddressed) draft; **domizilierte** ~ domiciled (domiciliated) bill;
~ **mit Dokumenten** documentary bill (draft); ~ **ohne Dokumente** clean draft; ~ **ohne Respektstage** fixed draft; ~ **mit drei Unterschriften** three-name paper *(US)*; ~ **mit beigefügten Verschiffungsdokumenten** arrival draft; ~ **mit Zinsvermerk** interest-bearing draft;
~ **akzeptieren** to give a draft due protection; ~ **nicht akzeptieren** to show dishono(u)r to a draft; ~ **ankaufen** to negotiate a draft; ~ **ankündigen (anmelden)** to advise a draft; ~ **ausstellen (begeben)** to make out (negotiate) a draft; **einer ~ guten Empfang bereiten** to meet a bill with due hono(u)r; ~ **einlösen** to take up a bill when due, to discharge a bill; ~ **honorieren** to show due protection to a draft; ~ **bei Vorzeigung honorieren** to hono(u)r a draft on sight; ~ **mangels Zahlung protestieren** to have a draft protested for nonpayment; ~ **mit Akzept versehen** to provide a bill with acceptance; ~ **zum Akzept vorlegen** to present a bill for acceptance.

Tratten|ankauf negotiation of a draft; ~**ankaufskredit** negotiation credit; ~**avis** advice of draft; ~**deckung** cover of draft; ~**inkasso** collection of drafts; ~**kopierbuch** *(chronologisch geordnet)* bill (bills discounted) register, *(nach Kunden geordnet)* bill book (ledger), *(Forderungswechsel)* notes receivable ledger *(US)*, *(Schuldwechsel)* notes payable register *(US)*; ~**kredit** acceptance credit; ~**umlauf** bills in circulation.

Traube grape, *(Menschenansammlung)* cluster, bunch;
~**n ernten** to gather (harvest) grapes; **in dichten ~n an den Eingängen stehen** to cluster around the entrances.

Traubensaft grape juice.

trauen to trust, *(riskieren)* to venture, to have the nerve;
seinen Augen nicht ~ not to believe one's eyes; **dem Frieden nicht** ~ not to like the look of it;
sich nicht ~, j. zu fragen not to dare to ask s. o.;
sich ~ **lassen** to undergo a marriage ceremony; **sich standesamtlich** ~ **lassen** to get married before the superintendent registrar *(Br.)*;
dem Glück ist nicht zu ~ fortune is fickle.

Trauer mourning, grief, sorrow;
in tiefer ~ in deep sorrow;
~ **ablegen** to come out of mourning; ~ **anlegen** to go into mourning; ~ **tragen** to be in mourning; **im Herzen** ~ **tragen** to be sad at heart; **Schwarz zum Zeichen der** ~ **tragen** to wear black as a token of mourning; **übergroße** ~ **zur Schau tragen** to profess extreme sorrow; **in tiefe** ~ **versetzen** to fill with deep grief;
~**anzeige** obituary [notice] *(Br.)*, funeral letter *(US)*; ~**fall** death; **wegen ~falls geschlossen** closed because of death; ~**feier**

funeral ceremony, burial service, obsequies; ~**feierlichkeiten** obsequies; ~**flor** mourning band, weeper; ~**gottesdienst** funeral service; ~**haus** house of mourning; ~**jahr** year of mourning, sad year; ~**kleidung** mourning apparel, black; ~**kleidung tragen** to be in black, to mourn; ~**liste** register of condolence; ~**marsch** funeral march; ~**papier** mourning paper; ~**rand** heavy frame, *(Anzeige)* thick (heavy) frame; ~**randpapier** black-edged paper; ~**spiel** tragedy; **ein richtiges ~spiel sein** to be a real shame; ~**wagen** mourning coach; ~**zeit** mourning time (period); **übliche ~zeit** regulation mourning; ~**zug** funeral procession.

Traufe, vom Regen in die ~ kommen to be out of the frying pan into the fire.

Traugottesdienst abhalten to officiate a marriage ceremony.

Trauma trauma.

Traum | auto ideal car; ~**beruf** dreamt-of profession.

träumen to dream;

von etw. ~ to let one's mind run upon s. th.; **mit offenen Augen** ~ to day-dream; **von großem Reichtum und Erfolg** ~ to have visions of great wealth and success.

Träumer day-dreamer.

Träumerei, politische utopianism.

Traum | fabrik *(Film)* dream factory; ~**gebilde** fantasy; ~**hochzeit** fairy-tale wedding; ~**land**, ~**welt** movieland, dreamland.

traurig sad, sorrowful, mournful, distressed, grieved;

~**es Ende finden** to come to a sad end; ~**e Erfahrung** painful experience; ~**es Ergebnis** poor result; ~**e Figur abgeben** to cut a poor figure, to look a sorry sight; ~**e Nachricht** sad piece of news; ~**e Verhältnisse** wretched circumstances.

Trau | ring wedding (church, marriage) ring; ~**schein** marriage licence, lines *(Br.)*.

Trauung marriage service, wedding ceremony, wedlock;

kirchliche ~ church marriage, **standesamtliche** ~ civil (registry) marriage, marriage in a registry office (in the office of a superintendent registrar, *Br.*);

~ **im kleinsten Kreis** private wedding;

~ **vollziehen** to celebrate (contract, solemnize) a marriage, to tie the knot.

Trauungsfeierlichkeit nuptial ceremony.

Trauzeuge witness to a marriage, best man;

~ **für j. sein** to stand up for s. o.

Trecker tractor, traction engine;

~**fahrer** traction driver.

Treffen meeting, gathering, conference, joining, hangout *(US sl.)*, *(mil.)* rencontre, action, affair, fight, *(pol.)* gathering, rally, convention;

informelles (zwangloses) ~ informal conference (gathering); **jährliches** ~ annual convention;

~ **im kleinem Kreis** small group meeting;

neue Truppen ins ~ führen to lead fresh troops into combat; **aus einem ~ als Sieger hervorgehen** to emerge victorious from an encounter.

treffen to meet, to gather, to visit *(US)*;

sich ~ to meet, to assemble, to gather, to visit with s. o. *(US)*; **Abkommen** ~ to come to an agreement (terms); **Auswahl** ~ to take one's choice; **Buchung** ~ to pass (effect) an entry; **j. empfindlich** ~ to touch s. o. to the quick; **Entscheidung** ~ to make a decision; **Feststellung** ~ to make a statement; **jds. Geschmack** ~ to hit s. one's fancy; **Nagel auf den Kopf** ~ to hit the nail on the head; **Nerv des Spionagerings** ~ to hit the nerve of the espionage ring; **auf Öl** ~ to strike oil; **ins Schwarze** ~ to hit the mark; **j. schwer** ~ to be a hard blow for s. o.; **sich häufig in der Straße** ~ to pass each other frequently in the street; **richtigen Ton** ~ to adopt the right note, to touch the right chord; **Verabredung** ~ to make (fix) an appointment, to arrange a meeting; **vorläufige Vereinbarung** ~ to make a provisional arrangement; **Vorbereitungen** ~ to make preparations; **Vorsichtsmaßregeln** ~ to take precautionary measures; **auf Widerstand** ~ to meet with resistance; **sich zufällig** ~ to bump into each other, to meet quite by chance, to drop upon (forgather) s. o., to knock up against s. o., to come across s. o.

treffend fitting, appropriate, apt, *(Bild)* well-captured;

~**e Bemerkung** fitting remark; ~**e Formulierung** apt words.

Treffer hit, success, go, do *(Australia, sl.)*, *(Lotterie)* prize, winning number;

~ **erzielen** to carry clout, to score a hit; **großen ~ erzielen** to hit it big.

Treffpunkt meeting place, junction, meet *(US sl.)*, place of meeting (assembly), tryst, rendezvous;

eleganter ~ classy venue; ~ **vielbeschäftigter Männer** busy haunts of men.

treffsicheres Urteil sound judgment.

Treib | anker drift (floating, drag) anchor; ~**eis** floating (drift) ice.

Treiben goings-on, bustle, happening, *(im Wasser)* flotation;

ausgelassenes ~ high jinks; **geschäftiges** ~ drive of business, hustle and bustle;

sich ins bunte ~ stürzen to plunge into the colo(u)rful medley.

treiben to float, to drift along, *(antreiben)* to urge, to press hard;

vor Anker ~ to be dragging anchor; **großen Aufwand** ~ to live in great style; **zum Äußersten** ~ to carry to extremes; **in die Enge** ~ to push into a corner; **Feind aus dem Land** ~ to drive the enemy out of the country; **Handel** ~ to carry on a business, to [ply a] trade; **schwunghaften Handel** ~ to have a roaring trade; **in einen Krieg** ~ to drift towards war; **Kurse (Preise) in die Höhe** ~ to send up (force, drive) prices; **realistische Politik** ~ to pursue a realistic course; **Schindluder mit jem.** ~ to play fast and loose with s. o.; **Skeptizismus ziemlich weit** ~ to carry scepticism to some length; **sein Spielchen mit jem.** ~ to play one's little game with s. o.; **seinen Spott mit jem.** ~ to make fun of s. o.; **stromaufwärts** ~ to tide up the river; **j. in den Tod** ~ to drive s. o. to death; **Tunnel durchs Gebirge** ~ to cut a tunnel through a mountain; **Vieh auf die Weide** ~ to drive cattle to the pasture; **vorwärts** ~ to flog along; **j. zum Wahnsinn** ~ to drive s. o. mad; **etw. zu weit** ~ to carry s. th. to extremes, to carry matters (push s. th.) too far;

sich ~ lassen to drift; **Dinge ~ lassen** to let s. th. drift, to let a matter drag on.

treibend floating.

Treib | gut flotsam, driftage; ~**haus** greenhouse, hothouse, glasshouse, conservatory *(Br.)*, stove *(Br.)*, forcing house *(Br.)*; ~**holz** driftwood; ~**jagd** battue *(Br.)*, drive *(US)*, *(Polizei)* round-up; ~**mine** floating mine; ~**netzfischdampfer** drifter; ~**netzfischen** drift netting; ~**öl** motor oil; ~**riemen** driving belt; ~**sand** drifting sand, quicksand; ~**satz** *(Rakete)* rocket motor.

Treibstoff fuel, petrol *(Br.)*, gasoline *(US)*, gas *(coll.)*;

fester ~ solid fuel;

~ **aus flüssigem Wasserstoff** liquid hydrogen fuel;

~ **einnehmen** to fuel [up], *(Schiff)* to fill up with petrol *(Br.)*, to bunker; **wenig ~ verbrauchen** to be high on fuel economy;

~**bedarf** fuel requirements; ~**depot** fuel-storage premises; ~**einnahme** fuelling; ~**einspritzung** *(Flugzeug)* contrainjection; ~**ersparnis** savings in fuel, fuel savings; ~**händler** dealer in gasoline *(US)*; ~**industrie** fuel economy (industry); ~**knappheit** fuel shortage; ~**lager** fuel dump (oil depot), fuel (petrol, *Br.*) storage; ~**lagerung** fuel storage; ~**monopol** fuel monopoly; ~**preis** fuel price; ~**preiserhöhung** fuel-price hike; ~**quellen** fuel resources; ~**steuer** petrol tax *(Br.)*, gasoline tax *(US)*; ~**steuererhöhung** petrol tax increase *(Br.)*; ~**tank** fuel (gasoline, *US*, petrol, *Br.*) tank; ~**verbrauch** fuel consumption, fuel usage; **sparsamer ~verbrauch** fuel economy; ~**verhältnis** fuel ratio; ~**verknappung** fuel shortage; ~**versorgung** fuel supply; ~**vorräte** fuel reserves; ~**zuteilung** fuel (petrol, *Br.*, gasoline, *US*) allowance, fuel allocation.

Treidel | mast towing post; ~**pfad** towing path.

Trend market trend, tendency;

~ **im Baugewerbe** trend in the building trade; ~ **im Versicherungsgeschäft** underwriting trend;

~ **der öffentlichen Meinung erkennen lassen** to mark the trend of public opinion; **augenblicklichen ~ mitmachen** to climb (jump) the bandwaggon *(US)*;

~**bestimmer** trend setter; ~**verlagerung** basic change in trend.

trennbar divisible, separable, *(Kupon)* detachable.

trennen to separate, to sever, to disconnect, to divide, to part, *(Kupon)* to detach, *(pol.)* to disunite, to segregate, *(Stromkreis)* to break, to disconnect, to open, *(Telefon)* to cut off, to disconnect;

sich ~ to part company, *(Ehepaar)* to become divorced, *(Geschäftspartner)* to dissolve partnership; **sich ~, ohne sich auf einen Antrag geeinigt zu haben** to break up without a motion being agreed on; **Ehe** ~ to dissolve a marriage; **sich als gute Freunde** ~ to part good friends; **von den übrigen Häftlingen** ~ to isolate from the other prisoners; **sich von einem Kind** ~ to part with one's child; **Kirche und Staat** ~ to disestablish the church; **das Wahre vom Falschen** ~ to winnow truth from falsehood; **Wort nach Silben** ~ to divide a word according to its syllables;

sich von seinem Geld schwer ~ können not to like to part with one's money.

Trenn | karton divider card; ~**linie** *(zum Anzeigenteil)* cut-off rule, *(Straße)* dividing (broken) line; ~**mauer** party wall, mutual wall *(Scot.)*; ~**schalter** disconnecting switch, insulating switch *(el.)*.

trennscharf *(Radio)* selective.

Trenn|schärfe *(Radio)* definition, selectivity; **~scheibe** glass panel, *(Auto)* glass partition; **~taste** disconnecting key.

Trennung disruption, dissolution, detail, separation, severance, *(Absonderung)* isolation, segregation, *(Abtrennung)* detachment, *(Eheleute)* separation, split-up;
notariell abgesprochene eheliche ~ notarial separation; **funktionelle ~** functional partition; **gerichtliche ~** judicial separation; **schmerzliche ~** terrible wrench; **verwaltungsmäßige ~** administrative separation;
~ der Gewalten division of powers; **~ von Kirche und Staat** disestablishment of the church, separation of church and state; **~ der Rassen** racial segregation; **~ von Tisch und Bett** legal (judicial) separation, separation from bed and board, limited divorce *(US)*; **~ von Verfahren** severance of actions;
~ von seiner Familie hinnehmen to submit to the separation of one's family.

Trennungs|entschädigung severance (separation, redundancy, *Br.*) allowance; **~gelder** severance benefit; **~linie** divisional (dividing) line, wall of partition; **durchgezogene ~linie** *(Straße)* continuous white line; **~plebiszit** separation note.

Trennungsstrich hyphen, cutoff point;
doppelter ~ *(Straße)* double white lines; **weißer ~** inside lane; **klaren ~ ziehen** to make a clear distinction.

Trennungs|stunde parting hour; **schriftliche ~vereinbarung** *(Eheleute)* deed of separation, separation deed (agreement); **~wand** partition wall, divisional wall; **~zeichen** *(Interpunktion)* dash, hyphen, division; **~zulage** separation allowance (maintenance) *(US)*, severance benefit *(US)*, redundancy pay *(Br.)*.

Treppe stairs (steps) *(Br.)*, stair, staircase;
drei ~n hoch three-pair *(Br.)*;
~ zum Erfolg ladder to success;
~ herauffallen *(fam.)* to get a rise, to be kicked upstairs; **j. die ~ herunterwerfen** to push s. o. downstairs; **eine ~ höher wohnen** to live one floor up.

Treppen|absatz platform, landing, footpace; **~aufgang** stairway, flight; **~beleuchtung** staircase lights; **~flucht** flight of stairs; **~geländer** handrail, bannister; **~haus** [cage of a] staircase; **~kante** nosing of a staircase; **~läufer** stair (venetian) carpet; **~stufe** stairstep; **~stufen austreten** to wear the steps down.

Tresor safe [deposit], strong room, treasury, safety vault;
diebessicherer ~ burglar-proof safe;
Wertpapiere in den ~ geben to deposit securities in safe custody *(Br.)*; **Schmuck im ~ haben** to have jewels in safe-keeping (safe custody, *Br.*);
~abteilung safe-deposit (custody, *Br.*) department; **~anlagen** safe-deposit (custody, *Br.*) facilities, vault, bank vault *(US)*.

Tresorfach safe [deposit], safe-deposit box (vault, *US*), strongbox;
~ mieten to rent a safe [deposit box];
~miete safe-deposit facilities (fee).

Tresor|guthaben safe-deposit balance; **~knacker** safe lifter, safeblower, safecracker; **~miete** safe-deposit fee (rent); **~raum** strongroom; **~schloß** safe lock; **~schlüssel** safe-deposit (strongroom) key; **~vermietung** letting of safes and safe-deposit boxes; **~versicherung** safe-deposit [box] insurance; **~vorrichtung** safe-deposit institution.

Tresse *(mil.)* stripe.

Tret|anker kick starter; **~anlasser** *(Motorrad)* foot starter.

treten, jem. auf die Hühneraugen to tread on s. one's corns; **in die Pedale ~** to tread the pedals of a bicycle.

Tretmine antipersonnel mine.

Tretmühle treadmill, jog trot;
in die ~ zurück back to the salt mines *(sl.)*;
in der ~ sein to keep (hold) one's nose to the grindstone, to grind the wind *(Br.)*, to be in a rut; **wieder in seiner ~ sein** to be back at the old grind; **wieder in die ~ zurückkehren** to get back into harness again *(fam.)*; **wieder in die berufliche ~ zurückkehren** to go back to the jogtrot of the office.

Treu und Glauben trust, good faith, equity;
auf ~ on trust, in good faith;
~ im Geschäftsleben (Geschäftsverkehr) good faith in business policy;
auf ~ hinnehmen to take on trust; **gegen ~ verstoßen** to act in breach of good faith, to contravene the first principles of equity;
auf ~ abgeschlossenes Geschäft bona fide transaction.

treu faithful, loyal, constant, *(Tonwiedergabe)* hi-fi *(coll.)*;
~ ergeben devotedly attached; **~ wie Gold** as true as gold;
seinem Eid ~ bleiben to keep one's oath; **seinen Grundsätzen ~ bleiben** to live up to one's principles; **seinem Vorsatz ~ bleiben** to stick to one's purpose; **seiner Frau ~ sein** to be faithful to one's wife;
~er Anhänger loyal supporter; **~ ergebener Freund** devoted friend; **zu ~en Händen** in trust; **~er Parteianhänger** loyalist, regular *(US)*; **~er Untertan** loyal subject; **~e Wiedergabe** faithful reproduction.

Treubruch breach (infraction) of faith, infidelity, defection.

Treue fidelity, loyalty, faithfulness, constancy, allegiance, *(Genauigkeit)* exactness, accuracy, *(Ton)* high fidelity;
eheliche ~ conjugal fidelity; **unverbrüchliche ~** unswerving faith;
seinem Herrn in hingebungsvoller ~ dienen to serve one's master devotedly; **seinen Freunden die ~ halten** to be constant to one's friends; **seinem Land die ~ halten** to remain loyal to one's country;
~bekenntnis profession of faith.

Treueid oath of allegiance (supremacy), test (loyalty, *US*) oath.

Treue|pflicht allegiance, loyalty, trust; **allgemeine ~pflicht** general duty of fidelity; **~pflichtverletzung** breach of trust; **~prämie** seniority benefit; **~rabatt** *(Ladengeschäft)* patronage discount *(US)*, *(Reedereigeschäft)* rebate; **~verhältnis** fiduciary relationship; **vertragliches ~verhältnis** privity of contract.

Treu|geber trustor *(US)*, grantor of trust, trust maker, settlor, donor, *(Sicherungsübereignungsvertrag)* beneficial owner; **~geber und ~nehmer** trustee and beneficiary; **~gut** trust [property], *(Sicherungsübereignungsvertrag)* trust capital, equitable lien; **~gut verwalten** to administer a trust.

Treuhand trust;
zur Stimmrechtsausübung bestellte ~ voting trust *(US)*;
~ mit Tätigkeitspflicht active trust; **~ ohne Verwaltungsfunktion** passive trust;
~abkommen trust engagement (agreement), *(UNO)* trusteeship agreement; **~abteilung** trust department (division); **~agentur für den Effektentransfer** nominees of a bank; **~anstalt** trust institution, public trustee *(Br.)*; **~bank** trust bank (company, *US*); **~begünstigter** equitable owner; cestui que trust, beneficiary; **~begünstigter auf Lebenszeit eines Dritten** cestui que vie; **~begünstigter bei einer Nutzungsüberlassung** cestui que use; **~bericht** trust report; **~bescheinigung** trust receipt *(US)*; **letztwillige ~bestellung** testamentary trust; **unwiderrufliche ~bestellung** irrevocable trust; **widerrufliche ~bestellung** revocable trust; **~beteiligung** trusteeship participation; **widerrufliche ~bindung** totten trust *(US)*; **~charakter** trustee character; **~dauer** trust period; **~eigentum** trust property, *(Sicherungsübereignungsvertrag)* equitable lien; **fingiertes ~eigentum** constructive trust; **gesetzlich vorgeschriebenes ~eigentum** statutory trust; **~eigentümer einer Liegenschaft** statutory owner; **~einkommen** trust income.

Treuhänder trustee [of a settlement], custodian, fiduciary [agent], bailee, trust officer, holder on trust, trustman, *(beschlagnahmten Vermögens)* sequester;
amtierender ~ managing trustee; **amtlich (behördlich) bestellter (staatlich eingesetzter) ~** conventional (official) trustee, public trustee *(Br.)*; **gerichtlich bestellter ~** receiver, judicial (court-appointed) trustee, manager *(Br.)*; **öffentlich bestellter ~** public trustee; **zur Stimmrechtsausübung bestellter ~** voting trustee *(US)*; **urkundlich bestellter ~** trustee under a deed, indenture trustee; **staatlich eingesetzter ~** public trustee; **einstweiliger ~** interim receiver; **gewillkürter ~** express trustee; **weisungsgebundener ~** bare trustee;
~ einer Familienstiftung private trustee; **als ~ Geltender** constructive trustee; **~ eines Grundstücksvertrages** escrow holder; **~ von Mündelvermögen** custodian trustee; **~ einer Nachlaßstiftung** testamentary trustee; **~ eines Pensionsfonds** pension-fund manager; **~ für die Verwaltung von Feindvermögen** Custodian of Enemy Property *(Br.)*, Alien Property Custodian *(US)*;
~ abberufen to remove a trustee; **weitere ~ bestimmen** to appoint new trustees; **~ einsetzen (ernennen)** to appoint a custodian (trustee); **~ entlasten** to discharge a trustee; **~ ernennen** to appoint a trustee; **als ~ fungieren** to trustee, to serve as trustee; **als ~ von Grundvermögen einer Offenen Handelsgesellschaft fungieren** to hold the property in trust for a partnership; **als ~ handeln** to act in a fiduciary capacity; **~ verantwortlich machen** to hold a trustee to account; **~ sein** to act as trustee; **einem ~ übergeben** to trustee, to garnishee; **Urkunde einem ~ übergeben** to place an instrument in escrow; **auf einen ~ übertragen** to vest in a trustee; **Vermögen auf einen ~ übertragen** to trustee an estate; **als ~ verwalten** to hold on trust; **als ~ zurücktreten** to resign from a trust;

~**abrechnung** trustee's accounts; ~**amt** office of trustee; ~**aufgaben** fiduciary duties; ~**ausschuß** board of (joint) trustees, trustee committee; ~**bestimmungen** trustee provisions; ~**depot** custody held for trustee, trust deposit; ~**eigenschaft** capacity to act a trustee, fiduciary (trustee) capacity; ~**entlastung** discharging a trustee; ~**fonds** trust fund; ~**fonds errichten** to place a fund in escrow; ~**funktionen wahrnehmen** to serve as custodian; ~**gesetz** trustee act *(Br.)*; ~**gremium** joint trustees, board of trustees; ~**haftung** liability of a trustee; ~**haftung bei Unterschlagung** quasi trustee.

Treuhänderin trust woman.

treuhänderisch fiduciary, in trust;
~ **halten** to hold in trust (escrow); ~ **verwalten lassen** to settle on a trust; **jds. Vermögensverwaltung** ~ **übernehmen** to accept the trusteeship of s. one's property; ~ **verwalten** to act as trustee, to hold on trust (in escrow); ~ **verwaltet werden** to be under (subject to) trust, to be held in a fiduciary capacity; ~**er Anteil** fiduciary interest; ~**e Buchführung** fiduciary accounting; ~**es Eigentum** trust capital, beneficial interest, equitable lien; ~**es Eigentum verschaffen** to deliver in trust; ~**e Funktionen** fiduciary duties; ~ **verwalteter Nachlaß** trust estate; ~**e Tätigkeit** fiduciary activity; ~ **geleitetes Unternehmen** Massachusetts trust; ~ **verwaltetes Vermögen** trust estate (fund); **in** ~**e Verwahrung nehmen** to take in trust; ~**e Verwaltung** trusteeship, trust administration; ~**er Verwaltung entziehen** to remove from a trust; ~**e Vollmachten** fiduciary powers.

Treuhänder|kaution trustee's security; ~**konto** trust (trustee's) account; **kreditorisch geführtes** ~**konto** trust credit account; ~**pflichten** trustee's duties; ~**rat** board of (joint) trustees, *(Vereinte Nationen)* Trusteeship Council.

Treuhanderrichtung creation of a trust;
testamentarische ~ creation of a trust by will; **unvollständige** ~ imperfect trust.

Treuhänderschaft trusteeship;
unter ~ **stellen** to place under trusteeship, to sequester.

Treuhänder|sitzung trustees' meeting; ~**status** trustee status; ~**tätigkeit** custodial service; ~**vergütung** remuneration of trustee; **eingegangene** ~**verpflichtung** trust undertaking; ~**vertrag** trust agreement, custodian's contract; ~**vollmacht** trustee's power.

Treuhand|fonds trust fund; ~**fonds mit freier Ertragsverwendung** expendable trust fund; ~**fonds auf Lebenszeit** protective trust *(Br.)*; ~**gebiet** trusteeship territory; ~**gebühren** trustee's fees; ~**gelder** trust fund (money); ~**geschäft** trust transaction.

Treuhandgesellschaft trust institution (company, *US*), trustee (auditing) company, corporate fiduciaries, auditor;
von einer ~ **verwaltet** trust-controlled;
~ **zur Kontrolle sicherungsübereigneter Waren** field warehousing organization *(US)*; ~ **zur Verwaltung öffentlicher Stiftungen** community trust *(US)*; ~ **zur Verwaltung einer Teilhaberversicherung** business life insurance trust; ~ **zum Zweck der Aktienausgabe** trustee under bond issue.

Treuhand|giro indorsement of trustee; ~**gut** trust [estate], *(Sicherungsübereignungsvertrag)* trust capital, equitable lien; ~**gut verwalten** to administer a trust; **gesetzliche** ~**haftung** trust in invitum; ~**indossament** trust endorsement; ~**kapital** settlement capital, capital money *(Br.)*; ~**kapitalbeiträge** trust capital money; ~**konto** trust (fiduciary, escrow, custodian) account; ~**kredit** loan made to a trustee; ~**nehmer** cestui que trust, beneficiary, bailee; ~**pflicht verletzen** to infringe a trust; ~**quittung** trust receipt *(US)*; ~**sonderkonto** special agency (trust) account; ~**sondervermögen** trust-and-agency fund; ~**staat** trustee state; ~**stelle** custodian office; **öffentlich-rechtliche (staatliche)** ~**stelle** trust corporation *(Br.)*, public trustee [office, *Br.*]; ~**stellung** trusteeship position, *(passiv)* naked (passive) trust; ~**system** trusteeship system; ~**urkunde** trust instrument (indenture, patent), covering deed; ~**vereinbarung** letter of trust, trust engagement (agreement); ~**vergütung** trustee's remuneration.

Treuhandverhältnis trust, trust (fiduciary) relation;
abstraktes ~ dry trust; **bedingtes** ~ contingent trust; **kraft Gesetzes entstandenes (gesetzliches)** ~ implied (involuntary) trust; **detailliert (genau) festgelegtes** ~ perfect (executed) trust; **gewillkürtes** ~ express (direct) trust; **spezialisiertes** ~ complete voluntary trust; **verdecktes** ~ secret trust; **teilweise verdecktes** ~ half-secret trust; **vermutetes** ~ implied trust; **gesetzlich vermutetes** ~ resulting (implied) trust;
~ **mit noch fehlender Treuhandübertragung** incompletely constituted trust; **reines** ~ **ohne besondere Verwaltungsaufgaben** instrumental (ministerial) trust; ~ **zur Vornahme eines einmaligen Auftrags** special trust;
~ **begründen** to trustee, to create (establish) a trust (trust relation[ship]).

Treuhandvermögen trust, trust estate (property, assets, fund), *(zu Lebzeiten des Verfügenden)* living trust *(US)*;
nach freiem Ermessen verwaltetes ~ discretionary trust *(Br.)*; **zweckgebundenes** ~ complete voluntary trust;
~ **eines Alterversorgungswerkes** pension-plan trust fund; ~ **mit besonderen Vollmachten** active trust;
nicht mehr zum ~ **gehören** to have ceased to be the subject of a trust; **für die Sicherheit des** ~**s Sorge tragen** to make the trust fund secure; ~ **übertragen** to vest trust property.

Treuhandvertrag fiduciary contract, bailment, escrow (trust) agreement, trust deed *(Br.)* (indenture, *US*, instrument);
~ **errichten** to declare a trust.

Treuhandverwaltung trusteeship, assigneeship, execution (accumulation) of a trust, personal trust *(US)*, trust administration;
auftragsgebundene ~ special trust; **auf den letzten Wunsch des Erblassers begründete** ~ precatory trust; **für einen Verschwender errichtete** ~ sheltering trust; **gemeinsame** ~ common trust; **lebenslängliche** ~ living trust *(US)*; **schlichte** ~ naked (passive, simple) trust, proprietary trust *(Scot.)*; **unvollständige** ~ imperfect trust; **weisungsgebundene** ~ ministerial trust;
~ **für bestimmte Begünstigte** personal trust, private trust; ~ **für Einzelgegenstände** particular trust; ~ **mit voller Freiheit in der Vermögensverwaltung** express active trust; ~ **mit besonderen Vollmachten** active trust, accessory trust *(Scot.)*; ~ **zum Zweck der Aktienausgabe** trustee under bond issue.

Treuhandzertifikat trust share, collateral trust certificate *(US)*.

treulos faithless, disloyal, *(verräterisch)* treacherous.

Treunehmer trustee, fiduciary debtor, beneficiary, bailee;
~**gesellschaft** corporate trust.

Tribunal tribunal, court of justice.

Tribüne *(Redner)* platform, rostrum, *(Zuschauer)* gallery, stand, grandstand;
~ **errichten** to erect a platform.

Tribut tribute, contribution, toll;
~ **des Fortschritts** penalty of progress;
einem Volk ~ **auferlegen** to lay a country under contribution; **hohen** ~ **an Menschenleben fordern** to take a heavy toll of human lives; ~ **zahlen** to pay a tribute; **seinen** ~ **zollen** to pay one's toll (penalty).

tributpflichtig tributary.

Trichter funnel, filler, *(Sprachrohr)* mouthpiece, megaphone;
Nürnberger ~ royal road to learning;
j. auf den ~ **bringen** to put s. o. on the scent; **auf den** ~ **gekommen sein** to have got the knack of it;
~**lautsprecher** cone (horn-type) loudspeaker.

Trick device, trick, trickery, dodge, knack, shuffle, artifice, doubling, fakery, fetch, wrinkle, lurk *(Br., sl.)*, *(Reklamestück)* gimmick, gag, stunt;
~**s** engineering, games;
gemeiner (übler) ~ mean trick; **rhetorische** ~**s** strategems of rhetoric; **schmutziger** ~ low-down trick;
~ **zur Ablenkung der Polizei** device to put the police off the scent; ~ **eines Betrügers** rascal's trick; **politische** ~**s und Kniffe** arts and wiles of politics;
sich einer Verpflichtung durch einen ~ **entziehen** to escape an obligation by a trick; **durch einen** ~ **erreichen** to get s. th. by a wangle; ~ **heraushaben** to have the knack of it; **auf den billigsten** ~ **hereinfallen** to fall for the cheapest trick; **alle** ~**s kennen** to be up to a dodge or two (all dodges); **zu einem** ~ **seine Zuflucht nehmen** to resort to tricks; **jeden nur erdenklichen** ~ **versuchen** to try every trick in the book; ~ **vorführen** to perform a trick;
~**aufnahme** *(Film)* trick shot; ~**betrüger** trickster; ~**diebstahl** ring dropping *(Br.)*.

Trickfilm *(Zeichentrick)* trick film, animated film;
~ **zeichnen** to animate a cartoon;
~**studio** animation studio; ~**zeichner** animator.

tricksen to trick, to feint, to wangle.

Trick|szene trick scene; ~**titel** animated title; ~**überblendung** *(Fernsehen)* split-screen effect, *(Film)* animation superimposition.

Trieb instinct, impulse, *(Psychopath)* compulsion, *(Verlangen)* desire, urge;
einem inneren ~ **folgen** to act on impulse; ~ **zum Verbrechen haben** to have criminal leanings; **von seinen niedrigen** ~**en beherrscht werden** to be dominated by one's instincts; **seine** ~**e zügeln** to curb (bridle) one's desire;

~**feder** mainspring; ~**feder von etw. sein** to be at the bottom of s. th.; ~**handlung** instinctive behavio(u)r; ~**kraft** driving force; ~**sand** quicksand; ~**wagen** rail car, shuttle (railway, *Br.*) car, tramcar *(Br.)*; ~**werk** *(Flugzeug)* gearing, power unit (plant), *(Panzer)* power plant.

triefen, von Blut to be stained with blood; **vor Freundlichkeit** ~ to gush with friendliness; **vor Nässe** ~ to be soaking wet; **von Schweiß** ~ to be dripping with perspiration.

Trift pasture, *(Weg zur Weide)* driveway, cattle track.

triftig cogent, plausible, weighty, valid, pleadable;
~**er Grund** sound (good) reason.

Triftigkeit cogency, weightiness, validity.

Trikotagen hosiery, knitted goods, knitwear.

Triller|haben to be not all there;
~**pfeife** police whistle.

trimmen to trim, *(Auto)* to tune (soup) up.

trinkbar fit to drink, drinkable, potable.

Trinken drinking;
gewohnheitsmäßiges ~ habitual drunkenness;
sich das ~ **angewöhnen** to take to drinking (the bottle); **j. zum** ~ **nötigen** to ply s. o. with drink.

trinken to drink;
einen ~ to raise one's elbow *(coll.)*; **Flasche leer** ~ to empty a bottle; **auf jds. Gesundheit** ~ to drink to s. one's health; **laufend** ~ to be fond of the bottle; **mehr** ~ **als man verträgt** to drink more than is good for one; **bis in die frühen Morgenstunden** ~ to carouse into the small hours of the morning; **in kleinen Schlucken** ~ to sip; **j. unter den Tisch** ~ to drink s. o. under the table; **übermäßig** ~ to drink to excess.

Trinker inebriate, habitual drunkard, alcoholic;
entwöhnter ~ reclaimed (reformed) drunkard; **starker** ~ heavy drinker; **unheilbarer** ~ incurable drunkard;
starker ~ **sein** to drink deep;
~**heilanstalt** home for incurables, asylum (institution) for inebriates, inebriate reformatory (asylum).

Trinkgelage spree, binge, carousal, drinking bout.

Trinkgeld fee, tip, perquisite, drink (throw) money, pourboire, beer money *(Br.)*, gratuity, gratification;
kein ~ no gratuities;
ganzen Tag für ein ~ **arbeiten** to work all day for a mere pittance; **jem. ein** ~ **aufnötigen** to force a tip into s. one's hand; **zusätzliche** ~**er erhalten** to get tips over and above one's wages; **jem. ein** ~ **geben** to cross s. one's hand with a piece of money, to pouch, to tip (fee) s. o.;
~**geben** tipping; **großzügiges** ~**geben** soldier *(sl.)*.

Trink|gewohnheiten drinking habits; ~**glas** tumbler; ~**halle** *(Bad)* pump room; ~**kur machen** to take the waters; ~**spruch** toast, rouse; ~**spruch ausbringen** to propose a toast; ~**stube** drinking (tippling) house; ~**wasser** fresh (drinking) water.

Triptyk, Triptik triptyque.

trist|e Gegend dismal place; ~**es Leben führen** to drag on a miserable (wretched) existence; ~**es Wetter** murky weather.

Tritt footstep, tread;
~ **in den Hintern** kick in the backside; ~**e im Schnee** footprints in the snow;
~ **verloren haben** to be out of step; **ohne** ~ **marschieren** *(auf Brücke)* to break step; **Tür mit einem** ~ **öffnen** to kick the door open; **falschen** ~ **tun** to miss one's step;
~**brett** running board, footboard, car step, pedal; ~**brettfahrer** bandwaggoner; ~**leiter** stepladder.

Triumph triumph, victory;
~ **der Naturwissenschaft** triumph of science;
~**bogen** triumphal arch; ~**geheul** shouts of triumph; ~**zug** triumph.

triumphieren, über j. to exult over s. o.; **nicht zu früh** ~ not to count one's chickens before they are hatched.

trivial trivial, fiddling, ordinary, common, trite, banal, hackneyed;
~**e Bemerkung** trite remark.

trocken dry, *(langweilig)* tedious, dry, dull;
noch nicht ~ **hinter den Ohren** still wet behind the ears;
j. ~ **sitzen lassen** to offer s. o. no refreshment;
~**en Auges zusehen** to watch without shedding tears; ~**es Brot** dry (stale) bread; **keinen** ~**en Faden am Leib haben** to have no dry stitch (thread) on one; ~**es Gedeck** meal excluding beverages; ~**er Humor** dry humo(u)r; ~**es Klima** dry climate; ~**e Lektüre** tedious lecture; ~**er Wechsel** promissory note; ~**er Witz** dry wit; ~**e Zahlen** dull figures.

Trocken|em, auf dem hard up;
im ~**en sein** to be out of the woods; **auf dem** ~**en sitzen** to be on the rocks, to be in low water(s) (stranded).

Trocken|anlage drying equipment; ~**apparat** drying train; ~**bagger** excavator; ~**batterie** dry battery.

Trockendock dry (graving) dock;
Schiff ins ~ **bringen** to dry-dock a ship; **ins** ~ **gehen** to dry-dock;
~**reparatur** dry-dock repair.

Trocken|eis dry ice; ~**element** dry cell; ~**farm** dry farm; ~**fäule** dry rot; ~**frachtbehälter** dry-cargo container; ~**frachter** dry-cargo carrier; ~**futter** provender; ~**fütterung** stall feeding; ~**gebiet** arid region; ~**gemüse** dehydrated vegetables; ~**gestell** drying frame, clothes horse; ~**gewicht** net (dry) weight; ~**heit** *(Klima)* dryness, aridity; **von der** ~**heit schwer betroffen** drought-stricken; ~**heitsperiode** run of dry weather; ~**kammer** drying chamber; ~**ladung** dry cargo.

trockenlegen to drain;
das ganze Land ~ to turn the whole country dry.

Trocken|legung drainage; ~**mauer** dry-stone wall, dry walling, pack wall; ~**milch** dry milk, milk powder; ~**periode** dry season, drought; ~**raum** drying room; ~**schleuder** extractor; ~**spiritus** white coal; ~**stempel** embossed stamp; ~**wäsche** roughdry clothes; ~**wirtschaft** dry farming; ~**zeit** dry season.

trocknen *(Früchte)* to dry, to dehydrate, *(Holz)* to season wood.

Trödel jumble, junk, trash, rubbish;
~**geschäft,** ~**laden** marine stores *(Br.)*, junk (jumble, *Br.*) shop, swagshop, jumble; ~**liese** slow coach, dawdler, slowpoke *(US)*; ~**markt** jumble (flea) market, rag fair, broker's row *(Br.)*.

trödeln to dawdle, to linger, to dillydally.

Trödelwaren second-hand goods, junk.

Trödler junk, wardrobe dealer, junkman, cadger, faker, peddler, broker *(Br.)*, higgler, *(Bummler)* laggard, poke *(US)*;
~**laden** junk (jumble) shop, swagshop, marine stores *(Br.)*;
~**markt** rag fair, broker's row *(Br.)*.

Trog trough, vat.

trollen, sich nach Hause to trot off home.

Trommel drum;
~ **für j. rühren** to beat the drum for s. o.;
~**feuer** drumfire, heavy barrage; ~**feuer von Fragen** volley of questions.

trommeln, jem. aus dem Bett to get s. o. out of bed; **nervös mit den Fingern auf den Tisch** ~ to beat the devil's tattoo.

Trommler drummer.

Trompeten|signal trumpet call; ~**stoß** trump, trumpet; ~**stoß zur Begrüßung** flourish of welcome; **etw. mit einem gewaltigen** ~**stoß veröffentlichen** to publish s. th. with a great flourish of trumpets.

Tropen|anzug lightweight suit; ~**ausführung** tropical finish; ~**ausrüstung** tropical kit.

tropenfest machen to tropicalize.

Tropen|gegend tropical country; ~**helm** tropical helmet, sun helmet, pith helmet, tropee; ~**klima** tropical climate; ~**krankheit** tropical disease.

Tröpfchen drop, droplet;
~**nebel** waterfog.

tröpfchenweise by drops, in driblets;
jem. eine Nachricht ~ **beibringen** to break the news gently to s. o.

tröpfeln to drip, to dribble, *(Besucher)* to trickle, *(Regen)* to be spitting with rain.

Tropfen, guter capital wine;
~ **auf dem heißen Stein** a drop in the ocean *(Br.)*, a pill to cure an earthquake;
steter ~ **höhlt den Stein** constant wearing wears away the stone;
~ **einnehmen** to take drops.

tropfen to drip, to drop;
von der Decke ~ to be dripping from the ceiling.

tropische|Hitze tropical heat; ~ **Störung** tropical disturbance.

Troß *(Gefolge)* followers, train, *(mil.)* baggage train *(Br.)*, impedimenta;
~ **mit sich führen** to have a crowd of followers.

Trosse hawser, towrope.

Trost, magerer cold comfort;
~ **in etw. finden** to draw consolation from s. th.; **aus etw.** ~ **schöpfen** to derive comfort from s. th.; **etw.** ~ **spenden** to offer a mite of comfort; **jds. Herzen** ~ **spenden** to pour comfort into s. one's heart.

trösten to comfort, to console;
sich kaum damit ~ **können** to draw little comfort from.

Tröster, schlechter job's comforter.

trostlos hopeless, desolate, bleak;
~**er Anblick** pathetic sight; ~**e Aussichten** bleak prospects; ~**e Gestalt** wretched figure; ~**e Verhältnisse** deplorable circumstances; ~**es Wetter** miserable weather.

Trostlosigkeit der Gegenwart desolation of the times.
Trostpreis consolation prize (stakes), booby prize.
Tröstung, geistliche ghostly (spiritual) comfort.
Trott trot, jogtrot, routine, groove, jag;
üblicher ~ rut;
alten ~ aufgeben to leave the beaten track; **seinen üblichen ~ beibehalten** to flow (travel) in the same old groove; **j. aus seinem gewohnten ~ bringen** to lift s. o. out of the rut; **wieder in den alten ~ zurückfallen** to get back to the jogtrot (old rut).
Trottel ninny, nincompoop, moron;
gutgläubiger ~ sucker.
trottelig clumsy, awkward, *(blöd)* moronic;
sich ~ benehmen to behave idiotically.
Trottoir foot pavement *(Br.)*, banquette *(US)*, side-walk *(US)*, flagging, foothpath *(Australia)*.
Trotz obstinacy, stubbornness;
einer Gefahr ~ bieten to defy a danger; **dem Schicksal ~ bieten** to fight against fate; **dem Sturm ~ bieten** to weather the storm.
trotzig obstinate, stubborn, *(Kind)* sulky.
Troygewicht troy weight.
trübe clouded, cloudy, nebulous, foggy, *(Licht)* dim, *(Sicht)* blurred;
~r Himmel overcast (cloudy) sky; **in ~r Stimmung sein** to be downcast, to have the blues *(US coll)*; **~s Wetter** murky (dull) weather; **~n Zeiten entgegensehen** to foresee gloomy days.
Trubel hubbub, bustle, *(Durcheinander)* fuss, rumpus *(coll.)*, *(Menschenmenge)* milling crowd, throng;
~ gesellschaftlicher Verpflichtungen whirl of social engagements, social whirl, racket;
sich in den ~ des Verkehrs stürzen to plunge into the hubbub of traffic.
Trüben, im ~ fischen to fish in troubled waters.
trüben to make cloudy (muddy);
jds. Heiterkeit ~ to damp s. one's spirits; **jds. Urteilskraft ~** to warp s. one's judgment; **jds. Verstand ~** to cloud s. one's mind.
Trübsal sorrow, grief;
~ blasen to be down in the dumps *(fam.)*, to have the blues *(US coll.)*, to be in the doldrums.
trübselig|e Gegend dismal place; **~es Wetter** gloomy weather.
trübsinnig melancholic, gloomy, drab.
Trübung cloudiness, turbidity, *(fig.)* shadow;
~ der diplomatischen Beziehungen disturbance of diplomatic relations.
Trudelfallschirm antispin parachute.
Trudeln *(Flugzeug)* tail spin, spinning.
trudeln *(Flugzeug)* to spin, *(Reifen)* to wobble.
trudelsicher nonspinning.
Trugbild phantasmagoria, phantasm, phantom.
trügerisch deceitful, deceptive, specious, fallacious;
~es Eis treacherous ice; **~e Hoffnung** illusory hope; **~es Spiel mit jem. treiben** to play s. o. false.
Trugschluß false conclusion, fallacy, sophism.
Truhe coffer, *(Radio)* console.
Trümmer debris, rubble, ruins, *(Schiff)* wreckage;
aus den ~n erstehen to rise from the ashes; **in ~ gehen** to break to pieces; **in ~ legen** to lay in ruins; **von ~n übersät sein** to be strewn with wreckage;
~beseitigung rubble clearance; **~feld** expanse of ruins; **~grundstück** bomb-damaged site; **~haufen** ruin, *(fig.)* wrack; **Stadt in einen ~haufen verwandeln** to turn a town into a shambles, to lay a city flat; **~verwertung** rubble salvage.
Trumpf trump;
seinen letzten ~ ausspielen to play one's last trump;
sich als ~as erweisen to come up trumps.
Trümpfe, seine ~ behalten to keep one's trumps in hand; **jem. die ~ aus der Hand nehmen** to steal s. one's thunder.
Trumpfkarte, seine ~ ausspielen to play one's trump card.
Trunk, dem ~ ergeben addicted to the bottle;
dem ~e fröhnen to take to the bottle, to be on the drink *(coll.)*.
trunken drunk, inebriated, intoxicated.
Trunkenbold drunkard, alcoholic, inebriate, soaker *(sl.)*.
Trunkenheit drunkenness, intoxication, inebriation;
gemeingefährliche ~ excessive drunkenness; **selbstverschuldete ~** voluntary drunkenness;
~ am Steuer driving while intoxicated *(US)*.
Trunksucht intemperance, inebriation;
der ~ verfallen to give o. s. over to drinking.
Trunksüchtiger inebriate, habitual drunkard, alcoholic.
Trupp gang, company, group, *(mil.)* section, detachment, party, *(Polizei)* squad;
~ Gefangener batch of prisoners.
Truppe gang, company, group, corps;
amphibische ~ landing party *(Br.)*.
Truppen troops, force;
einsatzbereite ~ effective troops; **entfaltete ~** extended troops; **getarnte ~** masked troops; **kampferprobte ~** troops seasonded by battle; **nicht motorisierte ~** nonmobile troops; **neue ~** fresh troops; **regierungstreue ~** loyalist troops; **reguläre ~** regular troops;
~ im Ausland forces stationed abroad;
~ aufbieten to order out troops; **~ aufstellen** to arrange (line up the) troops; **~ für den Einsatz ausbilden** to prepare troops for action; **~ ausheben** to call out (up, raise) troops, to levy an army; **~ per Schiff befördern** to transport troops by boat; **~ zum Gefecht bereitstellen** to prepare troops for action; **~ demoralisieren** to destroy the discipline of troops; **den ~ neuen Auftrieb geben** to put fresh heart into the troops; **~ aus der Frontlinie herausnehmen** to recall troops from the front; **~ inspizieren** to inspect troops; **~ konzentrieren** to concentrate troops; **~ aufmarschieren lassen** to assemble troops, to draw up; **~ beritten machen** to mount troops; **~ massieren** to mass troops; **~ an die Front schaffen** to move troops to the front; **~ stationieren** to station troops; **~ verladen** to embark troops; **~ verlegen** to evacuate (remove, move, shift) troops; **~ in die Bresche werfen** to fling troops into the fray; **~ an die Front werfen** to move troops to the front; **~ in die Schlacht werfen** to pitchfork troops into battle; **~ aus einer vorgeschobenen (unhaltbaren) Stellung zurücknehmen** to withdraw troops from an exposed position; **~ zusammenziehen** to consolidate (concentrate) troops, to gather troops together;
~abbau troop cuts (redeployment), forces reduction; **wechselseitiger ausgewogener ~abbau** Mutual Balanced Force Reduction (MBFR); **~abzug** withdrawal of forces (troops), manpower withdrawal; **~ansammlung, ~aufmarsch** concentration of troops, buildup; **~aushebung** levy, conscription; **~bereitstellung** assembly of troops, preparation of troops for battle; **~besichtigung** field day; **~betreuung** welfare of troops in the field; **~bewegung** movement of an army, dislocation, manoeuvre; **~einheit** element, unit; **~einsatz** troop commitment; **~einschiffung** embarkation of troops; **~entflechtung** disengagement of troops; **~entsendung** dispatch of troops; **~führer** troop leader; **~führung** *(Lehrfach)* applied tactics; **~gattung** branch of the service; **~gliederung** organization of troops; **~höchstgrenze** troop ceiling; **~kontingent** troop detachment, contingent; **voller ~kontingent** full quota of troops; **~körper** element, body, **~lager** compound; **~landungsboot** flat, landing craft; **~massierung vornehmen** to mass troops; **größere ~mengen heranführen** to bring up heavy forces; **~nachschub** reinforcements; **~offizier** line (regimental) officer; **~parade** parade, trooping the colo(u)rs, review; **~parade abnehmen** to review troops, to pass troops in review; **~reduzierung** reduction of forces, force (troop) reduction; **~schau** [military] review; **~schleier** curtain of troops; **~schule** branch school; **~standort** garrison; **~stärke** strength, forces capability; **~teil** unit, element, outfit; **sich bei seinem ~teil einfinden** to join one's unit; **~transport** troop transport (transportation); **~transporte im Geleitzug über den Ozean eskortieren** to convoy troopships across the Atlantic; **~transporter** troop carrier, trooper, troopship, transport vessel, personel carrier; **~transportflugzeug** troop carrier; **~transportschiff** liberty ship *(US)*; **~transportzug** troop train; **~übung** field exercise, manoeuvre, maneuver; **~übungsplatz** training area, camp, army training ground; **~unterkunft** barracks, billet; **~verband** body, task force; **feindliche ~verbände binden** to immobilize a body of troops; **~verbandsplatz** aid station, regimental aid *(local, US)*, aid post; **~verladung** entrainment, *(Flugzeug, Schiff)* embarkation; **~verlegung** troop redeployment; **~verminderung** reduction of forces; **~verringerung** run-down; **~verschiebung** troop redeployment, dislocation of troops; **~versorgung** subsistence of troops; **~vertrag** Forces Convention; **~verwendung** troop deployment; **~zusammenziehung** concentration of troops.
truppweise in troops.
Trust combination, combine, pool, business trust *(US)*;
in einem ~ zusammenfassen to trustify;
~anteilschein certificate of beneficial interest; **~bildung** trustification.
Tube, auf die ~ drücken to step on the gas *(US)*, to open the taps *(sl.)*.
Tuch cloth, *(Halstuch)* scarf, *(Kopftuch)* kerchief;
rotes ~ für j. sein to be a pet peeve for s. o.; **wie ein rotes ~ auf j. wirken** to be a red rag to s. o., to act like a red rag to a bull;

~**ballen** bale of cloth; ~**fabrik** cloth factory; ~**fabrikant** cloth manufacturer, clothier; ~**fühlung** *(mil.)* close touch (interval); **in ~fühlung mit jem. stehen** to rub shoulders with s. o.; ~**händler** wool(l)en draper; ~**handlung** draper's shop, dry-goods store *(US)*.

tüchtig capable, competent, skilled, skilful, hot and strong, efficient;
~ **arbeiten** to work hard; **in seinem Fach ~ sein** to have a good grasp of a subject; ~ **zulangen** to do justice to a meal, to tuck in; ~**er Appetit** hearty appetite; ~**er Arbeiter** skilled worker; ~**e Geschäftsfrau** efficient business woman; ~**e Kräfte** qualified personnel; ~**er Lehrer** capable teacher; ~**e Mahlzeit** square meal; ~**er Mensch** trojan; ~**en Schluck nehmen** to take a swig *(coll.)*; ~**e Sekretärin** efficient secretary; ~**e Tracht Prügel** sound thrashing.

Tüchtigkeit capability, capacity, competence, efficiency, skill;
berufliche ~ occupational efficiency.

Tücke malice, spite, perfidy, treachery, deceit;
~ **des Gesetzes** cobwebs (intricacies) of the law; ~ **des Objekts** general cussedness of things; ~**n des Schicksals** tricks of fortune.

tuckern *(Motorboot)* to put-put.

tückisch vicious, malignant, malicious, spiteful, *(hinterlistig)* sly, guileful;
~**er Blick** malignant glance; ~**e Handlung** piece of perfidy.

Tüftelarbeit tedious work.

tüfteln to fiddle, to puzzle.

Tugend, aus der Not geborene virtue made of necessity;
viele ~en haben to have many qualities; **Pfad der ~ wandeln** to follow the path of virtue;
~**bold** paragon of virtue, prig, goody *(US coll.)*.

tummeln, sich to romp about, to frolic.

Tummelplatz playground, stamping ground *(US coll.)*.

Tumor, bösartiger malignant tumo(u)r.

Tümpel slough, marshy pool, swamphole.

Tumult tumult, rumpus, uproar, disturbance, commotion, disorder, riot, rout, turmoil, whirl, clamo(u)r, hullabaloo, hurlyburly;
~ **erregen** to stir (kick up) a row, to cause a riot;
~**gesetz** Riot Act *(Br.)*; ~**risiko** risk of civil commotion; ~**schäden** riot damage; ~**schädengesetz** Riot Damages Act *(Br.)*.

tumultuarisch tumultuary, tumultuous, uproarious, riotous.

Tumultversicherung riot and civil commotion insurance.

Tun action, doing, activities;
verräterisches ~ treacherous activities;
sein ~ bemänteln to put a good face on one's actions.

tun, jds. Ansehen Abbruch to cast a slur on s. o.; **Fehltritt ~** to make a false step; **jem. einen Gefallen ~** to do s. o. a favo(u)r; **des Guten zuviel ~** to overdo things; **Mißgriff ~** to make a blunder; **treu seine Pflicht ~** to stand to one's duty; **recht daran ~** to do well; **das Seinige ~** to do one's part (one's level best); **überhaupt nichts ~** to omit to do a piece of work; **jem. Unrecht ~** to wrong s. o.; **etw. völlig unvorbereitet ~** to do s. th. with no preparation; **Wunder ~** to work wonders; **jem. etw. zuliebe ~** to do s. th. for s. one's sake;
~, was einem gefällt to do one's own thing;
es mit jem. zu ~ bekommen to get into hot water with s. o.; **mit der Exportabteilung zu ~ haben** to be connected with the export department; **mehr als genug zu ~ haben** to have enough on one's plate; **genügend zu ~ haben** to have one's work cut out *(fam.)*; **mit jem. zu ~ haben** to have dealings with s. o.; **mit jem. nichts zu ~ haben** to have no truck with (wash one's hands of) s. o., to have nothing to do with s. o.; **mit einer Sache nichts zu ~ haben** to have no hand in an affair, to have no concern with a matter; **mit einer Sache nichts mehr zu ~ haben** to wash one's hands of s. th.; **schrecklich viel zu ~ haben** to have a frantic amount to do; **Gartenhaus bauen, um etw. zu ~ zu haben** to build a summer house for s. th. to do; **es mit jem. zu ~ kriegen** to get into hot water with s. o.; **mit jem. nichts mehr zu ~ haben wollen** to cut all connections with s. o.; **mit bestimmten Transaktionen nichts zu ~ haben wollen** to refuse to touch certain transactions.

Tünche varnish, veneer, *(Anstrich)* wash, whitewash.

tünchen to wash, to paint.

Tunichtgut good-for-nothing (-naught).

Tunke, dicke ~ mit jem. sein to be hail-fellow-well-met with s. o.

tunlich feasible, practicable, expedient, advisable;
für ~ halten to think fit.

Tunlichkeit feasibleness, practicableness, practicability, expediency.

Tunnel tunnel, *(Unterführung)* underpass, subway;
~ **bohren** to drive a tunnel; **in einen ~ einfahren** to enter a tunnel; ~ **graben** to excavate a tunnel;
~**durchgang** underground crossing; ~**schacht** tunnel shaft.

Tüpfelchen dot, tittle;
bis aufs letzte ~ down to the last detail;
das ~ auf dem I the cherry on the cake.

Tür, feuerfeste fire door; **luftdichte ~** airtight door; **zugemauerte ~** blind door;
~ **aufbrechen** to force [open] a door, to wrench (pry, burst) a door open; ~ **aufstoßen** to fling open a door, to push a door open; **Politik der offenen ~ betreiben** to open the door to agreements on international affairs; **offene ~en einrennen** to flog a dead horse, to force an open door *(fam.)*; ~ **eintreten** to kick the door in; **mit der ~ ins Haus fallen** to blurt out everything; **überall offene ~en finden** to be welcome everywhere; **Gespräche hinter verschlossenen ~en führen** to hold talks behind closed doors; **j. zur ~ geleiten** to conduct s. o. to the door; **zur einen ~ hereingehen und zur anderen herauskommen** to go in at one door and out at the other; **zuerst vor der eigenen ~ kehren** to put one's house in order first; **an die ~ klopfen** to knock on (at) the door; ~ **zu weiteren Verhandlungen offenlassen** to leave the door open for further negotiations; ~ **öffnen** to answer the door; ~ **mit einem Drücker öffnen** to let o. s. in with a latch-key; **dem Mißbrauch ~ und Tor öffnen** to open a door to abuses; **der Verleumdung ~ und Tor öffnen** to lay o. s. open to calumny; **jem. den Stuhl vor die ~ setzen** to show s. o. the door, *(Mieter)* to put s. o. onto the street; **jem. die ~ verschließen** to lock the door against s. o.; ~ **an ~ mit jem. wohnen** to live next door to s. o.; **jem. die ~ vor der Nase zuschlagen** to shut the door in s. one's face.

Turbinen|antrieb turbine-powered; ~**auto** turbocar; ~**dampfer** turbine steamer; ~**flugzeug** turbine (turboprop) aircraft; ~**lokomotive** steam-turbine engine; ~**triebwerk** turbo-prop engine.

Turbo|jäger jet fighter; ~**propeller** jet propeller; ~**strahltriebwerk** turbojet engine.

turbulenter Verlauf turbulent course.

Tür|gitter grille; ~**glocke** door bell; **versenkbarer ~griff** *(Auto)* inset handle; ~**hüter** *(Hotel)* doorkeeper, commissionaire *(Br.)*; ~**klinke** door handle; **schon die ~klinke in der Hand haben** to be on the point of leaving; ~**klinken putzen** *(betteln)* to go begging from house to house, *(hausieren)* to peddle, to hawk, *(sammeln)* to canvass in (on) behalf of charity.

Turm tower;
drehbarer ~ *(Panzer)* revolving turret.

türmen *(sich davonmachen)* to clear off, to blow *(sl.)*, to hop it *(sl.)*, to skedaddle, to decamp, to skip, *(Gefangener)* to break jail, to escape;
sich ~ to heap (pile) up.

turmhoch towering, lofty;
über jeden Verdacht ~ erhaben sein to be above any suspicion; **jem. ~ überlegen sein** to tower above s. o.

turmhohe Wellen mountain-high waves.

Turm|uhr tower clock; ~**verlies** dungeon.

Turnier, in einem ~ ausscheiden to be knocked out in a tournament.

Turnus turn, rota, rotation [period], course;
im ~ by rotation, rotational; **in zweijährigem ~** biennially; **sich im ~ ablösen** to take turns; **im ~ ausscheiden** to retire by rotation; **in einem zweiwöchentlichen ~ erscheinen** to be published every other week.

turnusmäßig according to the order of sequence, at regular intervals, rotational, by rotation, rotatory;
~ **ausscheiden** to retire by rotation; **erfolgversprechende Nachwuchskräfte ~ versetzen** to rotate promising executives; ~ **wechseln** to alternate, to rotate in office;
~**er Vorstandswechsel** rotation of directors; ~**er Wechsel im Amt** rotation in office.

Tür|pfosten gatepost, door post; ~**plakat** front-end space; ~**riegel** bolt; ~**schild** door (name) plate; **automatischer ~schließer** door spring; ~**schließerin** *(Theater)* usherette, boxkeeper; ~**schloß** door lock; ~**schlüssel** door key; ~**schoner** finger plate; ~**schwelle** threshold; ~**steher** *(Hotel)* doorkeeper, janitor, concierge; ~**stopper** holdback; ~**verkleidung** *(Auto)* door panel.

Tuscheln whisper, whispering.

tuscheln, über j. to whisper against s. o.

Tüte [paper]bag;
~ **kleben** to be in clink *(sl.)*, to do one's time;
das kommt nicht in die ~ nothing doing.

Tuten toot, honk;
von ~ und Blasen keine Ahnung haben not to know the first thing about it.
tuten *(Autofahrer)* to blow (honk) one's horn, *(Lokomotive)* to toot.
Tütenpapier cap paper.
Tüttelchen iota.
TÜV|-Bescheinigung roadworthiness test certificate, MOT test certificate *(Br.)*; **~-Plakette** date-stamp registration letter.
Typ type, make, model, class, style, exponent, *(Baumuster)* type, design, *(Schlag)* type, kind, sort, exponent;
von südländischem ~ of Latin look;
entgegengesetzter ~ countertype; **gängiger ~** salable type; **komischer ~** queer bird, strange fellow; **netter ~** nice fellow; **~ eines Wissenschaftlers** typical scientist;
fünf neue ~en auf den Markt bringen to put five new models on the market; **jds. ~ sein** to be s. o. after one's (own) heart; **nicht jds. ~ sein** not to suit s. one's books; **lebensfremden ~ in einen Roman zeichnen** to overdraw a character in a novel.
Type *(fig.)* queer bird (fish), strange fellow, *(Schreibmaschine)* type, *(Schrift)* letter, character;
falsche ~ *(drucktechn.)* wrong fount.
typen to typify.
Typen|bescheinigung der Hersteller production certificate; **~beschränkung** simplification of designs; **~bezeichnung** standardization; **~bild** face; **~drucker** type printer; **~druckerei** stamp type set; **~hebel** *(Schreibmaschine)* type bar; **~material verteilen** to take down characters; **~muster** [representative] sample; **~normung** standardization; **~raddrucker** wheel printer; **~reiniger** *(Schreibmaschine)* type cleaner; **~schild** type plate, *(Motor)* name plate; **~setzmaschine** typesetting machine.
typisch typical, characteristic, exemplary, representative;
~er Engländer sein to be an Englishman to the fingertips; **~er Fall** a case in point; **~e Merkmale** *(Krankheit)* character-istic symptoms.
typisieren to standardize, to typify, to personalize.
Typisierung standardization, stylization, typification.
typografisch typographical;
~e Anstalt printing shop *(US)*; **~er Punkt** typographic point.
Tyrann tyrant, despot, oppressor, oppressive ruler.
Tyrannei, Tyrannenherrschaft tyranny, despotism.
tyrannisch despotic, tyrannical, hard-headed.
tyrannisieren to oppress, to tyrannize, to domineer.
tyrannisierend, auf ~e Art und Weise in an oppressive manner.

U

U-Bahn metropolitan (underground) railway *(Br.)*, tube railway *(Br.)*, tube *(Br.)*, Metro *(Br., coll.)*, underground railroad *(US)*, subway *(US)*, underground *(Br.)*;
mit der ~ fahren to go by tube (underground) *(Br.)*;
~ausgänge issues from the underground; **~bahnsteig** subway platform *(US)*; **~benutzer** subway rider *(US)*; **~fahrschein** tube fare (ticket) *(Br.)*; **~hof** subway (tube, *Br.*) station; **~linie** tube line *(Br.)*; **~netz** subway *(US)* (underground, *Br.*) system; **~station** tube station *(Br.)*, subway station *(US)*; **~wagen** subway car *(US)*; **~werbung** underground railway advertising *(Br.)*, subway advertising *(US)*; **~zug** underground train, tube train *(Br.)*.
U-Boot U-boat, submarine;
~ auf Unterwasserfahrt submarine boat moving undersea;
~begleitschiff corvette; **~bekämpfung** submarine defence (defense, *US*); **~bunker** submarine pen; **~falle** mystery (hush, decoy) ship, decoy; **~hafen** submarine base; **~jäger** chaser; **~krieg** submarine warfare; **~kriegführung** submarine warfare; **~mutterschiff** submarine tender; **~netz** submarine net; **~ortungssystem** submarine tracking system; **~rettungsschiff** submergence rescue ship; **~streitmacht** submarine force; **~stützpunkt** submarine base; **~turm** conning tower; **~werft** submarine shipyard.
U-Schätze short-time treasury bills.
Übel evil, ill, *(Mißstand)* trouble, evil, grievance;
das kleinere ~ the lesser evil, lesser of two evils; **soziales ~** social ill;
einem ~ auf den Grund gehen to get at the root of a trouble; **das kleinere ~ wählen** of two evils choose the less.
übel bad, rotten, nasty, ill;
gar nicht so ~ not so dusty *(fam.)*;
sich nicht ~ anlassen to be quite promising; **etw. ~ aufnehmen** to take it badly; **~ ausgehen** to end badly; **jem. ~ bekommen** *(Nahrungsmittel)* not to agree with s. o.; **sich heute ganz ~ fühlen** to be feeling rotten today; **j. ~ hereinlegen** to play a dirty trick on s. o., to pull a fast one on s. o. *(sl.)*; **~ beraten sein** to be ill advised; **~ dran sein** to be ill off; **jem. ~ gesinnt sein** to be ill disposed towards s. o.; **jem. beim Autofahren ~ werden** to feel sick in a car; **j. ~ zurichten** to beat s. o. up;
Verbrecher der ~sten Sorte sein to be a criminal of the first water.
üble | Erkältung nasty cold; **~ Gegend** tough neighbo(u)rhood; **~r Geruch** nauseating smell; **~ Gerüchte über j. im Umlauf** evil reports afloat about s. o.; **in eine ~ Geschichte geraten sein** to be mixed up in a nasty affair; **in ~ Gesellschaft geraten** to get into bad company; **~s Gesöff** wicked stuff; **~r Kunde** nasty fellow, ugly customer; **sich in einer ~n Lage befinden** to be in a plight (tight spot); **~r Laune sein** to be in a filthy mood; **~ Nachreden über j. verbreiten** to calumniate (slander) s. o.; **~r Ruf** ill (bad) repute; **~ Spelunke** low dive; **~s Subjekt** bad lot (egg) *(sl.)*; **~r Trick** dirty trick; **~s Wetter** nasty (rotten, awkward) weather; **sich in einem ~n Zustand befinden** to be in a bad state of repair (pretty mess).
Übles von jem. reden to speak badly (evil) of s. o.
übel | beleumdet ill-reputed, of ill fame; **~gesinnt** ill-disposed.
Übelkeit sickness, nausea, squeamishness;
jem. ~ verursachen to turn s. one's stomach.
übelnehmen, etw. to take umbrage (huff, pet) at s. th.; **Bemerkung äußerst ~** to take a remark in very bad part; **leicht ~** to have a disposition to take offence.
übelnehmerisch huffish, easily offended.
übelriechend noxious, foul, stinking, fetid.
Übelsein sickness, nausea.
Übelstand grievance, trouble, abuse, mischief;
einem ~ abhelfen to redress a grievance, to remedy an abuse.
Übel | tat misdeed, offence, misdemeanor, crime; **~täter** wrongdoer, evildoer, malefactor, misdemeanant.
übelwollen, jem. to be ill disposed towards s. o.
übelwollend evil-minded, malevolent.
Üben exercise, practice;
regelmäßiges ~ regular practice.
üben, sich to practice, to practise *(Br.)*, to train; **Geduld ~** to show patience; **sich in Höflichkeit ~** to practise politeness; **Klavier ~** to practise on the piano; **Kritik ~** to criticize; **Verrat ~** to commit an act of treachery.
Über-die-Verhältnisse-Leben dissaving.
überaltert obsolete, superannuated.
Überalterung excess of age, obsolescence, *(Person)* superannuation;
geplante ~ planned obsolescence;
~ der Bevölkerung aging of the population; **~ der Wirtschaftsgüter** industrial obsolescence.
Überangebot glut, oversupply, surplus stocks, excess offer, excessive (overhead) supply;
~ an Arbeitskräften labo(u)r glut, surplus manpower, overcrowded labo(u)r market, abundance of labo(u)r supply; **~ an Büroräumen** office glut; **~ an Waren** excessive supply.
überängstlich overanxious, panicky.
überanstrengen to overlabo(u)r, to overtax, to overstrain;
sich ~ to exert (overdo, overwork, overexert) o. s.; **seine Augen ~** to strain one's eyes, to play heavily upon the sight.
überanstrengt strained, exhausted.
Überanstrengung overwork, overexertion, fatigue, overtoil.
überantworten to surrender, to commit;
jem. eine Abteilung ~ to put s. o. in charge of a department; **Kind den Großeltern ~** to hand over a child to the grandparents.
Überantwortung *(Übeltäter)* surrender, commitment.
Überanzug overall.
überarbeiten to rework, to retouch, to finish, *(Buch)* to revise, *(noch einmal machen)* to work over, to remake;
sich ~ to kill o. s. with work, to overstrain o. s., to burn the candle at both ends; **Buch ~** to revise a book; **nochmals ~** to touch up; **Programm ~** to touch up a program(me).
überarbeitet overworked, *(Buch)* revised.
Überarbeitung *(Buch)* revision, revised edition, *(letzter Schliff)* finishing touch, retouch, *(Überanstrengung)* occupational fatigue, overwork;
~ eines Buches revision of a book.
Überbau encroachment, superstructure, projecting part.
überbauen to overbuild.
überbeanspruchen, j. to overtax (overwork) s. o.
Überbeanspruchung overemployment, overstress, overstrain, overexertion, *(Maschine)* overload;
~ des Kapitalmarktes crowding out of the capital market.
Überbedarf excessive demand.
über | belasten to overload; **~belastet** overtaxed, overburdened, *(Maschine)* overloaded; **~belegen** to overbook, to overcrowd.
überbelegt *(Haus)* overcrowded;
~e Wohnung crowded dwelling.
Überbelegung overcrowding.
überbelichten to overtime, *(beim Kopieren)* to overprint.
überbelichtet overexposed, too dense.
Überbelichtung overexposure.
überbeschäftigt overbusy.
Überbeschäftigung overemployment, overful employment *(US)*, hyperemployment.
überbesetzt overcrowded, overstaffed.
Überbesetzung | mit Arbeitskräften overmanning, overstaffing, featherbedding *(US)*; **~ von Arbeitsplätzen** restrictive labo(u)r practices;
personelle ~ abbauen to cut overmanning.
Überbestände excess stocks.
überbesteuern to overtax.
Überbesteuerung excessive taxation, overtaxation;
inflationsbedingte ~ overtaxation by inflation.
überbevölkert overpopulated.
Über | bevölkerung congestion of population, surplus population, overpopulation; **~bevorratung** overstocking.
überbewerten to overvalue, to overestimate, to set too high a value on, to overstate, *(Vermögen)* to overassess;
sich ~ to have an exaggerated sense of one's own importance; **jds. Fähigkeiten ~** to overrate s. one's abilities; **seine Tätigkeit nicht ~** to be modest about one's achievements.
überbewertet *(Wertpapier)* top-heavy;
~es Buch overrated book.
Überbewertung overvaluation, overestimate, *(Vermögen)* overassessment, *(Wertpapiere)* top-heaviness.
überbezahlen to overpay, to pay through the nose.
Überbieten higher bid, outbidding, overbid;
~ aus Konkurrenzgründen squeeze pricing *(US)*.
überbieten to bid up, to overbid, to outbid, to bid higher (in), to buy over one's head;
j. ~ to bid against s. o.; **Rekord ~** to beat a record.

Über|bietender, ~bieter outbidder.
Überbleibsel holdover, rest, remnants, rump, oddments, relic, fag end, hangover *(US)*, refuse *(Br.)*, *(Restbestände)* remainder, remains, *(Rückstand)* residue *(Br.)*, *(Speise)* leftover;
einige ~ some residuary odds and ends; **trauriges ~** snuff; **kümmerliche ~ verlorengegangener Traditionen** loose detritus of lost traditions *(coll.)*; **~ aus alter Zeit** survival of former times.
überblenden to fade, to dissolve;
von einer Szene in die andere ~ to fade one scene into another.
Überblendverschluß dissolving shutter.
Überblick view, review, survey, summary, *(ungefähre Vorstellung)* general account (idea);
allgemeiner ~ general survey; **flüchtiger ~** skim; **umfassender ~** comprehensive survey; **vollständiger ~** panorama;
kritischer ~ über jds. Gesamtwerk general review of s. one's works; **~ über die allgemeinen Lohnverhältnisse** community wage survey;
sich einen ersten ~ über ein Fachgebiet beschaffen to get a general idea of a subject; **~ geben** to outline; **allgemeinen ~ über jds. Arbeiten geben** to give a general view of s. one's works; **~ über ein Buch geben** to give a general idea of a book; **~ über die internationale Lage geben** to survey the international situation; **~ über ein Fachgebiet haben** to have a general knowledge of a field; **über die Anzahl seiner Bücher den ~ verloren haben** to have lost count of one's books; **~ über die Lage völlig verloren haben** to have completely lost track of things.
überblicken to survey, to review;
politische Lage im Augenblick nicht ~ to be out of touch with the political situation; **Situation sofort ~** to sum up the situation at a glance;
Sache nicht ~ können to be beyond s. one's grasp;
soweit ich die Lage ~ kann as far as I can see.
Überbord overside, overboard;
~ablieferung overside delivery; **~auslieferungsklausel** overside delivery clause; **~spülen** washing overboard; **~werfen** jettison.
überbringen to deliver, to hand over, to present, *(übermitteln)* to transmit;
Glückwünsche ~ to convey gratulations; **Nachricht ~** to deliver a message.
Überbringer bearer, deliverer, carrier, bringer, conveyer, *(Scheck)* bearer, *(Wechsel)* presenter;
auf den ~ lautend in bearer form; **durch ~** per bearer; **zahlbar an ~** payable to bearer;
~ dieses Briefes bearer of this letter; **~ schlechter Nachrichten** porter of ill news; **~ dieser Unterlagen** bearer of these presents; **~klausel** bearer clause; **~scheck** bearer check (cheque, *Br.*).
Überbringung delivery, surrender, *(Übermittlung)* transmission.
überbrücken to bridge (fill) a gap, to overbridge, to tide over;
Gegensätze ~ to reconcile differences; **Schwierigkeit ~** to bridge over a difficulty; **um die arbeitslose Zeit zu ~** to tide over a period of unemployment.
überbrückend, Kontinent nation-spanning.
Überbrückung bridge-over, tiding over, interim aid, stopgap;
j. bei der ~ von Schwierigkeiten helfen to hold out a hand to s. o.
Überbrückungs|darlehn bridge-over advance; **~fazilitäten** bridge-over facilities; **~finanzierung** temporary (interim) financing; **~gelder** stopgap money; **~hilfe** stopgap (interim) aid, gratuity; **~kredit** interim (tide-over) credit, accommodation (bridging, transitional, stopgap, hold-over, interim) loan; **~maßnahmen** bridging transactions, temporary (interim) measures; **~reserve** carryover; **~zahlungen** transitional payments.
überbürden, Kosten jem. to award the costs against s. o.; **j. mit Steuern ~** to overburden s. o. with taxes.
Überbürdung der Kosten auf die Staatskasse awarding the costs against the state.
über|dachen to roof; **~dauern** to outlive, to outlast, to outwear.
Überdecke bedspread.
überdecken *(Störsender)* to blanket;
mit einer Plane ~ to tilt.
Überdeckung excess cover (coverage).
überdenken to think over, to turn over in one's mind, to reconsider;
Politik ~ to rethink its policy.
überdosieren to overdose.
Überdosis overdose.
überdreht excentric, *(Kind)* overexcited.
Überdruck excess pressure, overpressure, *(Briefmarke)* surcharge, *(Buch)* surplus, surprint;
~anzug pressure suit.
überdrucken *(Postwertzeichen)* to surprint, to overprint.
Überdruck|kabine pressurized cabin; **~papier** transfer paper *(Br.)*; **~ventil** safety valve.
überdrüssig weary, tired of;
einer Sache ~ sein to be fed up with it *(coll.)*.
überdurchschnittlich above average (standard), supernormal;
~e Leistung outstanding performance; **~e Wohnung** above-average dwelling.
Übereifer overzeal, busybodyism, bustle.
übereifrig overeager, overkeen, bustling, busybodyish;
~ sein to be a good deal too zealous;
~er Mensch busybody.
übereignen to make over, to pass title, to transfer ownership, to assign, to alienate;
Grundstück ~ to convey land to a purchaser; **sicherheitshalber ~** to place in escrow.
Übereignung making over, transfer [of title], assignment, alienation, *(Grundstück)* conveyance;
bedingte ~ conditional conveyance; **fiduzarische ~** trust receipt *(US)*; **unentgeltliche ~** voluntary conveyance; **urkundliche ~** grant by deed;
~ eines Grundstücks conveyance of real estate, assignment of property; **~ durch eine Mittelsperson** mesne conveyance; **~ frei von allen Rechten** absolute conveyance;
~ vornehmen to make a conveyance.
Übereignungsurkunde deed of conveyance.
übereilt rash, precipitate, hurried;
~e Schlüsse ziehen to jump to conclusions.
Übereinanderkopieren *(Foto)* process.
Übereinkommen agreement, arrangement, understanding, convention, condition, stipulation, settlement, bond, *(Gläubigervergleich)* composition, compromise;
laut ~ as agreed upon;
gebündeltes ~ package settlement; **gegenseitiges ~** understanding; **internationales ~** international convention; **stillschweigendes ~** silent (tacit, implicit) agreement;
~ zur Steigerung der Produktivität productivity deal;
gewisses ~ jem. gegenüber aufrechterhalten to hold terms with s. o.; **~ bestätigen** to confirm an agreement; **~ kündigen** to denounce a treaty; **~ treffen** to enter into an agreement, to compact; **~ mit seinen Gläubigern treffen** to arrange (compound) with one's creditors.
übereinkommen to agree, to come to (enter into, make, reach) an agreement, to come to an understanding (to terms), to settle, to bargain, to stipulate.
Übereinkunft agreement, arrangement, compact, composition, convention, understanding, treaty;
in gegenseitiger ~ by mutual consent; **laut ~** by agreement; **laut allgemeiner ~** by general compact; **mangels ~** in default of agreement;
grundsätzliche ~ agreement in principle;
internationale ~ über den Eisenbahnfrachtverkehr International Agreement on Railway Freight Traffic;
zu einer ~ mit jem. gelangen to come to (arrive at) an agreement with s. o.; **~ mit jem. haben** to be in agreement with s. o.
übereinstimmen to agree, to be of accord (in accordance, in line with), to cotton, to hitch, to jibe *(US coll.)*, *(Bücher)* to [be] conform, to run with, to tally *(Br.)*, *(Konten)* to agree, to be in keeping with, *(Sachen)* to correspond, to be in agreement;
mit jem. ~ to share s. one's opinion, to be in agreement (key, agree) with s. o., to hold with s. o. (s. one's opinion); **mit der Beschreibung ~** to answer to description, *(Waren)* to correspond with the description; **gut ~** *(Farben)* to match (blend) well; **mit jem. hundertprozentig ~** to be in wholehearted agreement (see eye to eye) with s. o.; **miteinander ~** *(Konten)* to duplicate with one another; **nicht ~** to jar, to dissent, *(Debet- und Krediteintragungen)* to be out of balance, *(Konten)* to disagree, *(Zeugenaussagen)* to differ; **in einer Sache mit jem. ~** to join issue with s. o. on s. th. *(fam.)*; **mit jem. sofort ~** to fall in with s. one's view at once; **mit einer Vertragsbestimmung ~** to conform to a clause.
übereinstimmend conform[able], concordant, congruent, consistent, consonant, corresponding, accordant with (to), *(Bücher)* in conformity with, *(einmütig)* unanimous, *(gleichlautend)* identical;
~ gebucht booked in conformity; **nicht ~** discrepant;
mit Ihren Büchern ~ conformable to your books; **mit dem Muster ~** matching the sample; **mit dem Original ~** corresponding to the original;
~ buchen to enter (book) in conformity;
~e Buchung corresponding entry; **~e Meinung** consensus of

opinion; ~e **Meldungen** concurrent reports; **nach dem ~en Urteil der Sachverständigen** according to the unanimous judgment (concurrent views) of the experts; ~e **Zeugenaussagen** concordant depositions.

Übereinstimmung concurrence, concord, conformance, consonance, consensus, congruence, unity, union, agreement, accord, keeping, *(Einheitlichkeit)* uniformity, *(Konten)* conformity;
in ~ mit in conformity (accordance, concordance, keeping, line, *US*) with; **in ~ mit den Ausführungen des Vorredners** in keeping with the remarks of the previous speaker; **in ~ mit den Bedingungen** in accordance with the terms; **in ~ mit den Experten** according to the best authorities; **in ~ mit der Rechtssprechung** in accordance with prevailing cases in law; **in ~ mit der Tagesordnung** agreeable to the order of the day; **in vollständiger ~** in wholehearted agreement;
allgemeine ~ general agreement, contention, common consent; **farbliche ~** harmony of colo(u)rs; **gedankliche ~** notional agreement; **mangelnde ~** incongruity, disagreement; **zeitliche ~** synchronization;
~ **mit der Beschreibung** *(Waren)* correspondence with description; ~ **der Ereignisse** coincidence of events; ~ **mit dem Markenbild** brand identity; ~ **der Willenserklärungen** meeting of minds;
in ~ bringen *(Texte, Steuern)* to harmonize; **Einnahmen mit den Ausgaben in ~ bringen** to make the receipts tally with the expenses; **Konten in ~ bringen** to make accounts agree, to reconcile (tally, readjust) accounts; **Konten wieder in ~ bringen** to readjust accounts; **Rechnungen in ~ bringen** to agree accounts; ~ **erzielen** to reach an agreement; **in vielen Punkten zu einer ~ gelangen** to reach an agreement on many points; **in ~ mit den gesetzlichen Bestimmungen handeln** to conform to the provisions of the law; ~ **in der öffentlichen Meinung herbeiführen** to line up public opinion.

Überemission overissue.

überemissionieren to overissue.

überempfindlich | reagieren to overreact;
~e **Nerven haben** to be high-strung.

über | entwickeln to overdevelop; ~**erfüllen** to overfill.

überfahren to run (drive) over, to knock down, *(Stoppschild)* to overshoot;
j. ~ *(fig.)* to walk over s. o.; **Signal** ~ to ignore a signal; **Stoppschild** ~ to overshoot a stop signal;
beinahe vom Omnibus ~ worden sein to come very near to be knocked down by the bus; **um ein Haar ~ werden** to narrowly miss being run over.

Überfahrt passage, [channel] crossing *(Br.)*, transit;
ruhige ~ smooth passage; **schnelle ~** quick passage; **stürmische ~** rough passage;
bezahlte ~ für Einwanderer *(Australia)* nominated passage;
seine ~ abarbeiten to work one's passage; **seine ~ bezahlen** to pay for one's passage; **gute ~ haben** to have a smooth crossing (passage).

Überfahrtsgeld *(Fähre)* ferriage, fare, *(Schiff)* passage [money].

Überfahrtstelle traject.

Überfahrtsvertrag passage contract.

Überfall raid, robbery, holdup *(US)*, attack, do, onslaught, assault, *(auf ein Land)* invasion, aggression, descent, depredation, raid, inroad;
bewaffneter ~ highway robbery, armed robbery (raid), holdup *(US sl.)*; **militärischer ~** army raid;
~ **auf eine Bank** raid on a bank by armed men, bank robbery.

überfallen to attack, to assault, to hold up, to raid;
j. ~ to beat s. one's quarters; **Bankboten ~** to assault a bank messenger; **j. mit einer Bitte ~** to spring a request on s. o.; **j. mit einer Frage ~** to fire off (bombard) a question at s. o.; **feindliches Lager ~** to make a raid upon the enemy's camp; **Land ~** to raid a country; **Sparkasse ~** to make a raid on a savings bank; **Stadt ~** to assail a city; **j. mit einem neuen Vorschlag ~** to spring a new proposition on s. o.; **Zug ~** to hold up a train *(US)*;
von einer plötzlichen Schwäche ~ werden to be overcome by a sudden fit of weakness.

überfällig overdue, past-due, *(Flugzeug)* missing, *(Schiff)* out of time;
längst ~ long past due;
~ **sein** *(Wechsel)* to lie over;
~**er Wechsel** bill overdue, past-due bill *(US)*.

Überfälligkeit von Saisonware obsolescence of seasonal goods.

Überfall | kommando flying (riot, *US*) squad, raiding party; ~**kommando anrufen** to dial the police station, to send a riot call *(US)*; ~**nummer** emergency number; ~**ruf** emergency (riot) call; ~**versicherung** riot and civil commotion insurance, personal holdup insurance *(US)*; ~**wagen** police van (waggon), flying squad, squad car *(US)*.

Überfliegen, unerlaubtes overflight;
~ **eines Gebiets** flight over a territory; ~ **mit Handelsflugzeugen** commercial overflight.

überfliegen to fly over, to overfly;
Brief ~ to glance (skim) over a letter; **Buch ~** to skim through a book; **Gebiet ~** to fly over a territory; **in geringer Höhe ~** to buzz; **Ozean ~** to fly the ocean.

Überfliegungsrechte overflying rights.

überfließen to well over;
von Reichtum ~ to overflow with riches.

überflügeln to outpass, to outstrip, to surpass, to outflank, to outdistance;
seine Konkurrenz ~ to get the jump on one's competitors.

Überfluß abundance, overabundance, superabundance, overflow, oversupply, glut, overstock, plenty, surplus, store, exuberance, superfluity, *(Arbeitskräfte)* redundance, *(Reichtum)* wealth, *(Wohlstand)* affluence, abundance, opulence, luxury;
im ~ galore, abundant, thick; **zu allem ~** to crown all, to make matters worse;
reichlicher ~ plentiful supply;
~ **an Nahrungsmitteln** superabundance of food;
~ **an etw. haben** to abound in s. th.; ~ **an Bargeld haben** to have cash galore; ~ **an Geld haben** to be flush of (have oodles of) money; **im ~ leben** to live in abundance (plenty, clover, luxury); **im ~ vorhanden sein** to overabound;
~**gesellschaft** affluent (opulent) society, abundance economy.

überflüssig abundant, redundant, in excess, superfluous, surplus, *(unerwünscht)* unwanted, undesirable, *(unnötig)* needless, uncalled-for;
~**e Arbeit** unnecessary labo(u)r; ~**e Bemerkung** superfluity; ~**e Person** fifth wheel at the coach; ~**es Zimmer** spare room.

Überflußperiode affluent years.

überfluten to overflow, *(absichtlich)* to inundate, to flood, *(Markt)* to flood, *(Touristen)* to overrun;
Gebiet ~ to flood a region; **Land im Sommer ~** to flood the land in summer; **Markt ~** to flood the market.

überflutet under water.

Überflutung flood, overflow, submergence, inundation.

überfordern to overcharge, to overtask, to overtax, to surcharge;
jds. Geduld ~ to be straining the limits of s. one's patience; **Kind ~** to ask too much of a child.

Überforderung overcharge [claim], excessive charge (demand), surcharge, overtaxing;
betrügerische ~ fraudulent overcharge;
~ **eines Kindes** excessive demands on a child.

Überfracht overfreight, excess freight, *(Flugzeug)* excess luggage *(Br.)* (baggage, *US*).

überfragt sein to be stumped.

überfremden to bring under foreign control.

überfremdet foreign-controlled.

Überfremdung foreign control (influence), control by foreign capital.

überführen to convey, to transport, *(Flugzeugtransport)* to ferry, *(Geldmittel)* to transfer, *(Verbrecher)* to convict, to find guilty of a charge, to bring home;
j. ~ to bring a charge home to s. o., to prove s. one's guilt; **in städtischen Besitz ~** to municipalize; **in Gemeineigentum ~** to nationalize, to socialize, to communize; **in ein anderes Krankenhaus ~** to transfer to another hospital; **in die Privatwirtschaft ~** to denationalize, to hive off state industries.

überführt, aufgrund eigener Aussagen self-convicted;
~ **sein** to stand convicted.

Überführung transport, transfer, conveyance, *(mit Flugzeug)* ferry, *(Überbau)* viaduct, overhead way, bridge over the line, overbridge *(Br.)*, flyover *(Br.)*, *(Verbrecher)* conviction;
kreuzungsfreie ~ overpass; **schienengleiche ~** level *(Br.)* (grade, *US*) crossing;
~ **in städtischen Besitz** municipalization; ~ **in ein Gefängnis** commitment to prison; ~ **in Gemeineigentum** nationalization, socialization, communization; ~ **in die Privatwirtschaft** denationalization, hive-off of state industries; ~ **in die Zivilverwaltung** demilitarization.

Überführungs | dienst *(Flugzeug)* ferry; ~**flug** ferrying flight; ~**kommando** ferry command; ~**kosten** *(Auto)* destination charges; ~**route** *(Flugzeug)* ferry line; ~**stück** *(Straftäter)* exhibit.

Überfülle glut, overabundance, ful(l)ness, opulence, superabundance;
~ **schöner Dinge** milk and honey.
überfüllen to overcrowd, to cram, *(Gefäß)* to overfill;
Markt ~ to glut (overstock) the market.
überfüllt *(Gefäß)* overfilled, *(Lager)* overstocked, *(Markt)* glutted, *(Straße)* crowded, jammed, congested, blocked, *(Versammlung)* stuffed, packed [to capacity], mobbed;
mit Menschen ~ crammed with people;
restlos ~ **sein** to be packed and more than packed;
~**er Berufszweig** [over]crowded profession; ~**er Hafen** congested harbo(u)r; ~**er Zug** overcrowded (packed) train; ~**er Zuhörerraum** crowded audience.
Überfüllung crowded state, *(Verkehrsverstopfung)* congestion;
wegen ~ **geschlossen** house full, full up *(Br.)*;
~ **des Marktes** glut in the market.
überfüttern to overfeed, *(fig.)* to heap, to cram.
Übergabe delivery, deliverance, surrender, turning in, consignment, *(Auslieferung)* extradition, *(Besitzverschaffung)* delivery, tradition, transfer, *(Einreichung)* filing, handing in, *(mil.)* surrender, *(Vorlage)* submission, submittal, submitting;
bei ~ **zahlbar** cash on delivery; **bis zur** ~ pending delivery; **gegen** ~ **der Dokumente zahlbar** payable against surrender of documents;
bedingungslose ~ unconditional surrender; **fiktive (fingierte)** ~ symbolic[al] delivery; **gültige** ~ valid delivery; **mittelbare** ~ constructive delivery; **ordnungsgemäße** ~ authorized delivery; **tatsächliche** ~ manual (actual) delivery; **unsachgemäße** ~ improper delivery;
~ **des Beschuldigten zwecks Kautionsfreigabe** surrender by bail; ~ **der Dokumente** transmission of documents; ~ **einer Festung an den Feind** surrender of a fortress to the enemy; ~ **zu treuen Händen an einen Dritten** *(Urkunde)* delivery in escrow *(US)*; ~ **in Raten** delivery in instal(l)ments; ~ **einer Stadt** surrendering of a town; ~ **eines Straftäters** surrender of a criminal; ~ **der Ware an die Eisenbahn** delivery of the goods into the custody of the railway *(Br.)*;
zur ~ **auffordern** to summon to (demand) surrender;
~**aufforderung** summons to surrender; ~**bedingungen** terms of surrender, surrender terms; ~**bescheinigung** delivery receipt; ~**frist** time of delivery; ~**klausel** delivery clause; ~**lotse** handover controller; ~**ort** handing-over point; ~**pflicht des Verkäufers** seller's duty to deliver; ~**protokoll** *(mil.)* instrument of surrender; ~**verhandlungen** *(mil.)* negotiations for surrender; ~**verweigerung** refusal to make delivery; ~**wert** transfer value.
Übergang *(Fußgängerbrücke)* footbridge, *(Parteiwechsel)* conversion, *(Rechte)* transition, change, transfer, passage, *(Verkehr)* passage, crossing, *(Wechsel)* switch, change;
für den ~ as an interim; **ohne** ~ without introduction;
kein ~ no crossing; **schienengleicher** ~ level *(Br.)* (grade, *US*) crossing;
~ **von der Bahn auf die Busbenutzung** switch from rail to bus; ~ **des Eigentums** devolution of title, passing of property; ~ **für Fußgänger** pedestrian lines (crossing), zebra crossing; ~ **der Gefahr** passage (passing) of risk; ~ **auf die tote Hand** mortification *(Scot.)*; ~ **von der zweiten in die erste Klasse** change from second to first class; ~ **zur Konvertierbarkeit** removes to convertibility; ~ **zur Oppositionspartei** floor crossing *(Br.)*; ~ **zur Tagesordnung** proceeding (passing) to the order of the day; ~ **von Todes wegen** transfer on death, devolution upon death (of inheritance, *US*); ~ **von Verwaltungsbefugnissen** devolution of authority;
~ **zur Tagesordnung beantragen** to move the previous question.
Übergangs|abkommen transitional arrangement, transitory treaty; ~**bahnhof** junction, transit station, transfer depot *(US)*; ~**beschäftigung** change-over employment, temporary job; ~**bestimmungen** provisional regulations, temporary (transition, transitory, transitional) provisions; ~**entschädigung**, ~**geld** severance benefit (pay) *(US)*, redundancy payment *(Br.)*; ~**fahrkarte**, ~**fahrschein** excess (transfer, intermediate, *US*) ticket; ~**gesetz** validating (temporary) statute, provisional law; ~**hilfe** stopgap (interim) aid, redundancy pay *(Br.)*, *(Wehrpflichtiger)* gratuity; ~**jahr** transitional year; ~**kabinett** caretaker cabinet; **Land acht Monate als** ~**kabinett regieren** to run the country on a caretaker basis for eight months; ~**klausel** shifting clause; ~**konto** suspense (transit, transitory) account; ~**lösung** transitional solution; ~**mantel** interseasonal coat; ~**maßnahmen** transitional (temporary) measures; ~**mode** interseason fashion; ~**periode**, ~**phase** intervening (transitional, transitory) period, [period of] transition, passing phase, *(Lebensabschnitt)* change of life; ~**politik** devolution policy; ~**posten** suspense entries, *(transitorische Posten)* transitory (deferred) items *(US)*; ~**prozeß** process of transition; ~**punkt** crossing point, checkpoint; ~**regelung** temporary (transitional, provisional) arrangement; ~**regierung** provisional (transitional, caretaker) government, interregnum; ~**stadium** transitional stage; **sich in einem** ~**stadium befinden** to be in a state of transition; ~**station** junction, transit station, transfer depot *(US)*; ~**stelle** crossing point, crossover, turnpike; ~**streifen** *(Flugplatz)* shoulder; ~**tarif** interim rate; ~**verkehr** transit traffic; ~**vertrag** transitive covenant; ~**verwaltung** interim administration; ~**vorschriften** temporary (transitional) provisions; ~**wahrscheinlichkeit** transition probability; ~**wirtschaft der Nachkriegszeit** postwar transitional period; ~**zahlung** transitional payment; ~**zeit** transition[al] (intervening, transitory) period, [period of] transition; ~**zeit durchmachen** to undergo a transition; ~**zustand** transitional stage.
übergeben *(abliefern)* to turn in, to surrender, *(anvertrauen)* to commit, to consign, to entrust, *(einhändigen)* to hand in (over), to present, to give in, *(liefern)* to deliver, *(überlassen)* to give up to, to abandon, *(übertragen)* to transfer;
jem. ~ to give in charge of s. o.; **sich** ~ to be sick, to vomit, to throw up; **sein Amt dem neuen Vormund** ~ to resign a ward to a new guardian; **jem. etw. zum Aufbewahren** ~ to give s. th. in s. one's charge; **einer Bank Geld zum Aufbewahren** ~ to deposit money in a bank; **jem. etw. eigenhändig** ~ to deliver into s. one's hands; **jem. die Erledigung einer Angelegenheit** ~ to place a matter into s. one's hands; **Festung dem Feind** ~ to deliver [up] a fortress to the enemy; **den Flammen** ~ to consign to the flames; **jds. Fürsorge** ~ to commit to s. one's care; **jem. Geld zur Aufbewahrung** ~ to leave a sum of money in s. one's custody; **Geld direkt** ~ to hand over the money direct; **jem. dem Gericht** ~ to hand s. o. over to justice; **Geschäft seinem Nachfolger** ~ to turn over a business to one's successor; **jem. etw. zu treuen Händen** ~ to entrust to the care of (confide) s. th. to s. o., to deliver s. th. into s. one's charge; **jem. das Kommando** ~ to hand over the command to s. o.; **jds. Obhut** ~ to commit to the charge of s. o.; **der Öffentlichkeit** ~ to bring before the public; **Sachen dem Gastwirt zur Aufbewahrung** ~ to deliver goods into the personal custody of the innkeeper; **Sache dem Gericht** ~ to submit to the court for decision; **Sache einem Rechtsanwalt** ~ to put a matter into the hands of a lawyer; **Scheck einer Bank zum Einzug** ~ to lodge a cheque (check, *US*) with a bank for collection; **schlüsselfertig** ~ to turn it over ready to turn a key; **dem Verkehr** ~ to open to traffic; **jem. seine Visitenkarte** ~ to hand one's card to s. o.; **jem. Waren vertragsgemäß** ~ to bail goods to s. o.
Übergebot higher (further) bid, outbidding, overbid.
Übergebühr surcharge.
übergebührlich excessively, unduly;
jds. Zeit ~ **in Anpruch nehmen** to encroach upon s. one's time.
übergegangen passed, devolved upon;
seit vielen Generationen vom Vater auf den Sohn ~ **sein** to have been handed down from father to son for many generations.
Übergehen skip, *(Beförderung)* jump;
~ **bei letztwilliger Verfügung** preterition, pretermission.
übergehen to devolve upon, *(auslassen)* to omit, to leave out, *(Eigentum)* to devolve upon, to descend, to pass, *(Erben auslassen)* to pretermit, *(Farben)* to merge, to blend, *(Gefahr)* to pass, *(Lager wechseln)* to go over, *(Rechte)* to subrogate, *(vernachlässigen)* to neglect, to overlook, to disregard;
j. ~ to pass s. o. over, to omit s. o., to leave s. o. out; **auf j.** ~ *(Erbschaft)* to lapse to s. o.; **von der Bahn- zur Busbenutzung** ~ to switch from rail to bus; **j. bei der Beförderung** ~ to pass over s. one's head; **anderen bei der Beförderung** ~ to be put over s. one's head; **in jds. Besitz** ~ to pass into the possession of s. o.; **einige Buchseiten** ~ to skip some pages in a book; **auf die Erben** ~ to pass to (devolve upon) the heirs; **zum Feind** ~ to go over to the enemy; **zur Gegenpartei** ~ to change sides, to cross the floor of the house *(Br.)*, to flop over *(US)*, to rat; **in andere Hände** ~ to change (pass into other) hands; **seinen Hunger** ~ to ignore one's hunger; **kommentarlos** ~ to pass without remark (comment); **auf den Nachfolger** ~ to devolve upon the successor; **zur Opposition** ~ to cross the floor *(Br.)*, to flop over *(US coll.)*; **zum nächsten Punkt der Tagesordnung** ~ to proceed to the next business (next item on the agenda); **zur Republikanischen Partei** ~ to switch to the Republicans; **jds. Schwächen** ~ to slur over s. one's faults; **auf den ältesten Sohn** ~ to portion to the eldest son; **vom Vater auf den Sohn** ~ to descend from father to son; **Sache mit Stillschweigen** ~ to pass

over an affair with silence; **stufenweise** ~ to gradate; **zur Tagesordnung** ~ to pass (proceed) to the order of the day; **zu einem neuen Thema** ~ to pass on to a new subject; **beim Todesfall** ~ to pass on (devolve upon) death; **auf einen großen Verband** ~ to merge into a large organization; **beim Verkauf** ~ *(Eigentum)* to pass by sale; **in Verwesung** ~ to putrefy, to decay; **auf den Vizepräsidenten** ~ to devolve upon the vice-president.
Übergehung disregard, neglect *(bei Beförderung)* omission, *(Erben)* preterition, pretermission.
übergenau scrupulous, punctilious, precise.
übergenug enough and to spare.
übergeordnet subordinate, upper, paramount, overriding, *(Gericht)* superior, *(Recht)* senior;
jem. ~ **sein** to have authority over s. o.;
von ~er Bedeutung of overriding importance; **~e Behörde** higher (superior) authority; **~es Gericht** court above, superior (higher) court.
Übergepäck excess luggage *(Br.)* (baggage, *US*).
übergeschnappt off one's (touched in the) head, crazy;
völlig ~ as mad as a hatter.
Übergeschnapptheit, wissenschaftliche mad professordom.
übergetreten sein to be a convert.
Übergewicht overweight, overload, extra (surplus) weight, *(fig.)* preponderance, prevalence, predominance, *(Gepäck)* overfreight, luggage in excess *(Br.)*, excess luggage *(Br.)* (baggage, *US*);
militärisches ~ military superiority; **politisches** ~ political ascendancy;
~ **über j. gewinnen** to gain ascendance (the upper hand) over s. o.; ~ **haben** to preponderate.
Übergewinn excess (extra, surplus, *US*) profit;
~steuer excess profits duty (levy) *(Br.)*, supertax *(Br.)*, general excess profits tax *(US)*.
übergewissenhaft overscrupulous.
überglücklich extremely happy, delirious with joy.
übergreifen to encroach upon, to infringe, to overlap, *(Feuer)* to spread to, *(Seuche, Streik)* to spread;
in jds. Rechte ~ to encroach upon s. one's rights.
Übergriff encroachment, infringement, interference, incursion, invasion, inroad, impingement, *(Grundstück)* trespass;
~ **in jds. Rechte** infringement of (encroachment upon) s. one's rights.
übergroß extra-big, outsized.
Übergröße outsize, oversize, King size, overproportion, giant package;
~n *(Schrift)* display type;
keine ~n führen to stock no outsizes.
überhaben to have left over, *(überdrüssig sein)* to be sick of (fed up with) s. th.
Überhandnehmen prevalence, rampancy, spread, rapid growth;
~ **einer Krankheit** spread (progress) of a disease; ~ **von Mordfällen** prevalence of murder; ~ **des Verkehrs** traffic seizure.
überhandnehmen to be rampant, to grow rapidly, to be prevalent, to spread, to gather head, to be rife.
Überhang *(Baum)* overrun, overhang, overhanging branches, *(Buchung)* carryover, *(Geld)* surplus money, *(Geldmarkt)* glut of money, *(Lager)* surplus, overhang;
~ **der Aktiva** excess of assets; ~ **an Angeboten** surplus of offers; ~ **an Aufträgen** backlog of unfilled orders; ~ **der Ausgaben über die Einnahmen** excess of expenditures over revenues; ~ **von Büroräumen** office glut; ~ **an Investitionen** excess of capital investments; ~ **der Zahlungsausgänge** negative cashflow.
überhängen to overhang.
überhängend overhanging, *(Gebäudeteil)* cantilevering, projecting.
überhäufen to overwhelm, to load with, to overleap, to heap, *(Lager)* to overstock;
mit Arbeit ~ to snow under with work; **j. mit Ehrungen** ~ to shower hono(u)rs upon s. o.; **mit Fragen** ~ to pepper (plague, ply) with questions; **j. mit Komplimenten** ~ to heap compliments upon s. o.; **Markt** ~ to overstock (glut) the market; **mit Papieren** ~ to swamp with papers.
überhäuft *(Markt)* glutted, swamped;
mit Anträgen ~ **sein** to be snowed under with applications; **mit Arbeit** ~ **sein** to be over head and ears in work, to be snowed under with work; **mit Aufträgen** ~ **sein** to be overwhelmed with orders.
Überhäufung *(des Marktes)* glut.
überhaupt nicht not for nuts *(sl.)*;
~ **interessiert sein** not to be in the slightest degree interested.
überheblich overbearing, high-handed, arrogant, presumptuous;
~ **werden** to get above o. s.
Überheblichkeit arrogance, pride, overbearance, high-handedness.
überheizen to overheat.
überhitzen, Konjunktur to overheat (overtax) the economy.
überhitzte Konjunktur overtaxed (excessive) boom, overheated economy.
Überhitzung der Konjunktur overheating (overtaxing) of the boom.
überhöhen *(Kurve)* to bank, *(Schiene)* to superelevate.
überhöht excessive, exaggerated, *(Kurve)* superelevated, banked;
mit ~er Geschwindigkeit fahren to exceed the speed limit; **~e Kaution** excessive bail; **~er Preis** stiff (excessive, prohibitive) price; **künstlich ~er Preis** inflated price; **total ~e Rechnung** exorbitant bill.
Überhöhung *(Kurve)* bank, superelevation;
~ **der Preise** excessive prices (charges).
Überholen overtaking, passing;
falsches ~ improper passing;
~ **verboten** *(Straßenschild)* overtaking prohibited, do not pass, no passing *(US)*.
überholen to overtake, to pass, to overhaul, to recondition, to service *(US)*, to outpace, *(ausbessern)* to repair, *(übertreffen)* to outdo, to surpass, to outstrip;
j. ~ to get ahead of s. o., to have the heels of s. o., *(mit Auto)* to overtake s. o.; **andere Fahrzeuge auf der Straße** ~ to overtake other cars on the road; **sehr knapp** ~ to cut in; **links** ~ to overtake on the left; **Motor** ~ to overhaul the engine of a car; **Schiff** ~ to overhaul a cargo boat.
Überhol|fahrbahn acceleration lane; **~gleis** passing track; **~manöver** overtaking manoeuvre; **zum ~manöver hinter einem Lastwagen ansetzen** to pull out from behind a lorry; **bei seinem ~manöver vorankommen** to pick up on s. o. *(coll.)*.
überholt *(Automotor)* overhauled, reconditioned, *(veraltet)* out-of-vogue, dated, out of date, obsolete;
gründlich ~ **werden müssen** to need a drastic overhaul; ~ **sein** to grow obsolete, *(Rechte)* to become antiquated; **von den nachfolgenden Ereignissen** ~ **sein** to be outdated by the following events; **völlig** ~ **sein** *(Nachricht)* to be old rope (hat) *(coll.)*; **von jem.** ~ **werden** to take s. one's dust;
~es Auto reconditioned car; **~e Theorie** outdated theory.
Überholtsein, entwicklungsbedingtes *(Industrieprodukt)* technological obsolence.
Überholung overtaking, overtake *(Br.)*, pass, *(Ausbesserung)* overhaul, reconditioning;
umfassende ~ major overhaul;
Maschine einer sorgfältigen ~ **unterziehen** to subject a machine to a careful overhaul.
Überholungsarbeiten overhaul work.
überholungsbedürftig in need of repair.
Überholungskursus refresher course.
Überhol|verbot no overtaking (passing, *US*); **im ~verbot überholen** to overtake within a passing (overtaking, *Br.*) limit; **~vorgang** overtaking, passing; **während des ~vorgangs** while passing.
überhören, etw. to miss s. th.; **Bitten laufend** ~ to turn a deaf ear to entreaties.
überinvestieren to overinvest.
Überinvestition excessive investment, overinvestment.
überirdisch superterranean, superterrestial, unearthly;
von ~er Schönheit of divine beauty.
über|jährig superannuated; **~kandidelt** crackbrained, eccentric, crazy *(coll.)*, nutty *(coll.)*.
Überkapazität overcapacity, excess capacity;
betriebliche und personelle ~en abbauen to weed out the surplus plant and manpower; ~ **loswerden** to work off its excess capacity.
überkapitalisieren to overcapitalize.
überkapitalisiert overcapitalized, high-geared.
Überkapitalisierung overcapitalization, high gearing.
Überkleber overlay.
überkommen werden, von Schwäche to be overcome by a fit of weakness.
Überkompensation overcompensation.
überkonfessionell interdenominational.
Überkonjunktur overdone (over-taxed) boom.
über|korrekt overcorrect; **~kreditieren** to overcredit; **~kritisch** overcritical, hypercritical.
Über|kreuzverflechtungen in Aufsichtsräten interlocking directorates; **~ladegleis** transshipping line *(US)*.

überladen to overload, to overburden, to overcharge;
j. mit Arbeit ~ to overwork s. o., to overwhelm s. o. with work; **Tisch mit Gerichten** ~ to pile a table with dishes;
~ *(a.)* overloaded, overweighted;
~**e Anzeige** buckeye; ~**er Stil** florid style.
überlagern *(Rundfunkempfang)* to blanket, to heterodyne, to superimpose;
sich ~ to interfere.
überlagernd interfering.
Überlagerung interference, heterodyne.
Überlagerungs|empfang beat reception; ~**empfänger** heterodyne (heat) receiver; ~**frequenz** beat frequency.
Überland|bahn interurban railway (railroad, *US*), transcontinental railway; ~**bus** interurban bus, motor coach; ~**flug** cross-country flight, *(kurzer)* hop; ~**frachtsatz** truck rates *(US)*; ~**leitung** transmission (power) line, *(Telegrafenlinie)* cross-country telegraph line; ~**netz** grid *(Br.)*; ~**omnibus** cross-country (interurban) bus, motor coach; ~**post** overland mail; ~**sendung** trucking shipment; ~**straße** cross-country road, highway *(US)*; ~**strom** long-distance electricity supply; ~**tarif** truck rates; ~**transport** long-distance transport (haulage, *US*), trucking shipment *(US)*, long-distance goods traffic *(Br.)*; ~**transportgesellschaft** long-distance carrier, trucking agency (company, *US*); ~**verbindungen** overland links; ~**verkehr** interurban (long-distance road) traffic, overland transport, truck service; ~**verkehrslinie** trucking line; ~**versandkosten** trucking costs; ~**weg** overland route; ~**zentrale** long-distance power station; ~**zustellung** truck delivery *(US)*.
Überlänge eines Films exceptional length of a film.
überlappen to overlap.
überlappend|e Streuung *(Werbung)* overlapping circulation; ~**es Streuungsgebiet** *(Werbung)* overlapping situation.
Überlappung von Besteuerungsrechten overlap of taxing authority.
überlassen to let have, to leave, *(abtreten)* to yield, to cede, to assign, to remit, to relinquish, *(anvertrauen)* to commit, to entrust, *(übergeben)* to abandon, to hand over, to give up to, *(übertragen)* to transfer, *(unberechtigt)* to disclose;
entgeltlich ~ to sell for value (a consideration); **sich seinen Erinnerungen** ~ to give o. s. up to one's memories; **jds. Ermessen** ~ to leave to s. one's discretion; **formell** ~ to grant; **gegen Kasse** ~ to sell for cash; **käuflich** ~ to sell; **Land zum allgemeinen Gebrauch** ~ to dedicate land for public use; **leihweise** ~ to lend; **dem Leser das Urteil** ~ to leave to the reader to judge; **jds. Pflege** ~ to entrust to s. one's care; **Sache sich selbst** ~ to let a thing go hang; **Schiff der Versicherungsgesellschaft** ~ to abandon a ship covered by a policy to the underwriters (a property to the insurer); **j. sich selbst** ~ to leave s. o. to his devices; **Tratte der Bank zum Einzug** ~ to hand over a draft to a bank for collection; **wieder** ~ to redemise; **Zimmer** ~ to rent (let) a room; **etw. dem Zufall** ~ to leave s. th. to chance; **nichts dem Zufall** ~ to leave nothing to accident;
jem. ~ **bleiben** to rest with s. o.; **sich selbst** ~ **sein** to be left to one's own discretion (devices).
Überlassung handing over, delivery, *(Abtretung)* transfer, cession, assignment, *(Aufgabe)* abandonment, relinquishment, surrender;
schenkungsweise ~ donation; **unentgeltliche** ~ voluntary contribution, gratuitous transfer;
~ **von Land zum allgemeinen Gebrauch** dedication of land for public use; ~ **zur Nutznießung** assignment for beneficial use; ~ **eines Schiffes an die Versicherungsgesellschaft** abandonment of a ship to the underwriters; ~ **von Verschlußsachen an einen Unberechtigten** disclosure of classified information to an authorized person.
Überlassungsurkunde transfer deed.
überlasten to overburden, to overcharge, to overload, to load, to overweight, to overtask, to snow under;
Betrieb ~ to operate works above capacity; **sich finanziell** ~ to bite off more than one can chew; **steuerlich** ~ to overtax.
überlastet overburdened, overstrained, overweighted, *(Maschine, Stromnetz)* overloaded;
mit Arbeit ~ overwhelmed (snowed under) with work; **nervlich** ~ overstrung; **von Sorgen** ~ loaded with cares; **steuerlich** ~ burdened with taxation.
Überlastung overburden, overload, excess weight.
Überlastungsgeld excess luggage charge *(Br.)*.
überlaufen to turn one's coat, *(drucktechn.)* to run over, *(mil.)* to desert, to go over, *(Politiker)* to flop over *(US)*, to cross the floor of the house *(Br.)*, to rat *(sl.)*;
von Patienten ~ regularly besieged by patients; **von Touristen** ~ overrun with (full of, inundated with) tourists;
von Hausierern ~ **sein** to be pestered (plagued) by pedlers;
~**er Beruf** overcrowded profession.
überlaufend overflowing.
Überläufer *(mil.)* deserter, runaway, *(Parteipolitiker)* turncoat, defector, renegade, rat *(sl.)*, ratter *(sl.)*, flopper *(US)*.
Überlauf|kanal overflow drain; ~**ventil** bypass (overflow) valve.
überlaut too loud, stentorian, *(Sirene)* deafening.
Überleben|der Regierung government survival; ~ **des Tüchtigsten** survival of the fittest.
überleben to survive, to overlive, to outlive;
j. ~ to last s. o. out; **Erdbeben** ~ to survive an earthquake; **diese Nacht nicht** ~ not to last this night.
Überlebende|r survivor, outliver;
letzte ~ **einer großen Familie** sole remains of a large family.
überlebender|Ehegatte surviving spouse; ~ **Teil** *(Lebensversicherung)* surviving party.
Überlebens|ausrüstung survival equipment; ~**fähigkeit** ability to survive; ~**fall** survival, survivorship; **im** ~**fall** in case of survival.
überlebensgroß above life size.
Überlebens|kampf struggle to survive; ~**klausel** survivorship clause.
Überlebensrente two-life (survivorship, joint and survivor) annuity, joint pension, annuity on the last survivor;
einseitige ~ reversionary annuity; **gemeinsame** ~ joint (last) survivor annuity.
Überlebens|tafel survivorship tables; ~**vermutung** *(Lebensversicherung)* presumption of survival; ~**versicherung** survivors' (survivorship) insurance; **wechselseitige** ~**versicherung** joint life insurance.
überlebt antiquated, obsolete, out-of-date, outdated, old-fashioned;
sich ~ **haben** to have had one's days, to have survived one's usefulness; **zwei Kriege** ~ **haben** to have lived through two wars;
~**e Anschauungen** antiquated views; ~**es Prinzip** out-of-date principle.
Überlebtheit obsoleteness, out-of-dateness.
überlegen to consider, to think over, to reflect, to turn about, *(sich ausdenken)* to work (figure, *US*) out, *(nachdenken)* to ponder, to reflect;
jem. eine Decke ~ to put a blanket over s. o.; **noch einmal** ~ to reconsider; **das Für und Wider** ~ to weigh the pros and cons; **sich etw. genau** ~ to stop and think; **hin und her** ~ to consider from every angle; **sich eine Sache gründlich (reiflich)** ~ to think twice about s. th., to give a question mature deliberation (careful consideration); **sich seine Worte genau** ~ to weigh one's words;
~ *(a.)* superior, ascendant;
weit ~ streets ahead;
j. ~ **besiegen** to mop the floor with s. o.; **sich** ~ **fühlen** to feel superior; **jem.** ~ **sein** to outclass (outdistance, surpass) s. o., to be a cut above s. o., to have the edge on (over) s. o. *(sl.)*; **jem. entschieden** ~ **sein** to have a decided superiority over s. o.; **jem. turmhoch** ~ **sein** to be head and shoulders above s. o.; **jem. in keiner Weise** ~ **sein** to be no match for s. o., to have nothing on s. o. *(US)*; **zahlenmäßig** ~ **sein** to be stronger in point of numbers, to outnumber s. o.;
~**er Könner** unsurpassed expert; **mit** ~**en Kräften angreifen** to attack with superior forces; ~**es Lächeln** serene smile; **mit** ~**er Miene** with an air of superiority; **mit** ~**er Ruhe an etw. herangehen** to tackle a problem serenely.
Überlegener superior, top dog *(sl.)*.
Überlegenheit superiority, ascendancy, odds;
wirtschaftliche ~ economic superiority; **zahlenmäßige** ~ superiority in numbers;
jds. ~ **anerkennen** to hand it to s. o. *(US sl.)*.
überlegt considerate, deliberate, advisedly, *(jur.)* premeditated;
gut ~ well-advised; **reiflich** ~ deeply devised;
~ **handeln** to act deliberately;
~**es Handeln** considerate action; **wohl** ~**er Plan** deliberate plan; ~**es Urteil** deliberate judgment.
Überlegung deliberation, consideration, thought, premeditation, formed design;
bei nochmaliger ~ on second thought; **nach erneuter** ~ upon reflection; **nach reiflicher (sorgfältiger)** ~ on balance, after long deliberations; **nach weiterer** ~ upon further consideration; **ohne** ~ without premeditation; **vorsätzlich und mit** ~ with malice aforethought;

ernsthafte ~en active considerations; **liquiditätspolitische ~en** considerations of liquidity; **nebensächliche ~en** outlying considerations; **steuerliche ~en** tax considerations; **vorherige ~** preconsideration; **rein wirtschaftliche ~** reasons of economic efficiency;
~en über etw. anstellen to think about s. th.; **ohne Plan und ~ arbeiten** to work on a piecemeal plan; **in seine ~en mit einbeziehen** to include in one's consideration; **persönliche ~en außer acht lassen (zurückstellen)** to eliminate personal considerations.
Überlegungsfrist *(vor Streikverkündung)* cooling-off period, compulsory delay *(US)*.
überleiten to transfer;
auf Umwegen zu einer Frage ~ to lead up to a question in a roundabout way; **auf ein anderes Thema ~** to switch the talk to another topic.
Überleitung transition;
musikalische ~ *(Rundfunk)* bridge; **statistische ~** statistical transition.
Überleitungs|anzeige notice of transfer; **~bestimmungen** provisional regulations, transition(al) provisions; **~regelung** transitional regulation; **~vertrag** transitory agreement; **~vorschriften** transitional provisions.
überlesen to run (glance) over, to peruse, *(übersehen)* to look over;
Druckfehler ~ to overlook a printer's error.
überliefern to deliver, to hand over, to commit, to entrust, *(weitergeben)* to transmit;
der Nachwelt ~ to hand down to posterity.
überliefert traditional, handed down;
mündlich ~ transmitted by word of mouth.
Überlieferungen hereditary beliefs;
erstarrte ~ ironbound traditions; **mündliche ~** traditions; **schriftliche ~** written traditions.
Überliegegeld demurrage;
~klausel demurrage clause.
überliegen lassen to allow on demurrage.
Überliege|tage, ~zeit extra lay days, demurrage days, laying up.
Überliquidität surplus (excess) liquidity.
überlisten to dupe, to trick, to outsmart;
Polizei ~ to outwit the police; **psychologisch ~** to psyche out; **j. zu ~ trachten** to try it on s. o. *(sl.)*.
übermachen to remit, to transfer, *(vermachen)* to make over.
Übermacht superiority, supremacy, *(mil.)* superior forces;
allein gegen eine ~ with one's back to the wall;
wirtschaftliche ~ economic supremacy;
sich aufgrund der ungeheuren ~ ergeben to surrender in face of the tremendous superiority; **durch seine ~ überwältigen** to overcome by superior forces.
übermächtig powerful, superior;
~es Verlangen strong desire.
Übermachung *(Testieren)* making over, *(Überweisung)* transfer, provision, remittance.
übermannt, von Rührung overcome with emotion.
Übermaß excess, exorbitance, *(Textilien)* oversize;
im ~ in excess;
~ an Arbeit excess of work; **~ an Freude** extremity of joy; **~ an Vertraulichkeit** excessive familiarity;
im ~ produzieren to overproduce.
übermäßig excessive, exorbitant, inordinate, undue;
~ arbeiten to work too hard; **~ trinken** to drink to excess; **~ viel Öl verbrauchen** to be very heavy on oil;
~e Absatzausweitung overtrading; **~er Alkoholgenuß** excessive or intemperate use of intoxicants; **~e Arbeit** excessive labo(u)r; **~er Aufwand** extravagant expenses; **einer Sache ~e Bedeutung beimessen** to attach excessive importance to a matter; **~e Konkursquote** surplus dividend; **~ hohe Preise** exorbitant prices; **~es Rauchen** immoderate smoking; **~er Verbrauch** excess consumption; **~e Zinsen** exorbitant interest.
Übermensch superman.
übermenschlich, mit ~er Anstrengung in a superhuman effort; **~e Leistung** Herculean achievement; **~e Leistungen verlangen** to push the panic button *(sl.)*.
Über|minister overlord; **~ministerium** overlord ministry.
übermitteln to convey, to deliver, to communicate, to make known, to signal;
jem. etw. ~ to communicate s. th. to s. o.; **Auftrag ~** to transmit an order; **Botschaft ~** to transmit a message; **telegrafisch Geld ~** to transfer money by telegraph; **Glückwünsche ~** to convey greetings; **Nachrichten ~** to transmit news; **Nachricht telegrafisch ~** to telegraph a message.
übermitteltes Telegramm transmitted telegram.
Übermittler communicator, transmitter.
Übermittlung transmission, communication, conveyance;
fernschriftliche ~ teleprinter transmission; **telegrafische ~** telegraphic transfer; **unrichtige ~** incorrect transmission;
~ eines Angebots communication of an offer; **~ einer Botschaft** delivery of a message; **~ von Nachrichten** transmission of news.
Übermittlungs|gebühr remittance fee; **~kosten** communication cost.
übermüdet overweary, overtired, fagged-out.
Übermüdung overfatigue, overexertion;
geistige ~ brain fag.
Übermut boisterousness, exuberant spirits;
aus reinem ~ just for kicks;
~ tut selten gut pride goes before a fall.
übermütig boisterous, rollicking, frolicsome;
in ~er Laune full of fun, in high spirits.
Übernachfrage exaggerated (excess) demand;
~inflation demand-pull inflation.
übernachten to stay overnight (the night at), to put up;
bei einem Freund ~ to stay overnight at a friend's house; **unter freiem Himmel ~** to spend the night in the open air; **in einem Hotel ~** to stay (spend) the night at a hotel;
unentgeltlich ~ können to have a place to stay without cost.
übernächtigt tired out, overwatched;
~ aussehen to be bleary-eyed; **~ sein** to have had too little sleep.
Übernachtung overnight [stop (stay)];
einmalige ~en *(Hotel)* overnight guests;
Preis für ~ und Frühstück price for bed and breakfast.
Übernachtungs|geld travel(l)ing allowance; **~kosten** overnight expenses; **~möglichkeiten** overnight facilities (accommodation); **sich eine ~möglichkeit suchen** to fix up somewhere.
Übernahme assumption, undertaking, *(Amt)* taking over (up), takeover, entering up, assumption, *(Annahme)* acceptance, taking delivery, *(Besitznahme)* taking possession, vesting, *(Effekten)* takeover, underwriting, *(Erwerb)* acquisition;
erwartete ~ takeover prospect; **feste ~** *(Emission)* firm underwriting, underwriting guarantee;
~ von Aktien stock takeover; **~ eines Amtes** assumption of (entrance upon) an office; **~ in das Angestelltenverhältnis** transfer to the salary payroll; **~ einer Anleihe** negotiation of a loan; **~ einer Arbeit** undertaking a job; **~ einer Aufgabe** undertaking a task; **~ von Aufgaben des Verbraucherhaushaltes** built-in maid service *(US)*; **~ an Bord** taking on board; **~ von Dokumenten gegen Bezahlung** lifting of documents against payment; **~ einer Erbschaft** coming into (entrance upon) an inheritance; **~ einer Garantie** warranty promise; **~ eines Geschäftes** taking over a business; **~ der Geschäftsführung** takeover; **~ einer ausländischen Gesellschaft** adoption of a foreign corporation; **~ der Haftung** assumption of liability; **~ einer Hypothek** assumption of a mortgage; **~ auf dem Konsortialwege** outright purchase; **teilweise ~ der Kosten** absorption of part of the costs; **~ der Macht** assumption of power; **~ eines Ministeramtes** entrance upon a ministerial office; **~ eines Nachlasses** assumption of a succession; **~ der Regierung** assumption of power; **~ eines Risikos** assumption of a risk; **~ von Schulden** assumption of liabilities, taking over of debts; **~ des Selbstbehalts in festgesetzter Höhe** assumption of a specified amount of each loss; **~ durch den Staat** government takeover; **~ öffentlicher Unternehmen durch Privatfirmen** reserve takeover; **~ eines Verlustes** assumption of a loss; **~ einer Versicherung** underwriting of a policy; **~ einer Versicherung als Unterversicherer** subunderwriting; **~ eines Versicherungsrisikos** underwriting a risk;
~ eines Amtes ablehnen to decline an appointment; **j. um die ~ eines Ministeriums bitten** to invite s. o. to form a ministry; **~ einer Anleihe garantieren** to underwrite a loan; **sich zur festen ~ verpflichten** *(Konsortialmitglied)* to subscribe absolute; **sich nur zur ~ nicht plazierter Aktien verpflichten** to subscribe conditionally;
~abkommen purchase and sale agreement, *(Effektenemission)* underwriting contract (agreement); **~angebot** takeover offer (bid), tender offer *(US)*; **~angebot mittels Verkauf eigener Aktien** paper bid; **~angebot aus kartellrechtlichen Gründen verhindern** to prevent a takeover bid on antitrust grounds; **~bedingungen** conditions of acceptance, *(Konsortium)* underwriting conditions; **~bescheinigung** *(Spediteur)* confirmatory note *(US)*; **~beschluß** *(AG)* takeover resolution; **~betrag** *(Börse)* subscription quota; **~garantie** *(Emission)* underwriting guarantee; **~gebühr** *(Effekten)* takeover tax, underwriting fee; **konsortiales ~gegenangebot machen** to make an underwritten

share counterbid; **zweifelhafte ~geschäfte** takeover manoeuvres; **~gesellschaft** finance company; **~gesetz** adoptive act; **~konnossement** received-for-shipment bill of lading.

Übernahmekonsortium takeover consortium, board company, [underwriting] syndicat underwriters, underlying (original) syndicate *(US)*;

~ für nicht abgesetzte Bezugsrechte standby underwriter; **~ für Obligationen** bonding underwriters.

Übernahme|kurs negotiation (underwriting, taking-over) price, transfer price (rate) *(Br.)*; **~kursfestsetzung** transfer pricing; **~preis** contract (purchase, negotiation, takeover, taking-over) price, *(EG)* target price; **~provision** underwriting commission; **~rede** inaugural address *(US)*; **~risiko** takeover risk; **~schein** certificate of receipt, sales licence; **~spesen** underwriting fee; **~syndikat** underwriting syndicate; **~vertrag** acquisition (takeover) agreement, *(Effektenemission)* underwriting contract (agreement); **~vertrag für nicht abgesetzte Bezugsrechte** standby (underwriting) agreement.

über|national supranational; **~natürliches Ereignis** miracle; **~-natürliche Erscheinung** supernatural phenomenon.

übernehmen to undertake, to take up, to take on, to accept, *(abnehmen)* to accept, to take delivery, to receive, *(Arbeit)* to undertake, to take in hand, *(Schiff)* to hoist in;

sich ~ to overextend (overstrain, overreach, overtax) o. s., to tax one's powers too much, to burn the candle at both ends; **Absatz wörtlich aus einem anderen Buch ~** to borrow a passage word for word from another book; **Aktien ~** to take delivery of stock; **Amt ~** to enter upon (take, take upon o. s., undertake, assume) an office; **Angestellte eines anderen Betriebs ~** to take over employees of another firm; **Anleihe ~** to subscribe to a loan; **Anleihetranche ~** to take a portion of a loan; **Anteile ~** to take over shares; **Arbeit ~** to undertake a piece of work; **zusätzliche Arbeiten ~** to take on extra work; **neuen Aufgabenbereich ~** to enter upon new duties; **Auto von der Fabrik ~** to take over a car; **zur Beförderung als Reisegepäck ~** to check baggage *(US)*; **Besitz ~** to take possession; **Bürgschaft für j. ~** to go (stand) surety for s. o., to become (go, stand) bail for s. o.; **Dokumente ~** to take up the documents; **fest ~** to take firm; **sich finanziell ~** to bite off more than one can chew; **etw. freiwillig ~** to volunteer to do s. th.; **Führung eines Kommandos ~** to take the lead; **Garantie ~** to guarantee, to guaranty, to warrant, to undertake a guarantee; **Geschäft ~** to take over (succeed to) a business; **Geschäftsbesorgung ~** to undertake a business errand; **Geschäftsleitung ~** to assume the direction of a business; **Gesellschaft ~** to take over a company; **Gewähr ~** to undertake a guaranty, to guarantee, to warrant; **Hälfte der Kosten ~** to go halves with s. o.; **Hypothek [unter Anrechnung auf den Kaufpreis] ~** to assume a mortgage; **Inkasso von Wechseln ~** to attend to the collection of bills; **entstandene Kosten ~** to pay the costs incurred; **Kosten auf die Staatskasse ~** to charge an expense to the public debt; **Kosten des Unternehmens ~** to bear the costs of an undertaking; **Kostenerhöhungen teilweise ~** to absorb part of the cost; **Leitung ~** to assume the control, to take over the management, to take charge of; **Macht ~** come into power; **Ministerium ~** to enter a ministry; **Neuemissionen in größerem Ausmaß ~** to underwrite a large part of public new issues; **Personenbeförderung gegen Entgelt ~** to carry passengers for a consideration; **Präsidium ~** to take the chair; **Produktionskosten teilweise ~** to contribute in part to the expense of production; **Regierung ~** to take over the (assume the reign of) government; **Risiko ~** to take upon o. s. the risk, to entertain (incur) a risk; **volles Risiko ~** to assume (incur) all risks; **Schulden ~** to assume (shoulder) debts; **Selbstbehalt in festgesetzter Höhe ~** to assume a specified amount of each loss; **Sendung ~** to take over a broadcast from another station; **Straße ~** *(Kommunalverwaltung)* to adopt a road; **Unkostenposten ~** to absorb expenses; **Unternehmen mit Aktiven und Passiven ~** to purchase an enterprise as a going concern, to take over the assets and liabilities (accounts receivable and accounts payable, *US*) of a company; **Verantwortung ~** to assume (take the) responsibility; **Verbesserungen ~** to adopt improvements; **Verbindlichkeiten ~** to incur (assume) liabilities, to enter into engagements; **Verhandlungsleitung ~** to assume (take) the chair; **finanzielle Verpflichtungen ~** to enter into pecuniary obligations; **Versicherung unter Risikoteilung ~** to underwrite a risk; **Verteidigung ~** to assume the defense *(US)* (defence, *Br.*); **Vertretung ~** to take up an agency; **Vertrieb verschiedener Erzeugnisse ~** to take up a line of goods; **Vorsitz ~** to assume the chair (presidency); **Wertpapiere ~** to take delivery of stocks.

übernehmend|e Gesellschaft transferee company; **~er Spediteur** on-carrier.

Übernehmer *(Bauunternehmer)* contractor, *(Bezogener)* drawee, *(Empfänger)* receiver, party receiving, *(Käufer)* purchaser, *(Rechtsnachfolger)* assign, assignee, transferee, *(Warensendung)* consignee, *(Wechsel)* indorsee, acceptor;

~ eines Werkvertrages independent contractor.

übernommen *(Straße)* adopted;

fest ~ *(Buchhändler)* taken up outright;

~es Risiko assumed risk.

überordnen to give precedence, to superordinate;

jem. ~ to put over o. s.

Überorganisation overorganization.

überorganisieren to overorganize.

überörtlich supraregional, supralocal.

Überpari|ausgabe, ~emission issue above par, superior issue, above-par emission.

überparteilich nonpartisan, nonparty, neutral, crossbench *(Br.)*, across party lines;

~e Ernennungen vornehmen to cross the party line in making appointments.

überpenibel overparticular;

mit seiner Kleidung ~ sein to be too fussy about one's clothes.

Überpfändung excessive distraint.

überplanmäßig *(Bezüge)* extra, noncontractual, *(Stelle)* supernumerary, nonschedule.

Über|prämie bei Kündigung durch den Versicherungsnehmer short rate; **~preis** overprice, overcharge, excess (excessive) price, *(Preiszuschlag)* premium; **~preis verlangen** to overcharge; **~produktion** overproduction, surplus (excessive) production.

überproduzieren to overproduce.

überproportionale Kurssteigerung price rise out of proportion.

Überprovision overriding commission.

überprüfen to go over, to check up, to look into, to inspect, to control, *(auf Brauchbarkeit)* to test, *(Bücher, Konten)* to audit, to examine, to check, to verify, *(Maschine)* to overhaul, *(Person)* to screen, *(sorgfältig)* to scrutinize, *(überarbeiten)* to revise, *(untersuchen)* to investigate, to search, to screen;

Angelegenheit ~ to check up (look into) a matter; **Argumente noch einmal ~** to go through the arguments again; **Aussage ~** to verify a statement; **doppelt ~** to double-check; **Entscheidung ~** to reconsider a decision; **erneut ~** to re-examine, to give reconsideration, to take a fresh look at; **Flüchtling sorgfältig ~** to screen a refugee; **genau ~** to scrutinize, to overhaul, to cross-check; **Gepäck ~** to go through the luggage, to examine the baggage *(US)*; **Konten ~** to control (audit) accounts; **Rechnungen ~** to examine (look over) accounts, to check invoices; **sachverständig ~** to expert; **etw. sehr sorgfältig ~** to give s. th. a careful perusal, to go over (through) s. th. with a fine-tooth comb; **Wählerliste ~** to scrutinize an electoral list; **Wechsel ~** to inspect a check *(US)* (cheque, *Br.*).

Überprüfer checker, inspector, reviser.

überprüft audited, tested, *(behördlich)* attested *(Br.)*;

nicht ~ unaudited, untested; **behördlich nicht ~** unattested *(Br.)*.

Überprüfung examination, inspection, control, check-up, check, *(auf Brauchbarkeit)* testing, *(Bücher, Konten)* auditing, checking, verification, *(Maschine)* overhaul, *(Person)* screening, *(Überarbeitung)* revision, *(Untersuchung)* investigation, search, screening, *(Urteil)* review, revision;

amtliche ~ official search; **fachmännische ~** expert examination; **flüchtige ~** cursory inspection, once-over *(US sl.)*; **gewerbepolizeiliche ~** factory inspection; **nochmalige ~** revise, reexamination; **sorgfältige ~** narrow search, scrutiny; **stichprobenartige ~** snap check, spot checking;

~ des Adressenmaterials address revision; **betriebssichere ~ der Arbeitsabläufe** operational auditing; **~ einer Aussage** verification of a statement; **~ der Betriebssicherheit** safety inspection of factories; **~ der Betriebstätigkeit** operational audit; **~ der verschlüsselten Daten** coding verification; **~ von Frachtrechnungen** rate check; **~ des Gesundheitsattestes** examination of the bill of health; **~ der Gültigkeit einer Police** checking for coverage; **~ einer Kostenrechnung** review of costs; **~ der Managementfunktionen** management audit; **~ der Personalpolitik** personnel audit; **~ von Preisherabsetzungen** markdown revision; **~ durch die Rechtsmittelinstanz** review on appeal; **~ der Sicherheitsbestimmungen** *(Betrieb)* safety testing; **~ des finanziellen Status** means test *(Br.)*; **~ der Stichproben** sampling inspection; **~ der Tarifeinstufung** wage review; **~ einer Wählerliste** scrutiny of an electoral list; **~ von Werbeträgern** media research;

einer amtlichen ~ standhalten to stand an audit; **Lage laufend einer ~ unterziehen** to keep a situation under review; **~ des Wahlergebnisses verlangen** to demand a scrutiny.

Überprüfungs|ausschuß board of review, review board; **~befugnis** revisory powers; **~behörde** review board; **~bogen** check-off sheet; **~dienst für Buchhaltungssysteme** system of auditing services; **~kommission** vetting panel; **~kosten** cost of checking operation; **~recht** revisory powers; **~stelle** board of review; **~stelle für Sicherheitsrisiken** loyalty board; **~verfahren** screening process.

überquellen to flow, to abound;
von Zuschauern ~ to be overflowing with spectators.

überqueren to traverse, to transit, to cross;
Atlantik ~ to cross the Atlantic; **Straße ~** to cross a street; **Straße an einer falschen Stelle (verkehrswidrig) ~** to jaywalk; **Straßenkreuzung ~** to cross at an intersection.

Überquerung crossing, traverse;
verkehrswidrige ~ jaywalking.

überragen to overtower, to surpass, to overreach;
j. haushoch ~ to be head and shoulders (tower) above s. o.; **j. an Leistungen ~** to outstrip s. o. in performance.

überragend, pre-eminent, brilliant, excellent, prominent;
~e Notwendigkeit paramount necessity; **~e Persönlichkeit** outstanding personality.

überraschen to surprise, to astonish, to amaze;
Täter ~ to catch s. o. red-handed; **j. völlig ~** to take s. o. unawares;
lassen wir uns ~ let's wait and see.

überraschend surprising, astounding, amazing, unawares;
~er Anstieg surprise jump; **Tatsachen durch ~e Befragung eines Zeugen herausbekommen** to surprise the facts from a witness; **~er Besuch** unexpected visitor.

überraschenderweise for a wonder.

überrascht overtaken by surprise, surprised, astonished, amazed;
maßlos ~ open-mouthed;
in einer ungünstigen Lage ~ werden to be caught short by.

Überraschung surprise, amazement, astonishment, shock;
angenehme ~ pleasant surprise; **große ~** rum start;
~ über die Nachrichten amazement at the news;
jem. eine ~ bereiten to prepare a surprise for s. o.; **größte ~ hervorrufen** to strike all of a heap; **seine ~ überwinden** to get over one's surprise; **zu seiner ~ vernehmen** to hear to one's astonishment.

Überraschungs|angriff sneak (surprise) raid, surprise military action, shock action, *(Atomkrieg)* first strike; **~kandidat** dark horse; **~moment ausnutzen** to take advantage of the element of surprise; **~päckchen** surprise packet *(Br.)*, prize packet; **jem. mit einer ~reklame zuvorkommen** to steal s. one's thunder; **~taktik** surprise tactics; **~überfall** tip- (hit-) and-run raid.

überrechnen to run over (through), to figure upon.

überreden to persuade, to wheedle, *(durch Schmeicheleien)* to cajole, to coax;
j. zu etw. ~ to talk s. o. round; **j. zu einer Ferienreise nach Italien ~** to talk s. o. into having a holiday in Italy; **j. zum Kauf von etw. ~** to wheedle s. o. into buying s. th.; **jem. ~, einem 50 Pfund zu leihen** to prevail upon s. o. to lend one £ 50;
sich ~ lassen to come round.

Überreder persuader.

Überredung persuasion, suasion;
~ ohne Zwang und Kniffe fair persuasion.

Überredungskünste art of persuasion, persuasive powers, snow job *(sl.)*, *(Verkaufsgespräch)* sales talk, pitch;
~ fallenlassen to desert argument of persuasion; **seine ~ bei jem. spielen lassen** to persuade s. o.

Überredungskünstler coaxer.

überregional supraregional;
~e Presse national press; **~e Werbung** general (nation-wide) advertising.

überreich|ausgestattet lavishly provided with;
j. ~ beschenken to shower gifts upon s. o.

überreichen to present, to hand in (over), to submit, to give;
Beglaubigungsschreiben ~ to present one's credentials;
in der Anlage ~ wir Ihnen unsere Preisliste enclosed please find our price list.

überreichlich ample, superabundant, exuberant;
~ mit Vorräten versehen sein to be amply supplied with provisions.

Überreichung presentation;
~ seines Beglaubigungsschreibens presentation of one's credentials.

überreizt overexcited, *(Nerven)* overstrained, high-strung.

überrennen, Feind to overrun the enemy.

Überrest rest, remainder, trace, residue, remains, *(Spur)* vestige;
~e odd-come-shorts;
sterbliche ~e mortal remains;
~e alter Kultur traces (vestiges) of an ancient civilization; **~e eines Mahles** fragments of a meal.

Überrock upper coat, overcoat.

überrollen to roll over;
feindliche Schützengräben ~ to sweep over the enemy's trenches.

überrumpeln to take by surprise, to catch unawares;
j. ~ to turn s. one's flank, to catch s. o., to catch s. o. napping (flat-footed, *US coll.*).

Überrumpelung surprise, *(mil.)* surprise attack, blitzkrieg;
~ durch die Polizei police swoop.

überrunden, j. to run rings round s. o.

übersäen, Stadt mit Reklame to bill a town.

übersät, mit Landhäusern dotted with cottages;
mit Sternen ~er Himmel star-spangled sky.

übersättigen, Markt to glut (overstock) the market.

Übersättigung glut, oversaturation.

Überschall|atombomber supersonic nuclear bomber; **~beförderung** supersonic transport; **~flug** supersonic flight; **~fluglinie** supersonic airline; **~flugzeug** supersonic aircraft (airliner); **~geschwindigkeit** supersonic (hypersonic) speed (velocity); **mit ~geschwindigkeit fliegen** to fly at supersonic speed; **~knall** sonic boom (bang, *Br.*).

überschallknallfrei bang-free.

Überschall|linienflugverkehr, planmäßiger supersonic commercial service; **~verkehr** supersonic transport; **~verkehrsflugzeug** supersonic transport (airliner); **~welle** ultrasound; **~windkanal** supersonic wind tunnel; **~zeitalter** supersonic age.

überschatten to overshadow;
etw. ~ to cast a cloud on s. th.; **jds. Ruhm ~** to cast s. one's fame into the shade.

überschätzen to overestimate, to overvalue, *(Steuern)* to overrate, to overassess;
sich ~ to think too highly of o. s.; **seine Kräfte ~** to overrate one's strength; **sehr stark ~** to overestimate by very large margins.

Überschätzung overestimation, overvaluation, *(Steuer)* overassessment.

Überschau survey, review, synopsis;
kurze ~ geben to give a brief outline.

überschaubares Ausmaß manageable proportion.

Überschäumen der Konjunktur boiling over of the boom.

überschäumen to flow, to abound, *(Konjunktur)* to boil over.

Überschicht extra shift, overtime, extra time;
~en machen to work overtime.

überschießen to exceed, to be in excess, to surpass.

überschießender Betrag exceeding (surplus) amount.

überschlafen, etw. to consult (take counsel of) one's pillow, to sleep [up]on s. th.

Überschlag computation, estimation, estimate, statement, rough calculation, sketch, *(Kunstflug)* loop, *(beim Landen)* nose over;
im ~ roundly, rough[ly];
annähernder ~ approximate calculation; **reiner ~** fair estimate;
~ machen to [frame (make) an] estimate, to compute, to figure upon.

überschlagen to estimate, to compute, to figure upon, *(auslassen)* to pass, to leave out;
sich ~ *(Auto)* to overturn, to be overturned, to turn turtle, to turn over; **sich vor Diensteifer beinahe ~** to fall over o. s. for the service of s. o.; **Kapitel ~** to skip a chapter; **sich [bei der Landung] ~** *(Flugzeug)* to nose over; **sich vor Liebenswürdigkeit fast ~** to bend over backwards; **Mittagessen ~** to cut (skip) lunch;
grob ~ *(a.)* on (at) a rough estimate.

überschläglich round[ly], rough[ly];
~ kosten to cost in the rough.

Überschlagsrechnung rough estimate, rule of thumb.

überschlau superclever, smart-aleck.

überschnappen to go off one's rocker *(sl.)*.

überschneiden, sich to overlap, to intersect, to coincide, *(Veranstaltungen)* to clash; **sich mit jds. Interessen ~** to collide with s. one's interests.

überschneidend|e Interessen clashing (colliding) interests; **sich ~e Posten** overlapping items; **~es Streuungsgebiet** overlapping situation; **sich ~e Versicherungsansprüche** overlap of insurances; **sich zeitlich ~e Vorlesungen** overlapping lectures.

Überschneidung overlap[ping], *(Anzeigen)* duplicate coverage, *(Linien)* intersection;
~ **von Besteuerungsrechten** overlap of taxing authority; ~ **von Interessen** clash (collision) of interests; ~ **von Veranlagungszeiträumen** overlap of basic periods.
überschreiben to transmit, to transfer, *(umschreiben)* to transcribe;
jem. etw. ~ to settle s. th. on s. o.; **Geschäft auf seinen Sohn** ~ to make over the business to one's son; **Haus auf den Namen seiner Frau** ~ to enter a house in the name of one's wife; **dem Käufer ein Grundstück** ~ to convey land to the purchaser; **auf ein anderes Konto** ~ to transfer to another account.
Überschreibung transfer, *(Umschreibung)* transport, transcription;
~ **eines Grundstücks** transfer of property, conveyance of real estate.
Überschreibungsurkunde deed of conveyance.
Überschreiten transgression, overstepping, stretch;
~ **der Geschwindigkeitsgrenze** exceeding the speed limit *(Br.)*, speeding, speeding violation *(US)*; ~ **der Parkzeit** overtime parking; ~ **der Sendezeit** overrun of the allotted time;
~ **der Gleisanlage verboten** do not cross the tracks.
überschreiten to overstep, to transgress, to exceed, to surpass, to go (pass) beyond, to overstay;
seine Anweisungen ~ to exceed (transcend) one's instructions; **seinen Auftrag** ~ to override one's commission; **seine Befugnisse** ~ to overstep (transgress) one's competence, to exceed one's authority (powers); **seine Besuchszeit** ~ to overstay one's welcome; **benötigten Betrag** ~ to be in excess of the sum required; **sein Einkommen** ~ to overspend one's income; **seinen Etat** ~ to exceed one's budget, to overrun the constable; **Frist** ~ to exceed the prescribed period; **zulässige Geschwindigkeit (Geschwindigkeitsgrenze)** ~ to exceed the speed limit; **Gesetz** ~ to transgress (infringe) a law; **Grenze** ~ to cross the border; **Höchstgeschwindigkeit** ~ to speed; **seine Instruktionen** ~ to exceed one's instructions; **sein Konto** ~ to overdraw one's account (the badger, *Br.*), to make an overdraft; **sein Konto fortlaufend** ~ to run up overdrafts; **seinen Kredit** ~ to overdraw one's account, to strain (stretch, outrun) one's credit; **Kreditlinie** ~ to run over the credit limit *(Br.)* (line, *US*); **Landesgrenze** ~ to cross the frontier; **Limit** ~ to exceed a prescribed amount, to go beyond the limit; **40-Millionengrenze** ~ *(Umsatz)* to top the 40.000.000 mark; **Satzungsbefugnisse** ~ to act ultra vires; **Sendezeit** ~ to overrun the allotted time; **Termin** ~ to overrun the time allowed; **seine Urlaubszeit** ~ to overstay one's leave; **seine Vollmachten** ~ to act contra vires, to act beyond the scope of one's authority, to overstep (exceed) one's powers, to exceed one's authority, to override one's commission; **seinen Voranschlag** ~ to exceed one's estimate; **seine Zuständigkeit** ~ to transgress one's competence.
Überschreitung *(Gesetz)* transgression, infringement, *(Konto)* overdraft;
~ **der Amtsgewalt (Amtsbefugnisse)** abuse of powers (authority); ~ **der Arbeitszeit** special hours; ~ **der betrieblichen Arbeitszeit** overtime employment; ~ **einer garantierten Auflage** circulation bonus; ~ **verliehener Befugnisse** ultra-vires action, excess of granted powers; ~ **des Etats (Haushalts)** exceeding the budget; ~ **der Grenze** crossing of the frontier; ~ **der Höchstgeschwindigkeit** exceeding the speed limit *(Br.)*, speeding violation *(US)*; ~ **der angesetzten Kostenlinie** cost overrun; ~ **der Packzeit** overtime packing; ~ **der Satzungsbefugnisse** acting ultra vires; ~ **der Vollmacht** stretch (abuse) of authority, ultra-vires action; ~ **der Zuständigkeit** transgression of competence.
Überschrift *(Buch)* title, heading, *(Film)* caption, *(Zeitung)* headline, head, rubric;
ganzseitige ~ spread head; **knallende** ~ striking headline, catchline; **sensationelle** ~ scare headline; **zweizeilige** ~ two-line head;
~ **über die ganze Breite** crosshead;
~**en überfliegen** to scan the headlines; **mit einer** ~ **versehen** to caption, to entitle; **Kapitel mit einer** ~ **versehen** to head a chapter.
Überschuh galosh, overshoe.
überschuldet deep[ly involved] in debts, insolvent, *(Betrieb)* overextended, *(Grundstück)* encumbered;
völlig ~ **sein** to be encumbered with mortgages;
~**er Nachlaß** insolvent estate.
Überschuldung excessive indebtedness (encumbrance), overindebtedness, insolvency, *(Betrieb)* overextension.
Überschuldungsnachweis proof of insolvency.

Überschuß surplus, excess, overbalance, redundancy, *(Differenz)* margin, *(drucktechn.)* overrun, *(Ernte)* carryover, *(Ertrag)* gain, profit, *(Kasse)* over, surplus in the cash, *(Restbetrag)* remainder, overplus, *(Saldo)* balance;
buchmäßiger ~ book surplus; **aus Höherbewertung des Anlagekapitals erzielter** ~ revaluation (appraisal) surplus *(US)*; **im Zwangsversteigerungsverfahren erzielter** ~ capitalized surplus; **rechnerischer** ~ surplus as shown in the books; **reiner** ~ margin, net rest (earnings); **frei verfügbarer** ~ *(Haushalt)* free surplus, disposable [budget] surplus;
~ **der Aktiva über die Passiva** surplus of assets over liabilities; ~ **an Arbeitskräften** labo(u)r (manpower) surplus, surplus manpower (workers), redundancy of workers; ~ **der Dienstleistungsbilanz** surplus in the service balance; ~ **der Einfuhren** excess of imports over exports; ~ **der Einnahmen über die Betriebsausgaben** balance of revenue, excess of receipts over expenditure; ~ **in der Handelsbilanz** surplus in the balance of t
on invisibles (current account); ~ **der Zahlungsbilanz** surplus in the balance of payments, external surplus;
mit einem ~ **abschließen** to close with a profit; ~ **abwerfen** to yield a profit; **guten** ~ **abwerfen** to leave a good margin; ~ **aufweisen** to show a surplus; ~ **überweisen** to remit the balance;
~**angebot** surplus supply (to offer); ~**ansammlung** surplus accumulation; ~**besteuerung** surplus taxes; ~**betrag** surplus amount.
Überschüsse, haushaltsrechtliche budget surpluses; **landwirtschaftliche** ~ agricultural (farm) surpluses;
~ **der Bevölkerung** excess of births over deaths; ~ **der Einfuhrwirtschaft** excess of imports over exports; ~ **in der Exportwirtschaft** overbalance of exports, export surpluses; ~ **und Fehlbeträge** shorts and overs; ~ **der Landwirtschaft** agriculture surpluses.
Überschuß|einnahmen surplus receipts; ~**ernte** surplus crop; ~**erzeugnisse** excess produce, surplus goods, overage *(US)*; **[wirtschaftliches]** ~**gebiet** surplus area (state); ~**gesellschaft** abundance economy; ~**güter** surplus property (goods); ~**haushalt** budget surplus.
überschüssig surplus, over, redundant, in excess, exceeding, *(Kapital)* unemployed, idle;
~**e Arbeitskräfte** surplus manpower, redundant labo(u)r; ~**er Betrag** balance, surplus; ~**e Durchschläge** surplus copies; ~**e Erzeugnisse** overage, surplus products; ~**e Exemplare** surplus copies, overrun; ~**e Gelder** surplus funds; ~**e Gewinne** surplus profits; ~**e Kapazität** excess (surplus) capacity; **seine** ~**e Kapazität loswerden** to work off its excess capacity; ~**es Kapital** redundant capital; ~**e Kaufkraft** surplus of (excess) spending power; ~**e Kaufkraft abschöpfen** to mop up excess spending power; ~**er Verwertungserlös** *(Hypothekengläubiger)* surplus proceeds on sale; ~**e Vorräte** excess of provisions.
Überschuß|konto surplus account; ~**land** surplus state (nation, country); ~**politik** *(Steuerpolitik)* surplus budgeting; ~**position** excess position; ~**posten** surplus item.
Überschußprodukte surplus products (goods), overage *(US)*;
landwirtschaftliche ~ farm (agricultural) surpluses;
landwirtschaftliche ~ **subventionieren** to subsidize farm surpluses.
Überschuß|produktion surplus production; ~**situation** surplus situation; ~**verteilung** distribution of surplus; ~**verwertung** surplus utilization; ~**vortrag** *(Gesellschaft)* initial surplus; ~**wasser** surplus water; ~**wirtschaft** economy of abundance, abundance economy, affluent (opulent) society.
überschütten to pour over, to overwhelm, to load, to shower;
Neuankömmling mit Fragen ~ to shower questions upon a new arrival; **mit Geschenken** ~ to load (shower) with gifts; **j. mit Gunstbezeigungen** ~ to heap (load) s. o. with favo(u)rs.
überschüttet, mit Abend-Einladungen snowed under with invitations to dinner parties; **mit Arbeit** ~ snowed under with works; **mit Bewerbungsschreiben** ~ inundated with applications for a post; **mit Blumen** ~ smothered with flowers;
mit Angeboten ~ **werden** to be snowed under with offers.
Überschüttung overwhelming.
Überschwang rapture, exaltation;
im ~ **seines Herzens** out of the ful(l)ness of one's heart.
überschwemmen to flood, to overflow, *(Touristen)* to inundate, to overrun;
Markt ~ to swamp (glut, overstock) the market.
überschwemmt flooded;
mit Briefen ~ deluged with letters; **von Touristen** ~ inundated with tourists;
~**es Gebiet** swamp and overflooded land, flood plain.

Überschwemmung flood, flood waters, flooding, overflow, flow, [over]flood, deluge, spate *(Br.)*, inundation, *(Markt)* glut; **katastrophale** ~ disastrous flood; **plötzliche** ~ flash flood; **nicht vorhersehbare** ~ extraordinary flood;
~ **des Marktes** glut in the market; ~ **durch Touristen** inundation of tourists;
~ **in den Griff bekommen** to get flood waters under control; ~**en in den niedriggelegenen Stadtteilen hervorrufen** to cause floods in the low-lying parts of the town; **durch** ~**en Tausende von Haus und Hof vertreiben** to flood out thousands of people.
Überschwemmungs|gebiet swamp and overflooded land, flood plain; ~**gefahr** danger of flooding; ~**katastrophe** disastrous flood, flood disaster; ~**risiko** flood risk; ~**schaden** flood damage; ~**versicherung** flood insurance.
überschwenglich rapturous, rhapsodic, exuberant;
j. ~ **loben** to praise s. o. profusely;
~**er Dank** effusive thanks; ~**e Kritik** rave review.
Übersee, in, beyond sea, oversea(s);
nach ~ **gehen** to go overseas;
~**auftrag** overseas order; ~**ausgabe** overseas edition; ~**ausgaben** overseas spending; ~**ausstellung** overseas exhibition; ~**bank** oversea[s] bank; ~**bedarf** overseas demands; ~**bericht** overseas report; ~**dampfer** transoceanic steamer, ocean-going (transatlantic) liner; ~**darlehn** overseas loan; ~**erzeugnisse** colonial (overseas) products; ~**expedition** overseas expedition; ~**fracht** ocean freight; ~**gebiete** overseas territories; ~**geschäft** oversea trade, business overseas; ~**gespräch** overseas call; ~**hafen** transatlantic harbour; ~**handel** ocean (oversea, seaborne, foreign) trade, ocean traffic, maritime commerce; ~**hilfe** overseas aid; ~**investitionen** overseas investment.
überseeisch oversea[s], ocean, transoceanic, transmarine, transatlantic;
~**e Besitzungen** overseas possessions; ~**e Filiale** overseas branch; ~**e Gebiete** overseas territories; ~**er Handel** oversea (sea-borne) trade; ~**e Interessen** overseas interests; ~**er Markt** overseas market; ~**e Niederlassung** overseas branch; ~**e Vermögenswerte** overseas assets.
Übersee|kabel transatlantic cable; ~**koffer** steamer trunk; ~**kunde** overseas buyer; ~**kundschaft** overseas customers; ~**länder** overseas countries; ~**markt** oversea (colonial, *Br.*) market; ~**papier** foreign note-paper; ~**preise** oversea prices; ~**produkte** overseas products; ~**reise** transatlantic (foreign) voyage, oversea journey; ~**reisen** overseas travel; ~**reise machen** to go overseas; ~**rundfunkprogramm** overseas broadcast program(me); ~**schiff** oversea vessel; ~**schiffahrt** oversea navigation; ~**speditionsgeschäft** ocean forwarding; ~**spekulant** merchant adventurer; ~**tarif** transatlantic rate; ~**telegramm** cablegram; ~**transport** sea transit, ocean (overseas) shipment, transatlantic (ocean, *US*) transport; ~**umsätze** overseas sales; ~**verkehr** overseas operations (transport); ~**verpackung** maritime packing, packing for export; ~**versicherung** overseas insurance; ~**vertrag** overseas contract; ~**vertretung** overseas agency; ~**verwendung** assignment overseas; ~**werbung** overseas advertising; **steuerfreier** ~**zuschlag** tax-free overseas allowance.
übersehen, jem. komplett not to give s. o. the time of day; **Situation mit einem Blick** ~ to sum up the situation at a glance.
übersenden to turn in, to send, to forward, to convey, *(Geld)* to transmit, to remit, *(Waren)* to consign, to ship *(US)*;
in bar ~ to make remittance in cash; **Waren auf Spekulation** ~ to venture goods.
Übersender sender, *(Geld)* transmitter, remitter, remittancer, *(Waren)* consignor, forwarder, transmitter.
Übersendung sending, forwarding, dispatch, conveyance, *(Geld)* transmission, transmittal, remittance, *(Waren)* consignation, consignment, shipment *(US)*;
bei ~ **der Faktura** on transmitting the invoice.
Übersendungskosten transport (transportation, *US*) charges.
übersetzbar translatable, interpretable.
übersetzen to translate, to render, *(dolmetschen)* to interpret;
vom Blatt ~ to translate at sight; **englisches Buch ins Französische** ~ to translate an English book into French; **ins Englische** ~ to do into English; **aus dem Englischen ins Französische** ~ to render English into French; **in einer Fähre** ~ to pass over in a ferry; **falsch** ~ to mistranslate; **frei** ~ to translate with some latitude; **genau** ~ to translate closely; **ohne Genehmigung des Autors** ~ to translate without the sanction of the author; **viel** ~ to do many translations; **wortgetreu** ~ to translate word for word (literally, with the greatest fidelity); **sich gut** ~ **lassen** to translate well; **sich nicht** ~ **lassen** not to be capable of translation.

Übersetzer translator, interpreter;
beeidigter ~ sworn translator; **freiberuflicher** ~ free-lance translator; **öffentlich bestellter und vereidigter** ~ sworn translator.
Übersetztsein overcrowdedness.
Übersetzung translation, act of translating, rendering, version, *(Getriebe)* transmission, gear ratio, *(Schule)* prose *(Br.)*;
in höchster ~ with full gear;
annähernde ~ rough translation; **autorisierte** ~ authorized version; **falsche** ~ mistranslation; **freie** ~ free translation, imitation; **genaue** ~ close (near, exact) translation; **kleine** ~ small gear; **mündliche** ~ interpretation; **schlechte** ~ poor translation; **sinngemäße** ~ near translation; **ungenaue** ~ inaccurate (loose) translation; **maschinell unterstützte** ~ machine-aided translation; **wortgetreue** ~ faithful (close, literal) translation, metaphrase; **wortwörtliche** ~ word-for-word (verbal) translation;
~ **vom Englischen ins Deutsche** translation from English into German;
sich mit einer ~ **abquälen** to flounder through a translation; ~ **anfertigen** to do (make) a translation; **sich zur** ~ **eignen** to translate; **hervorragende** ~ **eines Buches liefern** to translate a work with finished skill.
Übersetzungs|aufgabe *(Schule)* translation exercise (task), version; ~**büro** translation agency, translating bureau *(US)*; ~**fehler** mistake in translation, misrendering; ~**gebühr** translation charge; ~**getriebe** transmission gear; **maschinelle** ~**hilfe** technical translation aid; ~**programm** *(Datenverarbeitung)* compiler; ~**rechte** translation rights; ~**schlüssel** *(Lehrer)* key for the use of teachers only; ~**übung** translation exercise (task); ~**verhältnis** gear ratio.
Übersicht survey, scheme, statement, roundup, review, table, schedule, *(Abriß)* sketch, outline, account, *(in Tafelform)* synoptical table, *(Zusammenfassung)* summary;
kurze ~ summary, short account, summary statement, abstract, profile; **Konjunkturabschwung mit Argusaugen notierende** ~ pin-point-the-downturn survey; **statistische** ~ statistical statement (table); **summarische** ~ summary statement; **tabellarische** ~ schedule; **vergleichende** ~ comparison table, synopsis;
~ **über die Beschäftigungsmöglichkeiten** employment possibilities picture; ~ **über die politische Lage** political survey; ~ **über die englische Literatur** outline of English literature; ~ **über den erzielten Reingewinn** statement of earned surplus;
~ **über die Finanzverhältnisse geben** to report the receipts and expenditures; ~ **völlig verloren haben** to be utterly confused.
übersichtlich clear, at a glance, synoptical;
~**e Anordnung** clear arrangement.
Übersichts|karte key (general, outline, skeleton) map; ~**konto** summary account; ~**plan** *(Betriebsanlage)* layout plan, plan of the installation (site); ~**skizze** sketch map; ~**tabelle** synoptic table, tabular summary; ~**tafel für Unterbringungsmöglichkeiten** accommodation chart.
übersiedeln to move, to remove.
übersiedelnd transmigratory.
Übersiedlung removal, relocation.
Übersiedlungs|beihilfe removal allowance; ~**gut** removal goods; ~**kosten** relocation expenses.
überspannen, Bogen to overdo it; **Fluß** ~ to span a river; **seine Forderungen** ~ to exaggerate one's demands.
überspannt extravagant, highflying, eccentric, kinky, wild, too-too *(coll.)*;
~**e Person** cracked (crazy) person, highflier; ~**e Pläne** highflown schemes; ~**e Vorstellungen** wild ideas.
überspielen to rerecord, to transfer;
Rolle ~ to overact; **auf ein Tonband** ~ to make a tape recording.
Überspielung rerecording, transfer.
überspitzte Forderungen overcharged claims, exaggerated demands (claims).
Übersprechen *(tel.)* crosstalk.
Überspringen skip.
überspringen *(bei der Beförderung)* to jump, *(Schulklasse)* to skip *(US)*;
anderen bei der Beförderung ~ to be promoted over s. one's head; **heikle Fragen** ~ to skip delicate questions;
Schüler Klassen ~ **lassen** to accelerate a pupil *(US)*.
überspülen, Deck to wash over the deck; **Ufer** ~ to flood its banks.
überspült, von den Wellen washed by the waves.
überstaatlich supranational.
überstanden tided over.

überstehen, Krankheit to recover from an illness; **Krise** ~ to weather a crisis; **Sturm** ~ to override a storm; **Tag mit Mühe** ~ to wear through a day; **viele harte Winter** ~ *(Haus)* to weather many bitter winters.
überstehender Umschlag extended cover.
übersteigen to exceed, to surpass, to outrun, to pass;
Bedarf ~ to be in excess of demand; **Buchwerte erheblich** ~ to be appreciably in excess of book values; **alle Erwartungen** ~ to exceed all expectations; **jds. Horizont** ~ to be beyond s. o.; **jds. Kräfte** ~ to be too much for s. o.; **Mauer** ~ to climb over a wall; **wertmäßig** ~ to exceed in value.
übersteigern *(Auktion)* to outbid, to overbid.
übersteigert excessive, exaggerated;
~**er Nationalismus** ultranationalism; ~**es Selbstbewußtsein** exaggerated sense of one's own importance.
Übersteigerung *(Auktion)* outbidding, overbid.
überstellen *(mil.)* to transfer;
dem Exekutionskommando ~ to deliver over to execution; **Strafgefangene** ~ to commit prisoners.
Überstellung *(mil.)* transfer;
~ **von Straftätern** commitment of prisoners, interstate reordition *(US)*.
Überstellungsbeschluß commitment order.
Übersteuer supertax.
übersteuern to overtax.
Überstimmen outvoting;
~ **eines Antrags** defeat of a motion.
überstimmen to vote down, to outvote, to defeat by vote, to countervote, to beat by a majority;
Antrag ~ to defeat a motion.
überstimmt werden to be defeated by a majority.
Überstrahlung *(Fernsehen)* bloom.
überstrapazieren, jds. Geduld to abuse s. one's patience; **seine finanziellen Mittel** ~ to overreach one's resources and finances.
überstreichen to wash over.
überströmen, von Dankbezeugungen to overflow with gratitude.
überströmt, von Touristen inundated with tourists.
Überstunde overtime, extra (excess) hour, overhour, overwork;
bezahlte ~**n** paid overtime; **geleistete** ~**n** overtime worked;
~**n im Speditionsgewerbe** shipping stretchouts *(US)*;
~**n abgelten** to pay for overtime; ~**n ablehnen** to jib at working overtime; ~**n machen** to put in an extra hour's work, to do (make, work, be on) overtime; **aus Prinzip keine** ~ **machen** not to work overtime on principle;
~**n machen lassen** to employ on overtime.
Überstunden|arbeit extra work, working overtime, overwork; ~**bezahlung** overtime [premium] pay, call-back pay, time and one-half pay; ~**forderung** overtime request; ~**geld** premium pay, overtime bonus (compensation, payment, premium); ~**gelder erhalten** to be paid extra for overtime; ~**genehmigung** overtime authorization; ~**gesuch** overtime request; ~**lohn** overtime wage (pay); ~**lohnsatz** overtime rate; ~**prämie** premium pay, overtime premium; ~**satz** overtime rate; **anderthalbfacher** ~**tarifsatz** overtime rate of time and a half; ~**verbot** overtime ban; ~**verdienste** overtime payments; ~**vergütung** overtime (premium) pay, overtime allowance, special allowance for irregular hours; ~**vorauszahlungsschema** prepayment plan *(US)*.
Überstundenzeit overtime hours;
einem Betrieb zugestandene ~ factory allowance of overtime; **zurückgehende** ~ outs in overtime;
~ **anrechnen** to reckon hours of overtime.
Überstunden|zulage, ~**zuschlag** overtime bonus (pay);
25%iger übertariflicher ~ time and a quarter.
überstürzen to rush into;
sich ~ to follow in rapid succession, *(Nachrichten)* to precipitate.
überstürzt headlong, precipitous, rash;
~ **handeln** to act with precipitation, to go off half-cocked *(US)*;
~ **urteilen** to rush to conclusions.
Überstürzung precipitance, precipitation, hurry-skurry.
Übertage|arbeiter surface hand (worker), surfaceman, pithead worker, topman; ~**bau** surface mining (working); ~**belegschaft** surface workers.
Übertara excess of tare.
übertariflich in excess of the wage scale;
~ **bezahlen** to pay in excess of standard rates;
~**e Bezahlung** payment in excess of standard rates, payment over and above the wage scale; ~**e Leistungszulage** merit increase.
überteuern to charge too much, to overcharge, to surcharge.
Überteuerung overcharge, surcharge, excessive prices.
Überteuerungszuschüsse high cost-of-living grants.
übertölpeln to dupe, to outwit.
Übertölpelung dupery.
übertourt overdriven.
Übertrag *(Buchführung)* carrying forward, carry forward *(Br.)*, carryover, holdover, balance carried (brought) forward, amount carried over, continued (transferred) account, *(Saldo)* balance, *(Umbuchung)* transfer entry, subtotal;
~ **auf Bilanzkonto** balance carried to balance sheet;
~ **machen** to carry over, to pass a transfer *(Br.)*, to effect a transfer [in the books]; ~ **in den Büchern vornehmen** to effect a transfer in the books.
übertragbar transferable, assignable, alienable, *(begebbar)* negotiable, *(übersetzbar)* translatable;
direkt ~ *(Krankheit)* contagious; **einfach** ~ negotiable without endorsement; **frei** ~ freely transferable; **nicht** ~ nontransferable, nondelegable, untransferable, not transferable, nonassignable, inalienable, not assignable, *(nicht begebbar)* not negotiable; **quasi** ~ quasi-negotiable;
nur urkundlich ~ **sein** to lie in grant;
~**e Stimme** transferable vote; ~**e Urkunde** negotiable instrument; **durch Indossament** ~**er Wechsel** negotiable bill.
Übertragbarkeit transferability, assignability, alienability, *(Begebbarkeit)* negotiability;
~ **eines Schecks ausschließen** to cross not negotiable.
übertragen *(abschreiben)* to transcribe, to copy, *(abtreten)* to transfer, to assign, to make an assignment, to alienate, to set over, to sign away (over), to negotiate, *(anvertrauen)* to commit, to entrust, *(Buchführung)* to carry forward (over, up), to post (bring) forward, to post up, *(Fernsehen)* to telecast, to televise, *(Grundstück)* to convey, to demise, *(Krankheit)* to communicate, to transmit, *(Kurzschrift)* to transcribe, *(als Relaisstation)* to relay, *(Rundfunk)* to broadcast, to transmit, *(übersetzen)* to translate, to render, *(verleihen)* to vest, *(vermachen)* to make over;
Aktien ~ to assign shares (stocks, *US*); **jem. ein Amt** ~ to receive s. o. into a charge; **jem. eine Angelegenheit** ~ to place a matter into the hands of s. o.; **Angelegenheit einem Rechtsanwalt** ~ to put a matter into the hands of a solicitor; **einem Architekten den Bau einer Brücke** ~ to entrust an architect with the construction of a bridge; **auf Band** ~ to record on tape; **seiner Bank die laufende Bezahlung seiner Steuern** ~ to commission one's bank to pay one's taxes; **Besitz** ~ to vest in possession; **blanko** ~ to assign in blank; **Blut** ~ to transfuse blood; **Buchung in das Hauptbuch** ~ to post a journal into the ledger; **direkt** ~ *(Rundfunk)* to transmit (broadcast) live; **Eigentum** ~ to pass a title; **aus dem Englischen ins Deutsche** ~ to render English into German; **in notarieller Form** ~ to convey by notarial deed; **formlos** ~ to negotiate by delivery only; **jem. Funktionen** ~ to devolve duties on s. o.; **Fußballspiel direkt** ~ to broadcast a football game live; **Geschäft auf seinen Sohn** ~ to make over the business to one's son; **durch Giro** ~ to endorse, to transfer by indorsement (endorsement); **Grundeigentum** ~ to transfer a title to land; **Grundstück notariell** ~ to grant land by deed; **im Hauptbuch** ~ to post up the ledger; **auf den Konkursverwalter** ~ to make an assignment for the benefit of one's creditors; **auf ein anderes Konto** ~ to transfer to another account; **jem. die Leitung einer Bank** ~ to invest the management of a bank in s. o.; **Manuskript ins reine** ~ to make a fair copy of a manuscript; **jem. ein Ministerium** ~ to call s. o. to office (to a ministry); **auf jds. Namen** ~ to register in s. one's name; **Patent** ~ to assign a patent; **Posten** ~ to carry forward an item; **Professur** ~ to endow with a professorship; **Recht** ~ to assign (transfer) a right; **Rechte auf einen Bevollmächtigten** ~ to delegate rights to a deputy; **Rede durch Rundfunk** ~ to broadcast a speech; **in Reinschrift** ~ to copy fair; **Saldo** ~ to extend (carry over) a balance; **Saldo von 100 £ auf ...** ~ to cover the balance of £ 100 into ...; **aus dem Stenogramm** ~ to transcribe, to write down from dictation; **Vermögen auf j.** ~ to devolve (hand over) property (deed one's estate) upon s. o.; **sein Vermögen auf seinen Sohn** ~ to deliver over one's property to one's son; **Vollmacht auf j.** ~ to delegate (vest) authority to (confer powers on) s. o.; **Zeichnung auf eine lithografische Platte** ~ to transfer a drawing to a lithographic plate; **Zuständigkeit** ~ to confer powers;
urkundlich ~ **werden** to pass by deed;
~ *(a.)* assigned, transferred;
direkt ~ *(Rundfunk)* live; **durch Satellit** ~ satellite-transmitted.
übertragende Gesellschaft transferor company.

Übertragender transferor, consignor, alienor, assignor, *(Wechsel)* endorser, indorser.

übertragene | Bedeutung figurative sense; ~ **Gerichtsbarkeit** delegated jurisdiction.

Übertragung *(Abschrift)* copying, *(Abtretung)* transfer, transference, assignment, assignation, delivery, *(Befugnisse)* delegation, devolution, *(Buchung)* transfer, entry, *(im Erbwege)* descent, livery, *(Fernsehen)* telecast, *(Grundbesitz)* conveyance, alienation, *(Korrekturen)* transcription, transfer, *(Rundfunk)* broadcast[ing], transmission, *(Stenogramm)* transcription, *(Übersetzung)* translation, rendering, *(Vermachung)* making over, vesting, *(Wertpapier)* negotiation;
an Bedingungen geknüpfte ~ conditional transfer (conveyance); **teilweise** ~ partial assignment; **uneingeschränkte** ~ absolute transfer; **unentgeltliche** ~ gratuitous transfer; **ungültige** ~ improper transfer; **unwiderrufliche** ~ irrevocable assignment; **blanko vorgenommene** ~ blank transfer *(Br.)*; **zu Zwecken der Erbschaftsregulierung vorgenommene** ~ transfer in contemplation of death; **wortgetreue** ~ literal transcript;
~ **von Aktien** transfer of shares (stocks, *US*); ~ **von Anteilen am Gesellschaftsvermögen** stock transfer; ~ **von Aufgaben** assignment of duties; ~ **vom Band** *(Rundfunk)* recorded broadcast; ~ **von Befugnissen** delegation of powers; ~ **vom Deutschen ins Englische** translation from German into English; ~ **von Eigentum** transfer of ownership (property, title), translation, bargain and sale; ~ **von Eigentum durch Staatsakt** conveyance by record; **drahtlose** ~ **elektrischer Energie** telemechanics; ~ **einer Fernsehsendung** transmission of a television program(me); ~ **einer Forderung** assignment of a debt, assignation of a claim; ~ **eines Geschäfts** transfer of a business; ~ **eines Gesellschafteranteils** assignment of a share in partnership; ~ **der Gesetzgebungsgewalt** delegation of legislative powers; **unentgeltliche** ~ **von Grundbesitz** voluntary conveyance; ~ **von öffentlichem Grundeigentum auf Privatpersonen** private land grant; ~ **von Grundstücksrechten** assurance of property, common assurance; ~ **in das Hauptbuch** posting up the ledger, ledger posting; ~ **einer Konferenz im Fernsehen** broadcast of a conference by television; ~ **der Konkursmasse** surrender of a bankrupt's property; ~ **einer Krankheit** communication (transmission) of a disease; ~ **an Ort und Stelle** conveyance in pais; ~ **eines Patents** assignment (conveyance) of a patent; ~ **eines Rechtes** assignment of a right, conveyance of title; ~ **einer stenografisch aufgenommenen Rede in Schreibmaschinenschrift** typewritten transcript of a speech; ~ **im Rundfunk** radio broadcast, broadcast (wireless) transmission; ~ **der beweglichen Sachwerte** *(Unternehmen)* bulk transfer *(US)*; ~ **eines Saldos** transfer of balance; ~ **des Schuldnervermögens mit dem Ziel der Gläubigerbenachteiligung** fraudulent transfer; ~ **des Treuhandvermögens** vesting of trust property; ~ **durch letztwillige Verfügung** disposition by will; ~ **von Vermögen** transfer (conveyance) of property; ~ **beweglichen Vermögens** grant of personal property; **unentgeltliche** ~ **beweglicher Vermögensgegenstände** voluntary transfer of personalty; ~ **von Vermögensgewinnen** transfer of capital gains; ~ **von Vertragsverpflichtungen** assignment of contractual obligations; ~ **der Verwaltungshoheit** cession of administration; ~ **von Zuständigkeiten** conferring of powers;
~ **in den Büchern vornehmen** to effect a transfer in the books.

Übertragungs | anweisung transfer order *(Br.)*; ~**anzeige** notice of assignment; ~**band** communication band; ~**bedingungen** terms of assignment; ~**beleg** transfer voucher; ~**bescheinigung** *(Aktien)* certification of transfer *(Br.)*; ~**datum** vesting date; ~**erklärung** deed of transfer, *(Treuhänder)* vesting declaration.

übertragungsfähig negotiable.

Übertragungs | fehler mistake in transcription; ~**formular** transfer form; **kombiniertes** ~- **und Vollmachtsformular** combined form of transfer and power of attorney; ~**gebühr** *(Aktien)* registration (transfer, *US*) fee; ~**hinweis** posting reference; ~**kabel** transmission cable; ~**leitung** transmission line; **[aktienrechtliche]** ~**quittung** transfer receipt; ~**raum** studio; ~**register** transfer book; ~**schein** transfer ticket (certificate); ~**spesen** transfer expense; ~**stempel** transfer stamp; ~**system** transmission system; ~**technik** communication engineering; ~**urkunde** [deed of] assignment, deed of conveyance, brief of title, vesting instrument (assent, deed) *(Br.)*, *(über Effektenverkäufe)* transfer deed (certificate, *Br.*), instrument of transfer, marked transfer *(Br.)*; ~**urkunde abstempeln** to stamp up the transfer; ~**verfügung** vesting order; ~**verlust** *(el.)* transmission loss; ~**vermerk** transfer entry, reference number; **üblichen** ~**vordruck rechtsgültig ausfüllen** to execute a common form of transfer; ~**wagen** mobile unit.

übertreffen to outrun, to outrival, to go one better, to excel;
j. ~ to be an improvement on s. o., to fly at a higher pitch than s. o.; **alles** ~ to whip creation, to top it all; **alles bisher dagewesene** ~ to bear the palm, to beat everything, to take the cake *(coll.)*; **Börsendurchschnittswerte** ~ to outrun the market average; **jds. Erwartungen** ~ to surpass s. one's expectations; **j. an Freundlichkeit** ~ to outdo s. o. in kindness; **an Geschwindigkeit** ~ to outspeed; **größen- und bevölkerungsmäßig** ~ to exceed in size and population; **gesamte Konkurrenz** ~ to excel (surpass) all rivals; **leistungsmäßig** ~ to outperform; **an Schlauheit** ~ to outwit, to outsmart *(US)*; **sich selbst** ~ to excel o. s., *(Schauspieler)* to top one's part; **j. spielend** ~ to knock s. one's head off *(coll.)*; **weit** ~ to outclass.

übertreiben to exaggerate, to outstep the truth, to overstate, to overshoot, to overdo, to go overboard, *(angeben)* to draw the long bow;
seine Bescheidenheit ~ to carry modesty too far; **ein bißchen** ~ to go it rather strong; **seine Künste** ~ to draw a streak; **eigene Sache** ~ to overstate one's case; **ganz schön** ~ to pile (put) it on, to come it a bit strong; **Schwierigkeit** ~ to magnify a difficulty.

Übertreibung exaggeration, overstatement, stretcher *(US sl.)*.

übertreten to contravene, to infringe, to transgress, to disobey, to trespass, *(Fluß)* to overflow its banks, *(Religion wechseln)* to turn, to change one's faith;
Anordnung ~ to act contrary to an order; **Bestimmungen** ~ to contravene the regulations; **zu einer anderen Partei** ~ to change sides, to turn one's coat *(Br.)*, to flop over *(US)*, to rat *(sl.)*.

Übertreter transgressor, trespasser, breaker, violator, contravener, infractor *(US)*, tort feasor;
~ **arbeitsrechtlicher Bestimmungen** labo(u)r law violator.

Übertretung infraction, misfeasance, contravention, transgression, misdemeano(u)r, violence, violation, *(Patent)* infringement, breach, *(Strafrecht)* slip, slight (summary, *US*) offence, violation *(US)*;
mit Geldstrafe belegte ~ pecuniary offence;
~ **von Anordnungen** infraction of regulations; ~ **von Polizeivorschriften** police offence (offense, *US*), breach of police regulations; ~ **der Steuerbestimmungen** tax offence (offense, *US*);
sich einer ~ **schuldig machen** to trespass against a law, to transgress a law, to commit a violation *(US)*.

Übertretungs | fall, im in case of noncompliance (contravention, transgression); ~**sache** summons case *(Br.)*.

übertrieben extreme, extravagant, highflying, fussy *(US)*;
leicht ~ mildly exaggerated; **maßlos** ~ grossly exaggerated; **nicht** ~ true to fact, literal;
~ **darstellen** to give an overdrawn account; ~ **streng zu jem. sein** to be too hard on s. o.;
~**e Ansichten** extreme opinions; ~**er Aufwand** extravagant expenses; ~**e Forderungen** exorbitant demands; ~**e Gebühren** excessive charges; **stark** ~**e Gerüchte** highly exaggerated rumo(u)rs; ~**e Vorsicht** overcaution.

Übertriebenheit extravagance, exaggeration.

Übertritt *(pol.)* defection, changing sides, ratting *(sl.)*, *(Religion)* conversion;
zum ~ **in eine andere Partei veranlassen** to convert to another party.

übertünchen to daub, to disguise.

übertrumpfen to surpass, to outdo, to go one better.

überversichern to overinsure.

überversichert sein to be overinsured, to be overcovered.

Überversicherung overinsurance, excess insurance, short interest.

übervölkert overpeopled, overpopulated, crowded, congested;
~**e Wohnungen** overcrowded dwellings.

übervoll brimful(l), overfull, crowded.

Übervollbeschäftigung overfull employment.

Übervorrat overstock.

übervorsichtig handeln to act overcautiously.

übervorteilen to overreach, to outbargain, to cheat, to push to the wall, to sting *(sl.)*;
j. ~ to overcharge s. o.

Übervorteilter fool, dupe.

Übervorteilung overreaching, taking undue advantage, *(Betrug)* defraud, defraudation, imposition;
flagrante ~ gross overcharge.

überwachen to supervise, to superintend, to overlook, to control, *(Detektiv)* to shadow, *(Nachrichtenverbindungen)* to monitor, *(Polizei)* to safeguard;
Druckvorgang ~ to see through the press, to supervise the printing; **Konten** ~ to control (audit) accounts; **j. laufend** ~ to

keep tabs on s. o., to keep s. o. under one's eye; **polizeilich** ~ to watch a suspect by police, to stake out *(coll.)*; **Preisanstieg** ~ to police the price increase; **schärfer** ~ to clamp down; **Schiffsbau** ~ to superintend the building of a ship; **Spesen genauestens** ~ to keep a strict account of (tabs on) expenses; **Stimmenabgabe** ~ to superintend an election; **j. streng** ~ to keep a sharp eye on s. o.; **Verkehr** ~ to control the traffic;
Maschinen zu ~ **haben** to be in charge of the machines.

Überwacher surveillant, supervisor.

überwacht controlled;
vom Geschäftsführer persönlich ~ under the personal superintendence of the manager;
polizeilich ~ **werden** to be under police supervision.

Überwachung observation, surveillance, control, supervision, superintendence, inspection, oversight, vigilance *(US)*, *(Rundfunksendung)* monitoring;
gerichtlich angeordnete ~ compulsory supervision; **betriebseigene** ~ internal (in-house) control; **finanzielle** ~ financial control; **polizeiliche** ~ police supervision, surveillance; **sanitäre** ~ sanitary control; **scharfe** ~ close supervision; **schärfere** ~ clampdown; **thermostatische** ~ thermostatic control;
~ **durch eingebaute Abhörgeräte** electronic surveillance; ~ **von drei Abteilungen** supervision of three departments; **betriebseigene** ~ **der Buchhaltung** accounting control; ~ **durch die Gesundheitsbehörden** sanitary inspection; ~ **der Grenzen** frontier control; ~ **des Kassenbestands** cash control; ~ **der Kreditfähigkeit** credit checking; ~ **eines Kredits** control of an advance, credit control; ~ **der Mietkosten** rent control; ~ **der Presse** control of newspapers; ~ **eingehender Rechnungen** invoice supervision; ~ **des Rechnungswesens** accounting, internal auditing; ~ **der Tarifpolitik im öffentlichen Bereich** public-sector pay control; ~ **von Telefongesprächen** supervision of calls; ~ **durch die Unternehmensleitung** managerial control; ~ **der Verschlüsselungsarbeit** coding control;
~ **des Nachtlebens schleifen lassen** to let down the bars *(US)*; ~ **verstärken** to clamp down.

Überwachungs|abteilung, technische safety engineering department; ~**anlagen** *(Rundfunk, Fernsehen)* monitoring system; ~**ausschuß** control (vigilance, *US*) commission, commission of control, supervisory (monitoring, watchdog) committee; ~**beamter** superintendent, supervisor, surveiller; ~**befugnis** power to control, supervisory powers (authority); ~**behörde** supervising authority, regulator; ~**behörde der Nachrichtendienste** intelligence oversight board *(US)*; ~**behörde für Rezeptgebühren** Prescription Pricing Authority *(Br.)*; **technischer** ~**dienst** technical control service; ~**fähigkeit** supervisory ability; **polizeiliches** ~**fahrzeug** surveillance squad; ~**funktionen** surveillance role, supervisory duties, regulatory job, oversight powers; ~**funktionen haben** to act as supervisor; ~**gerät** *(Rundfunk, Fernsehen)* monitor; ~**klinke** *(Telefonzentrale)* monitor jack; ~**kosten** cost of control, supervisory costs; ~**lücke** regulatory void; ~**methode** control method; ~**organ** supervisory organ; ~**pflicht** duty of supervision; ~**position** supervisory post; ~**raum** monitor room; ~**rolle** surveillance role; ~**satellit** spy satellite; ~**schiff** control vessel.

Überwachungsstelle board of control, supervisory (regulatory) agency, control office, regulator, *(Rundfunksendung)* monitoring station;
~ **für Aktienausgaben** stock registrar *(US)*; ~ **für Obligationsausgabe** bond registrar *(US)*.

Überwachungssystem supervisory system, *(Fernsehen, Rundfunk, Telefon)* monitoring system;
gegenseitiges ~ *(Regierung)* system of check and balance *(US)*.

Überwachungstätigkeit regulatory job, control, supervisory service;
finanzielle ~ financial control; **technische** ~ control engineering;
~**en ausüben** to exercise supervisory control.

Überwachungs|verfahren *(Rundfunk)* monitoring procedure; ~**verfügung** supervision order; ~**vorrichtung** *(Fernsehen, Rundfunk)* monitoring device; ~**zeit** machine attention time; ~**zentrum** control center *(US)* (centre, *Br.*); ~**zone** control zone.

überwältigen to overwhelm, to overpower;
Feind ~ to overcome the enemy;
sich vom Zorn ~ **lassen** to let one's anger get the better of one.

überwältigend|er Erfolg smashing success; ~**e Mehrheit** overwhelming (crushing) majority.

überwältigt overpowered, overwhelmed, stunned;
von Kummer ~ overburdened with grief;
von den Nachrichten ~ **sein** to be overpowered by the news; **völlig** ~ **sein** to be swept off one's feet; **von Müdigkeit** ~ **werden** to be overcome by fatigue.

überwälzen *(Steuer)* to shift, to pass.

Überwasser|fahrzeug surface ship (vessel); ~**geschwindigkeit** surface speed; ~**streitkräfte** surface forces.

überwechseln to go over;
vom Heer zum Anwaltsbüro ~ to leave the army for the law; **in ein anderes Lager** ~ to go over to the other camp, to rat *(sl.)*; **in eine andere Partei** ~ to turn one's coat *(Br.)*, to flop over *(US)*, to rat *(sl.)*;
Reisende in eine andere Klasse ~ **lassen** to transfer passengers from one class to another.

überweisen to remit, to transfer, to consign;
an einen Ausschuß ~ to refer (commit) to a committee; **durch eine Bank** ~ to pay (remit) through a bank; **brieflich** ~ to remit by letter; **Gegenwert** ~ to remit the proceeds; **Geld auf ein Konto** ~ to transfer money to an account; **Geldbetrag** ~ to remit a sum of money, to send a remittance; **einem Gericht** ~ to commit for trial; **Kunden** ~ to recommend customers; **Patienten an einen Facharzt** ~ to refer a patient to a specialist; **postwendend** ~ to remit by return of post *(Br.)* (returning post, *Br.*, returning mail, *US*); **für jds. Rechnung 1000 Dollar** ~ to remit $ 1000 for s. one's account; **Saldo** ~ to remit (pay in) the balance; **telegrafisch** ~ to cable, to transfer money by cable; **zur Verhandlung und Aburteilung** ~ to commit for trial.

überweisende Bank remittent bank.

Überweisender remitter, transmitter.

Überweisung remittance, transfer, *(an Ausschuß)* commitment, committal, *(an andere Behörde)* reference;
bargeldlose ~ credit transfer; **garantierte briefliche** ~ guaranteed mail transfer *(US)*; **postalische** ~ remittance by post, mail transfer *(US)*; **telegrafische** ~ telegraphic (cable) transfer, cable remittance;
~ **ins Ausland** sending money abroad, remittance (transfer of funds) abroad; ~ **des geschuldeten Betrages** remittance of the amount payable; ~ **in Übersee erzielter Einkünfte** remittance of overseas income; ~ **von Einwanderern** immigrant remittances; ~**en von Gastarbeitern** transfers by foreign employees; ~ **des Gegenwertes** remittance of proceeds; ~ **des Gehalts** transfer of salary; ~ **an ein anderes Gericht** remittal, remitter; ~ **eines Gesetzentwurfes** commitment of a bill; **schwebende** ~ **und Inkassi** float; ~ **auf ein Konto** transfer into an account; ~ **zu Lasten des Kreditkontos** credit transfer, bank giro *(Br.)*; ~ **durch die Post** remittance by post, mail transfer *(US)*; ~ **von einem Postscheckkonto auf das andere** inter-giro transfer; ~ **auf ausländische Postscheckkonten** transfer to foreign giro system; ~ **einer Provision** remittance of a commission; ~ **an den Rücklagenfonds** transfer to the reserve fund; ~ **eines Schecks zu Parikurs** par remittance *(US)*; ~ **in jeder frei konvertierbaren Währung** remittance in any convertible currency; ~ **an Zahlungs Statt** transfer in lieu of cash;
~ **eines Geldbetrages verzögern** to postpone the payment of an amount.

Überweisungs|abschnitt *(Bank)* transfer slip, *(Post)* postal check; ~**abteilung** transfer department; ~**anzeige** bank payment advice; ~**auftrag** remittance order, order for a bank, banker's order, transfer order *(Br.)*; ~**beleg** remittance slip; **Pfändungs- und** ~**beschluß** attachment *(US)* (garnishee) order, writ of attachment, decree of forthcoming *(Scot.)*; ~**beschränkungen** transfer restrictions; ~**buch** book of remittances; ~**empfänger** transferee, remittee; ~**formular** remittance form, transfer slip, *(Bank)* bank transfer form, girotransfer slip *(Br.)*, *(im Clearingverfahren)* transfer ticket, *(Postscheck)* transfer deposit form; ~**gebühr** charge for transmitting money, remittance fee; ~**genehmigung** transfer authorization; ~**konto** remittance account; ~**möglichkeit** transfer facility; ~**posten** amount remitted; ~**provision** transfer commission; ~**scheck**, ~**schein** transfer ticket (check), clearinghouse certificate; ~**schreiben** transmittal letter; ~**träger** remittance slip, transfer voucher (ticket); ~**verkehr** transfer business, interbank money transfer, clearing system.

überwerfen, sich mit jem. to fall out (break) with s. o.

überwiegen to overweigh, to outbalance, to prevail, to predominate.

überwiegend predominant, prevalent, preponderant;
~ **heiter** *(Wetter)* mainly bright;
~**e Mehrheit** overwhelming majority; ~**e Mode** prevailing fashion; ~**er Teil der Bevölkerung** majority of the population.

überwinden to overcome, to overpass, to surmount, *(Gefühle)* to subdue;

etw. ~ to get over s. th.; **j. ~** to fly at a higher pitch than s. o.; **sich ~, etw. zu tun** to bring o. s. to do s. th.;
Hindernis ~ to overcome (pass over) an obstacle; **Krise ~** to overcome a crisis; **mühelos ~** to take in one's stride; **Vorurteil ~** to outgrow a prejudice.
Überwindung reluctance, constant effort;
~ der Dollarlücke bridging the dollar gap.
überwuchert overgrown, undergrown.
überwunden, etw. ~ haben to be clear of s. th., to have got over s. th.;
~er Standpunkt outdated view.
Überzahl numerical superiority, *(Mehrheit)* majority;
der ~ weichen to yield to superior forces.
überzahlen to overpay, to pay too much for (through the nose).
überzählig surplus, excess, odd, over, superfluous, *(Beschäftigter)* supernumerary, redundant;
~es Geld overpayment, payment in excess, money to spare; **~e Warenbestände** surplus stocks.
überzahlte Steuer excess (overpaid) duty.
Überzahlung der Einkommensteuer excess payment of income tax.
überzeichnen, Anleihe to oversubscribe (cover) a loan, to subscribe a loan in excess.
überzeichnet oversubscribed;
~ sein *(Anleihe)* to be covered; **mehrfach ~ sein** to be subscribed several times;
~e Anleihe oversubscribed loan.
Überzeichnung oversubscription, subscription in excess, excess application *(Br.)*.
überzeugen to convince, to persuade, to satisfy;
Parlament ~ to carry the floor; **j. von der Wahrheit seiner Erklärung ~** to persuade s. o. of the truth of one's statement; **Widersacher schließlich ~** to talk over an opponent;
sich gern ~ lassen to be open to conviction; **sich von jem. ~ lassen** to buy s. one's line of thinking.
überzeugend cogent, conclusive;
nicht sehr ~ klingen not to carry much conviction;
~er Beweis convincing proof, conclusive evidence; **~e Beweiskraft** strength of an argument.
überzeugt, felsenfest ~ sein to tell the world; **fest ~ sein** to be absolutely convinced (positive); **von einer Sache ~ sein** to be conscious (convinced) of s. th.;
~er Nationalist ardent nationalist.
Überzeugung belief, conviction;
zur ~ des Gerichts to the satisfaction of the court;
politische ~ political opinions (conviction); **religiöse ~** religious conviction; **starke ~** strong feelings;
unumstößliche ~ von einer Schuld abiding conviction;
j. von seiner ~ abbringen to dissuade s. o.; **zu der ~ gelangen** to arrive at the conclusion; **aus innerer ~ handeln** to act up to one's conviction.
Überzeugungs|kraft persuasive force, power of suasion (suggestion); **~reklame** reason-why copy.
überziehen *(Flugzeug)* to stall, to overclimb, to pancake, to whipstall;
sich ~ *(Himmel)* to cloud over, to become overcast; **Bett frisch ~** to put fresh sheets on a bed; **sein Konto ~** to overdraw one's account (the badger, *Br., coll.*), to make overdrafts, to overcheck one's account *(US)*; **seinen Kredit ~** to outrun (overdraw) one's credit; **Land mit Krieg ~** to invade a country; **sich einen Mantel ~** to put on one's coat; **seine Redezeit ~** to overrun one's allotted time; **Sessel mit Leder ~** to cover a chair with leather; **mit Silver ~** to silver-plate.
Überzieher overcoat, topcoat, paletot, raincoat.
Überziehung overdraft;
~ des Bankkontos bank overdraft.
Überziehungs|finanzierung overdraft finance; **~grenze** overdraft limit; **vereinbarte ~grenze** agreed overdraft limit.
Überziehungskredit loan on overdraft, overdraft facilities, *(Handelsabkommen)* swing;
um Einräumung eines ~es einkommen to ask the banker for an overdraft; **einem Unternehmen einen ~ einräumen** to grant a firm overdraft facilities; **~ gewähren** to grant a credit by overdraft; **sich im Rahmen eines ~es halten** to be within the limit of an overdraft;
~satz base rate; **~zinsen** interest on overdraft.
Überziehungs|limit overdraft limit; **~möglichkeit** overdraft facilities; **~provision** commission on overdraft, overdraft commission (fee); **~recht** overdraft privilege; **~scheck** overcheque *(Br.)*, overcheck *(US)*; **~zeitraum** period of overdraft; **~zinsen** overdraft interest.
überzogen, sein Konto bis zu einer Höhe von 100 £ ~ haben to be overdrawn to the extent of £ 100;
~es Konto overdraft, overdrawn account; **~e Werbung** persuasive advertising, advertisement puff *(Br.)*.
Überzug cover, *(Kopfkissen)* slip.
üblich general, traditional, customary, conventional, usual, in use, *(normal)* standard, ordinary;
absolut ~ all in the day's work; **allgemein ~** in common use; **nicht ~** uncustomary;
~ sein to be the normal practice; **im allgemeinen ~ sein** to be common practice (general); **im ordentlichen kaufmännischen Leben ~ sein** to be consistent with sound commercial practice;
zu den ~en Bedingungen at the usual terms; **~e Begrüßung** usual welcome; **~e Gebühr** *(Bank)* usual charge; **~er Geschäftsablauf** usual course of employer's trade; **~e Geschenke** customary gifts; **~e Honorarregelung** *(Werbeagentur)* usual agency terms; **~er Lohn** prevailing rate, going wage; **~es Muster** conventional design; **~e Rechnung** ordinary bill; **~e Rechtsmängelgewährhaftung** usual covenant; **~er Schadensersatz** general damages; **im Verkehr ~e Sorgfalt** ordinary care (diligence); **~e Tagesordnung** ordinary business; **~e Tara** customary tare; **~es Verfahren** standard (common) practice; **im ~en Verfahren herstellen** to produce in the ordinary way; **~e Verspätung** habitual delay; **unter dem ~en Vorbehalt** under the usual proviso; **~er Wechselkurs** usual rate of exchange; **auf dem ~en diplomatischen Weg** through the usual diplomatic channels; **~er Wind** prevailing wind; **~e Zahlungsbedingungen** standard payment clauses, usual terms of payment; **~er Zinssatz** standard interest, conventional rate of interest.
üblicherweise as a general rule, by custom, in the ordinary course of things.
übrig spare, left on hand, left over, residual, residuary;
im ~en for the rest;
etw. für j. ~ haben to have a soft spot for (be fond of) s. o.; **nicht viel dafür ~ haben** not to be particularly interested in s. th.; **keine Zeit ~ haben** to have no time to spare; **jem. verflixt wenig ~ lassen** to leave s. o. precious little to do;
~es Europa rest of Europe; **mein ~es Geld** rest of my money; **~e Zeit** spare time.
übrig|behalten to keep over; **~bleiben** to remain, to be left over; **~bleibend** residual; **~geblieben** remaining, left.
Übung usance, use, usage, practice, custom, routine, *(Schule)* exercise, lesson;
aus der ~ out of practice, out of training, rusty;
bestehende ~ *(Gericht)* established practice; **militärische ~en** military exercises;
~ der Gastfreundschaft rites of hospitality;
in ~ bleiben to keep in training; **der zwischenstaatlichen ~ entsprechen** to conform to international standards; **nicht aus der ~ geraten** to keep one's hand in; **aus der ~ kommen** to train off; **es an der nötigen ~ fehlen lassen** to lack the necessary practice; **aus der ~ sein** to be out of practice, to have lost the knack of it; **an praktischen ~en teilnehmen** to attend a tutorial;
~ macht den Meister practice makes perfect.
Übungs|aufgabe exercise; **~buch** exercise book; **~flug** practice flight; **~flugzeug** trainer, penguin; **~gelände** training ground.
übungshalber for the sake of practice.
Übungs|hang nursery slope; **~kurs** training course; **~marsch** route march; **~platz** training field; **~schießen** *(mil.)* practice firing, target practice; **~stunde** study hour.
Ufer *(Fluß)* bank, *(Meer)* shore, seashore, beach;
am ~ gelegen by the riverside, riparian; **von ~ zu ~** *(Seeversicherung)* from shore to shore;
steil abfallendes ~ steep bank;
~ bespülen to lick the beach; **ans ~ gelangen** to win to the shore; **über das ~ treten** to flow over the banks, to overflow its banks;
~anlieger frontager, riparian; **~anliegerrecht** riparian rights; **~bauten** embankments; **~befestigung** river bank; **~bewohner** riparian, riparian owner (proprietor), *(Küste)* coaster; **~bezirk** waterfront; **~damm** embankment; **~geld** pierage; **~grundstück** waterfront property; **~linie** shore line.
uferlos endless, boundless, vast, unlimited;
~e Debatte endless debate.
Ufer|mauer quay; **~recht** riparian rights; **~staat** riparian state; **gemauerte ~straße** embankment.
Uhr watch, timepiece;
gegen die ~ against time;
sich automatisch aufziehende ~ self-winding (keyless) watch; **Punkt zwölf ~** twelve o'clock on the dot;
~ aufziehen to wind a watch; **sich in einem Rennen gegen die ~ befinden** to race against time; **jem. sagen, was die ~ geschlagen**

hat to tell s. o. what's what; **pünktlich um 5 ~ kommen** to come at the stroke of five; **~ reparieren** to fix (mend, repair) a watch; **nach der ~ sehen** to consult one's watch; **~ zurückstellen** to put the clock back;
seine ~ ist abgelaufen his sands are running out;
~armband watchband.
Uhrenvergleich time check.
Uhr | kette watch chain; **~macher** watchmaker.
Uhrzeiger watch hand;
entgegengesetzt zum ~ counterclockwise;
~ zurückstellen to put back a minute hand;
im ~sinn clockwise; **entgegen dem ~sinn** anticlockwise.
Uhrzeit vergleichen to synchronize watches.
UK | stellen *(mil.)* to exempt, to defer *(US)*;
~-Gestellter exempt, deferable *(US)*; **~-Stellung** exemption from military service, deferment *(US)*.
Ukas ukase, edict, decree.
Ulk lark, joke.
ulkiger Vogel queer bird, odd fish *(coll.)*.
Ultimatum ultimatum;
~ der Geschäftsführung management ultimatum;
einem Land ein ~ stellen to deliver an ultimatum to a country.
Ultimo end of the month;
per ~ for the monthly settlement; **bis ~ gültig** *(Börse)* good this month;
~abrechnung, ~abschluß, ~abwicklung monthly (end-of-month) settlement; **~anforderungen** monthly demands; **~ausgleich** end-of-month adjustment, *(Jahresende)* year-end adjustment; **~beanspruchung am Jahresende** year-end pressure; **~bedarf** monthly requirements; **~bedingungen** end-of-month terms; **~effekten** securities for future delivery; **~einflüsse** end-of-month influences; **~fälligkeiten** monthly accruals; **~geld** end-of-month settlement loan, last-day money; **~geschäft** business done for the monthly clearance, last-day business; **~kurs** end-of-the-month stock-exchange price; **~liquidation** end-of-month settlement, monthly settlement (regulation); **~preis** account price; **~regulierung** monthly settlement; **schwierige ~regulierung** heavy settlement; **~stand** end-of-month figures; **~wechsel** bill maturing at the end of the month.
Ultra *(pol.)* extremist;
~konservativer stick-in-the-mud, fog(e)y, Hunker *(US sl.)*, blimp *(Br.)*.
ultrakonservativ stick-in-the-mud, hunkerous *(US sl.)*.
Ultra | kurzwelle ultra-short wave, very high frequency, microwave; **~nationalist** hundred-percenter; **~radikaler** maximalist; **~schall** supersound.
ultraviolett, Patienten ~ bestrahlen irradiate a patient;
~e Strahlen ultraviolet rays.
umadressieren to readdress, to redirect, to reconsign, to change the address.
Umadressierung redirection, reconsignment.
umändern to change, to modify, to alter, to make over, to alternate *(US)*, *(Buch)* to recast, to restyle.
Umänderung conversion, change, alteration, modification.
umarbeiten to work over, to remake, to remodel, to restyle, to remanufacture, to make over *(US)*, to alternate, *(Buch)* to revise, to rewrite, *(Schneider)* to fashion, to translate;
Roman ~ to rewrite a novel; **Stück für den Rundfunk ~** to adapt a play for broadcasting.
Umarbeitung conversion, modification, remanufacture, *(Buch)* revision, *(für den Film)* adapt[at]ion;
~ eines Stückes für den Rundfunk adaptation of a play for broadcasting.
Umarmung embrace, hug.
Umbau rebuilding, reconstruction, renovation, structural alteration, *(umgebautes Gebäude)* altered section, *(Verwaltung)* turnover, reorganization, reform;
wegen ~s geschlossen closed for renovation;
~ in Appartementwohnungen conversion into flats; **~ von Handels- zu Kriegsschiffen** conversion of merchant ships into warships; **~ der Verwaltung** civil service reform *(Br.)*.
umbauen to rebuild, to reconstruct, to renovate, to convert, to carry out structural alterations, *(Verwaltung)* to reorganize, to reform;
in Appartements ~ to convert into flats; **Bühnenbild ~** to change the scenery; **Verwaltung ~** to reorganize (reform) the administration.
umbaufähig suitable for conversion.
Umbauten building alterations;
~ vornehmen to carry out structural alterations.

umbauter Raum enclosed area.
umbenennen to rename, to redesignate.
Umbenennung change of name.
umbesetzen to shake up, *(Theater)* to recast;
Kabinett ~ to [re]shuffle the cabinet; **Stelle ~** to appoint another person; **Vorstand ~** to make changes in the direction of a firm (membership of the board), to shake up the management *(coll.)*.
Umbesetzung *(Angestellte)* turnover, *(Regierung)* reshuffle, *(Vorstand)* shakeup, *(Rolle)* recast;
personelle ~en personnel shake-up;
~en im Kabinett reshuffle of the cabinet; **~ der Schlüsselpositionen in der Vorstandsspitze** reshuffling of top management, executive shuffle; **~en des Vorstands** management turnover, management changes, changes in the direction of a firm, change in the membership of the board, shake-up of the management *(coll.)*;
~ der Werbefachleute vornehmen to rotate advertising executives.
umbiegen to bend (turn) up, *(Buchseite)* to dog-ear.
umbilden to remodel, to refashion, to reorganize, to reshape;
Koalition ~ to reshuffle the coalition; **Regierung ~** to reshuffle (make changes in) the cabinet.
Umbildung recomposition, reorganization;
~ der Regierung [re]shuffle of the cabinet (government);
~ der Regierung vornehmen to [re]shuffle the cabinet (government).
umblättern to turn over the leaves.
umbrechen *(Buch, Zeitung)* to break the line, to make up, to copy-edit, to overrun.
umbringen to knock off, to put out of the way, to put over *(sl.)*, to top;
j. ~ to kill s. o., to put s. o. to death, to remove s. o. out of the way, to send s. o. to glory *(coll.)*, to bump off s. o. *(sl.)*; **sich ~** to blow out one's brains, to kill o. s.; **sich beinahe ~ für j.** to fall over backwards for s. o.; **meuchlerisch ~** to assassinate.
Umbruch radical change, *(pol.)* upheaval, revolution, *(drucktechn.)* copy editing, make-up, making up and imposing;
~ machen to break the line, to copy-edit, to make up;
~abzug page proof; **~korrekturen** final (second) revise, make-up proof; **~redakteur** copy editor, copyreader, make-up man; **~redaktion** desk.
umbuchen to transfer from one account to another, to rebook, to reverse an entry;
Flug ~ to change a flight reservation.
Umbuchung transfer, cross entry, rebooking, *(Flug)* change in a reservation, *(Stornierung)* reverse entry, reversal;
~ im Hauptbuch ledger transfer;
~ vornehmen to transfer from one account to another; **~ in den Büchern vornehmen** to effect a transfer in the books.
umdatieren to change the date.
Umdenken, völliges countermarch.
Umdenkungsprozeß rethinking, change in the outlook.
umdeuten to reinterpret, to give a new interpretation;
jds. Aussage zu einem Geständnis ~ to twist s. one's words into a confession of guilt.
Umdeutung new interpretation, *(Rechtsgeschäft)* conversion.
Umdeutungsmöglichkeit, beschränkte ~ eines Rechtsgeschäftes qualified conversion.
umdirigieren to redirect, to reconsign;
Kapitalströme ~ to switch the flow of capital; **Verkehr ~** to divert (deroute, *US*) traffic.
umdisponieren to change one's arrangements, to redispose, to reorganize.
Umdisposition redisposition, reorganization;
~en vornehmen to change one's arrangements.
umdrehen to turn round, *(umkehren)* to invert;
jem. den Hals ~ to wring s. one's neck; **jeden Pfennig zweimal ~** to look at every penny twice; **Schlüssel im Schloß ~** to turn the key in a lock; **jem. das Wort im Munde ~** to misinterpret s. one's words.
Umdrehung revolution, rev.
Umdruck reprint.
umdrucken to reprint.
Umdruck | originalpapiere master papers, **~papier** offset paper, transfer paper *(Br.)*; **~vervielfältiger** liquid duplicator.
umerziehen *(pol.)* to re-educate.
Umerziehung *(pol.)* re-education.
umfahren to take a roundabout way, to bypass, to [make a] detour;
j. ~ to run s. o. over;

Hindernis ~ to drive round an obstacle; **Welt** ~ to circumnavigate the world.
Umfahrt machen to make a roundabout way (detour).
Umfall *(Parlamentarier)* defection, ratting *(sl.)*.
Umfallen, zum ~ **müde** fit (ready) to drop.
umfallen to fall down, to droop, to drop to the ground, *(Auto)* to upset, to overturn, *(Parlamentarier)* to change sides, to cross the floor of the house *(Br.)*, to rat *(sl.)*;
wie die Fliegen ~ to drop like flies in the heat.
umfaltbar turndown.
Umfang *(Ausdehnung)* extent, scope, size, measure, *(Baum)* girth, circumference, *(Bedeutung)* amount, significance, *(Buch)* length, *(Fassungsvermögen)* capacity, bulk, volume, *(Fülle)* amplitude, abundance, *(Größe)* size, *(Größenordnung)* dimensions, content, *(Maßstab)* scale, *(Rauminhalt)* volume, *(Reichweite)* range, radius, scale, *(Stadt)* perimeter;
in beschränktem ~ on a limited scale; **in geringem** ~ in a lesser degree; **in großem** ~ in a large measure, on a large scale, large-scale, largely; **in vollem** ~ to the full extent;
~ **der Eigentumsrechte** quality of estate; ~ **der Einfuhr** scale of imports; ~ **der Ermessensbefugnis** scope of discretion; ~ **des Fertigungsprogramms** range of products; ~ **einer Garantie** extent of warranty (guarantee); ~ **der Geschäftsführungsbefugnisse** *(Bank)* banking power; ~ **der Haftung** accountability, extent of liability; ~ **der vorgenommenen Investitionen** volume of investments; ~ **des Nutzungsrechts** scope of licence; ~ **dessen, was die Öffentlichkeit weiß** body of public knowledge; ~ **eines Patents** scope of a patent; ~ **der Produktion** scale of production, range of products; ~ **der Revision** scope of audit; ~ **der Schadenersatzberechnung** measure of damages; ~ **des Schadens** extent of damage; ~ **der Sorgfaltspflicht** degree of care; ~ **der Steuervergünstigung** extent of taxation relief; ~ **der Vergünstigungen** scale of allowances; ~ **einer Versicherung** scope of a policy, coverage of an insurance; ~ **der Vertretungsmacht** scope of an agent's authority; ~ **einer Vollmacht** extent (scope) of a power of attorney;
~ **des Manuskripts berechnen** to copy-cast, to calibrate a copy; **Produktion in kleinerem** ~ **fortsetzen** to continue production on a smaller scale; ~ **von 400 Seiten haben** to contain 400 pages; **in vollem** ~ **haften** to be liable to the extent of one's property; **Geschäfte größeren** ~**s tätigen** to deal in big volumes; ~ **der Auswirkungen übersehen** to foresee the full extent of the consequences; ~ **der vorgesehenen Investitionen leicht verringern** to trim slightly the current rate of spending; **an** ~ **zunehmen** to grow in volume.
umfangreich ample, voluminous, large-scale, bulky, *(geräumig)* extensive, spacious;
~ **sein** to bulk;
~**e Aufträge** heavy orders; **über** ~**e Mittel verfügen** to have ample means at one's disposal; ~**e Reparaturen** extensive repairs; ~**e Vorkehrungen** ample precautions; ~**es Warenangebot** wide range of items.
Umfangs|berechnung, ~**schätzung** *(Manuskript)* copycasting.
umfassen to cover, to comprehend, to comprise, to include, to contain, *(mil.)* to envelop, to outflank, to encircle;
vier Abteilungen ~ to embrace four departments; **Fall nicht** ~ not to reach a case; **vier Schreibmaschinenseiten** ~ to hold four typewritten pages; **Zeitraum von einer Woche** ~ to cover a period of a week.
umfassend extensive, complete, full, copious, integrated, overall, catchall, global, blanket *(US)*;
~**e Änderungen** sweeping changes; ~**e Bibliothek** comprehensive library; ~**e Kenntnisse** extensive (complete) knowledge; ~**er Lohnanstieg** across-the-board (round-of-) wage increase; ~**e Meinungsumfrage** national opinion poll; ~**es Patent** complete (blanket, *US*), patent; ~**e Prüfung** comprehensive examination; ~**e Reformen** sweeping reforms; ~**es Studium** comprehensive studies; ~**e Untersuchung** extensive inquiry; ~**e Vollmachten** plenary (full) powers; ~**e Vorbereitungen** large preparations; ~**e Zugeständnisse** far-reaching concessions.
umfinanzieren to refinance, to refund.
Umfinanzierung refinancing, refunding.
umfirmieren to rename a firm.
Umfirmierung changing a firm's name.
umformen to reform, to remodel, to new-model, *(el.)* to transform, to convert.
Umformstation converter station.
umformulieren to redraft, to rephrase;
Frage ~ to restate a question.
Umformulierung redraft;
~ **einer Frage** restatement of a question.
Umformung reform, *(el.)* conversion, transformation.
Umfrage [opinion] poll, survey, field investigation, *(Auskunfteinholung)* inquiry;
betriebliche ~ employee-attitude survey; **postalische** ~ postal survey;
~ **zur Erforschung der öffentlichen Meinung** public opinion poll; ~ **bei den Fernsehzuschauern** viewer survey; ~ **anhand von Fragebogen** questionnaire survey;
~ **durchführen** to take a poll, to conduct a survey; ~ **halten** to make inquiries; **Ergebnis einer** ~ **veröffentlichen** to release a poll;
~**antwort** survey answer; ~**bogen** opinionnaire; ~**ergebnisse** poll ratings, result of a survey; **systematischer** ~**fehler** nonsampling error.
umfriedet fenced in, enclosed.
Umfriedung enclosure, fence.
umfunktionieren to remodel;
in ein Lazarettschiff ~ to turn into a hospital ship.
Umgang dealings, intercourse, relations, association;
beim ~ **mit Büchern** when working with books;
familiärer ~ familiarity; **gesellschaftlicher** ~ conversation, social interchange (intercourse); **vertraulicher** ~ confidential relationship;
auf seinen ~ **achten** to pick one's company; **keinerlei gesellschaftlichen** ~ **haben** to be cut off from all society; **mit niemandem** ~ **haben** to live in seclusion; **schlechten** ~ **haben** to keep bad company; **verbrecherischen** ~ **haben** to consort with criminals, to be linked by crime; **wenig** ~ **haben** not to mix much; ~ **mit jem. haben** to keep up acquaintance (company) with s. o.; ~ **mit feinen Leuten haben** to train with well-dressed people *(sl.)*; **gesellschaftlichen** ~ **pflegen** to socialize o. s.; **mit berühmten Persönlichkeiten vertraulichen** ~ **pflegen** to be intimate with the great; **täglichen** ~ **mit berühmten Schriftstellern pflegen** to live in daily intercourse with great writers.
umgänglich sociable, companionable, *(leicht zu behandeln)* affable.
Umgangsenglisch conversational English.
Umgangsformen manners, deportment;
angenehme ~ pleasing countenance; **betriebliche** ~ corporate etiquette; **geschäftliche** ~ business etiquette (manners); **gesellschaftliche** ~ social habits, etiquette; **gute** ~ urbanity; **strenge** ~ strict etiquette; **verbindliche** ~ pleasing personality.
Umgangssprache common parlance, colloquial (everyday) language.
umgarnen to mesh, to ensnare.
umgarnt entangled.
umgebaute Ställe converted mews *(Br.)*.
umgeben to enclose, to surround, to inclose, to encompass, to hem about, to encircle;
j. mit liebevoller Fürsorge ~ to take great care of s. o.; **Garten mit einem Zaun** ~ to fence in a garden;
von Geheimnissen ~ wrapped in mystery; **von Luxus** ~ surrounded by luxury.
Umgebung environs, environment, surroundings, surrounding countryside, vicinity, neighbo(u)rhood, region, medium, setting, way, precincts, *(Präsident)* entourage, suite;
in der unmittelbaren ~ in close vicinity;
abstoßende ~ ugly surroundings; **gesundheitsfördernde** ~ wholesome surroundings; **gewohnte** ~ element; **häusliche** ~ house environment; **kümmerliche** ~ mean surroundings; **ländliche** ~ country setting; **nahe** ~ vicinity; **nähere** ~ near surroundings, outskirts, purlieu; **ungewohnte** ~ novelty of surroundings; **wohnliche** ~ homely comfort;
~ **einer Stadt** environs of a town;
sich seiner ~ **anpassen** to fit o. s. into one's surroundings, to adjust o. s. to one's environment; **jem. aus einer gewohnten** ~ **herausnehmen** to take s. o. out of his sphere, to uproot s. o.
Umgegend environs, environment, neighbo(u)rhood.
umgehbar evadable, avoidable.
umgehen *(Bestimmungen)* to elude, to evade, to circumvent, to dodge, to avoid, to get round *(US)*, *(Gerücht)* to be abroad, to float about, *(Krankheit)* to stalk, *(spuken)* to haunt;
mit jem. ~ to deal (handle) with s. o.; **Bestimmungen** ~ to evade (get round, *US*) regulations; **brutal mit jem.** ~ to treat s. o. brutally; **Feind** ~ to outflank the enemy; **Frage** ~ to evade a question; **mit dem Gedanken** ~ to contemplate doing; **leichtfertig mit Vaters Geld** ~ to play fast and loose with father's money; **mit größeren Geldbeträgen** ~ to handle large sums of money; **Gesetz** ~ to dodge (evade, get round, *US*) a law; **grob mit jem.** ~ to treat s. o. roughly; **Großhandel** ~ to

eliminate wholesalers; **mit Kindern behutsam** ~ to be gentle with children; **leichtfertig mit etw.** ~ to play pitch and toss (trifle) with s. th.; **taktvoll mit den Leuten** ~ to show tact in dealing with people; **mit seinen Mitmenschen geduldig** ~ to show forbearance in dealing with people; **mit Mordgedanken** ~ to meditate murder; **Patent** ~ to circumvent a patent; **zu etwa 7 1/2%** ~ *(Börse)* to rule about 7 1/2 per cent; **mit seinen Sachen liederlich** ~ to be careless with one's things; **sparsam** ~ to economize, to husband; **Stadt** ~ to circumvent a town; **Steuern** ~ to dodge (evade) a tax; **Sumpf** ~ to by-pass a swamp; **großzügig mit einem Text** ~ to take liberties with a text; **Verkehr** ~ to by-pass (dodge) the traffic, to make a roundabout way (detour, *US*); **Vorschrift** ~ to get round a regulation *(US)*; **vorsichtig mit jem.** ~ to give s. o. a kid-glove treatment; **mit seinem Wahlkreis pfleglich** ~ to nurse one's constituency;
mit etw. ~ **können** to have a hand for s. th., to know how to handle s. th.; **mit Leuten** ~ **können** to know how to deal with people; **mit Maschinen** ~ **können** to know how to operate machines; **Anwesenheitsliste** ~ **lassen** to circulate an attendance list; **Brief** ~ **lassen** to let a letter circulate;
es ließ sich nicht ~ there was nothing else for it.
umgehend at your earliest convenience, immediate, forthwith, prompt, as soon as possible, by return of post (mail, *US*);
~ **beantworten** to answer by return of post (mail, *US*); ~ **Schritte ergreifen** to take immediate steps;
~**e Antwort** immediate replay; ~**e Auftragserledigung** prompt attention to an order.
Umgehung circumvention, evasion, avoidance, elusion, *(mil.)* flanking manoeuvre *(Br.)* (maneuver, *US*), *(Straße)* roundabout way, detouring *(US)*;
~ **von Devisenvorschriften** evasion of currency laws; ~ **eines Gesetzes** elusion of a law; ~ **des Großhandels** elimination of wholesalers; ~ **von Haftungsbestimmungen** avoidance of liability; ~ **des Militärdienstes** draft evasion *(US)*; ~ **eines Patents** circumvention of a patent; ~ **einer Steuer** avoidance of a tax, tax evasion (avoidance).
Umgehungs|bahn by-line; ~**bestimmungen** avoiding provisions; ~**geschäft** *(Konkurs)* transaction not protected; ~**straße** by-pass, by-road, sliproad, *(um eine Stadt)* circumferential expressway, circular road, *(Umleitung)* detour; **ringförmige** ~**straße** orbital road.
umgekehrt vice versa, conversely, opposite, turned, reverse;
im ~**en Fall** in the reverse case; **im** ~**en Verhältnis stehen** to be in inverse proportion to; **mit** ~**en Vorzeichen** with completely reversed premises.
um|gekippt upset; ~**gerechnet** converted.
umgesetzt werden|mit ... *(Börse)* to change hands at ...;
langsam ~ to be of slow sale; **rasch** ~ to yield an easy (quick, short) return.
Umgesiedelter resettled person.
umgestalten to reform, to reorganize, to alter, to modify.
Umgestaltung reform, reorganization.
um|gestürzt, ~**geworfen** upset.
umgewöhnen müssen, sich to have to adapt o. s. to circumstances.
umgliedern, Gesellschaft to reorganize (reshape, rehabilitate) a company.
Umgliederung einer Gesellschaft reshape (rehabilitation) of a company.
umgrenzen, jds. Befugnisse to define s. one's powers.
umgrenzt, genau clearly defined.
Umgrenzung enclosure.
umgründen, Gesellschaft to reorganize (reconstruct, *Br.*, rehabilitate) a company.
Umgründung|einer Gesellschaft reorganization (rehabilitation, reconstruction, *Br.*) of a company;
Gesellschaft durch ~ **sanieren** to reorganize (rehabilitate, reconstruct, *Br.)* a company.
Umgründungsbedingungen, den ~ **gerecht werden** to fulfil the terms of reconstruction.
umgruppieren to rearrange, to regroup, to redeploy, *(pol.)* to shuffle, to reshuffle, to shake up *(US)*;
Arbeitskräfte ~ to regroup labo(u)r; **Kabinett** ~ to reshuffle the cabinet.
Umgruppierung reorganization, redeployment, turnover, recomposition, shakeup *(US)*;
~ **von Arbeitskräften** regrouping of labo(u)r; ~ **in der Industrie** industrial regrouping; ~ **des Kabinetts** reshuffle of the cabinet.
umhauen, Baum to fell (cut) a tree; **j. glatt** ~ to bowl s. o. over, to knock s. o. down.

umher|gehen, in einem Park to stroll through a park; **in den Straßen** ~**irren** to wander around the streets; **in der Stadt** ~**jagen** to chase around town; **unruhig** ~**laufen** to fly around *(US)*.
Umherreisen touring.
umher|reisen to tour, to travel about; ~**schweifend** wandering.
umherstreifen to tramp;
plündernd ~ to maraud; **ziellos** ~ to wander about without any object.
umher|streunen to roam around (about); ~**streunend** *(Tier)* running at large; ~**wandern** to gad.
Umherziehen, im itinerant.
umherziehen to rove, to itinerate, to roam about, to wander, *(Wanderbühne)* to stroll.
umherziehend *(Gewerbe)* itinerant.
umhören, sich to inquire.
umhüllen, mit einer Decke to wrap up in a blanket; **sich mit einem Mantel** ~ to invest o. s. in one's coat.
umhüllt, von einem Geheimnis shrouded (wrapped-up) in secrecy.
Umhüllung wrapper, wrapping, cover.
umkämpft, hart ~ **sein** to be hotly contested.
Umkehr return, turning back, *(pol.)* about-face, volte-face, turnabout;
Feind zur ~ **zwingen** to force the enemy to retreat.
umkehrbar *(Beweislast)* reversible;
nicht ~ irreversible.
umkehren to return, to invert, *(Film)* to reverse, *(Schiff)* to put back;
Beweislast ~ to shift the burden of proof.
Umkehr|film reversible film; ~**grenzpunkt** *(Flugzeug)* point of no return; ~**probe [bei Indexzahlen]** reversal test; ~**schalter** reversing switch.
Umkehrung converse, inversion;
~ **der Beweislast** reversal of the burden of proof.
Umkehr|verfahren *(Foto)* reversal process; ~**wert** inverse value.
Umkippen overset.
umkippen to overturn, to topple over, *(Auto)* to turn over, to overturn, to upset, *(ohnmächtig werden)* to pass out *(US sl.)*.
umklammern to clasp, to clutch;
j. mit beiden Armen ~ to cling to s. o., to clasp both arms round s. o.; **Feind** ~ to encircle the enemy.
Umklammerung clutch, stranglehold, *(mil.)* pincer movement, encirclement, envelopment.
umklappbar *(Sitz)* collapsible, folding.
Umkleide|kabine, ~**raum** locker (dressing) room; ~**möglichkeit** accommodation for changing.
umkleiden, sich zum Abendessen to change for dinner; **mit schönen Worten** ~ to cover with euphemistic words.
umkommen to perish, to lose one's life, to die;
bei einem Erdbeben ~ to perish in an earthquake; **bei einem Flugzeugunglück** ~ to be killed in a plane crash; **gemeinsam** ~ to die in a common disaster; **vor Hunger fast** ~ to starve, to be simply starving;
etw. ~ **lassen** to let s. th. go bad.
Umkreis radius, way, compass;
im ~ within a radius of, in the limits.
umkreisen to circle around, to encircle, *(Sonne)* to revolve;
Mond ~ to orbit the moon.
umkrempeln, alles (total) to turn everything inside out; **alles** ~, **um ein verlorengegangenes Testament aufzufinden** to hunt high and low for a missing will; **Plan völlig** ~ to change a plan completely; **ganze Wohnung** ~ to turn an apartment upside down.
Umlade|bahnhof reloading station; ~**bühne** tran(s)shipping platform; ~**erklärung** tran(s)shipment entry; ~**gebühren** transfer (reloading) charges, charges for reloading (tran(s)-shipment); ~**genehmigung** tran(s)shipment permit; ~**geschäft** switching operations; ~**gleis** reloading (tran(s)shipping, *US*) line; ~**gut** goods for tran(s)shipment; ~**hafen** tran(s)shipping port; ~**klausel** tran(s)shipment clause; ~**konnossement** tran(s)-shipment bill of lading.
Umladen tran(s)shipping, transferring.
umladen to shift, to reload, to tran(s)ship, to ship, to reship;
zollpflichtige Waren ~ to tran(s)ship dutiable goods.
Umlade|platz reloading place, tran(s)shipment point; ~**recht** *(Bahn)* privilege of transit; ~**risiko** reloading (tran(s)shipment) risk; ~**schuppen** tran(s)shipment shed; ~**spedition** switching carrier; ~**spesen** transfer (reloading) charges; ~**station** transfer (shunting) station; ~**verkehr** tran(s)shipment traffic.
Umladung reloading, tran(s)shipment, transferring, reshipment;
ordnungsgemäße ~ due tran(s)shipment.

Umladungs|kosten transfer charges, tran(s)shipment expenses; ~**schein** tran(s)shipment bond, tran(s)shipment (delivery) note.

Umlage levy, charge levied on, rate *(Br.)*, contribution, *(Verteilung)* allocation, apportionment, encumbrance;
noch nicht bewilligte ~ unliquidated encumbrance; **rückständige** ~**n** delinquent special assessments *(US)*; **städtische** ~ assessment, rating, local tax, county rate *(Br.)*; **zusätzliche** ~ additional assessment; **zweckgebundene** ~ special assessment; ~ **für Anlieger** special assessment *(US)*; ~ **von Gemeinkosten** allocation (apportionment) of indirect cost; **Steuern und** ~**n** rates and taxes;
von einer ~ **befreien** to derate *(Br.)*; **sich an einer** ~ **nicht beteiligen** to contract out of payment of a levy; **Beiträge durch** ~ **erheben** to impose a contribution; ~**n herabsetzen** to reduce the rates; **j. zu einer** ~ **heranziehen** to rate (assess) s. o.;
~**befreiung** derating *(Br.)*; ~**behörde** assessment office, rating authority *(Br.)*; ~**bescheid** precept; ~**bestimmung** *(Feuerversicherung)* contribution clause; ~**bezirk** rating area *(Br.)*, assessment district; ~**erhebung** rating *(Br.)*, assessment; ~**ermäßigung** reduction of rates, rate reduction.

umlagefrei exempt from rates.

Umlage|kosten assessment (joint) costs; ~**liste** assessment roll (list); ~**pflicht** assessability, ratability; **von der** ~**pflicht befreit** rateless.

umlagepflichtig ratable, assessable;
~**er Grundbesitzer** ratepayer *(Br.)*.

Umlage|pflichtiger ratepayer *(Br.)*; ~**register** rate book.

umlagern *(Fracht)* to swift, to shift, *(Vorräte)* to restore;
Eingang ~ to crowd around an entrance; **Verkaufsstand** ~ to besiege a stand.

Umlagerung shift, *(Quoten)* redistribution, *(Vorräte)* restoring.

Umlagerungskaution *(Zoll)* removal bond.

Umlage|satz assessment instal(l)ment, rate of assessment (contribution); ~**schlüssel** cost allocation; ~**schuldner** assessee *(US)*; ~**stelle** assessment office, rating authority *(Br.)*; ~**veranlagung** rating *(Br.)*, assessment of landed property; ~**vereinbarung** assessment contract; ~**verfahren** assessment system; ~**verfahren einer Versicherung** contributory system of an insurance; ~**vermögen** assessment fund; ~**verpflichtung** special assessment bond; ~**zeitraum** assessment period.

Umlauf *(Geld)* circulation, currency, *(Kapital)* flotation, *(Rundschreiben)* circular [order], *(Waggon)* transit time, turn-round;
im ~ **[befindlich]** *(Geld)* circulating, in circulation, current, *(Kapital)* afloat, floating;
sich im ~ **befinden** to circulate, to be in circulation; **in** ~ **bringen** *(Geld)* to issue, to circulate, to put in circulation, *(Kapital durch Effektenausgabe)* to float, to set afloat; **falsches Geld in** ~ **bringen** to utter (put off) forged money, to put forged notes in circulation; **Gerücht in** ~ **bringen** to give currency to (spread) a rumo(u)r; **außer** ~ **kommen** to disappear from circulation; **im** ~ **sein** to be in circulation (current), to circulate, *(Gerücht)* to be bruited about, *(Waren)* to knock about, *(Wechsel)* to run; **nicht mehr im** ~ **sein** to be out of circulation; **außer** ~ **setzen** *(Banknoten)* to withdraw from circulation, *(Effekten)* to call in; **in** ~ **setzen** *(Geld)* to circulate, to set (put) in circulation, to emit, to issue, *(Gerücht)* to put about, to spread, to circulate, to give currency to, to float, *(Kapital durch Effektenausgabe)* to float; **Brief in** ~ **setzen** to circulate a letter; **Falschgeld in** ~ **setzen** to put off (utter) forged money.

Umlaufbahn orbit;
auf einer ~ orbiting;
feste ~ fixed orbit;
~ **um den Mond** lunar orbit;
~ **beschreiben** to orbit; **in eine niedrige** ~ **schießen** to park into a low orbit.

umlaufen to circulate, to be in circulation, to revolve, *(Effekten)* to float, *(Gerücht)* to spread, to turn, to float;
Brief ~ **lassen** to let a letter pass around.

umlaufend circulating, running, current, *(Effekten)* floating.

umlauffähig marketable, *(begebbar)* negotiable;
~ **sein** to constitute a good delivery.

Umlauf|fähigkeit marketability, negotiability; ~**fonds** revolving fund; ~**frist** currency, validity, life; ~**geschwindigkeit** *(Geld)* rate of turnover, velocity of circulation; **hohe (niedrige)** ~**geschwindigkeit haben** to circulate freely (slowly); ~**grenze** circulation limit; ~**kapital** circulating (floating, liquid, fluid, *US*) capital, circulating *(Br.)* (floating, current, fluid, *US*) assets, *(Betriebsmittel)* working (ready) capital; ~**kapitalverluste** losses of circulating capital; ~**kredit** revolving credit; ~**mappe** circulating file; ~**mittel** circulating media, operating fund, floating capital, current funds (assets); ~**pumpe** rotary pump; ~**rendite** current yield; ~**schreiben** circular [letter], tracer.

Umlaufvermögen circulating capital, current funds, liquid (floating, circulating, *Br.*, fluid, *US*, quick, *US*) assets, *(Bilanz)* current receipts, current receivables *(US)*;
kurzfristiges ~ *(Bilanz)* current (liquid) assets; **mittel- und kurzfristiges** ~ *(Bilanz)* medium-term and short-term assets; **normales** ~ regular working capital;
~ **abzüglich Verbindlichkeiten** net working capital;
sich in einem Anstieg des ~**s niederschlagen** to find its way into an increase of current assets.

Umlauf|wert *(Banknoten)* circulating value; ~**zeit** *(Geld)* currency, period of circulation, *(Güterwagen)* transit time, *(Hafen)* turn-round; ~**zettel** circular.

umlegbar turndown.

Umlege|kalender desk calendar; ~**mappe** flip-flop *(US)*.

umlegen to apportion, to allocate, to prorate, *(Depot)* to transfer, *(Feuerversicherung)* to contribute, *(Grundstücke)* to reallocate, *(Kommunalabgabe)* to rate *(Br.)*, to assess, *(Schalter)* to throw, to reverse, *(Schienen)* to relay, *(umbringen)* to put out of the way, to do s. o. in *(sl.)*, to put over *(sl.)*;
Betrag auf verschiedene Personen gleichmäßig ~ to apportion (allocate) a sum among several people; **jem. eine Decke** ~ to put a blanket around s. one's shoulders; **Gemeinkosten der Muttergesellschaft auf ihre Auslandstöchter entsprechend ihrem Umsatzanteil** ~ to allocate corporate overhead expenses to overseas subsidiaries in proportion to their share of sales; **Kosten** ~ to apportion the cost; **Stuhl** ~ to turn down a chair; **Telefongespräch** ~ to transfer a call; **Unkosten auf die Vereinsmitglieder** ~ to assess the members of the society with the expenses; **zeitlich** ~ to apportion on a time basis.

Umlegung allocation, apportionment, *(Feuerversicherung)* contribution, *(Kommunalabgabe)* rating *(Br.)*, assessment;
~ **der Anliegerkosten anhand der Straßenfront** front-foot rule; ~ **eines Betrages auf verschiedene Leute** allocation of a sum among several people; ~ **von Gemeinkosten** allocation of indirect costs; ~ **eines Telefongesprächs** transfer of a telephone call; ~ **von Unkosten** apportionment of costs.

Umlegungs|ausschuß assessment (rating, *Br.*) committee; ~**bestimmungen** *(Feuerversicherung)* contribution clause.

umleiten, umlenken to redirect, *(Kapitalströme)* to switch, to redirect, *(Verkehr)* to reroute, to divert *(Br.)*, to detour *(US)*, to deroute *(US)*;
Fluß ~ to divert a river.

Umleitung, Umlenkung *(Kapitalströme)* switch, redirection, *(Verkehr)* rerouting, by-pass, diversion *(Br.)*, derouting *(US)*, detour *(US)*, roundabout *(US)*;
~ **fahren** to take a by-pass, to make a detour *(US)*.

Umleitungs|schild diversion (detour, *US*) sign; ~**straße** by-pass, detour *(US)*; ~**system bei Verkehrsstauungen** emergency routing system.

umlernen to relearn, to reorientate o. s., to change one's views.

Umlernprozeß reorientation.

umliegend surrounding, neighbo(u)ring;
~**e Gegend** environs, surrounding countryside, surroundings.

ummauern to wall.

Ummeldegebühr registration fee.

ummelden to reregister.

Ummeldung reregistration.

ummodeln to reshape, to remodel, *(Arbeitsweise)* to alter;
gänzlich ~ to put into the melting pot.

umnachtet, geistig mentally deranged, insane.

Umnachtung, geistige mental derangement.

um|numerieren to renumber; ~**ordnen** to rearrange, to reorder.

Umorganisation reorganization, reconstruction *(Br.)*, rehabilitation, shake-up, turnover.

umorganisieren to reorganize, to rehabilitate, to shake up;
Unternehmen ~ to reshape (remodel) a company (corporation), to reconstruct a company *(Br.)*.

umpacken to pack up again, to repack, to repackage, *(Schiffsladung)* to break bulk.

Umplazierung reallocation.

umprägen to coin again, to recoin.

Umprägung recoinage.

umprogrammieren to rearrange the program(me).

umquartieren to remove to another quarter, *(Bevölkerung)* to evacuate, to rehouse, *(Soldaten)* to rebillet, to requarter;
Truppen ~ to shift troops.

Umquartierung removal, *(Bevölkerung)* rehousing, evacuation;
~ **ausgesiedelter Personen** rehousing of displaced people.

Umrahmung *(drucktechn.)* box.
umranden to edge, to border, *(drucktechn.)* to box in, *(auf Vordruck)* to mark with a circle.
Umrandung, fette thick frame; **schwarze ~** black frame.
umrangieren to shunt, to switch.
umräumen *(Möbel)* to shift furniture around.
umrechenbar convertible, reducible.
umrechnen to recalculate, *(Devisen)* to convert (reduce) to;
Pfunde in Franken ~ to reduce (convert) pounds to francs.
Umrechnung recalculation, *(Devisen)* conversion, reduction of money.
Umrechnungs|faktor conversion factor; **~formel** reduction formula.
Umrechnungskurs rate of exchange, exchange rate, conversion price (rate), parity;
zahlbar zu dem im Indossament vermerkten ~ payable as per indorsement *(Br.)*; **zum ~ von** at the parity (the current exchange) of;
amtlicher ~ official exchange rate; **fester ~** certain price, direct exchange; **günstiger ~** favo(u)rable exchange rate; **nomineller ~** nominal exchange rate.
Umrechnungs|regeln rules of conversion; **~satz** *(Devisen)* conversion rate, *(Papiere)* basis of exchange; **~schlüssel** conversion key; **~tabelle** ready reckoner, *(Börse)* cambist, table of exchange, conversion table (chart), *(Paritäten)* commutation table; **~verhältnis** exchange conversion ratio; **~wert** exchange value.
umreißen *(mit wenigen Worten)* to outline, to sketch;
Mauer ~ to pull down a wall; **Passanten ~** *(Auto)* to knock down a passenger.
umringen to gather (crowd) round.
Umriß outline, *(Stadt)* skyline, contour, profile, silhouette;
verschwommene ~e vague outlines;
Epoche in großen ~en schildern to give a rough outline of an epoch.
umrissen outlined;
klar ~ precise, clear-cut.
umrüsten *(Armee)* to re-equip, *(Maschine)* to reset.
umsatteln to enter upon a new career, to switch a job.
Umsatz turnover, sales, overturn *(US)*, *(Börse)* business, transactions *(US)*, movement, trading, *(Einnahmen)* return[s], market, profit, *(Lager)* stock turnover, stockturn, *(Verbrauch)* consumption, *(Werbeagentur)* billing;
ohne ~ no sales (movement), nothing doing, *(Börse)* no business [done];
sprungartig angestiegener ~ sales leap; **bankmäßiger ~** bank turnover; **direkter ~** direct sales; **durchschnittlicher ~** average turnover; **fakturierter ~** invoiced sales; **fingierter ~** dummy transactions, fictitious sales (turnover); **fremder ~** *(Konzernbilanz)* external sales; **geringer ~** thin market, *(Börse)* narrow (quiet) market, little business; **guter ~** brisk sales; **jährlicher ~** annual turnover (sales); **mengenmäßiger ~** quantity (physical) turnover, sales volume; **pro-Kopf ~** per capita sales (turnover); **rascher ~** quick returns; **reger ~** active turnover; **rückläufiger ~** receding (declining) sales; **schlechter ~** heavy market; **schneller ~** quick turnover, early returns; **schrumpfender ~** contracting turnover, *(Börse)* light trading; **steuerfreier ~** tax-exempt sales; **steuerpflichtiger ~** taxable turnover, trading adventure, *(Börse)* taxable transaction; **ungenügender ~** lack of sales; **unsichtbarer ~** invisible transactions;
~ des Betriebskapitals working-capital turnover; **~ im gesamten Firmenbereich** total sales effort of a company; **~ am Kassamarkt** spot sale; **~ an die Kundschaft** *(Konzernbilanz)* consolidated outside sales, external turnover (sales);
großen ~ erzielen to do a large turnover *(coll.)*; **~ machen** to turn over; **~ steigern** to roll up (increase) the sales; **für beschleunigten ~ Sorge tragen** to speed up the sales process;
~abbau undertrading; **~abschwächung** drop in sales; **~analyse** sales breakdown; **~angaben** facts about turnover; **~anstieg** upsurge in sales, increase in turnover; **sprungartiger ~anstieg** sales jump, jump in sales; **verstärkte ~anstrengungen** sales drive; **~anteil** share of turnover; **~aufgliederung, ~aufschlüsselung** sales breakdown; **~aufstellung** statement of turnover; **~ausfall** shortfall in sales; **~ausgleichssteuer** countervailing duty, import equalization tax; **~aussichten** sales prospects; **~ausweitung** expansion of sales (turnover), sales (turnover) expansion; **~belebung** increase in sales (turnover); **verstärkte ~bemühungen** increased sales efforts; **~besteuerung** taxation on sales; **~beteiligung** commission on sales effected, seller's commission; **~beteiligung des Absatzstabes** sales-force participation; **~betrag** business done; **~bewegung** sales activity.
umsatzbewußt sales-minded.
Umsatz|bilanz statement of sales done (cost of sales); **nachträglicher ~bonus** deferred rebate; **~chance** potential sales.
Umsätze sales, dealings, *(Börse)* transactions;
bei guten ~n with a brisk market;
bedeutende ~ important dealings; **flotte ~** brisk sales; **getätigte ~** *(Börse)* business done; **große ~** large returns, *(Börse)* good business; **hohe ~** *(Börse)* heavy trading; **konzerneigene ~** intercompany sales, interassociation transactions *(US)*; **laufende ~** current transactions; **mäßige ~** few dealings; **provisionspflichtige ~** commission sales; **rückläufige ~** *(Börse)* retrograde movement; **schwache ~** *(Börse)* light trading; **unsichtbare ~** invisible transactions; **verschiedenartige ~** *(Börse)* mixed turnovers;
~ im Dienstleistungsgeschäft sales of services; **~ im Einzelhandel** retail sales; **~ in Farbfernsehgeräten** colo(u)r-television sales; **~ im Gebrauchtwagenmarkt** used-car sales; **~ im Großhandel** wholesale trading; **~ in einer Höhe von mehreren Millionen Pfund** transactions amounting to several million pounds; **~ im Neuwagengeschäft** new-car sales; **~ der Modeindustrie** fashion-house turnover; **geringe ~ in Ölaktien** not much move in oil shares; **erste ~ zwischen 10 und 12 Uhr** *(Börse)* first board *(US)*; **hohe ~ durch die Vertreter im Außendienst** large returns from agents in the field; **~ in mündelsicheren Wertpapieren** gilt-edged sales *(Br.)*;
bei der Börseneröffnung mit lebhaften ~n beginnen to advance from start in brisk dealings; **befriedigende ~ erzielen** to trade at a satisfactory level of turnover; **gute ~ erzielen** to make good returns; **erhebliche ~ machen** to reach a respectable figure; **flotte ~ machen** to do a lively business; **glänzende ~ machen** to carry on a roaring trade; **überdurchschnittliche ~ machen** to do above the average trade; **~ steigern** to increase business (sales); **größere ~ tätigen** to make more sales, to do good business; **große ~ in ... tätigen** to deal in big volume, to do large business in ...; **~ verzeichnen** to be sold, to change hands; **ermäßigte Preise durch große ~ wettmachen** to sell at a low price and recoup o. s. by large sales.
Umsatz|entwicklung sales trend; **~ergebnis** sales results; **~erhöhung** rise in sales; **~erlös** gross profit on (income from) sales (turnover) proceeds; **~erlöse** *(Bilanz)* sales; **~erträge** sales revenue; **~erwartung** sales expectancy; **~flaute** stagnation in sales; **~förderung** sales promotion; **~garantie** sales guarantee; **~geschäft in der Automationsindustrie** automation sales; **~geschwindigkeit** rate (speed) of turnover, sales frequency, trading pace; **~gewinn** gross profit on sales, sales gain; **~gliederung** sales analysis (breakdown); **~grenze** sales limit; **~häufigkeit** rate of turnover; **~höhe** sales revenue; **~index** sales index; **~kapazität** sales potential; **~konto** unbroken account, active account; **~kontrolle** sales control; **~krise** sales crisis; **~kurve** sales curve; **~kurve in grafischer Darstellung** sales chart; **weiteres Absinken der ~kurve verhindern** to stem the downwards sales curve; **~lage** turnover situation.
umsatzlos without sales, *(Börse)* featureless, inactive, no sales;
~ sein to do no sales;
~es Guthaben dormant balance; **~es Konto** dead (inoperative, broken, dormant) account *(Br.)*, inactive account *(US)*.
umsatzmäßig überflügeln to outtrade.
Umsatz|maximierung sales revenue maximation; **~pacht** percentage lease; **~planung** sales planning; **~plus** sales plus; **~prämie** sales premium; **~prognose** sales forecast; **~provision** commission on sales effected, commission percentage on sales, seller's (selling, turnover) commission; **~provision gewähren** to allow a percentage on all transactions; **~prozentsatz** sales percentage, percentage of sales; **~quote** turnover rate; **~rekord** sales record; **~rückgang** decrease in (drop of) turnover, decline (falling off, fall, drop, letdown) in sales, falling off of sales, sales decline (reduction, dip); **rapider ~rückgang** slump in sales; **~rückgang aufweisen** to be on a downswing; **~schätzung** sales estimate; **~schrumpfung** decrease in sales; **~schwankungen** sales fluctuations, sales dip, slower business; **~schwund** shortfall in sales; **~spitzenreiter sein** to be at the top of the turnover list; **~statistik** sales (turnover) statistics.
umsatzsteigernd auswirken, sich to help sales.
Umsatzsteigerung increase in (expansion of) turnover, turnover (sales) increase, rising sales, growth in sales;
~ erzielen to roll up (boost) the sales;
durch ~en zu Gewinn gelangen to sell one's way into profit.
Umsatzsteuer turnover tax *(Br.)*, tax on turnover *(Br.)*, receipts tax, sales tax *(US)*, value-added tax *(Br.)*, vat *(Br.)*;

allgemeine ~ general sales tax *(US)*; **kumulative** ~ cascade tax; ~ **im Einzelhandel** retail sales tax; ~ **auf Güter des gehobenen Bedarfs** purchase tax *(Br.)*;
~ **abwälzen** to pass on vat *(Br.)*;
~**aufkommen** sales tax revenue *(US)*; ~**befreiung** exemption from turnover tax *(Br.)*; ~**bescheid** turnover-tax notice *(Br.)*; ~**erhöhung** vat increase *(Br.)*; ~**erklärung** turnover-tax return *(US)*; ~**erträge** vat receipts *(Br.)*.
umsatzsteuerfrei vat-exempt *(Br.)*.
Umsatzsteuer|freibetrag sales tax relief *(US)*; ~**rückerstattung** sales *(US)* (turnover, *Br.*) tax refund; ~**sätze** turnover tax rates *(Br.)*.
Umsatz|tantieme *(Vertreter)* bonus; ~**tief** sales crisis.
umsatzträchtiges Konto active (unbroken) account.
Umsatz|umfang turnover range; ~**verdoppelung** doubling of sales; ~**verlagerung** shifting of turnover; ~**verlust** shortfall of sales; ~**volumen** sales volume, volume of turnover; ~**voraussage** sales forecast; ~**wachstum** growth in sales, increase in turnover; ~**wachstumsrate** turnover growth rate; ~**welle** wave of selling; ~**werte** sales figures; **im** ~**wettrennen auf den zweiten Platz verweisen** to route in a sales race; ~**zahlen,** ~**ziffern** turnover rate (figures), rate of turnover, sales figures, data on sales, figures on sales volume; ~**zunahme** turnover increase, sales plus; ~**zuwachs** turnover gain, increase in turnover.
Umschalten switch[ing], *(Auto)* gear change.
umschalten to switch [over], *(Auto)* to change (shift) the gears, *(fig.)* to alter one's course, *(Stromrichtung)* to reverse;
auf kurzfristige Finanzierungsformen ~ to switch to shorter-term forms of financing; **auf ein anderes Programm** ~ to switch to another program(me).
Umschalter switch, *(Schreibmaschine)* shift key;
selbsttätiger ~ cutout.
Umschalt|hebel lever; ~**taste** *(Schreibmaschine)* shift key.
Umschaltung changeover, switch, *(Auto)* gear change.
Umschau lookout, *(Rundfunkprogramm)* topical magazine, *(Zeitschrift)* review;
~ **nach Fahrgästen** *(Taxi)* cruising;
nach jem. ~ **halten** to look out for s. o.
umschauen to look around.
umschichten to regroup, to shift;
Partei ~ to restructure a party; **Vermögenswerte eines Unternehmens** ~ to redeploy the assets of a company.
umschichtig by turns, *(Arbeitszeit)* in shifts;
~ **arbeiten** to work in shifts.
Umschichtung switch, shifting, regrouping, rearrangement, shake-up, turnover;
soziale ~ social upheaval;
~ **des Eigentums** redistribution of income; ~ **von Investitionen** redirection of investments; ~ **der Nachfrage** shift in the demand pattern; ~ **des Vermögens in Wachstumswerte** switch into growth stocks; ~ **von Vermögenswerten** redeployment of assets.
umschiffen to circumnavigate, to double, to round;
Klippe ~ *(fig.)* to weather.
Umschlag *(Brief)* envelope, *(Buch)* cover, dust jacket, *(Güter)* goods turnover, *(Kreuzband)* wrapper, *(Lager)* inventory turnover, *(Mappe)* folio, *(Schiff)* turnround, *(Umladung)* tran(s)shipment, reloading, *(Umsatz)* [rate of] turnover, sales, *(Wetter)* abrupt change, break, sudden change;
in verschlossenem ~ in a sealed envelope; **unter besonderem** ~ under separate cover;
frankierter ~ stamped envelope; **gummierter** ~ gummed envelope; **rascher** ~ quick sales;
~ **von im Huckepackverkehr eingesetzten Containern** tran(s)shipment of roll-on roll-off containers; ~ **eines Hafens** amount of traffic handled by a port; ~ **des Kapitals** capital turnover; **viermaliger** ~ **des Warenlagers im Jahr** stock turnover four times a year;
~ **adressieren** to address an envelope; **mit einem** ~ **versehen** to [put into an] envelope;
~**anlage** tran(s)shipment facility; ~**bahnhof** reloading station, marshal(l)ing yard; ~**bild** cover picture (subject); ~**deckel** cover.
umschlagen *(kentern)* to capsize, to heel over, to list, to overturn, *(Konjunktur)* to reach the turning point, *(umladen)* to reload, to tran(s)ship, *(umsetzen)* to turn over;
ins Gegenteil ~ to change completely; **plötzlich** ~ *(Stimmung)* to change all of a sudden.
Umschlag|fähigkeit der Forderungen receivables turnover; ~**fähigkeit des Warenbestandes** inventory turnover; ~**gebühr** tran(s)shipment charge; ~**geschäft** turnover business, sales transaction; ~**hafen** tran(s)shipment (tran(s)shipping) harbo(u)r, port of tran(s)shipment; ~**karton** cardboard covering; ~**kosten** reloading (tran(s)shipment) charges; ~**lager** turnover storage; ~**papier** cover stock, wrapping paper; ~**platz** tran(s)shipment point, transfer, place of tran(s)shipment, rail and water terminal.
Umschlags|anlage tran(s)shipment facilities; ~**arbeiten** handling operations; ~**bild** cover picture; ~**dauer** average inventory cycle.
Umschlagseite [front] cover;
innere ~ inside cover; **vierte** ~ back cover.
Umschlags|erlaubnis tran(s)shipment permit; ~**geschwindigkeit** rate of turnover, receivables turnover *(US)*.
Umschlagshäufigkeit turnover ratio;
~ **des Eigenkapitals** capital turnover ratio *(Br.)*, sales volume rate *(US)*, total assets turnover; ~ **der Forderungen** receivables turnover *(US)*; ~ **des Rohstofflagers** raw-materials turnover; ~ **der Vorräte** inventory turnover ratio; ~ **des Warenbestandes** finished-goods turnover.
Umschlags|kapazität handling capacity; ~**spediteur** switching carrier; ~**spesen** handling charges; ~**station** tran(s)shipment (tran(s)shipping) station; ~**verkehr** tran(s)shipment traffic; ~**zeichnung** cover design; ~**zeit** turnover period, *(Warentransport)* transit time; ~**zentrum** tran(s)shipment centre *(Br.)* (center, *US*).
umschließen to surround, to encircle, *(Kolumnen)* to reimpose;
Garten mit einer Mauer ~ to fence in a garden.
Umschließung encirclement, enclosure, *(Festung)* investment.
umschlossen, von Bergen locked in by mountains.
umschmeicheln, j. to cajole (flatter) s. o.
Umschreibegebühr *(Börse)* transfer stamp duty.
umschreiben to transcribe, to change an entry in the register, *(Aktien)* to transfer, *(Flugkarte)* to reroute, *(Grundstück)* to convey, to surrender, to alienate, *(mit Worten)* to circumscribe, to paraphrase, *(zurückgirieren)* to reindorse;
neues Arbeitsgebiet ~ to define a new field of activity; **Artikel** ~ to rewrite an article; **Flugschein** ~ to alter a ticket; **mit wenigen Worten** ~ to outline briefly;
Haus auf den Namen der Ehefrau ~ **lassen** to have a house transferred to one's wife.
Umschreibung paraphrase, circumlocution, circumscription, *(Aktien)* transfer, *(Flugkarte)* rerouting, *(Schriftstück)* transcription, *(Wertpapiere)* transfer, *(mit anderen Worten)* paraphrase;
~ **eines Grundstücks** alienation of an estate, conveyance of land, transfer of title to land; ~ **im Register** change of registration.
Umschreibungs|beamter registrar of transfer; ~**buch** *(AG)* transfer book *(Br.)*; ~**ersuchen** letters of request; ~**formular** transfer form; ~**gebühr** registration fee, *(Aktien)* transfer duty (tax, *US*); **Eintragungs- und** ~**gebühr** registration and transfer fee; ~**register** transfer register *(Br.)*; ~**stelle** *(Effekten)* transfer office (agent); ~**tag** transfer day *(Br.)*; ~**zertifikat** transfer warrant.
Umschrift *(Münze)* legend, [marginal] inscription, circumscription.
umschulden to refund fund debts, to convert, to refinance.
Umschuldung debt refunding (funding), conversion of debts;
längerfristige ~ conversion into medium-term debts;
~ **der kurzfristigen Kredite** funding of short-term borrowings;
~ **von Obligationen** refunding of bonds.
Umschuldungs|aktion funding operation; ~**angebot** conversion offer; ~**anleihe** conversion (funding) loan; ~**anspruch** conversion privilege; ~**bestimmungen** conversion provisions; ~**guthaben** conversion balance; ~**kasse** conversion office; ~**klausel** conversion feature; ~**kredit** conversion credit; ~**plan** funding system; ~**satz** conversion price; ~**tabelle** conversion table; ~**transaktion,** ~**vorgang** funding operation; ~**wesen** funding system.
umschulen to reeducate, to recondition, to retrain.
Umschulung reeducation, reconditioning, vocational (occupational) retraining, rehabilitation, conversion training;
berufliche ~ vocational reeducation (rehabilitation), occupational resettlement;
~ **auf einen zivilen Beruf** training for a trade, profession or vocation.
Umschulungs|beihilfe training allowance, rehabilitation relief; ~**lager** reeducation (rehabilitation) camp; **staatliches** ~**lager** government training center *(Br.)*; **berufliche** ~**leistungen** rehabilitation services; ~**programm** retraining program(me).
umschwärmt, von Jugendlichen mobbed by teenagers.

Umschweife indirect means;
ohne ~ in simple phrase (plain language), straight out, point-blank, plump *(coll.)*; **ohne weitere** ~ bluntly;
keine ~ **machen** to stop beating about the bush; **ohne** ~ **tun** to do without further ado.
Umschwenken turn, shunt, *(plötzlich)* tangent.
umschwenken to turn round, to wheel about, to flop, to veer, to shunt;
zur erfolgreichen Partei ~ to jump on the bandwaggon.
Umschwung turnabout, about-face, *(Börse)* reversal, turn, reaction, break, turn, reaction, *(Politik)* landslide, swingback *(US)*, reversal;
heftiger ~ rebound; **plötzlicher** ~ sudden change, revulsion; **völliger** ~ about-face;
ein ~ turn of the dice;
~ **im Denken** revolution in thought; ~ **des Glücks** turn of the tide; ~ **bei den Kommunalwahlen** local election swing; ~ **in den Lagerpositionen** reversal in stockpiling; ~ **der Liquiditätsverhältnisse** reversal of liquidity; ~ **der öffentlichen Meinung** swing of the pendulum; ~ **zu Ungunsten der Regierung** antigovernment (anti-the-men-in-power) swing;
~ **herbeiführen** to bring about a change; ~ **der öffentlichen Meinung mißachten** to ignore the rising tide of public opinion; ~ **verzeichnen** *(Börse)* to turn the corner *(US)*.
umsehen, sich to look around; **sich im Städtchen etw.** ~ to have a nose round in a town; **sich nach einer Stellung** ~ to look for a job.
umseitig on the next page.
umsetzbar realizable, salable, marketable, *(begebbar)* negotiable, convertible;
gut ~ good delivery; **nicht** ~ inconvertible, nonnegotiable;
~**es Papier** convertible security.
Umsetzbarkeit marketability, salableness, realizabilty, *(Begebbarkeit)* negotiability, convertibility.
umsetzen to sell, to dispose, to negotiate, *(Arbeitskräfte)* to transfer, to dislocate, *(drucktechn.)* to reset, *(realisieren)* to realize, *(Umsatz haben)* to turn over, to return;
Arbeitskräfte ~ to reallocate (dislocate) labo(u)r; **in bares Geld** ~ to convert into cash, to turn into money, to realize; **jährlich** ~ to have an annual turnover; **wöchentlich 2000 Pfund** ~ to turn over £ 2000 a week; **Plan in die Tat** ~ to put a plan into action.
umsetzfähig *(Arbeitskräfte)* mobile.
Umsetzfähigkeit *(Arbeitskräfte)* occupational mobility;
nicht vorhandene ~ occupational immobility.
Umsetzung, innerbetriebliche production transfer;
~ **von Arbeitskräften** dislocation of workers, reallocation of labo(u)r.
Umsetzungszuschuß relocation grant.
Umsichgreifen rampancy, spread.
Umsicht discretion, prudence, caution, vigilance, circumspection;
mit ~ **handeln** to act with discretion.
umsichtig prudent, cautious, long-sighted, far-sighted, vigilant, wary;
~ **handeln** to use discretion;
~**e Hausfrau** prudent housekeeper; ~**er Kaufmann** prudent business man.
umsiedeln to evacuate, to resettle, to transplant, to relocate.
Umsiedler repatriated person, evacuee, resettler;
~**gruppe** transplantation; ~**lager** evacuation (resettlement) camp.
Umsiedlung resettlement, transplantation, transfer, evacuation, relocation;
~ **von Bevölkerungsteilen** relocation of the population; ~ **der Einwohner** evacuation of inhabitants; ~ **mit Familie** family relocation.
Umsiedlungs | aktion resettlement scheme; ~**beihilfe** resettlement allowance (aid); ~**gebiet** evacuation area; ~**kosten** relocation expenses; ~**lager** evacuation camp; ~**plan** evacuation plan; ~**programm für Industriearbeiter** Resettlement Transfer Scheme *(Br.)*.
umsonst free of (without) cost, cost-free, costless, without payment, uncharged, gratis, gratuitous, *(Schaugeschäft)* free, cuffo, *(vergeblich)* futile, fruitless, in vain;
fast ~ for a mere song; **nicht** ~ not without good reason;
fast ~ **arbeiten** to work without pay; **etw.** ~ **bekommen** to have s. th. for keeps; **sich** ~ **bemühen** to lose one's labo(u)r; **fast** ~ **kaufen** to buy for a mere song; **völlig** ~ **sein** *(Bemühungen)* to be a complete waste of time; ~ **zu haben sein** to be had for the asking; **etw. völlig** ~ **tun** to go on a fool's errand;
~ **ist der Tod** no paternoster no penny.
Umsonstgeschäft machen to peddle a deadhead.
umsorgen, j. to take care of s. o.
umspannen to comprise, to cover, to embrace, *(el.)* to transform.
Umspannung *(el.)* transformation.
umspringen *(Wind)* to haul;
hart mit jem. ~ to deal with s. o. harshly; **nach Norden** ~ to veer round to North.
Umsprung *(von Nah- auf Fernaufnahme)* jump.
umspulen *(Film)* to reroll.
Umstand circumstance, factor, *(Lage)* position, state, conditions, *(Tatsache)* fact;
belastender ~ incriminating circumstance; **besonderer** ~ particular; **erschwerender** ~ aggravation; **fördernder** ~ contributing factor, contributory; **maßgebender** ~ determining factor; **unglücklicher** ~ unfortunate circumstance; **in der Sache begründeter wesentlicher** ~ material circumstance;
~ **in Rechnung stellen** to take a factor into consideration.
Umstände circumstances, surrounding facts, causes, matters, *(Einzelheiten)* details, particulars;
durch die ~ **bedingt** rendered necessary by circumstances; **falls unvorhergesehene** ~ **eintreten sollten** in case of a contingency; **in ähnlichen** ~**n** similarly situated; **in Anbetracht aller** ~ considering all circumstances; **in anderen** ~**n** in the family way; **ohne** ~ without formalities (ceremony); **sehr durch die** ~ **bedingt** highly conditional; **unter** ~**n** circumstances permitting; **unter allen** ~**n** at all hazards; **unter diesen** ~**n** in such a case; **unter den gegebenen (obwaltenden)** ~**n** under the prevailing circumstances; **unter keinen** ~**n** on no account;
soweit es die ~ **zulassen** circumstances permitting;
außergewöhnliche ~ exceptional circumstances; **belastende** ~ aggravating circumstances; **besondere** ~ particular circumstances; **besorgniserregende** ~ precarious circumstances; **erschwerende** ~ aggravating circumstances; **günstige** ~ favo(u)rable factors; **mildernde** ~ extenuating circumstances; **mitverursachende** ~ contributory causes; **nähere** ~ details, particulars; **preiserhöhende** ~ price-raising factors; **strafbegründende** ~ factors that constitute an offence; **strafverschärfende** ~ aggravating circumstances; **unberechenbare** ~ imponderables; **ungewöhnliche** ~ unusual circumstances; **unvorhergesehene** ~ unforeseen circumstances; **versicherungswichtige** ~ material representations; **wesentliche** ~ essentials; **wichtige** ~ adverse circumstances;
für die Beurteilung wesentliche materielle ~ **eines Falles** merits of a case; ~, **die die Entstehung einer Nation fördern** factors in the making of a nation;
sich den ~**n anpassen** to conform to the circumstances; **alle** ~ **darlegen** to go into details; **mildernde** ~ **gewähren** to allow extenuating circumstances; **nach den** ~**n handeln** to act according to events; **den** ~**n nach annehmen können** to have good grounds to suspect; ~ **machen** to cause inconvenience, to be ceremonious, to kick up a fuss; **jem.** ~ **machen** to give s. o. much trouble, to trouble s. o.; **keine langen** ~ **machen** to take the gloves off, not to let the grass grow under one's feet; **nicht viel** ~ **machen** to make short work (shrift, no fuss) of; **viel** ~ **wegen etw. machen** to make heavy weather of s. th.; **in anderen** ~**n sein** to be in a delicate condition (in the family way); **mildernde** ~ **zubilligen** to allow extenuating circumstances.
umständehalber owing to circumstances.
umständlich circumstantial, tortuous, *(zu genau)* particular, minute, detailed, *(verwickelt)* complicated, involved, intricate;
sehr ~ old-womanish;
~**e Erzählung** long-winded narrative; ~**e Schilderung** circumstanntial description.
Umständlichkeit eines Verfahrens circuity of an action.
Umstands | krämer slow coach, fusspot, fuss *(US)*; ~**wort** adverb.
Umstauen | an Bord handling on board; ~ **der Ladung** handling of cargo.
umstauen to shift (handle) the stowage.
umstehend printed overleaf, on the next page;
wie ~ as booked overleaf;
~**e Leute** onlookers, bystanders.
Umstehende bystanders.
Umsteige | fahrschein, ~**fahrkarte** detour (through, correspondence) ticket, transfer *(US)*; ~**möglichkeit** interchange service.
Umsteigen changing trains, transfer *(US)*.
umsteigen to change [for], to change trains;
aus Aktien in hochverzinsliche Obligationen ~ to switch out of stocks into high-yielding bonds; **in einen anderen Bus** ~ to change buses; **in Wachstumswerte** ~ to switch into growth stock;
alles ~! all change (out, *US*)!

Umsteigeplatz changeover, crossover.
Umsteiger detour (through, correspondence) ticket, transfer *(US)*.
Umsteigestation crossover, transfer station *(US)*.
umstellen to regroup, to reorganize, to readjust, to modify, *(anpassen)* to adapt, *(Außenhandelsgeschäft)* to switch, *(automatisieren)* to automatize, *(Betrieb)* to convert, to shift, to change over, to re-equip, *(Maschinen)* to reset, *(Produktion)* to switch, to turn over to, *(bei Währungsreform)* to convert, *(Wörter)* to transpose;
sich ~ to accommodate (accustom) o. s., to change one's attitude; **Beteiligungen** ~ to shuffle holdings; **von Dollar- auf Goldbasis** ~ to gear the dollar value of contracts to gold; **Fabrik auf Maschinenbetrieb** ~ to mechanize a factory; **Fabrikationsbetrieb** ~ to convert a factory, to adapt a factory to the production of other products; **Möbel** ~ to shift furniture about (around); **Produktion auf Konsumgüter** ~ to switch over production to consumer goods; **sich auf die Verbraucherbedürfnisse** ~ to gear to consumer needs; **Wirtschaft auf Friedensproduktion** ~ to reconvert industry to peacetime production.
Umstellung regrouping, reorganization, readjustment, modification, *(Anpassung)* accommodation, adaptation, *(Automatisierung)* automatization, automation, *(Betrieb)* change-over, shift, reorganization, reconversion, *(Maschinenbetrieb)* mechanization, *(Währungsreform)* conversion;
geldmarktpolitische ~en shift in monetary policy; **organisatorische ~en** organizational changes; **politische** ~ policy switch; ~ **von direkter auf indirekte Besteuerung** switch from direct to indirect taxation; ~ **von Beteiligungen** shuffle of holdings; ~ **des Effektenportefeuilles** switching of securities; ~ **des Fabrikationsbetriebes** adaptation of a factory to the production of other products; ~ **von Gas und Erdöl auf Kohle** conversion from gas and oil to coal; ~ **auf das Landleben** ruralization; ~ **auf Wachstumswerte** switch into growth stocks; ~ **im Wertpapierbesitz** changes in holdings, portfolio switch; ~ **der Wirtschaft auf Friedensproduktion** reconversion of industry.
Umstellungs|angebot conversion offer; **~beihilfe** adaptation allowance, block grant *(Br.)*; **~bestimmungen** conversion provisions; **~betrag** conversion amount; **~betrieb** plant in process of conversion; **~bilanz** conversion sheet; **~entschädigung** disturbance allowance; **~guthaben** conversion balance; **~konto** conversion account; **~kosten** changeover costs; **~kredit** reequipment (reorganization) credit; **~kurs** conversion price; **~maßnahmen** readjustment measures; **~prozeß** changing process; **~rechnung** conversion account; **~schema** restructuring scheme; **~schwierigkeiten** reconversion difficulties; **~zeit** set-up time.
Umstellzeichen *(Korrektur)* transpose.
umstimmen, j. to bring (win) s. o. round.
umstoßbar defeasanced, reversible.
umstoßen to overthrow, to upset, to overturn, *(Vertrag)* to abate, to make void, to invalidate, to annul, to rescind;
j. ~ to knock s. o. off his pins *(coll.)*; **Plan** ~ to upset a plan; **Testament** ~ to revoke a will; **Urteil** ~ to reverse (quash) a judgment; **Vertrag** ~ to avoid (invalidate, annul) a contract.
Umstoßung overthrow, invalidation, avoidance, abatement, reversal;
~ **eines Testaments** revocation of a will; ~ **eines Urteils** reversal of a judgment.
umstritten controversial, contested, in contestation, in dispute, moot;
nicht ~ noncontroversial;
~ **sein** to be in controversy;
~e Ansicht disputed opinion; **~e Frage** debatable (moot) point, vexed question.
umstrukturieren to restructure, to redeploy.
Umstrukturierung spadework, redeployment;
~ **von Grund auf** top-to-bottom restructuring; ~ **der Industrie** industrial restructuring; ~ **der Nachfrage** change in demand; ~ **der Nachfrage hervorrufen** to change the demand pattern.
Umstrukturierungsprozeß restructuring process.
umstufen to regrade.
Umstufung regrading.
Umsturz overthrow, upheaval, subversion, revolution, anarchy, bouleversement;
~ **der Verfassung** subversion of the constitution;
~ **planen** to plot against the government;
~bestrebungen revolutionary tendencies; **~bewegung** subversive movement.
Umstürzen *(Auto)* upset, overturn, turnover.
umstürzen *(Mauer)* to fall down, to tumble;
Auto ~ to upset (overturn) a car; **Gesellschaftsordnung** ~ to subvert the social order.
Umsturzklima schaffen to create a revolutionary climate.
Umstürzler revolutionist, subverter, overthrower, destructionist;
radikaler ~ demolitionist.
umstürzlerisch subversive, revolutionary.
Umsturz|partei revolutionary party; **~versuch** attempted overthrow.
Umtausch exchange, barter, *(Börse)* swap, *(Devisen)* conversion;
kein ~ all sales final, no goods exchanged; ~ **vorbehalten** subject to change;
~ **von Fertigwaren gegen Rohprodukte** exchange of finished goods against raw materials; ~ **zum Nennwert** conversion at face value; ~ **von Sicherheiten** substitution of collateral; ~ **von 5%igen in 4%ige Wertpapiere** conversion of 5-per-cent stock into 4-per-cents;
zwecks ~ **übergeben** to surrender for exchange;
~aktion conversion scheme; **~angebot** exchange offer, *(Wandelschuldverschreibung)* conversion offer.
umtauschbar exchangeable, *(Wertpapier)* convertible, commutable;
nicht ~ inconvertible.
umtauschen to change, to exchange, *(Börse)* to swap, *(Wertpapiere)* to commute, to convert;
Pfunde in Franken ~ to convert pounds into francs.
umtauschfähig exchangeable, returnable, *(Wertpapier)* convertible;
nicht ~ not returnable, inconvertible;
~e Aktie convertible stock.
Umtausch|fähigkeit convertibility; **~fahrschein** exchange ticket; **~formular** exchange form; **~frist** conversion period; **~kosten** costs of exchange; **~obligationen** refunding (redemption) bonds; **~preis** exchange price; **~recht** exchange privilege, option of exchange, *(Wandelschuldverschreibung)* conversion privilege; **~satz** *(Devisen)* conversion rate; **~spesen** cost of exchange; **~stelle** conversion office, exchange agent; **~stelle für fremde Sorten** bureau de change facilities; **~transaktion** conversion scheme, *(Devisen)* exchange operation; **~vergütung** conversion bonus; **~verhältnis** basis of exchange, *(Devisen)* conversion rate; **~verhältnis eins zu eins** *(Aktie)* share-for-share exchange; **~vorrecht** conversion privilege.
Umtriebe activities, machinations, practices, intrigues, stratagems, engineering *(coll.)*;
staatsfeindliche ~ subversive (unamerican, *US*) activities.
Umtrunk wassail;
vergnügten ~ **halten** to be merry in one's cups.
umtun, sich nach Arbeit to look for a job.
Umverpackung overwrap.
umverteilen to redistribute;
Arbeitskräfte ~ to reallocate labo(u)r.
Umverteilung redistribution;
~ **der Arbeitskräfte** reallocation of labo(u)r; ~ **der Bevölkerung** population redistribution; ~ **des Eigentums** redistribution of property.
Umwälz|anlage circulation equipment; **~pumpe** circulation pump.
Umwälzung changeover, overturn, upthrow, radical change, earthquake, landslide *(US)*;
soziale ~ social upheaval, cataclysm; **wirtschaftliche** ~ industrial revolution.
umwandelbar *(Anleihe)* convertible, *(Gesellschaft)* transformable, *(Strafe)* commutable;
nicht ~ inconvertible.
Umwandelbarkeit *(Anleihe)* convertibility, *(Strafe)* commutability.
umwandeln to form into, to transform, to convert, to turn, *(Rente)* to commute, *(Wertpapiere)* to convert, to reconvert;
Anleihe ~ to convert a loan; **in Bargeld** ~ to convert into cash money; **Einzelunternehmen in eine Gesellschaft** ~ to turn the business of a sole proprietor into a partnership; **Firma in eine Aktiengesellschaft** ~ to turn a firm into a joint-stock company, to convert a firm into a public company; **Gesellschaft** ~ to reorganize a company (corporation); **Grundstücksrechte in Geldansprüche** ~ to convert from rights in land to rights in money; **Handelsgesellschaft in eine Aktiengesellschaft** ~ to convert a partnership into a company (corporation); **Handelsschiffe in Kriegsschiffe** ~ to convert merchant ships into warships; **in Kapital** ~ to convert into capital; **voll**

eingezahlte Kapitalanteilsrechte in Aktien ~ to convert paid-up shares into stock; **Rente in eine Pauschalzahlung** ~ to commute an annuity into (for) a lump sum; **schwebende Schuld** ~ to fund the floating debt; **Todesstrafe** ~ to commute a death sentence; **unbewegliches in bewegliches Vermögen** ~ to convert realty into personalty (equity).

Umwandlung transformation, rearrangement, *(Rente, Strafe)* commutation, *(Wertpapiere)* conversion;
steuerbegünstigte ~ *(Firma)* tax-privileged reorganization;
~ **in eine steuerfreie Anlage** conversion into a nontaxable form; ~ **einer Anleihe** conversion of a loan; ~ **eines Einzelunternehmens in eine Gesellschaft** turning the business of a sole proprietor into a partnership; ~ **einer Gesellschaft** reorganization of a company (corporation); ~ **in eine Gesellschaft** conversion into a company (corporation); ~ **von Grundeigentum in bewegliches Eigentum** conversion in equity; ~ **einer offenen Handelsgesellschaft in eine Aktiengesellschaft** conversion of a partnership into a company (corporation); ~ **von Handels- in Kriegsschiffe** conversion of merchant ships into warships; ~ **voll einbezahlter Kapitalanteilsrechte in Aktien** conversion of shares into stock; ~ **von Kapitalgesellschaften** conversion of corporations; ~ **steuerpflichtiger Pfandbriefrenditen in steuerfreie Kapitalgewinne** bond washing; ~ **schwebender Schulden** conversion (funding) of debts; ~ **einer Todesstrafe in lebenslängliches Zuchthaus** commutation of a death sentence to life imprisonment; ~ **von unbeweglichem in bewegliches Vermögen** conversion of realty into personalty.

Umwandlungs | klausel convertibility clause; ~**prozeß** process of transformation, *(Industrie)* fluid state; **sich in einem** ~**prozeß befinden** to be in the process of being reorganized; ~**recht** *(Anleihe, Wandelschuldverschreibungen)* right of conversion, *(Gruppenlebensversicherung)* conversion privilege; ~**tabelle** conversion table; ~**wert** *(Lebensversicherung)* paid-up value.

umwechselbar *(Papiergeld)* convertible.

umwechseln to change, to exchange, *(Wertpapiere)* to convert; **ausländisches Geld** ~ to change foreign currency.

Umwechslung exchange, *(Wertpapiere)* conversion;
~ **von Banknoten in Gold** conversion of notes into gold.

Umwechslungs | kurs rate of exchange; ~**preis** *(zwischen Gold und Silber)* parity of value.

Umweg roundabout way, circuitous way, devious path, detour *(US)*, *(Bahn)* loop-line;
auf ~**en** in a roundabout fashion, indirectly, by indirections, by hints; **ohne** ~**e** straight to the point;
~**e** indirect means;
großer ~ long way round; **umständlicher** ~ roundabout route; **auf** ~**en erfahren** to hear through side channels (news in a roundabout way); **zur Vermeidung des Verkehrs einen** ~ **fahren** to take a devious route to avoid busy streets; ~ **von dreißig Kilometern fahren** to go twenty miles round; **j. einen** ~ **machen lassen** to take s. o. out of his way; **ohne** ~**e auf sein Ziel losgehen** to come straight to the point; ~ **machen** to detour *(US)*, to make a detour *(US)*, to take a roundabout way; **großen** ~ **machen** to go a long way round; **nur ein** ~ **von 10 km sein** to be only six miles out of the way;
~**strecke** indirect route, roundabout tour, detour *(US)*.

Umwelt environment, milieu;
feindliche ~ hostile environment, enemy world; **gegenständliche** ~ physical environment; **natürliche** ~ natural environment; **soziale** ~ social environment;
sich seiner ~ **anpassen** to adjust o. s. to one's environment; **seine** ~ **hinreichend kennengelernt haben** to have had a wide experience of men;
~**amt** environmental office; ~**ausschuß** environment panel; ~**auswirkungen** environment aspects.

umweltbedingt environmental;
aus ~**en Gründen** on environmental grounds.

Umwelt | bedingungen environmental conditions; ~**bedingungen aufrechterhalten** to get environmentally adjusted; ~**beeinflussung** environmental impact; ~**behörde** environment department, environmental office; ~**beobachtungssatellit** environmental monitoring satellite.

umweltbewußt conservation-minded, environment-conscious, ecology-minded.

Umwelt | bewußtsein ecology; ~**beziehung** ecological relationship; ~**demonstration** environment demonstration; ~**denken** environmental thinking; ~**einflüsse** environmental effect (factors, influences), *(Anlagegeschäft)* investment environment, *(Beruf)* work environment, job conditions; **sich von** ~**einflüssen freimachen** to get away from one's environment; ~**fachmann** environmentalist, environment man.

umweltfeindlich sein to be noxious to the environment.

Umwelt | forschung ecology; ~**frage** environmental issue.

umweltfreundlich ecological;
~ **sein** to be kind to the environment.

Umwelt | freundlichkeit ecology; ~**gebiet** environmental area; ~**gefahr** ecological hazard; ~**gestaltung** environment planning.

umweltgestört *(Soziologie)* maladjusted.

Umwelt | hygiene environment sanitation; ~**katastrophe** ecological disaster; ~**kommission** environmental health commission; ~**kontrolle** environmental control; ~**krise** environmental crisis; ~**minister** Minister for the Department of the Environment *(Br.)*, Secretary of State for Environment *(US)*; ~**ministerium** Ministry of the Environment *(Br.)*; ~**normen** environmental standards; ~**planung** environmental planning; ~- **und Bauleitplanung** physical planning *(US)*; ~**politik** environmental politics; ~**probleme** environmental problems (questions); ~**prognose** environment forecast; ~**programm** environment program(me); ~**schäden** environmental damage (penalties).

Umweltschutz environmental safety (protection);
den Anforderungen des ~**es entsprechen** to meet pollution standards;
~**abteilung** environmental department; ~**anordnungen** environmental regulations; ~**aufwendungen** environmental services *(Br.)*; ~**bestimmungen** environmental rules; ~**bewegung** environmentalist movement.

umweltschutzbewußt conservationminded.

Umweltschutz | fonds environmental defence fund; ~**gesetz** environmental protection law, Environmental Policy Act *(US)*; ~**gesetzgebung** environmental legislation.

Umweltschützler environmentalist, conservationist.

Umweltschutz | probleme environment problems; ~**programm** environment[al] program(me); ~**recht** environmental law; ~**vorschriften** environmental standards.

Umwelt | störung *(Soziologie)* maladjustment; ~**studie** environmental study; ~**veränderungen** environmental changes; ~**verbesserungsbehörde** council of environmental quality *(US)*; **durch die Familie bestimmte** ~**verhältnisse** family environment.

umweltverschmutzend pollutive.

Umwelt | verschmutzer polluter; ~**verschmutzung** environment[al] pollution; ~**verschmutzung durch die Industrie** industrial pollution; ~**wirkung** environmental effect; ~**wissenschaft** environmental science; ~**zone** environmental area.

umwerben, Kunden to solicit customers; **Verbraucherschaft** ~ to court the consumer.

Umwerfen upset, turnover.

umwerfen to upset, *(Auto)* to overturn, to overthrow, to tip over, *(Konkurs machen)* to go smash (to the wall, *Br.*);
j. ~ *(Nachricht)* to disturb s. o. greatly; **jds. Pläne** ~ to thwart s. one's plans.

umwerfend | komisch screamingly funny;
nicht gerade ~ no great shakes.

umwerten to revalue, to revaluate, to reassess, to transvalue.

Umwertung revaluation, transvaluation, reassessment.

umwickeln, mit einer Schnur to wrap about with a string; **mit Stroh** ~ to cover with straw.

umwittert, von Geheimnissen shrouded (veiled) in mystery.

umwölken, sich to cloud over, to become overcast.

umzäunen to fence in (up), to enclose with a fence.

Umzäunung hedge, enclosure, fence.

Umziehen move, remove, *(Kleider)* change of clothes.

umziehen to move house (one's lodgings), to remove, to shift (change) one's quarters (residence, lodgings), to pull up stakes *(US coll.)*, to dislodge;
sich zum Abendessen ~ to dress for dinner; **dauernd** ~ to move from place to place; **aufs Land** ~ to move to (remove into, *Br.*) the country.

umzingeln to encircle, to surround, to encompass.

Umzug shift, change of residence, remove *(Br.)*, removal [of furniture] *(Br.)*, house moving, move *(US)*, flit *(Br.)*, *(pol.)* demonstration, *(Festzug)* parade, procession;
historischer ~ pageant;
seinen ~ **bewerkstelligen** to have one's furniture removed *(Br.)*; ~ **durch die Stadt durchführen** to walk in procession through the streets; **sich um den gesamten** ~ **kümmern** to take care of the moving details; **im** ~ **begriffen sein** to be in process of removal, to be on the move; **jds.** ~ **übernehmen** to move s. o.; ~ **veranstalten** to go in a procession, to parade, to demonstrate; ~ **verbieten** to veto a procession.

Umzüge besorgen *(Spediteur)* to remove furniture.

Umzugs|anzeige notice of removal; **~beihilfe** assistance with removal expenses *(Br.)*, moving (removal, *Br.*) allowance; **~geld** allowance for removal *(Br.)*; **~ und Wohnungsgeld** removal and lodging grant *(Br.)*; **~geschäft** removal business *(Br.)*; **~gewerbe** household-moving industry; **~gut** removal goods *(Br.)*.

umzugshalber geschlossen closed for removal *(US)*.

Umzugs|hilfe relocation assistance; **~kosten** removal expenses (expenditure) *(Br.)*, removing expense *(Br.)*, moving expenses *(US)*; **innerbetriebliche ~kosten** rearrangement (relocation) expense; **~kostenbeihilfe, ~kostenersatz, ~kostenerstattung** allowance for removal *(Br.)*, removal allowance *(Br.)*, transfer allowance *(US)*; **~spediteur, ~unternehmen** remover, moving man *(US)*, removal contractor *(Br.)*, furniture [re]mover; **~tag** moving day; **~teilnehmer** processionist; **~versicherung** moving (furniture-in-transit) insurance.

unabänderlich unalterable, incommutable, *(Urteil)* irrevocable, irreversible.

unabdingbar inalterable, obligatory, indispensable;
~e Bestimmung mandatory clause *(US)*; **~es Recht** inalienable right, peremptory law; **~e Voraussetzung** essential prerequisite; **~es Vorrecht** absolute privilege.

un|abgebunden *(Beton)* green; **~abgefertigt** *(Gepäck)* undispatched, *(Schalterkunde)* unattended; **~abgerechnet** nondeducted.

unabhängig independent, self-reliant, self-supporting, self-employed, on one's own, free, irrespective of, voluntary, *(blockfrei)* nonaligned, *(getrennt)* severable, *(pol.)* independent, middle-of-the-road, cross-bench *(Br.)*, *(Schriftsteller)* free-lance, *(Staat)* autonomous, sovereign, self-governing; **wirtschaftlich ~** autarchic, autonomous, self-supporting;
~ machen to emancipate; **sich von seinen Eltern finanziell ~ machen** to end one's dependence on one's parents; **~ sein** to be one's own master (independent), to stand on one's own legs *(fam.)*; **finanziell ~ sein** to be of independent means; **von den öffentlichen Verkehrsmitteln ~ sein** to be independent of trains, trams and buses;
~es Bankwesen independent banking system; **~e Bundesbehörde** independent agency *(US)*; **~es Einzelhandelsgeschäft** independent outlet; **~e Fachgewerkschaft** independent union; **von der Höhe der Forderung und dem Umfang des belasteten Grundstücks ~e Hypothek** closed-end mortgage; **~er Journalist** free-lance [writer]; **~e politische Körperschaft** independent body politic; **~es Leben führen** to live a life of independence; **~er Preis** free price.

Unabhängiger self-employed person, *(pol.)* independent, freelance, cross bencher *(Br.)*, mugwump *(US sl.)*;
finanziell ~ person of independent means.

Unabhängigkeit independence, self-reliance;
finanzielle ~ comfortable independence; **politische ~** political independence; **richterliche ~** judicial independence; **wirtschaftliche ~** self-sufficiency, economic independence, autarchy, autarky;
seine ~ erreichen (erhalten) to gain (conquer, secure, reach) independence; **einer Kolonie die ~ gewähren** to raise a colony to the status of a substantive nation; **gewisse ~ erreicht haben** to have acquired a modest independence.

Unabhängigkeits|bewegung independence movement; **~erklärung** Declaration of Independence; **~forderung** quest for independence; **~gefühl** separatist sentiment; **~grad** degree of independence; **~krieg** war of independence; **~tag** date of independence, Independence Day *(US)*.

unabkömmlich nonavailable, unavoidably absent, indispensable, *(im Augenblick)* busy, *(mil.)* exempt from military service, deferred *(US)*, reserved, keyed;
~ sein to be unavoidably prevented; **~ gestellt werden** *(mil.)* to be in a reserved occupation, to be deferred *(US)*.

Unabkömmlichkeit nonavailability, indispensability;
berufliche ~ reserved occupation, occupational deferment *(US)*.

Unabkömmlichkeitsstellung exemption from military service, reserved occupation.

unablässig constant, persistent, continuous;
~ regnen to be raining without let-up; **~ bemüht sein** to be persistent in one's efforts;
~e Klagen incessant complaints.

unablösbar *(Effekten, Hypothek)* irredeemable, *(Etikett)* irremovable, undetachable, *(Renten)* perpetual, irredeemable, *(Zinsschein)* undetachable;
~e Anleihe consolidated fund; **~e Rente** irredeemable (perpetual) annuity.

unabsehbar|e Folgen unforseeable consequences; **~er Schaden** immeasurable (incalculable) loss; **auf ~e Zeit** for an unforeseeable length of time.

unabsetzbar irremovable, undeposable, *(steuerlich)* deductible.

Unabsetzbarkeit irremovability.

unabsichtlich nonintentional, indeliberate, undesigned, involuntary, *(versehentlich)* inadvertent.

unabtretbar nonassignable, unassignable, inalienable, untransferable.

Unabtretbarkeit nonassignability, inalienability.

unabweisliche Rechtsvermutung irrebuttable presumption.

unabwendbar unpreventable, unavoidable, unescapable;
~es Ereignis inevitable accident; **~e Gefahren** unavoidable dangers; **~e Ursachen** unavoidable cause; **~er Zufall** act of God.

unachtsam careless, inattentive, inadvertent, neglectful, off one's guard, *(Verkehrsteilnehmer)* negligent, careless;
~ sein to be off one's guard;
~e Bemerkung thoughtless remark.

Unachtsamkeit inattention, inadvertence, *(Fahrlässigkeit)* carelessness.

unadressiert undirected.

unaffektiert without pose.

unakzeptiert not accepted, unaccepted;
~er Wechsel dishono(u)red bill.

unanfechtbar clear, watertight, undeniable, above exception, *(endgültig)* absolute, *(Entscheidung)* nonappealable, inappealable, *(Testament)* incontestable, indisputable;
~e Argumente invulnerable argument; **~es Beweismaterial** incontestable evidence; **~er Vertrag** unavoidable contract.

Unanfechtbarkeit incontestability, nonappealability, indisputability, *(Vertrag)* unavoidableness.

Unanfechtbarkeitsklausel *(Versicherung)* noncontestable clause.

unangebaut uncultivated.

unangebracht wide of the mark, inappropriate, unsuitable, beside the point, unseasonable, unfitting, out-of-place, *(ungelegen)* inopportune;
völlig ~ sein to be completely out-of-place;
~e Sparsamkeit misplaced thrift.

Unangebrachtheit einer Diskussion unreasonableness of a discussion.

unangefochten unchallenged, *(Patent, Testament)* uncontested, undisputed;
~ bleiben to emerge unscathed.

unangemeldet not previously announced, unannounced, *(Forderung)* undeclared;
~ eingehen *(Waren)* to arrive without previous notice;
~es Vermögen property not returned (reported).

unangemessen inopportune, unreasonable, inappropriate, disproportionate, unsuitable, incommensurate, *(ungeeignet)* unsuitable, *(unzulänglich)* inadequate;
~e Bezahlung erhalten to work for a mere pittance; **~e Forderungen stellen** to make exorbitant demands; **~e Frist** unreasonable length of time; **~er Preis** unreasonable price; **~e Schadensersatzzuerkennung** excessive damages.

Unangemessenheit inadequacy, unsuitableness, *(Mißverhältnis)* incongruity;
~ der Rücklagen beanstanden to disclose a material inadequacy in the reserve.

unangenehm unpleasant, disagreeable, awkward, unpleasant, disagreeable, uncomfortable;
~ auffallen to attract unfavo(u)rable notice, to make a bad impression; **jem. sehr ~ auffallen** to notice s. o. with disgust; **~ werden** to become rather nasty;
~er Geruch offensive smell; **~e Geschichte** unpleasant affair; **~en Geschmack haben** to be distasteful (unpalatable); **~er Kerl** nasty fellow; **~er Kunde** awkward customer; **in einer ~en Lage sein** to be in an awkward situation (tight squeeze, predicament); **~e Sache** a bad job; **sehr ~e Sache** dirty business; **~e Situation überspielen** to pass off an awkward situation; **~es Subjekt sein** to be a bad penny; **~er Teil einer Aufgabe** dirty end of the stick.

Unangenehmes, sich ~ nicht anmerken lassen to put a bold face on s. th.

unangerührt, unangetastet untouched;
~ bleiben *(Rechte)* to remain unattached (undrawn);
~e Vorräte untouched provisions.

unangreifbar enchallengeable, incontestable, *(mil.)* unattackable, *(Ruf)* unassailable;
~e Rechte unimpeachable rights.

unannehmbare Forderungen unacceptable demands.

Unannehmlichkeiten inconveniences, annoyances, unpleasantness, discomfort, cross;
j. ~ aussetzen to put s. o. to inconvenience; **~ bekommen** to get into trouble; **jem. ~ ersparen** to spare s. o. trouble; **~ verursachen** to discommode, to incommode; **auf Kosten größter persönlicher ~ mit etw. fertig werden** to manage s. th. at great personal inconvenience; **sich ~ zuziehen** to get into hot water (trouble), to put o. s. out of the way.
unansehnlich unattractive, plain, homely *(US)*;
~e Kleidung shabby clothes; **~e Verpackung** unsightly packing.
unanständig indecent, improper, unseemly, gross, obscene, vulgar, *(unehrenhaft)* dishono(u)rable;
etwas ~ a bit near the knuckle *(fam.)*;
sich ~ benehmen to behave improperly (shockingly);
~es Betragen indecent behavio(u)r; **~e Reden führen** to talk smut; **~er Witz** off-colo(u)r (blue) joke; **~e Wörter** four-letter words.
Unanständigkeit indecency, impropriety, indelicate act, obscenity.
unantastbar irreproachable, inviolable;
~e Reserven untouchable reserves.
unanwendbar inapplicable.
Unanwendbarkeit inapplicability, inadaptability.
unappetitlich unappetiszing, unsavory, *(Person)* unprepossessing.
Unart bad habit (manners), *(Unhöflichkeit)* incivility.
unaufdringlich unobtrusive;
~es Parfüm discreet perfume; **~ gemusterter Stoff** discreetly patterned fabric.
unauffällig under plain cover, unobtrusive.
unauffindbar untraceable, undiscoverable, *(Postvermerk)* not found;
trotz aller Bemühungen ~ sein to resist all efforts to be tracked down.
unaufführbar unactable.
unaufgefordert unsolicited, unasked, unbidden, unrequested, of one's own accord.
unauf|geführt *(in Liste)* unlisted, *(Theaterstück)* unacted, unperformed; **~geklärtes Verbrechen** unsolved crime; **~geschnitten** *(Buch)* uncut; **~haltsamer Verfall** decay which cannot be stopped; **~hebbar** nonrepealable, uncancellable; **~hörlich** continual, unremitting; **~löslich** indissolvable, *(Ehe)* indissoluble.
unaufmerksam inattentive, inadvertent;
~er Fahrer careless driver.
unaufrichtig two-sided, insincere, double-faced.
unaufschiebbar urgent, pressing, not to be delayed;
~e Angelegenheit pressing business; **~er Verhandlungstermin** peremptory day; **~e Vollstreckung eines Todesurteils** unreprievable execution of a death sentence.
unausbleibliche Mißverständnisse inevitable misunderstandings.
unausführbar impracticable, unfeasible, inexecutable.
Unausführbarkeit impracticability, unfeasability.
unaus|gebaut unfinished; **~gebildet** unskilled, untrained; **~gefeilt** unpolished; **~geführt** unexecuted.
unausgefüllt blank, unfilled;
~ lassen to leave a blank (void);
~es Formular blank form; **~es Wechselformular** skeleton bill.
unausgeglichen *(Etat)* unbalanced, out of balance;
~es Bild *(Statistik)* unbalanced picture; **~e Bücher** unbalanced books; **~er Charakter** unstable character; **~er Haushalt** unbalanced budget; **~e Rechnung** unsettled bill; **~es Verhältnis zwischen Angebot und Nachfrage** disproportion of supply and demand; **~e Zahlungsbilanz** imbalance in payments.
Unausgeglichenheit *(Zahlungsbilanz)* imbalance.
unaus|gegorene politische Ideen half-baked policies; **~gelastet** *(Person)* not fully occupied, *(Produktionsanlage)* not working to capacity; **~genutzt** idle; **~gereift** immature, unripe; **~geschüttet** unappropriated; **~gesprochen** unsaid; **~gestattet** unfitted; **~gewogen** unbalanced.
Unausgewogenheit imbalance.
unaus|löschlich in jds. Herz eingegraben sein to be etched on s. one's heart (in acid); **~rottbare Krankheit** inveterate disease.
unaussprechlich beyond all expression, unspeakable;
~es Elend abject misery; **~er Name** tongue-twister, jawbreaker.
unausstehlich intolerable;
~er Kerl old so-and-so.
unausweichlich inevitable, unavoidable.
unbändig unrestrainable, uncontrollable;
von ~er Wut erfüllt sein to fly into an unrestrained rage.
unbare Belastungen noncash charges.
unbarmherzig ruthless, pittiless, merciless;
mit ~er Strenge with iron (inexorable) severity.
unbeabsichtigt unintended, undesigned, inadvertent;
scheinbar ~ by accident on purpose.
unbeachtet unnoticed, unobserved, disregarded;
Einwand ~ lassen to disregard an objection;
~er Schriftsteller neglected writer.
unbeachtlich off the mark, *(jur.)* irrelevant.
unbeanstandet unopposed, not opposed, without objection, *(Warensendung)* not rejected, unobjected;
~ durch die Zollkontrolle kommen to pass the customs without objection;
~e Ware not rejected goods.
unbeantwortet unanswered, unacknowledged, without reply;
~ bleiben to meet with no response.
unbearbeitet natural, in the native state, rough, unwrought, raw *(US)*, unmanufactured, unfinished, unmachined, unlabo(u)red, *(Geschäftsvorgang)* not yet taken up, not yet dealt with, *(Rechtssache)* pending;
~er Fall untreated case.
unbeaufsichtigt uncontrolled, without control, unattended.
unbebaubar untillable, uncultivable, *(Grundstück)* not suitable for development.
unbebaut *(Feld)* uncultivated, *(Grundstück)* unimproved, undeveloped, waste, vacant, open and unbuilt upon;
~ oder bearbeitet raw or processed;
~ bleiben *(Acker)* to lie waste;
~er Grund vacant plot, vacancy, open spaces *(Br.)*; **~e und bebaute Grundstücke** *(Bilanz)* real estate.
unbedacht improvident, thoughtless;
in einem ~en Augenblick in an unguarded moment; **~e Äußerung** thoughtless remark.
Unbedachtsamkeit improvidence, thoughtlessness.
unbedarft unexperienced.
unbedenklich absolutely reliable;
Angebot ~ annehmen to accept an offer without hesitation.
Unbedenklichkeits|bescheinigung clearance certificate, *(Zoll)* import certificate; **~überprüfung** *(Zoll)* objectionability test; **~zeugnis** *(Geleitschein)* navicert.
unbedeutend trifling, petty, fractional, distant, faint, jesting, peddling, inconsiderable, negligible, trivial, weightless, paltry, two-bit *(US)*, *(Börsenumsätze)* insignificant, *(Mensch)* noaccount;
völlig ~ nothing to write home about;
~e Angelegenheit smalltime affair, trivial matter; **aus ~em Anlaß** from a trifle; **~er Betrag** paltry (insignificant) sum; **~e Einzelheiten** minor details; **~er Fehler** petty fault; **~er Händler** petty dealer; **~e Kursveränderungen** fractional changes; **~e Person** nonentity, small beer, cipher, also-run *(sl.)*, peanut *(US)*; **~e Reparaturen** minor repairs; **~er Schaden** negligible (minor) damage; **~er Schriftsteller** undistinguished writer; **~e Schulden** paltry (petty) debts; **~e Stadt** one-horse (jerkwater, *US*) town; **~e Stellung** inferior position; **~er Unfall** minor accident; **~er Verlust** trivial (minor, insignificant) loss; **~er Wert** trifling value.
unbedingt unconditional, peremptory, absolute, altogether, must, all-out, *(auf jeden Fall)* by all means, *(uneingeschränkt)* unqualified, without reserve;
~e Annahme eines Wechsels unqualified acceptance of a bill; **~e Diät** strict diet; **~er Gehorsam** implicit obedience; **~e Verpflichtung** absolute liability; **jds. ~es Vertrauen besitzen** to have s. one's complete confidence; **~e Zustimmung** unqualified approval.
unbedruckt blank;
~er Rand margin; **~er Raum** blank space; **~e Seite** blank page.
unbeeidigt unsworn;
~e Zeugenaussage unsworn testimony.
unbeeindruckt lassen, j. to cut no ice with s. o. *(fam.)*.
unbeeinflußt without preoccupation, unbiassed.
unbeeinträchtigt uninjured, unimpaired, *(Eigentum)* undisturbe.
unbefahrbar impassable, impracticable, *(Wasserweg)* not navigable.
unbefangen without preoccupation, at ease, unprejudiced, *(Richter)* clean, impartial, unbiassed;
~er Beobachter unbiassed observer.
Unbefangenheit freedom from bias, impartiality, ease.
unbefestigt *(Stadt)* unfortified, unsecured, *(Straße)* unmetal(l)ed, unpaved;
~e Stadt open town.

un|befrachtet clear, empty; **~befriedigendes Ergebnis** unsatisfactory result; **~befriedigt** *(Schuldner)* unsatisfied.
unbefristet undated, having no limit, unlimited, for an unlimited period, for an indefinite time, *(Anleihe)* perpetual;
~er Lieferungsvertrag open-end contract.
unbefugt unauthorized, incompetent, without permission (authority), freewheeling;
~es Betreten eines Grundstücks trespass.
Unbefugte|r unauthorized person, trespasser;
~n ist der Eintritt verboten no unauthorized entry, no admittance except on business.
un|begabt untalented, ungifted; **~begeben** undisposed, unsold, still on hand, *(Anleihe)* not disposed of; **~beglaubigt** uncertified, unauthenticated, unaccredited, parol, unattested; **~beglichen** *(Rechnung)* unsettled, unpaid, unsatisfied, outstanding; **~begreiflich** inapprehensible, inconceivable, incomprehensible.
unbegrenzt indefinite, unlimited, timeless;
~er Kredit unlimited credit; **~e Möglichkeiten** boundless possibilities, unlimited opportunities; **der Höhe nach ~er Scheck** unlimited check *(US)* (cheque, *Br.*); **~e Zufallsstichproben** unrestricted random sampling.
unbegründet without merits, idle, groundless, unsolid, gratuitous, without good ground, unfounded;
Klage als ~ abweisen to dismiss a case on the merits; **[völlig] ~ sein** to be without foundation;
~er Anspruch bad claim; **~e Beschuldigungen** unsupported charges; **~es Gerücht** unfounded rumo(u)r.
unbegütert impecunious, not well off, without means.
Unbehagen uneasiness;
jds. ~ beschwichtigen to calm s. one's uneasiness.
un|behaglich uncomfortable, uneasy; **~behauen** in the log; **~behelligt** unmolested, undisturbed.
unbeherrscht|handeln to act without self-control;
~e Äußerung intemperate utterance.
Unbeherrschtheit lack of self-control, unrestraint.
unbehindert unentangled, *(Handel)* unrestricted;
~e Zufahrt unobstructed approach.
un|behobene Dividende unclaimed dividend; **~beholfen** unpractical, clumsy, wooden, unblemished, shiftless; **~beirrt** unswerving, steadfast, unwavering.
unbekannt unknown, nameless;
bisher ~ fresh;
völlig ~ sein to spring from obscurity;
~en Aufenthalts present address unknown; **~es Flugobjekt** unidentified flying object; **~e Gegend** unfamiliar district; **~e Größe** unknown quantity, *(fig.)* dark horse; **gänzlich ~er Ort** obscure locality; **~es Risiko** unknown risk; **~e Umgebung** strange surroundings.
Unbekannter unknown person, stranger.
un|bekömmlich *(Nahrung)* indigestible, unwholesome, *(Wetter)* ungenial; **~bekümmert** light-hearted, careless, uncareful, unclouded, happy-go-lucky, easy-going; **~beladen** unloaded, unladen, without cargo, *(Schiff)* light.
unbelastet *(Grundstück)* clear, unembarrassed, free and unencumbered, unincumbered, *(Haus)* unmortgaged, *(politisch)* with a clean record, *(sorglos)* free from care, lighthearted, free and easy;
~es Gewissen clear conscience; **in ~em Zustand** in no-load condition.
un|belästigt unmolested, scot-free; **~belebt** *(Markt)* slack, dull, dead, lifeless, inanimate, sluggish, *(Straße)* unfrequented, quiet, deserted, inactive.
Unbelebtheit *(Markt)* slackness, dullness, deadness.
un|beleckt von jeder Kultur untouched by civilization; **völlig ~belehrbar sein** not to listen to reason; **~belesen** unlettered; **~beleuchtet** unlit, unilluminated, unlighted; **~belichtet** *(Film)* unexposed; **~beliebt** unpopular, disliked.
Unbeliebtheit unpopularity;
sich über seine ~ klar werden to get next to s. o. *(sl.)*.
un|belohnt unrewarded, unrequited; **~bemannt** unmanned, pilotless.
unbemerkt unnoticed, undiscerned, unseen;
j. ~ verfolgen to shadow s. o.
unbemittelt without means, poor, impecunious;
gänzlich ~ destitute.
Unbemitteltheit lack of means.
unbenommen free, unrestrained;
es jem. ~ bleiben to be at liberty to.
unbenutzt unused, unavailed, *(Gebäude)* vacant, unoccupied, *(Kapital)* unemployed, dormant, idle.
unbeobachtet unobserved, unwitnessed;
~ bleiben to escape notice.
unbequem inconvenient, incommodious, uncomfortable;
jem. ~ werden to become a nuisance for (to) s. o.
Unbequemlichkeit lack of comfort, inconvenience;
geringfügige ~en little discomforts;
~en des Lebens auf dem Lande inconvenience of living far from town;
keine unbilligen ~en erleiden not to be unduly inconvenienced.
unberechenbar incalculable, incomputable, beyond computation, *(launisch)* wayward;
völlig ~ sein to be out of all count;
~e Umstände imponderables.
unberechnet free of charge, gratis, complimentary.
unberechtigt without justification, unauthorized, incompetent, not entitled, unwarranted, uncharged, unentitled, without authority, unlicensed, *(ungerechtfertigt)* unjustified;
~e Entlassung unlawful dismissal; **~e Forderung** unfounded claim; **~er Maklergehilfe** unauthorized clerk *(Br.)*; **~er Nachdruck** unauthorized (counterfeit) reprint, pirated edition, piracy; **~e Preisbindung** unreasonable restraint of trade *(US)*; **~e Zurückhaltung** unlawful detainer.
Unberechtigter unauthorized person.
unberichtigter *(Rechnung)* unpaid, unsettled, not settled, *(Schriftstück)* unrectified, incorrected.
unberücksichtigt unnoticed, disregarded, not taken into account, unconsidered;
~ bleiben to leave out of count; **~ lassen** to shelve.
unberufen! touch wood!
unberührt unaffected, *(Jungfrau)* chaste, virgin;
von einem Preisrückgang ~ bleiben not to be affected by a fall in prices; **j. völlig ~ lassen** to leave s. o. cold; **von einem Gesetz ~ werden** not to fall within the purview of a law;
~es Bett bed not been slept in.
unbeschadet within prejudice, saving, notwithstanding;
~ irgendwelcher Ansprüche without prejudice to any claims; **~ anderweitiger Bestimmungen** notwithstanding any clauses to the contrary.
unbeschädigt undamaged, not damaged, free of damage, sound, unhurt, in good condition, uninjured, unimpaired, *(Münze)* in mint condition, *(Schiff)* free from average.
unbeschäftigt free from business, disengaged, unengaged, unoccupied, off work, at leisure, idle, *(arbeitslos)* unemployed, out of work.
Unbeschäftigtsein disoccupation.
unbescheiden immodest, presumptuous;
~er Preis unreasonable price.
un|bescheinigt uncertified; **~beschnitten** *(drucktechn.)* rough.
unbescholten blameless, of good reputation, unblemished, fair, spotless;
~ sein to have no police record;
~e Frau innocent woman; **~e Person** person of unblemished character; **~er Ruf** unimpeachable reputation.
Unbescholtenheit integrity, virtue.
Unbescholtenheitszeugnis certificate of good behavio(u)r (character).
unbeschotterte Straße unmetal(l)ed road.
unbeschränkt unlimited, for an unlimited time, unrestricted, uncontrolled, unqualified, absolute;
~ haften to be liable without limitation;
~es Eigentumsrecht absolute ownership; **~es Giro** absolute indorsement; **~er Grundstückseigentümer** owner in fee simple; **~e Haftpflicht** unlimited (full) liability; **~e Monarchie** absolute monarchy; **~er Preis** unlimited price; **~ wirksames Recht** absolute right; **zeitlich ~e einstweilige Verfügung** perpetual injunction; **~e Verfügungsmacht** outright disposition; **~e Vollmacht** unlimited power of attorney, blank check *(US)* (cheque, *Br.*); **mit ~en Vollmachten ausgestattet** plenipotentiary.
unbeschrankter Bahnübergang level *(Br.)* (grade, *US*) crossing.
unbeschreibliches Durcheinander topsy-turvydom, shambles.
unbeschrieben blank;
~es Blatt *(fig.)* unknown quantity, dark horse.
un|beschrittene Pfade gehen to travel on new ground; **~beschwert** footloose, easy-going, easy in one's mind.
unbesehen unlooked at, without previous examination;
~ kaufen to buy unsight (sight unseen, *US*, a pig in a poke).
unbesetzt vacant, unoccupied, void, *(Rolle)* uncast, *(Telefon)* disengaged, clear *(US)*, *(Theater)* empty;
~ sein to fall vacant (void); **noch ~ sein** to be still open;
~er Omnibus empty bus; **~e Stelle** vacant situation, vacancy.

un|besiedelt unsettled, unplanted, uncolonized; ~**besiegbar** invincible; ~**besoldet** unsalaried, unpaid, *(ehrenamtlich)* honorary; ~**besonnen** heedless, blind, imprudent, thoughtless; ~**besorgt** unconcerned, with an easy mind; ~**besprochen** unventilated.

unbeständig unballasted, fickle, *(Markt)* unsteady, unsettled, *(Nachfrage)* variable, unsteady, *(pol.)* unstable, *(Preise)* fluctuating, irregular, *(Wetter)* broken, variable;
~**er Kurs** variable exchange; ~**e Valuta** fluctuating value.

Unbeständigkeit instability, unstableness, vicissitude, changeability, *(Markt)* unsteadiness, *(pol.)* instability.

unbestätigt unconfirmed, unacknowledged, uncorroborated;
~**es Akkreditiv** unconfirmed letter of credit; ~**en Meldungen zufolge** according to unofficial reports.

unbestechlich incorrupt, uncorrupted, incorruptible, unbribable, moneyproof, proof against corruption (bribes), not open to bribery;
~ **sein** to be above taking bribes.

Unbestechlichkeit incorruptibility.

unbestellbar undeliverable, *(Brief)* unclaimed, dead, *(Feld)* untillable, uncultivable;
Brief als ~ erklären to dead a letter;
~**er Brief** returned (dead) letter.

Unbestellbarkeitsmeldung advice of nondelivery.

un|bestellt not ordered, *(Brief)* undelivered; ~**besteuert** untaxed, tax-free; ~**bestimmbar** indeterminable.

unbestimmt uncertain, indefinite, unliquidated, general, rough, unset, vague;
der Höhe nach ~e Forderung unliquidated demand; ~**es Gefühl haben** to have a vague feeling; **auf ~e Zeit vertagen** to adjourn sine die.

Unbestimmtheit eines Vertrages uncertainty in a contract.

unbestochen clean-handed.

unbestraft unpunished, with a clean record;
~ **bleiben** to go unpunished, to escape scot-free.

unbestreitbar undeniable, incontestable, unassailable, clear, certain, indisputable, unchallengeable, beyond debate;
~**e Tatsache** established fact.

Unbestreitbarkeit indisputability.

unbestritten undisputed, uncontradicted, uncontested, undoubted.

unbeteiligt indifferent, uninterested, unconcerned, *(unparteiisch)* unbiassed, *(nicht verwickelt)* not involved;
~ **sein an** to have no part in, not to be participating, *(Unternehmen)* to have no shares in.

Unbeteiligte|r disinterested party, outsider, onlooker;
am Vertrag ~r stranger to a contract;
sich einem ~n anvertrauen to confide in a neutral person.

unbeträchtlich inconsiderable, trivial;
nicht ~e Summe considerable amount.

unbeugsam unbending, unyielding, unfaltering, inflexible;
~**er Wille** inflexible will.

un|bewacht unguarded, unwatched, *(Schranke)* keeperless; ~**bewaffnet** unarmed; ~**bewandert** unversed, ignorant, unskilled, unstudied.

unbeweglich real, *(Feiertag)* immovable, *(feststehend)* stationary, fixed;
~**e Sachen** immovables; ~**es Vermögen** real property, realty.

Unbeweglichkeit, wohnungsbedingte geographical immobility;
~ **des Vorstandes** lack of management mobility.

un|bewegtes Kundenkonto dormant (dead, broken) account; ~**beweisbar** unprovable; ~**bewertet** unvalued, *(nicht steuerlich abgeschätzt)* unassessed; ~**bewiesen** *(Forderung)* unproved, unproven, illiquid.

unbewirtschaftet not rationed, *(Devisen)* uncontrolled, *(Feld)* uncultivated, unmanaged;
zur Zeit ~ sein *(Hotel)* to be closed for the moment.

unbewohnbar unhabitable, untenantable, unfit for habitation;
verfallene Häuser für ~ erklären to condemn slum dwellings.

unbewohnt unoccupied, vacant, void, uninhabited, empty, *(entvölkert)* unpeopled, desolate, unpopulated, deserted, untenanted, tenantless *(US)*;
~**e Zeit** void period.

Unbewohntsein, zeitweiliges inoccupancy, unoccupancy, vacancy *(US)*.

unbewölkt unclouded, cloudless.

unbewußt unconscious, involuntary.

unbezahlbar prohibitively expensive, not to be paid for, *(unersetzlich)* beyond price, priceless, impayable, *(unschätzbar)* inestimable, invaluable;
~ **sein** to be worth its weight in gold.

unbezahlt unsettled, not settled, unsatisfied, unliquidated, unpaid, without pay, uncleared;
~ **bleiben** to lose one's debts; ~ **lassen** to leave unpaid;
~**e Arbeit** unremunerative work; ~**e Beschäftigung** unsalaried employment; ~**e Rechnungen** outstanding bills; ~**er Urlaub** leave without pay, payless vacation *(US)*; ~**e Waren** unpaid goods; ~**er Wechsel** dishono(u)red bill.

un|bezeichnet undesignated; ~**beziffert** unliquidated, without stint; ~**bezogen** *(Bett)* without sheets.

Unbilden des Wetters inclemency of the weather.

unbillig inequitable, unreasonable, oppressive, unfair, unjust;
~**e Härte** undue hardship; ~**es Verlangen** unreasonable demand.

Unbilligkeit iniquity.

unblutige Revolution unbloody revolution.

unbotmäßig disorderly, recalcitrant, insubordinate.

Unbotmäßigkeit incivism, recalcitration, insubordination.

unbrauchbar useless, of no use, inapplicable, *(Maschine)* unserviceable, unavailable, *(Material)* waste;
völlig ~ of no earthly use;
für ~ erklären *(Gebäude)* to condemn; ~ **machen** to destroy, to wreck, to disable; **völlig ~ sein** to be good for nothing; **für diese Arbeit völlig ~ sein** not to be suited for this kind of work;
~**e Methode** impracticable method; ~**er Plan** infeasible plan;
~**es System** impracticable method; ~ **gewordene Ware** spoilt goods.

Unbrauchbarkeit uselessness, obsolescence, inapplicability.

Unbrauchbarkeitserklärung *(Gebäude)* condemnation.

Unbrauchbarmachung destruction, wreckage.

unchiffriert in plain language, en clair.

Undank, grober gross ingratitude.

Undankbarkeit ingratitude;
mit ~ vergelten to lift up the heel against.

un|datiert dateless, undated, without date; ~**definierbar** indefinable; ~**deklariert** *(Zoll)* unentered, undeclared; ~**demokratisch** undemocratic; **seit ~denklichen Zeiten** from time immemorial.

undeutlich unclear, vague, inarticulate, *(Foto)* thin, *(Sicht)* blurred, hazy;
sich ~ erinnern to have a hazy recollection; ~ **sprechen** to speak indistinctly;
~**e Erinnerung** vague (faint) memory; ~**e Schrift** obscure writing.

undicht leaky, permeable, not watertight, pervious, *(Faß, Schiff)* leaky;
~**e Stelle** *(fig.)* leak.

Unding absurdity, preposterous thing.

un|diskutabel sein to be out of the question; ~**diszipliniert** undisciplined, tumultuary; ~**duldsam** intolerant.

Unduldsamkeit in Rassenfragen racial intolerance.

undurchdringlich impenetrable, thick;
~**er Dschungel** unpassable jungle; ~**es Geheimnis** profound mystery; ~**es Gesicht** poker face; **mit ~er Miene** with a deadpan stare *(coll.)*.

Undurchdringlichkeit eines Waldes density of a forest.

undurchführbar impracticable, unfeasible, impossible;
~**er Plan** impracticable (infeasible) scheme.

un|durchlässig impermeable, waterproof, *(Luft)* airproof, *(Schall)* soundproof; ~**durchschaubares Verhalten** obscure behavio(u)r; ~**durchsetzbar** unenforceable.

undurchsichtig nontransparent, *(fig.)* mysterious;
völlig ~ as clear as ditch water.

uneben uneven, rough, broken;
nicht ~ sein not to be so bad.

unebenbürtig of inferior rank.

Unebenheit des Bodens irregularity of ground.

unecht *(Farbe)* fading, not fast, *(fingiert)* fictitious, bogus, *(gefälscht)* counterfeit, false, faked, phony, straw, dummy, *(künstlich)* artificial, *(nachgemacht)* imitated, sham, mock, spurious, imitated;
~**e Banknote** spurious bank bill, dud *(sl.)*, bogus money *(US)*;
~**er Bruch** improper fraction; ~**e Perlen** false pearls; ~**er Schmuck** counterfeit jewels, imitation (imitated) jewelry.

unedle Motive base motives.

unehelich illegitimate, born out of wedlock, of illegitimate birth, love-begotten, unlawful, spurious, bastard, nameless, misbegotten, outside *(sl.)*;
~**es Kind** bastard child *(US)*.

Unehelichkeit illegitimacy.

Unehelichkeits|erklärung bastardization; ~**verfahren** bastardy process.

Unehre dishono(u)r;
in ~n verabschiedet *(mil.)* dishono(u)red;
seiner Familie zur ~ gereichen to bring disgrace (dishono(u)r) on one's family.
unehrenhaft dishono(u)rable, infamous;
~ entlassen cashiered;
~ handeln to be dishonest in one's dealings.
unehrerbietig disrespectful, irreverent.
unehrlich dishonest, unfair, untrue, foul;
~e Absichten disgraceful intentions; **~es Handeln** crooked dealings.
Unehrlichkeit dishonesty, improbity, unfairness, irrelevancy.
uneigennützig disinterested, altruistic, selfless, unselfish.
Uneigennützigkeit disinterest, altruism.
uneinbringlich uncollectible, irrecoverable, irredeemable, unenforceable;
~e Forderung bad debt; **~e Schulden** irrecoverable debts; **~er Verlust** irretrievable (irredeemable) loss.
Uneinbringlichkeit uncollectibility;
im Fall der ~ in default of payment.
uneingeladen erscheinen to crash a party *(coll.)*, to gatecrash.
uneingelöst *(Koupon)* uncollected, uncashed, *(unbezahlt)* unpaid, *(Wechsel)* unredeemed, dishono(u)red;
~e Abschnitte unredeemed coupons.
uneingeschränkt unreserved, free, unrestrained, unrestricted, unsparing, entire, all-out, unlimited, unqualified, without restriction (control), *(Konzession)* plenary *(US)*, *(Revisionsvermerk)* unqualified;
~e Annahme unqualified acceptance; **~er Kredit** unrestricted (unlimited) credit; **~es Lob verdienen** to deserve unstinted praise (full marks); **~er Prüfungsvermerk** unqualified report; **~er Schuldschein** absolute bond; **jem. ~es Vertrauen schenken** to trust s. o. unreservedly; **~e Vollmacht** plenary power; **~e Zustimmung** unqualified assent, unreserved compliance.
uneingesehenes Gelände unseen ground.
uneinheitlich unsettled, uneven, not uniform, *(Börse)* irregular, erratic;
~ sein *(Börse)* to make an irregular showing;
~es Bild bieten *(Börse)* to present a mixed showing.
Uneinheitlichkeit *(Börse)* irregularity.
uneinig divided, different, disunited, at variance;
~ sein to be at (in) disagreement (variance, at odds).
Uneinigkeit disunity, difference, disagreement, discord, jar.
un|einlösbar *(Bürgschaft)* irrepleviable, *(Papiergeld)* inconvertible, irredeemable; **~einnehmbare Festung** impregnable fortress; **~eins** at odds (variance, at issue) with; **~einträglich** unprofitable, unremunerative.
Uneinträglichkeit unprofitableness.
uneintreibbar irrecoverable, unenforceable;
~e Forderung debt dead in law.
uneinziehbar uncollectable.
unelastisch *(Angebot und Nachfrage)* rigid;
~e Nachfrage inelastic demand.
unempfänglich insensitive, insusceptible;
~ gegen Schmeicheleien immune (deaf) to flattery.
unempfindlich gegen Schmerzen insensitive to pain.
unendlich endless, never-ending, *(Bruch)* infinite;
auf ~ einstellen *(Fotoapparat)* to focus at infinity; **~ langsam vergehen** to pass terribly slowly;
~ viel Geld pots of money; **~e Mühe** tremendous difficulty; **~ schweres Problem** intricate problem; **~e Sorgen** no end of trouble.
Unendlicheinstellung *(Fotoapparat)* infinity setting.
Unendlichkeit des Weltalls deep of space.
unentbehrlich indispensable, irreplaceable, absolutely necessary.
unentgeltlich gratis, gratuitous, free of charge, without return (consideration, remuneration), *(ohne Gegenleistung)* voluntary, *(Zugabe)* as a free gift;
~ tätig sein to work without recompense;
~e Beratung free consultation; **~er Rat** gratuitous advice; **~e Übereignung** voluntary conveyance; **~er Vertrag** gratuitous contract; **~er Vertreter** gratuitous agent; **~er Verwahrer** gratuitous bailee; **~e Verwahrung** gratuitous bailment, naked deposit; **~ ausgeübte Vollmacht** naked authority; **~e Zuwendung** free gift, voluntary contribution, transfer payment *(US)*.
Unentgeltlichkeit gratuitousness.
unentschädigt uncompensated, unindemnified;
~ bleiben to get no redress for one's losses.
unentschieden undecided, abeyant, undetermined, unadjudged;
noch ~ dependent, pending;
~ ausgehen to end in a draw; **~ bleiben** to remain in suspense; **~ lassen** to abey; **~ sein** to be left in abeyance; **noch ~ sein** to be still in two minds, *(Prozeß)* to depend;
~er Mensch ditherer *(coll.)*.
Unentschiedenheit suspense, pendency, tie, poise.
unentschlossen undecided, tentative, on the fence, wavering, wishy-washy;
~ sein to vacillate, to be infirm of purpose, to lack decision, to chop and change, to hang back, to ride *(US)* (sit) on the fence, to straddle *(US)*;
~er Mensch irresolute person, fence rider (sitter) *(US)*.
Unentschlossenheit infirmity of purpose.
unentschuldbar inexcusable, unpardonable;
völlig ~ sein to be wholly indefensible.
unentschuldigt without valid excuse, without cause;
~ fehlen to be absent without leave;
~es Fehlen absent without leave, absenteeism.
unentwegt stalwart, unflinching, steadfast;
~ arbeiten to work steadily; **~ klingeln** *(Telefon)* to ring without let-up; **~ regnen** to rain incessantly.
unentwickelt immature, *(Land)* undeveloped;
~e Länder developing countries.
unentzifferbar undecipherable.
Unerbietigkeit disrespect.
unerbittlich implacable, iron, relentless.
unerfahren inexperienced, without experience, young, fresh, unacquainted, unseasoned, *(unreif)* green, callow;
geschäftlich ~ unpractised in business.
Unerfahrenheit inexperience, inacquaintance;
jds. ~ ausnutzen to trade upon (take advantage of) s. one's inexperience; **jugendliche ~ vorschützen** to plead the inexperience of youth; **etw. auf jds. ~ zurückführen** to put it down to s. one's inexperience.
un|erfindliche Gründe obscure reasons; **~erforscht** unexplored.
unerfreulich unpleasant, unwelcome;
~es Ergebnis disappointing result.
un|erfüllbar unrealizable, impossible; **~erfüllt** unfulfilled.
unergiebig *(Ernte)* poor, unprofitable, unproductive;
~er Boden barren (poor) soil; **~e Mine** unproductive mine.
Unergiebigkeit des Bodens poverty of soil.
unergründliche Tiefe des Meeres fathomless depth of the sea.
unerheblich immaterial, insignificant, irrelevant, trivial;
für den in Frage stehenden Punkt ~ sein not to be material to the point in question;
~e Änderungen slight changes; **~er Betrag** trifling sum; **~e Einwände** trivial objections; **~e Kosten** insignificant expenses; **~es Prozeßvorbringen** irrelevant allegation; **~er Schaden** trivial loss, negligible damage; **nicht ~e Verluste** considerable (heavy) losses; **~er Wert** trifling value.
Unerheblichkeit irrelevance, impertinence.
unerhoben not collected;
~e Dividende unclaimed dividend; **~e Steuer** unlevied tax.
unerhört outrageous, scandalous;
~er Fall unprecedented case; **~e Frechheit** outrageous insolence; **~es Glück** devil's own luck; **~er Preis** exorbitant (fabulous) price; **~er Reichtum** terrific wealth *(coll.)*.
unerkannt undiscerned, unrecognized, incognito;
~ bleiben to be safe from recognition.
un|erklärlich unexplainable, inexplicable; **~erläßlich** indispensible, obligatory, imperative.
Unerläßlichkeit must, indispensability, essentiality.
unerlaubt unauthorized, unlicensed, freewheeling, not permitted, *(ohne Konzession)* unlicensed, *(im bürgerlichene Recht)* tortious, unlawful, prohibited, *(ungesetzlich)* illicit, illegal, unlawful;
~er Alkoholausschank unlicensed saloon, speakeasy *(US)*; **~es Betreten ist verboten** no admittance except on business; **~e Beziehungen mit jem. unterhalten** to have illicit relations with s. o.; **~e Entfernung von der Truppe** *(mil.)* absence without leave; **~e Geschäfte machen** to indulge in illicit transactions; **~e Gewinne** illicit profits; **~er Handel** illicit trade; **~e Handlung** [personal] tort, actionable tort, tortious (unlawful, wrongful) act, *(auf schiffbaren Gewässern)* maritime tort; **~e Handlung begehen** to commit a tort; **~e Inbesitznahme** unlawful entry; **~er Nachdruck** pirated edition, piracy; **~es Streikpostensetzen** unlawful picketing; **~e Tarifvergünstigungen** discriminations; **~e Vergütung** illicit commission; **~es Wettgeschäft** illicit betting.
unerledigt unsettled, outstanding, undone, unperformed, *(Post)* unanswered;
~ bleiben to wait, to rest;

~e **Arbeit** arrears of work; ~e **Aufträge** backlog of orders, unfilled orders; ~er **Prozeß** pending action (lawsuit); ~e **Rechnungen** unsettled (unpaid) bills; ~e **Tagesordnungspunkte** carryover (unfinished) business.
Unerledigtes *(in den Akten)* pending files, *(Tagesordnung)* unfinished (carryover) business.
unermeßlich immense, vast, immeasurable;
~es **Vermögen** vast fortune.
un|erörtert undiscussed; ~**erprobt** *(Maschine)* untried, untested; ~**erreichbar** unattainable, inaccessible; ~**ersättlich** gluttonous, voracious, insatiable; ~**erschlossen** unexplored, virgin, *(Boden)* unexploited, *(Gelände)* undeveloped, *(Markt)* untapped; ~**erschöpflich** inexhaustible; ~**erschrocken** dauntless, unflinching, unafraid.
unerschütterlich unshaken, stalwart, steadfast, immovable, constant, inflexible;
~ **sein** to be as firm as a rock.
unerschwinglich unattainable, beyond one's means, out of one's reach, exorbitant;
~e **Kosten** enormous costs; ~er **Preis** prohibitive (exorbitant) price.
unersetzbar irreplaceable, unreplaceable.
unersetzlich irrecoverable, irreparable, irretrievable, irremediable;
keineswegs ~ **sein** to be not the only pebble on the beach.
unersitzbar imprescriptible.
Unersitzbarkeit imprescriptibility.
unerträglich beyond (past) endurance, unbearable, intolerable;
~ **heiß sein** to be unbearably hot.
unerwähnt unmentioned, unspoken of, untouched;
~ **lassen** to pass over, to leave out.
unerwartet without a moment's warning, unlooked for, unexpected, out of the blue sky, unforeseen;
~e **Ausgaben** contingencies, contingent expense; ~er **Besucher** surprise visitor; ~er **Gewinn** windfall profit; **auf** ~e **Schwierigkeiten stoßen** to meet with unexpected difficulties.
unerwidert *(Brief)* unanswered.
unerwiesen unproved, disputable, unproven.
Unerwiesenheit disputability, lack of proof.
unerwünscht unwanted, unwelcome;
völlig ~ welcome as snow in the harvest;
~er **Ausländer** undesirable alien.
unerzogen ill-bred.
unfachmännisch unprofessional, unskilled, inexpert.
unfähig incapable, inefficient, unfit, insufficient, unable, ineligible, not qualified, *(nicht befugt)* incompetent, not qualified, *(invalide)* disabled;
~ **zur Bekleidung eines öffentlichen Amtes** incapable of holding public office; ~ **zu zahlen** insolvent;
~ **machen** to incapacitate.
Unfähigkeit inability, incapability, inability, inefficiency, *(mangelnde Befugnis)* disqualification, incompetence, incompetency, *(Invalidität)* disability;
~ **zur Bekleidung öffentlicher Ämter** disqualification of a person for office, incapability of holding public office, ineligibility; ~ **Zeuge zu sein** incompetence to act as a witness.
unfair unfair, wrongful;
~e **Methoden** underhand methods.
Unfall accident, casualty, misadventure, mishap;
~ **ausgenommen** barring accident; **durch einen** ~ **aufgehalten** detained by accident; **im Falle eines** ~**s** in case of an accident; **außerberuflicher** ~ off-the-job (nonoccupational) accident; **bedauernswerter** ~ deplorable accident; **böser** ~ nasty accident; **dienstlicher** ~ industrial (on-the-job) accident; **ekliger** ~ disagreeable accident; **fürchterlicher** ~ wretched accident; **mittelbarer** ~ accident to third parties; **schrecklicher** ~ ghastly accident; **schwerer** ~ serious (bad) accident; **selbstverschuldeter** ~ accident due to one's own fault; **tödlicher** ~ accidental death, fatal accident; **unbedeutender** ~ minor accident; **unvermeidbarer** ~ inevitable (unavoidable) accident; **nicht zum Schadenersatz verpflichtender** ~ noncompensable accident; **auf Ermüdung zurückzuführender** ~ fatigue accident;
~ **mit Arbeitsausfall** lost-time accident; ~ **außerhalb der Arbeitszeit** nonoccupational (off-the-job) accident; ~ **innerhalb der Arbeitszeit** on-the-job (industrial, occupational) accident; ~ **mit tödlichem Ausgang** fatal accident, homicide by misadventure; ~ **mit dem Auto** motorcar *(Br.)* (motor-vehicle) accident; ~ **mit Verletzten** injury accident;
mit knapper Not einem ~ **entgehen** to just miss an accident; **bei einem** ~ **den Tod finden** to be killed in an accident; ~ **haben** to meet with (have) an accident, to come to grief, to sell out to the Yankees *(US coll.)*; ~ **verschuldet haben** to be at fault in an accident; **aus einem** ~ **herrühren** to result from an accident; ~ **der Polizei melden** to report an accident to the police; **gegen** ~ **versichert sein** to be insured against accidents; **in einen** ~ **verwickelt sein** to be involved in an accident; **bei einem** ~ **zugegen sein** to witness an accident; **gegen** ~ **sichern** *(Maschine)* to fence securely; **bei einem** ~ **sterben** to lose one's life in an accident; ~ **verhüten** to prevent an accident; ~ **verursachen** to bring about (cause) an accident; ~ **auf die Unvorsichtigkeit des Fahrers zurückführen** to impute an accident to the driver's carelessness; **einem** ~ **zuschreiben** to ascribe to an accident;
~**abteilung** *(Krankenhaus)* casualty department (ward); ~**analyse** accident analysis.
unfallanfällig accident-prone, prone to accidents.
Unfall|anfälligkeit accident proneness; ~**anzeige** notification of an accident, *(bei Versicherung)* immediate notice; ~**arzt** casualty doctor; ~**aufnahme** preliminary investigation of an accident; ~**ausgleich** accident indemnity (benefit); ~**ausrüstung** first-aid equipment.
unfallbedingt sein to result from an accident.
Unfall|begrenzung accident reduction; ~**beihilfe** accident payments; ~**bericht** report of an accident, accident record (report); ~**berichtsformular** accident-report form; ~**beteiligter** victim of an accident, accident victim; ~**buch** *(Betriebsunfälle)* accident book; ~**darstellung** version of an accident.
Unfälle, viele ~ **erlitten haben** *(Fluggesellschaft)* to have a bad record.
Unfall|entschädigung accident benefit (indemnity); **betriebliche** ~**entschädigung** workmen's *(Br.)* (workers', *US*) compensation; ~**entschädigungsgesetz für Staatsangestellte** Employee's Compensation Act *(US)*; ~**entschädigungsleistungen** compensation allowance; ~**ereignis** occurrence of an accident; ~**ermittlung** investigation of an accident; ~**fahrer** driver involved in an accident; ~**flucht** hit-and-run driving; ~**flucht begehen** to hit and run; ~**flüchtiger** hit-and-run driver; ~**fluchtsache** hit-and-run accident; ~**folgen** damage resulting from (results of) an accident; ~**forderung** accident claim.
unfallfrei accident-free;
~er **Fahrrekord** spotless accident record.
Unfallfürsorge accident welfare work.
unfallgefährdet accident-prone.
Unfall|gefährdung accident proneness (recidivism); **betriebliche** ~**gefährdung** occupational hazards; ~**gründe** accident causes.
Unfallhaftpflicht personal injury liability, *(Grundstückseigentümer)* occupier's liability;
~ **der Arbeitgeber** employer's liability;
sich auf das ~**geschäft konzentrieren** to concentrate on liability lines; ~**gesetz** Employer's Liability Act *(US)*; ~**versicherung** accident (casualty, *US*) insurance, third-party accident insurance *(Br.)*.
Unfall|haftung responsibility for an accident; ~**häufigkeit** accident frequency, frequency of accidents; ~**häufigkeitsziffern** accident frequency rates; **epidemieartige** ~**häufung** rash of accidents; ~**hilfstrupp** breakdown gang; ~**klinik** emergency hospital; ~**kolonne** breakdown gang; ~**kommando** emergency car, ambulance; ~**kosten** accident costs; ~**liste** list of accidents, death roll; ~**meldedienst** accident reporting service; ~**meldung** notice of accident, accident report; ~**meldung erstatten** to report an accident to the police; ~**neigung** accident proneness; ~**opfer** accident victim; ~**ort** place (scene) of accident; ~**police** accident policy; ~**protokoll** record of an accident; ~**puppe** dummy; ~**quelle** accident source; **tödliche** ~**quote** toll of death; ~**rate** accident rate; ~**reaktion** traumatic reaction; ~**rente** accident annuity, accident (injury, *Br.*) benefit; **betriebliche** ~**rente** compensation benefit; ~**rettungsdienst** ambulance service; ~**risiko** accident hazard (risk); ~**rückstellung** reserve for accidents; ~**sache** road accident case, runner; ~**schaden** accident (accidental) damage; ~**schadensmeldung erstatten** to draw up a report on an accident; ~**schadensversicherung** casuality insurance; ~**schilderung** version of an accident; ~**schuld** blame for an accident; ~**schuldiger** party at fault in an accident; ~**schutz** protection against accidents; ~**schutzmaßnahmen** crash safety precautions; ~**serie** chapter of accidents.
unfallsicher beyond reach of accident, accident-proof.
Unfall|station ambulance station, first-aid post (station), *(Krankenhaus)* casualty ward, emergency room; ~**statistik** recording of accidents, accident statistics; ~**statistik führen** to keep a record of road accidents; ~**stelle** scene of an accident; **typische** ~**stelle** accident black spot; ~**tag** date of injury.
Unfalltod casualty, death by misadventure, accidental death (killing);

schadensersatzpflichtiger ~ compensable death;
~ **erleiden** to lose one's life by accident;
~**police** accident policy.
Unfall|tote casualties; ~**tote und** ~**verletzte** the dead and the injured; ~**unterstützung** accident relief, *(für Arbeiter)* workmen's compensation *(Br.)*; ~**untersuchung** investigation of accidents; ~**ursache** cause of accident; **entscheidende** ~**ursache** supervening cause of an accident; ~**ursache sein** to be the cause of an accident; ~**ursachenforschung** accident analysis; ~**vergütung** *(Arbeiter)* [workmen's] compensation *(Br.)*; ~**verhütung** accident prevention, prevention of accidents.
Unfallverhütungs|maßnahmen ergreifen to provide against accidents; ~**tätigkeit** loss preventive work; ~**vorschriften** safety regulations.
Unfall|verletzter victim of an accident; ~**verletzung** injury caused by accident; ~**verlust** accidental loss; ~**verluste begrenzen** to reduce accident waste; ~**vermeidung** accident avoidance.
Unfallversicherung casualty insurance, [personal] accident insurance, *(Betriebsangestellte)* disability insurance *(US)*, disablement insurance *(Br.)*;
gewerbliche ~ industrial accident insurance, industrial injuries insurance *(Br.)*, workmen's compensation insurance *(US)*; **private** ~ personal accident insurance;
~ **abschließen** to insure against possible accidents.
Unfallversicherungs|bereich *(Betriebshaftpflichtversicherung)* zone of employment; ~**gesetz** workmen's compensation law (act, *Br.*); ~**leistung** accident benefit, *(Arbeiter)* workmen's compensation *(Br.)*; **allgemeine** ~**police** general accident policy; ~**prämie** casualty premium; **voller** ~**schutz** full third-party cover; **sozialer** ~**tarif** manual rates *(US)*; ~**vertrag** accident insurance contract.
Unfall|versorgung emergency treatment; ~**verzeichnis** list of accidents, death roll; ~**wagen** motor ambulance, ambulance car (wagon); ~**wahrscheinlichkeit** accident process; ~**zeitpunkt** time of accident; ~**zeitverlust** accident severity; ~**zeuge** witness of an accident; ~**ziffern** accident frequency (fatality) rates; **freiwillige** ~**zulage** accident benefit; ~**zusatzversicherungsklausel** double indemnity clause; ~**zwangsversicherung** compulsory accident insurance.
un|faßbar inconceivable, incomprehensible; ~**fehlbar** unfailing, unerring; ~**fein** indelicate, ungenteel; ~**fertig** unfinished, rough, uncompleted, *(Mensch)* half-baked, callow, unformed.
unflätig dirty, filthy, bawdy, obscene, smutty;
~ **schimpfen** to swear filthily;
~**e Sprache** filth.
un|förmig *(sperrig)* bulky; ~**frankiert** unstamped, [postage] unpaid, without prepayment, *(Fracht)* carriage forward *(Br.)*.
unfrei unfree, not free, covenanted, *(Sendung)* not prepaid, carriage forward *(Br.)*;
sich in jds. Gegenwart ~ **fühlen** to be embarrassed in s. one's presence; **Paket** ~ **schicken** to send a parcel unpaid.
unfreiwillig involuntary, *(gezwungen)* compulsory.
unfreundlich unfriendly, unkind, *(Börse)* cheerless, unfavo(u)rable;
~**er Empfang** rough welcome; ~**e Handlung** unfriendly act; ~**es Wetter** unpleasant (rough) weather.
Unfreundlichkeit unfriendliness, *(Börse)* cheerlessness, *(Wetter)* roughness, dullness.
Unfrieden discord, disharmony;
~ **zwischen zwei Menschen stiften** to make bad blood between two persons.
unfrisiert *(Bilanz)* undoctored, uncooked, *(Motor)* not tuned (souped, *sl.*) up.
unfruchtbar *(Acker)* unfertile, barren, bad, lean, thin, waste, *(Arbeit)* unproductive, *(Verhandlung)* fruitless, futile;
~ **machen** to sterilize;
auf ~**en Boden fallen** to fall on stony ground; **bei jem. auf** ~**en Boden fallen** to be lost with s. o.; ~**e Kritik** negative criticism; ~**e Tätigkeit** fruitless efforts.
Unfug mischief;
grober ~ public (common) nuisance, horseplay;
~ **treiben** to be full of mischief.
unfundiert groundless, unfounded, infirm, *(Schulden)* unfunded, floating, unconsolidated;
~**e Behauptung** unfounded allegation.
un|gangbar *(Weg)* impassable, *(Münze)* not current; ~**gastlich** unsociable, inhospitable.
ungeachtet notwithstanding, regardless, despite;
~ **gegenteiliger Bestimmungen** notwithstanding any provisions to the contrary.
ungeahndet unpunished.
ungeahnte Möglichkeiten undreamt-of-possibilities.
ungebeten self-invited, unasked;
~**er Gast** gatecrasher.
ungebildet vulgar, unrefined, rough, rude, uncultured, unpolished, untutored, uncultivated, gross, illiterate, ill-bred, uneducated;
~**e Masse** rough element of the population.
Un|gebildetheit incivility; ~**geborener** unborn person.
ungebräuchlich uncustomary, unusual, uncommon, unusable, unserviceable, disused;
~ **werden** to go (fall) out of use, to become unserviceable.
Ungebräuchlichkeit unserviceability, desuetude.
ungebraucht unused, fresh, *(Kapital)* dormant, idle, unemployed.
ungebrochen *(Rekord)* unbroken.
Ungebühr misconduct, impropriety;
~ **vor Gericht** contempt of court;
sich einer ~ **schuldig gemacht haben** to be in contempt.
ungebührlich improper, unseemly, disorderly, unbecoming, undue;
sich ~ **benehmen** to behave in an indecent manner; **j.** ~ **lange warten lassen** to make s. o. wait unduly long;
~**e Beeinflussung** undue influence; ~**es Benehmen** abusive behavio(u)r, misbehavio(u)r; ~**er Ton** unseemly tone.
ungebunden *(Buch)* unbound, in sheets, stitched, *(fig.)* unattached, unengaged, independent, go-as-you-please, *(Politik)* nonaligned, uncommitted, noncommitted, *(Politiker)* free-lance, free, independent, cross-bench *(Br.)*, middle-of-the-road;
~ **sein** *(Buch)* to be in sheets;
~**er Einzelhandel** independent retail trade; ~**es Leben führen** to live a life of independence; ~**er Preis** free price; ~**er Staat** nonaligned country; ~**e Wirtschaft** free enterprise.
Ungebundenheit *(Politik)* nonalignment.
ungedeckt uncovered, without cover (security), unbacked, *(Banknoten)* fiduciary, *(Rechnung)* unsettled, unpaid, *(Tisch)* unlaid;
~ **lassen** to leave uncovered;
~**es Konto** unsecured account; ~**er Kontokorrentkredit** uncovered advance; ~**er Kredit** insecured (uncovered) credit; ~**e Notenausgabe** fiduciary issue *(Br.)*; ~**er Notenumlauf** fiduciary circulation *(Br.)*; ~**es Papiergeld** uncovered (fiduciary, *Br.*) paper money; ~**er Personalkredit** fiduciary loan; ~**er Saldo** uncovered balance; ~**er Scheck** uncovered check *(US)* (cheque, *Br.*), rubber check *(US)*, bouncing cheque *(Br.)*; ~**e Schecks ausstellen** to issue bad checks *(US)* (cheques, *Br.*); ~**e Schuld** unsecured debts; ~**er Wechsel** bill not provided for, uncovered note (bill), kite *(Br.)*.
ungedruckt in manuscript, unprinted.
Ungeduld impatience.
ungeduldig impatient, restless, on edge.
ungeeignet unfit, incapable, inapt, unapt, inept, incapable, unqualified, ineligible, not qualified, ill-qualified, unsuitable, unsuited, inappropriate, *(Manuskript)* unavailable *(US)*;
beruflich ~ incompetent to do one's job; **für Besicherungszwecke** ~ *(Wertpapiere)* thrown out of loans; **charakterlich** ~ unfit to act; **für die menschliche Ernährung** ~ unfit for human consumption; **geschäftlich** ~ inapt for business; **als Getränk** ~ unfit for use as a beverage; **als Lehrer** ~ not suited for teaching; **für eine Stellung** ~ not qualified for a post;
für etw. schlechthin ~ **sein** to be thoroughly incompetent to do s. th.;
~**er Bewerber** applicant unsuited for a position; **im** ~**en Moment** at the most unsuitable time.
Ungeeignetheit inaptitude, insuitability, ineligibility, *(Verwaltung)* improvidence.
ungefähr approximate, about, general, roughly, rough, roundly, round about, round, say around *(US)*;
sich ~ **belaufen** to come to near to; ~ **kosten** to cost roughly (in the neighbo(u)rhood of); ~ **100 Dollar kosten** to cost $ 100 in the rough; ~ **stimmen** to be about right; ~ **1000 Pfund verlieren** to lose a sum in the neighbo(u)rhood of £ 1000;
~**er Bedarf** approximate requirements; ~**e Berechnung** rough calculation; ~**er Durchschnitt** rough average; ~**er Kostenüberschlag** rough estimate; ~**e Schätzung** rough guess; ~**e Vorstellung** rough idea; ~**er Wert** approximate amount (value).
un|gefährdet safe and sound; ~**gefährlich** harmless, not dangerous; ~**gefällig** disobliging, uncomplaisant, unaccommodating, unobliging.

ungefärbt undyed, uncolo(u)red;
~**er Bericht** unvarnished report.
un|gefaßt *(Edelstein)* unset; ~**gefragt** not asked for; ~**gefrühstückt** on an empty stomach; ~**gefütterter Briefumschlag** unlined envelope; ~**gegliedert** unorganized.
ungehalten annoyed;
~ **werden** to lose one's temper.
ungehemmt without restraint, unrestrained, unhampered.
ungeheuer enormous, vast, tremendous, giant.
ungeheure|n Durst haben to be terribly thirsty; ~ **Explosion** tremendous explosion; ~**r Fehler** blunder, howler *(sl.)*; ~ **Menge Geld** enormous (vast) amount of money; ~**r Reichtum** immense riches; ~**s Tempo** terrific pace.
ungeheuerlich monstrous, atrocious;
~**er Preis** outrageous price; ~**es Verbrechen** atrocious crime.
Ungeheuerlichkeit eines Verbrechens flagrancy of a crime.
ungehindert unimpeded, unhampered;
Grenze ~ passieren to cross the border without being hindered.
ungehobelt unpolished, homebred, inurbane;
~**e Manieren** uncouth manners.
ungehörig undue, improper, inept;
sich ~ benehmen to misbehave;
~**es Benehmen** incorrect behavio(u)r; ~**e Worte** offensive words (language).
Ungehörigkeit impropriety, impertinence, indecorum.
Ungehorsam civil disobedience, insubordination;
bewußter ~ wilful disobedience.
un|gehorsam disobedient, recalcitrant, *(mil.)* insubordinate; ~**gekündigt** not under notice; ~**gekünstelt** unstudied, unaffected, unsophisticated; ~**gekürzt** in full, *(Buchausgabe)* complete, uncondensed, unabridged.
ungelegen inconvenient, ill-timed, out of season, not in the picture;
jem. höchst ~ kommen not to suit s. one's book.
Ungelegenheit inconvenience;
sich in ~en bringen to put o. s. out, to be causing trouble for o. s.; **sich in finanzielle ~en bringen** to jeopardize one's finances; **jem. so wenig ~en wie möglich machen** to consult s. one's convenience.
un|gelegte Eier begackern to cross one's bridges before one comes to them; ~**gelenke Schrift** clumsy (awkward) writing.
ungelernt unskilled, common *(US)*, *(unausgebildet)* untrained;
~**er Arbeiter** unskilled workman; ~**e Arbeitskräfte** unskilled manpower, untrained labo(u)r *(Br.)*.
ungelüftet unventilated, unaired.
Ungemach hardship, trouble, adversity.
ungemischt unblended, unmixed, *(Metall)* unalloyed.
ungemünzt uncoined, in bars;
~**es Edelmetall** bullion.
ungemütlich uninviting, uneasy;
~ **für j. werden** to be getting too hot for s. o.
ungenannt anonymous, unnamed;
~**er Auftraggeber** undisclosed principal; ~**er Käufer** undisclosed buyer.
ungenau inaccurate, incorrect, inexact;
~ **übersetzen** to translate inaccurately;
~**e Angaben** inaccurate information; ~**e Übersetzung** inaccurate (loose) translation; ~**e Vorstellung** vague idea.
Ungenauigkeit incorrectness, inaccuracy, *(Testament)* uncertainty;
terminologische ~ terminological inexactitude;
~ **im Ausdruck** incorrect expression; ~ **einer Übersetzung** inaccuracy of a translation;
~**en scharf im Auge behalten** to always be on the watch for discrepancies.
ungeniert unembarrassed, shirt-sleeve, free and easy;
völlig ~ with perfect aplomb;
ganz ~ sein to feel at home.
Ungeniertheit easiness, ease of manner.
ungenießbar inedible, uneatable, *(Mensch)* disagreeable, unbearable, brackish;
~ **machen** to denature.
ungenügend insufficient, unsatisfactory, inadequate, incommensurate, scanty, *(Zeugnis)* poor (F, *US*) mark;
~ **ausgerüstet** inadequately provided; ~ **bemannt** *(Schiff)* undermanned; ~ **bezahlt** underpaid; ~ **frankiert** insufficiently prepaid; ~ **verstempelt** insufficiently stamped;
~ **für seine Arbeit bekommen** to be given a very poor mark (an F, *US*) for one's work;
~ **frankierter Brief** short-paid letter; ~**e Deckung** *(Wechsel)* insufficient funds; ~**e Vorräte** scanty supply.
ungenutzt unused, wasted, *(Betrieb)* lying idle, *(Kapital)* unemployed, idle;
~ **bleiben** to stand idle; **etw. ~ lassen** to lay s. th. up in a napkin; **Gelegenheit ~ verstreichen lassen** to let an opportunity slip; **Zeit ~ verstreichen lassen** to waste time;
~**e Begabung** wasted talent; ~**es Grundstück** unseated land; ~**e Kapazität** idle capacity; ~**er Saldo** dormant balance.
ungeöffneter Brief unopened letter.
ungeordnet disordered, disarranged;
~**e Verhältnisse** disorder, *(finanziell)* scattered finances.
un|gepanzert unprotected; ~**gepflastert** unpaved; ~**gepflegte Sprache** uncultivated language.
ungeprüft unexamined, unchecked, uninspected, untried;
~**e Bilanz** unaudited balance sheet; ~**e Bücher** unaudited accounts.
un|gerade odd, uneven; ~**geratener Sohn** wayward son.
ungerechnet not included, without, apart from, not counting;
Reisekosten ~ without reckoning the travelling expenses.
ungerecht inequitable, unjust, unequal, wrongful;
~**e Vermögensverteilung** unjust distribution of property; ~**e Versicherungssätze** inequitable rates.
ungerechtfertigt unjustified, unwarranted;
~**e Bereicherung** unjust enrichment; **Klage auf Herausgabe der ~en Bereicherung** action for money had and received; ~**es Urteil** unrighteous sentence.
Ungerechtigkeit injustice, inequity, injury, injustice;
offenbare ~ manifest injustice; **schreiende ~** gross (howling) injustice.
ungeregelt irregular, unregulated, go-as-you-please, *(nicht festgelegt)* unscheduled;
Schulden ~ lassen to leave debts unsettled;
~**e Freizeit** unscheduled free time.
un|gereimtes Zeug daherreden to talk rot; ~**gereinigt** unrefined; ~**gern** reluctantly, unwillingly, grudgingly, with a bad grace; ~**gerufen** unbidden; ~**gerührt** with dry eyes; ~**gerupft davonkommen** to get away with it; **besser ~gesagt bleiben** to be better left unsaid; ~**gesäumt** without delay, immediately; ~**geschätzt** unassessed, not rated; ~**geschehen machen** to undo.
Ungeschick lack of skill, mishap.
ungeschickt unskilled, clumsy, butterfingered, awkward;
etw. ~ anfassen to go about it the wrong way; **sich ~ benehmen** to behave imprudently.
ungeschliffen *(Edelstein)* uncut, *(fig.)* crude, unpolished, countrified;
~**er Diamant** rough diamond.
ungeschmälert unimpaired, undiminished, uncurtailed, unpractical, untutored, in full.
ungeschminkt dry, plain;
~ **sagen** to put it bluntly;
~**e Wahrheit** unvarnished (plain, naked) truth.
ungeschoren unpunished, scot-free;
~ **bleiben** to get away with it.
ungeschrieben|es Gesetz unwritten law; ~**e Verfassung** unwritten constitution.
un|geschuldet undue; ~**geschult** raw, unbred, unschooled, untrained; ~**geschützt** unprotected, unguarded, *(el.)* unscreened.
ungesellig unsociable, insociable, asocial;
~**es Wesen** disinclination to meet people.
ungesetzlich illegal, illicit, lawless, extralegal, illegitimate, unlawful, under the counter, black, wildcat;
für ~ erklären to illegitimate;
~**e Handlung** unlawful (wrongful) act.
Ungesetzlichkeit lawlessness, illegality;
mit dem Makel der ~ behaften to contaminate with illegality, to infect.
Ungesetzmäßigkeit begehen to trespass.
ungesichert unsecured, *(Notenausgabe)* uncovered, fiduciary;
~**es Darlehen** unsecured (personal) loan; ~**es Kontokorrentkonto** unsecured account, uncovered advance; ~**e Schuld** unsecured debt; ~**er Schuldschein** unsecured bond, plain bond; ~**e Schuldverschreibung** naked debenture *(Br.)*; ~**e Verbindlichkeit** unsecured liability.
ungesiegelt unsealed.
ungesittet ill-mannered, ill-bred, *(Volk)* uncivilized, wild.
ungestempelt unstamped;
~**e Briefmarke** undefaced stamp.
ungestört undisturbed, unmolested;
~ **sein** to be secure (safe) from interruption; ~ **verlaufen** to go off smoothly;
~**er Besitz** full possession, quiet enjoyment; ~**er Schlaf** sound sleep.

ungestraft unpunished;
~ **davonkommen** to get off scot-free.
Ungestüm, mit jugendlichem with youthful impetuosity.
ungestüm frantic, violent, vehement;
~**e Jugend** impetuous youth; ~**er Liebhaber** passionate lover.
ungesühnt unatoned, unexpiated;
~**es Verbrechen** unpunished crime.
ungesund unhealthy, unwholesome, injurious to health, unsound;
~**e Entwicklung der Konjunktur** unsound trend of the market; ~**es Klima** insalubrious climate.
ungetan bleiben to remain undone.
ungeteilt undivided, unseparated, entire;
~**e Erbengemeinschaft** privacy of estate, estate in common; **zur** ~**en Hand** jointly; ~**e Zustimmung** unanimous approval.
Ungeteiltheit entirety.
ungetilgt unredeemed, unacquitted;
~**e Schuld** uncrossed debt.
un|getragen unworn; ~**getrennt** undetached; ~**getreuer Beamter** disloyal officer, grafter *(US coll.)*.
ungetrübt clear, *(fig.)* undisturbed, unmixed;
~**e Tage der Freude** serene days of happiness.
un|geübt untrained; ~**gewechselt** unchanged.
ungewiß uncertain, unsure, trembling in the balance, *(unentschieden)* undecided, unsettled, *(zweifelhaft)* doubtful, dubious;
~ **sein** to hang in the balance;
auf ~**e Zeit verschieben** to postpone indefinitely.
Ungewisse|n, im all at sea;
j. im ~**n lassen** to keep s. o. in the dark; **im** ~**n sein** to be in the air, to hang in the balance; **Sprung ins** ~ **tun** to leap in the dark.
Ungewißheit uncertainty, dark, darkness, *(Risikoklasse)* uncertainty.
Ungewitter tempest, storm.
ungewogener Index unweighted index.
ungewöhnlich uncustomary, extra, extraordinary, out of the ordinary (off the beaten track), unusual, uncommon, out of the common (way);
~**e Auszeichnung** rare distinction; ~**e Begabung** remarkable talent; ~**es Format** unusual size; ~**e Gefahr** *(Dienstverhältnis)* extraordinary danger; ~**e Niederschlagsmenge** extraordinary rainfall; ~ **hoher Preis** extra high price; ~**e Umstände** unusual circumstances.
Ungewöhnlichkeit abnormality.
ungewohnt|er Anblick unfamiliar sight; ~**e Umgebung** strange surroundings.
ungewollt unintentional, inadvertent, unintended.
ungezählt uncounted;
~**e Möglichkeiten** innumerable possibilities; ~**e Stimme** unpolled vote.
ungezeichnet unmarked, unlabelled, *(Anleihe)* unsubscribed, *(Brief)* unsigned.
Ungeziefer vermin, insects, pest;
voller ~ **sein** to be vermin-infested.
ungeziemend unbecoming;
~**e Bemerkung** unsuitable remark.
ungezogen ill-mannered, uncivil;
~**es Kind** naughty child.
Ungezogenheit bad manners, unmannerliness, impertinence.
ungezügelt unbridled;
~**es Mundwerk** unbridled tongue.
ungezwungen unconstrained, unstrained, free, unrestrained, *(Atmosphäre)* free and easy, unstudied, casual, free-form, unforced;
völlig ~ go-as-you-please;
sich ~ **benehmen** to let one's hair down; ~ **mit jem. verkehren** to be at ease with s. o.
Ungezwungenheit ease.
ungiriert unendorsed, unindorsed, without indorsement.
unglaubhaft unbelievable, incredible;
~**e Geschichte** cock-and-bull story.
ungläubig incredulous, sceptical;
~ **lächeln** to smile disbelievingly.
unglaublich|e Behandlung scandalous treatment; ~**e Frechheit** outrageous impertinence; ~**es Glück haben** to be bloody lucky; ~**er Reichtum** fabulous wealth.
unglaubwürdig of suspect authority, unworthy of credit, untrustworthy, *(Dokument)* unauthentic;
~ **sein** *(Geschichte)* to pass belief; **als** ~ **verwerfen** to condemn as untrustworthy;
~**er Zeuge** incredible witness.
Unglaubwürdigkeit incredibility, unreliability, untrustworthiness.
ungleich odd, unequal, unlike, dissimilar, diverse, different;
von ~**er Güte** varying in quality.
ungleichartig different, divergent, dissimilar.
Ungleichgewichtigkeit disequilibrium, imbalance;
~**en der Einkommensverteilung mindern** to lessen the inequality of incomes.
Ungleichheit inequality, irregularity, disparity;
~ **der Einkommen** inequality of incomes.
ungleichmäßig irregular, unsteady, uneven;
~**er Lauf einer Maschine** irregular action of a machine; ~**e Verteilung** uneven distribution.
Unglück misfortune, bad luck, disaster, mischief, calamity, hard lines, ill;
nichts als ~ pure mischief; **vom** ~ **befallen** overtaken by disaster; **vom** ~ **verfolgt** dogged (pursued) by misfortune; **zu allem** ~ to make matters worse;
Mädchen ins ~ **bringen** to get a girl into trouble; ~ **für j. darstellen** to be hard lines on s. o. *(fam.)*; ~ **ertragen** to endure misfortune; ~ **haben** to be out of luck, to come to grief; ~ **herbeiführen** to draw on disaster; ~ **prophezeien** to croak disaster; **ins** ~ **rennen** to be riding for a fall; **j. ins** ~ **stürzen** to bring s. o. down; **sich ins** ~ **stürzen** to head for disaster; ~ **verhüten** to avert a catastrophe; ~ **voraussehen** to foresee a calamity;
ein ~ **kommt selten allein** misfortune never comes singly, it never rains but it pours.
unglücklich unhappy, unlucky, unfortunate, *(verzweifelt)* miserable, wretched;
~**e Bemerkung** unfortunate remark; ~**e Figur machen** to cut a sorry figure; ~**e Hand in Geschäften haben** to have bad luck in business; ~**e Liebe** unrequited love; ~**es Schicksal** adverse fortune; ~**e Wahl treffen** to make an untoward choice.
unglücklicherweise by mischance.
Unglücks|bote stormy petrel; ~**botschaft** bad tidings.
unglückselig|e Affäre unfortunate affair; ~**es Leben** miserable life.
Unglücks|fall disaster, calamity, casualty, fatality, misfortune; **durch** ~**fall** per misadventure; ~**jahr** disastrous year; ~**rabe** unfortunate man, jinx; **richtiger** ~**rabe sein** to be born under an unlucky star; ~**serie** sequence of calamities, run of misfortune; ~**stätte** scene of disaster; ~**stern** unlucky star; ~**tag** evil day, black-letter day.
Ungnade disfavo(u)r, disgrace;
in ~ **[gefallen]** out of favo(u)r, in bad *(US)*, in the doghouse *(US coll.)*;
sich auf Gnade und ~ **ergeben** to surrender at discretion; **in** ~ **fallen (geraten)** to fall out of favo(u)r (into contempt); **bei jem. in** ~ **sein** to be in bad odo(u)r with s. o., to be in s. one's bad graces (books), to be in disgrace with s. o.; **sich jds.** ~ **zuziehen** to incur s. one's disfavo(u)r.
ungnädig ungracious, surly;
j. ~ **empfangen** to give s. o. a cool welcome.
ungültig invalid, ineffective, [null and] void, *(aufgehoben)* cancelled, *(Eintrittskarte)* not available, unavailable, *(Gesetz)* inoperative, inept, *(Zahlungsmittel)* not current, uncurrent;
~ **wegen unklarer Fassung** void for uncertainty.
ungültig erklären, für to invalidate, to cancel, to rescind, to annul, to declare null and void, to defeat, to dissolve, to kill, *(Wertpapiere)* to call for validation;
Ehe ~ to nullify (annul) a marriage, to declare a marriage invalid; **Garantieversprechen** ~ to rescind a guaranty; **Gerichtsverfahren** ~ to annul judicial proceedings; **Paß** ~ to invalidate a passport; **Testament** ~ to set aside a will; **Urteil** ~ to set aside (vacate, quash, annul) a judgment; **Vertrag** ~ to invalidate an agreement (a contract); **Wahl** ~ to declare an election void.
ungültig machen to cancel, to [make] void, to avoid, to nullify;
Fahrkarte ~ to cancel a ticket; **Scheck durch Streichungen** ~ to obliterate the writing of a check *(US)* (cheque, *Br.*); **Vertrag** ~ to render a contract void, to vitiate a contract.
ungültig [geworden] sein *(Kreditbrief)* to have expired.
ungültig werden to become ineffective, *(Gesetz)* to become inoperative (invalid), to abate, *(Münze)* to be no longer legal tender;
durch Verjährung ~ to superannuate.
ungültig|es Akkreditiv invalid letter of credit; ~**e Forderung** stale claim; ~**e Stimme** spoilt vote; ~**er Stimmzettel** void voting paper; ~**es Testament** invalid will; ~**es Verfahren** void process; ~**er Vertrag** void (invalid) contract.

Ungültigkeit voidness, invalidity, nullity, illegitimacy, *(Eintrittskarte)* unavailableness, unavailability;
~ **wegen Formfehlers** voidness on account of an irregularity in the indorsement;
~ **geltend machen** to set up invalidity.
Ungültigkeits|bestimmung condition of avoidance; ~**erklärung** invalidation, annulment, cancellation, rescission, nullification, defeat, defeasance, illegitimation, legal extinction, *(Ehe)* annulment of marriage, decree of nullification; ~**erklärung einer Urkunde** cancellation of a deed; ~**faktoren** vitiating factors; ~**klausel** derogatory clause; ~**vereinbarung** backletters *(US)*.
Ungunst disadvantage, disfavo(u)r, disgrace;
zu meinen ~en in my disfavo(u)r; **zu jds. ~** to s. one's disadvantage;
zu jds. ~ sprechen to tell against s. o.
ungünstig unfavo(u)rable, unseasonable, *(wenig schmeichelhaft)* unflattering, unbecoming, *(Bilanz)* unfavo(u)rable, disadvantageous, adverse, *(Liegeplatz)* foul, *(Vertrag)* unprofitable;
~ **gegen j. aussagen** to evidence against s. o.; **sich ~ auswirken** to have an unfavo(u)rable effect;
~**e Belegenheit** ineligible location; ~**en Eindruck hinterlassen** to leave an unfavo(u)rable impression; **im ~sten Fall** at the worst; ~**er Kurs** unfavo(u)rable exchange rate; ~**e Lage** disadvantage; **sich eine ~e Meinung bilden** to form an unfavo(u)rable opinion; **unter ~em Vorzeichen** of no good omen, inauspicious; ~**e Witterungsverhältnisse** adverse weather conditions; **zu einer ~en Zeit** at an inopportune time, ill-timed.
unhaltbar untenable, unsustainable, *(Festung)* indefensible;
~**e Behauptung** unwarrantable assertion.
unhandlich unmanageable, unhandy, bulky.
unhäuslich sein not to be a homebody at all.
Unheil mischief, evil;
~ **ausbrüten** to meditate mischief; ~ **kommen sehen** to foresee disaster.
unheilbar past cure, incurable, past recovery;
~ **geisteskrank** of incurably unsound mind.
Unheilstifter mischief-maker.
unheimlich weird, creepy, eerie;
jem. ~ zumute sein to have an uncanny feeling;
~**es Durcheinander** utter confusion, shambles; ~ **viel Geld** lots (piles) of money; ~**e Geschwindigkeit** tremendous speed, awful lick; ~**en Hunger haben** to be terribly hungry.
unheizbar without a heating system.
unhöflich disobliging, impolite, inurbane, uncomplimentary;
~ **begegnen** to disoblige.
Unhöflichkeit impoliteness, incivility.
unhygienisch insanitary, unhygienic.
Uni varsity *(coll.)*, shop *(Br., sl.)*, U *(US sl.)*.
Uniform uniform, battle dress;
in großer ~ in full dress;
~ **anziehen** to join the forces, to sign up; ~ **ausziehen** to quit the service;
vorschriftsmäßige ~ und Ausrüstung order.
uniformierter Teil der Polizei uniformed branch of the police.
Uniform|rock tunic; ~**tragen** wearing of uniforms; ~**träger** person in uniform.
Unikum original.
uninformiert unposted, not up to date.
uninteressant as dry as a chip, void of interest;
sofort gänzlich ~ sein to be an instant writeoff.
uninteressiert incurious;
~ **sein** to take no part in it; **vollkommen ~ sein** to plead a five *(sl.)*; **sich an einer Frage ~ zeigen** to dissociate o. s. from a question.
Uninteressiertheit detachment.
Union, Interparlamentarische Interparliamentary Union.
unionistisch union, federal *(US)*.
Unions|priorität *(Patentrecht)* convention agreement; ~**vorrang** *(dipl.)* Union priority.
universal universal.
Universal|bank allround bank; ~**einstellung** universal adjustment; ~**erbe** universal successor (heir), sole heir (legatee, *US*), heir general *(US)*; ~**erbfolge** universal succession; ~**frachtdüsenflugzeug** all-cargo jet clipper; ~**frachtflugzeug** all-freight cargo plane; ~**genie** universal genius, allround man, allrounder *(US)*, Jack of all trades, fount of all knowledge *(coll.)*; ~**genossenschaft** multipurpose corporation; ~**küchenmaschine** galley slave *(coll.)*; ~**nachfolge** universal representation *(Scot.)*; ~**police** all-risks policy; ~**radar** general-purpose radar; ~**schlüssel** master key; ~**schraubenschlüssel** monkey wrench; ~**spediteur** all-purpose shipper; ~**sucher mit gekoppeltem Entfernungsmesser** view- and range-finder combined; ~**sukzession** universal legacy (representation) *(Scot.)*; ~**verkaufsrecht** sole right of selling, exclusive privilege; ~**vermächtnis** residuary (universal) legacy; ~**versicherung** all-in loss (comprehensive) insurance, *(Auto)* all-loss (risk) insurance; ~**werkzeug** all-purpose tool.
universell universal, multipurpose, all-purpose;
~**e baugeschäftliche Betreuung** allround banking.
Universität university, college;
auf der ~ gewesen college-bred; **außerhalb der ~** extramural; **gerade von der ~ gekommen** fresh from college; **innerhalb einer ~** intramural, introcollegiate;
staatlich geförderte ~ land-grant university;
~ **mit dem Recht der Promovierung** degree-granting university;
~ **besuchen** to be at university; ~ **in Oxford besuchen** to obtain one's education at Oxford; ~ **beziehen** to enter (go up) to the university, to come up *(Br.)*; **sich bei einer ~ einschreiben** to incorporate, to put one's papers in; **zur ~ gehen (kommen)** to come up [to the university]; ~ **besucht haben** to have had a university education, to be college-trained; **auf der ~ sein** to be at the university, to keep terms *(Br.)*; ~ **verlassen** to go down *(Br.)*; **von der ~ verweisen** to expel from college, to send down *(Br.)*, to rusticate.
Universitäts|abschluß, mit university-trained (-educated); ~**aufnahmeprüfung** college entrance (local, *Br.*) examination; ~**aufnahmeprüfung bestehen** to be classed *(Br.)*; ~**ausbildung** university (college) training (education); ~**beamter** university administrator; ~**behörden** university authorities; ~**betrieb** running of universities; ~**bibliothek** university library; ~**bildung** university education; ~**buchhandlung** university bookshop; ~**examen** university examination, academic examination (qualification), science degree; ~**ferien** vacation; **in die ~ferien gehen** to go down; ~**gebäude** university building; ~**gebühren bezahlen** to pay tuition at the university; ~**gelände** university campus; **auf dem ~gelände gelegen** on-campus; ~**grad** ordinary (academic, pass) degree; ~**institut** institute; ~**jahr** academic year; ~**jahre** college years; ~**kasse** university chest; ~**kreise** academic circles; ~**laufbahn** academic career; ~**leben** campus, academic world; ~**lehrer** university teacher, don *(Br.)*; ~**professor** university (college) professor; **sich auf eine ~prüfung vorbereiten** to read for a degree; ~**satzung** university statute; ~**sprecher** public orator *(Br.)*; ~**stadt** university (college) town; ~**stellung** academic position; ~**stipendium** fellowship; ~**studium** university (college) education, graduate study, academical training; **kostenloses ~studium** free university education; **ganztägiges ~studium absolvieren** to receive full-time instruction at a university; ~**tracht** cape and gown; ~**unruhen** campus disorders; ~**verwaltung** university administration; ~**verweisung** rustication, sending down *(Br.)*; ~**vorlesung** university (public) lecture; ~**vorlesung belegen** to enrol for a course of lectures; ~**wettkämpfe** inter-university sports; ~**zeit** college years.
Universum universe, cosmos, world.
un|kalkulierbares Risiko unexpectable risk; ~**käuflich** unpurchasable; ~**kaufmännisch** unbusinesslike, uncommercial.
unken to croak *(coll.)*.
unkenntlich unidentifiable;
~ **gemacht** disfigured;
~ **machen** to deface, to obliterate, to cancel, *(mil.)* to camouflage; **Urkunde ~ machen** to spoliate a document.
Unkenntlichmachen defacement, cancellation, obliteration;
~ **von Urkunden** spoliation of documents.
Unkenntnis ignorance, lack of knowledge, incognizance;
in ~ von ignorant of, unaware;
fahrlässige ~ constructive notice; **schuldhafte ~** culpable ignorance; **zwangsläufige ~** involuntary ignorance;
~ **des Gesetzes** ignorance of the law;
~ **nebensächlicher Umstände** accidental ignorance; ~ **tatsächlicher Umstände** ignorance of facts; ~ **wesentlicher Umstände** essential ignorance;
jds. ~ ausnutzen to trade upon s. one's ignorance; **sich auf ~ berufen** to plead ignorance; **j. in ~ lassen** to keep s. o. in ignorance (in the dark); **seine ~ offenbar werden lassen** to betray one's ignorance; ~ **vorschützen** to pretend ignorance; ~ **des Gesetzes vorschützen** to plead ignorance in excuse of one's conduct.
unklagbar unactionable, unenforceable.
unklar obscure, dark, not clear, vague, unclear, abstruse, foggy, hazy, non liquet, *(Ausdrucksweise)* muddy, confused, woolly, blurry, nebulous, *(Vertrag)* ambiguous;

j. im ~en lassen to leave s. o. in the dark; **im ~en gelassen werden** to be left up in the air;
~e **Antwort** vague answer.
Unklarheit unclearness, unclarity, darkness, *(Vertrag)* ambiguity;
alle ~en beseitigen to eliminate any unclear points.
un|kolonisiert unplanted; **~kompliziert** uncomplicated, simple; **~konsolidiert** unconsolidated; **~kontrollierbar** unmanageable.
unkontrolliert uncontrolled, unbounded;
seine Kinder völlig ~ aufwachsen lassen to allow one's children to run wild;
~e **Stichprobe** haphazard sample.
un|konventionell off-beat; **~konvertierbar** inconvertible.
Unkonvertierbarkeit inconvertibility.
unkörperlich immaterial, intangible, incorporeal, spiritual.
unkorrekt incorrect, improper, *(grammatikalisch)* wrong;
~e **Einkommensteuererklärung** false income-tax return.
Unkorrektheit impropriety;
~ **begehen** to cut corners.
unkorrigiert uncorrected.
Unkosten cost[s], expenses, expenditure, charges;
ab an (abzüglich) ~ charges to be deducted, less charges; **gegen Erstattung der** ~ with out-of-pocket expenses; **mit Einschluß aller** ~ all expenses included; **mit ~ verknüpft** involving expense; **nach Abzug aller** ~ all charges paid, expenses deducted; **unter Tragung der** ~ on payment of costs; **zur Deckung der** ~ in order to cover our expenses;
abnehmende ~ decreasing costs; **steuerlich absetzbare (abzugsfähige)** ~ *(Einkommensteuererklärung)* charges to be deducted, deductible expenses, permissible (tax) expenses; **abzurechnende** ~ off charges; **allgemeine** ~ overhead [charges], operating (indirect) expenses, factory cost, burden, oncost *(Br.)*; **zukünftig anfallende** ~ future costs; **im Gewerbebetrieb zwangsläufig anfallende** ~ expenses wholly and exclusively laid out for the purpose of the trade; **außerordentliche** ~ extra charges; **außerordentliche und betriebsfremde** ~ extraordinary and outside expenditure; **bare** ~ out-of-pocket expenses; **beträchtliche** ~ heavy costs (expenses); **bleibende** ~ basic expenditure; **diverse** ~ promiscuous charges, sundries; **durchschnittliche** ~ average expenses; **effektive** ~ primary cost; **einmalige** ~ nonrecurring expenditure; **entstandene** ~ expenditure occasioned, expenses accrued (incurred); **erhebliche** ~ considerable expenses; **feste** ~ standing expenses; **feststehende** ~ assured (fixed) costs, expenses covered; **generelle** ~ indirect cost; **gleichbleibende** ~ expense constants; **große (hohe)** ~ heavy expenses, large overhead *(US)*; **indirekte** ~ indirect expenses; **kapitalisierte** ~ capitalized expenses; **kleine** ~ petty expense, petties; **laufende** ~ current expense, standing expenses (charges), uneconomic cost, running costs (charges), general charges, cost in carrying business; **pauschalierte** ~ bunched cost; **personelle** ~ employment costs; **private** ~ private cost; **sonstige** ~ sundry expenses, sundries; **steigende** ~ rising cost; **übliche** ~ usual charges; **mit der Anschaffung verbundene** ~ purchase-related costs; **verschiedene** ~ sundry expenses, sundries; **voraussichtliche** ~ prospective costs; **im Etat vorgesehene** ~ expenses provided for in the budget; **wachsende** ~ growing expenditure; **zusammengefaßte** ~ pool cost; **zusätzliche** ~ additional expenses, added costs; ~ **der Agenturunterhaltung** agency costs; ~ **der Bürounterhaltung** office expenses; ~ **der Fabrikation** work-in- process burden; **laufende ~ der Geschäftsführung** expenses in carrying on business; ~ **der Verwaltung** administrative expenditure; ~ **der Zentrale** head-office expense;
~ **abbremsen** to put a stop to expenses; **als ~ abbuchen** to enter as expenses; **seine ~ abrechnen** to deduct one's expenses; ~ **abwälzen** to pass costs on; **seine ~ abziehen** to deduct one's expenses; ~ **aufschlüsseln** to break down expenses; ~ **aufteilen** to lump the expenses; **sich die voraussichtlich entstehenden ~ ausrechnen** to reckon the probable costs; **zu den ~ beitragen** to contribute towards the costs; **zu gleichen Teilen zu den ~ beitragen** to contribute equal shares to the expenses; **Konto mit sämtlichen ~ belasten** to charge an account with all the expenses; ~ **berechnen** to figure out (calculate) the expenses; ~ **bestreiten** to defray (bear) the expense; **sich an den ~ schlüsselmäßig beteiligen** to pool the expenses; ~ **bezahlen** to quit costs; **für ~ in Abzug bringen** to allow for costs; **als ~ buchen** to enter as expense; ~ **über ein Konto buchen** to charge an expense to an account; ~ **decken** to cover expenses; **seine ~ decken** to pay one's way, to get back one's expenses, to get out without a loss; **nicht einmal seine ~ decken (hereinbekommen)** not to clear one's expenses; ~ **erstatten** to refund (reimburse) the expenses; **für ~ aufzukommen haben** to be liable for expenses; ~ **niedrig halten** to keep (hold) down expenses, to control the expenditure; ~ **kalkulieren** to cost-account; ~ **raketenartig ansteigen lassen** to rocket costs; ~ **anwachsen lassen** to pile on the expense; ~ **machen** to involve expenses; **jem. ~ machen** to put s. o. to expense; ~ **drastisch reduzieren** to slash costs; **mit zusätzlichen ~ verbunden sein** to involve additional charges; ~ **senken** to reduce expenses (costs); **sich in ~ stürzen** to launch out [into expense], to put o. s. to charge, to go to expense; **sich in große ~ stürzen** to incur heavy expenses; **sich in die ~ von etw. mit jem. teilen** to go shares with s. o. in the expense of s. th., to share with s. o. in the costs; ~ **tragen** to foot the bill, to pay the piper; ~ **übernehmen** to pay costs (expenses); ~ **teilweise übernehmen** to go halves with s. o.; ~ **umlegen** to divide expenses in equal proportions, to allocate (apportion) the costs; ~ **auf die Vereinsmitglieder umlegen** to assess members of a society for expenses; **im Zeitpunkt der Entstehung als ~ verbuchen** to book expenses in the year of occurrence; ~ **verringern** to reduce (cut down) costs; ~ **verteilen** to spread the costs; ~ **über drei Jahre verteilen** to amortize costs over a period of three years; ~ **verursachen** to go to expense; **hohe ~ verursachen** to put to great (involve much) expense, to entail large expenditure;
~abrechnung anerkennen to allow costs; **~anfall** cost accruing.
Unkostenanteil expense portion, expense ratio, cost fraction, share of the expense, portion of the costs, *(Gemeinkostenanteil)* cost (overhead) rate;
jds. ~ ausrechnen to work out s. one's share of the expense; ~ **übernehmen** to pay one's proportion of the expenses.
Unkosten|aufgliederung expense classification, cost analysis, breakdown of costs, cost breakdown; **~aufstellung** expense account (invoice), specification of disbursements, statement of expenses; **~aufteilung** burden adjustment, cost allocation (distribution); **~aufwand** cost, outlay, expenditure; **unmittelbarer ~aufwand** direct expense; **~aufwand berechnen** to cost a job; **~auslagen** recoverable cost; **auf Tages- und ~basis beschäftigen** to retain on a per-diem-plus-expense basis; **~beitrag** contribution to the expenses, service charge; **~beitrag leisten** to contribute to the expenses; **~belastung** expense charge (burden), *(Versicherung)* expense loading *(US)*; **~belastung einer Abteilung** departmental charge; **~beleg** cost card (record, voucher); **~belege einreichen** to submit expense reports; **~berechnung** computation of costs, calculation of expenses, cost accounting, costing; **~bericht** cost report; **~beteiligung** sharing of costs, cost sharing; **~betrag** amount of expenses; **~buch** expense book.
unkostendeckend at their commercial cost.
Unkosten|deckung reimbursement of expenses; **~einschätzung** estimated costs; **~einstufung** expense classification; **~ersparnis** cost saving, *(Versicherung)* loading profit; **~erstattung** reimbursement (refund) of expenses, compensation for outlay incurred; **~etat** expense budget, return of expenses; **seinen ~etat erhöhen** to increase one's expenses; **~etat kürzen** to cut down expenses; **~faktor** expense factor; **~fonds** expendable (expense) fund; **~gebühr** service charge; **~hauptbuch** expenses ledger; **~herabsetzung** cutting down of expenses, cost cutting; **~kalkulation** cost estimate, computation of costs, calculation of cost; **~konto** expense account, account of expenses (expenditure); **auf ~konto belasten** to charge to expense.
Unkostenposten cost item, item of expense (expenditure);
~ **anerkennen** to allow an item of expenditure; ~ **übernehmen** to absorb expenses;
~anerkennung allowance of an item of expenditure.
Unkosten|rechnung expense invoice, account of charges (costs, expenses), bill of costs (charges, *US*); **~satz** expense ratio; **höchstzulässiger ~satz** expenditure (cost) rate; **~schätzung** estimated cost; **~senkung** cost cutting; **vergleichsweise ~situation** comparative costs; **~spezifizierung** breakdown of expenses; **~tabelle** cost chart, scale of charges; **~tarif** list of charges; **~überhang** excess of expenditure over revenue; **~umlage** levy of costs; **~umlage unter den Vereinsmitgliedern vornehmen** to assess members of a society for expenses; **~umlegung** apportionment of costs; **~vergütung** reimbursement (refund) of expenses; **~verringerung** cost reduction; **~verteilung** allocation of expense, cost distribution, *(Versicherung)* expense loading.
Unkraut, vom ~ überwuchert overrun with weeds;
von ~ befreien to weed; ~ **jäten** to hoe up weeds, to weed; **vom ~ überwuchert sein** to be running to weed;
~jäten weeding; **~vernichtungsmittel** weed killer; **~vertilgungsmittel** poison for killing weeds.

un|kritisch uncritical; ~**kulant** unaccommodating; ~**kultiviert** uncultivated, uncultured, rude, rough, unrefined, *(Land)* raw *(US)*.

unkündbar irrevocable, binding, *(Anleihe)* irredeemable, perpetual, nonredeemable, *(Beamter)* irremovable, *(Hypothek)* not to be foreclosed, *(Kapital)* noncallable, not subject to call, *(Rente)* perpetual, *(Schuld)* funded, consolidated, permanent; ~**e Pacht** perpetual lease; ~**e Schuldverschreibungen** irredeemable bonds, perpetual debentures; ~**e Stellung** permanent appointment (assignment, position); ~**e Vollmacht** irrevocable power of attorney.

Unkündbarkeit irredeemableness, irredeemability, *(Stellung)* permanency, irremovability.

unkundig ignorant, unacquainted;
des Lesens und Schreibens ~ sein to be illiterate (analphabetic);
der englischen Sprache ~ sein to have no knowledge of English.

unlängst yesterday, not long ago.

unlauter, sich ~er Mittel bedienen to use improper means; ~**er Wettbewerb** unreasonable restraint of trade, unfair [methods of] competition.

unlegiert unalloyed.

unleserlich illegible, unreadable, indecipherable;
~ **machen** to cancel, to deface, to obliterate.

Unleserlichkeit illegibility, defacement, obliteration.

un|leugbar undeniable, incontestable; ~**limitiert** unlimited, without stint; ~**liniert** unruled, unlined, plain; ~**liquidiert** unliquidated; ~**logisch** illogical.

unlösbar|er Knoten inextricable knot; ~**es Rätsel** unsolvable (insoluble) riddle.

Unlust disinclination, reluctance, miff, *(Börse)* slackness, flatness, dullness, deadness.

un|lustig reluctant, disinclined, *(Börse)* dull, slack, dead, flat; ~**manierlich** ill-mannered, unmannered; ~**männlich** effeminate, sissy *(coll.)*; ~**maskiert** with the mask off, undisguised.

Unmasse, Unmenge large (vast) quantity, host, world, multitude, loads *(coll.)*;
~ **Briefe** loads of letters; ~ **von Fehlern** mass of errors; ~ **von Fragen** shower of questions; ~ **Geld** oodles of money; ~ **von Getränken** lashings to drink; ~ **von Kindern** host of children; ~ **Menschen** a heap (millions) of people; ~ **von Zeugen** crowds of witnesses.

unmaßgeblich unauthoritative;
nach meiner ~en Meinung in my humble opinion.

unmäßig immoderate, unreasonable, excessive.

Unmensch monster, brute, beast, hellkite.

unmenschlich inhuman, brutal, beastly, cruel;
~**e Behandlung** inhuman treatment; ~**e Grausamkeit** wanton cruelty.

un|merklich indiscernible, imperceptible; ~**methodisch** unmethodical, touch-and-go, desultory; ~**militärisch** unmilitary.

unmißverständlich unmistakable, unequivocal, blunt, plain;
jem. ~ klarmachen to make it perfectly clear to s. o.; **seine Meinung ~ sagen** to speak one's mind bluntly; ~ **ausgezeichnet sein** to be marked in plain figures.

unmittelbar direct[ly], proximate, just (right, *US*) off, *(aus erster Hand)* immediate, first-hand, *(Fernsehen)* live;
~ **haftbar** primarily liable; ~ **nach** in the wake of, in the neck of; **nicht ~** at secondhand, indirect;
~ **bevorstehen** to be imminent; ~ **haftbar sein** to be personally (individually, primarily) liable;
~**er Abstammung** direct (immediate) descent; ~**er Arbeitsaufwand** direct labo(u)r costs; ~ **geleistete Arbeitszeit** direct labo(u)r; ~**e Belastung** direct charge; ~**er Besitz** actual (personal, physical) possession; ~**er Beweis** direct evidence; ~**er Boykott** primary boycott; ~**er Feuerschaden** direct loss by fire; ~**e Gefahr** immediate (imminent) danger; ~ **danebenstehende Häuser** proximate houses; ~**es Heimfallrecht** immediate reversion; ~**es Interesse** direct interest; ~**e Kenntnis** firsthand knowledge; ~**e Lohnkosten** direct wages; ~**er Materialaufwand** direct material costs; ~**er Nachbar** immediate neighbo(u)r; **in ~er Nachbarschaft** in the immediate (close) vicinity; ~**er Schaden** direct (proximate) damage; ~**es Unterstellungsverhältnis** direct-reporting agency system; ~**e Ursache** direct (immediate, proximate) cause; ~**e Verkaufskosten** direct selling costs; ~**e Werbesendung** direct circularizing (commercial); ~**er Zufahrtsweg** immediate approach; ~**er Zusammenhang** primary relationship.

unmöbliert unfurnished.

unmodern old-fashioned, unfashionable, out of fashion (date, vogue), unstylish, out of line, outmoded, superannuated, wet *(sl.)*;
bald ganz ~ on the way out *(coll.)*;
~ **werden** to go out of fashion (style, vogue), to pass.

unmöglich impossible, infeasible, unearthly *(coll.)*, *(lächerlich)* ridiculous, preposterous, grotesque;
absolut ~ absolutely impossible; **fast ~** next to impossible; **so gut wie ~** well-nigh impossible; **materiell ~** physically impossible; **rechtlich ~** legally impossible; **relativ ~** relatively impossible; **schlechterdings ~** downright impossible;
~ **aussehen** to look ridiculous; **sich ~ benehmen** to make an exhibition of o. s.; **es für ~ erklären** to put up a plea of impossibility; **etw. ~ machen** to bang the door on s. th.; **j. ~ machen** to make s. o. look ridiculous; **Vertrag ~ machen** to frustrate a contract;
~**e Leistung** impossible consideration; ~**e Situation** impossible situation; ~**er Vertrag** impossible (frustrated) contract; ~**e Vertragserfüllung** impossibility of performance of contract, frustration of contract; **zu einer ~en Zeit kommen** to come at an unearthly (ungodly) hour *(coll.)*.

Unmöglich|es unternehmen, etw. (Wirklichkeit werden lassen) to square the circle, to set the Thames on fire; **nach ~em verlangen** to cry for the moon, to ask for the moon and stars; ~**es versuchen** to make bricks without straw.

Unmöglichkeit, absolute absolute impossibility; **anfängliche ~** prior impossibility; **dauernde ~** permanent impossibility; **faktische ~** physical impossibility; **nachträgliche ~** subsequent (supervening) impossibility, *(Schuldrecht)* supervening frustration; **objektive ~** impracticability, *(Schuldrecht)* frustration; **offenbare ~** manifest impossibility; **praktische ~** practical impossibilty; **subjektive ~** inability; **teilweise ~** partial impossibility; **ursprüngliche ~** prior impossibilty, original frustration;
~ **der Vertragserfüllung** impossibility of performance of contract, frustration of contract;
~ **der Leistung einwenden** to put up a plea of impossibility.

unmontiert *(Klischee)* unmounted.

unmoralisch immoral, vicious;
~**e Lebensführung** vicious life.

unmündig infant, underage, under age, minor.

Un|mündiger infant, minor; ~**mündigkeit** infancy, tutelage, nonage, minority; ~**mut** irritation, annoyance, vexation, ill humo(u)r; **seinen ~mut verbergen** to hide one's displeasure.

un|nachgiebig incompliant, unyielding, tough, unfailing, hardshell *(US coll.)*, *(Material)* unbending, inflexible; ~**nachsichtig** strict, severe, unrelaxing; ~**nahbar** reserved, standoffish, inaccessible, ungetatable; ~**natürlich** unnatural, constrained, *(geziert)* affected.

unnotiert *(Börse)* not quoted, unquoted, unlisted *(US)*;
~**er Markt** curb (kerb, *Br.*) market; ~**e Werte** securities not quoted (listed, *US*) on the stock exchange.

unnötig unnecessary, needless, *(übertrieben)* fussy;
sich ~e Sorgen machen to worry needlessly.

unnumeriert unnumbered.

unnütz *(Geldausgabe)* useless, unprofitable;
sich als ~ erweisen to be found wanting; **sein Geld ~ verschwenden** to waste one's money to no purpose;
es ist ~ darüber zu sprechen it's no use talking about spilt milk;
~**e Person** fifth wheel at the coach.

unökonomisch uneconomical.

unordentlich untidy, slipshod, frowsy, *(ungeordnet)* disordered, disorderly;
~ **im Zimmer herumliegen** to be scattered about a room; **schrecklich ~ sein** to be in a dreadful mess;
~**er Schreibtisch** disorderly desk; ~**es Zimmer** untidy (disorderly) room.

Unordnung disorder, untidiness, disarray, *(Durcheinander)* confusion, mess, muddle, jumble, juggermugger;
in ~ not in order, off the hooks, wrong, out of gear;
wüste ~ wild disorder, huddle;
furchtbare ~ anrichten to jumble everything up; ~ **beseitigen** to clear up the mess; **Buchführung in ~ bringen** to muddle account books; **Haus in einer furchtbaren ~ hinterlassen** to leave a house in an awful mess; **in ~ sein** to become deranged.

unorganisiert disorganized, *(Gewerkschaft)* nonunion;
~**er Streik** wildcat strike.

unorthographisch misspelled, misspelt *(Br.)*.

unparlamentarisch unparliamentary.

unparteiisch nonpartisan, impartial, neutral, unprejudiced, dispassionate, indifferent, colo(u)rless, clean, without fear or favo(u)r, detached;
~**e Haltung hinnehmen** to maintain a neutral attitude; ~**er Vorsitzender** impartial chairman.

Unparteilichkeit impartiality, neutrality, detachment.
unpassend unsuitable, inept, *(Augenblick)* inconvenient, ill-timed;
~**e Bemerkung** inopportune remark; ~**e Zeit** unsuitable time.
unpassierbar impassable, impracticable.
unpäßlich out of sorts, indisposed, poorly *(coll.)*.
Unpäßlichkeit ailment, indisposition.
unpersönlich impersonal, distant, aloof.
unpfändbar nonforfeitable, exempt [from execution], privileged from distress, unseizable, not attachable, mace-proof *(US)*, nonleviable, void of seizable property;
~**er Besitz** exemption.
Unpfändbarkeit exemption from seizure (execution).
Unpfändbarkeits | bescheinigung execution returned, nulla bona *(US)*; ~**bestimmungen** exemption laws.
un | plazierbar unmarketable, unsalable; ~**plombiert** *(Zoll)* unplumbed; ~**polemisch** noncontroversial; ~**politisch** nonpolitical, apolitical, impolitical; ~**praktisch** unpractical, impractical, helpless.
unproduktiv nonproductive, unproductive, sterile, *(Kapital)* dead, idle;
~**er Verbrauch** unproductive consumption.
Unproduktivität unproductiveness, nonproductiveness.
un | profiliert undistinguished; ~**programmgemäß** nonscheduled.
Unproportionalität disproportion.
unproportioniert disproportionate.
unpünktlich unpunctual, *(Zug)* not as scheduled;
~ **zur Schule kommen** to be late (tardy, *US*) for school;
~**e Zahlungen** irregular payments.
un | qualifiziert unqualified; ~**quittiert** unreceipted.
Unrat filth, *(Abfall)* rubbish, refuse, garbage, dust.
un | rationell inefficient, wasteful; ~**real** unreal; ~**realistischer Reformer** starry-eyed reformer.
Unrecht injustice, wrong, tort;
vorsätzlich begangenes ~ positive wrong; **schreiendes** ~ flagrant injustice; **schweres** ~ deep wrong; **völkerrechtliches** ~ international delinquency;
j. zu ~ beschuldigen to accuse s. o. wrongly; ~ **erleiden** to suffer wrong; ~ **stillschweigend hinnehmen** to pocket wrongs; **Recht und ~ unterscheiden können** to know the difference between right and wrong; ~ **wiedergutmachen** to right a wrong; **jem. ein ~ zufügen** to do s. o. an injustice, to wrong s. o.;
besser ~ leiden als ~ tun better suffer ill than do ill.
unrecht wrong, *(unpassend)* inappropriate, unsuitable;
~ **haben** to be wrong;
zur ~en Zeit at an unsuitable moment.
unrechtmäßig wrongful, illegal, unlawful, lawless, false, wildcat, illegitimate;
~**e Gewinne** illegal profits.
Unrechtmäßigkeit illegitimacy, lawlessness, illegality.
Unrechtsbewußtsein guilty knowledge and wilfulness.
unredlich dishonest, unfair, dishono(u)rable, corrupt, in bad faith, mala fide, shady, crooked, unreliable, unsound, wildcat *(US)*;
~**e Verwaltung** corrupt administration; **auf ~e Weise** on the cross *(sl.)*.
Unredlichkeit dishonesty, corruptedness, shadiness, crookedness;
wegen ~ entlassen werden to be dismissed for being dishonest.
unreell dishonest, unreliable, unsound, unfair, wildcat *(US)*, underhand, crooked;
~**es Geschäft** dishonest business.
unregelmäßig casual, irregular, at odd times, inordinate;
~**e Zahlungen** irregular payments.
Unregelmäßigkeit anomality, irregularity;
~**en abschleifen** to plane away the irregularities; ~**en ausgleichen** to smooth irregularities; **sich ~en zuschulden kommen lassen** to commit an irregularity.
un | regierbar ungovernable; ~**reguliert** unregulated.
unreif unripe, crude, *(Mensch)* immature, green, young, bread-and-butter *(coll.)*;
~**e Ideen** half-baked ideas.
Unreife immatureness, callowness.
unrein unclean, dirty, foul, *(Edelstein)* impure, flawy, *(Luft, Wasser)* unclean, polluted;
etw. ins ~e schreiben to make a rough copy.
unrentabel unprofitable, unremunerative, not paying, unpayable, submarginal, losing, nothing to it.
Unrentabilität unprofitability, wastefulness.
unretouchiert not retouched (touched up).
unrettbar verloren sein to be irretrievably lost.
unrichtig incorrect, improper, inaccurate, untrue, *(irrtümlich)* false, mistaken, erroneous;
~ **adressieren** to misdirect;
~**e Angaben** *(Steuererklärung)* false statement, *(Versicherung)* misrepresentations; ~**e Darstellung des Sachverhalts** false recital of facts; ~**e Steuererklärung** false tax return.
Unrichtigkeit incorrectness, mistake;
fahrlässige ~ negligent misrepresentation; **offenbare** ~ obvious mistake;
~ **der Buchführung** incorrect accounting; ~ **einer Übersetzung** inaccuracy of a translation.
unromantisch down to earth.
Unruhe disturbance, agitation, *(Aufruhr)* riot, turmoil, earthquake, public disturbance, *(Börse)* flurry, flutter, *(Industriegebiet)* unrest, *(Sorge)* anxiety, vexation, worriment *(US)*;
innere ~ ferment, uneasiness, feeling of unrest; **innere ~n** civil commotion, riot, turmoil, public disturbance; **kurzdauernde** ~ *(Börse)* flurry *(US)*; **nervöse** ~ fidget; **politische ~n** political disturbances, intestinal disorders *(US)*, civil commotion; **spürbare** ~ articulate unrest;
große ~ am Geldmarkt money-market turmoil; ~ **einer Großstadt** hustle and bustle of a city;
j. von seiner ~ befreien to set s. one's mind at ease; ~ **in jds. Leben bringen** to muddle in s. one's life; **starke ~ über etw. empfinden** to have s. th. on one's conscience; **in ~ geraten** to grow uneasy; **soziale ~n hervorrufen** to create social unrest; ~**n niederschlagen** to suppress a riot; **in großer ~ sein** to be ill at ease; ~ **stiften** to stir up disorder, to make trouble, to make the fur fly; **j. in ~ versetzen** to worry s. o., to make s. o. uneasy;
~**herd** storm center *(US)* (centre, *Br.*), trouble spot *(coll.)*.
Unruhestifter troublemaker, broiler, rioter, disturber of the peace, firebrand, hellion *(US)*;
professioneller ~ professional agitator;
~ **auf einer Versammlung zum Schweigen bringen** to put down a heckler at a meeting.
Unruhestiftung criminal mischief.
unruhig hectic, unquiet, restless, agitated, knockabout *(US)*, *(ängstlich)* anxious, *(Bevölkerung)* restless, unsettled;
innerlich ~ uneasy;
~ **laufen** *(Motor)* to run unevenly (jerkily); ~ **schlafen** to have an uneasy sleep;
~**es Bild abgeben** *(Börse)* to give an uneven performance; ~**es Fernsehbild** unsteady picture; ~**es Gefühl** uneasy feeling; ~**e Lage** troubled waters; ~**er Lauf** *(Maschine)* uneven running; ~**es Leben führen** to lead a restless (knockabout, *US*) life; ~**es Publikum** restless audience; ~**es Stadtviertel** rough quarter of a town; ~**e Überfahrt** rough crossing; ~**e Wohnung** noisy apartment; **in einer ~en Zeit leben** to live in troublesome times.
un | rühmliches Ende finden to end ignominously; ~**sachgemäße Lagerung** careless storage; ~**sachlich** irrelevant, subjective, unobjective.
unsagbar inexpressible, untold, unspeakable, ineffable;
~**e Schmerzen** incredible pains.
unsaldiert unbalanced.
unsanft | mit jem. umgehen to handle s. o. roughly, to treat s. o. harshly; ~ **mit einem Betrunkenen umgehen** to manhandle a drunkard.
unsauber foul, impure, unwashed, *(Arbeitsausführung)* careless, untidy;
~**e Geschäfte** underhand dealings; ~**e Geschäftsmethoden** unfair business practices; ~**e Luft** impure air.
unschädlich inoffensive, harmless, innocuous, *(Industrie)* innoxious;
j. ~ machen to dispose of s. o., to put s. o. out of the way; **Minen ~ machen** to neutralize mines;
~**er Stoff** innocent material.
Unschädlichkeitszeugnis clearance certificate.
Unschädlichmachung *(Insekten)* destruction, *(Minen)* neutralization.
unscharf vague, nebulous, *(Bild)* out of focus, obscure, blurred, hazy, *(Rundfunkempfang)* broad;
Munition ~ machen to deactivate munition;
~**e Sendertrennung** clack of sensitivity.
un | schätzbar priceless, unpriced, unprizable, above (without) price, invaluable, inestimable; ~**scheinbar** inconspicuous, plain, ordinary; ~**schicklich** in bad (improper) form, unseemly, unbefitting, unbecoming.
Unschicklichkeit impropriety.
unschlagbar unrival(l)ed.
unschlüssig undecided, wavering, *(Beweis)* inconclusive, *(Klage)* demurrable, non liquet;

~ **bleiben** to stand suspended; ~ **sein** to hesitate, to be in two minds, to waver, to back and fill *(US)*;
~**e Klageerwiderung** irrelevant answer.
Unschlüssigkeit oscillation, hesitation, *(Beweis)* inconclusiveness.
Unschlüssigkeitseinrede general exception.
Unschuld innocence;
bewiesene ~ proven innocence;
~ **vom Lande** country innocent;
seine ~ **beteuern** to assert (insist on, protest) one's innocence, to plead not guilty; **jds.** ~ **beweisen** to prove s. o. to be innocent; **seine** ~ **nachweisen** to clear o. s. of a charge; ~ **vorschützen** to pretend innocence; **in einer Sache sich die Hände in** ~ **waschen** to wash one's hands of an affair.
unschuldig innocent, not guilty, guiltless, white-handed;
~ **im Sinne der Anklage** innocent of a charge; **so** ~ **wie ein neugeborenes Kind** as innocent as a new-born child; **völlig** ~ **aussehen** to look as if butter wouldn't melt in one's mouth; **sich für** ~ **erklären** to declare o. s. to be innocent; **j. im Zweifelsfall für** ~ **erklären** to give s. o. the benefit of the doubt; **j. für** ~ **halten** to presume s. o. innocent; ~ **sein** to have no hand in an affair; **nicht gänzlich** ~ **sein** to bear part of the responsibility; ~ **an einem Unfall sein** not to be at fault in an accident;
~**e Vergnügungen** innocent amusements.
Unschulds|beteuerung protestation of innocence; **kein ~lämmchen mehr sein** to be anything but the snow-white lamb; **~miene aufsetzen** to put on an innocent face.
unschwer zu erreichen easy to reach.
Unsegen curse.
unselbständig in a dependent capacity, nonindependent, dependent, subaltern, *(Staat)* subject;
~ **machen** to spoon-feed;
~**e Arbeit** wagework, employment work; ~ **Beschäftigter,** ~**e Erwerbsperson** salary (wage) earner; ~**es Beschäftigungsverhältnis** wage-earning employment.
Unselbständiger salary (wage) earner.
Unselbständigkeit lack of independency.
unseriös dubious, untrustworthy, slippery, wildcat *(US)*, chancy *(coll.)*;
~**er Bursche** chancy-looking fellow; ~**e Gesellschaft** dubious company; ~**e Methoden** wildcat methods.
unsicher uncertain, insecure, instable, unstable, dubious, doubtful, precarious, slippery, in the air, *(gefahrvoll)* dangerous, unsafe, *(schwankend)* shaky, dotty, *(ohne Selbstvertrauen)* diffident, *(ungenügend)* unsolid, *(unzuverlässig)* unreliable, undependable;
Stadt ~ **machen** to paint the town red; **Straßen** ~ **machen** to infest the streets;
~**e Aktien** wildcat stocks; ~**e Außenstände** bad *(US)* (doubtful) debts; ~**e Bürgschaft** straw bail; ~**e Existenz haben** to make a precarious living; ~**e Forderung** dubious (doubtful) claim; ~**e Kapitalanlage** insecure investment; ~**er Kredit** shaky (unsound) credit; ~**er Kunde** bad customer, dead beat *(US)*; **aus einer** ~**en Quelle** from an unreliable source; ~**e Schulden** uncertain debts; **in** ~**er Stellung** unstable; ~**es Unternehmen** dubious undertaking, fly-by-night corporation; ~**e politische Verhältnisse** unstable political situation; ~**es Wertpapier** unsafe paper; ~**e Wirtschaftslage** precarious economic situation.
Unsicherheit insecurity, unsteadiness, fog, *(Risikoklasse)* uncertainty, *(Währung)* instability;
berufliche ~ job insecurity; **konjunkturelle** ~ economic uncertainty;
~ **im Berufsleben** job insecurity; ~ **der Börse** unsettled state of the market; ~ **der politischen Lage** unstable political situation; ~ **auf den Straßen** unsafe conditions of the road.
Unsicherheitsfaktor element of uncertainty.
unsichtbar invisible, hidden, latent, secret;
sich ~ **machen** to vanish into thin air;
~**e Ausfuhr** invisible exports; ~**e Ausfuhren und Einfuhren** invisibles; ~**e Bestände** invisible supply; ~**er Handel** invisible trade, invisibles; ~**er Posten der Leistungsbilanz** invisible item of trade; ~**e Reserven** hidden (latent, secret) reserves; ~**e Tinte** invisible (sympathetic) ink.
Unsinn gammon and spinach, nonsense, rubbish, footle, fiddle-faddle, piffle, poppycock *(US coll.)*;
absoluter ~ flat nonsense; **blanker** ~ bare nonsense; **dummer** ~ blinking nuisance; **glatter** ~ pure nonsense, plumb nonsense *(coll.)*; **völliger** ~ perfect (rank) nonsense;
~ **machen** to fool around, to cut capers; ~ **reden** to talk rubbish (rot), to shoot the bull *(sl.)*.
unsinnig stupid, foolish, absurd;
~**e Forderungen** unreasonable demands; ~**e Menge Geld** tremendous amount of money; ~**er Preis** ridiculous (preposterous) price; **unter** ~**en Schmerzen sterben** to die in terrible agonies; ~**es Zeug** rubbish, balderdash, twaddle.
Unsitte vulgarity, bad habit, deplorable custom;
sich eine ~ **abgewöhnen** to break o. s. of a bad habit; **alte** ~**n aufgeben** to cast off the old Adam; **in seine alten** ~**n zurückfallen** to go back to one's old ways.
unsittlich immoral, indecent, improper;
~**er Antrag** indecent proposition.
Unsittlichkeit immorality, indecency.
unsolide unreliable, unsafe, untrustworthy, shaky, crank *(sl.)*, *(Konstruktion)* unstable, *(Lebensführung)* dissipated, loose;
~**r Charakter** fickle character; ~ **Finanzverhältnisse** unsound (wildcat) finances; ~ **Firma** unreliable firm, wildcat business house; ~**s Leben führen** to lead a fast life; ~**s Vorhaben** wildcat scheme.
Unsolidität unreliability, untrustworthiness.
un|sorgfältig careless; **~sortiert** unassorted, unsorted.
unsozial unsocial, unsociable, dissociable;
~**e Kündigung** unfair dismissal *(Br.)*; ~**es Verhalten** dissociality.
unstabil *(Börse)* soft, *(Konjunktur)* unstable, instable, fluctuating, unsettled, *(Schiff)* tender;
~**er Gesundheitszustand** precarious state of health.
un|ständig Beschäftigter casual worker; **~statthaft** inadmissible, impermissible.
unsterblich immortal;
sich ~ **blamieren** to make a complete fool of o. s.; **sich** ~ **in j. verlieben** to fall madly in love with s. o.
Unstern, unter einem ~ **geboren sein** to be born under an unlucky star.
unstet unsteady, wandering, restless, shifty, unbalanced unballasted, restless, knock-about *(US)*, *(Maschine)* intermittent, *(nicht seßhaft)* vagrant;
~ **umherirren** to roam about the world;
~**es Leben führen** to lead an unsteady life.
Unstetigkeit *(Film)* flutter.
un|stillbar *(Durst)* unquenchable, *(Hunger)* insatiable, unappeasable; **~stimmig** disagreeing, at variance, disunited.
Unstimmigkeit difference, disagreement, disconformity, friction, discrepancy;
kleine ~ slight variance;
~ **zwischen zwei Konten** discrepancy between two accounts; **kleine** ~**en haben** to tiff.
unstreitig, unstrittig without dispute, beyond controversy, undisputed, uncontested, unquestionable, incontestible, *(Rechtssache)* noncontentious.
Unsumme vast amount;
~ **Geldes** mint of money;
~**n kosten** to cost a mint (unholy amount) of money.
unsympathisch disagreeable, dislikable, alien;
j. äußerst ~ **finden** not to like the cut of s. one's jib *(sl.)*.
unsystematisch unsystematical, unmethodical;
~ **arbeiten** to work without system.
untadelig blameless, irreproachable, impeccable;
~ **gekleidet** immaculately dressed;
sich ~ **aufführen** to behave irreproachably;
~**er Ruf** stainless reputation.
Untat wrongdoing, outrage, atrocity;
~ **begehen** to commit an atrocity.
untätig inactive, idle, passive, inert, inoperative, vacant, *(Vulkan)* dormant;
~ **bleiben** to sit on one's hands; ~ **die Hände in den Schoß legen** to sit back and do nothing; ~ **sein** to sit at home, to rest on one's oars.
Untätigkeit idleness, inactivity, inaction, do-nothingness, inertia, rust;
~ **vor den Wahlen** pro-election paralysis;
zur ~ **verurteilt sein** to be reduced to inaction.
Untätigbleiben omission, nonperformance.
untauglich unfit, insufficient, inefficient, unqualified, incapable, unapt, inapt, inept, *(mil.)* disabled, ineligible, unfit, *(Schiff)* unseaworthy;
für ~ **erklären** to disqualify; ~ **machen** to incapacitate, to disable.
Untauglichkeit incapability, incapacity, invalidity, incompetency, inaptitude, disqualification, *(mil.)* ineligibility, unfitness;
~ **des Personals** incapacity of staff;
wegen ~ **entlassen werden** to be dismissed because of unfitness.
Untauglichkeitserklärung disqualification [for office].

untaxiert unvalued, *(Grundstück)* unassessed, unrated *(Br.)*.
unteilbar indivisible, unapportionable;
~**er Vertrag** entire contract.
Unteilbarkeit indivisibility.
unten below, at the bottom, *(im Haus)* downstairs, on the groundfloor;
nach ~ downward(s); **siehe** ~ see below;
~ **näher bezeichnet** hereinafter mentioned, undermentioned; ~ **erwähnt** undermentioned.
untenstehend [mentioned] below, at the foot of the page, following;
~ **finden Sie unsere Abrechnung** please find our account below.
unter | dem heutigen Datum under today's date; ~ **100 DM** for less than DM 100; ~ **der Hand verkaufen** to sell privately; ~ **dem Meeresspiegel** below sea level; ~ **dem Strich** *(Bilanz)* below the line; ~ **Tage** underground; ~ **uns gesagt** between you and me and the lamppost; ~ **dem üblichen Vorbehalt** with the usual proviso; ~ **Wasser** flooded;
~**e Beamtenlaufbahn** minor civil service; ~**es Gericht** court below.
Unter | abnehmer subpurchaser; ~**abschnitt** subsection, subsector, subparagraph, subclause; ~**abteilung** subsection, subdivision, subbranch, subcategory, subhead; ~**abteilungsleiter** subsection head; ~**agent** subagent; ~**agentur** subagency; ~**akkreditiv** ancillary letter of credit; ~**angebot** insufficient supply; ~**anspruch** subclaim; ~**auftrag** subcontract; ~**auftrag vergeben** to subcontract; ~**auftragnehmer** subcontractor; ~**ausschuß** subcommittee; ~**bau** basement, foundation, earthwork, *(Bahn)* substructure, subbase, groundwork, grounding.
unterbefrachten to refreight, to underfreight.
Unter | befrachter refreighter, underfreighter; ~**befrachtung** refreighting.
unterbelegt *(Hotel)* not full, *(Krankenhaus)* not fully occupied.
Unterbelegung insufficient occupation.
unter | belichten *(Foto)* to underexpose; ~**belichtet** underexposed.
Unter | belichtung underexposure; ~**beschäftigung** underemployment.
unterbesetzt, personell understaffed, shorthanded.
Unterbeteiligung subpartnership, *(Emissionsgeschäft)* subunderwriting.
Unterbett featherbed.
unterbevölkert underpopulated.
Unter | bevölkerung underpopulation; ~**bevollmächtigter** subagent; ~**bevollmächtigung** delegation of powers.
unterbewerten to underestimate, to undervalue, to underrate.
Unterbewertung underestimation, undervaluation, underratement.
unterbewußt subconscious, marginal.
Unterbewußtsein, etw. im ~ **ahnen** to feel s. th. subconsciously; **im** ~ **haften bleiben** to cling to the side of the mind; **in das** ~ **eindringen** to probe into the subconscious mind; **j. im** ~ **zuhören** to listen to s. o. with one's third ear.
unterbezahlt underpaid;
jämmerlich ~ miserably underpaid;
~ **sein** to work for a mere pittance.
Unter | bezahlung underpayment; ~**bezirk** subdistrict, civil township; ~**bibliothekar** sublibrarian; ~**bieten** *(Preise)* price cutting, *(auf dem Weltmarkt)* dumping.
unterbieten to undersell, to undercut, *(Auktion)* to underbid, *(Rekord)* to lower, *(Weltmarkt)* to dump;
Konkurrenten ~ to undercut a competitor in trade; **j. preislich** ~ to undercut price-wise, to cut s. one's prices; **Rekord** ~ to beat a record.
Unter | bieter undercutter, underbidder; ~**bietung** price cutting, undercutting; **bewußte** ~**bietung** price slashing, dumping; ~**bietungspreis** cut rate; ~**bilanz** adverse (short) balance, deficiency, deficit; **mit** ~**bilanz arbeiten** to work at a loss (deficit).
unterbinden to paralyse, to stop, to prevent, to forestall.
Unter | bindung prevention, paralysation, injunction; ~**bodenschutz** *(Auto)* undersealed body.
unterbrechen to interrupt, to discontinue, to break, to intermit, *(aussetzen)* to adjourn, *(Feuer)* to stop, to suspend, *(Gespräch)* to cut (chime, butt) in, to interrupt, *(Strom)* to break, to disconnect, to cut off, *(Telefon)* to cut off, to disconnect;
j. ~ to cut s. o. (take s. o. up) short, to speak in s. one's cast; **Handelsbeziehungen** ~ to interrupt the flow of commerce; **Prozeß** ~ to stop a case; **j. beim Reden** ~ to break in on a conversation; **Redner** ~ to interrupt a speaker; **seine Reise in X** ~ to break one's journey (stop over, *US*) at X; **Sitzung** ~ to adjourn (break up) a meeting, *(Gericht)* to suspend a hearing (proceedings); **j. sofort** ~ to take s. o. up sharp (short); **für eine Stunde** ~ to adjourn for an hour; **Verhandlung** ~ to suspend a hearing (proceedings); **Verhandlungen** ~ to stay (break off) negotiations; **Verjährung** ~ to interrupt prescription, to save (toll, *US*) the statute of limitations;
sich ~ **lassen** *(Abgeordneter)* to give way.
Unterbrecher *(el.)* circuit (contact) breaker;
~**stromkreis** make-and-break circuit.
Unterbrechung interruption, break, pause, interval, time, rupture, letup, discontinuance, *(el.)* disconnection, break, *(Gerichtsferien)* recess, *(Pause)* intermission, rest, *(Reise)* break, stoppage, stopover *(US)*, *(Sendung)* intermission, interval, *(Verhandlung)* adjournment;
mit ~ intermittently; **mit häufigen** ~**en** by easy stages; **ohne** ~ in a circle;
vorübergehende ~ temporary cessation, interruption;
~ **der Arbeit** suspension of employment, break from work, interruption in working hours; ~ **diplomatischer Beziehungen** suspension of diplomatic relations; ~ **der Geschäftstätigkeit** disruption of business activities, interruption of business; ~ **der Handelsbeziehungen** interruption of the flow of commerce; ~ **des Handelsverkehrs** derangement of trade; ~ **des Kausalzusammenhanges** intervening agency; ~ **eines Prozesses** abatement of proceedings; ~ **eines Redners** interruption of a speaker; ~ **einer Reise** interruption (break) of a journey, discontinuance of travel; ~ **einer Sitzung** adjournment of a meeting; **vorübergehende** ~ **des Strafvollzugs** temporary suspension of punishment; ~ **des Telefonverkehrs** disconnection of telephone lines; ~ **der Verbindungen** severance of communications; ~ **des Verfahrens** suspension (stay) of proceedings; ~ **der Verjährungsfrist** saving (interruption, suspension, tolling, *US*) the statute of limitations, interruption of the period of limitation (prescription); ~ **des Verkehrs** interruption (stoppage) of traffic, holdup;
zehn Stunden ohne ~ **arbeiten** to work ten hours without letup; ~ **der Debatte beantragen (verlangen)** to move to report progress; **nach einer kurzen** ~ **fortfahren** to continue after a short intermission; **mit** ~**en reisen** to travel with occasional rests.
Unterbrechungstag intermediate [day] *(Br.)*.
unterbreiten to submit, to present, to propound;
Offerten ~ to submit tenders; **Streitfall einem Schiedsrichter** ~ to submit a difference to an arbitrator; **jem. einen Vorschlag** ~ to make a proposal to s. o.; **einer Versammlung einen Vorschlag** ~ to present a plan to a meeting.
Unterbreitung submittal, submission, presentation;
~ **einer Frage zur schiedsrichterlichen Entscheidung** submission of a question to arbitration.
unterbringen *(im Haus)* to place, *(Kapital)* to invest, *(lagern)* to store, *(nächtigen)* to lodge, to accommodate, to house, to put (fix, *US*) up, to nestle, *(Truppen)* to billet, to quarter, *(verkaufen)* to realize, to sell, to find a market, to dispose of, *(Wertpapiere)* to digest, to place;
j. ~ to find a job (an employment) for s. o., to berth s. o., to place s. o. out *(US)*, *(anderweitig)* to ease into another job; **j.** ~ **und versorgen** to board and lodge s. o.; **Anleihe** ~ to negotiate (place, dispose of) a loan; **Anleihe zum Kurs von 98%** ~ to place a loan at 98 per cent; **Arbeiter** ~ to place workers; **Artikel bei einer Zeitung** ~ to place an article with a newspaper; **Buch in einem Verlag** ~ to place a book with a publisher; **j. bei sich [im Büro]** ~ to place s. o. in one's office; **Emission** ~ to place an issue; **seine Familie** ~ to house one's family; **j. bei einer Firma** ~ to find s. o. a situation in a firm; **Flüchtlinge** ~ to house refugees; **Geld** ~ to put out money; **Gepäck** ~ to stow (tuck) away luggage; **in einem Hotel** ~ to put up in a hotel; **Kind in einem Pflegeheim** ~ to place a child in a foster home; **jungen Mann** ~ to launch a young man in business; **am offenen Markt** ~ to sell in the open market; **j. eine Nacht** ~ to lodge s. o. over night; **über Pari** ~ to sell at a premium; **unter Pari** ~ to sell at a discount; **Sammlumg** ~ to house a collection; **Schiffbrüchige vorübergehend in einer Schule** ~ to lodge shipwrecked persons in a school; **j. sofort** ~ to house s. immediately; **Sohn gut** ~ to settle a son in his profession; **in Sozialwohnungen** ~ to accommodate in public housing; **j. in einer Stellung** ~ to find a situation for s. o., to get s. o. a job, to fix s. o. up *(US)*; **in einer Stunde** ~ to crowd in an hour; **mit Verlust** ~ to sell at a loss; **Wechsel** ~ to have a bill discounted, to discount a bill; **Wertpapiere beim Publikum** ~ to place securities with the public; **j. übers Wochenende** ~ to put s. o. up for the weekend; **nicht** ~ **können** to find no sellers; **Namen nicht** ~ **können** not to be able to place a name; **sich leicht** ~ **lassen** to sell readily.

Unterbringung *(Anleihe)* negotiation, placement, placing, *(Kapital)* investment, *(Lagerung)* storing, storage, *(Nächtigung)* finding accommodation, lodging, housing, putting up, *(Stellung besorgen)* placing in position, settlement, *(Truppen)* billet, quarters, *(Verkauf)* sale, disposal, realization;
zumutbare anderweitige ~ suitable alternative accommodation; **angemessene** ~ proper lodging; **auswärtige** ~ accommodation out of town; **behelfsmäßige** ~ temporary housing; **kostenlose** ~ free housing; **preiswerte** ~ accommodation provided at nominal rent; **verbesserte** ~ upgraded housing; **vorübergehende** ~ temporary housing; **zwangsweise** ~ compulsory detention;
~ **im Altersheim** part III accommodation *(Br.)*; ~ **von Arbeitnehmern** placing of employees; ~ **mit Bedienung** serviced accommodation; ~ **in einer Besserungsanstalt** Borstal training; ~ **in Einzelzimmern** single-room accommodation; ~ **von Flüchtlingen** housing of refugees; ~ **in einem Fürsorgeheim** welfare housing, Borstal training; ~ **in einer Heilanstalt** confinement in an asylum; ~ **im Hotel** hotel accommodation; ~ **in einem Jugendgefängnis** detention in a reformatory *(US)*; ~ **von Kindern in Pflegeheimen** placing of children in foster homes; ~ **für eine Nacht** a night's lodging; ~ **in Sozialwohnungen** accommodation in public housing; ~ **für Verheiratete** married accommodation; ~ **eines Wechsels** discounting a bill; ~ **in Werkswohnungen** company housing; ~ **von Wertpapieren beim Publikum** placing of securities with the public;
an der ~ **beteiligt sein** to participate in the placement of; **für anderweitige** ~ **sorgen** *(Vermieter)* to offer alternative accommodation.

Unterbringungs|möglichkeit accommodation; ~**zuschüsse** accommodation subsidies.

unterbrochen interrupted, *(Feuer)* suspended, stopped, *(Stromkreis)* broken, disconnected;
nicht ständig ~ intermittent;
~**e Beschäftigungszeit** interruption of employment.

Unter|deck lower deck; ~**deckung** insufficient funds, shoestring margin *(US)*; ~**deckung an Wohnungen** housing shortage; ~**deklaration** *(Zoll)* short entry; ~**delegierter** subdelegate.

unterdessen in testimony (virtue) whereof, in verification of which (writing).

Unterdruckbremse vacuum brake.

unterdrücken to tyrannize, to suppress, to oppress, *(Aufstand)* to crush, to smother, to burke, to quell, to break down all opposition, *(Rundfunksendung, Zensur)* to black out, *(verschleiern)* to conceal;
Angelegenheit ~ to hush up an affair; **Bericht** ~ to stifle a report; **Beweismaterial** ~ to suppress (conceal) evidence; **seine Empörung** ~ to choke back one's indignation; **seine Gefühle** ~ to bottle up one's feelings; **Minderheiten** ~ to oppress minorities; **wesentliche Tatsachen** ~ to conceal material facts; **Urkunde** ~ to suppress a document; **Veröffentlichung** ~ to suppress a publication; **Volk** ~ to keep a people down by force; **Wahrheit** ~ to suppress the truth.

Unterdrücker represser, suppressor.

Unterdruck|förderer vacuum tank; ~**kammer** low-pressure chamber; ~**messer** vacuum gauge.

unterdrückt suppressed, oppressed, *(Aufstand)* stifled;
~ **werden** to be under the hoof;
~**es Gelächter** stifled laughter; ~**e Minderheit** downtrodden minority; **mit** ~**er Stimme** in a suffocated voice.

Unterdrückte, sich der Sache der ~**n annehmen** to champion the oppressed.

Unterdrückung suppression, repression, *(Verheimlichung)* concealment, *(Zensur)* blacking;
widerrechtliche ~ iniquitous oppression;
~ **von Beweismaterial** suppression (concealment) of evidence; ~ **von Minderheiten** oppression of minorities; ~ **wesentlicher Tatsachen** concealment of material facts; ~ **eines Testamentes** suppression of a will; ~ **einer Urkunde** suppression (concealment) of a document; ~ **von Vermögenswerten** concealment of assets.

Unterdrückungspolitik policy of suppression;
~ **betreiben** to sit on the safety valve.

unterdurchschnittlich below the mark (standard, average), substandard.

untereinander heiraten to intermarry.

Unter|einteilung subdivision; ~**emission** inferior issue.

unterentwickelt underdeveloped, developing, backward;
geistig ~ mentally retarded;
~**e Gebiete** underdeveloped areas; ~**e Länder** developing countries.

Unter|entwickeltsein retardation; ~**entwicklung** underdevelopment, backwardation.

unterernährt undernourished, underfed, underbred.

Unterernährung deficiency of food, undernourishment, malnutrition, nutrition deficiency.

Unterfangen enterprise, undertaking, venture;
fruchtloses ~ wild-goose chase; **klippenreiches** ~ hazardous undertaking.

unterfertigen to undersign, to sign, to execute.

Unter|fertigter the undersigned, signatory; ~**fertigung** execution, signing.

unterfliegen, Radarkontrolle to duck radar control.

Unter|format subsize; ~**frachtvertrag** contract of recharter; ~**führer** *(mil.)* noncommissioned officer; ~**führung** subway, underpass *(US)*, dive *(Br.)*.

Untergang loss, decay, ruin, naught, *(jur.)* destruction, extinguishment, extinction, *(Schiff)* shipwreck, *(Statusverlust)* downfall;
teilweiser ~ partial destruction; **zufälliger** ~ accidential loss; ~ **eines Pfandes** extinguishment of lien; ~ **von Sachen** destruction of goods; ~ **der Sonne** setting of the sun; ~ **und Verderben** wrack and ruin; ~ **durch Vermischung** merger; ~ **des Vertragsgegenstands** destruction of the subject matter of contract;
zum ~ **beitragen** to help down; **vor dem** ~ **stehen** to be faced with ruin.

Unter|gebener subordinate, subaltern, inferior, vassal, *(verächtlich)* underling; ~**gebot** lower bid, underbid.

untergebracht placed;
fest ~ *(Börse)* digested;
nicht ~ **werden können** to find no sale; **gut** ~ **sein** to be well kept.

untergegangen *(Forderungen)* extinguished, *(Schiff)* lost at sea.

untergehen to go under (to ruin), to be on the decline, *(Ertrinkender)* to be drowned, *(Sachen)* to perish, *(Schiff)* to sink, to founder, to be lost, to go down (to wreck), *(vernichtet werden)* to be destroyed, *(Volk)* to be wiped out;
mit der gesamten Besatzung (Mann und Maus) ~ to be lost with all hands; **im Lärm** ~ to be swamped by the noise.

untergehende Sonne setting sun.

untergeordnet subordinate, subaltern, base, inferior, ancillary, minor, *(nebensächlich)* accessory, secondary, collateral, *(im Rang)* junior;
jem. ~ **sein** to be subordinate to s. o.;
~**er Angestellter** nonpolicy-making functionary, subordinate clerk; ~**e Aufgaben** ancillary duties; ~**er Beamter** inferior (subordinate, *US*) officer; **von** ~**er Bedeutung** of secondary importance; ~**e Beweistatsache** minor fact; ~**e Dienste** inferior (base) services; ~**e Dienststelle** subordinate office; ~**e Einzelheiten** minor details; ~**e Frage** subordinate question; ~**es Interesse** subordinate (minor) interest; ~**er Markt** secondary market; ~**es Problem** minor problem; ~**e Rolle spielen** to play a minor role, to play the second fiddle; ~**e Stellen** subordinate bodies; **in einer** ~**en Stellung sein** to be in an inferior subordinate) position; ~**e Tätigkeit** inferior services; ~**er Vorgesetzter** straw boss *(US)*.

Untergeordneter subordinate, secondary, inferior.

untergeschoben *(Kind)* supposititious, *(Urkunde)* spurious, forged, counterfeit.

Unter|geschoß basement, ground (first, *US*) floor, lower stor(e)y (floor); ~**gestell** *(Auto)* undercarriage, underframe, chassis, *(Beine)* underpinnings.

untergetaucht submersed.

Untergewicht short (shortage in) weight, underweight.

untergewichtig underweight.

untergliedern to subdivide, to split up, to break down.

Untergliederung subdivision.

untergraben to undermine, to abrade, to sap;
jds. Gesundheit ~ to shatter (impair) s. one's health; **jds. guten Ruf** ~ to undermine s. one's reputation.

Untergrund underground, substratum, subsoil;
felsiger ~ bedrock; **fester** ~ hard core;
auf festem ~ **errichten** to build on firm ground; **in den** ~ **gehen** *(pol.)* to go underground, to go into hiding.

Untergrundbahn underground *(Br.)*, tube [railway] *(Br., coll.)*, subway *(US)*, Metropolitan and District Railway *(Br.)*, the Metro *(Br.)*;
mit der ~ **fahren** to go (travel) by underground *(Br.)*;
~**benutzer** subway rider *(US)*; ~**netz** subway *(US)* (underground, *Br.*) system; ~**station** subway station *(US)*; ~**steig** subway platform *(US)*; ~**werbung** underground railway advertising *(Br.)*, subway advertising *(US)*.

Untergrund|bewegung underground movement, fifth column; **~film** underground film; **~kämpfer** undergrounder, fifth-column (front) man (columnist); **~literatur** underground literature; **~organisation** cover organization; **~presse** underground press; **~tätigkeit** undercover activities, fifth-column (subversive) activity.

Untergruppe minor group, *(Fertigung)* subassembly.

Unterhalt maintenance, [means of] support, subsistence, sustenance, livelihood, living, keep, keeping, *(an geschiedene Ehefrau)* alimony, aliment *(Scot.)*, *(Kostgeld)* board, *(Wartung)* maintenance, upkeep, *(Zahlung aus dem Nachlaß)* family allowance *(US)*;
zum ~ dienend alimentary;
angemessener ~ reasonable subsistence (maintenance), health and decency standard of living; **auskömmlicher ~** sufficiency; **ehelicher ~** matrimonial maintenance *(Br.)*; **freier ~** free board and lodging; **laufender ~** *(Geschiedene)* permanent alimony *(Br.)*; **notdürftiger ~** necessaries of life, bare necessities of life; **provisorischer (vorläufiger) ~** alimony pendente lite, temporary alimony *(US)*; **standesgemäßer ~** comfortable maintenance, maintenance suitable to s. one's station in life; **aus dem Nachlaß zu zahlender ~** family allowance *(US)*;
~ einer Familie maintenance of a family; **~ bei Getrenntleben** separate maintenance *(US)*; **~ und Instandsetzung** maintenance and repair; **~ während des Prozesses** alimony pendente lite;
für seinen ~ arbeiten to work for one's living; **gemeinsam für den ~ aufkommen** to share the maintenance; **zum ~ der Familie beitragen** to contribute to the family's keep; **jds. ~ bestreiten** to provide for s. o.; **seinen ~ selbst bestreiten** to support o. s., to earn one's living; **~ fordern** to claim maintenance; **~ gewähren** to provide maintenance, *(Ehefrau)* to pay alimony, to aliment; **Anspruch auf ~ haben** to be entitled to an allowance, *(Ehefrau)* to be entitled to alimony; **seinen ~ haben** to earn a livelihood; **auf ~ klagen** to sue for maintenance; **für seinen ~ aufkommen können** to pay one's way; **sich für seinen ~ abrackern müssen** to scrabble for one's livelihood; **für seinen ~ auf j. angewiesen sein** to be dependent upon s. o. for support; **~ für seine Ehefrau sicherstellen** to provide one's wife with alimony; **~ für seine Familie sicherstellen** to support one's family; **für seinen ~ sorgen** to provide for o. s.; **jds. ~ gegen Bezahlung einer Pauschale übernehmen** to farm out s. o.; **seinen ~ [selbst] verdienen** to earn a living (one's keep), to gain one's livelihood, to pay one's way, to support o. s.; **seinen ~ nicht verdienen** not to earn one's keep; **seinen ~ durch seiner Hände Arbeit verdienen** to earn a living by manual labo(u)r; **seinen ~ durch Stundengeben verdienen** to earn one's livelihood by giving lessons; **~ seiner Familie vernachlässigen** to neglect to maintain one's family; **~ zahlen** to pay alimony, to aliment; **~ zuerkennen** to award maintenance, to award alimony *(US)*.

unterhalten to maintain, to support, to keep, to nourish, *(amüsieren)* to entertain, to divert, to recreate, *(Betrieb)* to operate, *(instand halten)* to keep up (in repair), to maintain;
j. ~ to subsist (provide maintenance for) s. o.; **sich ~** to entertain o. s.; **sich mit jem. ~** to converse (talk) with s. o., to hold a discourse (talk) with s. o.; **sich selbst ~** to make one's own living, to keep o. s.; **Angehörigen gemeinsam ~** to jointly maintain a dependant; **j. angemessen ~** to keep s. o. amused; **Bankkonto bei jem. ~** to bank with s. o.; **Beziehungen ~** to maintain (entertain) relations; **diplomatische Beziehungen zu einem Land ~** to maintain diplomatic relations with a country; **freundschaftliche Beziehungen ~** to sustain friendly relations; **intime Beziehungen ~** to have sexual intercourse; **Briefwechsel ~** to keep up (carry on, maintain) a correspondence; **Eisenbahnlinie für den öffentlichen Verkehr ~** to maintain a railway (railroad, *US*); **sich auf Englisch ~** to talk in English; **vier Fabriken ~** to operate four factories *(US)*; **Familie ~** to maintain (keep, sustain, *US*) a family; **Feuer ~** to feed a fire; **Filiale ~** to maintain a branch; **Gebäude ~** to keep a building in repair; **Geschäft ~** to run a shop; **Geschäftsbeziehungen ~** to entertain business connections; **Geschäftsstelle ~** to maintain (run) an office; **sich glänzend ~** to have the time of one's life; **sich gut ~** to amuse o. s., to have a good time; **großes Haus ~** to keep (up) a large house, to entertain a great deal; **Kantine ~** to run a canteen; **Konto ~** to have (keep) an account; **auf öffentliche Kosten ~** to support at public expense; **umfangreiche Lager ~** to operate a network of depots; **Landeszentralbankguthaben ~** to have special deposits with the Bank of England *(Br.)*, to have a deposit account with the Federal Reserve Bank *(US)*; **aus öffentlichen Mitteln ~** to maintain at public expense; **sich politisch (über Politik) ~** to talk politics; **Reserven ~** to maintain reserves; **Straße ~** to maintain a road; **sich mit jem. im Vorbeigehen ~** to pass the time of day with s. o. *(coll.)*;
Frau und sieben Kinder zu ~ haben to have a wife and seven children to support (keep); **seine Eltern ~ müssen** to have one's parents to keep; **durch freiwillige Beträge ~ werden** to be supported by voluntary contributions; **aus öffentlichen Mitteln ~ werden** to be maintained at public expense, to live on the parish (town, *US*);
~ *(a.)* alimonied;
~e Versicherung insurance carried.

unterhaltend recreative.

Unterhalter conversationalist, entertainer, showmaster *(US)*;
hervorragender ~ vintage conversationalist.

unterhaltsabhängig, völlig wholly dependent.

unterhaltsam amusing, entertaining, diverting.

Unterhaltsanspruch right of support, *(Ehefrau)* claim of (right to) alimony, *(Kinder)* claim for (right to) maintenance, maintenance claim;
für die Ehefrau festgelegter ~ alimony awarded to a wife;
~ bestreiten to contest the alimony claim; **~ geltend machen (stellen)** to claim (recover) maintenance (alimony).

Unterhaltsbedürfnisse necessitous circumstances.

unterhaltsbedürftig necessitous, requiring maintenance;
~ werden to come (go) on the parish (upon the town, *US*).

Unterhalts|bedürftigkeit destitute or necessitous circumstances; **~befugnis** power of maintenance; **~beihilfe** subsistence (maintenance) allowance (grant), subsistence benefit.

Unterhaltsbeitrag maintenance allowance, *(an getrennt lebende Ehefrau)* alimony *(US)*;
laufender ~ permanent alimony *(US)*; **monatlicher ~** monthly allowance;
jem. einen jährlichen ~ von ... gewähren to make s. o. an allowance of ... a year.

unterhaltsberechtigt *(Ehefrau)* entitled to alimony, *(Kind)* entitled to maintenance;
~er Angehöriger dependant, beneficiary; **~e Familie** family dependent on s. o.

Unterhalts|berechtigter legal dependant, beneficiary; **~beschluß** *(Gericht)* maintenance order *(Br.)*; **~betrag** amount of maintenance, maintenance allowance, *(geschiedene Ehefrau)* alimony *(US)*; **laufender ~betrag** permanent alimony; **~betrug** alimony racket; **~empfänger** *(Sozialhilfe)* recipient of relief, welfare recipient; **~entzug** withholding means of support from dependants.

unterhaltsfähig able to earn (make a living).

Unterhalts|fähigkeit *(Scheidung)* faculties; **~fonds** alimentary trust, protective trust; **~forderung** claim for maintenance, maintenance claim; **~freibetrag** dependant relative allowance *(Br.)*; **~geld** national *(Br.)* (public, *US*) assistance; **vorläufiges ~geld** alimony pendente lite *(US)*; **~gesetz** support law; **~gewährung** granting of public *(US)* (national, *Br.*) assistance; **~klage** affiliation proceedings, alimony process, action for support *(US)*, *(uneheliches Kind)* bastardy case *(US)*; **~klage anstrengen** to sue for maintenance, *(uneheliches Kind)* to file an affiliation petition; **~kläger** plaintiff in a maintenance case; **~kosten** cost of living, living expenses, cost[s] of maintenance, *(Betrieb)* maintenance charges (expenses); **vorläufige ~kosten** interim alimony; **Beitrag zu den ~kosten leisten** to make contributions towards the cost of maintenance; **~lasten** *(Betrieb)* maintenance charges; **~leistung** maintenance allowance, *(an getrennt lebende Ehefrau)* separation maintenance, alimony, *(für die Dauer des hierüber geführten Prozesses)* temporary alimony *(US)*, alimony pendente lite *(US)*; **~mittel** upkeep, maintenance, means of subsistence; **ersichtlich keine ~mittel** no visible means of support; **unentbehrliche ~mittel** strict necessaries; **~pension** alimentary endowment; **~pflicht** legal obligation to support, liability to provide, maintenance obligation, duty to furnish support *(US)*, *(an geschiedene Ehefrau)* obligation to pay alimony, liability to support a wife *(US)*; **gesetzliche ~pflicht** legal obligation to support; **sich seiner ~pflicht entziehen** to evade one's legal obligations to support, to evade one's maintenance obligations.

unterhaltspflichtig liable to maintain (support);
~ sein to have a legal obligation to support, to be responsible for maintenance, *(für geschiedene Ehefrau)* to be under obligation to pay alimony.

Unterhalts|prozeß affiliation proceedings, alimentary (alimony, bastardy, *US*) process, bastardy proceedings *(US)*; **~rente** maintenance allowance; **lebenslängliche ~rente** permanent alimony; ~**rückstände** arrears of maintenance, maintenance arrears; ~**rückstände erlassen** to remit arrears of maintenance; ~**sache** affiliation (bastardy, *US*) case; ~**unterstützung** allowance, subsistence, grant.

Unterhaltsurteil order of filiation, maintenance order *(Br.)*, *(Vaterschaftsprozeß)* affiliation (bastardy, *US*) order;
~ **zugunsten der Kinder** court order for the maintenance of children.

Unterhalts|vereinbarung, rechtsverbindliche legally binding agreement for the maintenance of children; ~**verfahren** maintenance proceedings, *(Vaterschaftsprozeß)* affiliation (bastardy, *US*) proceedings; ~**verfügung** affiliation order; **vorsätzliche** ~**verletzung** wilful neglect to provide maintenance, nonsupport *(US)*.

unterhaltsverpflichtet liable to pay alimony (maintain, support).

Unterhalts|verpflichtung legal obligation (liability for) to support, affiliation responsibility, *(für die Ehefrau)* obligation to pay alimony *(US)*; ~**verpflichtungen schriftlich anerkennen** to sign a recognizance, to accept affiliation responsibilities; ~**vertrag** contract in respect of alimony, property settlement.

Unterhaltszahlung alimony (support) payment, payment for maintenance, maintenance allowance;
gesicherte ~ secured maintenance *(Br.)*; **laufende** ~**en** permanent alimony; **pauschalierte** ~**en** alimony in gross; **rückständige** ~ maintenance arrears; **ungesicherte** ~ unsecured maintenance *(Br.)*;
~ **an die Ehefrau** alimony granted to a wife; ~ **für geschiedene Ehefrau** estovers, compassionate allowance;
~**en von jem. verlangen** to come upon s. o. for alimony.

Unterhaltszusage maintenance bond.

Unterhaltszuschuß living allowance, maintenance (subsistence, cost-of-living) allowance, subsistence [money], maintenance grant, supplies;
~ **bewilligen** to grant an allowance; **jem. keinen** ~ **mehr gewähren** to cut off s. one's supplies; ~ **kürzen** to curtail an allowance; **seiner Tochter einen** ~ **zukommen lassen** to allow one's daughter a stipend; **jem. den** ~ **streichen** to stop s. one's allowance.

Unterhaltung *(Betrieb)* maintenance, *(Gespräch)* talk, conversation, discourse, *(Unterstützung)* maintenance, support, upkeep, keeping, sustenance, *(Vergnügen)* entertainment, amusement, distraction, diversion, resource, escape, bee *(US)*;
angeregte ~ spirited conversation; **langweilige** ~ flat (inanimate) conversation; **laufende** ~ current upkeep; **vertrauliche** ~ familiar discourse, converse;
~ **der Bahnanlagen** maintenance of way; ~ **von Gebäuden** building maintenance; ~ **eines Geschäftsbetriebes** doing business; ~ **und Instandsetzung** maintenance and repair; ~ **einer Kirche** support of a church; ~ **eines Kraftfahrzeuges** maintenance of an automobile; ~ **armer Krankenhauspatienten** in-maintenance; ~ **des Postverkehrs** operation of postal service; ~ **von Reserven** *(Bank)* maintenance of reserves; ~ **einer Spielbank** keeping a gambling house (place); ~ **von Straßen** upkeep of roads; ~ **der Straßen und öffentlichen Wege** maintenance of public roads and highways;
~ **anfangen** to break the ice; **sich an einer** ~ **beteiligen** to enter into a conversation; ~ **an sich reißen** to engross (monopolize) the conversation; **sich in eine** ~ **stürzen** to launch into a discussion; ~ **eines Mindestguthabens verlangen** to require a minimum balance.

Unterhaltungs|aufwand current maintenance, maintenance expenses (charges); ~**aufwand für ein Auto** car-mile revenue, automobile operating costs *(US)*; ~**aufwandskonto** maintenance expense account; ~**beilage** literary supplement, feuilleton; ~**blatt** family magazine; ~**film** entertainment film, feature; ~**gabe** conversational power; ~**industrie** entertainment field (world), show business; ~**konzert** entertainment concert.

Unterhaltungskosten maintenance cost (expense, charges), expenses of maintenance, [cost of] upkeep, upkeep expenses, *(Auto)* running expenses, automobile operating costs *(US)*, car-mile revenue, *(Gebäude)* carrying charges, *(Straßen)* upkeep of roads;
hohe ~ high carrying costs;
~ **eines Lastkraftwagens** motor-van expenses *(Br.)*;
~ **eines Autos tragen** to pay for the cost of keeping a car on the road.

Unterhaltungs|künstler entertainer, conversationalist, showmaster *(US)*; ~**lasten** *(Straßen)* maintenance charges; ~**literatur** literature of escape, escape reading (literature), fictional (light) literature, fiction, jolly stuff; ~**lokal** entertainment spot; ~**magazin** family magazine; ~**musik** light music; ~**orchester** band; ~**pflicht** maintenance obligation; ~**programm** entertainment show (schedule), comedy program(me), *(Rundfunk)* light program(me); ~**programm ziemlich langweilig finden** to think an entertainment rather slow; ~**roman** fiction; ~**sendung** light program(me); ~**sendung im Fernsehen** television entertainment; ~**stück** entertainment; ~**teil** *(Zeitung)* feuilleton, column *(US)*; **im** ~**ton schreiben** to write in conversational style; ~**zeitschrift** family magazine; ~**zentrum** entertainment complex, resource center *(US)* (centre, *Br.*); **allgemeiner** ~**zustand** general maintenance; ~**zyklus** maintenance cycle.

unterhandeln to negotiate, to treat with, to transact, *(mil.)* to parley with.

Unterhändler negotiator, delegate, *(mil.)* parliamentary, commisioner, *(Vermittler)* go-between, mediator.

Unterhandlung negotiation, transaction, treaty, *(mil.)* parley;
~**en abbrechen** to break off negotiations; **in** ~**en eintreten** to enter into negotiations; **in** ~**en stehen mit** to negotiate, to be in treaty with; **in** ~**en über den Ankauf eines Hauses stehen** to negotiate for the sale of a house; **seit einiger Zeit in** ~**en stehen** to have been negotiating for some time.

Unterhaus Parliament, lower house, Lower Chamber, House of Commons *(Br.)*, House of Representatives *(US)*, *(Einzelstaaten der USA)* House of Delegates, assembly;
fürs ~ **kandidieren** to stand for parliament *(Br.)*; **dem** ~ **zur Beratung vorlegen** to put before the house for consideration; **im** ~ **angenommen werden** to pass the House of Commons;
~**abgeordnete** member of parliament; ~**ausschuß** parliamentary (House, *Br.*) committee; ~**debatte** parliamentary debate; ~**kandidat** [parliamentary] candidate; ~**mitglied** member of the House of Commons (Parliament), M.P.; ~**vertagung** count-out *(Br.)*; ~**wahlen** general (parliamentary) elections.

unterhöhlen to undermine, to mine.

Unterholz underwood, undergrowth, understory *(US)*.

unterirdisch underground, subterranean;
~**er Gang** underground passage, subway; ~**e Gewässer** subterranean waters; ~**es Kabel** underground cable; **Land durch** ~**e Kanäle entwässern** to underdrain a country; ~**e Parkmöglichkeit** underground parking; ~**e Straße** underground road; ~**e Versuche** underground testing.

unterjochen to subject, to subjugate, to put under the yoke.

Unterjochung subjugation, conquest, enslavement.

unterkapitalisiert undercapitalized, low-geared.

Unterkapitalisierung undercapitalization, low gearing.

unterkellern to make a cellar under a house.

Unter|kellerung cellarage; ~**klasse** subclass; ~**kommen** accommodation, lodging, *(Beschäftigung)* employment, job, situation, post, *(Obdach)* shelter.

unterkommen to get a lodging, to find accommodation, *(Stellung finden)* to find employment (a job), to be taken on.
sehr gut ~ to find excellent quarters [at an inn].

Unter|kommission subcommission; ~**konto** subaccount, subsidiary account.

unterkriegen, j. to bring s. o. to heel;
sich ~ **lassen** to knuckle under; **sich nicht** ~ **lassen** to bob up like a cork, to pang-wangle *(sl.)*.

unterkühlt undercooled, *(Stil)* unimpassioned.

Unterkunft lodging, quarters, place, bed, accommodation, *(mil.)* quarterage, billet, *(Obdach)* shelter, housing, *(Wohnung)* abode, dwelling;
einschließlich ~ **und Verpflegung** found *(US)*; **ohne feste** ~ without abode;
billige ~ low-cost accommodation; **freie** ~ free quarter, quarters in kind; **kostenlos zur Verfügung gestellte** ~ rent-free accommodation; **jämmerliche** ~ miserable dwelling; **unzulängliche** ~ substandard housing; **vorübergehende** ~ temporary housing;
~ **und Verpflegung** bed and board, board and residence (lodging);
~ **für eine Nacht finden** to find lodging for a night; **jem.** ~ **geben** to put s. o. up; **für** ~ **sorgen** to arrange for accommodation; ~ **und Verpflegung stellen** to provide full board and accommodation.

Unterkunfts|gerät *(mil.)* barrack stores *(Br.)*; ~**hütte** refuge; ~**möglichkeit** accommodation; ~**raum** shelter, *(mil.)* quarters, cantonment area *(US)*; ~**verhältnisse** lodging conditions.

Unterlage foundation, groundwork, *(beim Arbeiten)* pad, *(Aufzeichnung)* record, *(Beleg)* voucher, *(Beweis)* proof, evidence, document, *(Kredit)* collateral *(US)*, security, *(technisch)* support, base plate;

gute ~ good grounding; **wasserundurchlässige** ~ waterproof sheet;
~ **zum Schreiben** desk pad.

Unterlagen data, information, papers, *(Quellen)* sources, references, *(Urkunden)* [supporting] documents, records, dossier; **amtliche** ~ official papers; **anerkannte** ~ approved vouchers; **außerbetriebliche** ~ external data; **einem Bericht beigefügte** ~ documents joined to a report; **einer Bewerbung beigefügte** ~ personal data and testimonials; **beizubringende** ~ documents required; **beweiserhebliche** ~ evidentiary documents; **buchungstechnische** ~ bookkeeping (accounting) records; **entsprechende** ~ pertinent data; **finanzielle** ~ financial records; **geschäftliche** ~ commercial documents; **statistische** ~ statistical data; **zur Verfügung stehende** ~ evidence available; **technische** ~ technical data; **urkundliche** ~ dossier; **vertrauliche** ~ confidential documents, sensitive material; **vollständige** ~ regular documents;
~ **für die Festsetzung des Haushalts** budget documents; ~ **einer Firma (Gesellschaft)** records of a corporation *(US)*; ~ **einer Kreditauskunftei** rating book; ~ **für eine Sitzung** documentation for a meeting;
~ **anfordern** to ask for the documents; ~ **aufbewahren** to preserve documents, to keep one's records; ~ **nach Zahlung einer Gebühr aushändigen** to hand out the papers on payment of a fee; ~ **beibringen (beschaffen)** to produce (procure, furnish) documents; ~ **durchnumerieren** to page the documents; **keine** ~ **haben** to have nothing to go upon; ~ **zu den Prozeßakten nehmen** to enter documents into the record; ~ **vernichten** to destroy documents; **alte** ~ **wiederfinden** to hunt up old records; **seinem Anwalt** ~ **zuleiten** to hand papers to one's solicitor; ~ **für eine wissenschaftliche Arbeit zusammenstellen** to collect material for a scientific work;
~**führung** keeping of records, record keeping; ~**prüfung** voucher audit; ~**verzeichnis** voucher register.

Unterlaß, ohne without intermission (letup), incessantly.

Unterlassen, schuldhaftes culpable neglect.

unterlassen to abstain, to refrain from, to desist, to neglect, to omit, to fail, *(Wettbewerb)* to cease and desist *(US)*;
feindselige Handlungen ~ to refrain from hostile actions; **Klage** ~ to forbear a suit; **nichts** ~ to leave no stone unturned;
~**e Berichterstattung** failure to render a report.

Unterlassung abstention, omission, forbearance, failure, neglect, nonaction, nonperformance, *(jur.)* default, *(Versehen)* overlook;
bei ~ in case of default;
vertraglich ausbedungene ~ negative condition; **fahrlässige** ~ passive negligence *(US)*; **pflichtwidrige** ~ nonfeasance, neglect; **strafbare** ~ penal neglect; **vorsätzliche** ~ wilful default;
pflichtwidrige ~ **einer Anzeige** negative misprision; ~ **der Geburtsanmeldung** concealment of birth; **Handlungen und** ~**en** acts and omissions; ~ **der Hilfestellung** failure to render aid; ~ **einer Klage** forbearance to sue; ~ **der erforderlichen Vorsichtsmaßregeln** neglect of proper precautions;
auf ~ **klagen** to sue for an injunction.

Unterlassungs|anordnung, ~**befehl** cease and desist order *(US)*; ~**bestimmung** negative term; ~**delikt** omission; **im** ~**fall** in case of noncompliance, in the event of default; ~**klage** injunction suit, *(Wettbewerbsrecht)* cease and desist order *(US)*; ~**pflicht** negative covenant (condition); ~**sünde** sin of omission; **endgültiges** ~**urteil** final injunction; **vorbeugendes** ~**urteil** cautionary judgment, preventive injunction; ~**verbot** injunction to restrain, *(Konkurrenzklausel)* cease and desist order *(US)*;**einstweiliges** ~**verbot** preliminary (interim) injunction; ~**verbot gegen eine Aktienübertragung** injunction restraining transfer; **vorbeugendes** ~**verfahren** quia timet proceedings; ~**verfügung** perpetual injunction; **vorbeugende** ~**verfügung** writ of prevention, quia timet injunction; ~**verfügung gegen Neubauerrichtung** denouncement of a new work *(US)*; ~**verpflichtung** restrictive condition, negative covenant; ~**versprechen** negative covenant.

unterlaufen *(Fehler)* to creep in, to occur.

unterlegen to put underneath, to underlay, *(drucktechn.)* to key;
anderen Sinn ~ to put another construction upon; **jds. Worten einen anderen Sinn** ~ to read another meaning into s. one's words;
~ *(a.)* inferior, *(besiegt)* defeated, losing;
jem. geistig ~ **sein** not to be able to hold a candle to s. o.; **jem. in keiner Weise** ~ **sein** to be in no way inferior to s. o.;
~**er Feind** defeated enemy; ~**e Partei** aggrieved (defeated) party.

Unterlegenheit, zahlenmäßige inferiority in numbers.

unterlegt underlaid.

Unterlieferant subcontractor, little master;
~**en der Raumfahrtindustrie** aerospace subcontractors;
Arbeit als ~ **ausführen** to carry out subcontracting work; **als** ~ **auftreten** to subcontract; **an** ~**en vergeben** to let out to subcontractors, to team *(sl.)*.

Unterlieferantentätigkeit subcontract work.

unterliegen to be subject, to underlie, *(Prozeßpartei)* to be unsuccessful, *(verlieren)* to be defeated, to lose [out];
einer vertraglichen Absprache ~ to fall within an agreement; **gesetzlichen Bestimmungen** ~ to come within the provisions (scope) of a law; **den nachfolgenden Bestimmungen** ~ to be governed by the following rules; **der Einkommensteuer** ~ to be liable to income tax; **der Entscheidung des Ministeriums** ~ to come (lie) within the purview of a ministry; **einer Genehmigung** ~ to be subject to an approval; **dem Gesetz** ~ to be amenable to the law; **der Preisbindung** ~ to be subject to a condition as to the price; **im Prozeß** ~ to lose (fail in) a suit; **einem Rechtsmittel** ~ to be subject to an appeal; **der Schweigepflicht** ~ to be sworn to secrecy; **mit 40 Stimmen** ~ to be 40 seats short of a majority; **der Übermacht** ~ to be overcome by superior forces; **einer genauen Untersuchung** ~ to be closely investigated; **noch Veränderungen** ~ to be subject to modifications; **der Verjährung** ~ to be barred by the statute of limitations; **der Versuchung** ~ to yield to temptation; **dem Zoll** ~ to be liable to customs (duty); **nicht jds. Zuständigkeit** ~ not to fall into s. one's province; **der Zuständigkeit eines Gerichts** ~ to come within the jurisdiction of a court; **einem Zweifel** ~ to be open to doubt; **keinem Zweifel** ~ to admit of no doubt.

unterliegend subjacent;
~**e Partei** aggrieved (unsuccessful, losing, defeated) party.

Unterlizenz sublicence;
~ **erteilen** to sublicense;
~**geber** sublicenser, sublicensor; ~**nehmer** sublicensee.

Untermakler intermediate broker.

untermalen, mit Musik to provide with a musical background.

Unter|malung background music; ~**maß** short measure.

untermauern to underpin, to support, to substantiate, *(fig.)* to support, to corroborate;
seinen Antrag mit einer eidesstattlichen Versicherung ~ to move an affidavit; **Behauptung mit Beispielen** ~ to support a statement with examples; **seine Beziehungen zu jem. finanziell** ~ to put one's relationship with s. o. on a paying basis.

Untermauerung supporting, underpinning.

Untermiete sublease, underlease, undertenancy;
Haus im Wege der ~ **pachten** to rent a house from a tenant; **Zimmer in** ~ **vergeben** to sublet a room; **in** ~ **wohnen** to be a subtenant (roomer, *US*), to lodge with s. o.

Untermieter undertenant, underlessee, sublettee, subtenant, lodger, roomer *(US)*;
geduldeter ~ **quasi tenant at sufferance;**
~ **nehmen** to take in lodgers (roomers, *US*); ~ **vermitteln** to write up a sublet.

Untermietverhältnis undertenancy, subtenancy.

unterminieren to countermine, to mine, to sap, to undermine.

Unterminierung, auf eine ~ **der Moral hinarbeiten** to tend to undermine morality.

Unternehmen enterprise, establishment, firm, concern, outfit, business, [business] undertaking *(Br.)*, *(AG)* company, corporation, *(mil.)* stunt, operation, expedition, *(Projekt)* project, *(Transaktion)* transaction, operation, business, *(Versuch)* attempt, *(Vorhaben)* venture, enterprise, *(Wagnis)* venture, adventure;
abhängiges ~ controlled concern; **hohe Gewinne abwerfendes** ~ business bonanza; **ähnliches** ~ business of similar nature; **alteingesessenes** ~ old-established firm; **anstrengendes** ~ arduous enterprise; **ausländische** ~ foreign enterprise; **in Betrieb befindliches** ~ going concern; **noch im Besitz der Gründerfamilie befindliches** ~ first concern; **befreundetes** ~ correspondent company; **beherrschendes** ~ controlling company; **beherrschtes** ~ controlled company (concern); **bestreiktes** ~ strike-bound factory; **beteiligtes** ~ participating company; **Endverbraucherwerbung betreibendes** ~ consumer advertiser; **privatwirtschaftlich betriebenes** ~ privately held company; **vom Staat betriebenes** ~ state-run company; **selbständig bilanzierendes** ~ accounting entity; **blühendes** ~ flourishing concern; **buchführendes** ~ accounting entity; **diversifiziertes** ~ multiple product firm; **dynamisches** ~ dynamic company; **nicht in den Konzernabschluß einbezogenes** ~ nonconsolidated affiliate; **gut eingeführtes** ~ well-established firm; **eingegliedertes** ~ integrated company; **höher**

eingestuftes ~ higher-grade corporation; **erfolgreiches** ~ prosperous enterprise, promising undertaking, ten-strike *(US)*, bonanza *(US)*; **erstklassiges** ~ first-rate (-class) firm, fair-dealing firm; **ertragreiches** ~ productive enterprise; **außerhalb der Konkurrenz fahrendes** ~ *(Schiffahrtsgesellschaft)* outsider; **finanzielles** ~ financial enterprise; **florierendes** ~ thriving operation; **fortschrittliches** ~ progressive organization, forward-looking company; **fruchtloses** ~ wild-goose chase; **führendes** ~ leading firm; **gut fundiertes** ~ sound firm; **breit gefächertes** ~ diversified corporation; **rationell geführtes** ~ efficiently managed firm; **treuhänderisch geleitetes** ~ business trust *(US)*, Massachusetts Trust *(US)*; **gemeinnütziges** ~ public institution, nonprofit corporation (enterprise), public-service enterprise *(US)*, *(Versorgungsbetrieb)* public utility, *(Stadt)* civil enterprise, *(wohltätige Einrichtung)* charitable institution (undertaking); **gemeinsames** ~ joint venture (adventure, *US*); **gemeinwirtschaftliches** ~ publicly-owned (public-service) enterprise, public company *(Br.)*; **gemischtwirtschaftliches** ~ mixed enterprise, quasi- (semi-) public corporation; **genossenschaftliches** ~ industrial cooperative society, cooperative association (enterprise); **geschäftliches** ~ business venture (enterprise, undertaking, unit), commercial (business) establishment; **finanziell gesundes** ~ sound business; **gewagtes** ~ risky business, speculative venture (enterprise); **gewerbliches** ~ manufacturing (commercial) establishment (enterprise), industrial (manufacturing) concern, productive (business) enterprise, industrial plant, commercial operator; **nicht gewerbliches** ~ nonprofit enterprise, noncommercial establishment; **gewerkschaftseigenes** ~ union enterprise; **gewinnbringendes** ~ profitable enterprise, paying concern; **großangelegtes** ~ undertaking of wide scope; **großes** ~ large establishment (concern); **gutgehendes** ~ prosperous enterprise; **halsbrecherisches** ~ ruinous project; **herrschendes** ~ controlling company; **industrielles** ~ industrial concern (corporation); **inländisches** ~ domestic enterprise; **kapitalintensives** ~ capital-oriented business, high-cost enterprise; **kapitalistisches** ~ capital venture, capitalistic enterprise; **kaufmännisches** ~ commercial establishment (undertaking), business undertaking, trading corporation; **kleinere und mittlere** ~ small and medium-sized businesses; **konsolidiertes** ~ consolidated company; **kontrolliertes** ~ controlled concern; **staatlich kontrolliertes** ~ state-controlled enterprise; **konzessioniertes** ~ licensed undertaking; **kreditaufnehmendes** ~ borrowing concern; **kreditsuchendes** ~ would-be borrower; **kriegerisches** ~ warpath; **laufendes (lebendes)** ~ operating (going) concern; **lebensfähiges** ~ viable scheme; **im öffentlichen Interesse liegendes** ~ business affected with a public interest; **marktbeherrschendes** ~ company (corporation) dominating the market, monopoly (monopolistic) enterprise; **mittelgroßes (mittleres, mittelständisches)** ~ medium-sized (small, *US*) business; **modebewußtes** ~ trendy entrepreneur; **monopolistisches** ~ monopolistic enterprise; **multinationales** ~ multinational company; **neugegründetes** ~ new establishment; **an der Börse nicht notiertes** ~ unquoted company, unlisted corporation *(US)*; **notleidendes** ~ failing company; **öffentliches** ~ public (public owned) enterprise; **örtliches** ~ local firm; **privates (privatwirtschaftliches)** ~ privately owned enterprise (establishment, undertaking); **durch den Krieg profitierendes** ~ war bridge *(US sl.)*; **renommiertes** ~ well-reputed firm; **rentables** ~ remunerative undertaking, paying concern; **riskantes** ~ speculative enterprise (venture), wildcat enterprise; **schwieriges** ~ heavy (laborious) undertaking, large order *(sl.)*; **solides** ~ solid business firm, sound business; **staatliches** ~ government[-owned] (publicly-owned) enterprise; **städtisches** ~ municipal enterprise; **steuerpflichtiges** ~ taxpayer corporation; **übernommenes** ~ absorbed company; **unrentables** ~ not paying business, business that does not pay; **unsicheres** ~ dubious undertaking, fly-by-night corporation *(US)*; **unsolides** ~ firm of speculators; **geschäftlich verbundenes** ~ associated company *(Br.)*; **mit Risiko verbundenes** ~ capital venture; **wirtschaftlich verbundene** ~ associated houses; **verstaatlichtes** ~ nationalized enterprise; **vertrauenswürdiges** ~ reliable firm; **verzweifeltes** ~ forlorn hope; **vielversprechendes** ~ promising enterprise, bonanza *(US)*; **waghalsiges** ~ plunge; **weltbekanntes** ~ world-renowned firm;

~ **mit breit gestreuten Absatzmärkten** multimarket company; ~ **im Eigentum der Arbeitnehmer** employee-owned corporation; ~ **mit einem hohen Ertragsmultiplikator** high-multiple company; ~ **mit überproportionalem Fertigungsprogramm** overdiversified company; ~ **zur Feststellung von Einschaltquoten** rating firm; ~ **im Familienbetrieb** family enterprise, family-owned business; ~ **der öffentlichen Hand** publicly-owned (state) enterprise, public corporation, public-sector undertaking, public business; ~ **der Konsumgüterindustrie** consumer-goods company; ~ **mit festgelegter Mindestzahl an Gewerkschaftsmitgliedern** percentage shop *(US)*; ~ **mit breitgestreutem Produktionsprogramm** multiproduct company, diversified concern (corporation); **städtisches** ~ **auf eigene Rechnung** force account; ~ **ohne eigene Rechtspersönlichkeit** unincorporated enterprise; ~ **der Schwerindustrie** heavy-industrial enterprise; ~ **mit Weltgeltung** world-renowned (universally known) firm; ~ **der gewerblichen Wirtschaft** corporate (commercial, trading) enterprise;

sein Vermögen in einem ~ **anlegen** to venture one's fortune in an enterprise; **Geld für ein** ~ **aufbringen** to put up the money for an undertaking; ~ **aufgeben** to abandon an enterprise, to shut the books; ~ **ausbeuten** to milk an enterprise *(US)*; **zum Erfolg eines** ~**s beitragen** to tend to the success of an enterprise; **Anteil an einem** ~ **besitzen** to have a concern (share) in a business; **sich an einem** ~ **beteiligen** to take up a partnership in a venture, to invest one's money in a business enterprise, to participate financially in an enterprise; **sich gemeinsam an einem** ~ **beteiligen** to share with s. o. in an undertaking; **sich mit Vermögenswerten an einem** ~ **beteiligen** to invest funds in a scheme, to embark on a new business undertaking; ~ **betreiben** to carry on an enterprise, to operate an undertaking *(US)*; **auf Gewinn gerichtetes** ~ **betreiben** to carry on business with a view to profit; **weltweites** ~ **betreiben** to operate in global spread; ~ **durchführen** to follow out an enterprise; **in ein** ~ **eintreten** to enter a firm; **mit seinem** ~ **Fehlschlag erleiden** to fail in one's undertaking; ~ **erweitern** to enlarge an establishment; **Kapitalmehrheit in einem** ~ **erwerben** to acquire a controlling interest in a concern; **Rendite in einem** ~ **erzielen** to put a company into the black *(US coll.)*; ~ **finanzieren** to finance the costs of an undertaking; ~ **finanzieren und dafür das Sagen haben** to pay the piper and call the tune; ~ **fördern** to encourage an enterprise; ~ **fortführen** to carry through an undertaking; ~ **zu Ende führen** to go through with an undertaking; ~ **gefährden** to endanger an undertaking; **zu den** ~ **mit dem besten Vorstand gehören** to be rated as one of the best-managed companies; ~ **gründen** to establish a business; **erhebliche Erfahrungen in der Leitung eines** ~**s haben** to be heavy on organizational management experience; **große Beträge in einem** ~ **investiert haben** to have large sums at stake in an enterprise; ~ **aus den roten Zahlen herausführen** to administer a company from red to black *(US coll.)*; **einem** ~ **seine Unterstützung angedeihen lassen** to confer one's patronage upon an undertaking; **erfolglose** ~ **fallen lassen** to bail out dud companies; ~ **leiten** to control an undertaking, to conduct a (manage the) business; ~ **liquidieren** to wind up a business; **an einem** ~ **beteiligt sein** to have a share in an undertaking (vested interest in a concern); **an einem** ~ **finanziell nicht beteiligt sein** to have no money interest in a concern; **neues** ~ **starten** to launch an enterprise; **hinter einem** ~ **stecken** to be the driving force behind the scenes; **Geld in ein** ~ **stecken** to invest money in a business; **sein ganzes Geld in ein** ~ **stecken** to sink all one's money in a concern; **Mittel zu einem** ~ **zur Verfügung stellen** to provide the money for a project; ~ **mit Aktiven und Passiven übernehmen** to purchase an enterprise as a going concern, to take over the assets and liabilities (accounts receivable and accounts payable, *US*) of a company; ~ **umorganisieren** to remodel a corporation; ~ **vom Kapitalmarkt verdrängen** to crowd out private borrowers from the capital market; ~ **vergrößern** to enlarge an establishment; **einem** ~ **den Todesstoß versetzen** to sign the death warrant for an enterprise *(fam.)*; **über das ganze** ~ **arbeitsmäßig verteilen** to redistribute workers throughout the company; ~ **weiterführen** to carry through an undertaking; **einem** ~ **zufließen** to accrue to an enterprise; **sich von einem** ~ **zurückziehen** to withdraw from an undertaking; **sich in einem großen** ~ **zusammenschließen** to merge into one large organization.

unternehmen to enterprise, to undertake, to take in hand, to go about, *(wagen)* to venture, to attempt;

Ausflug ~ to go on an excursion; **zu viele Dinge gleichzeitig** ~ to have too many irons in the fire; **nichts** ~ to hold one's hand; **nichts gegen j.** ~ to take no action against s. o.; **Reise** ~ to make (go on, undertake) a journey; **Schritte** ~ to take action (steps); **Schritte bei der Regierung** ~ to approach the government; **Spaziergang** ~ to go for a walk; **Stützungsaktion** ~ *(Börse)* to rescue (hold) the market; **Werbekampagne** ~ to run an advertising campaign; **zur rechten Zeit** ~ to time.

unternehmend enterprising, speculative.
Unternehmens | analyse, vertriebs- und marktpolitische marketing audit; **~beherrschung durch Holdinggesellschaften** pyramiding; **~berater** management counsel(l)or (consultant, adviser), consultant on business policy, brain truster *(US)*, *(Personalberater)* executive recruiter *(US)*; **~beraterverband** Association of Executive Recruiting Consultants *(US)*; **~beratung** management consulting (consultancy), *(Firma)* management consulting firm, consulting organization, *(Personalberatungsfirma)* executive *(US)* (search) firm; **~beratungsgesellschaft** management consulting firm (organization); **~bereich** corporate sector; **~bericht** annual (directors') report; **~beteiligung** firm's participation; **~bewertung** operations audit, management appraisal; **~bilanz** corporate balance sheet, company statement; **~erfolg** corporate success *(US)*; **finanzielles ~ergebnis** cashflow; **~ertrag veranschlagen** to estimate the gains of an enterprise; **geplanter ~erwerb** acquisition planning; **~finanzierung** business finance, business (corporate) financing; **~form** form (type) of enterprise; **~formen des Handelsrechts** forms of business organization; **~forschung** operations *(US)* (operational, *Br.*) research.
Unternehmensführung business management;
unterste ~ junior management; **zielgesteuerte ~** management by results;
~ unter Krisenbedingungen crisis management.
Unternehmens | funktion function of enterprise; **~gewinn** profit from operations *(US)*, company's surplus, corporate profit *(US)*, equity earnings; **~größe** company size; **~gründungen im Ausland** establishment of enterprises abroad; **~gruppe** group of companies, entrepreneurial group; **der Führung einer immer breiter gefächerten ~gruppe gerecht werden** to manage increased diversity; **~haftung** enterprise liability; **~kapital** equity capital; **~konzentration** business concentration; **~leiter** corporate head *(US)*, manager; **~leitung** company's (top executive, *US*) management, managing board.
unternehmenslustig enterprising, go-getting, full of go.
Unternehmens | optimum firm optimum; **~planspiel** operational game, business game; **~planung** management (corporate) planning; **langfristige ~planung** corporate planning *(US)*; **~politik** company (operations, management, corporate) policy, management strategy; **~rentabilität** overall (operational) profitability; **~risiko** business risk; **~sektor** business sector; **~sitz** business situs, domicile of a corporation, commercial domicile, headquarters; **~spitze** top management *(US)*; **~strategie** corporate strategy *(US)*; **~struktur** corporate structure, structure of a business; **~verband** association of enterprises; **~verbindung** interlocking relationships; **~verflechtung** enterprise affiliation, interlocking of several undertakings; **~vertreter** management representative; **staatliche ~verwaltung** National Enterprise Board *(Br.)*; **~wachstum** corporate growth *(US)*; **~zusammenschluß** corporate (conglomerate) merger, pool, business (contract, *US*) combination; **~zuschuß** company contribution; **~zweck** object of an enterprise, business edge.
Unternehmer entrepreneur, contractor, industrialist, factory owner, manufacturer, undertaker *(Br.)*, operator *(US)*, runner *(US)*, black-coat *(sl.)*, *(Arbeitgeber)* principal, employer;
ausländischer ~ foreign contractor; **Risiko eingehender ~** capital venturer; **exportinteressierter ~** prospective exporter; **geschickter ~** engineer; **selbständiger (unabhängiger) ~** private trader, independent contractor (entrepreneur), self-employer;
~ und Arbeitnehmer employer and employed;
~ansicht proprietorial outlook; **~begabung** managerial talent; **~betrieb** entrepreneurial company; **~disposition** entrepreneurial disposition; **~eigenschaften** managerial (entrepreneurial) qualities, entrepreneurial skill (capacity, ability); **~einkommen** entrepreneurial income; **~einstellung** proprietorial attitude; **~entwicklung** managerial process; **~erfahrung** general management experience; **~fonds** employer fund; **~funktionen** managerial (entrepreneurial) functions; **~garantie** contract bond; **~gewinn** business profit, producer's rent, wages (earnings) of management, residual payment; **temporärer ~gewinn** quasi-rent; **freie ~grundsätze** free-enterprise policies; **~gruppe** entrepreneurial (employer) group.
Unternehmerhaftpflicht *(gegenüber Angestellten)* employer's liability, contractor's liability;
~gesetz Employers' Liability Act *(US)*; **~versicherung** employer's liability (workmens' compensation, *US*) insurance; **~- und Sachschadenversicherung** contractors' (manufacturers') public liability and property damage liability insurance.
Unternehmerhaftung employers' liability.
Unternehmerin woman executive.
Unternehmerinitiative industrial initiative.
unternehmerisch enterprising, managerial, managemental, entrepreneurial;
sein Geld ~ arbeiten lassen to embark one's capital in trade; **sehr ~ eingestellt sein** to be a man of great enterprise; **~ veranlagt sein** to be gifted with entrepreneurial spirit;
~e Aufgabe company task; **~e Begabung** entrepreneurial instinct, managerial talent; **~e Eigenschaften** entrepreneurial ability; **~e Erfahrung** management experience; **~e Fähigkeiten** managerial talent; **~ eingestellte Firma** enterprising business firm; **~e Funktion** entrepreneurial function; **~es Geschick bei der Planung, Aushandlung und Durchführung von Neuabschlüssen** proven entrepreneurial flair in planning, negotiating and managing new business; **~ eingestellte Persönlichkeit** enterprising personality; **~es Risiko** entrepreneurial (business) venture.
Unternehmer | kaution contract (guarantee) bond, master bond *(US)*; **~kreise** industrial circles; **~laufbahn** management career; **~lohn** wages (earnings) of management; **~organisation** employers' association, entrepreneurial organization; **langfristige ~politik** corporate strategic research; **~reingewinn** net earnings of management, pure profit; **~risiko** business (entrepreneurial, contractor's) risk, *(Feuerversicherung)* special hazard; **~schaft** entrepreneurship, employers; **~schicht** class of entrepreneurs, employer (entrepreneurial) class, business category; **~schule** management school; **~schulung** management training; **~standpunkt** attitude of the management; **~tätigkeit** entrepreneurial activity.
Unternehmertum management, managerial system, entrepreneurial class (management), entrepreneurship *(US)*;
freies ~ free-enterprise industry;
~ und Arbeiterschaft capital and labo(u)r;
~ in arbeitsrechtlichen Auseinandersetzungen vertreten to represent management in labo(u)r disputes.
Unternehmer | unfallversicherung employers' liability insurance, workmen's compensation insurance *(US)*; **~verband** contractor (employer's, entrepreneurial) association, trade association *(US)*; **~vertreter** employers' representative; **~vertretung** managerial representation; **~vorrechte** managerial prerogatives; **~wagnis** business hazard, entrepreneurial (business) risk; **~wirtschaft** entrepreneurial system, enterprise economy *(US)*; **freie ~wirtschaft** free-enterprise system, multiopoly; **~zusammenschluß** business combination, combine.
Unternehmung undertaking, enterprise;
gemeinschaftliche ~ concerted action; **geschäftliche ~** commercial (trading) operation; **gewagte ~** speculative enterprise, speculative (business) venture; **staatliche ~** publicly-owned (public service) enterprise;
~en des Baustoffsektors building material producers *(US)*; **sich in eine ~ einlassen** to embark in (on) a project.
Unternehmungs | geist vigorous enterprise, push, initiative, gumption, go, getup *(US)*, pep *(US)*, *(Unternehmer)* entrepreneurial spirit; **großen ~geist haben** to have large powers of initiative; **~lust** pep *(US)*, go.
unternehmungslustig enterprising, aggressive, full of go (pep, *US*), go-ahead, up-and-coming;
~er junger Mann go-at-it young man.
Unteroffizier corporal, noncommissioned officer, NCO;
dienstältester ~ colo(u)r sergeant;
~ vom Dienst duty noncommissioned officer, noncommissioned officer in charge of quarters *(US)*.
Unteroffiziersgrad enlisted grade *(US)*.
unterordnen, sich to subordinate o. s., *(nachgeben)* to submit.
Unter | ordnung subordination, subjection; **~ordnungsverhältnis** vassalage; **~organisation** subsidiary organization, offshoot; **~pacht** subtenancy, sublease; **~pächter** subtenant, undertenant, sublessee, underlessee, portioner; **~pariausgabe** inferior issue, issue below par; **~pariausgabe von Aktien** issue of shares at a discount.
unterpfählen to strengthen with piles.
Unterpfand pledge, deposit, gage *(Br.)*;
als ~ für einen Kredit dienen to be deposited as underlying security; **als ~ geben** to [put in] pledge.
Unterpflasterbahn underground tramway, subway.
unterpflügen to turn (plough) under.
Unterposition subitem.
unterpriviligiert underprivileged.
Unter | priviligierter underdog; **~programm** *(Computer)* subroutine; **~putzschalter** *(el.)* flush switch.

Unterredung conversation, conference, talk, interlocution, palaver, *(Presse)* interview;
persönliche (vertrauliche) ~ private conversation;
~ **auf 12 Uhr ansetzen** to schedule a conference for 12 o'clock; **um eine** ~ **ersuchen** to ask for an appointment; **mit j. eine persönliche (private)** ~ **führen** to talk to s. o. in private; **jem. eine** ~ **gewähren** to grant s. o. an interview; ~ **haben** to confer; **mit jem. eine geheime (vertrauliche)** ~ **haben** to be closeted with s. o.

Unterrepräsentation underrepresentation.

Unterricht instruction, tuition, *(Schule)* school, lessons;
vom ~ **befreit** exempted from classes; **während des** ~**es** during school hours;
obligatorischer ~ compulsory class attendance; **programmierter** ~ program(m)ed instruction; **weiterführender** ~ continuation schooling;
~ **im Freien** outdoor classes; ~ **in einer Fremdsprache** foreign-language teaching; ~ **am Krankenbett** bedside teaching; ~ **mit Lehrfilmen** audio-visual instruction; ~ **an der Universität** unversity teaching;
~ **von jem. erhalten** to draw lessons from s. o.; **jem.** ~ **erteilen** to tutor (teach, lesson) s. o.; ~ **fortsetzen** to proceed with the lessons; ~ **geben** to hold classes, to teach; **guten** ~ **geben** to teach well; ~ **haben** *(einzeln)* to coach; **täglich fünf Stunden** ~ **haben** to have five hours of classes daily; ~ **nehmen** to take lessons; **bei jem.** ~ **nehmen** to take lessons from s. o.; ~ **schwänzen** to play truant (hooky, *US*); ~ **stören** to disturb the class; **am** ~ **teilnehmen** to attend classes; ~ **in einer Klasse übernehmen** to take a class; **durch** ~ **Geld verdienen** to earn a living by teaching; ~ **versäumen** to miss (be absent from) classes; **sich für den** ~ **vorbereiten** to prepare one's lessons, to do one's prep *(coll.)*.

unterrichten to guide, to instruct, *(benachrichtigen)* to inform, to advise, to brief, *(Unterricht erteilen)* to instruct, to teach, to give lessons, to school, to train;
sich ~ to acquaint (orient, instruct) o. s.; **j. von etw.** ~ to inform (advise, notify) s. o. of (acquaint s. o. with) s. th.; **j. über seine beabsichtigte Abreise** ~ to inform s. o. of one's intended departure; **Englisch** ~ to teach English, to give English lessons; **falsch** ~ to misinform, to misdirect; **j. laufend** ~ to keep s. o. posted (informed, up-to-date); **Leser** ~ to inform the readers; **Polizei von etw.** ~ to notify the police of s. th.; **j. über die Rechtslage** ~ to advise s. o. on legal points; **sich über den Sachverhalt** ~ to acquaint o. s. with the facts; **an einer Schule** ~ to teach in a school; **Schulklasse** ~ to instruct a class.

unterrichtet, falsch wrongly informed; **glänzend** ~ wise *(sl.)*; **glaubhaft** ~ credibly informed; **gut** ~ well-informed, posted; **nicht** ~ unposted, not up to date;
von etw. nicht ~ **sein** to have no information as to (not to have heard of) s. th.;
~**e Kreise** informed quarters, insiders.

Unterrichts | anstalt educational establishment; **private** ~**anstalt** private venture college; ~**briefe** correspondence lessons; **über** ~**erfahrungen verfügen** to have experience of teaching; ~**fach** subject of teaching, teaching discipline; ~**film** educational (instructional) film; ~**gruppe** set; ~**klassen** tutorial classes; ~**kursus im Fernsehen** television course; ~**methoden** teaching techniques; ~**minister** President of the Board of Education *(Br.)*; ~**ministerium** Ministry of Education *(Br.)*, Office of Education *(US)*; ~**programm** educational training program(me), *(Privatschule)* prospectus; ~**raum** lecture (class) room, *(Betrieb)* lecture room; ~**sprache** language of instruction; ~**stoff** subject matter; **auf den** ~**stoff der letzten Stunde eingehen** to go back to the last lesson; ~**stunde** hour, lesson, lecture, class, session, period *(US)*; ~**stunde versäumen** to miss a lesson; ~**vorbereitung** preparation for teaching; ~**wesen** education; ~**zeit** schooltime; ~**ziel** teaching object.

Unterrichtung instruction, *(Benachrichtigung)* information, advice, briefing, notice;
ohne vorherige ~ without prior notice;
gegenseitige ~ exchange of information; **gemeinsame** ~ assembly; **persönliche** ~ personal notice; **rechtzeitige** ~ due notice; **vertrauliche** ~ restricted (confidential, inside) information, dope *(sl.)*, stable push *(sl.)*; **vorherige** ~ notice in advance;
~ **der Polizei** notification of the police; ~ **über ein beabsichtigtes Strafverfahren** notice of intended prosecution.

Unterrock, jedem ~ **nachlaufen** to be always after a petticoat.

untersagen to inhibit, to forbid, to prohibit, to bar, to ban, to interdict;
gerichtlich ~ to enjoin, to grant an injunction; **Handelsverkehr mit dem Ausland** ~ to interdict trade with foreign nations.

untersagt forbidden;
das Betreten des Fabrikgeländes ist strengstens ~ no trespassing on the factory premises.

Untersagung inhibition, prohibition, interdict, enjoinment *(US)*;
~ **der Berufsausübung** disqualification of a person for office.

Untersatz stand, mat;
fahrbaren ~ **haben** to be on wheels.

Unterschallgeschwindigkeit subsonic flight.

unterschätzen to underestimate, to undervalue, to underrate, to depreciate;
Feindstärke ~ to underestimate the enemy's strength; **Gegner** ~ to underrate an opponent; **Stadtbevölkerung** ~ to understate the population of a city.

Unterschätzung underestimate, undervaluation, underrating, understatement.

unterscheiden to differentiate, to distinguish, to discriminate, to discern;
sich ~ to differ; **sich auffallend wohltuend** ~ to do con-trastingly well; **zwischen Fahrlässigkeit und Vorsatz** ~ to discriminate between negligence and premeditation;
zwischen zwei verschiedenen Dingen wohl ~ **können** to know a hawk from a handsaw; **zwischen Gut und Böse** ~ **können** to discern good and evil.

unterscheidend discriminatory, discriminating;
~**es Merkmal** distinctive mark (feature).

Unterscheidung difference, differentiation, determination, discrimination;
feine ~ refined distinction; **klare** ~ sharp distinction; **spitzfindige** ~ distinction without a difference; **strenge** ~ curious discrimination; **subtile** ~ fine distinction; **übertriebene** ~**en** overnice distinctions;
~ **zwischen Recht und Unrecht** determination between right and wrong.

unterscheidungsfähig *(Warenzeichen)* distinctive;
~**es Alter** *(Strafrecht)* age of discretion.

Unterscheidungsfähigkeit *(Warenzeichen)* distinctiveness.

Unterscheidungs | marke distinctive mark; ~**merkmal** distinction, distinctive feature, differential, discriminative feature, criterion, difference; ~**vermögen** discrimination, discernment, faculty of discrimination, judicial faculty.

Unterschicht lower stratum.

unterschieben to substitute, *(Kind)* to father;
jem. etw. ~ to father (impute) s. th. on s. o.; **jem. falsche Beweggründe** ~ to attribute false motives to s. o.; **Testament** ~ to forge a will; **jds. Worten einen anderen Sinn** ~ to read another meaning into s. one's words.

Unterschiebung eines Kindes substitution of a child.

Unterschied difference, distinction, gulf, *(zwischen Brief und Geld)* jobber's turn, *(Temperatur)* variation;
mit dem ~, **daß** except for the fact that; **ohne** ~ by wholesale; **ohne** ~ **der Staatszugehörigkeit** regardless of nationality;
nur ein rein äußerlicher ~ leather and prunella; **bemerkenswerter** ~ notable difference; **entschiedener** ~ decided difference; **feiner** ~ minute difference, nice distinction; **geringfügiger** ~ tweedledum and tweedledee; **soziale** ~**e** social distinctions; **weltweiter** ~ world of difference;
~**e steuerlicher Art** disparities in tax systems; **große** ~**e in den Auffassungen zweier Staatsmänner** wide gaps between the views of two statesmen; ~ **zwischen Einkaufs- und Verkaufspreis** margin; ~ **in den Frachtsätzen** difference in rates; ~ **im Preis** difference in price; ~ **in der Qualität** difference in quality; **ein** ~ **wie Tag und Nacht** as different as chalk and cheese;
~ **ausgleichen** to make up the difference; **keinen** ~ **ausmachen** to make no difference; ~ **feststellen** to discriminate; ~ **machen** to differentiate, to draw a distinction, to difference; **haarfeinen** ~ **machen** to make a hairline distinction; **keinen** ~ **machen** to be all the same.

unterschiedlich discriminatory, differential, wide, varying;
Personen ~ **behandeln** to discriminate between persons;
~**e Behandlung** discriminating treatment; ~**e Berichterstattung** disparities in the newspaper accounts; ~**e Kosten** variable costs (expenses); ~**er Meinung mit jem. sein** to differ with s. o.; ~**e Preise** varying prices; ~**es Preisniveau** difference in price levels; ~**e Produktionskosten** difference in cost of production; ~**e Sätze** differential rates; ~**er Verbrauch** consumption differential; ~**e Warenqualität** varying quality of goods.

Unterschiedsbetrag difference;
~ **begleichen** to pay the balance.

unterschiedslos indiscriminate, undiscriminating, random;
~ **behandeln** to treat equally; ~ **gelten** to apply to all alike.

Unterschieds|losigkeit indiscrimination; ~**merkmal** distinguishing mark, earmark; ~**schwelle** difference threshold (limen).
unterschlagen to embezzle, to defalcate, to misappropriate, to defraud, to peculate;
Beweismaterial ~ to suppress evidence; **Brief** ~ to intercept a letter; **Gelder** ~ to misapply funds; **öffentliche Gelder** ~ to misappropriate public funds; **in seinem Lebenslauf etw.** ~ to suppress a fact in one's curriculum; **Mündelgelder** ~ to embezzle the funds of a ward; **Neuigkeiten** ~ to hold back news; **10.000 Pfund** ~ to make defalcations to the extent of £ 10.000; **Testament** ~ to suppress a will; **Vereinsgelder** ~ to misappropriate a society's funds.
Unterschlager öffentlicher Gelder defaulter of property entrusted.
Unterschlagung embezzlement, constructive (equitable) fraud, misappropriation, defraudation, fraudulent conversion, conversion to one's own use, defalcation, peculation, jobbery;
~ **im Amt** malversation, extortion in office, depeculation; ~ **von Bankgeldern** abstraction (embezzlement) of bank funds; ~ **von Beweismaterial** suppression of evidence; ~ **von Briefen** interception of letters; ~ **von Geldern** conversion of funds to one's own use, misuse of funds; ~ **öffentlicher Gelder** misappropriation of public funds; ~ **von Schiffsgut** plunderage; ~ **eines Testaments** suppression of a will;
große ~en begehen to embezzle a large sum; **jem. der ~ bezichtigen** to hold s. o. liable for conversion; **sich ~en zuschulden kommen lassen, sich der ~ schuldig machen** to peculate, to be guilty of conversion.
Unterschlagungs|fall case of embezzlement; ~**summe** defalcation, embezzlement.
Unterschleif peculation, abstraction, malversation, embezzlement;
~**e begehen** to misappropriate public funds.
Unterschlupf refuge, hiding place, cache, covert, harbo(u)r, tabernacle, recess;
~ **für Terroristen** terrorist hideout;
~ **bei jem. finden** to find shelter with s. o.; **einem Flüchtling ~ gewähren** to conceal a fugitive; **einem Verbrecher ~ gewähren** to give harbo(u)r to (harbo(u)r) a criminal;
~**gewährung** concealment of a criminal.
unterschreiben to sign [one's name], to undersign, to subscribe, to make one's mark, to affix (append) one's signature, to set one's hand to;
blanko ~ to sign in blank (a blank document); **eigenhändig** ~ to sign in one's own hand, to autograph; **kritiklos (routinemäßig)** ~ to sign on the dotted line; **mit einem falschen Namen** ~ to subscribe a false name; **mit vollem Namen** ~ to sign in full; **Urkunde** ~ to subscribe one's name to a document.
unterschreiten, Betrag to fall below an amount.
unterschrieben undersigned, signed;
eigenhändig ~ under one's signature, autographic; **nicht** ~ unsigned, unsubscribed; **ordnungsgemäß** ~ duly signed; **von mir** ~ given under my hand;
~ **und versiegelt** under hand and seal.
Unterschrift signature, hand, subscription;
~ **fehlt** signature missing; **zweite ~ fehlt** further signature required; **laut meiner** ~ witness my own hand, as witness our hands; **ohne** ~ unsigned; ~ **unbekannt** signature unknown; ~ **ungenau** signature differs; ~ **unvollständig** incompletely signed; **zur ~ bereitliegend** open for signature;
anwaltschaftliche ~ counsel's signature; **beglaubigte** ~ attested signature; **echte** ~ genuine signature; **eigenhändige** ~ idiographic signature, sign manual; **gefälschte** ~ forged (fictitious) signature; **gemeinsame** ~ joint (multiple) signature; **nachträgliche** ~ deferred signature; **namentliche** ~ sign manual;
~ **eines Analphabeten** mark signature; ~ **des Ausstellers** drawer's signature; ~ **ohne Bevollmächtigung** unauthorized signature; ~ **durch Handzeichen** signature by mark; ~ **per Prokura** procuration signature; ~ **und Siegel** hand and seal; ~ **als Stellvertreter** proxy signature; ~ **ohne Vertretungsmacht** unauthorized signature; ~ **in Vollmacht** signature by procuration;
seine ~ anerkennen to declare a paper signed by o. s., to acknowledge one's signature; **seine ~ nicht anerkennen** to go back on (disown, refuse to recognize) one's signature; ~ **avalieren** to stand security for a signature; ~ **beglaubigen** to attest the signature of a document, to verify (certify, attest, authenticate) a signature; **Echtheit einer ~ bestätigen** to confirm the authenticity of a signature; **[Rechts]gültigkeit seiner ~ bestreiten** to deny one's signature; ~ **unter einer Urkunde bezeugen** to be witness to a deed; **seine ~ dazusetzen** to add one's signature; **seine ~ einlösen** to hono(u)r one's signature; ~ **für gefälscht erklären** to pronounce the signature to be a forgery; ~ **fälschen** to counterfeit (forge) a signature; ~ **geben** to sign; ~**en sammeln** to round up (gather) signatures, to get up a petition; **mit jds. ~ versehen sein** to bear s. one's signature; **seine ~ unter einen Brief setzen** to sign one's name to a letter; **seine ~ unter eine Urkunde setzen** to append one's signature to a document; ~ **tragen** to bear a signature; **seine ~ verleugnen** to go back on one's signature; **Urkunde mit ~ versehen** to sign a document; **zur ~ vorlegen** to submit for signature; **jem. eine Verordnung zur ~ vorlegen** to submit a decree to s. o. for signature; **j. zu einer ~ zwingen** to force s. o. to sign a paper.
Unterschriften|fälschung forgery of signatures; ~**folge** *(dipl.)* alternate; ~**karthotek** signature card file; ~**liste** signature book; ~**mappe** blotting book, due-date portfolio; ~**probe** facsimile signature; ~**verzeichnis** list of authorized signatures, signatory list, signature book.
Unterschriftleiter subeditor.
Unterschrifts|befugnis authority (power) to sign; ~**beglaubigung** attestation (verification, certification, confirmation) of signature; ~**benachrichtigung** notification of signatures.
unterschriftsberechtigt authorized (entitled) to sign;
~ **sein** to be of a proper age to sign, *(für eine Firma)* to sign on behalf of a firm, to be authorized to sign, to have power to sign.
Unterschrifts|berechtigter authorized signer; ~**berechtigung** authority to sign; ~**bestätigung** confirmation of signature; ~**fälscher** forger of a signature; ~**fälschung** forgery of signature, forged (fictitious) signature; ~**folge** *(Völkerrecht)* alternate; ~**leistender** subscriber to a document; ~**leistung** signing a document, signature; ~**mappe** signature folder; ~**probe** sample signature, facsimile (specimen) signature; ~**recht** authority to sign.
unterschriftsreif open for signature.
Unterschrifts|stempel facsimile signature; ~**tisch** signing table; ~**verzeichnis** signature book, signatory list, *(Bank)* list of authorized signatures, autograph album (book).
Unterschriftsvollmacht authority (authorization, power) to sign, signing power;
beschränkte ~ limited authority to sign;
jem. eine ~ geben to authorize s. o. to sign; ~ **haben** to sign on behalf of a firm.
Unterschrifts|vorlage specimen signature; ~**zeuge** attesting (subscribing) witness, witness to a deed (document).
Unterschuß shortfall, deficit.
unterschwellige Werbung subliminal advertising.
Unterseeboot submarine.
Unterseeboots|begleitschiff submarine parent ship; ~**bunker** submarine pen; ~**dienst** silent service *(US)*; ~**stützpunkt** submarine base.
Unterseefrachter cargo submarine.
unterseeisch submarine, undersea.
Unterseekabel undersea (submarine) cable.
Unterspalte *(Kassenbuch)* subdivision.
unterspülen, Damm to wash away the embankment.
unterspült, vom Meer undermined by the sea.
Unterstaatssekretär deputy undersecretary *(Br.)*;
ständiger ~ permanent undersecretary.
Unterstaatssekretariat undersecretaryship.
Unterstand *(mil.)* helter, dugout, watch box, pillbox *(sl.)*, funk hole *(sl.)*;
bombensicherer ~ bunker;
~ **für Taxifahrer** taxi-driver's shelter.
Unterste zuoberst kehren, das to turn everything topsy-turvy.
unterste|Etage bottom floor; ~ **Gehaltsstufe** minimum salary level.
unterstehen, jem. to be responsible (subordinate) to s. o.; **der Aufsicht eines Vormunds** ~ to be in the charge of a guardian; **einer Gerichtsbarkeit** ~ to be subject to a jurisdiction; **dem Innenministerium** ~ to come within the purview of the Home Office *(Br.)*; **jem. unmittelbar** ~ to be directly responsible to s. o.; **unmittelbar dem Vorstand** to report directly to the board of directors;
sich ~, etw. zu tun to have the impudence (cheek) to do.
unterstellen to presume, to assume, to impute, to insinuate, *(mil.)* to put in charge of, *(unterordnen)* to subordinate, to assign, to put under s. one's command;
schlüssig ~ to presume conclusively; **als wahr** ~ to proceed on the footing that it is true.

Unterstellmöglichkeit carport.

unterstellt|sein to be subordinated to;
~e Führungskraft managerial subordinate.

Unterstellung assumption, presumption, suggestion, supposition, *(Anspielung)* insinuation, innuendo, suggestion, *(mil.)* assignment, *(Unterordnung)* subordination, assignment, *(Verdacht)* presumption, imputation;
~ zu jds. Gunsten presumption in favo(u)r of s. o.; **unmittelbare ~ unter den Vorstandsvorsitzenden** *(Anzeige)* responsibility will be to the general manager.

Unterstellungsverhältnis, unmittelbares direct-reporting agency system.

unterstreichen to underline, to emphasize, to stress, to score under, to underscore, to point up, to highlight.

Unterstreichung emphasis, stress.

Unter|strömung undercurrent, underset; **~stufe** *(Schule)* lower form (grade, *US*).

unterstützen to [give] support, to back, to help, to encourage, to shove [up], to bolster, to stand by, to upbear, to get behind *(sl.)*, *(befürworten)* to advocate, *(begünstigen)* to favo(u)r, to patronize, to patron, to nourish, *(fördern)* to further, to promote, to boost, to sponsor, *(helfen)* to assist, to aid, to aid and assist, *(mil.)* to back up, to reinforce, *(mit Strebepfeilern)* to buttress, *(Wohlfahrt)* to relieve, to grant relief;
j. ~ to hold up the hands of s. o.; **Ansicht ~** to endorse an opinion; **Antrag ~** to second (support, back, carry, speak in support of) a motion; **die Armen ~** to relieve the poor; **befürwortend ~** to endorse, to advocate; **Bewerber ~** to back (bolster, second, endorse) a candidate; **Entschließung ~** to support a resolution; **j. finanziell ~** to back s. o. financially, to aid s. o. with money; **Flüchtlinge ~** to provide relief for refugees; **sich gegenseitig ~** to join hands with s. o., to log-roll *(US)*; **Gesuch ~** to second a petition; **Kandidaten ~** to go in for (back up, boost, support, endorse) a candidate; **politische Partei finanziell ~** to support (sustain) a political party; **neubegründete politische Partei ~** to identify o. s. with a new political party; **Plan ~** to promote a scheme; **mit Rat und Tat ~** to advise and assist; **staatlich ~** to subventionize; **Unternehmen ~** to encourage an enterprise; **Vorschlag ~** to give support to a proposal, to second a vote, to be in favo(u)r of a proposal; **Vorschlag stark ~** to come out strongly for a proposition; **mit staatlichen Zuschüssen ~** to subsidize, to subventionize.

unterstützendes Beweismaterial collateral (secondary) evidence.

Unterstützer supporter, backer, countenancer, *(Antrag)* seconder;
~ eines Wahlvorschlags assentor *(Br.)*.

unterstützt upborne, upheld, supported;
durch Spenden ~ voluntary; **staatlich ~** government sponsored, administration-supported, state-fed, grant-aided, bounty-fed;
~ werden to obtain relief; **von jem. ~ werden** to find a warm supporter in s. o.; **finanziell ~ werden** to receive financial support.

Unterstützung support, help, backing, *(Arbeitslose)* unemployment benefit, dole *(Br.)*, *(Förderung)* furtherance, encouragement, patronization, boost, promotion, support, arm, *(Fürsorge)* relief, *(Hilfe)* assistance, aid, lift, *(Sozialversicherungsleistung)* benefit, *(Spende)* contribution, sign-up, *(Unterhaltungsgewährung)* maintenance, alimony;
auf Ihre ~ angewiesen depending on you for support; **auf die ~ von Freunden angewiesen** dependent upon friends; **auf städtische ~ angewiesen** on the parish (town, *US*); **mit kommunaler ~** rate-aided *(Br.)*; **mit ~ von** with the support of, *(Rundfunkprogramm)* presented by courtesy of; **mit ~ aus staatlichen Mitteln** state-aided, bountyfed; **ohne ~** unbacked, unhelped, *(Wohlfahrtsempfänger)* unaided, unrelieved; **zur ~ ihrer Ziele** in furtherance of your aims;
anstaltsinterne ~ institutional (indoor) relief *(Br.)*; **von der Gewerkschaft ausgehandelte ~** union benefit; **bar ausgezahlte ~** cash assistance; **fachliche ~** technical aid; **finanzielle ~** pecuniary assistance, financial help (backing, aid), accommodation, *(durch kommunale Stellen)* municipal aid; **gegenseitige ~** mutual aid (assistance), log-rolling *(US)*; **geldliche ~** pecuniary assistance; **von der Gemeinde gewährte (gemeindliche) ~** parish relief, community support; **kommunale ~** rate aid *(Br.)*, parish relief; **laue ~** lukewarm support; **mangelnde ~** lack of support; **moralische ~** countenance, booster; **öffentliche ~** pauper (poor) relief *(Br.)*, public welfare (aid, assistance), outdoor relief *(Br.)*, public relief *(US)*; **politische ~** en-dorsement, political backing; **schwache ~** infirm support; **staatliche ~** government support (backing, assistance, aid), governmental assistance, grant, subsidy, subsidizing, subvention, state-aid, *(für Kommunalaufgaben)* municipal support, grant-in-aid *(US)*, Exchequer equalization grant *(Br.)*; **tatkräftige ~** strong-arm treatment; **technische ~** technical aid; **vorläufige ~** interim relief; **vorübergehende ~** temporary relief; **werbliche ~** advertising support; **wesentliche ~** material support; **projektgebundene wirtschaftliche ~** tied aid; **zuerkannte ~** affirmative relief; **zusätzliche ~** additional benefit;
~ durch die Aktionäre shareholder (stockholder, *US*) support; **~ durch Anstaltsfürsorge** indoor (institutional, *Br.*) relief; **~ eines Antrags** seconding a motion; **~ durch Arbeiterstimmen im ganzen Land** labo(u)r's national support; **~ der Armen** contribution to the poor, pauper (poor) relief *(Br.)*; **staatliche ~ für die Beschäftigung von Kurzarbeitern** temporary employment subsidy; **~ eines Bewerbers** backing up of a candidate; **~ für Familien mit abhängigen Familienangehörigen** aid to families with dependent children; **~ der obersten Führungskräfte durch Arbeitnehmervertreter** multiple management; **~ nicht im Armenhaus untergebrachter Fürsorgeempfänger** outdoor-relief *(Br.)*; **~ eines Gesetzentwurfes** backing (endorsement) of a bill; **werbliche ~ des Händlers** dealer-aid advertising; **~ der Industrie** encouragement of industry; **~ aus dem konservativen Lager** grassroots support; **~ durch die Luftwaffe** air support; **~ der Minderheit** minority support; **~ in Notfällen** emergency support; **staatliche ~ bei durch Dürre verursachten Notfällen** emergency drought assistance; **~ durch Öffentlichkeitsarbeit** public-relations support; **~ beider Parteien** bipartisan support; **~ von seiten der Regierung** government support; **~ durch die Werbewirtschaft** advertiser support; **~ aus Wirtschaftskreisen** business support; **~ bei der Wohnungsbeschaffung** subsidized housing;
j. um ~ angehen to call upon s. o. to give assistance; **seine Freunde um finanzielle ~ angehen** to lay one's friends under contribution; **sich um ~ bemühen** to gun for support *(US)*; **~ beziehen (erhalten)** to obtain (receive) state relief, to be (go) on the parish (town, *US*), to receive aid from a public poor fund, to be on relief, *(Arbeitsloser)* to draw unemployment benefit *(Br.)*, to receive unemployment compensation *(US)*, to be on (draw) the dole *(Br.)*; **j. um ~ bitten** to ask s. o. for a service; **~ für den Pfundkurs durchführen** to support the sterling rate of exchange; **~ einstellen** to pull the plug *(sl.)*; **~ empfangen** to go on relief rolls *(US)*; **minimale ~ erzielen** to obtain (pressgang) minimal support; **Geld zur ~ für Sozialfälle geben** to spend money in alms; **allgemeine ~ genießen** to enjoy popular support; **~ gewähren** to grant relief, to lend one's aid to, to ante *(sl.)*; **finanzielle ~ gewähren** to extend pecuniary assistance; **j. zur ~ heranziehen** to enlist the services of s. o.; **mit der vollen ~ eines Ausschusses rechnen können** to be solid with a committee; **jem. seine ~ angedeihen lassen** to lend countenance to s. o., to give s. o. a leg up; **einem Unternehmen seine ~ angedeihen lassen** to confer one's patronage upon an undertaking; **dem Roten Kreuz eine ~ zukommen lassen** to contribute to the Red Cross; **der Exportwirtschaft jedmögliche ~ zuteil werden lassen** to shore up export industries; **von ~en leben** to live on alms; **von staatlicher ~ leben** to live off government aid (assistance); **auf ~en angewiesen sein** to be dependent on alms; **auf jds. ~ angewiesen sein** to be dependent upon s. o. for support; **auf öffentliche ~ angewiesen sein** to be thrown upon the parish (on the town, *US*), to be a public charge; **auf die ~ seines Sohnes angewiesen sein** to be dependent on one's son's earnings; **sich zur ~ verpflichten** to pledge one's support; **durch ~en unterhalten werden** to be supported by voluntary contributions.

Unterstützungs|angebot offer of assistance; **~anspruch** *(Angehöriger)* right of support, *(Fürsorgeempfänger)* claim for benefit; **~ansprüche haben** to have a right of support; **~ansprüche stellen** to claim benefit; **~arbeiten** contributory labo(u)r; **~aufwendungen** relief expenditure.

unterstützungsbedürftig in need of assistance (relief), needy, indigent, poor;
~ machen to pauperize; **~ werden** to require relief, to come on the parish, to fall upon the town *(US)*.

Unterstützungsbedürftiger pauper, rate-aided person *(Br.)*.

unterstützungsberechtigt eligible for (entitled to) relief, relievable.

Unterstützungs|berechtigter welfare beneficiary, pauper *(US)*, rate-aided person *(Br.)*; **nicht ortsansässiger ~berechtigter** casual *(Br.)*, casual pauper *(US)*; **~berechtigter einer Versorgungsstiftung** beneficiary of a provident fund; **~berechtigung** entitlement to benefit, *(öffentlich)* eligibility for relief; **~bescheinigung** relief ticket; **kleiner ~betrag** small sum for relief; ~**einrichtung** welfare centre *(Br.)* (center, *US*), *(Betrieb)* pension fund; ~**empfänger** pauper *(US)*, welfare beneficiary, recipient of relief, taxeater, rate-aided person *(Br.)*; **alleinstehender ~empfänger** outpensioner; **vorübergehender ~empfänger** casual *(Br.)*, casual pauper *(US)*; ~**fall** *(Angelegenheit)* case, *(Empfänger)* public charge; ~**fonds** aid (sustention, benefit, benevolent, provident, subsidy) fund, alimentary trust, protective trust *(US)*, *(Fürsorge)* relief (welfare) fund; ~**fonds für die Belegschaft** staff provident fund; ~**fonds ausstatten** to allocate a poor fund; ~**formel** grant formula; ~**gelder** subsidies, subventions; ~**genossenschaft** benefit company *(Br.)*; ~**gesuch** application for relief; ~**höhe** level of relief.

Unterstützungskasse provident (benevolent, charity) fund, friendly society *(US)*, *(Fürsorge)* relief (poor, welfare) fund; **betriebliche** ~ staff provident fund; **Pensions- und** ~ pension trust;
~ **auf Gegenseitigkeit** mutual relief association.

Unterstützungs|käufe *(Börse)* support buying, supporting purchases; ~**konto** benevolent account; ~**kürzung** benefit cut.

Unterstützungsleistung benefit, grant;
~**en** *(Fürsorge)* public-aid benefits, *(Sozialversicherung)* social security benefits *(Br.)*, public assistance benefits *(US)*, subsistence benefits, benefit payments;
erneute ~ resumption of a grant; **festgesetzte** ~ definite benefit; **in Fortfall gekommene** ~ forfeited benefit; **lohnabhängige** ~ wage-related benefit.

Unterstützungs|normen, bundeseinheitlich festgelegte national basic standards of relief *(Br.)*; ~**periode** benefit period; ~**pflicht** legal obligation to support; ~**plan** *(Fürsorge)* relief plan, welfare system; ~**programm** aid (relief) program(me), *(Fürsorge)* welfare program(me); **ausländisches ~programm** foreign aid program *(US)*; **staatliches ~programm** state-aided program(me); ~**satz** benefit rate, rate of benefit; **normale ~sätze** *(öffentliche Fürsorge)* relief standards *(Br.)*; ~**scheck** benefit check *(US)* (cheque, *Br.*); ~**schema für die Zahlung von Kurzarbeiterzuschüssen** temporary employment subsidy scheme *(Br.)*; ~**stelle** relief office; ~**suchender** applicant for relief, relief applicant; ~**summe** grant, allowance, *(Betriebsunfall)* compensation; ~**system** system of support, *(Fürsorge)* relief (welfare) system; ~**umfang** scale of benefits; ~**unterlagen** case history; ~**verband** welfare association, poor law parish *(Br.)*; ~**verein** benevolent association (society, *Br.*), benefit company (society) *(Br.)*, relief association, provident (friendly) society *(Br.)*, benefit club *(Br.)*, slate club *(Br.)*; ~**verein auf Gegenseitigkeit** mutual (provident, *Br.*) society; ~**verpflichtungen** compulsory support commitments; ~**voraussetzungen** qualifications for benefit; ~**wohnsitz** social settlement.

unterstützungswürdig worthy of support.

Unterstützungszahlungen maintenance payments, grants, allowances, transfer payments *(US)*, *(Fürsorge)* relief payments, *(Sozialversicherung)* benefit payments, *(Wohltätigkeit)* charitable contributions;
~ **aus öffentlichen Mitteln** social security payments; ~ **im Todesfall** death benefit.

Unterstützungs|zeitraum benefit period, *(Betriebsunfall)* compensation period; ~**zusage** promise of help; ~**zustand** pauperdom, pauperage; ~**zweck** welfare purpose.

untersuchen to investigate, to inspect, to examine, to test, to go over, to go (inquire, look) into, to explore, *(durchsuchen)* to search, *(nachprüfen)* to verify, to check;
Angelegenheit ~ to inquire into a matter; **Außenhandel eines Landes** ~ to make a study of a country's foreign trade; **Auto auf seine Verkehrssicherheit** ~ to test a car for road safety; **Eigentumsverhältnisse einer Gesellschaft** ~ to investigate ownership of a company; **etw. eingehend** ~ to examine closely, to give s. th. a close examination; **Fall** ~ to make an inquiry into a case; **Fall nochmals** ~ to retry a case; **Fingerabdrücke** ~ to check fingerprints; **Gebäude** ~ to examine a building; **genau** ~ to scrutinize, to bolt out, to test; **Gepäck** ~ *(Zoll)* to search the luggage; **etw. gründlich** ~ to look into the inside of s. th., to examine a matter; **Ursachen eines Eisenbahnunglücks** ~ to investigate the causes of a railway accident; **Verbrechen** ~ to inquire into a crime; **zollamtlich** ~ to inspect, to jerque *(Br.)*; **sich ärztlich** ~ **lassen** to undergo a medical examination, to have a medical checkup.

Untersuchung investigation, inquiry, inspection, quest, *(Abhandlung)* treatise, paper, *(Forschung)* exploration, research, *(Leichenschau)* inquest, *(Prüfung)* examination, *(techn.)* testing, test, overhauling, *(Übersicht)* survey;
bei näherer ~ upon investigation;
amtliche ~ official (public, *Br.*) inquiry; **amtsärztliche** ~ medical inspection; **analytische** ~ analytical investigation; **brieflich angestellte** ~ mail survey *(US)*; **ärztliche** ~ physical (medical) examination, *(mil.)* medical *(sl.)*; **ausgedehnte ~en** extensive inquiries (researches); **betriebswissenschaftliche** ~ industrial research; **demoskopische** ~ field research, public opinion poll; **eingehende** ~ close investigation (examination), close-up, scrutiny, *(ärztlich)* checkup *(US)*; **sich über Jahre erstreckende ~en** inquiries extending over several years; **förmliche** ~ formal inquiry; **genaue** ~ curious investigation, scrutiny, test, research; **gerichtliche** ~ judicial inquiry, judicial investigation, inquisition; **gründliche** ~ close investigation, canvass, scrutiny, overhaul, general checkup *(US)*; **inoffizielle** ~ informal investigation; **kriminalpolizeiliche** ~ criminal investigation; **minutiöse** ~ minute examination; **oberflächliche** ~ cursory inspection; **öffentliche** ~ public examination (enquiry); **parlamentarische** ~ parliamentary inquiry; **polizeiliche** ~ police investigation; **psychiatrische** ~ psychiatric examination; **sorgfältige** ~ sifting; **äußerst sorgfältige** ~ hard-nosed scrutiny; **sorgsame** ~ field survey, study; **statistische ~en** statistical enquiries; **stichprobenartige** ~ accidental sampling; **systematische** ~ systematic investigation; **umfassende** ~ extensive inquiry; **wissenschaftliche** ~ scientific research (investigation), study; **zollamtliche** ~ customs examination.

Untersuchungs|beamter inquisitor, scrutator; **von der Regierung eingesetzter ~beamter** government investigator; ~**befehl** search warrant; ~**befund** examination report; ~**bericht** investigating (research) report; ~**bericht des Innenministeriums** Home Office inquiry; **kleinste ~einheit** *(Statistik)* elementary unit.

Untersuchungsergebnis findings [of a commission], report of inquiry, result of an investigation, test result;
amtliches ~ findings of an official report; **tabellenmäßig zu erfassendes** ~ quantitative survey;
seine ~se veröffentlichen to publish one's observations.

Untersuchungs|fall investigatory matter; ~**gefangener** person arrested (remanded in custody, detained for hearing, *US*), remand prisoner *(Br.)*, prisoner on remand *(Br.)*; **nicht vor Gericht gestellter ~gefangener** detention-without-trial prisoner; ~**gefangenen vorführen** to produce a prisoner; ~**gefängnis** remand prison, jail *(US)*, house of detention, goal, lockup *(US)*, tank *(sl.)*; ~**gegenstand** subject under investigation; ~**gericht** court of law, *(Geschworenengericht)* coroner's court; ~**grundsatz** inquisitorial system; ~**gruppe** research team.

Untersuchungshaft custody, detention of remand *(Br.)*, pre-trial detention *(US)*, imprisonment before (detention pending) trial;
in ~ detained for trial, remanded in custody;
dreimonatige ~ **absitzen** to be kept three months in prison awaiting trial; **sich in** ~ **befinden** to be held in custody; **in** ~ **behalten** to detain in custody; **in** ~ **bleiben** to be remanded in custody; **in** ~ **nehmen** to keep in custody until trial; **in** ~ **sein** to be imprisoned, to be on remand *(Br.)*; ~ **für eine Woche verlängern** to remand for a week; **aus der** ~ **vorgeführt werden** to be brought up on remand, to come out *(Br.)*; **in die** ~ **zurückschicken** to remand.

Untersuchungs|häftling detainee, remand prisoner *(Br.)*, prisoner on remand *(Br.)*, person detained for hearing *(US)*; ~**kommission** board of inquiry, fact-finding committee, commission (court) of inquiry; ~**kommission bilden** to form a commission for the purpose of investigation; ~**kosten** investigation costs; ~**methoden** research methods, methods of investigation; ~**protokoll** inquisition; ~**recht** *(auf hoher See)* [right of] search; ~**richter** committing (examining, investigating) magistrate, examining judge, inquisitor; ~**stab** research staff, investigatory force; **sich im ~stadium befinden** to be under investigation; ~**tätigkeit** investigating activity, investigations, investigative work; ~**verfahren** investigative process; ~**zimmer** *(Arzt)* examination room.

Untertage|arbeit underground work; ~**arbeiter** underground worker; ~**bau** underground mining (working); ~**streik** stay-down strike *(Br.)*.

Untertan subject, vassal;
britischer ~ British subject, subject to Britain; **eingebürgerter britischer** ~ naturalized British subject; **treuer (treu ergebener)** ~ loyal (devoted) subject.

untertan, sich j. ~ **machen** to subjugate s. o.; **jem.** ~ **sein** to be dependent on (subordinate to) s. o.

untertarifieren to underrate.

untertariflich below agreed wages;
~**er Lohn** subminimum wage.

untertauchen to dip, to dive, *(U-Boot)* to submerge;
im Straßengewühl ~ to dive into the streets; **zeitweilig** ~ to keep close for a while, to go bush.
unterteilen to subdivide, *(untergliedern)* to classify, to group;
statistisch ~ to break down.
Unterteilung subdivision, *(Statistik)* breakdown;
~ **in Sachgebiete** subject heading.
Untertitel catch title, subtitle, subheading.
Unterton undertone, undersong;
humorvollen ~ **haben** to have a thread of humo(u)r; **mit warnendem** ~ **sprechen** to sound a note of warning.
untertreiben to understate.
Untertreibung understatement.
untertunneln to tunnel.
Unter|überschrift subhead; ~**verband** local association, subassociation.
unterverfrachten to subcharter, to underfreight.
Unter|verfrachter underfreighter; ~**verkauf** subsale; ~**vermieten** subletting, underletting.
untervermieten to sublease, to sublet, to underlet, to underlease, to underrent.
Unter|vermieter sublessor, subletter, undertenant, underlessor; ~**vermieterverhältnis** undertenancy; ~**vermietung** sublease; ~**vermietungsrecht** right to sublet.
unterverpachten to underlet, to underlease, to sublet.
Unter|verpächter underlessor; ~**verpachtung** subleasing.
unterverpfänden to submortgage.
Unterverpfändung submortgage.
unter|versichern to underinsure; ~**versichert** underinsured.
Unterversicherung underinsurance.
Unterversicherungs|beteiligung subunderwriting commission; ~**klausel** standard average clause; ~**provision** subunderwriting commission.
Unter|vertrag subsidiary contract; ~**vertreter** subagent, underagent; ~**vertretung** subagency; ~**vollmacht** substitute power, subagency; ~**vollmacht erteilen** to delegate power (authority); ~**wanderer** plant *(Br., sl.)*.
unterwandern *(pol.)* to infiltrate;
Organisation ~ to infiltrate an organization.
Unter|wanderung einer Organisation infiltration of an organization; ~**wäsche** underwear, underclothes.
Unterwasser|fahrt *(U-Boot)* dive; ~**horchgerät** hydrophone; ~**jagd** underwater hunting; ~**kabel** subfluvial cable; ~**kurhotel** underwater resort hotel; ~**langstreckengeschoß** undersea long-range missile (ULM); ~**leitung** submarine conveyance *(el.)*; ~**ortungsgerät** sonar; ~**ortungssystem** submarine tracking system; ~**streitkräfte** submarine forces; ~**torpedo** subsurface torpedo; ~**tragflügel** submerged wing.
unterwegs on the way (go, *US*), *(Güter)* in transit, *(Schiff)* under way, *(Vertreter)* on tour, en route;
geschäftlich ~ on the road; **immer** ~ always on the move; **nach A** ~ *(Schiff)* bound for A;
j. ~ **absetzen** to drop s. o. on the way; ~ **anhalten** to stop in transit; ~ **sein** *(Reisender)* to be on the road (en route), *(Schiff)* to have way on, *(ganze Stadt)* to be up and about; **geschäftlich** ~ **sein** to travel on business; **aus beruflichen Gründen oder geschäftlich** ~ **sein** to travel for genuine business or professional reasons; **Drittel des Jahres** ~ **sein** to be on the road about a third of the time; **laufend** ~ **sein** to be always on the go; **pausenlos (ständig)** ~ **sein** to be on a merry-go-round, to live in the street; **in Scharen** ~ **sein** to be out in full force; **ganzen Tag** ~ **gewesen sein** to have been on all one's legs all day; ~ **verlorengegangen sein** to be lost in transit.
Unterwegskosten charges en route.
unterweisen to instruct, to direct, to indoctrinate, to brief, to train, to teach.
Unterweisung training, notice, direction, indoctrination, instruction, briefing, training.
Unterwelt underworld, the swell mob, gangsters *(US)*, gangland.
unterwerfen to subjugate, to prostrate, to subject, *(mil.)* to reduce;
sich ~ to yield submission, to submit, to knuckle under; **sich Bedingungen** ~ to submit to conditions; **sich einem Schiedsgericht** ~ to submit to arbitration; **sich einem Schiedsspruch** ~ to abide by an award; **wilde Stämme** ~ to subdue wild tribes; **sich den Verfahrensregeln** ~ to comply with the rules; **Waren einer genauen Untersuchung** ~ to submit goods to a careful examination; **der Zensur** ~ to submit to censorship.
Unterwerfung subjection, subjugation, prostration, surrender, conquest, yoke, *(sich unterwerfen)* lying down, acquiescence;
~ **unter ein Schiedsgericht** submission to arbitration.
Unterwerfungs|erklärung *(Schuldner)* statement of confession; ~**klausel** cognovit clause *(US)*, *(Hypothekenbrief)* sharp clause; ~**schuldschein** judgment note.
unterwertige Güter inferior goods.
unterworfen subject to, liable, *(Land)* subdued;
dem Gesetz ~ amenable to the law; **Kursschwankungen** ~ subject to price fluctuations;
der Mode ~ **sein** to be subject to changes in fashion; **der Zuständigkeit eines Gesetzes** ~ **sein** to come within the jurisdiction of a court.
unterwürfig obedient, subservient, submissive, cringing, servile;
~ **sein** to crawl, to stoop;
~**er Mensch** underling, servile person.
Unterwürfigkeit subservience, servility, cringingness, conformation.
unterzeichnen to sign, to undersign, to subscribe, *(Versicherungspolice)* to underwrite;
blanko ~ to sign in blank; **mit einem Kreuz** ~ to sign by a mark; **mit einem falschen Namen** ~ to subscribe a false name; **Notariatsvertrag** ~ to sign a legal agreement; **Urkunde** ~ to subscribe one's name to a document; **Vertrag** ~ to sign an agreement, *(pol.)* to ratify a contract.
Unterzeichner signer, signatory, *(Anleihe)* subscriber, *(Effektenemission)* underwriter;
~ **eines Vertrages** signatory to an agreement;
~**regierung** signatory government; ~**staat** signatory power (state), signatory *(Br.)*.
unterzeichnet undersigned, signed, subscribed;
~ **von** under the hand of; **von mir** ~ witness my hand;
~ **und gesiegelt** signed and delivered (sealed).
Unterzeichneter undersigned.
Unterzeichnung signing, signature, *(Anleihe)* subscription, *(Ratifikation)* ratification;
nachträgliche ~ deferred signature;
~ **eines Grundstücksvertrages** real-estate closing; ~ **einer Urkunde** execution of a deed; ~ **durch einen bevollmächtigten Vertreter** signature by an authorized representative;
zur ~ **ausliegen** to be open for signature (to subscription).
unterziehen, einer Besichtigung to subject to an examination; **einer Bewertung** ~ to value, to make an estimate; **Geschäfte einer Gesellschaft einer Nachprüfung** ~ to investigate the affairs of a company; **sich einer Kur** ~ to undergo a cure; **Maschine einer sorgfältigen Überholung** ~ to subject a machine to a careful overhaul; **einer Nachprüfung** ~ to reexamine; **sich einer Operation** ~ to undergo an operation; **sich einer Prüfung** ~ to go in for (undergo) an examination; **j. einer Prüfung** ~ to subject s. o. to an examination; **sich einer Sache** ~ to go in for s. th.; **sich einer völligen Umwandlung** ~ to go into the melting pot; **Ware einer sorgfältigen Überprüfung** ~ to submit goods to a careful examination; **Zeugen einem Verhör** ~ to question (interrogate) a witness.
unterzubringen, schwer *(Wechsel)* difficult to negotiate.
Untiefe port bar, shallows, shoal;
voller ~**n** shoaly.
untilgbar *(Anleihe)* irredeemable, unsinkable, *(Rente)* perpetual, permanent.
untragbar unbearable, intolerable;
~**e Kosten** prohibitive costs; ~**e Preise** prohibitive prices; ~**e Steuern** prohibitive taxes.
untrennbar inseparable, *(Koupon)* nondetachable.
untreu disloyal, derelict *(US)*, unfaithful;
seiner Frau ~ **sein** to be unfaithful to one's wife.
Untreue dishonesty, misapplication, fraud in law, infidelity, unfaithfulness, *(im Amt)* malpractice, *(Betrug)* constructive (equitable, legal) fraud, fraudulent breach of trust, misfeasance;
~ **begehen** to embezzle;
~**versicherung** surety insurance.
Untüchtigkeit unfitness, incapacity.
Untugend, sich eine ~ **abgewöhnen** to break a bad habit.
ununlich inexpedient, unfeasible, not feasible, impracticable.
Untunlichkeit von Steuererhebungen inexpediency of raising taxes.
un|überbrückbare Gegensätze irreconcilable differences; ~**überdachter Zuschauersitz** open stand, bleachers *(US)*; ~**überlegt** indeliberate, unweighted, unpremeditated, imprudent, impolitical; ~**übersehbarer Fehler** obvious mistake; ~**übersehbarer Schaden** incalculable loss.
unübersetzbar not translatable, untranslatable.
unübersichtlich unclear, obscure;
~**e Kurve** blind curve.

unübertragbar unassignable, inalienable, nontransferable, intransferable, *(auf den Namen lautend)* registered, *(Wertpapier)* nonnegotiable.
Unübertragbarkeit inalienability, unassignability, *(Wertpapiere)* nonnegotiability.
un|übertroffen unmatched, unparalleled, matchless; **~überwindlich** insurmountable.
unumgänglich indispensable, inevitable, imperative, material, unavoidable, material;
~e Klausel iron-clad clause.
Unumgänglichkeit absolute necessity.
unumschränkt full, without restraint, dictatorial, *(pol.)* absolute, autocratic;
~er Eigentümer absolute owner.
unumstößlich unalterable, inalterable, irrevocable;
~es Urteil irrevocable judgment.
unumstritten undisputed.
ununterbrochen without a break (interruption), ininterrupted, uninterrupted, continuous, endless, *(Besitzdauer)* unbroken;
~ geregnet haben to have been raining without a let-up; **~ reden** to talk nineteen to the dozen.
un|unterrichtet uninformed; **~unterschrieben** unsigned, not signed, unsubscribed.
unveränderlich invariable, stable, fixed, constant, eternal, *(Börse)* firm;
~e Kosten constant costs.
unverändert unaltered, unmodified, stationary, stable, *(Börse)* firm, unchanged, *(Kranker)* unimproved;
~ annehmen to adopt as it stands; **~ bleiben** to remain stationary; **fast ~ bleiben** *(Börse)* to mark time; **ziemlich ~ schließen** *(Börse)* to leave off without material alteration; **~ sein** *(Börse)* to be unchanged (without alteration);
~er Preis unchanged price.
un|verantwortlich irresponsible; **~verarbeitet** raw, crude, unmanufactured, unwrought, unfinished, in the native state, unprocessed *(US)*, *(fig.)* undigested.
unverausgabt unexpended, unspent;
~er Rest unspent rest.
unveräußerlich inalienable, unsalable, *(Grundbesitz)* in mortmain, entailed.
Unveräußerlichkeit inalienability, unsalableness.
Unveräußerlichkeits|verfügung *(Grundstück)* perpetuity; **~zeitraum** *(Grundstück)* perpetuity period.
unverbaubare Sicht unobstructed view.
unverbesserlich incorrigible, tough, vicious, incurable;
~er Optimist incorrigible optimist.
unverbessert uncorrected.
unverbindlich not binding, unaccommodating, without obligation, naked, without any commitment (engagement), *(kühl)* detached, noncommittal *(US)*;
~e Besichtigung free inspection; **~er Preis, ~es Preisangebot** prices subject to alteration, prices without commitment.
Unverbindlichkeit noncommitment.
unverblümt straight from the shoulder, blunt, in plain English, plump *(coll.)*;
~ reden to be very outspoken, to use plain language; **~ sagen** to plump; **ganz ~ mit jem. sprechen** to say hard things to s. o.; **~ mit jem. umgehen** to pick s. o. up sharply;
~e Antwort round answer.
un|verborgen unhidden, *(Fehler)* patent; **~verbraucht** unused, *(Kredit)* unconsumed; **~verbrieft** unchartered, *(Kredit)* unsecured.
unverbrüchlich steadfast, staunch, unswerving;
~ festhalten to stick to s. th.
un|verbürgt unwarranted, unauthenticated, unconfirmed; **~verdächtig** unsuspected; **~verdauliche Lektüre** indigestible reading; **~verdaut** undigested.
unverdient undeserved, unmerited, unearned, fluky *(sl.)*;
~es Lob unearned praise; **~er Wertzuwachs** unearned increment.
un|verdorben *(Fleisch)* free from taint, *(Lebensmittel)* untainted, *(Wasser)* unpolluted; **~verdrossen** untiring, unflagging; **~verdünnt** undiluted, *(Alkohol)* unwatered, neat; **~veredelt** unimproved; **~verehelicht** single, spouseless, unmarried; **~vereidigt** unsworn.
unvereinbar inconsistent, contradictory, repugnant, incompatible, irreconcilable, dissociable, incongruous, *(mit den eigenen Ansprüchen)* averse;
~ mit der Verfassung repugnant to constitutional law;
~ sein to clash;
~e Interessen incompatible interests.
Unvereinbarkeit incompatibility, contradiction, repugnancy, incompatibility, incongruity, inconsistency, contrariety, disparity;
~ von Interessen clash of interests; **~ von Zeitungsberichten über einen Unfall** disparities in the newspaper accounts of an accident.
unvererblich not inheritable.
Unverfallbarkeit nonforfeiture.
un|verfälscht sterling, good, genuine, undiluted, unmingled, unadulterated, undebased; **~verfänglich** harmless, straight-forward, noncommittal, plausible; **~verfolgbar** unenforceable.
unverfroren bold, outspoken, *(frech)* saucy, cheeky, fresh *(US)*, brazen-faced;
so ~ sein to have the neck *(sl.)*;
~er Bursche brazen-face, cheeky brat *(coll.)*.
Unverfrorenheit impudence, nerve *(coll.)*, neck;
etw. mit größter ~ vertreten to face it out.
un|vergänglich imperishable, undying, unfading, immortal; **~vergeßlich** unforgettable; **~verglast** unglazed.
unvergleichlich incomparable, matchless, unparallel(l)ed;
sich ~ besser fühlen to feel definetely better; **~ schön sein** to be of matchless beauty;
~es Ansehen unrival(l)ed reputation; **~e Möglichkeiten** incomparable possibilities.
unverhältnismäßig disproportionate, out of proportion, unequal;
~ klein extremely small;
~ hoher Preis excessive (exorbitant) price; **~ hohe Spesen** excessive costs.
Unverhältnismäßigkeit disproportion, disparity.
unverheiratet single, unmarried, *(Frau)* sole, discovert;
~e Tante maiden aunt.
Unverheiratet|e spinster; **~er** unmarried person, bachelor.
unverhofft unexpected, unforeseen;
~es Glück unhoped for piece of good fortune.
unverhohlen unveiled, unconcealed, *(freimütig)* candid;
jem. ~ seine Meinung sagen to give s. o. a good piece of one's mind.
unverhüllt undisguised, unveiled, unshrouded.
unverjährbar imprescriptible, not subject to the statute of limitations;
~er Anspruch indefeasible title.
unverjährt still valid, not barred by the statute of limitations.
unverkäuflich unsalable, unmarketable, unrealizable, unmerchantable, not merchantable, *(nicht zu verkaufen)* not for sale (to be sold);
~e Ladenhüter drug on (in) the market; **~e Ware** dead stock (commodities).
Unverkäuflichkeit unsalableness, unsalability.
unverkauft unsold, undisposed, unbought, remaining;
~ bleiben to remain on hand (unsold, on the shelf); **~ bei jem. liegenbleiben** to lie on s. one's hands;
~e Exemplare unsold copies.
un|verkennbar unmistakable, obvious; **~verkürzt** uncurtailed, unabbreviated, *(ohne Abzug)* without reduction, *(Text)* unabbreviated, unabridged; **~verladen geblieben** short-shipped.
unverlangt|es Manuskript unsolicited manuscript; **~e Reklame** unsolicited advertisement.
unverletzt unhurt, uninjured, unscathed, safe, *(Siegel)* unbroken.
Unverletzbarkeit, persönliche personal inviolability.
unverletzlich sacrosanct, inviolable, sacred.
Unverletzlichkeit immunity, *(Diplomat)* inviolability;
~ des Bankgeheimnisses inviolability of bank secrecy; **~ des Gesandtschaftsgebäudes** *(Völkerrecht)* franchise de l'hotel.
un|verletzt unhurt, uninjured, unscathed, intact; **~verlost** unallotted.
un|vermeidbar, ~vermeidlich inevitable, unavoidable, fortuitous;
~es Ereignis inevitable (unavoidable) casualty; **~e Katastrophe** unpreventable catastrophe; **~e Risiken** unavoidable hazards;
~er Unfall unavoidable accident.
Unvermeidbares, sich in ~ fügen to resign o. s. to the inevitable.
un|vermengt unmingled; **~vermietbar** untenantable; **~vermietet** untenanted, tenantless, unlet, *(leerstehend)* unoccupied, vacant, void.
unvermindert undiminished, unabated;
~e Geschwindigkeit undiminished speed.
unvermischt absolute, *(Spirituosen)* unblended, unadulterated, unmixed, pure, *(unlegiert)* unalloyed, *(Wein)* neatly;
~e Waren honest goods.

Unvermögen relative impossibility, inability, incapacity, disability, disqualification, *(Zahlungsunfähigkeit)* insolvency; **absolutes** ~ absolute disability; **voraussichtliches** ~ prospective inability;
~ **der Beibringung einer Urkunde** failing of record; ~ **der Regierung** impotence of the government; ~ **in seiner Sache zu entscheiden** inability of deciding in one's own case; ~ **zu zahlen** inability to pay, insolvency.
unvermögend without means, penniless, impecunious, destitute, *(unfähig)* incapable;
nicht ~ **sein** to be quite well-to-do.
Unvermögensfall, im in case of inability to pay (insolvency).
unvermutet unexpected, unforeseen, sudden;
~ **auf j. stoßen** to come upon s. o. unawares.
Unvernunft nonsense, foolishness, unreasonableness.
unvernünftig unreasonable, *(töricht)* senseless, stupid, foolish;
~**es Kind** silly child.
un|veröffentlicht unpublished; ~**verpachtet** untenanted; ~**verpackt** unpacked, unwrapped, in bulk, bulk, loose; ~**verpfändet** unpledged, unmortgaged, unencumbered; ~**verplant** unallocated, not budgeted for; ~**verputzt** unplastered; ~**verrichtet** unperformed; ~**verrichteterdinge** without success; ~**verrückbar** fixed, immovable, *(Grundsatz)* unshakable.
unverschämt impudent, impertinent, cheeky, pushing, saucy, fresh *(US)*;
so ~ **sein** to have the nerve (neck, *sl.*) to do; ~ **gegenüber jem. werden** to get fresh with s. o.;
~**es Benehmen** outragious behavio(u)r; ~**er Bursche** cheeky brat, brazen-face; ~**e Forderung darstellen** to be highway robbery; ~**es Glück haben** to be bloody lucky; ~**e Lüge** blatant (barefaced) lie; ~**er Preis** exorbitant (steep, outrageous) price; ~**es Schwein haben** to be damned lucky, to have the devil's own luck.
Unverschämtheit impertinence, impudence, cheek, insolence, nerve *(coll.)*, front, lip *(sl.)*;
einkalkulierte ~ premeditated insolence;
die ~ **haben** to have the face (cheek); ~**en überhören** to ignore rude remarks.
un|verschlossen *(Brief)* unsealed, *(Tür)* unlocked; ~**verschlüsselt** in plain language, en clair.
unverschuldet not in debt, without debts, *(Grundbesitz)* unencumbered, *(schuldlos)* blameless, without fault;
~**er Bankrott** simple (casual) bankruptcy.
unversehens unawares, unexpected.
unversehrt untouched, safe and sound, intact, *(Ware)* undamaged, sound, unhurt, safe;
völlig ~ unscathed.
Unversehrtheit sound condition, intactness;
territoriale ~ **eines Staates** integrity of an empire.
un|versetzbar not transferable; ~**versichert** uninsured, not insured, unassured, uncovered; ~**versiegelt** unsealed; ~**versöhnlich** irreconcilable, intransigent.
unversorgt unprovided for, unsettled, unsupplied, without means, *(ohne Pflege)* unattended;
~**e Haushalte** households not connected to the mains; ~**es Vieh** untended cattle.
Unverstand senselessness, stupidity, *(Gedankenlosigkeit)* thoughtlessness.
unverstandene Frau misunderstood woman.
unverständlich unintelligible, incomprehensible, obscure, insensible, *(Rundfunkempfang)* jammed, *(Worte)* indistinct;
~ **machen** to obscure the understanding; **jem. völlig** ~ **sein** to be Greek to s. o.
Un|verständlichkeit obscurity; ~**verständnis** lack of sense.
un|verstellbarer Sitz nonadjustable seat; ~**versteuert** duty off (unpaid), *(steuerfrei)* untaxed; ~**verstümmelt** unmutilated; **nichts** ~**versucht lassen** to leave no stone unturned; ~**vertauschbar** unexchangeable.
unverteilt undivided, undistributed, unallowed;
~**er Reingewinn** undistributed net profit, unappropriated earned surplus *(US)*.
un|verträglich unsociable, *(zänkisch)* quarrelsome, cantankerous; ~**vertretbar** untenable, indefensible, *(Anspruch)* unwarrantable; ~**verwässertes Aktienkapital** unwatered stock; ~**verwendbar** unemployable, unusable; ~**verwendete Etatsmittel** unexpended (unallotted) appropriations; ~**verwertbar** *(nicht begebbar)* not negotiable, *(nicht einlösbar)* inconvertible, *(nicht einziehbar)* uncollectable, *(nicht verkäuflich)* unsalable, unrealizable.
unverwertet unrealized;
~**e Aktien** unissued shares (stock, *US*).
unverwundet invulnerable, unwounded, unscathed.
unverwüstlich durable, everlasting, hard-wearing;
~ **sein** to be still bursting with energy;
~**er Optimist** never-say-no-diehard.
un|verzagt unabashed, undismayed, undaunted; ~**verzeihlicher Irrtum** unforgivable (inexcusable) mistake.
unverzerrt *(Fernsehbild)* undistorted;
~**e Schätzwerte** estimates free from bias.
unverzichtbar *(Anspruch)* unrenounceable.
unverzinslich bearing no (without, free of) interest;
~ **sein** to lie dormant;
~**es Darlehen** free loan; ~**es Konto** noninterest-bearing account; ~**e Papiere** noninterest-bearing securities; ~**e Schulden** passive debts.
unverzollt duty off (not paid, unpaid), unentered, uncustomed, *(unter Zollverschluß)* bonded, in bond;
~**e Ware** unentered goods; ~**er Wert** bonded value.
unverzüglich without delay (rest), forthwith, immediate[ly], instantaneous[ly], instantly;
sich ~ **auf den Weg machen** to set out at once; ~ **schreiben** to write without delay;
~**e Verlustanzeige** immediate notice.
unvollendet unfinished, incomplete;
~**e Straftat** inchoate offence.
unvollkommen defective, imperfect, half.
Unvollkommenheiten eines Erziehungssystems defects in a system of education.
unvollständig unfinished, incomplete, *(Rechtstitel)* defective;
~**er Bericht** fragmentary report; ~**es Geschäft** uncompleted transaction; ~**e Kenntnisse** smattering; ~**er Scheck** invalid check *(US)* (cheque, *Br.*); ~**e Urkunde** irregular document, inchoate instrument; ~**er Vertrag** incomplete contract; ~ **ausgefüllter Wechsel** inchoate bill.
Unvollständigkeit *(Berichterstattung)* diminution, *(eidesstattliche Erklärung)* insufficiency;
~ **eines Vertrages** incompleteness of a contract.
un|vollstreckt not executed; ~**vollzählig** incomplete; ~**vollziehbar** unenforceable; ~**vollzogen** executory.
unvorbereitet unprepared, unpremeditated, offhand, willy-nilly, *(Rede)* impromptu, extemporaneous, extemporary, extempore, off the cuff *(US)*;
~ **sprechen** to extemporize, to speak off the cuff *(US)*; **völlig** ~ **angetroffen werden** to be caught on the wrong foot;
~**e Rede** unprepared speech.
un|vordenklich, seit ~**vordenklichen Zeiten** from time immemorial; ~**voreingenommen** unbiassed, unprejudiced, detached, free from bias, uninfluenced, impartial.
Unvoreingenommenheit impartiality, freedom from bias.
unvorhergesehen unforeseen, unexpected, unlooked for;
~**es Ereignis** fortuitous (unforeseen) event; **falls** ~**e Ereignisse eintreten sollten** should unforeseen circumstances arise.
un|vorhersehbar unforeseeable, unpredictable; ~**vorschriftsmäßig** contrary to the rules, improper, irregular.
unvorsichtig imprudent, inadvertent, careless;
~**er Fahrer** reckless driver; ~**er Schritt** incautious step.
unvorstellbar unthinkable, unimaginable;
~**en Ausmaßes** of an inconceivable extent.
unvorteilhaft unfavo(u)rable, unprofitable, disadvantageous, gainless, lean, *(Kleidung)* unflattering;
~**e Bedingungen** unprofitable terms; ~**es Geschäft** losing bargain.
Unwägbarkeit imponderability;
mit den ~**en auf allen Märkten fertig werden** to perform against the odds in all the world areas.
un|wählbar ineligible; ~**wahr** untrue, untruthful, false.
Unwahrheit untruth, falsity;
vorsätzliche ~ falsehood.
unwahrscheinlich improbable, unlikely, tall *(coll.)*;
nicht ~ on the cards;
~ **schnell fahren** to have a fantastic speed;
~**e Geldbeträge ausgeben** to spend incredible sums of money;
~**es Glück haben** to have the luck of the Irish *(coll.)*.
Unwahrscheinlichkeit improbability, unlikelihood.
unwegsames Gelände impassable terrain.
un|weigerlich inevitable, unavoidable; ~**weit der Stadt** not far from the town.
Un|wert want of value; ~**wesen** nuisance, sinister activities.
unwesentlich inessential, unessential, immaterial, insignificant, unsubstantial, trifling, trivial, extrinsic, vain;
sich nicht ~ **bessern** to improve appreciably; **sich nur** ~ **unterscheiden** to differ only negligibly;

~er **Fehler** trifling error; ~e **Kleinigkeiten** trivial matters, trifles; ~e **Rolle in der Gesellschaft spielen** to occupy an insignificant place in society; ~e **Tatsachen** immaterial facts.
Unwesentliches weglassen to discard the unnecessary.
Unwetter tempest, thunder and lightning, stormy weather;
~**schäden** damage caused by storm.
unwichtig unimportant, unessential, insignificant, immaterial, unsubstantial;
für ~ halten to make nothing of it; **alle anderen Überlegungen ~ erscheinen lassen** to override all other considerations; **ziemlich ~ sein** to make not much difference;
~**er Verband** small-time organization.
Unwichtiges auslassen to omit inessentials.
unwiderlegbar irrebuttable, irrefutable, unanswerable, nonrebuttable;
~**es Beweismaterial**, ~**e Zeugenaussage** incontestable (irrefutable) evidence; ~**e Vermutung** irrebuttable presumption.
unwiderlegt unrefuted.
unwiderrufen unchallenged, unrescinded.
unwiderruflich irrevocable, irreversible, irrepealable, uncancellable;
~ **feststellen** to be quite positive;
~**es Akkreditiv** irrevocable letter of credit; ~**e Vereinbarung** binding agreement; ~ **letzte Vorstellung** definitely last performance.
Unwiderruflichkeit irrevocability, finality.
unwidersprochen uncontradicted, unopposed, unchallenged;
etw. ~ lassen to let s. th. pass unchallenged.
unwiderstehlicher Trieb *(Täter)* irresistible impulse.
unwiederbringlich irrecoverable, irretrievable, irreparable;
~**er Verlust** irretrievable loss.
Unwille indignation, reluctance, unwillingness;
~**n empfinden** to be indignant about; **j. mit ~n erfüllen** to possess s. o. with indignation; **mit ~n feststellen** to notice with indignation; **mit ~n tun** to do reluctantly (in bad grace).
un|willig indignant, angry, *(lustlos)* unwilling, reluctant; ~**willkürlich** mechanical, unconscious, involuntary, spontaneous, instinctive; ~**wirklich** unreal, fictitious.
unwirksam inoperative, ineffective, inefficacious, invalid, noneffective, nugatory, without effect, bad, *(nichtig)* null, void, *(verjährt)* stale;
für ~ erklären to declare null and void; ~ **machen** to invalidate, to render void; ~ **werden** to lapse, to become void (ineffective), to have ceased to have effect;
~**er Vertrag** void contract.
Unwirksamkeit inefficiency, insufficiency, *(gesetzlich)* legal invalidity, *(Nichtigkeit)* nullity;
~ **eines Vermächtnisses** extinguishment of a legacy.
Umwirksamkeits|erklärung repudiation, annulment; **absichtliche ~klausel** joker *(US)*.
Unwirksamwerden eines Gesetzes desuetude of a law.
unwirtlich desolate, deserted, unsociable.
unwirtschaftlich uneconomical, unproductive, anti-economic, unthrifty, inefficient, wasteful, *(nicht lohnend)* unremunerative;
~**e Güter** onerous goods; ~**e Steuer** nuisance tax.
Unwirtschaftlichkeit unthriftiness, wastefulness, unproductiveness, inefficiency.
unwissend ignorant, uninformed, rude, young.
Unwissenheit ignorance;
entsetzliche ~ woeful ignorance; **gänzliche ~** utter ignorance; **sich mit ~ entschuldigen** to plead ignorance; **j. in ~ lassen** to keep s. o. in ignorance; **seine ~ erkennen lassen (zur Schau stellen)** to display one's ignorance .
un|wissenschaftlich unscientific, unscholarly; ~**wissentlich** unconscious, unwitting; ~**wohl** seedy, under the weather, off colo(u)r.
unwürdig unworthy, undeserving;
seiner ~ derogatory to s. o., beneath s. o.; **eines Staatsmannes ~** unstatesmanlike;
einer hohen Stellung ~ sein not to comport with a high position.
Unzahl host of.
unzählig innumerable, uncountable, numberless, countless.
Unzeit, zur untimely, ill-timed, out of season, out of time, inopportune.
un|zeitgemäß inopportune, outmoded, old-fashioned, untimely; ~**zensiert** uncensored; ~**zerbrechlich** unbreakable; ~**zeremoniell** informal; ~**zertrennlich** inseparable friends; ~**ziemlich** improper, unseemly, unbecoming.
Unzierde eyesore.
unzivilisiert uncivilized, primitive, rude, wild.
Unzucht indecent liberties, indecency, debauchery, fornication, *(Männer)* sodomy, buggery, *(Tiere)* bestiality;
gewerbsmäßige ~ prostitution;
~ **treiben** to fornicate, to whore; **j. zur ~ verleiten** to seduce s. o.
unzüchtig indecent, obscene, lewd;
~**e Entblößung** indecent exposure; ~**e Schriften** indecent publications, pornography.
Unzüchtigkeit obscenity, lewdness.
unzufrieden discontent, malcontent;
mit jem. ~ sein to be dissatified (displeased) with s. o.; **ewig ~ sein** to be always grumbling; **mit seinem Gehalt ~ sein** to be dissatified with one's salary.
Unzufriedenheit *(pol.)* disaffection;
allgemeine ~ popular discontent; **soziale ~** social unrest;
~ **der Verbraucherschaft** consumer dissatisfaction.
unzugänglich inapproachable, unapproachable, out-of-reach, off-the-map, inaccessible, *(Mensch)* hard to deal with;
Bitten gegenüber ~ sein to turn a deaf ear to entreaties.
unzulänglich insufficient, inadequate, deficient, poor;
~**e Informationen** inadequate information; ~**e Mittel** inadequate means (resources); ~**e Mittel haben** to be deficient in means; ~**e Strafe** inadequate sentence; ~**e Vorräte** scanty supplies.
Unzulänglichkeit deficiency, insufficiency, inadequacy, defectiveness;
~**en** shortcomings.
unzulässig inadmissible, undue, *(verboten)* prohibited, unlawful, incompetent, out of order, defective;
für ~ erklären to rule out *(US)*; **Klage für ~ erklären** to dismiss (rule out, *US*) a case; **Berufung als ~ verwerfen** to disallow an appeal;
~**e Beeinflussung** undue influence; ~**e Bevorzugung von Konkursgläubigern** undue preference of one debtor over the others; ~**es Beweismaterial** incompetent evidence; ~**er Gebrauch** improper use; ~**e Klagenverbindung** misjoinder of actions; ~**es Rechtsgeschäft** unlawful act; ~**er Zeuge** incompetent witness; ~**e Zusammenrottung** unlawful assembly.
Unzulässigkeit inadmissibility, incompetence;
~ **der Ausübung eines Rechts** equitable estoppel; ~ **der Ausübung eines Rechts aufgrund eigenen Verhaltens** estoppel by conduct; ~ **von Beweismaterial** incompetence of evidence *(US)*; ~ **der Klage** barring of an action; ~ **einer Prozeßeinrede** technical estoppel; ~ **der Strafverfolgung** bar to trial.
unzumutbar unconscionable, unreasonable;
~**e Veräußerungsbehinderung** unreasonable restraint of alienation.
unzurechnungsfähig mentally defective, irresponsible, of unsound mind *(US)*, incompetent, *(wahnsinnig)* insane, nonsane;
für ~ erklärt certified *(Br.)*;
für ~ erklären to declare irresponsible, to certify s. one's insanity *(Br.)*, to stultify; ~ **sein** to be immune of criminal responsibility, not to be responsible, to be quite irresponsible;
für ~ erklärt werden to be certified insane *(Br.)*.
Unzurechnungsfähiger insane (irresponsible) person, person of unsound mind *(US)*, non compos mentis.
Unzurechnungsfähigkeit mental incapacity (incompetence) legal, insanity, nonsane memory, irresponsibility, unsoundness of mind *(US)*, lunacy;
altersbedingte ~ involutional insanity, senile dementia;
~ **bei Begehung strafbarer Handlungen** volitional insanity; ~ **wegen Geistesschwäche** mental incapacity; ~ **wegen Volltrunkenheit** insanity induced by intoxication;
~ **einwenden** to enter (put forward) a plea of insanity; ~ **vortäuschen** to simulate insanity.
unzureichend inadequate, unsatisfactory, insufficient, deficient;
~**e Aktiva** insufficient assets; ~**e Mittel** slender means; ~**e Nahrungsmittelvorräte** insufficient food supplies; ~**e Organisation** inadequate arrangement.
unzuständig not competent, *(Richter)* incompetent, unqualified;
sich für ~ erklären to disclaim competence, to decline jurisdiction; **Gericht für ~ erklären** to put in a plea in bar of trial;
~**er Gerichtsort** improper venue; ~**es Gerichtsverfahren** improper legal proceedings.
Unzuständigkeit noncompetence, *(Richter)* incompetence, want (lack) of jurisdiction;
sachliche ~ lack of jurisdiction over the subject matter;
Einwand der ~ des Gerichts erheben to put in a plea in bar of trial.

unzustellbar undeliverable, not known;
~**er Brief** dead letter.
Unzustellbarkeit, im Fall der in case of nondelivery.
unzuträglich unwholesome, unhealthy.
Unzuträglichkeit nuisance, *(Klima)* unwholesomeness.
unzutreffend unfounded.
Unzutreffendes streichen delete as required.
unzuverlässig unreliable, untrustworthy, incalculable, unsound, slippery, *(Firma)* windy, shaky, *(Untersuchung)* biassed;
~**e Firma** unreliable (shaky) firm; ~**e Freunde** fair-weather friends; ~**es Gedächtnis** treacherous memory; ~**er Kunde** shifty customer, bad customer (egg, *sl.*); ~**er Mensch** broken reed; **aus einer** ~**en Quelle** from an unreliable source; ~**er Zeuge** slippery witness.
Unzuverlässigkeit unreliability, untrustworthiness, improvidence, slipperiness, unsoundness, *(Firma)* shakiness, *(Parteipolitik)* mugwumpery *(US sl.)*, *(Test)* bias.
unzweckmäßig inappropriate, unsuitable;
~**e Bemerkung** inexpedient remark; ~**e Kleidung** unsuitable clothing.
unzweideutig unambiguous, univocal, unequivocal;
jem. ~ **zu verstehen geben** to make it quite clear to s. o.;
~**e Antwort** plain answer.
unzweifelhaft without dispute, beyond controversy, undoubtful;
~**e Tatsache** established fact.
üppig rank, rich, luxurious, luxuriant, exuberant, lavish, lush;
zu ~ **werden** to be getting too big for one's boots *(coll.)*;
~**er Busen** opulent bosom; ~**es Leben führen** to live from the fat of the land; ~**es Mal** sumptuous meal; ~**er Pflanzenwuchs** rampant vegetation; ~**es Trinkgeld** generous tip;
Üppigkeit exuberance, luxuriance, lavishness.
Urabstimmung plebiscite, *(Lohnkämpfe)* ballot (strike) vote, strike-vote meeting.
uralt as old as the hills;
~**er Witz** stale joke; **aus** ~**en Zeiten** from time immemorial.
Uraufführung first night (performance), *(Film)* release.
Urbanisation property development.
urbar arable, cultivated;
~ **machen** to cultivate, to reclaim, to subdue.
Ur|barmachung von Grund und Boden land reclamation, cultivation; ~**bevölkerung** aborigines; ~**einwohner** original inhabitant, native, aboriginal; ~**gestein** primary rocks.
Urgrund, auf den ~ **eines Themas stoßen** to get to the core of a subject.
Urheber originator, creator, author;
~ **von etw. sein** to be at the bottom of s. th.;
~**lizenz** copyright royalty.
Urheberrecht proprietary right, copyright, literary property, *(Gesetz)* copyright law, *(Patent)* patent right;
noch bestehendes ~ subsisting copyright; **erloschenes** ~ lapsed copyright; **zwischenstaatliches** ~ international copyright;
~ **an Bühnenwerken** dramatic copyright; ~ **an Werken der Tonkunst** musical copyright; ~ **an literarischen Werken** literary copyright; ~ **an ursprünglichen Werken** copyright of original works *(Br.)*;
~ **ablösen** to cancel a copyright; ~ **erwerben** to obtain the copyright; ~ **leugnen** to disclaim authorship; ~ **verlängern** to renew a copyright; ~ **verletzen** to infringe a copyright.
urheberrechtlich|geschützt copyright[ed]; ~ **nicht geschützt** uncopyrighted;
~ **schützen** to copyright; ~ **nicht mehr geschützt sein** to be in the public domain *(US)*;
~ **geschützte Auflage** copyright[ed] edition; ~ **geschützte Produktion** copyrighted production; ~**em Schutz unterliegen** to be copyrighted; ~ **geschütztes Werk** copyright work.
Urheberrechts|abkommen copyright deal (convention); ~**anspruch** claim to copyright; ~**eintragung** registration of a copyright; ~**erneuerung** renewal of copyright.
urheberrechtsfähig copyrightable.
Urheberrechts|gebühren copyright fees; ~**gesetz** Copyright Act *(Br.)* (Statute, *US*), law of copyright; ~**inhaber** copyright holder; ~**klage** copyright case; ~**lizenzen** royalties; ~**register** register of copyrights; ~**schiedsstelle** performing rights tribunal; ~**schutz** protection by copyright, copyright protection; ~**übertragung** assignment of copyright; ~**vereinbarung** copyright deal; ~**verfahren** copyright procedure; ~**verlängerung** renewal of copyright; ~**verletzung** infringement (breach) of a copyright, copyright infringement; **gegen j. wegen einer** ~**verletzung vorgehen** to sue s. o. for infringement of copyright; ~**vermerk** copyright notice *(US)*; ~**vertrag** publishing contract; ~**verzicht** abandonment of copyright.
Urheberrolle register of copyrights.
Urheberschaft authorship, paternity;
~ **ablehnen** to disclaim authorship; ~ **an einem Buch ableugnen** to repudiate the authorship of a book; ~ **anerkennen** to mother.
Urheberschutz copyright;
vorläufiger ~ ad-interim copyright;
~ **beantragen** to file an application for registration of copyright;
~**antrag** application for copyright; ~**eintragung** registration of copyright; ~**frist** term of copyright; ~**klausel** manufacturing clause *(US)*; ~**recht** copyright; **vorläufiges** ~**recht** ad-interim copyright.
Urkunde *(Beleg)* record, voucher, *(Beweismittel)* evidence, proof, *(Beweisurkunde)* written instrument, writing, title deed, *(Dokument)* document, deed, copy, paper, certificate, diploma, *(Satzung)* statute, charter, licence;
aufgrund vorliegender ~ by these presents; **durch** ~**n belegt** documentary; **zu** ~ **dessen** in witness thereof (whereof);
~**n** rolls, papers;
amtliche ~ public (official) document; **öffentlich aufbewahrte** ~ public record; **ausgefüllte** ~ complete instrument; **zur Sicherung des Eigentumsvorbehaltes ausgestellte** ~ conditional sales note; **ausländische** ~ foreign document; **authentische** ~ authentic paper; **begebbare** ~ negotiable instrument; **beglaubigte** ~ certified (exemplified) copy, authentic instrument, confirmed (authenticated) document *(US)*; **beiliegende** ~ appended document; **beizubringende** ~**n** documents required; **beschlagnahmte** ~ impounded document; **beweiserhebliche** ~ documentary evidence; **echte** ~ authentic paper (instrument, document); **eingetragene** ~ perfect instrument; **ergänzende** ~ supplemental instrument; **gefälschte** ~ fabricated (forged) document, false instrument (token); **abhanden gekommene** ~ lost instrument (document); **öffentlichen Glauben genießende** ~ official document; **gerichtliche** ~ judicial document; **eigenhändig geschriebene** ~ holograph; **gesiegelte** ~ specialty, sheepskin *(sl.)*; **nicht gesiegelte** ~ document under hand; **gültige** ~ effective instrument; **vorläufig hinterlegte** ~ escrow; **maßgebende** ~ authoritative document; **notarielle** ~ document drawn up before a notary, notarial deed; **öffentliche (öffentlich-rechtliche)** ~ official (public) document; **privatschriftliche** ~ private deed (document); **rechtserhebliche** ~ relevant document; **rechtsgültige** ~ valid deed; **rechtsverkörpernde** ~ title deed; **übertragbare** ~ assignable instrument; **unechte** ~ fabricated (forged) document; **uneingeschränkte** ~ clear title; **unerreichbare** ~ inaccessible document; **ungültige** ~ document that is not in [legal] order; **unvollständige** ~ irregular document, imperfect title, inchoate instrument; **verfälschte** ~ forged document (instrument); **verlegte** ~ lost paper; **einseitig verpflichtende** ~ deed poll; **vertrauliche** ~ privileged document; **als Beweis vorgelegte** ~ exhibit; **nur in einer Ausfertigung vorhandene** ~ single original; **vorliegende** ~ these presents; **wichtige** ~ valuable paper; **zusätzliche** ~ ancillary document; **amtliche** ~ **über die Einsetzung eines Nachlaßverwalters** letters testamentary; ~ **über die Gewährung von Zahlungsaufschub** letter of licence; ~**n zur Unterstützung eines Schriftsatzes** moving paper; ~ **über einen Verwahrungsvertrag** memorandum of deposit *(Br.)*; ~ **über die Zulassung zur Anwaltschaft** attorney's certificate;
~ **abändern** to alter an instrument (document); ~ **als echt anerkennen** to acknowledge a deed; **beglaubigte Abschrift einer** ~ **anfertigen** to exemplify a deed; **jem. eine falsche** ~ **aufschwatzen** to foist a spurious document on s. o.; ~ **aufsetzen** to draw [up] a deed (document), to engross a document; ~ **ausfertigen** to extend a deed, to execute an instrument; ~ **aushändigen** to deliver a deed (an instrument); ~ **ausstellen** to draw up a document; ~ **begeben** to deliver a document; ~ **einem Exposé beifügen** to append a document to a dossier; **mit** ~**n belegen** to support (evidence) by documents; ~ **berichtigen** to reform an instrument *(US)*; ~ **beschaffen** to supply a document; ~ **beseitigen** to destroy (make away with) a document; **Echtheit (Rechtsgültigkeit) einer** ~ **bestreiten** to challenge (dispute) the validity of a document; **durch** ~**n beweisen** to prove by documentary evidence; ~ **in eine rechtsgültige Form bringen** to settle a document; ~**n deponieren** to lodge records; ~ **in einen Prozeß einführen** to put in a document in a law case; ~**n bei Gericht einreichen** to lay papers on the table; ~ **zu den Prozeßakten einreichen** to enter a document into the record; ~ **einsehen** to inspect a document; ~ **eintragen** to register (record) a deed; ~ **entwerfen** to engross a document; ~ **für ungültig erklären** to defeat a deed (document);

~ **formgerecht errichten** to settle a document; ~ **fälschen** to fabricate (falsify) a document; ~ **zum Beweis heranziehen** to refer a document as proof; ~ **nicht herausgeben** to withhold a document; ~ **hinterlegen** to place an instrument in escrow, to lodge a document; ~**n kollationieren** to compare [two] documents; ~ **bei einer Bank aufbewahren lassen** to place documents on deposit with a bank; ~ **vom Notar aufnehmen lassen** to register a deed; ~ **beglaubigen lassen** to have a document authenticated; ~ **in Zeugengegenwart legalisieren lassen** to have a document witnessed; ~ **zu den Akten legen (nehmen)** to place a document on the record, to file a document; ~ **ungültig machen** to frustrate a deed; ~ **zu den Prozeßakten nehmen** to enter a document into the record; ~ **in gerichtliche Verwahrung nehmen** to impound a document; ~**n offenlegen** to disclose documents; ~ **paraphieren** to initial a document; **j. mittels einer ~ in Kenntnis setzen** to communicate a document to s. o.; ~ **siegeln** to seal a deed, to affix a seal to a document; ~**n seinem Anwalt übergeben** to deposit papers with one's lawyer; ~ **einem Treuhänder übergeben** to place an instrument in escrow; ~ **unterdrücken** to suppress a document; ~ **unterfertigen (unterschreiben)** to execute a legal document, to affix one's signature to a document; ~ **verfälschen** to forge a document; **Inhalt einer ~ verfälschen** to tamper with a document; ~**n vergleichen** to compare documents; **Vorlage von ~n verlangen** to call for production of documents; ~ **verlegen** to mislay a document; **einer ~ durch Siegelung Rechtskraft verleihen** to stamp one's approval on a document; **auf der Rückseite einer ~ vermerken** to endorse a document; ~ **mit Aktenzeichen versehen** to put a reference on a document; ~ **mit seinem Handzeichen versehen** to initial a document; ~ **mit einem Kennzeichen versehen** to earmark a document; ~ **mit einem Siegel versehen** to place (put) one's seal on a document; ~ **mit seiner Unterschrift versehen** to sign (set one's hand to) a document; ~**n verwahren** to keep papers in one's possession; ~**n vorlegen** to tender (produce, present) documents; **beweisstützende ~n vorlegen** to produce documents in support [of an allegation]; ~**n auf dem Amtsweg weiterleiten** to route documents; ~ **als Beweismaterial zulassen** to invoke a paper into court.

Urkunden|abschreiber engrosser; **wortgetreue ~abschrift** exact copy of a document; **unbefugte ~änderung** alteration of an instrument; ~**anhang** rider, appendix; ~**aufbewahrung** safe-keeping of documents; ~**ausfertigung** execution of a deed (instrument), engrossment; ~**aushändigung** delivery of deed; ~**auszug** abstract of title; **zu den Akten einzureichender ~auszug** memorial; ~**bearbeiter** documentalist; **bedingte ~begebung** conditional delivery; ~**beglaubigung** attestation (recording) of a deed; **amtliche ~beglaubigung** certifying of a document; ~**beseitigung** destruction (spoliation) of documents; ~**bestätigung** acknowledgment of a deed.

Urkundenbeweis written (documentary, intrinsic) evidence; **indirekter** ~ secondary documentary evidence; **mittelbarer** ~ external evidence;
~ **antreten** to put in a document; ~ **führen** to document, to prove by documents.

Urkunden|einsicht inspection of documents; ~**entwurf** draft document; ~**fälscher** forger of documents, falsifier, counterfeiter; ~**fälschung** falsifying a record, falsification (forgery) of documents (an instrument); ~**fälschung begehen** to falsify a document; ~**formular** law blank; ~**führung** keeping of records; ~**hinterlegung** depositing of documents, lodgment; ~**inhalt bekanntgeben** to give discovery to documents; ~**interpretation** construction of documents; ~**kassette** deed box; ~**kommission** record commission; ~**mahnbescheid** default summons *(Br.)*; ~**mappe** folder of a document; ~**material** documentary evidence (material); ~**prozeß** trial by record *(US)*; ~**prüfung** inspection of documents; ~**registrierung** deed registration; ~**rolle** register of deeds *(US)*; ~**sammelstelle** archives; ~**sammlung** collection of documents; ~**schluß** chirograph; ~**stempel** documentary (deed) stamp; ~**steuer** documents tax, *(Wechsel)* stamp duty; ~**text** four corners of an instrument; ~**tinte** indelible ink; ~**überprüfung** perusal of documents; ~**unterdrückung** suppression of deeds (documents), concealment (interception) of documents; ~**unterschlagung** abstraction (suppression) of documents; ~**verfälschung** tampering with documents; ~**verfasser** draftsman; ~**vergleich** comparision of documents; **falsche ~verlesung** misreading; ~**vernichtung** spoliation of documents; ~**vorlage** exhibition (production) of documents, transumpt *(Scot.)*; ~**vorlage anordnen** to make discovery of documents; ~**zeuge** subscribing witness; ~**zustellung** delivery of a deed.

urkundlich documentary, founded on documents, archival, *(verbürgt)* authentic;
~ **belegt** supported by documents, documented; **nicht ~ übertragbar** undeeded; **nur ~ übertragbar** in grant;
~ **beglaubigen** to witness, to certify; ~ **belegen** to support (evidence) by documents; ~ **nachgewiesen sein** to be founded on documents; **nur ~ übertragbar sein** to lie in grant; ~ **übertragen** to assign, to transfer;
~**er Beleg** documentary evidence; ~**e Belegung** documentation; ~**es Beweismaterial** documentary evidence; ~**e Erwähnung** documentation; ~**er Nachweis** documentation; ~**e Rechtsmittel** muniments.

Urkundsbeamter recording secretary, register, marshal, certifying officer, keeper of the records *(US)*, common sergeant *(Br.)*, actuary *(Br.)*, sheriff clerk *(Scot.)*, *(Notar)* notary [public];
~ **der Geschäftsstelle** registrar of the court, court registrar, clerk of the court's office *(US)*, master at common law *(Br.)*.

Urkundsperson certifying officer, commissioner for oaths *(Br.)* (deeds), *(Zeuge)* witness to a document (deed), attesting witness.

Urlaub holiday, leave, vacation *(US)*, *(Beamter, Soldat)* furlough, leave, *(Freizeit)* time off, *(Student)* exeat;
auf ~ on holidays (leave, vacation, *US*), *(Soldat)* on pass; **zusätzlich bewilligter** ~ additional leave; **bezahlter** ~ paid holidays (vacation, *US*), holidays (vacation, *US*) with pay, vacation pay *(US)*; **dreiwöchentlicher** ~ three-weeks holiday; **genehmigter** ~ leave of absence; **halbjähriger** ~ a six-month leave; **tariflicher** ~ holiday with pay, on-leave *(US)*; **unbegrenzter** ~ indefinite leave; **unbezahlter** ~ leave without pay, payless vacation *(US)*; **ungenehmigter** ~ absence without leave; **vierzehntägiger** ~ a fortnight's holiday; **vollbezahlter** ~ full-pay leave; **noch zustehender** ~ terminal leave;
~ **aus familiären Gründen** compassionate leave; ~ **von der Haftanstalt** ticket-of-leave system; ~ **von ganzen zehn Tagen** poor ten day's holiday; ~ **bis zum Wecken** night leave;
seinen ~ antreten to go on leave; ~ **aufteilen** to stagger the holiday; ~ **beantragen** to ask (apply) for leave; **dreitägigen ~ beantragen** to put in for three days' leave; ~ **vorzeitig beenden** to curtail one's holiday; **einen Monat ~ bekommen** to obtain a month's leave; **um einen dreitägigen ~ bitten (einkommen)** to put in for three days' leave (holiday); **auf (in) ~ gehen** to go on leave, to take a holiday; **eine Woche ~ genehmigen** to allow a week's holiday; **einem Beamten ~ gewähren** to grant furlough to a official; ~ **haben** to have a holiday; **vierwöchigen ~ haben** *(Beamter)* to have a four weeks furlough; ~ **dringend nötig haben** to want a holiday; **um seinen ~ kommen** to miss one's holiday; **jedesmal um seinen ~ kommen** to be done out of one's leave every time; ~ **machen** to be on holiday (one's holidays), to take a vacation *(US)*; **getrennten ~ machen** to take separate holidays; **seinen ~ nehmen** to take one's leave, to vacation *(US)*; **nicht genehmigten ~ nehmen** to break leave; **auf ~ sein** to be out on leave (away on holiday, on vacation, *US*); **genehmigten ~ verbringen** to be on leave of absence; **seinen ~ im Ausland verbringen** to spend one's vacation abroad *(US)*; **sich zu ~ verhelfen** to work it so that one has a vacation *(coll.)*; ~ **verlängern** to extend a leave (holiday); **im ~ verreisen** to get away for the holiday.

Urlauber holidayer, holidaymaker, vacationist *(US)*, vacationer *(US)*;
~**schiff** liberty boat; ~**strom** holiday crowds; ~**zug** leave train.

Urlaubs|abgeltung payment in lieu of vacation *(US)*, vacation allowance *(US)*; ~**abkürzung** curtailment of one's holidays; ~**anschrift** holiday address; ~**anspruch** leave entitlement, entitlement to holidays, holiday entitlement, vacation privilege (right) *(US)*; **viertägiger ~anspruch pro Monat** home leave earned at the rate of four days per calendar month; ~**anspruch haben** to be eligible for leave; ~**antritt** commencement of one's leave; ~**aufteilung** staggering of holidays.

urlaubsbedingte Schließung holiday (vacation, *US*) shutdown.

urlaubsberechtigt eligible for leave (vacation, *US*);
~ **sein** to be eligible for leave; **alle drei Jahre ~ sein** to have a furlough every three years.

Urlaubs|berechtigung vacation eligibility *(US)*; ~**bestimmungen** leave regulations, vacation provisions *(US)*; ~**- und Fürsorgebestimmungen eines Vertrages** vacation and welfare features of a contract *(US)*; ~**bezahlung** leave (holiday, vacation, *US*) pay; ~**buch** *(mil.)* leave book; **durchschnittliche ~dauer** average length of a holiday; ~**einrichtungen** holiday facilities; ~**entgelt** holiday remuneration vacation pay; ~**entschädigung** holiday pay, vacation compensation *(US)*; ~**etat** holiday budget; ~**fahrzeug** recreational vehicle; ~**foto** holiday snapshot;

~**gebiet** holiday region; ~**geld** payment during leave, leave (holiday, vacation, *US*) pay, holiday remuneration *(Br.)*; **zustehendes ~geld** accrued holiday remuneration; ~**geldrückstände** accrued holiday pay; ~**gesuch** application for leave of absence, request for a holiday, vacation request *(US)*; ~**gesuch einreichen** to apply (ask) for leave; ~**jahr** holiday year, *(Universität)* sabbatical year; ~**konjunktur** recreation boom; ~**liste** leave book (roster); ~**lohn** holiday pay, vacation compensation (pay) *(US)*; ~**ordnung** holiday schedule; ~**ort** resort, holiday spot *(US)*; **stark besuchter ~ort** crowded holiday resort; ~**paradies** holiday paradise; ~**plan** leave (vacation, *US*) schedule; **seine ~pläne mit einem anderen abstimmen** to fit in one's holidays with s. o. else; ~**politik** vacation policy *(US)*; ~**programm** holiday (vacation, *US*) program(me); ~**recht** vacation privilege *(US)*; **großzügige ~regelung** generous leave conditions; **großzügig bezahlte ~regelung** generous paid leave.

Urlaubsreise holiday travel (tour), vacation trip *(US)*;
bezahlte ~ holiday visit passage;
~ über ein Reisebüro buchen to go on holiday through a travel agency; **sich eine ~ leisten** to run a holiday.

Urlaubs|reisender vacationer *(US)*, vacationist *(US)*, holidayer, holidaymaker; ~**reservierung** holiday booking; ~**schein** *(mil.)* ticket of leave, furlough certificate *(US)*, [free] pass *(US)*; ~**sperre** stoppage of leave; ~**system** vacation policy *(US)*; ~**tag** day off; **bezahlte ~tage** days of paid vacation *(US)*; ~**überschreitung** overstaying of leave, *(mil.)* absence over leave, leave-breaking; ~**verfahren** vacation procedure *(US)*; ~**vergünstigung** furlough benefit; ~**vergütung** holiday remuneration, time off with pay; ~**vergütungsgesetz** Holidays with Pay Act *(Br.)*; ~**verkehr** holiday traffic; ~**verlängerung** extension of one's holiday (leave); ~**vertrag** contract for a holiday; ~**vertretung** holiday replacement *(Br.)*, vacation replacement *(US)*; ~**wesen** vacation system *(US)*; ~**zeit** holiday season (time), vacation period (season, time) *(US)*; ~**zeit aufteilen** to split vacations *(US)*; **seine ~zeit überschreiten** to overstay one's leave; ~**zulage** vacation time allotment *(US)*.

Urne *(Begräbnis)* urn, *(Wahl)* ballot box.

Urnen|beisetzung urn burial; ~**friedhof** cinerarium, cremation cemetery.

Urproduktion primary production (sector).

Ursache cause, *(Anlaß)* ground, reason, *(Beweggrund)* motive, *(Grund)* reason;
adäquate ~ adequate cause; **auslösende ~** occasional cause; **dazwischentretende ~** intervening cause; **eigentliche ~** ultimate cause; **entfernte ~** remote cause; **mitwirkende ~** instrumental cause; **unmittelbare ~** proximate (direct, immediate) cause; **nicht vorhergesehene ~** *(Betriebshaftpflicht)* unforeseen cause;
~ des Feuers cause of the fire; **~ und Wirkung** cause and effect; **kleine ~en, große Wirkung** every oak has been an acorn;
seine ~ haben in to originate in; **alle ~en haben, zu fürchten** to have every reason to fear; **~ eines Eisenbahnunglücks untersuchen** to investigate the cause of a railway accident.

Ursachenzusammenhang causality, proximate cause.

ursächlich causal, causative;
~**er Zusammenhang** causal connection, causative (proximate) cause.

Ursächlichkeit causation.

Urschrift original [text] script;
in einer ~ in a single copy;
~ des Frachtbriefes original waybill.

urschriftlich original, autographic.

Ursprung origin, origination, spring, well, fountain, parent, mother, source, growth, *(Ware)* nationality;
deutschen ~s of German extraction; **fremden ~s** of foreign growth; **lateinischen ~s** of Latin origin;
~ einer Sache germ of an idea;
seinen ~ haben in to originate, to derive.

ursprünglich original, primary;
~**es Angebot** original offer; ~**e Fassung** original version; ~**e Gesellschaftsziele** original aims of an association; ~**es Mißtrauen** initial distrust; ~**er Produktionsfaktor** primary factor of production; ~**e Schönheit** pristine beauty; ~**e Staatsangehörigkeit** original nationality; ~**e Unmöglichkeit** *(Vertrag)* original frustration; ~**e Vereinbarung** original agreement.

Ursprungs|angabe indication of origin; ~**anstalt** bank of issue; ~**auszeichnung** informative labelling; ~**bescheinigung** certificate of origin; ~**bezeichnung** mark of origin, informative labelling; ~**domizil** domicile of origin; ~**eintragung** *(Warenzeichen)* home registration; ~**hinweis** certification mark; ~**journal** book of original entry; ~**land** country of origin; ~**nachweis** certification mark; ~**ort** originating point, point of origin *(US)*; ~**patent** base (pioneer) patent; ~**vermerk** indication of origin; ~**wohnsitz** domicile of origin; ~**zeichen** mark of origin; ~**zeugnis** certificate of origin; ~**zustand** native state.

Urstoff primary matter.

Urteil judgment, adjudgment, *(Ansicht)* opinion, *(Beschluß)* judicial decision, decree, *(Ehescheidung)* decree absolute, *(Geschworene)* verdict, *(Meinung)* opinion, *(Schiedsspruch)* award, arbitration, *(Strafmaß)* sentence;
meinem ~ nach in my opinion; **nach dem allgemeinen ~** in the eyes of the world; **nach dem ~ von Sachverständigen** in the opinion of experts; **wie aus dem ~ hervorgeht** as appears from the judgment of the court;
abänderndes ~ disaffirmance of a judgment; **abgekürztes ~** summary judgment; **abgewogenes ~** deliberate judgment; **abschließendes ~** final sentence; **von der ständigen Rechtssprechung abweichendes ~** irregular judgment; **abweisendes ~** judgment of dismissal, adverse verdict; **anfechtbares ~** voidable judgment; **angefochtenes ~** appealed decree; **aus Rechtsgründen aufgehobenes ~** judgment quashed on a point of law; **ausgeglichenes ~** deliberate judgment; **ausländisches ~** foreign judgment; **nach der Entscheidung der unterlegenden Partei auszufüllendes ~** alternative judgment; **bedingtes ~** conditional judgment; **deklatorisches ~** declaratory judgment; **einstimmiges ~** unanimous decision; **endgültiges ~** definitive judgment; **verfahrenswidrig ergangenes ~** irregular judgment; **nach Klageverzicht ergehendes ~** judgment of retraxit; **bei unstreitigem Sachverhalt ergehendes ~** *(Geschworene)* judgment on a special verdict; **im Versäumnisverfahren erlassenes ~** default judgment; **erschlichenes ~** simulated judgment; **erstinstanzliches ~** judgment by the court of the first instance; **falsches ~** error in judgment; **freisprechendes ~** acquittal; **früheres (älteres) ~** prior (previous) judgment; **gerechtes ~** a just and lawful decision; **gesundes ~** good sense, clear judgment; **von der Geschworenenmehrheit getragenes ~** majority verdict; **hartes ~** harsh judgment, severe sentence; **inländisches ~** domestic judgment *(US)*; **irriges ~** misjudgment, erroneous judgment; **klageabweisendes ~** judgment of dismissal; **klares ~** definite judgment; **kontradiktatorisches ~** contradictory judgment; **kritisches ~** nice judgment; **letztinstanzliches ~** final judgment; **mildes ~** lenient sentence; **nichtiges ~** void judgment; **obsiegendes ~** favo(u)rable judgment; **parteiisches ~** one-sided judgment; **rechtsfehlerhaftes ~** erroneous judgment; **rechtskräftiges ~** final (nonappealable) judgment, legal decision, final decree, judgment at law (of recovery, *US*), *(Ehescheidung)* decree absolute; **noch nicht rechtskräftiges ~** judgment subject to appeal; **richterliches ~** adjudgment; **schuldrechtliches ~** judgment in personam; **strafhäufendes ~** cumulative sentence; **strenges ~** severe sentence; **subjektives ~** subjective judgment; **unrichtiges ~** false judgment; **der Aufhebung unterliegendes ~** reversible judgment; **dem Vollstreckungsaufschub unterliegendes ~** judgment liable to stay of execution; **verjährtes ~** dormant judgment; **vollstreckbares ~** enforceable judgment; **[wegen Verjährung] nicht mehr vollstreckbares ~** dormant judgment; **noch nicht vollstreckbares ~** unsatisfied judgment; **sofort vollstreckbares ~** self-executing judgment; **vorläufig vollstreckbares ~** judgment provisionally enforceable; **nicht vollstrecktes ~** unsatisfied judgment; **vorläufiges ~** provisional decree (judgment), *(Ehescheidung)* decree nisi; **vorschnelles ~** snap judgment;
~ zugunsten des Beklagten verdict for the defendant; **~ in der Berufung** judgment in error; **~ über Delikte in Idealkonkurrenz** concurrent sentence; **~ über Delikte in Realkonkurrenz** consecutive sentence; **~ eines nicht zuständigen Gerichts** foreign judgment; **~ dem Grunde nach** decision on merits; **~ zugunsten des Klägers** judgment given for the plaintiff; **klageabweisendes ~ ohne Sachentscheidung** dismissal without prejudice; **~ des Schwurgerichts** findings of the jury; **~ im Urkundenprozeß** summary judgment; **~ im abgekürzten Verfahren** summary judgment; **~ im unstreitigen Verfahren** consent judgment; **~ mit Wirkung für und gegen alle** judgment in rem;
erstinstanzliches ~ abändern to disaffirm the judgment of an inferior court; **sein ~ über etw. abgeben** to give one's opinion on s. th.; **~ anfechten** to appeal against a judgment; **~ annehmen** to acquiesce in a judgment; **~ aufheben** to set aside (quash, vacate, reverse, annul, suspend, recall) a judgment, to set aside a verdict; **~ in der Berufungsinstanz aufheben**

to reverse the judgment of the court below, to vacate a judgment on appeal; ~ **aus formellen Gründen aufheben** to quash a judgment on a technical point; ~ **in der zweiten Instanz aufheben** to uphold a decision on appeal; ~ **aus Rechtsgründen aufheben** to quash a judgemnt on a point of law; **sein** ~ **aufrechterhalten** to stick to one's verdict; ~ **aussetzen** to arrest a judgment; **Vollstreckung eines ~s aussetzen** to stay (suspend) a judgment; **Aussetzung eines ~s beantragen** to move an arrest of judgment; **sich aus einem ~ befriedigen** to satisfy a judgment; ~ **begründen** to set forth the reasons for a judgment; **über ein ~ beraten** to break a case; ~ **bestätigen** to affirm a judgment, to confirm a judgment, to approve a decision, to affirm (uphold) a decree (sentence); **sich ein ~ bilden** to form one's (make a) judgment; **sich ein ~ über j. bilden** to take s. one's measure, to measure s. o. with one eye; **Rechtsmittel gegen ein ~ einlegen** to appeal against a judgment (sentence); **sich eines ~s enthalten** to refrain from giving one's opinion; ~ **ergänzen** to amend a judgment; ~ **für nichtig erklären** to rescind (invalidate) a judgment; ~ **erlangen** to obtain a judgment; ~ **erlassen** to enter a (pass, render, give) judgment; ~ **zugunsten des Klägers erlassen** to pass a judgment for the plaintiff in a suit; ~ **erwirken** to recover (secure, obtain, procure) judgment; **günstiges ~ erwirken** to obtain a favo(u)rable sentence; ~ **gegen einen Schuldner erwirken** to obtain judgment against a debtor; ~ **fällen** to judge, to deliver (enter a, pass, hand down) judgment, to adjudicate, *(Strafprozeß)* to sentence, to pronounce a verdict; ~ **zu jds. Gunsten fällen** to give the case for s. o. against s. o.; ~ **zugunsten des Klägers fällen** to decide for (in favour of) the plaintiff; ~ **zuungunsten des Klägers fällen** to decide against the plaintiff; ~ **auf einen Schiedsspruch gründen** to found a judgment on an award; **selbst ein ~ haben** to judge for o. s.; ~ **kassieren** to invalidate a judgment; **ziemlich gutes ~ über etw. abgeben können** to be a fair judge of s. th.; ~ **vollstrecken lassen** to enforce a judgment by execution; **einem ~ nachkommen** to satisfy a judgment; ~ **sprechen** to give (render) judgment; ~ **der öffentlichen Meinung überlassen** to leave it to the country to judge; ~ **der Vorinstanz überprüfen** to review a judgment on appeal; ~ **umstoßen** to vacate (quash) a judgment; ~ **verkünden** to deliver (pass, pronounce, hand down) a judgment; ~ **öffentlich verkünden** to pronounce judgment in open court; ~ **vervollständigen** to perfect a judgment *(US)*; **jds. ~ verzerren** to warp s. one's judgment; ~ **vollstrecken** to execute a judgment (sentence), to carry out a judgment (sentence), to enforce a judgment; **dem ~ eines Gerichts vorgreifen** to prejudice the decision of a court; **jem. ein ~ zustellen** to notify s. o. of a decision.

urteilen to judge, to decide, to decree, to sentence;
anders ~ to take a different view; **nach Äußerlichkeiten** ~ to judge by externals (appearance); **zu früh** ~ to prejudge; **ohne vorherige Prüfung** ~ to prejudge; **in einer Sache letztinstanzlich** ~ to decide in the last instance.

Urteils|abänderung amendment of a judgment; **~abfassung** wording of a decision; **getreue ~abschrift** estreat *(Br.)*; **~anerkennung** confession of judgment; **~anfechtung** direct attack against a judgment; **~anfechtung im Nebenverfahren** collateral attack; **~aufhebung** falsifying (quashing of) a judgment; **~aufhebung in der Berufungsistanz** reversal of judgment; **~aufschiebung** ampliation; **vollstreckbare ~ausfertigung** judgment execution; **~auslegung** construction of a sentence; **~aussetzung** arrest (suspension) of judgment; **~aussetzung zur Bewährung** suspension of sentence on probation; **~aussetzung beantragen** to move an arrest of judgment; **~begründung** opinion of the court, finding of the court, judicial opinion; **gesonderte ~begründung** separate opinion; **~berichtigungsbeschluß** writ of error coram nobis; **~betrag** sum adjudged, face of judgment; **beglaubigter ~entwurf** judgment paper; **~ergänzung** amendment of a judgment; **~erneuerung** revival of judgment.

urteilsfähig discriminating.

Urteils|fällung [passing of] judgment, deliverance *(Scot.)*, rendition *(US)*; **~fällung aussetzen** to arrest (suspend) judgment; **~forderung** judgment debt; **~formel** operative provisions; **~gründe** reasons adduced, opinion, grounds for a judgment; **~jury** petty jury *(US)*; **~kraft** judicative power, *(Beurteilungsfähigkeit)* judgment, discernment, discrimination; **kaufmännische ~kraft** business judgment; **mangelnde ~kraft** lack (defect, want) of judgment.

urteilsreif ripe for judgment.

Urteils|reife maturity of judgment; **~sammlung** session of cases *(Scot.)*; **~schuld** judgment debt; **~schuldner** judgment debtor; **~spruch** judgment, sentence [report], *(Strafgericht)* verdict; **~tenor** clausula, operative part; **~überprüfung der Vorinstanz** review on appeal *(US)*; **~urkunde mit Ladungsnachweis** judgment roll.

Urteilsverkündung pronouncement (passing, delivery) of judgment, rendition *(US)*;
ausgesetzte ~ deferred sentence; **gesonderte** ~ separate opinion;
~ **aussetzen** to reserve (arrest, suspend) judgment, to defer a sentence.

Urteilsvermögen discretion, discernment;
ohne ~ uncritical;
gesundes ~ clear (sound) judgment; **kaufmännisches** ~ business judgment;
nicht genügend ~ **besitzen** to want judgment; **jegliches** ~ **verlieren** to lose all sense of judgment.

Urteils|vollstreckung judgment execution, enforcement of a judgment; **~zustellung** service of judgment.

Urtext original [manuscript];
im ~ in the original.

Ur|väterzeiten, seit from time immemorial; **~wahl** primary election *(US)*; **~wähler** elector; **~wählerversammlung** primary assembly; **~wald** virgin forest; **sich einen Weg durch den ~wald bahnen** to cut a pass through the jungle.

urwüchsig natural, original;
mit ~er Kraft with elemental force.

Ur|zeiten, vor in time out of mind; **~zustand** native state.

Usance usage, custom, rule, *(althergebrachter Brauch)* standing custom;
fremde ~n foreign rules; **kaufmännische ~n** usage of trade, custom of merchants; **lokale** ~ local custom; **völkerrechtliche ~n** comity of nations;
~bestimmung customary clause.

usancemäßig customary, according to custom (usance).

Usancenhandel trading in foreign exchange.

Usowechsel bill at usance.

Usurpation usurpation.

Usurpator usurper.

usurpieren to usurp.

usurpiert usurped, engrossed.

Utopia land of make-believe, Utopia.

Utopie Utopia, utopian scheme.

utopischer Plan utopian scheme.

Utopist Utopianist, Utopian.

V

V-Waffe flying bomb.
Vabanquespiel hazardous venture;
~ **betreiben** to take an inordinate risk.
Vagabund vagabond, landloper, hedge bird *(US)*, roamer, rover, tramp, tramper, rogue *(Br.)*, hobo *(US)*.
vagabundenhaft vagabondish.
Vagabunden|leben vagrancy, roving life; ~**leben führen** to lead a vagrant life; ~**manieren** vagabond habits; ~**sprache** flash, thieves' language; ~**tum** vagrancy, vagabondage.
Vagabundieren vagrancy.
vagabundieren to tramp, to vagabondize, to vagabond.
vagabundierend vagrant, fugitive, roaming.
vage|Antwort vague answer; ~ **Vorstellung** dim (hazy) idea.
vakant vacant, unoccupied;
~ **werden** to fall vacant.
Vakanz vacancy, vacant office, avoidance, voidance;
~ **in der Belegschaft** vacancy on the staff; **freie** ~**en für Stenotypisten und Kontoristen** good vacancies for typists and clerks; ~ **infolge Todesfalls** casual vacancy; ~ **im Vorstand** vacancy on the board of directors;
~ **ausschreiben** to advertise a vacancy; ~ **neu besetzen** to fill a vacancy;
~**rate** vacancy rate.
Vakuum vacuum, vacancy;
~**lampe** vacuum lamp; ~**röhre** vacuum tube, valve *(Br.)*.
vakuumverpackt vacuum-packed, airtight.
validieren to validate, to make valid;
Summe ~ **lassen** to place a sum (set off) against.
Validierung validation.
Valoren securities, shares, stocks *(US)*, *(Wertsachen)* valuables;
~**versicherung** registered mail insurance *(US)*.
valorisieren to valorize.
Valorisierung validation, valorization.
Valuta *(Devisen)* foreign exchange, *(Devisenkurs)* rate of exchange, exchange rate, *(Gegenwert)* consideration, equivalent, *(Hypothek)* mortgage money, *(Währung)* [monetary] standard, [standard] currency, medium of exchange, foreign notes and coins, *(Wert)* value, *(Wertstellung)* value (availability, *US*) date;
franko ~ free of payment; ~ **kompensiert** value compensated; **ausländische** ~ foreign currency (exchange); **deckungsfähige** ~ currency eligible to serve as collateral; **feste** ~ fixed (regular) rate, fixed standard; **gegenwärtige** ~ present rate; **goldwertige** ~ gold currency; **sichere** ~ sound (stable) currency; **unbeständige** ~ fluctuating standard; **unveränderliche** ~ fixed standard; **veränderliche** ~ uncertain rate;
~ **in Gold** value in gold;
~ **für einen Wechsel anschaffen** to give consideration for a bill; **in** ~ **zahlen** to pay in foreign currency; **für** ~ **zahlen** to pay for value received;
~**abschluß** currency transaction; ~**akzept** foreign currency bill; ~**änderung** currency change-over; ~**anleihe** currency bonds; ~**bescheinigung** estoppel certificate; ~**bestände** currency holdings; ~**bonds** currency bonds; ~**dumping** currency (foreign-exchange) dumping; ~**entwertung** currency depreciation, devaluation; ~**forderung** currency claim; ~**geschäfte** currency transactions; ~**gewinn** foreign-exchange earnings, exchange profit, currency gain; ~**guthaben** currency assets (balance), *(Bilanz)* balances with foreign bankers; ~**klausel** currency (value-given) clause; ~**knappheit** currency shortage; ~**konto** currency (exchange, *US*) account; ~**kredit** foreign currency loan; ~**kupon** coupon payable in foreign currency; ~**kurs** rate of exchange, exchange rate; ~**mangel** currency shortage; ~**notierung** quotation of [foreign] exchange [rates]; ~**obligationen** currency bonds; ~**papiere** foreign currency securities (stock); ~**politik** currency policy; ~**quittung** value received; ~**regulierung** currency regulation; ~**risiko** exchange risk; ~**schuld** currency claim.
valutaschwaches Land soft-currency country.
Valuta|schwankungen fluctuations in the rate of exchange, currency fluctuations; ~**schwierigkeiten** currency troubles; ~**spekulant** currency speculator; ~**spekulation** currency speculation.
valutastark with a high rate of exchange;
~**es Land** hard-currency country.
Valuta|tag value (availability, *US*) date; ~**umstellung** currency change-over; ~**verbindlichkeiten** currency liabilities; ~**verhältnis** monetary relationship; ~**verlust** exchange loss, currency loss (leakage); ~**versicherung** foreign currency insurance; ~**wechsel** currency bill *(Br.)*, currency draft; ~**zahlung** currency payment.
Valuten foreign exchange;
~**arbitrage** currency arbitrage, arbitration of exchange; ~**geschäft** dealing in foreign notes ands coins; ~**konto** foreign-currency (external, *Br.*) account; ~**kurs** rate of exchange.
valutieren to value, to state the value (fix the availability, *US*) date;
Buchungsposten ~ to fix the value of an entry.
Valutierung fixing of the value (availability, *US*) date;
~ **feststellen** to state the value (availability, *US*) date.
Valutierungstag value (availability, *US*) date.
Valvation valuation.
Valvations|tabelle valuation table; ~**wert** fixed rate of exchange.
valvieren to state the value.
Vamp vamp *(coll.)*.
Vandalismus vandalism.
variabel variable, fluctuating;
~ **notiert werden** to be quoted consecutively.
variabl|es Agio fluctuating premium; ~**er Betrag** variable fee; ~**e Kosten** variable expenses (cost); ~**er Kurs** variable exchange; ~**e Lohnabzüge** variable deductions; ~**er Marktwert** fluctuating market value; ~**e Notierung** consecutive (fluctuating) quotation; ~**e Preise** variable prices; ~**e Produktionsfaktoren** variable resources; ~**e Werte** securities quoted consecutively.
Variante variant, version, lection, different reading;
klimatisch bedingte ~ climatic variety;
~ **der jüngsten Zeit sein** to be a latter-day variation.
Varianzanalyse variance analysis, analysis of variance.
Variationskarte *(mar.)* variation chart.
Varieté variety [show], vaudeville [show] *(US)*, music hall *(Br.)*;
~**künstler** variety artist, vaudeville actor *(US)*, vaudevillist *(US)*; ~**nummer** variety act, stunt *(US)*; ~**programm** variety program(me); ~**stunde im Fernsehen** variety hour; ~**theater** variety theater (theatre, *Br.*), vaudeville theater *(US)*; ~**unterhaltung** variety entertainment; ~**vorstellung** variety (vaudeville, *US*) show, variety performance.
variieren to vary, to range, to fluctuate, *(Thema)* to diversify;
von zehn Schilling bis zu einem Pfund ~ to run (range) from ten shillings to a pound; **seinen Stil** ~ to vary one's style.
Vasall vassal, liege, retainer.
Vasallen|schaft vassalage; ~**staat** vassal (dependent) state, tributary; ~**verhältnis** vassalage.
Vater father, the old man;
geistiger ~ father figure; **treusorgender** ~ good provider *(coll.)*;
~ **Staat** Uncle Sam *(US)*;
sich als ~ **bekennen** to father; **auf seinen** ~ **kommen** to favo(u)r one's father *(coll.)*; **seit vielen Jahren vom** ~ **auf den Sohn übergegangen sein** to have been handed down from father to son for many generations;
~**ersatz** father substitute; ~**figur** father figure; ~**haus** parental home; ~**komplex** father complex.
Vaterland native (parent) country (land), fatherland, motherland, homeland, parent country;
zweites ~ country of one's adoption;
für sein ~ **fallen** to die for one's country; **sich um sein** ~ **verdient gemacht haben** to deserve well of one's country; **sein** ~ **verteidigen** to defend one's country.
vaterländisch patriotic, national.
Vaterlands|gefühl, aus prompted by patriotism; ~**liebe** patriotism, love of one's country; ~**verräter** traitor to one's country.
väterlich fatherly, ancestral, paternal, parental;
~**es Erbteil** patrimony; ~**e Fürsorge** paternal care; ~**es Geschäft** father's business; ~**e Gewalt** paternal authority; ~**es Vermögen** paternal property; ~**er Wechsel** parental contribution.
väterlicherseits on the father's side;
~ **verwandt** agnate.
Vatermord parricide.
Vaterschaft paternity, fatherhood;
~ **ableugnen** to deny paternity; ~ **eines Kindes anerkennen** to acknowledge the paternity of a child, to father, to recognize a natural child, to own a child; ~ **behaupten** to claim paternity; **jds.** ~ **feststellen** to affiliate a child to s. o., to determine s. one's paternity; ~ **eines Kindes feststellen** to affiliate a child; ~ **eines**

unehelichen Kindes feststellen to filiate; **auf Anerkennung der ~ klagen** to claim one's status; **jem. die ~ eines unehelichen Kindes zuschieben** to affiliate a child upon (to) a putative father.
Vaterschafts|anerkenntnis public acknowledgement of paternity; **~ermittlung, ~feststellung, ~nachweis** affiliation, paternity test, establishment of paternity; **~prozeß** affiliation (certification, bastardy, *US*) case (proceedings), paternity suit *(US)*; **~urteil** order of filiation, [af]filiation (bastardy, *US*) order; **~vermutung** presumption of paternity.
Vatersname family name, surname.
Vater|stadt native town, hometown; **~stelle an jem. vertreten** to act as father to s. o.; **~tag** Father's Day *(US)*.
Vegetarier vegetarian.
vegetarische|Kost vegetable diet; **~ Lebensweise** vegetarianism.
Vegetation, üppige luxuriant (lush, rank) vegetation.
vegetieren to vegetate, to live in wretched poverty.
Vehikel vehicle.
Ventil valve, *(fig.)* safety valve, vent, outlet;
~ **für überflüssige Kräfte** outlet for one's energies; ~ **für die Unzufriedenheit der Arbeitnehmer** safety valve for the discontent of the employees;
mit ~en kontrollieren (versehen) to valve.
Ventilation ventilation, aeration.
Ventilationsanlage ventilating system.
Ventilator ventilator, fan, vacuum fan;
~antrieb fan driving; **~flügel** vane of a fan blower.
Ventilgehäuse valve box.
ventilieren to ventilate, to air, to moot, to discuss;
Erhöhung um 15% ~ to broach the subject of a 15% rise; **Frage** ~ to ventilate (air, moot) a question; **Ursachen der Parteispaltung** ~ to ventilate the causes of the rift in a party.
Ventilsteuerung valve gear.
verabreden to agree upon, to stipulate, to fix, to concert, to appoint, to arrange;
sich ~ to make an appointment (a date, *coll.*), *(verschwören)* to conspire; **sich mit jem.** ~ to arrange to meet s. o.; **sich zum Abendessen** ~ to engage o. s. for dinner; **Zusammenkunft** ~ to arrange (fix) a meeting.
verabredet arranged;
heimlich ~ collusive; **stillschweigend** ~ understood; **vorher** ~ preengaged, preconcerted; **wie** ~ as agreed upon, stipulated; **sich mit jem. ~ haben** to have an appointment with s. o., to meet s. o. by appointment; **schon ~ sein** to have a previous appointment;
~e Sache put-up job, cut and dried; **zur ~en Zeit** at the appointed time.
verabredetermaßen according to previous arrangements, as agreed upon.
Verabredung appointment, engagement, tryst, concerted action, date *(coll.)*, conspiracy, *(Vereinbarung)* agreement, arrangement;
aufgrund vorheriger ~ owing to previous engagement; **nach** ~ by appointment;
anderweitige ~ previous engagement; **geschäftliche** ~ business meeting (appointment); **unerlaubte** ~ collusion;
~ **zu einer strafbaren Handlung** criminal conspiracy; ~ **zum Mittagessen** luncheon engagement; ~ **zum Mord** conspiracy to commit murder; ~ **zum Selbstmord** suicide pact; ~ **mit einem Unbekannten** blind date *(US)*;
~ **absagen (nicht einhalten)** to break an appointment (a tryst), to keep s. o. waiting; ~ **einhalten** to keep an appointment; ~ **mit jem. nicht einhalten** to stand s. o. up; **~en pünktlich einhalten** to be a strict timekeeper; ~ **haben** to have a date *(US coll.)* (an appointment); **keine ~ haben** to have nothing on; **seine ~en notieren** to list all one's engagements; **infolge einer früheren ~ an der Übernahme des Vorsitzes verhindert sein** to have been prevented by a previous engagement from taking the chair; ~ **treffen** to enter into an engagement, to fix (make) an appointment, to arrange to meet s. o., to meet s. o. by appointment; ~ **verpassen** to miss an appointment.
verabredungsgemäß as per arrangement.
verabreichen, Gift to administer poison.
verabsäumen to neglect, to omit;
es ~, j. zu benachrichtigen to fail to inform s. o.
verabscheuen to loathe, to detest, to abominate.
verabscheuens|wert loathsome, detestable, abhorrent, abominable; **seine Freunde in ~würdiger Weise ausnutzen** to exploit one's friends in an abominable way.
verabschieden *(Beamte)* to dismiss, to discharge, to retire, *(Offizier)* to place on the retired list, to gazette out, *(Truppen)* to disband, to demobilize;
sich ~ to take one's leave; **Gast schnell** ~ to speed a parting guest; **Gesetz** ~ to pass a bill; **sich mit einem Handschlag** ~ to take leave with a handshake; **Haushalt** ~ to vote the estimates; **Minister** ~ to relieve a minister of his office; **j. offiziell** ~ to bid an official farewell to s. o.; **sich umständlich** ~ to take a ceremonious leave; **unter Zahlung einer Pension** ~ to pension off.
verabschiedet *(Gesetz)* passed, *(Offizier)* on half-pay.
Verabschiedung send-off, *(Beamte)* discharge, dismissal;
~ **einer Gesetzesvorlage** passing (passage) of a bill, enactment of a law; ~ **des Haushalts** voting the estimates;
~ **eines Gesetzentwurfes im Parlament verschleppen** to obstruct the progress of a bill through the House of Commons.
verachten to despise, to disdain, to depreciate;
j. ~ to feel contempt for s. o.; **jede Schmeichelei** ~ to scorn flattery;
nicht zu ~ sein not to be sneezed (scoffed) at.
verächtlich contemptuous, despicable, disparaging, disdainful, depreciatory;
~er Blick disdainful look; **~e Gesinnung erkennen lassen** to reveal an abject character; **in ~er Weise von jem. sprechen** to refer to s. o. in terms of disparagement (disparaging terms).
verächtlichmachen to disparage, to bring in disrepute, to decry;
j. ~ to say black in one's eye, to cast a slur on s. one's reputation; **Konkurrenz** ~ to disparage competitors.
Verächtlichmachung disparagement;
~ **des Gerichts** contempt of court; ~ **der Konkurrenz** disparagement of competitors, defamation of a competitor's reputation; ~ **einer Person** defamation of s. one's character.
Verachtung contempt, disdain, scorn;
der öffentlichen ~ preisgeben hold up to public obloquy;
j. mit ~ strafen to show one's contempt for s. o.; **seine ~ zeigen** to make a lip.
veralbern, j. to ridicule (poke fun at) s. o.
verallgemeinern to generalize.
Verallgemeinerung generalization;
~en anstellen to generalize.
veralten to become obsolete, to go out of date, to get out of use, *(Gesetz)* to become antiquated.
Veralterung, geplante planned obsolescence.
Veralterungsabschreibung depreciation for obsolescence.
veraltet antiquated, obsolete, obsolescent, old-fashioned, superannuated, out-of-use (-date), stale, dated, disused, off the map, worm-eaten, timeworn, passé, *(Mode)* outmoded, out-of-fashion, out-of-vogue;
hoffnungslos ~ desperately dated, horse-and-buggy;
~ **sein** to grow obsolete;
~e Ansichten outmoded (moth-eaten) views; **~e Arbeitsmethoden** archaic working methods; **~er Ausdruck** archaism; **~e Ausgabe** outdated edition; **~er Kommentar** obsolete textbook; **~e Sache** model T Ford.
Veranda veranda[h], porch *(US)*, sun parlo(u)r;
offene ~ open (unroofed) veranda, stoop *(US)*.
veränderlich alterable, changeable, *(Börse)* variable, unsettled, *(Charakter)* fickle, unsteady, *(Wetter)* changeable, variable;
auf ~ zeigen *(Barometer)* to point to a change;
~es Agio fluctuating premium; **~e Kosten** running (variable) costs; **~er Kurswert** fluctuating market value.
Veränderlichkeit variability, instability, unsettledness.
verändern to alter, to change, *(abändern)* to modify, *(verschieben)* to shift;
sich ~ *(Kurs)* to fluctuate, *(Preise)* to undergo changes, to vary, *(Stellung wechseln)* to drop one's work; **von Grund auf** ~ to revolutionize; **sich leicht** ~ *(Kurse)* to shift slightly; **sich nachteilig** ~ to deteriorate, to fall off; **Sachlage** ~ to alter matters; **strukturell** ~ to convert; **sich vorteilhaft** ~ to change for the better; **seinen Wohnsitz** ~ to move, to change one's lodgings.
verändernd alternative.
verändert changed, different;
leicht ~ adapted;
j. sehr ~ finden to find a great change in s. o.; **sich sehr ~ haben** to have changed a lot (altered a great deal); **sich völlig ~ haben** to come back a changed man;
~e Umstände changed circumstances.
Veränderung alteration, change, *(Abänderung)* modification, *(Börse)* turn, *(Schwankung)* fluctuation, variation, *(Wende)* shift;
schnellen ~en unterworfen runaway;
bedeutende ~ serious alteration; **jahreszeitliche bedingte** ~ seasonal variation; **bemerkenswerte** ~ observable (noticeable)

change; **berufliche** ~ change of position (job); **friedliche** ~ *(Völkerrecht)* peaceful change; **geringfügige** ~**en** *(Kurs)* fractional changes, *(Warenzeichen)* colo(u)red imitation; **geschäftliche** ~**en** business changes; **gewaltsame** ~ *(Völkerrecht)* violent change; **mancherlei** ~**en** change of many sorts; **organisatorische** ~**en** organizational changes; **riskante** ~ *(Meinungsforschung)* risky shift; **strukturelle** ~**en** structural (textural) alteration (changes); **zukünftige** ~**en** changes ahead; ~**en im Anlagevermögen** capital gains and losses; ~**en in der Belegschaftszusammensetzung** personnel changes; ~ **der Erbanlagen** genetic engineering; ~ **der Firma** change of trade name; ~**en im Gesellschafterverhältnis** change in partnership; ~ **des Gesellschaftszweckes** alteration of objects clause; **kaum** ~**en im Gesicht einer Stadt** not much alteration in a town; ~ **der Grenze** changes in the frontier line; **werterhöhende** ~**en in der Grundstückssubstanz** ameliorating waste; ~**en im Kabinett** reshuffle of the government; ~**en in der Parteispitze** changes (reshuffle) in party leadership; ~ **der Satzung** amendment of charter, alteration in the articles of association; ~ **des Steuersatzes** variation of the tax rate; ~**en im Vorstand** management changes, change in the direction of a firm, change in the membership of the board; **dramatische** ~**en in der Weltlage** dramatic changes in the international situation; ~**en erleiden** to undergo changes; **noch** ~**en unterliegen** to be subject to modifications; **betrügerische** ~**en vornehmen** to tamper; **einige** ~**en vornehmen** to make some modifications.

veränderungshalber for a change.

Veränderungs|meldung change report; ~**sperre** development freeze.

verängstigen, j. to intimidate (cow) s. o.

verängstigt intimidated, scared, frightened, cowed.

verankern to anchor, to moor, to fasten, *(Recht)* to embody, to incorporate;
Vertrag gesetzlich ~ to embody a treaty in a law.

verankert anchored, moored, *(fig.)* embodied, incorporated;
in der Verfassung ~ laid down in the constitution;
~ **sein in** to be grounded in; **fest** ~ **sein** *(Gewohnheit)* to be solidly entrenched.

veranlagen to assess, to rate;
anteilsmäßig ~ to prorate, to assess *(US)*; **einkommenssteuerlich** ~ to assess income tax; **zur Erbschaftssteuer** ~ to assess death duties; **Gebäude steuerlich** ~ to assess a building; **Geschäftsgewinn mit einem höheren Steuersatz** ~ to assess a business profit at a higher rate; **steuerlich getrennt** ~ to assess separately; **zu hoch** ~ to overassess, to overrate; **körperschaftssteuerlich** ~ to assess to corporation tax; **zur Vermögenssteuer** ~ to assess property for taxation; **zusammen** ~ to assess jointly; **sich getrennt** ~ **lassen** to file separate returns; **sich zusammen** ~ **lassen** to file a joint return.

veranlagt inclined, prone, *(begabt)* talented, *(Grundstück)* extended, *(steuerlich)* assessed, rated *(Br.)*;
gut ~ highly gifted; **nicht** ~ unassessed; **unrechtmäßig** ~ illegally assessed;
praktisch ~ **sein** to have a practical turn of mind; **verbrecherisch** ~ **sein** to have criminal leanings; ~ **werden** to be taxed (assessed); **getrennt** ~ **werden** to be taxed separately; **aus steuerlichen Gründen getrennt** ~ **werden** to be treated as separated for tax purposes; **zu hoch** ~ **werden** to be overrated; ~**e Einkommensteuer** assessed (individual, *US*) income tax; **geistig gut** ~**er Schüler** highly gifted pupil; ~**e Steuer** scheduled (assessed) tax; ~**er Steuerbetrag** assessment; ~**e Summe** assessed amount; ~**er Wert** assessed (ratable) value (valuation, *US*).

Veranlagter taxpayer, ratepayer.

Veranlagung assessment, taxation, assessor's valuation, *(Begabung)* talent, gift, disposition, predisposition, *(Hang)* proclivity, leanings, *(Kommune)* rating *(Br.)*;
bei seiner ~ with his talents; **seiner ganzen** ~ **nach** temperamentally;
anteilmäßige ~ proportional (prorata) assessment; **bösartige** ~ *(Tier)* vicious propensity; **direkte** ~ direct assessment; **erbliche** ~ hereditary predisposition; **gemeinsame** ~ *(Ehegatten)* joint return; **gestaffelte** ~ graduated assessment; **getrennte** ~ *(Ehegatten)* separate assessment, splitting *(US)*; **herabgesetzte** ~ reduced assessment; **zu hohe** ~ overassessment, overrate; **krankhafte** ~ pathological predisposition; **kriminelle** ~ criminal leanings (disposition), general malice, criminalism; **künstlerische** ~ artistic bend; **nachträgliche** ~ subsequent assessment; **glückliche natürliche** ~ happy dispensation of nature; **zu niedrige** ~ underassessment; **ordnungsgemäße** ~ fair and proper legal assessment; **pauschale** ~ flat-rate assessment; **steuerliche** ~ assessed valuation, tax assessment; **überhöhte** ~ overassessment; **aufgrund von Schätzungen vorgenommene** ~ arbitrary assessment; **zusätzliche** ~ additional assessment;
~ **des Bruttoeinkommens** gross rating assessment; ~ **zur Einkommensteuer** assessment of income tax; ~ **durch die Gemeinde (zur Gemeindesteuer)** assessment of landed property, local assessment, rating *(Br.)*; **neue** ~ **zur Grundsteuer** new valuation for rating purposes *(Br.)*; **sofortige** ~ **wegen befürchteten Steuerausfalls** jeopardy assessment; ~ **zur Vermögenssteuer** assessment of property;
getrennte ~ **beantragen** to claim separate assessment; **neue** ~ **beantragen** to reopen an assessment; ~ **berichtigen** to revise an assessment; ~ **durchführen** to calculate (prepare) an assessment; **um getrennte** ~ **einkommen** to apply for separate assessment; **Einspruch gegen eine** ~ **einlegen** to appeal against a tax assessment; **Steuer durch** ~ **erheben** to levy a tax; ~ **in Abweichung von der Steuererklärung festsetzen** to raise an estimated assessment; **politische** ~ **haben** to have a head for politics; **falsche** ~ **vornehmen** to assess incorrectly; **durch eine** ~ **benachteiligt werden** to be aggrieved by an assessment.

Veranlagungs|behörde assessment (tax-writing) committee, valuation *(Br.)* (tax, *US*) commission; ~**bereich** area of assessment; ~**bescheid** notice of assessment, tax assessment note; ~**bestimmungen** methods of assessing taxable property; ~**betrag erhöhen** to increase the assessment; ~**bezirk** assessment district (area), taxing district; ~**einrichtungen** assessment machinery.

veranlagungsfähiger Personenkreis taxable persons.

Veranlagungs|gesetz assessment committee act; ~**grenze** assessment limit; **aus** ~**gründen** for the purpose of taxation; ~**grundlage** tax base, basis of assessment; ~**jahr** year of assessment, taxable year; **laufendes** ~**jahr** current period taxation; **vorhergehendes** ~**jahr** preceding period; ~**kosten** assessment costs; ~**liste** assessment list (roll), tax book, taxpayer's list; ~**methode** method of assessment, taxation method; ~**objekt** unit of assessment; ~**periode** assessment (taxable) period; ~**pflicht begründen** to make taxable.

veranlagungspflichtig assessable, taxable, subject to taxation, *(kommunal)* ratable;
~ **sein** to be taxed;
~**es Vermögen** taxable property.

Veranlagungs|pflichtiger taxable person; ~**prinzipien** methods of assessing taxable property; ~**richtlinien** rules of assessment, assessment directives; ~**rücklage** tax reserve; ~**satz** tax rate, rate of assessment; ~**stelle** taxation authority, special commissioners *(Br.)*, tax assessor *(Scot.)*; ~**tag** date of assessment; ~**verfahren** procedure of assessment, assessment; ~**vorschriften** assessment provisions; ~**wahlrecht** *(Einkommensteuer)* election; **im** ~**wege erhobene Steuern** assessed taxes; ~**wert** ratal, ratable value, assessed value (valuation, *US*); ~**wert eines Hauses** ratable value of a house; ~**zeitpunkt** date of assessment; ~**zeitraum** taxable (assessment) period, basic period, chargeable accounting period *(Br.)*, period of assessment.

veranlassen to give rise to, to prompt, to occasion, to induce, to draw on, to cause, *(verleiten)* to induce, to dispose,;
j. zu etw. ~ to move s. o. to do s. th.; **jem. zur Annahme einer Stellung** ~ to dispose s. o. to accept a position; **j. zu einem Entschluß** ~ to prompt s. o. to a decision; **j. zu dem Glauben** ~ to make s. o. think; **das Nötige** ~ to take the necessary steps.

veranlaßt under the inspiration, induced.

Veranlassung cause, occasion, instigation, inducement, room, provocation;
auf ~ **von** at the instigation of, under the inspiration of, by direction of, upon the recommendation (suggestion) of; **auf meine** ~ by my orders; **auf seine** ~ on his initiative; **aus gegebener** ~ should the occasion arise, for a particular reason; **ohne jede** ~ without any reason (provocation), unprovoked; **zur sofortigen** ~ for immediate attention; **zur weiteren** ~ for appropriate (further) action;
keine ~ no call for;
für eine Behauptung keine ~ **haben** to have no warrant for saying.

veranschaulichen to visualize, to illustrate.

Veranschaulichung visualization, illustration.

veranschlagen to [make an] estimate, to appraise, to evaluate, *(bewerten)* to value, to rate, *(steuerlich)* to assess, to rate;
Besitz auf 400.000 DM ~ to value (rate) a property at DM 400.000; **Druckkosten eines Auftrages** ~ to estimate a job of printing; **im Haushaltsplan** ~ to budget for; **hoch** ~ to value at a high rate *(US)*; **zu hoch** ~ to overrate, to overestimate; **Kosten** ~

to estimate the costs; **Neubaukosten** ~ to estimate the cost of a new house; **zu niedrig** ~ to underestimate, to underrate; **Reparaturkosten eines Hauses** ~ to estimate for the repair of a building; **Schaden auf 5 Pfund** ~ to value the damage [done] at five pounds.

veranschlagt valued, estimated, rated, assessed;
annähernd ~ on a rough calculation; **steuerlich** ~ assessed, rated;
~ **werden** to be calculated, to figure out at *(coll.)*;
~**er Betrag** estimated amount; ~**e Kosten** estimated cost; ~**er Wert** appraised (assessed) value; ~**e Zuschüsse** budgeted provisions.

Veranschlagung estimation, estimate, statement, *(Bewertung)* valuation, *(steuerlich)* rate, rating, assessment, taxation;
annähernde ~ approximate calculation;
~ **der Baukosten** building estimate; ~ **der Druckkosten** printing estimate.

veranstalten to arrange, to organize, to manage, to get up;
Auktion ~ to get up an auction; **Ausstellung** ~ to organize an exhibition; **Empfang** ~ to give a reception; **Meinungsumfrage** ~ to organize an opinion poll, to take a poll, to conduct a survey; **Sammlung** ~ to open a subscription, to pass the hat round; **Umzug** ~ to stage a procession; **Volkszählung** ~ to take a census.

Veranstalter promoter for the occasion, manager, organizer, *(Gastgeber)* host;
~ **einer Versammlung** promoter of a meeting.

Veranstaltung performance, function, activity, arrangement;
ausgelassene ~ racket; **außerschulische** ~**en** out-of-school activities; **betriebliche** ~ company social function; **festliegende** ~ fixture; **von den Angestellten finanzierte** ~ employee party; **gesellschaftliche** ~ special (social, active) event, function, festive affair, social activity (life), exhibition, entertainment, mix *(sl.)*, session *(sl.)*; **musikalische** ~ musical entertainment; **sportliche** ~ event; **überfüllte** ~ crush;
~ **einer Ausstellung** organization of an exhibiton; ~**en im Laufe des Jahres** events of the year;
viele gesellschaftliche ~**en besuchen** to go out a great deal; **sich von gesellschaftlichen** ~**en fernhalten** to estrange o. s. from social life; **auf einer großen** ~ **völlig verloren sein** to be lonely in the midst of a racket; **j. bei gesellschaftlichen** ~**en treffen** to see s. o. socially; **öffentliche** ~ **übertragen** to broadcast a public function.

Veranstaltungs|kalender calendar of events; ~**raum** cultural hall.

verantworten to answer (render account, stand, *US*) for;
sich ~ to defend o. s.; **Tat** ~ to justify an action;
Ausgaben zu ~ **haben** to be liable (responsible) for the expenditure; **sich für einen Vorfall zu** ~ **haben** to have to answer for an incident.

verantwortlich responsible, *(geschäftsführend)* acting, *(haftbar)* answerable, liable, responsible, accountable;
nicht ~ not responsible; **der öffentlichen Meinung** ~ responsible before public opinion; **strafrechtlich** ~ liable to penalty, chargeable; **voll** ~ legally responsible, wholly liable;
~ **machen** to hold accountable; **j.** ~ **machen** to hold s. o. responsible (liable), to pin responsibility on s. o.; **j. für den Kriegsausbruch** ~ **machen** to blame s. o. for the outbreak of a war; ~ **sein** to be obliged, to be liable, to answer; **nur dem Chef** ~ **sein** to be accountable to the boss only; **strafrechtlich nicht** ~ **sein** to be immune of criminal responsibility; **unmittelbar** ~ **sein** to be primarily responsible; **voll** ~ **sein** to be responsible for one's actions; ~ **zeichnen** to make o. s. responsible;
~**es Kapital** authorized capital; ~ **aufgeteilte Kostenkalkulation** responsibility costing; ~**er Leiter** acting manager; ~**er Redakteur** responsible editor; ~**e Stellung** fiduciary position, post of confidence (trust); ~**er Teilhaber** general (associated) partner.

Verantwortlichen, die the people responsible.

Verantwortlichkeit responsibility, *(Haftung)* liability, accountability, amenability, charge;
alleinige ~ undivided responsibility; **ministerielle** ~ responsibility and accountability of a minister, ministerial responsibility; **strafrechtliche** ~ penal liability *(US)*; **unternehmerische** ~ executive responsibilty; **volle** ~ full responsibility;
~ **der Betriebsführung** management accountability;
~ **delegieren** to delegate responsibility; **strafrechtlicher** ~ **unterliegen** to be liable to prosecution; **nicht strafrechtlicher** ~ **unterliegen** to be immune of criminal responsibility; **seine** ~ **zugeben** to admit one's responsibility.

Verantwortung responsibility, charge;
auf deine ~ on your head be it; **auf eigene** ~ on one's own responsibility, at one's own risk; **auf Ihre** ~ on your head be it, at your risk; **auf unsere** ~ under our guarantee; **mit** ~ **belastet** laden with responsibility;
behördliche ~ official responsibility; **berufliche** ~ job responsibility; **erhöhte** ~ additional responsibility; **hohe** ~ heavy responsibility; **persönliche** ~ personal (direct) responsibility; **schwere** ~ heavy load on one's shoulders; **strafrechtliche** ~ criminal liability;
~ **in Einkaufsfragen** purchasing responsibility; ~ **der weißen Rasse** the white man's burden;
~ **für etw. ablehnen** to disclaim (decline, assume no) responsibility for s. th.; ~ **für einen Unfall restlos ablehnen** to decline all responsibility for an accident; **jem. die** ~ **abnehmen** to exonerate s. o. from responsibility, to take a matter off s. one's hands; ~ **auf jem. abwälzen** to devolve the responsibility on (pass the buck to, *US*) s. o.; **sich** ~ **aufbürden** to saddle o. s. with responsibility; **jem.** ~ **auferlegen** to put responsibility on s. one's shoulders; **sich vor der** ~ **drücken** to shuffle out of the responsibility, to pass the buck *(US)*; **von der** ~ **entbinden** to indemnify; **sich der** ~ **entziehen** to evade (dodge, shirk) responsibility; **in die** ~ **des Autors fallen** to lie with the author; **jem. seine** ~ **klar machen** to awaken s. o. to his responsibilities; **schwere** ~ **tragen müssen** to have a great weight of responsibility; ~ **tragen** to bear the responsibility, to be responsible, to be in the driving seat, to take the can back *(fam.)*; ~ **für die Sicherheit der Passagiere tragen** to be responsible for the passengers' safety; ~ **übernehmen** to assume (incur) responsibility, to accept liability for; **schwere** ~ **übernehmen** to take on heavy responsibility; ~ **für j. übernehmen** to take s. o. in hand; ~ **gemeinsam übernehmen** to join together in responsibility; **gesamte** ~ **in einem Vorstandsbereich übernehmen** to resume responsibility in the overall operating management; **etw. auf eigene** ~ **unternehmen** to do s. th. on one's own [responsibility]; **zur** ~ **ziehen** to call to account, *(haftpflichtig machen)* to hold responsible (liable); **jem. die** ~ **zuschieben** to fasten (shift) the responsibility upon s. o., to pass the buck to s. o. *(US)*.

Verantwortungsbereich area (zone) of responsibility, responsibility basis, responsibilities, *(Kostenstellenrechnung)* responsibility basis;
seinen ~ **voll ausfüllen** to fill well one's responsibilities; ~ **dezentralisieren** to pass responsibility down the line; **in eine Stellung mit höherem** ~ **befördert werden** to be promoted to heavier responsibilities.

verantwortungsbewußt responsible.

Verantwortungsfreude zeigen to enjoy one's responsibilities.

verantwortungsfreudig ready to take responsibility.

Verantwortungsgefühl sense of responsibility.

verantwortungs|los irresponsible, wanton, without restraint, devil-may-care; ~**reiche Stellung haben** to have a very responsible position.

Verantwortungssinn, finanzieller financial responsibility.

verantwortungsvoller Posten post of trust, fiduciary position, responsible office.

veräppeln, j. to poke fun at (josh) s. o.; **sich selbst** ~ to kid o. s.

verarbeiten to process, to convert, to finish, *(aufarbeiten)* to work up, *(fabrizieren)* to manufacture, to turn into fabric, to fabricate;
Baumwolle zu Tuch ~ to work cotton into cloth; **Eisen zu Stahl** ~ to convert iron to steel; **maschinell** ~ to machine; **geliefertes Material** ~ to work up, to finish, to process.

verarbeitende Industrie processing (manufacturing, finishing) industry.

Verarbeiter processor.

verarbeitet finished, processed;
fest ~ hard-finished;
nicht ~**e Waren** unprocessed (unfinished) commodity (goods).

Verarbeitung mechanical treatment, *(Aufarbeitung)* working up, *(Ausführung)* workmanship, *(Industrie)* processing, finishing, manufacturing, manufacture, *(Lektüre)* digestion, *(Umarbeitung)* conversion;
in der ~ **begriffen** in process of completion;
erste ~ first processing; **gute** ~ good workmanship; **schlechte** ~ poor finish; **stapelweise** ~ *(Datenverarbeitung)* batch processing.

Verarbeitungs|abteilung processing department; ~**anweisung** processing prescription; ~**beschränkungen** processing restrictions; ~**bestand** work in process *(Br.)* (progress, *US*); ~**betrieb** processor of commodities, processing enterprise, endprocessing plant (enterprise), manufacturing business (enterprise, establishment, plant); ~**genehmigung** processing permit;

~**industrie** processing (finishing, manufacturing) industry; ~**kosten** processing expenses, conversion cost; ~**ort** place of manufacture; ~**preis** manufacturing price; **einer Reihe von** ~**prozessen unterwerfen** to route; **im** ~**stadium** in process of completion; ~**steuer** processing tax *(US)*; ~**stufe** stage of processing, processing stage; ~**verbot** processing (converting) prohibition; ~**verfahren** finishing process; ~**vorschrift** processing prescription; ~**zentrum** processing center *(US)* (centre, *Br.*).

verärgern, j. to annoy (irritate, vex, provoke, pique) s. o.

verärgert annoyed, angry, irritated, vexed;
sehr ~ as cross as two sticks *(coll.)*;
über j. ~ **sein** to be put out with s. o., to get mad at s. o. *(US fam.)*; **ziemlich** ~ **sein** to be anything but pleased.

Verärgerung annoyance, irritation, provocation, anger.

verarmen to fall (sink) into (be reduced to) poverty, to impoverish.

verarmt poverty-stricken, impoverished, in reduced circumstances;
völlig ~ destitute, reduced to destitution, plunged into poverty;
~ **sein** to be reduced to poverty, to live in penury; **völlig** ~ **sterben** to die in abject poverty;
~**e Familie** penurious family.

Verarmung impoverishment, pauperization.

verarschen, j. to have s. o. on, to make a sucker out of s. o.

Verästelung ramification, branching, offshoot;
~**en einer Verschwörung** ramifications of a plot;
Affäre in allen ~**en kennen** to know the ins and outs of a matter.

verauktionieren to sell at (by, *US*) auction.

verauktioniert werden to to come under the hammer, to be sold at (by, *US*) auction.

verausgaben to spend, to expend, to disburse, to lay out, to outlay;
sich ~ to spend beyond one's means, to run short of money, to overspend, to part with one's money, *(fig.)* to burn the candle at both ends.

verausgabt spent, disbursed;
nicht ~ unspent;
sich ganz ~ **haben** to have run out of cash.

Verausgabung spending, expenditure;
~ **von Mitteln** disbursement of funds.

verauslagen to spend, to disburse, to expend.

Verauslagung reimbursable expenses.

Veräußerer seller, disposer, alienor, alienator, releasor.

veräußerlich salable, alienable, disposable, sellable, *(übertragbar)* assignable, transferable, negotiable;
nicht ~ not for sale, inalienable, unassignable.

Veräußerlichkeit alienability, salability, negotiability.

veräußern to alienate, to alien, to dispose of, to sell, *(übertragen)* to assign, to transfer, to convey, to make over (off);
etw. ~ to make money out of s. th.; **privatrechtlich** ~ to sell s. th. by private treaty; **unter dem Wert** ~ to bargain away.

veräußert sold, disposed of.

Veräußerung alienation, sale, disposal, disposition;
freihändige ~ sale in the open market;
~ **des Betriebs** sale of plant; ~ **von Grundbesitz** disposal of land, mobilization, conveyance of real estate; ~ **an die tote Hand** alienation in mortmain, amortization; ~ **von Patentrechten** disposal of patent rights; ~ **des gesamten Vermögens** bulk sale *(US)*; ~ **mit dem Ziel der Gläubigerbenachteiligung** fraudulent assignment;
Schuldner an der ~ **seines Grundbesitzes verhindern** to restrain a debtor from selling his property.

Veräußerungs|anzeige advertisement of a sale; ~**bedingungen** clauses governing sale; ~**befugnis** power of sale (alienation, disposal), *(Grundstück)* ministerial powers *(Br.)*; ~**beschränkungen** limitations of the right to alienation, sales restrictions *(Br.)*; ~**beträge** cash receipts; ~**erlös** disposal proceeds, proceeds of sale; ~**genehmigung** sales permit; ~**geschäft** act of sale; ~**gewinn** profit on sale, sales profit, income from sale, capital gain from sales; ~**gewinn aus Investitionsgütern** capital profit; ~**preis** sales price; ~**sperre** prohibition to sell, stop order; ~**termin** date of disposal; ~**treuhand** trust for sale *(Br.)*; ~**verbot** prohibition to sell, conditions against alienation, restraint on alienation (upon anticipation, *US*), *(Zahlungseinstellung)* receiving order *(Br.)*; ~**verbot für den Gemeinschuldner** bankruptcy inhibition; ~**vollmacht** power of alienation (disposal); ~**wert** realization value; ~**zeitraum** time of disposal.

Verbalbeleidigung insult to s. one's hono(u)r.

verballhornen to distort, to warp.

Verbalnote *(dipl.)* note verbale.

Verband association, federation, confederation, syndicate, organization, union, society, league, combine, *(Arzt)* bandage, *(Flugzeug)* formation, *(mil.)* unit, group, formation, *(Versicherungsgesellschaften)* bureau *(US)*;
angeschlossener ~ affiliate, affiliated organization; **fliegender** ~ *(mil.)* flying unit; **gemeinnütziger** ~ nonprofitmaking organization; **internationaler** ~ international union; **karikativer** ~ charitable institution; **mechanisierter** ~ *(mil.)* mechanized force; **örtlicher (regionaler)** ~ regional association, local; **unwichtiger** ~ small-time organization;
~ **der Arbeitgeber** [etwa] Federation of Industries; ~ **der Erdölexportierenden Länder** Organization of Petroleum Exporting Countries (OPEC); ~ **der Europäischen Landwirtschaft** European Confederation of Agriculture; ~ **britischer Kapitalanlagegesellschaften** National Association of Investment Clubs *(Br.)*; ~ **der Kleinlebensversicherungen** Industrial Life Office Association *(Br.)*; ~ **mit eigenen Kontrollfunktionen** self-regulatory organization; **Internationaler** ~ **für Meinungsforschung** International Association for Public Opinion Research; ~ **zum Schutz des gewerblichen Eigentums** Union for the Protection of Industrial Property; ~ **der Steuerzahler** National Tax Association *(US)*;
sich einem ~ **anschließen** to affiliate with an association; **in geschlossenem** ~ **fahren** *(Schiff)* to sail in company (a convoy); **Anschluß an einen** ~ **finden** to affiliate with an association; **im** ~ **fliegen** to fly in formation; ~ **gründen** to form an association, to call an organization into existence.

Verbands|abkommen association agreement; ~**absatz** associative marketing *(US)*; ~**anmeldung** convention application; ~**anwalt** corporation lawyer *(US)*; ~**archiv** organization library; ~**beitrag** subscription to a trade association; ~**blatt** organ of a corporation.

verbandseigene Geschäfte interassociation transactions *(US)*.

Verbands|flug formation flight; ~**geschäft** associated store *(US)*; ~**kasse** fund of an association; ~**kasten** ambulance box, first-aid outfit (box), bandage case; ~**klage** representative action; ~**land** convention country; ~**leiter** association president; ~**marke** certification trademark *(Br.)*, collective mark *(US)*; ~**material** dressing material; ~**mitglied** syndicate (trade) member, member of an association; ~**mitgliedschaft** association membership; ~**organ** organ of a corporation, trade paper *(Br.)*; ~**päckchen** first-aid kit, *(mil.)* field dressing; ~**präsident** association president; ~**preis** association (combine) price; ~**priorität** convention priority; ~**satzung** articles of association; ~**staat** union state; ~**syndikus** association attorney, corporation lawyer *(US)*; ~**tag** congress of an organization; ~**tarif** *(Versicherung)* bureau rates; ~**vertrieb** associative marketing *(US)*; ~**vorsitzender** association president; ~**zeichen** collective (certification, *US*) mark, certification trademark *(Br.)*; ~**zeitschrift** organ of a corporation, trade paper *(Br.)*; ~**zeitschrift der Fernsehindustrie** television industry trade paper; ~**zugehörigkeit** association membership.

verbannen to exile, to proscribe, to forejudge, to relegate, to banish, to cast out;
j. ~ to send s. o. into exile; **j. aus seinem Vaterland** ~ to exile s. o. from his country.

verbannt werden, lebenslänglich to be sentenced to transportation for life.

Verbannter expatriate, exile.

Verbannung exile, ban, banishment, expulsion, deportment;
in die ~ **gehen** to expatriate o. s.; **in der** ~ **leben** to live in exile.

Verbannungsort exile.

verbarrikadieren to barricade, to block;
sich ~ to entrench o. s.

verbauen, jem. die Aussicht to obstruct s. one's view; **Haus völlig** ~ to make a mess of a house; **jds. Zukunftsaussichten** ~ to spoil (mar) s. one's future.

verbaut badly planned.

verbeamten, j. to give s. o. the rank of a civil servant.

verbeißen, sich in eine Aufgabe to become deeply involved in one's work, to get one's teeth into a job; **sich das Lachen** ~ to contain one's laughter; **sich den Zorn** ~ to stifle one's anger; **sich eine Antwort nicht** ~ **können** not to be able to suppress an answer.

verbergen to hide, to veil, to conceal, to disguise, to curtain, to dissemble, to niche;
sich ~ to be in hiding, to secrete o. s., to lie low; **seine Absichten vor jem.** ~ to mislead s. o. as to one's intentions; **seine Erregung** ~ to veil one's excitement; **seine Gefühle nicht** ~ to make no

disguise of one's feelings; **sein Gesicht in seinen Händen** ~ to bury one's face in one's hands; **seine Pläne** ~ to disguise one's plans; **sich vor der Polizei** ~ to hide from the police, to hide out *(US)*; **Schatz** ~ to hide away a treasure; **seine Sorgen hinter betont fröhlichem Auftreten** ~ to disguise one's sorrow beneath a cheerful appearance.

verbessern to better, to improve, to ameliorate, to correct, to rectify, to mend, *(Buchausgabe)* to revise, *(kritisch durchsehen)* to amend, to revise, to castigate;
sich ~ *(Kurse)* to improve, to experience an advance, *(Markt)* to look up, to change (take a turn) for the better, *(in der Rede)* to correct o. s.; **Beziehungen zu einem Land** ~ to improve (the) relations with a country; **Eintragung** ~ to rectify an entry; **Erfindung** ~ to perfect an invention; **falsch** ~ to miscorrect; **Fehler** ~ to correct a mistake; **sich finanziell** ~ to better o. s. (one's circumstances), *(durch Gehaltserhöhung)* to get a raise *(US)* (rise, *Br.*); **Gesetz** ~ to amend (emend) a bill; **Grundertragswert durch Bebauung** ~ to improve a lot by building on it; **Korrekturen** ~ to revise the proof sheet, to correct the press; **Kultivierungsmethode** ~ to improve on the mode of tillage; **Los der Arbeiter** ~ to better the conditions of the workers; **das Los der Armen** ~ to meliorate the lot (ameliorate the condition) of the poor; **Methode** ~ to rectify a method; **sich um 3 Punkte** ~ *(Kurs)* to gain 3 points; **Situation** ~ to better a situation, to mend matters; **Text** ~ to emend (castigate) a text.

verbessernd corrective.

verbessert improved;
~**e Auflage** revised [and improved] edition; ~**e Korrektur** revised proof; ~**es Modell von 1981** improvement design of 1981; **gesellschaftlich** ~**e Stellung** improvement in one's social conditions.

Verbesserung progress, advance, improvement, *(Berichtigung)* correction, rectification, *(Boden)* improvement, amelioration, melioration, betterment, *(Bucht)* revisal, revision, *(Gesetz)* emendation, amendment, *(Vervollkommnung)* perfection;
allerletzte ~**en** the very latest improvements; **ausgesprochene** ~ real improvement; **bauliche** ~**en** structural improvements, improvement of building *(US)*; **durchgreifende** ~**en** far-reaching improvements; **entwicklungsbedingte** ~**en** technological improvements; **merkliche** ~ marked improvement; **organisatorische** ~**en** organizational improvements; **patentfähige** ~ patentable improvement; **technische** ~**en** technological (technical) improvements; **treibstoffsparende** ~**en** fuel-economy improvements; **werterhaltende** ~**en** *(Gebäude)* necessary improvements;
~ **von Druckfahnen** correction of proof sheets; ~ **der Einkommensverhältnisse** income support; ~ **eines Fehlers** correction (rectification) of a mistake; ~ **der Handelsbilanz** amelioration (improvement) of the trade balance; ~**en der Ladeanlagen** betterments of loading facilities; ~ **des Lebensstandards** rise in the standard of living; ~**en auf der ganzen Linie** allround improvements; ~ **eines Patents** amendment of a patent; ~ **der Pensionsleistungen** pension improvements; ~ **im Pfundkurs** improvement in sterling exchange; ~**en nach dem Stand der Technik** technological improvements; ~ **der Tarifsätze** improvement in rates; ~ **eines Textes** castigation (emendation) of a text; ~ **der Verkehrs- und Wohnungsbedingungen** transportation and housing improvement; ~ **des Verwaltungsapparates** civil service reform; ~ **der Zahlungsbilanz** improvement in the balance of payments;
~ **erfahren** *(Kurs)* to show improvement, to experience an advance; **textliche** ~**en vornehmen** to amend a text.

Verbesserungs|antrag amendment; ~**antrag einbringen** to move an amendment; ~**auflage** *(Sanitätsbehörde)* improvement service *(Br.)*; ~**aufwand** cost of improvement.

verbesserungsbedürftig open to (capable of) improvement, improvable.

Verbesserungschancen, nur geringe ~ **versprechen können** to hold out little hope for recovery.

verbesserungsfähig reclaimable, subject to revision, open to improvement;
nicht mehr ~ incapable of improvement.

Verbesserungs|fähigkeit improvability; ~**investition** capital deepening; ~**patent** patent of improvement, improvement patent; **durch** ~**versuche verderben** to improve away; ~**vorschläge** suggestions for improvements, *(im Betrieb)* employee suggestion system; **patentfähige** ~**vorschläge** patentable improvements.

verbeugen, sich to bow, to bend, to make one's manners.

Verbeugung bow, reverence.

verbiestert annoyed, irritated, pigheaded.

verbieten to prohibit, to inhibit, to forbid, to bar, to interdict, to enjoin *(US)*;
Buch ~ to put a book on the index; **Handelsverkehr mit dem Ausland** ~ to interdict trade with foreign nations; **jem. den Mund** ~ to order s. o. to be quiet; **sich von selbst** ~ to be out of the question; **Theaterstück** ~ to ban a play; **Zeitung** ~ to suppress a journal (newspaper).

verbilligen to cheapen, to lower (bring down) a price.

verbilligt at a reduced price, cheap, lower-priced;
~**e Fahrkarte** cheap (reduced, reduced-rate, *Br.*) ticket; **zu** ~**en Preisen** at reduced prices; ~**er Schatzwechselankauf** *(Notenbank)* backdoor operation *(Br.)*; **zu** ~**em Tarif** at a reduced fare.

Verbilligung reduction in prices, price reduction, cheapening;
~ **der Geldmarktsätze** cheapening of money, drop in money market rates.

Verbinden von Erfindungselementen juxtaposition.

verbinden to link, *(Telefon)* to connect, to put through, *(vereinigen)* to unite, to associate, to combine, to join, *(Gesellschaften vereinigen)* to incorporate, to amalgamate, *(Waggons)* to couple, to link;
j. ~ *(tel.)* to put s. o. through; **sich** ~ to associate, to join, to enter into a partnership, to conjoin, to affiliate with *(US)*, *(pol.)* to confederate; **das Angenehme mit dem Nützlichen** ~ to mix (combine) business with pleasure; **durch eine Eisenbahnlinie** ~ to connect by a railway; **eng** ~ to weld; **zwei Fernsprechteilnehmer miteinander** ~ to connect two telephone subscribers; **Idee mit etw.** ~ to associate an idea with s. th.; **Insel mit dem Festland** ~ to join an island with the mainland; **mit einem Kanal** ~ to link with a canal; **Klagen miteinander** ~ to consolidate actions; **zwei Länder** ~ to bind two countries together; **sofort** ~ *(Telefon)* to put (pass) through at once; **zwei Städte durch eine Eisenbahnlinie** ~ to connect two towns by a railway (railroad); **Urlaub mit einer Geschäftsreise** ~ to combine one's holiday with a business trip; **zwei Wahllisten miteinander** ~ to combine two electoral lists; **Warenzeichen miteinander** ~ to associate trademarks;
sich mit jem. ~ **lassen** *(Telefon)* to get on to s. o.

verbindlich *(bindend)* binding, obligatory, mandatory *(US)*, *(entgegenkommend)* obliging, courteous, urban, civil, *(verantwortlich)* accountable, answerable, liable, obliged, *(zwingend)* compulsory;
allgemein ~ generally binding, all the world; **nicht** ~ without engagement, of no binding force;
für ~ **erklären** to declare to be binding; ~ **machen** to make binding, to commit; **jem. etw.** ~ **vorschreiben** to make s. th. mandatory (obligatory) upon s. o.; **für j.** ~ **zeichnen** to bind s. o.;
~**es Angebot** firm offer; ~**sten Dank** many thanks; ~**es Lächeln** friendly smile; ~**er Preis** operative price; ~**er Text** authentic text; ~**e Umgangsformen** urbanity; ~**es Wesen haben** to have an engaging manner.

Verbindlichkeit obligation, liability, engagement, commitment, duty, *(Entgegenkommen)* obligingness, *(Höflichkeit)* courtesy, *(bindende Kraft)* binding force, *(Versprechen)* assumpsit;
mit gegenseitiger ~ mutually binding; **ohne** ~ without prejudice (responsibility), free from (without) liability, *(Giro)* without recourse; **ohne jede** ~ without any commitment;
ausländische ~ foreign debt; **bedingte** ~ contingent obligation; **aufschiebend bedingte** ~ floating liability; **bestehende** ~ existing liability; **fällige** ~ matured liability; **innerhalb eines Jahres fällige** ~ current maturity; **festgestellte** ~ liquidated liability; **finanzielle** ~ pecuniary liability; **gemeinsame** ~ joint liability; **gesamtschuldnerische** ~ joint and several liability; **langfristige** ~ long-term liability (obligation), funded liability; **rechtsgültige** ~ valid obligation; **solidarische** ~ joint and several liability; **unbestrittene und unbedingte** ~ direct liability *(US)*; **unbesicherte** ~ unsecured liability; **der Höhe nach unbestimmte** ~ unliquidated unascertained liability; **vertragliche** ~ contractual obligation (liability); **sofort vollstreckbare** ~ pure obligation; **in Kürze fällig werdende** ~ maturing liability;
~ **mit Konventionalklausel** penal obligation; ~ **ohne Konventionalklausel** single obligation;
sich von einer ~ **befreien** to exempt o. s. from a liability, to rid o. s. of an obligation; ~ **eingehen** to enter into a commitment, to bind o. s.; **j. aus einer** ~ **entlassen** to release s. o. from an obligation; ~ **erledigen** to discharge an obligation; **sich von einer** ~ **freimachen** to repay an obligation; **einer** ~ **nachkommen** to discharge a liability; **von einer** ~ **zurücktreten** to retract from an engagement.

Verbindlichkeiten indebtedness, liabilities, *(Bilanz)* debts due, debts *(Br.)*, creditors, accounts payable *(US)*, payables *(US)*; **aufgelaufene, aber noch nicht fällige** ~ liability reserve; **ausgewiesene** ~ declared liabilities; **ausstehende** ~ outstanding liabilities; **befristete** ~ time liabilities; **nicht belegte** ~ unrecorded liabilities; **diskontfähige** ~ eligible liabilities; **eingefrorene** ~ blocked liabilities; **eingegangene** ~ debts incurred; **einklagbare** ~ debts enforceable at law; **entstandene (noch nicht fällige)** ~ *(Bilanz)* accrued liabilities *(US)*, accruals payable *(US)*; **sofort fällige** ~ sight liabilities, liabilities payable on demand (due on presentation); **feste** ~ fixed liabilities; **fremde** ~ third-party liabilities; **fundierte** ~ fixed liabilities; **nicht fundierte** ~ *(Pensionsplan)* past-service cost; **gleichbleibende** ~ fixed liabilities; **gleichrangige** ~ liabilities of equal priority; **hypothekarische** ~ mortgage debts (liabilities), mortgages payable *(US)*; **konsolidierte** ~ funded liabilities (debts); **kurzfristige** ~ short-term liabilities (obligations, indebtedness), quick (current) liabilities; **langfristige** ~ long-term (fixed) liabilities, long-term obligations; **laufende** ~ current engagements (liabilities); **mindestreservepflichtige** ~ *(Bank)* reserve-carrying liabilities, liabilities subject to reserve requirements; **mittel- und kurzfristige** ~ *(Bilanz)* accounts payable for goods received and services accepted *(US)*; **offene** ~ outstanding debts; **rechtsgültige** ~ valid obligations; **rücklagepflichtige** ~ liabilities subject to reserve requirements; **sichergestellte** ~ secured liabilities; **sonstige** ~ other charges (bonds), *(Bilanz)* liabilities other than above, sundry liabilities, other debts (liabilities, accounts payable, *US*); **innerhalb eines Jahres zu tilgende** ~ *(Bilanz)* current liabilities; **unbedingte und unbestrittene** ~ direct liabilities *(US)*; **ungesicherte** ~ unsecured liabilities; **voreheliche** ~ antenuptial debts; **fällig werdende** ~ maturing liabilities;
~ **aus Akzeptverpflichtungen** liabilities on account of acceptances; ~ **aus der Annahme gezogener Wechsel** *(Bilanz)* liabilities from the acceptance of bills; ~ **aufgrund der Ausgabe von Banknoten** bank-note liabilities; ~ **für weiterbegebene Auslandswechsel** liabilities for foreign bills negotiated; ~ **aus der Ausstellung eigener Wechsel** *(Bilanz)* notes payable *(US)*; ~ **gegenüber Banken** *(Bilanz)* accounts due to banks; ~ **aus der Begebung und Übertragung von Wechseln** *(Bilanz)* liabilities from the issue and endorsement of bills; ~ **an Beteiligungsgesellschaften** *(Bilanz)* creditors; ~ **aus Bürgschaften und Gewährleistungsverträgen** *(Bilanz)* liabilities arising from guarantee and warranty contracts; ~ **aus Depositenkonten** deposit liabilities; ~ **gegenüber Dritten** *(konsolidierte Bilanz)* liabilities to outsiders; ~ **und Eigenkapital** liabilities and shareholder's equity; ~ **zu Eigenkapitalverhältnis** debt equity ratio; ~ **aus Giroverpflichtungen** liabilities on account of endorsements; ~ **gegenüber Konzerngesellschaften** *(Bilanz)* indebtedness to affiliates *(US)*, intercompany liabilities; ~ **gegenüber Kreditinstituten** *(Bankbilanz)* liabilities to credit institutions, liabilities to banks; ~ **gegenüber Kunden** *(Bankbilanz)* current deposits and other accounts; ~ **mit einer Laufzeit von mindestens vier Jahren** *(Bilanz)* liabilities for a term of at least four years; ~ **aus Lieferungen und Leistungen** *(Bilanz)* trade creditors, accounts payable for purchases and deliveries *(US)*; ~ **juristischer Personen** corporate liabilities; ~ **gegenüber Sozialeinrichtungen** *(Bilanz)* loans from social and welfare funds; ~ **gegenüber verbundenen Unternehmen** *(Bilanz)* payables to affiliates; ~ **aus Warenlieferungen** *(Bilanz)* suppliers; ~ **aus noch nicht eingelösten Wechseln** liabilities upon bills, liabilities on account of acceptances, bills payable *(US)*; ~ **für weiterbegebene Wechsel** *(Bilanz)* liabilities for foreign bills negotiated;
kurzfristige ~ **abdecken** to meet short-term liabilities; **von** ~ **befreien** to acquit; ~ **eingehen** to enter into commitments, to contract (incur) liabilities, to assume obligations; **sich vertraglich übernommenen** ~ **entziehen** to back out of a contract; **seine** ~ **erfüllen** to meet one's liabilities (commitments, engagements); **seine** ~ **nicht erfüllen** to go back on one's engagements, to make default; ~ **gegenüber jem. haben** to be obliged to s. o.; **für** ~ **haften** to be liable for commitments; **seinen** ~ **nachkommen** to pay one's way, to meet one's obligations, to carry out (meet) one's engagements, to discharge (meet) one's liabilities; **seinen** ~ **nicht nachkommen** to fail to meet one's commitments, to make default; ~ **ordnen** to wind up liabilities; **seine** ~ **reduzieren** to scale down one's liabilities; ~ **übernehmen** to take over liabilities, to assume obligations; **kurzfristige** ~ **umschulden** to reschedule short-term debts; ~ **nach sich ziehen** to involve o. s. in debts (obligations).

Verbindung relation, connexion *(Br.)*, connection *(US)*, nexus, *(Bindeglied)* link, *(el.)* connection, *(Gelenk)* joint, *(Kontakt)* contact, liaison, *(Personenvereinigung)* association, society, *(pol.)* coalition, bond, coalescence, *(Rundfunk)* hookup, *(Studenten)* fraternity, *(Studentinnen)* sorority *(Br.)*, *(technisch)* assemblage, *(Telefon)* connexion *(Br.)*, connection *(US)*, call, *(im Text)* context, *(Vereinigung)* union, conjunction, *(Verkehr)* communication, connection, *(Verschmelzung)* amalgamation, merger, fusion;
briefliche ~ correspondence; **direkte** ~ *(Bahn)* direct communication; **durchgehende** ~ *(Bahn)* through connection; **eheliche** ~ matrimony, marriage bond; **enge** ~**en** close relations; **falsche** ~ *(Telefon)* wrong connection, crossed line; **familiäre** ~**en** family relations; **geheime** ~ secret society; **geschäftliche** ~**en** business relations (connections); **hergestellte** ~ established contact; **kürzeste** ~ straight line; **langjährige** ~ connexion *(Br.)* (connection, *US*) of long standing; **postalische** ~ postal communication; **unsichere** ~ rush wedding; **unterbrochene** ~ *(tel.)* broken connection; **weitverzweigte** ~**en** far-reaching connections (connexions, *Br.*);
~ **zu den Aktionären** stockholder (shareholder) communication; ~**en auf höchster Ebene** high-echelon connections; ~ **mit dem Feind** intelligence with the enemy; ~ **zwischen Gestern und Morgen** link between the past and the future; **dingliche** ~ **mit einem Grundstück** running with the land; ~ **zwischen Kirche und Staat** connection between church and state; ~ **von Klagen** joinder of actions; ~ **von Warenzeichen** association of trademarks;
~ **abbrechen** to break off correspondence; **alle** ~**en mit jem. abbrechen** to break off all communication with s. o.; **diplomatische** ~**en abbrechen** to sever one's diplomatic ties; ~**en anknüpfen** to make contacts; ~ **mit jem. aufnehmen** to contact (establish contact with) s. o., to liaise s. o.; **brieflich mit jem.** ~ **aufnehmen** to contact s. o. by mail; **geschäftliche** ~ **mit einer Firma aufnehmen** to open up a business connection with a firm; ~ **mit jem. aufrechterhalten** to keep terms (one's ties) with s. o.; ~ **bekommen** *(Telefon)* to get through; **keine** ~ **bekommen** *(Telefon)* to fail to get a connection; **in** ~ **bleiben** to keep in touch; **j. mit einer Angelegenheit in** ~ **bringen** to link s. o. with an affair; **j. mit einem Entführungsfall in** ~ **bringen** to suspect s. o. of having s. th. to do with a kidnapping; ~ **mit jem. eingehen** to enter into a combination with s. o.; **regelmäßige** ~ **einrichten** *(Bahn)* to establish a regular line; ~ **erhalten** *(Telefon)* to get through; **ausländische** ~**en haben** to have connections (connexions, *Br.*) abroad; **glänzende** ~**en haben** to be in with the best people; **gute** ~**en haben** to be well (influentially) connected; ~ **mit jem. haben** to be in touch with s. o.; ~ **mit jem. verloren haben** to be out of touch with s. o.; **mit jem.** ~ **halten** to keep in touch with s. o.; **mit der Presse** ~ **halten** to liaise with the press; ~ **herstellen** to establish contact, to reach out to; **neue** ~ **herstellen** to build up a new connection; **telefonische** ~ **herstellen** to complete a call, to put a call through; **gedankliche** ~ **zwischen zwei Dingen herstellen** to associate one thing with another; ~ **zwischen zwei Flüssen herstellen** *(Kanal)* to form a link between two rivers; **mit jem. in** ~ **kommen** to get on to (in touch, in contact with) s. o.; **seine** ~**en spielen lassen** to pull the wires (strings); ~ **lösen** to discontinue a connection; **alte** ~**en lösen** to break with old ties; ~ **pflegen** to nurse a connection; **geschäftliche** ~**en mit jem. pflegen** to transact with s. o.; **nur in** ~ **mit einer persönlichen Einladung gültig sein** to be valid only in conjunction with a personal invitation; **sich mit jem. in** ~ **setzen** to communicate with (contact) s. o.; **in** ~ **stehen** to be connected; **mit jem. brieflich in** ~ **stehen** to correspond with s. o.; **mit jem. in enger** ~ **stehen** to be in close contact with s. o.; **mit jem. in geschäftlicher** ~ **stehen** to have regular business relations with s. o.; **mit jem. laufend in** ~ **stehen** to communicate regularly with s. o.; **miteinander in** ~ **stehen** to be in touch, to communicate, to intercommunicate; ~ **trennen** *(Telefon)* to switch off; **mit jem. in** ~ **treten** to enter into relations (contact, connections) with s. o., to contact s. o., to get into touch (communication) with s. o., to intercommunicate with s. o.; **brieflich in** ~ **treten** to commence a correspondence, to contact s. o. by mail; ~**en unterbrechen** to disrupt communications; **telefonische** ~ **unterbrechen** to cut off a telephone connection; **über weitreichende** ~**en verfügen** to have far-reaching influence; ~ **mit jem. verlieren** to lose touch with s. o.; **wirtschaftliche** ~**en verstärken** to tighten economic bonds.

Verbindungs|abzeichen fraternity pin; ~**amt** liaison office; ~**aufgaben** liaison duties; ~**ausschuß** liaison committee; ~**bahn** junction line; ~**büro** liaison mission; ~**dose** *(el.)* junction box;

~**flugzeug** tiny airplane, jeep *(US)*; ~**gang** passage, *(Zug)* vestibule; ~**gleis** junction rail; ~**glied** communication (connection) link, organ of communication; ~**graben** *(mil.)* communication trench; ~**kabel** connection cable; ~**kanal** junction canal; ~**klemme** *(el.)* terminal; ~**kommando** *(mil.)* liaison detachment; ~**leitung** junction line; ~**linie** line of communication, communication line; **lebenswichtige** ~**linie** *(mil.)* lifeline; ~**mann** contact man, key man, intermediary, intermediate, liaison consultant (officer, man, *US*); ~**punkt** junction; ~**schnur** flexible cord; ~**stecker** *(el.)* connection plug; ~**stelle** liaison office, information department; ~**stück** tie; ~**tür** communicating door; ~**wege** communications.
verbissen grim, stubborn, dogged.
verbitten, sich to refuse to tolerate, not to permit, to beg, to decline, will not stand s. th.
verbittert embittered, bitter, sour;
~ **über das ständige Alleinsein** weary of living all alone.
verblassen to wane, *(Inschrift)* to wear away, *(Neuheit)* to wear off;
völlig ~ *(Farben)* to fade away to nothing.
verblassend, nicht *(Farbe)* unfading.
verblaßt washed out.
verblättern, Stelle in einem Buch to lose one's place in a book.
Verbleib whereabouts, stay;
zum ~ to be retained.
Verbleiben im Amt continuance in office.
verbleiben to remain, to dwell;
im Amt ~ to continue (remain) in office; **bei seiner Ansicht** ~ to abide by (persist in) one's opinion.
verbleibend|es Guthaben remaining credit balance; ~**er Rest** remainder; ~**er Schuldbetrag** balance due; ~**e Summe** rest.
verblenden to infatuate, to dazzle, to bind.
Verblendziegel face brick.
verbleuen, j. to give s. o. a good licking, to paddle s. o. *(US)*.
verblichen faded, discolo(u)red.
verblieben vestigial.
verblöden to go dotty, to become demented.
verblüffen to perplex, to consternate, to flabbergast, to amaze;
j. mit Fragen ~ to perplex s. o. with questions.
verblüffend amazing, astonishing, astounding.
verblüfft perplexed, bewildered, dazed, amazed.
Verblüffung, zu meiner großen to my great surprise.
verblümt in a roundabout way, sub rosa;
jem. ~ **zu verstehen geben** to drop s. o. a gentle hint.
verbluten to bleed to death.
verbockt pigheaded, stubborn, mulish.
verbodmen to hypothecate.
Verbodmung hypothecation.
verbohrt dense, dense-minded, one-track, obstinate, stubborn, pigheaded;
sich in die Idee ~ **haben** to be bent on (obsessed with) an idea.
Verbohrtheit density, obstinacy, stubbornness, obsession.
verborgen private, secret, latent, hidden, under cover;
nicht ~ manifest, overt, unconcealed;
jem. nicht ~ **bleiben** not to escape s. one's notice; **Flüchtling** ~ **halten** to conceal a fugitive; **seinen Kummer** ~ **halten** to keep one's sorrow to o. s.;
~**e Fähigkeiten** latent abilities; ~**e Machenschaften** clandestine machinations; ~**e Mängel** latent (hidden) defects; ~**er Platz** secluded place; ~**er Sinn** inner meaning.
Verborgenen, im ~ **leben** to live in seclusion (the shadow).
Verbot inhibition, prohibition, interdiction, ban, taboo, *(Gericht)* injunction;
auf Unterlassung gerichtetes ~ prohibitory injunction; **gerichtliches** ~ negative injunction; **gesetzliches** ~ statutory prohibition; **polizeiliches** ~ police ban; **staatliches** ~ government inhibition;
~ **der Beförderung spediteureigener Güter** commodities clause *(US)*; ~ **unterschiedlicher Behandlung** nondiscriminatory treatment; ~, **einen bestreikten Betrieb zu beliefern** hot-cargo ban; ~ **der Doppelbestrafung** double jeopardy clause; ~ **für Jugendliche unter 16 Jahren** *(Film)* X certificate *(Br.)*; ~ **der Leistung von Zahlungen an einen Dritten** garnishment; **nachbarliches** ~ **der Lichtbeschränkung** easement of light; ~ **der Praxisausübung** disbarment order; ~ **rückwirkender Strafgesetze** ex post facto clause; ~ **bestimmter Streikaktionen** blanket injunction; ~ **eines Streiks** ban of a strike; ~ **politischer Versammlungen** ban on political meetings; ~ **der Vorausverfügung** restraint upon anticipation *(US)*; ~ **der Warenursprungsfälschung** doctrine of unfair trade; ~ **des freien Wettbewerbs** restraint of trade; ~ **einer Zeitung** suppression of a newspaper;
~ **aufheben** to lift a prohibition (ban), to overturn a ban; ~ **erlassen** to impose a prohibition (ban); ~ **mißachten (überschreiten)** to ignore a prohibition.
verboten forbidden, prohibited, under a ban, *(unerlaubt)* illicit, illegal, unlawful;
Betreten des Grundstücks ~! trespassers will be prosecuted, no trespassing!; **Einfahrt** ~! no entry!; **Eintritt** ~! no admittance, keep out!; **Nachdruck** ~! copyright reserved!; **Rauchen** ~! no smoking!; **Überschreiten der Gleise** ~! do not cross the lines!; **Zettelankleben** ~! post no bills!; **Zutritt** ~! out of bounds *(Br.)*, off limits *(US)*!;
~**e Eigenmacht** illegitimate (unwarrantable) interference, private nuisance; ~**e Sonderprovision** secret commission; ~**es Thema berühren** to tread on forbidden ground; ~**e Transaktionen** illicit transactions; ~**e Versammlung** unlawful assembly; ~**e Verwandtschaftsgrade** *(Eheschließung)* forbidden degrees; ~**er Weg!** private way!
Verbots|bestimmungen prohibitory provisions; ~**gesetz** negative statute, prohibitory law; ~**gesetzgebung** prohibitory legislation; ~**grundsatz** principle of prohibition; ~**hinweis** prohibition notice; ~**liste** prohibited list, *(Ausfuhr)* positive list *(US)*; ~**schild** prohibitive sign; ~**verfügung** preventive (restrictive) injunction.
verbotswidrig unlawful.
Verbots|zeichen prohibition sign; ~**zone** prohibited zone.
verbrämen, Mord patriotisch to commit murder under the veil of patriotism.
verbrannt burned, burnt;
~**e Erde** *(mil.)* scorched earth.
Verbrauch consumption, expenditure;
beim augenblicklichen ~ at the present rate of consumption; **zum** ~ **im Inland** for home use; **zum sofortigen** ~ **bestimmt** for immediate consumption;
demonstrativer ~ conspicuous consumption; **durchschnittlicher** ~ average consumption; **erhöhter** ~ increased consumption; **geringerer** ~ low consumption, underconsumption; **gewerblicher** ~ industrial consumption; **inländischer** ~ internal consumption, home use *(Br.)*; **jährlicher** ~ annual consumption; **laufender** ~ current consumption; **mangelnder** ~ underconsumption; **normaler** ~ normal consumption; **örtlicher** ~ local consumption; **privater** ~ personal consumption, family use; **produktiver** ~ productive consumption; **pro-Kopf-**~ per capita consumption; **saisonbedingter** ~ seasonal consumption; **sparsamer** ~ low consumption, *(Auto)* economy run, *(Gasherd)* slow burn; **staatlicher** ~ government consumption; **täglicher** ~ everyday (daily) consumption; **übermäßiger** ~ excess consumption, waste; **üblicher** ~ normal consumption; **unproduktiver** ~ unproductive (final) consumption; **unterschiedlicher** ~ consumption differential; **zurückgegangener** ~ decreased consumption; **zusätzlicher** ~ additional consumption;
~ **der privaten Haushalte** consumption of private households; ~ **im Inland** home use (consumption, *Br.*); ~ **pro Kopf** per-capita consumption; ~ **von Staatsleistungen** government consumption;
~ **anregen** to stimulate consumption; ~ **drosseln** to curb (curtail) consumption; ~ **einschränken** to reduce consumption; **privaten** ~ **einschränken** to keep personal consumption down; **hohen** ~ **an Papier haben** to use a great deal of paper; ~ **steigern** to predispose (increase) consumption.
verbrauchen to consume, to use up, *(abnutzen)* to wear [out], *(ausgeben)* to spend, to spend up, to expend, *(benutzen)* to employ;
sich ~ to wear o. s. out, to ruin one's health; **j. so** ~ **wie er ist** to take s. o. for what he is; **sein ganzes Geld für den Haushalt** ~ to spend all one's money on housekeeping; **ganzes Lager** ~ to work up all the stock; **alle Mittel** ~ to exhaust the means; **viel Öl** ~ *(Motor)* to be heavy on (consume a lot of) oil; **übermäßig** ~ to waste, to squander; **vollständig** ~ to exhaust.
Verbraucher consumer, user, expender, *(Kunde)* customer, client, buyer;
gewerblicher ~ business (industrial) user, industrial (manufacturing) consumer; **inländischer** ~ domestic consumer; **letzter** ~ final (ultimate) consumer; **potenter** ~ high-income consumer; **potentieller** ~ prospective consumer *(US)*, prospect *(US)*;
Kostensteigerungen auf den ~ **abwälzen** to pass cost increases onto consumers; **Lohnkostenerhöhung auf die** ~ **abwälzen** to pass increased labo(u)r costs onto consumers; ~ **beraten** to advise (aid) the consumer; ~ **unmittelbar treffen** to fall directly onto the consumer;

~**abgabe** excise (consumption) tax; ~**abzahlungskredit** consumer instalment loan (credit); ~**aggressivität** militancy of consumers; ~**analyse** consumer research; ~**anreiz** induced consumption; ~**ansichten** consumer sentiments; ~**ansprüche** consumer demands; ~**anteil** consumer share; ~**anwalt** consumer advocate; ~**aufklärung** consumer guidance; ~**aufnahmebereitschaft** propensity to consume, consumer acceptance; ~**aufwand** consumer expenditure; ~**aufwendungen für Autoanschaffungen** consumers' actual car-buying performance; ~**ausgaben** consumer expenditure (spending); ~**ausschuß**, ~**beirat** consumer advisory council *(Br.)*; ~**bedarf** consumer demand; ~**bedürfnisse** consumer needs (demand), consumptive demand; **sich dem** ~**bedürfnis anpassen** to gear to consumer needs; ~**befragung** consumer research (survey, inquiry); **postalische** ~**befragung** consumer mail panel; ~**beratung** consumer counselling; ~**beratungsdienst** consumer advisory service; ~**beschwerden** consumer complaints; ~**betrieb** consumer enterprise; ~**bewegung** consumer movement.

verbraucherbewußt consumer-conscious.

Verbraucher|bewußtsein consumer consciousness; ~**boykott** consumer boycott; ~**einheit** consumer (spending) unit; ~**einkommen** consumer income; **frei verfügbares** ~**einkommen** discretionary income; ~**entscheidung** consumer decision; ~**erzeugnis** consumer product; ~**erziehung** consumer education; ~**feldzug** consumer crusade; ~**festpreis** fixed consumer price; ~**forschung** consumer research; ~**fragen** consumer questions.

verbraucherfreundlich consumer-conscious (-minded).

Verbraucher|freundlichkeit consumer consciousness; ~**genossenschaft** consumer cooperative; ~**gesellschaft** consumer society *(Br.)*; ~**gewohnheiten** consumer (consuming, buying) habits; **repräsentative** ~**gruppe** consumer panel (group), *(in Schlüsselposition)* key market; ~**handel** retail trade; ~**herrschaft** sovereignty of the consumer, consumers' sovereignty, consumerism; ~**hinweise** consumer information; ~**höchstpreis** retail ceiling price; ~**industrien** consumer goods industries; ~**informationen** consumer information; ~**informationszentrum** consumer center *(US)* (centre, *Br.*); ~**interesse** customer interest; ~**interesse hervorrufen** to excite a customer's interest; ~**interview** consumer interview; ~**irreführung** misleading of consumers; ~**kapital** consumer capital; ~**kategorie** consumer category; ~**käufe** consumer buying; ~**kaufkraft** consumers' ability to buy, spending capacity; ~**komitee** consumer board; ~**konjunktur** consumer prosperity; ~**kredit** consumption loan (credit); ~**kreditbeschränkungen** restrictions of consumer credits; ~**kreditwerbung** consumer credit advertising; ~**kritik** consumer criticism; ~**land** consumer nation, consuming country; ~**leitung** *(el.)* service line; ~**macht** consumer sovereignty; ~**markt** market of consumption, consumption (consuming) market; ~**menge** consumer quantity; **staatliches** ~**monopol** public consumption monopoly; ~**nachfrage** consumer purchasing (demand); ~**nachfrageübersicht** consumer buying survey; ~**optimismus** consumer optimism; ~**organisation** consumer organization; ~**orientierung** consumer information (orientation); ~**packung** economy size; ~**politik** consumer policy; ~**preis** consumer[s'] price, price to consumers; ~**preisindex** index of consumer prices, cost-of-living (consumer price) index; ~**preisniveau** retail price level; ~**psychologie** consumer psychology; ~**querschnitt** cross-section of the consumers; ~**reklame** consumer advertisement; ~**rente** consumer's surplus; ~**repräsentant** consumer activist; ~**risiko** consumer's risk; ~**schaft** consuming public, usership; **ländliche** ~**schaft** agricultural clientele; **der** ~**schaft Einblick in die Kaufneigungen geben** to let consumers in on the shopping tips; ~**schicht** class of consumers; ~**schutz** consumer protection; ~**schutzgesetz** consumer-protection act; ~**schutzstelle** consumer-protection office; ~**seite** consumer side; ~**staat** consuming state; ~**statistik** consumer statistics; ~**steuer** tax on consumption, consumption tax; ~**stichprobe** consumer sample; ~**streik** consumers' strike; ~**studien** consumer studies; ~**stufe** consumer level; ~**tagung** consumer assembly; ~**test**, ~**umfrage** consumer buying survey; ~**testgruppe** consumer panel; ~**überschuß** consumer affluence; ~**unterrichtung** consumer information; ~**untersuchungen** consumer studies; ~**verband** association for consumer research, consumers' association; ~**vereinigung** consumer organization; ~**verhalten** consumer behavio(u)r; ~**vertretung** consumer representation; ~**verzicht** deferred consumption; ~**wahl** consumers' choice; ~**werber** consumer advertiser; ~**werbung** consumer advertising; ~**wettbewerb** consumer contest; ~**wirtschaft** consumer economics; ~**wünsche** consumer wants (desires); ~**zeitschrift** consumer magazine (publication); ~**zentrum** consumer center *(US)* (centre, *Br.*); ~**zurückhaltung** consumer resistance.

Verbrauchs|abgabe customs duty, excise *(US)* (consumption) tax; ~**artikel** article of consumption, *(pl.)* consumption (consumer, convenience, *US*) goods; ~**aufwand** consumption expenditure, consumer spending; ~**ausgaben der privaten Haushalte** consumption of private households; **gesamtwirtschaftliche** ~**ausgaben** consumer expenditure; ~**ausweitung** increased consumption.

verbrauchsbedingte Abschreibung physical depreciation.

Verbrauchs|bereitschaft demand from consumers, consumer acceptance; **an der Grenze liegende** ~**bereitschaft** marginal propensity to consume; ~**beschränkungen** restrictions set on consumption; ~**bild** pattern of consumption; ~**einheit** consumption (consuming) unit, consumption standard; **frei verfügbares** ~**einkommen** discretionary income; ~**explosion** burst of consumption.

verbrauchsfertig ready for consumption.

Verbrauchs|freudigkeit propensity to consume; ~**funktion** consumption function; ~**gebiet** area of supply, consuming area (region); ~**gegenstände** articles of consumption, consumer (consumption) goods; ~**gewohnheiten** consuming habits, consumption patterns; ~**grenze** margin of consumption.

Verbrauchsgüter consumption (consumer, convenience, *US*, current) goods, goods of the first order (consumption), nondurable manufactures, perishables, perishable commodities; **aufwendige** ~ goods of conspicuous consumption; **gewerbliche** ~ industrial consumer goods; **haltbare** ~ consumer durables; **kurzlebige** ~ soft (nondurable, perishable) consumer goods, single-use goods, consumer nondurables; **langlebige** ~ long-life consumer goods;
~**bereich** consumer-goods sector; ~**forschung** consumer-goods research; ~**industrie** consumption goods industry; ~**konjunktur** consumer-goods boom; ~**markt** consumer market; ~**sektor** consumer-goods sector.

Verbrauchs|industrie consuming industry; ~**konjunktur aufrechterhalten** to maintain high consumption; ~**kontrolle** consumer clampdown; ~**kurve** consumption line; ~**land** consuming country; ~**lenkung** direction of consumption, consumption control; ~**markt** consuming market; ~**material** expendable items (stores) *(Br.)*; ~**menge** consumer (consumed) quantity; ~**nachfrage** consumer demand.

verbrauchsnah consumer-conscious;
~**e Investitionsgüter** consumer capital-type goods.

verbrauchsorientiert consumer-orientated.

Verbrauchs|orientierung consumer orientation; ~**planung** consumption planning; ~**preis** retail price, price to consumers; ~**prinzip der Besteuerung** benefit taxation; ~**quote** consumption ratio; ~**rate**, ~**satz** rate of consumption; ~**regelung** rationing of consumption; ~**rekord** consumption record; ~**reserven** consumptive power; ~**richtung** consumption trend; ~**rückgang** decreased (decrease, decline in, drop in, cut in) consumption; ~**sättigung** saturation of consumer demands; ~**schätzung** estimate of consumption; ~**schema** pattern of consumption, consumption pattern; ~**sektor** consumer-goods sector; ~**soll** nominal consumption; ~**stand** level of consumption; ~**steigerung** induced (increase in) consumption.

Verbrauchssteuer consumption (indirect) tax, excise *(Br.)* (customs) duty, use tax *(US)*;
mit einer ~ **belegen** to excise *(Br.)*;
zusätzliche ~**belastung** excess burden *(Br.)*.

verbrauchssteuerfrei unexcised, exempt from excise duty.

Verbrauchssteuerfreibetrag excise tax exemption *(US)*.

verbrauchssteuerpflichtig excisable;
nicht ~ unexcised.

Verbrauchs|struktur pattern of consumption, consumption pattern; ~**stufe** stage of consumption; ~**tarif** *(el.)* step rate; ~**trend** consumption trend; ~**umschichtungen**, ~**verlagerungen** shifts in consumption, consumption shifts; ~**wandlungen** changes in consumption; ~**waren** consumable (consumption, convenience, *US*, current) goods, nondurable manufactures, perishables; ~**welle** upsurge in consumption; ~**werbung** consumer advertising; ~**wert** consumption value; ~**wirtschaft** consumer economics (-goods industry); ~**zahlen**, ~**ziffern** consumption figures, rates of consumption; **hohe** ~**zahlen erreichen** to gallop to high consumption; ~**zunahme** increased consumption.

verbraucht spent, used up, out, obsolete, worn out, timeworn, *(Batterie)* finished, run-down.

Verbrechen crime, criminal act, indictable offence, outrage, malefaction, wrongdoing;

abscheuliches ~ ugly crime; **nicht aufgeklärtes** ~ unfathomed crime; **entehrendes** ~ infamous crime; **unter mehrere Gerichtszuständigkeiten fallendes** ~ continuous crime; **feststehendes** ~ patent offence; **flagrantes** ~ flagrant offence; **fortgesetztes** ~ continuing offence; **gemeines** ~ ugly crime; **gemeingefährliches** ~ felony, felonious act; **nachgewiesenes** ~ patent and established crime; **politisches** ~ political crime; **scheußliches** ~ hideous (atrocious) crime; **selbständiges** ~ substantive felony; **todeswürdiges** ~ hanging matter; **unaufgeklärtes** ~ unfathomed crime; **versuchtes** ~ attempted crime; **vollendetes** ~ completed (accomplished) offence; **nicht vollendetes** ~ inchoate crime;
~ **im Amt** misdemeano(u)r in office; ~ **gegen die Menschlichkeit** outrage (crime) against humanity; ~ **am untauglichen Objekt** abortive crime;
jem. ein ~ **anlasten** to impute a crime to s. o.; **j. zu einem** ~ **anstiften** to instigate (incite) s. o. to a crime, to put s. o. up to a crime; ~ **aufdecken** to detect a crime; ~ **begehen** to compound a felony, to commit (perpetrate, pull off, *sl.*) a crime; **schweres** ~ **begehen** to commit a serious crime; **j. aller nur möglichen** ~ **beschuldigen** to throw the boot at s. o.; ~ **mit dem Tode bestrafen** to punish a crime with death; **etw. als** ~ **bezeichnen** to denominate s. th. a crime; ~ **[ein]gestehen** to confess (own up to) a crime; **als** ~ **einstufen** to class as crime; **wegen eines** ~**s ermitteln** to investigate a crime; ~ **gestehen** to confess a crime; ~ **nicht begangen haben** to be innocent of a crime; **j. in ein** ~ **mit hineinziehen** to implicate s. o. in a crime; **einem** ~ **Vorschub leisten** to aid and abet; **jem. ein** ~ **nachweisen** to bring a crime home to s. o.; ~ **ungeschminkt offenbaren** to reveal the crime in all its nakedness; **jedes** ~**s fähig sein** to be capable of any crime; **in ein** ~ **verwickelt sein** to be implicated in a crime; **j. eines** ~**s schuldig sprechen** to find s. o. guilty of a crime; ~ **sühnen** to purge an offence, to pay the penalty of a crime; ~ **untersuchen** to inquire into a crime; ~ **verheimlichen** to prevaricate a crime; **j. zu einem** ~ **verleiten** to entice s. o. into committing a crime; ~ **vertuschen** to slur a crime; ~ **verüben** to perpetrate (commit) a crime, to compound a felony.

verbrechen to compound a felony, to perpetrate (commit) a crime;
etw. ~ to put one's foot in it, to be up to mischief.

Verbrechens|aufklärung crime detection; ~**begünstigung** abetment of crime; ~**bekämpfung** suppression of crime; ~**ermittlung** crime detection; ~**prozentsatz** crime rate; ~**schilderung** modus of an indictment; ~**statistik** criminal statistics; ~**tatbestand** constructive crime; ~**verhütung** prevention of crime, crime prevention; **der** ~**verhütung dienen** to act as a determent of crime; **unterstellter** ~**vorsatz** constructive malice; ~**ziffer** crime rate; ~**zunahme** increase in crime.

Verbrecher criminal, indictable offender, felon;
ausgebrochener ~ fugitive felon; **ausgekochter** ~ old lag; **auf freiem Fuß befindlicher** ~ loose criminal; **bewaffneter** ~ gangster, gunman *(US)*; **erstmaliger** ~ first offender; **gemeingefährlicher** ~ dangerous criminal, public enemy; **gesuchter** ~ person wanted; **gewohnheitsmäßiger** ~ goal bird; **hartgesottener** ~ tough criminal; **hingerichteter** ~ executed criminal; **jugendlicher** ~ teenage offender; **politischer** ~ political offender; **rückfälliger** ~ second offender, recidivist; **überführter** ~ convict; **unverbesserlicher** ~ hard case *(US)*; **verstockter** ~ hardened criminal; **zum Tode verurteilter** ~ criminal under sentence of death;
~ **anstiften** to instigate a malefactor; ~ **aufspüren** to spot a criminal; ~ **hart bestrafen** to inflict severe punishment on criminals; ~ **zur Strecke bringen** to nail down a criminal; ~ **fesseln** to truss up a criminal; ~ **fotografieren** to mug a criminal; **Umgang mit** ~**n haben** to be linked by crime; ~ **beobachten lassen** to study a criminal's movements; **einem flüchtigen** ~ **nachsetzen** to pursue a fugitive from justice; ~ **zu einer strafbaren Handlung provozieren** to entrap a criminal; ~ **schnappen** to land a criminal *(coll.)*; **abgefeimter (hartgesottener)** ~ **sein** to be old in crime (a hardened offender); ~ **in die Enge treiben** to run down a criminal; ~ **der Polizei übergeben** to surrender a criminal to the police; ~ **verfolgen** to trail a criminal; ~ **wegen Mordes verhören** to try a criminal for murder; ~ **vorführen** to make a criminal appear in court; **zum** ~ **gestempelt werden** to be label(l)ed a criminal;
~**album** rogues' gallery, picture gallery *(sl.)*.

Verbrecherbande gang of criminals, protection gang;
jugendliche ~ seven hundred *(sl.)*;
~ **aufrollen** to round up a gang of criminals; ~ **aufspüren** to locate a gang.

Verbrechergehilfe stall *(sl.)*.

verbrecherisch criminal, guilty, delinquent, felonious, outrageous;
~ **veranlagt** crime-prone;
wirklich ~ **sein** to be positive crime;
~**e Absicht** criminal intent; ~**e Anlage** criminal leanings; ~**e Anlagen haben** to have an instinct for crime.

Verbrecher|jagd hue and cry; ~**kolonie** penal settlement; ~**laufbahn** criminal career; ~**organisation** criminal organization; **auf dem** ~**pfad** on the shake *(sl.)*; ~**signalement veröffentlichen** to circulate the description of a criminal; ~**syndikat** syndicate; ~**tum** criminality; **berufsmäßiges** ~**tum** professional crime; **internationales** ~**tum** international gangsterism; ~**viertel** Hell's kitchen *(US sl.)*; ~- **und Vergnügungsviertel** tenderloin *(US sl.)*; ~**visage haben** to have the look of a gallows bird.

verbreiten to spread, to divulge, to disseminate, to circulate, to propagate, to vent, to disperse, to broadcast;
sich ~ to go, *(Gas)* to be diffused, *(Gerücht)* to fly about; **sich über etw.** ~ to enlarge upon (speak about) a subject; **sich im einzelnen darüber** ~ to hold forth on it in detail; **sich fächerförmig** ~ to fan out; **Falschgeld** ~ to utter false notes, to put false money in circulation; **sich über ein weites Gebiet** ~ to spread through a large area; **gerüchtweise** ~ to rumo(u)r; **Geschichte** ~ to bandy a story about; **Ideen** ~ to disseminate ideas; **Klatsch** ~ to gossip; **Licht** ~ to shed (radiate) light; **Meldungen** ~ to circulate news; **sich von Mund zu Mund** ~ to spread from mouth to mouth; **Nachrichten** ~ to propagate (circulate, spread, disperse) news; **falsche Nachrichten** ~ to circulate false news; **Nachricht über den Rundfunk** ~ to broadcast a piece of news; **Nachrichten über die ganze Welt** ~ to flash news across the world; **sich über die ganze Stadt** ~ to spread throughout the town; **sich langatmig über ein Thema** ~ to descant (deal at length) upon a subject; **sich ausführlich über seinen Vorschlag** ~ to elaborate one's proposal; **Wärme** ~ *(Ofen)* to radiate warmth.

verbreitern to enlarge, to broaden, to widen;
Straße ~ to widen a road.

Verbreiterung enlargement;
~ **einer Straße** widening of a road.

verbreitet prevalent, current, common;
allgemein ~ general, customary; **weit** ~ widespread, widely distributed, popular; **ganz weit** ~ all the way across; **über die ganze Welt** ~ world-wide;
~ **sein** to be prevalent (widespread); **nicht weit** ~ **sein** to be local; ~ **werden** to go about (round);
weit ~**es Blatt** widely read paper; **weit** ~**e Meinung** widely-held opinion; **weit** ~**er Niederschlag** rain over a large area.

Verbreitung incidence, spread, dispersal, propagation, *(Geruch)* diffusion, *(Nachrichten)* dissemination, proliferation, publication, *(Reklame)* propaganda, coverage, distribution, *(Zeitung)* circulation;
lauffeuerartige ~ grapevine telegraphy;
~ **einer verleumderischen Behauptung** publication of a libel; ~ **von Falschgeld** uttering false notes; ~ **einer Falschmeldung** dissemination of a false report; ~ **eines Gerüchts** dissemination (divulgation) of a rumo(u)r; **freie** ~ **von Ideen** free flow of ideas; ~ **von Klatschgeschichten** scandal mongering; ~ **einer Krankheit** spread of a disease; ~ **seiner persönlichen Meinung** spreading of one's views; ~ **von Nachrichten** circulation (dissemination) of news; ~ **von Rundfunknachrichten** broadcasting; ~ **unzüchtiger Schriften** circulation of obscene literature; ~ **des Wissens** increase of knowledge;
weite ~ **gefunden haben** to have general currency.

Verbreitungs|analyse circulation analysis; ~**dichte** circulation density; ~**gebiet** circulation area, covered sector, migratory grounds, habitat *(zool.)*; ~**ziffer** number of incidences.

verbrennbar combustible, inflammable.

verbrennen to burn, to go up in smoke, to incinerate, *(Leichen)* to cremate, *(Treibstoff)* to combust, *(versengen)* to scorch;
sich die Finger ~ *(fig.)* to burn one's fingers; **Gebäude zu Schutt und Asche** ~ to lay a building in ashes; **sich den Mund** ~ to drop a brick; **seine Schiffe hinter sich** ~ to burn one's boats (bridges) behind one.

Verbrennung burning, incineration, *(Heizung)* firing, heating, *(med.)* burn;
~ **ersten Grades** *(Unfallversicherung)* first-degree burn.

Verbrennungs|anlage incineration plant, incinerator; ~**gas** power gas; ~**kammer** combustion chamber; ~**motor** internal-combustion engine (motor); ~**ofen** incinerator, incineration plant; ~**öl** burning oil; ~**prozeß** process of combustion.

verbriefen to vest, to charter, to license, to attest, *(Schuldverschreibungen)* to secure by bond.

verbrieft chartered, licensed, *(aufgelassen)* transferred, conveyed;
~**e Forderung** bonded debt; ~**e Rechte** vested rights.
Verbriefung embodiment in a document.
verbringen to commit, *(verleben)* to spend;
in eine Anstalt ~ to confine into an asylum, to commit to a mental home; **seine Freizeit** ~ to spend one's leisure time; **Stunde mit Zeitunglesen** ~ to put in an hour reading newspapers; **ein paar angenehme Tage mit jem.** ~ to pass a few pleasant days with s. o.; **Winter im Ausland** ~ to spend the winter abroad.
Verbringung committal, transfer, transformation;
~ **in eine Anstalt** confinement into an asylum, committal to a mental home; ~ **an Bord** loading on board; ~ **eines Kindes zu Pflegeeltern** child placing; ~ **an Land** wharfage.
verbrüdern, sich to fraternize.
Verbrüderung fraternization.
Verbuchen posting, booking, entering.
verbuchen to post, to bring to book, to carry in books, to book, to enter, to record, to make an entry, *(Effekten)* to register;
als Ausgabe (Betrag über Handlungsunkosten) ~ to enter an amount in the expenditure; **neuen Höchstkurs** ~ to reach (register, establish) a new high (top), to rise into new high ground *(US)*; **Kursverbesserung** ~ to secure an advance; **jeden Posten einzeln** ~ to post each entry singly; **Posten im Hauptbuch** ~ to post up an item, to enter an item in the ledger; **Posten auf einem Konto** ~ to pass an item to an account; **Posten nachträglich** ~ to book an omitted item; **auf Reservekonto** ~ to put to reserve; **neuen Tiefstand** ~ to register a new low *(US)*.
Verbuchung posting, booking, entering, entry;
irrtümliche ~ erroneous entry; **nachträgliche** ~ post-entry.
Verbuchungs|datum value (availability, *US*) date; ~**kurs** bookkeeping rate; ~**termin** value (availability, *US*) date; **laufendes** ~**verfahren des Nettogewinns** current operating concept of net income.
verbummeln to fritter, to dawdle, to idle, to trifle, to loaf away, *(herunterkommen)* to come down in the world.
verbummelt frittered, idled, trifled, *(heruntergekommen)* seedy, dowdy;
~**er Nachmittag** fiddled afternoon; ~**er Student** lackadaisical student.
Verbund link, vertical combine (integration, *US*), compound;
~**anordnung** *(el.)* compound arrangement; ~**betrieb** *(el.)* compound power station.
verbunden joint, conjoint, conjunct, connected, tied up, *(verpflichtet)* obliged, liable, *(Wunde)* bound, bandaged;
durch eine Brücke ~ linked by a bridge; **mit dem Grundstück fest** ~ affixed to (running with) the land, incident to a piece of land; **miteinander** ~ interconnected;
sich jem. ~ **fühlen** to be indebted to s. o.; ~ **sein** to be connected, *(fig.)* to be incidental; **eng mit jem.** ~ **sein** to be hand in glove with s. o., to be bound up with s. o.; **mit jem. geschäftlich** ~ **sein** to entertain business relations with s. o.; **durch Heirat** ~ **sein** to be related by marriage; **durch vielerlei gemeinsame Interessen** ~ **sein** to be united by many common interests; **mit zusätzlichen Kosten** ~ **sein** to involve additional costs; **mit Schwierigkeiten** ~ **sein** to involve (entail) difficulties;
mit ~**en Augen** blindfold; **mit einer Reise** ~**e Ausgaben** expenses incidental to a journey; ~**e Kosten** composite cost; ~**e Leben** *(Lebensversicherung)* joint lives; ~**e Warenzeichen** associated trademarks.
verbünden, sich to join hands, to league (ally) o. s., *(Staaten)* to confederate, to ally, to form (enter into) an alliance.
Verbundenheit connection, attachment, solidarity;
in enger ~ *(Briefschluß)* affectionately yours;
innere ~ clubbiness.
verbündet allied, *(Staaten)* confederated, allied;
mit jem. ~ **sein** to be in league with s. o.
Verbündeter ally, associate, affiliate, confederate.
Verbund|fenster double-glazed window; ~**glas** laminated glass; ~**lokomotive** compound locomotive; ~**netz** *(el.)* grid; ~**produkte** joint products; ~**projekt** multipurpose project; ~**system** compound system; ~**tarif** joint rates; ~**werbung** tie-up (association) advertising; ~**wirtschaft** integrated economy, vertical trust (organization of industries), *(el.)* compound arrangement; **in** ~**wirtschaft arbeiten** to be economically integrated.
verbürgen, sich to vouch, to avouch, to undertake, to warrant, to guarantee, to stand surety, to bail, to furnish (give) security, to insure; **sich für j.** ~ to become bail (stand security, surety) for s. o.; **sich für einen Bericht** ~ to warrant a report; **sich für jds. Ehrlichkeit und Zuverlässigkeit** ~ to warrant s. o. an honest and reliable person (fellow); **Nachrichten** ~ to vouch news; **sich für die Richtigkeit seiner Angaben** ~ to vouch for the truth of one's statements; **sich für eine Schuld** ~ to answer for a debt; **sich für jds. Zahlungsfähigkeit** ~ to vouch for s. one's ability to pay.
verbürgt warranted, *(Meldung)* authentic, authorized, confirmed;
~**e Tatsache** established fact.
verbüßen, Freiheitsstrafe to serve (complete) a sentence, to do one's time.
Verbüßung einer Freiheitsstrafe serving (completion) of a sentence.
verbuttern to squander, to dissipate, to spend lavishly;
Geld in ein Haus ~ to put a lot of money into a house.
verchartern to charter, to let;
Schiff ~ to freight out a ship.
Vercharterung chartering.
Verdacht suspicion;
auf den ~ **hin** on the strength of; **im** ~ **stehen** under suspicion; **nicht unter** ~ **stehen** unsuspected; **unter dem Schatten eines** ~**s** under a cloud; **von jedem** ~ **befreit** clear of any suspicion;
begründeter ~ well-founded suspicion; **beunruhigender** ~ uneasy suspicion; **dringender** ~ strong suspicion; **grundloser** ~ groundless (gratuitous) suspicion; **hinreichender** ~ reasonable ground of suspicion; **nicht der leiseste** ~ not the slightest suspicion; **unbegründeter** ~ unfounded suspicion;
~ **einer strafbaren Handlung** indication of a criminal act; **ausreichender** ~ **der Zahlungsunfähigkeit** reasonable cause to believe a debtor insolvent;
~ **auslösen** to set the mental alarm off; **sich von einem** ~ **befreien** to clear the air; ~ **bestätigen** to confirm (verify) a suspicion; **j. in falschen** ~ **bringen** to slander s. o.; ~ **erregen** to arouse (be looked upon with, be creative of) suspicion; ~ **bei jem. erregen** to put s. o. on his guard; **in** ~ **geraten** to fall under suspicion; **leisen (vagen)** ~ **haben** to have a sneaking (kind of) suspicion; ~ **hegen** to entertain (harbo(u)r) a suspicion, to have a hunch; **jds.** ~ **verstummen lassen** to quiet s. one's suspicion; ~ **auf j. lenken** to fix (cast, throw) suspicion on s. o.; **jds.** ~ **auf sich lenken** to incur s. one's suspicions; ~ **rechtfertigen** to verify a suspicion; **sich von einem** ~ **reinigen** to purge o. s. from a suspicion; **sich von dem** ~ **eines Verbrechens reinigen** to clear o. s. of a crime; ~ **schöpfen** to smell a rat; **von jedem** ~ **befreit sein** to be clear of any suspicion; **im** ~ **stehen** to be suspected of (under suspicion); **wegen des** ~**s finanzieller Unregelmäßigkeiten verhaften** to take into custody on suspicion of financial impropriety; ~ **zerstreuen** to dispel a suspicion.
verdächtig suspicious, suspected, spotted, fishy *(sl.)*;
~ **klingen** to sound fishy *(sl.)*; **sich** ~ **machen** to cut a feather *(coll.)*, to run it out *(sl.)*; ~ **werden** to fall under suspicion;
~**er Gewohnheitsverbrecher** suspicious character; **politisch** ~**e Personen** political suspects; ~**e Umstände** suspicious circumstances.
verdächtigen, j. to cast (throw) suspicion on (suspect) s. o., to put the finger on s. o.; **j. bis zum Beweis seiner Unschuld** ~ to hold s. o. suspect until his innocence is proved; **j. des Mordes** ~ to suspect s. o. of murder.
verdächtigt suspected;
~ **werden** to fall under suspicion; **nicht mehr** ~ **werden** to be clear of suspicion;
~**e Person** suspicious person.
Verdächtigter suspicious person, suspect;
der Mittäterschaft ~ conjunct person;
~ **unter Polizeiaufsicht** suspected person under police surveillance.
Verdächtigung casting suspicion, backbiting, aspersion;
~ **wider besseres Wissen** malicious falsehood *(Br.)*;
j. durch abscheuliche ~**en kränken** to insult s. o. with odious suspicions.
Verdachts|grund ground for suspicion; ~**moment** suspicious fact; ~**person** suspect, suspicious person.
verdammen to curse, to condemn, to disapprove, *(schlechtmachen)* to disparage, to run down;
etw. heftig ~ to cry out against s. th.; **Theaterstück in Grund und Boden** ~ to tear a play to pieces.
verdammenswertes|Verbrechen detestable crime; ~ **Verhalten** damnable behavio(u)r.
verdammt damned, dashed, confounded, darned, bloody, blasted;
~ **und zugenäht** hang it, confound it, God damn it *(US)*;
~**er Kerl** goddamn fellow *(US)*; ~**er Narr** bloody fool.
Verdammung damnation.

verdampfen to vapo(u)r, to vapo(u)rise.
verdanken, jem. etw. to owe s. th. to s. o.; **seinen Eltern sehr viel** ~ to owe a great deal to one's parents; **sein Leben** ~ to owe one's life; **seiner Vorsicht** ~ to be due to one's caution.
verdattert flabbergasted, dumbfounded, stunned; **ganz** ~ **aussehen** to look [sadly] out of place; **ganz** ~ **sein** to feel cheap about, to be dumbfounded.
verdauen *(Börse)* to absorb, to digest; **seinen Lesestoff** ~ to digest what one reads.
verdaulich, leicht easy of digestion.
Verdauungsspaziergang machen to go for (take) a constitutional *(coll.)*.
Verdeck *(Auto)* hood, *(Autobus)* top (upper) deck, *(Lastwagen)* tarpaulin, *(Planwagen)* tilt, awning; **mit abnehmbarem** ~ soft-top; **ohne** ~ open-top *(US)*; **aufklappbares** ~ convertible roof; **zusammenklappbares** ~ folding roof; ~ **aufklappen (öffnen)** to lower the hood.
verdecken to conceal, to hide.
verdeckt concealed, hidden; **mit ~en Karten spielen** to hide one's cards; **~e Stellvertretung** undisclosed agency.
verdenken, jem. etw. nicht not to blame s. o. for s. th.
Verderb spoilage, decay, ruin, deterioration, naught, *(moralisch)* debasement, corruption, vitiation; **innerer** ~ inherent deterioration; **üblicher** ~ normal decay; **dem** ~ **ausgesetzt sein** to be of perishable nature.
Verderben ruin, doom; **in sein** ~ **rennen** to run straight for disaster; **j. ins** ~ **stürzen** to bring ruin upon s. o.
verderben to deteriorate, to spoil, to decay, to ruin, to wreck, *(schädlich beeinflussen)* to taint, to vitiate, *(Ernte)* to be ruined, *(Grundwasser, Luft)* to pollute, *(sittlich)* to stain, to taint, to corrupt, to debauch; **es mit jem.** ~ to fall out with s. o.; **Arbeit** ~ to botch a piece of work; **Getreide** ~ to ruin the grain; **jem. das Konzept** ~ to spoil (thwart) s. one's plans; **jem. die gute Laune** ~ to put s. o. in bad humo(u)r; **jds. Plan** ~ to upset s. one's applecart.
verderblich injurious, destructive, pernicious, poisonous, *(Ware)* perishable; **moralisch** ~ filthy, corruptive, pernicious; **nicht** ~ non-perishable; **~er Einfluß** corruptive influence; **~e Ladung** perishable cargo; **leicht ~e Waren** perishable goods (commodities); **~e Wirkung von Rauschgift** pernicious effect of narcotics.
Verderblichkeit, leichte perishableness, inherent deterioration.
verderbt foul, rotten, perverse, *(moralisch)* vicious, tough; **~er Text** corrupt text.
verdeutlichen to explicate, to explain, to eludicate, to point out.
Verdeutlichung explanation, explication, eludication; ~ **der Geschäftspolitik auf Vorstandsebene** policy information at corporate level.
verdichten to compress, *(Gas)* to condense; **sich** ~ *(Gerücht)* to increase, to heighten; **sich zur Gewißheit** ~ to become gradually a certainty.
Verdichtung agglomeration, compression.
Verdichtungsraum agglomeration area, *(Motor)* clearance space.
verdienen to earn, to gain, to pick up, to get, to make, to win, *(würdig sein)* to deserve, to merit; **Belohnung** ~ to merit reward; **gute Bezahlung** ~ to deserve good pay; **Bombengehalt** ~ to earn a packet of money; **sein Brot ehrlich** ~ to earn an honest penny; **im Schweiß der Arbeit sein Brot** ~ to sweat for one's bread; **sein tägliches Brot** ~ to win one's daily bread; **dick** ~ to rack up big sales; **40.000 Dollar im Jahr** ~ to get $ 40.000 a year; **Geld** ~ to make money; **Geld wie Heu** ~ to be simply coining money; **schweres Geld** ~ to line one's pockets, to earn big money; **genug** ~ to pay one's way, to make a good income, to do well; **an einem Geschäft** ~ to make a profit out of a transaction; **an einem Geschäft groß** ~ to be great gainer by a bargain; **gut** ~ to earn good money (a good living), to be in a good way of business, to have a good income; **Haufen Geld** ~ to make a pile (stacks) of money; **unsere Hilfe** ~ to deserve our help; **seinen Lebensunterhalt** ~ to make a (win one's) living, to earn one's livelihood, to get one's bread, to earn one's bread and butter; **seinen Lebensunterhalt durch Stundengeben** ~ to teach for a living; **nebenbei** ~ to make money on the side, to obtain a measure of economic independence; **netto** ~ to take home, to net; **netto 10.000 £ jährlich** ~ to clear ten thousand a year; **sich die Reise** ~ to work one's passage; **schlecht** ~ to be on the drab side; **schnell und bequem Geld** ~ to ride the gravy train *(sl.)*; **durch Schwarzarbeit** ~ to scab it; **schwer** ~ to make huge profits; **sich in einem Anwaltsbüro die Sporen** ~ to serve a hitch with a law firm; **Stange Geld** ~ to make a pile of money; **Strafe** ~ to deserve punishment; **sich sein Studium als Werkstudent** ~ to work one's way through college; **Vermögen** ~ to make a fortune; **Vertrauen** ~ to deserve merit; **viel mit etw.** ~ to make a lot of money out of s. th.; ~ **lassen** to keep in business.
Verdiener earner, breadwinner.
Verdienst *(Ansehen)* worth, *(Gewinn)* gains *(US)*, profit, gainings, makings, *(Lohneinkommen)* earnings, wages, *(Sporteln)* perquisites *(Br.)*, *(Verdienste)* merit, desert, credit; **aus eigenem** ~ in one's own right; **jds.** ~ **entsprechend** equal to s. one's merit; **nach** ~ worthily; **angemessener** ~ adequate wages; **durchschnittlicher** ~ average earnings (earned rate); **effektiver** ~ actual takings (earnings); **entgangener** ~ ceasing gain; **mein ganzer** ~ all I make by it; **garantierter** ~ guaranteed earnings; **geringer** ~ small profit; **großes** ~ feather in one's cap; **hervorragender** ~ sterling merit; **tariflicher** ~ standard wages, union rate; **zweifelhaftes** ~ dubious hono(u)r; **~e um sein Land** service to one's country; **~e um die Wissenschaft** services to science; **leichten** ~ **abgeben** to be a ready penny; **sich als** ~ **anrechnen** to count it one's glory, to take credit to o. s.; **geringere ~e als ein anderer aufweisen** to be inferior to s. o. in merit; **j. nach seinen ~en behandeln** to treat s. o. according to his merits; **vom** ~ **einbehalten** to deduct from the wages; **jds.** ~ **erwähnen** to notice s. one's services [in a speech]; **sich große ~e um etw. erwerben** to take great merit to o. s. for s. th.; **jds. ~e schmälern** to detract from s. one's merits; **jds. ~e in den Schatten stellen** to throw s. one's merits in the shade; **nach** ~ **behandelt werden** to get one's due; **nach seinem** ~ **eingeschätzt werden** to be judged according to one's deserts (merits); **~anteil** slice of earnings; **~ausfall** broken time, loss of trade (earnings), suspension of salary (earnings) *(US)*, *(Betriebsunfallfolgen)* future earnings; **~bescheinigung** wage certificate; **~durchschnitt** average earnings; **~kreuz** Distinguished Service Cross *(Br.)*; **geschätzte ~möglichkeiten** potential earnings; **gute ~möglichkeiten ausfindig machen** to hit upon a plan for making money; **~orden** order of merit; **~schmälerung** detraction from s. one's merits; **~sicherungsklausel** *(Akkordlohn)* standard wage maintenance clause.
Verdienstspanne profit margin, margin of profit; **geringe (schmale)** ~ narrow profit margin; **kaufmännische** ~ dealer markup; ~ **herabsetzen** to cut the margin.
Verdienst|staffelung graduation of wages; **~stufe** wage bracket (group).
verdienstvoll deserving; **~es Verhalten** meritorious conduct.
verdient, leicht lightly earned; **sauer** ~ hard-earned; **Gefängnisstrafe** ~ **haben** to deserve to be sent to prison; **sich um sein Land** ~ **gemacht haben** to deserve well of one's country; **sich um etw.** ~ **machen** to take great merit to o. s. for s. th.; **schwer ~es Geld** hard-earned money; **~e Transportkosten** earned freight.
Verdikt assize.
verdingen to put (farm) out; **sich** ~ to engage o. s. [as a servant], to go into (enter, take) service, to bind o. s., to hire o. s. out; **Arbeit** ~ to let out on contract; **einem Architekten einen Bau** ~ to allocate a building to an architect by contract; **sich als Knecht** ~ to enter service as a farmhand; **sich als Lehrling** ~ to bind o. s. as apprentice, to apprentice o. s.
Verdingung *(öffentliche Arbeiten)* placing of a contract by tender, contracting for work, *(Person)* hiring out, hire.
Verdingungs|ergebnis adjudication; **~kartell** contractual cartel.
verdolmetschen to interpret.
Verdolmetschung interpretership, interpretation.
verdonnern *(fam.)* to sentence, to fine.
verdoppeln to double, *(Einsatz)* to straddle; **sein Einkommen** ~ to double one's income; **sich mit der Zeit** ~ to double itself in time.
Verdopplung doubling.
verdorben spoiled, spoilt, damaged, unsound, tainted, rotten *(Br.)*, *(Frucht)* bad, *(Luft)* vitiated, polluted, *(sittlich)* corrupt, *(Wasser)* polluted, foul; **total** ~ rotten to the core; **~e Waren** perished (spoilt) goods.
verdorrt parched, scorched.

Verdrahtungsplan *(el.)* wiring diagram.
verdrängen to oust, to displace, *(Wasser)* to displace;
j. ~ to supplant s. o.; **j. aus dem Amt** ~ to supersede s. o. in office; **menschliche Arbeitskraft immer mehr** ~ *(Maschinen)* to replace human labo(u)r gradually; **unliebsame Begebenheit aus dem Gedächtnis** ~ to efface unpleasant memories of the past; **aus dem Besitz** ~ to dispossess; **Feind aus seinen Stellungen** ~ to drive the enemy out of his positions, to dislodge the enemy; **aus seinen Gedanken** ~ to dismiss all thoughts; **gewinnträchtigen Güterfernverkehr von den Straßen** ~ to price profitable long-distance freight traffic off the roads; **andere Interessen** ~ to push other interests into the background; **Konkurrenten aus einer Stellung** ~ to oust a rival from office; **private Kreditnehmer aus dem Kapitalmarkt** ~ to crowd debtors out of the capital market; **aus dem Markt** ~ to oust from the market; **Mieter aus der Wohnung** ~ to evict a tenant; **Waren aus dem Markt** ~ to price goods out of (oust goods from) the market.
verdrängt, von einem Konkurrenzbetrieb supplanted by a rival firm.
Verdrängung *(Schiff)* displacement, *(aus einer Stellung)* supplantation, *(aus einer Wohnung)* eviction;
~ **aus dem Besitz** dispossession; ~ **privater Kreditnehmer aus dem Kapitalmarkt** crowding debtors out of the capital market; ~ **eines Pächters** disturbance of tenure.
Verdrängungs|tonnage displacement tonnage; ~**tonne** displacement ton.
verdreckt covered with dirt (mud), dirty, filthy.
verdrehen *(Sinn)* to misinterpret, to warp, to distort, to wrest, to twist, to sophisticate, to chicane;
Recht ~ to pervert the course of justice; **Sinn eines Wortes** ~ to twist the meaning of a word; **Tatsachen** ~ to distort (screw) the facts; **Textstelle** ~ to warp the sense of a passage; **Wahrheit** ~ to twist (pervert) the truth.
verdreht *(fig.)* cracked, crazy, peculiar *(coll.)*, screwy *(US sl.)*;
j. ganz ~ **machen** to make s. one's head spin;
~**e Ansichten haben** to have crazy ideas.
Verdrehung distortion, perversion;
~ **der Tatsachen** distortion of the facts; ~ **eines Textes** distortion of a text; ~ **der Wahrheit** prevarication (perversion) of the truth.
verdreifachen to treble, to triple.
Verdreifachung triplication.
verdreschen, j. to give s. o. a warning, to lick s. o. *(sl.)*; **j. mörderisch** ~ to beat the daylight out of s. o.
verdrießen lassen, sich keine Mühe to leave no stone unturned.
verdrießlich annoyed, sullen, peevish, vexed;
~**es Gesicht** sullen face; ~**es Gesicht machen** to look annoyed.
ver|drossen annoyed, vexed, troubled, sullen, morose; ~**drucken** to misprint; **Mahlzeit** ~**drücken** to tuck in *(sl.)*; ~**druckt** incorrectly printed.
Verdruß trouble, vexation, annoyance, pet;
unaufhörlicher ~ incessant worries;
jem. laufend ~ **bereiten** to cause s. o. a lot of trouble.
verduften *(fam.)* to blow, to lam, to duck out *(US sl.)*, to hop the twig *(sl.)*, to beat it *(US sl.)*, to do a guy *(Br., sl.)*.
verdunkeln to obscure, to prevaricate, to camouflage, *(mil.)* to black (dim) out, to darken;
jds. Gemüt ~ to cloud s. one's mind.
verdunkelt, nicht undimmed.
Verdunkelung obscuration, prevarication, *(mil.)* blackout, blacking out, *(Straftat)* suppression of evidence;
teilweise ~ dim-out;
~ **des Sachverhalts** collusion of facts.
Verdunkelungs|gefahr danger of prejudicing the course of justice; ~**manöver** *(fig.)* collusion; ~**material** dark curtain (blacking-out) material; ~**übung** *(mil.)* trial blackout; ~**zeit** blackout time.
verdünnen to dilute, to thin, to weaken, to temper.
verdünnisieren, sich to beat it, to make o. s. scarce, to bunk, to duck out *(US sl.)*.
verdünnt diluted, thinned, watered-down;
~**e Zone** thinned-out zone.
Verdünnung dilution;
~ **der Kaufkraft** watering-down of purchasing power.
verdunsten to dry, to vaporize, to evaporate.
Verdunstung evaporation, vaporization.
Verdursten, am ~ **sein** to be parched with thirst.
ver|dursten to perish of thirst; ~**düstern** to darken.
verdutzt flabbergasted;
ganz ~ **sein** to be in a mist.
verebben *(Sturm)* to subside, to die down, to abate, to tail away.
Veredeler processer.
veredeln to process, to refine, to finish, to improve, to meliorate.
veredelt refined;
~**e Erzeugnisse** finished products, improved goods.
Veredelung finishing, processing, refining, refinement, melioration, culture aging, improvement, *(Garten)* graft, *(Lohnveredelung)* job processing, contract processing *(Br.)*.
Veredelungs|abteilung processing department; ~**betrieb** end-processing (finishing) plant, processing enterprise; ~**erzeugnisse** finished products, improved goods; ~**industrie** processing (finishing, refining) industry; ~**kosten** processing expenses; ~**land** processing country; ~**produkte** finished (processed) products, improved goods; ~**prozeß** finishing process; ~**steuer** processing tax *(US)*; ~**stufe** processing stage; ~**verfahren** finishing process; ~**verkehr** processing traffic, improvement trade; ~**wirtschaft** finishing (processing, refining) industry.
verehelichen, sich to marry, to get married.
Verehelichung solemnization of a marriage.
verehren to hono(u)r, to venerate;
jem. etw. ~ to make s. o. a present of s. th.; **j. hoch** ~ to entertain a high esteem for s. o.; **Künstler** ~ to admire an artist.
Verehrer hono(u)rer, venerator, admirer;
glühender ~ devotee;
~**briefe** fan letters.
verehrt hono(u)red, dear, esteemed.
Verehrung worship, veneration;
aus ~ **für j.** in homage to s. o.;
große ~ **für j. erkennen lassen** to profess a great esteem for s. o.;
jem. ~ **zollen** to pay reverence to s. o.
verehrungswürdig venerable, hono(u)rable.
vereidigen to administer an (put on, bind by) oath, to swear in, to adjure.
vereidigt|werden to be sworn in;
~**er Makler** sworn broker.
Vereidigung administration of an oath, adjuration, oath-taking ceremony, *(mil.)* attestation;
nach ordnungsgemäßer ~ being duly sworn;
auf die ~ **verzichten** to dispense with an oath.
Verein association, society, club, union;
im ~ **mit** in conjunction with;
eingetragener ~ registered *(Br.)* (incorporated, *US*) society, incorporated (registered) association (club), corporation *(Br.)*, membership corporation *(US)*; **nicht eingetragener (rechtsfähiger)** ~ unincorporated association (club), unregistered society *(Br.)* (membership association, *US*); **führender** ~ *(Sport)* flagship club; **gemeinnütziger** ~ nonprofit association, charitable organization, service club, collecting society *(Br.)*; **konzessionierter** ~ approved society; **rechtsfähiger** ~ registered (incorporated) club; **wohltätiger** ~ benevolent (charitable, friendly) society, charitable organization;
~ **mit Alkoholkonzession** registered club *(Br.)*; ~ **zur Förderung gegenseitiger (gemeinsamer) Interessen** fraternal (fraternity) association *(US)*; ~ **für Kapitalanlageinteressenten** investment club;
~ **auflösen** to disincorporate a club; **mit Freunden gemeinsam einen geselligen** ~ **aufziehen** to cooperate with friends in starting a social club; **aus einem** ~ **ausscheiden** to withdraw from a society (corporation, an association); **aus einem** ~ **ausschließen** to exclude (expel) from [membership of] a society; **aus einem** ~ **austreten** to withdraw from an association (society); **einem** ~ **beitreten** to become a member of (join) an association, to get into a club; **sich in einen** ~ **einkaufen** to join a society by redemption; ~ **eintragen lassen** to incorporate (register) an association (a society, a club).
vereinbar accordable, consistent, consonant, reconcilable, compatible;
mit dem Gesetz ~ consistent with the law; **miteinander** ~ compatible, consistent;
kaum ~ **sein** to be hardly compatible with.
vereinbaren to agree, to come to an agreement (arrangement), to arrange, to settle, to stipulate, to bargain;
Abfindung ~ to settle an amount of compensation; **Bedingungen** ~ to stipulate conditions; **Belohnung** ~ to stipulate a reward; **förmlich** ~ to indent; **Gehalt** ~ to appoint a salary; **monatliche Kündigung** ~ to agree upon a period of one month's notice; **Lieferfrist** ~ to stipulate a time for delivery; **erstklassige Materialverwendung** ~ to stipulate for the best material to be used; **Preis** ~ to agree about (stipulate) a price; **schriftlich** ~ to stipulate (agree) in writing; **stillschweigend** ~ to stipulate tacitly; **örtlich begrenzte Tarifverträge** ~ to bargain on a local basis; **Termin** ~ to agree upon (settle) a day, to fix a

date; **Treffpunkt** ~ to arrange (for) a meeting place; **vertraglich** ~ to stipulate by contract, to covenant; **Vertragsbestimmungen** ~ to set forth conditions in a contract; **vorher** ~ to prearrange; **von vornherein** ~ to pre-arrange; **Zahlungen auf Goldbasis** ~ to stipulate payment in gold; **vierteljährliche Zahlungen** ~ to stipulate that payment should be quarterly.

Vereinbarkeit compatibility, consistency.

vereinbart agreed, settled, stipulated, pactional;
es gilt als ~ it is understood; **falls (soweit) nicht anderweitig** ~ unless otherwise agreed; **früher als** ~ ahead of schedule; **nicht** ~ unarranged; **vertraglich** ~ stipulated by contract; **wie** ~ as stipulated (arranged); **wie vertraglich** ~ as provided in the contract;
~**e Bedingungen** conditions agreed upon; ~**es Darlehen** contractual loan; ~**er Preis** price agreed upon; **vertraglich** ~**er Preis** price agreed upon by arrangement; ~**e Qualität** stipulated quality; ~**e Schiedsgerichtsbarkeit** voluntary arbitration; ~**es Vorgehen** concerted action; ~**er Zeitpunkt** stated (specified) time; ~**er Zolltarif** conventional tariff.

Vereinbarung agreement, arrangement, stipulation, contract, condition, settlement, covenant, memorandum, league, terms, *(nach Anmeldung)* appointment, *(Völkerrecht)* accord;
aufgrund mündlicher ~ by parol; **entgegen früheren** ~**en** against previous arrangements; **gemäß der** ~ as per agreement; **im Wege freier** ~ by private treaty; **je nach** ~ as may be agreed; **laut** ~ as agreed (arranged); **mangels** ~ failing agreement; **mangels anderweitiger** ~ in the absence of any provision to the contrary, unless otherwise agreed; **nach** ~ by arrangement; **vorbehaltlich ausdrücklicher** ~ subject to express stipulation; **schriftlich abgefaßte** ~ memorandum of agreement; **ausdrückliche** ~ express agreement; **außergerichtliche** ~ out-of-court settlement; **beispielhafte** ~ pattern-making (-setting) agreement; **bestehende** ~ existing agreement; **bindende** ~ binding (obligatory) agreement; **eintragungspflichtige** ~ *(Kartellrecht)* registrable agreement; **entgegenstehende** ~**en** agreements not in accordance with; **sofort erfüllbare** ~ paction; **von den Parteien erzielte** ~ settlement arrived at by the parties; **schrittweise erzielte** ~**en** step-by-step deals; **feste** ~ fix up; **finanzielle** ~ financial arrangement; **der Betriebsschließung folgende** ~ post-shutdown arrangement; **formlose** ~ understanding; **frühere** ~ prior engagement; **gegenseitige** ~ mutual agreement; **geschäftliche** ~ business arrangement; **gesellschaftliche** ~ social agreement; **aufgrund einer Gerichtsanordnung getroffene** ~ judicial convention; **grundsätzliche** ~ agreement in principle; **gütliche** ~ amicable arrangement (settlement); **internationale** ~ international agreement; **kriminelle** ~ criminal organization; **lockere** ~ *(Kartellrecht)* loose combination *(US)*; **mündliche** ~ verbal (oral, parol) agreement, agreement by word of mouth; **nachträgliche** ~ subsequent agreement; **obligatorische** ~ obligatory pact; **privatschriftliche** ~ agreement under hand *(Br.)*; **gerichtlich protokollierte** ~ contract of record; **rechtsfähige** ~ incorporated association; **schriftliche** ~ agreement in writing, written agreement (memorandum); **schuldrechtliche** ~ contractual agreement; **stillschweigende** ~ implicit (silent, tacit) agreement; **ungesetzliche** ~ unlawful combination; **ungültige** ~ invalid agreement; **ursprüngliche** ~ original agreement; **verfassungsfeindliche** ~ seditious group; **vertragliche** ~ contractual arrangement (agreement); **völkerrechtliche** ~ convention, binding treaty; **vorausgegangene** ~ previous arrangement; **vorläufige** ~ interim (provisional) agreement, temporary (provisional) arrangement; **wettbewerbsbeschränkende** ~ restrictive trading agreement *(Br.)*; **zwischenstaatliche** ~ international convention;
~**en über den Austausch von Submissionsinformationen** information agreement; ~ **mit einer Bank** bank memorandum; ~ **über Befreiung vom Paßzwang** exchange of notes on the cancellation of passport requirements; ~ **zur Durchsetzung gebundener Wiederverkaufspreise** *(Kartellrecht)* agreement for collective enforcement of conditions as to resale prices; ~ **zur Einrichtung eines voll gewerkschaftspflichtigen Betriebs** approved closed-shop agreement; ~ **über gemeinsame Entschädigungsleistungen an unbeteiligte Dritte** *(Unfallversicherung)* third-party sharing agreement; ~ **mit der Finanzverwaltung** arrangement with the board of inland revenue; ~ **über die Fortführung des Geschäfts und die Liquidation des Schuldnervermögens unter Aufsicht eines Gläubigerausschusses** deed of inspectorship; ~ **über die Freistellung von Schadensersatzverpflichtungen** hold-harmless agreement; ~ **ohne Gegenleistung** naked contract; ~ **auf Gegenseitigkeit** reciprocal agreement; ~ **aufgrund einer Gerichtsanordnung** judicial convention; ~ **über das Getrenntleben** *(Ehegatten)* separation agreement, deed of separation *(Br.)*; ~ **mit den Gewerkschaften** trade-union agreement; ~ **einer Konkurrenzklausel** stipulation in restraint of trade; ~ **einer Konventionalstrafe** penal bond; ~ **über geteilte Machtausübung** power-sharing agreement; ~ **zwischen den Parteien** agreement between the parties; ~ **aufgrund schlüssigen Parteiverhaltens** agreement by inference from the conduct of the parties; ~ **über Preisbindung** resale price (price maintenance) agreement; ~ **pauschalierten Schadensersatzes** liquidated damages clause; ~ **eines Schiedsvertrages** arbitration agreement, submission to arbitration; ~ **der Steuerfreiheit** tax-free covenant *(US)*; ~ **über wechselseitiges Studium und Arbeit** work-study agreement; ~ **der Tarifpartner über gewerkschaftliche Zwangsbeiträge** agency shop agreement; ~ **über erneute Tarifverhandlungen** wage reopening clause; ~ **über Trennung von Tisch und Bett** separation from bed and board; ~ **auf Treu und Glauben** gentleman's agreement; ~ **einer Unterbeteiligung** subunderwriting agreement; ~ **zur Vermeidung der Doppelbesteuerung** double taxation agreement; ~ **über den Vorbehalt aller Rechte** nonwaiver agreement; ~ **mit dinglicher Wirkung** covenant held to touch and concern the land; ~ **über die Zahlungsmodalitäten** financial arrangement, financial agreement, stipulation of payment; **ausdrückliche** ~ **der Zulässigkeit des ordentlichen Rechtsweges** *(Schiedsgerichtswesen)* contracting-in; ~ **über Zusammenarbeit** cooperation agreement; ~ **über betriebliche Zusammenarbeit** collaboration deal;
~ **mit jem. abschließen** to enter into (conclude) an agreement with s. o.; ~ **aufheben** to abrogate an agreement; ~ **bestätigen** to confirm an agreement; ~ **zustande bringen** to bring about an agreement; ~ **durchführen** to carry out an agreement; ~ **nicht einhalten** to break an engagement; ~ **100%ig erfüllen** to keep to the letter of an agreement; ~ **erzielen** to reach (conclude, consummate) an agreement; **zu einer** ~ **gelangen** to reach (arrive at) an agreement; **zu einer endgültigen** ~ **gelangen** to come to a definite understanding; **zu einer gütlichen** ~ **gelangen** to make an amicable arrangement; **zu einer sofortigen** ~ **gelangen** to rush into a quick agreement; ~ **rechtsgültig gestalten** to constitute an indenture a valid, binding and legal agreement; **sich an eine** ~ **halten** to keep to (abide by, stand by) an agreement; ~ **mit jem. schließen** to make arrangements with s. o.; **in einer** ~ **begründet sein** to stem from an agreement; **mit jem. eine** ~ **treffen** to arrive at (reach) an agreement with s. o.; **schriftliche** ~ **treffen** to enter into a written agreement; **vorläufige** ~ **treffen** to make a provisional agreement; ~ **unter Druck unterzeichnen** to sign an agreement under duress; **an einer** ~ **nicht teilnehmen wollen** to ask to be left out of an agreement; **einer** ~ **zustimmen** to acquiesce in an agreement; **einer** ~ **nicht zustimmen** to dissent from an agreement.

vereinbarungsgemäß provided, as per agreement (arrangement).

vereinfachen to simplify, to short-circuit;
Dinge reihum ~ to simplify matters allround.

vereinfachte Rechnung short-cut computation.

Vereinfachung simplification;
zu große ~ oversimplification; **wirtschaftliche** ~ rationalization;
~ **eines Ausdrucks** reduction of an expression.

Vereinfachungsgründen, aus to simplify matters.

vereinheitlichen to unify, to standardize, to whip into line.

vereinheitlicht unified, standardized.

Vereinheitlichung unification, standard, standardization, simplification;
~ **der Ausrüstung** equipment standardization.

vereinigen to combine, to unite, to join, to gather, *(fusionieren)* to consolidate, to amalgamate, to merge, to pool, to fuse, *(gleichschalten)* to coordinate, *(pol.)* to unify, *(vergesellschaften)* to associate, to incorporate;
sich ~ to unite, to associate, *(Kräfte)* to join, to mingle, *(verbünden)* to ally, *(versammeln)* to assemble, to rally, to coalesce; **Familie wieder** ~ to reunite a family; **zwei Grundstücksparzellen** ~ to assemble two parcels of land; **Hypotheken** ~ to consolidate (pool) mortgages; **sich zu einer Koalition** ~ to form a coalition, to coalesce; **zwei Länder miteinander** ~ to unite one country with another; **Mehrheit der abgegebenen Stimmen auf sich** ~ to poll a majority of votes cast; **sich in einer Person** ~ *(Rechte)* to merge in one person; **Truppen** ~ to concentrate troops, to join forces; **sich zu gemeinsamem Tun** ~ to make a joint effort; **Verfahren** ~ to consolidate proceedings; **wieder** ~ to reunite.

vereinigt united, conjunct, conjoint, joint, associate, corporate, *(Kapital)* concentrated, consolidated;
~**e Fachgewerkschaft** amalgamated craft union.

Vereinigte Internationale Büros zum Schutz geistigen Eigentums United International Bureaux for the Protection of Intellectual Property.

Vereinigung *(Bund)* union, fraternity, conjunction, *(Körperschaft)* body, corporation, *(Menschenmenge)* assemblage, *(mil.)* rally, junction, *(Organisation)* organization, *(Verband)* federation, association, *(Verbindung)* confederacy, alliance, coalition, coalescence, *(Verein)* association, society, club, *(Verschmelzung)* consolidation, amalgamation, merger, fusion, pool;
berufliche ~ professional association; **gemeinnützige** ~ nonprofit (charitable) corporation (enterprise); **geschäftliche** ~ business league; **internationale** ~ international confederation; **korporative** ~ corporate body; **politische** ~ political assemblage; **wirtschaftliche** ~ economic union; **wohltätige** ~ benevolent society;
~ **der Arbeitgeberverbände** association of employers; ~ **zweier Börsenmitglieder an der Londoner Börse** market partnership *(Br.)*; ~ **zweier Eisenbahnlinien** junction of two railway (railroad, *US*) lines; ~ **zur Erzielung besserer Geschäftsmethoden** association of better business bureaus; ~ **zur Förderung der Wissenschaft** Association for the Advancement of Science; ~ **zu einer Genossenschaft** corporation; ~ **von Gläubiger und Schuldner in einer Person** confusion of rights *(US)*; ~ **von Hypotheken** pooling (consolidation) of mortgages, tacking; ~ **von Rechten in einer Person** merger of rights; ~ **von Verfahren** consolidation of proceedings; ~ **mehrerer Wahlstimmen auf einen Kandidaten** preferential voting; ~ **zu spekulativen Zwecken** bear pool.

Vereinigungs|freiheit freedom of association; **freies ~recht** principle of free association; **~recht aufheben** to rule out the right to associate.

vereinnahmen to collect, to receive, to take in;
devisenmäßig ~ to repatriate foreign exchange; **ausländische Anlagenerlöse devisenmäßig** ~ to repatriate earnings from foreign investments; **Wechsel** ~ to cash a bill.

Vereinnahmung collection;
devisenmäßige ~ foreign exchange repatriation.

Vereins|abend club night; **Zeit für die ~angelegenheiten aufwenden** to spend much time on the transaction of the society's business; **~auflösung** disincorporation; **~ausschluß** dismemberment; **~beitrag** dues, club dues (fees, money), subscription to a club; **~beitrag anfordern** to assess *(US)*; **~freiheit** freedom of association; **~funktionär** club officer; **~gebäude** club building; **~gelände** *(Sportverein)* home ground; **~gelder** association's funds; **~gelder unterschlagen** to misappropriate the society's funds; **~grundstück** club premises; **~gründung** organization of a club; **~gründung vorantreiben** to give a club the push-off; **~haus** club house; **~jahr** corporate year; **~kasse** funds of a society, society funds, treasury [of a club]; **~lokal** club premises; **~meier** clubmonger.

Vereinsmitglied clubmate, clubfellow, member of an association;
gastgebendes ~ host member; **neues** ~ recruit, new (freshman) member; **ständiges** ~ habitual member;
als ~ **aufnehmen** to enrol as a member of a club (society), to matriculate, to admit to fellowship; ~ **vorübergehend ausschließen** to suspend a member of a club; ~ **werden** to get into a club, to join an association, to become a member of an association;
~schaft membership in a club.

Vereins|raum clubroom; **~recht** clublaw, freedom of association; **~register** register of associations (of membership corporations); **ins ~register eintragen lassen** to incorporate a club; **~satzung, ~statuten** society's (club) rules, articles of agreement, regulations of a society, clublaw; **~sekretär** club manager; **~sperre** club embargo; **~tätigkeit** club activities; **~vermögen** club fund, association property; **~vorsitzender** club head; **~vorstand** executive committee of an association; **~zeremoniell** club etiquette *(US)*; **~zimmer** clubroom; **~zugehörigkeit** membership; **bestehende ~zugehörigkeit** effective membership of the society.

Vereinte Nationen United Nations Organization (UNO).

vereinte Kräfte combined (united) efforts.

vereinzelt singular, single, individual, isolated, detached, solitary;
~ **auftreten** to occur in isolated cases;
~e Fußgänger a few odd pedestrians; **~e Geschäfte** casual (spasmodic) transactions; **~e Häuser** scattered houses; **~e Regenschauer** occasional (scattered) showers; **~es Taxi** stray taxi; **~e Überfälle** sporadic raids; **~er Verkauf** sole transaction.

vereisen to ice (freeze) up, to ice (frost) over.

vereist frozen over, icy, *(Scheibe)* frosted, iced-up;
~e Straßen frozen roads.

Vereisung freezing up, *(Flugzeug)* icing, *(Straße)* icy condition.

vereisungsfrei ice-free.

Vereisungsgefahr danger of icing.

vereiteln to frustrate, to upset, to thwart, to baffle, to block, to obstruct, to torpedo, to circumvent, to foil, to hinder and delay;
durch einen Gegenauftrag ~ to countermine; **Plan** ~ to thwart (frustrate, foil) a plan; **Zwangsvollstreckung** ~ to obstruct process.

vereitelt frustrated.

Vereitelung frustration, circumvention, disappointment, discomfiture, prevention, bafflement;
~ **der Gläubigerbefriedigung** hindering and delaying creditors; ~ **eines Plans** defeat of a plan; ~ **der Vertragserfüllung** frustration of contract; ~ **der Zwangsvollstreckung** obstructing process.

verelenden to sink into poverty, to be reduced to misery.

verelendet pauperized, impoverished.

Verelendung pauperization;
~ **der Arbeiterklasse** impoverishment of the working class.

Verelendungstheorie theory of increasing misery, pauperization theory.

verengen, sich to [become] narrow; **Gewinnspanne** ~ to narrow the profit margin.

verengte Fahrbahn narrowed road.

Verengung constriction;
~ **des Geldmarktes** tightening of money conditions (the money market).

vererbbar inheritable, heritable, hereditable, hereditary, devisable, descendible.

vererben to leave, to bequeath, to will, *(Grund und Boden)* to devise, *(Krankheit)* to transmit, to propagate;
sich ~ to run in the family.

vererblich heritable, devisable, inheritable.

Vererbung descent, devise, *(biologisch)* inheritance.

verewigen to perpetuate, to eternize, to immortalize.

Verewigter deceased [person].

Verfahren *(Arbeitsvorgang)* operation, course, *(Behandlung)* treatment, *(Gericht)* procedure, proceeding(s), process, case, suit at law, lawsuit *(US)*, controversy, *(Handlungsweise)* deal, dealings, *(Herstellung)* process, method, technique, departure, *(Methode)* manner, method, plan, line, way, mode, *(Politik)* policy, *(Rechtsgang)* practice, *(Schema)* policy, system;
~ **eingestellt** case dismissed, *(Schwurgericht)* no bill; **in einem schwebenden** ~ pendente lite;
abgekürztes ~ summary proceeding; **aufeinander abgestimmtes** ~ concerted practices; **abgetrenntes** ~ separate trial; **abtrennbares** ~ separable controversy; **anhängiges** ~ case at law, proceedings instituted; **neu aufgenommenes** ~ new trial; **aufgeschobenes** ~ postponed trial; **schlampig ausgearbeitetes** ~ crude scheme; **beschleunigtes** ~ summary proceeding, speedup; **bewährtes** ~ established procedure; **dingliches** ~ proceeding in rem; **disziplinarisches** ~ disciplinary proceedings; **zwangsweise durchgeführtes** ~ compulsory process; **ehrliches** ~ fair play; **eigenmächtiges** ~ arbitrary action, highhandedness; **eingebürgertes** ~ custom, usance; **einheitliches** ~ standard practice, uniform procedure; **erprobtes** ~ well-tried method; **erstinstanzliches** ~ original process; **fehlerhaftes** ~ irregular proceedings; **einheitlich festgelegtes** ~ uniform procedure; **geheimes** ~ secret process, letters (trade) secret; **anhängig gemachtes** ~ instituted procedure; **gerechtes** ~ fair trial, just proceeding; **gerechtes und objektives** ~ fair and impartial trial; **gerichtliches** ~ legal proceedings, judicial process (action, proceedings), court proceedings; **gesetzlich geschütztes** ~ proprietary industrial process; **getrenntes** ~ separate action; **gewohntes** ~ familiar pattern; **industrielles** ~ know-how, industrial technique (process); **konkursrechtliches** ~ bankruptcy proceedings (procedure), proceedings in bankruptcy; **kontradiktorisches** ~ contentious business; **kostspieliges** ~ costly proceedings; **langwieriges** ~ lengthy process; **unter Formfehlern leidendes** ~ irregular proceedings; **mechanisches** ~ mechanical process; **mündliches** ~ verbal process; **neues** ~ new departure; **neuartiges** ~ novel method; **nichtiges** ~ void process; **nichtstreitiges** ~ noncontentious business; **ordentliches** ~ regular process, ordinary proceedings, *(Testament)* common form; **ordnungsgemäßes** ~ due process of law; **parlamentarisches** ~ parliamentary procedure; **patentfähiges** ~ patentable process; **patentiertes** ~ patented process; **rechtsgültiges** ~ validity of judicial proceedings;

rechtsstaatliches ~ due process of law; **redliches** ~ fair play; **schiedsgerichtliches** ~ arbitration procedure; **schleppendes** ~ drag; **schriftliches** ~ trial by certificate, written proceedings; **schwebendes** ~ pending action; **statistisches** ~ census procedure; **strafrechtliches** ~ criminal procedure (proceedings), trial prosecution; **streitiges** ~ adversary lawsuit, ligitation, defended trial; **summarisches** ~ summary proceeding (action, *Scot.*), *(fig.)* rough justice; **überholtes** ~ outmoded process; **[allgemein] übliches** ~ usual (routine) procedure, standard (general, common) practice, usage; **ungerechtes** ~ unfair hearing; **ungesetzliches** ~ illegal proceedings; **ungültiges** ~ void (irregular) process, mistrial; **unvorschriftsmäßiges** ~ undue proceedings; **verbessertes** ~ improved process; **gesetzlich vorgeschriebenes** ~ statutory proceedings; **wiederaufgenommenes** ~ new trial; **zivilrechtliches** ~ suit of a civil nature, civil action (proceedings);
~ **zur Anerkennung und Vollstreckung ausländischer Urteile** action on the judgment; ~ **in familienrechtlichen Angelegenheiten** domestic proceedings; ~ **bei der Aufstellung des Haushalts** budget (budgetary) procedure; ~ **bei der Aufstellung des Werbeetats** advertising budget procedure; ~ **zur besseren Ausnutzung elektronischer Datenverarbeitungsanlagen** time sharing of data-processing machines; ~ **zur Beilegung von Tarifstreitigkeiten** disputes procedure; ~ **wegen Besitzstörung öffentlicher Ländereien** information of intrusion; ~ **zur Beweisaufnahme** taking of evidence; ~ **in Ehesachen** matrimonial case (proceedings), divorce proceedings; ~ **nach Einweisung in eine Heilanstalt** post-commitment hearing *(US)*; ~ **vor dem Einzelrichter** trial at nisi prius; ~ **zwecks Erlaß einer einstweiligen Verfügung** civil suit for injunction; ~ **zur Festsetzung der Folgeprämie** renewal procedure; ~ **zur Feststellung eines Prioritätsrechtes** *(Patentrecht)* interference proceedings; ~ **zur Feststellung der Schadenshöhe** writ of inquiry [after judgment by default]; ~ **zur Feststellung des Schuldigen** fault-finding procedure; ~ **in Forderungspfändungen** process of garnishment, trustee process *(US)*; ~ **zur Freigabe von Geheimmaterial** declassification procedure; ~ **der freiwilligen Gerichtsbarkeit** noncontentious business; ~ **wegen unerlaubter Handlung** proceedings in tort; ~ **wegen Konzessionserschleichung** information in the nature of a quo warranto; ~ **wegen Mordes** homicide trial; ~ **in Nachlaßangelegenheiten** administration suit; ~ **in Nichtigkeitssachen** nullity suit; ~ **zur Offenlegung der Vermögensverhältnisse** equitable garnishment, supplementary proceedings *(US)*; ~ **vor dem Patentamt** patent-office procedure; ~ **eines integrierten Planungs-, Programmierungs- und Haushaltssystems** Planning-Programming-Budgeting System; ~ **nach der Prozeßordnung** judicial process (proceedings); ~ **bei Rechtshilfeersuchen** procedure for letters rogatory; ~ **zur Regelung eines Streitfalls** *(dipl.)* contentious procedure; ~ **zur Regelung arbeitsrechtlicher Streitigkeiten** disputes procedure; ~ **zur Regelung von Versicherungsansprüchen** claim procedure; ~ **in der Revisionsinstanz** proceedings in error; ~ **in Steuersachen** process in tax proceedings; ~ **in Warenzeichenangelegenheiten** trademark procedure; ~ **in Zivilsachen** civil proceedings (action, trial);
~ **abtrennen** to separate a case; ~ **ändern** to reverse a procedure; **Wiederaufnahme des ~s anordnen** to grant s. o. a new trial; ~ **anstrengen** to institute legal proceedings, to bring a suit; **neues** ~ **anwenden** to take a new departure; **sein übliches** ~ **anwenden** to follow one's standard practice; **neue** ~ **ausprobieren** to experiment with new methods; **gerichtliches** ~ **aussetzen** to stay *(US)* (suspend) the proceedings, to arrest judgment; **schwebendes** ~ **beeinträchtigen** to prejudice a fair trial; **nach einem besonderen** ~ **behandeln** to process; **gerichtliches** ~ **behindern** to prejudice the due course of justice; ~ **beschleunigen** to accelerate proceedings; **Rechtsgültigkeit eines ~s bestreiten** to object to the regularity of the proceedings; ~ **betreiben** to prosecute an action, to carry on a lawsuit; ~ **gegen j. in Gang bringen** to proceed (take out a process) against s. o.; ~ **vor das Schwurgericht bringen** to conclude to the country; ~ **durchführen** to proceed with a case, to carry on legal proceedings; **abgetrenntes** ~ **gegen j. durchführen** to try s. o. separately; **neues** ~ **einführen** to inaugurate a new system; **neue technologische** ~ **in der Industrie einführen** to make technical innovations in industry; **in ein laufendes** ~ **eingreifen** to publish comment on cases pending; ~ **einleiten** to institute proceedings, to strike an action off the roll; ~ **gegen j. einleiten** to order proceedings to be taken against s. o.; **gerichtliches** ~ **gegen j. einleiten** to institute legal proceedings against s. o.; ~ **wegen Amtsmißbrauchs einleiten** to take misfeasance proceedings; **gerichtliches** ~ **einstellen** to dismiss a case, to discharge any proceeding in court, to abate proceedings, to sist *(Scot.)*, *(Strafverfahren)* to lapse criminal proceedings *(Br.)*, to abate an action, to quash proceedings (the indictment); **gerichtliches** ~ **ermöglichen** to to authorize legal proceedings; ~ **eröffnen** to open a case; **ordnungsgemäßes** ~ **gegen j. eröffnen** to put together a plausible case against s. o.; ~ **in seltsamem Licht erscheinen lassen** to cast a gloom on the proceedings; ~ **ruhen lassen** to let a cast rest; **j. mit einem** ~ **bekannt machen** to introduce s. o. to a process; ~ **niederschlagen** to squash proceedings; **ordnungsgemäßes** ~ **sicherstellen** to regularize the proceedings; ~ **überprüfen** to review the proceedings; ~ **unterbrechen** to suspend the proceedings, to adjourn a trial; **einem** ~ **unterwerfen** to process; **sich einem schiedsrichterlichen** ~ **unterwerfen** to submit to arbitration; **verschiedene** ~ **vereinigen** to consolidate proceedings; ~ **verschleppen** to delay the proceedings; **auf ein** ~ **verzichten** to waive trial; **umgekehrtes** ~ **wählen** to reverse a process; **in einem schiedsgerichtlichen** ~ **tätig werden** to arbitrate between parties to a suit; **zu den Kosten des ~s verurteilt werden** to be condemned in (ordered to pay) the costs; ~ **wiederaufnehmen** to rehear, to reopen a case (judgment); ~ **in den vorigen Stand wiedereinsetzen** to reinstate (reopen) a case.

verfahren to proceed, to deal, to act;
sich ~ to lose one's way, to take the wrong road; **mit jem.** ~ to deal with s. o.; **enorm viel Benzin** ~ to spend a fortune on petrol; **nach den Bestimmungen** ~ to act according to the rules; **seine Schicht** ~ to finish one's task; **schonend** ~ to act with consideration; **streng mit jem.** ~ to treat s. o. with severity; **nach einem bestimmten System** ~ to go to work on a system; **streng nach den Vorschriften** ~ to deal strictly by the rules; **vorsichtig mit jem.** ~ to handle s. o. carefully;
~ *(a.) (verpfuscht)* muddled, wrecked;
total ~ **sein** to be a complete tangle.

Verfahrens|ablauf, formloser und schneller informal and speedy procedure; **~ablauf beschleunigen** to speed up trial proceedings; **~abschnitt** stage of a proceeding; **~änderung** change in process; **~angelegenheit** procedural matter; **~antrag** formal (procedural) motion, interlocutory application; **~anweisungen** *(Gericht)* general orders; **~anwendung** practical application of a process; **~art** mode of procedure; **~ausschuß** procedural committee; **~aussetzung** suspension (stay) of proceedings; **~aussetzung von Amts wegen** involuntary discontinuance; **~beginn** commencement of proceedings; **~beschluß** procedural order; **~bestimmungen** procedural provisions, general (standing) rules of court; **~einreden** bill of exceptions; **~einstellung** dismissal (stay) of proceedings, abatement of an action, sist *(Scot.)*, *(Strafverfahren)* nolle prosequi *(lat.)*; **einstweilige ~einstellung** suspension of proceedings; **~einwand** exception, plea in abatement; **~erfordernisse** procedural requirements; **~fehler** irregularity in the proceedings; **absichtlicher ~fehler** invited error; **~form** formal way of procedure; **~formen** forms of legal procedure; **~forschung** operational *(Br.)* (operations, *US*) research; **~fortsetzung** resumption of a trial, *(ruhendes Verfahren)* revival of an action; **~frage** matter of form, *(Gericht)* procedural question (matter), *(Parlament)* point of procedure (order); **Debatte über ~fragen beenden** to stop arguing about [questions of] procedure; **über ~fragen streiten** to argue about procedure; **~gang** course of procedure; **~gegenstand** subject matter, matter in issue; **~gründe** procedural grounds; **schwerwiegender ~irrtum** prejudicial error; **~kosten** legal (law) costs, costs of proceedings, expense of trial; **~kosten auferlegen** to condemn in (order to pay) the costs; **~kosten aufteilen** to allocate the costs.

verfahrensleitender Antrag originating motion.

Verfahrens|mangel irregularity (error) in the proceedings, legal irregularity; **durch Urteil geheilter ~mangel** aider by verdict; **~mangelheilung im Urteilswege** cure by verdict; **~manöver** procedural manoeuvre.

verfahrensmäßige Schwierigkeiten beseitigen to iron out procedural difficulties.

Verfahrens|mechanismus procedural machinery; **~methode** mode of proceeding; **~mißbrauch** abuse of the process in court; **~modus anwenden** to carry out a procedure; **sich einem ~modus vollinhaltlich anschließen** to buy a line completely; **~neuerungen** procedural innovations; **~nummer** processing number; **~ordnung** procedure, rules of practice, procedural rules, standing rules, Procedure Act *(US)*, Act of Adjournal *(Scot.)*; **strenge ~ordnung** stringent code of procedure; **~patent** process patent; **~protokoll** written proceedings; **~recht** procedural law, law of procedure *(Br.)*, procedural (adjective) law.

verfahrensrechtlich procedural;
~e Frage matter of form; **~e Schwierigkeiten beseitigen** to iron out procedural difficulties.
Verfahrens | regeln, gerichtliche general (standing) rules of court, practice of law, procedure, order *(Br.)*; **übliche ~regeln einhalten** to be according to an established pattern; **~regelung** procedure agreement; **~rüge** motion in error; **~streitigkeiten** procedural wrangling; **~taktik** procedural tactics; **~technik** process engineering.
verfahrenstechnisch technical, procedural;
~e Verbesserungen procedural improvements.
Verfahrens | trennung severance of an action; **~trick** procedural device; **~vereinbarung** procedure agreement; **formaler ~verstoß** legal irregularity.
Verfahrensvorschriften rules of practice (procedure), practice rules, procedural provisions;
allgemeine ~ general rules; **gerichtliche ~** general (standing) rules of the court;
~ erfüllen to comply with procedural requirements.
Verfahrensweise process, method, way of operating;
~ einführen to adopt a policy.
Verfall *(Ablauf)* expiration, expiry, *(Anspruch)* lapse, forfeiture, *(an Staat wegen fehlender Erben)* escheat, *(Fälligwerden)* maturity, *(Firma)* decline, descent, *(Gebäude)* dilapidation, disrepair, deterioration, decay, *(Hypothek)* foreclosure, *(Körper)* decline, decay, corruption, *(Kurse)* sudden fall, slump, nose dive, break *(US)*, *(Niedergang)* decadence, decline, breakup, waste, *(Pfand)* forfeiture, *(Prämie)* abandonment, *(Sitten)* deterioration, decadence, *(Vermögen)* dwindling assets, *(Wechsel)* maturity;
bei ~ when due, at (on) maturity, at the time of (on) expiration; **bei ~ zahlbar** payable on expiration (maturity); **bis zum ~** till maturity; **im ~ begriffen** on the go; **nach ~** *(Wechsel)* when overdue; **vor ~** before maturity, before [falling] due;
~ unbehobener Dividenden forfeiture of unclaimed dividends; **~ der Moral** depravation of morals; **~ eines Patents** forfeiture (expiration, lapse) of a patent; **~ einer Police** lapse of a policy; **~ der Sicherheitsleistung** bail jumping *(US)*; **~ eines Urheberrechts** lapse of a copyright;
~ aufschieben to defer (delay) maturity; **~ eines Wechsels ausrechnen** to compute a bill; **Wechsel bei ~ einlösen** to hono(u)r a bill when due; **in ~ geraten** *(Haus)* to [fall into] decay, to fall into disrepair, *(Moral)* to deteriorate; **in ~ geraten lassen** to waste; **bei ~ nicht honoriert werden** to lie over, to be dishono(u)red; **vor ~ zahlen** to pay (make payments) in advance, to pay in anticipation; **vor ~ zurückzahlen** to repay before the expiration of a period;
~buch debt book, maturity tickler (index, *US*), tickler diary, *(Wechsel)* bill diary *(Br.)*, bills payable (receivable) book *(US)*, note tickler *(US)*; **~buch für Akzepte** acceptance diary *(Br.)* (maturity tickler, *US*); **~datum** *(Ablaufdatum)* expiring (expiration) date, *(Fälligkeit)* due (maturity) date, date of maturity.
Verfallen decay, dilapidation.
verfallen *(Fahrkarte)* to expire, *(fällig sein)* to be due, *(fällig werden)* to become (fall) due, to mature, *(Haus)* to fall into decay (disrepair), to decay, to waste, to dilapidate, *(Optionsrecht, Versicherungspolice)* to expire, to lapse, *(Pfand)* to forfeit, to become forfeited, *(Sitten)* to deteriorate, to decay, to degenerate, *(ungültig werden)* to lapse, to cease to be valid;
dem Alkohol ~ to become addicted to alcohol; **in die alten Fehler ~** to slip back into one's old ways; **auf einen Gedanken ~** to hit upon an idea; **in Krämpfe ~** to be seized with cramp; **der Lächerlichkeit ~** to lay o. s. open to ridicule, to make a laughing-stock of o. s.; **in seinen alten Schlendrian ~** to travel in the same groove; **in Schweigen ~** to sink into silence; **dem Wahnsinn ~** to go insane; **zusehends ~** *(Kranker)* to sink fast; **für ~ erklären** to forfeit, *(Hypothek)* to foreclose (close down, *US coll.*) a mortgage; **Sicherheit für ~ erklären** to forfeit a security; **~ lassen** to waste; **Haus ~ lassen** to dilapidate a building; **Kaution ~ lassen** to forfeit a bond; **Patent ~ lassen** to drop (abandon) a patent;
~ *(a.) (abgelaufen)* expired, lapsed, *(beschlagnahmt)* confiscated, forfeited, *(wegen Erbenmangels)* escheated, *(fällig)* matured, due, overdue, back, payable, *(Haus)* decayed, dilapidated, tumbled down, tumble-down, *(Hypothek)* foreclosed, *(Patent)* void, *(Pfand)* forfeited, *(verjährt)* lapsed, barred by the statute of limitations;
~ sein to have lapsed (expired), *(baufällig)* to be in decay;
~e Karten expired tickets; **~es Patent** lapsed (expired) patent; **~e Pfänder** forfeited pledges; **~e Versicherungspolice** lapsed policy; **~er Wechsel** payable (matured) bill.
Verfallenlassen waste.
Verfalls | androhung, mit on pain of forfeiture; **~erklärung** confiscation, cancellation, *(Hypothek)* foreclosure; **~erscheinungen** symptoms of decay; **~klausel** acceleration (cancellation, forfeiture) clause; **~liste** aging schedule.
Verfallstag date of expiration (expiry), expiry (termination) date, *(Hypothek, Obligation)* law day, *(Wechsel)* date (day) of maturity, due date;
durchschnittlicher ~ *(Wechsel)* average due date;
~ eines Wechsels ausrechnen to compute a bill.
Verfalls | termin date of expiry, expiry (termination) date, time of payment; **~zeichen** sign of decay.
Verfallszeit time of payment, *(Wechsel)* maturity;
bis zur ~ till (until) due; **zur ~** when due, at (on) maturity, at the time of expiration;
kurze ~ short maturity; **mittlere ~** average due date;
vor ~ bezahlen to repay before expiration; **zur ~ nicht bezahlt werden** to lie over, to be dishono(u)red.
Verfallszustand state of decay.
verfälschen *(Banknoten)* to counterfeit, *(Münzen)* to debase, *(Text)* to corrupt, to sophisticate, *(Urkunde)* to forge, to falsify, to tamper with;
Bilanz ~ to doctor (cook, fake) a balance sheet; **Nahrungsmittel ~** to adulterate food; **Statistik ~** to falsify statistics; **Tatsachen ~** to juggle with the facts; **Text ~** to corrupt a text; **Urkunde ~** to forge a document.
Verfälscher falsifier, faker, sophisticator;
~ von Nahrungsmitteln adulterator.
verfälscht forged, falsified, *(Text)* corrupt, distorted;
~e Bilanz cooked (doctored) balance sheet; **~e Nahrungsmittel** adulterated food; **~e Urkunde** forged (false) instrument.
Verfälschung falsification, *(Banknoten)* counterfeiting, *(Bilanz)* doctoring, cooking, faking, *(Münzen)* debasement, *(Text)* distortion, corruption, *(Urkunden)* falsification, forgery;
einseitige ~ *(Befragung)* interview bias;
~ von Nahrungsmitteln adulteration of food; **~ eines Textes** corruption (sophistication) of a text.
Verfälschungsmittel adulterant.
verfangen, bei jem. nicht to have no effect on s. o.; **sich in etw. ~** to get caught (entangled) in s. th.; **sich in einem Lügennetz ~** to get entangled in a web of lies.
verfänglich tricky, embarrassing, *(schlüpfrig)* off-colo(u)r, risqué;
~e Frage captious question; **j. durch ~e Fragen in Verlegenheit bringen** to embarrass s. o. with indiscreet questions; **~e Situation** awkward situation.
verfassen to draft, to draw (make) up, to compose, to write, to compile;
Brief ~ to pen a letter; **Buch ~** to write (compose) a book; **Rede ~** to compose a speech.
Verfasser author, writer, composer, framer, *(Aussteller)* drafter, draftsman, draughtsman;
im Auftrag des ~s with the compliments of the author; **ohne ~** no single author;
alleiniger ~ sole author; **der gelehrte ~** the learned editor; **ungenannter ~** anonymous author;
~ biographischer Artikel personalist; **~ anonymer Briefe** poison pen; **~ einer Dissertation** dissertator; **~ von Flugschriften** pampleteer; **~ einer Resolution** resolutioner; **~ einer Urkunde** engrosser; **~ eines Wörterbuches** compiler of a dictionary, lexicographer;
sich als ~ bekennen to avow o. s. the author; **~ in Grund und Boden verurteilen** to pull an author to pieces;
~anteil royalty; **~eigenschaft** authorship; **~katalog** *(Bibliothek)* author catalog(ue); **~korrektur** author's proof; **~schaft** authorship.
verfaßt worded;
gerichtlich ~ in due form of law.
Verfassung constitution, fundamental law, charter, polity, *(Aufmachung)* make-up, *(Gesundheitszustand)* condition of health, way, *(System)* organization, system, *(Zustand)* condition, state, make, shape, trim, fix *(US)*;
in bester ~ as fit as a fiddle; **in guter ~** in [a] good state (condition, form), in good construction, in fine fettle; **in schlechter ~** out of condition; **in trauriger ~** in a wretched plight (terrible way), in bad shape;
brauchbare ~ workable constitution; **finanzielle ~** financial condition (position, status); **geistige ~** frame of mind; **körperliche ~** physical shape; **richtige ~** trim; **starre ~** rigid constitution; **unabänderliche ~** rigid constitution; **ungeschriebene ~** unwritten constitution;

finanzielle ~ im Fall einer Liquidation gone-concern position; **~ ändern** to amend a constitution; **~ annehmen** to adopt a constitution; **~ aufheben** to overthrow (abrogate) a constitution; **sich in einer unglaublichen ~ befinden** *(Gebäude)* to be in an indescribable state of disrepair; **unter eine ~ fallen** to come within the framework of a constitution; **sich nicht in der ~ fühlen** not to be in the state of mind; **einem Land eine ~ geben** to give a country a constitution; **gesündere finanzielle ~ erkennen lassen** to show a stronger position; **in erstklassiger ~ sein** to be as hard as nails *(fam.)*; **in ziemlich guter ~ sein** to be in fair condition; **in schlechter ~ sein** to be in a bad frame of mind, to be under the weather.

verfassunggebend constituent;
~e Gewalt constituent power; **~e Versammlung** National (Constituent) Assembly.

Verfassungs|abschnitt section of the constitution; **~änderung** constitutional amendment, change in (amendment, modification of) the constitution; **~änderungen** constitutional changes, changes in the constitution; **~anhang** schedule; **~anhänger** constitutionalist; **~ausschuß** constitutional convention (committee); **~beschränkung** constitutional limitation; **~beschwerde** constitutional complaint.

Verfassungsbestimmung constitutional provision;
automatische ~ self-executing constitutional provision;
unter ~en fallen to come within the framework of a constitution; **nach den ~en ernannt werden** to be constitutionally appointed.

Verfassungs|bruch violation (infringement) of the constitution; **~bruch begehen** to infringe the constitution; **~demokratie** constitutional democracy; **~eid** promissory oath; **~entwurf** draft constitution.

verfassungsfeindlich anticonstitutional, seditious.

verfassungsgemäß constitutional;
~e Mittel constitutional means; **~en Zustand wiederherstellen** to go back to civilian rule.

Verfassungs|gemäßheit constitutionality; **~gericht** constitutional court; **~gesetz** constitutional (fundamental) law; **~grundsatz** constitutional principle; **~grundsatz der Gleichberechtigung** equality clause *(US)*; **~konflikt** constitutional conflict.

verfassungskonform, etw. für ~ halten to find s. th. constitutional.

Verfassungskrise constitutional crisis.

verfassungsmäßig constitutional;
~ absegnen to give a constitutional rubber stamp;
~e Gewalt constitutional power; **~e Grundlage** constitutional basis; **~e Mittel** constitutional means; **~e Ordnung** constitutional order; **~ garantierte Rechte** constitutional rights; **~e Regierung** constitutional government; **~ vorgesehene Volksbefragung** constitutional referendum; **~en Zustand wiederherstellen** to go back to civilian rule.

Verfassungs|mäßigkeit constitutionality, validity of a statute; **~mäßigkeit eines Vertrages** validity of a treaty; **~problem** constitutional issue; **~recht** constitutional (organic, paramount) law, franchise; **~rechte aufheben** to exclude from the operation of the convention; **~rechtler** constitutionalist.

verfassungsrechtlich constitutionally, organic;
~ schützen to entrench in a constitution;
~e Auslegung constitutional statement; **aufgrund ~er Bedenken** on constitutional ground(s); **~e Beschränkungen** constitutional limitations.

Verfassungs|reform constitutional reform; **~schutz** [etwa] intelligence office; **~streit** constitutional conflict; **~system** constitutional system.

verfassungstreu constitutional.

Verfassungs|urkunde Constitutional Charter, Bill of Rights, Magna Charta *(Br.)*; **~vorschrift** constitutional formula.

verfassungswidrig unconstitutional.

Verfassungs|widrigkeit unconstitutionality; **~wirklichkeit** constitutional reality; **~zusatz** constitutional amendment.

verfaulen to rot, to mo(u)lder, to putrefy, to decay.

verfault putrid, putrefied, rotten, decayed, *(Obst)* unsound;
total ~ rotten throughout.

verfechtbar defensible, assertible, maintainable.

verfechten to advocate, to maintain, to contend, to champion, to stand up for;
Meinung ~ to advance (advocate) an opinion; **seine Rechte ~** to assert one's rights; **Zweiparteiensystem ~** to support the two-party system.

Verfechter defender, advocate, champion, supporter;
~ des Goldstandards goldbug *(US sl.)*; **~ eines harten Kurses** hardliner; **~ des Wettbewerbsgedankens** believer in competition.

verfehlen to miss, to fail;
seine Wirkung ~ to fail to have effect; **sein Ziel ~** to miss one's aim;
nicht zu ~ as big as a barndoor.

verfehlt amiss, abortive, miscarried;
~e Geschichte failure; **~es Leben** misspent life; **~e Politk** inappropriate policy.

Verfehlung delinquency, misconduct, failure, *(jur.)* misdemeanor, minor offence;
schwere ~ gross (wilful) misconduct;
~en im Amt malfeasance in office; **schwere ~ eines Angestellten** wilful misconduct of an employee.

verfeinden to estrange, to cause enmity;
sich ~ to become estranged; **Freunde ~** to turn one friend against the other.

verfeindet estranged, on bad terms;
mit jem. ~ sein to be at daggers drawn with s. o.

verfeinern to cultivate, to refine, to polish, to improve, to process, *(Umgangsformen)* to urbanize.

verfeinert refined, cultivated, *(Stil)* sophisticated.

Verfeinerung culture, refinery, refinement, improvement, cultivation, urbanization, elaboration, elevation.

verfemen to ostracize, to send to Coventry *(Br.)*.

verfertigen to fabricate, to manufacture, to make;
Brief ~ to compose a letter; **Liste ~** to draw up a list.

verfestigen, sich to solidify, to become rigid (firm).

verfeuern to burn as fuel;
seine ganze Munition ~ to fire away all one's ammunition.

verfilmen to film, to screen, to adapt to the screen, to picture, to cinematize, to picturize *(US)*;
Roman ~ to put a novel on the films;
sich gut ~ lassen to film well.

Verfilmung screening, film version, picturization *(US)*;
zur ~ geeignet screenable;
~ eines Theaterstücks photoplay.

Verfilmungsrechte screen (film) rights.

verfinstern, sich to darken, to obscure, *(Sonne)* to eclipse.

verflechten *(Motive)* to interweave, to intertwine, *(Unternehmen)* to integrate, to interlock, to interlace;
europäischen Markt ~ to integrate the European market; **zwei Unternehmen miteinander ~** to interlock two enterprises.

Verflechtung interlocking, interrelation, network, *(Themen)* interweavement, intertwinement, entwinement;
bei einer ~ von Umständen by a strange coincidence;
absatzmäßige ~ forward linkage; **außenwirtschaftliche ~en** foreign trade links; **kapitalsmäßige ~** capital interrelation; **produktionsmäßige ~en** interlocking arrangements of production; **vertikale ~** vertical combination; **wirtschaftliche ~** economic interdependence (integration);
~ von Interessen nexus of interests; **~ von Kapital** interlacing of capital; **~ der Kapitalmärkte** interpenetration of capital markets; **~ eines Konzerns** interlocking combine; **~ verschiedener Märkte** integration of markets; **~ verschiedener Unternehmen** interlocking of several undertakings; **~ in eine Verschwörung** involvement in a conspiracy; **~ der Weltmärkte** integration of world markets.

Verflechtungs|beziehungen, industrielle linkage; **~koeffizient** input-output coefficient; **industrielle ~struktur** input-output structure.

verfliegen *(Zeit)* to fly;
im Nu ~ to pass in no time.

verfließen *(Zeit)* to elapse, to go, to pass, to run.

verflixt plaguy *(coll.)*;
~e Geschichte unpleasant affair; **~er Kerl** devil of a fellow.

verflochten interlaced, interwoven, entwined, *(Unternehmen)* interlocked, interlinked, integrated;
in eine undurchsichtige Sache ~ sein to be entangled in a shady business;
sehr ~e Romanhandlung highly involved plot.

verflossen past;
~e Freundin ex-girl; **in ~en Jahren** in former (past) years.

verfluchen to curse, to damn, to cuss.

verflüchtigen, sich to take wings to itself.

verflüchtigend, sich schnell volatile.

verflüssigen to realize, to sell, *(Liquidität)* to ease, to increase the liquidity.

Verflüssigung *(Geldmarkt)* increasing liquidity.

Verflüssigungspolitik *(Geldmarkt)* policy of active ease.

Verfolg progress, continuation;
im ~ seiner Aufgaben in prosecution of his duties; **im ~ unseres Schreibens** referring to our letter, reverting to ours.

verfolgbar actionable, *(strafrechtlich)* punishable, indictable.

verfolgen to pursue, to follow, to chase, *(Detektiv)* to shadow, *(Interessen)* to look out for, *(Radar)* to track, *(schikanieren)* to persecute, to victimize;
j. ~ to be in pursuit of (pursue) s. o.; **Anklage ~** to prosecute an indictment; **Anspruch ~** to prosecute a claim; **j. in aufrührerischer Weise ~** to follow another person in a disorderly manner; **j. mit Bitten ~** to badger s. o. with requests; **energisch ~** to follow up; **gerichtlich ~** to prosecute an action; **j. gerichtlich ~** to institute legal proceedings against s. o.; **realistischen Kurs ~** to pursue a realistic course; **Linie ~** *(pol.)* to follow a line; **Markt ~** to watch the market; **Prozeß ~** to watch a case; **Sache genau ~** to keep a question under review; **Scheck ~** to trace a check *(US)* (cheque, *Br.*); **Spur ~** to hunt a track; **falsche Spur ~** to follow the wrong track; **Spur eines Verbrechers ~** to trace a criminal; **j. steckbrieflich ~** to search for a criminal; **strafrechtlich ~** to prosecute, to pursue *(Scot.)*; **Tagesereignisse ~** to keep track of current events; **neue Veröffentlichungen ~** to keep track of new publications; **weiter ~** to follow up; **Ziel ~** to pursue a goal.

Verfolger pursuer, persecutor, follower, tracker, shadow;
seine ~ abschütteln to shake off one's pursuers; **~ antreiben** to hound on pursuers; **seinen ~n davonreiten** to outride one's pursuers.

verfolgt prosecuted, hunted;
aus politischen Gründen ~ werden to be prosecuted for political reasons; **auf Schritt und Tritt ~ werden** to be shadowed everywhere; **steckbrieflich ~ werden** to be wanted by the police.

Verfolgter victim, persecutee;
zu Unrecht ~ underdog.

Verfolgung pursuit, pursuance, hunt, chase, persecution, *(Schikane)* victimization;
disziplinarische ~ disciplinary (punishment) measures; **sofortige ~** fresh pursuit; **strafrechtliche ~** criminal prosecution, persecution;
~ eines Mörders pursuit of a murderer; **weitere ~ einer Sache** follow-up;
~ aufgeben to let up on a pursuit; **~ aufnehmen** to take up the pursuit; **sich strafrechtlicher ~ aussetzen** to render o. s. liable to prosecution; **strafrechtliche ~ einleiten** to put a prosecution under way; **sich der gerichtlichen ~ entziehen** to evade (cheat) justice, to avoid prosecution; **~ und Verbannung erfahren** to live through persecution and exile; **schrecklichen ~en ausgesetzt sein** to suffer cruel persecutions; **Angeklagten außer ~ setzen** to discharge the accused (from prosecution); **strafrechtliche ~ veranlassen** to authorize prosecution.

Verfolgungs|jagd hot pursuit; **~jagd durchführen** to raise a hue and cry after s. o.; **~recht** *(Völkerrecht)* right of stoppage in transitu; **~verjährung** prescription; **~wahn** persecution mania, obsession.

verfrachten to freight, to charter, to consign, to transmit, to ship *(US)*, *(Schiff)* to charter, to ship, *(verladen)* to load;
Dieb in die grüne Minna ~ to hustle a thief into the van; **im ganzen ~** to charter by the lump; **in ein Taxi ~** to bundle s. o. into a taxi.

Verfrachter freighter, [ocean] carrier, carrier by sea, common carrier, forwarding agent, consignor, shipper *(US)*;
~ und Befrachter owner and charterer.

Verfrachtung freighting, freightage, consignment, forwarding, carriage of goods, shipping *(US)*, *(Schiff)* charter, chartering;
~ der Schiffe im ganzen charter by the lump; **~ auf Stückgüter** charter for a general cargo.

verfranzen, sich to get lost, *(Flugzeug)* to wander off its course.

Verfremdung alienation.

verfressen greedy, gluttonous, voracious;
~er Kerl glutton, gormandizer.

Verfressenheit gluttony, greediness, voracity.

verfrühen, sich to come too early.

verfrüht premature, too early, untimely;
~ einsetzen to begin too early;
~er Schneefall premature fall of snow.

verfügbar available, disposable, at one's disposal, at (on) call, ready, *(Kapital)* uninvested;
am Platz ~ spot delivery; **bei Abruf ~** ready for delivery; **immer ~** on tap; **nicht ~** unavailable; **uneingeschränkt ~** unconditionally available;
~ sein to be ready (available); **nicht immer ~ sein** not to be always at liberty;
~er Anschlagraum available sites; **~e Arbeitskräfte** supply of labo(u)r, manpower available; **~es Bargeld** cash in hand; **~es Eigenkapital** disposable capital; **frei ~es Einkommen [nach Steuern]** discretionary (disposable, personal) income; **~es Geld** cash in hand; **~e Guthaben** available funds; **alle ~en Hilfsmittel** all available resources; **~es Kapital** available capital, funds available; **frei ~e Kaufkraft** discretionary buying power; **~e Mittel** available means; **~er Reingewinn** available surplus; **frei ~er Überschuß** *(Haushaltsrecht)* disposable budget surplus; **~er Vermögensanteil** *(Testator)* disposable portion of property; **~e Vermögenswerte** ready assets; **sofort ~e Ware** stock in hand, disposable goods.

Verfügbarkeit availability, availableness, disposability.

verfügen to dispose, *(abheben)* to draw, *(anordnen)* to arrange, to direct, *(Behörde)* to order, to decree, *(besitzen)* to possess, *(Gericht)* to rule, to decide;
über j. ~ to have s. o. at one's disposal; **über Arbeitskräfte ~** to make a call on manpower; **über einen Betrag bei jem. ~** to draw value on s. o. for an account; **über gute Beziehungen ~** to have influential friends; **Gesetzesänderung ~** to dispose of an amendment; **gesetzlich ~** to decree, to enact; **über ein größeres Kapital ~** to be well provided with capital, to have large capital at one's disposal; **über ein Konto mittels Scheck ~** to draw on an account by check *(US)* (cheque, *Br.*); **über große Körperkräfte ~** to have great physical strength; **letztwillig (testamentarisch) ~** to make one's (dispose of by) will; **über eine Mehrheit ~** to be in control of (swing, *US*) a majority; **über reichliche Mittel ~** to possess ample means; **im Notfall über 5000 Dollar ~** to command $ 5000 in an emergency; **noch über Reserven ~** still to have some money on hand; **über gute englische Sprachkenntnisse ~** to have a sufficient command of English; **über Vermögen ~** to be possessed of property; **über seine Zeit ~** to be master of one's time;
über Geld ~ können to have money at one's disposal; **über sein Grundeigentum frei ~ können** to own the freehold; **über sein Vermögen frei ~ können** to have entire disposal of an estate, to be entire master of one's property; **j. über ein Konto ~ lassen** to authorize s. o. to operate on an account.

verfügt, es wird hiermit be it enacted by this.

Verfügung disposition, disposal, *(Anordnung)* direction, directive, regulation, instruction, provision, act, mandate, order, *(Testament)* terms, *(Verordnung)* decree, order, ordinance, process;
aufgrund gerichtlicher ~ by order of the court; **bis auf weitere ~** till further provisions; **durch ~ des Staates** by order of the government; **im Wege letztwilliger ~** by will; **laut ~** according to orders (directions), as directed (ordered), by command; **ohne letztwillige ~ verstorben** intestate; **zu Ihrer ~** at your disposal; **zur ~** on hand;
alleinige ~ entire use; **~ aufgehoben** rule discharged; **behördliche ~** decree, ministerial act; **einstweilige ~** restraining order *(Br.)*, interim (provisional, temporary, *US*, preliminary, special, interlocutory) injunction, extent, interlocutory mandamus *(Br.)*, *(Provinzbehörde)* provisional order *(Br.)*; **auf Unterlassung gerichtete einstweilige ~** cease-and-desist order, injunction to distrain; **globale einstweilige ~** *(Arbeitsrecht)* blanket injunction; **antragsgemäß erlassene ~** *(Richter)* rule of course; **freie ~** free disposal; **gerichtliche ~** court ruling, order of a court, judicial order (writ), mandatory writ, rule *(US)*; **berufungsunfähige gerichtliche ~** peremptory order; **zeitlich unbeschränkte gerichtliche ~** perpetual injunction; **vollzogene gerichtliche ~** executed writ; **gesetzliche ~** enactment, measure *(Br.)*; **bis zum Gerichtsurteil gültige ~** permanent injunction; **letztwillige ~** testamentary disposition (paper, instrument), last will and testament, *(über Grundbesitz)* devise, devising; **bedingte letztwillige ~** conditional devise; **noch zu erfüllende letztwillige ~** executory devise; **nicht wirksam gewordene letztwillige ~** lapsed devise; **mündliche letztwillige ~** nuncupative will, nuncupation; **unbedingte letztwillige ~** vested devise; **ungewöhnliche letztwillige ~** unnatural will; **ministerielle ~** departmental order; **polizeiliche ~** police ordinance; **prozeßleitende ~** rule to plead, preliminary measure; **rechtsgeschäftliche ~** voluntary disposition; **richterliche ~** judicial writ (decree), judge's order, court order, ruling, fiat *(Br.)*; **außerordentliche richterliche ~** prerogative writ; **befristete richterliche ~** temporary injunction *(US)*; **schriftliche ~** order in writing; **testamentarische ~** testamentary arrangement (disposition); **treuwidrige ~** breach of trust; **unentgeltliche ~** gratuitous transfer; **zwingend vorgeschriebene ~** mandatory provision *(US)*; **vorläufige ~** provisional injunction; **widerrechtliche ~en** illegal transactions;
~ gegen eine Aktienübertragung injunction restraining transfer; **einstweilige ~ mit gewisser Dauerregelung** interlocutory injunction; **einstweilige ~ zur Durchsetzung einer Konkurrenz-**

klausel restrictive injunction; ~ **über Eigentum** disposition of a property; ~ **über ein gutes Einkommen** enjoyment of a good income; ~ **des Finanzministeriums** treasury ruling; **letztwillige ~ ohne gesetzliche Formerfordernisse** testamentary paper; ~ **über den restlichen Grundbesitz** residuary devise; ~ **von hoher Hand** restraint of princes and rulers; ~ **unter Lebenden** disposition inter vivos; **einstweilige ~ wegen einer gegenständlichen Leistung** mandatory injunction, mandamus *(Br.)*; ~ **über sämtliche Rohstoffe** disposal of all material resources; ~ **über Sachwerte** disposition of property; ~ **über Stimmen** voting control; **einstweilige ~ in arbeitsrechtlichen Streitigkeiten** labo(u)r injunction; ~ **angesichts des Todes** transfer in contemplation of death; ~ **von Todes wegen** testamentary disposition, disposition by will, disposal of property, devise; ~ **auf Unterlassung** prohibitory injunction; ~ **im einseitigen Verfahren (ohne Anhörung der Gegenseite)** ex parte injunction; ~ **über bewegliches Vermögen** disposal of assets, personal settlement *(Br.)*; **gerichtliche ~ zur Vornahme (oder Unterlassung) einer Handlung** mandatory injunction, mandamus *(Br.)*; **weitere ~en abwarten** to wait for (await) further instructions; ~ **aufheben** to discharge an order; **einstweilige ~ aufheben** to discharge (dissolve, cancel) an injunction; **letztwillige ~ aufheben** to repeal a will; ~ **eines untergeordneten Gerichts aufheben** to quash the order of an inferior court; **einstweilige ~ beantragen** to file an application (ask for, seek) an injunction; ~ **befolgen** to comply with an order; **Weg der einstweiligen ~ beschreiten** to use an injunctive route; **gerichtliche ~ durchführen** to execute a writ; **Beschwerde gegen eine einstweilige ~ einlegen** to appeal against an injunction; ~ **erlassen** to emit (make, issue, enter) an order, to pass a decree; **einstweilige ~ erlassen** to grant (award) an injunction; **gesetzliche ~ erlassen** to enact a law; **einstweilige ~ zur Erhebung einer Feststellungsklage erlassen** to issue a show-cause order; **einstweilige ~ ohne mündliche Verhandlung erlassen** to grant an injunction ex parte; **gerichtliche ~ erwirken** to sue for a writ; **zur ~ haben** to have on one's hands; **Geld zur ~ haben** to have money at one's disposal; **große Geldbeträge zur ~ haben** to have large capital at one's disposal; **reichliche Mittel zur ~ haben** to be endowed with ample means; **zu jds. ~ halten** to hold at s. one's disposal; **Gegenwert zu jds. ~ halten** to hold the proceeds at s. one's disposal; **Geld zu jds. ~ halten** to hold money to the order of s. o.; **zur ~ des Käufers halten** to hold subject to the buyer's order; **auf Erlaß einer einstweiligen ~ klagen** to bring an action for an injunction; **zur ~ stehen** to be at disposal (available); **jem. zur ~ stehen** to be at s. one's disposal (command); **jem. finanziell zur ~ stehen** to put one's purse at s. one's disposal; **für besondere Zwecke zur ~ stehen** to be available on call; **jem. zur ~ stellen** to make available for s. o., to place at s. one's disposal (disposition, service); **sein Amt zur ~ stellen** to tender one's resignation; **Antrag auf Erlaß einer einstweiligen ~ stellen** to file an application for an injunction; **zum Ausgleich zur ~ stellen** to grant in return; **jem. sein Auto zur ~ stellen** to place (put) one's car at s. one's disposal; **Betrag wieder zur ~ stellen** to refund an amount; **jem. hinreichende Deckung zur ~ stellen** to furnish s. o. with funds; **sich freiwillig zur ~ stellen** to volunteer; **sich der Regierung zur ~ stellen** to tender one's services to the government; **notwendige Transportmittel zur ~ stellen** to provide the necessary transport; **der UNO Truppen zur ~ stellen** to assign troops to the United Nations; **ohne letztwillige ~ zu hinterlassen sterben** to die intestate; ~ **treffen** to make a disposition, to give an order, to dispose of; **15 Jahre zur ~ gestellt werden** *(Kredit)* to be for a term of 15 years; **sich einer richterlichen ~ widersetzen** to resist the authority of the court; ~ **zurückziehen** to recall a decree; **jem. eine ~ zustellen** to pass on an order to s. o.

Verfügungs | alter erreichen to reach vesting age; ~**befugnis** power of disposition (disposal), disposing power (capacity); ~**befugnis zur Einstellung von Arbeitskräften** disposition of appointment.

verfügungsberechtigt entitled (authorized, competent) to dispose, *(testierfähig)* able to devise property;
~ **sein** to have power to dispose, to be of disposing capacity (mind) *(US)*, to have the disposition of property.

Verfügungsberechtigter authorized agent.

Verfügungsberechtigung power of disposition, disposing capacity (mind) *(US)*;
jem. die ~ über ein Konto übertragen to authorize s. o. to operate on an account.

Verfügungsbeschränkung restraint of disposal, restraining powers;
~ **der Frau über Vorbehaltsgut** restraint upon anticipation; **auf einer ~ bestehen** to uphold a restraint; **unter ~en hinterlassen** to tie up an estate.

Verfügungs | einkommen disposal income; ~**entwürfe ausarbeiten** to prepare draft rules; ~**fähigkeit** competence to dispose of property, power of disposal; ~**freiheit** discretion.

Verfügungsgewalt disposing power, power of disposal;
freie ~ right to dispose; **internationale ~** international control; **unbeschränkte ~** full and absolute control, outright disposition;
~ **über ein Grundstück** disposition of a land;
~ **über sein Geld bekommen** to come into one's own money; **gesamte ~ haben** to have the entire disposal.

Verfügungs | handlung disposition; ~**klausel** dispositive clause.

Verfügungsmacht power of disposal (disposition), disposing power, disposal, control;
gemeinsame ~ joint control; **letztwillige ~** testamentary power; **unbeschränkte ~** outright disposition;
~ **über sein Geld bekommen** to come into one's own money.

Verfügungsrecht disposing capacity (mind), title, *(Abhebungsbefugnis)* drawing right, *(Erblasser)* power of disposal, *(Veräußerungsrecht)* power of sale;
freies ~ right to dispose, run; **handelsübliches ~** merchantable title;
~ **Arbeitskräfte einzustellen** disposition (power) of appointment; **ausschließliches ~ über den Nachlaß** exclusive power of an estate;
~ **haben** to have power to dispose; **sich das ~ an Waren vorbehalten** to reserve the right of disposal of goods.

Verfügungsunfähigkeit disability for legal action.

Verfügungsverbot restraint on alienation, *(gerichtliche Verfügung)* restraining order *(US)*, interdict[ion];
vorläufiges ~ charging (stop) order;
jem. ein gerichtliches ~ auferlegen to impose a judicial injunction upon s. o.

Verfügungsverfahren, einstweiliges injunctive process (suit).

verführen to seduce, to mislead, *(verlocken)* to entice, to tempt, to allure;
j. ~ to lead s. o. astray; **Arbeitskräfte zum Berufswechsel ~** to lure labo(u)r into other jobs; **j. zum Baden ~** to tempt s. o. to go for a swim; **Jungfrau ~** to betray a maiden; **Kunden zum Kauf ~** to allure customers to buy goods; **j. zu einem unsoliden Lebenswandel ~** to lead s. o. astray; **j. durch Schmeicheleien zum Kauf ~** to draw s. o. in to purchase by flattery; **j. zum Trinken ~** to encourage s. o. to drink.

Verführer seducer, Don Juan *(coll.)*, make-out artist *(sl.)*.

Verführerin vamp *(coll.)*.

verführerisch bewitching, seductive;
~**es Angebot** seductive (tempting) offer; ~**e Schönheit** ravishing beauty.

verführt seduced, *(verlockt)* tempted;
durch Geld zum Vaterlandsverrat ~ werden to be seduced by the offer of money into betraying one's country.

Verführung seduction, debauchment, *(Verlockung)* enticement, allurement, temptation;
~ **zum Geldausgeben** temptation to spend money; ~**en einer Großstadt** allurements of a big city; ~ **einer Minderjährigen** seduction of a minor; ~ **zur Unzucht** solicitation of chastity.

Verführungskünste seductive arts, wiles, charms;
jds. ~n erliegen to fall victim to s. one's wiles.

verfüttern to use as fodder, to feed.

Vergabe giving away;
freihändige ~ competitive bidding;
~ **von Aufträgen** placing of orders, allocation of contracts; ~ **öffentlicher Aufträge** awarding of contracts, contract award; ~ **zu Festpreisen** selling at fixed prices; **gleichzeitige ~ an mehrere Makler** general listing *(US)*; ~ **öffentlicher Mittel** appropriation of funds; ~ **von Paketlizenzen** block booking, mandatory package licensing; ~ **von Staatsaufträgen** government contracting; ~ **im Submissionswege** allocation by tenders;
~**ausschuß** committee of awards; ~**beamter** contracting officer; ~**experte** expert in contracting; ~**politik** contracting policy; ~**verfahren** bidding (contract-awarding) procedure.

vergafft haben, sich in j. to be smitten with s. o.

vergaloppieren, sich to drop a brick, to drop a clanger *(sl.)*, to pull a boner *(US sl.)*.

vergammeln to go to the dogs, to be on (hit) the skids *(US sl.)*, *(Lebensmittel)* to go bad.

vergangen bygone, past;
schnell ~ und vergessen sein to pass as a watch in the night; **mir ist die Lust völlig ~** I don't care a fig (tinker's damn);
~**e Generationen** past generations; ~**es Jahr** last year.

Vergangenes ruhen lassen to let bygones be bygones.
Vergangenheit past, antecedents, record, long-ago, *(gr.)* past tense, *(Hintergrundmaterial)* background, record;
dunkle ~ murky past; **einwandfreie** ~ clean record; **glorreiche** ~ *(Stadt)* glorious history; **politische** ~ public record, political background;
der ~ **angehören** to be over and done with; **sich zu sehr mit seiner** ~ **beschäftigen** to dwell too much upon one's past; ~ **haben** to have a history; **auf eine bewegte** ~ **zurückblicken** to have led an adventurous life.
vergänglich transitory, fleeting, passing, written in water, dross.
Vergaser | ersaufen lassen to flood the carburettor;
~**brand** fire in the carburettor; ~**motor** carburettor (petrol) engine.
Vergasung gasification, *(Auto)* carburetion;
bis zur ~ until you are blue in the face.
vergattern, j. to enjoin strictest secrecy upon s. o.; **Wache** ~ to instruct the guards.
vergeben to forgive, to pardon, *(Aufträge)* to allocate, to let out, to award, *(übertragen)* to bestow, to confer;
Amt an j. ~ to appoint s. o. an office; **Auftrag** ~ to place an order; **öffentlichen Auftrag** ~ to let out on (confer a) contract; **nach außerhalb** ~ to contract out; **Eintrittskarten** ~ to give away tickets; **Mittel für die Errichtung von Schulneubauten** ~ to appropriate funds for new school buildings; **sich nichts** ~ to stand on one's dignity; **Satzarbeiten** ~ to farm out composing; **Stipendium** ~ to award a scholarship; **in Submission (im Submissionswege)** ~ to let out by contract, to allocate by tenders; **Unterauftrag** ~ to contract out, to subcontract; **eheliche Untreue** ~ to condone a husband's infidelity; **seiner Würde etw.** ~ to compromise one's dignity;
alle Abende ~ **haben** to be dated up *(US)*; **Stelle zu** ~ **haben** to have a vacancy; **von jem.** ~ **werden** to be in the gift of s. o.; **für zehn Jahre** ~ **werden** *(Pacht)* to be tenable for ten years;
~ *(a.)* disposed;
nicht ~ undisposed; **noch nicht** ~ *(Stelle)* still vacant;
bereits ~ **sein** to have previous engagements; **noch nicht** ~ **sein** to be still vacant.
vergeblich vain, futile, fruitless, idle, unavailing, of no effect, useless;
sich ~ **bemühen** to try in vain;
~**e Anstrengungen** futile (vain) efforts.
Vergebung | eines Amtes appointment to an office; ~ **an das billigste Angebot** allocation to the lowest tenderer; ~ **von Arbeiten im Akkord** contract system *(US)*; ~ **von Arbeiten und Lieferungen** letting of works and supplies; ~ **von Aufträgen** placing of orders; ~ **im Submissionswege** allocation by tenders, awarding of contracts.
vergegenwärtigen, sich to visualize, to realize; **sich kürzliche Ereignisse** ~ to travel over recent events.
Vergehen minor offence (offense, *US*), misdemeanor, tort, misdoing, delinquency, delict, wrong[doing];
zur Last gelegtes ~ offence charged with; **geringfügiges** ~ minor offence, petty misdemeanor *(US)*; **politisches** ~ political offence; **schweres** ~ high crime, indictable offence *(Br.)*;
~ **im Amt** malfeasance, official misconduct; ~ **gegen die Devisenbestimmungen** currency offence; ~ **gegen den Rauschgifthandel** drug-trafficking offence; ~ **mit Todesfolge** misdemeanor manslaughter *(US)*;
~ **anzeigen** to report an offence; **sich eines** ~**s schuldig machen** to commit [make s. o. guilty of) a misdemeanor; **eines** ~**s angeklagt (bezichtigt) sein** *(mil.)* to be pegged.
vergehen to be drawing to a close, to wear off, to wither away, *(Frist)* to lapse, to run, *(Jahre)* to glide past, to go, to pass by, *(Zorn)* to blow off;
sich ~ to commit an offence against the law, to misdemean; **vor Angst fast** ~ to be scared stiff (in a blue funk); **vor Durst fast** ~ to be dying with thirst; **wie im Fluge** ~ to flee away; **vor Gram** ~ to pine away with grief; **vor Kälte** ~ to be nearly frozen; **langsam** ~ *(Zeit)* to wear away, to hang heavy on one's hand; **schnell** ~ to spin; **sich gegen die guten Sitten** ~ to outrage the rules of propriety;
jem. die Lust ~ **lassen** to sober s. o. up;
Dir wird das Lachen noch ~ you will laugh on the other side of your face.
vergeistigt spiritual, refined, sublimed.
vergelten to retort, to requite, to reward, to pay home;
jem. einen Dienst ~ to remunerate s. o.; **Gleiches mit Gleichem** ~ to give tit for tat; **Gutes mit Bösem** ~ to repay good with evil; **es jem. reichlich** ~ to reward s. o. generously;
das werde ich Dir ~ you will smart for it.
vergeltend retributive.
Vergeltung retribution, retaliation, reprisal, *(Belohnung)* reward, recompense, requital, return, *(Völkerrecht)* retorsion, retortion;
abgestufte ~ *(Atomwaffen)* controlled (flexible) response;
an jem. ~ **üben** to retaliate upon s. o., to pay s. o. back.
Vergeltungs | aktion reprisal (retaliatory) action; ~**feldzug** retaliatory raid; ~**maßnahmen** reprisals, retalioratory measures, retorsion, retaliations; **diskriminierende** ~**maßnahmen** *(Zoll)* discriminatory retaliation; ~**maßnahmen treffen** *(Zoll)* to retaliate; ~**potential** *(Atomwaffen)* strike-back capability; ~**schlag** saturation (retaliatory) raid, *(Atomwaffen)* second strike; ~**waffe** flying bomb; **im** ~**wege** by way of retaliation; ~**zoll** retaliatory tariff.
vergesellschaften to incorporate, *(kommunalisieren)* to municipalize, *(verstaatlichen)* to communize, to socialize, to nationalize *(Br.)*.
Vergesellschaftung incorporation, *(Kommunalisierung)* municipalization, *(Verstaatlichung)* communization, socialization, nationalization *(Br.)*.
Vergessen anheimfallen, dem to sink into oblivion.
vergessen to forget, *(liegenlassen)* to leave behind;
seine Pflichten ~ to neglect one's duty;
~ **werden** *(Skandal)* to blow over.
Vergessenheit, der ~ **anheimfallen** to lapse into obscurity, to pass into nothingness; **etw. der** ~ **entreißen** to rescue s. th. from oblivion; **in** ~ **geraten** to sink (subside) into oblivion, to lapse into obscurity, to pass out of one's mind.
vergeuden to waste, to squander, to play away, to dissipate;
Geld ~ to squander money; **Material** ~ to spoil materials; **Vermögen** ~ to dilapidate a fortune; **seine Zeit** ~ to waste one's time.
Vergeudetes throwaway.
Vergeudung waste, dissipation, squandering.
vergewaltigen to rape, to violate, to abuse, to ravish;
englische Sprache ~ to butcher (murder) Queen's English; **Volk** ~ to terrorize a nation.
Vergewaltigung rape, violation, abuse, ravishment;
~ **der Gerechtigkeit** outrage upon justice; ~ **der Minderheit** oppression of minorities.
vergewissern, sich to make sure of; **sich über die Wahrheit eines Berichts** ~ to satisfy o. s. of the truth of a report.
vergiften to poison, *(Luft, Wasser)* to pollute, to contaminate;
sich ~ to commit suicide by taking poison; **jds. Fantasie** ~ to poison s. one's mind; **jds. ganzes Leben** ~ to poison s. one's whole life; **Seele eines Kindes** ~ to pervert the mind of a child.
Vergiftung poisoning, *(Luft, Wasser)* pollution, contamination.
vergilbt yellowed, time-stained.
vergittern to grate, to lattice, *(mit Stangen)* to bar.
verglasen to glaze.
verglaster Blick glazed look.
Verglasung glasswork, *(Arbeit)* glazing.
Vergleich comparison, *(mit einem Einzelgläubiger)* accord, *(mit allen Gläubigern)* settlement, composition, compromise, reorganization *(US)*, *(Text)* collation, *(Übereinkommen)* arrangement, amicable arrangement, private agreement, adjustment;
im ~ **mit** compared with;
von den Erben abgeschlossener ~ settlement of inheritance; **mit den Konkursgläubigern abgeschlossener** ~ composition in bankruptcy; **von den Parteien abgeschlossener (erzielter)** ~ settlement arrived at by the parties inter se; **außergerichtlicher** ~ out-of-court composition (settlement), settlement out of court, extra-judicial settlement, accord and satisfaction, amicable arrangement, compromise; **gütlicher** ~ amicable adjustment; **schiedsgerichtlicher** ~ settlement by arbitration; **schiefer** ~ false analogy; **unpassender** ~ unapt comparison; **vorgeschlagener** ~ composition offered; **zwischenbetrieblicher** ~ inter-factory comparison;
außergerichtlicher ~ **mit seinen Gläubigern** composition by deed of arrangement; ~ **der Kosten** comparison of costs; ~ **vor Prozeßbeginn** pre-trial settlement; ~**e zwischen klagender Regierung und beklagter Privatpartei** consent decree *(US)*; ~ **zur Vermeidung des Rechtsweges** *(Haftpflichtversicherung)* nuisance settlement;
~ **ablehnen** to reject a composition; ~ **abschließen** to arrive at an accommodation (a composition), to effect (come to) a composition, to execute an accord; ~ **mit jem. abschließen** to arrange (make) a settlement with s. o.; **mit seinen Gläubigern einen** ~ **[ab]schließen** to come to terms with one's creditors, to compound (compose) with one's creditors; ~ **annehmen** to

agree to a settlement; ~ **anstellen** to draw a parallel; ~ **aufheben** to set aside a composition; ~ **aushalten** to stand (sustain) a comparison, to hold a candle to *(coll.)*, to be the peer of; **Rechtsstreitigkeit durch** ~ **beilegen** to settle a lawsuit amicably; ~ **bestätigen** *(Konkursrecht)* to confirm an arrangement; ~ **zustande bringen** to effect a settlement between two parties; ~ **durchführen** to satisfy an accord; **auf einen** ~ **eingehen** to enter into an arrangement; **durch** ~ **erledigen** to settle by compromise, to settle by consent, to compound; ~ **ermöglichen** to open a door to a settlement; ~ **erzielen, zu einem** ~ **gelangen** to come to (reach) an arrangement (agreement), to accord; ~ **perfekt machen** to finalize a settlement; ~ **schließen** to compromise, to compound, to come to terms (an arrangement); ~ **ziehen** to draw a comparison; **einem** ~ **zustimmen** to fall in with (assent to) an arrangement;
ein magerer ~ **ist besser als ein fetter Prozeß** to come to an arrangement is better than going to law, a lean compromise is better than a fat lawsuit.

vergleichbar comparable;
nicht ~ incomparable, incommensurate;
~**es Angebot von Konsumgütern** comparable supply of consumer goods; ~**er Zeitraum** comparable period.

Vergleichbarkeit comparability.

vergleichen to compare, *(rangmäßig)* to put on an equal footing, *(schlichten)* to settle, to adjust, *(Schriftstücke)* to collate, to check;
j. mit einem anderen ~ to put s. o. on the same level with s. o.; **sich** ~ to [arrive at a] compromise, to compound with, to make a composition, to settle, to enter into an agreement, to come to an arrangement (terms), to compromise; **sich mit jem.** ~ to get square with s. o.; **Abschrift mit dem Original** ~ to compare the copy with the original; **sich außergerichtlich** ~ to settle an affair out of court, to arrange privately; **Bücher** ~ to compare the books; **sich mit seinen Gläubigern** ~ to compound (compose) with one's creditors; **sich gütlich** ~ to make an amicable arrangement; **Konten** ~ to agree accounts; **Kontoauszug** ~ to audit an abstract of account; **seine Kräfte mit jem.** ~ to match one's strength with s. o.; **postenweise** ~ *(Buchführung)* to reconcile, to prick up items; **Saldo** ~ to ascertain the balance; **Uhrzeit** ~ to check the time; **Zahlen** ~ to check figures;
mit seinem letzten Buch nicht zu ~ **sein** not to be up to his last book.

vergleichend | gegenüberstellen to compare;
~**e Gewinn- und Verlustrechnung** comparative income statement; ~**e Rechtswissenschaft** comparative jurisprudence; ~**e Regierungslehre** comparative government; ~**e Übersicht** comparison table; ~**e Werbeaussage** comparative story; ~**e Werbung** comparative advertising.

Vergleichs | abkommen composition deed (settlement); ~**abschluß** reaching an agreement; **von einem** ~**abschluß in Kenntnis setzen** to serve with a notice of a deed of arrangement; ~**abschnitt** basic period; ~**angebot** composition offered, offer of compromise, settlement offer; ~**angebot ausschlagen** to reject a composition; ~**angebot machen** to offer a compromise; ~**anspruch** right to compound; ~**antrag** reorganization petition *(US)*, petition for arrangement (reorganization, *US*); ~**antrag stellen** to file a petition for an arrangement (reorganization, *US*); ~**ausschuß** conciliation (reorganization, *US*) committee; ~**basis** basis of comparison; ~**bedingungen** terms of arrangement (settlement, composition).

vergleichsbereit sein to be ready to compromise.

Vergleichs | bereitschaft willingness to come to a compromise; ~**bestätigung** confirmation of an arrangement (reorganization, *US*); ~**bilanz** comparative balance sheet, liquidating balance sheet; ~**bilanzberichtsformular** comparative balance sheet record form; ~**eröffnung** institution of composition (reorganization, *US*) proceedings; ~**experiment** control experiment; ~**fall** composition case; ~**forderung** liquidated demand; ~**formel** compromise formula; ~**frage** matter of arrangement; ~**gläubiger** creditor in a settlement; ~**grundlage** basis of comparison, principles of a settlement; ~**gruppen** matched samples; ~**index eines Werbewirksamkeitstestes** order-of-merit rating; ~**jahr** *(Statistik)* basic year; ~**konto** arrangement (reorganization, *US*) account; ~**liste** check list; ~**maßnahmen** reorganization measures; ~**maßstab** degree of comparison, yardstick; ~**maßstab für das Arbeitsbewertungsverfahren** job evaluation system *(US)*; ~**miete** equivalent rent; ~**muster** reference sample; ~**ordnung** Insolvent Law (Statute) *(US)*, Insolvency Laws, Deed of Arrangement Act *(Br.)*; ~- **und Schiedsgerichtsordnung** *(Handelskammer)* Rules of Conciliation and Arbitration; ~**periode** basic period; ~**plan** scheme of arrangement; ~**preise im Jahr 1979** survey prices of 1979; **abgestimmte** ~**proben** matched samples; ~**punkte** articles of agreement; ~**quote** liquidation dividend; ~**regelung** composition settlement; **gerichtliche** ~**regelung** liabilities adjustment order *(Br.)*; ~**regelung mit jem. treffen** to effect (arrive at) a compromise with s. o.; ~**sache** matter of arrangement; ~**schließender** compounder; ~**standard** comparison level; **abgestimmte** ~**stichproben** matched samples; ~**summe** composition, amount of compensation; ~**tabelle** comparison table, *(Tarife)* comparative rate schedule; ~**tabelle für das Arbeitsbewertungsverfahren** job evaluation scale *(US)*; ~**tarif** comparable rate; ~**termin** day of settlement, settlement date, *(Konkurs)* date of hearing, hearing date; ~**treuhänder** trustee under scheme; ~**urkunde** deed of composition (settlement), composition deed; ~**vereinbarung** settlement (compromise) agreement, conciliation scheme, composition agreement; ~**vereinbarung vor Prozeßbeginn** settlement before judgment, pre-trial settlement.

Vergleichs- und Sanierungsverfahren insolvency (composition, reorganization, *US*) proceedings, reorganization under Chapter X *(US)*;
außergerichtliches ~ voluntary arrangement, adjustment procedure; **gerichtliches** ~ compulsory winding-up;
~ **einer Gesellschaft** reorganization of a corporation *(US)*, reconstruction of a company *(Br.)*;
~ **beantragen** to file a petition for an arrangement (Chapter X proceedings, *US*); ~ **durchführen** to reconstruct a company *(Br.)*, to reorganize under Chapter X *(US)*; **im** ~ **sein** to be in bankruptcy reorganization *(US)*; **Antrag auf Eröffnung des** ~**s stellen** to file a petition for reorganization (apply for permission to reorganize) under Chapter X *(US)*.

Vergleichs | verfahrensspezialisten reorganization bar *(US)*; ~**verhandlungen führen** to carry on negotiations for a settlement; **in** ~**verhandlungen stehen** to come to terms of composition; ~**vertrag** deed of settlement, deed of composition, composition deed, *(Zwangsvergleich)* compulsory arbitration; ~**verwalter** estate manager, trustee under a deed, reorganization trustee *(US)*; ~**verwalterposition,** ~**verwalterschaft,** ~**verwalterstellung** equity receivership; ~**vorschlag** suggested compromise, compromise offer, composition offered, proposal (plan) for a composition (settlement), scheme of arrangement; **vernünftiger** ~**vorschlag** feasible method of liquidation; ~**vorschlag machen** to propose terms of a settlement, to file a plan; **im** ~**wege** by [way of] compromise (comparison).

vergleichsweise by [way of] comparison (compromise), by way of agreement, comparatively;
Streit ~ **beilegen** to compromise a dispute, to settle a case out of court;
~ **Ausgangsstellung** *(Tarifverhandlungen)* comparative advantage; ~ **Forderungsbefriedigung** compounding of claims; ~ **Regelung** compromise, settlement by agreement; ~ **Regelung vor Urteilsverkündung** settlement before judgment, pre-trial settlement; ~ **Regelung treffen** to make a composition; **einer** ~**n Regelung zustimmen** to agree (effect, arrive at) a compromise; ~ **Unkostensituation** comparative costs.

Vergleichs | wert *(Statistik)* comparative value, base value, *(Liquidationswert)* liquidation value; ~**zahlen** comparative (comparable) figures; ~**zeitraum** comparable (comparative, basic, corresponding) period; ~**ziffern** comparative figures; ~**zustimmungsformular** composition acceptance form.

Vergleichung collation, checking.

Vergleichungstag *(Börse)* settlement (cash) day, ticket day *(Br.)*.

verglichen compared with;
~**es Telegramm** collated telegram.

verglühen to smo(u)lder (die) out, *(Rakete)* to burn out.

Vergnügen amusement, pleasure, delight, recreation, entertainment, distraction, spree;
mit dem allergrößten ~ with all the pleasure in life, with the greatest of pleasure; **zum eigenen** ~ on a frolic of one's own; **harmloses** ~ innocent amusement; **herrliches** ~ terrific fun; **kein reines** ~ not at all beer and skittles *(Br.)*;
~ **an einem gescheiten Gespräch** feast of intelligent conversation;
jds. ~ **entscheidend beeinträchtigen** to detract much from s. one's pleasure; **großes** ~ **bereiten** to afford great pleasure; **etw. als** ~ **betrachten** to deem s. th. a pleasure; ~ **empfinden** to experience pleasure; **sein** ~ **haben** to pleasure; **nur dem** ~ **leben** to live only for enjoyment; **seinem** ~ **nachgehen** to pursue (follow) one's pleasure; **im** ~ **schwelgen** to wallow in pleasure.

vergnügen, sich to enjoy (divert, amuse) o. s.

vergnüglich entertaining, amusing, delightful, diverting.
vergnügt jolly, merry, gay, chipper *(US coll.)*;
äußerst ~ sein to be as merry as the day is long;
~es Dasein führen to lead a life of pleasure; **in ~er Stimmung sein** to be in high spirits; **sich einen ~en Tag machen** to make a great day of it; **~en Umtrunk halten** to be merry in one's cups.
Vergnügung delectation, spree;
heimliche ~en surreptitious pleasures; **nichtssagende ~en** empty pleasures; **weltliche ~en** earthly joys;
den ~en entsagen to take leave of pleasure; **seine ~en mit seinem Pflichtenkreis kollidieren lassen** to allow pleasure to interfere with duty; **~en ihren Reiz nehmen** to take the edge off pleasures.
Vergnügungs | ausschuß entertainment committee; **~betrieb** amusement caterer; **~branche** entertainment industry, show business; **~bummel machen (unternehmen)** to go pleasuring, to go on a spree (sporting, *sl.*); **~dampfer** pleasure boat, cruiser ship, cruiser, excursion steamer; **~etablissement** entertainment spot; **~fahrt** joy (thrill) ride, junket, *(zu Schiff)* pleasure cruising; **~fahrt unternehmen (machen)** to go for a ride, to joy-ride, *(Schiff)* to cruise for pleasure; **~gelände** amusement park, recreation site, pleasure grounds *(Br.)*.
vergnügungshalber for the fun of it.
Vergnügungs | industrie entertainment industry (world, field), show business; **~kommission** entertainment committee; **~lokal** pleasure house, palace, gaudy establishment, amusement place, cabaret, night club; **~park** fun (amusement) park, pleasure *(Br.)* (holiday) grounds.
Vergnügungsreise journey for pleasure, pleasure trip (travel), excursion, *(zu Schiff)* cruise;
kleine ~ jaunt;
~ auf öffentliche Kosten junket *(US)*;
~ unternehmen to travel for pleasure, *(zu Schiff)* to cruise, to go on a pleasure cruise.
Vergnügungs | reisender pleasure seeker, excursionist, tourist, pleasurer, *(zu Schiff)* cruiser; **öffentliche ~stätte** place of entertainment (amusement), entertainment spot; **verschiedene ~stätten aufsuchen** to go on a spree, to go places; **~steuer** entertainment duty *(Br.)*, admission (amusement) tax *(US)*; **~steuer niederschlagen** to drop the amusement tax *(US)*.
vergnügungssüchtig pleasure-seeking (-loving), intent on pleasure;
~er Mensch pleasure lover.
Vergnügungs | taumel racket; **~tour** round of pleasure; **~viertel** entertainment (amusement) center *(US)* (centre, *Br.*), the Street, night-life district; **billiges ~viertel** skid row *(sl.)*; **~wesen** entertainment world (field); **~zentrum** entertainment center *(US)* (centre, *Br.*); **~zug** excursion train; **Boot zu reinen ~zwecken vermieten** to let a boat for hire for the purpose of pleasure only.
vergolden to overgild, to gild, to gold-plate.
vergoldet gilded, gold-plated;
teilweise ~ parcel-gilt.
Vergoldung gold-plating (coating), gilt;
matte ~ dead gilding.
vergöttern to adore, to idolize, to idolatrize;
j. ~ to set s. o. on a pedestal.
Vergötterung worship, adoration, idolatry.
vergraben to bury, to hide;
sich ~ to hibernate, to live in seclusion; **sich ganz in seine Arbeit ~** to bury o. s. in one's work.
vergreifen, sich an etw. to misappropriate s. th.; **sich an anvertrautem Geld ~** to embezzle trust funds; **sich an der Kasse ~** to tamper with the cash; **sich im Ton ~** to use the wrong approach; **sich bei der Wahl seiner Mittel ~** to adopt the wrong means.
vergreisen to become senile.
vergreiste Bevölkerung overaged population.
vergriffen sold out, exhausted, out-of-stock, nonavailable, unavailable, *(Buch)* out-of-print;
~, Neuauflage vorgesehen out of print, reprint planned;
~ sein to be consumed (sold out, out-of-stock), *(Buch)* to be out-of-print; **schnell ~ sein** to be taken up readily.
vergrößern to enlarge, to expand, to extend, to augment, to aggrandize, to heighten, to increase, *(Foto)* to enlarge, to blow up, *(Haus)* to add to, to enlarge, *(Optik)* to magnify;
sich ~ *(Firma)* to branch out, *(Wohnung)* to move to a bigger plan; **seinen Besitz ~** to enlarge one's possessions; **Fotografie ~** to enlarge a photograph; **sein Gebiet ~** to extend one's territory; **sein Geschäft ~** to expand (enlarge) one's business; **sein Haus ~** to enlarge one's house; **Maßstab ~** to enlarge the scale; **proportional ~** to enlarge proportionally; **Schwierigkeiten ~** to aggravate (intensify) difficulties; **seinen Spesenetat ~** to increase one's expenditure; **Truppenzahl ~** to augment the strength of troops; **seinen Zuständigkeitsbereich ~** to extend one's jurisdiction;
sich gut ~ lassen *(Foto)* to enlarge well.
vergrößertes Negativ enlarged negative.
Vergrößerung enlargement, extension, expansion, increase, growth, accession, augmentation, amplification, addition, *(Vergrößern eines Fotos)* scaling up, scale-up;
fotografische ~ blow-up; **territoriale ~** territorial expansion;
~ der Belegschaft additions to the staff; **~ des Geschäfts** expansion (enlargement) of business; **~ eines Hauses** extension (addition) to a house; **~ der Kapazität** extension (expansion) of capacity; **~ des Maschinenparks** expansion of machinery; **~ des Risikos** increase in the risk; **~ des Sortiments** expansion of assortment, increase in range of goods; **~ des Vorstands** additions to the management.
Vergrößerungs | glas magnifying (reading, multiplying) glass, magnifier; **~linse** magnifying lens.
vergucken, sich in j. to fall for (be smitten with) s. o.
vergünstigt, zu ~en Preisen at reduced prices.
Vergünstigung favo(u)r, *(Erlaubnis)* permit, permission, licence, indulgence, *(Ermäßigung)* allowance, abatement, *(Vorteil)* benefit, advantage, *(Vorzugsbehandlung)* preferential treatment, preference, priority, privilege, courtesy, favo(u)r, *(Zugeständnis)* concession;
mit steuerlichen ~en tax-eating;
alleinige ~ entire benefit; **beitragsfreie ~en** noncontributing benefits; **betriebliche ~en** fringe benefits; **entsprechende ~en** like benefits; **steuerliche ~** tax privilege (concession, allowance, *Br.*, benefit, *Br.*, credit, *US*); **besondere tarifliche ~** package benefit, *(Eisenbahn)* reduced fare, *(Werbung)* special rates; **zusätzliche ~en** secondary benefits;
~en für leitende Angestellte executive perks *(Br.)*, perquisites *(sl.)*, fringe benefits *(US)*; **~en bei der Anwendung der Erbschaftssteuersätze** relief from the estate rate;
~en bei der Festsetzung von Kommunalabgaben beantragen to claim rating relief *(Br.)*; **~ durch etw. erfahren** to benefit by s. th.; **~en erhalten** to receive a preference; **keine ~en genießen** to have no preference; **tarifliche ~en genießen** to enjoy preferential treatment; **~en des Doppelbesteuerungsabkommens genießen** to qualify for double-taxation relief *(Br.)*; **~ gewähren** to concede (grant) a favo(u)r, to allow an abatement; **besondere ~en gewähren** *(Fluggesellschaft)* to offer special reductions; **einem Kunden besondere ~en gewähren** to grant special favo(u)rs to a customer; **finanzielle ~en gewähren** to distribute financial favo(u)rs; **jem. eine ~ zukommen lassen** to confer a benefit on s. o.; **~en aus dem Doppelbesteuerungsabkommen in Anspruch nehmen** to claim double-tax relief *(Br.)*.
Vergünstigungs | bereich, in einen ~bereich fallen to come within a benefit range; **~tage** respite; **~tarif** preferential tariff (rate); **~verbesserungen** benefit change; **~wesen** benefit plan; **Gratifikations- und ~wesen** fringe benefits program(me); **~zoll** preferential tariff, differential duty, imperial preference *(Br.)*.
vergüten to remunerate, to pay, to make good, *(belohnen)* to reward, to gratify, *(entschädigen)* to indemnify, to compensate, *(zurückerstatten)* to reimburse, to refund;
jds. Auslagen ~ to reimburse s. o. for his costs; **brieflich ~** to remit by mail *(US)*; **Diskont ~** to allow a discount; **Portoauslagen ~** to reimburse (refund) for postage incurred; **Reisekosten ~** to refund travel expenses; **Schaden ~** to make amends (good a damage), to compensate a loss; **jem. die Spesen ~** to indemnify s. o. for expenses incurred, to reimburse s. o. for his costs, to refund the expenses; **für Tara ~** to allow for tare; **telegrafisch ~** to transfer money by telegraph; **voll ~** to allow in full; **4% Zinsen ~** to allow 4 per cent interest.
vergütend compensative, compensatory.
vergütet paid for, stipendiary.
Vergütung remuneration, pay, payment, consideration, requital, *(Beihilfe)* allowance, benefit, *(Belohnung)* reward, rewarding, gratuity, *(besondere Bezüge)* emoluments, fringes, perquisites *(Br.)*, *(Entschädigung)* compensation, indemnification, *(Gratifikation)* bonus, *(Honorar)* fee, *(Rabatt)* allowance, *(Rückerstattung)* reimbursement, refund, refunded amount;
als ~ für Ihre Dienste as payment (remuneration) for your services; **gegen ~** on payment of, remunerated; **gegen ~ der baren Auslagen** for reimbursement of out-of-pocket expenses; **ohne ~** without giving compensation therefor;
von freiem Ermessen abhängige ~ facultative compensation; **angemessene ~** fair and reasonable compensation; **briefliche ~**

mail remittance *(US)*; **feste** ~ fixed remuneration; **zusätzlich zum Gehalt gewährte ~en** salary supplements (supplementation), fringe benefits *(US)*, perquisites *(Br.)*; **kassenärztliche** ~ panel doctor's fee; **sonstige ~en** any other considerations; **tägliche** ~ perdiem allowance, *(für Fahrtkosten)* travel(l)ing allowance; **besondere tarifliche** ~ package benefit; **telegrafische** ~ transfer remittance; **überdurchschnittliche** ~ above-average compensation; **übertarifliche** ~ compensation over and above the contractual wages; **unerlaubte** ~ illicit commission; **wiederkehrende ~en** periodic payments; **zugebilligte** ~ sum allowed; **zusätzliche** ~ supplementary compensation, additional benefit;

~ **für leitende Angestellte** executive compensation (bonus, fringes); **zusätzliche ~ für außerplanmäßige Arbeit** statutory pay, special allowance for irregular hours; ~ **für nicht verschuldeten Arbeitsausfall** delay allowance; **satzungsmäßige ~ für den Aufsichtsrat** statutory allowance to the board of directors; ~ **in bar** allowance in money; ~ **für Bruchwaren** breakage; ~ **für schnelle Entladung** dispatch money; ~ **für beschädigte Faßware** leakage; ~ **für den Firmenwert** allowance for goodwill; ~ **für Leergut** constructive allowance; ~ **für Nachtarbeit (Nachtschicht)** allowance for night duty; ~ **von Portoauslagen** refunding of postage; ~ **für kleinere Reiseunkosten** *(Schiff)* petty average; ~ **von Spesen** compensation for outlay incurred, reimbursement of charges; ~ **für eine Teilleistung** quantum meruit; ~ **für Überstunden** overtime allowance, special allowance for irregular hours; ~ **des Vorstands** remuneration of directors; ~ **von Zinsen** allowance of interest;

angemessene ~ einklagen to sue on a quantum meruit; **angemessene ~ für seine Arbeit erhalten** to receive [an] adequate remuneration for one's work; ~ **gewähren** to pay compensation; ~ **für Tara gewähren** to make allowance for the tare.

Vergütungs|angebot für Führungskräfte executive pay package; **~ansprüche** compensation demands; **~klausel** *(Treuhänder)* charging clause; **~möglichkeit** compensation device *(US)*; **~satz** rate of remuneration; **~sätze für Leihfahrzeuge** rental rate; **~satz für Überstunden** overtime rate of time and a half; **~tabelle** scale of remuneration; **~tarif** rate of remuneration; **~wesen** compensation field *(US)*.

verhackstücken, jem. etw. to spell s. th. out to s. o.

verhaften to [take into] custody, to imprison, to apprehend, to arrest, to place under arrest, to custody, to attach, to nab *(coll.)*, to nail *(sl.)*, to pinch *(sl.)*, to pull up (in) *(sl.)*, to tag *(sl.)*; **j.** ~ to put the snatch on s. o. *(sl.)*; **aufgrund von Beschuldigungen** ~ to arrest on charges; **erneut (wieder)** ~ to recommit to prison, to rearrest; **sofort** ~ to arrest immediately without warrant; **wegen des Verdachts finanzieller Unregelmäßigkeiten** ~ to take into custody on suspicion of financial impropriety; **vorübergehend** ~ to take into remand.

verhaftet under arrest;

Traditionen zutiefst ~ sein to be deeply rooted in tradition; **schon einmal ~ gewesen sein** to have had a previous arrest; ~ **werden** to be put (placed, held) under arrest.

Verhaftete|r arrested person;

~n zwecks Aburteilung dem Gericht übergeben to commit a prisoner for trial.

Verhaftung attachment, commitment, arrestment *(Scot.)*, arrestation, arrest, imprisonment, apprehension;

erneute ~ recommitment, recommittal; **ungerechtfertigte** ~ malicious arrest;

~ **ohne Haftbefehl** immediate arrest without a warrant; ~ **wegen Mordverdachts** arrest on suspicion of murder; ~ **im Strafverfahren** arrest in criminal cases;

~ **eines Verdächtigen anordnen** to warrant the arrest of a suspected criminal; **mehrere ~en vornehmen** to make several arrests; **sich der ~ widersetzen** to resist arrest.

Verhaftungswelle series of arrests.

verhallen, ungehört to meet with no response.

Verhalten demeano(u)r, behavio(u)r, [line of] conduct, bearing, attitude, goings-on *(coll.)*, approach, process, *(Verhaltensweise)* policy, dealing;

durch schlüssiges ~ by conduct;

aufeinander abgestimmtes ~ *(Kartellrecht)* restricted (concerted) practices, quasi agreement *(US)*; **achtloses** ~ *(Verkehrsteilnehmer)* negligence; **amoralisches** ~ evil conduct; **anständiges** ~ square dealing; **berufswidriges** ~ professional misconduct, malpractice; **diskriminierendes** ~ discriminatory conduct; **drohendes** ~ threatening attitude; **ehewidriges** ~ matrimonial offence, misconduct; **fahrlässiges** ~ active negligence; **faires** ~ sporting conduct; **fehlerhaftes** ~ fault; **gesetzwidriges** ~ illegal conduct; **gewinnsüchtiges** ~ profiteering; **bewußt gleichartiges** ~ *(Kartellrecht)* conscious parallelism of action *(US)*; **kaltes (kaltschnäuziges)** ~ cool behavio(u)r; **konkludentes** ~ implied consent; **korrektes** ~ correct behavio(u)r, just conduct, proprieties; **korruptes** ~ malversation; **kränkendes** ~ insulting behavio(u)r; **marktgerechtes** ~ action in conformity with the market; **nichtswürdiges** ~ contemptible conduct; **opportunistisches** ~ temporization; **ordnungsmäßiges** ~ right conduct, correct (orderly) behavio(u)r, proprieties; **ordnungswidriges** ~ misconduct, disorderly conduct; **provozierendes** ~ provoking a difficulty; **raffiniertes** ~ shifty behavio(u)r; **redliches** ~ clean hands; **rücksichtsloses und unsinniges** ~ wanton and reckless misconduct; **schuldhaftes** ~ fault; **sittenwidriges** ~ immoral conduct; **sittliches** ~ morality; **sozialwidriges** ~ unfair industrial practices *(Br.)*; **standesgemäßes** ~ professional conduct; **standes- und ehrenrühriges** ~ conduct unbecoming an officer and gentleman; **standeswidriges** ~ infamous behavio(u)r, malpractice, professional misconduct, *(Anwalt)* conduct unbefitting a solicitor *(Br.)*; **tadelnswertes** ~ demerit; **tierisches** ~ behavio(u)r of an animal; **unanständiges** ~ low-down behavio(u)r; **unbotmäßiges** ~ disorderly behavio(u)r, disorderliness; **undurchsichtiges** ~ ambiguous policy; **unehrenhaftes** ~ infamous behavio(u)r; **unerhörtes** ~ outrageous conduct; **ungehöriges (unziemliches)** ~ indecorous behavio(u)r, malpractice, misconduct; **fortgesetztes ungehöriges** ~ *(Angestellter)* history of misconduct; **unqualifiziertes** ~ *(Beamter)* poor behavio(u)r; **unsittliches** ~ indecency; **unsoziales** ~ dissociality; **untadeliges** ~ irreproachable conduct; **mit berufsethischen Grundsätzen unvereinbares** ~ conduct inconsistent with the standards; **verborgenes** ~ *(Psychologie)* covert behavio(u)r; **vernünftiges** ~ *(Wirtschaftstheorie)* rational behavio(u)r; **weiteres** ~ subsequent conduct; **standeswidriges ~ eines Anwalts** conduct discreditable to a barrister (unbefitting a solicitor, *Br.*); ~ **des Arbeitnehmers** employee attitude; **verdächtiges ~ bei Ausschußsitzungen** suspicious proceedings in committee meetings; ~ **einer Führungskraft** managerial behavio(u)r *(US)*; **schuldhaftes ~ eines Handelsvertreters** wilful misconduct on the part of an agent; ~ **auf dem Markt** market conduct; **unzumutbares ~ des Mieters** misconduct of a tenant; ~ **am Telefon** telephone manner; ~ **der Wählerschaft** voting behavio(u)r;

sein ~ ändern to change one's skin, to veer; **einer Firma korrektes ~ bescheinigen** to give a firm a clean bill of health; ~ **billigen** to uphold a conduct; **jds. ~ miserabel beurteilen** to take a poor view of s. one's conduct; **jds. ~ positiv beurteilen** to view s. one's conduct in a favo(u)rable light; **jds. ~ falsch deuten** to place s. one's conduct in a false light; **sich für sein ungebührliches ~ entschuldigen** to purge one's contempt; **jem. sein ~ vorschreiben** to enjoin a conduct upon s. o.

verhalten, sich to act, to conduct, *(Angelegenheit)* to stand; **sich ablehnend** ~ to take a negative attitude; **sich abwartend** ~ to wait and see, to maintain a passive attitude; **sich anständig (manierlich)** ~ to behave; **sich fair gegenüber jem.** ~ to deal fairly with s. o.; **sich konformgerecht** ~ to run true to form; **sich opportunistisch** ~ to temporize; **sich passiv** ~ to maintain a passive attitude; **sich ruhig (still)** ~ to keep quiet; **sich schäbig gegen j.** ~ to behave shabbily towards s. o.; **seine Schritte** ~ to stop short; **sich skeptisch** ~ to assume a sceptical attitude; **sich unauffällig** ~ to keep a low profile; **sich undiszipliniert** ~ to run riot; **sich vorschriftswidrig** ~ to commit irregularities; **sich vorsichtig** ~ to lie low;

~ *(a.)* with restraint;

mit ~er Stimme sprechen to speak in a subdued voice.

Verhaltens|änderung attitude change; **~anpassung** behavio(u)ral adaptation; **~anweisung** letter of instruction; **~beobachtung** behavio(u)r observation; **~dokumente** behavio(u)r documents; **~forscher** behavio(u)ral scientist, behavio(u)rist; **~forschung** behavio(u)ral science (study), behavio(u)r observation, investigation of behavio(u)r; **~grundsätze** code of conduct; **~kodex** code of conduct; **~kontrolle** behavio(u)r control; **~maßregeln** instructions for negotiations, rules of conduct; **ohne ~maßregeln** uninstructed; **~modell** behavio(u)r model; **~normen** standard of conduct; **völkerrechtliche ~normen** international standards.

verhaltensorientierte Unternehmenstheorie behavio(u)ral theory of a firm.

Verhaltens|psychologie behavio(u)r psychology; **~regeln** directive rules, *(ethisch)* ethics; **~skala** attitude scale; **~studie** attitude survey (study).

Verhaltensweise behavio(u)r pattern, course of conduct;

aufeinander abgestimmte ~ *(Kartellrecht)* concerted practice,

arrangement *(Br.)*; **wettbewerbsbeschränkende** ~ restrictive practices;
an einer bestimmten ~ **festhalten** to adhere to a line of conduct.
Verhaltenswissenschaft behavio(u)r science.
Verhältnis affair, liaison, *(Beziehung)* relation[ship], condition, rapport, *(Maßstab)* measure, unit of measurement, *(Quote)* quota, dividend, *(Vergleich)* proportion, rate, ratio;
im ~ **von** at the rate of, in the ratio of; **im** ~ **zu der geleisteten Arbeit** in proportion to the work done; **im** ~ **1 : 2** *(Bezug neuer Aktien)* in the proportion of one new share against every two old shares held; **im gleichen** ~ in equal proportion; **im umgekehrten** ~ in inverse ratio; **in angemessenem** ~ in due proportion; **in rein dienstlichem** ~ **stehend** of a strictly professional nature; **in freundschaftlichem** ~ on friendly terms; **in gespanntem** ~ on strained terms, at outs *(US)*; **in keinem** ~ **stehend** out of all proportion; **in richtigem** ~ proportionate; **nicht im** ~ **stehend** disproportionate, out of proportion;
besitzähnliches ~ quasi possession; **eheähnliches** ~ quasi marriage; **ehebrecherisches** ~ adulterous relationship; **eheliches** ~ conjugal relation; **enges** ~ close relationship; **festes** ~ definite ratio; **freundschaftliches** ~ friendly footing; **funktionierendes** ~ working relationship; **gespanntes** ~ strained relations, tense relationship, tension, out *(US)*; **gesundes** ~ healthy relationship; **gutnachbarliches** ~ good neigbo(u)rliness; **nießbrauchähnliches** ~ quasi usufruct; **obligatorisches** ~ contractual obligation; **persönliches** ~ personal relationship; **vertragliches**
~ contractual relationship; **vertragsähnliches** ~ quasi-contractual relationship; **verwahrungsähnliches** ~ quasi deposit;
~ **der Aktiva zu den Passiva** equity ratio; ~ **der flüssigen Aktiven zu den gesamten Verbindlichkeiten** ratio of current assets to total liabilities; ~ **zwischen Angebot und Nachfrage** ratio between supply and demand; ~ **zwischen Arbeitgeber und Arbeitnehmer** industrial relations *(US)*; ~ **auf dem Arbeitsmarkt** labo(u)r situation; ~ **geleisteter Arbeitsstunden zum Preis** work-time price ratio; ~ **von Eigen- zu Fremdkapital** equity position, credit ratio *(US)*; ~ **vom Gewinn zum Umsatz** sales profit ratio; ~ **zur Kundschaft** customer relations; ~ **der Mietparteien** landlord-tenant relationship; ~ **der finanziellen Mittel** financial ratio; **günstiges** ~ **des Nettoanteils** favo(u)rable equity position; ~ **der Netto- zur Bruttobelastung** proportion of the net load to the gross load; ~ **von Nettoumsatz zu Betriebskapital** working-capital turnover; ~ **von Obligationen und Vorzugsaktien zu Stammaktien** leverage; ~ **zwischen Prinzipal und Angestellten** relation of master to servants; ~ **der Rücklagen zu den Verbindlichkeiten** proportion of reserves to liabilities; ~ **der Sichteinlagen zu den Gesamteinlagen** ratio of time deposits to total deposits; ~ **von 60% Text zu 40% Anzeigenraum** 60 - 40 ratio of text advertising; ~ **zwischen Umlaufvermögen und kurzfristigen Schulden** current ratio, *(Kreditbeurteilung)* banker's ratio *(US)*; ~ **sämtlicher Verbindlichkeiten zum Eigenkapital** liabilities to worth ratio;
nach dem ~ **beitragen** to contribute proportionally; ~ **berechnen** to pro-rate; **in ein richtiges** ~ **bringen** to proportion; **engeres** ~ **zu seiner Umgebung zustande bringen** to bring o. s. into closer rapport with one's environment; **mit dem Lieferanten ein** ~ **haben** *(Köchin)* to walk out with a tradesman; **richtiges** ~ **zu seiner Arbeit haben** to have one's heart in one's work; **nach dem** ~ **der Beträge kürzen** to reduce pro rata; ~ **lösen** to break off an affair; **im** ~ **1 : 4 mischen** to mix in the ration of 1 : 4; **freundschaftliches** ~ **schaffen** to build up goodwill; **zum Einkommen in keinem** ~ **stehen** to be out of proportion to one's income; **zum Ergebnis in keinem** ~ **stehen** to bear no relation to the result; **im umgekehrten** ~ **stehen zu** to be in inverse proportion to; **in einem** ~ **1 : 1 stehen** to have a one-to-one relationship; **in freundschaftlichem** ~ **zueinander stehen** to be on an amicable footing; **Einfuhren nur im** ~ **zu den Ausfuhren zulassen** to allow imports in proportion to exports;
~**anteil** ratable (proportionate) share, quota, dividend; ~**klausel** average clause.
verhältnismäßig in proportion, proportionate, proportional, ratable, in equal ratio, pro rata, commensurable, *(vergleichsweise)* relatively, comparatively;
~ **wohlhabend** comparatively well-off;
Gewinne ~ **aufteilen** to prorate profits;
~**er Anteil** comparative (proportional) share; ~**e Aufteilung** prorata apportionment; ~**er Wert** relative value.
Verhältnismäßigkeit commensurableness, commensurability;
~ **einer Gerichtsentscheidung** balance of convenience.
Verhältnis|maßstab ratio, scale; **vergleichbare** ~**positionen** common ratio positions.
Verhältnisse *(persönliche Lage)* situation, position, conditions, *(Vermögenslage)* status, circumstances, means;
aus kleinen ~**n** from a humble cottage, of humble origin; **durch die** ~ **bedingt** modal; **in bescheidenen** ~**n** down, low; **in beschränkten** ~**n** in reduced (pinched) circumstances, near; **in glänzenden** ~**n** in flourishing circumstances; **in guten** ~**n** of good position, well circumstanced, well-off, in the green tree, sitting pretty, on easy street *(US)*; **unter den bestehenden (normalen)** ~**n** under existing (normal) conditions; **unter diesen** ~**n** under (in) these circumstances; **unter dem Druck der** ~ forced by circumstances; **unter normalen** ~**n** normally; **unter den derzeitigen steuerlichen** ~**n** with taxes as they now are;
angenehme ~ easy street; **ärmliche** ~ indigent circumstances; **berufliche** ~ professional status; **beschränkte** ~ narrow (pinched) circumstances *(coll.)*; **finanzielle** ~ financial conditions, *(Firma)* [financial] status; **häusliche** ~ home environment; **innenpolitische** ~ local political situation; **örtliche** ~ local conditions; **soziale** ~ social conditions; **vermögensrechtliche** ~ pecuniary circumstances; **wirtschaftliche** ~ economic conditions; **zerrüttete** ~ decayed circumstances, embarrassed business;
sich den ~**n anpassen** to adapt o. s. to circumstances; **sich schnell auf veränderte** ~ **einstellen** to adjust o. s. readily to changed circumstances; **sich eingehend nach jds.** ~**n erkundigen** to inquire into s. one's position; **früher in guten** ~**n gelebt haben** to have known better days; **in bedrängten (ärmlichen, dürftigen)** ~**n leben** to live in close quarters (poverty), to be poorly (badly) off, to be in straitened (narrow, needy) circumstances; **in bescheidensten** ~ **leben** to live upon a very small modicum; **in guten** ~**n leben** to be in good financial (easy) circumstances (well-off), to live at ease; **in jämmerlichen** ~**n leben** to live in misery and want; **in kleinen** ~**n leben** to be in narrow (pinched) circumstances; **in ordentlichen** ~**n leben** to live in decent conditions; **in unwürdigen** ~**n leben** to live in (a life of) degradation; **über seine** ~ **leben** to live beyond (above) one's means (income), to exceed (outrun) one's income, to overspend, to splurge *(fam.)*, to outrun (overrun) the constable *(Br.)*; **seinen** ~**n entsprechend leben** to live within one's means (purse); **sich mit ärmlichen** ~**n abfinden müssen** to have to reconcile o. s. to a life of poverty; **geänderten** ~**n Rechnung tragen** to face altered circumstances; **stabile** ~ **in der Wirtschaft wiederherstellen** to reorganize the economy on a stable basis.
Verhältnis|tabelle ratio chart; ~**wahl** proportional ballot (vote); ~**wahlsystem** proportionalism, proportional representation.
verhältniswidrig disproportionate.
Verhältnis|zahl, ~**ziffer** ratio, figure, proportion, coefficient, factor;
spezifische ~ *(Statistik)* specific rate.
verhandeln to confer, to hold a conference, to deliberate, to treat about, *(diskutieren)* to discuss, to hold discussions, to debate, to argue, *(Gericht)* to hear, to hold court, *(Strafgericht)* to try, *(Unterhandlungen führen)* to negotiate, to prosecute negotiations, to transact, to treat, to bargain;
über etw. ~ to be in debate, to traffic away s. th.; **gegen j.** ~ to try s. o.; **über den Ankauf eines Hauses** ~ to negotiate for the purchase of a house; **mit den Aufrührern** ~ to parley with the rebels; **unter Ausschluß der Öffentlichkeit** ~ to sit in camera, to hear a case in closed session (in chambers, *Br.*); **erneut** ~ *(Gericht)* to rehear (reargue, *US*) a case; **Fall** ~ to hear a case; **vor Gericht** ~ to try a case, *(Anwalt)* to plead; **rein geschäftsmäßig** ~ to deal at arm's length; **geschickt** ~ to play one's cards well; **gesondert gegen j.** ~ to try s. o. separately; **zur Hauptsache** ~ to deal with a case upon its merits; **mit dem Kläger** ~ to stipulate with the plaintiff; **mündlich** ~ *(Anwalt)* to plead a case, *(Gericht)* to hear an argument by counsel, to argue a case; **öffentlich** ~ to try at the bar; **über einen Preis** ~ to negotiate a price; **über eine Sache** ~ to proceed with (sit in judgment on) a case, to hear (proceed with)a case; **über eine Sache in allen Einzelheiten** ~ to discuss a matter in detail; **streitig** ~ to hold an argument; **über einen Tarifvertrag** ~ to bargain collectively; **in allen Einzelheiten über einen Vertrag** ~ to negotiate a contract in exhaustive detail; **über einen Vertragsabschluß** ~ to negotiate a contract; **mit dem Gegner über einen Waffenstillstand** ~ to parley with the enemy about an armistice; **über Zollfragen** ~ to debate the tariff question.
verhandelt dealt with;
~ **werden** *(Fall)* to come up for judgment; **öffentlich** ~ **werden** to be tried in open court; **nächste Woche** ~ **werden** to come up for hearing next week.
Verhandler negotiator, bargainer.

Verhandlung *(Beratschlagung)* counsel, deliberation, *(Besprechung)* conference, talk, parley, *(Debatte)* debate, discussion, argument, assize, *(vor Gericht)* judicial hearing, proceeding, *(mil.)* parley, *(Parteivortrag)* pleading, *(Strafverhandlung)* criminal proceedings, *(Unterhandlungen)* negotiation, transaction, treaty, passage;
in ~ under negotiation; **in nicht öffentlicher** ~ in chambers *(Br.)* (camera); **nach längeren** ~**en** after much discussion; **während der** ~**en** pending negotiations, *(Gericht)* pending the action; **zu** ~**en bereit** open to negotiations;
abgesonderte ~**en** separate negotiations; **abgetrennte** ~ *(Strafverfahren)* separate trial; **bevorstehende** ~**en** forthcoming negotiations; **bisherige** ~**en** negotiations hithertho; **erneute** ~ renegotiation, *(Gericht)* rehearing, revision, hearing de novo, *(Strafsache)* retrial; **festgefahrene** ~**en** deadlocked negotiations; **finanzielle** ~**en** financial talks; **im geheimen geführte** ~**en** secret (private) negotiations; **hinter den Kulissen geführte** ~**en** backstage negotiations; **gemeinsame** ~**en** collective bargaining; **gerichtliche** ~**en** forensic debates, court hearing, hearing in court, *(Strafverfahren)* trial of an action; **kontradiktorische** ~ contentious business, defended trial; **langwierige** ~**en** lengthy negotiations; **lohnpolitische** ~**en** wage negotiations; **mündliche** ~ *(Anwalt)* oral pleading, judicial hearing; **letzte mündliche** ~ final hearing; **nichtöffentliche** ~ closed-door hearing, hearing in camera (chambers, *Br.*); **nichtstreitige** ~ undefended suit; **nochmalige** ~ further consideration, *(Gericht)* rehearing, *(Strafgericht)* new trial, retrial; **öffentliche** ~ hearing in court, public hearing, *(parl.)* debate, *(Strafsache)* open (public) trial; **schwebende** ~**en** negotiations in progress; **sofortige** ~ trial instanter; **streitige** ~ defended trial (suit); **vertagte** ~ deferred hearing, postponed case; **intensiv vorbereitete** ~**en** cut-and-dried negotiations;
~**en über eine Anleihe** negotiations for a loan; ~ **über einen Antrag** hearing of an application; ~ **in Anwesenheit von Sachverständigen** trial with assessors; ~ **nach Augenscheinsnahme** trial by inspection or examination; ~ **unter Ausschluß der Öffentlichkeit** hearing in camera (chambers, *Br.*); ~ **zwischen Ausschüssen gesetzgebender Körperschaften** conference; ~**en über die Begrenzung der strategischen Kernwaffen** Strategic Arms Limitations Talks (SALT); ~ **einer Berufungssache** hearing of an appeal; ~**en auf höchste Ebene** top-level negotiations; ~ **vor den Einwanderungsbehörden** hearing before the immigration office *(US)*; ~ **vor dem Einzelrichter** sitting in closed sessions (camera, chambers, *Br.*), special term, trial before a single judge; ~ **vor einem voll besetzten Gericht** trial at bar; ~ **vor den Geschworenen** trial by the country (by jury); ~**en mit den Gewerkschaften** union negotiations; ~ **erster Instanz** first trial; ~**en über einen neuen Luftfrachttarif** airline bargaining; **gleichzeitige** ~ **mehrerer Rechtssachen** duplicity; ~ **über eine Sache** hearing of a case, *(Strafsache)* trial of an action, trying of a case; ~**en zwischen den Tarifpartnern** voluntary negotiations, collective bargaining; ~ **hinter verschlossenen Türen** closed-door hearing;
~**en abbrechen** to cut (break) off negotiations; ~**en abschließen** to terminate negotiations; **mündliche** ~ **absetzen** to cancel a hearing; **Termin zur mündlichen** ~ **anberaumen** to assign a day for (fix) a hearing in court (for a trial); **mündliche** ~ **anordnen** to put a case down for hearing; **zur** ~ **ansetzen** to set down for trial, to bring to hearing; **zur** ~ **anstehen** to be on the cause list (down for hearing); **nächsten Monat zur** ~ **anstehen** to be heard next month; ~**en aufnehmen** to take up negotiations, to open talks; ~**en mit jem. aufnehmen** to enter into an agreement with s. o.; ~ **aufrufen** to call a case *(Br.)*; **j. von der** ~ **ausschließen** to put s. o. out of court; ~ **aussetzen** to stay an action (proceedings); ~ **drei Tage aussetzen** to adjourn a case for three days; **sich für** ~**en aussprechen** to speak for negotiations; ~**en beginnen** to start negotiations; **durch** ~**en beilegen** to settle by negotiations; **einer mündlichen** ~ **bis zum Schluß beiwohnen** to sit a hearing out; ~**en zu einem erfolgreichen Abschluß bringen** to bring negotiations to a satisfactory conclusion; ~**en in Gang bringen** to set negotiations in motion; **sich durch** ~ **zur Hauptsache einlassen** to put in an appearance; ~**en einleiten** to initiate negotiations; **j. in die** ~**en einschalten** to call s. o. in on the negotiations; **in** ~**en eintreten** to engage in (initiate) negotiations; **in die** ~ **eintreten** *(Gericht)* to open the case; **in eine** ~ **eintreten** to open a discussion; **in** ~**en mit jem. eintreten** to enter into negotiations with s. o.; ~ **eröffnen** *(Gericht)* to open the case, *(Strafgericht)* to open the trial; ~**en eröffnen** to start negotiations; ~**en fortführen** to continue negotiations; ~ **fortsetzen** to proceed with a trial; ~**en führen (leiten)** to conduct (carry on, transact) negotiations; ~**en führen und abschließen** to transact negotiations; ~ **unter Ausschluß der Öffentlichkeit führen** to sit in camera, to hear a case in chambers *(Br.)*; **bei einer** ~ **den Vorsitz führen** to preside at a hearing; ~**en über einzeln ausgewählte Waren führen** to carry out negotiations on a selective product-by-product basis; ~**en hintertreiben** to prevent negotiations taking place; **zur** ~ **kommen** *(Strafverfahren)* to be up for trial; **nächste Woche zur** ~ **kommen** to come up for hearing next week; ~ **leiten** *(Gericht)* to proceed with a case; ~**en leiten** to conduct negotiations; ~**en pflegen** to be in treaty; ~ **schließen** to close the court; **zu bundesweiten** ~**en bereit sein** to be open to negotiate at national level; **mit jem. in** ~**en stehen** to be negotiating with s. o.; **schon geraume Zeit in** ~**en stehen** to be negotiating for some time; ~ **unterbrechen** *(Gericht)* to adjourn a trial; ~**en unterbrechen** to break off (stay) negotiations; ~**en unterstützen** to aid negotiations; ~ **vertagen** to adjourn (postpone) a hearing, to postpone a trial; ~ **eine Woche vertagen** to put off a case for a week; **Weg für** ~**en vorbereiten** to prepare the way for negotiations; **mündliche** ~ **wahrnehmen** to attend to a hearing, to plead; ~ **wiederaufnehmen** to open up judgment, *(Strafgericht)* to resume a trial; ~**en wiederaufnehmen** to resume negotiations; **mündliche** ~ **wiederaufnehmen** to continue a case.

Verhandlungs|ablauf hinziehen to drag out the negotiating process; ~**akten** records of the proceedings; ~**angebot** overture, bargaining offer; **gesamtes** ~**angebot** overall package; **vorläufiges** ~**angebot** tentative offer; ~**atmosphäre** negotiating atmosphere; ~**aufschub erzwingen** to force a suspension of the negotiations; ~**ausschuß** negotiating committee; **gemeinsamer** ~**ausschuß** joint negotiating panel; ~**basis** negotiation basis; ~**beginn** opening of negotiations.

verhandlungsbereit open to negotiate (to negotiations).

Verhandlungsbereitschaft willingness to negotiate.

Verhandlungsbericht transcript, protocol, report of the proceedings;
~**e** transactions, written proceedings;
mündlicher ~ verbatim report of the proceedings; **zusammengefaßter** ~ *(parl.)* summary of the debate.

Verhandlungs|bevollmächtigter plenipotentiary, authorized agent, *(Gewerkschaft)* bargaining agent; ~**buch** minutes, minute book; **während der** ~**dauer** during the process of negotiations; ~**delegation** negotiating group (team); ~**dolmetscher** conference interpreter; ~**erfahrung** bargaining experience; ~**erfolg** negotiating success; ~**eröffnung** opening of a case.

verhandlungsfähig negotiable;
~ **sein** to have a quorum.

Verhandlungs|fähigkeit negotiability, skills of negotiation, *(Beschlußfähigkeit)* quorum; ~**frieden** peace by negotiation; ~**führer** negotiator, *(Gericht)* recorder, *(Gewerkschaft)* bargaining agent; ~**führung** conduct of negotiations, *(Gericht)* conduct of a case; ~**gebühr** sitting fee *(Br.)*; ~**gegenstand** negotiating package, *(Gericht)* matter, case, *(parl.)* question; ~**gegenstände** [items on the] agenda; ~**geschick** negotiating skills, ability to negotiate; ~**gespräche gleich zum Beginn stark belasten** to get talks off to an awkward start; ~**gremium** negotiating (bargaining) body; **gemeinsames** ~**gremium** joint negotiating panel; ~**grundlage** basis for negotiations, negotiation basis; **gemeinsame** ~**grundlage finden** to find a common ground for negotiations; ~**gruppe** negotiating (bargaining) group; ~**instrument** bargaining counter; ~**kalender** *(Gericht)* calendar of causes, cause list *(Br.)*, trial docket *(US)*; ~**künste** skills of negotiations, negotiating skills; ~**leitung** chairmanship, *(Gericht)* conduct of a case; ~**leitung in einer Sitzung an sich reißen** to monopolize a meeting; ~**leitung übernehmen** to assume the chair; ~**liste** *(Gericht)* appearance docket, cause list *(Br.)*, trial docket *(US)*; ~**mitglied der Gewerkschaft** union negotiator; ~**niederschrift** written proceedings, record of the proceedings, minutes; ~**objekt** bargaining chip, bid for bartering; ~**ort** place of meeting, *(Gericht)* venue, trial site; ~**paket** package deal, contract (negotiating) package; ~**partei**, ~**partner** negotiator, negotiating party, *(Tarifvertrag)* bargainor, bargaining agent; ~**partner auf seiten der Industrie** industry negotiator; **als** ~**partner zur Aushandlung von Tariflöhnen und Arbeitsbedingungen vom Arbeitgeber anerkannt sein** to be recognized by an employer for the collective bargaining of wages and conditions; ~**pause** suspension of negotiations; ~**phase** bargaining round; ~**plan** negotiating plan; ~**position** negotiating (bargaining) position; **starke** ~**position** negotiating power; **günstigere** ~**position haben** to negotiate on better terms; ~**protokoll** minutes [of the proceedings], minute book,

(Gericht) written proceedings, record of the proceedings, transcript, *(parl.)* deliberations; **~protokoll führen** to keep records of the proceedings; **~punkte** bargaining counts (agenda); **~punkte festsetzen** to fix the agenda; **sich dem nächsten ~punkt zuwenden** to go on to the next item on the agenda; **~raum** *(Gericht)* court room, *(Hotel)* conference room.
verhandlungsreif *(Rechtssache)* ready for hearing, judiciable.
Verhandlungs|richtlinien rules of order; **~runde** round (set) of negotiations, *(Tarifvertrag)* bargaining round; **~saal** conference hall, *(Gericht)* court room; **~sache** matter of arrangement; **bei ~schluß** at the close of negotiation; **~schriftsatz** pleading, trial brief *(US)*.
Verhandlungsspielraum negotiating room, room for manoeuvre, *(Tarifverhandlungen)* bargaining room;
keinerlei ~ mehr haben to run out of negotiating room; **außerhalb des ~s liegen** to be outside the bargaining area; **im ~ liegen** *(Tarifverhandlung)* to be on the bargaining cards.
Verhandlungs|sprache official language; **~stärke** negotiating (bargaining) power; **~tag** *(Gericht)* trial date, juridical day; **pro ~tag** for one day in court; **~tage** paper days, days in court; **~taktik** negotiating tactics; **~tarif** bargaining tariff; **~teilnehmer** participant in a conference; **~termin** day fixed for trial, trial date, appearance (return) day, day of appearance, *(Insolvenz)* hearing date; **neuer ~termin** adjournment day; **~termin in einer Sache ansetzen** to fix a day for a hearing in court, to assign (appoint) a day for the trial, to put a case on the calendar *(US)*; **~tisch** conference (board, negotiating, bargaining, round) table; **am ~tisch vertreten sein** to have representatives at the bargaining table; **~trick** negotiating bluff; **~tür zuschlagen** to slam the negotiating door; **~unfähigkeit** inability to follow the proceedings; **~unlust überwinden** to break down bargaining intransigence; **~versuche** efforts of negotiation; **~vollmacht** negotiating power (right), power to negotiate, *(Tarife)* bargaining power; **~weg** negotiating route; **im ~wege** by private treaty (negotiation); **im ~wege regeln** to settle by negotiation; **~zimmer** *(Gericht)* hearing room, courtroom.
verhangen *(Himmel)* overclouded, overcast.
Verhängen imposition, infliction.
verhängen to impose;
Ausnahmezustand ~ to declare a state of emergency; **Ausnahmezustand über ein Gebiet ~** to proclaim a district; **Belagerungszustand ~** to declare a state of siege; **Embargo ~** to put an embargo on, to impose an embargo; **Geldstrafe gegen j. ~** to fine s. o., to inflict a fine on s. o.; **über j. den Konkurs ~** to adjudge (adjudicate) s. o. a bankrupt; **Kriegsrecht ~** to impose martial law; **Strafe gegen j. ~** to impose a penalty (inflict a punishment) on s. o.; **Todesstrafe ~** to pronounce a sentence of death; **Wagen mit schwarzen Tüchern ~** to drape a car with black cloth.
Verhängnis calamity, disaster, catastrophe;
jem. zum ~ werden to become s. one's undoing.
verhängnisvoll calamitous, fateful, fatal, disastrous;
sich ~ auf ein Land auswirken to be disastrous for a country; **~en Einfluß auf j. ausüben** to have a fatal influence over s. o.
verhängt *(Gebäude)* draped, *(Strafe)* imposed;
~e Zügel loose reins.
Verhängung|des Ausnahmezustands über ein Gebiet proclamation of a district; **~ des Kriegsrechts** imposition of martial law; **~ des Notstands** declaration of national emergency; **~ des Standrechts** proclamation of martial law; **~ einer Strafe** imposition of a penalty, infliction of a punishment.
verharmlosen to belittle, to make light of;
Gefahr einer Aufgabe ~ to minimize the danger of a task.
Verharmlosung belittlement, minimization.
verhärmt aussehen to look careworn.
verharren to persist;
bei einem Entschluß ~ to stick to one's decision; **bei seiner Meinung ~** to adhere to one's opinion, to stick to one's guns; **im Schweigen ~** to remain silent.
verhärten to harden, to indurate;
sein Herz ~ to harden one's heart.
verhärtete Front hardened front.
verhaspeln, sich in einer Rede to flounder through a speech.
verhaßt loathed, detested, hated;
j. ~ machen to bring s. o. into odium; **sich ~ machen** to make o. s. unpopular; **überall ~ sein** to be hated by everyone.
verhätscheln to pamper, to coddle, to wet-nurse;
Tier ~ to make a pet of an animal.
Verhau entanglement.
verhauen to give a licking, to leather *(coll.)*, *(Arbeit)* to bungle, to muff, to boss *(sl.)*;
sich gründlich ~ to be way off in one's calculation.
verheddern to tangle;
sich ~ to get o. s. mixed up; **sich in einer Rede ~** to become embarrassed (involved) in a speech.
verheeren to lay waste, to devastate, to desolate, to infest.
verheerend destructive, devastating, *(unmöglich)* ghastly, dreadful;
~ aussehen to look a sight; **sich ~ auf etw. auswirken** to wreak havoc on s. th.;
~er Sturm devastating storm.
Verheerungen devastation, havoc, desolation, destruction;
~ in den Straßen anrichten to play havoc in the streets.
verheften, Buch to transpose the sheets.
verheftet faulty stitching.
verhehlen to dissemble;
sich etw. nicht ~ to be well aware of it.
verheimlichen to conceal, to hide, to keep back, to suppress, to dissimulate;
jem. etw. ~ to hold out at s. o. *(US coll.)*; **Hehlerware ~** to receive stolen goods; **ausländische Vermögenswerte ~** to conceal foreign assets; **jem. die Wahrheit ~** to withhold the truth from s. o.
verheimlichte Vermögenswerte concealed assets.
Verheimlichung concealment, suppression.
verheiraten to marry off;
j. ~ to give s. o. in marriage; **sich ~** to get married, to match, to unite, to change one's condition; **sich mit jem. ~** to take s. one's hand in marriage; **sich gut ~** to make a match; **sich wieder ~** to remarry; **zwei Menschen ~** to join two persons in marriage; **Tochter ~** to get one's daughter off.
verheiratet married, at marriage estate, *(Tochter)* settled;
~e Frau spouse; **~er Mann** family man.
Verheiratetenzulage family allowance.
Verheirateter married man.
Verheiratung marriage, marrying, wedlock.
verheißungsvoll auspicious, favo(u)rable, promising.
verheizen to burn, *(Soldaten)* to send to the slaughter.
verhelfen, j. zu seinem Recht to see s. o. righted; **jem. zu einer Stellung ~** to find a post for s. o. (s. o. a job).
verherrlichen to glorify, *(mit Reklame)* to glamo(u)rize;
Krieg ~ to glorify war.
verhetzt instigated, incited.
Verhetzung incitation, instigation;
~ des Volkes demagogism, demagoguery.
verhext bedevil(l)ed, bewitched;
heute ist alles ~ there's a jinx (hoodoo) on everything today.
verhindern to prevent, to obstruct, to hinder, to balk, to foil, to provide against, to block, to impede, to frustrate;
Attacke auf die Staatskasse ~ to forestall a raid on the treasury; **Ausübung einer Dienstbarkeit ~** to obstruct an easement; **Pfändung ~** to buy out the execution; **jds. Pläne ~** to thwart (foil) s. one's plans; **Rechtsausübung ~** to prevent the exercise of a right; **Verabschiedung eines Gesetzentwurfes ~** to obstruct a bill; **Vertragserfüllung ~** to frustrate a contract; **Zwangsvollstreckung ~** to obstruct process;
Vollstreckung zu ~ suchen to hinder and delay.
verhindernd prohibitive.
verhindert prevented, windbound, wind-bound *(fig.)*;
anderweitig ~ prevented by previous appointments;
absolut ~ sein to be unavoidably prevented from doing s. th.;
~er Künstler would-be artist.
Verhinderung prevention, restraint, hindrance, impediment, frustration, obviation;
~ steuerlicher Belastungen tax shelter; **~ des Entstehens von Ersatzansprüchen** claim prevention; **~ von Lohnsteigerungen** wage restraint; **~ von Unfällen** prevention of accidents; **~ der Vertragserfüllung** prevention of performance, frustration of contract; **~ der Zwangsvollstreckung** obstructing process.
Verhinderungs|fall, im in case of prevention; **~gründe** frustrating factors.
verhöhnen to ridicule, to mock, to jibe at, to scoff;
j. öffentlich ~ to make a hostile demonstration against s. o.
Verhöhnung ridicule, mock, derision, jibe.
verhökern to huckster, to barter away.
Verhör interrogation, questioning, examination, screening, *(Gericht, Parlament)* hearing, trial;
nach stundenlangem ~ after hours of interrogation;
nochmaliges ~ reexamination; **verschärftes ~** third-degree practices;

beim ~ auspacken to squeal; **ins ~ nehmen** to question, to interrogate, *(Gegenanwalt)* to cross-examine; **j. ins ~ nehmen** to take s. one's examination; **Gefangenen einem ~ unterziehen** to take the examination of a prisoner; **einem scharfen ~ unterziehen** to put on the grill *(sl.)*; **zum ~ vorladen** to call in question; **einem ~ unterworfen werden** to be questioned [by the police].
verhören to interrogate, to question, to examine, to hear, to try, to put s. o. on trial.
Verhör | methoden, unmenschliche inhuman methods of interrogation; **~richtlinien** judges' rules.
verhört, nicht untried;
~ werden to undergo (be under) examination, to be on trial.
Verhörter interrogatee.
Verhörzwecke, zu ~n festgehalten detained for interrogation.
verhüllen to veil, to shroud, to curtain, *(bemänteln)* to cloak, to mantle;
sein Haupt ~ to hang one's head in shame.
verhüllt veiled, shrouded;
kaum ~e Drohung an almost open threat.
Verhungern starvation.
verhungern to die of hunger (starvation);
fast ~ to famish;
j. ~ lassen to starve s. o. to death; **j. am ausgestreckten Arm ~ lassen** to make s. o. sing small.
verhungert starved;
buchstäblich ~ literally famished.
verhunzen to muck up, to botch, to bungle, to make a hash of it;
Arbeit ~ to butcher a job; **englische Sprache ~** to murder King's English.
verhunzt hashed, butchered, bungled, *(verdorben)* spoilt, marred.
verhüten to prevent, to preserve, to protect.
verhütend preventive.
verhütten to smelt.
Verhüttung smelting.
Verhütung von Unfällen prevention of accidents.
Verhütungs | maßnahmen preventive measures; **~mittel** contraceptive.
verhutzeltes Weiblein wizened old woman.
verifizieren to authenticate, to verify, to check;
Betrag ~ to prove a sum.
Verifizierung verification;
~ durch Wiederholung *(Telegramm)* collation.
verirren, sich to go astray, to lose one's bearings.
verirrt lost, astray.
Verirrung, geistige aberration of the mind; **geschmacklose ~** lapse of taste.
verjagen to chase (drive) away;
Einbrecher ~ to frighten a burglar away; **Feind ~** to dislodge the enemy; **Menge ~** to disperse the crowd.
verjährbar prescriptable, subject to the statute of limitations.
Verjährbarkeit prescriptibility.
verjähren to become barred by the statute of limitations (statute-barred, invalid by prescription), to expire by limitation, to prescribe, to be in lapse, *(Vollmacht)* to become stale, to superannuate;
in vier Jahren ~ to be subject to a period of limitation of 4 years; **am Jahresende ~** to be barred at the end of the year.
verjährt prescriptive, barred by the statute of limitations, statute-barred, statute-run, time-barred *(US)*, barred by prescription, stale;
für ~ erklären to outlaw *(US)*; **~ sein** to be barred by the statute of limitations (statute-barred, barred by limitation); **längst ~ sein** to be all water under the bridge;
~er Anspruch unenforceable (outlawed, *US*) claim; **fast ~er Anspruch** stale demand; **~e Dienstbarkeit** nonapparent easement; **~e eidesstattliche Erklärung** stale affidavit; **~e Forderung** barred (unenforceable, outlawed, *US*) claim; **~er Scheck** stale cheque *(Br.)* (check, *US*); **~e Schuld** debt barred by the Statute of Limitations, stale (prescriptive, prescribed) debt; **~e Vollmacht** superannuated (stale) power of attorney.
Verjährung time limitation, statute of limitations, extinctive prescription, *(Vollmacht)* superannuation;
auf ~ beruhend prescriptive; **durch ~ ausgeschlossen** statute-barred (-run); **durch ~ zu Recht bestehen** ancient; **durch ~ erworben** prescriptive;
~ eines Anspruchs limitation of a claim; **~ einer Klage** limitation of action; **~ der Strafverfolgung** limitation of criminal proceedings; **~ eines Wechsels** prescription of a bill of exchange;
~ ausschließen to bar prescription; **sich auf ~ berufen, ~ geltend machen** to plead the statute of limitations (prescription); **~ einwenden** to set up the statute of limitations; **~ hemmen** to stop (suspend) the period of limitation; **durch ~ ungültig machen** to prescribe; **~ unterbrechen** to toll *(US)* (save) the statute of limitations, to interrupt prescription (the period of limitation, *Scot.*), to extend a term of prescription, to lift the bar; **der ~ unterliegen** to be subject to (fall under) the statute of limitation, to be statute-barred; **Folgen der ~ vermeiden** to save the statute of limitations; **in einem bestimmten Fall die Folgen der ~ vermeiden** to take a case out of the statute of limitations; **auf Geltendmachung der ~ verzichten** to waive the statute of limitations; **von der ~ betroffen werden** to be barred by the statute of limitations (statute-barred); **durch ~ ungültig werden** to be prescribed.
Verjährungsbestimmungen statutory limitations, statute of limitations, limitation provisions, provisions of the Limitation Act *(Br.)*;
gesetzliche ~ statutory provisions for limitation, statutory limitations;
~ von Garantiezusagen limitations written into warranties;
~ anwenden to apply the Limitation Act *(Br.)* (statute of limitations).
Verjährungseinwand plea of lapse of time;
einem ~ entgegenstehen to negative a defence under the statute of limitations; **~ erheben** to plead the statute of limitations (prescription); **~ gegen eine Forderung erheben** to bar a debt by the Statute of Limitations.
Verjährungsfrist statute (period) of limitation, limitation period, time (period) of prescription;
gesetzliche ~ statutory [period of] limitation;
~ vertraglich abkürzen to cut down the period of limitations; **~ wieder zum Laufen bringen** to recommence the limitation period; **~ hemmen (unterbrechen)** to toll *(US)* (save) the statute of limitations, to interrupt a statutory limitation; **~ verlängern** to extend the statute of limitations; **auf die Geltendmachung der ~ verzichten** to waive the statute of limitations.
Verjährungs | gesetz Limitation Act *(Br.)*; **~recht** statute of limitations; **~regeln** principles of prescription, principle of limitation; **~streitfrage** statute-of-limitations issue; **~tabelle** limitations table.
Verjährungsvorschriften, gesetzliche statutory limitations, limitation provisions, statute of limitations;
~ anwenden to apply the statute of limitations; **~ unterbrechen** to save (toll, *US*) the statute of limitations; **~ verlängern** to extend the statute of limitation; **durch ~ betroffen werden** to be barred by the statute of limitation.
Verjährungszeitraum statutory period, period of limitations, limitation period, time of prescription.
verkalkt old-fogyish, old-fogey.
Verkalktheit old fogydom.
verkalkulieren, sich to miscalculate.
Verkauf sale, selling, vending, disposal, disposition, *(Realisierung)* realization;
auf dem Bürgersteig zum ~ ausgelegt peddled on the pavement; **für den ~ zurechtgemacht** faked up for sale; **zum ~** for (on) sale, for disposal, on the market;
abgeschlossener ~ definite sale; **gebietsmäßig aufgeteilter ~** geographical distribution; **bedingter ~** conditional sale; **bedingungsloser ~** absolute sale; **betrügerischer ~ [mit der Absicht der Gläubigerschädigung]** bogus (fraudulent) sale; **direkter ~** direct sale; **zwangsweise durchgeführter ~** forced (sheriff's) sale; **fester ~** firm sale; **fiktiver ~** fictitious sale; **freihändiger ~** voluntary (private, off-hand) sale, private treaty, sale by private contract, *(Effekten)* sale in the open market, over-the-counter sale *(US)*; **rückgängig gemachter ~** countermanded sale; **gerichtlicher ~** judicial sale; **frei gestalteter ~** sale by private treaty; **kommissionsweiser ~** sale on consignment (commission), memorandum sale; **langsamer ~** *(Börse)* dull sales; **lebhafter ~** brisk sales; **leichter ~** quick sale, wrap-up; **privatrechtlicher ~** sale by private contract; **rascher ~** ready (quick) sale; **schwerer ~** dull sale; **Terminkauf- und ~** double option; **vollständiger ~** clearance sale; **vorrangiger ~** *(Effekten)* priority sale; **zwangsweiser ~** compulsory (judicial) sale;
~ auf Abzahlungsbasis instal(l)ment sale, hire purchase *(Br.)*, deferred-payment sale *(US)*; **~ von Aktien** selling off of stock, sale of shares; **~ vorbehaltlich sicherer Ankunft** sale to arrive (on arrival); **~ gegen Anschreiben** charge sale; **~ eines Anwartschaftsrechtes** catching a bargain; **~ mit Anzahlung** sale on account; **~ von Anzeigenraum** space selling; **~ wegen**

Aufgabe des Geschäfts winding-up (liquidation) sale; ~ **aufgrund einer Ausschreibung** sale by tender; ~ **auf Baisse** bear sale (selling, *Br.*), short sale *(US)*, going short *(US)*; ~ **gegen bar** cash sale, cash deal, cash (money) sale, *(Effekten)* spot sale; ~ **gegen Barzahlung und ohne Kundendienst** cash sale, sold over the counter, cash and carry *(US)*, *(Börse)* cash contract; ~ **gegen Barzahlung bei Lieferung** cash-on-delivery sale; ~ **in Bausch und Bogen** sale in gross, loose-leaf (bulk, *US*) sale, sale per aversionem (by the bulk); ~ **auf Besichtigung** sale on inspection; ~ **aus eigenen Beständen** *(Effekten)* long sale; ~ **von Debitoren** selling accounts receivable outright *(US)*, factoring; ~ **ohne Deckung** uncovered sale, bear sale (selling, *Br.*), [selling] short *(US)*, short sales *(US)*; ~ **zu Deckungszwecken** hedging sale; **freihändiger** ~ **von Effekten** sale in the open market; ~ **mit Eigentumsübergang** executed sale; ~ **unter Eigentumsvorbehalt** conditional sale (sales contract), sale subject to an unpaid seller's right of lien; ~ **zu Einzelhandelspreisen** sail at retail, retail sale; ~ **von Flugplätzen für Gruppenreisen** bulk-seat sale *(US)*; ~ **pro forma** sham (pro-forma) sale; ~ **im Freiverkehr** sale in the open market, over-the-counter sale *(US)*; ~ **nach Gewicht** sale according to weight; ~ **mit Gewinn** sale at a profit; ~ **zwecks Gewinnrealisierung** profit-taking sale; ~ **durch den Großhandel** wholesale, sale (selling) by wholesale; ~ **von Grundbesitz** sale of real property (realty); ~ **unter der Hand** private (underhand) sale; ~ **aus zweiter Hand** secondhand sale, resale; ~ **durch einen Hausierer** house-to-house selling; ~ **durch ein Kartell** pool selling; ~ **gegen Kasse** cash sale; ~ **laut Katalog** sale by description; ~ **aufgrund übersandten Katalogs** catalog(ue) (mail-order, *US*) sale; ~ **auf Kommissionsbasis** sale on consignment, consignment (memorandum) sale; ~ **auf Kreditbasis** credit[ing] sale; **direkter** ~ **an Kunden** *(Fabrik)* direct-to-customer selling; ~ **über den Ladentisch** over-the-counter sale; ~ **unter dem Ladentisch** under-the-counter sale; ~ **auf Lieferung** *(Börse)* forward sale, sale for forward (future, *US*) delivery, sale for account; ~ **zur sofortigen Lieferung** sale for prompt delivery; ~ **für zukünftige Lieferung** *(Börse)* sale for the account *(Br.)*; ~ **mit Lieferung nach Bezahlung** deposit sale; ~ **auf Lieferung am folgenden Tag** *(Börse)* regular sale; ~ **am offenen Markt** market overt; ~ **durch Mittelsleute** indirect selling *(US)*; ~ **nach Muster** sale by sample (to pattern); ~ **gegen Nachnahme** cash-on-delivery sale; ~ **an Ort und Stelle** sales on the spot; ~ **durch Postversand** catalog(ue) selling, direct-mail selling *(US)*, selling by direct mail *(US)*; ~ **zu einem festen Preis** outright sale; ~ **zu herabgesetzten Preisen** bargain sale; ~ **um jeden Preis** hard selling; ~ **unter Preis** sale under price, drive *(US)*; ~ **nur an Private** privately sold; ~ **nach Probe** sale by sample, sale on approval; ~ **zur Probe** sale on trial, memorandum sale; ~ **im Rahmen eines Kartells** pool selling; ~ **von Ramschware** rummage sale; ~ **gegen Ratenzahlung** instal(l)ment sale, hire purchase *(Br.)* (deferred-payment, *US*) sale; ~ **auf Rechnung** sale on account, invoiced sale; ~ **auf eigene Rechnung** sale for own account; ~ **auf feste Rechnung** outright sale; ~ **für fremde Rechnung** sale for third account; ~ **von Restauflagen** remainder sale; ~ **mit Rückgaberecht** sale and return, sale with right of redemption; ~ **und gleichzeitiger Rückkauf von Aktien** bed and breakfast operation *(Br.)*; ~ **mit Rückkaufsrecht** sale with privilege (option) of repurchase; ~ **beweglicher Sachen** sale of personal property, sale of chattels; ~ **nach dem Schneeballsystem** pyramid selling; ~ **durch Selbstbedienung** automatic selling; ~ **unter Selbstkosten** sale below cost, selling below cost (under price); ~ **zum Selbstkostenpreis** sale at cost price; ~ **aufgrund einer Sonderermächtigung** sale under a special power; ~ **am Sonntag** Sunday trading; ~ **unter Spekulation auf Baisse** bear sale (selling) *(Br.)*, short sale *(US)*, going short *(US)*; ~ **von Spezialartikeln** specialty selling; ~ **wie es steht und liegt** as is sale, sale with all faults; ~ **auf offener Straße** street vending; ~ **auf Termin** forward sale, selling forward; ~ **mit Verlust (zu Verlustpreisen)** losing (ruinous, sacrifice) sale, selling at a loss, *(Börse)* slaughtering; ~ **zu Verlustpreisen** selling at a loss; ~ **durch Versandgeschäft** catalog(ue) (mail-order, *US*) selling, selling by direct mail *(US)*; ~ **durch Vertreter** house-to-house selling; ~ **durch bestimmte Vertreter** selective selling; ~ **nach erfolgter Verzollung** duty-paid sale; ~ **unter Vorbehalt** conditional sales contract; ~ **mit Vorbehalt des Wiederkaufs** sale with option of repurchase; ~ **wie die Ware steht und liegt** as is sale; ~ **unberechtigt als Markenartikel ausgezeichneter Waren** passing off one's goods as those of another make *(US)*; ~ **feuerbeschädigter Waren** fire sale *(US)*; ~ **im Wege der Versteigerung** sale by *(Br.)* (at, *US*) auction; ~ **unter dem Wert** sacrifice sale; ~ **zum Wochenende** weekend sale; ~ **zu Wohltätigkeitszwecken** sale of work; ~ **auf Zeit** forward time (futures, *US*) sale; ~ **zu verschiedener Zeit und zu verschiedenen Preisen** *(Börse)* split sale; ~ **auf Ziel** credit sale; ~ **ab Zollager** sale ex bond; ~ **mit Zugaben** selling with premium, premium offer *(US)*; ~ **ohne Zugabe** selling without premium; ~ **in der Zwangsversteigerung** forced (sheriff's, execution) sale; ~ **ohne Zwischenhandel** direct selling (sale), sale to the market;

~ **abschließen** to effect (negotiate) a sale, to consummate a deal; **günstigen** ~ **abschließen** to conclude (close) a bargain; **zum** ~ **anbieten** to offer (put up) for sale; ~ **annullieren** to cancel (rescind) a sale; **zum** ~ **anstehen** to be on the auction block; ~ **anzeigen** to advertise a sale; **zum** ~ **aufgeben** to give a selling order; **zum** ~ **aufliegen** to be exposed for sale; **zum** ~ **ausbieten** to declare for public sale; **zum** ~ **auslegen (ausstellen)** to expose (put up, display, exhibit) for sale; **j. mit dem** ~ **betrauen** to entrust s. o. with the sale; ~ **einer Sache bewirken** to make sale of a thing; **zum** ~ **bringen** to put to sale; ~ **zum Abschluß bringen** to negotiate a sale; **mit dem** ~ **einhalten** to suspend the sale; ~ **einstellen** to suspend the sale, to stop selling; **sich zum** ~ **entschließen** to settle on selling; ~ **fördern** to promote sale; **zum** ~ **gelangen** to go on sale; **für den** ~ **herrichten** to adapt for sale; **zum** ~ **kommen** to be sold, to come into the market; ~ **rückgängig machen** to rescind a sale; **bei einem** ~ **mitwirken** to attend a sale; **zum** ~ **staatliche Finanzierungshilfe in Anspruch nehmen** to sell by working through government program(me)s; **zum** ~ **[auf dem Grundstücksmarkt] angeboten sein** to be in the [real-estate] market; **mit dem** ~ **von etw. beauftragt sein** to be entrusted with the selling (sale) of s. th.; **zum** ~ **stehen** to be up for sale; **zum** ~ **stellen** to expose (put up) for sale, to set up for public sale; ~ **tätigen** to negotiate (effect) a sale; **beim** ~ **übergehen** *(Eigentum)* to pass by sale; **zum** ~ **übernehmen** to take on sale; **jem. den** ~ **übertragen** to entrust s. o. with the sale; **vom** ~ **übrigbleiben** to be left over from a sale; **zum** ~ **angeboten werden** to come into the market; ~ **widerrufen** to avoid a sale; **zum freien** ~ **zulassen** to deration *(Br.)*; **vom** ~ **zurücktreten** to rescind a sales contract; **einem vom bevollmächtigten Vertreter getätigten** ~ **zustimmen** to ratify a sale made under power of attorney; **zum** ~ **zwingen** *(Börse)* to squeeze out.

Verkäufe selling, *(Börse)* sales, transactions;

sprungartig angestiegene ~ sales leap; **getätigte** ~ accrued sales; **auf Grund von Warenproben getätigte** ~ sales made on the basis of samples; **konzerneigene** ~ intercompany sales; **matte** ~ dull sales; **unbehinderte (unkontrollierte)** ~ unrestricted sales; **unregelmäßige** ~ *(Börse)* spasmodic selling; **vereinzelte** ~ scattered sellings;

~ **seitens des Auslandes** foreign liquidations; ~ **auf Baisse** bear sale (selling) *(Br.)*, selling stocks short *(US)*; ~ **an Dritte** *(Bilanz)* sales to others; ~ **von Effekten** sale of securities; ~ **im Einkaufszentrum** discount selling; ~ **zwecks Gewinnrealisation** profit-taking sales; ~ **gegen sofortige Kasse und Lieferung** spot trading *(US)*; ~ **innerhalb des Konzerns** intercompany sales; ~ **unter dem Ladentisch** under-the-counter sales; ~ **am offenen Markt** open-market sales; ~ **von Nostro-Effekten** sales from the portfolio; ~ **in Partien** sales by lots; ~ **zum Selbstkostenpreis** marginal sales; ~ **zur Überwindung des Steuertermins** tax sales (selling); ~ **in früherem Umfang** maintenance selling;

~ **weiterhin als Kassageschäfte abwickeln** to continue business on a cash basis; ~ **gut (glatt) aufnehmen** to take sales well; **zu ~n führen** to filter down to sales; **durch** ~ **gedrückt liegen** to be under selling pressure; ~ **erheblich steigern** to speed up the sales process; **seine** ~ **über eine Hausseperiode verteilen** to sell on a slice; ~ **unterhalb der abgesprochenen Preisgrenze vornehmen** to sell out of line; **Neigung zu ~n zeigen** to incline to sell.

Verkaufen selling;

~ **um jeden Preis** hard selling.

verkaufen to sell, to dispose, to vend, to value, to sell out *(sl.)*, *(absetzen)* to market, *(beliefern)* to supply, *(Börse)* to unload, to negotiate, *(realisieren)* to realize, *(umsetzen)* to turn over, *(verfügen)* to dispose of, *(Verkäufer sein)* to be behind the counter;

nicht zu ~ *(Effekten)* not to float; **schwer zu** ~ flat, heavy of sale; **zu** ~ for (on) sale, on offer, *(Anzeige)* to be sold;

jem. etw. ~ to hand s. o. a line; **sich** ~ to sell, *(Prostituierte)* to prostitute o. s.; **unter sich** ~ *(Auktion)* to knock out *(Br.)*; **auf Abruf** ~ to sell for delivery; **mit Abschlag** ~ to sell at reduced prices (a discount); **auf Abzahlung** ~ to sell on hire purchase (the deferred-payment system, *US*); **mit einem Agio** ~ to sell at a premium; **Aktien** ~ to realize shares (stocks); **Aktien aus einem großen Portefeuille** ~ to sell long stock; **anderweitig** ~ to sell elsewhere; **als Ausschuß** ~ to sell as rejects; **gegen bar (Barzahlung)** ~ to sell for cash (ready money, current payment); **in Bausch und Bogen** ~ to sell by bulk, to sell outright; **bestens (zum Bestpreis)** ~ to sell at the best possible rates; **Beteiligung** ~ to sell out one's shares of a business (an interest); **gegen entsprechende Bezahlung** ~ to sell for value; **billig** ~ to sell cheap, to sell at a low figure; **möglichst billig** ~ to go as low as possible; **billiger als die Konkurrenz** ~ to undersell, *(im Ausland)* to dump; **blanko (ohne Deckung)** ~ to go bear *(Br.)* (short, *US*); **Debitoren** ~ to factor; **en detail** ~ to sell [by] retail *(Br.)* (at retail, *US*); **mit einem Disagio** ~ to sell at a discount; **j. für dumm** ~ to sell s. o. a packet; **Effekten mit Verlust** ~ to slaughter stocks; **einzeln** ~ to sell separately; **ohne zu entladen** ~ to sell without breaking the bulk; **Ernte auf dem Halm** ~ to sell the crop standing; **seine Erzeugnisse auf dem ganzen Erdball** ~ to turn the world into a global market place; **fest** ~ to sell outright; **flaschenweise** ~ to sell by the bottle; **flott** ~ to do a brisk trade; **freihändig** ~ to sell offhand (by private contract, treaty); **im Freiverkehr** ~ to sell on the street (over the counter, *US*); **gerichtlich** ~ to sell by subhastation; **sein Geschäft** ~ to dispose of one's business; **seinen Geschäftsanteil** ~ to sell out one's share of a business (an interest); **wegen Geschäftsaufgabe zu** ~ on sale, owner retiring from business; **unter dem Gestehungspreis** ~ to sell below cost price; **nach dem Gewicht** ~ to sell by weight; **mit Gewinn** ~ to sell at a profit (premium, to advantage); **jem. gut gewogen** ~ to give s. o. full measure; **glänzend** ~ to sell to the best advantage; **sich glänzend** ~ *(Buch)* to be booming (a bestseller); **en gros** ~ to sell wholesale *(Br.)* (at wholesale, *US*); **auf der Grundlage der Barzahlung** ~ to sell on a spot basis; **gut** ~ to sell at a high figure, to come to a good market; **sich gut** ~ to be quick of sale, to sell well (quickly), to meet with a ready market, to be current; **auf dem Halm** ~ to sell the crop standing; **unter der Hand** ~ to sell by private bargain (privately); **gegen Kasse** ~ to sell for cash; **im kleinen** ~ to retail; **auf Kommissionsbasis** ~ to sell on commission; **auf Kredit** ~ to sell on credit, to sell on trust (tick, *Br.*); **im Laden** ~ to sell over the counter; **über den Ladentisch** ~ to sell over the counter; **lastenfrei** ~ to sell free from encumbrances; **leer** ~ to go short; **sich leicht** ~ to sell readily; **auf zukünftige Lieferung** ~ to sell forward (for future delivery, *US*, by anticipation, *US*); **loko** ~ to sell for spot delivery; **am offenen Markt** ~ to sell in the open market; **auf dem schwarzen Markt (schwarz)** ~ to sell on the black market; **Maschinen auf Abbruch** ~ to sell machinery as junk; **mehr** ~ to outsell; **meistbietend** ~ to sell to the highest bidder, to put up for sale; **in zu großen Mengen** ~ to oversell; **nach modernsten Methoden** ~ to streamline one's sales representation; **nach Muster** ~ to sell by sample; **an der Nachbörse** ~ to sell on the street (kerb market, *Br.*); **sich nicht** ~ to find no sale; **öffentlich** ~ to sell by (at, *US*) auction; **in kleinen Partien** ~ to sell in dribs and drabs; **partieweise** ~ to sell in lots; **pauschal** ~ to sell on a lump-sum basis; **pfandfrei** ~ to sell free of encumbrances; **auf Prämie** ~ to sell at option; **zu einem festen Preis** ~ to sell outright; **zu herabgesetztem Preis** ~ to sell at a reduced price; **zu den niedrigsten je erzielten Preisen** ~ to sell at an all-time low; **unter dem Preis** ~ to sell under price (the value), to undersell; **preiswert** ~ to sell at a low price; **auf Punkte** ~ to sell under the point system; **mit Rabatt** ~ to sell at a reduction; **im Ramsch** ~ to sell as a job lot; **sich rasch** ~ to find a ready market; **auf Rechnung** ~ to sell for account; **für fremde Rechnung** ~ to sell for third account; **mit Rückkaufsrecht** ~ to sell with right of redemption; **mit Schaden** ~ to sell at a loss; **sich schwer** ~ to go off heavily, to be a drug in the market; **unter Selbstkostenpreis** ~ to sell below cost price (at a loss); **zum Selbstkostenpreis** ~ to sell at cost price; **gegen Sicherheitsleistung** ~ *(Effektendifferenzgeschäft)* to sell on margin; **spottbillig** ~ to sell for a mere song; **seine Stimme** ~ to sell one's vote; **täglich zweihundertfünfzigtausend Stück** ~ to become permanent on sales of 250,000 a day; **stückweise** ~ to sell by the piece; **zum Subskriptionspreis** ~ to sell at the subscription price; **unter Taxe** ~ to sell at reduced prices; **auf Termin** ~ to sell forward (for the account, for the settlement, *Br.*, on future delivery, *US*); **teuer** ~ to sell at a high figure; **etw. zu teuer** ~ to make an overcharge on s. th.; **teurer** ~ to outsell; **[un]verpackt** ~ to sell [un]packed; **mit Verlust** ~ to sell at a loss (disadvantage, discount), to [sell at a] sacrifice; **aus einer Verlustposition** ~ to sell out of a loss situation; **ohne Vorbehalt** ~ to sell outright; **seinen ganzen Vorrat** ~ to sell out; **mit Vorteil** ~ to sell at a premium; **etw. vorteilhaft** ~ to sell s. th. to [good] advantage; **Waren** ~ to sell goods; **als zweitklassige Waren** ~ to sell goods under a secondary label; **im Wege der Auktion** ~ to sell by (at, *US*) auction (at the spear); **im Wege öffentlicher Versteigerung** ~ to sell by subhastation; **unter Wert** ~ to sell below cost price; **wertentsprechend** ~ to sell for value; **an Wiederverkäufer** ~ to sell to the trade; **unter dem Wiederverkaufspreis** ~ to sell at a price below the resale price, to sell below cost price; **wohlfeil** ~ to sell low; **sich wie warme Würstchen** ~ to sell like hot cakes; **auf Zeit** ~ to sell on credit; **auf Ziel** ~ to sell on time;

leerstehendes Haus zu ~ **haben** to have an empty house on one's hands; **sich gut** ~ **lassen** to meet with (find) a ready sale (market), to fetch a good price; **sich gut wieder** ~ **lassen** to have a better resale value; **sich leicht** ~ **lassen** to sell well, to meet with a ready market; **sich nicht** ~ **lassen** to fail to sell, to find no sale; **sich schlecht** ~ **lassen** to come to a bad market; **sich schwer** ~ **lassen** to be dull of sale, to be hard to sell, to run into heavy selling, to sell hard (heavily, badly);

mir kannst Du das nicht ~ go tell it to the marines *(sl.)*.

Verkäufer seller, vendor, vender, bargainer, bargainor, disposer, *(Abgeber)* giver, marketeer, *(Angestellter)* salesman, shop assistant *(Br.)*, salesperson, sales clerk *(US)*, counterman, shopman, *(Einzelhändler)* retailer, *(Ladenbesitzer)* shopkeeper, shop salesman, storekeeper *(US)*, *(Verkaufspersonal)* sales force (people), *(Vertreter)* sales representative, salesman, *(Wiederverkäufer)* dealer;

im nachstehenden ~ **genannt** *(Vertrag)* hereinafter called seller; **beratender** ~ merchandiser *(US)*; **gewerbsmäßiger** ~ common seller; **gutgläubiger** ~ bona-fide seller; **hervorragender (rasanter)** ~ high-powered salesman; **hochqualifizierter** ~ high-cost (-powered) salesman; **stummer** ~ dummy salesman, dispenser; **technischer** ~ sales engineer, technical sales representative; **[teilweise] noch unbefriedigter** ~ unpaid seller; **ungenannter** ~ undisclosed seller; **unseriöser** ~ carpet-bagging salesman; **mir unterstehende** ~ salesmen under my guidance; **unter Eigentumsvorbehalt verkaufender (veräußernder)** ~ conditional seller (vendor);

~ **im Außendienst** field agent, outside (travel(l)ing) salesman; **bester** ~ **dieser Branche** best seller in the trade; ~ **von Hehlerware** stuffer *(sl.)*; ~ **von Lastwagen** van salesman; ~ **einer Rückprämie** giver for a put *(Br.)*; ~ **von Spezialitäten** specialty salesman; ~ **von Stempelmarken** stamp distributor; **stummer** ~ **auf der Theke** counter display container; ~ **einer Vorprämie** taker for a call, seller of a call option *(Br.)*;

zusätzliche ~ **einstellen** to hire extra sales people; **Erfolg als** ~ **haben** to succeed in salesmanship; **zur Verfügung des** ~**s halten** to hold subject to the seller's order; **der geborene** ~ **sein** to be a born salesman; **nur** ~ **im Markt sein** to be all sellers; **als** ~ **tätig sein** to clerk *(US)*.

Verkäuferin saleswoman, shopgirl *(Br.)*, countergirl, shop assistant *(Br.)*, shopmaid *(Br.)*, shopwoman *(US)*, sales lady *(US coll.)*.

Verkäufer|jargon sales patter; ~**kartell** price ring; ~**leistung** salesman's performance; ~**markt** seller's market; ~**merkblatt** salesfolder; ~**pflichten** seller's obligations; ~**schulung** sales meeting; ~**stab** sales force *(US)*; ~**stellung** salesman position; ~**tätigkeit** sales performance; ~**typ** salesman type; ~**vereinigung** sales club.

verkäuflich salable, vendible, on (for) sale, on offer, *(absatzfähig)* marketable, merchantable, *(begebbar)* negotiable, *(realisierbar)* realizable;

frei ~ free on sale; **gut** ~ selling, highly salable, moving; **leicht** ~ current, easy to sell, easily disposed of, commanding a ready market; **nicht** ~ not for sale; **schlecht (schwer)** ~ hard to sell, slow of sale, not moving, dull, frozen;

~ **sein** to be for sale; **jederzeit** ~ **sein** to have a ready market for sale; **schwer** ~ **sein** to go off slowly, to be a drug on the market; ~ **überlassen** to sell;

schlecht ~**er Artikel** drug on the market; **schlecht** ~**es Buch** bad seller; **leicht** ~**e Ware** readily marketable staples.

Verkäuflichkeit salableness, salability, vendibility, *(Absatzfähigkeit)* merchantableness, marketability, *(Begebbarkeit)* negotiability.

Verkaufs|abkommen marketing (distribution) agreement; ~**abrechnung** *(Kommissionär)* sales note, account sales *(US)*; ~**abschluß** actual sale, sale completion, closing the sale; **beim** ~**abschluß** at the time of sale, on making the contract; **fester** ~**abschluß** outright sale; ~**abteilung** selling (sales, distribution) department; ~**agent** selling (sales, *US*, distributing) agent, market representative; ~**agentur** sales agency.

Verkaufsaktion sales representation (campaign);

~ **zu herabgesetzten Preisen** drive *(US)*; ~ **im Vorführungsraum** conference selling;

~ **durchführen** to deliver a sales representation.

Verkaufs|aktivität sales activity (measure); **~analyse** sales (market) analysis; **~angebot** announcement of sale, sales offer, offer [to sell, for sale]; **festes ~angebot** *(Börse)* firm offer; **~anlagen** sales facilities; **spezieller ~anlaß** sales event; **frühjahrsbedingter ~anstieg** spring sales sprint; **plötzlicher (sprunghafter) ~anstieg** jump (surge) in sales, sales jump.

Verkaufsanstrengungen selling (sales) efforts, sales push, sales promotional efforts (practices);
lückenlose ~ complete chain of sales efforts;
energische ~ unternehmen to push one's business; **seine ~ verstärken** to beef up one's sales operations.

Verkaufs|anweisung disposal instruction; **~anzeige** advertisement of a sale, for-sale ad *(US)*; **~apparat** slot machine, one-armed bandit *(US)*, *(Vertrieb)* sales administration (organization).

Verkaufsargument sales argument, selling point;
~e selling points, sales talk;
rationell ansprechendes ~ rational sales argument; **an das Gefühl appellierendes ~** emotional sales argument; **aufdringliche ~e** high-pressure selling arguments.

Verkaufsargumentation purchase proposition.

Verkaufsartikel, gewinnintensive higher-margin items; **teurer ~** big ticket; **zusätzlicher ~** sideline;
~ zurechtmachen to lick an article into shape.

Verkaufsauflage, durchschnittliche average net paid circulation.

Verkaufsauftrag *(Börse)* sell[ing] (sales) order, order to sell, sale application;
~ über eigene Aktien long order; **~ über eigene Effekten** long sale; **~ an mehrere Grundstücksmakler** open listing *(US)*;
~ erteilen to give a selling order.

Verkaufs|auftragsformular vendor's memorandum form; **~aufwendungen** selling expense; **~ausbildung** sales training; **~ausbildungskurs** sales training course; **~ausbildungsprogramm** sales training program(me); **~auslage** sales display; **~ausrüstung** sales kit *(US)*; **~aussage** sales message; **~außendienst** sales force; **~aussichten** sales prospects (outlook), marketing outlook; **~ausstellung** fair, exhibition, exposition *(US)*; **~automat** mechanical seller, automatic vending machine, vendor, automat *(US)*; **~basis** sales base; **~bedingungen** conditions of sale, sales conditions (terms, *US*), marketing conditions; **erschwerende ~bedingungen** onerous selling conditions; **~begabung** sales ability; **~belebung** revival of sale; **~beleg** sales slip (record); **~bemühungen** sales (marketing) efforts; **~berater** sales consultant, marketing adviser; **~berechtigung** right (power) to sell, selling right; **~bereich** sales area (region), marketing (trading) area.

verkaufsbereiter Veräußerer willing seller.

Verkaufs|bereitschaft readiness to sell; **~bericht** sales report; **~bescheinigung** sales sheet (ticket, *US*); **~beschränkung** restriction on sales, selling (sales) restrictions; **~beschränkungen für etw. festsetzen (anordnen)** to place restrictions on the sale of s. th.; **~bestätigung** sales confirmation; **~bezirk** sales (marketing) territory; **~brief** sales letter; **~bude** stand, stall, sales booth, concession stand; **~budget** sales budget; **~büro** sales (selling) office (agency), marketing agency, distribution center *(US)* (centre, *Br.*); **~chancen** sales prospects (possibilities), opening; **~darbietungen auf einer Rednerbühne** platform representations; **seine ~darbietungen den neuesten Erkenntnissen des Verkaufens anpassen** to streamline one's sales representation; **~datum** date sold *(US)*; **~delegation** sales mission; **~dezernat** sales section; **~diagramm** sales chart (curve); **~dichte** *(Einzelhandel)* sales density; **~direktor** sales manager; **unter ~druck liegen** to be under selling pressure; **~durchführung** sales performance; **~einrichtungen** sales devices, marketing facilities; **ambulante ~einrichtung** mobile selling unit; **~entwicklung** development of sales; **~erfahrung** sales (merchandising) experience; **industrielle ~erfahrungen** industrial sales background.

Verkaufserfolg market success;
~ eines Verkäufers sales pitch;
erwartete ~e sales expectancy.

Verkaufsergebnis sales results;
gesamtes ~ sales revenue; **hervorragende ~se** sales records; **rückläufige ~se** sales slump.

Verkaufserlaubnis sales permit, licence to sell.

Verkaufserlös proceeds of sale, sale proceeds, sales profit (receipts, returns), disposal value;
realisierbarer ~ *(Bilanz)* net realizable value *(Br.)*; **aus dem Anlagevermögen realisierte ~e** realized profit on fixed assets;
~ über einen Dreijahreszeitraum verteilen to prorate the sale over a three-year period.

Verkaufs|ermächtigung sales permit; **~ertrag** sales returns; **~erwägungen** sales considerations; **~erwartung** sales expectancy; **~etat** sales (selling-expenses) budget; **~fachleute** marketing people; **~fachmann** market-research (marketing) specialist.

verkaufsfähig merchantable, marketable, salable, merchandisable, *(begebbar)* negotiable;
~e Nettoförderung net merchantable production.

Verkaufs|fähigkeit salability, salableness, selling capacity, marketability, merchantability; **~faktura** sales invoice; **~feldzug** selling (sales, marketing) campaign, marketing drive.

verkaufsfertig ready for sale, salable.

Verkaufs|filiale [sales] branch; **betriebseigene ~filiale** manufacturer's own shop (outlet); **~finanzierung** marketing (sales) financing; **~fläche** sales floor, selling space; **~flaute** stagnancy of business (trade), period of dull sale.

verkaufsförderndes Ereignis sales event; **~e Gesamtmaßnahmen für einen Artikel** marketing of an article; **~e Idee** promotional idea; **~e Maßnahmen** promotional support *(US)*; **~e Mittel** sales promotion aids.

Verkaufsförderung sales promotion, commercial development, merchandising;
auf einen bestimmten Artikel abgestellte ~ product promotion *(US)*; **im Laden betriebene ~** in-store promotion *(US)*; **planmäßige ~** sales drive;
~ von Sammelartikeln continuity promotion *(US)*; **~ durch Warenauslage** visual merchandising;
~ vor dem Marktabsatz vornehmen to presell.

Verkaufsförderungs|etat sales-promotion budget *(US)*; **~hilfe** sales-promotion aid; **~maßnahmen** sales kit *(US)*; **~material** promotion matter *(US)*; **~mittel** point-of-purchase display; **~plan** sales-promotion campaign *(US)*, merchandising plan; **~verfahren** sales-promotion technique *(US)*.

Verkaufs|formalitäten sales terms *(US)*; **~forschung** marketing research; **~funktion** selling function; **~garantie** sales garantee.

Verkaufsgebiet sales (selling, marketing) area, area of destination, trading (selling) territory, *(Vertreter)* sales (travelling) territory;
ausländische ~e foreign markets; **eingegrenztes (enges) ~** narrow sales area; **natürliches ~** natural marketing area;
~ mit primärer Verantwortlichkeit *(Kartellrecht)* area of primary responsibility;
~e erschließen to open up new markets; **~ zurückerobern** to win back (recover) a market.

Verkaufs|gebühr sales charge; **~gegenstand** item, article of sale; **~gegenstände** saleswork; **~gegenstand beschädigen** to injure an article of merchandise; **~gelände** sales location; **~gelegenheit** sales opportunity; **günstige ~gelegenheit vorübergehen lassen** to lose a market; **~gemeinschaft** sales combine (group), marketing association; **~genehmigung** sales permit, licence to sell; **~genie** star (top) salesman; **~genossenschaft** cooperative selling (sales) association, marketing cooperative, *(Landwirte)* producer cooperative; **~geschäfte** sales transactions; **~geschäfte vermitteln** to negotiate contracts of sale; **~gesellschaft** sales association (company), agency company, distributing agency; **~gesellschaft von Firmenmänteln** shell company; **~gesichtspunkt** sales approach (angle); **~gesichtspunkte** selling points; **~gespräch** sales (dealer) talk, selling conversation; **~gewandtheit** [personal] salesmanship; **~gewicht** selling weight; **~gewinn** sales profit; **~gewohnheit** selling habit; **~grenze** sales limit; **~grundlage** sales base; **~gruppe** sales team; **~handbuch** sales manual; **~herrichtung** adapting for sale; **~hilfe** selling (display, dealer) aid, sales tool, promotion matter, visual; **~hinweis** sales notice; **~idee** sales idea; **~impuls** sales incentive; **~index** retail-price index; **~ingenieur** sales engineer; **~interesse** selling interest, inclination to sell; **~interessenten** would-be sellers; **~interview** sales interview; **~jahr** sales year; **~kalkulation** sales estimate; **~kampagne** sales campaign (drive); **~kanone** top (star) salesman; **~kapazität** sales capacity; **~kartell** sales syndicate, price ring; **~katalog** sale catalog(ue), shopping guide; **derzeit gültiger ~katalog** current catalog(ue); **~kommission** selling brokerage, commission on sales effected; **~kommissionär** selling agent, commission merchant, factor; **~konsortium** *(Emission)* selling group, underwriting (selling) syndicate; **~kontenbuch** sales ledger; **~kontingent** sales (market, marketing) quota; **regionales ~kontingent** territory quota; **~kontingentierung** rationing of sales; **~konto** sales (trading) account; **~kontor** selling agency; **~kontrolle** sales progress control, orderly marketing *(US)*; **~konzeption** marketing conception; **~konzession** licence (license, *US*) to sell; **~konzession für etw. haben** to be licensed to sell s. th.; ~**kosten** selling costs; **unmittelbare ~kosten** direct selling costs; ~-, **Verwaltungs- und allgemeine Kosten** *(Bilanz)* administrative and general selling expenses *(US)*; ~**kraft** shop assistant; ~**kunst** selling technique, salesmanship; ~**kurs** asked price, *(Devisen)* selling rate; ~**kurs ohne Deckungserhöhung** *(Börse)* exhaust price *(US)*; ~**kurve** sales curve (chart), distribution curve; ~**laden** shop *(Br.)*, store *(US)*; **betriebseigener (werkseigener) ~laden** own (industrial) retail store (shop); **an eine Firma gebundener ~laden** tie-up shop; ~**lager** stock, depot *(Br.)*; ~**land** country of origin; ~**lawine** avalanche of selling; ~**lehrgang** sales training course; ~**leistung** sales (market) performance, sales vigo(u)r; ~**leiter** sales executive (supervisor, manager, promoter), director of sales, *(Markenartikel)* brand manager; **einfallsreicher ~leiter** aggressive sales manager; ~**leitung** sales management; ~**lenkung** sales control, control of the market; ~**limit** selling limit; ~**liste** sales list; ~**literatur** sales literature; ~**lizenz** licence to sell, selling licence; ~**lokal** salesroom; ~**lücke** sales lag; ~**makler** selling broker; ~**mannschaft** sales force; ~**marge** profit margin; ~**markt** market, outlet; ~**messe** fair.

Verkaufsmethode sales (selling) method;
aggressive ~ high-pressure salesmanship; **anschauliche** ~ direct-to-point selling; **suggestive** ~ suggestion selling; **unaufdringliche** ~ low-pressure selling; **zielbewußte** ~ high-pressure salesmanship;
~ **zur Beschaffung postalischer Aufträge** direct-mail marketing.

Verkaufs|mischung sales mix *(US)*; ~**modalitäten** terms of sale, sale terms; ~**modell** mockup.

Verkaufsmöglichkeit sales opportunity, selling possibility, opening;
mit sicheren ~en certain to sell;
beschränkte ~en narrow market;
neue ~en entwickeln to develop selling; **dem Verleger überall ~en gewähren** to grant to the publisher on an open market basis; **sich ~en entgehen lassen** to miss a market; **für ~en auf Empfang stehen** to be an antenna for possible sales.

Verkaufs|monopol sales monopoly; ~**neigung** inclination (propensity) to sell; **steigende ~neigung** wave of selling; ~**netz** distribution network; ~- **und Kundendienstnetz** sales and service forces; ~**niederlage** stock, depot *(Br.)*; ~**niederlassung** sales branch (agency); ~**nota** bill of sale, prompt note, sales note *(US)*; ~**nummer** number; ~**objekt** subject of sale.

verkaufsoffener Sonnabend late-closing Saturday.

Verkaufs|offerte sales offer; ~**option** seller's option, option to sell, *(Börse)* put option; ~**order** sales (selling) order, sell order, order to sell; **limitierte ~order** selling stop order *(US)*; **Kauf- und ~orders zu verschiedenen Zeiten geben** *(Börse)* to scale *(US)*; ~**organisation** sales (selling) organization (agency), field sales force; ~**organisation einer Tochtergesellschaft** subsidiary sales organization; ~**organisator** sales organizer; ~**ort** point of purchase; ~**pavillon** kiosk, display stand; ~**personal** sales force (people, *US*, personnel), selling (sales) staff; ~**plan** plan of distribution, selling (distribution) plan, merchandising (selling) scheme; **strategischen ~plan ausarbeiten** to map out a sales strategy; ~**planung** sales planning, marketing planning (mix, *US*); ~**platz** point of purchase; ~**plus** sales plus.

Verkaufspolitik merchandising (sales, selling) policy, sales approach *(US)*, *(Verkäufer)* sales pitch, marketing;
aggressive ~ hard (high-pressure) selling; **individuelle** ~ direct marketing; **schöpferische** ~ innovative marketing; **selektive** ~ selective marketing; **übertriebene** ~ overselling; **zurückhaltende** ~ policy of restraint in sales;
~ **festlegen** to formulate a merchandising policy.

Verkaufs|position bargaining position; ~**potential** sales potential; ~**praktikant** sales trainee; ~**praktiken** sales techniques, marketing practices, sales promotional practices *(US)*; **reißerische ~praktiken** commercial rip-offs; **unlautere ~praktiken** unfair salesmanship; ~**prämie** sales premium, push money, spiff *(Br., sl.)*; ~**praxis** sales experience.

Verkaufspreis sales (selling, disposal, output) price, *(Börse)* asked (selling, realization) price, *(für Investmentanteile)* offering price, *(Marktwert)* market value;
festgesetzter ~ fixed selling price; **vom Hersteller festgesetzte ~e** prices laid down by the manufacturer; **höchster** ~ maximum selling price; **die Herstellungskosten nur wenig übersteigender** ~ close price;
~ **bei Eingang des Fahrzeugs am Versandort** on-truck sales price; ~ **bei Eintreffen der Ware** to-arrive sales price; ~ **ab Fabrik** manufacturer's sales price; ~ **einschließlich Fracht- und Entladungskosten** landed terms; ~ **ab Schacht** pithead price; **mit einem ~ auszeichnen** to mark with a selling price; ~ **für ein Grundstück festsetzen** to price a property; ~ **für ein Haus festsetzen** to set the price of a house; ~**e heraufsetzen** to up one's selling prices; ~ **kalkulieren** to calculate the selling price; **sich den ~ eines Hauses vorbehalten** to put a reserve price on a house;
~**berechnung** calculation of the selling price; ~**politik** pricing policy.

Verkaufs|prinzipien selling principles; ~**problem** marketing problem; ~**produkt** marketing (marketable) product; ~**produktion** marketable production; ~**prognose** sales forecast[ing].

Verkaufsprogramm marketing program(me);
gesamtes ~ range of goods; **globales** ~ overall selling plan; **sein ~ darauf abstellen** to tailor one's sales representation.

Verkaufs|projekt sales proposition; ~**proportion** sales proportion; ~**prospekt** sales brochure (literature), selling prospect; ~**provision** commission on sales effected, seller's (selling) commission, selling brokerage, commission paid on sales, *(Kapitalanlagegesellschaft)* underwriting provision; ~**psychologie** sales psychology; ~**punkte** selling points; ~**quittung** sales check *(US)*; ~**quote** sales quota, sales proportion; ~**rabatt** sales discount (allowance), rebate (rebatement) on sales; ~**raum** salesroom, saleroom *(Br.)*, warehouse room, wareroom, *(Produktenbörse)* commercial sale room; ~**rechnung** sale invoice, *(Einzelhandel)* bill, account, sales ticket *(US)*, *(Großhandel)* invoice, *(Kommissionsgeschäft)* sales account, account sales *(US)*; **fingierte ~rechnung** pro-forma account sales; ~**regulierung** sales control; ~**reinerlös** net sales proceeds; ~**reklame** sales promotion (publicity), consumer advertising, *(im Laden)* point of purchase advertising; ~**rekord** sales record; ~**resultat** sales results; ~**richtlinien** principles of selling; ~**richtung** destination of goods sold; ~**risiko** merchandising risk; ~**rückgang** fall (letdown, decline) in sales, sales drop; ~**saison** selling (marketing) season; ~**schätzung** sales estimate; ~**schein** sale sheet, sales warrant; ~**schlager** big (hot) seller, article of quick sale, draw-card, hit *(US)*, quick-selling line, *(Buch)* best seller, knockout *(sl.)*; **kein großer ~schlager sein** not to be a big runner; ~**schulung** sales test (training); ~**schwankungen** sales fluctuation; ~**schwierigkeiten** sales difficulties; **auf der ~seite** on the sales side; ~**signal** sell signal; ~**situation** sell condition; ~**soll-Quotenmethode** *(Werbeetat)* unit-of-sales method; ~**sollsumme** sales target; ~**spanne** margin on sales; ~**spesen** selling expenses, *(Kapitalanlagegesellschaft)* sales load, redemption cost; ~**spezialist** marketing specialist; ~**spielraum** *(Börse)* trading range; ~**stab** selling staff, sales force (people, *US*, personnel); ~**stab mit den neuesten Informationen versehen** to update the sales forces; ~**stand** stall, stand, sales booth, bulk, *(Zeitungen)* news-stand; ~**stand aufschlagen** to pitch; ~**ständer** rack, counter display container; **werbemäßiger ~standpunkt** advertising sales angle (approach).

verkaufsstark *(Anzeige)* sales-boosting.

Verkaufsstatistik sales (distributive) statistics.

verkaufssteigernde Anstrengungen sales promotional efforts *(US)*.

Verkaufssteigerung sales increase.

Verkaufsstelle sales agency (outlet, *US*), *(Einzelhandel)* retail outlet, *(Fahrkarten)* ticket office *(US)*, *(im Laden)* selling point, *(Vorverkauf)* booking *(Br.)* (box) office;
anerkannte ~ established retail outlet; **fabrikeigene** ~ manufacturer's sales branch; **fahrbare** ~ mobile shop, shopmobile;
~ **für ausrangiertes Heeresgut** army surplus store.

Verkaufs|stellung sales position; ~**steuer** purchase tax *(Br.)*, sales tax *(US)*; **Vertriebs- und ~steuerung** merchandise technique, merchandising; ~**stockung** slowing down of sales, stagnation in trade; ~**stopp** stop order; ~**stornierung** sales cancellation; ~**studie** marketing [research] study; ~**stunden** selling (shopping) hours; ~**summe** selling price; ~**syndikat** sales (sellers' cartel) syndicate; ~**system** selling plan; **bargeldloses ~system** credit coupon plan; ~**tage** selling days; ~**tätigkeit** sales performance (activity); **erfolgreiche ~tätigkeit** effective selling; **nichtpermanente ~tätigkeit** hawking; ~**team** sales team; ~**technik** salesmanship, sales (selling) technique; **energische ~technik** hard sell *(US)*; **rasante ~technik** high-pressure salesmanship.

verkaufstechnisch, hervorragende ~e Fähigkeiten marketing leadership.

Verkaufs|tendenz sales trend, trend of the market; ~**termin** on-sale (offering) date; ~**terminologie** marketing terminology; ~**tisch für Sonderangebote** bargain counter; ~**tour** sales trip; **bestimmte ~tournee** definite route; **feste ~tourneen festlegen** to build regular routes; ~**transaktion** sales transaction; ~**tratte** sales bill; **für den Einzelfall vorgesehene ~treuhänderschaft** ad hoc trust for sale; ~**trick** sales gimmicks *(US sl.)*; ~**tüchtigkeit** salesmanship; ~**überwachung** sales supervision; ~**umfang** sales volume, volume of trade; ~**umsatz** turnover; ~**umsatzplan** sales budget; ~**unkosten** sales (selling) expense, cost of sales, marketing costs, *(Versicherungsgesellschaft)* acquisition cost (expense); ~**unterlage** sales record; ~**unterstützung** sales aid; **bildliche** ~**unterstützung** visual aid; ~**unterstützung beim Einzelhandel** merchandising support; ~**urkunde** bill of sale; ~**veranstaltung** trade fair; ~**verband** selling group; ~**verbot** restraint on alienation, sales ban (prohibition); ~**vereinbarung** agreement for sale, selling arrangement; ~**verfahren** selling process; ~**verhalten** selling attitude; ~**verpackung** sales package; ~**verpflichtung** *(Börse)* commitment *(US)*; ~**versprechen** promise to sell; ~**vertrag** agreement for sale, sales contract, contract of sale, sales note *(US)*; ~**vertretung** sales agency; **alleinige** ~**vertretung** sole agency; ~**vollmacht** power of sale, authority to sell; ~**volumen** sales volume, volume of sales; ~**voraussage** sales forecast; ~**vorbereitung durch Vertriebsplanung** merchandising; ~**vorführung** sales demonstration; ~**vorgang** sales process; ~**vorschriften** conditions of sale; ~**wagen** mobile shop; ~**wege** channels of distribution; ~**welle** wave of selling, selling wave; ~**werbung** sales promotion (publicity), consumer advertising; **breitgestreute** ~**werbung** large-scale consumer advertising; ~**wert** sale (salable, marketable, selling) value, price, *(Haus)* free market value, fair cash market value; **gewöhnlicher** ~**wert** market selling value, salable value; **realisierbarer** ~**wert** net realizable value *(Br.)*; ~**wettbewerb** sales contest; **auf starke** ~**widerstände stoßen** to meet with stiff sales resistance; ~**wirkung** pull; ~**woche** white sale; ~**zahlen** sales (market) data; ~**zeiten** shop (business) hours; ~**zentrale** distribution center *(US)* (centre, *Br.*); ~**zettel** sales slip (ticket, *US*); ~**ziel** sales objective (target); ~**ziffern** sales data (figures); ~**zwang** compulsory sale.

verkauft sold, disposed of;
am meisten ~ best-selling; **bereits** ~ sold up; **freihändig** ~ over the counter; **gegen bar** ~ sold for cash; **meistbietend** ~ sold by auction; **nach Gewicht** ~ sold by weight; **nicht** ~ unsold; **verraten und** ~ **sein** to have been sold down the river; ~ **werden** to be sold, to sell, to go; **als Ganzes oder in Parzellen** ~ **werden** to be sold as a whole or in sections; **öffentlich** ~ **werden** to be sold in public;
~**e Auflage** total net paid circulation.

Verkehr traffic, *(Bahn)* service, *(Beförderung)* transport, transportation *(US)*, *(Beziehungen)* intercourse, dealings, truck, *(Börse)* trading, market, doing, dealings, *(Handel)* trade, commerce, *(Umgang)* association, intercourse, *(Umlauf)* circulation, *(Umsätze)* business, dealings, transactions, sales, *(Verbindung)* communication, *(Verkehrsdienst)* service;
außer ~ *(Banknoten)* withdrawn from circulation; **bei Eröffnung des** ~**s** *(Börse)* at the opening of the market; **für den** ~ **geeignet** trafficable; **für den öffentlichen** ~ **freigegeben** open to the public; **im freien** ~ *(Börse)* on the curb (kerb, *Br.*) market, in outside (unofficial, *Br.*) trading; **mit starkem** ~ **belastet** traffic-laden; **ordnungsgemäß in den** ~ **gebracht** *(Patent)* sent into the ordinary channels of trade; **vom** ~ **verstopft** congested with traffic;
amtlicher ~ interoffice dealings; **ausgedehnter** ~ extensive trade; **außerbörslicher** ~ off-board (over-the-counter, *US*) trading; **bargeldloser** ~ transfer business, clearing system, cashless payments; **nicht mehr zu bewältigender** ~ overflow traffic; **brieflicher** ~ correspondence; **diplomatischer** ~ diplomatic intercourse; **direkter** ~ direct (through) communication; **dritter** ~ congested traffic; **durchschnittlicher** ~ normal run of traffic; **ehebrecherischer** ~ adulterous intercourse; **ehelicher** ~ marital intercourse; **einspuriger** ~ one-way traffic; **entgegenkommender** ~ oncoming traffic; **fahrplanmäßiger** ~ regular (scheduled, *US*) service; **fließender** ~ fast-moving traffic; **freier** ~ free trade; **geringer** ~ *(Börse)* little doing (business); **gesellschaftlicher** ~ social intercourse, conversation; **gewerblicher** ~ commercial transport; **grenzüberschreitender** ~ goods traffic across the border; **großstädtischer** ~ big-city traffic (transport); **innerstaatlicher** ~ intrastate transport *(US)*; **innerstädtischer** ~ traffic in towns, local traffic; **lebhafter** ~ *(Börse)* lively dealings; **öffentlicher** ~ public transport (transportation, *US*); **ruhender** ~ stationary vehicles; **schwacher** ~ light traffic; **städtischer** ~ municipal transit; **starker** ~ heavy traffic, great deal of traffic on the road; **telegrafischer** ~ telegraphic communication; **umgeleiteter** ~ diverted traffic *(Br.)*, derouted traffic *(US)*; **verstopfter** ~ congested traffic; **vertrauter** ~ intercommunion; **vierspuriger** ~ four-lane traffic; **zähflüssiger** ~ slow-moving traffic; **geschäftlicher** ~ **mit feindlichen Ausländern** trading with the enemy; ~ **von Chartermaschinen** charter traffic; ~ **mit Grundstücken** property dealing; **persönlicher** ~ **mit den Kindern** *(bei Ehescheidung)* personal access to the children; ~ **im Stadtzentrum** downtown traffic *(US)*; ~ **in leicht verderblichen Waren** perishable traffic;
~ **mit jem. abbrechen** to break with s. o., to drop s. one's acquaintance; **jeden** ~ **mit jem. abbrechen** to break off all communication with s. o.; **Waren aus dem Zollager zum freien** ~ **abfertigen** to withdraw goods from warehouse for consumption; **gegen die Lähmung des gesamten** ~**s angehen** to stave off traffic paralysis; ~ **anhalten** to suspend the traffic; ~ **aufhalten** to delay (block, hold up) traffic; **mehr** ~ **aufnehmen** to move more traffic; ~ **glatt (ohne Schwierigkeit) aufnehmen** to cream off traffic; **dem** ~ **ausweichen** to dodge the traffic; ~ **behindern** to disturb (impede, block, congest, obstruct, hold up) traffic, to cause an obstruction; **fremdes Fahrzeug im** ~ **behindern** to obstruct another car; ~ **bewältigen** to handle (cope with) traffic; **in den** ~ **bringen** to put into circulation, to introduce, to market; **Banknoten in den** ~ **bringen** to issue bank notes; **Effekten in** ~ **bringen** to issue (market, *US*) securities; **Falschgeld in den** ~ **bringen** to utter false notes; **Münzen in** ~ **bringen** to put a coinage in circulation; **Ware in den** ~ **bringen** to put an article on the market; ~ **durcheinanderbringen** to dislocate traffic; **sich in den fließenden** ~ **einreihen** to filter into the streaming traffic, to get into the line of traffic; **in den** ~ **einschleusen** to channelize traffic; ~ **einstellen** to stop traffic; ~ **entwirren** to disentangle traffic; **Straße für den öffentlichen** ~ **freigeben** to open a road for traffic; **in den fließenden** ~ **hineinfahren** to cut in; ~ **lahmlegen** to obstruct the traffic; ~ **regeln** to direct (regulate, control) traffic; **aus dem** ~ **gezogen sein** *(Fahrzeug)* to be off the road; **außer** ~ **setzen** *(Banknoten)* to withdraw from circulation; **für den** ~ **sperren** to close to traffic; **im** ~ **stehen** to communicate; **mit jem. in brieflichem** ~ **stehen** to stand in correspondence; ~ **steuern** to channelize traffic; **vorsichtig durch den** ~ **steuern** to nose one's way through the traffic; **in den freien** ~ **überführen** *(Zollwaren)* to enter into the channels of distribution; **Straße dem** ~ **übergeben** to open a road for traffic; ~ **umgehen** to bypass traffic; ~ **umleiten** to divert traffic *(Br.)*, to detour *(US)*; ~ **unterbrechen** to intercept traffic; **aus dem** ~ **ziehen** *(Fahrzeug)* to take off the road (traffic), *(Geld)* to withdraw (recall) from circulation, *(Bargeld)* to immobilize; **Obligationen aus dem** ~ **ziehen** to retire bonds; **Auto zum** ~ **zulassen** to license a car.

verkehren *(Bahn, Bus)* to go, to run, to ply, to be operated, *(Handel treiben)* to trade, to traffic, *(Sinn)* to pervert, *(Umgang pflegen)* to keep company, to commerce, to consort, to have intercourse, to affiliate *(US)*;
mit jem. ~ to deal with s. o., to have dealings with s. o.; **nicht mit jem.** ~ not to be on visiting terms with s. o.; **brieflich mit jem.** ~ to correspond with s. o.; **fahrplanmäßig** ~ to run pretty well on time, to run on schedule *(US)*; **auf dem Fluß** ~ *(Fähre)* to ply the river; **freundschaftlich** ~ to be on a friendly footing (terms), to hobnob (intimately), to pal up; **ins Gegenteil** ~ to spell backward; **in der besten Gesellschaft** ~ to mix in the best society; **gesellschaftlich** ~ to mingle with the crowd; **mit intelligenten Leuten** ~ to associate with intelligent people; **in einem Lokal** ~ to frequent a restaurant (public house); **zwischen London und New York** ~ to trade between London and New York; **alle zehn Minuten** ~ to run every ten minutes; **heute nicht** ~ not to be running today; **pünktlich** ~ to run on time; **mit seinesgleichen** ~ to consort with one's equals; **mit jem. wie mit seinesgleichen** ~ to treat s. o. on a footing of equality; **Sinn ins Gegenteil** ~ to reverse the meaning; **stundenweise** ~ *(Bus)* to run every hour; **Tag und Nacht** ~ to run day and night; **in zwei Teilzügen** ~ to run in two sections; **ungezwungen mit jem.** ~ to be at ease with s. o.; **nur unregelmäßig** ~ to run by fits and starts; **zweimal wöchentlich** ~ to run twice a week; **zurückhaltend mit jem.** ~ to stand on ceremony with s. o.

Verkehrs|abgaben traffic duty; ~**abkommen** traffic arrangement, transport treaty; ~**abnahme** decrease in traffic; ~**abteilung** transportation (traffic) department; ~**abwicklung** traffic operation (handling); ~**achse** transport axis; ~**ader** thoroughfare, arterial road, *(Handel)* artery of commerce.

Verkehrsampel traffic lights (beacon, *Br.*, signals), signal light, stop-go light *(US)*, *(Hinweisschild)* signals ahead;
Zufahrt kontrollierende ~ access-control light; **versetzbare** ~ mobile traffic light;
sich nach einer ~ **richten** to comply with a traffic signal;
~**anlage** traffic-light control.

Verkehrs|amt tourist office (bureau, *US*); **~andrang** heavy traffic, rush hours; **morgendlicher ~andrang** morning's traffic crush; **mit einem großen ~andrang in den Sommermonaten rechnen** to prepare for heavy summer traffic; **~anhäufung, ~ansammlung** traffic congestion, congestion of traffic; **~anlagen** transportation facilities; **~anordnung** circulation pattern; **mehrstöckige ~anordnung** multilevel circulation pattern; **~anschauung** normal view; **öffentliche ~anstalt** transit company, common carrier *(US)*; **~apparat** communication (transportation) system.

verkehrsarm quiet;
~e Zeit slack hours.

Verkehrs|aufkommen traffic generation, volume of traffic, *(Verkehrswirtschaft)* transportation money; **~ausgaben** traffic expenditure, fares; **~auskunft** tourist information; **~ausschuß** transportation committee; **~band** *(Radio)* citizen's band; **gemeinwirtschaftliche ~bedienung** transport provision, common-carrier principle *(US)*.

verkehrsbedingtes Dahinschleichen crawling in traffic.

Verkehrs|bedingungen traffic conditions; **~bedürfnisse** traffic requirements, transportation needs.

Verkehrsbehinderung impediment to traffic, obstruction (disturbance) of traffic (trade), *(auf öffentlichen Straßen)* obstructing a highway;
vorsätzliche ~ wilful obstruction of traffic;
~ eines fremden Fahrzeugs obstruction of another car;
~ darstellen to obstruct a highway; **sich der ~ strafbar machen** to be guilty of obstruction.

Verkehrs|behörden transport authorities *(US)*; **~belegenheit** proximity to transportation; **~benutzung** traffic use; **~bericht** traffic news, motoring report on road conditions, *(Bahn)* traffic return; **~beschränkungen** traffic restrictions (restraints); **~bestimmungen** traffic regulations; **sich um ~bestimmungen einfach nicht kümmern** to be negligent of traffic rules; **~betrieb** transport service, transportation, *(Firma)* transport undertaking, transportation company; **öffentliche ~betriebe** public transport undertakings (operators); **städtische ~betriebe** city transports; **~bewältigung** handling of traffic, traffic handling (operation); **maximale ~bewältigung** maximum through-put of traffic; **~büro** tourist office (bureau, *US*); **~chaos** breakdown of communications, traffic snarl *(US)*, *(Bahn)* breakdown on the railway; **~delikt** traffic offence (violation), motoring offence *(Br.)*, traffic case *(US)*, moving violation *(US)*; **~dezernat** traffic department; **~dezernent** goods manager, freight handler, traffic director; **~dichte** traffic on a road, density of traffic, traffic density; **~dichte im Güterfernverkehr** freight density, density of freight; **~dichte im Personenverkehr** density of passengers, passenger density; **~dienst** point duty *(Br.)*; **regelmäßiger ~dienst** regular service; **~dienstleiter** passenger manager; **~direktor** traffic director; **~disziplin** courtesy of the road, road behavio(u)r, traffic discipline; **~durcheinander** dislocation of traffic, traffic jam; **~durchsage** *(Radio)* traffic announcement; **~einheit** *(Börse)* unit of trade; **~einnahmen** [revenue from] traffic, traffic receipts; **~einrichtung** transport equipment (facilities, installations), transportation facilities; **~endpunkt** terminus *(Br.)*, terminal *(US)*; **~engpaß** transport bottleneck; **~entwicklung** transport development, development of transportation; **explosionsartige ~entwicklung** traffic explosion; **~entwirrung** disentanglement of traffic; **~erfahrung** driving experience; **~erleichterungen** transport (transportation, *US*, traffic) facilities, derestrictions of traffic, *(Handel)* trade facilities; **~ermittlung** determination of traffic; **~erschwernisse** traffic restrictions (restraints), *(Handel)* trade restrictions; **~erziehung** road safety campaign, safety education, traffic education *(US)*, kerb drill; **~erziehungsprogramm** campaign for road safety; **~experte** transportation expert.

verkehrsfähig marketable, *(begebbar)* negotiable, *(Geld)* current;
nicht ~ nonnegotiable, nonmarketable.

Verkehrs|fähigkeit marketability, *(Begebbarkeit)* negotiability, *(Währung)* currency; **~fliegerei** commercial aviation; **~flughafen** [commercial] airport, civil airfield; **~flugzeug** civil airliner, transporter, commercial plane, transport aircraft (plane), passenger plane; **~fluß** flow of traffic; **~fluß behindern** to inconvenience traffic.

verkehrsfrei closed to traffic;
~e Zone pedestrian zone (precinct).

Verkehrs|frequenzband communication band, citizen's band; funk road-traffic broadcasting; **~funknetz** mobile radiotelephone scheme.

verkehrsgefährdet endangered by the traffic.

Verkehrs|gefährdung dangerous (reckless) driving; **wegen ~gefährdung angeklagt sein** to be charged with dangerous driving; **wegen ~gefährdung vorbestraft sein** to have a conviction for dangerous driving; **~gericht** magistrate's (traffic) court; **~gesellschaft** transit (communication) company, transportation agency *(US)*; **öffentliche ~gesellschaft** common carrier *(US)*; **~gesetz** Transport Act *(Br.)*, Road Traffic Act *(US)*; **~gesetzgebung** traffic legislation; **~gewalt** police power; **~gewerbe** traffic service (interests), transport (transportation, *US*) business; **~gleichung** quantity equation; **~größe** density (volume) of traffic, traffic density; **solide ~grundsätze** communicative justice; **~gunst** accessibility.

verkehrsgünstig accessible;
~ gelegen in a desirable location;
~ gelegene Stadt accessible town.

Verkehrs|gürtel belt line *(US)*; **~güter** shopping goods *(US)*; **~haftpflicht** liability of common carrier *(US)*; **~häufigkeit** frequency; **~hindernis** impediment (obstruction) on the road, *(Bahn)* obstruction on the line, *(Engpaß)* bottleneck; **~hinweis** motoring report on road conditions, traffic direction, *(Schild)* road sign; **~hubschrauber** traffic helicopter; **~hypothek** common-law (ordinary) mortgage; **~industrie** transport industries; **~information** motoring information; **~ingenieur** transport engineer; **~insel** safety island (isle, zone), street (traffic) island, refuge *(Br.)*; **~investitionen** capital expenditure on transport and communications; **~knotenpunkt** traffic junction (center, *US*, centre, *Br.*); **~kontrolle** control of traffic, traffic control, road check; **~kontrolleur** traffic warden *(Br.)*; **~koordination** coordination of traffic; **~kreisel** traffic circle *(US)*, roundabout *(Br.)*, rotary; **~lage** traffic (road) situation; **zufriedenstellende ~lage** adequacy of communications; **~lärm** traffic noise; **~last** *(Brücke)* live load; **~leben** traffic.

verkehrsleer empty of traffic.

Verkehrs|leistung volume of traffic, transport services; **~leiter** traffic director; **~lenkung** control of traffic, traffic control; **~licht** traffic light (signal); **~linie** life line, transportation line; **~linie betreiben** to operate an airline; **~luftfahrt** commercial airline, commercial (civil) aviation; **~luftfahrtabkommen** civil aviation agreement; **Internationale ~luftfahrtorganisation** International Civil Aviation Organization; **~maschine** transport aircraft; **~minister** Minister of Transport *(Br.)*, Transportation Minister *(US)*, Secretary of State for Transport *(Br.)* (Transportation, *US*), transport secretary *(Br.)*, Minister of Shipping and Transport *(Australia)*; **~ministerium** Ministry (Department) of Transport [and Aviation] *(Br.)*, Transportation Department *(US)*, Department of Transportation *(US)*.

Verkehrsmittel vehicle, *(pl.)* [means of] communication, conveyance, [means of] transportation *(US)*, transportation means *(US)*;
mit öffentlichem ~ by public transport;
billiges ~ jitney *(US)*; **öffentliches ~** public (transit) vehicle, public transportation *(US)*, common carrier *(US)*; **städtisches ~** city transportation *(US)*;
öffentliche ~ benutzen to ride in public transport; **von den öffentlichen ~n unabhängig sein** to be independent of trains, trams and buses;
~werbung transport (transportation, *US*) advertising, poster advertising.

Verkehrs|modernisierung modernization of communications; **gute ~möglichkeiten** ease of transport; **~monopol** transportation monopoly; **~nachfrage** traffic requirements, transportation needs; **~nachrichten** motoring report on road conditions.

verkehrsnah gelegen in a desirable location.

Verkehrs|netz communications (road) system *(Br.)*, transport network, transportation network *(US)*, *(Bahn)* network of railways (railroads, *US*); **sich über das ganze ~netz erstreckend** system-wide; **~nummer** *(Buchhandel)* transaction reference number; **~ökonom** transport economist; **~opfer** victim of a motor accident, *(pl.)* toll of the roads, casualty; **~ordnung** Highway Code *(Br.)*, Uniform Traffic Code *(US)*; **~- und Verkaufsordnung des Buchhandels** transaction and sale regulations of the book trade; **~plan** *(Bahnhof, Flugplatz)* timetable; **~planer** traffic engineer; **~planung** traffic (transport, transportation) planning *(US)*; **~podest** traffic policeman's raised platform, traffic control tower; **~politik** transport (traffic, transportation, *US*) policy; **gemeinsam ~politik treiben** to pool traffic; **~polizei** traffic-control squads *(US)*, traffic police *(coll.)*; **~polizist** traffic policeman (constable, officer, cop), police officer controlling traffic, point policeman *(Br.)*, pointsman *(Br.)*; **motorisierter ~polizist** speed cop *(US coll.)*, easy rider, wheeler *(sl.)*; **~posten** traffic post; ~**potential** traffic potential; ~**privilegien** privilege for communication; ~**problem** traffic (transportation) problem; ~**probleme** traffic problems; ~**prognose** traffic forecast; ~**projekt** transportation project; ~**provisionen** commission to agents; ~**radar** radar speedmeter; ~**recht** vehicle and traffic laws *(US)*; ~**redaktion** *(Rundfunk)* motoring unit; ~**regeler** traffic regulator; ~**regeln** rules of the road *(US)*, traffic rules *(US)*; ~**regelung** traffic regulation (duty), motor traffic management, controll[ing] of traffic, direction of the traffic, [road] traffic control; ~**regelung an einer Kreuzung** controlled crossing; ~**regelungssystem** traffic management system.

verkehrsreich crowded [with traffic], traffic-congested (-laden); ~**e Straße** congested street.

Verkehrs|reklamepächter franchise operator; ~**richter** police magistrate *(US)*; ~**richtung** direction of traffic; ~**risiko** traffic hazard; ~**route** trafficway, route for traffic; ~**rowdy** road hog; ~**rückgang** decrease in traffic; ~**rücksichtnahme** courtesy of the road; ~**sache** *(Gericht)* running-down action, runner; ~**sachverständiger** transportation expert; ~**schild** traffic (highway) sign; ~**schutzmann** traffic regulator (policeman, constable), point policeman *(Br.)*, police constable *(Br.)*, pointsman *(Br.)*, patrolman, traffic cop.

verkehrsschwache Zeit slack period, off-peak hours.

Verkehrsschwierigkeiten traffic difficulties.

verkehrssicher *(Auto)* roadworthy;
nicht ~ *(Auto)* unroadworthy, unsafe.

Verkehrssicherheit road safety, safety of traffic *(US)*, traffic safety *(US)*, *(Fahrzeug)* roadworthiness *(Br.)*;
der ~ **genügen** to meet the demands of road safety.

Verkehrssicherheits|gesetz Road Safety Act *(Br.)*; ~**plakat** road safety poster; ~**rat** National Safety Council *(US)*.

Verkehrs|signal traffic signal; ~**sitte** use and wont, general custom, usage, custom of the country, assuetude; **nach der** ~**sitte** according to custom; ~**situation** road situation; ~**spitze** peak traffic period, peak hours, rush hour; ~**sprache** professional language, jargon.

verkehrsstarke Zeit rush (heavy, *US*) hours, busy (peak) period.

Verkehrs|stärke traffic on the road; ~**statistik** traffic return (statistics); ~**statistiker** traffic taker.

Verkehrsstau congestion, traffic jam, jam in the street, traffic holdup;
~ **beseitigen** to ease the congestion in a street; ~ **entwirren** to disentangle the traffic; ~ **hervorrufen** to congest traffic.

Verkehrsstauung congestion point (spot), traffic jam (tangle, holdup, block), block in the (congestion of) traffic;
~**en ausweichen** to dodge the traffic; ~ **beheben** to ease the congestion in a street, to unjam traffic; ~ **herbeiführen** to congest the traffic.

Verkehrs|steuer road-fund tax, tax on freight transportation *(US)*; **kommunale** ~**steuer pro Hotelbett** local authority advalorem bed tax; ~**steuerung** control of traffic, traffic control; ~**stillegung** suspension of traffic, *(Flugverkehr)* suspension of air service; ~**stockung** traffic delay (congestion), congestion of traffic, traffic jam (block, holdup, tangle), tie-up, *(Bahn)* breakdown; ~**stollen** *(Kohlenbergbau)* travelling ways; ~**stopp** traffic stop; ~**störung** traffic block (holdup), road jam, jam in the street, *(Bahn)* breakdown, holdup, stoppage of the traffic; **zu** ~**störungen führen** to disturb traffic; ~**stoß** peak-hour traffic, rush-hour traffic; ~**strafe** motoring (traffic) fine *(Br.)*; ~**strafsache** traffic violation, traffic case *(US)*; ~**straße** thoroughfare, main (public) road, trafficway, highway, highroad *(Br.)*, service road; ~**straßenprogramm** highway program(me); ~**strecke** lines of communication; ~**streife** traffic (courtesy, police, mobile) patrol, traffic squad, street police, cop on the beat, cruiser *(US)*; **motorisierte** ~**streife** highway patrolman; ~**streik** strike of transport workers; ~**strom** traffic flow, stream (flow) of traffic; **sich in den** ~**strom einreihen** to cut (filter, *Br.*) into the line of traffic; **dem** ~**strom entgegenfahren** to travel against the traffic; ~**sünder** traffic offender, *(unachtsamer Fußgänger)* jaywalker *(coll.)*; ~**sünderkartei** central index of traffic offenders; ~**system** transportation system; ~**tafel** traffic sign; ~**tarif** transportation rate.

verkehrstauglich roadworthy.

Verkehrstauglichkeit roadworthiness.

verkehrstechnisch erschließen to open up to traffic.

Verkehrs|teilnehmer road (transport) user, *(Fußgänger)* foot passenger, pedestrian; ~**tod** fatality; ~**tote** victims of motor accidents, toll of the road, casualties; ~**träger** transportation undertaking, common carrier *(US)*; ~**transportleistung** volume of traffic; ~**trubel** bustling traffic.

verkehrstüchtig *(Fahrzeug)* roadworthy.

Verkehrs|tüchtigkeit roadworthiness; ~**turm** traffic [control] tower, dummy *(US sl.)*; ~**überschüsse** *(Bahn)* traffic balances; ~**übertretung** traffic violation *(US)*, *(Autofahrer)* driving (motoring, *Br.*) offence; ~**überwachung** traffic control.

verkehrsübliche|Geschäfte day-to-day business; ~ **Miete** open market rent; ~ **Sorgfalt** diligence usual in ordinary business; ~ **Straßenbenutzung** ordinary travel.

Verkehrs|umfang amount of traffic, traffic volume (density); ~**umleitung** diversion of traffic *(Br.)*, traffic diversion *(Br.)*, detour *(US)*.

verkehrsunfähig *(nicht absetzbar)* unmarketable, *(nicht begebbar)* nonnegotiable.

Verkehrsunfall street (road, traffic) accident, crash, *(pl.)* toll of the road;
~ **haben** *(Ehefrau)* to be going to have an unplanned baby; ~**quote** traffic-accident rate; ~**sache** running-down case; ~**statistik** road-accident figures; ~**verhütung** prevention of road accidents; ~**ziffer** highway (traffic) toll.

verkehrsungünstig gelegen not in a desirable location.

Verkehrs|unterbrechung stoppage of the traffic; ~**unternehmen** transit company, transportation enterprise (operation); **öffentliches** ~**unternehmen** public transport company (undertaking), public transportation company *(US)*, common carrier *(US)*; ~**unternehmer** common carrier *(US)*; ~**unterricht** traffic (road safety) instruction, *(Schule)* instruction in the highway code; ~**verband** *(konkurrierende Verkehrsunternehmen)* pool; ~**verbandsvertrag** pooling contract; ~**verbesserung** traffic improvement; ~**verbindung** [lines of] communication, communication line; ~**verbot** prohibition of traffic; ~**verdichtung** traffic congestion; ~**verein** tourist information agency, tourist office (bureau, *US*); ~**vereinbarungen [konkurrierender Verkehrsunternehmen]** pool; ~**verflechtung** interpenetration of traffic; ~**vergehen** traffic offence, traffic (moving) violation *(US)*, *(Autofahrer)* motoring *(Br.)* (driving) offence; ~**verhältnisse** traffic situation; ~**verlagerung** dislocation of traffic, traffic dislocation (shift), deflection of trade; ~**verletzung** traffic offence (infringement), traffic violation *(US)*, *(Autofahrer)* motoring (driving) offence; ~**verstopfung** traffic tie-up *(US)*, traffic jam (tangle, holdup); ~**verstoß** traffic infringement; ~**vorschriften** traffic (road) regulations, vehicle and traffic laws *(US)*; ~**wacht** road patrol, scout [car], *(ADAC)* Automobile Association patrol.

Verkehrsweg [service] road, [arterial] highway, traffic route, traffic artery (corridor), trafficway, [lines of] communication, communication lines;
öffentlicher ~ public highway (thoroughfare);
~ **für die Benutzung freigeben** to open (dedicate) a highway, to open a road for traffic.

Verkehrs|welle citizen's band; ~**werbung** tourist advertising, *(im Verkehrsmittel)* poster advertising; ~**werbungsunternehmen** traffic solicitor.

Verkehrswert market (sound, salable, trade, actual, fair, cash, attached business) value, going price, fair valuation;
echter ~ *(Erbschaftssteuer)* clear (open, *Br.*) market value;
~ **nicht erschlossenen Geländes** unimproved value *(US)*; ~ **eines Grundstücks** fair market price, fair (free) cash market value, current use value of land; ~ **einer Mine** commercial value of an ore; ~ **in unbeschädigtem Zustand** sound value;
~**schätzung** market appraisal.

Verkehrswesen transport matters, traffic management (communications) system, field of traffic, transportation *(US)*;
öffentliches ~ public transport (transportation, *US*);
~ **und Nachrichtenwesen** transport and communication;
staatliche Reglementierung des ~**s aufheben** to free the entry into the transportation market *(US)*.

verkehrswidrig contrary to traffic regulations, improper;
~ **über die Straße gehen** to jaywalk *(coll.)*.

Verkehrs|widrigkeit traffic violation; ~**wirrwarr** communication (traffic) snarl *(US)*; ~**wirtschaft** business of carrying goods, transport economics, transport[ation] industry, economics of road and rail transport; ~**wirtschaft steuern** to control transportation; ~**wirtschaftler** transport economist; ~**zähler** travel counter; ~**zählung** traffic census (count), travel counting; ~**zeichen** traffic signal (beacon, *Br.*, post, sign), road (direction) sign, control signal, *(automatisch)* robot, *(zur Aufhebung der Geschwindigkeitsbeschränkung)* derestrictive sign *(Br.)*, *(Wegweiser)* signpost; **internationale** ~**zeichen** international road signs; ~**zeichen mißachten** to disobey (fail to comply with) a traffic sign, *(falsche Straßenüberquerung)* to jaywalk *(coll.)*; **schwache** ~**zeit** slack hours; **starke** ~**zeit** rush hours; ~**zentrum** traffic center *(US)* (centre, *Br.*); ~**ziffern**

traffic return; ~**zulassung** road fund licence; ~**zunahme** increase in traffic, traffic increase; ~**zusammenballung** absolute standstill of traffic, congestion of traffic.
verkehrt wrong, false, *(verrückt)* crazy, wet *(US sl.)*;
~ **abbiegen** to take a wrong turning; **Sache ~ anfangen** to put the cart before the horse; **etw. ~ auffassen** to misunderstand s. th.; ~ **herum sein** to be queer;
~**e Adresse** wrong address; ~**e Richtung** wrong direction; ~**e Stoffseite** reverse side of a material; ~**e Vorstellung von etw. haben** to have a wrong idea about s. th.; ~**e Welt** upside-down world.
Verkehrten, an den ~ kommen to catch a tartar, to bark up the wrong tree.
Verkehrung ins Gegenteil complete reversal.
verkennen to misunderstand, to mistake, to misjudge;
jds. Motive ~ to misjudge s. one's motives; **nicht ~** to be fully aware of; **Schwierigkeiten der Lage nicht ~** not to underestimate the difficulty of the situation; **Tatsachen ~** to misapprehend the facts; **j. völlig ~** to misjudge s. o. completely.
Verkennung misjudgment, misapprehension, *(Unterschätzung)* underestimation;
~ **der Tatsachen** misapprehension of facts.
Verkettung von Umständen chain of events.
verketzern, j. *(pol.)* to brand s. o. a heretic.
verklagen to sue, to bring to justice (an action against), to exhibit a bill, to commence suit *(US)*;
j. ~ to go to law with s. o., to take legal proceedings (bring an action) against s. o., to action s. o., to sue s. o. at law, to bring s. o. into court, to institute an action against s. o.; **j. auf Bezahlung seiner Schulden ~** to summon s. o. for debts; **einzeln ~** to sue separately; **j. wegen Körperverletzung ~** to sue s. o. for civil injury; **wegen Nichterfüllung eines Vertrages ~** to sue for breach of contract[ual obligations], to sue for nonperformance; **wegen Patentverletzung ~** to bring an action for infringement of a patent; **auf Schadensersatz ~** to sue in court for damages; **wegen Schadensersatz aus unerlaubter Handlung ~** to sue in tort for conversion.
verklagt impleaded;
gemeinschaftlich ~ werden to be sued jointly;
~**e Partei** party sued, defendant.
verklaren to extend protest.
verklärtes Gesicht transfigured face.
Verklarung ship's (extended) protest, captain's report, maritime declaration, protest of the shipmaster;
~ **ablegen** to extend protest, to make oath upon average.
Verklarungsprotokoll deed of ship's protest.
verklausulieren to arrange (hedge) in (guard by) clauses, to clause, *(vertraglich festsetzen)* to stipulate.
verklausuliert hedged in by clauses, clausular;
nicht ~ with no strings attached.
Verklausulierung involved wording, *(vertragliche Festsetzung)* qualification, stipulation.
verkleben to stick together, to paper.
verkleckern, sein ganzes Geld to trifle away (squander) one's money; **seine Zeit ~** to fritter away one's time.
verkleiden to disguise, to masquerade, *(verschalen)* to board, *(vertäfeln)* to panel, to wainscot.
Verkleidung *(fig.)* disguise, mask, masquerade, *(techn.)* sheating, jacketing, casing, lining, *(Vertäfelung)* wainscot, panelling.
Verkleidungs|blech *(Flugzeug)* panel; ~**material** jacketing.
verkleinern to reduce in size, to attenuate, *(Leistung)* to belittle, to disparage, to derogate, *(Wert)* to depreciate, *(Zeichnung)* to scale down;
sich ~ to move to a smaller place; **Geschäft um die Hälfte ~** to reduce a business by half; **proportional ~** to scale down; **jds. Schuld ~** to extenuate s. one's guilt.
Verkleinerung diminution, reduction, *(Leistung)* belittlement, detraction, derogation;
proportionale ~ scaling down, reproduction on a small scale; ~ **der Belegschaft** cutback in staff; ~ **des Geschäftsumfangs** undertrading.
verklingen *(Begeisterung)* to ebb, to wear off, *(Film)* to fade out (away).
verknacken, j. zu Gefängnis to put s. o. behind bars (in clink, *sl.*).
verknallen, sich in j. to fall (go, *US coll.*) for s. o.
verknappen to run short, to become rare (scarce).
Verknappung shortage, scarcity, shortcoming, tightness, narrowness;
infolge zeitweiliger ~ owing to temporary scarcity;
kriegsbedingte ~ wartime shortage;
~ **an Arbeitskräften** labo(u)r shortage, scarcity of workers; ~ **der Barmittel** shortage of cash; ~ **der Devisenvorräte** shortage of currency, shortage of foreign exchange, foreign exchange stringency; ~ **am Geldmarkt** money stringency, tightness of the money market, tight money market; **staatlich gesteuerte ~ des Geldmarktes** fiscal stringency; ~ **der Kreditmittel** credit stringency; ~ **der Rohstoffvorräte** scarcity of raw materials;
unter größter ~ leiden *(Geldmarkt)* to be very stringent.
Verknechtung enslavement, sugjugation.
verkneifen, sich etw. to bite on the bits, to stifle s. th., to keep s. th. back; **sich eine Sekretärin ~** to do without the services of a secretary;
sich das Lachen kaum ~ können to hardly be able to keep one's face straight.
verknöchert old-fogyish (fogy), ossified, stuffy;
~**er Kerl** old fossil.
verknüpfen to connect, to fasten, to tie, to bind, to knot together;
Urlaub mit einer Geschäftsreise ~ to combine one's holiday (vacation, *US*) with a business trip.
verknüpft connected, associated;
mit Kosten ~ involving expenses.
Verknüpfung linkage, connection, association, nexus.
verkohlen *(fam.)* to spoof, to kid;
j. ~ to pull s. one's leg.
Verkohlung carbonization.
verkommen to dilapidate, to go to wreck and ruin, to rust, *(Garten)* to run wild, *(Gebäude)* to become dilapidated, *(Lebensmittel)* to waste, *(moralisch)* to become demoralized (corrupted), to debauch;
~ *(a.)* dilapidated, *(Garten)* overgrown, wild, *(Speisen)* bad, rotten;
moralisch ~ corrupted, degenerate, demoralized, debauched;
~**es Subject** reprobate.
verkorken to cork up.
verkorksen to botch, to butcher, to make a mess of, to mishandle, to queer *(sl.)*, to muck up *(sl.)*;
sich den Magen ~ to upset one's stomach.
verkorkste Angelegenheit muddle, mess, pretty kettle of fish *(sl.)*.
verkörpern to corporate, to personify, to impersonate, to body, to embody, to represent, to typify, to evidence, to be a representative of;
urenglische Eigenschaften ~ to be English to the core.
verkörpert represented, incorporated.
Verkörperung personification, embodiment, impersonation, representation, incarnation.
verköstigen to board.
Verköstigung board, food.
verkrachen, sich mit jem. to fall out with s. o., to part brass rags with s. o.
verkracht on bad terms;
~**e Existenz** failure in life, shipwrecked person.
verkraften to manage, to handle, to cope with, to tackle;
immer noch zunehmenden Arbeitsanfall ~ to cope with the growing amount of work; **Ausgabe ~** to afford an expense; **Verkehr ~** to cope with (handle) the traffic; **Verlust ~** to stand a loss.
verkrampft cramped, frustrated;
~**es Lachen** strained laugh.
Verkrampfung cramp.
verkriechen, sich to hide (hole, *US*) up, to poke o. s. up; **sich ins Bett ~** to slip off to bed *(coll.)*.
verkrümeln, sich to steal (sneak) away.
verkrüppeln to disable, to cripple, to maim;
~ **lassen** to dwarf.
verkrüppelt crippled, *(Baum)* dwarfed, stunted.
Verkrüppelung crippling, maiming.
verkühlen, sich to catch a chill.
verkümmern to shrivel up, *(Pflanze)* to die off, to wither away;
~ **lassen** to dwarf.
verkünden to announce, to make known, to manifest, to pronounce, to deliver, to read out, *(Gesetz)* to promulgate;
Abstimmungsergebnis ~ to announce the result of the poll; **Freispruch ~** to pronounce an acquittal; **öffentlich ~** to announce publicly, to make known by public proclamation, to proclaim [from the house tops], to publish; **jem. den Streit ~** to give s. o. third-party notice; **Tatsachen lauthals ~** to shout facts from the rooftops; **Todesurteil ~** to pronounce a death sentence; **Urteil ~** to render (deliver, pronounce) a judgment; **Versäumnisurteil ~** to deliver judgment by default.
Verkünder messenger, announcer.
verkündet *(Urteil)* pronounced, declared.

Verkündung publication, announcement, *(feierliche Mitteilung)* pronouncement, *(Veröffentlichung)* proclamation;
~ **eines Gesetzes** promulgation of a law; ~ **eines Strafurteils** pronouncement of a sentence; ~ **eines Urteils** deliverance (pronouncement) of a judgment.
verkuppeln to procure, to prostitute.
Verkuppelung procuration.
verkürzen to shorten, to limit, to abbreviate, *(Rechte)* to curtail, *(Text)* to abridge, *(vermindern)* to reduce, to diminish;
Arbeitszeit ~ to shorten one's working time; **Frist** ~ to abridge a time, to shorten a period; **Front** ~ to reduce the front; **um ein Jahr** ~ to cut a year off; **Legat** ~ to abate a legacy; **Löhne** ~ to cut wages; **seinen Urlaub** ~ to curtail one's holiday; **jem. die Zeit** ~ to help s. o. kill the time; **finanzielle Zuwendung** ~ to curtail an allowance of money.
verkürzt curtailed, *(Rente, Lebenserwartung)* curtate;
~**e Arbeitszeit** part-time employment, short time; ~**e Lebenserwartung** curtailed expectation of life.
Verkürzung shortening, abridgement, diminution, limitation, contraction, *(Lohn)* reduction, *(Rechte)* curtailment;
~ **der Arbeitszeit** shortening of working hours, reduction in hours of work; ~ **einer Bilanz** contraction of balance sheet; ~ **einer Frist** abridgement of time; ~ **seines Urlaubs** curtailment of one's holiday; ~ **eines Vermächtnisses** abatement of legacy; ~ **der Zollsätze** drop in the customs duty; ~ **der Zugfolge** curtailment of service.
Verlade|anlage loading plant (facilities), handling equipment, trucking facilities; ~**anweisung** *(Schiff)* sailing card; ~**anzeige** shipping advice; ~**arbeiter** loading hand, shipping worker, packer; ~**aufseher** loading officer, chief loader; ~**bahnhof** dispatching (loading) station; ~**bahnsteig** loading platform; ~**bedingungen** loading (shipping) conditions.
verladebereit *(Güter)* ready to dispatch (to be shipped, for shipment, *US*), *(Schiff)* on the berth, *(Transportmittel)* ready to take cargo.
Verlade|bescheinigung *(Schiff)* mate's receipt; ~**bestimmungen** loading regulations; ~**betrieb** tran(s)shipment plant; ~**brücke** loading bridge; ~**bühne** loading platform; ~**dauer** loading time (days); ~**dokumente** loading (shipping, *US*) documents, shipper's papers *(US)*; ~**einheit** unit load; ~**einrichtung** loading plant (gear), handling equipment; ~**fähigkeit** loadability; ~**flughafen** port of embarkation; ~**frist** loading days; ~**gebühren** loading (shipping, *US*) charges, loading costs; ~**gerät** loading gear; ~**gerüst** handling platform; ~**gewicht** loading (shipping) weight; ~**gleis** siding, sidetrack; **von zwei Spediteuren benutztes** ~**gleis** joint track; ~**hafen** loading (lading, shipping, *US*) port, port of loading (shipment, *US*); **letzter** ~**hafen** port arrived from; ~**kai** loading berth (quay, wharf); ~**klasse** freight category; ~**kosten** loading (stevedoring, shipping, *US*) charges; ~**kran** material-handling crane; ~**liste** freight list, shipping note *(US)*, shipper's manifest *(US)*; ~**mannschaft** loading crew (hands).
Verladen loading, lading.
verladen to lade, to load, to freight, to pack up, to embark, to ship *(US)*, *(im Flugzeug)* to emplane, *(versenden)* to consign, to forward, to dispatch, *(in Waggon)* to entrain;
auf Deck ~ to ship on deck; **in einen Eisenbahnzug** ~ to put aboard a [railroad] train *(US)*, *(Truppen)* to entrain; **Güter** ~ to take in freight; **auf Lastkraftwagen** ~ *(mil.)* to entruck; **lose** ~ to load (ship, *US*) in bulk; **in ein Schiff** ~ to stow cargo in a ship's hold; **Stückgut** ~ to load in (freight by) parcels; **Sturzgüter** ~ to load in bulk; **wieder** ~ to reload, to reship *(US)*;
~ *(a.)* loaded, freighted, laden, shipped *(US)*;
in nicht hinreichender Menge ~ short-shipped *(US)*; **sorgfältig** ~ handled (freighted) with care; **in Stückgut** ~ loaded in bulk.
Verlade|nachweis evidence of shipment *(US)*; ~**ort** place of loading, loading place (point, berth); ~**papiere** loading (shipping, *US*) documents, shipper's papers *(US)*; ~**platz** loading place (berth), goods platform, *(Schiff)* loading dock, wharf; **sicherer** ~**platz** safe loading place; ~**preis** forwarding expenses, loading charges, shipping price *(US)*.
Verlader [van] loader, lader, packer, cargo worker, freighter, consignor, shipper *(US)*, shipping agent *(US)*, *(in Waggon)* entrainer.
Verlade|rampe loading platform (ramp); ~**raum** *(Schiff)* ship's hold; ~**risiko** loading risk; ~**schein** consignment note, shipping note, shipping bill *(US)*, dispatch note *(Br.)*, bill of lading, *(Schiff)* certificate of receipt; ~**schluß** closure (closing) for cargo; ~**spediteur** loading carrier, shipping agent *(US)*; ~**spesen** loading (shipping, *US*) charges; ~**station** loading station; ~**stelle** place of shipment *(US)*, loading (shipping, *US*) point, loading berth (place); ~**streik** strike of stevedores; ~**system** loading system; ~**termin** date of loading (shipment, *US*); ~**vorrichtung** loading gear, loading equipment (tackle); ~**vorrichtung für Stückgut** unit loading device; ~**vorschrift** loading pamphlet; ~**zeit** loading days; ~**zeugnis** bill of lading, shipping certificate *(US)*.
Verladung loading, lading, *(Verschiffung)* embarkation, shipment, stowage, *(Versendung)* dispatch, consignment, shipment *(US)*, shipping *(US)*, *(Truppen auf Lastwagen)* entrucking;
nach ~ when shipped *(US)*; **zur** ~ **bereit** ready for loading (shipping, *US*);
fehlerhafte ~ improper stowage; **prompte** ~ prompt shipment *(US)*; **raumsparende** ~ commercial loading; **teilweise** ~ partial loading (shipment, *US*);
~ **auf Deck** shipment on deck; ~ **ohne Frachtbrief** overfreight; ~ **nach London** loading for London; ~ **von Stückgut** loading on the berth; ~ **von Stückgut ohne Aufschlag** free lighterage; ~ **mehrerer Stückgutladungen** multiple loading; ~ **von Sturzgütern** loading in bulk; ~ **von Truppen** entrainment, entraining; ~ **der Ware** loading of goods, merchandise shipment *(US)*, shipment of goods *(US)*.
Verladungs|frist loading time; ~**konnossement** bill of lading; ~**kosten** loading (forwarding) charges, shipping expenses *(US)*; ~**ort** place of loading; ~**papiere** shipping documents; ~**preis** forwarding expenses, shipping price *(US)*; ~**schein** bill of lading; ~**zeugnis** shipping certificate.
Verlag publishing house (firm, company, business), publisher, *(Verlegen)* publication, publishing;
im ~ **von** published by;
für einen ~ **arbeiten** to work for a publishing company; ~ **vor Schaden bewahren** to save the publisher harmless; ~ **gründen** to start out in publishing; **in** ~ **nehmen** to publish.
verlagern to shift, to switch, to displace, to pass on, *(Betrieb)* to evacuate, to remove, to dislocate, *(Industrie)* to relocate;
sich ~ *(Interessen)* to be switched over; **Aufträge** ~ to shift orders; **Bankinstitut** ~ to transfer a bank; **Beweislast** ~ to shift the burden of proof; **aufs Land** ~ to move to the country; **Produktionsschwerpunkt** ~ to shift product emphasis; **seinen Schwerpunkt in den kommerziellen Sektor** ~ to diversify into commercial markets.
Verlagerung shift, shifting, displacement, *(Betrieb)* evacuation, removal, relocation, dislocation;
~ **der Beweislast** shifting of the burden of proof; ~ **einer Industrie** relocation of an industry; ~ **des Schwerpunkts von militärischer auf zivile Luftfahrt** diversification away from military (and) into civilian aircraft; ~ **aus Steuergründen** relocation for tax purposes.
Verlagerungs|fachmann relocation specialist; ~**plan** relocation plan; ~**zuschuß** *(Betrieb)* removal grant, relocation assistance.
Verlags|abteilung publishing department; ~**agent** literary agent; ~**agentur** literary agency; **ohne** ~**angabe** no imprint; ~**ankündigung** notice of new publications; ~**anstalt** publishing house (firm, company), publisher; ~**artikel** publication; ~**auslieferung** publisher's delivery agency; ~**buchhandel** publishing trade (business); ~**buchhändler** [book] publisher, publishing bookseller, copy purchaser; ~**buchhandlung** publishing house; **neue** ~**erscheinungen** new publications.
verlagsfähig publishable.
Verlags|gemeinkosten publishers' overheads; ~**geschäft** publishing trade (business), economics of publishing; ~**gewerbe** publishing trade; ~**gewinn** publishing (publisher's) profit; ~**händler** *(Postversandhaus)* catalog(ue) company, mail-order wholesaler *(US)*; ~**haus** publishing house (firm, company), wholesaler *(US)*, book concern *(US)*; ~**kalkulation** publishers' calculation; ~**katalog** publisher's catalog(ue), list of publications; ~**konzern** publishing concern; ~**kosten** publishing expenses; ~**lektor** publisher's reader; ~**objekt** publication; ~**ort** town of publication; ~**preis** publishing price.
Verlagsrecht copyright;
~**e erloschen** out of copyright; **alle** ~**e bei ...** copyright © by ...; **internationales** ~ international copyright;
~ **ablösen** to commute a copyright; ~**e beantragen** to file an application for registration of copyright; ~ **besitzen** to own a copyright; ~ **erneuern** to renew a copyright; ~ **übernehmen** to copyright; ~ **verletzen** to infringe the copyright; ~ **wahren** to enter in the office of the Librarian of Congress *(US)*, to enter at Stationers' Company *(Br.)*.
verlagsrechtlich geschützt copyright[ed];
~**e Ausgabe** copyright edition, copyrighted publication; ~**e Produktion** copyrighted production; ~**e Veröffentlichung** copyrighted publication; ~**es Werk** copyrighted work.

Verlagsrechts | ablösung commutation of copyright; **~inhaber** copyright owner (proprietor).

Verlags | repräsentant publisher's representative; **~unternehmen** publishing house (company, firm); **~vermittler** literary agent; **~vermittlung** literary agency; **~veröffentlichung** publication; **~veröffentlichung ankündigen** to announce the publication of a book; **~vertrag** publishing agreement (contract); **~vertrag über ein Buch abschließen** to place a book with a publisher; **~vertreter** publisher's representative, book agent; **~werk** publication; **~wesen** publishing trade; **~zeichen** imprint.

Verlangen demand, request, claim, wish, *(Begierde)* appetite, desire, *(Sehnsucht)* longing, yearning, craving;
auf ~ by request, on demand (application), *(bei Voranzeigung)* on presentation, upon requisition; **auf ~ zahlbar** payable on demand; **bei ~ vorzuzeigen** to be shown upon request; **ausdrückliches ~** express request; **brennendes ~** itch; **dringendes ~** urge;
~ nach Vollkommenheit aspiration towards perfection;
jem. bei einem ~ recht geben to sustain s. o. in a demand; **großes ~ nach etw. haben** to have a great wish (be itching) for s. th.; **großes ~ nach Süßigkeiten haben** to be dying for some sweets; **jds. ~ nachkommen** to meet s. one's request; **auf ~ zahlen** to pay on demand.

verlangen to demand, to require, to request, to call (apply) for, to want, to claim, to arrogate, to assert, to exact, *(berechnen)* to charge, *(bestehen auf)* to insist on, *(ersehnen)* to long, to yearn;
~, was einem zusteht to claim one's due; **nach einem Arzt ~** to ask for a doctor; **jds. volle Aufmerksamkeit ~** to require s. one's full attention; **Bezahlung einer Schuld ~** to demand payment of a debt; **keine Eintrittsgebühr ~** to charge no entrance fee; **Filmrechte eines Buches ~** to ask for an option on the film rights of a book; **kurze Fristverlängerung ~** to request a brief delay; **Herausgabe des Eigentums ~** to require the surrender of property; **hohe Miete von jem. ~** to rent s. o. high; **geringe Miete von seinen Mietern ~** to rent one's tenants low; **seine Post ~** to call for one's mail; **Preisbindung ~** to maintain fixed resale prices; **Provision ~** to charge commission; **Rechnung ~** to ask for the bill; **spezifizierte Rechnung ~** to demand an itemized bill; **sein Recht ~** to claim one's right; **sein volles Recht ~** to want one's pound of flesh; **Schadenersatz ~** to claim (collect, demand) damages, to claim compensation; **Schadenersatz für geringere Lebenserwartung ~** to claim damages for loss of expectation of life; **Steuerherabsetzungen ~** to request diminution of taxes; **pro Tag ~** to charge a day; **j. am Telefon ~** to want s. o. on the telephone; **Unmögliches ~** to ask for the moon and stars; **viel ~** to set a high standard; **sehr viel von jem. ~** to require a great deal of s. o.; **zu viel ~** to overcharge; **zu viel von jem. ~** to be expecting too much of s. o.; **Zahlung ~** to request payment; **zusätzlich ~** to demand in addition (extra).

verlängerbar renewable, extendable.

verlängern to lengthen, *(Frist)* to extend, *(Wechsel)* to renew, to prolong;
sich ~ *(Abkommen)* to extend, to prolong; **Abonnement ~** to renew a subscription; **Arbeitszeit ~** to lengthen working hours; **Besuch ~** to prolong a visit; **Debatte ~** to protract a debate; **Gültigkeitsdauer einer Fahrkarte ~** to extend a ticket; **Kredit ~** to extend (renew) a credit; **Laufzeit eines Films ~** to hold a film over; **Leben ~** to lengthen life; **Lizenz ~** to renew a licence; **Pachtvertrag ~** to renew (extend) a lease; **Paß ~** to renew a passport; **Patent ~** to renew (extend) a patent; **Startbahn ~** to lengthen the runway; **stillschweigend ~** to renew by implication; **Urlaub ~** to extend (prolong) a leave; **Verjährungsfrist ~** to extend the statute of limitations; **Vertrag ~** to prolong (renew, extend) a contract; **Zahlungsfrist ~** to grant a respite.

verlängert extended, prolonged;
~ werden to be extended;
~er Arm der Regierung instrument of the government; **~er Mietvertrag** renewed lease; **~e Polizeistunde** extended hours; **~er Schuldschein** renewed note; **~er Urlaub** extended leave.

Verlängerung lengthening, continuation, *(Frist)* extension, *(Kredit)* renewal, *(Wechsel)* prolongation;
ausdrückliche ~ explicit extension; **automatische ~** automatic renewal; **stillschweigende ~** implicit (tacit) renewal;
~ der Abgabefrist filing extension; **~ eines Abkommens** extension of an accord; **~ eines Abonnements** renewal of a subscription; **~ der Amtsdauer** renewal of term of office; **~ der Arbeitszeit** extension (lengthening) of working hours; **~ der Aufenthaltsgenehmigung** extension of the residence permit; **~ einer Debatte** protraction of a debate; **~ einer Frist** extension of time; **~ der Gültigkeitsdauer** extension of validity; **~ der Laufzeit eines Darlehens** renewal of a loan, extension of credit; **~ der Lieferfristen** lengthening of delivery periods; **~ eines Mietvertrages** renewal of a lease; **~ eines Pachtvertrages** extension of a leasehold; **~ eines Passes** renewal of a passport; **~ eines Patents** renewal (extension of the life) of a patent; **~ der Rechtsmittelfrist** extension of time to appeal; **~ einer Sitzung** prolongation of a meeting; **~ seines Urlaubs** extension of one's holidays (leave); **~ der gesetzlichen Verjährungsfrist** extension of the statutory period of limitations; **~ eines Vertrages** prolongation of an agreement; **~ eines Visums** extension of visa; **~ der Zahlungsfrist** extension of payment;
um ~ der Zahlungsfrist einkommen to request an extension of payment; **~ der Zahlungsfrist erhalten** to obtain an extension of time for payment; **~ einer Frist erreichen** to get an extension of time; **~en zum Satz von 2% tätigen** to put through renewals at 2 per cent; **~ einer Frist zugestehen** to grant a delay; **einer ~ zustimmen** to agree to a renewal.

Verlängerungs | abkommen prolongation agreement; **~antrag** application for renewal; **~bedingungen** terms of continuation.

verlängerungsfähig protractile, *(Vertrag)* renewable;
~e Risikolebensversicherung renewable term [life] insurance.

Verlängerungs | frist period of extension; **~gebühr** *(Patent)* renewal fee; **~kabel** extension cable; **~klausel** *(Seeversicherung)* prolongation (continuation) clause; **automatische ~klausel** renewal clause; **~option** option to extend; **~police** renewal policy; **~prämie** renewal premium; **~protokoll** protocol of extension; **~provision** renewal commission; **~quittung** *(Versicherung)* renewal receipt; **~recht** right of renewal; **~schlüssel** extension key; **~schnur** extension cord; **~stück** extension piece, *(Wechsel)* allonge; **~stück anbringen** to paste an allonge to a bill; **~urkunde** charter by progress *(Scot. law)*; **~wechsel** renewal (continuation) bill; **~zeit** extra time; **~zeitraum** renewal period, period of extension; **~zettel** rider, *(Wechsel)* allonge.

verlangsamen to slow down, to slacken, to reduce;
seine Fahrt ~ to slow down, to cut down one's speed; **Konjunktur ~** to slow down the economy; **seinen Schritt ~** to slacken one's pace; **Tempo ~** to decelerate, to slow down, *(Schiff)* to slacken speed; **Wachstum der Industrie ~** to slow down industrial expansion.

verlangsamt | er Konjunkturanstieg slowdown in the recovery; **~e Konjunkturbewegung** economic slowdown, slowdown in economic activity.

Verlangsamung slowing down, slowdown, slackening, retardation;
~ des Inflationstempos (der Inflationsrate) slowdown in the rate of inflation; **~ der Konjunktur** slackening of the economic trend; **~ des Preisanstiegs** price slowdown.

verlangt wanted, in demand;
nicht ~ dull; **viel ~** a large order *(fam.)*;
~ werden to find a market; **nicht ~ werden** to go a begging.

Verlaß dependence;
auf ihn ist kein ~ there is no relying upon him.

Verlassen desertion, *(Räumung)* vacation, leaving;
befehlswidriges ~ *(mil.)* abandonment; **böswilliges ~** wife desertion, matrimonial offense (offence, *Br.*) of desertion, malicious abandonment; **grundloses ~** voluntary abandonment;
~ des letzten englischen Hafens final sailing; **~ des Saales** walkout;
j. zum ~ seines Grundstücks auffordern to warn s. o. off.

verlassen to leave, to quit, *(aufgeben)* to relinquish, to abandon, *(Frau und Kinder)* to desert, to abandon, *(im Stich lassen)* to abandon, to forsake;
sich auf j. ~ to rely on (depend upon, count, be reliant on) s. o., to place reliance (reckon) upon s. o.; **Frau und Kinder ~** to forsake wife and children; **sich auf sein Glück ~** to trust one's luck; **sich hundertprozentig auf etw. ~** to bet one's boots on s. th. *(sl.)*; **sich auf eine unzuverlässige Person ~** to lean on a reed; **j. plötzlich ~** to leave s. o. flat; **Schiff ~** to abandon a ship; **sich auf sich selbst ~** to paddle one's own canoe; **Universität ~** to go down from the university; **sich auf weiterhin gutes Wetter ~** to bank on the weather keeping up;
sich auf sich selbst ~ können to be self-reliant; **das Land ~ müssen** to have to leave the country;
darauf kannst Du Dich ~ depend upon it;
~ *(a.)* *(abgelegen)* lonely, remote, out-of-the-way, solitary, off the beaten track, *(Haus)* empty, derelict, *(hilflos)* forlorn, desolate, *(Land)* desolate, unmanned, *(Schiff)* abandoned, *(Straße)* deserted;
von allen guten Geistern ~ sein to be out of one's mind;
~e Gegend desolate region.

Verlassenheit desolation, forlornness, loneliness;
~ **einer Stadt** vacancy of a city.
verläßlich reliable, certain, constant, dependable, calculable;
~**er Mensch** reliable person; ~**e Quelle** reliable source; **aus einer ~en Quelle haben** to have from a reliable source.
Verläßlichkeitskaution fidelity guarantee.
Verlaub, mit if you will excuse me, with your permission.
Verlauf *(Ablauf)* course, go, way, lapse, run, progress, progression, *(Entwicklung)* development, *(Fluß)* course, trend, *(Tendenz)* trend, tendency, tenor, *(Vorgang)* progress;
im ~ in the course of, in progress; **im weiteren ~** later on, in the further course of events; **im ~ der Diskussion** in the course of the debate; **im ~ der Liquidation** in the course of liquidation; **im ~ der Zeit** with the passing of time; **nach ~ einer Woche** after the lapse of a week;
gewohnheitsmäßiger ~ routine; **zurückhaltender ~** self-effacing line;
natürlicher ~ der Dinge natural course of events; **unglücklicher ~ einer Expedition** unfortunate end of an expedition; **~ der Konjunktur** economic (cyclical) trend, business cycle; **~ einer Krankheit** development (progress) of a disease; **~ der Küstenlinie** trend of the coastline; **~ der Verhandlungen** course of negotiations;
~ abwarten to wait and see; **guten ~ nehmen** to make good progress; **seinen ~ nehmen** to run its course; **ungünstigen ~ nehmen** to take an unfavo(u)rable turn.
verlaufen *(Fluß, Straße)* to run, *(Zeit)* to lapse, to run, to pass; **sich ~** to mistake (miss) one's way, *(Hochwasser)* to drain away, *(Menschenmenge)* to scatter; **befriedigend ~** to turn out satisfactory; **nicht fahrplanmäßig ~** to be running behind schedule *(US)* (time); **wie geplant ~** to go according to plan; **glatt ~** to pass off well (smoothly), to go swimmingly (with a swing); **normal ~** to be proceeding as usual; **von Osten nach Westen ~** *(Grenze)* to range east and west; **parallel ~** to run parallel; **reibungslos ~** to go off without a hitch; **ruhig ~** to run smoothly; **im Sand ~** to peter out, to come to nothing; **tödlich ~** to have a fatal issue.
Verlaufsstruktur time path.
verlautbaren to pronounce, to proclaim, to promulgate, to make known, to issue a statement, *(enthüllen)* to disclose, to divulge; **amtlich ~** to make an official statement.
Verlautbarung pronouncement, statement, promulgation, proclamation, bulletin, declaration, notice;
amtliche ~ official announcement (news), magisterial pronouncement, communiqué; **öffentliche ~** public statement;
~ über die Entwicklung der Belegschaftssituation employment statement; **~ des Finanzministeriums** treasury minute; **~ eines Ministers** ministerial statement; **~ des Präsidenten** pronouncement of the President;
~ veröffentlichen to issue a communication.
verlauten to transpire, to be spread out (heard);
an bestimmten Stellen gerüchteweise ~ to be rumo(u)red in certain quarters;
etw. ~ lassen to give to understand.
verlautet, es it is learned (reported), by all accounts; **wie gerüchtweise ~** it is learned (reported), reportedly.
verleben, Sommer auf dem Lande to spend the summer in the country.
verlebt played-out.
verlegbar publishable, *(mil.)* mobile.
verlegen *(Bücher)* to publish, to print, to bring out, to edit, *(Fabrik)* to displace, *(Geschäft)* to remove, to relocate, to dislocate, *(elektrische Leitungen)* to instal, *(vertagen)* to defer, to put off, to postpone;
etw. ~ to misplace s. th.; **sich ~ auf** to go in for; **Bankinstitut ~** to transfer a bank; **beschleunigt ~** to rush into print; **sein Büro ~** to move one's office; **Fabrik in einen Vorort ~** to transfer a factory to a suburb; **sich wieder auf sein Geschäft ~** to devote o. s. anew to one's business; **etw. nach innen ~** to move s. th. indoors; **Kabel ~** to lay a cable; **Patienten in eine andere Station ~** to move a patient to another ward; **Schauplatz nach A ~** to locate the scene in A; **Schlüssel ~** to mislay a key; **Schulbücher ~** to edit books for use in schools; **Sitzung ~** to adjourn (postpone, put off) a meeting; **Termin ~** to postpone a date; **sich aufs Trinken ~** to take to the bottle; **Truppen ~** to remove (redeploy) troops; **Veranstaltung ~** to put off a function (performance); **sich auf den Vertrieb verschiedener Erzeugnisse ~** to take up a line of goods; **Vorlesung ~** to put off a lecture; **jem. den Weg ~** to block s. one's way; **seinen Wohnsitz ~** to change one's address, to shift one's quarters; **Zeitung ~** to publish a newspaper;
~ *(a.)* confused, embarrassed, red-faced;
nie um eine Antwort ~ sein to be never at a loss for an answer; **immer um Geld ~ sein** to be always short of money;
~**es Schweigen** awkward silence.
Verlegenheit dilemma, corner, mire, nonplus, embarrassment, scrape, quandary, puzzle, constraint, confusion, *(unangenehme Lage)* awkward situation;
in ~ embarrassed, entangled, aground;
finanzielle ~ embarrassment, financial difficulties, straits;
in ~ bringen to entangle, to inconvenience; **j. in ~ bringen** to give s. o. short notice; **in ~ geraten** to get into a fix; **j. aus einer ~ helfen** to help s. o. out of a predicament; **in ~ kommen** to get into a scrape; **in ~ sein** to be in a fix; **in finanzieller ~ sein** to be in low straits; **in großer ~ sein** to be hard put to it; **j. durch indiskrete Fragen in ~ setzen** to embarrass s. o. with indiscreet questions; **~ verursachen** to pose a dilemma; **vor ~ nicht aus und ein wissen** to squirm with embarrassment.
Verlegenheits|lösung makeshift (emergency) solution; ~**pause** awkward silence; ~**politik** policy of expediency.
Verleger publisher, editor;
Drucker und ~ printer and publisher;
~**broschur** publisher's brochure; ~**einband** publisher's binding; ~**geschäft** economics of publishing; ~**inkassostelle** publishers' encashment agency.
verlegerische Tätigkeit publishing.
Verlegerverband publishers' association.
verlegt|bei published (edited) by;
~ werden *(Gegenstand)* to get mislaid.
Verlegung adjournment, postponement, *(Betrieb)* removal, removal operation, evacuation, dislocation, transfer, *(Buch)* publication, publishing;
~ von Bahnschienen platelaying; **~ einer Fabrik** removal (transfer, relocation) of a factory; **~ einer Verhandlung** postponement of trial; **~ auf dem Luftwege** air move; **~ eines Termins** postponement of a date; **~ von Truppen** troop redeployment.
Verlegungskosten *(Betrieb)* removal expenses.
Verleih lending, hire, hiring, *(Film)* distribution, release;
Film für den ~ freigeben to release a film.
verleihbar grantable, loanable, lendable, conferable.
Verleiheinnahmen rental earnings.
verleihen to lend, to loan, to put out on loan, to let out, to rent, *(Film)* to distribute, to release, *(Orden)* to award;
jem. ein Amt ~ to appoint s. o. to an office; **Auszeichnung ~** to award a decoration; **Boot nur zu reinen Vergnügungszwecken ~** to let a boat for hire for the purpose of pleasure only; **einer Sache Dauer ~** to make s. th. last; **Ehrenbürgerrechte ~** to confer the freedom of a city on s. o.; **Geld auf Zinsen ~** to lend (put out) money at interest, to loan [out] *(US)*; **jem. einen akademischen Grad ~** to confer a degree on s. o.; **Konzession ~** to grant a licence; **gegen Miete ~** to hire; **jem. den Offiziersrang ~** to commission s. o.; **Pfründe ~** to collate (appoint) to a benefice; **Preis ~** to award a prize; **jem. Rechte ~** to vest s. o. with rights; **einem Gesetz Rechtskraft ~** to give effect to a law; **Satzung ~** to grant a charter; **jem. einen Titel ~** to bestow (confer) a title on s. o.; **einer Sache Würde ~** to lend dignity to s. th.
Verleiher lender, keeper, loaner *(US)*, *(von Rechten)* grantor, *(Filmgeschäft)* catering firm, distributor.
Verleih|firma *(Film)* catering firm, distributor; **ins ~geschäft einsteigen** to roll into renting; ~**gesellschaft** rental company; ~**kopie** distributing print; ~**system für bewegliche Wohnungseinheiten** motor home rental program(me).
Verleihung lending, *(Gewährung)* grant, conferment, *(Konzession)* concession, licence, *(Rechte)* vesting;
~ eines Amtes appointment to (dation of) an office; **~ eines akademischen Grades** conferment of a degree, graduation; **~ einer Konzession** granting a licence, public grant, *(Bank)* grant of a charter; **~ eines Preises** awarding a prize; **~ eines Rechtes** granting (vesting) a right; **~ der Rechtsfähigkeit** general franchise; **~ einer Würde** bestowal of a dignity.
Verleihungs|recht gift; ~**urkunde** charter, diploma, *(Offizier)* commission.
verleiten to induce, to entice, to incite, to inveigle;
Arbeiter zum Streik ~ to induce men to strike, to instigate workers to down tools; **zum Diebstahl ~** to solicit to larceny; **zu einem Fehler ~** to lead into a mistake; **j. zur Fehlinvestition ~** to inveigle s. o. into investing his money unwisely; **Soldaten zum Ungehorsam ~** to incite soldiers to rise against their officers; **j. zum Vertragsbruch ~** to procure s. o. to break his contract; **Zeugen zum Meineid ~** to suborn a witness;

sich ~ lassen to yield to impulse, to get fooled into doing; **sich zu einem Irrtum ~ lassen** to be induced by s. th. to commit an error.

Verleitung misguidance, inveiglement;
~ **zum Diebstahl** solicitation to larceny; ~ **zum Meineid** subordination of perjury; ~ **zur Patentverletzung** inducement of infringement; ~ **zum Vertragsabschluß** inducement to enter a contract; ~ **zum Vertragsbruch** inducing (procuring) breach of contract; ~ **zum Wechsel der Versicherung** twisting.

verlernen to forget, to unlearn.

Verlesen | des Protokolls reading the minutes; ~ **einer Zeugenaussage** deposition de bene esse.

verlesen to read out;
Bericht ~ to read a report; **Namen** ~ to roll-call, to call over; **Protokoll** ~ to read the minutes.

Verlesung reading;
~ **von Namen** roll call; ~ **des Protokolls** reading the minutes.

verletzbar damageable, vulnerable;
leicht ~ touchy, easily hurt.

verletzen to injure, to hurt, to violate, to infringe, to infract *(US)*, *(beleidigen)* to offend, *(beschädigen)* to damage, *(kränken)* to hurt, to cut, to wound, *(übertreten)* to break, to disobey, to contravene;
Abmachung ~ to break an agreement; **Anstandsgefühl** ~ to offend against decency; **Bestimmungen** ~ to contravene regulations, to be in violation of provisions; **Briefgeheimnis** ~ to break the secrecy of a letter; **Eid** ~ to violate an oath; **jds. Eigentum** ~ to trespass upon s. one's property; **jds. Gefühle** ~ to hurt s. one's feelings; **jds. Gerechtigkeitsgefühl** ~ to offend s. one's sense of justice; **guten Geschmack** ~ to overstep the lines of good taste; **Gesetz** ~ to break (offend against, contravene) the law; **Grenze** ~ to violate the frontier; **einfachste Grundsätze der Billigkeit** ~ to contravene the first principles of equity; **jds. Interessen** ~ to injure (impair, interfere with) s. one's interests; **jds. Intimsphäre** ~ to violate (trespass upon) s. one's privacy; **Neutralität** ~ to infract a neutrality; **Patent[recht]** ~ to infringe a patent right; **seine Pflicht** ~ to fail in (neglect) one's duty; **Postgeheimnis** ~ to break the secrecy of letters; **jds. Rechte** ~ to encroach (trespass) upon s. one's rights; **Regel** ~ to transgress a rule; **Siegel** ~ to break a seal; **jds. Stolz** ~ to hurt s. one's pride; **jds. Stolz empfindlich** ~ to cut s. o. to the quick; **Urheberrechte** ~ to infringe a copyright; **Verpflichtung** ~ to infringe an obligation; **Vertrag** ~ to break (violate) a contract, to transgress a treaty; **Vertragsbestimmungen** ~ to violate a clause, to break [through] the obligations of a contract; **Vorfahrt** ~ to violate the right of way; **Warenzeichen** ~ to infringe a trademark;
j. nicht ~ **wollen** to mean no offence.

verletzend offensive.

Verletzer *(Patentrecht)* infringing party, pirate;
~ **eines Patents** infringer of a patent, infringing party.

verletzt injured, wounded, hurt, punctured, *(beleidigt)* affronted, offended, hurt;
tödlich ~ fatally injured; **zutiefst** ~ cut to the quick;
schwer ~ **werden** to receive severe injuries;
~**e Eitelkeit** wounded vanity.

Verletzter injured (wronged) party, person (party) injured, the injured.

Verletzung injury, wound, hurt, violence, *(Beleidigung)* affront, hurt, offence, offense *(US)*, *(Beschädigung)* damage, *(Patentrecht)* infringement, *(Übergriff)* invasion, encroachment, *(Überschreitung)* infraction, transgression, *(Vertrag)* violation, transgression, breach, infraction;
unter ~ **von** in contravention of;
immer wieder auftauchende ~ continuous injury; **einklagbare** ~ private injury; **im Dienst erlittene** ~ injury sustained in the line of duty; **geringfügige** ~**en** minor injuries; **innere** ~**en** internal injuries; **lebensgefährliche** ~**en** critical injuries; **offenkundige** ~ public infringement; **schadensersatzerhöhende** ~**en** aggravation of the disability; **schuldhafte** ~ nonaccidental injury; **schwere** ~ serious injury; **äußerlich sichtbare** ~ visible injury; **tödliche** ~ fatal injury; **unfallbedingte** ~ injury caused by an accident, sudden or violent injury; **vorsätzliche** ~ wilful and malicious (wanton) injury;
~ **der Amtspflicht** official misconduct, breach (neglect) of duty, malfeasance, malversation; ~ **der Amtsverschwiegenheit** breach of official secrecy; **grobe** ~ **des Anstands** outrage upon morals (decency, *US*); ~ **der vorvertraglichen Anzeigepflicht** *(Versicherung)* nondisclosure; ~ **des Berufsgeheimnisses** breach (breaking) of professional secrecy; ~ **der Bestimmungen des Kartellgesetzes** Antitrust Act Violation *(US)*; ~ **des Briefgeheimnisses** breach of the secrecy of letters; ~ **des Bürgerrechts** enfranchisement; ~ **der Eidespflicht** violation of an oath; ~ **wesentlicher Formvorschriften** nonobservance of essential formalities; ~ **eines Gebrauchsmusters** infringement of registered design *(Br.)*; ~ **der Geheimhaltungspflicht** breach of confidence; ~ **eines Gesetzes** infraction (breach, contravention, violation) of a law; ~ **der Gewährleistungspflicht** breach of warranty; ~ **des Gleichberechtigungsprinzips** *(Verfassungsrecht)* discrimination; ~ **der Grundrechte** violation of the rights of a citizen; ~ **der Intimsphäre** invasion of (intrusion on) s. one's privacy, violation of privacy; ~ **des Luftraums** violation of airspace; ~ **der Menschenrechte** human rights violation; ~ **von Mitgliedschaftsrechten** absolute injury; ~ **der Neutralität** violation (infringement, infraction) of neutrality; ~ **eines Patents** infringement of a patent right; ~ **der ehelichen Pflichten** matrimonial offence; ~ **obliegender Pflichten** neglect (breach) of one's duties; ~ **moralischer Prinzipien** violation of the principles of morality; ~ **von jds. Rechten** encroachment on s. one's rights; ~ **einer Rechtspflicht** breach of legal duty; ~ **der öffentlichen Ruhe und Ordnung** violation of the peace; ~ **der Schweigepflicht** breach of professional secrecy; ~ **der Sonn- und Feiertagsruhe** breaking the Sabbath; ~ **der Sorgfaltspflicht** lack of care; ~ **der gesetzlich vorgeschriebenen Sorgfaltspflicht** negligence in law, statutory negligence *(US)*; ~ **der Standespflichten** breach of professional etiquette; ~ **von jds. Stolz** affront to s. one's pride; ~ **der Treuepflicht** breach of trust; ~ **durch einen Unfall** accidental injury, injury caused by accident; **vorsätzliche** ~ **der Unterhaltspflicht** wilful neglect to provide reasonable maintenance *(Br.)*, nonsupport *(US)*; ~ **des Urheberrechts** infringement (breach) of copyright; ~ **der Verfassung** infringement of the constitution; ~ **einer Verkehrsvorschrift** moving *(Br.)* (traffic, *US*) violation; ~ **eines Vertrages** infringement (violation, breaking) of a contract; **absichtliche** ~ **eines Vertrages** constructive breach; **fortgesetzte** ~ **eines Vertrages** continuing breach of contract; ~ **der Vertraulichkeit** violation of privacy, intrusion on (invasion of) s. one's privacy; ~ **des Völkerrechts** violation of an international law; ~ **der Vorfahrt** violation of the right of way; ~ **gesetzlicher Vorschriften** breach of the law; ~ **von Warenzeichenrechten** infringement of trademarks; ~ **einer vertraglichen Zusicherung** breach of warranty;
seinen schweren ~**en erliegen** to die as a result of one's severe injuries; ~ **eines Vertrages feststellen** to set up the breach; **unter** ~ **eines Rechts handeln** to act in contravention of a right; ~ **vorschützen** to allege an injury; **sich bei einem Unfall innere** ~**en zuziehen** to suffer internal injuries in an accident.

Verletzungs | absicht malicious intent; ~**handlung** injurious act.

verleugnen to deny, to disown, to repudiate;
Kind ~ to disown (disavow) a child; **sich selbst** ~ to betray one's principles; **seine Unterschrift** ~ to deny one's signature; **Urheberschaft** ~ to disclaim authorship.

Verleugnung denial, repudiation;
~ **eines Kindes** disownment (disavowal) of a child; ~ **von Tatsachen** denial of facts.

verleumden to slander, to defame, to calumniate, to blemish, to utter calumnies, to run down *(US)*;
j. ~ to asperse s. one's good name; **Unschuldigen** ~ to malign an innocent person.

Verleumder libeller, slanderer, calumniator, backbiter, detractor, *(pl.)* slanderous tongues.

verleumderisch defamatory, slanderous, libellous, detractive, foul-spoken;
~**e Bemerkungen machen** to speak disparagingly; ~**er Bericht** calumnious report; ~**e Beschuldigung** defamatory imputation; ~**es Material** defamatory material.

Verleumdung slander, libel, defamation, backbiting, stab in the back, calumny, calumniation, malediction, mudslinging, aspersion, disparagement;
bösartige ~ vicious slander *(coll.)*; **geschäftliche** ~ disparagement of a competitor; **strafbare** ~ criminal libel;
~ **im Geschäftsverkehr** trade disparagement;
~ **gegen j. begehen** to utter a libel against s. o.; **der** ~ **Tür und Tor öffnen** to give a handle for calumny; ~**en über j. verbreiten** to fling dirt at s. o. (s. one's reputation).

Verleumdungs | absicht intent to defame; ~**feldzug** smearing campaign, campaign of abuse; ~**klage** libel suit (action), defamatory action, action for libel (slander), action for the tort of defamation; ~**prozeß** defamation process; ~**taktik** smearing devices; ~**versuch** smear attempt.

verlieben, sich to fall in love; **sich in ein Kleid** ~ to take a fancy to a dress.

verliebt, in ein Auto mad about a car; **hoffnungslos** ~ head over heels in love.
verliehen vested.
verlieren to lose, to forfeit, *(Prozeß)* to be unsuccessful, to lose; **sich** ~ to go astray, to lose one's way, *(Begeisterung)* to subside, *(Eindruck)* to wear off, *(Menge)* to disperse, to scatter; **bei jem.** ~ to sink in s. one's estimation; **schlechte Angewohnheit** ~ to outgrow a bad habit; **etw. aus den Augen** ~ to lose track of s. th.; **in den Augen seiner Freunde** ~ to forfeit the good opinion of one's friends; **das Bewußtsein** ~ to faint; **an Boden** ~ to lose ground; **sich vom Boden der Wirklichkeit** ~ to lose one's hold on reality; **glatte tausend Dollar** ~ to lose a clear thousand dollars; **den Faden** ~ to lose the thread of one's discourse; **seine Fassung** ~ to lose one's balance (hair); **seinen Führerschein** ~ to forfeit one's driving licence *(Br.)*; **aus dem Gedächtnis** ~ to lose one's memory; **sehr viel Geld** ~ to drop a lot of money; **bei einem Geschäft** ~ to lose on a transaction; **Gültigkeit** ~ to be deprived of validity; **Krieg** ~ to lose the war; **Kundschaft** ~ to lose business; **Neuigkeitswert** ~ to wear off; **Prozeß** ~ to lose a lawsuit (case); **sich rasch** ~ to fade; **Recht** ~ to forfeit a right; **seinen guten Ruf** ~ to forfeit one's credit (reputation), to grow out of estimation; **Ruhegehaltsanspruch** ~ to forfeit one's pension; **Schlacht um die Gunst der öffentlichen Meinung** ~ to lose the battle for public opinion; **seine Stellung** ~ to lose (fall from) one's position, to lose one's job, to forfeit one's place; **seinen Verstand** ~ to take leave of one's senses; **an Wert** ~ to lose (go down) in value, to deteriorate;
gut ~ **können** to play the game.
Verlierer loser, unsuccessful party;
schlechter ~ **sein** to be a bad loser.
Verlies dungeon, hell;
finsteres ~ dark dungeon.
verloben, sich to become (get) engaged.
Verlobte intended wife, *(pl.)* engaged couple;
~ **aufbieten** to proclaim the banns.
Verlobter fiancé, betrothed.
Verlobung engagement, betrothal, affiance, espousals;
~ **[auf]lösen** to break an engagement, to declare an engagement off.
Verlobungs|antrag declaration, proposal; ~**anzeige** notice of engagement, engagement announcement; ~**feier** engagement celebration; ~**ring** engagement ring; ~**zeit** time of engagement.
verlocken to entice, to entrap, to allure, to inveigle;
j. zum Baden ~ to tempt s. o. to go for a swim; **zu Spekulationen** ~ to encourage speculation.
verlockend tempting, attractive, enticing, alluring;
~**es Angebot** tempting offer.
Verlockung enticement, attraction, inveiglement;
~ **zum Geldausgeben** temptation to spend money; ~**en einer Großstadt** allurements (attractions) of a big city; ~**en des Landlebens** seductions of country life;
einer ~ **nachgeben** to yield to a temptation; **gegen alle** ~**en gefeit sein** to be proof against all inveiglements.
verlogen lying, mendacious;
~**er Bursche** glib liar.
verlohnen, sich der Mühe nicht not to be worthwhile.
verloren lost, missing, ruined, done for, out the window *(sl.)*, *(hilflos)* forlorn, *(Kranker)* past help;
unwiederbringlich ~ past recovery, irrecoverable, *(Verpackung)* nonreturnable;
als ~ **betrachten** to give up for lost; **sich** ~ **geben** to throw in one's hand; **Spiel** ~ **geben** to give up the game for lost; **tausend Pfund** ~ **haben** to be the poorer by a thousand pounds; **in Gedanken** ~ **sein** to be wrapped up (lost) in thought; ~ **im Gedränge stehen** to be forlorn in the middle of the crowd;
~**es Buch** missing book; ~**e Gegenstände** lost property; ~**e Liebesmüh** wasted effort; **auf** ~**em Posten stehen** to fight a losing battle; ~**e Sache** forlorn hope; ~**er Sohn** prodigal son; ~**er Zuschuß** lost contribution.
verlorengegangen lost, missing;
völlig ~ **sein** to have gone right out of the window; **durch die Zeit** ~ **sein** to be lost in the mist of time;
~**e Gegenstände** lost property;
an ihm ist ein Schauspieler ~ he is cut out to be an actor.
Verlorengehen miscarriage.
verlorengehen to go astray, to get (be) lost, to be divested, *(Brief)* to miscarry, *(Schiff)* to go by the board, to founder.
verlosbar redeemable (callable) by lot.
verlöschen to go (die) out, *(Kerze)* to quench, *(Schrift)* to fade, *(Sterne)* to set;
flackernd ~ to flicker out.
verlosen to allot, to draw by lot, to dispose by lots, to lot out, to cast lots, *(Wertpapiere)* to raffle;
Pfandbriefe zur Rückzahlung ~ to redeem bonds by drawing;
Tombola ~ to raffle off.
verlost werden to be drawn.
Verlosung lottery, lottery drawing, allotment, prize drawing, *(Wertpapiere)* raffle;
jährliche ~ annual drawing;
Karten für die ~ **kaufen** to buy raffle tickets; ~ **veranstalten (vornehmen)** to draw a lottery, to run a raffle.
verlöten to solder, to plumb;
einen ~ to have a quick one *(coll.)*.
Verlust loss, sacrifice, *(Abgang)* wastage, waste, *(Defizit)* deficit, red *(US coll.)*, *(Konfiskation)* forfeiture, *(Leckage)* leakage, *(Nachteil)* disadvantage, detriment, *(Schaden)* damage, detriment, cost, *(Schwund)* shrinkage, *(Spiel)* losings, *(Todesfall)* bereavement, *(Verderb)* spoilage, waste;
bei ~ under pain (with forfeiture) of; **bei Eintritt eines** ~**es** in the event (upon the occurrence) of a loss; **einem** ~ **unterworfen** deprivable; **in** ~ **geraten** lost; **mit** ~ at a sacrifice (loss), at a loss; **nach Abschreibung aller** ~**e** after charging off all losses; **ohne** ~ wasteless; **ohne einen einzigen** ~ with a no-loss record; **ohne Rücksicht auf** ~**e** at all risks;
~**e** *(mil.)* casualties, losses;
abschätzbarer ~ estimable loss; **steuerlich absetzbarer (abzugsfähiger)** ~ loss available for relief, deductible loss; **steuerlich nicht absetzbarer** ~ loss not allowable; **absoluter** ~ dead loss; **nicht anerkannter** ~ *(Spediteur)* concealed loss; **steuerlich anerkannter** ~ taxable loss; **anteilsmäßiger** ~ proportional loss; **in der Bilanz ausgewiesener** ~ loss as shown in the balance sheet; **auf Brandstiftung beruhender** ~ incendiary loss; **beträchtlicher** ~ severe loss; **nicht betriebsbedingter** ~ nontrading loss; **buchmäßiger** ~ accounting (book) loss; **eingetretener (entstandener)** ~ incurred (actual) loss; **einmaliger** ~ nonrecurring loss; **empfindlicher** ~ considerable loss, deprivation; **endgültiger** ~ dead loss; **auf konzernfremde Gesellschaften entfallender** ~ *(Bilanz)* minority interest in losses; **durch Kursschwankungen entstandener** ~ exchange loss; **durch Nichtvermietung entstandener** ~ vacancy loss; **durch Preisherabsetzung (Preisheraufsetzung) entstandener** ~ markdown (markup) loss; **bei der Liquidation voraussichtlich entstehende** ~**e** total estimated deficiency from realization of assets; **durch Nichtvermietung von Räumen entstehender** ~ vacancy loss; **erkannter** ~ *(Spediteur)* known loss; **erlittener** ~ loss sustained; **erlittene** ~**e** *(mil.)* casualties; **ersetzbarer** ~ recoverable loss; **erwartete** ~**e** anticipated losses; **finanzieller** ~ pecuniary loss; **durch Exzedentenrückversicherung nicht gedeckter** ~ uninsured excess loss; **von der Versicherung voll gedeckter** ~ loss fully covered by insurance; **von der Versicherung nicht gedeckter** ~ loss not compensated by insurance; **versicherungsmäßig gedeckte** ~**e** losses recoverable under a contract of insurance; **nicht geschäftsbedingter** ~ nonbusiness loss; **gleicher** ~ even break; **großer** ~ heavy (severe) loss; **aus zweifelhaften Forderungen herrührende** ~**e** bad-debt losses *(US)*; **zufällig hervorgerufener** ~ casual loss; **landwirtschaftliche** ~**e** farm losses; **laufender** ~ operating loss; **mittelbarer** ~ consequential (constructive) loss; **Per-Saldo-**~ net loss; **reiner** ~ net (dead) loss; **schwerer** ~ heavy (severe) loss; **für den Konzernausgleich zur Verfügung stehender** ~ loss available for group relief *(Br.)*; **tatsächlicher** ~ actual loss; **aus dem Jahresertrag zu tilgende** ~**e** losses chargeable against the year; **totaler** ~ dead (outright) loss; **übermäßiger** ~ excess loss; **unbedeutender** ~ insignificant (trivial) loss; **unermeßlicher** ~ incalculable loss; **unersetzlicher** ~ irrecoverable (irretrievable, irredeemable) loss; **unerwarteter** ~ unanticipated loss; **unmittelbarer** ~ direct loss; **unwiederbringlicher** ~ dead loss; **steuerlich noch nicht verbrauchte** ~**e** unabsorbed losses; **nicht versicherter** ~ uninsured loss; **durch Brand verursachter** ~ loss by fire; **steuerlich nicht verwertbarer** ~ unrelieved loss *(Br.)*; **aus den Vorjahren vorgetragene** ~**e** losses brought forward from previous years; **vorweggenommener** ~ anticipated loss; **auf Abschreibungen im Anschaffungsjahr zurückzuführender** ~ loss arising from first-year allowance; **auf Autounfälle zurückzuführende** ~**e** motor accident casualties;
Gewinn und ~ profit and loss, losses and gains;
~**e aus dem Abgang von Gegenständen des Anlagevermögens** losses on retirement of fixed assets; ~ **überseeischer Absatzgebiete** loss of overseas markets; ~ **des Allmenderechts** extinguishment of common; **ein** ~ **nach dem anderen** loss on loss; ~ **der Arbeitsfähigkeit** loss of earning capacity; ~ **der Arbeitskraft des Ehegatten** loss of services of the spouse *(Br.)*; ~

des Arbeitsplatzes loss of employment; ~ **durch Auslaufen** loss by leakage; ~**e durch Betriebsunterbrechung** use and occupancy loss; ~**e aus Bürgschaftsverpflichtungen** surety losses; ~ **der bürgerlichen Ehrenrechte** forfeit of civil rights, infamy *(US)*; ~ **durch Feuer** losses caused by fire; ~ **aus zweifelhaften Forderungen** bad *(US)* (doubtful, *Br.*) debt losses, loss from bad *(US)* (doubtful, *Br.*) debts; ~ **im Geschäftsjahr** *(Versicherungsgesellschaft)* underwriting loss; ~**e der Gesellschaft** corporate losses *(US)*; ~ **durch allgemeine Havarie** average loss; ~ **in Höhe des Zeitwertes [des versicherten Gegenstandes]** actual loss; ~ **aus Kapitalanlagen** loss on investments; ~ **der Konzession** loss of franchise; ~ **der Kundschaft** loss of custom; ~ **aus Kursschwankungen** exchange loss; ~ **der Ladung** loss of cargo; ~**e der Landwirtschaft** farm losses; ~ **der Lebensgemeinschaft** loss of consortium *(Br.)*; ~**e an Menschenleben** loss of life; ~**e im Mietgeschäft** rental losses; ~ **bei Nachwahlen** by-election losses *(Br.)*; ~ **des Pensionsanspruches** disqualification of benefit, forfeiture of a pension; ~ **seines Ranges** forfeiture of a seniority rank (right); ~ **eines Rechtes** loss (forfeiture) of a right; ~ **auf See** marine loss; **vollständiger** ~ **des Sehvermögens** entire loss of sight; ~ **der Staatsbürgerschaft** forfeiture of citizenship, loss of nationality; ~ **auf dem Transport** loss in transit; ~ **aus einem Verkauf** sales loss; ~ **bei Verladungen** loss of shipments *(US)*; ~ **von Vermögenswerten** loss of property values; ~ **infolge nicht zustande gekommenen Vertragsabschlusses** loss of contract; ~ **der Voraussetzungen für ein öffentliches Amt** disqualification of a person for office; ~ **des Wahlrechts** withdrawal of franchise, disfranchisement; ~**e aus Wertminderungen oder dem Abgang von Gegenständen des Umlaufvermögens außer Vorräten** valuation adjustment on current assets other than inventories; ~ **aus Wertpapieranlagen** loss from securities holding; **schwere** ~**e am Wildbestand** heavy damage to wildlife; ~ **an Zeit und Lohn** broken time; ~ **der Zeugnisfähigkeit** disqualification from being a witness;

~**e abbuchen** to cut one's losses; ~ **abdecken** to cover (make good) a loss; ~ **abschätzen** to assess a loss; **mit** ~ **abschließen** to show (result in, close with) a loss; **Jahr mit** ~ **abschließen** to close a year in the red *(US coll.)*; **seine** ~**e abschreiben** to cut (charge off, deduct) one's losses; ~ **abwenden** to turn off a loss; **mit** ~ **arbeiten** to operate (run, carry on) at a loss, to run in the red *(US coll.)*; **mit schweren** ~**en arbeiten** to work out heavy deficits; ~**e auffangen** to absorb (cushion) losses; ~**e auffüllen** *(mil.)* to make good the casualties; **für einen** ~ **aufkommen** to be liable (responsible) for a loss; ~**e aufteilen** to share losses; ~**e aufweisen** to show a loss, to show red ink *(US coll.)*; ~ **ausgleichen** to make good (recoup) a loss, to make up for a deficit (deficiency), to make good a deficit; ~**e wieder ausgleichen** *(Börse)* to recover one's losses; ~ **ausweisen** to show a loss (deficit); **seine** ~**e ersetzt bekommen** to recover one's losses; **seinen** ~ **berechnen** to reckon up one's loss; ~**e berücksichtigen** to make allowance for losses; **sich an einem** ~ **beteiligen** to share in a loss; **mit** ~ **betreiben** to carry on at a loss; **vor** ~ **bewahren** to save from a loss; **als** ~ **buchen** to put down to loss; **ohne** ~**e davonkommen** to get off without a loss; ~ **decken** to make up for a deficiency, to make good a deficit, to cover a loss; ~ **wieder einbringen** to make up for a deficiency, to retrieve a loss; **mit** ~ **einkaufen** to buy at a loss; **j. für einen** ~ **entschädigen** to indemnify (compensate) s. o. for a loss; ~ **erfahren** to undergo (meet) a loss; **sich von seinen** ~**en erholen** to recover one's losses; ~ **erleiden** to sustain (meet with, incur, experience) a loss; **finanzielle** ~**e erleiden** to suffer in one's pocket money; **steuerlich anerkannten geschäftlichen** ~ **erleiden** to make a loss in a trade or business; **große** ~**e erleiden** to incur (suffer) severe losses, to lose heavily, to sustain heavy losses, to go heavily into the red *(US coll.)*; **bei der Briefbeförderung keine** ~**e erleiden** *(Postverwaltung)* to break even on letters; ~**e an der Börse erleiden** to meet with losses on the stock exchange; ~ **ermitteln** to ascertain a loss; ~ **ersetzen** to make amends, to repair a damage (loss); **jem. den** ~ **von etw. ersetzen** to pay s. o. the lost value of s. th.; ~ **erzielen** to notch up a loss; **in** ~ **geraten** to get lost; ~**e haben** to be out of pocket, to be in the red *(US coll.)*; **100 Dollar** ~**e haben** to be out by $ 100; **schwere** ~**e haben** to lose heavily, to be hard hit, to have a heavy loss, *(mil.)* to have a high death toll; **für** ~**e haften** to be liable for [a loss]; **sich für einen** ~ **schadlos halten** to retrieve a loss; ~**e durch Börsenspekulationen wieder hereinholen** to recoup one's losses in gaining on the stock market; **schwer unter seinen finanziellen** ~**en leiden** to be hard hit by one's financial losses; **geringe** ~**e hinnehmen müssen** to lose a little ground; ~ **in Kauf nehmen** to take a loss; **seine** ~**e durch An- und Verkauf reduzieren** *(Börse)* to average down (up); **geschäftliche** ~**e riskieren** to jeopardize one's business; ~ **von Tausenden von Arbeitsplätzen riskieren** to put thousands of jobs at risk; **sich vor** ~**en schützen** to save one's bacon, *(Börse)* to hedge; **einem** ~ **ausgesetzt sein** to be exposed to a loss; **am** ~ **beteiligt sein** to participate in a loss; **gegen** ~**e sicherstellen** to safeguard against losses; **j. in** ~**e stürzen** to run s. o. into losses; ~ **tragen** to bear (stand) a loss; ~ **anteilig tragen** to share a loss ratably; **Gewinne und** ~**e zu gleichen Teilen tragen** to share and share alike; **sich von jem. ohne** ~ **trennen** to break even with s. o.; **jds.** ~**e übernehmen** to reimburse s. o. for his losses; ~ **vergüten** to make up for a loss; ~ **verhüten** to cut a loss; **mit** ~ **verkaufen** to sell at a loss (discount, sacrifice, disadvantage, with a forfeit), to bargain away; ~**e gerade noch vermeiden** to break even; **seine** ~**e verniedlichen** to understate one's losses; ~**e mit den erzielten Einkünften verrechnen** to set the loss against earned income; ~**e verschleiern** to conceal losses; ~**e gleichmäßig über ein Jahr verteilen** to apportion losses evenly over a year; **finanzielle** ~**e des einzelnen Versicherungsnehmers auf alle verteilen** to spread the financial losses of insured members over the whole community; ~**e rückwirkend verwenden** *(Steuererklärung)* to relate back losses; ~ **verzeichnen** to record a loss; ~**e längerfristig vortragen** to carry forward long-term losses *(Br.)*; **mit einem** ~ **fertig werden** to cope with red ink *(US coll.)*; **mit** ~ **liquidiert werden** to wind up in the red *(US coll.)*; ~ **wettmachen** to repair a loss; ~ **zufügen** to cause a loss; **schweren** ~ **zufügen** to inflict a serious loss; ~ **steuerlich zurücktragen** to carry back a loss;

bei ~ **kann kein Ersatz geleistet werden** no refund if lost;

~**abschluß** losing bargain, *(Bilanz)* closing in the red *(US coll.)*, balance sheet that shows a deficit, deficiency statement *(US)*, *(Einzelgeschäft)* losing bargain; ~**abschluß tätigen** to close a year in the red *(US coll.)*; ~**abzug** loss relief, *(Steuer)* deductible loss; ~**anrechnung** *(Einkommensteuer)* loss relief *(Br.)*; ~**anteil** share in a loss, *(Bilanz)* loss; ~**anzeige** *(Versicherung)* notification (notice) of loss, immediate notice; ~**anzeige bei der Polizei abgeben** to notify the police of a loss.

verlustarm *(el.)* low-loss.

Verlust|artikel loss leader; ~**aufteilung** loss repartition, division of losses, *(Firma)* distribution of partnership loss; ~**auftrag** money-losing order.

verlustaufweisend showing a loss.

Verlustausgleich making up for losses, loss compensation, *(Einkommensteuer)* carryback *(US)*;

konzerninterner ~ group relief *(Br.)*; **voller und angemessener** ~ fair and full equivalent for a loss;

~ **herbeiführen** to offset earlier losses.

Verlustausgleichsbestimmungen carryback provisions *(US)*.

verlustausweisend showing a loss (deficit).

Verlust|begrenzung limitation of loss, loss limitation; ~**beitrag** deficiency contribution; ~**benachrichtigung** notification of a loss, *(Lloyd)* casualty sheet; ~**bericht** *(Versicherung)* damage report; ~**beteiligung** sharing a loss; ~**beteiligung bei gemeinschaftlicher Havarie** contribution to general average; ~**beträge ungesicherter Gläubiger** deficiency to unsecured creditors; ~**betrieb** plant working with a deficit, money-losing operation, money loser, *(Bahn)* loss-making traffic; **landwirtschaftlicher** ~**betrieb** submarginal farm; ~**betrieb verkaufen** *(Konzern)* to sell its losing line; ~**bilanz** adverse balance, balance sheet that shows a deficit, deficiency statement *(US)*; ~**bilanz aufstellen** to reckon up one's losses.

verlustbringend detrimental, losing, involving (causing) a loss; ~**es Geschäft** losing business.

Verlust|deckung covering a loss; ~**eintragung** red-ink entry *(US coll.)*; ~**ermittlung** calculation of a loss; ~**etat** budget that shows a deficit; ~**faktor** loss-producing factor; **steuerliche** ~**faktoren** revenue drains; **im** ~**fall** in case (the event) of loss; **wirtschaftliches** ~**gebiet** deficit area; ~**gefahr** risk; ~**geschäft** losing business, money-losing operation (order); **steuerliches** ~**geschäft** tax-loss selling; ~**geschäfte erleiden** to go flat with losing operations; ~**geschäftsabschluß** losing bargain; ~**höhe** amount of loss.

verlustieren, sich to amuse (divert) o. s.

verlustig deprived of;

für ~ **erklären** to declare forfeited; **eines Rechtes** ~ **gehen** to lose a right; **einer Sache** ~ **gehen** to be deprived of s. th.; **seiner Staatsbürgerschaft für** ~ **erklärt werden** to be deprived of one's nationality.

Verlustigerklärung forfeiture.

Verlust|jahr deficit year; ~**kalkulation** estimable loss; ~**konto** deficit (loss) account, account showing a debit balance; ~**liste**

death roll, casualty list (returns), *(Schiffe)* casualty book; ~**meldung** *(mil.)* deficiency report; ~**minderung** reduction in losses, mitigation of damage (loss); ~**nachweis** *(Feuerversicherung)* proof of loss; **während einer ~periode** at the time of loss; ~**preis** ruinous (losing, loss-making, sacrifice) price; ~**preise hinnehmen** to be loss-leading; **betriebliche ~quellen** operational deficiencies; ~**quellenrechnung** losses caused by operational deficiencies; ~**quote** percentage of loss, loss ratio; **Gewinn- und ~rechnung** profit and loss account (statement), income statement, statement of revenue and expenditure; **Gewinn- und ~rechnung in Staffelform** report form; **konsolidierte Gewinn- und ~rechnung** consolidated profit and loss (income) statement; **vergleichende Gewinn- und ~rechnung** comparative income statement; ~**reduzierung** reduction of losses.

verlustreich involving heavy losses;
~**es Jahr** deficit year.

Verlust|risiko risk of loss, downside risk, hazard; **jem. das ~risiko abnehmen** to guarantee s. o. from (against) a loss; ~**rücklage** loss reserve, reserve for contingencies; ~**rückstellungen** appropriation for losses; ~**rücktrag** *(Einkommensteuer)* loss carryback *(US)*; ~**rücktragszeitraum** carryback period *(US)*; ~**saldo** loss balance, debit (adverse) balance; ~**schätzung** estimable loss; ~**seite** loss side; ~**sendung** miscarriage of goods; ~**spanne** deficit margin; ~**spitze** marginal loss; ~**statistik** loss statistics; ~**steigerung** increased losses; ~**strom** *(el.)* leak; ~**stück** lost property, *(Wechsel)* lost bill of exchange; ~**tochter** loss-making subsidiary; ~**träger** money loser, loss maker; ~**übernahme** assumption of losses; ~**umlage** apportionment of losses; ~**verkauf** ruinous (sacrifice, losing) sale, *(von Anreizwaren)* loss selling; ~**verkäufe** lost sales; ~**verkauf tätigen** to sell at a sacrifice; ~**verschleierung** concealment of losses; ~**verteilung** division of losses; ~**verteilung zu Steuerzwecken** carryback *(US)*; ~**vorausschätzung** pre-estimate of loss; ~**vortrag** *(Einkommensteuererklärung)* carryover *(US)*, debt balance (loss, *Br.*) carried forward, tax-loss carry forward *(Br.)*; **zweijähriger ~vortrag** deduction of losses against two following years; ~**zahlen** loss figures; **in ~zahlen geraten** to slip into deficit, to run into red ink *(US coll.)*; ~**zeit** *(Betrieb)* dead time, *(Maschinendefekt)* idle (waiting) time; **betriebsbedingte ~zeit** delay (down, *US*) time; **unvermeidliche ~zeit** *(Maschinenausfall)* required idle time; ~**ziffern** *(mil.)* casualties; **in die ~zone geraten** to get into the red *(US coll.)*; **plötzlich in die ~zone geraten** to plunge into the loss column, to spurt (plunge) into red ink *(US coll.)*.

vermachbar disposable by will, devisable.

Vermachen devisal.

vermachen to leave, to give and bequeath, to will;
jem. in seinem Testament 10.000 Dollar ~ to have s. o. down in one's will for $ 10.000; **testamentarisch ~** to give and bequeath, to bequeath, to leave by will, *(Grundstück)* to devise by will.

vermacht bequeathed, left;
nicht testamentarisch ~ intestate.

Vermächtnis bequest, legacy, settlement, gift by will, *(von Grundbesitz)* devise;
in Teilbeträgen auszuzahlendes ~ annuity; **bedingtes ~** conditional devise; **aufschiebend bedingtes ~** executory devise (limitation); **betagtes ~** deferred legacy; **im voraus empfangenes ~** preferential legacy; **durch Tod des Bedachten erledigtes ~** lapsed legacy; **geistiges ~** intellectual heritage; **mündliches ~** will parole; **politisches ~** legacy; **überholtes ~** lapsed legacy; **unabdingbares ~** vested legacy; **unbedingtes ~** absolute legacy; **von einem Treuhänder zu verwaltendes ~** trust legacy; **wohltätiges ~** charitable bequest;
~ **nach Abzug der Nachlaßverbindlichkeiten** residuary legacy (gift); ~ **einer Anwartschaft** executory bequest; ~ **mit (unter) Auflage** contingent legacy, conditional devise, modal legatee; ~ **eines Geldbetrages** pecuniary legacy; ~ **von Grundbesitz** devise; ~ **bezüglich des gesamten Grundbesitzes** general devise; ~ **bezüglich einzelner Grundstücke** special devise; ~ **des Reinnachlasses** residuary bequest (legacy); ~ **des gesamten Vermögens des Erblassers** universal legacy;
~ **annehmen** to accept a legacy; ~ **ausschlagen** to disclaim a legacy; ~ **aussetzen** to bequeath to [a legacy], to bequest; **jem. ein ~ aussetzen (hinterlassen)** to leave a legacy to (make a settlement on) s. o.; ~ **einbehalten** to subtract a legacy; **kulturelles ~ erhalten** to preserve the heritage; ~ **kürzen** to abate the amount of a legacy; **von einem ~ profitieren** to be enriched by a legacy; ~ **widerrufen** to redeem (adeem) a legacy; ~**anfall** devolution of a legacy; ~**anspruch** interest of legatee; ~**aussetzung** bequeathal; ~**berechtigter** specific legatee, devisee; ~**erbe** real representative, legatee; ~**fortfall** extinguishment of legacy; ~**geber** legator; ~**kürzung** abatement of legacy; ~**nehmer** [specific] legatee, taker, beneficiary, real representative, *(Grundbesitz)* devisee, *(Restnachlaß)* residuary legatee; **alleiniger ~nehmer** sole legatee; ~**nehmer sein** to receive (come into) a legacy; ~**rücknahme** redemption of a legacy; ~**wegfall** lapse of a testamentary bequest; ~**widerruf** ademption of a legacy.

Vermachung, testamentarische ~ von Geld disposal of money by will.

vermählen, sich to marry, to get married.

Vermählte newly married (wedded) couple.

Vermählung marriage, wedding.

Vermählungsanzeige wedding card, *(Zeitung)* wedding announcement.

vermanschen to make a hash of;
Blatt Papier ~ to spoil a sheet of paper.

vermarken to mark the border.

Vermarktung cooperative marketing.

Vermarkung marking out of a claim.

vermascht *(el.)* interconnected.

vermasseln to abort *(sl.)*, to muck up *(sl.)*, to queer *(sl.)*, to botch, to hash, to mess, to spoil, to muck up *(sl.)*;
j. etw. ~ to queer s. one's pitch; **Arbeit ~** to gum up the works.

vermasselt, damit ist alles that tears it *(sl.)*.

vermehren to augment, to increase, *(ausdehnen)* to extend, *(vergrößern)* to enlarge;
sich ~ *(Bevölkerung)* to multiply, *(Tiere)* to propagate, to breed; **sich erneut ~** to increase in number again; **sich wie die Kaninchen ~** to multiply like rabbits; **sein Vermögen ~** to enlarge one's fortune; **Zahlungsmittelumlauf ~** to expand the currency.

vermehrt increased, enlarged;
~**e Auflage** enlarged edition; **mit ~er Kraft** with augmented force.

Vermehrung increase, augmentation, increasement, increment, improvement, *(Ausdehnung)* extension, *(Vergrößerung)* enlargement;
~ **der Bevölkerung** multiplication of the population; ~ **des Zahlungsmittelumlaufs** expansion of the currency.

vermeidbar avoidable.

vermeiden to evade, to avoid, to prevent, to shun, to shirk;
Beantwortung einer Frage ~ to evade answering a question; **Diskussion ~** to evade a discussion; **Doppelbesteuerung ~** to avoid double taxation; **Härten ~** to avoid anomalies; **unnötige Licht- und Heizungskosten ~** to economize on light and fuel; **Steuerzahlungen ~** to avoid (evade) paying taxes; **Zusammenstoß ~** to avoid colliding.

Vermeidung avoidance, evasion, prevention;
bei ~ von under pain of, at the peril of; **bei ~ des Ausschlusses** under penalty of foreclosure; **zur ~ weiterer Verluste bestimmt** stop-loss;
~ **von Bargeschäften** flight from cash; ~ **der Doppelbesteuerung** avoidance of double taxation; ~ **der Erbschaftssteuer** avoidance of estate duty; ~ **von Härtefällen** prevention of hardship; ~ **eines Konkurses** avoidance of bankruptcy proceedings.

vermeintlich putative, reputed, presumed, supposed;
~**er Arzt** pretended doctor; ~**er Erbe** presumptive heir; ~**er Täter** alleged culprit; ~**er Tod** presumptive death; ~**er Vater** putative father.

vermelden, nichts zu ~ haben to have no say in a matter.

Vermengung *(jur.)* confusion, commingelment, commixture.

vermenschlichen to humanize.

Vermenschlichung humanization.

Vermerk note, notice, notation, mention, memorandum, *(Buchung)* entry, *(Kontrollzeichen)* tick, *(auf Urkunde)* endorsement, *(auf Wechselrückseite)* enfacement;
kurzer ~ jotting;
~ **in den Büchern** entry in the books; ~ **auf einer Urkunde** indorsement on a document; ~ **auf der Vorderseite** *(Wechsel)* enfacement;
~ **machen** to [make a] note; **in den Büchern einen ~ machen** to make notation on the records (an entry in the books); **mit ~en versehen** to docket.

vermerken to [make a] note (record), to mark down, to item, to note, to endorse;
in den Büchern ~ to make an entry in the books; **Eingangsdatum ~** to mark the date of receipt; **am Rande ~** to margin, to marginalize; **etw. auf der Rückseite einer Urkunde ~** to endorse s. th. on a document; **etw. übel ~** to take s. th. amiss (offence at s. th.).

Vermerkspalte memorandum (annotation) column.
Vermessen survey, measurement, measuring;
neues ~ resurvey.
vermessen to take the measurements, to measure, *(Forstwirtschaft)* to scale, *(Rauminhalt)* to cube, *(Schiff)* to measure the tonnage;
sich ~ to presume; **erneut** ~ to resurvey, *(Schiff)* to remeasure; **Grundstück** ~ to survey a piece of land; **Rauminhalt** ~ to take the dimensions of a room; **sich aufgrund seines Reichtums** ~ to presume on one's wealth;
~ *(a.)* arrogant, presumptuous, presuming, impudent;
wie kann man so ~ **sein!** what a daring thing to do!;
~**es Unternehmen** bold undertaking.
Vermessenheit presumption, arrogance, audacity, impudent.
Vermesser surveyor.
Vermessung measurement, *(Grundstück)* [land] surveying, survey, *(Schiff)* tonnage measurement, *(aus dem Weltraum)* tracking;
allgemeine ~ inclusive survey; **amtliche** ~ ordnance survey *(Br.)*; **genaue** ~ detailed survey;
~ **eines Grundstücks** survey of land; ~ **der Küstengewässer** marine surveying; ~ **aus der Luft** aerial surveying.
Vermessungs|amt surveyor's office; ~**arbeiten** surveying, surveyancy; ~**aufnahme aus der Luft** photographic survey; ~**beamter** surveying officer, surveyor, land measurer (surveyor); ~**boot** surveying ship; ~**deck** tonnage deck; ~**flugzeug** aerial photomap plane; ~**gebühren** surveyor's (survey) charges; ~**gerät** measuring instrument; ~**gesellschaft** survey company; ~**gruppe** survey crew; ~**ingenieur** surveyor, land measurer, geometer, topographical engineer; ~**kosten** surveyor's fee; ~**länge** tonnage length; ~**marke** tonnage mark; ~**notizen** field notes; ~**protokoll** verification of survey; ~**punkt** monument; ~**schein** certificate of survey; ~**schiff** surveying ship; ~**stab** levelling (surveyor's) rod; ~**station** *(Weltraum)* tracking station; ~**tätigkeit** surveyance; ~**vorhaben** surveying project; ~**wesen** surveying, topographical engineering; ~**zeichen** bench mark.
vermiesen, jem. etw. to spoil s. one's fun, to mar s. one's joy.
vermietbar rentable, to let, hirable, tenantable, lettable *(Br.)*;
nicht ~ illocable.
Vermieten hiring, let, letting, leasing;
~ **möblierter oder nicht möblierter Zimmer** letting furnished or unfurnished rooms.
vermieten to let [out to tenants (on hire)], to let on (put out to) lease, to lease [out], to grant a lease, to put out on rental *(US)*, to hire out *(US)*, *(Schiff)* to charter;
etw. ~ to let s. th. out on hire; **zu billig** ~ to rent below the value; **Boot zu reinen Vergnügungszwecken** ~ to let a boat for hire for the purpose of pleasure only; **Geschäftsgrundstück** ~ to lease business property; **zu Geschäftszwecken** ~ to let at a full commercial rent; **Haus** ~ to let (lease, rent) a house; **Hausgrundstück zu Kostensätzen** ~ to let one's property at an economic rent; **jährlich** ~ to let at an annual rent; **Liegestühle** ~ to hire out deck chairs; **möbliert** ~ to let furnished lodgings; **Motorboote stundenweise** ~ to hire out motor-boats by the hour; **bewegliche Sachen** ~ to let out on hire; **zu teuer** ~ to rent too high, to overrent; **wieder** ~ to relet, to release; **möblierte Wohnung** ~ to let off a furnished flat *(Br.)*; **Wohnungen in einem Haus einzeln** ~ to let off a house in flats *(Br.)* (apartments, *US*); **Zimmer** ~ to take in lodgers, to let rooms; **Zimmer an Urlauber** ~ to rent (let, *Br.*) rooms to holidaymakers; **möbliertes Zimmer** ~ to let a furnished apartment;
zu ~ for hire (rent, *US*); **bezugsfertig zu** ~ to be let with immediate possession; **Haus teilweise zu** ~ *(Anzeige)* part of house to let; **Zimmer zu** ~ *(Aushang)* rooms for rent (to let, *Br.*); **Haus nicht** ~ **können** not to get a let for one's house; **sich gut** ~ **lassen** to let well.
Vermieter lessor, letter, hirer out, locator *(US)*, *(Hauswirt)* landlord, *(Verleiher)* keeper, lender;
~ **eines Apartments** lessor of a flat; ~ **einer Elendswohnung** slum landlord; ~ **und Mieter** landlord and tenant, *(pl.)* householders and lodgers; ~ **eines Schließfachs** hirer of a safe; ~ **einer Sozialwohnung** council landlord *(Br.)*.
vermieterfreundlich sein to be [heavily] balanced in the landlord's favo(u)r.
Vermieterhaftpflicht landlord's liability;
~**versicherung** landlord's (tenant's) liability insurance.
Vermieterin landlady.
Vermieter|pfandrecht lessor's warrant; ~**rechte** rights of a landlord; ~**verband** property owners' association; ~**verpflichtung** obligation of a landlord.
vermietet rented, leased, let, hired, for hire;
erstmals ~ first let; **nicht** ~ tenantless, *(Haus)* vacant;
zu 90% ~ **sein** to run at 90% occupancy; ~ **werden** to rent, to be let;
~**e Wohnung** rental apartment.
Vermietung letting *(Br.)*, let, lease, leasing, rental *(US)*, location, *(Sachen)* hiring out;
zentralüberwachte ~ management-supervised rental *(US)*;
~ **der Ausrüstung** equipment leasing; ~ **von Ausrüstungsgütern unter gleichzeitiger Rückmiete** sales leasing, sale-lease back; ~ **ganzer Betriebsanlagen** plant leasing; ~ **ganzer Fuhrparks** fleet leasing; ~ **von Industrieanlagen** plant leasing; ~ **von Kraftfahrzeugen** renting of cars; ~ **von Lastkraftwagen** truck leasing; ~ **von Safes (Schrankfächern)** safe hiring, safe-deposit facilities; ~ **unter Übernahme der Nebenleistungen** service leasing; **Anlagenerwerb durch eine Leasinggesellschaft und gleichzeitige** ~ **an den Verkäufer** sales-back leasing; ~ **möblierter Wohnungen** furnished lettings; ~ **von Zimmern** letting of rooms;
Verteilerschlüssel von Verkäufen zur ~ **veröffentlichen** to break out its sales-to-rental ratio for public display.
Vermietungs|aufwand letting expenses; ~**büro** lease monger, real-estate agency, estate agency *(Br.)*; ~**ergebnis** rental result; ~**geschäft** flat-letting business, rental deal; ~**provision** rental commission.
vermindern to diminish, to lessen, to depress, *(beeinträchtigen)* to impair, *(beschränken)* to curtail, to retrench, to cut [back, *US*], *(herabsetzen)* to reduce, to lower, to decrease;
sich ~ to decrease, to diminish; **Anbaufläche** ~ to reduce acreage; **seine Ausgaben** ~ to retrench one's expenses; **Gefahr eines Krieges erheblich** ~ to minimize the danger of a war; **seine Geschwindigkeit** ~ to lessen (slacken) one's speed, to slack up, to slow down; **jds. Gewinnbeteiligung** ~ to cut down s. one's profits; **sich um die Hälfte** ~ *(Einnahmen)* to drop by half; **Kapital** ~ to reduce capital; **Personal** ~ to reduce (axe, *Br.*) a number of officials; **seine Schulden** ~ to reduce one's debts; **jds. Verdienste** ~ to detract from s. one's merits, to lessen s. one's services.
vermindert|er Ertrag disminished (diminishing) returns; ~**es Kapital** impaired capital; ~**e Leistungsfähigkeit** reduced performance; ~**e Nachfrage** slackening demand; ~**er Umsatz** reduction in turnover; ~**e Zurechnungsfähigkeit** diminished responsibility.
Verminderung diminution, abatement, *(Ausgaben)* retrenchment, cut, *(Beeinträchtigung)* impairment, *(Wert)* decrease, shrinkage, reduction;
~ **der Anbaufläche** reduction of acreage; ~ **des Anlagevermögens** capital loss; ~ **der Einnahme** decrease in receipts; ~ **der Erwerbsfähigkeit** reduction of earning capacity; ~ **der Geschwindigkeit** slackening of speed; ~ **des Gewinns** drop-off in profits, profit decline; ~ **der Gewinnspanne** profit squeeze; ~ **des Kapitals** impairment (reduction, decrease) of capital; ~ **der Kosten** retrenchment of expenses; ~ **der Spannungen** lessening of tensions; ~ **der Truppenstärke** rundown of forces; ~ **der Verluste** reduction in losses; ~ **des Wertes** diminution in value, impairment of value.
verminen to mine, to lay mines, to torpedo.
vermint mined.
vermischen to mingle, to intermingle, to intermix, to compound, *(jur.)* to commingle, *(Rassen)* to cross, to interbreed;
Farben ~ to blend colo(u)rs; **Wein mit Wasser** ~ to water wine, to dilute wine with water.
vermischt mixed, mingled, *(Nachrichten)* miscellaneous columns;
~**e Aufsätze** miscellany; ~**e Einkünfte** miscellaneous income;
~**e Schriften** miscellaneous writings.
Vermischtes *(Zeitung)* miscellaneous.
Vermischung *(jur.)* confusion of goods, comminglement, commixture, intermixture of goods, adjunction;
~ **treuhänderisch gehaltener Geldbeträge** mixing of trust money.
Vermischungstheorie *(Bankgelder)* earmark rule.
vermissen to miss;
Durchhaltevermögen ~ **lassen** to fail in perseverance; **Urteilsvermögen** ~ **lassen** to want judgment.
vermißt lost, *(verschollen)* missing;
~ **werden** to be missing; **als** ~ **gemeldet werden** to be reported missing.
Vermißten|anzeige erstatten to report s. o. as missing; ~**dienst** search and rescue service.
Vermißter missing person, supposed deceased *(US)*.

vermitteln to mediate, to go between, to serve as a go-between, to act as intermediary, to intermediate, to interlope, *(beschaffen)* to procure, to obtain, *(pol.)* to intervene;
Anleihe ~ to negotiate a loan; **Arbeitskräfte** ~ to place workers; **Auftrag** ~ to procure an order; **jem. einen Briefpartner** ~ to supply s. o. with a pen friend; **Eindruck** ~ to create the impression; **j. an eine Firma** ~ to place s. o. with a firm; **Frieden** ~ to mediate peace; **Geschäft** ~ to introduce business, to negotiate a transaction; **Geschäfte in Wertpapieren** ~ to negotiate transactions in securities; **Heirat** ~ to make a match, to bring about a marriage; **Idee** ~ to convey an idea; **Kapitalinteressenten** ~ to procure funds; **jem. Kenntnis von etw.** ~ to impart knowledge of s. th. to s. o.; **jem. eine Stellung** ~ to find a post for s. o. (s. o. a job); **bei einem Streit** ~ to intervene in a dispute; **zwischen Vater und Sohn** ~ to intercede with the father for the son; **Versicherung** ~ to introduce an insurance; **Wertpapiergeschäfte** ~ to act as intermediary for the trading in securities; **Zusammentreffen** ~ to arrange a meeting.
vermittelnd intercessory, intermediary, interventional, intercessional, conciliatory;
~e Schritte unternehmen to mediate, to intercede.
vermittels by the agency of.
Vermittler middleman, mediator, intermediator, intermediate agent, intermediary, intermeddler, go-between, interagent, interceder, intercessor, intervener, conciliator, friendly arbitrator, *(Anleihen)* negotiator, *(Filmgeschäft)* casting director, *(Kommissionsgeschäft)* commission agent, *(Makler)* broker;
als ~ **auftreten** to act as an intermediary; ~ **ausschalten** to cut out the middleman; ~ **spielen** to mediate;
~ **verbeten** *(Zeitung)* only principals will be dealt with;
~amt mediatorship; **~provision** broker's (agent's) commission, brokerage; **~rolle** office of mediator.
Vermittlung mediation, intermediation, intercession, interposition, interagency, agency, *(Beschaffung)* procuring, *(Filmgeschäft)* casting directorate, *(Makler)* brokerage, *(pol.)* intervention, *(Streitbeilegung)* adjustment, settlement, *(Telefon)* telephone exchange, operator;
dank seiner ~ thanks to his intervention; **durch** ~ **von** through the medium (agency) of, by s. one's instrumentality; **mit freundlicher** ~ through the kind offices;
gewerbsmäßige ~ commercial agency;
~ **einer Anleihe** negotiation of a loan; ~ **von Arbeitskräften** placement of labo(u)r; ~ **einer Idee** conveyance of an idea; ~ **von Kapitalinteressenten** procurement of funds; ~ **einer Zusammenkunft** arrangement of a meeting;
seine ~ **anbieten** to offer one's good services; **sich jds.** ~ **bedienen** to accept the mediation of s. o.; **jds.** ~ **erbitten** to seek the good offices of s. o.
Vermittlungs|agent [soliciting] agent, middleman, mediator, *(Effektenmakler)* half-commission man *(Br.)*, *(Versicherung)* cash agent; **~aktion** mediatorship; **~angebot** offer of mediation; **~ausschuß** mediation commission, mediation (arbitration) committee, committee of conference *(US)*, conference committee *(US)*; **~büro** broker's office, *(für Arbeitskräfte)* placement agency *(US)*, employment bureau; **~dienste** good offices; **~dienst für Arbeitsstellen** placement service; **seine ~dienste anbieten** to offer mediation; **~gebühr** commission, *(Bank)* service charge, *(Makler)* brokerage; **~geschäft** agency (middleman's) business, brokerage, broking; **~geschäfte machen** to job; **~möglichkeit für Stellen** placement facilities; **~projekt** intermediary project; **~provision** commission; **~schrank** *(Telefon)* switchboard; **~stelle** liaison office, conciliation board, agency, *(für Arbeitslose)* labo(u)r contractor, employment agency (bureau), placement agency *(US)*; **~stelle für Sekretariatskräfte** secretarial employment agency; **~tätigkeit** conciliation services; **~verfahren** conciliation proceedings, offer of mediation, proposed compromise, arbitration procedure; **~vorschlag** conciliatory proposal, offer of mediation, proposed compromise; **~zeit** mediation period.
vermodern to mo(u)lder away.
vermöge|seiner Beziehungen due to one's connections; ~ **seiner Stellung** by virtue of his position.
Vermögen property, property and effects, fortune, commodities, *(Aktiva)* assets, *(Fähigkeit)* faculty, power, ability, capacity, *(Gesellschaft)* treasury, *(Kapital)* funds, means, *(Nachlaß)* estate, *(Reichtum)* wealth, riches, money, substance;
im ~ **der toten Hand** in mortmain;
abgesondertes ~ *(Ehefrau)* separate property; **abgetretenes** ~ assigned property; **Ertrag abwerfendes** ~ income-producing property; **von der Versicherungsgesellschaft anerkanntes** ~ admitted (net) assets; **in Effekten angelegtes** ~ funded property, securities portfolio; **in Grundstücken angelegtes** ~ capital invested in real property; **in Staatspapieren angelegtes** ~ funded property; **in Wertpapieren angelegtes** ~ property capital, securities (equity) portfolio, *(Kapitalanlagegesellschaft)* total investments, investment portfolio; **anmeldepflichtiges** ~ property to be reported (declared); **ansehnliches** ~ sizable (handsome) property (fortune); **aufzeichnungspflichtiges** ~ property to be recorded; **ausländisches** ~ foreign assets, foreign-owned property, foreign ownership, alien property; **bares** ~ liquid (cash) assets, cash capital, pecuniary property; **beachtliches** ~ sizable property, respectable competence; **hypothekarisch belastbares** ~ mortgageable property; **belastetes** ~ encumbered estate; **bescheidenes** ~ modest fortune; **beschlagnahmtes** ~ confiscated (requisitioned, blocked) property; **vom Feind beschlagnahmtes** ~ enemy-controlled property; **zum persönlichen Gebrauch bestimmtes** ~ personal chattels; **bewegliches** ~ personal chattels (property), goods and chattels, movables, movable goods (property, estate), personalty; **bewegliches und unbewegliches** ~ mixed property; **blockiertes** ~ frozen fund, blocked property; **brachliegendes** ~ funds lying idle; **bei einer Bank deponiertes** ~ property lodged with a bank; **eheliches** ~ matrimonial assets; **eigenes** ~ own property, independent means; **elterliches** ~ patrimony; **erbschaftssteuerfreies** ~ free estate, property exempt from estate duty; **erbschaftssteuerpflichtiges** ~ property liable to estate duty; **sofort erbschaftssteuerpflichtiges** ~ property without the instal(l)ment option; **ererbtes** ~ general inheritance *(US)*, estate of inheritance *(US)*; **voll erhaltenes** ~ unimpaired fortune; **ertragbringendes** ~ income-producing property; **ertragloses** ~ onerous property; **zu erwartendes** ~ fortune in reversion; **erworbenes** ~ acquired property; **während der Ehe erworbenes** ~ property acquired during marriage; **nach der Eheschließung erworbenes** ~ after-acquired property; **vom Gemeinschuldner nach Konkurseröffnung erworbenes** ~ property acquired after adjudication; **mühsam erworbenes** ~ hard-got fortune; **später erworbenes** ~ after-acquired property; **unrechtmäßig erworbenes** ~ ill-gotten property, property acquired by fraud; **feindliches** ~ alien (enemy) property; **flüssiges** ~ cash (liquid) property, quick (liquid) assets, money capital; **forstwirtschaftliches** ~ commercial woodland; **freies** ~ unencumbered assets; **das ganze** ~ all one's belongings, the whole of one's property; **gefährdetes** ~ impaired fortune; **gegenwärtiges** ~ present estate; **gegenwärtiges und zukünftiges** ~ present and future property; **gemeinsames** ~ common (joint) property; **gepfändetes** ~ seized assets; **gerettetes** ~ salvaged property; **geringfügiges** ~ *(Steuerformular)* unadmitted assets; **gesamtes** ~ aggregate property, entire fortune; **gesperrtes** ~ blocked property; **gewerbliches** ~ industrial (business) property; **greifbares** ~ tangible property; **großes** ~ ample (large, great) fortune, plenty of money; **grundsteuerpflichtiges** ~ rat(e)able property *(Br.)*; **hinterlegtes** ~ bailed property; **treuhänderisch hinterlegtes** ~ sheltering trust *(US)*; **immaterielles** ~ intangible property; **inländisches** ~ internal (domestic) property; **investiertes** ~ funds invested; **kleines** ~ small fortune; **konkursfreies** ~ unattachable property (assets), property exempt from distribution in bankruptcy; **landwirtschaftliches** ~ agricultural property; **lastenfreies** ~ unencumbered assets; **massefreies** ~ *(Konkursschuldner)* distrainable property; **mütterliches** ~ maternal property; **kein nennenswertes** ~ no property worth mentioning; **ganz nettes** ~ snug (decent) fortune; **öffentliches** ~ social capital (wealth); **persönliches** ~ private property (means), *(Gemeinschuldner)* personal assets, *(Gesellschafter)* individual assets; **pfändbares** ~ distrainable assets; **pfändungsfreies** ~ exempt (unattachable) property, unattachable (exempt) assets; **leicht realisierbares** ~ easily realizable assets; **nicht realisierbares** ~ unrealizable property; **restliches** ~ remaining property, residual assets; **schuldenfreies** ~ unencumbered estate; **sonstiges** ~ *(Bilanz)* other assets; **im Eigentum eines Ausländers stehendes** ~ foreign-owned property; **im Eigentum neutraler Staatsangehöriger stehendes** ~ neutral property; **für die Gläubiger [nicht] zur Verfügung stehendes** ~ [non]distributable property; **zur Schuldenbegleichung zur Verfügung stehendes** ~ property available for payment of debts; **steuerfreies** ~ tax-exempt property; **steuerpflichtiges** ~ taxable (dutiable) property; **umlaufendes** ~ current assets; **unbewegliches** ~ landed (immovable, *US*) property, immovables, real estate (assets), realty *(US)*, *(Bilanz)* capital (fixed, permanent) assets; **unschätzbares** ~ fortune impossible to estimate; **unübersehbares** ~ fortune impossible to estimate; **väterliches** ~ paternal property; **verbleibendes** ~ remaining property; **vererbliches** ~ assets per descent,

inheritable property; **vererbtes** ~ property escheated; **verfallenes** ~ dilapidated fortune; **verfügbares** ~ *(Erblasser)* disposable portion of property; **nicht vermachtes** ~ property undisposed of by will; **vermögenssteuerpflichtiges** ~ property liable to wealth (general property) tax; **verpfändbares** ~ mortgageable property; **verpfändetes** ~ pledged property; **als Sicherheit verpfändetes** ~ assets pledged as collateral, property charged as security for a debt; **aufgrund gerichtlicher Anordnung verwaltetes** ~ court trust *(US)*; **nach freiem Ermessen verwaltetes** ~ discretionary trust *(Br.)*; **treuhänderisch verwaltetes** ~ property held as trustee, trust estate (fund); **wohlfundiertes** ~ well-established fortune; **zinstragendes** ~ income-producing property; **zukünftiges** ~ future[-acquired] property, future estate; **zwangsverwaltetes** ~ estate by elegit; **zweckgebundenes** ~ restricted property;
~, **das unabhängig macht** independent fortune (means); ~ **einer Aktiengesellschaft** corporate assets *(US)*, corporate funds, treasury; ~ **der Arbeitslosenversicherung** Unemployment Trust Fund *(US)*; ~ **im Ausland** external property, assets held abroad; ~ **einer Bank** bank assets; ~ **der Ehefrau** wife's estate, dotal property, married woman's property; **persönliches** ~ **des Gemeinschuldners** personal assets; ~ **der Gesellschaft** assets of a company (partnership), *(AG)* corporate assets; ~ **der öffentlichen Hand** social capital (wealth); ~ **einer Kommune** general revenue fund; ~ **des Konkursschuldners** bankrupt's (bankruptcy) assets; ~ **einer Pensionskasse** pension fund assets; ~ **juristischer Personen** corporate assets (property), company (corporation) property; ~ **natürlicher Personen** personal assets (property); ~ **der Postsparkasse** postal savings fund *(US)*; ~ **in Sachform** tangible property (assets); ~ **einschließlich der Verbindlichkeiten** net assets; ~ **einer testamentarisch errichteten Vermögensverwaltung** property in a will trust;
sein ~ **angreifen** to make a dent in one's fortune; **sein** ~ **in Grundstücken anlegen** to put one's money into land; **sein ganzes** ~ **in Grundstücken anlegen** to lock up all one's capital in land; **sein** ~ **in einem Leibrentenvertrag anlegen** to invest one's money at life interest; **sein** ~ **in Wertpapieren anlegen** to invest one's money in stock; ~ **einer Pensionskasse in Aktien anderer Gesellschaften anlegen** to diversify pension funds into other companies' shares; ~ **anmelden** to declare (report) property; ~ **ansammeln** to amass a fortune, to hoard up a treasure; **kleines** ~ **ansammeln** to make a small fortune; **sein** ~ **unter seine Erben aufteilen** to divide one's property among one's heirs; **sein** ~ **aufzehren** to get through one's fortune, to live on one's capital; ~ **ausgeben** to spend a mint of money; **für jds. Erziehung ein** ~ **ausgeben** to give up a fortune for s. one's education; **kleines** ~ **für etw. ausgeben** to spend a small fortune on s. th.; **jds.** ~ **beschlagnahmen** to seize (take charge of) s. one's property; **gesamtes** ~ **beschlagnahmen** to levy on the entire property; ~ **besitzen** to be worth, to have property, to be a man of means; **großes** ~ **besitzen** to be in possession of a large fortune; **sein ganzes** ~ **für wohltätige Zwecke bestimmen** to dispose of one's fortune in (leave one's fortune, all one's money) to charity; **Pfändung in das bewegliche** ~ **wegen nicht bezahlter Pacht betreiben** to distrain chattels for nonpayment of rent; ~ **bewerten** to assess a property [for taxation]; ~ **bilden** to create wealth; **j. um sein** ~ **bringen** to trick s. one out of his fortune; **sein** ~ **durchbringen** to dice away (make, muddle away with, spend, run through, consume) one's fortune; **sein** ~ **in die Gütergemeinschaft einbringen** to bring one's property into the communal estate; **sein** ~ **einsetzen** to risk one's fortune; ~ **erben** to succeed to (come in for, come into possession of) a fortune, to fall heir to a (into) property; **mit einem Heimfallrecht belastetes** ~ **erben** to come into a reversion; **beträchtliches** ~ **erben** to come in for a pretty penny; **glänzendes** ~ **erben** to be heir to a splendid fortune; ~ **steuerlich erfassen** to list property for taxation *(US)*; **über jds.** ~ **den Konkurs eröffnen** to adjudge s. o. bankrupt; ~ **erwerben** to make a fortune, to come into property; **großes** ~ **erwerben** to acquire (amass) great wealth, to amass great riches; **sein** ~ **nach dem Kriege erwerben** to make one's fortune after the war; **sein** ~ **flüssigmachen** to realize one's property (assets); **über jds.** ~ **gehen** to be beyond s. o.; **zu** ~ **gelangen** to come to wealth (into property), to rise to affluence; **bedeutendes** ~ **haben** to have considerable means; **eigenes** ~ **haben** to have s. th. in one's own right (an independent income), to have a little independence of one's own; **kein** ~ **haben** to have nothing to depend upon (of one's own), to have no resources of one's own; **sein ganzes** ~ **in Aktien angelegt haben** to have all one's fortune in stocks *(US)*; **mit seinem ganzen** ~ **haften** to be liable without limitation (to the extent of one's property); ~ **des Konkursschuldners nicht zur Masse heranziehen** to disclaim property of a bankrupt; **großes** ~ **hinterlassen** to cut up well (fat); **sein** ~ **hinterlassen** to make over one's estate; **seiner Ehefrau sein** ~ **hinterlassen** to leave one's property to one's wife; **spielend zu einem** ~ **kommen** to step into a fortune; **unerwartet zu einem** ~ **kommen** to drop into a fortune; **völlig frei über sein** ~ **verfügen können** to be entire master of one's property, to have entire disposal of one's estate; **von seinem** ~ **leben** to live on prior (one's private) means; **Grundlage für ein** ~ **legen** to found a fortune; ~ **machen** to make (carve out, land) a fortune; **aus kleinen Gewinnen ein großes** ~ **machen** to raise a great estate out of small profits; ~ **für seine privaten Zwecke mißbrauchen** to funnel funds to one's own use; **sein** ~ **in einem Unternehmen riskieren** to venture one's fortune in an enterprise; **Reste seines ~s sammeln** to collect the wrecks of one's fortune; **ohne pfändbares** ~ **sein** to be judgment- (mace-, *US*) proof; **sein** ~ **aufs Spiel setzen** to cast one's bread upon the waters; **sein** ~ **als Sicherheit stellen** to pledge one's property; **jds.** ~ **auf ... taxieren** to rate s. one's fortune at ...; **sich von seinem ganzen** ~ **trennen** to give up all one's possessions; ~ **übertragen** to assign (alienate, transfer) property, to deed one's estate; ~ **auf j. übertragen** to devolve property upon s. o., to vest property in s. o., to hand over one's property to s. o.; **sein** ~ **auf seine Gläubiger übertragen** to surrender one's goods to one's creditors; **sein** ~ **auf den Konkursverwalter übertragen** to put one's property under the control of a trustee in bankruptcy; **sein unbewegliches in bewegliches** ~ **umwandeln** to convert one's realty into personalty; ~ **einer Treuhandverwaltung unterstellen** to put property into a trust; ~ **bei einem Geschäft verdienen** to make a fortune out of a business; **über ein großes** ~ **verfügen** to have a large capital at hand; **über kein eigenes** ~ **verfügen** to have no resources of one's own; ~ **vergeuden (verjubeln)** to dilapidate (run through) a fortune; **sich an fremdem** ~ **vergreifen** to take liberties with another person's property; **fast sein ganzes** ~ **verlieren** to lose the bulk of one's goods; **jem. sein** ~ **vermachen** to devise one's property, to make over one's estate to s. o.; **sein** ~ **testamentarisch vermachen** to transmit one's property by will; **sein** ~ **vermehren** to enlarge one's fortune; **sein** ~ **verprassen (verschleudern)** to dissipate one's fortune, to waste one's property (substance); **sein** ~ **verspielen** to gamble (dice) away one's money (fortune), to spend one's estate in gaming; **sein** ~ **unter seine Erben verteilen** to divide one's property among one's heirs; ~ **verwalten** to be in charge of an estate, to administer property, to act as trustee for s. one's property; **sein** ~ **verwetten** to spend one's estate in gaming; **auf sein** ~ **verzichten** to renounce one's property; **ins** ~ **vollstrecken** to levy execution on the property; **sein verlorenes** ~ **wiederbekommen** to recover one's fallen fortunes; **sein** ~ **wiedererwerben** to retrieve one's fortune; **beschlagnahmtes** ~ **zurückgeben** to restore confiscated property; ~ **zusammenscharren** to rake together wealth; **zu versteuerndes** ~ **zusammenstellen** to list assets *(US)*.

vermögen to be able (capable);
wenig bei jem. ~ to have little influence on s. o.

vermögend rich, wealthy, well-off, moneyed, possessed of property, opulent, well-to-do *(Br.)*;
~ **sein** to enjoy a fortune, to be worth money, to be in affluent circumstances; ~ **werden** to come to wealth;
~**er Mann sein** to be a man of substance.

Vermögens|abgabe capital (property) levy, conscription of wealth; **einmalige ~abgabe** one-for-all special contribution *(Br.)*; **~abschätzung** valuation (census) of property, *(Steuer)* appraisal, tax assessment; **~absonderung** separation of property; **~abtretung** assignment of property, *(im Konkursfall)* voluntary assignment; **~änderung** change of assets; **~änderung der volkswirtschaftlichen Gesamtrechnung** gross saving and investment accounts; **~anfall** accession to an estate, accretion; **~angabe** declaration of property; **~angelegenheiten** financial affairs; **~anhäufung** accumulation of wealth (property).

Vermögensanlage pecuniary investment, investment of one's capital;
~**n** capital assets;
sichere ~ safe investment, capital safety (security);
~ **in Industriewerten** industrial investment; ~ **im Interesse des Geschäftsbetriebes** trade investment *(Br.)*;
Einkommen aus einer ~ **beziehen** to derive income from an investment;
~**klassen** categories of investment.

Vermögens|anmeldung declaration of property; **~ansammlung** accumulation of wealth (property), capital accumulation;

~**anspruch** possessory title; ~**anteil** share in (slice of, proportion of) property, proprietary (ownership) interest; **freiverfügbarer** ~**anteil** *(Erblasser)* disposable portion; **j. von einem** ~**anteil ausschließen** to cut s. o. out of one's property; ~**anwachsung** increase in assets; ~**arten** types of property; ~**aufbau** asset structure; ~**aufgabe** relinquishment of one's property; ~**aufnahme** valuation of property, *(Steuer)* assessment of property; ~**aufsicht** property control (custodian); ~**aufstellung** statement (inventory, listing, *US*) of one's property, property statement (status), statement of assets and liabilities, *(Gemeinschuldner)* statutory statement of affairs *(Br.)*; **frisierte** ~**aufstellung** write-up *(US)*; ~**aufstellung einreichen** to file a schedule of assets and liabilities, to submit a statement of one's affairs; ~**aufzehrung** negative savings; ~**auseinandersetzung** partition (division) of an estate; ~**auskunft** status enquiry; **hintangehaltene** ~**auslieferung** *(Konkurs)* failing to deliver up property; ~**ausweis** statement of assets and liabilities, financial condition (position); ~**ballung** concentration of wealth; ~**begründer** creator of wealth; ~**belastung** charge on property *(Br.)*, encumbrance; ~**berater** property finance consultant, investment (estate) adviser, security (stock, *US*) analyst; ~**beratung** security advice, investment counselling; ~**beratungsgesellschaft** investment house (counselling firm); ~**beratungsvertrag** investment advisory agreement (contract); ~**berechnung** valuation of property, *(Steuer)* assessment of property; ~**beschlagnahme** distraint of property, *(Arrestverfahren)* seizure (attachment) of property; ~**besitz** ownership of wealth, possession of property; ~**besitzer** property owner; ~**bestand** *(Konkursfall)* available assets; ~**bestandteil** individual asset, property item; ~**besteuerung** taxation of property, *(verschärft)* conscription of wealth; **nicht ausgeschüttete** ~**beträge** *(Treuhänder)* undistributed funds; ~**bewegung** capital movement; ~**bewertung** valuation of property, property valuation, *(Steuer)* property appraisal, assessment of property; ~**bilanz** statement of one's property, property balance, statement of assets and liabilities, net asset position *(US)*, statement of financial position, *(Gemeinschuldner)* statutory statement of affairs *(Br.)*; ~**bildung** accumulation of capital (assets), wealth creation (formation); **betriebliche** ~**bildung** staff capital formation; ~**bindung** immobilization of funds; ~**defizit** deficiency of assets; ~**delikt** offence against property; ~**disposition** disposing (disposal) of property; **periodenübergreifender** ~**effekt** distributed lag; ~**einbuße** loss of property; ~**einlage** capital investment; ~**einnahmen,** ~**einkünfte** proprietor's (investment, unearned) income, income of property; **niedrige** ~**einstufung** downgrading of property; ~**einziehung** forfeiture of one's property, *(Fremdstaat)* confiscation; ~**einziehung eines Hochverräters** single escheat; ~**erfassung** registration of property; ~**erklärung** declaration of property, property statement; ~**erschleichung mittels vorsätzlicher Täuschung** obtaining property by false representation; ~**erträgnisse** rents, issues and profits, investment income, wealth flow; ~**erwerb** acquisition of property; **zukünftiger** ~**erwerb** future-acquired property.

vermögensfähig capable of personal property.

Vermögens|fonds, besonders bezeichneter particular fund; ~**fonds Treuhändern anvertrauen** to commit a fund to the care of trustees; ~**freigabe** release of property; ~**freigabe anordnen** to release an attachment; ~**freigabe nicht gestatten** to withhold release of property; ~**gattung** type of property; ~**gegenstand** asset, item of property, valuable (piece of) property asset; **rückerstatteter** ~**gegenstand** restituted property; ~**gegenstand veräußern** to dispose of an asset.

Vermögengegenstände items of property, assets;

beanspruchte ~ property subject to claim; **bewegliche** ~ goods and chattels; **entzogene** ~ affected property; **feststellbare** ~ identifiable property; **nicht körperliche (immaterielle)** ~ intangible assets, incorporeal hereditaments; **rückerstattete** ~ restituted property; **sicherungsübereignete** ~ hypothecated assets; **erworbene steuerpflichtige** ~ chargeable assets acquired; **veräußerte steuerpflichtige** ~ chargeable assets disposed of; **unpfändbare** ~ judgment- (mace-, *US*) proof property; **nicht der Kapitalgewinnsteuer unterliegende** ~ assets exempt from capital-gains tax; **vererbliche** ~ hereditaments *(US)*; **versicherbare** ~ insurable property;

~ **im Ausland** *(Bilanz)* assets held abroad, foreign assets (possessions) *(Br.)*;

~ **beseitigen** to abstract funds.

Vermögens|gerichtsstand forum rei sitae, place where the subject matter in controversy is situated; **reale** ~**güter** tangible assets; ~**haftung** financial liability; ~**hinterziehung** *(Gemeinschuldner)* fraudulent alienation (conveyance); ~**höhe** amount of assets; ~**interesse** interest in business, property (pecuniary) interest; ~**interesse haben** to have a money interest; ~**komplex** total estate (assets); ~**konfiskation** forfeiture of one's property, *(Fremdstaat)* confiscation; ~**konto** property account; ~**kontrolle** property control; ~**lage** financial condition (position), conditions, status, pecuniary circumstances; **Bericht über seine** ~**lage erstatten** *(Gemeinschuldner)* to state one's affairs; **seine** ~**lage verschleiern** to conceal one's financial conditions; ~**liquidation** liquidation of property; ~**liquidität** liquidity in assets.

vermögenslos impecunious, penniless, without means.

Vermögenslosigkeit indigence, impecuniosity, lack of funds.

Vermögensmasse fund, *(Konkurs)* mass of assets, assets of a bankrupt's estate, *(Nachlaß)* estate;

in pflichtgemäßem Ermessen zu verwaltende ~ discretionary settlement trust *(Br.)*;

~ **anderweitig anlegen** to convert funds to another purpose; ~ **des Gemeinschuldners aufbrauchen** to destroy the assets of the debtor; ~ **ordnen** to wind up an estate.

Vermögens|nachteil detriment to one's property, pecuniary detriment; ~**nachweis** evidence of means, property qualification, funds statement; ~**neubewertung** reassessment of property; ~**pfändung** attachment of funds (property); ~**pflegschaft** receivership, trusteeship of s. one's property; ~**position** financial condition (position), conditions; ~**rechnung** statement of one's property, property statement; ~**recht** right of property, property (proprietary) right.

vermögensrechtlich proprietary;

~**e Ansprüche** pecuniary claims; ~**e Streitigkeiten** pecuniary causes; ~**er Vorteil** pecuniary advantage.

Vermögens|regelung property settlement; ~**rente** benefit from property; ~**reserve** reserve fund, capital reserve; ~**rest** fragments of a fortune, remnants of a property; ~**rückgabe** restitution of property, restoration of confiscated property; ~**schaden** property tort (damage), pecuniary loss (damage), damage to (loss of) property, *(Unfall)* necessary injury; ~**schaden erfahren** to waste; ~**schadensversicherung** consequential loss insurance; ~**schätzung** valuation of property, *(Steuer)* property appraisal, assessment of property; ~**schichtung** classification of properties, distribution of wealth; ~**schöpfung** capital (wealth) formation; ~**schutz** protection of property; ~**sicherung** protection of an estate; ~**sperre** blocking of property; ~**status** statement of assets and liabilities.

Vermögenssteuer tax on property, wealth (personal, *US*, general property, *US*) tax, *(Doppelbesteuerungsabkommen)* capital tax;

proportional erhobene ~**n** proportional taxes; **fällige** ~ property tax payable *(US)*;

~ **auf Grundbesitz** general property tax *(US)*; ~ **auf bewegliches Vermögen** personal property tax *(US)*;

~ **erheben** to make a levy (levy taxes) on capital; **100 Pfund** ~ **für j. festsetzen** to rate s. one's property at £ 100 per annum; **zur** ~ **veranlagen** to assess property for taxation;

~**bescheinigung** property-tax receipt; ~**bestimmungen** property-tax provisions; ~**erklärung** listing property for taxation; ~**freibetrag** estate-duty credit *(Br.)*, exemption of property *(US)*; ~**liste** list of taxable property; ~**richtlinien** general property tax rules; **jährliche** ~**sätze** annual rates of property tax; ~**veranlagung** assessment of property; ~**vorauszahlungen** wealth tax prepayments.

Vermögens|stock capital reserve, fund; ~**strafe** administrative fine; ~**strategie** asset strategy; ~**struktur** financial structure.

Vermögensstück portion of property, asset;

~**e** effects, assets, items of property;

belastetes ~ encumbered estate; **hinterlegte** ~**e** bailed property; **verpfändete** ~**e** pledged property;

sich aus einem ~ **befriedigen** to satisfy a debt out of a property; ~**e beiseite schaffen** to abstract funds, to fraudulently remove property.

Vermögenssubstanz substance, total assets (estate);

~**steuer** capital levy.

Vermögensteil, festgelegter portion of property, *(erbrechtlich)* settled property; **testierfähiger (frei verfügbarer)** ~ disposable portion of property;

~ **aufgeben** to part with a property; **auf unwirtschaftliche** ~**e verzichten** *(Konkursverwalter)* to disclaim onerous property.

Vermögens|teilung division (partition) of an estate, *(Erbteilung)* partition of a succession *(Br.)*; ~**träger** property owner; ~**transaktion** capital transaction, money management operation; ~**überreste zusammensuchen** to gather together what was left of a fortune; ~**übersicht** statement of assets and liabilities (one's property), abstract of balance, listing of property *(US)*; ~**übersicht vorlegen** to file a schedule of assets and liabilities.

Vermögensübertragung alienation (assignment, deed, conveyance, transfer) of property, devolution (alienation) of property, transfer of wealth, cession of goods, grant of personal property;
anfechtbare ~ *(Gemeinschuldner)* voidable preference; **entgeltliche** ~ grant of personal property; **freiwillige** ~ *(auf Konkursverwalter)* voluntary assignment; **treuhänderische** ~ trust settlement; **nicht der Konkursanfechtung unterliegende** ~ settlement protected against avoidance; **zwangsweise** ~ *(Gemeinschuldner)* involuntary assignment;
~ **zwecks Gläubigerbenachteiligung** fraudulent transfer of property; **vollständige** ~ **auf einen Treuhänder zugunsten aller Gläubiger** conveyance to trustee for benefit of creditors generally, assignment for the benefit of creditors, general assignment *(US)*.

Vermögens|umschichtung regrouping of assets, reinvestment; ~**umverteilung** redistribution of property; ~**umwandlung** conversion in equity; ~**ungleichheit** inequality of wealth; ~**veränderung** change in assets; ~**veränderungskonto** investment account; ~**veräußerung** sale of property; ~**verbindlichkeit** capital liability; ~**verfall** financial collapse, dwindling assets; **in** ~**verfall geraten** to be verging on insolvency; ~**verfügung** disposal of property (assets), disposition of property.

Vermögensverhältnisse pecuniary circumstances, financial conditions (position), financial status, exhibit;
beschränkte ~ straitened circumstances; **günstige (gute)** ~ good (flourishing, easy) circumstances, good position; **meine** ~ my worldly circumstances; **schlechte** ~ reduced (straitened) circumstances; **zerrüttete** ~ decayed (broken) fortune;
~ **einer Firma** state of a commercial house;
seine ~ **offenbaren** *(Gemeinschuldner)* to discover one's assets; **seine** ~ **neu ordnen** to repair one's fortune; **in bedrängten** ~**n sein** to be in straitened circumstances; **seine** ~ **verschleiern** to conceal one's financial condition.

Vermögens|verkehrssteuer capital transfer tax *(Br.)*; ~**verlust** pecuniary loss, loss of wealth (property); ~**vermehrung** capital appreciation, increased wealth; ~**verschiebung** *(Statistik)* shifting of property, *(Gemeinschuldner)* fraudulent alienation, *(einzelner Gläubiger des Gemeinschuldners)* fraudulent preference; ~**verschlechterung** deterioration of the financial position; ~**verschleierung** concealing property, concealment of assets; ~**verschleuderung** consumption of a fortune; ~**versicherung** insurance of the rights of financial interest, pecuniary (property) insurance; ~**verteilung** distribution of property (wealth); **ungleiche** ~**verteilung** maldistribution of wealth; **bessere** ~**verteilung herbeiführen wollen** to look to a better distribution of wealth; ~**verwahrer** custodian.

Vermögensverwalter estate (money) manager, receiver, steward, fund administrator (manager), custodian of property, guardian of property, *(Geisteskranker)* receiver in lunacy, *(vom Gericht bestellter)* court-appointed trustee, judicial factor, equity receiver, *(Kapitalanlagegesellschaft)* portfolio manager, *(für Minderjährige bestellter Nachlaßverwalter)* administrator, *(Treuhänder)* trustee of a settlement, settlement (private) trustee;
vorläufiger ~ *(für Strafgefangenen)* interim curator;
~ **mit Geschäftsführungsbefugnis** receiver and manager *(Br.)*.

Vermögensverwaltung administration (custody, management) of property, property (money) management, stewardship, *(durch Bank)* investment management, *(Kapitalanlagegesellschaft)* portfolio management, *(Konkursverwalter)* receivership;
ausländische ~ alien property custodian *(US)*; **gesetzlich begründete** ~ statutory trust *(Br.)*; **für einen Verschwender eingesetzte** ~ spendthrift trust *(US)*; **zu Lebzeiten errichtete** ~ property in trust created inter vivos; **nach freiem Ermessen gehandhabte** ~ discretionary settlement trust *(Br.)*; **zusammengefaßte** ~**en** compound settlements;
~ **mit genehmigtem Substanzanbruch** wasting trust;
~ **anordnen** to appoint an administrator; ~ **haben** to have a fortune to manage; **jds.** ~ **treuhänderisch übernehmen** to accept the trusteeship of s. one's property.

Vermögensverwaltungs|gesellschaft property investment company; ~**konto** stewardship account.

Vermögens|verzeichnis statement (list, schedule) of assets and liabilities; ~**verzicht** renouncement of one's property; ~**verzinsung** investment return (yield).

Vermögensvorteil capital gain, pecuniary (financial) benefit, pecuniary advantage;
zwecks Erlangung eines ~**s** for pecuniary gain;
rechtswidriger ~ unjust enrichment;
~ **erlangen** to gain a pecuniary advantage; ~ **durch Betrug erlangen** to obtain property by false pretences.

Vermögenswert property value, financial worth, asset, *(Kapitalanlagegesellschaft)* net asset value;
umlagepflichtiger ~ contributing value.

Vermögenswerte pecuniary assets, property holdings, effects, resources *(coll.)*;
abschreibungsfähige ~ depreciable property *(US)*; **aussonderungsfähige** ~ equitable assets; **beitragspflichtige** ~ contributory values; **beschlagnahmefähige** ~ attachable assets; **betriebsnotwendige** ~ operating assets; **blockierte** ~ frozen assets; **effektive** ~ active assets; **eingefrorene (gesperrte)** ~ blocked property; **entzogene** ~ affected property; **erbschaftssteuerfreie** ~ assets relieved of estate duty; **feststellbare** ~ identifiable property; **fiktive (fingierte)** ~ fictitious assets; **flüssige** ~ moneyed capital, cash (liquid) assets; **freie** ~ unencumbered assets; **greifbare** ~ tangible assets; **immaterielle** ~ intangible assets, incorporeal property; **konvertierbare** ~ convertible assets; **kurzfristige** ~ current (limited-life) assets; **landwirtschaftliche** ~ agricultural assets; **liquide** ~ moneyed capital; **monetäre** ~ monetary assets; **pfändbare** ~ seizable assets; **pfändungsfreie** ~ exempt assets; **kurzfristig realisierbare** ~ liquid strength; **leicht realisierbare** ~ easily realizable assets; **nicht realisierbare** ~ unrealizable (dead) assets; **schwer realisierbare** ~ slow assets; **sonstige** ~ *(Bilanz)* other assets; **steuerpflichtige** ~ chargeable assets; **übertragbare** ~ negotiable kind of property; **umlagenpflichtige** ~ contributing values; **ihrem Wert nach ungewisse** ~ doubtful assets; **dem Substanzverzehr unterliegende** ~ wasting property; **verfügbare** ~ ready (disposable) assets; **frei verfügbare** ~ liquid assets; **als Sicherheit verpfändete** ~ assets pledged as collateral; **verschleierte** ~ concealed assets; **zweckgebundene** ~ earmarked assets;
~ **einer Aktiengesellschaft** corporate assets; ~ **im Ausland** external assets, assets held abroad; ~ **einer Bank** bank assets; ~ **des Gemeinschuldners** assets of a bankrupt's estate;
sich mit ~**n an einem Unternehmen beteiligen** to invest funds in a scheme; **unter vom Konkursgläubiger hinterzogene** ~ **einrangieren** to class as property transferred under fraudulent preference; ~ **eines Unternehmens anderweitig einsetzen** to redeploy the assets of a company; ~ **flüssigmachen** to realize assets; ~ **beiseite schaffen** to abstract funds; **ausländische** ~ **verheimlichen (verschleiern)** to conceal foreign assets.

vermögenswirksam asset-creating;
~**e Ausgaben** capital spending; ~**e Leistung** property-creating performance.

Vermögens|zuführung accession of property; ~**zunahme** increased wealth; ~**zusammenballung** concentration of wealth; ~**zusammenfassung** fund group; ~**zuwachs** accession of property, capital gain, capital appreciation *(Br.)*, *(Gesellschaft)* capital formation, *(Grundbesitz)* unearned increment.

vermummen, sich to disguise, to mask.

vermummt masked;
mit ~**em Gesicht** with one's face muffled up.

Vermummung disguise, masquerade.

vermurksen, etw. to make a mess (botch, hash) of s. th., to muck s. th. up *(Br.)*.

vermuten to presume, to assume, to suppose, to guess *(US)*, to reckon *(US)*;
Brandstiftung ~ to suspect arson.

vermutet supposed, presumed;
gesetzlich ~ implicit;
~**e Lebensgefahr** expectance (expectancy, expectation) of life; ~**er Wert** assumed value.

vermutlich presumable, probable, supposed;
sich ~ **irren** to be probably wrong;
~**e Ankunftszeit** expected time of arrival; ~**er Erbe** presumptive heir; ~**er Vater** putative father; ~**er Verlust** presumptive loss.

Vermutung assumption, presumption, supposition, guesswork, guess, *(Hypothese)* hypothesis, *(Spekulation)* surmise, conjecture, speculation, *(Verdacht)* suspicion, hunch *(coll.)*;
auf ~**en angewiesen** reduced to conjectures;
begründete ~ educated guess; **bloße** ~ random guess; **falsche** ~ false presumption, bad shot; **gesetzliche** ~ general presumption of law, artificial (legal) presumption; **kühne** ~ longish shot; **reine** ~ anybody's (wild) guess; **tatsächliche und gesetzliche** ~ mixed presumption; **unwiderlegbare** ~ conclusive (irrebuttable, nonrebuttable, absolute) presumption; **widerlegbare** ~ rebuttable (disputable) presumption;

~ **des erstversterbenden Älteren bei gemeinsamem Tod** law of commorientes; ~ **besseren Fachwissens** assumption of skill; ~ **einer Schenkung** presumption of a gift; ~ **einer Treuhandregelung** presumption of a trust; ~ **des Überlebens** presumption of survival; ~ **der entgeltlichen Übertragung** presumption of value; ~ **der Vaterschaft** presumption of paternity; ~ **der Vermögensentziehung** presumption of confiscation; ~ **im Zweifel zugunsten des Angeklagten** presumption of innocence; ~**en anstellen** to make conjectures; **wahrscheinlich zutreffende ~ anstellen** to make a shrewd guess; ~ **begründen (entstehen lassen)** to raise a presumption; **zu der ~ führen** to lead to the assumption; ~ **widerlegen (entkräften)** to rebut a presumption, to negative an inference.

vernachlässigen to neglect, to be disregardful (negligent), to leave in the cold *(coll.)*;
sich ~ to let o. s. go; **Anlagegüter** ~ to waste assets; **seine Arbeit** ~ to be negligent in one's work; **seine Familie völlig** ~ to neglect utterly one's family; **Gast** ~ to slight a guest; **seine Pflichten** ~ to fail in (neglect, be backward in) one's duty, to be derelict in one's duty *(US)*; **sein Studium** ~ to neglect one's studies.

vernachlässigt neglected, *(Anlagegut)* wasted, *(Kind)* unattended, *(Wertpapier)* inactive;
~**er Minderjähriger** neglected minor.

Vernachlässigung neglect, *(Pachtobjekt)* waste;
fahrlässige ~ voluntary waste; **schuldhafte** ~ dereliction, neglect by wilful abandonment;
~ **einer Amtspflicht** misprision; ~ **der Aufsichtspflicht** neglect of one's supervisory duties; ~ **notwendiger Gebäudereparaturen** permissive waste; ~ **seines Geschäfts** inattention to (neglect of) one's business; ~ **der elterlichen Pflichten** parental neglect; ~ **der Prozeßführung** default of defence; ~ **der Unterhaltspflicht** wilful neglect of reasonable maintenance *(Br.)*, nonsupport *(US)*; ~ **der Vormundschaftspflichten** guardian neglect; ~ **der erforderlichen Vorsichtsmaßnahmen** neglect of proper precautions.

vernarrt fond of;
völlig ~ wrapped up;
völlig in etw. ~ **sein** to be nuts (mad) about s. th.; **völlig in jem.** ~ **sein** to be smitten (infatuated) with s. o.

vernaschen, sein Geld to spend one's money on sweets; **Mädchen** ~ to lay a girl *(sl.)*.

vernebeln to screen by smoke;
Tatsachen ~ to obscure the facts.

Vernebelung smoke screen.

Vernehmen, sicherem ~ nach according to records, from what I understand.

vernehmen to question, to interrogate, to examine, to hear, *(hören)* to hear, to perceive;
j. ~ to put s. o. to trial; **zur Anklage** ~ to arraign; **eidlich** ~ to examine on oath; **Geräusch deutlich** ~ to hear a noise distinctly; **vorher** ~ to pre-examine; **Zeugen** ~ to interrogate a witness, to hear evidence, to call to the witness box (stand, *US*);
sich eindeutig dahin gehend ~ lassen to intimate quite clearly.

Vernehmer examiner, interrogator.

vernehmlich distinct, clear.

Vernehmung public examination, interrogation, questioning, *(Gemeinschuldner)* examination, *(Gericht)* trial, *(parl., Voruntersuchung)* hearing;
eidliche ~ examination on oath; **getrennte** ~ separate examination; **polizeiliche** ~ police interrogation, interrogation by a police officer; **richterliche** ~ judicial examination;
~ **zur Anklage** arraignment; ~ **durch den Einzelrichter** examination before a magistrate, private examination; ~ **des Gemeinschuldners** examination of a bankrupt; **nochmalige ~ nach dem Kreuzverhör** redirect examination; ~ **durch Stellen von Suggestivfragen** suggestive interrogation; ~ **von Zeugen** hearing of evidence, interrogation of witnesses; **direkte ~ eines Zeugen** direct examination; ~ **eines Zeugen durch den eigenen Anwalt** examination-in-chief; ~ **von Zeugen vor Verhandlungsbeginn** examination before trial;
~ **durchführen** to examine, to interrogate, *(parl.)* to hold a hearing.

Vernehmungsbeamter examiner, interrogator, interrogation officer.

vernehmungsfähig fit to undergo an examination.

Vernehmungs|protokoll examination, protocol, record of interrogation; ~**richter** examining judge (magistrate); **beauftragter ~richter** examiner in chancery; ~**termin** diet; **polizeiliche ~unterlagen** charge sheet; ~**zimmer** hearing room.

verneigen, sich vor jem. to bow to s. o.

verneinen to [answer in the] negative, to negate, to deny.

verneinend| den Kopf schütteln to shake one's head;
~**e Aussage** negative statement.

Verneinung denial, negation, negative answer.

Verneinungsfall, im in case of an answer in the negative.

vernichtbar *(anfechtbar)* voidable.

vernichten to annihilate, to destroy, to destruct *(US)*, to crush, *(anfechten)* to annul, to avoid, *(ausrotten)* to exterminate, to extirpate, to destroy, to tread under foot, to end, to put to death, *(Pflanzen)* to nip;
ganze Armee ~ to reduce an army to nothing, to wipe out a whole army; **Ernte** ~ to ruin the harvest; **jds. Hoffnungen** ~ to dash s. one's hopes; **durch Kritik** ~ to kill; **Kunstwerk** ~ to destroy a work of art; **jds. Pläne** ~ to ruin s. one's plans; **Stadt** ~ to raze a city to the ground; **Urkunden** ~ to destroy documents; **völlig** ~ to pulverize.

vernichtend slashing;
jem. einen ~en Blick zuwerfen to wither s. o. with a scornful look; ~**e Kritik** scathing (destructive) criticism; ~**e Niederlage** crushing defeat; ~**es Urteil über j. fällen** to make mincemeat of s. o.

vernichtet, vom Erbeben razed by earthquake; **von den Flammen** ~ destroyed by flames.

Vernichtung destruction, annihilation, making away, erasement, *(Ausrottung)* extirpation, extinction, extermination, *(Vertrag)* annulment, avoidance;
buchstäbliche ~ literal annihilation;
~ **von Akten** record destruction; ~ **eines Landes** ruin of a country;
seiner ~ entgegengehen to rush to one's own destruction.

Vernichtungs|bahn *(Sturm)* trail of destruction; ~**feldzug** extermination campaign; ~**feuer** *(mil.)* annihilating fire; ~**krieg** war of extermination, exterminatory war; ~**lager** extermination camp; ~**mittel** *(gegen Insekten)* insecticide, vermicide; ~**politik** policy of annihilation; **überschüssiges ~potential** *(Atomwaffenkrieg)* overkill capacity; **zum ~schlag ausholen** to deal the final bow; ~**verhandlung** *(Geheimsachen)* cremation certificate.

verniedlichen to euphemize, to play down, to minimize;
Problem ~ to play down an issue.

vernommen werden to be under examination.

Vernommener interrogatee.

Vernunft reason, rationality, sense, *(Begriffsvermögen)* understanding, intellectual capacity;
~ **annehmen** to listen to reason; **jem.** ~ **beibringen** to pound sense into s. o.; **j. zur ~ bringen** to bring s. o. back to his senses; ~ **walten lassen** to apply reason to; **jeder ~ Hohn sprechen** to be opposed to all reason;
~**ehe** marriage of convenience; ~**grund** rational argument; **auf ~gründe hören** to listen to reason; **sich von ~gründen leiten lassen** to take reason as one's guide.

vernünftig reasonable, sensible, thinking, *(umsichtig)* judicious, considerate, sober-minded, levelheaded, fair enough;
~ **klingen** to make sense, to sound reasonable (all right); **Sache ~ erscheinen lassen** to make doing a thing basic common sense;
~ **reden** to talk sense (wisdom); **mit jem.** ~ **reden** to have a straight talk with s. o.;
~**es Angebot** reasonable offer; ~**e Forderungen stellen** to be reasonable in one's demands; ~**e Idee** sensible idea; ~**er Preis** reasonable (moderate) price.

Vernunft|mensch rational person; ~**regel** rule of reason.

veröden to become desolate, to depopulate.

Verödung desolation, devastation, depopulation.

veröffentlichen to make public (known), *(ankündigen)* to announce, to issue, to vent, to send out, *(Buch)* to publish, to bring (get) out, to edit, to print;
etw. ~ to publicize (give publicity to) s. th., to give s. th. to the public; **durch Anzeigen** ~ to advertise, to insert; **Anzeige in der Zeitung** ~ to insert an advertisement in a newspaper; **Aufgebot** ~ to put up the banns; **Beförderung** ~ to gazette an appointment; **Brief vollinhaltlich** ~ to publish a letter in full; **Briefsammlung** ~ to edit a collection of letters; **Buch** ~ to publish (bring out, print) a book; **Buch unter eigenem Namen** ~ to publish a book under one's own name; **Buchkritiken** ~ to carry book reviews; **Gesetz** ~ to promulgate a law; **Nachrichten ohne Nachprüfung** ~ to publish news without vouching for its accuracy; **Roman in Fortsetzungen** ~ to serialize a novel; **mit einer Schlagzeile über die ganze Seite** ~ to banner; **Stellengesuche kostenlos** ~ to run free ads for job seekers *(US)*; **unüberlegt** ~ to rush into print; **Verordnung** ~ to promulgate (issue) a decree.

veröffentlicht published, printed out;
nach dem Tode des Verfassers ~ posthumous; **nicht** ~ unpublished; **wert,** ~ **zu werden** printable;
~ **sein** to be out (published); ~ **werden** to be published, to see the light of day, to come out; **endlich** ~ **werden** to limp into publication; **auf Kosten von Autor und Verleger** ~ **werden** to be published at joint expense of publisher and author;
~**e Werke** published books (works).
Veröffentlichung *(Ankündigung)* announcement, *(Anzeige)* advertisement, insertion, *(Buch)* publication, published work, appearance, issue, *(Herausgabe)* bringing out, publication, publishing, editing, edition, *(Pressenotiz)* release;
mit der Bitte um ~ **in Ihrem geschätzten Blatt** for favo(u)r of publication in your columns; **nicht zur** ~ **bestimmt** off the record *(coll.)*; **nicht zur** ~ **geeignet** unfit for publication;
amtliche ~ governmental publication; **ausführliche** ~ saturation release; **außerbetriebliche** ~ external publication; **druckschriftliche** ~ *(Patentrecht)* printed publication; **erneute** ~ republication; **monatlich erscheinende** ~ monthly publication; **regelmäßig erscheinende** ~ periodical; **exklusive** ~ class publication; **frühere** ~**en** prior publications; **gedruckte** ~ printed matter, print *(US)*; **urheberrechtlich geschützte** ~ copyright[ed] publication (production, *US*); **hochverräterische** ~ seditious libel; **industrielle** ~ industrial publication; **pornographische** ~ obscene (indecent, pornographic) publications; **rechtswirksame** ~ legal publication; **repräsentative** ~ prestige publication; **unzulässige** ~ undue publication;
~ **des Aufgebots** publication of the banns; ~ **im Bundesanzeiger** [etwa] advertisement in the Gazette *(Br.)*; ~ **in Fortsetzungen** serial publication, serialization; ~**en einer Gesellschaft** official records of a society; ~ **eines Gesetzes** promulgation of a law; ~ **von Informationsmaterial** information disclosure; ~ **eines Projektes** issuing a prospectus; ~ **ersten Ranges** top publication; ~ **einer Verordnung** issuance of an order; ~ **in der Zeitung** insertion of an announcement in a newspaper;
~ **im voraus bestellen** to subscribe for a publication; **vor der** ~ **durchsehen** to sub; ~ **vorübergehend einstellen** to suspend a publication; **zur** ~ **durch die Presse freigeben** to release to the press; ~ **für November planen** to schedule the publication for November; **für die** ~ **umschreiben** to ghost; ~ **untersagen** to suppress a publication; **durch die** ~ **rechtswirksam werden** to constitute legal publication.
Veröffentlichungs|blatt official gazette *(Br.)*; ~**datum** date of publication, publication [issue] date, *(für die Presse)* release date; ~**devise** publishing formula; ~**kosten** publishing expenses (costs); ~**recht** copyright; ~**rechte in Zeitschriften** magazine rights; ~**rechte in Zeitungen und Zeitschriften** serial rights; ~**termin** publication (issue) date, *(für die Presse)* release date.
verordnen to [pass a] decree, to order, to enact, to ordain, to issue an order, to institute, to decree, *(Arzt)* to prescribe;
jem. Tabletten ~ to prescribe tablets for s. o.
Verordnung decree, order, ordinance, enactment, mandate, edict, precept, *(Durchführungsbestimmung)* executive order *(US)*, appointment, *(EG)* regulation, *(Erlaß)* prescription, *(Vorschrift)* statute, regulation, rule, provision, direction, directive;
vorbehaltlich anderweitiger ~**en** except as directed otherwise; **ärztliche** ~ prescription; **aufgehobene** ~ enactment repealed; **einschränkende** ~ restraining statute; **geltende** ~ regulation in force; **außer Kraft getretene** ~ dead letter; **ministerielle** ~ departmental order; **neue** ~ re-enactment; **polizeiliche** ~ police ordinance; **städtische** ~ city regulation, bylaw; **strenge** ~ stringent regulation; **verkehrspolizeiliche** ~**en** road regulations; **die oben zitierte** ~ the above decree;
~ **über Änderungen der Verjährungsfristen** Prescription Act *(Br.)*; ~ **mit Gesetzeskraft** statutory instrument, special order *(Br.)*;
~ **anwenden** to make a decree operative; ~ **ausschreiben** *(Arzt)* to make out a prescription; **Durchführung einer** ~ **aussetzen** to stop the execution of a decree; ~ **befolgen** to comply with a regulation; ~ **zur Anwendung bringen** to bring a decree into operation; ~ **erlassen** to issue a decree (order, ordinance), to decree, to order; ~ **verabschieden** to pass an ordinance; ~ **jem. zur Unterschrift vorlegen** to submit a decree to s. o. for signature; ~ **zurückziehen** to recall a decree.
Verordnungs|blatt bulletin, official gazette *(Br.)*; ~**recht** subordinate legislation, administrative law; **auf dem** ~**wege** by decree.
verpachten to let [out to tenants], to let on (put out to) lease, to grant a lease, to let out on hire (for rent), to rent, *(Steuereinnahmen)* to farm out;
gewerbsmäßig ~ to let at a commercial rent; **Grundbesitz auf Zeit** ~ to demise an estate; **Hof** ~ to let a farm to a tenant; **jahrweise zur landwirtschaftlichen Nutzung** ~ to let on an annual agricultural tenancy, to lease for agricultural use; **zu normalen Sätzen** ~ to let at a full rent.
Verpächter lessor, leaser, locator *(US)*, ground landlord;
~ **und Pächter** landlord and tenant.
Verpächterin lessor company.
Verpächterpfandrecht an Vieh und Ernte landlord's right over crop and stocking, hypothec *(Scot. law)*.
verpachtet out, leased, let, rented;
~ **sein** to be rented on a lease;
~**e Grundstücke** let property.
Verpachtung lease, leasing, letting on lease, let, demise, location, *(Steuereinnahme)* farming out;
landwirtschaftliche ~ lease of a farm, farm lease;
~ **von Industrieanlagen** plant leasing.
Verpacken packaging, packing, package, boxing in (up).
verpacken to pack, to package, to wrap [up], *(Waren)* to embale;
geschenkmäßig ~ to giftwrap; **in Schachteln** ~ to box up; **seine Waren in Ballen** ~ to pack (bale) one's wares; **Waren sachgemäß** ~ to pack goods in the proper manner; **Waren für den Verkauf** ~ to box articles for sale;
sich leicht ~ **lassen** to pack easily.
Verpacker baler, packer, packing agent.
verpackt packed, made up for sale;
bahnmäßig ~ packed for railroad transport *(US)*; **dutzendweise** ~ packed by the dozen; **fest** ~ packed tight; **handelsüblich** ~ packed as usual in trade; **im Karton** ~ boxed; **seemäßig** ~ packed for exportation by sea;
lose oder ~ loose or in packages;
~**e Ware** package (packaged) goods.
Verpackung package, packaging, packing, casing, *(Packmaterial)* packing material, *(Papier)* wrapping;
~ **ausgenommen** exclusive of wrappings; ~ **wird besonders (gesondert) berechnet** packing extra; ~ **wird nicht berechnet** no charge is made for packing; ~ **nicht einbegriffen** not including packing; **einschließlich** ~ including (inclusive of) package, packing inclusive; **zuzüglich** ~ plus packing;
äußere ~ outer (external) packing; **fehlerhafte** ~ faulty packing; **gebrauchte** ~ empties; **handelsübliche** ~ customary packing; **mangelhafte** ~ defective (insufficient) packing; **maschinelle** ~ automatic (machine) packing; **seetüchtige** ~ seaproof (seaworthy) packing; **unsachgemäße** ~ improper packing; **unzureichende** ~ defective packing; **ursprüngliche** ~ original packing (wrapping); **verlorene** ~ nonreturnable packing, one-trip container *(US)*; **vorschriftsmäßige** ~ packing ordered; **wasserdichte** ~ waterproof packing; **wiederverwendbare** ~ reusable package; **zurückgesandte** ~ returned empties;
~ **von Paketen** make-up of packets; ~ **zum Selbstkostenpreis** packing at cost; ~ **zur einmaligen Verwendung** disposable packing;
~ **zurücksenden** packing to be returned.
Verpackungs|abteilung packing (packaging) department; ~**anweisungen** packaging instructions; ~**art** type of packing, package; ~**band** bale tie; ~**beilage** package insert *(US)*; ~**bestimmungen** packaging (packing) regulations; ~**betrieb** packing plant; **auf Exportversand spezialisierter** ~**betrieb** export packer; ~**erfordernisse** packaging requirements; ~**fachmann** packaging engineer *(US)*; ~**fehler** insufficient packing; ~**gewicht** tare, dead weight; **reines** ~**gewicht** actual tare; ~**gewicht bestimmen** to ascertain (allow for) the tare; ~**industrie** packaging industry; ~**kosten** packing charges (costs), cost of packing, packaging costs; ~**kosten abziehen** to allow for the tare; **mit den** ~**kosten belastet werden** to be debited with the charges for packing; ~**leinwand** balecloth; ~**maschine** parcel(l)ing machine; ~**material** packaging (wrapping) material, packaging, packing, boxing; ~**muster** package design; ~**normen** package-size standards; ~**pflicht** obligation to provide packing; ~**raum** packing (wrapping, shipping, *US*) room, packery; ~**richtlinien** packaging classifications; ~**sektor** packaging sector; ~**spezialist** packaging consultant; ~**system** method of packing; ~**technik** packaging engineering *(US)*; ~**test** package test; ~**verpflichtung** obligation to provide packing; ~**vorschriften** packaging instructions; ~**weise** type of packing; ~**zettel** packing slip; **schlechter** ~**zustand** bad (poor) packing.
verpanschen to adulterate.
Verpassen miss.
verpassen, Anschluß *(fig.)* to miss the bus; **Gelegenheit** ~ to miss one's chance; **Zug** ~ to miss a train.

verpatzen *(Schauspieler)* to corpse;
etw. ~ to make a hash (bad job, mess) of s. th.
verpesten to pollute, to foul, to contaminate, to taint;
Luft ~ to vitiate the air.
verpestet foul, tainted, polluted;
~e Luft vitiated (tainted) air.
verpetzen to squeal, to squeak;
j. ~ to tell tales about s. o.
verpfändbar pledgeable, mortgageable, pawnable.
verpfänden to [put in] pawn, to deliver for pawn, to pledge, to put in pledge, to bond, to gage, to hock *(US sl.)*, to pop *(Br., sl.)*, to put away *(sl.)*, *(Grundstück)* to hypothecate, to mortgage;
Effekten bei einer Bank ~ to pledge (hypothecate, *US*) securities with a bank for payment of a loan; **seine Ehre** ~ to give (pledge, pawn) one's hono(u)r; **erneut** ~ to repawn; **für etw. sein Leben** ~ to stake one's life on it; **als Sicherheit** ~ to deposit as security for an advance *(Br.)*, to deposit as collateral security *(US)*, to collaterate *(US)*; **weiter** ~ to repledge, to rehypothecate; **sein Wort** ~ to pass one's oath (word);
sich ~ **lassen** to take in pawn.
Verpfänder bailor, pawner, pawnor, pledger, pledgor *(US)*, mortgager, mortgagor, lienee.
verpfändet bonded, pledged, in pledge, in (at) pawn, pawned, in hock *(US sl.)*, *(Grundbesitz, Lombardierung)* hypothecated *(US)*, mortgaged, encumbered;
nicht ~ unpledged, unengaged, unmortgaged, unencumbered;
~ **sein** to be lying in pledge, to be at pawn (in pledge), to lie to (be at) gage, *(Grundbesitz)* to be mortgaged (encumbered);
~er Gegenstand pledge, pawn, thing pledged; **~e Gegenstände** pledged chattels; **~e Waren** goods lying in pledge, goods pledged; **~er Wechsel** pawned bill of exchange; **als Sicherheit ~e Wertpapiere** pledged securities, pawned stock *(US)*, collateral securities *(US)*.
Verpfändung pawn, pawnage, pawning, pledge, pledging, bailment of goods, affection, *(Grundbesitz, Lombardierung)* hypothecation;
formlose ~ general equitable charge; **widerrechtliche** ~ unlawful pledge;
~ **von Aktien** pledge of stocks; ~ **eines obligatorischen Anspruchs** mortgage of an equitable interest; ~ **von Außenständen** assignment of choses in action; ~ **ganzer Bestände** chattel mortgage, bulk mortgage *(US)*; ~ **landwirtschaftlichen Betriebsvermögens** agricultural charge *(Br.)*; ~ **der Buchforderungen** charge on book debts; ~ **beweglichen Eigentums** pledge of personal property; ~ **der Ernte auf dem Halm** crop mortgage; ~ **des Firmenwertes** charge on goodwill; ~ **restlicher Kapitaleinzahlungsansprüche** charge on uncalled share capital; ~ **einer Lebensversicherungspolice** charge on a life policy; ~ **von Mieteinkünften** charge for rent; ~ **noch nicht geleisteter Nachzahlungsaufforderungen** charge on calls made but not paid; ~ **eines Pachtgrundstückes** mortgage of a leasehold, mortgage on leasehold property, leasehold mortgage; ~ **eines Schiffes** bottomry; ~ **von Sicherheiten** pledging (hypothecation, *US*) of securities; ~ **von Waren** pledge (hypothecation) of goods;
gegen ~ **von Sicherheiten Geld leihen** to advance money (lend) on pawns, to borrow on collateral *(US)*; **aus der** ~ **lösen** to take out of pawn; ~ **von Wertpapieren vornehmen** to pledge (hypothecate, *US*) securities, to collaterate *(US)*.
Verpfändungs|bedingungen, langfristige attendant terms *(Br.)*; **~bestimmungen** terms of pledge; **~formular** charge form; **~urkunde** document of charge, memorandum (letter) of pledge, memorandum of lien *(Br.)*, bond, *(Hypothek)* mortgage deed, mortgage instrument, *(Kauf unter Eigentumsvorbehalt)* bailment lease, deed of trust, *(Obligationenanleihe)* covering deed, *(Warenrembours)* letter of hypothecation, hypothecation certificate *(US)*; **~vertrag** contract of pledge; **~wert** loan (collateral, hypothecation, hypothecary, *US*) value.
verpfeifen *(fam.)* to squeak *(sl.)*, to sell out *(sl.)*, to shop *(sl.)*, to put the finger on *(US sl.)*, to switch *(sl.)*, to peach *(sl.)*, to blow the gaff about *(fam.)*, to rat.
verpflegen to board, to feed, *(Lieferant)* to cater for, to victual, *(mil.)* to ration;
Angestellte ~ to cater for employees; **Armee** ~ to ration an army; **jem. für 4 Dollar täglich** ~ to keep s. o. for 4 dollars a day; **sich selbst** ~ to cook for o. s.
verpflegt werden, erstklassig to have a good feed.
Verpflegung board, keep, food, subsistence, *(Bewirtung)* entertainment, *(mil.)* rations, *(Truppenteil)* provisions;
in ~ *(Pferd)* at livery;
~ **von Angestellten** catering of employees; **Unterkunft und** ~ board and room (lodging); **freie** ~ **und Wohnung** free food and accommodation;
~ **empfangen** to draw rations; **bei jem. in** ~ **sein** to board (lodge) with s. o.; **volle** ~ **und Unterkunft stellen** to provide full board and accommodation.
Verpflegungs|amt food office, commissariat magazine, victual(l)ing office *(Br.)*; **~ausgabe** issue of rations; **~ausgabestelle** ration distribution point; **~ausschuß** kitchen committee; **~bombe** *(mil.)* ration delivery unit; **~depot** subsistence depot; **~einrichtungen** feeding (catering) facilities; **~empfang** reception of rations; **~geld** alllowance for board, meal (daily) allowance, board charges, *(mil.)* ration money; **tägliches ~geld** per diem pay, daily subsistence allowance; **~gutschein** victual(l)ing note *(Br.)*; **~kolonne** supply column; **~kosten** board, *(Kasino)* catering costs, *(mil.)* marching money, *(Schiff)* cost of maintenance; **~lager** subsistence stores, victual(l)ing yard *(Br.)*; **vorgeschobenes ~lager** *(mil.)* advance depot; **~marke** meal voucher; **~möglichkeiten** catering facilities; **~offizier** catering officer; **~portion** ration; **~satz** daily ration; **~schiff** victual(l)ing ship; **~sektor** catering field; **~stärke** *(mil.)* ration strength; **~station** victual(l)ing station; **~wesen** *(mil.)* logistics, commissariat; **~zug** supply train; **~zulage, ~zuschuß** meal (daily, maintenance, food) allowance.
verpflichten to bind, to commit, to engage, to obligate, to oblige, to put under an obligation;
sich ~ to covenant, to engage, to pledge (oblige) o. s., to undertake, to sign up; **j.** ~, **etw. zu tun** to make it binding on s. o. to do s. th.; **seinen Auftraggeber rechtlich** ~ to bind one's principal; **durch Bürgschaft** ~ to bind over; **sich ehrenwörtlich** ~ to pledge one's hono(u)r; **sich eidlich** ~ to bind o. s. under oath; **j. eidlich** ~ to bind s. o. by oath; **j. auf Geheimhaltung** ~ to bind s. o. to secrecy; **sich für drei Jahre** ~ to engage for three years; **neu** ~ to recruit afresh; **sich für die Saison** ~ to engage o. s. for the season; **Schauspieler für eine Rolle** ~ to engage an actor for a role; **zur Tragung der Kosten** ~ *(Urteil)* to carry costs; **sich zur Übernahme der Kosten** ~ to undertake to pay the costs; **sich zur Unterstützung** ~ to pledge one's support; **j. auf die Verfassung** ~ to swear s. o. in; **sich vertraglich** ~ to enter into a covenant, to bind o. s. by contract; **seine Zuhörer zum Stillschweigen** ~ to pledge one's hearers to secrecy.
verpflichtend binding, obligatory, mandatory *(US)*.
Verpflichtender obliger.
verpflichtet obligatory, obligated, liable, answerable, bound, obliged, engaged, attendant, *(verschuldet)* indebted;
einseitig ~ onerous; **gesamtschuldnerisch** ~ jointly and severally bound; **gesetzlich** ~ liable by law, legally bound; **moralisch** ~ morally bound, duty-bound; **nicht** ~ unengaged; **zum Schadenersatz** ~ liable to respond in damages, bound to allow indemnity; **zum Schweigen** ~ pledged to secrecy; **vertraglich** ~ liable under a contract (deed), indentured; **zwangsweise** ~ conscript;
sich ~ **fühlen** to feel under an obligation; ~ **sein** to lie under an obligation, to be under liability (duty); **jem. [gegenüber]** ~ **sein** to be under an obligation (obliged) to s. o.; **gesetzlich** ~ **sein** to be bound by law (statutorily obliged); **zu Steuerzahlungen** ~ **sein** to be liable to pay taxes; **vertraglich** ~ **sein** to be under a contract; **jem. weiterhin** ~ **sein** to remain under an obligation to s. o.; **zur Verschwiegenheit** ~ **werden** to be pledged to secrecy.
Verpflichteter debtor, party liable, obligor, covenanter.
Verpflichtung obligation, liability, bond, responsibility, commitment, debt, engagement, trust, sponsion, tie, *(Pflicht)* duty;
ohne ~ without obligation;
abhängige ~ dependent covenant; **abstrakte** ~ independent covenant; **akzessorische** ~ accessory contract; **allgemeine** ~ general obligation; **ältere** ~ prior obligation; **in der Zukunft anfallende** ~ prospective obligation; **ausdrückliche** ~ express covenant (obligation); **bare** ~ cash obligation; **bedingte** ~ contingent liability; **auf Billigkeit beruhende** ~ equitable obligation; **bestehende** ~ existing liability; **bereits bestehende** ~ pre-existing liability; **bindende** ~ binding commitment; **dingliche** ~ real obligation; **juristisch durchsetzbare** ~ perfect obligation; **einfache** ~ simple obligation; **vorher eingegangene** ~ pre-engagement; **einklagbare** ~ civil (perfect) obligation; **nicht einklagbare** ~ natural (imperfect) obligation; **einseitige** ~ imperfect obligation, naked bond; **stillschweigend enthaltene** ~ implied covenant; **entstandene** ~ liability accrued; **schwer zu erfüllende** ~ onerous obligation; **feierliche** ~ solemn undertaking; **ausdrücklich festgelegte** ~ express obligation;

freiwillige ~ voluntary undertaking; **frühere** ~ pre-engagement; **gesamtschuldnerische** ~ joint and several liability, joint and several obligation *(US)*; **gesellschaftliche** ~ social engagement (commitment); **gesetzliche** ~ statutory (perfect) obligation, statutory duty, legal liability; **durch Konventionalklausel gesicherte** ~ penal obligation; **harte** ~ rigid obligation; **hypothekarische** ~ mortgage obligation; **moralische** ~ moral consideration (obligation), ethical duty; **obligatorische** ~ equitable obligation; **öffentlich-rechtliche** ~ obligation under public law; **persönliche** ~ personal obligation (liability); **primäre** ~ primary obligation; **satzungsmäßige** ~ liability created by statute; **bindende schriftliche** ~ obligatory writing; **schuldrechtliche** ~ general covenant, civil obligation; **solidarische** ~ solidary obligation; **stillschweigende (mit übernommene)** ~ implied engagement (obligation); **unabdingbare** ~ absolute obligation (liability); **unabhängige** ~ simple obligation; **unbedingte** ~ pure obligation; **unbestrittene** ~ direct obligation; **unumgängliche** ~ imperative duty; **vertragliche** ~ obligation under a contract; **vertragsähnliche** ~ quasi-contract; **zusätzliche** ~ accessory obligation; **zwingende** ~ absolute obligation;
~ **zur Abnahme der Ware** obligation to accept the goods; ~ **zu zukünftigen Leistungen** affirmative covenant; ~ **zur Preisstabilität** price pledge; ~ **zur Sicherheitsleistung** injunction bond; ~, **sich der Substanzverringerung zu enthalten** obligation not to commit waste; ~ **zum Unterhalt** obligation to support (maintain); ~ **zu einer Unterlassung** negative covenant; ~ **zur Vornahme einer Handlung** obligation to perform;
~ **abgelten** to discharge an obligation; ~ **ablehnen** to decline a liability; ~ **annullieren** to deface a bond; ~ **auferlegen** to impose an obligation; **jem. eine** ~ **auferlegen** to lay (throw) s. o. under an obligation, to fasten an obligation on (make it obligatory upon) s. o.; ~ **aufheben** to nullify an obligation; **von einer** ~ **befreien** to exempt (free, release) from a liability; **von der** ~ **zur Leistung befreien** to discharge from performance; ~ **begründen** to create an obligation; **sich offen zu einer** ~ **bekennen** to make an open-ended commitment; **sich auf satzungsmäßige ~en berufen** to invoke the provisions of a statute; ~ **eingehen** to incur a liability (commitment), to enter into a bond (an obligation, undertaking), to commit o. s.; **bindende** ~ **eingehen** to enter into a binding agreement; ~ **einhalten** to fulfil(l) an obligation; **j. aus einer** ~ **entlassen** to discharge s. o. from an obligation; **j. aus einer vertraglichen** ~ **entlassen** to release o. s. from a contract; **j. von einer** ~ **entlasten** to exonerate s. o. from an obligation; **sich seiner** ~ **entledigen** to acquit o. s. of a duty; **sich einer** ~ **entziehen** to back out of (elude) an obligation; **sich einer** ~ **durch Vertragsabschluß entziehen** to contract o. s. out of an obligation; ~ **erfüllen** to discharge (redeem) an obligation; ~ **erhöhen** to enlarge a recognizance; **jem. eine** ~ **erlassen** to release s. o. from an obligation; ~ **haben** to lie under an obligation; ~ **loswerden** to get off a duty; **einer** ~ **nachkommen** to implement (satisfy) an obligation; **einer** ~ **nicht nachkommen** to infringe an obligation; ~ **auf sich nehmen** to shoulder a liability, to incur an obligation; ~ **übernehmen** to incur (assume) an obligation; **aus einer** ~ **entlassen werden** to obtain a release from an obligation; **sich aus einer** ~ **zurückziehen** to back out of an obligation.

Verpflichtungen liabilities, indebtedness;
angesichts der eingegangenen ~ given the made commitments; **aufgrund früherer** ~ owing to previous engagements; **ohne** ~ unbound;
aufgelaufene, aber noch nicht fällige ~ accrued liabilities; **außenpolitische** ~ foreign commitments; **bankinterne** ~ interbank obligations; **zeitlich befristete** ~ time liabilities; **eingegangene** ~ liabilities incurred; **für wohltätige Zwecke eingegangene** ~ deeds of covenant in favo(u)r of charities; **finanzielle** ~ pecuniary (financial) obligations, commitments; **gegenseitige** ~ mutual demands (covenants); **geschäftliche** ~ business commitments; **mit dem Diplomatenleben verbundene gesellschaftliche** ~ social obligations incident to life in the diplomatic service; **gesetzliche** ~ legal liabilities; **handelsvertragliche** ~ obligations under a trade agreement; **hypothekarische** ~ *(Hauptbuch)* mortgage payable *(US)*; **laufende kaufmännische** ~ ordinary business engagements; **kurzfristige** ~ current liabilities; **langfristige** ~ long-term obligations (engagements); **laufende** ~ running engagements, financial debts, trade liabilities; **mögliche** ~ contingent liabilities; **sonstige** ~ *(Bilanz)* other liabilities; **bedingte und spätere** ~ existing liabilities; **steuerliche** ~ tax liabilities; **finanzielle Leistungsfähigkeit übersteigende** ~ overcommitments; **vertragliche** ~ liabilities of contract, contractual commitments, treaty obligations; **völkerrechtliche** ~ international commitments; **voreheliche** ~ antenuptial debts; **wechselrechtliche** ~ liabilities upon bills;
~ **aus geleisteten Akzepten** *(Bilanz)* contingent liabilities in respect of acceptances; ~ **aufgrund der Ausgabe von Banknoten** bank-notes liabilities; ~ **aus abgetretenen Debitoren** accounts receivable discounted *(US)*; ~ **gegenüber Dritten** *(konsolidierte Bilanz)* liabilities to outsiders; ~ **bei anderen Etatstiteln** due to other funds; ~ **des Käufers** buyer's obligations, buyer's duties; ~ **der Kundschaft** customers' liabilities; ~ **der Kundschaft aus dokumentarischen Krediten und Rembourskrediten** customers' liabilities due to documentary and commercial credits; ~ **der Kundschaft aus Wechsel- und Garantieverbindlichkeiten** *(Bilanz)* customers' liabilities for acceptances and guarantees; ~ **der Öffentlichkeit gegenüber** public engagements; ~ **gegenüber Tochtergesellschaften** *(Bilanz)* owing to subsidiaries; ~ **aus einem Vertrag** obligations pursuant to a treaty; ~ **aus diskontierten Wechseln** contingent liabilities on account of endorsements on bills discounted; ~ **aus noch nicht eingelösten Wechseln** liabilities upon bills;
~ **anerkennen** to acknowledge liabilities; **sich** ~ **aufladen** to incur liabilities; **von** ~ **befreien** to release from obligations; **sich um seine** ~ **drücken** to get out of one's duties; ~ **eingehen** to contract (incur, assume) liabilities; **betriebliche** ~ **eingehen** to make corporate commitments; **seine** ~ **einhalten** to keep one's engagements; **seine vertraglichen** ~ **einhalten** to meet one's contract obligations; **sich finanziellen** ~ **entziehen** to repudiate financial obligations; **sich seinen** ~ **entziehen** to withdraw from one's engagements (obligations); **seine** ~ **erfüllen** to discharge one's liabilities, to carry out one's obligations, to meet one's commitments (engagements); **seine schriftlichen** ~ **erledigen** to attend to the correspondence, to do one's mail *(US)*; **große** ~ **gegenüber jem. haben** to be greatly indebted to s. o.; **verschiedene [finanzielle]** ~ **haben** to have various commitments; **alle** ~ **loswerden** to free o. s. from one's commitments; **seinen** ~ **nachkommen** to meet (settle) one's commitments, to meet (discharge) one's obligations (liabilities), to keep one's engagements, to satisfy one's creditors, *(Parteipolitik)* to toe the line; **seinen** ~ **nicht nachkommen** to fail to meet one's obligations (commitments), to avoid one's obligations, to [make] default; **seinen** ~ **pünktlich nachkommen** to meet one's obligations punctually; **seinen laufenden kaufmännischen** ~ **stets nachkommen** to be good for one's ordinary business engagements; **seinen** ~ **als Verkäufer nachkommen** to fulfil(l) one's obligations under a contract of sale; **durch** ~ **gebunden sein** to be under bond; ~ **übernehmen** to assume obligations (liabilities); **finanzielle** ~ **übernehmen** to enter into pecuniary obligations; ~ **unterliegen** to be liable; ~ **nach sich ziehen** to involve liabilities.

Verpflichtungseid promissory oath.

Verpflichtungserklärung bond, undertaking, pledge card, *(Zeuge)* binding over;
gesamtschuldnerische ~ joint and several bond; **schriftliche** ~ written undertaking;
schriftliche ~ **eines Anwalts** solicitor's letter of undertaking.

Verpflichtungs|geschäft executory contract; ~**klausel** *(Praktikant)* radius clause.

Verpflichtungsschein surety bond *(US)*, obligation;
gegenseitiger ~ reciprocal bond; **kaufmännischer** ~ promissory note; **persönlicher** ~ single bond; **wertloser** ~ straw bond;
~ **eines Treuhänders** receiver's bond;
~ **ausstellen** to give a bond.

Verpflichtungs|übernahme assumption of a liability; ~**urteil** writ of mandamus.

verpfuschen to bungle, to botch, to mess up, to muck up *(coll.)*, to make a muck of *(coll.)*;
immer alles ~ to keep on paying out small sums; **Arbeit** ~ to blunder work, to muck up a job *(fam.)*.

verplanen to budget.

verplant budgeted;
noch nicht ausgegebene, jedoch ~e Etatmittel unexpended appropriations; **noch nicht ausgegebener, jedoch bereits ~er Haushaltsüberschuß** unexpended balance; **~e Mittel** budgeted means.

Verplanungsrest unexpended balance.

verplappern, sich to let the cat out of the bag, to blab out a secret, to shoot off one's mouth *(US sl.)*.

verplempern to trifle, to chuck away;
Geld ~ *(fam.)* to spill money; **seine ganze Zeit** ~ to fritter (fool, peddle, loiter) away one's time.

verplomben to seal.
verprassen to guzzle away;
sein Vermögen ~ to dissipate one's fortune.
verproviantieren to supply with provisions, to provision, to [re]-victual;
sich ~ to take in supplies; **Flugzeug** ~ to cater an airplane; **Heer** ~ to furnish an army with supplies, to sustain an army; **Schiff** ~ to victual (supply) a ship.
verproviantiert, nicht unstored.
Verproviantierung supplying with provisions, provisioning, victual(l)ing;
~ **von Flugzeuggesellschaften** airline catering.
verprovisionieren, Gesamtumsatz to allow a percentage on all transactions.
verprügeln to give a sound thrashing, to paddle *(US)*.
verpuffen to come to nothing, to end in smoke.
verpuffte Werbung advertising falling flat.
verpulvern, sein Geld to fritter away one's money.
Verputz plaster, coating, finish;
~**arbeit** plastering.
verputzen to plaster over;
Mahlzeit ~ to tuck in, to polish off a meal *(sl.)*; **Wand** ~ to daub plaster on a wall.
verquer gehen, jem. to go against s. one's grain.
verquicken to mix up;
Interessen miteinander ~ to combine interests.
Verquickung, wirtschaftliche involvement in business.
verrammeln to barricade, to bar.
verrannt, in eine Sache obsessed by an idea;
sich völlig ~ **haben** to be on the wrong side of the post *(fam.)*.
Verranntheit obsession.
Verrat treason, treachery, betrayal, prodition;
regelrechter ~ rank treason;
~ **eines Freundes** going back on a friend; ~ **militärischer Geheimnisse** disclosure of military secrets;
~ **begehen** to commit an act of treachery; **nahe an** ~ **grenzen** to reach the dignity of treason.
verraten to betray, to sell out *(sl.)*, *(jur.)* to commit an act of treachery;
seine wahren Absichten ~ to show one's true colo(u)rs; **alles** ~ to spill the beans *(US sl.)*, to spill one's guts *(sl.)*; **Bestürzung** ~ to reveal great dismay; **Geheimnis** ~ to disclose a secret; **gute Sache** ~ to sell the pass; **Staatsgeheimnisse** ~ to betray state secrets; **Verschwörung** ~ to divulge a plot.
Verräter traitor, betrayer, *(pol.)* quisling, rat, *(Verbrecher)* squeaker, squealer *(sl.)*;
schändlicher ~ infamous traitor;
~ **in mehrerlei Hinsicht** manifold traitor;
zum ~ **werden** to turn traitor, *(pol.)* to rat; **an jem. zum** ~ **werden** to betray s. o.
Verräterei treachery, ratting.
verräterisch treacherous, treasonable, felonious, unfaithful;
in ~**er Absicht** with treasonable intent; ~**er Blick** revealing (betraying) look; ~**e Handlungsweise** foul play; **in** ~**er Weise** treasonably.
verrauschen *(Beifall)* to die down, to subside.
verrechnen *(im Clearingwege abrechnen)* to clear, *(ausgleichen)* to balance, *(belasten)* to charge up against, *(in Gegenrechnung bringen)* to compensate, to set off *(Br.)*, to offset *(US)*, *(verbuchen)* to pass (put, place) to account;
sich ~ to miscount, to miscalculate, to misreckon, to be out in one's calculation(s), to make a mistake; **sich gewaltig** ~ to be sadly mistaken; **Gewinn mit einem Verlust** ~ to set off (offset, *US*) a gain against a loss; **Kosten unmittelbar auf jede Abteilung** ~ to charge costs directly to the department; **jeden Posten** ~ to put to account every single item.
verrechnet, nicht uncleared;
sich ~ **haben** to be out in one's calculations (reckoning).
Verrechnung settlement, *(Belastung)* debiting, charging, *(Buchung)* placing to account, *(Gegenrechnung)* compensation, set-off *(Br.)*, offset *(US)*, *(im Verrechnungswege)* clearing;
nur zur ~ *(Scheck)* not negotiable, account payee only (crossing, *Br.*), payable only through the clearinghouse;
schwebende ~**en** clearing items;
~ **von Schecks** clearing of checks *(US)* (cheques, *Br.*); ~ **auf die Schuldsumme** appropriation of money [to a debt]; ~ **aus Zinsgründen** set-off for interest purposes;
~ **von Spekulationsverlusten mit Einkommensteuerpflichten gestatten** to allow losses in venture capital companies to set off against personal income-tax liabilities; **zur** ~ **zur Verfügung stehen** to be available for offset *(US)*.
Verrechnungs|abkommen clearing (offset, *US*) agreement; **dreiseitiges** ~**abkommen** tripartite clearing agreement; ~**bank** clearing member bank, clearinghouse agent (bank); ~**beleg** clearing voucher, *(Warenhaus)* drawback slip; ~**defizit** clearing deficit; ~**devisen** clearing (agreement) currency; ~**dollar** agreement (accounting, offset, *US*) dollar; ~**einheit** clearing (accounting) unit; **wechselkursfreie** ~**einheit** floating-value unit of account; ~**einrede** offsetting plea; ~**fonds** settlement fund; ~**forderungen** clearing claims; ~**geschäft** clearing operation (transaction), offsetting transaction *(US)*, *(im Konzern)* intercompany operation; ~**guthaben** clearing balance (assets); ~**gutschrift** *(Fluglinie)* exchange order; ~**kasse** clearing office, clearinghouse; ~**konto** offset *(US)* (clearing, current, drawing, running) account; ~**kredit** offset credit *(US)*; ~**kurs** making-up price, clearing rate, rate of exchange, *(im Konzern)* intercompany rate; ~**land** agreement (clearing, offset, *US*) country; ~**posten** clearing item; ~**preis** internal (intercompany) price; ~**raum** clearing area; ~**saldo** clearing balance, *(Scheckverkehr)* clearinghouse balance; ~**satz** specified rate of exchange; **nicht übertragbarer** ~**scheck** clearinghouse (nonnegotiable) check *(US)*, crossed cheque *(Br.)*, cheque only for account *(Br.)*, voucher check *(US)*, check for deposit only *(US)*; ~**scheck für Ausgleichsbeträge** redemption check *(US)*; ~**scheck einreichen** to present a cheque *(Br.)* (check, *US*) through the clearing; ~**schema** compensation scheme; ~**schlüssel** clearing ratio; ~**schuld** clearing debt; ~**spitze** clearing balance; ~**stelle** clearinghouse; ~**summe** clearings; ~**system** clearing system, *(Warenhaus)* drawback system; ~**tag** day of settlement; ~**verfahren** clearing mechanism (operation, system).
Verrechnungsverkehr clearing system (business, transactions);
allgemeiner ~ general clearing; **internationaler** ~ international clearings; **multilateraler** ~ multilateral clearing system.
Verrechnungs|vermerk *(auf Scheck)* crossing *(Br.)*; **allgemeiner** ~**vermerk** general crossing *(Br.)*; ~**vermerk nur zur Gutschrift des Empfängers** account payee only (crossing, *Br.*); ~**vorgang** clearing transaction; ~**vorschüsse** clearing advances; ~**währung** agreement (clearing) currency; **im** ~**wege** through clearing channels; ~**wert** trade-in value; ~**wesen** clearing system.
Verrecken, nicht ums not on my life.
verrecken to die wretchedly;
kümmerlich ~ to die in the last ditch;
eher will ich ~ I'll be blowed.
verregneter Sommer wet summer.
verreisen to go on a journey;
in den Ferien ~ to get away for a holiday; **geschäftlich** ~ to go away on business; **zu Lasten des Spesenkontos** ~ to travel on expense account; **nach M** ~ to leave for M; **oft** ~ to travel a good deal.
verreißen to pull (tear) to pieces, to slam *(coll.)*.
verreist away from home, out of town *(Br.)*;
geschäftlich ~ away on business; **übers Wochenende** ~ away over the weekend;
~ **sein** to be out of town.
verrenken, sich den Hals to twist one's neck; **sich die Zunge** ~ to twist one's tongue.
verrichten to perform, to discharge, to carry out, to execute, to effect, to act, to transact;
Dienst ~ to officiate; **sein Gebet** ~ to say one's prayers; **Schwerarbeit** ~ to slave, to drudge.
Verrichtung performance, transaction, execution, discharge;
kleine häusliche ~**en** little domestic offices; **tägliche** ~**en** daily routine.
Verrichtungsgehilfe vicarious officer (agent).
verriegeln to bolt, to bar, *(Bahnsignal)* to interlock;
Tür fest ~ to fasten a door.
Verriegelung *(Bahnsignal)* interlocking.
Verriegelungsschloß dead lock.
verringern to diminish, to reduce, to decrease, to extenuate, to attenuate, to pare down, *(Münzen)* to debase, *(im Wert)* to deteriorate;
sich ~ to go down, to reduce, to diminish; **Arbeitskräfte** ~ to reduce forces; **Ausgaben** ~ to cut down (retrench) one's expenses; **seine Chancen** ~ to muddle away one's opportunities; **seine Kosten** ~ to retrench one's expenses; **Personal radikal** ~ to axe a number of officials *(Br.)*; **Tempo** ~ to lessen one's speed, to slow down; **Unkosten** ~ to reduce costs; **jds. Zuschuß** ~ to cut s. one's allowance.
Verringerung reduction, diminution, decrease, *(Münzgewicht)* debasement;

~ **der Arbeitslosigkeit** decrease in unemployment; ~ **von Arbeitsplätzen** job reduction; ~ **der Arbeitszeit** reduction of working hours; ~ **des Geschäftsvolumens** business contraction; ~ **des Gewichts** diminution in weight; ~ **der Kapitalgüter** diminution of capital goods; ~ **des Personalbestandes** retrenchment of employees, reduction in (axing of, *Br.*) staff; ~ **der Rücklagen** cancellation of reserves; ~ **des Spesenvolumens** expense account cutback; ~ **des Wertes** decrease in value.

Verriß pulling to pieces, scathing criticism, slam *(coll.)*.

verrosten to rust, to corrode.

verrostet rusty, corroded.

verrottet putrid, *(Haus)* dilapidated, decayed.

verrucht abominable, wicked;
~**e Tat** atrocity.

verrückt insane, crazy, wild, mad, cracked, loony *(sl.)*, daft *(sl.)*, balmy, over the edge, off one's nut (head, top) *(sl.)*, screwy *(US sl.)*, nutty *(sl.)*, wet *(US sl.)*;
ein bißchen ~ off one's trolley (onion); **total** ~ as mad as a March hare, mad as a hatter, plumb crazy *(US sl.)*; **wie** ~ like one o'clock, like blazes, like all possessed *(US)*;
jem. ~ **machen** to addle s. one's wits; **j. mit törichten Fragen reinweg** ~ **machen** to drive s. o. to distraction with silly questions; ~ **sein** to be nuts *(sl.)*; **ein bißchen** ~ **sein** to be little off, to have a screw loose; **ganz** ~ **nach etw. sein** to be wild about s. th. *(coll.)*; **ganz** ~ **nach jem. sein** to be wild (daft, nuts) about s. o. *(sl.)*; ~ **spielen** to have one's tantrums; ~ **werden** to lose one's senses, to go off one's nut; **vor Angst** ~ **werden** to go out of one's mind with fear; **total** ~ **werden** to go haywire *(US sl.)*; **für** ~ **erklärt werden** to be declared a fool;
~**e Idee** crazy (daft, *coll.*) idea; ~**er Plan** crackbrained scheme.

Verrücktenanstalt madhouse, lunatic asylum.

Verrückter crackbrain, madman, lunatic, idiot;
sich wie ein ~ **aufspielen** to fling o. s. about like a madman; **wie ein** ~ **fahren** to drive like mad *(coll.)*.

Verruf disrepute, disparagement, discredit;
in ~ **bringen** to discredit, to bring into disrepute; **sein Regiment in** ~ **bringen** to be a dishono(u)r to one's regiment; **in** ~ **erklären** to boycott; **in** ~ **geraten** to fall into obloquy (discredit).

verrufen disreputable, ill-famed, notorious.

Vers|e in seine Rede einflechten to tag a speech with verses; **sich keinen** ~ **daraus machen können** not to be able to make head or tail of it.

Versagen failure, flunk, *(Maschine)* breakdown;
menschliches ~ human failure;
~ **einer Batterie** failure of a battery; ~ **eines Patents** withdrawal of a patent;
~ **der Lichtanlage, der Bremsvorrichtungen und des Treibstoffsystems anzeigen** to warn of any malfunction in the lighting, braking and fuel system; ~ **durch harte Arbeit vermeiden** to avert failure by hard work.

versagen to fail, to flunk, to flop *(sl.)*, *(ablehnen)* to decline, to refuse, *(Bremse)* to fail, *(Maschine)* to break down, to conk out, *(Schußwaffe)* to misfire;
jem. die Aufnahme ~ to deny s. one's admission; **sich eine Bemerkung nicht** ~ not to refrain from making a remark; **beruflich** ~ to fall down on the job *(coll.)*; **in einer Prüfung** ~ to fail (flunk, *sl.*) in an examination; **als Rechtsanwalt völlig** ~ to be a failure as a lawyer; **seine Zustimmung** ~ to withhold (refuse) one's consent.

Versager dud, flop *(sl.)*, washout *(sl.)*, oilcan *(sl.)*, turkey *(US sl.)*, breakdown, lame duck, lemon *(sl.)*, slouch *(US sl.)*, *(Waffe)* misfire;
~ **auf der Universität** college dropout *(coll.)*;
sich für einen ~ **halten** to suffer a feeling of failure; ~ **sein** to flunk, to flop *(sl.)*; **totaler** ~ **sein** to be a complete failure; **nach glänzendem Start zum** ~ **werden** to be a flash in the pan.

versagt engaged, booked, dated;
anderweitig ~ **sein** to have a previous engagement.

Versagung refusal, denial;
~ **der Eintragungsgenehmigung** nonregistration.

Versagungsfall, im in case of refusal.

Versalien capital letters;
in ~ **gedruckt** in capitals.

versalzen, jem. die Suppe to spoil s. one's fun.

versammeln to assemble, to muster, *(einberufen)* to convene, to convoke, *(mil.)* to rally, to assemble;
sich ~ to assemble, to meet, to hold a meeting, to gather, to congregate, *(pol.)* to rally; **seine Freunde um sich** ~ to gather one's friends together; **sich zu seinen Vätern** ~ to gather to one's fathers, to meet the majority.

Versammlung assembly, meeting, gathering, convention, congregation, assemblage, convocation, session, *(pol.)* rally, congress, convention, caucus *(US)*, *(Zuhörer)* audience;
auf einer öffentlichen ~ at a public gathering, in open assembly;
öffentlich abgehaltene ~ meeting in a public place; **privat abgehaltene** ~ meeting in a private place; **turnusmäßig aufeinanderfolgende** ~**en** rotatory assemblies; **außerordentliche** ~ special meeting, *(AG)* extraordinary general meeting; **beratende** ~ deliberative assembly, council, synod; **gut besuchte** ~ good turnout at the meeting; **einberufene** ~ called meeting; **formgerecht einberufene** ~ duly convened meeting; **kurzfristig einberufene** ~ meeting called at short notice; **erregte (hysterische)** ~ worked-up audience; **gelehrte** ~ learned body; **gemeinsame** ~ *(ECU)* Common Assembly; **gesetzgebende** ~ convention, legislative (general, *US*) assembly, General Court *(US)*; **glänzende** ~ constellation; **große** ~ numerous assembly; **konstituierende** ~ constituent assembly; **lärmende** ~ bear garden; **öffentliche** ~ public meeting, open assembly; **gesetzlich genehmigte öffentliche** ~ lawful public meeting; **ordentliche** ~ regular meeting; **politische** ~ political gathering (assembly, meeting, rally); **erregte politische** ~ tumultuous political meeting; **staatsgefährdende** ~ seditious meeting; **ständige** ~ permanent assembly; **morgen stattfindende** ~ the meeting to be held tomorrow; **stürmische** ~ rough house; **überfüllte** ~ packed meeting; **ungesetzliche** ~ unlawful meeting; **verfassunggebende** ~ constitutional convention, National (Constituent) Assembly; **vollzählige** ~ full assembly;
~ **der Aktionäre** meeting of shareholders (stockholders, *US*); ~ **der Europäischen Gemeinschaften** European Assembly; ~ **nachschußpflichtiger Gesellschafter** meeting of contributories; ~ **unter freiem Himmel** open-air meeting; **glänzende** ~ **begabter Persönlichkeiten** galaxy of talents;
~ **abhalten** to hold an assembly (a rally, a meeting, a gathering), to convene (keep) an assembly; ~ **entsprechend den vorgeschriebenen Regularien abhalten** to hold a meeting in accordance with the regulations; ~ **auflösen** to disperse a meeting, to dissolve a meeting (an assembly), to dismiss a congregation, *(gewaltsam)* to break up a meeting; **einer** ~ **beiwohnen** to attend a meeting; **über eine** ~ **berichten** to report (cover) a meeting; ~ **besuchen** to attend (turn out for) a meeting; ~ **auf Touren bringen** to work up the feelings of an audience; **große Anzahl von Anhängern in eine** ~ **dirigieren** to pack a meeting; ~ **einberufen** to convene (convoke, call, set up) a meeting (an assembly); **Resolution in einer** ~ **einbringen** to bring up a resolution in a meeting; ~ **für beendet erklären** to wind up a meeting; ~ **eröffnen** to call a meeting to order *(US)*; **sich von einer** ~ **fernhalten** to absent o. s. from a meeting; **zu früh zu einer** ~ **kommen** to arrive too early for a meeting; ~ **leiten, einer** ~ **präsidieren** to be in the chair, to preside at a meeting, to moderate an assembly; **öffentliche** ~ **leiten** to moderate a public meeting; **bei einer** ~ **anwesend sein** to attend (be present) at a meeting; **an einer** ~ **teilnehmen** to assist at (attend) a meeting; **einer** ~ **einen Vorschlag unterbreiten** to present a plan to a meeting; ~ **untersagen (verbieten)** to prohibit a meeting; ~ **verlassen** to walk out of a meeting; ~ **vertagen** to postpone (adjourn) a meeting.

Versammlungs|ablauf meeting procedure; ~**bericht** report on a public meeting; ~**beschlüsse** resolutions of a [public] meeting; ~**freiheit** freedom of assembly; ~**gesetz** Public Meeting (Order) Act *(Br.)*; ~**halle** convention (meeting) hall, assembly room, wigwam *(US sl.)*; ~**haus** *(Sekte)* meeting house; ~**leiter** chairman of a meeting, conference leader; ~**leitung** presiding at a meeting; ~**mehrheit** major part of an assembly; ~**ort** meeting place; ~**protokoll** minutes of a meeting; ~**prozedur** meeting procedure; ~**raum** assembly (common) room; ~**recht** right of assembly (public meeting); ~**teilnehmer** conference member, assembler, conventioner, convocator; ~**teilnehmer zum Kochen bringen** to work up the feelings of an audience; ~**termin festlegen** to appoint a meeting; ~**verbot** interdiction of a public meeting, ban of a gathering (on public meetings); ~**zelt** wigwam *(US sl.)*; ~**zweck** purpose of a meeting.

Versand forwarding, dispatch, dispatching, shipment *(US)*, shipping *(US)*, *(Absenden)* sending, *(Auslieferung)* delivery, *(durch Post)* posting *(Br.)*, mailing *(US)*, *(per Schiff)* shipment, *(Transport)* transport, transportation;
alleiniger ~ sole distributor; **binnenstaatlicher** ~ interstate shipment *(US)*; **kostenloser** ~ carriage-paid dispatch;
hafenüblicher prompter ~ customary dispatch; **sofortiger** ~ prompt forwarding (shipment, *US*); **verzögerter** ~ delay in dispatch; **zwischenstaatlicher** ~ interstate shipment *(Br.)*;

~ **auf Abruf** delivery upon request; ~ **per Bahn** dispatch (delivery, transport) by rail; ~ **von Belegexemplaren** sending of vouchers; ~ **frei Bestimmungsbahnhof** delivery free station of destination; ~ **an einen bestimmten Empfänger** straight shipment *(US)*; ~ **ab Fabrik** factory shipment *(US)*; ~ **frei Haus** delivered free at residence; ~ **auf dem Landwege** land transport; ~ **auf dem Luftwege** transportation (delivery) by air, air transport; ~ **gegen Nachnahme** charges forwarded *(Br.)*, cash *(Br.)* (collect, *US*) on delivery (C.O.D.); ~ **per Post** dispatch by mail; ~ **auf eigene Rechnung** adventure, shipped on consignment *(US)*; ~ **auf gemeinsame Rechnung** adventure in co; ~ **von Stückgut** shipment at less-than-carload lot *(US)*; ~ **am gleichen Tage** same-day delivery; ~ **auf dem Überlandwege** land transport, trucking shipment *(US)*;

~ **beschleunigen** to dispatch speedily, to expedite shipment *(US)*; **zum ~ bringen** to consign, to dispatch, to send, to forward, to ship *(US)*, *(per Post)* to post *(Br.)*, to mail *(US)*; **per Bahn zum ~ bringen** to consign by rail; **als Stückgut zum ~ bringen** to freight by parcels, to ship in carloads *(US)*; **in Teilsendungen zum ~ bringen** to ship goods by instalments *(US)*; **Waren an jem. zum ~ bringen** to ship goods to the consignation of s. o. *(US)*;

~**abteilung** delivery (forwarding, dispatch, postal) department, dispatch service, shipping department *(US)*, dispatching office; ~**abwicklung** dispatch of goods; ~**adresse** forwarding address; ~**angestellter** forwarding (dispatch, shipping, *US*) clerk; ~**anschrift** forwarding address; ~**anweisungen** instructions for dispatch, forwarding (packing, shipping, *US*) instructions; ~**anzeige**, ~**avis** advice note, notice of consignment, dispatch *(Br.)* (consignment, receiving) note, waybill *(US)*, forwarding advice, shipping advice (announcement, report) *(US)*, advice of shipment *(US)*; ~**arbeiter** dispatching clerk, shipping worker *(US)*; ~**artikel** package goods, *(ins Ausland)* exports; ~**auftrag** dispatch (shipping, *US*) order; ~**bahnhof** forwarding (dispatch, dispatching) station; ~**bedingungen** forwarding (shipping, *US*) terms; ~**behälter** package conveyer, shipping container *(US)*; **mehrfach verwendbarer** ~**behälter** container premium; ~**benachrichtigung** dispatch (consignment, receiving) note, notification of goods dispatched, shipping advice (note).

versandbereit ready for dispatch (shipment, *US*).

Versand|bereitstellungskredit packing credit *(Br.)*, anticipatory credit *(Br.)*; ~**bestätigung** declaration of shipment *(US)*; ~**betrieb** forwarding firm, shipment operation *(US)*, dispatch [service]; ~**buch** forwarding book, book of shipments *(US)*; ~**buchhandel** mail-order book trade; ~**büro** forwarding (shipping, *US*) agency, mailing office; ~**datum** date of dispatch; ~**dokument** transport document.

versanden to silt up.

versandfähig transportable, fit for shipment *(US)*;
nicht durch die Post ~ nonmailable *(US)*.

Versand|fähigkeit transportability; ~**fehler** miscarriage.

versandfertig ready for dispatch (shipment, *US*).

Versand|form manner of delivery; ~**formalitäten** shipping formalities *(US)*; ~**gebiet** shipping area *(US)*; ~**gebühren** mailing expenses *(US)*, forwarding (shipping, *US*) charges; ~**geschäft** catalog(ue) (mail-order, *US*) sale, direct-mail selling, mail-order business, *(Einzelhandel)* mail-order retailer, *(Transportunternehmen)* forwarding agency (firm), *(Versandhaus)* catalog(ue) distribution plant, mail-order firm *(US)*; **durch ~geschäft** mail-order *(US)*; ~**geschäftsartikel** package (catalog[ue]) goods; ~**geschäftsauftrag** catalog(ue) (mail-order, *US*) contract; ~**geschäftshausse** mail-order business boom *(US)*; ~**gewicht** shipment weight *(US)*; ~**großhändler** catalog(ue) (mail-order, *US*) wholesaler; ~**hafen** lading (loading, shipping, *US*) port, port of lading; **vereinbarter ~hafen** agreed port of shipment; ~**handel** catalog(ue) sale, direct-mail selling *(US)*.

Versandhaus catalog(ue) house, mail-order firm (house) *(US)*; ~**artikel** catalog(ue) (package) goods; ~**betrieb** mail-order firm (house), catalog(ue) distribution plant; ~**dienst** catalog(ue) service; ~**geschäft** catalog(ue) store (business), catalog(ue) selling, mail-order selling *(US)*; ~**katalog** trade (mail-order, *US*) catalog(ue), wish book *(coll.)*; ~**reklame** mail-order advertising *(US)*; **durch das ~system absetzen** to practise mail-order distribution *(US)*; ~**umsatz** mail-order (catalog[ue]) sales; ~**unternehmen** catalog(ue) (mail-order, *(US)* company; ~**werbung** mail-order advertising *(US)*; ~**wesen** catalog(ue) (mail-order, *US*) field.

Versand|karton mailing carton; ~**katalog** trade (mail-order, *US*) catalog(ue); **nur nach ~katalog verkaufen** to sell from one's catalog(ue); ~**kaution** transportation bond; ~**kiste** shipping crate *(US)*; ~**konto** shipment account *(US)*, shipping expenses account *(US)*; ~**kosten** forwarding (mailing, dispatch, transport) expenses, shipping costs (expenses, charges) *(US)*, transportation [charges] *(US)*, *(Bahn)* freight expenses, *(Lieferkosten)* cost of delivery, delivery costs (expenses); **niedrige ~kosten** low-cost transportation *(US)*; ~**lager** catalog(ue) distribution plant; ~**land** country of shipment *(US)*; ~**leiter** traffic manager; ~**leitung** traffic management; ~**liste** packing (freight) list, shipping bill *(US)*, memorandum (packing) note *(US)*; ~**markierung** shipping marks *(US)*; ~**mitteilung** forwarding note; ~**möglichkeiten** forwarding (shipping, *US*) facilities; ~**muster** shipping sample *(US)*; ~**nachweis** evidence of shipment *(US)*; ~**note** dispatch (consignment, receiving) note, shipping advice *(US)*, advice of shipment *(US)*; ~**ort** dispatch (forwarding, shipping, *US*) point, shipping place *(US)*, point (place) of shipment *(US)*; ~**papiere** documents, shipping documents (papers) *(US)*, shipper's papers *(US)*; **bar gegen ~papiere** cash against documents; ~**personal** *(Firma)* postal staff; ~**plan** forwarding schedule, schedule of shipment *(US)*; ~**prospekt ohne Umschlag** selfmailer *(US)*; ~**raum** shipping room *(US)*; ~**rechnung** expense (shipping, *US*, shipment, *US*) invoice; **kombiniertes Auftrags- und ~rechnungsformular** combination sales-order-shipper invoice form *(US)*; ~**rolle** dispatch (mailing, *US*) tube; ~**schein** consignment (receiving, dispatch) note, advice of shipment *(US)*, shipping ticket *(US)*; ~**spediteur** destination carrier; ~**spesen** forwarding expenses (charges), shipping expenses *(US)*; ~**station** dispatch (sending, forwarding) station, point of dispatch, shipping point *(US)*; ~**stelle** mailing (dispatch) office; ~**stück** parcel, package.

versandt forwarded, dispatched, shipped *(US)*;
unfrei ~ freepost;
in Waggonladungen ~ shipped in carloads *(US)*.

Versand|tasche American envelope; ~**termin** date of dispatch, mailing (shipping, *US*) date, date of shipment *(US)*, shipping time *(US)*; ~**unternehmen** dispatch, forwarding agency (firm), mail-order firm, catalog(ue) house; ~**vereinigung** shipping association *(US)*; **gemeinschaftliches ~verfahren** *(EG)* community transit arrangement; ~**verkauf** mail-order (catalogue, *Br.*) selling; ~**vermerk** note of dispatch; ~**verzögerung** delay in dispatch; ~**verzug** default in delivery; ~**vorschriften** forwarding (dispatch) regulations, shipping instructions *(US)*; ~**waren** forwarded (dispatched, shipped, *US*) goods; ~**wechsel** out-of-town (country) bill; ~**weg** forwarding route; ~**weise** method of dispatch (shipment, *US*); ~**werbung** package advertising, mail-order advertising; ~**zeit** mailing (shipping, *US*) time, time of shipment *(US)*; ~**ziel** place (point) of destination.

Versatzschlüssel *(Verschlüsselung)* transposition cipher.

versauen to butcher, to muck up *(coll.)*, to make a mess of.

versäumen to neglect, to miss, *(unterlassen)* to fail, to omit;
Anfang eines Films ~ to miss the beginning of a film; **Chance ~** to neglect (omit) an opportunity; **Frist ~** to fail to comply with a term; **Gelegenheit ~** to miss one's chance (the bus); **nichts ~** to leave no stone unturned; **Termin ~** to [make] default, to fail to appear; **Unterricht ~** to shirk school, to play truant (hooky, *US*); **Verabredung ~** to miss an appointment; **zu zahlen ~** to fail to pay; **Zug ~** to miss one's train;
nichts zu ~ haben to have plenty of time.

Versäumnis neglect, negligence, *(Abwesenheit)* nonattendance, miss, *(Termin)* default [of appearance], defaulting, *(Unterlassung)* failure, omission;
unverschuldetes ~ excusable neglect;
~ **der rechtzeitigen Geltendmachung einer Forderung** laches; ~ **eines Termins** default of appearence;
~**gebühr**, ~**kosten** fine for default, default fine.

Versäumnisurteil default judgment, decree pro confesso, decree in absence *(Scot.)*;
durch ~ verloren jactivous;
~ **beantragen** to move that a judgment by default be rendered; ~ **erlassen** to deliver judgment by default; ~ **gegen den Beklagten erlassen** to declare the defendant in default; **Prozeß durch ~ gewinnen** to win a case by default; ~ **gegen sich ergehen lassen** to suffer a default; **Prozeß durch ~ verlieren** to lose a case by default.

Versäumnisverfahren default procedure.

versäumte|Gelegenheit missed opportunity; ~ **Zeit einholen** to make up for lost time.

Versäumtes nachholen to make up leeway.

Verschachern einflußreicher Positionen influence peddling, spoils system *(US)*.

verschachern to barter (truck) away, to trade off.
verschachteln to pyramid, *(Kapital)* to interlock.
verschachtelt pyramided, interlocked;
~**e Unternehmen** interlocked enterprises.
Verschachtelung pyramiding, interlocking;
~ **des Aktienkapitals** interlocking stock ownership; ~ **verschiedener Unternehmungen** interlocking of several undertakings.
Verschachtelungs|struktur pyramided structure; ~**technik** pyramiding techniques.
Verschaffen procurement.
verschaffen to supply, to procure, to obtain, to provide, to find, to furnish;
sich ~ to obtain, to get; **Arbeit** ~ to provide (procure) employment; **Besitz** ~ to deliver possession; **Deckung** ~ to furnish with cover, to provide for payment; **jem. Deckung** ~ to furnish s. o. with cover, to supply s. o. with funds; **sich Eintritt** ~ to get admission; **Geld** ~ to find the money, to raise funds; **sich Genugtuung** ~ to get satisfaction; **sich absolute Gewißheit** ~ to make certain of; **sich selbst Recht** ~ to take the law into one's own hands; **jem. eine Stelle (Stellung)** ~ to find a job for s. o., to put s. o. onto a job; **sich durch Beziehungen eine Stellung** ~ to pull the wires for office; **einem Freund eine gute Stellung** ~ to manoeuvre (job) a friend into a good post; **sich einen Vermögensvorteil durch Betrug** ~ to obtain property by false pretences; **sich unter Vorspiegelung falscher Tatsachen** ~ to obtain by fraud; **sich einen Vorteil** ~ to gain an advantage.
verschalen, mit Brettern to board up, to plank.
verschalten *(el.)* to cross.
Verschalung timbering, planking, lining.
Verschalungsbretter weatherboarding.
verschämt shameful, abashed;
~**e Arme** humble poor.
verschandeln, Landschaft to disfigure the landscape; **Sprache** ~ to murder a language.
verschandelt disfigured, spoilt, marred;
~**e Sprache** murdered (butchered) language.
Verschandelung der Landschaft disfigurement of the landscape.
verschanzen to fortify, to entrench.
Verschanzung fortification, entrenchment.
verschärfen to tighten, to aggravate, to increase;
Beschränkungen ~ to intensify restrictions; **Bestimmungen** ~ to tighten restrictions; **Blockade** ~ to tighten a blockade; **Lage** ~ to aggravate a situation; **Liquiditätsbestimmungen** ~ to clamp down on liquidity; **Strafe** ~ to raise a fine; **Tempo** ~ to accelerate speed, *(fam.)* to step on the gas; **Zensurbestimmungen** ~ to tighten the censorship.
verschärfter Schadenersatz exemplary damages.
Verschärfung intensification, tightening, stiffening, aggravation, increase, *(Geschwindigkeit)* acceleration;
~ **der Blockade** tightening of a blockade; ~ **der Lage** aggravation of the situation; ~ **der Provisionsbestimmungen** tightening of commission provisions.
verschätzen, sich to be out in one's calculation(s) (estimate).
verschaukeln to diddle s. o., to do s. o. in the eye *(sl.)*.
verschenken to present, to gift;
fast ~ to give away for a mere song; **seine Gunst an j.** ~ to bestow one's favo(u)r on s. o.; **sein Herz** ~ to give one's heart.
verscherbeln to flog off.
verscherzen, sein Glück to spurn one's fortune.
verscheuchen to scare (frighten) away, to dissipate;
Zweifel ~ to dispel doubts.
verscheuern to trade away, to sell off.
verschicken to send off, to dispatch, to forward, to consign, to ship *(US)*, *(deportieren)* to deport, to exile, *(Post)* to post, to mail *(US)*;
massenhaft Einladungen ~ to send out invitations wholesale; **Kinder aufs Land** ~ to send the children into the country; **an die Mitglieder** ~ to mail out to members *(US)*; **Rechnungen** ~ to send out accounts (bills); **Waren als Eilgut** ~ to ship goods by express train; **Waren mit der Eisenbahn** ~ to send goods by rail.
Verschickung dispatching, consignment, forwarding, dispatch, shipping *(US)*, shipment *(US)*.
verschiebbar adjustable, *(zeitlich)* postponable;
sofort ~ *(mil.)* mobile.
Verschiebe|anlage shunting (switching) installation; ~**bahnhof** classification (railway-switching, marshalling, *US*) yard, switchyard, shunting (train order) station; ~**bahnhof für Personenwagen** coach yard; ~**gleis** classification (shunting) track; ~**lokomotive** shunter, switching engine, switcher.
Verschieben *(Waggons)* shunting, switching.
verschieben to shift, to move, *(aufschieben)* to put off, to hold over, to delay, to defer, to procrastinate, to shelve *(Br.)*, to table *(US)*, *(Kamera)* to pan, *(Truppen)* to redeploy, *(vertagen)* to postpone, to adjourn, *(Waggons)* to marshal, to shunt, to switch *(US)*, *(Waren)* to sell under the counter (on the black market);
sich ~ *(Wählerstimmen)* to turn over; **seine Abreise um eine Woche** ~ to defer one's departure for a week; **auf ein andermal** ~ to reserve for another time; **Entscheidung** ~ to procrastinate a decision; **Geld** ~ to finance away *(US)*; **etw. auf später** ~ to defer s. th. to a later date; **von einem Tag auf den anderen** ~ to put off from one day to the next; **Verhandlung um eine Woche** ~ to put a case off for a week; **bis auf weiteres** ~ to defer until further notice; **um eine Woche** ~ to postpone for a week; **auf einen späteren Zeitpunkt** ~ to defer to a later date; **Zug auf ein anderes Gleis** ~ to shunt a train to a siding.
Verschiebung shift, *(Aufschub)* deferment, deferral, *(Ladung)* displacement, *(Umgruppierung)* turnover, shake-up, *(Verlegung)* postponement, delay, *(Vertagung)* adjournment, putting off, *(Waggons)* shunting, switching, *(Wählerstimmen)* turnover;
zeitliche ~ time lag;
~ **der Ladung** shift of stowage; ~**en im Wechselkursgefüge** shift in the exchange rate;
j. gegen eine weitere ~ **beeinflussen** to determine s. o. against further delay.
verschieden different, diverse, distinct, miscellaneous, several, sundry, *(abweichend)* discrepant;
~ **wie Tag und Nacht** as different as chalk and cheese;
~ **beurteilen** to judge differently; **je nach Branche** ~ **sein** to differ from trade to trade; **sehr** ~ **sein** to differ widely; **total** ~ **sein** to be completely unalike;
~**e Anlagegüter** miscellaneous assets; ~**e Ausgaben** sundries, sundry expenses; ~**e Ausschußmitglieder** several members of a committee; ~**e Beteiligungen** miscellaneous investments; ~**e Debitoren** sundry debtors; **in den** ~**sten Farben** in all sorts of colo(u)rs; **bei** ~**en Gelegenheiten** on various occasions; **völlig** ~**e Geschmäcker haben** to differ widely in their tastes; **aus** ~**en Gründen** for various (a variety of) reasons; ~**e Interessen haben** to have different interests; **zu** ~**en Malen** several times; ~**er Meinung sein** to differ, to diverge; ~**e Muster** sundry samples; **unter** ~**en Namen polizeibekannt sein** to be known to the police under various names; ~**e Posten** miscellaneous items; ~**e Schuldbeträge** *(Bilanz)* sundry moneys owing; ~**ste Stellen** various places.
verschiedenartig different, miscellaneous, various, varied.
Verschiedenartigkeit diversification, diversity, variety.
Verschiedenes sundries, *(Buchung)* sundries journal, *(Katalog)* miscellaneous items, *(Tagesordnung)* any other (general) business, *(Zeitung)* miscellanies;
Spalte ~ miscellaneous column.
Verschiedenheit difference, inequality, odds, *(Mannigfaltigkeit)* diversity, variety, *(Ungleichheit)* disparity;
~ **der Staatsangehörigkeit** diversity of citizenship *(US)*; ~ **der Stellungen** disparity in position.
verschiffbar shippable.
verschiffen to ship, to freight, to send by water, to transport;
erneut ~ to reship.
Verschiffer shipper.
verschifft afloat, shipped;
~**e Waren** goods shipped.
Verschiffung shipping, shipment, water carriage, transport;
zur ~ **empfangen** received for shipment;
~ **erst bei eisfreiem Wasser** first open water.
Verschiffungs|anzeige advice of shipment, shipping advice; ~**auftrag** shipping order.
verschiffungsbereit ready for shipping.
Verschiffungs|bescheinigung certificate of shipment; ~**dokumente** shipping documents; **zahlbar gegen Aushändigung der** ~**dokumente** payable against surrender of shipping documents; ~**genehmigung** shipping permit; ~**gewicht** shipping (shipment) weight; ~**hafen** port of shipment, shipping port; ~**konnossement** ocean (shipped) bill of lading; ~**kosten** shipping (ocean) charges; ~**kredit** respondentia; ~**land** country of shipment; ~**order** broker's order; ~**ort** point of shipment, shipping point; ~**papiere** shipping documents; **durch** ~**papiere gedeckt** covered by shipping documents; ~**spesen** shipping charges (expenses); ~**tag,** ~**termin** date of shipment, shipping date; ~**tonne** shipping ton; ~**vorschriften** shipping instructions; ~**wert** shipping value.
verschimmeln to mould *(Br.)*, to mold *(US)*.

Verschiß, in ~ geraten to be sent to Coventry.
Verschlag cote, hutch, lean-to, closet, *(Kiste)* crate, *(Schiff)* locker, *(Schuppen)* shed.
verschlagen, mit Brettern to board up; **Buchseite ~** to lose one's place; **j. auf eine Insel ~** to strand s. o. on an island; **jem. die Sprache ~** to make s. o. speechless;
~ werden *(Schiffbruch)* to be cast away;
~ *(a.)* tricky, wily, cunning, furtive.
verschlampen, Akte to mislay a file;
Garten ~ lassen to let the garden grow wild.
verschlechtern to worsen, to impair, to deteriorate, to decline, to waste, *(Münzen)* to debase;
sich ~ to fall off in quality, to deteriorate, *(Gehaltsempfänger)* to get less pay, *(Wetter)* to become worse; **sich beruflich ~** to change one's position for the worse; **sich finanziell ~** to earn less; **Lage ~** to aggravate the situation; **sich immer mehr ~** to be going from bad to worse; **sich merklich ~** to deteriorate markedly; **Münzen ~** to debase coin; **Währung ~** to depreciate the currency; **Zahlungsbilanz ~** to worsen the balance of payment.
Verschlechterung deterioration, depreciation, setback, decline, *(Gesundheit)* change for the worse, impairment, *(Münze)* debasement;
böswillig verschuldete ~ voluntary waste;
~ der Beziehungen deterioration in relations; **~ des Geldwertes** decline in the value of money; **~ der Handelsbilanz** deterioration of the trade balance; **~ der Kaufkraft** deterioration of purchasing value of money, depreciation of the currency; **~ der Lage** aggravation of the situation; **~ der Qualität** deterioration of quality; **~ der Umweltbedingungen** environmental derogation; **~ durch Vernachlässigung** waste; **~ des Wechselkurses** exchange-rate depreciation; **~ der Zahlungsbilanz** worsening of the balance of payment; **~ im Zustand eines Kranken** deterioration in a patient's condition.
verschleiern to conceal, to cloak, to curtain, to disguise, to mask, to veil, *(mil.)* to screen, to camouflage;
Bilanz ~ to cook (doctor, fake, tamper with, window-dress) a balance sheet; **seine Motive ~** to veil one's motives; **wahre Sachlage ~** to conceal the true state of affairs; **Tatsachen ~** to disguise the facts; **seine Vermögenslage ~** to conceal one's financial conditions; **ausländische Vermögenswerte ~** to conceal foreign assets.
verschleiert veiled, *(Blick)* vague, *(Foto)* foggy;
~e Bilanz tampered (faked, cooked, doctored) balance sheet;
~e Vermögenswerte concealed assets.
Verschleierung concealment, disguise, *(Bilanz)* tampering, cooking, doctoring, window dressing, *(mil.)* camouflage, screening;
~ des Funkverkehrs deception signal traffic; **~ von Vermögenswerten** concealment of assets.
Verschleierungs|maßnahmen camouflage measures; **~strategie** strategy of ambiguity.
Verschleiß wear and tear, waste, erosion, attrition, deterioration;
dem ~ unterworfen subject to wear; **unter Berücksichtigung des ~es** allowing for wear and tear;
geplanter ~ built-in obsolescence; **normaler ~** natural wear and tear, equitable waste; **wirtschaftlicher ~** decline in economic usefulness;
~beanspruchung abrasive stress; **~beständigkeit** wear-resisting quality.
verschleißen to waste, to abrade, *(durch Korrosion)* to corrode;
sich ~ to wear out, to decline in economic usefulness.
verschleißend wearing.
Verschleiß|entschädigung indemnity for wear and tear; **~erscheinungen aufweisen** to show signs of wear; **~festigkeit** freedom from wear and tear, resistance to wear; **~geschwindigkeit** rate of wear; **~teil** working part; **~werkzeug** perishable tool.
verschleppen *(aussiedeln)* to displace, to deport, *(entführen)* to abduct, to kidnap, *(verzögern)* to obstruct, to practise obstruction, to delay, to play for time, to stall *(sl.)*, to postpone, to put off;
Debatte ~ to protract a debate; **Konkurs ~** to obstruct bankruptcy; **Kunstschätze ~** to take away treasures of art; **Prozeß ~** to protract a lawsuit, to delay the proceedings; **Verabschiedung eines Gesetzentwurfes ~** to obstruct the progress of (filibuster, table, *US*) a bill.
Verschlepper abductor.
verschleppt deported, displaced.
Verschleppter deportee, displaced person (DP).
Verschleppung delay, obstruction, protraction, dilatory tactics, procrastination, *(Deportation)* displacement, exilement, deportation, *(Entführung)* kidnapping, abduction, *(parl.)* obstructionism, filibuster;
~ einer Debatte protraction of a debate; **~ eines Konkurses** obstruction of bankruptcy; **~ eines Prozesses** protraction of a lawsuit, delay of the proceedings.
Verschleppungs|einwand vorbringen to plead laches as defence (defense, *US*) to a suit; **~manöver** dilatory manoeuvre, procrastination, *(pol.)* filibustering, stonewalling *(Australia)*; **~methoden** dilatory methods, *(pol.)* obstructive tactics (measures); **~politik** obstructionism, ca'canny; **~politik betreiben** to practise obstruction, to adopt a ca'canny policy; **~schriftsatz** frivolous plea; **~taktik** delaying tactics, dilatory policy, procrastination, filibuster *(US)*, stonewalling *(Australia)*; **~taktiker** filibusterer *(US)*; **~versuch** attempt to obstruct the proceedings.
verschleudern to undersell, to sell under the value (dirt-cheap), to barter (play) away, *(Vermögen)* to waste, to squander, to dissipate, *(auf dem Weltmarkt)* to dump;
seinen Besitz ~ to dissipate one's fortune; **Bestände ~** to slaughter (spill, *US*) stocks; **sein väterliches Erbteil ~** to squander one's estate; **sein ganzes Geld ~** to make ducks and drakes of one's money; **sein Vermögen ~** to dissipate one's fortune.
Verschleuderung underselling, selling at ruinous prices (under price), *(Vermögen)* dissipation, squandering, *(auf dem Weltmarkt)* dumping;
~ seines Vermögens dissipation of one's fortune.
verschließbar lockable.
verschließen to lock, *(mit Riegel)* to bolt;
sich vor jem. ~ to be extremly reserved with s. o.; **sich gegen etw. ~** to close one's mind to s. th.; **sich einem Argument gegenüber ~** to ignore an argument; **Brief ~** to seal a letter; **Geld im Koffer ~** to bestow money in a trunk; **sein Herz ~** to harden one's heart against; **sich einer Sache ~** to turn a deaf ear (close one's eyes) to s. th.; **Tür ~** to lock up a door; **mit einem Vorhängeschloß ~** to padlock.
verschlimmern to worsen, to aggravate;
sich ~ *(Krankheitszustand)* to grow from bad to worse; **Lage ~** to make the situation worse.
Verschlimmerung aggravation, deterioration, worsening.
verschlingen to swallow, to wolf, to devour;
ein Drittel des Jahresetats ~ to eat up a third of the annual budget; **mehr als die Einkünfte ~** to swallow up more than one's earnings; **viel Geld ~** to cost a mint of money; **sich zu einem Knoten ~** to become entangled (entwined) in a knot; **neuen Kriminalroman sofort ~** to devour a new detective novel.
verschlossen locked up, closed, *(Brief)* sealed, *(zurückhaltend)* uncommunicative, reserved;
~e Einlage sealed deposit; **~er Mensch** close customer; **~es Testament** sealed will; **hinter ~en Türen tagen** to sit behind closed doors (in camera, in chambers, *Br.*); **in ~em Umschlag** in a sealed envelope.
verschlucken to swallow, *(Silbe)* to slur over;
Fußtritte ~ *(Teppich)* to kill the sound of footsteps; **sehr viel Geld ~** to cost a mint of money.
Verschluß lock, *(Fotoapparat)* shutter, *(Riegel)* bolt, *(Zoll)* seal;
mit automatischem ~ self-locking; **unter ~** under seal; **unter zollamtlichem ~** bonded, in bond;
etw. unter ~ halten to keep s. th. locked up (under lock and key); **sorgfältig unter ~ halten** to keep carefully under wraps; **in ~ legen** to bond; **aus dem zollamtlichen ~ nehmen** to take out of bond.
Verschlüsseler cipher (code) clerk, cryptographer.
Verschlüsseln ciphering, *(Daten)* coding, *(tel.)* scramble.
verschlüsseln to code, to cipher, to encipher, to encode, *(tel.)* to scramble;
Nachricht ~ to write a message in code; **Telegramm ~** to code a telegram.
verschlüsselt in code, in cipher, *(tel.)* scrambled;
nicht ~ in plain language;
~e Meldung ciphered message; **~es Telegramm** cipher telegram; **~er Text** coded (cipher) text.
Verschlüsselung coding, ciphering, *(Telefongespräch)* scrambling.
Verschlüsselungs|abteilung ciphering service; **~gerät, ~maschine** *(Telefon)* privacy scrambler, converter *(US)*; **Telegramm ohne ~maschine verschlüsseln** to cipher telegrams by hand; **~raum** cipher room; **~unterlagen** cryptographic keys, cipher documents; **~zentrale** code center *(US)* (centre, *Br.*).

Verschluß | geschwindigkeit *(Fotoapparat)* shutter speed; **~mappe** classified file, *(Kurier)* pouch; **~marke** paper seal, sealing label; **~sache** *(mil.)* restricted matter *(US)*, classified information (material, matter) *(US)*; **~sachen unberechtigten Personen zugänglich machen** to disclose classified information to an unauthorized person; **~sachenverordnung** *(EURATOM)* security regulations; **~streifen** sealing tape; **zentrales ~system** central locking system; **~zeit** *(Fotoapparat)* shutter speed.

verschmachten to pine [away];
vor Durst ~ to be parched with thirst.

verschmähen to disdain, to scorn, to spurn.

verschmäht forsaken, jaded, deserted, jilted;
~er Bewerber spurned lover; **~e Liebe** unrequited love.

verschmelzen to amalgamate, to fuse, to merge, to consolidate, *(Farben)* to blend, to merge, *(techn.)* to weld, to fuse;
zu einem großen Unternehmen ~ to merge into one large organization.

Verschmelzung amalgamation, fusion, confusion, melting, merger, consolidation, affiliation;
~ von Konkurrenzfirmen horizontal integration; **~ der Mutter- mit der Tochtergesellschaft** downstairs merger; **~ branchenfremder Unternehmen** conglomerate merger; **~ zweier Werbeentwürfe** marriage of advertising ideas.

Verschmelzungsvertrag merger agreement.

verschmerzen, Verlust to get over a loss.

verschmiert smudged, smeared, *(Straße)* foul.

verschmitzt cunning, roguish;
~e Augen roguish eyes.

verschmutzen to soil, to get dirty, *(Luft, Wasser)* to pollute, to contaminate;
leicht ~ to spot easily.

verschmutzt dirty, soiled, *(Wasser)* polluted, contaminated;
nicht ~ unpolluted;
völlig ~ sein to be all over mud.

Verschmutzung pollution, contamination;
~ der Flüsse pollution (contamination) of rivers; **~ der Luft** pollution of the air; **~ der See** pollution of the sea.

Verschmutzungs | kontrolle pollution control; **~problem** pollution issue; **~schaden** pollution damage.

verschnaufen to recover one's wind (breath).

Verschnaufpause breather.

verschneit snowed over, snow-covered.

Verschnitt *(Alkohol)* blend.

verschnörkeln to adorn, to flourish.

verschnupft sein to be offended (piqued).

verschnüren to cord, to tie up, to wrap about with a string.

verschollen disappeared, missing, untraceable, presumed dead;
j. für ~ erklären to declare s. o. legally dead; **~ sein** to be missing;
~es Schiff missing ship.

Verschollener missing person, supposed deceased *(US)*.

Verschollenheit disappearance, want of appearance, presumption of death *(US)*;
~ eines Schiffes presumptive loss of a ship.

Verschollenheits | erklärung declaration of death; **~pfleger** curator absentis; **~pflegschaft** curatorship **~vermutung** presumption of death.

verschonen, j. to spare s. o.

verschönern to adorn, to embellish, to smarten up.

verschönert gilded.

Verschönerung embellishment, adornment, *(Haus)* renovation, face lifting *(sl.)*.

Verschönerungs | aktion beauty campaign; **~arbeiten** *(Wohnung)* voluntary improvements; **~aufwand** costs of improvement, expenses for embellishments.

verschont free, exempt;
vom Kriege ~ bleiben to be spared from the war.

verschossen *(Vorhang)* faded, discolo(u)red;
in j. ~ sein to be smitten with (go for, *US*) s. o.; **total in j. ~ sein** to be dead nuts on s. o.

verschrammt scratched.

verschränkt, mit ~en Armen with one's arms folded.

verschreckt scared stiff, frightened.

Verschreiben clerical error, slip of the pen.

verschreiben *(Arzt)* to prescribe, *(Besitz)* to make over, *(Leben)* to dedicate, to devote;
sich ~ to make a slip of the pen; **sich einer Sache mit allen Fasern seines Herzens ~** to throw (put) one's heart and soul into a business.

Verschreibung *(Abtretung)* assignment, *(Urkunde)* bond, deed;
ärztliche ~ prescription.

verschrien ill-reputed;
als Geizhals ~ sein to be a notorious miser.

verschroben odd, queer, crotchety, eccentric;
j. ~ machen to warp s. one's mind;
~e Vorstellung wry notion.

Verschrobenheit crotchetiness, quirk, twist.

verschrotten *(Schiff)* to scrap, to break up.

Verschrotter scrap merchant, *(Schiff)* ship breaker.

Verschrottung junking, *(Schiff)* shipbreaking, scrapping;
~ von Rüstungsmaterial physical destruction of armaments.

Verschublokomotive pug *(Br.)*.

verschüchtert intimidated, subdued, shy.

Verschulden negligence, blame, fault *(US)*, *(Vertragsverletzung)* default;
durch fremdes ~ through third-party negligence; **ohne ~** without fault *(US)*;
beiderseitiges ~ mutual contributory negligence, both-to-blame; **fahrlässiges ~** negligence; **geringes (geringfügiges) ~** slight fault; **grobes ~** gross negligence; **keinerlei ~** no degree of fault *(US)*; **konkurrierendes ~** contributory negligence; **leichtes ~** slight negligence; **mitwirkendes ~** contributory *(Br.)* (concurrent, comparative, *US*) negligence; **strafrechtliches ~** criminal negligence; **zum Schadenersatz verpflichtendes ~** actionable negligence; **zuzurechnendes ~** fault attributable to *(US)*; **~ der Ehefrau** wife's fault *(US)*;
für das ~ des Erfüllungsgehilfen verantwortlich machen to attribute the servant's negligence to the master; **frei von ~ sein** to be free from fault *(US)*.

verschulden to be to blame, to encumber with debts;
sich ~ to run into debt, to take on debts, to involve o. s. (get into) debt, to outrun the constable *(Br.)*, to run up a score *(Br.)*; **sich kurzfristig erheblich ~** to borrow heavily on a short-term basis; **sich erneut ~** to run into debt again; **sich total ~** *(Staat)* to plunge into debt; **sich ungewöhnlich ~** to go into debt at a record chip *(US)*; **sein Unglück selbst ~** to bring misfortune upon o. s.

Verschuldenshaftung tortious liability.

verschuldet indebted, in debt, embarrassed by (involved in) debts, hock, *(überschuldet)* encumbered, incumbered;
hoffnungslos (bis über die Ohren) ~ over head and heels in debt; **nicht ~** unindebted; **stark ~** heavily in debt, heavily indebted; **~ sein** to be in debt, to stand indebted; **bis übers Dach hinaus ~ sein** to be mortgaged up to the eyes; **bis zum Hals ~ sein** to be over head and heels in debt; **in höchstem Maße ~ sein** to be heavily in (overextended with) debts; **immer mehr ~ sein** to be becoming more and more indebted; **tief ~ sein** to be deeply involved in debt; **völlig ~ sein** to be encumbered with debts, to be immersed (plunged) in debt; **tief ~ sterben** to die greatly in debt.

Verschuldung debts contracted, floating debt, indebtedness, *(Schuldenmachen)* running into debt;
echte ~ net indebtedness; **erhebliche ~** excessive indebtedness; **nicht genehmigte ~** unauthorized borrowing; **hypothekarische ~** mortgage indebtedness; **kommunale ~** indebtedness of local authorities, municipal debts; **kurzfristige ~** short-term indebtedness (borrowing); **langfristige ~** fixed (long-term) indebtedness, long-term debts; **laufende ~** running debts; **mittelfristige ~** shorter-term debts; **staatliche ~** state indebtedness; **starke ~** heavy indebtedness; **zugelassene ~** *(Kommunalwesen)* legal debt margin;
öffentliche ~ durch Anleiheaufnahme bond indebtedness, deficit financing *(US)*; **~ bei den Banken** bank indebtedness; **~ der öffentlichen Hand (öffentlichen Haushalte)** public sector borrowing; **~ der Landwirtschaft** rural indebtedness; **~ auf der Verbraucherseite** consumer instalment debts;
~ geringfügig abbauen to trim a small slice off the debt; **~ scheuen** to be reluctant to go into debt; **kurzfristige ~ vergrößern** to expand the floating debt.

Verschuldungs | bilanz *(Gemeinschuldner)* balance of indebtedness, statement of affairs *(Br.)*; **~grad** debt-equity ratio, leverage factor; **großen ~grad aufweisen** to be highly leveraged; **~grenze** *(kommunales Rechnungswesen)* debt limit, limitation of indebtedness, borrowing limit; **~koeffizient** debt ratio, ratio of indebtedness to capital, debt-equity ratio; **~möglichkeit** borrowing capacity; **~rate** debt-equity ratio; **~saldo** net indebtedness; **~spielraum** *(Gemeinde)* legal debt margin; **~vorgang** incurring of debts.

verschütten to spill, to slop, *(Menschen)* to bury, to entomb.

verschüttet spilled, spilt *(Br.)*, *(Menschen)* buried, trapped, *(Stollen)* blocked;
von einer Lawine ~ sein to be buried in an avalanche.

verschwägert connected (related) by marriage, affiliated.
Verschwägerung relationship by marriage, alliance, affinity.
Verschweigen concealment, nondisclosure;
absichtliches ~ active concealment; **arglistiges (betrügerisches)** ~ fraudulent concealment;
~ **von Tatsachen** suppression of facts; ~ **wesentlicher Tatsachen** nondisclosure of material facts, failure to disclose material facts, material nondisclosure, material concealment; **absichtliches** ~ **von für die Versicherungsgesellschaft wesentlichen Umständen** material misrepresentation; ~ **der Wahrheit** suppression of the truth.
verschweigen to hide, to conceal, to suppress, to withhold;
ohne etw. zu ~ *(Versicherungsrecht)* utmost good faith;
arglistig ~ to conceal fraudulently; **wahre Sachlage** ~ to conceal the true state of affairs; **wesentliche Tatsachen** ~ to suppress material facts; **ausländische Vermögenswerte** ~ to conceal foreign assets.
verschwenden to squander, to waste, to lavish, to spend, to consume;
mit vollen Händen ~ to spend lavishly; **Vermögen** ~ to dissipate one's fortune, to squander an estate; **seine Worte** ~ to waste one's breath; **sein Zeit** ~ to waste one's time.
Verschwender waster, squanderer, dissipated man, dissipator, spendthrift, spender, waster, wastrel, prodigal.
verschwenderisch extravagant, thriftless, prodigal, spendthrift, fast-spending, profuse, unthrifty, lavish, wasteful, like water;
~ **ausgeben** to blow, to spend freely (lavishly); **j.** ~ **bewirten** to entertain s. o. lavishly; ~ **leben** to live in lavish style; ~ **umgehen** to be lavish with (wasteful of, prodigal of);
~**e Ausgaben** prodigal expenses; ~**es System** wasteful scheme.
verschwendet werden to run waste.
Verschwendung waste, wastage, profusion, extravagance, dissipation;
mutwillige ~ *(Pächter)* voluntary waste;
~ **von Energie** wastage (waste) of energy; ~ **öffentlicher Mittel** waste of public funds;
ziemliche ~ **sein** to be a bit of a waste; **durch** ~ **zusammenschmelzen** to dwindle by waste.
Verschwendungssucht extravagance, profligacy, squandermania, prodigality;
wegen ~ **entmündigt sein** to be adjudged incompetent to manage one's property because of propensity to waste one's capital.
verschwiegen discreet, secretive, close, counsel-keeping, *(nicht mitgeteilt)* suppressed, withheld;
~ **sein** to keep a secret, to keep counsel; ~ **wie das Grab sein** to be as tight as wax;
~**er Mensch** counsel keeper; ~**es Örtchen aufsuchen** to wash one's hands, to spend a penny *(Br.)*; **sich an einem** ~**en Plätzchen treffen** to meet at a secluded place.
Verschwiegenheit discretion, secrecy, reticence;
unter dem Siegel der ~ confidentially, bound to secrecy;
unter dem Siegel der ~ **mitteilen** to speak under the seal of confession; **sich auf jds.** ~ **verlassen** to confide in s. one's discretion; **j. zur** ~ **verpflichten** to enjoin silence on s. o., to swear s. o. to secrecy; **strenge** ~ **wahren** to observe strict secrecy.
Verschwiegenheitspflicht duty not to disclose confidential information, duty of secrecy.
verschwimmen to become blurred.
Verschwinden disappearance;
j. zum ~ **zwingen** to make a place too hot for s. o.
verschwinden to disappear, to vanish;
aus jds. Blickfeld ~ to dip down out of sight; **neben jem.** ~ to be overshadowed by s. o.; **auf Nimmerwiedersehen** ~ to disappear for good; **aus der Stadt** ~ to skip town; **in der Versenkung** ~ to quit the scene, to vanish in space;
Geheimmaterial ~ **lassen** to dispose of classified material.
verschwindend gering infinitely small.
verschwistern, sich *(Städte)* to become twinned.
verschwistert sein to be closely related.
verschwitzen, etw. völlig to forget all about it.
verschwitzt, völlig covered with perspiration.
verschwommen dim, hazy, *(Farbe)* muddy, *(Foto)* blurred, *(unklar)* nebulous, vague;
~ **werden** to fade;
~**e Erinnerung** vague memory, dreamy recollection; ~**e Idee** foggy idea.
verschwören, sich to form a conspiracy, to conspire, to plot; **sich einer Sache** ~ to devote o. s. to a cause.
verschworene Gemeinschaft sworn confraternity.
Verschwörer conspirator, plotter;
zu den ~**n gehören** to participate in a plot; **nicht zu den** ~**n gehören** to have no part in a plot;
~**gruppe** undercover group; **auf Dauer angelegte** ~**tätigkeit** continuing conspiracy.
Verschwörung conspiracy, plot, plotting, complot, confederacy;
als Hochverrat geltende ~ constructive treason *(Br.)*; **kommunistische** ~**en** communistic plots;
~ **des Schweigens** conspiracy of silence; ~ **zum Sturz der Regierung** conspiracy to overthrow the government;
seine Teilnahme an einer ~ **ableugnen** to disavow a share in a plot; ~ **anzetteln** to form a conspiracy, to devise (lay) a plot; ~ **aufdecken** to discover (uncover) a conspiracy (plot); ~ **aushecken** to hatch a plot; **sich an einer** ~ **beteiligen** to take part in a plot; ~ **gegen sich ergründen** to penetrate the plot against o. s.; **in eine** ~ **verwickelt sein** to be roped into (concerned in) a conspiracy, to be ensnarled in a plot; ~ **unterlaufen** to forestall a plot; **j. in eine** ~ **verwickeln** to draw s. o. into a conspiracy; ~ **wittern** to smoke out a plot, to smell a rat.
verschwunden disappeared, missing;
von der Landkarte ~ **sein** to have slid off the map.
Versehen inadvertency, mistake, slip, lapse, fault, *(Irrtum)* error, *(Nachlässigkeit)* negligence, oversight, overlook;
aus ~ by mistake (an oversight), inadvertently;
beiderseitiges ~ mutual mistake;
aus ~ **jds. Regenschirm mitnehmen** to walk off with s. one's umbrella.
versehen to provide, to furnish, to supply, to fill, to afford with, *(falsch machen)* to overlook, to neglect;
sich ~ to make a mistake; **mit Akzept** ~ to provide with acceptance; **Amt** ~ to hold an office; **Amt eines Richters** ~ to perform the duties of a judge; **mit Brandzeichen** ~ to brand, to burn; **mit Deckung** ~ to furnish with cover (funds); **jds. Dienst** ~ to take s. one's place, to do duty for s. o.; **mit Geld** ~ to keep in money; **mit Giro** ~ to indorse, to endorse; **Haushalt** ~ to look after the household; **mit Kleidung** ~ to provide with clothing; **mit Lebensmitteln** ~ to stock with provisions; **mit Mitteln** ~ to put in funds; **seine Pflichten** ~ to perform (attend to) one's duties; **Schriftstück mit seiner Unterschrift** ~ to append one's signature to a document; **Tür mit einem neuen Schloß** ~ to fit a door with a new lock; **überreichlich** ~ to oversupply; **Urkunde mit Beglaubigungsklausel** ~ to authenticate a document; **Urkunde mit Unterschrift** ~ to sign a document; **mit Vollmacht** ~ to invest (clothe) with power; **Wechsel mit Akzept** ~ to endorse (accept) a bill;
sich ~ **haben** to have made a mistake;
~ *(a.)* provided, furnished;
mit Etikett ~ labelled; **mit Geld wohl** ~ flush of money; **mangelhaft (unzureichend)** ~ scantily provided; **mit Unterschrift** ~ duly signed;
mit Gitterstäben ~ **sein** to be fitted with iron bars; **reichlich mit Mitteln** ~ **sein** to be flush of money, to have ample means; **mit jds. Unterschrift** ~ **sein** to bear s. one's signature;
wohl ~**es Lager** well-assorted stock.
versehentlich inadvertently, by mistake;
etw. ~ **tun** to do s. th. in error.
versehrt hurt, damaged, injured, *(invalide)* disabled.
Versehrten|geld injury benefit; ~**grad** degree of disability; ~**heim** soldier's home *(US)*; ~**hilfe** rehabilitation of the disabled; ~**rente** disablement annuity (pension), disability benefit, industrial disablement benefit *(Br.)*; ~**rente bei Schwerstbeschädigung** exceptionally severe disablement benefit *(Br.)*; ~**unterstützung bei Gliederverlust** dismemberment benefit.
Versehrter invalid, disabled.
Versehrtheit disablement.
verselbständigen *(Staatsbetrieb)* to hive off;
sich ~ to become independent.
Verselbständigung *(Industrie)* hiving off.
Verselbständigungsprozeß hiving-off process.
versenden to send off, to forward, to convey, to transport, to freight, to ship *(US)*;
ins Ausland ~ to export; **mit der Bahn** ~ to dispatch (send, forward) goods by rail; **als Eilgut** ~ to forward (ship) by express train *(Br.)*; **unter Frachtnachnahme** ~ to ship freight collect; **mit Luftpost** ~ to send by airmail; **mit der Post** ~ to post *(Br.)*, to mail *(US)*, to send off by post *(Br.)*; **Rechnungen** ~ to send in one's bills (out accounts); **Rundschreiben** ~ to circularize, to send out circulars; **Waren zu einem bestimmten Frachtsatz** ~ to rate goods *(US)*; **Ware in Teilladungen** ~ to ship goods by instal(l)ments; **auf dem Wasser** ~ to ship by sea, to convey by water.

Versender sender, forwarder, consignor, shipper *(US)*.

Versendung sending [off], forwarding, dispatch, sending out, consignment, conveyance, transport, transportation *(US)*, shipment *(US)*;
während der ~ in transit;
~ **mit der Bahn** consigment by goods train *(Br.)*; ~ **mit der Post** mailing, dispatch of mail, posting; ~ **von Rundschreiben** circularization, sending out of circulars; ~ **von Waren** sending of goods.

Versendungs|anzeige forwarding advice, dispatch note; **~art** mode of conveyance; **~kauf** sale by description, sales shipment *(US)*; **~kosten** transport (shipping, *US*) charges, transportation charges *(US)*; **~land** country of origin; **~ort** place of consignment.

versengen to scorch, to singe, *(Gas)* to parch.

versenkbar lowerable, *(Panzerkuppel)* disappearing, *(Schiff)* sinkable.

versenken *(Schiff)* to submerge;
sich in ein Buch ~ to become absorbed in a book; **Sarg in die Erde** ~ to lower a coffin into the ground; **sich selbst** ~ to scuttle o. s.

versenkt *(Schiff)* sunk, submerged, *(selbst)* scuttled.

Versenktisch drop compartment.

Versenkung *(Schiff)* submersion, kill, *(Theater)* trap door;
in der ~ **verschwinden** *(fig.)* to vanish into space.

Versenkvorrichtung *(Schreibtisch)* drophead.

versessen intent, fond of, crazy;
ganz ~ as keen as mustard;
auf etw. ganz ~ **sein** to be a whale for (wild to do) s. th., to be dead nuts about s. th.; **auf die Herbeiführung von Reformen völlig** ~ **sein** to sicken to bring about reforms.

versetzbar *(Beamter)* removable, *(Gegenstand)* pawnable.

Versetzen pawning, pledging.

versetzen to move, to shift, *(Angestellte)* to transfer, to assign, to move, to displace, *(Schüler)* to remove, to move up, to promote *(US)*, *(verpfänden)* to [put in] pawn, to pledge, to pop *(Br., sl.)*, to hock *(sl.)*, to put away *(sl.)*, to soak *(sl.)*;
j. ~ to stand s. o. up; **Angestellten in die Zentrale** ~ to relocate an employee; **j. in den Anklagezustand** ~ to commit s. o. for trial, to arraign s. o.; **Beamten** ~ to transfer a civil servant, to displace an officer; **Berge** ~ to move mountains; **jem. eins** ~ to give s. o. a sock in the jaw; **j. in einen Freudentaumel** ~ to send s. o. into raptures; **aus disziplinarischen Gründen** ~ to transfer for disciplinary reasons; **j. in die Lage** ~ to put s. o. in the position; **sich in jds. Lage** ~ to imagine o. s. in another's position; **Metalle** ~ to alloy; **in den nächstniedrigen Rang** ~ to demote to the rank below; **in den Ruhestand** ~ to pension off, to retire, to put on the retired list, to superannuate; **in den einstweiligen Ruhestand** ~ to put s. o. on half pay; **wegen Erreichung der Altersgrenze in den Ruhestand** ~ to retire under the age limit; **Schüler in eine höhere Klasse** ~ to promote a pupil to a higher class *(US)*; **strafweise** ~ to transfer for disciplinary reasons; **einem Unternehmen den Todesstoß** ~ to sign the death warrant for an enterprise *(coll.)*; **seine Uhr** ~ to pop one's watch *(sl.)*; **in den Wartestand** ~ to put on half pay.

versetzt transferred, moved, *(von Freundin)* stood-up *(coll.)*, *(Schüler)* promoted *(US)*, moved up *(Br.)*, *(verpfändet)* pledged, up the spout, in pop *(Br., sl.)*;
~ **werden** to get a transfer, *(Pfand)* to go up the spout, *(Schüler)* to be moved up; **zu einer Einheit** ~ **werden** to be posted to a unit; **nach Hause** ~ **werden** to be posted home; **nicht** ~ **werden** *(Schüler)* to have to repeat a year.

Versetzung *(Beamter)* transfer, transposal *(Br.)*, change, removal, displacement, *(Buchstaben)* transposition, *(mil.)* reassignment, transfer, *(Schule)* remove, promotion *(US)*;
~en personnel shifts, staff transfers;
betriebsbedingte ~ production transfer *(US)*, interplant transfer; **bevorstehende** ~ *(Diplomat)* pending assignment; **personelle ~en** personnel shifts;
~ **innerhalb einer Abteilung** intradepartmental transfer; ~ **von einer Abteilung in die andere** interdepartmental transfer; **turnusmäßige** ~ **leitender Angestellter** executive rotation; ~ **in den Anklagezustand** committal for trial, arraignment; ~ **von Arbeitskräften in andere Schichten** shift transfer; **~en innerhalb des Betriebes** personnel transfer; ~ **in den Ruhestand** retirement, retiring, superannuation, pensioning [off]; ~ **in den zeitweiligen Ruhestand** retirement on half pay; **zwangsweise** ~ **in den Ruhestand** compulsory retirement; ~ **in den Ruhestand wegen Arbeitsunfähigkeit** disability retirement; ~ **in den Wartestand** retirement on half pay, suspension from office;
um seine ~ **einkommen** to ask to be moved; **um seine** ~ **in den Ruhestand einkommen** to apply for retirement on a pension; **Voraussetzungen für die** ~ **in den Ruhestand erfüllen** to qualify for retirement on a pension; **seine** ~ **erhalten** *(mil.)* to get a shift; **auf innerbetriebliche laufbahnbedingte ~en zurückzuführen sein** to arise from an internal career development move.

Versetzungs|arten transfer types; **~gesuch** request to be moved; **~gremium** assignment panel; **~kosten** relocation expenses; **~zeugnis** *(Schüler)* promotion certificate.

verseuchen to contaminate, to infect, *(Luft)* to pollute.

verseucht polluted.

Verseuchung contagion, contamination, infection, *(Luft, Wasser)* pollution;
radioaktive ~ radioactive contamination;
~ **der Flüsse** contamination (pollution) of rivers; ~ **der Wasserversorgung** contamination of the water supply.

versicherbar insurable, assurable;
~es Interesse insurable interest; **~es Risiko** insurable risk.

Versicherer insurer, underwriter, *(Lebensversicherung)* assurer *(Br.)*;
als ~ **tätig sein** to sell (write) insurance.

versichern to insure, to underwrite, to write, *(behaupten)* to assert, *(bezeugen)* to declare, to assure, to aver, to avouch, to certify, *(Lebensversicherung)* to take out a life policy, to assure *(Br.)*;
sich jds. ~ to make sure of s. o.; **sich mit Abkürzung auf das 70. Jahr** ~ to take out an endowment policy maturing at the age of 70; **sich gegen Ansprüche Dritter** ~ to insure against third-party claims; **sich gegen Brandfolgeschäden** ~ to insure against loss of business profit following a fire; **an Eides Statt (eidesstattlich)** ~ to depose on oath, to file (subscribe, execute) an affidavit, to affirm *(US)*; **eidlich** ~ to affirm upon oath; **feierlich** ~ to asseverate; **sich gegen die Folgen der gesetzlichen Haftpflicht** ~ to insure against one's legal liability or damage to others; **gegen Haftpflicht** ~ to insure against third-party risks; **sein Haus gegen Feuer** ~ to insure one's house against fire; **zu hoch** ~ to overinsure; **höher** ~ to rate up; **Ladung** ~ to take a risk on a cargo; **sein Leben für £ 20.000** ~ to take out a life insurance policy (insure o. s.) for £ 20.000; **sich jds. Mitarbeit für das Rote Kreuz** ~ to enlist s. one's help for the Red Cross; **zu niedrig** ~ to insure below value, to underinsure; **zu einer niedrigen Prämie** ~ to insure at a low premium; **gegen Schaden** ~ to insure a loss; **Schiff für Hin- und Rückreise** ~ to insure a ship out and home; **Schiffsladung** ~ to insure a ship's cargo; **gegen eventuelle Unfälle** ~ to insure against possible accidents; **seine Unschuld** ~ to protest one's innocence; **bei einer Versicherungsgesellschaft** ~ to insure with an insurance office; **sich jds. Zustimmung** ~ to secure s. one's consent;
sich ~ **lassen** to take out an insurance [policy], to buy insurance, to have one's life assured *(Br.)*; **sein Leben bei einer Gesellschaft** ~ **lassen** to assure one's life with a company *(Br.)*;
~, **im guten Glauben gehandelt zu haben** to protest one's good faith.

versichert insured, assured *(Br.)*;
anderweitig ~ insured elsewhere; **laufend** ~ currently insured *(US)*; **nicht** ~ noninsured; **nicht gegen Havarie** ~ free from average; **über dem Wert** ~ overinsured; **unter dem Wert** ~ underinsured; **voll** ~ fully insured;
~ **sein können** to rest assured; ~ **sein** to be insured, to carry insurance *(US)*, to have coverage *(US)*, to be covered *(US)*; **gegen Diebstahl** ~ **sein** to be insured against theft;
~e Gefahr risk subscribed.

Versicherter insurant, insured [person], policyholder, insuree, *(Lebensversicherung)* assured *(Br.)*;
freiwillig ~ voluntary contributor *(Br.)*;
~ **bei Lloyds** Lloyd's underwriter *(Br.)*.

Versicherung insurance, assurance *(Br.)*, *(Erklärung)* declaration, statement, assurance, assertion, affirmation, pledge;
durch ~ **gedeckt** covered by insurance;
abgekürzte ~ term insurance; **abgelaufene** ~ expired insurance (policy); **noch nicht abgelaufene** ~ unexpired insurance; **abgelehnte** ~ declinature; **unter einem Jahr abgeschlossene** ~ short-period insurance; **abgetretene** ~ assigned insurance policy; **aufgeschobene** ~ *(Leben)* deferred assurance *(Br.)*; **aufgestockte** ~ extended insurance; **aufrechterhaltene** ~ insurance carried; **beitragsfreie** ~ paid-up insurance; **direkte** ~ direct insurance; **doppelte** ~ double insurance; **ehrenwörtliche** ~ solemn promise; **eidesstattliche** ~ affidavit, statutory declaration *(Br.)*; **eidliche** ~ adjuration; **eingeschränkte** ~ restricted coverage; **voll eingezahlte** ~ paid-up insurance; **fakultative** ~ optional insurance; **fällige** ~ matured insurance;

feierliche ~ solemn assertion, affirmation, asseveration; **freiwillige** ~ voluntary (nonmandatory) insurance; **führende** ~ leading underwriter;. **gegenseitige** ~ mutual insurance; **gesperrte** ~ blocked insurance; **gewinnbeteiligte** ~ participating insurance; **nicht gewinnbeteiligte** ~ nonparticipating insurance; **zu hohe** ~ overinsurance; **kombinierte** ~ combined policy; **kurzfristige** ~ term insurance; **noch laufende** ~ policy still in force; **mehrfache** ~ multiple-line system of insurance; **zu niedrige** ~ underinsurance; **obligatorische** ~ compulsory insurance; **prämienfreie** ~ paid-up (extended) policy; **prolongierte** ~ extended insurance; **staatliche** ~ state insurance; **unterhaltene** ~ insurance carried; **verfallene** ~ lapsed (expired) insurance; **vorausbezahlte** ~ prepaid insurance; **zusätzliche** ~ additional (supplementary, collateral) insurance;

~ **gegen Abbruchkosten** demolition cost insurance; ~ **mit ermäßigter Anfangsprämie** renewable insurance; ~ **leitender Angestellter** business insurance; ~ **für die Ausstattung eines Handelsreisenden** drummer floater *(US)*; ~ **gegen Bankeinbruch und Bankraub** bank burglary and robbery insurance; **globale** ~ **der Büroeinrichtung** office floater *(US)*; ~ **an Eides Statt** *(Zeuge)* declaration *(US)*, declaration in lieu of oath *(Br.)*; ~ **für die Einhaltung von Reallastverpflichtungen** ground rent insurance; ~ **gegen Entführungen** snatch insurance *(sl.)*; ~ **auf den Erlebensfall** ordinary long-term (endowment) insurance, master scheme with profits endowment assurance *(Br.)*; **gemischte** ~ **auf den Erlebens- und Todesfall** combined endowment and whole-life insurance; ~ **im Fall von Dauerinvalidität** permanent disability insurance; ~ **gegen Flugzeugentführung** hi[gh]jacking insurance; ~ **gegen Folgeschäden** consequential damages insurance; ~ **gegen alle Gefahren** insurance against all risks, all-risks insurance; ~ **auf Gegenseitigkeit** mutual insurance *(US)*; ~ **für entgangenen Gewinn im Wert gestiegener Grundstücke** leasehold insurance *(US)*; ~ **mit Gewinnbeteiligung** participating insurance; ~ **ohne Gewinnbeteiligung** insurance without profits; ~ **mit Gewinnbeteiligungsgarantie** guaranteed dividend policy; **private** ~ **gegen Haftpflichtschäden** third-party indemnity insurance; ~ **für Handlungsreisende** drummer floater *(US)*; ~ **des Interesses an rechtzeitiger Lieferung** insurance of delivery in time; ~ **für stationäre Krankenhausbehandlung** hospital benefit (hospitalization, *US*) insurance; **unbegrenzte** ~ **im Krankheitsfall** permanent health insurance, permanent sickness policy; ~ **gegen Kriegsgefahr** war risk insurance; ~ **gegen Kunstfehler** malpractice insurance; ~ **auf ein anderes Leben** insurance for the life of another; ~ **im Luftverkehr** air passengers' insurance; ~ **gegen Nichterneuerung der Konzession** licence insurance; ~ **für entgangenen Pachtgewinn** leasehold insurance *(US)*; ~ **mit ermäßigten Prämiensätzen** low-premium insurance; ~ **mit abgekürzter Prämienzahlung** insurance with limited premium; ~ **gegen aus Produzentenhaftung herrührenden Schäden** product liability insurance; ~ **gegen entgangene Provisionseinnahmen** commission insurance; ~ **gegen Raubüberfälle** personal holdup insurance; ~ **gegen Rechtsmängel beim Grundstückserwerb** guaranty-of-title insurance *(US)*; ~ **der Richtigkeit der Angaben** affirmative warranty; ~ **gegen besondere Risiken** contingency insurance; ~ **mit beschränktem Risiko** limited policy; ~ **gegen Schäden an unbewohnten Gebäuden** unoccupied buildings insurance; ~ **mit Selbsterhalt** contributory insurance; ~ **auf den Todesfall** straight life insurance, whole-life insurance, assurance payable at death *(Br.)*; ~ **gegen zusätzliches Transportrisiko** special insurance; **prämienfreie** ~ **mit gekürzter Versicherungssumme** paid-up policy of a reduced amount; ~ **gegen Wasserschäden bei Feuerlöschanlagen** sprinkler leakage insurance; ~ **auf Zeit (für eine bestimmte Zeitdauer)** term insurance;

durch eine ~ **abdecken** to cover by an insurance; **eidesstattliche** ~ **abgeben** to file a statutory declaration (an affidavit); **feierliche** ~ **abgeben** to make a solemn protestation, to assert solemnly; ~ **an Eides Statt abnehmen** to administer an affirmation *(US)*; ~ **abschließen** to effect (place, take out, arrange) an insurance; ~ **aufheben** to drop a policy; **aus einer** ~ **ausscheiden** to revoke an insurance contract; ~ **durch Eid bekräftigen** to swear an affidavit; ~ **decken** to cover (provide) an insurance; **jem. die** ~ **geben** to assure s. o.; ~ **übernehmen** to write insurance; ~ **unter Risikoteilung übernehmen** to underwrite a risk; ~ **unterhalten** to carry an insurance *(US)*; ~ **verlängern** to renew a policy; ~ **vermitteln** to introduce an insurance; **weniger Geld für ~en vorsehen** to cut back on insurances; ~ **wiederaufnehmen** to reinstate an insurance; ~ **zurückkaufen** to surrender an insurance policy.

Versicherungs|ablauf expiration of policy; **~ablaufregister** lapsed policies book; **~abneigung** disinclination to insure; **~abschätzung** insurance appraisal; **~abschluß** issuance of policy; **~abschlußbeleg** insurance slip *(Br.)*; **~abschlüsse** transactions at the insurance office; **~abschlüsse für Privatfahrzeuge** personal auto underwriting; **~abschlußkosten** initial expenses of an insurance; **~abteilung** insurance department; **~agent** insurance broker (agent), policy broker, writer; **~agentur** insurance office (agency); **~akquisiteur** insurance canvasser (travel(l)er); **~aktien** insurance shares (stocks, *US*); **~aktiengesellschaft** joint-stock insurance company, stock insurance corporation *(US)*; **~alter** age of insured, insured's age; **~angestellter** insurance clerk.

Versicherungsanspruch insurance claim;
anerkannter ~ admitted claim; **noch nicht entschiedener** ~ open claim;
~ **des Begünstigten** beneficial interest;
~ **regulieren** to adjust a claim; ~ **verpfänden** to pledge an insurance.

Versicherungsansprüche, sich überschneidende overlap of insurances;
~ **voll abdecken** to meet an insurance claim in full; ~ **einklagen** to sue on a policy; ~ **gegen einen fahrlässigen Autofahrer erheben** to claim against a negligent motorist; ~ **regulieren** to settle insurance claims.

Versicherungs|anstalt insurance company (office), insurance bank; **~anteilschein** insurance certificate.

Versicherungsantrag proposal of insurance, insurance application;
~ **entgegennehmen** to secure an application; ~ **erfüllen** to discharge an insurance contract; ~ **stellen** to propose to an insurance company.

Versicherungs|anwalt insurance solicitor (lawyer, *US*); **~anwärter** prospective insured; **~anzeige** immediate notice, discovery; **Voraussetzung einer ~anzeige erfüllen** to constitute notice to the insurance company; **~arten** classes of insurance; **bestimmte ~arten von Kraftfahrzeugen ablehnen** to decline certain types of motor risk; **~arzt** *(Krankenkasse)* panel doctor *(Br.)*; **~aspekte** elements of insurance; **~aufnahmeantrag** in-surance application; **~aufsichtsbeamter** Insurance Commissioner *(US)*; **~aufsichtsbehörde** insurance department, Bureau of Old-Age and Survivors Insurance *(US)*, insurance section *(Br.)*; **~aufsichtsgesetz** [etwa] Trustee Investment Act *(Br.)*, Federal Credit Union Act *(US)*; **~aufwertung** revalorization of an insurance; **~ausfall** loss of insurance premiums; **~ausmaß** scope of policy; **~beamter** officer of an insurance company, insurance officer (official); **~bearbeiter** insurance clerk; **~bedarf** insurance demand (needs).

Versicherungsbedingungen terms of a policy, policy provisions, insurance (policy) conditions, conditions of insurance;
allgemeine ~ standard provisions; **allgemeine** ~ **bei Lloyds** usual Lloyd's conditions;
~ **neu fassen** to redraw the lines.

Versicherungs|bedürfnisse insurance needs; **~beginn** commencement of an insurance, inception date of policy, policy inception; **~begrenzung** exclusion; **~begünstigter** insurance beneficiary; **~beitrag** insurance premium (contribution); **zurückgestellte ~beiträge** deferred insurance; **~beitrag anrechnen** *(Sozialversicherung)* to credit with a contribution; **~berater** actuarial consultant; **~beratung** actuarial consultation; **~berechtigter** beneficiary of insurance; **~bescheinigung** insurance certificate; **~bestand** insurance portfolio, *(Versicherungsgesellschaft)* business in force; **~bestätigung** binding (conditional) receipt, *(vorläufig)* covering (cover, *Br.*) note, slip *(Br.)*; **~besteuerung** insurance taxation; **~bestimmung** insurance clause; **~bestimmungen** insurance regulations, policy provisions, provisions of an insurance; **~betrag** amount insured, face amount insured by the policy; **~beträge fortzahlen** to pay premiums to date; **~betrieb** insurance business; **~betrug** insurance fraud, fraudulent claim; **Londoner ~börse** Lloyd's; **~bote** insurance messenger; **~branche** insurance sector (business), *(Einzelsparte)* insurance line; **~bürgschaft hinterlegen** to post an endowment bond; **~büro** insurance office (agency); **~darlehen** loan granted by an insurance company; **~dauer** term (period) of an insurance, insurance period; **noch nicht abgelaufene ~dauer** years to run; **~deckung** insurance coverage; **vorläufige ~deckung** binder, *(Feuerversicherung)* covering note; **~deckung von Haus zu Haus** warehouse-to-warehouse insurance; **~deckungsfonds** insurance fund; **~dokumente** insurance papers; **~einkommen**

underwriting income; ~**einnehmer** insurance collector; ~**entschädigung** insurance recovery; ~**entscheidung** underwriting decision; **gesetzliche** ~**erfordernisse** statutory insurance requirements; ~**ergebnis** underwriting result; ~**experte** actuary; ~**experte bei Bergungsschäden** salvage expert; ~**fach** insurance line; ~**fachmann** insurance expert, actuary.

versicherungsfähig insurable, assurable *(Br.)*;
nicht ~ uninsurable;
nicht ~**es Risiko** uninsurable risk.

Versicherungs|fähigkeit insurability; **Nachweis der** ~**fähigkeit** evidence of insurability satisfactory to company; ~**fall** insurance case, occurrence of the event insured against, event insured, maturity; **bei Eintritt des** ~**falles** in case (the event) of the loss; ~**fonds** insurance (benevolent, benefit) fund; ~**forderung anmelden** to give notice of claim; ~**form** type of insurance; ~**formular** insurance slip, covering form.

versicherungsfrei exempt from insurance;
~ **sein** *(Sozialversicherung)* to be outside the scope of the national insurance system *(Br.)* (relieved from security payments, *US*).

Versicherungs|geber insurer, insurance underwriter; **auf dem** ~**gebiet** in the field of insurance; ~**gebühren** insurance charges, *(Post)* insurance fee; ~**gegenstand** subject matter of the insurance, subject matter insured; ~**gehilfen** agents and servants; ~**genossenschaft** cooperative insurance society.

Versicherungsgeschäft insurance business (operation, transaction), underwriting [business];
~**e aller Art betreiben** to write all lines of insurance; ~ **einschränken** to withdraw underwriting capacity; ~ **tätigen** to underwrite.

Versicherungsgesellschaft insurance company (corporation, *US*), insurance office, insurers, office *(Br.)*, moneyed corporation *(US)*, *(in Form einer AG)* joint-stock insurance company, *(Lebensversicherung)* assurance company *(Br.)*, insurers, assurers *(Br.)*, *(Seeversicherung)* underwriters;
Wrack auswertende ~ abandonee; **betriebseigene** ~ captive insurance company; **rückversichernde** ~ direct-writing company; **universelle** ~ multiple-line company; **nicht verbandsangehörige** ~ nonorganization carrier; **zugelassene** ~ admitted insurance company; **in einem Kartellsystem zusammengeschlossene** ~**en** tariff companies *(Br.)*;
~ **auf Aktien** stock insurance company (insurer) *(US)*; **Bank und** ~ moneyed corporation *(US)*; ~ **auf Gegenseitigkeit** friendly society *(Br.)*, mutual insurance corporation *(US)* (company, society, office, *Br.*); ~ **mit Gewinnbeteiligung** mixed insurance company;
seine ~ **in Anspruch nehmen** to make a claim on one's insurance company; **bei einer** ~ **versichern** to insure with an insurance office.

Versicherungs|gesetz National Insurance Act *(Br.)*; ~**gewerbe** insurance trade (industry), insurance profession (business); **im** ~**gewerbe tätig sein** to be in the insurance business; ~**gewinn** underwriting profit; **nicht vereinbarter** ~**gewinn** uncovenanted benefit; **vertragsmäßiger** ~**gewinn** covenanted benefit; ~**grenze** maximum amount insured, *(Sozialversicherung)* exemption limit; ~**grundlage** insurance basis; ~**gruppe** class of risks; ~**gutachten** actuarial expertise; ~**haftung ausgeschlossen** warranted free; ~**höchstgrenze** line; ~**höhe** insured amount, amount of insurance; ~**holding gründen** to build an insurance holding company; ~**industrie** insurance industry; ~**inspektor** claim adjuster (inspector, agent), inspector of agents, new business inspector; ~**interesse** insurable interest; ~**interesse anerkannt** policy proof of interest (full interest admitted) clause; ~**interesse des Hypothekengebers** mortgage interest.

versicherungsinterne Vereinbarung inter-insurer agreement.

Versicherungs|jahr policy year; **erstes** ~**jahr** *(Selbstmordklausel)* first policy year; **schadensfreie** ~**jahre** previous claim-free years; ~**jurist** insurance lawyer; ~**kalkulation** actuarial calculation; ~**kalkulator** actuary; ~**kapital** insurance stock; ~**karte** ticket; **grüne** ~**karte** insurance green card; ~**kasse** insurance fund; **sein Abschlußexamen als** ~**kaufmann bestehen** to pass the qualifying examination of the Chartered Insurance Institute *(Br.)*.

Versicherungsklausel insurance clause;
nur die Ersthypothek begünstigende ~ noncontribution clause; ~ **über Ausschluß des Selbstbehalts** agreed-amount clause; ~ **zur Deckung aller vom Fahrzeughalter eingesetzten Kraftfahrzeuge** omnibus clause; ~ **gegen verborgene Mängel** *(Schiff)* Jason clause.

Versicherungs|kniffe insurance wrinkles; ~**konjunktur** underwriting cycle; ~**konsortium** syndicate of underwriters; ~**kontroverse** insurance dispute; ~- **und Finanzierungskonzern** insurance and financial service conglomerate; ~**kosten,** ~**lasten** cost of insurance, insurance charges (costs); ~**kredit** loan from an insurance company; ~**kunde** prospective insured; ~**kündigung** termination of an insurance contract; ~**kundschaft** insurance-buying public; ~**lage** insurance aspects.

Versicherungsleistung insurance benefit (payment);
neuartige ~**en** frills *(US)*;
inflationsunabhängige ~**en gewährleisten** to maintain insurance benefits in the event of inflation; **sich die gewünschten** ~**en selbst zusammenstellen** to select one's own table of benefits.

Versicherungs|makler insurance (policy, placing) broker; ~**marke** policy stamp, *(Sozialversicherung)* national insurance stamp *(Br.)*; ~**markt** insurance market; ~**markt für nicht haftpflichtbedingte Risiken** *(Kraftfahrzeug)* voluntary auto insurance market; ~**mathematik** actuarial science; ~**mathematiker** insurance technician, actuary; **amtlicher** ~**mathematiker** government actuary.

versicherungsmathematisch|einwandfrei actuarially sound;
~**es Defizit** actuarial deficit; ~**e Tabellen** actuarial tables.

Versicherungs|möglichkeit underwriting capacity; ~**nachlaß für unfallfreies Fahren** no-claim bonus *(Br.)*, selective driver plan *(US)*; ~**nachtrag** endorsement on insurance policy; ~**nachzahlung** *(Gegenseitigkeitsverein)* assessment *(US)*; ~**nehmer** insured [person], assured *(Br.)*, policyholder, policy owner, beneficiary, insurant, insurance consumer (holder); **gesunder** ~**nehmer** good life; **unfallhäufiger** ~**nehmer** bad insurance risk; ~**nummer** insurance number; ~**objekt** subject matter insured; ~**periode** period of insurance; ~**pflicht** insurance liability, compulsory insurance; **gesetzliche** ~**pflicht** statutory duty to insure.

versicherungspflichtig liable to pay insurance premiums;
nicht ~ **sein** *(Sozialversicherung)* to be outside the scope of the national insurance system *(Br.)* (relieved from security payments, *US*);
~**e Umstände** material representation.

Versicherungspflichtiger insurance contributor.

Versicherungspolice [insurance] policy, insurance certificate, policy of assurance *(Br.)*;
abgelaufene ~ expired insurance policy; **abtretbare** ~ assignable insurance policy; **für mehr als ein Jahr ausgestellte** ~ long-rate policy; **auf den Letztlebenden ausgestellte** ~ last survivor policy; **Selbstbehalt ausschließende** ~ fixed-amount policy; **beitragsfreie** ~ paid-up insurance policy; **berichtigte** ~ corrected policy; **erstklassige** ~ top-hat insurance policy; **gegliederte** ~ scheduled policy; **mit einem sachverständig geschätzten Inventar gekoppelte** ~ policy based on an inventory and value; **gewinnbeteiligte** ~ participating policy; **laufende** ~ floating policy; **nachschußfreie** ~ nonassessable policy *(US)*; **offene** ~ open policy; **prämienfreie** ~ paid-up insurance policy, nonassessable policy *(US)*; **prolongierte** ~ extended-term policy; **taxierte** ~ valued policy; **übertragbare** ~ transferable insurance policy; **ungültige (verfallene)** ~ lapsed policy; **unkündbare** ~ noncancellable policy; **vorläufige** ~ binder;
~ **für leitende Angestellte** top-hat policy; ~ **mit unwiderruflicher Bezugsberechtigung** nomination policy; ~ **unterhalb der Dauer eines Jahres** short-period policy; ~ **mit Gewinnberechtigung** participating policy; ~ **ohne Gewinnbeteiligung** nonparticipating policy; ~ **mit fester Laufzeit** time policy; **kurzfristige** ~ **für ein besonderes Risiko** special-risk policy; ~ **für automatische Sprinkleranlage** sprinkler leakage policy; ~ **für Straßenbenutzung** *(Autohändler)* road risk policy; ~ **mit frei vereinbartem Wert** agreed value policy; ~ **mit Wertangabe** valued policy; ~ **ohne Wertangabe** unvalued (open) policy; ~ **für eine bestimmte Zeit** time policy;
~ **aufrechterhalten** to keep a policy alive; ~ **ausstellen** to issue a policy; ~ **beleihen** to lend money on an insurance policy; **seine** ~ **bezahlen** to pay one's insurance; ~ **einlösen** to pay the first premium; ~ **erlangen** to procure a policy; ~ **erneuern** to renew an insurance policy; ~ **erwerben** to take out an insurance policy; ~ **kündigen** to drop a policy; ~ **zurückkaufen** to surrender an insurance.

Versicherungsprämie insurance premium (rate, *US*), policy premium, premium paid for insurance, rate of insurance *(US)*;
besonders festgesetzte ~ merit rate *(US)*; **jährlich steigende** ~ step-rate premium; **steuerbegünstigte** ~ premium qualifying for relief *(Br.)*; **verauslagte** ~ advanced premium;
~ **für Hin- und Rückreise** premium out and home; ~ **für Produzentenhaftung** product liability premium; ~ **für einen Zeitraum unter einem Jahr** short rate *(US)*;

~n im Abbuchungsverfahren bezahlen to initiate debits for payment of premiums; ~ fortzahlen to pay premiums to date.
Versicherungs|prämiensatz insurance rate *(US)*, insurance instalment; ~provision insurance commission; ~prüfer insurance examiner (auditor); ~publikum insurance-buying public; ~rate insurance instalment (rate, *US*); ~recht law of insurance, insurance law; ~reform insurance reform; ~regulierer insur-ance adjuster, claim agent (adjuster); ~reisender insurance traveller; bei der Pensionierung ausgezahlte ~rente retirement annuity; ~reserve für Verwaltungskosten reserve for management expenses; ~revisor insurance auditor; laufende ~risiken pending risks.
Versicherungsrisiko insurance (insurable) risk, hazard;
schlechtes ~ bad insurance risk; subjektives ~ moral hazard; zugewiesenes ~ assigned risk;
~ loswerden to come off risk.
Versicherungs|rückkauf *(Lebensversicherung)* surrender; ~rückkaufswert surrender value; ~sachverständiger insurance tester, claim adjuster, appraiser, *(Seeversicherung)* insurance surveyor, nautical assessor *(Br.)*; ~satz insurance rate *(US)* (premium); ungerechte ~sätze inequitable rates *(US)*.
Versicherungsschaden loss, damage, *(Schiff)* average;
~ nach Abzug der geretteten Waren salvage loss;
~ aufnehmen to assess the damage; ~ durch Besichtigung feststellen to adjust the average.
Versicherungsschein certificate of insurance, insurance certificate, ticket, policy of insurance, policy document;
typisierter ~ block policy; vorläufiger ~ insurance (cover) note, binder *(US)*, memorandum of insurance, slip *(Br.)*.
Versicherungsschema scheme for insurance.
Versicherungsschutz insurance protection (cover, umbrella), coverage;
~ vorübergehend aufgehoben out of benefit; doppelter ~ duplicated cover; kostenloser ~ free insurance; sofortiger ~ immediate benefit; geographisch unbeschränkter ~ liberty of the globe; zusätzlicher ~ *(Feuerversicherung)* extended coverage;
~ im gewerblichen Bereich commercial coverage; kein ~ bei Beschlagnahme free of capture and seizure; ~ gegen Naturkatastrophen natural-disaster coverage; ~ im Rahmen der Haus-zu-Haus Klausel *(Spediteur)* standard warehouse-to-warehouse clause;
~ aufrechterhalten to maintain an insurance in force; vorgesehenen ~ beschränken to restrict the cover provided; keinen ~ gewähren to withdraw coverage; ausreichenden ~ für ein Grundstück unterhalten to keep a property fully insured; rückwirkende ~klausel *(Seerecht)* lost or not lost.
Versicherungs|sektor insurance sector; ~sparte class of business, line of insurance; bestimmte ~sparte betreiben to write a class of business; bisher betriebene ~sparte weiter betreiben to continue insurance of a class written previously *(Br.)*; ~spesen saving via an insurance system; ~sprache insurance parlance; genormte ~sprache standardized wordings; ~statistik actuarial statistics; ~statistiker actuary.
versicherungsstatistisch actuarial;
~e Abteilung actuarial department.
Versicherungs|stempel policy stamp; ~steuer premium tax, policy duty, excise lien property tax *(US)*; ~stock insurance fund.
Versicherungssumme insurance [money], amount insured (of insurance), insured value, capital sum insured, *(Lebensversicherung)* reversion;
ausgezahlte ~ policy money; doppelte ~ bei Unfalltod double indemnity; erhöhte ~ increased limit; normale ~ standard limit; ungenügende ~ inadequate sum insured; für Rückversicherung vorgesehene ~ surplus line;
~ in Höhe von 10.000 £ ausgezahlt bekommen to receive £ 10.000 insurance.
Versicherungssyndikat underwriting syndicate.
Versicherungssystem insurance system (plan), system of insurance;
beitragspflichtiges ~ contributory insurance system; lohngekoppeltes ~ earnings-related insurance scheme; verschuldenfreies ~ *(Autoversicherung)* no-fault insurance plan *(US)*.
Versicherungs|tabelle table of insurance, actuarial table; ~tarif insurance rates (tariff); ~tätigkeit insurance operations (transactions); ~taxe insurance value; ~technik actuarial practice.
versicherungstechnisch actuarial;
~ einwandfrei actuarially sound;
~er Berater actuarial consultant.
Versicherungs|termin date of policy; ~träger insurer, assurer *(Br.)*, *(Seeversicherung)* insurance carrier, underwriter; staatlich genehmigter ~träger recognized insurer; ~umfang scope of policy, insurance coverage; ~unkosten cost of insurance; ~unterlagen insurance papers; ~unterlagenverzeichnis insurance register; ~unternehmen insurance company (corporation, *US*); ~unternehmer insurance carrier, [insurance] underwriter; ~urkunde policy (insurance) document; ~verband bureau company; ~- und Sparverein mutual reserve company; ~verein auf Gegenseitigkeit mutual insurance (assurance, *Br.*) company, fraternal insurance, benefit association *(Br.)*, mutual benefit society *(US)*, benefit (friendly, *Br.*, benevolent, *US*) society; betrieblicher ~verein employee benefit association; besondere ~vereinbarungen rider; ~verfall expiration (lapse) of a policy; ~verlängerung renewal of policy; ~verlust loss, underwriting deficit; ~verordnung state insurance regulations.
Versicherungsvertrag policy (insurance, coverage, underwriting) contract, contract of insurance, agreement to insure;
sich automatisch erneuernder ~ continuing policy;
~ zur Sicherstellung der Ausbildung endowment contract;
~ abschließen to arrange (conclude, enter into) an insurance, to take out a policy; ~ kündigen to give notice of cancellation of the insurance policy.
Versicherungs|verträge, Erlöse bis zu 50% in neuen ~verträgen steuerverbilligt anlegen to invest up to 50% in reserves for future underwriting; ~vertreter insurance canvasser (traveller, salesman, writer, agent); festangestellter ~vertreter industrial insurance agent; ~vertreter sein to sell (write) insurance; ~vertretung insurance office; ~voraussetzung prerequisite for insurance; ~vorauszahlung prepaid insurance; ~vorauszahlungskonto prepaid insurance account; ~vorschriften provisions of an insurance, policy provisions; ~vorvertrag slip, rider; ~wartezeit waiting period; ~wechsel insurance draft *(US)*; ~werber insurance canvasser; ~wert value insured, insurable (actuarial) value, full (actual cash) value, value in damages, face of policy; festgesetzter ~wert insurance (policy) value; ~wesen, ~wirtschaft insurance industry (business); genossenschaftliches ~wesen cooperative insurance; ~zahlung insurance recovery; ~zeit insurance period, period insured; beitragsfreie ~zeit paid-up insurance; ~zertifikat certificate of insurance, insurance certificate; ~zugang new business; ~zusammenschluß insurance merger; ~zuschlag additional insurance; ~zweig line of insurance, insurance line (branch); risikoreicher ~zweig high-risk line.
versickern to ooze away, to percolate, *(Interesse)* to wear off, to peter out.
versieben, es bei jem. to get in s. one's bad books.
versiegeln to [affix a] seal, to seal up (with lead).
versiegelt sealed, *(Testament)* mystic *(US)*;
unterschrieben und ~ given under hand and seal;
~er Brief sealed letter.
Versiegelung sealing;
gerichtliche ~ sealing by the proper officer.
Versiegen des Arbeitskräftereservoirs drying up of labo(u)r reserves *(US)*.
versiegen to exhaust, *(Arbeitskräftereservoir)* to dry up *(US)*, *(Einnahmen)* to close, to be cut off, to dwindle, to peter out.
versiert practised, experienced, conversant, smart, versed;
in einer Branche besonders ~ sein to be versed in a trade; in finanziellen Dingen ~ sein to be conversant with finance;
~er Anwalt full-fledged barrister; ~er Geschäftsmann smart businessman.
versilbern *(fam.)* to convert into cash (money), to turn into money, to realize;
Schuldnervermögen ~ to realize the debtor's property; sein Vermögen (Warenlager) ~ to turn one's stock into cash.
versilbert [silver-]plated.
Versilberung plating, *(Realisierung)* equitable conversion, convertibility into cash, cash realization;
erleichterte ~ ease of realization.
Versilberungskosten costs of realization.
versinken to go to the bottom, to sink down, *(Schiff)* to founder, to sink;
bis zu den Knien im Schnee ~ to sink up to one's knees in the snow; im Morast ~ to bog down in the mire; in einen tiefen Schlaf ~ to sink into a deep sleep.
versinnbildlichen to allegorize, to symbolize, to represent.
Version version;
amtliche ~ official version;
neue ~ einer alten Geschichte new lilt to an old song.

Versklavung enslavement, enthral(l)ment, servitude.
versoffen sodden, boozy *(coll.)*, *(Bergwerk)* submerged;
~ **sein** to be abdicted to the bottle (a slave to drink);
~**er Kerl** sot, boozer *(coll.)*.
versohlen, jem. das Fell to trim s. one's jacket.
versöhnen to conciliate, to reconcile, to heal;
sich ~ to bury the hatchet; **sich mit jem.** ~ to become (be) reconciled with s. o., to make it up with s. o.; **sich mit seinem Schicksal** ~ to reconcile o. s. to one's fate.
versöhnlich stimmen, j. to appease (placate, reconcile) s. o.
Versöhnung conciliation, reconciliation;
~ **der Parteien zustande bringen** to bring the parties together; ~ **herbeiführen** to bring about a reconciliation; ~ **zwischen zwei Menschen herbeiführen** to heal the breach between two persons.
Versöhnungs|gesten conciliatory gestures; ~**politik** policy of reconcilement.
versonnen lost in thought, pensive, thoughtful.
versorgen to provide, to supply, to furnish, to accommodate, to fit out, to fix up *(US)*, to heel *(US sl.)*, *(Familie)* to keep, to support, to maintain, to provide, *(Lager)* to stock, to make provision, to maintain, to find, *(mit Lebensmitteln)* to purvey, to cater, to victual *(Br.)*, *(Versicherungsbetrieb)* to serve, to service;
j. ~ to provide for (take care of) s. o.; **sich selbst** ~ to find for o. s., to cook for o. s.; **j. mit allem Erforderlichen** ~ to furnish s. o. with what he needs; **Geschäft mit Vorräten** ~ to stock a shop with supplies; **private Haushalte mit Elektrizität** ~ to supply electricity to domestic consumers; **Kind** ~ to look after a child; **seine Kinder** ~ to settle one's children; **Kranken** ~ to take care of a patient; **Ladengeschäft mit Waren** ~ to stock a shop with goods; **mit Lebensmitteln** ~ to stock (supply) with provisions; **Markt mit Waren** ~ to supply the market; **j. mit Nachrichten** ~ to furnish s. o. with information, to keep s. o. posted; **Schiff mit Vorräten** ~ to store (supply) a ship with provisions; **mit Vorräten für den Winter** ~ to stock up for the winter;
Frau und sieben Kindern zu ~ **haben** to maintain a wife and seven children.
Versorger provider, supplier, breadwinner, breadearner;
alleiniger ~ **seiner Familie sein** to be one's family sole support.
versorgt alimonied, supplied, provided for, furnished, *(Lager)* stocked, *(Tochter)* settled;
gut ~ well found; **personalmäßig gut** ~ well staffed;
~ **sein** to be provided for; **nicht** ~ **sein** *(Vieh)* to suffer from neglect; **seine Töchter gut** ~ **wissen** to see one's daughters comfortably fixed.
Versorgung supply, supplying, furnishing, procuration, provision, accommodation, *(Familienunterhalt)* maintenance, subsistence, sustenance, upkeep, support, *(mit Lebensmitteln)* catering, purveyance, victualling *(Br.)*, *(Lebensstellung)* establishment, place in life, settlement, good situation, *(mil.)* supply, provisioning, logistics, *(Pension, Rente)* pension;
ärztliche ~ medical attendance; **ausreichende** ~ adequate provision, sufficient supply of provisions; **kassenärztliche** ~ panel system *(Br.)*; **lebenslängliche** ~ life pension; **logistische** ~ logistical support; **soziale** ~ social services; **standesgemäße** ~ maintenance suitable to s. one's station in life; **ungenügende** ~ shortage of supply;
~ **der Bevölkerung** population supply; ~ **der Familienangehörigen** family protection (provision) *(Br.)*; ~ **mit Lebensmitteln (Nahrungsmitteln)** purveyance, victualling, food supply; ~ **aus der Luft** aerial (air) supply; **ärztliche** ~ **von Verkehrsopfern** emergency treatment;
dringend der ärztlichen ~ **bedürfen** to be in urgent need of medical supplies; **der öffentlichen** ~ **dienen** to constitute a public utility; **betriebliche Altersversorgung jetzt in die staatliche** ~ **einbeziehen** to contract into the state pension scheme; ~ **sicherstellen** to recruit supplies; **seine ausreichende** ~ **sicherstellen** to assure o. s. of adequate supply; ~ **unterbrechen** to black supply.
Versorgungs|abteilung, ~**behörde** war pensions administration, Veteran's Administration (Bureau) *(US)*; ~**achse** axis of supply; ~**aktien** public utilities; ~**amt** pension office; ~**anlagen** utility equipment; ~**anleihe** public utility bonds; ~**anspruch** claim to maintenance, *(Beamter)* pension claim; ~**anstalt** charitable institution, asylum, *(Altersversorgung)* pension fund, pension plan trust fund; ~**anwärter** pension applicant; ~**anwartschaft** eligibility for a pension, pension expectancy; ~**basis** supply base, base of supplies; **vorgeschobene** ~**basis** advanced base (depot); ~**bedarf** supply requirements; ~**bedingungen** provisions of supply.
versorgungsberechtigt entitled to maintenance, *(Beamter)* eligible for (entitled to) a pension;
~ **sein** to be participant in a pension scheme.
Versorgungs|bereich service area; ~**bestimmung** *(Testament)* maintenance clause.
Versorgungsbetrieb public utility [agency], utility company *(US)* (enterprise, corporation, establishment);
auf dem Gebiet der öffentlichen ~**e** in the field of public utilities;
~**e** *(Börse)* utilities *(US)*;
gemischter ~ quasi-public corporation; **integrierte** ~**e** integrated public utility system; **kommunaler** ~ municipally-owned (municipal) utility; **öffentlicher** ~ public utility company (corporation, *US*, establishment, undertaking), public service company (corporation, enterprise) *(US)*; **privater** ~ statutory undertaker *(Br.)*.
Versorgungs|bewilligung pension approval certificate; ~**bezüge** pensionable emoluments, superannuation benefits, income received from a pension, retirement income; ~**bombe** supply bomb; ~**dezernat** utility department; ~**dienst** public utility; ~**dienstalter** pensionable age; **Bereitstellung von** ~**diensten** public service *(US)*; ~**einheit** ancillary unit; ~**einrichtungen** utility equipment, *(Altersversorgung)* pension scheme; **lebenswichtige** ~**einrichtung** essential service; ~**empfänger** pensioner, beneficiary in a provident fund, recipient of a pension; ~**engpaß** bottle-neck in (shortage of) supplies, supply bottleneck; ~**fahrzeug** service van; ~**fall** public charge, case; ~**flugzeug** service plane; ~**fonds** provident (pension) fund; ~**freibetrag** old-age exemption, age relief; ~**gebiet** public utility field, supply area, *(el., Gas)* service area; ~**güter** supplies; **auf dem Transport befindliche** ~**güter** pipeline stocks; **gemeinschaftliche** ~**güter** common supplies; ~**industrie** public utility field, *(Börse)* public utilities *(US)*.
Versorgungskasse pension fund (plan);
beitragsfreie ~ company-financed (noncontributory) pension plan; **beitragspflichtige** ~ *(Betrieb)* contributory pension plan; **rechtlich selbständige** ~ legally independent pension fund.
Versorgungs|kette supply chain (line); ~**klemme** shortage in supply, supply difficulties; ~**kompanie** service company; ~**krise** critical supply situation; ~**lage** *(mil.)* logistic situation; **angespannte** ~**lage** tight supply situation; ~**lager** supply depot, victualling stores; **vorgeschobenes** ~**lager** advanced depot; ~**leistung** pension [payment]; **in der Zukunft zu erdienende** ~**leistungen** *(Pensionsplan)* future service cost; ~**leitung** supply pipe; ~**lücke** gap in supplies, famine; ~**mittel** means of subsistence; ~**modell** pattern of benefit; ~**monopol** supply monopoly; ~**netz** distribution (administrative) network, *(el.)* grid *(Br.)*; ~**ordnung** pension law; ~**pflicht** *(Spediteur)* common humanity doctrine; ~**plan** supply plan; ~**problem** supply problem, *(mil.)* logistical problem; ~**quelle** supply area, source of supply, *(Nachwuchs)* recruiting ground *(US)*; ~**regelung** superannuation provision; ~**rente** annuity, *(staatlich)* public (social, *US*, national, *Br.*) assistance; ~**satz** rate of pension, pension rate; ~**schiff** supply (replenishment, depot, victualling) ship; ~**schwierigkeiten** difficulties of supply; ~**staat** welfare state; ~**stand** level of supply; ~**stelle** supply center *(US)* (centre, *Br.*); ~**straße** supply line; ~**stützpunkt** supply base; ~**system** supply system, *(Altersversorgung)* retirement benefit system *(US)*; ~**system mit proportionalen Beiträgen und Leistungen** graduated pension scheme; **konkurrenzfähiges** ~**system einrichten** to provide benefits on competitive terms; ~**tarif** utility rates; ~**träger** pension fund; ~**truppen** support (services) troops; **privat betriebenes** ~**unternehmen** statutory company *(Br.)*; **öffentliches** ~**unternehmen** public utility company (corporation, establishment, society, undertaking); ~**vergütung** settlement allowance, retirement income, superannuation, pensionable emoluments; ~**verpflichtungen** pension obligations; ~**versicherung** endowment insurance; ~**wagen** supply waggon; ~**wege** channels of supply; ~**werk** pension plan (scheme); **innerbetriebliches** ~**werk** company-financed pension plan; ~**werte** *(Börse)* public utility bonds, utility shares (stocks, *US*), [public] utilities *(US)*; ~**wesen** service system; ~**wirtschaft** subsistence economy, public utilities, utility service.
verspäten, sich ~ to be late (behind time), *(Schiff, Zug)* to be overdue (behind schedule, *US*); **sich bei jem.** ~ to be held up at s. one's place.
verspätet late, belated, delayed, tardy *(US)*, *(Zug)* overdue, behind schedule *(US)*;
~ **zahlen** to be short in one's payment;
~**e Ankunft** late arrival; ~**e Lieferung** late (delayed) delivery.

Verspätung late arrival, delay, retardation, *(im Betrieb)* tardiness *(US)*;
mit ~ abfahren to leave too late; **~ haben** *(Zug)* to be late (overdue, behind time, schedule, *US*); **~ wiedereinholen** to make up for the time lost; **seine ~ auf die Wetterverhältnisse zurückführen** to explain that one has been delayed by the weather.
Verspätungs|prozentsatz *(Betrieb)* tardiness rate *(US)*; **~zinsen** interest on arrears; **~zuschlag** fine for default, default fine.
verspekulieren, sich to make a bad speculation, to lose money by bad investment.
versperren to obstruct, to bar, to bolt, to jam, to toll, *(zuschließen)* to lock away;
mit Barrikaden ~ to barricade; **Hafen ~** to blockade a port; **jem. den Weg ~** to bar s. one's way.
verspielen, sein Vermögen to gamble away one's fortune, to spend one's estate in gaming.
verspielt *(Kind)* frolicsome;
bei jem. ~ haben to get in s. one's bad books.
versponnen sein to live in the clouds.
verspotten to ridicule, to mock, to deride, to monkey;
alles ~ to turn everything into a jest.
Versprechen promise, assumpsit, undertaking, vow, pledge;
von vertraglich ausbedungenen Vorleistungen abhängiges ~ dependent promise; **absolutes ~** absolute promise; **akzessorisches ~** collateral promise; **ausdrückliches ~** express promise; **bedingtes ~** conditional promise; **bindendes ~** binding promise; **festes ~** seal; **formloses ~** assumpsit; **gemeinsames ~** joint promise; **leeres ~** vain promise; **notarielles ~** [etwa] promise under seal; **unbedingtes schriftliches ~** unconditional promise in writing; **unsittliches ~** unlawful promise; **vorbehaltsloses ~** unconditional promise;
~ ohne Gegenleistung gratuitous promise; **~ der Schadloshaltung** *(Dokumentenkredit)* indemnity;
jem. ein ~ abringen to screw a promise out of s. o.; **jem. mit einem ~ abspeisen** to fob s. o. off with a promise; **j. an sein ~ binden** to pin s. o. down to his promise; **~ brechen** to break a promise, to spin *(sl.)*; **~ einhalten** to make good on a pledge; **sein ~ nicht einhalten** to go back on (dishono(u)r) one's promise; **~ einlösen** to fulfil(l) a promise; **~ erfüllen** to deliver on a promise; **j. auf sein ~ festnageln** to pin (nail, hold) s. o. down to his promise; **sein ~ geben** to pledge one's faith; **sein ~ halten** to keep (perform) one's promise, to keep (be true to) one's word; **sich nicht an sein ~ halten** to have no respect for one's promise, to break one's vow, to be false to (go back from, break) one's word; **einem ~ nachkommen** to live up to a promise; **sein ~ zurücknehmen** to punk out.
versprechen, sich to stumble over a word; **sich etw. von jem. ~** to pin one's hopes on s. o.; **Erfolg ~** to bid fare to succeed; **erfolgreich zu werden ~** to look promising; **feierlich ~** to vow; **hoch und heilig ~** to give a solemn promise; **auf Treu und Glauben ~** to pledge one's word; **sich viel von etw. ~** to have high hopes for o. s.
Versprechens|empfänger promisee; **~geber** promisor; **~nehmer** promisee.
Versprecher slip (trip, lapse) of the tongue, *(Radio)* fluff.
Versprechungen, leere empty (court) promises, pie in the sky;
von jds. ~ nichts halten to take no stock in s. one's promises; **j. mit leeren ~ hinhalten** to feed s. o. with empty promises; **großzügig überall ~ machen** to make promises in profusion, to be liberal of promises.
Versprengtensammelstelle straggler post.
Versprengter *(mil.)* evader, straggler.
versprengter Truppenteil scattered body of troops.
versprühen, Geist to be scintillating with wit.
verspüren, Lust to be strongly inclined.
verstaatlichen to nationalize *(Br.)*, to transfer to state ownership, to put under government control, to socialize;
Eisenbahn ~ to take control of the railways; **Industrie ~** to effect nationalization of industry *(Br.)*; **Stahlindustrie ~** to nationalize the steel industry *(Br.)*.
verstaatlicht nationalized, socialized.
Verstaatlichung nationalization *(Br.)*, socialization;
drohende ~ nationalization threat *(Br.)*; **halbe ~** semi-nationalization *(Br.)*;
~ der Banken bank nationalization *(Br.)*; **~ der Flugzeugindustrie** aircraft nationalization *(Br.)*; **~ von Grund und Boden** land nationalization *(Br.)*; **~ der Industrie** nationalization of in-dustry *(Br.)*; **~ der Schiffahrtindustrie** shipbuilding nationalization *(Br.)*; **~ der Stahlindustrie** steel nationalization *(Br.)*;
~ der Stahlindustrie wieder aufheben to unscramble the steel industry; **der ~ entgehen** to stay free of government ownership; **von der ~ am meisten bedroht sein** to be in the front line of nationalization *(Br.)*.
Verstaatlichungs|absicht nationalization plan *(Br.)*; **~entschädigung** nationalization indemnity *(Br.)*; **~gesetz** Nationalization Act *(Br.)*.
verstädtern to urbanize, to deruralize.
Verstädterung urbanization.
Verstädterungsprozeß urbanization process.
Verstand sense, intelligence, intellect, head, understanding, reason, brains, mind, grey matter *(Br.)*;
bei klarem ~ compos mentis; **ohne klaren ~** off one's head *(US)*;
durchdringender ~ penetration, sharp discernment; **nüchterner ~** cold reason;
ausgezeichneten ~ besitzen to have an excellent understanding; **j. um den ~ bringen** to drive s. o. out of his senses (round the bend, *fam.*); **seinen ~ gebrauchen** to exercise one's wits, to use one's loaf *(fam.)*; **über jds. ~ gehen** to pass (be beyond) s. one's comprehension; **messerscharfen ~ haben** to have a mind as sharp as a razor; **soviel ~ haben** to know better than; **seinen ~ verloren haben, seines ~es beraubt sein** to be deprived of one's reason; **zu ~ kommen** to warm wise *(sl.)*; **sich eines scharfen ~es rühmen** to value o. s. on a keen intellect; **bei klarem ~ sein** to be in one's right mind; **bei vollem ~ sein** to be of sound mind; **~ verlieren** to lose one's wits (mind, senses).
verstanden *(Funkverkehr)* roger *(US sl.)*;
nur von Fachleuten ~ werden to be comprehensible only to specialists; **im ganzen Theater gut ~ werden** to make o. s. heard in every part of the house.
Verstandeskräfte intellectual (brain) powers;
seinen ~n entsprechend handeln to act according to one's lights; **von seinen ~n ungestört Gebrauch machen** to exercise one's mind fully and freely.
verstandesmäßig intellectual.
Verstandes|mensch intellectual, intellectualist, down-to-earth person; **~schwäche** mental weakness.
verständig intelligent, reasonable, wise, common-sense;
~es Alter age of discretion; **~er und umsichtiger Kaufmann** reasonable and prudent businessman.
verständigen to notify, to inform, to let know, to advise;
sich mit jem. ~ to come to (reach, effect) an agreement (understanding, a compromise) with s. o., *(in fremder Sprache)* to make o. s. understood to s. o.; **sich über alle strittigen Punkte ~** to settle all points of issue; **im voraus ~** to notify before-hand.
verständigerweise reasonably.
verständigt worden sein to be in the know (on notice, *US*).
Verständigung understanding, agreement, arrangement, accommodation, settlement, *(Mitteilung)* notification, information;
briefliche ~ written communication; **heimliche ~** collusion; **telefonische ~** telephone message, communication; **telegrafische ~** wire (telegraphic) advice;
~ durch Sichtzeichen *(mil.)* visual signal(l)ing; **mangelhafte ~ am Telefon** faulty telephone reception;
~ erzielen, zu einer ~ gelangen to reach (come to) an agreement, to come to an understanding.
verständigungsbereit ready to reach an understanding.
Verständigungs|bereitschaft *(dipl.)* goodwill; **~friede** negotiated peace; **~frieden** negotiated peace; **breite ~grundlage** large area of agreement (basis for negotiation); **~mittel** means of communication; **~politik** give-and-take policy, policy of appeasement (mutual understanding); **~sprache** working language; **~system** intercommunication system; **~weg** channel of communication.
verständlich comprehensible, understandable, intelligible, clear, apprehensible;
allgemein ~ popular; **leicht ~** easy to understand; **schwer ~** difficult to grasp, abstruse; **ohne weiteres ~** readily understood;
sich sowohl mündlich wie auch schriftlich überzeugend ~ machen können to be a first-class communicator face-to-face and on paper; **~ machen** to put over; **sich ~ machen** to make o. s understood; **sich jem. ~ machen** to get across to s. o.; **allgemein ~ sein** to be within everybody's grasp; **auch für jugendliche Leser ~ sein** to be within the capacity of young readers;
~e Aussprache haben to have a clear pronunciation.
Verständlichkeit *(tel.)* articulation.
Verständnis apprehension, comprehension, understanding, grip, grasp, *(Unterscheidungsvermögen)* discernment;

~ **für einander aufbringen** to understand one another; **sich jds. ~ entziehen** to elude s. one's understanding; **für eine Politik ~ gewinnen** to put over a policy; **für alles ~ haben** to be open to all views.
verständnislos lacking in understanding.
verständnisvoll understanding;
~ **handeln** to act with judgment.
verstärken to strengthen, to intensify, to reinforce, *(Radio)* to amplify, *(durch Träger)* to truss, to stiffen;
sich ~ to grow stronger; **seine Bemühungen ~** to redouble one's efforts; **Besatzung einer Garnison ~** to reinforce a garrison; **Blockade ~** to tighten up a blockade; **Druck ~** to increase pressure; **seine Eigenmittel ~** to strengthen one's own funds; **Flotte ~** to strengthen a navy; **Truppen ~** to reinforce the troops; **wirtschaftliche Verbindungen ~** to tighten economic bonds.
Verstärker *(Foto)* intensifier, *(Radio)* amplifier, *(Telefon)* repeater;
~**amt** repeater station; ~**stufe** stage.
verstärkt added, underlaid;
~**e Polizeistreifen** strengthening of patrols; ~**er Werbeeinsatz** sales drive.
Verstärkung strengthening, *(el.)* amplification, *(Foto)* intensification, *(Telefon)* booster;
~**en** *(Militär)* reinforcements;
laufende ~ der Geldmarktkontrolle progressive tightening of monetary control; ~ **der Polizeikräfte** police reinforcement; ~ **der gesellschaftlichen Stellung** status plus;
in aller Eile ~en heranschaffen to rush up reinforcements.
Verstärkungs|regler gain control; ~**reklame** institutional advertising.
verstaubt stuffy, fusty, old-hat.
verstauen to tuck away, *(im Schiffsraum)* to stow;
etw. ~ to stow s. th. away; **seine Einkäufe im Auto ~** to fill one's car with one's purchases; **erneut ~** to restow; **sein Gepäck im Gepäcknetz ~** to bestow (deposit) one's luggage (baggage, *US*) on the rack; **Ladung ~** to stow freight; **Ladung neu ~** to restow the cargo.
Verstauung stowage, stevedoring;
fehlerhafte (unsachgemäße) ~ improper stowage.
Verstauungskosten cost of stowage.
Versteck hiding [place], hide, hide-out *(coll.)*, place of hiding, covert, nook, subterfuge, stash, lurk, lurking (hoarding) place, nest, cache, den, mike, hideout *(US)*;
~ **mit jem. spielen** to play hide-and-seek with s. o.; **sein ~ verlassen** to come out of hiding.
Verstecken|vor den Gläubigern keeping house; ~ **von Verbrechern** harbo(u)ring of criminals.
verstecken to hide, to conceal, to stash, to keep shady *(sl.)*;
sich ~ to take to earth; **Geld unter der Matratze ~** to tuck the money away under the mattress; **sich hinter einem falschen Namen ~** to masquerade under a false name;
neben ihm mußt Du Dich ~ you are no match for him.
Versteckspiel hide-and-seek.
versteckt under cover, covered, hidden;
sich ~ halten to stay in concealment;
~**er Mangel** hidden (latent) defect; ~**e Offerte** hidden offer; ~**e Reserven** secret (hidden) reserves, cache; ~**e Vorräte** hidden supplies, cache.
verstehen to understand, to comprehend, to grasp, to catch, to conceive;
sich auf etw. ~ to know what's what, to be at home in s. th., to be a judge (connoisseur) of s. th.; **sich auf alles ~** to be up to anything; **etw. aus dem Effeff ~** to know one's stuff (onions), to be death on s. th. *(sl.)*; **Englisch ~** to know English; **kein Englisch ~** to have no knowledge of English; **falsch ~** to misunderstand; **sein Geschäft ~** to know one's onions (oil, oats); **etw. glänzend ~** to be a good hand at (have the knack of) it; **sich glänzend mit jem. ~** to get on well (be hand in glove, hit if off) with s. o.; **sein Handwerk ~** to know the ropes; **sich am Rande ~** to go without saying; **von einer Sache etw. ~** to be at home with (a dab at) s. th.; **sich nur schwer zu etw. ~** to agree with great reluctance;
zu ~ geben to intimate, to make s. o. understand, to put across the message.
verstehender Blick knowing look.
versteifen to strengthen, to stiffen, *(stützen)* to prop, to strut, to brace;
sich ~ *(Geldmarkt, Kurse)* to stiffen, to harden, to tighten, *(pol.)* to toughen, to stiffen; **sich darauf ~ Sprachen zu studieren** to be set on studying languages.
Versteifung *(Börse)* hardening, stiffening, *(pol.)* toughening, stiffening;
~ **des Geldmarktes** tightening of money conditions (market), pressure on the money market, stiffening of prices; ~ **der politischen Haltung** stiffening of the political attitude; ~ **der Kurse** firming up of (stiffening) prices; ~ **der Markttendenz** hardening of the market tendency;
~ **erfahren** to stiffen, to harden, to tighten.
Versteigerer, öffentlicher auctioneer, common crier.
Versteigern auctioneering.
versteigern, [öffentlich] to sell (put up) at *(US)* (by, *Br.*) auction, to sell by public sale (publicly, at the spear), to bring under the hammer, to auction [off];
gerichtlich ~ to sell by order of the court; **meistbietend ~** to knock down to the highest bidder;
~ **lassen** to put up at *(US)* (by, *Br.*) auction.
versteigert sold by auction, under the hammer;
~ **werden** to come under the hammer.
Versteigerung auction [sale], auctioneering, selling by auction, vendue *(US)*;
zur ~ anstehend on the block;
aufgeschobene ~ adjourned sale; **beschränkte ~** reserved bidding; **ordnungsgemäß durchgeführte ~** fair sale; **gerichtliche ~** sale under a court order, judicial sale *(Scot., US)*; **öffentliche ~** public auction, open (public) sale, subhastation;
~ **mit verstärktem Mindestgebot** dump bidding; ~ **bei Zuschlag unter Taxpreis (mit laufend erniedrigtem Anbietungspreis)** Dutch auction;
zur ~ anstehen to be up for auction (on the auction block); **zur ~ bringen** to put up at *(US)* (by, *Br.*) auction, to submit to public sale; ~ **fortsetzen** to open bids; **in die ~ geben** to auction off, to sell at *(US)* (by, *Br.*) auction; **auf einer ~ kaufen** to buy at auction; **zur ~ kommen** to be sold at *(US)* (by, *Br.*) auction; **zur ~ gebracht werden** to be put on the auction block.
Versteigerungs|ankündigung notice of sale by auction, auction notice (sign); ~**antrag** application for public auction; ~**bedingungen** terms of auction, auction terms; ~**erlös** proceeds of an auction, avails of a sale by auction *(US)*; **an Kapitän und Mannschaft verteilter ~erlös** lay system; ~**firma** auction company; ~**gebühren,** ~**kosten** lot money, auction fees (charges); ~**geschäft beleben** to spur auction activity; ~**limit** reserve price; ~**liste** auction bill, catalog(ue) of sale; ~**lokal,** ~**saal** auction mart (room), saleroom; ~**preis** auction price; ~**termin** auction day; ~**zeit** time of auction.
verstellbar adjustable.
verstellen to block, to bar, *(falsch stellen)* to misplace, *(techn.)* to adjust, to shift, to regulate, *(unkenntlich machen)* to disguise, to dissemble;
sich ~ to hide one's feelings, *(Krankheit vortäuschen)* to malinger; **Eingang mit Stühlen ~** to block the entrance with chairs; **seine Handschrift ~** to disguise one's handwriting.
verstellt obstructed, blocked;
~**e Stimme** disguised voice.
Verstellung disguise, dissimulation, masquerade, *(Liegestuhl)* adjustment.
Verstellvorrichtung adjusting device.
verstempeln to stamp;
Urkunde ~ to stamp a document.
verstempelt stamped;
nicht ~ unstamped; **ungenügend ~** insufficiently stamped.
Verstempelung stamping;
der ~ unterliegen to be subject to stamp duty *(Br.)* (tax, *US*).
Versteppung desertification.
versterben to pass away, to die;
schon früh ~ to come to an untimely end; **gleichzeitig ~** to die simultaneously.
versteuerbar taxable, dutiable;
als normales Einkommen ~ sein to be taxable as ordinary income.
versteuern to pay duty (taxes) on;
im Ausland erzielte Einkünfte ~ to pay taxes on income earned abroad; **als Einkommen ~** to report as income; **Geld ~** to declare money to the tax authorities; **normal ~** to pay tax at the basic rate; **mit einem höheren Satz ~** to tax at a higher rate; **normal zu ~ sein** to be taxable as ordinary income.
versteuernd, zu ~e Einkünfte taxable income.
versteuert duty (tax) -paid;
~**er Gewinn** profit after tax.
Versteuerung payment of taxes;
~ **nach England überwiesener Beträge** remittance basis *(Br.)*.
verstiegen high-flown, eccentric, extravagant.

verstimmen to disaffect, to put in bad humo(u)r, to disgruntle;
Börse ~ to depress the market.
verstimmt annoyed, out of sorts, *(Magen)* upset;
~**e Börse** depressed market.
Verstimmung resentment, indisposition, annoyance, disgruntlement, ill feeling, *(pol.)* shadow;
~ **der Börse** temporary reaction of prices;
leichte ~ **aufweisen** *(Börse)* to suffer a slight reaction; **seine** ~ **loswerden** to unload one's resentment.
verstockt obstinate, tough.
verstohlen furtive, stealthy, surreptitious, underhand, clandestine.
verstopfen *(Kanal)* to block, to clog, *(Ritze)* to fill up, *(Straße)* to block, to jam, to obstruct.
verstopft *(Ausgang)* obstructed, *(Kanal)* blocked, clogged, choked, *(Verkehr)* traffic-congested, obstructed, jammed;
abends am meisten ~ **sein** to become congested towards evening.
Verstopfung congestion, lock, traffic jam, blocking;
~ **der Luftwege** air congestion.
verstorben deceased, defunct, dead, late;
ohne letztwillige Verfügung ~ intestate;
~**er Teilhaber** deceased partner.
Verstorbener deceased person, departed, decedent *(US)*.
verstört haggard, stricken;
völlig ~ like a duck in a thunderstorm *(coll.)*.
Verstoß offence, infraction, breach, infringement, contravention, slip, violation;
gesellschaftlicher ~ social breach;
~ **gegen die Bebauungsvorschriften** contravention of building restrictions; ~ **gegen die Bestimmungen der Bankaufsichtsbehörde** violation of banking regulations; ~ **gegen die Betriebsordnung** shop infraction; ~ **gegen die Devisenbestimmungen** currency offence; ~ **gegen die Etikette** breach of etiquette; ~ **gegen die Geschäftsordnung** breach of order; ~ **gegen das Gesetz** contravention (infraction, breach) of the law; ~ **gegen die öffentliche Ordnung** political offence; ~ **gegen die Parkbestimmungen** parking violation *(US)*; ~ **gegen die Privilegien einer Körperschaft** breach of privilege; ~ **gegen die Regeln** breach of the rules; ~ **gegen die Satzungen** infringement of the statutes; ~ **gegen die guten Sitten** acting contrary to good morals; ~ **gegen die Sittlichkeit** public act of indecency; ~ **gegen die Standesregeln** breach of professional etiquette; ~ **gegen die getroffenen Vereinbarungen** violation of the covenant; ~ **gegen die Verkehrsvorschriften** moving *(Br.)* (traffic, *US*) violation; ~ **gegen einen Vertrag** breach of a contract; ~ **gegen die Zollbestimmungen** fiscal offence.
verstoßen to offend against, to violate, to infringe, to infract, to contravene, to transgress, *(Ehefrau)* to repudiate, to dismiss, *(verbannen)* to cast out, to expel;
seine Frau ~ to repudiate one's wife; **gegen den guten Geschmack** ~ to commit an offence against good taste; **gegen ein Gesetz** ~ to infract a law, to act in contravention of a law; **gegen die Gesetze der Höflichkeit** ~ to offend against the laws of courtesy; **gegen ungeschriebene Gesetze** ~ to transgress the bounds of decency; **Kind** ~ to disown a child; **gegen die Moralgesetze** ~ to offend morals; **gegen eine Regel** ~ to infringe a rule; **gegen die guten Sitten** ~ to act contrary to (offend) good morals (public policy); **gegen die Tradition** ~ to offend tradition; **gegen einen Vertrag** ~ to act in violation of a treaty.
Verstoßung *(Ehefrau)* dismissal, repudiation;
~ **eines Kindes** disownment of a child.
Verstreichen *(Frist)* expiration, expiry, *(Zeit)* lapse of time.
verstreichen *(Frist)* to expire, *(Zeit)* to lapse [away], to run, to go on, to pass;
Butter ~ to spread butter; **Fugen** ~ to fill the joints;
Frist ~ **lassen** to let the appointed time pass.
verstreuen, Papier auf dem Fußboden to scatter the floor with paper.
verstreut scattered, dotted about;
überall ~ all over the place;
~ **liegende Häuser** scattered houses.
verstrichen lapsed, expired.
verstricken to ensnare, to entangle, to intertwine, to ensnarl.
verstrickt, in ein Komplott ensnarled in a complot (conspiracy);
in ein Intrigenspiel ~ **sein** to be wrapped up in an intrigue; **in den Schlingen des Gesetzes** ~ **sein** to be caught in the meshes of the law.
Verstrickung entanglement, involvement.
Verstrickungsbruch *(Pfand)* breach of pound, rescue of goods distrained.
verstümmeln to mutilate, to dismember, to maim, *(Telegramm)* to mutilate;
Text ~ to garble a text.
verstümmeltes Telegramm mutilated telegram.
Verstümmelung mutilation, dismemberment, *(Funkspruch, Text)* garble.
Versuch trial, attempt, try, fling, stab *(sl.)*, *(Experiment)* experiment, *(Prüfung)* test, tryout *(US)*, *(Strafrecht)* attempt;
ehrenwerter ~ creditable attempt; **ernsthafter** ~ serious attempt; **fruchtloser** ~ ineffectual attempt; **gutgemeinter** ~ pious effort; **kümmerlicher** ~ little go *(sl.)*; **kurzfristiger** ~ short-term test; **nutzloser** ~ vain attempt; **schüchterner** ~ mild attempt; **stümperhafter** ~ humble attempt; **gemeinsam unternommener** ~ conjunct attempt; **vergeblicher** ~ futile attempt;
~ **einer strafbaren Handlung** attempted crime, criminal attempt, attempt to accomplish a crime; ~ **am lebenden Objekt** human experiment; ~ **am untauglichen Objekt** ill-judged attempt;
~ **anstellen** to make (try) experiments, to experiment; **weitere** ~**e mit einer Maschine anstellen** to put a machine to further trials; ~ **durchführen** to conduct a test, to experimentalize; **Tatbestand des** ~**s erfüllen** to constitute an act of attempt; ~ **machen** to to make an attempt (a shot at it); ~ **mit etw. machen** to have a try at s. th.; ~ **riskieren** to have a smack at s. th.; ~ **unternehmen** to make a trial, to have a crack; **weiteren** ~ **unternehmen** to have another go; ~ **zur Lösung eines Problems unternehmen** to attempt to solve a problem; **vom** ~ **zurücktreten** *(Strafrecht)* to abandon an attempt.
versuchen to attempt, to try, to test, to experiment;
etw. noch einmal ~ to have another go at s. th.; **alles Erdenkliche** ~ to make every endeavour; **es mit Güte und Strenge** ~ to try both leniency and severity; **mit allen Mitteln** ~ to try hard; **sich eine Stunde an der Reparatur des Rundfunkgerätes** ~ to have an hour's tinker at the radio set;
~, **mit etw. fertig zu werden** to put s. th. into one's pipe and smoke it *(coll.)*.
Versuchs|abteilung experimental (research) department; ~**anlage** research (pilot) plant, test facility; ~**anordnung** *(Statistik)* design; ~**anstalt** research (experimental) institute; ~**anstalt zur Erforschung von Feuerursachen** fire testing station *(Br.)*; ~**auftrag** trial order; ~**aufwand** experimental expense, research expenditure; ~**ballon** trial (sounding) balloon, feeler; ~**ballon steigen lassen** to fly a test balloon, to put (throw) out a feeler; **auf** ~**basis** on a pilot scale; ~**bedingungen** test conditions; ~**bericht** research report; ~**betrieb** pilot plant; ~**bohrungen** exploratory drilling; **spekulative** ~**bohrung** wildcat; ~**ergebnisse** research material, test results; ~**fabrik** research (pilot) plant; ~**fahrt** *(Auto)* trial run, *(Schiff)* trial trip; ~**fall** *(Prozeß)* test case; ~**farm** experimental farm; ~**fehler** experimental error; ~**feld** proving ground; ~**feld für Werbezwecke** test campaign; ~**feldzug** test (tryout, *US*) campaign; ~**flieger** test pilot; ~**flug** trial flight; ~**gebiet** testing area; ~**gelände** trial ground, proving ground, test site; ~**gruppe** experimental (research) group; ~**gut** experimental (pilot) farm; ~**handlung** *(Strafrecht)* attempt; ~**ingenieur** research engineer; ~**jahr** experimental year; ~**kampagne** test (tryout, *US*) campaign; ~**kaninchen** guinea pig *(Br.)*; ~**laboratorium** research laboratory; ~**markt** *(Werbung)* test market; ~**modell** working (experimental) model; ~**muster** experimental type; ~**objekt** test object; **betrieblicher** ~**plan** factorial design; ~**produktion** pilot production; ~**programm** pilot program(me); ~**projekt** pilot scheme (project); ~**prozeß** test case; ~**serie** pilot (test) series (lot); ~**stadium** experimental stage; **noch in einem** ~**stadium sein** to be in a tentative stage; ~**station** research plant, experimental station *(US)*; ~**straße** experimental road; ~**strecke** test track, pilot length; ~**tank** model tank; ~**tier** laboratory animal; ~**wagen** test car.
versuchsweise as an experiment, by way of trial, on approval (trial).
Versuchs|werbung advertising test; ~**zeit** testing period; ~**zweck** experimental purpose.
versuchter Mord attempted murder, assassination attempt.
Versuchung trial;
gegen ~ **nicht gefeit** open to temptation; **in der Stunde der** ~ in one's hour of trial;
~**en leichten Verdienstes** temptation of easy profit;
seinen ~**en erliegen** to fall a prey (yield) to temptations; **j. in** ~ **führen** to lead s. o. into temptation; **der** ~ **widerstehen** to withstand temptation.
versumpft sein to be caught up in a drinking bout.

versunken sunken, foundered, *(fig.)* immersed, engrossed, absorbed;
ganz in seine Arbeit ~ sein to be completely absorbed by (wrapped up in) one's work; **in seinem Buch ganz ~ sein** to be deep in one's book.

versüßen, sich das Leben to sweeten one's life.

vertagen *(aufschieben)* to delay, to defer, to adjourn *(US)*, to put off, to prorogate, to [lay on the] table *(US)*, *(Sitzung)* to adjourn, to postpone, to continue *(US)*;
sich ~ to prorogue, to recess, to stand over (adjourned), *(Gericht)* to rise; **Beratung einer Angelegenheit ~** to postpone consideration of a subject; **erneut ~** to readjourn; **sich in den großen Ferien ~** to wind up for the summer holidays, to adjourn over the holidays; **Hauptversammlung ~** to adjourn a general meeting; **Parlament ~** to prorogue (count out, *Br.*) the house; **Verhandlung ~** to adjourn a hearing; **Verhandlung für eine Woche ~** to put off a case for a week; **sich auf unbestimmte Zeit ~** to adjourn (recess) sine die.

vertagt adjourned, deferred, *(Parlament)* up;
~ werden to go over, to be adjourned;
~e Verhandlung postponed case.

Vertagung adjournment, deferment, deferral, continuance *(US)*, *(Gerichtsentscheidung)* rising, ampliation, *(parl.)* count out *(Br.)*, *(bis zur nächsten Sitzungsperiode)* prorogation, *(auf unbestimmte Zeit)* postponement;
dreitägige ~ adjournment of three days; **erneute ~** readjournment; **fehlerhafte ~** miscontinuance;
~ der Berufungsverhandlung respite of appeal; **~ einer Entscheidung** postponement of a decision, ampliation; **~ auf die nächste Legislaturperiode** prorogation; **~ einer Sache** *(Gericht)* rising of court, *(Strafsache)* discontinuance of proceedings, postponement of a trial; **~ einer Verhandlung** adjournment of a hearing; **~ zur Vorbereitung der mündlichen Verhandlung** general imparlance; **~ auf unbestimmte Zeit** *(Gericht)* adjournment sine die;
~ beantragen to move that the meeting be adjourned; **~ der Debatte beantragen** to move that the debate be adjourned; **~ einer Sitzung beschließen** to vote the adjournment of a meeting; **um ~ bitten** to move that a case may be adjourned; **Gesetzesantrag durch ~ zunichte machen** to count out the house *(Br.)*.

Vertagungs|anspruch right to adjourn; **~antrag** motion for adjournment (to adjourn), adjournment motion; **~antrag stellen** to move that the case be adjourned; **~beschluß** resolution for adjournment; **~frage** question of adjournment; **~liste** imparlance roll; **~recht** right to adjourn; **äußerster ~termin** adjournment deadline *(US)*.

vertäuen, Schiff to moor (make fast) a ship.

vertauschbar exchangeable, commutable.

Vertauschbarkeit exchangeability.

vertauschen to exchange, to barter, *(verwechseln)* to mix up, to confuse;
Plätze ~ to change places; **Räder untereinander ~** to change the wheels.

vertauscht taken by mistake;
mit ~en Rollen with reversed roles.

Vertäuung, Boot von der ~ lösen to untie a boat from the mooring.

verteidigen to defend, to vindicate, *(rechtfertigen)* to justify;
j. ~ to plead s. one's cause, to conduct the defence (defense, *US*) of s. o., to hold a brief for s. o. *(coll.)*; **sich ~** to defend one's life; **sich geschickt ~** to put up a clever defence *(Br.)* (defense, *US*); **sein Land ~** to fight in defence *(Br.)* (defense, *US*) of one's country; **seine Meinung ~** to uphold one's opinion; **Sache vor Gericht ~** to plead a case; **sich selbst ~** *(vor Gericht)* to answer, to defend, to plead one's cause, to conduct one's own defence *(Br.)* (defense, *US*); **jeden Zentimeter des Bodens ~** to contest every inch of ground.

Verteidiger *(Fürsprecher)* advocate, pleader, *(Recht)* defender, vindicator, *(Strafprozeß)* trial lawyer, lawyer (counsel) for the defense *(US)* (defence, *Br.*), pleader, *(Zivilprozeß)* attorney for the defendant (defense, *US*);
als ~ auftreten to defend s. o.; **~ bestellen** to designate a counsel for the defence *(Br.)* (defense, *US*); **gute ~ haben** *(Angeklagte)* to have able counsel.

verteidigt werden, von einem Anwalt to be defended by counsel.

Verteidigung defence *(Br.)*, defense *(US)*, vindication, *(mil.)* defensive, *(Strafgericht)* defense *(US)*, defence *(Br.)*, advocacy;
~ durch einen Anwalt defence *(Br.)* (defense, *US*) by counsel; **~ der vordersten Linien** forward strategy; **erfolgreiche ~ einer eroberten Stellung** holding of a captured position;
~ ablehnen to hold no brief for *(coll.)*; **zu seiner ~ anführen** to plead in one's defence *(Br.)* (defense, *US*); **j. in die ~ drängen** to force s. o. into a defensive position; **zur ~ seines Landes kämpfen** to fight in defence *(Br.)* (defense, *US*) of one's country; **~ niederlegen** to abandon the defence *(Br.)* (defense, *US*); **~ übernehmen** to assume the defence *(Br.)* (defense, *US*); **etw. zu seiner ~ vorbringen** to state s. th. in one's defence *(Br.)* (defense, *US*); **gute ~ vorbringen** to set up a good defence *(Br.)* (defense, *US*); **seine ~ vortragen** to state one's case.

Verteidigungs|abkommen mutual defence *(Br.)* (defense, *US*) agreement; **~abschnitt** *(mil.)* defensive sector; **~anlagen** defences; **~anleihe** defence *(Br.)* (defense, *US*) loan; **kostenlos übernommener ~auftrag** dock brief *(Br.)*; **insgesamt abgeschlossene ~aufträge** *(mil.)* overall negotiated defence *(Br.)* (defense, *US*) work; **~ausgaben** defence *(Br.)* (defense, *US*) spending (expenditure); **sich an einer ~ausschreibung beteiligen** to bid on defence *(Br.)* (defense, *US*) contracts; **~ausschuß** defence *(Br.)* (defense, *US*) committee; **~behörde** defence *(Br.)* (defense, *US*) agency; **~beitrag** defence *(Br.)* (defense, *US*) contribution; **~bereitschaft** preparedness for war; **~block zusammenbringen** to align nations against war; **~bündnis** defensive alliance, defence *(Br.)* (defense, *US*) pact; **~einwand** incidental plea of defence *(Br.)* (defense, *US*); **~etat** defence *(Br.)* (defense, *US*) (military) budget; **im ~fall** in case of war; **~folgekosten** defence- *(Br.)* (defense-, *US*) induced costs; **~forschung** defence *(Br.)* (defense, *US*) research; **~fragen** defence *(Br.)* (defense, *US*) matters; **~gebiet** defence *(Br.)* (defense, *US*) area; **~gürtel** defence *(Br.)* (defense, *US*) position; **~haushalt** military household; **~konzeption** defence *(Br.)* (defense, *US*) concept; **~kosten** defence *(Br.)* (defense, *US*) costs; **~krieg** defensive (defence, *Br.*, defense, *US*) war; **~line** line of defence *(Br.)* (defense, *US*); **letzte ~linie** last ditch defence *(Br.)* (defense, *US*); **zweite ~linie** *(Verrechnungsbanken)* second line of defence *(Br.)* (defense, *US*); **~maßnahmen** defensive measures; **~minister** Minister of Defence *(Br.)*, Defence Minister *(Br.)*, Secretary of State for Defense *(US)*, minister of state for defence *(Br.)* (defense, *US*); **~ministerium** Ministry of Defence *(Br.)*, Department of Defense *(US)*, Defense Department *(US)*, Department of National Defence *(Canada)*; **neue ~mittel vorbringen** to amend the defence *(Br.)* (defense, *US*); **~pakt** defence *(Br.)* (defense, *US*) treaty, defensive alliance; **~plädoyer** defence *(Br.)* (defense, *US*) speech; **~politik** defence *(Br.)* (defense, *US*) policy; **~rat** Defence Council *(Br.)*, Council of National Defense *(US)*; **~rede** apology; **~schrift** statement of defence *(Br.)* (defense, *US*), answering paper, defence; **~stellung** *(mil.)* defensive position (site); **~stellung beziehen** to stand on the defensive; **~system** retrenchment; **~taktik** defensive tactics; **~vorbringen** defensive allegation, defendant's answer, defence *(Br.)*, defense *(US)*; **~waffe** weapon of defence *(Br.)* (defense, *US*); **~werte** *(Börse)* defensive issues; **~zone** defensive zone, zone of defence *(Br.)* (defense, *US*); **~zustand** state of defence *(Br.)* (defense, *US*); **~zwecke** defence *(Br.)* (defense, *US*) purposes.

verteilbar distributable;
~er Gewinn available profit; **~e Quote** *(Konkurs)* liquidation dividend.

Verteilen division, dealing out, distribution.

verteilen to distribute, to dispense, to issue, to divide, to outportion, to give (deal) out, to partition, *(Aufgaben)* to assign, *(unter sich aufteilen)* to share, *(gleichmäßig)* to allot, to portion, to apportion, to allocate, *(Nachlaß, Konkursmasse)* to settle up, to appropriate;
Abzahlungsraten über mehrere Monate ~ to spread instal(l)ments over several months; **Anschaffungskosten eines Wirtschaftsgutes auf die Nutzungsdauer ~** to spread the costs of an asset over its useful life; **anteilig ~** to distribute pro rata; **Betrag auf verschiedene Leute gleichmäßig ~** to allocate (apportion) a sum amongst several people; **Dividende ~** to declare a dividend; **größere Dividende ~** to cut a melon *(US)*; **zusätzliche Dividende ~** to distribute an additional (supplementary) dividend; **Einkommen steuerlich auf mehrere Jahre ~** to spread out income over several years; **Erlös ~** to distribute the proceeds; **Geld gleichmäßig ~** to divide money equally; **Gerichtskosten anteilmäßig auf die Parteien ~** to apportion the costs to the sides; **Gewinne ~** to divide the profits; **Konkursmasse ~** to marshal the assets; **Kontingente ~** to allocate the shares in a quota; **Kosten ~** to allocate (apportion) costs; **Material ~** to give out material; **auf den ganzen Monat ~** to spread throughout the month; **Nachlaß ~** to distribute an estate; **neu ~** to redistribute, to re-allocate; **Risiko ~** to spread a risk; **steuerlich über das ganze Jahr ~** to spread over the entire

taxable year; **Steuerverlust über fünf Jahre** ~ to spread the impact of a tax loss over five years; **seine Stimme auf mehrere Kandidaten** ~ to split one's vote; **Unkosten über drei Jahre** ~ to amortize costs over a period of three years; **Verkäufe über eine Hausseperiode** ~ *(Börse)* to sell on a scale; **Verluste gleichmäßig** ~ to apportion losses evenly; **sein Vermögen unter seine Erben** ~ to divide one's property amongst one's heirs; **Zahlungen steuerlich über das ganze Jahr** ~ to spread payments over the entire taxable year.

Verteiler distributor, *(Gewerbe)* retail trade, dealer, *(Liste)* distribution list, *(Motor)* distributor, *(Straße)* distributory road; **~anlage** *(el.)* distributing mains; **~dose** *(el.)* distributing (junction) box; **großräumiges ~gebiet** large-scale distribution operation; **~gewerbe** business of distribution, distributive (distributing) trade; **~kartell** distribution cartel; **~kasten** *(el.)* distribution box; **~klemme** terminal; **~kopf** distributor head; **~liste** distribution (mailing, *US*) list; **~netz** distribution network; **~organisation** distributing organization; **~postamt** post-distributing (-separating, -sorting) office.

Verteilerschlüssel key of distribution, distribution key;
fester ~ specified formula; **über den Daumen gepeilter** ~ rule-of-thumb ratio;
~ **von Verkaufs- zu Mietabschlüssen öffentlich bekanntmachen** to break out its sales-to-rental ratio for public display.

Verteiler | staat distributive state; **~stelle** distributor, marketing board, *(Post)* distributing office; **~straße** distributory road; **~welle** *(Auto)* distributor shaft; **~wirtschaft** economics of distribution; **~zentrale** distribution center *(US)* (centre, *Br.*).

verteilt divided, allotted, apportioned;
nicht ~ unallotted, undivided.

Verteilung distribution, division, dispensation, share-out, *(Anordnung)* disposition, arrangement, *(Aufgaben)* assignment, *(el.)* distribution, *(mil.)* issuance *(US)*, issue, *(Streuung)* dispersal, *(Zuteilung)* allotment, allocation, partition, array, apportionment;
anteilsmäßige ~ pro-rata (proportional) distribution; **gerechte** ~ equitable (fair) distribution; **prozentuale** ~ percentage distribution; **schlechte (mangelhafte)** ~ maldistribution; **ungleichmäßige** ~ uneven distribution; **verhältnismäßige** ~ repartition;
~ **von Arbeitskräften** allocation of manpower; ~ **der Bevölkerung** distribution of population; ~ **einer Dividende** distribution (declaration) of dividend; ~ **des Einkommens** income distribution; ~ **der Geschäftsunkosten** overhead allocation; ~ **des Gesellschaftergewinns** distribution of partnership profit and loss; ~ **durch den Handel** physical distribution; ~ **durch einen ausgewählten Händlerkreis** selective distribution; **höchstzulässige** ~ **auf mehrere Jahre** *(Einkommensteuer)* maximum time apportionment; ~ **der Konkursmasse** distribution of assets (of a bankrupt), division of a bankrupt's estate; ~ **von Kontingenten** allocation of quotas; ~ **der Kosten** distribution (allocation) of expenses, apportionment (allocation) of costs, cost allocation; ~ **eines Nachlasses** distribution of a deceased's estate, distribution and partition *(US)*; ~ **von Nahrungsmitteln** dispensation of food; ~ **des Reingewinns** distribution of the net gain; ~ **des Risikos** spread of risk; ~ **der Steuerbelastung** incidence of taxation; ~ **einer Superdividende** cutting a melon *(US)*; ~ **von Truppenquartieren** quartering of troops; ~ **der Unkosten** allocation of expenses; ~ **des Volkseinkommens** distribution of wealth;
zur ~ **bringen** to distribute.

Verteilungs | amt *(Post)* post-distributing (-separating, -sorting) office; **~anordnung** *(Nachlaßgericht)* administrative order; **~anpassung** distributional adjustment; **~ansatz der Volkseinkommensberechnung** earnings-and-cost approach; **~apparat** *(Firma)* distributive facilities, *(Handel)* distribution network, distributive machinery; **örtlicher ~beschluß** *(Nachlaßgericht)* decree of locality *(Scot.)*; **~bogen** spread sheet; **~ und Abgangsfach** *(Post)* compartment for dispatch.

verteilungsfähig distributable.

Verteilungs | funktion allocative function; **~kampf** struggle for redistribution; **~kartell** distributing syndicate *(US)*; **~kosten** cost of distribution; **~methode** distribution method; **~netz** distribution network; **~plan** plan of distribution, *(Nachlaß)* scheme *(Br.)*; **~plan aufstellen** *(Konkursverwalter)* to marshal the assets; **~prozeß** process of distribution; **~quote** *(Konkurs)* liquidation dividend; **~schlüssel** distribution ratio (coefficient), key of distribution, basis of allocation; **über den Daumen gepeilter ~schlüssel** rule-of-thumb ratio; **~spielraum** scope for redistribution; **~stelle** marketing board, distribution agency, distributor; **~system** distribution (distributive, communication) system; **~termin** date of distribution; **festes ~verhältnis** fixed ratio.

verteuern to raise (increase, enhance) prices;
sich ~ to get dearer, to become more expensive.

Verteuerung advance (increase) in prices, price increase;
~ **der Lebenshaltungskosten** cost-of-living increase.

verteufeln to disparage.

verteufelt plaguy *(coll.)*;
~e Geschichte nasty business, go; **~es Glück** damned luck *(coll.)*; **~er Kerl** devil of a fellow.

vertiefen to deepen;
sich in etw. ~ to become engrossed in s. th.; **seine beruflichen Erfahrungen** ~ to add depth to one's career experiences; **sich in Gedanken** ~ to bury o. s. in one's thoughts; **sich in ein Gespräch** ~ to immerse o. s. in a conversation; **Kluft zwischen Armen und Reichen** ~ to widen the gulf between the rich and the poor; **sich in ein Thema** ~ to dive into a subject.

vertieft deepened, absorbed, engrossed, preoccupied, immersed;
in seine Arbeit ~ wrapped up in one's work; **in seine Lektüre** ~ absorbed in one's reading;
in etw. ~ **sein** to be engrossed (immersed) in s. th.; **in einen Brief** ~ **sein** to pore over a letter.

Vertieftsein immersion, engrossment.

Vertiefung depression, dip, trough, *(Nische)* recess, alcove.

vertikal vertical;
~e Preisbindung vertical price-fixing contract, fair trade (trading) *(US)*; **~er Zusammenschluß** vertical amalgamation (integration, combination, combine, merger).

Vertikal | aufstieg *(Rakete)* vertical ascent; **~konzern** vertical combination; **~struktur** vertical structure; **~trust** vertical trust.

vertilgen to annihilate, to exterminate, to extirpate;
Mahlzeit mit vier Gängen ~ to tuck into a four-course meal.

Vertilgungsmittel vermin killer, insecticide.

vertonen to set to music.

Vertonung musical setting;
~ **eines Films** sound recording.

Vertrackte, das ~ **an der Sache** the devil of it.

vertrackte Geschichte tricky situation.

Vertrag contract, covenant, *(Geschäftsabschluß)* transaction, *(Staatsvertrag)* treaty, pact, *(Übereinkommen)* convention, *(Urkunde)* deed, instrument, document, indenture, indent, *(Vereinbarung)* agreement, composition, compact, article;
auf ~ **gegründet** contractual; **aufgrund eines ~es** under an agreement (indenture); **bei Wirksamwerden des ~es** when the contract is effected; **durch** ~ **gebunden** bound by contract; **kraft ~es** by virtue of a treaty; **laut** ~ as by agreement, according to (as may be required by) contract; **vorbehaltlich eines noch abzuschließenden ~es** subject to formal contract; **während der Dauer des ~es** during the life of a contract;
abgeänderter ~ modified (amended) contract; **zugunsten der Gläubiger abgeschlossener** ~ deed for the benefit of creditors; **konkludent abgeschlossener** ~ implied contract; **zwischen Sonderorganisationen der UNO abgeschlossener** ~ interagency agreement; **abhängiger** ~ dependent contract; **akzessorischer** ~ accessory contract; **aleatorischer** ~ aleatory contract; **anfechtbarer** ~ voidable (impeachable) contract; **angemessener** ~ fair and reasonable contract; **annullierter** ~ cancelled (rescinded) contract; **atypischer** ~ innominate contract; **mit Preisgleitklausel ausgestatteter** ~ cost-of-living escalator contract; **Prozeßweg nicht ausschließender** ~ procedural contract; **bedingter** ~ executory agreement (contract), conditional contract; **befristeter** ~ temporary (conditional, terminable) contract; **einseitig begünstigender** ~ contract of benevolence; **bestehender** ~ existing contract; **beurkundeter** ~ specialty, special contract, contract under seal, instrument in writing; **bindender** ~ binding agreement; **einseitig bindender** ~ unilateral contract; **völkerrechtlich bindender** ~ binding treaty; **gültig bleibender** ~ contract that can be upheld; **deklaratorischer** ~ declaratory covenant; **als Grundlage dienender** ~ underlying contract; **dinglicher** ~ real contract (agreement, covenant); **dreijähriger** ~ 3-year contract; **einfacher (formloser)** ~ simple contract, contract (agreement) under hand *(Br.)*; **einklagbarer** ~ contract enforceable at law, legally enforceable contract; **nicht einklagbarer** ~ unenforceable contract; **einseitiger (einseitig bindender)** ~ unilateral (nude, one-sided, gratuitous) contract, contract of benevolence, deed poll; **endgültiger** ~ final contract; **entgeltlicher** ~ onerous contract; **beiderseits erfüllter** ~ executed covenant (agreement, contract); **noch nicht erfüllter** ~ executory (unfulfilled, open)

contract; **ordnungsgemäß errichteter** ~ contract drawn up in due form; **fairer** ~ *(Minderjähriger)* fair and reasonable contract; **fehlerhafter** ~ invalid (defective) contract; **fester** ~ standing contract; **fingierter** ~ fictitious (sham) contract (dealing); **formbedürftiger** ~ specialty (formal) contract, specialty [deed]; **formfreier** ~ parole agreement, simple (unsealed, informal) contract, agreement (contract) under hand *(Br.)*; **formgebundener** ~ specialty [contract]; **förmlicher** ~ solemn agreement, contract by deed, sealed instrument; **formloser** ~ agreement under hand, parole agreement; **gegenseitiger** ~ mutual (reciprocal) contract, *(zweiseitiger)* synallagmatic contract; **gemeinschaftlicher** ~ joint contract; **gemischter** ~ mixed contract (treaty); **ausdrücklich geschlossener** ~ express contract (covenant); **stillschweigend geschlossener** ~ implied contract (covenant), tacit agreement; **lästig gewordener** ~ burdensome contract; **objektiv unmöglich gewordener** ~ frustrated contract; **gültiger** ~ valid contract; **horizontaler** ~ horizontal contract; **individueller (höchstpersönlicher)** ~ personal contract; **internationaler** ~ international agreement; **interner** ~ private agreement; **kaufähnlicher** ~ quasi contract; **kündbarer** ~ [de]terminable contract; **langfristiger** ~ long-term contract; **lästiger** ~ burdensome contract; **laufender** ~ continuing (standing, running) contract; **leonischer** ~ leonine contract; **mehrseitiger** ~ multilateral agreement; **mündlicher** ~ verbal contract (agreement), parole agreement, oral contract; **neuer** ~ fresh (substituted) contract; **nichtiger** ~ void contract; **normativer** ~ lawmaking contract, *(Völkerrecht)* law (legislative) treaty; **notarieller** ~ sealed (specialty) contract, notarial deed, contract under seal; **obligatorischer** ~ consensual contract; **öffentlich-rechtlicher** ~ contract under public law; **ordnungsgemäßer** ~ binding contract; **paraphierter** ~ initialled contract; **rechtsgeschäftlicher** ~ *(Völkerrecht)* ordinary (contractual) treaty; **rechtsgültiger** ~ valid contract; **rechtsverbindlicher** ~ legally binding contract; **amtlich registrierter** ~ contract of record; **schlichter** ~ bare contract; **schriftlicher** ~ written (literal) contract, contract in writing (under hand, *Br.*), covenant; **schuldrechtlicher** ~ personal (obligatory) covenant; **schwebender** ~ executory contract (covenant); **seerechtlicher** ~ marine contract; **selbständiger** ~ independent contract; **sittenwidriger** ~ contract tainted with immorality, immoral contract; **stillschweigender** ~ implied contract; **synallagmatischer** ~ synallagmatic (mutual) contract, deed indented; **teilbarer** ~ divisible contract; **unbefristeter** ~ contract for an unlimited period; **unentgeltlicher** ~ gratuitous (naked, nude) contract (deed); **unerlaubter** ~ illegal contract; **ungeteilter** ~ entire contract; **ungewisser** ~ hazardous contract; **ungültiger** ~ invalid (void) contract; **aufgrund Gesetzes ungültiger** ~ contract rendered void by statute; **unmöglicher** ~ impossible contract; **unmoralischer** ~ immoral contract; **unrentabler** ~ unprofitable contract; **unselbständiger** ~ dependent contract (covenant); **unteilbarer** ~ indivisible contract; **einseitig unterzeichneter** ~ inchoate instrument (agreement); **unverbindlicher** ~ naked (nude) contract; **mit Treu und Glauben unvereinbarer** ~ unconscionable contract; **unvollständiger** ~ incomplete contract; **unwirksamer** ~ void contract; **schwebend unwirksamer** ~ [etwa] contract not yet completed; **unzumutbarer** ~ unreasonable contract; **verbindlicher** ~ firm contract; **auch für die Nachfolger verbindlicher** ~ transitive covenant; **gesetzlich verbotener** ~ contract prohibited by statute; **verletzter** ~ impaired contract; **verpflichtender** ~ onerous contract; **einseitig verpflichtender** ~ naked agreement, personal covenant, deed poll; **zweiseitig verpflichtender** ~ commutative contract, reciprocal contract *(Br.)*; **gegen die guten Sitten verstoßender** ~ contract offending public policy; **völkerrechtlicher** ~ treaty; **vorehelicher** ~ antenuptial settlement; **vorläufiger** ~ provisional contract (treaty), *(Grundstücksvorvertrag)* preliminary agreement, binder; **vorliegender** ~ present agreement; **wechselseitiger** ~ commulative contract; **widerrechtlicher** ~ illegal contract; **wirksamer** ~ executed contract; **wucherischer** ~ usurious contract; **zugrundeliegender** ~ underlying contract; **zweiseitiger** ~ synallagmatic (bilateral, mutual) contract (covenant), bipartite treaty;

~ **über den Abschluß eines Prämiengeschäfts** option contract; ~ **zwecks Ausschluß des ordentlichen Rechtsweges** *(Schiedsgerichtswesen)* exclusion agreement; ~ **auf der Basis zu erstattender Selbstkosten** cost reimbursable contract; ~ **zur Begründung eines dinglichen Eigentumsrechtes** estate contract; ~ **zugunsten Dritter** third-party beneficiary contract, contract for benefit of a third party (in consideration of another); ~ **über Entwicklungsvorhaben** developmental contract; ~ **zur Festlegung des Selbstbehalts** *(Rückversicherungsgeschäft)* surplus treaty; ~ **in gesiegelter Form** contract under seal, specialty; ~ **über die Fortführung des Geschäftes unter Gläubigeraufsicht** deed of inspectorship; ~ **mit nichtverbürgter Gegenseitigkeit** contract lacking mutuality; ~ **über Gegenstände des notwendigen Lebensbedarfs** contract for necessaries; ~ **mit weggefallener Geschäftsgrundlage** frustrated contract; ~ **vor Gesellschaftseintragung** pre-incorporation contract; ~ **auf Lebenszeit** life contract; ~ **über bestimmte Leistungen** certain contract; ~ **über selbständige Leistungen** independent contract; ~ **auf teilbare Leistungen** divisible contract; ~ **über eine unentgeltliche Leistung** gratuitous contract; ~ **mit ungleichen Leistungen** mixed contract; ~ **auf unteilbare Leistungen** entire contract; ~ **über mehrere Lieferungen** multiple-delivery contract; ~ **eines Minderjährigen** infant's contract; ~ **mit Preisfestsetzung nach den Kosten zuzüglich einer Leistungsprämie** cost-plus-incentive-fee contract; ~ **mit Preisfestsetzung nach den Kosten zuzüglich Verrechnung fester Zuschläge** cost-plus-a-fixed-fee contract *(US)*; ~, **der den Prozeßweg nicht ausschließt** procedural contract; ~ **in Schriftform** literal contract; ~ **zur Sicherstellung des notwendigen Lebensunterhalts** contract for necessaries; ~ **gegen die guten Sitten** contract offending public policy, immoral contract; ~ **mit Unterlassungsverpflichtung** negative covenant; ~ **über eine schlüsselfertige Wohnung** turn-key contract; ~ **zu Zwecken der Steuerhinterziehung** contract to defraud the revenue;

~ **abändern** to modify a contract; ~ **ablehnen** to disaffirm a contract; ~ **abschließen** to conclude (enter into) an agreement, to make (close) a contract; **förmlichen** ~ **abschließen** to make a deed; **schriftlichen** ~ **abschließen** to enter into a written agreement; ~ **unter Druck abschließen** to make a contract under duress; ~ **nicht anerkennen** to repudiate (deny) a contract (an agreement); ~ **anfechten** to rescind (void, avoid) a contract; **ungültigen** ~ **anfechten** to disaffirm an invalid contract; ~ **annehmen** to adopt (assume) a contract; ~ **annullieren** to annul (void, evacuate, vitiate) a contract, to invalidate a contract *(Br.)*; ~ **automatisch annullieren** to wash up a contract automatically; ~ **aufheben** to annul (avoid, cancel, set aside, dissolve, evacuate, reprobate, rescind) a contract, to rescind an agreement; ~ **in gegenseitigem Einvernehmen aufheben** to rescind a contract by mutual consent; ~ **aufkündigen** to give notice of termination of a contract; **völkerrechtlichen** ~ **aufkündigen** to renounce a treaty; ~ **auflösen** to sever (cancel, annul, rescind, invalidate) a contract; **Klausel in einen** ~ **aufnehmen** to embody a clause in a contract; ~ **aufrechterhalten** to keep a contract alive, to go on with a contract; ~ **aufsetzen** to draw up (write, prepare) a contract (an agreement), to make a deal; ~ **neu aufsetzen** to renegotiate a contract; ~ **ausfertigen** to draw up a contract (an agreement); ~ **aushandeln** to negotiate a contract; ~ **bis in die kleinsten Kleinigkeiten aushandeln** to negotiate a contract in exhausting detail; ~ **auslegen** to interpret a contract; ~ **beenden** to determine (terminate, discharge) a contract; ~ **als ungültig behandeln** to repudiate a contract; **einem bestehenden** ~ **beitreten** to intervene in an (become party to an) agreement, *(Völkerrecht)* to join a treaty; ~ **bestätigen** to affirm (ratify) a contract, to confirm a treaty; ~ **nicht bestätigen** to disaffirm a contract; ~ **als nichtig betrachten** to consider a contract void; ~ **brechen** to break (violate) a contract; ~ **zustande bringen** to form a contract; ~ **genau durchlesen** to read through a contract; **Klausel in einen** ~ **einfügen** to insert a clause into a contract, to embody (put) a clause in a treaty; ~ **eingehen** to enter into an agreement, to make a contract; ~ **einhalten** to hono(u)r a contract, to abide by an agreement; **in einen bestehenden** ~ **eintreten** to intervene in an agreement; **aus einem** ~ **entlassen** to release from a contract; ~ **entwerfen** to draft a contract (deed); **einem** ~ **die Geschäftsgrundlage entziehen** to frustrate a contract; ~ **erfüllen** to complete (execute, satisfy, fulfil(l), perform, carry out) a contract, to satisfy (implement) an agreement; ~ **bis zum letzten I-Tüpfelchen erfüllen** to live up to the letter of a contract; ~ **für nichtig (ungültig) erklären** to vitiate (invalidate) a contract, to set aside an agreement; ~ **erneuern** to renew a contract; **durch einen neuen** ~ **ersetzen** to supersede by a new contract; **unter einen** ~ **fallen** to fall within the scope of (be covered by, come under) an agreement; ~ **formulieren** to draw up (word) a contract; **zu einem** ~ **gelangen** to come to an agreement; ~ **genehmigen** to approbate an agreement (a contract); **aus einem schwebend wirksamen** ~ **haften** to be liable on an executory contract; **sich an einen ~ halten** to abide by an agreement; **einem ~ gemäß handeln** to act in conformity with a contract; **aus einem ~ herauskommen** to get out of a contract; **Rechtsgültigkeit eines ~es herbeiführen** to make a contract binding; **aus einem ~ (aufgrund eines ~es) klagen** to sue on a contract; **~ kündigen** to revoke a contract, to denounce a treaty; **~ mit vierteljährlicher Frist kündigen** to denounce an agreement with three month's notice; **~ (nicht) fristgemäß kündigen** to terminate a contract by (without) notice; **~ aus wichtigem Grunde kündigen** to terminate a contract for cause; **~ registrieren lassen** to enter a deed; **~ lösen** to dissolve an agreement; **~ machen** to make a contract; **zu einem rechtsgültigen, bindenden und gesetzmäßigen ~ machen** to constitute an indenture a valid, binding and legal agreement; **~ ungültig machen** to void (vitiate) a contract; **~ nachträglich unmöglich machen** to frustrate a contract; **unter ~ nehmen** to employ, to engage, to sign on, to recruit *(US)*, to hire *(US)*; **~ ratifizieren** to ratify a contract (treaty); **~ registrieren** *(Völkerrecht)* to register a treaty; **~ schließen** to enter into (conclude) a contract, to consummate an agreement, to covenant; **von wesentlicher Bedeutung für einen ~ sein** to be of essence for a contract; **an einem ~ beteiligt sein** to become party to an agreement; **durch ~ gebunden sein** to be bound by contract; **im ~ vorgesehen sein** to be provided for in a contract, to be covered by an agreement; **auf ~ stützen** *(Klage)* to sound in contract; **~ umstoßen** to void (vitiate) a contract; **~ unterzeichnen** to sign an agreement (a contract); **internationalen ~ gesetzlich verankern** to embody a treaty in law; **~ verklausulieren** to put hedges in a contract; **~ verlängern** to extend (prolong) a contract; **~ verletzen** to violate a contract (an agreement), to transgress a treaty; **sich durch einen ~ verpflichten** to bind o. s. by contract, to enter into a covenant; **unterschriftsreifen ~ vorlegen** to submit a contract all cut and dried, to draw up a contract for signature; **zu einem ~ gezwungen werden** to make a contract under duress; **~ widerrufen** to revoke (rescind) a contract; **~ zuerkennen** to award a contract; **von einem ~ zurücktreten** to recede (withdraw from, terminate) an agreement, to treat a contract as repudiated, to rescind a contract; **einem ~ zustimmen** to assent to (ratify) a contract.

Verträge, ungleiche *(Völkerrecht)* unequal treaties;
~ Minderjähriger infants' contracts; **Römische ~** *(EG)* Treaty of Rome.

vertragen *(Medizin)* to tolerate;
sich ~ *(vereinbar sein)* to be compatible, to comply, to harmonize; **sich mit jem. ~** to mix with s. o.; **Farbe nicht ~** to clash with a colo(u)r; **sich glänzend mit jem. ~** to get on splendidly (be hand in glove) with s. o.; **sich mit jem. gut ~** to hit it off with s. o.; **sich wie Hund und Katze ~** to lead a cat-and-dog life; **Kälte gut ~** to be able to stand the cold; **sich miteinander ~** to go together, to hitch *(coll.)*; **sich mit jem. nicht ~** not to be able to get on with s. o., to be out (at outs, *US*) with s. o.; **gehörigen Stiefel ~** to hold one's liquor well; **sich wieder mit jem. ~** to wipe out old scores (square o. s.) with s. o., to make it up with s. o.;
einen Puff (viel) ~ können to have broad shoulders, to be able to take a lot *(coll.)*.

vertraglich ex contractu, contractual, by contract;
~ gebunden bound by contract, articled; **~ vereinbart** by contract, conventional, stipulated; **wie ~ vereinbart** as provided in the contract; **~ nicht vereinbart** uncovenanted; **~ verpflichtet** liable under contract, covenanted, bound by contract, indented, indentured under articles; **~ vorgesehen** provided (appointed) by the articles;
sich ~ binden to bind o. s. by contract; **~ regeln** to stipulate by contract; **~ gebunden sein** to be bound by indenture; **~ verpflichtet sein** to be bound by a contract, to be under bond (an agreement); **~ vorgesehen sein** to be provided for in a contract; **etw. ~ übernehmen** to contract for s. th.; **~ vereinbaren** to stipulate in writing; **sich ~ verpflichten** to bind o. s. by contract, to contract for s. th., to enter into a covenant; **~ vorsehen** to specify in an agreement;
~e Abmachung agreement, stipulation; **~ begründete Ansprüche** claims based on contract, contractual claims; **~es Auslösungsrecht** contractual right to redeem; **~e Auswirkung** contractual force; **~e Bedingungen** conditions as per contract, terms; **gemäß den ~en Bestimmungen** in accordance with the provisions of the agreement; **~e Beziehungen** contractual relations; **~e Bindung** contractual relation; **~e Gegenleistung** valuable consideration; **~ vereinbarte Gütergemeinschaft** conventional community; **~es Güterrecht** contractual regime *(US)*; **~ geschuldete Leistung** contractual obligation, simple contract debt; **~ vereinbartes Mietverhältnis** contractual tenancy; **~e Regelung** contract settlement; **~e Schlußbestimmungen** conclusion; **~e Schutzvorschriften** contractual safeguards; **~es Treueverhältnis** privity of contract; **~e Verbesserungen** contract improvements; **~e Vereinbarung** contractual (treaty) arrangement; **~e Verpflichtungen** treaty obligations, contractual commitments (obligations); **seinen ~en Verpflichtungen nachkommen** to meet one's contract obligations; **~ vorgesehener Zahlungstermin** contractual due date; **innerhalb der ~ vereinbarten Zeit** within the period stipulated by contract.

verträglicher Mensch easy person to get on with.

Verträglichkeit easy temper, tractability, compatibility, sociability, good feeling.

Vertrags|ablauf determination (expiration, expiry) of a contract; **~ablehnung** contract rejection; **schriftliche ~abmachungen** articles of agreement; **~abreden** stipulation of a contract.

Vertragsabschluß formation of a contract, closing of contract, conclusion of (entering into) an agreement, negotiation, *(Bausparkasse, Versicherung)* business portfolio;
bei ~ at the making of a contract; **gültig nur bei ~** subject to contract; **im Falle des ~es** subject to contract; **zur Zeit des ~es** at the time of making the contract;
fahrlässiger ~ negligence in contract; **nicht zustande gekommener ~** loss of contract;
~ erzielen to land a contract; **Mißverständnisse beim ~ haben** to enter a contract under a misapprehension.

Vertragsabschrift copy of a contract;
~ herstellen to write out a copy of an agreement.

vertragsähnlich quasi-contractual;
~es Verhältnis quasi contract (contractual relationship); **Schadenersatzklage aus ~en Verhältnissen** common assumpsit.

Vertrags|änderung alteration (modification) of a contract, contract change; **~anfechtung** avoidance (vitiation, rescission) of contract; **~anfechtungsklage erheben** to bring an action for rescission of contract; **~angebot** offer, executory unilateral accord; **~angebot zurücknehmen** to revoke an offer; **~anlage** enclosure to an agreement; **~annahme** acceptance (adoption) of a contract; **~annahme durch Vornahme einer Handlung** acceptance by act; **~annullierung** avoidance (dissolution, rescinding) of a contract; **~anspruch** simple contract debt, contract claim; **~anteil** contractual share, *(Rückversicherung)* treaty quota; **~antrag** offer, proposal; **~art** type of contract; **~artikel** clause [in an agreement], stipulation; **~arzt** panel doctor.

Vertragsaufhebung dissolution (avoidance, cancellation, rescission, repudiation, evacuation) of a contract, contract cancellation;
von den Parteien vereinbarte ~ legal rescission;
~ unter Beibehaltung von Schadensersatzansprüchen qualified rescission;
auf ~ klagen to initiate proceedings for rescission of a contract.

Vertrags|aufkündigung notice of termination of treaty; **~auflösung** termination of a contract; **durch Gerichtsurteil bedingte ~auflösung** equitable rescission; **~aufsetzung** drafting a contract; **~ausfertigung** engrossment; **nachlässige ~ausführung** misfeasance; **~ausfüllung** implementation of an agreement; **~auslegung** construction of a contract, interpretation of a contract; **~auswirkungen** effect of a contract; **~autonomie** contractual autonomy.

Vertragsbedingungen contract[ual] terms, terms (conditions) as per (stipulations of) contract, terms of an agreement;
stillschweigende ~ implied conditions;
den ~ nicht entsprechen *(Waren)* not to be of the contract description; **~ erfüllen** to comply with (observe) the terms of a contract; **~ festsetzen** to stipulate the terms of a contract; **~ gutheißen** to endorse the terms of a settlement.

Vertrags|beendigung cessation of agreement, termination (discharge) of contract; **einverständliche ~beendigung** termination (discharge) by agreement; **~beendigung wegen Fortfalls der Geschäftsgrundlagen (objektiver Unmöglichkeit)** termination (discharge) by frustration; **~begriff** contractual term; **~beitritt** *(Völkerrecht)* adherence (accession) to a treaty; **~beitritt erklären** to accept an agreement; **~bekanntgabe** promulgation of a treaty; **~bereitschaft** willingness to contract; **~berichtigung** correction of a contract, rectification *(Br.)*; **~bestand** *(Bausparkasse)* business portfolio; **wesentlicher ~bestandteil** integral part of a contract; **~bestandteile** elements (features) of a contract; **~bestätigung** affirmation (confirmation) of a contract, confirmation note, homologation *(Scot.)*.

Vertragsbestimmung contract clause (provision);
~, **die Leerstehen eines Hauses gestattet** *(Versicherung)* vacancy clause.

Vertragsbestimmungen articles (terms) of an agreement, terms (provisions, articles, conditions, rules, stipulations, regulations) of a contract, contract (contractual) provisions (terms), *(Völkerrecht)* treaty provisions;
nach den ~ under (in accordance with) the articles; **vorbehaltlich der** ~ subject to the terms of a contract;
allgemeine ~ conditions laid down in an agreement; **besondere** ~ specification of a contract **ausdrücklich festgelegte** ~ express terms; **glasklare** ~ clear-cut provisions of a contract; **mutmaßliche** ~ implied terms; **stillschweigende** ~ implied conditions; **unvereinbarte** ~ repugnant clauses; **wesentliche** ~ substantial parts of a contract;
~ **abändern** to vary the terms of a contract; ~ **ausbedingen** to condition; ~ **nicht einhalten** not to conform to a clause, to break through the obligations of a treaty; **unter die** ~ **fallen** to come within the terms of a contract; ~ **festlegen** to set forth conditions in a contract; **sich an die** ~ **halten** to comply with the clauses (stand by the terms) of a contract; **zu den** ~ **des Eigentümers mieten** to lease on the landlord's terms; ~ **verletzen** to violate a clause.

Vertrags|beteiligte privies in respect of a contract; ~**bevollmächtigter** authorized representative; ~**beziehung** contractual relationship (relation); ~**brecher** covenant breaker.

Vertragsbruch breach (violation) of contract (covenant), rupture of an agreement, infraction of a treaty;
grundlegender ~ fundamental breach of contract; **teilweiser** ~ partial breach; **vorweggenommener** ~ anticipatory breach of contract;
~ **begehen** to act in violation of a contract (treaty); **sich auf** ~ **berufen** to set up a breach of contract; **j. zum** ~ **verleiten** to procure s. o. to break his contract.

vertragsbrüchig contract-breaking, defaulting;
~ **werden** to break a contract, to forfeit, to fail to keep an obligation;
~**e Partei** contract-breaker; ~**er Staat** treaty-breaking state.

Vertrags|brüchiger party in breach; **obligatorischer** ~**charakter** obligatory scope of a contract; ~**datum** contract date; ~**dauer** continuance (term) of a contract, contract (contractual) period, life of an agreement (contract); **während der** ~**dauer** during the life of a contract; ~**durchführung** contract execution; ~**einheit** entirety of a contract; ~**entwurf** draft contract (treaty), draft (tentative) agreement; ~**erbe** conventional heir *(US)*; ~**erfordernisse** formalities (requirements) of a contract; **wesentliche** ~**erfordernisse** essentials (essence) of a contract.

Vertragserfüllung fulfil(l)ment (performance, execution, discharge) of a contract, implement *(Scot.)*;
effektive ~ specific performance; **nachträglich unmöglich gewordene** ~ frustration of contract; **mangelnde** ~ failure to perform (of performance); **unmögliche** ~ impossibility of performance of contract, frustration of contract; **unterlassene** ~ *(Völkerrecht)* negative reprisal; **wesentliche** ~ substantial performance of a contract;
~ **durch den Erfüllungsgehilfen** vicarious performance;
~ **ablehnen** to repudiate a contract; ~ **wegen Minderjährigkeit ablehnen** to repudiate a contract during infancy; **j. zur** ~ **auffordern** to summon s. o. to perform a contract; ~ **nachträglich unmöglich machen** to frustrate the performance of a contract.

Vertragserneuerung renewal of contract (an agreement), contract renewal, revival of a contract, *(Verteidigungsaufträge)* renegotiation;
stillschweigende ~ tacit renewal of a contract.

vertragsfähig able (capable) to contract, [legally] competent to contract, able to enter into a contract.

Vertrags|fähigkeit competence (ability, capability) to contract, contractual capacity (power), responsibility *(US)*; ~**festsetzung** stipulation; ~**firma** contracting firm; **als** ~**folge darstellen** to count on a contract; ~**forderung** contract[ual] claim, simple contract debt; **nicht verbriefte** ~**forderung** debt by simple contract; ~**form** form of a contract, contract by form; ~**formalitäten** formalities of a contract; **handelsübliche** ~**formen** trade terms; ~**fortsetzung** renewal of a contract; ~**freiheit** freedom (liberty) of contract, contractual liberty; ~**frist** contract period; ~**gaststätte** tied house *(Br.)*; ~**gebiet** territory covered by a contract, *(Vertreter)* travel(l)ing territory; ~**gegenstand** subject matter of the agreement, contract goods; ~**gegner** contracting party, party to an agreement (contract).

vertragsgemäß pursuant to the contract, provided, conditional, [as may be required] by contract, according to contract, contractual, conventional, as agreed upon, stipulated, as per agreement;
~**e Anweisung** lawful order.

Vertrags|gläubiger contract creditor; ~**grundlage** basis of a contract (an agreement); **fortgefallene** ~**grundlage** frustrated fundamental purpose of a contract; ~**gültigkeit** validity of a contract (deed), force of an agreement; ~**hafen** treaty port; ~**haftung** contractual liability; ~**händler** appointed (recognized, licensed, authorized) dealer, distributor; **richterliche** ~**hilfe** protection order *(Br.)*; ~**hindernis** frustrating event; ~**hotel** *(Touristikunternehmen)* contract hotel; ~**hypothek** conventional mortgage; ~**inbegriff** essence of a contract; ~**inhalt** subject matter of an agreement, terms of contract; **stillschweigend vereinbarter** ~**inhalt** implications into a contract; **wesentlicher** ~**inhalt** essential terms, root of a contract, essence of an agreement; ~**interesse** valuable (good) consideration; ~**jahr** year of contract.

Vertragsklausel contract[ual] clause;
~**n** stipulations of a contract, *(Völkerrecht)* clauses in a treaty;
umstrittene ~ contentious clause in a treaty;
~ **respektieren** to respect a clause in a contract.

Vertrags|kommentierung note of an agreement; ~**kontingent** quota provided for in a contract; ~**kontrahenten** parties to a contract, contracting parties; ~**kündigung** contract cancellation, revocation of a contract; ~**land** contracting state, member (partner) country.

Vertragsleistung obligation under a contract, contractual obligation, consideration;
ausbedungene ~ obligation of a contract; **noch nicht erfüllte** ~**en** *(Bilanz)* uncompleted contracts; **gesetzwidrige** ~ illegal consideration; **hauptsächlichste** ~ primary obligation; **unmögliche** ~ impossible consideration;
~ **erzwingen** to enforce payment (performance) of a contract; **mit den** ~**en in Verzug kommen** to get behind with the performance of a contract, to fail to complete within contract time.

Vertrags|lieferant von Betriebskantinen industrial contract caterer, catering contractor; ~**lieferant von Filmgesellschaften bei Außenaufnahmen** location caterer; ~**lücke** loophole in a contract; ~**macht** treaty power (signatory).

vertragsmäßig contractual, conventionary, according to contract, stipulated;
~**er Gebrauch** intended use; ~**e Kündigungsfrist** statutory notice; **nicht** ~**e Lieferung** bad delivery.

Vertrags|menge contract supplies; ~**merkmale** features of a contract; ~**muster** contract pattern; ~**nachweis** evidence of a contract; ~**natur** essence of a contract; ~**netz** network of treaties; ~**niederschrift** *(Völkerrecht)* memorandum of agreement; **kurze** ~**niederschrift** note of memorandum; ~**offerte** offer, executory unilateral accord; ~**paragraph** item of a contract.

Vertragspartei contracting party, contractor, stipulator;
~**en** competent parties, contracting parties, parties to a contract;
im Irrtum befangene ~ mistaken party; **hohe** ~**en** High Contracting Parties; **unmittelbare** ~**en** parties and privies.

Vertrags|partner party to an agreement, contrahent, signatory, *(pl.)* contracting parties (partners); ~**periode** contractual period; ~**pfandrecht** conventional lien.

Vertragspflicht contractual obligation (duty), obligation pursuant to a treaty, obligation under a contract;
wesentliche ~ inherent covenant;
~ **aus der Aufrechterhaltung einer Versicherung** covenant to insure.

Vertrags|prämie stipulated premium; ~**preis** contract (target, firm) price; **zum** ~**preis** at the contract rate; ~**prinzip** [etwa] privity of law; ~**problem** contractual problem; ~**punkte** articles of an agreement, terms of a contract; ~**quote** contractual rate; ~**recht** law of contract.

vertragsrechtlich contractual.

Vertrags|regelung contract settlement; ~**regierung** government party to a convention; ~**restaurant** *(Bierverlag)* tied house *(Br.)*; ~**revision** revision of a treaty; ~**rücktritt** cancellation of a contract; ~**sammlung** treaty collection.

vertragsschließend signatory, contrahent;
~**e Teile** contracting parties, parties contracting.

Vertrags|schließender contractor, party; ~**schluß** making a contract, conclusion of an agreement, *(Schlußbestimmungen)* conclusion; **beim** ~**schluß** at the time of reaching agreement, when the contract was made; ~**schluß herbeiführen** to complete a contract; ~**schuld** contract debt; ~**schuldner** contract debtor; ~**schwierigkeiten** treaty troubles; **gleichgelagerte ~situationen** similarly based contract situations; ~**skizze** project; ~**sorte** *(Produktenbörse)* contract grade; ~**spediteur** contract carrier; ~**staat** contracting state, member country; ~**stempel** contract note *(Br.)*; ~**strafe** liquidated damages, penal sum (clause, obligation), maintenance fee *(US)*; ~**strafe verwirken** to forfeit a penalty; ~**streitigkeiten** disputes under a contract; ~**system** treaty system; ~**tarif** *(Bahn)* convention tariff; ~**teil,** ~**teilnehmer** party to an agreement (a contract), contracting party; ~**termin** contract date; ~**text** wording of a contract.

vertragstreu true to the contract;
~ sein to abide by an agreement;
~e Erfüllung faithful performance of contract; **~e Partei** observant party.

Vertrags|treue contractual fidelity, observance of a contract; ~**typ** contract type, type of contract (agreement); ~**umfang** extent of an agreement.

vertragsunfähig incapable of entering into (incompetent to make a) contract.

Vertrags|unfähigkeit incapacity to contract; ~**ungültigkeit** voidance of a contract ~**unterschrift** signature of a contract (treaty); ~**unterzeichnung** signing of a contract.

Vertragsurkunde covenant, contractual document, deed, written instrument, memorandum, evidence of a contract, contract;
hinterlegte ~ escrow; **in mehreren Ausfertigungen vorliegende ~** indenture;
~ aufsetzen to draw up a deed; **~ im Duplikat aufsetzen** to indent.

Vertrags|verbindlichkeiten contractual obligations, liabilities of a contract; ~**vereinbarung** contractual stipulation; **ausdrückliche ~vereinbarung** express term; ~**vereinbarung mit jem. schließen** to enter into a treaty with s. o.

Vertragsverhältnis contractual relation[ship];
im ~ mit under contract;
gesetzlich fingiertes ~ implied contract; **unmittelbares ~** privity of contract;
~ beenden to terminate a contract; **aus einem ~ entlassen** to leave out of an agreement; **~ fortsetzen** to go on with a contract; **~ herstellen** to establish privity of contract.

Vertrags|verhandlungen negotiations for a treaty, contract negotiations (talks); ~**verlängerung** contract renewal, prolongation of a contract; **stillschweigende ~verlängerung** tacit renewal; ~**verlängerungsklausel** renewal clause.

Vertragsverletzung contract violation, violation (breach, infringement) of a contract, default, *(Völkerrecht)* infringement (violation, infraction) of a treaty;
positive ~ collateral negligence;
für ~en agieren to fly in the face of treaties; **~ begehen** to break (violate) a contract, *(Völkerrecht)* to violate a treaty; **~ feststellen** to set up breach of contract; **über eine ~ hinwegsehen** to waive the break; **sich einer ~ schuldig machen** to become liable for a summons.

Vertragsverletzungsverfahren *(EG)* action for infringement of the treaty.

Vertragsverpflichtung contractual (treaty) obligation (commitment);
bindende ~en binding terms of a contract; **gegenseitige ~** concurrent conditions; **vom anderen unabhängige ~** severable contract obligation;
~ abschwächen to impair the obligation of a contract; **außerhalb seiner ~en tätig werden** to overstep the limits of one's contractual duties.

Vertrags|versicherung contract insurance; ~**versprechen** assumpsit; **unterstelltes ~versprechen** fictitious promise; ~**verzicht** disclaimer of contract; ~**vollmacht** power to contract; ~**vorbehalt** proviso, reservation; ~**vorbehalt aufnehmen** to enter a reservation in respect of a contract; ~**vorschlag** contract proposal; ~**vorschriften** rules (provisions) of contract; ~**vorteile** contract gains; ~**währung** currency of contract; ~**ware** contract goods; ~**werk** set of agreements; ~**werkstatt** tied garage *(Br.)*; ~**wert** contract value.

vertragswidrig contrary (in contravention) to an agreement, contrary to the terms of the contract (treaty), contract-breaking.

Vertrags|widrigkeit violation of contract, contravention of a treaty, *(bei Warenlieferung)* lack of conformity; ~**wille** intent of agreement (the parties); ~**wirkungen** effects of a contract; ~**zeit** contractual (contract) period, life of a contract; ~**ziel** contract goal; ~**zinsen** stipulated interest; ~**zölle** treaty (contractual, conventional) duties; ~**zusage** contractual undertaking (promise); ~**zusatz** marginal note, rider, supplement; ~**zuteilung** awarding of contract.

Vertrauen faith, confidence, trust, reliance, dependence, hope;
ganz im ~ between you and me and the lamppost (gatepost) *(coll.)*; **im ~** privately, confidentially; **im ~ auf** relying on, on the strength of; **vom ~ des Volkes getragen** supported by the people's confidence;
blindes ~ implicit faith; **erschüttertes ~** shaken confidence; **mangelndes ~** want (lack) of confidence, lack of faith; **übermäßiges ~** overconfidence; **unbeschränktes ~** unlimited credit; **volles ~** entire confidence;
~ des Anlagepublikums investor confidence; **~ der Gläubiger** creditor confidence; **~ der Kundschaft** customer confidence; **~ der Öffentlichkeit** public confidence; **~ in die Wirtschaftslage** business confidence;
jem. sein ~ aufdrängen to force one's confidence upon s. o.; **~ aussprechen** *(parl.)* to pass a vote of confidence; **~ ausstrahlen** to have the quality of inspiring confidence; **auf ~ beruhen** to rest upon credit; **jem. ~ einflößen** to inspire s. o. with confidence; **sich in jds. ~ einschleichen** to worm o. s. into s. one's confidence; **jem. ~ entgegenbringen** to repose confidence in s. o.; **jem. sein ~ entziehen** to withdraw one's confidence from s. o.; **jds. ~ erlangen** to obtain s. one's confidence; **~ erschüttern** to shake the confidence; **~ fassen** to feel one's legs; **jds. ~ genießen** to enjoy s. one's confidence; **als Politiker ~ genießen** to enjoy political trust; **jds. ~ mißbrauchen** to break s. one's faith; **jds. ~ rechtfertigen** to deserve (justify) s. one's confidence; **einem Tatsachenbericht ~ schenken** to trust an account of what has happened; **sein ~ in j. getäuscht sehen** to be deceived in s. o.; **sein ~ in j. setzen** to place confidence (put one's trust) in s. o.; **~ in jds. Worte setzen** to place dependence on s. one's word; **öffentliches ~ verlieren** to lose the confidence of the people; **ins ~ gezogen werden** to be made privy to it; **~ zu der Währung wiederherstellen** to restore confidence in the currency; **j. ins ~ ziehen** to let s. o. in on the secret, to take (admit) s. o. into one's confidence, to make s. o. privy.

vertrauen to trust, to rest (rely) upon, to have confidence, to set store by;
jds. Ehrlichkeit ~ to have trust in s. one's honesty.

vertrauenerweckend aussehen to look promising.

Vertrauens|amt position of trust; ~**antrag** motion for a vote of confidence; ~**anwalt** panel solicitor; ~**arzt** public health commissioner, medical examiner (referee, *US*); ~**arztsystem** contract service system *(Br.)*; ~**beweis** expression of confidence; ~**beziehung** fiduciary relation; ~**bruch** breach of faith (confidence), indiscretion, selling off (out) *(US sl.)*; ~**debatte** *(parl.)* confidence debate; ~**frage stellen** *(parl.)* to ask for a vote of confidence; ~**funktion** fiduciary nature; ~**grad** *(Vorhersage)* confidence figure; ~**journalist** lobby correspondent; ~**kredit** personal loan; ~**krise** crisis of confidence; ~**mann** private (confidential) agent, confidant, confidential person, *(Polizei)* police agent, *(Sprecher)* spokesman, *(Treuhänder)* trustee; ~**mann der Belegschaft** shop deputy (steward) *(US)*; **jds. ~mann sein** to be in the confidence of s. o., to be s. one's confidant; ~**mißbrauch** abuse of confidence (trust), jobbery; ~**order** discretionary order; ~**person** reliable (confidential) person, fiduciary, right-hand man; ~**posten** position of trust, confidential post (place), post of confidence (trust), fiducial office; ~**rabatt** confidential discount; ~**sache** confidential matter, matter of confidence; ~**schaden** loss incurred from breach of contract; ~**schadenversicherung** commercial insurance; ~**schüler** monitor, prefect *(Br.)*; ~**schwund** credibility gap, loss of confidence.

vertrauensselig trusting, dupable;
Dritten gegenüber zu ~ sein to become too confidential with strangers.

Vertrauensstellung confidential place (post), fiduciary position, position of trust, post of confidence (trust), responsible position (job);
einer ~ nicht gewachsen unfit for a position of trust; **in einer ~** in a fiduciary position;
~ innehaben to be in a position of trust.

Vertrauens|verhältnis confidential (fiduciary) relationship; **persönliches ~verhältnis** personal confidence; ~**verletzung** breach of trust; ~**verlust** drop in confidence; ~**votum** vote of confidence; ~**votum erhalten** to receive a vote of confidence; ~**werbung** public relations, *(durch Anzeigen)* institutional advertising; ~**wert einer Marke** brand preference.

vertrauenswürdig responsible, credible, trustworthy, sound, reliable, of safe discretion.

Vertrauenswürdigkeit trustworthiness, reliability, creditability.

vertraulich personal, in confidence, confidential, under the rose, under one's hat, sub rosa, closet, sub silentio, privy, *(allzu persönlich)* too familiar, chummy, *(Sitzung)* private;
streng ~ strictly confidential (off the record), private and confidential, in strict privacy, between you and me and the lamppost (gatepost);
sich ~ **äußern** to speak off the record; ~ **behandeln** to treat confidentially; **streng** ~ **behandeln** to treat in strictest confidence; **etw.** ~ **erfahren** to hear s. th. privately; **jem. etw.** ~ **erzählen** to tell s. o. s. th. on the quiet;
~**e Angaben** confidential data; ~**er Brief** private (confidential, personal) letter; **einem Freund** ~**e Dinge aus seinem Leben anvertrauen** to tell a friend intimate details of one's life; ~**es Gespräch** confidential talk; ~**e Information** private information; **während der Ehe erlangte** ~**e Kenntnisse** confidences communicated during their marriage; ~**e Mitteilung** confidential communication; ~**es Thema in einem Kreise abhandeln** to address a meeting on an off-the-record basis; **mit berühmten Persönlichkeiten** ~**en Umgang pflegen** to be intimate with the great.

Vertraulichkeit confidentiality, intimacy, privacy;
~**en** passages;
sich jem. gegenüber ~**en erlauben** to use freedoms (make free) with s. o.

vertraut familiar, intrinsic, conversant, intimate;
~ **mit** in the swim; **mit der jüngsten Entwicklung** ~ up-to-date, abreast of the times; **nicht** ~ unknown, unfamiliar, strange; **sich mit etw.** ~ **machen** to familiarize (acquaint) o. s. with s. th.; **sich mit dem Gedanken** ~ **machen** to get used to the idea; **mit allen Büroarbeiten** ~ **sein** to be familiar with all office routine; **gründlich mit etw.** ~ **sein** to have at one's finger tips; **mit einer Sache** ~ **sein** to be conversant with a matter; **mit einer Sache nicht** ~ **sein** to be unacquainted with s. th.; **mit jem. sehr** ~ **sein** to be hand in glove with s. o.; **mit etw. wieder ganz** ~ **sein** to be right back in s. th.; **mit einer Arbeit** ~ **werden** to get one's hand in;
auf ~**em Fuß mit jem. stehen** to be on familiar (intimate) terms with s. o.; **sich in** ~**en Gefilden bewegen** to be on familiar ground.

Vertrauter intimate (close) friend, familiar, confidant, repository, pal *(fam.)*, chum.

Vertrautheit familiarity, conversance;
mangelnde ~ unfamiliarity; **persönliche** ~ **mit dem Theater- und Fernsehleben** personalities of the stage and screen.

Vertrautsein, geringes ~ **mit einem Thema** slender acquaintance with a subject.

vertreiben to expel, *(Amtsinhaber)* to dislodge, *(aus dem Land)* to banish, to expel, to displace, to out, *(verkaufen)* to trade (deal) in, to sell, to market, *(Zeitungen)* to distribute;
aus dem Besitz ~ to dispossess of property, to eject, to oust; **Buch im Subskriptionswege** ~ to canvass a territory for a subscription book; **Eindringlinge aus dem Land** ~ to scour the invaders from the land; **Feind aus seinen Stellungen** ~ to drive (manoeuvre) the enemy out of his positions; **durch ein eigenes Filialnetz** ~ to peddle through its branch offices; **j. aus seinem Haus** ~ to pull up s. one's roots; **im Hausierhandel** ~ to peddle; **j. aus dem Heimatland** ~ to expatriate s. o.; **über ein Netz von 550 Vertragshändlern** ~ to sell through a network of 550 dealers; **Seeräuber** ~ to sweep pirates from the sea; **Wolken** ~ to drive away the clouds; **sich die Zeit** ~ to kill [the] time.

Vertreibung dispossession, displacement, expulsion, *(aus dem Land)* banishment, *(mil.)* dislodgement, *(Völkerrecht)* forcible transfer;
~ **aus dem Besitz** eviction, ejection, ouster; ~ **aus dem Heimatland** expatriation.

vertretbar *(ersetzbar)* replaceable, *(Sache)* fungible, *(zu vertreten)* maintainable, tenable, justifiable, pleadable, warrantable;
juristisch (rechtlich) ~ legally justifiable; **nicht** ~ untenable, indefensible; **sozial nicht** ~ unsocial, unsociable;
~ **sein** *(Theorie)* to hold water;
~**es Argument** valid argument; ~**e Ausgabe** warrantable outlay; ~**e Sachen** fungibles, fungible things; ~**er Standpunkt** supportable point of view.

Vertretbarkeit fungible nature, fungibility, *(vertragliches Einstehen)* warrantableness.

vertreten *(als Anwalt)* to advocate, to appear (plead) for, to defend, *(als Bevollmächtigter)* to represent, to act on behalf of, *(als Ersatzmann)* to substitute, to deputize, *(ersetzen)* to replace;
j. ~ to act (be agent, deputize, appear) for s. o., to supply s. one's place; **Ansicht** ~ to hold a view; **j. anwaltlich** ~ to plead s. one's cause, to act as counsel for s. o. *(Br.)*; **Beklagten** ~ to appear for the defence *(Br.)* (defense, *US*); **j. dienstlich** ~ to substitute (sit in) for s. o., to act as substitute for s. o.; **Firma allein** ~ to be sole agent for a firm; **sich die Füße** ~ to stretch one's legs; **vor Gericht** ~ to plead at the bar, to hold a brief *(Br.)*; **sich selbst [vor Gericht]** ~ to conduct one's own defence *(Br.)* (defense, *US*); **Gläubigerinteressen** ~ to represent the interests of the creditors; **seine Interessen** ~ to safeguard one's interests, to fight for one's own hand; **jds. Interessen** ~ to see to s. one's interests; **Kläger** ~ to appear for the plaintiff; **j. bis zu seiner Rückkehr** ~ to fill in until s. o. returns; **Sache** ~ to become the advocate of (uphold) a cause, *(vor Gericht)* to plead a case (cause); **jds. Sache** ~ to fight s. one's battle; **seine Sache vor Gericht gut** ~ to plead one's case well; **sich selbst** ~ to plead one's name (cause); **Standpunkt** ~ to hold the view; **seinen Standpunkt** ~ to state one's case; **Theorie** ~ to support a theory; **j. vorübergehend** ~ to stand in for s. o. temporarily, to supply s. one's place; **Wahlbezirk (Wahlkreis)** ~ to represent (sit for) a constituency; **jem. den Weg** ~ to block s. one's way; **ein Zehntel der Gesamtstimmrechte** ~ to represent one-tenth of the total voting rights; **ein Zehntel des eingezahlten Kapitals** ~ to hold one-tenth of the paid-up capital;
etw. zu ~ **haben** to be liable (answerable) for s. th.; **unerlaubte Handlungen seiner Beauftragten zu** ~ **haben** to be liable for the torts of one's agents; **Schulden seiner Frau zu** ~ **haben** to be liable for one's wife's debts; **sich** ~ **lassen** to find a deputy, to send (appoint) a proxy; **sich bei der Abstimmung** ~ **lassen** to vote by proxy; **sich anwaltlich** ~ **lassen** to appear by counsel *(Br.)*, to get a lawyer (barrister, *Br.*) to plead one's case;
~ *(a.)* represented, *(anwesend)* present;
anwaltlich ~ represented by counsel; **nicht** ~ unrepresented; **von keiner Partei zu** ~ no fault of the parties; **zu** ~ pleadable; **im Aufsichtsrat** ~ **sein** to be represented on the board; **am Verhandlungstisch** ~ **sein** to have representatives at the bargaining table; **zahlreich** ~ **sein** to be pretty thick on the ground;
im Parlament ~**e Parteien** parties represented in parliament.

vertretend representative.

Vertreter [authorized] agent, business agent, proxy, representative, attorney [in fact], *(Abgesandter)* delegate, deputy, *(Befürworter)* advocate, supporter, champion, *(Erfüllungsgehilfe)* vicarious agent, *(Ersatzmann)* deputy, substitute, *(einer Firma)* staff representative *(US)*, selling agent, factor, *(Händler)* dealer, *(Hausierer)* door-to-door salesman, peddler, *(Platzhalter)* locum tenens, *(Reisender)* commercial travel(l)er, travelling salesman, drummer *(US)*, runner *(US)*, sales (manufacturer's) representative, commercial *(Br.)*, distributor, solicitor *(US)*, road agent *(US)*;
als ~ in a representative capacity; **über einen** ~ through an agent;
alleiniger ~ exclusive (sole) agent; **amtlicher** ~ official representative; **anerkannter** ~ recognized agent; **auf Vorschußbasis arbeitender** ~ advance agent; **ausländischer** ~ representative abroad; **bestellter** ~ nominated representative; **ordnungsgemäß bestellter** ~ duly (lawfully) appointed (authorized) agent; **bevollmächtigter** ~ accredited (authorized, lawful) representative, proxy; **diplomatischer** ~ diplomatic agent (representative), *(ranghoher)* public minister *(US)*; **einstweiliger** ~ provisional representative; **erster** ~ top representative; **gemeinsamer** ~ joint agent; **gesetzlicher** ~ legal representative (agent), statutory guardian (agent), attorney, administrator at law *(Scot.)*; **hauptberuflicher** ~ full-time agent; **hochwertiger** ~ high-cost salesman; **konsularischer** ~ consular agent (representative); **nebenberuflicher** ~ part-time agent; **nomineller** ~ front; **örtlicher** ~ local agent, man on the spot; **parlamentarischer** ~ representative, member of parliament, deputy *(US)*; **persönlicher** ~ personal representative, private agent; **rechtmäßiger** ~ lawful (legal) representative; **selbständiger** ~ free-lance agent; **ständiger** ~ regular (appointed, ordinary) agent, general deputy; **typischer** ~ type; **unentgeltlicher** ~ gratuitous agent; **unseriöser** ~ carpet-bagging salesman;
~ **der Angestelltenschaft** employees' representative; ~ **der Anklage** public prosecutor, counsel for the prosecution, prosecuting attorney *(US)*; ~ **der Anteilseignerseite** representative of ownership, ownership representative; ~ **der Arbeitnehmerseite im Aufsichtsrat** labo(u)r representative on the board; **vollendeter** ~ **der alten Aristokratie** perfect type of the old aristocrat; ~ **mit begrenztem Aufgabenbereich** agent for a particular duty; ~ **im Außendienst** field agent; ~ **einer Bank**

representative of a bank; ~ **mehrerer Firmen** general salesman; ~ **des Fiskus** fiscal agent; ~ **der Geschäftsleitung** managing man; ~ **des Gesetzes** man of law; ~ **der Gewerkschaft** trade delegate, union representative, business agent *(US)*; ~ **öffentlicher Interessen** public representative; ~ **des flachen Landes** *(parl.)* country member; ~ **der Massenmedien** media person; ~ **der Presse** representative of the press; ~ **auf Provisionsbasis** traveller on commission; ~ **kraft Rechtsscheins** agent by estoppel; ~ **mehrerer Spediteure** joint agent; ~ **von Spezialartikeln** specialty salesman; ~ **des Staates** agent of the crown *(Br.)*; ~ **für die Tarifverhandlungen** bargaining agent; ~ **mit Untervertretern** travel(l)ing representative; ~ **der Verbraucherschaft** consumerite; ~ **der Versicherungsbranche** insurance investment salesman; ~ **ohne Vertretungsmacht** unauthorized agent, apparent (ostensible) agent; ~ **mit beschränkten Vollmachten** agent with limited powers; ~ **der Wirtschaft** commercial delegate;
~ **abberufen** to recall an agent; ~ **zu einer Konferenz abordnen** to send a representative to a conference; **Stadt als ~ bearbeiten** to canvass a town, to work a district; ~ **beschäftigen** to retain an agent; ~ **bestellen (bestimmen)** to appoint an agent (a representative), to appoint (authorize) a proxy; **Waren durch einen ~ bestellen** to order goods through an agent; ~ **einsetzen** to employ an agent; ~ **entsenden** to send a proxy (representative); ~ **ernennen** to appoint an agent; **als ~ fungieren** to act as deputy, to appear by proxy, to deputize for s. o.; **sich an einen ~ halten** to hold an agent; **als ~ handeln** to act in the capacity of an agent; ~ **sein** to travel for a firm; **jds. ~ sein** to deputize for s. o.; **freier ~ sein** to be a free agent; **typischer ~ des Zeitgeistes sein** to personalize the spirit of one's age; **zu jds. ~ ernannt werden** to be appointed s. one's substitute;
~**befugnisse** duties of an agent; ~**bereich** sales territory, distributorship; ~**bericht** sales (agent's) report, call slip; ~**bestellung** appointment of (appointing) an agent, *(Aufträge)* line, agent's order; ~**besuch** sales call, visit by a commercial travel(l)er; **nachfassender ~besuch** follow-up visit, call back; ~**besuch verbeten** no agents; ~**besuchskosten** sales-call costs.

Vertreterbezirk sales (travel(l)ing, agent's) territory, agency;
seinen ~ durcharbeiten to work one's territory intensively; **feste ~e einrichten** to set up regular territories for salesmen; **großen ~ haben** to travel over a large territory.

Vertreter|büro representative office (agency); ~**eigenschaft** representative capacity; ~**fixum** salesman's basic pay; ~**gebiet** sales region, sales (travelling) territory; ~**gebühr** agency fee; ~**kosten** agent's expenses; ~**leistung** salesman's performance; ~**organization** agency system; ~**provision** commission to salesman, agency (agent's) commission; ~**stab** sales staff (team), sales force *(US)*; ~**stellung** salesman position; ~**tagung** sales meeting; ~**tätigkeit** sales capacity, agency business (work); ~**typ** salesman type; ~**vereinigung** sales club; ~**verhältnis** agency (principal-agent) relationship; ~**versammlung** sales meeting; ~**vertrag** contract of agency, agency contract (agreement); ~**vollmacht** authority, power of an agent; ~**wagen** agency car; **in seiner ~zeit** during the course of one's agency; ~**zusammenkünfte** sales conventions.

Vertretung agency, representation, *(Abordnung)* delegation, *(im Amt)* substitution, *(Ersatz)* replacement, *(Geschäft)* agency business (office);
in ~ by proxy, acting as deputy, by attorney, in charge; **in dienstlicher** ~ in commission;
anteilsmäßige ~ proportional representation; **ausländische ~en** representations abroad; **ausschließliche** ~ exclusive agency; **auswärtige ~en** agents in the field, *(Diplomatie)* foreign missions, diplomatic representations; **berufliche ~ [in politischen Gremien]** functional representation; **berufsständische** ~ occupational representation, professional organization; **diplomatische** ~ diplomatic representation, foreign mission; **gerichtliche** ~ legal representation; **gerichtliche und außergerichtliche** ~ legal and general representation; **gesetzliche** ~ legal representation; **gewinnbeteiligte** ~ agency coupled with an interest; **konsularische** ~ consular agency; **örtliche** ~ local agent; **paritätische** ~ representation in equal numbers; **parlamentarische** ~ parliamentary representation; **vorübergehende** ~ substitution, supplying s. o.; **zusätzliche** ~ *(Reisender)* sideline;
~ **der Angestelltenschaft** employees' representation; ~ **der Anteilseigner** representation of ownership; ~ **durch einen Anwalt [bei Gericht]** appearance by attorney; **unrichtige ~ des Auftraggebers** misrepresentation of a client; ~**en im Ausland** representative offices abroad; ~ **der Betriebsführung** managerial representation; ~ **vor Gericht** legal representation; **berufliche ~ in politischen Gremien** functional representation in political bodies; ~ **von Interessen** representation of interests; ~ **seiner Interessen** safeguarding of one's interests; ~ **kraft Rechtsschein** agency by estoppel; ~ **ohne Vertretungsmacht** ostensible (unauthorized) agency; ~ **im Vorstand** board-level representation;
ausländische ~ aufheben to withdraw a mission; **mit seiner ~ einen erfahrenen Anwalt betrauen** to trust one's affairs to an experienced lawyer; ~ **einrichten** to establish an agency; ~ **niederlegen** to resign an agency; **mit einer ~ beauftragt sein** to hold a brief; **sich eine ~ sichern** to secure an agency; ~ **übernehmen** to act as substitute for s. o., to take up an agency; ~ **einer Firma übernehmen** to take up (accept) the agency of a firm; ~ **einer Sache vor Gericht übernehmen** to take a brief; **jem. eine ~ übertragen** to entrust s. o. with an agency; **zu jds. ~ bestimmt werden** to be appointed s. one's substitute.

Vertretungsbefugnis power of attorney (an agent, to represent), authority;
außerhalb seiner ~se handeln to act beyond the scope of one's authority (ultra vires, *Br.*); ~ **jederzeit widerrufen** to revoke an agent's authority at any time.

vertretungsberechtigt representative.

Vertretungs|berechtigter authorized representative (agent); ~**büro** representative office; ~**eigenschaft** representative capacity; ~**gebühr** agency cost (fee).

Vertretungsmacht [scope of] authority, power (authority) of an agent, procuration;
außerhalb des Rahmens der ~ beyond the scope of one's authority, ultra vires *(Br.)*; **im Rahmen seiner** ~ within one's power (the scope of one's authority);
ausdrücklich erteilte ~ express authority; **stillschweigend erteilte** ~ implied power; **fehlende** ~ lack (absence) of authority; **gesetzliche** ~ legal power, statutory agency; **mangelnde** ~ absence of authority; **scheinbare** ~ colo(u)r of (apparent, ostensible) authority, holding out; **tatsächliche** ~ actual authority; **unbeschränkte** ~ unlimited authority;
~ **im Einzelfall** actual authority; ~ **kraft Rechtsscheins** authority by estoppel;
außerhalb seiner ~ handeln to act ultra vires; **innerhalb (im Rahmen) seiner ~ handeln** to act within the scope of one's authority; **ohne ~ handeln** to conduct affairs without authority; **seine ~ überschreiten** to exceed one's powers (authority); **jem. scheinbare ~ zuordnen** to hold out s. o. *(Br.)*.

Vertretungs|monopol exclusive agency; ~**nachweis** grant of representation; **ausschließliches ~recht einer Gewerkschaft** union jurisdiction; ~**verhältnis** agency; ~**verhältnis aufheben** to revoke an agency; ~**verhältnis beenden** to terminate an agency; ~**vertrag** contract of agency; ~**vollmacht** power of attorney.

vertretungsweise by proxy, vicariously.

Vertrieb sale, selling, marketing, distribution, run;
direkter ~ direct selling (marketing); **genossenschaftlicher** ~ associative (cooperative) marketing;
[Güter]absatz und ~ distribution, marketing;
~ **von Anteilen** sale of shares; ~ **landwirtschaftlicher Erzeugnisse** agricultural market[ing]; ~ **mittels eigenen Fahrzeugparks** own-vehicle distribution; ~ **durch einen ausgewählten Händlerkreis** selective distribution (selling); ~ **von Industrieerzeugnissen** industrial marketing; ~ **auf dem Kommissionswege** consignment marketing; ~ **durch Vertreter** house-to-house selling;
~ **der Masse der Erzeugnisse beeinflussen** to account for the bulk of goods sold; ~ **eines Erzeugnisses übernehmen** to take up a line of goods.

vertrieben outcast, exiled, expelled, displaced.

Vertriebener displaced (expelled) person, refugee, outcast.

Vertriebs|abkommen marketing agreement; ~**absprache** distribution agreement; ~**abteilung** sales (marketing) department; ~**agentur** marketing agency; ~**analyse** sales (marketing) analysis; ~**anstrengungen** sales drive, marketing (selling) efforts; ~**anzeige** notice of sales; ~**apparat** marketing organization (machinery), distributive machinery, sales administration (organization); **leistungsfähiger ~apparat** marketing efficiency; **wachsende ~aufgaben** growing distribution task; ~**aufwand** expense of marketing (sale), marketing expenses (cost), distribution costs; ~**ausschuß** sales committee; ~**aussichten** marketing conditions (outlook), sales prospects; ~**bedingungen** marketing conditions, sales terms *(US)*; ~**berater** marketing adviser, sales consultant; **freiberuflicher ~berater** marketing consultant; ~**beratung** marketing consulting; ~**bereich** sales (distribution, marketing) area; ~**beschränkungen** sales restrictions.

vertriebsbewußt marketing-minded (orientated).

Vertriebs | büro selling agency; **sich immer mehr dem ~denken zuwenden** to grow in marketing mindedness; **~direktor** marketing director, merchandising manager; **~einrichtungen** distribution equipment, marketing facilities, sales devices; **~erfahrungen** marketing knowhow (experience); **~ergebnis** sales result; **~fachleute** marketing people, distributive salesmen; **~fachmann** marketing specialist (man, economist, expert), distributive salesman; **~fachmann im Angestelltenverhältnis** professional salesman; **~fähigkeit** selling capacity; **~finanzierung** market financing.

vertriebsfördernde Gesamtmaßnahmen für ein Gebiet marketing of an article.

Vertriebs | förderung sales promotion; **~funktionen** marketing functions; **~gebiet** sales territory, distribution outlet; **~gebiet erschließen** to make up a market; **~gemeinkosten** selling expenses; **verrechnete ~gemeinkosten** allocated sales overhead expenses; **~gemeinschaft** sales combine (syndicate, group); **~genossenschaft** cooperative marketing association; **~gesellschaft** trading (agency, marketing) company, sales organization (company, association), distributive (distributing) enterprise, distributing agency, marketing subsidiary (corporation, *US*); **~gesetzgebung** marketing legislation; **~gewinn** sales profit; **~idee** sales idea; **~ingenieur** salesman engineer, engineer salesman; **~kalkulation** sales estimate; **~kanäle** trade channels, channels and outlets; **~kartell** marketing cartel; **~kaufmann** sales promoter; **~kennzahlen** distribution indices; **~kontrolle** sales progress (marketing) control, orderly marketing *(US)*; **~kosten** cost (expense) of marketing, marketing (distribution, selling) costs (expense), cost of sales, sales expense; **~kostenanalyse** distribution cost analysis; **~kunde** marketing; **~lagerbestände** products for sale; **~leiter** sales (distribution) manager, marketing director (manager), *(für Markenartikel)* brand manager, *(Verlagshaus)* circulation manager; **~lenkung** controlled distribution; **~maßnahmen** marketing transactions; **~mathematik** mathematics of distribution; **~methoden** distribution (sales, marketing, selling) methods; **~möglichkeiten** distribution opportunities; **~monopol** sales monopoly; **~netz** distribution network; **~niederlassung** sales (distributive) agency; **~organisation** sales (merchandising) organization, distributor; **~personal** marketing personnel; **~plan** plan of distribution, distribution (sales) plan; **~planung** marketing mix *(US)*; **~politik** marketing (sales) policy; **erfolgreiche ~politik** merchandising efficiency; **schöpferische ~politik** innovative marketing; **~preis** selling price; **~produkt** marketing product; **~programm** distribution plan, marketing program(me); **~quote** sales quota; **~recht** selling rights, *(Bücher)* copyright; **alleiniges ~recht** sole right to sell; **alleiniges ~recht haben** to be sole agent; **~regelung** distribution agreement; **~schema** distribution system; **~schwierigkeiten** marketing difficulties; **~stelle** sales office, sales outlet *(US)*, distributing agency; **~steuerung** marketing control; **~- und Verkaufssteuerung** merchandising technique; **~struktur** structure of distribution; **~studie** marketing [research] study; **~system** selling plan, marketing (distribution) system; **zweigleisiges ~system** dual distribution *(US)*; **~tätigkeit** marketing activity (function), distribution service; **~technik** marketing technique; **~terminologie** marketing terminology; **~unkosten** selling (marketing) expenses; **~unterlagen** marketing data; **~unternehmen** distributive enterprise, distributing agency; **~unterstützung** selling (dealer) aid; **~verbot** sales prohibition; **~vereinbarung** marketing contract (agreement), distribution (selling) arrangement; **~verfahren** marketing procedure (process); **~verhältnisse** market[ing] conditions; **~vertrag** marketing contract; **~vertreter** distributor, selling agent; **~vorschlag** marketing proposal; **~vorschriften** conditions of sale, sales terms *(US)*; **~vorteile** marketing (distribution) advantages; **~wege** channels of distribution, sales (distribution) channels; **~wesen** marketing field, distribution; **genossenschaftliches ~wesen** cooperative marketing; **~zahlen** sales figures, marketing data; **~ziel** marketing goal (target).

vertrinken, ganzen Wochenlohn to spend a week's pay on booze *(Br., sl.)*.

vertrödeln to trifle, to fritter;
seine Zeit ~ to potter away one's time; **Zeit bei der Arbeit ~** to dawdle over one's work.

vertrösten, j. to put s. o. off; **seine Gläubiger mit leeren Versprechungen ~** to feed (put off) one's creditors with empty promises; **Kind ~** to console a child.

vertrusten to corner the market, to trustify, to pool.

Vertrustung trustification, pooling.

vertuschen to blanket, to hush (cover) up, to burke, to camouflage.

vertuschte Angelegenheit hush affair.

Vertuschung cover-up, camouflage.

verübeln, jem. etw. to resent s. one's doing.

verüben *(Verbrechen)* to commit, to perpetrate.

Verübung *(Verbrechen)* commitment, commission, perpetration.

verulken to make fun of;
j. ~ to pull s. one's leg, to kid s. o., to take the micky out of s. o. *(sl.)*.

Verulkung josh.

verunglimpfen to slander, to disparage, to defame, to denigrate, to blacken, *(politischen Gegner)* to smear;
Tote ~ to revile the memory of the dead.

verunglimpfend detractive.

Verunglimpfung slander, defamation, detraction, disparagement, denigration, *(politischer Gegner)* smear;
~ von Konkurrenzerzeugnissen disparagement of goods, slander of title, trade libel *(US)*; **~ Verstorbener** reviling the memory of the dead.

verunglücken to meet with an accident, *(Schiff)* to be lost, *(tödlich)* to perish;
mit dem Flugzeug ~ to be involved in a plane crash; **tödlich ~** to be killed in an (have a fatal) accident.

Verunglückter casualty, injured, victim.

verunreinigen to contaminate, to pollute.

Verunreinigung contamination, pollution;
~ verboten! commit no nuisance!

verunsichern, j. to disconcert (rattle, *US*) s. o.

verunsichert fühlen, sich to be disconcerted.

verunstalten to disfigure, to blemish, to deform, to deface.

verunstaltete Landschaft marred (disfigured) landscape.

Verunstaltung disfigurement, defacement, deformation;
~ der Landschaft a blot on the landscape; **~ durch Reklame** disfigurement by advertisement.

veruntreuen to misappropriate, to embezzle, to peculate, to defalcate, to job;
öffentliche Gelder ~ to misappropriate public funds; **Mündelgelder ~** to embezzle the funds of a ward; **Vereinsgelder ~** to misappropriate the society's funds.

Veruntreuer embezzler, defalcator, peculator.

Veruntreuung fraudulent conversion, wrongful abstraction, defalcation, embezzlement, peculation, jobbery, graft *(US)*, *(im Amt)* malversation;
~ öffentlicher Gelder defalcation, misappropriation of public funds;
~ begehen to defalcate; **~en in Höhe von 100.000 Pfund begehen** to make defalcations to the extent of £ 100.000.

Veruntreuungsversicherung fidelity insurance.

verursachen to cause, to occasion, to give rise to, to bring about, to draw on;
große Aufregung ~ to cause great excitement; **große Ausgaben ~** to entail great expense; **Kosten ~** to involve expenses; **jem. große Kosten ~** to put s. o. to great expense; **Skandal ~** to give rise to a scandal; **jem. Umstände ~** to give s. o. much trouble; **jem. große Unannehmlichkeiten ~** to put s. o. to great inconvenience; **Unfall ~** to be the cause of an accident.

Verursachungsprinzip law of causation, *(Umweltschutz)* causative principle.

verurteilen to damn, *(Gericht)* to condemn, to sentence, to convict;
j. in Abwesenheit ~ to condemn s. o. in absentia; **Beklagten zur Zahlung der Prozeßkosten ~** to condemn the defendant in costs; **aufgrund gefälschten Beweismaterials ~** to kangaroo *(US sl.)*; **Dieb zu einem halben Jahr Gefängnis ~** to sentence a thief to six months; **zu einer Geldstrafe ~** to [condemn to pay a] fine, to impose (levy) a fine; **jds. Handlungsweise ~** to disapprove of s. one's action; **j. aufgrund geringen Indizienmaterials ~** to condemn s. o. on slight evidence; **zur Leistung von Unterhaltszahlungen ~** to award alimony; **zum Tode ~** to condemn to death; **zur Zahlung eines hohen Schadensersatzes ~** to award heavy damages; **zivilrechtlich ~** to adjudge.

verurteilt condemned, sentenced;
rechtskräftig ~ sein to be prosecuted to conviction; **zum Scheitern ~ sein** to be doomed to failure; **~ werden** to be sentenced, to stand convicted; **in Abwesenheit ~ werden** to be sentenced by default; **zu den Kosten ~ werden** to be cast (ordered) to pay the costs; **rechtskräftig ~ werden** to be prosecuted to conviction; **zum Schadensersatz ~ werden** to be cast in damages; **zu lebenslänglichem Zuchthaus ~ werden** to get a life sentence.

Verurteilten hinrichten to dispatch a condemned man.
Verurteilter convict, person convicted;
lebenslänglich ~ lifer;
~ **mit Bewährung** probationer; ~ **mit erleichtertem Strafvollzug** first-class misdemeanant.
Verurteilung condemnation, conviction, sentence;
erneute ~ reconviction; **erste** ~ first conviction; **frühere** ~ former conviction; **rechtskräftige** ~ final sentence;
~ **des Angeklagten** conviction of the accused; ~ **wegen Rückfalls** second conviction; ~ **zum Schadensersatz** legal award; ~ **im Schnellverfahren** summary conviction; ~ **zum Tode** sentence of death, death sentence; ~ **zur Tragung der Kosten** order to pay the (judgment for) costs;
der Gefahr einer ~ **ausgesetzt sein** to be in jeopardy.
vervielfältigen to multiply, *(Drehbuch)* to micrograph, *(hektographieren)* to mimeograph, *(reproduzieren)* to reproduce, to process, *(Schriftsatz)* to manifold, to duplicate.
Vervielfältiger multiplier, reproducer.
vervielfältigter Brief process letter.
Vervielfältigung mimeographing, multiplication, duplication, *(Abzug)* duplicate, *(Film)* printing, *(Reproduktion)* reproduction;
~ **auf mechanischem Wege** mechanical reproduction.
Vervielfältigungs|apparat duplicator, duplicating machine, copying apparatus, manifold writer, manifolder, polygraph, copycat *(Br.)*; ~**arbeiten** manifolding; ~**büro** mimeographic department; ~**gerät**, ~**maschine** mimeograph, multigraph, manifolding (duplicating) machine, hectograph; ~**kosten** reproduction costs; ~**matrize** stencil; ~**methode** manifold system; ~**papier** manifold paper; ~**recht** copyright; ~**system** manifold system; ~**verfahren** autography, duplication.
vervollkommnen to bring to perfection, to round off;
sich in etw. ~ to improve in one's studies, to perfect o. s. in s. th.; **fremde Erfindung** ~ to refine upon another's invention; **Maschine** ~ to improve a machine, to introduce refinements into a machine.
Vervollkommnung perfection, advance, improvement, complement;
~ **der Betriebsausstattung** expansion in equipment; ~ **einer fremden Erfindung** refinement upon another invention; ~ **des Maschinenparks** expansion in machinery.
Vervollkommnungspatent improvement patent, patent for improvement.
vervollständigen to accomplish, to complete, to complement, to fill up, to make up, to piece out, to top off, *(abrunden)* to round off, to complement, *(Buchungen)* to enter up;
Buch durch Nachträge ~ to supplement a book; **Ladung** ~ to get full cargo; **sein Lager** ~ to replenish one's (lay in fresh) stock; **seine Sammlung** ~ to complete one's collection.
vervollständigende Tätigkeit follow-up work.
Vervollständigung completion, complement, supplementation;
~ **einer Sammlung** completion of a collection.
verwachsen *(Baum)* stunted, crooked, *(bucklig)* hunchbacked;
mit etw. völlig ~ **sein** to become deeply rooted in s. th.; **mit jem. eng** ~ **sein** to be hand in glove with s. o.
verwackeln, Aufnahme to have a photo spoiled (spoilt).
Verwählen *(tel.)* false (lost) call.
verwählen to dial a wrong number.
Verwahr ward;
in ~ **haben** to hold in custody.
verwahren to keep, to bail, to preserve, *(Wertpapiere)* to have (hold) in [safe] custody *(Br.)*, to hold in trust;
abgesondert ~ to keep separately; **sich energisch gegen etw.** ~ to raise a strong protest against s. th.; **für das Gericht** ~ to hold for the court; **sicher** ~ to have in safekeeping, to stow away; **sich gegen Verdächtigungen** ~ to protest against suspicions; **jem. etw. zu** ~ **geben** to entrust to s. one's care, to deposit s. th. with s. o.
Verwahrer keeper, person in charge, consignatory, bailee, guardian, *(Vermögenswerte)* depository, depositary, depositee, safekeeper, custodian;
entgeltlicher ~ bailee for reward; **treuhänderischer** ~ trustee; **unentgeltlicher** ~ gratuitous bailee;
als ~ **innehaben** to hold to bail;
~**staat** depositary government.
verwahrlosen to be neglectful of one's appearance;
~ **lassen** *(Pachtgrundstück)* to estrepe; **j.** ~ **lassen** to neglect s. o.; **Gebäude** ~ **lassen** to dilapidate a building.
verwahrlost dilapidated, down (out) at heel *(Br.)*;
~ **sein** to be in a state of neglect;
~**es Kind** neglected minor; ~**e Kinder** waifs and strays.
Verwahrloster neglected (seedy, dissipated) person.
Verwahrlosung limbo, neglect, *(Gelände)* dilapidation, *(Pachtgrundstück)* estrepement;
sittliche ~ dissipation.
Verwahr|staat depository state; ~**stück** vault deposit, custody item; ~**stücke für gemeinsame Hinterleger** custody held for joint deposition.
Verwahrung keeping, trust, custody, bailment, ward, charge, *(Effekten)* safekeeping, safe custody *(Br.)*, deposition, custodianship *(US)*, *(Protest)* protest;
in ~ on deposit, in trust;
amtliche ~ official custody; **gerichtlich angeordnete** ~ judicial deposit; **entgeltliche (gewerbliche)** ~ lucrative bailment; **gerichtliche** ~ impoundage, judicial sequestration; **unentgeltliche** ~ gratuitous bailment (deposit), naked deposit;
~ **durch das Gericht** impounding, sequestration; ~ **von Wertpapieren** deposit (safe custody) of securities;
jds. ~ **in einer Erziehungsanstalt anordnen** to order s. one's detention in a reformatory *(Br.)* (industrial, *US*) school; ~ **einlegen** to enter (lodge, make, raise) a protest; ~ **bei einer Regierung einlegen** to protest to a government; **in** ~ **geben** to deliver in trust, to deposit, to reposit, to give into custody (care), to lodge, to bail, to entrust (commit) to the custody; **jem. etw. in** ~ **geben** to give s. th. to s. o. to keep, to trust s. o. with s. th.; **jem. Geld in** ~ **geben** to lodge money with s. o.; **in gerichtliche** ~ **geben** to impound; **in** ~ **haben** to have in charge, to have (hold) in custody, to have s. th. in one's keeping; **öffentliche Urkunden in** ~ **haben** to have the legal custody of public records; **in** ~ **nehmen** to take charge of (into custody, in trust); **Urkunde in gerichtliche** ~ **nehmen** to impound (sequester) a document.
verwahrungsähnliches Verhältnis quasi-deposit.
Verwahrungs|beschluß *(Geisteskranker)* reception order; ~**bruch** rescue of goods restrained; ~**gebühr** custody fee, *(für zwangsvollstreckte Gegenstände)* possession money *(Br.)*; **einseitiges** ~**geschäft** bailment for the sole benefit of one party; ~**ort** depository, repository, place of custody; ~**quittung** safe-custody receipt; ~**schein** trustee's certificate *(Br.)*; **amtliche** ~**stelle** legal custodian; ~**stelle für treuhänderisch hinterlegte Wertpapiere** escrow depository; **gesetzliches** ~**verhältnis** involuntary deposit; **unentgeltliches** ~**verhältnis** gratuitous bailment; ~**vertrag** bailment, bailment agreement (contract), *(Effekten)* deposit, safe custody *(Br.)* (custodianship, *US*) contract; **entgeltlicher** ~**vertrag** bailment for hire; **unentgeltlicher** ~**vertrag** gratuitous (naked) deposit.
verwaiste Straßen deserted streets.
verwalten to administer, to administrate, to govern, *(Betrieb)* to manage, to conduct, to direct, to operate *(US)*, to control, to run, *(Feindvermögen)* to sequester, *(überwachen)* to superitend, to supervise, to control;
Amt ~ to hold (execute, serve) an office; **Archiv** ~ to keep the archives; **Depots** ~ to administer custodianship *(US)* (safe-custody, *Br.*) accounts; **Effekten** ~ to assume safe custody *(Br.)* (custodianship, *US*); **Geld** ~ to appropriate money; **getrennt** ~ to keep apart; **Haus** ~ to manage a house, *(Hausmeister)* to janitor for *(US)* (be caretaker of) a house; **Kasse** ~ to keep the cash; **Konkursmasse zugunsten der Gläubiger** ~ to administer an estate for the benefit of the creditors; **Konto** ~ to carry an account; **Nachlaß** ~ to administer upon an estate; **provisorisch** ~ to put into commission; **schlecht** ~ to maladminister, to mismanage, to misgovern, to misconduct; **treuhänderisch** ~ to act as trustee, to hold in trust; **jds. Vermögen** ~ to act as trustee for s. one's property, to be in charge of s. one's estate.
Verwalter person in charge, sequester, curator, *(Aufseher)* superintendent, intendant, *(Grundstück, Haus)* property manager, *(Hausmeister)* caretaker, janitor *(US)*, *(Landgut)* steward, bailiff *(Br.)*, *(Leiter)* manager, *(Nachlaß)* administrator, executor, *(Treuhänder)* trustee, custodian;
behördlich bestellter ~ official receiver, conventional trustee; **für die Durchführung eines Zwangsvollstreckungsbeschlusses bestellter** ~ receiver by way of equitable execution *(Br.)*; **gerichtlich eingesetzter** ~ judicial factor; **schlechter** ~ misgovernor; **sparsamer** ~ saving manager;
~ **einer Konkursmasse** assignee in bankruptcy, trustee of a bankrupt's estate, official receiver *(Br.)*; ~ **von Mündelvermögen** custodian trustee; **unredlicher** ~ **mit zwangsweiser Treuhänderhaftung** trustee ex maleficio; ~ **des Vermögens einer Kapitalsammelstelle** institutional fund manager;
als ~ **tätig sein** to administrate, to factor;
~**amt** administratorship, receivership, stewardship, trusteeship, custodianship.

verwaltet | werden, von jem. to be under the care of s. o.; **treuhänderisch ~ werden** to be under trust;
vom Staat (staatlich) ~er Fonds state-operated fund.

Verwaltung administration, intendance, superintendence, *(AG)* managing board, management, *(Behörde)* [administrative] authority, governing body, agency, *(Leitung)* management, dispensation, charge, conduct, control, direction, carriage, running, *(Staatsdienst)* civil service *(Br.)*, government, *(Treuhänder)* custodianship, trusteeship;
unter gerichtlicher ~ in chancery;
aufwendige ~ wasteful administration; **betrügerische ~** surreptitious management; **bundeseigene ~** federal administration; **finanzielle ~** finance administration; **gemeinsame ~** coadministration; **kommunale ~** municipal (local, *Br.*) government (authorities); **korrupte ~** corrupt administration; **öffentliche ~** public administration, civil service *(Br.)*, local administration (government); **schlechte ~** maladministration, poor management, mismanagement, misgovernment; **selbständige ~** self-government, independent government; **sparsame ~** economical administration; **städtische ~** local (municipal) government; **vorläufige ~** receivership; **zentrale ~** central (centralized) government;
~ von Aktienbeteiligung equity management; **~ eines Amtes** exercise of an office; **~ von Bagatellnachlässen** summary administration; **~ eines landwirtschaftlichen Betriebes** farm management; **~ öffentlich-rechtlicher Betriebe** public-business administration; **~ von Effekten** safe-deposit keeping, custodianship *(US)*; **~ des Fondsvermögens** *(Pensionkasse)* deposit administration; **~ von Fremdwährungsguthaben** currency exposure management; **~ öffentlicher Gelder** care of public money, handling of public funds; **~ von Kapitalanlagen** investment management; **~ des gesamten Nachlasses** general administration; **~ bisher nicht erfaßter Nachlaßgegenstände** grant of administration de bonis non; **~ des Obligationenvermögens** bond management; **~ eines Pensionsfonds** deposit administration; **~ und Förderung eines Pensionsfonds** pension administration and development; **~ der Staatsfinanzen** administration of the public revenue; **~ des Steuerressorts** tax management; **~ durch einen Treuhänder** trusteeship, trust administration; **~ ohne Treuhandfunktionen** passive trust; **~ eines Vermögens** administration of an estate (of property); **~ gesperrter Vermögen** alien property custodian *(US)*; **~ von Versicherungsrisiken** risk management; **~ von Währungsguthaben** reserve asset management; **~ eines Wertpapierdepots** portfolio management; **~ für europäische wirtschaftliche Zusammenarbeit** Economic Cooperation Administration; **~ von Zwischenanlagebeträgen** management of cash funds;
Leitung der ~ abgeben to pass on the administrative leadership; **in der ~ mitzureden haben** to have a voice in the management; **bestechliche ~ zum Teufel jagen** to throw out a corrupt regime; **in der öffentlichen ~ tätig sein** to be in the public service *(Br.)*; **auf schlechte ~ zurückzuführen sein** to be due to bad management.

Verwaltungs | abkommen administrative agreement (contract), interdepartment agreement; **zwischen Sonderorganisationen der UNO abgeschlossene ~abkommen** interagency agreement; **~abteilung** administrative division (department); **~akt** administrative (governmental, ministerial) act; **fehlerhafter ~akt** failure to act; **~amt** administration office, stewardship; **~angelegenheit** administrative matter, civil affair; **~angestellter** government employee; **~anordnung** administrative order (directive), government regulation; **~apparat** administration [machinery], administrative apparatus (setup, establishment, organization); **übersetzter ~apparat** overstaffed civil service *(Br.)*; **~apparat abbauen** to axe a number of officials *(Br.)*; **~arbeit** administrative work; **~arbeit eines Vereins** transactions of a society's business; **~aufbau** corporate structure.

Verwaltungsaufgaben administrative duties;
regierungsmäßige ~ governmental responsibilities;
~ durchführen to fulfil(l) a management roll; **mit allen ~ bestens vertraut sein** to be good at paper work; **~ wahrnehmen** to fulfil(l) a managing role.

Verwaltungs | aufsicht administrative supervision; **~aufwand** administrative expense (costs), staff and material expenditure; **~ausgaben** administrative expenses (expenditure, costs); **persönliche ~ausgaben** personal expenses; **sachliche ~ausgaben** material expenses; **~ausschuß** administrative board (committee, commission), executive (managing, prudential, *US*) committee; **~ausschuß einsetzen** to appoint an administrative board; **~ausschußverfahren** *(EG)* management committee; **~autonomie** self-government, home rule *(Br.)*.

Verwaltungsbeamter administrative (administration) officer (official), ministerial (civil service, *Br.*, civil, *US*) officer, administrant, magistrate *(US)*;
höchster ~ *(Universität)* registrar, *(allgemein)* chief magistrate, governor; **oberster ~** *(Gesellschaft)* company secretary *(Br.)*;
~ sein to be in the civil service *(Br.)*.

Verwaltungs | befugnisse übertragen to lodge administrative powers; **~behörde** administrative authority (body, agency, *US*), governmental body (agency) *(US)*, government, departmental agency; **nachgeordnete ~behörde** governmental subdivision; **~behörde für die Verkehrsluftfahrt** civil aeronautics administration; **~beirat** advisory (administrative) board, *(Kommunalwesen)* county board of supervisors; **~bereich** jurisdiction, competence; **~bericht** administrative report; **~beschwerde** appeal; **~bezirk** division, administrative district (area, unit), municipal (magisterial, *US*) district, administrative county *(Br.)*, administration area, riding *(Br.)*, township *(Br.)*, civil district, superintendency, intendancy; **in ~bezirke aufteilen** to regionalize; **~büro** [administrative] office; **~chef** chief magistrate.

Verwaltungsdienst administrative (civil, *Br.*) service;
höherer ~ administrative class, higher grade of the civil service *(Br.)*; **weisungsgebundener ~** ministerial services;
~leistungen erstellen to provide administrative services.

Verwaltungs | ebene tier *(Br.)*; **zweite ~ebene** second-tier authority; **~einheit** unit of administration, local division; **autonome ~einheiten** proprietary governments; **kommunale ~einheit** municipal (local, *Br.*) authority; **~einsparungen** economies in administration, civil service cuts *(Br.)*; **~entscheidung** administrative ruling; **~erfahrungen** administrative (management) experience; **~erlaß** ordinance, magisterial decree *(US)*; **~ermessen** administrative discretion; **~etat** administrative expense budget; **~examen** divisional examination; **~fach** administrative department; **~fachmann** business administrator; **~formalitäten** administrative formalities; **~funktionen** administrative (governmental) functions; **~gebäude** administration (administrative) building, *(AG)* business premises, management office; **~gebiet** administrative area (county, *Br.*), political subdivision; **~gebühr** *(Bank)* account-carrying (administrative) charge, *(Bearbeitung)* management charge, *(Behörde)* [administrative] fee, governmental fee, *(Investmentfonds)* management fee, service charge *(Br.)*, *(Lagerungskosten)* carrying charge *(US)*, *(Rückkauf einer Lebensversicherung)* surrender charge; **~gebührprämie** *(Kapitalanlagegesellschaft)* management fee bonus; **~gemeinkosten** administrative overheads; **~genie** administrative genius; **~gericht** administrative (legislative) court, *(UNO)* Administrative Tribunal; **~gerichtsbarkeit** administrative jurisdiction, disputed-claims office; **~geschäfte** administrative transactions; **~gesellschaft** administrative company, civil corporation, managing company, *(Kapitalanlagegesellschaft)* management company *(Br.)*; **~gremium** administrative board, administrative (governing) body; **~grenzen** limitations of an administration; **~grundsätze** principles of administration; **~handlung** administrative act; **nicht ordnungsgemäß zustande gekommene (fehlerhafte) ~handlung** failure to act; **~haushalt** administration expense budget; **~jahr** business year; **~kader** management cadre; **~karriere** management career; **~klage** administrative court action; **~komitee** *(ECU)* managing board; **~kompetenz** administrative jurisdiction; **~konto** management account; **~körper** administrative body (board), *(Betrieb)* management team, managerial staff.

Verwaltungskosten costs of administration, administrative costs (charges, expenditure, expenses), handling costs, *(je Abteilung)* direct department expenses, *(Betrieb)* cost of management, management expense, *(Investmentgesellschaft)* management fee, operating costs, service charge *(Br.)*;
~anteil overhead rate, *(Versicherung)* load[ing]; **~last** administration burden; **~zuschlag** margin, *(Versicherung)* load, loading.

Verwaltungs | kräfte administrative manpower (staff); **~macht** *(Völkerrecht)* administering authority; **~maschine** mechanics of government.

verwaltungsmäßig administrative, ministerial, managerial.

Verwaltungs | maßnahmen administrative action (measures), administration measures, governmental actions; **~maßnahmen in Schutz nehmen** to defend the course of the administration; **~methoden** *(Betrieb)* methods of management; **vielschichtige ~methoden** multilevel government; **~organ** administrative body (organ); **~organisation** management organization; **~personal** administrative personnel (staff); **~posten** administrative post, government situation; ~**praktiken** administrative practices; ~**prämie** management incentive, *(Kapitalanlagegesellschaft)* management fee bonus; ~**praxis** administrative practice.

Verwaltungsrat board of governors (directors), governing body, committee of management, executive committee, managing (outside, *US*) board, *(Europäische Investitionsbank)* administrative board, *(Institut)* board of trustees, prudential committee *(US)*, *(Universität)* regent *(US)*;
geschäftsführender ~ einer Aktiengesellschaft managing directors, board of directors; **gesetzlich vorgeschriebener ~** statutory board;
~ der unabhängigen Rundfunk- und Fernsehgesellschaften Independent Broadcasting Authority.

Verwaltungsrats|bezüge directors' fees; ~**mitglied** board member; **geschäftsführendes ~mitglied** managing director; ~**sitzung** board meeting; **anteilsmäßige ~vergütung** apportionment of director's remuneration; ~**vorsitzender** chairman of the board.

Verwaltungs|recht administrative law; **~- und Nutznießungsrecht des Ehemanns am Vorbehaltsgut der Ehefrau** marital control *(Br.)*; ~**reform** civil service reform *(Br.)*; **~reform durchführen** to reform an administration; ~**regionen** regional authorities *(Br.)*; ~**richter** administrative law judge, hearing officer *(US)*; ~**sachen** administration business; ~**schwierigkeiten** administrative difficulties; ~**sitz** administrative headquarters, registered office *(Br.)*; ~**spitze** management; **zentralgesteuerte ~spitze auflösen** to dismantle central management; ~**sprache** administrative terminology; ~**stelle** administrative board (agency), ministerial office; **höhere ~stufe** upper tier *(Br.)*; **zweistufiges ~system** two-tier system; ~**talent** administrative competence; ~**tätigkeit** administrative work (activity, service), governmental action (activity); ~**technik** administrative engineering.

verwaltungstechnisch administrative;
~e Maßnahmen administrative measures.

Verwaltungs|träger executive body; ~**umbau** civil service reform *(Br.)*; ~**unkosten** administrative expenses, *(Einkommensteuererklärung)* selling and administrative expense; **aufgeschlüsselte ~unkosten** administrative charges expended on the work to date; ~**vereinbarung** administrative arrangement, interdepartmental agreement; ~**verfahren** administrative procedure (proceedings); ~**verfügung** administrative ruling, executive order (ruling); **~verfügung erlassen** to give an administrative order; ~**verordnung** statutory order; ~**vertrag** management contract; ~**vorgang** administrative process; ~**vorschrift** administrative regulation, rule *(US)*.

Verwaltungsweg, auf dem through administrative channels;
im ~ zur Durchführung bringen to put into effect by administrative action; **~ einhalten** to act through the channels; **im ~ überprüfen** to review administratively.

Verwaltungs|wesen administration; ~**wissenschaft** administrative science; ~**zentrum** administrative center *(US)* (centre, *Br.*); ~**zweig** executive branch, administrative department.

verwandeln to convert, to change, to turn, to transform;
in verbrannte Erde ~ *(mil.)* to scorch; **Stadt in einen Trümmerhaufen ~** to turn a town into shambles; **Strafe ~** to commute a sentence; **j. völlig ~** to change s. o. completely.

Verwandlungs|flugzeug convertible aircraft, convertiplane; ~**künstler** quick-change artist.

verwandt related, kindred, affined, akin, *(entsprechend)* analogous, *(vertraut)* familiar, near;
mütterlicherseits ~ related on the mother's side; **nahe ~** near in blood, closely related; **in der Seitenlinie ~** related in the collateral line;
mit jem. ~ sein to be related (of kin) to s. o., to count kin with s. o. *(Scot.)*; **eng ~ sein** to be a first cousin with;
~e Gebiete allied subjects; **nicht ~e Person** stranger in blood.

Verwandte, engere near relatives; **entfernte ~** distant relations; **nächste ~** next of kin; **nahe ~** near relations;
~ in absteigender Linie lineal descendents; **~ in aufsteigender Linie** lineal ascendants; **~ in der aufsteigenden Seitenlinie** collateral ancestors;
einem ~n zufallen to revert to an ascendant (ascendent).

Verwandten|ehe intermarriage; ~**erbfolge** chain of succession.

Verwandter relation, relative, kin;
angeheirateter ~ in-law *(coll.)*; **entfernter ~** distant relative, side cousin; **naher ~** close relation; **unmittelbarer ~** lineal relative; **weitläufiger ~** distant relation, cater cousin;
~ in aufsteigender Linie ascendant; **~ in der direkten Linie** lineal kin; **~ von mir** connection of mine; **~ in der Seitenlinie** collateral [kin], collateral kinsman.

Verwandtschaft relations, relationship, affinity, cognation, line, kin, kindred, kinsfolk, cousinhood;
ohne ~ kinless;
nahe ~ near relation, nearness of relationship;
~ im vierten Grad relation in the fourth degree; **~ in gerader Linie** lineal consanguinity, relation by lineal descent; **~ mütterlicherseits** relation on the mother's side; **~ in der Seitenlinie** collateral consanguinity;
große ~ haben to have a large connection.

verwandtschaftlich kinsmanlike;
~e Beziehungen relationship, blood bond, kinship; **in ~e Beziehungen treten** to become connected.

Verwandtschafts|beziehung relationship; ~**grad** degree [of relationship], degree of consanguinity, line of ascent; **gleicher ~grad** equal degree; **verbotene ~grade** *(Ehe)* forbidden degrees; ~**linie** line; ~**nähe** proximity of blood; ~**verhältnis** privity of blood, kinship.

verwarnen to caution, to warn, to admonish, *(Polizei)* to fee, to reprimand;
j. erneut ~ to send s. o. a second notice; **jem. offiziell ~** to give s. o. a formal warning; **j. immer wieder ~** to warn s. o. over and over again.

Verwarnung warning, reprimand, admonition, *(Polizei)* fee, caution *(Br.)*;
erneute ~ second notice; **gebührenpflichtige ~** warning and fee *(Br.)*, motoring (traffic) fine *(Br.)*, fixed penalty notice, ticket *(US)*; **gerichtliche ~** special injunction; **rechtzeitige ~** fair warning;
gebührenpflichtige ~ wegen falschen Parkens parking fine, parking ticket *(US)*;
gebührenpflichtige ~ ausstellen to fee s. o., to give s. o. a ticket *(US)*; **gebührenpflichtige ~ in Höhe von 200 DM zahlen müssen** to be fined to the tune of £ 50.

verwaschen washed out, *(unbestimmt)* vague, wishy-washy.

verwässern to dilute, *(fig.)* to water down;
Aktienkapital ~ to water stock *(US)*; **Bestimmungen ~** to water down provisions; **Eigenkapital ~** to dilute the equity.

Verwässerung dilution;
~ des Aktienkapitals watering of stock *(US)*; **~ des Eigenkapitals** equity dilution.

verwechseln to mistake, to confuse, to mix up;
j. ~ to mistake s. o. for somebody else; **Daten ~** to confuse dates.

Verwechslung von Warenzeichen confusion of trademarks.

Verwechslungsgefahr possibility of confusion.

verwegen bold, audacious, daring.

verwehen to be blown over;
Straße ~ to drift a road.

verwehren, Zutritt to deny admittance.

verweichlichen to soften, to mollycoddle, to effeminate, to featherbed *(sl.)*.

verweichlicht effeminate, mollycoddle, womanish.

verweigern to refuse, to decline;
Annahme ~ to decline (refuse) acceptance; **Annahme einer Lieferung ~** to refuse to take delivery; **Annahme eines Wechsels ~** to dishono(u)r a draft by nonacceptance; **jem. eine Auskunft ~** to deny s. o. information; **jem. die Ausreise ~** to prohibit s. o. from leaving the country; **Bezahlung ~** to refuse payment; **Gehorsam ~** to be disobedient; **Giro ~** to refuse to back a bill; **jem. Hilfe ~** to refuse help to s. o.; **Kriegsdienst ~** to be a conscientious objector; **Lieferung ~** to withhold delivery, to withhold supplies from a dealer; **Nahrung ~** to reject food; **Patent ~** to refuse (withhold the grant of) a patent; **Warenannahme ~** to refuse goods; **Zahlung eines Wechsels ~** to dishono(u)r a draft by nonpayment; **Zutritt ~** to refuse admittance.

verweigert, Annahme *(Brief)* refused; **grundlos ~** unreasonably refused;
~e Patenterteilung patent barred.

Verweigerung refusal, denial;
~ der Annahme refusal to accept (of acceptance), nonacceptance; **~ des Gehorsams** insubordination, disobedience; **~ einer Genehmigung** disaffirmance, nonratification; **~ des Kriegsdienstes** conscientious objection; **~ weiterer Lieferungen** refusal to deal *(US)* (supply); **~ eines Patents** withholding the grant of a patent; **widerrechtliche ~ der Räumung** unlawful detainer; **~ der Unterstützung des eigenen Kandidaten** bolt *(US)*; **~ eines rechtsstaatlichen Verfahrens** denial of justice; **~ zwischenstaatlicher Wirtschaftsbeziehungen** nonintercourse of commercial relations; **~ der Zahlung** nonpayment, refusal to pay, *(Staat)* repudiation.

Verweigerungsfall, im in case of refusal.
verweilen to sojourn, to stay;
sich ~ to linger; **bei einem Thema** ~ to dwell upon a subject.
Verweis reprimand, admonition, animadversion, dressing-down, reprehension, snub, telling-off, rap on the knuckles *(Br.)*, going over *(US)*, *(Hinweis)* reference;
scharfer ~ rebuke; **schriftlicher** ~ discipline entry *(US)*; **strenger** ~ severe reprimand, lesson; **unbedeutender** ~ small one *(sl.)*;
~ **erteilen** to reprimand, to animadvert, to rebuke, to skin *(sl.)*, *(parl.)* to censure; **jem. einen ~ erteilen** to read s. o. a lesson, to rap s. o. over the knuckles; **einem Untergebenen einen scharfen ~ erteilen** to rebuke a subordinate; **einem ~ nachgehen** to look up a reference; **mit einem ~ versehen** to reference.
verweisen to refer to, to remit, *(im Buch)* to cross-reference, *(Gericht)* to defer;
an einen Ausschuß ~ to refer to a committee, *(Gesetzentwurf)* to commit a bill to a committee; **auf die gesetzlichen Bestimmungen** ~ to refer to the provisions of the law; **auf eine Fußnote** ~ to refer to a footnote; **an ein anderes Gericht** ~ to remove (transfer) a cause by change of venue; **an das untere Gericht** ~ to remit to a lower court; **j. des Landes** ~ to exile s. o., to expel s. o. from the country; **j. in seine Schranken** ~ to put s. o. in his place (box, *US*); **von der Schule** ~ to expel from school; **j. an die Sekretärin** ~ to refer s. o. to the secretary; **von der Universität** ~ to rusticate, to send down *(Br.)*.
Verweisstelle referent.
Verweisung reference, cross-reference;
~ **an einen Ausschuß** committal; ~ **an den Einzelrichter** special rule; ~ **an ein höheres Gericht** evocation; ~ **an ein unteres Gericht** remitter; ~ **an den Rechtspfleger** transfer to the master; ~ **einer Sache an ein anderes Gericht** transfer (removal) of a cause to another court, remittal; ~ **an einen Schiedsrichter** remission to arbitration; ~ **von der Universität** rustication, sending down *(Br.)*.
Verweisungs | beschluß order of removal; ~**beschluß an die untere Instanz** writ of trial *(Br.)*; ~**stelle** reference; ~**verfahren** removal proceedings; ~**zeichen** insertion (guiding, reference, referential) mark.
verwendbar serviceable, applicable, utilizable, appropriate, useful, suitable;
erneut ~ reusable; **nicht** ~ unsuitable; **vielseitig** ~ versatile, many-sided, allround.
Verwendbarkeit employability, usability, usefulness, applicability, serviceableness, appropriateness, *(Fernsehgerät für Farb- und Schwarzweißsendungen)* compatibility;
praktische ~ practicability; **vielseitige** ~ versatility.
verwenden to employ, to use, to dispose (make use) of, *(anlegen)* to invest, *(anwenden)* to apply for, *(ausgeben)* to appropriate, to expend, to spend;
nicht zu ~ useless, inefficient;
für sich ~ to take for one's own use; **sich für j.** ~ to intercede (put in a good word) for s. o.; **Aktien als Deckung** ~ to apply stocks as a collateral security *(US)*; **sich besonders für j.** ~ to recommend s. o. highly; **seine Englischkenntnisse gut** ~ to make good use of one's knowledge of English; **seine Freizeit** ~ to devote one's spare time; **Geld für die Bezahlung von Schulden** ~ to apply money for the payment of debts; **sein Geld zum Kauf von Büchern** ~ to spend one's money on books; **Geldbetrag** ~ to use a sum of money; **nur bestes Material** ~ to employ the best workmanship only; **nutzbringend** ~ to turn to good account, to put s. th. to a good use; **nützlich** ~ to use to good advantage; **für sich persönlich** ~ to divert to one's personal use; **5000 £ für Schulneubauten** ~ to appropriate £ 5000 for the new school buildings; **Sorgfalt** ~ to expend (bestow) care; **gehörige Sorgfalt** ~ to use diligence in business; **unrechtmäßig für sich** ~ to misappropriate, to convert to one's own use; **sein ganzes Vermögen für wohltätige Zwecke** ~ to dispose of one's fortune to charity; **für Werbezwecke** ~ to spend on advertising; **widerrechtlich** ~ to misapply; **Wohnung für einen anderen Zweck** ~ to alter the use of premises; **Zahlung zur Verkürzung der Zinsrückstände** ~ to apply payments to the reduction of interest; **viel Zeit** ~ to spend (put in) a lot of time; **zweckentsprechend** ~ to apply correctly.
verwendet, gut well-spent; **oft** ~ stock, stereotyped.
Verwendung employment, application, use, utilization, *(als Anlage)* investment, *(Eintreten für j.)* intercession, *(Person)* assignment, *(Zuweisung)* appropriation;
auf seine ~ hin through s. one's influence; **keiner bestimmten ~ zugeführt** unappropriated; **zur besonderen** ~ *(Offizier)* for special duty;
ausschließliche ~ exclusive use; **falsche** ~ misemployment; **gemeinwirtschaftliche** ~ use on a collective basis; **gesetzeswidrige** ~ *(Fonds)* improper investment; **gewerbliche** ~ industrial use; **gewöhnliche** ~ ordinary use; **mißbräuchliche** ~ improper use, misuse; **notwendige ~en** necessary outlay; **unrechtmäßige** ~ misappropriation; **vielseitige** ~ versatility; **widerrechtliche** ~ constructive taking, conversion; **wirtschaftliche** ~ economic application; **zukünftige** ~ future use;
~ **für das Anlagevermögen** capital outlay; **sinnvolle ~ von Arbeitskräften** appropriate placement of labo(u)r; ~ **von Ausweichfrachtsätzen** alternative application of freight rates; **unbefugte ~ eines Firmennamens** improper use of a firm's name; ~ **eines Fonds** use of a fund; ~ **des Gegenwertes** application of proceeds; ~ **des Gewinns** appropriation of profit; ~ **von Giftgas** application of poison gas; ~ **des Grundkapitals** use of funds; ~ **der Haushaltsmittel** appropriation of supply; ~ **im Innendienst** *(Diplomat)* home posting; ~ **im öffentlichen Interesse** public use *(US)*; ~ **der Lebensversicherungsgewinnanteile zur Hypothekentilgung** bonus reinforcement; ~ **von Mitteln** allocation of resources, employment (use) of funds; ~ **des Prämienerlöses zur Erhöhung der Versicherungssumme** paid-up addition; ~ **des Reinerlöses (Reingewinns)** disposition (appropriation) of net income (profits); ~ **von Steuereinnahmen** employment of tax receipts; ~ **für einen wohltätigen Zweck** charitable use;
~ **finden** to be employed as; **in der Industrie ~ finden** to take up an appointment in industry; **keine ~ haben für** to have no use for; **bei unsachgemäßer ~ schnell kaputtgehen** to wear out under rough usage.
Verwendungs | antrag application request; ~**auflage** tying of funds; ~**ausweis des Volkseinkommens** flow of funds approach; ~**bereich** field of application; ~**beschränkung** restriction in the use; ~**dauer** service life.
verwendungsfähig adaptable, usable, employable.
Verwendungsfähigkeit adaptability, employability, usability.
verwendungsgebundene Anleihe tied loan.
Verwendungs | grenze appropriation mark; ~**karte** classification card (record); ~**möglichkeiten** possibilities of use; ~**nachweis** statement of application of funds, statement of resources and their application *(US)*, source and disposition statement *(US)*; ~**nachweis eines Fonds** funds statement; ~**rechnung des Volkseinkommens** expenditure approach of the national income; **derzeitiger ~zweck** existing use; **vorgesehener ~zweck** intended use; **verschiedene ~zwecke haben** to have different uses.
verwerfen to reject, to negative, to ignore, to turn down, to throw out, to dismiss, to condemn, to damn, to reprobate;
Anspruch ~ to set aside a claim; **Berufung** ~ to disallow (dismiss) an appeal; **Gesetzesvorlage** ~ to reject a bill; **Klage** ~ to dismiss a case, to nonsuit; **Urteil aus Rechtsgründen** ~ to quash a judgment on a point of law.
verwerflich condemnable, reprehensible, *(abscheulich)* abominable, obnoxious.
Verwerfung *(Ansprüche)* setting aside, *(geol.)* faulting, *(Urteil)* quashing;
~ **der Berufung** dismissal of appeal.
Verwerfungs | linie fault line; ~**schein** rejection slip.
verwertbar exploitable, utilizable, *(einlösbar)* convertible, *(verkäuflich)* realizable, salable, negotiable, marketable;
gewerblich ~ new and useful;
nicht ~e Aktiva unmarketable assets; ~**e Kupons** collectable coupons.
Verwertbarkeit exploitability, usability, *(Verkäuflichkeit)* realizability, negotiability;
mangelnde ~ nonutility; **marktmäßige** ~ marketability.
verwerten to make use of, to use, to employ, to utilize, *(Altmaterial)* to recover, to retrieve, to salvage, *(ausbeuten)* to exploit, *(auswerten)* to evaluate, *(Effekten)* to realize;
etw. ~ to put to good account; **Abfallprodukte** ~ to utilize waste products; **Anregungen in einem Roman** ~ to use suggestions in a novel; **geschäftlich** ~ to commercialize; **Patent** ~ to work (exploit) a patent, to use a patented product; **Pfandgegenstände** ~ to realize objects seized; **Waren** ~ to realize (sell) goods; **Wechsel** ~ to negotiate a draft;
sich gut ~ lassen to fetch a good price; **sich leicht ~ lassen** to find a ready market; **sich schwer ~ lassen** to find no sale, to sell badly.
Verwertung *(Abfall)* salvage, recovery of waste, *(Ausnutzung)* utilization, exploitation, turning to account, *(Gebrauch)* employment, use, *(Verkauf)* realization, sale, equitable conversion;

bestmögliche ~ optimal use; **geschäftliche (gewerbliche)** ~ commercial exploitation, commercialization, industrial use; **praktische** ~ *(Erfindung)* reduction to practice; **zukünftige** ~ future use;
~ **von Abfallprodukten** utilization of waste products; ~ **eines gepfändeten Gegenstandes** realization of a pledge; ~ **eines Patents** working (exploitation, utilization) of a patent; **wirtschaftliche** ~ **von Rohstoffen** economic utilization of raw products; ~ **von Sicherheiten** realization of securities (properties);
keine ~ **für etw. haben** to have no use for s. th.

Verwertungs|anlage utilization plant; ~**antrag** disposal request; ~**erlös** realization proceeds; **überschüssiger** ~**erlös** surplus proceeds on sale; ~**genossenschaft** marketing cooperative; ~**gesellschaft** *(Urheberrecht)* utilization company; ~**klausel** realization clause; ~**kosten** costs of realization, exploitation cost; ~**möglichkeiten** possibilities of use; **von den vorhandenen** ~**möglichkeiten zu geringen Gebrauch machen** to spread a thing's use too thinly; ~**patent** utility patent *(US)*; ~**rechte** exploitation rights; ~**sperre** prohibition to sell; ~**zwang** compulsory exploitation.

verwesen to putrefy, to decay, to decompose.

Verweser administrator, sequester, stakeholder.

Verwesung putrefaction, decay, decomposition.

verwetten to wager, to stake, to bet.

verwickeln to entangle, to involve, to implicate, to embroil;
sich ~ to tangle, to become entangled; **Freund in eine üble Angelegenheit** ~ to involve a friend in a sorry business; **in einen Krieg** ~ to embroil in a war; **in einen Prozeß** ~ to involve in a lawsuit; **in eine Verschwörung** ~ to ensnare in a conspiracy; **sich in Widersprüche** ~ to get entrapped in one's own contradictions.

verwickelt entangled, embarrassed, involved, complex, *(schwierig)* intricate, reticular;
in ein anrüchiges Geschäft ~ **sein** to be entangled in a shady business; **in eine Sache** ~ **sein** to be mixed up in (connected with) an affair; **in einen Streit mit jem.** ~ **sein** to be embroiled with s. o.;
~**e Angelegenheit** complicated affair; ~**e Handlung** *(Roman)* intricate plot; ~**es Problem** knotty problem.

Verwickelter person involved.

Verwicklung knot, entanglement, involvement, *(Hineinziehung)* implication, embroilment, *(Roman)* embroglio, imbroglio;
außenpolitische ~**en** external entanglements;
~ **in einen Prozeß** involvement in a lawsuit.

ver|wildern to go native, *(Garten)* to grow wild, to become overgrown, *(Sitten)* to degenerate; ~**winden** to get over.

verwirkbar forfeitable.

Verwirkbarkeit forfeitableness.

verwirken to forfeit;
Kaution ~ to forfeit one's bail (bond); **sein Leben** ~ to forfeit one's life; **sein Stimmrecht** ~ to forfeit one's voting rights; **Vertragsstrafe** ~ to forfeit a penalty.

verwirklichen to realize, to effectuate, to put into practice, to carry out;
sich ~ to materialize, to take shape, to come true.

Verwirklichung realization.

verwirkt forfeited;
Aktienrechte für ~ **erklären** to forfeit shares; **Geldstrafe** ~ **haben** to be liable for a fine;
~**es Recht** forfeited right.

Verwirkung forfeit, forfeiture, laches;
~ **des Pensionanspruchs** forfeiture of a pension; ~ **eines Pfandes** forfeiture of a bond; ~ **eines Rechts** forfeiture of a right.

Verwirkungs|einrede estoppel by laches; ~**klausel** defeasance (forfeiture) clause.

verwirren to derange, to disarrange, to confound, to consternate, to baffle, *(beschämen)* to put out of face, *(blenden)* to dazzle;
völlig ~ to confuse completely, to take to town *(sl.)*.

verwirrende Fülle neuer Eindrücke confusing multitude of new impressions.

verwirrt upset, in a fog, hot and bothered, unhinged, *(verlegen)* embarrassed, discomfited, *(ratlos)* perplexed, dazed, bewildered, mazed;
völlig ~ out of countenance;
~ **sein** to be in a puzzle; **von den Nachrichten ganz** ~ **sein** to be taken aback by the news.

Verwirrung baffle, confusion, embarrassment, puzzle, gog, disorder;
geistige ~ mental aberration, disorder of the mind;
größte ~ **anrichten** to throw everything in confusion; **in** ~ **geraten** to get into a muddle; ~ **lösen** to unravel an entanglement; ~ **stiften** to stir up trouble, to perplex; **in** ~ **stürzen** to upset, to overset.

verwirtschaften to squander, to dissipate;
Firma ~ to let down a firm; **Gut** ~ to disable an estate.

verwischen to smear, to smudge, *(drucktechn.)* to slur;
Spur ~ to blind a trail; **Spuren eines Verbrechens** ~ to blur the traces of a crime.

verwischt smudged, smeared, blurred.

verwittern to weather.

verwittert weather-beaten, weathered.

Verwitterung decay.

verwitwet widowed;
~**e Frau** discovert woman.

verwöhnen to spoil, *(verhätscheln)* to mollycoddle, to pamper.

verwöhnt fastidious;
~ **sein** to be dainty about one's food;
~**eren Ansprüchen gerecht werden** to satisfy the highest demands; ~**er Geschmack** extravagant taste; ~**er Pudel** pampered poodle.

Verwöhnung featherbedding.

verworfen depraved, abject, profligate, corrupt, immoral.

Verworfenheit depravation, abjection, depravity, profligacy, turpitude;
moralische ~ moral turpitude.

verworren muddy, muddled, foggy, intricate;
~**er Kopf** scatterbrain; ~**e Lage** complicated situation; ~**es Zeug reden** to talk a lot of rubbish.

verwundbar vulnerable;
~**e Stelle** sore point.

verwunden to wound, to hurt, to injure.

verwunderlich astonishing, amazing, *(merkwürdig)* odd, strange.

verwundert surprised, astonished, amazed;
mit ~**en Blicken** wonderingly.

Verwunderung surprise, amazement, astonishment;
zu meiner größten ~ to my great surprise.

verwundet wounded;
tödlich ~ fatally injured;
schwer ~ **werden** to stop a packet *(sl.)*.

Verwundete wounded, casualty.

Verwundetenabzeichen Gold Stripe *(Br.)*, Purple Heart *(US)*.

Verwundung hurt, wound, injury;
leichte ~ **davontragen** to be slightly injured; **einer** ~ **erliegen** to die from a wound.

verwunschen bedevilled, bewitched.

verwünschen *(verfluchen)* to curse, to cuss *(sl.)*, to damn *(sl.)*.

Verwünschung curse, cuss, expletive, malediction;
in ~**en über j. ausbrechen** to launch into abuse of s. o.; **j. mit** ~**en überschütten** to curse s. o. with bell, book and candle, to pump abuses upon s. o.

verwürfeln *(tel.)* to scramble.

verwurzeln to strike root;
tief ~ to ingrain.

verwurzelt, tief deeply rooted.

verwüsten to devastate, to desolate, to make (play) havoc, to destroy, to destruct *(US)*, to harry;
ganzes Land ~ to lay waste to the whole country; **weite Landstriche** ~ to play havoc with large areas of the country.

verwüstet sein to be a wilderness.

Verwüstung havoc, devastation, desolation, destruction, strip *(US)*;
schwere ~**en verursachen** to cause havoc.

verzagen to fall in despondence, to despair, to give up hope.

verzagt despondent, down-hearted, weak-spirited.

verzählen, sich to miscount, to count wrong, to lose count.

Verzahnung close interrelationship, interdependence, tooth system.

verzanken, sich mit jem. to fall out with s. o.

verzankt sein to be at loggerheads.

verzapfen, Unsinn to talk rubbish, to talk through one's hat.

verzärteln to pamper, to wet-nurse, to mollycoddle;
Kind ~ to pet (coddle) a child.

verzaubern to cast a spell over, to bewitch, to enchant.

Verzehr consumption, eating;
für menschlichen ~ **ungeeignet** unfit for human consumption; **zum** ~ **an Ort und Stelle** for consumption on the premises; **Waren zum freien** ~ **einführen** to enter goods for consumption.

verzehren to consume, to eat, *(verbrauchen)* to spend, to expend;
sich ~ to waste away; **sich vor Gram** ~ to eat one's heart out *(coll.)*; **Mahlzeit im Freien** ~ to eat a meal out of doors; **sich vor Sehnsucht nach jem.** ~ to hanker after s. o.

verzehrt, vom Kummer wasted with grief.
verzeichnen to register, to list, to enter in a list, to record, to enrol(l), to chronicle, to schedule, to item, *(verzerren)* to misrepresent, to distort;
geringste Erderschütterungen ~ to register even the minutest tremors of the earth; **beachtliche Ergebnisse** ~ to achieve considerable results; **Gewinne** ~ to record gains; **kleine Gewinne** ~ to register small gains; **neuen Höchststand** ~ to register a new top; **Kursgewinn** ~ to score an advance; **Kurssteigerung von 17 Punkten** ~ to secure an advance of 17 points; **in einer Liste** ~ to enter in a list; **Niederlage** ~ to suffer a defeat; **neuen Tiefstand** ~ to establish a new low level; **mehrere Todesfälle** ~ to record several deaths;
Erfolg ~ **können** to score a success.
verzeichnet written down, registered, *(Börse)* quoted.
Verzeichnis *(amtliche Aufstellung)* register, registry, record, *(geschlossene Aufstellung)* specification, schedule, *(Gebührenordnung)* tariff, *(Güteverzeichnis)* classification, *(Inhaltsverzeichnis)* table of contents, index, *(Inventar)* inventory, bill, *(Katalog)* catalog(ue), *(Liste)* list, file, docket, account, *(Namenliste)* roll, *(Terminliste)* calendar, cause list;
laut anliegendem ~ as per enclosed statement;
alphabetisches ~ alphabetical list (index, catalog[ue]); **bibliographisches** ~ bibliographical notes; **tabellarisches** ~ table, schedule; **thematisches** ~ thematic catalog(ue);
~ **der Aktenstücke eines Prozesses** docket; ~ **der Aktiengesellschaften** registry of joint stock companies; ~ **der Aktionäre** share list, stock ledger (record, *US*), list of stockholders *(US)*; ~ **der Aktiva und Passiva** schedule of assets and liabilities; ~ **der Anlagenwerte** schedule of investments; ~ **der Anwesenden** record of attendances; ~ **der Aussteller** list of exhibitors; ~ **der hypothekarischen Belastungen** schedule of encumbrances; ~ **empfohlener Börsenwerte** list of recommendation, official list *(US)*; ~ **lieferbarer Bücher** list of books available; ~ **der Buchungsunterlagen** voucher register; ~ **der Debitoren** schedule of accounts receivable *(US)*; ~ **zollfreier Gegenstände** free list; ~ **der Gläubiger** schedule of creditors; **amtliches** ~ **anhängiger Grundstückssachen und Konkursfälle** register of pending actions *(Br.)*; ~ **von Grundstücksurkunden** title plant *(US)*; ~ **kreditfähiger Kunden** credit list; ~ **unsicherer Kunden** blackboard book; ~ **der Mitglieder** register of members; ~ **der Patentklassen** class index of patents; ~ **der benutzten Quellen** table of authorities consulted; ~ **vorzunehmender Reparaturen** *(Haus)* schedule of dilapidations; ~ **der abzulehnenden Risiken** *(Versicherung)* decline list; ~ **der beteiligten Schauspieler** credit list; ~ **nicht eingelöster Schecks** unpaid register; ~ **der Sofortsachen** special calendar; ~ **der Steuerzahler** tax roll; ~ **der säumigen Steuerzahler** *(Grundsteuer)* tax list; ~ **der Unterschriftsberechtigten** *(Bank)* mandate form; ~ **der einsatzbereiten Waggons** loading and unloading report; ~ **der Wahlberechtigten** register of electors; ~ **der ausgelegten Waren** show bill; ~ **versandter (verschiffter) Waren** shipping note (bill) *(Br.)*, invoice; ~ **neu erschienener Werke** list of new publications; ~ **börsengängiger Wertpapiere** the list, official list *(US)*; ~ **der Zollverschlußwaren** register of goods in bond; ~ **von Zwangsversteigerungsverfahren und Sequesteraussetzungen** register of writs and orders affecting land *(Br.)*;
~ **anlegen** to make a list, to draw up (take) an inventory; **in ein** ~ **aufnehmen** to enter (enrol(l), put into, add to) a list, to catalog(ue); **Posten in ein** ~ **aufnehmen** to enter an item in (on) the index; ~ **aufstellen** to draw up (make) a list, to prepare a schedule; **in ein** ~ **eintragen** to register, to docket, to endorse; ~ **führen** to keep a list.
verzeihen to excuse, to pardon, *(Ehepartner)* to condone;
jem. eine Beleidigung ~ to pardon s. o. an offence.
Verzeihung pardon, excuse, *(Ehescheidung)* condonation;
um ~ **bitten** to beg s. one's pardon; **jem.** ~ **gewähren** to grant s. o. pardon.
verzerren to warp, to wrest, *(tel.)* to distort;
ins Lächerliche ~ to caricature, to travesty; **Text** ~ to wrest (distort) a text; **jds. Urteil** ~ to warp s. one's judgment; **Wettbewerb** ~ to distort competition.
verzerrt|e Kosten distorted costs; ~**es Lächeln** wry smile.
Verzerrung *(fig.)* warp, *(Statistik)* bias, *(Telefon)* distortion, *(Zerrbild)* travesty, caricature, parody;
~ **nach oben** upward bias; ~ **des Wettbewerbs** distortion of competition, competitive distortion (imbalance).
verzetteln, sich to have too many irons in the fire; **seine Anstrengungen** ~ to dissipate one's efforts; **sich in routinemäßiger Arbeit** ~ to waste in routine work; **seine Zeit** ~ to fritter away one's time.
Verzicht abstention, waiver, release, renunciation, relinquishment, resignation, renouncement, abnegation, abandonment, sacrifice, quitclaim, cession;
ausdrücklicher ~ express waiver (release); **stillschweigender** ~ implied waiver;
~ **auf ein Abgeordnetenmandat** resignation of membership; ~ **zugunsten der Allgemeinheit** *(Urheberrecht)* dedication to the public *(US)*; ~ **auf ein Amt** laying down of an office; ~ **auf einen Anspruch** relinquishment (waiver, abandonment) of a claim; ~ **auf alle gegenwärtigen und zukünftigen Ansprüche** general release; ~ **auf ein Anwartschaftsrecht** release of expectancy *(US)*; ~ **auf die Aussageverweigerung im Falle der Selbstbeschuldigung** waiver of immunity; ~ **auf eine Benachrichtigung** waiver of notice; ~ **auf die Berufung** abandonment of appeal; ~ **auf ein Besteuerungsrecht** abandonment of taxing power; ~ **auf die Einrede der Verjährung** waiver of the statute of limitations; ~ **auf Einrede der Vorausklage** waiver by election of remedies; ~ **auf eine Erbschaft** renouncement (relinquishment) of succession, renunciation of an inheritance *(US)*, disclaimer of an estate; ~ **auf Genauigkeit** sacrifice of accuracy; ~ **auf eine Grunddienstbarkeit** abandonment of an easement; ~ **auf eine Kandidatur** withdrawal from a candidature; ~ **auf eine Kaution** surrender of a charter; ~ **auf die Mitgift** renunciation of dower; ~ **auf Nachweis eines versicherbaren Interesses** interest or no; ~ **auf ein Patent** surrender (abandonment) of a patent; **schriftlicher** ~ **auf Pfändungsschutz** waiver of exemption; ~ **auf ein Recht** release (relinquishment, resignation) of a right; ~ **auf einen Rechtsanspruch** abandonment of a legal title; ~ **auf eine Sicherheit** abandonment of security; ~ **auf ein Staatsamt** abandonment of a public office; ~ **auf die Staatsangehörigkeit** renunciation (renouncement) of citizenship *(Br.)* (nationality, *US*); ~ **auf den Thron** abdication of the throne; ~ **auf sein Vermögen** relinquishment (renouncement) of one's property; ~ **auf Verwertung unwirtschaftlicher Vermögensteile** *(Konkursverwalter)* disclaimer of onerous property; ~ **auf Vorlage von Unterlagen** waiver of presentation; ~ **auf Wechselprotest** waiver of protest; ~ **auf das Zeugnisverweigerungsrecht** waiver of privilege;
~ **leisten** to disclaim, to quitclaim, to relinquish, to release; **auf einen Anspruch** ~ **leisten** to waive (renounce, abandon) a claim; ~ **unterschreiben** to sign a waiver of claim, to file a disclaimer;
~**anzeige** notice of renunciation.
verzichtbar renounceable;
nicht ~ nonrenounceable.
verzichten to waive, to release, to renounce, to relinquish, to resign, to abnegate, to forgo;
auf Alkohol ~ to forbear to drink alcohol; **zugunsten der Allgemeinheit** ~ *(Urheberschutz)* to dedicate to the public *(US)*; **auf ein Amt** ~ to resign office; **auf einen Anspruch** ~ to waive (renounce, abandon) a claim, to renounce one's title; **auf Ausübung eines Rechtes** ~ to release a (waive one's) right; **auf ärztliche Betreuung** ~ to dispense with the doctor's services; **auf jds. Bürgschaft** ~ to release s. o. from bondage; **auf eine Erbschaft** ~ to renounce one's interests in an estate, to resign (relinquish) an inheritance *(US)*; **auf das Erscheinen von Zeugen** ~ to dispense with the calling of witnesses; **auf eine Ferienreise** ~ to go without a holiday; **auf eine Forderung** ~ to release (abandon) a claim; **auf Förmlichkeiten** ~ to dispense with formalities; **auf die Geltendmachung einer Einrede** ~ to waive a defence *(Br.)* (defense, *US*); **zugunsten seiner Kinder** ~ to deny o. s. for one's children; **auf alle Konkursansprüche** ~ to give up all one's claims upon the bankrupt; **auf sein Ministeramt** ~ to resign from the Cabinet; **auf die Nachlaßverwaltung** ~ to resign control of an estate; **auf ein Patent** ~ to drop a patent; **auf ein unberechtigtes Patent** ~ to surrender a patent; **auf Pfändungsschutz** ~ to waive the laws exempting limited amounts of personal property from levy; **auf ein Recht** ~ to disclaim a (waive a, relinquish one's) right; **auf einen Rechtsanspruch** ~ to waive a claim, to renounce one's title; **auf eine Sekretärin** ~ to do without the services of a secretary; **auf eine Sicherheit** ~ to abandon a security; **auf seine Staatsangehörigkeit** ~ to renounce one's nationality *(US)* (citizenship, *Br.*); **auf Teileinkünfte** ~ to relinquish one's right to part of the income; **auf sein Testamentvollstreckeramt** ~ to renounce to act as executor of an heir; **auf den Thron** ~ to abdicate (renounce one's claim to) the throne; **auf sein Vermögen** ~ to renounce one's property; **auf ein Vorrecht** ~ to waive a privilege; **auf das Wort** ~ to waive the right to speak; **lieber auf etw.** ~ **als einen so hohen Preis dafür zu zahlen** to prefer to go without rather than pay so dearly for it.
Verzichtender resigner, renouncer, disclaimer, disclaimant.

Verzichterklärung waiver, release, disclaimer, quitclaim, renunciation, notice of renunciation;
bindende ~ binding waiver;
~ **des Abwicklers auf Verwertung unrentabler Vermögensgegenstände** disclaimer of onerous property by liquidator;
~ **abgeben (unterschreiben)** to file a disclaimer, to sign a waiver (release); ~ **einreichen** to file a disclaimer.

Verzicht|erklärungsformular *(für Bezugsrechte)* renunciation form *(Br.)*; ~**handlung** act of disclaimer; ~**klausel** disclaimer clause; ~**leistender** waiver, disclaimer, renouncer, resigner.

Verzichtleistung waiver, quitclaim, release, resignation, renunciation, renouncement, disclaimer, abandonment;
~ **auf Sicherheiten** abandonment of securities; ~ **auf die Staatsangehörigkeit** renunciation of citizenship *(Br.)* (nationality, *US*); ~ **auf Wechselprotest** waiver of demand, notice and protest.

Verzicht|leistungsklausel waiver clause; ~**recht** *(Konkursverwalter)* right of disclaimer; ~**schreiben** *(von Aktionären auf Zuteilung junger Aktien)* letter of renunciation, renunciation form *(Br.)*; ~**urkunde** quitclaim deed, release, deed of renunciation (release).

verziehen *(wegziehen)* to change one's residence, to [re]move;
sich ~ *(Brett)* to warp, to wind, *(Einbrecher)* to make off, *(Menschenmenge)* to break up, to scatter, to disperse, *(Nebel)* to lift, to disperse, to dissolve; **sich ins Bett** ~ to turn in, to go between the sheets *(coll.)*; **sein Gesicht** ~ to make a wry face; **sich zu einem breiten Grinsen** ~ to widen into a broad grin; **Kind** ~ to spoil a child; **ohne eine Miene zu** ~ without batting an eyelid *(sl.)*.

verzieren to ornament, to garnish;
reich ~ to enrich.

Verzierung ornament, garnish, enrichment, embellishment, decoration, flower;
brich Dir nur keine ~ **ab** come down from your high horse.

ver|zimmern to timber; ~**zinken** to galvanize, to electroplate, *(verpfeifen)* to squeal, to squeak *(coll.)*.

verzinsen to pay interest;
sich ~ to yield (bear, carry) interest;
Einlagen mit 4% ~ to allow 4 per cent interest on deposits; **sich gut** ~ to earn good interest, to give a good (bring a fair) return on an investment; **sich hoch** ~ to yield high interest; **Kredit mit 12%** ~ to pay 12 per cent interest on a loan; **sich nicht** ~ to lie dormant; **mit 8%** ~ to grant an interest of 8 per cent; **sich mit 6%** ~ to bear interest at 6 per cent, to return six per cent.

verzinslich paying (bearing, yielding) interest;
fest ~ at a fixed rate of interest; **nicht** ~ free of interest;
~ **angelegt** funded; ~ **ausgeliehen** out at interest;
Geld ~ **anlegen** to put out money at interest; ~ **sein** to bear (carry) interest; **mit 8%** ~ **sein** to bear interest at 8 per cent; **gut** ~ **sein** to return good interest; **hoch** ~ **sein** to yield high interest; **niedrig** ~ **sein** to carry a low rate of interest; ~ **angelegt sein** to be out at interest;
~**es Darlehn** loan on interest; ~**es Kapital** interest-bearing capital; ~**e Papiere** interest-bearing securities; ~**e Schatzanweisungen für die Banken** treasury deposit receipts *(Br.)*.

Verzinsung *(Ertrag)* interest, yield, return, *(Zinssatz)* rate of interest, interest rate, *(Zinszahlung)* payment of (paying) interest;
durchschnittliche ~ average yield; **effektive** ~ effective rate of interest, net return (yield); **feste** ~ fixed interest; **gesetzliche** ~ legal rate of interest; **über handelsübliche Sätze hinausgehende** ~ interest in excess of reasonable commercial rates; **laufende** ~ flat (running, *Br.*) yield; **marktkonforme** ~ interest in conformity with the market; **reale** ~ real interest rate; **sinkende** ~ diminishing yield; **variable** ~ variable yield;
~ **der Anschaffungskosten** interest on capital account (outlay); ~ **des Eigenkapitals** return on common equity (net worth, *US*); ~ **des eingesetzten Kapitals** return on capital employed (investment); ~ **der Nationalschuld** national debt interest; **12%ige** ~ **des Nettovermögens** 12% return on net assets; ~ **der laufenden Schulden** interest on current debts; ~ **von Spareinlagen** interest paid for savings deposits;
achtprozentige ~ **abwerfen** to give 8 per cent; **zur** ~ **ausleihen** to put out at interest; **geringe** ~ **erzielen** to yield little.

verzogen *(Kind)* spoiled, spoilt;
falls ~ if moved, in case of change of address; **falls** ~, **zurück an Absender** if moved, return to sender; **unbekannt** ~ no trace, gone away, no address;
unbekannt ~**er Schuldner** absconding debtor.

verzögern to delay, to defer, to retard, to protract, to procrastinate, to lag, to slow (hang) up;
sich ~ to be protracted; **etw.** ~ to hold s. th. up; **absichtlich** ~ to drag one's feet; **Mittelbewilligung** ~ to delay its funding; **Verabschiedung eines Gesetzentwurfes** ~ to obstruct the progress (filibuster, table, *US*) a bill.

verzögert|e Behandlung delay [action], runaround *(US)*; ~**e Lieferung** delay in (delayed) delivery; ~**es Telegramm** delayed telegram; ~**e Vorlegung** delay in presentment.

Verzögerung delay [action], lag, retardation, protraction, procrastination;
ohne weitere ~ without further delay;
bürokratische ~ bureaucratic delay; **schuldhafte** ~ undue delay; **streikbedingte** ~ delay by strike; **unvermeidbare** ~ unavoidable delay; **vom Staat zu vertretende** ~ government-caused delay;
~ **abgewickelter Fertigungsaufträge** delay in settlement of long-term orders; ~ **eines Gesetzentwurfes** *(US Präsident)* pocket veto *(US)*; ~ **bei der Lieferung** delayed delivery; ~ **des U-Bahnverkehrs** holdup on the underground railway;
~ **erleiden** to be delayed, to suffer delay; **keine** ~ **zulassen** to admit (permit, brook) of no delay.

Verzögerungs|absicht intention to delay; ~**antrag** dilatory (guillotine) motion; ~**einwand** dilatory (sham) plea; ~**grund** delayer, stick; ~**manöver** dilatory manoeuvre, procrastination, *(parl.)* filibustering *(US)*, stonewalling *(Australia)*, *(Prozeß)* sham plea; ~**politik** Fabian policy, ca'canny method, obstructionism, delaying tactics; ~**relais** time-delay relay; ~**streifen** deceleration lane; ~**taktik** delaying (stalling) tactics; ~**taktik konterkarieren** to run up against stonewalling *(Australia)*; ~**zünder** *(el.)* delayed-action fuse.

verzollbar tollable, dutiable, subject to a duty.

verzollen to pay duty on, to custom, to declare, to take out of bond, *(Güter, Schiff)* to clear through the customs, to make a bill of entry, to enter at the customhouse;
bei der Ausfahrt ~ to clear outward; **zu niedrig** ~ to enter short; **Schiff bei der Einfahrt** ~ to clear customs entering in; **Waren** ~ to clear goods out of bond;
etw. zu ~ **haben** to have s. th. to declare.

verzollt cleared, duty-paid, out of bond;
~ **und Zoll bezahlt** cleared and customs duty paid;
~**e Waren** cleared goods; **niedrig** ~**e Waren** low-duty goods, low-rate articles; ~**er Wert** declared value.

Verzollung customhouse entry, clearance [through the customs], clearing, *(Zollbegleichung)* payment of duties;
nach ~ duty paid;
nachträgliche ~ post entry;
~ **am Bestimmungsort** bonded to destination;
zur ~ **angeben (anmelden)** to declare, to enter goods for customs clearance, to pass a customs entry; ~ **vornehmen** to enter at the customhouse, to effect customs clearance; **vorläufige** ~ **vornehmen** to lodge a prime entry.

Verzollungs|dokumente clearance papers; ~**kosten** clearance charges; ~**papiere** clearance papers; ~**vorschriften** bonding requirements; ~**wert** declared (customs) value.

verzückt enraptured, enrapt, in raptures, thrown into ecstasy.

Verzückung entrancement;
~**en** the jerks *(US)*;
in ~ **geraten** to go into raptures (ecstasy).

Verzug default, *(Verzögerung)* delay;
bei ~ upon default; **Gefahr im** ~ delays are dangerous; **im** ~ defaulting; **ohne** ~ forthwith, without delay;
~ **der ganzen Familie** pet of the whole family; ~ **des Mieters** tenant's default;
ohne ~ **ausführen** to carry out without delay; **sich im** ~ **befinden** to [make] default; **in** ~ **geraten** to default; **mit der Verzinsung und Amortisation seiner Hypothek in** ~ **geraten** to default in one's mortgage payments; **mit den Leistungen in** ~ **kommen** to fail to complete within contract time; **mit den Zahlungen in** ~ **kommen** to default in payment; **im** ~ **sein** to be in default (arrears), *(mit der Zahlung)* to delay payment; **in** ~ **setzen** to hold (put) in delay; ~ **wiedergutmachen** to cure a default.

Verzugs|aktie deferred share (stock, *US*); ~**fall** event of default; **im** ~**fall** in the event of default; ~**folgen** consequences of a delay; ~**gewährung** forbearance; ~**klausel** demurrage clause; **sich überall auswirkende** ~**klausel** *(Konsortialanleihe)* cross-default clause; ~**kosten** *(Schiff)* demurrage; ~**obligationen** preference bonds; ~**schaden** damage caused by delay; ~**schadensersatz** damages for delay; ~**strafe** penalty for delay; ~**tage** *(Wechsel)* days of grace; ~**woche** week of delay; ~**zeit** dead time; ~**zinsen** accumulated (penal, default, past-due) interest, interest on arrears, interest payable on default (delay, arrears, for detention); ~**zoll** differential (discriminating) duty.

verzweifeln to despair, to despond;
an der Menschheit ~ to despair of mankind.
verzweifelt|wenig precious little;
Geld ~ **nötig haben** to desperately need the money;
~**er Versuch** desperate attempt.
Verzweiflung despair, desperation;
in der größten ~ in the depth of despair;
selbst einen Engel zur ~ **bringen** to vex a saint; **j. in** ~ **stürzen** to plunge s. o. into despair; **j. zur** ~ **treiben** to drive s. o. to despair.
Verzweiflungs|akt desperate act; ~**schreie** wailings of despair.
Verzweigung ramification;
~ **einer Verschwörung** ramifications of a plot.
verzwickte Angelegenheit awkward business, intricacy.
Vesper meat tea.
Vestibül vestibule, anteroom.
Veteran veteran, ex-service man, old campaigner, *(Schnauferl)* vintage car.
Veterinär veterinary surgeon, vet.
Veto veto, negative;
aufschiebendes ~ suspensible (suspensory) veto; **begründetes** ~ veto message *(US)*; **eingeschränktes** ~ limited (negative) veto; **überstimmbares** ~ qualified veto *(US)*;
gegen eine Entscheidung sein ~ **einlegen** to veto a decision, to put (set) a (one's) veto on s. th.; ~ **gegen eine Ernennung einlegen** to protest against an appointment; ~ **überstimmen** to override a veto.
Vetorecht veto [power], right to veto;
absolutes ~ absolute veto; **aufschiebendes** ~ suspensible (suspensory) veto; **eingeschränktes** ~ qualified (limited, negative) veto;
sein ~ **ausüben** to exercise (interpose, impose) one's veto, to veto *(US)*; ~**e im Parlament behalten** to retain blocking powers in Parliament; ~ **haben** to have the power (right) of veto; **sich über ein** ~ **hinwegsetzen** to override a veto; **von seinem** ~ **Gebrauch machen** to interpose (exercise, use) one's veto; ~ **rückgängig machen** to reverse a veto; **über** ~**e verfügen** to hold veto powers.
Vetter, leiblicher ~ full cousin; **weitläufig verwandter** ~ remote cousin;
~ **ersten Grades** first (blood) cousin, cousin in the first remove;
~ **zweiten Grades** cousin twice removed; ~ **vom Lande** country cousin.
Vettern|schaft cousinhood; ~**wirtschaft** nepotism, partisanship, patronage system, favo(u)ritism, spoils system *(US)*; **nach** ~**wirtschaft riechen** to smell of nepotism.
Vexier|bild picture puzzle; ~**schloß** combination (permutation) lock; ~**spiegel** distorting mirror.
Vibrieren eines Flugzeugs wing flutter.
vibrieren to pulsate, *(Flugzeug)* to flutter, *(Stimme)* to vibrate, to tremble.
Videokassette video cassette.
Viecherei dirty trick, *(Schufterei)* grind.
Vieh stock, livestock, beast, *(Miststück)* brute, beast, swine;
richtiges ~ absolute beast;
verlaufenes ~ **einsperren** to impound stray cattle; ~ **stehlen** to lift cattle *(Br.)*; ~ **züchten** to raise cattle;
~**ausstellung** cattle show; ~**bestand** farm stock, livestock; ~**dieb** cattle chief, rustler *(US sl.)*; ~**diebstahl** cattle lifting *(Br.)*; ~**farm** stock farm; ~**frachtliste** cattle manifest; ~**futter** forage; ~**handel** cattle trade; ~**händler** cattle dealer (trader), livestock dealer *(US)*, drover; ~**herde** herd of cattle; ~**hüten** herding; ~**hüter** rancher, stockman *(Australia)*, stock raiser, ranchman *(US)*.
viehisch brutal, beastly, bestial;
j. ~ **behandeln** to treat s. o. brutally.
Vieh|knecht herdsman, stockman; ~**markt** cattle market; ~**pfändung wegen nicht bezahlter Pacht betreiben** to distrain cattle upon nonpayment of rent; ~**schaden** damage caused by cattle; ~**schranke** cattle guard; ~**seuche** cattle plague; ~**transport** cattle transport; ~**transportanhänger** cattle trailer; ~**transporter** stock carrier; ~**transportzug** cattle train; ~**treiber** trail drover; ~**verluste** losses of livestock; ~**versicherung** cattle (livestock) insurance; ~**waggon** livestock waggon, stockcar *(US)*, cattle truck (car, *US*); ~**weide** pasture; ~**wirtschaft**, ~**zucht** stockbreeding *(Br.)*, cattle (stock) farming (raising, *US*), animal husbandry, cattle-rearing, store farm *(Australia)*; ~**zucht betreiben** to breed (raise, *US*) stock; ~**zuchtbetrieb** stock farm; ~**züchter** cattle (stock) farmer, rancher, livestock ranger, stock raiser *(US)*, stockbreeder *(Br.)*, store farmer *(Scot.)*, storemaster *(Scot.)*; ~**zuchtgebiet** range land.
viel|bändig of many volumes, voluminous; ~**beschäftigter Anwalt** busy lawyer; ~**deutig** ambiguous.
vielfach multiple, manifold;
sich ~ **bewährt haben** to have proved its worth many times;
~**er Millionär** multimillionaire.
Vielfach|kabel multiple cable; ~**klinke** *(tel.)* multiple jack panel; ~**schalter** *(el.)* multiple switch; ~**stecker** *(el.)* multiway (manifold) plug.
Viel|fältigkeit diversity; ~**fraß** glutton; ~**fraß sein** to make a pig of o. s.
viel|gebildet allround; ~**gereist** travel(l)ed; ~**jährige Erfahrungen** many years' experience; ~**schichtig** multidivisional.
Vielschreiber penny-a-liner *(Br.)*;
~ **sein** to penny-a-line, to overwrite.
vielseitig versatile, many-sided, allround, of varied powers, multilateral;
~ **sein** to range widely;
~ **gebildet** allround; ~ **verwendbar** adaptable, versatile, multipurpose, manifold;
~**e Interessen** multiple interests; ~**e Kenntnisse** extensive knowledge; ~ **gebildeter Mensch** versatile person; ~**es Werkzeug** multipurpose tool; **auf** ~**en Wunsch** by popular request.
Vielseitigkeit versatility, diversification;
~ **des Produktionsprogramms** diversification of products.
Vielseitigkeitsausbildung versatility training.
viel|staatlich multinational; ~**streckig** multiroute; ~**stufiger Schalter** multiway switch; ~**vermögend** influential.
vielversprechend favo(u)rable, promising, likely-looking, fair;
~ **sein** to shape well;
die Sache sieht ~ **aus** it looks promising, the goose hangs high *(US coll.)*;
~**e Aussichten** rosy prospects; ~**es Unternehmen** promising enterprise.
Vielzahl multitude, plurality;
~ **von Abbildungen** wealth of illustrations;
~ **von Ämtern auf sich vereinigen** to hold a plurality of offices.
Vierachser four-axle vehicle.
Vierkreis *(el.)* phantom circuit.
vierfach|ausfertigen to quadruplicate;
~**e Ausfertigung** quadruplicate.
Vier|farbanzeige four-colo(u)r ad *(US)*; ~**farbendruck** four-colo(u)r (-process) printing; ~**felderwirtschaft** four-course system; ~**ganggetriebe** four-speed drive; ~**jahresplan** four-year plan; ~**kursfunkfeuer mit Sicht- und Höranzeige** *(Flugzeug)* visual aural range.
Viermächte|abkommen quadripartite agreement, *(Berlin)* Four Power Agreement; ~**ausschuß** four-power committee; ~**besprechung**, ~**konferenz** four-power talks (conference).
Vierradantrieb four-wheel drive.
vierschrötig square-built.
Viersitzer four-seater, four-passenger car.
vierspaltig four-columned.
Vierspänner coach-and-four.
vier|sprachig quadrilingual; ~**spurig** four-laned; ~**stöckiges Mietshaus** four-stor(e)y apartment house.
Vierstufenrakete four-stage rocket.
Viertaktmotor four-cycle (-stroke) engine.
Viertel quarter, *(Bezirk)* district, quarter, precinct, ward;
für ein ~ **des Preises** for one quarter (a quarter of) the price;
abgelegenes ~ outlying quarter; **akademisches** ~ 15 minutes grace; **elegantes (vornehmes)** ~ best parts, silk-stocking district *(US)*, gold coast *(US sl.)*; **nichteuropäisches** ~ township *(South Africa)*; **wohlhabendes** ~ high-income suburb;
~**dollar** quarter [dollar]; ~**finale** quarter final; ~**jahr** [calendar] quarter.
Vierteljahres|abonnement quarterly subscription; ~**abrechnung** *(Börse)* term settlement; ~**ausweis** *(Bank)* quarterly return *(Br.)*; ~**bericht** quarterly report (statement, return), *(Notenbank)* quarterly bulletin; ~**bezug** quarterly subscription; ~**bilanz** quarterly balance sheet; ~**dividende** quarterly dividend; ~**einlagen** three-months deposit; ~**endziffern** final-quarter's figures; ~**erträgnisse** quarter earnings; ~**frist** term; ~**gehalt** quarterly salary; ~**geld** three months' money; ~**miete** quarter's rent; ~**miete schulden** to owe a term of rent; ~**prämie** quarterly premium; ~**rate** quarterly payment, quarter's instalment; ~**schrift** quarterly [publication]; ~**tabelle** quarterly table; ~**zahlen** quarterly figures; ~**zahlung** quarterage; ~**zeitschrift** quarterly magazine (review).
vierteljährlich quarterly, every (by the) quarter;
~**e Kündigung** three months' notice; ~**e Mietzahlung** quarter's rent.

Viertelmorgen rood of land.
Viertelsaktie quarter stock *(US)*.
Viertelseite *(Reklameanzeige)* quarter page.
Viertelstunde quarter hour;
jem. eine unangenehme ~ bereiten to give s. o. a bad quarter of an hour.
Viertelstundenglocke quarter bell.
viertelstündlich schlagen to strike the quarter hours.
Viertkläßler fourth grader *(US)*.
Vierundzwanzigstunden|dienst 24-hour service; **~kredit** overnight (one-day) loan *(US)*.
Vierzigstundenwoche forty-hour week;
~ haben to work forty hours a week.
Vierzimmerwohnung four-room apartment.
Vignette vignette, ornament, mask, flower, printer's flourish.
Villa villa, country house, cottage.
villenähnlich villalike.
Villen|besitzer villa owner, cottager; **~kolonie** garden city; **~viertel**, **~vorort** villadom, residential district.
vinkulieren, Aktien to restrict shares.
Vinkulierung von Aktien restriction on [the right to transfer] shares.
Virtuose virtuoso.
Virtuosentum, Virtuosität virtuosity.
Viruskrankheit virus disease.
Visier visor, sight, *(Scharfschütze)* sniperscope;
mit offenem ~ kämpfen to be straightforward;
~stab *(Landvermessung)* surveyor's rod.
Vision, nächtliche night vision.
visionär visionary.
Visitation official inspection.
Visitationsrecht *(Schiffe)* right of approach.
Visite hinter sich bringen to come before the medical officer.
Visitenkarte visiting *(Br.)* (calling, *US*) card;
gemeinsame ~ collective card;
seine ~ bei jem. abgeben to leave one's card on s. o.
Visitenkartentäschchen card case.
visitieren to search, to rummage *(Br.)*.
visuell|es Gedächtnis visual memory; **~e Kommunikation** visual communication.
Visum visa;
~ für vorübergehenden Aufenthalt visitor's visa *(US)*;
~ ausstellen to issue a visa; **beim Konsulat ein ~ beantragen** to apply to the consul for a visa; **~ erhalten** to have one's papers viséed (visaed); **mit ~ versehen** to visa; **~ verweigern** to refuse a visa;
~ablehnung refusal of a visa; **~abteilung** visa department (office); **~antrag** application for visa; **~ausstellung** issuance of a visa; **~gebühr** visa fee; **~rangklasse** visa category; **~verlängerung** extension of visa; **~zwang aufheben** to abolish visas.
vital lively, vital;
sehr ~ sein to be full of life (beans);
zu ~er Bedeutung im täglichen Leben werden to become vital in one's daily life.
Vitalität vitality;
seine ~ verloren haben to be played out.
Vitamin vitamin;
mit ~en anreichern to vitaminize;
~mangel vitamin deficiency, poverty in vitamins.
vitaminreiche Lebensmittel protective food.
Vitamin|spritze vitamin shot; **~tabletten** vitamin tablets.
Vitrine display stand (cabinet), glass case, showcase.
Vize|gouverneur deputy governor; **~kanzler** vice-chancellor; **~konsul** deputy (vice-) consul; **~konsulat** vice-consulate; **~präsident** vice-president, deputy governor, veep *(US coll.)*; **geschäftsführender ~präsident** executive vice-president; **~präsidentschaft** vice-presidency, vice-chairmanship.
Vogel, komischer funny (queer) bird;
~ abschießen to carry the day, to steal the show; **einen ~ haben** to be crackbrained, to have bats in the belfry, to have a bee in one's bonnet *(sl.)*; **jem. einen ~ zeigen** to give s. o. the V-sign *(Br.)*;
friß ~ oder stirb sink or swim.
Vögel, jagdbare wild fowl.
vogelfrei outlawed, proscribed.
Vogel|perspektive bird's-eye view; **~scheuche** scarecrow; **wie eine ~scheuche aussehen** to look a sight; **~straußpolitik** ostrich policy; **~straußpolitik treiben** to bury one's head in the sand.
Vogt steward, bailiff, warden.
Vokabel|buch vocabulary; **~teil** vocabulary section.
Vokabular, aus seinem ~ streichen to drop from one's vocabulary.
Volk people, community, *(Masse)* crowd, masses, *(Nation)* nation, land, country, commonwealth;
aus dem ~e stammend derived from the grassroots;
arbeitendes ~ working classes; **das ~** ordinary people; **das auserwählte ~** God's peculiar (own) people; **ausgestorbenes ~** extinct nation; **fahrendes ~** wayfaring people; **das gemeine ~** the common people, common herd; **das niedere ~** the lower classes; **reiches ~** strong nation;
~ ausrotten to delete a nation; **~ um seine Meinung befragen** to appeal to the sense of the nation, to go to the country *(Br.)*; **unter das ~ bringen** to vulgarize; **im ganzen ~ Widerhall finden** to find a nation-wide response; **beim ~e liegen** *(Macht)* to reside in the people; **sich mit dem ~ gemein machen** to mix with the crowd; **dem souveränen ~ obliegen** to be vested in the people; **beim ~ beliebt sein** to be a favo(u)rite with the public; **sein Anliegen dem ~ unterbreiten** to take one's case to the people; **~ unterdrücken** to keep a people down by force.
Völkchen, lustiges merry crowd.
Völker|beschreibung ethnography; **~bund** Commonwealth (League) of Nations; **~bundsgemeinschaft** community of nations; **~bundspakt** Covenant of the League of Nations; **~familie** family of nations; **europäische ~familie** European family; **~gemeinschaft** international community, *(Britisches Weltreich)* commonwealth of nations; **~gruppe** group; **~krieg** international (public) war; **~kunde** ethnology.
völkerkundlich ethnological.
Völker|mord genocide; **~recht** law of nations, public (international) law; **~recht im Kriege** customs and usage of war; **~rechtler** internationalist, publicist.
völkerrechtlich under international law;
~e Anerkennung eines Staates recognition of a state; **~er Anspruch** international claim; **~e Haftung** international responsibility; **~e Verhaltensnormen** international standards.
Völkerrechts|abkommen, sofort gültiges transitory treaty; **~kommission** *(UNO)* International Law Commission; **~persönlichkeit haben** to be subject to international law; **~spezialist** internationalist, publicist; **~subjekt** international personality; **~verletzung** violation of an international law; **unmittelbar anzuwendender ~vertrag** self-executing treaty; **~vertrag ratifizieren** to acknowledge a treaty; **~vertrag registrieren** to register a treaty.
völkerrechtswidrig contrary to international law.
Völker|stamm race; **~wanderung** migration of the people.
völkisch ethnic, national.
volkreich populous, densely populated.
Volksabstimmung plebiscite vote, referendum;
~ über ein verabschiedetes Gesetz statutory referendum; **örtliche ~ über Gewährung von Schankkonzession** local option *(US)*;
durch ~ billigen to approve by plebiscite; **~ durchführen** to hold a plebiscite; **einer ~ unterbreiten** to submit to a plebiscite; **~ verlangen** to demand a poll.
Volks|aktie baby share *(Br.)*, penny stock *(US)*; **~aktionär** small shareholder; **~aufgebot** levée en masse, levy; **~aufklärung** public enlightenment; **~auflauf** crowd; **~auflauf zerstreuen** to scale a crowd *(Scot.)*; **~aufruhr** riot, popular tumult; **~aufruhr anzetteln** to stir up a people to rebellion; **~aufstand** popular uprising, popular insurrection, upheaval; **zu einem ~aufstand führen** to touch off a national uprising; **~aufwiegelung** rabble rousing; **~aufwiegler** agitator, demagog(ue), [political] rabble rouser; **~ausdruck** nonstandard expression; **~ausgabe** popular (cheap, paperback, reprint) edition, cheap reprint; **~ausrottung** genocide; **~bank** [etwa] credit union, people's bank; **~befragung** popular vote, direct government, referendum, plebiscite, *(Meinungsumfrage)* opinion (Gallup) poll; **~befragung bei Verfassungsänderungen** constitutional referendum; **~befragung durchführen** to hold a referendum; **~begehren** popular initiative, initiation, facultative (optional, nation-wide) referendum; **~belustigung** outdoor diversion; **~betrug** hoodwinking of a nation; **~bewegung** popular (national) movement; **~bibliothek** public (free) library; **~bildung** adult education.
Volksbildungs|heim community centre *(Br.)*; **~stätte** adult school; **~verein** lyceum *(US)*; **~werk** adult education courses, university extension.
Volks|blatt popular newspaper; **~buch** chapbook, popular book; **~bücherei** free (public) library; **~charakter** national character; **~demokratie** representative democracy.
volkseigener Betrieb nationalized *(Br.)* (socialized) enterprise.
Volks|eigentum public (state) property; **~eigentum sein** to be state-owned; **~einkommen** national income (dividend), na-

tional revenue *(US)*; ~**einkommen nach Einkommensarten** national income by distributive shares *(US)*; **allgemeines ~empfinden** common feeling; ~**entscheid** plebiscite, referendum; ~**erhebung** upheaval, popular insurrection, revolt, uprising; **zu einer ~erhebung führen** to touch off a national uprising; ~**erzählung** folk tale; ~**feind** public enemy *(US)*, enemy of the people; ~**fest** popular festival; ~**front** people's (popular) front; ~**frontbündnis** Socialist-Communist alliance, popular-front alliance; ~**führer** popular leader; ~**gesundheit** national health; ~**gesundheitspfleger** public health service; ~**gewühl** jam; **nach ~gruppen** ethnically oriented.

Volksgunst popularity, favo(u)r of the people;
sich um die ~ bemühen to bid for popular support; **nach ~ streben** to play to the gallery; **von einer Woge der ~ getragen werden** to ride on a wave of popularity.

Volks|haß national hatred; ~**held** popular (folk) hero, tribune; ~**herrschaft** popular government, people's democracy.

Volkshoch|schule [etwa] adult education courses, Workers Education Association *(Br.)*, night school, lyceum *(US)*, university extension classes; ~**schüler** [etwa] extension student, extramural student *(Br.)*.

Volkshochschul|kursus university extension course, further education course *(Br.)*, extramural work *(Br.)*; ~**lehrer** further-education teacher *(Br.)*; ~**zweig** extramural department *(Br.)*.

Volks|justiz lynch (mob) law; ~**kammer** lower house; ~**kommissar** commissar; ~**kommissariat** commissariat; ~**krieg** perfect war; ~**küche** communal (soup) kitchen; ~**kunde** folklore; ~**lebensversicherung** home service assurance *(Br.)*, prudential (industrial, *US*) insurance; ~**leidenschaft erregen** to inflame popular feeling; ~**lied** folk song; ~**meinung** public opinion, popular verdict; ~**menge** crowd, mass of people; **für die ~menge gut sichtbar sein** to stand in full view of the crowd; **im ~mund** vernacular; ~**musik** folk music; ~**partei** popular party; ~**polizei** people's police; ~**rede halten** to hold forth to the crowd, to harangue the mob; ~**redner** mob (stump, *US*) orator, tub thumper; ~**regierung** government of the people; ~**republik** People's Republic; ~**schädling** enemy of the people, public enemy *(US)*; ~**schicht** social stratum; ~**schichten** sections of the population; **ärmere ~schichten** poorer classes; ~**schlag** stock; ~**schriftsteller** popular writer; ~**schulbildung** elementary (primary) education; ~**schule** elementary (council, common, *US*) school, graded (district, primary) school *(US)*.

Volksschul|klasse first-grade class; **die ersten vier ~klassen** junior forms *(Br.)*; ~**lehrer** primary-school teacher, grade teacher *(US)*; ~**schüler** primary scholar, elementary student *(US)*; ~**unterricht** primary instruction, grades *(US)*; ~**unterricht erteilen** to teach in the grades *(US)*; ~**wesen** elementary education *(Br.)*, graded school system *(US)*, grades *(US)*.

Volks|seele, empörte infuriated population; ~**sitte** national custom, folklore; ~**souverän** sovereign people; ~**souveränität** popular sovereignty; ~**sprache** vernacular language; ~**stamm** race, tribe; ~**stimmung** sentiment of the people; ~**stück** folk play; ~**tanz** folk square dance; ~**tracht** traditional costume; ~**traditionen** national traditions; ~**trauertag** memorial day.

Volkstum folklore.

volkstümlich popular, vulgar, grassroots;
~ werden to gain in popularity;
~**er Preis** popular price; ~**e Redewendung** popular phrase.

Volkstümlichkeit popular appeal.

Volkstümlichkeitstabelle, jem. in den ~n Auftrieb geben to send s. o. soaring in the popularity charts.

volkstumsmäßig ethnic.

Volksunruhen communal disturbances.

volksverbunden populist, grassroots.

Volks|verführer demagog(ue); ~**vermögen** wealth of a nation, national wealth; ~**vermögensrechnung** national income accounting; ~**versammlung** popular assembly, public meeting; ~**versicherung** industrial assurance *(Br.)*, industrial (prudential) insurance *(US)*; ~**vertreter** people's representative, deputy *(US)*, delegate, member of Parliament; ~**vertretung** representative body of the people, representation, Parliament; ~**wagen** popular-priced car; ~**wille** will of the people; ~**wirt** political economist; **graduierter ~wirt** master of economics; ~**wirt mit akademischem Abschluß** academic economist.

Volkswirtschaft national (political) economy, economics;
angewandte ~ applied (political) economy; **autarke ~** self-contained economy; **geschlossene ~** closed economy; **antizyklisch gesteuerte ~** stop-go economics; **offene ~** open economy; **reine ~** pure economics;
~ ohne Außenhandel closed economy; **~ mit zurückgestauter Inflation** overloaded economy;
~ ernstlich gefährden to be gravely injurious to the national economy; **mit der allgemeinen Entwicklung der ~ nicht Schritt halten** to be out of phase with the national economy; **~ eines Landes steuern** to run a country's economy.

Volkswirtschaftler political economist.

volkswirtschaftlich economic[al];
~**e Anforderungen** economic wants; ~**e Arbeitskraft** national manpower resources; ~**e Entwicklung** economic progress; ~**e Ersparnisse** external benefit, national savings; **allgemeine ~e Fragen** general economic matters; ~**e Gesamtplanung** national economic planning; ~**es Gesamtprodukt** gross national product; ~**e Gesamtproduktion** national output; ~**e Gesamtrechnung** national income accounting (accounts), social accounting, blue book *(Br.)*; ~**es Gesamtvermögen** national capital equipment; ~**er Kapitalaufwand** national capital spending (accounts); ~**e Kosten** external costs; ~**e Notwendigkeit** economic necessity; ~**e Planung** national economic planning; ~**e Theorie** theory of political economy, economic theory.

Volkswirtschafts|abteilung economic unit; ~**kurs für Jungakademiker** postgraduate course in economics; ~**lehre** social (political) economy, economic science *(US)*, economics; **allgemeine ~lehre** pure economics; **angewandte ~lehre** applied economics; ~**multiplikator** international multiplier; ~**politik** social economics; ~**theorie** pure (political) economy, economic theory; ~**trend** path of the economy.

Volks|wohl public weal; ~**wohlfahrt** public welfare; ~**wohlstand** national well-being (prosperity); ~**zahl** population figure; ~**zählung** [population] census, return; ~**zählung vornehmen** to [take a] census.

Volkszählungs|beamter census taker; ~**bogen** census sheet; ~**ergebnis** census result; ~**formular** census paper; ~**verfahren** census procedure, enumeration process.

Volkszugehörigkeit nationality;
deutsche ~ German stock.

voll full, *(blau)* tight *(sl.)*, *(gedrängt)* crowded, *(vollständig)* outright, entire, complete, whole;
zum Bersten ~ crowded to overflowing; **brechend ~** jammed, jam-packed, crowded to capacity; **gerammelt ~** *(Bus)* packed to the door; **gestrichen ~** brimful, full to the brim; **zum Platzen ~** full to overflowing; **sehr ~** *(Autobahn)* much traffic;
~ ausgeschrieben in full [letters]; **~ beladen** loaded; **~ berechtigt** fully entitled; **~ berufsunfähig** wholly and permanently disabled; **~ beschäftigt** fully occupied (employed); **~ besetzt** *(Bus)* packed to the door, *(Hotel)* full up *(Br.)*, fully booked; **~ eingezahlt** *(Kapital)* fully paid [up]; **~ gedeckt** fully covered; **~ gezeichnet** fully subscribed; **~ haftbar** fully liable; **~ motorisiert** fully motorized; **~ wie eine Strandhaubitze** as drunk as a lord; **~ versichert** fully insured *(US)*;
j. ~ ansehen to look s. o. straight in the face; **j. für ~ ansehen** to take s. o. seriously; **j. ~ auszahlen** to pay s. o. outright; **~ bezahlen** to pay in full; **~ dasein** to be with it, to keep one's eye on the ball *(US sl.)*; **~ einzahlen** to pay up; **über sein Vermögen ~ verfügen können** to be entire master of one's property; **im ~en leben** to live on the fat of the land; **den Mund ~ nehmen** to boast, to brag; **aus dem ~en schöpfen** to draw on abundant resources; **~ sein** *(betrunken)* to be tight (drunk, intoxicated, plastered, *US sl.*); **~ ausgelastet sein** to be full up with business, *(Betrieb)* to be working to capacity; **~ gebunkert sein** to be full up with coal (oil); **~ verantwortlich sein** to be fully responsible, to be responsible for one's actions; **~ des süßen Weines sein** to have had a drop too much; **~ von jem. unterstützt werden** to find a warm supporter in s. o.;
~**e Adresse** full (complete) address; **~ eingezahlte Aktie** paid-up share, full-paid stock *(US)*; ~**er Arbeitslohn** full pay; ~**e Besatzung** full force of men, complement; ~**e Besetzung** full cast; **bei ~er Besinnung** fully conscious; ~**e Beteiligung zugesagt** full interest admitted; ~**er Betrag** entire amount; ~**e Betriebsleistung** full operating capacity; **mit ~en Bezügen pensioniert werden** to be retired on full pay; **in ~er Blüte stehen** to flower, *(fig.)* to have reached its peak; **um ein ~es Drittel herabsetzen** to reduce by a whole third; ~**er Dummheiten stecken** to play the fool all the time; ~**e Eigentumsrechte haben** to own outright; ~**es Einverständnis** express consent; ~**er Erfolg** complete success, hit *(US)*; **in ~em Ernst** in dead earnest; ~**er Fahrpreis** full fare; ~**er Fehler sein** to be teeming with mistakes; ~**es Gehalt** full salary (pay); **Taschen ~er Geld haben** to have one's pockets full of money; ~**e Geldbörse** well-lined purse; ~**es Gewicht** full weight; ~**e Gewißheit haben** to be quite certain; **in ~er Größe** in full length; **in ~er Größe malen** to paint life-size; ~**e Gültigkeit** *(ausländisches Urteil)* full faith

and credit; ~e **Haftung** full liability; ~es **Handelsgewicht** avoirdupois; ~es **Haus** *(Theater)* packed (full) house; ~es **Haus haben** *(Hotel)* to be fully booked, *(Theater)* to play to a capacity audience; ~es **Jahr** whole year; ~er **Jahresertrag** full annual value; **mit** ~er **Kraft** with might and main; ~e **Kraft voraus** full speed ahead; ~e **Ladung** full load (cargo); ~ **ausgeschriebener Name** name written in full, full name; ~e **Pension** board residence; ~es **Portemonnaie** well-lined purse; ~en **Preis zahlen** to pay full fare; ~e **Produktionskosten** total production cost; ~e **Risikoübernahme** *(Versicherung)* full risk (coverage); ~er **Satz Versandpapiere** complete set of shipping documents *(US)*; **in** ~em **Scheinwerferlicht** *(fig.)* in the limelight; ~er **Seitenpreis** full-page rate; ~ **bezahlte Stelle** full-time job; ~e **Stunde** solid hour; ~e **Summe** total [amount], entire sum; **sechs** ~e **Tage** six clear days; ~ **besetztes Theater** full (packed) house; ~es **Vertrauen** entire confidence; ~es **Vertrauen zu jem. haben** to have complete confidence in s. o.; ~e **Wahrheit** whole truth; ~e **Woche** whole week.

Voll|abschreibung writing-down allowance; ~**anschluß** *(Telefon)* standard subscriber connection; ~**arbeitskräfte** fully qualified workers.

Vollast full load.

vollauf zu tun haben to have one's hands full.

vollaufen lassen, sich to get tanked-up *(sl.)*; **j. mit Bier** ~ to prime s. o. with beer.

Voll|aussteuerung maximum level; ~**automatik** fully automatic system.

vollautomatisiert automated, fully automatic.

Voll|autotypie, rechteckige square half-tone; ~**bahn** standard-gauge railway; ~**belegung aller Anschlagstafeln** *(Anzeigenwesen)* full showing of all hoardings.

vollberechtigt fully qualified (authorized);
~es **Mitglied** full member.

Vollberechtigung full qualification.

vollbeschäftigt employed on full time, *(Betrieb)* fully occupied, working to capacity;
~ **sein** to be in full employment.

Vollbeschäftigter full-time worker (timer).

Vollbeschäftigung full employment, full-time job, hyper-employment;
~ **sicherstellen** to ensure full employment; **vom Status der** ~ **zur Kurzarbeit übergehen** to shift from full-time schedules to part-time; **der Konjunktur weltweit wieder zur** ~ **verhelfen** to drag the world economy up towards the full-employment path.

Vollbeschäftigungs|haushalt full-employment budget; ~**lücke** full-employment gap; ~**politik** full-employment policy (economy); ~**these** full-employment thesis; ~**ziel** full-employment target; ~**zustand in der Wirtschaft herbeiführen** to move the economy towards full employment; ~**zustand sofort wiederherstellen** to rush the economy back to full-employment levels.

vollbesetzt full up, crowded to capacity, packed, crammed.

Voll|besitz, im ~**besitz seiner geistigen Kräfte sein** to be in full possession of one's senses (of sound mind, *US*); ~**betrag** full amount.

vollbetriebsfähiger Zustand complete working order.

Voll|bezahlung full payment; ~**bremsung durchführen** to jam on the brakes.

vollbringen to accomplish, to achieve;
etw. Ungewöhnliches ~ to set the Thames on fire; **Wunder** ~ to perform wonders.

Voll|bürger voting and taxpaying citizen; ~**charter** affreightment; ~**dampf** *(Schiff)* full steam; ~**dampf voraus** full speed ahead; ~**druckhöhe** critical altitude; ~**dünger** compound fertilizer; ~**eigentum** legal title, estate in fee simple, absolute (full) ownership; ~**eigentümer** outright (general, sole and unconditional) owner; ~**einzahlung** payment in full; ~**einzahlung einer repartierten Zuteilung** payment in full on allotment.

vollelektrisch all-electric.

vollenden to accomplish, to fulfil(l), to achieve, to round off, *(beenden)* to bring to a close, to finish, to get over, to terminate, to execute, *(krönen)* to consummate, to crown;
seine Ausbildungszeit (Lehrzeit) ~ to finish one's apprenticeship.

vollendet perfect, ideal, downright, right as nails, consummate, *(beendet)* finished, complete;
nicht ~ inchoate, incomplete;
etw. ~ **beherrschen** to do s. th. to perfection;
~e **Leistung** outstanding achievement; ~e **Manieren** perfect manners; ~e **Tatsache** accomplished fact; ~es **Verbrechen** accomplished (completed) crime; **nicht** ~es **Verbrechen** inchoate crime.

Vollendung completion, finish, perfection, consummation, *(fig.)* accomplishment;
bei ~ **seines 18. Lebensjahres** at his coming of age; **mit künstlerischer** ~ with consummate art;
glorreiche ~ crowning; **höchste** ~ pink of perfection;
~ **einer Lebensarbeit** consummation of a life's work; ~ **eines Verbrechens** accomplishment of a crime; ~ **eines Versuchs** completion of an attempt;
der ~ **entgegengehen** to be nearing (progress towards) completion; **energisch der** ~ **zuführen** to push to completion.

Völlerei gluttony.

Vollgas full throttle;
mit ~ **arbeiten** to work at white-hot speed; ~ **geben** to depress the pedal fully, to step on the gas, to open out; **mit** ~ **in eine Kurve gehen** to take a bend at full speed;
~**sturzflug** power dive.

vollgedeckte Diebstahlsversicherung full-coverage theft insurance.

vollgefressen sein to be stuffed with food (blue around the gills, *sl.*).

Voll|gehalt *(Münze)* full value (standard); **im** ~**genuß seiner Rechte** in full enjoyment of one's rights.

vollgepfropft as full as an egg.

vollgestopft full to the brim, stuffed, crammed, *(Bus)* packed to the door, crammed, jam-packed, crowded to capacity (with people).

Voll|gewicht full weight; ~**giro** full (special, direct, *US*) indorsement.

vollgültig at full value, valid, sterling.

Voll|gummi solid rubber; ~**gummireifen** solid (rubber) tyre (tire, *US*); ~**haftung** full (unlimited) liability; ~**idiot** no end of a fool *(sl.)*, blank idiot *(sl.)*.

völlig full, entire, complete, outright, *(gründlich)* thorough, well;
mit seinen Kräften ~ **am Ende** utterly run down;
~ **recht haben** to be absolutely right; ~ **frei über sein Vermögen verfügen können** to be entire master of one's property; ~ **gleichgültig sein** not to care a damn; **etw.** ~ **Neues sein** to be a whole new ball game; ~ **übersehen** to overlook completely;
~es **Durcheinander** utter confusion, devil among tailors; ~e **Gewißheit** absolute certainty; ~e **Handlungsfreiheit** full liberty to act; ~e **Unkenntnis** complete ignorance; ~er **Unsinn** perfect nonsense; ~er **Versager** complete failure, dropout.

Vollindossament full (special, direct, *US*) indorsement, indorsement in full.

vollinhaltlich in all points;
Brief ~ **veröffentlichen** to publish a letter in full.

Voll|invalide fully disabled person; ~**invalidität** permanent disability, total incapacity.

volljährig major, of age, of full age, free;
~ **sein** to be of [full] age; **noch nicht** ~ **sein** to be under age; ~ **werden** to reach lawful age, to attain one's majority (full age), to attain to man's estate, to come of age, to write o. s. a man, to come to years of discretion.

Volljähriger adult;
~ **und Geschäftsfähiger** person of full age and capacity.

Volljährigkeit lawful (legal, full) age, majority, manhood;
bei ~ on (at) his coming of age.

Volljährigkeits|alter erreichen to come of age, to attain one's majority; ~**erklärung** express emancipation, emancipation from the authority of one's parents; **vorzeitige partielle** ~**erklärung** partial emancipation.

Volljährigwerden coming of age.

Voll|jurist sein to be versed (skilled) in law; ~**kasko** comprehensive plus collision *(US)* (coverage); ~**kaufmann** general merchant; ~**kettenfahrzeug** full-track vehicle.

vollklimatisiert fully air-conditioned.

Vollklischee complete block *(Br.)* (plate, *US*).

vollkommen entire, all-out, *(perfekt)* perfect in all things, accomplished, ideal, right as nails, down to the ground, out and out, positive *(coll.)*;
keineswegs ~ **sein** to be a long way off perfection;
~er **Markt** perfect market; ~e **Markttransparenz** perfect knowledge of a market.

Vollkommenheit perfection, consummateness;
höchste ~ acme of perfection.

Voll|kontingent full quota; ~**konvertibilität**, ~**konvertierbarkeit** full convertibility; ~**kornbrot** coarse-grained whole-meal (-wheat, *US*) bread; ~**kosten** full cost; ~**kostenkalkulation** full-cost pricing; ~**kostenprinzip**, ~**kostenrechnung** full-cost principle.

vollkritzeln, Papier to scrawl all over a paper.

Vollmacht power, full powers, authority, *(Auftrag)* mandate, *(Handlungsvollmacht)* proxy, procuration, *(Urkunde)* power (letter, *US*) of attorney (procuration), commission *(Scot.)*; **außerhalb des Rahmens seiner ~en** outside the scope of one's authority, ultra vires *(Br.)*; **im Rahmen seiner ~en** within the scope of one's authority; **in ~** by attorney; **kraft der mir erteilen ~** by virtue of my authority; **laut ~** as per power [of attorney]; **mit allen ~en ausgestattet** fully authorized; **mit gehöriger ~ versehen** duly authorized, vested with powers; **mit ~, den Umständen entsprechend zu handeln** invested with discretionary powers; **ohne ~** without authority, unauthorized; **abgeleitete ~en** derived powers; **angemaßte ~** self-authority; **antiinflationistische ~en** anti-inflation powers; **ausdrückliche ~** express authority; **betrügerisch ausgeübte ~** fraudulent appointment; **stellvertretend ausgeübte ~** vicarious power; **unentgeltlich ausgeübte ~** naked authority (power); **beglaubigte ~** authenticated power of attorney; **begrenzte (beschränkte) ~en** limited authority; **einfache ~** collateral (naked) powers (authority); **erloschene ~** terminated (superannuated) power of attorney, terminated authority; **ausdrücklich erteilte ~** express power; **für einen Einzelfall erteilte ~** power of attorney in a specific act; **stillschweigend erteilte ~** tacit procuration, implied authority; **durch schlüssiges Verhalten erteilte ~** agency by estoppel; **von vornherein erteilte ~** advance authority; **fehlende ~** absence of authority; **gesetzliche ~** lawful authority; **implizierte ~** implied powers (authority); **notarielle ~** authorized power of attorney; **offene ~** apparent authority; **ordnungsgemäße ~** rightful authority; **polizeiliche ~en** police powers; **reine ~** power simply collateral; **schlichte ~** naked authority; **schriftliche ~** written authorization (authority), authority in writing; **staatliche ~en** government powers; **stillschweigende ~** implied powers; **testamentarische ~** letters testamentary; **treuhänderische ~en** fiduciary powers; **umfangreiche ~en** large powers; **umfassende ~en** broad authority (mandate), full powers; **unanfechtbare ~** authority beyond exception; **unbeschränkte (unumschränkte) ~en** unlimited (discretionary, plenary, full) powers, full authority, full (general) power of attorney, carte blanche; **ungleichartige ~** hybrid power; **unwiderrufliche ~** *(Hauptversammlung)* irrevocable proxy *(US)*; **verlängerte ~** extended power; **vermutete ~** implied powers; **jederzeit widerrufliche ~** mere authority; **der Satzung nach zustehende ~en** incidental powers;
~ zur Abgabe der entscheidenden Stimme power to use a casting vote; **~ zum Abschluß von Tarifverhandlungen** bargaining power; **~ zum Abschluß eines Vergleichs** power to compromise; **~en zur Aburteilung im Schnellverfahren** summary powers; **~en für den Arbeitskräfteeinsatz** powers of direction of labo(u)r; **~ zur Auftragsvergabe auch außerhalb des Etatsjahres** contract authorization; **~ unter Ausschluß des Selbstkontrahierens** power (authority) coupled with an interest; **~ für die Betriebsleitung** operating authority; **~ für die Einbehaltung von Lohnsteuerbeträgen** withholding authorization; **~, über ein Konto zu verfügen** power to operate an account; **~ zur Kreditgewährung** lending power; **~en eines Liquidators** liquidator's power; **~en des Ministerpräsidenten** powers of the Prime Minister; **~ eines Pflegers (Verwalters)** receiver's authority; **~ mit dem Recht der Erteilung von Untervollmachten** power of substitution; **~en des Senats** senatorial powers; **~ zur vorzeitigen Steuereinziehung** commission of anticipation *(Br.)*; **~ eines Treuhänders** trustee's power; **~ zur Übertragung von Schuldverschreibungen** bond power;
jds. ~ abgrenzen to define (restrict) s. one's power; **~ urkundlich ausschlagen** to disclaim by deed a power; **j. mit ~ ausstatten** to vest (clothe) s. o. with power [under the deed of a trust]; **~ ausstellen** to execute a power of attorney; **~en austauschen** to exchange powers; **~en ganz nach Ermessen ausüben** to exercise powers discretionary (entirely at will); **jds. ~en begrenzen** to restrict (define) s. one's powers; **jds. ~en auf ein bestimmtes Gebiet beschränken** to confine s. one's authority within certain limits; **~ delegieren** to delegate authority; **jds. ~ einschränken** to restrict (narrow, place a restriction on) s. one's power; **mit ~ entsenden** to depute; **~ entziehen** to cancel procuration, to revoke a power of attorney; **~en erbitten** to seek authority; **~ erteilen** to vest with power, to empower, to authorize, to bestow (grant) a power of attorney, to appoint a proxy, *(Handlungsvollmacht)* to confer procuration; **jem. ~ erteilen** to confer (delegate) power of attorney on s. o., to give s. o. authority, to authorize (empower) s. o.; **jem. unumschränkte ~en erteilen** to give s. o. discretionary powers, to furnish s. o. with full power (a blank check, *US*, cheque, *Br.*); **jds. ~en festlegen** to define s. one's powers; **jem. ~ geben** to lodge power in s. one's hands; **jem. unbeschränkte ~ geben** to give a blank check (cheque, *Br.*) to s. o.; **der Regierung größere ~en für die Investitionssteuerung geben** to give the government greater say in steering investment; **~ haben** to be authorized to act, to have authority; **alle ~en haben** to act with full powers; **ausdrückliche ~en haben** to be endowed with express authority; **keine ~ haben** to hold no brief; **ordnungsgemäße ~ haben** to be duly authorized; **~ von jem. haben** to hold power of attorney from s. o.; **alle nur möglichen ~en erhalten haben** to be invested with full authority; **~en zur Erteilung von Deckungszusagen für bestimmte Versicherungssparten haben** to have authority to give cover for a class of business concerned; **~ zur Unterschriftsleistung haben** to be authorized to sign; **sich im Rahmen seiner ~ halten** to act within the actual limits of one's authority; **in ~ handeln** to act by procuration; **aufgrund von jds. ~en handeln** to act on s. one's authority; **ohne ~ zu haben handeln** to conduct affairs without authority; **in ~ kontrahieren** to contract as the agent of another; **Gebrauch von einer ~ machen** to exercise power of attorney; **seine ~ mißbrauchen** to abuse one's authority; **~ für die Verhandlungen mitbringen** to be authorized to negotiate; **um ~en nachsuchen** to seek authority; **seine ~ niederlegen** to divest o. s. of one's authority; **~en einer Delegation prüfen** to verify the credentials of a delegation; **mit ~en versehen sein** to be invested with full authority; **seine ~en überschreiten** to go beyond (act in excess, beyond the scope of) one's powers, to exceed one's authority, to override one's commission (leave), to act ultra vires *(Br.)*; **seine ~en übertragen** to delegate one's powers; **~en auf j. übertragen** to devolve powers onto s. o., to vest s. o. with authority; **in ~ unterschreiben** to sign by proxy (as attorney in fact); **Wechsel in ~ unterschreiben** to indorse a bill by procuration; **in ~ für j. unterschreiben** to sign for s. o.; **mit allen ~en versehen** to invest with full powers (authority); **seine ~ vorlegen** to produce one's authority (a power of attorney, proxy); **~ widerrufen** to revoke (cancel) a power of attorney, to revoke a proxy; **seine ~ zurückgeben** to divest o. s. of one's authority.

Vollmachten|austausch exchange of powers; **~überprüfung** examination of powers, *(dipl.)* certification of credentials.

Vollmacht|geber mandator, donor [of a power of appointment], granter of power, proxy giver, constituent, principal; **~geber und ~nehmer** principal and agent; **~nehmer** appointee, donee, proxy, mandatary.

Vollmachts|anweisung proxy statement; **~austausch** exchange of powers; **~ausübender** donee, appointee, proxy, mandatary; **~ausübung** execution of an authority, exercise of power; **Grenzen seiner ~befugnisse erreicht haben** to have exhausted one's mandate; **~beschränkung** limitation of authority, curtailment (restriction) of powers, restraining powers; **~delegierung** devolution of power; **~entzug** revocation of power, withdrawal of a power of attorney; **~erteilung** granting (delegation) of power, authorization; **~fehler** defect of authority; **~formular** form of proxy, mandate (authorization, proxy) form; **~grenzen** limits of authority; **~indossament** restrictive indorsement; **~inhaber** holder of a power of attorney; **unwiderrufliche ~klausel** irrevocable power of attorney clause; **~mißbrauch** abuse (misuse) of power; **~nachweis** warranty of authority; **~prüfung** certification of credentials; **~prüfungsausschuß** credentials committee; **~rücknahme** revocation of power, withdrawal of a power of attorney; **treuhänderische ~stellung** power in the nature of a trust; **~stimmrecht** proxy voting; **~überprüfung** examination of powers (proxies), *(dipl.)* certification of credentials.

vollmachtsüberschreitend ultra vires *(lat.)*.

Vollmachts|überschreitung excess of authority, excessive appointment, ultra-vires action *(Br.)*; **~übertragung** power to delegate, delegation of authority (powers); **~umfang** scope of authority, extent (extension) of power of attorney; **~umfang in einer Weisung genau festlegen** to outline a power in a mandate; **~urkunde** power (letter, *US*) of attorney, procuracy, certificate of authority, proxy; **~verhältnis** agency relationship; **~verhältnis begründen** to create an agency relationship; **~widerruf** revocation of proxy; **~zweck** purpose of agency.

vollmast flaggen to hoist a flag full mast.

Voll|matrose able-bodied seaman; **~milch** full-cream (unskimmed) milk; **~mitglied** *(EG)* full member; **~mitglied werden** to get full membership; **~mitgliedschaft** full membership; **~mond** full moon; **~mondgesicht** pudding face; **~pension** board and residence, room and board, full board *(Br.)*; **~pensionär** boarder; **~professor** full-fledged professor; **sich einen ~rausch holen** to get dead drunk; **~schiff** full-rigged ship.

voll|schlagen, sich den Bauch to eat one's fill; ~**schlank sein** to have a well-rounded figure.
vollschreiben, sechs Seiten to write six pages.
Vollsicht *(Auto)* full vision;
~**kanzel** *(Flugzeug)* clear-vision cockpit, greenhouse *(sl.)*; ~**kuppel** astrodome; ~**rückfenster** wrap-around rear window; ~**scheibe** *(Auto)* panorama windscreen (windshield, *US*), wrap-around windshield *(US)*.
Vollsitzung plenary (full) session (assembly).
Vollspur *(Bahn)* standard gauge.
vollspurig *(Bahn)* standard-gauge.
vollständig complete, *(ganz)* entire, whole, wholly, total, thorough, copious, from top to bottom, from hub to tire *(US)*, *(voll)* full, plenary;
in sich ~ self-contained;
~ **im unklaren** utterly at sea; ~ **unterhaltsabhängig** wholly dependent; ~ **verteilt** *(Nachlaß)* fully administered;
seinen Namen ~ **ausschreiben** to write one's name in full; **Sprache** ~ **beherrschen** to have a thorough command of a language; **j.** ~ **enterben** to cut s. o. off with a shilling; ~ **entmachten** to strip totally of any power; **j.** ~ **fertigmachen** to finish s. o. off; **Geschäft** ~ **allein leiten** to have complete charge of a business; ~ **einverstanden sein** to be utterly (in wholehearted) agreement; ~ **verrückt sein** to be downright mad; **sich** ~ **verändern** to change completely;
~**e Abhängigkeit** total dependency; ~**e Abschrift** full copy; ~**e Adresse** full address; ~**e Ausgabe** complete edition; ~**er Ausgleich** full settlement; ~**es Belegexemplar** complete voucher copy; ~**er Bericht** comprehensive (detailed, complete) report; ~**e Erklärung** full statement; ~**e Finsternis** utter darkness; ~**e Klagebeantwortung** full answer; ~**er Text** unabridged text; ~**er Unsinn** downright nonsense; ~**e Zahlung** payment in full; ~**er Zusammenbruch einer Bank** bank smash.
Vollständigkeit completeness, entirety;
keinen Anspruch auf ~ **erheben** not to claim completeness.
Vollständigkeits|erklärung *(Vorstand für Prüfer)* letter of representation, liability certificate *(US)*; ~**klausel** *(Testament)* perfect attestation clause; ~**satz** completion rate.
vollstellen, Zimmer mit unnötigen Möbeln to clutter a room with useless furniture.
vollstopfen to stuff, to cram, *(Bus)* to crowd, to jam;
j. bis zum Hals ~ to load s. o. down with s. th.; **seinen Koffer** ~ to jam one's clothes into a suitcase; **Schüler mit Daten** ~ to stuff a pupil with dates; **sinnlos** ~ to lumber up.
vollstreckbar enforceable, executory, valid;
nicht ~ unenforceable; **sofort** ~ sharp; **vorläufig** ~ provisionally enforceable;
Urteil für ~ **erklären** to issue a writ of execution, to put a judgment in force; ~ **sein** to be enforceable;
~**e Ausfertigung** special execution, authority to execute a deed; **erste** ~**e Ausfertigung** first authentic copy; ~**e Forderung** judgment debt; ~**en Schuldtitel haben** to have a writ of execution for service; ~**er Titel** enforced judgment; **nicht** ~**es Urteil** dormant execution; **vorläufig** ~**es Urteil** provisionally enforceable judgment; ~**e Urteilsausfertigung** judgment execution; **nicht** ~**es Vermögen** exempt (mace-proof, *US*) property.
Vollstreckbarkeit enforceableness, enforceability;
mangelnde ~ lack of execution; **vorläufige** ~ provisional enforceability;
~ **eines Urteils beantragen** to file a judgment.
Vollstreckbarkeits|anordnung für Urteile anderer Staaten extension of judgment *(Br.)*; ~**erklärung** writ of execution; ~**erklärung ausfertigen** to carry a judgment into execution; ~**verfahren** executory proceedings.
vollstrecken to execute, to carry out (into execution), to enforce, to abide and satisfy;
in jds. Eigentum ~ to distrain upon s. one's belongings; **gerichtliche Entscheidung** ~ to enforce an order; **in das Gesellschaftsvermögen** ~ to levy execution into the company's property; **aus einer Hypothek** ~ to foreclose on a mortgage; **wegen der Kosten** ~ to issue execution for the amount of the costs; **Testament** ~ to carry out the provisions of a will; **Todesurteil** ~ to execute s. o.; **aus einer Urkunde** ~ to execute a deed; **aus einem Urteil** ~ to execute the judgment of a court, to enforce a judgment by execution; **in das Vermögen** ~ to levy execution upon the property;
~ **lassen** to carry into effect.
Vollstrecker executor.
vollstrecktes|Urteil satisfied (enforced) judgment; **nicht** ~ **Urteil** unsatisfied (dormant) judgment.
Vollstreckung execution, enforcement, levy of execution;
der ~ **unterliegend** distrainable; **nicht der** ~ **unterliegend** exempt from execution, judgment-proof, mace-proof *(US)*; **von der** ~ **erfaßt** *(Grundstück)* delivered in execution;
durchgeführte ~ completed execution; **nur teilweise durchgeführte** ~ dormant execution; **erfolglose (fruchtlose)** ~ unsatisfied execution; **nachrangige** ~ junior execution; **noch nicht vollendete** ~ uncompleted execution;
~ **in einen bestimmten Gegenstand** special execution; ~ **wegen Mietschulden** distress for nonpayment of rent; ~ **in der Nacht** noctanter; ~ **durch Räumung** eviction by bailiff; ~ **in bewegliche Sachen** general execution; ~ **eines Schiedsspruchs** enforcement of an award; ~ **ausländischer Schuldansprüche** execution of foreign awards; ~ **gegen Sicherheitsleistung** execution of forthcoming bond; ~ **eines Todesurteils** execution of a death sentence; ~ **von Unterhaltsansprüchen** enforcement of supports *(US)*; ~ **aus einem Urteil** execution under (enforcement of) a judgment; ~ **einer gerichtlichen Verfügung** enforcement of an order; ~ **durch Versteigerung** execution sale *(US)*, execution by sale of debtor's chattels;
Einstellung der ~ **anordnen**, ~ **eines Urteils aussetzen** to grant a stay of execution, to stay (suspend) a judgment, to grant a respite, to stay the execution; ~ **beantragen** to sue for a distraint, to issue execution against; **Einstellung der** ~ **beantragen** to ask for a stay in execution; ~ **betreiben** to levy a distraint, to enforce a judgment by execution, to levy (put in) a distress on; ~ **gegen j. betreiben** to levy on s. one's estate (property, goods); ~ **in das bewegliche Eigentum wegen nicht bezahlter Miete betreiben** to distrain chattels for nonpayment of rent; ~ **aus einem Kostenurteil betreiben** to levy execution with respect to the costs; ~ **in den Pfandgegenstand betreiben** to levy against the pledged property; ~ **durchführen** to levy an execution, to put in an execution and levy; ~ **mangels Masse einstellen** to return an execution unsatisfied (nulla bona, *US*); ~ **vorübergehend einstellen** to suspend an execution temporarily; ~ **zu vereiteln suchen** to hinder and delay; **der** ~ **unterliegen** to be subject to distraint (execution); **nicht der** ~ **unterliegen** to be liable to stay execution, to be exempt from execution, to be judgment-proof (mace-proof, *US*); ~ **vornehmen** to put in an execution and levy.
Vollstreckungs|abwehrklage foreclosure suit (action) *(US)*; ~**abwehrklage erheben** to bring a foreclosure action *(US)*; ~**anordnung** writ of [general] execution (delivery, *Br.*), foreclosure order *(US)*, warrant of distress, *(auf Herausgabe einer Sache)* writ of delivery; ~**anordnung für Zahlungsaufforderungen eines Liquidators** balance order; ~**anspruch** right to foreclose; ~**antrag** bill of foreclosure; ~**anweisung wegen einer Geldschuld** writ of debt *(US)*; ~**aufschub** stay of execution, suspense, respite, *(Strafe)* suspension of execution, reprieve; ~**aufschub gewähren** to respite execution of a judgment; **dem** ~**aufschub unterliegen** to be liable to stay execution.
Vollstreckungs|auftrag, ~**bescheid** writ (judgment) of execution, warrant of distress, distress warrant, enforcement order, praecipe, fieri facias, elegit *(Br.)*;
~ **gegen einen Drittschuldner** extent in aid; ~ **aus Vermieterpfandrecht** landlord's warrant;
~ **ausstellen** to issue a writ of execution; ~ **beantragen** to file a praecipe for a writ of execution; ~ **erlassen** to execute a writ; ~ **erteilen** to issue execution against (a writ of execution).
Vollstreckungs|aussetzung stay (suspension) of execution, *(Strafvollzug)* respite of sentence; ~**beamter** execution (enforcement) officer, executioner, marshal *(US)*; ~**behinderung** obstructing process; ~**behörde** enforcement (enforcing) agency, law enforcement authority, sheriff *(US)*; ~**beschluß** writ of execution; ~**einstellung** suspension (stay) of execution; **vorläufige** ~**einstellung** forced respite; ~**erschleichung** malicious use in process.
vollstreckungsfähig enforceable, executory, distrainable, valid, *(Grundstücke)* foreclosable.
Vollstreckungsforderung judgment debt.
vollstreckungsfreies Vermögen exempt (mace-proof, *US*) property.
Vollstreckungs|gebühr sheriff's poundage *(US)*; ~**gläubiger** execution (executing, attaching, judgment, elegit) creditor, distraining party; **gutgläubiger** ~**gläubiger** bona fide judgment creditor; ~**gläubiger bei einer Forderungspfändung** garnisher; ~**handlung** execution; ~**instanz** enforcement agency; ~**klausel** order for the enforcement, enforcement order, final process, writ of delivery *(Br.)*; **neue** ~**klausel** writ of revivor; ~**klausel erteilen** to carry a judgment into execution; ~**kosten** sheriff's poundage *(US)*; ~**leiter** enforcement officer; ~**maßnahmen**

enforcement measures; ~**mißbrauch** abuse of distress (process), malicious abuse of legal process; **erleichterte ~möglichkeit** ease of enforcement; ~**organ** enforcement agency; ~**pfandrecht** execution lien; ~**schuld** judgment debt; ~**schuldner** judgment (execution) debtor, distrainee, person distrained.

Vollstreckungsschutz exemption from seizure (execution), *(Mieter)* relief against forfeiture;
~ **genießen** to be exempt from execution (judgment-proof, mace-proof, *US*);
~**gesetz** stay law, exemption law; ~**gesetzgebung** exemption laws.

Vollstreckungs | titel, ~**urteil** writ of execution, executory decree; ~**vereitelung** conveyance to defraud a creditor, fraudulent conveyance (alienation); ~**vereitelung begehen** to rescue goods restrained; ~**verfahren** procedure for execution, attachment (judgment) execution, enforcement (supplementary) proceedings, foreclosure proceedings *(US)*, executory process (proceeding), elegit *(Br.)*; ~**verfahren gegen einen Drittschuldner** attachment execution; ~**verjährung** *(Straftat)* limitation of criminal proceedings.

volltanken to fill up with petrol, to refuel.

Voll | tastatur *(Schreibmaschine)* full keyboard; ~**tonätzung** full-tone engraving; ~**treffer** flush blow, direct hit, teller *(sl.)*, sockdolager *(US sl.)*; ~**treffer landen** to hit the bull's-eye.

volltrunken drunk to the light *(sl.)*, stone blind *(sl.)*.

Volltrunkenheit, im Zustand der in a state of total intoxication.

Vollversammlung plenary meeting (assembly), plenum, *(UNO)* general assembly (meeting).

vollversichert fully insured *(US)*.

Voll | waise orphan; ~**waschmittel** heavy-duty detergent.

vollwertig up to standard, of good value, sterling, adequate, undepreciated, *(neuwertig)* practically new;
nicht ~ below standard;
j. nicht als ~en Menschen betrachten to regard s. o. as inferior.

Vollwertversicherung *(Auto)* full coverage collision insurance.

vollzählig in full force (strength), complete;
~ **erscheinen** to turn out in full strength;
~**er Satz Briefmarken** full set of stamps; ~**e Versammlung** full assembly, full house.

vollziehbar executable, enforceable.

Vollziehbarkeit enforceability, executability.

vollziehen to enforce, to perform, to fulfil(l), to carry out, to effect, to execute;
Ehe ~ to consummate a marriage; **Trauung** ~ to perform (solemnize, *Br.*) a marriage.

vollziehend executory, executive, executorial;
~**er Ausschuß** executive committee; ~**e Behörde** executive branch of government; ~**e Gewalt** executive [power (authority)]; ~**es Organ** executive agent, enforcement agency.

Vollzieher executor.

Vollziehung fulfil(l)ment, performance, execution;
~ **der Ehe** consummation of marriage.

Vollziehungs | ausschuß execution committee; ~**beamter** collector; ~**befehl** warrant.

vollzogen executed, carried out;
nicht ~ unexecuted;
~**e Ehe** consummated marriage; ~**e Schenkung** vested gift; ~**e gerichtliche Verfügung** executed writ.

Vollzug execution, enforcement.

Vollzugs | anordnung executive order; ~**anstalt** penal establishment (institution); ~**ausschuß** executive committee (council); ~**beamter** law enforcement officer, marshal, *(Haft)* jailer, gaoler, warder; ~**behörde** enforcing authority, enforcement agency; ~**bericht** *(Gerichtsvollzieher)* return; ~**bestimmungen** regulations of an executive department; ~**dienst** *(Strafe)* execution of punishment; ~**frist von vier Tagen** four-day order; ~**funktionen** executive functions; ~**gewalt** executive power; ~**klausel** enforcement order; ~**meldung** report of compliance; ~**organ** executive officer (agent), enforcement agency.

Volontär unsalaried clerk, improver, supernumerary, supernumerary clerk *(US)*, apprentice, volunteer, trainee *(US)*, *(Betriebsprüfer)* articled clerk;
als ~ **arbeiten** to volunteer;
~**zeit** training time on a job.

Volt volt;
~**stärke** bias.

Volumen volume, content, bulk, cubic capacity;
dem ~ **nach** in terms of volume.

volumenmäßig zunehmen to increase in volume.

vorab in advance, by way of advance.

Vor | abbescheid advance notice; ~**abdruck** advance copy, preprint copy for private use; **am ~abend großer Ereignisse** on the eve of great events; ~**abentscheidung** preliminary ruling (decision), interlocutory decision; ~**abinformation** advance notice (information); ~**abzug** previous deduction, *(drucktechn.)* advance sheet, *(Erbe)* deduction.

Vorahnung presentiment, hunch;
böse ~ misgiving; **düstere ~en** dim forebodings;
~ **haben** to feel in one's bones; **schlimme ~en haben** to have evil forebodings; ~**en eines Unglücks haben** to forebode disaster.

Voralarm blue alarm, early warning.

voran, schon weit well on one's way.

Voranfrage *(parl.)* previous question.

vorangehen to lead the way, *(Ansprüche)* to have precedence, to antecede.

vorangehend precedent.

vorangekommen, schon weit well on one's way;
gut ~ **sein** to have made a good start.

Vorankommen progress, way, getting on;
persönliches ~ personal progress;
jds. ~ **behindern** to cramp s. one's progress.

vorankommen to advance, to make headway, to progress, to be proceeding, to walk one's way forward, to be on the rise, to rise in the world;
beruflich ~ to grow, to get along, to make one's way; **im Blitztempo** ~ to get on like a house on fire; **erstaunlich** ~ to progress surprisingly; **gut** ~ to jog along comfortably, to be doing well, to make great progress; **mit seiner Arbeit gut** ~ to be well forward with one's work; **glänzend** ~ to progress by leaps and bounds, to get on first-rate; **langsam** ~ to move slowly; **wegen Nebels nur langsam** ~ to make little progress in a fog; **langsam, aber sicher** ~ to progress steadily; **in einer Sache gar nicht** ~ to make no strides with a task; **unwahrscheinlich schnell** ~ to get on like a house on fire; **schrittweise** ~ to advance by degrees; **in einer Stellung** ~ to rise to a higher rank; **ganzes Stück** ~ to cover a great deal of ground; **gesellschaftlich wieder ein Stück** ~ to climb a rung of the social ladder; **immer weiter** ~ to be on the up and up *(coll.)*.

vorankommend rising, progressing, advancing, sledding.

Vorankündigung preannouncement, advance (previous) notice, *(Film, Rundfunk)* trailer, preview, *(Theater)* underline;
ohne ~ without previous notice; **ohne jede** ~ at an hour's notice;
~ **einer Emission** [red-herring, *US*] prospectus.

Voranmelder *(Patentrecht)* prior applicant.

Voranmeldung [previous] announcement, notice in advance, *(Patentrecht)* prior (previous) application, *(Telefon)* personal (person-to-person, *US*) call;
telefonische ~ **aufgeben** to book a personal call.

Voranschlag estimate (calculation) of costs, rough (preliminary, previous) calculation, cost estimate, statement, *(Etat)* budget;
dem ~ **entsprechend** in accordance with the budget;
überschläglicher ~ preliminary estimate;
~ **der Betriebseinnahmen und -ausgaben** operating budget; ~ **für die Lohn- und Gehaltskosten** labo(u)r [budget] estimate; ~ **auf Wunsch** estimate on demand;
~ **aufstellen** to make a cost estimate; **sich auf das Doppelte des ~s belaufen** to come to double the estimate; ~ **einreichen** to put in an estimate; ~ **für ein Haus erstellen** to estimate the cost of a new house; ~ **machen** to make an estimate of the costs; **seinen** ~ **überschreiten** to exceed one's estimate (budget).

voranschreiten to progress;
gut ~ to make good progress.

voranstellen to prefix.

vorantreiben, seine Angelegenheiten to press ahead with s. th., to push one's affairs; **Dinge** ~ to expedite (crowd, *US*) matters; **Projekt** ~ to push (promote) a scheme.

Vor | anzeige previous (advance) notice, notice in advance, preliminary advice, announcement, *(Film)* trailer, preview, prevue, *(Prospekt)* [red-herring, *US*] prospectus; ~**arbeit** preparatory (preliminary) work, *(Kleinarbeit)* spadework; **allgemeine ~arbeiten** general preparations.

vorarbeiten to work in advance (preparation);
sich ~ to work one's way up.

Vorarbeiter foreman, overseer, overman *(US)*, master mechanic, taskmaster, gaffer *(Br.)*, poppy guy *(sl.)*, *(Bergbau)* pit boss, butty, *(Farm)* headman *(Br.)*;
~ **bei Streckenarbeiten** section boss *(US)*;
~**ausbildung** training of foremen; ~**stelle** foremanship, overseership.

Vorarbeiterin forewoman.

Voraus *(Erbschaft)* advancement, advance, preferential benefit *(US)*;
~ **an den Haushaltungsgegenständen** widow's chamber;
~ **erhalten** to receive an advance.
voraus, im in advance, beforehand, by anticipation;
im ~ abziehen to deduct in advance, *(Steuern)* to deduct at the source; **etw. im ~ ausbedingen** to stipulate s. th. in advance; **im ~ bestellen** to order in advance; **im ~ bezahlen** to pay in advance; **sich im ~ Sorgen machen** to run to meet one's troubles; **jem. ~ sein** to be one up on s. o.; **weit ~ sein** to be streets ahead; **seiner Zeit ~ sein** to be ahead of one's time; **im ~ tun** to anticipate; **sein Einkommen im ~ verbrauchen** to anticipate one's income; **im ~ verfügen** to predispose.
Voraus|abteilung *(mil.)* vanguard, advance party, spearhead; **~abtretung** assignment of future debts; **~abzug** prior deduction.
vorausbedingen to stipulate beforehead.
Vorausbenachrichtigung prenotification, advance warning, preliminary (previous) notice, warning, caveat.
vorausberechenbar precalculable;
~er Schaden speculative damage.
vorausberechnet ex ante.
Voraus|berechnung forecast, precalculation; **~berechnung eines Schadens** pre-estimate of damage; **~besprechung** *(Buch)* previous review.
vorausbestellen to order in advance, to pre-engage, to make reservations, *(Karten)* to book in advance, *(Neuerscheinung)* to subscribe, *(Tisch)* to bespeak;
Plätze ~ to reserve seats, to book in advance; **Zimmer ~** to book (reserve, *US*) rooms at a hotel.
Vorausbesteller *(Neuerscheinung)* subscriber.
Vorausbestellung advance order (booking), order[ing] in advance, reservation, *(Neuerscheinung)* subscription.
vorausbewerten *(Börse)* to discount.
vorausbezahlen to pay in advance (by anticipation, *US*, beforehand, before maturity), to make payments in advance, to prepay, to advance.
vorausbezahlt prepaid;
~er Betrag amount paid in advance; **~e Fracht** advance[d] freight.
Voraus|bezahlung prepayment, payment in advance, advance (anticipated, *US*) payment, foregift *(Br.)*; **~bilanz** proforma balance sheet; **~buchung** advance booking; **~buchungscharter** advance booking charter; **~buchungstarif** *(Fluglinie)* advanced purchasing excursion (apex) tariff; **~buchungstarif für Charterflüge** advance booking charter (ABC) tariff; **~datieren** dating forward, advance dating.
vorausdatieren to date in advance, to foredate, to antedate;
Wechsel ~ to postdate a bill.
vorausdatiert antedated.
Voraus|datierung dating forward, advance dating, antedating, anticipation; **~datum** advance date; **~denken** advanced thinking, foresight.
vorausdenkend foresighted.
vorausdisponieren to make arrangements in advance, *(Kaufmann)* to buy ahead.
Voraus|dispositionen arrangements made in advance; **~einkauf** advance purchase; **~empfang** *(Erbe)* advance[ment], preferential benefit; **als ~empfang anrechnen** to bring into hotchpot advances; **einem Kind den ~empfang geben** to advance a child.
vorausempfangen *(Erbe)* to receive in advance.
Voraus|entnahme prior withdrawal, preferential benefit *(US)*; **~entrichtung** prepayment; **~erhebung** collection in advance; **~exemplar** advance copy.
vorausfahrendes Fahrzeug vehicle in front.
Voraus|frachten im Ortsverkehr prepaid local freights; **~gabe** preliminary edition.
voraus|gehende Bemerkungen precursory remarks; **~gezahlt** prepaid, paid in advance; **Erfahrungen ~haben** to have the advantage of greater experience.
Voraus|haftung primary liability; **~information** preliminary information; **~kalkulation** advance calculation; **~kasse** cash before delivery; **~klage** preliminary injunction; **~kommando** *(mil.)* advance party, vanguard; **~konto** discount for prepayment; **~korrektur** pre-press correction; **~leistung** advanve performance, *(Zahlung)* payment in advance; **~lieferung** advance delivery; **~nahme** anticipation.
vorausplanen to budget;
alles ~ to plan everything ahead.
Voraus|planung advance planning, budget[ing]; **~prämie** advance premium; **~rechnung** invoice sent in advance.
Voraussage prediction, *(Marktforschung)* forecast, forecasting, *(Prophezeiung)* prophecy, prognosis, prediction;
entgegen allen ~n against all forecasts;
~ **der Börsenentwicklung** stock-market prediction;
~ **machen** to prognosticate, to predict.
voraussagen to forecast, to foretell, to predict;
zukünftige Entwicklung ~ to predict future development; **Erdbeben ~** to predict that there will be an earthquake; **Verlauf der Wirtschaftsentwicklung ~** to forecast the course of business; **Zukunft ~** to foretell the future.
Voraus|sagespanne prediction interval; **~schätzung** preassessment, prognosis; **~schau** forecast, forecasting, prognosis; **technische ~schau** technical forecasting; **~schau der Sparbewegungen** savings estimate.
vorausschauend farsighted, provident.
vorausschicken to send in advance, *(fig.)* to mention;
einer Rede einige Bemerkungen ~ to premise a speech with a few remarks.
voraussehbar foreseeable.
voraussehen to foresee, to anticipate;
Schwierigkeiten ~ to see things through a mist; **als sicher ~** to take for granted.
voraussetzen to assume, to presume, to suppose;
stillschweigend ~ to understand, to imply tacitly; **langjähriges Studium ~** to presuppose long years of study.
Voraussetzung prerequisite, precondition, qualification, requisition, requirement, *(Annahme)* supposition, presupposition;
unter der ~ on the assumption (understanding); **unter der stillschweigenden ~** with the implicit understanding;
allererste ~ number-one requirement; **finanzielle ~en** financial requirements; **gesetzliche (gesetzlich vorgeschriebene) ~en** statutory conditions, legal requirements; **gewerbepolizeiliche ~en** licensing requirements; **materielle ~en** substantive requirements; **personelle ~en** staffing requirements; **persönliche ~en** personal qualifications; **satzungsmäßige ~en** statutory requirements; **erforderliche steuerliche ~en** necessary fiscal conditions; **technische ~en** technical prerequisites; **unabdingbare ~en** mandatory requirements; **verfahrensrechtliche ~en** procedural requirements; **verfassungsmäßige ~en** constitutional requirements; **wesentliche ~en** essentials;
~en für einen Anspruch prerequisites for a claim; **~en für die Bekleidung eines öffentlichen Amtes** qualifications for a public office; **~en für den Betrieb von Rückversicherungsgeschäften** reinsurance requirements; **~en für die Börseneinführung** listing requirements *(US)*; **~en für die Eintragung** requirements of registration; **~ für bedingte Entlassung** *(Strafgefangener)* parole eligibility; **~en für die Erlangung der Doktorwürde** requisitions for a university degree; **~en für den Erwerb der Bürgerrechte** qualification of citizenship (nationality, *US*); **~en für den Erwerb der Mitgliedschaft** qualification for membership; **~ der Gegenseitigkeit** similar credit requirements *(US)*; **~en für die Genehmigung** licensing requirements; **~ für Unterstützungsleistungen** qualification for benefits; **~en einer Versicherungspolice** prerequisites of an insurance policy; **~en für die Zulassung** requirements for admission;
von falschen ~en ausgehen to take an argument from false premises; **~en erfüllen** to comply with the conditions (requirements); **berufliche ~en erfüllen** to hold the qualifications, to qualify [o. s.] for a job; **gesetzliche ~en erfüllen** to fulfil(l) the requirements of the law; **~en für die Arbeitslosenunterstützung erfüllen** to qualify for unemployment insurance; **~en der Bewährungshilfe erfüllen** to be eligible for parole; **~en für die Gewährung einer Pension erfüllen** to be eligible for a pension; **~en für die Staatsangehörigkeit erfüllen** to qualify for citizenship (nationality, *US*); **zur ~ haben** to presuppose; **den ~en der Wahl Genüge leisten** to qualify for the vote; **erforderliche ~en mitbringen** to have the necessary qualifications; **~en für eine Stellung mitbringen** to have the qualifications for a post; **nötige ~en für ein Amt nachweisen** to qualify for an office; **~en schaffen** to create the prerequisites.
Voraussicht foresight, prudence;
nach menschlicher ~ as far as can be anticipated.
voraussichtlich expected, probable;
~e Ankunftszeit expected time of arrival; **~er Bedarf** potential demand, anticipated requirements; **~er Käufer** prospective (potential) buyer, prospect *(US)*; **~e Kosten** prospective costs; **~ entstehende Kosten ausrechnen** to reckon the probable costs; **~er Kunde** prospective client, potential customer, prospect *(US)*; **~e zukünftige Leistungen** *(Invalidenversicherung)* probable future payments; **~er Verbraucher** prospective consumer; **~er Vorteil** prospective advantage.

Voraus|skonto discount for payment; ~**subskription** subscription reservation; ~**truppen** *(mil.)* advanced units; ~**unterrichtung** advance word; ~**veranlagung** advance assessment; ~**vereinbarung eines pauschalierten Schadensersatzes** preassessment of a loss; ~**verfügung über Vermögenserträge** anticipation of property; ~**vermächtnis** preference legacy; **etw. im Wege des ~vermächtnisses übertragen** to bequeath s. th. as a preference legacy; **grobe ~wahl treffen** to screen; ~**wechsel** advance bill.

vorauszahlbar prepayable, payable in advance.

Vorauszahlung advance (advanced, anticipated, *US*) payment, prepayment, payment in advance (by anticipation, *US*), amount paid in advance (advanced), *(Einkommensteuer)* instal(l)ment;
~ **auf Kapitalanteile** payment of calls in advance;
~ **leisten** to make a prepayment; ~ **verlangen** to ask payment in advance.

Vorauszahlungs|möglichkeiten prepayment facilities; ~**prämie** advance premium.

Voraus|ziehung einer Tratte anticipatory drawing of a draft; ~**zollsystem** Commonwealth preference *(Br.)*.

Vor|avis preliminary advice; ~**bahnhof** auxiliary station; ~**bau** colonnade, portico; **überdachter ~bau** porch.

vorbauen, einer Sache to provide against s. th.

vorbearbeiten to rough-work.

Vorbedacht forethought, premeditation, premeditated design;
mit ~ prepense, *(Strafrecht)* with malice aforethought.

vorbedacht intentional.

Vorbedeutung omen, portent, foretoken.

Vorbedingung condition precedent, precondition, stipulation, *(Voraussetzung)* prerequisite, qualification, requirement;
den ~en entsprechend eligible; **ohne** ~ unconditioned;
~ **für ein öffentliches Amt** qualification for a public office; ~**en für die Annahme als Auszubildender (Lehrling)** apprenticeship requirements; ~**en für die Policengültigkeit** conditions precedent to the policy;
den ~en entsprechen to qualify; **alle ~en erfüllen** to meet the requirements.

Vorbehalt exception clause, reservation, reserved power, condition, proviso, provision, caveat, stipulation, restriction;
mit ~ with a grain (pinch) of salt; **mit allem** ~ with all reservations; **mit dem** ~ with the reservation that, reserving; **ohne** ~ unconditionally, without reservation (reserve), outright; **ohne ~ versetzt** *(Schüler)* unconditioned; **unter** ~ under reservation (reserve, protest), subject to reservation; **unter dem** ~ under the proviso; **unter üblichem** ~ under usual reserve (the usual reservations, provisions), with (under) the usual proviso; **unter ~ des Eingangs** reserving due payment; **unter ~ meiner Rechte** without prejudice to my rights; **unter ~ sämtlicher Rechte** all rights reserved;
geheimer ~ mental reservation (reserve); **grundlegender** ~ fundamental reservation; **schriftlicher** ~ protest in writing; **vertragliche ~e** contractual safeguards;
~ **der Rechte** reservation of rights;
~ **anmelden** to make reservations; **mit ~ annehmen** to accept under protest; **ohne ~ annehmen** to accept without qualification (reservation, protest); ~ **aufheben** to abolish a reserve; **keine ~e aufweisen** to be clean; ~**e zum Ausdruck bringen** to express reservations; ~ **formulieren** to stipulate a reserve; **unter ~ handeln** to act under the proviso; ~ **machen** to make reservations (a proviso); **unter ~ unterzeichnen** to sign under reserve.

vorbehalten to reserve;
Änderungen ~ subject to alterations (qualifications); **Eingang** ~ due payment provided; **Irrtümer** ~ errors excepted; **Nachprüfung** ~ subject to inspection; **alle Rechte** ~ all rights reserved; **Zwischenverkauf** ~ subject to prior sale;
sich ~ to retain for o. s. (the right), to reserve, to retain; **sich das Eigentum** ~ to retain title; **sich seine Entscheidung** ~ to reserve one's decision; **sich ein Recht** ~ to reserve a right for o. s.; **sich alle Rechte einer Erfindung** ~ to reserve all rights in an invention; **Regreßansprüche** ~ to reserve the right of recourse.

vorbehaltlich subject to, under reserve, with [a] proviso, reserving, with reservation as to, excepting, save for;
~ **von Änderungen** subject to alterations (modifications, revisions); ~ **Artikel 1** save as provided in paragraph 1; ~ **anderer (anderweitiger) Bestimmungen** unless otherwise provided; ~ **der Bestimmungen im Paragraph 7** except as provided in section 7; ~ **des Eingangs** subject to payment; ~ **unvorhergesehener Ereignisse** barring unforeseen developments; ~ **der Genehmigung** subject to approval (ratification); ~ **der Rechte Dritter** reserving the rights of third parties; ~ **eines Vertragsabschlusses** subject to contract; ~ **der Vertragsbestimmungen** subject to the terms of the contract; ~ **Zahlungseingang** reserving due payment.

vorbehaltlos without reservation, down-the-line, unreserved, unconditional;
~ **annehmen** to accept without qualifications (reservations); **jds. Bedingungen ~ annehmen** to accept s. one's conditions without reserve; ~ **zustimmen** to agree without the slightest reservation;
~**es Angebot** unconditional offer; ~**e Annahme** outright acceptance.

Vorbehalts|erklärung reserve, reservation; ~**gut** *(Ehefrau)* extradotal property, separate estate (property), paraphernal property, paraphernalia; ~**gut für Ehefrau und Kinder** wife's equity; ~**kauf** conditional sale; ~**käufer** conditional purchaser; ~**klausel** reservation clause, proviso, saving clause, salvo, exception, reddendum, hedge clause *(US)*; ~**preis** reserve price; ~**recht** reservation, right reserved; ~**urteil** provisional judgment; ~**verkäufer** conditional vendor.

vorbeibenehmen, sich völlig to make an exhibition of o. s.

vorbeifahren to roll past.

vorbeiführen, nahe am Dorf *(Straße)* to pass close to the village.

Vorbeigehen, im by the way, in passing.

vorbeigehen to go by.

vorbeikommen to pop round, *(Vertreter)* to come round.

Vorbeimarsch march past;
~ **abnehmen** to take the salute of the troops.

vorbeimarschieren to march (rank) past, to parade, to defile.

vorbeischicken to send along.

vorbelastet sein *(Grundstück)* to carry prior encumbrances.

Vorbelastungen *(Grundstück)* prior encumbrances (charges);
standortbedingte ~ handicaps due to location.

Vorbemerkung preliminary remark, *(Buch)* introduction, preface, prefatory [note], foreword, *(Gesetz)* preamble, *(Vertrag)* representations.

vorbenannt aforesaid.

Vor|benutzer previous (prior) user; ~**benutzung** *(Patentrecht)* prior use; **offenkundige ~benutzung** public prior use; ~**beratung** previous consultation, preliminary discussion.

vorbereiten to prepare, to arrange, to fix up;
sich ~ to get ready, to prepare o. s., to train, *(ankündigen)* to be in the offing (air); **sich für die Abreise** ~ to prepare for departure; **Ansprache** ~ to prepare a speech; **sich für ein Examen** ~ to prepare o. s. (sit) for an examination; **sich geistig** ~ to get one's thoughts together; **Gesetzentwurf** ~ to draft a [parliamentary] bill; **j. auf eine schlechte Nachricht** ~ to prepare s. o. for bad news; **j. auf eine Prüfung** ~ to coach s. o. for an examination; **sich für den Rechtsanwaltsberuf** ~ to study for the bar; **Schriftsatz** ~ to draw up a writ.

vorbereitend preparatory, preliminary;
~**e Arbeiten** preparations; ~**er Ausschuß** preparatory committee; ~**e Maßnahmen** preliminary measures; ~**er Schriftsatz** brief.

vorbereitet cranked up;
schlecht ~ ill-prepared;
~ **sein auf** to be prepared for; **auf alles (alle Eventualitäten) ~ sein** to be prepared for all contingencies, to have one's finger on the trigger;
~**e Rede** prepared (set) speech.

Vorbereitung|en preparations, dispositions, arrangements;
in geheimer ~ in the wind;
berufliche ~ apprenticeship training; **innerbetriebliche** ~ inservice training; **kriegsähnliche ~en** warlike preparations; **letzte ~en** final preparations; **technische** ~ *(Buch)* forwarding; **umfassende ~en** large preparations;
~ **auf die Arbeitswelt** work preparation; ~ **des Haushalts** budgetary preparation, preparation of the budget; ~**en für ein Landungsunternehmen** prelanding operations; ~ **der Pensionierung** retirement planning; ~**en zum Sturz der Regierung** conspiracy to overthrow the government; ~ **auf den Unterricht** preparation for teaching; ~ **der mündlichen Verhandlung durch Schriftsätze** pleading;
alle ~en durcheinanderbringen to mess up all one's plans; **in ~ sein** to be in preparation; ~**en treffen** to make arrangements; **nächtliche ~en treffen** to make preparations overnight.

Vorbereitungs|arbeiten preliminary (preparatory) work; ~**dienst** preparatory training, training time on a job; ~**feuer** *(mil.)* softening-up fire; ~**gespräche** preliminary consultation; ~**handlung** *(Strafrecht)* preparation; ~**jahr** preparatory year; ~**kosten je Einheit** preparation unit costs; ~**kursus** preparatory course; ~**schule** preparatory *(Br.)* (fitting, *US*, vestibule, *US*, prep, *US sl.*) school; **im ~stadium** in the pipeline; **sich noch im ~stadium befinden** to be still in the drawing-board stage; ~**zeit** preparatory period, lead, *(Produktion)* make-ready time, *(Schulaufgaben)* preparation *(Br.)*, *(Wartezeit)* preparatory period.

Vorbericht premature (preliminary, preparatory) report.

vorberuflich preprofessional.

Vor|bescheid provisional decision, preliminary answer, interim order, *(Patentwesen)* interim action, prior notice; ~**besitzer** previous owner (holder), prepossessor; ~**besprechungen** preliminary talks (discussions), *(Buch)* previous review.

vorbestellen to order (book) in advance, to make reservations, *(Zeitung)* to subscribe, to take in;
Buch ~ to subscribe for a book; **Plätze** ~ to book in advance, to reserve seats; **Zimmer im Hotel** ~ to book (reserve, *US*) rooms at a hotel.

Vorbestellpreis subscription price.

Vorbestellung advance order, booking in advance, reservation *(US)*;
auf ~en verkauft sold on order;
umfangreiche ~en heavy booking (reservations, *US*).

Vorbestellungspreis subscription price.

vorbestraft previously convicted;
einschlägig ~ previously convicted; **nicht** ~ *(Angeklagter)* first offender;
~ **sein** to be known to the police, to have a police record (previous conviction); **mehrfach** ~ **sein** to already have several convictions recorded against o. s.; **nicht** ~ **sein** to have a clean record (no convictions); **wegen ...** ~ **sein** to have a conviction for ..., to have been convicted of a previous crime.

Vorbestrafter person convicted, convict, criminal, taint;
mehrfach ~ recidivist; **nicht** ~ first offender.

Vorbeuge|gesetz gegen Gewohnheitsverbrecher prevention of crimes act; ~**haft** preventive custody (detention) *(Br.)*; ~**maßnahmen** preventive measures.

vorbeugen to prevent, to forestall, to preclude;
einer Krankheit ~ to prevent a disease; **jedem Mißverständnis** ~ to preclude any misunderstanding.

vorbeugend precautionary, prohibitive, preventively;
~**e Instandhaltung** preventive maintenance; ~**e Maßnahme** preventive measures.

Vorbeugung prevention, obviation;
zur ~ **gegen Unfälle** in order to prevent accidents.

Vorbeugungs|maßnahmen preventive (precautionary) measures; ~**mittel** preventive.

Vorbilanz preliminary balance sheet, [preclosing] trial balance.

Vorbild paragon, mirror, archetype, model;
~ **an Selbstbeherrschung** model of self-control; ~ **von Treue** paragon of loyalty;
j. als ~ **hinstellen** to hold s. o. up as an example.

vorbilden, j. to give s. o. preparatory training.

vorbildlich exemplary, model, ideal;
~**er Schüler** exemplary pupil.

Vorbildung educational background;
juristische ~ legal training; **notwendige** ~ required qualification;
für etw. nicht die notwendige ~ **haben** to be unqualified for s. th., to lack the necessary qualifications.

Vor|bogen *(drucktechn.)* introductory matter; ~**börse** business before official hours.

vorbörslich before [official] hours.

Vorbote forerunner, messenger.

Vorbringen presentation, objection, *(Behauptung)* allegation, assertion, contention, *(Partei)* pleading, plea;
aussichtsreiches ~ good case; **irrelevantes** ~ irrelevant answer; **leichtfertiges** ~ frivolous defence; **materiellrechtliches** ~ meritorious defence; **substantiiertes** ~ particular averment, articulated pleading; **tatsächliches** ~ material allegation, matter in pais; **überflüssiges** ~ surplusage; **unerhebliches** ~ immaterial averment; **für die Entscheidung unerhebliches** ~ irrelevant allegation; **unzulässiges** ~ inadmissible defence; **rechtlich zulässiges** ~ legal defence;
~ **gegen wichtige Anklagepunkte** traverse of indictment or presentment; ~ **von Beweismaterial** production of evidence; ~ **neuen Beweismaterials** production of fresh evidence; ~ **gegen Teile der Klage** partial defence; **wesentliches** ~ **der Verteidigung** merits of the defence.

vorbringen to bring forward, to come up with, to submit, to present, *(behaupten)* to assert, to allege, *(Frage)* to propound, *(vor Gericht)* to plead, to contend, to object;
Ansicht (Meinung) ~ to advance (venture) an opinion; **Beschwerde** ~ to make a complaint; **Beweis** ~ to produce (adduce) evidence; **prozeßhindernde Einrede** ~ to estop; **Einrede der Unzurechnungsfähigkeit** ~ to enter a plea of insanity; **einredeweise** ~ to enter a plea, to set up a defence; **Einwand der Mittellosigkeit** ~ to plead poverty; **Entschuldigung** ~ to offer an excuse; **Gründe** ~ to state (put forward) reasons; **Klage** ~ to prefer a charge; **Krankheit als Grund** ~ to allege ill health as a reason; **wohlbekannte Tatsachen lediglich neu formuliert** ~ to dish up well-known facts in a new form; **zu seiner Verteidigung** ~ to state in one's defence.

vorbuchstabieren to spell out.

vordatieren to date forward (ahead), to foredate, antedate;
Scheck ~ to date a check *(US)* (cheque, *Br.*) ahead, to antedate a check *(US)* (cheque, *Br.*).

vordatiert antedated;
~**e Rechnung** antedated invoice; ~**er Scheck** antedated check *(US)* (cheque, *Br.*); ~**e Zeitung** antedated paper, bulldog (early-bird) edition *(US)*.

Vorder|achse *(Auto)* front axle, *(Bahn)* leading axle; ~**achsenantrieb** front-wheel drive; ~**ansicht** front view; ~**deck** main deck, foredeck; ~**front** frontage, front; ~**gebäude** front building.

Vordergrund foreground, *(Bühne)* downstage;
deutlich im ~ well to the fore;
in den ~ **rücken** to play up; **sich in den** ~ **schieben** to push o. s. forward; **sich in den** ~ **spielen** to keep o. s. in the foreground; **im** ~ **stehen** to be in the fore; **im Augenblick weitgehend im** ~ **stehen** to be very much on the map now; **in den** ~ **treten** to come into prominence (to the front);
~**programm** *(Computer)* foreground program(me).

Vorder|haus front of a house; ~**hausbewohner** frontager; ~**kajüte** forward cabin.

Vordermann predecessor, *(Wechsel)* prior (previous) endorser (holder), preceding indorser;
auf ~ **bringen** to line up, *(Parteimitglieder)* to whip into line; **j. auf** ~ **bringen** to make s. o. toe the line; **sich an den** ~ **halten** to have recourse against the preceding party.

Vorder|rad front wheel; ~**radantrieb** front-wheel drive; ~**radaufhängung** front-wheel suspension; ~**richter** judge of fact, trial judge *(US)*, lower (inferior, previous) court; ~**satz** premise; ~**schiff** foreship; ~**seite** right-hand (front) page, *(Münze)* face, obverse; ~**seite eines Gebäudes** face (front) of a building; **auf die ~seite eines Wechsels die Worte setzen ...** to enface a draft with the words ...; ~**sitz** *(Auto)* forward (front) seat; ~**sitztasche** seat back pocket; ~**tür** front door; ~**türgriff** *(Auto)* front-door handle; ~**zimmer** front room, foreroom *(US)*.

Vordiplom preliminary diploma.

Vordividende interim (initial, *Br.*) dividend, dividend on account.

vordrängen, sich to jump the queue (line).

Vordringen der See aufs Festland encroachments made by the sea upon land.

vordringen to advance, to forge ahead, to press forward;
mit einer Beschwerde bis zum Geschäftsführer ~ to work one's way through to the manager with one's complaint; **in unbekanntes Gebiet** ~ to penetrate into unknown territory.

vordringlich urgent, most important;
~ **behandeln** to give high priority (urgent attention); ~ **behandelt werden** to receive priority consideration, to have first priority;
~**e Aufgabe** priority task; ~**e Behandlung** priority attention (consideration); ~**e Sache** urgent case.

Vordringlichkeit priority, urgency.

Vordringlichkeitsliste priority list.

Vordruck [printed] form, [application] form, blank *(US)*;
~ **ausfüllen** to fill in (up, out, *US*, complete) a form;
~**satz** set of printed forms.

vorehelich prenuptial, antenuptial;
~**e Verbindlichkeiten** antenuptial debts.

Voreigentümer previous owner, predecessor in title.

voreilig hasty, precipitate, too previous;
sich ~ **entscheiden** to make a rash decision;
~**e Schlüsse ziehen** to jump to conclusions.

Voreiligkeit hastiness.

Voreindeckung covering purchases.

voreingenommen biassed, prejudiced, partial, prepossessed, one-sided;
politisch ~ warped in political principles;
~ **sein** to bias, to take a jaundiced view; **gegen j.** ~ **sein** to be prejudiced against s. o.; **überhaupt nicht** ~ **sein** to be free from all preoccupations.

Vor|eingenommenheit prejudice, interestedness, preoccupations, jaundice, bias; **alle ~eingenommenheiten über Bord werfen** to shake o. s. free from all bias; **~eintragung** preceding entry; **~eltern** forefathers, ancestors; **~empfang** *(Erbe)* advance[ment], preferential benefit *(US)*.
vorenthalten to hold back, to withhold;
jem. etw. ~ to withhold s. th. from s. o.; **Informationsmaterial** ~ to suppress information; **jem. seine Pension** ~ to suppress s. one's pension; **Teil einer Nachricht** ~ to kill a passage; **jem. etw. widerrechtlich** ~ to deforce s. th. from s. o.; **Zahlung** ~ to withhold payment; **seine Zustimmung** ~ to withhold one's consent.
Vorenthaltung withholding, detainer;
widerechtliche ~ unlawful detainer, deforcement;
~ **eines rechtsstaatlichen Verfahrens** denial of justice.
Vorentscheidung preliminary decision, interim order, interlocutory decree, precedent;
von einer ~ abweichen to overrule a previous decision; ~ **nicht akzeptieren** to overrule a precedent; **sich auf eine ~ berufen** to cite an authority.
Vorentwurf preliminary (rough) draft.
Vorerbe fiduciary heir, first devisee, heir of inventory (in tail);
Ehefrau als ~n einsetzen to leave property to one's wife for life with remainder to one's children; **befreiter ~ sein** [etwa] to have a general power to dispose of the property; **nicht befreiter ~ sein** [etwa] not to be competent to dispose of one's property; **jem. als befreitem ~n zufallen** to be left to s. o. without remainder to another.
Vor|erbeneinsetzung entailment; **~erbschaft** [etwa] particular estate, estate in tail; **~erfinder** prior inventor; **~erhebung** *(Statistik)* preliminary examination, exploratory survey.
vorerwähnt above-mentioned, aforesaid, afore-mentioned.
Vor|erzeugnis product for further processing, primary product; **~etat** current budget; **~examen** previous examination, preliminary *(US)*; **~fabrikation** *(Häuser)* prefabrication, prefab *(coll.)*.
vorfabrizieren to prefabricate.
vorfabriziert prefabricated, prefab *(coll.)*, *(Beton)* precast.
Vorfahr ancestor, forefather, ascendant, parent;
~en ancestry;
~e in gerader Linie lineal ancestor;
von einem gemeinsamen ~ abstammen to originate from a common ancestor.
vorfahren to drive up, *(Kamera)* to track in;
bei jem. ~ to drive up to (draw up at) s. one's house; **beim Bahnhofseingang** ~ to draw up at the station entrance; **vor dem Haupteingang** ~ to drive right up the front door;
sein Auto ~ lassen to order one's car.
Vorfahrt right of way, *(Kamera)* track-in;
~ **beachten** to yield right of way, *(Schild)* major road ahead.
vorfahrtsberechtigt major;
nicht ~ *(Güterzug)* inferior;
~ **sein** to have the right of way.
Vorfahrts|berechtigung vor anderen Zügen haben to carry top running priority over all other trains; **~recht** right of way, yield *(US)*; **~schild** priority sign; **~straße** major (through) road; **~zeichen** priority sign.
Vorfaktur proforma invoice.
Vorfall event, occurrence, incident, occasion;
ergreifender ~ touching incident.
vorfallen to occur, to happen, to take place.
Vor|fälligkeitsklausel prepayment clause; **~feier** precelebration.
Vorfeld forefield, *(Flugplatz)* apron;
im ~ *(fig.)* at the preliminary stage;
~ **einer Wahl** run-up to an election.
vorfertigen to prefabricate.
Vor|fertigung prefabrication; **~film** supporting film.
vorfinanzieren to prefinance, to provide interim financing.
Vorfinanzierung preliminary (advance) financing, prefinancing.
Vorfinanzierungskredit preliminary credit.
vorflunkern, jem. etw. to tell s. o. a fib, to taradiddle s. o.
Vor|fracht original freight; **~frage** preliminary question, *(parl.)* previous question; **~friedensvertrag** peace preliminaries.
vorfühlen *(mil.)* to seek contact;
bei jem. ~ to approach s. o.
Vorführ|apparat projection apparatus; **~dame** mannequin, model; **als ~dame fungieren** to model; **~dauer** *(Film)* running time.
vorführen to present, to show, to exhibit, to display, *(Auto)* to demonstrate, *(Film)* to project, to screen, *(Mode)* to model, to parade, *(Theaterstück)* to present, to show;
seine Künste ~ to show off; **dem Richter** ~ tbring up before the court; **Verbrecher** ~ to make a criminal appear in court, to arraign a prisoner; **Zeugen** ~ to produce a witness.
Vorführer *(Auto)* demonstrator, *(Film)* motion-picture operator, projectionist, movie man.
Vorführ|gebiet demonstration area; **~genehmigung** *(Film)* production permit; **~gerät** projection machine, projector; **~kabine** projection booth; **~mann** dressman; **~raum** projection room; **~termin** *(Fernsehen)* preview date.
Vorführung performance, play, *(Ausstellung)* exhibition, presentment, *(Auto)* demonstration, *(Film)* projection, production, showing, show, performance, *(Mode)* parade, show;
laufende ~ continuous performance; **musikalische** ~ musical performance; **öffentliche** ~ public demonstration; **praktische** ~ practical demonstration; **private** ~ private view; **zwangsweise** ~ compulsory attendance, *(Zeuge)* compulsory process;
~ **zur Aburteilung** gaol delivery; **private ~ eines Films** private view of a film; ~ **im Haftprüfungstermin** habeas corpus; ~ **schlechter Manieren** exhibition of bad manners; **polizeiliche ~ von Tatverdächtigen** identification parade, show-up line *(sl.)*, parade shed *(US)*; ~ **beim Untersuchungsrichter** arraignment;
~ **eines Zeugen** production of a witness.
Vorführungs|befehl bench warrant, letters of intimation *(Scot.)*, capias *(lat.)*; **~gelände** demonstration plot; **~maschine** demonstration machine; **~modell** demonstration model; **~raum** projection room, auditorium; **~rechte** performance rights; **alleiniges ~recht** *(Film)* exclusive film; **~zwecke** demonstration purposes.
Vorführwagen demonstration car.
Vorgabe standard, target, jump *(US)*;
~leistung standard [performance]; **~stunde** standard hour; **~zeit** *(Zeitstudie)* standard time for a given job, time standards; **~zeitermittlung** rate setting *(US)*.
Vorgang occurrence, event, course of events, proceedings, incidence, *(Akte)* precedent, record, matter, *(Geschäft)* transaction, previous correspondence, *(Verfahren)* process, precedence, authority, procedure, operation;
aktenmäßiger ~ subject of records; **steuerpflichtiger** ~ taxable transaction;
~ **anziehen** to quote a precedence; **geschäftlichen ~ aufzeichnen** to record a transaction; ~ **beschleunigen** to speed up a process; ~ **buchen** to make an entry of a transaction; ~ **zu seinen Akten nehmen** to place a report on one's files; **jem. einen ~ genauestens schildern** to tell exactly how it happened.
Vorgänger forerunner, foregoer, antecessor, *(Effekten)* previous holder, *(Recht)* predecessor;
~ **im Amt** precursor.
Vorgangsschreiben previous letter.
Vorgarten front garden (yard, *US*).
vorgaukeln, jem. etw. to lead s. o. up the garden path, to pull the wool over s. one's eyes.
Vorgeben einer falschen Persönlichkeit false personation.
vorgeben to pretend, to use as a pretext;
jem. etw. ~ to give s. o. odds; **Arzt zu sein** ~ to pretend to be a doctor; **dringende Geschäfte** ~ to use urgent business as a pretext; **im Interesse der Allgemeinheit zu handeln** ~ to profess to act in the interest of the general public; **Polizist zu sein** ~ to purport to be a police officer; **Unkenntnis** ~ to plead ignorance.
vorgebildet, beruflich professionally trained, skilled; **juristisch** ~ learned in the law;
~ **sein** to have basic knowledge; **fachlich ~ sein** to have had previous technical training.
Vorgebildeter, fachlich professional employee.
Vorgebirge foreland, head, cape.
vorgeblich pretended, alleged, so-called, colo(u)rable, would-be;
~er Zweck ostensible purpose.
vorgefaßte Meinung preconceived opinion, prejudice, bias.
vorgefertigt prefabricated.
Vorgefühl presentment, hunch, foreboding.
Vorgehen [line of] action, plan, proceeding, procedure;
abgekartetes ~ collusive action; **diplomatisches** ~ diplomacy; **eigenmächtiges** ~ unauthorized act; **gemeinsames** ~ concerted (joint) action; **gerichtliches** ~ court action; **gesetzwidriges** ~ unlawful act; **indirektes** ~ indirect action; **planvolles** ~ tactics *(mil.)*; **schlaues** ~ manoeuvre *(Br.)*, maneuver *(US)*; **unkluges** ~ impolicy; **verständnisvolles** ~ light hand; **vorsichtiges** ~ go-slow approach;
~ **eines Anspruchs** priority of a claim;
das weitere ~ genauestens bestimmen to dictate a line of action;
~ **billigen** to approve of an action.

vorgehen to proceed, to take action, to act, to adopt measures, *(sich ereignen)* to happen, to occur, to take place, *(Hypothek)* to have priority, *(Konkursforderung)* to have precedence, *(mil.)* to advance, to push forward, *(vorangehen)* to go in front;
allem ~ to take precedence of all others; **mit kühler Berechnung** ~ to act in a calculating manner; **energisch** ~ to take a strong position (stern steps); **gegen j.** ~ to proceed against s. o.; **gemeinsam** ~ to take joint action, to act in concurrence, *(Konkursfall)* to concur; **gerichtlich gegen j.** ~ to proceed (institute judicial (legal) proceedings) against s. o., to file a suit against s. o. *(US)*; **geschickt** ~ to operate with skill; **geschlossen** ~ to advance in close order; **jem. im Grundbuch** ~ to have priority over s. o. in one's claim on mortgaged property; **äußerst methodisch** ~ to dot and carry; **sehr methodisch** ~ to be very orderly; **am Tag drei Minuten** ~ *(Uhr)* to gain three minutes a day; **im Range** ~ to have precedence (priority), to rank before; **rücksichtslos** ~ to act ruthlessly; **in einer Sache** ~ to act in a case; **schrittweise** ~ to proceed by stages; **strafrechtlich gegen j.** ~ to start a prosecution against s. o.; **energisch gegen die Streikenden** ~ to take a tough line against the strikers; **summarisch** ~ to take summary proceedings; **unbarmherzig** ~ to take the gloves off; **ungeschickt** ~ to play one's cards badly (ill); **unorthodox** ~ to cut corners; **vorsichtig** ~ to tread with caution, to go easy, to hew close to the line *(US)*.
vorgehend precedent;
~**e Hypothek** prior mortgage; ~**er Hypothekengläubiger** prior mortgager; **im Range** ~**es Pfandrecht** senior lien.
Vorgehender, schonungslos no-quarter man.
Vorgehensweise line of proceeding.
vorgeladen summoned;
~ **sein** to be up for; **als Zeuge** ~ **sein** to be subpoenaed as a witness; ~ **werden** to receive a summons.
vorgelagert, dem Festland ~**e Insel** offshore island.
Vorgelände *(mil.)* foreground.
vorgelegt werden *(Wechsel)* to make appearance.
vorgelesen, genehmigt und unterschrieben read aloud, agreed to and signed.
vorgenannt before-mentioned, aforesaid.
vorgerückt advanced, forward;
im ~**en Alter** advanced in years; **in** ~**er Stimmung sein** to be in high spirits; **zu** ~**er Stunde** at a late hour.
Vorgeschichte case history, *(Person)* antecedents, background, personal history;
zweifelhafte ~ spotty record.
Vor|geschlagener nominee; ~**geschmack** taste.
vorgeschoben pretended, ostensible, dummy, sham, *(mil.)* advanced;
~**e Agentur** house agency; ~**er Geschäftsstand** advance command post; ~**e Person** man of straw, figurehead, nominee; ~**er Posten** advanced post.
vorgeschrieben prescribed, required, provided, obligatory, stipulated, formulary, compulsory;
gesetzlich ~ prescribed (required) by law; **wie im nachstehenden** ~ as hereunder prescribed;
~ **sein** to be the rule; **vom Gesetz** ~ **sein** to be required by law; ~**es Alter** statutory age; ~**er Anzug** regulation dress; ~**e Bescheinigung** qualifying certificate; ~**es Formblatt** prescribed form; **innerhalb der** ~**en Frist** within the stipulated period, in the required time; **in der** ~**en Frist liefern** to deliver within the stipulated time; ~**e Höhe** *(Mindestreserven)* prescribed level; **über das** ~**e Kapital verfügen** to have the money required; ~**e Menge** quantity required; ~**e Mindestreserven** *(Bank)* fractional (required, *US*) reserves; ~**e Plazierung** *(Anzeige)* prescribed position; ~**e Qualität** stipulated quality; ~**er Satz** prescribed rate.
vorgesehen specified, stipulated, provided, *(ausersehen)* designate;
gesetzlich ~ provided by statute; **nicht** ~ unprovided; **nicht anderweitig** ~ not otherwise provided; **wie** ~ as scheduled *(US)*;
~ **sein** to be slated *(US)*; **gesetzlich** ~ **sein** to be provided by law; **vertraglich** ~ **sein** to be provided for in a contract; **für etw.** ~ **werden** to be intended for s. th., to get credit for s. th.;
~**e Produktion** proposed production.
Vorgesellschaft predecessor company.
vorgesetzt superior;
~**e Behörde** supervising authority; ~**er Richter** supervising judge.
Vorgesetzte|r superior, senior [officer], [big] boss *(coll.)*, *(Betriebsinhaber)* master, employer, principal, chief;
mein ~**r** my senior officer; **oberster** ~**r** top brass; **unmittelbarer** ~**r** immediate superior; **untergeordneter** ~**r** straw boss *(US)*; **j. bei seinem** ~**n anzeigen** to put s. o. on the peg *(mil., sl.)*; **seinem** ~**n täglich Bericht erstatten** to report daily to one's chief.
Vorgesetzten|schulung supervisory training; ~**verhältnis** relationship between superior and subordinate.
vor|gestrig outmoded, outdated, old-fashioned; ~**getäuscht** artificial, simulated, sham; ~**getragener Saldo** balance carried forward; **sich zu weit** ~**gewagt haben** to have gone too far to withdraw.
vorgreifen to forestall, to anticipate;
jds. Entscheidung ~ to anticipate s. one's decision; **einer Frage** ~ to prejudice a matter.
vorgreifend anticipative.
Vorgriff anticipatory expenditure, anticipation, *(Etat)* advance, credit *(Br.)*;
im ~ **auf** in anticipation of;
steuerliche ~**e** anticipation of tax payments;
~ **auf den Haushalt** advance, credit *(Br.)*;
~**e auf seine Einnahmen machen** to anticipate one's income; ~ **auf das nächste Monatsgehalt vornehmen** to draw on one's next month's salary.
Vorgriffskontingent advance quota.
vorgriffsweise in anticipation.
Vorgründungs|bericht *(an Handelsregister)* statement in lieu of prospectus *(Br.)*; ~**gewinn** profit prior to incorporation; ~**vertrag** promotion agreement.
Vorhaben intention, plan, design, counsel, project, mind, purpose, contemplation, aim;
aussichtsloses ~ unlikely venture; **bestimmtes** ~ specific project; **finanziertes** ~ project financed; **schwebende** ~ pending projects;
j. von seinem ~ **abbringen** to put s. o. off his plan; ~ **durchführen** to execute (carry out) a plan; **einem** ~ **positiv gegenüberstehen** to look on a plan with favo(u)r; ~ **in Angriff nehmen** to engage in a project; **gegen ein** ~ **sein** to deprecate a scheme; **jds. Interesse für ein** ~ **wecken** to interest s. o. in a plan.
vorhaben to plan, to design, to be up to, to contemplate;
j. ~ to haul s. o. over the coals; **nichts** ~ to have nothing on; **nichts Besonderes** ~ to have nothing particular to do; **nichts Böses** ~ to intend no harm; **nichts Gutes** ~ to be up to no good.
Vor|hafen outer port, outport; ~**haftung** prior commitment.
Vorhalle entry, entrance hall, vestibule, anteroom, stoop *(US)*, *(Hotel)* lounge, *(Theater)* lobby.
vorhalten to censure, to rebuke, *(Vorräte)* to last;
jem. etw. ~ to rebuke s. o.; **jem. als Muster** ~ to hold s. o. up as an example.
Vorhaltungen rebuke, censure, *(dipl.)* representations, remonstrances;
jem. ~ **machen** to remonstrate with s. o.; **ernste** ~ **machen** to expostulate.
Vorhand first refusal (claim);
~ **haben** to have first refusal.
vorhanden existing, actual, effective, *(auf Lager)* in (on) stock, on hand, on tap, *(auf dem Markt)* on the market, *(verfügbar)* available;
nicht ~ nonexistent, null, *(Ware)* out of stock; **reichlich** ~ abounding, abundant;
~ **sein** to be in existence, to exist; **nicht mehr** ~ **sein** *(Firma)* to have ceased to exist; **reichlich** ~ **sein** to be abundant, to teem, to superabound;
~**er Anspruch** existing claim; ~**er Bedarf** effective demand; ~**es Kapital** effective capital; ~**e Vorräte** supplies on hand.
Vorhandensein existence;
gleichzeitiges ~ concomitance, concomitancy.
Vorhang, Eiserner *(pol.)* iron curtain; **eiserner** ~ *(Theater)* safety (fireproof) curtain; **geteilter** ~ tableau curtains;
~ **fallen lassen** to ring down; **mit einem** ~ **versehen** to curtain; ~ **vorziehen** to draw the curtain.
Vorhängeschloß padlock.
Vorhang|stange curtain pole; ~**stoffe** drapery *(US)*; ~**werbung** theatre-curtain advertising.
vorherbestimmt predestined, predeterminate, set.
Vorherbestimmung predestination, foredoom.
vorhergehend previous, preceding, prior;
~**er Absatz** preceding article (paragraph); **auf der** ~**en Seite** on the previous page.
Vorhergehender the foregoing.
vorherig previous, prior, precedent, preceding;
ohne ~**e Ankündigung** without previous notice; ~**e Benachrich-**

tigung notice in advance; ~er **Eigentümer** predecessor, previous owner; ~er **Preis** previous price; ~e **Verabredung** previous engagement; ~e **Vereinbarung** previous agreement, precontract.

Vorherrschaft predominance, domination, prevalence, superiority, ascendancy;
wirtschaftliche ~ economic domination;
~ **der Arbeitgeber** employer domination.

Vorherrschen prevalence;
~ **des Kleinbesitzes** small-holdings system; ~ **von Parteigeist** party spirit, faction; ~ **der weißen Rasse** white supremacy.

vorherrschen to prevail, to predominate.

vorherrschend prevailing, prevalent, predominant;
~e **Meinung** prevailing opinion.

Vorhersage prognostic, prognosis, [economic] forecasting;
langfristige ~ long-range forecasting;
~ **einer Depression** forecast of a slump; ~ **wirtschaftlicher Entwicklungen** business (economic) forecasting;
~ **machen** to forecast, to predict, to call the shots; ~ **über den Haufen werfen** to throw a prediction off;
~**änderung** forecast amendment; ~**dienst** forecasting service; **schlechte** ~**ergebnisse** poor forecasting records; ~**gebiet** *(Wetter)* reported area; ~**irrtum** forecasting error; ~**karte** forecast chart; ~**methode** forecasting method.

vorhersagen to forecast, to foretell, to predict;
Wetter ~ to forecast the weather.

Vorhersage|zeitraum forecast period; ~**zentrum** *(Wetter)* weather center *(US)* (centre, *Br.*).

vorheucheln, Krankheit to simulate (malinger) to be ill.

Vorhof forecourt, dooryard *(US)*.

Vorhut *(mil.)* vanguard, advance guard;
~**gefecht** vanguard action.

vorig previous, former;
~**er Monat** last month.

Vor|indikator leading indicator; ~**indossant** previous indorser; ~**instanz** lower (inferior) court, court below; ~**inventar** previous inventory.

Vorjahr last (previous, preceding, prior) year;
hinter dem ~ **zurückbleiben** to be off from last year.

Vorjahres|abschnitt preceding annual period; ~**abzüge** prior-period deductions; ~**dividende** last year's dividend; **hinter dem** ~**ergebnis zurückbleiben** to remain below year-ago levels; ~**gewinn berücksichtigen** to adjust prior year's profit; ~**modell** previous year's model; ~**monat** corresponding month of the previous year; ~**niveau** year-ago (previous year) level; ~**produktion** last year's output; ~**stand** level of the previous year; ~**umsatz** last year's turnover; **im** ~**vergleich** composed with the year before; ~**zahlen** year-end (year-end-before, *US*) figures; ~**zeit** period of last year.

vorjährig of last year;
~**e Belastungen** prior-year charges.

vorjammern, jem. etw. to hand s. o. a long tale of woe.

Vorkalkulation precalculation, preliminary calculation, estimation of cost, cost accounting.

Vorkalkulationskarte product cost card.

vorkalkulieren, Kosten hoch to establish standard cost at a high level.

vorkalkulierte Kosten standard (predetermined, scheduled, target) costs.

Vorkämpfer champion, promoter, pioneer;
~ **auf sozialem Gebiet** social activist.

Vorkasse payment in advance, advance payment;
gegen ~ against prepayment.

Vorkauf preëmption, first refusal.

vorkaufen to buy beforehand, to forestall, to preëmpt.

Vorkäufer preëmptor.

Vorkaufs|berechtigter preëmption claimant, preëmptor, preëmptioner; ~**berechtigung** preëmptive right; **Grundstück mit** ~**berechtigung besitzen** to settle upon land subject to preëmption *(US)*; ~**klausel** clause of preëmption, preëmption clause, first refusal clause *(US)*; ~**preis** preëmption price.

Vorkaufsrecht preëmption [right], first refusal, preferment, prior-purchase obligation, *(Grundstück)* option to purchase land;
einem ~ **unterliegend** preëmptible;
~ **einräumen** to give the right of first refusal; **durch Ausübung (im Wege) des** ~**s erwerben** to preëmpt, to obtain by preëmption; ~ **haben** to have [the] first refusal; **Haus mit** ~ **mieten** to rent a building with the option of purchase; **sich ein** ~ **vorbehalten** to reserve an option to acquire.

Vorkaufsvertrag binder, *(Grundstück)* covenant to convey.

Vorkehrungen arrangements, provisions, efforts, dispositions;
anschließende ~ follow-up arrangements;
~ **gegen Überschwemmungen** flood prevention;
~ **treffen** to make provisions, to make arrangements (dispositions), to arrange, to take precautions, to meet troubles half-way; **gesundheitliche** ~ **treffen** to sanitate; **notwendige** ~ **treffen** to take all due measures; ~ **gegen den Ausbruch von Krankheiten treffen** to take measures for the prevention of diseases; ~ **für die Deckung treffen** to make arrangements for cover; ~ **für die Herstellung treffen** to arrange for the manufacture; ~ **zur Schuldentilgung treffen** to make appropriation for the payment of debts; **nichts in seinen** ~ **vergessen** to provide for everything.

Vorkenntnisse previous knowledge, rudiments, elements;
~ **haben** to have previous (background) experience; **gute** ~ **haben** to be well grounded in the elements;
~ **erwünscht, aber nicht Bedingung** *(Anzeige)* previous experience is desired but not obligatory.

vorknöpfen, sich j. to take s. o. by the button (to task), to have a word with s. o. about s. th., to buttonhole s. o., to work on s. o.; **sich j. gründlich** ~ to give s. o. what for *(fam.)*.

Vorkommando advance party.

Vorkommen incidence, event, occasion, appearance, *(Lagerstätte)* deposit;
bei ~ on demand, *(Wechsel)* on presentation;
~ **von Öl** oil deposits.

vorkommen to occur, to take place, to happen, *(Mineralien)* to be found, to occur;
einem irgendwie bekannt ~ to seem to strike a chord; **sich zu fein** ~**, um mit anderen zu sprechen** not to have a word to throw at a dog; **nur in einem bestimmten Gebiet** ~ to be local; **sich gedemütigt** ~ to feel cheap; **sich wunder wie gescheit** ~ to think no small beer of o. s.; **häufig** ~ to be of frequent occurrence; **einem merkwürdig** ~ to seem to be rather strange; **jem. ganz natürlich** ~ to come to s. o. by nature; **jem. spanisch** ~ to be Greek to s. o.; **überall** ~ to have a very wide distribution; **immer wieder** ~ to happen again and again.

vorkommend incident;
natürlich ~ native.

Vor|kommnis event, occasion, happening, incident, incidence, occurrence; **keine besonderen** ~**kommnisse** nothing to write home about o. s., *(mil.)* nothing to report; ~**konferenz** preliminary consultation; ~**konnossement** through bill of lading; ~**konzession** preliminary concession (franchise, *US*); ~**korrektur** first proof, *(Lesen)* reading of the copy; ~**kosten** preliminary costing.

Vorkriegs|anleihe prewar loan; ~**ausfuhr** prewar export; ~**beteiligungen** prewar holdings; ~**drama** *(Theater)* drama of prewar vintage; ~**gepflogenheiten** prewar principles; ~**gewinn** prewar profits; ~**gewinnstandard** prewar standard of profits; ~**kaufkraft** prewar purchasing power; ~**leistung** prewar performance; ~**miete** prewar rent, standard rent *(Br.)*; ~**niveau** prewar price level; ~**position** prewar position; ~**preis** prewar price; ~**preisniveau** prewar price level; ~**schulden** prewar debts; ~**stand** prewar level; ~**vergleich** prewar comparison; ~**verhältnisse** prewar conditions; ~**volumen** prewar volume; ~**ware** prewar goods; ~**wert** prewar value; ~**zeit** prewar period, prewar era.

Vorkrisenmodell pre-crisis model.

vorkühlen to precool.

Vorkurs preparatory course.

Vorladegebühr fee for issue of a summons.

vorladen to summon, to issue a summons, to process, to cite;
amtlich ~ to convene; **jem. als Zeugen** ~ to subpoena s. o. to appear as witness;
jem. ~ **lassen** to take out a summons against s. o.

Vorladung summons, summoning, writ, process, monition, citation *(US)*, notification, interpellation;
gerichtliche ~ summons, notice of appearance; **nochmalige** ~ resummons; **persönliche** ~ peremptory writ; **polizeiliche** ~ police summons; **schriftliche** ~ letters citatory;
~ **des Angeschuldigten** criminal process; ~ **unter Beifügung von Urkunden** specially indorsed writ; ~ **des Beklagten** capias ad respondendum; ~ **eines Drittschuldners** summons to garnishee, garnishment; ~ **vor Gericht** judicial process; ~ **unter Strafandrohung** subpoena; ~ **bei Zahlungsbefehl** default summons *(Br.)*;
gerichtliche ~ **erhalten** to be served with a summons; ~ **gegen jem. erwirken** to take out a writ (summons) against s. o.; ~ **ergehen lassen** to issue (take out) a summons, to indorse a writ, *(unter Strafandrohung)* to hand out a subpoena; **einer**

gerichtlichen ~ Folge leisten to answer (obey) a summons; ~ **zustellen** to serve a subpoena; **jem. eine ~ zustellen** to serve s. o. with a summons.

Vorladungs|befehl precept, subpoena; ~**beschluß** original process; **von den ~pflichten entbunden sein** to be relieved of the terms of subpoena; ~**vollmachten einräumen** to grant subpoena powers.

Vorlage *(Einreichung)* filing, *(Kredit)* advance, *(Muster)* model, sample, pattern, *(parl.)* bill, motion, *(zum Schreiben)* copy, *(Text)* text, original, *(Unterbreitung)* submission, *(Wechsel)* presentation;
bei ~ on demand, at sight, when presented; **bei ~ zahlbar** payable on presentation; **gegen ~** on (upon) presentation; **genau nach beiliegender ~** matching the sample; **nur gegen ~ des Personalausweises** to be handed out only on presentation of the identity card; **zur ~ bei** for submission to;
kurzfristige ~ short-term advance; **mangelnde ~** failure of presentment; **reproduktionsreife ~** *(Anzeige)* finished art; **unstreitige ~** unopposed bill; **vorzeitige ~** pre-presentment;
~ zur Annahme (zum Akzept) presentment (presentation) for acceptance; **~ für eine Anzeige** copy for advertisement; **kurzfristige ~n der Banken** day-to-day advances from banks; **~ von Beweisen** submission of evidence; **~ von Bilanzen** production of balance sheets; **~ der Dokumente** presentation of documents; **~ der Geschäftsbücher** production of books; **~ eines Gesetzentwurfes** introduction of a bill; **~ des Haushaltsvoranschlages** appropriation request; **~ zum Inkasso** presentment for collection; **~ des Jahresabschlusses** presentation of the annual balance sheet; **~ von Mustern** submission of patterns; **~ einer Offerte** submission of an offer; **~ einer Rechnung** submission of account; **~ einer Rechtsfrage** reference of a matter in dispute; **~ eines Schecks** presentation of a check *(US)* (cheque, *Br.*); **~ bei einem Schiedsgericht** reference to a court of arbitration; **~ eines gefälschten Testaments** production of a forged will; **~ von Urkunden** exhibition (putting in) of documents; **~ falscher Urkunden** production of forged documents; **mangelnde ~ einer Urkunde** failure of record; **~ einer Urkunde bei Gericht** profert in curiam; **~ eines Werbeplans** presentation of a publicity campaign; **~ zur Zahlung** presentment for payment;
~ ablehnen *(parl.)* to drop (kill, reject) a bill; **bei ~ akzeptieren** to accept upon presentation; **~ der Unterlagen eines Falles beantragen** to move for papers; **~ durchpeitschen** to rush a bill through the house *(Br.)*, to railroad a bill through Congress *(US)*; **~ einbringen** to bring in (table) a bill; **~ der Friedensbevollmächtigung fordern** to ask for powers to conclude peace; **bei ~ honorieren** to hono(u)r on presentation; **mit einem Betrag in ~ treten** to advance an amount; **~ einem Ausschuß überweisen** to refer a bill to a committee; **~ unterstützen** to speak for (support) a motion; **~ verabschieden** to pass a bill; **aufgrund der ~ von Mustern verhandeln** to negotiate on the strength of samples; **~ verwässern** to water down a bill; **bei ~ zahlbar werden** to be payable on presentation; **~ zurückstellen** to lay a bill on the table, to table a bill *(US)*;
~**bericht** statement of a case; ~**beschluß** recordare *(US)*; ~**formular** presentation form; ~**frist** time of presentment (allowed for presentation).

Vorlagen|buch formulary; ~**entwurf** draft bill; ~**mißbrauch** colo(u)rable imitation.

Vorlage|ort place of presentation; ~**pflicht** liability to discover.

vorlagepflichtig liable to discover;
nicht ~ privileged from production (discovery).

Vorlage|provision overdraft commission; **~- und Einführungssystem** *(Versicherungsaufsichtsamt)* file and use system; ~**verzicht** waiving presentment; ~**verzug** delay in presentment; ~**zwang zwecks Augenscheinseinnahme** discovery and inspection.

vorlassen to admit, *(Vortritt lassen)* to give precedence;
Auto ~ to allow a car to pass.

Vorlast prior charge, earlier encumbrance;
~**en haben** to carry prior encumbrances.

vorlastig *(Schiff)* down by the head.

Vor|lauf vor der allgemeinen Preiserhöhung pacing the general increase of prices; ~**läufer** forerunner, foregoer, precursor.

vorläufig for the time being, provisional, preliminary, in the interim, interlocutory, provisory, temporary, tentative;
Beamten ~ seines Dienstes entheben to suspend an official;
~**es Abkommen** preliminary agreement; ~**e Abmachung** tentative agreement; ~**er Abschluß** provisional booking; ~**e Anmeldung** *(Patent)* provisional application; ~**e Anordnung** interim order, provisional arrangement, rule nisi *(Br.)*; ~**er Ausschuß** temporary committee; ~**er Bericht** interim report; ~**er Bescheid** preliminary answer; ~**e Beschlagnahme** provisional seizure; ~**e Beschreibung** *(Patent)* provisional specification; ~**e Bilanz** interim (tentative) balance sheet; ~**e Deckungszusage** provisional cover, binding slip (receipt), binder *(US)*; ~**e Dividende** interim (initial, *Br.*) dividend; ~**e Entscheidung** interim decree (order); ~**er Entwurf** preliminary scheme; ~**er Erschließungsplan** interim development; ~**er Konkursverwalter** interim factor, official receiver *(Br.)*; ~**es Konto** transit (provisional) account; ~**e Maßnahmen** preliminary (temporary) measures; ~**er Nachlaßverwalter** temporary receiver; ~**e Obligationen** provisional bonds; ~**e Quittung** interim receipt; ~**e Rechnung** provisional invoice; ~**er Rechtsschutz** interlocutory relief; ~**e Regierung** caretaker (provisional) government, interim cabinet; ~**er Schadensnachweis** preliminary proof; ~**e Stückelung** temporary denomination; ~**e Tagesordnung** provisional agenda; ~**e Tariferhöhung** interim increase in tariff; ~**es Urheberschutzrecht** interim copyright; ~**es Urteil** provisional judgment, interlocutory injunction, interim decree; ~**e Vereinbarung** interim (provisional) agreement; ~**er Versicherungsvertrag** binding slip, binder *(US)*; ~**er Vertrag** provisional contract.

Vorlaufzeit lead time.

vorlaut|e Bemerkung flippant remark; ~**es Wesen** forward manner.

Vor|leben *(Person)* antecedents, past [history] record, background; ~**legen** *(Gesuch)* filing, submission, submittal, exhibiting.

vorlegen to submit, to produce, to lay on the table, to put in, to file with, to exhibit, *(Frage)* to propound;
zum Akzept ~ to present for acceptance; **zur Ansicht ~** to display, to exhibit; **Bericht ~** to submit a report; **Betrag ~** to advance an amount (a sum); **Beweismaterial ~** to produce (adduce, exhibit) evidence; **zur Entscheidung ~** to submit for decision; **mehrere Entwürfe ~** to present several plans; **Frage dem Gericht ~** to submit a question to the court; **jem. zur Genehmigung ~** to submit for s. one's approval; **Gesetzentwurf ~** to introduce (table, *Br.*) a bill; **zum Inkasso ~** to present for collection; **Offerten ~** to tender, to make tenders; **seine Rechnung ~** to send in one's bill; **Scheck zur Bestätigung ~** to present a cheque for certification *(Br.)*; **tolles Tempo ~** to go at a breakneck pace; **Testament ~** to file a will; **gefälschtes Testament ~** to produce a forged will; **zur Unterschrift ~** to submit for signature; **Urkunde ~** to present a document; **Vergleichsvorschlag ~** to propose terms for a settlement, to file a plan; **Wechsel zur Annahme ~** to present a bill for acceptance; **wieder ~** to represent; **völlig neues Wörterbuch ~** to publish a completely new dictionary; **zur Zahlung ~** to present for payment.

Vorlegung production, presentation;
bei ~ zahlbar payable on presentation;
verzögerte ~ delay in presentment;
~ zur Annahme presentation for acceptance; **~ von Beweismaterial** production of evidence; **~ von Mustern** submission of samples; **~ zur Zahlung** presentation for payment.

Vorlegungs|frist time allowed for presentation; ~**nachweis** certificate of presentation; ~**tag** day of presentation.

vorleisten to pay in advance (by anticipation, *US*).

Vorleistung past consideration, *(Produktion)* intermediate input, *(Zahlung)* payment in advance (by anticipation, *US*), prepayment;
kalkulierbare ~ im Produktionsprozess input.

Vorleistungs|koeffizient production coefficient; ~**pflicht** liability to pay in advance.

Vorlesen reading, recital.

vorlesen to read aloud (out);
jem. etw. ~ to read s. th. to s. o.; **Bericht ~** to read a report; **Sitzungsbericht ~** to read the minutes; **unverständlich ~** to gabble over.

Vorleser reader, reciter;
~**amt** readership.

Vorlesung [university] lecture, reading, paper, class;
auf einem Fernsehband aufgenommene ~ videotape lecture; **dreistündige ~** three-hour lecture; **kleine ~** lecturette; **langweilige ~** tedious lecture, sleeper *(sl.)*; **leichte ~** snap course; **öffentliche ~** open lecture, prelection; **sich zeitlich überschneidende ~en** overlapping lectures; **uninteressante ~** dry lecture;
~ mit Lichtbildern lantern lecture; **~ auf der Volkshochschule** university extension lecture;

~ **vorzeitig abbrechen** to curtail a lecture; ~ **abhalten** to lecture to students; ~ **für Erstsemester abhalten** to teach at first year undergraduate level; ~ **belegen** to go in for (enro(l)l for, subscribe to) a course of lectures; ~**en besuchen** to attend lectures; **juristische ~en besuchen** to keep a term at an inn of court; ~**en regelmäßig besuchen** to be a constant attendant at a course of lectures; **bis zum Schluß einer ~ bleiben** to sit a lecture out; ~ **interessant finden** to think a lecture interesting; ~ **halten** to deliver (read) a lecture, to give a reading, to hold a course, to lecture, to prelect, to read a paper (a discourse); ~ **hören** to attend a course of lectures; **seine ~en in Buchform erscheinen lassen** to print one's lectures; **in einer ~ mitschreiben** to take notes to a lecture (lecture notes); ~ **ausführlich mitschreiben** to take good notes on a lecture; ~ **schwänzen** to cut a lecture; ~ **verhindern** to prevent a lecture taking place.

Vorlesungs|aufzeichnungen notes on a lecture; **seine ~aufzeichnungen überarbeiten** to write up one's notes on a lecture; ~**beginn** commencement of lectures; ~**boykott** boycott of lectures; ~**gebühr** lecture fee; ~**liste** lecture list; ~**plan** syllabus; ~**raum** lecture room (hall), lyceum; ~**reihe** course of lectures, lectureship; ~**reihe halten** to deliver a course of lectures; **aus alten Aufzeichnungen eine ~reihe zusammenschustern** to vamp up some lectures out of old notes; ~**saal** lecture hall (room); **anrechenbare ~stunde** credit hour *(US)*; ~**system** lecture system; ~**tag** day of presentation; ~**verzeichnis** [university] calendar, syllabus, lecture list, catalog *(US)*; ~**zyklus** course of lectures, syllabus.

Vorliebe fancy, inclination, leaning, partiality, relish, weakness *(coll.)*;
~ **für Musik** passion for music;
~ **für etw. haben** to be partial to (have a leaning towards) s. th.;
~ **für Schokolade haben** to have a great tooth for chocolate.

vorliebnehmen, mit etw. to put up with s. th.

Vorlieferant supplier.

Vorliegen, bei ~ besonderer Gründe in the event of special reasons.

vorliegen *(Anfragen)* to have come in, *(Auftrag)* to be in (at, on, *US*) hand, *(bearbeitet werden)* to be under consideration, *(Wortmeldung)* to be on the list of speakers;
jem. zur Einsichtnahme ~ to be submitted for s. one's kind inspection; **dem Gericht** ~ to be in court; **noch nicht** ~ not yet to have come in, *(Urteil)* not yet known; **dem Parlament** ~ to be up before Parliament;
etw. gegen j. ~ haben to have a charge against s. o.; **Beschwerde ~ haben** to have a complaint;
da muß ein Irrtum ~ there must have been a mistake.

vorliegend present, on hand, instant, available, in question;
nicht ~ nonextant, nonexistent;
~**e Exemplare** existing specimens; ~**er Fall** case in question (under review); ~**e Probleme** problems in question; ~**e Sache** matter in hand, business before us.

Vorlizenz interim licence.

vormachen to demonstrate, to show;
jem. ein X für ein U (blauen Dunst) ~ to take s. o. in, to throw dust in s. one's eyes;
jem. nichts ~ können not to be able to fool s. o.; **sich kein X für ein U ~ lassen** to be a strictly no-nonsense lady.

Vormachtstellung dominating position, supremacy, hegemony;
atomare ~ nuclear preponderance;
~ **einnehmen** to hold majority power; **seine ~ festigen** to tighten one's grip; ~ **als Händler wiedergewinnen** to refill its dealer forecourts.

Vormann prior party, previous (preceding) indorser (endorser);
sich an seinen ~ halten to have recourse against the preceding party.

Vormarkt für erstklassige Wertpapiere primary market.

Vormarsch, ungehinderter unchecked advance;
~ **von Ideen** onward march of ideas; ~ **eines Heeres** pressing forward of an army;
feindlichen ~ stoppen to check the enemy's advance;
~**straße** road of approach.

Vormerkbuch rough (memorandum) book, notebook, tickler *(US coll.)*.

vormerken to [make a] note, to jot down, *(zu den Akten nehmen)* to record, to put on the file;
j. für etw. ~ to put s. o. down for s. th.; **Plätze** ~ to book seats, to make reservations; **Recht** ~ to note a right on the record; **Sitzung in seinem Kalender** ~ to note a meeting in one's appointment book;
sich ~ lassen to have one's name registered, to put one's name down.

Vormerk|gebühr booking (reservation, *US*) fee; ~**kalender** tickler, scribbling diary *(Br.)*; ~**kartei** *(Buchhändler)* memorandum card index; ~**liste** waiting list.

Vormerkung note, memorandum, caveat, *(Eintragung)* registration, entry, *(Grundbuch)* priority notice *(Br.)*, inhibition *(Br.)*, caution *(Br.)*;
gleichlautende ~ note in conformity; ~ **zum Protest** *(Wechsel)* note for protest;
~ **eintragen lassen** to lodge (register) a caution with the registrar *(Br.)*, to note a right on the record, to put in a caveat; **in ~ nehmen** to record, to put (place) on the file; **gehörige ~ nehmen** to take due notice.

Vormerkungs|begünstigter *(Grundbuch)* cautioner; ~**berechtigter** preëmptioner; ~**gebühr** booking (reservation, *US*) fee.

vormilitärisch premilitary.

Vormittags|besuch morning call; **leichter ~imbiß** elevens; ~**sitzung** morning session; ~**unterricht** morning instruction; ~**zug** morning train.

Vormonat previous month.

Vormund guardian, custodian, parent, warden, tutor, curator;
befreiter ~ general guardian; **von den Eltern bestellter** ~ tutor nominate *(Scot.)*; **für einen bestimmten Fall bestellter** ~ curator ad hoc; **gerichtlich bestellter** ~ guardian by appointment of the High Court of Justice; **vom Wohnsitzgericht bestellter** ~ domestic guardian; **gesetzlicher** ~ statutory (natural) guardian, guardian by nature; **vom Mündel gewählter** ~ guardian by election; **selbst gewählter** ~ guardian by election; **natürlicher** ~ natural guardian; **testamentarischer** ~ testamentary guardian; **unbeschränkter** ~ general guardian;
~ **eines Minderjährigen** curator bonis; ~ **und Mündel** guardian and ward;
~ **bestellen** to appoint a guardian; **als ~ tätig sein** to guardianize; ~ **eines Kindes werden** to obtain custody of a child, to act in one's capacity as a guardian.

Vormundsbestellung appointment of a guardian, act of curatory *(Scot.)*.

Vormundschaft guardianship, chancery, tutelage, tutorship *(Louisiana)*, custodianship *(US)*;
unter ~ in care, under guardianship, in warden;
übertragene ~ dative tutelage;
~ **aufgrund letzwilliger Verfügung** testamentary guardianship; **unter ~ stehen** to be in ward (under guardianship, wardship); **j. unter ~ stellen** to admit s. o. under guardianship, to place s. o. under the care of guardian, to put s. o. under tutelage (in ward), to place a child under s. one's guardianship; ~ **für j. übernehmen** to take over s. one's guardianship.

vormundschaftlich custodial, curatorial, tutelary;
~**e Gewalt** tutelary authority; ~ **betreute Person** ward of a court.

Vormundschafts|amt wardency, curatorship; ~**bericht erstatten** to give an account of one's guardianship; ~**beschluß** care and protection order; ~**bestallung** court of protection bond; ~**gericht** court of domestic relations, orphans' court *(US)*, [etwa] Court of Protection *(Br.)*; ~- **und Nachlaßgericht** surrogate's court; **beim ~gericht um Übertragung seines Erbgutes nachsuchen** to sue out one's livery *(Br.)*; **vernachlässigte ~pflichten** guardian neglect; ~**richter** master in lunacy, orphan master; ~**rolle** tutelary role; ~**sachen** domestic relations; ~**verhältnis** guardianship.

Vormunds|einsetzung, testamentarische tutorship by will; ~**vergütung** guardian's allowance.

Vornahme undertaking, taking up, performance, execution;
~ **einer Falschbuchung** making a false entry; ~ **von Geschäften** entering into transactions; ~ **unzüchtiger Handlungen** defilement.

Vorname Christian (first, front, *US)* name, forename;
~ **und Zuname** full name;
sich telefonisch mit dem ~n anreden to be on a first-name phone-calling basis.

vornehm fashionable, grand, genteel, elevated, noble, polite, upper-crust;
nicht ~ non-U *(Br.)*;
~ **tun** to put on style, to do the grand (polite, *fam.*) thing;
~**e Dame** distinguished lady; ~**e Gegend** silk-stocking district *(US)*; ~**e Gesellschaft** high (polite) society; ~**e Gesinnung** noble-mindedness; ~**es Hotel** swell hotel; ~**ste Pflicht** first duty; **die ~e Welt** fashion, the elite.

vornehmen to undertake, to take in hand, to design;
sich etw. ~ to occupy o. s. (be busy) with s. th.; **sich j.** ~ to work on s. o.; **sich j. gründlich (richtig)** ~ to come down on s. o. like a ton of bricks, to talk to s. o. like a Dutch uncle, to put s. o.

through his paces; **Änderungen** ~ to make alterations; **Buchung** ~ to effect an entry; **sich ernsthaft** ~ to have a strong purpose; **Gegenbuchungen** ~ to make cross entries; **Inkasso eines Wechsels** ~ to undertake the collection of a bill; **Lieferung** ~ to effect (execute) delivery; **Nachtragsbuchung** ~ to make a supplementary (subsequent) entry; **sich eine Sache** ~ to deal with a case of business; **sich etw. für den nächsten Tag** ~ to make plans for tomorrow; **Umbuchung** ~ to effect a transfer in the books; **Umgruppierungen** ~ to regroup, to reshuffle; **sich zuviel** ~ to take too much on hand, to fly at too high game, to have to many irons in the fire.

Vornehmheit fashion, grand air.

vornehmlich first and foremost, in particular.

Vornehmtuerei airs and graces.

Vorort suburb;
grüne und schläfrige ~**e** leafy suburban backwaters;
zum ~ **machen** to suburbanize;
~**bahn** suburban line, suburban (local, district, *Br.*) railway; ~**bewohner** suburbanite, commuter *(US)*; ~**gespräch** *(tel.)* toll call; ~**straße** suburban street; ~**strecke** suburban section; ~**verkehr** suburban (local) traffic; ~**zug** local (accommodation, suburban, shuttle, *US*, way, *US*, commuter, *US*) train, peddler *(sl.)*; ~**zugverkehr** suburban train service.

Vorpatent prior patent.

vorpfänden, Wertpapierrechte to serve notice in lieu of distringas.

Vorpfändung seizure under a prior claim, *(Aktienanteile)* notice in lieu of distringas, stop notice.

Vorplatz square, court, *(Treppenhaus)* landing, *(in Wohnung)* land, stoop *(US)*, hallway *(US)*;
überdachter ~ porch.

Vorposten *(fig.)* outpost, *(mil.)* outlying picket, outsentry;
~ **ausstellen** to throw out pickets; ~ **einziehen** to call in an army's outposts;
~**boot** patrol (picket) boat; ~**gefecht** skirmish; ~**kette** stationary screen.

Vorprämie buyer's option *(Br.)*, call premium, premium for the call;
~ **kaufen** to buy a call option, to give for the call; ~ **verkaufen** to take for the call.

Vorprämien|geschäft option deal for the call, trading in calls *(Br.)*; ~**kurs** price of a call, call price.

vorpredigen, jem. die Notwendigkeit harter Arbeit to din into s. one's ears the importance of hard work.

Vor|produkte preliminary products, pre-products; ~**produktionskosten** starting-load costs; ~**programm** introductory program(me).

vorprogrammieren to preprogram(me).

Vor|projekt preliminary plan, pilot study; ~**prozeß** previous lawsuit; ~**prüfer** *(Patentamt)* primary examiner.

Vorprüfung *(Bücher)* preliminary audit, preaudit, *(Industrieprojekt)* feasibility study, *(Patentgesetz)* preliminary examination;
~ **bestehen** to pass a proficiency test.

Vorrang precedence, antecedence, primacy, *(Dringlichkeit)* priority, *(Gläubiger)* priority [of rank], rank in priority, ranking, *(Hypothek)* precedence, *(Pfandobjekt)* marshalling;
mit ~ **vor** with priority over;
zeitlicher ~ priority of date;
~ **eines Anspruchs** priority of a claim;
j. mit ~ **abfertigen** to deal with s. o. with priority; ~ **beanspruchen** to take the wall of s. o., to claim priority; **mit** ~ **behandeln** to give priority treatment; ~ **einräumen** to grant prior rank, to give priority to (the first place); **jem. den** ~ **einräumen** to give s. o. the first place, to yield precedence to s. o.; **Kundenwünschen** ~ **einräumen** to put customer demands first; **Dringendem den** ~ **geben** to put first things first; **einer Sache absoluten** ~ **geben** to raise s. th. into first priority; ~ **genießen** to have first priority; ~ **haben** to rank as preferential (in priority), to have precedence (the eminence), to antecede, to go before, to be top dog, to rank in, *(Verkehr)* to have the right of way; **jem. den** ~ **lassen** to take one's hat off to s. o.

vorrangig of prior rank, senior, paramount, preëminent, overriding;
kaum als ~ **angesehen werden** to have low priority; ~ **behandelt werden** to have first priority, to take preference;
~**er Auftrag** prior charge; ~**e Behandlung** priority attention (treatment); ~**e Belieferung** priority delivery.

Vorrangmeldung *(Fernsehen, Rundfunk)* priority item, flash.

Vorrangs|aktie preferential share, classified stock *(US)*; ~**behandlung** priority treatment.

vorrangsberechtigt senior, prior.

Vorrangs|gebiet priority area; ~**gespräch** *(tel.)* priority call; ~**gläubiger** prior (preceding) creditor; ~**hypothek** senior (underlying, *US*) mortgage; ~**liste** priority list; ~**pfandrecht** senior (underlying, *US*) lien; ~**stellung** position of priority, superiority, paramountcy, preëminence, *(pol.)* hegemony; **wirtschaftliche** ~**stellung** economic preëminence.

Vorrat provision, supply, stock [on hand], stockpile, bank, fund, store *(US)*, *(Lieder)* repertoire, repertory, *(Reserve)* reserve;
mit einem reichlichen ~ **versehen** loaded up with;
geringer ~ low stock, scanty supply; **heimlicher** ~ hoard; **reichlicher** ~ copious supply; **wirklicher** ~ visible supply;
~ **auf Lager** stock on hand; ~ **an Lesestoff** supply of reading matter;
jem. den ganzen ~ **abkaufen** to clear off s. one's stock; **seinen ganzen** ~ **abstoßen** to sell out; ~ **anlegen** to lay (take) in a supply, to stockpile, to lay in store *(US)*; **auf** ~ **arbeiten** to work on stock; **jds. ganzen** ~ **aufkaufen** to buy up s. one's stock; ~ **beschaffen** to supply with provisions; ~ **ergänzen** to stockpile, to restock *(US)*; **zu großen** ~ **haben** to be overstocked; **in** ~ **halten** to keep in stock; **seinen** ~ **loswerden** to get one's stock off; **auf** ~ **produzieren** to make for stock; **sich einen** ~ **zulegen** to stock up, to stockpile.

Vorräte supplies, holdings, provisions, receipts, *(Bilanz)* inventories, stocks, stock-in-trade;
bar aller ~ naked of all stocks; **hinlänglich mit** ~**n versehen** adequately stocked; **mit** ~**n überhäuft** overstocked; **ohne** ~ unstocked; **reichlich mit** ~**n versehen** heavily stocked;
aufgebrauchte ~ exhausted supplies; **ausreichende** ~ adequate supply of provisions (stocks); **bedeutende** ~ considerable stock; **erschöpfte** ~ depleted (exhausted) stocks; **frische** ~ new stock; **große** ~ substantial reserves; **knappe** ~ stock shortage; **mangelnde** ~ want of provisions (stocks); **reiche** ~ liberal provisions; **überschüssige** ~ excess of provisions; **unerschöpfliche** ~ inexhaustible supplies; **unzulängliche** ~ scanty supplies; **vorhandene** ~ supplies on hand;
~ **an Bord** ship's stores; ~ **an Lebensmitteln** food stocks;
~ **abbauen** to reduce stocks; ~ **angreifen** to touch supplies, to draw on stocks; ~ **anlegen** to lay in supplies, to build up stocks; **seine ganzen** ~ **aufbrauchen** to use up all one's supplies; ~ **auffüllen** to replace the stock, to replenish stocks (provisions), to restock *(US)*; **frische** ~ **aufnehmen** to refresh; ~ **bekommen** to obtain provisions; ~ **beschaffen** to supply with provisions; ~ **beschlagnahmen** to commandeer provisions; ~ **bestellen** to order supplies; ~ **bilden** to build up stocks (reserves), to stockpile, to restock *(US)*; ~ **für den Winter einlagern** to lay in store for the winter; ~ **ergänzen** to renew a stock of goods, to replenish provisions, to refill the stock; **keine** ~ **haben** to be out of stock; **knappe (zu wenig)** ~ **haben** to be in short supply, to be understocked; **umfangreiche** ~ **haben** to carry heavy stock; **zu wenig** ~ **haben** to be understocked; **ausreichende** ~ **im Haus haben** to have a good store of provisions in the house; ~ **horten** to hoard [supplies]; **mit seinen** ~**n pfleglich umgehen** to husband one's resources; **über** ~ **für durchschnittlich sechs Wochen verfügen** to have an average of six weeks' stocks on hand; **mit** ~**n versehen** to complete with provisions; **mit zu wenig** ~**n versehen** to understock; **Kaufhaus mit** ~**n versehen** to stock a warehouse with goods; **knapp an** ~**n werden** to run short of provisions (supplies); **auf** ~ **zurückgreifen** to draw on stocks;
~**bewertung** inventory pricing, inventory valuation, resource appraisal.

vorrätig stocked, stock, in (on) stock, on hand, carried in stock, in store *(US)*, available, *(Buch)* in print, *(Reserve)* in reserve;
nicht ~ out of stock; **nicht mehr** ~ sold out; **noch nicht** ~ *(Buch)* not yet in print;
~ **haben** to have (keep) in store, to carry in stock, to have on stock *(US)*; **Ersatzteil nicht** ~ **haben** to be out of a spare part; **Ware im Augenblick nicht** ~ **haben** to be short of an article; **[nicht]** ~ **sein** to be in [out of] stock;
stets ~**e Größe** stock size.

Vorrats|abbau inventory cutting (decumulation), reduction of stock; ~**aktie** reserved share (stock, *US*); ~**anfertigung** production for stock; ~**anlage**, ~**ansammlung** laying-in of provisions, inventory accumulation, stockpiling; ~**anstieg** inventory buildup; ~**auffüllung**, ~**aufstockung** stock accumulation, rebuilding of stocks; ~**auswahl** selection of stock; ~**behälter** storage bin; ~**bestand** carriage stock; ~**bewertung** inventory valuation (pricing), resource appraisal; ~**bewertung mit Hilfe des Rohgewinns** gross-profit method; ~**bewirtschaftung** inventory control; ~**bildung** building up of stocks, inventory accumulation (bildup), stockpiling; ~**buchung** provisional booking; ~**dispositionen**, ~**einkäufe** advance (stockpiling) purchases, stockpiling behavio(u)r, hedge buying; ~**durchschnitt** average stock; **durch ~engpässe aktionsunfähig sein** to be crippled by a loss of supplies; ~**ergänzungsgeschäft** restocking operations; ~**fach** *(Lesegerät)* read hopper; ~**gelände erwerben** to acquire land in advance of development; **städtisches ~gelände erwerben** to acquire land for expanding the site of a town; ~**haltung** holding of stocks, stockpiling, storing, stockkeeping; ~**investitionen** stock (inventory) investment; ~**kammer** store (stock) room, *(Küche)* pantry, larder; ~**käufe** advance (stockpiling) purchases, hedge buying; ~**käufe auf dem Stahlmarkt** steel hedging; ~**käufe tätigen** to buy in provisions; ~**keller** cellar storeroom; ~**kontingente** *(Emission)* quotas held in reserve, reserved quotas; ~**konto** cash reserve account; ~**kredit** stockpiling, storage credit; ~**lage** stock position.

Vorratslager stock of provisions, reserve stock, warehouse, storeroom *(US)*, *(Rohstoffe)* buffer stock;
natürliche ~ stores of natural resources;
~ **anlegen** to stockpile, to lay in a store of provisions; ~ **beschlagnahmen** to condemn stores.

Vorrats|lagerung stockpiling, stocking in advance; ~**planung** stock planning; ~**politik** stockpiling policy; **vorsichtige ~politik betreiben** to keep down an inventory; ~**polster** cushion of provisions; ~**raum** stock room, storeroom, magazine; ~**schiff** depot ship; ~**speicher** *(Getreide)* granary, corn loft *(Br.)*; ~**stelle** storage agency; ~**tank** storage (reserve) tank; ~**überhang** surplus stock (stockpiles); ~**vermögen** stock-in-trade, inventories, stocks; ~**verzeichnis** inventory list; ~**wirtschaft** stockpiling, inventory control.

Vorraum anteroom, lobby, vestibule, foyer.

vorrechnen, Kosten to calculate (work out) the costs.

Vorrecht preference, privilege, franchise, freedom, benefit, indulgence, peculiar, *(Gläubiger)* preferential right (claim), *(Krone)* prerogative, *(Vordringlichkeit)* priority;
mit einem ~ ausgestattet preferred; **mit besonderen ~en ausgestattet** privileged, franchised;
verfassungsmäßig begründetes ~ constitutional privilege; **berufliches** ~ professional privilege; **gegenseitig eingeräumte ~e** reciprocal privileges; **königliches** ~ royal prerogative; **unabdingbares** ~ absolute priority (privilege); **wirtschaftliche ~e** economic privileges;
~**e und Immunitäten** *(dipl.)* privileges and immunities; ~ **eines Parlaments** prerogative of a legislature;
jds. ~e antasten to encroach upon s. one's prerogatives; ~**e aufheben** to retrench privileges; ~ **beanspruchen** to claim a privilege; **j. eines ~es berauben** to debar s. o. of a right; ~**e beseitigen** to expropriate privileges; **in jds. ~e eingreifen** to invade s. one's privileges; ~ **einräumen** to grant (concede, accord) a privilege; **jds. ~e einschränken** to curtail s. one's privileges; ~**e genießen** to be privileged, to enjoy privileges; **besondere ~e genießen** to hold special privileges; **dieselben ~e genießen** to get in on the ground floor *(US)*; ~ **auf etw. haben** to have first call on s. th.; **sein ~ geltend machen** to interfere; ~ **mißbrauchen** to stretch a privilege; ~ **verleihen** to invest with a prerogative; **auf ein ~ verzichten** to surrender (waive) a privilege.

Vorrechts|aktien preference shares *(Br.)*, preferred stock *(US)*; ~**anleihe** preference loan; ~**forderung** preferential claim.

Vorrede prefatory remark, *(Buch)* preface, foreword, *(Gesetz)* preamble;
~ **schreiben** to preface.

Vor|redner preceding (previous, last) speaker; **der Herr ~redner** my hono(u)rable friend; **industrieller ~reiter** industrial leader.

Vorrichtung appliance, device, machine, apparatus, contrivance, mechanism, outfit;
~**en** facilities;
behelfsmäßige ~ rig; **mechanische ~en** mechanical devices; **praktische** ~ knock, clever contrivance; **sinnreiche** ~ ingenious device.

Vorrichtungspatent device patent.

Vorrücken *(mil.)* moving forward;
~ **einer Armee** progress of an army; ~ **nach dem Dienstalter** promotion by seniority;
~ **befehlen** to direct an advance to be made.

vorrücken *(Beamter)* to be promoted, *(mil.)* to advance, to move forward;
auf einen Platz ~ to progress towards a place; **auf die Stadt** ~ to proceed towards the town.

Vorsaal entry, entrance hall, vestibule.

Vorsaison preseason, off-season;
~**geschäft** early-season business.

Vorsatz purpose, interest, resolve, intent, *(Buchbinderei)* pastedown, *(Strafrecht)* contemplation, intent, malice;
mit ~ on purpose; **mit dem ~, zu töten** with intent to kill; **mit ~ und Überlegung** with malice aforethought (criminal intent);
fester ~ specific intent; **gemeinsamer** ~ common design; **strafrechtlicher** ~ criminal intent; **vermuteter** ~ implied malice; **wucherischer** ~ corrupt intent;
festen ~ fassen to make a firm resolution; ~ **haben** to intend; **den Geschworenen die Frage nach dem ~ der Täter vorlegen** to ask the jury whether the act was committed with intent;
~**blatt** *(Buch)* flyleaf.

Vorsätze, mit guten ~n gepflastert paved with good intentions; **seinen ~n treu bleiben** to keep to one's resolutions.

Vorsatzgerät add-on unit, adapter.

vorsätzlich intentional, deliberate[ly] of set (on) purpose, purposely, prepense, designed, with intent, voluntary, *(jur.)* malicious, with malice, aforethought, premeditated, *(strafrechtlich)* knowingly and wilfully;
nicht ~ unintended.
~**e Körperverletzung** malicious injury; ~**e Sachbeschädigung** malicious damage; ~**e Verkehrsbehinderung** wilful obstruction of traffic.

Vorsätzlichkeit wilfulness, maliciousness.

Vorsatz|linse *(Foto)* supplementary lens; ~**papier** *(Buchbinderei)* end paper; ~**papier einkleben** to paper up; ~**scheibe** *(Foto)* mask.

Vorschau outlook, forecast[ing], *(Film)* trailer, preview, prevue *(US)*;
~ **auf die Abendsendungen** summary of the evening program(me); ~ **auf die finanzielle Entwicklung** financial forecast;
~ **auf das kommende Jahr abgeben** to view the coming year;
~**bild** *(Fernsehen)* monitor picture; ~**wettrennen** forecasting race.

Vorschein, zum ~ kommen to emerge, *(Krankheit)* to become apparent.

vorschieben *(fig.)* to plead as an excuse, to use as a pretext, *(Riegel)* to put across.

vorschießen *(Auto)* to lurch (shoot) forward;
Geld ~ to advance (lay out) money.

Vorschlag proposal, proposition *(US)*, suggestion, *(Angebot)* offer, *(Empfehlung)* recommendation, *(Kanditat)* nomination, *(parl.)* motion;
auf ~ by (on) request, on the advice of, at the instance (upon the proposal) of;
geschäftlicher ~ business proposition; **praktischer** ~ practical proposal; **schriftlicher** ~ written representation; **unannehmbarer** ~ inadmissible proposal; **unverbindlicher** ~ speculative work; **zweckmäßiger** ~ practical suggestion;
~ **zur Güte** conciliatory proposal; ~ **zur Regelung der Auslandsschulden** foreign-debt proposal; ~ **der Verwaltungsstellen** administrative proposal;
~ **ablehnen** to refuse a proposal; ~ **annehmen** to adopt (subscribe to) a proposal, to accept a proposition; ~ **einstimmig annehmen** to carry a vote unanimously; ~ **gern annehmen** to welcome a proposal; ~ **günstig aufnehmen** to receive a proposal favo(u)rably; ~ **ausarbeiten** to project a scheme; **sich zugunsten eines ~s aussprechen** to express one's opinion in favo(u)r of a proposition, to pronounce o. s. in favo(u)r of a proposal, to pass a resolution in favo(u)r; **einem ~ beistimmen** to concur with a proposal; **über einen ~ beratschlagen** to deliberate a proposition; ~ **positiv beurteilen** to consider a proposal favo(u)rably; **in ~ bringen** to propose, to move; **Dividende in ~ bringen** to recommend a dividend; **sich für eine Stellung in ~ bringen** to offer o. s. for a post; **auf einen ~ näher eingehen** to consider the details of a proposal; **sich mit einem ~ einmischen** to strike in with a suggestion; ~ **einreichen** to file a plan, to enter a proposal; **sich zur Annahme eines ~ entschließen** to see fit to adopt a suggestion; ~ **einstimmig gutheißen** to accept a proposal with unanimous approval; **etw. gegen einen ~ einzuwenden haben** to object s. th. to a proposal; **mit einem ~ herausrücken** to come out with a suggestion; ~ **scheitern lassen** to kill a proposal; ~ **machen** to make (put forward, initiate) a proposal, to propose, to offer a suggestion, to suggest; **für einen ~ sein** to be in favo(u)r of a proposal; **in einen ~ übernehmen** to incorporate in a proposal; ~ **in einer Versammlung unterbreiten** to present a plan to a meeting; ~ **unterstützen** to give support to a proposal; ~ **kräftig unterstützen** to come out strongly for a proposition; ~ **verwerfen** to overrule (negative) a proposal; ~ **vorbringen** to set forth a proposal; ~ **in Erwägung ziehen** to entertain a proposal;

~ **in freundliche Erwägung ziehen** to give a proposal a kind reception; ~ **dem Vorstand zuleiten** to put a proposal to the board; **einem** ~ **zustimmen** to agree (consent, be favo(u)rable) to a proposal.

Vorschläge, folgenschwere far-reaching proposals; **ins einzelne gehende** ~ detailed estimates; **theoretische** ~ paper schedules; ~ **für eine Ausweitung des Handels** proposals for increasing trade between two countries; ~ **für neue Projekte** new venture proposals;
~ **ausarbeiten** to formulate proposals; ~ **unterbreiten** to submit proposals; **jem.** ~ **unterbreiten** to place proposals before s. o.

vorschlagen to propose, to propound, to suggest, to put forth, *(empfehlen)* to recommend;
zur Aufnahme ~ to propound for admission; **Hotel** ~ to recommend a hotel; **Kandidaten** ~ to nominate (propose) a candidate, to recommend a candidate for a post; **Konkursvergleich** ~ to present a petition for composition; **j. als Vorsitzenden** ~ to propose s. o. for chairman.

Vorschlagender proposer, propounder, presenter.

Vorschlags|annahme adoption of a proposal; ~**band** volume recommended; ~**entwurf** draft proposal; ~**liste** list of nominations, slate *(US)*; ~**liste für Ordenverleihungen** honours list *(Br.)*; ~**prämie** suggestion award; ~**recht** right of nomination; ~**tag für Kandidaten** nomination day; ~**wesen** suggestion program(me); **betriebliches** ~**wesen** employee suggestion system.

vorschnell precipitous, rash, hasty;
~ **urteilen** to jump to conclusions.

vorschreiben to enjoin, to order, to direct, to appoint, to dictate, *(Gesetz)* to provide;
jem. etw. ~ to make s. th. mandatory upon s. o.; **als Muster** ~ to set a copy.

Vorschrift *(Anweisung)* direction, instruction, order, charge, injunction, stipulation, notice, *(Mußvorschrift)* mandate, *(Richtschnur)* precept, rule *(US)*, line, *(Verordnung)* decree, prescript, provision, regulation;
aufgrund dieser ~ hereunder; **den gesetzlichen** ~**en nicht entsprechend** *(Arznei)* unofficial; **gegen die** ~**en** in contravention of the rules; **genau nach** ~ according to Hoyle; **laut** ~ in accordance with the regulations, to rule; **mangels gegenteiliger** ~ save as provided otherwise; **nach** ~ as prescribed (directed), as the law directs; **ungeachtet gegenteiliger** ~**en** notwithstanding any provisions to the contrary;
durch Parteivereinbarung abgeänderte (dispositive) ~**en** optional provisions; **aktienrechtliche** ~**en** principles of company (corporation, *US*) law; **allgemeine** ~**en** general rules; **arbeitsrechtliche** ~**en** labo(u)r legislation rules; **ärztliche** ~ prescription; **baupolizeiliche** ~**en** building regulations; **behördliche** ~**en** official regulations; **absolut bindende** ~ hard and fast rule; **dienstliche** ~**en** service instructions; **einschlägige** ~**en** relevant provisions; **endgültige** ~ final direction; **formelle** ~**en** formal rules; **geltende** ~**en** regulations in force; **gegen Steuerumgehungen gerichtete** ~**en** anti-avoidance provisions; **gesundheitsrechtliche** ~**en** health provisions; **gewerbepolizeiliche** ~**en** factory regulations; **innerstaatliche** ~**en** domestic regulations; **kartellrechtliche** ~**en** rules of a cartel; **konkursrechtliche** ~ rules of bankrupty; **patentamtliche** ~**en** patent rules; **polizeiliche** ~**en** police regulations; **postalische** ~**en** postal regulations; **steuerrechtliche** ~**en** fiscal provisions; **strenge** ~ absolute rule; **verfahrensrechtliche** ~**en** rules of procedure (practice, *US*), procedural rules; **verfassungsrechtliche** ~**en** constitutional requirements; **widersprechende** ~**en** conflicting rules; **die oben zitierte** ~ the above decree; **zwingende** ~ peremptory rule (provision);
~**en über** rules which govern; ~**en über die Abwicklung von Nachlässen im Rahmen der freiwilligen Gerichtsbarkeit** noncontentious probate rules *(Br.)*; ~**en über die Aufrechterhaltung des Versicherungsschutzes beim Rückkauf der Police** nonforfeiture provisions; ~**en über die Beförderungen** lines of promotion; ~**en über die Bildung der gesetzlich vorgeschriebenen Reserven** minimum reserve requirements *(US)*; ~ **über das Korrekturlesen** directions for correctors; ~**en eines Maklerausschusses** rules of a brokerage board; ~**en über den Marktverkehr** regulations restricting marketing practices; **gesetzliche** ~**en über Qualitätsprüfungen** *(Lebensmittel)* inspection laws; ~**en durch Rechtsverordnung** statutory orders; ~**en über den Straßenverkehr** road regulations; ~**en für gewerbliche Transportunternehmer** regulations of private carriers; ~**en über den Versand** shipping instructions *(US)*; **gesetzliche** ~**en über das Versicherungswesen** insurance legislation; ~**en eines Vertrages** provisions (terms) of a contract;
sich mit ~**en abfinden** to put up with regulations; **streng nach** ~**en arbeiten** to go slow, to work to rule *(Br.)*; ~ **aufheben** to abolish a provision, to set aside an order; ~**en ausführen** to carry out orders; ~ **zu weit auslegen** to stretch a rule; ~**en befolgen** to comply with regulations; ~**en berücksichtigen** to observe the rules; ~**en durchführen** to comply with legal requirements; ~**en einhalten** to adhere to instructions; **den** ~**en entsprechen** to comply with the requirements; ~**en erlassen** to prescribe regulations; **sich den** ~**en fügen** to comply with the rules; **sich genau an die** ~**en halten** to stick to the rules; **einer** ~ **entsprechend handeln** to live up to the rules; **den strengen** ~**en Genüge leisten** to comply with the strict requirements; ~ **lockern** to relax a rule; **durch amtliche** ~**en regeln** to regiment; **sich streng nach den** ~**en richten** to deal strictly by the rules, to rubberstamp; ~ **umgehen** to evade a rule; **gesetzliche** ~ **verletzen** to disobey a law; **gegen** ~**en für Charterfluggesellschaften verstoßen** to violate rules regarding charter operations; **einer** ~ **zuwiderhandeln** to contravene (disregard) an instruction, to infringe the provisions.

Vorschriften|buch manual; ~**fach** data case; ~**sammlung** directory, code.

vorschriftsgemäß according to instructions (directions), duly, in accordance with instructions.

vorschriftsmäßig regular, proper, formulary, normal, standard, in due form, according to regulations, to the book, as prescribed, correct;
~ **handeln** to act in accordance with the regulations; **sich** ~ **verhalten** to go by the book;
~**e Größe** regulation size; ~**e Kündigung** due and proper notice; ~**e Quittung** proper receipt; ~**e Uniform** regulation uniform; ~**e Verpackung** packing ordered.

vorschriftswidrig irregular, against the rules, contrary to regulations, *(Verkehr)* improper.

Vorschub aid, abetment, assistance;
~ **leisten** to encourage, to foster, to countenance, *(stillschweigend)* to connive; **jem.** ~ **leisten** to aid and abet s. o.; **dem Feinde** ~ **leisten** to aid and comfort the enemy;
~**leistung** aiding and abetting.

Vorschule preparatory (lower) school, infant school *(Br.)*.

Vorschul|erziehung preschool education; ~**programm** *(Rundfunk)* preschool broadcasting; ~**zentrum** preschool center *(US)* (centre, *Br.*).

Vorschuß advance, advanced money, advance money *(US)*, first stroke, *(Anwalt)* retainer, retaining fee, *(Rundfunk)* bill-board, *(Spesen)* imprest fund *(Br.)*;
als ~ by way of advance;
kurzfristiger ~ short-term loan, day-to-day advance; **ungedeckter** ~ uncovered advance; **zinsloser** ~ advance free of interest;
~ **in bar** cash advance;
auf ~ **arbeiten** to go in advance; ~ **bewilligen (genehmigen)** to grant an advance, to impress *(Br.)*; **um einen** ~ **bitten** to ask for an advance; ~ **erhalten** to obtain an advance of money; ~ **leisten** to advance; ~ **nehmen** to anticipate salary; ~ **verlangen** to ask for an advance; ~ **zurückzahlen** to repay an advance;
~**anweisung** advance note, bill of imprest *(Br.)*; ~**berechnung** computation of an advance; ~**bewilligung** grant of an advance; ~**dividende** interim (initial, *Br.*) dividend, dividend on account.

Vorschüsse *(Bilanz)* sums advanced;
geleistete ~ advances made; **an Betriebsangehörige geleistete** ~ advances to employees;
kurzfristige ~ **der Banken** day-to-day advances from banks; ~ **auf Waren** advances against merchandise; ~ **auf Wertpapiere** advances against securities;
~ **gewähren** to make advances *(US)*; **durch** ~ **gedeckt sein** to be covered by advances; ~ **zahlen** to advance funds.

Vorschuß|empfänger imprest accountant *(Br.)*; ~**genossenschaft** small-loan company; ~**höchstgrenze** maximum advance.

vorschüssige Rente annuity due.

Vorschuß|kasse loan office; ~**klausel** *(Konnossement)* red clause; ~**konto** advance (imprest, *Br.*) account, *(Kommunalbetrieb)* working capital fund; ~**leistungen zurückbekommen** to recover money advanced; ~**lorbeeren** advance publicity; ~**provision** overdraft commission; ~**verein auf Gegenseitigkeit** mutual loan society *(Br.)*; ~**wechsel** advance bill.

vorschußweise by way of (as an) advance (a loan, *US*).

Vorschuß|wesen imprest system *(Br.)*; ~**zahlung** previous payment, payment in advance (by anticipation, *US*); ~**zinsen** interest an advance.

vorschützen, Krankheit to pretend to be ill, *(mil.)* to malinger; **Unwissenheit** ~ to plead ignorance.

vor|schwatzen, jem. etw. to tell s. o. a rigmarole; **jem. ~schweben** to have in mind; **~schwindeln** to tell a fib.

vorsehen to stipulate, to provide, to prescribe, *(Mittel)* to destine, to earmark, *(planen)* to plan, to schedule *(US)*;
~ als to mark out for; **sich ~** to watch (look) out, to take care, to mind one's eye *(coll.)*; **zur Beförderung ~** to mark out for promotion; **im Etat ~** to budget for; **Gelder für einen bestimmten Zweck ~** to earmark funds; **sich vor einem Hund ~** to beware of a dog; **neue Maßnahmen ~** to plan new measures; **j. zum Nachfolger ~** to designate s. o. as one's successor; **für einen Notfall ~** to provide for an emergency; **Platz für j. ~** to reserve a place for s. o.; **für eine Schlüsselstellung ~** to earmark for a key position; **für Steuern ~** to make provisions for taxation; **Zahlungen auf Goldbasis ~** to stipulate payments in gold.

Vorsehung, der ~ in den Arm fallen to fly in the face of providence.

vorsetzen to put forward, *(Schüler)* to move up;
jem. ein gutes Essen ~ to serve s. o. a good meal; **jem. eine Lügengeschichte ~** to dish up a pack of lies to s. o.

Vorsicht caution, care, precaution, *(auf Kisten)* Beware!, Take care!, *(Umsicht)* prudence, *(Wachsamkeit)* vigilance;
mit aller gebotenen ~ with all due caution; **zur ~** as a precaution;
~ Ausfahrt! caution, concealed drive!, beware of traffic!; **~, frisch gestrichen!** wet (fresh, *US*) paint!; **~ Glas!** glass!; **~, bissiger Hund!** beware of the dog!; **~, nicht stürzen!** this side up!; **~ zerbrechlich!** fragile!; **~ am Zug!** stand back!;
besondere ~ additional (special) care; **übertriebene ~** over-caution;
mit äußerster ~ zu Werke gehen to use every precaution, to proceed with utmost caution; **~ walten lassen** to practise caution; **zur ~ mahnen** to warn; **zur ~ raten** to recommend caution; **jede ~ vergessen** to fling caution to the wind.

vorsichtig cautious, careful, circumspect, step by step, wary, *(wachsam)* vigilant, watchful;
~ anfassen to handle carefully; **j. sehr ~ behandeln** to handle s. o. with kid gloves; **sich ~ benehmen** to be guarded in one's behavio(u)r; **äußerst ~ disponieren** to show caution in placing of orders; **~ fahren** to drive carefully; **sehr ~ handeln** to use every precaution; **~ sein** to have a care *(Br.)*; **~ vorgehen** to proceed cautiously, to take in a reef;
~e Antwort guarded answer; **~e Berechnung** conservative (safe) estimate; **~er Fahrer** cautious driver; **~e Formulierung** careful wording; **~en Gebrauch machen** to use with discretion.

Vorsichtsankündigung *(Blocksystem)* cautionary card.

vorsichtshalber as a precaution.

Vorsichts|hinweis cautionary note; **~maßnahmen** measures of precaution, precautionary measures; **als ~maßnahme** by way of precaution; **~maßnahmen außer acht lassen** to neglect precautions; **~maßregeln treffen** to take precautions; **~motiv** *(Gelddispositionen)* precautionary motive.

Vorsignal *(Bahn)* distant signal.

vorsintflutlich horse-and-buggy, antediluvian;
~e Ansichten vertreten to hold antiquated views; **~e Einrichtung** model T Ford *(US)*.

Vorsitz chair, chairmanship, presidency;
unter dem ~ von ... under the presidency (chairmanship) of, presided over by, with ... in the chair;
turnusmäßig wechselnder ~ rotating chairmanship;
~ abgeben to pass the chair; **für den ~ abstellen** to second to the chair; **~ führen** to be in (occupy, preside over, fill the [speaker's]) chair; **bei einer Sitzung den ~ führen** to preside over (be chairman of) a meeting; **~ innehaben** to [occupy the] chair, to chair *(US)*; **~ niederlegen** to resign from the chairmanship; **~ übergeben** to pass the chair; **~ übernehmen** to assume the chair, to chair *(US)*, to take the lead; **~ turnusmäßig übernehmen** to take the chair according to the rota.

vorsitzen to preside, to be in (occupy) the chair, to chair *(US)*.

Vorsitzende|r chairman, president, presiding officer, *(Gericht)* sitting magistrate, presiding (senior, chief) judge, president, *(Parlament)* speaker, *(Vereinigung)* father *(Br.)*;
mit A als ~m with A in the chair;
Herr ~r! Mr. Speaker!;
geschäftsführender ~r executive vice-president *(US)*; **stellvertretender ~r** deputy (vice) president, deputy chairman; **unparteiischer ~r** impartial chairman;
~r des Aufsichtsrates chairman of the supervisory board; **~r des Börsenvorstands** chairman of the stock-exchange council; **~r der Fraktion** fraction leader; **~r mit Richterqualifikation** legally qualified chairman; **~r des Vorstandes** chairman of the managing (executive) board, president;
Entscheidung des ~n anrufen to appeal to the board; **sich der Meinung des ~n anschließen** to support the chair; **zum ~n berufen** to appoint as chairman; **zum ~n ernennen** to call to the chair; **als ~r fungieren** to act as chairman, to chair *(US)*, to preside over; **j. zum ~n vorschlagen** to propose s. o. for chairman; **j. zum ~n wählen** to call s. o. to the chair, to elect s. o. chairman; **sich an den ~n wenden** to address the chair; **~r werden** to rise to be chairman; **zum ~n bestellt werden** to be called to the chair[manship]; **zum ~n gewählt werden** to be voted in (moved into) the chair; **als ~r nominiert werden** to secure the appointment as president.

Vorsitzer des Aufsichtsrates president, chairman of the [supervisory] board.

Vorsommer early summer.

Vorsorge providence, forethought, provision against, provisory care, precaution;
genügende ~ adequate provision;
~ für eine gute Ausbildung seiner Kinder provision for the education of one's children; **~ für Berichtigungen** allowance for readjustment; **~ für die Zukunft** provision for the future;
~ treffen to provide against; **besondere ~ treffen** to make a special provision about; **für einen Notfall ~ treffen** to provide for an emergency;
~maßnahmen precautionary measures; **~motiv** *(Keynes)* precautionary motive.

vorsorgen to provide, to take precautions;
für den Winter ~ to make provisions for the winter.

Vorsorgeuntersuchung prophylactic checkup.

vorsorglich provident, [pre]cautionary, by way of precaution;
~e Maßnahmen precautionary measures, precautions.

Vorspalte preceding column.

Vorspann *(Film)* leader, trailer, curtain raiser, cowcatcher *(US sl.)*, *(Hörfunksendung)* billboard, *(Schauspielerverzeichnis)* credit;
~benennung *(Filmschauspieler)* screen credit; **~lokomotive** pilot engine.

vorspiegeln to make false pretences, to pretend, to delude;
jem. falsche Hoffnung ~ to raise false hopes in s. o.; **Krankheit ~** to feign illness, to pretend illness; **jem. Versprechungen ~, die man nicht halten will** to delude s. o. with promises one does not intend to keep;
jem. etw. ~ wollen to try to pull the wool over s. one's eyes.

Vorspiegelung pretence, delusion, *(Krankheit)* simulation;
~ der Eheschließung jactitation of marriage *(Br.)*; **~ falscher Tatsachen** cheat, fraudulent misrepresentation, false pretences (misrepresentation), false and misleading statement;
unter ~ falscher Tatsachen erlangen to obtain by fraud.

Vorspiel overture, prelude, *(Anfang)* prologue, prelude, *(für Prüfung)* audition, *(Theater)* curtain raiser (lifter);
~ zur Schlacht prelude to the battle.

vorspielen to play, *(bei Ausstellung)* to have an audition;
jem. Theater ~ to put on an act to s. o.

vorsprechen to come round, *(Theater)* to audition;
in einem Amt ~ to call at an office; **kurz bei jem. ~** to call (drop) in on s. o.

Vorspruch preamble.

Vorsprung advance, jump, *(Gebäude)* projecting angle, *(Küste)* headland, promontory, *(Sport)* start, advantage, lead;
klarer ~ vor anderen Bewerbern clear edge over other candidates;
~ vor jem. behalten to keep one's lead over s. o.; **jds. ~ einholen** to catch up with s. o.; **~ vor jem. erhalten** to get a lead start on s. o.; **~ vor seinen Verfolgern erzielen** to gain on one's pursuers; **~ vor den anderen haben** to be ahead of the others.

Vorstadium preliminary stage;
sich im ~ befinden to be in the pipeline.

Vorstadt suburb, suburbia;
schäbige ~ shanty-town;
~ausdehnung suburban extension; **~belegenheit** suburbia locality; **~bevölkerung** residents of the suburbs, villadom; **~bewohner** suburban inhabitant, suburbanite, *(pl.)* suburbia; **schon von weitem als ~bewohner zu erkennen sein** to have suburbia written all over one's face; **~gebiet** suburban area; **gut verdienendes ~gebiet** high-income suburb; **~geschäft** suburban shop (store, *US*); **~haus** suburban house; **~herkunft von weitem erkennen lassen (nicht verleugnen können)** to reflect suburbia strongly.

vorstädtisch suburban.

Vorstadt|restaurant suburban restaurant; **vornehmes ~viertel** genteel suburb, silk-stocking district *(US)*; **~welt** suburbia; **~wohngegend** residential suburb; **~wohnung** suburban residence (apartment); **ärmliche ~wohnung** poor suburban home.

Vorstand executive board (management), managing board, managers, governing body, officers, *(Bank)* governor, *(Stiftung)* board of trustees, managing committee, *(einzelnes Vorstandsmitglied)* director general, general executive, board member, governor, *(Vorsteher)* head;
außerhalb des Einflusses des ~s not within the compass of the board's jurisdiction;
beschlußfähiger ~ directors' quorum, quorum of directors; **gesamter ~** general management; **geschäftsführender ~** managing (executive) committee, managing board; **pensionsreifer ~** superannuated management; **unternehmerischer ~** aggressive management;
~ einer AG top executive management *(US)*; **~ eines Anwaltvereins** principal of the house; **~ einer Kopffiliale** area board; **seine Stimme für die Vorschläge des ~s abgeben** to cast one's vote for the presidency; **~ ansprechen** to refer to the board; **in den ~ aufnehmen** to elect to the board; **~ auswechseln** to change the management; **Bericht des ~s entgegennehmen** to receive the report of the managing board; **~ entlassen** to remove the board, *(einzelnen)* to remove a board member; **~ entlasten, dem ~ Entlastung erteilen** to discharge the directors from their responsibilities, to approve the directors' report; **in den ~ gelangen** to come onto the management scene; **neuen ~ haben** to be under new management; **sich beim ~ melden** to report to the manager; **im ~ vertreten sein** to have a voice in the management; **~ unter Druck setzen** to put pressure on the management; **dem ~ beratend zur Verfügung stehen** to supply management advice; **~ von Grund auf umstrukturieren** to structure one's management from scratch.
Vorstands|aktien management shares (stock, *US*); **~amt** managership; **~amt niederlegen** to resign a managership; **~analyse** directorate analysis; **~anwärter** board candidate; **~assistent** company secretary; **~aufgaben** duties of a director; **seinen ~aufstieg bewerkstelligen** to come onto the management scene; **~befugnisse** authority of directors, directors' powers; **~berater** management adviser (consultant); **~beratung** management consultancy; **~beratungsausschuß** management advisory committee; **~bereich** management control, board jurisdiction; **~bericht** report of the directors, directors' report; **~beschluß** judgment (resolution) of the board of directors, corporate *(US)* (board) resolution; **~bestellung** appointment of director; **~beteiligungen** directors' interests; **~bezüge** director's fees (emoluments, remuneration), executive salaries; **~bürgschaft** directors' guarantee; **Tätigkeit auf der ~ebene ausüben** to work at board level; **außerhalb des ~einflusses** not within the compass of the board's jurisdiction; **~enthebung** disqualification of a director; **~entlassung** removing an officer, amotion *(US)*; **~entlastung** approval of directors' acts, *(Wirtschaftsprüfer)* relief to officers; **~erfahrung** general management experience; **~erklärung über die Geschäftspolitik [für die Revisionsbeamten]** representation; **~ermessen** discretion of the directors; **~erweiterung** additions to management; **~etage** executive suite, city boardrooms, corporate boardrooms *(US)*; **~funktionen** management functions; **~genehmigung** board approval; **~gremium** management board; **~handlung** director's act; **~kandidat** board candidate; **~kasino** private dining room; **~kollege** fellow member of the board, fellow board member; **~konzeption** management concept; **~majorität besitzen** to have a majority on the board; **~mehrheit** board majority.
Vorstandsmitglied board member, member of the board [of directors], chief executive officer, member of the managing committee (management, executive board), director, top-management official, executive (inside, *US*) director, corporate officer *(US)*, top *(sl.)*;
ausscheidendes ~ retiring director; **lebenslänglich bestelltes ~** life director; **einfaches ~** ordinary director; **in Aussicht genommenes ~** director designate; **geschäftsführendes ~** acting (managing) director *(Br.)*, executive president *(US)*, general manager; **privat interessiertes ~** interested director; **kaufmännisches ~** commercial manager; **ordentliches ~** full member of the board; **säumiges ~** officer in default; **stellvertretendes ~** deputy board member, vice-member of the management, assistant director; **hauptamtlich tätiges ~** service director; **für den Verkauf verantwortliches ~** sales executive;
~ für Absatz und Vertrieb marketing executive; **~ für Finanzfragen** financial manager; **~ für Öffentlichkeitsfragen** public-relations director; **~ für Steuerfragen** tax manager; **~ eines Vereins** officer of a society;
~ abberufen to remove a director; **j. als ~ bestellen** to appoint s. o. [to be] manager; **pensionsreifes ~ bestellen** to appoint an over-age director; **~ sein** to act as director.
Vorstands|nachfolge executive succession; **~niveau** boardroom level; **~pension** directors' (top-hat, *sl.*) pension; **~position** board appointment, management position, directorship; **~position erreichen** to make it to the executive suite; **~posten** office of director; **~protokoll** board (corporation) minutes; **~qualität** boardroom quality; **~ressort** executive department, general management field in industry; **~sekretär[in]** assistant to a manager, executive (managerial) secretary; **~sitz** seat on a board, board seat, directorship; **~sitzung** directors' meeting, meeting of the [executive] board, meeting of directors, board meeting, executive session; **~spesen** director's expenses; **~spitze neu besetzen** to reshuffle its top team; **~sprecher** spokesman for the managing board; **~tantieme** director's percentage of profit; **seine ~tätigkeit beenden** to retire from one's full executive responsibility; **~vergütung** management fee, director's remuneration, remuneration of directors; **anteilsmäßige ~vergütung** apportionment of directors' remuneration; **~vertrag** management contract; **~verzeichnis** list (register) of directors; **~vorsitz** managing directorship; **~vorsitzender** board chairman, chairman of the [executive] board (board of management), chief executive [officer] *(US)*, president; **stellvertretender ~vorsitzender** executive vice-president; **seine Funktionen als ~vorsitzender abgeben** to relinquish one's duties as chairman; **dem ~vorsitzer unmittelbar unterstehen** to report directly to the president; **~wahl** board elections, corporate elections *(US)*; **~wechsel** management changes; **an ~weisungen gebunden sein** to serve at the pleasure of the board; **~zimmer** board room.
vorstehen to be at the head (in charge), to preside, *(Bauteile)* to project, to protrude, *(verwalten)* to manage, to direct, to administer;
einem Amt ~ to administer an office; **einem Geschäft ~** to manage a business; **einer Partei ~** to preside over a party.
vorstehend preceding, aforementioned, aforesaid, *(Bauteil)* protruding, projecting;
im ~en thereinbefore, hereinabove, heretofore.
Vorstehendes foregoing, the premises.
Vorsteher head, manager, director, governor, chief, master, headman, *(Bahnhof)* station master, *(Gefängnis)* warden, *(Schule)* headmaster, principal;
~ des Eichamts warden of the standards *(Br.)*; **~ der Treuhandabteilung** *(Bank)* trust officer.
Vorsteherin dame.
vorstellen *(neuere Artikel)* to introduce, *(Person)* to present *(US)*, *(Uhr)* to turn on, to put forward;
etw. ~ to be quite impressive; **sich ~** to imagine, to picture, to envisage, to visualize; **sich selbst ~** to introduce o. s. [by name], to make o. s. known; **sich bei jem. ~** to present o. s. to s. o.; **neuen Artikel ~** to introduce a new article in the market; **sich bei jem. im Büro ~** to report to s. o. in his office; **jem. einem Dritten ~** to introduce s. o. in s. one's presence; **Gesandten dem König ~** to present an envoy to the king; **sich persönlich ~** to come for an interview; **jem. das Törichte seines Verhaltens ~** to point out to s. o. the folly of his conduct; **Vortragenden ~** to introduce the lecturer to the audience.
vorstellig|bei in remonstrance with, remonstrative;
bei den Behörden ~ werden to apply to the authorities; **auf diplomatischem Wege ~ werden** to make diplomatic representations.
Vorstellung introduction, *(zwecks Anstellung)* interview, *(Aufführung)* performance, play, show, entertainment, presentation, *(Begriff)* idea, notion, conception, picture, fancy, imagination, *(bei Hofe)* presentation, *(Protest)* representation, remonstrance;
auf jds. dringende ~en at s. one's urgent request;
nur in der ~ bestehend aerial;
allgemeine ~ introduction all around; **schwach besuchte ~** poorly attended performance; **diplomatische ~en** diplomatic representations, remonstrances, remonstrations, intercession; **dringende ~en** urgencies; **durchgehende ~** *(Kino)* nonstop performance; **falsche ~** illusion, misconception; **feierliche ~** presentation ceremony; **geistige ~** mental image; **geschlossene ~** private (closed) performance; **lebhafte (lebendige) ~** lively idea; **nebelhafte ~** vague idea; **persönliche ~** employment interview; **persönliche ~ erwünscht** *(Anzeige)* personal attendance required; **romantische ~en** romantic visions; **seltsame ~** queer notion; **ungefähre ~** general idea; **vage ~** remote conception; **zweite ~** *(Theater)* second house;
~ eines neuen Artikels new-product introduction; **~ mit erster Besetzung** *(Theater)* star performance; **~ auf lange Sicht** long-range idea;

öffentliche ~ abbrechen to discontinue a public performance; **~ beginnen** to ring up the curtain; **j. zu einer persönlichen ~ einladen** to invite s. o. to come to a personal interview; **ernste ~en erheben** to remonstrate, to make representations, to represent against; **nur in jds. ~ existieren** to exist only in s. one's imagination; **~ geben** to give a performance; **~en in den größten Städten geben** to play the larger cities; **verschwommene ~ haben** to have a hazy idea; **ganz bestimmte ~ über seine Verwendungsmöglichkeiten haben** to be vocal about one's assignments; **sich keine ~ machen** to have no idea about s. th.; **~ bühnenreif machen** to get a show onto the stage; **~ widerlegen** to explode a notion;
~ fällt heute aus no performance to-night.

Vorstellungs|bild mental picture, image; **~bild eines Unternehmens in der Öffentlichkeit** corporate image *(US)*; **~kraft** imaginative power, imagination, ideality; **~verfahren** interlocutory proceedings; **~vermögen** representative faculty, thought, power to conceive.

Vorsteuer input tax;
~abzug deduction of input tax; **gezahlte ~beträge zurückverlangen** to reclaim paid taxes on all purchases of a business; **~einkommen** pretax income; **~gewinn** profit before tax; **~zahler** registered vat business.

Vorstoß dash, drive, *(mil.)* push, onrush, thrust, advance, *(Versuch)* attempt, try;
~ aufs Geratewohl wild pitch;
~ für die Freiheit unternehmen to make a dash for freedom; **~ wagen** to dare to advance; **~ in ein unbekanntes Land wagen** to venture into an unknown country.

vorstoßen *(mil.)* to forge ahead, to push forward;
in unerforschte Gebiete ~ to venture into unknown territory.

Vorstrafe previous (former) conviction, taint;
einschlägige ~ similar conviction;
~n haben to have been convicted of previous crimes.

Vorstrafen|register, ~verzeichnis police (criminal, prison) record, record of prior convictions, form *(sl.)*, *(mil.)* crime sheet; **~ haben** to have been convicted of previous crimes, to be known to the police.

vorstrecken, Geld to advance money.

Vorstudie preliminary study, *(Industrieprojekt)* feasibility study.

Vortag previous day.

Vortagsnotierung *(Börse)* quotation of the previous day.

vortäuschen to pretend, to sham, to simulate, to feign;
Betroffenheit ~ to put on an air of perplexity; **Krankheit ~** to pretend to be ill, to feign (simulate) illness, to malinger.

Vortäuschung einer Krankheit simulation of an illness.

Vorteil advantage, turn, benefit, use, capital, good, jump *(US)*, *(Gewinn)* profit, gain, market, account, *(Nutzen)* interest, *(Überlegenheit)* odds;
auf den eigenen ~ bedacht self-seeking; **zu meinem ~** at my hands; **zu seinem eigenen ~** for his own good; **zum gegenseitigen ~** to their mutual benefit;
seine ~e his assets;
alleiniger ~ über sole edge over *(fam.)*; **sich erst in der Zukunft auswirkende ~e** long-term benefits; **erheblicher ~** material benefit; **teuer erkaufter ~** dearly bought advantage; **aus der Freiheit der Presse erwachsende ~e** advantages accruing from the freedom of the press; **durch Amtsmißbrauch erworbene ~e** graft *(US)*; **geldwerte ~e** benefits of pecuniary conditions; **nicht geldwerte ~e** nonmonetary advantages; **materieller ~** pecuniary benefit; **möglicher ~** contingent advantage; **naturgegebene ~e** natural advantages; **offensichtlicher ~** patent (obvious) advantage; **persönlicher ~** personal benefit; **preislicher ~** price advantage; **wirtschaftlicher ~** economic advantage;
~e einer guten Ausbildung benefits of a good education; **~e und Nachteile** pros and cons;
~ ausnutzen to follow up an advantage; **jds. ungünstige Lage zu seinem ~ ausnutzen** to take s. o. at a disadvantage; **~ nicht ausnutzen** to surrender an advantage; **sich zu jds. ~ auswirken** to redound to (make for) s. one's advantage; **seinen eigenen ~ bedenken** to consult one's own advantage, to take care of number one; **~e bieten** to offer advantages; **bestimmte ~e einräumen** to grant certain facilities; **~e erbringen** to be advantageous; **~ vor jem. erringen** to get windward of s. o.; **sich verstellen, um einen ~ zu erzielen** to play booty; **~e genießen** to enjoy privileges; **zum ~ gereichen** to turn up trumps; **~ gewähren** to offer an advantage; **~e haben von** to benefit by; **großen ~ haben** to be quids in *(fam.)*; **~ vor jem. haben** to have the draw on (whip row of) s. o.; **jds. ~ im Auge haben** to study s. one's interests; **seinen eigenen ~ im Auge haben** to consult (have an eye to) one's own interest; **~e einer Urkunde in Anspruch nehmen** to accept a benefit under an instrument; **im ~ sein** to possess the deadwood *(US sl.)*; **jem. gegenüber im ~ sein** to have the edge (goods) on (over) s. o. *(sl.)*; **von ~ sein** to be profitable; **auf seinen ~ bedacht sein** to consult one's own interest, to know on which side one's bread is buttered, to have an eye to the main chance, to look (take care) after number one; **sich zu gegenseitigem ~ vereinigen** to pool issues *(US)*; **mit ~ verkaufen** to sell at a profit; **sich einen unfairen ~ verschaffen** to jump the gun *(sl.)*; **sich einen ~ gegenüber jem. verschaffen** to gain an advantage over (get the weather gauge on) s. o.; **sich ~e bei einflußreichen Leuten verschaffen** to make up to influential people; **~ wahrnehmen** to follow up an advantage; **seinen ~ rücksichtslos wahrnehmen** to press one's advantage, to drive a hard bargain; **~ ziehen** to profit (benefit) by, to take (suck) advantage of, to turn to account, to derive benefit, to find one's account in.

vorteilhaft advantageous[ly], profitable, profitably, well, favo(u)rable, remunerative, beneficial to business, *(Kaufpreis)* at the best price;
nicht ~ nonbeneficial; **für beide Teile ~** mutually profitable; **sein Geld ~ anlegen** to lay out one's money to advantage, to invest one's money to good account; **in einem Kleid sehr ~ aussehen** to look one's best in a dress; **~ einkaufen** to buy at a cheap rate; **~ sein** to be of benefit; **etw. ~ verkaufen** to sell s. th. to good advantage; **~ verwerten** to fetch a good price;
zu ~en Bedingungen on favo(u)rable terms; **~e Gemeindeabgaben** remunerative duties; **~es Geschäft** paying (profitable) business, bargain, catch, good deal *(US)*; **~e Kapitalanlage** profitable (remunerative) investment; **~er Kauf** bargain, good buy; **~e Sache** oyster; **sehr ~e Verzinsung** lucrative interest.

Vortrag *(Ansprache)* address, speech, lecture, *(Bericht)* report, *(Buchführung)* carryforward, carrying forward, brought (balance carried) forward, *(Gedicht, Musik)* recital, recitation, *(Radio)* talk, *(Umbuchung)* transfer in the books, *(Vorlesung)* lecture, *(Vortragsstil)* diction, elocution;
gehaltener ~ paper read before a society; **geistreicher ~** firework; **honorierter ~** paid lecture; **mündlicher ~** *(Anwalt)* oral pleading; **öffentlicher ~** declamation; **praktisch unveränderter ~** *(Bilanz)* virtually unchanged carryforward; **wissenschaftlicher ~** paper;
~ der Anklagebehörde statement of the prosecution; **~ auf Bilanzkonto** balance carried to balance sheet; **~ aus dem vorhergesehenen Geschäftsjahr** balance from previous business year, carryforward *(Br.)*; **~ mit Lichtbildern** lantern lecture; **~ aus alter Rechnung** balance carried forward from last account; **~ auf neue Rechnung** amount (account) carried (balance brought, carried) forward; **~ aus dem vorherigen Rechnungsjahr** amount brought in, carryforward *(Br.)*; **~ einer Rede** delivery of a speech; **~ einschließlich Reingewinn** net profits including balance; **~ des Sachverhalts** relation, pleading; **~ einer Summe** bringing forward of a sum; **~ auf Warentermingeschäfte** commodity carry scheme;
sich einen ~ anhören to attend (turn out to) a lecture; **~ halten** to read a paper, to deliver a lecture, to lecture on, to give an address, to dissert, *(berichten)* to report; **einem ~ ein paar Worte vorausschicken** to precede a lecture with a few words; **~ vornehmen** *(Bilanz)* to carry forward; **seinen ~ in die Länge ziehen** to water one's lecture.

vortragen to set forth, *(Anwalt)* to argue, to plead, to count, *(berichten)* to report, to state, *(buchen)* to carry forward (up), *(Gedichte)* to recite, *(Vorlesung halten)* to [give a] lecture, to read a paper, *(vorschlagen)* to propose;
allgemeinverständlich ~ to lecture lucidly on a subject; **Angelegenheit einem Ausschuß ~** to present a matter to a committee; **Beschwerde ~** to lodge (prefer) a complaint; **Betrag zu Lasten eines Kontos ~** to charge a sum to the debit of an account; **Effekten ~** to carry over stock; **Fall ~** to state (put) a case; **seinen Fall dem Gericht ~** to lay one's case before (submit the case to) the court; **Fall schriftlich ~** to submit a written statement of a case; **finanziell anstehende Fragen übersichtlich ~** to develop financial reporting; **Gedicht ~** to recite a poem; **materiellrechtlich ~** to plead to the merits; **Meinung ~** to offer an opinion; **nochmals ~** *(Anwalt)* to replead; **auf neue Rechnung ~** to carry forward (place) to new account; **Saldo ~** to carry forward the balance; **schlüssig ~** to appear, to plead a cause; **schriftlich ~** to state in writing; **unverzüglich ~** to plead instanter; **Verluste längerfristig ~** to carry forward long-term losses *(Br.)*; **seine Wünsche der Sekretärin ~** to state one's business to the secretary; **den Zuhörern seine Pläne ~** to develop one's plans to an audience;

gut ~ können to have a good delivery; **seine Sache durch einen Anwalt ~ lassen** to be heard by counsel *(Br.)*.
Vortragender lecturer, speaker, performer, discourser.
vortragender Rat councillor.
Vortrags|abend recital; **~art** delivery; **~folge** program(me), *(Universität)* series of lectures; **~honorar** lecture fee; **~kunst** speech technique, elocution; **~künstler** elocutionist; **~posten** item carried forward; **~raum** lecture room, auditorium; **~reihe** course (series) of lectures; **~reise** lecture circuit (tour), *(pol.)* speaking tour; **~reise unternehmen** to go on a lecture tour; **~saal** lecture hall (room), lyceum *(US)*, auditorium *(US)*; **~stück** piece; **~verpflichtung** speaking engagement; **~weise, ~stil** action, delivery; **~zyklus** course of lectures; **~zyklus halten** to give a course of lectures.
vortrefflich excellent, splendid, superb.
Vortriebsstrecke *(Bergwerk)* headway.
Vortritt antecedence, precedence;
~ haben to have precedence, to rank; **jem. den ~ lassen** to yield precedence to s. o.
Vortrittsrecht preaudience.
Vortrupp *(mil.)* vanguard advance unit.
vorübergegangen, nicht spurlos ~ sein to have left its mark.
vorübergehen to pass away.
vorübergehend temporary, transitory, passing;
~ geschlossen temporarily closed;
sich ~ aufhalten to make a short stay; **j. ~ vertreten** to supply s. one's place;
~e Anlagen current investment; **~e Einstellung** temporary posting; **schnell ~er Erfolg** short-lived success; **~e Erwerbstätigkeit** temporary employment; **~er Pensionär** transient lodger; **~e Produktion** change-over production.
Vorübergehender passer-by.
Vor|überlegungen preliminary considerations; **~übungen** introductory exercises; **~umsätze** intermediate transactions; **~untersuchung** preliminary hearing (investigation), prejudgment, pre-examination, *(Patentrecht)* preliminary examination, *(Strafrecht)* criminal (preliminary) investigation, precognition *(Scot.)*; **~untersuchung durchführen** to to precognosce *(Scot.)*; **~untersuchungen** preliminary findings.
Vorurteil bias, biased opinion, prejudice, warped judgment, prejudgment, preconceived idea, *(Urteil der Vorinstanz)* junior judgment;
frei von ~en unbiassed, large-minded; **in ~en befangen** trammelled in prejudices;
ausgeprägtes ~ strong prejudice; **örtlich begründete ~e** local prejudices *(US)*; **bürgerliche ~e** middle-class prejudices; **tief eingewurzeltes ~** ingrained prejudice; **offensichtliches ~** *(Schwurgericht)* actual bias; **persönliches ~** personal bias; **subjektives ~** *(Marktforschung)* bias;
j. mit ~en erfüllen to imbue s. o. with prejudices; **sich von ~en freimachen** to get the better of one's prejudices; **~ haben** to hug prejudice; **kein ~ haben** to hold no prejudice; **jem. seine törichten ~e nehmen** to disabuse s. o. of silly prejudices; **~en ausgesetzt sein** to be open to prejudices; **jds. ~e in Rechnung stellen** to work on s. one's prejudices; **~ überwinden** to outgrow (live down) a prejudice.
vorurteilslos free from bias, unbiassed, unprejudiced, enlightened.
Vorurteilslosigkeit impartiality, cando(u)r.
Vor|väter forefathers, ancestors; **~vereinbarung** preliminary contract, *(Völkerrecht)* preliminary agreement; **~vereinigung** quasi corporation; **~verfahren** preliminary (interlocutory) proceedings, pretrial procedure *(US)*; **~verfahrenskosten** preproduction costs; **~verhandlungen** preliminaries to a negotiation, preliminary talks.
Vorverkauf advance sale, *(Karten)* advance booking, booking in advance, *(Theater)* ticket agent, booking office;
im ~ bookable, box-office;
~ eines Produkts preselling;
~ übermäßig anheizen to advance sales excessively; **im ~ besorgen** to book in advance.
Vorverkaufs|gebühr booking fee; **~karte** advance ticket; **~kasse, ~stelle** booking (box) office.
vorverlegen to antedate, to put forward, *(Termin)* to accelerate.
Vor|verlegung acceleration; **~vermächtnis** executory use; **~vernehmung** *(Zeuge)* voire dire *(US)*, statement of proof *(Br.)*; **~veröffentlichung** prepublication, *(Patentrecht)* prior printed publication *(US)*; **~verpackung** prepackaging; **~versammlung** preliminary meeting; **~versicherung** preinsurance; **~versorgung** *(Erbe)* advance, preferential benefit *(US)*.
vorversterben to predecease.
Vor|verstorbener predeceased; **~versuch** pilot experiment.
Vorvertrag preliminary agreement (contract), precontract, *(Versicherung)* binder *(US)*, cover note, *(Völkerrecht)* preliminary (provisional) treaty;
~ für ein Grundstück agreement to sell land;
~ abschließen to precontract.
Vorvertragsniederschrift slip, memorandum.
vorwagen, sich zu weit to go out on a limb, to stick one's neck out *(sl.)*.
Vorwahl pre-election, preliminary election, preferential ballot, preference voting, primary election *(US)*, *(Telefon)* preselection;
endgültige ~ runoff election *(US)*.
Vorwählautomatik automatic preselector.
vorwählen *(tel.)* to preselect.
Vorwähler *(tel.)* preselector.
Vorwählnummer *(tel.)* dialling code, call prefix.
Vorwand pretext, pretence, colo(u)r, professed excuse, mask, veil, cover handle, blind, stalking horse, peg, subterfuge, come-off *(coll.)*;
unter dem ~ under the pretence (colo(u)r, guise of, plea that, the cloak); **unter dem ~, sich von seinem Anwalt beraten zu lassen** under the pretext of consulting one's lawyer;
unberechtigter ~ idle pretext;
als ~ dienen to serve as a pretext; **etw. unter dem ~ eines Freundschaftsdienstes tun** to do s. th. under the pretence of friendship.
vorwarnen to forewarn.
Vorwarnsystem *(Raketenabwehr)* warning system.
Vorwarnung advance warning, *(Luftschutz)* early warning.
vorwärts kommen *(Schiff)* to make way;
wegen des Nebels nur langsam ~ to make little progress in a fog; **trotz ungünstigen Wetters ~** *(Schiff)* to weather along.
vorwärts treiben to impel, to hurry up.
Vorwärtsbewegung progressive movement.
vorwärtsdrängen, sich rücksichtslos to muscle *(US coll.)*.
Vorwärtsgang forward gear.
vorwärtsgehen *(fig.)* to make progress.
Vorwärtskommen progress;
gesellschaftliches ~ rise in social position (status);
sein berufliches ~ beschleunigen to speed up one's business progress.
vorwärtskommen to grow, to advance, to gain ground, to do well, to get on [in the world], to make (progress on) one's way, to make progress, to get along, *(mit der Arbeit)* to make headway; **beruflich ~** to improve one's position, to progress, to get ahead; **nur langsam ~** to make little headway; **ruckweise ~** to get on (forward) by leaps and bounds.
vorwärtsschauend prospective, forward looking.
Vorwärtsstrategie *(mil.)* forward strategy.
Vorwärtsverteidigung *(mil.)* forward defence.
Vorweg|abzug deduction at source; **~anhebungen** prior increases; **~befriedigungsrecht** preferential right (claim), *(Nachlaßverwalter)* retainer of debts.
vorwegbehandeln to precondition.
Vorweg|belastung prior charge; **~bewilligung** grant of an advance; **~entnahme** preferential benefit *(US)*; **~finanzierung** advance to finance.
vorweggenommener Gewinnanteil *(Versicherung)* anticipated profit.
Vorweg|leistung advance payment, prepayment; **~nahme** forestalling, anticipation; **neuheitsschädliche ~nahme einer Erfindung** anticipation of an invention.
vorwegnehmen to forestall, to anticipate, *(Börse)* to discount; **Einwände ~** to preclude objections.
vorwegnehmend anticipative.
Vorwegpfändung seizure under a prior claim.
Vorwegweiser *(Autobahn)* route confirmation sign.
vorwegzunehmen, um das wichtigste to come to the most important items first.
vorweisen *(Karte)* to show, to present;
ausreichende Kenntnisse ~ können to have adequate qualifications.
vorwerfen, jem. etw. to reproach (rebuke) s. o., to hold s. th. against s. o.
vorwiegen, jem. etw. to weigh in front of s. o.
vorwiegend prevailing, preponderant;
~ Brief *(Börse)* sellers over.
Vorwort foreword, preface, preamble, prologue, *(Einleitung)* introduction;
~ für ein Buch schreiben to write a preface to a book.

Vorwurf reproach, censure, blame, rebuke, charge, obloquy, upbraiding.
Vorwürfe | ausräumen to rebut the charges; **beleidigende ~ gegen j. erheben** to lash s. o. with one's tongue; **jem. heftige ~ machen** to hurl reproaches at s. o., to slang s. o. *(fam.)*; **j. mit ~n überschütten** to heap reproaches upon s. o.
vorwurfsvoll reproachful, upbraiding.
vorzählen, jem. Geld to count money in s. one's presence (before s. o.).
Vorzeichen auspice, omen, portent, prognostic, presage;
böses ~ ill omen; **positives** ~ plus (positive) sign;
negatives ~ haben to have a negative cast; **etw. als gutes ~ werten** to take s. th. as a good omen.
vorzeigen to produce, to show, *(Wechsel)* to present, to sight;
seine Karte ~ to show (produce) one's ticket; **seinen Paß** ~ to produce one's passport;
sich kaum ~ können to be hardly fit to face company;
Fahrkarten ~! tickets please!
Vorzeiger *(Wechsel)* bearer, presenter, holder.
Vorzeigung exhibition, production, *(Wechsel)* presentation, sight;
bei ~ at sight, on presentation; **bei ~ rückzahlbar** repayable at call; **bei ~ zahlbar** payable at sight;
bei ~ zahlen to pay on demand.
vorzeitig premature, anticipated.
Vorzensur *(Presse)* censureship of the press.
Vorziehen von Bestellungen predating of orders.
vorziehen to favo(u)r, *(begünstigen)* to prefer, to give preferential treatment;
Bestellungen ~ to predate orders; **eine Sache einer anderen** ~ to give s. th. the preference over the other; **Sache zeitlich** ~ to deal with s. th. first; **Schüler** ~ to favo(u)r a pupil.
Vorzimmer waiting room, anteroom;
j. im ~ warten lassen to keep s. o. waiting in the anteroom;
~dame receptionist.
Vorzug advantage, preference, merit, asset, priority, virtue, *(Bahn)* relief (special) train, *(mil.)* pilot train;
großer ~ eines Planes great virtue of a scheme;
~ geben to prefer; **~ haben** to be privileged; **~ größerer Sicherheit haben** to have the advantage of being safer.
Vorzüge privileges;
besondere ~ *(Grundstück)* amenities;
materielle ~ und Annehmlichkeiten material comforts and pleasures; **~ und Nachteile eines Arbeitsplatzes** nonmonetary advantages and disadvantages;
~ eines Gesetzes erlangen to secure the immunities of a statute;
~ genießen to enjoy privileges; **~ schlecht beurteilen können** to be a poor judge of values.
vorzüglich first-class, prime, superior, superb, excellent, exquisite, *(auserlesen)* select, choice, first-rate;
~e Arbeit first-class work; **~e Beschaffenheit (Qualität)** superior (first-rate) quality; **~e Referenzen** first-class references; **~e Sorte** choice brand; **~e Ware** articles of first (superior) quality, choice commodities.
Vorzüglichkeit excellence, superbness, outstanding quality.
Vorzugsaktie preference (preferential, senior, priority, preferred) share *(Br.)*, preference (preferred, preferential, prior, debenture) stock *(US)*;
im Sanierungsverfahren ausgegebene ~n adjustment preferred stocks *(US)*; **mit zusätzlicher Gewinnbeteiligung (besonderer zusätzlicher Dividendenberechtigung) ausgestattete** ~ participating preferred stock *(US)*; **mit Umtauschrecht ausgestattete** ~ convertible preference share *(Br.)*; **nicht zu einer zusätzlichen Dividende berechtigte ~n** nonparticipating preference shares *(Br.)*, nonparticipating preferred stocks *(US)*; **zusätzlich gewinnberechtigte ~n** participating preferred ordinaries; **gewöhnliche** ~ preferred ordinary share *(Br.)*; **kumulative ~n** noncontingent preference shares *(Br.)*, cumulative preference stock *(US)*; **nicht nachschußpflichtige** ~ nonassessable preferred stock *(US)*; **nachzugsberechtigte** ~ cumulative preference share *(Br.)*; **rückkaufbare** ~ redeemable preference share *(Br.)* (preferred stock, *US*); **stimmberechtigte ~n** voting preferred stock *(US)*; **stimmrechtslose** ~ nonvoting preference share *(Br.)* (preferred stock, *US*); **zusätzliche ~n** cumulative preferred stock *(US)*;
~ mit Dividendenbezugsrecht cumulative preferred stock *(US)*; **~ ohne Dividendenbezugsrecht** noncumulative preferred stock *(US)*; **~ mit Dividendengarantie** share (stock, *US*) as preferred to dividends; **~n zweiter Klasse** second preferred stocks *(US)*; **~ ohne Nachbezugsrecht** noncumulative stock *(US)*; **~ mit Umtauschrecht** convertible preference share *(Br.)*, convertible preferred stock *(US)*.
Vorzugs | aktienzertifikat preference share certificate *(Br.)*; **~aktionär** preference (preferential, privileged) shareholder *(Br.)*, preferred (privileged, preference) stockholder *(US)*; **~angebot** exceptional (special, preferential, preference) offer; **~anleihe** preference (preferential) loan; **~anspruch** preference (preferential, priority, preferred) claim; **~ausgabe** preference issue; **~bedienung des Erstkommenden** *(Flugbuchungen)* first-come first-served basis; **~bedingungen** preferential terms; **~befriedigung** priority of payment; **~behandlung** preference, preferential (priority) treatment, *(Zoll)* discrimination, Imperial preference *(Br.)*; **steuerliche ~behandlung** discriminatory taxation; **~belieferung** priority delivery; **~berechtigter** priority permit holder; **~diskontsatz** preferential discount (prime lending, *US*) rate; **~dividende** participating (preference, preferential, preferred, *US*) dividend; **~dividende mit fester Verzinsung** preferred fixed dividend; **~forderung** preferential (privileged) claim; **~fracht** preference freight *(US)*; **~frachtsätze** *(Fluggesellschaft)* commodity rates; **~gebühr für Bestellformulare des Buchhandels** preferential fee for book-trade order forms; **~gläubiger** preferential (prior, preferred, secured) creditor; **Stellung eines ~gläubigers einnehmen** to rank as a preferential creditor; **~karte** privilege ticket; **~klausel** preference clause; **~kurs** preferential price; **~liste** priority list; **~obligationen** preference (priority) bonds, participating (senior) bonds; **~pfandrecht** prior lien; **~plazierung, ~platz** special (preferred, full, *US*) position; **~preis** bargain (exceptional, private, special, preferential) price; **~preis für Belegung mehrerer Regionalausgaben desselben Blattes** *(Anzeige)* combined edition discount; **~rabatt** special rebate[ment], promotion allowance, preferential discount; **~rangfolge** preferential priority; **~rate im Luftfrachtverkehr** commodity rate; **~recht** prior right, preferential claim (right), preference, priority, privilege; **mit einem ~recht ausgestattet** preferential; **~satz** specimen (preferential) rate, *(Anzeige)* preferred (exceptional) position; **~stellung** preferential (privileged) position, bull point *(coll.)*; **~stellung erhalten** to receive a preference; **~stimmrecht** preferential voting rights; **~tarif** preferential tariff (rate), Imperial preference *(Br.)*, *(Fluggesellschaft)* commodity rate, *(Werbung)* special rate; **~wahlsystem** preferential voting.
vorzugsweise by preference, preferably;
~ Befriedigung preferential treatment.
Vorzugs | zahlungen *(Konkurs)* preferential payments; **~zinssatz für erstklassige Firmen** key rate, prime [lending] rate *(US)*; **~zoll[tarif]** preferential tariff (duty), differential duty, Imperial preference *(Br.)*.
Vorzündung preignition, spark advance.
vorzuweisen haben, etw. to have s. th. under one's belt.
Vostroguthaben vostro (their, *US*) account.
votieren to vote.
Votum vote, opinion;
einstimmiges ~ solid (block) vote;
~ der Mehrheit prevailing opinion *(US)*;
sein ~ abgeben to cast one's vote.
vulgär vulgar, gross;
~e Sprache vulgar language.
Vulgärausdruck vulgarism.
Vulkan volcano;
erloschener ~ extinct volcano; **rauchender** ~ smoking volcano;
tätiger ~ active volcano; **untätiger** ~ dormant volcano;
~ausbruch eruption of a volcano, volcanic eruption.
vulkanisch vulcanic, volcanic;
~es Gestein volcanic rock.
Vulkanisierapparat vulcanizer.
vulkanisierbar vulcanizable.
Vulkanisierbetrieb tire *(US)* (tyre, *Br.*) vulcanizer.
vulkanisieren to vulcanize, to volcanize, to cap.
Vulkanisierung vulcanization, volcanization.

W

WC watercloset, convenience *(Br.)*.
Waage scales, weighing machine, *(Sternzeichen)* Libra;
~ **der Gerechtigkeit** scales of justice;
Zünglein an der ~ bilden to hold the balance, to tip the scales; **in der ~ halten** to keep in equilibrium; **sich die ~ halten** *(Gewinn und Verlust)* to be on a par; **auf einer ~ wiegen** to weigh on the scales.
Waagenmeister weighmaster, weigher.
waagerecht horizontal, even, flat.
Waagschale pair of scales, pan;
seinen Einfluß in die ~ bringen to throw one's weight about; **in die ~ werfen** to balance against.
wach awake, *(aufgeschlossen)* wide-awake, alert;
~ **bleiben** to stay awake; **sich mühsam ~ halten** to struggle to stay awake; **ganze Nacht ~ liegen** not to have a wink of sleep, to pass a wakeful night.
Wach|ablösung changing of the guard, relief of a sentry; ~**bataillon** guards battalion; ~**boot** patrol vessel, picket boat, watchboat; ~**buch** guard book.
Wache watch, guard, *(Begleitung)* escort, *(Gebäude)* guardhouse, *(mar.)* wake, *(mil.)* sentinel, warden, *(Polizei)* police station (office, *Br.*), station house *(US)*;
auf ~ on watch;
erste ~ first post *(mil.)*;
~ **einer Krankenschwester** nurse's post;
~**[n] aufstellen** to watch *(Br.)*; ~ **beziehen** to mount guard; ~**n einteilen** to watch, to assign watches; ~ **haben** to have the watch; ~ **halten** to keep [a] watch on (over), to watch; **draußen ~ halten** to be watching outside; ~ **herausrufen** to call out the guard; ~ **heraustreten lassen** to turn out the guard; **auf ~ stehen,** ~ **schieben** to be on guard duty; ~ **übernehmen** to keep guard.
Wachen watching;
~ **am Krankenbett** vigils at a sickbed.
wachen to wake;
bei einem Kranken ~ to sit with a sick person; **ganze Nacht ~** to pass a wakeful night, not to have a wink of sleep.
Wach|fahrzeug patrol boat (vessel), guard boat (ship); ~- **und Schließgesellschaft** security guards, Security Corps *(Br.)*; ~**habender** guard commander, watcher, *(Schiff)* watch header.
wach|habender Offizier watch officer; **seine Zuhörer ~halten** to hold the interest of one's audience.
Wach|haus guardhouse; ~**hund** watchdog, mastiff; **abgerichteter ~hund** attack dog; ~**hundfunktion** watchdog role; ~**lokal** guardroom; ~**mann** guard, sentinel, security man; ~**mannschaft** guards, watch, set of watchmen; ~**offizier** watch officer; ~**personal** security employees; ~**pflicht bei Tag und Nacht** watch and ward; ~**posten** guard, watch; ~**posten aufstellen** to station a sentinel; ~**posten vor einer Tür aufstellen** to plant a sentry before a door; ~**raum** guardroom.
wachrufen, Erinnerungen to awaken memories.
Wachs|in jds. Händen sein to be wax in s. one's hands; **bleich wie ~ werden** to go as pale as death;
~**abdruck** print of a seal in wax; ~**abdruck machen** to print a seal on wax.
wachsam watchful, vigilant, wary, wakeful.
Wachsamkeit vigilance, watch;
jds. ~ hintergehen to catch a weasel asleep; **in seiner ~ niemals nachlassen** to never take one's eyes off.
wachsen to grow, to increase, to expand, to extend, *(sich entwickeln)* to develop;
Fußboden ~ to wax the floor; **aus den Kleidern ~** to outgrow one's clothes; **über den Kopf ~** *(Arbeit)* to pile up; **zu schnell ~** to overgrow o. s.
wachsend growing, accumulative, increasing;
~**es Ansehen** growing reputation; ~**e Nachfrage** growing demand; ~**e Unkosten** growing expenditure; **mit ~em Wohlstand** with increasing prosperity.
Wachs|figurenkabinett waxworks; ~**kerze** wax; ~**matrize** recording stencil, *(Schallplatte)* wax record; ~**platte** stencil; ~**plattenabzug** stencilled copy.
Wachstube watchhouse, *(Polizei)* police station.
Wachstum growth, increase, expansion, augmentation;
nicht inflationär bedingtes ~ noninflationary growth; **durch Investitionen beeinflußtes ~** investment-led growth; **exportbeeinflußtes ~** export-led growth; **gestörtes geistiges ~** disturbed mental development; **gleichgewichtiges ~** balanced growth; **industrielles ~** industrial growth; **rapides ~** mushroom growth; **reales ~** real growth; **schnelles ~** quick growth;
~ **des Bruttoinlandsprodukts** growth in gross domestic product (gdp); ~ **der Industrie** industrial (industry) growth; ~ **eines Unternehmens** company growth; ~ **der Volkswirtschaft** economic growth, growth of the economy;
~ **finanzieren** to underwrite growth; **im ~ zurückgeblieben sein** to be stunted in growth; ~ **der Industrie verlangsamen** to slow down industrial expansion.
Wachstums|aktien growth stocks; ~**annahme** growth assumption; **kräftiger ~anstieg** strong burst of growth; **verzögerter ~anstieg** slowdown in the rate of advance; ~**aspekt** growth aspect; ~**aussichten** growth prospects; ~**behinderung** growth squeeze; **marginaler ~beitrag** marginal growth contribution; **erneute ~beschleunigung** re-acceleration of growth; ~**branche** growth sector; ~**chance** growth opportunity; ~**einreihung** growth ranking; ~**ende erreicht haben** to come to the end of the growth line; ~**faktor** *(Wertpapiere)* growth factor; ~**favoriten** growth favo(u)rites; ~**finanzierung** growth financing; ~**flaute** stagnation; ~**folge** sequence of growth; ~**fonds** performance fund, accumulation unit (growth) trust.
wachstumsfördernd growth-promoting.
Wachstums|gebiet growth zone (field, area); ~**gelegenheiten** growth opportunities; ~**grad** growth term; ~**grenze** growth limit; ~**impuls** impetus towards expansion; ~**industrie** growth (science-based) industry; **kein ~jahr** no-growth year; **langsames ~jahr** slow-growth year; ~**kapazität** capacity for growth; ~**krise** development crisis; ~**kurve** growth kurve; ~**markt** market growth; ~**mentalität** growth mentality; ~**messung** growth measurement; ~**modell** growth model; ~**möglichkeit** growth potential; **nicht genutzte volkswirtschaftliche ~möglichkeiten** national loss in potential output; ~**nachweis** growth record; ~**periode** growth era, growing season; **geringe ~periode** slow economic growth; **langfristige ~periode** long-term growth, period of prolonged growth; ~**phase** growth phase; ~**pol** growth pole; ~**politik** growth policy; ~**prognose** growth forecast; ~**programm** growth program(me); ~**prozeß** growth process, up-growth, process of growth; **wirtschaftlicher ~prozeß** economic growth march.
Wachstumsrate rate of growth, growth rate;
zum Stillstand führende ~ zero growth rate; **jährliche ~** year-to-year growth rate; **rückläufige ~** negative economic growth rate;
entwicklungsbedingte ~ des Bundessozialprodukts trend rate of gross national product growth; ~ **des Sozialprodukts** rate of economic growth, economic growth rate;
der Gesamtwirtschaft zu angemessenen ~n verhelfen to carry the whole economy to a decent growth rate.
Wachstums|reserven growth reserves; ~**rezession** growth recession; ~**schaden** crop damage.
wachstumsschwach slow-growing.
Wachstums|schwierigkeiten haben to outgrow one's strength; **noch immer an ~schwierigkeiten kranken** to be still suffering from growing pains; ~**sektor** growth sector; ~**situation** growth situation; ~**spirale** growth spiral; ~**stadien** stages of growth.
wachstumsstark growing strong.
Wachstums|tabelle growth rate table; ~**tempo** growth rate; ~**trend** growth performance; ~**verlangsamung** slowdown of the growth rate; ~**verluste** losses of the growth side; ~**vertrag** growth plan; ~**werte** growth stocks; **in ~werte umsteigen** to switch into growth stocks; ~**zeit** growing time; **beschleunigtes ~zentrum** accelerated growth center *(US)* (centre, *Br.*); ~**ziel** growth target; ~**zustand** vegetative stage.
Wachtafel log board *(Br.)*.
Wächter watch, watchman, guard, guardsman, *(Museum)* keeper, attendant;
~ **des öffentlichen Interesses** guardian of the public interest.
Wachtmeister *(Gericht)* tipster, court marshal *(US)*.
Wach|träume haben to daydream; ~**turm** observation tower, watchtower; ~**vergehen,** ~**verfehlung** neglect of duty while on guard; ~**wechsel** watch change.
Wackelkontakt *(el.)* tottering contact, loose connection.
wackeln to wobble, to shake, *(Regierung)* to totter.
wacker upright, honest, brave;
sich ~ halten to hold one's ground.
wack[e]lig shaky, unsteady, *(Auto)* rattly, ramshackle, *(Zaun)* loose;

nach einer langen Krankheit ziemlich ~ sein to be still a bit wobbly after a long illness;
~er alter Mann tottery old man; **~e Regierung** tottering government; **~er Stuhl** wobbly chair; **~es Unternehmen** shaky business.
Waffe weapon, persuader *(sl.)*;
mit vorgehaltener ~ at gunpoint;
blanke ~ cold steel; **geladene ~** loaded arm;
~ entladen to unload a firearm; **~ auf j. richten** to point a gun at s. o.; **als strategische ~ völlig nutzlos sein** to give zero value as a strategic weapon.
Waffen arms, weapons, ordnance;
konventionelle ~ conventional weapons; **primitive ~** primitive weapons; **stumpfe ~** *(fig.)* arms of courtesy; **vollautomatische ~** robot;
~ der Polizei police weapons; **~ mit maßgerecht begrenztem Wirkungskreis** tailored-effect weapons;
nach ~ abtasten to prowl *(sl.)*; **zu den ~ eilen** to fly to arms; **zu den ~ greifen** to be up in arms; **~ an ein Land liefern** to supply a country with arms; **~ niederlegen** to lay down one's arms, to ground arms; **Volk zu den ~ rufen** to call a people to arms; **j. mit seinen eigenen ~ schlagen** to hoist s. o. with his own petard, to beat s. o. at his own game; **~ tragen** to go armed, to carry arms; **~ wegwerfen** to abandon one's arms;
~abkommen arms agreement; **~amt** Ordnance Department *(US)*; **~ansammlung** arms buildup; **~appell** arms inspection; **~ausfuhr** export of arms; **~ausfuhrverbot** arms embargo; **~beschaffung** arms procurement; **unerlaubter ~besitz** unauthorized possession of weapons; **~depot** arms depot, arsenal; **~einfuhr** arms import; **~embargo** arms embargo; **~entwicklung** weapons development; **~etat** weapons budget; **~export** arms export; **~fabrik** armament plant, arsenal; **~fabrikant** armament maker.
waffenfähig fit to carry arms;
~ sein to bear arms.
Waffen|gebrauch use of arms; **~gefährte** comrade- (brother-) in-arms, companion at arms; **~geschäft** arms business (selling process); **ins internationale ~geschäft einsteigen** to move into the international arms market; **~gewalt** force of arms; **mit ~gewalt** with arms; **seinen Anspruch mit ~gewalt vertreten** to throw one's sword into the scale; **~handel** gun running, traffic (trade) in arms; **~händler** gun runner; **~handwerk** war (military) profession; **~handwerk erlernen** to learn the craft of war; **~hersteller** arms manufacturer; **~kammer** armo(u)ry; **~kontrollvereinbarung** arms control agreement; **~lager** arsenal, weapon stock, store of arms; **~lieferung** arms delivery (shipment); **~meldepflicht** gun registration; **~moratorium** arms moratorium; **~offizier** ordnance officer; **~produktion** weapons production; **~ruhe** truce, ceasefire, suspension of hostilities; **~schein** firearms certificate *(Br.)*, gun licence, licence to carry firearms; **~schmuggel** gunrunning; **~schmuggler** arms smuggler, gunrunner; **~schule** special service school; **~stillstand** armistice, cessation (suspension) of hostilities, ceasefire, truce; **über einen ~stillstand verhandeln** to hold a parley.
Waffenstillstands|abkommen armistice (ceasefire) agreement; **~abkommen einhalten** to preserve ceasefire; **~angebot** truce offer; **~bedingungen** armistice terms; **~beschluß** ceasefire resolution; **~delegation** truce delegation; **~kommission** armistice commission; **~konferenz** ceasefire conference; **~linie** ceasefire lines; **~tag** Remembrance Day; **~vereinbarungen** ceasefire arrangements; **~verhandlungen** negotiations for an armistice, armistice negotiations, parley; **~verhandlungen führen** to hold a parley; **~verletzung** ceasefire violation.
Waffen|system weapons system, weaponry; **~transporte** arms shipments; **~verkäufe** arms sales.
Wagen carriage, vehicle, conveyance, *(Auto)* car, automobile *(US)*, motorcar *(Br.)*, auto *(US)*, *(Bahn)* carriage, car, wag(g)on, *(Kutsche)* coach, *(Möbel)* van, *(Schreibmaschine)* carriage, *(Taxe)* taxi, cab;
frei auf den ~ free on the wag(g)on, free on truck *(Br.)*;
durchgehender ~ through carriage; **eigener ~** private car; **firmeneigener ~** company car; **frisierter ~** tuned (souped) car, hot rod *(US sl.)*; **gebrauchter ~** secondhand car; **wenig gefahrener ~** low-mil(e)age car; **in Zahlung genommener ~** traded-in car; **geschlossener ~** limousine, sedan *(US)*, coach *(US)*; **klimatisierter ~** air-conditioned car; **leichter ~** bulk wag(g)on; **letzter ~** *(Bahn)* end carriage; **mittelstarker ~** medium-powered car; **offener ~** open carriage, platform car, *(Auto)* roadster; **schneller ~** soup job *(sl.)*; **wirtschaftlicher ~** economy-sized car; **zugelassener ~** licensed car; **zweiräderiger ~** two-wheeled wag(g)on;
~ für leitende Angestellte executive-class car; **~ für gehobene Ansprüche** quality car; **~ mit Frontantrieb** front-wheel-drive car; **~ mit Heckmotor** rear-engine car; **~ zweiter Klasse** second-class carriage; **~ der Linie 17** route 17 car; **~ der Mittelklasse** intermediate-sized car; **~ der gehobenen Mittelklasse** car of the upper middle price range; **~ mit Musikkapelle** bandwag(g)on; **geschlossener ~ mit versenkbarem Verdeck** drophead coupé; **~ der Verkehrswacht** scout car *(Br.)*;
schleudernden ~ abfangen to pull a car out of a skid; **~ abschleppen** to pick up a car; **~ ins Ziel bringen** to bring a car home to the finish; **j. an den ~ fahren** to thwart s. one's plans, *(beleidigen)* to be offensive to s. o.; **seinen eigenen ~ fahren** to drive one's own car, to have a car of one's own; **~ vorsichtig nach Hause fahren** to nurse a car home; **seinen ~ kommen lassen** to order one's car round; **j. im ~ mitnehmen** to give s. o. a lift; **~ montieren** to assemble a motor car; **~ wieder in Betrieb nehmen** to take a car out of storage; **~ aus dem Dreck ziehen** to get the car out of a ditch.
wagen to venture, to [take the] risk, to hazard, to attempt;
sich aus dem Haus ~ to venture out of doors; **sich an die Herausgabe einer Zeitschrift ~** to try one's hand at editing a magazine.
wägen, seine Worte sorgfältig to weigh one's words.
Wagen|abteil compartment; **~achse** car axle; **~achskilometer** mil(e)age covered; **~aufbau** car body, coachwork; **~aufsatz** *(LKW)* superstructure; **~bauer** cartwright, coachmaker, carriage (van) builder; **~bedarf** truck requirements; **~besitzer** car owner; **~bremse** car brake, *(Bahn)* wag(g)on lock; **Gepäck auf dem ~dach unterbringen** to put the luggage at the (on) top of the car; **~depot** car pound, carpool *(US)*; **~dienst** car service; **~fähre** drive-on ferry; **~fahrt unternehmen** to go for a ride, to joy-ride; **~führer** *(Straßenbahn)* motorman; **~geld** *(Bahn)* truckage; **~gestell** chassis; **~halle** *(Auto)* garage, *(Straßenbahn)* train shed *(Br.)*, car shed *(US)*; **~haltung** keeping a car; **~hebebühne** lifting platform; **~heber** car (lifting) jack; **fahrbarer ~heber** garage trolley jack; **~heizung** car heating; **~klasse** class of vehicle, *(Bahn)* class; **~knappheit, ~mangel** *(Bahn)* shortage of rolling stock, carriage shortage; **~kolonne** string (column, queue) of cars, *(Verpflegung)* supply column; **~ladeschein** manifest; **~ladung** cart, cart (coach) load, wag(g)onload, carload lot *(US)*; **gemischte ~ladung** mixed carload *(US)*; **ganze ~ladungen von Plunder** wag(g)onloads of rubbish; **~ladungsgut** raw goods, carload freight *(US)*; **~ladungstarif** carload rate *(US)*; **~lampe** carriage lamp; **~meister** wag(g)on master; **~miete** car rental; **~nummer** car (registration) number; **~papiere** *(Auto)* driving papers, registration slip; **~park** *(Bahn)* rolling stock, *(Firma)* fleet of cars (motorcars), fleet of vehicles, automobile pool, delivery equipment, *(Taxiunternehmen)* fleet of taxis; **~pferd** cart horse; **~pflege** care of a car, car service *(US)*; **~plane** canvas, tarpaulin, awning; **~rad** wag(g)on wheel; **~remise** coach house; **~rückgabe** return of a car; **~rücklauf** *(Schreibmaschine)* carriage return; **~schuppen** car shed, coach house, *(Straßenbahn)* train *(Br.)* (car, *US*) shed, *(Omnibusse)* garage; **~spur** trace, rut; **~standgeld** *(Bahn)* demurrage, truckage; **~tritt** footplate; **~typ** car type; **~unterstand** carport *(US)*; **~verdeck** top, hood *(Br.)*; **~verleiher** jobmaster *(Br.)*; **~vermietung** car hire *(Br.)*, rent-a-car *(US)*; **~vermietung für Selbstfahrer** drive-yourself service; **~waschanlage** car-wash (washing) bay; **~wechsel** change of carriage.
wagenweise by cartloads.
Waggon wag(g)on, [railway] carriage, railway car *(Br.)*, railroad car *(US)*, *(Güter)* goods van (vehicle) *(Br.)*, freight car *(US)*, boxcar *(US)*, box wag(g)on *(Br.)*;
ab ~ ex wag(g)on; **frei ~** free on rail; **im ~ transportierbar** wag(g)onable;
abgefertigte ~s cars handled *(US)*; **beim Fahren abgehängter ~** slip carriage (coach); **ausrangierter ~** defective car; **beladene ~s** cars loaded *(US)*, loaded wag(g)ons *(Br.)*; **eigener ~** home car, *(Spediteur)* owned car *(US)*; **außerhalb eingesetzter ~** off line car *(US)*; **im Nahverkehr eingesetzter ~** commuter car *(US)*; **einsatzbereiter ~** serviceable car *(US)*; **nicht einsatzfähiger ~** unserviceable car *(US)*; **erster ~** front carriage; **erster Klasse ~** first-class railway carriage; **gedeckter (geschlossener) ~** freight car *(US)*, covered wag(g)on *(Br.)*, boxcar *(US)*, box wag(g)on *(Br.)*; **heizbarer ~** heater car; **leerer ~** idler, deadhead; **offener ~** open railway car *(Br.)*, truck *(Br.)*, freight car *(US)*, flat car *(US)*, platform car *(US)*; **auf Kilometerbasis vermieteter ~** mil(e)age car *(US)*; **vorbestellter ~** private line car *(US)*;
~ einer anderen Gesellschaft foreign car *(US)*; **~ ohne Platform** blind car; **~ für Stückgutladungen** package car *(US)*;

~ **abkuppeln** to detach a coach *(Br.)* (car, *US*) from a train; **zwei ~s aneinanderkuppeln** to couple two railway coaches *(Br.)*; ~ **anhängen** to hitch a carriage *(Br.)* (car, *US*) onto the train; **zusätzliche ~s anhängen** to put on more coaches *(Br.)* (cars, *US*); ~ **ausladen** to unload a wag(g)on (freight car, *US*); ~ **beladen** to stow (load on) a wag(g)on, to fill a truck *(Br.)*; **~s stellen** to supply cars *(US)*; ~ **vollstopfen** to pack a carriage with passengers;

~auftrag carload order *(US)*; **~bau** car building *(US)*; **~bedarf** truck requirements *(Br.)*; **~beförderung** wag(g)onage; **~bestand** wag(g)on stock, rolling stock; **gesamter ~bestand** car ownership *(US)*; **~depot** car depot; **~fabrik** car builders, railcar plant *(US)*; **~fracht** bulk (carload, *US*) freight (rate); **~frachtsatz** bulk (carload, *US*) freight (rate), flatcar rate *(US)*; **~gestellung** car supply *(US)*, truck supply *(Br.)*; **~heizung** heated car service; **~industrie** railroad industry *(US)*; **~kipper** car tipper; **~knappheit** car shortage *(US)*.

Waggonladung bulk cargo, load of a wag(g)on *(Br.)*, truckload *(Br.)*, wag(g)onload *(Br.)*, wag(g)on lot *(Br.)*, carload (carlot) shipment *(US)*, carloading *(US)*, carload lot *(US)*, trainload, carload *(US)* (carlot) shipment;

in ~en versandt shipped by truckloads *(Br.)* (carloads, *US*); **gemeinsame ~** consolidated carload freight *(US)*; **volle ~** full truckload *(Br.)*;

Frachtsätze für ~en zur Anwendung bringen to handle a shipment as a truckload *(Br.)* (carload, *US*); **in ~en versenden** to ship in carlots *(US)* (carloads, *US*, truckloads, *Br.*).

Waggonladungs|fracht carload freight *(US)*, truckload freight *(Br.)*; **~minimum** carload amount *(US)*; **~satz** carload rate *(US)*, truckload rate *(Br.)*.

Waggon|liegegelder car service *(US)*, demurrage [charges]; **~miete** rail car leasing *(US)*; **~nummer** track number *(Br.)*, car number *(US)*; **~park** car equipment; **gesamter ~park** cars on line *(US)*; **~rücklauf** carriage return *(Br.)*; **~sendung** carloading *(US)*, carlot shipment *(US)*, truckload *(Br.)*; **~standgeld** demurrage [charges], car service *(US)*; **~tarif** carlot (carload, *US*, truckload, *Br.*) rate; **~verschiebung** shunting of a wag(g)on.

waggonweise versandt shipped in wag(g)onloads (carloads, *US*), shipped by truckloads *(Br.)*.

Wagnis venture, risk, hazard, enterprise, throw;

gemeinsames ~ joint venture;

~ **eingehen** to run a risk; **sich auf kein ~ einlassen** to take no risks;

teilweise ~abgabe *(Rückversicherungsgeschäft)* cession; **~zuschlag** bonus risk.

Wahl election, returning, poll, ballot, voting, *(Alternative)* alternative, *(Auswahl)* selection, choice, *(Güteklasse)* quality, grade, option, *(Parlament)* election, returning, poll, ballot, *(Wahlstimme)* vote, voting;

am Vorabend der ~ on election eve; **aus freier ~** of one's own choice; **durch ~ bestimmt** elective; **im Hinblick auf die ~en** with an eye on the elections; **nach ~** at one's option; **nach Käufers ~** optional with the buyer; **nach ~ des Verkäufers** seller's option; **von Bedeutung für die ~en** electorally significant; **zweiter ~** second-grade;

allgemeine ~en general elections; **angefochtene ~** contested *(US)* (disputed) election; **anstehende (bevorstehende) ~** elections in the offing; **aufregende ~** cliffhanger election *(sl.)*; **direkte ~** direct election (nomination, voting); **einstimmige ~** solid vote; **engere ~** short list, second (final, additional) ballot; **für ungültig erklärte ~** invalidated election; **erste ~** prime goods, *(Qualität)* first quality; **freie ~** free choice, option; **freie ~en** free elections; **geheime ~** ballot, voting by ballot, secret vote; **knapp gewonnene ~** squeeze-through election; **indirekte ~** indirect election; **knappe ~** close election; **konkurrenzlose ~** unopposed return; **örtliche ~** local option, primary *(US)*; **übliche ~** regular election; **hart umstrittene ~** closely contested election; **unmittelbare ~** direct vote; **unregelmäßige ~** irregular return; **öffentlich vorgenommene ~** open voting, vote by open ballot; **zweite ~** irregulars, *(Waren)* seconds;

freie ~ des Arbeitsplatzes free movement of labo(u)r; **~en zum Aufsichtsrat** board election; **~ ohne Gegenkandidaten** uncontested election; **~ durch Handaufheben** vote by show of hands; **~ des Lieferortes** right to choose the place of delivery; **~ mit Namensaufruf** vote by roll-call; **~en zum Parlament** parliamentary elections; **~en in der Provinz** provincial elections; **~ durch Wahlmänner** election by electors; **~ des richtigen Zeitpunkts** timing; **~ durch Zuruf** vote by acclamation;

gleichzeitig auf Bundes- und Landesebene ~en abhalten to hold simultaneous elections on state and national level; **~en unter internationaler Aufsicht abhalten** to hold elections under international supervision; **in geheimer ~ abstimmen** to vote by ballot; **Gültigkeit einer ~ anfechten** to challenge (question, contest, *US*) an election; **allgemeine ~en ansetzen** to call a general election; **von der ~ ausschließen** to disfranchise; **~en ausschreiben** to call a new election, to go to the country *(Br.)*; **sich bei der ~ in etwa auszahlen** to bring some electoral dividends; **~ beeinflussen** to sway the elections; **~ entscheidend beeinflussen** to turn an election; **über die ~en berichten** to cover the elections; **Gültigkeit einer ~ bestreiten** to deny the validity of an election; **~ durchführen** to hold an election; **~ für ungültig erklären** to declare an election void, to invalidate an election, to cancel a vote; **vorschriftswidrige ~ für ungültig erklären** to void an irregular election; **~ eröffnen** to open the ballot; **25% der Stimmen bei der ~ erzielen** to poll as much as 25% in an election; **zu Veränderungen bei ~en führen** to swing elections; **freie ~ ärztlicher Leistungen garantieren** to guarantee a free choice among all the medical services available; **zur ~ gehen (schreiten)** to go to the poll, to flock to the polls; **~ knapp gewinnen** to win an election with a narrow margin; **freie ~ haben** to have freedom of choice; **keine ~ haben** to have no option (alternative, choice); **siegreich aus einer ~ hervorgehen** to carry an election; **bei einer ~ kandidieren** to stand for (run in) an election; **in die engere ~ kommen** to be put on the short list; **freie ~ lassen** to give the refusal; **bei der ~ schlagen** to outpoll; **nicht dem Druck der öffentlichen Meinung kurz vor den ~en ausgesetzt sein** to be free of election-eve pressure; **jem. bei der ~ behilflich sein** to play the electoral hand for s. o.; **in der ~ der Mittel nicht zimperlich sein** not to be nice about the means; **zur ~ von jem. schreiten** to proceed to elect s. o.; **zur engeren ~ stehen** to be on the short list; **sich zu einer ~ stellen** *(Abgeordneter)* to stand for parliament (a constituency); **seine ~ treffen** to make one's option (choice); **sorgfältige ~ treffen** to make a careful choice; **in einer ~ unterliegen** to be defeated in an election; **Nachprüfung der ~ verlangen** to demand a scrutiny (recount); **~en verlieren** to lose the elections; **~ vornehmen** to take a vote; **j. zur ~ vorschlagen** to nominate s. o. as a candidate; **j. zur ~ als Vizepräsidenten vorschlagen** to draft s. o. as vice-presidential candidate; **zur ~ zulassen** to enfranchise;

~abkommen electoral cartel (pact, arrangement); **~abmachungen** electoral arrangements; **~agent** election (electioneering, polling) agent, electioneer; **~agitation** electioneering; **~agitator** electioneerer; **~akt** voting, polling, election, elective act; **~akten** election returns, tally sheet *(US)*; **~alter** voting (legal) age; **~alternative** election option; **~amt** elective office.

Wählamt automatic telephone exchange.

Wahl|amtsleiter registrar of voters, returning officer *(Br.)*; **~analyse** analysis of a vote; **~anfechter** contestant of election returns; **~anfechtung** election contest *(US)* (petition), petition against a return.

Wählapparat dialling apparatus.

Wahl|aufruf election address, manifest; **~auseinandersetzung** electoral showdown; **~ausgang** result of the elections; **~ausgang entscheidend beeinflussen** to turn an election; **~auslösungsmoment** election trigger; **~ausschreibung** calling an election, going to the country *(Br.)*, writ *(Br.)*; **~ausschuß** election (electoral) committee, returning board *(US)*; **~aussichten** elective (electoral, election) chances (prospects); **~aussichten untersuchen** to canvass the prospective vote in an election; **~ausweis** registration card; **~auswertung** interpretation of election returns.

wählbar eligible, pollable, votable;

nicht ~ noneligible, ineligible.

Wählbarkeit eligibility.

Wählbarkeitsvoraussetzungen eligibility requirements.

Wahl|beamter elector official; **~beauftragter** election commissioner; **~beeinflussung** electoral corruption, vote rigging; **aus ~beeinflussungsgründen handeln** to play to the voting galleries; **~behinderung** obstruction of polling; **~beisitzer** polling clerk, returning officer *(Br.)*; **~beitrag** assessment *(US)*, campaign expenses; **~bekanntmachung** election notice.

wahlberechtigt entitled to vote, pollable, votable, constituent, *(wählbar)* elective, eligible [for election];

nicht ~ voteless; **passiv ~** elegible for election;

~e Bevölkerung constituent population.

Wahlberechtigte|r qualified voter (elector), constituent, legal voter, freeman;

alle ~n erfassen to poll all adult citizens.

Wahl|berechtigung franchise, qualification for election, eligibility of voting, right to vote; **amtlicher ~bericht** election returns;

~**beschwerde** election petition *(Br.)* (contest, *US*); ~**bestechung** bribery at elections, electoral corruption, corrupt practices.

Wahlbeteiligung poll, votes registered, electoral (votes) participation, percentage of voting, turnout *(fam.)*, *(einzelner)* voting;
was die ~ angeht in terms of vote turnout;
geringe (schlechte) ~ small poll; **hohe (starke) ~** heavy poll.

Wahl|betrieb *(Telefon)* dial system; ~**betrug** vote manipulation, electoral practices.

Wahlbezirk polling (electoral) district, electoral division (area), election precinct (district, *US*), electorate, [parliamentary] borough *(Br.)*, constituency *(Br.)*, congressional (senatorial) district *(US)*;
kommunaler ~ ward; **städtischer ~** borough, city ward *(Br.)*; **umstrittener ~** marginal constituency *(Br.)*;
~ mit knapper Stimmenmehrheit marginal constituency *(Br.)*; **zuständiger ~ eines Wählers** legal voting residence;
~ bearbeiten to canvass an electorate; **in neue ~e einteilen** to redistrict *(US)*; **sich um seinen ~ kümmern** to nurse one's constituency, to look after one's fence *(US)*.

Wahl|bezirksabgrenzung, manipulierte gerrymandering; ~**bonbon** electioneering sweeteners; ~**boykott** boycott of the elections; ~**bündnis** electoral (election) alliance, electoral pact; ~**bündnispartner** electoral ally; ~**büro** elective office; ~**chancen** elective (electoral, *US*) chances; ~**dauer** voting hours; ~**einspruch** objection to elections, election contest *(US)* (petition, *US*).

Wählen polling, poll, election, voting;
zum ~ gehen to go to the polls, to poll.

wählen to go to the polls, to poll, to record one's vote, to elect, *(abstimmen)* to vote, *(auswählen)* to choose, to select, to opt, to pick out, *(Telefon)* to dial;
j. ~ to vote s. o.; **Abgeordneten ~** to return a member of parliament; **für ein Amt ~** to elect for (to) an office; **j. zum Anführer ~** to choose s. o. for their leader; **neuen Aufsichtsrat ~** to elect a new board; **durch Aufstehen ~** to vote by rising to one's feet; **einstimmig ~** to vote unanimously; **falsch ~** to dial a wrong number; **gut ~** to make a good choice; **durch Handaufheben ~** to vote by show of hands; **hintereinander ~** to vote in an uninterrupted sequence; **auf vier Jahre ~** to elect for a term of four years; **Kandidatenliste ~** to vote the straight ticket; **nicht lange ~** not to pick and choose; **liberal ~** to go liberal; **Liste ~** to vote a ticket; **aus ihrer Mitte ~** to elect from among themselves; **bei der Nachwahl einen liberalen Kandidaten ~** to go liberal at the by-election; **nicht ~** to abstain from voting; **Nummer ~** *(Telefon)* to dial a number; **ins Parlament ~** to return to Parliament; **zum Präsidenten ~** to elect s. o. to be president, *(Versammlung)* to vote into the chair; **j. mit Stimmenmehrheit ~** to return s. o. by a majority of votes; **kleineres Übel ~** to choose the lesser evil; **zum Vorsitzenden ~** to move (vote) into the chair, to elect as chairman; **seinen Wohnsitz ~** to elect domicile at a place, to choose (elect) one's residence; **seine Worte sorgfältig ~** to pick one's words carefully.

Wahlenthaltung abstention from voting.

wahlentscheidende Vereinbarung vote-switching arrangement.

Wähler voter, vote, elector, constituent, *(Telefon)* selector;
berechtigter ~ qualified elector; **prosaisch eingestellter ~** bread-and-butter voter; **eingetragener ~** registered voter, registered qualified elector *(US)*, legally qualified voter; **gemeindesteuerpflichtiger ~** scot and lot voter; **ländlicher ~** agricultural voter; **nicht parteigebundener ~** mobile voter; **parteiloser ~** floating voter, floater, float *(US)*; **wehrdienstleistender ~** service voter *(Br.)*; **nicht im Wahlkreis wohnender ~** outvoter;
~ bearbeiten to canvass for votes; **~ beeinflussen** to manipulate voters; **unentschiedene ~ bei umkämpften Entscheidungen beeinflussen** to cast the swing vote on split decisions; **~ an die Wahlurne bringen** to get out the vote; **sich erst am Wahltag als ~ registrieren lassen** to register on election day itself;
~**anlage** *(Telefon)* selector plant; **vorübergehende** ~**ansiedlung** colonization *(US)*; **schwankender** ~**anteil** floating vote; ~**ausschuß** electoral body; ~**befragung** election survey; ~**bescheinigung** precept.

wählerbewußt vote-conscious.

Wähler|durchschnitt, repräsentativer cross-section of electors; ~**einrichtung** *(tel.)* dial instrument.

Wahlerfolg electoral performance.

Wahlergebnis election results (returns), vote, outcome of the elections;
angefochtenes ~ contested *(US)* (disputed) election; **knappes ~** narrow voting margin, close election;
~ anfechten to dispute (contest, *US*) an election; **~ bekanntgeben** to declare the poll (results of an election), to return; **~ manipulieren (verfälschen)** to manipulate election returns; **~ überprüfen** to check (scrutinize) election returns; ~**se verfälschen** to manipulate election returns, to doctor election results; **Nachprüfung der ~se verlangen** to demand a scrutiny (recount); **~ veröffentlichen** to return the result of the poll.

Wähler|gefolgschaft electoral following; **bei der nächsten Wahl die freie ~gemeinschaft wählen** to vote for the independents next election; ~**gewohnheiten** voting habits (instincts); ~**gruppe** group of voters; ~**identifizierungsproblem** voter-recognition problem; ~**initiative** initiative.

wählerisch particular, fastidious, dainty, choosy, squeamish, nice, finical, kid-glove;
~ sein to pick and choose, to be choosy; **in der Auswahl seiner Freunde äußerst ~ sein** to be particular as regards one's choice of friends.

Wählerkollegium electoral college *(US)*.

Wahlerlaubnisschein precept.

Wählerliste [electoral] list, registration list, list (registrar) of voters, voting (check, *US*) list, poll-[book], parliamentary (electoral) register;
in die ~ eintragen to poll; **sich in die ~ eintragen** to register o. s. [on the voting list], to poll; **~ nachprüfen** to scrutinize (recount) an electoral list; **in der ~ eingetragen sein** to be registered as an elector.

Wähler|meinung verdict of the electors; ~**nummer** *(tel.)* telephone digit; ~**reaktion** voter reaction; ~**registrierung** voting (voter) registration; ~**schaft** electorate, constituency, electoral panel, constituent body, body of voters; **nicht parteigebundene ~schaft** floating vote, floaters; **~schaft korrumpieren** to corrupt the electorate; ~**scheibe** *(tel.)* dial disk, fingerplate; ~**schwund** electoral rot; ~**stamm** electoral clientele; **nicht feststehende ~stimme** floating vote; **~stimmen erhalten** to poll; ~**stimmung** sentiment of electors, voter sentiment; ~**sucher** *(tel.)* allotter; **~umschwung herbeiführen** to swing votes; ~**unterstützung** electoral support; ~**vereinigung** voters' (constituency) association; ~**verhalten** voting behavio(u)r; ~**versammlung** election meeting, nominating convention; ~**verzeichnis** registrar of voters, electoral register, voter registration roll; **nicht den ~willen repräsentierend** *(pol.)* unrepresentative.

Wahlfach elective (optional, special, facultative) subject, elective *(US)*, optional *(US)*.

wahlfähig entitled to vote, *(wählbar)* eligible;
nicht ~ ineligible;
~ sein to be eligible for election;
~**es Alter** voting age; **in ~em Alter sein** to be eligible to vote.

Wahlfähigkeit franchise, *(Wählbarkeit)* eligibility.

Wahlfälschung vote manipulation.

Wahlfeldzug electoral (election, *US*) campaign, canvass;
aufregender ~ rousing campaign; **aussichtsloser ~** shoestring campaign; **mit kleinen Beträgen finanzierter ~** chickenfeed campaign;
~ der Opposition opposition campaign;
~ beginnen to start campaigning; **~ durchführen** to electioneer, to campaign; **Redner in einem ~ einsetzen** to put an orator in requisition in a political campaign; **~ gegen j. führen** to campaign against s. o.; **~ leiten** to conduct a campaign; **~ vorbereiten** to build up a campaign.

Wahlfeldzugs|ausschuß campaign committee; ~**diskussion** campaign debate; ~**gelder** campaign finances; ~**kosten** campaign debts; ~**leiter** campaign manager; **für ~zwecke** for political campaign use.

Wahl|ferien election recess; ~**feststellungen** *(Gericht)* alternative findings; ~**fonds** campaign (caucus, *US*) fund, barrel *(US)*.

wahlfrei facultative, *(Schule)* optional, elective *(US)*.

Wahlfreiheit free voting.

Wahlgang polling, ballot, proxy *(US)*;
im ersten ~ in (on) the first ballot;
zweiter ~ second voting;
zum zweiten ~ schreiten to hold a second ballot.

Wahl|geheimnis secrecy of the vote (ballot); ~**gelder** campaign finances; ~**gerichtsstand** concurrent jurisdiction; ~**geschäft** voting business; ~**geschenke** campaign gifts, vote-winning goodies, electoral blessings; ~**gesetz** election law, Representation of the People Act *(Br.)*; ~**gewinne** balloting rewards; ~**gremium** electoral body; ~**handlung** poll, vote, elective act; ~**heimat** country of one's adoption, adopted country; ~**helfer** poller, precinct worker *(US)*; ~**hilfe** support in an election;

~**interessen** electoral concerns; ~**jahr** election year; ~**kabine** ballot box, polling booth; ~**kampagne** election campaign, campaign trail, electioneering.

Wahlkampf electoral (election, elective, *US*, electioneering, political) campaign, electoral, election fight, contest *(Br.)*, run *(US)*; **von drei Parteien bestrittener** ~ three-cornered contest; **rückhaltsloser** ~ open campaigning;
~ **für die Präsidentschaft** presidential campaign;
Redner in einem ~ **einsetzen** to put an orator in requisition in a political campaign; ~ **führen** to wage a campaign, to electioneer; **Partei in den** ~ **führen** to lead a party into the election campaign; **in einem** ~ **unterliegen** to be defeated at an election; ~ **vorbereiten** to plan a campaign;
~**argumente** campaign arguments; ~**ausgaben** campaign spending; ~**beauftragter** election agent; ~**beginn** campaign start; ~**beteiligter** campaign partner; ~**finanzierung** financing of a campaign, campaign financing; ~**fonds** campaign chest (fund), election fund, barrel *(US)*; ~**gelder** campaign money; ~**geschenke** campaign gifts, vote-winning goodies; ~**geschenkkorb** campaign basket; ~**hilfe** campaign aid; ~**kasse** campaign coffer; ~**kosten** election expenses; **unlautere** ~**methoden** campaign abuses; ~**organisation** campaign organization; ~**reise** whistle stop tour *(US)*; ~**reise durchführen** to make a canvass of a constituency; ~**schatulle** campaign chest; ~**schriften** campaign documents; ~**schulden** campaign debts; ~**slogan** rallying (election, battle) cry; ~**spende** political campaign contribution; ~**technik** politicking *(US)*; ~**thema** election issue; ~**transparent** campaign banner; ~**trubel** election push; ~**versprechen** campaign pledge; ~**vorbereitungen treffen** to gear up for election campaign; ~**zeiten** campaign time; **für** ~**zwecke** for political campaign use.

Wahlkandidat [parliamentary] candidate;
sich als ~ **bewerben** to figure for an election; ~ **bleiben** to remain on the ballot; **sich als** ~ **aufstellen lassen** to run for an election; **als** ~**en vorschlagen** to put up for an election.

Wahl|kandidatenaufstellung open primary *(US)*; ~**karte** voting ticket, *(Stimmschein)* ballot; ~**kollegium** electoral college *(US)*; ~**komitee** election (electoral) committee, board of elections, returning board; ~**kommissar** registrar of votes, voting steward, returning officer *(Br.)*; ~**konsul** honorary (elective) consul; ~**kontingent** electoral quota; ~**kontrolle** vote checking; ~**körperschaft** elective (constituent) body, body of electors; ~**korruption** bribery at election.

Wahlkreis constituency *(Br.)*, constituency (election) district, election precinct *(US)*, electoral division (district), parliamentary (returning) borough *(Br.)*, electorate, representative district *(US)*;
beeinflußter ~ pocket borough *(Br.)*; **ländlicher** ~ agricultural constituency; **städtischer** ~ parliamentary borough *(Br.)*; **vernachlässigter** ~ rotten borough *(Br.)*;
~ **mit knapper Mehrheit** marginal constituency;
~ **bearbeiten** to canvass an electorate; **sich um einen** ~ **bewerben** to get in for a constituency *(Br.)*; ~ **kontrollieren** to pocket a borough *(Br.)*; **sich um seinen** ~ **kümmern** to nurse one's constituency; ~ **vertreten** to sit for (represent) a constituency;
~**änderung** constituency revision; ~**apparat** constituency organization; ~**arbeiten** constituency work, working a constituency; ~**einteilung** dividing a state in election divisions, *(betrügerisch)* gerrymandering; ~**ergebnis** constituency poll; **ständige** ~**kommission** Permanent Boundary Commission *(Br.)*; ~**leiter** precinct captain *(US)*; ~**revision** constituency revision; ~**schiebungen vornehmen** to gerrymander; **willkürliches** ~**system** gerrymandered electoral system; ~**verpflichtungen** constituency duties.

Wahl|kugel ballot; **schwarze** ~**kugel** blackball; ~**leiter** voting steward, returning officer *(Br.)*.

Wahlliste list of voters (electors), electoral list (register), pollbook, polling list, ticket *(US)*, slate *(US)*;
abgeänderte ~ mutilated ballot;
~ **durchsprechen** to caucus; **sich in die** ~ **eintragen** to register o. s.; **j. auf die** ~ **setzen** to put s. o. on the slip; ~ **überprüfen** to scrutinize an electoral list; **zwei** ~**n miteinander verbinden** to combine two electoral lists.

Wahl|listenprüfer registrar of voters, revising barrister; ~**lokal** ward room, polling station (place), poll *(US)*; **bei Eröffnung der** ~**lokale** at the opening of the poll; ~**lokomotive** vote catcher (getter).

wahllos indiscriminate, indiscriminating, at random;
~ **herausgreifen** to choose at random.

Wahl|mache electioneering manoeuvre, claptrap; ~**machenschaften** electoral practices; ~**macher** vote manipulator, [ward] heeler *(US)*; ~**manifest** manifest (election) ticket; ~**manipulation** manipulation of an election; ~**mann** delegate, constituent, elector *(US)*; ~**männerkollegium** electoral college *(US)*; ~**männerstimme** electoral count *(US)*; ~**männerversammlung** primary election *(US)*, convention; ~**manöver** electioneering manoeuvre, gerrymandering; ~**maschine** voting machine; ~**methode**, ~**modus** mode of election; ~**monarchie** elective monarchy; ~**monat** month of electioneering; ~**müdigkeit** electoral apathy; **Ergebnis der** ~**müdigkeit sein** to reflect apathy among the voters.

wahlmündig werden to come of voting age.

Wahl|mündigkeit coming of voting age; ~**niederlage** election (electoral) defeat; ~**niederlage erleiden** to be defeated (meet with a defeat) at the polls; ~**nötigung** electoral duress; ~**organ** electoral body; ~**ort** polling place (station), poll *(US)*; ~**parole** rallying (banner) cry, catchphrase; ~**periode** election period, term of office; ~**periode des Senats** senatorial term; **sich für eine dritte** ~**periode zur Verfügung stellen** to run for a third term; ~**pflicht** electoral duty; ~**pflicht bei Kommunalwahlen** compulsory voting in local elections.

wahlpflichtig of voting age.

Wahl|plakat election poster (placard); ~**plattform** platform.

wahlpolitische Maßnahmen electoral politics.

Wahl|praktiken electoral practices; **rechtswidrige** ~**praktiken** illegal practices *(Br.)*; ~**prognose** electing forecasting; ~**programm** election (electioneering) program(me), election manifesto, election plan, [campaign] platform *(US)*, ticket *(US)*, *(Abgeordnete)* position paper; ~**proklamation** election manifesto; ~**propaganda** electioneering propaganda, canvassing, stump *(US)*; ~**propaganda treiben** to beat the election drums, to electioneer, to campaign, to stump *(US)*; ~**protest** petition against the return *(Br.)*, election petition *(Br.)*, election contest *(US)*; ~**protokoll** election returns; ~**protokollführer** polling clerk; ~**prüfer** supervisor (judge, *US*) of election, election auditor (commissioner, *US*), scrutineer; ~**prüfung** canvass, verification of powers, scrutiny of an electoral list; ~**prüfungsausschuß** election (electoral) committee; ~**prüfungsbeamte** revising assessors *(Br.)*; ~**quotient** election quotient, electoral ratio; ~**raum** polling station (place).

Wahlrecht right of choice, suffrage, right of vote, privilege of voting, elective franchise *(US)*, *(bezüglich Auszahlungsmodalität)* option, optional right, *(Versicherung)* right of change;
aktives ~ franchise; **allgemeines** ~ poll, universal suffrage, parliamentary (elective) franchise; **ausgeübtes** ~ *(Einkommensteuer)* election made; **beschränktes** ~ restricted suffrage; **passives** ~ eligibility;
~ **beim Empfang der Versicherungsleistung** optional modes of settlement; ~ **der Frauen** women's suffrage; ~ **einer Geldstrafe** option of a fine; ~ **auf beitragsfreie Lebensversicherung** extended-term insurance; ~ **des Schiffseigners** ship's option; ~ **der Witwe** *(Nachlaß)* widow's election;
~ **ausüben** to exercise one's voting rights, to elect; ~ **nicht ausüben** to abandon an option, *(pol.)* to abstain from voting; **aktives** ~ **besitzen** to be qualified to vote, to have the franchise *(Br.)*; ~ **entziehen** to exclude from the poll, to deprive of the right to vote, to disfranchise; **Vorbestraften das** ~ **entziehen** to debar persons who have been convicted of crime from voting at elections; ~ **erhalten** to be enfranchised; **ausschließliches** ~ **haben** to have an exclusive voice in an election; **jem. das [passive]** ~ **nehmen** to exclude s. o.from the poll, to disfranchise s. o.; ~ **verleihen** to enfranchise.

Wahlrechts|entziehung, ~**verlust** withdrawal of franchise, disfranchisement; ~**verleihung** enfranchisement.

Wahl|rede electoral address, address to the voters, election speech, stump oratory (speech); ~**reden halten** to electioneer, to stump a district *(US)*; ~**redner** election speaker, campaigner, stump orator *(US)*, stumper *(US)*; **als** ~**redner durchs Land ziehen** to stump through the country *(US)*; ~**reform** electoral reform; ~**reformgesellschaft** electoral reform society; ~**register** election register, voter-registration roll; ~**reise** electioneering tour, campaign trail; ~**resultat** election results (returns), result of the vote; ~**rummel veranstalten** to make a racket at election time; ~**runde** round of the balloting.

Wählscheibe *(tel.)* finger disk (plate), preselection dial.

Wahlschein electoral vote certificate, ticket, voting paper, *(Briefwahl)* mail ballot;
amtlicher ~ official ballot; **ungültiger** ~ void voting paper, scratch ticket;
seinen ~ **ungültig machen** to spoil one's ballot paper;
~**wähler** outvoter.

Wahl|schiebung gerrymandering, traffic in votes; **~schiebung begehen (vornehmen)** to rig (gerrymander, *US*) an election, to traffic in votes; **~schlacht** election campaign (battle); **~schlager** election battle (rallying) cry, election stunt; **~schuld** alternative obligation; **~schwindel** ballot-box stuffing *(US)*.

Wahlsieg electoral victory (triumph), election victory;
überwältigender ~ landslide sweep;
~ der Linksparteien left-wing election victory;
~ erringen to defeat at the polls; **großen ~ erringen** to poll heavily, to sweep the board; **~ überlassen** to concede *(US)*.

Wahl|sieger, als ~sieger eingestuft expected to win; **~slogan** election battle (rallying) cry; **~sonderzug** campaign train; **~sorgen** electoral troubles; **~spende** campaign contribution; **~sprengel** constituency, electoral precinct *(US)*; **~spruch** device, motto, slogan; **~spruch eines Schiffes** name of a ship; **~stärke** voting strength; **~statistik** election statistics.

Wahlstimme [electoral] vote, suffrage;
abgegebene ~ ballot; **in Stellvertretung abgegebene ~** proxy vote *(US)*; **erschlichene ~** faggot vote; **unsichere ~** close vote; **~n der Armee** army vote; **~n der Landbevölkerung** rural votes; **~n auszählen** to count the votes, to open the letters; **einem Kandidaten seine ~ geben** to give one's suffrage to a candidate; **meiste ~n haben** to head the poll; **~n kaufen** to buy a borough *(Br.)*; **~n sammeln** to electioneer; **~n überprüfen** to scrutinize (recount) votes; **~n auf sich vereinigen** to poll; **~n verschieben** to package votes; **~n werben** to canvass, to solicit votes.

Wahlstimmen|prüfer scrutineer; **~prüfung, ~untersuchung** scrutiny of the votes cast; **~verlustgeschäft** vote loser; **~verschiebung** packaging (shift) of votes, turnover; **~werber** canvasser; **~werbung** canvass of votes.

Wahl|stimmrecht voting right; **~stratege** electoral strategist; **~studium** elective (facultive) study; **~system** system of voting, elective (electoral, voting) system; **~tag** [general] election (polling) day; **~taktik festlegen** to settle strategy for election; **~taktiker** electioneer, electoral strategist; **~täuschung** deception of voters; **~teilnahme der Streitkräfte** service voting; **~termin** general election day, election hour; **~termin ansetzen** to call a new election, to go to the country *(Br.)*; **im Wettlauf mit dem ~termin liegen** to be in a race against the election clock; **~thema** election issue, chosen topic; **~trommel schlagen** to beat the election drums; **~umtriebe** electioneering practices.

wahlunfähig not entitled to vote;
passiv ~ incapable of being elected, ineligible.

Wahlunfähigkeit, passive inability of being elected, ineligibility.

Wahl|unkosten campaign expenses; **~unruhen** riots during the elections; **~urne** ballot (voting) box, polls *(US)*; **zur ~urne gehen** to go to the polls *(US)*.

Wählverbindung *(Fernschreiber)* automatic call.

Wahl|verfahren manner of voting, electoral procedure; **ruhiger ~verlauf** quiet elections; **~vermächtnis** alternate legacy; **~vermögen** electiveness; **~versammlung** election meeting, elective assembly, rally, caucus; **~versprechen** election campaign promise, election pledge, plank *(US)*; **~verteidigung** defence by counsel; **~verwandtschaft** affinity; **~voraussetzungen erfüllen, den ~voraussetzungen Genüge leisten** to qualify for the vote (an election); **~vorbereitungen** hustings; **~vordruck** printed ballot; **~vorgang** polling, balloting, elective (electoral) process; **~vorschlag** nomination of candidates; **~vorschlag einer freien Wählergemeinschaft** nomination paper.

Wahlvorschläge|entgegennehmen to receive nominations; **~ versenden** to mail out ballots *(US)*.

Wahl|vorschlagsliste nomination petition; **~vorsitzender** registrar of votes, voting steward, presiding officer *(Br.)*; **~vorstand** elective (electoral) committee, returning board *(US)*; **~vorsteher** registrar of votes, voting steward, returning (presiding) officer *(Br.)*.

wahlweise optional, at will, alternatively.

Wahlzählung vote counting (count), poll, scrutiny of votes.

Wählzeichen dial signal (tone).

Wahl|zeit election period (time), voting hours; **~zelle** polling (voting) booth; **~zensus** property qualification to vote.

Wahlzettel ballot, ticket, ballot (voting, *Br.*) paper;
abgeänderter ~ multilated ballot;
~ ohne Abänderung clean ticket;
~ durch Streichungen abändern to scratch a ballot *(US)*.

Wahlzyklus vote cycle.

Wahn craze, mirage, illusion, delusion;
in einem ~ befangen sein to labo(u)r under a delusion; **jds. ~ zerstören** to shatter s. one's illusions.

Wahnsinn mental alienation, insanity, madness, lunacy, dementia;
an der Grenze des ~s on the verge of madness;
heller ~ sheer madness, plain folly;
in ~ verfallen to go mad.

wahnsinnig insane, mad, delirious, crazy, *(ungemein)* terribly, awfully;
~ beschäftigt awfully busy; **~ teuer** horribly (terribly) expensive;
~ schnell fahren to drive like a madman; **~ machen** to derange, to render insane; **noch ~ werden** to be going out of one's mind; **~e Angst haben** to be in a blue funk *(coll.)*; **~e Kopfschmerzen** splitting headache.

Wahnsinniger insane person, madman, lunatic.

Wahn|verbrechen insane crime; **~vorstellung** insane delusion, hallucination; **~witz** utter madness.

wahr true, real, veritable, *(richtig)* proper, correct;
sich als ~ herausstellen to prove true;
~er Freund sincere friend; **~e Geschichte** true story; **sein ~es Gesicht zeigen** to show one's true colo(u)rs; **~es Glück sein** to be most fortunate; **~er Hagel von Fragen** hail of questions; **~e Pracht** real treat; **~e Wohltat** absolute bliss.

wahren to guard, to protect;
Anstand ~ to preserve decency, to observe the proprieties; **Frist ~** to comply with a term; **Geheimnis ~** to guard a secret; **das Gesicht ~** to save one's face; **jds. Interessen ~** to protect (safeguard) s. one's interests; **Recht ~** to reserve the right; **Regreßrecht ~** to preserve recourse; **Schein ~** to keep up appearances;
seinen eigenen Vorteil zu ~ wissen to look after one's own interests.

wahrhaft lächerlicher Preis ridiculous price.

wahrhaftig honest, truthful, veracious.

Wahrheit truth, verity;
um der ~ zu dienen in the interest of the truth;
einfache und reine ~ pure and simple (downright) truth; **feststehende ~** established truth; **die ganze ~** the whole truth; **grausame ~** grim truth; **ungeschminkte ~** naked (home) truth; **unverblümte ~** unvarnished truth;
~ in der Werbung truth in advertising;
~ eines Berichtes anzweifeln to doubt the truth of a report; **~ beschönigen** to put a gloss on the truth; **~ einer Aussage bestätigen** to attest to the truth; **~ beweisen** to prove the truth; **bei der ~ bleiben** to keep (stick) to the truth, to draw it mild *(coll.)*; **schriftstellerisch für die ~ eintreten** to dedicate one's pen to truth; **~ entstellen** to twist the truth; **~ erfahren** to learn the truth; **über etw. die unverblümte ~ erfahren** to get the lowdown on s. th. *(sl.)*; **~ erkennen** to discern the truth, to see the light *(fam.)*; **zur ~ ermahnen** to admonish to tell the truth; **mit der vollen ~ herausrücken** to come clean *(sl.)*; **der ~ nahekommen** to be near the mark; **es mit der ~ nicht so genau nehmen** to stretch the truth; **jem. die ~ sagen** to pitch it straight to s. o., to tell s. o. the straight of it *(US)*; **reine ~ sagen** to tell the plain truth, to say a mouthful *(sl.)*, to level *(sl.)*; **ohne von der ~ überzeugt zu sein** *(Prospekt)* to be without belief in its truth; **j. von der ~ seiner Erklärung überzeugen** to persuade s. o. of the truth of one's statement; **~ von der Lüge unterscheiden** to winnow the truth from falsehood; **~ seiner Angaben verbürgen** to vouch for the accuracy of one's statement; **~ verdrehen** to prevaricate, to twist the truth; **~ verheimlichen** to suppress the truth; **seine Augen vor der ~ verschließen** to shut one's eyes (close one's ears) to the truth; **jem. ein paar ~en an den Kopf werfen** to tell s. o. a few home truths; **jem. die ~ aus der Nase ziehen** to corkscrew the truth out of s. o.;
die ~ liegt in der Mitte the truth is somewhere inbetween; **so tun, als ob man die ~ gepachtet habe** to act as if one has a monopoly of the truth.

Wahrheitsbeweis justification, defence of truth *(US)*;
~ antreten to prove the truth of one's statement(s), to prove that the statement was substantially true; **~ für beleidigende Äußerungen antreten** to prove that the defamatory words were true in substance and in fact.

Wahrheits|droge truth drug; **~ermittlung** ascertainment of the truth; **~gehalt einer Aussage bestätigen** to attest the truth of a statement; **~gehalt von Schriftsätzen eidlich bestätigen** to verify pleadings in an action.

wahrheitsgetreu true, faithful, literal;
~e Angaben true statement; **~er Bericht** true report.

Wahrheitsliebe veracity.

wahrheits|liebend veracious; **~widrig** contrary to the truth.

wahrnehmbar preceptible, perceivable, noticeable, visible, apprehensible, external;
mit dem bloßen Auge ~ visible to the naked eye.

wahrnehmen to discern, to see;
dienstliche Aufgaben ~ to carry out official functions; **Gelegenheit** ~ to seize an opportunity; **erstbeste Gelegenheit** ~, **etw. zu erledigen** to take an early opportunity to do s. th.; **Interessen** ~ to safeguard (protect) interests; **Termin** ~ *(Anwalt)* to attend a hearing.
Wahrnehmung notice, apprehension, perception;
in ~ **berechtigter Interessen** on a privileged occasion; **übersinnliche** ~ extrasensory perception; **unterschwellige** ~ subliminal perception;
~ **von Aufgaben** exercise of functions; ~ **einer Gelegenheit** improvement of an occasion; ~ **von Interessen** safeguarding (protection) of interests; ~ **berechtigter Interessen** justification and privilege, privilege by reason of occasion *(Br.)*; ~ **seiner eigenen Interessen** maintenance of one's rights; ~ **der Regierungsgeschäfte** administration of the government; ~ **eines Vorrechts** exercise of a privilege;
j. mit der ~ **seiner Geschäfte beauftragen** to entrust s. o. with the care of one's business.
Wahrnehmungsbereich der Gerichte presence of the court.
Wahrsagen fortune-telling.
wahrsagen to foretell;
jem. ~ to read s. one's fortune; **jem. aus der Hand** ~ to read s. one's palm; **aus den Karten** ~ to tell fortunes from cards.
Wahrsager fortune-teller, *(aus der Hand)* palmist, chiromancer.
Wahrsagerei fortune-telling, palmistry.
Wahrsagergewerbe the fortune-telling racket.
Wahrsagerin wisewoman.
Wahrsagerzelt *(Jahrmarkt)* fortune teller's (mitt, *sl.*) camp.
wahrscheinlich likely;
nicht sehr ~ to be pretty remote.
Wahrscheinlichkeit likelihood, plausibility, probability;
mit größter ~ most probably;
bedingte ~ conditional probabilty; **an Sicherheit grenzende** ~ utmost probability, moral certainty; **statistische** ~ posterior probability.
Wahrscheinlichkeits|auswahl probability sampling; **~beweis** presumptive (probable) evidence (proof), moral evidence; **~beweisführung** probable reasoning; **~faktor** probability factor; **~fehler** probable error; **~grad** degree of probability; **~kurve** probability curve; **~prüfung** probability check; **~rechnung** calculation of probabilities, *(math.)* probability calculus, theory of probabilities; **~verhältnis** probability relation; **~verhältnistest** probability ratio test.
Wahrspruch *(Schwurgericht)* verdict.
Wahrung protection, safeguarding, maintenance, observance;
unter ~ **unserer Rechte** without prejudice to our rights, with an express salvo of our rights; **unter** ~ **seines Standpunkts** under adherence to one's point of view;
~ **des Anstands** observance of the proprieties; ~ **seiner Interessen** maintenance of one's rights, safeguarding (protection) of s. one's interests.
Währung currency, exchange, [money] standard, value;
in deutscher ~ in German currency; **in der** ~ **des Landes** in the legal currency of the country;
in gängiger ~ **zahlbar** payable in currency;
abgewertete ~ devalued (depreciated) currency, bad money; **gesetzlich anerkannte** ~ legal tender, lawful money *(US)*; **auf dem Grundsatz Mark gleich Mark aufgebaute** ~ commodity standard *(US)*; **aufgewertete** ~ revalued currency; **ausländische** ~ foreign standard (currency), offshore currency; **nicht in Gold einlösbare** ~ irredeemable currency; **elastische** ~ elastic currency (money), automatic (flexible, adjustable) currency; **sich entwertende** ~ depreciating currency; **entwertete** ~ depreciated currency; **feste** ~ hard (stable) currency; **fiktive** ~ token money; **fremde** ~ foreign currency; **gebundene** ~ controlled currency; **nur durch Aktiva der Emissionsbank gedeckte** ~ asset currency *(US)*; **für Ziehungen normalerweise geeignete** ~ *(Weltwährungsfonds)* normally drawable currency; **staatlich gelenkte** ~ controlled currency; **gemeinsame** ~ convention money; **gesetzliche** ~ legal tender, lawful money *(US)*; **staatlich gesteuerte** ~ managed currency; **gesunde** ~ sound (hard) currency, sound money; **harte** ~ hard (stable, strong, scarce) currency; **hinkende** ~ limping standard; **inländische** ~ home currency; **kontrollierte** ~ flexible currency; **frei konvertierbare** ~ free (freely convertible) currency; **nicht frei konvertierbare** ~ inconvertible paper currency; **nicht frei konvertierbare und transferierbare** ~ blocked currency; **[behördlich] manipulierte** ~ managed currency; **monometallistische** ~ single standard *(US)*; **notleidende** ~ depreciated currency; **regulierte** ~ flexible currency; **staatlich regulierte** ~ managed currency; **schwache** ~ weak (soft) currency; **sichere** ~ sound currency; **stabile** ~ stable (hard) currency; **stabilisierte** ~ stabilized standard; **überbewertete** ~ overvalued currency; **unstabile** ~ currency instability; **unterbewertete** ~ undervalued currency; **US-**~ United States currency; **veränderliche** ~ fluctuating standard; **weiche** ~ soft (weak) currency; **wichtigste** **~en** major currencies; **zerrüttete** ~ dislocated exchange;
~en der Europäischen Gemeinschaft EEC currencies; ~ **mit Golddeckung** currency backed by gold; ~ **mit verschiedenen Wechselkursen** currency with multiple exchange rates;
~ **abwerten** to devalue a currency; **~en angleichen** to adjust currencies; ~ **aufwerten** to revalue a currency; ~ **entwerten** to deface the currency; ~ **korrumpieren** to debauch the currency; ~ **manipulieren** to manipulate the currency; ~ **sanieren** to restore a currency; ~ **stabilisieren** to re-establish the currency; ~ **stützen** to support a currency; **englische** ~ **stützen** to peg the rate of sterling exchange; ~ **verschlechtern** to deface (deprave) the coinage (currency), to lower (debase) the currency; **Vertrauen in die** ~ **wiederherstellen** to restore confidence in the currency; **ihre ~en in einem festen Block zusammenschweißen** to weld their currencies into a tight bloc.
Währungs|abkommen monetary (currency) agreement, monetary convention; **Washingtoner ~abkommen** Smithonian Agreement *(Br.)*; **~abteilung** foreign exchange department; **~abwertung** currency (exchange) depreciation, depreciation of currency, devaluation; **~anarchie** monetary anarchy; **~änderung** currency change-over; **~änderungsklausel** currency clause; **~angleichung** currency adjustment; **~anleihe** [foreign] currency loan; **~aufruhr** monetary turmoil; **~aufwertung** appreciation of a currency, currency revaluation, currency appreciation, exchange appreciation; **~ausgleich** equation of exchange (currency), exchange equation, quantity equation; **~ausgleichsfonds** Exchange Equalization Fund *(US)*, Exchange Equalization Account *(Br.)*; **~ausgleichszollzuschlag** exchange compensation duty; **~ausschuß** monetary committee, national monetary commission; **~ausweitung** currency expansion; **~bank** bank of issue; **~behörden** monetary (financial) authorities; **~beirat** monetary council; **~bereich** currency (monetary) area; **~beschränkungen** currency (monetary) restrictions; **~bestimmungen** currency (monetary) regulations; **~beziehungen** exchange arrangements; **~block** currency bloc; **~buchhaltung** currency accounting; **~chaos** monetary chaos; **~deckung** backing of notes; **~disparitäten** currency disparities; **~dumping** currency dumping; **~einflüsse** monetary influences; **~einheit** monetary unit (standard), primary money; **ausländische ~einheit** foreign currency unit; **~entwertung** currency depreciation; **~experte, ~fachmann** currency economist; **~flucht** currency evasion; **Internationaler ~fonds** International Monetary Fund; **~fragen** questions of currency, currency problems, monetary policy; **~garantie** exchange risk guarantee; **~gebiet** currency (monetary) area, monetary scene; **~gefährdung** jeopardizing of currency; **~geld** standard money; **~gesetz** currency law; **~gesetzgebung** currency legislation; **~gesundung** currency reform; **~gewinn** exchange profit, monetary (currency) gain; **~gold** stock of monetary gold; **~guthaben** foreign currency balance, reserve assets; **~hoheit** monetary sovereignty; **~hüter** monetary official; **~hypothek** mortgage on the currency; **~inflation** monetary inflation; **~instanzen** monetary authorities; **~kapazitäten** monetary leaders; **~katastrophe** monetary disaster; **~klausel** currency (exchange, standard) clause; **~kompetenz** monetary competence *(US)*; **~konferenz** monetary conference; **~konto** foreign-exchange account; **gegenseitiges ~konto** mutual currency account; **~konvertibilität** convertibility of currency; **~korb** basket unit of account (currencies); **~kredit** foreign currency loan; **~krise** monetary (currency) crisis, crisis in the money market; **feste ~kurse** pegged exchange rates; **~kursstabilität** exchange stability; **~lage** monetary situation; **~manipulation** currency manipulations, manipulation of the currency; **~maßnahmen** monetary measures; **~mechanismus** monetary system; **~münze** standard coin; **~neuordnung** monetary (currency) reform; **~option** currency option; **~organ** monetary body; **~panik** money panic; **~parität** equivalence of exchange, par value (parity) of a currency; **seine ~parität langsam ändern** to crawl one's parity; **~parität neu festsetzen** to re-establish the parity; **~politik** currency (monetary) policy; **deflatorische ~politik** deflationary policy.
währungspolitisch|e Befugnisse monetary powers; **Hilfe bei ~en Fragen angedeihen lassen** to help s. o. with the currency side; **~e Größe** monetary variable; **erforderliche ~e Maßnahmen treffen** to carry out the monetary policy of a country.

Währungs|problem [foreign] currency problem; ~**raum** free currency area; ~**reform** monetary (currency) reform; ~**reserve** *(Notenbank)* monetary *(US)* (currency) reserve, *(Bilanz)* official reserves, *(Welternährungsfonds)* pool; ~**risiko** foreign-exchange (currency) risk; ~**sanierung** monetary rehabilitation, re-establishment of currency; ~**scheck** foreign currency check *(US)* (cheque, *Br.*); ~**schlange** currency snake, snake system, floating block; **Europäische ~schlange** European Snake; **unerwarteter ~schnitt** currency windfall; ~**schuldner** *(Bilanz)* foreign currency debtors.
währungsschwach monetarily weak;
~**es Land** country with a low monetary standard (soft currency), weak- (soft-) currency country.
Währungs|schwankungen currency fluctuations; ~**schwierigkeiten** monetary (currency) difficulties, currency troubles; ~**schwund** monetary erosion; ~**seminar** monetary seminar; ~**sicherung** safeguarding of the currency; ~**sicherungsklausel** exchange clause; ~**situation** monetary situation; ~**souveränität** monetary sovereignty; ~**spekulant** currency speculator (operator, *US*), exchange speculator; ~**spekulation** currency (exchange) speculation; ~**spezialist** money expert, currency economist; ~**stabilisierung** currency (monetary) stabilization; ~**stabilisierungsfonds** currency (foreign exchange) stabilization fund; **dem ~stabilisierungsfonds überweisen** to deposit in [to] to the currency stabilization fund; ~**stabilität** stability of the currency, currency (monetary) stability; ~**standard** monetary standard; ~**standard senken** to lower the title of the coinage.
währungsstarkes Land strong-currency country.
Währungs|statistik monetary statistics; ~**struktur** monetary structure; ~**system** currency (monetary) system; **internationales ~system** international monetary system (standard).
währungstechnische Maßnahmen monetary techniques.
Währungs|umrechnungstabelle conversion table; ~**umstellung** currency conversion, currency change-over, currency reform; ~**union** monetary union; ~**unsicherheit** monetary uncertainty; ~**verbindlichkeit** currency liabilities; ~**verfall** depreciation (dislocation) of the currency, currency erosion; ~**verfassung** monetary constitution; ~**verhältnisse** currency conditions; ~**verlust** monetary (currency, exchange) loss; ~**verschlechterung** deterioration (debasement) of currency; ~**vorteile** advantages of exchange; ~**wirbel** currency gyration; ~**zusammenbruch** collapse of a currency, monetary collapse; ~**zwangskurse** forced rate of exchange.
Wahrzeichen landmark;
~ **guten Betriebsklimas sein** to stand for good staff relations.
Waise orphan.
Waisen|geldzahlungen orphan's allowance; ~**haus** orphan asylum, orphanage; ~**kind** orphan child, charity child; ~**knabe** orphaned boy; **gegen ihn ist er der reinste ~knabe** he can't hold a candle to him; ~**rente** orphan's pension, survivor's benefit *(US)*; ~**schule** charity school; ~**zusatzrente** *(Sozialversicherung)* child's insurance benefit *(US)*.
Wald forest, timber *(US)*;
im tiefen ~ deep in the wood; **von ~ umgeben** environed with forests;
undurchdringlicher ~ dense forest;
~ **von Schiffsmasten** forest of masts;
den ~ vor lauter Bäumen nicht sehen to be unable to see the wood for trees;
~**abholzung** deforestation; ~**anpflanzung** forestry plantation; ~**anteil** woodland proportion; ~**beschädigung** forest damage; ~**besitz** forest property; ~**bestand** forest cover; ~**bewohner** forest dweller; ~**brand** forest fire.
Wäldchen grove, coppice, hurst.
Wälder forest land, forestry;
sich kilometerweit hinziehende ~ forests stretching for miles and miles;
~ **abholzen** to cut down forests.
Waldesinneren, im in the heart of the forest.
Wald|fläche forest area; ~**gebiet** forestry land, forest land, woodland; ~**gemälde** forest interior; ~**grundstück** forested land, wood, woodlands; ~**honig** wild honey.
waldig woody.
Wald|land wooded (forested) land, woodland; ~**lichtung** opening, clearance, cut; ~**nutzung** commercial forestry; ~**rand** wood margin, edge of a forest; **am ~rand** on the fringe[s] of a forest; ~**schutzgebiet** forest reserve *(US)*.
Waldung wood, woodland.
Wald|weg cart road, track through the forest; ~**wirtschaft** forestry.

Walfang whaling, whale fishing (fishery).
Walfänger whale fisherman.
Walfang|flotte whaling fleet; ~**hafen** whaling port; ~**industrie** whaling industry, whalery *(US)*; ~**schiff** whaler; ~**station** whaling station.
Walfisch whale;
~**tran** whale (train) oil, blubber.
Wall earth filling, embankment, *(Bollwerk)* bulwark, *(Festung)* rampart;
~ **aufschütten** to fill an earth ridge; **mit einem ~ umschließen** to wall around.
Wall|fahrer pilgrim; ~**fahrt** pilgrimage.
Wallung, in in boil;
in ~ geraten to fly into a (boil with) rage; **Wasser in ~ versetzen** to make the water bubble.
Walmdach hip roof.
walten, seines Amtes to officiate;
Gnade ~ lassen to show mercy.
Walze trundle;
auf der ~ on the bum;
immer wieder die alte ~ always the same old cant;
auf die ~ gehen to take to the road.
Walzeisen plate iron.
wälzen to roll;
sich ~ to wallow; **sich zum Ausgang** ~ *(Menge)* to surge along to the exit; **sich in seinem Blute** ~ to welter in one's blood; **sich vor Lachen** ~ to split one's sides with laughter; **sich schlaflos im Bett** ~ to toss and turn in one's bed; **sich vor Schmerzen auf dem Boden** ~ to writhe on the ground with pain; **Schuld auf j. anderen** ~ to lay the blame on s. o. else.
Walzen|straße train, roller mill; **kontinuierliche ~straße** continuous mill; ~**strecke** train.
Wälzer, dicker tome, ponderous volume.
Walz|stahl rolled steel; ~**werk** rolling mill, train; ~**werkarbeiter** roller.
Wand wall, curtain, *(Barriere)* barrier;
mit dem Rücken gegen die ~ up against the wall;
blinde ~ blank wall; **schallabsorbierende** ~ tormentor; **schräge** ~ slanting wall; **spanische** ~ holding screen;
gegen eine ~ von Vorurteilen anrennen to run up against a wall of prejudices; ~ **bezwingen** to climb a face; **j. an die ~ drücken** to push (pin) s. o. against the wall; **gegen eine ~ reden** to speak to the wall; **Mitteilung an die ~ schlagen** to nail up a notice on the wall; **j. an die ~ spielen** to steal a march on s. o.; **alle anderen gegen die ~ spielen** to steal the show; **j. an die ~ stellen** to shoot (execute) s. o.; **weiß wie eine ~ werden** to grow as white as a sheet; **an die ~ gedrückt werden** to go to the wall; **Bild an die ~ werfen** to project a picture on the screen; **mit dem Kopf durch die ~ wollen** to run one's head against the wall (full tilt at everything);
~**anschluß** *(el.)* wall socket; ~**apparat** wall telephone; ~**arm** wall bracket; ~**behang** hangings; ~**beleuchtung** wall illumination; ~**bretter** wallboard.
Wände, die ~ hochgehen to go up the wall *(sl.)*; **leeren ~n predigen** to preach to deaf ears; **in seinen eigenen vier ~n völlig gelöst sein** to feel very relaxed in one's own home.
Wandel|im Absatzweg change in distribution; ~ **in der Volksstimmung** shift in the popular mood;
sich dem ~ der Zeit anpassen to adapt o. s. to the changing times; **grundsätzlichen ~ erfahren** to undergo a fundamental change;
~**anleihe** convertible loan; ~**flugzeug** convertiplane; ~**gang** aisle, walk, [box] lobby, foyer; ~**halle** lobby, *(Theater)* foyer.
wandeln to walk, to stroll;
sich ~ to change.
wandelndes Konversationslexikon sein to be a walking library.
Wandel|obligationen, ~verschreibungen convertible debentures (bonds, *US*).
Wander|arbeiter seasonal (itinerant, migrant, migratory) worker, okie *(US sl.)*, shuffler *(sl.)*; ~**ausrüstung** hiking kit; ~**ausstellung** travel(l)ing (touring) show, travel(l)ing exhibition, flying exhibition *(US)*; ~**bibliothek, ~bücherei** circulating (package, travel(l)ing, mobile, *Br.*) library, bookmobile *(US)*; ~**bühne** touring (travel(l)ing) theatre, road (fit-up, touring) company *(US)*.
Wanderer wanderer, tramp, travel(l)er, hiker;
ewiger ~ a rolling stone.
Wandergewerbe itinerant (pedlar's) trade, nonestablished retail trade, [itinerant] peddling, itinerant trading, business of peddling, pedlary;
~ **betreiben** to peddle;

~**schein** pedlar's license *(US)* (certificate, *Br.*), hawker's licence; ~**treibender** travel(l)ing (itinerant, *US*) vendor, pedlar *(Br.)*, peddler *(US)*, hawker, itinerant (transient) merchant, itinerant salesman (dealer).

Wander|jahre, nach vielen ~jahren seßhaft werden to settle down after years of roaming; ~**karte** trail map; ~**leben** migratory (itinerant) life; ~**leben führen** to tramp; **von der ~lust gepackt werden** to get itchy feet.

Wandern walking, wayfaring.

wandern to wander, to travel, to tramp it, to hike, *(Blick)* to roam;
durch den ganzen Bezirk ~ to walk the whole district; **über den Himmel** ~ *(Scheinwerfer)* to traverse the sky; **in den Papierkorb** ~ to land in the wastepaper basket, to go limbo; **über die ganze Welt** ~ to roam about the world.

wandernd itinerant, wayfaring, travel(l)ing, vagrant.

Wanderpreis challenge cup, itinerant trophy.

Wanderschaft, auf der on the road;
auf ~ gehen to go on a tramp; **auf der ~ sein** to tramp; **immer auf der ~ sein** to roam up and down the road aimlessly.

Wanderschule ambulatory school.

Wandersmann wayfaring man, wayfarer.

Wander|stab walking staff; ~**tag** *(Schule)* excursion day; ~**truppe** touring (fit-up, road, *US*) company.

Wanderung wandering, walk, walking tour, ramble, hike, migration, tramp;
saisonbedingte ~ seasonal migration.

Wanderungs|bilanz net migration change; ~**gewinn** growth due to migration, net migration gain; ~**saldo** net migration change; ~**verlust** loss due to migration, net migration loss.

Wander|vogel rolling stone; ~**zirkus** travel(l)ing circus.

Wand|flächenreklame outdoor publicity; ~**fliese** wall tile; ~**gekritzel** graffiti; ~**gemälde** wall painting; ~**heizung** panel heating; ~**kalender** wall calendar, sheet almanac; ~**klappbett** turnup bed; ~**leuchte** wall lamp.

Wandlung *(beim Kauf)* cancellation of a sale, redhibition *(US)*;
zur ~ berechtigend redhibitory *(US)*;
geistige ~ conversion; **große** ~ *(fig.)* sea change;
~ **wegen Gewährleistungsbruches** redhibition for breach of warranty *(US)*;
zur ~ berechtigen to give rise to redhibition *(US)*; **auf ~ klagen** to maintain a redhibitory action *(US)*, to sue for conversion.

wandlungsfähig able to shift focus;
~**er Schauspieler** versatile actor.

Wandlungs|fähigkeit ability to shift focus; ~**fehler** redhibitory defect (vice) *(US)*; ~**klage** redhibitory action *(US)*, rescissory action *(Scot.)*; ~**klage erheben** to bring an action for rescission *(Scot.)*, to sue for conversion; ~**recht begründen** to maintain a redhibitory action *(US)*; ~**verfahren** redhibitory suit *(US)*.

Wand|malerei mural (wall) painting; ~**plakat** wall poster; ~**platte** panel *(Br.)*, pan; ~**protest** *(Wechselrecht)* [etwa] householder's protest; ~**schalter** *(el.)* wall box; ~**schild** wall sign; ~**schirm** screen *(US)*; **eingebauter ~schrank** built-in cupboard; **großer ~spiegel** pier glass; ~**stecker** wall plug; ~**tafel** blackboard; ~**täfelung** wainscot; ~**telefon** wall telephone; ~**teppich** tapestry carpet; ~**verkleidung** facing on a wall, wall lining (facing); ~**zeitung** wall newspaper.

wankelmütig fickle, unsteadfast, variable, volatile.

Wanken staggering, faltering;
Einzelhandel durch Aufgabe von Rabattmarken ins ~ bringen to rock the retail trade by dropping trade stamps.

wanken to totter, to stagger, to waver, to teeter *(US)*;
in seinem Entschluß ~ to falter in one's decision; **beim Erdbeben** ~ to rock in the earthquake; **in seinen Grundfesten** ~ *(Staat)* to rock in its foundation.

wankend shaking, swaying, *(Gebäude)* rocking, swaying, *(Staat)* tottering, shaky;
in seinen Entschlüssen ~ werden to begin to falter in one's decisions;
~**e feindliche Linien** wavering lines of the enemy.

Wanne *(Foto)* tank, tub.

Wanze *(el.)* bug;
flach wie eine ~ as flat as a pancake;
~ **in einem Zimmer anbringen** to bug a room.

Wappen coat of arms, crest;
~**blume** state flower *(US)*.

wappnen, sich gegen etw. to fortify o. s. against s. th.

Ware *(einzelnes Stück)* article, parcel [of goods], *(Erzeugnis)* product, *(Handelsware)* merchandise, *(Kurszettel)* offers, sellers, *(Sammelbegriff)* goods, articles, commodity, [sale] wares, stuff;
mit einer ~ handeln to deal in an article; **Preis einer ~ auf ... herabsetzen** to bring down the price of an article to ...

Waren goods, commodities, stock, articles, products, *(Warenart)* line;
nicht abgeholte ~ uncollected goods; **abgepackte** ~ packaged goods; **abrufbereite** ~ goods actually ready for immediate delivery; **absatzfähige** ~ marketable commodity; **leicht absetzbare** ~ fast-moving goods; **schwer absetzbare** ~ hard-to-move (slow-moving) products; **sicher abzusetzende** ~ articles certain to sell; **angebotene** ~ goods for sale; **vom Zoll angehaltene** ~ goods stopped at the customhouse; **anmeldepflichtige** ~ *(Zoll)* goods to declare; **annehmbare** ~ goods in fair condition; **in beiliegender Rechnung aufgeführte** ~ goods specified in the annexed invoice; **auserlesene** ~ choice goods (articles), picked goods; **ausgeführte** ~ exported goods; **wieder ausgeführte** ~ reexports; **offen ausgelegte** ~ open display; **ausgestellte** ~ merchandise displayed; **im Schaufenster ausgestellte** ~ articles shown in the window; **zum Verkauf ausgestellte** ~ goods exhibited for sale; **ausgesuchte** ~ choice goods (articles); **ausgezeichnete** ~ price-labelled (marked) goods; **avisierte** ~ advised goods; **bearbeitete** ~ processed goods; **nicht auf Lager befindliche** ~ items not stocked; **unterwegs befindliche** ~ goods afloat, merchandise in transit; **auf dem Luftwege beförderte** ~ merchandise consigned by air; **in der Herstellung begriffene** ~ goods in process; **täglich benötigte** ~ necessary articles; **nach Maß berechnete** ~ measurement goods; **beschädigte** ~ damaged goods; **vom langen Liegen im Laden beschädigte** ~ shop-worn (shop-soiled) merchandise; **auf dem Transport beschädigte** ~ goods damaged in transit; **beschlagnahmte** ~ confiscated (seized) goods; **vom Zoll beschlagnahmte** ~ goods held up at customs; **bessere** ~ superior articles; **bestellte** ~ goods ordered; **zur Ausfuhr bestimmte** ~ goods intended for export; **beim Kaufabschluß bestimmte** ~ specific goods; **bewirtschaftete** ~ quota (rationed) goods, rationed (scarce) commodity; **nicht bewirtschaftete** ~ nonrationed goods, commodities not under control; **nicht mehr bewirtschaftete** ~ derationed goods; **falsch bezeichnete** ~ falsely marked merchandise; **bezogene** ~ purchased merchandise; **bezugsbeschränkte** ~ rationed (quota) goods; **preislich billigere** ~ lower-priced goods; **deklarierte** ~ declared goods; **nicht deklarierte** ~ undeclared goods; **verkehrswidrig als Gepäck deklarierte** ~ contraband baggage; **devisenschwache** ~ soft goods; **devisenstarke** ~ hardgoods; **disponible** ~ disposable goods, stock on hand; **effektive** ~ actual goods ready for immediate delivery; **eingebürgerte** ~ well-introduced articles; **eingeführte** ~ imported goods; **gut eingeführte** ~ popular make, well-kown merchandise (commodities), established products; **unverzollt eingeführte** ~ uncustomed merchandise; **eingehende** ~ incoming goods, receipts; **eingelagerte** ~ stockpiled commodities, stored goods, goods (merchandise) in storage, goods in warehouse; **einheimische** ~ home-made (inland) commodities, domestic goods; **nicht einwandfreie** ~ faulty goods; **erstklassige** ~ good-class (superior) articles, first-rate goods; **noch zu erzeugende** ~ future goods; **etikettierte** ~ labelled (branded) goods; **exportierte** ~ exported goods; **fakturierte** ~ invoiced goods; **nicht unter Tarif fallende** ~ exempt commodities; **fehlende** ~ missing goods, short interest; **fehlerfreie** ~ goods free from fault, faultless goods; **fehlerhafte** ~ defective goods; **feinere** ~ better description; **fertiggestellte** ~ finished (fully manufactured) goods; **feuergefährliche** ~ inflammable cargo; **flüssige** ~ wet goods; **freigegebene** ~ goods taken out of pledge, derationed goods; **gangbarste** ~ leading articles; **gängige** ~ current articles, marketable products; **gebrauchte** ~ secondhand goods; **gediegene** ~ sterling goods; **gefahrbringende (gefährliche)** ~ hazardous goods, dangerous articles; **von Natur aus gefährliche** ~ goods dangerous in themselves; **maschinell gefertigte** ~ machine-made products; **in Auftrag gegebene** ~ merchandise on order, ordered goods; **in Zahlung gegebene** ~ trade-in goods; **im Preis gehaltene** ~ price-maintained commodities; **gekaufte** ~ store goods *(US)*; **auf Kredit gekaufte** ~ goods bought on credit; **erst nach Preisvergleich gekaufte** ~ shopping goods *(US)*; **spontan gekaufte** ~ impulse goods (items) *(US)*; **gekennzeichnete** ~ marked goods; **gelagerte** ~ stored goods; **vermischt gelagerte** ~ commingled goods; **gelieferte** ~ goods sold and delivered; **noch nicht gelieferte** ~ undelivered goods; **beim Zoll nicht gemeldete** ~ undeclared goods; **gemischte** ~ mixed goods; **genormte** ~ standardized commodities; **gepackte** ~ packaged goods; **gepfändete** ~ distrained (seized) goods; **aus Brandschäden (Seeschäden) gerettete** ~ salvage stock; **geringwertige** ~ low-quality goods; **geschmuggelte** ~ smuggled goods; **nicht**

geschmuggelte ~ innocent goods; **durch Einfuhrzölle geschützte** ~ protected articles; **dem Kunden in Rechnung gestellte** ~ goods billed to customer; **zur Schau gestellte** ~ merchandise displayed; **frisch gestohlene** ~ hot goods; **gesuchte** ~ articles in demand; **gleichwertige** ~ goods of the same standard; **greifbare** ~ tangible goods, merchandise on hand; **halbfertige** ~ semi-finished goods; **begrenzt haltbare** ~ goods with limited shelf life; **handgefertigte** ~ handmade products; **havarierte** ~ goods damaged by sea water; **heiße** ~ hot goods; **im Preis herabgesetzte** ~ reduced (marked-down) merchandise, markdowns; **fabrikmäßig hergestellte** ~ manufactured commodities, manufactured (machine-made) goods; **im Gefängnis (von Strafgefangenen) hergestellte** ~ prison- (convict-) made goods; **maschinell hergestellte** ~ machine-made goods; **von Nichtgewerkschaftlern hergestellte** ~ tainted goods *(Br.)*; **serienmäßig hergestellte** ~ mass- (volume-) produced goods; **hochqualifizierte (hochwertige)** ~ high-quality (-grade) goods; **importierte** ~ imported goods; **inflationsempfindliche** ~ inflation-prone goods; **katalogisierte** ~ catalog(u)ed goods; **käufliche** ~ goods for sale; **konkurrenzfähige** ~ competitive products; **konsignierte** ~ consignment goods; **kontingentierte** ~ quota (rationed) goods; **nicht kontingentierte** ~ nonquota goods; **kriegswichtige** ~ strategic goods; **nicht kriegswichtige** ~ nonstrategic goods; **lagerfähige** ~ storable goods; **lebenswichtige** ~ goods of vital necessity, essential goods; **lieferbare** ~ goods on hand (fit for acceptance); **sofort lieferbare** ~ spots, spot goods; **lieferfähige** ~ goods fit for acceptance; **unter Zollverschluß liegende** ~ goods in bond; **lose** ~ unpacked (bulk) goods; **mangelhafte** ~ faulty (defective) goods; **markenpflichtige** ~ coupon goods; **nicht marktkonforme** ~ down-market goods; **minderwertige** ~ goods of inferior workmanship, low-class (low-quality) goods, inferior products (goods), inferior goods, trumpery wares, wastrel; **modische** ~ novelties, up-to-date merchandise; **notleidende** ~ distress merchandise; **patentierte** ~ patented articles (products), proprietary articles; **preisgebundene** ~ price-controlled (price-bound) merchandise, price-fixed goods; **preisgeschützte (preisstabile)** ~ price-maintained goods (commodities); **preiswerte** ~ cheap line, good value; **rationierte** ~ allocated (quota, rationed) goods; **leicht realisierbare** ~ readily marketable staples; **reduzierte** ~ as-is merchandise; **reelle** ~ good articles; **retournierte (zurückgesandte)** ~ returned goods; **rollende** ~ rolling freight; **schlechte** ~ faulty articles, inferior products; **schwimmende** ~ floating goods; **sicherungsübereignete** ~ pledged goods (merchandise); **sortierte** ~ graded commodity; **sperrige** ~ bulky goods; **nicht sperrige** ~ goods of small bulk; **spottbillige** ~ sacrificed goods; **im Eigentum des Verkäufers stehende** ~ existing goods; **zum Verkauf stehende** ~ goods for sale; **steuerpflichtige** ~ taxable class of goods (commodity); **tarierte** ~ tared goods; **tiefgekühlte** ~ frozen goods; **trockene** ~ dry goods; **übereignete** ~ assigned goods; **unter Eigentumsvorbehalt überlassene** ~ merchandise on memorandum *(US)*, memorandum goods *(US)*, goods on commission; **übersandte** ~ forwarded (shipped, *US*) goods; **übriggebliebene** ~ remnants, oddments; **schnell umschlagbare** ~ fast-moving (-selling) goods (items); **unbestellte** ~ goods not ordered; **unbezahlte** ~ unpaid goods, goods left on our hands; **unfertige** ~ rough goods; **unsortierte** ~ nongraded products; **unterdurchschnittliche** ~ substandard goods; **der Preisüberwachung unterliegende** ~ price-controlled articles; **unterversicherte** ~ underinsured goods; **unverderbliche** ~ nonperishable merchandise, nonperishables; **unverkäufliche** ~ dead commodity (stock), dud stock, drug in the market, unsalable articles (items); **unvermischte** ~ honest goods; **unverpackte** ~ unpacked (bulk) goods; **unversicherte** ~ uninsured goods; **unverzollte** ~ uncustomed goods; **noch unverzollte** ~ unentered goods; **verarbeitete** ~ processed goods; **verbrauchsnahe** ~ goods close to the customer; **leicht verderbliche** ~ goods which perish, perishable goods (commodity), perishables, highly perishable products, bona peritura; **nicht verderbliche** ~ nonperishable goods; **verdorbene** ~ spoilt (perished) goods; **verfügbare** ~ available (disposable) goods, stock on hand; **in Kommission vergebene** ~ goods on commission, memorandum goods *(US)*; **schnell vergriffene** ~ goods selling like wildfire (hot cakes, *Br.*, hot dogs, *US*); **verkäufliche** ~ marketable commodities; **langsam verkäufliche** ~ slow-moving merchandise, sleeper *(US)*; **leicht verkäufliche** ~ fast-moving (-selling) goods; **schlecht verkäufliche** ~ slow-selling goods; **schwer verkäufliche** ~ unsalable goods, articles hard to get rid of; **verkaufsfähige** ~ marketable products; **nach dem Stück verkaufte** ~ piece goods; **nicht verladene** ~ short interest; **vermischte** ~ mixed lot; **verpackte** ~ packaged goods; **verpfändete** ~ goods lying in pledge, pledged (mortgaged) goods; **verplombte** ~ leaded goods; **versandfertige** ~ goods ready for delivery; **versandte** ~ forwarded goods; **in Behältern versandte** ~ container-shipped goods; **auf Rechnung versandte** ~ goods shipped on account *(US)*; **verschiffte** ~ goods shipped; **mit Gewerkschaftsetikett versehene** ~ union label goods *(US)*; **versicherte** ~ insured goods; **versteigerte** ~ auctioned goods; **vertretbare** ~ fungible things, representative commodities; **in beiliegender Rechnung verzeichnete** ~ goods specified in the invoice attached; **verzollte** ~ cleared goods, goods out of bond; **hoch verzollte** ~ high-duty goods; **nicht verzollte** ~ uncleared goods; **noch nicht verzollte** ~ unentered goods; **niedrig verzollte** ~ low-rate articles, low-duty goods; **vorrätige** ~ goods on hand, available goods; **ständig vorrätige** ~ open stock; **vorzügliche** ~ choice commodities, articles of superior quality; **vom langen Liegen im Laden wertgeminderte** ~ shopworn merchandise; **wertlose** ~ trash, poor truck *(US)*; **zerbrechliche** ~ fragile goods; **zollfreie** ~ duty-free articles (goods), free (uncustomed) goods; **zollhängige** ~ goods in the process of clearing, uncleared goods; **zollpflichtige** ~ dutiable (bonded) goods; **zugkräftige** ~ articles of quick sale, popular articles; **zurückgehende** ~ returnable goods; **zurückgelegte** ~ lay-away *(US)*; **zurückgenommene** ~ returns inward; **zurückgesandte** ~ returned goods, returns outward; **zurückgesetzte** ~ old stock, damaged goods, as-is merchandise; **zurückgewiesene** ~ rejected goods;

~ **zur Ansicht** merchandise sent on approval (for inspection, show); ~ **mittlerer Art und Güte** merchandise quality, medium-quality goods, seconds; ~ **von kriegswichtiger Bedeutung** strategic goods; ~ **mit hoher Gewinnspanne** higher-margin merchandise; ~ **ausländischer Herkunft** goods of foreign origin; ~ **auf Kredit** merchandise on account; ~ **auf Lager** warehouse goods; ~ **aus den Ländern des British Commonwealth** Empire products; ~ **der Lebensmittelindustrie** prepared foodstuffs; ~ **mit gleichbleibenden Preisen** price-maintained articles; ~ **in hoher Preislage** high-cost merchandise; ~ **mittlerer Preislage** medium-priced goods; ~ **niedriger Preislage** low-priced goods; ~ **bester Qualität** high-class goods; ~ **minderwertiger Qualität** thirds; ~ **mittlerer Qualität und Güte** merchantable quality, medium-quality goods; ~ **von schlechter Qualität** poor-quality goods; ~ **zweiter Qualität** seconds; ~ **mit geringer Umsatzgeschwindigkeit (Umschlaghäufigkeit)** slow-moving goods (stock), sleeper *(US)*; ~ **mit hoher Umschlaggeschwindigkeit** fast-moving (-selling) goods; ~ **mit hohen Verkaufspreisen** high-priced commodity; ~ **aus der Vorkriegszeit** prewar goods; ~ **unter Zollverschluß** bonded goods;

~ **im Durchgangsverkehr abfertigen** to convey goods in transit; ~ **auf einer Liste abhaken** to keep tally of goods; ~ **abnehmen** to take delivery of (accept, collect the) goods; ~ **in großen Posten abnehmen** to take up goods to a large amount; ~ **abrufen** to recall goods; ~ **abschätzen** to make a valuation of goods, to value goods; ~ **absetzen** to dispose (get off, place) goods, to push one's wares; ~ **flott (leicht) absetzen** to sell goods easily; ~ **abstoßen** to sell off goods; ~ **im Durchgangsverkehr abwickeln** to convey goods in transit; ~ **mit einem 10%igen Abschlag vom Normalpreis (unter Preis) anbieten** to offer goods at 10 per cent off the regular price; ~ **auf dem Markt anbieten** to put an article on the market; **seine** ~ **anpreisen** to puff one's wares *(Br.)*; ~ **aufdrängen** to push goods; **jem. minderwertige** ~ **aufdrängen** to impose inferior goods upon s. o.; ~ **aufkaufen** to corner the market; ~ **glatt aufnehmen** *(Börse)* to absorb all offerings; **jem.** ~ **aufschwindeln** to palm off goods on s. o.; ~ **in Partien aufteilen** to parcel out goods; ~ **zum Verkauf ausbreiten** to spread (sort) out goods for sale; ~ **dem Frachtführer aushändigen** to place goods in the custody of the carrier; ~ **ausklarieren** to clear goods out of bond; ~ **auslegen** to flourish goods, to lay out goods, to set out articles; ~ **ausliefern** to have goods delivered; ~ **im Fenster ausstellen** to display goods in the window; ~ **auszeichnen** to price (tally) goods, to ticket goods with prices; ~ **billiger auszeichnen** to mark down goods; ~ **frei Achse befördern** to cart goods; **gute** ~ **für sein Geld bekommen** to get good value for one's money; **verlorene** ~ **wertmäßig ersetzt bekommen** to recover the value for lost merchandise; ~ **für den Käufer bereitstellen** to place goods at the buyer's disposal; ~ **bestellen** to order goods; ~ **über einen Vertreter bestellen** to order goods through a representative; ~ **bewerten** to value goods; **in** ~ **bezahlen** to pay in kind, to truck *(Br.)*; ~ **beziehen** to receive (obtain, procure, purchase) goods; **seine** ~ **außerhalb beziehen** to get commodities (supply o. s. with articles) from abroad; ~ **an Bord bringen** to deliver the goods on board; **jem.** ~ **ins Haus bringen** to deliver goods to s. one's address; **seine schlechten ~ unter die Leute bringen** to foist one's wares upon the public; ~ **auf den Markt bringen** to launch a new product, to introduce goods into the market; ~ **im Ausland billig auf den Markt bringen** to dump goods on foreign markets; **seine ~ [beim Zoll] deklarieren** to make a declaration, to make an entry of (enter) goods; ~ **deponieren** to warehouse goods; **sich mit ~ eindecken** to supply o. s. with goods; **über den Bedarf mit ~ eindecken** to overstock a shop; ~ **einführen** to bring in goods; ~ **in ein Land einführen** to introduce goods into a country; ~ **zum freien Verkehr einführen** to enter goods for consumption; ~ **einlagern** to lay in goods; **zu viel ~ einlagern** to overstock a shop; ~ **in einen Karton einpacken** to put goods in a carton; ~ **nach Güteklassen einstufen** to grade goods; **seine ~ empfehlen** to recommend one's wares; **Einfuhrzoll auf ~ erheben** to levy a duty on goods; ~ **auf einer Auktion erwerben** to buy goods at the sales; ~ **etikettieren** to docket (label) goods; ~ **feilbieten** to expose goods for sale; **billige ~ feilbieten** to show a cheap line of goods; ~ **feilhalten** to expose goods for sale; **gegen Zahlung ~ freigeben** to release goods against payment; ~ **führen** to have goods in stock, to have (keep) an article in stock, to deal in (stock) an article; **alle Arten von ~ führen** to stock varied goods; **ausländische ~ führen** to handle foreign goods; **Verhandlungen über einzeln ausgewählte ~ führen** to carry on negotiations on a selective product-by-product basis; ~ **nicht mehr führen** to be out of an article; ~ **in Kommission geben** to deliver goods on sale or return; ~ **auf Lager haben (halten)** to carry goods in stock, to stock an article; ~ **im Augenblick nicht auf Lager (vorrätig) haben** not to stock an article, to be short of an article; ~ **für den Verkauf herausstellen** to get up articles for sale; ~ **hereinbekommen** to receive (obtain) goods; ~ **der verschiedensten Beschaffenheit herstellen** to manufacture goods in various qualities; ~ **massenhaft herstellen** to turn out large quantities of goods; ~ **horten** to hoard goods; ~ **auf einer Auktion kaufen** to buy goods at the sales; ~ **auf Termin kaufen** to buy on terms; ~ **kennzeichnen** to identify goods by marks; ~ **konditionieren** to condition goods; ~ **lagern** to store (lay in) goods; ~ **unter Zollverschluß lagern** to have goods bonded; ~ **verabfolgen lassen** to have goods delivered; ~ **liefern** to supply with (deliver) goods; ~ **auf Kredit liefern** to supply goods on credit, to grant credit terms; ~ **an einen Kunden liefern** to serve a customer with goods; ~ **lombardieren** to lend money on goods, to hypothecate goods; ~ **wieder in Besitz nehmen** to repossess goods; ~ **an Bord nehmen** to take goods on board; ~ **in Kommission nehmen** to take goods on a consignment basis; ~ **auf Kredit nehmen** to take goods on credit; ~ **auf Lager nehmen** to put goods in stock, to lay in goods; ~ **am Kai niederlegen** to place goods on the dock; ~ **billiger notieren** to mark down the prices of goods; ~ **pfänden** to distrain upon (seize) goods; ~ **prüfen** to examine the goods; ~ **retournieren** to return articles; ~ **per Expreß schicken** to send goods by fast train; ~ **per Nachnahme schicken** to send goods cash (collect, *US*) on delivery; **sich ~ sichern** to assure o. s. with goods; **mit (auf) seinen ~ sitzenbleiben** to be left with goods, to hold the bag *(US)*; ~ **sortieren** to grade goods; ~ **in Rechnung stellen** to bill goods; ~ **zu niedrig in Rechnung stellen** to underbill goods *(US)*; ~ **auf einem Stand zur Schau stellen** to set out goods on a stall; ~ **taxieren** to value (make a valuation of) goods; ~ **übereignen** to assign goods; **jem. ~ vertragsmäßig übergeben** to bail goods to s. o.; **Laden mit ~ übersättigen** to overstock a shop; ~ **auf Spekulation übersenden** to venture goods; ~ **umsetzen** to turn out goods; ~ **unterbewerten** to set too low a valuation on goods; ~ **einer genauen Untersuchung unterziehen** to submit goods to a careful examination; ~ **auf dem Markt eines anderen Landes verbringen** to introduce goods into the commerce of another country; ~ **verkaufen** to clear goods; **als zweitklassige ~ verkaufen** to sell under a secondary label; ~ **in Ballen verkaufen** to sell in bales; ~ **nach dem Dutzend verkaufen** to sell articles by the dozen (sets of a dozen); ~ **unberechtigt als Markenartikel verkaufen** to pass off goods as those of another make *(US)*; ~ **verpacken** to wrap up goods; **seine ~ in Ballen verpacken** to pack up one's wares, to make up one's goods in bales; ~ **für den Verkauf verpacken** to box articles for sale; **seinen ~ einen ausgezeichneten Ruf verschaffen** to build up a good reputation for one's goods; ~ **mit der Eisenbahn versenden** to send goods by rail; ~ **zu einem bestimmten Frachtsatz versenden** to rate goods *(US)*; ~ **ins Landesinnere versenden** to intern goods; ~ **auf dem Seeweg versenden** to ship goods by sea; **seine ~ unter falschem Warenzeichen vertreiben** to pass off one's goods as those of another make *(US)*; **Annahme von ~ verweigern** to refuse goods; ~ **verwerten** to realize goods; ~ **verzollen** to clear goods at the customhouse; ~ **an eine neue Adresse weiterbefördern** to reconsign goods; ~ **über Bord werfen** to jettison goods; ~ **auf den Markt werfen** to throw goods on the market, *(im Ausland)* to dump goods on a foreign market; **in ~ zahlen** to pay in kind; ~ **im Schaufenster zeigen** to expose goods in a shop window; **beschädigte ~ wieder zurechtmachen** to render goods marketable; ~ **zurücknehmen** to take goods back; ~ **unmittelbar zuschicken** to dispatch goods direct;

~**abgabe** supply of goods, sale; ~**abgabe für Inlandswaren** excise duty *(Br.)*; ~**abkommen** commodity (goods) agreement; ~**abnahmeverpflichtung** obligation to accept goods; ~**abruf** calling-forward notice; ~**absatz** marketing (sale) of goods, commodity marketing; ~**absatzorganisation** merchandising organization; ~**abschluß** commodity contract; ~**absender** consignor, shipper *(US)*; ~**absendung** dispatch of goods; ~**abteilung** goods *(Br.)* (merchandising) department; ~**adreßzettel** label, docket; ~**akkreditiv** commercial letter of credit; ~**akzept** trade acceptance, mercantile paper; ~**analyse** product analysis; ~**anforderung** command of goods.

Warenangebot [merchandise] offerings, supply of goods, pitch; **billiges ~** bait; **mannigfaltiges ~** wide range of items, varied assortment of goods; **preisgünstiges ~** bargain sale.

Warenanhäufung backup of goods.

Warenannahme receiving (acceptance) of goods, product acceptance, *(Annahmestelle)* receiving room;

~ **verweigern** to refuse goods;

~**abteilung** receiving division (department); ~**schein** receiving sheet; ~**stelle** receiving department.

Waren|anordnung merchandise arrangement; ~**anpreisung** commercial puff *(Br.)*, styling *(US)*; ~**anreiz** merchandise appeal; ~**art** article; ~**aufnahme** inventory taking, stocktaking, *(im Markt)* product acceptance; ~**aufseher** freight conductor; ~**aufstellung zusenden** to deliver specification of goods; ~**auftrag** buyer's order, line; ~**aufzug** hoist, freight elevator *(US)*; ~**ausfuhr** visible exports, export[action] [trade]; ~**ausfuhr zu Schleuderpreisen** dumping; ~**ausfuhrgenehmigung** export licence, licence outwards; ~**ausgang** outgoing goods (stock); ~**ausgangsbuch**, ~**ausgangsjournal** sales journal (register), sales day book; ~**ausgangskonto** sales account; ~**auslage** display of goods, *(im Laden)* interior display, *(im Schaufenster)* window display; ~**auslage verwandter Artikel** related-item display; ~**auslieferungsanweisung** order sheet (slip); ~**auslieferungslager** supply store, local supply station, repository, solus.

Warenaustausch exchange of commodities (goods), *(Tauschhandel)* barter trade;

freier ~ free trade of goods; **zwischenstaatlicher ~** international bartering;

~**abkommen** barter agreement; ~**verhältnis** commodity terms of trade.

Waren|auswahl merchandise selection; **bedingte ~auswahl** tentative selection *(US)*; ~**auszeichner** marker of goods; ~**auszeichnung** marking of goods, mark; ~**automat** vending (selling) machine, mechanical seller; ~**avis** advice of goods; ~**ballen** bale, package; **wöchentlich 1000 ~ballen produzieren** to put out 1000 bales weekly; ~**barometer** commodities indicator; ~**bedarf** goods request, required (requirement in) goods, demand; ~**bedarfsdeckung** commodity coverage; ~**beförderung auf Schiffen regulärer Linien** liner transport; ~**begleitpapiere** goods invoice; ~**begleitschein** consignment note, bill of delivery, shipping note *(Br.)*; ~**beilage** enclosure; ~**beleihung** lending on goods; ~**belieferung** supply of goods; ~**beschädigung** injury suffered by goods; ~**beschaffung** assembly, procurement of merchandise, merchandise procurement.

Warenbeschaffungs|amt supply office; ~**journal** requisition journal; ~**kosten** purchasing (merchandise procurement) cost; ~**kredit** purchase-money loan; ~**plan** merchandise plan (budget).

Waren|beschlagnahme detention of goods; ~**beschreibung** trade description, description of commodities; **schriftliche ~beschreibung** bill of sight.

Warenbestand merchandise inventory, stock[-in-trade], remainder in goods, merchandise on hand, store, carriage stock;

veränderlicher ~ shifting stock of merchandise;

~ **am Monatsanfang** merchandise at the beginning of the month;

~ **ergänzen** to replace the stock.

Warenbestände storage on hand, stocked goods, goods in stock, wares and merchandise, inventories;

~ **zum Anschaffungs- oder niedrigerem Marktpreis angesetzt** inventories at the lower-of-cost-or-market.

Warenbestands | abschreibung inventory writedown; ~**anreicherung** inventory accumulation; ~**aufnahme** stocktaking, inventory taking (proceedings); ~**konto** inventory (stock, *Br.*) account; ~**liste** inventory list; ~**prüfung** distributor audit.

Warenbestellbuch order book.

Warenbestellung order for goods;
~ **aus dem Ausland** indent, export order; ~ **eines bestimmten Markenerzeugnisses** closed indent;
~ **aufgeben** to put goods on order; ~ **für London aufgeben** to order goods from London; ~**en entgegennehmen** to take orders for future delivery.

Waren | bevorschusser factor; ~**bevorschussung** warehouse loan, commodity advance, advance against products, factoring, *(Bilanz)* selling accounts receivable outright *(US)*; ~**bevorschussung vornehmen** to advance against products; ~**bewegung** merchandise movement; ~**bewertung** evaluation of goods, merchandise (inventory) valuation; ~**bewirtschaftung** commodity control, rationing of goods; ~**bewirtschaftungsmaßnahmen** rationing arrangements; ~**bezeichnung** description of goods, description (denomination) of commodities, merchandise (trade) description, commercial mark, distinctive name *(US)*, *(Bahn)* billing reference; **falsche** ~**bezeichnung** false trade description; ~**bezieher** importer; ~**bezug** procurement of goods; ~**bezug zu verbilligten Preisen** cooperative purchasing; ~**bezugsprämie** trading stamp; ~**bezugsschein** purchase (purchasing) permit; ~ **und Dienstleistungsbilanz** balance of trade in goods and services, balance of payments on current account; ~**bonuskredit** commercial acceptance credit; ~**börse** produce (commodity) exchange, commodity market; ~**börsenausschuß** commodity commission; **überseeisches** ~**börsengeschäft** merchanting *(Br.)*; ~**buchhaltung** merchandise accounting; ~**deckung** commodity coverage; ~**deklaration** specification [of merchandise]; ~**depot** goods depository, warehouse *(US)*; ~**diskont** trade discount; ~**dollar** commodity dollar; ~**dumping betreiben** to dump goods; ~**durchfuhr** transit of goods; ~**eigentümer** owner of the goods, holder of stocks; ~**eigentümer sein** to own commodities.

Wareneinfuhr entry (importation) of goods, import of commodities, introduction of goods into a country;
unerlaubte ~ clandestine import of goods;
~ **in handelsüblichen Mindestmengen** importation of goods in minimum commercial quantities;
~**bilanz** balance of merchandise imports.

Waren | eingang goods received, incoming goods (stocks), arrival of goods, stock receipt; ~**eingänge** purchase, goods received, incoming goods (stocks); ~**ein- und** ~**ausgang** purchase and sale of goods; ~**eingang bestätigen** to sign for the goods.

Wareneingangs | abteilung receiving department; ~**bescheinigung** delivery receipt, receiving slip; ~**bestätigung** delivery verification; ~**buch,** ~**journal** purchase book (journal ledger), supplier's (goods-bought) ledger; ~**konto** purchase (goods-purchased) account; ~**meldung** receiving report; ~**rechnung** purchase account; ~**schein** receiving slip; ~**stelle** receiving room; ~**überwachung** delivery supervision.

Wareneinkauf offtake, [merchandise] purchase.

Wareneinkaufs | angebot basket of available commodities; ~**buch** goods-bought (-purchased) ledger (journal); ~**genossenschaft** cooperative wholesale society, *(Einzelhandel)* retail coop; ~**konto** goods-purchased ledger; ~**system** merchandise planning.

Waren | einlagerung storage of goods, warehousing; ~**einstandspreis** cost price; ~**einstufung** merchandise classification, classification of goods; ~**einteilung nach Güteklassen** grading of commodities; ~**einzelhandel** retail trade (merchandising); ~**einzelhändler** retailer, retail trader; ~**einzelspanne** commercial margin per item, markup; ~**empfang bestätigen** to sign for the goods; ~**empfänger** receiver of goods, consignee; ~**empfangsbestätigung,** ~**empfangsschein** receipt for goods, receiving ticket, delivery receipt; ~**entlohnung** truck [system] *(Br.)*, store pay *(US)*; ~**ersatz** replacement of goods; ~**etikette** trade label, ticket; ~**etikettierung** label(l)ing of goods; ~**fluß** flow of merchandise; ~**forderungen** *(Bilanz)* trade debtors, merchandise (trade accounts) receivables *(US)*; ~**forschung** product research; ~**freigabe gegen Bezahlung** release of goods against payment; ~**gattung** line, description, sort (kind, class) of goods; **steuerpflichtige** ~**gattung** taxable class of goods; **verschiedene** ~**gattungen führen** to stock varied goods; ~**gebiet** category of goods; ~**genossenschaft** consumer cooperative; ~**geschäft** commercial transaction, transaction in goods; ~**geschäfte machen** to trade in goods; ~**gewinn** trading profit; ~**gläubiger** trade (merchandise, mercantile) creditor; **einfacher** ~**gläubiger** *(im Konkurs)* ordinary unsecured creditor; ~**gruppe** category of goods, group of merchandise, inventory group; ~**gruppenspanne** merchandise-category [profit] margin; ~**gruppenstatistik** merchandising statistics; ~**güterstruktur** commodity pattern; ~**gütezeichen** quality label; ~**gutschein** voucher exchangeable for goods, shopping cheque *(Br.)* (check, *US*); ~**handbuch** merchandise manual; ~**handel** commodity trading, mercantile business, [business of] merchandising, merchandise (goods) trade, trade in products; ~**handel betreiben** to merchandise, to merchant; ~**handelsbilanz** merchandise trade balance; ~**handelsüberschuß** merchandise trade surplus; ~**händler** commodity dealer.

Warenhaus stores *(Br.)*, department *(US)* (departmental, *Br.*, multiple) store, universal providers *(Br.)*, bulk store *(Australien)*, *(Lagerhaus)* warehouse;
frei ~ delivered in stores;
billiges ~ limited-price variety store; **großes** ~ supermarket *(US)*; **voll sortimentiertes** ~ full-line department store *(US)*;
~**aktien** store shares *(Br.)*, department store shares *(US)*; ~**bilanz** department balance; ~**buchhandel** departmental store bookselling (booksellers); ~**dieb** shop-lifter; ~**diebstahl** shoplifting; ~**direktor** merchandising director; ~**einkäufer** departmental buyer; ~**filiale** department-store branch *(US)*; ~**kette** supermarket (department store, *US*) chain; ~**konzern** stores group *(Br.)*, department store group *(US)*; ~**lizenz** department-store licence; ~**umsätze** department store sales *(US)*; ~**verkäufer** store clerk *(US)*; ~**versicherung** warehouseman's liability insurance.

Waren | hortung hoarding (retention) of goods; ~**inventar** inventory of goods, merchandise inventory; ~**katalog** catalog(ue) of merchandise; ~**kauf** sale of goods; ~**kenntnis** knowledge of goods; ~**kennzeichen** merchandise mark; ~**kennzeichnung** label(l)ing, marking; ~**kennzeichnungsgesetz** Trade Description Act *(Br.)*; ~**klasse** class of goods; ~**klasseneinteilung** international classification of goods; ~**knappheit** shortage of goods, stock (merchandise) shortage; ~**konjunktur** commodity boom; ~**konkurrenz** industrial competition; ~**kontingent** goods quota; ~**kontingentierung** allocation of quotas, quota system; ~**konto** goods (merchandise) account; ~**kontobuch** book of merchandise; ~**kontrolle** merchandise control, quality inspection; ~**korb** *(Statistik)* basket of available commodities, market basket, shopping bag.

Warenkredit commercial (commodity, omnibus, *Br.*, mercantile) credit, commodity loan, commercial loan, credit in goods, produce loan, *(Lieferant)* supplier's (trade, *US*) credit;
kurzfristiger ~ self-liquidating advance (credit), self-liquidating loan *(US)*; **mittelfristiger** ~ medium-term commercial credit;
~**abteilung** commercial credit department; ~**bearbeiter** commercial credit man *(US)*; ~**brief** commercial letter of credit; ~**bürgschaft** commercial credit guarantee; ~**fazilitäten** produce facilities; ~**genossenschaft** industrial cooperative society *(Br.)*; ~**gesellschaft** consumer credit agency; ~**konto** produce loan account; ~**wechsel** trade note receivables *(US)*.

Waren | kunde merchandising technique, commodity economics; ~**ladung** commodity cargo.

Warenlager warehouse, merchandise (inventory) stock, goods on hand, *(Lagerhaus)* depot, repository, magazine, packing house, warehouse, storehouse, *(Lagerraum)* storeroom, stock room, *(Vorrat)* stock-in-trade, assortment (stock) of goods, packing house *(US)*, *(Warenhof)* goods yard;
sein ~ **absetzen** to make one's market; ~ **wieder auffüllen** to renew a stock of goods; ~ **besitzen** to own commodities; ~ **bewerten** to appraise a stock of goods; **im** ~ **festlegen** to lie up in stocks; **im** ~ **stark investiert haben** to carry heavy stocks; ~ **räumen** to weed a stock of goods; ~ **umschlagen** to turn over stock;
~**funktion** merchandising function; ~**haltung** stockkeeping, stockpiling, warehousing; ~**haus** storeroom, warehouse; ~**raum** merchandise storage space.

Waren | lagerung storage of goods, commercial storage, warehousing; ~**lieferant** supplier [of goods], contractor, purveyor (furnisher) of goods.

Warenlieferung delivery (supplying) of goods, goods delivery;
~**en** *(Bilanz)* payable to suppliers *(US)*;
~**en auf Abzahlungsbasis** supplies on a hire-purchase *(Br.)* (deferred-payment, *US*) basis; ~ **längsseits Schiff** delivery of goods alongside the ship;
~ **beanstanden** to reject goods delivered; ~**en zurückhalten** to withhold supply of goods from a dealer.

Warenlieferungsvertrag contract for the delivery of goods.

Waren | liste list of products; ~**liste liberalisieren** to liberalize a list of items; ~**lohn** truck [wages] *(Br.)*, store pay *(US)*; ~**lohnsystem** truck system *(Br.)*; ~**lombard** hypothecation of goods, commodity collateral loan *(US)*, advances against [hypothecation of] merchandise *(US)*; ~**lombardkredit** revolving credit; ~**makler** produce (merchandise) broker; ~**mangel** want (scarcity) of goods, *(Börse)* scarcity of (few) offerings; ~**markt** commodity (produce) market.

Warenmenge amount (quantity) of goods;
angebotene ~ pitch; **nicht zum Handel geeignete** ~**n** noncommercial quantities; **dem Markt zur Verfügung stehende** ~ visible supply.

Waren | merkmale, äußerliche descriptive standards; ~**messe** show of goods, merchandising show; ~**muster** commercial sample, pattern; ~**neubewertung** remarking of merchandise; ~**niederlage** depository of goods, magazine, warehouse; ~**normen** product standards; ~**normung** standardization of commodities, commercial standardization; ~**note** prompt note.

Warenpartie parcel, package (shipment) of goods, lot, consignment [of merchandise];
gesonderte ~**n** detached parcels of goods; **zweitklassige** ~ cheap line;
große ~ **verkaufen** to pitch a large consignment; **verlorene** ~ **wiederfinden** to trace lost goods.

Warenpaß *(Schiff)* navicert.

Warenposten [merchandise) item, lot;
nicht auf Lager befindliche ~ out-of-stock item;
~ **mit kleinen Fehlern (zweiter Wahl)** job lot;
~ **losschlagen** to work off a stock of goods.

Warenprämie trade premium.

Warenpreis commodity price, price of goods;
~**e neu auszeichnen** to remark merchandise; **angemessenen** ~ **einklagen** to sue for a reasonable price of goods; ~ **erhöhen** to enhance the prices of goods; ~ **herabsetzen (heruntersetzen)** to mark (bring) down the price of an article, to lower the price of goods; ~**e in die Höhe treiben** to puff up goods;
~**hausse** commodity boom; ~**prognose** commodity price forecasting.

Warenprobe sample [of merchandise], pattern of trade, pattern reference, specimen;
kostenlose ~ free trial (sample); **zurückbehaltene** ~ reference pattern;
~ **zum Selbstkostenpreis** self-liquidating premium, self-liquidator;
~**n zusammenstellen** to make up samples.

Waren | probenverteilung free-gift (novelty) advertising; **willkürliche** ~**probenverteilung** caravan test; ~**prüfer** merchandise checker, quality inspector *(Br.)*; ~**prüfstelle** merchandise testing bureau; ~**prüfung** quality control (inspection, *Br.*); ~**prüfungsamt** merchandise testing bureau; ~**qualität** qualities of merchandise (commodities, goods); ~**rabatt** trade premium (discount), merchandise allowance; ~**raum** wareroom; ~**rechnung** goods account, invoice; **spezifizierte** ~**rechnung** bill of parcels, detailed (itemized) account; ~**rechnungspreis** billed price of merchandise *(US)*; ~**reichweite** commodity coverage; ~**reserve** stockpile; ~**reste** remnants, oddments; ~**rest zurückhalten** to hold over the rest of the goods; ~**retouren** goods returned, return sales; ~**risiko** sales risk; ~**rohgewinn** gross profit on sales, gross trading profit; ~**rohgewinnaufschlag** inventory markup; ~**rückgabe** return of goods, merchandise return, ~**schein** dock warrant, consignment note; ~**schuld** commercial debt; ~**schulden** *(Bilanz)* trade debts, trade accounts payable *(US)*; ~**schuldner** debtor.

Warensendung consignment [of merchandise], package (parcel, shipment, *US*) of goods, lot;
~**en** *(Post)* fourth class matter *(US)*;
ausgehende ~**en** outgoing shipments of merchandise *(US)*; **eingegangene** ~**en** goods (merchandise) received *(US)*; **eingehende** ~**en** incoming shipments of merchandise *(US)*; **gemischte** ~**en** miscellaneous collections of goods, mixed goods; **kreditierte** ~ credit shipment;
neue ~ **von Hüten erhalten** to receive a new lot of hats; ~ **ab heute versichert haben** to hold a consignment covered as from today; ~ **per Eilgut schicken** to send a consignment by passenger train; ~ **stichprobenartig überprüfen** to check samples, to spotcheck the shipment *(US)*.

Waren | sicherheit commodity collateral; ~**skonto** trade discount, merchandise allowance; ~**sorte** category of goods, grade (commodity) description.

Warensortiment line (assortment) of goods (products), assortment of merchandise, merchandise assortment (line);
breit gestreutes ~ broadly diversified product lines; **unvollständiges** ~ broken assortment;
sein ~ **auffächern** to diversify one's product lines; **mit einem** ~ **ausstatten** to assort with a stock of goods.

Waren | speicher [commercial] warehouse, storehouse, magazine, depot; ~**spezialisierung** [commodity] specialization; ~**statistik** merchandising statistics; ~**stempel** trademark, brand; ~**ströme** trade currents; ~**struktur** pattern (range) of goods; ~**stückpreis** average revenue; ~**tarif** commodity tariff; ~**tausch** barter, bartering, trading; ~**technik** commercial engineering.

Warentermin | börse commodity forward exchange; ~**geschäft** [trading-in] commodity futures *(US)*; ~**handel** dealings in commodity futures *(US)*; ~**händler** commodity future trader.

Waren | test consumer test, product test[ing]; ~**testaktion** merchandising operation; ~**transaktion** merchandising operation, merchandise transaction; ~**transit** transit of goods, passage; ~**transport** transport of merchandise, goods transport; ~**transportversicherung** marine (shipping, *US*) insurance; ~**übereignung** merchandise transfer; **innerbetriebliche** ~**übereignungen** interplant transfers *(US)*; ~**überfluß**, ~**überschuß** surplus of goods, overage; ~**überprüfung** quality inspection *(Br.)*, merchandise control; ~**überprüfungsvorschriften** inspection laws; ~**umsatz** merchandise turnover, commodity sales, turnover of merchandise, sales turnover, momentum of sales *(US)*; **schneller** ~**umsatz** rapid turnover of goods; ~**umsatzsteuer** sales (turnover, transactions, purchase, *Br.*) tax; ~**umschlag** movement of goods; ~**umschlagsplatz** trading post *(US)*; ~**unterscheidung** product differentation; ~**verbindlichkeiten** commercial commitments, accounts payable *(US)*; ~**verbrauch** commodity consumption; ~**verkauf** sale of goods, commodity (commercial) sale.

Warenverkaufs | buch book of sales, sales journal (book); ~**konto** sales (trading) account; ~**steuer** retail sales tax *(US)*.

Warenverkehr movement of freight (goods, commodities), trade (traffic) in goods, [slow-]goods traffic *(Br.)*, merchandise traffic, visible trade, flow of commodities;
freier ~ free movement of goods; **grenzüberschreitender** ~ frontier-crossing goods traffic; **innergemeinschaftlicher** ~ *(EG)* intra-community trade;
~ **und Dienstleistungsverkehr** trade and services, goods and service transactions, exchange of goods and services; ~ **und Dienstleistungsverkehr mit dem Ausland** foreign trade and service transactions; ~ **und Kapitalverkehr** goods and capital movement;
~ **liberalisieren** to liberalize trade.

Waren | verknappung shortage of goods, stock (merchandise) shortage, shortage of merchandise; ~**vermittler** middleman; ~**verpackung** wrapping; ~**verpfändung** pledge (hypothecation) of goods; ~**versand** consignment (shipping, *US*, sending, dispatch, shipment, *US*) of goods, commercial (merchandise) shipment *(US)*; ~**versand auf dem normalen Postweg durchführen** to send goods regularly by surface *(Br.)*; ~**verschleuderung** *(auf dem Weltmarkt)* dumping; ~**versender** consignor; ~**versendung** consignment of goods; ~**versicherung** insurance of merchandise; ~**verteilung** distribution of goods; ~**vertrieb** distribution of goods, commodity marketing; ~**vertrieb im großen** sales transacted at large; ~**vertriebsorganisation** merchandising organization; ~**verzeichnis** list of commodities (products), [merchandise] inventory, stock book, inventory of goods, commodity code (classification), *(Faktur)* invoice, manifest, *(Schiff)* ship's manifest; **Internationales** ~**verzeichnis für den Außenhandel** Standard International Trade Classification; ~**verzollung im Zollager** clearance of goods from warehouse; ~**vorrat** stock of merchandise, stock-in-trade, stock on hand, merchandise (stock) investment, stocked goods; ~**vorräte abbauen** to liquidate an inventory; **umfangreiche** ~**vorräte haben** to carry heavy stock; ~**vorschüsse** advances against [hypothecation of] merchandise; ~**vorschüsse** commodity standard; ~**wechsel** commercial (mercantile, trade, sales, business, *US*) paper, trade bill (acceptance), mercantile (commodity, sales, *US*) bill; **diskontfähiger kurzfristiger** ~**wechsel** good trade paper; ~**werbung** product advertising; **zwanglose** ~**werbung** soft sell *(US)*; ~**wert** goods (commodity) value; ~**wettbewerb** commodity competition.

Warenzeichen trademark, trade-mark *(Br.)*, brand, trade name, *(Gütezeichen)* manufacturer's (certification) mark, make;
mit einem ~ **versehen** branded;

anerkanntes ~ trademark with a good name; **ausländisches** ~ foreign trademark; **bereits bestehende** ~ previously existing trademarks; **eingetragenes** ~ registered trademark; **nicht eingetragenes** ~ unregistered (common-law, *US*) trademark; **geschütztes** ~ registered trademark; **international geschütztes** ~ international trademark; **irreführendes** ~ deceptive mark; **nachgemachtes** ~ forged trademark; **spezifisches** ~ distinctive mark; **im Eigentum einer Tochtergesellschaft stehendes** ~ trademark owned by a subsidiary; **unterscheidungskräftiges** ~ distinctive trademark; **verbundene** ~ associated trademarks *(Br.)*;
~ **anmelden** to register a trademark; ~ **benutzen** to use a trademark; ~ **besitzen** to own a trademark; ~ **einprägen** to stamp a manufacturer's name on his goods; ~ **eintragen** to register a trademark; **als** ~ **eintragen lassen** to have a trademark registered at the Board of Trade; ~ **im Register löschen** to cancel a trademark registration; ~ **nachahmen** to pirate a trademark; ~ **miteinander verbinden** to associate trademarks; ~ **verletzen** to infringe a trademark; **mit** ~ **versehen** to brand, to label; **seine Waren unter falschem** ~ **vertreiben** to pass off one's goods as those of another make; ~**abteilung** trademark section; ~**anmeldung** application for registration of trademarks; **eingetragener** ~**benutzer** registered user; ~**benutzung** use of a registered trademark; ~**benutzungsrecht** trademark rights; **eingetragener** ~**besitzer** registered user *(Br.)*; ~**eintragung** register of trademark, trademark registration; **täuschend ähnliche** ~**fälschung** colo(u)rable imitation; ~**gebühren** trademark registration fees; ~**gesetz** Trademark Registration Act *(US)*, Merchandise Marks Act *(Br.)*; ~**inhaber** trademark owner, proprietor (owner) of a registered trademark; ~**lizenz** trademark licence; ~**löschung** cancellation of trademark registration.

Warenzeichenrecht trademark law;
~**e** trademark rights;
~ **überschreiben lassen** to assign a trademark; **jds.** ~ **verletzen** to appropriate unlawfully s. one's trademark, to infringe s. one's trademark.

Warenzeichen|register trademark registry; ~**rolle** registry of trademarks; **in der** ~**rolle löschen** to remove a trademark from the register; ~**schutz** protection of trademarks, trademark protection; ~**schutzgesetz** Trademark Registration Act; ~**verfälschung** imitation of trademarks, colo(u)rable imitation; ~**verletzung** infringement (misappropriation) of a trademark; ~**verwechslung** confusion of trademarks; ~**vorschriften** trademark rules of practice *(US)*.

Waren|zettel docket, label, mark; ~**zoll** customs duty; ~**zufuhr** supply (arrival) of goods; ~**zugänge** incoming stocks; ~**zurückhaltung** withholding supply of goods from a dealer; **mangelhafter** ~**zustand** defective conditions of the goods; ~**zustellung** delivery of goods.

warm hot, warm;
sich ~ **anziehen** to put on warm clothes; **jem. etw.** ~ **empfehlen** to recommend s. th. highly to s. o.; **sich j.** ~ **halten** to stand in with s. o.; **sich eine geschäftliche Aussicht** ~ **halten** to keep a business report warm; **Mahlzeit** ~ **halten** to keep a dish hot; **seine Gäste** ~ **werden lassen** to thaw out one's guests;
~**er Umschlag** fomentation.

Wärme|bedingungen thermic conditions; ~**dämmung** heat insulation; ~**einbruch** invasion of warm air; ~**einheit** heat unit; ~**energie** heat (thermal) energy; ~**gehalt** heat content; ~**leistung** heat output; ~**leitfähigkeit** thermal conductivity; ~**menge** quantity of heat.

wärmen, sich am Feuer to warm o. s. at the fire.

Wärme|schutz thermic protection; ~**vergütung** *(Metall)* heat-treatment; ~**verlust** loss of heat.

Wärmflasche hot-water bottle, warming pan.

Warm|halteplatte dish-warmer (heater); ~**laufen** *(Motor)* warmup.

warmlaufen lassen *(Motor)* to warm up.

Warmluft warm air;
~**front** warm front; ~**heizung** hot-air heating; ~**rohr** hot-air pipe.

Warmwasser|anschluß haben to have hot-running water; ~**bereiter** water heater; ~**hahn** warm (hot) [-water]tap; ~**heizung** hot-water heating; ~**speicher** hot-water reservoir.

Warn|anlage warning device; ~**blinkanlage** emergency traffic signal.

warnen to caution, to warn, to admonish;
j. vor einer Gefahr ~ to give warning of danger to s. o.; **vor Übergriffen** ~ to sound a warning note to those who would go too far; **j. vorher** ~ to tip s. o. off.

warnend|es Beispiel [warning] example; ~**en Ton anschlagen** to sound a note of warning.

Warn|feuer *(mar.)* warning light; ~**flagge** red flag; ~**gebiet** danger zone; ~**kreuz** *(Bahn)* warning cross; ~**lampe** alarm lamp; ~**leuchte** telltale lamp; ~**licht** warning light; ~**lichtschalter** *(Auto)* emergency blinker signal; **einige** ~**schüsse abgeben** to fire some warning shots; ~**signal** warning (alarm) sign, *(Bahn)* signal, fusee *(US)*, *(Luftschutz)* on signal, *(Schiff)* cautionary signal; ~**streik** warning (token) strike.

Warnung warning, caution, alarm, *(Mahnung)* admonition, notice, *(Vorbehalt)* caveat;
vorherige ~ premonition;
~ **vor einer Gefahr** danger warning;
jem. eine ~ **zukommen lassen** to pass on a warning to s. o.; ~ **in den Wind schlagen** to disregard a warning.

Warn|vorrichtung alarm (warning) device, warner; ~**zeichen** monitor, warning sign; ~**zeit** warning period.

Warptrosse warp.

wartbar maintainable.

Wartbarkeit maintainability.

Warte, von meiner ~ **aus** from my point of view.

Wartebahn *(Flugzeuge)* holding (landing) pattern;
von der ~ **abrufen** to call off a holding (from the landing) pattern; **auf der** ~ **fliegen** to orbit; **auf die** ~ **schicken** to put on a holding (send in the landing) pattern, to stack up.

Warte|flughöhe holding altitude; ~**funkfeuer** holding radio beacon; ~**geld** *(Beamter)* half pay, *(Schiff)* demurrage; **auf** ~**geld setzen** to put on half pay; ~**halle,** ~**häuschen** streetcar (bus, tram, *US*) shelter; ~**kosten** opportunity (alternative) costs; ~**kreisbahn** *(Raumfahrt)* parking orbit; ~**liste** waiting list, *(Anzeigenwesen)* issue waiting list, *(Flugzeug)* standby; **j. auf die** ~**liste setzen** to put s. o. on the waiting list.

warten to wait for, *(pflegen)* to nurse, to attend, *(Anlage)* to maintain;
auf seine Abholung ~ to wait to be collected; **auf eine Erbschaft** ~ to wait for a dead man's shoes; **Flughafen** ~ to maintain an airport; **auf eine günstige Gelegenheit** ~ to bide one's opportunity, to lie low *(sl.)*; **mit dem Mittagessen auf j.** ~ to wait dinner for s. o.; **geschlagene zwei Stunden** ~ to wait two hours on end;
ungeduldig ~, **bis man dran ist** to fume because one is kept waiting; ~, **bis man dran kommt** to wait one's turn;
auf sich ~ **lassen** to hang fire; **j.** ~ **lassen** to keep s. o. waiting, to make s. o. wait; **sein Auto laufend** ~ **lassen** to have one's car serviced regularly; **j. lange** ~ **lassen** to let s. o. cool his heels; **j. vergeblich** ~ **lassen** to turn s. o. down; **lange auf den Bus** ~ **müssen** to have a long wait for the bus.

Wärter keeper, tender, *(Gefängnis)* warden, *(Pfleger)* caretaker, attendant, *(Wächter)* watchman.

Warte|raum waiting room, restroom, *(Flugplatz)* departure lounge, *(Flugzeuge)* holding area; ~**raum vor Kopfbahnsteigen** head house; ~**saal** waiting room (hall); ~**schlange** queuing line *(Br.)*, queue *(Br.)*, line-up *(US)*; ~**schlangentheorie** waiting-line (queuing, *Br.*) theory; ~**schleife** *(Flugzeug)* holding (landing) pattern; ~**schleife ziehen** to circle for landing (on a landing pattern); ~**signal** amber-light signal; ~**stand** temporary retirement, half-pay; **in den** ~**stand versetzen** to place on half-pay; ~**standsbeamter** half-pay officcer; ~**stellung** *(mil.)* standby position, wait-and-see attitude, *(Raumschiff)* holding position; ~**theorie des Zinses** abstinence theory of interest; ~**zeit** period of waiting, waiting period, time of waiting, wait, gap, *(für Anwartschaft)* qualifying (waiting) period, *(Flugzeugplatz)* standby time, *(Maschine)* down (waiting) time, *(Produktionsprozeß)* idle time, *(Schiff)* demurrage, *(Streik)* cooling-off period, *(Versicherung)* initial waiting period, *(Zeitstudie)* attendance time; ~**zeitprobleme** *(Verkehr)* congestion problems; ~**zimmer** anteroom, reception (waiting) room.

Wartung maintenance [service], upkeep, servicing, *(Maschine)* attendance, *(Pflege)* care, attendance, nursing;
laufende ~ current maintenance (upkeep);
~ **eines Fahrzeugs** maintenance of an automobile; ~ **eines Flugzeugs** servicing an aircraft; ~ **der Mietgegenstände** rental maintenance.

Wartungs|abkommen maintenance contract; ~**anlagen** maintenance facilities; ~**aufwand** maintenance charges; ~**dienst** maintenance service; ~**etat** maintenance budget; ~**ingenieur** service (maintenance) engineer; ~**kosten** cost of servicing, cost of upkeep, maintenance charges (costs), current maintenance; ~**kräfte** maintenance workers; ~**miete** maintenance leasing; ~**personal** maintenance personnel (employees), maintenance people (staff); ~**zyklus** maintenance cycle.

Wasch|anlage, automatische car wash; ~**anstalt** laundry, washhouse; ~**automat** automatic washing machine.

waschbar washable, *(Farben)* fast;
~**es Material** wash goods.

Wasch|becken washhand basin (stand) washbowl *(Br.)*; ~**beutel** overnight bag; ~**bottich** washing tub; ~**brett** washboard.

Wäsche laundry, wash;
~ **aufhängen** to hang out the laundry; ~ **zum Trocknen aufhängen** to put linen out to dry; **frische** ~ **aufziehen** to put on fresh sheets; ~ **waschen** to launder; **seine schmutzige** ~ **in aller Öffentlichkeit waschen** *(fig.)* to wash one's dirty linen in public; **regelmäßig seine** ~ **wechseln** to change one's underwear regularly;
~**ausfahrer** bobtail driver; ~**beutel** laundry bag.

waschecht amerikanisch as American as apple pie.

Waschechter out-and-outer.

Wäsche|fabrik underwear factory; ~**geschäft** lingerie shop (store, *US*); ~**gestell** clothes horse; ~**kammer** linen room; ~**klammern** clothes pegs; ~**korb** hamper; ~**leine** [hang-]clothes line.

waschen *(Erz)* to wash, to clean;
Auto ~ to give the car a wash; **seine Hände in Unschuld** ~ to wash one's hands of it; **für fremde Leute** ~ to take in washing; **außerhalb** ~ **lassen** to send one's laundry out; **sich gut** ~ **lassen** to wash well.

Wäscherei laundry;
in der ~ at the wash;
etw. in die ~ **geben** to send s. th. to the wash.

Wäsche|schleuder spin drier; ~**schrank** linen cupboard (press); ~**trockner** drying machine, clothes (hot-air) drier; **eingewebtes** ~**zeichen** name tape.

Wasch|flüssigkeitsbehälter washing-liquid bottle; ~**frau** laundress; ~**gelegenheit** washing facilility, lavatory; ~**kessel** wash boiler; ~**kommode** washstand; ~**küche** washhouse, *(dichter Nebel)* pea-soup fog; ~**lappen** wash rag *(US)*, face cloth, *(fig.)* milksop, sissy *(sl.)*; ~**lederhandschuh** wash glove; ~**maschine** washer, washing machine; ~**mittel** detergent; ~**möglichkeit** wash place; ~**pulver** washing powder; ~**raum** washroom, lavatory, rest room; ~**salon** public laundry, launderette, laundromat *(US)*; ~**schüssel** washbowl; ~**tag** washing day; ~**trommel** drum (cylinder) washer; ~**weib** gossip, chatterbox; ~**zettel** *(Buch)* dope, clip sheet, blurb *(US)*; ~**zettel schreiben** to blurb *(US)*; ~**zettelverfasser** blurb writer *(US)*; ~**zeug** toilet things; ~**zuber** washing tub.

Wasser, am ~ **gelegen** water-front; **bei auflaufendem** ~ when the tide rises; **mit** ~ **versorgt** watered; **vom** ~ **eingeschlossen** water-bound; **vom reinsten** ~ *(Brillant)* of the first water;
ablaufendes ~ ebbing (receding) tide; **auflaufendes** ~ rising (incoming) tide; **fließendes** ~ running water; **an die Oberfläche gebrachtes** ~ developed waters; **aus Bewässerungsprojekten gewonnenes** ~ irrigation (reclamation, *US*) water; **offenes** ~ open water; **sauberes** ~ clean (pure) water; **schales** ~ ditch water; **seichtes** ~ shallow water; **stehendes** ~ dead (stagnant) water; **verschmutztes** ~ polluted water;
jem. das ~ **abgraben** to cut the ground from under s. one's feet; **an jem. wie** ~ **ablaufen** *(Vorwürfe)* to run off s. o. like water of a duck's back; **wie aus dem** ~ **gezogen aussehen** to look like a drowned rat; **Boot zu** ~ **bringen** to launch a boat; ~ **einnehmen** *(Schiff)* to water [ship]; **über das große** ~ **fahren** to cross the Atlantic; **ins** ~ **fallen** to come to naught, to fall flat; ~ **fassen** *(Lokomotive)* to water; ~ **in den Wein gießen** to damp s. one's spirits, to throw cold water on s. th.; **das** ~ **bis zum Halse stehen haben** to be in deep waters; **j. über** ~ **halten** to keep s. o. going; **sich über** ~ **halten** *(fig.)* to stay afloat, to keep one's head above water (afloat), to tide it over; **sich mit eigenen Mitteln über** ~ **halten** to rub along with one's means of support; **sich nur mit Mühe über** ~ **halten können** to have difficulties in making both ends meet; **jem. nicht das** ~ **reichen können** not to be fit to hold a candle to s. o.; **mit** ~ **kühlen** to water-cool; **jem. das** ~ **im Munde zusammenlaufen lassen** to make s. one's mouth water, to bring the water to s. one's mouth; **am** ~ **liegen** to lie at a river; **Wein mit** ~ **mischen** to dilute wine with water; ~ **mit einem Sieb schöpfen** to waste one's efforts; **nahe am** ~ **gebaut sein** to be easily moved to tears; **mit allen** ~**n gewaschen sein** to know a thing or two; ~ **auf jds. Mühle sein** to be grist to s. one's mill; **Schlag ins** ~ **sein** to be a fiasco; **unter** ~ **setzen** to float; **bei Brot und** ~ **sitzen** to be in jug, to do a stretch *(Br.)*; **auf beiden Schultern** ~ **tragen** to serve two masters; ~ **ins Meer tragen** to carry coals to Newcastle; **über fließendes** ~ **verfügen** to have water on tap; **mit** ~ **versorgen** to serve (supply) with water; **stille** ~ **gründen tief** still waters run deep;
~**abfluß** water outlet; ~**ableitung aus öffentlichen Gewässern** appropriation of water; ~**abzugsgraben** field ditch; ~**ader** water vein; ~**amt** water authority; ~**anschluß haben** to be on the water mains; ~**armut** aridity, dryness; ~**aufbereitungsanlage** water treatment plant; ~**ballast** water ballast; ~- **und Kanalbauamt** Commissioner of Sewers *(Br.)*; ~**bauingenieur** water-supply (hydraulic) engineer; ~**bauwesen** water-supply (hydraulic) engineering; ~**becken** basin; ~**bedarf** water requirements; ~**behälter** water cistern; ~**benutzungsrecht** water privilege.

wasser|beschädigt damaged by water; ~**beständig** waterproof, water-resistant.

Wasserbuch water-rights register.

Wässerchen, er sieht aus, als ob er kein ~ **trüben könnte** he looks if butter wouldn't melt in his mouth.

Wasserdepot *(Bahn)* water (watering, *US*) depot.

wasserdicht impermeable to water, waterproof;
~ **sein** to hold water;
~**e Abteilung** *(Schiff)* watertight compartment.

Wasser|druck water pressure; ~**dunst** water vapo(u)r; ~**durchlaß** culvert.

wasserdurchlässig permeable.

Wasser|eimer bucket, pail; ~**enthärtungsanlage** water softener; ~**entnahmerecht** water privilege; ~**fahrzeug** watercraft, vessel, boat; ~**fall** waterfall; **wie ein** ~**fall reden** to talk nineteen to the dozen; **jds.** ~**fall stoppen** to turn off s. one's water *(sl.)*; **in** ~**farben malen** to paint in water-colo(u)rs; ~**faß** water cask; ~**flughafen** marine airport, water aerodrome *(Br.)*; ~**flugzeug** seaplane, hydroplane, waterplane, aeroboat, floatplane; ~**flut** inrush of water; ~**fracht** carriage by water, water-borne transport, *(Gebühr)* freight, waterage *(Br.)*; ~**frachtführer** water carrier; ~**frachtkosten** freight, waterage *(Br.)*.

wassergekühlt water-cooled.

Wasser|geld water rates *(Br.)*, water charges *(US)*; ~**graben** ditch, drain, water gang; ~**grundstück** waterfront property; ~**hahn** water cock; ~**haushalt** water balance (resources); ~**höhe** water level, watermark; **wieder normale** ~**höhe haben** *(Fluß)* to be down; ~**hose** waterspout, wind spout, twister *(US coll.)*.

wässerig wishy-washy;
jem. den Mund ~ **machen** to make s. one's mouth water.

Wasser|kanne water pitcher (jug); ~**kante** watersite; ~**karte** hydrographic card; ~**kessel** kettle; ~**klosett** water closet, convenience *(Br.)*; ~**kopf haben** *(Verwaltung)* to be top-heavy; ~**kraft** water power; ~**kraftstrom** hydro-electric power; ~**kraftwerk** hydro-electric power station; ~**kühlmantel** water jacket; ~**kühltank** water cooler; ~**kühlung** *(Auto)* water cooling; ~**landflugzeug** amphibian plane; ~**lauf** water course; ~**leitung** water pipe (main); ~**lieferung** water supply; ~**linie** waterline; **mit** ~**linien versehen** *(Notenpapier)* water-lined; **unterhalb der** ~**linie** underwater; ~**mangel** water shortage (famine); **strömende** ~**masse** flood, water flow.

wassern *(Flugzeug)* to water, to alight (touch down) on water, *(Raumkapsel)* to splash down.

wässern to water, *(Felder)* to submerge, *(Foto)* to rinse.

Wasser|nehmen *(Schiff)* watering; ~**nutzungsrecht** *(Mühle)* water power, water right; ~**oberfläche** surface (top) of water, water surface; **unterhalb der** ~**oberfläche** under water; ~**oberfläche kräuseln** to wimple (ripple) the lake; ~**pfütze** puddle, pool; ~**pumpe** water pump; ~**rationierung** rationing of water; ~**recht** right of water; ~**reservoir** reservoir; ~**rinne** *(Straße)* gutter; ~**rohr** water pipe (tube); ~**rohrbruch** break in the water mains, [water]pipe failure; ~**rohrbruchversicherung** burst water-pipes insurance; ~**sack** water pocket; ~**säule** head of water; ~**schaden** damage caused by water, water damage; ~**schadensversicherung** water-damage insurance; ~**scheide** watershed *(Br.)*, water divide.

wasserscheu sein to be a water funk *(coll.)*.

Wasser|schlauch hose, waterskin; ~**schlauch auf das Feuer richten** to play a hose on the fire; ~**schutzgebiet** water conservation area; ~**schutzpolizei** waterside (river) police; ~**ski** water-skiing; ~**spiegel** water level; **über dem** ~**spiegel** above water; **unter dem** ~**spiegel** below water; ~**sport** pleasure boating; ~**spülung** *(WC)* flushing.

Wasserstand watermark, water level;
beim höchsten ~ at full tide;
niedriger ~ low watermark.

Wasserstands|anzeiger water (tidal) gauge; ~**marke** water mark; ~**meldung** water-level bulletin.

Wasser|stelle watering place; ~**stiefel** Wellington (hip) boot; ~**stoffbombe** thermonuclear bomb, H- (hell-) bomb *(sl.)*; ~**straße** waterway, navigable road.

Wasserstraßen|amt Waterways Board *(Br.)*; **~netz** inland waterways system; **~verkehr** inland waterways traffic; **~verkehrsordnung** Inland Rules of the Road *(US)*.
Wasser|tank water tank, cistern; **~tankwagen** water carrier; **auslotbare ~tiefe** sounding; **~tiefe mit einem Lot messen** to fathom the depth of the water; **~träger** water-bearer; **~transport** water carriage, conveyance by water; **~turbine** water wheel, hydraulic turbine; **~turm** water tower (house); **~uhr** water clock (meter).
wasserundurchlässig waterproof.
Wasserung *(Flugzeug)* alighting on water, *(Raumkapsel)* splashdown.
Wasser|untersuchung water sampling; **~verbrauch** water consumption; **~verbraucher** water user; **~verdrängung** *(Schiff)* displacement; **~verschluß** waste trap; **~verschmutzung** water pollution; **~versorgung** water supply (service), *(städtische)* town waterworks; **nahegelegene ~versorgung** nearness to water supply; **~versorgungsanlagen** waterworks; **~versorgungsgesetz** Water Resources Act; **~vorrat** water resources; **~waage** level; **~wagen** water wag(g)on (cart).
Wasserweg waterway, water route, riverway, road;
auf dem ~ on the (by) water;
auf dem ~ befördern to send by water;
öffentlicher ~ public river; **schiffbarer ~** channel.
Wasser|welle water wave; **~werfer** *(Polizei)* water cannon; **~werk** waterworks, water company; **~wirtschaft** water engineering, water-supply industry (service).
Wasserwirtschafts|amt water board (authority), Water Resources Board *(Br.)*; **~ingenieur** water-power engineer; **~unternehmen** water undertaking.
Wasser|wüste waste (expanse) of water, wilderness of sea, watery waste; **~zähler** water meter; **~zapfstelle** standpipe; **~zeichen** *(Banknote)* watermark, paper mark; **mit einem ~zeichen versehen** to watermark; **~zeichenpapier** security paper, watermarked paper, filigreed paper; **~zins** water rate; **~zufluß** water feeder; **gewaltiger ~zufluß** flush.
watscheln, über die Straße to waddle across the road.
Watt shore lands, tideland, foreshore, *(el.)* watt.
Watte cotton wool *(Br.)*, absorbent cotton *(US)*;
j. in ~ packen to handle s. o. with kid gloves.
wattieren to wad, to pad.
wattierter Umschlag padded envelope.
Wattierung padding, wadding.
Watt|lampe, sechziger 60-watt light-bulb; **~leistung** wattage; **~messer** wattmeter; **~stunde** watt-hour; **~stundenzähler** watt-hour meter, wattmeter; **~zahl** wattage.
Weberei weaving mill;
~erzeugnis woven product.
Web|fehler weaving fault; **einen ~fehler haben** to be nuts; **~stuhl** loom; **~waren** textiles, soft goods.
Wechsel *(Abwechslung)* change, alternation, turn, *(Austausch)* exchange, barter, *(Bilanz)* bills in hand, bill holdings, bills receivable *(US)*, *(monatliche Geldzuwendung)* [personal] allowance, *(regelmäßiger Personenaustausch)* shift, *(Tratte)* bill [of exchange], draft, paper, *(Übergang)* switch, *(Umschwung)* reversal;
bei Ablauf des ~s when the bill matures; **in buntem ~** in medley succession; **in ewigem ~** in constant alternation;
abgelaufener ~ bill overdue; **akzeptierter ~** accepted bill; **nicht akzeptierter ~** unaccepted bill, bill dishono(u)red by nonacceptance; **angekaufter ~** discounted bill; **angenommener ~** bill of acceptance; **noch nicht vollständig ausgefüllter ~** inchoate bill *(Br.)*; **ausgestellter ~** issued (drawn) bill; **auf Usozeit ausgestellter ~** bill at usance; **ausländischer ~** bill in foreign currency, foreign bill (note); **ausstehende ~** *(Bilanz)* bills outstanding; **avalierte ~** backed (guaranteed) bill of exchange; **bankfähiger ~** bankable (eligible, *US*) bill, eligible paper *(US)*; **nicht bankfähiger ~** nonnegotiable paper, noneligible bill *(US)*; **in Kraft befindlicher ~** subsisting bill; **begebener ~** negotiated (drafted) bill (note); **durch Effekten besicherter ~** security bill, collateral note *(US)*; **tiefgreifender beständiger ~** radical state of flux; **bezahlter ~** discharged bill; **bundesbankfähiger ~** bill eligible for rediscount *(US)*; **diskontfähiger ~** bankable (discountable) bill (note), eligible bill of exchange, eligible paper *(US)*; **nicht diskontfähiger ~** unbankable paper, noneligible paper *(US)*; **diskontierter ~** discounted bill (note); **nicht diskontierter ~** undiscounted bill; **vorzeitig diskontierter ~** note receivable discounted; **domizilierter ~** domiciliated (domiciled, addressed, indirect) bill; **eigener ~** promissory note, note of hand *(Br.)*; **begebbarer eigener ~** negotiable note; **inländischer eigener ~** inland note; **trassiert eigener ~** house draft (bill); **eingelöster ~** hono(u)red bill; **nicht eingelöster ~** unpaid (dishono(u)red) bill; **vor Verfallzeit eingelöster ~** anticipated bill of exchange, retired bill *(US)*; **einwandfreier ~** approved bill; **den Anforderungen der Notenbank entsprechender ~** eligible paper (bill) *(US)*; **erstklassiger ~** first-rate bill, first-class (white) paper, fine *(Br.)* (prime, *US*) bill; **fällige ~** *(Bilanz)* notes (bills) payable *(US)*; **fälliger ~** bill due, expired (matured, payable) bill; **in Kürze fällige ~** bills about to mature; **noch nicht fälliger ~** unexpired bill; **falscher ~** forged bill, counterfeited bill of exchange; **fauler ~** worthless (queer) bill; **feiner ~** fine *(Br.)* (prime, *US*) bill, first-class (good) paper; **fiktiver (fingierter) ~** bogus (proforma) bill, fictitious bill, windmill; **im Außenhandel gebrauchter ~** outland bill *(Br.)*; **gefälschter ~** forged bill, counterfeited bill of exchange; **durch Werterhöhung gefälschter ~** raised bill *(US)*; **zur Annahme geschickter ~** bill out for acceptance; **nicht dokumentarisch gesicherter ~** clean bill; **durch Effekten gesicherter ~** security bill; **durch Verpfändung von Vieh gesicherter ~** cattle paper; **nach dato zahlbar gestellter ~** draft after date; **gezogener ~** drawn bill, draft; **auf das Ausland gezogener ~** foreign bill; **gegen Getreideverschiffungen gezogener ~** grain bill; **auf die eigene Niederlassung gezogener ~** house bill, pig on pork *(Br.)*; **girierter ~** indorsed (made, *Br.*) bill; **noch nicht girierter ~** original bill; **handelsfähiger ~** negotiable bill; **honorierter ~** hono(u)red bill; **indossierter ~** indorsed (made, *Br.*) bill; **inländischer ~** domestic bill of exchange; **kurzfristiger ~** short-dated (-sighted) bill, short[-dated] exchange, short paper, short-term note; **landeszentralbankfähiger ~** rediscountable (eligible, *US*) bill; **langfristiger ~** long[-dated] bill, long draft, finance bill; **laufende ~** bills in circulation (to mature); **auf den Inhaber lautender ~** bill made out to bearer; **auf Order lautender ~** bill made out to order; **auf englische Pfund lautender ~** sterling bill; **auf eine fremde Währung lautender ~** foreign currency bill; **lombardierter ~** bill pledged as security for an advance, pawned bill; **monatlicher ~** *(Student)* monthly allowance; **normaler ~** ordinary bill; **notleidender ~** dishono(u)red bill, bill held over, bill in suspense (distress); **offener ~** blank bill; **protestierter ~** bill noted for protest, dishono(u)red (protested) bill; **quittierter ~** receipted bill of exchange; **rediskontierter ~** rediscounted bill *(Br.)*; **regelmäßiger ~** course turn; **reiner (schlichter) ~** clean bill of exchange; **sicherungsübereigneter ~** pawned bill of exchange; **stetiger ~** constant change; **trassierter ~** draft, drawn bill; **trockener ~** promissory note, note of hand; **domizilierter trockener ~** domicilated promissory note; **solidarischer trockener ~** joint promissary note; **turnusmäßiger ~** rotation; **überfälliger ~** bill overdue, past due bill (note); **durch Indossament übertragbarer ~** negotiable bill; **umlaufender ~** circulating bill; **unbegebbarer ~** nonnegotiable bill; **unbezahlter (uneingelöster) ~** dishono(u)red (unpaid) bill, bill in suspense; **uneingelöster ~** bill in suspense; **ungedeckter ~** uncovered bill (note), bill not provided for, kite *(Br.)*; **unsicherer ~** dubious paper; **unterschriebener ~** signed bill; **unverstempelter ~** unstamped bill; **verfallener ~** matured (past due) bill, bill payable; **verlorengegangener ~** lost bill of exchange; **verpfändeter ~** pawned bill of exchange; **verstempelter ~** stamped bill; **vorausdatierter ~** postdated bill; **vorgekommener ~** bill presented for payment; **zum Akzept vorzulegender ~** acceptance bill; **zur Zahlung vorzulegender ~** payment bill; **weiterbegebener ~** negotiated (rediscounted) bill; **fällig werdender ~** bill to mature; **im Ausland zahlbarer ~** foreign bill; **an den Inhaber zahlbarer ~** bill payable to bearer; **in London zahlbare ~** enfaced papers *(Br.)*; **an Order zahlbarer ~** bill payable to order; **in englischen Pfunden zahlbarer ~** sterling bill; **zu zahlende ~** bills payable; **zentralbankfähiger ~** rediscountable (eligible, *US*) bill, eligible paper *(US)*; **nicht zentralbankfähiger ~** noneligible paper *(US)*; **zurückgenommener ~** returned bill; **zurückgewiesener ~** rejected bill;
~ gegen Abtretung der Warenforderung bill on goods, value bill; **turnusmäßiger ~ im Amt** rotation in office; **~ in politischen Ansichten** shift in political opinions; **~ des Arbeitsplatzes** change of employment; **~ in mehrfacher Ausfertigung** bills in a set; **~ einer Bankfiliale** branch bill; **~ der halben Belegschaft innerhalb eines Jahres** turnover of fifty per cent in a year; **~ in der Betriebsführung** change in the management, management turnover; **~ zum Diskont** bill for discount; **~ gegen Dokumente** bill of exchange against documents; **~ mit Dokumenten** documentary draft; **~ in Duplikat** set of exchange; **~ des Gerichtsstandes** change of venue; **~ dritter Güter** third-class paper; **~ ohne Indossament** single-name paper *(US)*; **~ zum Inkasso** bill to be encashed (for encashment), bill for

collection; ~ **der Jahreszeiten** rotation of the seasons; ~ **mit Laufzeit** time bill (draft); ~ **mit bestimmter Laufzeit** time note (bill, draft), time paper; **störender ~ in den Lebensgewohnheiten** dislocation; ~ **in der Leitung** change in the management; ~ **der Mode** shift of fashion; ~ **mit anhängenden Papieren** bill with documents attached; ~ **auf Plätze des europäischen Kontinents** continental bills *(Br.)*; ~ **in der Regierung** change in the cabinet (of the government); ~ **und Schecks** bills and checks *(US)* (cheques, *Br.*); ~ **auf Sicht** bill payable at sight (on demand), demand draft; ~ **auf kurze Sicht** short (short-sighted) bill, short paper; ~ **von Tag und Nacht** alternation of day and night; ~ **mit nur einer Unterschrift** single-name paper *(US)*; ~ **mit zwei Unterschriften** double-name paper *(US)*; **eigener ~ mit Unterwerfungsklausel** cognovit note *(US)*; ~ **im Vorstand** change in the management (directorate), management change; ~ **in ausländischer Währung** bill in foreign currency, currency bill *(Br.)*; ~ **über empfangene Ware** bona-fide bill; **häufiger ~ von kaltem zu warmem Wetter** frequent transition from cold to warm weather; ~ **der Wohnung** change of address; ~ **mit unrichtigem Wortlaut** wrongly drafted (worded) bill; ~ **auf die Zukunft** bill of exchange on the future;

~ **abgeben** to dispose of a bill; ~ **abweisen** to refuse (reject) a bill; ~ **akzeptieren** to accept (hono(u)r) a bill; ~ **nicht akzeptieren** to dishono(u)r a bill by nonacceptance; ~ **nicht annehmen** to refuse the acceptance of a bill; **Deckung für einen ~ anschaffen** to provide cover for a bill; ~ **aufkaufen** to buy up (do, *Br.*) bills; ~ **zu hohem Diskont aufkaufen** to shave *(US sl.)*; ~ **ausfertigen** to make out (issue) a bill; ~ **doppelt ausfertigen** to draw a bill of exchange in duplicate; **Verfalltag eines ~s ausrechnen** to compute a bill; ~ **ausstellen** to make out a bill of exchange (note), to give a bill of exchange; **laufenden ~ ausstellen** to make out a bill payable thirty days (d/d); ~ **auf j. ausstellen** to draw a bill on s. o.; ~ **in zwei Ausfertigungen ausstellen** to draw bills in sets of two; ~ **an Order ausstellen** to make a bill payable to order (to s. o.); ~ **avalieren** to guarantee a bill; ~ **avisieren** to advise a bill; ~ **begeben** to issue (give, negotiate) a bill, to discount a bill; **ungedeckten ~ begeben** to fly a kite *(Br.)*; ~ **begleichen** to discharge (hono(u)r, meet) a bill; **Inkasso eines ~s besorgen** to attend to the collection of (undertake to collect) a bill; ~ **bezahlen** to take up (hono(u)r, meet pay) a bill; **mit einem ~ bezahlen** to pay by means of a bill; ~ **vor Fälligkeit bezahlen** to take up a bill under rebate[ment] *(Br.)*; **für einen ~ bürgen** to act as surety for a bill; ~ **decken** to furnish a bill with security, to provide cover for a bill, to answer a bill of exchange, to hono(u)r a bill; ~ **diskontieren** to discount a bill, to take up a bill under rebate *(Br.)*; ~ **domizilieren** to domiciliate a bill; ~ **durchstreichen** to cancel a bill; ~ **einkassieren** to collect (cash) a bill; **Zahlung eines ~s einklagen** to sue on a bill; ~ **einlösen** to hono(u)r (answer) a bill of exchange, to meet (cash, draw in, pay, take up, discharge, clear, retire, remit) a bill, to hono(u)r a draft, to make good on a note; ~ **nicht einlösen** to leave a bill unpaid (unprotected), to dishono(u)r a bill; ~ **bei Fälligkeit einlösen** to collect (take up) a bill (draft) when due, to protect a bill at maturity, to pay a bill of exchange at maturity; ~ **vor Fälligkeit einlösen** to anticipate (retire) a bill; ~ **unter Protesterhebung einlösen** to pay a bill under protest; ~ **bei Verfall einlösen** to hono(u)r (protect) a bill at maturity; ~ **vor Verfall einlösen** to anticipate a bill; ~ **zum Diskont (Zahlung) einreichen** to offer (tender) a bill for discount; ~ **einziehen** to collect (cash) a bill; ~ **fälschen** to forge a bill, to forge a promissory note; ~ **garantieren** to guarantee (guaranty) a bill; ~ **aus der Hand geben** to deliver a bill; ~ **zum Inkasso geben** to have a bill collected; ~ **mangels Zahlung zu Protest geben** to have a bill protested for want of payment; **mit der Bezahlung eines ~s in Verzug geraten** to default in paying a note; ~ **girieren** to endorse (indorse, circulate) a bill; **Rückseite eines ~s girieren** to inscribe across the face of a bill; ~ **Eingang vorbehalten gutschreiben** to enter a bill short; ~ **im Umlauf haben** to keep bills afloat; ~ **zum Diskont hereinnehmen** to accept a bill for discount; ~ **zum Einzug hereinnehmen** to accept bills for collection (discount); ~ **honorieren** to take up (hono(u)r, redeem, cash, meet) a bill, to pay due hono(u)r to a draft, to answer a bill of exchange; ~ **nicht honorieren** to leave a bill unprotected (unpaid), to dishono(u)r a bill, to return a bill unpaid; ~ **indossieren** to endorse (indorse) a bill; ~ **kassieren** to collect (cash) a bill, to take up a bill; ~ **von einer Bank diskontieren lassen** to lodge a note in a bank for discount; ~ **Not leiden lassen** to keep a bill in suspense; ~ **platzen lassen** to dishono(u)r a bill; ~ **zurückgehen lassen** to return a bill protested; ~ **unbezahlt zurückgehen lassen** to return a bill unpaid; ~ **lombardieren** to pledge a bill as security for a loan, to pawn a bill; ~ **zahlbar machen** to domiciliate a bill, to make a bill payable; ~ **prolongieren** to hold over a bill, to extend (renew) a bill of exchange, to grant a renewal (accord a respite for payment) of a draft, to enlarge the payment of a bill; ~ **protestieren** to protest a bill, to note [down] a bill (draft); ~ **mangels Annahme protestieren** to protest a bill for nonacceptance; ~ **mangels Zahlung protestieren** to protest a bill for nonpayment; ~ **rediskontieren** to rediscount a bill; ~ **retournieren** to return a bill to drawer; ~ **schützen** to hono(u)r (protect) a bill; ~ **in Umlauf setzen** to give currency to (issue) a bill; ~ **sperren** to stop a bill; ~ **an Order stellen** to make a bill payable to order; ~ **zahlbar stellen** to domiciliate a bill; **Betrag durch ~ übermachen** to return an amount by bill of exchange; ~ **zum Inkasso übernehmen** to undertake the collection (cashing) of a bill; ~ **überprüfen** to inspect a bill; ~ **zum Inkasso übersenden** to remit a bill for collection; ~ **übertragen** to remit a bill; ~ **unterschreiben** to sign a bill; ~ **verlängern** to prolong (renew, hold over) a bill; ~ **mit Bürgschaft versehen** to furnish a bill with security (surety), to guarantee (guaranty) a bill; ~ **mit Giro versehen** to indorse a bill; ~ **mit Protestvermerk versehen** to note a protest; ~ **mit Sicht versehen** to sight a bill; ~ **mit einem Zusatz versehen** to enface a bill with a memorandum; ~ **verstempeln** to furnish a bill with a stamp; **Annahme eines ~s verweigern** to dishono(u)r a bill, to dishono(u)r a draft by nonacceptance; ~ **vorausdatieren** to antedate a bill; ~ **zur Annahme vorlegen** to present a bill (draft) for acceptance; ~ **zur Einlösung vorlegen** to present a bill for payment, to collect on a note; ~ **erneut vorlegen** to represent a bill; ~ **zur Zahlung vorlegen** to collect on a note, to present a bill for payment; **Inkasso eines ~s vornehmen** to undertake the collection of a bill; ~ **zur Annahme vorzeigen** to present a bill for acceptance; ~ **zur Zahlung vorzeigen** to present a bill for payment; ~ **weitergeben** to negotiate a bill; ~ **ziehen** to draw (value, make out, issue, pass) a bill; ~ **auf lange (kurze) Zeit ziehen** to draw at long (short) date; ~ **zurückrufen** to withdraw a bill; ~ **mit Akzept zurückschicken** to return a bill accepted; ~ **mit Protest zurückschicken** to return a bill of exchange protested; ~ **zurückübertragen** to endorse back a bill of exchange;

~**abrechnung** discount liquidation; ~**abschrift** copy (transcript) of a bill; ~**abteilung** bill (discount) department; ~**agent** bill broker; ~**agio** discount, premium on exchange; ~**akzept** acceptance of a bill, *(Warenakzept)* trade acceptance; ~**akzeptant** acceptor of a bill; ~**allonge** rider; **nachträgliche ~änderung** material alteration of a bill *(Br.)*; ~**anhang** rider; ~**annahme** acceptance of a bill; **bedingte ~annahme** conditional acceptance; **verweigerte ~annahme** default of acceptor, dishono(u)red acceptance; ~**annahme verweigern** to dishono(u)r a bill; ~**arbitrage** arbitration of exchange, arbitrage in bills [of exchange], bill jobbing *(Br.)*, jobbing in bills *(Br.)*; ~**arbitrage über drei oder mehrere Plätze** cross exchange *(Br.)*; ~**arbitrageur** jobber in bills; ~**archiv** bill file; ~**ausfertigung** drafting of a bill; **zweite ~ausfertigung** second [of exchange] bill; ~**ausgabe** issue of a bill of exchange, issuance of notes; ~**aussteller** drawer (giver) of a bill, maker, notemaker *(US)*; ~**ausstellung** issue of a bill of exchange; ~**badbehandlung** *(fig.)* hot-cold treatment; ~**balg** changeling; ~**bank** acceptance house, exchange bank; ~**begebung** negotiating (negotiation, delivery of) a bill of exchange; ~**besitzer** billholder, holder of a note, noteholder; ~**bestände** *(Bilanz)* bills in hand, billholdings, bill case *(Br.)*, paper holdings (discounts), bills receivable *(US)*; ~- **und Scheckbestände** drafts and cheques in hand *(Br.)*; **unmittelbare ~beteiligte** immediate parties to a bill; ~**betrag** value; ~**beziehung** mutual relation, interrelation; **in ~beziehung stehen** to correlate; ~**bezogener** drawer of a bill, payor; ~**blankett** blank (skeleton) bill.

Wechselbuch bill book (ledger), draft book *(Br.)*, note register *(US)*, notebook, discount ledger, bills-receivable book *(US)*, *(Verfallbuch)* bills-payable book *(US)*;

~ **für Inkassowechsel** bills for collection book.

Wechselbürge giver of guaranty, guarantor for a bill, surety of a bill, bill surety, backer.

Wechselbürgschaft guarantee (guaranty, surety, backing) of a bill of exchange, collateral acceptance, aval;

~ **leisten (übernehmen)** to back (guarantee the due payment of) a bill, to guarantee a bill of exchange, to act as surety for a bill; **mit ~ versehen** to provide a bill with guarantee (guaranty, *US*).

Wechsel|büro money broker (dealer), bureau de change; ~**courtage** exchange brokerage, bill brokerage *(Br.)*.

Wechseldebitoren billholdings, bills receivable *(US)*;

~**buch** bills-receivable book (journal) *(US)*; ~**konto** bills-receivable account *(US)*.

Wechsel|deckung cover of a bill; ~**depot** deposit of bills.
Wechseldiskont discount of a bill, bill discount;
noch nicht verdienter ~ unearned discount;
~**abzug** rebate[ment] on bills (items) not due; ~**geschäft** bill discounting.
Wechsel|diskontierer bill discounter, *(Bank)* discount banker; ~**diskontierung** bill discounting (brokerage, *Br.*), taking up bills under rebate *(Br.)*.
Wechseldiskont|kredit acceptance (discount) credit; ~**satz** bill discount (bank, *Br.*, rediscount, *US*) rate.
Wechsel|domizil domicile of a bill; ~**drittausfertigung** third of exchange; ~**duplikat** duplicate [of exchange], duplicate bill, second [of exchange]; ~**eingangsbuch**, ~**eingangsregister** bill register; ~**einlösung** hono(u)ring (retirement, retiring of, payment of) a bill; ~**einlösung bei Fälligkeit** payment in due course; ~**einlösung vor Verfall** anticipation (retirement) of a bill; ~**einziehungsdienst** collection service; ~**einzug** collection of a bill; ~**erneuerung** renewal of a bill; ~**erstausfertigung** first of exchange.
wechselfähig entitled to draw a bill.
Wechsel|fähigkeit capacity to contract by bill; ~**fälle** chops and changes; ~**fälle des Schicksals** weathers, vicissitude of fortune; ~**fälligkeit** time of payment of a bill; ~**fälscher** bill forger, forger of a bill; ~**fälschung** bill forgery, forgery (forging) of bills; ~**fieber** intermittent fever; ~**finanzierung** bill finance; ~**folge** alternation, rotation.
Wechselforderung bill claim, claim arising from a bill;
~**en** *(Bilanz)* billholdings, bills outstanding, notes (bills) receivable *(US)*;
~ **einklagen** to sue [for claims] on a bill of exchange; ~ **einziehen** to collect a bill.
Wechselformular blank (skeleton) bill, skeleton note;
noch nicht vollständig ausgefülltes ~ inchoate bill;
~ **ausfüllen** to fill out a bill.
Wechsel|frist usance, days of grace; ~**garantie** bill guarantee (guaranty, *US*); ~**geber** maker [of a bill]; ~**geld** change, *(Kleingeld)* small coin (change, money), divisional currency, coins *(US)*, subsidiary coinage, fractional money *(US)*, money of exchange, fractional coins (currency, paper money) *(US)*; **zu wenig ~geld herausgeben** to shortchange *(US)*; ~**geldbetrug** ringing the changes.
Wechselgeschäft *(Devisen)* exchange business, agiotage, *(Wechsel)* bill discounting (brokerage) *(Br.)*;
~ **betreiben** to carry on exchange business.
Wechsel|gesetz Bills of Exchange Act *(Br.)*, Negotiable Instrument Law *(US)*; ~**getriebe** transmission gear; ~**girant** endorser of a bill; ~**giro** endorsement, indorsement; **volles** ~**giro** special endorsement; ~**gläubiger** holder of a bill of exchange, bill creditor; ~**haftung** liability on a bill; ~**handel** bill *(Br.)* (note, *US*) brokerage; ~**händler** bill *(Br.)* (note, *US*) broker; ~**indossament** endorsement; ~**indossierung** backing a bill; ~**inhaber** bearer (holder) of a bill of exchange, holder of a note, noteholder, billholder, bill creditor, payee; **rechtmäßiger** ~**inhaber** holder in due course, bona-fide holder for value without notice.
Wechselinkasso collection of bills (drafts), draft (note) collection;
~ **besorgen** to attend to the collection of (undertake to collect) a bill;
~**geschäft** bills discounting, discounting of bills; ~**liste** list of bills for collection.
Wechsel|intervention *(Annahme)* acceptance for hono(u)r (supra protest), *(Zahlung)* payment for hono(u)r (supra protest); ~**journal** bills register, bills-payable (receivable) book *(US)*; ~**klage** action on a [dishono(u)red] bill; ~**klage erheben** to sue on a bill; ~**kontingent** discount limit; ~**konto** bills account, liability ledger, exchange account *(US)*, account of exchange *(US)*; ~**kontrahenten** parties to a bill of exchange; ~**kontrakt** bond of exchange; ~**kopie** copy of a bill, second (third) of exchange; ~**kopierbuch** discount (bills) register, bill copying (draft, *Br.*) book; ~**kosten** bill charges (brokerage, *Br.*).
Wechselkredit acceptance (bill) credit;
offener ~ paper credit;
~**brief** marginal letter of credit, marginal credit *(Br.)*.
Wechselkreditoren billholdings, bills payable *(US)*;
~**konto** bills-payable account *(US)*.
Wechselkurs rate of exchange, exchange (trading) rate, course of exchange *(Br.)*;
amtlicher ~ official exchange rate, official fixed rate of exchange, currency; **ausländischer** ~ foreign exchange rate; **bewegliche** ~**e** free (freely fluctuating) exchange rates; **feste** ~**e** fixed exchange rates; **flexibler (freier, freigegebener, gleitender)** ~ floating (flexible) exchange rate, flexible parities, floating currencies (rates); **gespaltene** ~**e** multiple exchange rates; **gestützter** ~ pegged exchange rate; **günstiger** ~ favo(u)rable exchange rate; **inoffizieller** ~ parallel rate of exchange; **periodisch korrigierter** ~ crawling peg; **Londoner** ~ London rate; **multiple** ~**e** multiple exchange (currency) rates; **schwankende** ~**e** fluctuating exchange rates; **stufenflexibler** ~ sliding parity (peg); **üblicher** ~ usual rate of exchange; ~ **unverändert** exchange the same;
~ **der augenblicklichen Verrechnungseinheit** present unit of account exchange rate;
~**e anpassen** to adjust the exchange rates; ~ **freigeben** to float the exchange rate; ~ **niedrig halten** to hold down the exchange rate; ~**e in der festgelegten Währungsparität halten** to peg their exchange rates at par; ~**e neu ordnen** to realign the exchange rates; ~ **sichern** to cover (fix, hedge) the exchange rate; ~ **stabilisieren** to peg the exchange;
~**änderung** exchange-rate change, parity change; **stufenweise** ~**änderung** crawling (dynamic) peg; **vorsichtige** ~**änderung** discretionary crawling peg; ~**arbitrage** arbitration of exchange, exchange arbitration; ~**arbitrageur** arbitrageur; ~**aufwertung** currency appreciation; ~**bandbreite** margin of the exchange rates; ~**berechnung** computation of exchange.
wechselkursfreie Verrechnungseinheit floating value unit of account.
Wechselkurs|freigabe floating rates of exchange; **gemeinsame** ~**freigabe** block floating; ~**garantie** exchange-rate guarantee; ~**gefüge** exchange-rate structure; ~**gewinn** exchange-rate profit; ~**liste** list (course, *Br.*) of exchange; ~**neuordnung** realignment of exchange rates; ~**notierung** quotation of exchange rates; ~**politik** exchange-rate policy; ~**relationen** exchange-rate relationships; ~**richtlinien** exchange-rate guidelines; ~**risiko** foreign exchange risk; ~**satz** *(Weltwährungsfonds)* par exchange rate; **angestrebte** ~**sätze** target exchange rates; ~**satz des Pfundes stützen** to peg the sterling exchange rate; ~**schwankungen** movement (fluctuations) in [exchange] rates, currency fluctuations; ~**stabilität** exchange stability; ~**stützung** pegging the exchange; ~**system** exchange-rate system (regime); **gleitendes** ~**system** system of floating exchange rates; ~**überwachung** exchange-rate surveillance; ~**veränderungen** changes in exchange rates; **gemeinsamer** ~**verbund** floating block; ~**vereinbarung** exchange-rate arrangement; ~**vergleich** compound arbitration of exchange; ~**zettel** list of exchange, record of foreign exchange rates *(US)*, course of exchange *(Br.)*.
Wechsel|laufzeit currency of a bill; ~**lombard** lending on bills; ~**makler** bill discounter, note *(US)* (bill and note, discount, exchange) broker, exchange dealer; ~**makler sein** to job in bills *(Br.)*; ~**marke aufkleben** to furnish a bill with a stamp; ~**markt** discount market; ~**material** commercial papers.
wechseln to exchange, to change, to shift;
Briefe ~ to correspond; **seine Diät** ~ to vary one's diet; **Eigentümer** ~ to change hands; **Geld** ~ to change money; **Lager** ~ *(pol.)* to switch sides, to rat *(sl.)*; **miteinander** ~ to alternate; **seine Stellung** ~ to change one's position; **Szene** ~ to shift the scene; **turnusmäßig** ~ to rotate; **Wohnung** ~ to move to another house; **ein paar Worte mit jem.** ~ to exchange a few words with s. o.
wechselnd varying;
~ **bewölkt** cloudy with bright intervals; **ständig** ~ rotating.
Wechsel|nehmer taker (payer) of a bill, payee; ~**notierungen** foreign-exchange rates; ~**obligationen** convertible bonds.
Wechselobligo discount ledger, bill diary, *(Bilanz)* discounts outstanding *(Br.)*, bills payable *(US)*;
~ **aus Akzeptverbindlichkeiten der Kundschaft** customers' liabilities on account of acceptances;
~**buch** bill book (diary), discount (bill discounted, *US*, liability) ledger.
Wechsel|ordnung Bills of Exchange Act *(Br.)*, [etwa] Uniform Negotiable Instrument Act *(US)*; ~**parität** parity of exchange; **feste** ~**parität** mint par of exchange, comparative bullion content *(Br.)*; ~**pensionsgeschäft** pledging of bills; ~**portefeuille** portfolio of bills, bills in hand, billholdings, bill case *(Br.)*; ~**prima** first [of exchange]; ~**prolongation** renewal (prolongation) of a bill of exchange, extension of note.
Wechselprotest bill protest;
~ **mangels Annahme** protest for nonacceptance; ~ **zwecks weiterer Sicherheit** *(bei Zahlungsunfähigkeit des Akzeptanten)* protest for better security *(Br.)*; ~ **mangels Zahlung** protest for nonpayment;

~ **einlegen (erheben)** to enter protest of a bill, to protest (note) a bill; ~ **aufnehmen lassen** to have a bill noted (protested); ~**anzeige** notice of dishono(u)r (protest, *US*); ~**frist** time for protesting a bill of exchange; ~**kosten** cost of protest; ~**urkunde** protest.

Wechsel|provision exchange commission, bill brokerage *(Br.)*; ~**prozeß** summary procedure on bills of exchange; ~**rahmen** *(Foto)* mat, passe-partout; ~**rechnung** bill (banker's exchange) account; ~**recht** law of exchange.

wechselrechtliche Klage summary procedure on bills of exchange.

Wechsel|registratur bill file; ~**regreß** recourse to the endorser; ~**reiter** kiteflyer, bill jobber *(Br.)*, jobber in bills *(Br.)*; ~**reiterei** drawing and redrawing, jobbing [in bills] *(Br.)*, bill jobbing *(Br.)*, kiteflying *(Br.)*, cross firing *(Br.)*; ~**reiterei betreiben** to draw and redraw bills, to trade in bills, to fly a kite *(Br.)*; ~**rembours** acceptance (documentary) credit; ~**respekttage** day of respite; ~**rückgabe** return of a bill to drawer; ~**schicht** rotating shift; ~**schulden** debts founded on bills, paper debts, *(Bilanz)* bills (notes) payable *(US)*; ~**schuldner** bill debtor.

wechselseitig alternate, mutual, reciprocal, vice versa.

Wechsel|sekunda second [of exchange]; ~**sendung** remittance of a bill; ~**serie** set of bills of exchange; ~**skandal** note scandal; ~**spannung** *(el.)* alternating voltage; ~**spekulant** bill jobber *(Br.)*; ~**spekulation** jobbing in bills of exchange *(Br.)*, bill jobbing *(Br.)*; ~**spesen** discount expenses *(US)*, bill charges; ~**sprechanlage** *(tel.)* intercom; ~**sprechbetrieb** *(tel.)* intercommunication system; ~**stelle** [money] exchange; ~**stempel** bill stamp; ~**steuer** stamp duty (tax); ~**steuermarke** bill stamp; ~**streuung** *(Anzeigen)* staggered schedule; ~**strom** *(el.)* alternating current; **mit** ~**strom laufen** to operate on AC; ~**stromanlage** alternating current plant.

wechselstrombetrieben AC-operated.

Wechsel|stube currency exchange, dealing room; ~**summe** value; ~**text** wording of a draft (bill); ~**trassierung** drawing (issue) of a bill of exchange; ~**überweisung** bill remittance; ~**umlauf** bills in circulation, circulation of bills, outstanding notes; ~**unterricht** *(Schule)* shift work; ~**unterschrift** signature on a bill; ~**valuta** exchange standard; ~**verbindlichkeiten** bills outstanding *(Br.)*, bills (notes) payable *(US)*; ~**verbundener** party to a bill of exchange, acceptor; ~**verfall** maturity of a bill; ~**verfallbuch** bill (bills payable, *US*) book, bills payable journal *(US)*, maturity tickler, bills discounted ledger (register, *US*); ~**verfalltag** maturity date; ~**verjährung** prescription of a bill of exchange; ~**verlängerung** renewal (prolongation) of a bill; **notarieller** ~**vermerk über erfolglose Wechselvorlage** noting of a bill; ~**verpflichteter** party to a bill of exchange, person liable on a bill, bill debtor; **unmittelbar** ~**verpflichteter** party primarily liable; ~**verpflichtungen** liabilities upon bills, *(Bilanz)* bills (notes) payable *(US)*; ~**verpflichtungen gegenüber Banken** notes due to banks; ~**verrechnungssystem** note-paying system; ~**vordruck** bill form; ~**vorgänger** prior party to a bill; ~**vorlage** presentment of a bill; **besondere** ~**vorlage** special presentation; **rechtsgültige** ~**vorlage** good presentment; ~**vormann** prior party to a bill; ~**wähler** swinging voter, floating vote, float *(US)*.

wechselweise alternative.

Wechsel|wirkung interaction, reciprocation, interplay; **in** ~**wirkung bringen** to correlate; ~**wirtschaft** *(Ackerbau)* alternate husbandry, shift (rotation) of crops; ~**wirtschaft treiben** to practise rotation on a field, to rotate crops; ~**wucher** bill usury; ~**zahlung** payment by bill of exchange; ~**zins** discount.

wecken to knock up;

jds. Interesse für etw. ~ to arouse s. one's interest for s. th.

Wecker alarm-clock;

jem. auf den ~ **fallen** to get on s. one's nerves; **jem. mit ständigen Bitten auf den** ~ **fallen** to weary s. o. with requests; ~ **auf 6 Uhr stellen** to set the alarm clock for six o'clock.

Weck|glas preserve jar; **telefonischer** ~**ruf** alarm call, shot, waking call; ~**signal** *(mil.)* rouse *(Br.)*.

Weg way, path, passage, lane, alley, *(Besorgung)* errand, channel, *(Methode)* manner, means, plan, method, *(Reiseroute)* route, *(Straße)* road, street;

am ~**e gelegen** at the roadside; **auf diplomatischem** ~ through diplomatic channels; **auf direktem** ~**e** by collateral hand; **auf friedlichem** ~ by peaceful means; **auf gütlichem** ~**e** amicably; **auf gerichtlichem** ~**e** by legal steps; **auf halbem** ~ midway; **auf offiziellem** ~**e** through official channels; **auf dem richtigen** ~**e** on the right track; **auf schriftlichem** ~**e** in writing; **auf dem** ~**e zur Arbeit** on the way to work; **im** ~**e öffentlicher Bekanntmachung** by public announcement; **im** ~**e der Klage** by bringing an action; **im** ~**e der Verordnung** by way of regulation; **vom rechten** ~ **ab** astray;

abschüssiger ~ precipitous path; **ausgetretener** ~ well-beaten way, trail, path; **befahrener** ~ frequented road; **direkter** ~ outright course; **getrennte** ~**e** several (separate) ways; **langer** ~ far (long) cry; **sein letzter** ~ his last journey; **öffentlicher** ~ public way (highway, thoroughfare), road; **nicht öffentlicher** ~ private road; **steiniger** ~ stony road; **ein gutes Stück** ~ a good way; **üblicher** ~ beaten track; **verbotener** ~! *(Schild)* no thoroughfare!; ~ **von zwanzig Minuten** twenty minutes' walk; ~**e des Handels** channels of trade; ~ **der Pflicht** path of duty; ~ **zum Ruhm** avenue to fame; ~ **ins Verderben** road to ruin; **unergründliche** ~**e der Vorsehung** inscrutable ways of providence;

j. von seinem ~ **abbringen** to lead s. o. out of his way; **vom rechten** ~**e abkommen** to go off the beaten track; **jem. einen** ~ **abnehmen** to do an errand for s. o.; ~ **abschneiden** to intercept; **jem. den** ~ **abschneiden** to block s. one's way; ~ **bahnen** to pave the way, to blaze a trail; **sich einen** ~ **bahnen** to cut one's way; **sich durch den Schlamm einen** ~ **bahnen** to plough (plow, *US*) one's way through the mud; **sich einen** ~ **durch die Menge bahnen** to open a way (hustle) through the crowd; ~ **beschildern** to signpost a trail; **neue** ~**e beschreiten** to apply new methods; **j. auf den rechten** ~ **bringen** to put s. o. in the right way; **j. wieder auf den richtigen** ~ **bringen** to bring s. o. back to the straight and narrow; **jem. den** ~ **ebnen** to pave the way for s. o., to make things smooth for s. o.; **sich auf friedlichem** ~**e einigen** to settle a matter out of court; **völlig neue** ~**e einschlagen** to strike out untrodden paths; **jem. auf halbem** ~ **entgegenkommen** to meet s. o. halfway; **seinen eigenen** ~ **erkennen** to find one's running legs; **sich nach dem** ~ **erkundigen** to ask the (inquire one's) way; **auf krummen** ~**en erreichen** to get on the crook, to worm; **kürzesten** ~ **fahren** to go by the nearest (shortest) road; **Mittel und** ~**e finden** to contrive ways and means; **seinen** ~ **fortsetzen** to proceed on one's way; **j. einen gefährlichen** ~ **führen** to take s. o. into dangerous waters; **jem. einen Ratschlag mit auf den** ~ **geben** to give s. o. a piece of advice to take with him; **jem. aus dem** ~**e gehen** to give s. o. a wide berth, to run away from (fight shy of, steer clear of) s. o.; **seinen** ~ **gehen** to make one's way in life; **seinen eigenen** ~ **gehen** to go one's own way, to strike out a line on one's own, to take one's own course; **neue** ~**e gehen** to strike out untrodden paths; **der Arbeit aus dem** ~**e gehen** to shirk work; **ausgetretene** ~**e gehen** to keep to the beaten track; **einer Entscheidung aus dem** ~**e gehen** to evade a decision; **einer Sache aus dem** ~**e gehen** to give s. th. a miss; **seinen** ~ **ganz allein gehen** to pull a lone oar; **seinen** ~ **zu Ende gehen** to walk the last mile; **den** ~ **allen Fleisches gehen** to go the way of all the earth (things); ~ **des geringsten Widerstands gehen** to take the line of least resistance; **auf schlimme** ~**e geraten** to fall into bad ways; **großes Stück** ~**es zurückgelegt haben** to have covered quite a distance; ~ **und Steg kennen** to know a region like the back of one's hand; **jds.** ~ **kreuzen** to cross s. one's path; **in die** ~**e leiten** to set afoot (on foot), to bring about, to start the ball rolling; **sich auf den** ~ **machen** to sally out, to go on one's way, to take the road, to push off *(coll.)*, to set off for; **seinen** ~ **machen** to pike along, to fight (make) one's way, to carve out a career for o. s., to get on in the world; **Schwierigkeiten aus dem** ~**e räumen** to remove obstacles; **seinen** ~ **heimwärts richten** to shape one's course homeward; **jem. im** ~**e sein** to be in s. one's way; **auf dem besten** ~**e sein, sich finanziell zu ruinieren** to be heading for financial disaster; **auf dem besten** ~**e sein, Millionär zu werden** to be in a fair way of becoming a millionaire; **auf dem falschen** ~ **sein** to be on the wrong track; **auf dem richtigen** ~ **sein** to be on the beam; **auf dem** ~ **zur Arbeit sein** to be on one's way to work; **auf dem** ~ **der Besserung sein** to be on the mend; **jem. im** ~ **stehen** to be in s. one's road, to be a hindrance for s. o.; **einer Sache im** ~**e stehen** to be a countercheck to s. th.; **sich selbst im** ~**e stehen** to be one's own enemy; **nicht auf halbem** ~ **stehenbleiben** to go the whole hog, to shoot the works *(sl.)*; **sich bedachtsam einen** ~ **suchen** to pick one's steps; **jem. nicht über den** ~ **trauen** not to trust s. o. round the corner; **verschlungene** ~**e des Kongresses überwinden** to wind its way through congress; ~ **zu einer späteren Einigung verbauen** to bar the way to a later agreement; **beharrlich seinen** ~ **verfolgen** to keep to one's course; **jem. den** ~ **verstellen** to block s. one's way; **jem. den** ~ **zum Bahnhof zeigen** to direct s. o. to the station.

weg gone, *(abwesend)* away;

in einem ~ nonstop, in one go; **weit** ~ well away;

über seinen Kummer ~ **sein** to have got over one's grief; **völlig** ~ **sein** to be flabbergasted, *(begeistert)* to be in raptures, to knock o. s. out *(sl.)*.

wegbegeben, sich to remove o. s. from a place.
Wegbereiter pioneer, trail blazer, waymaker.
wegbleiben to be omitted (left out), *(Kunde)* to drop off;
von einer Versammlung ~ to stay away from a meeting.
wegbringen to bring (take) away, to clear off.
Wege|abkürzung short cut, cutoff *(Br.)*; ~**abweichungsklausel** *(Warenverkehr)* deviation clause; ~**bau** road making (building); ~**benutzer** road user; ~**beschaffenheit** state of the roads, road conditions; ~**biegung** road bend, curve; ~**einmündung** road junction; ~**gabelung** fork of a road; **sich an einer** ~**gabelung befinden** to be at the parting of the ways; ~**gebühr** wayleave rent, road toll, *(Beamter)* travelling expenses, *(Notar)* mil(e)age; ~**geld** deadheading pay, *(Landstraße)* turnpike money, *(Zeuge)* travelling allowance, mil(e)age; ~**gerechtigkeit** wayleave *(Br.)*, right of way, easement of access; ~**kreuzung** crossroads, road intersection *(US)*; ~**lagerer** highway robber, footpad, waylayer; ~**lagerpatent** shot-gun patent *(US)*; ~**markierung** road marking.
wegen on the grounds (account) of, *(Aktenzeichen)* re.
Wegenetz road network.
wegengagieren to attract away;
mit dem Angebot höherer Bezahlung ~ to lure away with an offer of better pay; **Arbeitskräfte direkt von der Universität** ~ to recruit on campus *(US)*.
Wegerecht right of way, wayleave *(Br.)*, easement of access (way);
gesetzlich begründetes ~ way of necessity; **eingetragenes** ~ toll traverse; **öffentliches** ~ public right of way.
Wegerechts|gebühr wayleave rent; ~**vorbehalt** reservation of a right of way.
Wege|stunde von hier, eine an hour from here; ~**tonne** marking buoy; ~**zeichen** waymark, guide; ~**zeit** traveltime; ~**zoll** toll, turnpike money.
wegfahren *(Auto)* to drive away, *(Schiff)* to leave, to sail, *(verreisen)* to go away.
Wegfall lapse, *(Abschaffung)* abolition, cessation, *(Auslassung)* omission;
bei ~ **dieser Bedingungen** should these regulations no longer exist;
~ **einer Bedingung** forfeiture of a condition; ~ **eines Erben** lapse of an heir; ~ **der Gegenleistung** failure of consideration; ~ **der Geschäftsgrundlage** [etwa] frustration of contract; ~ **von Sonderabschreibungen beim Grundstücksverkauf** recapture of excess depreciation upon sale of property; ~ **eines Vermächtnisses** lapse of testamentary bequest;
in ~ **kommen** to cease to exist.
wegfallen to cease to exist, *(aufgehoben werden)* to be abolished, *(Bestimmungen)* to become void, to be cancelled, *(Vermächtnis)* to lapse;
~ **lassen** to cut, to kill *(US)*.
wegfliegen to leave by plane, *(Flugzeug)* to take off.
Weggang departure.
weggeben to dispose, to hand over, to send away, *(schenken)* to give away.
weggehen to leave, to go away, to depart, *(Ware)* to go off;
entrüstet ~ to shake the dust off one's feet; **ohne besonderen Grund** ~ to leave for no particular reason; **heimlich** ~ to take French leave; **reißend (wie warme Semmeln)** ~ to go off rapidly, to sell like hot cakes (dogs, *US*); **schnell** ~ to be selling fast; **unbefriedigt** ~ to go and whistle.
weggetragen, tot ~ **werden** to be carried away with the heels foremost.
weggetreten! *(mil.)* dismiss *(Br.)*!, dismissed *(US)*!;
zeitweise völlig ~ to have fits of inattention.
weggeworfen, als nutzlos ~ **werden** to be dumped into limbo;
~**es Geld** waste of money.
Weggeworfenes throwaway.
weghaben, etw. to have the knack of it; **etw. schnell** ~ to cotton on to s. th. quickly; **Erkältung** ~ to have caught a cold.
wegkommen to get away;
am besten dabei ~ to have the best of it; **finanziell gut** ~ to do very nicely; **schlecht** ~ to come out at the little end of the horn *(US)*; **am schlechtesten** ~ to get the worst of it.
Wegkrümmung bend in a path.
weglassen to omit, to leave out.
Weglassung leaving out, omission;
~ **wesentlicher Inhaltsteile** omission of important contents.
weglaufen to run off (away), to make away, to take to flight (to one's heels.
Weglegen putting away.
weglegen to put away, *(Akten)* to file away.
wegloben, j. to give s. o. a golden handshake.
Wegnahme taking away, privation, requisition, *(Beschlagnahme)* seizure, confiscation, requisition, capture;
erneute ~ retaking; **widerrechtliche** ~ unlawful taking, asportation;
~ **als Selbsthilfe** recaption.
wegnehmen to withdraw, to take away, to seize, *(konfiszieren)* to confiscate, to seize, to requisition;
jem. den Parkplatz ~ to nab s. one's parking place.
wegputzen *(Mahlzeit)* to polish off, to tuck in *(sl.)*.
wegradieren to erase.
Wegrand wayside, roadside.
weg|räumen to clear, to remove; **Brücke** ~**reißen** to sweep (wash) away a bridge; ~**schaffen** to remove, to do away with, to bring (clear, carry) away, to get rid of.
Wegscheide crossroads, bifurcation, road fork.
wegschicken to dispatch, to send away;
j. ~ to dismiss s. o..
weg|schleichen to steal (sneak) away; **Brücke** ~**spülen** to wash off a bridge.
wegstecken to tuck away;
schnell ~ to pop away.
weg|stehlen, sich to lurk away; ~**steuern** to tax away.
Wegstrecke stretch of a road, distance, mil(e)age;
schlechte ~! bad road ahead!; **zurückgelegte** ~ distance covered.
weg|tragen to carry away; ~**treiben** to break adrift.
Weg|überführung overpass, viaduct; ~**unterführung** underpass, subway.
wegwaschen to purge away.
Wegweiser direction post (sign), road sign (post), signpost, finger post, finger board *(US)*, *(fig.)* pilot, pioneer, index;
~**tafel** guide board.
Wegwerfartikel throwaway product.
wegwerfbar disposable, expendable.
Wegwerfbehälter one-trip container *(US)*.
wegwerfen to throw (cast) away (to the dogs), to kiss goodbye;
Geld ~ to throw money down the drain.
wegwerfende Handbewegung disparaging gesture.
Wegwerf|güter disposables; ~**packung** one-way package.
weg|wischen to wipe off; ~**ziehen** to move.
Wegzug removal, *(Br.)* move.
weh sore, bad;
sich ~ **tun** to hurt o. s.; **jem. in der Seele** ~ **tun** to cut s. o. to the quick.
wehen to blow, *(Töne)* to drift, to float;
Fahne ~ **lassen** to fly a flag.
weh|klagen lamentation, jeremiad; ~**leidig sein** to be a whiner.
Wehmut woefulness, nostalgia, melancholy.
wehmütig lächeln to smile wistfully.
Wehr *(Wasserbau)* weir;
sich gegen etw. zur ~ **setzen** to offer resistance to s. th.;
~**auftrag** defense (defence, *Br.*) order; ~**beitrag** defence (defense, *US*) contribution; ~**bereitschaft** readiness for defence (defense, *US*); ~**bezirk** military district, county association *(Br.)*.
Wehrdienst military (colo(u)r, national) service;
zum ~ **eingezogen** enlisted in the army, conscript, drafted *(US)*; **seinen** ~ **ableisten** to serve with the armed forces (colo(u)rs), to do one's military service, to hitch *(US sl.)*; **sich vom** ~ **drücken** to evade military service; **aus dem** ~ **entlassen** to demob, to muster out *(US)*; ~ **leisten** to serve in the army (in the armed forces, with the colo(u)rs); **zum** ~ **pressen** to commandeer; **sich erneut zum** ~ **verpflichten** to reup *(sl.)*; **aus dem** ~ **entlassen werden** to be separated from the service (demobilized);
~**befreiung** draft exemption *(US)*; ~**beschädigung** disability incurred in the line of duty; ~**entlassener** separatee *(US)*; ~**erfassung** enlistment order; ~**pflicht** liability for military service.
wehrdienstpflichtig liable to military service.
Wehrdienstpflichtiger conscript, enlistee, draftee *(US)*.
wehrdiensttauglich, für ~ **erklären** to pass for military service.
Wehrdienst|verhältnis status; ~**verweigerer** conscientious objector, draft dodger (resister) *(US)*; ~**verweigerung** conscientious objection, draft dodging (resistance) *(US)*; ~**wesen** conscriptive system; ~**zeit** active service.
Wehrdisziplinaranwalt provost-marshal.
wehren, sich to resist, to refuse, to reject; **den Anfängen** ~ to nip things in the bud; **sich gegen einen Angriff** ~ to resist an attack; **sich gegen einen Gedanken** ~ to refuse to accept an idea; **sich mit Händen und Füßen** ~ to fight tooth and nail; **sich mit**

Händen und Füßen gegen ein Projekt ~ to have set one's face like a flint against a plan;
sich nicht ~ **können** to be powerless to resist.
Wehrersatz|kommando local recruiting office; ~**soldat** enlisted specialist *(US)*; ~**verwaltung** recruiting administration.
Wehr|ertüchtigung premilitary training; ~**etat** defence (defense, *US*) budget.
wehrfähig fit for active service, able-bodied.
Wehr|fähigkeit fitness for military service; ~**hoheit** military sovereignty; ~**kraftzersetzung** demoralization of the armed forces.
wehrlos defenceless, unarmed, helpless;
dem Feinde ~ **ausgeliefert sein** to be a sitting duck for the enemy; **einer Sache** ~ **ausgesetzt sein** to be at the receiving end of s. th.
Wehrpaß small (military service) book, certificate of service.
Wehrpflicht, allgemeine general (universal) subscription, universal draft (military camp) *(US)*, national service *(Br.)*;
seiner ~ **genügen** to put in one's term of military service; **zur Ableistung der** ~ **einberufen werden** to be called up for military service;
~**erfassung nach Musterung** selective service *(US)*; ~**gesetz** National Service Act *(Br.)*.
wehrpflichtig liable to military service;
~**er Jahrgang** draft age class *(US)*.
Wehr|pflichtiger conscript, conscriptee *(US)*, draftee *(US)*; **hunderttausend** ~**pflichtige pro Jahr** annual intake of 100,000 National Service men *(Br.)*; ~**pflichtsystem** selective service system *(US)*; ~**sold** soldier's (active service, army, military) pay, *(Marine)* navy pay; ~**stammrolle** muster (nominal) roll; ~**strafrecht** military law.
wehruntauglich unfit for military service;
für ~ **erklären** to disqualify s. o. for military service.
Wehr|urlaub draft leave *(US)*; ~**wirtschaft** defence (defense, *US*) economy; ~**zweige** armed service.
Wehwehchen pain in one's little finger, little finger ache.
Weib woman;
zänkisches ~ termagant, shrew, bitch *(coll.)*, vixen.
Weiber|feind, erklärter professed woman-hater; ~**geschwätz** gossip; ~**regiment** petticoat government; **hinter jedem** ~**rock her sein** to be always hanging on to s. one's skirt.
weibisch womanish, effeminate, unmanly.
weiblich|e Arbeitskräfte female labo(u)r; ~**es Geschlecht** female sex, womankind; ~**e Linie** female line, distaff side; ~**e Logik** woman's reason; ~**es Wesen** petticoat.
Weiblichkeit, holde gentle sex.
Weibsbild petticoat;
hübsches ~ a pretty piece *(sl.)*.
weich soft, weak;
so ~ **wie Samt** soft as velvet;
sich ~ **betten** to feather one's nest; **Wasser** ~ **machen** to soften water; **allmählich** ~ **werden** to relent gradually;
~**e Landung** smooth landing; ~**e Luft** balmy air; ~**e Tour** soft sell; ~**e Währung** soft currency; ~**e Werbemasche** soft sell in advertising.
Weichbild precincts, outskirts.
Weiche switch, points, *(el.)* bandpass filter, *(Rohrpost)* guide;
~**n für eine Entwicklung stellen** to initiate a development; ~ **umstellen** to reverse the switches.
Weicheisen soft iron.
Weichen der Kurse fall in stocks.
weichen to yield, to give way, *(Kurse)* to decline, to drop, to ease off, to recede, to go down, to [be on the] fall;
nicht von jds. Seite ~ not to leave s. one's side; **nicht von der Stelle** ~ not to budge an inch; **der feindlichen Übermacht** ~ to yield to the superior forces of the enemy.
weichend *(Kurse)* receding, dropping, easy;
~**e Preise** falling (retroactive) prices.
Weichen|signal target; ~**steller** pointsman *(Br.)*, switchman *(US)*, switch tender *(US)*, shunter; ~**stellung** shunting, switch.
Weich|holz soft wood; ~**ling** mollycoddle, milkshake, softy *(fam.)*; ~**macher** *(Waschmittel)* softening agent, softener; ~**währungsland** soft-currency country.
Weide pasture, grass[land], willow, grazing;
auf der ~ out on feed;
auf der ~ **sein** to be at grass; **auf die** ~ **stellen (treiben)** to put out to graze (pasture), to turn out to grass;
~**fläche** meadow land, pasture, pastoral property; ~**gerechtigkeit** common of pasture, commonage; ~**koppel** paddock; ~**land** cattle range, meadow land, pasture, grassland.
Weiden graze.
weiden [lassen] to pasture, to graze;
sich an etw. ~ to feast one's eyes on s. th.;
seine Schafe auf dem Dorfanger ~ **lassen** to pasture one's sheep on the village common.
Weide|pacht occupation licence; ~**pflock** picket pin.
Weiderecht common of pasture, pasturage, herbage *(Br.)*;
~**e** grazing rights;
gemeinsames ~ intercommonage, common appurtenant, cattle gate *(Br.)*; **dinglich gesichertes** ~ common appendant.
Weidewirtschaft pasture farming.
weigern, sich einstimmig to refuse with one voice; **sich entschieden** ~ to set one's face against; **sich grundsätzlich** ~ to refuse on principle.
Weigerung refusal, no, denial;
willkürliche ~ arbitrary refusal.
Weigerungsfall, im in case of refusal.
weihen, sein Leben der Wissenschaft to dedicate one's life to science; **sich völlig einer Sache** ~ to be wholly devoted to a cause.
Weiher pond, pool.
Weihnachten Christmas, Xmas *(coll.)*;
schneefreie ~ green Christmas; **weiße** ~ white Christmas;
~ **zu Hause verbringen** to spend Christmas at home.
Weihnachts|abend Christmas eve; ~**ausgaben** Christmas expenses; ~**baum** Christmas tree; ~**baum schmücken** to decorate a Christmas tree; **alte** ~**bräuche bewahren** to keep Christmas in the old style; **betriebliche** ~**feier** staff Christmas party; **zweiter** ~**feiertag** Boxing Day *(Br.)*; ~**freibetrag** tax-free Christmas bonus; ~**geschenk** Christmas gift (present); ~**geschenkliste** gift list; ~**glocken** Christmas bells; ~**gratifikation** Christmas bonus; ~**karte** Christmas card; ~**lied** Christmas carol; ~**lotterie** Christmas draw; ~**mann** Father Christmas *(Br.)*; ~**markt** Christmas shopping; ~**nummer** Christmas number; ~**päckchen** Christmas box; ~**paket** Christmas package; ~**schmuck** Christmas decorations; ~**tag** Christmas Day; ~**zeit** Christmas time.
Weilchen, ein wee, a little while.
Weiler hamlet.
Wein, offener wine from the cask; **verschnittener** ~ blended wine; ~ **ohne Bouquet** empty wine; **junger** ~ **in alten Schläuchen** new wine in old bottles;
mit ~ **bewirten** to wine; **jem. reinen** ~ **einschenken** to tell s. o. the plain truth, to make a clean breast of it, to talk turkey *(US)*; ~ **keltern** to press the grapes; ~ **lesen** to gather in the vintage, to harvest the grapes; ~ **panschen** to adulterate wine; **zu viel** ~ **trinken** to overindulge in wine; ~ **und Wasser vermischen** to dash wine with water;
~**anbaugebiet** winegrowing district; ~**bau** winegrowing, viniculture, viticulture; ~**bauer** winegrower; ~**berg** vineyard.
weinen to cry, to weep, to turn on the waterworks *(fam.)*;
sich die Augen aus den Kopf ~ to cry one's heart out; **Krokodilstränen** ~ to shed crocodile tears.
weinerliche Stimme whining voice.
Wein|ernte, ~**ertrag** vintage; ~**faß** wine cask; ~**flasche** wine bottle; **einer** ~**flasche den Hals brechen** to crack a bottle of wine; ~**gegend** winegrowing region; ~**geschäft** wineshop; ~- **und Spirituosengeschäft** off-licence *(Br.)*; ~**handel** wine trade; ~**händler** wine merchant, vintner, cooper *(Br.)*; ~**handlung** wineshop, winehouse; ~**karte** wine list; ~**keller** wine cellar (vault); **in jds.** ~**keller tüchtig aufräumen** to punish s. one's cellar; ~**kellner** winewaiter, cellarman, butler; ~**kelterung** vinification; ~**kenner sein** to have a good palate for wines; ~**kiste** case of wine; ~**krug** pitcher; ~**kühler** wine cooler; ~**lager** wine vault; ~**laubverzierung** vignette; ~**lesezeit** vintage; ~**lokal** wine restaurant; ~**panschen** adulteration of wine; ~**steuer** wine duty; ~**stock** grapevine; ~**traube** wine-grape; ~**verfälschung** adulteration of wine; ~**verkäufer** retail dealer in wine, cooper *(Br.)*; ~**vorrat** stock of wine.
Weise manner, fashion, way, method, *(Melodie)* melody, air, tune;
auf anständige oder unredliche ~ by fair means or foul; **auf irgendeine** ~ by some means or other; **in förmlicher** ~ by deed;
in keinster ~ not in the least;
volkstümliche ~ popular tune;
auf recht ungewöhnliche ~ **reich werden** to get rich by devious ways.
weisen, Kind aus der Schule to expel a child from school; **aus dem Lande** ~ to expel s. o.; **von der Universität** ~ to rusticate, to send down *(Br.)*; **Verdacht von sich** ~ to repudiate a suspicion; **jem. den Weg** ~ to show s. o. the way.
Weiser pundit.

weise | r werden to grow in wisdom;
~s Urteil wise judgment.
Weisheit wisdom;
alte ~ old saying;
der ~ letzter Schluß the whole answer;
seine ~en für sich behalten to mind one's own business; **mit seiner ~ am Ende sein** to be at one's wit's end (at the end of one's tether).
Weisheits | brunnen fountain of wisdom; **~krämer** smart aleck, wiseacre, know-all *(Br.)*, wise guy *(US)*.
weismachen, jem. etw. ~ wollen to pull s. one's leg, to hoodwink (fool) s. o., to tell s. o. a yarn *(coll.)*, to throw s. o. a long line *(US)*; **sich selbst etw. ~ wollen** to overestimate one's own importance;
mir kannst du das nicht ~ go tell it to the marines *(sl.)*.
weiß white;
Wand ~ streichen to paint a wall white; **Mohren ~ waschen** to milk the pigeon;
~es Blatt Papier blank sheet of paper; **~e Farbe** white; **~er Fleck auf der Landkarte** blank space on the landscape; **~er Kreis** *(Wohnungswirtschaft)* decontrolled area; **~e Mäuse sehen** to see rats (pink elephants) *(sl.)*; **~er Rabe** rare bird; **~e Stellen lassen** *(drucktechn.)* to white out; **~e Woche** white sale.
weissagen to prophesy, to forebode, to predict.
Weissagung prophecy, foreboding, prediction.
Weiß | blech white iron, tin plate; **dünnes ~blech** tagger; **~blechplatte** tin sheet; **j. zum ~bluten bringen** to bleed s. o. white; **~brötchen** French roll; **~buch** *(pol.)* White Book (Paper).
Weißer white [man, person, *US*].
weißglühend white-hot.
Weißglut white heat;
j. zur ~ bringen to get s. o. into a rage; **in ~ geraten** to become livid with anger.
Weiß | metall white alloy; **~näherei** plain work; **~raum** *(drucktechn.)* white space; **~warenhändler** linen draper.
Weisung instruction, order, direction, directive, guidance;
auf ~ von by direction of; **auf ~ und für Rechnung** by order and for account of; **bis auf weitere ~en** until further orders; **laut ~** according to (in accordance with, as per) instructions;
ausdrückliche ~en strict instructions; **telegrafische ~en** telegraphic orders;
kreditpolitische ~en des Finanzministeriums directions of the treasury *(Br.)*, treasury directives *(Br.)*; **~ an den Rechtspfleger** precipe;
von ~en abweichen to deviate from (contravene) instructions; **~en ausführen** to carry out orders; **~ befolgen** to comply with (follow) an instruction; **~en einholen** to ask for directions (instructions); **~en erhalten** to receive instructions; **jem. eine ausdrückliche ~ erteilen** to instruct s. o., to give s. o. a strict charge; **~en geben** to order and direct; **sich haarscharf an seine ~en halten** not to depart by a hair's breadth from one's instructions; **sich nicht an seine ~en halten** to go flat against one's orders; **gegen strikte ~en handeln** to act in the face of direct orders; **über seine ~en hinausgehen** to go beyond one's instructions; **den ~en seines Auftraggebers Folge leisten** to comply with one's principal's instructions; **sich nach bestimmten ~en richten** to proceed on certain lines; **~en unterworfen sein** to be subject to directions.
Weisungsbefugnis authority to instruct.
weisungsgebunden subject to directions, *(Behörde)* ministerial *(Br.)*.
weisungsgemäß according to (in accordance with, as per) instructions, as directed (instructed);
~ handeln (verfahren) to act according to directions.
weit vast, wide, broad;
~ und breit far and wide, widely;
bei ~em out and away; **~ fortgeschritten** far advanced; **nicht ~ her** no great shakes *(coll.)*, nothing to write home about; **~ hergeholt** farfetched; **~ nach Mitternacht** long past midnight; **~ verbreitet** widely held;
~ vom Thema abkommen to travel out of the record; **Klappe ~ aufreißen** to brag, to be a big-mouth; **es im Leben ~ bringen** to get on in life; **zu ~ gehen** to overshoot the mark, to go too far, to strain a point; **mit einem Scherz zu ~ gehen** to carry a joke too far; **~ abgeschlagen an letzter Stelle liegen** to be dead last; **~ davon entfernt sein** not to have the slightest intention; **zu ~ herumgekommen sein** to have been all over the place; **zu ~ treiben** to overdo; **sich zu ~ vorwagen** to stick one's neck out *(sl.)*; **~ von sich weisen** to reject emphatically; **~ entfernt wohnen** to live far away;
~ und breit war niemand zu sehen there wasn't a soul to be seen;
in ~en Abständen at long intervals; **~e Auslegung** broad (liberal) interpretation; **in ~er Ferne liegen** to be in the remote future; **~en Horizont haben** to have a broad outlook; **in ~en Kreisen bekannt sein** to be widely known; **~e Reise** long journey; **~e Verbreitung** wide distribution.
weitab liegen to be a great distance off.
Weitblick long sight;
geschäftlicher ~ business acumen.
weitblickend far-sighted, long-sighted.
Weite distance, *(Kleidungsstück)* width, *(Landschaft)* vastness, expanse, extent;
grenzenlose ~ des Ozeans unlimited expanse of the ocean.
weiter further, *(zusätzlich)* additional;
nicht ~ können to be at a stop;
~e Angaben further particulars; **bis auf ~e Anweisung** until further notice; **unter ~er Bezugnahme auf meinen Brief** with further reference to my letter; **in ~e Einzelheiten eintreten** to go into further details; **ohne ~e Umstände** without further ado.
Weiterarbeit continued production.
weiterarbeiten to keep on working.
Weiter | ausbildung continuation (follow-up) training; **zur ~ausfuhr kaufen** to purchase for tran(s)shipment; **~beförderer** on-carrier.
weiterbefördern *(Briefe)* to forward, to reforward, to send on, *(umadressieren)* to redirect.
Weiterbeförderung forwarding, subsequent transport, *(Umadressierung)* redirection;
zur ~ to be forwarded.
weiterbefrachten to underfreight, to recharter.
Weiterbefrachtung recharter.
weiterbegeben to negotiate further.
Weiter | begebung eines Schecks further negotiation of a check *(US)* (cheque, *Br.*); **~behandlung** further treatment, processing; **~behandlungsgebühr** processing fee; **~benutzung** *(Patent)* continued use, continuation of use *(US)*; **~besprechung einer Sache abbrechen** to cut off an argument; **~bestand einer Firma** continuance of a firm; **~bestehen** continuance, continued existence; **~bestehen des Klageanspruchs** survival of action.
weiterbestehen to continue to exist, to remain in existence.
Weiterbildung further education *(Br.)* (training), *(im Betrieb)* inservice (inplant, continuous) training;
berufliche ~ continuation education, advanced vocational training;
~ leitender Angestellter, ~ von Führungskräften executive training.
Weiterbildungs | möglichkeiten possibilities for further education, *(beruflich)* vocational training facilities; **~programm** development program(me).
weiterempfehlen to recommend.
Weiterentwicklung development, progress, advance.
weitererzählen to repeat s. th. heard.
weiteres, bis auf until further notice, by implication;
ohne ~ wirksam werden to become automatically operative.
weiterfahren to drive on, to proceed, to go on.
Weiterfahrt *(Schiff)* proceeding.
weiterfliegen to continue its flight.
weiterführen to pursue, to continue;
Firma ~ to continue a firm.
Weiterführung *(Firma)* continuation.
Weitergabe forwarding, transmission, passing on;
~ eines Auftrages passing on of an order; **~ von Handelswechseln** rediscounting of commercial bills; **~ von Informationen** conveying of information; **~ von Nachrichten** transmission of news.
Weitergeben von Falschgeld passing counterfeit money.
weitergeben to pass on, to transmit, *(Wechsel)* to negotiate;
Gesuch ~ to pass on a petition; **gestiegene Kosten ohne Verschlechterung der Wettbewerbssituation ~** to pass on rising costs without becoming uncompetitive; **an den Nachbarn ~** to pass s. th. on to one's neighbo(u)r.
Weitergeber transferor.
weitergegebener Wechsel rediscounted (negotiated) bill.
Weitergehen, Menge zum ~ auffordern to get the crowd to move on; **von der Polizei zum ~ aufgefordert werden** to be hurried on by the police.
weitergehen to move on, to go on (ahead).
Weitergeltung continuation;
~ von Bestimmungen continued application of provisions.
Weitergeltungsklausel overreaching clause.
weiterhelfen, jem. to give s. o. a shove.
weiterkämpfen to keep on fighting.

Weiterkommen, berufliches occupational opportunities.
weiterkommen *(beruflich)* to progress;
irgendwie ~ to jog on somehow; **einfach nicht** ~ to be completely stuck.
weiterlaufen *(Gehalt)* to be continued, *(Maschine)* to keep running.
weiterleiten to pass on, to transmit onward, to dispatch, to handle, *(Bahn)* to forward;
etw. an j. ~ to pass s. th. on to s. o.; **Brief** ~ to redirect a letter; **Kredit** ~ to channel a credit; **an die zuständige Stelle** ~ to refer to the appropriate quarter; **Telefongespräch** ~ to forward a call.
Weiterleitung passing on, handling, *(Fracht)* reconsignment, retransmission;
zur ~ for onward transmission;
~ **eines Kredits** channel(l)ing of a credit; ~ **eines Telefongesprächs** call forwarding; ~ **eines Telegrammes** transmission (translation) of a telegram.
Weiterleitungsstelle *(Bahn)* forwarding office.
weitermachen to go along, to continue, to proceed;
gleich ~ to follow on; **unbeirrt** ~ to soldier on *(fam.)*; **unverdrossen** ~ to peg on.
weiterreden to go on, to keep talking.
Weiterreise continued voyage.
weiter|schicken, ~senden to send on, to forward, to redirect, *(Rundfunk)* to continue broadcasting;
Waren an die neue Adresse ~ to reconsign goods.
Weiter|sendung *(Briefe)* forwarding, redirection, *(Waren)* reconsignment; **~übertragung** sub delegation.
Weiterungen inconvenience, complication, unpleasant consequences.
weiterverarbeiten to process, to finish.
weiterverarbeitende Industrie processing (finishing) industry.
Weiterverarbeiter processor, processing firm.
Weiterverarbeitung processing, finishing, aftertreatment;
automatische ~ process automation.
Weiterverarbeitungs|betrieb processing company, end-processing plant, processor; **~erzeugnis** processing product.
weiterveräußern to resell.
Weiterveräußerung resale.
weiterverbreiten to propagate.
Weiterverbreitung propagation.
weiterverfolgen, Sache to follow s. th. through.
Weiterverfolgung eines Planes pursuance of a plan.
Weiterverfrachter forwarder, underfreighter.
weitervergeben to sublet, to underlet, to job out *(Br.)*.
Weiterverkauf reselling, resale.
weiterverkaufen to resell.
Weiterverladung onward shipment.
weitervermieten to sublet, to underlet.
Weitervermietung subletting.
weiterverpachten to sublease.
Weiterverpachtung sublease.
weiterverpfänden to repledge.
weiterversenden to reforward, to redispatch.
weiterversichern to continue one's insurance.
Weiterversicherung, freiwillige voluntarily (continued) insurance.
weiterverwendbare Packung secondary-usage package.
weiterwissen, nicht mehr to be at the end of one's tether.
weiterwursteln to muddle on.
weiterzahlen to continue to pay.
Weiterzahlung continuation of payments.
Weitflug distance flight.
weitgehend large, extensive, to a large extent;
~ **berücksichtigen** to take into account to a large extent; **jds. Verlust** ~ **decken** to go far towards making up for s. one's loss; **~e Auslegung** broad interpretation; **~e Preissenkungen** sweeping reductions in prices; **~e Reformen** sweeping reforms; **~e Unterstützung** large support; **~es Verständnis** general understanding; **~e Vollmachten** plenary (large) powers; **~e Vorschläge** far-reaching proposals.
weit|gereist travel(l)ed; **~gespannte Interessen** wide interests; **~herzige Ansichten** broad views.
weitläufig spacious, ample, *(genauestens)* in full detail;
über ~e Beziehungen verfügen to have a far-reaching influence; **~e Schilderung** lengthy description; **~er Verwandter** distant relative.
weitreichend long-range, wide-ranging;
~e Reformen sweeping reforms; **~e Verbindungen** far-reaching connections; **~e Vollmachten** plenary powers.
weitschweifig long-winded, prolific, redundant, verbose, wordy, lengthy.
Weitschweifigkeit verbosity, *(Klagevortrag)* prolixity, redundancy.
weitspurig *(Bahn)* broad-gauged.
Weitstreckenflug long-distance flight.
weitverbreitet widespread, widely held;
~e Erscheinung wide-spread phenomenon; **~e Meinung** widely held opinion; **~e Zeitung** widely read newspaper, newspaper with a wide circulation.
Weitverkehr long-range communication.
weitverzweigt wide-branched (-ramified).
Weitwinkel wide angle;
~kamera panorama camera; **~objektiv** wide-angle lens.
weitzeilig *(Schreibmaschine)* double-spaced.
Weizen wheat, corn *(Br.)*;
loser ~ bulk wheat;
Spreu vom ~en scheiden to sift the chaff from the wheat; **Internationales ~abkommen** International Wheat Agreement; **~anbau** wheat growing, corn growing *(Br.)*; **~börse** wheat pitch *(US)*, wheat pit *(US)*, corn exchange *(Br.)*; **~ernte** wheat crop (harvest); **gute ~ernte** good yield of wheat; **~feld** wheat field; **~gürtel** wheat zone *(US)*; **~handel** trade in wheat; **~kartell** wheat combine; **~knappheit** wheat shortage; **~lieferungen** supplies of wheat, wheat shipments; **~markt** wheat (corn, *Br.*) market; **~mehl** wheat flour; **~saatgut** seed wheat; **~sendung** wheat shipment; **~stroh** wheaten straw; **~überschuß** wheat glut.
welk withered, faded.
Wellblech corrugated iron.
Welle wave, *(fig.)* trend, line, *(mil.)* echelon, *(Schaft)* tree;
grüne ~ *(Straßenverkehr)* linked (synchronized) traffic lights; **die neue** ~ the new trend; **schaumgekrönte ~n** white-crested waves; **weiche** ~ soft line, *(pol.)* soft pedal;
~n der Empörung waves of indignation;
in einander folgenden ~n angreifen to attack in waves; **hohe ~n schlagen** to cause quite a stir; **auf einer ~ senden** to broadcast on a wavelength; **hilfslos in den ~n treiben** to be tossed about by the waves; **in den ~n umkommen** to be drowned at sea.
Wellen|band wave band; **~bereich** waveband coverage; **~berg** crest of a wave, *(Konjunktur)* peak; **~brecher** breakwater, splashboard; **~einstellknopf** tuning knob.
wellenförmig wavelike, wavy, rippled, undulatory, undulating, corrugated in waves;
~e Beschaffenheit undulation; **~e Unebenheit** wave.
Wellenkonferenz frequency tuning planning conference.
Wellenlänge wave length;
~ **absorbieren** to pirate a wave length; **auf eine bestimmte** ~ **einstellen** to tune in; **gleiche** ~ **mit jem. haben** to be on common ground with s. o.
Wellen|plan frequency plan; **~rand** undulated frame; **~schalter** *(Rundfunkgerät)* wave changer (switch); **~schlag** wash; **~schwund** fading; **~skala** tuning scale; **~tal** trough of the sea; **~tal der Konjunktur** economic trough; **~verteilung** frequency allocation.
Wellpappe corrugated pasteboard (cardboard).
Welt, am Ende der off the map; **bis ans Ende der** ~ to the world's end; **von aller** ~ **verlassen** alone and forelorn;
die Dritte ~ the third world, developing countries; **freie** ~ free world; **gesamte** ~ world at large, international community; **die große** ~ the fashionable world, top drawer, the four hundred *(US)*; **literarische** ~ literary set; **verkehrte** ~ upside-down world; **vornehme** ~ rank and fashion;
~ **der Wissenschaften** scientific world, realm of science;
~ **beherrschen** to hold sway over the world; **die** ~ **nicht gerade einreißen** to be no great shakes, not to be the sort ever to set the Thames on fire; **der** ~ **entsagen** to foresake the world; **Licht der** ~ **erblicken** to see the light; **alles in der** ~ **für etw. geben** to give one's ears for s. th.; **einer** ~ **von Vorurteilen gegenüberstehen** to be confronted with a multitude of prejudices; **in die** ~ **hinausziehen** to fare out; **nicht gleich die** ~ **kosten** not to cost the earth; **der ganzen** ~ **zugänglich machen** to be a window to the world; **durch ~en getrennt sein** to be poles apart; **in der ganzen** ~ **tätig sein** to operate world-wide; **Gerücht in die** ~ **setzen** to set a rumo(u)r afloat; **allein und auf sich gestellt in die** ~ **entlassen werden** to be decanted into the world;
das ist der Lauf der ~ such is life; **dem Mutigen gehört die** ~ fortune favo(u)rs the bold.
weltabgeschieden secluded, isolated, remote.
Welt|abkommen universal convention; **~agrarmarkt** international agricultural market; **~all** universe, cosmos; **~ansicht**

world concept; ~**anschauung** outlook on life; ~**arbeitsamt** International Labo(u)r Office; ~**arbeitskonferenz** International Labo(u)r Conference; ~**arbeitsrecht** international labo(u)r code; ~**aufrüstungswirtschaft** international rearmament economy; ~**ausstellung** international (universal, world) exhibition, world fair; ~**bank** International Bank of Reconstruction and Development; ~**bedarf** world requirements (demands).

welt | beherrschend world-dominating; ~**bekannt** world-renowned; ~**berühmt** world-famous.

Weltbevölkerung world population.

weltbewegend earth-shaking.

Welt | bewegendes, nichts no great shakes, nothing to write home about; ~**blatt** paper of world-wide circulation; ~**bühne** world stage; ~**bund** world alliance; ~**bürger** cosmopolitan, citizen of the world; ~**bürgertum** cosmopolitanism; ~**energieverbrauch** world energy consumption; ~**ereignis** event of international importance; ~**ernährungsprogramm** world food program(me); **nichts ~erschütterndes** nothing to make a song about; ~**erzeugung** world production; ~**exportmarkt** world export market; ~**fernsprechdienst** global phone service; ~**firma** firm of world-wide importance; ~**flüchtlingsorganisation** International Refugee Organization; ~**flugreise** round-the-world jaunt.

weltfremder Reformer starry-eyed reformer.

Welt | geltung world reputation; ~**gerichtshof** Permanent Court of International Justice; ~**geschehen** theater (theatre, *Br.*) of life; ~**geschichte** universal history; ~**gesundheitsorganisation** World Health Organization; ~**gewandtheit** urbanity; ~**gewerkschaftsbund** World Federation of Trade Unions; ~**handel** world (international) trade, international commerce.

Welthandels | durchschnitt average figure of world trade; ~**konferenz der Vereinten Nationen** United Nations Conference on Trade and Development; ~**lage** world trading pattern; ~**nation** world trader; ~**preis** world price; ~**schranken** barriers to world trade; ~**stadt** world trade position; ~**ströme** flow of world trade; ~**volumen** volume of world trade; ~**währung** world trading currency; ~**zentrum** world trade center *(US)* (centre, *Br.*).

Welt | herrschaft domination of the world, world domination; ~**kapazität** global capacity; ~**karte** international map, map of the world; ~**kartell** world cartel; ~**klugheit** sophistication; ~**knappheit** world shortage; ~**konferenz** world (international) conference; ~**kongreß** world congress; ~**krieg** world war; ~**kugel** globe; ~**lage** state of the world, international situation.

weltlich mundane, profane.

Welt | liquidität world liquidity; ~**macht** world power; ~**machtpolitik** imperialism; ~**mann** man of the world.

Weltmarkt world market;
~**monopol** global monopoly; ~**notierung** international quotation; ~**preis** world market (international) price, *(Öl)* posted price; ~**rohstoffe** world-market raw materials.

Weltmaßstab, im in world terms.

Weltnahrungsmittel | handel world trade in food; ~**knappheit** world food shortage; ~**versorgung** world food supplies; ~**vorräte** world food reserves.

Welt | öffentlichkeit the world at large; ~**organisation** international (world-wide) organization; ~**organisation für geistiges Eigentum** World Intellectual Property Organization; ~**patent** universal patent; ~**politik** world politics; ~**postkarte** foreign postcard; ~**postverein** International Postal Union; ~**postvertrag** Universal Postal Convention; ~**preisindex für Stapelware** Moody Index *(US)*; ~**preisniveau** international price level; ~**presse** world press; ~**produktion** world production (output).

Weltraum outer space;
unendlicher ~ endless space;
~**erkundung** space exploration; ~**fahrer** space travel(l)er; ~**fahrt** space travel; ~**forschung** space research (exploration); ~**funkdienst** space service; ~**labor[atorium]** space lab, skylab; **bemanntes ~laboratorium** manned orbiting laboratory; ~**nachrichtenwesen** space communication; ~**odyssee** space odyssey; ~**rakete** space rocket; ~**recht** outer space law; ~**roman** space fiction; ~**reise** space trip; ~**satellit** space (orbiting) satellite; ~**sender** space-borne transmitter; ~**sonde** voyager spacecraft; ~**station** orbiting (space) platform; ~**vertrag** space treaty; ~**zeitalter** space age; ~**zentrum** space flight center *(US)* (centre, *Br.*).

Welt | regierung world-government; ~**reise** round-the-world tour (cruise), tour round the world; ~**reise machen** to go round the globe, to go for a trip (travel, journey) round the world, to take a trip (make a journey) round the world; ~**revolution** world revolution; ~**rezession** world recession; ~**ruf** international (world-wide) reputation; ~**sicherheitsrat** Security Council; ~**spartag** World Savings Day; ~**sprache** world (universal) language; ~**staat** world state; ~**stadt** metropolis, world capital, cosmopolis, cosmopolitan city; ~**stadtatmosphäre** cosmopolitan atmosphere; ~**stellung** great position in the world; ~**umsatz** world turnover.

weltumspannend universal, global, world-wide;
~**e Interessen** world-wide interests.

Weltuntergangs | prophet doom prophet; ~**stimmung** air of impending doom; ~**töne anschlagen** to take on apocalyptic tones.

Welt | uraufführung world premiere; ~**urheberrechtsabkommen** Universal Copyright Convention; ~**verband** world association, international union; ~**verband für Reisebüros** World Association of Travel Agencies; ~**verbesserer** do-gooder, utopian; **kein ~verbesserer sein** not to be out to reform the world; ~**verbrauch** world consumption; ~**verkehr** international traffic; ~**währung** world currency.

Weltwährungs | behörde International Monetary Authority; ~**fonds** International Monetary Fund; ~**konferenz** international monetary conference; ~**reserven** world monetary reserves, international (world) liquidity; ~**system** world monetary system.

weltweit throughout the world, world-wide, global;
~ **auseinander sein** to be poles apart;
~**e Finanzkrise** world-wide financial crisis; ~**er Unterschied** world of difference.

Weltwirtschaft international (world, global) economics, world (world-wide) economy.

Weltwirtschafts | gipfel world economic summit; ~**kommission** World Economic Commission; ~**konferenz** World Economic Conference; ~**krise** world[-wide] depression, great depression, world slump; ~**lage** world economic situation (conditions); **neue ~ordnung** *(UN)* New International Economic Order; ~**system** world economic system.

Wende *(Börse)* turn;
konjunkturelle ~ economic turnaround;
~**kreis** *(Auto)* turning circle.

Wendeltreppe spiral (circular, winding, wall) staircase.

Wendeltreppenstufe winder.

Wenden U-turn;
~ **verboten!** U-turns not allowed!

wenden *(Flugzeug)* to yaw, *(Schiff)* to round, to wind;
sich ~ *(Flut)* to be on the turn; **sich an j.** ~ to approach (contact) s. o., to call on (apply to) s. o.; **sich von jem.** ~ to turn away from s. o.; **kein Auge von jem.** ~ not to take one's eyes off s. o.; **sich bittend an j.** ~ to cast o. s. upon s. one's kindness; **sich hauptsächlich an den Fachmann** ~ *(Buch)* to be intended mainly for the expert; **sich zum Guten** ~ to turn out well; **sich gegen eine höhere Instanz** ~ to have recourse to a higher court; **jem. den Rücken** ~ to turn one's back on s. o.; **sich scharf gegen etw.** ~ to object strongly against; **sich vertrauensvoll an j.** ~ to confide in s. o.; **Zeit auf etw.** ~ to spend time on s. th.

Wendepunkt turning point, landmark, *(pol.)* turnaround, *(Theater)* crisis;
konjunktureller ~ business turning point, economic turnabout (turnaround); **politischer** ~ turn in policy;
~ **der Gesamtertragskurve** extensive margin; ~ **eines Konjunkturzyklus** business cycle turning; ~ **in jds. Laufbahn** turning point in s. one's career;
~ **in seinem Leben erreichen** to reach a turning point in one's life; **am unteren** ~ **sein** to be in the general bottoming area.

Wende | radius turning radius; ~**verbot** U-turns not allowed.

wendig manoeuvrable *(Br.)*, maneuverable *(US)*, *(geistig)* nimble, agile, flexible, versatile.

Wendigkeit manoeuvrability *(Br.)*, maneuverability *(US)*, *(geistige)* nimbleness, versatility, wit, mental sharpness.

Wendung turn;
neue ~ new spin *(US)*;
~ **zum Schlechteren** turn for the worse;
dem Gespräch eine andere ~ **geben** to change the subject; **einer Sache eine ganz andere** ~ **geben** to put a new face on the business; **glückliche** ~ **nehmen** to take a fortunate turn.

wenig lightly, little;
~ **gefragt** easy, down;
sich nicht ~ **ärgern** to be pretty annoyed; ~ **von jem. halten** to have a poor opinion of s. o.; **j.** ~ **interessieren** not to interest s. o. greatly; ~ **erfreulich sein** to be rather disappointing; ~**er werden** to ebb; **immer** ~**er werden** to be gradually melting away; **ein** ~ **Geduld** some patience; **sehr** ~ **Geld haben** to have very

little money; ~ **oder gar keine Hilfe** little or no help; ~ **Nachfrage** little demand; **in ~en Tagen** in a few days; ~ **Zeit haben** to be pressed for time.

Wenigkeit, meine my humble self.

Wenigstfordernder lowest taker.

Werbe|abschluß für öffentliche Verkehrslinien line sale; **~absicht** advertising purpose; **~abteilung** advertising *(Br.)* (advertisement, *US*, publicity, promotion, *US*) department, *(Bank)* new business department, *(Versicherung)* canvassing department; **~abteilungsleiter** director of advertising; **~adreßbuch** advertising directory.

Werbeagentur advertising (publicity, ad, *US*) agency, advertisement contractor;
anerkannte ~ recognized (accredited) agency; **eigene** ~ house agency;
~ **beschäftigen** to retain an agency.

Werbeakquisiteur canvasser, space salesman *(US)*, advertising agent (solicitor, *US*).

Werbeaktion advertising (canvassing, publicity) campaign, promotion exercise *(US)*;
begleitende ~ accessory (auxiliary) advertising; **kombinierte** ~ tie-up advertising;
~ **in den Massenmedien durchführen** to run a media campaign.

Werbe|aktiva advertising assets; **bezahlte ~ankündigung** *(Rundfunk)* paid announcement; **~ansprache** advertising approach; **~ansprache auf dem Wege über das Kind** kid appeal; **~anspruch** claim; **~anstrengung** advertising (propaganda) effort; **~anteil** advertising share; **~antwort** return, postal *(Br.)* (mail, *US*) advertising; **~antwortdienst** business-reply service; **~antwortkarte** business-reply card; **~anzeige** advertisement, ad *(US)*, notification; **~appell** advertising appeal; **~arbeit** advertising activities, publicity work, publicity, canvassing; **~argument** advertising angle; **~argument im Text** copy point; **~artikel** publicity (promotion, *US*) article, advertised article (product), novelty, *(Zeitung)* advertising editorial; **~atelier** commercial (art) studio; **~auftrag** advertisement order.

Werbeaufwand publicity expenses, advertising investment (expenditure), promotional expense *(US)*, *(Einkommensteuererklärung)* professional expenditure;
~ **pro Minute** *(Fernsehen)* cost of time;
80% seines ~s im Fernsehsektor einsetzen to allocate 80% of its ad budget to television *(US)*.

Werbe|ausgabe advertising edition; **~ausgaben** advertising expenditure (costs), publicity expenses; **~auslage** display, advertising layout *(US)*; **~aussage** advertising (sales) message, story, *(unbezahlte)* plug; **vergleichende ~aussage** comparative story; **~auswüchse** advertising extravagance; **~bauten** display kiosks; **~behauptung** claim; **~beigabe** dealer help; **~beilage** advertising supplement, stuffer *(US)*; **~beispiel** example of advertising; **~beitrag** advertising contribution; **~berater** advertising consultant; **fachmännische ~beratung** expert advertising advice; **~bereich** advertising area; **~beruf** advertising profession; **~bestimmungen** advertising regulations (provisions); **~botschaft** advertising (sales) message, story, *(unbezahlte)* plug; **~bräuche** advertising practices; **~brief** sales letter; **nachfassender ~brief** follow-up letter; **~broschüre** leaflet, brochure; **kleine ~broschüre** booklet; **~büro** advertising agency (contractors), publicity bureau (office), *(für Arbeitskräfte)* recruiting office; **~chef** *(Theater)* press agent *(US)*; **~dienst** advertising (publicity) service; **~direktor** advertising (publicity) director (manager); **~drucksache** advertising matter, broadsheet, broadside.

Werbedurchsage radio (spot) announcement, commercial spot;
betriebliche ~ company radio commercial; **eingeblendete** ~ straight commercial; **kurze** ~ radio spot;
~ **für ein Nebenprodukt** trailer, hitchhike.

Werbe|effekt advertising effect[iveness]; **kurze ~einblendung** chain break, spot announcement *(US)*; **~einnahmen** advertising revenue; **fortgesetzter ~einsatz** continuity in advertising; **verstärkter ~einsatz** sales drive; **lokale ~einschaltung** cut-in advertisement; **zugkräftiges ~element** interest factor; **~entwurf** advertising design; **~erfahrung** advertising experience; **~erfolg** advertising result, publicity success; **~erfolgskontrolle** advertising control, keying of advertisements *(US)*; **~erfolgskontrolle durchführen** to test the advertising impact; **~erinnerung ohne Gedächtnisstützen** pure recall.

Werbeetat advertising [expense] budget, advertising appropriation *(US)*, *(Werbeagentur)* account;
aufgeschlüsselter ~ mechanical budget *(US)*; **bewilligter (genehmigter)** ~ appropriation for advertising, advertising budget (appropriation, *US*);
~ **aufteilen** to assign advertising expenditure; ~ **verantwortlich bearbeiten** *(Agentur)* to handle an account; ~ **gekürzt haben** to be down in advertising.

Werbe|ethik advertising standard; **~exemplar** complimentary copy.

Werbefach, im ~ **tätig sein** to be in the advertising line; **~blatt** advertising paper; **~leute** admen *(US)*; **führende ~leute** advertising executives; **~mann** publicity (advertising) man, adman *(US)*, advertising expert (specialist, executive, engineer, *US*), publicist, publicity expert; **freie Künstler beschäftigender ~mann** art buyer; **~verband** advertising association; **~zeitschrift** advertising publication.

Werbe|fahne, vom Flugzeug gezogene airplane banner; **~faltblatt** booklet, leaflet, *(für Spezialauflagen)* rack folder; **~feindlichkeit** antipathy to advertising.

Werbefeldzug publicity (sales, advertising, media) campaign, publicity stunt, canvass, drive, tryout *(US)*;
örtlich begrenzter ~ local campaign; **erfolgversprechender** ~ cream campaign; **regionaler** ~ zone campaign; **überregionaler** ~ national campaign;
~ **für Kapitalanlagen** investment sales drive;
~ **erfolgreich abschließen** to bring a campaign to a successful issue; **großangelegten** ~ **durchführen** to conduct a wide publicity campaign; ~ **starten** to launch an advertising campaign.

Werbefernsehanzeige television advertisement.

Werbefernsehen commercial (pay, *US*) television, television advertising;
privates ~ independent television.

Werbefernseh|gebühr television advertisement duty; **~gesellschaft** commercial television company; **~lizenz** commercial television franchise; **~station** commercial television station.

Werbefigur advertising figure (character).

Werbefilm advertising film (screen), propaganda (publicity) film, commercial spot;
einminütiger ~ minute movie *(US)*; **kurzer** ~ quickie, spotfilm;
~ **mit eingeblendeten Händleradressen** open-end commercial;
~rolle budget film.

Werbe|firma advertising contractor, *(auf Außenwerbung spezialisiert)* outdoor advertising firm; **~fläche** advertising space, poster panel, *(angestrahlte)* floodlight advertisement; **~flächenpächter in öffentlichen Verkehrsmitteln** advertising operator; **~flugblatt** dealer broadside; **~flugzeug** advertising aeroplane; **~fonds** advertising budget (appropriation, *US*); **~förderung** advertising promotion; **~forschung** advertising (media) research; **~foto** commercial photo.

Werbefunk advertising commercial, commercial broadcasting (radio), broadcast (radio) advertising;
~plan time schedule; **~schluß** closing; **~sendung** commercial program(me), *(kostenlose)* plug; **~sendung mehrerer Firmen** participating program(me); **~station** commercial station.

Werbe|funktion advertising function; **~funkvertreter** station representative; **~gag** publicity gag, promotion gimmick *(US)*; **~gebiet** advertising field, *(Nachwuchs)* recruiting ground; **~gebühren** advertising rates; **~geschenk** advertising article, free (business, specialty, goodwill) gift; **~geschenkartikel** advertising novelty; **~geschenkverteilung** business gift-giving, free-gift advertising; **~gesellschaft** advertising company (corporation); **~gesichtspunkt** advertising angle (approach); **~gespräch** sales talk (chat); **~gestalter** art designer; **~grafik** commercial (advertising) art; **~grafiker** industrial artist, art (advertising) designer; **~großanlage** spectacular; **~grundaussage** basic message; **~haushalt** advertising budget (appropriation, *US*); **~idee** advertising idea; **~industrie** advertising industry; **~instruktionsfilm** demonstrational film; **~instrument** advertising medium; **~investitionen** advertising investments; **~jargon** advertising argot; **~journal** advertising journal.

Werbekampagne advertising (marketing, sales, publicity, media) campaign, publicity stunt, drive, canvass, publicity effort, tryout *(US)*;
über Rundfunksender ausgestrahlte ~ broadcast media campaign; **langfristig geplante** ~ preplanned advertising; **großangelegte** ~ elaborate campaign; **gegenwärtig laufende** ~ current advertising;
~ **mit beigefügtem Kupon** coupon scheme;
bei einer ~ **Rabattsätze ausnutzen** to buy advertising at a discount.

Werbe|kolonne team of canvassers; **~konzeption** advertising concept, media conception; **~kosten** advertising (publicity) expense (expenditure, outlay, costs), media cost; **~kostenpauschale** standard deduction for expenses *(US)*; **~kraft** publicity (attention, *US*) value, advertising appeal, selling power,

(Blickfänger) eye catcher; ~**kurzfilm** spotfilm, quickie; ~**kurzspiel** advertising sketch; ~**läufer mit Rückenplakat** sandwich man; ~**leiter** publicity (advertising) manager (director), publicity representative (director), promotion manager *(US)*; ~**literatur** advertising literature; ~**manager** publicity representative; ~**manuskript** advertising matter; ~**mappe** publicity kit; ~**masche** publicity gag; **weiche** ~**masche** soft sell in advertising; **periodisch unterbrochene** ~**maßnahmen** intermittent ad campaign *(US)*.

Werbematerial advertising (publicity) material, advertising article *(US)*, promotion matter (material) *(US)*, promotional literature *(US)*, *(für Händler)* advertising (dealer) aids, *(Vertreter)* sales kit *(US)*;
an den Haustüren verteiltes ~ house-to-house advertising; **bei der Einführung verwendetes** ~ introductory material;
~ **für Dienstleistungsbetriebe** service packaging; ~ **für den Fremdenverkehr** tourist publicity material; ~ **für den Händler** dealer aids, package.

Werbe|medien communication (advertising) media; ~**methoden** publicity (advertising) methods; **neuartige** ~**methoden** original way of advertising; ~**minute** *(Fernsehen)* commercial minute; ~**mitteilung** advertising message, business press; ~**mittel** advertising medium (device), medium [for advertising], vehicle for advertising, *(pl.)* advertising media, *(Geldmittel)* advertising budget (appropriations, *US*); **provisionsfähige** ~**mittel** commissionable media; ~**mittel als Verkaufshilfe** dealer aids; ~**möglichkeiten** advertising horizons; ~**motiv** advertising motive (motif); ~**motto** [advertising] slogan; ~**müdigkeit** oversaturation with advertising; ~**muster** trial (free) sample.

werben to advertise, to campaign, to solicit, to publicize, to make propaganda, to promote *(US)*, *(aufdringlich)* to boost, to plug, to puff *(Br.)*;
j. für etw. ~ to win s. o. over; **Abonnenten** ~ to solicit subscriptions; **Arbeitskräfte** ~ to recruit workers *(US)*; **für seine Erzeugnisse** ~ to push one's products; **um jds. Gunst** ~ to court s. one's favo(u)r; **Hotelgäste** ~ to tout for a hotel; **Inserate** ~ to canvass advertisements; **intensiv** ~ to push; **Kunden** ~ to tout, to solicit (canvass, acquire, drum up, *US*) customers; **um ein Mädchen** ~ to court a girl; **Mitglieder** ~ to enlist members; **Nachwuchs** ~ to hunt (recruit, *US*) junior executives; **für eine Sache** ~ to make propaganda for s. th.; **Soldaten** ~ to enlist (recruit, *US*) soldiers; **Stimmen** ~ to canvass for (solicit) votes; **Stimmen für den konservativen Kandidaten** ~ to canvass for the conservative candidate; **Subskribenten in einem Bezirk** ~ to canvass a territory for a subscription [of a book], to solicit subscriptions in a district; **in einem Wahlbezirk Stimmen** ~ to canvass a district.

Werbe|nachricht advertising news (message); ~**nachweis** advertising record.

werbend productive, promotional *(US)*;
~**e Aktiva** earning assets; ~**e Anlage** profitable investment; ~**e Ausgaben** productive expenses; ~**er Betrieb** *(Kommunalwesen)* public utility; ~**es Kapital** working (interest-bearing) capital; ~**e Tätigkeit** productive activity.

Werbe|neuheit advertising novelty; ~**nummer** complimentary (presentation) copy; ~**offensive** propaganda offensive; ~**offizier** recruiting officer *(US)*, recruiter *(US)*; ~**pavillon** advertising pavilion; ~**plakat** placard, poster; ~**plakat in öffentlichen Verkehrsmitteln** car card; ~**plan** campaign plan, schedule, advertising program(me), prospectus; ~**planvorlage** presentation; ~**politik** advertising policy; ~**preis** cut-rate (knockdown, early-bird, introductory) price; ~**programm** advertising (publicity) program(me); ~**prospekt** booklet, handbill, [propaganda] leaflet, handout, promotional literature, *(einseitig bedruckt)* broadsheet, broadside, *(Gesellschaftsgründung)* prospectus; ~**psychologie** psychology of advertising.

Werber canvasser, advertiser, solicitor, propagandist, crimp, *(Arbeitskräfte)* recruiter *(US)*, recruiting officer *(US)*.

Werbe|rabatt advertising (promotion, *US*) allowance, rebate; ~**recht** advertising law; ~**rummel** puffing publicity *(Br.)*, ballyhoo *(US)*; ~**rundschreiben** advertising circular; ~**sache mit Rückantwort** self-mailer; **degressive** ~**sätze** graded advertising rates; ~**schau** advertising display; ~**schild** sign, billboard, facia; ~**schlacht** advertising battle; ~**schlagwort** advertising slogan; ~**schreiben** sales letter, prospectus; ~**schrift** brochure, publicity document, prospectus, pamphlet, [propaganda] leaflet; ~**schulungsleiter** missionary salesman; ~**seite** advertising page; ~**sektor** advertising sector.

Werbesendung [broadcast] commercial, broadcast production;
für ~**en gesperrt** blocked-out;
eingeblendete ~ integrated commercial; **unmittelbare** ~ direct commercial;
~ **für Nebenprodukte** trailer, hitchhike; ~ **zur gleichen Tagesstunde jeden Wochentag** across-the-board [broadcasting].

Werbe|serie, ständig wiederholte rotation; ~**silhouette** sky sign; ~**sketch** advertising sketch; ~**slogan** advertising slogan; ~**spezialist** advertising specialist; ~**spot** spot announcement, advertising spot, commercial, filmlet; **kurzer** ~**spot** quicky, spotfilm; ~**spruch** advertising slogan, catch-phrase, jingle; ~**spruchband** banner, streamer; ~**standpunkt** advertising angle (approach); ~**stelle** advertising agency, official publicity bureau; ~**stil** brand image, graphic design; ~**strategie** advertising strategy (tactics); ~**streifband** advertising tape; ~**studio** advertising (commercial, art) studio; ~**tarif** advertising (advertisement, *Br.*) rates; ~**tätigkeit** advertising activities, propaganda; ~**technik** mechanics of advertisement, publicity technique; ~**teil** *(Zeitung)* advertising side (page); **motorisiert durchgeführter** ~**test** caravan test.

Werbetext advertising slogan, [advertising] copy, advertising matter (text);
aggressiver ~ competitive copy; **außergewöhnlicher** ~ creative copy; **begründender** ~ reason-why copy; **herabsetzender** ~ disparaging (knocking-down) copy;
~ **verfassen** to sloganize, to compose copy;
~**abfassung** copywriting.

Werbe|texter copywriter, sloganeer *(coll.)*, ad writer *(US)*; ~**thema** advertising theme (slogan).

Werbeträger [advertising] medium, medium (vehicle) for advertising, advertising vehicle, *(pl.)* communication media;
überregionale ~ national media;
~ **für die Verbrauchswerbung** consumer advertising medium; **Anzeigen bei verschiedenen** ~**n unterbringen** to place advertisements in various media;
~**analyse** media analysis; ~**auswahl** selection of media; ~**bewertung** media evaluation; ~**forschung** media survey (research).

Werbe|trommel rühren to make propaganda, to boost, to drum *(US)*, *(mil.)* to beat up for recruits; **eigene** ~**trommel rühren (schlagen)** to be self-advertising; ~**unkosten** advertising (publicity) expenses (costs); ~**unterlagen** advertising matter, promotional material; ~**unternehmen** advertising business (enterprise, contractor), commercial undertaking; ~**unterstützung** advertising support; ~**usancen** advertising practices; ~**veranstaltung** publicity event; ~**verband** advertising association; ~**verbot** ban on publicity; ~**verkäufe** promotional selling; ~**versuchsfeldzug** test campaign; ~**vitrine** showcase; ~**vorbereitung** advertising research; ~**vorhaben** advertising plan; ~**vorlage** [advertisement] copy; ~**vorspann** *(Sendung)* warmup; ~**wagen** advertising van; ~**wert** advertising (publicity, promotional, *US*) value; ~**wertprüfung** pretest, media research; ~**wesen** publicity, advertising business; ~**wettbewerb** advertising competition (contest).

werbewirksam effective in advertising.

Werbe|wirksamkeit ad effectiveness *(US)*; ~**wirksamkeitsanalyse** advertising effectiveness survey, audience measurement; ~**wirksamkeitstest** *(Anzeige)* association test; ~**wirkung** advertising effectiveness, attention value; **eigene** ~**wirkung** *(Ware)* self-appeal; **kumulierte** ~**wirkung** accumulated advertising effectiveness; ~**woche** propaganda week; ~**zeichner** advertising artist (cartoonist), advertising designer; ~**zeichnung** advertising design (drawing); **käufliche** ~**zeit** *(Rundfunk)* advertising time; ~**zeiten** *(Rundfunk)* availabilities; ~**zeitschrift** advertising publication; ~**zensur** advertising censorship; ~**zettel** throwaway, handbill, leaflet; ~**ziel** advertising purpose; ~**zuschuß des Herstellers** advertising allowance; **zu** ~**zwecken** for advertising purposes; **seinen** ~**zweck konkret ansprechen** to detail one's advertising object.

werbliche Unterstützung advertising support.

Werbung advertising, advertisement *(Br.)*, propaganda, publicity, promotion *(US)*, copy, *(Anwerbung)* enrolment, enlistment, recruiting *(US)*, *(Aufträge)* soliciting, *(Stimmen)* canvassing, *(Verkaufsförderung)* sales promotion;
aggressive ~ disparaging copy, competitive advertising *(US)*; **anreißerische** ~ puffing advertising *(Br.)*; **ansprechende** ~ appealing advertising; **redaktionell aufgemachte** ~ editorial advertisement, editorial *(sl.)*; **aufklärende** ~ reason-why advertising; **an ethischen Gesichtspunkten ausgerichtete** ~ ethical advertising; **belehrende** ~ educational advertising; **betrügerische** ~ deceptive advertising; **bezahlte** ~ paid advertising; **direkte (direkt gestreute)** ~ direct advertising; **diskriminierende** ~ discriminatory advertising; **überregional**

durchgeführte ~ nation-wide (across-the-board) advertising; **einführende** ~ original advertisement; **eingeblendete** ~ tie-in advertising; **erzieherische** ~ educational copy; **firmenbetonte** ~ institutional advertising; **fremdsprachige** ~ foreign-language advertising; **geballte** ~ mass advertising; **gefühlsbestimmte** ~ sense-appeal copy; **gelegentliche** ~ opportunity advertising; **gemeinsame** ~ association (cooperative) advertising; **auf Massenwirkung gerichtete** ~ mass-emotional appeal; **auf einen bestimmten Personenkreis gerichtete** ~ selective appeal; **direkt gestreute** ~ direct advertising; **gezielte** ~ selective advertising; **gleichgerichtete** ~ coordinated advertising; **großzügige** ~ large-scale advertising; **herabsetzende** ~ disparaging (knocking-down, competitive) copy; **im eigenen Betrieb hergestellte** ~ inhouse advertising; **irreführende** ~ misleading advertisement (advertising); **kostspielige** ~ expensive advertising; **lautere** ~ truth in advertising, advertising ethics; **marktschreierische** ~ puffing advertising *(Br.)*; **nachfassende** ~ follow-up advertising; **redaktionelle** ~ editorial publicity; **kostenlose redaktionelle** ~ write-up *(US)*, free puff *(Br.)*; **reißerische** ~ loud publicity, harmless puffing *(Br.)*; **schwungvolle** ~ dynamic advertising; **täuschende** ~ misleading advertisement; **überregionale** ~ national (nation-wide) advertising; **überzogene** ~ persuasive advertising, advertisement puff *(Br.)*, harmless puffing *(Br.)*, wide advertising; **ungewöhnliche** ~ offbeat advertising; **ungezielte** ~ nonselective advertising; **unlautere** ~ puff; **unterschwellige** ~ subliminal advertising; **unwahre** ~ false advertising; **zwei miteinander verbundene** ~**en** tie-in; **vergleichende** ~ competitive (comparative) advertising; **in rascher Folge wiederholte** ~ high-pressure advertising; **wirksamste** ~ advertising pulling the best results; **zielbewußte** ~ systematic advertising; **zugkräftige** ~ audience builder; **zusätzliche** ~ accessory (supplementary) advertising;

~ **bei Aktienkunden** stock touting *(US)*; ~ **von Arbeitskräften** recruiting of labor *(US)*; ~ **durch Ausgabe von Warenproben** sample advertising; ~ **in Berufskreisen** professional advertising; ~ **auf Bundesebene** national advertising; **direkte** ~ **durch Drucksachenversand** direct-mail advertising *(US)*; ~ **mit größter Durchschlagskraft** advertising pulling the best results; ~ **im Einzelhandelsgeschäft** point-of-sale (purchase) advertising; ~ **innerhalb des Einzelhandelsgeschäfts** inside-the-store advertising; ~ **in Fachzeitschriften** trade-paper advertisement; ~ **in Farben** colo(u)r advertising; ~ **für den Fremdenverkehr** tourist advertising; ~ **für Gelegenheitskäufe** bargain-sale advertising; ~ **für Grundstücksbeteiligungen** syndicate advertising; ~ **für Industrieerzeugnisse** industrial advertising; ~ **am Kaufort** point-of-purchase advertising; ~ **mit Kennziffern** keyed advertising; ~ **beim Kunden** direct advertising; ~ **im Ladeninnern** inside-the-store advertising; ~ **mit Lockartikeln** bait advertising; ~ **in der Luft** air advertisement, aerial (skyline) advertising; ~ **für Markenerzeugnisse** brand advertising; ~ **in gedruckten Medien** print advertising; ~ **von Mitgliedern** membership drive; ~ **durch Musterverteilung** sampling, free trial, free-gift (novelty) advertising; ~ **durch Plakate** outdoor (billboard, *Br.*) advertising; ~ **durch Postversand** direct-mail advertising (promotion, *US*); ~ **mit dem [niedrigen] Preis** price advertising; ~ **in der Presse** press (newspaper) advertising; ~ **im Rundfunk** broadcast advertising; ~ **für Sonderangebote** bargain-sale advertising; ~ **in der Straßenbahn** streetcar advertising; ~ **in den Tageszeitungen** newspaper advertising; ~ **in Verbindung mit einem Fernsehprogramm** program(me) advertising; ~ **für den Verbraucher** consumer advertising; ~ **am Verkaufsort** point-of-purchase advertising; ~ **an der Verkaufsstelle** point-of-purchase advertising; ~ **an einem Verkehrsknotenpunkt** head-on position; ~ **in eigenen Verkehrsmitteln** self-operation; ~ **in öffentlichen Verkehrsmitteln** travel(l)ing display; ~ **am Verkehrsstrom** outdoor advertising; ~ **durch Verteilung von Geschenkartikeln** novelty (free-gift) advertising;

~ **betreiben** to advertise, to solicit for custom (orders); **auffällige** ~ **betreiben** to beat (thump) the drum; ~ **durchführen** to publicize, to advertise; ~ **unterbringen** to place advertising; **großzügige** ~ **veranstalten** to advertise widely.

Werbungs|aufwand *(steuerlich)* professional expenditure (outlays), business allowance *(US)*; ~**konto** complimentary account; ~**kosten** promotion and advertising costs *(US)*, publicity costs (expenses), promotional expenses *(US)*, *(Handelsunkosten)* overhead [expense], *(steuerlich)* professional outlays (expenditure), business allowance, class A deductions *(US)*; **für** ~**kosten abziehen** to allow for professional expenditure; ~**kostenpauschale** overall allowance for professional expenditure; ~**mittel** advertising media, publicity aids; ~**mittler** publicity agent, space buyer (broker); ~**verfahren** publicity method; ~**vermittler** advertising agent; ~**zusatz** accessory (auxiliary, supplementary) advertising; ~**zwecke** advertising purposes, promotions.

Werbungtreibender [business] advertiser.

Werdegang career, background, record, curriculum vitae;
akademischer ~ academic background; **beruflicher** ~ professional background (record), business career, employment history, job specification *(US)*; **kaufmännischer** ~ business training background; **politischer** ~ political background;
sich auf den beruflichen ~ **positiv auswirken** to be a good step career-wise; **beruflichen** ~ **mitteilen** to write with career details; **von ausschlaggebender Bedeutung für jds.** ~ **sein** to be determinent for s. one's career.

Werden, im in progress.

werfen to throw, to toss;
sich ~ *(Holz)* to warp, to wind; **Argument in die Waagschale** ~ to bring an argument to bear; **sein Auge auf etw.** ~ to have one's eye on s. th.; **alle Bedenken hinter sich** ~ to have no scruples; **jem. Beleidigungen an den Kopf** ~ to hurl insults at s. o.; **Bilder an die Wand** ~ to project pictures on the screen; **Bomben** ~ to drop bombs; **sich aufs Briefmarkensammeln** ~ to go in for stamp-collecting; **Effekten auf den Markt** ~ to unload securities upon the public; **Feind aus der Stellung** ~ to dislodge the enemy; **Flinte ins Korn** ~ to chuck up the sponge; **jem. ins Gefängnis** ~ to thrust s. o. into prison; **mit dem Geld nur so um sich** ~ to fling one's money about one; **Geld aus dem Fenster** ~ to throw money down the drain; **das Handtuch** ~ to toss in the towel; **jem. einen Knüppel zwischen die Beine** ~ to put a spoke in s. one's wheel; **ganzen Krempel vor die Füße** ~ to chuck up the whole thing; **helles Licht** ~ to cast a bright light; **ungünstiges Licht auf j.** ~ to cast an unfavo(u)rable light on s. o.; **Los** ~ to cast lots; **sich mit Macht auf etw.** ~ to launch o. s. upon s. th.; **jds. Pläne über den Haufen** ~ to upset s. one's applecart; **sich in Schale** ~ to spruce o. s. up; **Waren auf den Markt** ~ to throw goods onto the market; **ein paar Zeilen aufs Papier** ~ to jot down a few notes.

Werft dockyard, shipyard, shipwright's wharf, *(Flugzeug)* workshop;
leistungsschwache ~ lame-duck yard;
~**anlage** wharfing, dock facilities; ~**arbeiter** dock worker, docker, yardman, shipyard worker, longshore-man *(US)*, roustabout *(US)*; ~**besitzer** wharf owner, wharfinger, shipwright; ~**gebühren** wharfage; ~**halle** *(Flugzeug)* hangar; ~**liegezeit** shipyard period; ~**reparatur** shipyard repair; ~**stillegung** yard closure.

Werk *(Arbeit)* work, labo(u)r, *(schriftstellerische Arbeit)* writing, *(Buch)* edition, *(Erzeugnis)* piece of work, product, production, *(Fabrik)* works, factory, establishment, facility, mill *(Br.)*, plant *(US)*, *(Leistung)* performance, achievement, *(Tat)* act, action, deed, *(Unternehmen)* enterprise, establishment, undertaking, *(Werkanlage)* installation;
ab ~ ex (loco) factory, ex works (mill);
beschädigtes ~ damaged edition; **erschienene** ~**e** published works; **fehlerhaftes** ~ erroneous edition; **neu in Betrieb genommenes** ~ newly established plant; **gesammelte** ~**e** collected works; **herausgegebenes** ~ publication; **für den Urheberschutz in Frage kommende** ~**e** copyrightable material; **mildtätige** ~**e** works of charity; **nachgelassenes** ~ posthumous work; **sämtliche** ~**e** complete works; **sechsbändiges** ~ six-volume work; **stillgelegtes** ~ mill out of work *(Br.)*; **umfangreiches** ~ voluminous work; **veröffentlichte** ~**e** published books; **vollautomatisches** ~ fully automated plant; **wissenschaftliches** ~ scientific work; **wohltätiges** ~ good work; **zweitklassiges** ~ inferior piece of work;
~ **eines Augenblicks** a matter of a moment; ~ **der Bildhauerkunst** sculpture; ~**e der Literatur, der Wissenschaft und der Kunst** literary, scientific and artistic works; ~ **im Stehsatz** *(drucktechn.)* dead job; ~ **der Tonkunst** musical work;
~ **in Lieferungen abnehmen** to take a work in parts; ~ **besichtigen** to go over a factory; ~ **demontieren** to pluck up a plant; **ans** ~ **gehen** to set to work; **vorsichtig zu** ~**e gehen** to feel one's way, to bid for safety, to tread lightly, to set about s. th. gingerly; ~ **in Betrieb nehmen** to open a factory; **neues** ~ **in Betrieb nehmen** to commission a new factory; ~ **schließen** to shut down a factory; **ins** ~ **setzen** to set on foot, to get up; **Drucklegung eines** ~**es überwachen** to see a work through the press; ~ **verlegen** to relocate a plant; **für seine guten** ~**e belohnt werden** to be rewarded for one's good deeds;
~**arbeitszeit** working hours; ~**aufnahme** industrial photo; ~**bahn** factory railway; ~**bank** bench; ~**bankarbeiter** bencher.

werkeigen factory-owned.
Werk|fahrer factory driver; **~feuerwehr** company fire brigade; **~fotograf** factory photographer.
werkfremd external.
Werk|führer foreman, shop superintendent *(US)*; **~führerposten** foremanship; **~fürsorge** factory welfare; **~halle** shopfloor; **~lieferungsvertrag** cost-plus contract *(US)*; **~lohn** wage(s); **~meister** [shop] foreman, overseer, head (master, *US*) workman, shop master, master mechanic *(US)*; **~pause** rest pause (period).
Werks|abnahme quality inspection; **~angehörige** employees, company staff; **~anlage** factory, works, [industrial (company)] plant *(US)*; **~anlagen** operating facilities, works installations, *(Bilanz)* plant and equipment, plant assets; **~anlagen im Bau** *(Bilanz)* installations under construction; **~anschluß** *(Bahn)* private siding; **~ansicht** general view of a plant; **~arzt** factory doctor, plant physician.
Werksatz *(drucktechn.)* bookwork.
Werks|ausnutzung plant utilization; **~ausrüstung** factory equipment; **~besichtigung** factory (plant) visit; **~bezugschein** store order; **~bibliothek** industrial library; **~direktor** works (plant) manager; **~einrichtungen** *(Bilanz)* plant and equipment; **~erhaltung** plant maintenance *(US)*; **~erweiterung** works (plant) expansion, plant addition; **~ferien** vacation shutdown *(US)*, works holidays; **~gelände** plant grounds, works (factory) area, factory premises; **~grundstück** plant site, millsite *(Br.)*; **~kantine, ~küche** factory canteen, tommy shop (store, *US*), catering department, factory snackshop *(US)*; **~kapazität** plant capacity; **~kontrolle** plant supervision; **~küchenberater** catering adviser; **~laden** company store *(US)*, in-plant shop *(Br.)*; **~leistung** operating performance; **~leiter** supervisor in a factory, factory (plant, *US*) manager, works supervisor, works manager *(Br.)*; **~leitung** plant *(US)* (works, factory) management; **~nummer** *(Arbeiter)* badge number; **~ordnung** factory order; **langfristige ~politik** company strategy; **~prüfer** quality inspector; **~prüfung** quality inspection; **~rente** company-paid annuity; **~schließung** plant shutdown; **~schrift** *(drucktechn.)* body type; **~schutz** plant protection, works (plant, *US*, industrial) police; **~sicherheit** industrial safety; **~siedlung** company town (colony) *(US)*.
Werk|sparen collective (industrial) saving, company saving system; **~sparkasse** company savings bank; **~spionage** industrial espionage, factory spying.
Werksplanung layout, plan.
Werkstatt workshop, shop *(Br.)*, laboratory workroom, *(Fabrik)* machine shop, assembly hall, *(Künstler)* studio, atelier;
fahrbare ~ travel(l)ing workshop; **mechanische ~** machine shop;
Fabrik oder ~ industrial hereditaments;
~arbeit shopwork; **~arbeiter** shopworker, shopman; **~auftrag** shop order *(Br.)*; **~ausbildung** workshop (vestibule, *US*, inplant, *US*) training; **~bedarf** workshop supply; **~geschicklichkeit** shop craft; **~kosten** workroom costs; **~leiter** workshop manager; **~montage** shop assembly; **~trupp** maintenance party; **~vertreter** manufacturer's agent *(US)*; **~wagen** maintenance truck; **~wagenheber** garage jack; **~zeichnung** working drawing.
Werkstätten- und Pflegedienst after-service for customers.
Werkstoff [raw] material, artificial material;
~anforderung material requisitioned; **~bearbeitung** materials handling; **~bedarf** material requirements; **~bedarfsplanung** direct materials budget; **~behandlung** materials handling; **~bestand** raw materials inventory; **~bestandskosten** direct goods account; **~durchlauf** materials flow; **~eigenschaft** property of material; **~einsparung** savings of raw material; **~empfangsbescheinigung** material-received report *(US)*; **~entnahmeschein** material requisition slip; **~ermüdung** material fatigue; **~ersatz** raw-material substitution; **~festigkeit** tensile strength; **~prüfung** material control (testing); **~umstellung** raw-material substitution.
Werk|straße factory roadway; **~stück** component, piece, workpiece; **~stückzeichnung** component drawing; **~student, ~schüler** half-timer, sandwich student; **sich sein Studium als ~student verdienen** to work one's way through college.
Werks|unfall industrial accident; **~uniform** work uniform; **~veredelung** plant processing; **~verkehrsverband** Traders' Road Transport Association; **~verlegung** relocation of a plant; **~vertreter** manufacturer's agent; **~vorschrift** works specification; **~wohnung** company dwelling (flat, house), employee home, cottage; **~zeitung** staff (plant, company) magazine, house organ; **~zentrale** *(tel.)* business switchboard.
Werktag working (lawful, business, secular) day, workday, weekday;
~ oder Arbeitstag secular or business day.
werktäglich, werktags on weekdays, daily.
Werktags|beschäftigung secular business; **~kleidung** work(a)day clothes; **~schankkonzession** six-day licence.
werktätig working, practical, labo(u)ring, on employment;
~e Bevölkerung working-class population, working classes.
Werktätige working-class population, labo(u)ring classes.
Werk|tätiger labo(u)ring (working) man; **~tisch** worktable, workbench; **~unterricht** manual training *(US)*, *(Tischler)* sloyd, sloid; **Achtung ~verkehr!** *(Schild)* caution! factory vehicles!
Werkvertrag contract to manufacture (for work and service), *(Reparaturen)* bailment for repair;
~ zu einem Pauschalpreis lump-sum contract;
~ mit jem. abschließen to contract with s. o.
Werkzeug tool, instrument, gear, stock in trade, *(fig.)* organ, puppet, creature, instrument;
~e *(Bilanz)* tools, furniture and fixtures;
berufsübliche ~e simple tools; **geeignetes ~** convenient tool; **willenloses ~** innocent agent;
~e zur Berufsausübung tools of trade; **~-, Betriebs- und Geschäftsausstellung** *(Bilanz)* toolings, furniture and fixture; **willenloses ~ eines Diktators** mere creature of a dictator; **~e, Instrumente und Geräte** tooling and instruments;
mit ~en bearbeiten to tool; **ohne ~e arbeiten** to make bricks without straw; **an seinem ~ etw. auszusetzen haben** to quarrel with one's tools; **willenloses ~ aus jem. machen** to make a cat's paw of s. o.; **jds. ~ mißbrauchen** to play tricks with s. one's tools; **bloßes ~ eines Verbrechers sein** to be a mere tool (instrument) in the hands of a criminal;
~auflage tool rest; **~ausrüstung** outfit of tools, tool equipment; **~ausstattung** *(Auto)* tool case, tool kit *(US)*; **~fabrik** tool shop, toolmaker; **~halter** tool carrier; **~industrie** machine tools industry; **~kasten** box of tools, tool case, toolbox, workbox; **~kosten** tooling costs; **~macher** toolbuilder, toolmaker; **~maschine** machine tool; **~maschinenindustrie** machine-tool industry; **~maschinenspezialist** toolmaker; **~miete** tools rent; **~sammlung** assortment of tools; **~schrank** tool cabinet; **~stahl** tool steel; **~tasche** *(Auto)* tool case (bag); **kleine ~tasche** wallet, flat leather bag; **~versicherung** tool insurance; **~zeichnung** working drawing.
Wermut vermouth.
Wermutstropfen wormwood.
Wert value, worth, *(Bedeutung)* amount, significance, *(Gegenwert)* equivalent, *(Güte)* quality, *(Kostbarkeit)* valuableness, *(Münze)* standard, *(Preis)* price, rate, *(Schätzung)* appreciation, *(Vermögen)* asset, *(Vorzug)* merit, desert, asset, virtue, good, *(Wertstellung)* value (availability, *US*) date, *(Wichtigkeit)* importance, store;
an ~ in value; **an ~ verloren** diminished in value; **dem ~ nach** ad valorem; **dem nominellen ~ entsprechend** by tale; **im ~e von** valued at; **ohne ~** unworthy; **ohne praktischen ~** of no practical value; **über ~** above value; **unter ~** below value; **von geringem ~** uncostly, of small value; **von gleichem ~** equivalent, of the same value; **von hohem ~** of great value (price);
~ 1. März value (due) 1st of March; **~ erhalten** *(auf Wechsel)* value received; **~ in bar erhalten** value received in cash; **~ heute** value from today;
abgeleiteter ~ imputed value; **abgeschriebener ~** depreciated value; **steuerlich voll abgeschriebener ~** written down value; **abnehmender ~** diminishing value; **absoluter ~** absolute value; **anerkannter ~** fair market value; **angegebener ~** *(Zoll)* declared value; **angemessener ~** fair and reasonable (just) value; **angenommener ~** assumed value; **willkürlich angenommener ~** arbitrary (fictitious) value; **angerechneter ~** imputed value; **zu hoch angesetzter ~** exaggerated value; **annähernder ~** approximate value; **ausmachender ~** *(Effekten)* cost of securities; **äußerer ~** face value; **behaupteter ~** hold-up value; **berechtigter ~** justified value; **berichtigter ~** absorption value; **bestätigter ~** certified value; **bleibender ~** lasting value; **buchmäßiger ~** accounting (book) value; **deklarierter ~** declared (registered) value; **dokumentarischer ~** documentary value; **durchschnittlicher ~** average (mean, effective) value; **effektiver ~** *(el.)* effective value; **eingebildeter ~** estimated value; **erhöhter ~** enhanced value; **durch Warenknappheit erhöhter ~** scarcity value; **erklärter ~** stated value; **errechneter ~** computed value; **fester ~** stable value; **festgelegter ~** *(Versicherungspolice)* agreed value; **gerichtlich festgesetzter ~** extended value; **gesetzlich festgesetzter ~** statutory value;

festgestellter ~ stated value; feststellbarer ~ ascertainable value; fiktiver ~ fictitious value; finanzieller ~ monetary value; gängiger ~ fair market value; garantierter ~ warranted value; gegenwärtiger ~ present (today's) value; gemeiner ~ fair market (principal, *Br.*) value; gemessener ~ measured value; geschätzter ~ valuation, estimated value; lagemäßig gestiegener ~ *(Grundstück)* plottage value; gleicher ~ equal worth; greifbarer ~ tangible value; häufigster ~ *(Statistik)* mode; hypothetischer ~ hypothetical value; ideeller ~ sentimental value; immaterieller ~ intangible value; innerer ~ intrinsic (true) value, *(Geld)* domestic value, *(Mensch)* intrinsic worth, human quality; innerlicher ~ intrinsic value; jetziger ~ present value; kapitalisierter ~ earning-capitalized value, capitalized value; körperlicher ~ physical value; kritischer ~ critical value; künstlerischer ~ artistic merit; laufender ~ current value; möglicher ~ potential value; moralischer ~ moral value; nomineller ~ nominal value; objektiver ~ real value; realer ~ effective value; durch sofortigen Verkauf realisierbarer ~ salvage value; rechnungsmäßiger ~ *(Versicherung)* actuarial value; reiner ~ net worth *(US)*; restlicher ~ residual value; seltenster ~ antimode; statistischer ~ statistical value; steuerbarer (steuerlicher, steuerpflichtiger) ~ ratable *(Br.)* (taxable) value, assessable value *(Br.)* (valuation, *US*); subjektiver ~ subjective value; tatsächlicher ~ effective (real, actual) value; unerheblicher ~ trifling value; ungefährer ~ approximate value; unverzollter ~ bonded value; ursprünglicher ~ sterling (original) value; veranlagter ~ assessed (ratable, *Br.*) value; veranschlagter ~ imputed (estimated) value; frei vereinbarter ~ *(Versicherungspolice)* agreed value; verhältnismäßiger ~ relative value; verminderter ~ diminished (reduced) value; vernünftiger ~ prudent (sound) value; versicherbarer ~ insurable (insurance) value; versicherungsmathematischer ~ actuarial value; vollwirtschaftlicher ~ net social benefit; wirklicher ~ intrinsic value, true value; wirtschaftlicher ~ industrial (economic) value; zollpflichtiger ~ dutiable value; zufälliger ~ *(Grundstück)* adventitious value of land; zukünftiger ~ future value; zweifacher ~ double value; berichtigter erklärter ~ des Aktienkapitals für Berechnung der Kapitalsteuer adjusted declared value for the computation of capital levy; ~ des Anlagevermögens value of fixed assets; ~ der Arbeit price of labo(u)r; ~ in bar value in cash; ~ als Bauerwartungsland development value of land; ~ erschlossenen Baulands developed value of land; ~ der Beeinträchtigung nuisance value; ~ zum Einzug *(Wechselvermerk)* only for collection; tatsächlicher ~ der Ersatzbeschaffung replacement cost depreciated; ~ einer guten Erziehung the objective value of education; ~ laut Faktura value as per invoice; ~ in Geld monetary value; wirtschaftlicher ~ eines Geschäftes general standing of a business; beitragspflichtiger ~ zur großen Havarie contributory general value; ~ heute value from today; ~ einer nachgewiesenen Konkursforderung proof value; ~ nach dem Niederstwertprinzip market price; ~ der umlaufenden Noten currency circulation; ~ in Rechnung *(auf Wechsel)* value in account; ~ des Streitgegenstands value of matter (amount) in controversy; ~ der einzelnen Stücke denominational value; ~ einer Summe summation value; ~ eines Treuhandvermögens trust asset (settlement) value; wirtschaftlicher ~ eines Unternehmens value of a plant in successful operation; ~ bei Verfall value when due (on expiration, on maturity); ~ des landwirtschaftlichen Vermögens agricultural value; ~ in Waren received value; effektiver ~ einer Ware actual cost of goods; ~ der geretteten Waren *(Versicherung)* salvage value; ~ bei Wiedererlangung repossession value; ~ einer Zeugenaussage weight of testimony; ~ im beschädigten Zustand damaged value; ~ im unbeschädigten Zustand sound value;

~ [bei der Verzollung] angeben to declare the value; unter dem ~ angeben to enter short; ~ beeinträchtigen to impair (diminish) the value; nach dem ~ befrachten to freight ad valorem; seinen ~ behalten to maintain its value; einer Sache geringen ~ beilegen to set little store by s. th.; einer Sache ~ beimessen to attach value to s. th.; einer Sache geringen ~ beimessen to set a low value (little store) on s. th.; einer Sache großen ~ beimessen to set great store on s. th.; einer Sache zu hohen ~ beimessen to set too high a value on s. th.; keinen oder nur geringen ~ beimessen to have little or no use for; ~ berechnen to compute (calculate) the value; hohen ~ besitzen to be of great value; keinerlei ~ besitzen to be worthless; ~ bestimmen to appraise; doppelten ~ bezahlen to pay double the value; unter dem ~ bieten to underbid; unter ~ deklarieren to enter short; jds. ~ einschätzen to take s. one's number; ~ seines Zeitaufwands hoch einschätzen to set a high value on one's time; ~ erhöhen to improve the value, to appreciate; sich im ~ erhöhen to increase in value; ~ ermitteln to assess the value, to appraise s. th., to make a valuation; im ~ fallen to fall in value; ~ festsetzen to assess (fix) a value, to set value upon s. th.; an ~ gewinnen to improve, to gain; in der Öffentlichkeit an ~ gewinnen to be rising in the estimation of the public; geringen ~ haben to be of inferior quality; im ~ gewonnen haben to have increased (gone up) in value; im ~ herabsetzen to discount, to depreciate in value; ~ einer Anlage heraufsetzen to write up the value of an asset; vollen ~ aus einer Sache herausholen to get the full value of a th.; etw. für ein Viertel des ~es kaufen to buy s. th. at a quarter of the price; großen ~ legen to attach great importance (store) to; ~ schätzen to appraise (estimate, assess) the value; im ~ schwanken to fluctuate in value; im ~ gestiegen sein to show an appreciation; im ~ sinken to depreciate, to recede; im ~ steigen to increase (advance, improve) in value, to appreciate; im ~ erheblich steigen to appreciate greatly; im ~ übersteigen, an ~ übertreffen to outvalue, to exceed in value; unter ~ verkaufen to sell below price (at an underrate); unter dem fakturierten ~ verkaufen to sell at a loss on the invoice; dem ~ entsprechend verkaufen to sell for value; an ~ verlieren to deteriorate, to lower (lose, drop, fall) in value, to damage; fortlaufend an ~ verlieren to go down in value all the time; wirtschaftlich an ~ verlieren to decline in economic usefulness; unter dem ~ vermieten to rent below value; [im] ~ vermindern to reduce the value, to debase; sich im ~ verringern to decline in value; an ~ zunehmen to improve (appreciate) in value.

wert valuable, worth, *(geschätzt)* esteemed, valued;
keinen Deut ~ not worth a fig (straw); nicht viel ~ not up to much, *(Person)* no great shakes *(sl.)*; nichts ~ worthless, of no value, good for nothing, pretty good rot *(sl.)*; keinen Pfifferling ~ not worth a tinker's damn (curse, brass farthing, penny, rap, shucks); 10 Pfund ~ valued at £ 10; der Rede ~ worth mentioning (speaking of); nicht der Rede ~ nothing to speak of (write home about);
es nicht für ~ befinden not to think it important enough; ~ sein to be worth, *(Geld)* to exchange for; etw. ~ sein to sell at a price; nicht das Druckpapier ~ sein not to be worth the paper it is printed on; Geld ~ sein to be worth money; sein Geld ~ sein to be worth one's salt; der Mühe ~ sein to be worth the trouble; nicht der Mühe ~ sein not to be worth-while, not to be worth the candle (trouble); keinen Schuß Pulver ~ sein not to be worth powder and shot; einer Sache ~ sein to be deserving of s. th.; eines Versuchs ~ sein to deserve a try; viel ~ sein to be a considerable step forward; soviel ~ sein wie vor zehn Jahren to go as far as ten years ago.

Wert|abfall drop in value; ~abnahme decrease in (deterioration of) value; ~abschätzung value appreciation; ~abstufung graduation in value; ~analyse value analysis; ~änderungsgewinn reappraisal surplus.

Wertangabe declaration (statement) of value, *(deklarierter Wert)* declared value (valuation);
zu hohe ~ declaration above value; zu niedrige ~ undervaluation; zollpflichtige ~ declared value;
~formular *(Seeschadensversicherung)* declaration form.

Wert|annahme *(für Schecks)* valuing; ~ansatz indicated value, valuation, appraisal; ~ansatz nach Anschaffungskosten value at cost; ~ansätze der Einzelbilanzen valuations entered in the individual balance sheets; zu verschiedenen ~ansätzen gelangen to arrive at different valuations; ~ansetzung valuation, appraisal; ~anstieg increase in value; ~anzeige declaration of value; ~arbeit qualified work, excellent (superior) workmanship; ~aufstockung appreciation in value, revalorization; ~ausgleich value adjustment; ~ausgleich bei Grundstückstausch owelty of exchange; ~ausgleich bei Naturalteilung owelty of partition; ~ausgleichszahlung *(Kriegsschäden)* value payment; ~beeinträchtigung impairment of value; nach dem formellen ~begriff in terms of the technical value; ~bemessung *(für Stempelsteuer)* adjudication; ~berechnung valuation, evaluation, appraisal, estimate, assessment of value; ~berechnung einer Obligation bond valuation; ~berechnungsskala valuation tariff.

Wertberichtigung adjustment [of value], value adjustment, *(Bilanz)* qualifying *(US)* (valuation) reserve;
aufgelöste ~en adjustments released; steuerliche ~en appreciation for tax purposes;
~ für Abnutzung accumulated (accrued) depreciation, adjustment for wear and tear; ~ des Anlagevermögens depreciation reserve, accumulated depreciation on fixed assets; ~ der Devisenvorräte foreign-exchange adjustments; ~ der Lagerbestände (des Vorratsvermögens) inventory reserve, *(volkswirt-*

schaftliche Gesamtrechnung) inventory valuation adjustment; **~en der Vorjahresbilanz** prior year adjustments; **~ für Wertänderung** asset valuation reserve; **~ auf Wertpapiere** value adjustment on securities;
für ~en Vorsorge treffen to allow for adjustments; **~ bei den gesetzlichen Rücklagen vornehmen** to reconcile one's earned surplus *(US)*.

Wertberichtigungs|aktie bonus share; **~buchung** reversing (adjustment) entry; **~größe** valuation item; **~klausel** stable value clause; **~konto** contra (absorption, adjustment-of-property, offset, valuation) account; **~posten** valuation item; **~posten auf Anlagen** reserve for depreciation; **~posten für Substanzverzehr** reserve for depletion.

wertbeständig stable, of stable (fixed in) value;
~ sein to have a fixed value;
~e Anlagegüter fixed capital goods; **~e Währung** stable currency.

Wert|beständigkeit stability of value, fixed value; **~bestimmung** valuation, *(Schätzung)* evaluation, appraisal, appraisement; **steuerliche ~bestimmung** assessment; **~bezeichnung** denomination; **~bezeichnung einer Obligation** bond valuation; **~brief** registered (insured, *Br.*, money, *US*) letter; **~deklaration** *(Zoll)* declared valuation.

Werte valuables, *(Aktiva)* assets, *(Anlagen)* investment, *(Wertpapiere)* securities, stocks, *(Ziffern)* figures, data;
ausländische ~ foreign stocks, foreigners; **bereinigte ~** adapted figures; **beschlagnahmefähige ~** attachable assets; **börsengängige ~** dividend-paying (marketable, stock) securities; **chemische ~** chemical issues; **an der Börse eingeführte (börsennotierte) ~** quoted (listed, *US*) securities; **elektrische ~** electrical data; **künstlich erhöhte ~** inflated values; **feste ~** firm stock *(US)*; **festverzinsliche ~** fixed-interest (fixed-yield, income-bearing) securities; **führende ~** [market] leaders, trading favo(u)rites, leading descriptions (shares) *(Br.)*; **seit je führende ~** traditional leaders on prices; **gangbare ~** salable stocks; **gehaltene ~** firm stock *(US)*; **gehandelte ~** negotiable stocks; **im Freiverkehr gehandelte ~** open-market papers, curb stocks, *(US)*; **international gehandelte ~** international (interbourse, *Br.*) securities; **telefonisch gehandelte ~** telephone (curb) stocks *(US)*; **variabel gehandelte ~** securities quoted consecutively; **greifbare ~** tangible assets; **heimische ~** home descriptions; **immaterielle ~** *(Bilanz)* intangible assets; **internationale ~** international (interbourse, *Br.*) securities; **lokale ~** local securities; **marktgängige ~** securities dealt in for cash; **mündelsichere ~** gilt-edged (trustee) securities *(Br.)*, trustee (widow and orphan) stocks *(US)*; **niedrigstehende ~** low-grade securities; **amtlich notierte ~** quoted (listed, *US*) securities *(US)*; **amtlich nicht notierte ~** unquoted (unlisted, *US*, offboard, *US*) securities; **selten notierte ~** uncurrent securities; **notleidende ~** suffering securities; **risikoreiche ~** high-risk issues; **sichere ~** sound stocks; **spekulative ~** speculative investments; **unkündbare ~** irredeemable securities; **unverzinsliche ~** noninterest-bearing securities; **verlangte ~** stocks wanted; **verschiedene ~** *(Bilanz)* sundry (miscellaneous) securities; **im Depot verwahrte ~** valuables for safe custody; **wirtschaftliche ~** capital assets;
immaterielle ~ von Bedeutung intangibles of value;
~ abstoßen to shake out stocks; **~ festlegen** to lock up a stock; **auf guten ~n sitzenbleiben** to hold sound stocks.

Wert|einbuße loss of value; **~einheit** unit of value.

werten to value, to rate, *(abschätzen)* to appraise, *(auswerten)* to evaluate, *(würdigen)* to appreciate;
zu hoch ~ to overrate; **jds. Leistung ~** to rate s. one's performance.

Werterhaltung *(Anlagefonds)* preservation of capital.

Werterhöhung rise (improvement, increase) in value, value increase, *(Grundstück)* appreciation, improvement *(US)*, increment;
~ des Anlagevermögens capital appreciation *(Br.)*; **~ von Geschäftsgebäuden** improvement of business premises *(US)*; **~ eines Hauses** improvement of a house *(US)*;
~en an einem Grundstück vornehmen to appreciate (improve, *US*) a property; **~en auf Industriegrundstücken vornehmen** to improve industrial premises *(US)*.

Wert|ermäßigung released valuation; **~ermittlung** ascertainment (determination) of value, *(Schätzung)* appraisal, appraisement, [assessed] valuation; **~errechnung** computation of value; **~ersatz** compensation, indemnification.

werteschaffend productive;
~e Arbeitslosenfürsorge productive unemployment relief.

Wertetabelle *(Computer)* truth table.

Wert|faktor factor of value; **~festsetzung, ~feststellung** value (valuation) assessment; **~fortschreibung** adjustment of real estate; **~fracht** ad-valorem rate; **~frachtzuschlag** valuable-cargo surcharge; **~gebühr** *(Post)* registration fee *(Br.)*; **~gegenstand** object (item) of value, valuable thing (item); **~gegenstände verwahren** to take charge of valuable articles; **~gegenständeversicherung** art property and jewellery insurance; **~gestaltung** value engineering; **~gleichheit** parity; **oberste ~grenze** maximum value; **~grundlage** valuation (cost) basis, *(für Steuerberechnung)* adjusted basis; **~herabsetzung** reduction in value, released valuation, depreciation; **~klasse** class; **~klausel** valuation clause; **~korrekturposten** valuation item.

wertlos worthless, valueless, of no value, tin-pot, peddling, vain, dross, frivolous, idle, without worth, paltry, twopenny *(Br.)*, catchpenny *(Br.)*, half-penny *(Br.)*, threepenny *(Br.)*, two-bit *(US)*, refuse, *(Fernsehen)* unfit for transmission, *(nutzlos)* useless, futile, pointless, *(unbedeutend)* trifling;
praktisch ~ of no practical value; **ziemlich ~** of little amount; **völlig ~ machen** to deprive of all value; **praktisch ~ sein** to be of little amount; **~ werden** to lose its value; **als ~ erachtet werden** to go for nothing;
~e Bürgschaft straw bail; **~e Sache** cherry stone; **~e Sicherheit** dead security; **~er Verpflichtungsschein** straw bond; **~es Zeug** trash, junk, stuff, fiddlestick.

Wert|losigkeit worthlessness, paltriness, *(Nutzlosigkeit)* uselessness; **~marke** ad-valorem stamp.

wertmäßig in terms of value, in value terms, ad valorem;
~ anordnen to arrange in order of value; **verlorene Sache ~ ersetzt bekommen** to recover the value of a lost article; **~ übertreffen** to exceed in value; **~ zunehmen** to be on the increase.

Wert|maßstab unit (standard) of value; **~maßstab für aufgeschobene Leistungen** standard of deferred payments; **schwankende ~stäbe** promiscuous standards; **~messer** standard of value; **gemeinsamer ~messer** common denominator.

Wertminderung depreciation (reduction, shrinkage, diminution) in value, impairment of value, value decrease, deterioration, discount, *(Grundstück)* injurious affection, waste, *(Versicherung)* sentimental damage, loss in value;
wirkliche ~ actual depreciation;
~ der Vorräte *(Bilanz)* inventory price decline;
~ erfahren to fall (decline) in value, to suffer a depreciation, *(Grundstück)* to waste; **einer ~ ausgesetzt sein** to be liable to deteriorate in value.

Wertminderungs|abschlag deducted depreciation; **~konto** depreciation account; **~reserve** depreciation reserve; **~rückstellung** accrued depreciation.

Wert|nachlaß *(Erbschaftssteuer)* value relief; **~nachnahme** payment on delivery; **~objekt** valuable; **~päckchen** insured box *(Br.)*; **~paket** insured *(Br.)* (registered, numbered, sealed) parcel; **als ~paket** by insured parcel post *(Br.)*; **~paketgebühr** insured box rate *(Br.)*.

Wertpapiere securities, commercial papers, shares, stocks, bonds, descriptions *(Br.)*, *(Bilanz)* investments;
ablösbare ~ redeemable securities; **absetzbare ~** marketable securities; **vom Markt aufgenommene ~** digested securities *(US)*; **vom Markt noch nicht aufgenommene ~** undigested securities *(US)*; **aufgerufene ~** securities called for repayment; **ausgegebene ~** securities issued; **über (unter) dem Nennwert ausgegebene ~** securities issued above (below) par; **ausgeloste ~** drawn bonds; **mit zusätzlicher Dividendengarantie ausgestattete ~** assumed bonds; **auf den Inhaber ausgestellte ~** bearer bonds (securities); **ausländische ~** foreign [currency] securities, foreigners; **auslosbare ~** callable (redeemable) securities, lottery bonds; **von Börsenvorschriften befreite ~** exempted securities; **begebbare ~** negotiable instruments; **nicht begebbare ~** nonnegotiable securities; **beleihungsfähige ~** assessable securities; **beliehene ~** pledged securities *(Br.)*, pawned (hypothecated) stock *(US)*; **am Sanierungsverfahren nicht beteiligte ~** nonassented bonds (securities, stock); **bevorrechtigte ~** senior securities; **börsenfähige (börsengängige) ~** marketable securities (stocks), quoted (listed, *US*) securities; **börsengängige ~** quoted investments *(Br.)*; **nicht börsengängige ~** unquoted investments *(Br.)*, unlisted securities *(US)*; **deckungsstockfähige ~** securities eligible to serve as collateral; **devisenbewirtschaftete ~** Exchange Control Act securities *(Br.)*; **diverse ~** miscellaneous (sundry) securities; **dividendenberechtigte ~** dividend-paying (equity) securities, securities entitled to a dividend; **erst an zweiter Stelle dividendenberechtigte ~** junior securities *(US)*; **dreiprozentige ~** three-percents;

an der Börse eingeführte ~ securities quoted (listed, *US*) on the stock exchange; **gut eingeführte** ~ seasoned securities; **eingetragene** ~ registered securities *(Br.)*; **erstklassige** ~ first-class (gilt-edged, *Br.*) stocks, prime papers, blue chips *(US)*; **ertragbringende** ~ income-producing stocks; **ertragssteuerfreie** ~ tax-exempt securities; **für Steuerrücklagen erworbene** ~ tax reserve certificates *(US)*; **festverzinsliche** ~ fixed-interest [bearing] securities (bonds), percents; **steuerfreie festverzinsliche** ~ tax-free fixed interest securities; **an der Börse gehandelte** ~ securities dealt in on the stock exchange; **im Freiverkehr gehandelte** ~ outside *(Br.)* (unlisted, *US*) securities, curb stocks *(US)*; **international gehandelte** ~ internationals, interbourse securities *(Br.)*; **lebhaft gehandelte** ~ active securities; **selten gehandelte** ~ inactive securities; **telefonisch gehandelte** ~ telephone (curb) stocks *(US)*; **auf Zeit gehandelte** ~ securities negotiated for future delivery *(US)*; **gemeinsame** ~ securities jointly owned; **außer Kurs gesetzte** ~ called bonds; **gesperrte** ~ restricted securities; **gezogene** ~ drawn bonds; **an der Börse handelbare** ~ securities negotiable on the stock exchange, negotiable securities; **nicht handelbare** ~ nonmarketable securities; **heimische** ~ home descriptions *(Br.)*; **hinterlegte** ~ securities deposited; **im Sammeldepot hinterlegte** ~ assented bonds (stock, *US*); **als Sicherheit hinterlegte** ~ securities lodged as collateral; **hochspekulative** ~ wildcat securities; **hochwertige** ~ high-grade securities, blue chip *(US)*, representative stocks *(US)*; **inländische** ~ home securities, home stocks *(Br.)*; **internationale** ~ internationals, interbourse securities *(Br.)*; **kaufmännische** ~ commercial instruments; **konvertierbare** ~ convertible securities; **kündbare** ~ callable bonds, dated stocks; **kursfähige** ~ stocks quoted (listed, *US*) on the stock exchange; **auf den Inhaber lautende** ~ bearer bonds; **auf den Namen lautende** ~ registered securities; **lieferbare** ~ good-delivery securities; **lombardfähige** ~ securities eligible to serve as collateral *(US)*; **lombardierte** ~ pledged securities, pawned stock *(Br.)*, securities held as collateral *(US)*, collateral securities *(US)*, hypothecated stocks *(US)*; **marktfähige** ~ marketable (negotiable) securities (stocks), negotiable stocks, open-market papers; **marktgängige** ~ securities dealt in for cash; **mündelsichere** ~ gilt-edged *(Br.)* (trustee) securities (investments) *(Br.)*, gilts *(Br.)*, trustee (widow and orphan) stock *(US)*, trust investments *(US)*, *(Börsenbericht)* gilt-edged list *(Br.)*; **nachschußpflichtige** ~ assessable securities; **mit Verlust notierende** ~ investment in default, decliners *(Br.)*; **notierte** ~ quoted (listed, *US*) securities; **[amtlich] nicht notierte** ~ outside (not listed) securities *(US)*, kerb (curb, *US*) stocks; **an der Börse nicht notierte** ~ unquoted (nonquoted) investments *(Br.)*; **in Pfund notierte** ~ sterling securities; **notleidende** ~ suffering securities; **plazierte** ~ digested securities *(US)*; **leicht realisierbare** ~ readily marketable securities; **sofort realisierbare** ~ liquid securities; **gut renommierte** ~ seasoned securities; **sparkassenfähige** ~ savings-bank securities; **spekulative** ~ speculative securities (investments); **steuerbegünstigte** ~ tax-privileged securities; **steuerfreie** ~ tax-exempt bonds (securities) *(US)*, tax exempts *(US)*; **stimmberechtigte** ~ voting securities; **stimmrechtslose** ~ nonvoting securities; **tarifbesteuerte** ~ securities subject to standard tax; **übertragbare** ~ transferable securities; **durch Indossament übertragbare** ~ negotiable instruments; **nicht umlauffähige** ~ nonmarketable securities; **umtauschfähige** ~ convertible securities; **unkündbare** ~ irredeemable securities, *(langfristig)* longs; **unverzinsliche** ~ noninterest-paying stock; **mit Rückerwerbsverpflichtung veräußerte** ~ securities held under agreement to repurchase; **ohne Deckung verkaufte** ~ shorts; **verkehrsfähige** ~ negotiable instruments; **nicht verkehrsfähige** ~ nonmarketable securities; **verlosbare** ~ redeemable securities; **verloste** ~ lottery bonds; **vernachlässigte** ~ inactive (neglected) stocks *(US)*; **[als Sicherheit] verpfändete** ~ pledged securities *(Br.)*, pawned stock *(Br.)*, hypothecated stock *(US)*, securities held as collateral *(US)*; **verwahrte** ~ securities held in safe custody; **verzinsliche** ~ interest-bearing securities; **nicht zinstragende** ~ noninterest-paying stock; **zum Börsenhandel zugelassene** ~ quoted (listed, *US*) securities; **zweitklassige** ~ second-class papers;

~ **des Anlagevermögens** long-term investments *(US)*; **börsengängige** ~ **zu Anschaffungskursen** *(Bilanz)* quoted investments (marketable securities) at cost; ~ **elektrisch betriebener Bahnen** traction securities; ~ **von äußerst spekulativem Charakter** cats and dogs *(US)*; ~ **im Depot** securities on deposit; ~ **mit zeitweilig gesperrter Dividendenauszahlung** deferred securities; ~ **mit vereinbartem Einlösungstermin** redeemable securities; ~ **mit festem Ertrag** fixed-yield securities; ~ **mit schwankendem Ertrag** variable-yield securities; ~ **von Lagerhausgesellschaften** dock stocks *(Br.)*, warehouse stocks *(US)*; ~ **mit kurzer Laufzeit** short-term securities; ~ **mit geringstem Nominalwert** baby bonds *(US)*; ~ **mit hoher Rendite** high-yield securities; ~ **mit variabler Rendite** variable-yield securities; ~ **mit hoher Sicherheit** trustee investments *(Br.)*, widow and orphan stock *(US)*; **nicht übertragbare** ~ **zu Steuerrücklagezwecken** tax reserve certificates *(Br.)*; ~ **des Umlaufvermögens** *(Bilanz)* temporary investment, marketable securities *(US)*; ~ **mit Vorzugsrechten** senior securities; ~ **mit steuerfreien Zinserträgnissen** nontaxable securities *(US)*;

~ **abtreten** to assign securities; **sein Geld in ~n anlegen** to invest one's money in stock; **sein Geld in mündelsicheren ~n anlegen** to invest one's money in a safe stock; ~ **zur Börsenzulassung anmelden** to qualify securities for sale to the public; ~ **ausgeben** to issue (put out, bring out) bonds; ~ **über (unter) dem Nennwert ausgeben** to issue securities at a premium (discount); ~ **zum Nennwert ausgeben** to issue securities at par; **in Kost gegebene** ~ **auswechseln** to commute securities; ~ **mit Sperre belegen** to stop bonds; ~ **beleihen** to lend money on stock, to pawn stock *(Br.)*, to hypothecate securities *(US)*; ~ **bereinigen** to validate securities; ~ **besitzen** to hold securities; **seine Anlagen hauptsächlich in ~n decken** to invest primarily in securities; ~ **durchhalten** to carry securities in safe custody *(Br.)*; ~ **an der Börse einführen** to introduce (market, list, *US*) securities on the stock exchange; ~ **ins Depot einliefern (legen)** to deposit securities, to place securities in safe custody (deposit, *US*); ~ **über pari emittieren** to issue securities at a premium (discount); ~ **für kraftlos erklären** to retire (invalidate) securities; **verlorengegangene** ~ **für kraftlos erklären** to cancel securities; ~ **ins Depot geben** to place securities in safe custody *(Br.)*, to place securities into a deposit *(US)*; **sein Geld in vierprozentigen ~n angelegt haben** to have one's money in four percents; ~ **zur Verfügung halten** to earmark securities; **mit ~n handeln** to handle stocks and bonds; ~ **hereinnehmen** to borrow (take in) stock; ~ **hinterlegen** to deposit securities; ~ **als Sicherheit hinterlegen** to deposit (lodge) stocks as underlying security; ~ **lombardieren lassen** to have securities hypothecated; ~ **lombardieren** to grant a loan against (hypothecate, *US*) securities, to advance money (borrow) on securities, to pawn stock *(Br.)*; ~ **zinslos lombardieren** to loan stock flat; ~ **aus einem Depot nehmen** to withdraw securities from a deposit; ~ **in Kommission nehmen** to take securities on a commission basis; ~ **an der Börse notieren** to quote (list, *US*) securities on the stock exchange; **lombardierte** ~ **realisieren** to sell out securities; **mit ~n eingedeckt sein** to be long of stock *(Br.)*; ~ **übertragen** to transfer stocks; ~ **verpfänden** to pledge (hypothecate, *US*) securities; ~ **im Depot verwahren** to hold securities for safekeeping; ~ **zu 9% auf Kredit verwahren** to carry securities at 9 per cent; ~ **zeichnen** to make an application for stocks; ~ **in Erwartung einer Kurssteigerung zurückhalten** to be on the long side of the market *(US)*; ~ **zurückkaufen** to redeem (repurchase) securities.

Wertpapier|absatz placement of securities, security sales; ~**abteilung** securities (stock, *Br.*) department; ~**analyse** security analysis; ~**angebot** securities offerings.

Wertpapieranlage investment [in securities], security (portfolio) investment;

sonstige ~n *(Bilanz)* other investment securities;

~**berater** security analyst, investment consultant; ~**beratung** investment counselling (advice); ~**beratungsvertrag** investment advisory agreement; ~**formular** investment application form.

Wertpapier|anschaffungspreis cost of securities; ~**arbitrage** stock arbitrage; ~**art** category of securities; ~**aufruf** retirement of securities; ~**aufstellung** statement of securities deposited, *(Investmentfonds)* portfolio description; ~**ausgabe** issue of securities, delivery of stocks; ~**beleihung** pledging of securities, hypothecation of securities for a loan *(US)*; ~**berater** stock (security) analyst; ~**beratung andienen** to offer security advice; ~**bereinigung** validation of securities; ~**besitz**, ~**bestand** security ownership, security (share, stock, *US*) holdings, *(Bilanz)* holdings of securities, investment (equity, security) portfolio; ~**besitzer** security holder; ~**beteiligungen** equity holdings; ~**börse** stock exchange (market).

Wertpapier|depot, ~**deponierung** deposit of securities, securities deposit, depositor's custody, security deposit account *(US)*; **sein** ~ **zu Tageskursen in mündelsicheren Papieren anlegen** to switch one's portfolio of assets into gilts at current rates of interest *(Br.)*;

~**abteilung** safe-custody department; ~**verwaltung** portfolio management.

Wertpapier|druck bond printing; ~**eingang** securities received; ~**emission** security issue, issue of securities; **von der Muttergesellschaft verbürgte** ~**emission** underlying security; ~**emissionskonsortium** underwriting syndicate; ~**ersterwerb** original acquisition of securities, buying the memorandum; ~**erträge** security income, income from securities; ~**erträge kapitalertragssteuerfrei erhalten** to receive income from securities without deduction of income tax; ~**fachmann** security (stock) analyst; ~**fonds** securities fund; ~**fonds einer Investmentgesellschaft** investment [company] portfolio; ~**gattung** class of securities; ~**gebühr** insured box rate *(Br.)*; ~**geschäft** securities business, *(einzelnes)* transaction in securities; **steuerfreies** ~**geschäft** tax-free transaction; ~**geschäft am Bankschalter** over-the-counter market *(Br.)*; ~**gesetz** Uniform Negotiable Instruments Act *(US)*; ~**gewinne** profit taking; ~**guthaben** securities holdings; ~**handel** trading in securities, security trading (dealings, jobbing, *Br.*); **nachbörslicher** ~**handel** secondary distribution of securities, over-the-counter business (trade) *(US)*; ~**händler** security trader, securities dealer, jobber in securities *(Br.)*, stockbroker; ~**händler sein** to handle stocks and bonds, to job *(Br.)*; ~**hinterlegung** depositing of securities; ~**inhaber** depositor, registered holder *(Br.)*, stockholder; ~**kauf** purchase of securities; ~**kauf zu verschiedenen Zeiten** scale buying *(US)*; **breitgestreute** ~**käufe tätigen** to go into a broader list of equities; ~**kommissionsgeschäft** stock transaction for third account; ~**konto** security account; ~**kredit** advance on securities, collateral loan *(US)*; ~**kundschaft** investing public; ~**kurs** price quotation; ~**kurszettel** exchange (price) list, list of market quotations, stock market report *(US)*; ~**lieferung entgegennehmen** to take delivery of stocks; ~**lombard** lending on securities, collateral loan business *(US)*, *(einzelnes Geschäft)* stock loan; ~**markt** securities market; ~**markt bis in seine Grundfesten erschüttern** to rock the securities market to its foundations; ~**mitteilungen** securities bulletin; ~**notierungen** securities quotations; ~**paket** block of shares; ~**pensionsgeschäft** carrying-over business; ~**plazierung** placing securities with the public; ~**portefeuille** holdings of securities, portfolio of investments (securities), investment (equity) portfolio; ~**recht** negotiable instruments law *(US)*; ~**rendite** security yield, investment saving; ~**rücklage** security reserve fund; ~**sammelkonto** general deposit; ~**sondervermögen** indenture trust; ~**sparen** investment saving; ~**spitze** fractional amount, fraction, odd lot *(US)*; ~**steuer** stamp duty (tax, *US*), securities tax; ~**stückelung** denomination; ~**tausch** exchange of securities; ~**termingeschäfte,** ~**terminhandel,** ~**transaktionen** trading in security futures *(US)*, forward transactions in securities; securities market transactions; ~**übertrag** stock transfer; ~**umlauf** circulation of securities; ~**umsatzsteuer** securities transfer tax *(US)*; ~**umschreibung** transfer of shares *(Br.)* (stock, *US*); ~**umtausch** conversion of securities; ~**unterbringung** placing of securities with the public; ~**verkäufe** sale of securities; ~**verkäufe zur Bezahlung der Einkommensteuer** tax selling of securities; ~**verkäufe an Private** private placement of securities; ~**verkehr** trading in securities; ~**vermögen** securities (equity, investment) portfolio; **gesamtes** ~**vermögen** *(Kapitalanlagegesellschaft)* total investments; ~**verwahrungsversicherung** securities insurance; ~**verwaltung** portfolio management; ~**verzeichnis** statement of securities deposited; ~**zinsen** interest on securities; ~**zulassung** *(Börse)* admission of securities to the stock exchange, listing of securities *(US)*.

Wert|police valued policy; ~**rückgang** depreciation, fall (drop, decline, reduction) in value.

Wertsachen valuable articles (things), valuables;
im Depot verwahrte ~ valuables for safe custody;
seine ~ **zur Aufbewahrung ins Depot geben** to place one's valuables in the bank, to deposit valuables in safe custody *(Br.)*; ~ **dem Hotelgeschäftsführer zur Aufbewahrung übergeben** to deposit valuables with the manager for safe keeping;
~**aufbewahrung** valuables for safe custody *(Br.)*; ~**versicherung** registered mail insurance *(Br.)*; **vom Aufenthaltsort unabhängige** ~**versicherung** world-wide insurance *(US)*.

wertschätzen to hold in high esteem.

Wertschätzung appreciation, personal estimation, respect, esteem, account, valuation, count, regard, *(Abschätzung)* appraisal, appraisement, valuation;
sich steigernder ~ **in der Öffentlichkeit erfreuen** to be rising in the estimation of the public; **seiner** ~ **Ausdruck verleihen** to express one's appreciation.

Wertschätzungserklärung, jds. ~**en geringen Glauben schenken** to attach little faith to s. one's profession of esteem.

Wert|schöpfung creation of value, *(Sozialprodukt)* net value added, added valuation; **nicht ausgeglichene** ~**schöpfung** unbalanced addition; ~**schwankungen** value fluctuations, fluctuations in value; ~**schwankungen unterliegen** to fluctuate in value; ~**sendung** consignment of valuables, *(Geldsendung)* remittance; ~**sicherung** value guarantee; ~**sicherungsklausel** escalator clause; ~**siegel** quality label; ~**skala** table of values.

wertsteigernde Aufwendungen valuable improvements.

Wertsteigerung appreciation (rise, increase, enhancement) in value, value increase, *(Grundstück)* betterment, appreciation in value, valuable improvement, unearned increment;
prozentual festgelegte ~ fixed-percentage value increment; **durch Bebauungsmöglichkeit hervorgerufene** ~ value added by zoning *(US)*;
~ **nur buchmäßig existierender Aktien** phantom appreciation; **unverdiente** ~ **des Grundstücks** unearned increment; ~ **bei Zusammenlegung verschiedener Parzellen** plottage increment *(US)*;
~ **erfahren** to increase (appreciate) in value; ~ **eines Geländes durch Bebauung erzielen** to improve a lot by building on it.

Wertsteigerungs|gewinn general benefit; ~**möglichkeiten** appreciation possibilities.

Wert|stellungstermin value *(Br.)* (availability, *US*) date; ~**stempel** revenue stamp; ~**steuer** ad-valorem tax *(US)*; ~**stück** valuable [thing]; ~**system durch Indexkopplung** monetary correction; ~**tarif** declared [valuation] rate; ~**taxe** estimate of value; ~**theorie** commercial theory.

Wertung estimation, valuation, *(Sport)* score, classification, points.

Wertungs|system system of classification; ~**zeit** *(Statistik)* original period.

Wert|unterschied discrepancy in value; ~**urteil** value judgment, comment; **zulässiges** ~**urteil** fair comment; ~**urteil über eine Arbeit fällen** to pass judgment on a work; ~**veränderungen** *(Bilanz)* additions and improvements; ~**verbesserung** *(Grundstück)* valuable improvement, betterment; **dauernde** ~**verbesserung** permanent improvement; ~**verhältnis** *(Bilanz)* ratio.

Wertverlust depreciation in (loss of) value, value depreciation;
ständiger ~ downward float;
~ **durch Abnutzung** waste;
~ **erleiden** to drop (lose, diminish, go down) in value.

Wertverminderung reduction in value, value depreciation;
absichtlich herbeigeführte ~ voluntary waste;
~ **erfahren** to lose in value.

Wert|verringerungsverlust, ~**verschlechterung** depreciation (decrease) in value, value depreciation; ~**verschlechterung durch Grundstücksbelastung** *(Aktie)* equity dilution; ~**verschleuderung** waste; ~**versicherung** insurance of value; ~**versicherungspolice** valued policy.

wertvoll valuable, precious;
sehr ~ of great worth;
für ~ **halten** to set store by; ~ **für j. sein** to be of value to s. o.; **sehr** ~ **sein** to possess great value; ~**er werden** to increase in value, to improve;
~**e Besitzgegenstände** prize possessions; ~**e Dienste** valuable services; ~**e Ladung** valuable cargo.

Wertzeichen *(Post)* [postage] stamp;
~**automat** stamp-dispensing machine; ~**fälschung** forgery of stamps; ~**papier** laid paper.

Wertzeugnis, kombiniertes ~ **und Ursprungszeugnis** Combined Certificate of Value and Origin *(Br.)*.

Wertzoll ad-valorem [rate of] duty, ad-valorem tariff, duty charged by the weight;
gemischter ~ compound (mixed) duty;
~**satz** ad-valorem rate of duty.

Wert|zunahme appreciation, valuable improvement; ~**zuschlag I** *(Luftfracht)* valuation charge; ~**zuschlag II** value surcharge.

Wertzuwachs increase in value, appreciation, plus value, *(Grundbesitz)* increment, betterment, added value, general benefit, valuable improvement, *(Kapitalanlagegesellschaft)* appreciation;
auf Meliorationen beruhender ~ drainage benefit; **nachgewiesener** ~ recorded appreciation; **unverdienter** ~ unearned increment;
~ **pro Anteil** *(Investmentfonds)* unit value; ~ **eines Grundstücks** appreciation of real estate, increment value of land; ~ **durch erhöhte Preise** price increment.

Wertzuwachs|abgabe betterment levy; ~**betrag** amount of appreciation; ~**möglichkeiten** appreciation possibilities; ~**steuer**

für Grundstücke property increment tax, increment value duty, land value (betterment, *Br.*) tax; **10%ige ~steuer für an den Verpächter zurückfallenden Besitz** reversion [value] duty *(Br.)*.

Wesen being, entity, *(Benehmen)* manners, conduct, *(Hauptinhalt)* substance, *(Veranlagung)* charakter, nature;
im innersten ~ at heart; **mit dem ~ übereinstimmend** in character;
ängstliches ~ timid creature; **freundliches ~** pleasant manner; **geselliges ~** social animal; **gewinnendes ~** congenial manners; **geziertes ~** constrained manner; **verbindliches ~** smooth exterior; **vernunftbegabtes ~** intellectual being;
~ eines Vertrages character of a contract;
innerstes ~ ausmachen to be at the heart of s. th.; **ganz und gar amerikanischem ~ entsprechen** to be thoroughly in the American vein; **zu jds. ~ gehören** to be part of s. one's nature; **zum ~ der Demokratie gehören** to be an intrinsic feature of democracy; **einnehmendes ~ haben** to have a pleasing personality, to have engaging manners; **sich im ~ völlig verändert haben** to have substantially changed; **gereiztes ~ an den Tag legen** to show temper; **viel ~s um j. machen** to fuss over s. o.; **nicht viel ~s von etw. machen** to make nothing of s. th.

Wesensart nature, trait, characteristic.

wesensfremd out of character.

Wesens | gleichheit *(Patentrecht)* identity; **~merkmal** criterion, characteristic feature, character; **~zug** vein, strain; **ungewöhnliche ~züge eines politischen Programms** unusual features in a political program(me).

wesentlich material, essential, *(beträchtlich)* substantial, substantive, integral, fundamental, *(unerläßlich)* vital, *(wichtig)* important;
sich ~ besser fühlen to feel considerably better;
keine ~e Änderungen no great change; **~e Angaben** material data; **~er Beitrag** substantial contribution; **~er Bestandteil** essential part (element), *(Grundstück)* immovable fixture; **~e Bestimmungen** material terms; **~e Eigenschaft** essential quality; **~e Eigenschaften eines Charakters** traits in character; **~er Einwand** material issue; **in den ~en Fragen zu einer Einigung gelangen** to reach a general agreement on fundamentals; **~er Inhalt eines Buches** substance (meat) of a book; **~e Interessen** vital interests; **~e Prozeßbehauptung** material allegation; **~e Punkte** elements; **sich in den ~en Punkten geeinigt haben** to be in substantial agreement; **~e Tatsache** material fact; **~er Teil** essential part; **~er Testamentsinhalt** essence of a will; **~e Umstände** essentials; **für die Beurteilung ~e innere Umstände eines Falles** merits of a case; **~er Unterschied** fundamental difference; **kein ~er Unterschied** no appreciable difference; **~e Veränderung** *(Urkunde)* material alteration; **~e Vertragsbestandteile (Vertragserfordernisse)** integral parts, essentials of a contract; **~e Vertragserfüllung** substantial performance; **~er Vertragsfehler** defect of substance; **~er Vertragsinhalt** essential term; **~er Vorteil** positive (substantial, real) advantage.

Wesentlich | es essence, marrow, principal matter, quick;
das ~e nicht begreifen to miss the point; **das ~e einer Sache berühren** to strike the key note; **zum ~en kommen** to get down to brass tacks; **sich im ~en einig sein** to be in substantial agreement; **das ~e verstehen** to catch the gist.

Wespennest, in ein ~ stechen to wake snakes, to stir up a nest of hornets, to bring a hornet's nest about one's ears.

Weste waistcoat *(Br.)*, vest *(US)*;
blütenweiße ~ clean sheet, spotless reputation;
sich eine reine ~ bewahren to keep one's nose clean *(US)*; **blütenweiße ~ haben** to be without a spot on one's reputation; **reine ~ haben** to come with clean hands; **keine reine ~ haben** to have a blot on one's escutcheon.

West | en *(pol.)* West, Occident;
mit dem ~en liiert sein to be linked with the West;
~europa Western Europe; **~europäische Union** Western European Union; **~grenze** western boundary; **Ost-~-Handel** East-West trade; **~mächte** Western Powers.

Westentasche waistcoat pocket;
Stadt wie seine ~ kennen to know a town like the back of one's hand.

Westentaschen | diktator tin-pot Napoleon *(sl.)*; **~format** [vest-] pocket size; **im ~format** in petticoats; **~kreuzer** pocket battleship.

Western western, oats opera *(sl.)*, oater *(sl.)*.

West | kurs western course; **~küste** west coast.

westlich occidental, western;
~en Charakter geben to westernize.

Wettannahme betting pool (shop).

Wettbewerb contest, competition, rivalry, *(Prüfung)* competitive examination;
auf ~ eingestellt competitive; **auf der Grundlage des ~s** on a competitive basis; **außer ~** noncompetitive; **unter Bedingungen des freien ~s** under fully competitive conditions;
außerpreislicher ~ nonprice competition; **existenzgefährdender ~** cutthroat competition; **freier ~** fair (pure, open) competition; **funktionsfähiger ~** workable competition *(US)*; **gemeinsamer ~** cooperative competition; **gesteigerter ~** heightened competition; **industrieller ~** industry competition; **internationaler ~** trade competition between countries; **lauterer ~** fair competition; **lebhafter ~** heavy competition; **monopolitischer ~** monopolistic competition; **mörderischer ~** cutthroat competition; **offener ~** free-for-all *(coll.)*; **regulierter ~** administered competition; **ruinöser ~** ruinous competition; **scharfer ~** keen (severe, cutthroat) competition; **starker ~** severe competition; **uneingeschränkter ~** perfect (pure) competition *(US)*; **unerlaubter ~** unfair trade *(US)*, restrictive business practices *(Br.)*; **unlauterer ~** fraudulent (mean, unfair, unfair methods of) competition, unreasonable restraint of trade, restrictive business practices *(Br.)*; **wirtschaftlich unsinniger ~** destructive competition; **unvollkommener ~** imperfect competition; **verschärfter ~** intensified competition; **vollkommener ~** atomistic (perfect, pure) competition;
~ ausschalten to eliminate competition; **aus einem ~ ausscheiden** to drop out of a contest; **von einem ~ ausschließen** to disquality from a contest; **öffentlichen ~ ausschreiben** to put up for competition, to invite tenders (public competition); **sich an einem ~ beteiligen** to go in for a competition, to contest for a prize; **unlauteren ~ betreiben** to engage in unfair competition; **~ einschränken** to restrict (restrain) competition (trade); **im ~ Kopf an Kopf liegen** to compete head on; **zum ~ angemeldet sein** to be entered in a competition; **im ~ nicht zu schlagen sein** to defy all competition; **im ~ stehen** to compete, to contest; **an einem ~ teilnehmen** to enter the lists; **in ~ treten** to enter into (go in for) competition, to compete, to rival; **mit jem. in ~ treten** to compete (enter into rivalry) with s. o.; **~ verfälschen** to falsify competition; **~ verzerren** to distort competition; **von scharfem ~ bedrängt werden** to be up against stiff competition.

Wettbewerber contestant, competitor, rival, contester;
preisdrückender ~ cut-price competitor;
~ mit unlauteren Geschäftsmethoden cutthroat competitor.

Wettbewerberschaft competitorship.

Wettbewerbs | abkommen covenant not to compete; **formlose ~abrede** hono(u)rable understanding, agreement in restraint of trade *(US)*; **~abteilung** competition department; **~anreiz** competitive boost; **~ausschluß** exclusivity stipulation; **~basis** competitive basis; **~bedingungen** terms (conditions) of competition; **ungleiche ~bedingungen** imperfect competition; **~behinderung** prevention of competition; **~behörde** *(EG)* competition department.

wettbewerbsbeschränkend anticompetitive, unreasonable *(Br.)*;
~e Maßnahmen restrictive practices; **~e Nebenabrede** ancillary restraint; **~e Vereinbarung** covenant in restraint of trade, restrictive trading agreement.

Wettbewerbsbeschränkung competitive restraint (restriction), restraint of competition, restraining of trade, restrictive practices;
unzulässige ~ unreasonable restraint of trade *(Br.)*; **vertragliche ~en** loose-knit combinations.

Wettbewerbsbeschränkungs | vereinbarung agreement restraining trade; **~vertrag** contract in restraint of trade.

Wettbewerbs | bestimmungen competition rules; **~charakter** competitive nature; **~drohung** competitive threat; **~druck** competitive pressure, stress of competition; **~eifer** competitive zeal; **~einheit** competitive unit; **~einschränkung** competitive limitation; **~element** competitive element; **~erfordernisse** competitive requirements.

wettbewerbsfähig competitive, able to compete, able to meet competition, capable of competing;
~er Preis competitive price.

Wettbewerbs | fähigkeit competitive ability (capacity, strength), competitiveness, capacity to compete; **~fähigkeit auf allen vom Preis unabhängigen Gebieten** nonprice competitiveness; **~fähigkeit auf dem Preisgebiet** price competitiveness; **~freiheit** freedom of competition, free competition; **unvollkommene ~freiheit** imperfect competition; **~geist** competitive spirit; **~gesellschaft** competitive society; **~gesetz** Unfair Trade Practice Act *(US)*; **~gründe** competitive reasons; **auf ~grundlage** on a competitive basis; **~handlungen** competitive acts (activity); **~intensität** intensity of competition; **~kampf**

strain of competition; ~**kartell** combination in restraint of trade; ~**klausel** competitive (restraint, competition) clause, *(für Teilnehmer an innerbetrieblichen Berufsausbildungskursen)* radius clause; ~**klima** competitive climate; ~**lage** competitive situation (position); ~**lohn** competitive wage; ~**markt** competitive market.

wettbewerbsmäßig auf dem Markt durchsetzen, sich to hold one's own in competitive markets.

Wettbewerbs|maßnahmen competitive moves; ~**mechanismus** mechanism of competition; **lautere** ~**methoden** fair trade practices; **ungleiche** ~**methode** imperfect competition *(US)*; **unlautere** ~**methoden** unfair methods of competition, unfair practices *(US)*; ~**möglichkeiten** competitive abilities; ~**nachteil** competitive disadvantage.

wettbewerbsneutral sein to remain neutral regarding competition.

Wettbewerbs|politik competition policy; ~**position** competitive position; ~**preis** competitive price; ~**problem** competitive problem; ~**prüfung** competitive examination; ~**rabatt** price shading; ~**recht** right to compete, competition law; ~**regeln** competition rules, trade practice rules *(US)*, trade regulations *(US)*, fair-trade rules *(US)*; ~**risiko** risk from competition; ~**situation** competitive atmosphere (situation, position); ~**spielraum** competitive range; ~**stärke** competitive strength (edge); **seine** ~**stärke demonstrieren** to demonstrate one's competitive muscle; ~**stellung** competitive position (situation); **starke** ~**stellung** competitive edge; ~**stimmung** competitive mood; ~**strategie** competitive strategy; ~**system** competitive system; ~**tarif** competitive rate; ~**tätigkeit** competitive activity (acts, practices); ~**teilnehmer** contestant, contestor, competitor, rival; ~**ungleichheit** competition imbalance; ~**verbot** restraint clause, restraint of trade, *(Angestellter)* restrictive covenant; **jem. ein** ~**verbot auferlegen** to restrain s. one's freedom to work; ~**verbotsklausel** restraint clause; ~**verbotsvertrag**, ~**verbotsvereinbarung** agreement in restraint of trade, restraint agreement; ~**verfälschung** falsification of competition; ~**verhältnisse** competitive conditions; ~**verhinderung** restraint of competition; ~**vertrag** contract in restraint of trade.

wettbewerbsverzerrend competitive-distorting.

Wettbewerbs|verzerrungen distortion of competition, competitive distortions (imbalance); ~**voraussetzungen schaffen** to pry open to competition; ~**vorteil** competitive advantage; **im** ~**wege** on a competitive basis.

wettbewerbswidrig contrary to fair competition.

Wettbewerbswirtschaft, [intensive] [highly] competitive economy (business world).

Wett|buch betting book, handbook; **berüchtigte** ~**bude hochgehen lassen** to knock over a reputed bookmaking parlo(u)r *(sl.)*; ~**büro** betting house.

Wette bet, wager;
gemeinsame ~ wagering transaction;
~ **mit gleichem Einsatz** even bet;
~ **abschließen** to lay (make) a wager; **einige erfolgreiche** ~**n abschließen** to pull off some good things at the races; ~ **anbieten** to make (lay) a bet (wager); ~ **annehmen** to take up a wager (bet), to take on (accept) a bet; ~ **eingehen** to make a bet; **hohe** ~ **eingehen** to go a bundle; **angenommene** ~ **eintragen** to make a book; ~ **gewinnen** to win a bet; ~ **halten** to hold a wager; **auf dem Rennplatz einige** ~**n legen** to go to the races and have a flutter; ~ **teilweise woanders plazieren** to lay off a bet; **sich gegen den Verlust einer** ~ **sichern** to hedge against a bet.

Wetteifer competition, contention, rivalry.

wetteifern to compete, to contend;
mit jem. ~ to vie with s. o.; **mit jem. um den ersten Platz** ~ to contend with s. o. for the first place.

Wetteinsatz bet, stake;
durch höheren ~ **gekennzeichnet** long;
~ **erhöhen** to go better.

Wetten betting.

wetten to bet, to lay (make) a wager, to punt;
seinen letzten Heller ~ to bet one's last dollar; **seinen Kopf darauf** ~ to stake one's life on it; **auf ein Pferd** ~ to back a horse; **soundsoviel auf ein Pferd** ~ to lay so much on a horse.

Wettender better.

Wetter, gelegentlicher casual better.

Wetter *(Bergbau)* air, intake, *(Witterung)* weather, sky;
bei jedem ~ come rain or shine; **falls das** ~ **es zuläßt** weather permitting; **vom** ~ **beschädigt** weather-beaten;
bedrohliches ~ ugly weather; **feuchtes** ~ muggy days; **mildes** ~ moderate weather; **miserables** ~ damnable (vile) weather; **nebliges** ~ foggy weather; **scheußliches** ~ disagreeable (wretched) weather; **schlagende** ~ mine gas, foul air, fire-damp explosion; **schlechtes (stürmisches)** ~ foul weather; **schönes** ~ Queen's weather; **anhaltend schönes** ~ continuance (long spell) of fine weather; **stürmisches** ~ windiness of the weather; **trügerisches** ~ treacherous weather; **unbeständiges** ~ variable weather; **veränderliches** ~ uncertain weather; **winterliches** ~ wintry weather;
vom ~ **abhängen** to turn on the weather; **dem** ~ **aussetzen** to weather; **j. um gutes** ~ **bitten** to make amends to s. o.; **über das** ~ **schimpfen** to inveigh against the weather; **auf gutes** ~ **stoßen** *(Schiff)* to make good weather; ~ **vorhersagen** to forecast the weather.

wetterabhängig sein to feel under the weather *(coll.)*.

Wetter|abhängigkeit der Ernte dependence of the crop upon the weather; ~**abteilung** *(Grube)* ventilating district; ~**amt** weather bureau, meteorological office; ~**analyse** weather analysis; ~**änderung** variation (change) in the weather; **plötzliche** ~**änderung** break in the weather; **auf eine** ~**änderung hoffen** to hope for a break in the weather; ~**anomalie** weather anomaly; ~**ansage** weather forecast; ~**ansager** weather caster *(US)*; ~**aussichten** weather outlook; ~**ballon** meteorological balloon; ~**bedingungen** weather conditions; ~**beeinflussung** weather modification; ~**beobachter** meteorologist, aerographer *(US)*; ~**beobachtung** meteorological observation; **mündliche** ~**beratung** *(Pilot)* meteorological briefing; ~**bericht** weather report (forecast), bulletin; ~**bericht bringen** to carry a weather forecast; ~**besserung** weather improvement; ~**dach** canopy, *(Schutzdach)* shelter, penthouse; ~**deck** *(Schiff)* weather deck.

wetterdicht weathertight.

Wetter|dienst weather service; ~**ecke** bad-weather area; ~**entwicklung** sequence of the weather; ~**ergebnisse** weather data; ~**fahne** wind vane, *(pol.)* trimmer *(Br.)*, fair-weather friend.

wetterfest weathertight, weatherproof.

Wetterfront front.

wetterfühlig sein to feel under the weather *(coll.)*.

Wetter|führung *(Grube)* ventilation; ~**hahn** weathercock, vane; ~**karte** weather chart (map); ~**lage** atmospheric conditions, weather situation; ~**leuchten** sheet (summer) lightning, wildfire, fireflaught *(Scot.)*; ~**leuchten am politischen Horizont** clouds on the political horizon; ~**mantel** waterproof overcoat, trench coat, raincoat; ~**meldung** meteorological message, weather forecast; ~**meßinstrument** radiosonde.

wettern, gegen etw. to rave (fulminate) against s. th.

Wetter|nachrichten meteorological message, weather forecast (report); ~**periode** spell of weather; ~**prophet** weather forecaster (caster, *US*), weatherman; **als erfolgreicher** ~**prophet gelten** to become famed as a weather prophet; ~**satellit** weather (meteorological) satellite; ~**schacht** *(Grube)* ventilation shaft, ventilator, windhole, monkey; ~**scheide** divide; ~**schiff** ocean weather ship; ~**seite** weather side; ~**sonde** dropsound; ~**station** weather station, meteorological office; **schwimmende** ~**station** weatherdrome; ~**störung** atmospheric disturbances; ~**straße** *(Bergbau)* airway; ~**strecke** *(Bergbau)* windway; ~**sturz**, ~**umschlag** abrupt change of the weather; ~**unbilden** rigo(u)rs of the weather; **den** ~**unbilden ausgesetzt** exposed to weather; **gegen** ~**unbilden geschützt werden müssen** to need protection against the weather; ~**veränderung** weather (meteorological) change; **auf eine** ~**veränderung hoffen** to hope for a break in the weather; ~**verhältnisse** the elements, weather (atmospheric) conditions; ~**verschlechterung** deterioration of the weather; ~**versicherung** weather insurance.

Wettervorhersage weather forecast, forecast of the weather, aeromancy;
langfristige ~ long-sighted (-range) weather forecast; **mittelfristige** ~ medium-term meteorological forecast;
~ **machen** to forecast the weather;
amtliche ~**stätte** weather bureau; ~**zentrum** weather center *(US)* (centre, *Br.*).

Wetter|warnung warning of bad weather; ~**warte** meteorological office, observatory; ~**wechsel** change of the weather, weather change.

wetterwendisch fickle, volatile, capricious;
~**er Mensch** weathercock, whiffler.

Wetter|winkel storm area, *(pol.)* storm center *(US)* (centre, *Br.*); **über der** ~**zone** *(Flugzeug)* above the weather.

Wett|gebühr stake [money]; ~**gemeinschaft** betting group; **unerlaubte** ~**geschäfte** illicit betting; ~**gewinn** betting win, winnings; ~**gewinnsteuer** race-betting tax; ~**kampf** competition, match, prize fight; ~**kampfstätte** competition site; ~**karte** policy slip *(US)*; ~**kurs** odds.

Wettlauf| um die Präsidentschaft race for the presidency; ~ **um Subventionen zur Erhaltung der Wettbewerbsposition** competitive subsidy race; ~ **mit der Zeit** race against time;
im ~ mit dem Wahltermin liegen to be in a race against the election clock.
Wettlokal betting shop, poolroom *(US)*.
wettmachen to make up for, to compensate;
ermäßigte Preise durch große Umsätze ~ to sell at a low price and recoup o. s. by large sales; **Produktivitätszunahme ~** to outrun increases in productivity; **Verlust ~** to make up for a loss.
Wett| police wager policy; ~**preis** prize, wager; ~**quoten herabsetzen** to reduce the odds; ~**rennen** race; ~**rennen im Weltraum** space race; ~**rüsten** arms race; ~**schein** betting slip; ~**schulden** betting debts; ~**spiel** match; ~**steuern** race-betting tax.
Wettstreit contest, competition, rivalry;
sich mit jem. auf einen ~ einlassen to agree to compete (enter into rivalry) with s. o.; **in friedlichem ~ stehen** to contend in friendly rivalry; ~ **veranstalten** to run a contest.
Wett| teilnehmer taker of a bet; ~**tip** racing tip; ~**tips geben** to tout *(US)*; ~**vertrag** gambling (gaming, wager) contract; ~**zettel** betting slip.
Whisky mit einem Schuß Sodawasser whisky and splash.
Wichs gala dress, regalia, wampum *(US sl.)*;
sich in ~ werfen to dress up to kill.
Wicht goblin, gnome, dwarf;
elender ~ wretched creature.
wichtig important, momentous, essential, influential, material, relevant, great, vital, *(aktuell)* front-page;
sich für ~ halten to think no small beer of o. s.; **sich ~ machen (tun)** to put on a face of importance, to splurge, to put on side, to give o. s. airs;
~**e Angelegenheit** momentous affair; ~**er Betrieb** essential industry; ~**e Entscheidung** momentous decision; ~**er Grund** just cause; ~**er Mann** man of influence; ~**e Miene aufsetzen** to put on a face of importance; ~**e Person** v.i.p., mugwump *(US)*.
Wichtigeres zu tun haben to have other fish to fry.
Wichtigkeit importance, moment, worth, interest, *(Tragweite)* momentousness, weight, consequence;
von äußerster ~ of utmost importance; **von größter (höchster) ~** of first-rate (primary, prime) importance;
einer Sache ~ beimessen to attach importance to a matter; ~ **einer Angelegenheit hervorheben** to point out a matter of chief interest.
Wichtigste essential(s);
kurz das ~ erwähnen to hit the high spot.
wichtigster Kunde key customer.
Wichtigtuer boaster, swaggerer, braggart, bustler, whippersnapper, pooh-bah, lineshooter *(sl.)*, fuss *(US)*.
Wichtigtuerei splurge, show-off, bragging, boasting, bumbledom.
Wickel *(Umschlag)* wrap, pack, compress;
j. beim ~ halten to hold s. o. by the scruff of the neck;
wie ein ~kind behandeln to mollycoddle.
wickeln to wind, to spool, *(med.)* to bandage, to dress, to bind;
j. um den kleinen Finger ~ to twist s. o. round one's little finger;
in ein Paket ~ to wrap up.
Wicklung *(el.)* winding.
Wider, das Für und the pros and cons;
~**druck** reiteration, second printing, *(Inserat)* backing up;
~**druckform** inner form.
Widerhall echo, reverberation;
starker ~ in der Öffentlichkeit wide publicity;
begeisterten ~ finden to meet with enthusiastic response; **im ganzen Volk ~ finden** to find a nation-wide response.
widerhallen to echo, to reverberate.
Widerklage cross complaint (demand, action, suit, *US*), counterclaim, counterplea, countercharge, countersuit *(US)*, reconvention;
~ **erheben** to cross-sue, to plead a counterclaim, to cross-petition;
~**antrag** bill of particulars.
Wider| kläger plaintiff in the cross, counterclaimant; ~**lager** buttress.
widerlegbar rebuttable, refutable, confutable, inconclusive;
nicht ~ irrefutable, irrebuttable.
Widerlegbarkeit inconclusiveness.
widerlegen to rebut, to refute, to disprove, to confute;
Anklagepunkte ~ to disprove the points of a charge; **Vorstellung ~** to explode a notion.
Widerlegung rebuttal, refutal, confutation, refutation.
widerlich repulsive, nauseating, awkward, cross;
j. ~ finden not to be able to stand s. o.; **sich selbst ~ finden** to kick o. s. *(sl.)*;
~**e Angelegenheit** can of worms *(US)*; ~**e Ansicht** repulsive (nauseating) sight; ~**er Kerl** nasty fellow, stinker *(sl.)*; ~**er Vorschlag** repugnant proposal.
Widerling stinker *(sl.)*.
widernatürlich unnatural, perverse, perverted.
widerrechtlich wrongful, unlawful, illegal, illegitimate, usurpingly;
sich ~ aneignen to usurp; ~ **betreten** to trespass; ~ **von einem Grundstück vertreiben** to disseize (dispossess) of an estate; ~ **verwenden** to misappropriate;
~**e Aneignung** conversion, misappropriation; ~**e Besitznahme** *(Grundstück)* unlawful entry; ~**es Betreten** trespass.
Widerrechtlichkeit wrongfulness, illegality.
Widerrede contradiction, backchat *(coll.)*.
Widerruf recall, revocation, repeal, retraction, *(Aufträge)* countermand, cancellation, withdrawal, *(Dementi)* disavowal, *(jur.)* disclaimer;
bis auf ~ until cancelled (countermanded), *(Beamtenposition)* during Her Majesty's pleasure, *(Inserat)* till forbid; **bis auf ~ gültig** good (valid) until recalled (cancelled);
allgemeiner ~ general revocation; **geheimer ~** counterdeed; **öffentlicher ~** disclaimer;
~ **eines Angebotes** revocation (withdrawal) of an offer; ~ **des Auftragsverhältnisses** revocation of an agency; ~ **einer Genehmigung** withdrawal of a permit; ~ **eines Geständnisses** retraction of a confession; ~ **einer Konzession** withdrawal (cancellation) of licence; ~ **einer Nutzungserlaubnis** determination of will; ~ **einer Schenkung** return of a gift; ~ **einer Stimmrechtsermächtigung** revocation of a proxy; ~ **der Strafaussetzung** revocation of probation; ~ **eines Testaments** countermand (revocation) of a will; ~ **eines Testamentswiderrufes** republication; ~**kraft gerichtlicher Verfügung** judicial revocation; ~ **eines Vermächtnisses** ademption (revocation) of a legacy; ~ **eines Vertretungsverhältnisses** renunciation (revocation) of an agency; ~ **eines Verzichts** retraction of a renunciation; ~ **einer Vollmacht** revocation of a power of attorney; ~ **einer Zeugenaussage** retraction of a deposition.
widerrufen to call back, to annul, to revoke, to abrogate, to unmake;
Auftrag ~ to countermand (cancel, withdraw) an order; **Behauptung ~** to retract a statement; **Beschuldigung ~** to retract an accusation (a charge); **frühere Erklärung öffentlich ~** to recant a former declaration; **Garantiezusage ~** to cancel a guarantee; **Geständnis ~** to retract a confession; **Konzession ~** to revoke a licence; **Telegramm ~** to kill a telegram, to recall a wire; **Testament ~** to countermand (cancel, revoke) a will; **Vereinbarung ~** to annul an agreement; **Vertretungsbefugnis jederzeit ~** to revoke an agent's authority at any time; **Vollmacht ~** to revoke a power, to withdraw (revoke) a power of attorney;
nicht ~ unrepealed; **sofern nicht vorher ~** unless previously withdrawn.
widerruflich repealable, revocable, *(absetzbar)* removable, dative, *(Auftrag)* countermandable, *(vom Eigentümer)* at the pleasure of the owner, *(auf Probe)* on probation;
jederzeit ~ precarious, ambulatory;
etw. ~ benutzen dürfen to enjoy the precarious use of s. th.;
~**er Kreditbrief** revocable letter of credit; ~**es Testament** ambulatory will.
Widerruflichkeit revocability;
~ **eines Amtes** uncertainty of tenure.
Widerrufs| anzeige notice of revocation; ~**befugnis** power of revocation (to revoke); **schriftliche ~erklärung** notice of revocation in writing; ~**klausel** repeating clause.
Wider| sacher adversary, opposer, enemy; **sich gegen alle ~sacher behaupten** to hold one's own against all comers; ~**schein des Feuers** reflection of the fire.
widersetzen to resist, to oppose;
sich dem Gesetz ~ to defy the law; **sich einer Sache mit allen Fasern seines Herzens ~** to oppose s. th. out and out; **sich einer richterlichen Verfügung ~** to resist the authority of a court; **sich der Verhaftung ~** to resist arrest; **sich jds. Willen ~** to resist s. one's will.
widersetzlich insubordinate.
Widersetzlichkeit insubordinate conduct, insubordination.
widersinnig absurd, preposterous.
Widersinnigkeit absurdity, preposterousness, incongruity.
widerspenstig recalcitrant, disobedient, contumacious.

Widerspenstigkeit refractoriness, recalcitrance, contumacy.
widerspiegeln to reflect, to mirror;
öffentliche Meinung ~ to be a reflex of public opinion.
Widerspiel der Kräfte action and counteraction.
widersprechen to contradict, to oppose, to controvert, to gainsay;
jem. ~ to fly in the face of s. o.; **sich** ~ to jar, *(Zeugenaussagen)* to be at variance, to disagree; **einer Behauptung** ~ to contradict (gainsay) a statement; **einer Handlung** ~ to object to an action; **dem gesunden Menschenverstand** ~ to be in contradiction to common sense; **einem Plan** ~ to oppose a scheme.
widersprechend contradictory, repugnant;
~e Ansichten clash of opinions; **~e Aussagen** conflicting declarations (statements); **einander ~e Berichte** discrepant accounts; **einander ~e Erklärungen** contradictory statements; **sich ~e Gesetze** conflicting laws; **sich ~e Meldungen** contradictory reports; **~e Zeugenaussagen** conflicting evidence.
Widerspruch *(Einspruch)* opposition, protest, objection, *(bei Eintragungen)* discrepancy, *(Gegensatz)* contradiction, incoherence, repugnancy, inconsistency, *(zweier Gesetze)* antinomy, *(Patentanmeldung, Warenzeichen)* opposition;
im ~ counter; **im** ~ **stehend** repugnant; **ohne** ~ without a dissentient voice;
absoluter ~ *(Zeugenaussagen)* positive discrepancy; **innerer** ~ contradiction in terms; **offener** ~ flagrant contradiction;
~ **in einer Zeugenaussage** discrepancy in the deposition of a witness;
~ **einlegen** to lodge a protest, to file an objection; ~ **erheben** to interpose (make) an objection, to oppose; ~ **herausfordern** to be open to objection; **keinen** ~ **hervorrufen** to raise no objection; ~ **nicht ertragen können** to be intolerant of opposition; **in sich selbst ein** ~ **sein** to be self-contradictory; **einem** ~ **stattgeben** to sustain an objection; **im** ~ **stehen** to contravene, to be inconsistent (in contradiction, repugnant), not to be consistent with; **im** ~ **zu jem. stehen** to be at discord with s. o.; **im** ~ **zueinander stehen** *(Zeugenaussagen)* to be at variance, to disagree, to be out of tune (repugnant); **auf scharfen** ~ **stoßen** to run into stiff opposition.
Widersprüche | verschiedener Berichte variance between reports;
~ **in den Zeugenaussagen** conflict of evidence;
auf immer neue ~ **stoßen** to detect more and more contradictions; **sich in** ~ **verwickeln** to entrap o. s. into contradicting.
widersprüchlich inconsistent, contradictory, incompatible, repugnant, cross;
~ **sein** *(Zeugenaussagen)* to differ.
Widersprüchlichkeit incompatibility, contrariety.
Widerspruchs | freiheit *(Meinungsforschung)* consistency; **~geist** contradictiousness.
widerspruchslos without opposition, deplano;
~ **hinnehmen** to swallow it without a murmur.
widerspruchsvoll incongruous, inconsistent.
Widerstand resistance, opposition, defiance, *(Hindernis)* obstacle;
bewaffneter ~ armed resistance; **entschlossener** ~ obstinate resistance to an attack; **hartnäckiger** ~ stout (stiff, stubborn) resistance; **heftiger** ~ sturdy resistance; **passiver** ~ passive resistance, civil disobedience;
~ **im Kongress** congressional opposition; ~ **der Kundschaft** customer resistance; ~ **bis zum letzten Mann** last-ditch resistance; ~ **der Regierung** administration opposition; ~ **gegen die Staatsgewalt** obstructing (obstruction of) a constable *(Br.)* (a police officer, *US*), in the performance (execution) of his duties; ~ **gegen Vollstreckungsbeamte** obstructing process, deforcement *(Scot.)*; ~ **der Wähler** voter resistance;
an allen Frontabschnitten heftigem ~ **begegnen** to meet with strong opposition all along the front; **jeden** ~ **beseitigen (brechen)** to break down all opposition, to break the back of (bring down all) resistance; **jds.** ~ **brechen** to overcome s. one's resistance; **feindlichen** ~ **brechen** to wear (break) down the enemy's resistance; **Weg des geringsten ~es einschlagen** to take (follow) the line of [the] least resistance; **der Polizei** ~ **entgegensetzen** to resist the police; **dem feindlichen Vorrücken** ~ **entgegensetzen** to dispute an advance of the enemy; **jds.** ~ **herausfordern** to put s. o. on the spot; **keinen** ~ **leisten können** to be powerless to resist; ~ **leisten** to oppose, to offer resistance; **dem Feind heftigen** ~ **leisten** to oppose a rigorous resistance to (make a stand against) the enemy; **keinen** ~ **leisten** to lie down; **einer feindlichen Landung** ~ **leisten** to dispute a landing by the enemy; **nur scheinbar** ~ **leisten** to offer only a token resistance; ~ **gegen polizeiliche Anordnungen leisten** to obstruct the police in the execution of their duties; ~ **gegen einen Staatsbeamten leisten** to oppose (obstruct, deforce, *Scot.*) an officer in the execution of his duty; ~ **gegen die Staatsgewalt leisten** to bid defiance to a policeman, to obstruct an officer *(US)* (constable, *Br.*) performing his duties, to resist arrest; **auf** ~ **stoßen** to meet with resistance (opposition), to encounter opposition; **auf eisernen** ~ **stoßen** to bite on granite; **auf heftigen** ~ **stoßen** to meet with a stiff opposition; ~ **überwinden** to wear down the opposition; **jeden** ~ **überwinden** to drive all before one; **jeden weiteren** ~ **unterdrücken** to silence all further opposition.
Widerstände, sich gegen alle ~ **durchsetzen** to hold one's way in spite of all obstacles; **seine Pläne gegen alle** ~ **durchsetzen** to have everything one's own way; **jds.** ~ **gegen einen Vorschlag ignorieren** to disregard s. one's objections to a proposal.
widerstandsfähig durable, stable, *(Börse)* resistant, strong;
nicht ~ **sein** to be powerless to resist; **sehr** ~ **sein** *(Börse)* to show strong resistance; ~ **werden** *(Börse)* to pick up strength.
Widerstands | fähigkeit hardness, durability, tenacity, *(Börse)* resistance, strength, strong attitude, *(Material)* endurance, strength; **~fähigkeit der Preise** price resistance; **~fähigkeit zeigen** *(Kurse)* to show strong resistance; **~gruppe** resistance (underground) group; **~kämpfer** resistance fighter, undergrounder; **~kraft** staying power, stamina, power of resistance; **jds. ~kräfte aufzehren** to destroy s. one's powers of resistance; **über große ~kräfte verfügen** to have great powers of endurance.
Widerstandslinie *(mil.)* defence line;
letzte ~ line of last resistance;
~ **aufbauen** *(Börse)* to form a base pattern, to bottom (base) out; ~ **überwinden** *(Börse)* to break a resistance level.
widerstandslos without resistance, nonresistant, unresisted.
Widerstands | nester pockets of resistance, defensive posts; **~organisation** resistance organization; **~schwelle** *(Börse)* resistance level.
widerstehen to resist;
einem Angriff ~ to outstand an assault; **dem Sturm** ~ to withstand the storm.
Widerstreben reluctance, antagonism.
widerstreben, jds. Charakter to go against s. one's grain.
widerstrebend reluctant, opposing, resisting.
Widerstreit conflict, clash, antagonism, hostility;
mit jem. in ~ **geraten** to come into conflict with s. o.; **mit etw. im** ~ **stehen** to clash with s. th.
widerstreitende | Interessen incompatible (conflicting, clashing) interests; ~ **Meinungen** clashing opinions.
widerwärtig nasty, horrid, disgusting, cross, awkward;
sich ~ **benehmen** to behave disgustingly;
~er Anblick nauseating (repulsive) sight; **~er Kerl** nasty fellow, stinker *(sl.)*.
Widerwärtigkeiten des Lebens the fret and fume (little vexations) of life.
Widerwille repugnance, disgust, aversion, dislike;
mit größtem ~n with utmost reluctance;
jem. ~n einflößen to fill s. o. with disgust; **~n empfinden** to sicken, to feel disgusted; **mit ~n an seine tägliche Arbeit gehen** to go about one's daily work reluctantly; **~n gegen fette Speisen haben** to loathe greasy food.
widerwillig unwilling, reluctant, with bad grace;
einem Befehl äußerst ~ **nachkommen** to be very reluctant to comply with an order.
widmen to dedicate, to inscribe, to devote;
jem. seine größte Aufmerksamkeit ~ to listen to s. o. with profound interest; **sich erneut ganz dem Geschäft** ~ to devote o. s. anew to business; **sich mit allen Kräften einem Projekt** ~ to fling o. s. into a project; **sein Leben der Kunst** ~ to devote one's life to art; **sich einer Sache** ~ to give o. s. up to s. th.; **Straße dem öffentlichen Verkehr** ~ to dedicate a highway; **sich seinen Studien** ~ to apply o. s. to one's studies; **jem. seine Zeit** ~ to devote one's time to s. o.
Widmung inscription, *(Eigentum)* tacit dedication;
ohne ~ undedicated;
gewohnheitsrechtliche ~ common law dedication; **handschriftliche** ~ handwritten dedication;
~ **eines Grundstücks zur öffentlichen Sache** preservation of land for public benefit; ~ **als öffentliche Straße** dedication of a highway;
~ **in ein Buch schreiben** to write a dedication in a book.
Widmungsexemplar complimentary (presentation) copy.
widrige Umstände adverse circumstances.

widrigenfalls failing which, in default whereof.
Wiederabdruck reimpression, reprint.
wiederabdrucken to reprint.
wiederaberkennen, Staatsbürgerschaft to denaturalize.
Wiederaberkennung der Staatsbürgerschaft denaturalization.
wieder|absagen to cancel, to countermand; **~absenden** to redispatch; **~abtreten** to reassign, to retrocede.
Wieder|abtretung reassignment, retrocession; **~anfang** *(Schule)* reopening; **~angleichung** realignment; **~ankauf** repurchase; **~anklage** reaccusation.
wiederanklagen to reaccuse.
Wiederanlage reinvestment;
~ des Erlöses (von Erträgen, des Gewinns) reinvestment of proceeds, ploughing (plowing, *US*) back of earnings (profits); **automatische ~ der Erträge** automatic reinvestment of income; **~ von Öldollarströmen** recycling (downstream investment) of petrodollars; **sofortige ~ von Spekulationsgewinnen** pyramid scheme;
~aufgabe recycling job; **~beträge** reinvested earnings; **~fonds** recycling fund; **~möglichkeiten** recycling facilities; **~plan** recycling plan; **~quote** reinvestment ratio; **~rabatt** *(Kapitalanlagegesellschaft)* reinvestment discount; **~recht** reinvestment privilege.
Wiederanlaufen der Konjunktur, gezügeltes restrained recovery in economic activity.
wiederanlegen *(Geld)* to reinvest, *(Gewinn)* to plough (plow, *US*) back, *(Öldollar)* to recycle.
Wieder|annäherung *(Politik)* rapprochement; **~annahme** reacceptance; **~annahme eines früheren Namens** resumption of a former name.
wiederannehmen, alten Namen to resume an old name.
wiederanpassen, Löhne to readjust wages.
Wiederanpassung readjustment.
Wiederanschaffung replacement.
Wieder|anschaffungswert replacement value; **~ansiedlungsraum** relocation center *(US)*.
wiederanstellen to re-engage, to re-employ, to reinstate, to reappoint, to rehire *(US)*.
Wieder|anstellung re-employment, re-engagement, reappointment, rehiring *(US)*, reinstatement; **konjunktureller ~anstieg** economic upturn, *(Rezession)* pickup.
wiederanwenden to reapply.
Wieder|anwendung reapplication; **~anziehen der Konjunktur** cyclical recovery; **~anziehen der Kurse** recovery of the market.
wiederanziehen *(Kurse)* to recover.
Wiederaufbau reconstruction, rehabilitation, recovery;
wirtschaftlicher ~ industrial rehabilitation (reconstruction); **~ eines Anwesens** rebuilding of premises; **~ eines Betriebes** plant rehabilitation; **~ eines Gewerbebetriebs** reconstruction of works; **~ in der Nachkriegszeit** postwar rehabilitation; **~ einer Partei** reorganization of a party; **~ der Wirtschaft** economic (industrial) reconstruction, industrial resurgence (rehabilitation);
jem. beim ~ helfen to aid s. one's recovery;
~anleihe reconstruction (rehabilitation) loan; **~arbeit** reconstruction work; **~ausschuß** reorganization committee; **~bank** Reconstruction Finance Corporation *(US)*; **Internationale ~bank** International Bank for Reconstruction and Development; **~darlehn** reconstruction loan.
wiederaufbauen to reconstruct, to rehabilitate;
Gebäude ~ to rebuild a house, to restore a [ruined] building.
Wiederaufbau|finanzierung reconstruction financing; **~- und Finanzierungsgesellschaft** Reconstruction Finance Corporation *(US)*; **~kosten** *(Grundbesitz)* reproduction (replacement) cost of real estate; **~kredit** reconstruction credit (loan); **~maßnahmen** recovery measures; **~mittel** funds for reconstruction; **~phase** period of reconstruction (recovery); **~plan** scheme of reconstruction; **wirtschaftlicher ~plan** reorganization (reconstruction) plan; **~police** reinstatement policy; **wirtschaftliches ~problem** industrial rehabilitation problem; **~programm** reconstruction program(me); **Europäisches ~programm** European Recovery Program(me); **wirtschaftliches ~programm** economic recovery program(me).
Wiederaufbereitungsanlage reprocessing plant;
~ für Atommüll nuclear waste reprocessing plant.
wieder|aufblühen to revive, to reflourish; **~auffinden** to recover.
Wiederaufflackern öffentlicher Unruhen recrudescence of civil disorders.
wieder|aufflackern to flare up again, *(Aufstand)* to recrudesce; **~aufflammen** *(fig.)* to recrudesce, *(Holzstoß)* to be flaming up again.
Wiederaufforstung reafforestation.
wiederauffrischen, sein Englisch to refurbish (brush up) one's English; **Erinnerungen ~** to refresh memories.
Wieder|auffrischung refreshment, revival, brush-up; **~aufführung** rerun.
wiederauffüllen, Reservefonds to build up (replenish the) reserves; **seine Vorräte ~** to replenish one's stock.
Wiederauffüllung|des Kapitals von Aktienbanken reassessment of bank stocks; **~ des Lagers** replenishment of stock, replacement of the inventory; **~ der Vorräte** revictualling.
wiederaufgenommenes Verfahren new trial, retrial.
wiederaufheben to abolish, to abrogate, *(Gesetz)* to repeal; **Steuer ~** to rescind a tax.
Wiederaufhebung abrogation, repeal, rescission, abolishment; **~ eines Gesetzes** repeal of a law; **~ der Preiserhöhung** markup cancellation; **~ einer Steuer** rescission of a tax.
wiederaufkommen to revive, *(Mode)* to come into fashion again.
wiederaufladen, Batterie to recharge a battery.
Wiederaufleben *(Aufruhr)* recrudescence, *(Markt)* revival, recovery;
~ der Bürgerunruhen recrudescence of civil disorder; **~ einer verjährten Forderung** revival of a debt barred by the statute of limitations; **~ der Inflation** inflation revival; **~ einer Versicherung** reinstatement of an insurance.
wiederaufleben *(Aufruhr)* to recrudesce, *(Markt)* to revive, to recover, *(Streit)* to flare up again, to recrudesce, *(Vertrag)* to revive;
alte Sitten ~ lassen to resurrect an ancient custom; **widerrufenes Testament ~ lassen** to revive a will; **Versicherung ~ lassen** to reinstate an insurance; **Vertrag ~ lassen** to revive a contract.
Wiederauflebenlassen|einer Versicherung reinstatement of an insurance; **~ eines Vertrages** revival of a contract.
Wiederauflebensklausel revival clause.
wiederauflegen to republish.
Wiederaufnahme *(Klinik)* readmission;
~ des Anleihezinsendienstes resumption of the service of a loan; **~ der Arbeit** resumption of (return to) work; **~ diplomatischer Beziehungen** re-establishment of diplomatic relations; **~ der Dividendenzahlungen** resumption of dividends; **~ der Geschäftstätigkeit** resumption of business; **~ der Goldzahlungen** resumption of specie payments; **~ von Prämienzahlungen** reinstatement of an insurance policy; **~ eines lange nicht mehr gespielten Stücks** revival of a play; **~ des Verfahrens (der Verhandlung)** reopening a case, new trial, revivor; **~ von Verhandlungen** renewal of negotiations, renegotiation exercise; **~ der Zahlungen** resumption of payments; **~ von Zuschußzahlungen** resumption of a grant;
~ des Verfahrens anordnen to grant a new trial; **einer Verkehrsgesellschaft die ~ des Omnibusverkehrs gestatten** to enable a company to resume normal bus service;
~antrag petition in (suggestion of) error, bill of revivor, further consideration *(Br.)*; **durch außergewöhnliche Umstände bedingter ~antrag** extraordinary motion of new trial; **~fall** case for new trial; **~genehmigung** certificate of assize; **~klausel für Lohnverhandlungen** wage reopening clause; **~verfahren** reopening a case, rehearing, new trial, retrial; **~verfahren beantragen** to file a motion for a new trial.
wiederaufnehmen, Arbeit to resume work; **diplomatische Beziehungen ~** to re-establish diplomatic relations; **Debatte ~** to renew a debate; **Geschäftstätigkeit ~** to resume business; **in eine Klinik ~** to readmit into hospital; **Korrespondenz mit jem. ~** to resume correspondence with s. o.; **Prozeß ~** to revive an action; **seine Tätigkeit ~** to resume one's activities; **Verfahren ~** to reopen a case, to resume proceedings; **Verhandlungen ~** to resume negotations; **Zahlungen ~** to resume payments; **Zinsendienst einer Anleihe ~** to resume the service of a loan.
wiederaufrüsten to rearm.
Wiederaufrüstung rearmament;
moralische ~ moral rearmament.
Wiederaufschwung economic recovery, revival, upswing; **konjunktureller ~** economic recovery, upturn in business; **~ der Wirtschaft** economic rebounds.
Wieder|aufstieg resurgence; **~auftauchen** recurrence, *(pol.)* comeback, *(U-Boot)* surfacing.
wiederauftauchen *(Person)* to turn up, to reappear, *(Thema)* to crop up again, to come back to the surface, *(Zweifel)* to come back.
wiederaufwerten to revaluate, to revalorize *(US)*.
Wieder|aufwertung revaluation, revalorization *(US)*; **~ausbürgerung** denaturalization; **~ausfuhr** re-export[ation].

wiederausführen to re-export, to reship.
Wieder|ausfuhrgüter re-exports; ~**ausfuhrhandel** re-export (entrepot) trade; ~**ausfuhrverbot** re-export prohibition; ~**ausgabe** *(Banknoten)* reissue.
wiederausgeben *(Banknoten)* to reissue.
wiederbefestigen, sich *(Börse)* to recover, to revive.
Wiederbefestigung *(Börse)* recovery, revival.
wiederbegeben to reissue.
Wiederbeginn recommencement, *(Schule)* reopening;
~ **des Gerichtsbetriebes** opening of the courts.
wiederbeginnen to commence again, to recommence, *(Schule)* to reopen;
Arbeit ~ to resume work.
Wiederbegründung des Wohnsitzes resumption of residence.
wiederbekommen to recover, to get back;
sein Geld ~ to recover one's money; **sein ganzes Vermögen** ~ to recover (retrieve) one's fallen fortunes.
wiederbeladen to reload.
wiederbeleben to revitalize;
j. ~ to recall s. o. to life; **sich** ~ *(Börse)* to revive, to recover; **Kapitalmarkt** ~ to revitalize the capital market; **Konjunktur** ~ to revive economic activity; **Partei** ~ to resuscitate a party.
Wiederbelebung *(Börse)* recovery, revival;
konjunkturelle ~ trade revival;
~ **alten Brauchtums** revival of an old custom; ~ **der Inflation** inflationary revival; ~ **des Kapitalmarktes** revitalization of the capital market; ~ **der Nachkriegszeit** postwar economic recovery; ~ **des Verbrauchermarktes** revival of consumption; ~ **der Wirtschaft** trade (economic) revival, trade recovery, revival (reanimation, recovery) of trade; ~ **des Wohnungsbaumarktes** recovery in housing;
~ **der Investitionstätigkeit auslösen** to trigger an investment recovery.
Wiederbelebungs|phase take-off phase; ~**versuche bei jem. machen** to attempt to restore s. o. to life.
Wiederbelieferung resupply.
wiederbeschaffen to replace, to repurchase.
Wiederbeschaffung replacement, repurchase.
Wiederbeschaffungs|bedarf replacement needs; ~**kosten** replacement (reproduction, repurchase) cost, cost of reproduction; ~**praxis** replacement practice; ~**preis** replacement price; ~**programm** replacement program(me); ~**satz** replacement rate; ~**wert** replacement-cost standard (value), market price *(US)*.
wiederbeschäftigen to re-employ, to re-engage, to rehire *(US)*.
Wiederbeschäftigung re-employment, re-engagement, rehiring *(US)*.
wiederbesetzen to reoccupy;
Lehrstuhl ~ to fill a vacant chair.
Wiederbesetzung reoccupation.
wiederbesiedeln to recolonize, to resettle.
Wieder|besiedlung resettlement, recolonization; ~**besitzergreifung** re-entry; ~**bestallung** reappointment.
wiederbevölkern, sich to repopulate.
Wiederbevölkerung repopulation.
wiederbezahlen to refund, to reimburse, to repay.
Wiederbezahlung refunding, reimbursement.
wiederbringen to restore, to return.
Wieder|bringung restoration; **genauer (getreuer)** ~**druck** facsimile reprint; ~**einbau** reinstalment, reinstallation.
wiedereinberufen to resummon, to reconvene.
Wiedereinberufung reconvention.
wiedereinbringen to recover, to repair;
Verlust ~ to retrieve (make up for) a loss; **vollständig** ~ to recoup.
Wiedereinbringung eines Verlustes recovery of a loss.
wiedereinbürgern to repatriate.
Wiedereinbürgerung repatriation.
wiedereindecken, sich to replenish one's supply.
wiedereinfallen, jem. to come back to s. o.
Wiedereinfuhr reimportation;
zollfreie ~ duty-free return;
~**genehmigung** bill of stores.
wiedereinführen to reintroduce, to re-establish, *(Ware)* to reimport;
Wertpapiere ~ to reintroduce securities to the stock exchange.
Wiedereinführung reintroduction, *(Waren)* reimportation;
~ **der Todesstrafe** return of the death penalty; ~ **von Wertpapieren** reintroduction of securities to the market.
Wiedereingang|von Geldbeträgen returns; ~ **einer versehentlich geleisteten Zahlung** recovery of payment made by mistake.
wiedereingesetzt werden *(Eigentümer)* to be in remitter.
wiedereingliedern to resettle, to rehabilitate;
Straftäter ~ to resettle offenders.
Wiedereingliederung resettlement, rehabilitation;
berufliche ~ vocational rehabilitation (resettlement); **berufliche und soziale** ~ rehabilitation and resettlement; **wirtschaftliche** ~ industrial rehabilitation;
~ **von Berufsunfähigen** rehabilitation of disabled men, disablement resettlement; ~ **von Straftätern** resettlement of offenders.
Wiedereingliederungsfonds resettlement fund;
~ **des Europarates für nationale Flüchtlinge und Bevölkerungsüberschüsse** Council of Europe Resettlement Fund for National Refugees and Overpopulation.
wiedereinlagern to rewarehouse.
Wieder|einlagerung rewarehousing ~**einlassungskarte** return check; ~**einlieferung** recommittal.
wiedereinlösen to redeem, *(Pfand)* to take out of pawn.
Wieder|einlösung redemption; ~**einlösung eines Pfands** redemption of a pledge; ~**einnahme** recapture.
wiedereinnehmen, seinen Platz to resume one's place; **Stadt** ~ to recapture a city.
Wieder|einräumung des Besitzes resumption of possession; ~**einreiseerlaubnis** re-entry permit.
wieder|einrenken to straighten out; ~**einrichten** to reorganize, to re-establish, *(Wohnung)* to refurnish; ~**einschiffen** to reembark.
Wiedereinschiffung re-embarkation.
wiedereinschlafen *(Briefwechsel)* to peter out.
wiedereinsetzen to restore, to reinstate, to reinstall, to reappoint, to rehabilitate;
jem. in seinen Besitz ~ to re-establish s. o. in his possession; **Herrscher** ~ to restore a prince to the throne; **Verfahren in den vorherigen Stand** ~ to reinstate a case, to restore to its original condition.
Wiedereinsetzung reinstal(l)ment, reappointment, reinstatement, reconstitution, restoration, *(in frühere Rechte)* rehabilitation;
~ **nach Versäumnisurteil bewilligen** to open a default *(US)*.
wiedereinstellen to re-employ, to re-enlist, to re-engage, to rehire *(US)*, to hire back *(US)*;
sich ~ to turn up again; **Angestellten** ~ to restore an employee in his old post; **Arbeiter** ~ to reinstate workers.
Wiedereinstellung re-employment, re-engagement, reinstatement, re-enlistment, rehiring *(US)*, reappointment;
~ **aus dem Wehrverhältnis Entlassener** reinstatement in civil employment.
Wiedereinstellungs|empfehlung re-engagement recommendation; ~**verfügung** reinstatement order.
Wiedereintrag re-entry.
wiedereintragen to re-enter, to reregister.
Wiedereintragung reregistration, re-entry.
wiedereintreten to re-enter, *(mil.)* to re-enlist;
in die Verhandlung ~ to reopen a hearing.
Wiedereintritt re-entrance, re-entry, *(mil.)* re-enlistment, *(Ereignis)* recurrence, *(Satellit)* re-entry;
~ **in die Schule** going back to school; ~ **in die Verhandlung** reopening of a hearing.
Wieder|eintrittsbahn *(Raumschiff)* re-entry trajectory; ~**einweisung** recommittal; ~**entdeckung** rediscovery.
wiederergreifen to reseize.
wiedererhalten to recover, to retrieve, to get back;
Besitz ~ to repossess.
Wiedererhaltung recovery.
wiedererholen to recover.
Wiedererkennen *(Anzeige)* recognition.
wiedererkennen, sich to recognize each other.
Wiedererkennungstest recognition test, *(mit zusätzlicher Kontrolle)* controlled recognition test.
wiedererlangbar recoverable, repleviable.
Wiedererlangbarkeit recoverableness.
wiedererlangen to reacquire, to recover, to resume, *(gepfändeten Gegenstand)* to replevy;
seinen Besitz ~ to recover possession by law; **sein Eigentum** ~ to recover title; **seine Rechte** ~ to redeem one's rights; **sein verlorenes Vermögen** ~ to recover one's fallen fortune.
Wiedererlangung recovery, reacquisition, getting back;
gesetzliche ~ recovery at law;
~ **des Eigentums** recovery of title; ~ **des Führerscheins** removal of disqualification; ~ **eines gepfändeten Gegenstands** replevin; ~ **eines Grundstücks** recovery of land; ~ **gestohlener Güter**

recovery of stolen goods; ~ **einer verlorenen Sache** recovery of a lost article; ~ **seines Vermögens** retrieval of one's fortune; ~ **einer versehentlich geleisteten Zahlung** recovery of payment made by mistake.
wiederernennen to reappoint.
Wiederernennung reappointment.
Wiedereroberung des Marktes recapture of the market.
wiedereröffnen to reopen;
Geschäft ~ to resume business; **Verhandlung** ~ to resume a trial.
Wieder|eröffnung der Börsen reopening of the security exchanges; ~**eröffnung der Verhandlung** resumption of a trial; ~**errichtung gewerblicher Anlagen** reconstruction of works; ~**errichtungskosten** replacement cost; ~**erscheinen** reappearance.
wiedererscheinen to reappear, *(Zeitung)* to resume publication; **Buch** ~ **lassen** to republish a book.
wiedererstatten to restore, to restitute, to replace, *(Steuern)* to refund;
jem. seine Auslagen ~ to reimburse s. o. for his costs.
Wiedererstattung restitution, restoration, *(Steuern)* refunding, *(Summe)* repayment;
~ **von Auslagen** reimbursement of expenses incurred.
Wieder|erteilung new issue, reissue; ~**erwerb** reacquisition.
wiederfinden to find, to recover;
sein Selbstvertrauen ~ to regain one's self-confidence; **verlorene Warenpartie** ~ to trace lost goods.
Wiederflottmachung eines Schiffes refloating a ship.
Wiedergabe *(Bericht)* account, report, description, *(Herstellung)* reproduction, *(Musikstück)* interpretation, *(Rückgabe)* restitution, return, presentment, *(Schallaufzeichnung)* playback, *(Übersetzung)* translation, rendition;
freie ~ paraphrase; **genaue** ~ faithful reproduction, *(Bericht)* exact account; **klangliche** ~ sound reproduction; **mechanische** ~ mechanical reproduction; **naturgetreue** ~ *(Bild)* fidelity, *(Ton)* high fidelity; **wörtliche** ~ verbatim account; **wortwörtliche** ~ **einer Rede** word-for-word repetition of a speech; ~ **einer Rundfunkübertragung** recorded broadcast; ~ **eines Zitats** quotation of a passage;
es mit der ~ **von Tatsachen nicht besonders genau nehmen** to relate facts with considerable latitude;
~**gerät** playback unit; ~**gerät für Farbfernsehfilmbänder** colo(u)r videotape player; ~**qualität** quality of reproduction; ~**taste** playback button; ~**treue** reproduction fidelity.
wiedergeben to give back, to restore, to return, to restitute, *(abspielen)* to play back, *(beschreiben)* to describe, to give a description, *(herstellen)* to reproduce, *(übersetzen)* to translate, to render, *(zitieren)* to quote;
einem Angestellten seine alte Stellung ~ to restore an employee in his old place (post); **beschlagnahmtes Eigentum** ~ to restore confiscated property; **Eigentum dem rechtmäßigen Eigentümer** ~ to return property to its rightful owner; **Ereignisse genauestens** ~ to describe a course of events precisely; **Freiheit** ~ to restore freedom; **Gedicht vollendet** ~ to recite a poem perfectly; **zuviel gezahltes Geld** ~ to return an overpaid amount; **Geschichte falsch** ~ to falsify a story; **Meinung einer Menschenmenge** ~ to voice the feelings of a crowd; **Musik verzerrt** ~ to give a distorted reproduction of a piece of music; **Stelle** ~ to reproduce a passage; **wortgetreu** ~ to report fully.
Wiedergeburt new birth.
Wiedergesundung recovery;
~ **der Wirtschaft** business recovery.
wiedergewählt, mit überwältigender Mehrheit overwhelmingly reelected.
wiedergewährung renewed grant.
wiedergewinnen to recover, to recuperate, to regain, *(Material)* to reclaim, *(mil.)* to make up for lost ground;
seine Autorität ~ to recover one's authority; **seine Fassung** ~ to regain one's composure.
Wiedergewinnung recovery, recuperation, retrieval, *(Material)* reclamation, recovery, salvage;
~ **eines Grundstücks** recovery of land; ~ **eines Marktes** regaining of a market; ~ **von Nebenprodukten** recovery of byproducts.
Wiedergewinnungsverfahren process of recovery.
wiedergutgebracht recredited.
wiedergutmachen to restitute, to repair, to recompense, to redeem, to make good, to make amends (it up), to right, to indemnify;
Schäden ~ to redress injuries; **Unrecht** ~ to repair a wrong; **Verluste** ~ to make up for a loss, to recover one's losses.
Wiedergutmachung restitution, restoration, reparation, retrieval, indemnification, amends, redress, *(Buße)* atonement money;
als ~ in satisfaction of;
~ **eines Verlusts** recoupment (recovery) of a loss.
Wiedergutmachungs|abkommen reparations agreement, restitution treaty; ~**angelegenheiten** restitution case; ~**anspruch** restitution claim; ~**berechtigter** restitutee; ~**kommission** Reparation Committee; ~**leistungen** restitution (reparation) payments; **Wohlfahrts- und** ~**organisation der UN** United Nations Relief and Rehabilitation Administration; ~**plan** reparation scheme; ~**sache** restitution case; ~**zahlungen leisten** to pay reparations.
wiedergutzumachen, nicht irreparable, irretrievable.
Wiederheirat remarriage.
wiederheiraten to marry again, to remarry.
wiederherrichten *(Haus)* to redecorate, *(Straße)* to repair, to mend.
wiederherstellen to re-establish, to restore, to renovate, to restitute, *(Rechte)* to redintegrate, to reinstate;
Frieden ~ to restore peace; **Gebäude** ~ to restore a [ruined] building, to rebuild a house; **Kredit eines Unternehmens** ~ to re-establish a firm's credit; **Öffentlichkeit** ~ *(Gericht)* to restore publicity, to resume the trial in public; **öffentliche Sicherheit und Ordnung** ~ to restore public order; **Vollbeschäftigungszustand sofort** ~ to rush the economy back to full-employment levels; **früheren Zustand** ~ to restore the state of things; **ursprünglichen Zustand** ~ to restore in status quo ante.
Wiederhersteller repairer.
Wiederherstellung re-establishment, restoration, readjustment, repair, reparation, replacement, restoration, refection;
~ **eines Gebäudes** repair to (restoration of) a building; ~ **der Gesundheit** restoration from sickness; ~ **der ehelichen Lebensgemeinschaft** restitution of conjugal life; ~ **eines verfallenen Patents** restoration of a lapsed patent; ~ **von Rechten** restitution of rights; ~ **ehelicher Rechte** restitution of conjugal rights; ~ **der öffentlichen Sicherheit und Ordnung** restoration of (return to) public order; ~ **des internationalen Vertrauens** recovery of international credit; ~ **des ursprünglichen Zustands** restoration to its original condition.
Wiederherstellungs|anspruch restitutory right; ~**kosten** rehabilitation expenses, repairs (replacement) costs, costs of repairs; ~**urteil** writ of execution.
wiederherzustellen, nicht not to be repaired, irreparable.
wiederholen to repeat, *(Anzeige)* to rotate, *(Klasse)* to review, *(kurz zusammenfassen)* to recapitulate;
Fehler ~ to repeat a mistake; **Forderung** ~ to renew a claim; **Sendung** ~ to repeat a performance, to rebroadcast; **sich** ~ *(Ereignis)* to recur, to happen again; **stereotyp** ~ to stereotype; **Telegramm** ~ to repeat a telegram; **wortwörtlich** ~ to repeat literarily.
wiederholt time and again, time without number, repeatedly;
~**e Aufforderungen** repeated requests; ~**e Bitten** entreaties.
Wiederholung repetition, *(Film)* retake, *(Rückblende)* cutback, *(Rundfunk)* repeat, *(Schule)* review, *(Stichproben)* replication, *(Theater, Wahlen)* rerun, *(Zusammenfassung)* recapitulation, sum-up, summary;
~ **einer Beleidigung** libel's repetition; ~ **einer Werbeserie** rotation of a commercial.
Wiederholungs|anzeige repeat [ad], rerun; ~**aufnahme** *(Film)* retake; ~**auftrag** *(Reklame)* repeat order; ~**besuch** callback; ~**druck** reprint; **im** ~**fall** in case of repetition, *(Straftäter)* in case of a fresh offence; ~**honorar** repeat fee; ~**impfung** booster shot; ~**kurs** review (refresher, *US*) course; ~**prüfung** make-up *(coll.)*; ~**rabatt** *(Anzeige)* series discount; ~**schalter** *(Plattenspieler)* repeat switch; ~**sendung** *(Fernsehen)* rerun, *(Rundfunk)* rebroadcast, repeat performance, rediffusion; ~**spiel** replay; ~**stichprobe** duplicate sample; ~**taste** *(Computer)* repeat key.
Wieder|inbesitznahme retaking, resumption of possession, *(Grundstück)* re-entry, regress; ~**inbetriebnahme** *(Straße)* reopening; ~**indienststellung** *(Schiff)* recommissioning.
wiederindossieren to reindorse.
Wieder|ingangsetzung reactivation, *(Maschine)* restarting; ~**inkrafttreten** revival, *(Gesetz)* taking effect again; ~**inkrafttreten eines widerrufenen Testaments** revival of a revoked will; ~**inkurssetzung von Münzen** remonetization; ~**instandsetzung** refit, reconditioning, *(Haus)* repair; ~**instandsetzungskosten** repairs, cost of repair, reconditioning charge; ~**kauf** repurchase, resale, redemption; ~**käufe** repeat business.
wiederkaufen to repurchase, to rebuy, to buy back.

Wieder|käufer repurchaser; ~**kaufspreis** repurchase (redemption) price; ~**kaufsrecht** redemption right; **mit ~kaufsrecht verkaufen** to sell with option of repurchase; ~**kehr** comeback, recurrence, return, *(Jubiläum)* anniversary.
wiederkehren to return, to recur.
wiederkehrend recurrent, recurring;
nicht ~ nonrecurrent; **regelmäßig** ~ repetitive, periodical, circuit;
~**e Ausgaben** recurring expenses; ~**e Einkünfte** regular income; ~**e Nutzungen** recurring revenues; ~**e Zahlungen** revolving (periodical) payments.
wiederkommen to come back, to return.
Wiederlieferung short delivery.
wieder|prägen to recoin; ~**schicken** to send back.
Wiedersehens|fest feiern to kill the fatted calf; ~**treffen** reunion.
wieder|übernehmen to reassume; ~**übertragen** to reassign, to retransfer; ~**vereinigen** to reunite, to redintegrate; ~**vereinigt** reunited.
Wiedervereinigung reunification, redintegration.
Wiedervereinigungsprozeß process of reunification.
Wiederverfilmung remake.
wiederverfrachten to recharter, to reship.
Wiederverfrachtung recharter, reshipment.
wiederverheiraten, sich to marry again, to remarry.
Wieder|verheiratung second marriage, remarriage; ~**verkauf** resale, reselling.
wiederverkaufen to sell again (by, at, retail), to resell, to retail.
Wiederverkäufer reseller, dealer's buyer, *(Einzelhändler)* retailer, retail dealer, *(Zwischenhändler)* middleman;
Lieferung nur an ~ supplied to trade only;
an ~ abgeben (verkaufen) to sell to the trade;
~**preis** resale (trade, dealer's, retail) price; ~**rabatt** distributor (trade) discount.
wiederverkäuflich resalable.
Wiederverkaufs|bestimmungen trade terms; ~**gewinn** resale profit; ~**preis** [fixed] retail (reserved, resale, dealer's resale, trade) price; ~**recht** right to resell; ~**skonto** trade discount; ~**vereinbarung** resale agreement; ~**wert** resale value.
wiederverladen to reload, to reship *(US)*.
Wiederverladung reloading, reshipment *(US)*.
wiedervermieten to relet, *(an Untermieter)* to sublet, to underlet.
Wieder|vermietung reletting; ~**veröffentlichung** republication.
wiederverpachten to regrant.
wiederverpacken to repack, to regrant *(Br.)*.
Wiederverpackung regrant *(Br.)*.
wiederverpfänden to rehypothecate.
Wiederverpfändung rehypothecation *(US)*.
wiederverpflichten *(mil.)* to re-enlist.
Wieder|verpflichtung *(mil.)* re-enlistment; ~**versendung** reshipment; ~**vertagung** readjournment.
wiederverwendbare Packung dual-usage package.
wiederverwenden to reuse, to re-employ, *(Müll)* to recycle.
Wieder|verwendung reuse, re-employment, re-enlistment; ~**verwertung** reutilization, *(Müll)* recycling.
wiedervorbringen to bring up again.
Wieder|vorführung *(Film)* rerun; ~**vorlage** return reference, resubmission; ~**vorlagemappe** calendar (follow-up, tickler) file; ~**vorlageverfahren** follow-up system.
Wiederwahl re-election, return;
seine ~ betreiben to plan to seek re-election; **sich zur ~ aufstellen lassen** to run for re-election; **sich turnusmäßig zur ~ stellen** to stand for re-election in rotation.
wieder|wählbar eligible for re-election; ~**wählen** to re-elect.
Wieder|zulassung readmission, readmittance; ~**zusammenfassung** regrouping.
wiederzusammentreten to reconvene, to reassemble.
wiederzustellen *(Prozeßakten)* to return.
Wiederzustellung der Prozeßakten return of records.
Wiege, von der ~ bis zur Bahre from cradle to grave;
~ **der schönen Künste** home of the fine arts; ~ **der westlichen Zivilisation** cradle of Western culture;
~**brücke** weighbridge; ~**geld**, ~**gebühr** weighing cost, weighage *(Br.)*; ~**karte** scale ticket; ~**löscher** rocker blotter; ~**meister** weighmaster.
wiegen, brutto to weigh in the gross; **j. in falschen Hoffnungen** ~ to lull s. o. with false hopes; **Kind in den Schlaf** ~ to rock a child to sleep; **mehr** ~ to outweigh; **nachdenklich seinen Kopf** ~ to shake one's head pensively; **j. in Sicherheit** ~ to lull s. o. into a false sense of security; **12 Tonnen brutto** ~ to weigh in at 12 tons.
Wiege|schein weight note; ~**stempel** weight stamp; ~**zettel** weight slip.

Wiese meadow, grassland, pasture [field].
Wiesel, flink wie ein fast as a hare, like a streak of lightning.
Wiesenparzelle green-field site.
Wild, erlegtes kill; **jagdbares** ~ fair game, beast of the chase;
~ **hegen** to preserve game.
wild wild, savage, like the devil, *(wütend)* raging, furious, mad;
~ **und gefährlich** *(Verbrecher)* unruly and dangerous;
alles ~ durcheinanderwerfen to make a complete muddle of everything; **j. ~ machen** to put s. one's monkey up, to get s. one's goat *(sl.)*; ~ **um sich schlagen** to lash out wildly; **ganz ~ auf etw. sein** to be crazy (mad) about s. th.; **ganz ~ werden** to see red;
~**er Anschlag** fly posting, sniping; **Publikum in ~e Begeisterung versetzen** to raise an audience to absolute frenzy; ~**er Boden** virgin soil; ~**er Buchmacher** unlicensed bookmaker; ~**e Ehe** concubinage; **in ~er Flucht** in a headlong flight; ~**er Handel** under-the-counter (illicit) trade; ~**er Kerl** wild fellow; ~**es Kind** wild (unruly) child; ~**er Mann** bugaboo, bugbear; ~**e See** tempestuous sea; ~**e Spekulation** wildcat finances; ~**er Stamm** savage tribe; ~**er Streik** outlaw (wildcat, hit-and-run) strike; ~**er Streiker** wildcat striker; ~**es Tier** wild animal; ~**es Treiben** whirl, goings-on; ~**e Triebe** rank shoots; ~**e Vermutungen** wild guesses; ~**es Zelten** unauthorized camping.
Wild|bach torrent; **freie ~bahn** wildlife; **in freier ~bahn** in the wild; ~**bestand** stock of game; ~**bret** game.
Wilde|r savage;
wie zehn nackte ~ angeben to shoot a line *(sl.)*; **sich wie ein ~r gebärden** to act like a madman; **wie die ~n hausen** to be living in savagery.
Wilderer poacher.
Wildern poaching.
wildern, in jds. Revier to go out poaching on a neighbo(u)r's land.
Wild|falle buckstall; ~**gatter** paddock; ~**gehege** game preserve, live park, vivary *(Br.)*; ~**gehegereservat** free warren.
wildgeworden running wild.
Wildhüter game warden, gamekeeper *(Br.)*, preserver *(Br.)*.
Wildnis wilderness.
Wild|park preserve, game reserve, live park; ~**reservat** wildlife refuge, game preserve; **wie eine ~sau fahren** to drive like a madman; ~**schaden** damage caused by game; ~**schutzgebiet** wildlife sanctuary.
Wildwest|film western, oater *(sl.)*, oats (horse) opera *(sl.)*; ~**roman** Wild West novel; ~**schau** Wild-West show, rodeo.
Wilhelm, den dicken ~ markieren to act the big cheese; **seinen Friedrich ~ darunter setzen** to put one's John Hancock on it *(US)*.
Wille will, intention, volition, *(Absicht)* purpose, *(Begehren)* wish, design;
aus freiem ~n voluntary, of one's own accord; **beim besten ~n nicht** not for the life of me;
eiserner ~ iron will *(fam.)*; **erklärter** ~ declared intention; **auf das Eingehen gesetzlicher Verpflichtungen gerichteter** ~ intention to create legal obligations; **letzter** ~ last will and testament; **unbändiger** ~ unbending will;
wirklicher ~ des Erblassers intendment of testator; ~ **des Gesetzgebers** legislative intent;
schon den guten ~n anerkennen to take the will for the deed; **jem. seinen ~n aufzwingen** to enforce one's will upon s. o.; **seinen ~n äußern** to give expression to one's will; **guten ~n beweisen** to show willing *(sl.)*; **seinen ~n dokumentieren** to give expression to one's will; **nach seinem freien ~n handeln** to have free agency; **seinen ~n kundtun** to communicate one's intention, to make known one's pleasure; **jem. seinen ~n lassen** to give s. o. way to work his will, to let s. o. have his way; **jem. zu ~n sein** to yield (submit) to s. o.; **seinen guten ~n unter Beweis stellen** to prove one's good will; **etw. aus freiem ~n tun** to do s. th. of one's own volition.
willenlos will-less, involuntary;
jem. ~ die Führung überlassen to submit meakly to s. one's leadership;
~**e Handlung** involuntary action; ~**es Werkzeug** mere tool (instrument).
Willens|änderung change of mind; ~**akt** spontaneous act; ~**äußerung** expression of one's will; **freie und ungehinderte ~ausübung** free exercise of independent will; **freie ~bestimmung** free will; ~**einigung** *(Vertragsschluß)* meeting of minds; **mangelnde ~einigung** absence of assent; ~**entscheidung** volition; **freie ~entschließung** one's own accord.
Willenserklärung expression of one's will, declaration of intention;

einseitige ~ unilateral declaration; **hoheitliche** ~ act of state; **politische** ~ policy statement; **rechtsgeschäftliche** ~ legal act, act of party; **stillschweigende** ~ implied intention;
~ **abgeben** to express (declare) one's intention.
Willens | fähigkeit willing faculty; ~**freiheit** freedom of the will, free will; ~**handlung** voluntary act; **unbeeinflußte** ~**handlung** mere motion; ~**kraft** will power, volitional faculty, backbone; ~**kundgebung** communication of intention; ~**mangel** defective intention; **allgemeine** ~**richtung** general intent; ~**übereinstimmung** mutual assent, meeting of minds, consensus ad idem *(lat.)*; **fehlende** ~**übereinstimmung** absence of assent.
willfahren to comply with, to accede to;
jds. Bitte ~ to accede to s. one's wish; **jds. Launen** ~ to gratify s. one's whims.
willfährig compliant, complaisant, obsequious, obliging, docile, manageable, willing, ready to act;
sich ~ **verhalten** to behave compliantly;
~**er Arbeiter** willing worker.
Willfährigkeit willingness, compliance.
Willkommen welcome;
eisiges ~ wintry greeting.
willkommen, jem. ~ **heißen** to bid s. o. welcome, to extend a welcome to s. o.
Willkommensschmaus veranstalten to kill the fatted calf.
Willkür arbitrariness, highhandedness, *(Ermessen)* discretion;
jds. ~ **ausgeliefert sein** to be put to (be at) s. one's mercy;
~**akt,** ~**handlung** discretionary action, arbitrary act (action), despotic act; ~**herrschaft** arbitrary government, despotism, high hand, tyranny; ~**justiz** Star-Chamber justice.
willkürlich arbitrary, wanton, *(unbegründet)* gratuitous, without good ground;
~**e Annahme** ungrounded assumption; ~**e Anwendung** arbitrary use; ~**e Auswahl treffen** to choose at random; ~**e Entscheidung** arbitrary decision; ~**e Kündigung** arbitrary notice; ~**er Nullpunkt** *(Statistik)* arbitrary origin; ~**er Preis** arbitrary price.
Willkürlichkeit arbitrariness, license, licence.
wimmeln to swarm, to be crowded with, to teem with people;
von Fehlern ~ to be teeming with mistakes.
wimmern to wail, to whimper;
vor Schmerzen ~ to wail with pain.
wimmernd wailing.
Wimpel pennon, pennant, streamer, guidon, pelmet, whip.
Wimper, nicht mit der ~ **zucken** not to turn a hair (stir an eyelid, move a muscle).
Wind, gegen den into the teeth of the wind, up; **in den** ~ **geschrieben** written on water;
auflandiger ~ onshore wind; **durchdringender** ~ piercing wind; **günstige** ~**e** prosperous (fair, friendly) winds; **heftiger** ~ high wind; **umspringender** ~ baffling wind; **ungünstiger** ~ contrary wind; **wechselnde** ~**e** variable winds;
frischer ~ **in den Segeln** *(fig.)* second wind;
dem ~ **aussetzen** to wind; ~ **von etw. bekommen** to get an inkling (hold, wind) of s. th.; **frischen** ~ **in etw. bringen** to make things hum; **sein Mäntelchen nach dem** ~**e hängen** to sail with every shift of the wind, to turn one's coat; **jem. den** ~ **aus den Segeln nehmen** to take the wind out of s. one's sails (the thunder out of s. one's approach); **der Kritik den** ~ **aus den Segeln nehmen** to disarm criticism; **in den** ~ **reden** to waste one's words; **in den** ~ **schlagen** to cast (fling) to the winds; **Rat in den** ~ **schlagen** to throw advice away, to set advice at nought; **sich wie der** ~ **verbreiten** *(Nachricht)* to spread like wildfire; **jem.** ~ **vormachen** to pull the wool over s. o.; **in alle** ~**e verstreut werden** to be blown to the four winds;
wissen, woher der ~ **bläst** to know how the land lies;
~**abnahme** abating of the wind; ~**änderung** change of wind; ~**beutel** whiffler, windbag; ~**blende errichten** to erect a protection against the wind; ~**bö[e]** gust [of wind]; ~**bruch** wind shake, windbreak, blow down *(US)*.
windbrüchig windfallen.
Winddruck wind pressure;
~**messer** wind gauge, anemometer.
Windel napkin *(Br.)*, nappy *(coll.)*, diaper *(US)*;
noch in den ~**n liegen** *(fig.)* to be still in swaddling clothes.
windelweich schlagen to reduce to pulp.
winden *(Blumen)* to bind, *(Garn)* to reel, to wind;
sich ~ to wind, to bend, *(Bach)* to meander, to brook; **sich wie ein Aal** ~ to wriggle like an eel; **sich durch eine Menschenmenge** ~ to worm one's way through the crowd; **sich vor Schmerzen** ~ to writhe with pain; **sich durch ein Tal** ~ *(Straße)* to weave through a valley.

Winderosion wind erosion.
Windeseile, mit in no time, in a jiffy, like a house on fire.
Wind | fahne anemoscope; ~**fang** *(Haus)* fly, airtrap, porch.
windgeschützt windproof;
~**e Stelle** lee.
Wind | geschwindigkeit wind speed; ~**hose** wind spout, dust devil, tornado.
windig windy, *(fig.)* shaky, unreliable, phony *(US sl.)*;
~**e Ausrede** flimsy excuse; ~**e Ecke** drafty corner.
Wind | jacke windcheater *(Br.)*; ~**jammer** windjammer; ~**kanal** wind tunnel; ~**laterne** hurricane lamp; ~**licht** storm lantern; ~**mühle** windmill; **gegen** ~**mühlen kämpfen** to tilt at windmills; ~**mühlenflügel** windmill sail.
windrichtig windway.
Wind | richtung wind direction; **in** ~**richtung** before the wind; ~**richtungsanzeiger** *(Flugplatz)* wind indicator; ~**rose** wind rose; ~**schatten** lee; **im** ~**schatten eines Busses fahren** to drive leeward of a bus; ~**schutzscheibe** windscreen *(Br.)*, windshield *(US)*; ~**schutzscheibe belüften** to demist the windscreen *(Br.)* (windshield, *US*); ~**seite** weather (wind) side; ~**stärke** wind force, wind speed; ~**stoß** gust, squall, flurry, flaw, waff *(Br.)*; **heftiger** ~**stoß** windflow.
Windung winding, twist, *(Fluß, Weg)* bend, turn, meander, winding, *(Krümmung)* wriggle;
~**en einer Straße** ins and outs of a street.
windwärts windward.
Windwiderstand wind drag.
Wink hint, intimation, cue, tip, inkling, nudge, nod, wrinkle, office *(sl.)*;
verstohlener ~ oblique hint;
~ **mit einer Flagge** wave of a flag; ~ **mit der Hand** wave of the hand; ~ **mit dem Zaunpfahl** broad hint;
jem. einen ~ **geben** to tip s. o. off, to give s. o. a wrinkle, to nudge s. o.; **jem. verstohlen einen** ~ **geben** to tip s. o. the wink; **jem. auf den leisesten** ~ **zur Verfügung stehen** to be at s. one's beck and call; ~ **verstehen** to take up the cue.
Winkel angle, *(Ecke)* corner, nook, cranny;
im entlegendsten ~ at a remote place, off the beaten track; **stiller** ~ recess, retreat, quiet nook; **toter** ~ blind (dead) angle, dead space, blind area;
~ **von 30 Grad** angle of 30 degrees;
in jedem ~ **nach etw. suchen** to search for s. th. in every nook and corner (cranny); **sich in einen** ~ **verkriechen** to creep into a corner;
~**advokat** hedge lawyer, pettifogger, pettifogging (hedge) lawyer, hack attorney, guttersnipe *(US)*, shyster *(US sl.)*; ~**aufträge durchführen** to bucket orders; ~**bankier** keeper of a bucket shop; ~**börse** bucket shop *(US)*; ~**börsenspekulant** speculator outside the stock exchange, bucketeer *(US)*; ~**konsulent** shyster *(US sl.)*; ~**makler** outside (street, *US*) broker, guttersnipe *(US)*, bucketeer *(US)*; ~**messer** protractor; ~**zug** wimple, tergiversation, prevarication, doubling; **durch einen geschickten** ~**zug** by a clever dodge; ~**züge** tricks, ins; ~**züge machen** to prevaricate, to tergiversate, to shuffle, to dodge.
winken, mit der Hand to wave one's hand; **dem Kellner** ~ to signal to the waiter; **einer Taxe** ~ to hail a taxi; **jem. mit dem Zaunpfahl** ~ to drop s. o. a broad hint.
Winker *(Auto)* traffic (direction) indicator, hand signal;
automatisch abschaltender ~ self-cancelling direction indicator;
~**arm** indicator arm.
winkt, ihm ~ **ein Geldpreis** he can expect a cash prize; **ihm** ~ **eine Tracht Prügel** he is in for a good hiding.
winseln, um Gnade to cringe for mercy.
Winter, im tiefsten in the depth (deep, heart) of winter; **mitten im kalten** ~ in the dead of winter;
strenger ~ hard winter;
durch den ~ **füttern** to winterfeed; **über den** ~ **hinweghelfen** to tide over the winter;
~**arbeitslosigkeit** winter-induced unemployment; ~**aufenthalt** winter abode; ~**ausrüstung** *(Auto)* winter equipment; ~**bewohner** winter resident; ~**fahrplan** winter timetable (schedule) *(US)*.
winterfest machen, Auto to winterize a car.
Winter | garten winter garden, conservatory *(Br.)*; ~**gäste** winter visitors; ~**getreide** winter crop; ~**katalog** winter catalog(ue); ~**kurort** winter resort; ~**lager** winter stock, *(mil.)* winter quarter.
winterlich | er Spitzenbedarf winter peak in demand; ~**es Wetter** wintry weather.

Winter|pause layoff in winter; ~**quartier** *(mil.)* winter quarters; ~**quartier beziehen** to go into winter quarters; ~**sachen** winter clothes; ~**saison** winter season; ~**schlaf halten** to hibernate, to den up *(US)*; ~**schlußverkauf** winter sales *(US)*, January sales *(Br.)*; ~**semester** winter term; ~**sport** winter sports; ~**sportplatz** winter sport (ski) resort; ~**vorräte anlegen** to lay in supplies (stores) for the winter; ~**weizen** winter wheat; ~**wetter** wintry weather.

Winzer winegrower;
~**fest** vintage festival; ~**genossenschaft** winegrowers' co-operative.

winzig tiny, wee, teeny, miniscule;
~ **klein** teeny-weeny;
~**er Unterschied** minute difference.

Wirbel whirl, twirl, *(fig.)* fuss, ado, to-do, *(im Wasser)* vortex, eddy, whirlpool;
~ **der Ereignisse** whirligig of events; ~ **gesellschaftlicher Veranstaltungen** vortex of the season;
zu einem ziemlichen ~ **im Dörfchen führen** to cause quite a stir in the village; ~ **machen** to stir the pot; **viel** ~ **machen** to make heavy weather; ~ **auf der Trommel schlagen** to roll the drum;
~**sturm** whirlwind, cyclone, tornado, twister *(US)*, hurricane, whirlicane, vortex.

wirbelsturmartig tornadic.

Wirbel|sturmzentrum eye of a storm, storm center *(US)* (centre, *Br.)*; ~**wind** whirlwind, whirlblast.

Wirken activity, functioning, operation, performance;
segensreiches ~ fruitful work.

wirken to be active, to function, *(Gesetz)* to operate, to be effective, *(weben)* to weave;
anspornend ~ to be encouraging; **wie ausgestorben** ~ to look deserted; **berauschend** ~ to have an intoxicating effect; **als Bremse** ~ to serve as brake; **stark auf Frauen** ~ to have a great appeal for women; **sehr jugendlich** ~ to have a very youthful appearance; **lächerlich** ~ to lay o. s. open to ridicule; **nachhaltig auf j.** ~ to make a lasting impression on s. o.; **schnell** ~ to have a prompt effect; **auf j. wie ein rotes Tuch** ~ to make s. o. see red; **Wunder** ~ to work miracles.

wirkend acting.

wirklich factual, real, actual, substantial, effective, intrinsic, true, genuine;
~ **verbrecherisch sein** to be a positive crime;
~**er Bedarf** effective demand; **nur den** ~ **Bedürftigen helfen** to help only the worthy poor; ~**er Bestand** *(mil.)* effective strength; ~**es Einkommen** real income; ~**er Künstler** real artist; ~**er Vorfall** matter of fact; ~**er Vorrat** visible supply; ~**er Wert** true (intrinsic, effective) value.

Wirklichkeit reality, actual fact, actuality, truth;
in ~ in effect;
rauhe ~ the hard facts;
sich auf den Boden der ~ **stellen** to start from reality; **in die** ~ **umsetzen** to materialize, to realize; ~ **werden** to come true, to materialize; **in die** ~ **zurückkehren** to come down to earth.

wirklichkeitsbezogen down-to-earth.

Wirklichkeitsflucht escapism.

wirklichkeitsfremd starry-eyed, unreal;
~**er Mensch** escapist *(US)*.

wirklichkeitsgetreu true to nature.

wirklichkeitsnah realistic, bread-and-butter-minded, down-to-earth;
~**es Programm** bread-and-butter program(me).

Wirklichkeitssinn common (horse, *US*) sense.

wirksam effective, operative, efficient, effectual, efficacious, *(gültig)* valid;
automatisch ~ automatically effective; **sehr** ~ powerful; **sofort** ~ immediately effective;
~ **bleiben** to remain in effect (operative); ~ **sein** to be operative (in force); ~ **werden** to take effect, to come into force (operation), to become operative; **wieder** ~ **werden** to revest;
~**e Blockade** effective blockade; **automatisch** ~**e Rückversicherung** treaty reinsurance; ~**e Schritte ergreifen** to take effectual steps; ~**e Unterstützung** effective support.

Wirksamkeit effectiveness, operative effect, operation, impressiveness, value, validity;
~ **der Verkaufstätigkeit** sales vigo(u)r;
in ~ **treten** to come into force; ~ **verlieren** to be deprived of effect, to become inoperative, to lose in presence.

Wirksamkeits|grad eines Gesetzes efficiency of a law; ~**prüfung** *(Anzeige)* impact test; ~**verhältnis** efficiency ratio.

Wirksamwerden coming into force.

wirksamwerdend executory.

Wirkung effect, operation, action, *(Anzeige)* appeal, *(Eindruck)* impression, impact, *(Ergebnis)* result;
mit ~ **vom** with effect from; **mit** ~ **vom 1. Juli** effective July 1st; **mit dinglicher** ~ touching the land; **mit geringer** ~ to little purpose; **mit sofortiger** ~ effective immediately, for immediate release; **ohne die geringste** ~ like water off a duck's back;
aufschiebende ~ delaying (suspensory) effect; **beschränkte** ~ limited operation; **bindende** ~ binding effect; **dramatische** ~ dramatic effect; **gesetzliche** ~ legal effect, operation of law; **kumulative** ~ cumulative effect; **nachteilige** ~**en** detrimental (disadvantageous) effects; **psychologische** ~ psychological impact; **rechtliche** ~ legal effect; **rechtserzeugende** ~ constitutive effect; **starke** ~ powerful effect; **verheerende** ~ destructive effect;
Ursache und ~ cause and effect;
packende ~ **eines Theaterstücks** grip of a play on the audience;
~ **eines Vertrages** operation of a contract;
~**en ausgleichen** to offset the effects; ~ **ausüben** to produce an effect; **starke** ~ **ausüben** to make a strong impression; **ohne** ~ **bleiben** to cut no ice; **richtig zur** ~ **bringen** to highlight; ~**en erzielen** to make inroads, to tell upon; ~ **haben** to operate as; **unter der** ~ **einer Droge stehen** to be under the influence of a drug; **seine** ~ **tun** to take effect; **seine** ~ **nicht verfehlen** to strike home; **in der** ~ **verpuffen** to run out of gas; ~ **zeitigen** to come home; **gewünschte** ~ **zeitigen** to have the desired effect; **nachhaltige** ~**en zeitigen** to have a bandwaggon effect; **schnelle** ~ **zeitigen** to operate quickly;
kleine Ursache, große ~ little strokes fell great oaks.

wirkungsarm feeble.

Wirkungs|bereich sphere of action, scope of activities, *(Gesetz)* sphere of operation; ~**gebiet** circle, sphere of influence, line; ~**grad** efficiency term, *(Anzeige)* sales impact, *(Maschine)* efficiency.

Wirkungskreis province, scope, purview, line, sphere of business (activity);
beschränker ~ limited sphere of activity; **umfassender** ~ far-flung activities;
~ **finden** to find an opening; **außerhalb seines üblichen** ~**es tätig werden** to be off (out) of one's beat.

wirkungslos inefficient, ineffective, inefficacious, ineffectual, of no effect;
~ **verpuffen** to fall flat;
~**e Maßnahme** inefficient measure.

Wirkungs|losigkeit inefficiency; ~**möglichkeit** impact; ~**radius** *(Atombombe)* efficient range; ~**stätte** place of activity, vineyard.

wirkungsvoll efficacious;
sehr ~ of great virtue;
für am ~**sten gehalten werden** to be judged most potent;
~**e Blockade** effective blockade; ~**e Strafe** effectual punishment.

Wirkungs|weise mode of operations; ~**wert** *(Anzeige)* sales impact.

Wirkwaren hosiery.

wirr wild, scattered, foggy, *(verworren)* confused, *(wirrköpfig)* scatterbrained;
völlig ~ **sein** to be in a muddle;
~**e Geschichte** rigmarole; ~**es Gestrüpp** tangled thicket; ~**es Zeug reden** to talk nonsense.

Wirrkopf scatterbrain, muddlehead, puzzlehead.

Wirrnis entanglement, confusion.

Wirrwarr din, chaos, jumble, puddle, derangement, pie, turmoil, clutter, huddle, upset;
~ **von Stimmen** babel of voices, hubble-bubble.

Wirt *(Gastgeber)* host, entertainer, *(Hauswirt)* landlord, *(Hotel)* hotelkeeper, padrone, *(Restaurant)* innkeeper, publican *(Br.)*, saloonkeeper *(US)*;
~ **und seine Gäste** landlord and his guests;
~ **machen** to act the host.

Wirtin *(Zimmerwirtin)* landlady.

Wirtschaft economy, economics, economic system, *(Gastwirtschaft)* public house *(Br.)*, inn, restaurant, alehouse, tavern, pub *(Br.)*, saloon *(US)*, *(Haushalt)* household, *(Landwirtschaft)* farm;
autarke ~ self-contained economy; **einheimische** ~ domestic economy; **expansive** ~ growing economy; **extensive** ~ extensive cultivation; **freie** ~ free (uncontrolled) economy, private enterprise [system]; **gelenkte** ~ controlled (draft, directed, governed) economy; **gesamte** ~ economy as a whole; **gesamteuropäische** ~ whole European economy; **gesteuerte** ~ guided economy; **von parlamentarischen Ausschüssen gesteuer-**

te ~ economy run by parliamentary-committee government; **gesunde** ~ sound economy; **gewerbliche** ~ industrial economy, trade and industry, manufacturing trade; **gewerkschaftsfreie** ~ unorganized economy; **volumenmäßig gleichbleibende** ~ stable-volume industry; **inflationistische** ~ inflation boom; **sich integrierende** ~ economy in process of integration; **integrierte** ~ integrated economy; **intensive** ~ intensive economy; **investitionsvorsichtige** ~ slow-to-invest businessmen; **kapitalistische** ~ capitalist economy; **konzertierte** ~ planned economy; **krisenanfällige** ~ economy prone to crisis; **krisenfeste** ~ crisis-proof economy; **unter Arbeitermangel leidende** ~ undermanned industry; **liberalisierte** ~ liberal trade; **mitbestimmte** ~ industrial democracy; **mittelständische** ~ medium and small-scale enterprises, small business *(US)*; **öffentliche** ~ public sector of the economy; **ölabhängige** ~ oil-based economy; **ortsansässige** ~ local economy; **polnische** ~ topsyturvydom; **preiskontrollierte (preisüberwachte)** ~ price-controlled economy; **private** ~ private business sector, private enterprise; **reglementierte** ~ regimented economy; **rückläufige** ~ slowdown in business, economic slump, subsiding boom; **sparsame** ~ economization, husbandry; **stabile** ~ stable economy; **überhitzte** ~ overheated (excessive) boom; **unterbesetzte** ~ undermanned economy; **wettbewerbsfähige** ~ competitive economy; **zerrüttete** ~ dislocated economy;

~ **im Tagesspiegel** businessman in the news;

überhitzte ~ **abkühlen** to cool off an overheated economy; ~ **anheizen** to heat up the economy; ~ **ankurbeln** to foster trade, to boost (enliven) business, to pep up the economy, to stimulate industry, to prime the pump *(US)*, to give the economy a shot in the arm *(US coll.)*; ~ **großen Belastungen aussetzen** to place great strains on the economy; ~ **betreiben** to keep an inn; ~ **führen** to [run a] farm, to be engaged in farming; **j. die** ~ **führen** to keep house for s. o.; **der** ~ **eine Konjunkturspritze geben** to give the economy a shot in the arm *(US coll.)*; **in die** ~ **gehen** to enter private business; **Vollbeschäftigungszustand in der** ~ **herbeiführen** to move the economy towards full employment; ~ **lähmen** to paralyse business; **in einer** ~ **anschreiben lassen** to run up a score at a public house *(Br.)*; ~ **auf Hochtouren laufen lassen** to keep the economy in high gear; ~ **geldflüssig machen** to put the economy on a richer monetary diet; ~ **eines Landes reglementieren** to regulate the industries of a country; ~ **sanieren** to revitalize the economy; **in der** ~ **eine Rolle spielen** to make o. s. a great factor in the economy; **der** ~ **neue Aufgaben stellen** to provide new avenues for industry; ~ **überfordern** to overstrain the economy; **aus dem politischen Bereich in der Lebensmitte in die** ~ **überwechseln** to swap politics for business in mid-career; ~ **umstellen** to switch production (its economy), to reconvert industry; ~ **wiederbeleben** to revive economy.

wirtschaften to keep house, to manage, *(Landwirt)* to farm; **geschickt** ~ to housewife; **großzügig** ~ to be free with one's money; **schlecht** ~ to mismanage; **sparsam** ~ to husband one's money, to look into economies, to cut and contrive, to live (operate) economically, to economize, to practise economy; **äußerst sparsam** ~ to be careful of one's small savings; **in die eigene Tasche** ~ to line one's pocket, to job; **aus dem vollen** ~ to have ample means at one's disposal;

gut ~ **können** to be a good housekeeper; **sehr gut** ~ **können** to be an excellent manager.

wirtschaftlich *(ertragabwerfend)* profitable, yielding a return, remunerative, paying, commercial, *(leistungsfähig)* efficient, *(sparsam)* saving, economical, money-saving, thrifty, *(volkswirtschaftlich)* economic[al];

~ **bedrängt** economically-beleaguered;

sein Geld ~ **anlegen** to invest one's money profitably; ~ **arbeiten** *(Maschine)* to work economically; ~ **gestalten** to rationalize; ~ **sein** to be on a profitable basis; ~ **tätig sein** to be in trade (business); ~ **mit etw. umgehen** to be economical with s. th.;

~**e Abkühlung** cyclical slowdown; ~**e Abkühlung herbeiführen** to cool the economy; ~**e Angaben** economic (business) data; ~**e Angliederung** economic assimilation (attachment); ~**e Anpassung** economic adjustment; ~**e Anspannung** economic strains; ~**es Arbeiten** economical operation; ~**e Auftragsgröße** economic order quantity; ~**e Ausdehnung** economic expansion; ~**er Ausgleich** economic adjustment; ~**e Aussichten** business prospects; ~**e Autarkie** economic self-sufficiency; ~**e Bedeutung** commercial prominence; ~**e Bedingungen** economic terms; ~**e Belange** trade concerns, economic interests; ~**e Belastung** economic handicap; ~**er Berater** economic adviser (consultant), industrial counsel(l)or; ~**er Berufsverband** trade association; ~**e Besprechungen** trade conference (talks); ~**er Betrieb** economical operation, profitable enterprise; ~**e Beweggründe** economic motives; ~**e Beziehungen** economic relations; ~**e Bindungen** business ties; ~**e Blüte** business boom; ~**en Druck ausüben** to exercise economic pressure; ~**e Durchdringung** economic penetration; ~**es Eigentum** business ownership; ~**e Eingliederung** economic integration; ~**e Einheit** economic whole (entity); ~**e Entwicklung** economic (commercianl) development, trade lead; ~**er Erfolg** commercial success; ~**e Erwägungen** economic policy; **sich von** ~**en Erwägungen leiten lassen** to be guided by financial considerations; ~**er Fachausdruck** economic (trade) term; ~**e Fähigkeiten** trade ability; ~**e Festsetzung** trade foothold; ~**er Fortschritt** economic progress; ~**es Gebiet** economic field; **auf** ~**em Gebiet** in the economic field, in economic matters; **auf** ~**em und sozialem Gebiet** in the economic and social fields; ~**e Gegebenheiten** economical realities; ~**e Geldanlage** profitable investment; ~**e Gesichtspunkte** economic angles (aspects, factors); ~**es Grundgesetz** economic principle; **gesunde** ~**e Grundlage** sound economic basis; ~**e Haushaltsführung** economical housekeeping; ~**e Herausforderung** economic challenge; ~**e Hilfe** commercial leg-up; ~**er Hintergrund** business background; ~**e Integrierung** economic integration; ~**e Interessen** commercial interests; ~**e Konkurrenz** trade rivalry; ~**e Konzentration** industrial concentration; ~**e Kräfte** economic forces; ~**e Lage** business situation, *(Schuldner)* financial position; ~**e Lebensdauer** economic (useful) life; ~**e Leistungsfähigkeit** economic vitality (performance, efficiency), industrial efficiency, profit-earning capacity; ~**e Machtstellung** economic power; ~**e Maßnahmen** economic actions; ~**e Misere** economic gloom; ~**es Motiv** profit motive; ~**er Niedergang** economic downturn; ~**e Notlage** economic distress, financial embarrassment; ~**e Nutzungsdauer** economic (useful) life; **vor großen** ~**en Problemen stehen** to be faced with great financial problems; ~**er Querschnitt** industrial cross-section; ~**er Reibungskoeffizient** economic friction; ~**e Repressalien** economic reprisals; ~**er Rückschlag** economic dip; ~**er Ruin** economic ruin; ~**e Sanierung** reorganization; ~**e Sanktionen** economic sanctions; ~**e Schlüsselstellung** key industrial emporium; ~**e Situation** economic situation; ~**e Stagnation** economic stagnation; **vom** ~**en Standpunkt** economically speaking; ~**e Stellung** trade (business) position; ~**e Tagesfragen** bread-and-butter economic issues; ~**e Tätigkeit** business activity; ~**er Tätigkeitsbericht** survey of economic activities; ~**es Tief** depression, low; ~**e Überhitzung** overheating of the boom; ~**e Überlegenheit** economic superiority; ~**e Überlegungen** trade reasons; ~**e Übermacht** economic supremacy; ~**e Umwälzung** commercial revolution; ~**e Unabhängigkeit** economic independence, *(Land)* [economic] autarchy; ~**e Unsicherheit** economic uncertainty; ~**es Unternehmen** business (mercantile) establishment, business (commercial) enterprise, industrial undertaking; ~**e Vereinigung** commerce association; ~**e Verflechtung** economic interdependence, web of business; ~**e Waffe** trade weapon; ~**er Wagen** economy-sized car; ~**er Wert** economic issue (worth); ~**e Werte** economic assets; ~**er Wiederaufbau** industrial reconstruction (rehabilitation); ~**e Wiederbelebung** economic recovery; ~**e Wiedereingliederung** industrial rehabilitation; ~**es Zentrum** industrial centre *(Br.)* (center, *US*); ~**e Zukunft** economic course; ~**e Zusammenarbeit vertiefen** to intensify economic cooperation; ~**er Zusammenbruch** business collapse; ~**er Zusammenschluß** economic fusion; ~**e Zwangsläufigkeiten** economic determinism; ~**er Zweck** commercial purpose.

Wirtschaftlichkeit economical operation, economics, profitability, economic efficiency, effectiveness, profitableness, *(Maschine)* commercial efficiency, *(Rationalisierung)* rationalization, *(Sparsamkeit)* thriftiness, economy;

von Filialgründungen abhängige ~ branch-factory economy; ~ **im Betrieb** economy in operation, operating efficiency.

Wirtschaftlichkeits|berechnung economic appraisal, calculation of profitability; ~**koeffizient** operating ratio; ~**prinzip** economy-of-effort principle; ~**prüfung** efficiency audit, *(Auto)* economy run; ~**untersuchung** economic research.

Wirtschafts|abkommen trade convention (pact), commercial treaty, business agreement (contract), economic agreement; ~**ablauf** economic process, business cycle; ~**abordnung** trade delegation; ~**abschwächung** downward business trend, economic slowdown; ~**abteilung** industrial section, *(Schiff)* cabin department; ~**ähnlichkeit** economic resemblance; ~**akademie** commercial college; ~**analyse** economic analysis; ~**ankurbelung** enlivening of business, pump priming *(US)*; ~**anpassung**

economic adjustment; ~**anstieg** advance of the economy, growth in economic activity, upswing; ~**anwalt** businessman's (economist-) lawyer; ~**anzeigenblatt** industrial advertiser; ~**apparat** economic system; ~**artikel** *(Zeitung)* city article *(Br.)*; ~**atlas** economic atlas; ~**aufbau** economic buildup (reconstruction); **sich mit den vordringlichsten ~aufgaben beschäftigen** to tackle the urgent needs of the economy; ~**aufschwung** economic impetus (upturn), upturn in business, [trade] recovery, revival; ~**auftrag** commercial order; ~**ausblick** outlook for the economy; ~**ausdehnung** economic expansion, expansion of trade; ~**ausdruck** trade (economic) term; ~**ausgaben** household expenses; ~**ausgleich** economic adjustment; ~**ausschuß** economic council; **~- und Sozialausschuß** *(EG)* Economic and Social Council; ~**aussichten** business (economic) prospects; ~**ausweitung** economic expansion; ~**autarkie** economic independence (self-sufficiency), autarchy; ~**barometer** economic indicator; ~**bedarf** household requirements; ~**beeinflussung** economic influences; ~**behörde** economic agency; ~**beihilfe** subsidy, grant, *(Lebenshaltungskosten)* cost-of-living bonus; ~**beirat** council of economic advisers; ~**belange** trade concerns, economic interest; ~**belebung** economic (trade, industrial) recovery, recovery of business; ~**belebung durch Anhebung des Preisniveaus** reflation; **Möglichkeiten der Regierung zur ~belebung durch inflationäre Mittel beschneiden** to trim off the government's reflationary margin; ~**beobachter** economic observer; ~**berater** business (economic, trade) consultant, consultant economist, industrial counsel(l)or, economic adviser, efficiency expert; ~**beratungsausschuß** council of economic advisers; ~**beratungsfirma** economic consultancy; ~**bereich** sector of the economy, field of business activity, industrial domain; ~**bericht** economic (commercial, business) report, commercial advice; ~**berichte des Handelsministeriums** board-of-trade returns *(Br.)*; ~**berichterstatter** economic correspondent; **kriegsbedingte ~beschränkungen abbauen** to dismantle wartime controls; ~**besprechung** trade (industrial) conference; ~**besprechungen** trade talks; ~**bestimmungen** commercial regulations; ~**betrieb** commercial establishment, industrial unit, business enterprise; ~**betrieb der öffentlichen Hand** state (government) enterprise; ~**bevormundung** industrial patronage; **innergemeinschaftliche ~beziehungen** *(EG)* intra-community economic relations; **enge ~beziehungen herstellen** to establish close economic relations; ~**bilanz** trade balance; ~**bild** economic picture; ~**blatt** business paper; ~**block** economic (trading) bloc, commercial grouping; ~**blockade** economic blockade; **konjunkturelle ~blüte** cyclical boom; ~**boß** big pot in the business world; ~**boykott** economic boycott; ~**buch** housekeeping book; ~**büro** trade bureau; ~**bürokratie** corporate bureaucracy *(US)*; ~**chaos** economic chaos; ~**debatte** economic debate; ~**delegation** trade delegation; ~**demokratie** industrial democracy; ~**denken** economic thought (thinking); ~**depression** business depression; ~**dichte** density of distribution of firms; ~**dienststelle** economic agency; ~**diktator** production chief *(Br.)*; ~**doktrin** economic doctrine; ~**dynastie** economic dynasty; ~**einflüsse** economic influences; ~**einheit** economic entity (unity), *(Betrieb)* self-contained unit; ~**englisch** commercial (business) English; ~**entwicklung** economic development, trade lead; ~**epoche der Rezession zurechnen** to put the recession tag on a period; ~**erfolg** industrial accomplishment, commercial success; ~**erholung** economic (booming) recovery, upturn in business; **abnehmender ~ertrag** diminishing returns; **staatlicher ~etat** national economic budget; ~**expansion** business expansion, economic growth; ~**experte sein** to be an expert on (in) economics; ~**fachkräfte der Regierung** administration economists; ~**fachmann** economic expert; ~**fachschule** school of commerce; ~**faktoren** economic factors.

wirtschaftsfeindlich antibusiness *(US)*, anticommercial.

Wirtschafts|festigung economic stabilization; ~**finanzierung** financing of industry; ~**finanzierungsgesellschaft** industrial finance company; ~**flaute** depressed economy, trade recession, dip; ~**fluß** flow of trade; ~**förderung** business (trade) promotion, promotion of trade; ~**förderungsprogramm** national plan *(Br.)*; **regionale ~förderungsstelle** Regional Industrial Development Board *(Br.)*; ~**form** economic system; **gemischte ~form** mixed economy, middle way; ~**forscher** research economist; ~**forschung** economic research; ~**forschungsinstitut** institute for economic research, economic research institute; ~**fortschritt** economic progress; ~**forum** economic forum; ~**frage** economic subject; ~**fragen** economic questions (issues, problems); ~**freiheit** free economy.

wirtschaftsfreundlich probusiness *(US)*;
~ **sein** to be nice to businessmen.

Wirtschafts|frieden industrial peace; ~**führer** captain (leader) of industry, business (industrial) leader, merchant prince; ~**führung** economic leadership, business (economic) management, *(Ehefrau)* housekeeping, *(Ehemann)* husbandry; **einwandfreie ~führung** good husbandry; ~**funktion** economic function; ~**fürsorge** industrial welfare; ~**gebäude** farm building (office, *Br.*), farmyard (agricultural, estate) building, outhouse, farmery *(Br.)*, farmtown *(Scot.)*; ~**gebiet** economic territory (area), trading area, *(Fachgebiet)* sector of economy; **einheitliches ~gebiet** self-contained industry; ~**gefälle** interindustry differential; ~**gefüge** economic structure; ~**geld** household expenses, housekeeping money; **beim ~geld Überschüsse erzielen** to make one's pickings out of the housekeeping money; **Europäische ~gemeinschaft** Common Market Community; **Erwerbs- und ~genossenschaft** industrial and provident (cooperative purchasing, industrial cooperative) society *(Br.)*; ~**geographie** economic (industrial, commercial) geography; ~**geräte** household appliances; ~**geschehen** economic process; ~**geschichte** history of the economy, economic (business) history; ~**gesetzgebung** economic laws; ~**gespräche** economic talks; ~**gipfel** economic summit; ~**gruppe** trade group (section), economic group.

Wirtschaftsgüter economic (business) goods, *(Bilanz)* economic assets;
nicht buchungsfähige ~ nonledger assets; **einheimische** ~ domestic goods; **im Abzahlungswege erworbene** ~ assets acquired on hire purchase; **gebrauchte** ~ secondhand assets; **geringwertige** ~ small-ticket items; **körperliche** ~ tangible assets; **kurzlebige** ~ short-lived (wasting) assets; **langlebige** ~ consumer durables, permanent assets; **nicht realisierbare** ~ dead assets; **schwer realisierbare** ~ slow assets; **unkörperliche** ~ intangible assets;
~ **des Anlagevermögens** capital assets; ~ **mit überhöhtem Buchwert** watered assets *(US)*; ~ **mit beschränkter Lebensdauer** limited-life assets.

Wirtschaftshilfe economic aid (assistance, support), foreign aid; **nach dem Kriege gewährte** ~ postwar economic aid; **projektfreie** ~ untied aid; **projektgebundene** ~ tied aid;
einem Land ~ gewähren to pump economic aid into a country.

Wirtschafts|hochschule school of economics, business school, business college; ~**imperialismus** economic imperialism; ~**imperium** industrial (trade) empire; ~**impulse** economic incentives; ~**index** index of general business activity; ~**informationen** business news; ~**infrastruktur** economic infrastructure; ~**ingenieur** commercial (industrial) engineer, engineer manager; ~**integration** economic integration; ~**interesse** business (economic, commercial) interests; ~**isolationismus** economic isolation; ~**jahr** [company's] financial *(Br.)* (fiscal, *US*) year; ~**journalist** business journalist, trade journal writer; ~**jurist** businessman's lawyer, economist-lawyer; ~**kabinett** economic cabinet; ~**kalamität** economic woes; ~**kammer** chamber of commerce; ~**kampf** trade competition, economic warfare; ~**kapazität** industrial capacity; ~**kartell** business cartel; ~**katastrophe** economic disaster; ~**kenntnisse** commercial knowledge, business experience (knowledge); **seine ~kenntnisse vertiefen** to broaden one's business outlook; ~**klub** economic club *(US)*; ~**kommentar** economic commentary; ~**kommissar** *(EG)* industry commissioner.

Wirtschaftskommission economic committee;
~ **für Afrika** Economic Commission for Africa (ECA); ~ **der Vereinten Nationen für Europa** Economic Commission for Europe (ECE); ~ **für Lateinamerika** Economic Commission for Latin America (ECLA).

Wirtschafts|konferenz economic conference; **internationale ~konferenz** International Trade (Economic) Conference; ~**kontrolle** business (economic, industrial) control; **staatliche ~kontrolle** state control; ~**konzentration** concentration of economic power; ~**konzern** business concern; ~**körper** economic entity; ~**korrespondent** business reporter, economic correspondent; ~**kraft** economic strength (power), *(Land)* economic resources (strength); ~**kredit** commercial credit; ~**kreise** business community, commercial circles (community), segments of business community, economic front, business circles, traders; **führende ~kreise** industry management; ~**kreislauf** business cycle, circular flow of the economy, economic circulation; ~**krieg** economic (industrial) warfare, trade (white) war; ~**kriegführung** economic warfare; ~**krise** economic (commercial) crisis, business (economic) depression, business downturn, economic wrench, slump, trade depression; **von den Auswirkungen der ~krise besonders betroffen sein** to be deep in depression.

Wirtschaftslage economic (business) situation, economic conditions (picture), market;
allgemeine ~ general level of business; **schwierige ~** economic plight;
~ ernst beurteilen to take a grave view of the economic situation.

Wirtschafts|leben economic life, business [life]; **im europäischen ~leben** on the European business scene; **~leben einer Gegend entscheidend beeinflussen** to control the economic life of a region; **~lehre** political economy (science); **~lehre der außenwirtschaftlichen Beziehungen** international economics; **~leistung** economic performance; **~lenkung** economic control, state (government) control, controlled economy, guidance of trade *(US)*, *(Planwirtschaft)* dirigism, planned economy; **administrative ~lenkung** central economic planning, economic manipulation; **staatliche ~lenkung** government economic manipulation (management); **~liberalismus** economic liberalism; **~liquidität** liquidity of the economy; **~literatur** trade literature; **~macht** economic power; **~magazin** economic review, business publication; **~märkte** industrial markets, business outlets; **~messe** commercial exhibition; **~minister** Minister of Economics, Minister of Economic Affairs *(Br.)*; **~ministerium** Department of Economic Affairs *(Br.)*, Department of Commerce *(US)*, Commerce Department *(US)*; **~modernisierung** modernization of the economy; **~monopol** industrial monopoly; **~moral** commercial morality, business ethics; **~nachrichten** industrial (commercial, business, city) news, business intelligence, economic survey; **~nachrichten schwerpunktartig hervorheben** to highlight financial news; **~nachrichtenagentur** economic news agency; **~nationalismus** economic nationalism; **~normen** trade standards; **~oberschule** commercial college; **~offensive** economic offensive; **~ordnung** economic order (system); **freiheitliche ~ordnung** free economic system; **kapitalistische ~ordnung** capitalistic order; **~organisation** trade (industrial) organization; **~periode** economic period; **~phase** economic cycle; **~philosophie** philosophy of business; **~plan** economic plan, budget; **staatliche ~planung** national economic (central) planning, planned (directed) economy, statism.

Wirtschaftspolitik economic (commercial) policy;
[anti]zyklische ~ countercyclical compensatory government policy, cyclical budgeting; **kontinuierliche ~** economic continuity; **produktionsorientierte ~** forestalling; **regionale ~** regional industrial policy;
~ mittels steuerlicher Maßnahmen functional finance, compensatory fiscal policy; **~ und Sozialpolitik** economic and social policy;
~ in den Griff bekommen to keep tabs on the state of the economy; **ausgeglichene ~ betreiben** to remain on an even keel; **restriktive ~ betreiben** to hold a restrictive economic course; **stabile ~ betreiben** to stabilize the economy; **antiinflationistische Maßnahmen in der ~ ergreifen** to build antiinflationary forces into the economy.

Wirtschaftspolitiker economic policymaker.

wirtschaftspolitisch political- (politico-) economic;
~e Abteilung economic-policy department; **~er Ausschuß** economic-policy committee; **~e Entscheidungen** economic-policy decisions; **~e Entschlüsse** anticyclical policy resolutions; **aus ~en Gründen** for [anti]cyclical reasons; **~es Instrumentarium** instrument of economic policy, economic-policy tools; **~e Lage** economic (cyclical) situation; **~e Maßnahmen** economic measures; **indikatorgebundene ~e Maßnahme** formula flexibilty; **~e Probleme** economic[-policy] problems; **~e Situation** economic situation; **~e Sofortmaßnahmen** discretionary stabilizer; **~e Tagesordnung** economic-policy agenda; **~er Teil** *(Zeitung)* financial columns (page), city news *(Br.)*; **~es Ziel** economic-policy goal; **~e Zielsetzungen** economic targets.

Wirtschafts|potential economic potential; **~präferenz** economic preference; **~presse** financial press, trade newspapers; **~pressedienst** economic news agency; **~problem** economic question; **~prognose** economic forecast, business outlook; **~programm** economic (industrial) expansion program(me); **~projekt** industrial project; **~propaganda** trade publicity; **~prospekt** trade folder; **~prozeß** economic process.

Wirtschaftsprüfer, [beeidigter (öffentlich zugelassener)] auditor, chartered (incorporated, *Br.*) accountant, [certified] public (independent) accountant *(US)*;
~ ganztägig beschäftigen to employ a private accountant on a full-time basis;
~ausbildung accountancy qualification; **~bericht** audit (auditor's) report, report of a public accountant; **~beruf** profession of accounting, accountancy profession; **~gebühren** accountant's fee; **~praxis** accountancy practice.

Wirtschaftsprüfung auditing, public accounting.

Wirtschaftsprüfungs|dienst accountancy service; **~gesellschaft** auditing company, accountancy firm, auditors; **~wesen** public accountancy.

Wirtschafts|psychologie industrial psychology; **~rat** council of economic advisers *(US)*; **Europäischer ~rat** Organization for European Economic Cooperation (OEEC); **~- und Sozialrat der Vereinten Nationen** United Nations Economic Council; **~raum** trading (trade, marketing) area, market, economic domain (area, region), *(Schiff)* service space; **~räume** offices; **~realismus** economic realism; **~recht** commercial law; **~rechtler** economist lawyer; **~redakteur** financial (economist, city, *Br.*) editor; **~reform** economic reform; **~region** economic (planning) region; **~reich** industrial empire; **~ressort** economics portfolio; **~restriktionen** restraint of trade; **~revolution** industrial revolution; **~rezession** economic recession; **~rückgang** trade backsliding, depression of trade; **~rückschlag** economic setback; **~sabotage** industrial (economic) sabotage; **~sachverständiger** economic expert, industrial counsel(l)or; **~sanierung** revitalization of the economy; **~sanktionen** economic sanctions; **gehobenere ~schichten** higher industrial classes; **~schlichter** trade arbitrator; **~schrifttum** trade literature; **~seite haben** *(Zeitung)* to carry a financial page *(Br.)*; **~sektor** sector of economy; **~seminar** business seminar; **~situation** state of the economy; **~sparte** line of commerce; **~spion** industrial spy, keek *(US sl.)*; **~spionage** economic (industrial) espionage; **~sprache** language of economics, economic terminology; **~stabilität** economic stability; **~statistik** business (economic) statistics, census of business; **~stelle** economic agency, *(Bewirtschaftung)* rationing board; **~stellung** business (trade) position; **~steuerung durch Überredung** jaw boning; **~stockung** economic stagnation, stagnation of business; **~strategie** economic strategy; **~struktur** business (economic) structure, economic setup *(US)*, structure of business; **alle ~stufen** all parts of the economy.

Wirtschaftssystem economic structure (system, regime, setup, *US*), industrial system (order);
autarkes ~ autarchy; **einheitliches ~** integrated economy; **freiheitliches ~** free enterprise (economic) system; **kapitalistische ~e** capitalistic economics;
~ eines Landes economics of a country;
das europäische ~ durcheinanderbringen to disturb the economy of Europe; **~ umstrukturieren** to reconstruct the economic system.

Wirtschafts|tagung economic conference, industrial gathering; **~tätigkeit** economic activity; **~teil** *(Zeitung)* financial (business-page) columns, city news *(Br.)*; **~tendenz** economic trend; **~terminologie** economic (business) terminology; **~theoretiker** economic theorist; **~trend** economic (business) trend; **~treuhänder** conventional trustee; **~überschuß** earned surplus; **~umschau** business roundtrip; **~umschwung** changes in the underlying trend, turn (break) of the market; **~union** economic union; **~unterhändler** trade negotiator.

Wirtschaftsunternehmen business (commercial) enterprise, commercial establishment, trading (business) concern;
kommunales ~ public utility; **monopolistisches ~** monopolistic enterprise;
~ der öffentlichen Hand state (government) enterprise, public corporation.

Wirtschafts|untersuchungsprogramm economic research program(me); **~verband** trade organization (association), business (industrial, US) association; **~verbindungen** trade connections; **~verbrechen** economic crime, white-collar crime *(US)*, economic offence; **~verbrecher** white-collar criminal *(US)*; **~vereinigung** trade organization (association), commercial association; **~verfassung** economic constitution (structure), economic system; **~verflechtung** economic interdependence; **~vergehen** economic offence, white-collar crime *(US)*; **~verhältnisse** business conditions; **gesunde ~verhältnisse** sound economic conditions; **~verhandlungen** trade conference (discussions, negotiations); **~verkehr** economic intercourse, trade, commerce, *(mit anderen Bundesländern)* intrastate commerce *(US)*; **~verlauf** cyclical trend, trend of business conditions; **~vertrag** trade agreement, business contract; **~vertreter** commercial representative; **~volumen** overall economic potential; ~**vorhaben** industrial project; ~**vorrechte** economic privileges (priorities); ~**vorschau** business outlook (prognosis), economic forecasting (outlook); ~**vorschlag** economic project; ~**vorteil** trade advantage; ~**wachstum auf 4% beschränken** to limit economic growth to four per cent; ~**wachstumspolitik** growth mentality; ~**wachstumsrate** growth rate; ~**weg** farm road; ~**welt** business community; ~**werbung** commercial (industrial, business) advertising; ~**wissenschaft** political economy, economics, economic science; ~**wissenschaften studieren** to be taught economics; ~**wissenschaftler** economist.

wirtschaftswissenschaftlich economic.

Wirtschafts|wörterbuch business (commercial) dictionary, lexicon of business; ~**wunder** economic miracle; ~**zahlen** economic data (figures); ~**zar** economic overlord; ~**zeitschrift**, ~**zeitung** trade (economic, commercial) journal (magazine, publication), industrial magazine, business review, trade paper (newspaper), financial press; ~**zentrum** trade (commercial) center *(US)* (centre, *Br.*), center *(US)* (centre, *Br.*) of trade; ~- **und Finanzzentrum** trade and financial capital; ~**ziele** economic aims; ~**zone** trade area; ~**zusammenschluß** economic union; ~**zweck** commercial (business) purpose.

Wirtschaftszweig sector of economy, industry, commercial line, line of business (commerce), trade group, branch of trade;
von Bodenschätzen abhängige ~**e** resource-based industries; **einzelstaatlicher** ~ *(EG)* home industry; **neuer** ~ new industry; **nichtindustrielle** ~**e** nonindustrial activities;
bedeutender ~ **sein** to be big business.

Wirtschaftszyklus business cycle, cycle of economy.

Wirtshaus inn, pothouse, taphoue, tap room, public house *(Br.)*, pub *(Br.)*, tavern, bush;
konzessioniertes ~ licensed house *(Br.)*;
ins ~ **gehen** to go round to the pub *(Br.)*;
~**genehmigung** publican's (liquor) licence; ~**leben** pubcrawling; ~**schild** tavern sign; ~**stube** tap room, bar parlo(u)r.

Wisch wisp, bumf *(Br., sl.)*, rag, clott for wiping, scrap of paper, waste paper, trashy writing.

wischen to wipe, to brush;
jem. eine ~ to cuff (clout, land) s. o. one; **sich die Stirn** ~ to wipe one's forehead, to mob one's brow; **im ganzen Zimmer Staub** ~ to dust the whole room.

Wisch|lappen dishcloth; ~**tuch** wiper.

Wißbegierde curiosity, inquisitiveness, thirst for knowledge.

wißbegierig inquisitive, curious;
~**er Mensch** inquiring mind.

Wissen knowledge, learning;
mit seinem ~ **und Willen** with his privity and consent; **nach bestem** ~ **und Gewissen** to the best of one's knowledge and belief, upon information and belief *(US)*; **wider besseres** ~ against one's better judgment;
bißchen ~ smack of knowledge; **hart erarbeitetes** ~ hard-acquired knowledge; **globales** ~ allround knowledge; **großes** ~ great store of knowledge; **oberflächliches** ~ smattering of knowledge; **praktisches** ~ know-how; **profundes** ~ profound knowledge; **umfassendes** ~ universal (extensive) knowledge; **unendliches** ~ depth of knowledge;
umfassendes ~ **haben** to be an allround scholar; **mit seinem** ~ **prahlen** to put all one's knowledge in the window; **aus dem Schatz seines** ~**s schöpfen** to draw on one's rich store of knowledge; **sein** ~ **zur Schau stellen** to air one's knowledge; **großes** ~ **zeigen** to disclose great learning.

wissen to know, to be aware of, to understand, to be informed, to have learned, *(sich vergegenwärtigen)* to remember;
keinen Ausweg mehr ~ to be at the end of one's tether; **in seinem Fach Bescheid** ~ to be well versed in a subject; **in einer Sache genauestens Bescheid** ~ to know the ins and out of a case; **sofort Bescheid** ~ to read while one runs; **in der Welt Bescheid** ~ to know a thing or two; **direkt von jem.** ~ to have it straight from s. o.; **aus eigener Erfahrung** ~ to know from one's own experience; **genau** ~ to be positive (thoroughly) acquainted; **Geschenk zu schätzen** ~ to appreciate a gift; **mit Kindern umzugehen** ~ to have a way with children; **nicht** ~ to be ignorant; **gar nichts über etw.** ~ to be quite in the dark about s. th.; **aus guter Quelle** ~ to have it on good authority; **nicht weiter** ~ to flounder;
~, **wo der Barthel den Most holt** to know where one's bread is buttered, to know one's onions (oil, oats); ~, **wie weit man gehen kann** to know one's distance; ~, **was es geschlagen hat** to know the time of the day; ~, **wie der Hase läuft** to know how the land lies (where the wind blows); **nicht** ~, **worauf jem. hinaus will** not do know, what s. o. is driving at; **alles** ~, **was beim Nachbarn vorgeht** to know all one's neighbo(u)r's proceedings; ~, **was j. im Schilde führt** to know s. one's little game; ~, **wo der Schuh drückt** to know where the shoe pinches; ~, **was man zu tun hat** to see one's way clear; **nicht** ~, **was man zuerst tun soll** to be puzzled what to do next; **genau** ~, **welchen Weg man einschlagen muß** to see one's way;
etw. genau ~ **wollen** to be inquisitive of s. th.; **von etw. nichts** ~ **wollen** to turn a deaf ear to s. th.; **unbedingt** ~ **wollen** to be determined to know.

wissender Blick knowing look.

Wissensbereich range of knowledge, ken.

Wissenschaft science;
im Bereich der ~ in the domain of science;
angewandte ~ applied science; **exakte** ~ exact science; **reine** ~ pure science; **schöne** ~**en** polite learning;
~ **von der Zukunft** science of future, futurology;
~**en fördern** to promote science; **nicht in den Bereich der** ~ **gehören** to fall outside the province of science; **sein Leben im Dienst der** ~ **opfern** to die a martyr in the cause of science; **sich der** ~ **verschreiben** to devote o. s. to science.

Wissenschaftler scientist, man of science, scholar;
als hervorragender ~ **anerkannt sein** to win eminence as a scientist; **als** ~ **gewertet werden wollen** to have pretensions to be considered a scholar.

wissenschaftlich scientific;
~ **ausgebildet** scientifically trained;
~**e Abhandlung** scientific work; ~**es Antiquariat** scientific antiquarian bookselling; **nachgewiesene** ~**e Befähigung** professional qualification in economics; ~**er Berater** scientific adviser; ~**e Beratergruppe** scientific advisory panel; ~**e Betriebsführung** scientific management; ~**e Bildung** scientific attainments; ~**e Forschung** scientific research; ~**er Fortschritt** scientific advance; **nach** ~**en Grundsätzen aufgestellter Tarif** scientific tariff; ~ **betriebene Landwirtschaft** scientific farming; ~**e Tätigkeit** back-room work; ~**e Zeitschrift** scientific periodical.

Wissenschafts|Ministerium Education Department *(Br.)*; ~**rat** scientific and technical advisory committee.

Wissens|darbietung, imponierende imposing display of one's knowledge; ~**drang,** ~**durst** thirst (hunger) for (pursuit of) knowledge.

wissensdurstig sein to be hungry for knowledge.

Wissens|gebiet field (branch) of knowledge, province; **uferloses** ~**gebiet** unlimited field of knowledge; **unbekannte** ~**gebiete** out-of-the-way items of knowledge; ~**schatz** thesaurus, store of knowledge; **seinen** ~**stand erweitern** to increase one's knowledge; **bewältigter** ~**stoff** acquired knowledge; ~**wertes** a thing or two; ~**zweig** branch of knowledge, discipline, art.

wissentlich conscious, knowingly, wiltingly, *(vorsätzlich)* intentional, deliberate, wilfully, scienter.

wittern *(böse Absicht)* to suspect, to sense;
Morgenluft ~ to see a ray of hope; **Unrat** ~ to smell a rat.

Witterung, im Freien der ~ **ausgesetzt** exposed to the weather;
milde ~ mild weather;
~ **aufnehmen** to follow the scent; ~ **von etw. bekommen** to get the wind of s. th.; **feine** ~ **für etw. haben** to have a good nose for s. th.; **bei jeder** ~ **spazierengehen** to go out in all weathers.

witterungsbeständig weatherproof, *(Stahl)* stainless.

Witterungs|einflüsse weather conditions; ~**umschlag** complete change of the weather, meteorological change; ~**unbilden** inclemencies of the weather; ~**verhältnisse** weather patterns.

Wittum jointure, free-bench, frank bank *(Br.)*, dower *(US)*;
seiner Frau ein ~ **aussetzen** to settle a jointure upon one's wife.

Witwe widow, [feme] discovert, dowager *(Br.)*, relict;
~ **mit einem Pflichtteilsnießbrauch** tenant in dower.

Witwen|abfindung compensation paid to a widow; ~**anteil** jointure, dower interest *(US)*, dower *(US)*; ~**geld** widow's allowance; ~- **und Waisengeld** compassionate allowance; ~**geld festsetzen** to assign a dower *(US)*; ~**kasse** widow's fund; ~**leibgedinge** dower; ~**nießbrauch** free-bench, estate by the curtesy; ~**nießbrauch nach Ortsgebrauch** dower by custom; ~**pension** widow's pension (bounty); ~**pflichtteil** right of dowry, widow right, widow-bench, election dower; ~**rente** widow's annuity (pension), survivor's benefit *(US)*, widow's benefit, *(Sozialversicherung)* national insurance widow's allowance; **kleine** ~**spende** the widow's mite; ~**stand** widowhood, viduage; ~**teil einräumen** to endow; ~**tracht** widow's weeds; ~**versicherung** widow's insurance.

Witwer widower;
~ **mit Nießbrauchrecht am Grundstücksnachlaß** tenant by the curtesy.

Witz joke, *(witzige Bemerkung)* wisecrack, jest, witticism; **abgedroschener (abgestandener) ~** worn joke, chestnut *(coll.)*; **trockener ~** dry wit; **unanständiger ~** dirty (risqué) joke; **uralter ~** wheeze *(sl.)*;
keine anstößigen ~e erzählen to keep the party clean; **etw. als ~ hinstellen** to pass s. th. off as a joke; **primitive ~e machen** to grin through a horse collar; **~ auf jds. Kosten machen** to crack a joke at s. one's expense; **vor Geist und ~ nur so sprühen** to scintillate with wit and humo(u)r; **~ verstehen** to see a joke;
der ~ daran ist the funny thing about it;
~blatt humo(u)rous (comic, funny) paper; **~bold** joker, wisecracker, wag; **~figur** funny sight; **~figuren zeichnen** to draw funny figures.
witzig funny, comic, jocular, *(geistreich)* witty;
~er Einfall funny idea.
witzlos unwitty, *(sinnlos)* pointless, useless;
völlig ~ sein to be of no use at all.
Witz|seite *(Zeitung)* funnies *(US sl.)*; **~zeichnung** cartoon.
Woche, angebrochene broken week; **Weiße ~** white sale; **wohlfeile ~** bonus week;
eine ~ nach Ankunft within a week of one's arrival; **eine ~ in London** up for a week *(Br.)*;
nur jede zweite ~ arbeiten to knock work off one week out of two; **~ Urlaub bekommen** to obtain a week's leave; **bis zur nächsten ~ bleiben** to stand over till next week; **ganze ~ durcharbeiten** to work out the week; **Tag in der ~ frei haben** to have one day out a week; **sich auf nächste ~ vertagen** *(parl.)* to rise next week; **nächste ~ verhandelt werden** to come up for hearing next week; **für eine ~ zurückstellen** to remand for a week.
Wochen|abonnement *(Bahn)* season (commuter, *US*) ticket; **~abschluß** weekly return, weekly statement; **am ~anfang** in the early part of the week; **halbe ~arbeit** half work; **~arbeitszeit** hours worked per week; **~arbeitszettel** time sheet; **~ausgabe** weekly edition; **~ausweis** weekly statement (return, *Br.*); **~ausweis einer Girostelle** clearinghouse statement; **~ausweis der Notenbank** Return for the week *(Br.)*, Treasury Statement *(US)*; **~beihilfe** maternity benefit; **~bericht** weekly report, *(Rundfunk)* newsreel *(Br.)*; **~bett** childbed, lying-in; **~bettkosten** costs of lying-in; **~blatt** weekly [newspaper (gazette)], local weekly; **~einnahme** weekly receipts.
Wochenend|asyl weekend retreat; **~aufenthalt** weekend stay; **~auftrag** weekend order; **~ausflug** weekend trip; **~ausflug aufs Land** weekend visit to the country; **~ausflügler** weekend tripper *(Br.)*; **~ausgabe** weekly edition.
Wochenende weekend;
sich ein arbeitsfreies ~ leisten to treat o. s. to a good weekend holiday; **~ mit Freunden verbringen** to spend the weekend with friends; **~ in London verbringen** to be spending the weekend in town *(Br.)*.
Wochenend|erholung weekend recreation; **~fahrkarte** weekend ticket; **~geschäft** Saturday business; **~haus** weekend cottage (shack), lodge; **sich in seinem ~haus an der See aufhalten** to use one's seashore cottage; **~karte** weekend ticket; **~presse** Sunday papers; **~programm** weekend entertainment; **günstiger ~tarif** special weekend rates; **~umsätze** weekend sales; **~urlaub zu Hause** homecoming weekend; **~urlauber** weekender, weekend tripper *(Br.)*; **~zeitung** weekend paper.
Wochen|geld weekly allowance, *(Börse)* weekly fixtures, weekly money, *(Mutter)* maternity benefit (allowance, relief); **~hilfe** *(Mutter)* maternity benefit (allowance, relief), childbirth allowance; **~index** weekly index; **~karte** weekly season (commuter, *US*) ticket.
wochenlang hintereinander for weeks on end.
Wochenlieferung weekly delivery.
Wochenlohn weekly pay (wages, salary);
seinen ~ erhalten to receive one's week's wage[s]; **jem. seinen ~ vorenthalten** to deprive s. o. of a week's pay;
sich mit maximal 30 DM ~anstieg zufriedengeben to accept a maximum wage increase of £ 6 a week; **~empfänger** weekly wage earner.
Wochen|markt weekly market, open-air market, market day; **~mindestlohn** minimum weekly wage; **~pendler** weekly commuter; **~pflegerin** visiting nurse; **~prämie** weekly premium; **~produktion** weekly output; **~rate** weekly instal(l)ment; **~rechnung** weekly bill; **~schau** newsreel, news (topical) film (picture), topical *(US)*; **~schrift** weekly publication; **~spielplan** *(Kino)* weekly program(me); **~tag** weekday; **normaler ~tag** legal day.
wöchentlich weekly, hebdomadal;
zweimal ~ twice a week;
~ abrechnen to settle accounts once a week; **~ 80 DM abwerfen** to bring in DM 80 a week; **~ erscheinen** to be published weekly, to be issued in weekly parts;
~e Kündigung seven days' (a week's) notice; **~e Zahlung** weekly payment.
Wochen|überblick digest of the week's news, weekly review; **~übersicht** weekly review; **~umsatz** weekly sales; **~umsatz von 200 Pfund haben** to turn over £ 200 a week; **~unterstützung** weekly benefit; **durchschnittlicher ~verdienst** average weekly earnings.
wochenweise by the week;
~ bezahlt werden to be paid by the week.
Wochen|zeitschrift weekly [newspaper]; **~zeitung** weekly [paper].
Wöchnerin woman in childbed, maternity case.
Wöchnerinnen|abteilung maternity ward; **~heim** maternity home.
Woge wave, breaker, surge;
haushohe ~n towering breakers;
~n der Begeisterung surge of excitement.
wogen *(Getreidefeld)* to ripple, to undulate, *(Meer)* to surge, to heave.
Wohl, das allgemeine general welfare, public welfare (weal); **das öffentliche ~** public good (welfare, weal);
sich um das ~ seines Landes verdient machen to work for the good of the country; **um das eigene ~ bedacht sein** to take care of number one; **auf jds. ~ trinken** to drink a health to s. o., to propose a toast for s. o.; **auf das ~ des Brautpaares trinken** to pledge the bride and bridegroom.
wohl well, happy, at ease (home);
sich nicht recht ~ fühlen to be uncomfortable; **sich nach Herzenslust ~ sein lassen** to indulge o. s. to one's heart's content.
wohlabgewogen well-weighted.
Wohl|abgewogenheit judiciousness; **körperliches ~befinden** physical comfort, well-being; **um jds. ~befinden besorgt sein** to be solicitous for s. one's welfare.
wohl|begründet well-founded (-established); **~behalten** safe and sound; **~bekannt** familiar, well-acquainted; **~besetzt** *(Lager)* well-stocked; **~bestallt** well-established, duly installed; **~bewandert** well-versed; **~durchdacht** well-contrived.
Wohlergehen, materielles economic welfare;
Interesse am ~ des Landes haben to have a stake in the country; **sich um das ~ der Nation Sorgen machen** to be mindful of the nation's welfare.
wohlerhalten in a sound state;
gut und ~ in good order and well-conditioned.
wohlerwogenes Risiko perceivable risk.
wohlerworben well-stablished, vested;
~e Rechte *(Verfassung)* vested rights.
wohlerzogen well-mannered.
Wohlfahrt welfare, prosperity, *(Unterstützung)* social service, poor relief *(Br.)*;
öffentliche ~ public welfare *(US)*, public charity; **soziale ~** social welfare *(US)*;
sich um die öffentliche ~ verdient machen to work for the welfare of the nation.
Wohlfahrts|amt relief office, welfare agency (authority) *(US)*, National Assistance Board *(Br.)*; **~ausgaben** welfare expenditure; **~ausschuß** public welfare committee; **~beamter** welfare worker, relief officer *(Br.)*, district visitor *(US)*; **~behörde** relief office, National Assistance Board *(US)*; **~einrichtung** welfare center *(US)* (centre, *Br.*), charitable institution, settlement [house].
Wohlfahrtsempfänger welfare recipient (beneficiary), recipient of national assistance *(Br.)*, taxeater, pauper *(US)*;
zum ~ machen to pauperize; **~ sein** to live on charity, to be on the parish *(Br.)* (town, *US*); **~ werden** to be put on public assistance rolls *(US)*;
~liste relief role.
Wohlfahrts|fonds public welfare (benefit) fund, community chest *(US)*; **~fonds für Angestellte** employees' benefit fund; **~funktionen** welfare functions; **~indikator** welfare indicator; **~kasse** relief fund; **~küche** soup kitchen; **~marke** charity stamp, semipostal; **~organisation** charitable organization; **~- und Wiedergutmachungsorganisation der Vereinten Nationen** United Nations Relief and Rehabilitation Administration; **~pflege** charity; **öffentliche ~pflege** welfare (charity) work, district visiting *(US)*; **~programm** welfare program(me); **~speisungen vornehmen** to provide meals free; **~staat** welfare state.

wohlfahrtsstaatlich welfarist.

Wohlfahrts|system welfarism, welfare statism; ~**tätigkeit** welfare (philanthropical) activities; ~**theorie** welfare economics; ~**unterstützung** public (poverty, poor, *Br.*) relief, welfare check *(US)* (cheque, *Br.*, payment); ~**unterstützung beziehen** to receive aid under a pauper law *(US)*; ~**unterstützungsempfänger** welfare recipient (beneficiary), taxeater, pauper *(US)*, recipient of national assistance *(Br.)*; ~**verband** welfare organization; ~**verein** provident society *(Br.)*.

wohlfeil cheap, inexpensive, at a cheap (low) rate, at a moderate charge;
~ **kaufen** to buy at a low rate; ~ **werden** to go down.

wohlfundiert financially strong (sound).

Wohlgefallen delight, pleasure;
sich in ~ **auflösen** to end up in smoke, to come to nothing.

wohlgefälliges Leben führen to walk with God.

wohlgeraten well-turned, *(Kind)* well-bred.

Wohlgeruch essence, perfume.

wohlgesonnen sein, jem. to feel warm (be well inclined) towards s. o.

wohlhabend affluent, pecunious, well-off, prosperous, wealthy, well-to-do *(Br.)*, in easy circumstances, silk-stocking *(US)*, well-heeled *(sl.)*, lace-curtain *(Irish sl.)*;
sich selbst als ~ **bezeichnen** to put o. s. forward as a wealthy man; **als** ~ **gelten** to be reputed to be wealthy; ~ **sein** to be on easy street; **verhältnismäßig** ~ **sein** to be in relative ease; **endlich wird er** ~ prosperity is dawning on him; **zu den** ~**en Leuten zählen** to be comfortably off; **verhältnismäßig** ~**er Mann** man of means; ~**es Viertel** silk-stocking district *(US)*.

Wohlhabenheit pecuniosity, easy street *(coll.)*, easy circumstances, affluence;
~ **der Arbeiterklasse** worker affluence; ~ **der gehobeneren Bevölkerungsschicht** executive class prosperity.

wohlig pleasant, cozy, snug.

Wohlleben high living.

Wohlmeinender do-gooder.

wohlproportioniert sein to have a well-proportioned form.

Wohlsein well-being, good health;
zum ~ here's to you, your health, cheers, cheerio *(Br., coll.)*; **um jds.** ~ **besorgt sein** to have s. one's welfare at heart.

Wohlstand wealth, fortune, prosperity, economic well-being, sun;
enorm gestiegener ~ vastly increased prosperity; **wirtschaftlicher** ~ circumstantial prosperity;
~ **der Verbraucher** consumer wealth;
~ **eines Landes erschöpfen** to drain a country of its wealth; **im** ~ **leben** to be affluent, to live in comfortable circumstances (easy street, *coll.*); **in großem** ~ **leben** to lie in the full swing of prosperity; **vom allgemeinen** ~ **abhängig sein** to be bound up with the welfare of the community.

Wohlstands|effekte des Außenhandels gains of trade; **soziale** ~**funktion** social welfare function *(US)*; ~**gesellschaft** affluent society; ~**index** prosperity index; ~**mehrung** increase of prosperity; ~**merkmale** evidence of prosperity; ~**niveau** level of prosperity; ~**steigerungen** social benefits; ~**zunahme** influx of wealth.

Wohltat benefit, benevolence, boon;
~ **fürs Auge** relief to the eye;
jem. ~**en erweisen** to confer benefits on s. o.

Wohltäter benefactor, patron, patronizer;
öffentlicher ~ public friend; **ungenannter** ~ unnamed benefactor;
sich als ~ **aufspielen** to put on the guise of benevolence.

wohltätig charitable, benevolvent, beneficent, eleemosynary, philanthropic;
~ **sein** to dispense charity;
~**e Anwandlung** charitable impulse; ~**e Spende** charitable contribution, contribution for the poor, contribution to charity; ~**e Stiftung** charitable foundation (establishment, institution, trust), eleemosynary corporation; ~**es Unternehmen** charitable (benevolent) enterprise; ~**er Verein** benevolent society; ~**er Zweck** charitable use, charitable (benevolent) purpose; **für** ~**e Zwecke bestimmt sein** to go to charity; **für** ~**e Zwecke spenden** to dispense charity.

Wohltätigkeit charity, beneficence, benefaction, benevolence, bounty;
falsch angebrachte ~ misdirected (misplaced) charity; **kritiklose** ~ indiscriminate charity; **private** ~ private charity;
~ **zur Linderung der Kriegsnot** war charities *(Br.)*;
von der ~ **der Gemeinde leben** to live on charity, to come on the parish (town, *US*); **von der** ~ **seiner Mitmenschen leben** to subsist on other men's charity; **sich der** ~ **widmen** to devote o. s. to charity.

Wohltätigkeits|anstalt charitable establishment (institution); ~**ausschuß** care committee, charity commission; ~**ball** charity ball; ~**basar** charity (bring-and-buy) bazaar, rummage (jumble) sale; ~**beitrag leisten** to contribute to a work of charity; ~**einrichtung** charitable establishment, benevolent (charitable) institution, charitable endowment; ~**fonds** charity (benevolent) fund, community chest *(US)*; **auf dem** ~**gebiet beispielhaft sein** to subscribe liberally to charity; ~**komitee** distress committee; ~**konzert** benefit concert; ~**organisation** charity (voluntary) organization; ~**stiftung** charitable trust; ~**transfer einer Volkswirtschaft** charity market; ~**überlegungen anstellen** to entertain charitable sentiments; ~**veranstaltung** benefice (charity) performance, performance in aid of the poor, friendly lead *(Br.)*, *(Theater)* benefit performance; ~**verein** charitable organization, fraternal (benefit, friendly, *Br.*, benevolent) society, benefit association (club) *(Br.)*, Charity Organization Society *(Br.)*, *(staatlich anerkannt)* approved society *(Br.)*; ~**verein auf Gegenseitigkeit** mutual benefit association; ~**vorstellung** charity performance; ~**zweck** charitable use; **jem. wie üblich etw. für seine bevorzugten** ~**zwecke zur Verfügung stellen** to come down to s. one's favo(u)rite charity.

wohl|tuende Erscheinung pleasing figure; ~**überlegt** deliberate, measured, calculated; ~**unterrichtete Kreise** well-informed circles; ~**verdient** well-deserved.

Wohlverhalten good behavio(u)r (conduct).

Wohlwollen goodwill, good feeling, grace, *(Gunst)* favo(u)r, patronage;
für das erwiesene ~ for past favo(u)rs;
sich das ~ **durch Schmeicheleien erkaufen** to purchase favo(u)r with flattery; **jds.** ~ **erringen** to gain s. one's goodwill; **jem. sein** ~ **zu erkennen geben** to throw the handkerchief to s. o.

wohlwollend friendly, benevolent, benign, favo(u)rable;
nicht ~ unfriendly;
j. ~ **behandeln** to look on s. o. with a favo(u)rable eye; **einer Sache** ~ **gegenüberstehen** to be friendly to a cause, to be favo(u)rably inclined towards s. th.; **j.** ~ **auf die Schulter klopfen** to give s. o. a pat on the shoulder;
~**er Freund** well-wisher; ~**e Neutralität** benevolent neutrality.

Wohn|anlage apartment building, flatted house *(Br.)*; ~**baracke** barracks, hut; ~**baudarlehen** housing loan; ~**bauten** residential buildings; ~**bedarf** housing requirements; **vorübergehend** ~**berechtigter** licensee; ~**berechtigung** residence permit; **ebenerdig gelegener** ~**- und Versorgungsbetrieb** accommodation arranged all on one floor; ~**bevölkerung** resident population; ~**bezirk** residential district (zone); **übervölkerter** ~**bezirk** warren, densely populated quarter.

Wohnblock apartment block, housing estate, block of flats *(Br.)*;
für die Errichtung von ~**s freigegeben sein** to be zoned for multiple-dwelling use *(US)*;
~**fertigungsmethode** site prefabrication; ~**straße** residential street.

Wohn|boot houseboat; ~**dichte** housing density; ~**diele** lounge; ~**einheit** accommodation (residential) unit; **vorgefertigte** ~**einheit** prefabricated housing module.

Wohnen im Ausland living abroad, absenteeism.

wohnen to live, to dwell, to reside, to quarter, to home, *(als Mieter)* to room *(US)*;
bei jem. ~ to stay with s. o.; **in A.** ~ to have one's residence in A.; **im Ausland** ~ to reside abroad; **außerhalb (auswärts)** ~ to live out of town; **um die Ecke herum** ~ to live close at hand (round the corner); **bei den Eltern** ~ to live with one's parents; **irgendwo in der Gegend von London** ~ to live somewhere London way; **im Haus** ~ *(Angestellter)* to live in; **hoch** ~ to live high up; **auf dem Lande** ~ to dwell in the country; **zur Miete** ~ to stay in private lodgings, to live as a lodger, to be a tenant, to lodge, to room *(US)*; **mietfrei in einem Haus** ~ to live in a house rent-free; **möbliert** ~ to live in furnished apartments *(US)* (lodgings); **ganz in der Nähe** ~ to live nearby, to live round the corner; **ein paar Schritte vom Bahnhof entfernt** ~ to live within a few seconds run of the station; **im zweiten Stock** ~ to have one's quarters on the second floor; **im Stockwerk darüber** ~ to live overhead; **fünf Straßen weiter** ~ to live five blocks from here; **umsonst** ~ to have free quarters, *(Hotelgast)* to be a guest of the management; **in bedrängten Verhältnissen** ~ to live in cramped conditions; **vorübergehend** ~ to stay, to lodge; **eine Zeitlang** ~ to tabernacle; **zusammen** ~ to live (room, *US*) together;

j. mietfrei ~ lassen to let s. o. occupy a property without charging him rent.

Wohn|erlaubnis residence permit; **~fläche** floor space (area), housing space.

Wohngebäude residential premises (building), dwelling house, *(Mietshaus)* mansions *(Br.)*, apartment house (building), block of flats *(Br.)*;
~steuer inhabited house duty, house tax (duty, *Br.*); **~verbesserungen** improvements in dwellings; **verbundene ~versicherung** householder's comprehensive insurance; **~zuschüsse** improvement grants.

Wohngebiet housing area, residential district (zone), habitat; **neuerschlossenes ~** addition, development *(US)*.

Wohngegend residential area (district, section, neighbo(u)rhood, zone);
bevorzugte ~ select part of a city; **billige ~** low-rent residential district; **bürgerliche ~** middle-class residential area; **gute ~** fashionable quarters; **reiche ~** sugar fill *(sl.)*; **teure ~** high-rent residential district; **vornehme ~** high-class residential area (center, *US*, centre, *Br.*), centre of fashionable residence, silk-stocking ward *(US)*;
~ einer Stadt residential parts of a city;
in einer guten ~ leben to live at a good address, to be in a good neighbo(u)rhood.

Wohngeländeverbesserung improvement of dwellings.

Wohngeld *(Zuschuß)* rent allowance;
von einer individuellen Bedürftigkeit abhängig gemachtes ~ single-means tested housing subsidy;
Mieterschutz- und ~gesetz Housing Rents and Subsidies Act *(Br.)*; **~programm** [etwa] assisted housing program *(US)*.

Wohn|gelegenheit dwelling (housing) accommodation; **~gemeinschaft** residential community, flatsharing *(Br.)*; **~grundstück** residential property (real estate, premises, house), home site (lot, *US*); **sein Geld in ~grundstücken anlegen, ~grundstücke erwerben** to invest in house property; **~grundstücksschätzung** dwelling appraisal.

wohnhaft ordinarily resident, residing, dwelling, domiciled, living;
ehemals ~ late of; **im Ausland ~** resident abroad.

Wohnhaus [dwelling] house, domestic (residential) building, *(Mehrfamilienhaus)* multiple dwelling, *(Studenten)* hostel *(Br.)*, dormitory *(US)*;
herrschaftliches ~ residence, mansion;
~ mit dazugehörigem Landsitz messuage; **~ einer Siedlungsgesellschaft** coöperation apartment house;
~errichtung house construction; **~komplex** housing complex; **~modernisierung** house modernization; **~steuer** house duty (tax, *Br.*).

Wohn|heim lodginghouse, hostel *(Br.)*, dormitory *(US)*, rooming house *(US)*; **~heimunterbringung** hostel accommodation *(Br.)*; **~hochhaus** tower block *(Br.)*; **~hotel** apartment hotel *(US)*, service flats *(Br.)*; **mit dem allerneuesten ~komfort** with all modern conveniences; **~küche** kitchen-cum-living-room; **~küchendrama** kitchen-sink drama; **~kultur** style (appreciation) of living.

Wohnlage residential section (area);
in günstiger ~ in a desirable location;
teure ~ high-rent residential section (district).

Wohn|landschaft landscaped interior; **~laube** summerhouse.

wohnlich comfortable, snug, cosy.

Wohn|mobil mobile home; **~möglichkeiten** residential (living, dwelling) accommodations, housing facilities.

Wohnort domicile, abode, place of residence, [dwelling] place, abiding place, legal residence, inhabitancy, inhabitation;
gegenwärtiger ~ actual residence; **ständiger ~** permanent abode;
~ im Ausland residence abroad.

Wohn|ortswechsel change of address (residence); **~partei** tenant, lodger, occupant; **~quartier** living quarter.

Wohnraum residential (housing) space, houseroom, *(Wohnzimmer)* sitting (living) room;
nicht bewirtschafteter ~ uncontrolled (unrestricted) dwelling; **preisgebundener ~** rent-controlled housing; **unmöblierter ~** unfurnished accommodation; **vermieteter ~** rented accommodation; **zusätzlicher ~** additional housing;
~ mit nachgewiesenem Eigenbedarf premises required for landlord or a member of his family;
neuen ~ beschaffen to rehouse; **~ freigeben** to derequisition; **ausreichenden und geeigneten anderen ~ nachweisen** to offer suitable alternative accommodation; **~ zur Verfügung stellen** to house;
~beschaffung housing accommodation; **~beschaffung für Kriegsversehrte** veterans' housing.

wohnraumbewirtschaftet sein to be subject to the Rent Restriction Act *(Br.)*.

Wohnraum|bewirtschaftung housing (rent, *Br.*) control; **~bewirtschaftung aufheben** to derequisition housing *(Br.)*; **~bewirtschaftungsgesetz** Rent Restriction Act *(Br.)*; **~dichte** housing density; **~durchschnitt** average accommodation; **~erstellung** creation of dwellings; **~gestaltung** residential accommodation; **~zuteilung** lodging (housing) allocation; **~zweck** residential use.

Wohnrecht, kostenloses ~ right of habitation *(Louisiana)*; **vorübergehendes ~** *(Hausangestellte)* license;
~ haben to have a settlement, to belong *(US)*; **lebenslängliches ~ besitzen** to remain in a house during lifetime.

Wohn|schlafzimmer bed-sitting room, bed-sitter *(Br.)*; **~siedlung** residential settlement, housing development (estate); **soziale ~siedlung** council estate *(Br.)*.

Wohnsitz [dwelling] place, residence, place of abode, seat, settlement, habitation, inhabitancy, lodgings;
mit ~ in domiciled in; **ohne festen ~** of no fixed abode, without permanent home, unsettled;
abgeleiteter ~ derived domicile; **abhängiger ~** domicile of dependence *(Br.)*; **bleibender ~** country; **dienstlicher ~** official residence; **gemeinsamer ehelicher ~** matrimonial home (domicile); **gesetzlich erforderlicher ~** legal residence (domicile), domicile by operation of law, necessary domicile; **erwählter ~** domicile of choice; **durch Heirat erworbener ~** domicile by operation of law; **faktischer ~** de facto domicile; **fester ~** fixed (settled) abode, established (settled) place of residence, foundation, fixed residence, establishment; **gewillkürter ~** elected domicile, bona fide residence, domicile of choice; **gewöhnlicher ~** ordinary residence *(Br.)*; **natürlicher ~** domicile of origin; **örtlicher ~** domestic domicile; **ständiger ~** permanent abode, actual (fixed) residence; **steuerlicher ~** residence for tax purposes, ordinary residence *(Br.)*; **zweiter ~** secondary residence;
~ im Ausland foreign residence; **~ in einer Gemeinde** municipal domicile; **~ der gewerblichen Niederlassung** commercial domicile, domicile of corporation; **~ zur Zeit der Eheschließung** matrimonial domicile;
seinen ~ aufgeben to abandon a domicile, to vacate (relinquish, abandon) one's residence; **seinen ~ aufschlagen** to take up one's dwelling; **seinen ~ vorübergehend im Ausland aufschlagen** to take up temporary residence abroad; **seinen ~ begründen** to set (take) up one's abode, to fix (choose) one's residence in (elect domicile at) a place, to settle down, to [establish a] domicile; **seinen ~ erneut begründen** to resume possession of one's domicile; **seinen ~ haben** to reside, to domicile, to inhabit; **seinen ständigen ~ haben** to be permanently resident; **~ oder gewöhnlichen Aufenthalt haben** to be resident in; **seinen ~ außerhalb (innerhalb) eines zum Sterlingblock gehörenden Landes haben** to be resident outside (inside) the Scheduled Territories *(Br.)*; **sich ohne festen ~ herumtreiben** to float around *(US)*; **jds. ~ in London notwendig machen** to involve s. one's living in London; **seinen ~ nehmen** to settle down; **seinen ~ verlegen** to change (transfer) one's residence, to change one's domicile (lodgings); **nach dem Recht des ~es beurteilt werden** to be governed by the law of domicile;
~änderung change of residence (abode); **~anschrift** residence (home) address; **~aufgabe** abandonment of domicile; **~arten** types of domicile; **~begründung** establishment of residence; **~berechtigter** person domiciled here, individual resident, *(ohne Staatsangehörigkeit)* nonnational resident *(US)*; **~bestimmung** designation of abode; **~eigenschaft zur Unterstützungsvoraussetzung machen** to make residence a condition of relief; **~erfordernis** residence qualification (requirements); **~erfordernisse für Wahlberechtigte** residential qualifications for voters; **~gerichtsstand** forum domicili; **~staat** country of established residence, *(Deportierter)* country whence he came; **~veränderung** change of abode (residence), remove, removal; **~verlegung** transfer of residence, change (transfer) of domicile; **~wechsel** change of abode (residence).

Wohn|standard housing standard; **~stätte** abidal, rest, tent; **ständige ~stätte** permanent home; **~straße** residential street; **~stube** sitting (living, *US*) room.

Wohnung dwelling, lodging[s], quarters, habitation, housing, house, place, abode, home, *(Etage)* flat *(Br.)*, apartment *(US)*, *(Unterbringung)* living accommodation, *(Wohnsitz)* residence, domicile, [place of] abode;
ohne ~ dishoused;

abgeschlossene ~ separate dwelling, self-contained flat *(Br.)*; **zumutbare anderweitige** ~ suitable alternative accommodation; **behagliche** ~ nest; **staatlich bereitgestellte** ~**en** publicly-provided housing; **betriebsnahe** ~ home close to work; **nicht bewirtschaftete** ~ unrestricted (uncontrolled) dwelling; **vom Eigentümer bewohnte** ~ owner-occupied dwelling; **sofort bezugsfähige** ~ lodging ready to move into; **billige** ~ low-cost housing (accommodation); **Dreizimmer**-~ three-room apartment *(US)*; **eheliche** ~ matrimonial home; **eigene** ~ self-contained flat *(Br.)*, individual apartment *(US)*; **freifinanzierte** ~ private-sector flat *(Br.)*, privately financed housing unit (dwelling); **öffentlich geförderte** ~ subsidized housing; **im weißen Kreis gelegene** ~ decontrolled premises; **ruhig gelegene** ~ flat *(Br.)* (apartment, *US*) in a quiet neighbo(u)rhood; **in Teilwohnungen umgebaute große** ~ converted flat *(Br.)*; **größere** ~ living quarters; **industriell hergestellte** ~ factory-built housing; **herrschaftliche** ~ state apartment *(US)*; **kleine** ~ flatlet *(Br.)*; **leerstehende** ~ idle tenement, vacant flat *(Br.)*; **möblierte** ~ furnished apartment *(US)* (flat, *Br.*, dwelling), chambers; **schlüsselfertige** ~ house ready for immediate occupancy; **schmutzige** ~ dunghill; **im Eigentum stehende** ~ condominium apartment *(US)*; **steuerbegünstigte** ~ tax-privileged accommodation; **überbelegte** ~ overcrowded dwelling; **überdurchschnittliche** ~ above-average dwelling; **unsoziale** ~ substandard dwelling; **unterbelegte** ~ undercrowded dwelling; **den Mieterschutzbestimmungen unterliegende** ~ rent-controlled flat *(Br.)*; **unzulängliche** ~ substandard housing; **von der Stadt vermietete** ~ council house *(Br.)*; **vorfabrizierte** ~ prefabricated housing module, prefab housing; **vorübergehende** ~ lodge; **werkseigene** ~ company flat *(Br.)*, company-owned dwelling, industrial dwelling, employee home;
~ **für gehobenere Ansprüche** higher-bracket flat *(Br.)* (apartment, *US*), upper-level housing; ~ **beim Arbeitgeber** living-in; ~ **mit Bedienung** serviced accommodation, service flat *(Br.)*, apartment hotel *(US)*; ~ **mit eigenem Eingang** self-contained flat *(Br.)* (unit); ~ **außerhalb des Hauses** *(Hausangestellte)* living out; ~ **mit allem modernen Komfort** flat *(Br.)* (apartment, *US*) with all modern conveniences; **drei leerstehende** ~**en in einem Mietshaus** *(Annonce)* three vacancies in an apartment house *(US)*; ~ **mit Zimmern in verschiedenen Stockwerken** duplex apartment *(US)* (flat, *Br.*);
aus einer ~ **ausziehen** to move out of a flat *(Br.)*, to vacate an apartment *(US)*; **dringend eine neue** ~ **benötigen** to desperately need rehousing; ~ **beschaffen** to provide (procure) housing; ~ **besitzen** to occupy an apartment *(US)* (flat, *Br.*); **eigene** ~ **besitzen** to live in a flat *(Br.)* (apartment, *US*); **seiner Familie eine** ~ **besorgen** to house one's family; **sich selbst eine** ~ **besorgen** to make one's own housing arrangements; **j. sofort eine** ~ **besorgen** to house s. o. immediately; **neue** ~ **beziehen** to move into new rooms; ~ **einrichten** to furnish a flat *(Br.)* (an apartment, *US*); **Möbel aus einer** ~ **entfernen** to unfurnish an apartment *(US)* (flat, *Br.*); ~**en finanzieren** to finance houses (apartments, *US*, flats, *Br.*); **seine** ~ **in A haben** to reside at A; ~ **im zweiten Stock haben** to have one's quarters on the second (third, *US*) floor; ~**en aus der Mieterschutzgesetzgebung herausnehmen** to remove dwellings from control *(Br.)*; ~ **neu herrichten** to refurbish an apartment *(US)* (flat, *Br.*); ~ **mieten** to rent a flat *(Br.)* (apartment, *US*); **möblierte** ~ **mieten** to rent a furnished apartment *(US)* (flat, *Br.*); ~ **mieten und die Möbel übernehmen** to rent a flat *(Br.)* (apartment, *US*) and take over the furniture; ~ **möblieren** to furnish a flat *(Br.)* (apartment, *US*); **andere** ~ **nehmen** to change one's quarters; ~ **räumen** to quit the premises; **neue** ~ **in Aussicht stellen** to hold out the prospect of a new flat; ~ **suchen** to look for an apartment *(US)* (flat, *Br.*), to house-hunt, to flat-hunt *(Br.)*; **elterliche** ~ **verlassen** to leave the parental home; ~ **vermieten** to rent an apartment *(US)*, to let a flat *(Br.)*; ~**en in einem Haus einzeln vermieten** to let off a house into apartments *(US)* (flats, *Br.*); **seine** ~ **wechseln** to move [one's lodgings], to change one's address, to change (shift) one's quarters; **seine** ~ **zweckentfremden** to alter the use of one's premises, to convert rooms to office use.

Wohnungs|amt housing office, National Housing Agency *(US)*; ~**amtsangestellter** housing officer; ~**amtsleiter** housing executive; ~**angabe**, ~**anschrift** address; ~**angebot** housing stock (supply); ~**anteil** *(Stadtbezirk)* residential segment; **mit Mitteln des sozialen Wohnungsbaus finanzierter** ~**anteil** council-rented housing tenure *(Br.)*; ~**anzeiger** directory, housing advertiser; ~**art** type of dwelling; ~**ausschuß** housing committee.

Wohnungsbau housebuilding, home building *(US)*, residential (housing, apartment) construction, housing;
billiger ~ low-cost home construction; **freifinanzierter** ~ privately financed dwellings, private residential construction *(US)*; **öffentlicher (gemeinnütziger)** ~ public housing; **sozialer** ~ low- (moderate-) income housing, federally financed low-cost housing *(US)*, council housing *(Br.)*; **steuerbegünstigter** ~ tax-favo(u)red housing construction;
~ **der öffentlichen Hand** public housing;
freifinanzierten ~ **ankurbeln** to lure private landlords back into the market; ~ **fördern** to stimulate housebuilding;
~**behörde** Housing Department *(Br.)*, National Housing Agency *(US)*; ~**darlehn** housing loan; ~**etat** spending on housing; ~**experte** housing analyst (expert); ~**feldzug** housing campaign; ~**finanzierung** financing of housing, [housing and] home financing *(US)*; ~**finanzierungsgesellschaft** housing and finance association; **staatliche** ~**förderung** subsidized housing; ~**förderungsgesetz** Housing Subsidies Act *(Br.)*, housing aid bill *(US)*; ~**genehmigung** home-building permit; ~**genossenschaft** housing cooperative; **gemeinnützige** ~**gesellschaft** housing society (association) *(Br.)*; ~**gesetz** housing law, National Housing Act *(Br.)*; ~**hilfe** subsidized housing; ~**hypothek** residential mortgage; ~**investitionen** capital expenditure on housebuilding; ~**konjunktur** housing upturn (boom); ~**kontingent** housing department allocation *(Br.)*; ~**kredit** housing loan (credit); ~**krise** housing crisis; ~**maßnahmen** prudential affairs; **neue** ~**methoden** housing innovations; ~**minister** Minister of Housing *(Br.)*; ~**ministerium** Housing Administration *(US)*, Ministry of Housing and Local Government *(Br.)*; ~**- und Städtebauministerium** Secretary of Housing and Urban Development; ~**mittel** funds for housing; ~**politik** housing policy; ~**prämie** housing bonus; ~**prognose** residential building outlook; ~**programm** housing program(me); ~**projekt** housing (scheme) development plan *(Br.)*; **von der Bundesregierung finanziertes soziales** ~**projekt** federally financed low-cost housing project *(US)*; **staatliches** ~**projekt** public housing project; ~**sektor** housebuilding sector, housing industry; ~**statut** housing ordinance; **gemeinnütziger** ~**verband** housing association *(Br.)*; ~**vorhaben** housing scheme (development plan); ~**wesen** residential [housing] construction; ~**wirtschaft** home building industry *(US)*.

Wohnungs|bedarf housing requirements (needs, demand); ~**bedingungen** housing conditions; ~**behörde** housing office (authority); ~**beihilfe** housing assistance (aid), lodging allowance (assistance), allowance for rent (quarters); ~**beihilfesystem** housing-assistance scheme; ~**beratung** housing counsel(l)ing; ~**beratungsstelle** Central Housing Advisory Committee *(Br.)*; ~**beschaffung** subsidized housing; ~**beschaffungskredit** housing credit; ~**bestand** total dwellings; ~**bestandsaufnahme** housing inquiry; **den** ~**bestimmungen nicht genügen** to be statutorily unfit; ~**bewirtschaftung** housing control; ~**darlehen für Instandsetzungszwecke** home-improvement loan; ~**defizit** housing shortage; ~**dichte** housing density; ~**diskriminierung** housing discrimination; ~**eigentum** residential property, condominium apartment *(US)*, freehold flat *(Br.)*; ~**eigentümer** owner of a freehold flat, condominium apartment owner *(US)*; ~**einbauten des Mieters** domestic fixtures; ~**einbruch** flat *(Br.)* (apartment, *US*) breaking; ~**einbruchsversicherung** residence burglary insurance; ~**einheit** dwelling (housing) unit; **neu angefangene** ~**einheiten** housing starts; **vorfabrizierte** ~**einheiten** factory-built (modular) housing; ~**einrichtung** household furnishings, home furnishings *(US)*; ~**entschädigung** housing assistance (allowance); ~**erhebung** census of housing; ~**finanzierung** financing of housing, housing finance (aid), [housing and] home financing *(US)*; ~**finanzierungsgesellschaft** housing and home financing agency *(US)*; ~**finanzierungshilfe** housing aid; ~**frage** housing question; ~**geld** rent allowance, living-out allowance; ~**geldzuschuß** lodging money (allowance), allowance for room (quarters, rent); ~**geldzuschuß gewähren** to allow for quarters; ~**genossenschaft** housing cooperative; ~**gesellschaft** housing society; **kostenlose** ~**gestellung** free housing; ~**gesuche** accommodation wanted; ~**inhaber** lodger, tenant, occupier, roomer *(US)*, renter *(Br.)*, *(Haushaltungsvorstand)* householder; ~**instandsetzung** housing rehabilitation; ~**kauf** housing deal; ~**käufer** purchaser of an apartment *(US)* (flat, *Br.*); ~**knappheit** housing shortage; ~**kosten** housing costs; ~**kostenzuschuß** overnight allowance; ~**krise** housing crisis; ~**makler** accommodation broker, house agent *(Br.)*, real-estate broker *(US)*; **übliche** ~**maklergebühr** normal charges paid to agent for letting; ~**mangel** housing shortage.

Wohnungsmarkt housing market;
bewirtschafteter ~ controlled housing; **krisenhafter** ~ housing crisis;
~**lage** housing position (scene).
Wohnungs|miete rent of a premise, rent of dwellings, apartment *(US)* (residential) rent, housing (home, *US*) rental; **freifinanzierte** ~**miete** private rent; **hohe** ~**miete** high housing rent; ~**mietzuschuß** rent subsidy; ~**müll** house (residential) refuse; ~**nachweis** housing office, accommodation registry *(Br.)*; ~**neubauten** housing starts; ~**not** scarcity (shortage) of housing, housing shortage (famine, problem); ~**nutzung** occupation of a dwelling; ~**problem** housing problem; ~**programm** housing program(me); ~**projekt** apartment *(US)* (flat, *Br.*) project; ~**qualität** housing quality; **fehlender** ~**raum** housing gap; ~**recht** law of landlord and tenant; ~**schwierigkeiten** housing difficulties; ~**situation** housing position; ~**standard** housing standard; ~**statistik** housing statistics; ~**suche** house (flat, *Br.*) hunting; **auf** ~**suche gehen** to house-hunt, to flat-hunt *(Br.)*; **bei der** ~**suche behilflich sein** to assist in finding [living] accommodation; ~**suchender** house-hunter, flat-hunter *(Br.)*, *(Eigenheim)* home seeker; ~**tausch** exchange of dwellings; ~**tür** outer door; **seine** ~**tür schließen** to sport one's oak *(Br.)*; **gemeinnütziges** ~**unternehmen** housing society (association) *(Br.)*; ~**verhältnisse** lodging (housing) conditions, living accommodation; **beengte (beschränkte)** ~**verhältnisse** close quarters, crowded conditions; ~**vermieter** landlord; ~**vermietung** flat-letting business *(Br.)*; ~**vermittlung** house agency, accommodation registry *(Br.)*; ~**verordnung** housing ordinance; ~**versicherung** residence insurance; ~**verwalter** housing manager; ~**verwaltung** housing management; ~**wechsel** change of address (residence), shift, flit *(Br.)*; ~**wesen** housing; **ländliches** ~**wesen** rural housing; ~**wesen und Stadtentwicklung** housing and urban development; ~**wirtschaft** housing industry, *(Bewirtschaftung)* housing control; ~**zählung** census of housing; ~**zuschuß** lodging money (allowance), accommodation (housing) allowance, housing subsidy; ~**zuweisung** lodging (housing) allocation; ~**zuweisungsschein** lodging bill; ~**zwangswirtschaft** housing (rent, *Br.*) control; ~**zwangswirtschaft aufheben** to derequisition housing *(Br.)*; **für** ~**zwecke ungeeignet** unfit for habitation.
Wohnverhältnisse housing conditions, living (dwelling) accommodation;
beengte (beschränkte) ~ overcrowded conditions, close quarters.
Wohnviertel residential area (district, zone), living quarter (section), housing estate;
im ~ **gelegen** uptown;
zentral gelegenes ~ downtown area *(US)*; **heruntergekommenes** ~ blighted area; **vornehmes** ~ affluent area, silk-stocking ward *(US)*.
Wohnvorort bedroom community *(US)*, dormitory suburb.
Wohnwagen caravan *(Br.)*, mobile home, house wag(g)on, house trailer *(US)*;
motorisierter ~ motorhome;
im ~ **leben** to caravan *(Br.)*;
~**anhänger** caravan *(Br.)*, trailer *(US)*; ~**benutzer**, ~**besitzer** caravaneer *(Br.)*, caravaner *(Br.)*, trailerite *(US)*; ~**park** caravan park (site) *(Br.)*, trailer park *(US)*; **fester** ~**platz** caravan stand *(Br.)*, pitch; ~**stadt** trailer camp (court) *(US)*.
Wohn|weise, asoziale substandard living; ~**wert** residential amenity; ~**zelt** living tent; ~**zentrum** residential community; ~**zimmer** living (sitting) room, parlo(u)r; **ebenerdiges** ~**zimmer** drawing room on a level with the garden; ~-**Schlafzimmer** bed-sitting room *(Br.)*; ~**zimmermöbel** parlo(u)r furniture; **für** ~**zwecke hinreichend geeignet sein** to be reasonably fit for habitation.
Wolf, hungrig wie ein as hungry as a hunter;
~ **im Schafspelz** a wolf in sheep's (lamb's) clothing, lamb in the skin, snake in the grass;
wie durch den ~ **gedreht sein** to be aching all over.
Wölfe, mit den ~**n heulen** to follow in the cry, to howl with the pack *(fam.)*.
Wolke cloud, *(Edelstein)* flaw;
~**n auflösen** to dissipate clouds; **in den** ~**n schweben** to be in the clouds; **wie aus allen** ~**n gefallen sein** to be flabbergasted.
Wolken|bank bank of clouds; ~**bruch** cloud burst, torrents of rain, torrential rain.
wolkenbruchartig torrential.
Wolken|decke cloud cover, blanket of clouds; **geschlossene** ~**decke** canopy of clouds; ~**dichte** density of clouds; ~**echo** *(Radar)* cloud return; ~**fetzen** shreds of clouds, scud.
wolkenfrei cloudless, no clouds.
Wolken|guß, von einem ~**guß überrascht werden** to be caught in a shower; ~**höhe** height of clouds; ~**höhenmesser** ceilometer; ~**karte** cloud map; ~**kratzer** skyscraper; ~**kuckucksheim** cloudland, Cloud-Cuckoo-Land.
wolkenlos cloudless, unclouded, fair, no clouds.
Wolken|obergrenze cloud top; ~**streifen** plume of cloud; ~**untergrenze** cloud base.
wolkig nebulous, cloudy, clouded, overcast.
wollartig woolly.
Woll|ballen wool bale; ~**börse** wool hall *(Br.)*; ~**decke** wool(l)en blanket, rug *(Br.)*.
Wolle, in der ~ **gefärbt** *(fig.)* dyed in the wool;
sich mit jem. in der ~ **haben** to be out (at outs, *US*) with s. o.
wollene Kleidung wool(l)ens.
Woll|ertrag, jährlicher wool clip; ~**handel** wool trade; ~**händler** wool merchant (stapler); ~**industrie** wool(l)en industry; ~**produktion** woolgrowing; ~**stoff** wool, wool(l)en.
Wollust lust, voluptuousness, wantonness.
wollüstig lustful, voluptuous, lecherous, lewd, wanton.
Wollüstling debauchee, lecher, sensualist.
Woll|waren wool(l)en goods; ~**warengeschäft** wool(l)en drapery; ~**zeug** wool(l)en.
Wonne, wahre bliss of luxury;
in eitel ~ **schwimmen** to be blissfully happy;
~**proppen** roly-poly, little lump of sweetness; ~**schauer** thrill of delight.
Wort word, *(Ausdruck)* expression, term, *(Parlament)* floor;
auf mein ~ upon my conscience; **aufs** ~ at a word; **im wahrsten Sinne des** ~**es** in the true sense of the word; **in** ~ **und Schrift** written and spoken; **in** ~ **und Tat** in word and deed; **in wenigen** ~**en** in brief; **mit eindringlichen** ~**en** with great insistence; **mit lobenden** ~**en** in terms of praise;
abgeleitetes ~ derivative word; **ärgerniserregende** ~**e** offensive language; **aufmunternde** ~**e** pep talk; **schwer auszusprechendes** ~ jawbreaker, tongue-twister; **beleidigende** ~**e** defamatory (injurious) words, words actionable in themselves; **böse** ~**e** sharp words; **einführende** ~**e** introduction, introductory words; **einschränkende** ~**e** *(Testament)* words of limitation; **erfundenes** ~ coined word; **freundliche** ~**e** kind words; **rechtsverbindliche, beim Kauf gebrauchte** ~**e** words of purchase; **geflügeltes** ~ familiar quotation, household name, current saying, dictum; **gegebenes** ~ pledged word; **geläufiges** ~ waif word; **gegenstandslos gewordene** ~**e** vestigal words; **hochtrabende** ~**e** big words; **unheilvoll klingende** ~**e** black words; **leere** ~**e** mere talk, empty words, wind; **letzte** ~**e** dying words; **neugeprägtes** ~ new-coined word; **rechtsgestaltende** ~**e** operative words; **seine tatsächlichen** ~**e** his exact words; **teilnehmende** ~**e** sympathetic words; **unanständige** ~**e** indelicate words, rank language; **unmißverständliche** ~**e** overt words; **unzüchtige** ~**e** four-letter (Saxon) words; **veraltetes** ~ archaism; **vielsagendes** ~ comprehensive word; **zornige** ~**e** hot (cross) words; **zusammengesetztes** ~ compound word;
erstes ~ **einer neuen Seite** prima *(Br.)*; **letzte** ~**e eines Sterbenden** expiring words of a dying man;
das ~ **an j. abgeben** to give the floor to s. o.; **jem. das** ~ **abschneiden** to cut s. o. short; **j. mit schönen** ~**en abspeisen** to put s. o. off with fair (pay s. o. in empty) words; **mit packenden** ~**en beschreiben** to describe vividly; **ums** ~ **bitten** to ask for (demand) the floor *(US)*, to try to catch the speaker's eye *(Br.)*; **sein** ~ **brechen** to dishono(u)r (break) one's word; **ein** ~ **dazwischenwerfen** to slip a word in; **ab und zu ein** ~ **dazwischenwerfen** to thrust a word in now and then; **gutes** ~ **für j. einlegen** to put in a good word for s. o.; **sein** ~ **nicht einlösen** to go back on one's word; ~ **einschieben** to edge a word in; ~ **einwerfen** to put a word in; **jem. das** ~ **entziehen** to closure s. o., to rule s. o. out of order; **das** ~ **ergreifen** to address the house, to speak, to take the floor *(US)*; **in einer Versammlung das** ~ **ergreifen** to address a meeting (the house); **das** ~ **zur Tagesordnung ergreifen** to rise to a point of order; **das** ~ **erhalten** to have (be given) the word (floor, *US*), to catch the speaker's eye *(Br.)*; **jem. das** ~ **erteilen** to call upon s. o. to speak, to give the floor to s. o. *(US)*, *(Abgeordnetem)* to recognize a member *(US)*; **mit keinem** ~ **erwähnen** not to speak a word of it; **in** ~**e fassen** to word, to voice, to phrase; **in andere** ~**e fassen** to make s. th. read differently; **keine** ~**e finden** to be speechless; **das große** ~ **führen** to monopolize (engross) the conversation; **sein** ~ **geben** to give one's word; **nichts auf jds.** ~**e geben** not to rely on s. o.; **jem. gute** ~**e geben** to talk nicely to s. o.; **hochtrabende** ~**e gebrauchen** to speak in a pretentious language; **unfreundliche** ~**e gebrauchen** to say rude things; ~

falsch gebrauchen to misuse a word; **jem. aufs ~ gehorchen** to obey s. o. to the letter; **das ~ haben** to have the floor *(US)* (ear) of the house, to be on the floor *(US)*; **das letzte ~ haben** to have the last word (say-so in a matter); **ein ~ mitzureden haben** to be qualified to speak *(fam.)*, to have a say in a matter; **sein ~ halten** to be true to one's word, to keep one's faith; **~ aus dem Griechischen herleiten** to derive a word from the Greek; **zu ~ kommen** to get a word in edgeways, to get a hearing; **auf das richtige ~ kommen** to hit on the right word; **~ fallen lassen** to drop a hint; **seinen ~en Taten folgen lassen** to suit the action to the word, to back up one's words with action, to make words with deeds; **ein ~ mit sich reden lassen** to listen to reason; **~ löschen** *(Satzmaschine)* to kill a word; **jem. schöne ~e machen** to speak s. o. fair; **sich zu ~ melden** to ask leave to speak (for the floor, *US*), to try to catch the speaker's eye *(Br.)*, to rise up; **das ~ nehmen** to take the floor *(US)*; **j. beim ~ nehmen** to hold s. o. to his word; **es sehr genau mit seinen ~en nehmen** to speak by the card; **jem. das ~ aus dem Mund nehmen** to take the words out of s. one's mouth; **jds. ~e für bare Münze nehmen** to take s. one's words at their face value; **~ prägen** to mint a word; **ernstes ~ mit jem. reden** to talk to s. o. like a Dutch uncle; **offenes ~ mit jem. reden** to speak frankly with s. o.; **ein ~ aus dem Zusammenhang reißen** to divorce (take) a word out of its context; **j. mit seinen eigenen ~en schlagen** to beat s. o. at his own game; **mit den ~en schließen** to conclude (wind up) by saying; **einleitende ~e schreiben** to preface; **~ mit großen Anfangsbuchstaben schreiben** to write a word with an initial (a capital) letter; **auf die Rückseite eines Wechsels die ~e setzen** to enface a draft with the words; **~ in Anführungsstriche setzen** to put a word in quotation marks; **das entscheidende ~ sprechen** to have the say-so in a matter, to boss the show *(US sl.)*; **verletzende ~e sprechen** to speak daggers; **kein ~ mehr miteinander sprechen** to be no longer on speaking terms; **zu seinem ~ stehen** to stick to one's word; **jem. das ~ im Munde umdrehen** to misinterpret s. one's words; **~e in Taten umsetzen** to translate talk into action; **sich in einer Fülle von ~en verheddern** to lose o. s. in verbiage; **keine ~e verlieren** to lose no words; **sein ~ verpfänden** to pass one's word; **j. mit schönen ~en vertrösten** to put s. o. off with fine words; **auf das ~ verzichten** to waive one's right to speak; **seine ~e sorgfältig wählen** to cull one's words, to be nice in the choice of words; **ein paar ~e mit jem. wechseln** to have a few words with s. o.; **in wenigen ~en zusammenfassen** to put in a nutshell;
~abstand spacing; **~akzent** word stress; **~armut** paucity of words; **~artbezeichnung** part-of-speech label; **~bank** word bank; **~bedeutung** meaning of a word, *(eigentliche)* literal meaning of a word; **~bedeutung forcieren** to strain the meaning of a word, to contort a word out of its ordinary meaning; **~-für-~-Bestätigung** verbatim confirmation; **~betonung** word accent; **~bildung** wordbuilding, word formation; **~bildungselement** combining form; **~bruch** breach of promise.

wortbrüchig werden to break (go back on) one's word.

Wörtchen, ein ~ mitzureden haben to have a say in a matter; **mit jem. ein ernstes ~ reden** to give s. o. a lick with the rough side of one's tongue.

Wortentziehung order to relinquish the floor *(US)*.

Wörterbuch dictionary, thesaurus;
elektronisches ~ computerized dictionary; **klassisches ~** standard dictionary; **wandelndes ~** walking dictionary;
~ der Handelssprache commercial (business) dictionary;
~ neu bearbeiten to revise a dictionary; **~ auf den neuesten Stand bringen** to update a dictionary; **~ konsultieren, in einem ~ nachschlagen** to consult (look up in) a dictionary; **~ verfassen** to compile a dictionary;
~definition dictionary definition; **~herausgeber** editor of a dictionary; **~herstellung** dictionary making; **~tätigkeit** dictionary work; **~verfasser** dictionary maker, lexicographer; **~zettel** dictionary slip.

Wort | ergreifung, zweite second speech; **~erteilung** recognition of a member *(US)*.

Wörterverzeichnis vocabulary list.

Wort | folge word order; **~führer** speaker, spokesman, prolocutor, mouthpiece, *(Jury)* foreman; **~gebühr** *(Telegramm)* telegraph (telegram) rate; **~gefecht** dispute, battle (war) of words, wordy warfare; **~gemälde** word picture; **~geplänkel** skirmish.

wortgetreu literal, verbatim, verbal, close;
~ übersetzen to translate word for word; **~ wiedergeben** to report fully;
~e Abschrift einer Urkunde exact (verbal) copy of a document; **~er Bericht** verbatim; **~e Übersetzung** close translation.

wort | gewandt eloquent, *(negativ)* glib; **~karg** laconic, taciturn.

Wort | klauber word-catcher, word splitter, verbalist; **~klauberei** word-catching, hair (word) splitting, verbalism, quibble; **~klauberei treiben** to quibble; **~krieg** wordy warfare.

Wortlaut tenor, text, wording, purport, phraseology;
nach dem ~ eines Gesetzes by the terms of an act;
amtlicher ~ official text; **authentischer ~** authentic text; **genauer ~** face, exact term;
~ einer Buchung narration of an entry; **~ einer Resolution** wording of a resolution; **genauer ~ einer Urkunde** face of an instrument; **~ eines Vertrages** wording of a contract;
~ eines Gerichtsbeschlusses aushandeln *(Anwalt)* to settle an order *(Br.)*; **folgenden ~ haben** to read as follows; **sich genau an den ~ halten** to stick to the text; **in vollem ~ zitieren** to quote verbatim.

wörtlich verbal, literal;
nicht ~ *(Übersetzung)* free;
Satz ~ auffassen to understand a phrase literally; **etw. ~ nehmen** to take in its literal sense;
~e Übersetzung verbatim translation; **~e Wiedergabe** verbatim record; **~es Zitat** word-for-word quotation.

Wort | malerei word painting; **~meldung** request for leave to speak; **vorbehaltene ~meldung** reserved speech; **~neuschöpfung** neologism; **~protokoll** verbatim report of the procedings.

wortreich wordy, verbose;
sich ~ bedanken to be profuse in one's thanks;
~e Erklärung wordy explanation.

Wort | reichtum verbosity; **~reihenfolge** word order; **~sammlung** thesaurus; **~schatz** word power, vocabulary; **seinen ~schatz vergrößern** to add to one's vocabulary; **~schöpfung** coinage; **~schwall** flood (volley, torrent, stream) of words, verbosity, tirade, verbiage; **j. mit einem ~schwall überschütten** to talk at s. o.; **~spiel** play upon words, wordplay, crank, pun; **~spiel machen** to pun (play) upon a word; **~stamm** radical; **~stellung** word order; **~streit** dispute, argument, quarrel, controversy; **~tarif** *(Telegramm)* word rate; **~umstellung** transposition of words; **~verdreher** prevaricator, wrestler; **~verdrehung** prevarication, crank, equivocation, distortion; **~verwechslung** confusion of terms, misuse of words; **~verzeichnis** verbal index; **falsche ~wahl** verbal error; **~wechsel** argument, dispute, contest; **heftiger ~wechsel** snap; **~wechsel mit jem. haben** to become involved in an argument with s. o.

wortwörtlich verbal, literal, verbatim;
Vertrag ~ auslegen to stick to the letter of an agreement; **~ nehmen** to take in a literal sense; **alles ~ nehmen** to be literal-minded; **~ übersetzen** to translate word for word;
~e Übersetzung verbatim (verbal, word-for-word) translation; **~er Verhandlungsbericht** verbatim report of the proceedings.

Wort | zeichen *(Warenzeichenrecht)* slogan trademark; **Inhalt aus dem ~zusammenhang entnehmen** to guess the meaning from the context; **~zusammensetzung** compound word.

Wrack shipwreck, wreck, abandoned ship, *(Mensch)* broken-down (worn-out) person, crock *(coll.)*;
von der Mannschaft aufgegebenes (herrenloses) ~ derelict, unclaimed wreck;
~ abbrechen to wreck off a ship; **~ flottmachen** to float a wreck; **nur noch ein ~ sein** to be a mere wreck of one's former self; **treibendes ~gut** wreckage, wrecked cargo, flotsam, jetsam; **~teil** wrecking, piece of wreckage; **treibende ~teile** floating timbers of a wreck; **~tonne** wreck buoy; **~trümmer** wreckage.

Wucher usury, extortion, extortionate charge, exorbitance;
~ treiben to practise usury;
~bedingungen usurious conditions; **~darlehen** usurious loan; **~einwand** defense *(US)* (defence, *Br.*) of usury.

Wucherer usurer, usurious person, excess profiteer, profitmonger, hawk, horseleech, loan shark *(US)*;
von ~n ausgebeutet werden to be in the hands of moneylenders.

Wucher | geschäft usurious trade (transaction), profiteering, unconscionable bargain (transaction); **gewissenloses ~geschäft** catching bargain; **~gesetz** usury law; **~gesetzgebung** usury legislation; **~gewinn** excess profit; **~grenze** usurious limit.

wucherisch usurious, profitmongering;
~ aufkaufen to forestall;
~es Gewerbe usurious trade; **~er Vertrag** usurious contract.

Wuchermiete usurious rent, rack rent *(Ireland)*.

wuchern to run wild, to go rampant;
mit seinen Pfunden ~ to make the most of one's talents.

wuchernd rampant, rank, *(üppig)* luxuriant.

Wucher | preis ransom (cutthroat, exorbitant, extortionate, usurious, famine) price; **~preis bezahlen** to pay through the

nose *(coll.)*; ~**preis von 100 Pfund bezahlen** to pay for s. th. to the tune of £ 100; ~**vertrag** usurious contract; ~**zinsen** illegal (usurious, exorbitant, excessive) interest, usury; **zu ~zinsen ausleihen** to lend on usurious interest.
Wuchsaktie growth share.
Wucht weight, force, thumper *(coll.)*;
mit voller ~ at full tilt;
~ **eines Angriffs widerstehen** to bear the brunt of an attack;
das ist eine ~ that's smashing (marvel(l)ous).
wuchtige Möbel massive furniture.
Wühlarbeit *(pol.)* underhand (subversive) activities.
wühlen, gegen j. to agitate against s. o.; **in alten Dokumenten wühlen** to quarry among old documents; **im Gelde** ~ to be wallowing (rolling) in money; **im Schmutz** ~ to wallow in filth; **in seinen Unterlagen nach einem verlorengegangenen Testament** ~ to be rooting among piles of paper for a missing will; **in alten Wunden** ~ to open old sores.
Wulstreifen clincher (beaded) tyre (tire, *US*).
wund sore, chafed, raw;
sich die Füße ~ **laufen** to be run off one's feet, to get sore feet;
sich die Finger ~ **schreiben** to write until one's fingers ache;
~**er Punkt** weak point; **Finger auf jds. ~e Stelle legen** to put one's finger on s. one's weak point; ~ **geriebene Stelle** sore.
Wunde, lebensgefährliche vital wound;
alte ~n wieder aufreißen to open old sores; **jem. eine** ~ **beibringen** to wound s. o.; **in einer** ~ **unnötig herumwühlen** to pile on the agony; **seinen Finger auf die offene** ~ **legen** to put one's finger on the bad place, to lay one's finger on the evil; **tiefe ~n schlagen** *(Krieg)* to cause disaster and suffering; **an seinen ~n sterben** to die from one's injuries.
Wunder wonder, miracle, marvel;
absolutes ~ positive miracle;
~ **an Ausdauer** marvel of perseverance; ~ **an Gelehrsamkeit** prodigy of learning; ~ **der modernen Technik** marvels of modern science;
~ **bewirken** to work wonders; **sein blaues** ~ **erleben** to be in for a surprise; **beinahe an ein** ~ **grenzen** to be little short of a miracle;
~ **vollbringen** to work wonders (miracles), to wring water from a flint.
wunderbar marvel(l)ous, wonderful, on top of the world;
~**es Essen** excellent food; ~**e Fügung** unfathomable fate; ~**e Stimme** beautiful (glorious) voice.
Wunder|kind infant (child) prodigy, child genius; ~**knabe** boy wonder; ~**land** wonderland, fairyland.
wunderlich whimsical, curious *(coll.)*;
etw. ~ **sein** to be kind of queer.
wundern, sich to be astonished, to be surprised;
sich nicht genug ~ **können** not to get over it.
Wunder|tat prodigy; ~**täter** miracle worker, wonderworker; ~**werk** wonderwork, miracle.
Wunsch wish, will, request;
auf ~ by request, on application; **auf** ~ **gegen besondere Berechnung** optional at extra cost; **auf allgemeinen** ~ by popular request; **je nach** ~ as desired (required); **von dem** ~ **geleitet** moved by the desire; **von dem** ~ **getrieben** actuated by the desire;
frommer ~ pious wish;
jem. jeden ~ **von den Augen ablesen** to anticipate s. one's wishes;
nach ~ **ausfallen** to answer expectations; **auf eigenen** ~ **ausscheiden** to retire from a firm at one's own request; **einem** ~ **nachkommen** to comply with a wish; **gegen seinen** ~ **pensioniert werden** to be compulsorily retired;
~**bild** ideal, vision; ~**denken** wishful thinking.
Wünsche| der Verbraucher wants of the customers;
seine ~ **befriedigen** to please o. s.; **den ~n auf halbem Wege entgegenkommen** to meet the wishes halfway; **den ~n einer neuen Publikumsschicht entsprechen** to cater to a new public; **um jds.** ~ **zu erfüllen** in order to comply with s. one's wishes; ~ **seiner Kunden unverzüglich erledigen** to meet one's customers' wishes without delay; **seine** ~ **formulieren** to postulate one's wishes; **keinerlei** ~ **haben** to want for nothing; **jds.** ~ **beiseite schieben** to override s. one's wishes; **jds. ~n Rechnung tragen** to comply with s. one's wishes; **seine herzlichen** ~ **übermitteln** to convey one's sincere wishes.
Wünschelrute wishing (magic) wand, divining (dipping) rod, dowser's (dowsing) rod;
mit der ~ **gehen** to work the twig.
Wünschelrutengänger water finder, water witch *(US)*.
wünschen to wish, to want, to desire, to request;
jem. Glück ~ to wish s. o. well;
viel zu ~ **übrig lassen** to leave much to be desired.
wünschenswert eligible, desirable;
~ **sein** to be desirable (an asset).
Wunscherfüllung wish fulfilment.
wunschgemäß after one's own heart, in accordance with one's desire.
Wunsch|handlung imaginative activity; ~**konzert** request program(me); ~**liste** want list.
wunschlos glücklich sein to be perfectly happy.
Wunsch|traum wish (pipe, *US*) dream; ~**vorstellung** wishful thinking; ~**zettel** list of wishes.
Würde dignity, rank, stateliness, gravity, elevation;
in voller ~ full-fledged; **ohne Beeinträchtigung der** ~ without derogation from dignity;
richterliche ~ judgeship, bench;
zu den höchsten ~n aufsteigen to attain the highest hono(u)rs;
der ~ **berauben** to discrown; **seine** ~ **bewahren** to retain one's dignity; **es unter seiner** ~ **finden, sich zu beschweren** to be too proud to complain; **es unter seiner** ~ **halten, ein Hilfsangebot anzunehmen** to disdain an offer of help; **zu hohen ~n kommen** to advance to high rank; **in Amt und ~n sein** to be in an established position; **unter jds.** ~ **sein** to be beneath s. one's dignity; ~ **zur Schau stellen** to deport o. s. with dignity; **seiner** ~ **Abbruch tun** to derogate from one's dignity; **seine** ~ **vergessen** to lay aside one's dignity; **einer Sache** ~ **verleihen** to lend dignity to s. th.; **jem. die** ~ **eines Doktors verleihen** to confer a doctorate on s. o.
würdelos undignified;
sich ~ **benehmen** to demean o. s.
Würdenträger dignitary, bigwig *(sl.)*, *(hoher)* cordon bleu;
alle ~ **des Landes** the whole dignity of the country.
würdig worthy, worth, dignified;
~ **auftreten** to deport o. s. with dignity; **einer Sache** ~ **sein** to be deserving of s. th.; **j.** ~ **vertreten** to be s. one's adequate substitute;
~**e alte Dame** dignified old lady.
würdigen to estimate, to acknowledge, *(Beweis)* to appreciate;
j. keiner Antwort ~ not to deign to answer s. o.; **Erfindungshöhe** ~ *(Patent)* to appreciate the inventive step; **gebührend** ~ to give due weight; **neue Symphonie** ~ to write an appreciation of a new symphony; **jds. Verdienste** ~ to pay tribute to s. one's merits.
Würdigung estimation, valuation, *(Beweise)* appreciation, summing-up, *(Buch)* appreciation;
bei aller ~ **seiner Verdienste** with due respect to s. one's merits;
nach sorgfältiger ~ **aller Gründe** after close consideration of all reasons;
dankbare ~ sincere appreciation; **kritische** ~ critical appraisal;
~ **vornehmen** to carry a tribute.
Wurf toss, pelt;
glücklicher ~ lucky hit (shot); **großer** ~ grand gesture, great success, ten-strike *(US)*;
alles auf einen ~ **setzen** to put all one's eggs in one basket.
Würfel dice, bones, cube;
falscher ~ loaded dice;
~ **fälschen** to load a dice; ~ **spielen** to play dice, to shoot craps *(US)*; **mit falschen ~n spielen** to cog;
wenn die ~ **gefallen sind** when the dice are cast (chips are down, *Br.*);
~**becher** dicebox.
würfeln to play dice, to shoot craps *(US)*;
um den ersten Einsatz ~ to cast dice for the first throw.
Wurf|geschoß missile, projectile; ~**leine** *(mar.)* hauling line;
~**sendungen** direct-mail advertising.
Würgegriff stranglehold, choking grip;
sich dem ~ **des Filmverleihgeschäfts entziehen** to stay out of the clutches of major distributors.
würgen to choke, to strangle;
an einer Arbeit ~ to sweat over a piece of work.
Würger strangler, butcher.
Würgespuren traces of strangulation.
Wurm des Gewissens pangs of conscience.
Würmer, jem. die ~ **aus der Nase ziehen** to worm a secret out of s. o.
wurmstichig worm-eaten.
Wurst wider Wurst diamond cut diamond.
Würstchen, heißes hot dog.
Würze savo(u)r, spice, zest.
Wurzel grassroots, *(Ursprung)* well;
üble Machenschaften mit der ~ **ausrotten** to destroy evil practices root and branch; ~ **eines Übels bloßlegen** to strike at the root of the evil; **Übel bei der** ~ **packen** to get down to the root of the trouble; ~**n schlagen** to strike (take) root.

wurzeln, tief in der Erde to be rooted deeply in the ground.
würzen, Rede mit klassischen Zitaten to pepper a speech with classic quotations.
Wust von Arbeit mess of work.
wüst waste, desolate, desert;
~**es Durcheinander** devil among the tailors, topsy-turvydom, haywire *(US sl.)*; ~**es Gelage** drunken revel, carouse; ~**es Leben führen** to lead a dissolute life; ~**e Unordnung** wild disorder.
Wüste desert, wild waste;
trostlose ~ howling wilderness; **unbewohnte** ~ houseless desert; ~ **durchqueren** to traverse a desert; **Land zur** ~ **machen** to lay waste a country; **in die** ~ **geschickt werden** to be send off into the wilderness.
Wüstengebiete desert areas (land);
rückständige ~ backward deserts;
~ **bewässern** to irrigate deserts.
Wüsten|karawane desert caravan; ~**randgebiet** desert fringe; ~**schiff** ship of the desert; ~**volk** desert tribe.
Wüstling libertine, lecher, roué, debauchee.
Wut rage, fury, wrath, heat;
seine ~ **am Büroboten auslassen** to vent one's anger on the office boy; **j. in** ~ **bringen** to work s. o. into a rage, to put s. o. into a passion (s. one's monkey up); **in** ~ **geraten** to get off the deep end, to fly into a rage, to flare up, to lose one's temper; **fürchterliche** ~ **haben** to be absolutely furious; **richtige** ~ **im Bauch haben** to be hopping mad *(coll.)*; **seiner** ~ **Luft machen** to giver utterance to one's rage (vent to one's anger); **vor** ~ **platzen** to explode with rage, to hit the ceiling; **vor** ~ **schäumen** to fret and fume, to snort with rage.
Wutanfall flare-up, wax *(sl.)*;
mit einem ~ **antworten** to answer in a fit of temper; ~ **bekommen** to have a fit, to fly off the handle *(coll.)*.
Wut|ausbruch explosion of wrath; **seine Zuhörer in** ~**ausbrüche hineinsteigern** to lash one's listeners into a fury.
wüten to rave, to foam, to fume, *(Menschenmenge)* to riot, *(Sturm)* to cause havoc;
ganzen Tag ~ *(Unwetter)* to rage all day.
wütend furious, angry, wild, raging;
j. ~ **anschreien** to scream at s. o. furiously; **auf j.** ~ **sein** to be furious (burnt up, *US*) at s. o.; ~ **werden** to fly into a temper (passion), to see red *(sl.)*.
wutentbrannt wild with rage.
Wüterich hothead, tartar.
Wutgeheul ausstoßen to give a howl of rage.
wutschnaubend in a towering rage.

Z

Zacke point, *(Felsen)* peak, *(Kamm)* tooth, *(Mauer)* merlon, *(Radar)* pip.

zackig indented, notched, *(Bergspitze)* jagged, *(Soldat)* snappy, brisk;
~ **grüßen** to salute smartly.

zäh tough, wiry, *(hartnäckig)* stubborn, tenacious;
~ **wie Leder** as tough as leather;
~ **an seiner Ansicht festhalten** to be tenacious of one's opinion; ~**er Bursche** tough guy; ~**es Leben haben** to have nine lives; **auf** ~**en Widerstand stoßen** to meet with dogged (stubborn) resistance.

zähflüssig | sein *(Verhandlungen)* to progress sluggishly;
~**er Verkehr** crawling traffic.

Zähigkeit stamina, toughness, wiriness.

Zahl number, figure, cipher, numeral, *(Betrag)* amount, *(Stelle)* digit;
in geringer ~ in small numbers; **in großen** ~**en** in large numbers; **in roten** ~**en** in debt (the red, *US coll.*), in the ketchup *(US sl.)*; **in runden** ~**en** in round figures (numbers); **mit nicht begrenzter** ~ **auszugebender Anteile** *(Kapitalanlagegesellschaft)* open-end; **abgerundete** ~**en** rounded numbers (figures); **amtliche** ~**en** official figures; **beliebige** ~ arbitrary number, *(Computer)* random number; **bereinigte** ~**en** revised figures; **einstellige** ~ one-digit number; **statistisch erfaßbare** ~**en** numbered scale; **ins Auge fallende** ~**en** salient figures; **finanzielle** ~**en** financial figures; **fortlaufende** ~**en** consecutive numbers; **gerade** ~ even number; **undeutlich geschriebene** ~ blind figure; **laufende** ~ consecutive (running) number; **neueste** ~**en** latest figures; **rote** ~**en** red products, red figures; **statistische** ~**en** statistical data; **teilbare** ~ divisible (reducible) number; **unbenutzte** ~ dead number; **ungerade** ~ odd number; **von der Handelskammer veröffentlichte** ~**en** released Board-of-Trade figures; **vielstellige** ~ large figure; **vierstellige** ~ four-digit number; **vorläufige** ~**en** provisional figures; **zulässige** ~**en** admissible numbers; **zusammengesetzte** ~ composite number; **zweistellige** ~ two-digit number;
zunehmende ~ **von Antragstellern** bulge of applicants; ~ **der Anwesenden** number of people present; ~ **der Arbeitslosen** unemployment level; ~ **der Beschäftigten** number of persons employed; ~ **der beförderten Briefe** letter traffic; ~ **der Eheschließungen pro Kopf der Bevölkerung** marriage rate; ~ **der verkauften Eintrittskarten** gate; ~ **der Erwerbspersonen** working population; ~**en des Meinungsumschwungs** swing figures; ~ **des Postzustellbezirks** postal district number; ~ **der abgegebenen Stimmen** number of votes recorded;
weiter mit roten ~**en arbeiten** to be still operating in the red *(US coll.)*; **rote** ~**en aufweisen** to show red ink *(US coll.)*; **auf** ~**en basieren** to assess on figures; **Betrieb in die roten** ~**en bringen** to administer a company from black to red *(US coll.)*; ~**en einsetzen** to fill in the figures; ~ **der Anwesenden feststellen** to tell the noses, to count heads (the house); **in die roten** ~**en geraten** to run into the red *(US coll.)*, to spurt red ink *(US coll.)*; **mit** ~**en jonglieren** to juggle with figures; **mit** ~**en gut umgehen können** to be smart at (have a head for) figures; ~**en schätzen** to eyeball the figures; **seine** ~**en überprüfen** to reckon (scan) one's figures; **an** ~ **übertreffen** to outnumber; **um die** ~ **vollzumachen** to make up the number.

zahlbar payable, dischargeable, prestable *(Scot.)*, *(fällig)* due, mature, *(Wechsel)* domiciled;
bei Abruf (auf Anforderung) ~ payable on demand; **bei Antragstellung** ~ payable on application; **bei Auftragserteilung** ~ cash with order; **im Ausland** ~ payable abroad; **bei ausländischen Banken** ~ payable with banks abroad; **bei der X-Bank** ~ payable at the X-bank; **in bar** ~ terms cash, cash down; **ohne vorherige Benachrichtigung** ~ payable on demand; **bei Bestellung** ~ payable on application; **in Devisen** ~ payable in currency; ~ **zuzüglich Einzugsspesen** *(Wechsel)* payable with exchange; **bei Erhalt** ~ payable on receipt; **bei Fälligkeit** ~ cash at maturity, payable when due; **bei Herrn X** ~ payable with Mr. X; **an den Inhaber** ~ payable to bearer; **netto Kasse** ~ net (spot) cash; **bei Lieferung** ~ cash (collect, *US*) on delivery (C.O.D.), payable on delivery; **an Order** ~ payable to order; **postnumerando** ~ payable later (afterwards); **pränumerando** ~ payable in advance; **in monatlichen Raten** ~ payable in monthly instal(l)ments; **an unseren Schaltern** ~ payable at our counters; **bei Sicht** ~ payable on demand (at sight, on presentation); **dreißig Tage nach Sicht** ~ payable thirty days after sight; **sofort** ~ spot [cash]; **sofort ohne Abzug** ~ terms strictly net cash; **in vier Terminen** ~ payable in four instal(l)ments; **an den Überbringer** ~ payable to bearer; **auf Verlangen** ~ payable on demand (presentation); **vierteljährlich** ~ payable quarterly; **im voraus** ~ payable in advance; **bei Vorlage** ~ payable at sight; **am Wohnsitz des Empfängers** ~ payable at address of payee;
~ **sofort ohne Abzug** terms strictly net cash; ~ **bei Aushändigung der Begleitpapiere** payable against surrender of shipping documents; ~ **zuzüglich Einzugsspesen** payable with exchange *(US)*; ~ **zu dem im Indossament vermerkten Umrechnungskurs** payable as per indorsement *(Br.)*; ~ **zum Verkaufskurs der einziehenden Bank für Sichtwechsel auf London** payable at the collecting bank's selling rate for sight drafts on London; ~ **bei Verschiffung** cash on shipment; ~ **gegen Vorlage des Personalausweises** payable upon submission of proof of indentity;
für ~ **erklären** to declare payable; **Wechsel** ~ **machen** to make a bill payable; **am 15. des nächsten Monats** ~ **sein** to be payable on the 15th prox; ~ **stellen** *(Wechsel)* to domiciliate, to domicile, to make payable; **bei einem Dritten** ~ **stellen** to make payable by a third party; ~ **werden** to become (fall) due, to mature; **bei Vorlage** ~ **werden** to be payable on presentation.

Zahlbarstellung *(Wechsel)* domiciliation.

Zählblatt tally sheet (card).

zahlen to pay, to make payment, *(Schuld voll begleichen)* to pay off, to clear, to discharge, to liquidate;
als Abfindung (Abstand) ~ to pay by way of compensation; **auf Abschlag** ~ to pay by instal(l)ments; **[in] bar** ~ to pay cash down (in cash, ready money, on the spot), to put down the money; **seinen Beitrag** ~ to pay one's contribution; **zusätzlichen Betrag** ~ to pay an additional amount; **Betrag in voller Höhe** ~ to pay an amount in full; **keine Dividende** ~ to omit (default, pass, *US*) a dividend; **Dividende vom Kapital** ~ to pay a dividend out of capital; **bei Erhalt** ~ to pay on receipt; **für die Fahrt** ~ to pay the fare; **bei Fälligkeit** ~ to pay at maturity; **vor Fälligkeit** ~ to pay in advance (anticipation); **fristgerecht** ~ to pay on maturity; **Höchstpreise** ~ to pay top prices; **jem. ein Honorar** ~ to fee s. o., to pay a fee to s. o.; **als Intervenient** ~ to pay for hono(u)r; **Jahresmiete im voraus** ~ to pay the rent annually in advance; **aus der Konkursmasse** ~ to pay out of the trust estate; **langsam** ~ to be slow in paying; **teures Lehrgeld** ~ to pay dearly for one's experience; **bei Lieferung** ~ to pay upon delivery; **am Monatsende** ~ to settle at the end of the month; **in Monatsraten** ~ to pay in monthly instal(l)ments; **in klingender Münze** ~ to pay in hard cash; **in Naturalien** ~ to pay in kind; **an jds. Order** ~ to pay to the order of s. o.; **mittels Postanweisung** ~ to pay by postal money order; **postnumerando** ~ to pay on receipt; **pränumerando** ~ to make payment in advance; **jeden Preis für etw.** ~ to pay anything for it; **pünktlich** ~ to pay punctually, to pay when due (on time), to be exact in one's payments; **ganz pünktlich** ~ to pay on the dot; **Rate** ~ to pay an instal(l)ment; **im ganzen oder in Raten** ~ to pay in full or by instal(l)ments; **Rechnung** ~ to settle an account (a bill); **Restbetrag** ~ to pay the balance; **in Sachwerten** ~ to pay in kind; **bei Sicht** ~ to pay at sight; **sofort** ~ to pay on the spot; **später** ~ to defer payment; **Steuerforderung unter Einlegung von Widerspruch** ~ to pay a tax demand under protest; **4000 DM an Steuern** ~ to pay DM 4000 in taxes; **Strafe** ~ to pay a fine; **Strafporto** ~ to pay extra postage; **teilweise** ~ to make part payment; **unbar** ~ to pay by cheque *(Br.)* (check, *US*); **Unterhalt** ~ to pay alimony; **vereinbarungsgemäß** ~ to pay as agreed; **zu viel** ~ to overpay, to pay too much; **vierteljährlich** ~ to pay by the quarter; **im voraus** ~ to make payment (pay) in advance; **unter Vorbehalt** ~ to pay with reservation; **bei Vorlage** ~ to pay on presentation; **Wechsel** ~ to meet a bill, to pay due hono(u)r to a draft; **wöchentlich** ~ to pay by the week; **Zeche** ~ to pay the piper; **zwangsweise** ~ to pay money under coercion;
~ **Sie an mich** *(Scheck)* pay self;
noch zu ~ payable, receivable;
nicht im Stande sein zu ~ to be unable to pay (insolvent);
Kinder ~ **die Hälfte** children half price.

zählen to count, to tell, to enumerate *(addieren)* to reckon [up], to count, *(sich belaufen)* to number, to amount to;
auf j. ~ to count (rely, bank) on s. o.; **zu den Besten** ~ to stand in the forefront; **Bevölkerung** ~ to take a census; **jem. jeden Bissen**

in den Mund ~ to grudge s. o. the food he eats; **400.000 Einwohner** ~ *(Stadt)* to number 400.000 inhabitants; **an den Fingern** ~ to count on one's fingers; **jem. zu seinen besten Freunden** ~ to count s. o. among (reckon s. o.) one's best friend; **zu jds. Freunden** ~ to number among s. one's friends; **herausgegebenes Geld** ~ to count one's change; **zu den Großmächten** ~ to rank among the Great Powers; **auf jds. Hilfe** ~ to reckon upon s. one's help; **nach Millionen** ~ *(Vermögen)* to run into millions; **zu den führenden Persönlichkeiten** ~ to reckon among the leaders; **richtig** ~ to keep count; **zu den großen Schriftstellern** ~ to range with the great writers; **Stimmen** ~ *(parl.)* to tell the votes; **Tageskasse** ~ to count the daily receipts; **Volk** ~ to [take a] census.

Zahlen|akrobatik betreiben to juggle with figures; **~angaben** data, figures; **~angaben gewinnen** to gather figures; **~aufstellung** numerical statement; **~beispiel** numerical example.

zahlend|es Mitglied paying member; **~er Passagier** revenue passenger.

Zahlen|feld *(Computer)* digit display; **~folge** numerical order, series; **schlechtes ~gedächtnis haben** to have a bad memory for figures (dates); **~gleichung** numerical equation; **~größe** numerical quantity; **~kode** cipher code; **~kolonne** column (group) of figures; **lange ~kolonnen zusammenrechnen** to add up a long column of figures; **~kolumne** column of figures; **~lotterie** Genoese lottery; **~lotto** lotto, numbers pool, bingo, policy *(US)*; **illegales ~lotto** policy racket *(US)*.

zahlenmäßig numerical;
~ überlegen sein to have the advantage in (of) numbers, to outnumber; **~ übertreffen** to exceed in numbers; **~ zunehmen** to increase in numbers;
~e Mehrheit numerical majority; **~e Überlegenheit** superiority in numbers; **~es Verhältnis** numerical proportion.

Zahlenmaterial data, figures;
behördliches ~ government data; **gesamtes** ~ full run of figures; **zuverlässiges** ~ material of hard figures;
~ in einer international vergleichbaren Weise aufbereiten to bring data to internationally comparable standards; **entsprechendes ~ zur Verfügung haben** to have data to work on.

Zahlen|mensch man of figures; **~reihe** column of figures; **~schloß** combination lock; **~sinn** head for figures; **~stempel** numbering stamp; **~symbol** numerical symbol; **~system** numerative (number) system; **~übersicht** statistical table, records; **~verdrehung** transposition; **~verhältnis** numerical proportion (ratio); **vollständiges ~werk** full figures; **~wert** numerical value; **~wert überprüfen** to verify the figures.

Zahler, pünktlicher prompt payer; **säumiger** ~ defaulter, dilatory (slow, tardy) payer, negligent customer;
pünktlicher ~ sein to be exact in one's payments (a good payer), to pay promptly; **schlechter ~ sein** to be slow in payments.

Zähler counter, enumerator, *(Gas, Elektrizität)* counter meter, demand meter, recorder, *(Stimmen)* teller, scrutineer;
~ ablesen to read a meter;
~ableser meter reader; **~ablesung** meter reading; **~stand** meter reading; **~tafel** meter board.

Zählfehler miscasting.

Zahlkarte money order, *(Postanweisung)* postal order.

Zählkarte score card, *(Bevölkerung)* census paper.

Zahl|kasse cash desk; **~kellner** headwaiter.

zahllos countless, innumerable, without number, numberless, vast.

Zahlmeister paymaster, disbursing officer, *(Marine)* purser;
~büro, ~ei pay office, spirit room *(sl.)*; **~gehilfe** pay clerk *(US)*.

zahlreich numerous, a great many;
~ anwesend sein to be present in a great number.

Zählscheibe recording disk.

Zahlstelle paying agent (office), fiscal (paying) agent, *(Arbeitsplatz)* cashier's (cash) desk, *(Bankverkehr)* paying banker (bank), collecting banker, *(Filiale)* subbranch, *(Postamt)* office of payment *(Br.)*, *(Wechsel)* domicile, official payee;
~ für Kupons ist die ... Bank coupons payable at the ... bank; **als ~ angeben** to indicate as paying agent.

Zahlstellen|geschäft, zum ~geschäft zugelassen sein to be in good marking name *(Br.)*; **~verzeichnis** list of paying agents; **~wechsel** domiciled (branch) bill of exchange, branch (domiciled) bill.

Zählstrich tally.

Zahltag *(Börse)* settling (account) day, day of account, *(Hausangestellte)* term *(Br.)*, *(Löhne)* day of payment, cash day, payday *(Br.)*, *(mil.)* quarter (eagle, *sl.*) day;
letzter ~ final date [for payment].

Zahltisch pay desk.

Zahlung payment, paying, scot, *(Schulden)* discharge, liquidation, settlement, clearance, *(Unkosten)* disbursement;
an ~s Statt for value, in lieu of payment; **auf ~ wartend** receivable; **gegen bare** ~ for current payment; **gegen ~ eines Betrages** in consideration of payment of a sum; **gegen ~ der Gebühren** upon payment of charges; **gegen ~ einer Lizenzgebühr** on a royalty basis; **mangels** ~ failing payment, for want (on default, in default) of payment; **mangels ~ protestiert** protested for nonpayment; **mangels ~ zurück** returned for nonpaying; **vorbehaltlich der** ~ payment provided; **zur ~ aufgefordert** called upon to pay;
~ eingestellt payment stopped; **~ erfolgt gleichzeitig per Post** payment is in the mail *(US)*; **~ erhalten** paid, received; **~ gesperrt** *(Scheck)* payment countermanded; **~ sofort** cash terms [of sale], spot;
abschlägige ~ payment on account; **laufend anfallende ~en** periodic payments; **anteilige** ~ prorata payment; **aufgeschobene** ~ deferred payment; **außerordentliche** ~ extra payment; **ausstehende ~en** outstanding debts; **avisierte ~en** amounts advised; **bargeldlose** ~ cashless payment *(US)*; **eingegangene ~en** payments received; **einmalige** ~ single sum (payment), lump-sum payment; **endgültige** ~ direct payment; **erste** ~ initial payment, first instal(l)ment; **erzwungene** ~ compulsory payment; **fällige ~en** due payments; **fingierte** ~ fictitious (sham) payments; **fristgemäße** ~ payment in due time; **geleistete ~en** payments made; **nicht geleistete ~en** delinquent payments; **nach Steuerabzug geleistete ~en** franked payments *(Br.)*; **zeitlich gestaffelte ~en** staggered payments; **gestundete** ~ deferred payments; **große ~en** large payments; **kapitalähnliche** ~ payment of a capital nature; **körperschaftssteuerfreie ~en** franked payments *(Br.)*; **laufende ~en** current (regular) payments; **massierte ~en** block of payments; **monatliche ~en** monthly payments; **multilaterale** ~ multilateral payment; **nachträgliche** ~ further (additional) payment; **zu niedrige** ~ underpayment; **ordnungsgemäße** ~ payment in due course; **periodische ~en** periodic[al] payments; **prompte** ~ prompt payment; **proratarische** ~ progress payment; **pünktliche** ~ punctual payment; **regelmäßige ~en** periodic[al] payments; **rechtzeitige** ~ due payments; **rückständige ~en** [payment in] arrears; **sofortige** ~ cash (immediate) payment, spot [cash]; **steuerfreie** ~ tax-free payment; **telegrafische** ~ telegraphic money order, cable transfer; **terminbedingte ~en** payments owed on fixed days; **überfällige** ~ overdue payment; **übertarifliche ~en** payments in excess of standard rates; **unregelmäßige ~en** irregular payments; **verspätete** ~ delayed payment; **verweigerte** ~ payment refused; **vierteljährliche ~en** quarterly payments, *(Dividenden)* quarterly disbursements; **vollständige** ~ payment in full; **vorherige** ~ advance (anticipated, *US*) payment; **widerrufene** ~ countermand payment; **[regelmäßig] wiederkehrende ~en** periodical (regular, revolving) payments; **zurückgestellte** ~ postponed payment;
vergleichsweise ~ einer Abfindung lump-sum (composition, compromise) payment; **~ auf Abruf** payment on demand; **~ ohne Anerkennung einer Rechtspflicht** ex gratia payment; **~ bei Auftragserteilung** cash with order; **~ gegen Aushändigung der [Verschiffungs]dokumente** payment against documents; **~ durch eine Bank** banker's payment; **~ im Bankverkehr** interbank payments; **~ in bar** payment in cash (ready money); **~ nach Belieben** payment as you feel inclined; **~ ohne Bestimmung** indefinite payment; **~ in Devisen** foreign payment; **~ gegen Dokumente** cash against documents; **~ zugunsten eines Dritten** payment on behalf of a third party; **~ ehrenhalber** payment for hono(u)r; **~ bei Eingang der Waren** payment must be made upon delivery of the goods; **~ bei Fälligkeit** payment when due; **~ vor Fälligkeit** advance (anticipated, *US*) payment; **freiwillige ~ des Gemeinschuldners** voluntary payment of a bankrupt; **~ in Gold** specie payment; **~en aus dem Kapital** principal payments; **~ gegen Kasse** payment in cash; **~ bei Kaufabschluß** payment on completion of purchase; **~en an die Kirche** oblations *(Br.)*; **~ mit rückwirkender Kraft** retroactive payment; **~ bei Lieferung** cash (payment) on delivery; **sofortige ~ bei Lieferung** spot cash; **~ gegen Nachnahme** cash *(Br.)* (collect, *US*) on delivery; **~ zum Parikurs** parity payment; **~ erfolgt in Pfund** payment will be made in pounds; **~ gleichzeitig per Post** payment is in the mail *(US)*; **~ auf dem Postwege** remittance by post; **~ unter Protest** payment supra protest; **~ in Raten** payment by instal[l]ments, instal[l]ment payment; **~ in bequemen Raten** easy payments; **~ gegen offene Rechnung** clean payment; **~en mit dem Recht der Steuereinbehaltung** payments within the charge; **~ in**

Sachwerten payment in kind; ~ **mittels Scheck** payment by cheque *(Br.)* (check, *US*); ~ **aufgrund arglistiger Täuschung** involuntary payment; ~ **aufgrund einer Trennungsvereinbarung** payments made under a separation agreement; ~**en aufgrund einer gerichtlichen Verfügung** court-order payments; ~ **auf Verlangen** payment upon request; ~ **ohne Verpflichtung** gratuitous payment; ~**en aufgrund vertraglich eingegangener Verpflichtungen** payment under deed of covenant; ~ **am Vierteljahresultimo** quarterly disbursement (payment); ~ **im voraus** advance (anticipated, *US*) payment; ~ **unter Vorbehalt** payment under reserve; ~ **durch Wechsel** payment by way of a bill; ~ **bei Wechselvorlage** payment on demand; ~ **binnen einer Woche nach Rechnungsdatum** payment within seven days of invoice date; ~ **zu einem späteren Zeitpunkt** deferred payment; ~ **Zug um Zug** contemporaneous payment; ~ **einer Zusatzsteuer** surtax payment; ~**en für wohltätige Zwecke** payments to charity;

~ **ablehnen** to decline (refuse) payment; ~ **anmahnen** to dun for payment; ~ **annehmen** to accept payment; **an ~s Statt annehmen** to take in (for value); **Etatstitel zur ~ anweisen** to pass an account for payment; **zur ~ auffordern** to demand (request) payment; **j. zur ~ auffordern** to call on s. o. to pay; **mit der ~ aufhören** to terminate (put off) payment; ~ **aufschieben** to postpone (defer, delay) payment; ~ **ausführen** to effect payment; ~ **vorübergehend aussetzen** to stop (suspend) payment; ~ **beitreiben** to exact payment, to collect debts; ~ **gerichtlich beitreiben** to enforce payment by legal proceedings; ~ **bescheinigen** to receipt a payment; **auf ~ bestehen** to insist on payment; **auf sofortiger ~ bestehen** to demand prompt payment; ~ **zur Begleichung einer bestimmten Schuld bestimmen** to apply a payment to a particular debt; **mit der ~ im Rückstand bleiben** to default on one's payment; **auf ~ drängen** to press for payment; ~ **in Dollars durchführen** to settle payment in dollars; **seine ~en einhalten** to keep payments, to keep up one's credit; ~**en nicht einhalten** to default; ~ **eines Wechsels einklagen** to sue on a bill; **Wechsel zur ~ einreichen** to tender a bill for discount; **seine ~en einstellen** to stop payments, to default, to become (declare o. s.) insolvent, to suspend (cease) payment of one's debts, to fail, to waddle out of the alley *(Br., sl.)*, *(Bank)* to cease (stop) payment; ~**en eintreiben** to exact payment; ~**en entgegennehmen** to receive payments; **sich einer ~ entziehen** to evade payment; ~ **erleichtern** to facilitate payment; ~ **von jem. erzwingen** to compel s. o. to pay; **vierteljährliche ~en festsetzen** to stipulate that payment should be quarterly; ~ **fordern** to demand payment; **Waren gegen ~ freigeben** to release goods against payment; ~ **garantieren** to guarantee payment; **in ~ geben** to deliver in payment, to trade in *(US)*, to give in payment *(Louisiana)*; **seinen 1980er Ford für das neueste Modell in ~ geben** to trade in one's 1980 Ford car for a new model *(US)*; **mit seinen ~en in Rückstand geraten** to fall behind with one's payments; **mit den ~en in Verzug geraten** to default [in payment]; **mit der ~ eines Wechsels in Verzug geraten** to default in paying a note; **zu zusätzlichen ~en heranziehen** to assess for additional payment; **zur ~ hereingeben** to lodge for payment; ~ **hinausschieben** to delay (defer, postpone) payment; **j. mit der ~ hinhalten** to keep s. o. waiting for funds; **auf ~ klagen** to sue for payment; **mit den ~en in Verzug kommen** to default [in payment]; ~ **leisten** to make (effect, carry out) payment, to pay; **einmalige ~ leisten** to commute; **steuerabzugsfähige ~en leisten** to make payments under deduction of tax; ~ **vor Fälligkeit leisten** to anticipate payment; **j. zur ~ mahnen** to call on s. o. to pay; **in ~ nehmen** to receive (accept) in payment; **Auto in ~ nehmen** to take a car in part exchange, to trade in a used car *(US)*; ~ **auf der Rückseite eines Kreditbriefes notieren** to record a payment on the reverse side of a letter of credit; **Wechsel mangels ~ protestieren** to protest a bill for nonpayment; ~ **quittieren** to receipt a payment; **mit seinen ~en im Rückstand sein** to be behind in (behindhand with) one's payments, to be in arrears; **mit einer ~ in Verzug sein** to delay in making payment; ~ **sicherstellen** to secure payment; ~ **sistieren** to stop payments; **für ~ sorgen** to provide for payment; ~ **stunden** to grant (allow) a respite, to grant a delay for payment, to extend the terms of payment; **als ~ einen Scheck übersenden** to send a cheque *(Br.)* (check, *US*) in settlement; ~ **verbuchen** to enter an item in the ledger; **vierteljährliche ~en vereinbaren** to stipulate that payment should be quarterly; ~**en auf Goldbasis vereinbaren** to stipulate payments in gold; ~ **verlangen** to request payment; ~ **Zug um Zug verlangen** to require payment on delivery; **konzerninterne ~en zeitlich verschieben** to delay intra-group payments; ~**en über mehrere Jahre verteilen** to space (spread) payments over several years; **zur ~ eines hohen Schadenersatzes verurteilen** to award heavy damages; ~ **verweigern** to refuse payment; ~**en zur Verkürzung von Zinsrückständen verwenden** to apply payments to the reduction of interest; ~ **vorenthalten** to withhold payment; **Scheck zur ~ vorlegen** to present a check *(US)* (cheque, *Br.*) for payment; **Wechsel zur ~ vorlegen** to present a bill for payment, to collect on a note; ~**en in Pfund vornehmen** to settle payments in pounds; **zur ~ herangezogen werden** to be called upon to pay; ~ **wiederaufnehmen** to resume payment; ~**en während der Untersuchung zurückstellen** to hold up payment pending inquiries; **zur ~ zwingen** to enforce payment.

Zählung counting, reckoning, *(Aufzählung)* numeration, enumeration, *(von Stimmen)* telling votes;
~ **der Weltbevölkerung** world census;
~ **durchführen** to take a count, *(Bevölkerung)* to take a census; **j. bei der ~ übergehen** to leave s. o. out on the count.

Zahlungs|abkommen monetary agreement, *(Schuldner)* payments agreement, arrangement for an extension of time; **zweiseitiges ~abkommen** bilateral transfer agreement, bipartite clearing agreement (arrangement); ~**abkommen treffen** to arrange for an extension of time; ~**abschnitt** counterfoil, stub; ~**absicht** intention to pay; ~**adresse** *(Wechsel)* domicile; ~**anforderung** application for payment; ~**anforderungen am Kassenschalter** counter (cash) requirements; ~**angebot** offer to pay, tender of payment, *(Auktion)* bid; ~**anordnung** order to pay; ~**anspruch** pecuniary claim, liquidated demand; ~**ansprüche befriedigen** to meet demands for payment.

Zahlungsanweisung order to pay (for payment), pay ticket (voucher, *Br.*), payment voucher, warrant for payment, *(Bank)* pay bill *(Br.)*, banker's order, *(Behörde)* appropriation of funds, disbursement voucher, *(Postanweisung)* postal (post-office) order, *(Zahlkarte)* money order *(Br.)*, postal money order *(US)*, postal note *(Canada)*;
~**en** payment instructions;
bedingte ~ conditional order to pay; **fällige ~en** warrants payable *(US)*; **kommunale ~** municipal (county) warrant;
~ **des Stadtkämmerers** town warrant;
~ **ausstellen** to pass an account for payment; **keine ~ vorliegen haben** to have no instruction to pay.

Zahlungs|anzeige advice of payment; ~**art** mode of payment.

Zahlungsaufforderung demand for payment, requisition, request for money (payment), notice (order) to pay, *(Kommunalabgaben)* demand note *(Br.)*, *(Mahnschreiben)* dun, *(Nachzahlung auf nicht eingezahlte Aktien)* call, *(Notar)* requisition *(Scot.)*; **dringende ~** dunning letter, dun; **gerichtliche ~** debtor's summons; **persönliche ~** personal demand;
~ **mit Konkursandrohung** bankruptcy notice;
~ **belegen** to specify application of one's payment; **j. eine ~ zukommen lassen** to draw on s. o.

Zahlungsaufforderungsschein demand note, *(Aktiennachzahlung)* call ticket.

Zahlungsaufschub indulgence, respite [for (delay of, prolongation of, extension of) payment], *(Moratorium)* moratorium, moratory;
dreitägiger ~ für einen Wechsel a three day's grace for payment of a bill;
~ **bewilligen (gewähren)** to indulge a debtor, to respite, to extend the terms of (grant a delay in) payment; **um ~ bitten (nachsuchen)** to ask for a respite, to request an extension; ~ **erlangen** to get an extension for (obtain a delay in) payment.

Zahlungsauftrag order [for payment (to pay)], payment order, *(Bank)* banker's order;
unwiderruflich erteilter ~ unconditional order;
~ **an eine Bank** order on a bank;
~ **eines Kunden durchführen** to make payment for a customer; ~ **stornieren** to countermand a payment.

Zahlungs|ausgang outpayment; ~**ausgleich** clearance, clearing, settlement, *(international)* exchange equilibrium, *(Bank für internationalen Zahlungsausgleich)* settlement of accounts; ~**aussichten** payments outlook.

Zahlungsbedingungen terms [of payment], payment conditions; **zu günstigen ~** by easy payments, on favo(u)rable terms; **gewöhnliche ~** ordinary dealings; **übliche ~** standard payment clause; **besonders vereinbarte ~** memorandum dating *(US)*;
~ **erleichtern** to facilitate terms of payment; **zu erleichterten ~ kaufen** to buy on easy terms.

Zahlungs|befehl default summons, summons to pay; ~**befreiung** exemption from payment; ~**begünstigter** beneficiary of a payment; ~**beleg** receipt for payment, [pay] voucher; ~**berechtigter** payee; ~**bereitschaft** willingness to pay,

(Solvenz) liquidity, solvency; **~bescheinigung** receipt for payment, acquittance; **~- und Transferbeschränkungen** exchange restrictions on payments and transfers; **~bestätigung** receipt for payment.

Zahlungsbilanz balance of payments;
aktive ~ favo(u)rable balance of payments, credit balance; **ausgeglichene** ~ equilibrium of the balance of payments; **globale** ~ overall balance of payment; **negative (passive)** ~ adverse (debit, deficit) balance of payments; **positive** ~ surplus balance of payment; **unausgeglichene** ~ disequilibrium in the balance of payment, imbalance in payment;
~en im Gleichgewicht halten to keep international payments in balance; ~ **verschlechtern** to worsen the balance of payments; **~ausgleich** balance-of-payments adjustment; **~bild** balance-of-payments picture; **~darlehen** balance-of-payments loan; **~defizit** [balance of] payments deficit, external deficit; **internationales ~defizit** deficit balance of international payments; **~disziplin** payments balance discipline; **~entwicklung** trend in the balance of payment; **~finanzierung** balance-of-payments financing; **~gleichgewicht** equilibrium of the balance of payments; **~hilfe** balance-of-payments aid; **~kosten** balance-of-payments costs; **~kredit** balance-of-payments credit; **~krise** balance-of-payments crisis; **~lücke** balance-of-payments gap; **~position** balance-of-payment position; **~problem** balance-of-payments problem (question); **~saldo** balance-of-payments current account; **~schwankungen** swings in the balance of payments; **seiner ~schwierigkeiten mit deflationistischen Maßnahmen Herr werden** to deflate its way out of its balance of payments; **entspannte ~situation** relaxed balance-of-payments situation; **~theorie** balance-of-payments theory; **~überschuß** [balance-of-]payment surplus, surplus in the payment balance, external surplus; **~ungleichgewicht** disequilibrium in the balance of payments, balance-of-payment disequilibrium; **~verpflichtungen** balance-of-payments burden; **~verschlechterung** worsening of the balance of payments; **~vorteile** balance-of-payments benefits.

Zahlungs|bürge voucher; **~eingang** *(Zahlungsbilanz)* money receivable; **~eingänge** takings, receipts, payments received, inpayment; **~einstellung** commercial failure, suspension (stoppage) of payments, stop payment, insolvency, default, abandonment of business; **~einwand** objection to payment; **~empfänger** recipient of a payment, payee.

Zahlungserleichterungen facilities for payment, easy terms;
unter ~ by easy payment;
~ **anbieten** to offer facilities for payment.

Zahlungs|ermächtigung authorization to pay; **~ersuchen** application for payment.

zahlungsfähig able to pay [one's debts], good, [financially] sound, solvent, in the black *(US coll.)*, substantial, responsible;
~ **sein** to be a good pay (in funds);
~e Firma sound business house, solvent merchant; **~er Schuldner** solvent debtor.

Zahlungsfähigkeit ability (capacity) to pay, solvency, responsibility;
seine ~ **nachweisen** to justify bail; **sich für jds.** ~ **verbürgen** to vouch for s. one's ability to pay.

Zahlungsfreigrenze *(Devisenbeschaffung)* quota allowed.

Zahlungsfrist term, time of payment, prompt, *(gewährter Aufschub)* extension of time, *(Nachfrist)* grace period;
mit bestimmter ~ time;
durchschnittliche ~ average collection period; **übliche ~en** conventional terms;
~ **bei Auftragsplazierung und Zahlungsregulierung vor der Saison** seasonal dating *(US)*;
~ **einhalten** to comply with a term, to pay at maturity; ~ **einräumen (gewähren)** to defer (respite) payment; **einem Schuldner** ~ **gewähren** to allow a debtor time to pay; ~ **verlängern** to extend the time for payment;
~verlängerung extension of time.

Zahlungs|garant für Auslandsaufträge confirming house *(Br.)*; **~garantie** payment guarantee, guaranty of collection *(US)*; **~gebaren** payment performance; **~genehmigung** authorization to pay; **~gepflogenheiten** paying habits; **~geschäfte** payment transactions; **~guthaben** credit balance.

zahlungshalber as payment.

Zahlungs|haushalt cash budget; **~hindernis** bar to payment; **~klausel** facility for payment clause.

zahlungskräftig able to purchase, good, [financially] sound, solvent, responsible;
~es Unternehmen sound business firm.

Zahlungs|leistung payment; **~leistungsverbot** garnishment.

Zahlungsmittel circulating (currency) medium, instrument of payment, medium of exchange, money, currency;
ausländische ~ foreign money; **bargeldlose** ~ deposit currency, credit instruments; **im Umlauf befindliche** ~ circulation; **gesetzliches** ~ legal coin (tender, *Br.*), common tender, lawful money (currency) *(US)*; **beschränkt gültige** ~ limited legal tender *(Br.)*;
eigene ~ **in fremder Hand** foreign-held balance;
als ~ **anbieten** to tender; **als gesetzliches** ~ **gelten** to be legal tender (lawful money, *US*), to be receivable; **zum gesetzlichen** ~ **machen** to monetize; **gesetzliches** ~ **sein** to be legal tender (lawful money, *US*), to be receivable, to be admitted in payment;
~abschnitte notes; **~aufschub** forbearance; **~einheit** monetary unit; **~gesetz** Currency and Bank Notes Act *(Br.)*; **~schöpfung** creation of means of payments.

Zahlungsmittelumlauf total money in circulation, currency;
vermehrter ~ debt monetization, currency expansion;
~ **ausweiten** to expand the currency; ~ **einschränken** to deflate a currency;
~erhöhung debt monetization.

Zahlungsmittel|versorgung currency supply; **~volumen** volume of currency.

Zahlungs|modalitäten terms [of payment], facilities of payment, modalities of payment; **erleichterte ~modalitäten** easier way to pay; **~modus** method (manner) of payment; **gute ~moral haben** to be exact in one's payments (a good pay, *US*); **schlechte ~moral haben** to be slow in payment (paying); **~moratorium** payments moratorium; **~nachweis** evidence (record) of payment; **~nachweisbuch** voucher register; **~ort** place of payment, *(Wechsel)* domicile; **~ort angeben** to specify a place of payment; **~periode** pay period; **~pflicht** liability to pay, financial responsibility, pecuniary obligation.

zahlungspflichtig liable, answerable, responsible;
ummittelbar ~ primarily liable (responsible).

Zahlungs|pflichtiger debtor, payor, assessee; **~plan** payment plan, *(Ratenzahlung)* hire-purchase *(Br.)* (deferred-payment, *US*) plan, *(Tilgung)* redemption plan; **~rate** collection rate; **~raum** currency area; **~regelung** payments arrangement; **~relation** *(Außenhandel)* terms of payment; **~reserve** reserve for payments to be made; **~restriktionen** exchange restrictions; **~rückstände** arrears, delinquent (outstanding) payments, outstanding debts; **~scheck** cash cheque *(Br.)*; **~schreiben** cash (dunning) letter; **~schuldner** debtor.

Zahlungsschwierigkeiten payment trouble, embarrassment, pecuniary difficulties;
sich in ~ **befinden, in** ~ **sein** to be in low straits (hard up for money), to be in embarrassed circumstances; **in** ~ **geraten** to get into debt, to run into financial difficulties.

Zahlungssperre stoppage of payments, stop payment;
Auftrag zur ~ **geben** to [give an order to] stop payment; ~ **über ein Konto verhängen** to block an account.

Zahlungs|stockung delayed payment; **~stopp** stoppage of payments, stop payment; **~struktur** payments pattern; **~surrogat** auxiliary currency, representative money *(US)*; **multilaterales ~system** multilateral system of payments; **~tag** pay day.

Zahlungstermin day (time) of payment, *(vierteljährliche Miete)* quarter (rent) day, *(Verfalltag)* day of maturity;
äußerster (letzter) ~ final date of payment; **mittlerer** ~ average due date; **vereinbarter** ~ contractual due day;
seine ~e einhalten (pünktlich erledigen) to be punctual in one's payment; ~ **nicht einhalten** to transgress payment; **seine ~e nie einhalten** to be always behind with one's payments; ~ **vereinbaren** to agree on a date for payment; ~ **verlängern** to grant a respite.

Zahlungs|überschuß payments surplus; **~unausgeglichenheit** payments imbalance.

zahlungsunfähig unable to pay [one's debts], insolvent, defaulting *(Br.)*, bankrupt, nonsolvent, *(Bank)* failing circumstances, illiquid;
zum Zeitpunkt der Gläubigerbegünstigung ~ insolvent at the time of preference;
sich für ~ **erklären** to declare o. s. a bankrupt (one's insolvency), to give one's effects to one's creditors, to hammer *(Br.)*, *(Münzen)* to decry; ~ **sein** to be unable to pay, to be in a state of insolvency (out of funds); **beinahe** ~ **sein** to be verging on insolvency; ~ **werden** to become insolvent, to fail in business, to default; **für** ~ **erklärt werden** to be struck from the list, to be gazetted bankrupt, to be hammered on the exchange *(Br.)*;

~er **Schuldner** insolvent [debtor], defaulting (bad, poor) debtor, defaulter *(Br.)*.
Zahlungsunfähiger insolvent [debtor], bad debtor, defaulter *(Br.)*, [adjudicated] bankrupt.
Zahlungsunfähigkeit inability to pay one's debts, [commercial] insolvency, failure, default, nonsolvency;
allgemein bekannte ~ open insolvency; **kaufmännische** ~ commercial insolvency;
~ **einer Gemeinde** municipal default; ~ **einer Gesellschaft** company's default;
~ **bekanntmachen** to hammer a defaulter *(Br.)*.
Zahlungs|unfähigkeitserklärung declaration of inability to pay one's debts; **Europäische ~union** European Payments Union; **~verbindlichkeit** financial obligation.
Zahlungsverbot stop order, freezing of payments;
endgültiges ~ garnishee order absolute; **vorläufiges** ~ garnishee order nisi;
~ **an den Drittschuldner** garnishment, garnishee (third-party, *US*) order, trustee process *(US)*;
~ **an den Drittschuldner erlassen** to garnish; ~ **erwirken** to stop payment; ~ **gegen j. erwirken** to issue a stop order against s. o.
Zahlungsvereinbarung payment agreement (arrangement), stipulation of payments, financial arrangements.
Zahlungsverkehr payment transactions, payment system, money transfers;
allgemeiner ~ general payments; **bargeldloser** ~ general clearing, clearing system, cashless payments *(US)*; **internationaler** ~ foreign-exchange arrangements, international payments;
~ **mit dem Ausland** foreign (external) payments transactions.
Zahlungsvermögen ability to pay, solvency, responsibility.
zahlungsverpflichtet liable to pay.
Zahlungsverpflichteter payer.
Zahlungsverpflichtung liability to pay, financial responsibility;
~en liabilities, commitments, engagements, money payable; **ausländische ~en** foreign commitments; **unaufschiebbare** ~ *(Kreis)* involuntary indebtedness;
~en auferlegen to subject to financial burden; **seine ~en einhalten** to meet one's commitments; ~ **nicht einhalten** to duck a payment; **sich einer** ~ **entziehen** to evade payment; **~en routinemäßig genehmigen** to rubberstamp commitments; **einer** ~ **nachkommen** to retire an obligation; **seinen ~en nachkommen** to keep up one's payments; **seinen ~en pünktlich nachkommen** to be exact (punctual, prompt) in one's payments.
Zahlungsversäumnis failure to pay.
Zahlungsversprechen promise to pay [the debt of another], undertaking to pay;
gesamtschuldnerisches ~ joint and several bond (note, *US*); **schriftliches** ~ benefit certificate, due bill *(US)*.
Zahlungs|verweigerung nonpayment, refusal to pay, declined payment, *(Staat)* repudiation of debts; **schikanöse ~verweigerung** vexatious refusal to pay; **~verzug** default of payment, delay in payment; **in ~verzug geraten (kommen)** to make default; **im ~verzug sein** to delay payment; **~vollmacht** authorization to pay; **~vorgang** payment; **~weg** method of payment; **~weise** manner (method, form, terms) of payment; **~widerruf** countermand of payments; **~woche** settling week.
Zahlungsziel respite, grace period;
offenes ~ open terms;
~ **einräumen** to grant a respite; ~ **um drei Wochen verlängern** to postpone the day of payment by three weeks.
Zahlungszusage promise to pay.
Zähl|vorrichtung, ~werk numerator, counter, meter, totalizator;
~ **eines Drehkreuzes** toll collector.
zahm tame, docile, tractable;
j. ~ **kriegen** to bring s. o. to heel *(coll.)*; ~ **mit jem. umgehen** to deal mildly with s. o.;
~e Kritik mild criticism.
zähmen to domesticize, to tame;
seine Wut ~ to restrain one's anger; **seine Zunge** ~ to hold one's tongue.
Zahn tooth, *(Geschwindigkeit)* lick, *(Zahnrad)* cog;
steiler ~ peach of a girl, smasher;
~ **der Zeit** tooth of time;
einen gehörigen ~ **draufhaben** to be riding hell for leather (going at breakneck speed); **jem. auf den** ~ **fühlen** to feel s. one's pulse; **kaum für einen hohlen** ~ **reichen** not to be able to keep a sparrow alive; **noch einen** ~ **zulegen** to step on the gas;
~antrieb gear drive; **~arzt** dental surgeon.
zahnärztliche Behandlung dental treatment.
Zähne, falsche store teeth *(US coll.)*;
sich die ~ **ausbeißen** to gnaw a file; **jem. die** ~ **ausschlagen** to punch s. one's teeth in; **mit langen ~n essen** to nibble at one's food; **mit den ~n knirschen** to grind (gnash) one's teeth; ~ **mit Jacketkronen versehen lassen** to have one's teeth capped; **bis an die** ~ **bewaffnet sein** to be armed to the teeth; **jem. die** ~ **zeigen** *(fig.)* to show (pull) s. one's teeth; **seine** ~ **zusammenbeißen** to clench one's teeth.
Zahn|klinik, fahrbare travelling dental clinic; **~radbahn** rock (cogwheel) railway; **~radgetriebe** toothed wheel gearing.
Zange tongs, pliers;
etw. nicht einmal mit der ~ **anfassen** not to touch s. th. with a barge pole; **jem. in der** ~ **haben** to have s. o. cornered; **j. in die** ~ **nehmen** to put the screws on s. o.
Zangen|bewegung *(mil.)* pincers movement; **reinste ~geburt** tough job.
Zank quarrel, squabble, wrangle, jar, discordance, breeze;
~ **mit jem. suchen** to try to pick a quarrel with s. o.;
~apfel apple of discord, bone of contention, debatable ground.
zanken to scold, to quarrel, to squabble, to bicker;
sich mit jem. ~ to have words with s. o.; **sich um einen Strohhalm** ~ to find a quarrel over a straw.
Zänker quarrel(l)er, squabbler, bickerer.
zänkisch querulous, cantankerous, quarrelsome.
Zankteufel termagant, vixen, virago, shrew.
Zapfen tap, *(Stift)* pin, *(Welle)* pivot, journal.
zapfen, Benzin to fill petrol.
Zapfen|lager journal (pivot) bearing; **~loch** pivot hole; **~streich** *(mil.)* call to quarters, tattoo, last post *(Br.)*, tap *(US)*.
Zapf|hahn tap, faucet *(US)*, *(Auto)* hose nozzle; **~säule** *(Tankstation)* filling (petrol, *Br.*, gasoline, *US*) pump.
zappelig fidgety, restless;
~ **sein** *(Prüfling)* to have the jitters *(sl.)*.
Zappeligkeit fidgetiness, nervousness, jitters *(US sl.)*.
Zappelliese fidgeter.
zappeln, vor Ungeduld to fidget with excitement;
jem. ~ **lassen** to have s. o. on a string, to tantalize s. o., to keep s. o. on tenterhooks.
zappenduster pitch-dark.
zart delicate, tender, frail, fragile, slight, *(Stoff)* flimsy, filmy, delicate;
~es Alter tender age; **~e Bande knüpfen** to form a sentimental attachment; **~e Behandlung** kid-glove treatment; **~es Geschlecht** gentle sex; **~e Gesundheit** frail (fragile) health; **jem. einen ~en Wink geben** to give s. o. a subtle hint.
zartbesaitet sensitive, highly strung.
Zartgefühl delicacy, discretion;
ohne ~ indelicate;
mit ~ **vorgehen** to go about things with great delicacy.
Zartheit delicacy, *(Stoff)* flimsiness.
zärtlich tender, fond, loving;
~er Brief affectionate letter; **~e Mutter** loving mother.
Zaster dibs *(sl.)*, tin *(sl.)*, dust *(sl.)*, stumpy *(Br., sl.)*, dough *(Br.)*, spondulics *(US)*;
~ **haben** to have plenty of chips *(US sl.)*.
Zauber witchcraft, charm, spell, glamo(u)r, *(Theater)* hullabaloo, fuss;
wie durch ~ as if by magic;
fauler ~ eyewash, baloney, boloney, humbug, sham, pony *(US sl.)*, monkey business;
jds. ~ **erliegen** to fall victim to s. one's charm; ~ **lösen** to break a spell; **ganzen** ~ **leid sein** to be fed up with the whole business; **dem** ~ **nicht trauen** to look a bit fishy to s. o.; **wie ein** ~ **wirken** to work like a charm;
unter einem ~bann stehen to be under a spell.
Zauberei magic, witchcraft.
Zauberer medicine man, wizard, magician, sorcerer.
Zauber|flasche magic bottle; **~formel** magic formula, open sesame.
Zauberin witch.
Zauber|kasten trick box; **~kraft** magic; **~künstler** wizard, juggler, illusionist, warlock; **~kunststück** sleight of hand, conjuration; **~land** wonderland, fairyland.
zaubern, Essen to conjure up a meal; **Lächeln auf jds. Gesicht** ~ to produce a smile upon s. one's face;
~ **können** to work miracles.
Zauber|reich der Musik magic realm of music; **~trick** conjurer's trick, conjuration.
Zauderer hesitator, procrastinator, temporizer.
Zaudern temporization, procrastination, putting-off *(sl.)*;
ohne ~ unhesitatingly, without hesitation.

zaudern to hesitate, to hang back, to temporize, to procrastinate.
zaudernde Politik hesitancy, Fabian policy.
Zaum bridle;
einem Pferd den ~ anlegen to bridle a horse; **j. im ~ halten** to keep a tight rein on s. o.; **seine Leidenschaften im ~ halten** to bridle one's passions; **seine Zunge im ~ halten** to hold (guard) one's tongue.
Zaun fence, hedge;
jenseits des ~es outside of the fence;
elektrischer ~ electric fence; **lebender ~** quickset [hedge]; **schikanöser ~** spit fence;
Krieg vom ~ brechen to unleash a war; **Streit vom ~ brechen** to pick a quarrel; **Grundstück mit einem ~ umgeben** to fence in a piece of land;
~gast looker-on, onlooker, unconcerned spectator; **~gast sein** to sit on (ride, *US*) the fence; **~latte** picket; **~lücke** gap in a fence.
Zebrastreifen zebra crossing (stripes).
Zechbruder pot companion, toper, tippler, boon companion (fellow).
Zeche *(Bergbau)* coal mine, coalpit, pit, colliery, *(Rechnung)* reckoning, score, restaurant bill, damage *(sl.)*;
abgebaute ~ exhausted mine; **aufgelassene ~** shutdown mine; **getrennte ~** Dutch treat; **unrentable ~** marginal mine;
~ mit großen Betriebsunfallquoten pit with a poor safety record;
~ bewettern to vent a coal mine; **~ bezahlen** to stand the treat (shot), to foot the bill, to pay the piper; **sich auf die kostengünstigeren ~n konzentrieren** to concentrate on the mines operating most economically; **große ~ machen** to run up a big bill; **~ prellen** to bilk, to duck out *(US sl.)*, to lam, to take the powder *(sl.)*; **~ stillegen** to shut down a mine.
zechen to carouse, to booze;
bis in die frühen Morgenstunden ~ to carouse until the small hours.
Zechen|abstimmung pithead ballot; **~arbeiter** pitman, coalminer; **~besitzer** coal owner (operator), mine owner; **~distrikt** coal district; **~förderung** coal output; **~gesellschaft** mining company; **~halde** dump; **~kohle** mine coal; **~preis** pit-head price; **~produzent** coal producer; **~stillegung** pit closure, mine closure (shutdown); **~unfall** mining accident; **~vorstand** mining board.
Zecher boozer, drinker, tippler, merrymaker.
Zecherei, Zechgelage drinking bout, binge, spree, drunk, carousal, compotation, high time *(sl.)*, tear *(US sl.)*.
Zech|kumpan pot companion; **~preller** bilker; **~prellerei begehen** to bilk, to take a powder *(sl.)*, to lam *(sl.)*; **~schulden haben** to have drinking debts; **~tour** pub crawl, spree, binge; **~tour machen** to pub-crawl, to go on a binge (spree).
Zedent surrender, surrenderer, alienator, assignor, transferrer, conveyer, cedent, grantor *(US)*, *(Indossent)* indorser, endorser;
freiwilliger ~ volunteer, voluntary conveyer.
zedierbar assignable, alienable, transferable.
zedieren to assign, to make an assignment, to alienate, to convey away, to transfer, to surrender, to cede.
Zedierung assignment, transfer, alienation, cession.
Zehen, auf ~ gehen to walk on tiptoe; **jem. auf die ~ treten** to tread on s. one's toes (kibes).
Zehner|gruppe, ~klub *(Zentralnotenbanken)* group of ten, Paris Club; **~system** decimal system.
zehnfacher Jahresbetrag ten year's purchase.
Zehn|fingerblindschreiben touch system; **~jahresfeier** decennial; **~jahresplan** ten-year plan; **~plattenspieler** automatic changer.
Zehnt|abgabe vom Gewerbeertrag personal tithes; **~ablösung** commutation of tithes.
Zehntausend, die oberen cream of society, upper ten, top drawer *(sl.)*, the four hundred *(US)*, fashion, the elite;
in die ~e gehen to run into five figures.
Zehntelstelle decimal.
Zehnter tenth, tithe.
zehren, von seiner Erinnerung to reminisce; **von jds. Gesundheit ~** to undermine s. one's health; **an jds. Herzen ~** to be gnawing at s. one's heart; **an jds. Kraft ~** to waste s. one's strength; **von seinem guten Namen ~** to live on one's name; **von seinen Vorräten ~** to use up all one's supplies.
Zehrpfennig travelling money.
Zeichen sign, mark, *(Anzeichen)* indication, evidence, token, *(Buchstabe)* character, *(Computer)* bit, *(Diktat)* reference, re, *(Kennmelodie)* signature tune, *(Signal)* sign, signal, *(Waren)* brand, trademark, mark;
als ~ meiner Dankbarkeit as token of my gratitude; **als ~ meiner Wertschätzung** as a mark of my esteem; **im ~ von** in the light of; **mit ~ und Nummern versehen** marked and numbered; **unter einem glücklichen ~** under a lucky star;
breitlaufende ~ expanded letters; **charakteristisches ~** characteristic sign; **willkürlich gewähltes ~** arbitrary trademark; **grafische ~** key symbols; **unser ~** *(Brief)* our file number; **untrügliches ~** unmistakable sign;
~ des Alters sign of old age; **~ einer Krankheit** symptoms of a disease; **~ von Liebenswürdigkeit** patent of gentility *(fam.)*; **~ zum Sammeln** *(mil.)* rallying sign; **~ konjunktureller Verschlechterung** signs of slowdown; **~ von Wohlstand** evidence of prosperity; **~ und Wunder** signs and wonders; **~ der Zeit** sign of the times;
etw. als günstiges ~ betrachten to regard s. th. as a favo(u)rable omen; **~ einbrennen** to brand; **jem. ein ~ geben** to signal to s. o.; **in einem Buch ein ~ machen** to mark a place in a book; **seines ~s Drucker sein** to be printer by trade; **~ von Unverschämtheit sein** to partake of insolence; **im ~ der Baisse stehen** to be marked by a decline of prices; **unter dem ~ technischen Fortschritts stehen** to be marked by technological progress; **Schwarz zum ~ der Trauer tragen** to wear black as a token of mourning;
~block drawing block (pad); **~brett** drawing board; **~büro** drawing office; **~dichte** horizontal spacing, *(Computer)* bit density; **~erklärung** explanation of (key to) signs, legend; **~feder** drawing pen; **~geber** signal transmitter; **~gebung** indication, signalling; **~gerät** drawing instrument, *(numerisch gesteuertes)* plotter; **~karton** art (fashion, drawing) board; **~kode** character code; **~lehrer** art teacher (master, *Br.*); **~maßstab** plotting scale; **~papier** drawing (drafting, plotting, Bristol) paper, *(starkes)* cartridge paper; **~rolle** *(Warenzeichen)* register of trademarks; **~saal** art room; **~schlüssel** key; **~schrift** charactery; **~schutz** protection of trademarks; **großzügige ~setzung** open punctuation; **strikte ~setzung** close punctuation; **~sprache** finger (sign) language; **~stift** drawing pencil, crayon; **~tinte** marking ink; **~trickfilm** animated cartoon, cartoon film; **~unterricht** drawing lesson; **~wiedergabe** *(Terminal)* character definition.
Zeichnen, freihändiges freehand drawing;
~ nach Modellen object drawing.
zeichnen *(entwerfen)* to design, to draw, to plot, *(schildern)* to describe, to depict, *(Unterschrift)* to sign, to subscribe, *(Waren)* to mark, to brand;
j. ~ to draw a picture of s. o.; **Aktien ~** to take up (subscribe for) shares (stock, *US*), to make an application for shares *(Br.)*, to apply for shares *(Br.)*; **Anleihe ~** to subscribe [to] a loan; **auf eine Ausgabe ~** to subscribe to an issue; **Betrag für wohltätige Zwecke ~** to subscribe a sum to charity; **in blanko ~** to sign in blank; **für eine Firma ~** to sign on behalf of a firm; **gemeinsam ~** to sign jointly; **fünf Gesellschaftsanteile ~** to subscribe for five shares of a company; **ein Gesicht ~** *(Schicksal)* to leave one's mark on a face; **Kapital ~** *(Konsortium)* to underwrite; **Landkarte ~** to map; **in verkleinertem Maßstab ~** to draw on a reduced scale; **maßstabsgerecht ~** to draw to scale; **in unserem Namen zu ~** to sign on our behalf; **nach der Natur ~** to draw from nature; **per Prokura ~** to sign per procuration; **verantwortlich ~** to be responsible (take the responsibility) for; **in Vollmacht ~** to sign as attorney-in-fact.
Zeichner drawer, designer, *(Bauzeichner)* draftsman, *(Effekten)* applicant, *(Wertpapiere)* subscriber, applicant for shares *(Br.)*; **berücksichtigter ~** *(Wertpapiere)* allottee; **potentieller ~** prospective subscriber; **technischer ~** industrial designer, draftsman, draughtsman;
~ einer Anleihe subscriber to a loan.
zeichnerische Darstellung graphic representation.
Zeichner|kreis category of subscribers; **~liste** list of subscribers.
Zeichnung drawing, design, device, *(Effekten)* subscription, application *(Br.)*, *(Entwurf)* draft, outline, *(Grundriß)* plan, *(Illustrierung)* illustration, *(Muster)* design, *(Schatzwechsel)* tender, *(Skizze)* sketch, *(Unterschrift)* signature;
zur ~ aufgelegt open for subscription;
bedeutende ~en important sums subscribed; **grafische ~** graph; **maßstabsgetreue ~** protraction, scale drawing; **öffentliche ~** issue to the public; **produktionsreife ~** finished art work; **technische ~** technical drawing;
~ von Aktien subscription to shares (stocks, *US*); **~ von Kapitalanteilen** capital stock subscription;
~ von jem. anfertigen to draw a picture of s. o.; **Öffentlichkeit zur ~ von Aktien auffordern** to invite applications for shares *(Br.)*; **Öffentlichkeit zur ~ einer Anleihe auffordern** to invite the public to subscribe to a loan, to offer a loan for subscription to

the public; **Anleihe zur ~ auflegen** to bring out (invite tenders for) a loan; **zur ~ aufliegen** to be offered (open) for subscription; **bei ~ voll einzahlen** to pay fully by subscription; **~ schließen** to close a subscription; **~ auf eine lithografische Platte übertragen** to transfer a drawing to a lithographic stone.

Zeichnungsangebot tender, offer for subscription, subscription offer;
~ auf öffentliche Anleihen tender for public loans; **~ mit unbestimmten Kurs** tender system *(Br.)*;
~ auf eine Anleihe abgeben to tender for a public loan; **zur Abgabe von ~en auffordern** to invite tenders for a loan.

Zeichnungs|aufforderung invitation to subscribe, subscription offer; **~bedingungen** underwriting conditions, terms of subscription; **~befugnis** authorization to sign; **~beginn** opening of the subscription.

zeichnungsberechtigt authorized (entitled) to sign, *(Bezugsrechte)* entitled to subscribe;
~ sein to have authorization to sign, *(Bezugsberechtigung)* to have the right to subscribe.

Zeichnungs|berechtigter signing clerk, *(Bezugsrecht)* allottee; **~berechtigung** authorization to sign, signing authority, *(Bezugsberechtigung)* application right *(Br.)*, subscription privilege (right) *(US)*; **~berechtigung auf junge Aktien ausüben** to subscribe to new shares (stock, *US*), to acquire new shares *(Br.)*; **~bescheinigung** subscription (application, *Br.*) receipt; **~betrag** subscription money, amount subscribed, application money *(Br.)*; **ausstehende ~beträge** subscription receivables *(US)*; **~bevollmächtigter** signing clerk; **~bogen** subscription list; **~buch** subscriber's ledger; **~einladung** subscription offer; **~ergebnis** subscription level; **~formular** application form *(Br.)*, subscription form (blank) *(US)*; **~frist** subscription period; **~gebühr** signing fee; **~grenze** *(Rückversicherung)* writing (underwriting) limit; **~höchstgrenze** *(Versicherung)* line; **~jahr** year of subscription; **~kurs** rate of subscription, subscription rate (price), *(Ausgabekurs)* issue price; **~liste** subscription list, list of applicants *(Br.)*; **~offerte** tender; **~preis** issue price; **~prospekt** underwriting prospectus; **~recht** subscription (application, *Br.*) right; **~schein** subscription (stock allotment, *US*) warrant; **~schluß** closing of subscriptions; **~stelle** bank of issue; **~tag** date of subscription; **~unterlagen** subscription records *(US)*; **~vertrag** option agreement, subscription contract; **~vollmacht** authorization to sign, signatory power; **~williger** potential subscriber; **~zuweisung** *(Bezugsrecht)* allotment.

zeigen to show, *(anzeigen)* to indicate, to mark, *(ausstellen)* to display, to exhibit, *(vorführen)* present, to demonstrate;
sich ~ to make one's appearance, to appear, to turn up, to show one's face; **Aktivität ~** to display activity; **Besserung ~** *(Kurse)* to show an improvement (advance); **sich erkenntlich ~** to acknowledge, to own with gratitude; **sich sehr erstaunt ~** to be much surprised; **mit dem Finger auf j. ~** to point one's finger at s. o.; **sein wahres Gesicht ~** to show one's true colo(u)rs; **nicht das geringste Interesse ~** not to show the slightest interest; **Kampfbereitschaft ~** to show fight; **sich im besten Licht ~** to put one's best foot forward; **seine Macht ~** to demonstrate one's power; **sich öffentlich ~** to appear in public; **jem. die kalte Schulter ~** to give s. o. the cold shoulder; **seinen Unmut ~** to let one's annoyance be felt; **jem. seine Verachtung ~** to let s. o. feel one's contempt; **jem. den Weg ~** to point s. o. the way;
~, was man kann to give a taste of one's quality; **jem. ~, wie es gemacht wird** to put up to the time of the day *(sl.)*;
sich ein Zimmer ~ lassen to ask to be shown the room.

Zeiger *(Meßinstrument)* needle, indicator, hand, *(Waage)* tongue, needle;
~ vorstellen to put the hand on;
~anzeige pointer reading; **~ausschlag** *(Radar)* needle deflection.

Zeile line, *(Fernsehen)* scanning line;
nach der ~ bezahlt penny-a-line; **zwischen den ~n** interlinear, interlineal;
blinde ~ *(drucktechn.)* blank line; **eingerückte ~** indented line; **versteckte ~** transposed line; **volle ~** full line; **nicht volle ~** short line;
mit voller ~ abschließen to make lines even; **neue ~ anfangen** to start a new line; **~ ausschließen** to adjust a line to word-space; **~ aussparen** to leave a line blank; **nach der ~ bezahlen** to pay by the line, to penny-a-line; **~ einfügen** to insert a line; **zwischen den ~n einfügen** to interline; **~ einrücken** to indent a line; **bei jedem Absatz die erste ~ einrücken** to indent the first line of each paragraph; **~ mit Spatien füllen** *(drucktechn.)* to end a break; **~ halten** to straighten (keep to) the line; **jem. ein paar ~n hinterlassen** to leave s. o. a note; **~n auslaufen lassen** to space out the lines; **zwischen den ~n lesen** to read between the lines; **~n schinden** to penny-a-line; **jem. ein paar ~n schreiben** to drop s. o. a line, to knock off a line or two to s. o. *(sl.)*; **schnell ein paar ~n schreiben** to write a few hurried lines; **~ wegschicken** *(Satzmaschine)* to transfer a line;
nach der ~ bezahlter Journalist penny-a-liner *(Br.)*.

Zeilen|ablenkung horizontal deflection; **~abstand** [interlinear] space; **~abtastung** *(Fernsehen)* scanning; **~auffüllung** line filling; **~ausgang** end of a line; **~ausschluß** justification; **~breite** line length, measure; **~drucker** line printer; **~durchschuß** *(drucktechn.)* reglet; **nicht reguläre ~einheit** odd-linage unit; **~feststeller** *(Fernsehgerät)* vertical hold, *(Schreibmaschine)* space lever; **~frequenz** *(Fernseher)* line frequency; **~honorar** penny-a-line payment, linage, space fee *(US)*; **~länge** length of line; **~maß, ~messer** line measure, type scale, printer's gauge; **~preis für Inserate** advertisement cost per line, agate line rate *(US)*; **~rücklauf** *(Fernsehen)* line flyback; **~schinder** penny-a-liner *(Br.)*, hack, garreteer; **~schinderei** penny-a-linerism; **~sprungverfahren** interlaced scanning; **~steuerung** *(Fernsehen)* line control.

zeilenweise bezahlen to penny-a-line, to pay by the line.

Zeilen|zahl *(Fernsehen)* picture line standard; **~zwischenräume** leads.

Zeit time, *(Frist)* term, *(Stadium)* stage, phase, *(Stunden)* hours, *(Zeitraum)* period, space of time, spell;
auf ~ forward, on term (credit), for time; **auf unbegrenzte ~** in perpetuity; **auf unbestimmte ~** for an indefinite period, sine die; **da die ~ erfüllt war** in the ful(l)ness of time; **für eine bestimmte ~** for a fixed (definite) period, for a stated term; **im Laufe der ~** in the course of time; **in absehbarer ~** within reasonable time; **in der ersten ~** during the first weeks; **in früherer ~** at an early period; **in guten wie in schlechten ~en** for richer, for poorer; **in der heutigen ~** as times go; **in dieser reiselustigen ~** in these locomotive days; **in der hierfür vorgesehenen ~** in the prescribed time; **innerhalb der vorgeschriebenen ~** within the required time; **seit dieser ~** since then; **zu jeder beliebigen ~** at any time; **zu einer bestimmten ~** at a given time; **zu der betreffenden ~** at the time in question; **zu einer genehmen ~** at a convenient time; **zu nachtschlafender (einer unmöglichen) ~** at an unearthly (ungodly) hour *(coll.)*; **zu sehr ungelegener ~** at a most inconvenient time; **zu einer ungünstigen ~** in an evil hour; **zur ~** for the time being, at present; **zur festgesetzten ~** at the fixed (stated) time; **zur gegebenen ~** at the appropriate time, in due course; **zur rechten ~** in due course (time), in season, timely;
~ spielt keine Rolle *(Inserat)* time is no object;
nicht ausgenutzte ~ dead time; **für Botengänge benötigte ~** runaround time; **bestimmte ~** designated time; **fahrplanmäßige ~** regular (scheduled, *US*) time; **festgesetzte ~** time specified, stated (fixed) time; **flaue ~** slack period; **fragliche ~** time in question; **freie ~** free (leisure, spare) time, time off, free moment; **genaue ~** correct time; **gerichtsfreie ~** court vacations; **geschäftslose ~** dead season, dead time of the year, slackness of the market; **nie kommende ~** Greek Kalends; **bestimmbare künftige ~** determinable future time; **eine ewig lange ~** a month of Sundays; **mitteleuropäische ~** Central European Time; **osteuropäische ~** Eastern European Time; **schlechte ~en** hard (slack) times, blue period; **sitzungsfreie ~** nonterm; **standgeldfreie ~** free allowance time; **stille (tote) ~** dull time, off-season, *(Bekleidungsindustrie)* pinocle season *(sl.)*, *(Lohnausfall)* dead time; **tolle ~en** wild times; **turbulente ~en** unquiet times; **übrige ~** remainder of the day, spare time; **unmögliche ~** unearthly (ungodly) hour *(coll.)*; **unvordenkliche ~** time immemorial, time out of mind (memory), remote ages; **üppige ~en** flush times; **vertraglich vereinbarte ~** time as provided in the contract; **frei verfügbare ~** leisure time; **längst vergangene ~** far-away times, bygone age; **verkehrsschwache ~en** slack hours; **verkehrsstarke ~** busy period, rush hours; **verlorene ~** *(Produktionsausfall)* idle time; **verstreichende ~** time elapsing; **viel ~** plenty of time; **wunderbare ~** swell time; **~ außergewöhnlichen Aufstiegs (Aufschwungs)** boom-and-bust *(US coll.)*; **~en geringster Belastung** off-peak hours; **~en größter Belastung** peak hours; **~en wirtschaftlicher Blüte** prolonged boom, boom years; **~ nach Börsenschluß** afterhours; **~en der Gesetzlosigkeit** lawless times; **~ des Humanismus** the new learning; **beste ~ des Jahres** pride of the season; **~ zwischen den Jahren** limbo period; **~ seines Lebens** all one's lifetime; **kurze ~ in der Oppostion** spell in opposition; **~ der Weinlese** vintage season; **~ der Zustellung** time of service;

seine ~ abdienen *(Lehrling)* to serve one's apprenticeship (time); **genaue ~ angeben** to state a precise time; **sich der ~ anpassen** to adjust o. s. to the times, to serve the time; **~ zum Besuch einer Filmvorführung aufbringen** to afford time for a cinema; **verlorene ~ aufholen** to make up for lost time; **auf die ~ aufpassen** to watch the time; **Erinnerungen an vergangene ~en austauschen** to exchange old memories; **~ sehr knapp bemessen** to cut it fine; **seine ~ dauern** to take one's time; **ganze ~ nur ans Geschäft denken** to be businessman all the time; **miserable ~ durchmachen** to have one's dog days; **schwere ~en durchmachen** to pass (live) through hard times; **versäumte ~ einholen** to make up for lost time; **seine ~ einteilen** to schedule (map out) one's time; **zur fahrplanmäßigen ~ eintreffen** to arrive at the scheduled time *(US)*; **glänzenden ~en entgegensehen** to be in for a period of prosperity; **aufregende ~en erleben** to have a lively time of it; **schlechte ~en erleben** to come on bad times; **in der halben ~ erledigen** to do it in half the time; **zur vorgegebenen ~ eröffnen** to open on schedule; **~ und Ort für die nächste Sitzung festlegen** to arrange time and place for the next meeting; **~ gewinnen** to buy (save) time; **sich mit der ~ daran gewöhnen** to get used to it; **~ haben** to have some time free; **viel freie ~ haben** to have time on one's hands; **scheußliche ~ haben** to have the devil of a time; **wenig ~ haben** to be pinched for time; **sich zu allen ~en bewährt haben** *(Verfahren)* to stand the test of time; **sich seit ewigen ~en nicht gesehen haben** not to have seen each other for ages; **beste ~ hinter sich haben** to have seen better days; **miese ~ hinter sich haben** to have had a thin time; **~ zum Lesen haben** to have leisure for reading; **längste ~ seines Lebens im Gefängnis verbracht haben** to have spent the greater part of one's life in prison; **gerade ~ haben, einen zu nehmen** to have just time for a quick one; **auf ~ kaufen** to buy on credit (account), *(Terminkauf)* to buy forward (for future delivery, *US*); **über seine ~ verfügen können** to dispose of one's time; **sich ~ lassen** to drag one's feet; **etw. ~ verstreichen lassen** to wait a while; **in seiner freien ~ viel lesen** to fill one's free time with reading; **mit der ~ mitgehen** to keep up with the times; **jds. ~ in Anspruch nehmen** to engross s. one's time; **seine ~ gut nutzen** to improve (make the best) of one's time; **jem. zur gegebenen ~ schreiben** to write s. o. in due course; **allerhöchste ~ sein** to be well past time; **in ganz kurzer ~ fertig sein** to finish in no time; **vor einer schweren ~ stehen** to fall on hard times; **jem. die ~ stehlen** to make inroads upon (eat up all) s. one's time; **~ totschlagen** to murder (kill) time; **~ zu gewinnen trachten** to stall for time, to temporize; **festgesetzte ~ überschreiten** to overrun the time stipulated; **schlechte ~en gut überstehen** to ride out bad times, to weather a storm; **herrliche ~en verbringen** to have the time of one's life (a field day of it); **seine ~ lesend verbringen** to put in one's time reading; **seine ~ verbummeln** to dawdle (laze) away one's time; **über freie ~ verfügen** to have time off; **~ vergleichen** to check the time; **seine ~ vergeuden** to waste (misemploy one's) time; **auf ~ verkaufen** *(Terminverkauf)* to sell forward (for future delivery, *US*); **seine ~ verplanen** to plan out one's time; **~ verplaudern** to talk away the time; **seine ~ verplempern** to fiddle (loiter, linger, fool, peddle) away one's time, to mess around *(sl.)*; **auf unbestimmte ~ verschieben** to postpone to a later day, to defer sine die; **~ verschwenden** to waste time, to burn daylight; **sich auf unbestimmte ~ vertagen** to adjourn sine die; **seine ~ verträumen** to dream (doze) away one's time; **seine ~ vertrödeln** to fiddle (lounge) away one's time, to piddle, to kick one's heels; **viel ~ für etw. verwenden** to expend much time on s. th.; **herrliche ~en vorhersagen** to preach glad tidings; **für die kommende ~ vorsorgen** to provide for the future; **richtige ~ für seine Ankunft wählen** to time one's arrival rightly; **auf bessere ~en warten** to await a turn of one's luck; **Geld für schlechte ~en zurücklegen** to put away for a rainy day; **auf unbestimmte ~ zurückstellen** to shelve *(Br.)*, to lay on the table *(US)*; **seine Schulden in der vereinbarten ~ zurückzahlen** to discharge one's liabilities within the agreed period;
~ ist Geld time is money; **andere ~en andere Sitten** other times, other manners; **kommt ~, kommt Rat** time will tell (bring the answer), all in good time;
~ablauf lapse (passage, efflux) of time, elapsed time, *(Fristablauf)* expiration of time (period); **eingebaute ~ablaufskala** built-in time indicator scale; **~abschnitt** distance (segment) of time, period, era, spell, epoch; **~absprachen für Zahlungen** datings *(US)*; **in regelmäßigen ~abständen** at regular time intervals, periodically.

Zeitalter era, epoch;
unser ~ the age we live in;
~ der Entdeckungen age of discovery; **~ der Hausindustrie** cottage period; **~ der Industriekonzerne** trust-stage; **~ der audiovisuellen Unterrichtsmethode** audiovisual age;
einem ~ seinen Stempel aufdrücken to leave an impress upon one's age.

Zeit|angabe date, *(Einladung)* exact date and time; **ohne ~angabe** undated; **~ansage** *(Rundfunk)* time check; **telefonische ~ansage** speaking clock; **mit Werbung verbundene ~ansage** time signal; **~arbeit** job leasing; **auf ~arbeitsgrundlage** on a part-time basis; **~arbeitskräfte** part-time workers, temporary staff; **~aufnahme** *(Film)* slow-motion picture, *(Foto)* time exposure; **~aufnahmebogen** time-study sheet; **~aufstellung** time sheet; **~aufteilung** time apportionment.

Zeitaufwand sacrifice of time, time spent;
erforderlicher ~ amount of time required;
Wert seines ~s sehr hoch einschätzen to set a high value on one's time; **jem. unnützen ~ ersparen** to save s. o. hours of hanging around; **mit großem ~ verbunden sein** to take up a great deal of time.

Zeit|ausgleich time allowance; **~ausnutzungsgrad** time efficiency; **~basis** base period.

zeitbedingt temporal, seasonal.

Zeit|bedingtheit temporality, seasonalty; **keinen ~begriff haben** to have no notion of time; **~berechnung** timing, computation of time; **~berechnungsfehler** parachronism; **~beschränkung** time limit.

zeitbeständig timeless, ageless.

Zeit|bestimmung dating, stipulation as to time; **~bombe** time bomb; **~charter** *(Schiff)* time charter[party]; **~dauer** duration, period, length (tract) of time, time quantitiy; **~dokument** document of the times; **~druck** pressure of time; **unter ~druck stehen** to be pressed for time; **~durchschnitt** average time; **~einheit** unit of time; **~einlage** *(Bankwesen)* time deposit; **~einteilung** allocation of time, time budget (management), scheduling one's time; **avandgardistische ~epoche** go-ahead times; **~ereignis** event; **~ersparnis** economy (saving) of time, timesaver; **~fahrkarte** season (commutation, *US*) ticket; **~faktor** time element; **festgelegter ~faktor** *(Leistungsbewertung)* recorded time value; **~folge** chronological order, time sequence; **~fracht** time freight, *(Schiff)* time charter; **~frachtvertrag** time charterparty; **~frage** matter of time; **~freiwilliger** *(mil.)* irregular.

zeitfremd behind the times.

Zeitfunk topical.

zeitgemäß opportune, seasonable, timely, well-timed, *(modern)* up (down) to date, topical, present-day;
~ sein to be in tune with the times;
~er Leitartikel timely editorial.

Zeitgenosse contemporary, coeval;
leicht zu nehmender ~ easy person to get on with; **primitiver ~** square; **spendabler ~** tow line; **leicht zu überzeugender ~** pushover *(sl.)*; **unangenehmer ~** trying person to deal with, tough (nasty) customer;
seinen ~n voraus sein to be ahead of (born before) one's time.

zeitgenössischer|Bericht temporary record of events; **~ Stil** contemporary style.

zeitgerecht at the proper time, timely, in due time;
~ fertig werden to be finished on schedule.

Zeit|geschäft time bargain (purchase), negotiation for time, call *(Br.)*, forward deal (operation, transaction), dealing for the account *(Br.)*, business in futures *(US)*, privilege *(US)*; **~geschäft in Devisen** forward exchange operation, future exchange *(US)*; **~geschehen** current affairs; **~geschichte** contemporary history; **~geschmack** prevailing taste.

Zeitgewinn gain of time, gained time;
auf ~ arbeiten to buy additional time; **nur einen kurzen ~ erzielt haben** to be living on borrowed time; **um ~ verhandeln** to temporize.

Zeit|grenze time limit; **~häufigkeitsstudie** ratio delay study.

zeitig aufstehen to be an early riser.

zeitigen, ein Ergebnis to produce a result.

Zeitkarte season (commutation, *US*) ticket, commuter fare *(US)*, contract *(sl.)*.

Zeitkarten|inhaber season-ticket holder, commuter *(US)*, daily breader *(Br.)*; **~tarif** commutation rates *(US)*; **~verkehr** multiple ride traffic, commutation passenger traffic *(US)*.

Zeitkauf forward (future, *US*) purchase, put and call *(US)*.

zeitknapp pressed (pushed, pinched) for time.

Zeit|kontrolle timekeeping; **~kontrolleur** time clerk, timekeeper; **~kritik** *(Rundfunk)* current affairs commentary, topical comment; **eine ~lang** for a while; **eine ~lang ertragen** to endure for a season; **~länge prüfen** *(Film)* to time the script.

zeitlebens all one's life.
zeitlich temporary, temporal, in time, *(weltlich)* worldly;
~ **begrenzt** limited in time; ~ **geordnet** chronological;
~ **aufeinander abstimmen** to synchronize;
~**er Abstand** time interval, distance; ~**e Abstimmung** timing; ~**e Anordnung** time series, chronology; ~**e Beschränkung** time limit; ~**er Entscheidungsraum** time horizon; ~**e Güter** temporalities; ~**es Nebeneinander** simultaneousness; ~**e Reihenfolge** chronological order; ~ **beschränkte Revision** partical audit; ~**e Verzögerung** time lag.
Zeitloch time lag.
Zeitlohn task (time, *US*) wage, time rate *(US)*;
reiner ~ straight time pay;
~**arbeit** daywork, timework; ~**satz** time rate *(US)*; ~**zettel** labo(u)r time ticket.
Zeit- und Akkordlöhne time and piece wages.
zeitlose Kunst timeless art.
Zeitlupe *(Film)* slow motion.
Zeitlupen|aufnahme slow-motion picture, photochronograph; ~**kamera** slow-motion camera; **im** ~**tempo arbeiten** to work at a leisurely space; ~**verfahren** slow-motion technique; ~**wiederholung** slow-motion replay.
Zeit|mangel, aus for want (lack) of time; ~**messer** timer, chronometer.
zeitnah up-to-date, topical.
Zeit|nehmer timekeeper, timer; ~**norm** task time, *(im Arbeitsprozeß)* standard time *(US)*; **in** ~**not geraten** to cut (run) it fine; **in** ~**not sein** to be pressed for time; ~**pacht** lease on time, leasehold, tenancy from year to year, term in gross; ~**pächter** tenant for years; **steuerliche** ~**phase verschieben** to alter the timing of the payment of a tax; ~**plan** timetable, schedule; **gedrängter** ~**plan** busy (tight) schedule; ~**planung** time schedule, timing; ~**police** time (term) policy; ~**präferenz** time preference; ~**präferenzrate** rate of time preference; ~**prämie** time premium.
Zeitpunkt point of time, time, moment, date;
zu einem festgesetzten ~ at a given time; **zum gegebenen** ~ at the appropriate (proper) time; **zum gegenwärtigen** ~ at the present time, now; **zum günstigsten** ~ on the crest of the wave; **zum jeweiligen** ~ for the time being; **zum vertraglich vereinbarten** ~ at the time provided by the contract;
zum ~ **der Eheschließung** at the time of marriage; **zum** ~ **der Klageerhebung** at the time the action is brought; **zum** ~ **der Testamentserrichtung** at the time of making the will;
bestimmter ~ certain time, specified date, particular instant; **richtig bestimmter** ~ timing; **geeigneter** ~ apt time; **günstiger** ~ opportunity; **kritischer** ~ juncture; **maßgeblicher** ~ material time; **frühest möglicher** ~ earliest practicable date; **spätmöglichster** ~ superior limit;
~ **des Inkrafttretens** effective date; ~ **der Lieferung** delivery date, date of dispatch; ~ **des Vertragsabschlusses** time of conclusion of the contract (of contracting);
richtigen ~ **abwarten** to bide one's time; **für einen späteren** ~ **aufheben** to keep for a later date; **richtigen** ~ **bestimmen** to time; ~ **festlegen** to specify (appoint) a time; **geeigneten** ~ **festsetzen** to decide on a fit time; ~ **für die Zahlung vereinbaren** to agree on a date for payment; **richtigen** ~ **zum Verkauf verpassen** to overstay one's market *(US)*.
Zeitraffer stop (quick) motion, *(Gerät)* quick-motion camera; ~**aufnahme** quick-motion picture, time-lapse shooting; ~**aufnahmeverfahren** time-lapse photography.
zeitraubend time-consuming, timetaking.
Zeitraum period of time, stretch, time limit, date, interval;
im ~ **eines Jahres** during the course of a year;
absehbarer ~ measurable space of time; **angemessener** ~ reasonable length of time; **steuerlich bedeutsamer** ~ relevant period; **fester** ~ fixed period; **festgesetzter** ~ fixed period; **kurzer** ~ short period; **mietfreier** ~ rent-free period; **rechtserheblicher** ~ material period;
~ **als Rezession definieren** to put the recession tag on a period; **sich über einen** ~ **von fünf Wochen erstrecken** to extend over a period of five weeks; ~ **von fünfzig Jahren überblicken** to look back over a distance of fifty years.
Zeit|rechnung era, chronology; ~**reihe** *(Statistik)* time series; ~**reihendiagramm** time series diagram; ~**relais** deferring (time-delay) relay; ~**rente** annuity certain, temporary (terminable) annuity; ~**schalter** time switch; ~**schloß** time lock.
Zeitschrift journal, periodical [newspaper], magazine, review, *(Verband)* bulletin;
reich bebilderte ~ glossy magazine; **bildende** ~ educational magazine; **elegante** ~ slick paper *(sl.)*; **monatlich erscheinende** ~ monthly; **wöchentlich erscheinende** ~ weekly paper; **hochqualifizierte** ~ highly selective magazine; **illustrierte** ~ illustrated paper (magazine); **juristische** ~ law review; **kritische** ~ critical review; **minderwertige** ~ pulp *(US)*; **technische** ~ technical publication (journal); **vereinzelte** ~ odd number; **wissenschaftliche** ~ scientific (learned) periodical, scientific journal; **einmalig zugesandte** ~**en** transient periodicals *(US)*; **Zeitungen und** ~**en** *(Post)* newspaper post, second-class mail *(US)*;
~ **abonnieren** to subscribe for (take in, *Br.*) a magazine; **Seite in einer** ~ **belegen** to place a page in a magazine; ~ **durchblättern** to leaf through a magazine; ~ **herausgeben** to [edit (manage) a] magazine; ~ **einzeln kaufen** to buy a periodical by the number; ~**en vertreiben** to distribute periodicals.
Zeitschriften|abonnement magazine subscription; ~**abonnent** subscriber (taker, *Br.*) of a periodical; ~**artikel** magazine article; **jem. einen** ~**aufsatz zuschreiben** to father a magazine article on s. o.; ~**beitrag** contribution to a magazine; ~**druck** magazine printing; ~**handel** magazine business; ~**händler** magazine salesman; ~**herausgeber** periodicalist; ~**katalog** periodical catalog(ue); ~**leserkreis** magazine's readership, magazine audience; ~**markt** magazine field; ~**mitarbeiter** magazinist; **neueste** ~**nummer** current issue of a magazine; ~**reklame** magazine advertisement; ~**saal** newsroom; ~**ständer** newspaper rack, canterbury *(Br.)*; ~**verleger** periodicalist; **geeignet für eine** ~**veröffentlichung** magazinable; ~**werber** magazine canvasser (solicitor, *US*); ~**werbung** magazine (periodical) advertising.
Zeitsichtwechsel sight bill.
Zeitspanne period of time, time limit (span, period, lag);
gedeckte ~ *(Versicherung)* period covered by the policy; **kurze** ~ short span of time; **unproduktive** ~ winter;
~ **erhöhter Gefahr** *(Versicherung)* apprehensive period; ~ **von drei Jahren** lapse of three years.
zeitsparend timesaving.
Zeit|sprung *(in Erzählung)* leap of time; ~**stempel** time-stamping clock; ~**strömung** tide of events, trend; **der** ~**strömung folgen** to follow the fashion; ~**stück** thesis play; ~**studie** time study.
Zeitstudien|berater timekeeper, timer *(US)*; ~**ergebnisse** time-study data; ~**ingenieur** time-study engineer; ~**mann** time-study observer; ~**methode** time-study technique.
Zeit|tafel timetable, chronological table; **ortsgebundene** ~**tafel über die Abfertigung von Briefpost** localized first-class letter posting timetable; ~**überschreitung** overrun; ~**uhr** timepiece.
Zeitung newspaper, paper, journal, newssheet, print;
von den ~**en aufgebauscht** got up by the press;
amtliche ~ bulletin, gazette; **wenig angesehene** ~ paper of no standing; **deutschsprachige** ~ German-language newspaper; **eingegangene** ~ defunct paper; **nicht öffentlich erscheinende** ~ private press; **täglich erscheinende** ~ daily [paper]; **wöchentlich erscheinende** ~ weekly newspaper (gazette); **unter Zensur erscheindende** ~**en** papers under censorship; **führende** ~ leading (key) paper; **gebündelte** ~**en** baled news; **die heutigen** ~**en** today's papers; **illustrierte** ~ pictorial, illustrated paper; **schlecht informierte** ~ paper deprived of news; **inländische** ~**en** national press; **meistgelesene** ~ most widely read paper; **rechtseingestellte** ~ right-wing paper; **regierungsfeindliche** ~ antigovernment newspaper; **vordatierte** ~ antedated paper; **weitverbreitete** ~ widely read newspaper, newspaper with a wide circulation;
~ **im Kleinformat** tabloid; ~**en aller Schattierungen** newspapers of every shade; ~ **im Weltformat** blanket sheet; ~**en und Zeitschriften** newspapers and periodicals, newspaper post *(Br.)*, *(Post)* second-class matter (mail) *(US)*;
~ **abbestellen** to give up (discontinue, stop) a newspaper; ~ **abonnieren** to take in *(Br.)* (subscribe for, *US*) a newspaper; **j. in den** ~**en angreifen** to go for s. o. in the papers; **bei einer** ~ **arbeiten** to be a newspaper man; ~ **aufschlagen** to open (unfold) a newspaper; **aus der** ~ **ausschneiden** to clip out of a newspaper; ~**en austragen** to deliver newspapers, to hand the papers round, to do a newspaper round; ~ **beschlagnahmen** to suppress a paper; ~ **bestellen** to take in *(Br.)* (subscribe for, *US*) a newspaper; ~ **drucken** to print [off] a newspaper; ~ **durchblättern** to scan a newspaper; **in eine** ~ **einrücken** to insert (put) in a newspaper; ~ **entfalten** to unfold a newspaper; **aus den** ~**en erfahren** to gather from the papers; **durch alle** ~**en gehen** to go the round of the papers; ~ **gründen** to get a newspaper afloat, to establish a newspaper; **in der** ~ **gestanden haben** to be stated in the newspaper, to have figured in the press; ~ **halten** to take [in] *(Br.)* (subscribe for, *US*) a newspaper; ~ **herausgeben** to publish (issue, run) a newspaper;

in einer ~ inserieren to advertise in a newspaper; **~ konfiszieren** to seize a paper; **seiner ~ eine Nachricht zukommen lassen** to file an item of information to one's newspaper; **bei einer ~ mitarbeiten** to be on the staff of a newspaper; **~ redigieren** to edit a newspaper; **für ~en schreiben** to write for the press; **bei einer ~ beschäftigt sein** to be on the staff of a newspaper (a newspaperman); **an einer ~ finanziell beteiligt sein** to own stock in a paper *(US fam.)*; **Annonce in die ~ setzen** to put an advertisment (a notice) in the papers; **in den ~en stehen** to figure (be) in the papers; **durch die ~ suchen** to advertise for; **Herausgabe einer ~ vorübergehend untersagen** to suspend a newspaper; **in den ~en erwähnt werden** to figure in the press; **den ~en zuspielen** to leak into press.

Zeitungs|ablage newspaper rack; **~abonnement** subscription [to a newspaper]; **~abonnent** subscriber [to a newspaper]; **~agentur** news agency; **~annonce, ~anzeige** insertion, [press] advertisement, newspaper (news) advertisement, press announcement, ad *(US)*; **erfahrener ~apparat** practised organization of a paper; **~archiv** archive, morgue *(US)*.

Zeitungsartikel [newspaper] article, news item;
alarmierender ~ panicky article; **groß aufgemachter ~** feature article; **dreispaltiger ~** three-column article; **auf der nächsten Seite fortgesetzter ~** turnover *(Br.)*, runover; **günstiger ~** writeup, spread *(sl.)*; **hetzerischer ~** incendiary article; **signierter ~** signed article; **wegen Platzmangels zurückgestellter ~** crowded-out article;
~ beisteuern to contribute newspaper articles; **~ wegen Platzmangels nicht bringen** to crowd out an article; **~ vor Veröffentlichung durchsehen** to sub-edit an article; **~ herunterhauen** to knock off an article for a newspaper (magazine); **kurzen ~ schreiben** to paragraph; **~ streichen** to kill an article; **~ unterbringen** to get an article into a paper; **~ zurechtschustern** *(fam.)* to fake (toss up) a newspaper article; **aus früheren ~n ein Buch zusammenschustern** to tag old articles together to make a book; **~ zusammenstreichen** to cut down (shorten) an article; **jem. einen ~ zuschreiben** to fasten an article on s. o.; **einem ~ zustimmen** to approve of the content of an article.

Zeitungs|auflage newspaper circulation, run; **tatsächlich abgesetzte ~auflage** net paid circulation; **~ausschnitt** press (newspaper) cutting *(Br.)* (clipping, *US*), cutting from a newspaper *(Br.)*, scrap, cut; **~ausschnittsbüro** [press-]clipping bureau *(Br.)*, press-cutting service *(US)*, clipping agency *(Br.)*; **~ausschreibung** newspaper competition; **~austragen** newspaper delivery; **~austräger** newspaper boy, newsboy; **~beilage** supplement, *(Reklame)* insert *(US)*, inset; **~beitrag** contribution [to a newspaper]; **seine Einkünfte durch ~beiträge verbessern** to augment one's income by writing for the newspapers; **~bericht** [newspaper] report, story, newspaper account; **alter ~bericht** vintage newspaper account; **verzerrte ~berichte** distorted newspaper accounts; **~berichterstatter** newspaper correspondent, reporter; **~berichterstattung** [newspaper] reporting; **~besitzer** newspaper owner, newspaper proprietor, press proprietor, newspaperman; **~bestellung** subscription; **~beteiligung** newspaper stake; **~betrieb** newspaper plant; **~bezug** subscription [to a newspaper]; **~branche** news business; **~bude** kiosk, newsstall *(Br.)*, newsstand *(US)*; **~druck** newspaper work; **~druckerei** news house *(Br.)*; **~drucksache** newspaper post *(Br.)*, second-class mail *(US)*; **~ente** *(fam.)* mare's nest, newspaper hoax; **altes ~exemplar** back number; **~expedition** newspaper dispatch office; **~format** newspaper size; **~geld** paper bill; **~geld einziehen** to call for the newspaper money; **~geld monatlich kassieren** to collect the money for the newspaper once a month; **~händler** news vendor (agent, dealer), newsman; **~herausgeber** news editor; **~indiskretionen** newspaper leaks; **~industrie** newspaper industry; **~inserat** insertion, [newspaper] advertisement, ad *(US)*; **~interesse** newspaper attention; **~interview** newspaper (press) interview; **~junge** newsboy, paperboy, newsy *(US)*; **~katalog** *(Anzeigenwesen)* rate book; **~kiosk** newspaper kiosk *(Br.)*, newsstand *(US)*, newsstall *(Br.)*, bookstall, news dealer *(US)*; **am ~kiosk kaufen** to buy at the news dealer *(US)*; **~könig** newspaper magnate, press lord *(Br.)*; **~konzern** newspaper syndicate, newspaper group; **zu einem ~konzern zusammenschließen** to syndicate newspapers; **~kopf** mast head, top; **~korrespondent** correspondent, news reporter; **gute ~kritiken bekommen** to have a good press; **~leser** newspaper reader (audience), newsreader; **von Interesse für den ~leser** newsworthy; **~lesezimmer** newsroom; **~mann** newspaperman, journalist, reporter, correspondent; **~meldung** newspaper announcement (report), press report; **~meldung freigeben** to release news; **~nachricht** newspaper report, news item; **~nachricht abgeben** to provide matter for a newspaper; **~nachrichten aus aller Herren Länder erhalten** to receive dispatches from all parts of the world; **~notiz** item of news, press (news) item, notice; **~nummer** copy; **alte ~nummer** back (backlog) number; **~papier** newsprint; **in ~papier einwickeln** to wrap up in a newspaper; **~porto** newspaper rate; **~post** newspaper post *(Br.)*, second-class mail *(US)*; **~raster** newsprint screen; **~redakteur** newspaper editor; **~redaktion** editorial board; **~reklame** newspaper advertising; **ganzseitige ~reklame** full-page advertisement *(Br.)*; **~reporter** reporter, correspondent, newspaperman, item man *(US)*; **~rückfrage** press query; **~schreiber** reporter, correspondent, newspaper writer, newspaperman, journalist, columnist; **~spalte** newspaper column; **~sprache** journalese; **~stand** newsstall *(Br.)*, kiosk *(Br.)*, newsstand *(US)*, bookstall; **am ~stand kaufen** to buy at the news dealer *(Br.)*; **~ständer** newspaper rack; **~stelle** newspaper service; **~stil** newspaper writing, journalese, newspaper style; **~stoß** file; **~streik** newspaper strike; **~syndikat** newspaper syndicate; **~text** newspaper copy; **~titel** title of a newspaper; **~träger** newsboy, delivery man; **~trust** newspaper syndicate; **~überschrift** headline, newspaper headline; **~überschriften auslösen** to make the papers; **~überschriften überfliegen** to take a glance at the newspaper headlines; **~verkäufer** news vendor (dealer), newsman, newspaperman, news hawk (butcher) *(US)*; **~verkaufsstelle** newsroom *(US)*, newspaper kiosk *(Br.)*; **~verleger** newspaper publisher *(US)* (owner), newspaperman; **~verlegerverband** Newspaper Society *(Br.)*; **~vertrieb** distribution of a newspaper; **~viertel** Fleet Street *(Br.)*; **~werbung** press advertisement; **~werbung unter Kennziffer** keyed advertising; **~wesen** newsprinting, press, business of printing, journalism, fourth estate; **~wirtschaft** newspaper industry; **~zustelldienst** newspaper delivery.

Zeit|unterschied difference in time; **~vergeudung** time-wasting; **~verlust** loss (waste) of time, delay; **ohne jeden weiteren ~verlust** without further loss of time; **glatter ~verlust** pure waste of time; **~verschiebung** time shift; **~verschluß** *(Foto)* time shutter; **~verschwendung** waste (wastage, dilution) of time; **~versicherung** term insurance; **~- und Reiseversicherung** mixed policy *(Br.)*; **~versicherungspolice** time policy.

Zeitvertreib diversion, amusement, play, entertainment, sport, fun;
jugendlicher ~ diversions of youth;
sich zum ~ mit Politik beschäftigen to play at (dabble in) politics; **nach einem ~ Ausschau halten** to seek diversion.

Zeit|verzögerung time lag; **keine ~verzögerung zulassen** to allow of no delay; **~vorgabe** time allowance; **~vorsprung vor jem. haben** to have a start over s. o.; **~vorverlegung** daylight saving; **richtige ~wahl** timing; **~wegschreiber** *(Auto)* tachograph.

zeitweilig temporary, provisional, *(gelegentlich)* occasional, intermittent;
~ beschäftigt seasonal, *(nicht ganztägig)* part-time;
Beamten ~ des Dienstes entheben to suspend an official;
~ zollfreie Einfuhr temporary admission; **~e Erwerbsunfähigkeit** temporary disability; **~e Geldknappheit** money pinch; **Beamten in den ~en Ruhestand versetzen** to put an official on half pay; **~es Verfügungsrecht** special property.

Zeit|wende new era; **~wert** present (current, market) value; **niedriger ~wert** lower market value; **~wertprinzip** cost method of valuation; **~zeichen** *(Rundfunk)* time signal, pip; **~zone** time zone (belt, *US*); **~zünder** time (delay) fuse.

Zelle *(Batterie)* cell, element, *(im Flugzeugrumpf)* bay, *(Gefängnis)* prison cell;
elektrolytische ~ voltaic cell; **fotoelektrische ~** photoelectric cell; **politische ~** cell; **schalldichte ~** soundproof booth; **kommunistische ~n in einer Industriestadt** communist cells in an industrial town;
in einer Gewerkschaft ~n bilden to set up cells in a trade union.

Zellen|gefängnis cell house; **~genosse** fellow prisoner; **~haft** confinement in a prison cell.

Zellstoffindustrie cellulose industry.

Zelluloseindustrie wood-pulp industry.

Zellwolle cellulose, staple fibre.

Zelt tent, *(Ausstellung)* marquee, pavilion;
in ~en under canvas;
~ abbrechen to break up camp; **seine ~e abbrechen** to fold up one's tent, to pack up; **~ abschlagen** to strike a tent; **~ aufschlagen** to pitch a tent;
~aufstellung pitching a tent; **~ausrüstung, ~ausstattung** camping gear (equipment); **~bahn** awning, fly, *(mil.)* ground sheet *(Br.)*; **~bett** canopy (camp) bed; **~bewohner** camper.

Zelten camping.
zelten to camp out, to tent.
Zelt|lager camp; **im ~lager wohnen** to camp out; **~leinwand** canvas; **~liege** camp bed; **~öffnung** opening of a tent; **~pflock** tent peg; **~plane** tarpaulin, awning; **~platz** camping ground (site, place); **~platzeinkünfte** income from a camping site; **~platzgebühren** camping fees; **~reihe** *(mil.)* line *(Br.)*; **~stange** tent pole.
Zement, schnellbindender quick-setting cement;
~boden cement floor; **~fabrik** cement works; **~industrie** cement industry.
Zenit|seiner Laufbahn zenith of one's career; **~ seiner Machtstellung** summit of s. one's power.
zensieren to expurgate, to [examine as] censor, *(kritisieren)* to criticize, *(Schule)* to mark, to grade, to blue-pencil;
Nachrichten ~ to exercise censorship over news.
zensiert|sein to be censored;
~e Stelle censored passage.
Zensor censor, expurgator.
Zensorenamt censorship.
Zensur censorship, censure, wrap, *(Schule)* score, marks, grade; **der ~ unterworfen** censorable; **von der ~ freigegeben** passed by the censor; **von der ~ gestrichen** deleted by the censor; **gute ~en in der Schule erhalten** to make good marks at school; **~ aufheben** to lift censorship; **bessere ~en erhalten** to receive higher grades; **durch die ~ gehen** to be censored; **der ~ unterwerfen** to apply censorship; **von der ~ durchgelassen werden** to pass the censor;
~behörde Board of Censors, Office of Censorship; **~bestimmungen** censorship regulations; **~bestimmungen verschärfen** to tighten up the censorship.
Zensurenkonferenz *(Schule)* reports conference.
Zensurlücke *(Zeitung)* deletions due to the censor.
zensurpflichtig must be submitted (subject) to the censor, censorable.
Zensur|stelle obliterated passage; **~stelle für Neuveröffentlichungen** watch and ward society *(US)*; **~stempel** censorship stamp; **~vorschriften** censorship regulations; **~vorschriften für Zeitungen erlassen** to clamp a ban on newspapers.
Zentner cental, hundredweight;
kleiner ~ short hundred;
~last *(fig.)* poundage; **wie eine ~last auf jds. Seele liegen** to weigh heavily on s. one's mind.
zentral central, pivotal;
~ gelegen sein to be very central;
~er Einkauf central buying; **~es Einkaufsbüro** *(Konzern)* syndicate buying office; **~e Figur** actor of character; **~ gelegenes Geschäft** central area shop; **~er Kapitalmarktausschuß** capital market committee; **~e Leitung** central management (administration); **~es Notenbankinstitut** central note-issuing bank; **das ~e Problem sein** to be the crux of the matter; **~ gelegenes Reisebüro** downtown ticket office *(US)*; **~e Schichtungsstelle** central arbitration committee *(Br.)*; **~e Verkehrssteuerung** *(Eisenbahn)* central traffic control.
Zentral|ablage centralized filing, central file; **~agentur** central agency; **~antenne** community (shared) antenna (aerial); **~archiv** central registry, *(Bibliothek)* main reference library; **~aufsichtsbehörde** central control agency; **~auskunftsstelle** central information office; **~ausschuß** central executive committee (commission); **~bank** central bank, Bank of England *(Br.)*, Federal Reserve Bank *(US)*.
zentralbankfähig eligible for rediscount.
Zentralbank|geld high-powered money, federal funds *(US)*; **der Wirtschaft ~geld zuführen** to inject central bank money into the economy; **~geldmenge** monetary base; **~guthaben** legal (minimum, *US*) reserve, safety fund *(US)*; **~guthaben der öffentlichen Hände** public deposits; **~institut** central bank, Federal Reserve Bank *(US)*; **~politik** central bank (Federal Reserve Bank, *US*) policy; **~rat** Federal Reserve Board *(US)*, Federal Advisory Council *(US)*, Board of Governors of the Federal Reserve System *(US)*; **~ratsmitglied** federal reserve agent; **~reserven** Bank of England (Federal Bank, *US*) reserves; **~system** Federal Reserve System *(US)*.
Zentral|behörde central authority (agency, *US*); **~bezugsgenossenschaft** cooperative buying office; **~büro** headquarters, head (front, central) office.
Zentrale principal establishment, headquarters, main *(US)* (head, front, principal, home) office, *(Artilleriestand)* fire control center *(US)* (centre, *Br.*), *(Befehlszentrale)* nerve center *(US)* (centre, *Br.*), *(el.)* central power station, *(Kriegsschiff)* control station, *(Omnibus)* bus depot, *(Rundfunk)* studio, *(techn.)* control room, central, *(Telefon)* switchboard, telephone exchange, chief operator *(US)*;
nicht an die ~ gekoppelt *(Datenverarbeitung)* off-line;
~ einer Behörde headquarters of an agency; **~ zu Hause** home office;
seine ~ haben to have its headquarters at, to headquarter; **auf die ~ zurückschalten** to switch back to the studio; **Angestellten in die ~ zurückversetzen** to relocate an employee.
Zentral|einkäufer central buyer, *(Warenhaus)* departmental buyer; **~einkaufsbüro** *(Konzern)* syndicate buying office *(US)*; **~flughafen** central airport; **~genossenschaft** cooperative wholesale society *(Br.)*.
zentralgesteuerte Verwaltungsspitze auflösen to dismantle central government.
Zentral|gewalt central power; **~gewerkschaftsfunktionär** national union officer *(US)*; **~gewerkschaftsverband** national union *(US)*; **~heizung** central heating.
Zentralisation centralization.
zentralisieren to centralize.
zentralisierter Einkauf centralized purchase, central buying.
Zentralisierungstendenz centralizing tendency.
Zentralismus centralism, federalism *(US)*.
zentralistisch centralistic, unitary, federal *(US)*.
Zentral|kartei, ~kartothek central (master) file (registry); **~kasse** clearinghouse; **~katalog** *(Bibliothek)* union catalog(ue); **~kommission, ~komitee** central commission (committee); **~konto der Regierung bei der Staatsbank** Exchequer *(Br.)*; **~markthändler** wholesaler, wholesale receiver *(US)*; **~notenbank** central bank, Federal Reserve Bank *(US)*, Bank of England *(Br.)*; **~organ** central executive body; **~organisation** head organization; **~organisation für den Fremdenverkehr** British Travel and Holiday Association; **~punkt** center *(US)*, centre *(Br.)*, central core; **~regierung** centralized (central) government; **~registratur** master (central) file (registry); **~staat** unitary state; **~stelle** central [agency, *US*], central office, center *(US)*, centre *(Br.)*; **~thema** central issue; **~unkosten** overhead, establishment charges, burden; **~verband** umbrella (central) association, central organization; **~verwaltung** central administration; **~wert** median.
zentrieren to center.
Zentrifugalkraft centrifugal force.
Zentrum middle, *(Handel)* emporium, *(Hochburg)* repository, *(pol.)* center *(US)*, centre *(Br.)*, *(Stadt)* centre *(Br.)*, downtown *(US)*;
~ des Handels commercial center *(US)* (centre, *Br.*), emporium, center *(US)* (centre, *Br.*) of commerce, staple, entrepôt, mart;
im ~ des Interesses stehen to be the focus of attention.
zerbombt bomb-shattered;
~e Gebiete blitzed areas.
zerbrechen to fall to pieces, to shatter, to smash, to break, to disrupt;
sich über etw. den Kopf ~ to rack one's brains about s. th.
zerbrechlich fragile, delicate, breakable, liable to breakage;
Vorsicht ~! handle with care, fragile!
Zeremonie ceremony, exercises *(US)*;
~ absolvieren to go through a ceremony.
Zeremoniell ceremony, solemnity;
mit gebührendem ~ with due ritual;
diplomatisches ~ protocol; **starres ~** hidebound etiquette.
zeremoniell ceremonial, solemn;
~e Notwendigkeiten pomp and circumstance, formalities, rites.
Zeremonienmeister master of ceremonies, marshal, emcee *(coll.)*.
zerfahren absent-minded, muddleheaded;
~er Mensch scatterbrain; **~e Straße** rutted street.
Zerfall *(Gebäude)* decay, ruin, *(geistig)* decadence, *(Staat)* collapse, decay;
radioaktiver ~ radioactive disintegration.
zerfallen *(Gebäude)* to fall apart, to decay, to go to ruin, *(Staat)* to collapse, to decay;
in zwölf Kapitel ~ *(Buch)* to be divided into four chapters; **zu Staub ~** to crumble to dust; **in Stücke ~** to crumble (tumble) to pieces;
mit jem. ~ sein to have broken with s. o.; **mit sich selbst ~ sein** to be at odds with o. s.
zerfetzen to tear in shreds, to tatter;
j. in der Luft ~ to tear s. o. apart limb by limb.
zerfleischen, sich gegenseitig to tear each other to pieces; **sich in Selbstvorwürfen ~** to torment o. s. with self-reproach.
zerfließen, unter den Händen *(Geld)* to melt away in one's hands;
vor Mitleid ~ to melt with pity.

zerfressen, Eisen to corrode iron; **Stoff** ~ *(Motten)* to eat up the material;
~ *(a.)* corroded;
von Motten ~ moth-eaten.
zerfurchte Straße furrowed (rutted) road.
zergehen to dissolve.
zergliedern to dissect, to dismember, *(analysieren)* to analyse, to break down *(US)*.
Zergliederung dissection, *(Analyse)* analysis, breakdown *(US)*;
kritische ~ autopsy;
~ **einer Bilanz** analysis sheet, breakdown of a balance sheet *(US)*; ~ **eines Landes** dismemberment of a territory.
Zerhacker *(el.)* inverter, vibrator.
zerkleinern to cut, to crush, to break.
Zerkleinerungsmaschine crusher, crushing mill, breaker.
zerklüftet *(Küste)* fissured, fractured.
zerknirscht remorseful, crestfallen, penitent;
völlig ~ **sein** to be full of remorse.
Zerknirschung crestfallenness, repentance, penitence.
zerknüllen, etw. in der Hand to crumple s. th. in one's hand.
zerkratzen to scrab, to scrape, to score.
zerlegbar knockdown, dismountable, separable, detachable, takedown;
~**e Antenne** sectioned antenna (aerial).
zerlegen to disassemble, to dismount, *(Maschine)* to take down (to pieces), to dismantle;
in Bestandteile ~ *(für Transportzwecke)* to knock down; **etw. in zwei Teile** ~ to divide s. th. into two parts.
zerlegt knocked down.
Zerlegung *(Maschine)* dismantling, dismantlement, disassembly;
~ **eines Arbeitsvorganges** elemental breakdown.
zerlesen *(Buch)* well-thumbed.
zerlumpt in tatters, tattered, ragged, in rags.
zermalmen to crush, to pound, to pulverize.
zermalmt, von einer Lawine crushed by an avalanche.
zermürben to wear out, *(mil.)* to demoralize;
Gegner ~ to soften an enemy.
zermürbend wearing, killing, trying.
zermürbt werden to come to pieces.
Zermürbung attrition.
Zermürbungs|krieg war of attrition; ~**politik** policy of attrition.
zernieren *(mil.)* to blockade, to besiege, to invest.
Zernierung *(mil.)* blockade, siege, investment.
zerpflücken to slash;
Argument ~ to tear an argument to pieces (shreds), to knock the bottom out of an argument; **Theorie** ~ to pick a theory to pieces.
zerplatzen *(Ballon)* to burst, to bust, *(Granate)* to burst, to explode.
zerquetschen to crush, to squash, to squelch;
Finger in der Tür ~ to crush one's fingers in the door; **Träne** ~ to squeeze a tear *(coll.)*.
Zerrbild caricature, mockery, takeoff *(coll.)*, distorted image;
~ **der Gerechtigkeit** travesty of justice.
Zerreißen eines Testaments tearing a will.
zerreißen to tear, *(Bindungen)* to disrupt, to break off, to sever, to rupture, *(Hose)* to rip, *(wildes Tier)* to maul;
Brief in Stücke ~ to tear a letter into shreds; **sich förmlich** ~, **um...** to fall over backwards to...; **seine Ketten** ~ to burst one's fetters; **Wolken** ~ to rive the clouds;
sich vor Wut ~ **können** to be bursting with rage.
Zerreiß|festigkeit tensile strength; ~**grenze** breaking limit.
Zerreißprobe tensile strength test, *(fig.)* endurance test, ordeal;
mit der Presse zu bestehende ~ ordeal with the press;
~ **für eine Freundschaft darstellen** to try a friendship to the breaking point; **schreckliche** ~ **bestehen müssen** to go through a terrible ordeal.
zerren to drag, to haul, to wrest, *(schleppen)* to tug;
j. vor Gericht ~ to bring s. o. into court; **jem. die Kleider vom Leib** ~ to rip s. one's clothes off; **an jds. Nerven** ~ to jar on s. one's nerves; **an die Öffentlichkeit** ~ to bring before the public; **j. in den Schmutz** ~ to fling dirt at s. o.; **Sträfling aus seinem Versteck** ~ to drag a prisoner out of his hiding place.
zerrinnen *(Vermögen)* to melt (dwindle) away;
jem. zwischen den Fingern ~ to run through s. one's fingers like water; **zu nichts** ~ *(Pläne)* to end up in smoke, to come to nothing.
zerrissen torn, ripped, tattered;
~**e Hose** torn trousers; **politisch** ~**es Land** country disrupted politically; ~**e Nebelschwaden** wisps of mist.
Zerrspiegel distorting mirror.
zerrütten to ruin, to destroy, to disorder, to disorganize;
Ehe ~ to wreck a marriage; **Finanzen** ~ to shatter finances; **geistig** ~ to derange the mind; **Währung** ~ to dislocate the currency.
zerrüttet disordered, *(Verstand)* deranged;
~**e Ehe** ruined (broken) marriage; ~**e Familienverhältnisse** broken home; ~**e Finanzen** shattered finances; ~**e Gesundheit** wretched (worn-out) health; ~**e Nerven** shattered nerves; ~**e Vermögensverhältnisse** decayed circumstances; ~**e Währung** dislocated (depreciated) currency.
Zerrüttung disorganization, disintegration, *(Ehe)* breakdown;
soziale ~ social malady; **unheilbare** ~ *(Ehe)* irretrievable breakdown;
~ **des Geistes** mental derangement; ~ **der Währung** dislocation of the currency.
Zerrüttungsprinzip *(Ehescheidung)* concept of breakdown.
zerschellen to shatter, to smash, *(Flugzeug)* to crash, *(Schiff)* to split, to wreck;
an den Felsen ~ to pound on the rocks.
zerschlagen to smash to pieces, *(Angriff)* to break up;
sich ~ *(Plan)* to come to nothing, to end up in smoke; **Ernte** ~ to beat down (batter) the harvest; **Fensterscheibe** ~ to shatter a windowpane; **jem. jeden Knochen im Leib** ~ to break every bone in s. one's body; **Organisation** ~ to disrupt an organization; **Spionagering** ~ to smash a spy ring; **Staat** ~ to disintegrate a state; **Teller** ~ to break a plate.
Zerschlagung von Industriebetrieben industrial disruption.
zerschmettern to crush, to shatter, to smash to pieces.
zerschneiden to cut [up];
jem. das Herz ~ to pierce s. o. to the core.
zerschossen riddled with bullets.
zersetzen *(chemisch)* to corrode, *(fig.)* to poison, to corrupt, to undermine;
sich ~ to decompose; **Gemeinschaft** ~ demoralize a community; **Moral der Truppe** ~ to destroy the discipline of troops; **Staat** ~ to undermine the power of a state.
zersetzend poisoning, *(politisch)* subversive;
~**e Kritik** destructive criticism; ~**e Tätigkeit** subversive activity.
Zersetzung disintegration, sedition, decay, subversion;
verfassungsverräterische ~ subversion of the constitution;
~ **der Moral** corruption of morale principles, vitiating the public taste; ~ **der Wehrkraft** destroying the discipline of troops, demoralization of the troops.
Zersiedlung urban sprawl, ribbon development *(Br.)*;
~ **der Landschaft** despoliation of the landscape.
zersplittern to splinter, to shiver, to shatter;
seine Kräfte ~ to dissipate one's strength; **Partei** ~ to splinter a party; **Truppen** ~ to scatter troops.
zersplittert shattered, *(Familie)* fragmented, *(Partei)* disunited, splintered;
~**e Stimmen** scattered votes.
Zersplitterung *(pol.)* disunion, cleavage;
~ **von Stimmen** scattered votes; ~ **von Truppen** dispersal of troops.
zersprengen, seine Ketten to burst one's fetters; **Menschenmenge** ~ to disperse (break up) the crowd.
zerspringen to splinter, to smash, to shatter, *(Geschoß)* to burst, to explode;
in tausend Stücke ~ to fly to bits.
zerstoben, in alle Richtungen scattered to the four winds.
zerstochen, von Mücken eaten all over by midges.
zerstören to annihilate, to demolish, to dilapidate, to undo, to tread under foot, *(mil.)* to destroy, to devastate;
durch Bomben völlig ~ to coventrate, to coventrize; **Ernte** ~ to ruin the crop; **jds. Gesundheit** ~ to ruin s. one's health; **jds. Hoffnungen** ~ to shatter s. one's hopes; **Kunstwerk** ~ to destroy a work of art; **mutwillig** ~ to vandalize; **ganzen Stadtteil** ~ to destroy (consume) the whole district.
zerstört, vom Feuer devastated by fire; **von der Flut** ~ overwhelmed by a flood; **total** ~ *(Gebäude)* wholly destroyed;
~**e Stadt** destroyed city.
Zerstörung annihilation, devastation, demolition, destruction, strip *(US)*, *(mar.)* kill;
durch das Feuer angerichtete ~ destruction caused by the fire; **große** ~**en** great devastations; **rücksichtslose** ~ wanton destruction; **totale** ~ root-and branch destruction; **vorsätzliche** ~ malicious destruction;
~ **eines Bauwerks** destruction of a building; ~ **durch Bomben** coventrization; ~ **einer Stadt durch ein Erdbeben** destruction of a town by an earthquake.

Zerstörungs|trupp *(mil.)* demolition party; ~**wut** vandalism.
zerstreuen to scatter, to disperse, to dissipate, *(ablenken)* to detract;
jem. ~ to take s. one's mind off things; **sich** ~ to disperse, *(sich ablenken)* to divert, to recreate; **sich bei seiner Lektüre angenehm** ~ to find a wholesome distraction in reading; **Menge** ~ to disperse the crowd; **Zweifel** ~ to dispel doubts.
zerstreut *(fig.)* absent-minded, scatterbrained;
weit ~ widely scattered;
~ **liegende Häuser** scattered houses; ~**er Mensch** scatterbrain.
Zerstreutheit absence of mind, absentmindedness.
Zerstreuung dissipation, *(Ablenkung)* distraction, diversion, escape, entertainment, sport, *(Volksmenge)* dispersion;
seinen Gästen allerlei ~**en bieten** to offer one's guests a variety of entertainments.
zerstritten, miteinander fallen out with each other;
~ **sein** to be at variance, to have fallen out with;
~**e Partei** split-up party.
zerstückeln *(Grundbesitz)* to parcel out, to divide into small sections, *(Land)* to dismember, to disintegrate.
Zerstückelung dismemberment, disintegration.
zerteilen to divide, to cut into pieces;
Wolken ~ to part the clouds.
Zertifikat certificate, warrant;
~ **einer Kapitalanlagegesellschaft** certificate of interest *(US)*, unit *(Br.)*;
ausgefülltes ~ **abgeben** to hand in a completed certificate; ~ **ausstellen** to certify.
Zertifikats|besitz holding of units *(Br.)*; ~**besitzer** *(Kapitalanlagegesellschaft)* certificate holder *(US)*, unitholder *(Br.)*; ~**preis** price of units *(Br.)* (certificates, *US*).
zertrampeln to trample all over, *(niedertrampeln)* to crush.
zertrümmern to smash, to shatter, to pound, to disrupt;
Fensterscheibe ~ to smash a windowpane; **jem. den Schädel** ~ to crack s. one's skull.
zertrümmert smashed, shattered, broken, demolished, wrecked.
zerwühlen to root up, *(Bett)* to rumple.
Zerwürfnis variance, disagreement, difference, quarrel.
Zession assignment of claim (chose in action), assignation, cession, alienation, conveyance, transfer;
offene ~ absolute assignment; **stille** ~ equitable assigment; **zu Besicherungszwecke vorgenommene** ~ assignment by way of security;
stille ~ **aller Buchforderungen** unregistered general assignment of book debts.
Zessionar assignee of a debt (in fact), assign, cessionary, transferee, grantee *(US)*.
zessionsfähig assignable, alienable.
Zessions|fähigkeit assignability; ~**urkunde** deed of transfer, transfer deed, [deed of] assignation, assignment, quitclaim *(US)*; ~**vertrag** assignment agreement.
Zeter und Mordio hullabaloo, hue and cry, shindy *(coll.)*;
~ **schreien** to cry blue murder, to scream the place down.
zetern to scold, to whine, to wail, to yell.
Zettel slip, *(Adressenanhänger)* label, ticket, tag, *(kurze Notiz)* note, *(Plakat)* bill, placard, poster, *(Prospekt)* leaflet, handbill, pamphlet *(US)*;
herausgerissener ~ scrap of paper;
~ **aufkleben** to bill, to post bills, to stick (set) up bills, to placard; **etw. auf einem** ~ **notieren** to jot s. th. down on a slip of paper; ~ **ankleben verboten!** post no bills!;
~**ankleben** billing, bill sticking; ~**ankleber** billposter, billsticker, placarder *(US)*; ~**bank** bank of issue; ~**kartei**, ~**katalog** card catalog(ue); ~**kasten** memorandum (slip) box, card-index box, pigeonhole, filing cabinet; ~**system** card system; ~**wahl** ballot.
Zeug stuff, things, *(Plunder)* junk, rubbish, trash;
dummes ~ fiddle, nonsense; **ungenießbares** ~ rotten stuff; **ungereimtes** ~ neither rhyme nor reason; **wertloses** ~ stuff and nonsense, trash;
jem. etw. am ~**e flicken** to find fault with s. o.; **mit jem. scharf ins** ~ **gehen** to give s. o. a talking-to; **das** ~ **dazu haben** to have the makings of, to have good stuff in one, to be cut out for; **sich für j. ins** ~ **legen** to go all out for s. o.; **sich tüchtig ins** ~ **legen** to put one's shoulder to the wheel, to put a bit of elbow grease in it *(coll.)*, to pitch in *(US)*; **dummes** ~ **reden** to talk through one's hat, to talk double Dutch; **kümmerliches** ~ **verkaufen** to sell poor stuff;
brüllen, was das ~ **hält** to shout at the top of one's voice.
Zeugamt *(mil.)* Ordnance Department *(US)*, ordnance office, arsenal, depot.
Zeuge witness, deponent, attestor, attestant, voucher, evidence, confirmor;
nach Angabe der ~**n** according to the witnesses; **vor** ~**n** in the presence of witnesses;
abgelehnter ~ challenged witness; **abreisefertiger** ~ going witness; **ausgebliebener** ~ defaulting witness; **unentschuldigt ausgebliebener** ~ contumacious witness; **aussagepflichtiger** ~ compellable witness; **beeidigter** ~ sworn witness; **befangener** ~ challengeable witness; **von der beklagten Partei benannter** ~ witness for the defence; **zur Aussageverweigerung berechtigter** ~ privileged witness; **berufssachverständiger** ~ witness from the profession; **eigener** ~ friendly witness; **nicht erschienener** ~ defaulting witness; **falscher** ~ false witness; **freiwilliger** ~ independent witness; **geschäftsfähiger** ~ competent witness; **gezwungener** ~ witness against himself; **glaubwürdiger** ~ credible (reliable, trustworthy) witness; **interessierter** ~ interested witness; **käufliche** ~**n** knights of the post; **noch lebender** ~ still living witness; **meineidiger** ~ perjured (forsworn) witness, straw man; **mittelbarer** ~ intermediate witness; **neutraler** ~ outside (disinterested) witness; **parteiischer** ~ interested (hostile, swift) witness; **sachverständiger** ~ expert (skilled) witness, witness from the profession; **übereifriger** ~ swift witness; **unzuverlässiger** ~ slippery witness; **vereidigter** ~ witness on oath, sworn witness, deposer; **verläßlicher** ~ unimpeachable witness; **zur Aussage nicht verpflichteter** ~ privileged witness; **voreingenommener** ~ swift (adverse, interested, prejudiced) witness; **wichtiger** ~ material witness; **wichtigster** ~ key witness;
~ **ohne Aussageverweigerungsrecht** compellable witness; ~ **der Gegenpartei (Gegenseite)** hostile (adverse) witness; ~ **vor Gericht** witness in court; ~ **der Staatsanwaltschaft** witness for the prosecution (the Crown, *Br.*); ~ **bei der Unterschriftsleistung** attesting (subscribing) witness; ~ **der Verteidigung** defence (defense, *US*) witness;
~**n ablehnen** to challenge (object to, protest, take exception to) a witness; ~**n anhören** to hear the evidence; ~**n aufrufen** to call to witness (into the witness box); **als** ~**n ausfragen** to draw out a witness; **als** ~ **aussagen** to bear witness, to testify, to [give] evidence, to take the stand *(US)*; **als** ~ **unter Eid aussagen** to make oath and depose; **als** ~ **falsch aussagen** to give false testimony; ~**n bearbeiten** *(fam.)* to get at a witness; ~**n beibringen** to produce (adduce) a witness; **j. als** ~**n benennen** to call s. o. to witness (in evidence); ~**n bestechen** to suborn (bribe, buy) a witness; ~**n zur Stelle bringen** to bring forward a witness; ~**n einschüchtern** to intimidate a witness; ~**n einvernehmen** to interrogate a witness; **Einspruch gegen einen** ~**n erheben** to challenge a witness; **dem** ~**n seine Kosten erstatten** to reimburse the witness for his expenses; **als** ~ **bei der Abfassung eines Testaments fungieren** to attest (witness) a will; ~**n gegenüberstellen** to confront witnesses; **j. als** ~**n laden** to call s. o. as witness, to summon s. o. to appear as a witness; ~**n unbeeidigt lassen** to leave a witness unsworn; ~**n erneut vernehmen lassen** to recall a witness; **als** ~ **bei einer Testamentserrichtung mitwirken** to witness (attest) a will; **durch** ~**n nachweisen** to show by testimony; ~**n ins Gegenkreuzverhör nehmen** to reexamine a witness, to cross-examine; ~**n präparieren** to prime a witness; ~ **sein** to witness, to testify, to evidence; ~**n stellen** to produce a witness; ~**n genauestens unterrichten** to prime a witness; ~**n vereidigen** to swear in a witness; ~**n vernehmen** to hear (examine, question, inspect) the witnesses, to take the testimony; **j. als** ~**n vernehmen** to take s. one's evidence, to interrogate s. o. as a witness, to put s. o. on the stand *(US)*; ~**n gerichtlich vernehmen** to examine a witness in a court of law; ~**n kommissarisch vernehmen** to hear a witness on commission; ~**n verwirren** to corner a witness; ~**n erneut vorführen** to reproduce a witness; ~**n zwangsweise vorführen** to compel the attendance of a witness; **j. als** ~**n vorladen** to summon (subpoena) s. o. as a witness; **ungewollt** ~ **werden** to become an unwilling witness; **als** ~ **aufgerufen werden** to be called on to give evidence; **einem** ~**n gegenüber gestellt werden** to be confronted with a witness; **als** ~ **vereidigt werden** to be sworn in as a witness; ~**n zwingen, sich an die Tatsachen zu halten** to pin a witness down to facts.
zeugen to beget, to propagate, to generate;
für j. ~ to give evidence for s. o.; **von großem Verständnis** ~ to bespeak of great understanding.
Zeugen|ablehnung impugnment of (objection to, exception to) a witness; ~**anwesenheit** attendance of a witness; ~**aufruf** calling of witnesses.
Zeugenaussage deposition, testimony, evidence, statement made by a witness;

nicht beeidigte ~ unsworn testimony, declaration *(US)*; **belastende** ~ incriminating evidence; **bestätigende** ~ corroborative evidence; **beweiserhebliche** ~ material evidence; **sich deckende (übereinstimmende)** ~ concordant depositions; **eidliche** ~ testimony under oath; **falsche** ~ false testimony (evidence); **glaubhafte** ~ reliable evidence; **meineidige** ~ perjured evidence; **mündliche** ~ oral evidence; **positive** ~ positive statement; **schriftliche** ~ written (proof of) evidence, deposition; **unbeeidigte** ~ unsworn statement of a witness, declaration *(US)*; **unterschriebene** ~ jurat *(Br.)*; **unwahre** ~ untrue statement; **widersprechende** ~ conflicting evidence, divergent testimonies;
~ **aufnehmen** to take proof *(Br.)*; ~**n für ein Verfahren auswerten** to apply the testimony to a case; **einer** ~ **keine Bedeutung beimessen** to discredit the evidence of a witness; **falsche** ~ **machen** to give false evidence; ~ **zu Protokoll nehmen** to enter a deposition on record; **Erklärung durch** ~**n untermauern** to produce testimony to a statement; **schriftliche** ~ **vor Gericht verlesen** to open a deposition; ~ **widerrufen** to withdraw (retract) testimony.

Zeugen|bank witness box (stand, *US*); ~**beeinflussung** tampering with a witness; **vom Verdacht der** ~**beeinflussung freigesprochen werden** to be purged of partial counsel; ~**befragung** examination of a witness; **eidliche** ~**befragung** examination on oath; ~**befragung durch den eigenen Anwalt** examination in chief; ~**benennung** calling to testify, specification of witnesses; ~**bestechung** subornation (corruption, bribing) of a witness; ~**beweis** testimonial proof, witnessing, proof by the evidence of witnesses; ~**eid** judicial oath; ~**einschüchterung** intimidation of witnesses; ~**einvernahme** oral evidence, interrogation of a witness, hearing of evidence; ~**formel** attestation clause; ~**gebühr**, ~**geld** witness fee (expenses), conduct money, mileage *(US)*; ~**gebühr zahlen** to reimburse a witness for his expense; **in** ~**gegenwart erklären** to declare before witnesses; ~**ladung** summons, *(unter Strafandrohung)* subpoena; **jem. eine** ~**ladung zustellen** to subpoena s. o. as witness; ~**manipulation** tampering with a witness; ~**nötigung** coercion (intimidation) of a witness; **jem. die** ~**qualifikation nehmen** to disqualify s. o. as (from being a) witness; ~**schaft bei der Testamentserrichtung** attestation of a will.

Zeugenstand witness box (stand, *US*);
vom ~ **abtreten** to stand down *(US)*; ~ **betreten** to take the stand *(US)*; **im** ~ **sein** to be in the box.

Zeugen|stuhl witness chair; ~**stuhl einnehmen** to take the stand *(US)*; ~**vereidigung** swearing [in] of a witness.

Zeugenvernehmung hearing (examination, interrogation) of a witness;
eidliche ~ examination on oath; **erste** ~ examination-in-chief, direct examination;
~ **durch die benennende Partei** direct examination; ~ **vor Verhandlungsbeginn** examination before trial;
in die ~ **eintreten** to hear the witnesses.

Zeugen|vorführung bringing forward (production) of a witness; ~**vorladung** witness summons.

Zeugnis *(Abgangszeugnis)* leaving certificate, *(Aussage)* attestation, testimony, evidence, voucher, *(Bescheinigung)* certificate, attestation, record, *(Bescheinigung für Angestellte)* written character, credentials, testimonial, *(Schule)* marks, report, credit *(US)*, grade *(US)*, card *(US)*;
zum ~ **dessen** in witness whereof (thereof);
gefälschtes ~ bogus certificate; **gutes** ~ *(Schüler)* good report; **gute** ~**se** good references;
~ **vom Hörensagen** mediate testimony; ~ **der mittleren Reife** [etwa] certificate of secondary education *(Br.)*, high-school certificate (graduation) *(US)*; ~ **der Vergangenheit** records of the past;
~ **ablegen** to bear evidence (testimony, witness); **falsches** ~ **ablegen** to bear false witness; ~ **ausstellen** to furnish (hand in) a certificate; ~ **für einen Angestellten ausstellen** to give a testimonial to an employee; ~ **beibringen** to produce a certificate; **erstklassige** ~**se haben** to bear the highest credentials; **sich ein** ~ **ausstellen lassen** to obtain a certificate; **schlechtes** ~ **mitbringen** to bring home bad marks; **gutes** ~ **vorlegen** to deliver a certificate of good character; **seine** ~**se vorlegen** to show one's testimonials, to present one's credentials;
~**abschrift** copy of a testimonial.

zeugnisfähig competent to give evidence.

Zeugnis|fähigkeit competence to give evidence; ~**heft** *(Schule)* report book.

zeugnisunfähig incapable of giving evidence.

Zeugnis|unfähigkeit disqualification from being a witness, incapability of giving evidence; ~**verweigerung** refusal to give evidence.

zeugnisverweigerungsberechtigt sein to be privileged from testifying.

Zeugnis|verweigerungsberechtigter privileged witness; ~**verweigerungsrecht** immunity from witness, privilege of witness; **auf das** ~**verweigerungsrecht verzichten** to waive a privilege.

Zeugung begettal, generation, procreation.

Zickzackkurs zigzag course, seesaw policy, traverse, tack;
konjunkturpolitischer ~ stop and go;
im ~ **fahren** to zigzag.

Zickzack|kurve der Preisbewegung prices switchback; ~**linie** zigzag line; ~**zaun** worm fence.

Ziegel, feuerfeste refractory brick, firebrick;
~ **brennen** to burn bricks; **Dach mit** ~**n decken** to tile a roof; ~**brenner** tile burner; ~**mauer** brick wall; ~**rohbau** brickwork; ~**stein** brick.

Zieh|brücke drawbridge; ~**brunnen** well.

ziehen to draw, to pull, *(anbauen)* to grow, *(Auto)* to haul, *(Lotterie)* to draw, *(Schiff)* to tow;
auf j. ~ to draw against s. o.; **per Appoint** ~ to draw per appoint; **per netto Appoint** ~ to draw the exact amount; **jds. Aufmerksamkeit auf sich** ~ to draw s. one's attention to o. s.; **auf eine Bank** ~ to draw on a bank; **Bargeld eines Landes aus dem Verkehr** ~ to draw away the specie of a country, to drain a country of money; **Bilanz** ~ to strike a balance; **Blicke auf sich** ~ to catch the people's eye; **seine Brieftasche** ~ to unclutch one's wallet; **Diskussion in die Länge** ~ to protract a debate; **in Erwägung** ~ to take into consideration; **Folgen nach sich** ~ to have consequences; **gegenseitig aufeinander** ~ to draw on each other, to fly kites *(Br.)*; **Geld aus dem Verkehr** ~ to withdraw money from circulation; **seine Geldbörse** ~ to fork out *(coll.)*; **j. ins Gespräch** ~ to include s. o. in the conversation; **Handbremse** ~ to pull the hand brake; **seinen Hut** ~ to raise one's hat; **j. durch den Kakao** ~ to pull s. one's leg, to kid s. o.; **Konsequenzen** ~ to take the consequences; **in den Krieg** ~ to go to war; **sich in vielen Kurven auf den Berg** ~ to wind its way up the mountains in serpentines; **den kürzeren** ~ to come off second best (badly); **etw. ins Lächerliche** ~ to hold s. th. up to ridicule; **aufs Land** ~ to move to the country; **sich in die Länge** ~ *(Verhandlungen)* to be of a protracted nature; **Lehre aus etw.** ~ to take s. th. as a lesson; **nach links** ~ *(Auto)* to pull over to the left; **das große Los** ~ to win the first prize, *(fig.)* to be in the luck; **Lotterielos** ~ to draw a lottery; **nach sich** ~ to carry with it; **nicht** ~ *(fig.)* to cut no ice; **Niete** ~ to draw a blank; **Nutzen** ~ to turn to account, to profit by, to derive (make) profit from; **nur geringen Nutzen aus etw.** ~ to get only a small profit for one's money; **Perlen auf eine Schnur** ~ to thread pearls; **j. zu Rate** ~ to ask s. one's advice; **j. zur Rechenschaft** ~ to call s. o. to account; **alle Register** ~ to go all out *(coll.)*; **Saldo** ~ to strike a balance, to cast accounts; **Scheck auf j.** ~ to draw upon s. one's account; **Schlüsse** ~ to draw conclusions; **Schlußstrich unter eine Sache** ~ to let bygones by bygones; **j. auf seine Seite** ~ to win s. o. over; **Sichtwechsel auf j.** ~ to draw on s. o. at sight; **Starter** ~ to pull the starter; **am gleichen Strang** ~ to be in the same boat; **Summe** ~ to add up; **zur Verantwortung** ~ to hold s. o. responsible; **Verhandlungen in die Länge** ~ to prolong negotiations, to drag out the negotiating process; **aus dem Verkehr** ~ to take off the road, *(Geld)* to withdraw from circulation, *(Schiff)* to put out of commission; **j. ins Vertrauen** ~ to let s. o. in on a secret; **aus allem Vorteil** ~ to turn everything to account; **auf Wache** ~ to mount guard; **Wechsel auf j.** ~ to value a bill upon (draw a bill of exchange on) s. o.; **Wechsel auf lange Sicht** ~ to draw at long date; **Wein auf Flaschen** ~ to bottle wine; **durch die Welt** ~ to roam the world; **sich durch das ganze Werk** ~ to run through the entire composition; **in ein anderes Zimmer** ~ to change one's room.

Ziehung *(Effektenauslosung, Wechsel)* drawing, draft, *(Lottozahlen)* draw;
inklusive ~ cum drawing; **ohne** ~ ex drawing;
~ **der Lose** prize drawing; ~ **von Schecks auf durch noch nicht eingegangene Inkassi vorgetäuschte Guthaben** kiting cheques *(Br.)*.

Ziehungs|avis draft advice; ~**ermächtigung** *(Weltwährungsfonds)* drawing authorization (right); ~**liste** drawing list; ~**plan** lottery scheme; ~**rechte** *(Weltwährungsfonds)* drawing rights; ~**tag** drawing day.

Ziel destination, goal, object, target, aim, intent, end, purpose, will, terminus, *(Lieferzeitpunkt)* term of delivery, *(Limit)* limit, *(Zahlungsfrist)* prompt, credit;

auf ~ on credit, *(Börse)* forward; **auf ~ gekauft** bought on credit; ~ **gegen drei Monate** at three months' credit (prompt); **mit kurzem** ~ on a short-term basis; **30 Tage** ~ 30 days' credit; **um zum ~ zu gelangen** for the attainment of one's purpose; ~ **wie gewöhnlich** at the usual date;
gegensätzliche ~e cross purposes; **hochgestecktes** ~ big game; **höchsterreichbares** ~ top notch; **konjunkturpolitisches** ~ economic policy goal; **kurzes** ~ short date; **langes** ~ long date; **politisches** ~ political goal; **alle möglichen politischen ~e** all manner of political goals; **vordringliches** ~ No. 1 target; **leicht zerstörbares** ~ *(mil.)* sitting duck;
~ **heftiger Kritik** target of bitter criticism; ~ **drei Monate** three months' credit, at three months's prompt; ~ **auf lange Sicht** long-term aim;
jem. offene ~e einräumen to grant s. o. open account terms; ~ **erreichen** to get through; **sein ~ erreichen** to achieve (gain) one's purpose, to work one's will, to attain one's end, to carry one's point, to effect one's purpose; **sein ~ nicht erreichen** to fail in one's object, to fall short of one's target; **sein ~ sicher erreichen** to come safe to port; ~ **seiner Wünsche erreichen** to touch the goal of one's desire; **Kopf an Kopf durchs ~ gehen** to finish neck and neck; **als Letzter durchs ~ gehen** to come in at the tail end; **als Zweiter durchs ~ gehen** to land second; **durch List und Tücke ans ~ gelangen** to whip the devil round the stump; **jem. drei Monate ~ gewähren** to grant s. o. three months' credit; **sein ~ erreicht haben** to have got one's way; **über das ~ hinausschießen** to overshoot the mark, to overreach one's purpose; **auf ~ kaufen** to buy on credit; **weder Maß noch ~ kennen** to know no bounds; **auf krummen Wegen zum ~ kommen** to work the oracle *(Br.)*; **rasch zu seinem ~ kommen** to find a quick way of doing s. th.; **gerade aufs ~ losgehen** to come straight to the point; **kurz vor dem ~ aufgeben müssen** to fail with one's goal in sight; ~ **unter Beschuß nehmen** to engage a target; ~ **wettbewerbsbedingter Preisnachlässe sein** to be the target of competitive discounting; **auf ein ~ abgestimmt sein** to be purpose-directed; **sich ein hohes ~ setzen** to aim high, to hitch one's waggon to a star; **sein ~ durch Tricks zu erreichen suchen** to resort to tricks to gain one's end; **sein ~ verfehlen** to miss one's aim; ~ **verfolgen** to pursue a goal; **auf ~ verkaufen** to sell forward; **ohne ~ verreisen** to set out with no particular destination; **seine ~e zurückschrauben** to lower one's sights; **automatisch auf das ~ zusteuern** *(Rakete)* to home;
~**anflug** approach flight, *(Rakete)* homing; ~**anfluggerät** *(Rakete)* homing device; ~**anflugradar** approach surveyance radar; ~**angaben** target data; **automatische ~ansteuerung** *(Rakete)* homing guidance; ~**ansteuerung vornehmen** *(Rakete)* to home; ~**auffassung** *(Radar)* target pickup; ~**bahnhof** station of destination, nearest railway station *(US)*; ~**bereich** target range; ~**fluggerät** homing device; ~**flughafen** port of destination; ~**flugkörper** homing vehicle; ~**fotokamera** photo-finish camera; ~**funktion** objective function; ~**gebiet** *(Bomben)* impact area; ~**gebiet nicht erreichen** to undershoot its target range; ~**gerät** *(Bomber)* bombsight; ~**größe der Bevölkerung** population target; ~**größenbestimmung** target setting; ~**gruppe** target group, target audience; ~**gruppenkombination von Medien** media audience combination; ~**hafen** port of destination; ~**landung** precision landing.
ziellos desultory, aimless, purposeless, objectless.
Ziel|ort final destination; ~**peilung** homing; ~**plan** end-state plan; ~**posten** goal post; ~**preis** *(Spediteur)* basing rate; ~**projektion** target projection; ~**punkt** *(Spediteur)* basing point; **neuer ~punkt** tee.
Zielscheibe butt, *(mil.)* target;
~ **des Gespötts** laughing stock;
als ~ des Spotts dienen to stand the roast; **j. zur ~ seines Spottes machen** to bring s. o. into derision, to use s. o. for sport.
Ziel|schiff target ship; ~**setzung** target, goal setting, objective.
zielstrebig purposeful, determined, resolute.
Ziel|strebigkeit dermination, determinateness, determinacy, tenacity of purpose; ~**suche** *(mil.)* homing guidance; ~**suchkopf** homing head; ~**vernichtung** target destruction; ~**verschiebung** goal displacement; ~**vorstellung regionalen Wachstums** directional grid; ~**wegverfolgung** *(Rakete)* missile tracking; ~**wurf durchführen** to pinpoint.
ziemen, sich to be befitting, to befit.
ziemlich|ausführlich at some length; ~ **gesucht** in tolerable demand;
~ **hoch sein** *(Rechnung)* to foot up pretty high;
~**e Anzahl** fair number; ~**e Arbeit** lot of work; ~**e Strecke** quite a distance; ~**e Zeit dauern** to take some time.
Zierbuchstabe ornamental (swash) letter.
Zierde decoration, ornament, *(fig.)* pearl;
~ **seines Berufsstandes** ornament of one's profession;
seiner Partei zur ~ gereichen to do credit to one's party.
zieren to embellish, to garnish, to grace;
sich ~ to make bones about, to give o. s. airs and graces, to plume o. s., *(herumreden)* to beat about the bush.
Zier|garten ornamental garden; ~**leiste** *(drucktechn.)* headpiece, border; ~**muster** ornamental design; ~**pflanzen** ornamental plants; ~**rand** fancy frame *(US)*.
Ziffer cipher, figure, number, digit, *(in einem Abkommen)* paragraph, sub-item, subsection;
in Worten und ~n in figures and words;
amtliche ~n official return; **undeutlich geschriebene ~** blind figure; **von der Handelskammer veröffentlichte ~n** released Board-of-Trade figures;
~**n über den Leserkreis von Zeitschriften** magazine-reading figures; ~**n des Wirtschaftsministeriums** commerce department figures *(US)*;
in ~n angeben to express in figures; ~**n einsetzen** to fill in the figures; **in rote ~n geraten** to plunge into the loss column, to run in red ink *(US coll.)*; ~**n zu Vergleichszwecken modifizieren** to modify figures for the sake of comparability;
~**blatt** dial (hour) plate, face of a clock.
Ziffern|kode code; ~**kontrolle** *(Computer)* digit control; **elektronisches ~lesegerät** figure-reading electronic device.
ziffernmäßig numerical, by figures.
Ziffern|material, amtliches government data; **zum Vergleich mit den Ausgabeplänen geeignetes ~material der Staatseinnahmen zur Verfügung stellen** to provide revenue figures to measure against the expenditure; ~**rechenanlage** digital computer; ~**sprache** numeral language; ~**stelle** digit [position]; ~**telegramm** cipher (code) telegram.
Zigarette cigarette, *(billige)* fag, gasper *(Br., sl.)*;
~ **ausdrücken** to crush out a cigarette.
Zigaretten|anzünder cigar lighter; ~**dose** tin of cigarettes; ~**etui** cigarette case; **auf eine ~länge zu jem. kommen** to come to s. o. for a smoke; ~**marke** brand of cigarettes; ~**päckchen** packet of cigarettes; ~**pause** smoke break; ~**stummel** stub, cigarette end, butt, stump of a cigarette; ~**töter** extinguisher.
Zigarillo whiff.
Zigarren|rauch fume of cigars, whiff of a cigar; ~**spitze** cigar holder.
Zigeuner gipsy;
~**leben** knockabout life.
Zimmer room, chamber, apartment *(Br.)*, *(in Untermiete)* lodgings, digs *(Br., coll.)*;
~ **zu vermieten** rooms (apartments) to let;
angebautes ~ extension room; **angrenzende ~** adjacent rooms; **aufgeräumtes ~** tidy room; **nicht aufgeräumtes ~** disorderly room; **dunkles ~** poorly illuminated room; **freies ~** *(Hotel)* vacant room, vacancy *(US)*; **nach außen gelegenes ~** outward room; **nach hinten gelegenes ~** back apartment *(Br.)*; **oben gelegenes ~** upstairs room; **gemietetes ~** lodging room; **ausreichend großes ~** room of adequate size; **ineinandergehende ~** rooms which open into each other; **enges kleines ~** poky little room; **klimatisiertes ~** air-conditioned room; **leeres ~** empty room; **möbliertes ~** lodging(s), furnished apartment (room); **dürftig möbliertes ~** poorly furnished room; **nebeneinanderliegende ~** *(Hotel)* communicating rooms; **reserviertes ~** reservation; **unaufgeräumtes ~** untidy room; **unmöbliertes ~** unfurnished room; **verfügbares ~** *(Hotel)* vacant room;
~ **mit Dusche und Kochnische** economic apartment *(Br.)*; ~ **nach hinten** back room; ~ **im oberen Stock** upstairs room; ~ **nach vorn** front room; ~ **mit fließendem Wasser** room with running water;
~ **abbestellen** to cancel a room in a hotel; ~ **abteilen** to partition off a room; **fünf ~ anbauen** to add five rooms to a house; ~ **aufräumen** to tidy up a room; ~ **ausmessen** to take the dimensions of a room; ~ **für j. bereithalten** to hold a room in readiness for s. o.; ~ **bereitstellen** to chamber; ~ **besorgen** provide with a room; **jem. ein ~ besorgen** to find (get) s. o. a room; ~ **in einem Hotel bestellen** to book (engage, reserve) rooms at a hotel; ~ **in Ordnung bringen (herrichten)** to settle a room, to set a room straight; ~ **desinfizieren** to fumigate a room; ~ **durcheinanderbringen** to stack *(sl.)*; **eigenes ~ haben** to have a room of one's own; **j. in ein ~ hereinführen** to introduce s. o. into a room; **in seinem ~ herumkramen** to fiddle about in one's room; ~ **hüten** to stay indoors; ~ **lüften** to admit fresh air into a room, to ventilate a room; ~ **mieten** to take a room (lodgings), to rent a room; ~ **putzen** to dress a room; ~ **räumen** to clear a room; **an sein ~ gefesselt sein** to be a prisoner in one's

room; **aus dem ~ stürmen** to fling out of the room; **sich ein ~ suchen** to look for a room; **~ mit jem. teilen** to share a room with s. o.; **~ mit Möbeln überladen** to crowd a room with furniture; **~ vermieten** to take in lodgers, to let lodgings; **möblierte ~ vermieten** to let furnished apartments, to let furnished rooms; **an Studenten ~ vermieten** to board students; **~ mit Möbeln vollstopfen (überladen)** to lumber a room with furniture; **~ vorausbestellen** to book (reserve, *US*) rooms at a hotel; **in einem möblierten ~ wohnen** to live in chambers *(Br.)*; **~ zweckentfremden** to convert a room to office use;
~antenne indoor aerial (antenna); **~aufteilung in einem Gebäude** disposition of rooms in a building; **~ausmaße, ~größe** measurements (contents) of a room; **~bedienung** room service; **~bestellung** booking of rooms, hotel reservation; **~decke** ceiling; **~dekoration** upholstery; **~einrichtung** furniture; **~flucht** set of rooms, suite, *(Hotel)* hotel suite; **~gebühr** room fee; **~genosse** fellow lodger, room-mate, chum *(US)*; **jds. ~genosse sein** to share a room with s. o.; **~herr** lodger, roomer *(US)*; **~kellner** bedroom waiter; **~lautstärke** *(Radio)* moderate volume; **verbrauchte ~luft** frowst; **~mädchen** chambermaid, housemaid; **~mann** carpenter; **~mannsarbeit** carpentry; **~miete** rent for a room, lodging money; **~mieter** tenant, lodger; **~nachbar** next-door neighbo(u)r; **~nummer** room number; **~ofen** stove; **~pflanze** indoor plant; **~preis** room rates, room fee, *(im Hotel)* tariff at a hotel, hotel tariff; **~preise in einem Hotel erfragen** to enquire about terms for a stay at a hotel; **~reservierung** booking of rooms, hotel reservation; **~reservierung im Griff behalten** to keep track of reservations; **~schlüssel** room key; **~suche** room hunting; **auf ~suche sein** to be on the lookout for digs *(Br.)*; **~tarif** hotel charges; **~telefon** room telephone; **~temperatur** inside (room) temperature; **~theater** cellar (little, *Br.*) theatre; **~vermieter** landlord, lodging letter; **~vermieterin** landlady; **~vermietung** letting of rooms, *(ohne Frühstück)* European plan *(US)*; **~vermittlung** accommodation registry *(Br.)*.

zimperlich finical, finicking, gingerly, squeamish, *(wehleidig)* soft, cissy *(Br., sl.)*, sissy *(US sl.)*;
nicht ~ sein not to be overnice.

Zimperliese prig, softy, sissy *(US sl.)*.

Zimt *(fig.)* stuff;
furchtbaren ~ reden to talk rubbish (nonsense).

Zink|blech zinc plate; **~hütte** zinc works; **~klischee** zinc block.

Zinn|aktien tin shares; **~erz** tin ore; **~grube** tin mine, stannary *(Br.)*.

Zins interest, use money *(sl.)*, *(Miete)* rent, rental, *(Tributleistung)* tribute;
landesüblicher ~ customary interest; **originärer ~** natural interest rate;
antizipative ~abgrenzung deferred interest; **~abkommen** agreement on interest rates; **~abschnitt** cut, interest warrant (coupon); **~abzug** discount; **~änderung** change in interest rates; **~anpassung** adjustment of interest, interest-rate adjustment; **~anspruch** interest due (receivable, *US*); **~anspruch gegen den Treuhänder** equitable rate of interest; **~arbitrage** interest arbitrage; **~auflauf** accrual of interest; **~auftrieb** rise in interest rates; **~aufwand** interest paid (cost, expense, expenditure); **~ausfall** loss of interest; **~ausgleich** adjustment of interest, interest rate adjustment; **~ausgleichsleistung** interest differential subsidy; **~ausgleichssteuer** interest equalization tax *(US)*; **~außenstände** outstanding interest, interest on arrears, interest receivable *(US)*; **~ausstattung** interest rate.

zinsbar for rent, *(zinstragend)* yielding interest;
~ anlegen to put out at interest.

Zins|bedingung terms of interest; **~befestigung** hardening of interest rates.

zinsbegünstigt sein to benefit from preferential interest rates.

Zins|beihilfen interest subsidies; **~belastung** interest burden (charges, statement); **~beleg** interest voucher; **~berechnung** working out (computation of) interest, interest statement; **genaue ~berechnung** accurate interest; **~berechnung durchführen** to ascertain interest; **~berichtigung** adjustment of interest; **~bescheinigung ausstellen** *(Bank)* to provide a customer with a signed certificate; **~bestandteil** interest component; **~betrag** amount of interest; **~bogen** coupon sheet, talon *(Br.)*; **~bonus** interest premium.

zinsbringend interest-bearing;
~ anlegen to put out at interest;
~e Kapitalanlage interest-bearing investment.

Zins|buch *(Pacht)* rent-roll, rental; **~darlehn** loan bearing interest; **~diskrepanz** interest differential; **~dotierung** interest allocation; **~druck** pressure of interest rates; **~eingang, ~eingänge** interest received (accrued); **~einkommen** interest (unearned) income; **~einlagen** deposits on current accounts; **~empfindlichkeit** interest sensitivity.

Zinsen interest, use money *(sl.)*, *(Bilanz)* interest charges;
auf ~ on interest; **auf ~ ausgeliehen** out at interest; **franko ~** without interest, no interest charged, flat; **mit ~** plus interest; **mit Ausnahme der ~** exclusive of interest; **mit Berechtigung auf ~** with interest; **ohne ~** ex interest, flat; **zu gesetzlichen ~** at legal interest; **zu niedrigen ~** at a low rate of interest;
ablösliche ~ redeemable interest; **steuerlich abzugsfähige ~** protected interest; **anfallende ~** accruing interest; **angefallene ~** accrued (accumulated) interest; **einem Konto angelastete ~** interest debited to an account; **aufgelaufene [noch nicht fällige] ~** accrued interest; **aufgelaufene [und fällige] ~** accumulated interest; **auflaufende ~** accruing interest; **ausstehende ~** interest receivable *(US)*; **berechnete ~** interest charged; **auf der Basis von 360 Tagen berechnete ~** ordinary interest *(US)*; **auf der Basis von 365 Tagen berechnete ~** exact interest *(US)*; **Unkosten gerade deckende ~** compensatory interest; **einfache ~** simple interest; **noch nicht eingegangene ~** *(Bilanz)* earned interest not collected; **eingekommene ~** interest paid; **entstandene, noch nicht fällige ~** *(Bilanz)* accrued interest payable *(US)*; **entstehende ~** accruing interest; **erhaltene ~** interest received; **erhöhte ~** increased interest; **fällige ~** interest payable (due), outstanding interest; **feste ~** fixed interest; **fundierte ~** consolidated interest; **gegenseitige ~** reciprocal interest; **gesetzliche ~** statutory interest, legal interest rate; **gestaffelte ~** equated (graduated) interest; **gegenseitig in Rechnung gestellte ~** reciprocal interest; **gestundete ~** deferred interest; **gewöhnliche ~** simple (ordinary, *US*) interest; **gezahlte ~** interest paid; **jährlich gezahlte ~** yearly interest paid; **zu Lasten des Kapitals gezahlte ~** interest paid out of the capital; **gleitende ~** sliding rate of interest; **gutgeschriebene ~** credited interest; **halbjährliche ~** semiannual interest; **hohe ~** dear money, high interest; **jährliche ~** annual interest, interest per annum; **kalkulatorische ~** imputed interest; **landesübliche ~** customary rate of interest; **laufende ~** current (running) interest; **marktgerechte ~** interest in conformity with the market; **niedrige ~** low interest; **reine ~** true interest; **rückständige ~** back (unpaid, outstanding arrears of) interest, interest in arrears; **satzungsmäßige ~** statutory interest; **steuerfreie ~** tax-free interest; **transitorische ~** deferred interest; **überfällige ~** past-due interest; **überhöhte ~** exorbitant interest; **übliche ~** interest as usual, conventional interest; **unversteuerte ~** untaxed interest; **variable ~** variable interest; **vereinbarte ~** conventional interest; **vertragliche ~** stipulated interest; **vorteilhafte ~** beneficial (lucrative, *US*) interest; **vorweggenommene ~** anticipated interest; **fällig werdende ~** accruing (accrual of) interest; **wucherische ~** usurious interest; **zurechenbare ~** imputed interest;
Kapital und ~ principal and interest;
~ und zinsähnliche Aufwendungen interest and similar expenses; **~ auf ein Bankguthaben** bank-deposit interest; **gezahlte ~ auf Bausparverträge** building society interest received; **~ aus Buchforderungen** accrued accounts receivable *(US)*; **~ in Form von festverzinslichen Schuldverschreibungen** funding debenture interest *(Br.)*; **~ von der Hauptsache** interest on principal; **~ aus Kapitalanlagen** interest on investments; **~ aus Kontokorrenten** interest on fluctuating overdrafts; **~ für langfristige Kredite** long-term interest rates; **~ von einem Postsparkassenbuch** post-office savings bank interest *(Br.)*; **~ zum Satz von 4%** interest at the rate of 4 per cent; **~ von Sparguthaben** interest on deposits with a trustee savings bank; **~ auf gewährte Vorschüsse** *(Bilanz)* interest on advances credited (payable on advances);
~ abwerfen to yield (draw) interest; **~ anpassen** to adjust interest rates; **sein Geld auf ~ ausleihen** to loan (lend) on (put out) one's money at interest; **~ ausrechnen** to cast (work out, compute) interest; **~ belasten** to charge interest; **9% ~ berechnen** to charge 9 per cent interest; **~ vierteljährlich berechnen** to compound interest quarterly; **~ bei Fälligkeit bezahlen** to keep down interest; **9,5% ~ für einen Kredit bezahlen** to pay 9,5 per cent interest on a loan; **~ laufend bezahlen** to pay interest when due; **~ bringen** to earn interest; **~ einbringen** to bring in (yield) interest; **~ erheben** to charge interest; **~ errechnen** to ascertain (work out, compute) interest; **auf ~ geben** to put out at interest; **6% ~ gewähren** to grant an interest of 6 per cent; **von den ~ seines Vermögens leben** to live on the interest received from one's capital; **hohe ~ zahlen müssen** to sit at a high interest; **~ zum Kapital schlagen (kapitalisieren)** to capitalize interest; **auf ~ ausgeliehen sein** to

be out at interest; ~ **senken** to reduce the interest rate; ~ **[gegenseitig] in Rechnung stellen** to charge interest [on both sides]; ~ **tragen** to yield interest; **5% ~ tragen** to bear interest at the rate (carry an interest) of 5 per cent; ~ **vergüten** to allow interest; ~ **zahlen** to pay interest; **hohe ~ zahlen** to pay high interest rates;
~**aufstellung** statement of interest, interest statement.
Zinsendienst payment of interest, interest expenditure, *(Anleihe)* loan service;
~ **einer Anleihe durchführen** to service a loan; ~ **einer Anleihe wiederaufnehmen** to resume the service of a loan.
Zins|entwicklung trend of interest rates; ~**erhöhung** increase of the rate of interest; ~**erleichterungszusage** interest-relief grant; ~**ermäßigung** rebate[ment] of interest, reduction of the interest rate; ~**erneuerungsschein** talon, renewal coupon; ~**errechnung** calculation of interest; ~**ersparnisse** interest savings; ~**ertrag** interest yield.
Zinserträge income from interest, interest, interest earned;
noch nicht eingegangene ~ *(Bilanz)* interest earned not collected; **transitorische** ~ *(Bilanz)* unearned interest; **noch nicht versteuerte** ~ interest not taxed before receipt.
Zins|ertragsbilanz interest income balance; ~**ertragszahlen** interest earned figures; ~**erwartungen** interest rate expectation.
Zinseszins interest upon interest, compound (surplus) interest; **mit ~ zurückzahlen** *(fig.)* to return with usury;
~**abschreibungsmethode** compound interest method of depreciation; ~**basis** compound interest basis; ~**betrag** compound amount; ~**formel** compound interest formula; ~**rechnung** compound calculation (computation) of interest; ~**satz** compound rate; ~**wert** compound present value.
Zins|fächer interest rate range; ~**fälligkeitstag**, ~**fälligkeitstermin** interest-due date; ~**festbetrag festlegen** to set margins *(US)*.
Zinsforderungen interest due (receivable, *US*);
entstandene [noch nicht fällige] ~ *(Bilanz)* accrued interest receivable *(US)*; **wucherische** ~ excessive interest charges.
Zinsformel formula for compound present value.
zinsfrei free of (ex) interest, interest-free, noninterest-bearing, flat, *(Grundstück)* allodial, rent-free;
~ **ausleihen** to lend free of interest.
Zinsfreigabe decontrol of interest rates.
Zinsfuß rate of interest, interest (bank) rate;
amtlicher ~ bank (discount, *US*) rate; **gesetzlicher** ~ legal [rate of] interest; **gleitender** ~ sliding rate of interest; **höchstzulässiger** ~ maximum interest; **üblicher** ~ interest as usual; **vereinbarter** ~ conventional rate of interest;
~ **von 4% auf 5% erhöhen** to raise the interest from 4 per cent to 5 per cent.
Zins|garantie guaranteed interest; ~**gefälle** margin between rates of interest, gap in interest rates, interest differential; ~**gefälle einebnen** to level the interest differential; ~**gefüge** structure of interest rates, interest-rate structure; ~**gleitklausel** sliding rate of interest clause.
zinsgünstig at a low (favo(u)rable) rate of interest.
Zins|gutschrift crediting of interest, interest crediting; **stolz wie ein ~hahn** as proud as Punch; ~**haus** leasehold building, flatted (apartment) house; ~**herabsetzung** *(Diskontsatz)* reduction in the discount (bank, *Br.*, rediscount, *US*) rate; ~**höchstsätze** interest-rate ceiling; ~**höhe** amount of interest; ~**hypothek** interest-bearing mortgage; ~**kapital** interest-bearing capital; ~**klausel** interest clause; ~**konditionen** interest rates; ~**konto** interest account; ~**kosten** interest cost; ~**kupon** [interest] coupon, interest voucher (warrant), cut, talon; ~**last** burden of interest, interest charges (burden); ~**leiste** talon; ~**liberalisierung** liberalization of interest rates.
zinslos noninterest-bearing, free of (without) interest, flat, idle, passive, *(ohne Miete)* rentless, rent-free;
~**er Kredit** loan without interest.
Zins|marge interest margin; ~**mehraufwand** net interest paid; ~**mehrertrag** additional interest income; ~**nachlaß** interest rebate, interest relief; ~**niveau** interest [rate] level; ~**niveau niedrig halten** to keep down interest; ~**note** interest statement; ~**nummern** interest (red) numbers, decimals *(Br.)*, products *(Br.)*; **schwarze ~nummern** black products *(Br.)*; ~**periode** interest-paying period.
zinspflichtig interest-bearing, *(Pacht)* for rent.
Zins|politik interest rate policy; ~**rate** interest rate, instal(l)ment interest; ~**rechnung** computation (calculation) of interest; ~**register** *(Pacht)* rent-roll, rental; ~**rendite** interest yield; ~**risiko** interest rate risk; ~**rückgang** fall in interest rates.
Zinsrückstände outstanding (unpaid, back) interest, arrears of interest, interest in arrears;
~ **kapitalisieren** to fund interest arrears; ~ **auflaufen lassen** to allow the back interest to accumulate.
Zins|saldo balance of interest, interest balance; ~**sammelkonto** collectible interest account.
Zinssatz rate of interest, [interest] rate, interest charges;
der einem Wertpapier aufgedruckte ~ nominal rate; **vertraglich ausbedungener** ~ contract rate of interest; **derzeitiger** ~ going rate of interest; **effektiver** ~ effective rate, basis; **gesetzlicher** ~ legal interest rate; **gleitender** ~ sliding rate of interest; **höchstzulässiger** ~ maximum interest; **hoher** ~ high rate of interest; **marktgängiger** ~ market-related interest rate; **progressiver** ~ progressive rate; **von der Zentralbank regulierter** ~ administered rate of interest; **üblicher** ~ conventional rate of interest; **vereinbarter** ~ **contract interest; wucherischer** ~ exorbitant rate;
~ **für Bankdepositen** deposit rates; ~ **für Debitoren** debtor interest rate; ~ **für Dreimonatsgeld** short-term rate of interest; ~ **im Fixgeschäft** loaning rate *(US)*; ~ **für von den Banken aufgenommene Gelder** rate on interbank loans; ~ **für überzogene Konten** overdraft rate; ~ **für langfristige Kredite** long-term interest rate; **effektiver** ~ **von Wertpapieren** basis of securities; ~ **für festverzinsliche Wertpapiere** coupon rate;
~ **herabsetzen** to lower (reduce) the rate of interest; ~ **heraufsetzen** to increase (raise) the rate of interest; **Zahlungen zur Verkürzung des ~es verwenden** to apply payments for the reduction of interest.
Zinssätze, anziehende attractive rates of interest; **nachlassende** ~ slide in the interest rates;
~ **allmählich senken** to edge interest rates down; ~ **weiter senken** to ease down interest rates.
Zinssatz|änderungen interest rate changes; ~**entwicklung** interest rate development.
Zinsschein interest coupon (ticket, warrant), counterfoil;
anhängender ~ attached coupon; **getrennter** ~ detached coupon; **notleidende ~e** outstanding coupons;
verfallene ~e ablösen to detach coupons due; ~**e aufbieten** to summon coupons; **Stücke ohne ~e handeln** to sell bonds exclusive of coupons.
Zins|schwankungen fluctuations in interest rates; ~**senkung** reduction of [the] interest [rate], cut in interest rates; ~**senkungstendenz** downward tendency in interest rates; ~**situation** interest-rate situation; ~**spanne** margin [between the rates] of interest, *(Bank)* margin of profit, profit margin; ~**spiegel** interest-rate level; ~**stabilisierung** interest stabilization; ~**staffel** equation of interest; ~**struktur** interest-rate structure; ~**subvention** subsidy of interest; ~**tabelle** interest table, table of interest, ready reckoner; ~**tag** quarter day; ~**termin** interest date; **zum ~termin ablösen** to redeem at an interest date.
zinstragend bearing interest, interest-bearing;
~ **anlegen** to invest advantageously;
~**es Konto** interest-bearing account.
Zins|überschuß interest surplus (earnings); ~**umwandlung** conversion of interest; ~**verbilligung** cheapening of interest rates, interest reduction, interest rebate; **entstandene [noch nicht fällige]** ~**verbindlichkeiten** accrued interest payable *(US)*; ~**vereinbarung** agreement on interest rates; ~**vergünstigung** interest-rate relief; ~**vergütung** allowance for interest, rebate[ment]; **Wertpapiere ohne ~vergütung veräußern** to sell stocks flat; ~**vergütungsschein** interest certificate; ~**verlust** loss on interest; ~**versprechen** *(Wechsel)* interest clause; ~**verzug** default of interest; ~**vorauszahlung** anticipatory interest, prepayment of interest, interest collected in advance, ~**vorauszahlungen leisten** to pay interest in advance.
zinsweise as interest.
Zins|wucher usury; ~**wucherer** loan shark *(US)*; ~**zahlen** red (interest) numbers, products *(Br.)*; ~**zahlung** payment of interest, interest payment; ~**zahlungen steuerlich geltend machen** to claim relief for interest paid; **mit den ~zahlungen in Verzug sein** to make default in the payment of interest; ~**zuschüsse** interest rate subsidy, interest-relief grants; ~- **und Tilgungszuschüsse** subsidies for interest and redemption.
Zipfel tip, tag, *(geographisch)* tongue of land, spit, promontory;
etw. beim richtigen ~ anfassen to tackle s. th. the right way.
zirka about, approximately, round, roundabout, in the neighbo(u)rhood of *(US)*.
Zirkapreis approximate price.
Zirkel circle, pair of compasses;
exklusiver ~ elite circle; **literarischer** ~ literary coterie (circle);

Entfernung mit dem ~ abgreifen to measure a distance with a pair of compasses; **Quadratur des ~s erreichen** to square the circle; **einem ~ zur Zierde gereichen** to be an ornament to a circle; **alles mit dem ~ messen** to be overmeticulous;
~**kasten** drawing set.
Zirkular circular [letter];
~**kreditbrief** circular letter of credit; ~**note** *(dipl.)* circular note; ~**scheck** traveller check *(US)* (cheque, *Br.*).
Zirkulation currency, circulation.
zirkulieren to circulate, to circuit, *(Gerücht)* to spread about;
~ **lassen** to put in circulation, to pass round.
zirkulierend current, running, circulating, floating, afloat.
Zirkus circus, hippodrome, *(Affäre)* carryings-on;
ganzen ~ satt haben to be sick of the whole business; **richtigen ~ veranstalten** to make a circus of o. s.;
~**arena** circus; ~**clown** clown, whiteface *(US)*; ~**direktor** ringmaster; ~**manege** circle; ~**vorstellung** circus show; **riesengroßes** ~**zelt** the big top.
Zischen pig's whisper.
zischen *(Publikum)* to hiss;
einen ~ to wet one's whistle.
Zisterne water cistern, raintank.
Zitat citation, quotation, quote;
mit ~en gespickt crammed (interlarded) with quotations; **abgedroschenes ~** tag; **falsches ~** misquotation; **unpassendes ~** unapt citation; **wörtliches ~** contextual (word-by-word, textual, verbatim) quotation, word-for-word citation;
~**e bei einer Rede anbringen** to use quotations in a speech, to pepper (intersperse) a speech with quotations.
Zitatenschatz book (thesaurus) of quotations.
zitierbar citable, quotable;
nicht ~ unquotable.
zitieren to quote, to cite, to bring up;
aus einer Entscheidung ~ to quote from a case, to cite an authority; **falsch ~** to misquote, to misallege; **j. vor Gericht ~** to summon s. o., to cite s. o. before the court; **Stelle aus einem Buch ~** to quote from a book; **wörtlich ~** to quote literally (verbatim).
Zitierung einer Gerichtsentscheidung citation of a decided case (of a decision).
Zittern shake, tremble, thrill.
zittern to shake, to tremble, to vibrate, to flutter, to wobble *(coll.)*, *(Erde)* to quake, *(Maschine)* to chatter, *(Nadel)* to flicker;
vor jem. ~ to be terrified of s. o.; **vor Angst ~** to shake in one's shoes (boots); **vor Erregung ~** to pulsate with excitement; **am ganzen Körper ~** to tremble all over; **in der Mittagshitze ~** *(Luft)* to quiver in the midday heat; **vor jds. Zorn ~** to fear s. one's anger.
zitternd | und bebend quaking all over;
~**e Stimme** trembling voice.
Zivil, in in plain (private) clothes.
zivil | er Alternativdienst civilian alternative service; ~**er Bevölkerungsschutz** civil defense *(US)*; ~**er Preis** moderate (reasonable) price; ~**e Versorgungsgüter** civilian supplies.
Zivil | anzug plain clothes; ~**beamter** civil servant; ~**bedarf** civilian requirements; ~**behörde** civil office, civilian authority; ~**bevölkerung** civilian population, *(mil.)* noncombatants; ~**bevölkerung in Kriegsaktionen einbeziehen** to bring war home to the people; ~**bevölkerung aus der Stadt evakuieren** to vacate the civilians from the city; ~**courage haben** to have the courage of one's conviction; **überhaupt keine ~courage besitzen** not to have an ounce of courage; ~**dienststelle** civil office; ~**ehe** civil marriage; ~**gerichtsbarkeit** civil justice (jurisdiction), plea side; ~**internierter** civilian detainee, repatriate.
Zivilisation civilization;
fern aller ~ outside the pale of civilization;
der ~ zugänglich machen to civilize; ~ **vorantreiben** to reduce the black area.
Zivilisationsgrenze, jenseits der outside the pale of civilization.
zivilisierbar cultivable.
zivilisieren to civilize, to cultivate, to humanize.
zivilisiert civilized.
Zivilist civilian, citizen *(US)*, civvy *(sl.)*.
Zivil | kammer civil (plea) side; ~**klamotten** civvies *(Br.)*; ~**kleidung** civilian (plain) clothes; **im ~leben** in civilian life (civvy street, *Br.*); ~**liste** Civil List *(Br.)*, privy purse *(Br.)*; ~**luftfahrt** civil aviation; ~**luftfahrtbehörde** Aeronautics Board *(US)*; ~**person** civilian.
Zivilprozeß common-law action (cause, suit), civil action (suit), suit at law *(US)*, lawsuit;
~**abteilung** plea side; ~**ordnung** rules of civil practice, General Practice Act *(US)*; ~**recht** law of procedure, rules of civil procedure *(US)*; ~**verfahren** common-law procedure.
Zivil | recht common (civil, private) law; ~**rechtler** common lawyer.
zivilrechtlich civil-law;
j. ~ verfolgen to bring a suit against s. o.;
~**e Abteilung** civil side; ~**e Haftung** civil liability (responsibility); ~**e Klage** civil (common-law) action, suit at law, lawsuit; ~**es Verfahren** civil proceedings.
Zivil | rechtsfall civil case; ~**rechtspflege** civil justice; **vom Militär gestützte rechts angesiedelte ~regierung** military-backed right-wing civilian government; ~**sache** civil (common law) action, lawsuit; ~**stand** civil rank; ~**trauung** civil marriage; ~**verbrauch** private use; ~**verfahren** proceedings in civil cases, common cause (suit), civil suit (trial); ~**verwaltung** civil government (administration, service, *Br.*); ~**verwaltungsreform** civil service reform *(Br.)*.
Zofe lady's-maid, waiting girl (maid).
Zögerer procrastinator, putter-off *(sl.)*.
Zögern hesitation, faltering, dilatoriness, retard, delay;
ohne ~ unhesitating; **ohne schuldhaftes ~** *(jur.)* without undue delay;
ohne ~ handeln to act without hesitation.
zögern to hesitate, to falter, to linger, to dawdle, to delay, to procrastinate, *(schwanken)* to waver, to shilly-shally;
nicht lange ~ not to let the grass grow under one's feet.
zögernd shilly-shally, hesitant, tentative;
~**en Schrittes** haltingly.
Zögling pupil, scholar.
Zölibat celibacy.
Zoll customs [duty], duty, tariff, toll, dues, *(Längenmaß)* inch, *(Zollbehörde)* customs authorities;
aus dem ~ gekauft bought in bond; **aus dem ~ verkauft** sold in bond; **mit hohem ~ belastet** bearing a heavy duty; **vom ~ eingezogen** confiscated by the customs authorities;
ausländischer ~ foreign tariff; **binnenländischer ~** internal customs; **diskriminierender ~** discriminatory tariff; **einheitlicher ~** uniform duty, single-schedule tariff; **zu erhebender ~** duty chargeable; **nach dem Gewicht erhobener ~** duty charged by the weight, poundage; **gemischter ~** compound (mixed) duty; **gestaffelter ~** differential (discriminating) duty; **gleitender ~** flexible (sliding-scale) tariff; **kombinierter ~** compound duty; **pauschalierter ~** unascertained duty; **spezifischer ~** specific duty; **suspendierter ~** suspended tariff; ~ **auf landwirtschaftliche Erzeugnisse** agricultural tariff; **jeder ~ ein Künstler** an artist in his every fibre; ~ **mit Rabatt** short duty;
beim ~ abfertigen to effect customs clearance, to clear through the customs; **Waren beim ~ abfertigen** to clear goods, to take goods out of bond; **Waren beim ~ angeben** to enter goods at the customhouse; ~ **aufheben** to repeal a duty; **Waren vom ~ ausnehmen** to take the duty off goods; **mit ~ belegen** to [rate in the] tariff; ~ **beseitigen** to eliminate customs duty; ~ **bezahlen** to pay duty on, to pay [the] customs; **Schiff beim ~ deklarieren** to pay the duties of a vessel, to clear a ship; **Waren beim ~ deklarieren** to make an entry of goods, to enter goods at the customhouse; **beim ~ durchgehen** to pass through the customs; ~ **einnehmen** to take toll; ~ **entrichten** to pay duty on (the toll), to clear the customhouse; ~ **erheben** to levy (collect) customs duty; ~ **erlassen** to remit a duty; ~ **festsetzen** to assess duty; **aus dem ~ freigeben** to remove the seals from a package; ~ **hinterziehen** to defraud the revenue; **sein Gepäck durch den (vom) ~ abfertigen lassen** to clear one's luggage through the customs; ~ **auf etw. legen** to lay a duty upon s. th.; ~ **passieren** to get (clear, pass) through the customs; **durch den ~ schmuggeln** to smuggle through the customs; **beim ~ sein** to be in the customs service; **dem ~ unterliegen** to be subject to duty; **keinem ~ unterliegen** to be exempt from duty; ~ **zahlen** to pay customs duties; **der Natur seinen ~ zahlen** to pay the toll to nature;
~ **geht zu Lasten des Empfängers** duty for consignee's account.
Zölle, durch ~ im Preis erhöht tariff-raised; **mit hohen ~n belastet** tariff-ridden;
binnenländische ~ internal customs;
~ **und Abgaben** duties, imposts and excises *(US)*; ~ **und Gebrauchssteuern** customs and excise duties *(Br.)*;
~ **abbauen** to reduce tariffs; ~ **abschaffen** to abolish customs duties; ~ **beseitigen** to eliminate customs duties; ~ **einführen** to introduce customs duties; ~ **erhöhen** to increase the tariff; ~ **senken** to lower the tariff; ~ **vergüten** to refund duties.

Zoll|abandonnierung abandonment of goods; ~**abbau** reduction of tariff, tariff cutting (reduction); ~**abbauprozeß** tariff-cutting process; ~**abfertigung** customs examination (entry), customs permit, *(Schiff)* [customs] clearance, clearance through the customs; ~**abfertigung vornehmen** to effect [customs] clearance.

Zollabfertigungs|antrag stellen to enter for customs clearance; ~**formular** customs declaration form; ~**gebühren** clearance charges, customs clearance fee; ~**hafen** port of entry; ~**kosten** costs of [customs] clearance, clearance charges; ~**papier** clearance (customs) paper, customs documents (documentation); ~**schein** customhouse permit, customs permit, customs certificate, clearing certificate, *(Schiff)* bill of sufferance *(Br.)*; ~**stelle** customhouse, customs declaration and receiving office, customs clearinghouse, receiver's office for the customs.

Zollabgabe customhouse duty (charges), customs [duty];
keiner ~ unterliegen to be exempt from duty.

zollabgabenpflichtig subject to customs duty.

Zoll|abkommen customs convention, tariff treaty (agreement); **Allgemeines ~- und Handelsabkommen** General Agreement on Tariffs and Trade (GATT); ~**abschaffung** elimination of customs duties; ~**abschätzung** customs valuation; ~**abschätzungsverfahren** customs valuation procedure; ~**abteilung** customs department; ~**agent** customs (customhouse) broker, customs agent; ~**agentur** customs agency.

Zollamt customhouse, customs (revenue) office, collector of customs and excises *(Br.)*, Bureau of Customs *(US)*, tariff board *(US)*;
beim ~ nicht angegeben unentered;
Schiff beim ~ deklarieren to pay the duties of a vessel, to clear a ship.

zollamtlich|erklärt declared; ~ **erledigt** customs cleared; ~ **verwahrt** in bond, bonded;
~ **deklarieren** to declare; **Waren ~ deklarieren** to enter goods at the customhouse (customs); **Schiff ~ durchsuchen** to search (rummage, *Br.*) a ship; **sich ~ abfertigen lassen** to clear through the customs, to effect customs clearance; **sein Gepäck ~ abfertigen lassen** to clear one's luggage through the customs; ~ **versiegeln** to docket;
~**e Abfertigung** customs clearance; ~**e Abfertigung übernehmen** to clear goods through the customs; ~**e Bescheinigung** customs certificate, [customs] permit; ~**e Durchsuchung** customs examination, search, rummage *(Br.)*; ~**e Einfuhrbestätigung** customs import certificate; ~**e Erlaubnis** customs permission; ~**e Untersuchung** customs examination (inspection); ~**er Verschluß** bond.

Zoll|amtsbescheinigung customs certificate; ~**änderung** duty change, tariff amendment; ~**änderungsgesetz** Tariff Amendment Act *(US)*; ~**angabe** customs declaration, customhouse entry, entry at the customhouse, *(vorläufige)* bill of sight; **zu hohe ~angabe** overentry; ~**angelegenheiten** tariff matters; ~**angleichung** tariff adjustment; ~**anhänger** protectionist; ~**anhebung** tariff increase; ~**anmeldung** customs declaration (entry), *(Einlagerung unter Zollverschluß)* entry for warehousing; ~**anschluß** customs union; ~**anschlußgebiet** customs enclave; ~**antrag** bill of entry; ~**anwendung** application of a tariff; ~**anwendungsgebiet** customs territory; ~**aufhebung** removal (abolition) of a tariff; ~**aufschlag** additional (extra) duty; ~**aufseher** customs inspector, customs overseer, locker, landwaiter *(Br.)*, surveyor of the customs *(US)*, *(Schiff)* tidewaiter; ~**aufsicht** customs supervision; **der ~aufsicht unterliegen** to be under control of customs officers; ~**aufsichtsstelle** customhouse; ~**ausfuhrerklärung**, ~**ausgangserklärung** declaration *(Br.)*, declaration (clearance, entry) outwards, outward manifest, customs specification *(Br.)*; ~**auskunft** tariff information; ~**ausland** territories outside the tariff jurisdiction; ~**auslieferungsschein** customs warrant; ~**ausschlußgebiet** free zone *(US)* (trade area), foreign trade zone *(US)*, customs-free zone; ~**aussetzung** suspension of customs duties; ~**autonomie** autonomous tariff [system]; ~**aval** customs guarantee; ~**bahnhof** customs station.

Zollbeamter customs officer (official), customhouse officer *(US)*, inspector, jerquer *(Br.)*, revenue agent *(US)*, customs guard *(US)*, searcher, *(im Hafen)* landwaiter *(Br.)*, boarding clerk (officer) *(Br.)*, coast waiter *(Br.)*;
~ **im Küstenhandel** coastwaiter, landing waiter;
~ **sein** to be in the customs service.

Zoll|bedienstete customs officers; ~**befreiung** exemption from duties; ~**begleitschein** bond note, customs passbook, customhouse pass, bond warrant *(Br.)*, transire *(Br.)*, customs certificate, warrant; ~**begleitscheinheft** carnet; ~**begünstigung** preferential treatment, preferentialism, imperial preference *(Br.)*; ~**begünstigungsliste** free list; ~**begünstigungstarif** preferential tariff; ~**behandlung** customs clearance, tariff (customs) treatment; **benachteiligende ~behandlung** tariff discrimination.

Zollbehörde customs [authorities];
oberste ~ Bureau of the Customs *(US)*, Collector of Customs and Excises *(Br.)*; **untere (untergeordnete) ~** subordinate customs station.

Zoll|belastung tariff burden; ~**benachrichtigung** customs letter; ~**benachrichtigung über Warenverlagerungen** cart note; ~**berechnung** duty computation; ~**beschau** customs examination; ~**bescheinigung** customs certificate, bond note, transire *(Br.)*, *(Schiff)* clearance certificate; ~**beschränkung** tariff restriction; **keinerlei ~beschränkungen unterliegen** not to be subject to customs restrictions; ~**bestimmungen** customs (tariff) regulations; **neue ~bestimmungen erlassen** to impose new duties; **den ~bestimmungen unterwerfen** to subject to tariff; ~**beteiligter** declarant; ~**bewertung** customs valuation, appraisal; ~**bewertungsbeamter** general appraiser; ~**bewilligung** customs permit; ~**bezirk** customs (frontier) district; **~- und Steuerbezirk** collection area; ~**boot** customs craft, revenue cutter; **keinen ~breit zurückweichen** not to budge an inch; ~**brücke** toll bridge; ~**bürgschaft** customs bond; ~**büro** customhouse; ~**buße** customs penalty.

Zolldeklaration [customs] declaration, customhouse entry (clearance), declaration of entry, customs entry, entry [at the customhouse], report *(Br.)*, bill of entry *(Br.)*, *(bei Einlagerung unter Zollverschluß)* entry for warehousing, *(Schiff)* captain's entry;
vorläufige ~ bill of sight, prime entry;
~ **für den Eigenverbrauch** entry for home use; ~ **für zollfreie Waren** entry for duty-free goods;
~ **abgeben** to enter at the customhouse.

Zoll|delikt customs offence; ~**depot** locked warehouse, *(Zolleigenlager)* bonded warehouse.

zolldick inch.

Zoll|dienst customs (international revenue) service; **im ~dienst einsetzen** to introduce to revenue service; **im ~dienst tätig sein** to be in the customs service; ~**direktion** customs authorities; ~**diskrepanz** tariff discrepancy; ~**diskriminierung** discrimination in the customs duties; ~**dokumente** customs documents, clearance papers; ~**durchgangsschuppen** transit shed; ~**durchgangsstelle** customs office en route; ~**durchlaßschein** transshipment bond (delivery note), excise bond, transire *(Br.)*; **mit ~durchlaßschein passieren** to have a permit for transire *(Br.)*; ~**durchsucher** searcher, finder; ~**durchsuchung** customs examination, search, rummaging *(Br.)*; ~**durchsuchung durchführen** to search, to rummage *(Br.)*, to jerque *(Br.)*; ~**durchsuchungsbefehl** search warrant, writ of assistance; ~**eigenlager** bonded warehouse; ~**einfuhrerklärung** customs bill of entry, duty-paid entry, home value declaration, customs specification *(Br.)*, declaration inwards *(Br.)*, inward manifest, jerque note *(Br.)*; ~**einfuhrstatistik** customs import statistics; ~**eingangsdeklaration** customs bill of entry, home value declaration, declaration inwards *(Br.)*, inward manifest; ~**eingangsschein** customs entry, bill of entry *(Br.)*; ~**einlagerer** bonder; ~**einlagerung** bonding; ~**einnahmen** customs revenue (receipts); ~**einnahmeziffern** customs figures; ~**einnehmer** collector of the customs, tollkeeper, toll collector, tollgatherer, pikeman; ~**einschlußgebiet** bonded area.

zollen, jem. Beifall to applaud s. o.; **jem. Bewunderung ~** to stand in admiration before s. o.; **jem. Dank ~** to express one's gratitude to s. o.; **einer Sache Tribut ~** to pay tribute to s. th.

Zollentrichtung payment of customs duties.

zollerhebend tariff-raising.

Zoll|erhebung levying of customs; ~**erhöhung** increase of customs duties, tariff increase (hike).

Zollerklärung [customs] declaration, customhouse clearance (entry), customs entry, entry [at the customhouse];
~ **mit zu niedrigem Wert** undervaluation;
~ **abgeben** to enter at the customs, to pass a customs entry.

Zoll|erlaß remission of duty, abatement; ~**erlaubnisschein** clearance certificate, bill of sight, customs (customhouse) permit; ~**erledigung** [customs] clearance; ~**erleichterung** customs facilities; ~**ermäßigung** reduction of rates (duty), tariff reduction; ~**erstattung** duty drawback, refund of duty; ~**etikett für Postpakete** green label *(Br.)*; ~**fahnder** landwaiter *(Br.)*, searcher *(Br.)*, preventive officer *(Br.)*, revenue officer *(US)*; ~**fahndung** customs (preventive, *Br.*) service, preventive investigation *(Br.)*, revenue cutter service *(US)*; ~**fahndungs-**

beamter preventive officer *(Br.)*, landwaiter *(Br.)*, searcher *(Br.)*, revenue officer *(US)*; ~**fahndungsdienst** customs (preventive, *Br.*, investigation, internal revenue, *US*) service, customs investigation, revenue cutter service *(US)*, coast guard *(US)*; ~**fahndungsstelle** investigative unit (agency); ~**fahrzeug** revenue cutter, coast-guard cutter *(Br.)*; ~**faktura** legalized (customs) invoice; ~**festsetzung** assessment of duties, tariffication; ~**flagge** revenue (coast guard, *US*) flag; ~**flughafen** airport of entry; ~**formalitäten** customs formalities; ~**formalitäten erledigen** to clear [through the] customs, to attend to the customs formalities, *(vorweg)* to pre-clear customs; **über** ~**fragen diskutieren** to debate the tariff questions.

zollfrei free of customs duty, customs-exempt (-free), exempt from duty (taxes), nondutiable, duty-free, free of duty;
etw. ~ **einführen** to import s. th. free of duty (duty-free); ~ **sein** to be exempt from duties, to be duty free; **zur Einfuhr** ~ **zulassen** to grant duty-free importation;
~**e Einfuhr** duty-free admission; ~**er Hafen** free port; ~**e Rohstoffe** duty-free raw materials; ~**er Staat** tariff-free country; ~**er Verkehr** free trade; ~**e Waren** free (uncustomed) goods; ~**e Wiedereinfuhr** duty-free return; ~**er Zugang** tariff-free access.

Zollfrei|betrag duty-free allowance; ~**gabe** release from bond, customs permit; ~**gabeschein** [customs] permit, stamp (dandy, *Br.*) note, *(für Verbringung in ein anderes Warenlager)* removal bond; ~**gebiet** free-trade area (zone, *US*), customs-free zone; ~**hafen** free port; ~**heit** exemption from duty; **befristete** ~**heit** admission temporaire; ~**laden** tax-free shop; ~**lager** storage warehouse, bonded warehouse (store, *Br.*), bond *(Br.)*; ~**liste** free list; ~**schein** [customs] permit, *(freie Durchfahrt)* tran(s)shipment bond (delivery note), transire *(Br.)*; ~**schein für im Lande verbleibende Waren** permit for home consumption.

Zoll|garantie customs bond; ~**garantie leisten** to deposit the duty [payable]; ~**gebiet** customs territory (area, district); **gemeinsames** ~**gebiet** *(EG)* common customs territory; ~**gebühren** customhouse fees (charges), customs charges, customs duties; ~**gebührenrechnung** bill of customs; ~**gefüge** tariff structure; ~**geleitschein** bill of sufferance, [customs] permit, transire *(Br.)*; ~**gemeinschaft** customs union; ~**gericht** customs court *(US)*.

zollgeschützt tariff-protected (-fed).

Zollgesetz tariff law (act, *US*);
~**entwurf** tariff bill; ~**geber** tariff maker; ~**gebung** tariff laws (legislation).

Zoll|gewahrsam customs custody; ~**gewicht** customs tare (weight); ~**grenzbezirk** customs (collection) district; ~**grenzdienst** border (customs) service; ~**grenze** border, frontier; ~**grenzstelle** frontier control point, customs post; ~**gut** bonded (dutiable) goods; ~**gut abfertigen** to clear goods at the customhouse; **privates** ~**gutlager** bonded warehouse; ~**hafen** point of entry, bonded port; ~**halle** customs hall, customs floor.

zollhängige Waren goods in process of clearing.

Zoll|harmonisierung *(EG)* harmonization of customs duties; ~**haus** customhouse, tollhouse; ~**hinterzieher** defrauder; ~**hinterziehung** defraudation of the revenue (customs), revenue fraud, evasion of customs duties; ~**hinterziehung begehen** to defraud the revenue, to evade customs duty; ~**hof** customs yard; ~**höhe** tariff level; ~**hoheit** customs sovereignty, tariff (customs) jurisdiction; ~**inhaltserklärung** customs declaration; ~**inland** customs area; ~**inspektor** customs inspector, examiner, locker *(Br.)*, surveyor *(US)*, *(Küstenverkehr)* landwaiter *(Br.)*, coastwaiter *(Br.)*; ~**kai** legal quay, *(Freihafenkai)* sufferance wharf; ~**katalog** tariff information catalog(ue); ~**kaution** customs *(Br.)* (entry) bond; ~**kaution zurückerhalten** to obtain a refund of the money deposited; ~**keller** bonded vaults; ~**kommission** tariff commission; ~**konferenz** tariff conference; ~**konstruktion** tariff structure; ~**kontingent** tariff[-rate] quota.

Zollkontrolle customs examination (inspection);
~ **passieren** to effect customs clearance, *(Schiff)* to enter out at the customhouse; **einer** ~ **unterliegen** to be subject to the control of the excise.

Zoll|krieg tariff war (battle); ~**kürzungen** tariff reductions, reduction of duties; ~**kutter** revenue cutter, coast-guard cutter *(US)*; ~**lager** bonded store, bonded warehouse, storage warehouse; **öffentliches** ~**lager** Queen's warehouse *(Br.)*, public store *(US)*; ~**lagerfrist** bonded (warehouse) period; ~**landeplatz** customs berth; ~**makler** customhouse (customs) broker; ~**mauer** tariff (trade) wall; ~**mauern gegen ausländische Produkte errichten** to raise tariff walls against foreign goods; ~**meldepflichtiger** person liable to duty.

Zöllner tollkeeper, customs officer (official), surveyor *(US)*; **berittener** ~ ride officer.

Zoll|niederlage locked (customs) warehouse, general-order (public, appraiser's, bonded, *Br.*) store, *(Zolleigenlager)* bonded (storage) warehouse, bond *(Br.)*, entrepôt; ~**nomenklatur** tariff nomenclature; ~**ordnung** custom-house regulations; ~**papiere** clearance papers, customs documents, *(für vorübergehende Einfuhr)* temporary importation papers; ~**passierschein** docket, landing order *(Br.)*, bill of sufferance *(Br.)*, *(Auto)* triptych; ~**passierscheinheft** international customs pass; ~**personal** officials in the customs, customhouse (customs) officials, customs people; **Waren von der** ~**pflicht ausnehmen** to take the duty off goods.

zollpflichtig liable to pay customs duties, liable to duty, dutiable, leviable, tariff-bound, customable, tollable, nonexempt, liable to custom duties;
~ **machen** to tariffize;
~**e Waren** dutiable (bonded) goods.

Zoll|pflichtigkeit dutiability; ~**plombe** [customhouse (lead)] seal; ~**plombe abnehmen** to remove the seal; ~**politik** tariff (customs) policy.

zollpolitisch|e Entwicklung tariff development; ~**e Forderungen** *(Wahlprogramm)* tariff plank; **zeitweise zu** ~**en Vergünstigungen berechtigt sein** to be eligible for a tariff commission recommendation of mandatory relief.

Zoll|position heading on the customs tariff, tariff heading (item); ~**posten** customs post; ~**präferenz** tariff (imperial, *Br.*) preference; ~**präferenzen genießen** to enjoy preferential treatment; ~**protektionismus** tariff protection; ~**prüfung** customs examination (inspection), rummaging *(Br.)*; ~**prüfungsbescheinigung** inspection certificate; ~**quittung** customhouse (customs) receipt, certificate of the customhouse, docket *(Br.)*; ~**quittungsbuch** toll book; ~**rechnung** customhouse note, account of customs; **Brüsseler** ~**rat** Customs Cooperating Council (CCC); ~**recht** tariff legislation.

zollrechtliche Behandlung customs treatment.

Zoll|reform tariff reform; ~**reformer** tariff reformer; ~**regal** toll.

zollregelnd tariff-regulating.

Zoll|regelung tariff regulation; ~**register** customs tariff; ~**repressalien** retaliatory measures; ~**revision** customs examination (inspection), rummaging *(Br.)*; ~**rückgabeschein** customs debenture, debenture certificate; ~**rückvergütung** [duty] drawback, customs rebate *(US)*, bonification; ~**sache** customs matter; ~**sachverständiger** examiner, general appraiser *(US)*; ~**satz** tariff [rate], rate of customs (duty), customs rate; **vertragsmäßiger** ~**satz** conventional tariff; **autonome** ~**sätze** autonomous (unilateral) tariff rates; ~**sätze herabsetzen** to reduce the customs duties; ~**schalter** customs desk; ~**schein** clearance certificate, customhouse certificate (bond, note), customs receipt (permit), *(Schiffsproviant)* victualling bill *(Br.)*; ~**scheinbuch**, ~**scheinheft** passbook, passbook *(Br.)*; ~**schiff** revenue cutter, coast-guard cutter *(US)*; ~**schranke** turnpike, tollgate, toll bar, customs barrier, pike *(US coll.)*; ~**schranken** *(hoher Zolltarif)* tariff (customs) wall (barriers), hostile tariff; ~**schranken abbauen** to eliminate customs barriers; ~**schuppen** locked warehouse, customs (bonded) shed, bonded store *(Br.)*; ~**schutz** tariff protection; **mittelbaren** ~**schutz genießen** to benefit from incidental tariff protection; ~**schutzschranken** tariff (customs) wall.

Zollsenkung reduction of rates (customs duties), tariff reduction (cut, cutback), customs duty reduction;
über die ausgehandelte Formel hinausgehende ~**en** deeper-than-formula tariff deductions; **lineare** ~**en** across-the-board customs reduction;
~**en synchronisieren** to phase in tariff reductions.

Zoll|senkungsabkommen tariff-cutting agreement; ~**senkungsformel** tariff cutting formula; ~**siegel** [custom-house] seal; ~**spediteur** customs expediter; ~**speicher** locked warehouse, appraiser's (public, customs, general order, bonded, *Br.*) store, *(Zolleigenlager)* bonded (customs) warehouse; ~**spesen** customhouse charges; ~**station** customs station, customs post, customhouse, *(für Straßengebühren)* toll booth, tollhouse; ~**statistik** customs statistics; ~**stelle** customhouse; ~**stempel** duty mark; ~**stock** yardstick, folding (foot) rule, inched staff; ~**strafe** customs penalty; ~**straße** customs route; ~**streife** customs control squad; ~**streitverfahren** tariff issue; ~**stundung** deferral of customs duties; ~**system** tariff system, customs regime; ~**tara** customs tare.

Zolltarif tariff [duty], customs tariff (regime), *(Katalog)* tariff information catalog(ue);
laut ~ as per tariff;
abgestufter ~ graded tariff; **allgemeiner** ~ full rates of customs duties; **anzuwendender** ~ applicable tariff; **ausgehandelter** ~ conventional tariff; **autonomer** ~ autonomous tariff [system]; **degressiver** ~ decreasing tariff; **dehnbarer (flexibler)** ~ flexible tariff; **eigener** ~ separate tariff; **einheitlicher** ~ single-schedule tariff **gemeinsamer** ~ *(EG)* common customs tariff; **gemischter (kombinierter)** ~ compound (mixed) tariff; **gleitender** ~ sliding-scale tariff; **gültiger** ~ tariff in force; **spezifischer** ~ specific tariff; **vereinbarter** ~ conventional tariff;
~**e angleichen** to harmonize customs tariffs; ~ **festsetzen** to fix the tariff;
~**abbau** tariff reduction; ~**änderung** tariff revision; ~**änderungen** tariff changes; ~**angleichung** harmonization of customs tariffs; ~**begünstigung** tariff (imperial, *Br.*) preference; ~**buch** tariff information catalog(ue), book (schedule) of rates.

Zolltarifierung customs classification, tariff, tariffication.

Zolltarif|satz rate of customs duties, tariff charge; ~**schema** tariff nomenclature; ~**senkung** tariff reduction (rollback), *(GATT)* Kennedy round; ~**sitzung** tariff session; ~**vereinbarung** conventional tariff system; ~**verfahren** tariff procedure.

Zoll|übereinkommen customs convention; ~**übertretung** customs offence; ~**union** customs union; **einer** ~**union beitreten** to enter into a customs union; ~**union bilden** to institute a customs union; ~**unionsteilnehmer** constituent territory of a customs union; ~**unterschied** tariff differential; ~**untersuchung** customs examination (inspection), *(Schiff)* search, rummage *(US)*, rummaging *(Br.)*; ~**verband** customs (tariff) union; ~**veredelung** processing in bond; ~**verein** tariff union; ~**vereinbarung** tariff agreement, conventional tariff system; ~**verfahren** customs (tariff) procedure; ~**vergehen** customs offence (violation), fiscal offence; ~**vergünstigung** preferential tariff, sufferance; ~**vergütung** duty (customs) drawback; ~**verhandlungen** tariff negotiations; ~**vermerk** customs visa; ~**verordnung** customs act (regulation).

Zollverschluß [customhouse, customs] seal;
außerhalb des ~**es** out of bond; **unter** ~ **lagernd** bonded, in bond;
unter ~ **bringen** to warehouse, to bond; **unter** ~ **einlagern, in** ~ **legen** to store in a warehouse, to warehouse (bond) goods; **unter** ~ **lagern** to remain in bond; **unter** ~ **lassen** to leave in bond; **in** ~ **legen** to [place under (put into)] bond; **im** ~ **liegen** to be in bond; **aus dem** ~ **nehmen** to release from (take out of) bond; **unter** ~ **nehmen** to take in bond;
~**schein** warehouse bond; ~**system** warehousing (warehouse) system; ~**verzeichnis** register of goods in bond; ~**vorschriften** bonding requirements; ~**waren** bonded goods; ~**wesen** warehouse (warehousing) system.

Zoll|vertrag tariff treaty; ~**verwahrung** warehousing; ~**verwaltung** customs authorities, customhouse officials; ~**verzeichnis** customs tariff (regime); ~**vorlage** tariff bill; ~**vormerkschein** excise bond, bond (customs) note; **unter** ~**vormerkschein zugelassen werden** to be admitted in bond; ~**vorschriften** customs (tariff) regulations; ~**vorteil** tariff advantage; ~**vorzugsabkommen** tariff preference agreement; ~**vorzugsgebiet** preferential tariff area; ~**vorzugssatz,** ~**vorzugstarif** preferential rate of duty, preferential (imperial, *Br.*) tariff; ~**wache** coast guard; ~**wachschiff** revenue cutter, coast-guard cutter *(US)*; ~**wert** tariff (dutiable, customs) value; ~**wertermittlung** customs valuation, appraisal; ~**wertüberprüfer** reappraiser; ~**wesen** customs; ~**zugeständnis** tariff concession; ~**zugeständnisliste** *(GATT)* schedule of concessions; ~**zuschlag** additional duty; ~**zuwiderhandlung** customs violation.

Zone zone, *(Landstrich)* area, region, belt, *(Verkehrsabschnitt)* stage;
in ~**n eingeteilt** zoned;
atomwaffenfreie ~ atom-free (denuclearized) zone; **entmilitarisierte** ~ demilitarized zone; **erste** ~ *(Fahrkarte)* first stage; **gemäßigte** ~ temperate zone; **heiße** ~ torrid zone; **hindernisfreie** ~ *(Flughafen)* end-cleared zone; **kalte** ~ frigid zone; **neutrale** ~ neutral zone; **tote** ~ *(Radar)* gap, *(Radio)* dead zone, blind spot; **verbotene** ~ forbidden zone; **militärisch verdünnte** ~ limited-force zone; **wirtschaftlich vereinigte** ~**n** economically fused zones; **windstille** ~ doldrums;
~ **mit Geschwindigkeitsbegrenzung** restricted area; ~ **für Kurzparker** limited parking zone;
nach ~**n einteilen** to zone.

Zonenabgrenzung zoning.

zonenartig zonal.

Zonen|behörden zonal authorities; ~**einteilung** zoning, zonation, *(Verkehrsbetrieb)* division into fare stages; ~**fahrkarte** zone ticket; ~**gebühr** *(Telefon)* zone area rate; ~**gliederung** zonal organization; ~**grenze** frontier, demarcation line; ~**plan** *(Werbung)* zone plan; ~**präsident** divisional chairman; ~**preis** zone price *(US)*; ~**preisverfahren** zone pricing *(US)*; ~**randgebiet** border area; ~**tarif** rate scale, *(Verkehr)* interline fare, *(Versorgungsbetrieb)* zone tariff (system, rates) *(US)*; ~**vertreter** zoning official; ~**wähler** *(Telefon)* zone selector; ~**zeit** zone time; ~**zusammenschluß** zone merger.

zoologischer Garten zoo, zoological gardens.

Zopf, alter wiggery, pedant[ry].

Zorn rage, anger, fury, wrath, heat, passion;
blaß vor ~ white with anger;
jds. ~ **dämpfen** to tone down s. one's anger; **in** ~ **geraten** to fly into a passion;
~**ausbruch** outburst, fit of anger.

zornentbrannt boiling with rage.

zornig furious, angry, mad.

Zote smutty (filthy, blue) joke.

Zoten bad language;
~ **erzählen** to talk smut;
~**reißer** bawdy joker.

Zubehör accessories, appurtenance, appendix, appendage, paraphernalia, trappings, material, pertinents, *(Inventar)* fittings, fixtures;
mit allem ~ with all convenience;
landwirtschaftliches ~ agricultural fixtures; **technisches** ~ tools and machinery;
~ **bei Bedarf** optional extras;
~ **entfernen** to remove fixtures; ~ **werden** to become a fixture;
~**fertiger** component maker; ~**industrie** accessories industry; ~**liste** inventory of fixtures; ~**tasche** *(Fotoapparat)* gadget bag; ~**teile** accessories.

Zuber tub.

zubereiten to prepare, to get ready, to cook.

zubilligen to allow, to grant, to accord, to concede;
Fristverlängerung ~ to grant extension of time, to accord a respite; **Schadensersatz** ~ to award damages; **mildernde Umstände** ~ to allow mitigating circumstances; **Vorrecht** ~ to concede a privilege; **einem Schuldner Zahlungsfrist** ~ to indulge a debtor, to allow a debtor time to pay.

Zubilligung concession, allowance, grant;
unter ~ **von Bewährungsfrist** on probation;
~ **von Schadensersatz** award of damages; ~ **mildernder Umstände** allowing mitigating circumstances.

zubinden, Sack to tie a sack.

zubringen to spend, to pass;
Nacht im Freien ~ to spend a night in the open (out of doors).

Zubringer access (feeder) road, local service line, feeder line;
~**bus** airport bus; ~**dienst** feeder service; **öffentlicher** ~**dienst** local haulage (line service); ~**dienst mit Kraftfahrzeugen** *(Flugplatz)* door-to-door airport limousine service; ~**fahrzeug der Eisenbahn** railway's collecting vehicle *(Br.)*; ~**flug** feeder flight; ~**flugzeug** feeder liner (plane, machine); ~**kosten** hauling costs; ~**leitung** *(Rundfunk)* transmission line; ~**linie** *(Bahn)* local service line, jerkwater railroad *(US)*, *(Fluglinie)* feeder [line]; ~**straße** access (feeder) road; ~**verkehr** feeder service; ~**zug** feeder (shuttle) train *(US)*, jerkwater *(US coll.)*.

Zubuße allowance, *(zu einem Kux)* contribution.

zubuttern to chip in, to kick in *(US sl.)*;
durch einen Nebenverdienst zu seiner Rente ~ to boost one's pension by making a few pennies on the side.

Zucht *(Anbau)* cultivation, growing, *(Aufzucht)* breeding, rearing, *(Disziplin)* discipline, morale;
eiserne ~ an iron hand; **strenge** ~ strict discipline;
in ~ **halten** to keep under discipline; **in** ~ **und Ordnung halten** to keep a tight rein on s. th.; **j. in die** ~ **nehmen** to discipline s. o.;
~**bestimmungen** breeding regulations.

Züchten breeding.

züchten to breed, to rear, to raise.

Züchtergenossenschaft breeding company.

Zuchthaus house of correction, convict prison *(Br., bis 1948)*, penal servitude *(Br.)*, state prison *(US)*, penitentiary *(US)*, *(Strafe)* imprisonment with hard labo(u)r;
lebenslängliches ~ penal servitude for life, life sentence;
im ~ **sitzen** to do a stretch *(sl.)*; **mit einem Bein im** ~ **stehen** to have one foot in goal; **zu fünf Jahren** ~ **verurteilen** to condemn (sentence) to five years hard labo(u)r; **zu lebenslänglichem** ~ **verurteilt werden** to get a life sentence;
~**arbeit** convict labo(u)r.

Zuchthäusler convict, jailbird *(coll.)*;
entsprungener ~ lamster *(sl.)*; **auf Bewährung entlassener** ~ lagger;
~**bande** gang of convicts.
Zuchthausstrafe penal servitude, infamous punishment, imprisonment with hard labo(u)r, reclusion *(Louisiana)*;
lebenslängliche ~ life imprisonment, lifer.
Zuchtherde pedigree herd.
züchtig modest, virgin.
züchtigen to chastise, to chasten, to correct, to punish;
j. ~ to punish s. o. corporally.
Züchtigung corporal punishment, correction, discipline, castigation;
gesetzlich zulässige ~ lawful correction.
zuchtlos disorderly, without discipline, undisciplined;
~**es Leben führen** to lead a dissipated life.
Zucht|losigkeit disorderliness, debauchery; **gestrenger** ~**meister sein** to be a strict disciplinarian; ~**mittel** means (measures) of coercion; ~**perle** culture[d] pearl; **unter jds.** ~**rute stehen** to be under s. one's thumb; ~**tier** breeding animal.
Züchtung breeding, culture, propagation.
Zuchtvieh breeding stock.
zucken to twitch, to jerk;
in den Fingern ~ to be itching; **mit den Schultern** ~ to shrug one's shoulders; **nicht mit der Wimper** ~ without turning a hair, without batting an eyelid, not to flinch once.
zücken, Geldbeutel to unstring one's purse.
Zucker|anbau sugar cultivation; ~**ankaufstelle,** ~**börse** sugar exchange, sugar board *(Br.)*; ~**brot und Peitsche** the stick and the carrot; **vom** ~**brot zur Peitsche übergehen** to switch from sweet talk to arm twisting; ~**fabrik** sugar works; ~**guß** icing; ~**handel** sugar trade; ~**industrie** sugar[-cane] industry; ~**krankheit** diabetes; **kein** ~**lecken** *(fam.)* no picnic; ~**raffinerie** sugar refinery; ~**sack** sugar bag; ~**steuer** sugar tax.
zudecken, j. mit Fragen to pester s. o. with questions; **j. mit einem Mantel** ~ to cover s. o. up with a blanket; **mit dem Mantel der christlichen Nächstenliebe** ~ to draw a curtain over s. th.
Zudrang der Gläubiger run of creditors.
zudringlich officious, too familiar, off base *(sl.)*;
einem Mädchen gegenüber ~ **werden** to make advances to (a pass at, *sl.*) at (get fresh with, *US coll.*) a girl;
~**e Fragen** impertinent questions.
Zudringlichkeit importunity.
zudrücken, ein Auge to turn a blind eye, to stretch a point; **jem. die Gurgel** ~ to throttle (strangle) s. o.
zueignen to inscribe, to dedicate;
sich ~ to appropriate; **sich in rechtswidriger Absicht** ~ to appropriate unlawfully, to take and carry away.
Zueigner dedicator.
Zueignung dedication, appropriation, inscription.
Zueignungsabsicht, rechtswidrige constructive taking, intent to steal.
zueinander gehören to belong together.
zuerkannt awarded, allocated, attributed;
im Schiedswege ~**e Abfindung** award of compensation; ~**e und fällige Entschädigung** accrued compensation; ~**er Schadensersatz** awarded damages; **rechtlich** ~**er Schadenersatz** *(Versicherung)* legal award.
zuerkennen to adjudicate, to adjudge, to admeasure, to acknowledge, to grant, *(zuteilen)* to allocate, to award;
jem. eine Belohnung ~ to confer a reward on s. o.; **jem. eine Eigenschaft** ~ to credit s. o. with a quality; **akademischen Grad** ~ to confer a degree; **jem. einen Preis** ~ to award (adjudge) a prize to s. o.; **Schadenersatz** ~ to award (adjudge) damages; **jem. einen Titel** ~ to bestow a title upon s. o.; **Unterhalt** ~ to award maintenance, to award alimony *(US)*.
Zuerkennung attribution, adjudgment, adjudication, awarding, admeasurement, acknowledgement;
~ **einer Belohnung** conferment of a reward; ~ **eines akademischen Grades** graduation; ~ **eines Preises** award of a prize; ~ **von Schadensersatzansprüchen durch staatliche Schadensregulierungsausschüsse** adjudication of claims of national claims commissions; ~ **von Unterhalt** award of maintenance, award of alimony *(US)*.
Zuerkennungsverfahren adjudication process.
Zuerstentnahme|der älteren Vorräte und Bilanzierung zum jeweiligen Buchwert *(Lagerbewertung)* first-in, first-out *(US)*, fifo; ~ **der neuen Vorräte und Bilanzierung zum jeweiligen Buchwert** last-in, first-out, lifo.
Zuerstkommender first comer.
zufahren, direkt auf j. to drive straight at s. o.
Zufahrt access, approach, entryway, drive, driveway *(US)*.
Zufahrts|bake entrance beacon; ~**kanal** entrance channel; ~**rampe** approach ramp, drive-on; ~**recht** right of access; ~**rinne** entrance channel; ~**straße** accommodation (occupation, access, feeder) road; ~**straßen zum Flughafen blockieren** to clog the roads leading to the airport; ~**weg** drive, entryway, driveway *(US)*, access road, carriage drive; **unmittelbarer** ~**weg** immediate approach.
Zufall chance, hazard, accident, coincidence, luck, *(Ereignis)* event, occurrence, incident;
durch reinen ~ by [a] mere chance; **vom** ~ **bestimmt** haphazard; **bloßer** ~ pure accident; **glücklicher** ~ fortune, lucky chance, fluke, stroke of luck, piece of good luck, break *(US)*; **purer** ~ mere coincidence; **unabwendbarer** ~ fortuitous event, Act of God, act of providence; **unglücklicher** ~ mischance, piece of ill luck; **unvermeidbarer** ~ casualty, inevitable (unavoidable) accident;
es dem ~ **überlassen** to let chance play its part; **nichts dem** ~ **überlassen** to leave nothing to accident (chance);
wie der ~ **es wollte** as luck would have it.
Zufälle|des Lebens side-shows of life;
von ~**n abhängen** to depend on contingencies.
Zufallen durch Erbschaft devolution, descent.
zufallen to go (fall) to, to vest;
jem. ~ to go to s. o., to accrue to (result, devolve upon) s. o.; **dem Arbeitgeber** ~ to accrue to the employer; **jem. als Aufgabe** ~ to fall to s. one's lot; **im Erbgang** ~ to accrue by way of succession; **dem ältesten Sohn** ~ to portion to the eldest son; **jem. bei der Teilung** ~ to fall to s. one's share.
zufällig casual, haphazard, incidental, by accident, accidental, fortuitous, random;
nicht ~ nonaccidental; **rein** ~ by a pure fluke, purely coincidental (by chance);
jem. ~ **treffen** to run into (knock against, stumble across, forgather) s. o.;
~**e Bekanntschaft** chance acquaintance; ~**es Ereignis** fortuitous event, contingency; ~**er Kunde** chance customer; ~**es Zusammentreffen** coincidence, chance meeting.
Zufälligkeit coincidence, accidentality, fortuitousness, contingency.
Zufallsabweichung *(Statistik)* deviation.
zufallsähnliche Stichprobenverfahren quasi-random sampling.
Zufalls|anfangszahl *(Statistik)*andom start; ~**anordnung** *(Statisk)* random order; ~**auswahl** random sampling (selection), lottery sampling.
zufallsbedingt fortuitous, accidental, due to chance;
~**e Schwankungen** chance fluctuations.
Zufalls|bedingung casual condition; ~**bekanntschaft** chance acquaintance, casual pickup; ~**einnahmen** windfall receipts; ~**ergebnis** accidental result; ~**fehler** *(Statistik)* accidental (random) error; ~**haftung** hazardous liability; ~**handlung** inadvertent action; ~**moment** *(Statistik)* chance factor; ~**stichprobe** random sample, probability sampling; ~**stimme** snap vote; ~**streubereich** *(Statistik)* random range; ~**streuung** *(Statistik)* random variation; ~**treffen** incidental (chance) meeting; ~**verteilung** random distribution; ~**zahlen** random sampling numbers.
zufassen to lend a hand, *(Chance wahrnehmen)* to jump at an opportunity.
zufliegen *(Tür)* to shut with a bang, to slam;
auf etw. ~ to fly towards (head) for s. th.
zufließen *(Einkommen)* to accrue, to issue;
einem Hilfsfonds ~ to flow into a relief fund; **dem Meer** ~ to flow into the sea; **einem Unternehmen** ~ to accrue to an enterprise.
Zuflucht refuge, shelter, anchor, resort, retreat, subterfuge, harbo(u)rage, asylum;
~ **zu den Waffen** appeal to the arms;
~ **gewähren** to harbo(u)r; **einem entsprungenen Gefangenen** ~ **gewähren** to shelter an escaped prisoner; **seine** ~ **nehmen** to take refuge (shelter), to resort to; **zu Ausreden** ~ **nehmen** to have recourse to excuses; **seine** ~ **zu Lügen nehmen** to fall back on lies; **seine** ~ **zu den Waffen nehmen** to appeal to the arms; ~ **suchen** to seek shelter (refuge); **an einer Freistätte** ~ **suchen** to seek sanctuary.
Zufluchts|hafen port (haven) of refuge; ~**land** asylum, refuge, repair, retreat, franchise, harbo(u)r, haven of rest, home, mike; ~**ort** harbo(u)r, refuge, place of hiding; ~**ort zur Entspannung** escape hatch; ~**ort für politische Flüchtlinge** sanctuary for political refugees; ~**stätte** asylum, sanctuary, harbo(u)rage, retreat.

Zufluß afflux, *(Geld, Waren)* supply, influx, inflow, *(See)* inlet;
~ **ausländischer Geldbeträge** inflow of foreign currency;
~**gebiet** river basin.
zuflüstern, jem. etw. to whisper s. th. to s. o., to drop a word in s. one's ear.
zufrieden content, happy, pleased, satisfied;
glücklich und ~ as happy as a lark;
mit sich selbst äußerst ~ **sein** to be very well pleased with o. s., **mit wenigem** ~ **sein** to be content with little;
~**es Dasein führen** to live in peace and content; ~**es Lächeln** complacent smile.
Zufriedenheit content, satisfaction;
mit einem Ausdruck von ~ with a look of contentment; **berufliche** ~ job satisfaction; **innere** ~ inner contentment;
~ **mit dem Wahlergebnis** satisfaction over the results of the election;
jds. ~ **beeinträchtigen** to alloy s. one's happiness; **Problem zur allgemeinen** ~ **lösen** to solve a problem to the satisfaction of everyone.
zufriedenlassen, j. to leave s. o. in peace (alone).
zufriedenstellen to satisfy, to please, to gratify, to content.
zufriedenstellend satisfactory, gratifying;
~ **laufen** *(Auto)* to perform satisfactorily;
alle Teile ~**e Abmachung** mutually satisfactory agreement; ~**e Fortschritte** satisfactory progress; ~**en Nachweis erbringen** to establish to the satisfaction.
Zufriedenstellung satisfaction, contentment, gratification;
~ **des Kunden** customer satisfaction.
zufriedenzustellen, schwer hard to please.
zufrieren to freeze over.
zufügen, Schaden to [cause] damage, to inflict damage, to harm; **jem. Schaden** ~ to inflict damage on s. o.; **jem. Schmerzen** ~ to cause s. o. pain; **schweren Verlust** ~ to inflict a serious loss.
Zufuhr supply, delivery, *(Lebensmittel)* provisions, *(Wareneingänge)* arrivals, imports, importation;
geregelte (ständige) ~ continuous supply; **gesicherte** ~ assured supply; **schwache** ~ scanty supply;
~ **frischer Meeresluft** influx of fresh air from the sea;
jem. die ~ **abschneiden** to cut off s. one's supply.
zuführen to supply, *(fig.)* to channel;
auf das Dorf ~ *(Straße)* to lead to the village; **einer Einheit Versorgungsgüter** ~ *(mil.)* to provision a unit; **Frage einer vernünftigen Lösung** ~ to find a satisfactory solution for a problem; **der Industrie neue Arbeitskräfte** ~ to introduce new labo(u)r force into industry; **Kunden** ~ to introduce (bring) customers; **jem. künstliche Nahrung** ~ to feed s. o. artificially; **den Rücklagen** ~ to transfer to reserves, to carry (add) to the reserve fund; **jem. seiner verdienten Strafe** ~ to punish s. o. as he deserves; **einem Unternehmen frisches Blut** ~ to put new life in an enterprise.
Zufuhr|gleis entry line; ~**stockung** interruption of supply.
Zuführung supply;
~ **zur Gewinnrücklage** addition to reserve, addition to retained earnings *(US)*; ~**en zu den Rückstellungen für das Kreditgeschäft** *(Bankbilanz)* allocations to provisions for possible loan losses.
Zuführungsleitung lead-in wire.
Zug draft, draught *(Br.)*, *(Bahn)* train, *(Eigenart)* trait, characteristic, trick, *(Fahrzeug)* convoy, *(Festzug)* procession, parade, *(Gesichtsausdruck)* line, look, *(Klingel)* bellpull, *(Kontur)* line, outline, *(Linie)* stroke, *(mil.)* platoon, *(Neigung)* bent, propensity, inclination, bias, *(Rahmen)* frame, framework, *(Reihe)* file, column, row, flock, *(Richtung)* trend, tendency, *(Ruck)* jerk, tug;
bei Ankunft des ~**es** on arrival of the train; **im** ~**e der Neugestaltung** in the course of reorganization; **mit einem** ~ at one go;
abfahrender ~ outgoing train; **angekommener** ~ in train; **aufgehaltener** ~ delayed train; **bezeichnender** ~ telling point; **charakteristischer** ~ characteristic feature; **direkter (durchgehender, D-)** ~ nonstop (direct, through, corridor, express, vestibule, *US*) train; **im Nahschnellverkehr eingesetzter** ~ local express (rapid transit, *US*) train; **entgleister** ~ wrecked train; **stadteinwärts fahrender** ~ down train *(US)*, train to town; **fahrplanmäßiger (pünktlich einlaufender)** ~ ordinary (regular, scheduled, *US*) train; **Fern-D-**~ extra-fare train; **gemischter** ~ mixed train; **geschickter** ~ clever stroke (move); **gläserner** ~ observation train *(US)*; **langsamer** ~ slow (parliamentary, *Br.*) train; **leichter** ~ light draft (draught, *Br.*); **pünktlicher** ~ scheduled train *(US)*; **superschneller** ~ advanced passenger train; **sympathischer** ~ nice trait; **überfüllter** ~ overcrowded (packed) train; **auf einer Hauptstrecke verkehrender** ~ mainline train; **versöhnlicher** ~ redeeming feature; **verspäteter** ~ delayed train; **vollgestopfter** ~ jam-packed train; **zuschlagspflichtiger** ~ limited train;
~ **ins Blaue** mystery train; ~ **mit Dampferanschluß** boat-load train *(Br.)*; ~ **zur größeren Einheit** move towards the bigger unit; ~ **der Gefangenen** line of prisoners; ~ **mit angehängtem Güterwaggon** mixed train; ~ **mit zwei Lokomotiven** double-headed train; ~ **für den öffentlichen Personenverkehr** public service train; **wesentlicher** ~ **einer Politik** essential feature of s. one's policy; ~ **mit Postbeförderung** mail train; ~ **mit Speisewagen** train with dining car; **allgemeiner** ~ **nach dem Süden** general southward trend; ~ **mit beschränkter Waggon- und Personenzahl** limited train *(US)*, limited *(US)*; ~ **der Zeit** trend of the times; ~ **um** ~ hand on hand, *(Schritt für Schritt)* step by step, *(als Vergeltung)* tit for tat;
~ **ablassen (abwinken)** to dispatch (flag) a train; **aus einem fahrenden** ~ **abspringen** to jump out of a moving train; **Geschäftsvorgänge** ~ **um** ~ **abwickeln** to carry out transactions one after the other; ~ **anhalten** to stop a train; ~ **durch Winkzeichen anhalten** to wave a train to a halt; ~ **auflösen** to split up a train; **auf einen** ~ **aufspringen** to hop a train *(US)*; ~ **ausrauben** to hold up a train *(US)*; **aus einem** ~ **aussteigen** to step (get) off a train; **in einem** ~ **austrinken** to empty one's glass in one go; **j. an den** ~ **begleiten** to see s. o. off; **D-**~ **benutzen** to travel express; ~ **ohne Fahrkarte benutzen** to jump a train; ~ **bereitstellen** to make up a train [of cars]; ~ **aufs Abstellgleis bringen** to dock a train, to put a train on the siding; ~ **zum Entgleisen bringen** to wreck a train; **neuen** ~ **in den Fahrplan einfügen** to schedule a new train *(US)*; **Mittagessen im** ~ **einnehmen** to have lunch on the train; **in einen** ~ **einsteigen** to go aboard (board, *US*) a train; ~ **erreichen** to make (catch, save) a train; **mit dem** ~ **fahren** to take a (travel by) train; ~ **fehlleiten** to misroute a train; **dem** ~ **seines Herzens folgen** to follow the prompting of one's heart; **keinen** ~ **haben** *(Ofen)* not to draw well; **seine Klasse im** ~ **haben** to keep one's pupils on their toes; ~ **zur Verschwendung haben** to live in lavish style; **sich einen** ~ **heraussuchen** to look up a train (for a train in the timetable); **sich in einen** ~ **hineindrängen** to push (force) one's way into a train; **zum** ~**e kommen** to get a word in, *(tätig werden)* to be given a chance; ~ **ausfallen lassen** to cancel (annul) a train; ~ **entgleisen lassen** to wreck a train; ~ **genau nach dem Fahrplan fahren lassen** to time a train; **j. nicht zum** ~**e kommen lassen** to shunt s. o., not to give s. o. a chance; **am** ~ **sein** to be one's turn; **j. aus dem** ~ **stoßen** to red-light s. o. *(sl.)*; ~ **überfallen** to hold up a train; ~ **verpassen** to lose (miss) a train; ~ **um eine Stunde vorlegen** to shift a train one hour ahead; ~ **aus dem Verkehr ziehen** to take off a train.
Zug um Zug | zu erfüllende Bedingungen concurrent conditions; ~ **Bezahlung** cash on delivery.
Zugabe *(Gewichtsauffüllung)* makeweight, surplus, *(Künstler)* added performance, *(Prämie)* [direct] premium, giveaway *(US)*, addition, bonus, gratuitous article, free gift, extra, *(Theater)* encore, *(Zeitung)* supplement, *(Zuzahlung beim Tausch)* boot money;
als ~ additionally, into the bargain, give-in;
~ **gegen eingesandten Kupon** mail-in premium *(US)*;
um eine ~ **bitten** to encore; **als** ~ **gewähren** to throw into the bargain;
~**angebot [für Händler]** [dealer] premium offer *(US)*; ~**artikel** [advertising] premium, loss leader *(US)*; ~**gutschein** free-gift coupon; **sich für** ~**kupons aussprechen** to vote one's preference on mail-in coupons; ~**produkt** premium product; ~**unwesen** giveaway and sampling practice; ~**werbeplan** gift enterprise system; ~**werbung** [free] gift advertising; ~**werbung in Sammelform** continuity premium; ~**wesen** selling with premium, premium promotion, premium selling, gift giving.
Zug|abfertiger train dispatcher; ~**abfertigung** train dispatch; ~**abfertigungsbeamter** train dispatcher; ~**abgänge** departure of trains; ~**abstand** headway; ~**abteil** compartment; ~**anfang** front (fore) part of a train.
Zugang access, admittance, approach, *(Anwachsen)* accrual, *(Eingang)* entrance, entry, entryway, gateway, *(Grundstück)* egress, *(Lager)* incoming stocks, quantity received, *(Vermehrung)* increase;
freier ~ *(Politik)* access; **geheimer** ~ secret entrance; **kein** ~! no admittance (entrance)!; **sicherer** ~ *(Gewerbeordnung)* safe access, means of access; **ungehinderter** ~ right of free entry; ~ **verboten!** no admittance!; **zollfreier** ~ tariff-free access;
~ **an Devisen** accrual of exchange; **bequemer** ~ **zu Energiequellen** proximity to power; **freier** ~ **für den Handel** open door;

~ **zu einer Höhle** entrance to a cave; ~ **zu Informationen** access to information; ~ **zum Kapitalmarkt** access to the capital market; ~ **zum Meer** outlet (access) to the sea, sea access; ~ **bei den Spareinlagen** inflow into savings accounts; ~ **auf einem Sparkonto** accumulation of savings;
~ **drosseln** to choke off; **schwer zu jem.** ~ **finden** to find it hard to get to know s. o.; ~ **haben** to have access to; **freien** ~ **haben** to go in and out; **jederzeit** ~ **bei jem. haben** to have s. one's ear; **freien** ~ **zu etw. haben** to have the run of s. th.; **freien** ~ **in einem Haus haben** to have the run of a house; **freien** ~ **zum Kapitalmarkt haben** to gain access to capital; ~ **zu den Unterlagen einer Gesellschaft haben** to have access to the books of a company; **sich selbst** ~ **verschaffen** to let o. s. in; **sich betrügerisch** ~ **verschaffen** to obtain entry by fraud; **sich gewaltsam** ~ **zu einer Versammlung verschaffen** to push one's way into a meeting; **dem öffentlichen** ~ **verschließen** to close off to the public.
zugange sein, mit etw. to be busy with s. th.
Zugänge *(Belegschaft)* accessions, additions, *(Bibliothek)* accessions, *(Bilanz)* subsequent additions, accruals, *(Einnahmen)* receipts, *(Hotel)* new registrations, *(Klub)* new members, *(Krankenhaus)* new admissions, *(Kreditbuchungen)* credit entries, *(Waren)* arrivals, incoming goods;
ausländische ~ accession of funds from abroad;
~ **auf dem Arbeitsmarkt** new entrants onto the labo(u)r market; ~ **an Bausparverträgen** investment inflow; ~ **zum Einstandspreis** *(Lager)* additions at cost.
zugänglich admissible, accessible, open to, approachable, get-at-able, *(fig.)* amenable, come-at-able *(coll.)*;
allgemein ~ publicly available, on hand; **frei** ~ open-door; **jedermann** ~ within reach of all; **leicht** ~ easy of access (approach), within easy reach; **der Öffentlichkeit nicht** ~ not open to the public; **einem Rat** ~ amenable to advice; **schwer** ~ difficult of access; **Vernunftsgründen nicht** ~ unamenable to reason;
~ **machen** to make (render) available; **sich j. mit Bestechung** ~ **machen** to approach s. o. with bribes; **unerlaubtes Informationsmaterial** ~ **machen** to disclose information; **der Öffentlichkeit** ~ **machen** to throw open to the public; **allgemein** ~ **sein** *(Patent)* to be in the public domain *(US)*; **der Bestechung** ~ **sein** to be open to bribes; **jedermann** ~ **sein** to be open to all; **sonnabends kostenlos** ~ **sein** to be open free on Saturdays.
Zugänglichkeit approachability, accessibility, *(fig.)* amenability, get-at-ability.
Zugangs|behinderung encroachment of access; ~**jahr** year of acquisition; ~**liste** accession book; ~**möglichkeit** availability of access; ~**nummer** accession number; ~**prozeß** *(Bevölkerung)* birth process; ~**rate** accession rate; ~- **und Abgangsrate** *(Belegschaft)* replacement rate; ~**recht** right (easement) of access; ~**straße** access road; ~**verzeichnis** accession record; ~**weg** access [route].
Zug|anordnung train order, flimsy; ~**anschluß** train connection; ~**anschluß haben** to connect with a train; ~**artikel** draw, price leader, eye appeal (catcher, stopper), flat catcher, article of quick sale, puller *(sl.)*; ~**auflösung** breaking up of a train; ~**auflösung nach Warenklassen** classification switching; ~**aufsichtsbeamter** train dispatcher; ~**ausfall** annulment of a train; ~**beanspruchung** tensile stress; ~**begleiter** train conductor (guard, *US*); ~**begleitpersonal,** ~**besatzung** train staff (crew, *US*); ~**brücke** drawbridge; ~**dichte** density of trains.
Züge *(Gesichtszüge)* features, lineament;
in kurzen ~**n** in short, briefly, in a nutshell;
etw. in groben ~**n darlegen** to explain s. th. in general terms; **etw. in großen** ~**n darstellen** to draw a rapid picture of s. th.; **sein Leben in vollen** ~**n genießen** to enjoy life to the full; **in den letzten** ~**n liegen** to be breathing one's last; **in kräftigen** ~**n skizzieren** to sketch with firm strokes.
zugeben to admit, to concede, to acknowledge, to confess, *(draufzahlen)* to throw into the bargain, to give in, to give to boot, *(einsehen)* to recognize;
seinen Fehler ~ to acknowledge the corn, to admit that one was in the wrong; **nicht** ~ to disallow; **seine Schuld** ~ to admit one's guilt, to confess o. s. guilty.
zugedachte Aufgabe, jem. work assigned to s. o.
zugeflüstert, das hat man mir a little bird told me.
zugefroren frozen, icebound.
zugegen present;
bei einer Sitzung ~ to attend a meeting.
zugehen *(Brief, Ware)* to come to hand, to reach, *(Koffer)* to close, to lock;
nicht mit rechten Dingen ~ to be somewhat fishy; **dem Ende** ~ to be drawing to a close; **auf die offene Tür** ~ to go up to the open door; **auf den Winter** ~ to be getting on for winter;
~ **lassen** to send, to forward.
Zugehfrau cleaning woman, cleaner, charwoman *(Br.)*.
zugehören to belong (appertain) to, to be member to.
zugehörig appertaining, pertinent, appropriate, belonging, accessory, appurtenant;
j. als ~ **betrachten** to count s. o. in;
~**e Grundstücke** plots of land belonging to it.
Zugehöriger des linken Flügels left-winger.
Zugehörigkeit adherence, *(Betriebsangehöriger)* belongingness, company seniority *(US)*, *(Verein)* membership;
politische ~ political leaning;
~ **zu einer Gewerkschaft** union membership; ~ **zum Gemeinsamen Markt** Common Market membership; ~ **zu einer Partei** party affiliation.
Zugehörigkeits|dauer continuation rate; ~**dauer zu einem Betrieb** length of service in a company, company seniority *(US)*; ~**gefühl** sense of belonging.
Zug|einlauf arrival of a train; ~**einschränkungen** curtailment of service.
zugeknöpft *(fig.)* tight-lipped, reticent;
völlig ~**er Mensch sein** to be as close as an oyster.
Zügel rein, brake, curb;
jem. ~ **anlegen** to keep s. o. in check; **jem. in die** ~ **fallen** to stop s. o.; **jem. an einem strengen** ~ **führen** to run s. o. hard; ~ **straff in der Hand halten** to keep a stiff rein, to keep a tight hold on s. th.; ~ **der Regierung halten** to hold the reins of government, to govern; **j. am langen** ~ **laufen lassen** to let s. o. have his head; ~ **locker lassen** to keep a slack rein; ~ **schleifen lassen** to loosen the reins; ~ **behutsam aber fest in die Hände nehmen** to bring a gentle but firm hand into the management.
zugelassen admitted, licensed, authorized, recognized, permitted, *(Bank)* located, *(Flugzeug)* airworthy, *(qualifiziert)* qualified;
amtlich ~ authorized, certified, certificated, accredited; **an der Börse** ~ admitted to (quoted at, listed at, *US*) the stock exchange; **gesetzlich** ~ permitted by law, legally qualified; **nicht** ~ unadmitted, unlicensed, unauthorized, unallowed, *(Aktie)* not quoted, unlisted *(US)*; **zur Prüfung** ~ admitted to a competitive examination (to sit for an examination); **staatlich** ~ certified;
als Anwalt ~ **sein** to be admitted as attorney *(US)* (solicitor, *Br.*, to the bar); **zur Wahl** ~ **sein** to be qualified to vote; **als Bürge** ~ **werden** to be admitted as bail;
~**er Beweis** admissible evidence; ~**e Gesellschaft** chartered (registered) company; ~**es Gewerbe** lawful trade; **amtlich** ~**er Makler** certified (inside, *Br.*) broker; ~**er Patentanwalt** chartered patent agent *(Br.)*, patent attorney *(US)*; ~**es Unternehmen** licensed undertaking; ~**er Verkaufsvertreter** licensed dealer; ~**e Versicherungsgesellschaft** admitted company; ~**er Vertreter** recognized agent; ~**er Wähler** qualified elector (voter); ~**er Wirtschaftsprüfer** chartered accountant *(Br.)*, certified [public] accountant *(US)*.
Zugelassener admittee *(US)*.
zügellos unrestrained, unbounded, *(ausschweifend)* wanton, lewd;
~**es Verhalten** dissolute conduct.
Zügellosigkeit unrestraint, dissipation, wildness, libertinism.
zügeln *(Konjunktur)* to curb;
seine Emotionen ~ to dam up one's feelings; **seinen Unmut** ~ to pull in one's horns.
Zügelung curb, curbing, restraint, lid *(US)*.
zugemauert walled-up.
Zug|ende rear of the train; ~**entgleisung** train wreck.
zu|gerechnete Fahrlässigkeit imputed negligence; ~**geschlagen** *(Auktion)* gone; ~**geschnitten auf** tailor-made for, adapted to; **auf das Verbraucherbedürfnis** ~**geschnitten sein** to be geared to consumer needs; ~**geschrieben** imputed, attributed, ascribed; **sich einer anderen Gruppe** ~**gesellen** to join another group; ~**gesellt** associate; ~**gesicherte Eigenschaft** fitness for purpose, warranted qualification; **sich** ~**gespitzt haben** to have come to a pass; ~**gesprochenes Telegramm** telegram by telephone, phonogram.
zugestanden admitted, acknowledged;
nicht ~ unacknowledged, unadmitted;
~**e Eigenschaften** warranted qualities, ~**e Tatsachen** conceded facts.
Zugeständnis confession, concession, acknowledgement, *(Prozeß)* admission, *(Zoll)* concession;
bei gegenseitigen ~**sen** by mutual concessions (compromise);

nachteiliges ~ damaging admission; **preisliches** ~ price concession; **steuerliches** ~ tax concession; **tarifliche ~se** tariff concessions; **weitreichende ~se** wide-reaching concessions; **belastendes ~ von Tatsachen** incriminating admission; **~se auf dem Zollgebiet** tariff concessions;
~se aussetzen *(Zoll)* to withhold a concession; **~ machen** to stretch a point, to make concessions.
zugestehen to concede, to admit, to yield, to own up, to grant; **Frist ~** to accord a respite, to grant extension of time; **jem. eine Kontoüberziehung nur zögernd ~** to be sticky about letting s. o. have an overdraft; **jem. einen Punkt ~** to yield a point to s. o.
zugestellt delivered, *(Ladung)* made known, served;
ordnungsgemäß ~ duly served; **persönlich ~** *(Ladung)* summoned personally.
zugetan sein, jem. to be attached to (fond of) s. o.; **dem Alkohol ~ sein** to be given to drinking; **der holden Weiblichkeit ~ sein** to be a ladies' man.
zugeteilt allotted, allocated, assigned, rationed;
ganz (teilweise) ~ fully (partly) allotted;
~er Bausparer advanced (borrowing) member *(Br.)*.
Zugewanderter newcomer.
zugewiesen assigned.
Zugewinn *(Ehegatten)* property acquired during the marriage; **~gemeinschaft** community of goods.
zugezogen sein, neu to be a newcomer in a community.
Zugezogener incomer, newcomer.
Zug|fähre train ferry; **~fahrt absichern** to protect a train; **~festigkeit** tensile strength, breaking strain.
Zugfolge train service, train schedule *(US)*;
~ ändern to alter the running of trains; **~ zusammenstellen** to make up a train of cars;
~verkürzung curtailment of service.
Zug|führer train driver, conductor, chief guard *(Br.)*; **~gespräch** *(tel.)* train call; **~glocke** pull bell.
zügig *(Abfertigung)* swift, brisk;
~ arbeiten to work steadily; **~ fahren** to drive smartly; **~ vorankommen** to make headway (good progress); **~ abgefertigt werden** to be dealt with swiftly;
~er Arbeiter steady worker.
Zug|katastrophe *(Unfallversicherung)* train wreck; **~kontrolle** train control; **~kraft** tractive (traction) power, *(Verkaufsartikel)* attention value, draw, pull, attraction, *(Werbung)* advertising appeal; **~kraft von zwanzig Tonnen** pull of twenty tons; **viel an ~kraft eingebüßt haben** to have lost much of its appeal.
zugkräftig attractive, popular, appealing;
sehr ~ sein to have universal appeal;
~er Artikel popular article, draw; **~e Werbung** audience builder.
Zug|maschine traction engine, [motor] tractor; **~meldedienst** train signal(l)ing service; **~mittel** draw; **~nummer** drawing card *(US)*; **~personal** train staff, train crew *(US)*, crew of a train *(US)*; **~pferd** trace horse, draft horse, drafter *(US)*, *(fig.)* drawing card; **~pflaster** *(med.)* blister.
zugreifen to grab for, *(sich bedienen)* to help o. s., *(helfen)* to lend a helping hand;
bei einem Angebot sofort ~ to jump at an offer; **mit beiden Händen ~** to jump at; **rasch ~** to intervene quickly; **tüchtig ~** to tuck in.
Zugriff seizure, quick action, *(Datenverarbeitung)* access;
fester ~ firm grip;
sich dem ~ der Polizei entziehen to flee from the police; **für den ~ offenstehen** to be up for grabs *(sl.)*.
Zugriffs|möglichkeit access to s. one's resources; **~zeit** *(Datenverarbeitung)* access time.
zugrunde gehen to go under, to perish, to decay, to go up *(US coll.)*, to go to pieces, to go to wrack and ruin, to wrack, *(Weltreich)* to pass away;
an einer Krankheit ~ to perish of an illness.
zugrunde|legen to take as basis; **~ liegen** to be at the bottom; **~ liegend** underlying, basic.
zugrunde richten to ruin, to undo, to mar, to destroy, to wreck, to bring to grief, to do up *(US sl.)*;
j. erbarmungslos ~ to smite s. o. hip and thigh; **Firma ~** to ruin a firm; **andere leichtherzig ~** to ruin others with a light heart; **Partei ~** to wreck a party; **sich selbst ~** to cut one's throat.
Zug|schaffner train inspector, guard *(Br.)*, conducter *(US)*, guard of a train *(Br.)*, king *(sl.)*, kayducer *(US sl.)*; **~schranke** railway gate; **~seil** hauling cable; **~tafel** train indicator; **~telefon** train telephone; **~tier** draught animal; **~unglück** train disaster, railway (railroad, *US*) accident.
zugunsten|von for the use and benefit (in aid) of, on behalf (in favo(u)r) of;
~ eines Dritten for the benefit of a third party;
~ des Angeklagten entscheiden to find for the defendant.
zugute halten to make allowances for;
sich auf etw. ~ to pride (plume) o. s. on s. th.
zugute kommen to benefit, to inure to the benefit.
Zug|verbindung train connection; **gute ~- und Omnibusverbindungen** good train and bus connections.
Zugverkehr train service, service (running) of trains;
stündlicher ~ hourly service of trains;
~ zwischen zwei Plätzen einrichten to run a service of trains between two places; **~ einschränken** to cut (curtail) the train service.
Zug|vogel bird of passage, passage bird; **~vorrichtung** traction (hoisting) gear; **~wache** railway (train) guard; **D-~-Wagen** pullman car; **~wechsel** change of trains.
zugweise *(mil.)* in platoons.
Zugzusammen|stellung making up a train, assembling of railway cars; **~stoß** train collision, railway collision.
Zuhälter bully, procurer, pimp, panderer, fancy man.
Zuhälterei pandering, procuring;
von der ~ leben to live on immoral earnings.
zuhauen to hit, *(Bruchsteine)* to dress, *(Tür)* to slam, to bang.
Zuhilfenahme, unter with the aid of;
~ der Waffen recourse to the arms.
Zuhören, hauptsächliche Aufgabe im ~ sehen to be primarily a listener.
zuhören, jem. to lend one's ear to s. o.; **jem. geduldig ~** to bear with s. o.; **sehr genau ~** to listen with both ears; **gespannt ~** to listen with all one's ears; **konzentriert ~** to listen with deep interest; **nur mit halbem Ohr ~** to listen with one ear, to be a half-listener; **im Unterbewußtsein ~** to listen with one's third ear;
gut ~ können to be a good listener.
Zuhörer listener, hearer, auditor, *(pl.)* audience, attendance, turnout, tip *(sl.)*;
aufmerksamer ~ interested (attentive) listener;
~ einer vorausgegangenen Sendung inherited audience;
seine ~ begeistern to kindle the interest of an audience; **aufmerksame ~ finden** to find an attentive audience; **seine ~ nicht mehr zu fesseln vermögen** to lose the power of holding one's audience; **seine ~ zum Stillschweigen verpflichten** to pledge one's hearers to secrecy; **seine ~ in Begeisterung versetzen** to carry one's audience with one;
~analyse audience analysis; **~beteiligung** audience participation (turnover); **~frage** question from the floor; **~raum** audience box (chamber), auditorium; **überfüller ~raum** crowded audience.
Zuhörerschaft audience, attendance, listeners, auditory;
anspruchsvolle ~ critical audience; **aufmerksame ~** eagerly listening assembly; **dürftige ~** slim audience;
große ~ anlocken to draw large audiences; **~ zu stürmischem Beifall hinreißen (mitreißen)** to bring down the house, to sweep one's audience along with one; **~ schätzen** to reckon the size of an audience.
Zukäufe additional purchase;
seine ~ über eine Baisseperiode verteilen to buy on a scale.
zukaufen to buy in addition;
zu seinen Beständen monatlich ~ to add to one's holdings monthly.
Zukaufs|plan, ~programm acquisition program(me).
zukommen *(Gebühren)* to be due, *(schicken)* to send on, to forward;
auf j. ~ to come up to s. o., to approach s. o., to contact s. o.; **auf sich ~ lassen** to wait and see; **seinem Sohn 1000 DM im Jahr ~ lassen** to make one's son an allowance of DM 1000 a year; **jem. eine Nachricht ~ lassen** to send word to s. o.; **seiner Tochter ein Nadelgeld ~ lassen** to allow one's daughter a stipend; **jem. eine Vergünstigung ~ lassen** to confer a benefit on s. o.
Zukunft future;
in ~ *(Vertragstext)* hereafter; **in der fernen ~** in the distant future; **der ~ vorbehalten** deferred;
ferne ~ remote future; **freudlose ~** dark future; **nächste ~** immediate future; **nahe ~** near future;
~ eines Unternehmens business future;
große ~ haben to have a great future, to have fine prospects before one; **für die ~ beseite legen** to lay up in lavender; **sich über die ~ keine Gedanken machen** to be unconcerned about the future; **sich um jds. ~ große Sorgen machen** to have fear for s.

one's future; **jds. ~ in leuchtenden (schillernden) Farben malen** to hold out bright prospects to s. o., to lure s. o. with bright prospects, **in Hinblick auf die ~ planen** to plan with relation to the future; **seine ~ sicherstellen** to provide (make provisions) for the future; **für die ~ seiner Familie sorgen** to make provisions for one's familiy; **jem. eine glänzende ~ in Aussicht stellen** to lure s. o. with bright prospects; **~ vorausplanen** to map a future; **~ voraussagen** to forecast the future; **jem. eine glänzende ~ voraussagen** to predict a brilliant future for s. o.; **jem. eine glänzende ~ vorgaukeln** to dangle bright prospects to s. o.; **für die ~ vorsorgen** to save in anticipation of the future; **sich an jds. ~ interessiert zeigen** to profess an interest in s. one's future.

zukünftig future, prospective, ulterior;
~er Anwalt intending lawyer; **~e Aufträge** future orders; **~er Käufer** prospective buyer; **~e Konjunktur** business future; **~er Kunde** prospective client (customer), prospect *(US)*; **~es Vermögen** future estate, future-acquired property; **~e Verpflichtung** prospective obligation; **~e Verwertung** future use; **~e Zugänge** future additions.

Zukünftiger, mein my intended (husband).

Zukunfts|aussichten eines Unternehmens future prospects of an undertaking; **glänzende ~aussichten haben** to make out for a brilliant future; **europäisches ~bild entwerfen** to envisage a Europe of the future; **~chancen der Raumfahrtindustrie** space outlook; **seine ~chancen vertun** to ruin one's future; **~forschung** futurology, future research; **düstere ~pläne** dim vistas of the future; **~pläne machen** to make plans for the future; **~planung** forward planning work; **industrielle ~planung** private planning; **~prognose** prognostication into the future; **~projekt** future project; **~roman** science fiction; **~schau** future outlook; **~sicherungen treffen** to provide (make provisions) for the future; **ungewisse ~träume** dim vistas of the future; **~weichen stellen** to gear the future.

Zuladung additional load.

Zulage extra pay, surplus, *(Gehaltserhöhung)* rise *(Br.)*, advance, increase, raise *(US)*, *(Gratifikation)* extra pay, bonus, *(Nadelgeld)* pin money, *(Ortszulage)* residential allowance, local bonus, *(Taschengeld)* allowance;
generelle ~ blanket subsidy; **ruhegehaltsfähige ~** pensionable allowance;
~ für den Auslandsaufenthalt *(Diplomat)* foreign service allowance; **~ im Fall einer notwendig werdenden Dauerpflegschaft** constant-attendance allowance; **~n für Familienangehörige** increase for dependants; **~ für behinderte Kinder** handicapped children allowance; **~n für die gestiegenen Lebenshaltungskosten** allowance for cost of living, cost-of-living bonus;
~ bekommen to get a rise *(Br.)*; **~ geben** to give a rise *(Br.)*, to raise a salary *(US)*; **seinem Sohn eine ~ von 1000 DM im Jahr gewähren** to make one's son an allowance (to allow one's son a stipend) of DM 1000 a year;
~staffel scale of allowances.

zulassen to admit, to allow, to permit, *(dulden)* to suffer, *(Konzession gewähren)* to license, to charter;
Anwalt ~ to admit an attorney (a solicitor, *Br.*) to practise law, to license a lawyer, to call to the bar; **als Arzt ~** to license to practise medicine; **zwei Auslegungen ~** to admit of two interpretations; **keine Ausnahme ~** to admit no exception; **Auto ~** to license a motor vehicle, to register (take a) a car's number; **Bank ~** to charter a bank; **Berufung ~** to grant leave to (allow an) appeal; **Berufung nicht ~** to dismiss an appeal; **Beweis ~** to admit in evidence; **zum Börsenhandel ~** to admit for quotation on (list at, *US*) the stock exchange; **keine Diskussion über etw. ~** to admit no discussion on s. th.; **Film ~** to release a film; **als Gastwirt ~** to license to keep an inn; **Journalisten zu einer Gerichtsverhandlung ~** to admit reporters to a trial; **Kaution ~** to grant bail; **Klage ~** to sustain an action; **Konkursforderung ~** to admit (allow) a claim; **Medikamente zum Verkauf ~** to approve a medicine; **zu einer Prüfung ~** to permit (admit) to sit for an examination; **Steuer ~** to authorize the levy of a tax; **Urkunde als Beweismittel ~** to invoke papers in court; **Verkauf ~** to authorize a sale; **keine Verzögerung ~** to permit no delay; **Wertpapiere zur Börse ~** to qualify a security for sale to the public, to quote (list, *US*) a security; **wieder ~** to readmit, to reinstate.

zulässig admissible, allowable, permissible, available, allowed, receivable, *(Parlament)* in order;
gesetzlich ~ permitted by law, legal;
Klage für ~ erklären to declare an action admissible; **Rechtsweg für ~ erklären** to allow legal proceedings; **~ sein** *(Berufung)* to be appealable, *(Klage)* to lie in action; **rechtlich ~ sein** to be good in law;
steuerlich ~e Abschreibungen capital allowance; **~er Beweis** admittable (admissible) evidence; **~e Forderung** allowable claim; **~es Gesamtgewicht** *(Auto)* licensed weight; **~e Geschwindigkeit** speed limit.

Zulässigkeit admissibility, permissibility;
~ eines Beweises admissibility of evidence; **~ einer Eintragung** registrability; **~ des Rechtswegs** admissibility of legal action; **~ einer Klage feststellen** to declare an action admissible.

Zulässigkeitsvermerk *(nicht einklagbarer Vertrag)* sufficient memorandum (note).

Zulassung entrance, admission, admittance, *(Börse)* quotation, listing *(US)*, *(Genehmigung)* leave, allowance, permit, *(Immatrikulation)* entrance, entering, *(Klub)* admission, *(Konzession)* licence, approval, charter, permit, permission, concession, allowance;
aufgrund einer ~ under a licence;
amtliche ~ licensing; **ärztliche ~** licence to practise as a doctor; **bauaufsichtliche ~** building permit (licence); **einstweilige (vorübergehende) ~** temporary admission;
~ zum Anwaltsberuf (zur Anwaltschaft) admission as solicitor *(Br.)* (attorney, *US*, to the bar); **~ der Berufung** leave to appeal; **offizielle ~ zum Börsenhandel** official quotation (listing, *US*); **~ von Effekten** admission of securities; **~ zum Geschäftsbetrieb** letters of business *(Br.)*, commercial privilege, licence to operate; **~ eines Kraftfahrzeugs** licensing of a motor vehicle, new car registration; **~ für Personenbeförderung** passenger certificate; **~ von Personenkraftwagen** passenger-car registration; **~ der Presse** admission of the press; **~ zur Promotion** grace; **~ als Rechtsanwalt** admission to the bar *(Br.)* (as attorney, *US*); **~ eines Rechtsmittels** writ of review; **~ der Revision** leave to appeal; **~ zum Studium** access to studies; **~ zur zollfreien Wiedereinfuhr** duty-free admission;
~ beantragen to apply for a licence (concession), to seek admission; **~ zur Börse beantragen** to apply for official quotation *(Br.)*, to qualify with the U.S. Securities and Exchange Commission *(US)*; **sich eine ~ erschleichen** to obtain a licence under false pretences; **einem Arzt die ~ erteilen** to license a doctor to practise medicine; **~ erwerben, sich eine ~ geben lassen** to take out a licence (permit); **~ gewähren** to grant a concession (charter); **um ~ nachsuchen** to apply for permission, to seek admission; **zur ~ berechtigt sein** to have the privilege of being admitted; **~ widerrufen** to revoke a licence.

Zulassungs|alter entry age; **~anspruch** right of admission; **~antrag** *(Verein)* application for admission, membership application; **~ausschuß** eligibility (admission) committee; **~ausschuß für Kassenärzte** medical practices committee; **~ausweis** registration certificate (card); **~beamter** admission officer; **~bedingungen** rules for (terms of) admission; **erleichterte ~bedingungen** easing of admission requirements; **~bedingungen erfüllen** to be eligible for admission; **~behörde** licensing authority.

zulassungsberechtigt admissible, qualified, eligible.

Zulassungs|berechtigung admissibility, eligibility, qualification; **~bescheid** *(Börseneinführung)* official listing notice *(US)*; **~bescheinigung** licence, permit; **~bescheinigung eines Flugzeugs** certificate of airworthiness; **~beschränkungen** entrance restrictions, *(Kfz)* licensing restrictions; **~bestimmungen** terms of admission; **~erfordernisse** qualification requirements.

zulassungsfähig eligible for admission, *(Aktien)* negotiable on the stock exchange, qualified to list *(US)*.

Zulassungs|frist period of qualification; **~gebühr** entrance (admission) fee, *(Auto)* registration fee; **vorläufige ~genehmigung** temporary registration; **~gesuch** application for admission; **~karte** admission ticket; **~nummer** registration number *(Br.)*, licence number *(US)*, permit number; **~ordnung** licensing regulations; **~ort** location *(US)*; **~papiere** car (driving) papers, car licence *(US)*, registration certificate; **Fahrzeug von der ~pflicht befreien** to exempt a vehicle from the obligation to register.

zulassungspflichtig in need of (subject) to a licence (to approval).

Zulassungs|prüfung entrance (previous) examination, admission test, test paper *(Br.)*, *(Staatsdienst)* competitive examination, *(Universität)* matriculation examination *(Br.)*; **~prüfung bestehen** to pass the entrance examination; **~quote** admission quota; **~schein** ticket of admission, permit; **~schild** *(Auto)* number plate, licence plate *(US)*; **~staat** *(Auto)* state of registration; **~statistik** *(Kfz)* car-registration statistics; **~stelle** admission board, registration office, *(Börse)* Secretary of the Share and Loan Department *(Br.)*, Committee on Stock List

(US), (Kraftfahrzeuge) traffic commissioner *(Br.)*; ~**stempel** *(TÜV)* date-stamp registration letter; ~**urkunde** registration certificate; ~**verfahren** admittance process, qualification procedure, *(Lizenzierung)* licensing procedure; ~**verweigerung** nonadmission; ~**voraussetzungen** requirements (terms) for admission, qualification (entrance) requirements, *(Vereine)* membership requirements; **gewerbepolizeiliche ~voraussetzungen** licensing requirements; ~**voraussetzungen erfüllen** to be eligible for admission, *(Anwalt)* to qualify for the bar; ~**wettbewerb** competitive (entrance) examination; ~**zeichen** registration mark.

Zulauf rush, crowd, throng;
großer ~ large custom, run;
großen ~ haben to have a great run (large custom), to be very popular, to be much run after (all the go), *(Anwalt, Arzt)* to have a large practice, *(Theaterstück)* to have a powerful draw, to be a box-office success *(US)*, *(Vortragender)* to draw a full house;
~**menge** flow rate.

zulegen, sich etw. to give o. s. a treat, to acquire (treat o. s. to, equip o. s. with) s. th.; **sich einen Bart ~** to sport a beard; **sich einen Bauch ~** to develop a paunch; **sich eine Erkältung ~** to catch a cold; **jem. am Gehalt ~** to raise s. one's salary *(US)*, to increase s. one's pay; **bei einem Geschäft fünfhundert Pfund ~** to lose five hundred pounds on a deal; **sich einen Namen ~** to adopt (assume) a new name; **sich einen neuen Rock ~** to treat o. s. to a new coat; **am Tempo ~** to step up the pace (on the gas, *coll.*).

Zulegung eines Namens adoption of a name.

Zuleitungs|draht *(Antenne)* lead-in; ~**kabel** supply cable.

zuliebe, jem. etw. ~ tun to do s. th. to please s. o.

Zulieferant, Zulieferer [component] supplier, subcontractor;
als ~ arbeiten to carry out subcontracting work, to subcontract.

Zulieferungs|auftrag subcontract; ~**auftrag an j. vergeben** to subcontract s. th. out to s. o.; ~**betrieb** manufacturing subsidiary, feeder plant, component supplier, supplier company, mill-supply house (firm) *(Br.)*; ~**industrie** supplying (ancillary) industry, supplier's trade, supply business; ~**material** fabricating material; ~**programm** supply program(me); ~**tätigkeit** subcontracted work; ~**teile** fabricating parts; ~**vertrag** subcontract; ~**werk der Rüstungsindustrie** defence supplier.

zumachen *(Geschäft)* to be closing down, to close down, to shut up, *(Loch)* to fill;
ganze Nacht kein Auge ~ not to sleep a wink all night; **Filiale ~** to close down a branch office; **Tür ~** to shut the door; **vorübergehend ~** to close temporarily.

zumauern to wall (brick) up.

zumessen to admeasure, to apportion, to allocate;
Belohnungen ~ to mete out rewards; **Strafe ~** to inflict (mete out) punishment.

Zumessung einer Strafe admeasurement of a punishment.

zumutbar reasonable.

zumuten to expect, to ask, to exact, to demand;
sich zuviel ~ to overtax (overtask) one's strength, to take too much on one's shoulder, to bite off more than one can chew.

Zumutung unreasonable demand.

Zunahme increase, advance, rise, step-up *(US)*, *(Vermehrung)* augmentation, aggrandizement, increment, *(Wachstum)* accession, accretion, growth, *(Wertzuwachs)* increment, gain;
entsprechende ~ proportional increase; **leichte ~** slight increase; **rapide ~** mushroom growth; **ständige ~** steady increase; **~ des Anlagevermögens** increase in fixed assets, gain in assets; **~ der Arbeitslosigkeit** increase (rise) in unemployment; **merkliche ~ der Autoverkäufe** marked increase in car sales; **~ der Bevölkerung** population increase; **~ des Bruttoinlandsprodukts** gross domestic product growth; **~ der Einkünfte** increase in receipts; **~ des Geschäfts** growth of business; **~ der Gewinne** rise in profits; **~ des Kinderprozentsatzes** increase in child population; **~ der Kosten** increasing costs; **~ des Notenumlaufs** increase of notes in circulation; **~ des Reiseverkehrs** travel growth; **~ der Rücklagen** growth of reserves; **~ der Spareinlagen** growth of savings deposits; **~ der Spartätigkeit** increase in savings; **~ des Verbrauchs** increase in consumption; **~ des Verkehrs** increase in traffic;
in der ~ begriffen sein to be increasing;
~**faktor** growth factor; ~**rate** growth rate, rate of increase.

Zuname surname, last (family) name, cognomen.

Zünd|anlage ignition system; ~**batterie** ignition battery; ~**einstellung** ignition timing.

zünden to kindle, to light, *(Auto)* to spark, to ignite, *(Begeisterung hervorrufen)* to inspire enthusiasm, *(vom Blitz)* to strike;
bei ihm wird es nun endlich ~ the penny will drop with him at last.

zündend|e Rede stirring speech; ~**e Worte** rousing words.

Zunder punk, tinder;
~ bekommen to catch it *(sl.)*; **wie ~ brennen** to burn like tinder.

Zünder ignitor, *(Sprengstoff)* fuse.

Zunderholz touchwood, punk *(US)*.

Zünd|flamme *(Gasboiler)* pilot burner; ~**funke** spark; ~**holzschachtel** matchbox; ~**kabel** distribution cable; ~**kerze** spark *(US)* (sparking, *Br.*) plug; ~**punkteinstellung** ignition timing; ~**schloß** ignition lock; ~**schlüssel** ignition key; ~**schnur** fuse; ~**stromkreis** ignition circuit.

Zündung spark, ignition;
schlecht funktionierende ~ reluctant starter;
~ zurückstellen (vorstellen) to retard (advance) the spark.

Zündverstellkabel ignition lever.

Zündwaren|monopol match monopoly; ~**steuer** duty on matches *(Br.)*, tax on lighting materials *(US)*.

Zunehmen, im ~ begriffen sein to be on the increase.

zunehmen to increase, to advance, to augment, *(Gewicht)* to put on weight, *(Mond)* to wax, *(Tage)* to grow longer, *(Umsatz)* to pick up, *(wachsen)* to grow;
beängstigend ~ to increase at a fearful rate; **beträchtlich ~** to grow considerably; **explosionsartig ~** to mushroom; **ständig ~** to go on increasing; **stark ~** *(Aufträge)* to come in strong; **an Stärke ~** to gain in strength; **im Wert ~** to improve [in value], to appreciate in value; **wertmäßig durch kumulierte Zuwächse ~** to build up by the addition of increments; **zahlenmäßig ~** to increase in numbers.

zunehmend increasing, advancing;
mit ~em Alter with advancing years; ~**e Erträge** increasing returns; ~**e Geschwindigkeit** accelerated velocity; ~**e Gewitterneigung** increasing tendency to thunderstorms; ~**e Kosten** increasing costs.

zuneigen, sich jem. to bend to s. o.; **jds. Ansicht ~** to fall in with s. o.; **sich dem Ende ~** to draw to a close.

Zuneigung affection, attachment, liking;
aufrichtige ~ entire affection; **eheliche ~** marital affection; **gegenseitige ~** mutual affection; **natürliche ~** natural affection; **Platz eines anderen in jds. ~ einnehmen** to displace s. o. in s. one's affection; **~ für j. empfinden** to have an inclination towards s. o.; **sich jds. ~ erschleichen** to wind o. s. into s. one's affection; **~ für jem. gefaßt haben** to have an attachment for s. o.

Zunft [craft] guild, corporation, fellowship, society;
~ der Journalisten brotherhood of journalists; **~ der Kritiker** critical fraternity; **~ der Taschendiebe** light-fingered gentry; ~**geist** party-spirit, sectarianism, caste feeling; ~**haus** hall; ~**meister** warden *(Br.)*; ~**mitglieder** liverymen *(Br.)*; ~**recht** exclusive privilege; ~**wesen** guild system.

zünftige Ausrüstung proper gear (outfit).

Zunge tongue, *(Rechenschieber)* sliding scale, *(Waage)* tongue, needle, pointer;
lästerliche ~n wagging tongues; **lose ~** unbridled tongue; **jem. auf der ~ brennen, etw. zu erzählen** to be dying to tell s. o.; **geläufige ~ haben** to have the gift of the gab; **schwere ~ haben** to have a slurred speech; **spitze ~ haben** to have a sharp tongue; **etw. auf der ~ liegen haben** to have s. th. at the tip of one's tongue; **seine ~ hüten** to hold (guard) one's tongue; **mit doppelter ~ reden** to speak with forked tongue, to be two-faced; **sein Herz auf der ~ tragen** to wear one's heart on one's sleeve; **sich die ~ verbrennen** to open one's mouth too wide.

züngeln *(Flammen)* to flicker, to lick.

Zungenbrecher tongue twister, jawbreaker.

zungenbrecherisch jawbreaking.

Zungenfertigkeit volubility.

Zünglein an der Waage tip of the scales;
~ bilden to hold the balance, to be the makeweight.

zunichte machen to frustrate, to knock on the head, to upset;
jds. Hoffnungen ~ to squash (kill, cut) s. one's hopes; **Plan praktisch ~** to kick the crutches from under a scheme; **jds. Pläne ~** to ruin (frustrate) s. one's plans, to upset s. one's applecart; **jds. Werk ~** to mar s. one's work.

zunichte werden to come to nought, to end up in smoke.

zunicken, jem. to give s. o. a nod.

zunutze machen, sich to utilize, to take advantage of, to turn to account (to one's profit);
sich die Gutgläubigkeit eines Kunden ~ to trade on the credulity of a client; **sich eine Idee ~** to cash in on an idea.

zuordnen to attribute, to allocate.
Zuordungs|problem assignment problem; ~**test** association test.
zupacken, kräftig to knuckle down.
zuraten, jem. zu einem Hauskauf to recommend s. o. to buy a house.
zurechenbar attributable, chargeable, imputable;
nicht ~ *(Einkünfte)* nonattributable;
~**e Einkünfte** attributable income; ~**e Kenntnis** imputed notice.
Zurechenbarkeit chargeability, imputability;
~ **der Kenntnis des Erfüllungsgehilfen** sole actor doctrine.
zurechnen *(addieren)* to add to, *(zuschreiben)* to impute, to ascribe;
~ **zu** to reckon (number) to;
Gewinne steuerlich ~ to attribute (allocate) profits; **einem Konto** ~ to debit (charge to) an account; **Zinsen zum Kapital** ~ to add interest to the capital.
Zurechnung addition, *(Dotierung)* allocation, *(fig.)* imputation, attribution;
unter ~ **von** adding; **unter** ~ **aller Kosten** including all charges; **steuerliche** ~ **von Gewinnen** attribution of profits.
zurechnungsfähig responsible, of sane memory (sound mind, *US*), accountable, competent;
nicht ~ not responsible, out of one's head *(US)*, non compos mentis, unaccountable.
Zurechnungsfähigkeit responsibility, sound mind *(US)*, mental capacity, accountability, competence, power, *(strafrechtlich)* discretion, criminal responsibility (liability), *(Unterscheidungsvermögen)* discernment;
bedingte ~ limited responsibility; **eingeschränkte (verminderte)** ~ diminished responsibility.
Zurechnungssystem *(Körperschaftssteuer)* imputation system *(Br.)*.
zurechtbiegen to lick into shape;
verfahrene Angelegenheit ~ to set things straight.
zurechtfinden, sich to find one's place (way about); **sich gut** ~ to shake down nicely; **sich tastend** ~ to feel one's way; **sich überhaupt nicht mehr** ~ not to be able to see what's what; **jem. sich** ~ **helfen** to keep s. o. straight.
zurechtgewiesen werden to be put on the carpet *(Br.)*.
zurechtkommen to manage, to get on;
mit jem. gut ~ to get on with s. o., to have a way with s. o.; **mit etw.** ~ to get into the knack of s. th.; **ganz gut allein** ~ to do well enough on one's own; **mit einer Arbeit** ~ to get on with a job; **auch ohne Geldmittel** ~ to manage in spite of lack of funds; **mit den Leuten** ~ to get along (have a winning way) with people.
zurechtlegen, sich eine Ausrede to have a pretext ready.
zurechtmachen to doctor, to cook, *(Bilanz)* to fake up, to doctor, *(Buch)* to get up, to edit;
sich ~ to tidy o. s., to make o. s. up, to smarten, to do s. o. up; **Kabine** ~ to trim a cabin; **beschädigte Waren wieder** ~ to render goods marketable.
zurechtschustern, Zeitungsartikel to fake a newspaper article.
zurechtsetzen, jem. den Kopf to bring s. o. to reason.
zurechtweisen to reprimand, to rebuke, to carpet *(Br.)*;
j. ~ to pull s. one's nose, to put s. o. in his place, to relegate s. o., to have s. o. on the mat, to talk to s. o.; **j. gehörig (scharf)** ~ to talk to s. o. like a Dutch uncle, to pull up stakes with s. o. *(US)*, to tell off *(mil., sl.)*.
Zurechtweisung reprimand, correction, setdown, rebuke, tingle *(coll.)*.
zurechtstutzen to fudge up.
Zureden, gütliches moral suasion *(Br.)*.
zureden, jem. gut to encourage (persuade) s. o.
Zurichtebogen *(drucktechn.)* register sheet, overlay.
Zurichten punishmeant *(coll.)*.
zurichten to prepare, to fit up, *(appretieren)* to finish, *(Setzerei)* to dress, to range, to overlay, to make ready, *(techn.)* to adjust, to fit;
j. übel ~ to beat s. o. up.
Zu|richter *(drucktechn.)* assistant minder, *(metallurgisch)* dresser; ~**richterei** adjusting (dressing) shop; ~**richtung** fitting up, *(Satz)* make ready, *(techn.)* bed, dressing, making ready.
zürnen, jem. to bear a grudge against s. o.
Zurschaustellen display, exposure, exhibition;
sittenwidriges ~ indecent exhibition.
Zurschaustellung display, exposure, exhibition, parade;
aufdringliche ~ **seines Reichtums** vulgar display of one's wealth.
zurück back, *(im Rückstand)* in arrears, behindhand, *(zurückgesandt)* returned;
hin und ~ out and home.
zurückabtreten to reassign.
zurückbegeben to negotiate back;
sich ~ to return.
zurückbegleiten to escort back.
zurückbehalten to keep (hold) back, to detain;
Eigentum ~ to retain property; **Lohnsteuer** ~ to withhold a tax from wage payment; **sicherheitshalber** ~ to distrain; **Teile des Geldes** ~ to retain part of the money; **Ware** ~ to detain goods; **restliche Ware** ~ to hold over the rest of the goods.
Zurückbehaltung withholding, recoupment, retention;
unberechtigte ~ forcible detainer, detinue;
~ **von Waren** retention of goods.
Zurückbehaltungsberechtigter lienor.
Zurückbehaltungsrecht retainer, lien on goods, equitable (special) lien, retaining lien;
allgemeines ~ general (common-law) lien; **gerichtlich festgestelltes** ~ judgment lien *(US)*; **gesetzliches** ~ lien by operation of law, statutory (common-law) lien; **gewerbliches** ~ mechanic's (artisan's) lien; **gleichrangige** ~**e** *(Seeversicherung)* concurrent liens;
~ **an Aktien** charging lien; ~ **eines Anwalts an den Akten** attorney's charging (retaining) lien; ~ **der Banken** bank's lien *(Br.)*; ~ **des Frachtführers** carrier's lien; ~**an einem bestimmten Gegenstand** special lien; ~ **des Handwerkers** artisan's (mechanic's) lien; ~ **des Kommissionärs** lien of factor of common law; ~ **an einem Scheck** lien on a cheque (check, *US*); ~ **des Spediteurs** carrier's lien; ~ **des Verkäufers** seller's lien; ~ **aus Werklieferungsvertrag** materialman's lien;
kaufmännisches ~ **ausüben** to stop goods in transit; ~ **des Gastwirts ausüben** to seize s. one's personal effects; ~ **an Aktien erhalten** to retain a lien on shares; ~ **an einer Ladung haben** to have a lien upon a cargo; ~ **an einer Sache geltend machen** to lay a lien on s. th.
zurückbekommen to get back, to regain, to recover;
seine Auslagen ~ to recover one's disbursements; **verlorenen Gegenstand** ~ to recover a lost article; **sein Geld** ~ to recover one's money; **Vorschußzahlungen** ~ to recover money advanced.
zurückbelasten to charge back.
zurückbeordern to order back;
jem. auf seinen Posten ~ to order s. o. back to his post.
Zurückberufung *(dipl.)* recall.
Zurückberufungsschreiben letter of recall.
zurückbezahlen to pay back, to repay, to refund, to reimburse, to discharge, to clear, to wipe off;
erste Hypothek ~ to pay off the first mortgage *(Br.)*; **seine Schulden** ~ to discharge one's liabilities.
Zurückbezahlung repayment, refunding, reimbursement, discharge.
zurückbeziehen to relate back.
Zurückbeziehung auf das Datum des Konkurseröffnungsantrages relating back to the date of filing the petition of bankruptcy.
Zurückbeziehungsgrundsatz *(Konkurs)* rule of relation back.
zurückbezogen retrospective.
Zurückbleiben eines Kulturzweiges culture lag.
zurückbleiben to drop behind, to lag, to stay behind, *(hinter Flugformation)* to straggle, *(Rest)* to be left over, *(überleben)* to survive, *(Umsätze)* to fall short;
hinter den Erwartungen ~ to fall short of expectations; **nicht hinter der Lebensführung der Nachbarn** ~ to keep up with the Joneses; **hinter dem Vorjahr** ~ *(Produktion)* to drop off from last year; **als Waise** ~ to be orphaned; **hinter der Zeit** ~ to be behind the times.
zurückbleibend residuary.
zurückblenden *(Film, Roman)* to pull back.
zurückbringen, j. auf sein eigentliches Anliegen to bring s. o. back to his actual business; **Goldabflüsse aus dem Ausland** ~ to repatriate gold; **wieder auf den vorigen Stand** ~ to restore to a level.
zurückdatieren to antedate, to date back.
Zurückdatierung antedating, *(Wechsel)* backvalue dating.
zurückdenken to recall, to remember, to recollect.
zurückdrängen, Einfluß des linken Flügels to break the left-wing grip; **Feind** ~ to press back the enemy; **Menge** ~ *(Polizei)* to push back the crowd.
Zurückdrängung moving back.
zurückerhalten to recover, to get back;
Besitz ~ to recover possession by law; **sein Geld** ~ to recover one's money; **sein verlorenes Vermögen** ~ to recover one's lost fortune; **Zollkaution** ~ to obtain a refund of the money deposited.

zurückerlangen to recover, to get back, to regain;
Eigentum ~ to recover title; **sein Vermögen** ~ to retrieve one's fortune.
Zurückerlangung recovery, getting back;
~ **des Eigentums** recovery of title; ~ **seines Vermögens** retrieval of one's fortune.
zurückerobern to reconquer, to recover, to retake.
zurückerstatten to give back, to return, to reimburse, to refund, to restitute, to restore, to render;
Auslagen ~ to refund the expenses (disbursements); **Geld** ~ to refund money, to pay back, to repay, to reimburse; **Geld dem Eigentümer** ~ to restore money to the owner; **zuviel gezahltes Geld** ~ to return an overpaid amount; **Portoauslagen** ~ to refund the cost of postage, to reimburse for postage incurred; **gerechtfertigte Spesen** ~ to refund properly incurred expenses.
Zurückerstattung restitution, restoration, *(Geld)* reimbursement, refund[ing], repayment;
~ **des Kaufpreises** refund of the purchase price.
zurückerwerben to reacquire.
zurückfahren to go back by train (bus, car), *(mit Fahrzeug)* to drive back.
zurückfallen, an die Familie to return to the family; **in schlechte Gewohnheiten** ~ to relapse into bad habits; **in den Müßiggang** ~ to lapse back into idleness; **stark** ~ *(Aktien)* to be a little high back; **an den Vorbesitzer** ~ to revert to the previous owner.
zurückfallend revertible.
zurück | finden, zu sich selbst to regain one's peace of mind; **~fliegen** to fly back; **~fließen** to reflux, to flow back; **~fordern** to claim back, to reclaim, to revindicate, to redemand.
Zurückforderung reclamation, revindication.
zurückführbar reducible, traceable.
zurückführen *(in die Heimat)* to repatriate;
auf etw. ~ to put down to s. th.; **Kapital** ~ to repatriate capital; **auf Kindheitserfahrungen** ~ to trace back to a childhood experience; **Kontoüberziehung** ~ to reduce an overdraft; **Krankheit auf Verschmutzung** ~ to attribute a disease to filth; **auf ein Minimum** ~ to reduce to a minimum; **Problem auf eine einfache Formel** ~ to reduce a problem to a simple formula; **Unfall auf die Unvorsichtigkeit des Fahrers** ~ to impute an accident to the driver's carelessness; **j. auf den rechten Weg** ~ to lead s. o. back to the straight and narrow; **j. auf den Weg der Pflicht** ~ to reclaim s. o. to a sense of his duty.
Zurückführung reduction, *(in die Heimat)* repatriation;
~ **einer Kontoüberziehung** reduction of an overdraft; ~ **in den Zivilberuf** resettlement.
zurückgeben to give back, to return, to restore, to restitute, to redeliver, to render;
seine Ausrüstung ~ to turn in one's equipment; **geliehene Bücher** ~ to restore (return) borrowed books; **beschlagnahmtes Eigentum** ~ to restore confiscated property; **erobertes Gebiet** ~ to recede conquered territory; **gestohlene Gegenstände** ~ to restore stolen goods; **zuviel gezahltes Geld** ~ to return an overpaid amount; **Scheck an den Aussteller** ~ to refer a cheque (check, *US*) to the drawer; **jem. sein Selbstvertrauen** ~ to restore s. one's confidence; **Vermögensgegenstand dem rechtmäßigen Eigentümer** ~ to return property to its rightful owner; **seine Vollmacht** ~ to divest o. s. of one's authority.
zurückgeblieben backward, slow, inept, unapt;
geistig ~ retarded.
Zurückgebliebener *(geistig)* dodo, backward child;
wirtschaftlich ~ economic laggard.
Zurückgebliebensein retardation.
zurückgedrängt back on one's heels.
zurückgefordert, nicht unreclaimed, donated stock *(US)*.
zurückgegangen *(Geschäft)* diminished;
im Preis ~ gone down in price.
zurückgegebene Gründeraktie donated stock *(US)*.
zurückgehalten | es Schiff detained ship; **~e Wut** suppressed anger.
Zurückgehen *(Ausgaben)* diminution, decrease, *(Flut)* abatement, subsidence, *(Handel)* recession, *(Preise)* decline, fall, drop.
zurückgehen to go back, *(Aufträge)* to go down, to drop, *(Einnahmen)* to fall off, *(Feind)* to retreat, to give way, to fall back, *(Flut)* to ebb, *(Handel)* to slacken, to recede, *(Hochwasser)* to subside, to abate, *(Konjunktur)* to dip, to move backwards (downwards), *(Kurse, Preise)* to [be on the] decline, to fall off, to give way, to recede, to decrease, to diminish, to drop, to go down, *(mil.)* to lose ground, to retreat, *(Praxis)* to drop off, *(Temperatur)* to fall, to drop, *(Unternehmen)* to go down, *(im Wert)* to deteriorate;
weit in die Geschichte ~ to go far in history; **auf den Krieg** ~ to date to from the war; **um zwei Punkte** ~ to drop (recede) two points; **Tag um Tag** ~ to be declining daily; **volumenmäßig** ~ to fall in volume terms;
~ **lassen** to send back, to return.
zurückgehend declining;
~e Waren returnable goods.
zurück | gekehrt, nicht unreturned; **~gelegte Entfernung** distance covered; **~gesandt** returned.
zurückgesetzt neglected, ignored, *(Ware)* marked-down, reduced in price;
~e Waren old stock.
zurückgestellt *(mil.)* deferred *(US)*, *(Mittel)* earmarked;
~ **werden** to go over, to be adjourned, *(Geld)* to be reserved, *(mil.)* to be deferred;
~e Investitionsvorhaben deferral of investment program(me)s; **~er Pfändungsauftrag** dormant execution.
Zurückgestellter *(Wehrdienst)* conscript exempted provisionally, deferrable *(US)*.
zurück | getreten resigned, retired; **~gewähren** to return, *(Geld)* to refund, to reimburse; **~gewiesene Waren** rejected goods.
Zurückgewinnung recovery.
zurückgezahlt repaid *(US)*;
nicht ~ unrepaid.
zurückgezogen quiet, secluded, close, private, retired;
sich ~ **haben** to be out of business; **völlig** ~ **leben** to live a secluded life (out of the world), to live in seclusion;
~er Antrag abandoned motion.
Zurückgezogenheit seclusion, privacy, retreat.
zurückgirieren to reindorse.
zurückgreifen to fall back upon, to take recourse to, to hark back;
auf einen Fonds ~ to resort to a fund;
auf seine Ersparnisse ~ **können** to have a sum put by to fall back upon.
zurückhalten to keep (hold) back, *(jur.)* to detain, to restrain, *(Käufer)* to hold back;
sich ~ to stand back, to efface (withhold, restrain) o. s., to keep one's distance; **Aktien in Erwartung von Kurssteigerungen** ~ to hold stocks for a rise; **seinen Ärger** ~ to suppress one's anger; **seinen Ärger nicht** ~ to give vent to one's anger; **seine Gefühle** ~ to bottle up one's feelings; **sich in jds. Gegenwart betont** ~ to show constraint in s. one's presence; **Informationen** ~ to keep (hold) back (suppress)information; **seine Kräfte** ~ to pull one's punches; **mit seiner Meinung** ~ to reserve one's judgment, to keep one's counsel; **die Menschenmenge** ~ to hold the crowd back; **sich mit der Verwirklichung geplanter Kapazitätsausweitungen** ~ to hold back on bringing new capacity; **restliche Ware** ~ to hold over the rest of the goods; **etw. wissentlich** ~ to keep s. th. in the background.
zurückhaltend reserved, standoffish, distant, passive, buttoned-up, icy, *(Börse)* flat, dead, dull, inactive, stagnant, *(Käufer)* reluctant, cautious;
sich sehr ~ **über einen Plan äußern** not to show much enthusiasm for a plan; ~ **disponieren** to show caution in placing orders; ~ **schreiben** to write with restraint; **sehr** ~ **sein** to keep one's distance; **mit seinem Lob sehr** ~ **sein** to be sparing with one's praise; ~ **sprechen** to speak with constraint;
~e Stimmung reserve of manner, *(Börse)* reserved (dull) tendency.
Zurückhaltung keeping back, constraint, ice, distance, retention, reserve, *(Behaltung)* detention, detainment, *(Bescheidenheit)* shyness, coyness, *(Börse)* stagnancy, stagnation, flatness, dullness, inactivity, *(Einbehaltung)* retention, *(Käufer)* restraining, restraint, hesitation, reluctance, *(Schiff)* detainment, *(Selbstbeherrschung)* restraint;
persönliche ~ self-effacement; **staatliche** ~ reluctance of the state; **weise** ~ prudent silence;
~ **eines Gesetzentwurfs** pocket veto *(US)*; **widerrechtliche** ~ **von Grundbesitz** forcible detainer; ~ **von Informationen** suppression of information; ~ **bei Neuanlagen** caution over new investment; ~ **eines Schiffes** detention of a ship; ~ **bei den Stahlausfuhren** steel export restraint; ~ **auf der Verbraucherseite** consumer caution, consumer resistance; ~ **am Wochenende** *(Börse)* pre-weekend caution; ~ **von Zahlungen** withholding of payments;
sich ~ **auferlegen** to hold one's fire, to put restraint upon o. s., to maintain an attitude of reserve, to know one's place; **sich** ~ **bei der Auftragserteilung auferlegen** to show caution in placing orders; **seine beruflich anerzogene** ~ **als leitender Angestellter aufgeben** to shed one's upright executive control; ~ **üben** to exercise reserve; ~ **bei der Verwirklichung bereits geplanter**

Kapazitätsausweitungen üben to hold back on bringing in planned new capacity; **in politischen Fragen ~ zeigen** to keep in the background on a political matters.
zurückholen, Kapitalien aus dem Ausland to repatriate funds.
zurückkaufen to repurchase, to buy back, to rebuy, *(Börse)* to buy in, *(Pfänder)* to redeem;
frühere Emissionen ~ to retire outstanding issues; **Sicherheit** ~ *(Treuhänder)* to redeem a security; **Versicherungspolice** ~ to surrender an insurance policy.
zurückkehren to return, to come again, *(Emigrant)* to re-emigrate, *(Schiff)* to put back;
zu seinem früheren Gesprächsthema ~ to recur to a former subject, to return to one's muttons; **so schnell wie möglich nach Hause** ~ to make the best of one's way home; **in seine Heimat** ~ to go back to one's native land, to return home; **langsam** ~ *(Erinnerung)* to come back gradually; **auf einen Posten** ~ to return to a position.
Zurückkommen recurrence.
zurückkommen, auf ein Angebot to refer to s. one's offer; **zum ursprünglichen Eigentümer** ~ to return to the original owner; **immer wieder auf etw.** ~ to harp upon the same string; **nie mehr** ~ to have gone for good and all; **unter Protest** ~ to return under protest; **auf eine Sache später noch einmal** ~ to return later to a subject, to revert to a matter in due course; **auf ein Thema** ~ to go back (return) to a subject; **immer wieder** ~ to come back like a bad penny.
zurücklassen, sein Gepäck am Bahnhof to leave one's luggage (baggage, *US*) at the station.
zurücklegen to lay aside (by, up), to put (set) by, to store up, to pigeon-hole, *(zweckbestimmt)* to earmark for;
Antrag zunächst ~ to shelve a petition; **Entfernung** ~ to cover a distance; **Geld für sein Alter** ~ to lay aside money (be saving) for one's old age; **Geld für unvorhergesehene Ereignisse** ~ to reserve money for unforeseen contingencies; **Hälfte seines Monatsgehalts** ~ to save half of one's salary every month; **Karten** ~ to reserve tickets; **für einen Notfall (Notgroschen)** ~ to put away for a rainy day; **Strecke in Etappen** ~ to cover a distance by stages; **ein gutes Stück Weges** ~ to cover a distance; **Teil seines Einkommens** ~ to set aside a part of one's income; **wöchentlich ganz beachtlich vom Lohn** ~ to save a nice little sum out of one's wages each week; **Ware** ~ to store (lay up, away, *US*) goods.
Zurücklegung putting aside, *(Geld)* saving.
zurückmelden, sich to report one's return;
sich vom Urlaub ~ to report back from leave.
Zurücknahme taking back, withdrawal, retraction, revocation;
~ **eines Antrags** withdrawal of a motion; ~ **einer Bewerbung** withdrawal of an application; ~ **eines Einspruchs** withdrawal of an opposition; ~ **einer Klage** withdrawal (discontinuance) of action (one's suit, *US*); ~ **einer Konzession** revocation (withdrawal) of a licence; ~ **einer Kündigung** withdrawal of a notice; ~ **einer Lizenz** revocation of a licence; ~ **eines Patents** revocation of a patent; ~ **einer Satzung** revocation of a charter; ~ **einer Schenkung** revocation of a donation; ~ **eines Strafantrages** withdrawal of a charge; ~ **eines Vertragsangebots** revocation of an offer; ~ **einer Vollmacht** revocation (withdrawal) of a power of attorney.
zurücknehmen to take back, to revoke, to withdraw, to retract, *(Gas)* to throttle;
Anschuldigung ~ to retract an accusation; **Antrag** ~ to revoke (withdraw) a motion; **Auftrag** ~ to cancel (countermand) an order; **beleidigende Äußerung** ~ to withdraw an offending expression; **Berufung** ~ to withdraw an appeal; **Einspruch** ~ to withdraw opposition; **Entscheidung** ~ to rescind a decree; **leere Flaschen** ~ to take empty bottles back; **Klage** ~ to withdraw an action, to relinquish (discontinue) a suit *(US)*; **Konzession** ~ to withdraw a concession, to revoke a grant; **Kündigung** ~ to withdraw a notice; **Lizenz** ~ to vacate a charter, to revoke a licence; **auf ein Niveau** ~ to reduce to a level; **Patent** ~ to revoke a patent; **Satzung** ~ to vacate a charter; **Strafantrag** ~ to withdraw a charge; **Truppen aus einer vorgeschobenen (unhaltbaren) Stellung** ~ to withdraw troops from an exposed position; **Versprechen** ~ to take down a pledge; **Vertragsangebot** ~ to revoke an offer; **Vollmacht** ~ to revoke a power of attorney; **unverkaufte Waren** ~ to take back unsold goods.
zurück|pfeifen, seinen Hund to whistle one's dog back; **~reisen** to travel back; **j. vom Abgrund ~reißen** to rescue s. o. from the edge of a precipice.
zurückrufen to recall, to call back, *(Wechsel)* to withdraw;
j. ~ to order s. o. home; **sich ins Gedächtnis** ~ to recall to memory; **ins Leben** ~ to bring back to life.
zurückschicken to send back, to return;
Wechsel mit Akzept ~ to return a bill accepted; **Wechsel mit Protest** ~ to return a bill protested.
zurück|schieben, jem. einen Eid to tender back an oath to s. o.; **~schlagen** *(mil.)* to strike back, to retaliate; **Überflüsse der Öllánder in den weltwirtschaftlichen Kreislauf ~schleusen** to recycle the oil countries' surpluses into the world economy.
zurückschrauben, Ansprüche to reduce (moderate) one's claims;
Preise ~ to reduce (roll back, *US*) prices.
zurückschrecken, vor etw. to shy away from s. th.; **vor nichts** ~ to hesitate (stop) at nothing.
zurücksenden to return, to send back, to resend, to remand.
Zurücksendung sending back, reconsignment, remand.
zurücksetzen to discriminate, *(Auto)* to reverse, to back, *(Preise)* to lower, to reduce;
Gast ~ to slight a guest.
Zurücksetzung discrimination, disregard, slight;
~ **der Preise** price reduction;
j. auf eine ~ schonend vorbereiten to let s. o. down gently.
zurückstecken to back down, to take in sails, to change one's tune;
mit seinen Ansprüchen ~ to come down a peg or two, to set one back *(US)*.
zurückstehen|hinter to be inferior;
hinter jem. ~ müssen to get the dirty end of the stick.
zurückstellen to set back, *(auf die lange Bank schieben)* to pigeonhole, to shelve, to put into cold storage, *(Geld bereitstellen)* to earmark, *(Reservekonto)* to reserve, to set aside [as reserve] *(US)*, *(vertagen)* to postpone, to adjourn, to defer, to waive, *(Waren)* to lay (set) aside;
j. ~ to discriminate against s. o.; **Angelegenheit** ~ to let a matter lie over; **Angelegenheit bis zur nächsten Sitzung** ~ to hold a matter over until the next meeting; **Antrag** ~ to lay a motion on the table *(US)*; **Beantwortung eines Gesuchs** ~ to postpone an answer to a request; **Bericht auf später** ~ to pigeonhole a report for future consideration; **Buch auf seinen Platz** ~ to return a book to its place; **Entscheidung** ~ to defer (reserve) a decision; **Frage auf einen späteren Zeitpunkt der Sitzung** ~ to postpone a question until later in the meeting; **Gesetzesvorlage** ~ to shelve (table, *US*) a bill; **eigene Interessen** ~ to sink one's interests, to put one's personal interests last; **vom Militärdienst** ~ to exempt (defer, *US*) from military service; **Sache für eine Woche** ~ to postpone a matter for a week; **Sacherörterung** ~ to postpone consideration of a subject; **etw. auf später** ~ to defer s. th. to a later date; **für Steuern** ~ to make provision (allow) for taxation; **Thema** ~ to shunt a subject; **als unentbehrlich** ~ *(mil.)* to exempt from service, to defer *(US)*; **bis auf weiteres** ~ to defer until further notice.
Zurückstellung *(Benachteiligung)* discrimination against, *(Bilanz)* allowance, provision, reserve, *(Verschiebung)* postponement, adjournment, deferment, *(Zweckbestimmung)* earmarking;
berufsbedingte ~ *(mil.)* occupational deferment *(US)*;
~ **für Abschreibungen** depreciation allowance; ~ **für Betriebsunfälle** industrial accident reserve; ~ **für Devisenverluste** allowance for exchange fluctuations; ~ **für Inventarergänzungen** provision for inventory reserves; **besondere ~ für Notfälle** naked reserve *(US)*; ~ **für nicht vermietete Räume** allowance for vacancies; **~en für Reparaturen und Erneuerungen** provision for deferred repairs and renewals; ~ **von persönlichen Überlegungen** elimination of personal considerations; ~ **vom Wehrdienst** deferment from military service *(US)*, postponement of national service *(Br.)*; ~ **einer Zahlung** deferment of a payment;
mit der ~ eines Antrags einverstanden sein to allow a motion to lie over.
zurückstoßen, Mitmenschen to hold off people.
Zurückströmen reflux.
zurückströmen *(Geld aus dem Ausland)* to flow back, *(Menschenmenge)* to stream back.
zurückstufen to downgrade;
tariflich ~ to demote.
Zurückstufung downgrading, demotional classification change, demotion *(US)*.
zurück|telegrafieren to wire back; **~tragen** to carry back; **~trassieren** to draw back, to redraw; **~treiben** to repel, to repulse.
zurücktreten to retire, to resign, to vacate office, to withdraw, to declare off, *(Minister)* to resign from the cabinet, to step down;
vor jem. ~ to make way for s. o.; **hinter dem Allgemeinwohl** ~ to come second to the general welfare; **von einem Amt** ~ to tender

one's resignation from a post, to vacate office; **von seinem Amt als Vormund** ~ to resign a ward to a new warden; **für einen anderen** ~ to step aside; **von einem Auftrag** ~ to cancel an order; **von einem Dienstvertrag** ~ to repudiate a contract of service; **von einer Forderung** ~ to abandon a claim; **von einem Geschäft** ~ to rescind a bargain; **von der Geschäftsführung** ~ to resign from the management; **geschlossen** ~ to resign in a body; **zu jds. Gunsten** ~ to stand aside (withdraw) in favo(u)r of s. o.; **von einem Kauf** ~ to repudiate (retire, cancel) a purchase; **von seinem Posten** ~ to resign one's position; **von einem Recht** ~ to waive a right; **turnusmäßig** ~ to retire by rotation; **von einer Verbindlichkeit** ~ to retract from an engagement; **unter Verdachtsumständen** ~ to resign under a cloud; **vom Versuch** ~ to abandon an attempt; **von einem Vertrag** ~ to terminate (withdraw from, repudiate, rescind, recede from) a contract.

zurückübersetzen to retranslate.

Zurückübersetzung retranslation.

zurückübertragen to retrocede, to retransfer, to reassign, to reconvey.

Zurückübertragung retrocession, reassignment, retransfer, reconveyance.

zurücküberweisen to transfer back.

zurückverfolgen, seine Abstammung bis auf eine alte normannische Familie to trace one's descent back to an old Norman family; **Ereignis bis zu seinem Ursprung** ~ to trace an event to its origin; **Spur eines Verbrechers bis M** ~ to trace a criminal to M.

zurückverfrachten, jem. sofort to shove s. o. straight back.

zurückvergüten to reimburse, to repay, to make refund;
Portospesen ~ to reimburse (refund) the cost of postage, to refund the postage cost; **Provision** ~ to return a commission.

Zurückvergütung refund, reimbursement, *(Spediteur)* advance billing.

zurück|verkaufen to sell back; **wieder ~verladen** to reload, to reship *(US)*; **~verlangen** to claim (demand) back, to reclaim; **~verlegen** *(Front)* to withdraw.

zurückversetzen *(mil.)* to degrade, *(Schule)* to put back into a lower class, to demote, to send back to a lower form;
Angestellten in die Zentrale ~ to relocate an employee.

zurückversetzt fühlen, sich in die Schulzeit to carry o. s. back to one's schooldays.

Zurückversetzung in die Zentrale relocation.

zurückverweisen to refer back to, *(an niederes Gericht)* to remand, to remit, *(an eine Kommission)* to recommit;
Fall ~ to remand a case; **Fall zur Rechtsmittelabhilfe** ~ to throw a case back for remedy; **Fall zur erneuten Verhandlung** ~ to send a case back to the lower court for revision; **Gesetzesvorlage an einen Ausschuß** ~ to recommit a bill.

Zurückverweisung remittal of record, relegation, rejection, *(Gericht)* remand;
~ **eines Gesetzentwurfes** recommitment of a bill.

zurückverwiesen deferred;
~e Sache remitted case.

zurückweichen to shrink back, to stand back, *(mil.)* to fall back, to give ground;
vor einer Aufgabe ~ to shrink (flinch) from a duty.

zurückweisen to reject, to refuse, to disallow, *(abschlägig bescheiden)* to rebuff, *(Beschuldigung)* to cast back, *(Schuldanerkenntnis)* to repudiate;
Angebot ~ to refuse an offer; **Angebot schroff** ~ to reject an offer bluntly; **Anmeldung** ~ *(Patentrecht)* to refuse an application; **Ansinnen** ~ to repel a suggestion; **Argument** ~ to overrule an argument; **Berufung** ~ to dismiss an appeal; **Beschwerde** ~ to ignore (dismiss)a complaint; **jds. Forderungen** ~ to repudiate (dismiss) s. one's claims; **staatliche Forderungen** ~ to balk government demands; **Geschenk** ~ to decline a present, to repudiate a gift; **Gesetzentwurf** ~ to throw out a bill; **j. an der Grenze** ~ to turn s. o. back at the border; **aus verfahrensrechtlichen Gründen** ~ to dismiss on procedural grounds; **Kandidaten** ~ to turn down a candidate; **Klage** ~ to nonsuit; **Klage als unbegründet** ~ to dismiss a claim on its merits; **kostenpflichtig** ~ to dismiss with costs; **Rechnung als unrichtig** ~ to disallow an account; **Rechtsmittel** ~ to reject an appeal; **Scheck** ~ to return (reject, dishono(u)r) a cheque (check, *US*); **als unbegründet** ~ to dismiss for want of sufficient grounds; **Vorschlag** ~ to turn down a proposal; **Wechsel** ~ to dishono(u)r a bill.

Zurückweisung *(Ablehnung)* rejection, refusal, exclusion, *(abschlägiger Bescheid)* rebuff, repulse, *(Ansprüche)* setting aside, *(Nichtanerkennung)* repudiation, *(Patentanmeldung)* refusal;
kostenpflichtige ~ dismissal with costs;
~ **von Ausländern** exclusion of aliens; ~ **der Berufung** dismissal of appeal; ~ **einer Einrede** disallowance of a plea; ~ **einer Gesetzesvorlage** recommitment of a bill; ~ **einer Klage** nonsuit; ~ **des gesamten Klagevorbringens** plea of the general issue; ~ **einer Konkursforderung** rejection of proof; ~ **einer Patentanmeldung** refusal of a patent; ~ **einer Stimmrechtsermächtigung** rejection of proxy; ~ **eines Zeugen wegen Unglaubwürdigkeit** impeachment of a witness;
~ **einer Klage beantragen** to file a rebuttal with a court; ~ **erfahren** to meet with a rebuff.

Zurückwerfen der Invasionstruppen rollback of the invading army.

zurückwerfen to pull (roll) back, *(Lichtstrahl)* to reflect, to echo;
Feind ~ to repulse (revert) the enemy.

zurückwirken to retroact, to have retroactive effect.

zurückzahlbar repayable, refundable, returnable;
al pari ~ repayable at par; **nicht** ~ nonreturnable.

zurückzahlen to pay back, to repay, to quit, to reimburse, to refund, to return, to restitute, to wipe off, to remit;
jem. seine Auslagen ~ to reimburse s. o. for his (refund s. one's) expenses; **Dollarschuld von 5,4 Millionen** ~ to retire 5,4 million dollar in debt; **zuviel gezahltes Geld** ~ to return an overpaid amount; **Hypothek** ~ to pay off (repay, wipe off) a mortgage; **Kredit** ~ to repay (redeem) a loan; **jem. mit gleicher Münze** ~ to pay s. o. back in his own coin; **seine Schulden** ~ to discharge (pay off, repay) one's debts, to get out from under; **vor Verfall** ~ to repay before the expiration of a period.

Zurückzahlung repayment, refund, reimbursement, discharge.

Zurückziehen [zur Beratung] *(Geschworene)* retirement;
~ **aus dem Geschäft** retiral, retirement from office.

zurückziehen to withdraw, to retract, *(Geld)* to recall, to call in, *(Einspruch)* to subduct, *(Truppen)* to draw off;
sich ~ to withdraw, to draw back, to retire, to give ground, to seclude o. s. from society, to sit back, to box o. s. up, *(mil.)* to retreat, to beat a retreat, to withdraw; **sich von jem.** ~ to dissociate o. s. from s. o.; **Akkreditiv** ~ to revoke a letter of credit; **Angebot** ~ to retract a bid, to withdraw an offer; **Anklage** ~ to nolle-pros; **Aufträge** ~ to cancel (countermand) orders, *(Börse)* to shorten commitments; **sich zur Beratung** ~ to retire for deliberation; **sich von der Bühne** ~ to give up acting, to quit the stage *(US)*; **Einladung** ~ to cancel an invitation, to put off one's guests; **sich gänzlich** ~ to drop out of things entirely; **seine Genehmigung** ~ to revoke one's consent (a grant); **sich geordnet** ~ *(mil.)* to effect a retreat in good order, to retire within one's lines; **sich völlig aus der Geschäftsführung** ~ to drop all operational duties; **sich aus dem Geschäftsleben** ~ to quit (retire from) business; **sich in sein Haus** ~ to confine o. s. to one's house; **sich in seine Kabine** ~ to retire to one's cabin; **seine Kandidatur** ~ to withdraw one's candidature; **Klage** ~ to withdraw an action, to drop one's litigation; **seinen Kongreßsitz aufgeben und sich** ~ to vacate one's seat in Congress by resignation; **Kredit** ~ to withdraw a credit; **sich mit zweimonatlicher Kündigung aus einer Vereinbarung über die Vorstandsbesetzung** ~ to drop out of the management arrangement on 60 days' notice; **sich aus dem öffentlichen Leben** ~ to withdraw from the world; **sich ins Privatleben** ~ to retire from the world; **sich aus dem Rüstungsgeschäft teilweise** ~ to reduce one's reliance on defence (defense, *US*) contracts; **sich aus einer Sache** ~ to drop out of s. th., to backtrack; **sich in sich selbst** ~ to turn in on o. s.; **sich von einem Unternehmen** ~ to withdraw from an undertaking, to backtrack; **Vorhänge** ~ to open the curtains; **sich in einen Wald** ~ *(mil.)* to fall back upon a forest; **sich von der Welt** ~ to detach o. s. from the world; **sich für eine Woche zur Erholung** ~ to go in retreat for a week.

Zurückziehung withdrawal, revocation, cancellation, *(vom Geschäft)* retirement, retiral, *(Kreditbrief)* revoking, *(mil.)* retreat;
~ **von Anlagekapital** disinvestment *(US)*; ~ **erteilter Aufträge** countermanding of orders given; ~ **eines Erlasses** retraction of a decree; ~ **eines Kandidaten** withdrawal of a candidate; ~ **einer Lizenz** revocation of a licence; ~ **einer Vollmacht** revocation of power.

zurückzuführen, allein *(Unfall)* exclusive of all other causes;
~ **sein** to be ascribable.

Zuruf cry, call, *(Beifall)* acclamation, cheers;
durch ~ **abstimmen** to vote by acclamation.

Zurverfügungstellung|von Kredit credit accommodation; ~ **der Ware** tender of goods.

Zusage answer in the affirmative, assurance, *(Annahme)* acceptance, *(Versprechen)* promise, pledge, word, *(Zustimmung)* consent, assent;

bindende ~ binding promise; **mündliche** ~ parol promise; **vorläufige** ~ tentative assent;
~ **eines Kredits** advance commitment, standby credit; ~**n bei Vertragsabschluß** promissory representations;
~ **einhalten** to make good on a pledge; **zahlreiche** ~**n auf eine Einladung erhalten** to receive numerous acceptances to one's invitation; ~ **geben** to give an undertaking; **seine** ~ **halten** to keep one's promise; **anderweitigen** ~**n nachkommen müssen** to have previous engagements.

zusagen to answer in the affirmative, *(gefallen)* to please, *(versprechen)* to promise, to pledge;
jem. ~ to be congenial to s. o.; **auf eine Einladung** ~ to promise to come; **jem. schnelle Hilfe** ~ to promise s. o. to help quickly; **jem. etw. auf den Kopf** ~ to tell s. o. outright; **jem. überhaupt nicht** ~ not to be at all to s. one's liking.

zusagende Antwort answer in the affirmative, affirmative reply.

zusammen together, jointly;
~ **ein neues Haus bauen** to throw together to build a house; **alles** ~ **bezahlen** to pay the piper.

Zusammenarbeit collaboration, cooperation, mutual support, liaison, *(zweier Firmen)* working affiliation, *(mil.)* combined operation;
betriebliche ~ staff cooperation; **koordinierte** ~ teamwork; **technische** ~ technical collaboration; **unternehmerische** ~ interindustry cooperation *(US)*; **wirtschaftliche** ~ economic cooperation;
enge ~ **zwischen einzelnen Abteilungen** close liaison between departments; ~ **von Betrieb und Belegschaft** employee cooperation; ~ **der Gewerkschaft mit der Unternehmerschaft** union-management cooperation; ~ **der Notenbanken** central bank cooperation; ~ **in Steuersachen** fiscal cooperation; ~ **der Verwaltungen** administrative cooperation; ~ **auf dem Währungsgebiet** monetary cooperation; ~ **im Wege des Kompromisses** give-and-take;
sich zur ~ **bereitfinden** to feel cooperative; **wirtschaftliche** ~ **vertiefen** to intensify economic cooperation.

zusammenarbeiten to join hands with s. o., to work together, to collaborate, to cooperate, to concert;
einverständlich ~ to be in the same camp; **eng miteinander** ~ to run (work) in double harness, to work hand-in-glove; **geschäftlich mit jem.** ~ to do business with s. o.; **gut** ~ to pull well together.

zusammenarbeitend cooperative.

zusammenballen to congest, to concentrate, to mass, *(wirtschaftlich)* to conglomerate, to concentrate, *(Gewitterwolken)* to bank (loom) up;
sich ~ *(Schnee)* to pack down hard; **sich über jem.** ~ to loom over s. o.; **sich in den Städten** ~ to concentrate in cities.

Zusammenballung congestion, agglomeration, *(wirtschaftlich)* conglomerate, conglomeration, concentration;
industrielle ~ concentration of industries;
~ **von Arbeitskräften** localization of labo(u)r; ~ **von Kapital** concentration of capital; ~ **wirtschaftlicher Macht** concentration of economic power; **große** ~**en in den Städten** large urban concentrations.

Zusammenbau fitting together, assembly, assemblage.

zusammenbauen *(Maschine)* to assemble, to mount, to set up;
Garage aus einem alten Hühnerhaus ~ to knock up a garage out of an old hen-house.

zusammenbeißen, Zähne to clench one's teeth.

zusammenbekommen *(Geld)* to scrape together.

zusammenberufen to call together, to convene, to convoke;
Gläubiger ~ to summon creditors.

Zusammenberufung calling together, convocation, summons;
~ **der Gläubiger** convocation (summoning) of creditors.

zusammenbleiben to stay together.

zusammenbrauen to cook up;
sich ~ *(Gewitter)* to be brewing.

zusammenbrechen to fall, to collapse, to break down, to go to pieces, *(fallieren)* to fail [in business], to break down, to crash, to smash, to go bankrupt, to fold *(Br.)*, *(Verhandlungen, Verkehr)* to collapse, to break down, *(Wirtschaftssystem)* to bog down;
beinahe ~ *(Verkehr)* to reach near-collapse; **in einer Krisenzeit** ~ to fail during a depression; **unter der Last der Beweise** ~ to break down under the weight of the evidence; **sich überarbeiten und** ~ to break down from overwork.

zusammenbringen to gather, to congregate;
j. mit jem. ~ to introduce s. o. to s. o.; **zerstrittene Familienmitglieder** ~ to reconcile estranged members of a family; **Geld** ~ to raise money; **Vermögen** ~ to amass a fortune.

Zusammenbruch collapse, debacle, fall, *(Bankrott)* breakdown, failure, ruin, collapse, smash, blowup *(US)*, *(Börse)* crash, smash, *(Verhandlungen)* breakdown, *(Verkehr)* collapse, breakdown;
kurz vor dem ~ on one's last legs;
endgültiger ~ final crisis; **finanzieller** ~ financial failure (collapse), breakdown, insolvency; **seelischer** ~ crackup *(sl.)*; **völliger** ~ smash; **wirtschaftlicher** ~ business collapse;
~ **des Aktienmarktes** stock-market crash; ~ **einer Bank** bank failure, collapse of a bank; ~ **des Eisenbahnverkehrs** breakdown of the railway; ~ **einer Firma** breakdown of a firm; ~ **des Fraktionszwanges** collapse of the whipping system; ~ **der Landwirtschaft** agricultural bust; ~ **des Marktes** collapse of the market; ~ **des Pfundes** sterling collapse; ~ **der Produktion** production breakdown; ~ **einer Produktionsanlage** equipment breakdown; ~ **eines Reiches** fall (disruption) of an empire; ~ **eines Unternehmens** collapse of an enterprise; ~ **der Weltmarktpreise** world price collapse;
von jds. finanziellem ~ **betroffen sein** to be involved in s. one's ruin; **kurz vor dem geschäftlichen** ~ **stehen** to be on the brink of ruin, to face the collapse of one's business; **finanziellen** ~ **überwinden** to recover after a business failure; **in jds.** ~ **mit hereingerissen werden** to be involved in s. one's ruin.

zusammenbündeln to bundle.

zusammendrängen, sich to throng, to crowd together; **Leute in einem Korridor** ~ to jam the passage with people; **sich in den letzten Tagen** ~ to be concentrated into the last few days.

Zusammenfall von Ereignissen coincidence of events.

zusammenfallen to collapse, to clash;
zeitlich ~ to concur, to coincide, to be contemporaneous.

zusammenfalten to double up;
Brief ~ to fold a letter;
sich ~ **lassen** to fold.

zusammenfassen to sum up, to subsume, to summarize, to give a summary, *(abkürzen)* to abridge, to condense, *(Artilleriefeuer)* to concentrate, *(integrieren)* to integrate, *(miteinander verbinden)* to amalgamate, to concentrate, to unite, to combine, to coordinate, to pool, *(Versicherungsvertrag)* to abstract;
Aufträge ~ to pool orders; **Aussprache** ~ to summarize a discussion; **verschiedene Begriffe unter einem Oberbegriff** ~ to class different terms under a general term; **Beweisergebnis** ~ to sum up the evidence; **Bilanz** ~ to consolidate a balance sheet; **seine Gedanken** ~ to collect one's thoughts; **Hypotheken** ~ to tack mortgages; **inhaltlich** ~ to pick up (resume) the threads of a conversation; **Klagen** ~ to consolidate actions; **in einem Konzern** ~ to bracket together in a group; **kurz** ~ to brief, to summarize; **noch einmal** ~ to recapitulate; **Sicherheiten** ~ to tack securities; **in Stichworten** ~ to sum up in key words; **wiederholend** ~ to resume, to recapitulate; **in wenigen Worten** ~ to put it in a nutshell.

zusammenfassend comprehensive, recapitulatory, the long and the short of it, synoptic;
~**er Bericht** comprehensive report, summary account; ~**e Darstellung** summary; ~**e Wiederholung** recapitulation.

Zusammenfassung summing up, summary, subsumption, resumé, conspectus, precis, *(Buch)* synopsis, *(mehrere Pläne)* composite, *(Rechtsfall)* syllabus, *(Schriftwerk)* condensation, *(Truppen)* concentration, *(Übersicht)* roundup;
gewerkschaftliche ~ unionization; **kurze** ~ boildown; **vertikale** ~ vertical combination; **wiederholende** ~ recapitulation;
~ **der Ausgaben** pool of expenditure; ~ **des Beweisergebnisses** summing up of the evidence; ~ **von Erfindungselementen** *(Patentrecht)* aggregation; **wirtschaftliche** ~ **von Gewerbezweigen** amalgamation of industries; ~ **von Lizenzen** package licensing; ~ **der wichtigsten Nachrichten über Entwicklungen auf dem Euromarkt** Eurobond market roundup; ~ **des Sachverhalts** summary of the facts; ~ **von Sicherheiten** tacking of securities; ~ **verschieden ausgestatteter Staatsanleihen** unification of different state loans; ~ **eines Urteils** headnote; ~ **für eine neue Werbeidee** briefing of a new advertising idea; ~ **des Wichtigsten** capital write-up;
~ **geben** to give a summary, to sum up, to recapitulate.

zusammen|finden, sich to come together, to collect, to gather; ~**flicken** to patch together; ~**fügen** to combine, to tie.

Zusammenfügung joinder, *(techn.)* assembly, assemblage.

Zusammenführung von Familien reunion of families.

zusammengedrängt tight, condensed;
auf engstem Raum ~ crowded together in a minimum of space.

zusammengefaßt summarized, summary, *(abgekürzt)* abridged, condensed, abbreviated, concise;

~er **Angriff** combined attack; ~er **Ausbildungsgang** summary of one's education; ~e **Bilanz** consolidated (summarized, condensed) balance sheet; ~e **Daten** integrated data; ~er **Haushaltsplan** summarized budget; ~e **Unkosten** pool costs; ~er **Verhandlungsbericht** summary of a debate.
zusammengehen to make common cause.
zusammengehören to be fellows, *(Dinge)* to match.
zusammengehörig related, allied, tied up.
Zusammengehörigkeit solidarity, fellowship.
Zusammengehörigkeitsgefühl sense of togetherness, solidarity, fellowship feeling, team spirit;
instinktives ~ der Presse freemasonry of the press.
zusammengenommen, alles all things considered, all-in-all.
zusammengepackt packed.
zusammengepfercht, wie Heringe in einer Büchse packed liked sardines in a tin;
~ **sein** to be cramped for room; ~ **wohnen** to live in close quarters (cramped conditions).
zusammengeraten, heftig to have a fierce argument.
zusammengeschlossene Berufsverbände amalgamated craft unions.
zusammengesetzt composite, compound, comprised, complex, sectional;
~e **Nachfrage** composite demand; ~es **Wort** compound word.
zusammen|gestellt assorted; ~**gestoppelt** patchy; ~**gewürfelt** ill-assorted.
zusammenhalten to hold together;
seine Gedanken ~ to keep track of one's thoughts; **sein Geld** ~ to take care of one's money; **wie Pech und Schwefel** ~ to be as thick as thieves.
Zusammenhang connection, connexion *(Br.)*, nexus, *(Textstelle)* context, *(Wechselbeziehung)* interrelation;
aus dem ~ gerissen out of context; **in diesem** ~ in this context; **nach dem textlichen** ~ [con]textual;
logischer ~ coherence; **ununterbrochener** ~ efficient intervening cause; **ursächlicher** ~ chain of causation, causality, proximate (legal) cause; **kein ursächlicher** ~ remote cause; **wirtschaftlicher** ~ economic relationship;
Wort aus dem ~ reißen to divorce a word from its context; **Dinge im ~ sehen** to see things together; **im ~ stehen** to connect; **sofern sich aus dem ~ nichts anderes ergibt** unless the context requires otherwise.
zusammenhängen to be linked (joined) up;
früher mit dem Festland ~ to have been formerly joined to the continent.
zusammenhängend connected, interrelated, coherent;
logisch ~ coherent; **untereinander** ~ interdependent, interrelated;
mit den Verpflichtungen im diplomatischen Dienst ~ incident to life in the diplomatic service;
~e **Grundstücke** contiguous plots of land.
zusammenhanglos incoherent, disconnected, loose.
zusammenhauen, Libretto to throw a textbook together.
zusammenheften to file;
Akten ~ to link records; **Papiere** ~ to clip papers together.
zusammenkaufen to buy up, *(Börse)* to forestall the market, to corner.
zusammenklappbar collapsible;
~ **sein** to fold.
zusammen|klappen to fold up, *(physisch)* to break down, to drop, to collapse; ~**kleben** to gum together; ~**klucken** to stick together; ~**knoten** to knot together; **Papier ~knüllen** to ruffle (rumple up) paper.
zusammenkommen to meet, to collect, to forgather, to come together, to congregate, to assemble, *(zur Abstimmung)* to whip in, *(Kongreß)* to convene, *(Umstände)* to combine;
in regelmäßigen Abständen ~ to meet periodically; **mit den verschiedensten Leuten** ~ to touch elbows with many sorts of people.
zusammenkoppeln, Raumschiffe to link up spaceships; **Waggons** ~ to couple railway coaches.
zusammenkratzen, Geld to scrape up a sum of money; **ein paar Pfennige** ~ to scrabble the pennies together, to scrape up a sum of money.
Zusammenkunft gathering, meeting, conference, convention, assembly, *(Beratung)* conference, *(Verabredung)* appointment;
geheime ~ secret assembly (meeting); **persönliche** ~ private interview; **regelmäßige** ~ periodical meeting; **zwanglose** ~ informal meeting, get-together;
~ **ausgesuchter Diskussionsmitglieder** panel meeting *(US)*; ~ **von Gewerkschaftsmitgliedern** labo(u)r causus;
~ **abhalten** to meet, to hold a rally; ~ **festsetzen** to make an appointment, to appoint a day; ~ **verabreden** to arrange a meeting.
Zusammenkunftsort junction, meeting place, venue.
Zusammenlaufen von Straßen convergence of streets.
zusammenlaufen to crowd (flock) together;
alle Fäden in seiner Hand ~ haben to pull the strings.
Zusammenleben living together, companionship;
eheähnliches ~ common-law marriage; **eheliches** ~ matrimonial cohabitation; **harmonisches** ~ intercommunity.
zusammenleben to live together, to keep house together, to cohabit;
wie Eheleute ~ to live and cohabit together as husband and wife; **mit dem Ehemann** ~ to live with the husband; **wie Mann und Frau** ~ to live as man and wife.
zusammenlegbar collapsible, folding, dismountable, knock-down.
zusammenlegen *(Anleihe)* to consolidate, *(Decke)* to fold up, *(Firmen)* to amalgamate, to merge, to fuse, to unite, *(Verwaltungen)* to centralize, to integrate, *(für gemeinsame Zwecke)* to club together for;
Aktien ~ to amalgamate shares; **Aktienkapital** ~ to write down (off) capital; **Geld** ~ to pool money (funds); **Grundstücke** ~ to incorporate a field into an estate; **auf einen Haufen** ~ to heap together; **Konten** ~ to pool accounts; **für einen gemeinsamen Zweck** ~ to club together.
Zusammenlegung consolidation, amalgamation, conversion, merging, merger, fusion, *(Verwaltungen)* centralization, integration;
~ **von Aktien** reserve split-up; ~ **des Aktienkapitals** writing down (off) of capital; ~ **des Grundkapitals** reduction of share capital *(Br.)* (capital stock, *US*); ~ **von Grundstücken** incorporation of a field into an estate; ~ **des Kapitals** merger of funds; ~ **von Konten** pooling of accounts;
~ **des Aktienkapitals vornehmen** to write down (off) capital.
zusammennageln to nail together (up).
zusammennehmen, alle seine Kräfte to muster up all one's strength; **seinen ganzen Mut** ~ to pluck up one's courage.
zusammenpacken, seine Sachen to pack up one's things.
zusammenpassen to match, to harmonize, to go with, to agree; **gut** ~ to match well.
zusammenpassend matching, matchable;
schlecht ~ ill-matched.
zusammenpferchen, Menschen to pen people up, to crowd people together.
Zusammenpferchung von Menschen herding of people.
zusammenpfuschen, Vertrag to huddle up an agreement.
Zusammenprall crash, clash, collision.
zusammenprallen to clash, to crash, to collide;
mit jem. ~ to bump into s. o.
zusammen|pumpen, sich to borrow from various sources; ~**quetschen** to pinch.
zusammenraffen to snatch up, to scrape together;
sich ~ to pick up spirit.
Zusammenrechnen casting, cast, footing, addition.
zusammenrechnen to cast accounts (up figures), to add up, to total, to reckon (sum) up;
Einkünfte nicht ~ *(Steuer)* to treat income separately; **Spalte** ~ to cast a column of figures; **Summe** ~ to compute a sum.
Zusammenrechnung adding up, addition, casting, footing up.
zusammen|reimen, sich nicht not to make sense; **sich ~reißen** to pull o. s. together; **sich ~rotten** to form (gather) into a mob, to band together, to riot, to gang up *(sl.)*.
Zusammenrottung unlawful (riotous, rebellious) assembly, rout;
wegen ~ angeklagt werden to be charged with riotous behavio(u)r.
zusammen|rufen to assemble, to convene, to convoke, to call, *(Parlament)* to summon; ~**sacken** to drop, to collapse; ~**schalten** *(Sender)* to hook (link) up.
Zusammenschaltung *(Sender)* hookup, linkup.
Zusammenschau conspectus, view, synopsis.
zusammenschießen to riddle with bullets, *(Artillerie)* to batter down;
Geld ~ to club together, to pool funds; **sein Kapital** ~ to join stock with s. o., to pool funds.
zusammenschlagen to smash to pieces, to beat up;
j. ~ to beat s. o., to make mincemeat of s. o.; **Hacken** ~ to click one's heels; **Hände über dem Kopf** ~ to throw up one's hands.
zusammenschließen to combine, to incorporate, to merge, to pool;

sich ~ to amalgamate, to merge, to combine, to line up, *(politisch)* to federate, to unite, to join [forces], to fuse, *(Verbrecher)* to gang up *(sl.)*; **sich mit jem.** ~ to enter into a combination with s. o.; **Arbeiter in einer Gewerkschaft** ~ to unite workers in a trade union; **Firmen** ~ to consolidate companies; **zu einheitlichem Handeln** ~ to line; **sich zu einem Kartell** ~ to join a cartel; **sich in einem großen Unternehmen** ~ to merge into one large organization; **sich zu einem Verein** ~ to club.

Zusammenschluß federation, union, integration, *(Firmen)* amalgamation, consolidation, combination, concentration, combine, merger, fusion, *(Kartell)* pool, pooling, *(Kettenläden)* chain, *(Verband)* association, organization;
erneuter ~ rebuilding; **horizontaler** ~ horizontal amalgamation, horizontal integration; **industrieller** ~ industrial merger; **lockerer (kartellähnlicher)** ~ contract (loose) combination *(US)*; **machtpolitischer** ~ concentration of powers; **organisierter** ~ organization; **politischer** ~ political union, coalition; **ungesetzlicher** ~ unlawful combination; **vertikaler** ~ vertical merger (integration, amalgamation); **wettbewerbsbeschränkender** ~ combination in restraint of trade; **wirtschaftlicher** ~ *(Einzelindustrien)* economic fusion (union), amalgamation of industries, *(Europa)* economic integration;
~ **von Aktiengesellschaften** consolidation of corporations, corporate merger; ~ **von Banken** merger (incorporation) of banks, bank merger; ~ **zu einem Bund** federalization; ~ **von Fernsehstationen** television linkup; ~ **von Landwirtschaftsbetrieben** farm merger; ~ **von Rundfunksendern** hookup of broadcasting stations, chain; ~ **branchenfremder Unternehmen** conglomerate merger; ~ **zu einem gemeinsamen Zweck** joint enterprise.

Zusammenschlüsse, ungesetzliche criminal syndicalism;
~ **auf kapitalistischer Basis** close combinations *(US)*.

zusammenschmelzen *(Vorräte)* to melt away, to dwindle, *(zusammenschließen)* to weld.

zusammenschreiben to write in one word, *(zusammenstellen)* to compile;
aus anderen Büchern ~ to copy from various sources; **Grundstücksparzellen** ~ to incorporate a field into an estate, to assemble two parcels of land; **Hypotheken verschiedenen Ranges** ~ to tack mortgages; **Rechnung** ~ to make out a bill; **sich ein Vermögen** ~ to make a fortune by one's pen.

Zusammenschreibung | von Grundstücksparzellen incorporation of a field into an estate, assemblage of two parcels of land; ~ **von Hypotheken** consolidation (tacking) of mortgages.

Zusammenschreibungs | befugnis für Hypotheken power of consolidation; ~**kosten** assemblage.

zusammenschrumpfen *(Einkommen)* to shrink, *(Vorräte)* to dwindle, to diminish, to run short.

zusammenschustern, aus alten Aufzeichnungen eine Vorlesungsreihe to vamp up some lectures out of old notes.

zusammenschweißen to weld;
seine Belegschaft ~ to hold one's staff together; **Währungen zu einem festen Block** ~ to weld currencies into a tight bloc.

Zusammensein companionship, meeting;
betriebliches ~ company togetherness; **geselliges** ~ social gathering;
geselliges ~ **über mehrere Tage** house party.

zusammensetzbares Haus prefabricated (frame, *US*) house, prefab *(Br.)*.

zusammensetzen to compound, to compose, *(Maschine)* to assemble, to mount, to fit together;
sich ~ to get together, to sit down; **sich** ~ **aus** to be composed (consist) of.

Zusammensetzung composition, compound, make-up, constitution, formation, arrangement of parts, *(Maschine)* assembly, assemblage;
patentfähige ~ patentable combination, juxtaposition *(Br.)*, aggregation;
~ **eines Ausschusses** constitution of a committee; ~ **eines Gerichts** combination (composition) of a court; ~ **der Hörerschaft** audience composition; ~ **des Kabinetts** make-up (composition) of the cabinet; ~ **des Publikums** audience profile (composition); ~ **der Repräsentativauswahl** sample set-up; ~ **des Sortiments** assortment composition, merchandise mix *(US)*; ~ **eines Vereins** make-up of a society.

zusammensinken *(Gebäude)* to collapse, to cave in.

zusammensitzen, eine Stunde bei einer Flasche Portwein to spend an hour over the discussion of a bottle of port.

zusammensparen to economize;
Geld für eine Reise ~ to save up money for a holiday.

Zusammenspiel interplay, teamwork.

zusammenstauchen, j. to give s. o. a dressing down (what for, *coll.*), to pan s. o. *(US coll.)*.

zusammenstecken, die Köpfe to put heads together.

Zusammensteckspiel jigsaw puzzle.

zusammenstehen, in Menschentrauben to stand in knots.

Zusammenstellen von Tatsachen abstracting of facts.

zusammenstellen to compile, to make up, to survey, *(drucktechn.)* to make ready, *(gruppieren)* to combine, to group, *(klassifizieren)* to classify, to assort, to group, *(Kleidungsstücke)* to combine, *(spezifizieren)* to specify;
Ausschuß ~ to set up (constitute, appoint) a committee; **Bericht** ~ to make up (prepare) a report; **Buch** ~ to compile a book; **Büchersendung** ~ to parcel up a consignment of books; **Geschworenengericht** ~ to strike (pack) a jury; **Katalog** ~ to compile a catalog(ue); **Ladung** ~ to assort a cargo; **Liste** ~ to make (build) up a list; **paragraphenweise** ~ to arrange articles in groups; **passend** ~ to match, to assort; **nach Posten** ~ to sort; **Programm** ~ to arrange a program(me); **nach Qualitäten** ~ to grade; **Rechnung** ~ to make out a bill; **Register** ~ to compile an index; **in einer Tabelle** ~ to compile (dress) a table; **Tatsachen** to marshal facts; **Unterlagen** ~ to prepare documents; **statistische Unterlagen** ~ to compile statistical information; **Wahlergebnisse** ~ to count the votes; **Warenproben** ~ to make up samples; **Warensortiment** ~ to make up an assortment; **Wörterbuch** ~ to compile a dictionary; **Zugfolge** ~ to assemble (make up) a train of cars, to marshal a train.

Zusammenstellung compilation, combination, composition, arrangement, make-up, *(Aufstellung)* statement, schedule, *(Klassifizierung)* classification, grouping, assortment, *(Übersicht)* roundup, survey, *(Zug)* marshalling;
patentfähige ~ patentable combination, aggregation, juxtaposition *(Br.)*; **produktionsreife** ~ *(Anzeige)* layout; **statistische** ~ statistical information (compilation, table), returns; **tabellarische** ~ schedule, table, summarizing sheet, summary, summarizing account; **typische** ~ representative collection; **vergleichende** ~ comparative statement, comparison table;
~ **von Anleihekonsortien** syndication of loans; ~ **der gesetzlich gewährten Einkommensteuerfreibeträge** notice of coding *(Br.)*; ~ **von Fachkräften** pool of technical manpower; ~ **der einzelnen Geschäftstransaktionen** transaction summary; **trügerische (parteiische)** ~ **eines Geschworenengerichts** packing (striking) of a jury; ~ **eines Katalogs** compilation of a catalog(ue); ~ **der Kosten** cost schedule; ~ **des Leserkreises** audience composition; ~ **von Lesestoff** reading list; ~ **von Monatsberichten** making up of monthly reports; ~ **der Neuigkeiten einer Woche** digest of the week's news; ~ **eines Programms** arrangement of a program(me); **klägerische** ~ **des Prozeßmaterials** main issue of a suit; ~ **der häufigsten Unfallursachen** survey of the most frequent causes of accidents; ~ **statistischer Unterlagen** compilation of statistics; **optimale** ~ **eines Wertpapierdepots** portfolio selection; ~ **eines Wörterbuches** compilation of a dictionary; ~ **einer [Zeitungs]seite** page layout;
~ **prüfen** to examine a statement.

zusammensteuern, für gemeinsame Zwecke to club together for.

zusammenstoppeln to patch up, to cobble together.

Zusammenstoß collision, hit, smash, smash-up, crash, clash, pile-up, run-in, running down, impingement, jostle, *(mil.)* encounter, engagement;
im ~ *(Schiff)* afoul;
bewaffneter ~ clash of arms; **frontaler** ~ head-on crash (collision);
~ **in der Luft** mid-air collision; **heftiger** ~ **mit der Polizei** violent clash with the police; ~ **auf See** collision of ships, foul; **schweren** ~ **mit einem Diskussionsteilnehmer haben** to have angry passages with an opponent in a debate; ~ **vermeiden** to avoid colliding.

zusammenstoßen to collide, to come into collision, to clash, to run into, to hurtle, *(Auto)* to pile up, to crash, *(mil.)* to encounter, to join forces with, *(Schiffe)* to run foul of each other (afoul), to foul;
mit einem Auto ~ to meet another car, to bump a car; **frontal** ~ to meet (strike, collide) head-on; **frontal mit dem Landungssteg** ~ **(kollidieren)** to collide with a ship head on a pier; **am Heck** ~ to collide end-on; **krachend** ~ to smash into each other.

Zusammenstoßklausel *(Schiff)* collision (running-down) clause.

zusammenstreichen *(Manuskript)* to cut down, to blue-pencil;
Etat ~ to slash a budget.

zusammenströmen, aus allen Gegenden to flock in from all quarters.

Zusammen | stückelung piecing together; ~**sturz** fall, collapse.

zusammenstürzen to collapse, to fall down (into disrepair);
wie ein Kartenhaus ~ to collapse like a house of cards.
zusammentragen to compile;
Informationsmaterial ~ to gather information.
Zusammentragungsmaschine *(Buchbinderei)* gatherer.
Zusammentreffen meeting, conference, concourse, *(Zusammenfallen)* coincidence;
zeitliches ~ concurrence; **zufälliges** ~ chance meeting; **ungewöhnliches** ~ **von Ereignissen** unusual conjunction of circumstances (events), conjuncture; ~ **von Inflation und Rezession** slumpflation; ~ **von Umständen** combination of circumstances.
zusammentreffen to concur, to meet, to coincide;
mit jem. ~ to meet s. o.; **zeitlich** ~ to coincide.
zusammentreiben to muster;
Vieh ~ to round up cattle.
Zusammentreten des Hauses zu einer Kommission beantragen *(parl.)* to call a committee of the whole House *(Br.)*.
zusammentreten to convene, to meet, *(parl.)* to assemble, to unite;
automatisch ~ to meet as of right; **zu einer Konferenz** ~ to have a conference; **wieder** ~ *(parl.)* to reconvene; **in regelmäßigen Zeitabschnitten** ~ to meet at regular intervals.
Zusammentritt meeting, assembly, convention, array;
~ **der Gläubiger** meeting of creditors; ~ **einer Konferenz** meeting of a conference.
zusammentrommeln to drum up, *(Parteimitglieder)* to whip together.
zusammentun, sich to unite, to join, to associate; **seine Ersparnisse** ~ to pool one's savings; **sich geschäftlich** ~ to associate with others in business.
Zusammenveranlagung *(Ehegatten)* joint return;
~ **von Nachlaßgegenständen** *(Erbschaftssteuer)* aggregation of assets.
zusammenwachsen to coalesce;
aus einigen Städten ~ *(Staat)* to grow out of a few towns.
zusammenwerfen to lump together, to pool;
sein Geld ~ to pool one's resources, to club together; **Patente** ~ to pool patents; **Posten** ~ to lump items together.
Zusammenwirken co-operation, cooperation *(US)*, collaboration, concerted action, coaction, united efforts, *(Umstände)* concurrence;
geheimes ~ quiet collaboration; **planvolles** ~ *(Kartellrecht)* unity by design;
unvorhergesehenes ~ **von Umständen** unforeseen concourse of circumstances.
zusammenwirken to cooperate, to collaborate;
mit jem. ~ to act in concert with s. o.
zusammenwirkend cooperative, cooperant.
Zusammenwohnen living together, cohabitation.
zusammenwohnen to live together, to cohabit, to hive, to flatshare *(Br.)*;
mit jem. ~ to take up one's quarters with s. o.; **eng** ~ to live in close quarters.
Zusammenzählen adding up, casting [up] of figures.
zusammenzählen to add [up figures], to count, to number, to tot, to totalize, to foot up *(US)*;
Beiträge ~ to total the amounts.
Zusammenzählung adding up, casting [up] of figures, summation.
zusammenziehen to concentrate, *(Bilanz)* to consolidate, *(Text)* to condense, to abridge;
mit jem. ~ to share rooms with s. o., to flatshare with s. o.; **sich in den Städten** ~ to concentrate in the cities; **Truppen** ~ to concentrate troops.
Zusammenziehen von Kräften buildup.
Zusammenziehung concentration, *(Bilanz)* consolidation;
~ **von Truppen** concentration (assembly) of troops.
Zusatz *(Abänderung)* appendant, alteration, amendment, *(Anhang)* appendage, appendix, addendum, addition, annex, insertion, *(zu einem Antrag)* rider, *(Befügung)* adjunct, opposition, *(Beimischung)* admixture, temper, *(Beimischung von Metall)* alloy, *(Einschaltung)* insertion, *(Ergänzung)* supplement, *(Gerät)* backup, *(Gesetzentwurf)* rider, *(Lebensmittel)* additive, *(med., Öl)* additive, *(Nachschrift)* postscript, *(Nachtrag)* supplementation, *(zum Testament)* codicil, *(Versicherungspolice)* endorsement, rider, addendum, *(Vertrag)* clause, reservation, *(Zubehör)* appurtenance;
als ~ additionally;
~ **abzeichnen** to initial an alteration; **einem Vertrag einen** ~ **hinzufügen** to insert (put) a clause into a contract; ~**abgabe** special levy, surtax; ~**abkommen** supplementary agreement (convention), additional agreement; ~**aggregat** additional set, booster; ~**anmeldung** *(Patent)* additional application; ~**antrag** amendment to an amendment, *(bei Gericht)* supplemental bill; ~**antrag einbringen** to move (table, *Br.*) an amendment; ~**artikel** subsequent clause, schedule, appendix, additional (amending) article, *(Gesetz)* rider, *(zur Verfassung)* first (constitutional) amendment *(US)*; ~**aufträge** additional orders; ~**ausbildung** additional training; ~**ausfuhrvergütung** export bounty; ~**ausstattung** *(Auto)* optional (extra, *US*) equipment; ~**batterie** booster battery; ~**bedingungen** added (additional) clauses, additional conditions, *(Feuerversicherung)* added charges; ~**beitrag** additional contribution; ~**belastung** additional load; ~**bericht** additional (supplementary) report; ~**bestimmung** additional clause, additional provision, companion provision, supplementary ordinance (provision); ~**betrag** additional sum (amount); **berufliche** ~**bezeichnung** addition; ~**darlehen** additional loan; ~**dividende** cumulative (extra, additional) dividend, superdividend, bonus; ~**dokument** supplemental instrument, supplement document, rider; ~**einrichtung** special device; ~**erfindung** additional invention; ~**erklärung** supplemental statement; **eidliche** ~**erklärung** supplemental affidavit; ~**erklärung bei der Eigentumsübergabe** secondary conveyance; ~**etat** supplementary estimate, deficiency bill *(US)*; ~**fahrkarte**, ~**fahrschein** excess fare (ticket); ~**farbe** supplementary colo(u)r; ~**finanzierung** supplementary financing; ~**fracht** surplus freight; ~**frage** *(Parlament)* supplementary (supplemental) question; ~**frist** additional time; ~**gebühr** additional charge, extra fee, *(Post)* surcharge; ~**gerät** attachment, standby, adapter, accessory desk; ~**gesetz** supplemental act; ~**haushalt** supplementary budget; ~**kapital** fresh capital; ~**karte** extra fare; ~**kasse** additional insurance; ~**klausel** added (additional, superimposed) clause, *(Versicherung)* endorsement, rider; ~**kontingent** supplementary allowance; ~**kredit** additional (supplementary) credit; ~**kredit gewähren** to supplement a credit; ~**ladung** filler freight, *(Auto)* supercharge; ~**leistung** additional contribution.
zusätzlich additional, in addition, supplementary, supplemental, cumulative, extra, odd, to boot, auxiliary, ancillary, added, accessory, further;
halben Tag ~ **arbeiten** to work an extra half day; **durch Ablieferung journalistischer Beiträge** ~ **verdienen** to supplement one's income by journalism; ~ **berechnet werden** to be charged for extra;
~**e Angaben** supplemental data, further details (information); ~**er Anspruch** supplemental claim; ~**e Anzeige** additional insertion; ~**e Arbeitslosenunterstützung** supplementary unemployment insurance; ~**e Aufträge** additional orders; ~**e Aufwendungen** *(Prozeß)* extra cost; ~**e Bewilligung** supplementary grant; ~**e Deckung** additional cover; ~**e Dienstleistungen** ancillary services; ~**e Einkünfte** supplementary (extra) income; ~**e Einnahme** *(Bilanz)* other receipts; ~**e Einwendungen** supplemental plea; ~**e Entschädigung** supplemental compensation; ~**er Etat** supplementary estimate, deficiency bill; ~**e Etatbewilligung** supplemental appropriations; ~**e Forderung** supplementary claim; ~**e Frist** additional time, additional respite; ~**e Information** supplementary information; ~**es Kapital** fresh capital; ~**e Kopie** blind carbon copy; ~**e Kosten** extra charges, supplementary costs; **mit** ~**en Kosten verbunden sein** to involve additional costs; ~**er Kredit** additional (further) credit; **um** ~**en Kredit nachsuchen** to ask for further credit; ~**e Leistung** additional contribution; ~**e Leistungen zum Selbstkostenpreis** additions at cost; ~**e Lieferungen** fresh supplies; ~**e Lohnzahlungen** wage supplements; ~**er Omnibus** extra bus; ~**es Parteivorbringen** supplemental pleading; ~**es Personal** ancillary (auxiliary) personnel; ~**e Schicht** relief (swing) shift *(US)*; ~**er Schriftsatz** supplemental answer; ~**e Sicherheit** additional security; ~**e Spesen** additional charges; ~**e Steuer** surtax, supertax; ~**e Versicherung** collateral insurance; ~**er Versicherungsschutz** *(Feuerversicherung)* extended coverage; ~**e Vorschriften** complementary rules; ~**e Werbung** supplementary (accessory, follow-up, auxiliary) advertising; ~**e Zuteilung** supplementary allowance.
Zusatz|licht *(Theater)* booster light; ~**lieferung** additional delivery; ~**lohn** wage supplement, *(Prämie)* bonus, fringe benefits; ~**maschine** *(Bahn)* booster; **mit einem** ~**mittel versehen** *(Benzin)* to dope; ~**nachfrage** competitive demand; ~**nahrung** supplementary nutrition, interval feeding *(US)*; ~**name** addition; ~**patent** improvement (supplementary, supplemental) patent, patent of addition; ~**police** additional

(supplementary) policy; ~**prämie** extra (supplementary) premium; ~**protokoll** supplementary (additional) protocol; ~**provision** additional commission; ~**rakete** booster racket; ~**rechnung** supplementary invoice, supplementary allowance.
Zusatzrente additional annuity, supplementary allowance, *(Sozialversicherung)* supplementary pension *(Br.)*;
bruttolohnbezogene ~ earnings-related additional pension; ~ **für Angehörige** supplementary benefit; ~ **für dauernde Beschäftigungsunfähigkeit** unemployability supplement; ~ **für die Ehefrau** *(Sozialversicherung)* wife's insurance benefit *(US)*; **betriebliche** ~**n zur staatlichen Altersversorgung gewähren** to provide occupational benefits in addition to those provided by the state.
Zusatz|rentenversicherung supplementary pension insurance *(Br.)*; ~**schicht** swing (relief) shift *(US)*; ~**steuer** supertax, surtax, additional (excess-profits, *US*) tax; ~**strafe** cumulative punishment; ~**stück** *(Wechsel)* rider; ~**system** backup system; ~**tarif** penalty rate, penalty tariff; ~**tarif in Notstandsfällen** emergency charge; ~**test** additional test; ~**triebwerk** booster engine; ~**übereinkommen** supplementary agreement; ~**unterstützung** supplementary payment (relief), *(Sozialversicherung)* additional benefit; ~**urkunde** schedule, rider, endorsement; ~**veranlagung** additional assessment; ~**vereinbarung** additional agreement; ~**vergünstigungen** fringe benefits; ~**vergütung** supplemental compensation, extra pay; **für Bankangestellte übliche** ~**vergütungen** usual banking fringe benefits; ~**vermächtnis** additional (cumulative, accumulative) legacy; ~**vermerk** superimposed clause; ~**verpflegung ausgeben** to issue additional rations; ~**versicherung** additional (supplementary, complementary) insurance; ~**versicherung für Krankenhausaufenthalt** hospitalization *(US)* (hospital benefit) insurance; ~**versorgung** additional benefit; ~**vertrag** additional agreement, accessory contract, *(internationale Abmachung)* protocol, *(Versicherung)* endorsement, rider; ~**visum** additional visa; ~**vorschlag** amendment; ~**wahl** by-election; ~**werbung** auxiliary advertising; ~**wette** added money; ~**zinsen** extra interest.
zuschalten *(el.)* to connect, *(Fernsehstation)* to link up, *(Rundfunkstation)* to hook up.
zuschanden arbeiten, sich to work one's fingers to the bone.
zuschanden machen, jds. Hoffnungen to wreck s. one's hopes; **jds. Pläne** ~ to thwart s. one's plans, to upset s. one's applecart.
zuschanzen, einem Freund einen guten Posten to manoeuvre a friend into a good position.
zuschauen to watch, to look on.
Zuschauer spectator, onlooker, looker-on, bystander, turnout, *(Augenzeuge)* eye witness, *(Fernsehen)* viewer, onlooker, looker-on, *(pl.)* the audience (public), gallery;
stehender ~ standee; **teilnahmsloser** ~ cold spectator; **unbeteiligter** ~ unconcerned spectator; **untätiger** ~ passive spectator; **zahlender** ~ spectator who pays, paying spectator; ~ **durch Seilabsperrung ausschließen** to rope out the spectators; ~ **elektrisieren** to thrill the listeners; ~ **sein** to look on;
~**analyse** audience analysis; ~**befragung** audience survey; ~**menge** audience, cluster of spectators; ~**messung** audience rating; ~**platz** seat; **auf einem billigen** ~**platz sitzen** to sit in the bleachers *(US coll.)*; ~**plätze** *(Kino)* seating capacity; ~**ränge** terraces; ~**raum** *(Theater)* auditorium, audience box, house; ~**schaft** audience; ~**terrasse** observation desk; ~**tribüne** public gallery, platform, scaffold; ~**umfrage** *(Fernsehen)* viewer survey; ~**zahl** attendance figure; **sinkende** ~**zahlen** falling gates.
zuschicken to send, to forward, to dispatch;
mit der Post ~ to post, to mail *(US)*; **jem. Ware unmittelbar** ~ to dispatch goods direct to s. o.
zuschieben, jem. einen Eid to put s. o. on his oath; **jem. ein Kind** ~ to father a child on s. o.; **jem. die Schuld** ~ to lay the blame at s. one's door; **jem. die Verantwortung** ~ to saddle the responsibility on s. o., to pass the buck *(US)*.
zuschießen to contribute, to invest additional funds, *(subventionieren)* to subsidize;
jem. wütende Blicke ~ to look daggers at s. o.
Zuschlag extra (supplementary) charge, surcharge, addition, additional charges, *(Auftragserteilung)* acceptance of tender, award, awarding a contract, *(Auktion)* acceptance of a bid, knocking down, knockdown, fall of the hammer, *(Erhöhung)* increase, augmentation, *(Fahrkarte)* extra fare, *(bei Fracht)* primage, *(durch das Gericht)* adjudication, *(Gratifikation)* bonus, premium, *(zum Lohn)* extra pay, allowance, bonus, *(Post)* late-letter fee, surcharge, *(Steuer)* surtax, supertax, late fee, *(techn.)* extra allowance;
außertariflicher ~ payment over and above the wage scale; **verdienstbezogener** ~ earnings-related supplement;
~ **für außerplanmäßige Arbeiten** call-back pay; ~ **für schwierige Arbeiten** job-difficulty allowance; ~ **für maschinelle Bearbeitung** machining allowance; ~ **zur Erzielung eines gewogenen Indexes** *(Statistik)* loading; ~ **für abhängige Familienangehörige** increase for dependants; ~ **zu den Lagerhauskosten** warehousing surcharges; ~ **an den Meistbietenden** sale (allocation, allotment) to the highest bidder; **hundertprozentiger** ~ **für Nacht- und Feiertagsarbeit** double time; ~ **für Sonderplazierung** *(Inserat)* surcharge for special position; ~ **bei Steuerzwangsvollstreckung** tax certificate *(US)*; ~ **an den Submittenten** acceptance of tender, awarding a contract; ~ **wegen Überfüllung des Hafens** congestion surcharge; ~ **für Überstunden** overtime pay; ~ **zum Verbraucherpreis** addition to price; ~ **für die Witwe mit Kindern** widowed mother's allowance *(Br.)*;
mit ~ **belegen** to surcharge; ~ **berechnen** to make an extra charge; ~ **bezahlen** to pay an extra charge; **für eine Lieferung den** ~ **erhalten** to secure (get, obtain) a contract; **sofortigen** ~ **erhalten** to bid off; ~ **erteilen** to award a contract, to accept a tender, *(Auktion)* to knock down, to strike off; ~ **verlangen** to make an extra charge.
zuschlagen to adjudicate, to allocate, *(Auftrag)* to award the contract, *(Auktion)* to knock down, to strike off, *(Gericht)* to adjudicate;
Auftrag einer Firma ~ to award a contract to a firm; **Buch** ~ to shut a book; **hart** ~ to strike hard; **Kiste** ~ to nail a box; **einem Kunsthändler** ~ to knock down to an art dealer; **dem Meistbietenden** ~ to allot to the highest bidder; **Tür** ~ to bang (slam) a door.
Zuschlags|bescheinigung *(Zwangsversteigerung)* certificate of sale; ~**beschluß**, ~**erteilung** awarding a contract, acceptance of tender, adjudication, *(Auktion)* knockdown; ~**fahrkarte**, ~**fahrpreis** excess fare (ticket); ~**fracht** extra (additional) freight.
zuschlagsfrei without surcharge.
Zuschlags|frist time of adjudication; ~**gebühr** surcharge, additional (excess) fee; ~**hammer** sledge hammer; ~**kalkulation** job order (distributive) cost accounting, target pricing; ~**karte** additional ticket, excess (extra) fare; ~**kosten** *(Buchführung)* retail cost; ~**methode** retail method.
zuschlagspflichtig liable to extra payment;
~**es Gepäck** extra luggage *(Br.)*, excess baggage *(US)*.
Zuschlags|porto excess postage, surcharge; ~**prämie** extra premium, *(Versicherung)* loaded premium; ~**preis** price of adjudication; ~**preis erheben** to excess *(Br.)*; ~**steuer** additional tax, surtax, supertax; ~**steuer erheben** to surtax; ~**submission** winning bid *(US)*; **niedrigster** ~**wert** *(Konkursverfahren)* lowest price; ~**zahlung** additional (extra) payment; ~**zoll** additional duty.
zuschließen to lock;
Laden ~ to shut up shop.
zuschneiden to fashion;
auf eine bestimmte Länge ~ to cut to size.
Zuschnitt *(fig.)* style, fashion, *(Kleidungsstück)* cut, *(Persönlichkeit)* caliber, calibre *(Br.)*;
im großen ~ on a grand scale, in a great style;
~ **seines Lebens** pattern of one's life;
den ~ **und die Nerven für politische Auseinandersetzungen haben** to have both the style and the stomach for political strifes.
zuschnüren to cord;
jem. die Kehle ~ to strangle s. o., *(wirtschaftlich)* to cut s. one's throat.
zuschreibbar attributable, ascribable, imputable.
zuschreiben to ascribe, to attribute, to impute, *(widmen)* to dedicate;
jem. etw. ~ to credit s. o. with s. th.; **einem Autor** ~ to impute to an author; **seinen Erfolg harter Arbeit** ~ to attribute one's success to hard work; **jds. Erfolge seinem Glück** ~ to put s. one's success down to luck; **einer bestimmten Person einen Artikel** ~ to fasten an article onto a particular person; **den Rücklagen** ~ to add (transfer) to the reserve fund; **einer Sache große Bedeutung** ~ to attach great importance to a matter; **jem. ein Stück** ~ to pose a play to s. o.; **einem Unfall** ~ to ascribe to an accident; **Unfall der Unvorsichtigkeit des Fahrers** ~ to impute an accident to the driver's carelessness; **sich als Verdienst** ~ to take credit to o. s.;
sich selbst ~ **müssen** to have to blame o. s.
Zuschreibung value adjustment, writing up, attribution;
~ **der Vaterschaft** affiliation.

zuschreiten, tüchtig to put one's best foot forward.
Zuschrift letter, notice, writing;
amtliche ~ official communication;
~en aus dem Leserkreis letters to the editor; **zahlreiche ~en aus der Öffentlichkeit** flood of mail from the public.
Zuschuß allowance, benefit, pecuniary aid, *(Beitrag)* contribution, *(Exportprämie)* export bounty, bounty on exportation, premium, *(Stipendium)* stipend, *(Unterhaltszuschuß)* allowance, allocation;
finanzieller ~ financial contribution; **zur freien Verfügung gewährter** ~ bloc grant; **nach Köpfen gezahlter** ~ capitation grant; **jährlicher** ~ annual grant; **nichtvermögenswirksamer** ~ nonasset-creating subsidy; **öffentlicher** ~ subvention, grant-in-aid *(US)*, subsidy; **persönlicher** ~ personal allowance *(Br.)*; **staatlicher** ~ governmental subsidy, subvention, state (government) grant; **steuerabzugsfähiger** ~ tax-deductible contribution; **verlorener** ~ lost contribution;
~ **zur Ausbildung** education maintenance grant (allowance); ~ **des Bundes** federal grant *(US)*; ~ **für die Einstellung von Jugendlichen** youth employment subsidy *(Br.)*; ~ **in Kapitalform** capital grant; ~ **zu den Lebenshaltungskosten** cost-of-living allowance; ~ **zum Universitätsstudium** grant towards the cost of university education;
ohne ~ **auskommen** to pay one's way; ~ **bei der Regierung beantragen** to put in a claim for grant; **jem. den monatlichen** ~ **beschneiden** to cut down s. one's monthly allowance; **jem. einen** ~ **bewilligen** to make a grant to s. o., to grant an allowance; **um die Bewilligung eines ~es einkommen** to put in a claim for a grant; **staatlichen** ~ **erhalten** to receive a state grant; ~ **gewähren** to allow, to make (grant) an allowance, *(Staat)* to pay (give) a subsidy; **seinem Sohn einen jährlichen** ~ **in Höhe von 1000 DM gewähren** to make one's son an allowance of DM 1000 a year; **für einen** ~ **in Frage kommen** to be eligible for a grant; **seiner Tochter einen** ~ **zukommen lassen** to allow one's daughter a stipend; ~ **zu den Unterhaltskosten leisten** to make a contribution towards the cost of maintenance; **jem. den** ~ **sperren** to stop s. one's allowances; ~ **widerrufen** to revoke a grant;
~antrag application for a grant; **~bedarf** subsidy requirements; **~bedingung** condition of grant.
zuschußbedürftig subsidizable.
Zuschuß | betrag additional amount; **~betrag für Familienangehörige** *(Arbeitslosenversicherung)* dependant's allowance; **~betrieb** subsidized (supply) undertaking; **~bogen** *(Druckerei)* extra sheet, oversheet.
Zuschüsse, durch staatliche ~ **unterstützt** grant-aided, bounty-(state-) fed;
außerordentliche ~ exceptional grants; **bare** ~ cash grants; **innerstaatliche** ~ grant-in-aids;
~ **im Krankheitsfall** subsidized medical scheme;
staatliche ~ **erhalten** to be subsidized by the state; ~ **erzwingen** to extort contributions; **durch** ~ **unterstützen** to subsidize, to subventionize.
Zuschuß | empfänger nominee, grantee, recipient of an allowance; **~kasse** benefit fund; **betriebliche ~kasse** pension plan, trust fund; **~tafel** scale of allowances; **~verfahren** grant-making procedure.
zuschustern, jem. etw. to put s. o. in the way.
Zusehen, bei näherem on closer inspection.
zusehen to watch, to look on;
tatenlos ~ to stand idly by, to sit on one's hands.
zusenden to send on, to consign, to forward;
mit der Post ~ to post, to mail *(US)*.
Zusendung consignment, sending, forwarding, delivery;
~ **mit der Post** posting, mailing *(US)*.
zusetzen *(bedrängen)* to press, to urge, *(verlieren)* to lose, to be a loser;
jem. mit Bitten ~ to badger s. o. with requests; **jem. mit Fragen** ~ to plague (pester) s. o. with questions; **jedes Jahr hunderte von Dollar** ~ to be hundreds of dollars out-of-pocket each year; **wöchentlich zehn Pfund** ~ to lose at the rate of ten pounds a week.
zusichern to assure, *(gewährleisten)* to warrant, to guarantee;
jem. ein bestimmtes Gehalt ~ to assure s. o. a definite salary.
Zusicherung assurance, promise, seal, covenant, *(Gewährleistung)* warranty, guaranty *(US)*, guarantee *(Br.)*;
auf die ~ **hin** on the undertaking;
~en *(bei Versicherungsabschluß)* representations;
ausdrückliche ~ express warranty; **positive** ~ *(Versicherungsrecht)* affirmative warranty; **vertragliche** ~ warranty in the contract;
~ **des ungestörten Besitzes** warranty of quiet enjoyment; ~ **einer Eigenschaft** undertaking as (warranty) of quality; **ausdrückliche** ~ **der Herstellerfirma** warranty of fitness; ~ **in tatsächlicher Hinsicht** affirmation of fact; ~ **angemessener Löhne [bei Auftragsvergabe]** fair wage clause; ~ **durchschnittlicher Qualität** warranty of quality (merchantability) *(Br.)*; ~ **der Richtigkeit der gemachten Angaben** affirmative warranty; **~en des Versicherungsnehmers** insurance warranties; ~ **über die Vornahme bestimmter Handlungen** *(Versicherungsrecht)* executory warranty;
~en [nicht] einhalten to fill (break) the warranty; ~ **erhalten** to obtain a guarantee; **jds.** ~ **blindlings glauben** to believe s. one's naked assertion.
Zusicherungs | abrede warranty; **~klausel** *(Versicherung)* attestation (signature) clause.
zuspitzen, sich to come to a head, to become more and more critical.
Zuspitzung der Lage increasing gravity of a situation.
zusprechen, dem Alkohol zu sehr to be too fond of the bottle; **jem. begütigend** ~ to calm s. o. down; **Erbschaft** ~ *(Gericht)* to award an inheritance; **Kind bei der Scheidung** ~ to grant custody of child; **einer Mahlzeit tüchtig** ~ to do full justice to a meal; **jem. Mut** ~ to encourage s. o.; **Schadenersatz** ~ to adjudge (award) damages; **Telegramm** ~ to telephone a message; **jem. Trost** ~ to comfort (console) s. o.
Zusprechung adjudication, award.
Zuspruch reception, approval, popularity;
besänftigender ~ soothing words; **großer** ~ plenty of customers; **lobender** ~ pat on the back;
sich großen ~s erfreuen *(Restaurant)* to be very popular with the public; **großen** ~ **finden** *(Film)* to meet with general approval; **großen** ~ **haben** to have a good custom, *(Arzt)* to be very popular, *(Film)* to meet with general approval, *(Hotel)* to be much frequented.
Zustand condition, state, form, make, *(Geistesverfassung)* frame of mind, *(Haus)* repair, *(Lage)* situation, position, *(pol.)* status;
in betriebsfähigem ~ in operating condition; **in betrunkenem** ~ while intoxicated; **in einwandfreiem** ~ in apparent good order and condition; **in gut erhaltenem** ~ in a good state of preservation; **in erstklassigem** ~ in first-rate order, *(Grundstück)* in good heart; **in gebrauchsfähigem** ~ in serviceable condition, in commission; **in gegenwärtigem** ~ in the present state; **in gutem** ~ in a good state, in good working order, good conditioned, in a state of good presentation, well conditioned, in good fix *(US)*, *(Haus)* in good repair; **in gutem und betriebsfähigem** ~ in good working condition; **in handelsfähigem** ~ in merchantable condition; **in heruntergekommenem** ~ in a dilapidated (rundown) condition; **in ordnungsgemäßem** ~ in good order and condition; **in schadhaftem** ~ at a damaged state; **in schlechtem** ~ in bad order, at a damaged state, *(Haus)* in bad repair, *(Waren)* ill-conditioned, out of condition; **in seetüchigem** ~ *(Schiff)* in navigable condition, sea-worthy; **in tadellosem** ~ *(Waren)* in sound condition; **in untauglichem** ~ on the blink *(US sl.)*; **in verpachtungsfähigem** ~ available for letting; **in wohnlichem** ~ in tenantable repair;
einwandfreier ~ **zugesichert** well-warranted;
abnormer ~ irregularity; **baulicher** ~ state of repair; **beschädigter** ~ damaged condition; **betriebsfähiger (betriebsbereiter)** ~ working order; **bewohnbarer** ~ tenantable (habitable) repair; **einwandfreier** ~ trim, *(Waren)* perfect condition; **fahrbereiter** ~ roadworthy condition; **fehlerloser** ~ faultless condition; **früherer** ~ status quo ante; **gegenwärtiger** ~ status quo; **gesetzloser** ~ anarchy; **hoffnungsloser** ~ hopeless condition, blank; **kriegsähnlicher** ~ warlike conditions; **lieferfähiger** ~ deliverable state (condition); **mangelfreier** ~ perfect condition; **neuwertiger** ~ as new; **ordnungsgemäßer** ~ apparent good order, *(Pachtgrundstück)* tenantable repair; **räumlicher** ~ spatial structure; **schlechter** ~ bad condition, *(Haus)* disrepair; **seelischer** ~ mental state; **unangenehmer** ~ down; **unbearbeiteter** ~ native state; **unbeschädigter** ~ sound condition; **unerträglicher** ~ intolerable state of affairs; **unhygienischer** ~ insanitation; **vermietungsfähiger** ~ tenantable repair; **voriger** ~ status quo ante; **vorzüglicher** ~ high (prime) condition; **wrackähnlicher** ~ quasi-derelict;
~ **eines Fahrzeugs** condition of a vehicle; ~ **der Geistesschwäche** mental bondage; ~ **vor der Verarbeitung** raw stock; **schlechter** ~ **der Verpackung** bad state of packing; **mangelhafter** ~ **der Ware** defective condition of the goods; ~ **der Zahlungsunfähigkeit** state of insolvency;
Haus in bewohnbarem ~ **halten** to keep a house in habitable repair; **in ordnungsgemäßem** ~ **halten** to keep in good repair; ~

der Handlungsunfähigkeit in einem Unternehmen herbeiführen to produce a state of deadlock in a firm; **in angetrunkenem ~ sein** to be under the influence of alcohol; **in gut erhaltenem ~ sein** to be in good state of repair; **in erstklassigem ~ sein** to be in fine whack; **in einem ~ völliger Erschöpfung sein** to be in a state of exhaustion; **in einwandfreien ~ versetzen** to put in repair; **in vollbetriebsfähigen ~ versetzen** to put in full working order; **früheren ~ wiederherstellen** to restore the status quo ante.

Zustände state of affairs, conditions, *(Umstände)* circumstances;
geordnete ~ proper state of affairs;
chaotische ~ im Bahnbetrieb hervorrufen to reduce the railway system to chaos; **~ kriegen** to have a fit.

zustande bringen to accomplish, to work it, to achieve, to manage, to effect, to bring to pass, to bring off *(fam.)*;
Friedensvertrag ~ to negotiate peace; **Geschäft ~** to secure a business; **so gut wie nichts ~** to accomplish just about nothing; **Vereinbarung ~** to reach (bring about) an agreement.

zustande kommen *(Gesetz)* to be passed, *(Plan)* to materialize, *(stattfinden)* to happen, to take place, to come to pass;
nicht ~ to fail.

Zustandebringen achievement.

Zustandekommen taking place, realization, *(Pläne)* materialization;
~ von Beschlüssen adoption of resolutions.

zuständig competent, *(fachlich berechtigt)* qualified, *(gehörig)* appertaining, *(Gericht)* having jurisdiction, competent, cognizant, *(maßgebend)* proper, appropriate, *(verantwortlich)* responsible, competent;
nicht ~ incompetent, not competent;
sich in einer Sache für ~ erklären to declare o. s. competent, to assume jurisdiction over a case; **sich für nicht ~ erklären** to disclaim competence; **für etw. ~ sein** to have charge of s. th. (s. th. under one's umbrella), *(Gericht)* to have cognizance (jusrisdiction); **ausschließlich ~ sein** to have exclusive jurisdiction in all cases; **für die Berufung ~ sein** to have appellate jurisdiction; **in erster Instanz ~ sein** to have original jurisdiction; **nicht ~ sein** to have no jurisdiction; **örtlich ~ sein** to lay the venue; **sachlich ~ sein** to have jurisdiction over the subject matter;
~er Beamter official in charge; **~e Behörde** competent (proper) authority; **~es Gericht** competent court; **~er Gerichtsort** venue; **~es Postamt** serving post office; **~er Richter** competent judge; **von ~er Seite hören** to be informed by experts; **~e Stelle** responsible (proper) quarters; **sich an die ~e Stelle wenden** to apply to the proper quarter.

Zuständigkeit competence, responsibility, province, sphere, *(Ausschuß)* reference, *(Befugnisse)* powers, *(Gericht)* jurisdiction, capacity, cognizance, *(Wirkungskreis)* province, sphere, line, scope of authority;
außerhalb der ~ extra vires; **außerhalb gerichtlicher ~ liegend** extrajudicial; **außerhalb unserer ~** outside our reference; **innerhalb meiner ~** within my province;
allgemeine ~ general jurisdiction; **ausschließliche ~** exclusive jurisdiction (competence); **begrenzte ~** limited jurisdiction; **bundesgerichtliche ~** removal jurisdiction *(US)*; **einzelrichterliche ~** summary jurisdiction; **erstinstanzliche ~** original jurisdiction; **fremde ~** foreign jurisdiction; **hilfsweise gegebene ~** auxiliary jurisdiction; **inländische ~** national jurisdiction *(Br.)*; **innerstaatliche ~** domestic jurisdiction; **konkurrierende ~** concurrent (coördinate) jurisdiction; **mangelnde ~** want of jurisdiction; **mehrfache ~** concurrent jurisdiction; **örtliche ~** forum, territorial (venue) jurisdiction, magisterial precinct *(US)*; **sachliche ~** full jurisdiction, jurisdiction in rem (over the subject matter); **steuerliche ~** tax jurisdiction; **unmittelbare ~** direct jurisdiction; **wahlweise ~** concurrence of jurisdiction;
~ in Berufungssachen appellate jurisdiction; **~ in Ehesachen** matrimonial jurisdiction; **~ für den Erlaß von Verwaltungsvorschriften** regulatory function; **allgemeine ~ eines Gerichts** general jurisdiction of a court; **~ in Nachlaß- und Vormundschaftssachen** probate jurisdiction; **örtliche ~ für einen Prozeß** locality of a lawsuit; **~ als Rechtsmittelinstanz** supervisory control (jurisdiction); **~ in bürgerlichen Rechtsstreitigkeiten** civil jurisdiction; **~ in Steuersachen** tax jurisdiction; **~ in Strafsachen** criminal jurisdiction; **~ in arbeitsrechtlichen Streitigkeiten** industrial jurisdiction; **~ für völkerrechtliche Vertragsabschlüsse** treaty-making power;
~ ablehnen to refuse jurisdiction; **~ begründen** to establish jurisdiction; **örtliche ~ begründen** to lay the venue; **~ eines Gerichts begründen** to confer jurisdiction on a court; **~ bestreiten** to plead (challenge) incompetence; **im Rahmen seiner ~ bleiben** to keep within one's proper sphere; **in jds. ~ fallen (gehören)** to come under the cognizance of s. o., to fall within the competence of s. o.; **unter die ~ eines Gerichtes fallen** to come within the jurisdiction (fall under the cognizance) of a court; **nicht zu jds. ~ gehören** not to fall in s. one's province; **nicht zur ~ eines Ausschusses gehören** to be outside the reference of a committee; **zur ~ eines Gerichts gehören** to come within the jurisdiction (fall within the cognizance) of a court, to be cognizable by a court; **in jds. ~ liegen** to lie within s. one's competence; **außerhalb jds. ~ liegen** to be beyond s. one's cognizance; **im Rahmen der ministeriellen ~ liegen** to be in the gift of a minister; **seine ~ überschreiten** to transgress (exceed) one's competence, to act in excess of one's powers; **~ verneinen** to disclaim competence.

Zuständigkeits|ausweitung extension of jurisdiction; **~begrenzung** limitation of jurisdiction (authority); **glaubhafte ~begründung** colo(u)rable invocation of jurisdiction.

Zuständigkeitsbereich sphere of responsibility, purview, scope, powers, *(Ausschuß)* terms of reference;
~ eines Gerichts jurisdiction (verge, competence) of a court; **örtlicher ~ eines Richters** territory of a judge;
etw. von seinem ~ abgeben to spin off some of its areas of jurisdiction; **~ erweitern** to extend jurisdiction; **in jds. ~ fallen** to fall within s. one's province; **zum ~ eines Gerichtes gehören** to be within the competence (jurisdiction) of a court; **im ~ des Innenministeriums liegen** to come within the purview of the Home Office *(Br.)*; **seinen ~ vergrößern** to extend one's jurisdiction.

Zuständigkeits|beschränkung limitation of authority (jurisdiction); **~einwand** jurisdictional plea; **~erfordernisse** jurisdictional facts; **~erklärung** assumption of authority; **~erweiterung** extension of jurisdiction; **~frage** question of privilege, jurisdictional question; **über die ~frage entscheiden** to decide the point; **~grenze** ambit.

zuständigkeitshalber for reasons of competence.

Zuständigkeits|katalog *(Verfassung)* enumerated powers *(US)*; **~klausel** *(Völkerrecht)* jurisdictional clause; **~streit** conflict of jurisdiction, jurisdictional dispute; **~überschreitung** excess of jurisdiction, *(Parlament)* breach of privilege; **~vereinbarung** jurisdiction[al] clause; **~verteilung** distribution of responsibilities.

zustatten kommen to come in handy, *(jem.)* to stand in s. one's stead.

zustecken, jem. etw. to slip s. th. into s. one's hands.

zustehen to appertain, to be due (belong) to, *(Eigentum)* to reside;
rechtlich 50% des Gewinns ~ to be lawfully entitled to 50% of the profit; **jem. nicht ~** to have no right to do s. th.

zustehend, mehreren Gläubigern ~e Hypothek participating mortgage; **~es Protokoll** due protocol; **noch ~er Urlaub** terminal leave.

zusteigen, in einen Bus to get on a bus; **in ein Flugzeug ~** to board a plane;
Passagiere ~ lassen to take on passengers.

Zustell|abteilung *(Warenhaus)* traffic department; **~anschrift** address for service *(Br.)*, mailing address *(US)*; **~bereich, ~bezirk** postal district (zone), walk, *(Spediteur)* cartage limit.

Zustelldienst delivery service (operation);
buchhändlerischer ~ bookseller-trade delivery service; **eigener ~** individually owned delivery;
gemeinsamer ~ mehrerer Firmen consolidated delivery system *(US)*; **~ an Sortimenter-Kommittenten** delivery service to retail bookseller agents.

zustellen *(Brief, Waren)* to deliver, to distribute, to effect service, *(Rechnung)* to send;
Abschriften ~ to serve copies; **jem. einen gerichtlichen Eröffnungsbeschluß ~** to serve a process on s. o.; **Klage ~** to serve a writ; **Konkurseröffnungsbeschluß ~** to serve with a bankruptcy notice; **jem. eine Kündigung ~** to serve notice on s. o.; **jem. eine Ladung ~** to serve s. o. with a summons (process on s. o.); **Pakete ~** to deliver parcels; **Pfändungsbeschluß ~** to give notice of distraint, to serve a writ of attachment upon s. o.; **jem. einen Schriftsatz ~** to serve a writ on s. o.; **dem Schuldner ~** to serve upon a debtor; **Telegramm ~** to deliver a telegram; **Urkunde ~** to deliver a deed; **jem. eine gerichtliche Verfügung ~** to serve a warrant on s. o.; **jem. eine Vorladung ~** to serve s. o. with a summons, to serve a citation (notice) upon s. o.; **wöchentlich nur einmal ~** to settle on a scheduled weekly delivery service.

Zusteller deliverer, *(Gericht)* person who serves, process server.

Zustell|gebühr charge for delivery, delivery charge, *(Paket, Telegramm)* portage, *(Spediteur)* carrier's charge, terminal charges, cartage; **~postamt** delivery office.

Zustellung delivery, consignment, *(Gericht)* service, serving, notice;
binnen zwei Wochen nach ~ within two weeks of service; **im Zeitpunkt der** ~ at the time of delivery;
ersatzweise ~ *(Gericht)* substituted service, notice in lieu of service; **erste** ~ general post delivery; **fehlende** ~ default of service; **freie** ~ free delivery system *(US)*; **gerichtliche** ~ delivery of a writ; **kostenlose** ~ free delivery; **letzte** ~ late-fee post; **öffentliche** ~ *(Gericht)* notice by advertisment in the press, service by publication *(US)* (advertisement) in the press, substituted service *(US)*; **ordnungsgemäße** ~ due service, due delivery, *(Gericht)* proper service; **nicht ordnungsgemäße** ~ irregularity in service, defective notice; **persönliche** ~ *(Gericht)* personal (direct) service; **portofreie** ~ free delivery; **verspätete** ~ postal delay; **vollständige** ~ constructive service of process; **ersatzweise vorgenommene** ~ substituted service;
~ **durch die Bahn** railway delivery; ~ **durch Eilboten** express delivery service *(Br.)*, by special delivery *(US)*; ~ **an den Empfänger** delivery to addressee; ~ **einer Erklärung** service of notice; ~ **von Gerichtsdokumenten** service of process; ~ **frei Haus** free (store-door) delivery; ~ **von Haus zu Haus** door-to-door pickup and delivery; ~ **der Klageschrift** service of process (writ of summons); ~ **einer Kündigung** service of notice; ~ **mit Luftpost** delivery by air; ~ **von Paketen** parcel delivery; ~ **eines Pfändungs- und Überweisungsbeschlusses** service of a garnishee order, garnishee summons; ~ **durch die Post** postal (mail, *US*) delivery, postal service, service by mail *(US)* (post, *Br.*); ~ **eines Schriftsatzes** notice of motion; ~ **eines Schriftsatzes zur Fortsetzung des Verfahrens** notice to proceed; ~ **einer Urkunde** delivery of a deed; ~ **von Vorrangpost am gleichen Tage** same-day priority date post door-to-door service; ~ **im Zivilprozeß** service of legal proceedings;
ersatzweise ~ **annehmen** to accept service *(Br.)*; **sich auf verspätete** ~ **berufen** to plead postal delay; ~ **nachweisen** to prove delivery, to aver notice; ~ **vereiteln** to obstruct process, to impede the service of process; ~ **an den Beklagten vornehmen** to serve the defendant.

Zustellungs|adresse, ~**anschrift** address for service *(Br.)*, mailing address *(US)*; ~**art** mode of process; ~**beamter** process server, warrant officer *(US)*, messenger at arms *(Scot.)*; **von der Partei beauftragter** ~**beamter** special bailiff *(Br.)*; ~**benachrichtigung** advice of delivery; ~**berechtigter** person authorized to give notice; ~**bescheinigung** *(Klage)* notice of action, *(Urteil)* notice of judgment; ~**bestätigung** return of service; **fehlerhafte** ~**bestätigung** *(Gerichtsvollzieher)* false return; ~**bevollmächtigter** authorized recipient.

Zustellungsdienst delivery system (service, operation), mail service *(US)*;
eigener ~ individually owned delivery; **gemeinschaftlicher** ~ cooperative delivery;
Abhol- und ~ pickup and delivery service;
~ **innerhalb 24 Stunden** overnight delivery; ~ **von Eilsendungen am gleichen Tag** same-day express post door-to-door service; **gemeinsamer** ~ **mehrerer Firmen** consolidated delivery system *(US)*; **freier** ~ **auf dem Land** rural-fee delivery.

Zustellungs|erklärung, beeidigte affidavit of service; ~**gebühr** charge for delivery, service fee, *(Post)* delivery fee, *(Spediteur)* terminal charges, cartage; ~**kosten** delivery costs (expenses), charges for delivery, *(Spediteur)* carrier's charges, cartage, hauling costs; ~**mangel** defective notice, irregularity in service; ~**nachweis** averment of notice, proof of service; ~**organ** process server, special bailiff *(Br.)*; ~**ort** place of delivery; ~**postamt** office of delivery; ~**schema der Post** scheme for the mail service; ~**tag** day of service; ~**urkunde** *(Urteil)* writ of summons; ~**vereitelung** obstruction (impeding the service) of process; ~**vermerk mit Rechnungslegung** special indorsement of a writ *(Br.)*; ~**vertreter** authorized recipient; ~**weg** *(Post)* delivery route; ~**wesen** delivery system, mail service *(US)*; ~**wohnort** address for service *(Br.)*, mailing address *(US)*; ~**zeiten** times of delivery.

zusteuern *(beitragen)* to contribute, *(Schiff)* to head (steer, make) for;
auf den Konkurs ~ to steer near receivership, to drift towards bankruptcy, to be on the brink of ruin; **auf einen Krieg** ~ to be heading for a war.

zustimmen to agree, to approve, to affirm, to accede, to fiat, *(vorher)* to consent, to assent;
einer Ansicht ~ to endorse an opinion; **einem Betrug im geheimen** ~ to connive at a fraud; **halbherzig** ~ to consent half-heartedly; **jds. Handlungsweise** ~ to endorse s. one's actions; **einer Heirat** ~ to approve of a marriage; **nachträglich** ~ to agree subsequently; **nicht** ~ to disagree, to disaffirm, to decline; **einer Preisherabsetzung** ~ to consent to a reduction of price; **einer vergleichsweisen Regelung** ~ to agree to a compromise; **einer Sache** ~ to give one's fiat to s. th.; **einer Sache formell** ~ to agree formally; **einer Vereinbarung** ~ to acquiesce in an agreement; **einem Vergleich** ~ to assent to an arrangement; **einem vom bevollmächtigten Vertreter getätigten Verkauf** ~ to ratify a sale made under power of attorney; **einem Vorschlag** ~ to agree (consent) to a proposal; **einem Vorschlag nur bedingt** ~ to give a scheme one's qualified approval.

zustimmend affirmative, approving, positive;
~**e Antwort** answer in the affirmative; ~**er Beschluß** consent decree; ~**es Nicken** nod of assent.

Zustimmender assenter, assentient.

Zustimmung agreement, affirmation, approval, approbation, advice and acceptance, placet, consent, imprimatur, green light, *(Abkommen)* ratification, *(Beifall)* applause, *(Ermächtigung)* assent;
mangels ~ failing consent; **mit** ~ with the advice and consent; **mit allseitiger** ~ by common consent (assent), consentaneous; **mit staatlicher** ~ with government blessing;
Schweigen bedeutet ~ silence gives consent;
ausdrückliche ~ express (explicit) consent (ratification, permission); **bedingte** ~ qualified approval; **einhellige** ~ unanimous consent; **elterliche** ~ parental assent; **stillschweigend erteilte** ~ implicit (tacit) assent, implied consent (ratification); **ungern erteilte** ~ defensive acceptance; **fehlende** ~ want of assent; **gemeinsame** ~ convention, common consent; **ministerielle** ~ ministerial approval; **mündliche** ~ verbal agreement, oral consent; **nachträgliche** ~ sanction; **notgedrungene** ~ reluctant consent; **prompte** ~ ready consent; **schriftliche** ~ assent in writing, written consent; **seine** ~ light of one's countenance; **sofortige** ~ lightning-like approval; **uneingeschränkte** ~ unreserved assent; **gesetzlich vermutete** ~ implied assent; **volle** ~ unreserved compliance; **vorbehaltslose** ~ consent without reserve; **vorherige** ~ prior consent, previous approval;
~ **der Aktionäre** shareholders' (stockholders', *US*) approval; ~ **zu einer Ansicht** adoption of an opinion; ~ **zu einem Geschäftsabschluß** adoption of a transaction; ~ **der Gläubiger zu einem Schuldenregulierungsplan** deed of accession; ~ **der Mehrheit** majority approval; ~ **des Parlaments** parliamentary approval, House approval *(Br.)*; ~ **des Parteiführers zu einer Kandidatur** coupon *(Br.)*; ~ **der Umweltschutzbehörden** environmental approval; ~ **zur Zulässigkeit eines Rechtseinwandes** joinder in demurrer;
von jds. ~ **abhängen** to be subject to s. one's approval; **jem. seine** ~ **abringen** to prevail upon s. o. to consent; **seine** ~ **bezeigen** to mark one's approval; ~ **einholen** to secure agreement; **jds.** ~ **erhalten** to meet with s. one's approval, to obtain s. one's consent; **seine** ~ **erteilen** to yield (signify) one's consent, to pass one's approbation; ~ **finden** to pass muster; **allgemeine** ~ **finden** to meet with general approval; **begeisterte** ~ **finden** to win raves *(fam.)*; ~ **der Wähler finden** to win voter acceptance; ~ **geben** to [give one's] consent, to go along with; **sofort seine** ~ **geben** to give a ready consent; **seine** ~ **zu erkennen geben** to sign one's consent; ~ **herbeiführen** to secure the assent; ~ **des Kongresses herbeiführen** to win Congressional acceptance; **seine** ~ **von einer Bedingung abhängig machen** to agree subject to one qualification; **auf** ~ **stoßen** to meet with approval; **seine** ~ **versagen (verweigern)** to withhold (refuse) one's consent, to refuse assent, to veto; **seine** ~ **widerrufen** to withdraw one's consent.

zustimmungsbedürftig requiring consent, in need of approval;
~ **sein** to require consent.

Zustimmungserklärung, formlose statutory declaration of assent; **schriftliche** ~ written assent.

zustoßen to happen, to meet with;
falls mir etw. ~ **sollte** in case of an accident.

Zustrom inflow, influx, *(Besucher)* stream, resort, inrush.

zustürzen, auf j. to descend upon s. o.

zutage|fördern *(Bergbau)* to exhaust, *(Geheimnis)* to bring to light; ~ **liegen** to be obvious (evident); ~ **treten** to emerge, *(Bergbau)* to crop out, to outcrop.

Zutaten trimmings.

zuteil werden, jem. to fall to s. one's share; **jem. eine Vergünstigung** ~ **lassen** to grant s. o. a privilege.

zuteilen to assign, to allocate, to allot, to apportion, to deal (measure, portion) out, to dispense, *(Gericht)* to adjudicate, to adjudge, *(rationieren)* to ration, *(verteilen)* to distribute;
Aktien voll ~ to allot shares to all applicants; **jem. ein tüchtiges**

Stück Arbeit ~ to cut out work for s. o.; **Bausparer** ~ to advance a borrowing member; **Devisen** ~ to allocate foreign exchange; **j. einer Dienststelle** ~ to assign s. o. to an office; **Frequenzen** ~ to allocate frequencies; **Lebensmittel** ~ to ration food; **durch Los** ~ to lot out; **neu** ~ to reallocate; **Quoten** ~ to allocate the shares in a quota; **jem. etw. reichlich** ~ to lavish s. th. on s. o.; **Sonderziehungsrechte** ~ *(Internationaler Währungsfonds)* to allocate special drawing rights.

Zuteilender assignor, allotter.

Zuteilung allocation, allotment, dispensation, granting, assignment, *(Bausparer)* advance, *(mil.)* attachment, *(Quote)* quota, share, *(Rationierung)* rationing, *(Verteilung)* distribution, *(Zuschuß)* allowance;

anteilsmäßige ~ prorata distribution; **gleichmäßige** ~ apportiomen; **knappe** ~ scant allowance; **monatliche** ~ monthly ration; **prozentuale** ~ percentage distribution; **repartierte** ~ scaled-down allotment; **volle** ~ full quota, *(Akten)* allotment of shares (stocks, *US*) to all applicants; **zusätzliche** ~ supplementary allowance;

~ **von Aktien** allotment (allocation) of shares (stocks, *US*); ~ **eines Bausparers** advancement of a borrowing member; ~ **von Brennholz** allotment of estovers; ~ **von Devisen** allocation of currency, foreign exchange allocation (allotment); ~ **von Frequenzen** allocation of frequencies; ~ **von Gratisaktien** melon cutting *(US)*; ~ **von Lebensmitteln** food ration (allowance); ~ **von Mitteln** appropriation of funds;

von der ~ **ausschließen** to preclude from allotments; ~ **knappstens bemessen** to cut an allocation as fine as possible; ~ **in solcher Höhe in Anspruch nehmen** to pay so much on an allotment; **Antrag auf** ~ **von Aktien stellen** to make application for shares (stocks, *US*); **der** ~ **unterliegen** *(Börse)* to be subject to allotment.

Zuteilungs|anspruch allotment right; ~**antrag** *(Börse)* application for allotment, application for shares *(Br.)*, letter of application *(Br.)*; ~**anzeige** letter of allotment *(Br.)*, certificate of allotment *(US)*, allotment certificate (letter, *Br.*, notice, *US*); ~**ausschuß** allocation commission (committee), allotment committee; ~**benachrichtigung** certificate of allotment *(US)*, allotment letter *(Br.)*; ~**bericht** return of allotments; ~**betrag** allotment money; ~**beschränkungen** restrictions on allotments; ~**empfänger** recipient of an allowance, allocatee, allottee; ~**formalitäten** application formalities; ~**frist** time of allotment; ~**karte** ration book (card); ~**kurs** allotment rate, tender price; ~**kürzung** ration cut; ~**liste** allotment sheet; ~**periode** ration period, *(Sonderziehungsrechte)* basic period; ~**plan** allocation scheme; ~**quote** ratio of allotment, share, quota; ~**schein** certificate of allotment *(US)*, allotment letter *(Br.)*; ~**stelle** allocator; ~**system** quota system; ~**umfang** scale of allowances.

zutragen, sich to occur, to happen, to transpire *(coll.)*.

Zuträger whisperer, talebearer, telltale, informer.

Zuträgerei whispering, talebearing, taletelling.

zuträglich beneficial, *(Klima)* wholesome, healthy, salutary.

Zutrauen trust, confidence.

zutrauen, jem. etw. to believe s. o. capable of s. th., not to put it past s. o.; **sich eine Aufgabe** ~ to nerve o. s. to a task; **sich nichts** ~ to be distrustful of one's own capabilities; **jem. jedes Verbrechen** ~ to hold s. o. capable of any crime; **sich zuviel** ~ to take on too much.

zutraulich confiding, trusting.

zutreffen to apply, to be (hold) true, to hold good, to prove right; **für alle Angestellten** ~ to apply to all employees; **auf einen Fall** ~ to be applicable to a case; **genau auf j.** ~ to fit s. o. perfectly.

zutreffend to the point, pointed;

absolut ~ just to a minute, right on the dot.

zutreffendenfalls if the answer is in the affirmative.

zutreiben, Kunden to tout customers.

zutrinken, jem. to raise one's glass to s. o.

Zutritt admission, admittance, access, approach, entry;

freier ~ ingress;

~ **gestattet** in limits *(US)*; ~ **unentgeltlich** admittance free; ~ **verboten!** no trespassing (admittance)!, private!, no admittance!, *(mil.)* out of bounds *(Br.)*, off limits *(US)*;

freien ~ **behindern** to beset; ~ **erhalten** to gain access; ~ **erlangen** to gain admission; ~ **gewähren** to admit, to grant s. o. admission; **freien** ~ **zu etw. haben** to have free admission, to be made free of s. th.; **freien** ~ **zu einem Haus haben** to have the run of a house; **Unbefugten ist der** ~ **verboten** no admittance except on business; **j.** ~ **verschaffen** to gain s. o. admittance; ~ **verwehren** to deny admittance; ~ **verweigern** to refuse admittance.

zutrittsberechtigte Person licensee by invitation.

Zutrittsberechtigter licensee by invitation.

Zutrittsrecht easement of access, right to access.

zuverlässig reliable, trustworthy, trusty, certain, faithful, creditable, steady, sure, dependable, authentic, thick-and-thin, *(pol.)* blue, true;

absolut ~ **sein** to be as good as one's word; **als absolut** ~ **gelten** to pass for a man of absolute reliability;

~**e Angaben** reliable data, exact figures; **Brief einem** ~**en Boten anvertrauen** to send a letter by a sure messenger; ~**e Firma** reliable firm; ~**er Kunde** loyal customer; ~**er Mann** reliable man, trustee; ~**e Quelle** trustworthy source, good (reliable) authority; **von** ~**er Seite wissen** to have it on good authority.

Zuverlässigkeit reliability, trustworthiness, credit, certainty, faithfulness.

Zuverlässigkeits|fahrt reliability trial; ~**probe** endurance test; ~**prüfung** reliability trial; ~**rekord** record of reliability; ~**überprüfung** reliability test, *(Personal)* screening, security clearing.

Zuversicht confidence, trust, hope;

~ **der Verbraucher** consumer confidence;

seine ~ **wiedergewinnen** to regain one's confidence.

zuversichtlich confident, assured, sanguine;

~ **sein** to be in good heart.

Zuvielbeträge in der Kasse cash overs *(US)*.

Zuvorkommen compliance.

zuvorkommen to forestall, to anticipate, to take before the bound;

jem. ~ to get in ahead of s. o., to steal a march upon s. o.; **einer Attacke auf die Staatskasse** ~ to forestall a raid on the treasury *(coll.)*; **einem Einwand** ~ to obviate (preclude) an objection; **einer Gefahr** ~ to anticipate a danger; **der Konkurrenz** ~ to forestall a competitor; **mit einer Überraschungsreklame** ~ to steal somebody's thunder; **jem. im Weltraum** ~ to beat s. o. into space.

zuvorkommend obliging, complaisant, accommodating, gracious;

Kunden ~ **bedienen** to accommodate a client.

Zuvorkommenheit obligingness, complaisance, accommodation, *(Höflichkeit)* politeness, courtesy, civility.

Zuwachs accession, growth, augmentation, accretion, accruement, increase, increment, *(Einkommen)* gain, *(Gebiet)* expansion, accession, *(Grundstück)* unearned increment, added value;

jährlicher ~ annual growth;

~ **und Verminderung des Anlagevermögens** capital gains and losses; ~ **der Linken** left-wing gain; ~ **an Mitgliedern** increase in members;

~ **bekommen haben** to have had an addition to the family.

Zuwächse, voraussichtliche assets likely to accrue, dependencies.

zuwachsen *(anfallen)* to accrue, *(Weg)* to overgrow.

Zuwachs|jahr, kein no-growth year; ~**potential** growth potential.

Zuwachsrate rate of growth (increment), growth (accession) rate;

zum Stillstand führende (keine) ~ zero growth rate; **voraussichtliche** ~ prospect of growth rate; **17%ige** ~ 17% rate increase, growth rate of 17%;

~ **der Geldmenge** monetary growth rate;

hohe ~ **haben** to enjoy a fast rate of growth.

Zuwachs|steuer property increment (betterment, *Br.*) tax; ~**vorhersage** increase (growth) forecast; ~**wert** *(Grundstück)* increment value, added value, betterment.

Zuwahl co-optation, coöptation.

zuwählen to co-opt, to coöpt.

Zuwanderung immigration;

~ **wissenschaftlicher Führungskräfte** brain gain.

zuwartende Haltung wait-and-see policy.

zuwege bringen to accomplish, to jockey, to manage, to pull off *(fam.)*.

zuweisbar assignable.

zuweisen to assign, to appropriate, to apportion, to allocate, to allot;

Arbeit ~ to place in work; **Arbeitskräfte** ~ to allocate manpower; **jem. eine Aufgabe** ~ to assign a task (allot duties) to s. o.; **Betrag den Rücklagen** ~ to allocate an amount to the reserve fund; **Fall** ~ to assign a case; **Land** ~ to assign land; **Mittel** ~ to appropriate (earmark) funds; **Pflichtenkreis** ~ to allocate duties; **den freien Rücklagen** ~ to appropriate to free reserve, to allocate to the reserve fund; **dem Unterstützungsfonds** ~ to allocate to the poor fund.

Zuweisung assignation, assignment, appropriation, allotment, allocation, attribution;
arbeitsamtliche ~ direction order; **besondere** ~ special allocation; **staatliche** ~ government grant; **unentgeltliche** ~ voluntary allowance; **zweckgebundene** ~ specific grant;
~ **von Arbeitskräften** allocation of labo(u)r (manpower); ~ **von Aufgaben** assignment of a task; ~ **von Fernsehkanälen** allocation of channels; ~ **im vertikalen Finanzbereich** rate deficiency payment; ~ **an den betrieblichen Gewinnbeteiligungsfonds** allocation to staff profit sharing; ~ **an das Kapitalkonto** transfer to capital account; ~ **von Land** assignment of land; ~ **von Mitteln** appropriation of funds; **detaillierte** ~ **von Mitteln** itemized (segregate) appropriation, earmarking; ~ **an die Pensions- und Wohlfahrtskasse** allocation to staff pension and provident fund; ~ **einer Rechtssache aufgrund der Geschäftsordnung** assignment of action; ~ **an den Rücklagenfonds** allocation to reserve fund, reserve allocation; ~ **für einen Sonderbericht** *(Chefredakteur)* assignment; ~ **an den Tilgungsfonds** sinking-fund contribution ~ **des Verantwortungsbereichs** assignment of responsibility.

zuwenden to allocate, to allot, to make an allowance, to apportion, to bestow, *(Fonds)* to contribute;
jem. etw. ~ to make a gift of s. th. to s. o.; **sich neuen Anlagemöglichkeiten** ~ to switch investments; **sich seiner Arbeit** ~ to turn to one's work; **sich ganz wissenschaftlichen Arbeiten** ~ to devote o. s. to science; **jem. seine Aufmerksamkeit** ~ to bestow one's attention upon s. o.; **sich einem anderen Beruf** ~ to take up a new profession; **jem. geschenkweise** ~ to make a gift of s. th. to s. o.; **sich einem anderen Gesprächsthema** ~ to switch the talk to another topic; **jem. seine Gunst** ~ to dispense one's favo(u)r to s. o.; **jem. etw. letztwillig** ~ to bequeath (devise) s. th. to s. o.; **sich der Politik** ~ to go in for politics; **dem Roten Kreuz** ~ to contribute to the Red Cross; **den Rücklagen** ~ to allocate to the reserve fund; **sich dem kommerziellen Sektor intensiver** ~ to diversify into commercial markets; **jem. eine größere Summe** ~ to bestow a considerable sum upon s. o.; **sich einem anderen Thema** ~ to turn to another topic.

Zuwendung allocation, allowance, allotment, bestowal, *(Belohnung)* gratification, gratuity, advancement, *(Fonds)* contribution, *(Geschenk)* gift, donation, money present, *(Immobiliarvermächtnis)* devise, *(Mobiliarvermächtnis)* bequest;
für gemeinnützige Stiftungen anerkannte ~**en** gifts held to be valid charitable trusts; **nicht als gemeinnützig anerkannte** ~**en** gifts held to be not charitable; **außerordentliche** ~**en** exceptional grants; **bedingungslose** ~ outright gift; **einmalige** ~ nonrecurring allowance; **fiduziarische** ~ voluntary trust; **finanzielle** ~ allowance, grant; **freigebige** ~ gift to charity; **freiwillige** ~ unasked (voluntary) contribution; **laufende** ~**en** periodical contributions; **letztwillige** ~ gift by will, testamentary gift, legacy of residue, residuary bequest; **staatliche** ~ subsidy, subvention, state contribution, grant-in-aid *(US)*; **steuerfreie** ~ tax-free gift; **steuerpflichtige** ~ taxable gift; **testamentarische** ~ legacy, bequest; **unentgeltliche** ~ donation, gratuitous payment (settlement), voluntary gift (contribution); **mit einer Auflage verbundene** ~ onerous gift; **wöchentliche** ~ weekly allowance;
~**en an den Flüchtlingsfonds** donations to the fund for refugees; ~ **zur Landschaftsverbesserung** gift for the benefit of a locality; ~ **aus öffentlichen Mitteln** grants-in-aid *(US)*, state contribution; ~**en aus der Staatskasse** exchequer equalization grants *(Br.)*; ~ **von einer Stiftung** settlement money; ~ **von Todes wegen** testamentary gift, gift mortis causa *(US)*; ~ **von Vermögenswerten** settlement of property;
finanzielle ~**en hereinholen** to shake the money tree; **finanzielle** ~**en für künstlerische Belange kürzen** to cut down money for the arts.

zuwerfen, jem. einen Blick to cast a glance at s. o.; **jem. einen Kuß** ~ to blow a kiss to s. o.

zuwiderhandeln to contravene, to counteract, to offend, to infringe;
Bestimmungen ~ to contravene the regulations, to infringe provisions; **baupolizeilichen Bestimmungen** ~ to violate building codes; **einer Weisung** ~ to disregard a direction.

Zuwiderhandelnder contravener, offender, trespasser.

Zuwiderhandlung contravention, noncompliance, nonobservance, offence, infringement, violation, trespass;
~**en gegen baupolizeiliche Anordnungen** building-code violations.

zuwiderlaufen to be in opposition;
dem Zweck ~ to be contrary to the purpose.

zuwinken to wave (signal) to s. o.

zuzahlen to pay in addition, to make an additional payment.

zuzählen to add to.

Zuzahlung additional payment, *(Effekteninhaber)* assessment;
~ **geleistet** assessment paid.

zuziehen to consult, to call in, *(einwandern)* to immigrate, *(sich niederlassen)* to settle down, to take up one's abode, *(Wohnung)* to move in;
sich ~ to incur, to catch, to get; **Anwalt** ~ to consult a lawyer (an attorney, *US*); **sich jds. Haß** ~ to incur s. one's hatred; **sich eine Krankheit** ~ to contract (catch, get) an illness; **sich Kritik** ~ to expose o. s. to criticism; **Sachverständigen** ~ to call in an expert; **Spezialisten** ~ to call in a specialist; **sich eine Strafe** ~ to make o. s. punishable; **sich Unannehmlichkeiten** ~ to get into trouble (hot water); **Vorhänge** ~ to draw the curtains; **j. als Zeugen** ~ to call s. o. as witness.

Zuziehung calling in, consultation;
unter ~ **von Zeugen** in the presence of witnesses;
~ **eines Anwalts** consultation (employment) of a lawyer; ~ **eines Sachverständigen** calling in of an expert.

Zuzug arrival, *(Einwanderung)* immigration.

zuzüglich plus, adding, add to this;
~ **Einzugsspesen** with exchange *(US)*; ~ **Nebenkosten** plus extras; ~ **der Spesen** including the expenses; ~ **Stückzinsen** and interest.

Zuzugsgenehmigung entry and registry permit, residence permit.

zuzu|rechnen sein to be attributable; ~**schreiben** to be due to.

Zwang duress, coercion, constraint, necessity, necessitation, compulsion, *(Gewalt)* force, violence, *(Hindernis)* fetter, *(sittliche Verpflichtung)* moral obligation, bondage;
unter ~ involuntary, under duress; **staatlichem** ~ **unterworfen** state-enforced;
ökonomischer ~ economic necessity; **physischer** ~ physical compulsion; **psychischer** ~ undue influence, mental duress;
~ **zu Deckungskäufen** squeezing the shorts *(US)*, bear squeeze *(Br.)*; ~ **der Mode** tyranny of fashion; ~ **der Notwendigkeit** bonds of necessity; ~ **der Verhältnisse** pressure of circumstances;
sich keinen ~ **antun** to suit o. s., not to stand on ceremony; **dem Gesetz** ~ **antun** to pervert the law; **einem Text** ~ **antun** to twist the meaning of a text; **unter** ~ **aussagen** to bear witness under duress; ~ **auf jem. ausüben** to bring pressure to bear on s. o.; **unter widerrechtlichem** ~ **handeln** to act under duress (coercion, pressure, protest); **unter dem** ~ **der Verhältnisse stehen** to be under the pinch of necessity; **Vertrag unter** ~ **unterschreiben** to make a contract under duress.

zwanglos free, informal, free-form, unbuttoned, familiar, relaxed, at ease, casual, unconventional;
sich völlig ~ **benehmen** to behave free and easy;
~**e Atmosphäre** relaxed atmosphere; ~**e Besichtigung** free inspection; ~**er Besuch** informal call; **in** ~**er Folge erscheinen** to be published in no particular order; ~**es Gespräch** informal conversation; ~**es Wochenendgespräch** country house chat; ~**es Zusammensein** informal gathering (meeting).

Zwanglosigkeit informality, relaxation, familiarity, ease.

Zwangs|abgabe compulsory contribution (levy, delivery); ~**abkommen mit Kunden eines bestreikten Betriebes** hot cargo agreement; ~**ablieferung** compulsory delivery; ~**abtretung** involuntary assignment; ~**abwicklung** forced execution, compulsory bankruptcy; ~**aktion** *(Völkerrecht)* enforcement action; ~**anheuerung** impressment; ~**anheuerung von Matrosen** pressing seamen; ~**ankauf von Grundstücken** compulsory land purchase; ~**anleihe** forced (compulsory) loan, postwar credit *(Br.)*; ~**anwendung** act of coercion; ~**arbeit** hard (compulsory, forced) labo(u)r, penal (involuntary) servitude.

Zwangsarbeiter slave (forced) labo(u)rer;
ausländischer ~ displaced person;
~ **einsetzen** to exploit slave labo(u)r;
~**lager** slave labo(u)r (concentration) camp.

Zwangs|aufenthalt detention; ~**auflage** requisition; ~**auflösung** compulsory dissolution (winding-up), involuntary liquidation; ~**aufnahme** compulsory membership; ~**ausgleich** compulsory settlement; ~**aushebung** *(mil.)* levy, conscription, draft *(US)*; ~**ausverkauf** forced (compulsory) sale; ~**beitrag** compulsory contribution; ~**beiträge zur Sozialversicherung** social security taxes *(US)*; **von der Zahlung von** ~**beiträgen befreit sein** to be exempt from payment of contributions; ~**beitreibung** compulsory collection; ~**beitritt** compulsory membership; ~**beurlaubung** suspension.

zwangsbewirtschaften to ration, to allocate;
Wohnungsmarkt ~ to control housing.

zwangsbewirtschaftet rationed, *(Häuser)* rent-controlled.

Zwangsbewirtschaftung rationing (standby) control;
~ **der Arbeitskräfte** compulsion of labo(u)r; ~ **der Mieten** rent control;
der ~ **unterwerfen** to ration, to allocate, to control.

Zwangs|einquartierung quartering, billeting; ~**einsatz** compulsory service; ~**eintragung** compulsory incorporation; ~**einweisung in eine Nervenheilanstalt** admittance to a mental hospital under compulsory power; ~**einziehung** mandatory redemption; ~**enteignung** compulsory surrender (purchase, *Scot.*), expropriation, eminent domain *(US)*; ~**enteignungsrecht** right of eminent domain *(US)*; ~**entziehungsanstalt** reformatory.

zwangsernährt force-fed.

Zwangs|ernährung forced (forcible) feeding; ~**etatisierung** compulsory budgeting.

zwangsevakuieren, Bevölkerung to relocate the population.

Zwangs|evakuierung relocation of the population; ~**geld** compulsory levy, administrative fine, *(Zwangswährung)* managed (fiat, *US*) money; ~**gemeinschuldner** involuntary bankrupt; ~**glattstellung** compulsory realization, forced evening up *(US)*; ~**haft** detention, *(Vorbeugehaft)* preventive detention *(Br.)*; ~**haftpflichtversicherung** compulsory insurance against third-party risks; ~**handlung** act of coercion; ~**herrschaft** dictatorship, despotism; ~**hypothek** judicial (distress-sale) mortgage, execution lien; ~**idee** obsession; ~**industrialisierung** forced-draft industrialization; ~**innung** guild; ~**jacke** strait jacket; **in die** ~**jacke stecken** to lag; ~**kartell** compulsory syndicate; ~**kartellisierung** compulsory cartelization; ~**konkurs** involuntary bankruptcy; ~**konkurs beantragen** to file an involuntary petition; ~**kontingent** mandatory quota; ~**konversion** compulsory (involuntary) conversion; ~**kurs** involuntary conversion, forced circulation, forced rate (course, *Br.*) of exchange.

Zwangslage duress, constraint, dilemma, predicament, exigency, quandary, Hobson's choice;
geldmarkttechnische ~ money squeeze; **physische** ~ physical necessity; **unausweichliche** ~ fine force;
in einer ~ **handeln** to act under constraint (duress); **in einer** ~ **sein** to be in a dilemma (between the devil and the deep blue sea); **j. in eine** ~ **versetzen** to lay (put) s. o. under the necessity.

zwangsläufig inevitable, unavoidable, necessary, mandatory;
~ **scheitern** to be bound to fail;
~**es Ereignis** inevitable accident.

Zwangs|läufigkeit, wirtschaftliche economic determinism; ~**leistung** compulsory service; ~**lektüre** must reading; ~**liquidation** involuntary liquidation, compulsory (adjudicated) winding up, forced liquidation, winding up by the court; ~**liquidator** liquidator in winding up by the court.

zwangsliquidieren to wind up compulsorily.

Zwangs|lizenz compulsory licence, licence of right *(Br.)*; ~**lotse** compulsory pilot; ~**maßnahmen** measures of coercion, coercive (compulsory, enforcement) measures, *(Sanktionen)* sanctions, *(Völkerrecht)* enforcement action; ~**maßnahmen anwenden** to employ means of coercion; ~**methoden** coercive (strong-arm) methods *(US)*; ~**methoden anwenden** to employ means of coercion; ~**mieter** statutory (assigned) tenant; ~**mitgliedschaft [in einer Gewerkschaft]** compulsory [union] membership; ~**mittel** compulsory means, means of coercion.

zwangspensioniert compulsorily retired.

Zwangs|pensionierung compulsory retirement on a pension; **die auf 70 Jahre abgestellte** ~**pensionierung abschaffen** to abolish the compulsory retiring age to 70; ~**psychose** compulsive insanity; ~**publikum** shotgun audience; **gesetzlich nicht ganz berechtigte** ~**quarantäne** shotgun quarantine.

zwangsräumen to eject, to evict.

Zwangs|räumung actual eviction, ejection, ejectment; ~**räumung wegen Mietschulden** eviction for nonpayment of rent; ~**räumung gegen einen Mieter durchführen** to eject (dispossess, evict, oust) a tenant; ~**räumungsauftrag** dispossess warrant; ~**regelung** mandatory settlement; ~**regime** dictatorship, despotism; ~**registrierung** compulsory incorporation; ~**regulierung** coercion, forced execution; ~**rekrutierung** impressment.

zwangsrepatriieren, Gastarbeiter to send foreign workers home compulsorily.

Zwangs|repatriierung forced repatriation; ~**schlichtung** compulsory arbitration; ~**sparen** forced (compulsory) saving, compulsory deposit scheme; ~**sterilisierung** forced sterilisation; ~**tarif** *(Bahn)* lawful (legal) rate; ~**übereignungsbeschluß** vesting order *(Br.)*; ~**überstunden** compulsory overtime; ~**umrechnungskurs** forced rate (course) of exchange, involuntary conversion; ~**umsiedler** displaced person; ~**veranlagung** arbitrary assessment; ~**verfahren** compulsory process, civil enforcement proceedings *(US)*; ~**vergleich** compulsory (forced) arbitration, compulsory settlement (liquidation), *(Konkurs)* composition in bankruptcy, *(Liquidation)* enforced (compulsory, involuntary) liquidation; ~**vergleichsantrag** involuntary reorganization petition; ~**verhör** third degree; ~**verkauf** compulsory (judicial) sale, sale by order of the court, forced sale, compulsory surrender *(Scot.)*, *(Börse)* execution under the rules; **gerichtlich bestätigter** ~**verkauf** confirmation of sale; ~**verkäufe durchführen** *(Börse)* to execute under the rules; ~**verkaufswert** forced-sale value.

zwangsverpflichtet conscript.

Zwangsverpflichtung conscription, impressment.

zwangs|verschicken to deport; ~**verschickt** displaced.

Zwangsverschickung displacement, deportation.

zwangsverschleppt displaced.

Zwangsverschleppter displaced person.

zwangsversichert sein *(Sozialversicherung)* to be inside the scope of the national insurance system *(Br.)*.

Zwangsversicherter compulsorily insured person.

Zwangsversicherung compulsory insurance.

zwangsversteigern to sell by public auction, to bring to the hammer.

Zwangsversteigerung execution *(US)* (compulsory, forced, public, judicial, *Scot.*) sale, execution by sale of debtor's chattels, distress sale, hammer, sheriff's sale *(Br.)*, *(Grundstücke)* foreclosure, foreclosure sale *(US)*;
gerichtlich angeordnete ~ forced sale by order of the court;
ordnungsgemäß durchgeführte ~ fair sale;
~ **eines Grundstückskomplexes** lumping sale;
Aussetzung der ~ **anordnen** to order the reopening of a foreclosure *(US)*; ~ **fortsetzen** to reopen foreclosure *(US)*.

Zwangsversteigerungs|beschluß foreclosure decree *(US)*; ~**erlös** proceeds of foreclosure sale *(US)*; ~**kosten** cost of foreclosure *(US)*; ~**verfahren** foreclosure suit *(US)*; ~**verfahren einstellen** to stay foreclosure of a mortgage *(US)*; ~**vermerk** receiver's certificate.

zwangsverwalten to sequester;
Schuldnervermögen ~ to administer a debtor's estate summarily.

Zwangsverwalter receiver, receiver by way of equitable execution *(Br.)*, *(Grundstück)* sequester, sequestrator of land;
behördlich bestellter ~ official receiver; **gerichtlicher** ~ sequester; **vorläufiger** ~ official receiver *(Br.)*;
~**einsetzung** equitable execution.

Zwangsverwaltung compulsory administration, *(Grundbesitz)* sequestration, poinding of the ground, real poinding, *(Konkurs)* receivership *(Br.)*;
erneute ~ re-extent;
~ **mit Veräußerungsbefugnis** equitable execution;
~ **aufheben** to desequester; **Gesellschaft unter** ~ **stellen** to put a corporation under receivership (sequestration).

Zwangs|verwaltungsbeschluß compulsory administration order, receiving order *(Br.)*; ~**verwertung eines Patents** compulsory exploitation (working) of a patent.

zwangsvollstrecken to levy, to issue execution, *(auf Grund einer Hypothek)* to foreclose *(US)*, to execute a mortgage;
gegen einen Schuldner ~ to distrain upon a debtor.

Zwangsvollstreckung levy [of execution], execution, enforcement of a judgment, seizure of goods by the sheriff, diligence *(Scot. law)*;
der ~ **unterliegend** subject to execution, distrainable, foreclosable; **im Wege der** ~ by way of execution; **nicht der** ~ **unterliegend** exempt from execution, judgment- (mace-) proof *(US)*;
noch nicht beendete ~ uncompleted execution; **im Gange befindliche (gerade stattfindende)** ~ execution in force and operating; **nur teilweise durchgeführte** ~ dormant execution; **erfolglose** ~ unsatisfied execution; **durch Pfändung vorgenommene** ~ execution levied by seizure;
~ **in das Gesellschaftsvermögen** execution against a company; ~ **aus einer Hypothek** execution (foreclosure, *US*) of a mortgage, mortgage foreclosure *(US)*; ~ **wegen Steuerrückständen** tax sale of property; ~ **in das bewegliche Vermögen** general execution; ~ **in das unbewegliche Vermögen** execution levied upon the property, foreclosure *(US)*; ~ **durch Wegnahme** execution levied by seizure;
~ **durch Zahlung abwenden** to satisfy an execution; **Einstellung der** ~ **anordnen** to grant a stay of execution; ~ **aussetzen** to stay execution; ~ **beantragen** to issue execution against; **Einstellung**

der ~ **beantragen** to ask for a stay of execution; ~ **betreiben** to levy a distress (execution on goods), to issue execution against; ~ **aus einer Hypothek betreiben** to execute (foreclose on, *US*) a mortgage; ~ **aus dem Kostenurteil betreiben** to levy (issue) execution with respect to the (for the amount of) costs; ~ **durchführen** to seize goods under process, to put in an execution and levy, to seize property on an execution; ~ **einstellen** to discharge process of execution, *(vorläufig)* to stay execution; ~ **mangels Masse einstellen** to return an execution nulla bona; **der** ~ **unterliegen** to be subject to the lien of a judgment, to be subject to foreclosure proceedings *(US)* (to distraint, to execution); **nicht der** ~ **unterliegen** to be liable to stay execution; ~ **vereiteln** to obstruct process; ~ **vornehmen** to put in an execution and levy; **im Wege der** ~ **verkauft werden** to be sold under execution.

Zwangsvollstreckungs|anordnung decree of strict foreclosure, foreclosure decree; ~**anspruch** right to foreclose; ~**antrag** action for poinding, bill of foreclosure *(US)*; ~**aussetzung** stay of execution; ~**beschluß** warrant of attachment, foreclosure decree *(US)*, foreclosure order *(US)*, decree of strict foreclosure *(US)*; ~**freibetrag für Heimstätten** homestead exemption *(US)*; ~**gebühren** sheriff's poundage; ~**gläubiger** execution creditor; ~**klage** hypothecary action, action for foreclosure *(US)*, foreclosure action (suit) *(US)*; ~**klage erheben** to bring a foreclosure action *(US)*; ~**klausel** writ of execution; ~**kosten** costs of execution; ~**verfahren** executory process, process of distraint, judgment execution, foreclosure proceedings (action) *(US)*; ~**verfahren betreiben** to bring a foreclosure action *(US)*; ~**verkauf** distress sale, forced sale by order of the court.

Zwangs|vorführung *(Zeuge)* compulsory attendance (process); ~**vorstellung** obsession, insane delusion; **von der** ~**vorstellung befallen arbeitslos zu werden** obsessed by fear of unemployment; ~**währung** forced currency, fiat standard (money) *(US)*, managed currency.

zwangsweise compulsory, under compulsion, obligatory, by force, forcibly, under constraint;
~ **ausheben** to impress, *(mil.)* to conscribe; **sich** ~ **Zugang zu einem Haus verschaffen** to force one's way into a house; ~ **pensioniert werden** to be compulsorily retired; ~ **zahlen** to pay money under coercion;
~ **Einhaltung von Gewerkschaftsbeträgen durch den Betrieb** compulsory checkoff of labor *(US)* (trade-union, *Br.*) dues; ~ **Entfernung eines Mieters** dispossession (eviction) of a tenant; ~ **Entlassung** mandatory removal; ~ **Unterbringung** compulsory detention; **zur Gläubigerbefriedigung** ~ **vorgenommene Vermögensübertragung auf einen Treuhänder** involuntary assignment for the benefit of creditors.

Zwangswirtschaft [state-]controlled economy, totalitarian economy, *(Bewirtschaftung)* rationing, *(Planwirtschaft)* planned economy;
~ **abbauen (aufheben)** to decontrol; **unter** ~ **stellen** to control; **Kapital der** ~ **unterwerfen** to conscript capital.

Zwangswohnsitz necessary domicile.

Zweck purpose, view, objective, turn, *(Absicht)* mind, intention, wile, *(Bestimmung)* intended use, *(Ziel)* object, aim, end, goal; **einem doppelten** ~ **dienend** dual purpose; **für einen besonderen** ~ **hergestellt** tailored for a special purpose; **für wohltätige** ~**e** for charitable causes, for a charitable object, for [the benefit of] charity; **für die** ~**e der Praxis** for all practical purposes; **mit dem** ~ with a view to; **nur für öffentliche** ~**e vorgesehen** exclusively for public purposes; **zu einem bestimmten** ~ for a set purpose; **zu betrügerischen** ~**en** for fraudulent purposes; **zu gewerblichen** ~**en** for commercial (industrial) purposes, for the purpose of trade;
beabsichtigter ~ intended purpose; **steuerlich begünstigter** ~ tax-favo(u)red purpose; **erlaubter** ~ lawful purpose; **gemeinnütziger** ~ public purpose; **landwirtschaftliche** ~**e** farming purposes; **mildtätiger** ~ charitable purpose; **öffentlicher** ~ governmental (municipal) purpose; **produktive** ~**e** productive purposes; **seelsorgerische** ~**e** pious uses; **wohltätige** ~**e** benevolent (charitable) purposes;
~ **eines Briefes** object of a letter; ~ **einer Gesellschaft** object of a company; ~ **einer Klage** object of an action;
sein Vermögen für wohltätige ~**e bestimmen** to leave one's money to charity; **einem guten** ~ **dienen** to serve a good cause; **privaten** ~**en dienen** to serve some private ends; **zweierlei** ~**en dienen** to perform a double service, to serve two purposes; **seinem** ~ **entfremden** to estrange; **dem** ~ **entsprechen** to serve (answer) a purpose; ~ **erfüllen** to serve the purpose, to do the trick *(sl.)*; **seinen** ~ **erreichen** to achieve (gain, effect) one's purpose (object); **eigens zu diesem** ~ **kommen** to come for this purpose; **für eigene** ~**e mißbrauchen** to divert for one's own use; **für wohltätige** ~**e stiften** to put one's hand in one's pocket; **seinen** ~ **verfehlen** to miss one's aim; **für einen nützlichen** ~ **verwenden** to press into a useful purpose; **zu unerlaubten** ~**en verwenden** to misapply, to misappropriate; **für einen bestimmten** ~ **vorsehen** to appropriate, *(Gelder)* to earmark; **Geldmittel unerlaubten** ~**en zuführen** to misappropriate funds;
~**abgabe** special rate; ~**bau** functional building; ~**bauten** special purpose (functional) buildings; ~**bestätigung** letter of charge *(Br.)*.

zweckbestimmen to appropriate;
Beträge ~ to earmark funds for a purpose.

zweckbestimmt appropriated, earmarked, *(Gebäude)* functional;
~**e Architektur** functional architecture.

Zweckbestimmung destination, purpose, appropriation, imputation;
ausdrückliche ~ **[durch Gesetzgeber]** specific (express) appropriation; **gesonderte** ~ segregated appropriation;
~ **von Geldbeträgen (Mitteln)** earmarking of funds; ~ **des Gesellschaftsvertrages** objects clause; ~ **durch den Schuldner** appropriation by debtor; ~ **von Steuereinnahmen** dedication of tax revenues; ~ **von Zahlungen** application (imputation, appropriation) of payments;
~ **einer Zahlung festlegen** to appropriate a payment.

Zweckbestimmungs|absicht intention to appropriate; ~**befugnis** *(Kongreß)* power of the purse *(US)*; ~**klausel** objects clause.

zweckbetont functional, *(nützlich)* utilitarian.

zweckbewußt purposive.

Zweckbindung project tying;
~ **von Steuererträgen** earmarking of taxes.

zweckdienlich convenient, pertinent, expedient, serviceable, to the purpose, useful, suitable;
~ **für j. sein** to serve s. one's turn;
~**e Angaben** relevant information.

Zweckdienlichkeit instrumentality, fitness for a particular purpose, expediency.

Zwecke brad, peg.

zweckentfremden to misappropriate, to divert, to misuse;
Mittel ~ to divert funds; **Wohnung** ~ to convert rooms to office use.

zweckentfremdete Mittel diverted funds.

Zweckentfremdung misappropriation, misuse;
~ **eines Fonds** diversion of a fund; ~ **einer Wohnung** conversion of rooms to office use.

zweckentsprechend suitable, appropriate, expedient;
~ **sein** to fulfil the purpose in view, to answer the purpose.

Zweckfahrzeug utility vehicle.

zweckgebunden tied, *(Erträge)* committed, *(Mittel, Steuer)* earmarked, *(Zuschuß)* specific;
nicht ~ uncommitted, not earmarked;
~**e Anleihe** tied loan; ~**e Einnahmen** restricted receipts; ~**es Konto** earmarked account; **nicht** ~**er Kredit** no-purpose loan; ~**e Mittel** appropriated (earmarked) funds; ~**e Mittelzuweisung** itemized (aggregated) appropriation; ~**e Rücklage** appropriated surplus *(US)*, surplus reserve *(US)*; ~**es Vermögen** restricted property; ~**er Vermögensteil** earmarked asset.

zwecklos purposeless, of no use, useless, aimless, pointless, *(vergeblich)* futile, idle;
absolut ~ of no mortal use;
~ **sein** to be of no avail.

Zwecklosigkeit purposelessness, aimlessness.

zweckmäßig expedient, appropriate, proper, practical, rational, advisable, wholesome, *(zeitlich)* opportune;
nicht ~ **sein** not to be advisable;
~**e Behebung einer Schwierigkeit** expedient solution of a difficulty.

Zweckmäßigkeit expedience, *(Wohnung)* convenience;
~ **der Genehmigung eines Gesuches bezweifeln** to question the propriety of granting a request.

Zweckmäßigkeits|erwägung, wirtschaftlichen ~**erwägungen entsprechen** to suit economic conveniences; ~**frage** question of expediency; **aus** ~**gründen** as a matter of convenience, on grounds of expediency.

Zweck|meldung inspired news item; ~**möbel** functional furniture; ~**optimismus** wishful thinking; ~**sparen** target saving; ~**stil** functionalism; ~**verband** *(Kommunalverwaltung)* joint board *(Br.)*, joint authority *(Br.)*, *(Versicherungswesen)* rating bureau; ~**vermögen** trust-and-agency fund; **verbundene** ~**vermögen** related funds.

zweckwidrig inexpedient, inappropriate, unsuitable;
~**e Verwendung öffentlicher Gelder** misappropriation of public funds.
Zweckzuweisung block grant, specific grant.
Zweiachser four-wheeler.
zweibahnig two-lane.
Zweibettzimmer double bedroom.
zweideutig | reden to double-talk;
~**er Witz** risqué joke.
Zweideutigkeit ambiguity, equivocality.
Zweidrittelmehrheit two-third majority;
~ **auf die Beine bringen** to muster a two-third majority; ~ **im Senat sicherstellen** to secure the assent of two thirds of the senate.
Zweidrittelseite two-third page.
zweifache Ausfertigung duplicate.
Zweifach | geschäft twig branch *(US)*; ~**stecker** *(el.)* two-pin plug; ~**steuerung** *(Flugzeug)* dual control.
Zwei | familienhaus semi-detached (two-family) house, duplex [house] *(US)*; ~**farbendruck** two-colo(u)r process.
Zweifel doubt, scruple;
ohne ~ and no mistake;
begründeter (berechtigter) ~ reasonable (legitimate, rational) doubt; **nicht der geringste** ~ no earthly doubt;
~ **ausräumen (beheben)** to remove a doubt; ~ **bekommen** to have second thoughts; ~ **beseitigen** to dispel doubts, to settle a query; **alle** ~ **beseitigen** to clinch an argument; **letzte** ~ **beseitigen** to remove the last doubts; ~ **hegen** to entertain doubts; **keinen** ~ **hegen** to make no doubt; **j. über etw. nicht im** ~ **lassen** to leave s. o. in no doubt about s. th.; **keinen** ~ **an seiner Einstellung lassen** to make one's meaning perfectly plain (clear); **von vielen** ~**n zerrissen sein** to be tossed on an ocean of doubts; ~ **verbannen** to dispel doubts; ~ **zerstreuen** to dissipate doubts; **in** ~ **ziehen** to call in question; **Behauptung in** ~ **ziehen** to throw discredit upon a statement; **jds. Motive in** ~ **ziehen** to impeach s. one's motives; **jds. Worte in** ~ **ziehen** to doubt (question) s. one's words.
zweifelhaft doubtful, dubious, hedge, open to question, *(fragwürdig)* suspicious, equivocal, shady, queer *(coll.)*, *(Schulden)* uncertain, doubtful, bad *(US)*;
etw. ~ **erscheinen lassen** to cast miscredit on s. th.;
~**e Auskunft** vague information; ~**e Forderung** *(hinsichtlich Rechtsanspruch)* doubtful claim, *(hinsichtlich Zahlung)* doubtful (bad, *US*) debt; ~**es Geschäft** shady business; ~**es Gesicht machen** to look sceptically; ~**es Kompliment** left-handed compliment; ~**e Persönlichkeit** suspicious character; ~**er Rechtstitel** doubtful title; **Zeitungsberichte in äußerst** ~**em Ruf erscheinen lassen** to throw serious discredit on the newspaper accounts; **von** ~**em Wert** of debatable merit.
zweifeln, an jds. Fähigkeiten to doubt s. one's abilities; **an der Wahrheit eines Berichts** ~ to doubt the truth of a report.
Zweifelsfall, im in case of doubt;
im ~ **zu jds. Gunsten entscheiden** to give s. o. the benefit of the doubt; ~ **erledigen** to settle a doubtful case.
Zweifelsfälle beseitigen, alle to exclude all possibilities of doubt.
Zweig twig, sprig, branch, arm, *(Familie)* branch;
~**abteilung** branch section (department, establishment), affiliate[d institution].
Zweiganggetriebe two-speed gear.
Zweig | bahn branch line (railway, *Br.*, railroad, *US*), secondary line, branch; ~**bank** branch [bank]; ~**betrieb** subsidiary (branch) plant, affiliated organization; ~**büro** sub-office; ~**geschäft** branch, branch business (establishment, store, *US*), subsidiary retail business, chain store *(US)*; ~**geschäftsstelle** district registry *(Br.)*; ~**gesellschaft** affiliated society, subsidiary (affiliated) company (corporation), ramification, local branch, regional office.
zweigleisig double-tracked;
~**e Bahn** double line; ~**e Strecke bauen** to double-track.
Zweig | linie branch; ~**niederlage,** ~**niederlassung** branch depot (house, establishment, office); **ausländische** ~**niederlassung** foreign branch; ~**niederlassung in der Provinz** *(Bank)* provincial branch; ~**organisation** branch organization, affiliate *(US)*; ~**postamt** branch post-office, post-office substation; ~**station** *(Bahn)* junction, branch station; ~**stelle** branch office (establishment), suboffice, local branch, *(Bank)* sub-branch, *(Werkstatt)* service depot, agency office; ~**stellen unterhalten** to maintain branches, to operate branch offices; ~**stellennetz** network of branches; ~**unternehmen** branch [establishment], branch house; ~**verein** branch, branch (affiliated) society.

Zweihundert | jahrfeier bicentennial celebration; ~**meilenzone** 200-mile zone.
Zweijahresvertrag two years' contract.
zweijährig biennial.
Zwei | kammersystem bicameral system, bicameralism; ~**kampf** mutual affray, single combat, duel.
zweiköpfige Familie familiy of two.
zweimonatlich bimonthly;
~**e Veröffentlichung** bimonthly [publication].
Zweimonats | geld two months' time deposit *(US)*; ~**schrift** bimonthly.
zweimotorig bimotored, *(Flugzeug)* twin- (two-) engined.
Zweiparteien | ausschuß bipartisan committee, ~**system** two-party (biparty, *US*) system.
Zweiphasenstrom two-phase current.
zweiphasig *(el.)* quarter-phase.
Zweischichtenbetrieb double-shift working.
zweischichtig belegt double-shifted.
zweischneidig *(fig.)* double-edged.
zweiseitig bilateral, bipartite;
~**e Anzeige** double-page spread; ~**es Handelsabkommen** bilateral trade agreement; ~**er Vertrag** bilateral contract.
Zweisitzer two-seater, *(geschlossen)* coupé, *(offen)* roadster.
zweisitzig two-seated.
Zweispalten | journal two-column journal; ~**tarif** two-column tariff.
zweispaltig half-measure;
~ **gedruckt** printed in double columns.
zweisprachig bilingual;
~**e Ausgabe** diglot.
Zweispur *(Tonband)* dual track.
zweispurig two-lane, *(Bahn)* double-tracked;
~**e Bahn** double line.
zweistellig two-digit;
~**e Zahl** two-figure (-place) number; **gut und gern** ~**e Zahlen erreichen** to be well into double figures.
zweistöckig two-storey, double-storied, *(Bus)* double-decked.
Zweistufenrakete two-stage racket.
zweistufig two-stage, two-tier;
~**es Stichprobenverfahren** double sampling.
zweistündige Besprechung conference lasting two hours.
Zweitaktmotor two-cycle motor, two-stroke engine.
Zweitausfertigung *(Urkunde)* duplicate document, second deliverance, *(Wechsel)* second [of exchange];
~ **einer Klage** concurrent writ; ~ **eines Vollstreckungsurteils** alias writ;
~ **einer Urkunde anfertigen** to make a copy of a deed.
Zweit | ausgabe *(Zeitung)* second edition; ~**bogen** second sheet.
zweite | Ausfertigung *(Wechsel)* second; ~**r Buchhalter** junior clerk; ~ **Etage** second storey *(Br.)* (story, *US*), third floor *(US)*; **aus** ~**r Hand** at second hand, secondhand; ~ **Hypothek** second (junior) mortgage; ~**s Ich** alter ego; ~**r Klasse** second-class; ~**r-Klasse-Wagen** second-class carriage; ~**r Mann** number-two man; **jeden** ~**n Montag** on alternate Mondays; ~**s Programm** *(Fernsehen)* second program(me), *(Computer)* alternate program(me); ~ **Wahl** medium quality; ~**r Wahlgang** second ballot.
Zweiter, als ~ **durchs Ziel gehen** to land second.
Zweit | erwerb secondhand purchase; ~**fahrzeug** second car; ~**hypothek** second mortgage.
zweitklassig common, inferior, second-rate, secondary, mediocre, second, second-class (-level);
als ~**e Ware verkaufen** to sell goods under a secondary label; ~**es Werk** inferior piece of work.
Zweit | korrektur revised proof; ~**mädchen** between-maid *(Br.)*.
Zweitonner two-ton lorry, two-tonner *(US)*.
zweitrangig second-rate, inferior, below standard, second-level, second-class (-tier), secondary, subordinate, *(fam.)* one-horse *(US)*;
~ **werden** to fall into the second rank;
~**e Angelegenheit** matter of secondary importance; ~**es Provinznest** one-horse town *(US coll.)*; ~**e Ware** inferior goods;.
Zweitschrift [duplicate] copy, counterpart, duplicate, second delivery;
~ **anfertigen** to copy.
Zweit | schuldner secondary debtor; ~**stimme** second vote.
zweitverpflichtet secondarily liable *(US)*.
Zweit | wagen second car; ~**wohnsitz** second domicile; ~**wohnung** second (additional) home.
zweiwöchentlich fortnightly.

Zweiwochenurlaub a fortnight's holiday.
Zwerg dwarf, midget, Tom Thumb;
lächerlicher ~ nobody;
~betrieb infinitesimal industry *(US)*, hole in the wall *(sl.)*; **~schule** one-room school house, all-age school.
Zwickmühle dilemma, squeeze, quandary, fix;
in einer ~ sitzen to be on the horns of a dilemma.
Zwiebelfisch *(drucktechn.)* pie, wrong font (fount, *Br.*).
zwiebeln, j. to give s. o. hell.
Zwiegespräch dialogue, conversation, talk.
Zwielicht twilight, dusk;
ins ~ geraten to lay o. s. open to suspicion.
zwielichtig dubious, shady, fishy;
~er Charakter shady character; **~e Gruppen** twilight groups; **~e Sache** funny business.
Zwiespalt conflict, dilemma;
in einen ~ geraten to be on the horns of a dilemma; **mit sich selbst im ~ sein** to be at odds with o. s.
zwiespältiger Eindruck mixed impression.
Zwietracht discord, dissunion;
~ säen to make mischief between; **~ zwischen Freunden stiften** to set friends at variance.
Zwillings|bereifung dual tyres; **~kinderwagen** duostroller *(US)*; **~paar** pair of twins; **~triebwerk** twin engine.
zwingen to force to, to coerce, to compel, to constrain;
j. zu etw. ~ to lay s. o. under a necessity (an obligation); **sich zu harter Arbeit ~** to force o. s. to work hard; **zu Deckungskäufen ~** to squeeze; **Feind zur Schlacht ~** to force an action on the enemy; **Festung zur Übergabe ~** to reduce a stronghold to surrender; **zur Geldaufnahme ~** to necessitate borrowing; **j. zu einem Geständnis ~** to force s. o. into a confession; **sich selbst ~** to flog o. s.; **j. zu einer Unterschrift ~** to force s. o. to sign a paper; **zur Zahlung ~** to compel payment.
zwingend cogent, compulsory, obligatory, binding, peremptory, coercive, forcible, mandatory;
~er Beweis conclusive evidence; **~e Beweisgründe anführen** to clinch arguments; **~es Gesetz** imperative law, mandatory statute; **~e Gründe** cogent (coercive) reasons; **~e Kraft** cogency; **~e Maßnahmen** coercive measures; **~e Schlußfolgerungen** stringent conclusion.
Zwirnsfaden, an einem ~ hängen to hang by a single thread (by the eyelids).
Zwischen|abkommen interim deal, temporary agreement; **~abrechnung** intermediate account; **~abschluß** interim accounts (statement); **~akt** interact; **~aktmusik** interlude; **~aktvorhang** tab; **~anlage** temporary investment; **kurzfristige ~anlage** cash funds; **~anleihe** interim loan; **kurzfristige ~ansage** *(Rundfunk)* continuity; **~antrag** interlocutory application; **~artikel** *(Zeitung)* padding; **~aufenthalt** transitory stay, stopover *(US)*; **mit kurzem ~aufenthalt reisen** to whistle-stop *(US)*; **~ausschuß** interim committee; **~ausschüttung** interim distribution; **~ausweis** temporary certificate, *(Bilanz)* interim return; **~bahn** *(Raumschiff)* parking orbit; **~belastung** mesne encumbrance; **~bemerkung** interruption, incidental remark; **~benutzung** intervening use; **~bericht** [ad-]interim report, *(Nachlaßverwalter)* intermediate account; **~bescheid** intermediate reply, interim reply (note), *(Gericht)* interlocutory decree; **~bescheinigung über eine abgeschlossene Versicherung** cover note; **~besitzer** temporary possessor.
zwischenbetrieblich intercompany;
~er Vergleich inter-factory comparison.
Zwischen|bilanz interim balance sheet, interim financial statement, struck balance *(Br.)*, interim earnings (cut-off) statement *(US)*; **~bilanzbuch** trial balance book; **~bilanzierung** interim financial reporting; **~blatt** *(Anzeigewesen)* interleaf; **~buchhandel** intermediary bookseller; **~deck** lower (berth, between) deck, steerage; **~deckpassagier** steerage passenger; **als ~deckpassagier reisen** to go (travel) steerage; **~dividende** interim dividend, dividend on account; **~eintragung** intervening (suspense) entry; **~entscheid** interlocutory decree; **~entscheidung** interlocutory decision (judgment); **~ergebnis** interim result; **~examen** intermediate examination, collection *(Br.)*, preliminary *(US)*; **~fall** incident; **ohne ~fälle verlaufen** to take place without disorder, to go off swimmingly (without a hitch); **~feststellungsklage** interpleader; **~finanzierung** interim (intermediate) financing; **~frage** incidental question, question thrown in, *(parl.)* interpellation; **~frage gestatten** to give way; **~frage stellen** to interpellate; **~gericht** entrée; **~geschoß** entresol, mezzanine; **~gewinn** middleman's profit; **~girant** intermediate indorser; **~handel** transit, transient (middleman's) business, intermediary (intermediate) trade, jobbing *(US)*; **~handel ausschalten** to eliminate the middleman; **~handel treiben** to job *(US)*; **~händler** transient vendor, in-between, go-between, intermediary, purchasing agent, independent middleman, broker, merchant shipper, jobber *(US)*; **kurzfristige ~hilfe** short-term interim; **~holding** intermediate (interposed) holding company; **~jahreszeit** between season; **~kalkulation** interim calculation; **~käufer** intermediate buyer; **~konto** interim (suspense, deferred) account; **~kosten** interlocutory costs; **~kredit** intermediate (interim, temporary) credit, interim (bridging) loan; **~lager** housing of goods, housage, intermediate depot *(mil.)*; **~lager für Halbfabrikate** intermediate store; **~lagergebühr** housage; **~lagerung** storage in transit; **~landestelle** stopover place; **~landung** stopover *(US)*; **ohne ~landung** nonstop; **~lösung** interim solution (measure); **~mahlzeit** snack; **~makler** intermediate broker, functional middleman.
zwischenmenschliche Beziehungen human relations.
Zwischen|nutzung intervening use; **~pause** break; **~platte** *(Ausziehtisch)* table leaf; **~produkte** intermediate goods (products), intermediary; **~prüfung** intermediate (term) examination, collection *(Br.)*, preliminary *(US)*; **~quittung** interim (accountable, provisional, temporary) receipt.
Zwischenraum space, clearance, interspace, break, *(drucktechn.)* blind space, spacing;
zu großer ~ wide gap; **variabler ~** *(Setzen)* justified space; **zeitlicher ~** time interval;
~ vermindern *(drucktechn.)* to close up;
~taste *(Schreibmaschine)* space key.
Zwischen|rechnung interim bill; **~regelung** provisional arrangement; **~regierung** interregnum, interim cabinet, caretaker government, interim rule; **~ruf** interruption; **durch ~rufe aus dem Konzept bringen** to heckle; **~rufer** heckler; **~rufer aus dem Saal entfernen lassen** to eject an agitator from a meeting; **~schaltung** insertion *(el.)*; **~schein** provisional bond (certificate, scrip), script, scrip certificate *(Br.)*, interim certificate *(US)*; **~sender** relay transmitter; **~spediteur** intermediate carrier, subagent, transit agent; **~spiel** interlude, intermezzo.
zwischenstaatlich intergovernmental, international, interterritorial, interstate *(US)*;
~e Beratungen intergovernment consultations; **~e Beziehungen** interstate relations; **~e Einrichtung** intergovernmental agency; **~er Handel** interstate commerce *(US)*; **~e Handelsschranken** interstate trade barriers; **~es Komitee für Europäische Auswanderung** Intergovernmental Committee for European Migration; **~e Organisationen** intergovernmental bodies; **~e Regierungskonferenz** intergovernmental conference; **~e beratende Schiffahrtsorganisation** Intergovernmental Maritime Consultative Organization; **~er Versand** interstate shipment.
Zwischen|stadium intermediate stage; **~station** intermediate station (depot, *US*), waystation *(US)*; **~stecker** *(el.)* adapter; **~stellung** intermediate position; **~stock** mezzanine, entresol; **~stufe** intermediate stage; **~summe** subtotal; **~texte schreiben** to do titles; **~titel** subtitle, half title, *(Film)* caption; **~träger** telltale, talebearer, intelligencer, go-between, confidential agent; **~überschrift** cross heading; **~urteil** interlocutory (interim) decree, judgment at interim, preceding judgment, prejudication, interlocutor, interlocution, interlocutory sentence; **~verdienst** middleman's profit; **~verfahren** mesne process *(US)*, interlocutory hearing; **~verfügung** interlocutory (interim) order, *(Richter)* intermediate order, mesne process, intermediate order; **~verfügung für abgetrennte Verfahren** summons and severance; **~verhör** interlocutory hearing; **~verkauf vorbehalten** subject to prior sale; **~verkäufer** intermediate seller; **~verkehr** intercommunication; **~vertrag** provisional contract; **~vertreter** intermediate agent; **~vorhang** *(Theater)* carpenter scene; **~wahl** mid-term (off gear) election; **~wand** partition wall, internal partition; **~wand ziehen** to wall off part of a room; **~wert** intermediate value; **~zeile** space line, interline; **~zeilenabtastung** *(Fernsehen)* interlaced scanning.
zwischenzeilig interlineal, interlinear.
Zwischenzeit time interval, interim period;
in der ~ in the interim.
zwischenzeitlich interim, in the meantime, intermediate, mesne;
~e Erledigung provisional handling.
Zwischen|zeugnis interim reference; **~ziel** *(mil.)* phase line; **~zinsen** mesne (intermediate, interim) interest; **~zustand** intermediate stage.
Zwist quarrel, dispute, *(Uneinigkeit)* discord;
alten ~ begraben to bury the hatchet; **~ mit jem. haben** to be at discord (have an argument) with s. o.

witschern, einen to wet one's whistle.
wölfstundenschicht twelve-hour shift.
yklisch cyclical;
~**er Haushaltsausgleich** cyclical budgeting; ~**e Konjunkturschrumpfung** cyclical contraction of general business activity; ~**en Kontraktionen unterworfen sein** to contract cyclically; ~**es Steuersystem** incentive taxation; ~**e Veränderung** business-cycle change; ~**e Wirtschaftspolitik** cyclical budgeting.

Zyklon cyclone, depression, low.
Zyklus cycle;
~ **von Vorlesungen** course of lectures.
Zylinder zylinder, *(Hut)* top hat;
sich in einem ~ bewegen to play within a cylinder;
~**block** cylinder block; ~**deckel** top of a cylinder; ~**hut** silk (high, top) hat, topper, shiner *(coll.)*, plug *(US)*; ~**kolben** cylinder piston; ~**mantel** jacket.

PRESSESTIMMEN

DIE WELT – Nr. 287 Dezember 1981

Die ganze Sprache soll es sein . . .

R. von Eichborns großes englisch-deutsches Wörterbuch

Die Sprache enthüllt Seele und geistige Potenz eines Volkes. Sie bleibt und wandelt sich trotzdem fortwährend. Der Sprachschatz vermittelt in den Wörtern Instrumente zur Aufhellung des Daseins in seiner ganzen Vielfalt. Ein Wörterbuch kann deshalb geistesgeschichtlichen Rang besitzen, wenn es ihm gelingt, den Reichtum der differenzierten Gedankengänge und Aussagen einer Sprache bis in die letzten Verästelungen zu verzeichnen. Als ein Werk von solchem Rang darf man das kürzlich erschienene „Wörterbuch Englisch – Deutsch" von Reinhart von Eichborn getrost bezeichnen; im Frühjahr 1982 wird die entsprechende deutsch-englische Ausgabe folgen.

Der vorliegende große Wurf ist die Frucht 35jähriger Forschungsarbeit – ein Kompendium, das den Sprachschatz aus Wirtschaft, Recht, Verwaltung und Verkehr nahezu vollständig wiedergibt. Hinzu kommt aber noch – das ist das Novum am altbewährten neuen Eichborn – die Umgangssprache der angelsächsischen Welt.

Reinhart von Eichborn hat seit 1946 Wörterbücher verfaßt, zunächst im Auftrag der damaligen Militärregierung in Stuttgart, die ihn drängte, ein Spezialwörterbuch für Wirtschaft und Handel herauszugeben. Der Verfasser begann bescheiden mit kleinen Auflagen in der Deutschen Verlags-Anstalt in Stuttgart; denn noch war der Zugang zur angelsächsischen Fachliteratur zu schwierig. Dann stellte ihm eine Spende der US-Regierung für ihre studierenden Soldaten Hunderte von einschlägigen Werken zur Verfügung, und aus England erhielt Eichborn bald die führenden Lexika. Auch konnte er nun ständig „Business Week", „Fortune", die „Financial Times" und den „Economist" auswerten. So erschienen drei Auflagen des „Spezialwörterbuchs" in der DVA, und ein Mann hatte sich eine neue Lebensaufgabe gestellt. Danach kam Eichborns „Wirtschaftswörterbuch" in vier Auflagen und 32000 Exemplaren bei Econ heraus.

In der jetzigen Ausgabe nun findet das Wörterbuch mit mehr als 250000 Eintragungen seine Vollendung. Der Verfasser verwendet als Prinzip für die alphabetische Einordnung eines Wortes den „Grad seiner Selbständigkeit". Hier wird das Wörterbuch zur angewandten Sprachforschung: Die Einordnung von Einzelbegriffen in das Gesamtgefüge der Sprache und des von ihr geprägten nationalen Geistes erfordert unablässige vergleichende Einsichten, den täglichen Umgang mit Prioritäten und Bedeutungswandlungen.

Besonderes Augenmerk legt der Autor auf die Phraseologie. Dafür seien nur zwei Beispiele angeführt: „capital" und „house". Jeweils über 500 Eintragungen ranken sich um die beiden Grundbegriffe und erschöpfen jede ihrer möglichen Differenzierungen. Eichborn hat aber auch „dem Volk aufs Maul geschaut"; er nahm zahlreiche Slang-Ausdrücke in sein Werk auf, während indes allzu modische Eintagsfliegen keine Gnade fanden. So ist das Soziologenchinesisch nur spärlich berücksichtigt, was den Autor jedoch nicht gehindert hat, über 300 Eintragungen um die Vokabeln „social" und „society" zu versammeln.

Die Erweiterung des früheren Wirtschaftswörterbuches um die Umgangssprache muß als Krönung des Eichbornschen Lebenswerkes angesehen werden. Dem Verfasser ist es gelungen, die fast unbegrenzten Variationsmöglichkeiten einzelner Begriffe so kompakt wie erschöpfend aufzuführen, wobei er gelegentlich zur rascheren Orientierung des Benutzers zusammengesetzte Begriffe unter beiden Wortteilen separat verzeichnet.

Das schwierige Problem der sachlichen Äquivalenz hat Eichborn glänzend gemeistert. Man kennt die oft sinnentstellenden Versuche von Wörterbüchern, etwa unser „Landgericht" in fremde Sprachen zu übersetzen. Auch hier beweist der Autor, wie souverän er die angelsächsische Welt im Griff hat – ihren geistigen Aufbau, ihre Verwaltung und Justiz, ihre politische Organisation und die Einrichtungen des gesellschaftlichen Lebens. Da eine völlige Äquivalenz nur selten besteht, sind analoge Wortbildungen in Klammern mit dem Zusatz „etwa" versehen. Abweichungen zwischen dem Englischen und Amerikanischen sind mit (BR) bzw. (US) gekennzeichnet.

Wir haben nun den Mini-Eichborn, den „kleinen" und den „großen" Eichborn. Die Fachkritik hat mit ihrem Lob nicht gegeizt: „Bestseller" – „unentbehrliches Requisit" – „uneingeschränkt empfehlenswerte Investition" – „alles zu finden, was zur Umgangssprache des modernen Menschen gehört" – „das Standardwerk schlechthin". Der Eichborn ist sprichwörtlich geworden. Gelehrte und Studenten, Praktiker aus Wirtschaft und Recht, Vertreter von Verwaltung und Verkehr, Forscher und schlichte Briefschreiber, Unternehmen und Behörden, Politiker und Schriftsteller und nicht zuletzt die öffentlichen Bibliotheken – sie alle werden auf dieses Lebenswerk von Reinhart von Eichborn nicht verzichten können.

Hermann M. Goergen

Frankfurter Allgemeine – Nr. 68 März 1982

Eichborn hat dem Wörterbuch als Motto einen Satz des großen britischen Journalisten, Kritikers und Aufklärers Samuel Johnson vorangestellt: Wörterbücher sind wie Uhren, die schlechteste ist besser als gar keine; und auch die beste wird nie ganz genau gehen. Mit diesem Motto zieht der Autor nicht nur ein weises und von britischen Understatement zeugendes Resümee von fünfunddreißig Jahren Beschäftigung mit der so überaus lebendigen und wandlungsfähigen englischen Sprache, er übt zugleich auch freundliche Nachsicht mit den Rezensenten. Denn es gibt kaum etwas Schwierigeres als die Besprechung eines Wörterbuches, zumal eines so umfassenden. Dennoch: wenn man ein paar Wochen lang mit dem Eichborn zur Hand englische und amerikanische Publikationen gelesen hat oder wenn man Stichproben etwa an Hand von Langenscheidts Handbuch der englischen Wirtschaftssprache vornimmt, zeigt sich, wie vorzüglich dieses Wörterbuch ist. Es ist eine Freude für alle, die sich seit Jahren über schludrige Übersetzungen englischer oder amerikanischer Bücher und Texte aus dem Bereich Wirtschaft ärgern oder enttäuscht in manchem „normalen" Wörterbuch blättern. Das gilt vor allem deswegen, weil hier erkennbar viele Bücher und Zeitschriften ausgewertet worden sind und über die Fachbegriffe hinaus nun auch Umgangssprachliches Eingang gefunden hat. Mit dem Großen Eichborn ist aus dem vormaligen Wirtschaftswörterbuch eine Institution von Rang und Qualität geworden. Zu bedauern ist allenfalls, daß auch dieses Wörterbuch ein Zeichen für die zunehmende Spezialisierung in unserer Zeit ist. Der Durchschnittsmensch kommt bekanntlich mit einem Vokabular von etwa 300 Wörtern aus. In Zeitungen und auch in Fachbüchern reicht etwa der zehnfache Wortschatz aus, der Große Eichborn enthält 250000 Eintragungen. Angefangen hat Eichborn 1946 mit einem kleinen Spezialwörterbuch für Handel und Wirtschaft im Auftrag der amerikanischen Militärregierung, das bei der Deutschen Verlags-Anstalt erschien und drei Auflagen erlebte. Als Wirtschaftswörterbuch im Econ Verlag kamen dann weitere vier Auflagen hinzu, außerdem eine Parallelausgabe als „Business Dictionary" bei Prentice Hall in New York. Es folgt im letzten Jahr zunächst der Kleine Eichborn, der es im englisch-deutschen Teil auf etwa 140000 Stichwörter brachte, und nun der Große Eichborn, der im Sommer mit dem deutsch-englischen Teil komplettiert wird. Eines spricht an dieser Erfolgsgeschichte für sich selbst: Der Eichborn gehört mit zu den am häufigsten gestohlenen Büchern in deutschen Bibliotheken.

J. Jürgen Jeske

German-American Trade News May-June 1982

A language reflects both the soul and the mind of a people. It endures and yet manages to change and renew itself through the years. As a vehicle for describing the human condition in its infinite variety, a truly excellent dictionary sometimes manages to achieve a reputation of its own in intellectual history. Only time can make such judgements, but the work under review will certainly find an important niche in offices and libraries in the United States and Europe. Mr. von Eichborn's work will find a welcome and appreciative audience among those who require a comprehensive up-to-date dictionary for the world of modern business and commerce. This volume is the culmination of 35 years of work and research by the author, whose name is virtually synonymous with the field of economics and business dictionaries in Germany. This dictionary contains an astounding total of 250,000 entries from the vocabulary of economics, business, finance, law, administration, and transportation. One example of the author's meticulous research and attention to the nuance of language should suffice: under the entry for "capital" are 500 German translations covering every conceivable substantive or metaphorical use of the term. Even the author's obvious aversion to trendy phrases or sociological jargon has not hindered him from offering the translator 300 nouns and adjectives under the entries for "society" and "social". Professors and students, lawyers, economists, businessmen and researchers alike will find Eichborn's new dictionary an indispensible reference work. The German-English version will also appear this year.